SYSTEM … RNS

No.	Pattern									
1	LEFT-RIGHT	c[illegible]	[illegible] 4-5	[illegible] 2-3	[illegible] 3-8	[illegible] 1-2	[illegible] 1-2	州 2-4	順 1-11	傾 2-11
		conceptual space	扱 3-3	級 6-3	歓 11-4	街 3-9	町 5-2	翻 12-6	髄 10-9	伺 2-5
2	UP-DOWN	clear space	示 1-4	二 1-1	三 1-2	言 1-6	公 2-2	谷 2-5	父 2-2	多 3-3
		conceptual space	芳 3-4	合 2-4	響 11-9	桑 2-8	系 1-6	雀 4-7	券 6-2	春 5-4
		horizontal line	寺 3-3	空 3-5	文 2-2	亭 2-7	忘 2-5	学 5-3	索 4-6	義 3-10
		frame element	古 2-3	点 2-7	免 2-6	早 4-2	尭 2-6	当 3-3	南 2-7	支 2-2
3	ENCLOSURE		進 3-8	辻 4-2	起 7-3	延 3-5	魅 8-7	直 1-7	匕 1-1	止 2-2
			旬 2-4	載 6-7	刀 1-1	司 1-4	可 2-3	戒 4-3	鳥 7-4	馬 6-4
			麻 3-8	圧 2-3	尾 3-4	病 5-5	石 2-3	考 4-2	着 7-5	斗 2-2
			間 8-4	岡 2-6	風 2-7	向 3-3	肉 4-2	凶 2-2	山 2-1	画 2-6
			医 2-5	臣 3-4	匿 2-9	丑 2-2				
			回 3-3	国 3-5	田 3-2	日 3-1	目 3-2	四 3-2	皿 3-2	
4	SOLID	1 top line	下 3-1	耳 6-1	雨 8-1	子 3-1	凸 5-1	口 3-1	亜 7-1	爾 14-1
		2 bottom line	上 3-2	七 2-2	亡 3-2	丘 5-2	由 5-2	自 6-2	坐 7-2	重 9-2
		3 through line	中 4-3	十 2-3	手 4-3	本 5-3	求 7-3	乗 9-3	毛 4-3	粛 11-3
		4 others	人 2-4	九 2-4	女 3-4	火 4-4	犬 4-4	成 6-4	寿 7-4	為 9-4

THE **KODANSHA KANJI** DICTIONARY

THE **KODANSHA** **KANJI** DICTIONARY

講談社漢英字典

Editor in Chief
JACK HALPERN

Kodansha USA

This dictionary is based on the *New Japanese-English Character Dictionary,* copyright © Jack Halpern, first published in Japan by Kenkyusha, Ltd. in 1990.

Published by Kodansha USA, Inc., 451 Park Avenue South, New York, NY 10016

Distributed in the United Kingdom and continental Europe by Kodansha Europe, Ltd.

Printed in South Korea through Dai Nippon Printing Co., Ltd.
22 21 20 19 18 17 16 15 14 13   12 11 10 9 8 7 6 5 4 3 2 1
ISBN 978-1-56836-408-7

Jacket design by Andrew Lee

Library of Congress Cataloging-in-Publication Data

The Kodansha Kanji dictionary / Editor in Chief, Jack Halpern.—Updated and revised ed.
pages cm
Text in English and Japanese.
"This up-to-date revision of the New Japanese-English Character Dictionary, originally published in 1990, includes an additional 886 Joyo Kanji and Jinmei Kanji characters that were not present in the first edition."
Includes indexes.
ISBN 978-1-56836-408-7
1. Japanese language—Dictionaries—English. 2. Chinese characters—Dictionaries—Japanese. I. Halpern, Jack, 1946- II. Title: New Japanese-English Character Dictionary.
PL677.5.N73 2013
495.6'321—dc23

2013004560

www.kodanshausa.com

To Michal

Every other author may aspire to praise; the lexicographer can only hope to escape reproach...

SAMUEL JOHNSON (1709-1784)
AUTHOR OF DICTIONARY OF THE ENGLISH LANGUAGE (1755)

全ての執筆者は称賛を追い求める。
辞書編纂者が願うのは非難を免れることのみ。

サミュエル・ジョンソン (1709-1784)
「英語辞典」(1755年) の著者

CONTENTS
目 次

APPENDIXES

INDEXES

EDITORIAL STAFF
編集スタッフ

Editor in Chief

Jack Halpern	CEO, The CJK Dictionary Institute Research Fellow, Institute of Modern Culture, Showa Women's University

Editorial Consultants

Kusuo Hitomi	President, Showa Women's University
Eleanor H. Jorden	Mary Dolon Alger Professor of Linguistics, Cornell University
Masaaki Nomura	Director, Department of Computational Linguistics, The National Language Research Institute (Japan)
Akiyasu Todo	formerly Professor of Chinese Literature at University of Tokyo and Waseda University

Associate Editors

Masato Asada	M.A., University of Tokyo
Michael Carr	Ph.D., University of Arizona
Chikasada Harada	Professor, Showa Women's University
Yukio Ishikawa	M.A., Keio University
Asako Kaneko	Assistant Professor, Showa Women's University
Masako Nakamura	B.A., Hiroshima University
Michael Staley	Editor, Kodansha Ltd.
Kay Yokota	Coeditor of the Revised Edition

Editorial Assistants

Kurt Easterwood	Harumi Iida	Chikako Imoto	Takane Ito
JeanPaul Jenack	Keith Johnson	Kazuyoshi Kawakami	Ryoun Kobayashi
Christine Lamarre	Peter H. Liu	Russel Marcus	Susumu Miyazawa
Yuko Momose	Kimiko Morishita	Ryoko Murase	Tazuko Nagae
Setsuo Nara	Harumi Nishimoto	Aki Ono	Junko Osaki
Xianhua Piao	Jack Plimpton	Meryl Schaffer	Junko Suzuki
Kazuko Suzuki	Midori Tajima	Yuriko Takagi	Hiroko Takahashi
Noriko Yamamoto	Tsuneo Yatagai	Tadashi Yumiketa	

Keyboarding

Michal Halpern	Yoshie Miura	Taeko Moriguchi	Haruko Oasa
Kumiko Suga	Nobuko Suzuki	Keiko Uchida	Chieko Yokoe
Toshiko Yoshida			

Chief of Software Development

Nicola Mettifogo	Director of Automated Typesetting, The CJK Dictionary Institute
Tyler Reid	Senior Software Engineer, The CJK Dictionary Institute

Programming and Computer Consultants

Shoichi Fujita, Yasuhiro Hasegawa, Koki Kondo, Toshio Otsuka

Graphics Designer

Toyoko Kon

Secretarial and Clerical Assistants

Chiaki Fujinawa	Junko Higuchi	Keiko Ikuta	Miyuki Masuda
Hikaru Matsumoto	Keiko Matsuoka	Keiko Matsushima	Teruko Miyake
Kumiko Nakagawa	Sachiko Shibata	Kazuto Shioiri	Chieko Takahata
Mitsuko Yanagisawa			

FOREWORD
緒言

This up-to-date revision of the **New Japanese-English Character Dictionary,** originally published in 1990, includes an additional 886 Jōyō Kanji and Jinmei Kanji characters that were not present in the first edition.

As Dr. Kusuo Hitomi mentions in his foreword to the first edition, kanji play a profound role in the Japanese language, constituting the foundation upon which the Japanese people communicate concepts and beliefs. During the Meiji era, when new products and ideas were rapidly being introduced to Japan from abroad, the ability to create new words using kanji characters allowed these new concepts to penetrate Japanese society with relative ease. Encountering new characters and kanji compounds naturally tests our allegorical reasoning skills.

To fully comprehend the meaning of a kanji compound, one must first understand the meaning of each component. For example, the meaning of 売電 'selling electricity' consists of 売 'sell' and 電 'electricity', so that the meaning of the whole is clear from the meanings of the components, even for compounds *not* listed in the dictionary. But this dictionary does not restrict itself to such obvious cases. For example, for 早 it gives the meaning 'abbrev. of 早稲田大学 Waseda University' and for 明 it gives 'abbrev. of 明治大学 Meiji University'. This enables the user to comprehend that 早明戦 means 'Waseda-Meiji (baseball) game', rather than "early bright war." Similarly, only by knowing that the first character of 雀荘 'mahjong club' is derived from 麻雀 'mahjong' does the meaning of that compound become clear.

Communication methods have changed drastically since the late twentieth century. Today virtually everyone communicates by email, alleviating the difficulty of having to write kanji characters or even to understand them in depth. But do the characters that pop up with such ease on our screens accurately convey the concepts we intend? Are we even expressing our own thoughts? I do hope that Japanese people will also make greater efforts to genuinely grasp the Japanese language and its writing system.

For many years I taught Japanese to foreigners—or should I say, to non-native speakers. The truth is that kanji constitute a huge hurdle for Japanese-language learners, especially those from outside the Sinosphere. When it comes to learning kanji, many people simply give up. On the other hand, there are those who become captivated by kanji and consider them to be enjoyable as well as quite logical.

I have often heard statements like "Sentences written in hiragana only are actually harder to read," "If you know the kanji you can guess the general meaning, even if you don't understand the context," or, "When I visited Taiwan, I was able to get around by reading the kanji." Here, I would like to recount my experience as a teacher who has long served as an interface between the Japanese language and such enthusiastic language learners.

I first met Jack Halpern back in 1980, when I was in the midst of coauthoring a new textbook for beginners called *Japanese for Busy People*. I was striving to develop an organized, easy-to-understand way to explain the Japanese language system, which is so completely different from those of Indo-European languages. While struggling to describe advanced grammatical points in a cogent manner, I decided to avoid the easy path of makeshift explanations that would later be inconsistent with those given at higher levels of learning. It was sometimes necessary to refer to the grammar of classical literature when contemporary grammar of the spoken language did not help.

Meanwhile, Jack Halpern was eagerly undertaking the study of kanji, but, as he pointed out, no kanji dictionaries existed that were easy to use for nonnative learners of Japanese. He had taken it upon himself to develop a solution to this fundamental problem. He and I agreed that teaching methods and materials should not be based on the conventional wisdom of teachers who are native speakers of Japanese. We felt that there was an acute need for materials that offer an easy-to-understand system, and that put particular emphasis on the specific challenges faced by nonnative learners. Such thinking, now commonplace, was not widespread back then. Jack Halpern and I had discovered a common mission. To achieve our goals, I went into textbook publishing, while he headed down the painstaking road toward completion of a kanji dictionary based on new principles.

The author explains the user-friendliness of this dictionary in detail, so I need not reiterate it here. There is one feature, however, that I would like to draw special attention to. Looking up kanji is a challenging task for anyone, but nonnative learners of Japanese have particular difficulty with old character forms and kanji variants. In traditional character dictionaries, looking up kanji, especially old forms and variant forms, is fraught with difficulties and requires a good knowledge of radicals. In contrast, this dictionary provides several search methods and indexes that enable even beginners to look up both simple and complex character forms with equal ease.

This kanji dictionary is unrivaled in terms of both quantity and quality. It is a groundbreaking guide and a reliable authority that anticipates the particular challenges faced by beginners struggling to surmount the barriers posed by kanji. Moreover, for those who have already tasted the charm of kanji, it will surely provide an inexhaustible source of joy. I am convinced that this dictionary will fully satisfy the needs of kanji learners the world over.

March 2013
Tokyo

SHIGEKO MIYAZAKI
Chair of the Board, The Association for Japanese-Language Teaching (AJALT)

FOREWORD TO THE FIRST EDITION
第一版緒言

An isolated island country lying off the eastern edge of the continental land mass of Asia, Japan has, since ancient times, developed a distinctive culture and history of her own while maintaining relations with her Asian neighbors. Chinese characters, which were introduced to Japan from ancient China, gave birth to a new set of phonetic characters known as kana. Although both these forms of script have thereafter been used side by side to write the Japanese language, the Chinese characters have always played a central role, serving as the chief medium of communicating ideas in a broad spectrum of fields ranging from philosophy and scholarship to the literary arts and ethics.

The introduction of Chinese characters made it possible for the Japanese to learn about religious ideas from the Buddhist classics and gave them a new means for expressing subtle emotional nuances. Eventually evolved a script, unprecedented in history, in which kana and kanji blend to produce a powerful means of conveying meaning in a concise and effective manner. The adoption of advanced Western thought, culture, social institutions, and technology that took place during the rapid modernization after the Meiji Restoration gave rise to a need for coining countless neologisms to express new concepts. Such items as 文明 ぶんめい 'civilization', 経済 けいざい 'economics', and 手続 てつづき 'procedure' are only a few examples of the innumerable words whose coinage was made possible by the word-forming ability of Chinese characters.

This uniquely Japanese writing system, while playing a role as a most beneficial and distinctly *human* medium of communication, has blossomed into a treasure of Japanese culture and tradition. In this manner, the Chinese characters have served as an extremely convenient set of symbols—the central pillar of the evolution of Japan's culture; in fact, they are the very symbol of Japan's membership in the "Kanji Sphere of Culture" [Sinosphere]—a community of nations sharing a common heritage based on Chinese characters.

Though Japan has experienced many ups and downs during the period of more than one hundred years that has elapsed since the Meiji Restoration, she has successfully pulled through to attain a high level of economic growth, and now even stands at the forefront of science and technology. As Japan has come to occupy an important position in world affairs, a rapidly increasing number of people and nations in every corner of the globe are turning to her as a focus of intense interest and active concern. This trend, which is likely to accelerate as the world undergoes increased internationalization, is clearly apparent in the sharp rise, both at home and abroad, in the number of non-Japanese studying Japanese in recent years. As Japan heads into the twenty-first century, organizations engaged in Japanese-language education are vigorously preparing to accommodate the growing demand by training more teachers, improving teaching methods, developing improved teaching materials, and implementing Japanese-language proficiency examinations.

All this notwithstanding, one of the central problems in Japanese-language education today is, as pointed out by Shigeko Miyazaki, chair of the board of the Association for Japanese-Language Teaching, the almost total lack of truly effective dictionaries for learners. A mere translated version of existing Japanese-Japanese dictionaries is hardly adequate for meeting the needs of the foreign student. More than anything else, there is now an urgent need for the publication of effective dictionaries that squarely address these needs.

The original motive force for the compilation of this dictionary sprung from the editor's own arduous experiences in struggling with traditional methods of rote memorization and the excessive burden which these place on the memory. Based on voluminous data sources and modern linguistic theory, this work is designed to meet the special needs of the non-Japanese student, while serving as a linguistically accurate, useful work of reference even for native Japanese.

This dictionary also introduces a new method of looking up characters known as the System of Kanji Indexing by Patterns (SKIP), which enables one to locate entries rapidly without previous knowledge of kanji elements. Character meanings and compound words are arranged in a manner that shows how each character functions as a word-building element, and an analysis of the differences between homophones (words pronounced alike but written differently) and kanji synonyms is presented. We are confident that students of Japanese using this dictionary will make rapid progress in their studies by deepening their knowledge and understanding of kanji, and will be completely gratified with its effectiveness.

In accordance with the founding principles of Showa Women's University, we endeavor to educate women to be "aware, intelligent, and fair-minded." Over the long years of our existence, we have striven to cultivate young women who will play an important role in society and, at the same time, have endeavored to contribute to research on and the advancement of culture. The Institute of Modern Culture, which is affiliated with the university and has been actively engaged in promoting cultural research, recognized that kanji is the key to the healthy growth of Japanese culture and literature. The Institute recognized the import of the new dictionary, and consequently proceeded, under the direction of Jack Halpern as editor in chief, to embark upon the long years of research necessary for its compilation.

To bring a project of this magnitude and complexity to successful completion required a high degree of scholarly expertise, the latest computer photocomposition technology, and advanced system design and software engineering. Furthermore, the layout and design of the dictionary had to be carefully executed to achieve maximum ease of use while satisfying a broad spectrum of diversified needs. To accomplish these objectives required an inestimable number of man-hours, painstaking labor, and capital funding on a major scale. If not for these coordinated efforts, this work would not have seen the light of day.

On this day, as we present the world with this new work, it is our duty to record our everlasting gratitude to Jack Halpern, the chief editor and central figure responsible for seeing this project through, for his outstanding achievement in producing a work that represents a significant departure from traditional character-dictionary lexicography. It is our great fortune that Jack Halpern, who eagerly devoted himself to the project while overcoming innumerable difficulties, should have become captivated by the rhythmical tones of the Japanese language and so intrigued by the Chinese characters as to embark upon their serious study. The day will surely come when he will be widely recognized for promoting the study of kanji throughout the world.

I would like to express my heartfelt appreciation to the distinguished scholars who served as editorial consultants, including Professor Eleanor Jorden, Professor Akiyasu Todo, Professor Masaaki Nomura, Professor Chikasada Harada, and others for their most valuable advice and cooperation. Sincere gratitude also goes to the Dictionary Department of Kenkyusha as well as to the technical staff engaged in computer photocomposition at the Toppan Printing Company for rendering their outstanding efforts. I also wish to sincerely thank the many organizations, foundations, and individuals who have made financial contributions to the project for their unlimited understanding and moral support.

I am convinced that this dictionary will make a major contribution to both the teaching and learning of Japanese. It is, furthermore, my earnest hope that this work will help promote understanding of Japan among the people of the world, and thereby stimulate further international economic and cultural exchange.

March 1990
Tokyo

Kusuo Hitomi
President of Showa Women's University

PREFACE
序言

Nearly a quarter of a century has passed since the first edition of this work, the **New Japanese-English Character Dictionary** (NJECD), was published by Kenkyusha in 1990. This groundbreaking dictionary, which has gained a solid reputation in the Japanese-language education community throughout the world, has become a standard reference work.

This revised edition, **The Kodansha Kanji Dictionary** (KKD), has the same goal as its predecessor: to provide the user with a thorough understanding of how kanji are used in contemporary Japanese. This is achieved by providing instant access to a wealth of useful information on the meanings, readings, and compounds for each entry character up to the advanced level and beyond.

Furthermore, this edition meets the urgent need for a comprehensive kanji dictionary based on the revised **Jōyō Kanji** list promulgated in November 2010. The most important feature of the revised edition is the addition of 821 new entries, bringing the total to 4408 character entries (excluding cross-references) covering all the kanji in the official **Jōyō Kanji** and **Jinmei Kanji** lists and beyond.

State-of-the-art typesetting technology was combined with computational lexicography to produce a work that aims to serve as a highly effective learning aid. Like **The Kodansha Kanji Learner's Dictionary: Revised and Expanded** (KKLD), this revised edition includes various features to help learners study kanji effectively, including core meanings for a deeper understanding of kanji, and the renowned SKIP system for rapid lookup.

The present work was compiled by **The CJK Dictionary Institute,** whose mission is to create large-scale lexical resources for CJK languages (Chinese, Japanese, Korean) and to publish high-end dictionaries and software for learners of Japanese, Chinese, and Arabic. The work represents the latest addition to the **Kanji Integrated Tools** (KIT), a series of dictionaries and software applications for mastering the Japanese writing system (eleven have been published altogether).

On this auspicious occasion, it is my sincere hope that the revised edition will serve as an up-to-date, easy-to-use reference, thereby promoting better communication between Japan and the rest of the world.

March 2013
Saitama, Japan

Jack Halpern
Editor in Chief

ACKNOWLEDGMENTS
謝辞

The Kodansha Kanji Dictionary is the second edition of the **New Japanese-English Character Dictionary** published by Kenkyusha in 1990. The two editions were compiled with the enthusiastic cooperation of some 120 staff members, part-time assistants, and outside consultants over a period of some eighteen years.

First and foremost, I wish to extend my heartfelt gratitude to the late Professor Kusuo Hitomi, former president of Showa Women's University, whose personal support of and unshaken faith in the project saw the first edition of this dictionary through the most difficult times both financially and logistically.

Special recognition is due to the distinguished scholars, editorial consultants, and editors without whose generous contributions this dictionary would not have seen the light of day. My gratitude goes to Professor Masaaki Nomura, for helping establish editorial policy; Dr. Michael Carr, Professor Chikasada Harada, and Assistant Professor Asako Kaneko, for critically proofreading the entire manuscript of the first edition; Professor Eleanor H. Jorden, a world authority on Japanese language studies, for her valuable suggestions; and finally, internationally renowned kanji scholar Professor Akiyasu Todo and Japanese-language authority Professor Haruhiko Kindaichi, for offering their warm recommendations.

Special thanks are due to Masato Asada, Masako Nakamura, Toshiko Yoshida, Chieko Yokoe, Ryoko Murase, Midori Tajima, Kurt Easterwood, Xianhua Piao, and other editors and proofreaders for their devotion to the tasks of semantic analysis, compilation of data, and the meticulous checking of sources, and validation of the data. In addition, dozens of consultants, computer programmers, keyboard operators, and secretarial and clerical personnel have worked on both editions at one time or another during its eighteen years of progress.

I also wish to thank the many others who have made substantial contributions to the arduous tasks of proofreading, compiling, and managing the revised edition, including but not limited to Michael Staley, the editor in charge of the project at Kodansha; Kay Yokota, for her painstaking efforts in compiling hundreds of new entries; Chikako Imoto, for her meticulous attention in proofreading; Naoyuki Takeshita, for his help in creating user-defined fonts of excellent quality; Xanthe Smith Serafin, a highly competent translator, for her contribution; Kimiko Morishita, who devoted careful attention to managing the project; and Ken Lunde, Senior Computer Scientist at Adobe Systems and a world authority on CJK information processing, for his inexhaustible assistance in customizing our fonts and guidance in using InDesign.

I also wish to thank the many organizations and individuals that have made substantial contributions to the dictionary, especially the staff members in charge of the project at Kodansha USA, and those who have contributed to the scholarly accuracy of the dictionary or have assisted in other ways, including Kokugo Mondai Kyogikai former president Nobutane Kiuchi, Japan Foundation, National Language Research Institute, Japan Research Corporation chairman Kazuo Noda, Professor Takao Suzuki, and Shigeko Miyazaki, chair of the Association for Japanese-Language Teaching.

I want to express my gratitude to the team of programmers who contributed to this project, but most of all to Tyler Reid and Nicola Mettifogo for their invaluable assistance in developing the data processing programs and sophisticated page composition system that made this dictionary a reality.

To bring a project of this magnitude to successful completion required large-scale contributions and financial assistance from many quarters. I wish to express my deep appreciation to the approximately 150 individuals, private organizations, corporations, and foundations that recognized the import of the dictionary and selflessly offered continuous support without seeking personal returns.

I also wish to express my sincere thanks to Vice Chairman Sohei Nakayama and First Subcommittee Chairman Naohiro Amaya, both of the National Council on Educational Reform, who have given their wholehearted support and assistance in raising funds for the project, and to Kiyotaka Kurokawa, Yasuo

Ushioda, Yoichiro Yamamura, and Russel Marcus for their active cooperation in the fund-raising effort and for their continuous moral support.

I am indebted to the hundreds of reference works such as dictionaries, encyclopedias, books, magazines, and newspapers that were used as sources or for reference in the compilation of this dictionary.

Finally, to my wife, Michal, who for long years devoted superhuman efforts to the project and has seen it through the most difficult of times, goes my everlasting gratitude and appreciation.

March 2013
Saitama, Japan

Jack Halpern
Editor in Chief

INTRODUCTION
序説

The Kodansha Kanji Dictionary (KKD) enables the user to gain an in-depth understanding of how kanji are used in contemporary Japanese by providing quick and easy access to a wealth of useful information on the meanings, readings, and compounds for each entry character.

A unique and valuable feature is the **core meaning,** a concise keyword that defines the most dominant meaning of each character, which is followed by detailed meanings that clearly show how a few thousand basic building blocks are combined to form countless compound words.

Clear, complete, and accurate **character meanings,** illustrated by numerous compounds and examples, are grouped around the core meaning in a logically structured manner that allows them to be perceived as an integrated unit. A unique feature of this dictionary is the full guidance it provides for distinguishing between easily confused characters such as synonyms, homophones, and orthographic variants.

Another unique feature is the **System of Kanji Indexing by Patterns** (SKIP), a system that enables the user to locate characters as quickly and as accurately as in alphabetical dictionaries.

Modern linguistic theory has been effectively integrated with sophisticated information technology to produce a powerful tool that can be used by learners and educators with equal ease. For the first time, users have at their fingertips a wealth of information on kanji that is linguistically accurate, easy to use, and carefully adapted to their practical needs.

Thanks to these and other features, this is the most in-depth and most comprehensive kanji-English dictionary ever compiled.

JAPANESE TODAY

The emergence of Japan as an economic and industrial superpower has had a major impact on her role in world affairs. More than ever before, businesspeople, students, diplomats, and scientists are faced with a growing need to communicate with Japan in her own tongue. In fact, statistics show that the number of Japanese-language students in the world has been rising rapidly.

Japanese is considered a difficult language. Some characteristics which justify this classification are a grammatical structure that is radically different from that of the European languages, complicated levels of formality, and what could be safely termed the most complex writing system devised by man. Consequently, the non-Japanese learner must invest considerably more time and effort to master Japanese than most other foreign languages.

THE STUDY OF KANJI

The Japanese writing system is composed of two phonetic syllabaries, called ***hiragana*** and ***katakana,*** and thousands of Chinese characters, called ***kanji.*** Kanji have three basic properties: form, sound, and meaning. Many characters are of complex shape, some having more than twenty or even thirty strokes. Almost all characters may be pronounced according to their Chinese-derived ***on*** reading(s), or one of several native Japanese ***kun*** readings, and each reading may have numerous meanings. Moreover, since many words are pronounced the same but written differently (homophones), the Japanese writing system is complex and requires considerable effort to learn.

But the effort is well worthwhile. Kanji have the ability to generate hundreds of thousands of compound words from a basic stock of a few thousand units.

They form a network of interrelated parts that function as an integrated system, not as an arbitrary set of disconnected symbols. The few character dictionaries for nonnative speakers presently available for nonnative speakers fail to systematically address that most elusive, yet undoubtedly most important, aspect of kanji: their meanings, especially their meanings as word-building elements.

Millions of people are learning Japanese in some 15,000 schools and organizations throughout the world. Although the number of Japanese-language students has been rising at a rapid pace, effective learning aids for truly mastering kanji have not been available.

A NEW DICTIONARY APPROACH

The primary goal of this dictionary has been set high: to create a practical tool that enables the learner to gain an *in-depth* understanding of the most frequently used kanji in contemporary Japanese. This was achieved by making full use of the most recent advances in linguistic science, computational lexicography, and digital publishing technology.

Based on a systematic approach and a firm theoretical foundation, this dictionary is designed to meet in full the specific needs of non-Japanese users. We have avoided the path of least resistance taken by other works: that is, compiling lists of words and presenting only dry facts such as readings and stroke-counts, while sidestepping the difficult task of presenting accurate character meanings. This dictionary not merely accurately records the linguistic facts about kanji, but also strives to present them in a manner that gives the user insight into how they function as a system.

This dictionary offers various unique features that clearly distinguish it from past works. It departs from tradition in three important ways.

Accurate character meanings The **core meaning,** a concise keyword that provides a clear grasp of the most fundamental concept for each character, is followed by clear and detailed character meanings arranged in a manner that shows how they are interrelated. Each meaning is followed by compounds and examples that show how they are formed from their constituents. Moreover, the degree of importance for each meaning is indicated for four levels of study.

Efficient indexing system The SKIP indexing system enables even beginners to locate entries quickly and with ease. Since it can be mastered in a very short time, this dictionary is an extremely convenient lookup tool. In addition, five other lookup methods, such as the Radical Index and the On-Kun Index, assure maximum convenience to the user.

Precise distinctions A unique feature of this dictionary is the detailed treatment of the differences and similarities between closely related characters. This includes the fine distinctions between kanji synonyms (形 'shape' vs. 状 'form'), usage notes indicating the differences between homophones (**あく** written 開く 'open' or 空く 'become vacant'), and labels that show the differences between orthographic variants (希 vs. 稀 in the sense of 'rare').

Many other features, such as traditional and Chinese character forms, detailed stroke order diagrams, an attractive user-friendly design, and appendixes that give a wealth of reference information distinguish this as the most in-depth Japanese-English character dictionary ever compiled.

COVERAGE AND SOURCES

This dictionary offers a detailed treatment of the meanings and functions of the most frequently used kanji in present-day Japanese, with particular emphasis on contemporary usage and newspapers. It contains 4408 main entry characters and approximately 65,000 senses for some 50,000 words, word elements, and illustrative examples.

Entry Characters The entries include (1) the 2136 characters in the official **Jōyō Kanji** list, which are widely used in the media and education, (2) the 861 characters in the official **Jinmei Kanji** list, used in names, (3) 345 non-jōyō and radical entries, (3) 1066 nonstandard forms, and (4) 1050 **cross-reference** entries. These cover more than 99% of the most frequently used characters, which is adequate for meeting the needs of the serious learner.

Compound Words Our general approach in selecting **compound words** has been to include the ones most useful to the user, based on the following criteria:

1. High-frequency compounds based on statistics compiled by the National Language Research Institute in the official survey **A Study of Uses of Chinese Characters in Modern Newspapers.**
2. All compounds normally written in kanji that are listed in **Ten Thousand Graded Japanese Words** (一万語語彙分類集), published by Senmon Kyōiku Shuppan.
3. Thousands of additional compounds necessary for illustrating the meanings of (1) the new characters

added to the revised **Jōyō Kanji** and **Jinmei Kanji** and (2) the many characters not in those lists.
4. Numerous other compounds, including rare ones, useful to intermediate and advanced learners, selected on the basis of their ability to illustrate the entry character's meaning.

In principle, the above criteria ensure that all high-frequency words and word elements important to the learner are covered. However, to keep the dictionary from getting too bulky, the following limitations were applied:

1. Kanji can be combined to form countless compound words by affixation. Only typical examples of these innumerable compounds (e.g., 校正済 こうせいずみ 'proofreading completed' from 校正 + 済) are given, since it is easy to infer their meanings.
2. Many nouns are turned into verbs by adding する, into adjectival nouns by adding な, into adverbs by adding に, and so on. The part of speech selected was based on importance and on its ability to illustrate the entry character's meaning.

This policy is sometimes misunderstood by those who compare dictionaries on the basis of the number of words included. Let it be clear: the primary emphasis has been on completeness in terms of quality, rather than comprehensiveness in terms of quantity; that is, to include compounds that directly contribute to an understanding of character meaning.

Character Readings The following types of **character readings** are given:

1. All **approved readings** (those in the Jōyō Kanji list) and their derivatives when necessary.
2. **Unapproved readings** (those not in the Jōyō Kanji list), including many rare ones.
3. **Name readings,** used exclusively in proper names.
4. Numerous common as well as many rare readings for characters not in the Jōyō Kanji list.

An important feature of this dictionary is the descriptive approach it takes to the selection of readings, which includes validating occurrences in the living language while avoiding the common practice of including readings merely on the authority of sources. For example, though various dictionaries claim that 茄 has the *on* reading ケ, this is nothing more than a historical ghost copied from outdated dictionaries. On the other hand, we have included readings, such as マン for 幡 and ジャン for 雀, that rarely if ever appear in dictionaries but are actually frequently used in contemporary Japanese.

Character Meanings The analysis of character meanings was inseparably linked to the analysis of kanji synonyms. As Ladislav Zgusta, the world-renowned authority on lexicography, has pointed out, the lexicographer cannot really know the precise meaning of a word unless it is examined in comparison and in contrast with its near-synonyms. In this dictionary, the analysis of kanji synonyms was firmly based on such a policy, which served as a powerful technique for establishing character meanings of high precision and clarity.

An important contribution of this dictionary is that it lists many compounds and character meanings, and sometimes even readings, that have never appeared in *any* character dictionary, including comprehensive dictionaries for native speakers. For example, character dictionaries report that 雀 means 'sparrow' and has an *on* reading of ジャク and a *kun* reading of すずめ. In actual fact, 雀 is frequently used in the sense of 'mahjong' in compounds such as 雀卓 じゃんたく 'mahjong board' and 雀荘 じゃんそう 'mahjong club'. Neither the reading ジャン, nor the meaning 'mahjong', nor any of these compounds are recorded in any of several dozen dictionaries that were surveyed in the late 1980s. In another survey conducted a quarter of a century later (late 2012), we have still not found a single dictionary that lists 'mahjong' as a meaning for 雀.

COMPILATION METHODS

There are two traditions in dictionary-making: the *prescriptive* approach, which aims to establish standards of proper usage, and the *descriptive* approach, which aims to objectively report what established usage is. Unlike most previous works, this dictionary is committed to the descriptive approach and modern linguistic theory. It aims to record usage as it actually occurs in the living language, not to report the results of previous works (though in the case of archaic meanings this is not always possible).

The compilation project was carried out through an interdisciplinary effort under the guidance of Japanese-language scholars from the United States and Japan. Great pains have been taken to ensure accuracy and clarity, while paying careful attention to detail. Each meaning was written afresh, the result of an exhaustive semantic analysis, using such techniques as componential analysis and the study of near-synonyms.

Although statistical data and other dictionaries served as our guidelines, the final authority in the selection of an item was the evidence of the living language itself. This has led to some very interesting results. For example, we have found that the heavy reliance of existing character dictionaries and textbooks on classical Chinese sources has resulted in their inclusion of many old and archaic meanings, while newer meanings are often inaccurate or totally missing.

The extensive use of computational lexicography at every stage of the compilation process has ensured a high level of accuracy and the implementation of editorial policy in a consistent manner.

HISTORY OF PROJECT

Years of struggling with self-study using traditional methods of rote memorization inspired the editor in chief to embark upon the compilation of a new dictionary based on a systematic approach. He began the work with the help of two assistants while residing in Kobe in 1974. Lack of funds brought the project to a halt several times. In 1980 a donation by Konosuke Matsushita enabled the project to proceed in earnest. This was followed by grants from Showa Women's University and many private individuals and organizations. The editor then joined the Institute of Modern Culture at Showa Women's University as a research fellow, and for several years the university provided financial assistance.

The first edition of this dictionary, the **New Japanese-English Character Dictionary** (NJECD), was published by Kenkyusha in 1990, and soon became established as a standard reference work for the study of kanji. This revised edition was published in 2013 by Kodansha USA under the current title, **The Kodansha Kanji Dictionary** (KKD).

The compilation project cost over two million U.S. dollars (which excludes publisher's expenses such as printing, marketing, and distribution) and required nearly 100 man-years to complete. In all, some 120 persons have contributed in one way or another to the completion of this project over a period of nearly twenty years.

Scholars well versed in Chinese, Japanese, and English linguistics, experienced lexicographers, as well as other experts have directly contributed to the accuracy of its contents, and Japanese-language authorities in the U.S. and Japan have confirmed its scholarly accuracy and lent their enthusiastic support and recommendations.

The dictionary project has also benefited from the support of various government organs, educational organizations, and government officials such as Japan's former prime minister Yasuhiro Nakasone, the Japan Foundation, the National Council on Educational Reform, the National Institute for Japanese Language and Linguistics, the Board of the Association for Japanese-Language Teaching, the Society for Teaching Japanese as a Foreign Language, and the National Language Society of Japan.

KANJI INTEGRATED TOOLS

The first edition of this dictionary (NJECD) was the first step in a series of computer-edited dictionaries and software applications for the study of kanji known as the **Kanji Integrated Tools** (KIT). The KIT project was first launched with the establishment of the **Kanji Dictionary Publishing Society** (KDPS) in 1993 under the auspices of the Institute of Modern Culture at Showa Women's University. The Society, headed by Showa Women's University president Professor Kusuo Hitomi, was financed by the university and other organizations. It was directed by the Editorial Committee, which included Japanese-language education specialists such as Professor Osamu Mizutani, the former president of the Society for Teaching Japanese as a Foreign Language.

The use of the latest computational lexicography techniques ensures that all KIT dictionaries and applications are tightly integrated and of consistent quality. KIT derivatives spread over a wide range, including teaching and learning aids such as learner's dictionaries, electronic dictionaries, and iOS applications. To date, the following dictionaries have been published:

1.	New Japanese-English Character Dictionary	NJECD	Kenkyusha	1990	Japanese market edition
2.	New Japanese-English Character Dictionary	NJECD-NTC	NTC	1993	international edition
3.	New Japanese-English Character Dictionary	NJECD-EB	Nichigai Associates	1995	electronic book edition
4.	The Kodansha Kanji Learner's Dictionary	KALD	Kodansha International	1999	learner's edition

5.	The Kodansha Kanji Learner's Dictionary	KALD-ED	CASIO	2007	electronic dictionary edition
6.	Japanese-Romanian Gakushu Kanji Dictionary	KALD-RM	Polirom	2008	Romanian edition
7.	The Kodansha Kanji Learner's Dictionary for iOS	iKALD	The CJK Dictionary Institute	2012	iOS edition
8.	The Kodansha Kanji Learner's Dictionary	KKLD	Kodansha USA	2013	revised and expanded
9.	The Kodansha Kanji Dictionary	KKD	Kodansha USA	2013	new edition of NJECD
10.	The Kodansha Kanji Learner's Dictionary	iKKLD	The CJK Dictionary Institute	2013	iOS edition of KKLD
11.	The Kodansha Kanji Dictionary	iKKD	The CJK Dictionary Institute	2013	iOS edition of KKD

In the next phase, a series of foreign-language editions, such as Portuguese, Spanish, German, French, and Indonesian editions of this dictionary, will be published, as well as other useful learning aids such as smartphone applications will be developed (see www.kanji.org for details).

Through these activities, we aim to offer a comprehensive solution to the diverse needs of learners, educators, and researchers. We invite scholars around the world to contribute to this ongoing effort.

FEATURES OF THIS DICTIONARY
本字典の特徴

Below is a description of the principal features of this dictionary, with emphasis on how they are useful to the learner. See the **Introduction** on p. 19a for a discussion of the dictionary's aims. To derive maximum benefit from the dictionary, consult also the **Guide to the Dictionary** on p. 41a, which describes the entry format in detail and supplements the information here.

1 UNDERSTANDING

The learner of Japanese must not only become familiar with the complex shapes and many readings of numerous characters, but must also understand their meanings as independent words and as components of compound words. Although this dictionary serves as an effective tool for looking up unknown words and characters, it does not aim to be a mere lookup tool. Of equal importance is the in-depth manner in which it treats meaning.

Past works have largely limited their treatment to character forms, readings, and compound words, whereas this dictionary includes many unique features that enable the user to gain a full, systematic understanding of the meanings and functions of each character.

1.1 Core Meaning

1.1.1 Concise English Keyword A striking feature of this dictionary is the presentation of a **core meaning** for each entry character. This is a concise keyword that provides a clear grasp of the central or most fundamental concept that links the principal senses of a character into a single conceptual unit.

Consider **KEEP**, one of the core meanings of 留:

▶KEEP
❶ cause to remain in a given place or condition:
　ⓐ **KEEP in place, keep from moving, keep in position**
　ⓑ **KEEP in custody, detain**
　ⓒ **KEEP for future use, leave behind**

By grasping that the central concept represented by 留 is **KEEP**, one can immediately see that such seemingly unrelated ideas as "keep in place" and "detain" are merely variants of the same basic concept. The core meaning thus *integrates* widely differing senses into a single conceptual unit.

The core meaning is useful to the learner in five ways:

1. It serves as a concise keyword that conveys the character's most fundamental meaning.
2. It acts as the central pivot that links the principal meanings of a character to each other.
3. It provides an instant grasp of the meaning and function of the character as a word-building element.
4. It helps illustrate the differences and similarities between *kun* homophones and easily confused characters.
5. It is easy to memorize, since it conveys a character's meaning as a concise thought package.

A brief glance at the character meanings makes the above relationships clear, thanks to the use of **CAPITAL** letters both for the core meanings and for the **core words** (words in a character meaning that correspond to a core meaning).

The core meaning is unique to the **Kanji Integrated Tools** (KIT). Since it functions as a concentrated thought package that appeals to the learner's powers of association, it is widely praised by students and educators as an effective learning aid.

1.1.2 Linguistic Background Because of the very important role that the core meaning plays as a feature of this dictionary, it may be of interest to the user to know some of the underlying theoretical principles.

The core meaning is often the direct, psychologically most dominant meaning—the meaning that might occur to a native speaker if presented with the character in isolation. It is a psychological unit, a basic notion of a character's meaning that conveys, in the famous linguist Edward Sapir's words, its "conceptual kernel." Linguistically, it is not normally possible to isolate any sense of a word or character that will make it possible to derive all its other senses. Often, it is not even possible to trace the origin of each sense historically and show how the individual senses relate to the character's original meaning. The core meaning is thus not necessarily the original meaning of the character, though it often is.

The core meanings were established by performing an exhaustive analysis of the lexical meaning and word-building function of each character. Each meaning component was carefully analyzed and compared with those of the other members of the same synonym group in order to determine the most precise English term that conveys the meaning, function, and subtle nuances in contrast with those of other closely related characters.

The core meaning for a given character may be viewed as the center of a circle representing that word's area of meaning. One or more other circles represent the areas of meaning of the words or word elements that can be written with that character, as illustrated below.

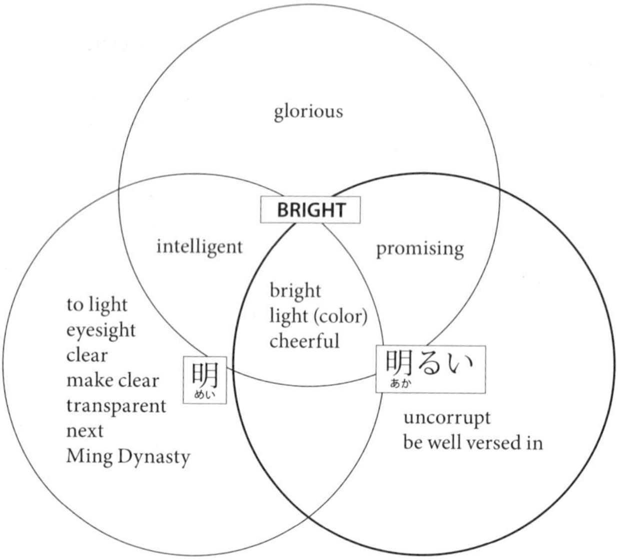

The core meaning is often given by the English word (as *bright*) for which the area of overlap of the circles is greatest. Although the meanings of a Japanese word (as 明るい あかるい) or word element (as 明 めい) may differ from the core meaning in various details, the central concept they represent is essentially the same, as can be seen in the illustration above.

1.2 In-Depth Meanings

A central feature of this dictionary is the in-depth manner in which it treats meaning. Not only are the character meanings clear, complete, and accurate, but they include meanings found only in KIT dictionaries.

The principal features that contribute to clarity of meaning are:

1. The core meaning.
2. Clear and accurate character meanings.
3. The ordering of senses in a manner that shows their interrelatedness.
4. Numerous illustrative compounds.

The precisely worded character meanings are presented in a manner that shows exactly how each character is used as a word element, and how the hundreds of thousands of compound words in Japanese can be generated from a stock of a few thousand building blocks.

1.3 Interrelatedness

To provide the learner with a clear understanding of character meaning, the meanings are presented in a manner that shows the **interrelatedness** between individual senses. Four features achieve this aim:

1. The capitalized **core words** make the relation between senses instantly obvious.
2. The **senses are ordered** in a manner that shows their interrelatedness.

3. The **sense division numbers** establish a logical hierarchy between character senses.
4. The **explanatory glosses** (e.g., "(of a vehicle)") show how the senses differ from one another, while the **supplementary glosses** (e.g., "—said esp. of God") provide additional discrimination.

Together these features help integrate the senses so that they can be perceived as a structured unit, rather than as an arbitrary list.

1.4 Order of Senses

Unlike traditional dictionaries, which usually order senses chronologically, this dictionary presents the senses in a **cogent order that shows their interrelatedness.** The core meaning serves as the basis of organization, and the various senses are grouped around it in clusters so that they can be perceived as a logically structured, psychologically integrated unit.

留, for example, has several distinct senses, but they are clustered around the core word **KEEP** in a way that shows their differences and similarities, greatly reducing the burden of memorization. If the senses were arranged as shown in the left column below, they would appear to be an arbitrary list, rather than a structured unit.

Arbitrary List	**Expansion from Core**
ⓐ keep from moving	**KEEP** in place
ⓑ detain	**KEEP** in custody
ⓒ leave behind	**KEEP** for future use

1.5 Degree of Importance

The **degree of importance** of each sense is indicated by typographical differences and labels for four levels of study (see **§17.3** on p. 50a for details). This enables beginner, intermediate, and advanced learners to use the dictionary with equal facility.

1.6 Glosses

In order to improve the user's understanding of character meanings, the English equivalents are often accompanied by **explanatory glosses,** which further clarify the meanings, as well as **supplementary glosses,** which supplement the equivalent by restricting its range of application, by describing its grammatical function, and so on. See **§17.4** on p. 50a and **§17.6** on p. 51a for details.

1.7 Compounds and Examples

The meanings of each character are normally illustrated by numerous high-frequency compounds that provide useful examples of each sense. All the compounds needed for the intermediate level, and numerous compounds for the advanced level, are given.

Unlike in other dictionaries, the compounds are classified by meaning in a way that clearly shows how they are formed from their constituent parts, which makes it easy to infer the meanings of unlisted compounds.

A new feature of this revised edition is the **subsense indicators,** which are tiny letters that show the beginning of a new subsense group in the compounds list. This makes it obvious how the entry character contributes its meaning to each compound.

Another useful feature of this dictionary is that it often lists compounds in which the entry character does not appear in the initial position, as 演奏 under 奏. This helps the user understand the word-building function of the entry character in a variety of contexts.

1.8 Compound Formation

The formation of a compound word is normally self-evident from the manner in which the compounds are grouped by meaning (**§1.7**). When the relationship between the components of a compound is not clear, a literal translation of the compound is sometimes given in parentheses, e.g., 忘年会 **ぼうねんかい** 'year-end party' ("forget-the-year party"). When a more detailed explanation is required, a **compound formation article** describes the etymology (origin or development) of the compound and/or explains how its constituent characters contribute to the meaning of the whole. This helps the user get a better understanding of the word-formation function of kanji, and also provides interesting sidelights on the historical circumstances that gave rise to the concept represented by the word.

1.9 Discriminating Synonyms

1.9.1 Kanji Synonyms The words of a language form a closely linked network of interdependent units. The meaning of a word or expression cannot really be understood unless its relationships with other closely related words are taken into account. In English, for example, such words as *kill, murder,* and *execute* share the meaning of 'put to death', but they differ considerably in usage and connotation. The ability to distinguish between such words not only allows one to gain a fuller understanding of their individual shades of meaning, but also helps one write with greater clarity and precision.

A special feature of this dictionary, presented for the first time in the first edition, is the complete guidance it offers for the precise distinctions between **kanji synonyms,** or characters of similar meaning. Since a proper understanding of the meanings of each character is essential for the effective mastery of the Japanese vocabulary, this will be of considerable benefit to the serious student. The kanji synonyms serve as a powerful learning aid for the following reasons:

1. They show the differences and similarities between closely related characters.
2. They act as a network of cross-references for quickly locating any synonym group member.
3. They act as a simple kanji thesaurus.
4. They provide the educator with a valuable source of reference data.

1.9.2 Powerful Learning Aid The SYNONYMS headwords show how the members of a synonym group *resemble* each other, while the keywords show how they *differ* from each other. Together, they serve as a powerful learning tool. Let us see how this helps the learner gain an in-depth understanding of the character 破:

破
1478

COMPOUNDS

❶ⓐ [original meaning] **BREAK, smash**
ⓑ **BREAK through, penetrate**

a 破壊する はかいする break (down), destroy, wreck
破片 はへん fragment, broken piece, scrap
破損 はそん damage, breakdown
破砕する はさいする crush, smash, crack to pieces
破滅 はめつ ruin, destruction, wreck, collapse, downfall
爆破 ばくは blasting, blowing up, explosion
難破 なんぱ shipwreck
打破する だはする break down, overthrow, abolish

b 突破する とっぱする break [smash] through; surmount; exceed
看破する かんぱする see through, penetrate, read (another's thoughts)
⋮

❷ **BREAK the enemy, defeat**
撃破する げきはする defeat, rout; destroy
論破する ろんぱする refute, defeat in argument
連破する れんぱする defeat one's enemy in succession

SYNONYMS

❶ⓐ **break**
破 BREAK → 1478
拉ぐ crush → 0372
崩 CRUMBLE → 2863
挫 SPRAIN → 0519
壊 BREAK DOWN → 0934
毀す break down → 2246
折 BREAK OFF → 0297
割る crack → 2284
裂 SPLIT → 3331
砕 CRUSH UP → 1458
摧 CRUSH UP → 0849
潰す CRUSH → 0919

ⓑ **penetrate**
透 PASS THROUGH → 3854
貫 PENETRATE → 3112
破 break through → 1478
滲 PERMEATE → 0862

As illustrated above, the core meaning and English equivalents show that the central concept represented by 破 is **BREAK.** Referring to sense ❶ⓐ of the SYNONYMS section, which corresponds to sense ❶ⓐ of the COMPOUNDS section, we find the headword **break,** which indicates the meaning *shared* by the group members. By comparing the individual keywords, such as 壊 BREAK DOWN and 折 BREAK OFF, we can see how they *differ* from each other.

To gain an even deeper understanding of the subtle differences in meaning, turn to the entries indicated by the arrow → and compare the character meanings and illustrative compounds for each group member with each other. This will show that, for example, whereas 破 means to break in general, 折 implies the application of a sudden force to such things as branches and bones, 崩 denotes breaking into small pieces, and so on.

Studying the meanings of closely related characters together, rather than as isolated units, provides a good understanding of their distinctive features and stimulates interest, thus increasing learning effectiveness. Moreover, the kanji synonyms help the student write with greater precision.

1.9.3 Simple Kanji Thesaurus The SYNONYMS sections and **Appendix 13. List of Kanji Synonym Groups** make it possible to use this dictionary as a **simple kanji thesaurus.** This helps the user find characters from their meanings. For example, to find characters related to *break,* consult the entries in the SYNONYMS section for 破 or under **break** in Appendix 13, where such synonyms as 砕 CRUSH UP and 崩 CRUMBLE can be found.

2 READING

The student learning how to read contemporary Japanese faces several difficulties, such as the need to identify thousands of characters, many of which have complex shapes, as well as the need to learn their numerous readings and meanings.

In addition to being a learner's dictionary, this work also has been designed as a *reader's* dictionary. The various features described below enable the reader to locate the readings and meanings of unknown characters and compounds with little effort.

2.1 Efficient Indexing System

The lack of an efficient scheme for ordering kanji has long been a source of frustration to learners and native speakers alike. Looking up characters by traditional radicals, or by most alternative systems, is both laborious and unreliable.

A major feature of this dictionary, unique to KIT dictionaries, is the speed and facility with which entries can be looked up. The **System of Kanji Indexing by Patterns** (SKIP) classifies each character under four easy-to-identify geometrical patterns: ◧**1** left-right, ⬒**2** up-down, ☐**3** enclosure, and ■**4** solid. Within each group the characters are further subdivided to achieve maximum access speed.

Designed for efficiency and ease of use, SKIP enables the user to locate entries as quickly and as accurately as in alphabetical dictionaries. Since the system can be learned by beginners in a short time, many Japanese-language educators consider it an important advance in kanji lexicography, and a growing number of electronic dictionaries have implemented it as part of their retrieval systems.

2.2 Six Lookup Methods

To assure maximum convenience to the user, this dictionary provides a choice of six methods of looking up characters:

1. The **Pattern Index** allows characters to be quickly located from their SKIP numbers (p. 2014).
2. The **Scan Method** is a shortcut for locating some characters almost instantly (p. 1798).
3. The **On-Kun Index** lists the characters in *a-i-u-e-o* order (五十音順) by both their *on* and *kun* readings (p. 1945).
4. The **Radical Index** lists the characters by their traditional radicals (p. 1988).
5. The **List of Kanji Synonym Groups** (Appendix 13) enables the user to find characters from their meanings (p. 1875).
6. The **Direct Method** allows characters to be located without using any index (p. 1797).

2.3 System of Guides

The various guides in the margins of the page have been carefully designed to facilitate the speedy location of entry characters.

2.4 Character Readings

A distinctive feature of Japanese is that each character has one or more **readings.** This refers to one of several sequences of speech sounds associated with a character; that is, to the Chinese-derived pronunciation, or *on* reading, and the native Japanese pronunciation, or *kun* reading. See **§2.3** on p. 1776 for details.

行 **コウ ギョウ アン い(く) ゆ(く) -ゆ(き) -ゆき**
0246 **-い(き) -いき おこな(う)** ㊔ やす なみ なめ
つら みち たか

Seven kinds of readings are given: principal readings, *on* readings, *kun* readings, special readings, unapproved readings, name readings, and Chinese readings. These are presented in a logical order by type of reading and degree of importance, with various symbols and typefaces to distinguish approved readings from unapproved ones, *on* from *kun,* and other categories.

This dictionary presents all contemporary readings, including approved and unapproved ones, as well as readings used only in names and important historical and archaic ones when necessary. The coverage is adequate for the advanced learner or scholar reading contemporary, classical, or technical texts.

See **§3 Character Readings** on p. 42a for details.

2.5 Character Forms and Styles

This dictionary presents several types of character forms and one calligraphic style, methodically checked by experts to ensure their accuracy.

1. The **standard form** is the form given in the official **Jōyō Kanji** and **Jinmei Kanji** lists, which are widely used in the media, government, and education.
2. The **nonstandard form** is the traditional variant used in prewar literature and in names. **Appendix 12** lists 390 variant forms, including important variants of Jinmei Kanji and all variants appearing in the Jōyō Kanji list.

3. The **Chinese form** is the official simplified Chinese form(s) used in the People's Republic of China.
4. The **square style** (楷書 かいしょ), given in the last frame of the stroke-order diagram, is the standard calligraphic style used in handwriting.

For the sake of the advanced user, the coverage of character forms is quite extensive (though not exhaustive), rendering this dictionary fully adequate for reading both contemporary and classical Japanese. The Chinese form is useful for learners of Chinese and for reference.

2.6 Easily Confused Forms

Some characters, such as 幣 へい 'currency' and 弊 へい 'evil practice', are very similar in form but unrelated in meaning. Some of these are so similar that even native speakers tend to confuse them. Such characters are cross-referenced to each other in the NOTE section. A new feature of this revised edition is that these characters are followed by their core meanings, which aids the user to easily grasp their differences.

2.7 Kana and Romanization

In the first edition of this dictionary, all character readings and Japanese words were transcribed in the Hepburn system of romanization (a description of kana and romanization is given in **Appendix 5. Kana and Romanization**). Times have changed and the use of kana has become the norm. In this revised edition, all readings, headwords, and compounds are given in kana.

2.8 Stroke Counting

The ability to count strokes accurately helps the user (1) write the characters correctly, (2) use the SKIP system effectively, and (3) look up characters in other character dictionaries based on radicals or stroke-count. The following information is provided:

1. **Stroke-count data** is given for each entry character.
2. The principles of stroke counting are explained in **Appendix 3. How to Count Strokes,** along with charts to help speed up the counting process.
3. Difficult-to-count characters are cross-referenced at common *incorrect* stroke-count locations.

2.9 Cross-Reference Network

An extensive **network of cross-references** directs the user to a wealth of information useful to both the learner and the educator. This includes cross-references to synonyms, homophones, variant forms, compound formation and usage articles, orthographic variants, incorrect SKIP locations, and more. See also **§21 Cross-Reference Entries** on p. 54a.

3 WRITING

The student learning how to write Japanese faces several difficulties, such as the large number of characters and their complex shapes, the need to learn the correct stroke order, a high degree of orthographic variation, and the large number of easily confused homophones. In addition to being a reader's dictionary, this work has also been designed to serve as a *writer's* dictionary. The features that make it a convenient tool for writing are described below.

3.1 Stroke-Order Diagrams

To write a character in the proper form, it is necessary to learn the stroke order. The **stroke-order diagrams,** in which the last frame shows the full character in the standard square style, indicate the stroke order.

The stroke-order diagrams were thoroughly checked for accuracy. Unlike in other reference works, which rely heavily on cross-referencing, the order of writing is presented stroke by stroke to ensure maximum convenience to the user.

3.2 Discriminating Homophones

3.2.1 *Kun* Homophones Japanese has numerous ***kun* homophones.** These are *kun* words that are pronounced the same but written differently, and that usually differ in meaning, as shown below.

上る	**のぼる**	go up (steps, a hill)
登る	**のぼる**	climb, scale
昇る	**のぼる**	ascend, rise (up to the sky)

Writing in Japanese often involves uncertainty over orthography. Although *on* homophones, such as 機構 きこう 'mechanism' and 帰港 きこう 'returning to the harbor', are very common, they are not likely to be confused since each character conveys a distinct meaning.

On the other hand, *kun* homophones are easily confused, even by native speakers, and pose special problems to the learner. Not only can each character have many *kun* readings, but many *kun* words can be written with a bewildering variety of characters. Unlike *on* homophones, many *kun* homophones are close or even identical in meaning. Often the differences may be subtle and a source of confusion.

For example, 解ける and 溶ける (**とける**) are interchangeable in the sense of 'melt, thaw' but not in the sense of 'come loose', which is always written 解ける. On the other hand, 柔らかい and 軟らかい (**やわらかい**) both have identical meanings. The concept of homophones in Japanese is not unlike variant spellings of such English words as *judgment* and *judgement*, which are identical in meaning.

Because of these complications, students learning how to write Japanese are often at a loss when attempting to select a character for a particular context. Unfortunately, dictionaries sometimes disagree with each other on how to differentiate between *kun* homophones, and in some cases they confuse the user by lumping the meanings of a group of homophones into a single entry with no indication of how to differentiate between them.

3.2.2 Usage Notes To help the serious student overcome the special problems posed by homophones in Japanese, this dictionary provides complete guidance on the differences between the vast majority of one-character *kun* homophones in current use. Since homophones are a source of confusion to Japanese and non-Japanese alike, this feature should prove to be of great value to the student.

丘
4307

USAGE

【おか】

丘
[sometimes also 岡] hill, hillock, mound

岡
① [usu. 丘] hill, hillock, mound
② [sometimes also 傍-] [in compounds] outsider, third party, bystander

陸
land, shore

傍-
[usu. 岡] outsider, third party, bystander

★丘 and 岡 have the same meaning. The former is used in both common nouns and place names, while the latter is used chiefly in the writing of proper names.

HOMOPHONES

おか
岡 HILL →3719
陸 LAND →0659
傍 BESIDE →0166

The **usage note** conveniently brings together, in a single entry, the meanings for every member of a homophone group, along with other information that helps deepen understanding. As can be seen from the above example, by comparing the English equivalents the user can accurately grasp the differences and similarities in shades of meaning and in usage between easily confused homophones.

The usage notes, a special feature of this dictionary, show precisely in which sense each homophone is used. They not only provide a better understanding of the often subtle differences between easily confused homophones, but also help the learner write with greater precision.

In addition, the usage notes present all kinds of useful information. This includes **orthographic labels** that show the interchangeability between orthographic variants (e.g., 丘 and 岡 in the sense of 'hill'), occasional **illustrative examples** that further clarify the differences between easily confused homophones, and **supplementary notes** (preceded by ★) that provide additional information. Referring to the **cross-references** in the HOMOPHONES section enables the user to gain a deeper understanding by studying the compounds and examples for each homophone.

3.2.3 Cross-References To help the user locate homophones quickly, the HOMOPHONES section lists groups of homophones and their entry numbers. These act as a network of cross-references for quickly identifying and locating each member of a group from any of the others.

A new feature of this edition is that homophone cross-references are followed by their core meaning, which allows the user to immediately identify their differences without consulting the corresponding entry character. By using these cross-references to compare the meanings and compounds for each homophone, the user can grasp the often subtle differences between them.

See also **§14 Homophones Section** on p. 48a for details.

3.3 Discriminating Variants

An important characteristic of the Japanese script is its variable orthography. For example, 先 is interchangeable with 尖 in such compounds as 尖兵 (=先兵) せんぺい 'advance detachment', but not in 先頭 せんとう 'forefront'. Two or more characters that are partially or completely interchangeable in this manner are referred to as **orthographic variants.** One is normally the phonetically *replaced* character (尖) while the second is the phonetic *replacement* character (先).

An important feature of this dictionary is the special attention it pays to discriminating between orthographic variants. This is particularly useful to the advanced student, since a knowledge of orthographic variants helps write with greater precision. The **orthographic labels** indicate the degree and type of orthographic variation, as illustrated below.

箱 3362 【はこ 箱】
①ⓐ [sometimes also 函] [also suffix] **BOX, case, chest, bin**
ⓑ counter for **BOX**es
⋮
② *slang* railway car
⋮
③ *slang* shamisen

函 3724 【はこ 函】 [now usu. 箱] **BOX**, case, mailbox

The orthographic labels serve three purposes:

1. To indicate the degree of interchangeability between orthographic variants (e.g., [sometimes also 函] versus [now usu. 箱] above).
2. To specify the sense(s) in which the orthographic variants are interchangeable. In the above illustration, 箱 and 函 are interchangeable in the sense of 'box'.
3. To serve as a cross-reference to the orthographic variants of the entry character, enabling the user to study their differences and similarities.

The meanings and format of the orthographic labels, which are mostly self-explanatory, are explained in detail in **§19.1 Orthographic Labels** on p. 52a.

3.4 *Okurigana* Endings

The *kun* readings in the entry-head data include parentheses that indicate ***okurigana*** endings in conformity with the official rules published by the Ministry of Education, Culture, Sports, Science and Technology, as explained in **Appendix 6.** The headwords and compounds also follow these rules when applicable. Important nonstandard variations are sometimes given.

4 OTHER FEATURES

4.1 Character Importance

The **degree of importance** of the entry character is indicated in various ways. This enables the user to know the relative importance of each character, and helps the teacher compile graded lessons.

1. The **frequency ranking** is given for each entry character. This is the relative frequency of occurrence of a character based on a survey conducted by the Agency for Cultural Affairs in 2010 (see p. 1850 for details).
2. The **grade** indicates the entry type (such as Jōyō Kanji or Jinmei Kanji) and the school grade during which the character is taught. A grade of 1 to 6 indicates a character in the 1006 **Education Kanji** taught in the six elementary school grades.
3. **Appendix 10** lists the top 1000 characters by **frequency ranking,** along with their core meanings. This is useful to both the learner and the teacher.

4.2 Reference Data

The dictionary presents reference and classification information of practical value to the user. This includes the frequency ranking, the character code (Unicode), the stroke count, the radical, and the grade. See p. 44a for details.

4.3 System of Labels

Existing character dictionaries and textbooks often include obsolete, archaic, and rare meanings without any indication to that effect. This dictionary provides a system of labels that indicate the temporal status, etymology, orthography, style, function, level of formality, etc., for each sense. These labels clearly distinguish basic and frequent meanings from rare and archaic ones, and provide the user with practical guidance on the style and usage associated with each sense. The various labels are described in **§19 Labels** on p. 52a.

4.4 Linguistic Functions

Each character may have various grammatical or syntactic **functions.** An important function of kanji is their role as **word elements;** that is, their ability to form numerous compound words by being combined with each other. Words can be formed by adding an **affix** (suffix or prefix) to a base, or by joining **combining forms** with each other. For example, -済 **-ずみ** 'completed' is attached to 点検 **てんけん** 'inspection' to yield 点検済 **てんけんずみ** 'inspection completed'. Kanji also function as **free forms,** which are words used independently. These terms are explained in **§17.7** on p. 51a.

Affixes, combining forms, and free forms can be combined with each other in various ways, the most important of which are shown below.

combining form + combining form	外 + 人 → 外人
combining form + free form	来 + 年 → 来年
free form + suffix	外国 + 人 → 外国人
prefix + free form	明 + 年度 → 明年度
free form + free form	日本 + 料理 → 日本料理

Note that free forms, combining forms, and affixes are basically distinct functional categories, but a character in any given sense may act in more than one of these capacities. In addition, the dictionary indicates other functions such as abbreviations, function words, counters, units, titles, numerals, phonetic substitutes, and symbols.

A distinctive feature of this dictionary is the indication of the function of each character meaning. A system of labels and the entry layout clearly distinguish the meanings of free forms from the meanings of word elements, as well as other categories. It is worth noting that this is the first dictionary offering a detailed analysis in English of the word-building function of one-character *kun* words and word elements, resulting from several years of conducting a full-scale analysis of how these homophones are used.

The indication of word-formation function in this dictionary is quite useful to the learner. Understanding the role of each character in the formation of compound words not only makes it possible to learn new words more effectively, but also allows one to infer the meanings of compound words not listed in the dictionary.

4.5 Character Etymology

This dictionary presents the following information on radicals and character etymology.

1. The **radical** and **radical number** are given for each entry character. Since radicals often function as semantic components, this aids in understanding the character's etymology, and is also useful for looking up characters in other dictionaries.
2. The RADICAL section describes the function of the entry character as a radical, giving such details as the radical number, standard and variant forms, and description of the radical's meaning and function. See **§7 Radical Section** on p. 44a for details.
3. The traditional radicals of **lost-radical** characters are given in the **Radical Index.**
4. The **Quick Reference Radical Chart** gives convenient access to information on radicals, including the parent and variant forms, stroke-counts, and radical names.
5. The **original meaning,** which is the first meaning associated with a character after its formation in China (or rarely Japan), is often given, especially when it helps clarify the character's meaning.
6. The **nonstandard forms** include the traditional form, which is the older form from which the standard form is derived.

4.6 User-Friendliness

Another feature of this dictionary is a layout that is visually attractive. Typographical design with the aid of cutting-edge typesetting technology was employed to achieve a harmonious blend of font styles and weights using Adobe's InDesign software (Adobe's Myriad and Minion fonts were used for English and Kozuka Mincho for Japanese). Some of the world's leading font designers have contributed to this effort, which has resulted in an aesthetically pleasing design that stimulates a desire to browse and explore.

EXPLANATORY CHART

凡 例 図 表

The **Explanatory Chart** shows the various parts of the character entry. The lightface numerals refer to the section numbers of the **Guide to the Dictionary** on p. 41a, where the format of each section is explained in detail.

ENTRIES AND GUIDES

1	entry number guide	1.1-1
2	page number guide	1.1-2
3	SKIP number guide	1.1-3
4	entry character	1.3
5	entry number	1.5
6	SKIP number	1.6

CORE MEANINGS

7	core meanings	2

CHARACTER READINGS

8	principal reading	3-1
9	*on* readings	3-2
10	*kun* readings	3-3
11	unapproved readings	3-5
12	name readings	3-6
13	Chinese reading	3-7
14	special reading	3-4

CHARACTER FORMS AND STYLES

15	standard form	4-1
16	nonstandard forms	4-2
17	Chinese form	4-3
18	*kokuji*	4-3
19	square style	4-4

REFERENCE DATA BOX

20	radical	5-1
21	grade	5-2
22	Unicode	5-3
23	strokes	5-4
24	frequency ranking	5-5

STROKE-ORDER DIAGRAM

25	stroke-order diagram	6

RADICAL SECTION

26	parent radical	7

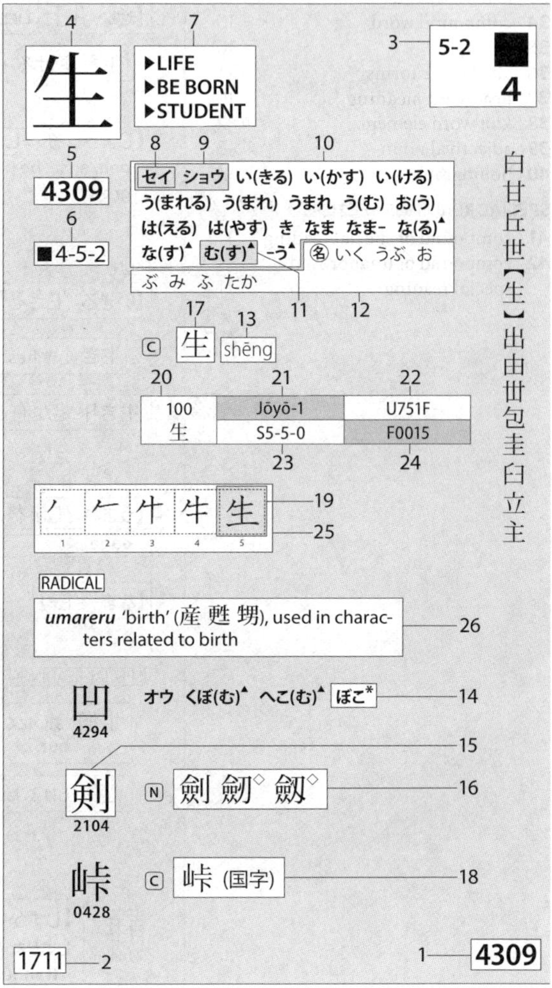

COMPOUNDS SECTION		
27	character meanings	8
28	compound word	8
INDEPENDENT SECTION		
29	INDEPENDENT headword	9
30	headword meaning	9
31	example	9
32	alternative reading	9
KUN SECTION		
33	KUN headword	10
34	compound word	10
35	example	10
36	alternative forms	10-1
37	headword meaning	10
38	*kun* word element	10-2
39	adjectival noun	10-3
40	homograph	10-4
SPECIAL READINGS SECTION		
41	compound of special reading	11
42	compound of unapproved special reading	11

COMPOUNDS

❶ⓐ (act of being alive) **LIFE, existence** — 27
ⓑ (interval between birth and death) **LIFEtime, life**

a 生命 せいめい life — 28

INDEPENDENT

29 30

【せい 生】 **LIFE, living;** [humble] **I**

生を享ける せいをうける be born, live — 31

32

【しょうじる (=しょうずる) 生じる(=生ずる)】 happen, arise, be produced; produce, create, cause; grow

KUN

【いきる 生きる】 — 33

a 生き いき freshness; stet — 34

生き甲斐が有る いきがいがある worthwhile living — 35

36 37

【うまれ 生まれ, 生】 [also suffix] **birth; origin, lineage**

【なま- 生-】 — 38

SPECIAL READINGS

生憎▲ あいにく unfortunately, unluckily; I am sorry, but… — 42

芝生 しばふ lawn, turf — 41

静
2164

【しずか 静か】
しずかな 静かな **QUIET, silent, still; calm, tranquil, gentle, quiet** — 39

泥
0384

【どろ¹ 泥】
❶ **MUD, mire, slush, dirt** — 40

SYNONYMS SECTION

43	SYNONYMS headword	12.2-1
44	synonym group	12.2-2
45	kanji synonym	12.2-3
46	synonym keyword	12.2-4
47	cross-reference	12.2-5

USAGE SECTION

48	USAGE headword	13.2-1
49	usage article	13.2-2
50	kanji heading	13.2-2
51	English equivalent	13.2-2
52	illustrative example	13.2-3
53	supplementary note	13.2-5

HOMOPHONES SECTION

54	HOMOPHONES headword	14
55	homophone group members	14-1
56	cross-reference	14-2

戦
2242

SYNONYMS

❶ⓐ fight and war — 43

45 46 47

闘 FIGHT →4136
戦 WAR →2242
征 go on a military expedition →0349 — 44

生
4309

USAGE

❶【うむ】 — 48

49

産む — 50

51

(produce offspring) give birth to, bear offspring, beget, breed; spawn

彼女は子供を五人産んだ かのじょはこどもをごにんうんだ She gave birth to five children

生む 52
① have children
② produce, bring forth, give rise to, yield

彼女は子供を五人生んだ かのじょはこどもをごにんうんだ She has five children

★These verbs share the meaning of giving birth. 産む, the more common form, refers to the physical act of bearing offspring, while 生む is used in the more abstract sense of having children. The principal use of 生む is in the sense of producing or giving rise to.

53

HOMOPHONES

いきる 活 ACTIVE →0460 — 54
いかす 活 ACTIVE →0460 — 56
いける
活 ACTIVE →0460
埋 BURY →0484 — 55

COMPOUND FORMATION SECTION		
57	COMPOUND FORMATION headword	15.2-1
58	compound formation article	15.2-2
NOTE SECTION		
59	cross-reference note	16-1
60	supplementary note	16-2
CHARACTER MEANINGS		
61	level 1 equivalents	17.3
62	sense division number	17.2
63	subsense division letter	17.2
64	level 2 equivalent	17.3
65	subsense	17.2
66	explanatory gloss	17.4
67	equivalent	17.5
68	level 3 equivalent	17.3
69	subject guide phrase	17.4
70	definition	17.5-1
71	main sense	17.2
72	comma	17.2
73	semicolon	17.2
74	free form	17.7-1
75	parenthetical adjunct	17.5-4

COMPOUND FORMATION

❶【先生 せんせい】 — 57

先生 'teacher; doctor' is a scholar (生 ⓬ⓐ) who studied ahead (先) of others. — 58

NOTE

➡ see also USAGE notes at 産 4089 and 成 4352 — 59

★ 生 is said to have a total of more than 200 readings, which is more than any other character. — 60

生

▶**LIFE**
▶**BE BORN**
▶**STUDENT** — 61

COMPOUNDS

62 63

❶ⓐ (act of being alive) **LIFE, existence** — 64

ⓑ (interval between birth and death) **LIFEtime, life** — 65

66 67

❷ⓐ (living organisms) **LIFE, living things**

ⓑ bio-, -zoic — 68

69 70

❺ [formerly 棲 せい or 栖 せい] (of animals) (occupy a habitat) **inhabit, live**

❼ (bring into existence) **produce, give rise to** — 71

72 73

⓬ⓐ [also suffix] **STUDENT**, **pupil**; **scholar**

INDEPENDENT

— 74

【せい 生】 **LIFE, living;** [humble] **I**

生を享ける せいをうける be born, live

KUN

【いける 生ける】

② [formerly also 活ける] **arrange** (**flowers**) — 75

76 level 4 equivalent 17.3
77 supplementary gloss 17.6
78 affix 17.7-2
79 combining form 17.7-3

COMPOUNDS AND EXAMPLES

80 subsense indicator 18.2
81 Japanese word or phrase 18.1-1
82 kana reading 18.1-1
83 English equivalent 18.1-1
84 compound word 18.1
85 example 18.1

LABELS

86 functional label 19.2
87 subject label 19.4
88 etymological label 19.3-1
89 orthographic label 19.1
90 part-of-speech label 19.2-1
91 status label 19.3

融
2303
❹ [archaic] **bright, glowing** — 76

渋
0625
❶ **ASTRINGENT, puckery, rough** —said esp. of the taste of unripe persimmons — 77

著
2869
❶ⓐ **AUTHOR, write, publish**
ⓑ [suffix] **AUTHORed by, by** — 78
86

87
長
3163
❽ *music* major — 79
長調 ちょうちょう major key

頂
0164
KUN
【いただく 頂く】
[humble]
ⓐ **RECEIVE HUMBLY, accept with thanks, be given, be favored with**
ⓑ **eat, drink**

80 81 82 83
a 頂き いただき windfall, unexpected gain; unauthorized borrowing

頂き物 いただきもの gift, present — 84

この本を頂いても良いですか このほんをいただいてもいいですか Can I have this book?
85

88
二
2421
❶ⓐ [original meaning] **TWO, second**

89 90
融
2303
【とかす 融かす】 [now usu. 解かす] *vt* melt (snow or ice), thaw (out)
氷を融かす こおりをとかす melt ice

91
小
0007
⓭ⓐ [humble] I
ⓑ suffix indicating humility on part of speaker
a 小生 しょうせい I

NONSTANDARD ENTRIES

CROSS-REFERENCE ENTRIES

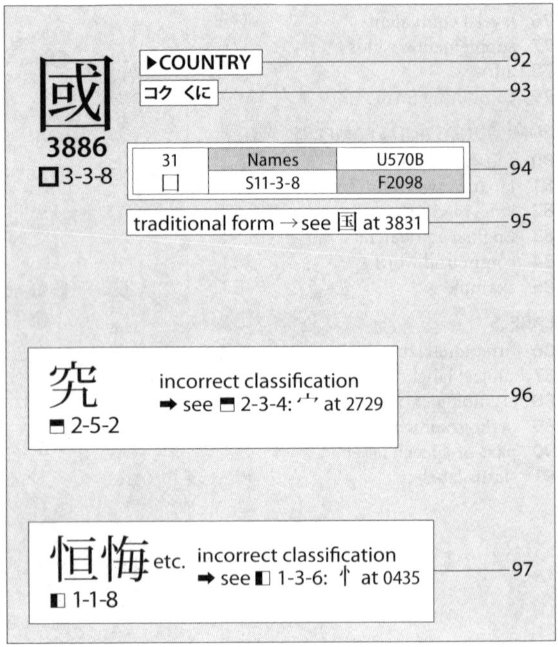

GUIDE TO THE DICTIONARY
凡例

The aim of this **Guide to the Dictionary** is to describe the various conventions used in the dictionary, including the entry format, as well as to define the meanings of technical terms, labels, glosses, and the like. The **Guide** deals mostly with *presentation,* with a primary emphasis on format. How this information is useful to the user is treated in **Features of This Dictionary** on p. 25a.

The **Explanatory Chart** on p. 35a describes the entry layout, while the meanings of symbols and abbreviations are given in **Abbreviations and Symbols** on p. 55a. The appendixes and indexes are described in their respective introductions.

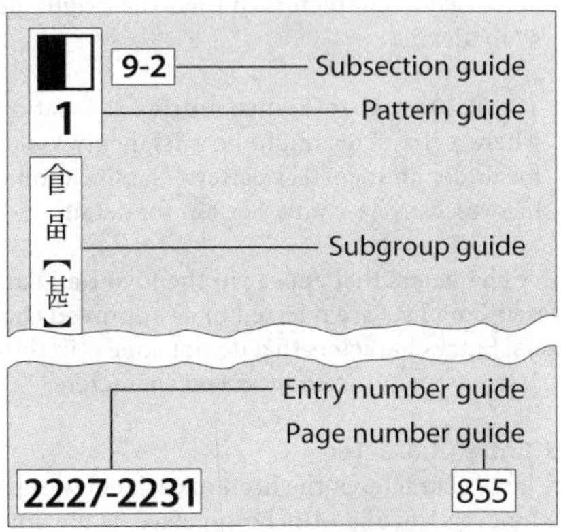

1 ENTRIES AND GUIDES

1.1 Guides

The various **guides** printed in the outer corners and margins of the page have been carefully designed and laid out to facilitate the speedy location of entries.

1. The **entry number guide** in the lower, outer corner of a page consists of numerals that indicate the entry number range for that page. Use it for locating a character when the entry number is known.

2. The **page number guide** consists of boldface numerals centered at the bottom of each page. In the introductory pages, page numbers are followed by the letter **a.** Entry numbers, not page numbers, are used in cross-references to entry characters.

3. The **SKIP guides,** which consist of the **subsection, pattern,** and **subgroup** guides, are described in **§2.7** on p. 1793.

1.2 Types of Entries

This dictionary contains a total of 5458 entries classified into six types. The first five types consist of the 4408 **main entries,** while the sixth type is the 1050 **cross-reference entries.**

1. The 2136 characters in the official **Revised Jōyō Kanji** list (改定常用漢字表) published in 2010, widely used in the mass media, government, and education. This represents an increase of 191 characters over the previous list published in 1981 (1945 characters).

2. The 861 characters in the **Jinmei Kanji** list (人名用漢字表) revised in 2010, an official list of kanji approved for use in personal names. This represents a major revision—an increase of 695 characters—over the first edition of this dictionary.

3. The 221 **non-Jōyō** characters neither in the Jōyō Kanji list nor in the Jinmei Kanji list.

4. The 1066 **nonstandard entries.** See **§4** and **§20** for details.

5. The 124 **radical entries** are entries that are either radicals or radical variants which are rarely if ever used as characters in their own right. See **§7** for details.

6. The 1050 **cross-reference entries** at locations where a character might be mistakenly looked for under an incorrect pattern classification or incorrect stroke-count. See **§21** for details.

Entry characters that appear in the Jōyō Kanji and Jinmei Kanji lists are referred to as **approved characters.** Entry characters that do not appear in those lists are referred to as **unapproved characters.**

1.3 Entry Character

The large character at the head of each entry, set in the modern Kozuka Mincho typeface, is the **entry character.**

愛	Entry character
3133	Entry number
⬒2-4-9	SKIP number

1.4 Entry-Head Data

The **entry-head data** consists of the entry character (**§1.3**), the entry number (**§1.5**), the SKIP number (**§1.6**), the core meaning (**§2**), the character reading(s) (**§3**), the nonstandard form(s) (**§4**), the Chinese form(s) (**§4**), the reference data box (**§5**), and the stroke-order diagram (**§6**). Each item is described in the section indicated in parentheses.

1.5 Entry Number

The boldface numeral below the entry character is the **entry number,** which uniquely identifies the entry characters throughout the dictionary, the appendixes, and the indexes for reference and cross-reference. The entry number appears as a four-digit, zero-padded numeral (e.g., **0023,** rather than **23**).

1.6 SKIP Number

The **SKIP number** of the entry character, which appears below the entry number, consists of the **pattern symbol** followed by hyphenated numerals used to locate characters according to SKIP rules, e.g., ◧1-2-5 for 体. See **§2.4** on p. 1789 for details.

2 CORE MEANINGS

The **CAPITALIZED** words preceded by the symbol ▶ convey the **core meaning** or core meanings of the entry character.

日
3759

▶DAY
▶SUN
▶JAPAN

The core meaning is one of the central features of this dictionary. It represents the fundamental concept(s) linking the principal senses of a character.

3 CHARACTER READINGS

The kana appearing immediately below the core meanings represent the **readings** of the entry character. *On* readings are given in katakana whereas *kun* readings are given in hiragana.

優
0200

ユウ ウ▲ やさ(しい) すぐ(れる) まさ(る)▲
㊔ まさ すぐる ゆたか

Seven types of readings are given:

1. **Principal readings** The first reading given is the most common or representative reading of a character. The principal reading is nearly always the *on* reading, but for characters that do not have an *on* reading, the *kun* reading is used.

2. **Approved *on* readings** The Sino-Japanese or Chinese-derived reading, given in katakana, that appears in the Jōyō Kanji list. *Approved* applies only to characters in that list.

3. **Approved *kun* readings** The native Japanese reading, given in hiragana, that appears in the Jōyō Kanji list. *Approved* applies only to characters in that list. ***Okurigana*** (kana endings) conforming to the official rules are shown in parentheses. If a *kun* reading includes a hyphen, it functions only as a word element.

4. **Special readings** In exceptional cases, a component of what is considered a **special reading** (see **§11**) in the Jōyō Kanji list can be isolated as a reading in its own right. For example, the 凹 in 凸凹 でこぼこ can be isolated as having the reading ぼこ. Such a reading is similar to an ordinary *kun* reading, and is marked by an asterisk (e.g., ぼこ*).

5. **Unapproved readings** Marked by a solid triangle (▲), this is a reading that is not listed in the Jōyō Kanji list but is sufficiently important to merit inclusion in this dictionary (e.g., 仏 フツ▲). The distinction between approved and unapproved readings (and thus the ▲ symbol) applies only to characters in the Jōyō Kanji list.

6. **Name readings** These readings, called ***nanori*** (名乗り), appear to the right of the symbol ㊔ and are used almost exclusively in personal, family, and place names, not in ordinary words. All such readings, both *kun* and *on*, are given in hiragana.

   If a name reading and an ordinary (nonname) reading are pronounced the same but differ only in *okurigana*, as in 偲ぶ and 偲 for しのぶ, only the ordinary reading is given. Similarly, if a reading or a derived reading (such as 行き ゆき from 行く ゆく) can be used in both names and ordinary words, it is listed only among the ordinary readings.

7. **Chinese readings** The romanized transcription following the Chinese form(s) is the **Chinese reading,** the standard pronunciation(s) of the character in the People's Republic of China given in the official Pinyin system of romanization.

4 CHARACTER FORMS AND STYLES

Character form refers to the skeletal framework or delineation of the figure formed by a character. The entry-head data includes three character forms and one calligraphic style.

剣 Ⓝ 劍 劒◇ 劔◇
2104

事 Ⓝ 亊◆
4384

1. **Standard form** The large character at the head of main entry characters. For approved characters, this is the officially sanctioned, widely used form.

2. **Nonstandard form** A variant form other than the standard form of approved characters or a variant form other than the traditional form of unapproved characters.

   Three kinds of nonstandard forms are given: the traditional form, the alternative forms, and the handwritten abbreviation, in that order.

   1. **Traditional form** is, in principle, the full unsimplified form introduced by the Chinese dictionary 康熙字典 こうきじてん in 1716. Although this dictionary places great emphasis on presenting precise character forms, the traditional forms given are sometimes slightly different from the original form because modern fonts introduce barely noticeable differences in stroke style, such as 配 as opposed to 配.
   2. **Alternative forms** (identified by ◇) refer to variant forms other than the traditional form, including one of the five "permitted forms" (許容字体) given in the Jōyō Kanji list (identified by ◈). Alternative forms always follow the traditional form.
   3. The **handwritten abbreviation,** marked by a solid diamond symbol ◆, is a simplified form used in handwriting.

   For approved characters, the nonstandard forms appear to the right of the symbol Ⓝ. For unapproved characters, the traditional form is given as the large main entry character, while the other nonstandard forms appear to the right of the symbol Ⓝ.

   See also **§20 Nonstandard Entries.**

3. **Chinese form** The Chinese form(s) appears immediately to the right of the symbol Ⓒ. This is the official simplified Chinese form(s) used in the People's Republic of China.

臨 Ⓒ 临 lín
2059

Sometimes the entry character was created in Japan on the model of Chinese characters but is not used in Chinese. This is called ***kokuji*** (国字) and is presented in the following format:

峠 Ⓒ (国字)
0428

In the rare cases that a *kokuji* was "exported" to Chinese, this is presented as follows:

腺 Ⓒ 腺 xiàn (国字)
1309

4. The **square style** (楷書 かいしょ), given in the last frame of the stroke-order diagram, is the standard calligraphic style used in handwriting.

5 REFERENCE DATA BOX

The **reference data box** gives reference and classification data.

日
3759

72	Jōyō-1	U65E5
日	S4-4-0	F0003

The reference data box consists of five items:

1. **Radical** The **radical** and traditional **radical number** for the entry character. If the form of the radical differs considerably from the parent radical, then a variant form similar to the form actually appearing in the character is given.

   The radical given for **lost-radical** characters is a new radical based on the simplified form of the entry character (see **§3** on p. 1981). It is distinguished by a white triangle (△) following the radical number.

会
2512

9△	Jōyō-2	U4F1A
人	S6-2-4	F0026

2. **Grade** The entry characters are divided into the following categories:
   - *a.* **Jōyō + number** One of the 1006 characters in the **Education Kanji** list (学年別漢字配当表) revised in 1989, which must be learned in the six years of elementary school. The number *n* indicates the one of the six school grades during which the character is taught.
   - *b.* **Jōyō** A character in the Jōyō Kanji list but not in the Education Kanji list; that is, a character taught in grades 7 to 9.
   - *c.* **Non-Jōyō** An entry character that is neither in the Jōyō Kanji list nor in the Jinmei Kanji list.
   - *d.* **Names** A character in the Jinmei Kanji list published in 2010.
   - *e.* **Radical** An entry character used only as a radical but not as a word or word element.
   - *f.* **Nonstandard** A nonstandard entry character.
3. **Unicode** A "**U**" followed by a hexadecimal number indicates the code assigned to the entry character by the Unicode character encoding standard.
4. **Strokes** Hyphenated numerals consisting of (1) the total stroke-count, (2) the stroke-count of the radical portion, and (3) the stroke-count of the nonradical portion. The total of the second and third parts equals the first part.
5. **Frequency ranking** A number that indicates the frequency of occurrence of the entry character based on a statistical survey published in 2010 (see p. 1850 for details).

6 STROKE-ORDER DIAGRAM

The **stroke-order diagram** shows the order in which the strokes of the entry character should be written. The order of writing is presented stroke by stroke, and tiny numerals indicate the position of each stroke in the sequence. Stroke-order diagrams are given for all Jōyō Kanji entries.

生
4309

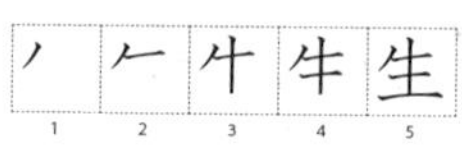

7 RADICAL SECTION

This section describes the function of the entry character as a radical.

人
4175

RADICAL
hito 'person' (仄 以 來), used in characters related to human beings
Left variant: 亻 ***ninben*** (仏 仁 代)
Top variant: 𠆢 ***hitoyane*** (今 令 会)

The RADICAL section is given for the 214 entry characters that are traditional radicals, referred to here as **parent radicals.**

The first line contains the radical name in Japanese, the English "name" of the radical, example characters, and an explanation of the meaning or function of the radical as a character-forming element. Each of the other lines lists **variants** of the parent radical, and consists of a caption (such as "Left variant") that often indicates the normal position of the radical within the character, the variant form(s), the variant name in Japanese, and example characters.

If the entry character is a **radical variant,** it appears at its own SKIP location with a cross-reference to the parent radical:

亻
4181

▶***NINBEN***

9	Radical	U4EBB
亻	S2-2-0	F0000

radical variant → see 人 at 4175

See also **Appendix 7. The Radicals.**

8 COMPOUNDS SECTION

This section lists the meanings of the main entry character as an *on* word element. Each sense is nearly always accompanied by compounds and examples and their English equivalents, arranged in an order that shows their semantic interrelatedness.

生
4309

COMPOUNDS

❶ⓐ (act of being alive) **LIFE, existence**
ⓑ (interval between birth and death) **LIFE-time, life**
a 生命 せいめい life
生保(=生命保険) せいほ(=せいめいほけん) life insurance

If a character meaning has more than one sense, these are subdivided by sense division numbers. See **§17** and **§18** for details on meanings and compounds.

9 INDEPENDENT SECTION

This section lists the meanings of the entry character as an independent *on* word (free form). The INDEPENDENT **headword** consists of a one-character *on* word, with or without particles, auxiliaries, or inflections, that can be used on its own. Thus 害がい and 害する がいする are treated as separate entries. Each meaning is often accompanied by examples and their English equivalents.

害
2826

INDEPENDENT

【がい 害】**HARM, evil, ill effect; damage**
飲酒の害 いんしゅのがい ill effects of drinking
【がいする 害する】**HARM, injure, damage**

The absence of the INDEPENDENT section indicates that the entry character is not commonly used as an independent word.

10 KUN SECTION

This section lists the meanings of the entry character as a *kun* word or word element. The senses are arranged in an order that shows their semantic interrelatedness, and are usually accompanied by compounds and examples and their English equivalents.

行
0246

KUN

【いく 行く】
① **GO, proceed, leave for; attend; visit**
行き着く いきつく arrive at, get to
⋮
【-ゆき -行き, -行】[suffix] **bound for, for**
東京行きの列車 とうきょうゆきのれっしゃ train (bound) for Tokyo

The KUN **headwords** are presented in the following format:

1. If a headword has two readings or written forms, they are listed separated by a comma. The first, like -行き above, is usually more common than the second.
2. If a KUN headword includes a hyphen, it functions only as a word element (affix or combining form) in all its senses. In the example above, -行き functions as a word element in the final position.
3. If a *kun* word is an adjectival noun (*na*-adjective), the KUN headword in the heavy square brackets 【 】 does not include な, but is followed on the next line by a headword in boldface (but not in brackets) that does include な.

静
2164

【しずか 静か】
しずかな 静かな **QUIET, silent, still; calm, tranquil, gentle, quiet**

Adjectival nouns can also be used as adverbs by replacing な with に. These forms are not necessarily listed separately.

4. If two KUN headwords have the same written form but differ in function (*homographs*), they are treated separately and distinguished by small superscript numerals, e.g., **どろ¹**, **どろ²**.

11 SPECIAL READINGS SECTION

This section lists compound words having **special readings** and their English equivalents. A special reading applies to words composed of two or more characters when the reading of the word as a whole is unrelated to the normal readings of the individual characters. For example, 明日 'tomorrow' is read あした, though 明 and 日 cannot be independently read as あ or あし or した.

Approved special readings are those listed in the appendix to the Jōyō Kanji list; **unapproved special readings,** followed by a superscript solid triangle (▲), are those that are not.

生
4309

SPECIAL READINGS
芝生 しばふ lawn, turf
生憎▲ あいにく unfortunately, unluckily; I am sorry, but...

12 SYNONYMS SECTION

This section lists groups of kanji synonyms and their English keywords for the principal senses of main entry characters:

戦
2242

SYNONYMS
❶ⓐ **fight and war** — Kanji synonym
闘 FIGHT →4136
戦 WAR →2242
征 go on a military expedition →0349
ⓑ **warfare and rebellions** — SYNONYMS headword
戦 WAR →2242
軍 war →2582
役 war →0288
陣 battle →0545 — Synonym group
乱 rebellion →1611
変 uprising →2569 — Synonym group member
闘 FIGHT →4136
❷ **game**
技 game →0292 — Synonym keyword
戦 match →2242
【たたかう】
② **compete** — Cross-reference
競 COMPETE →2322
戦う contest →2242
闘 FIGHT →4136
争 CONTEND →2523

12.1 Aims and Definitions

Synonyms, or **kanji synonyms,** refers to characters of similar or related meaning (see **Appendix 13** for a detailed definition). As a rule, kanji synonyms refer to the relationship between *on* word elements, but important independent *kun* words, and, more rarely, independent *on* words are also included.

This section has two principal aims:

1. To enable the user to study the differences and similarities of synonym group members by (*a*) indicating the semantic relationship between them and (*b*) bringing together their English keywords into a single article.
2. To act as a network of cross-references that enables the user to quickly locate the meanings and the compounds or examples for any member of a synonym group from any of the others. This allows the user to fully understand the differences between closely related characters.

12.2 Section Format

The SYNONYMS section consists of five elements:

1. The SYNONYMS **headword** at the head of each synonym group is an English word or phrase that concisely expresses the semantic relationship (usually the shared meaning) between the members of a synonym group.

   Synonym headwords are preceded by circled numbers and letters that point to the corresponding sense(s) in the COMPOUNDS section (black circles) and the KUN or INDEPENDENT sections (white circles). The solid black and white circles (● ○) refer to unnumbered senses.

2. The **synonym group** is a collection of two or more kanji synonyms. The members of a synonym group are normally presented in order of semantic relatedness.

3. The **kanji synonym** is a Japanese word or word element that is a member of a synonym group.

4. The **synonym keyword** is a concise English equivalent that most aptly represents that sense of a kanji synonym which is relevant to that synonym group. This is usually identical with one of the core meanings (in **SMALL CAPITALS**), or with an English keyword that is not a core meaning (in lowercase), of the entry character for that kanji synonym.

5. The **cross-reference** consists of an arrow → followed by an entry number referring to where that kanji synonym appears as a main entry character, enabling the user to study each kanji synonym in more detail.

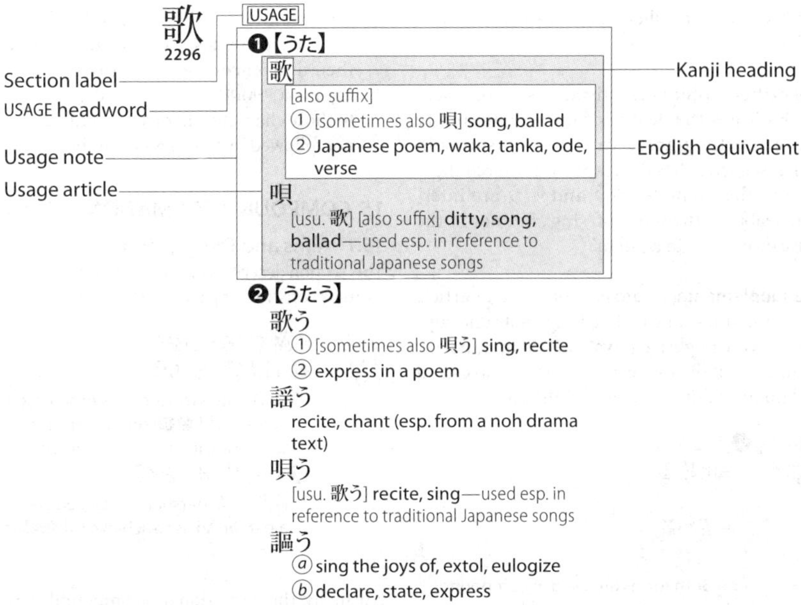

13 USAGE SECTION

13.1 Aims and Definitions

This section discriminates between the meanings of **homophones** by bringing together their English equivalents into a single article.

Homophones and homophone groups as used in this dictionary are defined as follows:

1. The term **homophone** as used in this dictionary refers to a member of a group of *kun* words or word elements, often etymologically related, that are pronounced alike but written differently and that often have different meanings. The term refers mostly to *kun* homophones or their derivatives.

2. **Homophone groups** usually consist of *kun* words or word elements that are pronounced the same but written differently and that usually differ in meaning, as in あく written as 開く, 空く, or 明く. Occasionally, easily confused compounds like 制作 and 製作 (both せいさく) are also included.

In addition to homophones, the USAGE section sometimes deals with easily confused synonymous words that are similar in meaning but written and pronounced differently; e.g., 森 もり 'thick woods' and 林 はやし 'small woods'.

As a rule, usage notes appear at the entry for the most common or important group member. The cross-references in the HOMOPHONES (**§14**) and NOTE (**§16**) sections enable the user to locate usage notes from the other group members, as well as to get a deeper understanding of the differences between homophones by studying the examples for each group member.

13.2 Section Format

Each group of homophones is treated in a separate subsection referred to as a **usage note.** This consists of the following elements:

1. The **usage headword** is the reading shared by the members of the homophone group (*okurigana* not shown). The usage notes are numbered sequentially by black-circled numbers.

2. The **usage article** gives the meanings for each group member. The kanji headings are followed by the English equivalents, which are (with minor exceptions) identical to the equivalents for the corresponding KUN headword.

3. **Illustrative examples** occasionally further clarify the differences between easily confused homophones. These are only given in the rare cases that the examples for the corresponding KUN

headwords are insufficient to fully explain these differences.

4. The **orthographic label,** given in square brackets, indicates the degree of interchangeability between orthographic variants and shows in which sense(s) these variants are interchangeable. In the example, 歌う and 唄う are interchangeable in the sense of 'sing', but not in the sense of 'express in a poem'.

5. The **supplementary note** is a comment or article that sometimes appears in a usage note and supplements the English equivalent(s). It may include an analysis of the usage of various examples and explain their differences and similarities:

止
3659
❹【-とめる】
-止める
⋮
-留める
⋮
★Both forms are used in compounds in the sense of kill, but -留める is preferred in the word 仕留める しとめる 'kill, shoot dead'. とめる is not used independently in this sense.

See also **§14 Homophones Section** and **§16 Note Section.**

14 HOMOPHONES SECTION

This section lists groups of homophones and their entry numbers for cross-reference, enabling the user to locate information about any group member from any of the others. The term **homophone** is defined in **§13 Usage Section.**

日
3759
HOMOPHONES
ひ 陽 SUN →0764
あさひ
旭 RISING SUN →3697
朝日 →2130, 3759

The HOMOPHONES section can be used in three ways:

1. Each group member is followed by its *first* core meaning as an entry character, which occasionally may not match the homophone's meaning as a KUN headword. Comparing the core meanings provides an understanding of each homophone's fundamental meaning.
2. The HOMOPHONES sections form a network of cross-references that point to the entry characters for each group member. Comparing the meanings and compounds of each group member provides a deeper understanding of their differences and similarities.
3. The HOMOPHONES section provides cross-references to those characters in orthographic labels that are not followed by their entry numbers.

15 COMPOUND FORMATION SECTION

15.1 Aims and Description

This section describes how a compound word is formed from its constituent parts and/or gives its etymology:

得
0577
COMPOUND FORMATION
❶【得意 とくい】
得意 'one's forte, etc.' is to satisfactorily achieve (得 ❸ⓑ) one's desires (意) and take pride in one's achievements.
❷【説得 せっとく】
説得する 'persuade' is to persuade (説) a person so as to achieve (得 ❸ⓑ) one's ends.

Normally, the formation of a compound word is self-evident because the compounds and examples are grouped by meaning (see **§18.2**). If the semantic relationship between the constituents of a compound is obscure, the COMPOUND FORMATION section explains how the constituents are combined by describing the meaning of each component or by presenting a brief etymology (account of origin and/or development).

As a rule, a compound formation article appears at the entry for the most relevant character. It can be located from the other characters through the cross-references in the NOTE section (**§16**).

15.2 Section Format

The formation and/or etymology of each compound word or group of related compound words are treated in a separate subsection, which consists of the following elements:

1. The COMPOUND FORMATION **headword** is the Japanese compound word(s) that is the subject of the compound formation article that follows. When there are two or more compound formation articles, the headwords are numbered sequentially by black-circled numbers.

2. The **compound formation article** explains the formation and/or etymology of a compound word whose formation may not be clear. The sense division numbers and letters within the article refer to the relevant sense in the COMPOUNDS or KUN sections. In the example, "得

❸ⓑ" refers to sense ❸ⓑ in the COMPOUNDS section of 得.

16 NOTE SECTION

This section consists of various cross-references and/or explanatory notes.

生
4309

NOTE
➡ see also USAGE notes at 産 4089 and 成 4352
➡ see COMPOUND FORMATION for 生涯 しょうがい →涯 0623
★ 生 is said to have a total of more than 200 readings, which is more than any other character.

There are two kinds of notes:

1. The **cross-reference note,** introduced by the arrow ➡, directs the user to another entry that should be consulted for further information, such as usage notes, compound formation articles, or another NOTE section.

   朝
   2130
   ➡ see USAGE note at 旭 3697

   次
   0058
   ➡ see also USAGE note at 接 0607

2. The **supplementary note,** introduced by the symbol ★, provides additional information, such as supplementary remarks on the usage, form, orthography, reading, etc., of the entry character:

   幅
   0694
   ★ Though 幅 and 巾 4217 are distinct characters, the latter is also used as an abbreviation of the former.

The supplementary note also directs attention to characters of similar form that are easily confused. These characters are always cross-referenced to each other, as shown below.

末
4317
NOTE
★ do not confuse with 未 NOT YET →4318

未
4318
NOTE
★ do not confuse with 末 LAST PART →4317

Each character is followed by its first core meaning, which clarifies their differences.

17 CHARACTER MEANINGS

The detailed presentation of character meanings is one of the principal features of this dictionary. **Character meaning** is defined as the meaning of an *on* word element, a KUN headword, or an INDEPENDENT *on* headword. The meanings, which consist of explanatory glosses and English equivalents, may be preceded by sense division numbers, functional labels, status labels, or subject labels, and are sometimes followed by supplementary glosses. Each of these elements is described below.

17.1 Order of Senses

The senses are arranged in an order that shows their semantic interrelatedness; an English keyword, often a **core word** such as **LIFE** in the example below, serves as the basis of organization, and the various senses are grouped in clusters in a manner that shows how they are interrelated.

The senses of a compound or example are normally presented in order of descending frequency or importance.

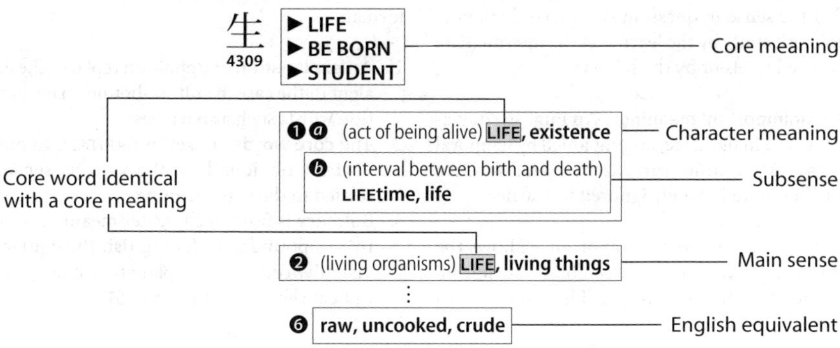

17.2 Sense Division

The character meanings are often subdivided by a system of black-circled sense division numbers (such as ❶ and ❷), subsense division letters (such as ⓐ and ⓑ), and semicolons and commas in a manner that shows the semantic relationship between the senses and subsenses (see example above). The senses of compounds and examples are subdivided only by semicolons.

If the COMPOUNDS section has only one **main sense** that is not subdivided into **subsenses,** that sense is identified by a solid black circle ●.

17.3 Degree of Importance

The degree of importance is divided into four levels, indicated by various typographical devices and labels as shown below.

弘
0223

▶ **DISSEMINATE** —— Level 1

COMPOUNDS

❶ **DISSEMINATE, spread, teach (esp. Buddhism)** —— Level 2

❷ ⓐ great, grand —— Level 3

ⓑ [original meaning, now rare] extensive, broad vast —— Level 4

Level 1: Core meaning—The most important sense, which is essential for the beginner, provides a basic understanding of the character.

Level 2: Important meaning—An English equivalent displayed in boldface signifies an important, usually high-frequency, sense. For Jōyō Kanji, these senses are essential for beginning and intermediate learners.

Level 3: Lightface meaning—An English equivalent in the COMPOUNDS section printed in lightface signifies that the sense in question is sufficiently important to merit study by the learner at the intermediate to advanced levels or by the scholar.

Level 4: Unimportant meaning—An English equivalent displayed in lightface, accompanied by temporal labels (**§19.3**), signifies rare, archaic and obsolete senses. These can be safely ignored by learners.

The indication of degree of importance allows the user to easily distinguish between basic, advanced, rare, and archaic meanings. This manner of presentation enables both the beginner and the advanced student to use the dictionary with equal ease, and helps the compiler of teaching materials to prepare graded lessons. This dictionary thus serves both as a practical learning tool and as a useful teaching aid.

17.4 Explanatory Gloss

Explanatory glosses supplement the equivalents in order to clarify their meanings. These are of two kinds. The **subject guide phrase** is a brief parenthetical phrase beginning with "of" that restricts the equivalent, especially as a typical subject of an intransitive verb.

伸
0079

❷ (of stock prices) **rise**

The **explanation** is a description, rather than a translation, of the meaning or grammatical function. If necessary, a full lexicographic **definition** is given.

折
0297

【おる 折る】

① (separate through the application of a sudden bending force) **BREAK OFF (as a branch), break (a bone), snap (in two), split**

17.5 The English Equivalent

The **English equivalent** or **equivalent,** the central part of the character meaning, refers to synonymous or nearly synonymous words or phrases that are an English translation of a Japanese word or word element (see **§17** for illustration).

The first word of the equivalent (sometimes modified by a qualifying word or phrase) is the **English keyword,** a concise English equivalent that most aptly represents the most fundamental concept of a sense or group of senses. Often this is a **core word,** which is usually identical to a core meaning.

The English equivalent is presented in the following format:

1. An **explanation** or **definition** replaces the equivalent in the case of culture-bound terms or function words such as particles.
2. The **core words** are set in **CAPITALS** to make it visually obvious how the various senses are related to the core meaning.
3. **Boldface** is used in character meanings (but not in compounds) to distinguish the equivalents visually from other explanatory matter, and to indicate level 2 importance (**§17.3**).

4. **Parenthetical adjuncts** sometimes accompany the equivalent to indicate a typical object of a transitive verb, a subject of a verb, and the like.

17.6 Supplementary Gloss

Introduced by a dash, the **supplementary gloss** typically consists of a phrase, beginning with "said of" or "used in," that supplements the equivalent by restricting its range of application, by describing its grammatical function, and so on.

渋
0625

【しぶい 渋い】
① **ASTRINGENT, puckery, rough**—said esp. of the taste of unripe persimmons

17.7 Linguistic Functions

This dictionary places special emphasis on indicating in an explicit manner the linguistic **function** of words and word elements, especially their morphological function as free forms, combining forms, and affixes.

1. **Free form** (or **word**) refers to any entry that can be used on its own, including independent *on* words, most *kun* words, and almost all compound words.
2. **Affix** refers to a word element added to a *base form* to create a new word. Affixes are normally single characters added to two-character compound words, but counters, units, titles, and various function words normally function as affixes and may be attached to one-character words.
3. **Combining form** refers to a word element *other than* an affix that can form a new word by combining with one or more words or word elements. Although combining forms and affixes are functionally distinct, some combining forms or free forms can sometimes also function as affixes.

On the whole, the function is clear from the entry format and the various labels. The details of the format are presented below:

1. Any character meaning in the COMPOUNDS section functions as a combining form, unless it is preceded by the label [prefix] or [suffix], in which case it is used exclusively as an affix.
2. Most KUN headwords can be used both as free forms and as combining forms. If a meaning is preceded by the label [in compounds], it is used only as a combining form; if it is preceded by [prefix] or [suffix], it is used exclusively as an affix. If a KUN headword includes a hyphen, it is only used as a combining form or affix (see **§10**).
3. INDEPENDENT headwords always function as free forms (independent *on* words).
4. In the COMPOUNDS section, the labels [also prefix] and [also suffix] indicate that the meaning is used both as an affix and as a combining form; in the KUN section these labels indicate that the meaning is used both as a free form and as an affix.

In the example below, 著 acts as a combining form (by default) in the sense of 'author, write', as a suffix in the sense of 'authored by', and as an independent word in the sense of 'literary work':

著
2869

COMPOUNDS
❶ⓐ **AUTHOR, write, publish**
ⓑ [suffix] **AUTHORed by, by**
a 著作する ちょさくする write, author
⋮
b 三島由紀夫著 みしまゆきおちょ authored by Mishima Yukio

INDEPENDENT
【ちょ 著】 literary work, book
. . . の著 …のちょ book written by…

In addition, various other grammatical and syntactic functions, such as part of speech, are indicated by the functional labels (**§19.2**). Words and word elements can also function in other capacities, such as numerals, counters, abbreviations, phonetic substitutes, and symbols. Though these are not explicitly distinguished by labels, various keywords and explanations such as "abbrev. of" and "counter for" make this clear.

18 COMPOUNDS AND EXAMPLES

18.1 Section Format

Each sense of a character meaning is usually illustrated by compounds and examples. **Compound** or **compound word** refers to a combination of two or more words or word elements having their own lexical meaning that together function as a single word (e.g., 携行する けいこうする 'carry along, bring'). **Example** refers to a word other than a compound or to an illustrative phrase or sentence (e.g., 杖を携える つえをたずさえる 'carry a stick in one's hand').

The compounds and examples are presented in the following format:

1. A Japanese word or phrase is followed by the kana reading and the English equivalent. The format of the equivalent generally follows that of the character meanings (**§17**).

2. Characters used in compounds and examples are sometimes followed by a superscript *x* (ˣ), which indicates that the character in question is not one of the main entry characters in this dictionary.
3. With rare exceptions, compounds in which the entry character appears in the initial position (as 吹奏 under 吹) precede those in which it appears in the final position (as 鼓吹 under 吹).
4. Sometimes a literal translation of the compound is given in parentheses, e.g., 忘年会 ぼうねんかい 'year-end party' ("forget-the-year party").

18.2 Subsense Indicators

The compounds and examples are grouped by meaning in a manner that shows how they are formed from their constituent parts; that is, they are grouped together under the same main sense that they illustrate.

If a **main sense** is divided into **subsenses,** the compounds are listed under the same main sense and subdivided into groups by subsense. In principle, within each (sub)sense group, compounds in which the entry character appears in the initial position precede those in which it does not.

The **subsense indicators,** which consist of tiny letters to the left of the compounds, indicate the beginning of a new subsense group; that is, the compounds from that point onwards illustrate only the subsense(s) indicated by the tiny letters.

効
1617

COMPOUNDS

ⓐ EFFECT, efficacy (esp. of drugs), virtue
ⓑ (state of being operative or in force) **EFFECT, effectiveness, validity**

a 効果 こうか effect, efficacy; result
効率 こうりつ efficiency
⋮
ab 効力 こうりょく effect, efficacy; effect (as of a law), validity
有効な ゆうこうな effective, valid
無効 むこう invalidity, ineffectiveness
b 発効する はっこうする become effective, take effect, come into force

In the example, the tiny ***a*** indicates that 効果 and 効率 illustrate subsense ⓐ; the ***ab*** that 効力, 有効な, and 無効 illustrate both subsenses ⓐ and ⓑ; and the ***b*** that 発効する illustrates subsense ⓑ.

19 LABELS

A labeling system including orthographic, functional, status, and subject labels provides guidance on etymology, style, function, level of formality, etc.

19.1 Orthographic Labels

The **orthographic label** indicates the orthographic variant(s) of a word or word element:

盲
2547

❷ [also 妄 2509] (not based on reason) **BLIND, reckless, aimless**

Orthographic variants are two or more characters that are partially or completely interchangeable in a given sense. For example, 盲 is interchangeable with 妄 in certain compounds but not in others. The orthographic labels indicate the degree of interchangeability of variants for specific senses and serve as a cross-reference to the orthographic variants of the entry character, enabling the user to study their differences and similarities.

An important role of the orthographic labels is to indicate the degree of interchangeability between **phonetically replaced characters** and **phonetic replacement characters.** This dictionary covers all commonly used replaced characters, as well as many rare ones too. Study the examples below.

風
3730

❿ [formerly also 諷 ふう 2005] **insinuate, hint, satirize**
風刺 ふうし satire, sarcasm
風喩 ふうゆ hint, insinuation, allegory

諷
2005

❶ [now usu. 風 3730] **INSINUATE, hint, satirize**
諷刺 ふうし satire, sarcasm
諷喩 ふうゆ hint, insinuation, allegory

In the entry for 風, the label indicates that 風, a phonetic *replacement* character, is now commonly used but that 諷, a phonetically *replaced* character, may formerly have been used in some compounds and examples. In the entry for 諷, the label [now replaced by] indicates that 諷 may now be replaced by 風 in all compounds and examples, not just those given in the dictionary.

The meanings of the orthographic labels, explained below, are mostly self-evident. In the chart, "now" and "formerly" refer mainly to the postwar and prewar periods, respectively; "archaic" is explained in **§19.3.**

Label	Explanation
[rarely also *B*]	*A* is common; *B* is extremely rare or archaic
[sometimes also *B*]	(1) *A* is common; *B* is unusual or rare (2) *A* is now common; *B* is now also sometimes used
[also *B*]	*A* and *B* are more or less equally common
[now also *B*]	(1) *A* and *B* are used interchangeably in some compounds and examples (2) *A* and *B* are now more or less equally common
[usu. *B*]	*A* is unusual or rare; *B* is common
[now usu. *B*]	(1) *B* replaces *A* in most compounds and examples (2) *B* is now common
[formerly *B*]	*A* is now common; *A* was not formerly used, or B may formerly have been used in all compounds and examples
[formerly also *B*]	*A* is now common; *A* and *B* have both been used, or *B* may formerly have been used in some compounds and examples
[now replaced by *B*]	*A* may now be replaced by *B* in all compounds and examples
[now always *B*]	*A* is extremely rare or archaic; *B* is common

19.2 Functional Labels

Functional labels indicate various grammatical and syntactic functions associated with a sense. These are of four kinds: part of speech, usage, word formation, and miscellaneous.

1. **Part-of-speech labels,** set in italics, are sometimes given. These include *particle, pronoun, demonstrative, vi* (intransitive verb), and *vt* (transitive verb). The part of speech is usually made clear by the wording of the equivalent. Labels appear mostly when it is necessary to eliminate ambiguity.

2. The **usage label,** enclosed in square brackets, indicates how a word or word element is used, especially its syntactic function and the grammatical construction in which it normally appears. These labels do not have a fixed form. Typical ones include [in the form of...] (form in which the word is normally used), [followed by...], and [in negative constructions].

3. The **word-formation label,** enclosed in square brackets, indicates the function of a form as a word element (affix or combining form). The absence of a word-formation label before the equivalent of an *on* word element indicates that the character functions as a combining form in that sense. The absence of such a label before the equivalent of a KUN headword indicates that that headword functions as an independent word that may or may not also function as a combining form in that sense.

   The following labels appear: prefix, also prefix, suffix, also suffix, also prefix and suffix, verbal prefix, verbal suffix, in compounds. If a label does not begin with "also," the function is exclusive. Thus, [prefix] means the sense is used only as a prefix.

4. **Miscellaneous functional labels,** such as [auxiliary] and [emphatic], are used to indicate various functions.

19.3 Status Labels

The **status label** restricts the sense to a particular time, level of style, or level of formality. Status labels are of four kinds.

1. The **etymological label,** which appears in the form [original meaning], indicates that the sense was the first meaning of the character after its formation. Though etymological labels appear quite often, the treatment of original meanings is not exhaustive.

2. The **temporal label,** enclosed in square brackets, restricts the accompanying sense to a particular time. The absence of a temporal label indicates that the sense is current in Modern Japanese.

   Temporal labels (see illustration in **§17.3**) include [rare] (infrequent in Modern Japanese), [archaic] (used especially in the classics), and [obsolete] (rarely, if ever, used in the classics).

3. The **stylistic label,** set in italics, restricts the sense to a particular level of style. The following labels

appear: *literary* (language of literature), *elegant* (language of poetry), *colloq* (spoken language), *slang* (extremely informal), and *vulgar* (social taboo).

4. The **formality label,** enclosed in square brackets, restricts the sense to a particular level of formality. The following labels appear: [honorific] (elevating subject's status), [humble] (lowering subject's status), [polite] (*desu-masu* style), and [belittling] (showing contempt or abuse).

19.4 Subject Labels

The **subject label,** in italics, identifies the field to which the sense applies. It is often an abbreviation, as *chem* for "chemistry." These abbreviations are listed with their full forms in **Abbreviations and Symbols** on p. 55a.

20 NONSTANDARD ENTRIES

The nonstandard forms of main entry characters are treated as separate entries referred to as **nonstandard entries.** These are of three types: (1) the traditional form, (2) the alternative forms, and (3) the handwritten abbreviation (see **§4** for details).

收
0065

▸**TAKE IN**
シュウ おさ(める) おさ(まる) ㊔ おさむ のぶ かず

66	Names	U6536
攵	S6-4-2	F0000

traditional form → see 収 at 0031

The entry characters are followed by their core meanings (**§2**), readings (**§3**), and the reference data box (**§5**) at their own SKIP locations with a cross-reference to their corresponding standard forms, as shown above.

21 CROSS-REFERENCE ENTRIES

Character entries appearing at an *incorrect* SKIP location with a cross-reference to the entry at the correct location are referred to as **cross-reference entries.**

究
⬒2-5-2

incorrect classification
➡ see ⬒2-3-4: ⺳ at 2729

Cross-reference entries can be distinguished by the words "incorrect classification" or "incorrect stroke count," and by the absence of entry numbers and explanatory matter organized into sections. They consist of (1) the entry character, (2) a description of the incorrect location, and (3) a cross-reference to the correct location.

Cross-reference entries are of two kinds: **single-character** and **multiple-character.** These are described in detail at **§2.6** on p. 1793.

ABBREVIATIONS AND SYMBOLS
略語・記号表

ABBREVIATIONS

anat	anatomy
astron	astronomy
biol	biology
bot	botany
chem	chemistry
colloq	colloquial
elec	electricity
geol	geology
gram	grammar
hist	historical
math	mathematics
phys	physics
psychol	psychology
vi	intransitive verb
vt	transitive verb

SKIP SYMBOLS AND ABBREVIATIONS

etc.	in cross-reference entries, other characters of similar structure
p	incorrect pattern classification (in **Pattern Index**)
ps	incorrect pattern classification and stroke-count (in **Pattern Index**)
s	incorrect stroke-count (in **Pattern Index**)
SKIP	System of Kanji Indexing by Patterns
◧1	left-right pattern
⬒2	up-down pattern
▣3	enclosure pattern
■4	solid pattern
▔1	top line (solid subpattern)
▁2	bottom line (solid subpattern)
◫3	through line (solid subpattern)
□4	others (solid subpattern)

SYMBOLS IN ENTRY-HEAD DATA

▶	core meaning
Ⓒ	Chinese form(s) and reading(s)
(国字)	*kokuji* (character created in Japan)
Ⓝ	nonstandard form(s)
㊔	reading(s) used only in names
( )	encloses *okurigana* of *kun* readings
1, 2	*kun* readings of exactly the same form
◇	alternative form
◆	handwritten abbreviation
◈	official alternative form
-	reading used as word element
*	special reading that can be isolated
▲	unapproved reading

REFERENCE DATA BOX

△	new radical based on simplified character form
S	stroke-count information
F	frequency ranking
U	Unicode

OTHER SYMBOLS AND MARKS

【 】	encloses KUN or INDEPENDENT headwords
❶❷...	numbered sense in COMPOUNDS section
ⓐⓑ...	subsense division letters in COMPOUNDS section
①②...	numbered sense in KUN or INDEPENDENT headword
ⓐⓑ...	subsense division letters in KUN or INDEPENDENT headword
●	unnumbered sense in COMPOUNDS section
○	in SYNONYMS section, points to unnumbered sense of subentry headwords
▲	unapproved special reading in SPECIAL READINGS section
×	character not found as an entry character
°	lost radical (in Radical Index)
★	supplementary note in USAGE and NOTE sections
➡, →	introduces cross-references
§	precedes section numbers in cross-references
=	precedes alternative forms/readings
( )	1. *okurigana* endings 2. explanatory glosses 3. optional omissions (*A(B)* = *A* or *AB*) 4. alternative forms/readings
[ ]	1. most labels 2. alternatives (*A[B]C* = *AC* or *BC*)
/	1. sometimes indicates alternatives 2. separates sentences
—	introduces supplementary glosses
-	KUN headword used as word element
‹ ›	encloses English equivalents in explanatory text
:	coordinates two parts of an English equivalent

THE **KODANSHA KANJI** DICTIONARY

◧ 1
LEFT-RIGHT
左右型

刂 ▶*RITTŌ*

0001
◧ 1-1-1

18	Radical	U5202
刂	S2-2-0	F0000

radical variant → see 刀 at 3642

丷 ▶*HACHIGASHIRA*

0002
◧ 1-1-1

12	Radical	U4E37
丷	S2-2-0	F0000

radical variant → see 八 at 3644

儿 ▶*NINNYŌ, HITOASHI*

0003
◧ 1-1-1

10	Radical	U513F
儿	S2-2-0	F0000

RADICAL

ninnyō or ***hitoashi*** 'legs' (元 兆 兢), used for character classification

八 ▶EIGHT

ハチ や や(つ) やっ(つ) よう

0004
◧ 1-1-1

12	Nonstandard	U516B
八	S2-2-0	F0000

traditional form → see 八 at 3644
radical variant → see 八 at 3644

⺌ ▶*NAOGASHIRA*

0005
◧ 1-1-2

42	Radical	U2E8C
⺌	S3-3-0	F0000

radical variant → see 小 at 0007

川 ▶RIVER

セン かわ

Ⓒ 川 chuān

0006
◧ 1-1-2

47	Jōyō-1	U5DDD
川	S3-3-0	F0109

radical variant → see 巛 at 0009

丿 川 川 (stroke order 1 2 3)

COMPOUNDS

❶ⓐ [original meaning] **RIVER**
ⓑ [rare] counter for **RIVER**s

a 河川 かせん rivers
山川 さんせん mountains and rivers
b 三川 さんせん three rivers

❷ unclassified compounds
川柳 せんりゅう short humorous verse, satirical poem

KUN

【かわ 川】 [sometimes also 河]
ⓐ **RIVER, stream, brook**
ⓑ **suffix after names of (esp. Japanese) RIVERs**

a 川上 かわかみ upstream, upriver
川瀬 かわせ rapids, shallows of a river
小川 おがわ brook, streamlet
b 江戸川 えどがわ Edo River

SPECIAL READINGS

川原(=河原) かわら dry riverbed, river beach

SYNONYMS

❶ⓐ **rivers and streams**
川 RIVER → 0006
河 RIVER → 0394
江 large river → 0257
渓 mountain stream → 0628
流 stream → 0529

USAGE

【かわ】

川

[sometimes also 河]

ⓐ river, stream, brook

ⓑ suffix after names of (esp. Japanese) rivers

河

[usu. 川]

ⓐ river, stream

ⓑ suffix after names of (esp. foreign) rivers

HOMOPHONES

かわ 河 RIVER →0394

NOTE

➡ see COMPOUND FORMATION for 川柳 せんりゅう →柳 1115

小

▶SMALL

ショウ ちい(さい) こ- お- さ-▲ ㊔ ささ

Ⓒ 小 xiǎo

0007

1-1-2

42	Jōyō-1	U5C0F
小	S3-3-0	F0035

亅 小 小 (stroke order 1 2 3)

RADICAL

chiisai 'small' (少 尖 尠×), used in characters related to smallness

Top variants: ⺌ ⺍× ***naogashira*** (当 尚 単)

COMPOUNDS

❶ⓐ [also prefix] [original meaning] (less in size, extent or quantity) **SMALL, little, minor, short, tiny, miniature, minute**

ⓑ (less in intensity) **SMALL**, slight

a 小国 しょうこく small nation, lesser power

小説 しょうせつ novel, story, fiction

小史 しょうし short history

小額 しょうがく small denomination

小アジア しょうあじあ Asia Minor

小規模 しょうきぼ small-scale

小東京 しょうとうきょう miniature Tokyo, epitome of Tokyo

小数 しょうすう decimal (fraction)

大小 だいしょう large and small; size; long and short swords

縮小する しゅくしょうする reduce, curtail, cut down

中小企業 ちゅうしょうきぎょう small-to-medium-sized enterprises

最小 さいしょう the smallest, minimum

b 小破 しょうは slight damage

❷ⓐ (less in importance) **SMALL, minor, petty**

ⓑ (of low rank) **SMALL**, petty, lesser, lower

ⓒ **SMALL**-minded, narrow-minded, timid

a 小前提 しょうぜんてい minor premise

小事 しょうじ trifle

小委 しょうい subcommittee

小学校 しょうがっこう elementary [primary] school

小学生 しょうがくせい schoolchild, schoolboy, schoolgirl

過小評価する かしょうひょうかする underestimate, underrate

b 小市民 しょうしみん lower middle class

小身 しょうしん humble position

c 小心な しょうしんな timid, coward

小主観 しょうしゅかん small ego

❸ⓐ abbrev. of 小学校 しょうがっこう: **elementary school, grade school**

ⓑ **suffix after names of elementary schools**

a 小一 しょういち first-year student of an elementary school

同小 どうしょう the above-mentioned elementary school

b 佃小 つくだしょう Tsukuda Elementary School

❹ [humble] my little, my humble, our humble

小生 しょうせい I

小社 しょうしゃ my company; little shrine

小店 しょうてん my little shop

❺ junior, younger, young, little

小弟 しょうてい my foolish brother; I

小児 しょうに little child, infant

小ケネディー しょうけねでぃー Kennedy Jr.

❻ urine

小用 しょうよう urination; small matter

小水 しょうすい urine, urination

INDEPENDENT

【しょう 小】**SMALLness; small size, small; short month; child**

小の月 しょうのつき month with 30 days or less

小二十円 しょうにじゅうえん 20 yen for children

大は小を兼ねる だいはしょうをかねる The greater serves for the lesser

KUN

【ちいさい 小さい】**SMALL, little, tiny; minute, fine; trifling, petty; slight; young, little**

小さな ちいさな noun adjective form of 小さい ちいさい

【こ- 小-】[also prefix]

①ⓐ (less in size or quantity) **SMALL, little, short**

ⓑ (less in intensity) **SMALL, light, slight**

a 小型(=小形)の こがたの small-sized, small; pocket (dictionary)

小物 こもの small articles, gadget

小鳥 ことり small [little] bird

小麦 こむぎ wheat

小唄 こうた ditty, ballad

小屋 こや cottage, hut, cabin; playhouse

小切手 こぎって check
小口 こぐち small lot, small sum [amount]; end, edge
小幅 こはば single breadth, narrow range
小指 こゆび little finger, pinkie; little toe
小文字 こもじ lowercase letter
b 小雪 こゆき light snowfall
小声 こごえ low voice, whisper

②ⓐ (of secondary importance) **secondary, sub-**
ⓑ [belittling] **SMALL, petty, little**
a 小売り こうり retail, sale in small quantities
小売店 こうりてん retail store
小分け こわけ subdivision
b 小僧 こぞう priestling; servant boy; kid, brat
小役人 こやくにん petty official

③ [emphatic preceding adjectives or verbs] **a little, slightly, very**
小戻す こもどす (of the market) rally a little
小恥ずかしい こはずかしい a little shameful
小高い こだかい slightly elevated

④ **nearly, almost**
小一時間 こいちじかん nearly one hour

【お- 小-】little, nice; a little
小川 おがわ brook, streamlet
小琴 おごと small koto
小父さん おじさん man; Mister, Uncle
小母さん おばさん (middle-aged) lady
小暗い おぐらい dusky

【さ- 小-】 [also prefix] *elegant* **little, nice**
小百合 さゆり lily
小夜曲 さよきょく serenade

SPECIAL READINGS
小豆 あずき adzuki bean
小波▲ さざなみ [also 漣 or 細波] ripples, wavelets
小火▲ ぼや small fire

SYNONYMS
❶ⓐ small and tiny
小 SMALL → 0007
豆- miniature → 2442
微 SLIGHT → 0788
細 MINUTE → 1689
寸 A BIT OF → 3652

❷ⓐ unimportant
細 MINUTE → 1689
微 SLIGHT → 0788
小 SMALL → 0007
末 last in importance → 4317

❸ schools
校 SCHOOL → 1166
学 EDUCATIONAL INSTITUTION → 3162
院 INSTITUTION → 0544
塾 PRIVATE SCHOOL → 3546
大 UNIVERSITY → 4224
高 high school → 2601
中 junior high school → 4262
小 elementary school → 0007
園 kindergarten → 3914

❹ humble prefixes
小 my little (*humble*) → 0007
弊 our [my] humble → 3583
拙 my humble → 0373
愚 my foolish → 3513

USAGE
【さ-】
小-
[also prefix] *elegant* little, nice
早-
young, supple

HOMOPHONES
こ-
子 CHILD → 4196
児 CHILD → 3153
娘 DAUGHTER → 0488
仔 OFFSPRING → 0038
さ- 早 EARLY → 3042
さざなみ
漣 RIPPLES → 0859
小波 → 0007, 0388
細波 → 1689, 0388

NOTE
➡ see also USAGE note at 子 4196

忄

0008
◧ 1-1-2

▶ ***RISSHINBEN***

61	Radical	U5FC4
忄	S3-3-0	F0000

radical variant → see 心 at 0011

巛

0009
◧ 1-1-2

▶ ***MAGARIGAWA***

47	Radical	U5DDB
巛	S3-3-0	F0000

RADICAL
magarigawa 'river' (巡), used for character classification
Variant: 川 ***sanbongawa*** (州)

少
◧ 1-1-3

incorrect classification
➡ see ■4-4-4 at 4278

水

▶WATER

スイ みず みず- ㊔ みな み

Ⓒ 水 shuǐ

0010

1-1-3

85	Jōyō-1	U6C34
水	S4-4-0	F0146

亅 水 水 水
1 2 3 4

RADICAL

mizu 'water' (永 沓 氷), used in characters related to water flow, liquids or water bodies

Left variant: 氵 *sanzui* (決 演 法)

Bottom variant: 氺 *shitamizu* (泰 求 滕×)

COMPOUNDS

❶ [also suffix]

ⓐ [original meaning] **WATER, cold water**

ⓑ body of **WATER**, waters

ⓒ the fifth of the five elements: **WATER** (→see APPENDIX 8)

a 水道 すいどう water service [supply]; channel
水準 すいじゅん level, standard; water level
水中 すいちゅう in the water
水面 すいめん surface of the water
水力 すいりょく waterpower, hydraulic power
水蒸気 すいじょうき steam, water vapor
海水 かいすい seawater
地下水 ちかすい underground water

b 水産物 すいさんぶつ marine products
水域 すいいき water area, waters

❷ [also suffix] (liquid or water solution) **WATER**, lotion, liquid, fluid; soda
水銀 すいぎん mercury, quicksilver
石灰水 せっかいすい lime water
化粧水 けしょうすい toilet water [lotion]

❸ **hydrogen**
水素 すいそ hydrogen
水爆 すいばく hydrogen bomb
炭水化物 たんすいかぶつ carbohydrates

❹ **Wednesday**
水曜(日) すいよう(び) Wednesday
月水金 げっすいきん Mondays, Wednesdays and Fridays

❺ Mercury
水星 すいせい Mercury

INDEPENDENT

【すい 水】 Wednesday; shaved ice; the fifth of the five elements: **WATER**

KUN

【みず 水】

①ⓐ **WATER, cold water**

ⓑ [in compounds] **liquid, WATERy**

a 水洗い みずあらい washing with water
水着 みずぎ bathing [swimming] suit
水色 みずいろ sky blue, turquoise
雨水 あまみず rainwater

b 水飴 みずあめ starch syrup

② *sumo* break
水入りの相撲 みずいりのすもう sumo match with a break

③ **damper, wet blanket, barrier**
水を注す みずをさす pour water (into); estrange (people); throw cold water
水入らずで みずいらずで by ourselves [themselves]

【みず- 水-】 [prefix] **WATER**
水資源 みずしげん water resources
水仕事 みずしごと scrubbing and washing, kitchen work
水商売 みずしょうばい bar and restaurant business; chancy trade

SYNONYMS

❶ⓐ **kinds of water**
水 WATER →0010
湯 HOT WATER →0747
汽 STEAM →0309
氷 ICE →0043
淵 DEEP WATER →0732

❷ **liquid**
液 LIQUID →0622
汁 fluid →0227
水 WATER →0010

❸ **lighter elements**
水 hydrogen →0010
酸 OXYGEN →1968
窒 NITROGEN →2853
塩 chlorine →0774
臭 bromine →3261
硫 SULFUR →1519
炭 carbon →2806

❹ **days of the week**
日 Sunday →3759
月 Monday →3674
火 Tuesday →4273
水 Wednesday →0010
木 Thursday →4261
金 Friday →2552
土 Saturday →4211

USAGE

【みず】

水

①ⓐ water, cold water

ⓑ [in compounds] liquid, watery

② *sumo* break

③ damper, wet blanket, barrier

瑞-

young and fresh, vigorous

HOMOPHONES

みず 瑞 AUSPICIOUS OMEN → 1302

心

▶HEART

シン こころ -ごころ ㊔ むね まこと み

Ⓒ 心 xīn

0011

1-1-3

61	Jōyō-2	U5FC3
心	S4-4-0	F0063

RADICAL

kokoro 'heart' (必 忍 恥), used in characters related to emotions, thought or intellect

Left variant: 忄 ***risshinben*** (性 情 悩)

Bottom variant: ⺗ ***shitagokoro*** (恭 慕)

COMPOUNDS

❶ⓐ **HEART, mind, spirit, feelings, emotions, thoughts**

ⓑ [also suffix] sense, motive

a 心情 しんじょう one's heart, one's feelings

心身 しんしん mind and body

心理 しんり mental state, mentality; psychology

心配 しんぱい anxiety, concern, worry, uneasiness; good offices

心境 しんきょう frame of mind, mental attitude [state]

心中 しんちゅう heart, mind, true motives

心中 しんじゅう lovers' suicide, double suicide

関心 かんしん concern, interest

安心する あんしんする have one's heart at ease, feel easy, be relieved

熱心 ねっしん enthusiasm, zeal, fervor, earnestness

感心する かんしんする admire, be deeply impressed

初心 しょしん one's original intention [object]

良心 りょうしん conscience

決心する けっしんする make up one's mind, decide

苦心 くしん pains, efforts, hard work

以心伝心 いしんでんしん silent [tacit] understanding, empathy

孝心 こうしん filial devotion [affection]

好奇心 こうきしん curiosity

b 愛国心 あいこくしん patriotism, nationalism

公徳心 こうとくしん sense of public duty, public spirit

❷ [also suffix] [original meaning] **HEART** (the organ)

心臓 しんぞう heart

心電図 しんでんず electrocardiogram

心不全 しんふぜん heart failure

狭心症 きょうしんしょう angina pectoris

衝心 しょうしん heart failure

脂肪心 しぼうしん fatty heart

❸ⓐ (central part) **HEART, center, core**

ⓑ [formerly also 腎 じん 3511] **HEART of a matter, vital point**

ⓒ (machine part) center

a 中心 ちゅうしん center, middle

都心 としん heart [center] of a city

核心 かくしん core, heart

重心 じゅうしん center of gravity, centroid

遠心力 えんしんりょく centrifugal force

外心 がいしん circumcenter, outer center

b 肝心な かんじんな vital, essential, main

c 心棒 しんぼう axle, shaft, arbor

心無し研削 しんなしけんさく centerless grinding

❹ [usu. 芯 2744] core (of fruit); wick; lead (of a pencil); padding

心抜き器 しんぬきき corer

花心 かしん center of a flower

灯心 とうしん (lamp) wick

替え心 かえしん spare lead

帯心 おびしん sash padding

INDEPENDENT

【しん 心】

① **HEART, core; vitality; marrow**

心から しんから from the bottom of one's heart; by nature

心は良い男 しんはよいおとこ a good man at heart

心が疲れる しんがつかれる tired to the bone; be mentally fatigued

② [usu. 芯 2744] **core (of fruit); wick; lead (of a pencil); padding**

心を入れる しんをいれる pad (a sash)

林檎の心 りんごのしん core of an apple

蠟燭の心 ろうそくのしん wick of a candle

鉛筆の心 えんぴつのしん lead of a pencil

KUN

【こころ 心】

①ⓐ [also suffix] **HEART, mind, spirit, soul; thoughts, ideas**

ⓑ **attention, mind, interest**

a 心構え こころがまえ mental attitude; preparation

心当たりが有る こころあたりがある have an idea [a clue]

真心 まごころ sincerity, true heart

子供心 こどもごころ child's naive [juvenile] mind

b 心を配る こころをくばる give attention

心する こころする mind, take care, be attentive

心掛ける こころがける bear in mind; try, endeavor, intend

心掛け こころがけ (mental) attitude; attention

② (emotional state) **HEART, feelings, emotion**

心を動かす こころをうごかす move one's heart; impress, touch (a person's heart)

心残りだ こころのこりだ feel sorry, regret

心細い こころぼそい helpless, forlorn; lonely

心安い こころやすい intimate, familiar

心持ち こころもち feeling, mood; slightly

心行く迄 こころゆくまで to one's heart's content

心強い こころづよい reassuring, heartening

気心 きごころ temper, disposition

恋心 こいごころ one's love

③ⓐ **(true) HEART, wholeheartedness, sincerity**

ⓑ (generous disposition) **sympathy, HEART, consideration**

a 心から こころから from the bottom of one's heart

心尽くし こころづくし kindness, consideration, solicitude

心を向ける こころをむける turn one's thoughts to

心無い こころない thoughtless; cruel; inconsiderate

b 心遣い こころづかい consideration, anxiety

手心を加える てごころをくわえる use one's discretion, take into consideration

④ⓐ mind, intention, will, inclination

ⓑ frame of mind, mood

a 心積もり こころづもり intention, expectation

下心 したごころ underlying motive, secret intention

⑤ **meaning, essence; answer (to a riddle)**

心得 こころえ knowledge, information; instructions

歌の心 うたのこころ true meaning of a poem, spirit of a poem

【-ごころ -心】 **spirit, soul; disposition, turn of mind**

大和心 やまとごころ the Japanese spirit

歌心 うたごころ poetic turn of mind, feel for poetry

SPECIAL READINGS

心地 ここち feeling, mood

SYNONYMS

❶ⓐ psyche

心 HEART → 0011

霊 SPIRIT (soul) → 3480

魂 SOUL, spirit → 1346

魄 SOUL → 1570

腹 heart → 1308

衷 INNER HEART → 2600

襟 inner mind → 1599

胸 breast → 1187

懐 BOSOM → 0942

神 MIND → 1143

気 SPIRIT (consciousness) → 3960

精 SPIRIT (mind) → 1729

❷ internal organs

心 HEART → 0011

肺 LUNG → 1147

胃 STOMACH → 3171

腸 INTESTINES → 1307

肝 LIVER → 1045

胆 GALLBLADDER → 1150

腎 KIDNEY → 3511

❸ⓐ middle

中 MIDDLE → 4262

央 CENTER → 4322

心 HEART → 0011

核 NUCLEUS → 1162

❹ central parts

核 NUCLEUS → 1162

仁 kernel → 0021

心 core → 0011

芯 CORE → 2744

【こころ】

② **feeling**

感 SENSE (feeling) → 3514

情 EMOTION → 0583

心 HEART → 0011

気 spirits → 3960

USAGE

【しん】

心

① heart, core; vitality; marrow

② [usu. 芯] core (of fruit); wick; lead (of a pencil); padding

芯

[sometimes also 心] core (of fruit); wick; lead (of a pencil); padding

NOTE

➡ see COMPOUND FORMATION for

以心伝心 いしんでんしん → 以 0045

衝心 しょうしん → 衝 0893

小

▸ *SHITAGOKORO*

0012

◧ 1-1-3

61	Radical	U2E97
小	S4-4-0	F0000

radical variant → see 心 at 0011

灬

▸ *REKKA*

0013

◧ 1-1-3

86	Radical	U706C
灬	S4-4-0	F0000

radical variant → see 火 at 4273

火

◧ 1-1-3

incorrect classification

➡ see ■4-4-4 at 4273

旧

▸FORMER

キュウ

Ⓝ 舊 舊 Ⓒ 旧 jiù

0014

◧1-1-4

72△	Jōyō-5	U65E7
日	S5-4-1	F0916

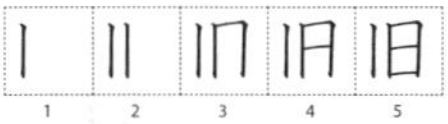

COMPOUNDS

❶ⓐ [also prefix] **FORMER, ex-, old-time, old**
ⓑ old, ancient, antique, old-fashioned, bygone

a 旧夫 きゅうふ former husband
旧居 きゅうきょ former residence
旧軍人 きゅうぐんじん ex-soldier
旧制 きゅうせい old system, old style
b 旧株 きゅうかぶ old stock
旧弊な きゅうへいな old-fashioned, conservative
旧式 きゅうしき old style, old type
新旧の しんきゅうの old and new
復旧する ふっきゅうする be restored, recover
懐旧 かいきゅう longing for the old days

❷ old acquaintance
故旧 こきゅう old acquaintance

❸ old calendar, lunar calendar
旧暦 きゅうれき old [lunar] calendar
旧正月 きゅうしょうがつ New Year's Day in the lunar calendar

INDEPENDENT

【きゅう 旧】**old things, original or FORMER state, old times; old [lunar] calendar; old stock**
旧に復する きゅうにふくする be restored to the former state

【きゅうの 旧の】old, **FORMER**
旧の三月 きゅうのさんがつ March according to the old calendar

SYNONYMS

❶ⓐ former
旧 FORMER → 0014
元 former → 2428
故 OLD (earlier time) → 1466
前 previous → 2819
嘗て previously → 3230
曽 previously → 2632
先 former → 3046
既 ALREADY → 1498

ⓑ old
古 OLD (not new) → 2495
老 OLD (not young) → 3963
故 OLD (of the past) → 1466
旧 old → 0014

❸ calendars
暦 CALENDAR → 3747
新 new calendar → 2239
旧 old calendar → 0014

必

▸WITHOUT FAIL

ヒツ かなら(ず) ㊔ さだ さだむ

Ⓒ 必 bì

0015

◧1-1-4

61	Jōyō-4	U5FC5
心	S5-4-1	F0283

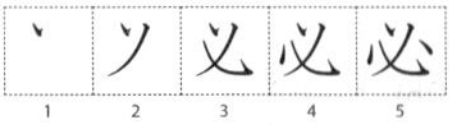

COMPOUNDS

❶ [original meaning] **WITHOUT FAIL, certainly, surely; inevitable**
必須の ひっすの indispensable, essential
必要 ひつよう need, necessity
必死 ひっし inevitable death; desperation
必需 ひつじゅ necessary
必然の ひつぜんの inevitable, necessary
必然的 ひつぜんてき inevitable
必至の ひっしの inevitable, necessary
必勝 ひっしょう certain victory

❷ must, required, compulsory, worthwhile
必読書 ひつどくしょ required reading
必見の物 ひっけんのもの something that deserves attention; a must
必修科目 ひっしゅうかもく required subject
必着 ひっちゃく (of mail) to be delivered (without fail)

INDEPENDENT

【ひっする 必する】warrant, guarantee

KUN

【かならず 必ず】**WITHOUT FAIL, certainly, surely, invariably, always, necessarily**
必ずしも かならずしも not always, not all

SYNONYMS

❶ certain
必 WITHOUT FAIL → 0015
確 CERTAIN → 1571
筈 OUGHT TO → 3318

❷ need and necessity
要 required → 3263
必 must → 0015
須 MUST → 0700
需 DEMAND → 3472
入 necessary → 4177
用 needed for (a specific use) → 3694

州

◧1-1-5

incorrect classification
➡ see ◧1-2-4: 刂 at 0064

1

灯 incorrect classification
➡ see ◧1-4-2: 火 at 1019
◧1-1-5

忙忙 incorrect classification
➡ see ◧1-3-3: 忄 at 0248
◧1-1-5

児 incorrect classification
➡ see ⬒2-5-2: 旧 at 3153
◧1-1-6

承 incorrect stroke-count
➡ see ◧1-1-7: フ at 0016
◧1-1-6

快 incorrect classification
➡ see ◧1-3-4: 忄 at 0289
◧1-1-6

灼灼 incorrect classification
➡ see ◧1-4-3: 火 at 1036
◧1-1-6

承

▶**AGREE TO**
ショウ うけたまわ(る) う(ける)▲ ㊔ つぐ よし
Ⓒ 承 chéng

0016
◧1-1-7

64	Jōyō-5	U627F
手	S8-4-4	F0949

ㇷ 了 子 手 手 承 承 承
1 2 3 4 5 6 7 8

COMPOUNDS

❶ **AGREE TO, consent, accept**
承諾する しょうだくする consent, assent, agree, accept
承知する しょうちする consent [agree] to; permit; forgive; know, understand
承認 しょうにん approval, recognition
承服 しょうふく consent, acceptance
了承 りょうしょう acknowledgment, understanding

❷ **succeed to, take over, inherit; receive**
承継 しょうけい succession
承前 しょうぜん continued (from the previous text)
継承する けいしょうする succeed to, accede to, inherit
伝承 でんしょう tradition, legend

❸ second stanza in a Chinese quatrain
起承転結 きしょうてんけつ introduction, development, turn and conclusion (of a Chinese quatrain)

KUN

【うけたまわる 承る】[humble] **hear, listen to, be told; know, understand; receive (a command)**
承りましょう うけたまわりましょう I'll listen to you respectfully
承れば うけたまわれば from what I am told

【うける 承ける】[usu. 受ける] inherit, get
親の気質を承ける おやのきしつをうける inherit one's parent's disposition

SYNONYMS

❶ **agree and approve**
賛 APPROVE OF → 3484
可 APPROVE → 3687
認 RECOGNIZE → 1948
諾 CONSENT → 1974
承 AGREE TO → 0016
肯 ASSENT → 3072
容 tolerate → 2832

❷ **succeed**
継 SUCCEED → 1720
承 succeed to → 0016
嗣 inherit → 2153

HOMOPHONES

うける
受 RECEIVE → 3076
享 ENJOY → 2545
請 REQUEST → 1983

NOTE

➡ see USAGE note at 受 3076

炉炊 incorrect classification
➡ see ◧1-4-4: 火 at 1079
◧1-1-7

性怪 etc. incorrect classification
➡ see ◧1-3-5: 忄 at 0353
◧1-1-7

胤

▶**PROGENY**
イン たね ㊔ つぐ つぎ かず
Ⓒ 胤 yìn

0017
◧1-1-8

130	Names	U80E4
月	S9-4-5	F2689

COMPOUNDS

❶ⓐ **PROGENY, descendant, posterity**
ⓑ descent, lineage
a 落胤 らくいん illegitimate child, love child
後胤 こういん descendant, scion
皇胤 こういん [archaic] Imperial descendant [posterity]
b 胤裔× いんえい [archaic] descendant, successor

❷ [original meaning, now archaic] succeed to, inherit

KUN

【たね 胤】[now usu. 種] **paternal blood, offspring**
胤違い たねちがい half brother, half sister

SYNONYMS

❶ⓐ descendant

孫 GRANDCHILD, descendant →0492
胤 PROGENY →0017
末 posterity →4317

HOMOPHONES

たね 種 VARIETY →1560

NOTE

➡ see USAGE note at 種 1560

畑炮 incorrect classification
➡ see ◧1-4-5: 火 at 1131
◧1-1-8

恒悔 etc. incorrect classification
➡ see ◧1-3-6: 忄 at 0435
◧1-1-8

鬥 incorrect classification
➡ see ◧1-5-5: 𨈑 at 1497
◧1-1-9

帰 incorrect classification
➡ see ◧1-2-8: 刂 at 0148
◧1-1-9

烟 incorrect classification
➡ see ◧1-4-6: 火 at 1180
◧1-1-9

悩悟 etc. incorrect classification
➡ see ◧1-3-7: 忄 at 0501
◧1-1-9

焔 incorrect classification
➡ see ◧1-4-7: 火 at 1216
◧1-1-10

情惨 etc. incorrect classification
➡ see ◧1-3-8: 忄 at 0581
◧1-1-10

順

0018
◧1-1-11

▸ORDER
▸OBEY

ジュン ㊔ より よし ゆき のり のぶ むね

Ⓒ 顺 shùn

181	Jōyō-4	U9806
頁	S12-9-3	F0975

丿 丿丨 川 川𠂆 ... 順 (stroke order 1–12)

COMPOUNDS

❶ [also suffix] **ORDER, sequence, turn**

順番 じゅんばん order, turn
順序 じゅんじょ order, sequence; system, procedure
順位 じゅんい order, rank, precedence
順順に じゅんじゅんに by turns, in order
順路 じゅんろ suggested route (for visitors), way round
筆順 ひつじゅん stroke order (in writing Chinese characters)
道順 みちじゅん route, itinerary
手順 てじゅん procedure, program, process
先着順 せんちゃくじゅん order of arrival
年齢順に ねんれいじゅんに by priority of age
ＡＢＣ順に えーびーしーじゅんに in alphabetical order

❷ⓐ [also 遵 3929] **OBEY, follow, submit to**
ⓑ obedient, gentle
ⓒ [also 馴 2290] tame, domesticate

a 順守する じゅんしゅする observe, obey, follow, conform to
順法 じゅんぽう law observance
随順する ずいじゅんする obey meekly, faithfully follow (one's master)

b 順逆 じゅんぎゃく obedience and disobedience, right or wrong
恭順 きょうじゅん obedience, submission
温順 おんじゅん obedience, gentleness, docility

c 順応 じゅんのう adaptation, accommodation, adjustment
順化 じゅんか acclimation

❸ favorable, satisfactory, right

順調 じゅんちょう favorable condition, smooth progress
順風 じゅんぷう favorable wind
順当な じゅんとうな proper, right, reasonable
順境 じゅんきょう favorable circumstances [condition]

INDEPENDENT

【じゅん 順】**ORDER, sequence, turn**
順に じゅんに in order, by turns

SYNONYMS

❶ order

序 ORDER (sequence/arrangement) →3803
順 ORDER (sequence) →0018
次 order (sequence) →0058
番 NUMERICAL ORDER →3416
秩 ORDER (methodical arrangement) →1489

❷ⓐ obey

守 observe →2697
遵 OBEY →3929
順 OBEY →0018
隷 be subordinate to →2201
従 FOLLOW →0498

❸ good

1

丿

良 GOOD →4373
善 GOOD →2921
好 FAVORABLE →0240
順 favorable →0018
佳 FINE →0096
美 BEAUTIFUL →2817

煤
◧1-1-11
incorrect classification/ stroke-count
➡ see ◧1-4-9: 火 at 1292

焼焰 etc.
◧1-1-11
incorrect classification
➡ see ◧1-4-8: 火 at 1255

愉惰 etc.
◧1-1-11
incorrect classification
➡ see ◧1-3-9: 忄 at 0706

熇
◧1-1-12
incorrect classification
➡ see ◧1-2-11: 刂 at 0183

煙煩 etc.
◧1-1-12
incorrect classification
➡ see ◧1-4-9: 火 at 1292

慎慨 etc.
◧1-1-12
incorrect classification
➡ see ◧1-3-10: 忄 at 0790

鬧
◧1-1-13
incorrect classification
➡ see □3-10-4: 鬥 at 4140

慣慢 etc.
◧1-1-13
incorrect classification
➡ see ◧1-3-11: 忄 at 0843

煽熄 etc.
◧1-1-13
incorrect classification
➡ see ◧1-4-10: 火 at 1338

憤憧 etc.
◧1-1-14
incorrect classification
➡ see ◧1-3-12: 忄 at 0897

憐
◧1-1-15
incorrect classification/ stroke-count
➡ see ◧1-3-12: 忄 at 0901

憾憶 etc.
◧1-1-15
incorrect classification
➡ see ◧1-3-13: 忄 at 0942

燃燎 etc.
◧1-1-15
incorrect classification
➡ see ◧1-4-12: 火 at 1375

燥燦 etc.
◧1-1-16
incorrect classification
➡ see ◧1-4-13: 火 at 1390

燿燻 etc.
◧1-1-17
incorrect classification
➡ see ◧1-4-14: 火 at 1406

爆
◧1-1-18
incorrect classification
➡ see ◧1-4-15: 火 at 1415

懐
◧1-1-18
incorrect classification
➡ see ◧1-3-16: 忄 at 0993

鬪
◧1-1-19
incorrect classification
➡ see □3-10-10: 鬥 at 4141

爐
◧1-1-19
incorrect classification
➡ see ◧1-4-16: 火 at 1420

爛
◧1-1-20
incorrect classification
➡ see ◧1-4-17: 火 at 1427

鬭
◧1-1-23
incorrect classification/ stroke-count
➡ see □3-10-15: 鬥 at 4142

鬮
◧1-1-24
incorrect classification
➡ see □3-10-15: 鬥 at 4142

孔
◧1-2-1
incorrect stroke-count
➡ see ◧1-3-1: 子 at 0205

从
0019
◧1-2-2

▸**FOLLOW**

ジュウ ショウ ジュ したが(う) したが(える)
㊔ より つぐ

9	Nonstandard	U4ECE
人	S4-2-2	F0000

traditional form →see 從 at 0498

仏
0020
◧1-2-2

▸**BUDDHA**
▸**FRANCE**

ブツ フツ^ ほとけ ㊔ さとる
Ⓝ 佛 Ⓒ 佛 fó fú

9	Jōyō-5	U4ECF
亻	S4-2-2	F0704

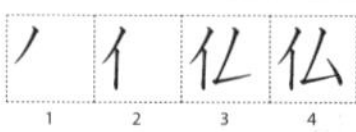

COMPOUNDS

❶ⓐ BUDDHA, Sakyamuni
ⓑ Buddhism
ⓒ [also suffix] **Buddhist image**

a 仏陀 ぶっだ Buddha
神仏 しんぶつ gods and Buddha; Shinto and Buddhism
b 仏教 ぶっきょう Buddhism
念仏 ねんぶつ Buddhist invocation, prayer to Amitabha
c 仏像 ぶつぞう image of Buddha; Buddhist statue
仏壇 ぶつだん family Buddhist altar
石仏 せきぶつ stone Buddhist image
三尊仏 さんぞんぶつ image of the three honorable ones
大仏 だいぶつ great statue of Buddha

❷ⓐ FRANCE
ⓑ French (language)

a 仏印 ふついん French Indochina
日仏 にちふつ Japan and France
b 仏文学 ふつぶんがく French literature
仏英辞典 ふつえいじてん French-English dictionary

❸ the deceased, departed soul
成仏する じょうぶつする enter Nirvana, attain Buddhahood; die

INDEPENDENT

【ぶつ 仏】BUDDHA; Buddhism
【ふつ 仏】FRANCE

KUN

【ほとけ 仏】**BUDDHA; Buddhist image; the deceased, departed soul**
仏様 ほとけさま Buddha; deceased person

SYNONYMS

❶ⓐ Buddha
仏 BUDDHA →0020
釈 Sakyamuni →1876
ⓑ religions and sects
仏 Buddhism →0020
法 Buddha's teachings →0391
禅 ZEN →1306
儒 CONFUCIANISM →0197
道 Taoism →3888
ⓒ images
像 IMAGE →0187
仏 Buddhist image →0020
偶 figure →0150

❷ⓐ European countries
英 ENGLAND →2782
独 GERMANY →0471
仏 FRANCE →0020
伊 ITALY →0052
葡 PORTUGAL →2902
西 Spain →4333
蘭 the Netherlands →3031
希 Greece →2543
露 Russia →3495
白 Belgium →4305

仁 ▸BENEVOLENCE

ジン ニ ニン▲ ㊔ ひと ひとし よし まこと ひろし まさ きみ さと のり

0021 Ⓒ 仁 rén

1-2-2

9	Jōyō-6	U4EC1
亻	S4-2-2	F1100

Stroke order: 1 ノ 2 亻 3 亻一 4 仁

COMPOUNDS

❶ BENEVOLENCE, the perfect virtue, humaneness, compassion, kindness, love, mercy (a basic Confucian precept)
仁愛 じんあい benevolence, charity
仁術 じんじゅつ benevolent act
仁義礼智信 じんぎれいちしん the five Confucian virtues (benevolence, justice, courtesy, wisdom and sincerity)
仁徳 じんとく benevolence, goodness
仁義 じんぎ humanity and justice; moral code; formal greeting among gamblers

❷ benevolent personage
仁者 じんしゃ man of virtue
御仁 ごじん personage

❸ kernel, core; karyosome
杏仁 きょうにん apricot stone
核仁 かくじん nucleus

❹ two (people)
仁王(=二王) におう the two Deva kings

INDEPENDENT

【じん 仁】BENEVOLENCE (→❶); nucleolus
身を殺して仁を為す みをころしてじんをなす do an act of benevolence at the sacrifice of oneself

SYNONYMS

❶ tender feelings for others
仁 BENEVOLENCE →0021
慈 compassion →2949
情 sympathy →0583
悲 mercy →3448
哀 PITY →2568
憐 PITY →0945

❸ central parts
核 NUCLEUS →1162
仁 kernel →0021
心 core →0011

芯 CORE → 2744

化

0022

1-2-2

▶CHANGE INTO

カ ケ ば(ける) ば(かす)

Ⓝ 化 Ⓒ 化 huà

21	Jōyō-3	U5316
ヒ	S4-2-2	F0102

ノ 亻 亻⺊ 化

1 2 3 4

COMPOUNDS

❶ⓐ **CHANGE INTO, transform into, turn into, convert**

ⓑ **change (a person) for the better, convert, influence**

a 化石 かせき fossil, fossil remains; petrifaction
化成 かせい chemical synthesis, transformation
化合 かごう chemical combination
消化 しょうか digestion; assimilation; consumption
同化 どうか assimilation
変化 へんか change, transformation, variety; declension

b 文化 ぶんか culture
感化する かんかする influence, exert influence, inspire
教化する きょうかする enlighten, educate, civilize

❷ [also suffix]

ⓐ (cause to become) **-ize, -ify, make into**

ⓑ (become) **-ize, become transformed, turn into**

a 強化 きょうか strengthening, intensification, build-up, reinforcement
液化 えきか liquefaction
浄化する じょうかする purify, cleanse
近代化 きんだいか modernization
コンピュータ化 こんぴゅーたか computerization

b 酸化 さんか oxidation
激化する げきか(=げっか)する intensify, become aggravated
悪化する あっかする worsen, aggravate, deteriorate
軟化 なんか softening; weakening (of the market)

❸ **CHANGE [transform] oneself INTO, take the form of; disguise oneself**

化粧品 けしょうひん cosmetics
化身 けしん Buddhist incarnation, reincarnation
権化 ごんげ incarnation, embodiment
変化 へんげ goblin, ghost

❹ abbrev. of 化学 かがく: **chemistry**

化工 かこう chemical engineering
化繊 かせん synthetic fiber

INDEPENDENT

【かする(=かす) 化する(=化す)】 **CHANGE INTO,** transform into; convert (by virtuous example), influence

徳を以て化する とくをもってかする influence by means of one's virtue

KUN

【ばける 化ける】 **CHANGE [transform] oneself INTO, take the form of; disguise oneself**

化け物 ばけもの monster; ghost
お化け おばけ apparition, specter, ghost
女に化ける おんなにばける change into a woman, assume the shape of a woman

【ばかす 化かす】 **bewitch, deceive; transfigure**

狐に化かされる きつねにばかされる be deceived by a fox

SYNONYMS

❶ & ❷ **change and replace**

変 CHANGE → 2569
替 REPLACE → 3457
代 SUBSTITUTE → 0034
迭 ALTERNATE → 3818
更 change → 4355
改 change → 0287
易 change → 3064
化 CHANGE INTO, -ize → 0022
遷 undergo transition → 3932
転 turn into → 1872
換 EXCHANGE → 0716
交 INTERCHANGE → 2508

❸ **disguise**

装 dress up → 3327
化 change oneself into → 0022

COMPOUND FORMATION

【文化 ぶんか】

文化 'culture' is influencing (化 ❶ⓑ) by means of culture (文).

NOTE

➡ see COMPOUND FORMATION for 羽化 うか → 羽 0265

仇

0023

1-2-2

▶FOE

キュウ あだ あだ(する) かたき

Ⓒ 仇 chóu

9	Non-Jōyō	U4EC7
亻	S4-2-2	F2043

COMPOUNDS

ⓐ **FOE, enemy**

ⓑ [rare] enmity, resentment, grudge

a 仇敵 きゅうてき bitter enemy
ab 仇怨 きゅうえん foe, enemy; grudge, hatred
b 復仇 ふっきゅう revenge

報仇 ほうきゅう revenge, retaliation

KUN

【あだ 仇】

①ⓐ **FOE, enemy**

ⓑ **revenge, retaliation**

ab 仇を討つ あだをうつ revenge, take revenge

② **malice, ill will, hostility**

恩を仇で返す おんをあだでかえす return evil for good

③ harm

仇となる あだとなる have a harmful result, backfire

【あだする 仇する】

① harm; injure

罪の無い人に仇する つみのないひとにあだする harm innocent people

② oppose, be hostile to

【かたき 仇】 [also 敵]

ⓐ **enemy, FOE**

ⓑ **revenge, retaliation**

a 仇同士 かたきどうし mutual enemies

b 父の仇を討つ ちちのかたきをうつ avenge one's father

SYNONYMS

ⓐ enemy

敵 ENEMY → 2340

仇 FOE → 0023

HOMOPHONES

かたき 敵 ENEMY → 2340

NOTE

➡ see USAGE note at 敵 2340

仂

0024

◧ 1-2-2

▶WORK

ドウ はたら(く)

9	Nonstandard	U4EC2
亻	S4-2-2	F0000

handwritten form → see 働 at 0172

化

0025

◧ 1-2-2

▶CHANGE INTO

カ ケ ば(ける) ば(かす)

9	Nonstandard	U5316
亻	S4-2-2	F0000

traditional form → see 化 at 0022

仔

◧ 1-2-2

incorrect stroke-count

➡ see ◧ 1-2-3: 亻 at 0038

艹

0026

◧ 1-2-2

▶*KUSAKANMURI*

140	Radical	U2EBF
艹	S4-4-0	F0000

radical variant → see 艸 at 0241

厶厶

0027

◧ 1-2-2

▶NEIGHBOR

リン とな(る) となり

28	Nonstandard	U53B8
ム	S4-2-2	F0000

traditional form → see 隣 at 0961

双

0028

◧ 1-2-2

▶SET OF TWO

ソウ ふた Ⓝ もろ なみ

Ⓝ 雙 Ⓒ 双 shuāng

29△	Jōyō	U53CC
又	S4-2-2	F1240

フ ヌ 双 双

1 2 3 4

COMPOUNDS

❶ⓐ [original meaning] **SET OF TWO (identical things such as hands), pair, both, two**

ⓑ counter for pairs

a 双肩 そうけん both shoulders

双生児 そうせいじ twins

双方 そうほう both sides [parties]

b 双眼鏡 そうがんきょう binoculars

一双 いっそう a pair

❷ comparison, match

双璧 そうへき two matchless authorities [jewels]

無双 むそう matchless, peerless

❸ [usu. 叢 3243] crowd together, meet in large numbers

双書(=叢書) そうしょ series, library

INDEPENDENT

【そう 双】 pair

双の手 そうのて both hands

KUN

【ふた 双】 [in compounds] **SET OF TWO, pair**

双子 ふたご twins

双葉 ふたば bud, cotyledon

SYNONYMS

❶ two

二 TWO → 2421

弐 TWO (in legal documents) → 3961

双 SET OF TWO → 0028

対 pair → 1025

偶 COUPLE → 0150

両 BOTH → 4331

HOMOPHONES

ふた 二 TWO → 2421

NOTE

➡ see USAGE note at 二 2421

比

0029

1-2-2

▸**COMPARE**

ヒ くら(べる) ㊔ これ

Ⓒ 比 bǐ

81	Jōyō-5	U6BD4
比	S4-4-0	F0585

一 匕 比 比 (stroke order 1 2 3 4)

RADICAL

kuraberu or ***hi*** 'compare' (毘), used for character classification

COMPOUNDS

❶ⓐ **COMPARE (with), contrast**

ⓑ [also 譬 3613] **COMPARE to, liken**

ⓒ (something of comparable standing) **comparison, match, equal**

a 比較 ひかく comparison

比較的 ひかくてき comparatively, relatively

対比する たいひする contrast, compare

b 比喩 ひゆ simile, metaphor, allegory

比類 ひるい parallel, equal, match

c 無比の むひの incomparable, matchless, unparalleled

❷ [original meaning] **rank, line up**

比翼 ひよく wings abreast; single garment made to look double

比肩する ひけんする equal, rank with, compare favorably

❸ [also suffix] **ratio**

比例 ひれい proportion, ratio

比率 ひりつ ratio, percentage

正比 せいひ direct ratio

容積比 ようせきひ volume ratio

❹ [also prefix] (of physical constants) **specific**

比熱 ひねつ specific heat

比重 ひじゅう specific gravity, density; relative importance

比電荷 ひでんか specific charge

❺ **Philippines**

比島 ひとう the Philippines

比日 ひにち the Philippines and Japan

❻ used phonetically for *bi* in the transliteration of Sanskrit Buddhist terms

比丘 びく Buddhist priest

INDEPENDENT

【ひ 比】**comparison, match, equal; ratio; the Philippines**

比を見ない ひをみない be unique [unrivaled]

比を求める ひをもとめる obtain the ratio

【ひする 比する】**COMPARE**

KUN

【くらべる 比べる】[sometimes also 較べる] **COMPARE, contrast**

比べ物にならない くらべものにならない be no match for

背比べ せいくらべ comparison of statures

SYNONYMS

❶ⓐ **compare**

比 COMPARE → 0029

較 COMPARE → 1939

譬 COMPARE TO → 3613

校 COLLATE → 1166

照 check against → 3506

対 OPPOSE (contrast) → 1025

参 refer → 2563

❷ **arrange**

並 LINE UP → 2793

比 rank → 0029

列 arrange in a row → 1018

陳 lay out (for exhibit) → 0656

羅 spread out → 3244

揃える arrange properly → 0719

整 PUT IN ORDER → 3562

理 put in order → 1220

❸ **rate**

率 RATE → 2625

割 rate → 2284

比 ratio → 0029

歩 percentage → 3071

❺ **Asian countries**

日 JAPAN → 3759

緬 Myanmar → 1758

老 Laos → 3963

華 CHINA → 2841

蒙 Mongolia → 2938

鮮 Korea → 2355

泰 Thailand → 3193

越 Vietnam → 4108

印 India → 1023

竺 INDIA → 3248

比 Philippines → 0029

USAGE

【くらべる】

比べる

[sometimes also 較べる] compare, contrast

較べる

[usu. 比べる] compare, contrast

HOMOPHONES

くらべる 較 COMPARE → 1939

切

▸CUT

セツ　サイ　き(る)　-き(る)　き(り)　-き(り)　-ぎ(り)　き(れる)　-き(れる)　き(れ)　-き(れ)　-ぎ(れ)

0030

1-2-2

Ⓝ 切◇ Ⓒ 切 qiē qiè

18	Jōyō-2	U5207
刀	S4-2-2	F0157

一 七 切 切
1 2 3 4

COMPOUNDS

❶ [formerly also 截 せつ 4092] [original meaning] **CUT, sever**
切断する せつだんする cut (off), sever
切開 せっかい incision, section
切除する せつじょする cut off, excise
切腹 せっぷく harakiri, suicide by disembowelment
半切 はんせつ half size

❷ⓐ **keen, acute, intense**
ⓑ eager, earnest, ardent
a 切実に せつじつに acutely, keenly, earnestly; sincerely, heartily
痛切な つうせつな keen, acute, poignant
b 切望 せつぼう earnest desire, eager wish
切切と せつせつと eagerly, earnestly, with emotion

❸ⓐ **in close contact, fitting closely, to the point**
ⓑ **urgent, pressing, close**
a 親切な しんせつな kind, friendly, obliging
適切な てきせつな appropriate, adequate, proper
懇切な こんせつな kind, cordial; exhaustive
b 切迫した せっぱくした urgent, pressing, imminent
切羽詰まって せっぱつまって under the pressure of necessity
大切な たいせつな important, weighty; valuable

❹ **everything, all**
一切の いっさいの all, entire, whole
合切 がっさい all (together), altogether

INDEPENDENT

【せつ 切】 label on switches: OFF
切—入 せつにゅう OFF-ON (marking on switches)
【せつなる 切なる】 earnest, eager; keen, acute
【せつに 切に】 earnestly, eagerly, fervently
【せつない 切ない】 **painful, trying, distressing**

KUN

【きる 切る】
①ⓐ **CUT, slice, carve**
ⓑ [sometimes also 伐る] **CUT down (trees), fell, chop down**
ⓒ [formerly also 剪る] **prune, trim, shear**
ⓓ [formerly also 截る] **CUT (flat things such as cloth or paper)**
a 切り離す きりはなす cut [chop] off, sever, detach
切り捨てる きりすてる cut down, cut away; omit
切手 きって postage stamp
切符 きっぷ ticket
切っ先 きっさき [sometimes also 鋒] point of a blade [sword]; tone of argument, force of an attack
b 切り倒す きりたおす fell (a tree)

② [also 斬る] **CUT (a person) with a sword, cut down, kill**
試し切り ためしぎり trying out a new sword (on someone)
裏切る うらぎる betray, turn traitor, double-cross

③ (separate from the main body) **CUT off, break away**
切符を切る きっぷをきる punch a ticket, rip off a coupon
封切り ふうきり release, first run, premiere

④ **perform an action as if by CUTting**
波を切る なみをきる cut one's way through the waves
踏切 ふみきり railroad crossing
皮切り かわきり beginning, start

⑤ⓐ (discontinue an action) **CUT off, pause, break off, turn off, hang up**
ⓑ **CUT [sever] connection with**
a 切り替える きりかえる switch, change, renew
思い切る おもいきる resign oneself to, give up; resolve, determine
打ち切る うちきる put an end to, break off, finish
b 縁切り えんきり severing off connections

⑥ **CUT off [divide] by or as if by a partition**
締切(=〆切) しめきり closing day, deadline; Closed, No Entrance
仕切る しきる partition, divide, mark off; settle accounts; *sumo* toe the mark

⑦ fall short of, be below
千円を切る せんえんをきる be less than 1000 yen

⑧ **perform an action boldly**
切り札 きりふだ trump (card), last resort
踏み切る ふみきる make a bold start, take a plunge; take off; *sumo* step out of the ring
見得を切る みえをきる pose, assume a posture; make a defiant [proud] gesture

⑨ drain (water)
水切り みずきり drainer; cutwater, forefoot; ducks and drakes

【-きる -切る】 [verbal suffix]
① **finish, be through**
読み切る よみきる finish reading, read through

②ⓐ **perform an action thoroughly**
ⓑ **perform an action decisively**
a 張り切る はりきる be in high spirits, be enthusiastic; stretch to the full
疲れ切る つかれきる be tired out, be exhausted

人 亻 十 厶 又 上【七】丬 メ ㅓ

b 言い切る いいきる declare, assert; finish saying

【きり 切り】**limits, bounds, end; the lowest [worst]; last part (of a noh or kabuki play); last piece (on a noh or kabuki program)**

切りが無い きりがない be endless [boundless]

ピンから切り迄 ぴんからきりまで of all sorts, of a wide range

大切り おおぎり last piece on the program; close, conclusion; large chop

【-きり -切り】**CUTter**

缶切り かんきり can opener

爪切り つめきり nail clipper [nipper]

【-ぎり -切り】[also suffix] **way of CUTting**

微塵切りにする みじんぎりにする cut into fine pieces

四つ切り よつぎり cutting in four; quarter

【きれる 切れる】

① **be CUT off, break, snap, burst, collapse**

切れた縄 きれたなわ broken rope

切れ端 きれはし fragment, scrap

② **be CUT [injured], become fissured**

切れ目 きれめ rift, gap, break; end, pause, interval

手が切れた てがきれた I cut my hand

③ wear, be worn out

裾が切れる すそがきれる get frayed at the hem

擦り切れる すりきれる wear out, become seedy

④ **break off, be interrupted**

途切れる とぎれる break, pause, be interrupted

息切れする いきぎれする get short [out] of breath, be winded

⑤ **CUT [sever] connection with**

手切れ てぎれ severance of connections; solatium for severing connections

⑥ **run out, expire, terminate**

期限が切れた きげんがきれた The term has expired

ガソリンが切れる がそりんがきれる run out of gas

⑦ **CUT** (well), be keen, be sharp

切れるナイフ きれるないふ sharp knife

⑧ sharp, smart, able

切れる男 きれるおとこ able [competent] man

⑨ fall short of, be below

元値が切れる もとねがきれる be below the cost

【-きれる -切れる】[verbal suffix] **be able to do, be able to finish**

飲み切れますか のみきれますか Can you drink it all up?

やり切れない やりきれない be unbearable, be too much

食べ切れない程のパン たべきれないほどのぱん more bread than one can eat

【きれ 切れ】

① **sharpness, CUTting quality**

切れ味 きれあじ sharpness, cutting quality

切れが悪い きれがわるい be dull [blunt]; thick, viscous

② [also 布] **cloth**

切れの帽子 きれのぼうし cloth hat

③ **piece, bit, strip, slice**

切れ切れの きれぎれの fragmentary, intermittent

板切れ いたきれ piece of wood, scrap lumber

【-きれ -切れ】**counter for strips or slices**

ケーキ一切れ けーきひときれ a piece of cake

二切れのパン ふたきれのぱん two slices of bread

【-ぎれ -切れ】[also suffix]

① **expiration of, depletion of**

品切れ しなぎれ absence [exhaustion] of stock

時間切れ じかんぎれ expiration of the allotted time

② fragments from writings by famous historical figures

高野切れ こうやぎれ fragments from the old literary work kept at Koyasan

SYNONYMS

❶ **cut**

切 CUT → 0030
薙ぐ MOW DOWN → 3010
剪 PRUNE → 2886
削 CUT BY CHIPPING → 1837
挽く GRIND, saw → 0511
断 CUT OFF → 1885
截 CUT OFF → 4092
裁 CUT OUT → 4090
斬 CUT WITH A SWORD → 1874
割 cut with a knife → 2284
剖 DISSECT → 2103
刈る CLIP → 0032
伐 CUT DOWN → 0046

❷ⓐ **extreme in degree**

酷 SEVERE → 1967
強 STRONG → 0574
凄い tremendous → 0145
重 HEAVY → 4390
高 HIGH → 2601
深 DEEP → 0636
大 BIG → 4224
厳 SEVERE → 4079
激 intense → 0955
極 EXTREME → 1243
痛 bitter(ly) → 4071
切 keen → 0030
甚 EXTREMELY → 3271
祁 EXTREMELY → 1447
超 super- → 4107

頗る EXCEEDINGLY →1552

ⓑ eager

懇 EARNEST →3606

切 eager →0030

摯 SERIOUS →3556

篤 DEVOTED →3371

熱 HOT →3555

USAGE

❶【きる】

切る

①ⓐ cut, slice, carve

ⓑ [sometimes also 伐る] cut down (trees), fell, chop down

ⓒ [formerly also 剪る] prune, trim, shear

ⓓ [formerly also 截る] cut (flat things such as cloth or paper)

② [also 斬る] cut (a person) with a sword, cut down, kill

③ (separate from the main body) cut off, break away

④ perform an action as if by cutting

⑤ⓐ (discontinue an action) cut off, pause, break off, turn off, hang up

ⓑ cut [sever] connection with

⑥ cut off [divide] by or as if by a partition

⑦ fall short of, be below

⑧ perform an action boldly

⑨ drain (water)

伐る

[now usu. 切る] cut down (trees), fell, chop down

剪る

[now usu. 切る] prune, trim, shear

截る

[now usu. 切る] cut (flat things such as cloth or paper)

斬る

① [also 切る] cut (a person) with a sword, cut down, kill

② criticize severely, attack

❷【-ぎれ】

-切れ

[also suffix]

① expiration of, depletion of

② fragments from writings by famous historical figures

-裂れ

[also suffix] fragment (of old textile), strip

HOMOPHONES

きる

伐 CUT DOWN →0046

剪 PRUNE →2886

截 CUT OFF →4092

斬 CUT WITH A SWORD →1874

-ぎれ 裂 SPLIT →3331

きっさき

鋒 POINT OF A BLADE →2172

切っ先 →0030, 3046

COMPOUND FORMATION

【大切 たいせつ】

大切な 'important, etc.' originally referred to a state of extreme (大) urgency (切 ❸ⓑ).

収

0031

1-2-2

▶TAKE IN

シュウ おさ(める) おさ(まる) ㊔ おさむ のぶ かず

Ⓝ 收 Ⓒ 收 shōu

29△	Jōyō-6	U53CE
又	S4-2-2	F0468

丨 丩 㕛 収 (1 2 3 4)

COMPOUNDS

❶ⓐ TAKE IN, gather in, absorb

ⓑ collect materials and record [write down]

ⓒ [formerly also 蒐 2942] **collect**

a 収容する しゅうようする accommodate, receive (guests)

収納 しゅうのう storing; harvesting; receipt

収穫 しゅうかく harvest; harvesting

収着 しゅうちゃく sorption

吸収 きゅうしゅう absorption, assimilation; merger

買収 ばいしゅう buying up, purchasing; bribing

回収する かいしゅうする collect, recover; withdraw

b 収録する しゅうろくする collect, record, write down

収集する しゅうしゅうする collect, gather, accumulate

c 徴収する ちょうしゅうする collect taxes [payment]

❷ⓐ (take possession of, esp. in payment) **TAKE IN, receive, accept**

ⓑ take possession by force, confiscate, seize

ⓒ [original meaning] **TAKE IN** a prisoner, take into custody

a 収入 しゅうにゅう income, earnings, receipts

収益 しゅうえき profit, earnings, proceeds, returns

収賄 しゅうわい acceptance of a bribe, corruption

収得する しゅうとくする take possession of

領収 りょうしゅう receipt

b 収用 しゅうよう expropriation

押収する おうしゅうする seize, confiscate

没収 ぼっしゅう confiscation, seizure, forfeiture

接収 せっしゅう requisition, takeover, seizure

c 収監する しゅうかんする confine in jail, imprison

❸ income, receipts, revenue

収支 しゅうし incomings and outgoings, earnings and expenses

増収 ぞうしゅう increased income [revenue]; increased yield
月収 げっしゅう monthly income
税収 ぜいしゅう yield of taxes, tax revenues

❹ shrink; converge
収縮する しゅうしゅくする contract, shrink
収斂×する しゅうれんする be astringent, contract; converge
収差 しゅうさ aberration
収束 しゅうそく convergence

❺ **bring to order [settlement]**
収拾する しゅうしゅうする get under control, save (the situation)

KUN

【おさめる 収める】

①ⓐ **gain, obtain, reap**
ⓑ **achieve, attain**
a 勝利を収める しょうりをおさめる win, gain a victory
b 成果を収める せいかをおさめる achieve success

② collect materials and record [write down]
情報を収めた本 じょうほうをおさめたほん book containing the information

③ [also 納める] put (back) in place, replace
元の所へ収める もとのところへおさめる put (a thing) back in its place

④ [also 納める] accept
どうぞお収め下さい どうぞおおさめください Please accept it

【おさまる 収まる】

① **be put (back) in place, be restored**
箱に収まる はこにおさまる be stored in a box

②ⓐ **be settled, be brought to a settlement**
ⓑ calm down (as of the wind)
a 収まり おさまり conclusion, end, settlement
争いが収まる あらそいがおさまる be settled
b 台風が収まった たいふうがおさまった The typhoon spent itself out

SYNONYMS

❶ⓐ **take in**
収 TAKE IN →0031
摂 TAKE IN →0799
喫 INGEST →0668
吸 SUCK →0234

ⓑ & ❶ⓒ **gather**
集 COLLECT →3445
蒐 COLLECT →2942
聚 COLLECT →3479
収 collect →0031
採 GATHER →0606
采 GATHER →3077
萃 GATHER →2882
湊 come together →0743

❷ⓐ **get**
得 ACQUIRE →0577
拾 PICK UP →0454
獲 obtain →0959
収 TAKE IN →0031
取 TAKE →1613

❷ⓐ **receive**
受 RECEIVE →3076
享 ENJOY →2545
領 receive →1567
収 TAKE IN →0031
納 ACCEPT →1652
貰 GET →3219
戴 RECEIVE HUMBLY →4093
頂 RECEIVE HUMBLY →0164
拝 have the honor to receive →0360

ⓑ **take forcibly**
奪 ROB →2956
拐 KIDNAP →0365
収 take possession by force →0031

❸ **pay and earnings**
給 PAY →1708
賃 WAGE →3341
料 FEE →1644
俸 SALARY →0128
禄 RETAINER'S STIPEND →1264
収 income →0031

HOMOPHONES

おさめる
納 PAY →1652
治 GOVERN →0393
修 CULTIVATE →0138

おさまる
納 PAY →1652
治 GOVERN →0393
修 CULTIVATE →0138

NOTE

➡ see USAGE notes at 納 1652 and 徵 0841

刈

0032

1-2-2

▶**CLIP**

ガイ▲ カイ▲ か(る)

Ⓝ 苅 Ⓒ 刈 yì

18	Jōyō	U5208
刂	S4-2-2	F2037

COMPOUNDS

● [original meaning, now rare] **CLIP**, crop, mow, cut down

刈除する かいじょする mow, cut off, remove

KUN

【かる 刈る】

ⓐ (cut grass, hair or the like by sharp instrument) **CLIP, crop, cut, shear, mow, prune, trim**

ⓑ **reap, crop, harvest**

a 刈り込む かりこむ prune

刈り取る かりとる mow, cut down, reap, harvest

刈り立ての かりたての newly mown, newly cropped (head), just clipped

草刈り くさかり mowing, mower

羊毛を刈る ようもうをかる shear sheep

b 刈り入れ かりいれ harvest, reap

稲刈り いねかり rice reaping

SYNONYMS

【かる】

ⓐ **cut**

切 CUT →0030

薙ぐ MOW DOWN →3010

剪 PRUNE →2886

削 CUT BY CHIPPING →1837

挽く GRIND, saw →0511

断 CUT OFF →1885

截 CUT OFF →4092

裁 CUT OUT →4090

斬 CUT WITH A SWORD →1874

割 cut with a knife →2284

剖 DISSECT →2103

刈る CLIP →0032

伐 CUT DOWN →0046

ⓑ **harvest**

採 PICK →0606

摘 PICK →0851

穫 HARVEST →1598

刈る reap →0032

USAGE

【かる】

刈る

ⓐ (cut grass, hair or the like by sharp instrument) clip, crop, cut, shear, mow, prune, trim

ⓑ reap, crop, harvest

狩る

hunt

駆る

① drive (a car), urge (a horse) on, spur on

② prompt, inspire

HOMOPHONES

かる

狩 HUNT →0474

駆 DRIVE →2293

艹

▸*KUSAKANMURI*

0033

◧ 1-2-2

140	Radical	UFA5D
艹	S4-4-0	F0000

radical variant → see 艸 at 0241

代

0034

◧ 1-2-3

▸**SUBSTITUTE**
▸**GENERATION**
▸**CHARGE**

ダイ タイ か(わる) か(わり) -が(わり) か(える) よ しろ[1] しろ[2] ㊔ より のり

Ⓒ 代 dài

9	Jōyō-3	U4EE3
亻	S5-2-3	F0042

ノ 亻 仁 代 代
1 2 3 4 5

COMPOUNDS

❶ⓐ [original meaning] **SUBSTITUTE, replace, represent, act for another, alternate**

ⓑ **SUBSTITUTE**, deputy, representative, proxy

a 代用する だいようする substitute, use for another

代行する だいこうする act for another, execute (business) for another

代表する だいひょうする represent, stand for; typify

代理人 だいりにん representative, deputy, proxy

代議 だいぎ popular representation

代議士 だいぎし member of the Diet [House of Representatives]

代打 だいだ pinch-hitting; pinch hitter

代替エネルギー だいたいえねるぎー alternative [substitute] energy

代謝(=新陳代謝) たいしゃ(=しんちんたいしゃ) metabolism; renewal, regeneration

代名詞 だいめいし pronoun

交代する こうたいする relieve (a person), take turns, alternate

b 師範代 しはんだい acting instructor

城代 じょうだい deputy castellan, keeper of the castle

❷ⓐ **GENERATION, lifetime**

ⓑ counter for **GENERATION**s, descendants or reign periods

ⓒ suffix for range of a person's age in ten-year periods: -ies

a 代代 だいだい generation after generation

世代 せだい generation

b 一代 いちだい one generation, lifetime

初代 しょだい first generation, founder

四代目の店主 よんだいめのてんしゅ shopkeeper of the fourth generation

徳川三代家光 とくがわさんだいいえみつ Iemitsu, third in the Tokugawa line

c 二十代の男 にじゅうだいのおとこ man in his twenties

❸ⓐ **age, era, times**

ⓑ suffix indicating years spanning a specific period: **-ies, the...-hundreds**

ⓒ geological era

a 時代 じだい age, era, period; antiquity
現代 げんだい present age, modern times, today
古代 こだい ancient times, antiquity, remote ages
年代 ねんだい age, era, period; date

b 千九百年代 せんきゅうひゃくねんだい the 1900's

c 中生代 ちゅうせいだい Mesozoic era

❹ [also suffix] (price charged) **CHARGE, fare, rate, fee, price, rent**
代金 だいきん charge, fee, price
ホテル代 ほてるだい charge for staying at a hotel
無代 むだい free of charge
タクシー代 たくしーだい taxi fare
地代 じだい land rent, rental
部屋代 へやだい room rent

❺ abbrev. of 代表電話 だいひょうでんわ: main telephone number
大代４６５－１１１１ だいだいよんろくごのいちいちいちいち Contact 465-1111 (main number)

INDEPENDENT

【だい 代】**GENERATION**; charge, fee, bill
代が変わる だいがかわる be succeeded, change hands
お代を払う おだいをはらう pay the bill
親の代 おやのだい one's parents' generation

KUN

【かわる 代わる】**SUBSTITUTE, be substituted for (a person), take the place of**
代わる代わる かわるがわる by turns, alternately
父親に代わって言う ちちおやにかわっていう speak for one's father
...に代わって …にかわって for..., in place of..., instead of...
機械が人力に代わる きかいがじんりょくにかわる Machinery takes the place of human labor

【かわり 代わり】

①ⓐ **substitution, SUBSTITUTE**
ⓑ **SUBSTITUTE, deputy, proxy**

a 父の代わりとして ちちのかわりとして in place of one's father

b 身代わり みがわり substitution; substitute, stand-in; scapegoat

② **compensation, exchange**
お代わり おかわり second helping
歩く代わりに走る あるくかわりにはしる run instead of walk

③ though...on the other hand
高価な代わりに持ちが良い こうかなかわりにもちがよい Though it is expensive, on the other hand it will last a long time

【-がわり -代わり】[suffix] **SUBSTITUTE, replacement**
住所録代わり じゅうしょろくがわり substitute for an address book

【かえる 代える】**SUBSTITUTE, use in place of, replace (something) with (another)**
代え かえ substitute, proxy
...に代えて …にかえて instead of..., in place of...
Ｂさんを Ａさんに代える びーさんをえーさんにかえる substitute Mr. A for Mr. B

【よ 代】

① **era of rule, age**
大正の代 たいしょうのよ Taisho era
明治天皇の代に めいじてんのうのよに under the rule of Emperor Meiji

② reign, rule
君が代 きみがよ Imperial reign; title of Japanese national anthem

【しろ[1] 代】**cost, CHARGE; rice seedling; material, ingredient**
代物 しろもの *slang* thing, stuff; business; guy
薬の代 くすりのしろ cost of medicine
飲み代 のみしろ drinking money
苗代 なわしろ bed for rice seedlings, rice nursery

【しろ[2] 代】[in compounds]

① margin, blank, allowance
糊代 のりしろ overlap width; margin to paste up
研削代 けんさくしろ grinding allowance

② **SUBSTITUTE, symbol**
身の代金 みのしろきん ransom
御霊代 みたましろ something worshiped as a symbol for the spirit of the dead

③ share, portion
取り代 とりしろ one's share, portion

SYNONYMS

❶ⓐ **substitute**
代 SUBSTITUTE →0034
摂 ACT AS REGENT →0799

❶ⓐ **change and replace**
変 CHANGE →2569
替 REPLACE →3457
代 SUBSTITUTE →0034
迭 ALTERNATE →3818
更 change →4355
改 change →0287
易 change →3064
化 CHANGE INTO, -ize →0022
遷 undergo transition →3932
転 turn into →1872

換 EXCHANGE → 0716
交 INTERCHANGE → 2508

❷ⓐ **generation**
代 GENERATION → 0034
世 generation → 4308

❸ⓐ **long time periods**
時 TIME → 1155
代 age → 0034
紀 ERA → 1628
世 AGE → 4308
朝 dynastic period → 2130
期 period → 2139
劫 KALPA → 1435

❹ **fee and price**
料 FEE → 1644
代 CHARGE → 0034
賃 CHARGES → 3341
銭 money paid → 2159
費 EXPENSE → 3221
価 PRICE → 0095
値 price → 0123

HOMOPHONES

かわる
替 REPLACE → 3457
換 EXCHANGE → 0716
変 CHANGE → 2569

かわり
替 REPLACE → 3457
換 EXCHANGE → 0716
変 CHANGE → 2569

かえる
替 REPLACE → 3457
換 EXCHANGE → 0716
変 CHANGE → 2569

かえ
替 REPLACE → 3457
換 EXCHANGE → 0716
変 CHANGE → 2569

よ 世 WORLD → 4308

NOTE

➡ see USAGE notes at 変 2569 and 台 2498 and 世 4308
➡ see COMPOUND FORMATION for 代謝(=新陳代謝) たいしゃ(=しんちんたいしゃ) → 謝 2048

付

0035
◧ 1-2-3

▶**ATTACH**
フ つ(ける) -つ(ける) -づ(ける) つ(け) つ(け)- -つ(け) -づ(け) -づけ つ(く) -づ(く) つ(き) -つ(き) -つき -づ(き) -づき

Ⓒ 付 fù

9	Jōyō-4	U4ED8
亻	S5-2-3	F0248

Stroke order: ノ 亻 仁 付 付 (1 2 3 4 5)

COMPOUNDS

[sometimes also 附 0410]

❶ⓐ **ATTACH, append, add to, affix**
ⓑ **ATTACHed, additional, supplementary**
ⓒ [original meaning] **ATTACH itself to, stick to, adhere to**

a 付記する ふきする add, write in addition
付加する ふかする add, supplement
添付する てんぷする attach, append, annex
貼付する ちょうふ(=てんぷ)する stick, paste, append

b 付録 ふろく appendix, supplement
付言 ふげん postscript, additional remarks
付図 ふず attached map, appended figure [graph]
付則 ふそく additional rules, bylaw

c 付着する ふちゃくする adhere [cling] to, agglutinate; cohere

❷ **be ATTACHed to, belong to, be affiliated with; be incidental to**
付属する ふぞくする be attached to, belong to
付随する ふずいする accompany, be incidental to, be annexed to
付帯の ふたいの incidental, accessory, collateral

❸ abbrev. of 付属校 ふぞくこう or 付属病院 ふぞくびょういん: **ATTACH**ed [affiliated] school, hospital in affiliation
東大付 とうだいふ school attached to the University of Tokyo

❹ⓐ **deliver, hand over, grant**
ⓑ entrust, commit to

a 付与する ふよする give, grant, allow, bestow
寄付する きふする contribute, donate
交付 こうふ delivery, grant, transfer, service
給付する きゅうふする make a presentation, grant, pay
送付する そうふする send, remit
配付する はいふする distribute, deal out

b 付託する ふたくする commit to, refer to, submit to

❺ **adjacent, near to**
付近 ふきん neighborhood, environs, vicinity

INDEPENDENT

【ふ 付(=附)】 appendix; supplement

付年表 ふねんぴょう appendix: chronological table

【ふする 付する(=附する)】ATTACH, append, add to, affix; commit [submit] to, refer to; consign to, dispose of

KUN

【つける 付ける】[sometimes also 附ける]

① **ATTACH, affix, stick, fasten, add (on), append; set, put (one thing on another)**
付け加える つけくわえる add
付け足す つけたす add on, append
くっ付ける くっつける join, attach; paste, glue
着付け きつけ dressing, fitting
コップに口を付ける こっぷにくちをつける put one's lips to a glass

② **apply, put on**
薬を付ける くすりをつける apply medicine

③ **leave a mark on**
染みを付ける しみをつける stain, blot, smudge

④ **write, make an entry**
付け込む つけこむ take advantage of; make an entry
帳簿に付ける ちょうぼにつける enter in a book

⑤ⓐ **give, impart, direct (one's attention)**
ⓑ **set (a price)**
a 元気を付ける げんきをつける give courage to, encourage
裏付け うらづけ guarantee, endorsement; support, backing; substantiation, proof
貸し付け かしつけ loaning
b 値段を高く付ける ねだんをたかくつける put a high price on

⑥ **provide (a person) with an attendant, place a person in attendance (on)**
護衛を付ける ごえいをつける provide (a person) with a bodyguard

⑦ **follow, trail, shadow**
後を付ける あとをつける follow, tag along

⑧ **kindle, set (fire)**
付け木 つけぎ spill (piece of wood for lighting)

⑨ **load, put on, dish up**
干し草を付けた馬 ほしくさをつけたうま horse loaded with hay

⑩ **settle, bring to terms**
話を付ける はなしをつける settle a matter; negotiate, arrange

⑪ [in the form of 付けて つけて] **refer to, relate to, connect with**
それに付けても それにつけても in this connection

⑫ **unclassified compounds**
受付 うけつけ receipt, reception, acceptance; receptionist, information clerk; information office [desk]

【-つける -付ける】

① **be accustomed [used] to**
読み付けている よみつけている be accustomed to reading

② **perform an action vigorously [vehemently]**
叱り付ける しかりつける scold away, rebuke strongly, bawl out
やっ付ける やっつける *colloq* attack, beat; let someone have it; kill

③ **perceive, detect**
聞き付ける ききつける hear, catch (the sound)

【-づける -付ける】[verbal suffix] **give, impart, provide with**
位置付ける いちづける locate, position
関係付ける かんけいづける connect with, relate to

【つけ 付け】**bill; account, credit**
付けを払う つけをはらう pay a bill
付けで買う つけでかう buy on credit

【つけ- 付け-】

①ⓐ **ATTACHed, fixed**
ⓑ **external (medicine)**
a 付け紐 つけひも sash attached to child's clothes
b 付け薬 つけぐすり external medicine

② **false (mustache), sham**
付け髭× つけひげ false mustache [beard]

【-つけ -付け】**one's favorite, accustomed**
行き付けの場所 いきつけのばしょ one's favorite place

【-づけ -付け, -付】

① **ATTACHing, affixing**
糊付け のりづけ pasting

② [suffix] **dated**
八日付 ようかづけ dated the eighth

【つく 付く】[sometimes also 附く]

①ⓐ **ATTACH itself to, stick (to), adhere (to); be connected with**
ⓑ **come in contact with, touch, reach**
a 結び付き むすびつき connection, relation, alliance
くっ付く くっつく stick (to), cling, adhere
噛み付く かみつく bite [snap] at
b 近付く ちかづく approach, near, get near; get acquainted
追い付く おいつく overtake, catch up with

② **be ATTACHed to, belong to, join, associate with; take up the cause of**
付き合う つきあう keep company with, get along with
付き合い つきあい friendship, association
敵に付く てきにつく take the side of the enemy

③ **gain (weight, power), become proficient, grow (wise)**
肉が付く にくがつく gain [put on] weight

④ **attend on, go with, accompany**

付き添う つきそう accompany, attend on, escort

⑤ **be installed, be built**

電話が付いた でんわがついた A telephone was installed

⑥ **be written, be registered**

帳面に付いている ちょうめんについている be written [entered] in a book

⑦ **be perceived [detected]**

目に付く めにつく catch one's eye, attract one's attention

気付く きづく notice, become aware of, find out

⑧ **catch fire, be ignited**

火が付く ひがつく catch fire, be ignited

⑨ **take (root)**

根が付く ねがつく take [strike] root

⑩ **cost, amount to**

安く付く やすくつく come cheaper

⑪ be lucky

付いている ついている be in luck

⑫ **be settled, be established**

話が付く はなしがつく come to terms, reach agreement

【-づく -付く】 [verbal suffix]

① **gain**

調子付く ちょうしづく warm up; be elated, be puffed up

② be absorbed in

演劇付く えんげきづく be absorbed in a play

③ **become**

元気付く げんきづく become heightened in spirits, get encouraged; recover one's strength

【つき 付き】

① **ability to stick, impression** (quality of printing)

付きが良い つきがよい stay well (on)

② attendant, escort; attendance

お付き おつき attendant; attendance

③ ease of kindling

火付きが悪い ひつきがわるい be slow to kindle

④ luck

付きが変わった つきがかわった My luck changed

【-つき -付き, -付】 [also suffix]

① **with, including**

バス付きの部屋 ばすつきのへや room with bath

期限付きの きげんつきの with a fixed time, with a deadline

② **appearance, state, condition**

顔付き かおつき face, countenance; expression, look

目付き めつき look in one's eyes, expression

【-づき -付き, -付】 [suffix] **ATTACHed to**

大使館付き武官 たいしかんづきぶかん military officer attached to the embassy

SYNONYMS

❶ⓐ & ❶ⓑ add to

付 ATTACH →0035

附 ATTACH →0410

加 ADD →0042

追 add →3840

添 ADD TO →0641

ⓒ stick

着 STICK →4110

貼 STICK →1904

付 attach itself to →0035

附 attach itself to →0410

❹ⓐ transfer

譲 CEDE →2080

渡 hand over →0746

付 deliver →0035

附 deliver →0410

USAGE

❶【つける】

付ける

[sometimes also 附ける]

① attach, affix, stick, fasten, add (on), append; set, put (one thing on another)

② apply, put on

③ leave a mark on

④ write, make an entry

⑤ⓐ give, impart, direct (one's attention)

ⓑ set (a price)

⑥ provide (a person) with an attendant, place a person in attendance (on)

⑦ follow, trail, shadow

⑧ kindle, set (fire)

⑨ load, put on, dish up

⑩ settle, bring to terms

⑪ [in the form of 付けて つけて] refer to, relate to, connect with

⑫ unclassified compounds

附ける

[usu. 付ける] same as 付ける

着ける

① (cause to arrive) bring (a vehicle or boat) alongside, put ashore, berth

② put on clothes, don, wear, be dressed

③ (place a person in a position) settle, settle [seat] a person, situate, steady

④ set about, start, commence

就ける

① install [place] a person in a position

② [formerly 即ける] enthrone

③ make (a person) study under (a teacher)

即ける

[now usu. 就ける] enthrone

【イ】 ⺅ 力 ラ ヲ レ

点ける
light, turn [switch] on
漬ける
① pickle (vegetables), salt, preserve
② immerse, steep, soak, dip

❷【-づけ】
-付け
① attaching, affixing
② [suffix] dated
-漬け
[also suffix]
ⓐ pickles
ⓑ pickling with, preserving in

❸【つく】
付く
[sometimes also 附く]
①ⓐ attach itself to, stick (to), adhere (to); be connected with
ⓑ come in contact with, touch, reach
② be attached to, belong to, join, associate with; take up the cause of
③ gain (weight, power), become proficient, grow (wise)
④ attend on, go with, accompany
⑤ be installed, be built
⑥ be written, be registered
⑦ be perceived [detected]
⑧ catch fire, be ignited
⑨ take (root)
⑩ cost, amount to
⑪ be lucky
⑫ be settled, be established
附く
[usu. 付く] same as 付く
着く
①ⓐ arrive at, reach, come to hand
ⓑ (succeed in touching) reach, come in contact with, touch
② (come to rest in a position) settle, settle [seat] oneself, become situated, settle down (in a place)
就く
①ⓐ set about a task, set out, enter upon, take up (a position), assume (office), enter (a business)
ⓑ set out, start, leave
② [formerly 即く] ascend to (the throne)
③ study under (a teacher)
即く
① [now usu. 就く] ascend to (the throne)
② be in immediate [close] contact, be based on
点く
be lighted, be switched on, go on

HOMOPHONES

つける
附 ATTACH → 0410
着 PUT ON → 4110
就 SET ABOUT → 2129
即 IMMEDIATE → 1439
点 POINT → 2587
漬 PICKLE → 0861
-づけ 漬 PICKLE → 0861
つく
附 ATTACH → 0410
着 PUT ON → 4110
就 SET ABOUT → 2129
即 IMMEDIATE → 1439
点 POINT → 2587

仙

0036

1-2-3

▶**IMMORTAL MOUNTAIN FAIRY**
セン せんと▲ ㊔ のり そま ひさ
Ⓒ 仙 xiān

9	Jōyō	U4ED9
⺅	S5-2-3	F1115

丿 亻 仆 仙 仙 (1 2 3 4 5)

COMPOUNDS

❶ⓐ **transcendent IMMORTAL FAIRY living in the MOUNTAINs and capable of performing miracles, Taoist immortal, supernatural being**
ⓑ **hermit, recluse**
a 仙人 せんにん immortal mountain fairy; hermit, unworldly person
仙術 せんじゅつ fairy magic
仙境 せんきょう fairyland, enchanted land
神仙 しんせん supernatural being
b 酒仙 しゅせん hermit who enjoys drinking; son of Bacchus

❷ master (as of an art)
歌仙 かせん master [major] poet

❸ unclassified compounds
仙骨 せんこつ sacrum
水仙 すいせん narcissus

KUN

【せんと 仙】 cent
五十仙 ごじゅっせんと 50 cents

SYNONYMS

❶ **religious persons**
聖 SAINT → 3509
仙 IMMORTAL MOUNTAIN FAIRY → 0036

仕

0037

1-2-3

▶SERVE
▶DO

シ ジ つか(える) ㊔ つこう

Ⓒ 仕 shì

9	Jōyō-3	U4ED5
亻	S5-2-3	F0195

丿 亻 仁 仕 仕

1 2 3 4 5

COMPOUNDS

❶ **SERVE (under), take service under, enter the government service**

仕官 しかん entering the government service; find service with (a lord)

奉仕 ほうし attendance, service

出仕する しゅっしする enter the service of; attend (one's office)

❷ used for し as the second (continuative) base of the verb する: **DO**

仕事 しごと work, employment, business

仕立て したて tailoring, dressmaking

仕方 しかた way, method, means

仕方が無い しかたがない have no choice; it is no use; cannot bear

仕手 して doer; protagonist in a noh drama; operator, speculator

仕組み しくみ construction; arrangement; plan, plot

仕上げ しあげ finish, elaboration, completion

仕返し しかえし doing over, tit for tat, revenge

仕合わせ しあわせ [also 幸せ, formerly also 倖せ] happiness, blessing; good fortune

仕入れる しいれる lay in, stock

仕入れ しいれ purchasing, stocking

仕送りする しおくりする supply, provide; send money to

仕舞い しまい end, conclusion, close

給仕 きゅうじ office boy, page (boy), waiter; service at table

INDEPENDENT

【し 仕】government service

仕を致す しをいたす leave the government service

KUN

【つかえる 仕える】**SERVE (under), take service under, enter the service of the shogunate**

宮仕え みやづかえ court service

夫に良く仕える おっとによくつかえる be devoted [attentive] to one's husband

神に仕える かみにつかえる serve God

二君に仕えず にくんにつかえず not serve two masters

SYNONYMS

❶ **work**

働 WORK → 0172

稼 WORK (for a living) → 1572

労 LABOR → 3155

勤める serve (in an office) → 2287

仕 SERVE → 0037

❷ **do and act**

為 DO → 4395

仕 DO → 0037

致す DO HUMBLY → 1668

行 ACT → 0246

作 WORK → 0077

HOMOPHONES

しあわせ

幸せ → 2755

倖せ → 0134

仕合わせ → 0037, 2511

NOTE

➡ see USAGE note at 幸 2755

➡ see COMPOUND FORMATION for 仕合わせ しあわせ → 合 2511

仔

0038

1-2-3

▶OFFSPRING

シ こ

Ⓒ 仔 zǐ zǎi zī

9	Names	U4ED4
亻	S5-2-3	F2329

COMPOUNDS

[now usu. 子]

❶ **animal OFFSPRING**

仔虫 しちゅう larva

胎仔 たいじ (nonhuman) embryo, fetus

同腹仔 どうふくし litter

❷ **small, minute**

仔細 しさい particulars, details; reasons, circumstances

KUN

【こ 仔】[now usu. 子] **animal OFFSPRING such as a puppy, cub or roe**

仔牛 こうし calf

仔犬 こいぬ puppy

SYNONYMS

❶ **offspring**

子 CHILD → 4196

仔 OFFSPRING → 0038

孤 orphan → 0426

嫡 LEGITIMATE CHILD → 0839

息 son → 3278

男 son → 3147

惣 eldest son →3452
娘 DAUGHTER →0488
女 daughter →4226
姫 DAUGHTER OF NOBLE BIRTH →0489

HOMOPHONES

こ
子 CHILD →4196
児 CHILD →3153
娘 DAUGHTER →0488
小 SMALL →0007

NOTE

➡ see USAGE note at 子 4196

他

0039
1-2-3

▶**OTHER**
タ ほか
Ⓒ 他 tā

9	Jōyō-3	U4ED6
亻	S5-2-3	F0325

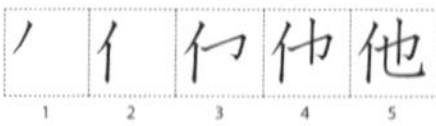

COMPOUNDS

❶ⓐ [also prefix] **OTHER, another**
ⓑ OTHERs, other people

a 他方 たほう other side [hand]
他意 たい other intention, secret purpose, ulterior motive
他人 たにん another person, other people; stranger
他国 たこく foreign countries, another province
他年 たねん some other year, some day
他府県 たふけん other prefectures
他者 たしゃ another person, other people
他面 ためん other side; while, whereas; on the other hand

b 他殺 たさつ homicide, murder
排他的な はいたてきな exclusive, clannish

❷ transitive verb
自他 じた oneself and others; transitive and intransitive

INDEPENDENT

【た 他】**OTHERs, other people; other things, the rest**
他の言に惑わされる たのげんにまどわされる be led astray by others' opinion
その他 そのた the others, the rest

KUN

【ほか 他】[also 外] **something OTHER than, the rest**
他の ほかの other, another, different, else
他ならぬ ほかならぬ nothing but, no other than
山田他 やまだほか Yamada and others [et al.]

SYNONYMS

❶ⓐ other
他 OTHER →0039
余 other →2535
別 ANOTHER →1434

HOMOPHONES

ほか 外 OUTSIDE →0215

NOTE

➡ see USAGE note at 外 0215

㐰

0040
1-2-3

▶**INDIVIDUAL**
▶**GENERAL COUNTER**
コ カ

9	Nonstandard	U500B
亻	S5-2-3	F0000

handwritten form →see 個 at 0132

氺

0041
1-2-3

▶***SHITAMIZU***

85	Radical	U6C3A
水	S5-5-0	F0000

radical variant →see 水 at 0010

加

0042
1-2-3

▶**ADD**
カ くわ(える) くわ(わる) ㊔ ます
Ⓒ 加 jiā

19	Jōyō-4	U52A0
力	S5-2-3	F0239

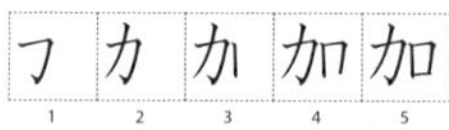

COMPOUNDS

❶ⓐ ADD, append
ⓑ ADD to, increase
ⓒ *math* **ADD, sum up**

a 加速 かそく acceleration
加速度 かそくど acceleration
加味する かみする tinge with, add to

b 追加する ついかする add, append, supplement
増加 ぞうか increase, gain, rise

c 加算 かさん addition
加減 かげん addition and subtraction; degree, extent; adjustment

❷ affect, influence, inflict
加工 かこう processing, manufacturing
加害者 かがいしゃ assailant, assaulter

❸ join, take part in, participate
加盟 かめい participation, affiliation
加入金 かにゅうきん admission fee
加担(=荷担) かたん assistance, support, participation
参加する さんかする participate, join, take part in

❹ used phonetically for *ka*, esp. in place names, as:
ⓐ Canada

ⓑ California

a 日加 にっか Japan and Canada

b 加州 かしゅう State of California

INDEPENDENT

【か 加】 **ADD**ition, plus; Canada

KUN

【くわえる 加える】 *vt* **ADD, append; add, sum up, increase; include, count in; inflict (an injury on), give**

付け加える つけくわえる add

五に六を加えよ ごにろくをくわえよ Add six to five

仲間に加える なかまにくわえる include in the circle

圧力を加える あつりょくをくわえる press, apply pressure to

【くわわる 加わる】 *vi* **join in, participate; gain (in), grow, increase**

会議に加わる かいぎにくわわる take part in a conference

暑さが加わる あつさがくわわる get hotter

SYNONYMS

❶ⓐ add to

付 ATTACH →0035

附 ATTACH →0410

加 ADD →0042

追 add →3840

添 ADD TO →0641

ⓑ increase

加 add to →0042

増 INCREASE →0836

殖 MULTIPLY →1253

倍 DOUBLE →0122

ⓒ add

加 ADD →0042

足す add →2714

〆る SUM →4179

❸ participate and join

参 PARTICIPATE →2563

与 take part in →4229

加 join →0042

入 ENTER →4177

❹ⓐ North American countries

米 AMERICA →4342

加 Canada →0042

氷

▸ICE

ヒョウ こおり ひ こお(る)▲

Ⓝ 冰 Ⓒ 冰 bīng

0043

◧ 1-2-3

85	Jōyō-3	U6C37
水	S5-4-1	F1369

亅 亅 氵 氺 氷 (1 2 3 4 5)

COMPOUNDS

ⓐ ICE

ⓑ turn into **ICE**, freeze

a 氷晶 ひょうしょう ice crystal

氷河 ひょうが glacier

氷山 ひょうざん iceberg

氷雪 ひょうせつ ice and snow

樹氷 じゅひょう trees covered with ice

製氷 せいひょう ice making

b 氷点 ひょうてん freezing point

氷結する ひょうけつする freeze, congeal

KUN

【こおり 氷】 [also suffix] **ICE, shaved ice**

氷枕 こおりまくら ice pillow

氷水 こおりみず ice water; shaved ice

氷菓子 こおりがし frozen sweet, ice candy

ぶっ欠き氷 ぶっかきごおり chipped ice

【ひ 氷】 **ICE, hail**

氷雨 ひさめ *elegant* hail; chilly rain (esp. in autumn)

【こおる 氷る】 [now usu. 凍る] freeze

→see 凍 0146 for compounds

SYNONYMS

ⓐ kinds of water

水 WATER →0010

湯 HOT WATER →0747

汽 STEAM →0309

氷 ICE →0043

淵 DEEP WATER →0732

ⓐ kinds of frozen water

氷 ICE →0043

雪 SNOW →3431

HOMOPHONES

こおる 凍 FREEZE →0146

NOTE

➡ see USAGE note at 凍 0146

★ do not confuse with 永 ETERNAL →2436

癶

▸*HATSUGASHIRA*

0044

◧ 1-2-3

105	Radical	U7676
癶	S5-5-0	F0000

RADICAL

hatsugashira 'spread legs' (発 登 癸×), used for character classification

以

▸TO THE…OF
▸BY MEANS OF
イ もっ(て)▲

0045
1-2-3

Ⓒ 以 yǐ

9	Jōyō-4	U4EE5
人	S5-2-3	F0128

丨 レ レ レ丿 以
1 2 3 4 5

COMPOUNDS

❶ [formerly also 已 4185] directional preposition placed before localizers to indicate the point of reference in compounds related to direction, time or range: **TO THE…OF, -ward**

以東 いとう to the east of, eastward
以上 いじょう or more than, not less than; beyond; the above-mentioned; now that; that's all
以来 いらい as of, since then, from that time on
以下 いか or less than, not more than, under; and downward; the following
以外に いがいに except for, excluding
以内 いない within, less than
以前 いぜん before, ago, since
以降 いこう on and after, hereafter
以後 いご after this, from now on, in future; after that, thereafter

❷ **BY MEANS OF, with, using**

以心伝心 いしんでんしん silent [tacit] understanding, empathy

❸ reason, cause

所以▲ ゆえん reason, grounds

KUN

【もって 以て】 **with, BY MEANS OF; because of; with this**

以ての外 もってのほか outrageous, preposterous, scandalous
以てする もってする do by the use of
以て瞑×すべし もってめいすべし You ought to be content with this
小刀を以て殺す こがたなをもってころす kill (a person) with a knife
山高きを以て やまたかきをもって because the mountain is high

SYNONYMS

❶ **direction indicators**

至 to → 2707
-行き bound for → 0246
-向け (bound) for → 3790
迄 UP TO → 3967
以 TO THE…OF → 0045
自 from → 4338
来 since → 4366
而 DIRECTION WORD → 2520

COMPOUND FORMATION

【以心伝心 いしんでんしん】

以心伝心 'silent [tacit] understanding, empathy', is to convey (伝) one's thoughts or feelings (心) by means of (以 ❷) thoughts (not words).

NOTE

➡ see COMPOUND FORMATION for 所以 ゆえん → 所 1056

伐

▸CUT DOWN
バツ き(る)▲

0046
1-2-4

Ⓒ 伐 fá

9	Jōyō	U4F10
亻	S6-2-4	F1936

丿 亻 仁 代 伐 伐
1 2 3 4 5 6

COMPOUNDS

❶ **CUT DOWN (trees), fell, chop down**

伐採する ばっさいする lumber, fell, deforest
伐木 ばつぼく felling, cutting, logging
濫伐(=乱伐)する らんばつする deforest indiscriminately, cut down [fell] trees recklessly
盗伐 とうばつ secret felling of trees

❷ **CUT DOWN (one's enemies), strike down, send a punitive expedition against, attack**

殺伐な さつばつな bloody, savage, warlike
征伐 せいばつ subjugation, conquest
討伐 とうばつ suppression (of a rebellion), punitive expedition

KUN

【きる 伐る】 [now usu. 切る] **CUT DOWN (trees), fell, chop down**

木を伐る きをきる fell a tree

SYNONYMS

❶ **cut**

切 CUT → 0030
薙ぐ MOW DOWN → 3010
剪 PRUNE → 2886
削 CUT BY CHIPPING → 1837
挽く GRIND, saw → 0511
断 CUT OFF → 1885
截 CUT OFF → 4092
裁 CUT OUT → 4090
斬 CUT WITH A SWORD → 1874
割 cut with a knife → 2284
剖 DISSECT → 2103
刈る CLIP → 0032
伐 CUT DOWN → 0046

❷ **conquer and suppress**

征 CONQUER → 0349

討 SUPPRESS BY ARMED FORCE → 1846
伐 CUT DOWN → 0046
鎮 QUELL → 2210
靖 PACIFY → 1546

HOMOPHONES

きる
切 CUT → 0030
剪 PRUNE → 2886
截 CUT OFF → 4092
斬 CUT WITH A SWORD → 1874

NOTE

➡ see USAGE note at 切 0030

仲

0047

◧ 1-2-4

▶**INTERMEDIARY**
▶**PERSONAL RELATIONS**

チュウ なか ㊔ なかば

Ⓒ 仲 zhòng

9	Jōyō-4	U4EF2
亻	S6-2-4	F0656

ノ 亻 仆 仃 仲 仲
1 2 3 4 5 6

COMPOUNDS

❶ **INTERMEDIARY, middleman, mediator**
仲介者 ちゅうかいしゃ intermediary, mediator, agent
仲裁人 ちゅうさいにん arbitrator, mediator

❷ occupying an intermediate position:
ⓐ middle [second month] of a season
ⓑ middle [second-born] brother
a 仲秋(=中秋) ちゅうしゅう mid-autumn, August according to the old calendar
b 仲兄 ちゅうけい second brother
伯仲する はくちゅうする be equal to

KUN

【なか 仲】

① **PERSONAL RELATIONS, relationship, (familiar) terms, fellowship, friendship**
仲が良い なかがよい be on good terms
仲良くする なかよくする become friendly with, make friends with
仲間 なかま company, fellow, comrade, associate
仲直り なかなおり reconciliation
恋仲 こいなか love relationship

② **INTERMEDIARY, go-between**
仲に入る なかにはいる act as an intermediary
仲買 なかがい brokerage; middleman
仲買人 なかがいにん broker
仲立ち なかだち intermediation
仲居 なかい parlormaid, waitress

③ [in compounds] inner, middle
仲見世通り なかみせどおり shopping street in the precincts of a shrine [temple]

SPECIAL READINGS

仲人 なこうど go-between, matchmaker

SYNONYMS

❶ **mediating and mediators**
紹 INTRODUCE → 1691
介 MEDIATE → 2463
媒 INTERMEDIATE → 0686
仲 INTERMEDIARY → 0047

❷ **between**
中 MIDDLE → 4262
仲 intermediate → 0047
間 BETWEEN → 4122
際 inter- → 0874

【なか】

① **personal relations**
縁 RELATION → 1754
交 INTERCOURSE → 2508
好 friendship → 0240
仲 PERSONAL RELATIONS → 0047
誼 FRIENDSHIP → 1977
絆 BONDS → 1686

HOMOPHONES

なか 中 MIDDLE → 4262

COMPOUND FORMATION

❶【伯仲 はくちゅう】
伯仲する 'be equal to' is a situation where it is difficult to determine which is the firstborn brother (伯) and which is the second-born brother (仲 ❷ⓑ).

❷【仲居 なかい】
仲居 'parlormaid, waitress' is a person who is (居) an intermediary (仲 なか ②) between the customer and the kitchen.

NOTE

➡ see USAGE note at 中 4262

伝

0048

◧ 1-2-4

▶**TRANSMIT**

デン つた(わる) つた(える) つた(う) -づた(い) つて* ㊔ つとむ ただ

Ⓝ 傳 Ⓒ 传 chuán zhuàn

9	Jōyō-4	U4F1D
亻	S6-2-4	F0237

ノ 亻 亻 仁 伝 伝
1 2 3 4 5 6

COMPOUNDS

❶ⓐ (convey from one person or place to another) **TRANSMIT, convey, pass on, communicate, initiate**
ⓑ (pass down by inheritance) **TRANSMIT, hand down**

c (disseminate information or religious teachings) **spread, propagate, TRANSMIT, teach**
d [original meaning] **TRANSMIT by stages, relay**

a 伝達する でんたつする transmit, convey, communicate; propagate
伝染 でんせん contagion, infection, communication (of a disease)
伝言 でんごん verbal message, word
伝授する でんじゅする instruct, initiate
中国伝来の ちゅうごくでんらいの imported [transmitted] from China
直伝 じきでん direct initiation
b 伝統 でんとう tradition, convention
伝説 でんせつ legend, folk tale
伝承する でんしょうする hand down, tell from generation to generation
以心伝心 いしんでんしん silent [tacit] understanding, empathy
遺伝 いでん hereditary transmission
c 伝道 でんどう gospel preaching, missionary work, evangelism
宣伝 せんでん publicity, propaganda; advertisement
d 駅伝 えきでん post-horse, stagecoach; long-distance relay race

2 *phys* **TRANSMIT**, conduct, convey
伝導 でんどう conduction, transmission
伝声管 でんせいかん voice pipe, speaking tube

3a [also suffix] biography
b tale, story, fable
a 伝記 でんき biography
列伝 れつでん series of biographies
ナポレオン伝 なぽれおんでん life of Napoleon
b 外伝 がいでん supplementary story; lateral biography

4 [also suffix] commentary, exposition
古事記伝 こじきでん Commentary on Kojiki (Ancient Chronicles)

INDEPENDENT

【でん 伝】 *colloq* way, manner, trick
いつもの伝で いつものでんで as usual, as is often the case

KUN

【つたわる 伝わる】 **be TRANSMITted [conveyed], spread, be propagated; be handed down, go [come] down, descend; go along, follow**
ニュースが伝わった にゅーすがつたわった The news went around
代代伝わる だいだいつたわる be transmitted [handed down] from generation to generation
屋根を伝わって歩く やねをつたわってあるく walk over the roof

【つたえる 伝える】

①ⓐ (convey from one person or place to another) **TRANSMIT, convey, pass on, communicate, initiate**
ⓑ (pass down by inheritance) **TRANSMIT, hand down**
ⓒ (disseminate information or religious teachings) **spread, propagate, TRANSMIT, teach**
a 命令を伝える めいれいをつたえる pass the word
b 言い伝え いいつたえ tradition, legend
c キリスト教を伝える きりすときょうをつたえる introduce Christianity

② *phys* **TRANSMIT, conduct, convey**
熱を伝える ねつをつたえる conduct heat

【つたう 伝う】 **go along, follow**
伝って登る つたってのぼる climb up, shin up

【-づたい -伝い】 [also suffix] **along**
川伝いに かわづたいに along a river
磯伝いに いそづたいに along the beach
海岸伝い かいがんづたい along the coast

【つて 伝】 intermediary, introducer, connection
良い伝が有る よいつてがある have a good connection

SPECIAL READINGS

伝馬船 てんません lighter, jolly (boat)
手伝う てつだう help, assist, lend a hand
手伝い てつだい help; assistant
お手伝い おてつだい help, assistance; maid
お手伝いさん おてつだいさん maid, house maid

SYNONYMS

1a & 1b transmit and deliver
伝 TRANSMIT → 0048
逓 RELAY → 3852
届ける DELIVER → 3820
達 deliver → 3893

c make widely known
布 SPREAD → 3691
流 spread → 0529
伝 spread → 0048
広 spread → 3769
弘 DISSEMINATE (esp. Buddhism) → 0223
及 REACH TO → 4192

3a records
記 written account → 1843
録 RECORD → 2186
譜 SYSTEMATIC RECORD → 2068
誌 records → 1950
史 HISTORY → 4324
伝 biography → 0048

3a history
史 HISTORY → 4324
伝 biography → 0048

歴 PERSONAL HISTORY → 3748

COMPOUND FORMATION

【伝統 でんとう】

伝統 'tradition, convention' is that which is handed down (伝 ❶ⓑ) through one's ancestry or lineage (統).

NOTE

➡ see COMPOUND FORMATION for
以心伝心 いしんでんしん → 以 0045
遺伝 いでん → 遺 3928

伏

0049

◧ 1-2-4

▸PROSTRATE

フク　ふ(せる)　ふ(す)

Ⓒ 伏 fú

9	Jōyō	U4F0F
亻	S6-2-4	F1032

ノ 亻 仁 什 伏 伏
1 2 3 4 5 6

COMPOUNDS

❶ [original meaning] **PROSTRATE (oneself), fall prostrate, lie down, bend down**
平伏する へいふくする prostrate oneself (before), kiss the ground
起伏 きふく ups and downs, undulations
倒伏 とうふく falling down

❷ [also 服 1090] **submit to, yield to**
屈伏 くっぷく submission, surrender
降伏 こうふく surrender, submission
折伏 しゃくぶく preaching down

❸ **lie in concealment, hide**
伏兵 ふくへい ambush, troops in ambush
伏線 ふくせん preparation, foreshadow
雌伏 しふく remaining in obscurity, lying low, biding one's time
潜伏 せんぷく concealment, hiding; latency
埋伏歯 まいふくし impacted tooth

INDEPENDENT

【ふくする 伏する】 **PROSTRATE**; yield to
威に伏する いにふくする yield to power

KUN

【ふせる 伏せる】
①ⓐ **turn downward, lay upside down, turn over**
ⓑ put something over (another)
ⓒ **lay under the ground**
a 身を伏せる みをふせる lie face down
説き伏せる ときふせる argue down, persuade, convince
b 鶏に籠を伏せる にわとりにかごをふせる coop hens
c 待ち伏せる まちぶせる lie in wait, ambush, conceal oneself in ambush
② **keep secret**
伏せ字 ふせじ omission, blank, asterisk

【ふす 伏す】 **PROSTRATE, fall prostrate, lie down, bend down**
伏し目 ふしめ downcast look
ひれ伏す ひれふす prostrate oneself before a person

SYNONYMS

❶ **lie down**
伏 PROSTRATE → 0049
臥 LIE DOWN → 1825
寝る lie down → 2925

❷ **submit and surrender**
服 SUBMIT → 1090
伏 submit → 0049
屈 bend in submission → 3821
降 surrender → 0548

❸ **hide**
隠 HIDE → 0873
蔽 COVER → 2991
伏 lie in concealment → 0049
潜 LURK → 0922
匿 CONCEAL → 3735
忍 perform by stealth → 2750

USAGE

【ふせる】
伏せる
①ⓐ turn downward, lay upside down, turn over
ⓑ put something over (another)
ⓒ lay under the ground
② keep secret
臥せる
① lie down
② be confined to one's bed, be sick in bed

❶【ふす】
伏す
prostrate, fall prostrate, lie down, bend down
臥す
same as 臥せる ふせる

HOMOPHONES

ふせる 臥 LIE DOWN → 1825
ふす 臥 LIE DOWN → 1825

伍

0050

◧ 1-2-4

▸RANK

ゴ ㊔ いつ　くみ　あつむ

Ⓒ 伍 wǔ

9	Names	U4F0D
亻	S6-2-4	F1728

COMPOUNDS

❶ⓐ **RANK, file, line**
ⓑ (members of the same group) **RANKs, rank and file, squad, group**

a 隊伍 たいご ranks, line array, formation
落伍(=落後)する らくごする straggle, drop out of line, fall out of the ranks
先頭伍 せんとうご leading file
b 伍長 ごちょう corporal; foreman

❷ five—used in legal documents and checks
金伍千円也 きんごせんえんなり 5000 yen

❸ [archaic]
ⓐ military unit of five soldiers (in Zhou Dynasty China)
ⓑ unit of administration consisting of five houses
a 伍伯 ごはく leader of a military unit of five soldiers

INDEPENDENT

【ご 伍】 five (→❷); military unit of five soldiers; **RANK**, file, line
伍を重ねる ごをかさねる double the ranks

【ごする 伍する】 **RANK** with, associate with

SYNONYMS

❶ⓐ linear arrangements
伍 RANK →0050
列 ROW →1018
行 LINE (esp. of print) →0246
欄 COLUMN →1419

ⓑ groups
群 GROUP (of any kind) →1942
班 SQUAD →1182
軍 team →2582
組 group (of people) →1693
陣 lineup →0545
連 set →3849
族 common-interest group (*slang*) →1195
党 PARTY →3190
隊 PARTY (organized group) →0762
団 BODY →3791
伍 ranks →0050

❷ five
五 FIVE →4244
伍 five (in legal documents) →0050

仰

0051

1-2-4

▶LOOK UP

ギョウ コウ あお(ぐ) おお(せ) おっ(しゃる)▲

Ⓒ 仰 yǎng

9	Jōyō	U4EF0
亻	S6-2-4	F1026

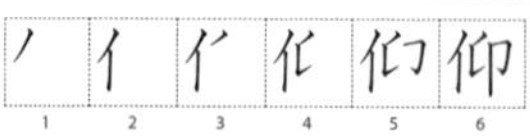

COMPOUNDS

❶ [original meaning] **LOOK UP, face upward**
仰視する ぎょうしする look up
仰角 ぎょうかく angle of elevation
仰臥 ぎょうが lying face up
仰天する ぎょうてんする be astounded

❷ **LOOK UP to, respect, revere**
仰望する ぎょうぼうする look up to, revere
信仰する しんこうする believe in, have faith

KUN

【あおぐ 仰ぐ】 **LOOK UP, face upward; look up to, respect; turn to, ask for; drink**
仰ぎ見る あおぎみる look up
仰向け あおむけ facing upward
師と仰ぐ しとあおぐ look up to (a person) as one's preceptor
助言を仰ぐ じょげんをあおぐ ask for advice
毒を仰ぐ どくをあおぐ take poison

【おおせ 仰せ】 **statement, wishes or command of a superior**
仰せに従って おおせにしたがって in obedience to your wishes, as you say
仰せつかる おおせつかる be ordered, be appointed

【おっしゃる 仰しゃる】 honorific verb equiv. to 言う いう: say, tell, speak, talk; call
お名前は何と仰しゃいますか おなまえはなんとおっしゃいますか What is your name, sir?

SYNONYMS

❶ see and look
見 SEE →3151
看 WATCH →3992
察 INSPECT →2961
窺 WATCH FURTIVELY →3002
瞥 GLANCE AT →3592
目 look →3777
観 VIEW →2359
覧 LOOK OVER →3538
眺 LOOK OUT OVER →1503
望 LOOK AFAR →3408
仰 LOOK UP →0051
顧 LOOK BACK →2394
視 REGARD →1223

❷ respect
敬 RESPECT →2136
尊 HONOR →2920
畏 respect →3170
欽 REVERE →2124
仰 look up to →0051
崇 REVERENCE →2864
尚 VALUE HIGHLY →2774
重 set value on →4390
拝 WORSHIP →0360
慕 ADORE →2970

伊

▸PHONETIC [i]
▸ITALY
イ ㊔これ よし ただ
Ⓒ 伊 yī

0052
◧1-2-4

9	Names	U4F0A
亻	S6-2-4	F0420

COMPOUNDS

❶ **used PHONETICally for *i*, esp. in proper names**
伊太利 いたりー Italy
伊呂波 いろは *iroha*, the Japanese syllabary [alphabet]

❷ⓐ **ITALY**
ⓑ Italian (language)
a 日独伊 にちどくい Japan, Germany and Italy
駐伊 ちゅうい stationed in Italy
b 日伊辞典 にちいじてん Japanese-Italian dictionary

❸ [archaic]
ⓐ this
ⓑ he

INDEPENDENT

【い 伊】 **ITALY**

SPECIAL READINGS

伊達者 だてしゃ dandy, coxcomb, beau

SYNONYMS

❶ **phonetic [i]**
伊 PHONETIC [i] →0052
斐 PHONETIC [i] →3449

❷ⓐ **European countries**
英 ENGLAND →2782
独 GERMANY →0471
仏 FRANCE →0020
伊 ITALY →0052
葡 PORTUGAL →2902
西 Spain →4333
蘭 the Netherlands →3031
希 Greece →2543
露 Russia →3495
白 Belgium →4305

仮

▸TEMPORARY
カ ケ かり かり-
Ⓝ 假 Ⓒ 假 jiǎ jià

0053
◧1-2-4

9	Jōyō-5	U4EEE
亻	S6-2-4	F1079

ノ 亻 仁 仮 仮 仮
1 2 3 4 5 6

COMPOUNDS

❶ **TEMPORARY, provisional, transient**
仮設の かせつの provisional, temporary; hypothetic
仮眠 かみん nap, doze
仮定 かてい assumption, supposition
仮説 かせつ hypothesis
仮称 かしょう temporary name
仮寓 かぐう temporary residence
仮死 かし suspended animation, apparent death
仮性近視 かせいきんし false nearsightedness, pseudomyopia

❷ **fake, false, sham, feigned, pseudo**
仮面 かめん mask, disguise
仮装 かそう disguise, fancy dress
仮名 かめい pseudonym, alias
仮病 けびょう feigned illness

❸ borrow, avail oneself of, allow
仮借無き かしゃくなき merciless(ly)

KUN

【かり 仮】 **provisional, TEMPORARY; assumed**
仮に かりに provisionally, tentatively; for example; supposing that
仮の親 かりのおや expedient parent, foster parent
仮の名 かりのな assumed name, alias

【かり- 仮-】 [also prefix] **TEMPORARY, provisional**
仮橋 かりばし temporary bridge
仮住まい かりずまい temporary residence
仮契約 かりけいやく provisional contract
仮溶接 かりようせつ tack welding

SPECIAL READINGS

仮名(=仮字▲) かな kana, Japanese syllabary
仮令▲ たとえ even if, granting that

SYNONYMS

❶ **temporary**
仮 TEMPORARY →0053
暫 for the time being →3553

❷ **false**
虚 FALSE →4017
仮 fake →0053
偽 sham →0149
擬 imitation →0969
義 artificial →2948

件

▸MATTER
ケン くだん▲
Ⓒ 件 jiàn

0054
◧1-2-4

9	Jōyō-5	U4EF6
亻	S6-2-4	F0244

ノ 亻 亻 亻 仁 件
1 2 3 4 5 6

COMPOUNDS

ⓐ **MATTER, affair, case, incident, item**
ⓑ **counter for cases or affairs**
a 一件 いっけん matter, affair, item

用件 ようけん matter (of business), things to be done
人件費 じんけんひ personnel expenses, labor cost
条件 じょうけん condition; item, proviso
事件 じけん affair, incident, case, event
案件 あんけん matter, case, item
要件 ようけん important matter; necessary condition
別件 べっけん separate case, another matter
b 件数 けんすう number of cases or items
五十件 ごじっけん 50 cases, 50 items

INDEPENDENT

【けん 件】**MATTER, affair, case**
例の件 れいのけん the matter you have been talking about

KUN

【くだん 件】the aforesaid **MATTER**
件の一件 くだんのいっけん the aforesaid matter, the matter in question

SYNONYMS

ⓐ **affair**
事 AFFAIR →4384
儀 affair →0191
件 MATTER →0054

ⓑ **general counters**
丁 MISCELLANEOUS COUNTER →4155
個 GENERAL COUNTER →0132
箇 COUNTER FOR ITEMS →3348
点 counter for articles →2587
件 counter for cases →0054

伎

▶PERFORMER

キ ギ* ㊔くれ

Ⓒ 伎 jì

0055

1-2-4

9	Jōyō	U4F0E
亻	S6-2-4	F2091

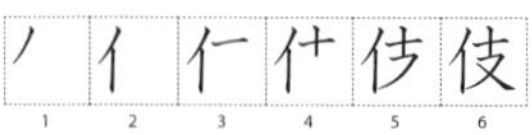

COMPOUNDS

❶ **PERFORMER, actor**
伎楽 ぎがく ancient mask show
歌舞伎 かぶき kabuki

❷ [now also 技 ぎ 0292] [original meaning] **skill, ability, craft, art**
伎倆(=技量) ぎりょう skill, ability, capacity

SYNONYMS

❶ **performers**
優 ACTOR →0200
俳 actor →0126
伶 MUSICIAN →0075

伎 PERFORMER →0055

休

▶REST

キュウ やす(む) やす(まる) やす(める)

Ⓒ 休 xiū

0056

1-2-4

9	Jōyō-1	U4F11
亻	S6-2-4	F0811

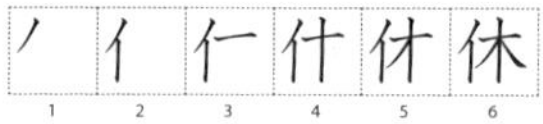

COMPOUNDS

❶ⓐ [original meaning] **REST, repose, relax**
ⓑ abbrev. of 休暇 きゅうか or 休業 きゅうぎょう: **holiday, vacation, suspension of business, day off**
a 休憩 きゅうけい rest, repose
休息 きゅうそく rest, repose
休養 きゅうよう rest, recuperation, relaxation
休止 きゅうし pause, standstill, dormancy; rest
休日 きゅうじつ holiday, day off
休暇 きゅうか holiday, vacation
休業 きゅうぎょう suspension of business
休火山 きゅうかざん dormant volcano
本日休診 ほんじつきゅうしん Office Closed Today (sign at doctor's office)
b 連休 れんきゅう consecutive holidays
週休 しゅうきゅう weekly holiday
定休 ていきゅう regular holiday
臨休 りんきゅう extra [special] holiday
産休 さんきゅう maternity leave

❷ **suspend, discontinue; cancel**
休演する きゅうえんする suspend performance
休会 きゅうかい adjournment, recess (of the Diet)
休戦 きゅうせん truce, armistice
休講 きゅうこう cancellation of lecture (for the day)
休校 きゅうこう temporary closure of school
休学 きゅうがく leave of absence (from school)
運休 うんきゅう suspension of (bus) service
閑話休題 かんわきゅうだい to return to the subject

❸ tranquil, peaceful
休戚 きゅうせき weal and woe

INDEPENDENT

【きゅうす 休す】cease, come to an end
万事休す ばんじきゅうす It's all up [over] (with us)/ Nothing can be done now

KUN

【やすむ 休む】**REST, take a rest, repose; suspend, discontinue; be absent; go to bed, retire**
休み やすみ rest, recess; suspension; vacation, holiday; absence
お休みなさい おやすみなさい good night
昼休み ひるやすみ noon recess, lunch break

夏休み なつやすみ summer vacation

【やすまる 休まる】 [sometimes also 安まる] **feel RESTed; be set at ease**

体が休まる からだがやすまる be [feel] rested

【やすめる 休める】 **REST, give a rest; suspend; set (a person's mind) at ease; lay land fallow**

骨休め ほねやすめ relaxation, recreation

気休め きやすめ soothing, consolation

SYNONYMS

❶ⓐ rest

休 REST →0056

息 rest →3278

憩 TAKE A REST →3590

歇 TAKE A REST →2243

ⓑ holiday

休 holiday →0056

暇 leave of absence →1275

❷ discontinue

絶 BREAK OFF →1711

廃 ABOLISH →3902

断 CUT OFF →1885

止 STOP →3659

休 suspend →0056

停 suspend →0156

已む CEASE →4185

USAGE

【やすまる】

休まる

[sometimes also 安まる] feel rested; be set at ease

安まる

[usu. 休まる] feel rested; be set at ease

HOMOPHONES

やすまる 安 PEACEFUL →2695

NOTE

➡ see COMPOUND FORMATION for 閑話休題 かんわきゅうだい →閑 4123

任

0057

◧1-2-4

▶**OFFICE**
▶**LEAVE TO**

ニン まか(せる) まか(す) ㊔ じん つとむ たか ひで と とう

Ⓒ 任 rèn rén

9	Jōyō-5	U4EFB
亻	S6-2-4	F0390

1	2	3	4	5	6
ノ	亻	仁	仟	任	任

COMPOUNDS

❶ⓐ OFFICE, duties, official post
ⓑ duty, responsibility
ⓒ take a duty upon oneself, assume responsibility

a 任期 にんき one's term of office

就任 しゅうにん assumption of office, inauguration

辞任 じにん resignation

留任 りゅうにん remaining in office

赴任する ふにんする proceed to a new post

解任 かいにん release from office, dismissal, discharge

b 任務 にんむ duty, part, function; mission

責任 せきにん responsibility, liability

重任 じゅうにん heavy responsibility, important duty; reappointment

c 担任する たんにんする be in charge of, take (a class) under one's charge

歴任する れきにんする hold various posts successively

❷ person holding an OFFICE

主任 しゅにん person in charge, head, chief

後任 こうにん successor, replacement

❸ⓐ appoint (to an office), nominate, place
ⓑ appointment, nomination

a 任命 にんめい appointment, nomination

任用する にんようする appoint, employ

選任する せんにんする select and appoint, assign [nominate] a person to a post

b 常任 じょうにん permanent appointment

❹ⓐ LEAVE (up) TO, entrust to, entrust with
ⓑ LEAVE a matter TO take its own course, leave a person to himself, leave alone

a 任意の にんいの optional, voluntary, discretionary; arbitrary

委任する いにんする entrust, delegate, commit

信任 しんにん confidence, trust, credence

一任する いちにんする leave (a matter) to (a person), entrust (a person) with the task (of)

b 任侠 にんきょう chivalrous spirit, siding with the weak

放任する ほうにんする leave (a matter) to take its own course, leave (a person) to himself

❺ profess [claim] to be, pose

自任 じにん pretension

INDEPENDENT

【にん 任】 **OFFICE**, duties, official post; duty, responsibility; person of sufficient competence for the task

任を果たす にんをはたす fulfill [discharge] one's duty [duties]

その任ではない そのにんではない not be fit for the task

【にんじる(=にんずる) 任じる(=任ずる)】 appoint, nominate, place; take a duty upon oneself, assume responsibility; profess [claim] to be, pose

KUN

【まかせる 任せる】LEAVE (up) TO, entrust to, entrust with; leave a matter to take its own course, leave a person to himself, leave alone
運を天に任せる うんをてんにまかせる resign oneself to one's fate, leave to chance
人任せ ひとまかせ leaving matters up to others
【まかす 任す】 same as 任せる **まかせる**
万事君に任す ばんじきみにまかす I leave everything in your hands

SYNONYMS

❶ⓐ work and employment
務 DUTY → 1505
任 OFFICE → 0057
役 SERVICE (esp. public) → 0288
勤 SERVICE (employment) → 2287
業 WORK → 3227
職 EMPLOYMENT → 1803
労 LABOR → 3155
ⓑ responsibility
務 DUTY → 1505
任 duty → 0057
責 RESPONSIBILITY → 3115
分 one's part → 2466
❸ⓐ appoint
任 appoint → 0057
補 appoint → 1529
挙 NOMINATE → 3106
❹ⓐ commit
託 ENTRUST → 1845
托 ENTRUST → 0252
預 DEPOSIT → 1317
委 COMMIT → 3160
任 LEAVE TO → 0057
嘱 CHARGE WITH → 0881

住

1-2-4

incorrect stroke-count
➡ see 1-2-5: 亻 at 0086

次

0058
1-2-4

▶NEXT
ジ シ つ(ぐ) つぎ ㊔ つぐる
Ⓝ 次 Ⓒ 次 cì

76	Jōyō-3	U6B21
欠	S6-4-2	F0138

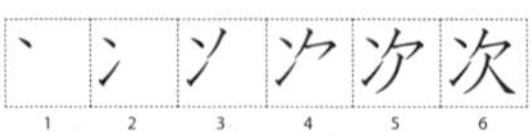

COMPOUNDS

❶ [also prefix] **NEXT, following, subsequent**
次回 じかい next time
次期 じき next term
次号 じごう next issue
次週 じしゅう next week
次年度 じねんど next (fiscal) year
❷ NEXT in order or rank:
ⓐ second
ⓑ secondary, sub-, vice, deputy, assistant
a 次男 じなん second son
次女 じじょ second daughter
次位 じい second rank, second place
b 次類 じるい subgenus
次官 じかん vice-minister, undersecretary
次長 じちょう assistant director
次席 じせき next in rank, associate
副次的な ふくじてきな secondary
❸ⓐ order, sequence, arrangement
ⓑ *math* (degree) **order, degree**
ⓒ suffix indicating numerical order or number of times
a 次第 しだい order; circumstances, reasons; as soon as
次第に しだいに gradually, by degrees
順次 じゅんじ order, turn; gradually
序次 じょじ order, sequence
席次 せきじ order of seats, seating precedence; class standing
目次 もくじ table of contents
b 次元 じげん dimension
高次の こうじの of high order
二次方程式 にじほうていしき quadratic equation, equation of the second degree
c 一次の いちじの first, primary; *math* linear, of the first degree
第二次世界大戦 だいにじせかいたいせん World War II
❹ *chem* prefix indicating a low state of oxidation or low oxygen content: **hypo-, sub-**
次亜硫酸 じありゅうさん hyposulfurous acid
次酸化炭素 じさんかたんそ carbon suboxide
❺ [rare]
ⓐ lodge, take a rest
ⓑ inn, post town
b 旅次 りょじ inn, hotel

KUN

【つぐ 次ぐ】rank NEXT to, come next [after]
次いで ついで next, secondly; subsequently
相次ぐ あいつぐ succeed one another
取り次ぐ とりつぐ act as agent; transmit; answer the door
【つぎ 次】
① NEXT, following
次次に つぎつぎに one after another, in succession
② post town

東海道五十三次 とうかいどうごじゅうさんつぎ
fifty-three stages on the Tokaido highway in former Japan

SYNONYMS

❶ next

次 NEXT → 0058
明 next → 1060
翌 THE FOLLOWING → 3307
来 the coming → 4366

❷ⓐ second

乙 SECOND → 4145
次 second → 0058
後 AFTER (latter) → 0431
中 MIDDLE → 4262

ⓑ subordinate

副 SECONDARY → 2230
次 secondary → 0058
従 subordinate → 0498
亜 SUB- → 4354
準 QUASI- → 3541
半 semi- → 4313
准 JUNIOR → 0143
助 assistant → 1440

❸ⓐ order

序 ORDER (sequence/arrangement) → 3803
順 ORDER (sequence) → 0018
次 order (sequence) → 0058
番 NUMERICAL ORDER → 3416
秩 ORDER (methodical arrangement) → 1489

ⓒ kinds of numbers

数 NUMBER (mathematical unit) → 2245
員 fixed number → 2822
号 NUMBER (numerical designation) → 2675
番 No. → 3416
第 ORDINAL NUMBER PREFIX → 3298
-目 ordinal number suffix → 3777
次 numerical order suffix → 0058
桁 DIGIT → 1165

USAGE

【つぎ】

次
① next, following
② post town

継ぎ
a patch

HOMOPHONES

つぐ

継 SUCCEED → 1720
接 CONTACT → 0607
注 POUR → 0383
つぎ 継 SUCCEED → 1720

NOTE

➡ see also USAGE note at 接 0607

冲

0059

◧ 1-2-4

▶OFFING

チュウ おき

15	Nonstandard	U51B2
冫	S6-2-4	F0000

traditional form → see 沖 at 0307

冴

0060

◧ 1-2-4

▶CRISP AND CLEAR

ゴ さ(える)

15	Nonstandard	U51B4
冫	S6-2-4	F0000

traditional form → see 冴 at 0087

冰

0061

◧ 1-2-4

▶ICE

ヒョウ こおり ひ こお(る)

15	Nonstandard	U51B0
冫	S6-2-4	F0000

traditional form → see 氷 at 0043

次

0062

◧ 1-2-4

▶NEXT

ジ シ つ(ぐ) つぎ ㊔ つぐる

76	Nonstandard	U6B21
欠	S6-4-2	F0000

traditional form → see 次 at 0058

决

0063

◧ 1-2-4

▶DECIDE

ケツ き(める) -ぎ(め) き(まる) ㊔ さだむ

15	Nonstandard	U51B3
冫	S6-2-4	F0000

traditional form → see 決 at 0308

孜

◧ 1-2-4

incorrect stroke-count
➡ see ◧ 1-3-4: 孑 at 0284

防阪

◧ 1-2-4

incorrect stroke-count
➡ see ◧ 1-3-4: 阝 at 0320

州

0064

◧ 1-2-4

▶STATE

シュウ す ㊔ くに

Ⓒ 州 zhōu

47	Jōyō-3	U5DDE
川	S6-3-3	F0488

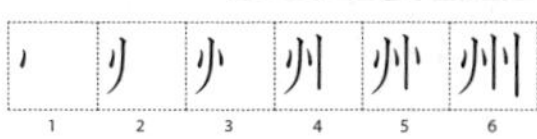

COMPOUNDS

❶ⓐ **STATE (as of the U.S. or Brazil), province (of Canada)**
ⓑ **suffix after names of STATEs**

a 州政府 しゅうせいふ state government
州立大学 しゅうりつだいがく state-run college
州都 しゅうと state capital
b テキサス州 てきさすしゅう State of Texas
リオ・デ・ジャネイロ州 りおでじゃねいろしゅう State of Rio de Janeiro

❷ⓐ (unit of administration in former Japan) **province**
ⓑ unit of administration in ancient China roughly equiv. to modern province

a 信州 しんしゅう Shinshu, Shinano
本州 ほんしゅう Honshu (the main island of Japan)

❸ [formerly also 洲 しゅう 0467] continent
豪州 ごうしゅう Australia
六大州 ろくだいしゅう the Six Continents

INDEPENDENT

【しゅう 州】 **STATE**
州の花 しゅうのはな state flower

KUN

【す 州】 [formerly also 洲] **sandbar, shallows, shoal**
三角州 さんかくす delta
砂州 さす sandbar, sandbank
座州する ざすする strand, run aground

SYNONYMS

❶ **territorial divisions**
州 STATE → 0064
県 PREFECTURE → 3269
府 URBAN PREFECTURE → 3824
道 district of Hokkaido → 3888
都 METROPOLIS OF TOKYO → 2120
省 province in China → 3100
郡 COUNTY → 1858

【す】
◯ **shoals**
瀬 SHALLOWS → 0995
州 sandbar → 0064
礁 REEF → 1588

◯ **elevations in water**
島 ISLAND → 4103
州 sandbar → 0064
礁 REEF → 1588
洲 SANDBAR → 0467

USAGE

【す】
州
[formerly also 洲] sandbar, shallows, shoal

洲
[now usu. 州] sandbar, shallows, shoal

HOMOPHONES

す 洲 SANDBAR → 0467

収

0065
1-2-4

▶**TAKE IN**
シュウ おさ(める) おさ(まる) ㊔ おさむ のぶ かず

66	Names	U6536
攵	S6-4-2	F0000

traditional form → see 收 at 0031

佃

0066
1-2-5

▶**CULTIVATED RICE FIELD**
デン つくだ
Ⓒ 佃 diàn tián

9	Names	U4F43
亻	S7-2-5	F2938

KUN

【つくだ 佃】 **CULTIVATED RICE FIELD**
佃煮 つくだに preserved food boiled in soy

SYNONYMS

【つくだ】
◯ **cultivated fields**
畑 FIELD → 1131
畠 FIELD → 3186
牧 PASTURE → 1083
園 GARDEN → 3914
田 RICE FIELD → 3775
佃 CULTIVATED RICE FIELD → 0066
圃 VEGETABLE GARDEN → 3871

伯

0067
1-2-5

▶**OLDER SIBLING OF PARENT**
▶**COUNT**
ハク ㊔ えき ひろ のり ほ お
Ⓒ 伯 bó bǎi

9	Jōyō	U4F2F
亻	S7-2-5	F1137

ノ	亻	亻'	𠆢	伯	伯	伯
1	2	3	4	5	6	7

COMPOUNDS

❶ **OLDER SIBLING OF one's PARENT, uncle, aunt**
伯父 はくふ(=おじ) uncle (older than one's parent)
伯母 はくぼ(=おば) aunt (older than one's parent)

❷ firstborn brother, older brother
伯仲する はくちゅうする be equal to

❸ⓐ **COUNT, earl**
ⓑ **title after names of COUNTs or earls**

a 伯爵 はくしゃく count, earl
b 前島伯 まえじまはく Count Maejima

❹ⓐ master of an art

❻ title after names of artists
a 画伯 がはく great artist, master painter
❺ abbrev. of 伯耆× ほうき, old name for west Tottori Prefecture
伯備線 はくびせん Hakubi Line (West Tottori-Okayama Railway)
❻ Brazil
日伯 にっぱく Japan and Brazil
❼ [rare] horse trader
伯楽 はくらく horse trader

INDEPENDENT

【はく 伯】COUNT

SPECIAL READINGS

伯父 おじ uncle (older than one's parent)
伯母 おば aunt (older than one's parent)

SYNONYMS

❶ **siblings of parents**
叔 YOUNGER SIBLING OF PARENT → 1622
伯 OLDER SIBLING OF PARENT → 0067
❸ **noblemen**
公 duke → 2468
侯 marquis → 0109
伯 COUNT → 0067
子 viscount → 4196
男 baron → 3147

NOTE

➡ see COMPOUND FORMATION for 伯仲 はくちゅう → 仲 0047

伴

0068

1-2-5

▶**ACCOMPANY**
ハン バン ともな(う) ㊔ とも
Ⓝ 伴 Ⓒ 伴 bàn

9	Jōyō	U4F34
亻	S7-2-5	F1257

Stroke order: 1 2 3 4 5 6 7

COMPOUNDS

❶ (go along with) **ACCOMPANY, go with, attend on**
伴奏 ばんそう accompaniment
伴食大臣 ばんしょくだいじん nominal [figurehead] minister
お相伴 おしょうばん participation
同伴する どうはんする accompany, go with
随伴する ずいはんする attend, accompany, follow
❷ [original meaning] companion, mate
伴侶 はんりょ companion

KUN

【ともなう 伴う】(go together with) **ACCOMPANY, go with, attend;** (occur together with) **accompany, go hand in hand with, follow**
友達を伴って ともだちをともなって accompanied by a friend
相伴う あいともなう accompany, go hand in hand
時勢に伴って じせいにともなって in step with the times

SYNONYMS

❶ **accompany**
伴 ACCOMPANY → 0068
添 accompany → 0641
陪 ACCOMPANY A SUPERIOR → 0655
侍 ATTEND UPON → 0094
従 FOLLOW → 0498
随 FOLLOW → 0765

位

0069

1-2-5

▶**RANK**
▶**POSITION**
イ くらい[1] くらい[2] ぐらい
Ⓒ 位 wèi

9	Jōyō-4	U4F4D
亻	S7-2-5	F0381

Stroke order: 1 2 3 4 5 6 7

COMPOUNDS

❶ [also suffix] **RANK, place, grade, position, station**
地位 ちい position, status, post, social standing
順位 じゅんい order, rank, precedence
上位 じょうい higher rank, precedence
優位 ゆうい superiority, predominant position
首位 しゅい first place, leading position
学位 がくい academic degree
第一位 だいいちい first place, foremost rank
正二位 しょうにい senior grade of second rank
従三位 じゅさんみ second grade of the third rank of honor
❷ [original meaning] **POSITION, location, place; direction**
位置 いち position, place
機位 きい position of aircraft
方位 ほうい direction, bearing
転位 てんい transposition, displacement
定位 ていい normal position; orientation
❸ⓐ decimal place, digit
ⓑ suffix after decimal places
a 百位 ひゃくい the hundreds (digit)
b 小数第五位 しょうすうだいごい five decimal places
❹ **level, standard of quality**
水位 すいい water level
単位 たんい unit
品位 ひんい dignity, grace, nobility; grade, quality
❺ **term of respect**
各位 かくい gentlemen, sirs

❻ *theology* person, hypostasis
三位一体 さんみいったい the Trinity
❼ⓐ spirits of the dead
ⓑ counter for spirits
a 先祖の位牌× せんぞのいはい ancestral tablet

KUN

【くらい¹ 位】**RANK, grade; dignity; the throne; decimal place**
位の高い人 くらいのたかいひと person of high rank
位する くらいする rank, be ranked; be located
位に就く くらいにつく ascend to the throne
一の位 いちのくらい the units

【くらい², ぐらい 位】
① **about, approximately**
十分位 じっぷんぐらい about ten minutes
これ位の大きさ これくらいのおおきさ about this size
② particle indicating comparison or extent: **as…as, like**
これ位 これぐらい this much
東京タワー位高い とうきょうたわーぐらいたかい as high as Tokyo Tower
どの位 どのくらい how much
お前位馬鹿な奴はいない おまえぐらいばかなやつはいない It would be hard to find an idiot like you
③ **at least**
お礼位言っても良さそうだ おれいぐらいいってもよさそうだ He might at least thank me
④ particle indicating that speaker thinks lightly of subject; sooner…than; at all
バスを使う位なら自転車に乗ろう ばすをつかうくらいならじてんしゃにのろう I'd just as soon ride my bike as take the bus

SYNONYMS

❶ **class**
級 GRADE → 1630
段 grade → 1471
位 RANK → 0069
階 RANK → 0761
身 social status → 4368
格 STATUS → 1161
等 CLASS → 3321
流 class → 0529
層 STRATUM → 3920
❷ **places and positions**
所 PLACE → 1056
処 place → 3764
場 PLACE (for specific activity) → 0678
地 PLACE (particular location) → 0236
席 meeting place → 3865
位 POSITION → 0069
点 POINT → 2587
座 place → 3868

【くらい²】
① **approximately**
約 APPROXIMATELY → 1632
概 GENERAL → 1322
大 in substance → 4224
-頃 ABOUT → 0163
位 about → 0069
-方 about → 2459
-程 …or thereabouts → 1524
辺り thereabouts → 3761

佚

▶LOST
イツ
Ⓒ 佚 yì

0070
1-2-5

9	Non-Jōyō	U4F5A
亻	S7-2-5	F0000

COMPOUNDS

[now usu. 逸 3872]
❶ **LOST**, missing
佚書 いっしょ lost book
散佚する さんいつする be lost and scattered
❷ indulge in idle pleasure
佚楽 いつらく idle pursuit of pleasure
安佚 あんいつ (idle) ease, idleness, indolence

SYNONYMS

❶ **losing and loss**
失 LOSE → 4325
喪 lose → 3504
逸 LET SLIP → 3872
損 LOSS, lose → 0801
佚 LOST → 0070

似

▶RESEMBLE
ジ に(る)
Ⓒ 似 sì shì

0071
1-2-5

9	Jōyō-5	U4F3C
亻	S7-2-5	F0673

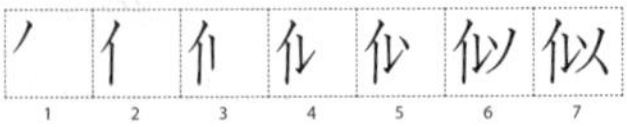

COMPOUNDS

● [original meaning] **RESEMBLE, be similar**
類似する るいじする resemble, be alike, be similar
酷似 こくじ close resemblance
相似 そうじ similarity, resemblance
近似する きんじする approximate to, resemble closely
疑似コレラ ぎじこれら suspected case of cholera, para-cholera

KUN

【にる 似る】**RESEMBLE, be alike, be similar**
- 似ている にている look like, resemble
- 似せる にせる imitate, copy; forge
- 似顔 にがお likeness, portrait
- 似顔絵 にがおえ portrait, likeness
- 似通う にかよう resemble closely
- 似合う にあう befit, suit; match well
- 似合いの にあいの becoming, suitable; well-matched
- 不似合い ふにあい inaptitude, incongruity

SPECIAL READINGS

- 真似▲ まね imitation, mimicry

SYNONYMS

❶ resemble
- 似 RESEMBLE → 0071
- 類 be similar → 2275

住

▶LIVE

ジュウ す(む) す(まう) -ず(まい)

Ⓝ 住 Ⓒ 住 zhù

0072

1-2-5

9	Jōyō-3	U4F4F
亻	S7-2-5	F0289

Stroke order: 丿 亻 亻 仁 住 住 住 (1 2 3 4 5 6 7)

COMPOUNDS

❶ⓐ LIVE, reside, dwell, inhabit
ⓑ housing, residence, house, dwelling
- *a* 住民 じゅうみん residents, dwellers
- 住居 じゅうきょ house, dwelling, residence
- 住所 じゅうしょ one's dwelling, address
- 住職 じゅうしょく Buddhist priest, chief priest
- 在住する ざいじゅうする live, reside, dwell
- 居住する きょじゅうする live, dwell, reside
- 移住する いじゅうする migrate, immigrate; move
- *b* 住宅 じゅうたく housing, dwelling house, residence
- 住宅地 じゅうたくち residential district
- 公住 こうじゅう apartment house built by the Japan Housing Corporation
- 衣食住 いしょくじゅう food, clothing and shelter, the necessities of life

❷ abbrev. of 住職 じゅうしょく: Buddhist priest
- 先住 せんじゅう previous priest; previous resident

❸ [original meaning] stop (an action), stand
- 行住座臥 ぎょうじゅうざが the four cardinal behaviors (walking, stopping [standing], sitting and lying); daily life

INDEPENDENT

【じゅう 住】living; dwelling, shelter

KUN

【すむ 住む】(of people) **LIVE, reside, dwell**
- 住み家(=栖、住み処) すみか residence
- 住み着く すみつく settle, take up residence

【すまう 住まう】**dwell, LIVE, reside in**
- 住まい すまい living; dwelling, house

【-ずまい -住まい】
ⓐ [suffix] **living**
ⓑ **dwelling, residence**
- *a* 団地住まい だんちずまい living in a housing complex
- *b* 仮住まい かりずまい temporary residence

SYNONYMS

❶ⓐ reside
- 住 LIVE → 0072
- 居 RESIDE → 3822
- 棲 INHABIT (said of animals), live → 1246
- 栖 INHABIT (said of animals), live → 1170
- 生 inhabit → 4309
- 植 colonize → 1247

ⓑ houses
- 家 HOUSE → 2827
- 屋 HOUSE → 3842
- 軒 house → 1851
- 戸 HOUSEHOLD → 2429
- 宅 DWELLING HOUSE → 2698
- 居 residence → 3822
- 邸 STATELY RESIDENCE → 1451
- 住 housing → 0072
- 庵 HERMITAGE → 3876

USAGE

【すむ】

住む
(of people) **live, reside, dwell**

栖む
[usu. 棲む] (of animals) **inhabit, live**

棲む
[sometimes also 栖む] (of animals) **inhabit, live**

HOMOPHONES

すむ
- 棲 INHABIT → 1246
- 栖 INHABIT → 1170

何

▶WHAT
▶HOW MANY

カ なに なん なに- なん- ㊔ が あが

Ⓒ 何 hé

0073

1-2-5

9	Jōyō-2	U4F55
亻	S7-2-5	F0051

ノ 亻 亻 仃 佢 佢 何
1 2 3 4 5 6 7

【亻】 冫 孑 阝 刂

COMPOUNDS

● **WHAT, which**

幾何学 きかがく geometry

誰何する すいかする challenge (an unknown person), ask a person's identity

KUN

【なに, なん 何】 **WHAT, which, whatever**—used also in the formation of various interrogative pronouns

何だか なんだか somewhat, a little; somehow; what's what

何時ですか なんじですか What time is it?

何言ってるんだ なにいってるんだ What's the idea [story]?

何か なにか something, some, any

何彼と なにかと in various ways

何等 なんら whatever; (not) any, (not) in any way

何で なんで why, what for

何と なんと what; how

何しろ なにしろ anyhow, at any rate; as you know

何より なにより above all, before everything else

何でも なんでも anything, whatever

何て なんて what, how; What.../How...!

何とか なんとか somehow or other, one way or another

何と無く なんとなく in some way, somehow

何とも なんとも not ... at all; nothing

何気無く なにげなく casually, as if nothing had happened

何者 なにもの who, what kind of man

何故 なにゆえ why, how

何事 なにごと whatever, what

何卒 なにとぞ please (be so kind as to)

【なに-, なん- 何-】 [also prefix]

① **HOW MANY**

何度 なんど how many degrees; how many times

何人 なんにん how many people

② **several, some, odd**

何十 なんじゅう several tens

何百 なんびゃく several hundred, hundreds

何千 なんぜん several thousand, thousands

何時間 なんじかん several hours

SPECIAL READINGS

何故▲ なぜ why, for what reason

何故か▲ なぜか for some reason (or other)

何故なら▲ なぜなら because

何時も▲ いつも always, usually; inevitably

如何▲ いかが how; what

如何▲(=奈何▲) いかん what; how

如何に▲ いかに how, in what way

SYNONYMS

● **interrogatives**

奈 interrogative forming element → 2759

那 interrogative forming element → 1047

何 WHAT → 0073

誰 WHO → 1986

【なに-】

① **how many**

幾 HOW MANY → 4403

何- HOW MANY → 0073

② **some**

幾- SOME → 4403

何- several → 0073

数 several → 2245

或る A CERTAIN → 3978

COMPOUND FORMATION

【幾何学 きかがく】

幾何学 'geometry' derives from 幾何, which originally meant 'how many'. The Chinese used these characters to phonetically transliterate the word *geometry*.

伽

0074

1-2-5

▸**PHONETIC [ga]**

カ ガ キャ とぎ

Ⓒ 伽 jiā gā qié

9	Names	U4F3D
亻	S7-2-5	F2283

COMPOUNDS

● **used PHONETICally for *ga, ka, kya,* esp. in the transliteration of Sanskrit Buddhist terms**

伽藍(=伽檻×) がらん Buddhist temple, cathedral

KUN

【とぎ 伽】

① **keep company by talking before sleep**

お伽噺× おとぎばなし fairy tale, nursery tale

子供の伽をする こどものとぎをする amuse a child

② nursing

病人の伽 びょうにんのとぎ taking care of a sick person

③ ancient custom of staying in bed with a noble person to "entertain" him

夜伽 よとぎ staying in bed with a noble person to "entertain" him

SYNONYMS

● **phonetic [k]/[g]**

迦 PHONETIC [ka] → 3982

珈 phonetic [kō] → 1138

伽 PHONETIC [ga] → 0074

瓦 phonetic [ga] → 4288

祇 phonetic [gi] → 1459

伶

0075

1-2-5

▶**MUSICIAN**

レイ ㊔ りょう

Ⓒ 伶 líng

9	Names	U4F36
亻	S7-2-5	F0000

COMPOUNDS

❶ [original meaning] **MUSICIAN, court musician, performer of court music, minstrel; actor**

伶人 れいじん minstrel, court musician

伶官 れいかん court musician

伶優 れいゆう actor

❷ [now always 怜 0356] clever, quick-witted, bright, nimble

伶俐(=怜俐) れいり cleverness, sagacity

SYNONYMS

❶ **performers**

優 ACTOR → 0200

俳 actor → 0126

伶 MUSICIAN → 0075

伎 PERFORMER → 0055

佐

0076

1-2-5

▶**ASSIST**

▶**FIELD OFFICER**

サ ㊔ すけ たすく

Ⓒ 佐 zuǒ

9	Jōyō	U4F50
亻	S7-2-5	F0455

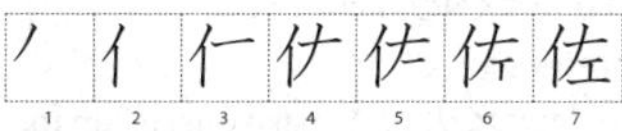

COMPOUNDS

❶ **ASSIST, aid, second**

佐幕派 さばくは supporters of the shogun

補佐(=輔佐)する ほさする assist, help

❷ (military officer or rank below 将 しょう 0551 (general officer) and above 尉 い 2119 (company officer) roughly equiv. to colonel or major (U.S. ranking)) **FIELD OFFICER**

佐官 さかん field officer

大佐 たいさ (army) colonel, (navy) captain

中佐 ちゅうさ (army) lieutenant colonel, (navy) commander

少佐 しょうさ (army) major, (navy) lieutenant commander

SYNONYMS

❶ **help**

助 HELP → 1440

佑 HELP (said esp. of God) → 0083

祐 DIVINE HELP → 1146

援 AID → 0715

佐 ASSIST → 0076

補 assist → 1529

輔 ASSIST → 1963

済 RELIEVE → 0634

❷ **military officers and ranks**

曹 SERGEANT → 3414

尉 COMPANY OFFICER → 2119

佐 FIELD OFFICER → 0076

将 GENERAL OFFICER → 0551

督 COMMANDER → 3471

帥 COMMANDER IN CHIEF → 1642

作

0077

1-2-5

▶**MAKE**

▶**WORK**

サク サ つく(る) つく(り) -づく(り)

Ⓒ 作 zuò zuō

9	Jōyō-2	U4F5C
亻	S7-2-5	F0067

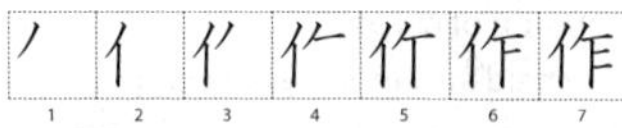

COMPOUNDS

❶ⓐ **MAKE, produce, manufacture**

ⓑ something made; **MAKE**

a 作成する さくせいする make, produce, draw up, frame, prepare

作製 さくせい manufacture, production

製作 せいさく manufacture, production

工作 こうさく handicraft; construction, building; maneuvering

試作 しさく trial manufacture

b 家作 かさく house for rent

造作 ぞうさく fixtures; features

❷ⓐ **compose (a literary or musical work), create, write**

ⓑ [also suffix] **(literary or artistic) WORK, composition, production**

ⓒ [suffix] made by, authored [composed] by, produced by

a 作品 さくひん (piece of) work, performance, product

作家 さっか writer, novelist, author

作曲する さっきょくする compose, write music

作者 さくしゃ author, writer, playwright

作文 さくぶん composition, essay; writing

b 原作 げんさく original (work)

名作 めいさく masterpiece, fine work

創作 そうさく creation, production; fiction writing

大作 たいさく monumental [great] work, major work

傑作 けっさく masterpiece, magnum opus; blunder

代表作 だいひょうさく representative work

c 川端康成作 かわばたやすなりさく written [authored] by Kawabata Yasunari

❸ⓐ **WORK, do, perform, function**

❻ **action, behavior**
a 作業 さぎょう work, operation
作用 さよう action, operation, function; effect
作動する さどうする operate, function, work; run, go
操作する そうさする operate, manipulate, handle
b 作法 さほう manners, etiquette, decorum
動作 どうさ action, movement; bearing, behavior
発作 ほっさ fit, attack, seizure
造作無く ぞうさなく without difficulty

❹ⓐ **raise crops, cultivate, farm**
❻ [also suffix] **crop, harvest, yield**
a 作物 さくもつ crops
作付 さくづけ planting
耕作 こうさく cultivation, farming
連作 れんさく repeated cultivation; story made up by several writers working on it in turn
輪作 りんさく rotation of crops
畑作 はたさく dry field farming, dry field crop
b 作柄 さくがら harvest, crop; quality (of an artistic production)
稲作 いなさく rice crop; raising rice plants
豊作 ほうさく good [abundant] harvest
不作 ふさく bad harvest, crop failure
平年作 へいねんさく average crop

❺ **contrive, scheme**
作戦 さくせん tactics, strategy; (military) operations, maneuvers
作為 さくい artificiality, intention; commission (of a crime)

❻ promote, arouse, awaken
作興する さっこうする promote; awaken, arouse, enhance
振作 しんさく promotion, enhancement, awakening

INDEPENDENT

【さく 作】**(literary or artistic) WORK, composition, production; authorship; crop, harvest, yield**
作が悪い さくがわるい have a poor crop
会心の作 かいしんのさく work after one's heart

KUN

【つくる 作る】
①ⓐ **MAKE (out of materials), form, prepare**
ⓑ [sometimes also 創る] **create, bring into being**
ⓒ **MAKE (as a document), make out, compose, frame, draw up**
ⓓ **form (an organization), organize, found, establish**
ⓔ **prepare food, cook; slice (raw fish)**
a 形作る かたちづくる form, shape, make, mold
ab 作り出す つくりだす make, turn out, create
c 詩を作る しをつくる compose a poem
d 新内閣を作る しんないかくをつくる form a new Cabinet
e 刺身を作る さしみをつくる slice (raw fish)
② **raise crops, cultivate, grow, till**
庭で作った野菜 にわでつくったやさい vegetables grown in one's yard
③ **foster, cultivate (a person's character), build up**
良い習慣を作る よいしゅうかんをつくる cultivate a good habit
④ **MAKE [touch] up, apply cosmetics; trim**
酷く作った顔 ひどくつくったかお face with heavy makeup
⑤ **MAKE up (a story), invent, fabricate**
作り話 つくりばなし fable, fiction
作り泣き つくりなき make-believe crying
作り笑い つくりわらい forced laugh

【つくり 作り】
① **MAKE, physique, features**
顔の作り かおのつくり features of the face
② **MAKEup**
濃い作り こいつくり heavy makeup
③ ***sashimi*, sliced raw flesh (esp. of fish)**
お作り おつくり *sashimi*, sliced raw flesh (esp. of fish)

【-づくり -作り】
① (build of the body) **MAKE, physique**
細作りの人 ほそづくりのひと slender person
② **suffix indicating material composition**
粘土作りの ねんどづくりの made of clay
③ **affectation, pretense**
若作りにする わかづくりにする make oneself up to look younger
④ **sliced raw fish, *sashimi***
生け作り(=活け作り) いけづくり freshly-killed fish served whole with its meat cut in slices

SYNONYMS

❶ⓐ **make**
作 MAKE → 0077
造 MAKE → 3856
成 FORM → 4352
工 MANUFACTURE → 4190
製 MANUFACTURE → 3478
産 PRODUCE → 4089
調 PREPARE → 1973
組む ASSEMBLE → 1693
構 CONSTRUCT → 1325

❷ⓐ **create**
創 CREATE → 2283
作 compose → 0077
綴 COMPOSE → 1746
生 produce → 4309
発 START → 3174

起 generate →4099

❷ⓐ **compose**

著 AUTHOR →2869
作 compose →0077
書く WRITE →3292
筆 write →3317

❸ⓐ **do and act**

為 DO →4395
仕 DO →0037
致す DO HUMBLY →1668
行 ACT →0246
作 WORK →0077

❹ⓐ **farm and plant**

植 PLANT →1247
栽 PLANT (saplings) →4087
培 CULTIVATE →0558
耕 TILL →1659
作 raise crops →0077
農 farm, FARMING →3345
蒔 SOW →2935
播 SOW →0906

USAGE

❶【つくる】

作る

①ⓐ make (out of materials), form, prepare
ⓑ [sometimes also 創る] create, bring into being
ⓒ make (as a document), make out, compose, frame, draw up
ⓓ form (an organization), organize, found, establish
ⓔ prepare food, cook; slice (raw fish)
② raise crops, cultivate, grow, till
③ foster, cultivate (a person's character), build up
④ make [touch] up, apply cosmetics; trim
⑤ make up (a story), invent, fabricate

造る

①ⓐ make (as an object that requires time and skill), manufacture, fabricate, fashion
ⓑ build (ships or buildings), construct
② make (wine), brew
③ coin, mint

創る

[usu. 作る] create, bring into being

❷【つくり】

作り

① make, physique, features
② makeup
③ *sashimi,* sliced raw flesh (esp. of fish)

造り

ⓐ making, building, constructing (as buildings or ships)
ⓑ make, structure, construction

❸【-づくり】

-作り

① (build of the body) make, physique
② suffix indicating material composition
③ affectation, pretense
④ sliced raw fish, *sashimi*

-造り

[also suffix]
ⓐ make, structure; style of building
ⓑ building, constructing, developing

HOMOPHONES

つくる
造 MAKE →3856
創 CREATE →2283
つくり 造 MAKE →3856
-づくり 造 MAKE →3856

伺

▶INQUIRE
シ うかが(う)
Ⓒ 伺 sì cì

0078
◧ 1-2-5

9	Jōyō	U4F3A
亻	S7-2-5	F2018

1 2 3 4 5 6 7

COMPOUNDS

[humble]

❶ **INQUIRE [ask] after (a person's health)**

奉伺する ほうしする inquire after (someone's health)

❷ⓐ **call on (a superior), pay a visit**
ⓑ wait upon, attend on, serve

ab 伺候する しこうする pay one's respects, make a courtesy call; wait upon (a nobleman)

KUN

【うかがう 伺う】[humble]

①ⓐ (put a question) **INQUIRE (about), ask**
ⓑ (request information) **INQUIRE [ask] after (a person's health)**

a 伺い うかがい question, inquiry; consulting the oracle; call, visit
御意見を伺う ごいけんをうかがう ask the opinion of (a superior)
b 伺いを立てる うかがいをたてる inquire of, ask for someone's opinion; invoke an oracle
暑中伺い しょちゅううかがい inquiry after a person's health in the hot season

② **call on (a superior), call at, pay a visit**

何時お伺いしましょうか いつおうかがいしましょうか When shall I call on you?

③ **hear, be told**

...と伺った …とうかがった I heard that...

SYNONYMS

❷ⓐ **visit**

訪 VISIT →1860
参 VISIT A HOLY PLACE →2563
詣 VISIT A HOLY PLACE →1918
寄 call at →2856
伺 call on →0078

【うかがう】

①ⓐ **inquire**

問 QUESTION →4117
詰 question closely →1920
聞く ask →4127
質 query →3483
尋ねる INQUIRE →2918
訊 INQUIRE →1842
伺う INQUIRE (*humble*) →0078
諮 CONSULT →2009
詢 ASK FOR ADVICE →1917

伸

0079

1-2-5

▶**STRETCH**

シン　の(びる)　の(びやか)　の(ばす)
の(べる)　の(す)▲　㊔ のぶ　ただ

Ⓒ 伸 shēn

9	Jōyō	U4F38
亻	S7-2-5	F0940

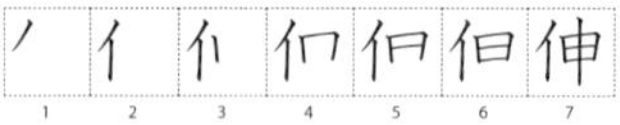

COMPOUNDS

❶ⓐ [original meaning] **STRETCH, elongate, extend, spread**
ⓑ expand, grow, develop

a 伸縮 しんしゅく expansion and contraction
伸張 しんちょう expansion, elongation
b 伸展する しんてんする expand, extend

❷ (of stock prices) **rise**

急伸 きゅうしん sudden rise (said esp. of stock prices), jump
続伸する ぞくしんする continue to rise

❸ [sometimes also 申 4319] **say, mention**

追伸 ついしん postscript

KUN

【のびる 伸びる】*vi*

①ⓐ **STRETCH, lengthen, extend, spread**
ⓑ **expand, increase, grow, develop, advance**

a 伸び のび stretching, elongation; development, growth; spread (as of paint)
背伸び せのび stretching one's back
b 伸び悩む のびなやむ be held in check, fail to grow
伸び率 のびりつ growth rate; coefficient of extension
伸び伸び のびのび at ease

② **spread (as of paint)**

良く伸びるクリーム よくのびるくりーむ easily-spreadable cream

③ **be exhausted, be knocked out**

殴られて伸びる なぐられてのびる be knocked out cold

【のびやか 伸びやか】**carefree; comfortable**

伸びやかに育つ のびやかにそだつ grow up naturally

【のばす 伸ばす】*vt*

①ⓐ **STRETCH, elongate, extend, spread**
ⓑ **expand, let grow, develop**

a 引き伸ばす ひきのばす stretch out, elongate; enlarge (photographs)
b 才能を伸ばす さいのうをのばす develop one's ability

② **straighten**

体を伸ばす からだをのばす stretch (unbend) oneself

③ **dilute**

スープを伸ばす すーぷをのばす thin soup with water

④ **knock out**

伸ばしてしまえ のばしてしまえ Knock him out!

【のべる 伸べる】[also 延べる]

ⓐ **extend, STRETCH out (one's arm)**
ⓑ spread out (bedding)

a 手を差し伸べる てをさしのべる extend one's arm, hold out one's hand
差し伸べる さしのべる stretch out (one's hand), extend (one's arm)
b 床を伸べる とこをのべる spread [make] a bed

【のす 伸す】gain influence, rise in power; go further, extend one's journey; **STRETCH**, spread; *slang* knock out, send (a person) sprawling

伸し上がる のしあがる stand on tiptoe; raise oneself to (a higher position); act important
党勢を伸す とうせいをのす extend the strength of a party

SPECIAL READINGS

欠伸▲ あくび yawn

SYNONYMS

❶ⓐ **expand**

脹 SWELL →1265
膨 EXPAND →1380
張 SPREAD →0573
氾 SPREAD OUT →0226
広げる spread (out) →3769
拡 ENLARGE →0366
伸 STRETCH →0079
延 EXTEND →3812

ⓑ **grow**

成 grow up →4352

長 grow (up) →3163
生 grow →4309
育 grow →2544
発 develop →3174
伸 expand →0079
展 UNFOLD →3862

USAGE

❶【のびる】
伸びる
vi
①ⓐ stretch, lengthen, extend, spread
ⓑ expand, increase, grow, develop, advance
② spread (as of paint)
③ be exhausted, be knocked out
延びる
vi
① extend (in space or time), be extended, be prolonged
② be postponed, be delayed

❷【のび】
伸び
①ⓐ stretching, elongation
ⓑ development, growth
② spread (as of paint)
延び
① extension
② postponement

❸【のばす】
伸ばす
vt
①ⓐ stretch, elongate, extend, spread
ⓑ expand, let grow, develop
② straighten
③ dilute
④ knock out
延ばす
vt
① extend (in space or time), prolong, spread
② postpone, delay, defer

❹【のびのび】
伸び伸び
at ease
延び延び
repeated delays, dragging on and on

❺【のべる】
伸べる
[also 延べる]
ⓐ extend, stretch out (one's arm)
ⓑ spread out (bedding)
延べる
① [also 伸べる]
ⓐ extend, stretch out (one's arm)
ⓑ spread out (bedding)
② postpone, delay

HOMOPHONES

のびる 延 EXTEND →3812
のび 延 EXTEND →3812
のばす 延 EXTEND →3812
のべる 延 EXTEND →3812

体

0080

▶BODY
▶FORM

タイ テイ からだ

Ⓝ 體 軆 躰◇ Ⓒ 体 tǐ tī

1-2-5

9△	Jōyō-2	U4F53
亻	S7-2-5	F0055

Stroke order: 1 丿 2 亻 3 亻一 4 什 5 休 6 休 7 体

COMPOUNDS

❶ⓐ [also suffix] (physical organism) **BODY, corpse**
ⓑ counter for dead bodies [corpses]

a 体力 たいりょく physical strength, strength of one's body
体質 たいしつ physical constitution
体内 たいない interior of the body
体操 たいそう gymnastics, physical exercise
体重 たいじゅう body weight
体育 たいいく physical training [education]
体温 たいおん body temperature
体温計 たいおんけい (clinical) thermometer
体長 たいちょう body length (of animals)
身体 しんたい body
人体 じんたい human body
一体 いったい one body; a style, a form; (why, what) on earth, (what, why) in the world
自体 じたい one's own body; itself
全体 ぜんたい whole (body), whole span
肉体 にくたい body, flesh
焼死体 しょうしたい charred body
遺体 いたい remains, body, corpse
脂肪体 しぼうたい corpus adiposum
b 死体三体 したいさんたい three corpses

❷ abbrev. of 体育 たいいく: physical education
体協 たいきょう Japan Amateur Sports Association
国体 こくたい National Athletic Meet

❸ⓐ (main part, esp. of a vehicle) **BODY, framework**
ⓑ (main or essential part) **substance, reality, real thing**

a 車体 しゃたい car body, chassis; frame (of a bicycle)
機体 きたい fuselage, body (of an airplane); machine
解体 かいたい dismantling (a machine), scrapping; dissolution, disorganization; dissection

b 体言 たいげん indeclinable parts of speech in Japanese, substantive
主体 しゅたい main part; subject
実体 じったい substance, essence
本体 ほんたい substance, thing itself; object of worship; main part
大体 だいたい outline, substance; generally, roughly, on the whole

❹ [also suffix]
ⓐ (physical object or mass) **BODY, object, substance**
ⓑ *geometry* **BODY**, solid body, figure

a 体積 たいせき (cubic) volume, capacity
物体 ぶったい body, physical solid, object, substance
固体 こたい solid, solid matter
気体 きたい gas, vapor, gaseous body
天体 てんたい heavenly body
有機体 ゆうきたい organism, organic body
立体 りったい solid (body), cube
b 六面体 ろくめんたい hexahedron

❺ (organized entity) **BODY, organization**
団体 だんたい group, party, body, corps; corporation, organization
自治体 じちたい self-governing body [community]
組織体 そしきたい body, organization

❻ [also suffix]
ⓐ **(characteristic) FORM, shape**
ⓑ (outer appearance) **FORM, appearance**
ⓒ (manner of expression) **style, FORM**
ⓓ (mode of existence) **FORM**, system

a 体系 たいけい system, organization
字体 じたい character form, type
具体的な ぐたいてきな concrete, definite, specific
正体 しょうたい one's natural [true] shape; consciousness
b 体貌 たいぼう appearance
体裁 ていさい decency, form, style, appearance
風体 ふうてい(=ふうたい) appearance, looks; posture
世間体 せけんてい appearance (in the eyes of society), decency
職人体の男 しょくにんていのおとこ man of workmanlike appearance
c 文体 ぶんたい (literary) style
書体 しょたい penmanship style, calligraphic style
ですます体 ですますたい *desu-masu* style (in Japanese grammar)
d 政体 せいたい form [system] of government

❼ **learn from experience**
体得する たいとくする realize, learn (from experience), comprehend, master
体験する たいけんする experience, go through, (actually) feel

❽ counter for images of Buddhist or Shinto deities
仏像二体 ぶつぞうにたい two images of Buddha

❾ *math* field
実数体 じっすうたい real number field

INDEPENDENT

【たい 体】 **BODY**; form, style; substance, essence; *math* field
体を交わす たいをかわす dodge, parry
体を成す たいをなす take form [shape]

【たいする 体する】 bear in mind, obey, comply with
社長の意を体する しゃちょうのいをたいする comply with the wishes of the company president

【てい 体】 appearance, air; condition, state
然有らぬ体で さあらぬていで with a nonchalant air
中止の体 ちゅうしのてい state of standstill

KUN

【からだ 体】 **BODY, physique; health**
体造り からだづくり physical culture
体付き からだつき one's figure
体が強い からだがつよい have a strong constitution, be in good health

SYNONYMS

❶ **body**
体 BODY → 0080
身 BODY (esp. vs. mind) → 4368
肉 FLESH → 3966
屍 CORPSE → 3843
尸 CORPSE → 4198
骸 DEAD BODY → 2301

❸ⓑ **essential content**
実 substance → 2765
体 substance → 0080
味 contents → 0325

❹ⓐ **object**
物 THING → 1084
品 ARTICLE → 2795
体 BODY → 0080

ⓑ **bodies**
体 BODY → 0080
塊 LUMP → 0775
球 BALL → 1219

❺ **organized bodies**
会 SOCIETY → 2512
協 association → 0103
団 BODY → 3791
体 BODY → 0080
組 union → 1693
労 workers' union → 3155
連 federation → 3849
講 fraternity → 2046
院 INSTITUTION → 0544

❻ⓐ **form**
形 SHAPE → 1050
状 FORM (external) → 0322
体 FORM (characteristic) → 0080
姿 FIGURE → 3264
ⓑ **appearance**
容 APPEARANCE → 2832
貌 APPEARANCE → 1958
姿 FIGURE → 3264
相 PHASE → 1120
体 FORM (outer appearance) → 0080
色 COLOR → 2522
風 air → 3730

但

▶PROVIDED THAT
タン ただ(し) ㊔ たじ
Ⓒ 但 dàn

0081
◧1-2-5

9	Jōyō	U4F46
亻	S7-2-5	F2020

1 2 3 4 5 6 7

COMPOUNDS

● abbrev. of 但馬 たじま, old name for north Hyogo Prefecture
播但線 ばんたんせん Bantan Line (railway in Hyogo Prefecture)

KUN

【ただし 但し】**PROVIDED THAT, on condition that, however, but, only**
但し書き ただしがき proviso, conditional clause
但し付き ただしつき conditional
但し...に就いてはこの限りではない ただし…についてはこのかぎりではない Provided that the same shall not apply to…
彼は約束はする、但し履行はせぬ かれはやくそくはする, ただしりこうはせぬ He makes promises, but he does not keep them

SYNONYMS

【ただし】
◯ **conditional conjunctions**
但し PROVIDED THAT → 0081
然し however → 3456

低

▶LOW
テイ ひく(い) ひく(める) ひく(まる)
Ⓒ 低 dī

0082
◧1-2-5

9	Jōyō-4	U4F4E
亻	S7-2-5	F0619

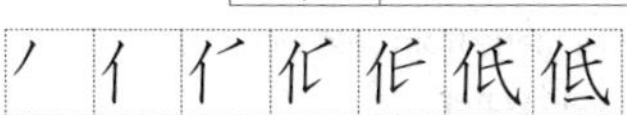
1 2 3 4 5 6 7

COMPOUNDS

❶ⓐ [original meaning] (having little height) **LOW**
ⓑ **LOWer, bring down**
a 低地 ていち low ground, lowlands
低空 ていくう low altitude
高低 こうてい high and low
b 低下する ていかする fall, sink, lower, go down
低頭 ていとう bowing low
❷ [also prefix]
ⓐ (below average in degree) **LOW**
ⓑ **LOW-priced, inexpensive**
a 低音 ていおん low-pitched sound, bass
低温 ていおん low temperature
低能 ていのう low intelligence
低気圧 ていきあつ low pressure, atmospheric depression
最低の さいていの lowest
b 低価 ていか low price
低廉な ていれんな cheap, inexpensive
低賃金 ていちんぎん low wages
❸ (of inferior social standing) **LOW, humble, vulgar**
低級 ていきゅう low grade, low class, vulgar
低俗な ていぞくな vulgar
❹ [formerly 彽 0350] linger, wander
低回(=彽徊)する ていかいする linger, loiter, wander

INDEPENDENT

【てい 低】**LOW**
高より低へ こうよりていへ from high to low

KUN

【ひくい 低い】**LOW, short** (stature); (of inferior social standing) **low, humble; in a low voice [key]**
低くする ひくくする lower, bring down
身長の低い人 しんちょうのひくいひと short person
【ひくめる 低める】**LOWer, bring down**
【ひくまる 低まる】**be LOWered, come down**

SYNONYMS

❶ⓐ **low**
低 LOW → 0082
下 lower → 4186
ⓑ **lower**
低 lower → 0082
下 bring down → 4186
❷ⓐ **less in degree**
弱 WEAK → 1499
軽 LIGHT → 1909
微 SLIGHT → 0788
低 LOW → 0082
薄 THIN → 3004
浅 SHALLOW → 0464

厌 FAINT →3664
❷ **inexpensive**
安 INEXPENSIVE →2695
廉 CHEAP →3911
低 low-priced →0082
❸ **lowly**
卑 MEAN →3270
下 of low rank →4186
低 LOW →0082

佑

0083
1-2-5

▶**HELP**
ユウ ウ ㊔ すけ たすく
Ⓒ 佑 yòu

9	Names	U4F51
亻	S7-2-5	F2224

COMPOUNDS

ⓐ [original meaning] **HELP, succor, protect**—said esp. of God
ⓑ [also 祐 1146] divine **HELP**, heavenly assistance [protection]
a 佑助 ゆうじょ help, divine help
b 天佑 てんゆう grace of Heaven, providential help

SYNONYMS

● **help**
助 HELP →1440
佑 HELP (said esp. of God) →0083
祐 DIVINE HELP →1146
援 AID →0715
佐 ASSIST →0076
補 assist →1529
輔 ASSIST →1963
済 RELIEVE →0634

佛

0084
1-2-5

▶**BUDDHA**
▶**FRANCE**
ブツ フツ ほとけ ㊔ さとる

9	Names	U4F5B
亻	S7-2-5	F0000

traditional form →see 仏 at 0020

伴

0085
1-2-5

▶**ACCOMPANY**
ハン バン ともな(う) ㊔ とも

9	Nonstandard	U4F34
亻	S7-2-5	F0000

traditional form →see 伴 at 0068

住

0086
1-2-5

▶**LIVE**
ジュウ す(む) す(まう) -ず(まい)

9	Nonstandard	U4F4F
亻	S7-2-5	F0000

traditional form →see 住 at 0072

冴

0087
1-2-5

▶**CRISP AND CLEAR**
ゴ さ(える)
Ⓝ 冴 Ⓒ 冱 hù

15	Names	U51B4
冫	S7-2-5	F2315

COMPOUNDS

● [original meaning, now rare] ice-cold, freezing; freeze
冴寒 ごかん extreme cold

KUN

【さえる 冴える】
①ⓐ **be CRISP AND CLEAR, be crystal-clear (as on an ice-cold winter night), be bright, be vivid**
ⓑ **be clearheaded, be wide-awake, be fresh**
a 冴え返る さえかえる be exceedingly clear; be keenly cold
冴えた色 さえたいろ bright color
b 冴え冴えした顔 さえざえしたかお fresh complexion, cheerful look
頭の冴え あたまのさえ bright intelligence
眼が冴える めがさえる be wakeful, be wide-awake
② be ice-cold, be chilly
冴えた夜 さえたよる crisp and cold night
③ become skilled, be dexterous
腕の冴え うでのさえ skill, dexterity

SYNONYMS

【さえる】
①ⓐ **clear**
透 TRANSPARENT →3854
澄 LIMPID →0915
清 CLEAR (liquid) →0635
明 CLEAR (unclouded) →1060
朗 CLEAR (sky) →1679
冴える CRISP AND CLEAR →0087

冷

0088
1-2-5

▶**COLD**
レイ つめ(たい) ひ(える) ひ(や) ひ(ややか) ひ(やす) ひ(やかす) さ(める) さ(ます) ㊔ りょう
Ⓒ 冷 lěng

15	Jōyō-4	U51B7
冫	S7-2-5	F0663

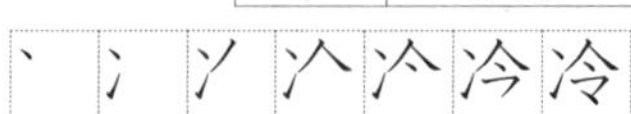
1 2 3 4 5 6 7

COMPOUNDS

❶ⓐ **COLD, chilled**
ⓑ [original meaning] **cool, chill, refrigerate**
a 冷気 れいき cold air; cold, chill
冷害 れいがい damage from cold weather
冷水 れいすい cold water
冷戦 れいせん Cold War

寒冷 かんれい cold, coldness, chilliness
b 冷房 れいぼう air conditioning
冷凍 れいとう freezing, cold storage
冷却 れいきゃく cooling, refrigeration
冷蔵 れいぞう cold storage
冷蔵庫 れいぞうこ refrigerator
水冷 すいれい water cooling

❷ COLDhearted, dispassionate
冷酷な れいこくな cruel, unfeeling, coldhearted
冷血な れいけつな cold-blooded, coldhearted, heartless
冷笑 れいしょう derisive smile, sneer
冷評 れいひょう sarcasm, sneer, jeer
冷静な れいせいな cool, calm, cool-headed, dispassionate

KUN

【つめたい 冷たい】COLD (to the touch), chilly; coldhearted, cold-blooded
冷たさ つめたさ coldness; coldheartedness
冷たい戦争 つめたいせんそう cold war

【ひえる 冷える】*vi* cool down, grow COLD; feel chilly
冷え ひえ chilling
冷え込む ひえこむ get colder, get chilled
冷え症 ひえしょう oversensitivity to cold
寝冷え ねびえ cold [chill] caught while sleeping

【ひや 冷や】cool drinking water; COLD sake; [in compounds] **cold, chilled**
冷や飯 ひやめし cold rice; cold treatment [shoulder]
冷や汗 ひやあせ cold sweat
お冷や一杯 おひやいっぱい a glass of water

【ひややか 冷ややか】
ひややかな 冷ややかな COLD, chilly; frigid, indifferent
冷ややかさ ひややかさ coldness; frigidity, indifference
冷ややかな態度 ひややかなたいど cold attitude

【ひやす 冷やす】cool, chill, refrigerate
冷やし中華 ひやしちゅうか chilled Chinese noodles
頭を冷やす あたまをひやす cool one's head

【ひやかす 冷やかす】banter, chaff, jeer at; window-shop, browse
冷やかし ひやかし banter, chaff, raillery; window-shopping, browsing

【さめる 冷める】*vi*
ⓐ **cool off, get COLD**
ⓑ **cool down, subside, flag, be dampened**
a スープが冷めた すーぷがさめた The soup has cooled
b 興冷め きょうざめ being wet-blanketed; skeleton at the feast

【さます 冷ます】*vt*
① **cool, let cool**
熱冷まし ねつさまし antifebrile, antipyretic
② **dampen, spoil**
興を冷ます きょうをさます spoil a person's pleasure, be a wet-blanket

SYNONYMS

❶ⓐ cold
冷 COLD → 0088
寒 COLD (weather) → 2894
涼 COOL → 0633
凜 SEVERELY COLD → 0195
ⓑ reduce the temperature
凍 FREEZE → 0146
冷 cool → 0088

HOMOPHONES

さめる
覚 PERCEIVE → 3217
醒 AWAKE → 2033
さます
覚 PERCEIVE → 3217
醒 AWAKE → 2033

NOTE

➡ see USAGE note at 覚 3217

冶

▶WORK METALS
ヤ
Ⓒ 冶 yě

0089
◧ 1-2-5

15	Jōyō	U51B6
冫	S7-2-5	F2418

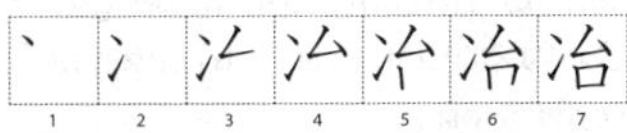

COMPOUNDS

❶ WORK METALS: smelt forge, cast
冶金 やきん metallurgy
❷ train, cultivate
陶冶する とうやする train, cultivate, educate
❸ sexy, seductive, bewitching
艶冶な えんやな beautiful and sexy, seductive

SPECIAL READINGS

鍛冶 かじ (=たんや) forging; smith

SYNONYMS

❶ work metals
錬 REFINE (crude metals) → 2185
煉 REFINE (crude metals) → 1297
鍛 FORGE → 2206
鋳 CAST → 2170
焼き annealing → 1256
冶 WORK METALS → 0089

イ【冫】扌阝リ

NOTE

★ do not confuse with 治 GOVERN →0393

况 0090
◧1-2-5

▸CONDITIONS
キョウ ま(して)

15	Nonstandard	U51B5
冫	S7-2-5	F0000

traditional form →see 況 at 0395

孤
◧1-2-5

incorrect stroke-count
➡ see ◧1-3-6: 子 at 0426

阻附 etc.
◧1-2-5

incorrect stroke-count
➡ see ◧1-3-5: 阝 at 0408

児
◧1-2-5

incorrect classification
➡ see ⬒2-5-2: 旧 at 3153

侮 0091
◧1-2-6

▸INSULT
ブ あなど(る)
Ⓝ 侮 Ⓒ 侮 wǔ

9	Jōyō	U4FAE
亻	S8-2-6	F2183

COMPOUNDS

ⓐ [original meaning] **INSULT, humiliate, make a fool of**

ⓑ **despise, disdain, hold in contempt, make light of**

a 侮辱する ぶじょくする insult, treat with contempt
侮言 ぶげん words of insult

b 侮蔑 ぶべつ contempt, scorn
軽侮する けいぶする look down upon, despise, disdain

KUN

【あなどる 侮る】**despise, disdain, hold in contempt, make light of**
侮り あなどり contempt, scorn
侮り難い敵 あなどりがたいてき formidable enemy

SYNONYMS

ⓐ **disgrace**
恥 SHAME →1664
羞 shame →4106
辱 HUMILIATE →3400
侮 INSULT →0091
罵 ABUSE →3233
汚 defile →0258
誹 SLANDER →1978
譏 SLANDER →2069

ⓑ **disdain**
侮 despise →0091
軽 make light of →1909
蔑 DESPISE →2969
嘲 SCOFF AT →0878

併 0092
◧1-2-6

▸TOGETHER
ヘイ あわ(せる) しか(し)▲
Ⓝ 併 Ⓒ 并 bìng bīng

9	Jōyō	U4F75
亻	S8-2-6	F1437

COMPOUNDS

❶ [also 並 2793] **TOGETHER, collectively, simultaneously, side by side**
併用する へいようする use together [jointly]
併発 へいはつ concurrence
併記する へいきする line up together (in writing)
併呑 へいどん annexation, merger
併殺 へいさつ double play

❷ [original meaning] **join TOGETHER, combine, unite**
合併する がっぺいする combine, unite, merge
兼併する けんぺいする join together, unite

KUN

【あわせる 併せる】[sometimes also 合わせる] (bring two or more things together) **join TOGETHER, combine, merge**
併せて あわせて collectively, all together; in addition, besides
併せ持つ あわせもつ own (something) as well
二つの会社を併せる ふたつのかいしゃをあわせる merge two companies

【しかし 併し】[also 然し] however, but, nevertheless

SYNONYMS

❶ **together**
共 JOINT →3045
同 together →3707
併 TOGETHER →0092
並 side by side →2793
兼 CONCURRENTLY →2850
倶 TOGETHER →0125

❷ **combine**
合 COMBINE →2511
結 TIE →1706
統 UNITE →1710
括 LUMP TOGETHER →0449
総 integrate →1743
併 join together →0092
綜 INTEGRATE →1744

纏める PUT TOGETHER → 1814

HOMOPHONES

あわせる

合 COMBINE → 2511

会 MEET → 2512

遭 MEET WITH → 3917

NOTE

➡ see USAGE note at 合 2511

依

0093

◧ 1-2-6

▶DEPEND ON

イ エ よ(る)▲ ㊔ よ

ⓒ 依 yī

9	Jōyō	U4F9D
亻	S8-2-6	F1076

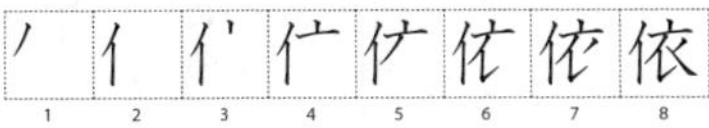

COMPOUNDS

❶ⓐ DEPEND ON, rely on

ⓑ be based on

a 依存する いぞん(=いそん)する depend on, rely on

依嘱する いしょくする entrust with

依頼する いらいする request, make a request; entrust, commission; rely on, depend on

帰依 きえ faith, devotion; conversion

b 依拠 いきょ basis, grounds; dependence

依願退職 いがんたいしょく retirement at one's own request

❷ as it used to be

依然として いぜんとして as ever, as before

KUN

【よる 依る】

① **DEPEND ON**, rely on, hang on

成功は忍耐の如何に依る せいこうはにんたいのいかんによる Success depends upon perseverance

② do by (means of), resort to, have recourse to

彼らの助力に依って かれらのじょりょくによって by dint of their help

SYNONYMS

❶ⓐ rely on

頼 RELY ON → 2041

依 DEPEND ON → 0093

HOMOPHONES

よる

拠 GROUNDS → 0369

因 CAUSE → 3792

由 REASON → 4311

寄 CONTRIBUTE → 2856

NOTE

➡ see USAGE note at 因 3792

侍

0094

◧ 1-2-6

▶ATTEND UPON

▶SAMURAI

ジ さむらい はべ(る)▲ ㊔ ひと

ⓒ 侍 shì

9	Jōyō	U4F8D
亻	S8-2-6	F1190

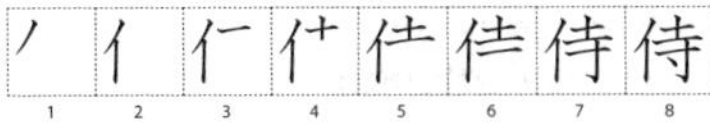

COMPOUNDS

● ATTEND UPON, wait upon, serve

侍女 じじょ lady attendant

侍従 じじゅう chamberlain

侍医 じい court physician, personal physician

陪侍 ばいじ attending on the nobility; retainer

近侍 きんじ attendant

KUN

【さむらい 侍】[also suffix] **SAMURAI, warrior; man of resolution and ability**

若侍 わかざむらい young samurai

犬侍 いぬざむらい shameless [depraved] samurai

田舎侍 いなかざむらい country samurai

【はべる 侍る】**ATTEND UPON**, wait upon, serve

美女を侍らす びじょをはべらす be waited upon by a beauty

SYNONYMS

● accompany

伴 ACCOMPANY → 0068

添 accompany → 0641

陪 ACCOMPANY A SUPERIOR → 0655

侍 ATTEND UPON → 0094

従 FOLLOW → 0498

随 FOLLOW → 0765

【さむらい】

○ soldiers and warriors

兵 SOLDIER → 3158

卒 private → 2549

士 MILITARY MAN → 4213

武 warrior → 3979

侍 SAMURAI → 0094

価

0095

◧ 1-2-6

▶PRICE

▶VALUE

カ あたい

Ⓝ 價 ⓒ 价 jià jiè

9	Jōyō-5	U4FA1
亻	S8-2-6	F0418

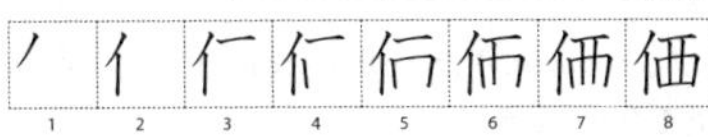

【亻】十 孑 阝

COMPOUNDS

❶ [original meaning] (monetary value) **PRICE, cost**
価格 かかく price, cost
物価 ぶっか prices (of commodities)
高価な こうかな expensive, high-priced
米価 べいか price of rice
定価 ていか fixed [set] price
❷ [also suffix] **VALUE, worth, merit**
価値 かち value, merit
評価する ひょうかする evaluate, appraise
声価 せいか reputation, fame
栄養価 えいようか nutritive value
❸ⓐ valence
ⓑ counter for valence
a 数価 すうか valence
原子価 げんしか (atomic) valence
多価 たか polyvalence
b 二価の にかの divalent

KUN

【あたい 価】 **PRICE, cost**
価千金の あたいせんきんの priceless, invaluable

SYNONYMS

❶ **fee and price**
料 FEE →1644
代 CHARGE →0034
賃 CHARGES →3341
銭 money paid →2159
費 EXPENSE →3221
価 PRICE →0095
値 price →0123
❷ **value**
値 VALUE →0123
価 VALUE →0095

HOMOPHONES

あたい 値 VALUE →0123

NOTE

➡ see USAGE note at 値 0123

佳 0096

▸**FINE**
カ ㊔ よし けい
Ⓒ 佳 jiā
1-2-6

9	Jōyō	U4F73
亻	S8-2-6	F1400

ノ 亻 亻 仁 件 佳 佳 佳 (1–8)

COMPOUNDS

❶ (of superior quality) **FINE, good, excellent**
佳作 かさく fine work
佳境 かきょう most interesting part, climax
佳品 かひん choice [excellent] article
佳味 かみ fine [good] taste; delicious food
❷ [original meaning] (of pleasing appearance) **FINE(-looking), beautiful**
佳人 かじん beautiful woman
佳麗 かれい beauty
佳景 かけい fine [beautiful] view
絶佳の ぜっかの superb (landscape)
❸ [also 嘉 2953] happy, auspicious, lucky, good
佳節 かせつ happy [auspicious] occasion
佳辰 かしん happy [auspicious] occasion

INDEPENDENT

【か 佳】 beauty, superbness
風光佳なり ふうこうかなり The scenery is fine

SYNONYMS

❶ **good**
良 GOOD →4373
善 GOOD →2921
好 FAVORABLE →0240
順 favorable →0018
佳 FINE →0096
美 BEAUTIFUL →2817
❷ **beautiful**
美 BEAUTIFUL →2817
彪 MAGNIFICENT →4115
綺 BEAUTIFUL →1734
娃 BEAUTIFUL →0419
佳 FINE →0096
瑶 EXQUISITE →1301
麗 OF GRACEFUL BEAUTY →2672
艶 CHARMING →2403
妙 of marvelous beauty →0280
華 MAGNIFICENT →2841
絢 GORGEOUS →1705
斐 florid →3449

侃 0097

▸**FORTHRIGHT**
カン ㊔ ただ ただし あきら つよし すなお なお やす
Ⓒ 侃 kǎn
1-2-6

9	Names	U4F83
亻	S8-2-6	F0000

COMPOUNDS

● **FORTHRIGHT, straightforward, straight and bold**
侃侃諤×諤×の かんかんがくがくの outspoken (dispute), straightforward
侃侃たる かんかんたる straight and bold (manner of speaking)

SYNONYMS

● **purehearted**

純 PURE → 1649
淳 PUREHEARTED → 0626
清 clean → 0635
潔 IMMACULATE → 0920
廉 INCORRUPT → 3911
敦 HONEST → 2128
惇 SINCERE → 0588
直 straightforward → 3649
侃 FORTHRIGHT → 0097

供

0098
◧ 1-2-6

▶OFFER
キョウ ク クウ▲ グ▲ そな(える) とも -ども
Ⓒ 供 gōng gòng

9	Jōyō-6	U4F9B
イ	S8-2-6	F0342

丿 亻 仁 什 册 供 供 供
1 2 3 4 5 6 7 8

COMPOUNDS

❶ⓐ (put at another's disposal) **OFFER, present, submit**
ⓑ **supply, deliver, furnish**
a 供覧 きょうらん display, show
提供する ていきょうする offer, tender; sponsor (a show)
試供品 しきょうひん sample, specimen
b 供給する きょうきゅうする supply, furnish, provide
供与する きょうよする offer, present, submit
供出 きょうしゅつ delivery of allotment to the government
供米 きょうまい delivery of rice to the government; rice delivered to the government

❷ [original meaning] **OFFER (sacrifices to a god), dedicate, sacrifice**
供物 くもつ offering
供養 くよう memorial service
供米 くまい rice offered to a god
供御 くご emperor's meal
人身御供 ひとみごくう human sacrifice, victim

❸ confess, depose
供述 きょうじゅつ testimony, statement; confession
自供する じきょうする confess, depose

❹ [formerly 饗 3616] treat, provide dinner for, entertain, banquet
供応 きょうおう treat, feast, banquet
供宴 きょうえん banquet, feast, dinner

❺ accompany, follow, go with
供奉する ぐぶする accompany, be in attendance

INDEPENDENT

【きょうする 供する】**OFFER**, present, submit; furnish, provide

KUN

【そなえる 供える】**OFFER (to a god), make an offering**
供え そなえ offering
供え物 そなえもの offering
墓に花を供える はかにはなをそなえる offer flowers on a tomb

【とも 供】**attendant, retinue**
供回り ともまわり train of attendants, retinue
お供する おともする go with, accompany, follow

【-ども -供】**plural suffix**—now used only in 子供 こども without implying plurality
子供 こども child, kid; son, daughter

SYNONYMS

❶ⓐ & ❷ **offer**
供 OFFER (to a person or god) → 0098
献 OFFER (esp. to a superior) → 2240
納 offer (as to a god) → 1652
提 PRESENT → 0720
貢 offer tribute → 2838
奉 DEDICATE → 3167
捧 OFFER RESPECTFULLY → 0594

ⓑ **supply**
供 supply → 0098
給 SUPPLY → 1708
納 deliver goods to a customer → 1652

【とも】
◯ **servants**
僕 MANSERVANT → 0185
奴 SLAVE → 0217
隷 UNDERLING → 2201
臣 RETAINER → 3806
従 follower → 0498
供 attendant → 0098

HOMOPHONES

そなえる 備 PROVIDE → 0165
そなえ 備 PROVIDE → 0165
とも
友 FRIEND → 3670
共 JOINT → 3045
朋 COMRADE → 1092
-ども 共 JOINT → 3045

NOTE

➡ see USAGE notes at 備 0165 and 友 3670 and 共 3045

例

0099
◧ 1-2-6

▶EXAMPLE
レイ たと(える)
Ⓒ 例 lì

9	Jōyō-4	U4F8B
イ	S8-2-6	F0490

【亻】 十 子 阝

1

丿 亻 亻 仃 仃 伢 例 例
1 2 3 4 5 6 7 8

亻 十 孑 阝

COMPOUNDS

❶ⓐ [also suffix] (something representative) **EXAMPLE, instance, case**
ⓑ previous EXAMPLE, precedent

a 例題 れいだい example, exercise
例文 れいぶん illustrative sentence, example (sentence)
一例 いちれい example, instance, case, illustration
範例 はんれい example
実例 じつれい example, instance, concrete case
用例 ようれい example, illustration (of the use of a word)
特例 とくれい special case [example]; exception
具体例 ぐたいれい concrete example

b 例外 れいがい exception
類例 るいれい similar example, parallel
先例 せんれい precedent, former example
前例 ぜんれい precedent; above example
判例 はんれい (judicial) precedent

❷ⓐ established practice, custom, usage
ⓑ regular, usual, established

a 恒例 こうれい regular ceremony, established custom
慣例 かんれい custom, usage, precedent
家例 かれい family usage [practice, custom]
常例 じょうれい usual practice, common usage, established custom

b 例会 れいかい regular meeting
例年 れいねん normal year, average year
例日 れいじつ regular day
例刻 れいこく regular time

❸ conventions, rules

条例 じょうれい regulations, rules, law
凡例 はんれい introductory remarks, explanatory notes, legend

❹ put side by side, compare

比例 ひれい proportion, ratio

INDEPENDENT

【れい 例】**EXAMPLE, instance; precedent; practice, custom, habit**
例を挙げる れいをあげる cite an example
例の れいの usual; that, (the one) in question

KUN

【たとえる 例える】**illustrate, give an EXAMPLE**
例え(=喩え、譬え) たとえ metaphor, simile, allegory
例えば たとえば for example

SYNONYMS

❶ example

例 EXAMPLE →0099
型 TYPE →3266

❷ⓐ custom

慣 HABITUAL PRACTICE →0843
例 established practice →0099
習 CUSTOM →3306
風 manners →3730
俗 popular custom →0119
癖 HABIT →4080
弊 EVIL PRACTICE →3583

ⓑ constant

定 fixed →2770
恒 CONSTANT →0438
常 REGULAR →3203
例 regular →0099

USAGE

【たとえる】

例える
illustrate, give an example

譬える
[also 喩える] compare to, liken, speak figuratively

喩える
[also 譬える] compare to, liken, speak figuratively

HOMOPHONES

たとえる

譬 COMPARE TO →3613
喩 METAPHOR →0671

使

▶USE
▶ENVOY

シ つか(う) つか(い) -つか(い) -づか(い)

0100

Ⓒ 使 shǐ

1-2-6

9	Jōyō-3	U4F7F
亻	S8-2-6	F0180

丿 亻 亻 仁 仨 佢 使 使
1 2 3 4 5 6 7 8

COMPOUNDS

❶ⓐ USE, make use of, employ
ⓑ abbrev. of 使用者 しようしゃ: employer

a 使用する しようする use, employ, apply
使用人 しようにん employee; servant
使途 しと how money is spent
使役 しえき employment, service; *gram* causative
行使する こうしする use, employ, exercise
駆使する くしする use freely, have good command of

b 労使 ろうし labor and management

❷ⓐ [also suffix] **ENVOY, messenger, emissary, ambassador, delegate**
ⓑ servant

a 使節 しせつ envoy, ambassador

使者 ししゃ messenger
使命 しめい mission, appointed task
大使 たいし ambassador
公使 こうし minister, attaché
特使 とくし special envoy [messenger]
天使 てんし angel
遣唐使 けんとうし Japanese envoy to Tang China
b 使丁 してい servant

KUN

【つかう 使う】

①ⓐ **USE, make use of, employ, handle**
ⓑ **employ, keep (in one's employ)**

a 使い古す つかいふるす wear out (a thing) by use
使いこなす つかいこなす manage, handle, acquire command of
使い分ける つかいわける use properly, know how to use properly
使い物にならない つかいものにならない be no use
使い手 つかいて user, consumer; (fencing) master
使い捨ての つかいすての throwaway (articles)
魔法使い まほうつかい magician, sorcerer
b 人を使う ひとをつかう employ, take a person in one's service

② [usu. 遣う] **spend, USE (time or money)**
金を使う かねをつかう spend money

【つかい 使い】 mission, errand; messenger, emissary
使いをやる つかいをやる send a messenger

【-つかい, -づかい -使い】 [also suffix]
① **trainer, tamer**
蛇使い へびつかい snake charmer
象使い ぞうつかい elephant trainer
② **servant, employee**
小間使い こまづかい lady's maid, housemaid
召し使い めしつかい servant

SYNONYMS

❶ⓐ use
使 USE →0100
用 EMPLOY →3694

❷ⓐ agents
使 ENVOY →0100
偵 SPY →0157

【つかう】
①ⓑ **employ**
雇 EMPLOY →2454
用 EMPLOY →3694
使う employ →0100
傭 HIRE →0181
役 press into service →0288

USAGE

❶【つかう】
使う
①ⓐ use, make use of, employ, handle
ⓑ employ, keep (in one's employ)
② [usu. 遣う] spend, use (time or money)
遣う
① [sometimes also 使う] spend, use (time or money)
② be anxious, worry
③ use (language properly), spell
④ manipulate

❷【-つかい】
-使い
[also suffix]
① trainer, tamer
② servant, employee
-遣い
① spending, spending money
② worrying, being anxious
③ use (of language), spelling
④ manipulating

HOMOPHONES

つかう 遣 DISPATCH →3908
-つかい 遣 DISPATCH →3908

COMPOUND FORMATION

【使命 しめい】
使命 'mission, appointed task' refers to the orders (命) or duties assigned to an envoy (使 ❷ⓐ).

NOTE

➡ see COMPOUND FORMATION for 使節 しせつ →節 3336

侑

0101
◧ 1-2-6

▸URGE TO EAT
ユウ 名 いく ゆき すすむ たすく あつむ
Ⓒ 侑 yòu

9	Names	U4F91
亻	S8-2-6	F0000

COMPOUNDS

● [archaic] **URGE** someone **TO EAT** or drink, assist with a meal
侑觴× ゆうしょう urging one to drink more good wine during a banquet
侑食 ゆうしょく dining with a superior, assisting at dinner

SYNONYMS

● urge
勧 URGE →2334
催 PRESS FOR →0178
促 HASTEN →0118
誘 INDUCE →1952
励 ENCOURAGE →1438

侑 URGE TO EAT → 0101

侠 **0102** 1-2-6

▶**CHIVALRY**

キョウ きゃん ㊔ ちか たもつ さとる いさむ

9	Nonstandard	U4FA0
亻	S8-2-6	F0000

traditional form → see 俠 at 0110

隹 1-2-6

incorrect classification
➡ see 4-8-2 at 4383

協 **0103** 1-2-6

▶**COOPERATE**

キョウ ㊔ かの やす かなう

Ⓝ 恊 㤼◆ Ⓒ 协 xié

24	Jōyō-4	U5354
十	S8-2-6	F0570

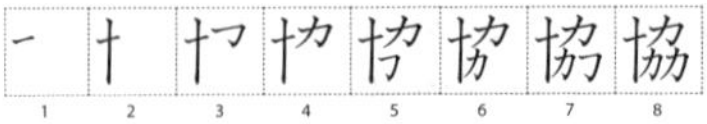

COMPOUNDS

❶ⓐ [original meaning] **COOPERATE, collaborate, work together; be in harmony**

ⓑ [also suffix] abbrev. of 協会 **きょうかい** or 協同組合 **きょうどうくみあい**: **association, cooperative**

a 協力する きょうりょくする cooperate, collaborate, work together
協同 きょうどう cooperation, collaboration, association
協調 きょうちょう cooperation, harmony
協賛 きょうさん support, cooperation
協奏曲 きょうそうきょく concerto

b 協会 きょうかい association, society
世界ボクシング協 せかいぼくしんぐきょう World Boxing Association
農協 のうきょう agricultural cooperative
生協 せいきょう cooperative association [society]
日米協 にちべいきょう Japan United States Cultural Exchange Association

❷ⓐ **reach an agreement, agree upon, make an agreement**

ⓑ abbrev. of 協議会 **きょうぎかい**: conference, council

a 協議 きょうぎ conference, deliberation
協議会 きょうぎかい conference, council
協商 きょうしょう entente, agreement
協約 きょうやく pact, convention, agreement
協定 きょうてい agreement, pact
妥協 だきょう compromise, agreement, understanding

b 経協 けいきょう Management Conference

SYNONYMS

❶ⓐ **cooperate**

協 COOPERATE → 0103
携 join hands → 0796
調 harmonize → 1973

ⓑ **organized bodies**

会 SOCIETY → 2512
協 association → 0103
団 BODY → 3791
体 BODY → 0080
組 union → 1693
労 workers' union → 3155
連 federation → 3849
講 fraternity → 2046
院 INSTITUTION → 0544

❷ⓐ **promise**

約 PROMISE → 1632
締 CONCLUDE (a treaty) → 1761
協 reach an agreement → 0103
契 MAKE AN AGREEMENT → 3267
盟 ALLIANCE → 3468
誓 VOW → 3424

㤼 **0104** 1-2-6

▶**COOPERATE**

キョウ ㊔ かの やす かなう

24	Nonstandard	U2B753
十	S8-2-6	F0000

handwritten form → see 協 at 0103

孤 1-2-6

incorrect stroke-count
➡ see 1-3-6: 孑 at 0426

限降 1-2-6

incorrect stroke-count
➡ see 1-3-6: 阝 at 0475

便 **0105** 1-2-7

▶**CONVENIENT**
▶**POST**
▶**EXCRETA**

ベン ビン たよ(り)

Ⓒ 便 biàn pián

9	Jōyō-4	U4FBF
亻	S9-2-7	F0907

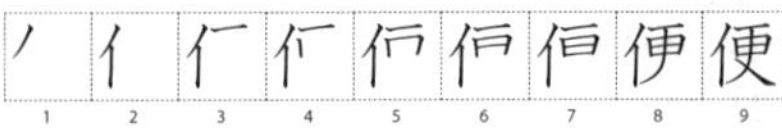

COMPOUNDS

❶ⓐ [original meaning] **CONVENIENT, expedient, handy**

ⓑ **CONVENIENT time for an action, opportunity, chance**

a 便利な べんりな convenient, handy, useful
便宜 べんぎ convenience, facility
便覧 べんらん(=びんらん) handbook, manual

便法 べんぽう convenient method, shortcut, expedient
不便な ふべんな inconvenient
方便 ほうべん expedient, instrument
b 便乗する びんじょうする take advantage of an opportunity; go on board
❷ⓐ (postal material) **POST, mail, letter**
ⓑ [also suffix] **POSTal service, postal delivery, mail**
a 便箋 びんせん letter paper, stationery, writing paper
郵便 ゆうびん mail service, mail, postal matter
別便 べつびん separate post
b 航空便 こうくうびん airmail
第一便 だいいちびん first delivery
❸ (feces or urine) **EXCRETA, excrement, feces, urine**
便所 べんじょ lavatory, bathroom
便秘 べんぴ constipation
便器 べんき toilet bowl, urinal
大便 だいべん feces, excrement
小便 しょうべん urine
❹ⓐ [also suffix] **transportation service, flight**
ⓑ counter for public transport runs or flights
a 定期便 ていきびん regular service
下り便 くだりびん outbound train, down train
貨物便で かもつびんで by freight
b 日航五百便 にっこうごひゃくびん JAL flight No. 500
一日三便 いちにちさんびん three flights [runs] per day
❺ relax, rest, be at ease
便衣 べんい convenient clothes, ordinary clothes
❻ [archaic] flatter, curry favor
便佞× べんねい flattery, adulation

INDEPENDENT

【べん 便】
① convenience, facilities, accommodation
便を図る べんをはかる administer to the convenience of, provide facilities
交通の便 こうつうのべん transportation facilities
②ⓐ feces, excrement
ⓑ abbrev. of 便所 べんじょ: toilet
a 便をする べんをする evacuate the bowels
【べんする 便する】 make **CONVENIENT**, provide facilities
【べんじる(=べんずる) 便じる(=便ずる)】 serve the purpose, will do
【びん 便】 **POST, mail; postal service; opportunity, chance; flight**
便の有り次第 びんのありしだい on the first opportunity
次の便 つぎのびん next post; next flight

KUN

【たより 便り】 **news, tidings; correspondence, letter, communication**
便りをする たよりをする write a letter
花便り はなだより news [first tidings] of the cherry blossoms

SYNONYMS

❶ⓐ **suitable**
適 SUITABLE → 3918
当 proper → 2701
宜 RIGHT → 2763
便 CONVENIENT → 0105
❷ **mail**
郵 MAIL → 2121
便 POST → 0105
❸ **excreta**
便 EXCRETA → 0105
尿 URINE → 3801
汗 SWEAT → 0256

俄

0106

▶**SUDDEN**
ガ にわか
Ⓒ 俄 é

1-2-7

9	Names	U4FC4
亻	S9-2-7	F2611

COMPOUNDS

● **SUDDEN, abrupt**
俄然 がぜん suddenly, all of a sudden, abruptly

KUN

【にわか 俄】
①ⓐ **SUDDEN, abrupt**
ⓑ **hasty**
a 俄に にわかに suddenly, at once; offhand
俄雨 にわかあめ (rain) shower
b 俄仕込み にわかじこみ hasty preparation
俄勉強 にわかべんきょう cramming
② improvised, impromptu
俄狂言 にわかきょうげん impromptu skit, (theatrical) farce

SYNONYMS

● **sudden**
急 SUDDEN → 2595
激 sudden → 0955
暴 sudden → 3138
俄 SUDDEN → 0106
頓 SUDDEN → 1320
勃 SUDDENLY → 1839
突 abruptly → 2772

1

保

▸PRESERVE

ホ ホウ^ たも(つ) ㊔ やす やすし まもる

Ⓒ 保 bǎo

0107

1-2-7

9	Jōyō-5	U4FDD
亻	S9-2-7	F0218

亻 子 阝

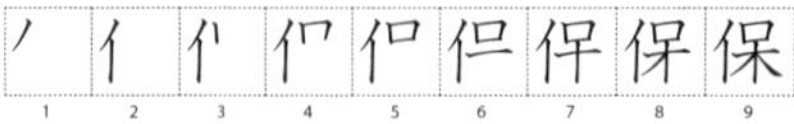

COMPOUNDS

❶ⓐ (maintain unchanged) **PRESERVE, maintain, keep, conserve, retain, hold**

ⓑ (maintain in good condition) **PRESERVE, keep up, maintain**

a 保持する ほじする maintain, preserve, retain
保有する ほゆうする possess, maintain
留保する りゅうほする reserve, withhold, keep back
確保する かくほする secure, make sure of, ensure

b 保存する ほぞんする preserve, conserve, maintain, store, keep
保管する ほかんする take custody [charge] of, keep
保温 ほおん keeping warm, heat insulation
保安 ほあん preservation of public peace
保健 ほけん (preservation of) health, sanitation
保全 ほぜん integrity, preservation
保線 ほせん track maintenance

❷ⓐ [original meaning] (maintain in safety) **PRESERVE, protect, defend, shield, guard**

ⓑ **care for, look after;** [formerly 哺 0478] **nurse, suckle**

a 保護する ほごする protect, safeguard, preserve, look after
保護者 ほごしゃ guardian; protector
保身 ほしん self-protection

b 保母 ほぼ nurse, kindergarten teacher
保育(=哺育) ほいく nurture, upbringing; lactation, nursing
保育園 ほいくえん day-care center

❸ⓐ **insure, guarantee, ensure**

ⓑ abbrev. of 保険 ほけん: **insurance**

a 保険 ほけん insurance
保証する ほしょうする (assume responsibility for) guarantee, vouch for, certify
保証人 ほしょうにん guarantor
保障する ほしょうする (ensure that an undesirable condition does not occur) guarantee, secure, ensure
安保(=安全保障条約) あんぽ(=あんぜんほしょうじょうやく) Japan-U.S. Security Treaty
担保 たんぽ security, mortgage

b 生保(=生命保険) せいほ(=せいめいほけん) life insurance
損保(=損害保険) そんぽ(=そんがいほけん) damage insurance

❹ abbrev. of 保守 ほしゅ: the conservatives
保革 ほかく conservatives and reformists
保無(=保守系無所属) ほむ(=ほしゅけいむしょぞく) conservative without party affiliation

❺ shop employee, shop
酒保 しゅほ canteen, PX

❻ unit of ten houses in a neighborhood
隣保館 りんぽかん settlement house

❼ [also 堡 ほ, ほう 3500] fort
橋頭保 きょうとうほ(=きょうとうほう) bridgehead, beachhead

INDEPENDENT

【ほする 保する】 guarantee, secure

KUN

【たもつ 保つ】 (maintain unchanged) **PRESERVE, keep, maintain, hold;** (maintain in good condition) **preserve, maintain, support, sustain**
命を保つ いのちをたもつ preserve life
平和を保つ へいわをたもつ maintain [preserve] peace

SYNONYMS

❶ **preserve**
留 KEEP →3189
保 PRESERVE →0107
持 uphold →0447

❷ **protect**
守 PROTECT (by watching over) →2697
護 PROTECT (by safeguarding) →2079
庇 PROTECT (by shielding) →3802
衛 GUARD →0938
警 GUARD AGAINST →3595
防 defend →0320
番 WATCH →3416
保 PRESERVE →0107
看 CARE FOR →3992

USAGE

【ほしょうする】

保証する
(assume responsibility for) guarantee, vouch for, certify

保障する
(ensure that an undesirable condition does not occur) guarantee, secure, ensure

NOTE

➡ see COMPOUND FORMATION for 保険 ほけん →険 0658

係

▶CONNECT
▶PERSON IN CHARGE

ケイ かか(る) かかり -がかり かか(わる)▲

0108

Ⓒ 系 xì jì

◧ 1-2-7

9	Jōyō-3	U4FC2
亻	S9-2-7	F0285

ノ 亻 仁 ⺅ 俘 係 係 係 係
1 2 3 4 5 6 7 8 9

COMPOUNDS

[formerly also 繋 3612]

❶ⓐ (have a relationship with) **CONNECT, be connected with, relate to, interrelate**

ⓑ CONNECTion, relation

a 係累 けいるい family ties, dependents
係争 けいそう dispute, contention; lawsuit
係属 けいぞく pendency (of a legal case); relationship
関係 かんけい relation, relationship, connection
連係 れんけい connection, linking, contact

b 係数 けいすう *math* coefficient

❷ **CONNECT, tie up, fasten, moor**

係留 けいりゅう mooring, anchorage
係船 けいせん mooring a ship

KUN

【かかる 係る】

① **affect, concern, involve**

面目に係る問題 めんぼくにかかるもんだい problem concerning one's honor

② *gram* modify

係り かかり relation, connection (esp. in grammar)
係り結び かかりむすび relation, connection (esp. in grammar)
副詞は動詞に係る ふくしはどうしにかかる Adverbs modify verbs

③ is the work of, is done by

これは浅田氏に係る小説だ これはあさだしにかかるしょうせつだ This novel is the work of Mr. Asada

【かかり 係】[sometimes also 掛]

ⓐ **PERSON IN CHARGE, official in charge, clerk**

ⓑ **charge, duty, post**

a 係員 かかりいん clerk in charge
係長 かかりちょう chief clerk
係官 かかりかん official in charge

b 係の人 かかりのひと person in charge
係をする かかりをする be in charge

【-がかり -係】[sometimes also -掛] [suffix] **PERSON IN CHARGE, official in charge, clerk**

案内係 あんないがかり clerk at the information desk
会計係 かいけいがかり accountant, treasurer
受付係 うけつけがかり reception clerk

【かかわる 係わる】[also 関わる]

① **be concerned in, be involved**

係わり かかわり relation, connection
事件に係わる じけんにかかわる be involved in a case

② **influence (adversely), affect**

命に係わる いのちにかかわる be threatening to one's life, be a matter of life and death

SYNONYMS

❶ⓐ **relate**

関 CONCERN →4129
係 CONNECT →0108
絡 INTERLINK →1709
渉 HAVE RELATIONS WITH →0638
連 LINK →3849
聯 LINK →1797

❷ **join**

結 TIE →1706
繋 CONNECT →3612
縛 BIND →1779
綴 BIND →1746
繃 BIND UP →1787
束 TIE UP →4369
梱 PACK →1205
連 LINK →3849
係 CONNECT →0108
接 join →0607

【かかり】

ⓐ & 【-がかり】 **person in charge**

係 PERSON IN CHARGE →0108
-方 person in charge →2459
員 MEMBER (of a staff) →2822

USAGE

【かかわる】

係わる
[also 関わる]
① be concerned in, be involved
② influence (adversely), affect

関わる
[also 係わる] same as 係わる

拘わる
adhere to, stick to

HOMOPHONES

かかる

掛 SET →0596
懸 SUSPEND →3632
架 LAY ACROSS →3178
繋 CONNECT →3612
罹 FALL ILL →3239

かかり 掛 SET →0596
-がかり 掛 SET →0596
かかわる
関 CONCERN →4129
拘 ARREST →0367

NOTE

➡ see also USAGE note at 掛 0596

侯

0109

1-2-7

▶FEUDAL LORD

コウ

Ⓒ 侯 hóu hòu

9	Jōyō	U4FAF
亻	S9-2-7	F1994

丿 亻 亻⺈ 亻⺈ 亻⺈ 亻⺈ 亻⺈ 侯 侯 (1–9)

COMPOUNDS

❶ⓐ FEUDAL LORD, daimyo
ⓑ honorific title after names of FEUDAL LORDs [daimyos]
a 諸侯 しょこう feudal lords
王侯 おうこう princess, royalty, crowned heads
b 仙台侯 せんだいこう Lord of Sendai
❷ⓐ marquis
ⓑ title after names of marquises
a 侯爵 こうしゃく marquis
b 黒田侯 くろだこう Marquis Kuroda

INDEPENDENT

【こう 侯】 lord, daimyo; marquis

SYNONYMS

❶ nobility
爵 RANK OF NOBILITY →3143
公 nobleman →2468
侯 FEUDAL LORD →0109
❷ noblemen
公 duke →2468
侯 marquis →0109
伯 COUNT →0067
子 viscount →4196
男 baron →3147

NOTE

★ do not confuse with 候 SEASON →0133

侠

0110

1-2-7

▶CHIVALRY

キョウ きゃん ㊔ ちか たもつ さとる いさむ

Ⓝ 俠 Ⓒ 侠 xiá

9	Names	U4FE0
亻	S9-2-7	F2678

COMPOUNDS

ⓐ CHIVALRY, gallantry
ⓑ chivalrous, gallant
a 任侠 にんきょう chivalrous spirit, siding with the weak
義侠 ぎきょう chivalry, generosity
b 侠客 きょうかく chivalrous person, self-styled humanitarian

KUN

【きゃん 侠】
① **tomboyishness**
お侠 おきゃん (of young women) being tomboyish [pert]; tomboy, pert girl
②ⓐ **CHIVALRY**
ⓑ a chivalrous person

SPECIAL READINGS

侠気(=男気) おとこぎ chivalrous spirit, chivalry

SYNONYMS

ⓑ brave
勇 BRAVE →2592
侠 chivalrous →0110
赳 VALIANT →4100
驍 VALIANT →2327
敢 bold →2142
豪 bold and unrestrained →2657
雄 HEROIC →1271
壮 heroic →0263
義 chivalrous →2948
凜 gallant →0195

俣

0111

1-2-7

▶BIFURCATION

また

Ⓒ 俣 yǔ

9	Names	U4FE3
亻	S9-2-7	F2235

KUN

【また 俣】 [usu. 股, sometimes also 叉] [in compounds]
BIFURCATION, fork (as of a body of water)
二俣 ふたまた bifurcation; *slang* two-timing
水俣病 みなまたびょう Minamata disease

SYNONYMS

【また】
◯ **furcation**
叉 FORK →4194
俣 BIFURCATION →0111
股 CROTCH →1093
岐 forked road →0285

HOMOPHONES

また
股 CROTCH →1093
叉 FORK →4194

NOTE

➡ see USAGE note at 股 1093

俚

▶RURAL

リ

Ⓒ 俚 lǐ

0112

◧ 1-2-7

9	Non-Jōyō	U4FDA
亻	S9-2-7	F0000

COMPOUNDS

● [now also 里 4356] [original meaning] **RURAL, rustic, vulgar**

俚謡 りよう ballad, folk song

俚言 りげん dialect; slang

俚諺 りげん traditional [folk] saying, proverb

俚耳 りじ public ears

SYNONYMS

● **vulgar and unrefined**

俗 vulgar → 0119

卑 MEAN → 3270

賤 MEAN → 1993

鄙 MEAN → 2338

俚 RURAL → 0112

里 rural → 4356

粗 COARSE → 1683

野 rustic → 1877

蛮 barbaric → 2638

俐

▶CLEVER

リ

Ⓒ 俐 lì

0113

◧ 1-2-7

9	Names	U4FD0
亻	S9-2-7	F0000

COMPOUNDS

● **CLEVER, bright, sharp-witted**

俐巧(=利口)な りこうな clever, bright, sharp, shrewd

伶俐(=怜悧) れいり cleverness, sagacity

SYNONYMS

● **intelligent and wise**

賢 WISE → 3518

俊 brilliant → 0117

鋭 SHARP → 2171

敏 NIMBLE → 1675

叡 PROFOUNDLY WISE → 2405

智 wise → 3458

慧 INTELLIGENT → 3485

怜 CLEVER → 0356

悧 CLEVER → 0505

俐 CLEVER → 0113

哲 SAGACIOUS → 3402

明 clear-sighted → 1060

聡 SHARP-WITTED → 1750

侶

▶COMPANION

リョ ロ▲ ㊔ かね かぬ

Ⓒ 侣 lǚ

0114

◧ 1-2-7

9	Jōyō	U4FB6
亻	S9-2-7	F2225

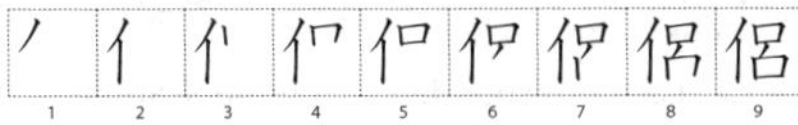

COMPOUNDS

● **COMPANION, mate**

伴侶 はんりょ companion

僧侶 そうりょ bonze, Buddhist priest

学侶 がくりょ scholar-monk

SYNONYMS

● **friends and associates**

僚 COLLEAGUE → 0186

輩 FELLOW → 3482

朋 COMRADE → 1092

友 FRIEND → 3670

侶 COMPANION → 0114

信

▶BELIEVE
▶MESSAGE

シン ㊔ のぶ しの まこと しげ あき とし

Ⓒ 信 xìn

0115

◧ 1-2-7

9	Jōyō-4	U4FE1
亻	S9-2-7	F0126

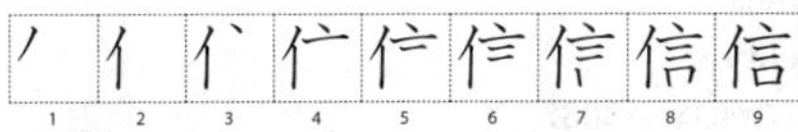

COMPOUNDS

❶ⓐ **BELIEVE, trust, have confidence in**
ⓑ **BELIEVE in (God), have faith**

a 信託 しんたく trust

信用 しんよう trust, credit, confidence

信頼 しんらい reliance, confidence, trust

自信 じしん self-confidence

不信 ふしん distrust, discredit

確信 かくしん firm belief, conviction

b 信仰 しんこう faith, belief, conviction

信者 しんじゃ believer, adherent

信心深い しんじんぶかい religious, devout

信教 しんきょう religion, faith

❷ [original meaning] fidelity, faith, sincerity

信義 しんぎ fidelity, faith, loyalty

威信 いしん prestige, dignity, authority

背信 はいしん breach of faith [trust], betrayal

❸ⓐ **MESSAGE, signal, news, tidings**

ⓑ **written communication or MESSAGE, letter, telegram**

a 信号 しんごう signal; traffic light
受信 じゅしん reception (of radio waves); receipt of a message
混信 こんしん jamming, interference, cross talk
交信 こうしん exchange of messages, communications
花信 かしん tidings of flowers, information about flowers for viewing
通信 つうしん correspondence, communication, information
b 返信 へんしん reply, answer
短信 たんしん brief note [letter], brief message
私信 ししん private note [letter]
電信 でんしん telegraph, telegram

❹ abbrev. of 信用 しんよう or 信託 しんたく: credit, trust
信金 しんきん credit union [guild]
投信 とうしん investment trust

❺ abbrev. of 信濃 しなの, old name for Nagano Prefecture
信州 しんしゅう Shinshu, Shinano
信越 しんえつ Nagano and Niigata

INDEPENDENT

【しん 信】 trust, credit, confidence; fidelity, faith, sincerity
信を問う しんをとう make an appeal to the confidence of

【しんじる(=しんずる) 信じる(=信ずる)】 **BELIEVE, trust; believe in, have faith in**

SYNONYMS

❷ **fidelity**
忠 LOYALTY → 3087
義 faith → 2948
孝 FILIAL PIETY → 3973
悌 BROTHERLY LOVE → 0507
誠 SINCERITY → 1922
実 faithfulness → 2765
信 fidelity → 0115
操 constancy → 0948
節 moral integrity → 3336

❸ⓐ **information**
報 information → 2133
信 MESSAGE → 0115
訃 NEWS OF DEATH → 1827

ⓑ **written communications**
状 LETTER → 0322
文 LETTER → 2458
翰 LETTER → 2198
書 letter → 3292
信 written communication → 0115
電 telegram → 3465

牒 OFFICIAL NOTICE → 1299

侵

▶INVADE
シン おか(す)
Ⓝ 侵 Ⓒ 侵 qīn

0116
1-2-7

9	Jōyō	U4FB5
亻	S9-2-7	F1221

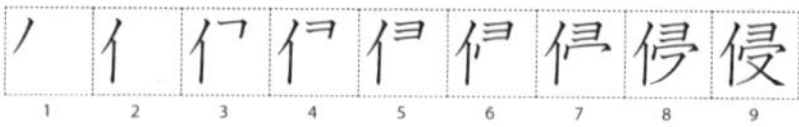

COMPOUNDS

ⓐ (enter by force) **INVADE, raid**
ⓑ (intrude upon) **INVADE, infringe on, violate**

a 侵略 しんりゃく invasion, aggression
侵入 しんにゅう invasion, raid, trespass, intrusion
侵犯 しんぱん invasion; violation
b 侵食 しんしょく infringement, violation
侵害 しんがい infringement, violation
不可侵条約 ふかしんじょうやく nonaggression treaty

KUN

【おかす 侵す】
ⓐ (enter by force) **INVADE, raid**
ⓑ (intrude upon) **INVADE, infringe on, violate**
a 国境を侵す こっきょうをおかす invade the frontier district, violate the border
b 権利を侵す けんりをおかす infringe upon someone's right

SYNONYMS

ⓐ **attack**
攻 ATTACK → 0286
撃 STRIKE → 3552
襲 RAID → 3633
侵 INVADE → 0116
爆 bomb → 1415

USAGE

【おかす】
侵す
ⓐ (enter by force) invade, raid
ⓑ (intrude upon) invade, infringe on, violate
犯す
① offend against, violate, infringe upon, commit (a crime), sin against
② rape, violate, deflower
冒す
①ⓐ risk, brave, defy
ⓑ (risk the danger of using a great person's name) assume (another's name); bear
② affect, attack, afflict

HOMOPHONES

おかす
犯 OFFENSE → 0229

冒 RISK → 3088

NOTE

➡ see also USAGE note at 浸 0530

★ do not confuse with 浸 SOAK → 0530

俊 0117

◧ 1-2-7

▸BRILLIANT PERSON

シュン ㊔ とし さとし すぐる たかし

Ⓒ 俊 jùn

9	Jōyō	U4FCA
イ	S9-2-7	F1150

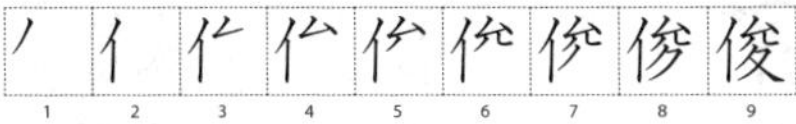

COMPOUNDS

❶ⓐ [original meaning] **BRILLIANT [talented] PERSON, genius**

ⓑ [sometimes also 駿 2304] **brilliant, talented, bright**

a 俊秀 しゅんしゅう genius, prodigy

俊才 しゅんさい genius, person of exceptional talent

俊英 しゅんえい talent, genius; gifted person

b 俊傑 しゅんけつ genius, hero

俊童 しゅんどう brilliant boy, infant prodigy

俊敏な しゅんびんな keen, quick-witted

❷ [also 駿 2304] swift-footed, fleet-footed

俊足 しゅんそく fleet speed; fast runner; brilliant person

SYNONYMS

❶ⓐ **wise and talented persons**

哲 sage → 3402

賢 wise man → 3518

博 DOCTOR → 0170

秀 genius → 3152

俊 BRILLIANT PERSON → 0117

才 person of talent → 4218

通 well-informed person → 3855

ⓑ **intelligent and wise**

賢 WISE → 3518

俊 brilliant → 0117

鋭 SHARP → 2171

敏 NIMBLE → 1675

叡 PROFOUNDLY WISE → 2405

智 wise → 3458

慧 INTELLIGENT → 3485

怜 CLEVER → 0356

悧 CLEVER → 0505

俐 CLEVER → 0113

哲 SAGACIOUS → 3402

明 clear-sighted → 1060

聡 SHARP-WITTED → 1750

促 0118

◧ 1-2-7

▸HASTEN

ソク うなが(す)

Ⓒ 促 cù

9	Jōyō	U4FC3
イ	S9-2-7	F1353

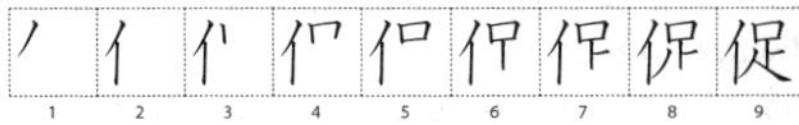

COMPOUNDS

❶ (cause to act with haste) **HASTEN, urge, hurry, press (for)**

促進する そくしんする promote, spur on, facilitate

促成 そくせい growth promotion

催促する さいそくする press for, urge, demand

督促状 とくそくじょう demand note, dunning letter [note]

❷ shorten, contract

促音 そくおん assimilated sound (double consonant represented by small っ in Japanese)

KUN

【うながす 促す】 **HASTEN, accelerate, stimulate; urge, press, call for**

発達を促す はったつをうながす accelerate development

注意を促す ちゅういをうながす call a person's attention (to)

SYNONYMS

❶ **urge**

勧 URGE → 2334

催 PRESS FOR → 0178

促 HASTEN → 0118

誘 INDUCE → 1952

励 ENCOURAGE → 1438

侑 URGE TO EAT → 0101

❶ **hurry**

急 HURRY → 2595

促 HASTEN → 0118

俗 0119

◧ 1-2-7

▸POPULAR

ゾク

Ⓒ 俗 sú

9	Jōyō	U4FD7
イ	S9-2-7	F1360

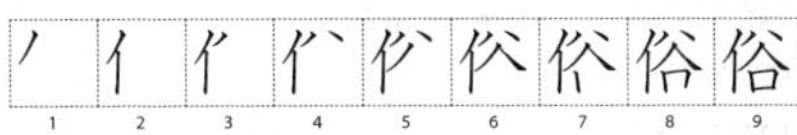

COMPOUNDS

❶ⓐ **POPULAR, folk, common**

ⓑ **vulgar, low**

a 俗説 ぞくせつ common saying, popular version

俗称 ぞくしょう popular [common] name

俗習 ぞくしゅう popular custom, usage

俗語 ぞくご slang
通俗 つうぞく popularity, conventionality
b 俗っぽい ぞくっぽい common, vulgar
俗悪 ぞくあく vulgarity, inelegance
低俗な ていぞくな vulgar

❷ [original meaning] **POPULAR custom, folk custom, folkways, convention**
風俗 ふうぞく manners, customs; popular [public] morals
習俗 しゅうぞく manners and customs, folkways
民俗 みんぞく folk customs, folkways
良俗 りょうぞく good custom

❸ⓐ **worldly, mundane; worldliness**
ⓑ secular
a 俗事 ぞくじ worldly affairs
俗人 ぞくじん layman, man of the world
俗情 ぞくじょう worldly-mindedness, worldliness
俗世間 ぞくせけん the workaday world
脱俗 だつぞく unworldliness
世俗の せぞくの common, worldly
b 俗名 ぞくみょう secular name
還俗 げんぞく return to secular life, secularization

INDEPENDENT

【ぞく 俗】 worldliness, vulgarity; laity
俗に ぞくに commonly, vulgarly

SYNONYMS

❶ⓐ **public**
公 PUBLIC → 2468
俗 POPULAR → 0119
巷 the public → 3097
ⓑ **vulgar and unrefined**
俗 vulgar → 0119
卑 MEAN → 3270
賤 MEAN → 1993
鄙 MEAN → 2338
俚 RURAL → 0112
里 rural → 4356
粗 COARSE → 1683
野 rustic → 1877
蛮 barbaric → 2638

❷ **custom**
慣 HABITUAL PRACTICE → 0843
例 established practice → 0099
習 CUSTOM → 3306
風 manners → 3730
俗 popular custom → 0119
癖 HABIT → 4080
弊 EVIL PRACTICE → 3583

❸ⓐ **worldly**
世 worldly → 4308
俗 worldly → 0119

侮
0120
◧ 1-2-7

▸INSULT
ブ あなど(る)

9	Names	UFA30
亻	S9-2-7	F0000

traditional form → see 侮 at 0091

侵
0121
◧ 1-2-7

▸INVADE
シン おか(す)

9	Nonstandard	U4FB5
亻	S9-2-7	F0000

traditional form → see 侵 at 0116

孫
◧ 1-2-7
incorrect stroke-count
➡ see ◧ 1-3-7: 孑 at 0492

陷
◧ 1-2-7
incorrect stroke-count
➡ see ◧ 1-3-8: 阝 at 0663

院除 etc.
◧ 1-2-7
incorrect stroke-count
➡ see ◧ 1-3-7: 阝 at 0543

倍
0122
◧ 1-2-8

▸TIMES
▸DOUBLE
バイ ㊔ ます
Ⓒ 倍 bèi

9	Jōyō-3	U500D
亻	S10-2-8	F0961

1	2	3	4	5	6	7	8	9	10
ノ	亻	亻'	亻亠	亻亣	亻立	倍	倍	倍	倍

COMPOUNDS

❶ **TIMES, -fold**
倍数 ばいすう multiple
倍率 ばいりつ magnification, magnifying power; rate of competition (in examinations)
三倍 さんばい three times, triple
数倍 すうばい several times (as large)

❷ⓐ **DOUBLE**
ⓑ **DOUBLE, multiply, increase**
a 倍増 ばいぞう redoubling
倍額 ばいがく double amount
倍加 ばいか doubling
人一倍働く ひといちばいはたらく work twice as hard as others
b 倍大 ばいだい double size

INDEPENDENT

【ばい 倍】 DOUBLE

倍にして返す ばいにしてかえす repay double the original amount

【ばいする 倍する】**DOUBLE**, be doubled; increase

SYNONYMS

❶ -fold

倍 TIMES → 0122
重 -fold → 4390

❷ⓐ compound

複 COMPOUND → 1565
倍 DOUBLE → 0122
重 DUPLICATE → 4390

ⓑ increase

加 add to → 0042
増 INCREASE → 0836
殖 MULTIPLY → 1253
倍 DOUBLE → 0122

値

▶VALUE

チ ね あたい

Ⓒ 値 zhí

0123

1-2-8

9	Jōyō-6	U5024
亻	S10-2-8	F0699

1	2	3	4	5	6	7	8	9	10
ノ	亻	仁	仕	什	佰	佰	值	值	値

COMPOUNDS

ⓐ VALUE, worth, merit

ⓑ [also suffix] *math* **VALUE**

a 価値 かち value, merit
数値 すうち numerical value

b 絶対値 ぜったいち absolute value
平均値 へいきんち mean value

KUN

【ね 値】[also suffix] **price, cost**

値が張る ねがはる be expensive
値段 ねだん price
値上げ ねあげ price hike
値打ち ねうち value, worth
値切る ねぎる beat down the price, bargain
値引き ねびき reduction in price, discount
高値 たかね high price
仕入れ値 しいれね cost price

【あたい 値】

ⓐ **VALUE, worth, merit**

ⓑ *math* **VALUE**

a 値する あたいする be worth, deserve, merit
一読の値が有る いちどくのあたいがある be worth reading

b Xの値 えっくすのあたい value of *x*

SYNONYMS

● value

値 VALUE → 0123
価 VALUE → 0095

【ね】

○ fee and price

料 FEE → 1644
代 CHARGE → 0034
賃 CHARGES → 3341
銭 money paid → 2159
費 EXPENSE → 3221
価 PRICE → 0095
値 price → 0123

USAGE

【あたい】

値

ⓐ value, worth, merit
ⓑ *math* value

価

price, cost

HOMOPHONES

あたい 価 PRICE → 0095

俺

▶I

エン▲ おれ

Ⓒ 俺 ǎn

0124

1-2-8

9	Jōyō	U4FFA
亻	S10-2-8	F0474

1	2	3	4	5	6	7	8	9	10
ノ	亻	仁	仐	伕	伕	俺	俺	俺	俺

KUN

【おれ 俺】**I**—intimate first person pronoun used by men; though usu. expressing intimacy, it sometimes has vulgar overtones

俺達 おれたち we
俺が俺がの連中 おれがおれがのれんちゅう ego-driven men

SYNONYMS

【おれ】

○ first person pronouns

私 I (*polite*) → 1432
我 SELF → 4362
己 ONESELF → 4188
身 ONE'S PERSON → 4368
僕 I (*familiar*) → 0185
俺 I (*intimate*) → 0124
吾 I (*elegant*) → 3060
予 I (*pompous*) → 2477
余 I (*pompous*) → 2535
麿 I (*archaic*) → 3949
朕 IMPERIAL WE → 1185
自 SELF → 4338

倶

0125

1-2-8

▶TOGETHER

グ ク とも(に)

Ⓝ 倶 Ⓒ 俱 jù jū

9	Names	U4FF1
亻	S10-2-8	F2263

〔亻〕 冫 阝 刂

COMPOUNDS

❶ [original meaning] **TOGETHER**

倶発 ぐはつ concurrence (of offenses)

不倶戴天の敵 ふぐたいてんのてき bitter enemy

❷ **used phonetically for *ku***

倶楽部 くらぶ club

倶梨伽羅紋紋 くりからもんもん tattoo

倶舎宗 くしゃしゅう *Kusha* sect

INDEPENDENT

【ぐする 倶する(=具する)】 possess; take (retainers) with (one), be followed by

KUN

【ともに 倶に】 [now usu. 共に] **TOGETHER**

倶に天を戴かず ともにてんをいただかず cannot live together under the canopy of heaven

SYNONYMS

❶ **together**

共 JOINT → 3045

同 together → 3707

併 TOGETHER → 0092

並 side by side → 2793

兼 CONCURRENTLY → 2850

倶 TOGETHER → 0125

HOMOPHONES

ともに 共 JOINT → 3045

NOTE

➡ see USAGE note at 共 3045

俳

0126

1-2-8

▶HAIKU

ハイ

Ⓒ 俳 pái

9	Jōyō-6	U4FF3
亻	S10-2-8	F1444

COMPOUNDS

❶ **HAIKU, 17-syllable poem**

俳句 はいく haiku

俳人 はいじん haiku poet

俳壇 はいだん haiku world

俳諧(=誹諧) はいかい *haikai,* (humorous) haiku

❷ [original meaning] **actor**

俳優 はいゆう actor, actress

❸ [archaic] jest, joke

俳謔× はいぎゃく joke

SYNONYMS

❶ **poetry**

詩 POETRY → 1924

歌 Japanese poetry → 2296

俳 HAIKU → 0126

句 HAIKU → 3685

❷ **performers**

優 ACTOR → 0200

俳 actor → 0126

伶 MUSICIAN → 0075

伎 PERFORMER → 0055

倣

0127

1-2-8

▶COPY AFTER

ホウ なら(う)

Ⓒ 仿 fǎng

9	Jōyō	U5023
亻	S10-2-8	F2384

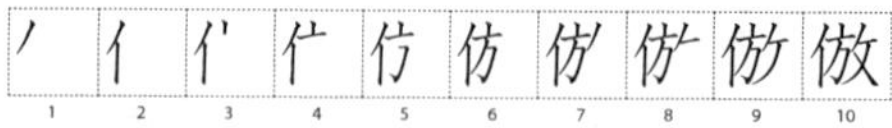

COMPOUNDS

● **COPY AFTER, copy from, imitate**

模倣(=摸倣)する もほうする imitate, copy

KUN

【ならう 倣う】 **COPY AFTER, copy from, imitate, follow an example**

前例に倣う ぜんれいにならう follow [copy after] a precedent

以下これに倣う いかこれにならう The undermentioned to follow this example

SYNONYMS

● **imitate**

擬 IMITATE → 0969

倣 COPY AFTER → 0127

摸 PATTERN AFTER → 0797

模 pattern after → 1326

肖 MODEL → 2733

象 represent → 2647

HOMOPHONES

ならう 習 LEARN → 3306

NOTE

➡ see USAGE note at 習 3306

俸

0128

1-2-8

▶SALARY

ホウ

Ⓒ 俸 fèng

9	Jōyō	U4FF8
亻	S10-2-8	F2620

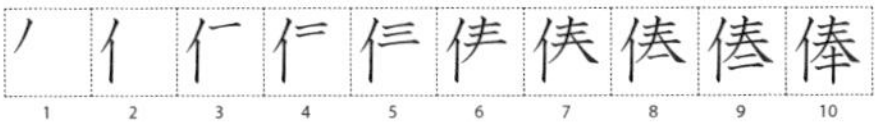

COMPOUNDS

● **SALARY, pay**

俸給 ほうきゅう salary, pay
俸禄 ほうろく retainer's stipend, official pay [salary]
年俸 ねんぽう annual salary
減俸 げんぽう salary cut
五号俸 ごごうほう fifth grade salary
増俸 ぞうほう increase in salary, raise

INDEPENDENT

【ほう 俸】 **SALARY**, pay

俸を食む ほうをはむ receive a salary

SYNONYMS

● **pay and earnings**

給 PAY → 1708
賃 WAGE → 3341
料 FEE → 1644
俸 SALARY → 0128
禄 RETAINER'S STIPEND → 1264
収 income → 0031

俵

0129

1-2-8

▶STRAW SACK

ヒョウ たわら

Ⓒ 俵 biào

9	Jōyō-5	U4FF5
亻	S10-2-8	F2144

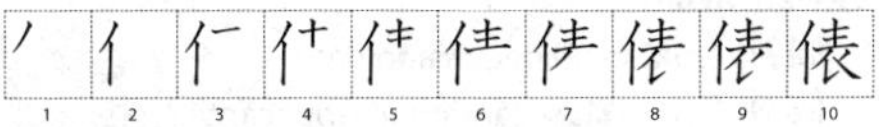

COMPOUNDS

ⓐ **STRAW SACK [bag], sack**
ⓑ counter for sackfuls or straw bags

a 土俵 どひょう sumo (wrestling) ring; sandbag
b 俵数 ひょうすう number of straw sacks [bags]
二俵 にひょう two straw sacks

INDEPENDENT

【ひょう 俵】 **STRAW SACK**

KUN

【たわら 俵】 **STRAW SACK [bag]; sumo ring**

米俵 こめだわら (straw) rice bag

SYNONYMS

ⓐ **bags**

俵 STRAW SACK → 0129
袋 BAG → 3201
鞄 BAG (for carrying) → 2248
包 wrapper → 3684
胞 MEMBRANOUS SAC → 1148

倹

0130

1-2-8

▶FRUGAL

ケン つま(しい)▲

Ⓝ 儉 Ⓒ 俭 jiǎn

9	Jōyō	U5039
亻	S10-2-8	F2881

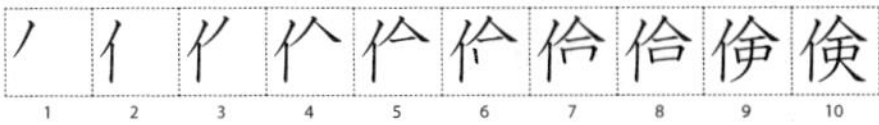

COMPOUNDS

❶ **FRUGAL, thrifty, economical, sparing**

倹約 けんやく economy, frugality, thrift
勤倹 きんけん diligence and thrift
節倹 せっけん economy, frugality, thrift

❷ modest, humble, unpretentious

恭倹 きょうけん respectfulness and modesty

KUN

【つましい 倹しい】 **FRUGAL**, economical, thrifty, sparing

倹しさ つましさ frugality
倹しく暮す つましくくらす live frugally

SYNONYMS

❶ **economizing and economy**

省 SAVE → 3100
節 economize → 3336
倹 FRUGAL → 0130

倦

0131

1-2-8

▶TIRE OF

ケン あぐ(ねる) う(む) あ(きる)

Ⓝ 倦 Ⓒ 倦 juàn

9	Names	U5026
亻	S10-2-8	F2779

COMPOUNDS

ⓐ **TIRE OF, be weary of**
ⓑ **become tired [weary]**

a 倦厭する けんえんする weary of
b 倦怠 けんたい fatigue, languor, weariness

KUN

【あぐねる 倦ねる】 [also suffix] **TIRE OF**, weary of, be at a loss

思い倦ねる おもいあぐねる think something over and over, rack one's brains
攻め倦ねる せめあぐねる be unable to mount a successful offensive

【うむ 倦む】 grow **TIRE**d **OF**, lose interest in

倦み疲れる うみつかれる grow tired (of doing something)

【あきる 倦きる】 [usu. 飽きる, sometimes also 厭きる] grow **TIRE**d **OF**, lose interest in

SYNONYMS

ⓐ & 【あぐねる】 **tire**

疲 TIRED →4063
労 fatigue →3155
倦 TIRE OF →0131
厭 TIRE OF →3745

HOMOPHONES

あきる
飽 SATIATED →2148
厭 TIRE OF →3745

NOTE

➡ see USAGE note at 飽 2148

個

▸INDIVIDUAL
▸GENERAL COUNTER
コ カ▲

0132

Ⓝ 个◇ 𠆩◆ Ⓒ 个 gè gě

1-2-8

9	Jōyō-5	U500B
亻	S10-2-8	F0567

丿 亻 亻 们 们 們 們 個 個 個
1 2 3 4 5 6 7 8 9 10

COMPOUNDS

❶ [sometimes also 箇 こ 3348] [original meaning] **INDIVIDUAL, single unit, single person or thing**
個個に ここに individually, separately
個有の こゆうの peculiar, inherent, characteristic
個室 こしつ private room, single room
個別的に こべつてきに individually, severally, singly
個人 こじん individual
個性 こせい individuality
個展 こてん personal exhibition
各個 かっこ one by one

❷ **GENERAL COUNTER for things or articles**
個数 こすう number of articles
一個 いっこ one, a piece
林檎三個 りんごさんこ three apples
十個 じっこ ten articles

❸ [usu. 箇 か 3348] **item, place**
個所 かしょ place, spot, point; part
個条書き かじょうがき itemization

INDEPENDENT

【こ 個】INDIVIDUAL
個と全 ことぜん individual and the whole

SYNONYMS

❶ **one**
一 ONE →4148
壱 ONE (in legal documents) →2723
片- ONE OF TWO →4272
隻 ONE OF A PAIR →3426
単 SINGLE →2805
個 INDIVIDUAL →0132

❷ **general counters**
丁 MISCELLANEOUS COUNTER →4155
個 GENERAL COUNTER →0132
箇 COUNTER FOR ITEMS →3348
点 counter for articles →2587
件 counter for cases →0054

NOTE

➡ see USAGE note at 箇 3348

候

▸SEASON
▸SEASONAL WEATHER
コウ そうろう

0133

Ⓒ 候 hòu

1-2-8

9	Jōyō-4	U5019
亻	S10-2-8	F0929

丿 亻 亻 们 㑇 佢 伫 佮 候 候
1 2 3 4 5 6 7 8 9 10

COMPOUNDS

❶ **SEASON, time of year**
候鳥 こうちょう migratory bird
時候 じこう season, time of the year

❷ **SEASONAL WEATHER, climate, weather**
天候 てんこう weather
気候 きこう climate, weather; season
測候所 そっこうじょ weather station

❸ **indication, sign, symptom; condition**
兆候(=徴候) ちょうこう symptom, sign; omen
症候 しょうこう symptom

❹ **wait, await**
候補 こうほ candidacy, candidate
候補者 こうほしゃ candidate, applicant

❺ inquire after, greet
斥候 せっこう scout, patrol, reconnoitering soldier
伺候する しこうする pay one's respects, make a courtesy call; wait upon (a nobleman)

INDEPENDENT

【こう 候】SEASON, time of year; seasonal weather
厳寒の候 げんかんのこう the coldest season [weather]

KUN

【そうろう 候】**classical verbal suffix equiv. to -ます**
候文 そうろうぶん epistolary style (i.e., the style employing the そうろう form)
候調 そうろうちょう epistolary style
書き候 かきそうろう (have the honor) to write
居候 いそうろう hanger-on, parasite

SYNONYMS

❶ **time periods**
時 TIME →1155
季 SEASON (quarter) →3161
候 SEASON (time of year) →0133

頃 TIME →0163
暇 FREE TIME →1275
般 period of time →1670
刻 POINT OF TIME →1619
間 INTERVAL →4122
隙 GAP →0826
期 TERM →2139
節 SEASON →3336

❷ **weather**
候 SEASONAL WEATHER →0133
天 weather →4250
晴 FINE WEATHER →1234

❸ **signs**
候 indication →0133
徴 SYMPTOM →0841
症 symptom (of a disease) →4065
気 sign →3960
兆 OMEN →0264

COMPOUND FORMATION

【居候 いそうろう】
居候 'hanger-on, parasite' was formerly the polite form of 居る いる 'be', which was extended to mean 'one who is always around, one who feeds on others'. 候 そうろう is a classical verbal suffix indicating politeness.

NOTE

➡ see COMPOUND FORMATION for
測候所 そっこうじょ →測 0744
候補者 こうほしゃ →補 1529
★ do not confuse with 侯 FEUDAL LORD →0109

倖

▶GOOD FORTUNE
コウ しあわ(せ) ㊔ ゆき さち
Ⓒ 幸 xìng

0134
◧ 1-2-8

9	Names	U5016
亻	S10-2-8	F2576

COMPOUNDS

[now replaced by 幸 2755]

❶ⓐ [original meaning] **GOOD FORTUNE, good luck**
ⓑ **happiness, well-being, felicity**
a 射倖心 しゃこうしん speculative spirit
僥×倖 ぎょうこう good fortune, luck, lucky chance
ab 薄倖 はっこう unhappiness; sad fate, misfortune
❷ [archaic] be in the good graces of (one's ruler); bestow favor upon
倖臣 こうしん favorite courtier

KUN

【しあわせ 倖せ】[now usu. 幸せ or 仕合わせ] **happiness, blessing; GOOD FORTUNE**

SYNONYMS

❶ⓐ & 【しあわせ】 **good fortune**
吉 LUCKY →2691
嘉 HAPPY →2953
祥 AUSPICIOUS →1184
瑞 AUSPICIOUS OMEN →1302
禎 PROPITIOUS OMEN →1305
幸 GOOD FORTUNE →2755
福 FORTUNE →1303
倖 GOOD FORTUNE →0134

HOMOPHONES

しあわせ
幸せ →2755
仕合わせ →0037, 2511

NOTE

➡ see USAGE note at 幸 2755
➡ see COMPOUND FORMATION for 仕合わせ しあわせ →合 2511

倫

▶MORALS
リン ㊔ とも みち のり ひとし
Ⓒ 伦 lún

0135
◧ 1-2-8

9	Jōyō	U502B
亻	S10-2-8	F1514

1	2	3	4	5	6	7	8	9	10
ノ	亻	亻	亼	亼	伶	侖	侖	倫	倫

COMPOUNDS

❶ⓐ **MORALS, ethics, moral rules, code of conduct**
ⓑ human relations, esp. as conceived by feudal ethics
a 倫理 りんり ethics, morals, code of conduct
倫理学 りんりがく ethics, moral philosophy
不倫な ふりんな immoral, illicit
人倫 じんりん humanity, morality; human relations
破倫 はりん immorality; incest
b 五倫 ごりん moral rules to govern the five human relations; the five cardinal principles of morality
❷ peer, match, equal
比倫 ひりん peer, match, equal
絶倫の ぜつりんの matchless, peerless
❸ used phonetically for *ron*
倫敦 ろんどん London

INDEPENDENT

【りん 倫】peer, equal
倫を絶する りんをぜっする incomparably excellent

SYNONYMS

❶ⓐ **moral principles**
倫 MORALS →0135
道 the way of moral conduct →3888

倆

▶SKILL

リョウ

Ⓒ 俩 liǎ liǎng

0136

1-2-8

9	Non-Jōyō	U5006
亻	S10-2-8	F0000

COMPOUNDS

● [now usu. 量 3119] **SKILL**

技倆(=伎倆) ぎりょう skill, ability, capacity

SYNONYMS

● **art**

技 SKILL → 0292
倆 SKILL → 0136
術 PRACTICAL ART → 0575
芸 ART → 2738
道 the way of an art → 3888

● **skill**

力 POWER → 4178
能 ABILITY → 1676
技 SKILL → 0292
倆 SKILL → 0136
腕 skill → 1269
才 TALENT → 4218

借

▶BORROW

シャク か(りる)

Ⓒ 借 jiè

0137

1-2-8

9	Jōyō-4	U501F
亻	S10-2-8	F0964

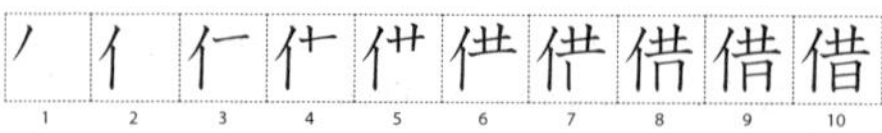

COMPOUNDS

❶ **BORROW, get a loan**

借金する しゃっきんする borrow money, run into debt
借用 しゃくよう borrowing, loan
借家 しゃくや house for rent, rented house
借款 しゃっかん loan
貸借 たいしゃく lending and borrowing, debt and credit, loan
拝借する はいしゃくする borrow
賃借する ちんしゃくする hire, lease

❷ by way of a makeshift, temporarily

借問す しゃくもんす Let me ask you…
仮借無き かしゃくなき merciless(ly)

KUN

【かりる 借りる】 **BORROW, get a loan; hire, rent; buy on credit**

借り かり borrowing; debt, loan
借り集める かりあつめる borrow money from many people
借り出す かりだす borrow, make a loan of
間借り まがり renting a room

SYNONYMS

❶ **lend and borrow**

借 BORROW → 0137
債 DEBT → 0177
貸 LEND → 3213
融 finance → 2303

修

▶CULTIVATE
▶REPAIR

シュウ シュ おさ(める) おさ(まる)

㊔ おさむ のぶ なが さね なお

Ⓒ 修 xiū

0138

1-2-8

9	Jōyō-5	U4FEE
亻	S10-2-8	F0680

COMPOUNDS

❶ **CULTIVATE (one's intellect or character), improve oneself, foster, pursue, study, train, practice**

修養する しゅうようする cultivate one's mind, improve oneself
修道院 しゅうどういん monastery, convent
修了 しゅうりょう completion (of a course)
修行 しゅぎょう training, study; ascetic practices
修験者 しゅげんじゃ ascetic (living in the mountains)
修学旅行 しゅうがくりょこう school excursion
修士 しゅうし Master, master's degree
研修 けんしゅう study and training
履修 りしゅう completion (of a course), taking (a course)
必修の ひっしゅうの required, compulsory

❷ **REPAIR, mend, rectify**

修正 しゅうせい amendment, revision, correction; retouch
修理 しゅうり repair, mending
修復 しゅうふく restoration
修繕する しゅうぜんする mend, repair
改修する かいしゅうする repair, improve
補修 ほしゅう repair, mending

❸ [original meaning] trim, decorate

修飾する しゅうしょくする decorate, ornament; *gram* modify
修辞法 しゅうじほう rhetoric

❹ compile, edit

修史 しゅうし compilation of a history
監修 かんしゅう (editorial) supervision

❺ used phonetically for *shu* in the transliteration of Sanskrit Buddhist terms

阿修羅 あしゅら *Asura* (fighting demon)

❻ perform (religious rites)

修祓× しゅうふつ(=しゅうばつ) expel [exorcise] evil spirits (by Shinto rituals)

INDEPENDENT

【しゅうする 修する】perform (religious rites)

法会を修する ほうえをしゅうする perform a Buddhist mass

KUN

【おさめる 修める】

① **CULTIVATE, pursue, practice, study; master, complete**

学を修める がくをおさめる pursue knowledge [one's studies]

② order (one's life)

身を修める みをおさめる order one's life

【おさまる 修まる】**govern oneself, conduct oneself well**

素行が修まらない そこうがおさまらない conduct oneself loosely, be dissolute

SYNONYMS

❶ **cultivate**

修 CULTIVATE → 0138
養 FOSTER (one's intellect) → 2998
練 TRAIN → 1738
錬 REFINE → 2185
鍛 train → 2206
磨 POLISH → 3946
琢 POLISH → 1222

❷ **repair**

直す FIX → 3649
修 REPAIR → 0138
繕 MEND → 1802

❺ **phonetic [s]/[sh]**

沙 phonetic [sha] → 0311
刹 phonetic [setsu] → 1620
遮 phonetic [sha] → 3916
叉 phonetic [sha] → 4194
世 phonetic [se] → 4308
須 phonetic [shu] → 0700
修 phonetic [shu] → 0138
西 phonetic [su] → 4333
相 phonetic [sō] → 1120
薩 phonetic [satsu] → 3016

HOMOPHONES

おさめる

納 PAY → 1652
収 TAKE IN → 0031
治 GOVERN → 0393

おさまる

納 PAY → 1652
収 TAKE IN → 0031
治 GOVERN → 0393

NOTE

➡ see USAGE note at 納 1652
➡ see COMPOUND FORMATION for 履修 りしゅう → 履 3933

倒

0139

◧ 1-2-8

▶**TOPPLE**

トウ たお(れる) -だお(れ) たお(す)

Ⓒ 倒 dǎo dào

9	Jōyō	U5012
亻	S10-2-8	F0640

(stroke order 1–10)

COMPOUNDS

❶ⓐ **TOPPLE, tumble down, fall over, fall, collapse**
ⓑ **cause to TOPPLE, overturn, overthrow, knock down**

a 倒木 とうぼく fallen tree
倒壊する とうかいする collapse, be destroyed, crumble
卒倒する そっとうする faint, fall unconscious, swoon
転倒する てんとうする tumble, fall down; invert, reverse; upset

b 倒産 とうさん insolvency, bankruptcy; breech birth
倒閣する とうかくする overthrow the cabinet
倒幕 とうばく overthrowing the shogunate
打倒する だとうする overthrow, knock down, defeat

❷ⓐ **upside-down, inverted**
ⓑ **turn upside down**

a 倒立 とうりつ handstand
倒影 とうえい inverted image
倒錯 とうさく perversion, inversion

b 倒置 とうち turning upside down; *gram* inversion

❸ **indicates emphasis of action**

圧倒する あっとうする overwhelm, overpower, crush
罵倒する ばとうする denounce, condemn, abuse
傾倒する けいとうする devote oneself to, set one's mind toward; admire
抱腹絶倒する ほうふくぜっとうする double up with laughter

❹ **unclassified compounds**

面倒な めんどうな troublesome, worrisome; difficult

KUN

【たおれる 倒れる】

① **fall over, TOPPLE, tumble down, collapse**

後に倒れる うしろにたおれる fall backward

② **succumb, break down, fall senseless**

③ⓐ **go to ruin**

ⓑ **go bankrupt**

a 共倒れ ともだおれ falling together, joint bankruptcy

内閣が倒れた ないかくがたおれた The cabinet was overthrown

④ [formerly 斃れる] fall down dead, perish, die

行き倒れ いきだおれ person dying [dead] on the street

【-だおれ -倒れ】

① **bad debt, loss, financial ruin**

貸し倒れ かしだおれ irrecoverable debt

食い倒れ くいだおれ bringing ruin upon oneself by extravagance in food

② showy but worthless, deceptive

看板倒れ かんばんだおれ gorgeous in appearance but poor in substance

【たおす 倒す】

① **bring down, fell, knock down, throw to the ground**

押し倒す おしたおす push down

②ⓐ **overthrow, ruin**

ⓑ **defeat**

b 拝み倒す おがみたおす entreat (a person) into consent, win over by persuasive entreaty

③ [formerly 斃す] **kill**

④ fail to pay

踏み倒す ふみたおす trample down; bilk, shirk payment

⑤ [in compounds] make a show of, sham

見掛け倒し みかけだおし deceptive appearance, mere show

SYNONYMS

❶ **descend and fall**

落 FALL → 2907

墜 DROP DOWN → 3578

降 DESCEND → 0548

下 go down → 4186

倒 TOPPLE → 0139

ⓑ **overturn**

覆 OVERTURN → 3386

翻 TURN OVER → 2391

反 turn over → 3663

顛 TURN [roll] OVER → 2317

転 turn [roll] over → 1872

倒 TOPPLE → 0139

轢 RUN OVER → 2095

❷ⓐ **opposite**

対 OPPOSITE → 1025

反 COUNTER → 3663

逆 REVERSE → 3835

倒 upside-down → 0139

USAGE

❶【たおれる】

倒れる

① fall over, topple, tumble down, collapse

② succumb, break down, fall senseless

③ⓐ go to ruin

ⓑ go bankrupt

④ [formerly 斃れる] fall down dead, perish, die

斃れる

[now usu. 倒れる] fall down dead, perish, die

❷【たおす】

倒す

① bring down, fell, knock down, throw to the ground

②ⓐ overthrow, ruin

ⓑ defeat

③ [formerly 斃す] kill

④ fail to pay

⑤ [in compounds] make a show of, sham

斃す

[now usu. 倒す] kill

HOMOPHONES

たおれる 斃 FALL DOWN DEAD → 3593

たおす 斃 FALL DOWN DEAD → 3593

倭

▶ANCIENT NAME FOR JAPAN

ワ イ カ やまと ㊔ しず まさ かず やす

ⓒ 倭 wō

0140

1-2-8

9	Names	U502D
イ	S10-2-8	F2119

COMPOUNDS

● **ANCIENT NAME FOR JAPAN**

倭人 わじん ancient name for Japanese

倭寇× わこう Japanese corsairs

INDEPENDENT

【わ 倭】**ANCIENT NAME FOR JAPAN**

KUN

【やまと 倭】

ⓐ [also 大和] *elegant* **ANCIENT NAME FOR JAPAN**

ⓑ [usu. 大和] [prefix] Japanese

a 倭建命 やまとたけるのみこと name of a mythical hero

SYNONYMS

● & 【やまと】ⓐ **Japan**

日 JAPAN → 3759

和 JAPAN → 1450

邦 JAPAN → 1051

国 Japanese → 3831

倭 ANCIENT NAME FOR JAPAN → 0140

HOMOPHONES

やまと 大和 →4224, 1450

倶 ▶TOGETHER
グ ク とも(に)

0141 1-2-8

9	Nonstandard	U5036
亻	S10-2-8	F0000

traditional form →see 俱 at 0125

併 ▶TOGETHER
ヘイ あわ(せる) しか(し)

0142 1-2-8

9	Nonstandard	U5002
亻	S10-2-8	F0000

traditional form →see 併 at 0092

偶 1-2-8
incorrect stroke-count
➡ see 1-2-9: 亻 at 0150

健 1-2-8
incorrect stroke-count
➡ see 1-2-9: 亻 at 0152

准 ▶JUNIOR
ジュン
Ⓒ 准 zhǔn

0143 1-2-8

15	Jōyō	U51C6
冫	S10-2-8	F2539

Stroke order 1–10

COMPOUNDS

❶ [also prefix] (of secondary rank) **JUNIOR, assistant**
准教員 じゅんきょういん junior [assistant] teacher
准尉 じゅんい warrant officer
准看護婦 じゅんかんごふ junior nurse

❷ grant permission, permit, sanction, authorize, allow
批准 ひじゅん ratification

SYNONYMS

❶ **subordinate**
副 SECONDARY →2230
次 secondary →0058
従 subordinate →0498
亜 SUB- →4354
準 QUASI- →3541
半 semi- →4313
准 JUNIOR →0143
助 assistant →1440

❷ **permit**
許 PERMIT →1862
免 license →2565
准 grant permission →0143
允 GIVE CONSENT →2476

凌 ▶SURPASS
リョウ しの(ぐ)
Ⓒ 凌 líng

0144 1-2-8

15	Names	U51CC
冫	S10-2-8	F2403

COMPOUNDS

❶ [now also 陵 りょう 0660] **SURPASS, outdo, outshine**
凌駕する りょうがする surpass, exceed, outshine, outdo

❷ rise high, soar aloft
凌雲の りょううんの rising up high; rising in the world

❸ [now also 陵 りょう 0660] insult, offend
凌辱する りょうじょくする insult, disgrace; rape

KUN

【しのぐ 凌ぐ】
ⓐ **SURPASS, outdo, outshine**
ⓑ **get through, pull over; endure, bear**
a 壮者を凌ぐ そうしゃをしのぐ put young men to shame
b 雨風を凌ぐ あめかぜをしのぐ take shelter from wind and rain

SYNONYMS

❶ & 【しのぐ】 ⓐ **excel**
勝 EXCEL →1268
抜 STAND OUT →0290
擢んでる stand out →0973
超 SURPASS →4107
越 GO BEYOND →4108
凌 SURPASS →0144
駕 outdo →3236

凄 ▶UNCANNY
セイ すご(い)▲ すご(む)▲ すさ(まじい)▲
Ⓒ 凄 qī

0145 1-2-8

15	Jōyō	U51C4
冫	S10-2-8	F1474

Stroke order 1–10

COMPOUNDS

❶ **UNCANNY, dreadful, terrible, fierce**
凄惨 せいさん ghastliness, gruesomeness
凄絶な せいぜつな fierce, violent

❷ [original meaning] **chilling, chilly, cold**
凄艶 せいえん chillingly beautiful

KUN

【すごい 凄い】

ⓐ **UNCANNY, dreadful, terrible, fierce**
ⓑ **incredible, amazing, excellent, great**
ⓒ (great in degree) **tremendous, terrific, extreme**
a 凄味 すごみ weirdness, ghastliness, dreadfulness
物凄い ものすごい ghastly, weird; terrible, tremendous
b 凄腕 すごうで go-getter, resourceful person
c 凄く すごく very, extremely, tremendously
【すごむ 凄む】threaten, intimidate
【すさまじい 凄まじい】dreadful, terrible, fierce; tremendous, terrific, extreme

SYNONYMS

❶ **fear**
怖 FEARFUL → 0353
凄 UNCANNY → 0145
恐 FEAR → 3283
惧 FEAR → 0581
慄 TREMBLE WITH FEAR → 0791
兢 BE IN FEAR → 1971
惶 BE AFRAID → 0708
畏 BE OVERAWED → 3170
臆 FEEL TIMID → 1397
怯える BE FRIGHTENED → 0355
【すごい】
ⓒ **extreme in degree**
酷 SEVERE → 1967
強 STRONG → 0574
凄い tremendous → 0145
重 HEAVY → 4390
高 HIGH → 2601
深 DEEP → 0636
大 BIG → 4224
厳 SEVERE → 4079
激 intense → 0955
極 EXTREME → 1243
痛 bitter(ly) → 4071
切 keen → 0030
甚 EXTREMELY → 3271
祁 EXTREMELY → 1447
超 super- → 4107
頗る EXCEEDINGLY → 1552

凍

0146
◧1-2-8

▸**FREEZE**
トウ こお(る) こご(える) い(てる)▲ し(みる)▲
Ⓒ 冻 dòng

15	Jōyō	U51CD
冫	S10-2-8	F1589

1	2	3	4	5	6	7	8	9	10
丶	冫	冖	冫…	冫…	冫…	冫…	冫…	凍	凍

COMPOUNDS

ⓐ (turn solid because of cold) **FREEZE, congeal**
ⓑ (be harmed by cold or frost) **FREEZE**, be frostbitten
a 凍結 とうけつ freezing
冷凍 れいとう freezing, cold storage
不凍港 ふとうこう ice-free port
b 凍死する とうしする freeze to death
凍害 とうがい frost damage
凍傷 とうしょう frostbite

KUN

【こおる 凍る】[formerly also 氷る] **FREEZE, congeal**
凍り付く こおりつく freeze
【こごえる 凍える】**be frozen, be chilled**
凍え死ぬ こごえしぬ freeze to death
【いてる 凍てる】*literary* **FREEZE**
凍て付く いてつく freeze
【しみる 凍みる】**FREEZE**, congeal

SYNONYMS

ⓐ **solidify and coagulate**
固 solidify → 3830
凝 CONGEAL → 0198
結 form into a mass → 1706
凍 FREEZE → 0146
ⓐ **reduce the temperature**
凍 FREEZE → 0146
冷 cool → 0088

USAGE

【こおる】
凍る
[formerly also 氷る] freeze, congeal
氷る
[now usu. 凍る] freeze

HOMOPHONES

こおる 氷 ICE → 0043
しみる
染 DYE → 3181
滲 PERMEATE → 0862

NOTE

➡ see also USAGE note at 染 3181

凉

0147
◧1-2-8

▸**COOL**
リョウ すず(しい) すず(む)

15	Names	U51C9
冫	S10-2-8	F0000

traditional form → see 涼 at 0633

隅随

◧1-2-8

incorrect stroke-count
➡ see ◧1-3-9: 阝 at 0760

陸険 etc.

◧1-2-8

incorrect stroke-count
➡ see ◧1-3-8: 阝 at 0655

帰

0148

1-2-8

▶**RETURN**

キ かえ(る) かえ(す)

Ⓝ 歸 皈 Ⓒ 归 guī

18	Jōyō-2	U5E30
刂	S10-2-8	F0270

COMPOUNDS

❶ **RETURN, come back, go back, take one's leave**

帰着する きちゃくする return, come back; arrive at, result in

帰還する きかんする return, come home, be repatriated

帰国する きこくする return to one's country

帰京 ききょう returning to Tokyo

帰路 きろ homeward journey, return circuit

帰宅する きたくする come [return] home

復帰する ふっきする return, be restored, revert

❷ⓐ **settle in place, conclude**

ⓑ settle in one place, be brought together, unite

a 帰結 きけつ conclusion, end, result

帰一する きいつする be united into one

帰納法 きのうほう inductive method

❸ **follow, yield to, pledge allegiance to**

帰順 きじゅん submission, return to allegiance

帰化 きか naturalization

帰依 きえ faith, devotion; conversion

INDEPENDENT

【き 帰】RETURNing

【きする 帰する】come to, result in, attribute; fall into

KUN

【かえる 帰る】[sometimes also 還る]

ⓐ **RETURN (to one's original position), come back, come home**

ⓑ **go back [home], take one's leave**

a 帰り道 かえりみち the way back, return trip

お帰りなさい おかえりなさい Hello!/Welcome back

日帰りする ひがえりする return on the same day, make a day's trip

家に帰る いえにかえる come back home

ab 帰り かえり return, coming back; going home

b 帰れ かえれ Get out!/Go home!

【かえす 帰す】**let (someone) RETURN, see out, send (someone) home, dismiss**

生徒を帰す せいとをかえす dismiss the pupils

SYNONYMS

❶ **return**

帰 RETURN →0148

還 RETURN →3945

回 turn back →3793

廻 turn back →3833

戻る RETURN →2441

復 RETURN TO →0701

❷ **settle**

着 settle (down) →4110

帰 settle in place →0148

落 be concluded →2907

USAGE

【かえる】

帰る

[sometimes also 還る]

ⓐ return (to one's original position), come back, come home

ⓑ go back [home], take one's leave

還る

[usu. 帰る] same as 帰る

返る

① be restored to, return to (the original state)

② be given back

反る

vi turn over, become overturned

HOMOPHONES

かえる

還 RETURN →3945

返 RETURN →3797

反 COUNTER →3663

かえす

返 RETURN →3797

反 COUNTER →3663

NOTE

➡ see also USAGE note at 返 3797

偽

0149

1-2-9

▶**FALSIFY**

ギ いつわ(る) にせ

Ⓝ 僞 Ⓒ 伪 wěi

9	Jōyō	U507D
亻	S11-2-9	F1327

COMPOUNDS

ⓐ [original meaning] **FALSIFY, forge, deceive**

ⓑ **falsehood, lie**

ⓒ false, forged

a 偽造 ぎぞう forgery, fabrication

偽証 ぎしょう perjury

b 真偽 しんぎ truth or falsehood; authenticity

虚偽 きょぎ falsehood, lie, fallacy

c 偽善 ぎぜん hypocrisy

偽名 ぎめい false name
偽印 ぎいん false [forged] seal

KUN

【いつわる 偽る】
ⓐ (state untruthfully) **FALSIFY, misrepresent, lie**
ⓑ [formerly also 詐る] (cause to believe a falsehood) **FALSIFY, deceive, cheat**
ⓒ **feign, pretend**
a 偽り いつわり lie, falsehood, fabrication
c 大学生と身分を偽る だいがくせいとみぶんをいつわる misrepresent oneself as a university student

【にせ 偽】 [also prefix] **sham, imitation, fake, forgery**
偽物 にせもの sham, imitation, fake, forgery
偽札 にせさつ counterfeit paper money
偽君子 にせくんし sham gentleman

SYNONYMS

ⓐ **deceive**
欺 DECEIVE → 2138
騙 DECEIVE → 2314
詐 SWINDLE → 1896
惑 mislead → 3461
拐 defraud → 0365
偽 FALSIFY → 0149
詭 TRICK → 1919

ⓑ **falsehood**
偽 falsehood → 0149
嘘 LIE → 0880

【にせ】
◯ **false**
虚 FALSE → 4017
仮 fake → 0053
偽 sham → 0149
擬 imitation → 0969
義 artificial → 2948

USAGE

【いつわる】
偽る
ⓐ (state untruthfully) falsify, misrepresent, lie
ⓑ [formerly also 詐る] (cause to believe a falsehood) falsify, deceive, cheat
ⓒ feign, pretend
詐る
[now usu. 偽る] (cause to believe a falsehood) **falsify**, deceive, cheat

HOMOPHONES

いつわる 詐 SWINDLE → 1896

偶

▶BY CHANCE
▶COUPLE
グウ たま▲

0150
Ⓒ 偶 ǒu
1-2-9

9	Jōyō	U5076
亻	S11-2-9	F1464

丿 亻 仆 仴 仴 但 偶 偶 偶 偶 偶 (1–11)

COMPOUNDS

❶ **BY CHANCE, accidentally, by coincidence, unexpectedly**
偶然に ぐうぜんに by chance, accidentally, by coincidence
偶発的な ぐうはつてきな accidental, contingent
偶詠 ぐうえい impromptu poem, poem written at the moment of inspiration
偶成の ぐうせいの fortuitous, contingent
偶感 ぐうかん random thoughts, chance impressions

❷ⓐ **COUPLE, pair**
ⓑ **mate, spouse**
a 偶力 ぐうりょく couple (of forces)
対偶 たいぐう contrapositive; spouse, companion
b 配偶者 はいぐうしゃ spouse, mate

❸ *math* **even, even number**
偶数 ぐうすう even number
奇偶 きぐう odd and even numbers

❹ [original meaning] (wooden) **figure, idol, image**
偶像 ぐうぞう idol, image
土偶 どぐう earthen [clay] figure

KUN

【たま 偶】 **rare occasion**
偶に たまに occasionally, on rare occasions
偶偶 たまたま by chance, accidentally

SYNONYMS

❷ⓐ **two**
二 TWO → 2421
弐 TWO (in legal documents) → 3961
双 SET OF TWO → 0028
対 pair → 1025
偶 COUPLE → 0150
両 BOTH → 4331

❹ **images**
像 IMAGE → 0187
仏 Buddhist image → 0020
偶 figure → 0150

偏

▶ONE-SIDED

ヘン　かたよ(る)

Ⓝ 偏 Ⓒ 偏 piān

0151

1-2-9

9	Jōyō	U504F
亻	S11-2-9	F1681

COMPOUNDS

❶ⓐ [original meaning] (occurring on one side) **ONE-SIDED, uneven, unbalanced**

ⓑ (favoring one side) **ONE-SIDED, biased, partial, unfair, prejudiced**

a 偏頭痛 へんずつう headache on one side, migraine
偏在 へんざい uneven distribution
偏食 へんしょく unbalanced diet

b 偏執狂 へんしつきょう(=へんしゅうきょう) monomaniac
偏見 へんけん prejudice, biased view, narrow view
偏重する へんちょうする attach too much importance, overemphasize
偏愛 へんあい partiality, favoritism

❷ⓐ (deviating from normal) **eccentric, deviating**

ⓑ (deviating from circular) eccentric

a 偏屈 へんくつ eccentricity, obstinacy, narrow-mindedness
偏差値 へんさち deviation (value)

b 偏心 へんしん eccentricity

❸ [sometimes also 扁 3728] left-side radical of Chinese characters, left radical
偏旁 へんぼう left and right radicals
人偏 にんべん *ninben*, 'person' radical (亻)

❹ countryside
偏土 へんど remote region

INDEPENDENT

【へん 偏】left-side radical of Chinese characters
「偏」の偏は人偏と言う へんのへんはにんべんという The left-side radical of 偏 is called *ninben*

【へんする 偏する】be **ONE-SIDED**, be partial; deviate

KUN

【かたよる 偏る】

ⓐ **be ONE-SIDED, be prejudiced, be partial, be unfair**

ⓑ **deviate**

a 偏った考え かたよったかんがえ partial [one-sided] view, prejudice

b 偏り かたより deviation, offset; polarization
偏りシリンダー かたよりしりんだー offset cylinder

SYNONYMS

❶ⓐ one side
片- one side →4272
偏 ONE-SIDED →0151
頗 one-sided →1552

ⓑ inclining toward
偏 ONE-SIDED →0151
傾 incline toward →0174

USAGE

【かたよる】

偏る
ⓐ be one-sided, be prejudiced, be partial, be unfair
ⓑ deviate

片寄る
concentrate on one side [place], go aside

HOMOPHONES

かたよる 片寄る →4272, 2856

NOTE

➡ see COMPOUND FORMATION for 偏執狂 へんしつきょう (=へんしゅうきょう) →執 2114

健

▶ROBUST

ケン　すこ(やか)　㊔ たけ　たけし　たつ　たける　やす　たて　つよし　まさる　やすし

Ⓒ 健 jiàn

0152

1-2-9

9	Jōyō-4	U5065
亻	S11-2-9	F0703

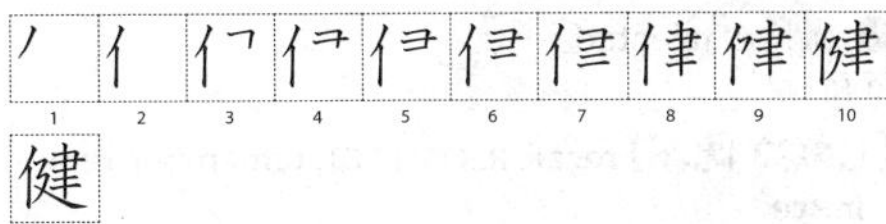

COMPOUNDS

❶ (strong and in good health) **ROBUST, healthy, sound, strong**
健康な けんこうな healthy, sound, well
健保(=健康保険) けんぽ(=けんこうほけん) health insurance
健在だ けんざいだ be well, be in good health
健全 けんぜん health, soundness
健脚の けんきゃくの strong in walking
強健な きょうけんな robust, healthy, strong
保健 ほけん (preservation of) health, sanitation
穏健な おんけんな moderate, temperate, sound
剛健な ごうけんな strong and sturdy, virile; manly

❷ be strong in, be good at
健筆 けんぴつ powerful [facile] pen
健忘 けんぼう forgetfulness, short memory
健闘する けんとうする fight bravely; make strenuous efforts

KUN

【すこやか 健やか】

すこやかな 健やかな **healthy, sound**

健やかな体 すこやかなからだ healthy [sound] body

SPECIAL READINGS

健気な▲ けなげな praiseworthy, admirable; brave

SYNONYMS

❶ strong

強 STRONG → 0574

壮 VIGOROUS → 0263

丈 STOUT → 4227

健 ROBUST (healthy) → 0152

逞しい ROBUST (sturdy) → 4004

康 HEALTHY → 3877

旺 ENERGETIC → 1061

潑 LIVELY → 0917

❶ healthy

康 HEALTHY → 3877

健 ROBUST → 0152

生 health → 4309

偲

▶RECOLLECT

サイ シ しの(ぶ)

Ⓒ 偲 sī cāi

0153

1-2-9

9	Names	U5072
亻	S11-2-9	F2958

COMPOUNDS

● [archaic] talented

KUN

【しのぶ 偲ぶ】 **recall, RECOLLECT, remember, reminisce**

故人を偲ぶ こじんをしのぶ think of the dead

昔を偲ばせる品 むかしをしのばせるしな things reminiscent of bygone days

SYNONYMS

【しのぶ】

○ **remember**

憶 REMEMBER → 0944

覚える COMMIT TO MEMORY → 3217

記 commit to memory → 1843

追 reminisce → 3840

顧 LOOK BACK → 2394

偲 RECOLLECT → 0153

HOMOPHONES

しのぶ 忍 BEAR → 2750

NOTE

➡ see USAGE note at 忍 2750

脩

▶DRIED MEAT

シュウ ㊔ おさむ なが おさ のぶ ゆう すけ

Ⓒ 修 xiū

0154

1-2-9

130	Names	U8129
月	S11-4-7	F3094

COMPOUNDS

❶ⓐ [original meaning] **DRIED MEAT**

ⓑ DRIED MEAT or ham as gift to teacher in lieu of salary in ancient times

b 束脩 そくしゅう tuition; ham as gift to teacher in lieu of tuition

❷ [rare] **long**

脩竹 しゅうちく tall bamboo

SYNONYMS

❶ meat

肉 FLESH → 3966

身 meat → 4368

脩 DRIED MEAT → 0154

側

▶SIDE

ソク がわ かわ そば▲

Ⓒ 侧 cè zè zhāi

0155

1-2-9

9	Jōyō-4	U5074
亻	S11-2-9	F0363

1	2	3	4	5	6	7	8	9	10	11
ノ	亻	亻	们	们	相	俱	俱	俱	側	側

COMPOUNDS

❶ⓐ (one of two or more opposing parts) **SIDE, part**

ⓑ (lateral surface) **SIDE, flank**

a 右側 うそく(=みぎがわ) right side

b 側聞(=仄聞)する そくぶんする learn by hearsay

側面 そくめん side, flank

側壁 そくへき side wall

船側 せんそく side of a ship

❷ surroundings, vicinity

側近者 そっきんしゃ close associate, aide

君側 くんそく vicinity of a lord

KUN

【がわ 側】 [also suffix] **SIDE, part; vicinity; those around one; case (of a watch)**

側の者 がわのもの people around one

どちらの側 どちらのがわ which side

西側 にしがわ west side; west European countries and America

内側 うちがわ inside, interior

裏側 うらがわ back [reverse, other] side, wrong side

敵側 てきがわ enemy's side

反対側 はんたいがわ opposite side; opponents' side
消費者側 しょうひしゃがわ consumers' side
銀側の時計 ぎんがわのとけい silver watch

【かわ 側】[also suffix] **SIDE, part**
左っ側 ひだりっかわ left side
上っ側 うわっかわ upper side; surface

【そば 側】[sometimes also 傍] **SIDE**, vicinity
側に そばに by the side of
側女 そばめ mistress, concubine

SYNONYMS

❶ **side**
側 SIDE → 0155
脇 SIDE → 1188
方 side → 2459
辺 -side → 3761
面 side → 2590
傍 BESIDE → 0166
横 SIDEWAYS → 1350

USAGE

【そば】
側
[sometimes also 傍] side, vicinity
傍
[usu. 側] side, vicinity

HOMOPHONES

そば 傍 BESIDE → 0166

停

0156
◧ 1-2-9

▶**HALT**
テイ と(める)▲ と(まる)▲
Ⓒ 停 tíng

9	Jōyō-4	U505C
亻	S11-2-9	F1165

Stroke order: 1–11

COMPOUNDS

❶ⓐ (make a temporary stop) **HALT, pause, stop**
ⓑ **be at a standstill, remain inactive**
a 停留する ていりゅうする halt, stop
停止 ていし stop, halt; suspension
停車 ていしゃ stoppage (of a vehicle)
b 停滞 ていたい stagnation, accumulation; arrearage

❷ abbrev. of 停留所 ていりゅうじょ: **stopping place, stop, station**
バス停 ばすてい bus stop
電停 でんてい tram stop

❸ **suspend, discontinue**
停学 ていがく suspension from school
停職 ていしょく suspension from office
停戦 ていせん cease-fire, armistice
停電 ていでん stoppage of electric power, power failure
調停する ちょうていする mediate, arbitrate, make peace

❹ [formerly 碇 1538] anchor
停泊する ていはくする anchor, moor

KUN

【とめる 停める】[now usu. 止める] (bring a vehicle to a temporary halt) **stop (a bus or train), bring to a HALT, brake**
車を停める くるまをとめる bring a car to a halt

【とまる 停まる】[now usu. 止まる] (of vehicles) **roll to a stop, stop (at a station)**
停まらずに行く とまらずにいく run without stopping, run past

SYNONYMS

❶ⓐ **stop**
止 STOP → 3659
停 HALT → 0156
駐 park → 2297

❷ **places for landing or stopping**
港 PORT → 0737
湊 PORT → 0743
津 HARBOR (*elegant*) → 0466
駅 STATION → 2292
停 stopping place → 0156

❸ **discontinue**
絶 BREAK OFF → 1711
廃 ABOLISH → 3902
断 CUT OFF → 1885
止 STOP → 3659
休 suspend → 0056
停 suspend → 0156
已む CEASE → 4185

HOMOPHONES

とめる
止 STOP → 3659
留 KEEP → 3189
泊 STAY OVERNIGHT → 0389

とまる
止 STOP → 3659
留 KEEP → 3189
泊 STAY OVERNIGHT → 0389

NOTE

➡ see USAGE note at 止 3659

偵

▶SPY

テイ ㊔ さだ

Ⓒ 侦 zhēn

0157

1-2-9

[亻] ヒ 阝 丁

9	Jōyō	U5075
亻	S11-2-9	F1480

丿 亻 亻' 亻⺊ 亻' 佔 侦 偵 偵 偵 偵 (1–11)

COMPOUNDS

❶ **SPY, detect, scout, investigate**

偵察 ていさつ scouting, reconnaissance

偵知 ていち [rare] spying, investigating

内偵する ないていする make secret inquiries, scout

❷ [original meaning] **SPY**

密偵 みってい spy, emissary

探偵 たんてい detective work; detective, sleuth

SYNONYMS

❶ **spy**

偵 SPY → 0157

探 spy on → 0613

❷ **agents**

使 ENVOY → 0100

偵 SPY → 0157

偏

▶ONE-SIDED

ヘン かたよ(る)

0158

1-2-9

9	Nonstandard	U504F
亻	S11-2-9	F0000

traditional form → see 偏 at 0151

偉

▶GREAT

イ えら(い) ㊔ ひで いさむ より

0159

1-2-9

9	Nonstandard	U5049
亻	S11-2-9	F0000

traditional form → see 偉 at 0167

條

▶ARTICLE

ジョウ ㊔ えだ

0160

1-2-9

75	Names	U689D
木	S11-4-7	F0000

traditional form → see 条 at 2726

假

▶TEMPORARY

カ ケ かり かり-

0161

1-2-9

9	Nonstandard	U5047
亻	S11-2-9	F0000

traditional form → see 仮 at 0053

倦

▶TIRE OF

ケン あぐ(ねる) う(む) あ(きる)

0162

1-2-9

9	Nonstandard	U5026
亻	S11-2-9	F0000

traditional form → see 倦 at 0131

頃

▶TIME

▶ABOUT

ケイ▲ ころ ごろ -ごろ

Ⓒ 顷 qǐng

0163

1-2-9

181	Jōyō	U9803
頁	S11-9-2	F0561

丿 ヒ ヒ一 ヒ丆 ヒ丆 ヒ丙 ヒ百 ヒ百 ヒ頁 ヒ頁 頃 (1–11)

COMPOUNDS

● [archaic] moment, instant, short **TIME**

頃刻 けいこく short moment

KUN

【ころ, ごろ 頃】

①ⓐ **TIME, approximate time**

ⓑ **right TIME (for doing something)**

a この頃 このごろ now, these days; lately

もう彼が帰る頃だ もうかれがかえるころだ It's about time for him to come home

b 食べ頃 たべごろ right time for eating

② [in compounds] **convenience, suitability**

頃合いの ころあいの suitable, handy

手頃な てごろな handy, convenient

③ **unclassified compounds**

身頃 みごろ body of a garment

【-ごろ -頃】 [also suffix] **ABOUT, around, toward**

十八世紀の終わり頃 じゅうはっせいきのおわりごろ toward the end of the eighteenth century

八時頃 はちじごろ about eight o'clock

SYNONYMS

● **short time periods**

頃 moment → 0163

瞬 INSTANT → 1594

秒 SECOND → 1462

分 MINUTE → 2466

時 hour → 1155

暫 SHORT WHILE → 3553

【ころ】

①ⓐ **time periods**

時 TIME → 1155

季 SEASON (quarter) → 3161

候 SEASON (time of year) → 0133

頃 TIME → 0163

暇 FREE TIME → 1275
般 period of time → 1670
刻 POINT OF TIME → 1619
間 INTERVAL → 4122
隙 GAP → 0826
期 TERM → 2139
節 SEASON → 3336

【-ごろ】

◯ **approximately**

約 APPROXIMATELY → 1632
概 GENERAL → 1322
大 in substance → 4224
-頃 ABOUT → 0163
位 about → 0069
-方 about → 2459
-程 …or thereabouts → 1524
辺り thereabouts → 3761

階隊 etc.

incorrect stroke-count
➡ see 1-3-9: 阝 at 0760

1-2-9

頂

▶**SUMMIT**
▶**RECEIVE HUMBLY**
チョウ いただ(く) いただき

0164

1-2-9

Ⓒ 顶 dǐng

181	Jōyō-6	U9802
頁	S11-9-2	F1119

Stroke order: 1–11

COMPOUNDS

❶ⓐ (highest part) **SUMMIT, top, peak, apex, vertex**
ⓑ (mountain top) **SUMMIT, peak**

a 頂点 ちょうてん apex, peak
絶頂 ぜっちょう summit, peak, climax
有頂天 うちょうてん exaltation, ecstasy
山頂 さんちょう summit

b 頂上 ちょうじょう summit, peak, top; climax
登頂する とうちょうする climb to the summit

❷ⓐ [original meaning] top of the head, crown
ⓑ head

a 頭頂 とうちょう *anat* vertex, parietal

b 円頂 えんちょう tonsured head; priest; round top

❸ **RECEIVE HUMBLY, accept with thanks**

頂戴する ちょうだいする [humble] receive, accept, take; eat, drink

KUN

【いただく 頂く】 [sometimes also 戴く]

① [humble]
ⓐ **RECEIVE HUMBLY, accept with thanks, be given, be favored with**
ⓑ **eat, drink**
ⓒ **trouble someone to do something, have something done**

a 頂き いただき windfall, unexpected gain; unauthorized borrowing
頂けない いただけない unapprovable, unsatisfactory
頂き物 いただきもの gift, present
有り難く頂く ありがたくいただく accept (a thing) with thanks
この本を頂いても良いですか このほんをいただいてもいいですか Can I have this book?

b 酒も煙草も頂きます さけもたばこもいただきます I both drink and smoke
十分頂きました じゅうぶんいただきました I have had enough

c 今晩来て頂きたい こんばんきていただきたい I hope you will come this evening
お茶を入れて頂けませんか おちゃをいれていただけませんか May I trouble you for a cup of tea?

② have over, be presided over by, live under (a ruler)

指導者として頂く しどうしゃとしていただく have (a person) as one's leader
彼らは女王を頂く かれらはじょうおうをいただく They have a queen over them

③ wear (a crown); be crowned (with snow)

雪を頂いた山 ゆきをいただいたやま snow-crowned mountain

【いただき 頂】 **SUMMIT, peak, top**

SYNONYMS

❶ⓐ **tops**

上 upper part → 4212
頂 SUMMIT → 0164
頭 HEAD → 2019

ⓑ **mountain parts**

頂 SUMMIT → 0164
峰 PEAK → 0494
嶺 RIDGE → 3013
峠 MOUNTAIN PASS → 0428
崖 CLIFF → 2862
壁 wall-like structure → 3601

❸ **receive**

受 RECEIVE → 3076
享 ENJOY → 2545
領 receive → 1567
収 TAKE IN → 0031
納 ACCEPT → 1652
貰 GET → 3219
戴 RECEIVE HUMBLY → 4093
頂 RECEIVE HUMBLY → 0164

拝 have the honor to receive →0360

USAGE

【いただく】

頂く

[sometimes also 戴く]

① [humble]

ⓐ receive humbly, accept with thanks, be given, be favored with

ⓑ eat, drink

ⓒ trouble someone to do something, have something done

② have over, be presided over by, live under (a ruler)

③ wear (a crown); be crowned (with snow)

戴く

[usu. 頂く] same as 頂く

HOMOPHONES

いただく 戴 RECEIVE HUMBLY →4093

備

▸PROVIDE

ビ そな(える) そな(わる)

Ⓒ 备 bèi

0165

1-2-10

9	Jōyō-5	U5099
イ	S12-2-10	F0483

Stroke order: 1–12

COMPOUNDS

❶ⓐ [original meaning] **PROVIDE for [against], prepare for [against], get ready**

ⓑ preparations, preparedness

a 備考 びこう explanatory note, remarks (for reference)

備蓄 びちく saving for [against] emergency, storing

準備する じゅんびする provide for [against], prepare for [against]

b 予備 よび reserve, spare; preparation, preliminaries

警備 けいび guard, defense

軍備 ぐんび military preparations, armaments

防備 ぼうび defense, defensive preparations

❷ⓐ PROVIDE (with), equip, fit

ⓑ be PROVIDED with, be equipped with

a 備品 びひん fixtures, furnishings

設備する せつびする equip [provide] (with)

整備 せいび maintenance, servicing, preparation

装備 そうび equipment, outfit

b 完備した かんびした fully-equipped, perfect, complete

具備する ぐびする be endowed [equipped] with, possess

❸ old name for south Okayama and east Hiroshima prefectures

備後 びんご old name for east Hiroshima Prefecture

KUN

【そなえる 備える】

①ⓐ **PROVIDE for, make preparations for, stock**

ⓑ **PROVIDE with, furnish**

a 備え そなえ provision, preparation; defense

万一に備える まんいちにそなえる provide against contingencies

b 備え付ける そなえつける provide with, furnish, fit with

② [also 具える] possess, be endowed with

資格を備える しかくをそなえる have a qualification (for)

【そなわる 備わる】 **be PROVIDED [furnished] with**

名実共に備わる めいじつともにそなわる live up to one's name

自然に備わる人格 しぜんにそなわるじんかく one's natural dignity

SYNONYMS

❶ⓐ prepare

備 PROVIDE →0165

調 PREPARE →1973

❷ equip and install

据える INSTALL →0602

敷 LAY →2345

架 LAY ACROSS →3178

装 FIT OUT →3327

設 SET UP →1863

備 PROVIDE →0165

USAGE

❶【そなえる】

備える

①ⓐ provide for, make preparations for, stock

ⓑ provide with, furnish

② [also 具える] possess, be endowed with

供える

offer (to a god), make an offering

❷【そなえ】

備え

① provision, preparation

② defense

供え

offering

HOMOPHONES

そなえる 供 OFFER →0098

そなえ 供 OFFER →0098

傍

▶**BESIDE**
ボウ かたわ(ら) わき▲ おか-▲ はた▲ そば▲

0166

Ⓒ 旁 páng 傍 bàng

◧ 1-2-10

9	Jōyō	U508D
亻	S12-2-10	F1362

COMPOUNDS

● [sometimes also 旁 2598] **BESIDE, by, by the side, nearby; side**
傍観者 ぼうかんしゃ bystander, onlooker
傍系の ぼうけいの collateral, subsidiary, affiliated
傍受 ぼうじゅ interception, tapping
傍線 ぼうせん side line, underline
傍聴 ぼうちょう hearing; attendance
傍若無人な ぼうじゃくぶじんな overbearing, arrogant, audacious
路傍 ろぼう roadside, wayside
近傍 きんぼう neighborhood

KUN

【かたわら 傍ら】**BESIDEs, while; side**
傍らに寄る かたわらによる step aside
勉強の傍ら音楽を聞く べんきょうのかたわらおんがくをきく listen to music while studying

【わき 傍】[now usu. 脇]
①ⓐ side
ⓑ the other way, another place
a 傍に置く わきにおく lay aside
b 傍視 わきみ looking aside
② supporting actor [role]
傍役 わきやく supporting actor [role]

【おか- 傍-】[usu. 岡] outsider, third party, bystander
傍目八目 おかめはちもく Onlookers can see [read] the game far better than the players themselves

【はた 傍】bystander, outsider
傍の者達 はたのものたち bystanders, onlookers

【そば 傍】[usu. 側] **side, vicinity**
傍に そばに by the side of

SYNONYMS

● **side**
側 SIDE → 0155
脇 SIDE → 1188
方 side → 2459
辺 -side → 3761
面 side → 2590
傍 BESIDE → 0166
横 SIDEWAYS → 1350

● **near**
近 NEAR → 3798
隣 neighboring → 0961
傍 BESIDE → 0166
旁 BESIDE → 2598
沿 ALONG → 0386

【かたわら】
○ **additionally**
亦 ALSO → 2504
兼 CONCURRENTLY → 2850
又 also, and → 4158
而うして and → 2520
及び and → 4192
並びに and also → 2793
傍ら besides → 0166
尚 STILL → 2774
更に furthermore → 4355
且つ AS WELL → 4297

USAGE

【わき】
傍
[now usu. 脇]
①ⓐ side
ⓑ the other way, another place
② supporting actor [role]

脇
① [formerly also 傍]
ⓐ side
ⓑ the other way, another place
② [formerly also 傍] supporting actor [role]
③ [also 腋]
ⓐ armpit
ⓑ armhole

腋
[also 脇]
ⓐ armpit
ⓑ armhole

HOMOPHONES

わき
脇 SIDE → 1188
腋 ARMPIT → 1266

おか-
岡 HILL → 3719
丘 HILL → 4307
陸 LAND → 0659

はた 端 END → 1564
そば 側 SIDE → 0155

NOTE

➡ see also USAGE notes at 丘 4307 and 端 1564 and 側 0155

1

偉

▶**GREAT**

イ えら(い) ㊔ ひで いさむ より

Ⓝ 偉 Ⓒ 伟 wěi

0167

1-2-10

[亻] 十 阝

9	Jōyō	U5049
亻	S12-2-10	F1573

COMPOUNDS

a (of superior character) **GREAT, grand**

b [original meaning] (of large size) **GREAT**, towering

a 偉大な いだいな great, mighty, grand
偉人 いじん great man
偉業 いぎょう great work [achievement]
偉勲 いくん great achievement
偉観 いかん grand sight
魁偉な かいいな gigantic, large-boned and impressive

b 偉丈夫 いじょうふ towering [great] man; hero

INDEPENDENT

【い 偉】 [rare] **GREAT**ness
偉とするに足る いとするにたる Credit is due to one

KUN

【えらい 偉い】

①ⓐ **GREAT, grand; famous, eminent**

ⓑ [sometimes also 豪い] **remarkable, extraordinary**

a 偉さ えらさ greatness; remarkableness
偉い人 えらいひと great man, extraordinary character
偉がる えらがる be self-important, be conceited
お偉方 おえらがた dignitary, exalted personalities

b 偉物 えらぶつ extraordinary [able] character

② [sometimes also 豪い] **awful, serious**
ど偉い どえらい terrible, very serious

SYNONYMS

a **great**
偉 GREAT (of superior character) → 0167
大 BIG → 4224
宏 GRAND (large in scale) → 2728
壮 GRAND (having grandeur) → 0263
豪 MAGNIFICENT → 2657
雄 HEROIC → 1271
碩 EMINENT → 1555

USAGE

【えらい】
偉い
①ⓐ great, grand; famous, eminent
ⓑ [sometimes also 豪い] remarkable, extraordinary
② [sometimes also 豪い] awful, serious

豪い
[usu. 偉い]
① remarkable, extraordinary
② awful, serious

HOMOPHONES

えらい 豪 GREAT MAN → 2657

傑

▶**OUTSTANDING PERSON**

ケツ ㊔ すぐる たかし ひで

0168

1-2-10

9	Nonstandard	U5091
亻	S12-2-10	F0000

traditional form → see 傑 at 0175

僅

▶**A LITTLE**

キン わず(か) ㊔ よし

0169

1-2-10

9	Nonstandard	U50C5
亻	S12-2-11	F0000

traditional form → see 僅 at 0176

僅

1-2-10

incorrect stroke-count
➡ see 1-2-11: 亻 at 0176

博

▶**EXTENSIVE**
▶**DOCTOR**

ハク バク ㊔ ひろ ひろし はか とおる

Ⓝ 博 Ⓒ 博 bó

0170

1-2-10

24	Jōyō-4	U535A
十	S12-2-10	F0852

COMPOUNDS

1 **EXTENSIVE (knowledge), wide (learning), well-informed, learned**
博士 はくし doctor, Ph.D.
博物学 はくぶつがく natural history
博物館 はくぶつかん museum
博覧 はくらん extensive reading, wide knowledge
博覧会 はくらんかい exhibition, fair, exposition
博愛主義 はくあいしゅぎ philanthropy, humanity
博識 はくしき extensive knowledge
博学 はくがく extensive learning, erudition, wide knowledge
該博な がいはくな extensive (knowledge), profound (learning)

2 abbrev. of 博士 はくし: **DOCTOR, Ph.D.**

医博 いはく doctor of medicine, M.D.
文博 ぶんはく doctor of literature

❸ abbrev. of 博覧会 はくらんかい exposition, expo
万博 ばんぱく world fair
宇宙博 うちゅうはく Space Expo

❹ gamble
博徒 ばくと gambler
賭博 とばく gambling

INDEPENDENT

【はくする 博する】 gain, win, enjoy
名声を博する めいせいをはくする earn fame, achieve reputation

SPECIAL READINGS

博士 はかせ expert, learned man; doctor, Ph.D.

SYNONYMS

❶ **wide and extensive**
広 WIDE → 3769
紘 WIDE-RANGING → 1650
博 EXTENSIVE → 0170
恢 EXTENSIVE → 0436
浩 VAST → 0525
洸 VAST (expanse of water) → 0462
滉 DEEP AND VAST → 0811
曠 SPACIOUS → 1411
闊 BROAD → 4135

❷ **wise and talented persons**
哲 sage → 3402
賢 wise man → 3518
博 DOCTOR → 0170
秀 genius → 3152
俊 BRILLIANT PERSON → 0117
才 person of talent → 4218
通 well-informed person → 3855

❸ **public display**
展 exhibition → 3862
博 exposition → 0170

愽

0171
1-2-10

▶**EXTENSIVE**
▶**DOCTOR**
ハク バク ㊔ ひろ ひろし はか とおる

24	Nonstandard	U535A
十	S12-2-10	F0000

traditional form → see 博 at 0170

隔隙 etc.

1-2-10

incorrect stroke-count
➡ see 1-3-10: 阝 at 0826

働

0172
1-2-11

▶**WORK**
ドウ はたら(く)
Ⓝ 仂◆ Ⓒ 働 dòng (国字)

9	Jōyō-4	U50CD
亻	S13-2-11	F0491

Stroke order: ノ 亻 亻 仁 仟 佰 佰 佰 俥 俥 俥 働 働 (1–13)

COMPOUNDS

ⓐ [original meaning] **WORK, labor, serve**
ⓑ **WORK** for, act, be active

a 労働 ろうどう (manual) labor, toil
稼働(=稼動) かどう working, work; operation (of a machine)
実働時間 じつどうじかん actual working hours
重労働 じゅうろうどう heavy labor

b 共働 きょうどう *biol* coaction
協働 きょうどう cooperation

KUN

【はたらく 働く】 **WORK, labor; do, act, commit; operate, function**
働き はたらき work, labor; activity, function; ability, talent
働き手 はたらきて worker, breadwinner
働き掛ける はたらきかける work on someone; begin to work
下働き したばたらき subordinate work; underworker
共働き ともばたらき working together (for a living), working in double harness
悪事を働く あくじをはたらく do evil, commit a crime
ブレーキが働く ぶれーきがはたらく The brakes function

SYNONYMS

ⓐ **work**
働 WORK → 0172
稼 WORK (for a living) → 1572
労 LABOR → 3155
勤める serve (in an office) → 2287
仕 SERVE → 0037

傲

0173
1-2-11

▶**ARROGANT**
ゴウ おご(る)▲
Ⓒ 傲 ào

9	Jōyō	U50B2
亻	S13-2-11	F2366

Side index: 亻 阝 刂 九

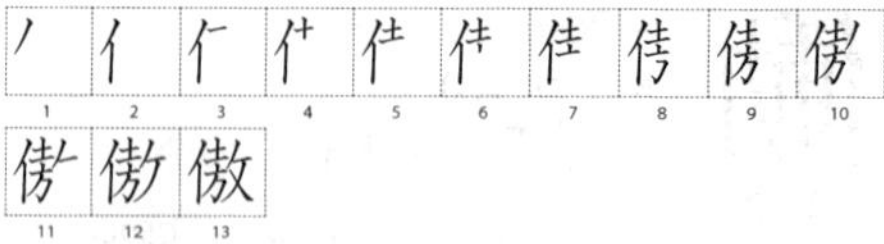

【亻】 阝 刂 九

COMPOUNDS

● **ARROGANT, proud, haughty**

傲慢な ごうまんな arrogant, haughty, insolent
傲然と ごうぜんと arrogantly, haughtily
傲岸な ごうがんな arrogant, haughty
倨×傲 きょごう arrogance, pride
驕×傲 きょうごう arrogance, pride

KUN

【おごる　傲る】 be **ARROGANT**, be proud, be haughty

SYNONYMS

● **boasting and arrogance**

誇 BOAST → 1921
慢 ARROGANT → 0844
傲 ARROGANT → 0173

傾

▸INCLINE

ケイ　かたむ(く)　かたむ(ける)　かし(げる)▲

Ⓒ 倾 qīng

0174

◧ 1-2-11

9	Jōyō	U50BE
亻	S13-2-11	F1019

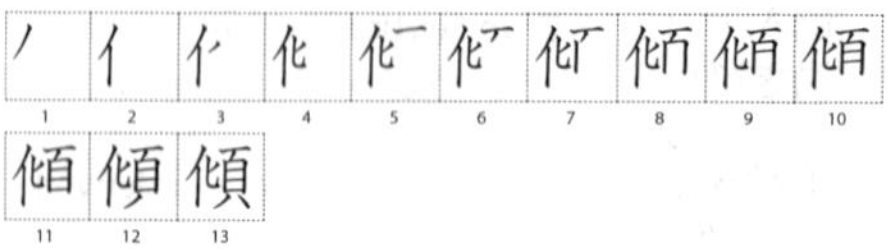

COMPOUNDS

❶ⓐ [original meaning] **INCLINE, lean, tilt, slant**
ⓑ inclination, tilt

a 傾斜する けいしゃする incline, slant, tilt
傾度 けいど inclination
傾角 けいかく (angle of) inclination
b 前傾 ぜんけい forward inclination [tilt]

❷ⓐ **INCLINE toward, be inclined to, tend to, lean to**
ⓑ (trend toward) inclination, tendency

a 傾向 けいこう tendency, trend; disposition
ab 左傾 さけい tendency [inclination] to the left
右傾する うけいする lean to the right

❸ devote oneself to, concentrate on

傾倒する けいとうする devote oneself to, set one's mind toward; admire
傾聴 けいちょう listening closely
傾注 けいちゅう devotion, concentration

❹ topple, bring down, cause the downfall of

傾城 けいせい courtesan, harlot; beautiful woman
傾国 けいこく beautiful woman; courtesan

KUN

【かたむく　傾く】 *vi* **INCLINE, lean, tilt, slant; incline toward, be inclined to, tend to; decline, be sinking; decline, fall**

傾き かたむき inclination, slope; tendency, trend
傾いた家運 かたむいたかうん fortunes on the wane [decline]
悪に傾く あくにかたむく be inclined to evil
日が西に傾く ひがにしにかたむく The sun declines westward

【かたむける　傾ける】 *vt* **INCLINE, lean, tilt, slant; devote oneself to, concentrate on; ruin, squander**

首を傾ける くびをかたむける incline one's head
愛情を傾ける あいじょうをかたむける fix one's affection on
身代を傾ける しんだいをかたむける squander one's fortunes

【かしげる　傾げる】 *vt* **INCLINE, lean, tilt**

首を傾げる くびをかしげる put one's head on one side

SYNONYMS

❶ⓐ **obliqueness and inclining**

斜 OBLIQUE → 1878
傾 INCLINE → 0174

❷ⓐ **inclining toward**

偏 ONE-SIDED → 0151
傾 incline toward → 0174

ⓑ **tendency**

向 tendency → 3790
性 NATURE → 0357
勢 trend → 3542
傾 inclination → 0174
潮 TIDE → 0916
流 CURRENT → 0529

❸ **concentrate on**

注 CONCENTRATE → 0383
傾 devote oneself to → 0174

COMPOUND FORMATION

【傾国　けいこく】

傾国 'beautiful woman; courtesan' derives from an ancient Chinese legend of a beautiful siren that brought on the downfall (傾 ❹) of a nation (国) with her voluptuous charms.

傑

▸OUTSTANDING PERSON

ケツ　㊔ すぐる　たかし　ひで

Ⓝ 傑 Ⓒ 杰 jié

0175

◧ 1-2-11

9	Jōyō	U5091
亻	S13-2-11	F1810

丿 亻 亻 亻 亻 亻 亻 亻 亻 傑 傑 傑 傑

1 2 3 4 5 6 7 8 9 10 11 12 13

COMPOUNDS

❶ [original meaning] **OUTSTANDING PERSON, hero, great man, master**

傑物 けつぶつ great man, outstanding figure
豪傑 ごうけつ hero, great [extraordinary] man
女傑 じょけつ heroine, lady of character
怪傑 かいけつ man of extraordinary talent, wonder man
英傑 えいけつ great man, hero, master mind

❷ **outstanding, remarkable, extraordinary**

傑作 けっさく masterpiece, magnum opus; blunder
傑出する けっしゅつする excel, stand out
傑人 けつじん outstanding person

SYNONYMS

❶ **great persons**

豪 GREAT MAN →2657
傑 OUTSTANDING PERSON →0175
雄 hero →1271
匠 CRAFTSMAN →3711
聖 great master →3509

❷ **conspicuous**

著 CONSPICUOUS →2869
顕 MANIFEST →2274
卓 PROMINENT →2561
傑 outstanding →0175

❷ **excellent and superior**

優 SUPERIOR →0200
絶 without match →1711
卓 PROMINENT →2561
快 splendid →0289
妙 MARVELOUS →0280
秀 EXCELLENT →3152
英 DISTINGUISHED →2782
尤 outstanding →3755
傑 outstanding →0175
穎 TALENTED →2036
逸 exceptional →3872
名 first-rate →2693
上 of upper grade →4212

僅

0176

1-2-11

▶**A LITTLE**

キン わず(か) ㊔ よし

Ⓝ 僅 Ⓒ 仅 jǐn jìn

9	Jōyō	U50C5
亻	S13-2-11	F2245

丿 亻 亻 亻 亻 亻 亻 亻 亻 亻 僅 僅 僅

1 2 3 4 5 6 7 8 9 10 11 12 13

COMPOUNDS

ⓐ **A LITTLE, a few**
ⓑ **slight, marginal**
ⓒ **only, merely**

a 僅少 きんしょう a few, a little, trifling
b 僅差 きんさ narrow [slim] margin
c 僅僅 きんきん merely, no more than

KUN

【わずか 僅か】

ⓐ **A LITTLE, a few**
ⓑ **slight, marginal**
ⓒ **only, merely**

c 人生僅か五十年 じんせいわずかごじゅうねん Life is short

SYNONYMS

ⓐ **few**

少 LITTLE →4278
寡 FEW →2957
乏 SCANTY →2432
薄 meager →3004
微 SLIGHT →0788
寸 A BIT OF →3652
僅 A LITTLE →0176
些 A BIT →3251

債

0177

1-2-11

▶**DEBT**
▶**BOND**
サイ

Ⓒ 债 zhài

9	Jōyō	U50B5
亻	S13-2-11	F1132

丿 亻 亻 亻 亻 亻 亻 亻 亻 亻 債 債 債

1 2 3 4 5 6 7 8 9 10 11 12 13

COMPOUNDS

❶ **DEBT, liability**

債権 さいけん credit, claim
債務 さいむ debt, obligation, liabilities
負債 ふさい debt, liabilities
減債 げんさい partial payment of a debt

❷ [also suffix] **BOND, debenture, loan**

債券 さいけん bond, debenture
社債 しゃさい debenture, corporation bond
国債 こくさい national bonds; national debt [loan]
起債 きさい flotation of a loan, issue of bonds

公債 こうさい public bond; public loan

SYNONYMS

❶ **lend and borrow**

借 BORROW → 0137
債 DEBT → 0177
貸 LEND → 3213
融 finance → 2303

❷ **securities**

株 STOCK → 1172
債 BOND → 0177

催

0178

1-2-11

▶**HOLD AN EVENT**
▶**PRESS FOR**

サイ もよお(す)

Ⓒ 催 cuī

9	Jōyō	U50AC
亻	S13-2-11	F1098

COMPOUNDS

❶ **HOLD AN EVENT [a meeting], give (a dinner), sponsor**

催事場 さいじじょう event hall
開催する かいさいする hold an event, open (an exhibition)
共催 きょうさい joint auspices, cosponsorship
主催 しゅさい sponsorship, promotion

❷ⓐ **PRESS FOR, urge, hasten**
ⓑ excite, stimulate, arouse, induce

a 催促する さいそくする press for, urge, demand
催告 さいこく notification, demand
b 催涙弾 さいるいだん tear-gas bomb
催眠 さいみん hypnotism
催淫剤 さいいんざい aphrodisiac

KUN

【もよおす 催す】**HOLD AN EVENT [a meeting], give (a dinner), put on (a show); feel like**

催し もよおし event, festivities, function, gathering; auspices; opening, holding (a meeting)
会を催す かいをもよおす hold a meeting
涙を催す なみだをもよおす be moved to tears

SYNONYMS

❶ **hold an event**

催 HOLD AN EVENT → 0178
挙 hold a function → 3106

❷ⓐ **urge**

勧 URGE → 2334
催 PRESS FOR → 0178
促 HASTEN → 0118
誘 INDUCE → 1952
励 ENCOURAGE → 1438
侑 URGE TO EAT → 0101

傷

0179

1-2-11

▶**WOUND**

ショウ きず いた(む) いた(める)

Ⓒ 伤 shāng

9	Jōyō-6	U50B7
亻	S13-2-11	F0828

COMPOUNDS

❶ⓐ [also suffix] **WOUND, injury, bruise, scar**
ⓑ **WOUND, injure, hurt; damage**

a 傷病 しょうびょう injuries and sickness
負傷する ふしょうする be injured [wounded], get hurt
重傷 じゅうしょう heavy [serious] wound, severe injury
打撲傷 だぼくしょう bruise, contusion
b 傷害 しょうがい injury, bodily harm
殺傷 さっしょう killing and wounding
損傷 そんしょう damage, injury

❷ be grieved at heart, be **WOUND**ed, be pained

傷心 しょうしん heartbreak, grief
感傷 かんしょう sentiment, sentimentality
愁傷 しゅうしょう grief, lamentation, condolence

❸ **slander, abuse**

中傷 ちゅうしょう slander, libel

KUN

【きず 傷】

① **WOUND, injury, bruise, scar**

傷口 きずぐち wound
傷跡(=傷痕) きずあと scar, cicatrix
傷付ける きずつける wound, injure, damage; hurt (a person's feelings), disgrace (one's family name)
傷付く きずつく get injured, be wounded [bruised]; be (emotionally) hurt
掠り傷 かすりきず scratch, graze, slight wound
古傷 ふるきず old wound, scar; past misdeed

② [formerly also 疵] **defect, flaw, crack, fault, weak point**

傷物 きずもの defective article; deflowered girl

【いたむ 傷む】

① **be damaged, be spoiled, wear out**

傷み いたみ damage, injury, bruise; wear; rot
傷んだ家 いたんだいえ damaged house

② **rot, spoil**
傷んだトマト いたんだとまと rotten tomatoes
【いためる 傷める】**damage, spoil**
花を傷める はなをいためる spoil a flower

SPECIAL READINGS
火傷▲ やけど(=かしょう) burn

SYNONYMS
❶ⓐ injury
傷 WOUND → 0179
創 wound (cut) → 2283
-擦れ sore → 0971
ⓑ harm and damage
害 HARM, damage → 2826
損 damage → 0801
傷 WOUND → 0179
❷ grieve
慨 DEPLORE → 0790
嘆 SIGH → 0773
悼 MOURN → 0587
傷 grieve → 0179
悲 feel sad → 3448
悄 BECOME DISPIRITED → 0506

USAGE
【きず】
傷
① wound, injury, bruise, scar
② [formerly also 疵] defect, flaw, crack, fault, weak point
疵
[now usu. 傷] defect, flaw, crack, fault, weak point

HOMOPHONES
きず 疵 DEFECT → 4067
いたむ
痛 PAIN → 4071
悼 MOURN → 0587
いためる 痛 PAIN → 4071

NOTE
➡ see also USAGE note at 痛 4071

僧 0180

◧ 1-2-11

▶**BONZE**
ソウ
Ⓝ 僧 Ⓒ 僧 sēng

9	Jōyō	U50E7
亻	S13-2-11	F1134

Stroke order: 1–13

COMPOUNDS
ⓐ [also suffix] [original meaning] **BONZE, Buddhist monk, priest**
ⓑ [original meaning] *saṃgha*, Buddhist order or community
a 僧侶 そうりょ bonze, Buddhist priest
僧職 そうしょく priesthood
僧院 そういん monastery, temple
禅僧 ぜんそう Zen priest [monk]
尼僧 にそう nun, sister; (Buddhist) priestess
小僧 こぞう priestling; servant boy; kid, brat
破戒僧 はかいそう sinful priest, depraved monk
b 僧伽 そうぎゃ *saṃgha*

INDEPENDENT
【そう 僧】monk, priest, **BONZE**
僧になる そうになる become a monk

SYNONYMS
ⓐ clergymen
僧 BONZE → 0180
坊 Buddhist priest → 0274
尼 BUDDHIST NUN → 3767
父 FATHER → 2467

傭 0181

◧ 1-2-11

▶**HIRE**
ヨウ やと(う)
Ⓒ 佣 yòng

9	Names	U50AD
亻	S13-2-11	F2772

COMPOUNDS
ⓐ [now usu. 用 3694] **HIRE, employ**
ⓑ HIRE (as a boat), charter
a 傭兵 ようへい mercenary soldier, hireling
傭人 ようにん employee
雇傭する こようする employ, hire
被傭者 ひようしゃ employee
b 傭船 ようせん chartered ship

KUN
【やとう 傭う】[now usu. 雇う]
ⓐ **HIRE, employ**
ⓑ **HIRE (as a boat), charter**
a 傭い やとい employee; employment
傭 やとい government employee

SYNONYMS
ⓐ employ
雇 EMPLOY → 2454
用 EMPLOY → 3694
使う employ → 0100
傭 HIRE → 0181
役 press into service → 0288

HOMOPHONES

やとう 雇 EMPLOY → 2454
やとい 雇 EMPLOY → 2454

NOTE

➡ see USAGE note at 雇 2454
★ do not confuse with 庸 MEDIOCRE → 3881

傳

0182
1-2-11

▶TRANSMIT
デン つた(わる) つた(える) つた(う) -づた(い) つて ㊔ つとむ ただ

9	Names	U50B3
亻	S13-2-11	F0000

traditional form → see 伝 at 0048

際障 etc.

1-2-11

incorrect stroke-count
➡ see 1-3-11: 阝 at 0873

臨

0183
1-2-11

▶BE PRESENT AT
リン のぞ(む)

30	Nonstandard	U81E8
口	S13-3-10	F0000

handwritten form → see 臨 at 2059

鳩

0184
1-2-11

▶PIGEON
キュウ はと ㊔ やす おさむ
Ⓒ 鸠 jiū

196	Names	U9CE9
鳥	S13-11-2	F2143

COMPOUNDS

❶ **PIGEON, dove, carrier pigeon**
鳩舎 きゅうしゃ pigeon house
鳩信 きゅうしん communication by carrier pigeon
❷ huddle like **PIGEON**s, herd together
鳩首する きゅうしゅする go into a huddle

KUN

【はと 鳩】 [also suffix] **PIGEON, dove**
鳩派 はとは doves, soft-liners
伝書鳩 でんしょばと carrier [homing] pigeon

SYNONYMS

❶ **birds**
鷹 HAWK → 3955
鷗 GULL → 2370
烏 CROW → 4088
雀 SPARROW → 3117
燕 SWALLOW → 3142
鴻 LARGE WILD BIRD → 0977
鳳 MALE PHOENIX → 3749
凰 FEMALE PHOENIX → 3738
鵬 MYTHICAL HUGE BIRD → 1416
鶏 CHICKEN → 2221
酉 ROOSTER → 4358
隼 FALCON → 3427
鳩 PIGEON → 0184
鷲 EAGLE → 3598
鳶 BLACK KITE → 3919
鶴 CRANE → 2326
鷺 HERON → 3621
鵜 CORMORANT → 2067
鴨 DUCK → 1582
雁 WILD GOOSE → 3741

僕

0185
1-2-12

▶I
▶MANSERVANT
ボク しもべ▲
Ⓒ 仆 pú pū

9	Jōyō	U50D5
亻	S14-2-12	F0454

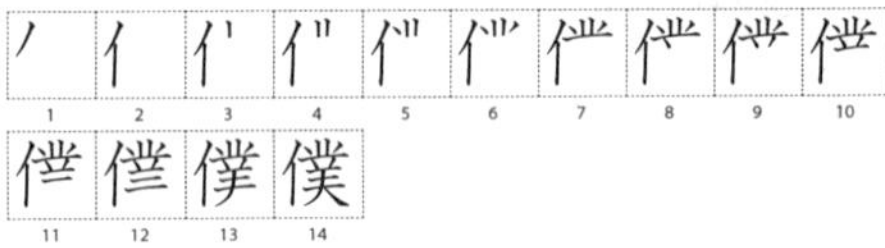

COMPOUNDS

❶ **I, myself**—familiar first person pronoun used by men in addressing inferiors or peers
僕達 ぼくたち we
❷ [original meaning] **MANSERVANT, servant, menial**
忠僕 ちゅうぼく faithful servant
従僕 じゅうぼく servant, attendant
家僕 かぼく manservant, house boy
下僕 げぼく servant, your humble servant
公僕 こうぼく public servant

INDEPENDENT

【ぼく 僕】 I (→❶)
僕の ぼくの my

KUN

【しもべ 僕】 **MANSERVANT**, servant
忠実な僕 ちゅうじつなしもべ faithful servant

SYNONYMS

❶ **first person pronouns**
私 I (*polite*) → 1432
我 SELF → 4362
己 ONESELF → 4188
身 ONE'S PERSON → 4368
僕 I (*familiar*) → 0185
俺 I (*intimate*) → 0124
吾 I (*elegant*) → 3060
予 I (*pompous*) → 2477
余 I (*pompous*) → 2535
麿 I (*archaic*) → 3949
朕 IMPERIAL WE → 1185

自 SELF →4338

❷ **servants**

僕 MANSERVANT →0185
奴 SLAVE →0217
隷 UNDERLING →2201
臣 RETAINER →3806
従 follower →0498
供 attendant →0098

NOTE

★ do not confuse with 撲 DEAL A BLOW →0903

僚

▶COLLEAGUE

リョウ ㊔ あきら

Ⓒ 僚 liáo

0186

◧ 1-2-12

9	Jōyō	U50DA
亻	S14-2-12	F1222

COMPOUNDS

❶ [original meaning] **COLLEAGUE, associate, co-worker, companion**

僚友 りょうゆう comrade, colleague, fellow worker
僚機 りょうき consort plane
同僚 どうりょう colleague, associate, comrade, fellow official

❷ **official**

閣僚 かくりょう cabinet members
官僚 かんりょう government official(s); bureaucracy, officialdom
幕僚 ばくりょう staff, staff officer

SYNONYMS

❶ **friends and associates**

僚 COLLEAGUE →0186
輩 FELLOW →3482
朋 COMRADE →1092
友 FRIEND →3670
侶 COMPANION →0114

❷ **officials**

官 GOVERNMENT OFFICIAL →2766
吏 OFFICIAL →4351
僚 official →0186
司 officiator →3648
役 executive →0288
事 officer →4384

像

▶IMAGE

ゾウ ㊔ かた

Ⓒ 像 xiàng

0187

◧ 1-2-12

9	Jōyō-5	U50CF
亻	S14-2-12	F0431

COMPOUNDS

❶ⓐ **optical IMAGE**

ⓑ [also suffix] **mental IMAGE, image**

ⓒ *math* **IMAGE**

a 影像 えいぞう image; shadow, phantom
映像 えいぞう (TV) picture, image; reflection
画像 がぞう portrait, likeness
現像する げんぞうする develop (film)
実像 じつぞう real image
虚像 きょぞう virtual image

b 心像 しんぞう mental image
想像する そうぞうする imagine
日本人の外人像 にほんじんのがいじんぞう the Japanese image of foreigners

c 鏡像 きょうぞう reflected image; *math* image by inversion

❷ [also suffix] (sculptured or painted likeness) **IMAGE, likeness, figure, statue; picture, portrait**

仏像 ぶつぞう image of Buddha; Buddhist statue
肖像 しょうぞう portrait, likeness
マリア像 まりあぞう image of the Virgin Mary
銅像 どうぞう bronze statue [image]
自画像 じがぞう self-portrait

INDEPENDENT

【ぞう 像】**IMAGE**, statue; optical image; *math* image
自由の女神の像 じゆうのめがみのぞう Statue of Liberty

SYNONYMS

❶ⓐ **image**

像 IMAGE →0187
影 SHADOW →2381

❷ **images**

像 IMAGE →0187
仏 Buddhist image →0020
偶 figure →0150

USAGE

【ぞう 像 象】

★像 is easily confused with 象, to which it is similar in shape, sound and meaning. 像, always read ぞう, has the core meaning IMAGE, i.e., a reduplication of appearance such as an optical image or a sculptured likeness. 象 refers to the outer appearance or manifestation of a thing, i.e., 'phenomenon', in which sense it is always read しょう. In the sense of elephant, 象 is always read ぞう. Both characters share the meaning 'mental image', as in the 心像 しんぞう 'mental image' and 心象 しんしょう 'image, mental picture'.

【亻】 阝

僞 0188

▶FALSIFY
ギ いつわ(る) にせ

9	Names	U50DE
亻	S14-2-12	F0000

1-2-12 traditional form → see 偽 at 0149

僱 0189

▶EMPLOY
コ やと(う)

9	Nonstandard	U50F1
亻	S14-2-4	F0000

1-2-12 traditional form → see 雇 at 2454

僧 0190

▶BONZE
ソウ

9	Names	UFA31
亻	S14-2-12	F0000

1-2-12 traditional form → see 僧 at 0180

隣

1-2-12 incorrect stroke-count
➡ see 1-3-12: 阝 at 0929

儀 0191

▶CEREMONY
ギ ㊔ よし のり
Ⓒ 仪 yí

9	Jōyō	U5100
亻	S15-2-13	F0953

1-2-13

ノ 亻 亻' 亻" 亻ᐟ 亻ᐟ 亻ᐟ 亻ᐟ 亻ᐟ 亻ᐟ 亻ᐟ 亻ᐟ 儀 儀 儀 (stroke order 1–15)

COMPOUNDS

❶ⓐ CEREMONY, rite, ritual
ⓑ [original meaning] (polite behavior) **CEREMONY**
a 儀式 ぎしき ceremony, rite, ritual
婚儀 こんぎ wedding ceremony
葬儀 そうぎ funeral service [rites]
b 儀礼 ぎれい etiquette, courtesy
礼儀 れいぎ etiquette, courtesy, propriety, manners
行儀 ぎょうぎ manners, behavior

❷ⓐ [suffix] (miniature representation) **model, globe**
ⓑ (example to be followed) model, paragon
a 地球儀 ちきゅうぎ globe (of the world)
b 儀典 ぎてん formality, (diplomatic) rite
律儀 りちぎ honesty, faithfulness, loyalty

❸ [suffix] measuring instrument, apparatus (esp. for astronomical applications)
経緯儀 けいいぎ theodolite
水準儀 すいじゅんぎ leveling instrument, surveyor's level

❹ⓐ affair, matter, case
ⓑ [suffix] as for
a 余儀 よぎ another method; another problem
難儀 なんぎ hardship, trouble
b 私儀 わたくしぎ as for me, I

INDEPENDENT

【ぎ 儀】 CEREMONY; affair, matter, case
婚礼の儀 こんれいのぎ wedding ceremony
其の儀に就いて そのぎについて about the matter

SYNONYMS

❶ⓐ **ceremonies and festivities**
式 CEREMONY → 3785
儀 CEREMONY → 0191
典 formal ceremony → 3253
礼 RITE → 1012
斎 religious ritual → 2622
会 Buddhist ceremony → 2512
祭 FESTIVAL → 3311
ⓑ **etiquette**
礼 ETIQUETTE → 1012
儀 CEREMONY → 0191

❷ⓐ **prototype**
型 TYPE → 3266
儀 model → 0191

❸ **machines and tools**
機 MACHINE → 1365
械 MECHANICAL CONTRIVANCE → 1203
具 IMPLEMENT → 3159
器 INSTRUMENT → 3367
儀 measuring instrument → 0191
鏡 OPTICAL INSTRUMENT → 2219
董 OLD TOOL → 2911

❹ⓐ **affair**
事 AFFAIR → 4384
儀 affair → 0191
件 MATTER → 0054

億 0192

▶HUNDRED MILLION
オク ㊔ やす
Ⓒ 亿 yì

9	Jōyō-4	U5104
亻	S15-2-13	F0824

1-2-13

丿 亻 亻 亻 亻 亻 亻 亻 倍 倍 倍 倍 億 億 億
1 2 3 4 5 6 7 8 9 10 11 12 13 14 15

COMPOUNDS

❶ **HUNDRED MILLION (10^8)**

億万長者 おくまんちょうじゃ billionaire

一億 いちおく 100,000,000

❷ multitude, astronomical figure

億兆 おくちょう multitude; [archaic] the people, the masses

巨億 きょおく millions, vast fortune

INDEPENDENT

【おく 億】**HUNDRED MILLION (10^8)**

SYNONYMS

❶ **large numbers**

百 HUNDRED → 2519

千 THOUSAND → 4219

万 TEN THOUSAND → 3653

億 HUNDRED MILLION → 0192

兆 TRILLION → 0264

京 ten quadrillion → 2546

NOTE

➡ see COMPOUND FORMATION for 億劫 おっくう, おっこう → 劫 1435

價

0193

◧ 1-2-13

▶**PRICE**
▶**VALUE**

カ あたい

9	Names	U50F9
亻	S15-2-13	F0000

traditional form → see 価 at 0095

儉

0194

◧ 1-2-13

▶**FRUGAL**

ケン つま(しい)

9	Names	U5109
亻	S15-2-13	F0000

traditional form → see 倹 at 0130

凜

0195

◧ 1-2-13

▶**SEVERELY COLD**

リン

Ⓝ 凛 Ⓒ 凛 lǐn

15	Names	U51DC
冫	S15-2-13	F2664

COMPOUNDS

❶ **SEVERELY COLD**

凜冽×たる りんれつたる piercing cold

❷ **gallant; brave**

凜凜しい りりしい gallant, brave, manly, dignified

勇気凜凜 ゆうきりんりん full of spirit, in high spirit

❸ [archaic] awe-inspiring, fearful

INDEPENDENT

【りんたる 凜たる】brave, gallant

SYNONYMS

❶ **cold**

冷 COLD → 0088

寒 COLD (weather) → 2894

涼 COOL → 0633

凜 SEVERELY COLD → 0195

❷ **brave**

勇 BRAVE → 2592

俠 chivalrous → 0110

赳 VALIANT → 4100

驍 VALIANT → 2327

敢 bold → 2142

豪 bold and unrestrained → 2657

雄 HEROIC → 1271

壮 heroic → 0263

義 chivalrous → 2948

凜 gallant → 0195

凛

0196

◧ 1-2-13

▶**SEVERELY COLD**

リン

15	Names	U51DB
冫	S15-2-13	F0000

traditional form → see 凜 at 0195

隣險 etc. incorrect stroke-count
➡ see ◧1-3-13: 阝 at 0961

◧ 1-2-13

儒

0197

◧ 1-2-14

▶**CONFUCIANISM**

ジュ

Ⓒ 儒 rú

9	Jōyō	U5112
亻	S16-2-14	F2025

丿 亻 亻 亻 亻 亻 亻 亻 亻 亻 亻 亻 亻 儒 儒 儒
1 2 3 4 5 6 7 8 9 10 11 12 13 14 15 16

COMPOUNDS

❶ⓐ **CONFUCIANISM**
ⓑ Confucian, Confucianist, Confucian scholar

a 儒教 じゅきょう Confucianism

儒仏 じゅぶつ Confucianism and Buddhism

b 儒者 じゅしゃ Confucianist

❷ learned scholars

大儒 だいじゅ great scholar

❸ dwarf

侏×儒 しゅじゅ dwarf

INDEPENDENT

【じゅ 儒】Confucianist; **CONFUCIANISM**

SYNONYMS

❶ⓐ religions and sects
- 仏 Buddhism → 0020
- 法 Buddha's teachings → 0391
- 禅 ZEN → 1306
- 儒 CONFUCIANISM → 0197
- 道 Taoism → 3888

凝

▶CONGEAL

ギョウ こ(る) こ(らす)

Ⓒ 凝 níng

0198

◧ 1-2-14

15	Jōyō	U51DD
冫	S16-2-14	F1505

COMPOUNDS

❶ CONGEAL, coagulate, solidify
- 凝結する ぎょうけつする congeal, coagulate, solidify
- 凝固する ぎょうこする solidify, coagulate, congeal
- 凝着 ぎょうちゃく adhesion
- 凝血 ぎょうけつ blood clot
- 凝脂 ぎょうし solidified oil
- 凝乳 ぎょうにゅう curd, curdled milk
- 凝縮 ぎょうしゅく condensation

❷ with fixed attention, with concentration
- 凝視 ぎょうし stare, steady gaze
- 凝議 ぎょうぎ (earnest) deliberation, consultation

KUN

【こる 凝る】*vi* **grow stiff; be absorbed in, be crazy for; be elaborate**
- 凝り こり stiffness (in the shoulders)
- 凝り性 こりしょう fastidiousness, perfectionism
- 凝った装飾 こったそうしょく elaborate ornaments
- 凝り固まる こりかたまる be fanatical; coagulate, clot
- 肩が凝る かたがこる feel stiff in the shoulders

【こらす 凝らす】*vt* **concentrate, strain, elaborate; have stiffness (in the shoulders)**
- 瞳を凝らす ひとみをこらす strain one's eyes
- 趣向を凝らす しゅこうをこらす elaborate a plan

SYNONYMS

❶ solidify and coagulate
- 固 solidify → 3830
- 凝 CONGEAL → 0198
- 結 form into a mass → 1706
- 凍 FREEZE → 0146

隱

◧ 1-2-14

incorrect stroke-count
➡ see ◧ 1-3-14: 阝 at 0987

償

▶RECOMPENSE

ショウ つぐな(う)

Ⓒ 偿 cháng

0199

◧ 1-2-15

9	Jōyō	U511F
亻	S17-2-15	F1450

COMPOUNDS

ⓐ [original meaning] (award compensation) **RECOMPENSE, compensate, indemnify, repay**

ⓑ (meet by payment) **RECOMPENSE, pay**

- *a* 償却 しょうきゃく repayment, refundment
- 報償 ほうしょう recompense, compensation
- 補償 ほしょう compensation, indemnity
- 賠償 ばいしょう indemnity, compensation, recompense
- 弁償 べんしょう compensation, indemnification
- 代償 だいしょう vicarious compensation
- *b* 償還 しょうかん repayment, refunding, reimbursement
- 無償 むしょう gratuitous, free

KUN

【つぐなう 償う】**RECOMPENSE, make up for, atone for**
- 償い つぐない recompense, indemnity, atonement
- 損失を償う そんしつをつぐなう recompense for a loss

SYNONYMS

ⓐ compensate
- 償 RECOMPENSE → 0199
- 賠 COMPENSATE → 1991
- 酬 RECIPROCATE → 1941
- 報 REQUITE → 2133

ⓑ pay
- 払う PAY → 0225
- 納 PAY (to the authorities) → 1652
- 済 settle accounts → 0634
- 支 pay out → 2473
- 賦 INSTALLMENT → 1992
- 償 RECOMPENSE → 0199

優 0200

▶SUPERIOR
▶ACTOR

ユウ ウ▲ やさ(しい) すぐ(れる) まさ(る)▲

㊔ まさ すぐる ゆたか

Ⓒ 优 yōu

1-2-15

9	Jōyō-6	U512A
亻	S17-2-15	F0437

COMPOUNDS

❶ⓐ (far above average) **SUPERIOR, excellent, dominant, predominant**
ⓑ *math* **SUPERIOR**, major
ⓒ (school mark) Excellent, A

a 優秀な ゆうしゅうな excellent, superior, best
優良品 ゆうりょうひん excellent articles
優等生 ゆうとうせい honor student, prize pupil
優越 ゆうえつ superiority, supremacy
優越感 ゆうえつかん superiority complex
優勝する ゆうしょうする win the victory [championship]
優先 ゆうせん preference, priority
優勢 ゆうせい superiority, lead, predominance
優性形質 ゆうせいけいしつ dominant character
b 優弧 ゆうこ superior [major] arc
c 全優の学生 ぜんゆうのがくせい straight A student

❷ **ACTOR, actress, performer**
俳優 はいゆう actor, actress
女優 じょゆう actress
名優 めいゆう great actor
声優 せいゆう radio actor; dialogue speaker (in dubbing)

❸ **kindly, gracious, gentle, kind, cordial**
優遇 ゆうぐう favorable treatment, warm reception
優待する ゆうたいする treat kindly, receive hospitably, give special consideration

❹ graceful, elegant, delicate
優美な ゆうびな graceful, elegant, refined
優雅 ゆうが elegance, grace
優艶な ゆうえんな beautiful, charming

❺ slowly, leisurely
優柔不断 ゆうじゅうふだん indecisiveness, vacillation

❻ used phonetically for *u*, esp. in the transliteration of Sanskrit Buddhist terms
優曇華 うどんげ *Udumbara*, name of a legendary tree which is thought to blossom once in 3000 years

INDEPENDENT

【ゆう 優】**SUPERIOR**ity; (school mark) Excellent, A
【ゆうに 優に】well, sufficiently, amply, fully; in a graceful manner
優に三時間は掛かる ゆうにさんじかんはかかる It takes a good three hours

KUN

【やさしい 優しい】
①ⓐ **gentle, tender, sweet**
ⓑ **kindhearted, kind**
a 優男 やさおとこ man of gentle manners
優しい声 やさしいこえ soft voice
b 優しくする やさしくする be kind to, treat kindly
② graceful, delicate

【すぐれる 優れる】[formerly also 勝れる]
① **be SUPERIOR to, be excellent, be better than, surpass**
優れて すぐれて exceedingly, conspicuously, by far
優れた学者 すぐれたがくしゃ eminent scholar
② [usu. in negative constructions] **be fine, feel well**
気分が優れない きぶんがすぐれない not feel well

【まさる 優る】[usu. 勝る] **excel, be better than, surpass**
優るとも劣らない まさるともおとらない not at all inferior to

SYNONYMS

❶ⓐ **excellent and superior**
優 SUPERIOR → 0200
絶 without match → 1711
卓 PROMINENT → 2561
快 splendid → 0289
妙 MARVELOUS → 0280
秀 EXCELLENT → 3152
英 DISTINGUISHED → 2782
尤 outstanding → 3755
傑 outstanding → 0175
穎 TALENTED → 2036
逸 exceptional → 3872
名 first-rate → 2693
上 of upper grade → 4212

❷ **performers**
優 ACTOR → 0200
俳 actor → 0126
伶 MUSICIAN → 0075
伎 PERFORMER → 0055

❸ **kind**
厚 KIND → 3726
篤 cordial → 3371
懇 cordial → 3606
慈 AFFECTIONATE → 2949
温 warmhearted → 0740

渥 GRACIOUS →0731
優 kindly →0200

❹ **elegant**
雅 ELEGANT →1532
淑 GRACEFUL →0639
優 graceful →0200
粋 REFINED →1645
彬 REFINED AND GENTLE →1201

【やさしい】
①ⓐ **gentle**
優しい gentle →0200
穏 MILD →1578
柔 SOFT →2591

USAGE

❶【やさしい】
優しい
①ⓐ gentle, tender, sweet
ⓑ kindhearted, kind
② graceful, delicate
易しい
easy, simple

❷【すぐれる】
優れる
[formerly also 勝れる]
① be superior to, be excellent, be better than, surpass
② [usu. in negative constructions] be fine, feel well
勝れる
[now usu. 優れる] same as 優れる

HOMOPHONES

やさしい 易 EASY →3064
すぐれる 勝 WIN →1268
まさる 勝 WIN →1268

NOTE

➡ see also USAGE note at 勝 1268

儲

▶PROFIT
チョ もう(ける) もう(かる) ㊔ そえ

0201
1-2-15

9	Nonstandard	U5132
亻	S17-2-15	F0000

traditional form →see 儲 at 0202

儲

▶PROFIT
チョ もう(ける) もう(かる) ㊔ そえ
Ⓝ 儲 Ⓒ 储 chǔ

0202
1-2-16

9	Names	U5132
亻	S18-2-16	F1727

COMPOUNDS

❶ store up, accumulate, amass, lay aside
儲蓄(=貯蓄)する ちょちくする save (money), lay aside

❷ [original meaning] heir
儲位 ちょい heirship

KUN

【もうける 儲ける】
① **PROFIT, make a profit, gain, earn**
儲け もうけ profit, earnings
儲け話 もうけばなし get-rich-quick scheme, money-making scheme
儲け物 もうけもの good bargain, unexpected profit, windfall, godsend
金儲け かねもうけ making money
丸儲け まるもうけ clear profit
ぼろ儲け ぼろもうけ easy profit, easy money
② have [bear, beget] (a child)

【もうかる 儲かる】 **be PROFITable, yield a profit**
風が吹けば桶屋が儲かる かぜがふけばおけやがもうかる Any event can have unexpected consequences

SYNONYMS

【もうける】
① **profit**
利 PROFIT →1431
益 PROFIT →2849
儲ける PROFIT →0202
得 GAIN →0577

儼

▶SOLEMN
ゲン

0203
1-2-17

9	Nonstandard	U2044A
亻	S19-2-17	F0000

traditional form →see 儼 at 0204

儼

▶SOLEMN
ゲン
Ⓝ 儼 Ⓒ 俨 yǎn

0204
1-2-20

9	Non-Jōyō	U513C
亻	S22-2-20	F0000

COMPOUNDS

● [now replaced by 厳 4079] **SOLEMN, majestic, dignified-looking**
儼然たる げんぜんたる solemn, grave, majestic, stern

INDEPENDENT

【げん 儼(=厳)】 severeness, strictness, rigor
儼として げんとして strictly

SYNONYMS

● **dignified**
荘 DIGNIFIED →2814
威 dignified →4394
儼 SOLEMN →0204
厳 solemn →4079

粛 solemnly → 4400

孔

▶OPEN HOLE

コウ ク▲ あな▲ ㊔よし く とおる

Ⓒ 孔 kǒng

0205

1-3-1

39	Jōyō	U5B54
子	S4-3-1	F1310

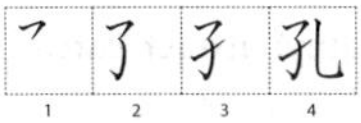

COMPOUNDS

❶ [also suffix] **OPEN or bottomless HOLE, opening, aperture**

鼻孔 びこう nostrils
気孔 きこう pore, stoma
瞳孔 どうこう pupil
穿孔 せんこう perforation, punching; rupture
排水孔 はいすいこう scupper (hole); osculum

❷ Confucius, Confucianism, Confucian

孔子 こうし Confucius
孔門 こうもん Confucian school

❸ peacock

孔雀 くじゃく peacock

INDEPENDENT

【こう 孔】OPEN HOLE

孔を穿つ こうをうがつ pierce a hole

KUN

【あな 孔】[usu. 穴] **OPEN** or bottomless **HOLE**, opening, aperture, perforation

針の孔 はりのあな needle's eye
毛孔 けあな pores (of the skin)

SYNONYMS

❶ **holes and cavities**

穴 HOLE → 2682
洞 CAVE → 0455
窟 CAVE → 2923
窪 HOLLOW → 2962
腔 BODY CAVITY → 1267
孔 OPEN HOLE → 0205
口 MOUTH → 4189
坑 PIT → 0277
堀 DITCH → 0561
溝 CHANNEL → 0810
壕 TRENCH → 0966
濠 MOAT → 0975
凹 concavity → 4294

❷ **Confucius and Confucianists**

孔 Confucius → 0205
子 the Master (Confucius) → 4196
孟 MENCIUS → 2760

HOMOPHONES

あな 穴 HOLE → 2682

NOTE

➡ see USAGE note at 穴 2682

幻

▶PHANTOM

ゲン まぼろし

Ⓒ 幻 huàn

0206

1-3-1

52	Jōyō	U5E7B
幺	S4-3-1	F1338

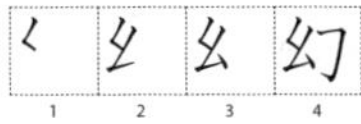

COMPOUNDS

❶ **PHANTOM, phantasm, fantasy, illusion, hallucination, vision**

幻像 げんぞう phantom, vision, illusion
幻肢 げんし phantom limb
幻影 げんえい vision, phantom, illusion
幻想 げんそう fantasy, illusion
幻覚 げんかく illusion, hallucination
幻聴 げんちょう auditory hallucination
幻滅 げんめつ disillusionment
変幻自在の へんげんじざいの ever-changing, phantasmagoric

❷ bewitch, bewilder, create an illusion

幻術 げんじゅつ magic, witchcraft
幻惑 げんわく bewitching, fascination
夢幻 むげん dream; vision; fantasy

KUN

【まぼろし 幻】**PHANTOM, apparition, phantasm; illusion, hallucination, vision, dream**

幻を追う まぼろしをおう pursue phantoms

SYNONYMS

❶ **illusory mental images**

夢 DREAM → 2939
幻 PHANTOM → 0206

❷ **charm**

魅 CHARM → 4131
幻 bewitch → 0206
媚 FAWN UPON → 0687

引

▶DRAW

イン ひ(く) ひ(き) ひ(き)- -び(き) ひ(ける)

Ⓒ 引 yǐn

0207

1-3-1

57	Jōyō-2	U5F15
弓	S4-3-1	F0166

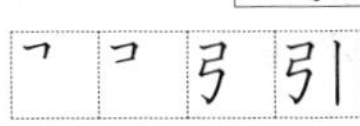

1

弓 幺 【引】

COMPOUNDS

❶ⓐ [original meaning] (pull toward one) **DRAW, pull, haul, tug**
ⓑ (extend in length) **DRAW** out, stretch
a 引力 いんりょく gravitation
引航する いんこうする tug, tow
牽引する けんいんする pull, draw, haul
強引な ごういんな overbearing, coercive
b 延引 えんいん delay, postponement

❷ⓐ (cause to move, as by leading) **DRAW (toward), draw in, call in**
ⓑ **DRAW** a person to act: entice, induce, seduce
ⓒ lead, guide, take along
a 引火する いんかする ignite, catch fire
引見する いんけんする receive, favor (a person) with an interview
我田引水 がでんいんすい seeking one's own interests
吸引 きゅういん suction, absorption, aspiration; attraction
b 誘引 ゆういん enticement, inducement, attraction
c 引率する いんそつする lead, command
引導 いんどう guidance; address to a departed soul
引致 いんち arrest, custody

❸ **quote, cite, refer to**
引用 いんよう quotation, citation
引照 いんしょう reference
引喩 いんゆ allusion
索引 さくいん index

❹ **withdraw, retire**
引退する いんたいする retire, go into retirement

❺ take upon oneself, accept
引責する いんせきする take responsibility upon oneself

❻ introduction, foreword
小引 しょういん brief foreword

KUN

【ひく 引く】

①ⓐ [formerly also 曳く or 牽く] **DRAW, pull, haul, tug;** [formerly also 曳く] **drag, trail**
ⓑ (cause to retreat) **DRAW** in, pull in
a 引 ひく PULL (marking on doors)
引っ張る ひっぱる pull, draw; drag
引き上げる ひきあげる draw [pull] up; promote; increase
引き出す ひきだす draw out; lure out
引き分け ひきわけ draw; drawn game [match]
引き摺る ひきずる drag along; trail
引き止める ひきとめる detain, keep
引き攣る ひきつる have a cramp
引き戻す ひきもどす bring back; pull back; restore
引き締める ひきしめる tighten; brace oneself; cut down
引き締め ひきしめ tightening
弓を引く ゆみをひく draw a bow
船を引く ふねをひく tow a boat
b 手を引く てをひく wash one's hands of; lead by the hand

② [formerly also 惹く]
ⓐ **DRAW (attention or sympathy), attract, catch**
ⓑ **catch (a cold)**
a 引き付ける ひきつける attract, charm, keep at hand; have a convulsive fit
客引き きゃくひき touting; tout, barker, pander
注意を引く ちゅういをひく draw attention
b 風邪を引いている かぜをひいている have a cold

③ⓐ **DRAW (off) (water), tap, conduct, lead (a stream through a field)**
ⓑ **lay on (gas or water), install (a telephone)**
a 川から水を引く かわからみずをひく draw water off a river
b 電話を引く でんわをひく install a telephone

④ **DRAW** (a line or diagram)
図面を引く ずめんをひく draw a plan

⑤ **DRAW lots**
福引き ふくびき lottery
籤引 くじびき drawing of lots

⑥ [also 退く]
ⓐ **retreat, withdraw**
ⓑ **retire, resign**
a 引っ込む ひっこむ draw back, retire; sink, fall in
駆け引き かけひき bargaining; tactics
後へ引く あとへひく retreat, recede
b 役所を引く やくしょをひく leave office, resign one's post in an office

⑦ [also 退く] subside, abate, go down
熱が引いた ねつがひいた The fever has abated

⑧ **subtract, deduct, deduce; allow discount**
引き算 ひきざん subtraction
三引く二は一 さんひくにはいち Three minus two equals one
割引 わりびき discount, reduction

⑨ **quote, cite, refer to**
例を引く れいをひく cite an example

⑩ **look up, consult (a dictionary)**
生き字引 いきじびき walking dictionary

⑪ lay on, apply, oil
油を引く あぶらをひく oil

⑫ **succeed to, take over**
引き継ぐ ひきつぐ take over, hand over; succeed to, inherit
引き継ぎ ひきつぎ taking over (someone's duties)

引き受ける ひきうける undertake; answer for, guarantee
引き取る ひきとる take over, receive; retire
皇室の血を引いている こうしつのちをひいている be descended from the Imperial House

⑬ **lift, steal**
万引き まんびき shoplifting; shoplifter

⑭ **unclassified compounds**
取り引き とりひき transaction, dealings

【ひき 引き】

① [sometimes also 抽-] **DRAWing**
引き出し ひきだし drawer; withdrawal (of money)

② patronage, backing, pull
良い引きが有る よいひきがある have a strong pull

【ひき- 引き-】 [sometimes 引っ ひっ- or 引ん- ひん-] **emphatic verbal prefix**
引き払う ひきはらう clear out, move out
引っ越し ひっこし moving (to a new residence)
引っ繰り返る ひっくりかえる be overturned, fall over; capsize; be reversed
引っ捕らえる ひっとらえる capture, arrest, seize
引っ付く ひっつく stick (to), cling, adhere
引ん剝く ひんむく peel, strip
引き続き ひきつづき continuously, without a break
引っ切り無しに ひっきりなしに incessantly, continually, without a break
引き換えに ひきかえに in exchange for

【-びき -引き】 [also suffix]

① **coated with**
ゴム引きの ごむびきの rubber-coated

② **discount**
一割引き いちわりびき 10% off

【ひける 引ける】 *vi* **close, be over, break up; feel small, become self-conscious**
引け ひけ defeat, reverse; close (esp. of stock market)
引け時 ひけどき closing time (of school)
引け目 ひけめ drawback, weakness
学校が引けてから がっこうがひけてから after school
気が引ける きがひける feel small, become self-conscious

SYNONYMS

❶ⓐ pull
引 DRAW → 0207
曳 DRAW → 4348
牽 DRAW → 2621
惹 DRAW ATTENTION → 2903
抽 DRAW OUT → 0359
抜 PULL OUT → 0290
控える HOLD BACK → 0600
扣える HOLD BACK → 0250
寄せる DRAW NEAR → 2856

❷ⓒ lead and escort
率 LEAD → 2625
引 lead → 0207
導 GUIDE → 3587
連 take along → 3849

❸ quote
引 quote → 0207
挙 cite → 3106

【ひく】

⑧ **subtract**
減 subtract → 0733
引く subtract → 0207
控 HOLD BACK → 0600
扣 HOLD BACK → 0250

USAGE

❶【ひく】

引く
①ⓐ [formerly also 曳く or 牽く] draw, pull, haul, tug; [formerly also 曳く] drag, trail
ⓑ (cause to retreat) draw in, pull in
② [formerly also 惹く]
ⓐ draw (attention or sympathy), attract, catch
ⓑ catch (a cold)
③ⓐ draw (off) (water), tap, conduct, lead (a stream through a field)
ⓑ lay on (gas or water), install (a telephone)
④ draw (a line or diagram)
⑤ draw lots
⑥ [also 退く]
ⓐ retreat, withdraw
ⓑ retire, resign
⑦ [also 退く] subside, abate, go down
⑧ subtract, deduct, deduce; allow discount
⑨ quote, cite, refer to
⑩ look up, consult (a dictionary)
⑪ lay on, apply, oil
⑫ succeed to, take over
⑬ lift, steal
⑭ unclassified compounds

挽く
① grind (meat or coffee)
② saw, cut with a saw

弾く
play on (stringed instruments)

轢く
run over (with a vehicle), knock down

牽く
[now usu. 引く, sometimes also 曳く] draw, pull, haul, tug

惹く
[now usu. 引く]

ⓐ draw (attention or sympathy), attract, catch
ⓑ catch (a cold)

退く
[also 引く]
①ⓐ retreat, withdraw
ⓑ retire, resign
② subside, abate, go down

曳く
[now usu. 引く]
ⓐ [sometimes also 牽く] draw, pull, haul, tug
ⓑ drag, trail

❷【ひき】
引き
① [sometimes also 抽-] drawing
② patronage, backing, pull

抽-
[usu. 引き] drawing

HOMOPHONES

ひく
弾 PROJECTILE →0697
退 RETREAT →3838
惹 DRAW ATTENTION →2903
挽 GRIND →0511
轢 RUN OVER →2095
牽 DRAW →2621
曳 DRAW →4348
ひき 抽 DRAW OUT →0359

NOTE

➡ see also USAGE note at 上 4212
➡ see COMPOUND FORMATION for 駆け引き かけひき →駆 2293

叩

▸KNOCK
コウ たた(く) はた(く)
Ⓒ 叩 kòu

0208
1-3-2

30	Non-Jōyō	U53E9
口	S5-3-2	F1167

COMPOUNDS

❶ **KNOCK, rap, beat, strike, hit**
叩扉する こうひする knock on a door; visit someone
叩解 こうかい beating (of pulp fibers)
叩音 こうおん rap, rapping sound
打叩 だこう tapping

❷ **kowtow, touch one's forehead to the ground**
叩頭 こうとう kowtow, deep bow

KUN

【たたく 叩く】
①ⓐ **KNOCK, rap, beat, strike, hit**
ⓑ **pound (meat)**
a 叩き割る たたきわる smash, break into pieces
叩きのめす たたきのめす knock down, beat up, give a good beating
叩き起こす たたきおこす rouse (someone) out of bed
叩き台 たたきだい springboard [basis] for discussion
肩叩き かたたたき shoulder massage; urging (of an employee) to retire
蝿×叩き はえたたき flyswatter
袋叩きにする ふくろだたきにする gang up on, beat up
手を叩く てをたたく clap one's hands
尻を叩く しりをたたく spank; urge (someone to action), encourage (someone)
b 叩き たたき minced raw fish [meat]
鯵×の叩き あじのたたき minced horse mackerel
② **attack, criticize severely**
③ **drill, discipline, train**
叩き込む たたきこむ drill [drive, hammer] into
叩き上げる たたきあげる to work one's way up (through the ranks)
④ **KNOCK** down [reduce] the price, discount
叩き売り たたきうり sacrifice sale
買い叩く かいたたく beat down the price
⑤ speak idly
陰口を叩く かげぐちをたたく backbite, talk behind someone's back
軽口を叩く かるくちをたたく crack jokes
無駄口を叩く むだぐちをたたく talk idly

【はたく 叩く】
①ⓐ slap, swat, strike
ⓑ dust, beat
a 引っ叩く ひっぱたく slap; spank
b 叩き はたき duster
絨×毯×を叩く じゅうたんをはたく beat (the dust out of) a carpet
② use up (money)
有り金を叩く ありがねをはたく spend all one's money

SYNONYMS

❶ **strike**
打 STRIKE →0224
撲 DEAL A BLOW →0903
殴 BEAT (strike a person) →1099
蹴 KICK →2074
撃 STRIKE →3552
挌 STRIKE (a person) →0448
撞 STRIKE (a ball or bell) →0905
撥ねる strike (knock down) →0907
当てる HIT →2701
叩 KNOCK →0208
拍 BEAT (strike repeatedly) →0361
搏 BEAT (throb) →0794

叶

0209

1-3-2

▸BE FULFILLED

キョウ ギョウ かな(う) かな(える)

㊔ かのう かの やす

Ⓒ 叶 yè xié

30	Names	U53F6
口	S5-3-2	F2166

KUN

【かなう 叶う】

① (of a wish) **BE FULFILLED, be realized, be granted**

叶わない かなわない be unable, be beyond one's power

叶わぬ時の神頼み かなわぬときのかみだのみ Man turns to God in times of trouble

望みが叶う のぞみがかなう have one's wish realized

② **be able to, can (do)**

【かなえる 叶える】**grant (a request), fulfill (expectations), answer (a person's prayer)**

希望を叶える きぼうをかなえる fulfill one's hopes

SYNONYMS

【かなう】

① **accomplish**

達 ATTAIN →3893
遂 ACCOMPLISH →3892
成 ACHIEVE →4352
徹 GO THROUGH →0894
破 carry through with →1478
叶 BE FULFILLED →0209

HOMOPHONES

かなう

適 SUITABLE →3918
敵 ENEMY →2340

NOTE

➡ see USAGE note at 適 3918

叱

0210

1-3-2

▸SCOLD

シツ しか(る)

Ⓝ 叱 Ⓒ 叱 chì

30	Jōyō	U20B9F
口	S5-3-2	F2168

1	2	3	4	5
丨	ㄇ	口	口一	叱

COMPOUNDS

● [original meaning] **SCOLD, reprehend, reproach**

叱咤×する しったする scold, give a scolding; command

叱責する しっせきする reproach, scold, reprove

叱正 しっせい correction (of errors)

KUN

【しかる 叱る】**SCOLD, rebuke, reprove, call down, bawl out**

叱られる しかられる be scolded [reproved]

叱り付ける しかりつける scold away, rebuke strongly, bawl out

SYNONYMS

● **blame and accuse**

責 BLAME →3115
叱 SCOLD →0210
詰 REPRIMAND →1920
難 find fault with →2310
批 CRITICIZE →0294
劾 EXPOSE CRIMES →1618
弾 impeach →0697

叮

0211

1-3-2

▸COURTEOUS

テイ

Ⓒ 叮 丁 dīng

30	Non-Jōyō	U53EE
口	S5-3-2	F0000

COMPOUNDS

● [now replaced by 丁 4155] **COURTEOUS**

叮嚀(=丁寧)な ていねいな polite, courteous

SYNONYMS

● **courteous**

寧 COURTEOUS →2959
鄭 COURTEOUS →2379
叮 COURTEOUS →0211
嚀 COURTEOUS →0965
丁 courteous →4155

叫

0212

1-3-2

▸SHOUT

キョウ さけ(ぶ)

30	Nonstandard	U2F839
口	S5-3-2	F0000

traditional form →see 叫 at 0233

叱

0213

1-3-2

▸SCOLD

シツ しか(る)

30	Nonstandard	U53F1
口	S5-3-2	F0000

traditional form →see 叱 at 0210

切

0214

1-3-2

▸CUT

セツ サイ き(る) -き(る) き(り) -き(り) -ぎ(り) き(れる) -き(れる) き(れ) -き(れ) -ぎ(れ)

18	Nonstandard	U2F850
刀	S5-2-3	F0000

alternative form →see 切 at 0030

1

外

▶OUTSIDE
ガイ ゲ そと ほか はず(す) はず(れる)
と-▲ ㊔ と との

0215 1-3-2

Ⓒ 外 wài

36	Jōyō-2	U5916
夕	S5-3-2	F0097

ノ ク タ 列 外

COMPOUNDS

❶ⓐ (outer side) **OUTSIDE, exterior; out, outer**
ⓑ [also suffix] (beyond the boundary) **OUTSIDE, without, beyond**

a 外部の がいぶの outside, outer, external
外野 がいや outfield; outsiders
外角 がいかく outside corner; external angle
外見 がいけん outward appearance
外科 げか (department of) surgery
外出 がいしゅつ going out, outing
外食する がいしょくする eat out
外気 がいき open [fresh] air
外面 がいめん exterior, outside, surface

b 意外な いがいな unexpected, unforeseen, surprising
郊外 こうがい suburbs, outskirts
案外 あんがい contrary to one's expectations, unexpectedly
以外に いがいに except for, excluding
内外 ないがい inside and outside; approximately
海外 かいがい overseas, abroad
. . . の範囲外に …のはんいがいに beyond the scope of…
予想外の よそうがいの unexpected, unforeseen

❷ⓐ **foreign, external**
ⓑ abbrev. of 外務省 がいむしょう: **Ministry of Foreign Affairs**

a 外国 がいこく foreign country
外人 がいじん foreigner, alien
外車 がいしゃ imported car
外為 がいため foreign exchange
外交 がいこう diplomacy, foreign relations
外務 がいむ foreign affairs
外貨 がいか foreign currency [money]; foreign [imported] goods
外来語 がいらいご loanword, foreign word
在外の ざいがいの overseas

b 外相 がいしょう Minister of Foreign Affairs

❸ **leave out, exclude**
除外する じょがいする exclude, make an exception of
疎外 そがい estrangement, alienation

❹ maternal, mother's
外祖父 がいそふ maternal grandfather
外姓 がいせい mother's family name

❺ unorthodox, unofficial, off-the-record
外道 げどう heresy, paganism, pagan
外史 がいし unofficial history

KUN

【そと 外】 **OUTSIDE, exterior; open air, outdoors**
外側 そとがわ exterior, outside
外回り そとまわり circumference, periphery; outside work; outer track (of a two-way belt line)
外で遊ぶ そとであそぶ play outdoors
家の外 いえのそと outside the house

【ほか 外】
① [also 他] **something other than, the rest**
外の ほかの other, another, different, else
外ならぬ ほかならぬ nothing but, no other than
山田外 やまだほか Yamada and others [et al.]
② some other place, **OUTSIDE**
外で ほかで elsewhere, somewhere else
外を探す ほかをさがす search somewhere else
③ **OUTSIDE, beyond, besides; except, but**
恋は思案の外 こいはしあんのほか Love and reason do not go together
その外 そのほか besides, in addition; the rest, others
そうする外は無い そうするほかはない There is nothing for it but to do so

【はずす 外す】 **take off, remove, undo, detach; miss, let go, fail; avoid, dodge, slip away; leave out, exclude**
眼鏡を外す めがねをはずす take off one's glasses
取り外す とりはずす remove, dismantle
機会を外す きかいをはずす miss a chance
席を外している せきをはずしている be not at one's desk
予定から外す よていからはずす exclude from the schedule

【はずれる 外れる】
① **come off, get out of place, slip out, be separated**
ボタンが外れている ぼたんがはずれている be unbuttoned
② **miss, go wide, fail**
外れ はずれ end, verge; miss, failure
並外れの なみはずれの out of the ordinary, far above the average
③ be contrary to, be against
道理に外れた どうりにはずれた contrary to reason

【と- 外-】 **OUTSIDE**, outer
外様 とざま one not included in the favored group, outsider; outside daimyo

SYNONYMS

❶ **outside**

外 OUTSIDE → 0215
表 SURFACE → 3083
面 FACE → 2590

❷ⓐ foreign

外 foreign → 0215
異 foreign → 3195

【はずす】

◯ eliminate

却 ELIMINATE → 1436
排 EXCLUDE → 0593
払う CLEAR AWAY → 0225
剥 PEEL OFF → 2105
耘 WEED → 1661
削 cross out → 1837
抹 wipe off → 0370
省 leave out → 3100
脱 REMOVE → 1225
去 take away → 2678
外す take off → 0215
除 RID OF → 0546
撤 WITHDRAW → 0912

【はずれる】

① come off

脱 get out of place → 1225
外れる come off → 0215
剥 PEEL OFF → 2105

② deviate

逸 deviate → 3872
外れる miss → 0215

USAGE

【ほか】

外

① [also 他] something other than, the rest
② some other place, outside
③ outside, beyond, besides; except, but

他

[also 外] something other than, the rest

HOMOPHONES

ほか 他 OTHER → 0039

NOTE

➡ see COMPOUND FORMATION for
案外 あんがい → 案 2824
外為 がいため → 為 4395

夘

0216

1-3-2

▸THE HARE

ボウ う ㊔ しげ しげる

26	Nonstandard	U5918
卩	S5-2-3	F0000

traditional form → see 卯 at 0231

奴

0217

1-3-2

▸SLAVE
▸GUY

ド やつ▲ やっこ▲

Ⓒ 奴 nú

38	Jōyō	U5974
女	S5-3-2	F1183

Stroke order: く 女 女 奴 奴 (1 2 3 4 5)

COMPOUNDS

❶ SLAVE, serf, manservant, menial

奴隷 どれい slave, servant
農奴 のうど serf
黒奴 こくど black slave

❷ derogatory suffix for persons performing a menial action

売国奴 ばいこくど traitor
守銭奴 しゅせんど miser, slave of money

❸ fellow, **GUY**

奴輩 どはい fellows, guys

KUN

【やつ 奴】 *slang*

①ⓐ GUY, fellow, chap
ⓑ thing; things, matter

a 奴等 やつら those guys, they
黒い奴 くろいやつ *derogatory* nigger; black one

② third person pronoun

【やっこ 奴】 servant, footman; **GUY**, fellow, chap; tofu [bean curd] cut in cubes

奴さん やっこさん guy, fellow, chap; footman, attendant

SPECIAL READINGS

彼奴▲ あいつ that guy, he, she; that one

SYNONYMS

❶ servants

僕 MANSERVANT → 0185
奴 SLAVE → 0217
隷 UNDERLING → 2201
臣 RETAINER → 3806
従 follower → 0498
供 attendant → 0098

【やつ】

①ⓐ fellow

奴 GUY → 0217
漢 FELLOW → 0808
輩 FELLOW (*belittling*) → 3482
徒 fellows → 0499
棒 tough guy → 1237
坊 COLLOQUIAL PERSON SUFFIX → 0274
屋 colloquial person suffix → 3842
物 character → 1084

② **third person pronouns**
彼 THIRD PERSON PRONOUN (*neutral*) → 0346
氏 third person pronoun (*polite*) → 3669
奴 third person pronoun (*slang*) → 0217

好 1-3-2
incorrect stroke-count
➡ see 1-3-3: 女 at 0240

功 0218 1-3-2

▶**MERIT**
コウ ク いさお▲ ㊔ いさ つとむ かつ のり
Ⓝ 刅 Ⓒ 功 gōng

19	Jōyō-4	U529F
力	S5-2-3	F0931

COMPOUNDS

ⓐ **MERIT(s), meritorious deed [service]**
ⓑ **success, achievement, result, fruit**
a 功績 こうせき meritorious deed, achievement
功労 こうろう meritorious deed, (distinguished) services
功名 こうみょう great exploit; distinction, fame
功罪 こうざい merits and demerits
功徳 くどく virtue, merits of one's pious acts
功力 くりき merits [influence] of one's pious acts or religious practice
年功 ねんこう long service, years' [long] experience
勲功 くんこう distinguished services, merit
戦功 せんこう merit of war
b 功利主義 こうりしゅぎ utilitarianism
成功 せいこう success

INDEPENDENT

【こう 功】**MERIT**(s), meritorious deed [service]; success, achievement, result, fruit
功を争う こうをあらそう claim credit, contend for distinction
功を奏する こうをそうする succeed

KUN

【いさお 功】[also 勲] *elegant* **MERITorious service, merit**

SYNONYMS

ⓐ **accomplishment**
績 ACHIEVEMENTS → 1788
功 MERIT → 0218
勲 MERITORIOUS SERVICE → 3560

HOMOPHONES

いさお 勲 MERITORIOUS SERVICE → 3560

NOTE

➡ see USAGE note at 勲 3560

★ do not confuse with 巧 SKILLFUL → 0219

巧 0219 1-3-2

▶**SKILLFUL**
コウ たく(み) たく(む)▲ **うま(い)**▲
㊔ いさお よし
Ⓒ 巧 qiǎo

48	Jōyō	U5DE7
工	S5-3-2	F1624

COMPOUNDS

● **SKILLFUL, ingenious, clever**
巧妙な こうみょうな skillful, ingenious, clever
巧拙 こうせつ skill, dexterity, workmanship
巧者 こうしゃ skillful [ingenious] person
巧言 こうげん flattery
技巧 ぎこう art, craftsmanship, technical skill; trick
精巧な せいこうな elaborate, exquisite, ingenious
悧巧(=利口)な りこうな clever, bright, sharp, shrewd

INDEPENDENT

【こう 巧】**SKILLFUL**ness, dexterity
巧を誇る こうをほこる be of excellent workmanship

KUN

【たくみ 巧み】**skill, dexterity, ingenuity**
巧みな たくみな skillful, clever, cunning
巧みな手段 たくみなしゅだん clever trick
【たくむ 巧む】[in negative constructions] contrive
巧まぬ技巧 たくまぬぎこう artless art
【うまい 巧い】[also 上手い or 旨い] **SKILLFUL**, clever; splendid, excellent
巧さ うまさ skillfulness, ingenuity
巧い絵 うまいえ excellent picture [painting]
英語が巧い えいごがうまい speak English well

SYNONYMS

● **skillful**
巧 SKILLFUL → 0219
能 able → 1676

USAGE

【たくみ】
巧み
skill, dexterity, ingenuity
匠
artisan; woodworker, carpenter

HOMOPHONES

たくみ 匠 CRAFTSMAN → 3711
うまい
旨い → 2516
甘い → 4306
上手い → 4212, 4267

NOTE

➡ see also USAGE note at 旨 2516
★ do not confuse with 功 MERIT → 0218

㓛

0220

1-3-2

▶**MERIT**

コウ ク いさお ㊔ いさ つとむ かつ のり

18	Nonstandard	U34DB
刀	S5-2-3	F0000

traditional form → see 功 at 0218

刊

0221

1-3-2

▶**PUBLISH**

カン

Ⓒ 刊 kān

18	Jōyō-5	U520A
刂	S5-2-3	F0729

一 二 干 刋 刊
1 2 3 4 5

COMPOUNDS

ⓐ [also suffix] **PUBLISH**
ⓑ **publication, edition, issue**

a 刊行 かんこう publication
発刊 はっかん publication, issue
未刊の みかんの unpublished
既刊の きかんの already published
隔月刊 かくげつかん published bimonthly
創刊号 そうかんごう inaugural number, first issue
b 週刊 しゅうかん weekly publication, weekly
朝刊 ちょうかん morning edition [paper]
夕刊 ゆうかん evening edition [paper]

INDEPENDENT

【かん 刊】PUBLISHed by [in]…
昭和三年刊 しょうわさんねんかん published in 1928

SYNONYMS

ⓐ **print and publish**
刷 PRINT → 1623
印 print → 1023
植 typeset → 1247
刊 PUBLISH → 0221
版 PUBLISHING → 1082
載 PUT IN PRINT → 4091
掲 display in writing → 0597
幀 BOOKBINDING → 0695

ⓑ **editions**
版 edition → 1082
刊 publication → 0221
訂 revision → 1829
刷 printing → 1623

NOTE

★ do not confuse with 刑 PENALTY → 1024

幼

0222

1-3-2

▶**VERY YOUNG**

ヨウ おさな(い)

Ⓒ 幼 yòu

52	Jōyō-6	U5E7C
幺	S5-3-2	F1078

㇛ 幺 幺 幻 幼
1 2 3 4 5

COMPOUNDS

❶ⓐ **VERY YOUNG, infant**
ⓑ **infantile, immature**

a 幼児 ようじ young child, infant
幼女 ようじょ baby girl
幼時 ようじ childhood, infancy
幼年 ようねん infancy, childhood
b 幼稚な ようちな childish, infantile, crude
幼稚園 ようちえん kindergarten

❷ [original meaning] **young child, child**
長幼 ちょうよう young and old
老幼 ろうよう old people and children

INDEPENDENT

【よう 幼】abbrev. of 幼稚園 ようちえん: kindergarten; infancy

KUN

【おさない 幼い】**VERY YOUNG, infant; childish, infantile**
幼子 おさなご baby, infant, child
幼馴染み おさななじみ childhood friend
幼心 おさなごころ child's mind; innocent heart

SYNONYMS

❶ **young**
若 YOUNG → 2785
弱 young → 1499
少 young → 4278
青 youthful → 3084
幼 VERY YOUNG → 0222
稚 CHILDISH → 1543

❷ **child**
児 CHILD (of any age) → 3153
子 CHILD → 4196
童 CHILD (young person) → 2639
幼 young child → 0222
坊 SONNY → 0274

弘

0223

1-3-2

▶**DISSEMINATE**

コウ グ ひろ(まる) ひろ(める) ㊔ ひろし ひろむ みつ

Ⓒ 弘 hóng

57	Names	U5F18
弓	S5-3-2	F1300

COMPOUNDS

❶ **DISSEMINATE, spread, teach (esp. Buddhism)**

弘報(=広報) こうほう (public) information, public relations

弘法 ぐほう spreading Buddhist teachings

❷ⓐ great, grand

ⓑ [original meaning, now rare] extensive, broad, vast

a 弘誓 ぐぜい Buddha's great vows

弘大な こうだいな grand, magnificent, vast

b 弘遠な こうえんな vast and far-reaching

KUN

【ひろまる 弘まる】[usu. 広まる] **spread, be diffused, be in general circulation, become popular**

【ひろめる 弘める】[usu. 広める] **spread, DISSEMINATE; extend, broaden, widen**

SYNONYMS

❶ **make widely known**

布 SPREAD → 3691

流 spread → 0529

伝 spread → 0048

広 spread → 3769

弘 DISSEMINATE (esp. Buddhism) → 0223

及 REACH TO → 4192

HOMOPHONES

ひろまる 広 WIDE → 3769

ひろめる 広 WIDE → 3769

NOTE

➡ see USAGE note at 広 3769

打

▶STRIKE

ダ う(つ) う(ち)- だーす▲

Ⓒ 打 dǎ dá

0224

◧ 1-3-2

64	Jōyō-3	U6253
扌	S5-3-2	F0345

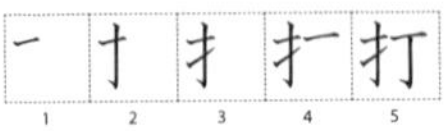

COMPOUNDS

❶ [also prefix] [original meaning] **STRIKE, hit, beat**

打撃 だげき blow, strike; batting, hitting

打撲 だぼく blow, stroke

打診 だしん sounding, tapping; percussion

打電 だでん sending a telegram

打楽器 だがっき percussion instrument, traps

殴打する おうだする give a blow, beat, strike

❷ *baseball*

ⓐ **hit, bat**

ⓑ [also suffix] **hit, base hit**

a 打線 だせん batting line-up

打者 だしゃ batter, hitter

打席 だせき batter's box; one's turn at bat

安打 あんだ safe hit, base hit

代打 だいだ pinch-hitting; pinch hitter

b 打率 だりつ batting average

長打 ちょうだ long hit

本塁打 ほんるいだ home run

適時打 てきじだ timely hit

❸ **used in verbal compounds to add euphony**

打開 だかい break, development, a new turn

打倒する だとうする overthrow, knock down, defeat

打算 ださん calculation, self-interest, selfishness

打算的 ださんてき calculating, self-centered

打破する だはする break down, overthrow, abolish

INDEPENDENT

【だ 打】*baseball* batting

打のチーム だのちーむ team excellent in batting

KUN

【うつ 打つ】

①ⓐ **STRIKE, hit, beat, give a blow, thrash**

ⓑ (of a clock) **STRIKE (the hour)**

ⓒ (impress upon) **STRIKE, move, impress**

a 打ち込む うちこむ strike [drive] into, ram down; devote oneself to, be absorbed in

打ち上げる うちあげる launch, shoot up; (of waves) dash, wash up [ashore]; finish, close

鞭打つ むちうつ whip, lash, give the rod; spur on

b 三時を打つ さんじをうつ strike three

c 心を打つ こころをうつ impress (a person), touch (a person's) heart

② perform an action by striking, as:

ⓐ **drive in (a nail), affix**

ⓑ cut off (a person's head)

ⓒ water, sprinkle

ⓓ **play (as a game of go)**

ⓔ till (the soil)

ⓕ **make something by striking**

a 銘打つ めいうつ engrave an inscription; call [designate] itself

b 打ち首 うちくび decapitation, beheading

c 打ち水 うちみず watering, sprinkling

d 碁を打つ ごをうつ play (a game of) go

e 田を打つ たをうつ till [plow] a rice paddy

f 刀を打つ かたなをうつ temper [forge] a sword

③ perform an action (as if by striking), as:

ⓐ **send (a telegram)**

ⓑ **pay (money on a contract)**

ⓒ perform, run

a 電報を打つ でんぽうをうつ send a telegram

b 手付けを打つ てつけをうつ advance money (on a contract)

c 芝居を打つ しばいをうつ give [present] a play; play a trick, put up a false show

仕打ち しうち (unfavorable) treatment, (cool) attitude

投げ打つ なげうつ [also 抛つ] fling away, abandon

④ [usu. 撃つ, sometimes also 討つ] **attack, STRIKE, assault**

不意を打つ ふいをうつ make a surprise attack, take (a person) unawares

挟み打ち はさみうち attack on both sides [flanks], pincer attack

追い打ち おいうち attacking the routed enemy, pursuit

【うち- 打ち-】 verbal prefix adding euphony or emphasis

打ち出す うちだす set out [forth], work out, hammer out; strike out, emboss; announce

打ち切る うちきる put an end to, break off, finish

打ち合わせる うちあわせる make arrangements, prearrange; strike against

打ち合わせ うちあわせ preliminary [previous] arrangement, preliminaries

打ち消す うちけす deny, negate, contradict

打ち消し うちけし negation, denial

打ち明ける うちあける confide in (someone), reveal, disclose

【だーす 打】 dozen

三打 さんだーす three dozen

SYNONYMS

❶ strike

打 STRIKE → 0224

撲 DEAL A BLOW → 0903

殴 BEAT (strike a person) → 1099

蹴 KICK → 2074

撃 STRIKE → 3552

挌 STRIKE (a person) → 0448

撞 STRIKE (a ball or bell) → 0905

撥ねる strike (knock down) → 0907

当てる HIT → 2701

叩 KNOCK → 0208

拍 BEAT (strike repeatedly) → 0361

搏 BEAT (throb) → 0794

USAGE

【うつ】

打つ

①ⓐ strike, hit, beat, give a blow, thrash

ⓑ (of a clock) strike (the hour)

ⓒ (impress upon) strike, move, impress

② perform an action by striking, as:

ⓐ drive in (a nail), affix

ⓑ cut off (a person's head)

ⓒ water, sprinkle

ⓓ play (as a game of go)

ⓔ till (the soil)

ⓕ make something by striking

③ perform an action (as if by striking), as:

ⓐ send (a telegram)

ⓑ pay (money on a contract)

ⓒ perform, run

④ [usu. 撃つ, sometimes also 討つ] attack, strike, assault

撃つ

① fire, shoot, discharge

② [sometimes also 打つ or 討つ] attack, strike, assault

討つ

① kill (with a sword or spear)

②ⓐ suppress by armed force, put down [attack] the enemy, send a punitive expedition

ⓑ [usu. 撃つ, sometimes also 打つ] attack, strike, assault

HOMOPHONES

うつ

撃 STRIKE → 3552

討 STUDY → 1846

なげうつ

抛つ → 0364

投げ打つ → 0300, 0224

払

0225

1-3-2

▶CLEAR AWAY
▶PAY

フツ はら(う) -はら(い) -ばら(い)

Ⓝ 拂 Ⓒ 拂 fú

64	Jōyō	U6255
扌	S5-3-2	F0785

一 十 扌 扎 払 (1 2 3 4 5)

COMPOUNDS

❶ [original meaning] **CLEAR AWAY, sweep away, wipe away**

払拭する ふっしょくする wipe out [away], dispel, cast aside (worries, etc.)

払底 ふってい shortage

❷ clear up, dawn

払暁 ふつぎょう dawn

KUN

【はらう 払う】

①ⓐ (remove something undesirable) **CLEAR AWAY, sweep away, brush off, prune**

ⓑ [also verbal suffix] (drive off) **clear out, drive away, expel, exorcise**

a 払い除ける はらいのける brush off, sweep away

払い落とす はらいおとす shake off, brush off

足払い あしばらい tripping up

取り払う とりはらう clear away, remove

b 追い払う(=追っ払う) おいはらう(=おっぱらう) drive away, expel, exorcise
　露払い つゆはらい herald; heralding, ushering
　厄払い やくばらい exorcism
　焼き払う やきはらう clear away by burning, reduce to ashes

② (dispose of supplies on hand) clear out, sell off, dispose of
　払い下げる はらいさげる sell, dispose of

③ (clear a debt) **PAY, settle accounts**
　払い はらい payment; account, bill
　払い戻す はらいもどす pay back
　払い込む はらいこむ pay in, pay up
　勘定を払う かんじょうをはらう pay a bill, settle one's account

④ **PAY (attention), give heed**
　注意を払う ちゅういをはらう pay attention (to)

⑤ (go away) clear out, leave, quit
　引き払う ひきはらう clear out, move out
　出払う ではらう be all out

【-はらい, -ばらい -払い】

① [also suffix] **PAYment, settlement**
　支払い しはらい payment, payout, defrayment
　延べ払い のべばらい deferred payment
　分割払い ぶんかつばらい payment in installments

② **emphatic verbal suffix**
　酔っ払い よっぱらい drunkard, boozer
　掻っ払い かっぱらい pilferer; pilfering

SYNONYMS

❶ **clean and wash**
　洗 WASH →0465
　漱 RINSE →0865
　拭 WIPE →0453
　滌 WASH →0854
　濯 RINSE →0978
　浴 BATHE →0533
　浄 cleanse →0457
　粛 PURGE →4400
　清 CLEAR →0635
　払 CLEAR AWAY →0225
　掃 SWEEP →0611

【はらう】

①ⓐ **eliminate**
　却 ELIMINATE →1436
　排 EXCLUDE →0593
　払う CLEAR AWAY →0225
　剝 PEEL OFF →2105
　耘 WEED →1661
　削 cross out →1837
　抹 wipe off →0370
　省 leave out →3100
　脱 REMOVE →1225
　去 take away →2678
　外す take off →0215
　除 RID OF →0546
　撤 WITHDRAW →0912

ⓑ **drive out**
　斥 EXPEL →3690
　排 EXCLUDE →0593
　追 chase away →3840
　退 cause to retreat →3838
　駆 drive away →2293
　逐 DRIVE OUT →3848
　払う clear out →0225

③ **pay**
　払う PAY →0225
　納 PAY (to the authorities) →1652
　済 settle accounts →0634
　支 pay out →2473
　賦 INSTALLMENT →1992
　償 RECOMPENSE →0199

此

1-3-2

incorrect stroke-count
➡ see 1-4-2: 止 at 1017

氾

0226

1-3-2

▸**SPREAD OUT**

ハン

Ⓒ 泛 fàn

85	Jōyō	U6C3E
氵	S5-3-2	F2862

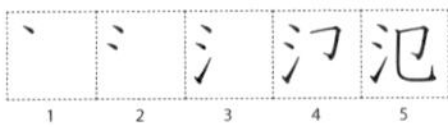

COMPOUNDS

❶ **SPREAD OUT, overflow**
　氾濫 はんらん flooding, overflowing, inundation

❷ extensive, wide-ranging

SYNONYMS

❶ **expand**
　脹 SWELL →1265
　膨 EXPAND →1380
　張 SPREAD →0573
　氾 SPREAD OUT →0226
　広げる spread (out) →3769
　拡 ENLARGE →0366
　伸 STRETCH →0079
　延 EXTEND →3812

汁

0227
◧ 1-3-2

▸**JUICE**
▸**SOUP**
ジュウ しる -しる
Ⓒ 汁 zhī

85	Jōyō	U6C41
氵	S5-3-2	F1544

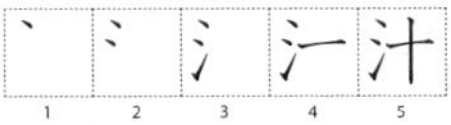

COMPOUNDS

❶ⓐ JUICE, sap
ⓑ SOUP, broth

a 汁液 じゅうえき juice
果汁 かじゅう fruit juice
b 一汁一菜 いちじゅういっさい simple meal
肉汁 にくじゅう meat juice, gravy

❷ [original meaning] **fluid, body fluid, liquid**
胆汁 たんじゅう bile, gall
墨汁 ぼくじゅう India ink, black writing fluid

KUN

【しる 汁】**JUICE, sap; soup, gravy; pus; profit yielded through another person's effort**
蜜柑の汁 みかんのしる mandarin orange juice
澄まし汁 すましじる clear soup
甘い汁を吸う あまいしるをすう make a good thing out of (something)

【-しる -汁】[suffix] **SOUP**
味噌汁 みそしる *miso* soup
野菜汁 やさいじる vegetable soup

SYNONYMS

❶ drinks
汁 JUICE, SOUP → 0227
乳 MILK → 1823
酒 ALCOHOLIC DRINK → 0532
茶 TEA → 2808
珈 COFFEE → 1138
醇 UNDILUTED WINE → 2001
酎 SHOCHU → 1852

❷ liquid
液 LIQUID → 0622
汁 fluid → 0227
水 WATER → 0010

汀

0228
◧ 1-3-2

▸**STRAND**
テイ チョウ みぎわ なぎさ
Ⓒ 汀 tīng

85	Names	U6C40
氵	S5-3-2	F3122

COMPOUNDS

● STRAND, beach, waterside, shore
汀線 ていせん shoreline, coastline
汀洲 ていしゅう sandbar, islet in a stream; shoreline

KUN

【みぎわ 汀】**STRAND, beach, waterside, shore**
汀に寄せる細波 みぎわによせるさざなみ ripples beating upon the seashore

【なぎさ 汀】[usu. 渚] **STRAND, beach, waterside, shore**
汀伝い なぎさづたい along the shore

SYNONYMS

● &【みぎわ】&【なぎさ】shores and watersides
畔 WATERSIDE → 1472
-辺 -side → 3761
浜 BEACH → 0523
岸 SHORE → 2777
浦 SEASIDE → 0524
渚 STRAND → 0637
磯 ROCKY BEACH → 1587
汀 STRAND → 0228

HOMOPHONES

なぎさ 渚 STRAND → 0637

NOTE

➡ see USAGE note at 渚 0637

犯

0229
◧ 1-3-2

▸**OFFENSE**
ハン ボン▲ おか(す)
Ⓒ 犯 fàn

94	Jōyō-5	U72AF
犭	S5-3-2	F0620

COMPOUNDS

❶ⓐ [also suffix] **OFFENSE, crime**
ⓑ counter for OFFENSEs

a 犯罪 はんざい offense, crime
犯行 はんこう criminal act, crime, offense
防犯 ぼうはん crime prevention
初犯 しょはん first offense
過失犯 かしつはん careless offense
b 前科三犯 ぜんかさんぱん previously convicted three times

❷ⓐ offend against, violate, infringe
ⓑ [also suffix] **offender, criminal**

a 犯則 はんそく transgression, violation (of the law)
侵犯 しんぱん invasion; violation
違犯(=違反) いはん violation (of the law), infringement; breach
不犯 ふぼん strict observance of the Buddhist commandment that all priests should be celibate
b 犯人 はんにん criminal, offender

戦犯 せんぱん war criminal
共犯 きょうはん accomplice, confederate, partner, associate
殺人犯 さつじんはん murderer
知能犯 ちのうはん intellectual criminal

KUN

【おかす 犯す】

① **offend against, violate, infringe upon, commit (a crime), sin against**
犯し難い おかしがたい dignified
法を犯す ほうをおかす violate the law
罪を犯す つみをおかす commit a crime

② **rape, violate, deflower**
女を犯す おんなをおかす rape a girl

SYNONYMS

❶ **crimes and offenses**
犯 OFFENSE →0229
罪 CRIME →3224
凶 atrocious crime →3679

❷ⓐ **violate**
違 VIOLATE →3907
破 BREAK →1478
犯 offend against →0229
反 act contrary to →3663
悖 GO AGAINST →0503
背 go against →3182

HOMOPHONES

おかす
侵 INVADE →0116
冒 RISK →3088

NOTE

➡ see USAGE note at 侵 0116

比 1-3-2
incorrect stroke-count
➡ see 1-2-2: 匕 at 0029

収 1-3-2
incorrect stroke-count
➡ see 1-2-2: 丩 at 0031

以 1-3-2
incorrect classification
➡ see 1-2-3: 𠂉 at 0045

北 0230 1-3-2

▶**NORTH**
ホク きた
Ⓒ 北 běi

21	Jōyō-2	U5317
匕	S5-2-3	F0232

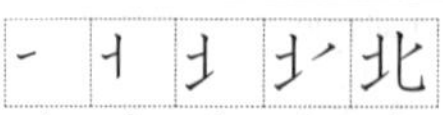

COMPOUNDS

❶ **NORTH**
北部 ほくぶ north, northern part
北欧 ほくおう Northern Europe, Scandinavia
北爆 ほくばく bombing the North (Vietnam)
北東 ほくとう northeast
北極 ほっきょく North Pole
北緯 ほくい north latitude
北方 ほっぽう north, northward; northern district

❷ [original meaning] **turn one's back on**
敗北 はいぼく defeat, setback

❸ abbrev. of 北海道 ほっかいどう: Hokkaido district
北大 ほくだい Hokkaido University

KUN

【きた 北】[also prefix] **NORTH**
北口 きたぐち north exit
北側 きたがわ north side, north bank
北半球 きたはんきゅう Northern Hemisphere

SYNONYMS

❶ **cardinal points**
東 EAST →4385
西 WEST →4333
北 NORTH →0230
南 SOUTH →2584
巽 SOUTHEAST →3329
艮 NORTHEAST →4330

卯 0231 1-3-2

▶**THE HARE**
ボウ う ㊔ しげ しげる
Ⓝ 夘 Ⓒ 卯 mǎo

26	Names	U536F
卩	S5-2-3	F2600

COMPOUNDS

● fourth sign of the Oriental zodiac: **THE HARE**—(time) 5-7 a.m., (direction) east, (season) February (of the lunar calendar) (→see APPENDIX 8)
卯月 ぼうげつ second month of the lunar calendar

KUN

【う 卯】fourth sign of the Oriental zodiac: **THE HARE** (→●)
卯月 うづき fourth month (of the lunar calendar), April
卯の花 うのはな flower of the deutzia; bean curd refuse

SYNONYMS

● **rabbit**
兎 RABBIT →4374
卯 THE HARE →0231

印 incorrect stroke-count
➡ see ◧1-4-2: ⺤ at 1023
◧1-3-2

吃 0232 ◧1-3-3

▶STAMMER
キツ ども(る)
Ⓒ 吃 chī

30	Non-Jōyō	U5403
口	S6-3-3	F3018

COMPOUNDS

❶ [original meaning] **STAMMER, stutter**
吃音 きつおん stammering
❷ [now also 喫 0668] **be subjected to, suffer, incur**
吃水 きっすい draft, sea gauge
吃驚する きっきょうする be astonished
❸ [now replaced by 喫 0668] urgent, pressing
吃緊の きっきんの very important, urgent

KUN

【どもる 吃る】**STAMMER, stutter**
吃りながら どもりながら stammering(ly), stuttering(ly)

SPECIAL READINGS

吃逆 しゃっくり hiccup
吃驚 びっくり surprise, amazement, astonishment

SYNONYMS

❶ **stagnate**
滞 STAGNATE → 0815
淀む STAGNATE → 0621
澱 SETTLE → 0954
渋 NOT GO SMOOTHLY → 0625
吃 STAMMER → 0232

叫 0233 ◧1-3-3

▶SHOUT
キョウ さけ(ぶ)
Ⓝ 叫 Ⓒ 叫 jiào

30	Jōyō	U53EB
口	S6-3-3	F0939

Stroke order: 1–6

COMPOUNDS

● [original meaning] **SHOUT, cry (out), shriek, scream, yell**
叫喚 きょうかん shout, cry, scream
叫号する きょうごうする [rare] cry aloud
絶叫する ぜっきょうする exclaim, ejaculate, scream, shout

KUN

【さけぶ 叫ぶ】**SHOUT, scream, cry; advocate**
叫び さけび shout, cry, scream
叫び声 さけびごえ shout, outcry
泣き叫ぶ なきさけぶ cry, scream, wail
改革を叫ぶ かいかくをさけぶ cry loudly for a reform

SYNONYMS

● **give out a call**
叫 SHOUT → 0233
号 holler → 2675
喝 SHOUT AT → 0554
喚 call out → 0666
呼 CALL → 0324
鳴 CRY → 0831
吠 BARK → 0269

吸 0234 ◧1-3-3

▶SUCK
▶BREATHE IN
キュウ す(う)
Ⓝ 吸 Ⓒ 吸 xī

30	Jōyō-6	U5438
口	S6-3-3	F0857

Stroke order: 1–6

COMPOUNDS

❶ [original meaning] **SUCK, suck in, absorb**
吸収 きゅうしゅう absorption, assimilation; merger
吸着 きゅうちゃく adsorption
吸引する きゅういんする suck (in), absorb, aspirate; attract
吸塵 きゅうじん dust vacuuming
吸血鬼 きゅうけつき vampire
吸盤 きゅうばん sucker, sucking disk
❷ **BREATHE IN, inhale**
吸入する きゅうにゅうする inhale, breath in; suck (in); imbibe
吸気 きゅうき inhalation of air; air breathed in
呼吸 こきゅう breathing, respiration

KUN

【すう 吸う】**inhale, BREATHE IN; smoke; suck, sip, absorb; draw**
吸い出す すいだす suck [draw] out; aspirate
吸い物 すいもの Japanese style soup
吸い殻 すいがら cigarette butt
煙草を吸う たばこをすう smoke a cigarette

SYNONYMS

❶ **take in**
収 TAKE IN → 0031
摂 TAKE IN → 0799
喫 INGEST → 0668
吸 SUCK → 0234
❷ **breathe and blow**
息 BREATH → 3278

氕 breath →3960
吸 BREATHE IN →0234
呼 breathe out →0324
吹 BLOW →0272

吐

▶SPEW
ト は(く)
Ⓒ 吐 tǔ tù

0235
1-3-3

30	Jōyō	U5410
口	S6-3-3	F1080

丨 口 口 口一 口十 吐
1 2 3 4 5 6

COMPOUNDS

❶ [original meaning] **SPEW, vomit**
吐出 としゅつ spew, vomit, disgorge
吐血 とけつ vomiting blood
吐息 といき sigh, long breath
嘔×吐 おうと vomiting
音吐朗朗と おんとろうろうと in a clear voice

❷ (spew out words) express, speak out
吐露する とろする express one's mind

KUN

【はく 吐く】**SPEW, vomit; exhale; emit, send forth; express, utter, give vent to; confess, own**
吐き出す はきだす spew, vomit, disgorge
吐き気 はきけ nausea
息を吐く いきをはく exhale, breathe out
煙を吐く けむりをはく emit smoke
意見を吐く いけんをはく give one's opinion
私が彼を吐かせてやる わたしがかれをはかせてやる I will have it out of him

SYNONYMS

❶ **discharge from mouth**
吐 SPEW →0235
吹 BLOW →0272

❶ **emit**
出 PUT OUT →4310
発 EMIT →3174
放 radiate →1058
排 DISCHARGE →0593
射 SHOOT →1850
噴 SPOUT →0879
吐 SPEW →0235
湧 WELL UP →0749

地

▶GROUND
▶PLACE
チ ジ
Ⓒ 地 dì de

0236
1-3-3

32	Jōyō-2	U5730
土	S6-3-3	F0036

一 十 土 圠 地 地
1 2 3 4 5 6

COMPOUNDS

❶ [also suffix]
ⓐ (solid surface of the earth) **GROUND, earth, land**
ⓑ (functionally distinguished tract) **land, GROUND, soil**

a 地面 じめん surface, ground, land
地下の ちかの underground, subterranean
地震 じしん earthquake
地上に ちじょうに on the ground; on earth
地階 ちかい basement, cellar
地図 ちず map, atlas
地理 ちり geographical features, topography; geography
地盤 じばん ground, foundation, base
地形 ちけい geographical features, topography
地質 ちしつ geological features; nature of the soil
土地 とち land
高地 こうち high ground, plateau, heights
湿地 しっち damp ground, swamp
耕地 こうち arable land, farm land
扇状地 せんじょうち alluvial delta

b 地主 じぬし landlord, landowner
地目 ちもく classification of land category
地価 ちか price [value] of land
宅地 たくち land for housing, residential land
敷地 しきち (building) site, (plot of) ground, lot
空き地 あきち unoccupied ground, vacant lot
分譲地 ぶんじょうち (building) lots for sale

❷ⓐ [original meaning] (surface of the world, as distinguished from heaven) **earth**
ⓑ **Earth, the Earth**

a 地獄 じごく hell; inferno
地平線 ちへいせん horizon
天地 てんち heaven and earth; top and bottom
大地 だいち ground, earth, solid earth

b 地球 ちきゅう the Earth
地殻 ちかく crust (of the earth)
地軸 ちじく axis of the earth
地動説 ちどうせつ heliocentric [Copernican] theory
地磁気 ちじき terrestrial magnetism

❸ⓐ [also suffix] (particular location) **PLACE, grounds, position**

ⓑ [also suffix] (particular region) **PLACE, locality, region, district**
ⓒ of that **PLACE** or region
ⓓ abbrev. of 地方 ちほう: district

a 地点 ちてん spot, point, place
各地 かくち every place, various parts [areas] (of the country)
基地 きち base
団地 だんち (public) housing development
現地 げんち actual place [locale]
当地 とうち this place [locality], here
番地 ばんち lot [house] number, address
余地 よち room, space, margin
墓地 ぼち graveyard, cemetery, burial grounds
爆心地 ばくしんち center of explosion

b 地元 じもと local end, local area
地名 ちめい place name
産地 さんち place of production; place of birth
辺地 へんち remote place
寒冷地 かんれいち cold [northern] district
遠隔地 えんかくち distant place

c 地酒 じざけ locally brewed sake
地卵 じたまご homegrown eggs, local eggs
地唄 じうた ballad, folk song

d 地裁 ちさい district court

❹ (main surface or background, as in a painting) **GROUND, background**
地金 じがね ore; ground metal; one's true character
地肌 じはだ one's skin; surface of the ground; texture
地色 じいろ ground color
白地 しろじ white (back)ground
下地 したじ ground work, prearrangement; grounding, making
無地 むじ solid color

❺ⓐ **one's GROUND, one's stand, one's place, one's position**
ⓑ **state of one's emotions**

a 地位 ちい position, status, post, social standing
地歩 ちほ one's stand, foothold, position
見地 けんち standpoint, viewpoint
窮地 きゅうち predicament, difficult situation, dilemma
実地 じっち actuality, reality; practice
境地 きょうち state, stage; field, ground

b 心地 ここち feeling, mood
意地 いじ nature, disposition; will power, backbone

❻ **natural, in its natural [original] form, inherent**
地力 じりき one's own strength
地声 じごえ natural voice
地髪 じがみ natural hair
地味な じみな plain, sober, unpretentious
地道な じみちな steady, straight, fair
素地 そじ inclination, makings; grounding, foundation
生地(=素地) きじ one's true color [character]; (plain) cloth, texture; unglazed pottery

❼ [also suffix] **fabric, texture, cloth, material**
服地 ふくじ cloth, dress material, clothing fabric
裏地 うらじ lining (cloth), material for lining
厚地 あつじ thick cloth
織地 おりじ fabric, texture
タオル地 たおるじ toweling
プリント地 ぷりんとじ printed cloth

❽ descriptive [narrative] part (as opposed to dialogue); choric part (in noh or *utai* singing)
地謡 じうたい chorus in *utai* singing

INDEPENDENT

【ち 地】

①ⓐ (solid surface of the earth) **GROUND, earth, land**
ⓑ (surface of the world, as distinguished from heaven) earth

a 足を地に付けて あしをちにつけて with one's feet planted on the ground, with steady steps

b 地の果て ちのはて end of the earth

② (particular location) **PLACE, grounds, position**
地の利 ちのり vantage ground, advantageous position
景勝の地 けいしょうのち place of scenic beauty

③ lower **PLACE**, bottom
天と地 てんとち top and bottom; heaven and earth

【じ 地】

① (solid surface of the earth) **GROUND**, earth, land
地を均す じをならす level the ground

② (particular region) **PLACE**, locality, region, district
地の卵 じのたまご farm-fresh eggs, local eggs

③ captured territory in the game of go

④ (main surface or background, as in a painting) **GROUND**, background
地を赤で塗る じをあかでぬる paint the ground in red

⑤ descriptive [narrative] part (as opposed to dialogue); choric part (in noh or *utai* singing)
地の文 じのぶん descriptive [narrative] part

⑥ fabric, texture, cloth, material
地の詰んだ じのつんだ of close texture

⑦ natural form, original condition
地が出る じがでる show one's true colors, betray oneself

⑧ actuality, reality
地で行く じでいく carry (a story) into actual practice

SYNONYMS

❶ **land and soil**

土 SOIL → 4211
地 GROUND → 0236
壌 ARABLE SOIL → 0933
泥 MUD → 0384
陸 LAND → 0659
埴 CLAY → 0562

❸ⓐ **places and positions**

所 PLACE → 1056
処 place → 3764
場 PLACE (for specific activity) → 0678
地 PLACE (particular location) → 0236
席 meeting place → 3865
位 POSITION → 0069
点 POINT → 2587
座 place → 3868

ⓑ **areas and localities**

地 PLACE → 0236
方 locality → 2459
辺 VICINITY → 3761
域 BOUNDED AREA → 0559
区 DISTRICT → 3681
領 TERRITORY → 1567
帯 BELT → 3191
圏 SPHERE → 3904

❺ⓐ **standpoint**

地 one's ground → 0236
立 standpoint → 2486

❻ **natural**

地 natural → 0236
野 wild → 1877
粗 crude → 1683
原 in the original state → 3733

❼ **fabric**

布 CLOTH → 3691
地 fabric → 0236
巾 CLOTH → 4217

舛

▶ ***MASU***

0237

1-3-3

136	Radical	U821B
舛	S6-6-0	F3155

RADICAL

masu 'dancing' (舜), used for character classification
Bottom variant: 舛 ***maiashi*** (舞)

妃

▶ **PRINCESS**

ヒ ㊔ き きさき

ⓒ 妃 fēi

0238

1-3-3

38	Jōyō	U5983
女	S6-3-3	F1773

COMPOUNDS

● (wife of a member of the Imperial or Royal family)
PRINCESS, queen, empress; consort (as of an emperor)

妃殿下 ひでんか Her Imperial Highness
王妃 おうひ queen, empress
后妃 こうひ queen consort, empress, queen
親王妃 しんのうひ Imperial princess

INDEPENDENT

【ひ 妃】 **PRINCESS**, consort (one rank below the empress)

SYNONYMS

● **wives of rulers**

后 EMPRESS → 3701
妃 PRINCESS → 0238
室 wife (esp. of persons of rank) → 2802

如

▶ **AS**

ジョ ニョ ごと(し)▲ ㊔ なお ゆき

ⓒ 如 rú

0239

1-3-3

38	Jōyō	U5982
女	S6-3-3	F1164

COMPOUNDS

❶ **AS, like, as if, such as**

如上の じょじょうの above-mentioned
如実に にょじつに truly, realistically
如是 にょぜ thus, so, like this
如来 にょらい Buddha
不如意の ふにょいの contrary to one's wishes, hard up, pressed for money

❷ **suffix added to modifiers (noun adjectives or adverbs) to express a state**

突如 とつじょ suddenly, unexpectedly
欠如 けつじょ lack, shortage
躍如たる やくじょたる vivid, graphic, lifelike

KUN

【ごとし 如し】 **like, AS, as if**

如く ごとく like, as if
. . . の如し …のごとし be like, be as if, seem

SPECIAL READINGS

如何▲ いかが how; what
如何▲(=奈何▲) いかん what; how
如何に▲ いかに how, in what way
如何にも▲ いかにも indeed, really; as if

SYNONYMS

❶ similar
類 similar →2275
様 like →1332
如 AS →0239
-通り as →3855
云 SUCH →2430

❷ modifier suffixes
然 MODIFIER FORMING SUFFIX →3456
乎 MODIFIER FORMING SUFFIX →4316
如 modifier suffix →0239
爾 adjective suffix →4407
的 ADJECTIVAL SUFFIX →1444

好

0240
1-3-3

▶LIKE
▶FAVORABLE
コウ この(む) す(く) よ(い)▲ い(い)▲
㊔ よし
Ⓒ 好 hǎo hào

38	Jōyō-4	U597D
女	S6-3-3	F0252

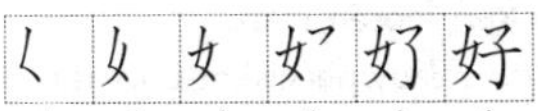

1 2 3 4 5 6

COMPOUNDS

❶ [original meaning] **LIKE, be fond of, love**
好学 こうがく love of learning
好物 こうぶつ favorite dish
好角家 こうかくか sumo fan, wrestling enthusiast
愛好者 あいこうしゃ lover (of music), fan
同好会 どうこうかい association of like-minded persons; club

❷ⓐ [also prefix] **FAVORABLE, good, fine**
ⓑ good-looking, beautiful
a 好調 こうちょう favorable [good] condition
好機 こうき favorable opportunity, good chance
好況 こうきょう brisk market, prosperity
好意 こうい goodwill, favor, kindness
好感 こうかん good feeling, good impression
好評 こうひょう favorable criticism [comment], public favor
好影響 こうえいきょう favorable influence
好都合な こうつごうな favorable, fortunate
絶好の ぜっこうの splendid, grand, best, golden
b 好男子 こうだんし handsome man
格好(=恰好) かっこう suitability, moderateness (in price); shape, form; appearance, manner

❸ friendship, friendly relations
好誼× こうぎ warm friendship
親好 しんこう friendship, good fellowship
友好的な ゆうこうてきな friendly, fraternal

KUN

【このむ 好む】 LIKE, be fond of, prefer
好み このみ taste, liking; choice; wish; fashion
好ましい このましい desirable, welcome, nice, pleasant

【すく 好く】 LIKE, be fond of, love
好き すき liking, fondness; fancy; taste
好きだ すきだ like, be fond of, love
好き好む すきこのむ like, be fond of
好き嫌い すききらい likes and dislikes, taste
好き好き すきずき a matter of taste
物好き ものずき curiosity, eccentricity; curiosity seeker

【よい 好い】 [now usu. 良い] same as 良い よい
お人好し おひとよし good-natured person; credulous person
→see 良 4373 for other compounds

【いい 好い】 [now usu. 良い] colloquial form of 好い よい
好い加減 いいかげん moderate, right; random, not thorough, vague

SYNONYMS

❶ love and like
愛 LOVE →3133
恋 LOVE (the opposite sex) →2602
好 LIKE →0240
慕 ADORE →2970
惚れる FALL IN LOVE →0584
玩 cherish →1085

❷ⓐ good
良 GOOD →4373
善 GOOD →2921
好 FAVORABLE →0240
順 favorable →0018
佳 FINE →0096
美 BEAUTIFUL →2817

❸ personal relations
縁 RELATION →1754
交 INTERCOURSE →2508
好 friendship →0240
仲 PERSONAL RELATIONS →0047
誼 FRIENDSHIP →1977
絆 BONDS →1686

HOMOPHONES

よい
良 GOOD →4373
善 GOOD →2921

いい 良 GOOD → 4373

NOTE

➡ see USAGE note at 良 4373

艸

0241

1-3-3

▶ ***KUSA***

140	Radical	U8278
艸	S6-6-0	F2794

RADICAL

kusa 'plants', used in characters related to plants or their qualities

Top variants: 艹 艹 艹 ***kusakanmuri*** (花 芯 夢)

巧

1-3-3

incorrect stroke-count
➡ see 1-3-2: 工 at 0219

帆

0242

1-3-3

▶ **SAIL**

ハン ほ

Ⓝ 帆 帆 Ⓒ 帆 fān

50	Jōyō	U5E06
巾	S6-3-3	F1716

COMPOUNDS

❶ [original meaning] **SAIL, canvas**

帆船 **はんせん** sailing vessel, sailboat
機帆船 **きはんせん** motor-powered sailboat
順風満帆 **じゅんぷうまんぱん** smooth sailing, sailing before the wind

❷ⓐ **SAIL**, set sail
ⓑ **SAIL**boat

a 帆走 **はんそう** sailing by boat
出帆 **しゅっぱん** sailing, departure
b 帰帆 **きはん** returning sailboat
孤帆 **こはん** solitary sailboat

KUN

【ほ 帆】**SAIL**

帆影 **ほかげ** sight of a sail
帆柱(=檣×) **ほばしら** mast
帆掛け船 **ほかけぶね** sailing ship, sailboat
帆前船 **ほまえせん** sailing ship
白帆 **しらほ** white sail

帆

0243

1-3-3

▶ **SAIL**

ハン ほ

50	Nonstandard	U3836
巾	S6-3-3	F0000

traditional form → see 帆 at 0242

帆

0244

1-3-3

▶ **SAIL**

ハン ほ

50	Nonstandard	U5E06
巾	S6-3-3	F0000

traditional form → see 帆 at 0242

弛

0245

1-3-3

▶ **SLACKEN**

シ ゆる(む) ゆる(める) たる(む) たゆ(む)

Ⓒ 弛 chí

57	Names	U5F1B
弓	S6-3-3	F2723

COMPOUNDS

● **SLACKEN, slack, loosen, relax**

弛緩 **しかん** relaxation; atony
弛張熱 **しちょうねつ** remittent fever
一張一弛 **いっちょういっし** tension and relaxation

KUN

【ゆるむ 弛む】[usu. 緩む] *vi*
ⓐ **SLACKEN, slack, loosen, relax**
ⓑ **be assuaged, abate, moderate, ease off**

【ゆるめる 弛める】[usu. 緩める] *vt*
ⓐ **loosen, unloose, unfasten**
ⓑ **ease (up), mitigate, moderate**

【たるむ 弛む】**SLACKEN, slack, loosen, sag**

弛み **たるみ** slack, sag; slackness, letdown

【たゆむ 弛む】**SLACKEN**, loosen, relax

弛み無い **たゆみない** steady, persistent, unceasing

SYNONYMS

● **loosen**

弛 SLACKEN → 0245
緩 SLACK → 1757

HOMOPHONES

ゆるむ 緩 SLACK → 1757
ゆるめる 緩 SLACK → 1757

NOTE

➡ see USAGE note at 緩 1757

行

0246

1-3-3

▶ **GO**
▶ **ACT**
▶ **LINE**

コウ ギョウ アン い(く) ゆ(く) -ゆ(き) -ゆき -い(き) -いき おこな(う) ㊔ やす なみ なめ つら みち たか

Ⓒ 行 xíng háng

144	Jōyō-2	U884C
行	S6-6-0	F0018

RADICAL

gyō 'road', used in characters related to roads or paths

Enclosure: 行 *gyōgamae* (術 衛 街)

COMPOUNDS

❶ⓐ **GO, walk, travel**
ⓑ [also suffix] trip, journey
a 行進する こうしんする march, parade
行列 ぎょうれつ procession, queue; matrix
徐行 じょこう going slowly
旅行 りょこう travel, trip
歩行 ほこう walk, walking
流行 りゅうこう fashion; prevalence
平行 へいこう parallelism, parallel; going side by side; occurring together
b 行幸 ぎょうこう imperial visit
行脚 あんぎゃ pilgrimage; walking tour; tour
箱根行 はこねこう trip to Hakone

❷ⓐ (perform an action) **ACT, do, carry out, perform, conduct**
ⓑ (something done) **ACT, action, deed**
a 行動 こうどう action, conduct, behavior
行為 こうい act, deed, conduct, transaction
行政 ぎょうせい administration
行事 ぎょうじ event, function
実行 じっこう practice, action; execution
b 非行 ひこう delinquency, misdeed, misdemeanor
悪行 あくぎょう misdeed, wicked act

❸ (personal behavior) **conduct, behavior**
行儀 ぎょうぎ manners, behavior
品行 ひんこう (moral) conduct, behavior, deportment
言行 げんこう speech and conduct
奇行 きこう eccentric conduct

❹ⓐ **LINE (esp. of print), row**
ⓑ counter for **LINE**s or columns
a 行間 ぎょうかん between the lines
行数 ぎょうすう linage, number of lines
行中 ぎょうちゅう in the middle of a line
別行 べつぎょう separate line, another row
b 三行 さんぎょう three lines

❺ **religious austerities, self-discipline, asceticism**
行者 ぎょうじゃ ascetic, pilgrim, devotee
修行 しゅぎょう training, study; ascetic practices
苦行 くぎょう asceticism, hard spiritual exercises

❻ **business establishment, firm**
銀行 ぎんこう bank
洋行 ようこう foreign firm (in preliberation China)
興行 こうぎょう public entertainment, show business

❼ **publish**
刊行する かんこうする publish
発行する はっこうする publish, issue; issue (bank notes)
単行本 たんこうぼん separate volume, independent volume

❽ⓐ abbrev. of 銀行 ぎんこう: bank
ⓑ counter for banks
a 行員 こういん bank clerk
行務 こうむ bank business
当行 とうこう our bank
b 三行 さんこう three banks

❾ *gyosho,* semicursive style of Chinese characters
行書 ぎょうしょ semicursive style of Chinese characters
行体 ぎょうたい semicursive characters

❿ **party, suite**
一行 いっこう party, suite

⓫ abbrev. of 行政 ぎょうせい: administration
行革(=行政改革) ぎょうかく(=ぎょうせいかいかく) administrative reform
行官庁 ぎょうかんちょう Administrative Management Agency

⓬ [also suffix] a style of Chinese poetry
琵琶行 びわこう Biwa Song

⓭ one of the five natural elements (or phases) that constitute the universe in Chinese philosophy
五行 ごぎょう the five elements
諸行 しょぎょう all earthly things

⓮ [original meaning] **crossroads, road**
行程 こうてい distance, journey

⓯ designed for carrying while walking, portable
行火 あんか bed warmer, foot warmer
行灯 あんどん paper-enclosed oil lantern

INDEPENDENT

【こう 行】 party, suite; journey; a style of Chinese poetry
行を共にする こうをともにする join the party

【ぎょう 行】 **LINE (esp. of print), row; religious austerities, asceticism;** ***gyosho*** (→❾)
行を改める ぎょうをあらためる start a new paragraph
朝夕の行 あさゆうのぎょう morning and evening services

【ぎょうずる 行ずる】 train; practice asceticism

KUN

【いく 行く】
① **GO, proceed, leave for; attend; visit**
行き いき(=ゆき) going
行き着く いきつく arrive at, get to
行き先 いきさき(=ゆきさき) one's destination
行き過ぎる いきすぎる go too far, go to extremes
行き過ぎ いきすぎ going too far
行き渡る ゆきわたる(=いきわたる) spread all over, pervade
行き来 いきき comings and goings, traffic

日 土 夕 女 中 工 巾 弓 【彳】 忄 扌 氵 丬 犭 习 彐 饣 巳

行き違い いきちがい crossing, missing each other; misunderstanding

余所行きの よそゆき(=よそいき)の formal (language); best (clothes)

②ⓐ **GO [fare] (well), turn out**

ⓑ **GO well, turn out well, proceed satisfactorily**

ⓒ *slang* **ejaculate, come**

a 旨く行かない うまくいかない go badly, be unsuccessful

b 満足が行く まんぞくがいく be satisfied

③ [following the TE-form of verbs]

ⓐ auxiliary indicating change in progress: **turn, grow**

ⓑ auxiliary indicating continuation of action: **GO on, continue**

a 段段夜が明けて行った だんだんよがあけていった Night melted into day

b どうにか食って行く どうにかくっていく manage to keep body and soul together

【ゆく 行く】 literary form of 行く いく

行き帰り ゆきかえり going and returning, both ways

行方 ゆくえ one's whereabouts

【-ゆき -行き, -行】 [suffix] **bound for, for**

東京行きの列車 とうきょうゆきのれっしゃ train (bound) for Tokyo

【-いき -行き, -行】 [suffix] **bound for, for**

大阪行 おおさかいき for Osaka

【おこなう 行う】 **ACT, do, perform; practice, carry out; hold (a meeting)**

行い おこない act, action, deed; conduct, behavior

行われる おこなわれる be done, be practiced; take place

SYNONYMS

❶ⓐ **go and come**

行 GO →0246
徠 COME →0576
往 GO ON →0348
出 go to →4310
参 go somewhere →2563
来 COME →4366
通 go to and from →3855
向 head toward →3790
赴 PROCEED TO →4095
嚮 GO TOWARD →3610

ⓑ **journey**

旅 TRAVEL →1153
行 trip →0246
遊 tour →3896
巡 tour around →3781

❷ⓐ **do and act**

為 DO →4395
仕 DO →0037
致す DO HUMBLY →1668
行 ACT →0246
作 WORK →0077

❷ⓐ **execute**

執 EXECUTE →2114
行 ACT →0246
履 FULFILL →3933
施 CARRY OUT →1103
践 IMPLEMENT →1938
果たす effect →4377
遂 ACCOMPLISH →3892

ⓑ **acts**

行 ACT →0246
挙 NOTEWORTHY ACT →3106
業 deed →3227

❸ **behavior**

行 conduct →0246
挙 deportment →3106
動 behavior →2232

❹ⓐ **linear arrangements**

伍 RANK →0050
列 ROW →1018
行 LINE (esp. of print) →0246
欄 COLUMN →1419

❽ⓐ **bank**

銀 bank →2156
行 bank →0246

❾ **styles of Chinese characters**

楷 SQUARE STYLE →1282
行 *gyosho* →0246
草 *sosho* →2813

【-ゆき】

◯ **direction indicators**

至 to →2707
-行き bound for →0246
-向け (bound) for →3790
迄 UP TO →3967
以 TO THE...OF →0045
自 from →4338
来 since →4366
而 DIRECTION WORD →2520

USAGE

【ゆく】

行く
literary form of 行く いく

逝く
depart this life, pass away, die

❶ 【いく】

行く
① go, proceed, leave for; attend; visit
②ⓐ go [fare] (well), turn out

ⓑ go well, turn out well, proceed satisfactorily

ⓒ *slang* ejaculate, come

③ [following the TE-form of verbs]

ⓐ auxiliary indicating change in progress: turn, grow

ⓑ auxiliary indicating continuation of action: go on, continue

逝く
depart this life, pass away, die

HOMOPHONES

いく 逝 DEPART THIS LIFE →3850
ゆく 逝 DEPART THIS LIFE →3850

NOTE

➡ see also USAGE note at 平 4291

行 0247

▶*GYŌGAMAE*

144	Radical	U884C
行	S6-6-0	F0000

◧ 1-3-3 radical variant →see 行 at 0246

忙 0248

▶BUSY

ボウ いそが(しい) せわ(しい)▲

Ⓝ 忙 Ⓒ 忙 máng

61	Jōyō	U5FD9
忄	S6-3-3	F1473

◧ 1-3-3

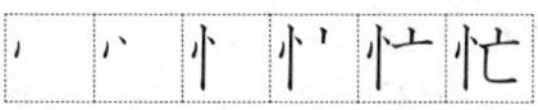

1 2 3 4 5 6

COMPOUNDS

● BUSY, occupied

忙殺される ぼうさつされる be very busily occupied, be worked to death
多忙な たぼうな busy
繁忙である はんぼうである be busy, be fully occupied

INDEPENDENT

【ぼう 忙】BUSYness
忙を厭わず ぼうをいとわず despite one's busyness

KUN

【いそがしい 忙しい】BUSY, occupied, engaged
忙しさ いそがしさ busyness
仕事で忙しい しごとでいそがしい be busy with one's work

【せわしい 忙しい】restless, fidgety; BUSY
忙しさ せわしさ busyness
忙しげな せわしげな looking restless
気忙しい きぜわしい restless, fidgety, fussy

SYNONYMS

● busy
忙 BUSY →0248
繁 bustling →3536
慌てる FLURRIED →0707

忙 0249

▶BUSY

ボウ いそが(しい) せわ(しい)

61	Nonstandard	U5FD9
忄	S6-3-3	F0000

◧ 1-3-3 traditional form →see 忙 at 0248

扣 0250

▶HOLD BACK

コウ ひか(える) ひか(え)

Ⓒ 扣 kòu

64	Non-Jōyō	U6263
扌	S6-3-3	F0000

◧ 1-3-3

COMPOUNDS

❶ [now replaced by 控 0600] HOLD BACK part of something, deduct, subtract
扣除 こうじょ (tax) deduction, subtraction

❷ button

KUN

【ひかえる 扣える】[now replaced by 控える]
① (keep in check) HOLD BACK, keep
②ⓐ (refrain from) HOLD BACK (from), restrain oneself, refrain
ⓑ be moderate, be sparing
③ be in waiting, wait
④ note down, write down, take notes

【ひかえ 扣え】[now replaced by 控え]
① note, memo; counterfoil, stub
② duplicate, copy
③ waiting; reserve, substitute, alternate
④ prop, stay

SYNONYMS

❶ subtract
減 subtract →0733
引く subtract →0207
控 HOLD BACK →0600
扣 HOLD BACK →0250

【ひかえる】
① pull
引 DRAW →0207
曳 DRAW →4348
牽 DRAW →2621
惹 DRAW ATTENTION →2903
抽 DRAW OUT →0359
抜 PULL OUT →0290
控える HOLD BACK →0600
扣える HOLD BACK →0250
寄せる DRAW NEAR →2856

② restrain
制 CONTROL (restrain) →1624

禁 PROHIBIT → 3469
限 LIMIT → 0475
抑 SUPPRESS → 0301
束 TIE UP → 4369
縛 BIND → 1779
控える HOLD BACK → 0600
扣える HOLD BACK → 0250
渋る hang [hold] back → 0625

HOMOPHONES

ひかえる 控 HOLD BACK → 0600
ひかえ 控 HOLD BACK → 0600

NOTE

➡ see USAGE note at 控 0600

扱 0251

1-3-3

▸HANDLE

ショウ▲ あつか(う) あつか(い)

N 扱 C 扱 xī

64	Jōyō	U6271
扌	S6-3-3	F1160

一 十 扌 扌 扨 扱 (1 2 3 4 5 6)

KUN

【あつかう 扱う】

① [original meaning] (manipulate with the hands) **HANDLE, manipulate, work**

粗末に扱う そまつにあつかう handle (a thing) roughly
機械を扱う きかいをあつかう work a machine, handle a tool
上手に扱う じょうずにあつかう handle skillfully

②ⓐ (deal with) **HANDLE (a matter), deal with, treat, manage**

ⓑ (trade in) **HANDLE (goods), deal in**

a 問題を扱う もんだいをあつかう deal with [handle] a matter
取り扱う とりあつかう handle, deal with, treat; deal in; handle, manipulate, operate; conduct; accept, take in
薬を扱う くすりをあつかう deal in medicines

b 扱わない品 あつかわないしな goods not in one's line

③ (treat a person in a particular way) **HANDLE, receive, entertain**

人を公平に扱う ひとをこうへいにあつかう deal justly with a person

【あつかい 扱い】

① [also suffix] (manipulation with the hands) **handling, manipulation, operation**

扱い方 あつかいかた how to handle, way with (an animal)
ボール扱いが巧い ぼーるあつかいがうまい be good at handling a ball

②ⓐ [also suffix] (dealing with a matter) **handling, managing, processing**

ⓑ [suffix] **handling (something) as, regarding (something) as equivalent to**

a 取り扱い とりあつかい handling, dealing, treatment; trading, selling; handling, manipulation, operation; acceptance, service

b 小荷物扱い こにもつあつかい parcel consignment
出席扱い しゅっせきあつかい regard as equivalent to attendance
他人扱いにする たにんあつかいにする treat (a person) as a stranger

③ **treatment of a person, reception, service**

客扱い きゃくあつかい hospitality, entertainment; service

SYNONYMS

【あつかう】

① **handle**

扱う HANDLE → 0251
馭 HANDLE → 2282
操 MANIPULATE → 0948
揮 WIELD → 0717
運 control movement skillfully → 3894

②ⓐ **deal with**

扱う HANDLE → 0251
処 DEAL WITH → 3764
辦 DISPOSE OF → 2028
措 dispose of → 0610
置 take proper steps → 3222

③ **treat and welcome**

遇 TREAT → 3889
待 treat → 0434
扱う HANDLE → 0251
款 treat cordially → 2135
接 receive → 0607
迎 WELCOME → 3796

托 0252

1-3-3

▸RECEPTACLE
▸ENTRUST

タク

C 托 tuō

64	Names	U6258
扌	S6-3-3	F2972

COMPOUNDS

❶ⓐ **RECEPTACLE [base] for holding an object**

ⓑ place [hold] in the hand

a 托子 たくし(=たくす) teacup saucer
茶托 ちゃたく teacup saucer
花托 かたく (of plants) receptacle, torus

b 托鉢 たくはつ religious mendicancy, begging bonze

❷ [also 託 1845] **ENTRUST (a person with a thing), place (a thing) in someone's charge, commit, ask**

托卵 たくらん brood parasitism
委托する いたくする entrust with, charge with, consign
一蓮托生 いちれんたくしょう sharing the same fate

INDEPENDENT

【たくす 托す】[usu. 託す] **ENTRUST** (a person with a thing); anchor (one's hope); convey (one's feelings) in (verse)

SYNONYMS

❶ vessels and receptacles
盤 dish → 3533
鍋 POT → 2202
釜 IRON POT → 2610
鼎 TRIPOD CAULDRON → 4405
臼 MORTAR → 4341
碓 MORTAR → 1537
托 RECEPTACLE → 0252
皿 PLATE → 4286
盆 TRAY → 2581
膳 LEGGED TRAY → 1381
杯 CUP → 1066
鉢 BOWL → 2144
椀 WOODEN BOWL → 1250
碗 CERAMIC BOWL → 1539
丼 LARGE BOWL → 4323

❷ commit
託 ENTRUST → 1845
托 ENTRUST → 0252
預 DEPOSIT → 1317
委 COMMIT → 3160
任 LEAVE TO → 0057
嘱 CHARGE WITH → 0881

NOTE

➡ see COMPOUND FORMATION for 托鉢 たくはつ → 鉢 2144

池

0253
◧ 1-3-3

▸POND
チ いけ
Ⓒ 池 chí

85 氵	Jōyō-2 / S6-3-3	U6C60 / F0744

COMPOUNDS

❶ⓐ [also suffix] [original meaning] **POND, pool**
ⓑ reservoir
a 池畔 ちはん edge of a pond
池沼 ちしょう ponds and swamps
養殖池 ようしょくち fish pond
b 貯水池 ちょすいち reservoir
用水池 ようすいち reservoir
電池 でんち electric cell, battery

❷ inkstone well
墨池 ぼくち inkstone well, inkhorn

KUN

【いけ 池】**POND, pool; reservoir; inkstone well**
溜め池 ためいけ reservoir, irrigation pond, cistern
古池 ふるいけ old pond

SYNONYMS

❶ⓐ lakes and marshes
沢 MARSH → 0313
沼 MUDDY POND → 0398
湖 LAKE → 0736
池 POND → 0253
潟 LAGOON → 0921

汎

0254
◧ 1-3-3

▸OVERALL
ハン
Ⓒ 泛 fàn

85 氵	Jōyō / S6-3-3	U6C4E / F2745

COMPOUNDS

❶ⓐ OVERALL, general, universal, versatile
ⓑ [prefix] **pan-**
a 汎論 はんろん general remarks; outline
汎愛 はんあい philanthropy
汎用 はんよう generic, general-purpose, all-purpose, universal, versatile
汎用型コンピュータ はんようがたこんぴゅーた mainframe computer
b 汎神論 はんしんろん pantheism
汎アメリカ主義 はんあめりかしゅぎ Pan-Americanism

❷ [now usu. 範 3360] extensive, wide-ranging
広汎な こうはんな extensive, wide-ranging, comprehensive

SYNONYMS

❶ general
総 GENERAL → 1743
惣 GENERAL → 3452
汎 OVERALL → 0254

汝

0255
◧ 1-3-3

▸THOU
ジョ なんじ ㊔ な
Ⓒ 汝 rǔ

85 氵	Names / S6-3-3	U6C5D / F2359

口 土 夕 女 中 工 巾 弓 彳 忄 扌 【氵】 丬 犭 习 扌 亻 E

COMPOUNDS

❶ **THOU**, you

爾汝 じじょ addressing someone familiarly in the second person or without using a title

KUN

【なんじ 汝】[sometimes also 爾] **THOU, you**

汝の隣人を愛せよ なんじのりんじんをあいせよ Love thy neighbor

汝自身を知れ なんじじしんをしれ Know thyself

SYNONYMS

❶ **second person pronouns**

君 YOU (*familiar*) →3974

汝 THOU →0255

爾 thou →4407

貴 you (*honorific*) →3220

卿 you (*archaic*, *honorific*) →0769

USAGE

【なんじ】

汝

[sometimes also 爾] thou, you

爾

[usu. 汝] thou, you

HOMOPHONES

なんじ 爾 THAT →4407

汗

0256

1-3-3

▸SWEAT

カン あせ

Ⓒ 汗 hàn hán

85	Jōyō	U6C57
氵	S6-3-3	F1172

Stroke order: 1 2 3 4 5 6

COMPOUNDS

❶ **SWEAT, perspiration**

汗腺 かんせん sweat gland

汗顔 かんがん sweating from shame

汗血 かんけつ sweat and blood

発汗する はっかんする perspire, sweat

冷汗 れいかん cold sweat

❷ [rare] khan, chieftain

ジンギス汗 じんぎすかん Genghis Khan

KUN

【あせ 汗】**SWEAT, perspiration**

汗掻き(=汗っ掻き) あせかき(=あせっかき) one who perspires freely, great sweater

汗臭い あせくさい smelling of sweat

汗だくで あせだくで bathed in perspiration, dripping with sweat

汗ばむ あせばむ become slightly sweaty

汗を掻く あせをかく sweat, perspire

冷や汗 ひやあせ cold sweat

SYNONYMS

❶ **bodily secretions**

乳 MILK →1823

精 sperm →1729

汗 SWEAT →0256

涙 TEAR →0528

唾 SALIVA →0553

❶ **excreta**

便 EXCRETA →0105

尿 URINE →3801

汗 SWEAT →0256

江

0257

1-3-3

▸INLET

コウ え ㊔ ごう

Ⓒ 江 jiāng

85	Jōyō	U6C5F
氵	S6-3-3	F0290

Stroke order: 1 2 3 4 5 6

COMPOUNDS

ⓐ [original meaning] **large river**

ⓑ suffix after names of large rivers

ⓒ Yangtze River (name of longest river in Asia)

a 江上 こうじょう bank of a large river

江山 こうざん [rare] rivers and mountains

江湖 こうこ general public, the world ("rivers and lakes")

b 揚子江 ようすこう Yangtze River

c 江河 こうが Yangtze and Yellow rivers

長江 ちょうこう Yangtze River, Changjiang River

KUN

【え 江】**INLET, cove**

入り江 いりえ inlet, cove, creek

SYNONYMS

ⓐ & ⓑ **rivers and streams**

川 RIVER →0006

河 RIVER →0394

江 large river →0257

渓 mountain stream →0628

流 stream →0529

【え】

○ **inlets and bays**

江 INLET →0257

浦 coastal indentation →0524

湾 BAY →0748

峡 narrows →0427

汚

0258

◧ 1-3-3

▶DIRTY

オ けが(す) けが(れる) けが(らわしい) よご(す) よご(れる) きたな(い)

Ⓝ 污 汙 Ⓒ 污 wū

85	Jōyō	U6C5A
氵	S6-3-3	F1151

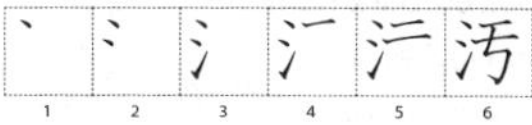

COMPOUNDS

❶ⓐ DIRTY, contaminated, defiled

ⓑ (make or become unclean) **DIRTY, soil, defile; become dirty, become defiled**

a 汚水 おすい dirty [filthy] water, sewage

汚物 おぶつ dirt, filth, impurities

b 汚染 おせん pollution, contamination

❷ (bring dishonor upon) **defile, disgrace, corrupt, dishonor**

汚職 おしょく (official) corruption, bribery

汚名 おめい bad name, ill fame, disgrace

汚点 おてん disgrace, flaw; stain, blot

汚濁 おだく(=おじょく) corruption

KUN

【けがす 汚す】 (bring dishonor upon) **defile, disgrace, dishonor, desecrate;** [humble] **be given a position**

名声を汚す めいせいをけがす defile one's reputation

女を汚す おんなをけがす defile [deflower] a woman

末席を汚す まっせきをけがす have the honor of being a member

【けがれる 汚れる】 (become unclean) **become DIRTY, become defiled, be stained;** (be contrary to honor or rules) **be defiled, get corrupted, be stained**

汚れ けがれ dirt, uncleanliness; impurity, disgrace

汚れた手 けがれたて dirty hand, blood(-stained) hand

汚れた一生 けがれたいっしょう dirty [sinful] life

【けがらわしい 汚らわしい】 **DIRTY, filthy; detestable**

汚らわしい身形 けがらわしいみなり dirty getup [appearance]

見るのも汚らわしい みるのもけがらわしい be detestable to look at

【よごす 汚す】 (make unclean) **make DIRTY, soil, defile;** (bring dishonor upon) **defile, corrupt, dishonor**

服を汚す ふくをよごす soil one's clothes

面汚し つらよごし disgrace, shame

【よごれる 汚れる】 (become unclean) **become DIRTY, become defiled**

汚れ よごれ dirt, filth

汚れ物 よごれもの laundry

【きたない 汚い】 (unclean) **DIRTY, soiled;** (contrary to honor or rules) **dirty, foul, base, obscene; niggardly**

汚らしい きたならしい dirty-looking, squalid

汚いやり方 きたないやりかた dirty trick

口汚い くちぎたない foulmouthed

金に汚い かねにきたない stingy, mean [greedy] about money

SYNONYMS

❶ⓐ dirty

汚 DIRTY → 0258

濁 TURBID → 0953

ⓑ & 【よごす】 dirty

汚 DIRTY → 0258

染 contaminate → 3181

❷ disgrace

恥 SHAME → 1664

羞 shame → 4106

辱 HUMILIATE → 3400

侮 INSULT → 0091

罵 ABUSE → 3233

汚 defile → 0258

誹 SLANDER → 1978

譏 SLANDER → 2069

汐

0259

◧ 1-3-3

▶TIDE

セキ しお Ⓝ うしお

Ⓒ 汐 xī

85	Names	U6C50
氵	S6-3-3	F2699

COMPOUNDS

ⓐ TIDE, ebb tide

ⓑ [original meaning, now archaic] **evening TIDE**

a 潮汐 ちょうせき ebb and flow, tide

KUN

【しお 汐】 [usu. 潮]

①ⓐ **TIDE, current**

ⓑ **seawater**

a 汐干狩り しおひがり shell gathering (at low tide)

b 汐汲み しおくみ drawing water from the sea; person who draws water from the sea

② **TIDE** (in the archaic sense of 'favorable occasion'), opportunity, chance

汐合い しおあい chance, opportunity

SYNONYMS

ⓐ running water

流 CURRENT → 0529

潮 TIDE → 0916

汐 TIDE → 0259

瀬 rapids → 0995

滝 WATERFALL → 0813

洪 FLOOD → 0461

渦 WHIRLPOOL →0735

HOMOPHONES

しお 潮 TIDE →0916

NOTE

➡ see USAGE note at 潮 0916

汲 0260

▶DRAW WATER

キュウ く(む)

1-3-3

85	Nonstandard	U6C72
氵	S6-3-3	F0000

traditional form →see 汲 at 0310

汙 0261

▶DIRTY

オ けが(す) けが(れる) けが(らわしい) よご(す) よご(れる) きたな(い)

1-3-3

85	Nonstandard	U6C59
氵	S6-3-3	F0000

traditional form →see 汚 at 0258

汚 0262

▶DIRTY

オ けが(す) けが(れる) けが(らわしい) よご(す) よご(れる) きたな(い)

1-3-3

85	Nonstandard	U6C61
氵	S6-3-3	F0000

traditional form →see 汚 at 0258

壮 0263

▶VIGOROUS
▶GRAND

ソウ ㊔ たけ たけし まさ つよし もり

Ⓝ 壯 Ⓒ 壮 zhuàng

1-3-3

33	Jōyō	U58EE
士	S6-3-3	F1566

丨 1 丬 2 丬 3 丬一 4 壮 5 壮 6

COMPOUNDS

❶ⓐ VIGOROUS, robust, strong, able-bodied, energetic

ⓑ [original meaning] **VIGOROUS** young man, prime of life

a 壮健な そうけんな vigorous, healthy, robust
強壮な きょうそうな robust, strong, vigorous

b 壮年 そうねん prime of life
壮丁 そうてい young man of conscription age
少壮 しょうそう youth

❷ⓐ (having grandeur) **GRAND, magnificent, splendid**

ⓑ heroic, ambitious, brave, dauntless

a 壮観 そうかん grand sight, magnificent view
壮大な そうだいな grand, magnificent, grandiose
壮麗な そうれいな grand, magnificent, splendid, imposing
豪壮な ごうそうな grand, magnificent, splendid
宏壮な こうそうな grand, magnificent, imposing

b 壮烈な そうれつな heroic, brave
壮挙 そうきょ grand scheme, heroic [daring] attempt
壮士 そうし desperado, brave, swashbuckler
壮途 そうと ambitious embarkment
勇壮な ゆうそうな brave, heroic
悲壮な ひそうな pathetic, tragic

INDEPENDENT

【そう 壮】 vigor; lofty ambition, courage
壮とする そうとする admire [approve of] a person's courage

SYNONYMS

❶ⓐ strong

強 STRONG →0574
壮 VIGOROUS →0263
丈 STOUT →4227
健 ROBUST (healthy) →0152
逞しい ROBUST (sturdy) →4004
康 HEALTHY →3877
旺 ENERGETIC →1061
溌 LIVELY →0917

❷ⓐ great

偉 GREAT (of superior character) →0167
大 BIG →4224
宏 GRAND (large in scale) →2728
壮 GRAND (having grandeur) →0263
豪 MAGNIFICENT →2657
雄 HEROIC →1271
碩 EMINENT →1555

ⓑ brave

勇 BRAVE →2592
侠 chivalrous →0110
赳 VALIANT →4100
驍 VALIANT →2327
敢 bold →2142
豪 bold and unrestrained →2657
雄 HEROIC →1271
壮 heroic →0263
義 chivalrous →2948
凜 gallant →0195

兆 0264

▶OMEN
▶TRILLION

チョウ きざ(す) きざ(し) ㊔ よし とき

Ⓒ 兆 zhào

1-3-3

10	Jōyō-4	U5146
儿	S6-2-4	F1325

ノ ソ 丬 兆 兆 兆
1 2 3 4 5 6

COMPOUNDS

❶ **OMEN, sign, indication, symptom; foreboding**
兆候(=徴候) ちょうこう symptom, sign; omen
前兆 ぜんちょう omen, sign
吉兆 きっちょう good omen, lucky sign

❷ⓐ **TRILLION (10^{12})**
ⓑ astronomical figure, multitude
a 八兆円 はっちょうえん eight trillion yen
b 億兆 おくちょう multitude; [archaic] the people, the masses

❸ [original meaning, now obsolete] line pattern on the back of a tortoise shell used for divination in ancient China

INDEPENDENT

【ちょう 兆】**OMEN, sign; trillion (10^{12})**
不吉の兆有り ふきつのちょうあり have an ill omen

KUN

【きざす 兆す】**show signs [symptoms] of**
【きざし 兆し】**OMEN, sign, symptom**
凶事の兆し きょうじのきざし omen of disaster

SYNONYMS

❶ **signs**
候 indication →0133
徴 SYMPTOM →0841
症 symptom (of a disease) →4065
気 sign →3960
兆 OMEN →0264

❷ⓐ **large numbers**
百 HUNDRED →2519
千 THOUSAND →4219
万 TEN THOUSAND →3653
億 HUNDRED MILLION →0192
兆 TRILLION →0264
京 ten quadrillion →2546

USAGE

❶【きざす】
兆す
show signs [symptoms] of
萌す
germinate, sprout; spring up, dawn

❷【きざし】
兆し
omen, sign, symptom
萌し
germination, sprouting; dawning

HOMOPHONES

きざす 萌 GERMINATE →2871
きざし 萌 GERMINATE →2871

羽

0265
1-3-3

▶**FEATHER**
▶**WING**
ウ は わ はね
Ⓝ 羽 Ⓒ 羽 yǔ

124	Jōyō-2	U7FBD
羽	S6-6-0	F0761

radical variant →see 羽 at 0266

丁 习 习 羽 羽 羽
1 2 3 4 5 6

COMPOUNDS

❶ [original meaning] **FEATHER, plumage**
羽毛 うもう feathers, plumage, down

❷ **WING (of birds or insects), ala**
羽翼 うよく wings; assistance
羽化 うか emergence (of insects)

❸ abbrev. of 出羽 でわ, old name for west Tohoku district
奥羽 おうう Ou, old name for Tohoku district

❹ [rare] fifth note of the pentatonic scale (→see APPENDIX 8)

INDEPENDENT

【う 羽】[rare] fifth note of the pentatonic scale

KUN

【は 羽】
① **FEATHER, plumage**
羽衣 はごろも robe of feathers
② **WING, ala**
羽蟻× はあり winged ant
羽音 はおと flapping [whirring] of wings
羽撃く はばたく flap the wings, flutter
③ **used phonetically for *ha***
羽織 はおり Japanese half coat, *haori*

【わ 羽】**counter for birds or rabbits**
一羽 いちわ one bird [rabbit]
三羽 さんば three birds [rabbits]

【はね 羽】**FEATHER, plume; wing, ala;** [also 羽根] **fan, blade**
羽布団 はねぶとん feather quilt

SYNONYMS

❶ **hair**
毛 HAIR (of any kind) →4264
髪 HAIR (on the head) →3528
辮 PLAIT →2085
羽 FEATHER →0265
眉 EYEBROW →3991
鬚 BEARD →3539

❷ **wings**
翼 WING (of birds or aircraft) →3379
羽 WING (of birds or insects) →0265
葉 plane →2912

口 土 夕 女 巾 工 巾 弓 彳 忄 扌 氵 丬 彐 ヨ 【羽】 竹 臼

【わ】

◯ **counters for animals**

匹 COUNTER FOR ANIMALS → 3680
頭 counter for large animals → 2019
羽 counter for birds → 0265
疋 counter for animals → 4292

COMPOUND FORMATION

【羽化 うか】

羽化 'emergence (of insects)' is the process of becoming transformed (化) into a winged (羽 ❷) creature.

NOTE

★ The pronunciation of 羽 わ when used as a bird counter depends on the preceding syllable as follows: 一羽 いちわ, 二羽 にわ, 三羽 さんば 四羽 よんわ, 五羽 ごわ, 六羽 ろくわ (=ろっぱ), 七羽 ななわ, 八羽 はちわ (=はっぱ), 九羽 きゅうわ, 十羽 じゅうわ (=じっぱ).

羽 0266

1-3-3

▶**FEATHER**
▶**WING**
ウ は わ はね

124	Nonstandard	UFA1E
羽	S6-6-0	F0000

traditional form → see 羽 at 0265

RADICAL

hane 'wing' (翰 翳 翅×), used in characters related to wings, feathers or related actions
Variant: 羽 *hane* (習 翁 翔)

竹 0267

1-3-3

▶**BAMBOO**
チク たけ ㊔ たか
Ⓒ 竹 zhú

118	Jōyō-1	U7AF9
竹	S6-6-0	F0773

1	2	3	4	5	6
ノ	㇐	𠂉	𥫗	𥫗	竹

RADICAL

take 'bamboo', used in characters related to bamboo or bamboo products
Top variant: ⺮ *takekanmuri* (第 策 答)

COMPOUNDS

❶ BAMBOO

竹馬の友 ちくばのとも childhood friend, old playmate
竹材 ちくざい bamboo
竹林 ちくりん bamboo grove

❷ BAMBOO writing tablets used for recording history in ancient China

竹簡 ちくかん bamboo writing strip
竹帛× ちくはく history

❸ [rare] BAMBOO wind instruments, as: flute, pipe, *sho* (Japanese mouth organ)

糸竹 しちく musical instruments

KUN

【たけ 竹】BAMBOO

竹細工 たけざいく bamboo work
竹製 たけせい made of bamboo
竹馬 たけうま(=ちくば) stilts

SPECIAL READINGS

竹刀 しない bamboo sword

SYNONYMS

❶ **bamboo**

竹 BAMBOO → 0267
笹 BAMBOO GRASS → 3301
篠 DWARF BAMBOO → 3376

❷ **writing strips**

簡 bamboo writing strips → 3380
竹 bamboo writing tablets → 0267

COMPOUND FORMATION

【竹馬 たけうま(=ちくば)】【竹馬の友 ちくばのとも】

竹馬 'stilts' are so called because they resemble a bamboo (竹 ❶) horse (馬). 竹馬の友 'childhood friend, old playmate' refers to friends (友) that used to play together with stilts.

⺮ 0268

1-3-3

▶***TAKEKANMURI***

118	Radical	U2EAE
⺮	S6-6-0	F0000

radical variant → see 竹 at 0267

臼

1-3-3

incorrect stroke-count
➡ see 1-4-3: 臼 at 1049

吠 0269

1-3-4

▶**BARK**
バイ ハイ ベイ ほ(える)
Ⓒ 吠 fèi

30	Non-Jōyō	U5420
口	S7-3-4	F2307

COMPOUNDS

❶ **BARK, bay, howl, roar, cry**

犬吠 けんばい barking (of a dog)
狗吠 くはい barking (of a dog)

❷ used phonetically for *bai* or *bei* in the transliteration of Sanskrit Buddhist terms

吠舎 ばいしゃ *Vaiśhya*
吠瑠璃 べいるり *vaidūrya,* lapis lazuli

KUN

【ほえる 吠える】

①ⓐ (of animals) **BARK, bay, howl, roar, cry**
ⓑ (of people) **yell, shout, cry**

a 吠え声 ほえごえ bark, bay, howl
吠え付く ほえつく bark at and chase
吠猿 ほえざる howler monkey
遠吠え とおぼえ howling (of a dog or wolf)
b 吠え面 ほえづら tearful face
会議で吠える かいぎでほえる yell at a meeting

② (of wind or waves) howl, roar
風が吠えている かぜがほえている the wind is howling

SYNONYMS

❶ **give out a call**
叫 SHOUT → 0233
号 holler → 2675
喝 SHOUT AT → 0554
喚 call out → 0666
呼 CALL → 0324
鳴 CRY → 0831
吠 BARK → 0269

吻

▶PROBOSCIS
フン
Ⓒ 吻 wěn

0270
◧1-3-4

30	Names	U543B
口	S7-3-4	F2368

COMPOUNDS

ⓐ **PROBOSCIS, nose, snout, muzzle, trunk, beak**
ⓑ **lip(s)**

a 口吻 こうふん proboscis, muzzle, snout; way of speaking, intimation
黄吻 こうふん young and inexperienced person ("yellow beak")
b 吻合 ふんごう concurrence, coincidence; anastomosis, inosculation
接吻 せっぷん kiss

INDEPENDENT

【ふん 吻】**PROBOSCIS**, snout, trunk

SYNONYMS

ⓐ **front parts of head**
顔 FACE → 2277
面 FACE → 2590
額 forehead → 2273
顎 chin → 2276
頬 CHEEK → 2043
吻 PROBOSCIS → 0270

吟

▶RECITE
ギン
Ⓒ 吟 yín

0271
◧1-3-4

30	Jōyō	U541F
口	S7-3-4	F1953

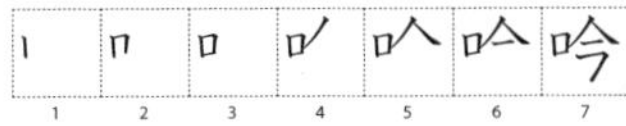

COMPOUNDS

❶ⓐ **RECITE (a poem), chant, intone**
ⓑ compose (a poem)
ⓒ [also suffix] poem

a 吟詠 ぎんえい reciting [chanting] a poem; poem
吟唱(=吟誦)する ぎんしょうする recite, chant
詩吟 しぎん reciting Chinese poems
b 苦吟 くぎん laborious composition
沈吟 ちんぎん painstaking elaboration on one's poem; groaning in distress
c 病中吟 びょうちゅうぎん poems composed in one's sickbed

❷ **examine carefully**
吟味する ぎんみする examine closely, scrutinize

❸ moan, groan
呻×吟する しんぎんする moan, groan

INDEPENDENT

【ぎん 吟】recital, chanting (a poem); poem
【ぎんじる(=ぎんずる) 吟じる(=吟ずる)】**RECITE**, chant (a poem); compose (a poem)

SYNONYMS

❶ⓐ **recite**
吟 RECITE → 0271
誦 RECITE → 1951
唱 chant → 0555
読 READ → 1943
詠 RECITE POETRY → 1894

吹

▶BLOW
スイ ふ(く)
Ⓒ 吹 chuī

0272
◧1-3-4

30	Jōyō	U5439
口	S7-3-4	F0917

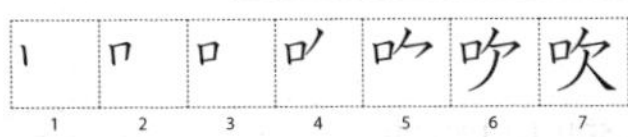

COMPOUNDS

ⓐ **BLOW on, play on a wind instrument**
ⓑ [original meaning] **BLOW, breathe out**

a 吹奏 すいそう playing wind instruments
鼓吹する こすいする inspire, inculcate, advocate
b 吹鳴する すいめいする blow (a whistle)

KUN

【ふく 吹く】
①ⓐ **BLOW, breathe out**
ⓑ **BLOW (as a trumpet), play on a wind instrument**

a 吹き込む ふきこむ blow into, breathe into
吹き出す ふきだす blow out; begin to blow

b 笛吹き ふえふき flute player

② (of wind) **BLOW**

吹き荒れる ふきあれる blow violently

吹き溜まり ふきだまり snowdrift, drift of dust [sand]

③ (of germs or buds) sprout

芽吹く めぶく bud

④ brag

吹聴する ふいちょうする make public, announce

ほら吹き ほらふき boaster, braggart

SPECIAL READINGS

吹雪 ふぶき snowstorm

息吹 いぶき breath

SYNONYMS

❶ⓐ play music

奏 PLAY MUSIC → 3185

弾 play on (stringed instruments) → 0697

吹 BLOW → 0272

ⓑ discharge from mouth

吐 SPEW → 0235

吹 BLOW → 0272

❶ⓑ breathe and blow

息 BREATH → 3278

気 breath → 3960

吸 BREATHE IN → 0234

呼 breathe out → 0324

吹 BLOW → 0272

USAGE

【ふく】

吹く

①ⓐ blow, breathe out

ⓑ blow (as a trumpet), play on a wind instrument

② (of wind) blow

③ (of germs or buds) sprout

④ brag

噴く

spout, emit, spurt, gush out

HOMOPHONES

ふく 噴 SPOUT → 0879

COMPOUND FORMATION

【鼓吹 こすい】

鼓吹 was originally a kind of ancient military or court music in which drums (鼓) and wind instruments (吹 ❶ⓐ) were used. 鼓吹する 'inspire, inculcate, advocate' derives from the idea of drumming up or rousing a person's emotions.

吸

0273

1-3-4

▶SUCK
▶BREATHE IN

キュウ す(う)

30	Nonstandard	U5438
口	S7-3-4	F0000

traditional form → see 吸 at 0234

吃

1-3-4

incorrect stroke-count
➡ see 1-3-3: 口 at 0232

吸

1-3-4

incorrect stroke-count
➡ see 1-3-3: 口 at 0234

坊

0274

1-3-4

▶SONNY
▶COLLOQUIAL PERSON SUFFIX

ボウ ボッ-

Ⓒ 坊 fāng fáng

32	Jōyō	U574A
土	S7-3-4	F1156

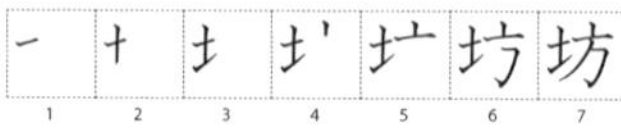

COMPOUNDS

❶ SONNY, boy, sonny boy

坊や ぼうや sonny, sonny boy, boy

坊ちゃん ぼっちゃん sonny, boy; Master Daring; greenhorn, baby

凸坊 でこぼう mischievous boy, imp

❷ COLLOQUIAL PERSON SUFFIX: indicates endearment, intimacy or derision, as the English "Jimmy boy" for James or such nicknames as "fatso" for a fat person

赤ん坊 あかんぼう baby

春坊 はるぼう nickname for such names as Haruo or Haruko

朝寝坊 あさねぼう late riser, sleepy head

けちん坊 けちんぼう miser, niggard, stingy fellow

食いしん坊 くいしんぼう glutton

風来坊 ふうらいぼう wanderer, vagabond, hobo

見栄坊 みえぼう fop, swell, dude, coxcomb

❸ colloquial suffix for children's games or various actions

隠れん坊 かくれんぼう hide-and-seek

通せん坊 とおせんぼう barring (a person's) way

立ちん坊 たちんぼう being kept standing

❹ⓐ Buddhist priest [monk], bonze

ⓑ title after names of Buddhist priests

ⓒ [also suffix] priest's residence

a 坊主 ぼうず Buddhist priest [monk], bonze; shaven head; sonny, sonny boy, boy

坊さん ぼうさん Buddhist priest

御坊 ごぼう Reverend
b 武蔵坊 むさしぼう Reverend Musashi
c 僧坊 そうぼう priest's living quarters in a Buddhist temple
宿坊 しゅくぼう priest's quarters; visitor's lodgings in a temple
本因坊 ほんいんぼう Honinbo Lodge in Jakko Temple; grand champion of go

❺ city quarter, streets
坊間 ぼうかん all over town

INDEPENDENT

【ぼう 坊】Buddhist priest [monk], bonze; priest's residence
坊の主 ぼうのあるじ master of the priest's quarters
師の坊 しのぼう master priest

SYNONYMS

❶ **child**
児 CHILD (of any age) →3153
子 CHILD →4196
童 CHILD (young person) →2639
幼 young child →0222
坊 SONNY →0274

❷ **fellow**
奴 GUY →0217
漢 FELLOW →0808
輩 FELLOW (*belittling*) →3482
徒 fellows →0499
棒 tough guy →1237
坊 COLLOQUIAL PERSON SUFFIX →0274
屋 colloquial person suffix →3842
物 character →1084

❹ⓐ **clergymen**
僧 BONZE →0180
坊 Buddhist priest →0274
尼 BUDDHIST NUN →3767
父 FATHER →2467

NOTE

➡ see COMPOUND FORMATION for 赤ん坊 あかんぼう →赤 2719

坂

▶SLOPE

ハン さか ㊔ ばん

Ⓒ 坂 bǎn

0275

◧ 1-3-4

32	Jōyō-3	U5742
土	S7-3-4	F0586

Stroke order: 1–7

COMPOUNDS

● [original meaning] **SLOPE, incline, hill**
急坂 きゅうはん steep hill [slope]
登坂 とはん climbing a slope [hill]

KUN

【さか 坂】**SLOPE, incline, hill**
坂道 さかみち slope
上り坂 のぼりざか ascent, upward slope

SYNONYMS

● **hills**
丘 HILL →4307
畝 RIDGE →1857
岡 HILL →3719
台 heights →2498
坂 SLOPE →0275
阪 slope →0321
塚 MOUND →0675
阜 MOUND →3254
陵 high mound →0660
稜 RIDGE →1545

USAGE

【さか】
坂
slope, incline, hill
阪
slope, incline, hill

★Both forms have the same meaning, but the latter is now used almost exclusively in the writing of names.

HOMOPHONES

さか 阪 OSAKA →0321

均

▶EVEN

キン なら(す)* ㊔ ひとし

Ⓒ 均 jūn

0276

◧ 1-3-4

32	Jōyō-5	U5747
土	S7-3-4	F1215

Stroke order: 1–7

COMPOUNDS

ⓐ **EVEN, uniform, equal, same, symmetrical, well-balanced**

ⓑ [original meaning] **make EVEN, level**
a 均一な きんいつな uniform, equal, even
均等の きんとうの equal, uniform
均質 きんしつ homogeneity
均分 きんぶん equal division
均勢 きんせい balance [equilibrium] of power, uniformity
b 均整(=均斉) きんせい symmetry
均衡 きんこう balance, equilibrium
平均 へいきん average, (arithmetical) mean; equilibrium, balance

KUN

【ならす 均す】

①level, make **EVEN**, roll

土を均す つちをならす level the ground

②average

均し ならし average

SYNONYMS

ⓐ same and uniform

等 EQUAL →3321

平 equal →4291

均 EVEN →0276

斉 UNIFORM →2548

同 SAME →3707

一 same →4148

HOMOPHONES

ならす

慣 HABITUAL PRACTICE →0843

馴 BECOME TAME →2290

NOTE

➡ see USAGE note at 慣 0843

坑

0277

1-3-4

▶PIT

コウ

Ⓒ 坑 kēng

32	Jōyō	U5751
土	S7-3-4	F2582

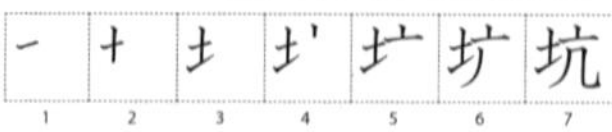

COMPOUNDS

❶ⓐ PIT (of a mine), mine-pit, mine

ⓑ [original meaning] **PIT**, shaft

a 坑口 こうこう pithead, minehead

坑外で こうがいで out of the pit

坑夫 こうふ miner

坑内 こうない mine-pit, shaft

坑底 こうてい mine-pit bottom

鉱坑 こうこう mine, shaft, pit

炭坑 たんこう coal-mine, coal pit

b 坑道 こうどう tunnel, pit; (mine) level; shaft

❷ [rare] bury alive

坑儒 こうじゅ burying Confucian scholars alive

INDEPENDENT

【こう 坑】 mine **PIT**, mine

SYNONYMS

❶ⓐ mine

坑 PIT →0277

鉱 MINE →2145

礦 MINE →1606

山 mine →3658

ⓑ holes and cavities

穴 HOLE →2682

洞 CAVE →0455

窟 CAVE →2923

窪 HOLLOW →2962

腔 BODY CAVITY →1267

孔 OPEN HOLE →0205

口 MOUTH →4189

坑 PIT →0277

堀 DITCH →0561

溝 CHANNEL →0810

壕 TRENCH →0966

濠 MOAT →0975

凹 concavity →4294

舛

0278

1-3-4

▶*MAIASHI*

136	Radical	U821B
舛	S7-7-0	F0000

radical variant → see 舛 at 0237

妨

0279

1-3-4

▶HINDER

ボウ さまた(げる)

Ⓒ 妨 fáng

38	Jōyō	U59A8
女	S7-3-4	F2044

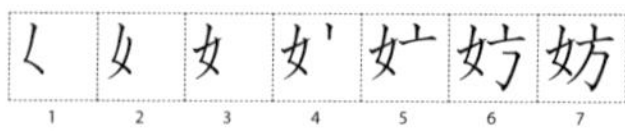

COMPOUNDS

● HINDER, interfere with, disturb, obstruct, impede

妨害する ぼうがいする disturb, hinder, obstruct, hamper, impede, interfere

妨害放送 ぼうがいほうそう radio jamming

KUN

【さまたげる 妨げる】 **HINDER, interfere with, disturb, obstruct, impede; preclude**

妨げ さまたげ hindrance, obstruction, disturbance

睡眠を妨げる すいみんをさまたげる disturb one's sleep

重任を妨げない じゅうにんをさまたげない Reappointment is not precluded

SYNONYMS

● obstruct and hinder

遮 INTERRUPT →3916

塞 STOP UP →2924

阻 OBSTRUCT →0411

沮 OBSTRUCT →0399

奄 OBSTRUCT (by covering) →2757

妨 HINDER →0279

障 hinder →0875

碍 STAND IN THE WAY →1536

害 stand in the way →2826

梗 STOP UP → 1204

妙

▶MARVELOUS

ミョウ たえ▲

Ⓒ 妙 miào

0280

◧ 1-3-4

38	Jōyō	U5999
女	S7-3-4	F0806

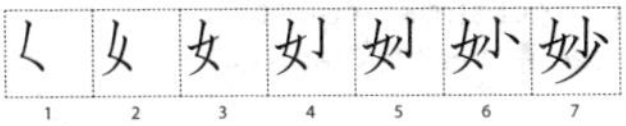

COMPOUNDS

❶ⓐ (causing wonder) **MARVELOUS, wonderful, miraculous**

ⓑ [original meaning] **of MARVELOUS beauty, exquisite, charming, subtle**

ⓒ (of incredible excellence) **MARVELOUS, superb, excellent; adroit, ingenious**

a 妙薬 みょうやく miracle drug, golden remedy
絶妙な ぜつみょうな miraculous, exquisite, superb

b 妙法蓮華経 みょうほうれんげきょう Lotus Sutra
妙味 みょうみ subtle charm, beauty
美妙な びみょうな elegant, exquisite
微妙な びみょうな subtle, delicate

c 妙案 みょうあん bright idea, excellent plan
妙技 みょうぎ wonderful skill; stunt
巧妙な こうみょうな skillful, ingenious, clever

❷ (arousing marvel) **strange, odd, queer, singular**
奇妙な きみょうな strange, queer, odd
珍妙な ちんみょうな queer, odd, fantastic

❸ youthful, young and beautiful
妙齢の みょうれいの young, blooming

INDEPENDENT

【みょう 妙】**mystery, miracle, wonder; cleverness, adroitness; strangeness**
妙な みょうな strange, queer, funny
妙を得ている みょうをえている clever, skillful
妙に思う みょうにおもう think strange
造化の妙 ぞうかのみょう the mystery of creation

KUN

【たえ 妙】

たえなる 妙なる **exquisite, excellent; delicate; charming**
妙なる調べ たえなるしらべ sweet tune, enchanting melody

SYNONYMS

❶ⓐ miraculous
妙 MARVELOUS → 0280
魔 magic(al) → 3953

ⓑ beautiful
美 BEAUTIFUL → 2817
彪 MAGNIFICENT → 4115
綺 BEAUTIFUL → 1734
娃 BEAUTIFUL → 0419
佳 FINE → 0096
瑶 EXQUISITE → 1301
麗 OF GRACEFUL BEAUTY → 2672
艶 CHARMING → 2403
妙 of marvelous beauty → 0280
華 MAGNIFICENT → 2841
絢 GORGEOUS → 1705
斐 florid → 3449

ⓒ excellent and superior
優 SUPERIOR → 0200
絶 without match → 1711
卓 PROMINENT → 2561
快 splendid → 0289
妙 MARVELOUS → 0280
秀 EXCELLENT → 3152
英 DISTINGUISHED → 2782
尤 outstanding → 3755
傑 outstanding → 0175
穎 TALENTED → 2036
逸 exceptional → 3872
名 first-rate → 2693
上 of upper grade → 4212

❷ abnormal
変 ABNORMAL → 2569
奇 UNUSUAL → 2756
畸 UNUSUAL → 1533
怪 MYSTERIOUS → 0354
妖 MYSTERIOUS → 0282
妙 strange → 0280
異 not ordinary → 3195
珍 curious → 1135

妊

▶BECOME PREGNANT

ニン はら(む)▲

Ⓝ 姙◇ Ⓒ 妊 rèn

0281

◧ 1-3-4

38	Jōyō	U598A
女	S7-3-4	F1632

COMPOUNDS

ⓐ [original meaning] **BECOME PREGNANT, conceive**

ⓑ pregnant, expectant

a 妊娠する にんしんする become pregnant, conceive
避妊 ひにん contraception
懐妊 かいにん pregnancy, conception
不妊 ふにん sterility

b 妊婦 にんぷ pregnant woman

妊産婦 にんさんぷ pregnant women and nursing mothers

KUN

【はらむ 妊む】 **BECOME PREGNANT**, conceive
子供を妊む こどもをはらむ become pregnant, conceive

SYNONYMS

● **conceive**
妊 BECOME PREGNANT → 0281
娠 CONCEIVE → 0490

妖

0282
◧1-3-4

▶**MYSTERIOUS**
ヨウ あや(しい)
Ⓒ 妖 yāo

38	Jōyō	U5996
女	S7-3-4	F1814

COMPOUNDS

❶ **MYSTERIOUS, strange, unusual**
妖怪 ようかい ghost, apparition, phantom, goblin
妖精 ようせい fairy, elf, sprite
妖婆 ようば witch, hag
妖術 ようじゅつ black magic, witchcraft, sorcery
妖気 ようき ghostly [unearthly, weird] air [atmosphere]

❷ **enchanting, bewitching, seductive**
妖女 ようじょ enchantress, vamp
妖艶な ようえんな fascinating, voluptuous

KUN

【あやしい 妖しい】 [also 怪しい] **strange, MYSTERIOUS; uncanny**

SYNONYMS

❶ **abnormal**
変 ABNORMAL → 2569
奇 UNUSUAL → 2756
畸 UNUSUAL → 1533
怪 MYSTERIOUS → 0354
妖 MYSTERIOUS → 0282
妙 strange → 0280
異 not ordinary → 3195
珍 curious → 1135

HOMOPHONES

あやしい 怪 MYSTERIOUS → 0354

NOTE

➡ see USAGE note at 怪 0354

妒

0283
◧1-3-4

▶**BE JEALOUS**
ト ねた(む) ねた(ましい) そね(む) や(く) や(ける)

38	Nonstandard	U5992
女	S7-3-4	F0000

traditional form → see 妬 at 0337

姉

◧1-3-4

incorrect stroke-count
➡ see ◧1-3-5: 女 at 0336

姊

◧1-3-4

incorrect stroke-count
➡ see ◧1-3-5: 女 at 0338

孜

0284
◧1-3-4

▶**MAKE DILIGENT EFFORTS**
シ ㊔ あつ つとむ ただす あつし まもる はじめ すすむ
Ⓒ 孜 zī

39	Names	U5B5C
子	S7-3-4	F0000

COMPOUNDS

● **MAKE DILIGENT EFFORTS**
孜孜 しし assiduously, diligently

SYNONYMS

● **exert oneself**
努 EXERT → 3154
勉 ENDEAVOR → 4113
励 make efforts → 1438
勤 work diligently → 2287
尽 use all one's strength → 3786
精 put one's heart into → 1729
孜 MAKE DILIGENT EFFORTS → 0284

岐

0285
◧1-3-4

▶**DIVERGE**
キ ギ* ㊔ みち また
Ⓒ 歧 岐 qí

46	Jōyō	U5C90
山	S7-3-4	F1443

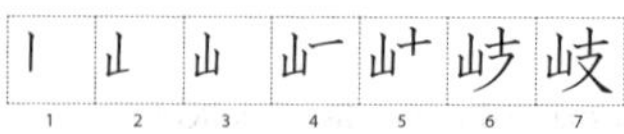

COMPOUNDS

❶ⓐ **DIVERGE, branch off, ramify, fork**
ⓑ [original meaning] **forked road, branch road**
a 分岐 ぶんき divergence, ramification, forking
分岐点 ぶんきてん junction
多岐 たき many branches, many divergences
b 岐路 きろ forked road, crossroad

❷ **unclassified compounds**
岐阜県 ぎふけん Gifu Prefecture

三岐代表 さんぎだいひょう representative of Gifu and Mie prefectures

SYNONYMS

❶ⓐ diverge

岐 DIVERGE →0285
分 branch off →2466

ⓑ ways and routes

道 WAY (path) →3888
径 PATH →0347
軌 TRACK →1832
線 LINE →1760
澪 WATERWAY →0957
途 WAY (route) →3853
路 ROAD →1936
筋 wayside →3319
通り street →3855
街 city street →0702
辻 CROSSROADS →3958
岐 forked road →0285
巷 THE STREETS →3097

❶ⓑ furcation

叉 FORK →4194
俣 BIFURCATION →0111
股 CROTCH →1093
岐 forked road →0285

攻

▶ATTACK

コウ せ(める) ㊔ おさむ

Ⓒ 攻 gōng

0286

1-3-4

66	Jōyō	U653B
攵	S7-4-3	F0698

Stroke order: 1–7

COMPOUNDS

❶ⓐ ATTACK, take the offensive
ⓑ ATTACK, offensive, offense

a 攻撃 こうげき attack, assault; criticism; *baseball* batting
攻勢 こうせい offensive, aggression
攻略 こうりゃく capture, conquest; invasion
正攻法 せいこうほう regular tactics for attack

b 攻守 こうしゅ offense and defense; batting and fielding
速攻 そっこう swift attack
反攻 はんこう counterattack, counteroffensive

❷ specialize, study

攻究 こうきゅう investigation, research
専攻する せんこうする major in, specialize in

INDEPENDENT

【こう 攻】*baseball* batting

KUN

【せめる 攻める】ATTACK, take the offensive

攻め せめ [also suffix] attack, offensive, bombardment; batting
攻め込む せめこむ attack and invade
攻め滅ぼす せめほろぼす attack and overthrow, utterly destroy
質問攻め しつもんぜめ barrage of questions

SYNONYMS

❶ attack

攻 ATTACK →0286
撃 STRIKE →3552
襲 RAID →3633
侵 INVADE →0116
爆 bomb →1415

❷ learn and study

学 STUDY →3162
考 study →3962
習 LEARN →3306
研 RESEARCH →1456
究 STUDY EXHAUSTIVELY →2729
攻 specialize →0286

USAGE

❶【せめる】

攻める
attack, take the offensive

責める
① blame, condemn, censure, accuse, criticize, reproach
② torture, persecute
③ urge, press; tease

❷【せめ】

攻め
① [also suffix] attack, offensive, bombardment
② batting

責め
① responsibility
② blame
③ [also suffix] torture, persecution

HOMOPHONES

せめる 責 RESPONSIBILITY →3115
せめ 責 RESPONSIBILITY →3115

改

▶REFORM

カイ あらた(める) あらた(まる)

Ⓒ 改 gǎi

0287

1-3-4

66	Jōyō-4	U6539
攵	S7-4-3	F0421

Stroke order: 1–7

COMPOUNDS

❶ⓐ **REFORM, renew, rectify, correct, revise, amend**
ⓑ **change, convert, modify**
ⓒ **redo, renew**

a 改善する かいぜんする improve, ameliorate
改新 かいしん renovation, reformation
改革 かいかく reform, reformation
改正 かいせい revision, amendment
改築 かいちく remodeling, rebuilding
b 改名 かいめい changing a name
改行する かいぎょうする change lines [paragraphs]
c 改選 かいせん reelection
改葬 かいそう reburial

❷ **examine, inspect**
改札 かいさつ ticket examination

KUN

【あらためる 改める】 **REFORM, rectify, correct; renew, redo; change, alter; revise, improve; examine**
改めて あらためて again, over again, anew; formally
悔い改める くいあらためる repent, be penitent
稿を改める こうをあらためる rewrite a manuscript
切符を改める きっぷをあらためる examine tickets

【あらたまる 改まる】 **be renewed, be renovated; change, be improved, be REFORMed; stand on ceremony, become formal**
改まった あらたまった formal, ceremonious
年が改まる としがあらたまる The new year comes round

SYNONYMS

❶ⓐ **reform**
改 REFORM → 0287
革 REFORM → 3099
更 RENEW → 4355
新 make new → 2239

❶ⓐ **correct**
正 RIGHT → 4296
直す correct → 3649
訂 REVISE → 1829
改 REFORM → 0287
矯 RECTIFY → 1586
匡 RECTIFY → 3710

ⓑ **change and replace**
変 CHANGE → 2569
替 REPLACE → 3457
代 SUBSTITUTE → 0034
迭 ALTERNATE → 3818
更 change → 4355
改 change → 0287
易 change → 3064
化 CHANGE INTO, -ize → 0022
遷 undergo transition → 3932
転 turn into → 1872
換 EXCHANGE → 0716
交 INTERCHANGE → 2508

ⓒ **repeating and repetition**
再 ANOTHER TIME → 4332
又 AGAIN → 4158
復 repeat → 0701
重 DUPLICATE → 4390
畳 reduplicate → 3205
改 redo → 0287
-換える redo → 0716
-直す repetition suffix → 3649
-返す do over → 3797

役

0288

1-3-4

▶**SERVICE**
ヤク エキ ㊔ え まもる
Ⓒ 役 yì

60	Jōyō-3	U5F79
彳	S7-3-4	F0322

Stroke order: 1 2 3 4 5 6 7

COMPOUNDS

❶ⓐ **SERVICE, public service, duty, official post, office**
ⓑ **executive, officer, public servant, official, director, person in charge**

a 役所 やくしょ public [government] office
役場 やくば public office
役柄 やくがら nature [quality] of one's office, one's position
役目 やくめ duty, function; role
役員 やくいん officer, leader, director
役人 やくにん government official
b 下役 したやく subordinate official
助役 じょやく assistant official; deputy mayor; deputy station-master
重役 じゅうやく director, executive
取締役 とりしまりやく director

❷ⓐ **press into SERVICE, enlist one's service, employ**
ⓑ **unpaid SERVICE, exacted labor, work, corvée**
ⓒ **military SERVICE, army duty**

a 使役 しえき employment, service; *gram* causative
労役 ろうえき labor, work, toil
雑役 ざつえき miscellaneous services, odd jobs
懲役 ちょうえき penal servitude, imprisonment with hard labor
b 役務 えきむ labor, service
役牛 えきぎゅう work cattle
c 兵役 へいえき military service
退役する たいえきする retire from military service

予備役 よびえき service in the first reserve

❸ **SERVICE, serviceability, usefulness, utility**

役立つ やくだつ be of use, serve a purpose

役立てる やくだてる put to use, make use of, turn to account

❹ [also suffix] **role, part, cast**

役割 やくわり assigning [allotment of] parts; part, role, duty

役者 やくしゃ actor, actress

配役 はいやく cast (of a play)

悪役 あくやく villain (of the piece)

主役 しゅやく leading part, starring role

脇役 わきやく supporting actor [role]

顔役 かおやく influential man, boss

メフィストフェレス役 めふぃすとふぇれすやく part of Mephistopheles

❺ war, battle, expedition

戦役 せんえき war, battle

❻ scoring hand of cards or mahjong tiles

手役 てやく hand of cards which scores as it is

❼ [also 軛 やく 1873] yoke

共役 きょうえき *math* conjugation

INDEPENDENT

【やく 役】

①ⓐ **office, post, position**

ⓑ **role, part; duty, function**

a 役に就く やくにつく assume office, be appointed to a post

役を勤める やくをつとめる hold an office; act (as), play the part (of)

b オセロの役を演じる おせろのやくをえんじる act [play] the part of Othello

仲人の役を買って出る なこうどのやくをかってでる offer one's service as a matchmaker

② **SERVICEability, usefulness, utility, help**

役に立つ やくにたつ be useful, be helpful

役に立たない やくにたたない be useless, be of no avail

③ scoring hand of cards or mahjong tiles

【えき 役】 war, battle, expedition

西南の役 せいなんのえき the Satsuma Rebellion

SYNONYMS

❶ⓐ & ❷ⓑ **work and employment**

務 DUTY → 1505

任 OFFICE → 0057

役 SERVICE (esp. public) → 0288

勤 SERVICE (employment) → 2287

業 WORK → 3227

職 EMPLOYMENT → 1803

労 LABOR → 3155

ⓑ **officials**

官 GOVERNMENT OFFICIAL → 2766

吏 OFFICIAL → 4351

僚 official → 0186

司 officiator → 3648

役 executive → 0288

事 officer → 4384

❷ⓐ **employ**

雇 EMPLOY → 2454

用 EMPLOY → 3694

使う employ → 0100

傭 HIRE → 0181

役 press into service → 0288

❸ **benefit**

利 ADVANTAGE → 1431

益 BENEFIT → 2849

為 SAKE → 4395

用 use(ful) → 3694

役 SERVICE → 0288

❺ **warfare and rebellions**

戦 WAR → 2242

軍 war → 2582

役 war → 0288

陣 battle → 0545

乱 rebellion → 1611

変 uprising → 2569

闘 FIGHT → 4136

徃

◧1-3-4

incorrect stroke-count

➡ see ◧1-3-5: 彳 at 0352

快

0289

◧1-3-4

▶**PLEASANT**

カイ こころよ(い)

Ⓒ 快 kuài

61 忄	Jōyō-5 S7-3-4	U5FEB F0912

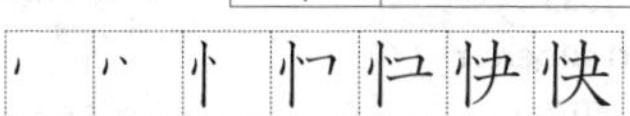

1 2 3 4 5 6 7

COMPOUNDS

❶ [original meaning] **PLEASANT, agreeable, comfortable, delightful, jolly**

快感 かいかん agreeable sensation, comfort

快適な かいてきな comfortable, pleasant, agreeable

快楽 かいらく pleasure, enjoyment

快削鋼 かいさくこう free-cutting steel

愉快な ゆかいな pleasant, delightful, joyful

不快な ふかいな unpleasant, disagreeable

❷ [also prefix] **splendid, fine, good**

快挙 かいきょ brilliant achievement, heroic deed [feat]

快晴 かいせい fine weather, fair and clear weather

快男児 かいだんじ fine fellow, spirited fellow

❸ **fast, speedy, rapid, quick**
快速 かいそく high speed; fast (local) train
快走 かいそう fast running, fast sailing
快足の かいそくの quick of foot, fast
特快 とっかい special fast (local) train
軽快な けいかいな light, nimble, quick; cheerful

❹ **recover, convalesce**
快方 かいほう convalescence
快復 かいふく recovery (from illness)
全快 ぜんかい complete recovery

❺ sharp
快刀 かいとう *literary* sharp sword

INDEPENDENT

【かい 快】 pleasure, delight, enjoyment
快を貪る かいをむさぼる enjoy oneself to the full

KUN

【こころよい 快い】 **PLEASANT, agreeable, comfortable, delightful, refreshing**
快さ こころよさ pleasantness, comfortableness
快く こころよく cheerfully, comfortably; gladly, willingly

SYNONYMS

❶ **pleased and pleasant**
楽 pleasurable → 3505
欣 JOYFUL → 1057
爽 REFRESHING → 4402
快 PLEASANT → 0289
朗 CHEERFUL → 1679
愉 PLEASED → 0710
悦 DELIGHTED → 0501
嬉しい GLAD → 0890
喜 HAPPY → 2889
歓 JOYOUS → 2342
驩 JOYOUS → 2333

❷ **excellent and superior**
優 SUPERIOR → 0200
絶 without match → 1711
卓 PROMINENT → 2561
快 splendid → 0289
妙 MARVELOUS → 0280
秀 EXCELLENT → 3152
英 DISTINGUISHED → 2782
尤 outstanding → 3755
傑 outstanding → 0175
穎 TALENTED → 2036
逸 exceptional → 3872
名 first-rate → 2693
上 of upper grade → 4212

❸ **fast**
速 QUICK → 3851
早 QUICK → 3042
疾 fast → 4064
快 fast → 0289
急 rapid → 2595
迅 SWIFT → 3780
敏 NIMBLE → 1675
即 IMMEDIATE → 1439
捷 AGILE → 0609

❹ **cure and recover**
療 TREAT → 4078
治 CURE → 0393
医 cure → 3715
癒 HEAL → 4081
快 recover → 0289

抜

0290

1-3-4

▶**PULL OUT**
▶**STAND OUT**

バツ ぬ(く) -ぬ(く) ぬ(き) ぬ(ける) ぬ(かす) ぬ(かる)

Ⓝ 拔 Ⓒ 拔 bá

64	Jōyō	U629C
扌	S7-3-4	F0495

Stroke order: 一 丁 扌 扌 扐 扐 抜 (1–7)

COMPOUNDS

❶ [original meaning] **PULL OUT, draw out, extract, remove**
抜歯 ばっし tooth extraction
抜糸 ばっし removal [extraction] of stitches
抜刀 ばっとう drawing a sword; drawn sword
抜本的な ばっぽんてきな radical, drastic
不抜の ふばつの indomitable, unswerving

❷ **single out, select, pick out, extract, excerpt**
抜擢 ばってき selection, choice
抜粋 ばっすい extract, excerpt, selection
選抜する せんばつする select, choose, pick out

❸ **STAND OUT [above], rise above, surpass, excel**
抜群の ばつぐんの preeminent, outstanding
奇抜な きばつな novel, unconventional, extraordinary
卓抜する たくばつする excel, surpass, stand high, be distinguished
海抜 かいばつ above sea level

KUN

【ぬく 抜く】
①ⓐ **PULL OUT, draw out, extract**
ⓑ remove, take out (a stain)
ⓒ **leave out, omit, skip**
a 引き抜く ひきぬく pull [draw] out, extract; single [pick] out, choose, recruit
b 色抜き いろぬき decolorization

c 手を抜く てをぬく scamp [skimp] one's work, cut corners

② single out, select, pick out, extract, excerpt
抜き刷り ぬきずり offprint

③ **outstrip, surpass, excel**
抜きん出る ぬきんでる [sometimes also 擢んでる] excel, stand out, be preeminent

④ pierce, shoot through
踏み抜く ふみぬく tread (a nail) into the sole of one's foot; tread through (the floor)

【-ぬく -抜く】 [verbal suffix]

① **perform an action to the end, stick it out**
生き抜く いきぬく live through
踊り抜く おどりぬく dance away

② be in a complete state of (distress)
困り抜く こまりぬく be in great trouble

【ぬき 抜き】 [also suffix]

① **leaving out, omission**
挨拶は抜きで あいさつはぬきで without compliments [greetings]
夕食抜きで ゆうしょくぬきで without having supper

② beating (in a match)
五人抜き ごにんぬき beating five opponents in a row

【ぬける 抜ける】 **come [fall] out [off], escape; leave, quit, withdraw, be left out, be missing; be dull-witted, be mentally deficient; go by [through], pass through;** [in compounds] **surpass, excel**
抜け毛 ぬけげ fallen hair, combings
抜け出す ぬけだす get [slip] out of, break loose
抜け道 ぬけみち byroad, secret passage; loophole, excuse
会を抜ける かいをぬける withdraw from a society [meeting]
一行抜けている いちぎょうぬけている A line is left out
彼は抜けている かれはぬけている He is a bit soft in his head
ずば抜けた ずばぬけた outstanding, prominent, distinguished

【ぬかす 抜かす】 **leave out, omit, skip;** *slang* **have the impudence to say**
二頁抜かす にぺーじぬかす skip two pages
何を抜かす なにをぬかす None of your cheek!

【ぬかる 抜かる】 **commit a blunder, make a slip**
抜かり ぬかり slip, blunder, oversight

SYNONYMS

❶ **pull**
引 DRAW → 0207
曳 DRAW → 4348
牽 DRAW → 2621
惹 DRAW ATTENTION → 2903
抽 DRAW OUT → 0359
抜 PULL OUT → 0290
控える HOLD BACK → 0600
扣える HOLD BACK → 0250
寄せる DRAW NEAR → 2856

❷ **choose**
選 CHOOSE → 3931
撰 choose → 0911
択 SELECT → 0299
採 PICK → 0606
摘 pick out → 0851
擢 SINGLE OUT → 0973
抜 single out → 0290
汰 SIFT OUT → 0312

❸ **excel**
勝 EXCEL → 1268
抜 STAND OUT → 0290
擢んでる stand out → 0973
超 SURPASS → 4107
越 GO BEYOND → 4108
凌 SURPASS → 0144
駕 outdo → 3236

【ぬく】

①Ⓒ **omit**
漏 omit → 0860
脱 leave out by mistake → 1225
抜く leave out → 0290
欠 missing → 2481

HOMOPHONES

ぬきんでる
擢 SINGLE OUT → 0973
抜きん出る → 0290, 4310

NOTE

➡ see COMPOUND FORMATION for 抜群 ばつぐん → 群 1942

扶

0291

◧ 1-3-4

▶**LEND SUPPORT TO**

フ たす(ける)▲ ㊔ すけ たすく

Ⓒ 扶 fú

64	Jōyō	U6276
扌	S7-3-4	F2040

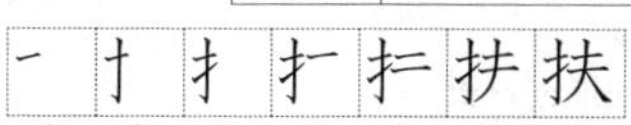

1 2 3 4 5 6 7

COMPOUNDS

ⓐ **LEND SUPPORT TO, support, hold up, sustain**

ⓑ [original meaning, now archaic] support with the hand, hold up

a 扶養する ふようする support, maintain
扶助する ふじょする support, sustain
扶育 ふいく bringing up (children)

口 土 夕 女 子 山 工 己 彳 忄 【扌】 氵 犭 阝 丩 丬

KUN

【たすける 扶ける】[now usu. 助ける] help, aid, assist
- 扶け起こす たすけおこす help a person to his [her] feet
- 家計の扶け かけいのたすけ assistance in supporting a family

SYNONYMS

ⓐ **support**
- 支 SUPPORT →2473
- 擁 SUPPORT →0949
- 扶 LEND SUPPORT TO →0291
- 賛 back up →3484

HOMOPHONES

たすける 助 HELP →1440

NOTE

➡ see USAGE note at 助 1440

技

0292

1-3-4

▶**SKILL**

ギ わざ

Ⓒ 技 jì

64	Jōyō-5	U6280
扌	S7-3-4	F0487

一 十 扌 扌 扌 抆 技 (1 2 3 4 5 6 7)

COMPOUNDS

❶ [sometimes also 伎 0055] [original meaning] **SKILL, ability, craft, art**
- 技術 ぎじゅつ technique, art, skill; technology
- 技能 ぎのう skill, ability, capacity
- 技師 ぎし engineer, technician
- 技量 ぎりょう skill, ability, capacity
- 技巧 ぎこう art, craftsmanship, technical skill; trick
- 競技 きょうぎ match, contest, game; sporting event
- 演技 えんぎ acting, performance
- 特技 とくぎ one's special ability [talent], one's special skill [art]
- 実技 じつぎ practical technique [skill]

❷ game, sport, pastime
- 球技 きゅうぎ ball game
- 国技 こくぎ national sport game

INDEPENDENT

【ぎ 技】**SKILL**, ability, craft, art
- 入神の技 にゅうしんのぎ skill of superhuman level

KUN

【わざ 技】

① **SKILL, ability, craft, art**
- 技を磨く わざをみがく improve one's skill

② *judo*
- ⓐ trick
- ⓑ half point

SYNONYMS

❶ **art**
- 技 SKILL →0292
- 倆 SKILL →0136
- 術 PRACTICAL ART →0575
- 芸 ART →2738
- 道 the way of an art →3888

❶ **skill**
- 力 POWER →4178
- 能 ABILITY →1676
- 技 SKILL →0292
- 倆 SKILL →0136
- 腕 skill →1269
- 才 TALENT →4218

❷ **game**
- 技 game →0292
- 戦 match →2242

USAGE

【わざ】

技
- ① skill, ability, craft, art
- ② *judo*
  - ⓐ trick
  - ⓑ half point

業
- work, act, deed

HOMOPHONES

わざ 業 WORK →3227

把

0293

1-3-4

▶**GRIP**

ハ ワ

Ⓒ 把 bǎ bà

64	Jōyō	U628A
扌	S7-3-4	F1822

一 十 扌 扌 扌 扌 把 (1 2 3 4 5 6 7)

COMPOUNDS

❶ⓐ [original meaning] **GRIP, grasp, seize, hold**

ⓑ a **GRIP**, a handle
- *a* 把握する はあくする grip, grasp; understand, grasp
- 把持する はじする grasp, hold, grip
- *b* 把手 はしゅ(=とって) handle, knob

❷ **counter for bundles or sheaves**
- 薪二把 たきぎにわ two bundles of firewood

SYNONYMS

❶ⓐ **take**
- 把 GRIP →0293
- 握 GRASP →0714
- 捉 GRASP →0518
- 執 SEIZE →2114

摑む GRASP → 0848
捕 CATCH → 0514
取 TAKE → 1613
持 HOLD → 0447
ⓑ **handles**
柄 HANDLE → 1111
手 handle → 4267
把 GRIP → 0293

NOTE

★ As a counter for bundles, 把 is read わ, ば or ぱ depending on the preceding syllable → see also note at 羽 0265

批

0294

1-3-4

▶**CRITICIZE**
ヒ
Ⓒ 批 pī

64	Jōyō-6	U6279
扌	S7-3-4	F1014

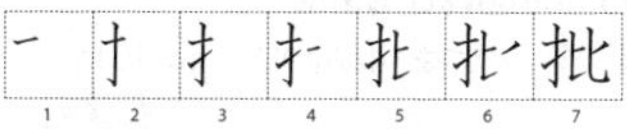

COMPOUNDS

❶ **CRITICIZE, comment, review**
批評 ひひょう criticism, comment
批難(=非難) ひなん criticism, blame
批評家 ひひょうか critic, reviewer
批判 ひはん criticism, comment
批議する ひぎする blame, criticize
❷ ratify, sanction
批准 ひじゅん ratification
批准書 ひじゅんしょ instrument of ratification

SYNONYMS

❶ **blame and accuse**
責 BLAME → 3115
叱 SCOLD → 0210
詰 REPRIMAND → 1920
難 find fault with → 2310
批 CRITICIZE → 0294
劾 EXPOSE CRIMES → 1618
弾 impeach → 0697
❶ **comment upon**
批 CRITICIZE → 0294
評 COMMENT → 1895

抒

0295

1-3-4

▶**DESCRIBE**
ジョ
Ⓒ 抒 shū

64	Non-Jōyō	U6292
扌	S7-3-4	F3317

COMPOUNDS

● [now usu. 叙 1834] **DESCRIBE, narrate, depict, explain**
抒情 じょじょう description of feelings, lyricism
抒情詩 じょじょうし lyric poem [poetry]

SYNONYMS

● **describe**
叙 DESCRIBE → 1834
抒 DESCRIBE → 0295
描 DEPICT → 0591
写 portray → 2493

抗

0296

1-3-4

▶**RESIST**
コウ
Ⓒ 抗 kàng

64	Jōyō	U6297
扌	S7-3-4	F0809

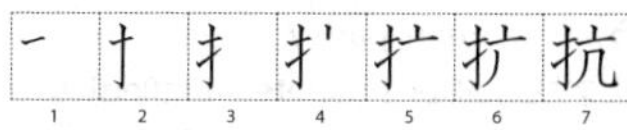

COMPOUNDS

ⓐ [original meaning] **RESIST, defy, oppose**
ⓑ [prefix] anti-
a 抗争 こうそう dispute, resistance
抗議 こうぎ protest, remonstrance, objection
反抗 はんこう resistance, opposition, defiance
抵抗する ていこうする resist, oppose, defy
対抗する たいこうする oppose, antagonize, rival; counteract
不可抗力 ふかこうりょく act of god, irresistible force
b 抗日 こうにち anti-Japanese
抗生物質 こうせいぶっしつ antibiotic
抗ヒスタミン剤 こうひすたみんざい antihistamine

INDEPENDENT

【こうする 抗する】**RESIST**, defy

SYNONYMS

ⓐ **resist**
抗 RESIST → 0296
抵 RESIST → 0377
耐 WITHSTAND → 1634
対 OPPOSE → 1025
反 COUNTER → 3663
逆 rebel → 3835
撥 REPEL → 0907
叛 REBEL → 1469

1

折

▶BREAK OFF
▶FOLD

セツ お(る) おり お(り) -お(り) お(れる)

0297 Ⓒ 折 zhé shé

1-3-4

64	Jōyō-4	U6298
扌	S7-3-4	F0823

一 十 扌 扌 扩 扩 折 (1 2 3 4 5 6 7)

口 土 夕 女 子 山 工 己 彳 忄 【扌】 氵 犭 阝 ...

COMPOUNDS

❶ⓐ (separate through the application of a sudden bending force) **BREAK OFF (as a branch), break (a bone), snap (in two), split**

ⓑ (weaken, as in spirit) break down, (cause to) lose heart

a 折半 せっぱん halving
折衷 せっちゅう compromise, eclecticism
骨折 こっせつ bone fracture
b 折衝 せっしょう negotiation, parley
挫折する ざせつする fail, be frustrated [baffled]

❷ FOLD
折角 せっかく with much trouble; specially

❸ bend
曲折 きょくせつ bending, winding; zigzags
屈折 くっせつ bending, turn; refraction

❹ turn (to the right or left)
右折する うせつする turn to the right
左折する させつする turn to the left

❺ chastise, criticize severely
折檻×する せっかんする chastise, correct, spank (a naughty boy)

❻ die
夭×折 ようせつ premature death

KUN

【おる 折る】

① (separate through the application of a sudden bending force) **BREAK OFF (as a branch), break (a bone), snap (in two), split**
歯を一本折る はをいっぽんおる break a tooth
へし折る へしおる smash, shatter

② **FOLD**
折り重ねる おりかさねる fold back [up]
折り紙 おりがみ folded paper; the art of paper folding

③ **bend, turn back**
折り曲げる おりまげる bend, double, turn up [down]
折り返す おりかえす turn back; turn up
折り返し おりかえし turn, turning point; return (trip), shuttle (service); lapel

④ yield, give in
折り合い おりあい mutual relations; compromise

⑤ **BREAK OFF**, quit
枝折り しおり [usu. 栞] bookmark; guidebook
筆を折る ふでをおる break off writing

【おり 折, 折り】

① **occasion, time, chance, opportunity**
折折 おりおり sometimes, occasionally, once in a while
折悪しくして おりあしくして inopportunely, unseasonably
折りに触れて おりにふれて on opportunity, occasionally
時折 ときおり sometimes, occasionally

② small wooden box
折り箱 おりばこ small wooden box
折り詰め おりづめ food packed in a small wooden box
菓子折り かしおり box of cakes

【-おり -折り】

① **counter for number of FOLDings**
二つ折り判の本 ふたつおりばんのほん books in folio

② counter for small boxes of food
寿司一折り すしひとおり a box of sushi

【おれる 折れる】 *vi* **break, snap; be FOLDed, be doubled; turn (to the right or left); give in, yield**
折れ目 おれめ crease, fold
折れ曲がる おれまがる be folded
折れ合う おれあう make concessions, come to an agreement
ぽきんと折れる ぽきんとおれる snap, break with a snap
左に折れる ひだりにおれる turn to the left

SYNONYMS

❶ⓐ break
破 BREAK → 1478
拉ぐ crush → 0372
崩 CRUMBLE → 2863
挫 SPRAIN → 0519
壊 BREAK DOWN → 0934
毀す break down → 2246
折 BREAK OFF → 0297
割る crack → 2284
裂 SPLIT → 3331
砕 CRUSH UP → 1458
摧 CRUSH UP → 0849
潰す CRUSH → 0919

❷ & 【おる】 ② fold
折 FOLD → 0297
畳む FOLD UP → 3205

❸ & 【おる】 ③ bend
曲 CURVE → 4340
彎 CURVE (become bow-shaped) → 3634

屈 BEND → 3821
折 bend → 0297
勾 be bent → 3660
歪 DISTORT → 3095

【おり】

① **occasions**

際 OCCASION → 0874
折 occasion → 0297
時 timely occasion → 1155
機 OPPORTUNITY → 1365
節 time → 3336

USAGE

【おる】

折る

① (separate through the application of a sudden bending force) break off (as a branch), break (a bone), snap (in two), split
② fold
③ bend, turn back
④ yield, give in
⑤ break off, quit

織る

weave

HOMOPHONES

おる 織 WEAVE → 1801

しおり

栞 BOOKMARK → 3285
枝折り → 1073, 0297

COMPOUND FORMATION

❶【折衝 せっしょう】

折衝 'negotiation, parley' originally referred to breaking (折 ❶ⓑ) the brunt of an enemy attack (衝), but now refers to settling a dispute by negotiation.

❷【折角 せっかく】

折角 'with much trouble; specially' originally referred to folding (折 ❷) the corners (角) of one's hood in ancient China. How it acquired its current meaning is not clear.

NOTE

★ do not confuse with 析 ANALYZE → 1072

抄 ▶EXCERPT

ショウ

Ⓒ 抄 chāo

0298

◧ 1-3-4

64	Jōyō	U6284
扌	S7-3-4	F2528

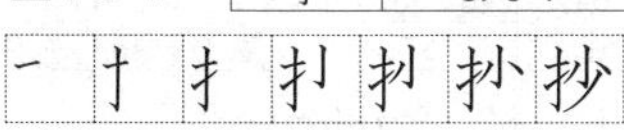

COMPOUNDS

❶ⓐ **EXCERPT, extract, abridge, select**

ⓑ [also suffix] **EXCERPT, selection, summary, abridgment**

a 抄出する しょうしゅつする take excerpts
抄録 しょうろく quotation, summary
抄訳 しょうやく abridged translation
抄本 しょうほん extract, abstract

b 平家物語抄 へいけものがたりしょう Abridged Version of the Historic Romance of the Taira Family

❷ⓐ annotate, append notes

ⓑ [suffix] annotation, commentary

a 抄物 しょうもの(=しょうもつ) commentary

b 史記抄 しきしょう Commentary on Shiki

❸ copy, transcribe

手抄 しゅしょう manual copying; excerption; excerpt

❹ manufacture paper

抄紙 しょうし paper making

INDEPENDENT

【しょう 抄】EXCERPT

【しょうする 抄する】EXCERPT, quote

SYNONYMS

❶ⓐ **abridge**

要 SUMMARIZE → 3263
抄 EXCERPT → 0298
約 CONTRACT → 1632
略 omit → 1501

択 ▶SELECT

タク

Ⓝ 擇 Ⓒ 择 zé zhái

0299

◧ 1-3-4

64	Jōyō	U629E
扌	S7-3-4	F1272

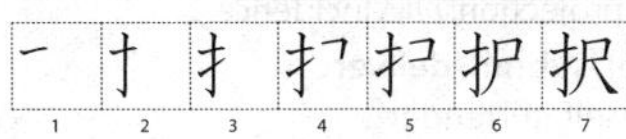

COMPOUNDS

● [original meaning] **SELECT, choose, pick out**

選択する せんたくする select, choose
採択する さいたくする adopt, select
二者択一 にしゃたくいつ choosing an alternative

SYNONYMS

● **choose**

選 CHOOSE → 3931
撰 choose → 0911
択 SELECT → 0299
採 PICK → 0606
摘 pick out → 0851
擢 SINGLE OUT → 0973
抜 single out → 0290
汰 SIFT OUT → 0312

投

▶THROW
▶SEND IN
トウ な(げる) -な(げ)
Ⓒ 投 tóu

0300
1-3-4

64	Jōyō-3	U6295
扌	S7-3-4	F0438

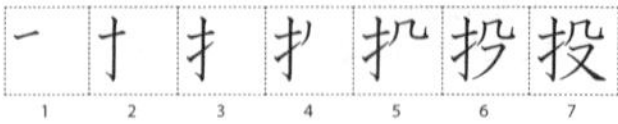

COMPOUNDS

1 a [original meaning] **THROW, cast, throw down**
b **THROW**ing, throw
c **THROW** oneself into (a river, etc. to commit suicide)
d *baseball* **pitch, pitching**

a 投下 とうか throwing down, dropping, airdrop; investment
投棄する とうきする abandon, give up, throw away
投石 とうせき throwing stones
投擲×する とうてきする throw
b 第一投 だいいっとう first throw
c 投身 とうしん suicide by drowning or jumping from a high place
d 投手 とうしゅ pitcher
投球 とうきゅう throwing a ball, pitching
投打 とうだ pitching and batting
力投 りきとう all-out pitching
好投 こうとう good [nice] pitching
完投する かんとうする pitch a whole game

2 abbrev. of 投手 とうしゅ: pitcher
投飛 とうひ pitcher's fly

3 **project (an image), cast**
投影 とうえい cast shadow; projection
投射 とうしゃ projection; *phys* incidence

4 a **SEND IN [to], submit, deliver**
b submit oneself, surrender

a 投書 とうしょ contribution, letter (from a reader)
投稿 とうこう contribution (to a magazine)
投票する とうひょうする vote, cast a ballot
投資 とうし investment
投入する とうにゅうする invest; throw into
b 投降する とうこうする surrender (to the enemy)

5 prescribe (medicine)
投薬 とうやく prescription, medication
投与する とうよする prescribe medicine, administer (medicine)

6 fit in with, agree with, be suited to the occasion
投合 とうごう agreement, coincidence
投機 とうき speculation, venture

7 stay over, stop over
投宿する とうしゅくする put up at a hotel

INDEPENDENT

【とう 投】 pitching strength
投に優る とうにまさる surpass in pitching strength

【とうじる(=とうずる) 投じる(=投ずる)】 **THROW, cast, pitch; send in [to]; launch into, join; invest, spend on; catch on, hit, seize on the situation**

KUN

【なげる 投げる】 **THROW, cast, pitch; throw [give] up, abandon; sell at a loss**
投げ なげ throw, throwing; giving up; shake-out
投げ飛ばす なげとばす fling away
投げ出す なげだす throw out; throw [give] up, abandon, leave off
投げ売り なげうり bargain [sacrifice] sale
投げ打つ なげうつ [also 抛つ] fling away, abandon
身投げ みなげ suicide by drowning or jumping from a high place

【-なげ -投げ】 [also suffix] *sports* **THROW, throwing**
ハンマー投げ はんまーなげ hammer throw
背負い投げ せおいなげ back throw
上手投げ うわてなげ *sumo* trick of throwing the opponent over oneself; *baseball* overhand throw

SPECIAL READINGS

投網 とあみ casting net

SYNONYMS

1 a **throw**
投 THROW → 0300
抛 TOSS → 0364
放 toss → 1058

4 a **send**
送 SEND → 3837
投 SEND IN → 0300
回 send round → 3793
遣 DISPATCH → 3908
派 DISPATCH → 0456

HOMOPHONES

なげうつ
抛つ → 0364
投げ打つ → 0300, 0224

抑

▶SUPPRESS
ヨク おさ(える)
Ⓒ 抑 yì

0301
1-3-4

64	Jōyō	U6291
扌	S7-3-4	F1189

COMPOUNDS

1 a (hold down) **SUPPRESS, repress, restrain**

ⓑ (put down forcibly) **SUPPRESS, bring under control**

a 抑制する よくせいする control, suppress, inhibit
抑止する よくしする deter, check, hold back
抑留 よくりゅう detainment, detention, internment, arrest
b 抑圧する よくあつする oppress, repress, suppress
抑鬱 よくうつ depression, dejection

❷ **lower, tone down**
抑揚 よくよう rising and falling (of tones), intonation

KUN

【おさえる 抑える】

①ⓐ (hold down) **SUPPRESS, repress, restrain, control, hold down; check, curb, stop; keep back, withhold**
ⓑ (put down forcibly) **SUPPRESS, subdue, bring under control**

a 抑え おさえ check, defense, suppression; control
抑え難い おさえがたい irrepressible, uncontrollable
b 反乱を抑える はんらんをおさえる stifle a rebellion

② catch, arrest
警官に抑えられる けいかんにおさえられる be caught by a policeman

SYNONYMS

❶ⓐ **restrain**
制 CONTROL (restrain) → 1624
禁 PROHIBIT → 3469
限 LIMIT → 0475
抑 SUPPRESS → 0301
束 TIE UP → 4369
縛 BIND → 1779
控える HOLD BACK → 0600
扣える HOLD BACK → 0250
渋る hang [hold] back → 0625

HOMOPHONES

おさえる 押 PUSH → 0371
おさえ 押 PUSH → 0371

NOTE

➡ see USAGE note at 押 0371

抛

0302
◧ 1-3-4

▶**TOSS**
ホウ なげう(つ) ほう(る)

64	Nonstandard	U629B
扌	S7-3-4	F0000

traditional form → see 抛 at 0364

拘

0303
◧ 1-3-4

▶**ARREST**
コウ かか(わる)

64	Nonstandard	U6285
扌	S7-3-4	F0000

traditional form → see 拘 at 0367

扱

0304
◧ 1-3-4

▶**HANDLE**
ショウ あつか(う) あつか(い)

64	Nonstandard	U6271
扌	S7-3-4	F0000

traditional form → see 扱 at 0251

拒

◧ 1-3-4

incorrect stroke-count
➡ see ◧ 1-3-5: 扌 at 0368

扱

◧ 1-3-4

incorrect stroke-count
➡ see ◧ 1-3-3: 扌 at 0251

没

0305
◧ 1-3-4

▶**SINK**
ボツ
Ⓝ 沒 Ⓒ 没 méi mò

85	Jōyō	U6CA1
氵	S7-3-4	F1391

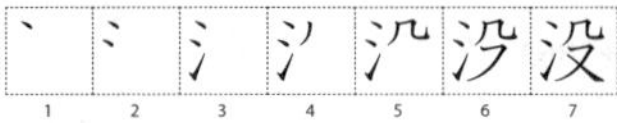

COMPOUNDS

❶ⓐ [original meaning] **SINK into the water, submerge; sink below the horizon**
ⓑ **SINK into the ground, subside, fall in**

a 水没する すいぼつする sink, submerge
沈没する ちんぼつする sink, go to the bottom
日没 にちぼつ sunset
b 埋没する まいぼつする be buried; fall into oblivion
陥没する かんぼつする sink, fall, cave in

❷ⓐ disappear, vanish, go out of sight, hide
ⓑ make disappear, hide, efface

a 出没する しゅつぼつする make frequent appearances; haunt
b 没却する ぼっきゃくする discard and ignore, lose sight of (an objective)
没我 ぼつが selflessness

❸ **be sunk in thought, become absorbed in**
没頭する ぼっとうする be absorbed in
没入する ぼつにゅうする be immersed in (one's work), be absorbed in

❹ [formerly also 歿 1078] **die, perish**
没後 ぼつご after one's death
没年 ぼつねん year of death
戦没する せんぼつする be killed in action

❺ [prefix] lacking in, not, un-
没常識 ぼつじょうしき lack of common sense
没個性 ぼつこせい lack of individuality

❻ reject, discard
没書 ぼっしょ rejected manuscript

❼ confiscate

没収 ぼっしゅう confiscation, seizure, forfeiture

INDEPENDENT

【ぼつ 没】rejected manuscript; [formerly also 歿 1078] indicates date of death

没にする ぼつにする reject (a manuscript), turn down (a proposal)

昭和三年没 しょうわさんねんぼつ died 1928

【ぼっする 没する】**SINK**, be immersed in; sink below the horizon; disappear, hide; ignore (someone's merits); reject; confiscate; [formerly also 歿する] die

SYNONYMS

❶ⓐ sink

沒 SINK → 0305
沈 SINK → 0306
潜 SUBMERGE → 0922
溺 DROWN → 0805

ⓑ collapse

陥 FALL IN → 0547
落 FALL → 2907
崩 CRUMBLE → 2863
没 SINK → 0305

❷ⓐ disappear

消 disappear → 0531
没 disappear → 0305

❹ die

死 DIE → 4334
萎 WITHER → 2872
没 die → 0305
亡 DECEASE → 4210
殉 DIE A MARTYR → 1177
歿 DIE → 1078
去 pass away → 2678
逝 DEPART THIS LIFE → 3850
斃 FALL DOWN DEAD → 3593
枯 WITHER → 1113

❺ terms of negation

不 NOT (negation) → 4242
非 IS NOT (contrariety) → 1101
無 WITHOUT (nonexistence) → 2648
没 lacking in → 0305
欠 LACK → 2481
否 OR NOT → 3058
未 NOT YET → 4318
莫 NOT → 2839
勿 DO NOT → 3661

NOTE

➡ see USAGE note at 不 4242

沈

0306

1-3-4

▸SINK

チン ジン▲ しず(む) しず(める)

N 沉 C 沉 chén 沈 shěn

85	Jōyō	U6C88
氵	S7-3-4	F1048

Stroke order: 1–7

COMPOUNDS

❶ⓐ SINK, submerge, go down

ⓑ [original meaning] (cause to) **SINK, submerge**

a 沈没する ちんぼつする sink, go to the bottom

沈下 ちんか subsidence, sinking

沈澱 ちんでん precipitation, settlement

沈滞 ちんたい stagnation, dullness

浮沈 ふちん rise and fall, ebb and flow; ups and downs

b 撃沈する げきちんする attack and sink a ship

❷ⓐ be sunk in thought, become absorbed in

ⓑ (sink into depression) **depressed, melancholy**

a 沈潜する ちんせんする sink into deep thought; sink to the depths

沈思 ちんし meditation, deep thought

b 沈鬱な ちんうつな melancholy, gloomy

❸ⓐ quiet, calm, tranquil

ⓑ **quiet, still**

a 沈静 ちんせい stillness, tranquility, slackness

b 沈着 ちんちゃく composure, self-possession

沈黙 ちんもく silence, reticence, taciturnity

❹ kind of aromatic tree

沈丁花 じんちょうげ(=ちんちょうげ) (sweet-smelling) daphne

KUN

【しずむ 沈む】**SINK, submerge, go down; set; sink into depression, be downcast; be losing (in a game of mahjong)**

沈んだ心 しずんだこころ depressed heart, low spirits

船が沈んだ ふねがしずんだ A ship sank

日が沈む ひがしずむ The sun sets

【しずめる 沈める】

ⓐ **SINK, send to the bottom, submerge**

ⓑ **SINK** oneself into (a chair), lower oneself

ⓒ **SINK** down in the world, go to ruin

a 敵艦を沈める てきかんをしずめる sink an enemy ship

b 椅子に身を沈める いすにみをしずめる sink into a chair

c 苦界に身を沈める くがいにみをしずめる become a prostitute

SYNONYMS

❶ sink

没 SINK →0305
沈 SINK →0306
潜 SUBMERGE →0922
溺 DROWN →0805

❷ⓑ sad and depressed

悲 SAD →3448
悄 BECOME DISPIRITED →0506
哀 sorrowful →2568
愁 MELANCHOLY →3508
鬱 GLOOM →3625
陰 gloomy →0657
沈 depressed →0306
寂 LONESOME →2855
淋しい LONESOME →0632
惨 MISERABLE →0585

HOMOPHONES

しずめる

鎮 QUELL →2210
静 QUIET →2164

NOTE

➡ see USAGE note at 静 2164

沖

0307

◧1-3-4

▸OFFING

チュウ おき

Ⓝ 沖 Ⓒ 冲 chōng chòng

85	Jōyō	U6C96
氵	S7-3-4	F1085

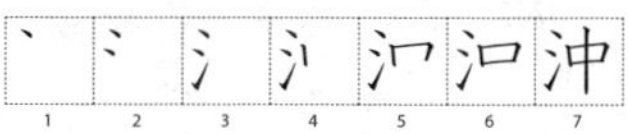

COMPOUNDS

❶ rise straight to heaven, soar to the skies

沖天 ちゅうてん rising to heaven

❷ wash away

沖積層 ちゅうせきそう alluvium

INDEPENDENT

【ちゅうする 沖する】 rise straight to heaven

KUN

【おき 沖】 [also suffix] **OFFING, offshore, open sea**

沖合い おきあい offing, offshore
沖釣り おきづり offshore fishing
二キロ沖 にきろおき two kilometers offshore

SYNONYMS

【おき】

◯ **sea**

海 SEA →0459
洋 OCEAN →0468
沖 OFFING →0307
灘 OPEN SEA →1006

決

0308

◧1-3-4

▸DECIDE

ケツ き(める) -ぎ(め) き(まる) ㊔ さだむ

Ⓝ 決 Ⓒ 决 jué

85	Jōyō-3	U6C7A
氵	S7-3-4	F0175

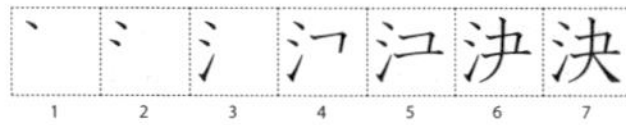

COMPOUNDS

❶ⓐ (make up one's mind) **DECIDE, determine, fix**
ⓑ (pronounce judgment) **DECIDE, resolve, settle**
ⓒ **decision**

a 決定 けってい decision, settlement, conclusion
決意 けつい resolution, determination
決心 けっしん determination, resolution, decision
解決 かいけつ solution, settlement

b 決算 けっさん settlement of accounts
決勝 けっしょう decision (of a contest)
決議 けつぎ resolution, decision

c 判決 はんけつ judicial decision, judgment, sentence
可決する かけつする approve [adopt] a bill
裁決 さいけつ decision, ruling
多数決 たすうけつ decision by majority

❷ decisively, resolutely

決行 けっこう decisive action
決然たる けつぜんたる decisive, resolute, determined

❸ [original meaning] break, burst, rip—said esp. of dikes

決壊 けっかい rip, break
決裂 けつれつ breakdown, rupture

❹ [formerly also 蹶 2073] spring to one's feet, rouse oneself

決起する けっきする rise to action, spring up

❺ [formerly also 訣 1861] separate, part, bid farewell

決別 けつべつ separation, farewell

❻ [formerly also 訣 1861] secrets (as of an art), knack

秘決 ひけつ secret, key

INDEPENDENT

【けつ 決】 decision, vote

決を採る けつをとる take a vote

【けっする 決する】 come to a decision, be settled; break, give way (as of dikes)

【けっして 決して】 **never, by no means, not at all**

KUN

【きめる 決める】 [sometimes also 極める]

① **DECIDE, determine, fix**

自分で決める じぶんできめる decide by oneself

② **agree upon, arrange**

取り決め とりきめ decision, agreement

③ (bring to a conclusion) **settle, conclude**

決め付ける きめつける scold, take (a person) to task
決め手 きめて decisive factor, clincher; trump card, winning move

【-ぎめ -決め】 [usu. -極め] **indicates periods of time (esp. months)**

【きまる 決まる】 [sometimes also 極まる]

① **be DECIDEd [fixed], be settled, be arranged**
決まり きまり settlement, conclusion; rule, regulation; custom
十五日と決まっている じゅうごにちときまっている The date is fixed for the 15th of the month

② **be certain [sure], be a matter of course**
雨が降るに決まっている あめがふるにきまっている It is sure to rain
行かないに決まっている いかないにきまっている Of course I won't go

SYNONYMS

❶ⓐ decide
決 DECIDE →0308
断 RESOLVE →1885
定 FIX →2770

ⓑ judge
判 JUDGE →1441
裁 JUDGE →4090
鑑 APPRAISE →2226
評 evaluate →1895
審 TRY →2985
決 DECIDE →0308
視 REGARD →1223

❷ resolutely
敢 BOLDLY →2142
断 resolutely →1885
決 decisively →0308

USAGE

❶【きめる】
決める
[sometimes also 極める]
① decide, determine, fix
② agree upon, arrange
③ (bring to a conclusion) settle, conclude
極める
[usu. 決める] same as 決める

❷【-ぎめ】
-決め
[usu. -極め] indicates periods of time (esp. months)
-極め
[sometimes also -決め] same as -決め

❸【きまる】
決まる
[sometimes also 極まる]
① be decided [fixed], be settled, be arranged
② be certain [sure], be a matter of course
極まる
[usu. 決まる] same as 決まる

HOMOPHONES

きめる 極 EXTREME →1243
-ぎめ 極 EXTREME →1243
きまる 極 EXTREME →1243

汽

0309

1-3-4

▶STEAM

キ

Ⓒ 汽 qì

85	Jōyō-2	U6C7D
氵	S7-3-4	F2138

Stroke order: 1–7

COMPOUNDS

● STEAM, vapor
汽車 きしゃ (steam) train
汽船 きせん steamship
汽圧 きあつ steam pressure
汽缶 きかん boiler
汽笛 きてき steam whistle
汽水 きすい brackish water

SYNONYMS

● kinds of water
水 WATER →0010
湯 HOT WATER →0747
汽 STEAM →0309
氷 ICE →0043
淵 DEEP WATER →0732

● gas and vapor
気 GAS →3960
空 AIR →2767
汽 STEAM →0309

汲

0310

1-3-4

▶DRAW WATER

キュウ く(む)

Ⓝ 汲 Ⓒ 汲 jí

85	Names	U6C72
氵	S7-3-4	F2136

COMPOUNDS

❶ [original meaning] **DRAW (WATER), scoop up, ladle, pump**
汲水 きゅうすい drawing [pumping] up water

❷ be busy, be occupied
汲汲としている きゅうきゅうとしている think only of, be absorbed in

KUN

【くむ 汲む】

①ⓐ **DRAW WATER, ladle, scoop up, pump**

ⓑ **pour (a drink) into a cup [glass]**

a 汲み取る くみとる draw [dip] up, drain; take into consideration

汲み立ての くみたての freshly drawn

汲み干す くみほす drain out, pump dry

水汲み みずくみ drawing water

b 茶汲み ちゃくみ serving tea (to guests); someone who serves tea

② **consider, sympathize with**

意を汲む いをくむ enter into a person's feelings

SYNONYMS

❶ **take from water**

撈 DREDGE → 0908

掬 SCOOP UP → 0599

汲 DRAW WATER → 0310

HOMOPHONES

くむ 酌 POUR WINE → 1854

NOTE

➡ see USAGE note at 酌 1854

沙

0311

◧ 1-3-4

▶SAND

サ シャ▲ すな▲ ㊔ まさご

Ⓒ 沙 shā

85	Jōyō	U6C99
氵	S7-3-4	F1295

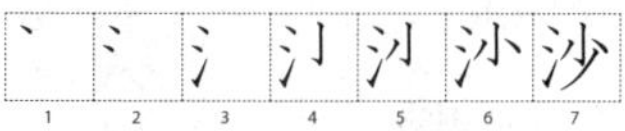

COMPOUNDS

❶ [now usu. 砂 さ 1457]

ⓐ [original meaning] **SAND (of granular constitution), tiny gravel or pebbles**

ⓑ **SANDy plain, the sands**

a 沙丘 さきゅう sand dune, sand hill

b 沙漠 さばく desert

❷ **wash, sift, sort**

沙汰 さた instructions; notice, tidings, rumor; affair

御無沙汰しております ごぶさたしております I haven't seen you for a long time

❸ **used phonetically for** *sha,* **esp. in the transliteration of Sanskrit Buddhist terms**

沙弥 しゃみ Buddhist novice, *śrāmaṇera*

沙門 しゃもん wandering Buddhist monk, *śramaṇa*

沙翁 さおう Shakespeare

KUN

【すな 沙】 [usu. 砂] **SAND, grit**

SYNONYMS

❶ⓐ **sand**

砂 SAND (fine) → 1457

沙 SAND (granular) → 0311

❸ **phonetic [s]/[sh]**

沙 phonetic [sha] → 0311

刹 phonetic [setsu] → 1620

遮 phonetic [sha] → 3916

叉 phonetic [sha] → 4194

世 phonetic [se] → 4308

須 phonetic [shu] → 0700

修 phonetic [shu] → 0138

西 phonetic [su] → 4333

相 phonetic [sō] → 1120

薩 phonetic [satsu] → 3016

HOMOPHONES

すな 砂 SAND → 1457

COMPOUND FORMATION

【沙汰 さた】

沙汰 'instructions, etc.' originally meant to sift out (沙 ❷) impurities from rice by washing (汰), and was extended to mean distinguishing between good and evil. When a superior makes a judgment to determine good or evil, he informs or instructs his subordinates to that effect. By this roundabout logic, 沙汰 came to mean instructions or tidings, giving rise to the expression 御無沙汰しております ごぶさたしております, literally "I have not (無) presented you with my humble (御) tidings (沙汰) or greetings," i.e., I have not seen you for a long time.

NOTE

➡ see USAGE note at 砂 1457

汰

0312

◧ 1-3-4

▶SIFT OUT

タ タイ▲

Ⓒ 汰 tài

85	Jōyō	U6C70
氵	S7-3-4	F1889

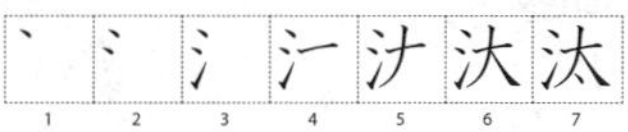

COMPOUNDS

● **SIFT OUT**

淘×汰する とうたする select, weed out, screen, sift; dismiss, cashier

自然淘×汰 しぜんとうた natural selection

沙汰 さた instructions; notice, tidings, rumor; affair

SYNONYMS

● **choose**

選 CHOOSE → 3931

撰 choose → 0911

択 SELECT → 0299

採 PICK → 0606

摘 pick out → 0851

擢 SINGLE OUT → 0973

抜 single out → 0290

汰 SIFT OUT → 0312

口 土 夕 女 子 山 工 己 彳 忄 扌 【氵】 犭 阝 丩 丬

NOTE

➡ see COMPOUND FORMATION for 沙汰 さた → 沙 0311

沢 0313

▶**MARSH**

タク さわ

Ⓝ 澤 Ⓒ 泽 zé

1-3-4

85 氵	Jōyō	U6CA2
	S7-3-4	F0569

1 2 3 4 5 6 7

COMPOUNDS

❶ [original meaning] **MARSH, swamp**

沼沢 しょうたく marsh, swamp

❷ **plentiful, abundant**

沢山 たくさん large quantity, plenty, abundance

潤沢 じゅんたく abundance, plenty

贅ˣ沢 ぜいたく luxury, extravagance

❸ luster, gloss, brightness

光沢 こうたく luster, gloss, polish

色沢 しきたく [rare] luster and color

❹ favor, benefit, grace, blessing

恩沢 おんたく favor, benefit

徳沢 とくたく grace, blessing

余沢 よたく blessings, benefits

KUN

【さわ 沢】**MARSH, swamp; valley, dale**

沢辺 さわべ edge of a swamp

沢地 さわち marshy land

一ノ倉沢 いちのくらさわ Ichinokura Valley

SYNONYMS

❶ **lakes and marshes**

沢 MARSH → 0313

沼 MUDDY POND → 0398

湖 LAKE → 0736

池 POND → 0253

潟 LAGOON → 0921

❷ **plentiful**

百 numerous → 2519

沃 FERTILE → 0315

万 myriad → 3653

多 MANY → 2694

豊 PLENTIFUL → 3344

沢 plentiful → 0313

穣 YIELDING ABUNDANTLY → 1597

裕 ABUNDANT → 1530

饒 ABUNDANT → 2280

富 RICH → 2892

❸ **luster**

艶 gloss → 2403

沢 luster → 0313

沌 0314

▶**PRIMEVAL CHAOS**

トン

Ⓒ 沌 dùn zhuàn

1-3-4

85 氵	Names	U6C8C
	S7-3-4	F2895

COMPOUNDS

● **PRIMEVAL CHAOS**

混沌 こんとん [sometimes also 渾沌] chaos

SYNONYMS

● **disordered**

紛 CONFUSED → 1648

乱 DISORDERED → 1611

錯 MIXED UP → 2187

混 mixed up → 0631

雑 mixed up → 1752

沌 PRIMEVAL CHAOS → 0314

沃 0315

▶**FERTILE**

ヨク ヨウ▲

Ⓒ 沃 wò

1-3-4

85 氵	Jōyō	U6C83
	S7-3-4	F3268

1 2 3 4 5 6 7

COMPOUNDS

❶ (of land or soil) **FERTILE, rich**

沃土 よくど fertile [rich] soil, fertile land

沃野 よくや fertile fields [plains]

肥沃な ひよくな fertile, productive

❷ iodine

沃素 ようそ iodine

沃化 ようか iodination

SPECIAL READINGS

沃度丁幾▲ よーどちんき iodine tincture

SYNONYMS

❶ **plentiful**

百 numerous → 2519

沃 FERTILE → 0315

万 myriad → 3653

多 MANY → 2694

豊 PLENTIFUL → 3344

沢 plentiful → 0313

穣 YIELDING ABUNDANTLY → 1597

裕 ABUNDANT → 1530

饒 ABUNDANT → 2280

富 RICH → 2892

没

0316

◧1-3-4

▶**SINK**

ボツ

85	Nonstandard	U6C92
氵	S7-3-4	F0000

traditional form → see 沒 at 0305

沉

0317

◧1-3-4

▶**SINK**

チン ジン しず(む) しず(める)

85	Nonstandard	U6C89
氵	S7-3-4	F0000

traditional form → see 沈 at 0306

汚

◧1-3-4

incorrect stroke-count

➡ see ◧1-3-3: 氵 at 0258

注

◧1-3-4

incorrect stroke-count

➡ see ◧1-3-5: 氵 at 0401

汲

◧1-3-4

incorrect stroke-count

➡ see ◧1-3-3: 氵 at 0260

狂

0318

◧1-3-4

▶**CRAZY**

キョウ くる(う) くる(おしい) くる(わす) くる(わせる)

Ⓒ 狂 kuáng

94	Jōyō	U72C2
犭	S7-3-4	F1124

1 2 3 4 5 6 7

COMPOUNDS

❶ [original meaning] **CRAZY, mad, insane**

狂気の きょうきの insane, mad, crazy

狂人 きょうじん lunatic, maniac

狂犬病 きょうけんびょう rabies

狂的な きょうてきな insane, fanatic

発狂する はっきょうする go mad, become insane [crazy]

❷ [suffix] (enthusiastic fan) **maniac, fanatic, fan, enthusiast**

殺人狂 さつじんきょう homicidal maniac

映画狂 えいがきょう cinema enthusiast, movie fan

窃盗狂 せっとうきょう kleptomaniac

偏執狂 へんしつきょう(=へんしゅうきょう) monomaniac

❸ raging, wild, furious

狂奔する きょうほんする rush around, run madly about, run wild; make frantic efforts, be very busy (in)

狂喜 きょうき wild joy, ecstasy

❹ comical, funny, jocular, humorous

狂言 きょうげん noh farce, comic interlude in a noh drama; kabuki play; sham, put-up job

狂歌 きょうか comic [satirical] tanka

KUN

【くるう 狂う】 **become insane [CRAZY], go mad; become crazy about (someone); go wild, rave; get out of order, be upset; warp, get warped**

狂い死に くるいじに death in madness

狂い くるい warp, deviation; aberration

女に狂う おんなにくるう run mad after a girl

荒れ狂う風 あれくるうかぜ raging wind

時計が狂っている とけいがくるっている My watch is not right

【くるおしい 狂おしい】 **driving mad, distracting; bordering on insanity**

狂おしい思い くるおしいおもい maddening thought

【くるわす 狂わす】 **drive CRAZY [mad]; put out of order**

【くるわせる 狂わせる】 **drive CRAZY [mad]**

番狂わせ ばんくるわせ upsetting of arrangements, upset, surprise

SYNONYMS

❷ **mania and maniacs**

痴 infatuated → 4072

狂 maniac → 0318

魔 maniac → 3953

熱 fever → 3555

❸ **extreme in power**

激 VIOLENT → 0955

荒 WILD → 2810

狂 raging → 0318

烈 VEHEMENT → 3286

猛 FIERCE → 0653

NOTE

➡ see COMPOUND FORMATION for 偏執狂 へんしつきょう (=へんしゅうきょう) → 執 2114

犹

0319

◧1-3-4

▶**DELAY**

ユウ ユ なお

94	Nonstandard	U72B9
犭	S7-3-4	F0000

traditional form → see 猶 at 0757

防

0320

◧1-3-4

▶**PREVENT**

ボウ ふせ(ぐ)

Ⓒ 防 fáng

170	Jōyō-5	U9632
阝	S7-3-4	F0618

口 土 夕 女 子 山 工 己 彳 忄 扌 氵 犭 【阝】 丬 丬

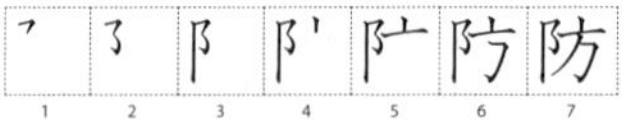

COMPOUNDS

❶ⓐ PREVENT, hold in check, keep away, shut out
ⓑ PREVENTing, -proof, anti-

a 防止する ぼうしする prevent, hold in check
防除 ぼうじょ pest control, extermination
防災 ぼうさい disaster prevention
消防 しょうぼう fire fighting, prevention and extinction of fires
予防 よぼう prevention, protection, precaution
b 防火 ぼうか fire prevention, fireproof
防音 ぼうおん soundproof
防水 ぼうすい waterproof
防虫剤 ぼうちゅうざい insecticide, vermicide
防腐剤 ぼうふざい antiseptic

❷ⓐ defend, guard against, protect, resist
ⓑ defense

a 防衛する ぼうえいする defend, protect, safeguard, shield
防備 ぼうび defense, defensive preparations
防御 ぼうぎょ defense, protection, safeguard
防戦 ぼうせん defensive battle
b 国防 こくぼう national defense

❸ [original meaning] **dike**
堤防 ていぼう bank, embankment, dike

❹ abbrev. of 周防 すおう, old name for east Yamaguchi Prefecture
防長 ぼうちょう old name for Yamaguchi Prefecture

INDEPENDENT

【ぼう 防】defense, protection

KUN

【ふせぐ 防ぐ】[formerly also 禦ぐ]
① **PREVENT, keep off, ward off**
伝染を防ぐ でんせんをふせぐ prevent infection
② **defend, protect, resist**
侵略を防ぐ しんりゃくをふせぐ defend against an invasion

SYNONYMS

❶ prevent
防 PREVENT → 0320
止 STOP → 3659

❷ protect
守 PROTECT (by watching over) → 2697
護 PROTECT (by safeguarding) → 2079
庇 PROTECT (by shielding) → 3802
衛 GUARD → 0938
警 GUARD AGAINST → 3595
防 defend → 0320
番 WATCH → 3416
保 PRESERVE → 0107
看 CARE FOR → 3992

❸ embankment
堤 EMBANKMENT → 0681
防 dike → 0320
堰 DAM → 0676

USAGE

【ふせぐ】
防ぐ
[formerly also 禦ぐ]
① prevent, keep off, ward off
② defend, protect, resist
禦ぐ
[now usu. 防ぐ] same as 防ぐ

HOMOPHONES

ふせぐ 禦 WARD OFF → 3561

阪 0321

▸OSAKA
ハン さか
Ⓒ 阪 bǎn

1-3-4

170	Jōyō	U962A
阝	S7-3-4	F0855

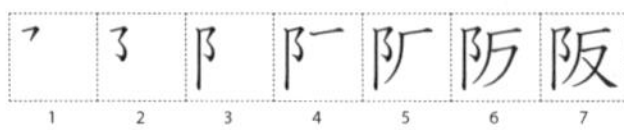

COMPOUNDS

❶ OSAKA
阪神 はんしん Hanshin, Osaka and Kobe
阪大 はんだい Osaka University
阪急デパート はんきゅうでぱーと Hankyu Department Store
来阪する らいはんする come to Osaka

❷ [original meaning] slope, incline, hill

KUN

【さか 阪】**slope, incline, hill**—now used almost exclusively in the writing of names
大阪府 おおさかふ Osaka Prefecture

SYNONYMS

❶ Kansai cities
阪 OSAKA → 0321
神 Kobe → 1143
京 KYOTO → 2546
洛 KYOTO → 0463

❷ hills
丘 HILL → 4307
畝 RIDGE → 1857
岡 HILL → 3719
台 heights → 2498
坂 SLOPE → 0275
阪 slope → 0321
塚 MOUND → 0675
阜 MOUND → 3254

陵 high mound →0660
稜 RIDGE →1545

HOMOPHONES

さか 坂 SLOPE →0275

NOTE

➡ see USAGE note at 坂 0275

收 1-3-4

incorrect stroke-count
➡ see 1-2-4: 丬 at 0065

状

0322

1-3-4

▶**FORM**
▶**CONDITION**
▶**LETTER**

ジョウ

Ⓝ 狀 Ⓒ 状 zhuàng

94	Jōyō-5	U72B6
犬	S7-4-3	F0299

丨 丬 丬 丬 壮 状 状 (1–7)

COMPOUNDS

❶ⓐ [original meaning] **(external) FORM, shape, appearance**
ⓑ [also suffix] **-FORM, in the form of, -shaped, -like**

a 形状 けいじょう shape, form, configuration
環状の かんじょうの ring-shaped, circular
波状 はじょう wave, undulation
球状 きゅうじょう shape of a globe, globular shape
b 帯状の おびじょう(=たいじょう)の belt-shaped
ガス状の がすじょうの gaseous, gasiform
液状の えきじょうの liquefied

❷ **(actual) CONDITION, state, situation, circumstances**
状態 じょうたい state, condition, appearance, situation, aspect
状況 じょうきょう state of affairs, conditions, circumstances
現状 げんじょう present condition
商状 しょうじょう market condition
症状 しょうじょう symptom
病状 びょうじょう condition of a disease [patient]
罪状 ざいじょう offense, charges

❸ [also suffix]
ⓐ **LETTER, note, card**
ⓑ **official document [paper], official LETTER, certificate, warrant**

a 書状 しょじょう letter, note
賞状 しょうじょう certificate of merit
招待状 しょうたいじょう letter of invitation
年賀状 ねんがじょう New Year's card
公開状 こうかいじょう open letter
b 信任状 しんにんじょう credentials, letter of credence
免状 めんじょう license, diploma
令状 れいじょう warrant, writ
遺言状 ゆいごんじょう will, testament

❹ **describe, narrate**
白状 はくじょう confession
名状する めいじょうする describe

INDEPENDENT

【じょう 状】**CONDITION**, state; letter, epistle
この状持参の者 このじょうじさんのもの the person bearing this letter

SYNONYMS

❶ **form**
形 SHAPE →1050
状 FORM (external) →0322
体 FORM (characteristic) →0080
姿 FIGURE →3264

❷ **states and situations**
態 STATE →3529
調 TONE →1973
様 MODE →1332
相 PHASE →1120
状 CONDITION →0322
況 CONDITIONS →0395
景 business conditions →3118
勢 course of events →3542
境 SITUATION →0835
局 current situation →3800
情 ACTUAL CONDITIONS →0583
訳 circumstances →1865

❸ⓐ **written communications**
状 LETTER →0322
文 LETTER →2458
翰 LETTER →2198
書 letter →3292
信 written communication →0115
電 telegram →3465
牒 OFFICIAL NOTICE →1299

ⓑ **certificates**
証 CERTIFICATE →1899
券 CERTIFICATE →3256
状 official document →0322
免 license →2565

呪

0323

1-3-5

▶**SPELL**

ジュ シュウ▲ のろ(う) まじな(う)▲

Ⓝ 咒 Ⓒ 咒 zhòu

30	Jōyō	U546A
口	S8-3-5	F1885

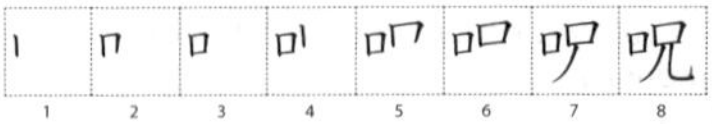

COMPTABLE

口 土 女 子 山 巾 弓 彳 忄 扌 氵 犭 阝

COMPOUNDS

● **SPELL, incantation, curse, charm**

呪縛 じゅばく spell
呪文 じゅもん spell, charm
呪術 じゅじゅつ magic, sorcery; spell
呪符 じゅふ amulet, charm
呪詛× じゅそ curse, hex
神呪 しんじゅ mystic spell, *dhāraṇi*

INDEPENDENT

【じゅ 呪】**SPELL**, incantation, curse, charm; *Buddhism* dharani, mantra

KUN

【のろう 呪う】
ⓐ **curse, put a curse on**
ⓑ **detest intensely**
a 呪い のろい curse, spell

【まじなう 呪う】
ⓐ pray against disaster [illness]
ⓑ curse, put a curse on
ⓒ treat illness with prayer
a 呪い まじない spell, incantation, charm, magic formula

SYNONYMS

● **pray and worship**

祈 PRAY →1086
祷 PRAY →1224
願 pray →2320
拝 WORSHIP →0360
祀 WORSHIP AS GOD →1448
崇 REVERENCE →2864
斎 OBSERVE RELIGIOUS ABSTINENCE →2622
呪 SPELL →0323

呼

▶**CALL**
コ よ(ぶ)
Ⓒ 呼 hū

0324
1-3-5

30	Jōyō-6	U547C
口	S8-3-5	F0315

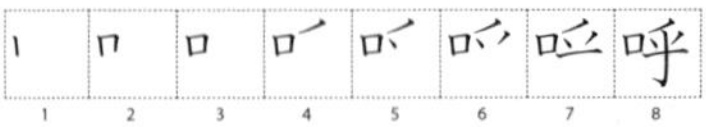

COMPOUNDS

❶ (cry out in a loud voice) **CALL, call out to**

呼応する こおうする hail to each other, act in concert
呼号する ここうする cry out, proclaim
指呼する しこする beckon
点呼 てんこ roll call
歓呼する かんこする cheer, cry out

❷ (attach a name to) **CALL**, name

呼称する こしょうする call, name
称呼 しょうこ appellation, designation

❸ [original meaning] **breathe out, exhale**

呼吸する こきゅうする breathe, respire
呼気 こき exhalation

KUN

【よぶ 呼ぶ】
①ⓐ (cry out) **CALL, call out to**
ⓑ (summon) **CALL, send for, invite**
a 呼び掛ける よびかける call to; appeal to
呼び出す よびだす call, summon; page
b 呼び出し よびだし call, calling out, summons
呼び寄せる よびよせる call, summon, send for, call together
医者を呼ぶ いしゃをよぶ call the doctor
② **CALL, give a name to**
呼び名 よびな given name, popular name
呼び捨てにする よびすてにする call by the first name, use a name without a title
③ bring about, give rise to
呼び起こす よびおこす awake, arise; call to mind

SYNONYMS

❶ **give out a call**

叫 SHOUT →0233
号 holler →2675
喝 SHOUT AT →0554
喚 call out →0666
呼 CALL →0324
鳴 CRY →0831
吠 BARK →0269

❷ **name**

呼 CALL →0324
言う call →2440
称 name →1491

❸ **breathe and blow**

息 BREATH →3278
気 breath →3960
吸 BREATHE IN →0234
呼 breathe out →0324
吹 BLOW →0272

【よぶ】
①ⓑ **call and invite**

呼ぶ CALL →0324
喚 CALL →0666
召 SUMMON →2494
招 INVITE →0374

味

0325

1-3-5

▶TASTE

ミ あじ あじ(わう) ㊔ うま

Ⓒ 味 wèi

30	Jōyō-3	U5473
口	S8-3-5	F0149

1	2	3	4	5	6	7	8
｜	冂	口	口一	口二	吽	味	味

COMPOUNDS

❶ **TASTE, flavor**
味覚 みかく sense of taste
調味 ちょうみ seasoning, flavoring
風味 ふうみ flavor, taste

❷ⓐ (quality of attracting interest) **TASTE, interest, flavor, charm, beauty**
ⓑ **TASTE, savor, appreciate, enjoy**
a 趣味 しゅみ hobby, interest, taste
興味 きょうみ interest
妙味 みょうみ subtle charm, beauty
b 味読する みどくする appreciate a book
吟味 ぎんみ close examination, scrutiny

❸ⓐ suffix attached to the stem of adjectives or words inflected like adjectives: a dash of, a flavor, a touch, a tinge
ⓑ suffix of nominalization like -さ or *-ness*
a 赤味 あかみ a tinge of red
滑稽味が有る こっけいみがある tinged with humor
b 深味 ふかみ depth, profundity
嫌味 いやみ disagreeableness

❹ⓐ **tasty food, nourishment; condiments**
ⓑ counter for foods or condiments
a 味噌 みそ *miso*, bean paste; flattery
滋味 じみ savoriness; rich food, nourishment
b 七味 しちみ *shichimi* (a kind of spice)

❺ **contents, substance; meaning**
正味の しょうみの net, full, clear
意味 いみ meaning, intention, significance, purport

❻ **feeling, sensation**
気味 きみ feeling, sensation; a touch [tinge] (of)
地味な じみな plain, sober, unpretentious

❼ **companion, fellow, mate**
味方 みかた friend, ally, one's side
一味 いちみ fellow conspirators, gang

❽ used phonetically for *mi*
三味線 しゃみせん shamisen (Japanese three-stringed musical instrument)

KUN

【あじ 味】**TASTE, flavor; relish, pleasure; experience; sentiment (of the market)**
味な あじな clever, witty, strange
味付け あじつけ seasoning
味気無い あじけない(=あじきない) wearisome, insipid
後味 あとあじ aftertaste
文学の味 ぶんがくのあじ the pleasures of literature
女の味を知る おんなのあじをしる have carnal knowledge (of a woman)
場味 ばあじ market sentiment

【あじわう 味わう】**TASTE, savor; appreciate, enjoy**
味わい あじわい taste, flavor
味わい知る あじわいしる taste and know
読書の面白味を味わう どくしょのおもしろみをあじわう appreciate the pleasures of reading

SYNONYMS

❷ⓐ **flavor and elegance**
趣 FLAVOR →4111
味 TASTE →0325
風 elegance →3730
品 refinement →2795

ⓑ **taste**
味 TASTE (savor) →0325
嘗める TASTE (have a taste) →3230
舐める TASTE (have a taste) →1669

❺ **essential content**
実 substance →2765
体 substance →0080
味 contents →0325

COMPOUND FORMATION

【正味 しょうみ】
正味 'net, full, clear' refers to the correct (正) content (味 ❺), i.e., the net amount, as in 正味重量 しょうみじゅうりょう 'net weight'.

NOTE

★ do not confuse with 昧 DARK →1105

咏

0326

1-3-5

▶RECITE POETRY

エイ よ(む) ㊔ うた なが

30	Nonstandard	U548F
口	S8-3-5	F0000

traditional form →see 詠 at 1894

咊

0327

1-3-5

▶HARMONIOUS
▶PEACE
▶JAPAN

ワ オ やわ(らぐ) やわ(らげる) なご(む) なご(やか) ㊔ かず より やす やわら やまと たか よし かつ とも

30	Nonstandard	U548A
口	S8-3-5	F0000

traditional form →see 和 at 1450

口 【土】 女 子 山 巾 弓 彳 忄 扌 氵 犭 阝

坪

0328

1-3-5

▶*TSUBO*

ヘイ▲ つぼ

Ⓝ 坪 Ⓒ 坪 píng

32	Jōyō	U576A
土	S8-3-5	F1833

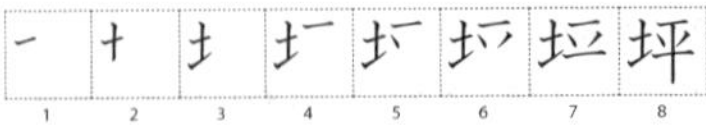

COMPOUNDS

● [original meaning, now obsolete] **level ground**

KUN

【つぼ 坪】*TSUBO*:

ⓐ **unit of sq. measure equiv. to approx. 3.3 sq. m or 36 sq. *shaku* (尺), used esp. for measuring land area**

ⓑ unit of cubic measure equiv. to approx. 6000 liters or 216 cubic *shaku* (尺), used esp. for measuring earth

a 十坪 とつぼ 10 *tsubo*

建て坪 たてつぼ floor space

SYNONYMS

【つぼ】

ⓐ **area units**

坪 *TSUBO* (3.3 sq. m) → 0328

歩 *bu* (3.3 sq. m) → 3071

畝 *se* (0.99 ares) → 1857

反 *tan* (9.9 ares) → 3663

町 *cho* (99.2 ares) → 1430

坦

0329

1-3-5

▶LEVEL

タン ㊔ ひろ やす やすし ひろし しずか ゆたか ひろむ ひら あきら ひとし かつ

Ⓒ 坦 tǎn

32	Names	U5766
土	S8-3-5	F2655

COMPOUNDS

❶ [original meaning] **LEVEL, flat, even**

坦坦 たんたん level, flat; uneventful

平坦 へいたん flat, level, even

❷ calm and open [frank]

虚心坦懐 きょしんたんかい with an open mind, frank, candid

SYNONYMS

❶ **flat**

平 FLAT → 4291

扁 FLAT → 3728

坦 LEVEL → 0329

坪

0330

1-3-5

▶*TSUBO*

ヘイ つぼ

32	Nonstandard	U576A
土	S8-3-5	F0000

traditional form → see 坪 at 0328

姆

0331

1-3-5

▶GOVERNESS

ボ うば

Ⓒ 姆 mǔ

38	Non-Jōyō	U59C6
女	S8-3-5	F0000

COMPOUNDS

● [now replaced by 母 4287] **GOVERNESS, female teacher; wet nurse**

保姆 ほぼ nurse, kindergarten teacher

KUN

【うば 姆】[now always 乳母] **wet nurse**

HOMOPHONES

うば

乳母 → 1823, 4287

姥 OLD WOMAN → 0420

NOTE

➡ see USAGE note at 姥 0420

姑

0332

1-3-5

▶MOTHER-IN-LAW

コ しゅうとめ しゅうと

Ⓒ 姑 gū

38	Non-Jōyō	U59D1
女	S8-3-5	F2148

COMPOUNDS

❶ [original meaning] **MOTHER-IN-LAW**

舅×姑 きゅうこ parents-in-law

❷ **awhile; for the time being**

姑息 こそく makeshift, stopgap, temporizing

❸ unclassified compounds

梯姑(=梯梧) でいご Indian coral tree

KUN

【しゅうとめ 姑】**MOTHER-IN-LAW**

嫁姑の仲 よめしゅうとめのなか relationship between bride and mother-in-law

【しゅうと 姑】same as 姑 しゅうとめ

小姑 こじゅうと(=こじゅうとめ) sister-in-law

SPECIAL READINGS

慈姑 くわい arrowhead (root), esp. *Sagittaria trifolia* var. *edulis*

SYNONYMS

❶ **in-laws**

婿 SON-IN-LAW → 0689

嫁 daughter-in-law → 0780

姑 MOTHER-IN-LAW →0332

妹

▶YOUNGER SISTER
マイ いもうと
Ⓒ 妹 mèi

0333
◧1-3-5

38	Jōyō-2	U59B9
女	S8-3-5	F1143

COMPOUNDS

● [original meaning] **YOUNGER SISTER**
姉妹 しまい(=きょうだい) sisters
義妹 ぎまい sister-in-law
弟妹 ていまい younger brothers and sisters
実妹 じつまい one's true (younger) sister
令妹 れいまい your younger sister

KUN

【いもうと 妹】**YOUNGER SISTER**
妹娘 いもうとむすめ younger daughter
妹分 いもうとぶん protégée

SYNONYMS

● **siblings**
妹 YOUNGER SISTER →0333
姉 OLDER SISTER →0336
兄 OLDER BROTHER →2676
弟 YOUNGER BROTHER →2537

姓

▶SURNAME
セイ ショウ
Ⓒ 姓 xìng

0334
◧1-3-5

38	Jōyō	U59D3
女	S8-3-5	F1263

COMPOUNDS

❶ⓐ **SURNAME, family name**
ⓑ **SURNAME** conferred by emperor in ancient times
a 姓名 せいめい full name
同姓 どうせい same surname
旧姓 きゅうせい one's former name, née
改姓する かいせいする change one's family name
百姓 ひゃくしょう farmer, peasant
b 氏姓制度 しせいせいど former naming system
❷ clan, caste
四姓 しせい the four castes (of India)
百姓 ひゃくせい common people

INDEPENDENT

【せい 姓】**SURNAME, family name**
姓が変わる せいがかわる assume a new surname

SYNONYMS

❶ **name**
名 NAME →2693
銘 name (inscribed by maker) →2158
姓 SURNAME →0334
氏 FAMILY NAME →3669
称 APPELLATION →1491
題 TITLE →4139
号 DESIGNATION →2675

COMPOUND FORMATION

【百姓 ひゃくしょう】
百姓 'farmer, peasant' originally meant 100 (百) surnames (姓 ❶ⓐ), i.e., the masses or peasantry.

始

▶BEGIN
シ はじ(める) -はじ(める) はじ(まる)
Ⓒ 始 shǐ

0335
◧1-3-5

38	Jōyō-3	U59CB
女	S8-3-5	F0303

COMPOUNDS

❶ **BEGIN, start, open**
始動 しどう starting (machines)
始業式 しぎょうしき opening ceremony of the school term
開始する かいしする begin, commence, open
創始する そうしする initiate, create, found
❷ⓐ **BEGINning, inception, start, origin**
ⓑ (source of something) **BEGINning, origin; first, starting**
a 始末する しまつする manage, deal with, dispose of; put in order
始終 しじゅう from beginning to end, at all times
年始 ねんし beginning of the year; New Year's greetings
終始 しゅうし from beginning to end, always
原始的な げんしてきな primitive, primeval
b 始発 しはつ first departure; starting station

KUN

【はじめる 始める】*vt* **BEGIN, open, start, originate; set about, embark on**
始め はじめ (act or point of commencement) beginning, start; (source) beginning, origin
始めて はじめて begin and... (TE-form of 始める はじめる)
始め(=初め)に はじめに in the beginning; early in (spring)
手始め てはじめ beginning, start, outset

口 土 【女】 子 山 巾 弓 彳 忄 扌 氵 犭 阝

御用始め ごようはじめ resumption of office business after the New Year recess

【-はじめる -始める】[verbal suffix] **BEGIN to perform an action**

雨が降り始めた あめがふりはじめた It has begun to rain

勉強し始める べんきょうしはじめる begin to study

【はじまる 始まる】*vi* **BEGIN, commence, start, open; originate; arise, break out**

始まり はじまり beginning

始まらない はじまらない It's no use

SYNONYMS

❶ **begin**

始 BEGIN →0335

-出す begin to do →4310

-掛ける start doing →0596

発 START →3174

起 start →4099

就 SET ABOUT →2129

開 OPEN →4121

創 initiate →2283

肇 ORIGINATE →3474

❷ **beginnings**

緒 OUTSET →1742

序 INTRODUCTORY PART →3803

端 start →1564

始 beginning →0335

初 beginning →1433

元 ORIGIN →2428

本 origin →4314

根 ROOT →1167

源 SOURCE →0806

HOMOPHONES

はじめ 初 FIRST →1433

はじめて

初 FIRST →1433

甫 BARELY →4363

COMPOUND FORMATION

【始末 しまつ】

始末する 'manage, deal with, etc.' is to deal with something from beginning (始 ❷ⓐ) to end (末).

NOTE

➡ see USAGE note at 初 1433

姉

0336

1-3-5

▶**OLDER SISTER**

シ あね

Ⓝ 姊◇ Ⓒ 姊 zǐ

38	Jōyō-2	U59C9
女	S8-3-5	F0998

く 夂 女 女' 女亠 女亡 女市 姉
1 2 3 4 5 6 7 8

COMPOUNDS

❶ **OLDER SISTER**

姉妹 しまい(=きょうだい) sisters

実姉 じっし one's true (older) sister

義姉 ぎし older sister-in-law

令姉 れいし your older sister

同母姉 どうぼし uterine sisters, sisters of the same mother

❷ title of respect for female peers or seniors

諸姉 しょし you (feminine plural), you ladies

貴姉 きし term of respect in addressing ladies or another's older sister

KUN

【あね 姉】**OLDER SISTER**

姉上 あねうえ older sister

SPECIAL READINGS

姉さん ねえさん older sister; waitress, girl; miss

SYNONYMS

❶ **siblings**

妹 YOUNGER SISTER →0333

姉 OLDER SISTER →0336

兄 OLDER BROTHER →2676

弟 YOUNGER BROTHER →2537

妬

0337

1-3-5

▶**BE JEALOUS**

ト ねた(む) ねた(ましい)▲ そね(む)▲ や(く)▲ や(ける)▲

Ⓝ 妒 Ⓒ 妒 dù

38	Jōyō	U59AC
女	S8-3-5	F1991

く 夂 女 女一 女丆 女石 妬 妬
1 2 3 4 5 6 7 8

COMPOUNDS

● **BE JEALOUS, be envious**

妬心 としん jealousy

嫉妬 しっと jealousy

KUN

【ねたむ 妬む】[also 嫉む] **BE JEALOUS, be envious**

妬み ねたみ jealousy, envy

【ねたましい 妬ましい】[also 嫉ましい]

ⓐ **enviable**

ⓑ **jealous, envious**

【そねむ 妬む】[also 嫉む] **BE JEALOUS,** be envious

【やく 妬く】[usu. 焼く] burn with jealousy, be envious

焼き餅を妬く やきもちをやく be jealous

【やける 妬ける】[usu. 焼ける] **BE JEALOUS,** burn with jealousy

SYNONYMS

❶ **jealous and envious**

嫉 JEALOUS →0783
妬 JEALOUS →0337
羨 ENVIOUS →2951

USAGE

❶【ねたむ】
妬む
[also 嫉む] be jealous, be envious
嫉む
[also 妬む] be jealous, be envious

❷【ねたましい】
妬ましい
[also 嫉ましい]
ⓐ enviable
ⓑ jealous, envious
嫉ましい
[also 妬ましい] same as 妬ましい

HOMOPHONES

ねたむ 嫉 BE JEALOUS →0783
ねたましい 嫉 BE JEALOUS →0783
そねむ 嫉 BE JEALOUS →0783
やく
焼 BURN →1256
灼 SCORCH →1036
やける 焼 BURN →1256

NOTE

➡ see also USAGE notes at 嫉 0783 and 焼 1256

姉

0338
◧ 1-3-5

▶**OLDER SISTER**
シ あね

38	Nonstandard	U59CA
女	S8-3-5	F0000

alternative form →see 姉 at 0336

孤

0339
◧ 1-3-5

▶**SOLITARY**
コ

39	Nonstandard	U5B64
子	S8-3-5	F0000

traditional form →see 孤 at 0426

岬

0340
◧ 1-3-5

▶**CAPE**
コウ▲ みさき
Ⓒ 岬 jiǎ

46	Jōyō	U5CAC
山	S8-3-5	F2104

1	2	3	4	5	6	7	8
丨	山	山	山	山冂	山冃	山日	岬

COMPOUNDS

❶ [rare] **CAPE**, promontory
岬角 こうかく promontory; *anat* promontory

❷ [original meaning, now archaic] **ravine, glen**

KUN

【みさき 岬】
ⓐ **CAPE, promontory, headland**
ⓑ **suffix after names of CAPEs**
a 潮岬 しおのみさき Cape Shio
b 三浦岬 みうらみさき Miura Point, headland of Miura

SYNONYMS

❶ **points of land**

岬 CAPE →0340
崎 PROMONTORY →0569
埼 promontory →0560

岨

0341
◧ 1-3-5

▶**STEEP**
ソ
Ⓒ 岨 qū

46	Non-Jōyō	U5CA8
山	S8-3-5	F0000

COMPOUNDS

ⓐ [now replaced by 阻 0411] **STEEP**
ⓑ [original meaning, now archaic] **STEEP mountain, rocky mountain**
a 嶮岨(=険阻)な けんそな steep (mountain pass), precipitous

SYNONYMS

ⓐ **steep**

険 STEEP →0658
嶮 STEEP →0937
岨 STEEP →0341
急 steep →2595
峻 high and steep →0495

帖

0342
◧ 1-3-5

▶**NOTEBOOK**
ジョウ チョウ
Ⓒ 帖 tiē tiě tiè

50	Names	U5E16
巾	S8-3-5	F2284

COMPOUNDS

❶ [now also 帳 ちょう 0572] **NOTEBOOK, book, register**
画帖 がじょう picture album
手帖 てちょう pocketbook, memo

❷ **model of calligraphy for copying**
法帖 ほうじょう copybook printed from the works of old masters of calligraphy

❸ counter for quires (of paper), folding screens, volumes of Japanese folding books, etc.
和紙三帖 わしさんじょう three quires of Japanese paper

❹ [usu. 畳 じょう 3205] counter for tatami or (straw) mats

六帖の部屋 ろくじょうのへや six-mat room

INDEPENDENT

【じょう 帖】Japanese folding book

SYNONYMS

❶ **notebook**

帳 NOTEBOOK → 0572
帖 NOTEBOOK → 0342
簿 RECORD BOOK → 3387
籍 REGISTER → 3394

口 土 女 子 山 巾 【弓】 彳 忄 扌 氵 犭 阝

弦

▶**STRING**

ゲン つる ㊔ いと

Ⓒ 弦 xián

0343

1-3-5

57	Jōyō	U5F26
弓	S8-3-5	F1931

COMPOUNDS

❶ [sometimes also 絃 1685]

ⓐ **STRING or chord of a musical instrument**

ⓑ counter for **STRING**s [chords]

ⓒ [original meaning] bowstring

a 弦楽器 げんがっき stringed instruments

調弦 ちょうげん tuning

b 一弦琴 いちげんきん one-stringed instrument, monochord

三弦 さんげん three-stringed instrument, shamisen

❷ **STRINGed instrument, the strings**

弦楽 げんがく string music

弦歌 げんか singing and (string) music

管弦 かんげん wind and string instruments

❸ *geometry* chord; hypotenuse

弦材 げんざい *civil engineering* chord member

補弦 ほげん supplementary chord

正弦 せいげん sine (of an angle)

❹ quarter (of the moon)

弦月 げんげつ crescent moon

上弦 じょうげん first quarter, dichotomy

下弦の月 かげんのつき waning moon

INDEPENDENT

【げん 弦】**STRING** (of musical instrument); *geometry* chord; bowstring

ギターの弦 ぎたーのげん guitar string [chord]

KUN

【つる 弦】**bowstring**

弦音 つるおと sound of a vibrating bowstring

弓弦 ゆみづる(=ゆづる) bowstring

SYNONYMS

❶ⓐ **ropes and lines**

綱 ROPE (esp. of fiber) → 1735
絃 STRING → 1685
縄 ROPE (esp. of straw) → 1756
緒 cord → 1742
組 braid → 1693
索 cable → 3105
鎖 CHAIN → 2213
線 LINE → 1760
紐 STRING → 1647
弦 STRING → 0343

❷ **musical instrument**

管 wind instrument → 3349
弦 string instrument → 0343

❸ **lines and line segments**

線 LINE → 1760
弧 ARC → 0430
弦 chord → 0343
径 DIAMETER → 0347
辺 side → 3761

NOTE

➡ see COMPOUND FORMATION for 正弦 せいげん → 正 4296

弥

▶**PHONETIC [mi]**

ミ▲ ビ▲ や いや▲ ㊔ わたる ひさ ひさし みつ ひろ

Ⓝ 彌 Ⓒ 弥 mí

0344

1-3-5

57	Jōyō	U5F25
弓	S8-3-5	F0909

COMPOUNDS

❶ **used PHONETICally for *mi*, esp. in the transliteration of Sanskrit Buddhist terms**

弥勒× みろく *Maitreya* (a *bodhisattva*)

阿弥陀 あみだ *Amitābha;* lottery; wearing a hat on the back of the head

❷ fill up, patch up

弥縫 びほう patching up

❸ [original meaning, now rare] reach for, extend, pervade, spread

弥久 びきゅう extending over a long time

KUN

【や 弥】[in compounds] **all the more, increasingly**

弥生 やよい third month (of the lunar calendar), March

【いや 弥】*elegant* all the more, increasingly

弥増す いやます increase all the more

SYNONYMS

❶ **phonetic [m]**

弥 PHONETIC [mi] → 0344
摩 phonetic [ma] → 3938
昧 phonetic [mai] → 1105
蜜 phonetic [mitsu] → 2958
勿 phonetic [mot] → 3661
牟 PHONETIC [mu] → 2518

弧 0345

1-3-5

▶**ARC**

コ

57 弓	Nonstandard	U5F27
	S8-3-5	F0000

traditional form → see 弧 at 0430

彼 0346

1-3-5

▶**THIRD PERSON PRONOUN**

ヒ かれ かの か(の)▲

Ⓒ 彼 bǐ

60 彳	Jōyō	U5F7C
	S8-3-5	F0053

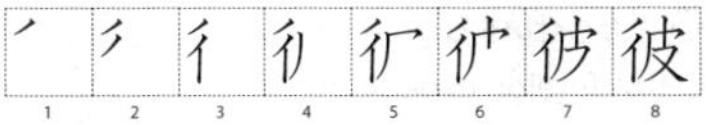

COMPOUNDS

❶ **THIRD PERSON PRONOUN, the other party, he, she**

彼我 ひが he [she] and I, they and we, both sides

❷ **that, the other**

彼岸 ひがん equinoctial week; the other shore

KUN

【かれ 彼】**he; boyfriend, lover**

彼等 かれら they
彼氏 かれし he; lover, beau

【かの 彼】[in compounds] **THIRD PERSON PRONOUN**

彼女 かのじょ she; one's sweetheart

【かの 彼の】*literary* that

彼の地 かのち that place, there

SYNONYMS

❶ **& 【かれ】 third person pronouns**

彼 THIRD PERSON PRONOUN (*neutral*) → 0346
氏 third person pronoun (*polite*) → 3669
奴 third person pronoun (*slang*) → 0217

❷ **this and that**

本 THIS → 4314
爾 THAT → 4407
其れ THAT → 3255
彼 that → 0346
今 THIS (week, etc.) → 2464
当 THE PRESENT → 2701
該 the said → 1916
同 the same → 3707
之 this → 4228
是 this → 3090
此 THIS → 1017
斯 THIS → 2140

径 0347

1-3-5

▶**PATH**
▶**DIAMETER**

ケイ ㊔ みち

Ⓝ 徑 逕 圣◇ Ⓒ 径 jìng

60 彳	Jōyō-4	U5F84
	S8-3-5	F1881

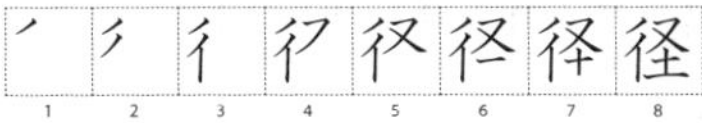

COMPOUNDS

❶ [original meaning] **(narrow) PATH, footpath, shortcut**

径路 けいろ path; process
捷径 しょうけい path, lane
山径 さんけい mountain path
小径 しょうけい path, lane

❷ **DIAMETER**

直径 ちょっけい diameter
半径 はんけい radius, semidiameter
口径 こうけい caliber, bore; diameter

❸ straight, direct

直情径行 ちょくじょうけいこう straightforwardness

INDEPENDENT

【けい 径】**DIAMETER**

径の大きい けいのおおきい of large diameter

SYNONYMS

❶ **ways and routes**

道 WAY (path) → 3888
径 PATH → 0347
軌 TRACK → 1832
線 LINE → 1760
澪 WATERWAY → 0957
途 WAY (route) → 3853
路 ROAD → 1936
筋 wayside → 3319
通り street → 3855
街 city street → 0702
辻 CROSSROADS → 3958
岐 forked road → 0285
巷 THE STREETS → 3097

❷ **lines and line segments**

線 LINE → 1760
弧 ARC → 0430
弦 chord → 0343
径 DIAMETER → 0347

口 土 女 子 山 巾 弓 【彳】 忄 扌 氵 犭 阝

口 土 女 子 山 巾 弓 【彳】 忄 扌 氵 犭 阝

辺 side → 3761

❷ **width**

幅 WIDTH → 0694

員 girth → 2822

径 DIAMETER → 0347

往

0348

1-3-5

▶**GO ON**

オウ

Ⓝ 徃 徍 Ⓒ 往 wǎng

60	Jōyō-5	U5F80
彳	S8-3-5	F1285

Stroke order: 1–8

COMPOUNDS

❶ⓐ **GO ON, proceed, move ahead, go by**

ⓑ **GO ON to the next world, pass away**

a 往復 おうふく going and returning; round trip

往来 おうらい come-and-go, traffic; road, street

往診 おうしん doctor's visit to a patient, house call

右往左往する うおうさおうする go this way and that

一往(=一応) いちおう once; in outline; tentatively; for the time being

b 往生する おうじょうする pass away; be at a loss

❷ **bygone days, ancient days**

往時 おうじ bygone days

往古より おうこより from ancient times, from times immemorial

既往症 きおうしょう previous illness, medical history

❸ **now and then**

往往 おうおう sometimes; often

SYNONYMS

❶ⓐ **go and come**

行 GO → 0246

徠 COME → 0576

往 GO ON → 0348

出 go to → 4310

参 go somewhere → 2563

来 COME → 4366

通 go to and from → 3855

向 head toward → 3790

赴 PROCEED TO → 4095

嚮 GO TOWARD → 3610

❷ **old times**

昔 FORMER TIMES → 3086

往 bygone days → 0348

NOTE

➡ see COMPOUND FORMATION for 一応(=一往) いちおう → 応 3804

征

0349

1-3-5

▶**CONQUER**

セイ Ⓝ ゆき いく まさ ゆく

Ⓒ 征 zhēng

60	Jōyō	U5F81
彳	S8-3-5	F1396

Stroke order: 1–8

COMPOUNDS

❶ **CONQUER, subjugate (the enemy), attack, assault, invade**

征服 せいふく conquest, subjugation

征伐 せいばつ subjugation, conquest

征討 せいとう subjugation, conquest

❷ⓐ **go on a military expedition, go to war, go to the front, lead a punitive force, invade**

ⓑ military expedition, expeditionary force

a 征夷大将軍 せいいたいしょうぐん Commander in Chief of the Expeditionary Force Against the Barbarians

遠征 えんせい (punitive) expedition, invasion; tour

出征する しゅっせいする go to war

b 外征 がいせい foreign expedition

❸ [original meaning] go on a journey, travel

征途に上る せいとにのぼる go on a military expedition; start on a journey

INDEPENDENT

【せいする 征する】 attack the rebellious, subjugate

SYNONYMS

❶ **conquer and suppress**

征 CONQUER → 0349

討 SUPPRESS BY ARMED FORCE → 1846

伐 CUT DOWN → 0046

鎮 QUELL → 2210

靖 PACIFY → 1546

❶ **win**

勝 WIN → 1268

克 OVERCOME → 2540

剋 OVERCOME → 4097

征 CONQUER → 0349

破 BREAK → 1478

凱 TRIUMPH → 2286

❷ⓐ **fight and war**

闘 FIGHT → 4136

戦 WAR → 2242

征 go on a military expedition → 0349

彽

0350

◧ 1-3-5

▶WANDER ABOUT

テイ

Ⓒ 低 dī 祇 dī

60	Non-Jōyō	U5F7D
彳	S8-3-5	F0000

COMPOUNDS

● [now replaced by 低 0082] **WANDER ABOUT, linger**

彽徊(=低回)する ていかいする linger, loiter, wander

彽徊趣味(=低回趣味) ていかいしゅみ dilettantism

SYNONYMS

● **wander**

浪 WANDER → 0527

遊 move about freely → 3896

漂 drift about → 0857

流 drift → 0529

彽 WANDER ABOUT → 0350

徊 MOVE TO AND FRO → 0432

徃

0351

◧ 1-3-5

▶GO ON

オウ

60	Nonstandard	U5F83
彳	S8-3-5	F0000

traditional form → see 往 at 0348

徃

0352

◧ 1-3-5

▶GO ON

オウ

60	Nonstandard	U5F80
彳	S8-3-5	F0000

traditional form → see 往 at 0348

怖

0353

◧ 1-3-5

▶FEARFUL

フ こわ(い) こわ(がる) お(じる)▲

Ⓒ 怖 bù

61	Jōyō	U6016
忄	S8-3-5	F0938

Stroke order: 1–8

COMPOUNDS

● [original meaning] **fear, be afraid of**

畏怖 いふ awe, fear, dread, fright

恐怖 きょうふ fear

KUN

【こわい 怖い】[also 恐い] **FEARFUL, scary, uncanny; be afraid**

怖さ こわさ fear, dreadfulness

怖怖 こわごわ timidly, gingerly

怖い顔 こわいかお angry look, grim face

犬が怖い いぬがこわい be afraid of dogs

【こわがる 怖がる】[also 恐がる] **be afraid of, be frightened**

怖がり こわがり timidity; coward

【おじる 怖じる】be frightened, be scared

怖じ気 おじけ fear, fright

物怖じ ものおじ timidity

SYNONYMS

● & 【こわい】 **fear**

怖 FEARFUL → 0353

凄 UNCANNY → 0145

恐 FEAR → 3283

惧 FEAR → 0581

慄 TREMBLE WITH FEAR → 0791

兢 BE IN FEAR → 1971

惶 BE AFRAID → 0708

畏 BE OVERAWED → 3170

臆 FEEL TIMID → 1397

怯える BE FRIGHTENED → 0355

USAGE

❶ 【こわい】

怖い

[also 恐い] fearful, scary, uncanny; be afraid

恐い

[also 怖い] same as 怖い

強い

tough, hard, stiff

❷ 【こわがる】

怖がる

[also 恐がる] be afraid of, be frightened

恐がる

[also 怖がる] same as 怖がる

HOMOPHONES

こわい

恐 FEAR → 3283

強 STRONG → 0574

こわがる 恐 FEAR → 3283

怪

0354

◧ 1-3-5

▶MYSTERIOUS

カイ ケ▲ あや(しい) あや(しむ)

Ⓝ 恠 Ⓒ 怪 guài

61	Jōyō	U602A
忄	S8-3-5	F1114

Stroke order: 1–8

COMPOUNDS

❶ [also prefix] **MYSTERIOUS, strange, unusual, suspicious, suspicious-looking**

怪奇 かいき mystery, wonder

怪異な かいいな mysterious, marvelous, grotesque

怪盗 かいとう mysterious thief
怪聞 かいぶん strange rumor, scandal
怪事件 かいじけん mystery case
怪文書 かいぶんしょ mysterious document; subversive literature
怪人物 かいじんぶつ mysterious person

❷ exceptional; extraordinary man
怪力 かいりき Herculean strength
怪傑 かいけつ man of extraordinary talent, wonder man

❸ monster, ghost, goblin, demon
怪獣 かいじゅう monster; beast
怪物 かいぶつ monster; ghost, goblin, bogey; mysterious figure
怪談 かいだん ghost story
妖怪 ようかい ghost, apparition, phantom, goblin

❹ used phonetically for *ke*
怪我 けが injury, wound; accident

INDEPENDENT

【かい 怪】 mystery, wonder; apparition, specter
怪中の怪 かいちゅうのかい mystery of mysteries

【け 怪】 evil spirit
物の怪 もののけ evil spirit, specter; supernatural thing

KUN

【あやしい 怪しい】
ⓐ **doubtful; suspicious**
ⓑ [also 妖しい] **strange, MYSTERIOUS; uncanny**
ⓒ clumsy, awkward
a 怪しげな あやしげな questionable, doubtful, suspicious
c 怪しい手付きで あやしいてつきで with clumsy hands, clumsily

【あやしむ 怪しむ】 **suspect, be suspicious; doubt; wonder, marvel**
怪しむに足りない あやしむにたりない It is no wonder (that)

SYNONYMS

❶ abnormal
変 ABNORMAL → 2569
奇 UNUSUAL → 2756
畸 UNUSUAL → 1533
怪 MYSTERIOUS → 0354
妖 MYSTERIOUS → 0282
妙 strange → 0280
異 not ordinary → 3195
珍 curious → 1135

❸ supernatural and evil beings
鬼 DEVIL → 3291
魔 DEMON → 3953
怪 monster → 0354
霊 SPIRIT → 3480
精 SPIRIT → 1729

【あやしむ】
○ **doubt**
疑 DOUBT → 1970
怪しむ suspect → 0354

USAGE

【あやしい】
怪しい
ⓐ doubtful; suspicious
ⓑ [also 妖しい] strange, mysterious; uncanny
ⓒ clumsy, awkward
妖しい
[also 怪しい] strange, mysterious; uncanny

HOMOPHONES

あやしい 妖 MYSTERIOUS → 0282

怯

0355

1-3-5

▸BE FRIGHTENED
キョウ おび(える) ひる(む)
Ⓒ 怯 qiè

61	Non-Jōyō	U602F
忄	S8-3-5	F1874

COMPOUNDS

● cowardly, timid, afraid
怯懦× きょうだ cowardice, timidity
怯弱 きょうじゃく cowardice, timidity
卑怯 ひきょう cowardice, meanness, unfairness
卑怯者 ひきょうもの coward

KUN

【おびえる 怯える】 **BE FRIGHTENED (by), be terrified (by), be scared (of)**
怯え上がる おびえあがる be frightened to death, tremble in fear
怯えた顔で おびえたかおで with a scared look
その光景に怯える そのこうけいにおびえる be frightened at the sight

【ひるむ 怯む】 flinch, wince, quail, falter, hesitate
怯む事無く ひるむことなく without hesitation, undaunted (by)
血を見て怯む ちをみてひるむ flinch at the sight of blood

SPECIAL READINGS

悪怯れる わるびれる [usu. in negative constructions] be timid, be shy, flinch

SYNONYMS

【おびえる】
○ **fear**
怖 FEARFUL → 0353
凄 UNCANNY → 0145
恐 FEAR → 3283
惧 FEAR → 0581

懍 TREMBLE WITH FEAR → 0791
兢 BE IN FEAR → 1971
惶 BE AFRAID → 0708
畏 BE OVERAWED → 3170
臆 FEEL TIMID → 1397
怯える BE FRIGHTENED → 0355

怜

0356
◧ 1-3-5

▶CLEVER
レイ レン ㊔ さと さとし さとる
Ⓒ 怜 lián

61	Names	U601C
忄	S8-3-5	F2932

COMPOUNDS

● [rarely also 伶 れい 0075] **CLEVER, quick-witted, bright, nimble**
怜悧(=伶俐) れいり cleverness, sagacity

SYNONYMS

● **intelligent and wise**
賢 WISE → 3518
俊 brilliant → 0117
鋭 SHARP → 2171
敏 NIMBLE → 1675
叡 PROFOUNDLY WISE → 2405
智 wise → 3458
慧 INTELLIGENT → 3485
怜 CLEVER → 0356
悧 CLEVER → 0505
俐 CLEVER → 0113
哲 SAGACIOUS → 3402
明 clear-sighted → 1060
聡 SHARP-WITTED → 1750

性

0357
◧ 1-3-5

▶NATURE
▶SEX
▶-ITY
セイ ショウ さが▲
Ⓒ 性 xìng

61	Jōyō-5	U6027
忄	S8-3-5	F0080

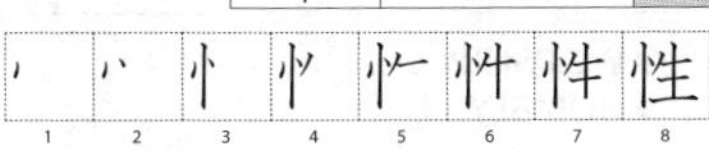

COMPOUNDS

❶ⓐ [original meaning] **one's NATURE, inherent nature, innate quality, character, temperament, disposition**
ⓑ [suffix] **NATURE, propensity towards, habit**
a 性格 せいかく character, personality
性質 せいしつ nature, temperament, character; (characteristic) property, quality
性悪な しょうわるな ill-natured
性向 せいこう inclination, disposition
性急な せいきゅうな impatient, quick-tempered; hasty
個性 こせい individuality
天性 てんせい nature, one's innate disposition
根性 こんじょう nature, spirit, temper; will power; guts
習性 しゅうせい habit, (one's) way
b 肥満性 ひまんしょう tendency to be obese
苦労性 くろうしょう worry habit, pessimistic nature

❷ⓐ **essential NATURE (of things), intrinsic quality, natural property, characteristic**
ⓑ suffix indicating quality, state or degree: **-ITY, -ness**
ⓒ *Buddhism* **NATURE**; that which belongs to a substance independent of external influences
a 性能 せいのう performance, capacity, efficiency
属性 ぞくせい attribute, property
人間性 にんげんせい human nature, humanity
慢性の まんせいの chronic
b 生産性 せいさんせい productivity
可能性 かのうせい possibility
安定性 あんていせい stability
アルカリ性 あるかりせい alkalinity
爆発性 ばくはつせい explosiveness
c 仏性 ぶっしょう Buddha nature

❸ⓐ (male or female classification) **SEX**
ⓑ (sexual intercourse) **SEX, sexuality, sexual desire**
ⓒ **gender**
a 性別 せいべつ distinction of sex; gender
男性 だんせい male, man
b 性欲 せいよく sexual desire, lust
性的 せいてき sexual
性行為 せいこうい sexual act, intercourse
性教育 せいきょういく sex education
c 中性 ちゅうせい neuter gender
女性名詞 じょせいめいし feminine noun

INDEPENDENT

【せい 性】
①ⓐ **one's NATURE, disposition**
ⓑ **essential NATURE, inherent quality**
a 人の性は善なり ひとのせいはぜんなり Man is naturally good
b 水の性 みずのせい properties of water
②ⓐ (male or female classification) **SEX**
ⓑ (sexual intercourse) **SEX, sexuality, sexual desire**
ⓒ gender
a 性の区別 せいのくべつ distinction of the sexes
性の自由 せいのじゆう sexual freedom

【しょう 性】
①ⓐ **NATURE**, disposition, temperament, character
ⓑ *Buddhism* **NATURE** (→ ❷ⓒ)
a 性の悪い犬 しょうのわるいいぬ ill-tempered dog, vicious dog

b 性に合う しょうにあう be congenial, agree with one
② quality, state
性の良い しょうのよい of good quality

KUN

【さが 性】one's **NATURE**, one's way, custom
女の性 おんなのさが the ways of women

SYNONYMS

❶ⓐ & ❷ⓐ nature and character
性 NATURE → 0357
気 temperament → 3960
質 QUALITY → 3483
品 grade of excellence → 2795
柄 CHARACTER → 1111
格 (good) character → 1161
ⓑ tendency
向 tendency → 3790
性 NATURE → 0357
勢 trend → 3542
傾 inclination → 0174
潮 TIDE → 0916
流 CURRENT → 0529
❷ⓑ nominalizers
所 PARTICLE OF NOMINALIZATION → 1056
事 nominalization word → 4384
子 NOUN SUFFIX → 4196
性 -ITY → 0357
❸ⓑ sex
性 SEX → 0357
情 (illicit) love → 0583
春 love → 3184
色 lust → 2522
淫 LEWD → 0624

NOTE

➡ see COMPOUND FORMATION for
慢性 まんせい → 慢 0844
機動性 きどうせい → 機 1365

口 土 女 子 巾 弓 彳 忄 【扌】 氵 犭 阝

拇

0358
1-3-5

▶**THUMB**
ボ
Ⓒ 拇 mǔ

64 扌	Non-Jōyō	U62C7
	S8-3-5	F0000

COMPOUNDS

● [now also 母 4287] [original meaning] **THUMB**
拇指 ぼし thumb
拇印 ぼいん thumbprint

SYNONYMS

● **hand and arm**
手 HAND → 4267
腕 ARM → 1269
肘 ELBOW → 1044
掌 PALM → 3215
指 FINGER → 0452
拇 THUMB → 0358
拳 FIST → 3295

抽

0359
1-3-5

▶**DRAW OUT**
チュウ ひき-▲
Ⓒ 抽 chōu

64 扌	Jōyō	U62BD
	S8-3-5	F1701

Stroke order: 1–8

COMPOUNDS

● [original meaning] **DRAW OUT, extract**
抽出する ちゅうしゅつする extract, abstract, educe
抽選(=抽籤) ちゅうせん drawing of lots
抽象的 ちゅうしょうてき abstract

KUN

【ひき- 抽-】[usu. 引き] drawing
抽出し ひきだし (desk) drawer

SYNONYMS

● **pull**
引 DRAW → 0207
曳 DRAW → 4348
牽 DRAW → 2621
惹 DRAW ATTENTION → 2903
抽 DRAW OUT → 0359
抜 PULL OUT → 0290
控える HOLD BACK → 0600
扣える HOLD BACK → 0250
寄せる DRAW NEAR → 2856

HOMOPHONES

ひき-引 DRAW → 0207

NOTE

➡ see USAGE note at 引 0207
➡ see COMPOUND FORMATION for 抽象 ちゅうしょう → 象 2647

拝

0360
1-3-5

▶**WORSHIP**
▶**HUMBLY**
ハイ おが(む)
Ⓝ 拜 Ⓒ 拜 bài

64 扌	Jōyō-6	U62DD
	S8-3-5	F1144

Stroke order: 1–8

COMPOUNDS

❶ⓐ (render religious reverence to) **WORSHIP, pay reverence to, pay one's respects**

ⓑ (feel an adoring reverence for) **WORSHIP, adore**
a 拝殿 はいでん front shrine, hall of worship
参拝する さんぱいする worship, pay reverence at, visit a shrine [temple]
礼拝 れいはい(=らいはい) worship; church service
b 拝金 はいきん money worship, worship of mammon
拝外的な はいがいてきな pro-foreign, xenophilous
崇拝 すうはい worship, adoration
❷ bow in veneration, make a bow
拝礼 はいれい worship
遥拝する ようはいする worship from afar
三拝九拝する さんぱいきゅうはいする kowtow, bow many times
❸ⓐ **HUMBLY, respectfully, reverentially**—honorific term expressing humility in reference to an action of the speaker
ⓑ **honorific term used in salutations**
a 拝見する はいけんする have the honor of seeing, see, look at, inspect
拝借する はいしゃくする borrow
拝聴する はいちょうする listen attentively [respectfully]
拝受する はいじゅする receive [accept] (humbly)
b 拝啓 はいけい Dear Sir, Dear Madam
拝復 はいふく in reply to your letter; Dear Sir, Dear Madam
❹ [humble]
ⓐ have the honor to receive
ⓑ have the honor to see [meet]
a 拝命 はいめい receiving an official appointment
拝領する はいりょうする receive (from a superior), be bestowed
b 拝眉する はいびする have the pleasure of seeing (a person)
拝顔の栄 はいがんのえい honor of seeing (a person)

INDEPENDENT

【はい 拝】term of humility used after one's name (chiefly by males) in letters
山本太郎拝 やまもとたろうはい your humble servant Taro Yamamoto

【はいする 拝する】
① bow in veneration, make a bow
神前に拝する しんぜんにはいする bow to a god in veneration
② [humble]
ⓐ have the honor to receive
ⓑ have the honor to see
a 大命を拝する たいめいをはいする receive an Imperial command
b お顔を拝する おかおをはいする have the honor to see his (Majesty's) face

KUN

【おがむ 拝む】**bow in veneration, make a bow, WORSHIP; pay one's respects with joined hands, entreat, solicit;** [humble] **see, have a look**
拝み倒す おがみたおす entreat (a person) into consent, win over by persuasive entreaty
拝ませる おがませる let a person have a look; allow to worship
伏し拝む ふしおがむ kneel down and worship, drop to one's knees

SYNONYMS

❶ⓐ **pray and worship**
祈 PRAY →1086
祷 PRAY →1224
願 pray →2320
拝 WORSHIP →0360
祀 WORSHIP AS GOD →1448
崇 REVERENCE →2864
斎 OBSERVE RELIGIOUS ABSTINENCE →2622
呪 SPELL →0323
ⓑ **respect**
敬 RESPECT →2136
尊 HONOR →2920
畏 respect →3170
欽 REVERE →2124
仰 look up to →0051
崇 REVERENCE →2864
尚 VALUE HIGHLY →2774
重 set value on →4390
拝 WORSHIP →0360
慕 ADORE →2970
❷ **bow**
礼 courtesy bow →1012
拝 bow in veneration →0360
❸ⓐ **respectful**
恭 RESPECTFUL →3109
謹 RESPECTFULLY →2045
奉 reverentially →3167
拝 HUMBLY →0360
❸ⓐ **humble**
謙 HUMBLE →2044
遜 HUMBLE →4041
拝 HUMBLY →0360
❹ⓐ **receive**
受 RECEIVE →3076
享 ENJOY →2545
領 receive →1567
収 TAKE IN →0031
納 ACCEPT →1652
貰 GET →3219
戴 RECEIVE HUMBLY →4093

頂 RECEIVE HUMBLY → 0164
拝 have the honor to receive → 0360

拍

▶BEAT

ハク ヒョウ

Ⓒ 拍 pāi

0361

1-3-5

64	Jōyō	U62CD
扌	S8-3-5	F1597

1	2	3	4	5	6	7	8
一	十	扌	扌'	扌'	拍	拍	拍

COMPOUNDS

❶ [also 搏 はく 0794] [original meaning] (strike repeatedly or rhythmically) **BEAT, clap (one's hands), throb**

拍手 はくしゅ applause, clapping
拍車 はくしゃ spur, rowel spur
拍動 はくどう pulsation, pulsebeat
脈拍 みゃくはく pulse, pulsation

❷ⓐ **BEAT, rhythm, time**
ⓑ counter for **BEAT**s or number of syllables in Japanese words

a 拍子 ひょうし time, beat, rhythm; chance, the moment
手拍子 てびょうし beating time with the hand; careless move
三拍子 さんびょうし simple triple time
b 三拍 さんぱく three beats, three syllables

INDEPENDENT

【はく 拍】**BEAT**
拍を数える はくをかぞえる count beats

SYNONYMS

❶ **strike**

打 STRIKE → 0224
撲 DEAL A BLOW → 0903
殴 BEAT (strike a person) → 1099
蹴 KICK → 2074
撃 STRIKE → 3552
挌 STRIKE (a person) → 0448
撞 STRIKE (a ball or bell) → 0905
撥ねる strike (knock down) → 0907
当てる HIT → 2701
叩 KNOCK → 0208
拍 BEAT (strike repeatedly) → 0361
搏 BEAT (throb) → 0794

❷ **musical elements**

韻 RHYME → 2279
律 RHYTHM → 0433
拍 BEAT → 0361
調 TONE → 1973
呂 ancient musical note → 2713

披

▶OPEN OUT

ヒ

Ⓒ 披 pī

0362

1-3-5

64	Jōyō	U62AB
扌	S8-3-5	F1737

1	2	3	4	5	6	7	8
一	十	扌	扌	扩	扩	披	披

COMPOUNDS

❶ **OPEN OUT (one's heart), reveal**

披講 ひこう introduction of poems at a poetry party
披露する ひろうする announce, introduce; [original meaning, now archaic] open one's heart
披瀝する ひれきする express (one's opinion), reveal (one's thoughts)
お披露目(=お広め) おひろめ début

❷ [original meaning] open and read, unseal, unfold, unroll

披見する ひけんする open and read, peruse (a letter)
直披 ちょくひ(=じきひ) confidential letter

SYNONYMS

❶ **reveal**

発 reveal → 3174
露 EXPOSE → 3495
曝 EXPOSE → 1410
晒す EXPOSE → 1156
暴 disclose → 3138
披 OPEN OUT → 0362
顕 MANIFEST → 2274
現 cause to appear → 1218

❷ **open**

開 OPEN → 4121
展 UNFOLD → 3862
披 open and read → 0362

抱

▶HUG

ホウ だ(く) いだ(く) かか(える)

Ⓝ 抱 Ⓒ 抱 bào

0363

1-3-5

64	Jōyō	U62B1
扌	S8-3-5	F0584

1	2	3	4	5	6	7	8
一	十	扌	扌	扚	扚	抱	抱

COMPOUNDS

❶ [formerly also 捧 0594] [original meaning] **HUG, embrace, hold in one's arms, enfold**

抱擁する ほうようする embrace, hug, hold in one's arms
抱卵 ほうらん incubation
抱腹絶倒する ほうふくぜっとうする double up with laughter

介抱する かいほうする nurse, care for

❷ (harbor a thought or feeling) **HUG, cherish, entertain**

抱懐する ほうかいする harbor, cherish, entertain

抱負 ほうふ aspiration, ambition

辛抱 しんぼう patience, endurance, forbearance

KUN

【だく 抱く】HUG, embrace, hold in one's arms

抱っこする だっこする hold (a child) in one's arms, hug

抱き合う だきあう hug, embrace

抱き締める だきしめる embrace closely, cuddle, hug

【いだく 抱く】harbor (suspicion), entertain (hope), cherish, HUG (a belief); hold in one's arms, hug

疑いを抱く うたがいをいだく harbor suspicion

【かかえる 抱える】hold in one's arms; employ, hire

抱え かかえ armful; employee

抱え込む かかえこむ hold in one's arm, take upon oneself

抱き抱える だきかかえる hold, carry, embrace (in one's arms)

召し抱える めしかかえる employ, engage

SYNONYMS

❶ **embrace**

抱 HUG →0363

擁 embrace →0949

❷ **hold in the mind**

持 HOLD →0447

抱 HUG →0363

懐 embosom →0942

抛

0364

◧ 1-3-5

▸TOSS

ホウ なげう(つ) ほう(る)

Ⓒ 抛 pāo

64	Non-Jōyō	U629B
扌	S8-3-5	F0000

COMPOUNDS

[now replaced by 放 1058]

ⓐ [original meaning] **TOSS, throw, let fly**

ⓑ **TOSS away, throw away, cast away**

a 抛物線 ほうぶつせん parabola

b 抛棄 ほうき abandonment, resignation

抛擲×する ほうてきする abandon, give up, quit

KUN

【なげうつ 抛つ】 [also 投げ打つ] **fling away, abandon**

【ほうる 抛る】 [usu. 放る]

ⓐ **TOSS, throw, fling, cast**

ⓑ **throw up, neglect**

SYNONYMS

ⓐ **throw**

投 THROW →0300

抛 TOSS →0364

放 toss →1058

HOMOPHONES

なげうつ 投げ打つ →0300, 0224

ほうる 放 LET GO →1058

NOTE

➡ see USAGE note at 放 1058

拐

0365

◧ 1-3-5

▸KIDNAP

カイ

Ⓝ 拐◇ Ⓒ 拐 guǎi

64	Jōyō	U62D0
扌	S8-3-5	F2297

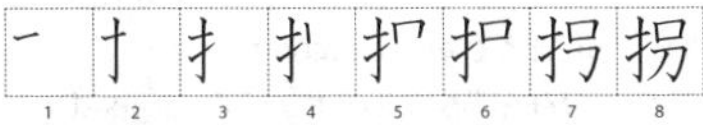

COMPOUNDS

❶ **KIDNAP, abduct**

拐取する かいしゅする abduct (legal term)

誘拐 ゆうかい kidnapping, abduction

❷ **defraud, swindle, abscond**

拐帯 かいたい abscondence with money

SYNONYMS

❶ **take forcibly**

奪 ROB →2956

拐 KIDNAP →0365

収 take possession by force →0031

❷ **deceive**

欺 DECEIVE →2138

騙 DECEIVE →2314

詐 SWINDLE →1896

惑 mislead →3461

拐 defraud →0365

偽 FALSIFY →0149

詭 TRICK →1919

拡

0366

◧ 1-3-5

▸ENLARGE

カク ひろ(がる)▲ ひろ(げる)▲ ㊔ ひろ

Ⓝ 擴 Ⓒ 扩 kuò

64	Jōyō-6	U62E1
扌	S8-3-5	F1061

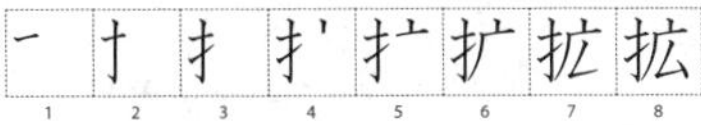

COMPOUNDS

● [original meaning] **ENLARGE, expand, magnify, widen, extend**

拡大する かくだいする magnify, enlarge, expand

拡張する かくちょうする expand, extend, enlarge

拡散 かくさん scattering, diffusion

拡声器 かくせいき (loud)speaker, megaphone
拡充 かくじゅう expansion, amplification
軍拡 ぐんかく expansion of armaments

KUN

【ひろがる 拡がる】[usu. 広がる] *vi*
ⓐ spread out, stretch, unfold
ⓑ expand, extend
ⓒ spread, reach, go about
b 拡がり ひろがり extent, expanse, stretch, spread
c 火が燃え拡がった ひがもえひろがった The fire spread

【ひろげる 拡げる】[usu. 広げる] *vt*
①ⓐ spread (out), outstretch
ⓑ unfold, unroll, open
a 地図を拡げる ちずをひろげる spread a map
b 拡げた腕 ひろげたうで outstretched arms
繰り拡げる くりひろげる roll out, unfold, spread out; develop
② widen, **ENLARGE**, expand, extend

SYNONYMS

● **expand**
脹 SWELL →1265
膨 EXPAND →1380
張 SPREAD →0573
氾 SPREAD OUT →0226
広げる spread (out) →3769
拡 ENLARGE →0366
伸 STRETCH →0079
延 EXTEND →3812

HOMOPHONES

ひろがる 広 WIDE →3769
ひろげる 広 WIDE →3769

NOTE

➡ see USAGE note at 広 3769

拘

▶**ARREST**
コウ かか(わる)▲
Ⓝ 拘 Ⓒ 拘 jū

0367
◧1-3-5

64	Jōyō	U62D8
扌	S8-3-5	F1811

COMPOUNDS

❶ [sometimes also 勾 3660] [original meaning] **ARREST, detain, confine**
拘留 こうりゅう penal detention up to 30 days
拘禁する こうきんする detain, confine, imprison
拘置 こうち detention, confinement, arrest
拘束 こうそく restriction, restraint, binding
拘引 こういん arrest, custody

❷ restrain, restrict the freedom of
拘泥する こうでいする adhere to (laws and rules), stick to (conventions)

KUN

【かかわる 拘わる】**adhere to, stick to**
. . . にも拘わらず …にもかかわらず in spite of…, regardless of…

SYNONYMS

❶ **catch a criminal**
捕 CATCH →0514
逮 CATCH A CRIMINAL →3875
拘 ARREST →0367
勾 ARREST →3660

❶ **imprison and confine**
拘 ARREST →0367
禁 confine →3469
留 keep in custody →3189
置 place in custody →3222
錮 IMPRISON →2182

HOMOPHONES

かかわる
係 CONNECT →0108
関 CONCERN →4129

NOTE

➡ see USAGE note at 係 0108

拒

▶**REFUSE**
キョ こば(む)
Ⓝ 拒 Ⓒ 拒 jù

0368
◧1-3-5

64	Jōyō	U62D2
扌	S8-3-5	F1410

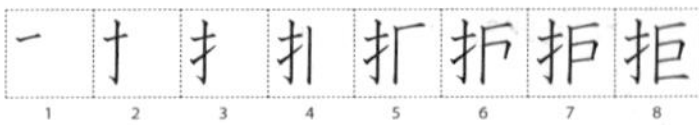

COMPOUNDS

❶ **REFUSE, reject, deny**
拒絶する きょぜつする refuse, reject, deny
拒否する きょひする deny, reject
拒止 きょし refusal
峻拒 しゅんきょ flat refusal, stern rejection

❷ resist, repel
抗拒する こうきょする resist, oppose

KUN

【こばむ 拒む】**REFUSE, decline, deny; prevent**
支払いを拒む しはらいをこばむ refuse payment, decline to pay
入場を拒む にゅうじょうをこばむ deny (a person) admission

SYNONYMS

❶ **refuse and reject**
拒 REFUSE →0368

断る refuse → 1885
否 SAY NO → 3058
却 reject → 1436

拠 0369

▶GROUNDS
キョ コ よ(る)▲
N 據 C 据 jù jū

1-3-5

64	Jōyō	U62E0
扌	S8-3-5	F0920

COMPOUNDS

❶ **GROUNDS, base, basis, foundation; authority**
拠点 きょてん strongpoint, base
根拠 こんきょ grounds, basis, authority
本拠 ほんきょ base, stronghold, headquarters
論拠 ろんきょ grounds [basis] of an argument
典拠 てんきょ authority
証拠 しょうこ proof, evidence

❷ occupy, take possession of, hold one's ground
拠守 きょしゅ defense
占拠 せんきょ occupation, exclusive possession
割拠する かっきょする hold one's own ground

❸ [also 醵 きょ 2087] contribute money to a common purpose
拠出 きょしゅつ donation, contribution
拠金 きょきん contribution, subscription

KUN

【よる 拠る】
① **be based on, be grounded on**
辞書に拠れば じしょによれば based on [according to] the dictionary
② occupy (a fortress), hold
天険に拠る てんけんによる hold a mountain fortress

SYNONYMS

❶ **basis**
基 BASE → 3312
本 BASIS → 4314
素 ELEMENT → 3108
礎 foundation → 1595
底 BOTTOM → 3827
根 ROOT → 1167
拠 GROUNDS → 0369

❷ **occupy**
占 OCCUPY → 2496
拠 occupy → 0369
領 take possession of → 1567
専 take exclusive possession of → 3272

HOMOPHONES

よる
依 DEPEND ON → 0093
因 CAUSE → 3792
由 REASON → 4311
寄 CONTRIBUTE → 2856

NOTE

➡ see USAGE note at 因 3792

抹 0370

▶WIPE
マツ
C 抹 mǒ mā mò

1-3-5

64	Jōyō	U62B9
扌	S8-3-5	F2386

COMPOUNDS

❶ⓐ (remove by rubbing) **WIPE off, wipe out, erase, strike out**
ⓑ (spread over) **WIPE** over [on], coat with, paint over
a 抹殺する まっさつする erase, strike out; deny, ignore; do away with, liquidate
抹消する まっしょうする erase, strike out
b 塗抹する とまつする coat with, paint over
一抹 いちまつ a touch of, a tinge of

❷ pulverize, powder
抹茶 まっちゃ powdered tea
抹香 まっこう incense powder, incense
抹香臭い まっこうくさい sound religious, smack of religion

SYNONYMS

❶ⓐ **eliminate**
却 ELIMINATE → 1436
排 EXCLUDE → 0593
払う CLEAR AWAY → 0225
剝 PEEL OFF → 2105
耘 WEED → 1661
削 cross out → 1837
抹 wipe off → 0370
省 leave out → 3100
脱 REMOVE → 1225
去 take away → 2678
外す take off → 0215
除 RID OF → 0546
撤 WITHDRAW → 0912

ⓑ **spread**
散 SCATTER → 2137
布 SPREAD → 3691
敷く LAY → 2345
舗 PAVE → 2177

塗 APPLY ON A SURFACE → 3523
抹 wipe over → 0370
撒 SCATTER → 0909

❷ break into small pieces
砕 CRUSH UP → 1458
抹 pulverize → 0370

押

▶PUSH

オウ お(す) お(し)- お(っ)- お(さえる)

Ⓒ 押 yā

0371

1-3-5

64	Jōyō	U62BC
扌	S8-3-5	F0521

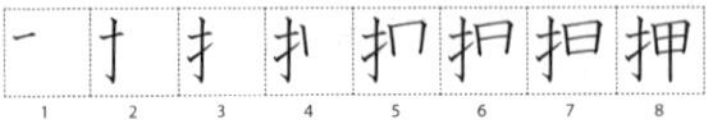

COMPOUNDS

❶ⓐ [original meaning] **PUSH** or press downward
ⓑ (fix a seal) **seal, stamp**
ⓒ seal, signature

a 押下する おうかする depress, press down (a computer key)
b 押印する おういんする seal, affix a seal
押捺 おうなつ sealing (a document)
c 花押 かおう signature, written seal

❷ perform an action by force, take by force
押収 おうしゅう seizure, confiscation
押送する おうそうする transfer (a convict), escort

❸ to rhyme
押韻 おういん rhyme, rhyming

KUN

【おす 押す】

①ⓐ (force to move) **PUSH, press, thrust, shove**
ⓑ [formerly also 圧す] **press down, press; compress, squash**

a 押し おし pushing, push; self-confidence, impudence; fall (in prices)
押 おす PUSH (marking on doors)
押し上げる おしあげる push up, boost
押し返す おしかえす push back, force back
押し釦× おしぼたん push-button
押し屋 おしや commuter train packer
押しも押されもせぬ おしもおされもせぬ of established reputation
後押し あとおし pushing; support, backing
b 押し潰す おしつぶす squash, crush, flatten

② (force to act) **PUSH [force] oneself; push a person (to do something)**
押して おして forcibly, by compulsion; importunately
押し売り おしうり coercive touting, importunate peddling [peddler]
押し問答 おしもんどう bandying words, haggling, argument
中押し ちゅうおし one-sided game, victory by a wide margin (in go)
病気を押して行く びょうきをおしていく go in spite of illness

③ [sometimes also 捺す] **fix a seal, stamp**
スタンプを押す すたんぷをおす stamp

④ overwhelm, have an edge over

⑤ perform an action though it is not necessary, make doubly sure
念を押す ねんをおす call attention to, make sure of, emphasize
駄目を押す だめをおす make sure

⑥ put (gold) leaf over, gild
手押し ておし hand gilding

⑦ (of prices) sag, drop, fall
押し目 おしめ weakness, relapse, scale-down

【おし- 押し-】 [verbal prefix]

① **PUSH (oneself or others) to perform an action**
押し付ける おしつける press against; force, compel
押し通す おしとおす push through, carry it through, hold out to the end
押し切る おしきる have one's own way, push one's way through
押し掛ける おしかける force oneself upon (a person), go uninvited

② emphatic verbal prefix
押し並べて おしなべて generally
押し隠す おしかくす conceal, cover up
押し黙る おしだまる keep silent, clam up
押し寄せる おしよせる advance on, rush for, push to one side

【おっ- 押っ-】 **emphatic verbal prefix**
押っ立てる おったてる raise, set up
押っ始める おっぱじめる begin

【おさえる 押さえる】

① **press down, hold down, force down**
押さえ おさえ weight, paperweight; rear guard
押さえ込む おさえこむ immobilize, pin down

② **stop up, cover**
耳を押さえる みみをおさえる hold one's ears

③ⓐ seize (goods), distrain, levy distress on
ⓑ seize, secure

a 差し押さえ さしおさえ attachment, seizure, distraint
b 証拠を押さえる しょうこをおさえる seize [secure] evidence

SYNONYMS

❶ⓐ push
押 PUSH → 0371
突く THRUST → 2772

圧 apply pressure → 3688
挨 PUSH → 0510
按 HOLD DOWN → 0444
ⓑ mark
印 imprint → 1023
押 seal → 0371
劃 MARK OFF → 2378
画 mark off → 3723
捺 AFFIX A SEAL → 0603

【おす】
① ⓐ **force to move**
推 propel → 0612
駆 DRIVE → 2293
押す PUSH → 0371
② **compel and press**
圧 PRESSURE → 3688
迫 PRESS → 3815
強 force → 0574
押す PUSH → 0371

USAGE

❶【おす】
押す
① ⓐ (force to move) push, press, thrust, shove
ⓑ [formerly also 圧す] press down, press; compress, squash
② (force to act) push [force] oneself; push a person (to do something)
③ [sometimes also 捺す] fix a seal, stamp
④ overwhelm, have an edge over
⑤ perform an action though it is not necessary, make doubly sure
⑥ put (gold) leaf over, gild
⑦ (of prices) sag, drop, fall
推す
① infer, deduce, conjecture, surmise, guess
② recommend, propose, nominate
圧す
[now usu. 押す] press down, press; compress, squash
捺す
[usu. 押す] affix a seal, stamp

❷【おし】
押し
① pushing, push
② self-confidence, impudence
③ fall (in prices)
圧し
① pressing down
② weight
③ authority, commanding presence

❸【おさえる】
押さえる
① press down, hold down, force down
② stop up, cover
③ ⓐ seize (goods), distrain, levy distress on
ⓑ seize, secure
抑える
① ⓐ (hold down) suppress, repress, restrain, control, hold down; check, curb, stop; keep back, withhold
ⓑ (put down forcibly) suppress, subdue, bring under control
② catch, arrest

❹【おさえ】
押さえ
① weight, paperweight
② rear guard
抑え
ⓐ check, defense, suppression
ⓑ control

HOMOPHONES

おす
推 INFER → 0612
圧 PRESSURE → 3688
捺 AFFIX A SEAL → 0603
おし 圧 PRESSURE → 3688
おさえる 抑 SUPPRESS → 0301
おさえ 抑 SUPPRESS → 0301

拉

0372

◧ 1-3-5

▶**ABDUCT**
ラ ラツ▲ ロウ▲ ひし(ぐ)▲ ひし(げる)▲ ひしゃ(げる)▲

Ⓒ 拉 lā lá lǎ

64	Jōyō	U62C9
扌	S8-3-5	F1713

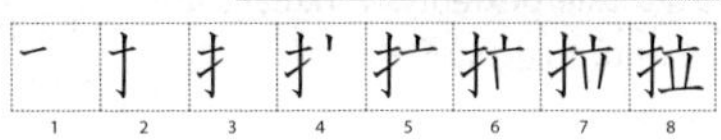

COMPOUNDS

❶ **ABDUCT, kidnap**
拉致 らち abduction, kidnapping
❷ **used phonetically for *ra***
拉麺 らーめん ramen, Chinese-style soup noodles
拉丁 らてん Latin
亜拉毘亜 あらびあ Arabia

INDEPENDENT

【らっする 拉する】**ABDUCT**, kidnap

KUN

【ひしぐ 拉ぐ】
ⓐ crush, squash
ⓑ discourage
a 取り拉ぐ とりひしぐ crush

b 打ち拉がれる うちひしがれる be stricken [overcome, overwhelmed] (with grief, etc.); be utterly defeated

【ひしげる 拉げる】 be crushed, be squashed, be flattened

【ひしゃげる 拉げる】 same as 拉げる ひしげる

SYNONYMS

【ひしぐ】

◯ **break**

破 BREAK → 1478
拉ぐ crush → 0372
崩 CRUMBLE → 2863
挫 SPRAIN → 0519
壊 BREAK DOWN → 0934
毀す break down → 2246
折 BREAK OFF → 0297
割る crack → 2284
裂 SPLIT → 3331
砕 CRUSH UP → 1458
摧 CRUSH UP → 0849
潰す CRUSH → 0919

拙

▶CLUMSY

セツ つたな(い)

Ⓒ 拙 zhuō

0373

1-3-5

64	Jōyō	U62D9
扌	S8-3-5	F1783

COMPOUNDS

❶ **CLUMSY, unskillful**

拙劣な せつれつな clumsy, awkward, unskillful
拙速主義 せっそくしゅぎ rough-and-ready method
巧拙 こうせつ skill, dexterity, workmanship

❷ [humble] my humble, my poor

拙者 せっしゃ I
拙宅 せったく my home, my humble abode

INDEPENDENT

【せつ 拙】 clumsiness; [humble] I

巧と拙 こうとせつ skillfulness and clumsiness

KUN

【つたない 拙い】 **CLUMSY, unskillful; incompetent, inexperienced; unfortunate (in war)**

拙い文章 つたないぶんしょう poor writing

SYNONYMS

❷ **humble prefixes**

小 my little (*humble*) → 0007
弊 our [my] humble → 3583
拙 my humble → 0373
愚 my foolish → 3513

招

▶INVITE

ショウ まね(く) ㊔ あき

Ⓒ 招 zhāo

0374

1-3-5

64	Jōyō-5	U62DB
扌	S8-3-5	F1162

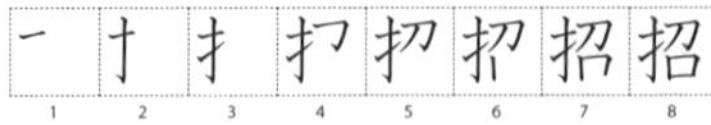

COMPOUNDS

ⓐ **INVITE**

ⓑ [original meaning] beckon (with the hand), call

a 招待 しょうたい invitation
招宴 しょうえん invitation to a party; party
招請国 しょうせいこく inviting country, host nation

b 招集する しょうしゅうする call, summon, convene
招致 しょうち summons, invitation
招聘× しょうへい invitation; engagement

INDEPENDENT

【しょうじる(=しょうずる) 招じる(=請じる、招ずる、請ずる)】 **INVITE**; usher in

KUN

【まねく 招く】 **INVITE; beckon, call; engage (someone's services); bring about, incur, cause**

招き まねき invitation, engagement
災いを招く わざわいをまねく bring calamity upon oneself

SYNONYMS

● **call and invite**

呼ぶ CALL → 0324
喚 CALL → 0666
召 SUMMON → 2494
招 INVITE → 0374

拓

▶OPEN UP

タク ひら(く)▲ ㊔ ひろ つげ

Ⓒ 拓 tuò tà

0375

1-3-5

64	Jōyō	U62D3
扌	S8-3-5	F1729

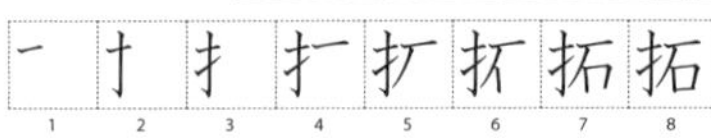

COMPOUNDS

❶ **OPEN UP (farmland or new frontiers), clear land, reclaim, develop**

拓殖 たくしょく colonization, exploitation
開拓 かいたく reclamation, opening up, clearing; exploitation
干拓 かんたく land reclamation by drainage

❷ copy by rubbing, make rubbings from inscriptions on stone

拓本 たくほん rubbed copy

魚拓 ぎょたく fish print

❸ abbrev. of 拓殖 たくしょく: colonization

拓大 たくだい Takushoku University

拓銀 たくぎん Takushoku Bank

KUN

【ひらく 拓く】 [usu. 開く] **OPEN UP** (land), clear, reclaim, develop

荒れ地を拓く あれちをひらく open up unbroken land

自分の道を拓く じぶんのみちをひらく hew one's way out

SYNONYMS

❶ **reclaim**

拓 OPEN UP →0375

墾 RECLAIM →3602

開 OPEN →4121

❷ **copy**

写 COPY →2493

謄 TRANSCRIBE →1398

複 duplicate →1565

拓 copy by rubbing →0375

HOMOPHONES

ひらく

開 OPEN →4121

啓 ENLIGHTEN →3434

NOTE

➡ see USAGE note at 開 4121

担 0376

▶**BEAR ON SHOULDER**
▶**UNDERTAKE**

タン かつ(ぐ) にな(う)

Ⓝ 擔 Ⓒ 担 dān dàn

◧1-3-5

64	Jōyō-6	U62C5
扌	S8-3-5	F0662

Stroke order: 1–8

COMPOUNDS

❶ [original meaning] **BEAR [carry] ON one's SHOULDER, shoulder, bear**

担架 たんか stretcher

❷ **UNDERTAKE (a task), take (a job) upon oneself**

担当する たんとうする undertake, be in charge of

担保 たんぽ security, mortgage

担任する たんにんする be in charge of, take (a class) under one's charge

負担 ふたん burden, charge, responsibility

分担 ぶんたん partial charge, allotment

❸ assist, help

加担(=荷担) かたん assistance, support, participation

KUN

【かつぐ 担ぐ】 **shoulder, carry [BEAR] ON one's SHOULDER; have as (president of), have (a person) over; be superstitious; take in, play a trick on**

担ぎ かつぎ carrier

担ぎ上げる かつぎあげる carry up

担ぎ屋 かつぎや superstitious person; black-market peddler

. . . を担いで …をかついで with (a person) at the head

【になう 担う】 **BEAR [carry] ON one's SHOULDER, shoulder; UNDERTAKE, take upon oneself**

担い手 にないて bearer, carrier

責任を担う せきにんをになう shoulder responsibility

SYNONYMS

❶ **bear**

負 BEAR (on the back) →2594

荷 carry on shoulder →2840

担 BEAR ON SHOULDER →0376

支 SUPPORT →2473

❷ **undertake**

負 BEAR →2594

担 UNDERTAKE →0376

抵 0377

▶**RESIST**

テイ

Ⓒ 抵 dǐ

◧1-3-5

64	Jōyō	U62B5
扌	S8-3-5	F1370

Stroke order: 1–8

COMPOUNDS

❶ **RESIST, withstand, oppose, stand up to**

抵抗する ていこうする resist, oppose, defy

❷ **be equivalent to, correspond to**

抵当 ていとう mortgage, security

❸ [formerly also 牴 1134 or 觝 1892] collide with, touch

抵触 ていしょく conflict; contradiction; incompatibility

❹ **generally, mostly**

大抵 たいてい generally, mostly, for the most part

SYNONYMS

❶ **resist**

抗 RESIST →0296

抵 RESIST →0377

耐 WITHSTAND →1634

対 OPPOSE →1025

反 COUNTER →3663

逆 rebel →3835

撥 REPEL → 0907
叛 REBEL → 1469

抜

0378

1-3-5

▶**PULL OUT**
▶**STAND OUT**

バツ　ぬ(く)　-ぬ(く)　ぬ(き)　ぬ(ける)　ぬ(かす)　ぬ(かる)

64	Names	U62D4
扌	S8-3-5	F0000

traditional form → see 抜 at 0290

拂

0379

1-3-5

▶**CLEAR AWAY**
▶**PAY**

フツ　はら(う)　-はら(い)　-ばら(い)

64	Names	U62C2
扌	S8-3-5	F0000

traditional form → see 払 at 0225

抱

0380

1-3-5

▶**HUG**

ホウ　だ(く)　いだ(く)　かか(える)

64	Nonstandard	U62B1
扌	S8-3-5	F0000

traditional form → see 抱 at 0363

拐

0381

1-3-5

▶**KIDNAP**

カイ

64	Nonstandard	U62D0
扌	S8-3-5	F0000

alternative form → see 拐 at 0365

拒

0382

1-3-5

▶**REFUSE**

キョ　こば(む)

64	Nonstandard	U62D2
扌	S8-3-5	F0000

traditional form → see 拒 at 0368

注

0383

1-3-5

▶**POUR**
▶**CONCENTRATE**

チュウ　そそ(ぐ)　さ(す)▲　つ(ぐ)▲

Ⓝ 注　Ⓒ 注 zhù

85	Jōyō-3	U6CE8
氵	S8-3-5	F0478

1 2 3 4 5 6 7 8 (stroke order: 注)

COMPOUNDS

❶ **POUR, pour into, pour on, inject**
注入する ちゅうにゅうする pour into, inject
注水 ちゅうすい flooding; douche
注射 ちゅうしゃ injection, shot
注油 ちゅうゆ oiling, lubrication

❷ abbrev. of 注射 ちゅうしゃ: injection, shot
筋注 きんちゅう intramuscular injection
静注 じょうちゅう intravenous injection

❸ **CONCENTRATE (on), pay attention to**
注意 ちゅうい attention, care, advice
注意深い ちゅういぶかい careful, cautious; discreet
注目 ちゅうもく attention, notice
注視 ちゅうし steady gaze, close observation
傾注 けいちゅう devotion, concentration

❹ [formerly also 註 1893]
ⓐ **annotate, explain with notes**
ⓑ **annotation, explanatory notes, comment**
a 注釈 ちゅうしゃく annotation, note, comment
注解 ちゅうかい annotation, explanatory notes
注記 ちゅうき annotation, commentary
b 頭注 とうちゅう headnote
脚注 きゃくちゅう footnote
評注 ひょうちゅう commentary, notes and comments

❺ [formerly also 註 1893] **write down, take notes of, record**
注進する ちゅうしんする inform, make a report
注文する ちゅうもんする order, place an order; request

❻ [formerly also 註 1893] abbrev. of 注文 ちゅうもん: order
発注する はっちゅうする place an order
受注する じゅちゅうする receive an order

INDEPENDENT

【ちゅう　注(=註)】**annotation, explanatory note, comment**

【ちゅうする　注する(=註する)】annotate, comment

KUN

【そそぐ　注ぐ】**POUR into, pour on; irrigate, sprinkle; flow into (the sea); concentrate (on), pay attention to**
注ぎ込む そそぎこむ pour into, instill
注意を注ぐ ちゅういをそそぐ pay attention
力を注ぐ ちからをそそぐ concentrate one's effort (on something)

【さす　注す】[usu. 差す]
① **POUR** (into), fill up
器に水を注す うつわにみずをさす fill a pitcher with water
② color

【つぐ　注ぐ】**POUR out, pour in, fill**
注ぎ込む つぎこむ pour in [into]; invest in
注ぎ口 つぎぐち spout

SYNONYMS

❶ **flow and drip**
流 FLOW → 0529

注 POUR → 0383
濫 overflow → 0990
溢 OVERFLOW → 0807
漏 LEAK → 0860
滴 DROP → 0866
泌 SECRETE → 0390
瀝 DRIP → 0996

❸ **concentrate on**

注 CONCENTRATE → 0383
傾 devote oneself to → 0174

❹ⓐ **explain**

説 EXPLAIN → 1949
明 make clear → 1060
釈 ELUCIDATE → 1876
詮 EXPOUND → 1923
講 expound → 2046
解 CLARIFY → 1913
注 annotate → 0383

ⓑ **explanatory remarks**

注 annotation → 0383
評 COMMENT → 1895

HOMOPHONES

さす

差 DIFFERENCE → 4104
指 FINGER → 0452
刺 STAB → 1625
挿 INSERT → 0517
射 SHOOT → 1850
止 STOP → 3659

つぐ

接 CONTACT → 0607
継 SUCCEED → 1720
次 NEXT → 0058

NOTE

➡ see USAGE notes at 差 4104 and 接 0607
➡ see COMPOUND FORMATION for 注文 ちゅうもん → 文 2458

泥

0384

◧ 1-3-5

▶**MUD**

デイ どろ¹ どろ² ㊔ ひじ

Ⓒ 泥 ní nì

85	Jōyō	U6CE5
氵	S8-3-5	F1421

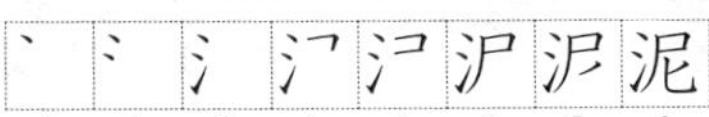

COMPOUNDS

❶ⓐ [original meaning] **MUD, mire**

ⓑ something with the consistency of **MUD**

a 泥土 でいど mud, mire
泥水 でいすい(=どろみず) muddy water, liquid mud
泥濘× でいねい mud, slush, mire; muddy road
雲泥の差 うんでいのさ great difference (as between clouds and mud)

b 泥炭 でいたん peat
金泥 きんでい(=こんでい) gold paint

❷ lose one's senses

泥酔する でいすいする get dead drunk

❸ stick to (old traditions), adhere

拘泥する こうでいする adhere to (laws and rules), stick to (conventions)

INDEPENDENT

【でい 泥】**MUD**

泥の像 でいのぞう mud image

KUN

【どろ¹ 泥】

① **MUD, mire, slush, dirt**

泥沼 どろぬま bog; swamp (of difficulties)
泥んこ どろんこ mud, morasses of mud
顔に泥を塗る かおにどろをぬる fling mud at, bring disgrace [dishonor] on

② **unclassified compounds**

泥棒 どろぼう thief, crook

【どろ² 泥】[in compounds] [also suffix] **petty thief, sneak thief, pilferer**

泥縄 どろなわ expediency coming too late (like making a rope after finding the thief)
こそ泥 こそどろ sneak, pilferer
自動車泥 じどうしゃどろ auto [car] thief

SYNONYMS

❶ⓐ **land and soil**

土 SOIL → 4211
地 GROUND → 0236
壌 ARABLE SOIL → 0933
泥 MUD → 0384
陸 LAND → 0659
埴 CLAY → 0562

【どろ²】

◯ **thieves**

盗 thief → 3309
泥 petty thief → 0384
賊 BANDIT → 1932

泳

0385

◧ 1-3-5

▶**SWIM**

エイ およ(ぐ)

Ⓒ 泳 yǒng

85	Jōyō-3	U6CF3
氵	S8-3-5	F1548

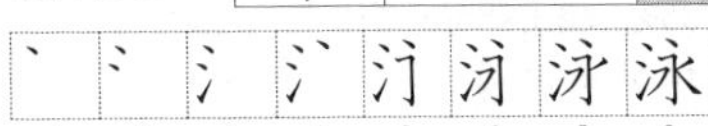

口 土 女 子 山 巾 弓 彳 忄 扌 【氵】 犭 阝

COMPOUNDS

a [original meaning] **SWIM**

b **SWIM**ming

a 泳法 えいほう swimming style

水泳 すいえい swimming

b 競泳 きょうえい swimming race

背泳 はいえい backstroke

継泳 けいえい relay swimming

KUN

【およぐ 泳ぐ】[sometimes also 游ぐ] **SWIM;** (figuratively) **swim, get along**

泳ぎ およぎ swimming

平泳ぎ ひらおよぎ breast stroke

人波を泳ぐ ひとなみをおよぐ wade through a crowd

時流に乗って泳ぐ じりゅうにのっておよぐ swim with the current

SYNONYMS

a **move through water**

泳 SWIM → 0385

游 SWIM → 0750

渉 wade → 0638

遡 GO UPSTREAM → 4040

漕 ROW → 0864

USAGE

【およぐ】

泳ぐ

[sometimes also 游ぐ] swim; (figuratively) swim, get along

游ぐ

[usu. 泳ぐ] swim; (figuratively) swim, get along

HOMOPHONES

およぐ 游 SWIM → 0750

沿

0386

1-3-5

▶**ALONG**

エン そ(う) -ぞ(い)

Ⓒ 沿 yán

85	Jōyō-6	U6CBF
氵	S8-3-5	F1255

Stroke order: 1–8

COMPOUNDS

1 **ALONG, alongside**

沿道 えんどう along the route

沿線の えんせんの along a railway line

沿海 えんかい coast, shore

沿岸 えんがん coast, shore

2 follow (a tradition)

沿革 えんかく history, annals

KUN

【そう 沿う】

ⓐ **lie ALONG (a river), follow along**

ⓑ be in line with (a policy)

a 路線に沿って ろせんにそって along the route [line]

b 対外政策に沿って たいがいせいさくにそって in line with the foreign policy

【-ぞい -沿い】[also suffix] **ALONG**

川沿いに かわぞいに along the riverside

山沿いの地方 やまぞいのちほう mountainous region

南岸沿い なんがんぞい along the southern coast

SYNONYMS

1 **near**

近 NEAR → 3798

隣 neighboring → 0961

傍 BESIDE → 0166

旁 BESIDE → 2598

沿 ALONG → 0386

USAGE

【そう】

沿う

ⓐ lie along (a river), follow along

ⓑ be in line with (a policy)

添う

① accompany, go along with, stay with

② marry

③ meet (someone's wishes), suit

④ add to, increase

HOMOPHONES

そう 添 ADD TO → 0641

COMPOUND FORMATION

【沿革 えんかく】

沿革 'history, annals' is following (沿 **2**) a tradition and reforming (革) it, i.e., the annals of change.

沸

0387

1-3-5

▶**BOIL**

フツ わ(く) わ(かす)

Ⓒ 沸 fèi

85	Jōyō	U6CB8
氵	S8-3-5	F2026

Stroke order: 1–8

COMPOUNDS

● (undergo boiling) **BOIL**

沸騰する ふっとうする boil, seethe, bubble

沸点 ふってん boiling point

煮沸 しゃふつ boiling

KUN

【わく 沸く】*vi*

① **BOIL, grow hot**
沸きが早い わきがはやい quick to warm up
沸き上がる わきあがる boil up; break out, arise; seethe, be in uproar
② **BOIL over (with excitement), seethe, be excited**
沸き返る わきかえる seethe, be in uproar; boil up
【わかす 沸かす】*vt*
① **BOIL, make hot**
湯沸かし ゆわかし kettle, water heater
② **excite, stimulate**
観衆を沸かす かんしゅうをわかす excite the spectators

SYNONYMS
● **cook**
煮 BOIL (cook by boiling) →3460
沸 BOIL (undergo boiling) →0387
炊 COOK →1080
蒸 STEAM →2936
焼く cook by fire →1256
揚げる fry in deep fat →0722
煎 ROAST, DECOCT →2950

USAGE
【わく】
沸く
vi
① boil, grow hot
② boil over (with excitement), seethe, be excited
湧く
①ⓐ well up, spring forth, gush out
ⓑ (of emotions or ideas) well up, gush out, spring up, appear
② (of insects) breed, be hatched

HOMOPHONES
わく 湧 WELL UP →0749

波 0388
▶**WAVE**
ハ ポ▲ なみ
Ⓒ 波 bō
▯1-3-5

85	Jōyō-3	U6CE2
氵	S8-3-5	F0542

Stroke order: 1–8

COMPOUNDS
❶ⓐ [also suffix] [original meaning] **WAVE**
ⓑ *phys* **WAVE**
a 波浪 はろう waves, billows
波紋 はもん ripple; stir, sensation
波止場 はとば wharf, quay
波瀾×(=波乱) はらん disturbance, troubles; fluctuation
風波 ふうは wind and waves, rough seas, storm
b 波動 はどう wave motion, undulation
波長 はちょう wavelength
電磁波 でんじは electromagnetic waves
電波 でんぱ electromagnetic waves, radio waves
短波 たんぱ shortwave
音波 おんぱ sound waves
光波 こうは light waves
❷ⓐ **something that occurs in WAVEs**
ⓑ counter for events occurring in **WAVE**s
ⓒ spread like **WAVE**s
a 寒波 かんぱ cold wave
b 第三波スト だいさんぱすと the third wave of strikes
c 波及する はきゅうする be propagated; extend, spread; affect
❸ⓐ used phonetically for *ha* and closely related sounds
ⓑ Poland
a 波羅蜜 はらみつ *pāramitā*, entrance into Nirvana
b 日波 にっぽ Japan and Poland

KUN
【なみ 波】**WAVE, billow, ripple; fluctuations, rise and fall; wave motion, undulation; wrinkles**
波乗り なみのり surfriding, surfing
波打つ なみうつ undulate, heave, surge; be wavy
津波 つなみ tsunami, tidal wave
人波 ひとなみ surging crowd
横波 よこなみ side wave; *phys* transverse wave
老いの波 おいのなみ wrinkles

SPECIAL READINGS
小波▲(=細波▲) さざなみ [also. 漣] ripples, wavelets

SYNONYMS
❶ **waves**
波 WAVE →0388
浪 BILLOW →0527
漣 RIPPLES →0859
❸ⓐ **phonetic [ha]**
巴 phonetic [ha] →4246
波 phonetic [ha] →0388

HOMOPHONES
さざなみ
漣 RIPPLES →0859
小波 →0007, 0388
細波 →1689, 0388

泊 0389
▶**STAY OVERNIGHT**
ハク と(まる) と(める) ㊔ とま
Ⓒ 泊 bó pō
▯1-3-5

85	Jōyō	U6CCA
氵	S8-3-5	F1066

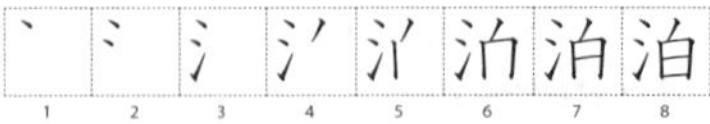

COMPOUNDS

❶ⓐ STAY OVERNIGHT, lodge, stay at
ⓑ counter for number of overnight stays

a 宿泊 しゅくはく lodging
外泊 がいはく staying out overnight
民泊 みんぱく private residence temporarily taking lodgers

b 一泊 いっぱく overnight stay
三泊四日の旅 さんぱくよっかのたび trip of four days and three nights

❷ stay at anchor, anchor a ship
泊地 はくち anchorage, berth
停泊 ていはく anchorage, mooring
仮泊 かはく temporary anchoring

❸ simple, plain
淡泊(=淡白)な たんぱくな light (color, taste); plain, simple; indifferent

❹ [original meaning] shallow body of water
漂泊する ひょうはくする roam, drift about, wander
梁山泊 りょうざんぱく gathering place of ambitious men

INDEPENDENT

【はく 泊】overnight stay
泊を重ねる はくをかさねる stay long

KUN

【とまる 泊まる】

① **STAY OVERNIGHT, lodge, stay at**
泊まり とまり stopover, stay; night duty; anchorage
素泊まり すどまり staying overnight without board

② **stay at anchor**
港に泊まる みなとにとまる stay at anchor

③ be on night duty
泊まり番 とまりばん night duty

【とめる 泊める】

① **lodge, give shelter, accommodate**
友達を泊める ともだちをとめる put a friend up for the night

② anchor a ship

SYNONYMS

❶ⓐ stay
滞 STAY → 0815
頓 STAY IN PLACE → 1320
留 STAY → 3189
逗 STAY → 4005
駐 STATIONED → 2297
屯 STATION TROOPS → 4268
在 reside temporarily → 3704
泊 STAY OVERNIGHT → 0389
宿 LODGE → 2858
寓 stay temporarily → 2893

HOMOPHONES

とまる
止 STOP → 3659
留 KEEP → 3189
停 HALT → 0156

とまり 止 STOP → 3659

とめる
止 STOP → 3659
留 KEEP → 3189
停 HALT → 0156

COMPOUND FORMATION

【梁山泊 りょうざんぱく】
梁山泊 'gathering place of ambitious men' refers to a shallow body of water (泊 ❹) near Mt. Ryozan (梁山), since ambitious men would gather there.

NOTE

➡ see USAGE note at 止 3659

泌

▶SECRETE
ヒツ ヒ
Ⓒ 泌 mì bì

0390
1-3-5

85	Jōyō	U6CCC
氵	S8-3-5	F2308

COMPOUNDS

● [original meaning] **SECRETE**
泌尿器 ひにょうき urinary organs
分泌 ぶんぴつ(=ぶんぴ) secretion
内分泌腺 ないぶんぴせん endocrine gland

SYNONYMS

● **flow and drip**
流 FLOW → 0529
注 POUR → 0383
濫 overflow → 0990
溢 OVERFLOW → 0807
漏 LEAK → 0860
滴 DROP → 0866
泌 SECRETE → 0390
瀝 DRIP → 0996

法

▶LAW
▶METHOD
ホウ ハッ- ホッ- のり▲ ふらん▲ ㊔ つね
Ⓒ 法 fǎ

0391
1-3-5

85	Jōyō-4	U6CD5
氵	S8-3-5	F0113

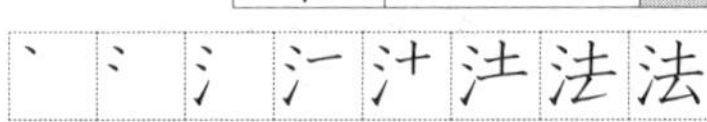

COMPOUNDS

❶ⓐ [also suffix] **LAW, rule, act, code of laws**
ⓑ **LAW(s) (as of an art), principle, rule**
ⓒ abbrev. of 法学(部) ほうがく(ぶ): **LAW** (department)

a 法律 ほうりつ law
法令 ほうれい laws and ordinances, statute
法学 ほうがく law, jurisprudence
法学部 ほうがくぶ law department [school]
法廷 ほうてい law court
法的 ほうてき legal, legalistic
法規 ほうき laws and regulations
法案 ほうあん bill, legislative proposal
法人 ほうじん legal person, corporation
法典 ほうてん code of laws, statute
法度 はっと law, ordinance, prohibition
憲法 けんぽう constitution, constitutional law
違法の いほうの illegal, unlawful
刑法 けいほう criminal law, penal code
国際法 こくさいほう international laws
農地法 のうちほう Agricultural Land Law
騒音防止法 そうおんぼうしほう Noise Abatement Act

b 法則 ほうそく law, rule
画法 がほう laws [canons] of painting

c 法博 ほうはく Doctor of Law

❷ LAWs of propriety, rules of etiquette
作法 さほう manners, etiquette, decorum
礼法 れいほう courtesy, etiquette, manners

❸ [also suffix] **METHOD, way, manner, system, process, technique**
方法 ほうほう method, way; system; scheme, means; process, procedure; plan
手法 しゅほう technique, mechanism, style
療法 りょうほう method of treatment, cure, remedy
製法 せいほう method of manufacture, process of preparation, recipe
生活法 せいかつほう way of life, art of living
教授法 きょうじゅほう method of teaching
銅アンモニア法 どうあんもにあほう cuprous ammoniacal process

❹ⓐ **Buddha's teachings, Buddha's doctrine, dharma, Buddhism; religious tenets**
ⓑ religious rites, ceremony, service

a 法王 ほうおう pope
法主 ほっす(=ほうしゅ, ほっしゅ) high priest (of a Buddhist sect)
仏法 ぶっぽう Buddhism
説法 せっぽう (Buddhist) sermon, preaching, moralizing

b 法事 ほうじ (Buddhist) memorial service
法要 ほうよう (Buddhist) memorial service

❺ [suffix] *gram* mood
仮定法 かていほう subjunctive mood
不定法 ふていほう infinitive mood

❻ model
法帖 ほうじょう copybook printed from the works of old masters of calligraphy

INDEPENDENT

【ほう 法】
① **LAW, rule, regulation**
法を守る ほうをまもる observe the law
② **METHOD**, way
旨い法を考え出す うまいほうをかんがえだす devise a crack method
③ Buddha's teachings, dharma
法を説く ほうをとく preach the truth
④ manners, etiquette
法に適う ほうにかなう conform to the rules of etiquette
⑤ reason
そんな法は無い そんなほうはない That's against reason/That's absurd
⑥ divisor, modulus, modulo
六は五を法として十一と合同である ろくはごをほうとしてじゅういちとごうどうである Six is congruent to eleven, modulo five
⑦ *gram* mood
法と時制 ほうとじせい mood and tense

KUN

【のり 法】 [sometimes also 則] **LAW, rule, regulation; model, pattern; religious doctrine; sacred teachings of Buddha**
法を越える のりをこえる violate the laws of nature

【ふらん 法】 franc
百法 ひゃくふらん 100 francs

SYNONYMS

❶ⓐ & ❶ⓑ **laws and rules**
法 LAW → 0391
律 LAW → 0433
典 CANON → 3253
憲 CONSTITUTION → 3001
令 ordinance → 2489
則 RULE → 1831
矩 RULE → 1475
規 REGULATION → 1231
紀 discipline → 1628

❸ **way and style**
風 MANNER → 3730
様 MODE → 1332
方 WAY → 2459
途 WAY → 3853
法 METHOD → 0391

流 STYLE →0529
式 STYLE →3785
調 TONE →1973

❹ⓐ **religions and sects**
仏 Buddhism →0020
法 Buddha's teachings →0391
禅 ZEN →1306
儒 CONFUCIANISM →0197
道 Taoism →3888

USAGE

【のり】
法
[sometimes also 則] law, rule, regulation; model, pattern; religious doctrine; sacred teachings of Buddha
則
[usu. 法] same as 法

HOMOPHONES

のり 則 RULE →1831

NOTE

➡ see COMPOUND FORMATION for 魔法瓶 まほうびん →魔 3953

泡

0392
1-3-5

▶**BUBBLE**
ホウ あわ
Ⓝ 泡 Ⓒ 泡 pào pāo

85	Jōyō	U6CE1
氵	S8-3-5	F1932

COMPOUNDS

❶ [original meaning] **BUBBLE, foam**
泡沫 ほうまつ bubble, foam, froth
泡沫会社 ほうまつがいしゃ bubble company, fly-by-night concern
発泡 はっぽう foaming, effervescence
気泡 きほう air bubble, bubble
水泡 すいほう bubble, foam

KUN

【あわ 泡】[sometimes also 沫] **BUBBLE, foam**
泡立つ あわだつ bubble, foam
泡盛 あわもり millet brandy
石鹸×の泡 せっけんのあわ lather, soapsuds

SYNONYMS

❶ **small water masses**
滴 DROP →0866
雫 DROP →3430
泡 BUBBLE →0392
沫 BUBBLE →0397

USAGE

【あわ】
泡
[sometimes also 沫] bubble, foam
沫
[usu. 泡] bubble, foam

HOMOPHONES

あわ 沫 BUBBLE →0397

治

0393
1-3-5

▶**GOVERN**
▶**CURE**
ジ チ おさ(める) おさ(まる) なお(る) なお(す) Ⓝ はる おさむ
Ⓒ 治 zhì

85	Jōyō-4	U6CBB
氵	S8-3-5	F0174

COMPOUNDS

❶ⓐ **GOVERN, administer, rule over, reign over**
ⓑ **GOVERNment, rule, administration**
a 治国 ちこく government
治世 ちせい reign, rule, regime, dynasty
自治 じち self-government, autonomy
統治 とうち rule, government, reign
明治 めいじ Meiji era
b 治下の ちかの under the rule of
政治 せいじ government, administration, politics
内治 ないち(=ないじ) home administration
法治 ほうち constitutional government
文治 ぶんち civil administration

❷ bring under control, manage, control
治具 じぐ jig
治産 ちさん property management
治水 ちすい flood control

❸ **public order, peace**
治安 ちあん public peace and order
治乱 ちらん war and peace
治平 ちへい peace and tranquility
退治 たいじ subjugation, subdual; extermination; crusade

❹ⓐ **CURE, treat, heal**
ⓑ **CURE**, recovery
a 治療 ちりょう medical treatment [cure]
治癒 ちゆ healing, cure, recovery
主治医 しゅじい physician in charge
不治の ふじの incurable, fatal
b 根治 こんじ(=こんち) complete [radical] cure
湯治 とうじ hot spring cure, taking healing baths

INDEPENDENT

【じする 治する】CURE, heal; rule; conserve
【ち 治】peace, public order
治に居て乱を忘れず ちにいてらんをわすれず We must not forget war in peace

KUN

【おさめる 治める】
ⓐ **GOVERN, rule over, reign over, manage**
ⓑ **bring under control, put down, suppress, pacify, quell**
a 国を治める くにをおさめる govern a country, manage a state
b 暴動を治める ぼうどうをおさめる quell a disturbance
【おさまる 治まる】
① **be in peace, be GOVERNed well**
国が治まる くにがおさまる Peace reigns in the country
② **be CUREd, be relieved (of pain)**
痛みが治まる いたみがおさまる A pain is cured
【なおる 治る】**be CUREd, get well, recover**
治り なおり recovery
傷が治った きずがなおった The wound has healed up
【なおす 治す】**CURE, heal**
風邪を治す かぜをなおす cure a cold

SYNONYMS

❶ⓐ **govern**
治 GOVERN →0393
統 rule →1710
ⓑ **government**
政 POLITICAL ADMINISTRATION →1468
治 government →0393
❸ **peace**
和 PEACE →1450
安 public peace →2695
治 public order →0393
❹ **cure and recover**
療 TREAT →4078
治 CURE →0393
医 cure →3715
癒 HEAL →4081
快 recover →0289

HOMOPHONES

おさめる
納 PAY →1652
収 TAKE IN →0031
修 CULTIVATE →0138
おさまる
納 PAY →1652
収 TAKE IN →0031
修 CULTIVATE →0138
なおる 直 STRAIGHT →3649
なおす 直 STRAIGHT →3649

COMPOUND FORMATION

【治具 じぐ】
治具 'jig' is a phonetic rendering of *jig*, i.e., a device for holding or guiding (治 ❷) a tool (具).

NOTE

➡ see USAGE notes at 直 3649 and 納 1652
➡ see COMPOUND FORMATION for 明治 めいじ →明 1060
★ do not confuse with 冶 WORK METALS →0089

河

0394
◧ 1-3-5

▸**RIVER**
カ かわ ㊔ こう
ⓒ 河 hé

85	Jōyō-5	U6CB3
氵	S8-3-5	F0609

Stroke order: 1–8

COMPOUNDS

❶ [original meaning] **RIVER, large river**
河川 かせん rivers
河流 かりゅう stream
河口 かこう river mouth, estuary
河岸 かし riverside; fish market
運河 うんが canal
銀河 ぎんが Milky Way; galaxy
暴虎馮×河 ぼうこひょうが foolhardy courage
❷ the Yellow **RIVER**, the Huanghe River
河北 かほく north of the Yellow River; Hebei (Province)
黄河 こうが the Yellow River

KUN

【かわ 河】[usu. 川]
ⓐ **RIVER, stream**
ⓑ **suffix after names of (esp. foreign) RIVERs**
a 河底 かわぞこ riverbed
b アマゾン河 あまぞんがわ Amazon River

SPECIAL READINGS

河原 かわら dry riverbed, river beach
河童▲ かっぱ water sprite, *kappa;* excellent swimmer
河豚▲ ふぐ *fugu,* globefish, swellfish

SYNONYMS

❶ **rivers and streams**
川 RIVER →0006
河 RIVER →0394
江 large river →0257
渓 mountain stream →0628
流 stream →0529

HOMOPHONES

かわ 川 RIVER →0006

NOTE

➡ see USAGE note at 川 0006

➡ see COMPOUND FORMATION for 暴虎馮×河 ぼうこひょうが →暴 3138

況

▶CONDITIONS

キョウ ま(して)▲

Ⓝ 况 Ⓒ 况 kuàng

0395

1-3-5

85	Jōyō	U6CC1
氵	S8-3-5	F0789

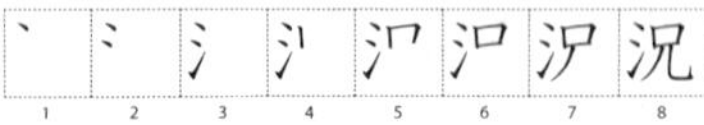

COMPOUNDS

❶ CONDITIONS, condition, situation, state of affairs

状況 じょうきょう state of affairs, conditions, circumstances

戦況 せんきょう war situation, progress of a battle

近況 きんきょう recent condition [situation]

実況 じっきょう actual conditions

概況 がいきょう general condition [situation], outlook

好況 こうきょう brisk market, prosperity

市況 しきょう market conditions, tone of the market

不況 ふきょう depression, slump, recession

盛況 せいきょう prosperity, boom, success

❷ compare

比況 ひきょう comparison

KUN

【まして 況して】to say nothing of; not to mention; [in negative constructions] let alone, much less

SYNONYMS

❶ states and situations

態 STATE →3529

調 TONE →1973

様 MODE →1332

相 PHASE →1120

状 CONDITION →0322

況 CONDITIONS →0395

景 business conditions →3118

勢 course of events →3542

境 SITUATION →0835

局 current situation →3800

情 ACTUAL CONDITIONS →0583

訳 circumstances →1865

泣

▶CRY

キュウ な(く)

Ⓒ 泣 qì

0396

1-3-5

85	Jōyō-4	U6CE3
氵	S8-3-5	F0943

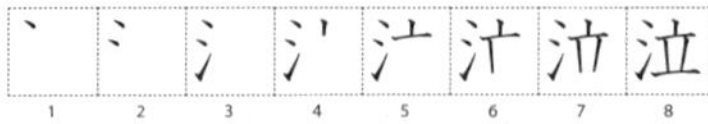

COMPOUNDS

● [original meaning] **CRY, weep, sob**

泣訴する きゅうそする implore with tears in one's eyes

号泣する ごうきゅうする wail, lament

感泣する かんきゅうする weep with emotion, be moved to tears

KUN

【なく 泣く】**CRY, weep, sob**

泣き なき weeping, lamenting

泣き顔 なきがお tear-stained face

泣き声 なきごえ tearful voice, crying

泣き叫ぶ なきさけぶ cry, scream, wail

咽び泣く むせびなく sob, be choked with tears

SYNONYMS

● cry and sigh

泣 CRY →0396

嘆 SIGH →0773

歎 SIGH →2344

USAGE

【なく】

泣く

cry, weep, sob

鳴く

(of animals, birds or insects) cry, chirp, ululate, howl, yelp, meow

HOMOPHONES

なく 鳴 CRY →0831

沫

▶BUBBLE

マツ あわ ㊔ わ

Ⓒ 沫 mò

0397

1-3-5

85	Names	U6CAB
氵	S8-3-5	F2759

COMPOUNDS

❶ BUBBLE, foam

泡沫 ほうまつ bubble, foam, froth

泡沫会社 ほうまつがいしゃ bubble company, fly-by-night concern

❷ [original meaning] **splash, spray**

飛沫 ひまつ splash, spray

飛沫感染 ひまつかんせん droplet infection

KUN

【あわ 沫】 [usu. 泡] **BUBBLE**, foam

SPECIAL READINGS

飛沫 しぶき splash, spray
泡沫 うたかた *elegant* bubbles (floating on water); transience, evanescence

SYNONYMS

❶ **small water masses**
滴 DROP → 0866
雫 DROP → 3430
泡 BUBBLE → 0392
沫 BUBBLE → 0397

HOMOPHONES

あわ 泡 BUBBLE → 0392

NOTE

➡ see USAGE note at 泡 0392

沼

0398
◧ 1-3-5

▶MUDDY POND
ショウ ぬま
Ⓒ 沼 zhǎo

85	Jōyō	U6CBC
氵	S8-3-5	F1212

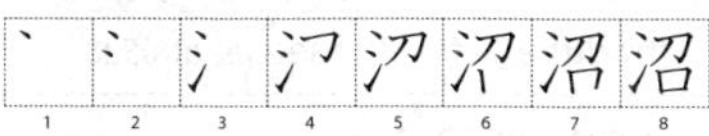

COMPOUNDS

● [original meaning] **MUDDY POND, low-lying lake, swamp, marsh, bog**
沼沢 しょうたく marsh, swamp
沼気 しょうき marsh gas, methane
湖沼 こしょう lakes and marshes

KUN

【ぬま 沼】 **MUDDY POND, low-lying lake, swamp, marsh, bog; suffix after names of muddy ponds**
沼地 ぬまち swampland, bogland, marshland
泥沼 どろぬま bog; swamp (of difficulties)
長沼 ながぬま Lake Naganuma

SYNONYMS

● **lakes and marshes**
沢 MARSH → 0313
沼 MUDDY POND → 0398
湖 LAKE → 0736
池 POND → 0253
潟 LAGOON → 0921

沮

0399
◧ 1-3-5

▶OBSTRUCT
ソ はば(む)
Ⓒ 沮 jǔ jù

85	Non-Jōyō	U6CAE
氵	S8-3-5	F0000

COMPOUNDS

[now replaced by 阻 0411]

❶ (prevent the progress or passage of) **OBSTRUCT**, impede, hinder, check
沮止 そし obstruction, check, hindrance
沮害 そがい obstruction, check, impediment, hindrance

❷ be dejected, lose heart
沮喪 そそう loss of spirit, dejection

KUN

【はばむ 沮む】 [now replaced by 阻む] **OBSTRUCT, impede, hinder, check, prevent**

SYNONYMS

❶ **obstruct and hinder**
遮 INTERRUPT → 3916
塞 STOP UP → 2924
阻 OBSTRUCT → 0411
沮 OBSTRUCT → 0399
奄 OBSTRUCT (by covering) → 2757
妨 HINDER → 0279
障 hinder → 0875
碍 STAND IN THE WAY → 1536
害 stand in the way → 2826
梗 STOP UP → 1204

HOMOPHONES

はばむ 阻 OBSTRUCT → 0411

NOTE

➡ see USAGE note at 阻 0411

油

0400
◧ 1-3-5

▶OIL
ユ ユウ▲ あぶら
Ⓒ 油 yóu

85	Jōyō-3	U6CB9
氵	S8-3-5	F0937

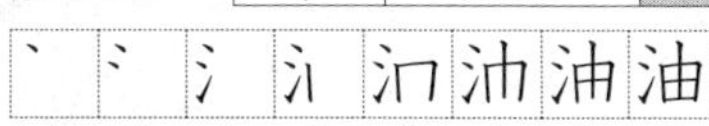

COMPOUNDS

❶ [also suffix]
ⓐ **OIL, animal oil, vegetable oil**
ⓑ (petroleum or petroleum derivative) **OIL, petroleum**

a 油脂 ゆし fats and oils
油断 ゆだん negligence, carelessness, inattentiveness
醤油 しょうゆ soy sauce
サラダ油 さらだゆ(=さらだあぶら) salad oil
オリーブ油 おりーぶゆ olive oil

b 石油 せきゆ petroleum, oil
重油 じゅうゆ fuel oil
灯油 とうゆ kerosene, lamp oil

原油 げんゆ crude oil
潤滑油 じゅんかつゆ lubricant, lubricating oil

❷ abundantly
油然と ゆうぜんと gushingly, copiously

KUN

【あぶら 油】**OIL, animal oil, vegetable oil**
油絵 あぶらえ oil painting
油気 あぶらけ greasiness, oiliness
油を売る あぶらをうる loaf, idle away one's time
油を絞る あぶらをしぼる extract oil by pressing; give a person a severe talking-to
胡麻油 ごまあぶら sesame (seed) oil
大豆油 だいずあぶら soy bean oil

SYNONYMS

❶ⓐ fats and oils
油 OIL → 0400
脂 FAT → 1190
肪 ANIMAL FAT → 1089
膏 FAT → 2658
蠟 WAX → 1818

❶ⓐ seasonings
糖 SUGAR → 1777
塩 SALT → 0774
酢 VINEGAR → 1910
醋 VINEGAR → 2002
油 OIL → 0400
醬 FERMENTED SAUCE → 3569
噌 MISO → 0882
蜜 HONEY → 2958

ⓑ kinds of fuel
炭 COAL, CHARCOAL → 2806
薪 FIREWOOD → 3009
油 OIL → 0400

USAGE

【あぶら】
油
oil, animal oil, vegetable oil
脂
[formerly also 膏] fat, grease, lard, blubber; greasy substance
膏
[now usu. 脂] fat, grease; greasy substance

HOMOPHONES

あぶら
脂 FAT → 1190
膏 FAT → 2658

COMPOUND FORMATION

【油断 ゆだん】
油断 'negligence, carelessness, inattentiveness', a Buddhist term found in the Nirvana Sutra, is derived from an ancient tale of a monarch that has his retainer hold a pot full of oil so as to test his powers of concentration. If the retainer should be so careless as to let even a single drop of oil (油 ❶ⓐ) spill, he would have his life cut off (断), that is, he would be put to death. In this way, 油断 came to signify carelessness or inattentiveness.

注
0401
1-3-5

▶POUR
▶CONCENTRATE
チュウ そそ(ぐ) さ(す) つ(ぐ)

85	Nonstandard	U6CE8
氵	S8-3-5	F0000

traditional form → see 注 at 0383

泡
0402
1-3-5

▶BUBBLE
ホウ あわ

85	Nonstandard	U6CE1
氵	S8-3-5	F0000

traditional form → see 泡 at 0392

泪
0403
1-3-5

▶TEAR
ルイ なみだ

85	Nonstandard	U6CEA
氵	S8-3-5	F0000

traditional form → see 涙 at 0528

泝
0404
1-3-5

▶GO UPSTREAM
ソ さかのぼ(る)

85	Nonstandard	U6CDD
氵	S8-3-5	F0000

traditional form → see 遡 at 4040

狗
0405
1-3-5

▶DOG
ク いぬ
Ⓒ 狗 gǒu

94	Non-Jōyō	U72D7
犭	S8-3-5	F2465

COMPOUNDS

● [original meaning] **DOG (esp. of small variety)**
走狗 そうく running dog; dupe, tool, cat's paw
羊頭狗肉 ようとうくにく using a better name to sell inferior goods, crying wine and selling vinegar
天狗 てんぐ *tengu,* long-nosed goblin; braggart

KUN

【いぬ 狗】[now usu. 犬]
① **DOG (esp. of small variety)**
喪家の狗 そうかのいぬ feeling lost like a stray dog
② **spy**
警察の狗 けいさつのいぬ police spy

口 土 女 子 山 巾 弓 彳 忄 扌 【氵】 犭 阝

SPECIAL READINGS

狗尾草 えのころぐさ foxtail, *Setaria viridis*

SYNONYMS

● **dog**

犬 DOG → 4275
狗 DOG → 0405
戌 THE DOG → 4350

HOMOPHONES

いぬ

犬 DOG → 4275
戌 THE DOG → 4350

NOTE

➡ see USAGE note at 犬 4275
➡ see COMPOUND FORMATION for 羊頭狗肉 ようとうくにく → 羊 2708

狙

0406

◧ 1-3-5

▶**AIM**

ソ ねら(う)

ⓒ 狙 jū

94	Jōyō	U72D9
犭	S8-3-5	F1126

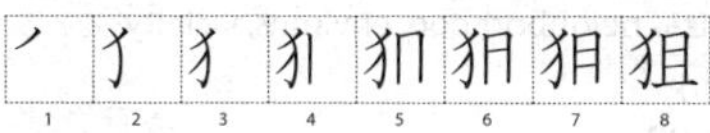

COMPOUNDS

● **AIM, take aim, target**

狙撃 そげき shooting, sniping

KUN

【ねらう 狙う】

ⓐ **AIM at, aim for, take aim, target**
ⓑ **be after, seek**
ⓒ eye, watch for

a 狙い ねらい aim, target, mark; aim, purpose, objective
狙い撃ち ねらいうち shooting, sniping
狙い澄ます ねらいすます take careful aim
穴狙い あなねらい aiming for a lucky break

b 命を狙う いのちをねらう seek [be after] someone's life

c 付け狙う つけねらう stalk, keep watch on

SYNONYMS

● **target**

的 TARGET → 1444
標 MARK → 1347
狙 AIM → 0406
目 aim → 3777

狐

0407

◧ 1-3-5

▶**FOX**

コ きつね

94	Nonstandard	U72D0
犭	S8-3-5	F0000

traditional form → see 狐 at 0472

阿

0408

◧ 1-3-5

▶**PHONETIC [a]**

ア お- おもね(る) ㊔ くま おか

ⓒ 阿 ā ē

170	Names	U963F
阝	S8-3-5	F0792

COMPOUNDS

❶ⓐ **used PHONETICally for *a*, esp. in the transliteration of names, foreign words or Sanskrit Buddhist terms**

ⓑ the letter *a* (in esoteric Buddhism symbolizes the unity of the world)

a 阿片 あへん opium
阿弥陀 あみだ *Amitābha;* lottery; wearing a hat on the back of the head
阿修羅 あしゅら *Asura* (fighting demon)

b 阿字 あじ the letter *a* (in esoteric Buddhism)
阿吽× あうん alpha and omega; inhalation and exhalation

❷ flatter, fawn upon, toady, favor

阿諛× あゆ flattery
阿世 あせい [rare] timeserving

❸ **fool, simpleton**

阿呆 あほう fool, idiot

❹ prefix for conveying intimacy

阿兄 あけい my dear brother
阿Q正伝 あきゅうせいでん The True Life of Ah-Q

❺ Africa

南阿共和国 なんあきょうわこく Republic of South Africa

❻ abbrev. of 阿波 あわ, old name for Tokushima Prefecture

阿南市 あなんし Anan City

❼ [archaic] hook-shaped object, bent

❽ [original meaning, now archaic] recesses of a mountain

INDEPENDENT

【あ 阿】 the letter *a* (in esoteric Buddhism *a* is mother of all sounds and represents the unity of the world)

KUN

【お- 阿-】 [also 御-] **prefix for conveying intimacy, esp. before names of women**

阿父様 おとうさま Father
阿国 おくに Okuni (female name)

【おもねる 阿る】 **flatter, fawn upon, toady**

大衆に阿る たいしゅうにおもねる sell out to the masses

SYNONYMS

❶ⓐ phonetic [a]

亜 PHONETIC [a] → 4354
阿 PHONETIC [a] → 0408

❺ continents

亜 Asia → 4354
阿 Africa → 0408
欧 EUROPE → 1098
米 AMERICA → 4342
豪 Australia → 2657

HOMOPHONES

お- 御 GENERAL HONORIFIC TERM → 0703

NOTE

➡ see USAGE note at 御 0703

陀

0409

1-3-5

▶**PHONETIC [da]**

ダ

Ⓒ 陀 tuó

170	Names	U9640
阝	S8-3-5	F1653

COMPOUNDS

● used PHONETICally for *da*, esp. in the transliteration of Sanskrit Buddhist terms

陀羅尼 だらに *dhāraṇi*, mystic Buddhist incantation
御陀仏 おだぶつ dying; ruining oneself, falling through
阿弥陀 あみだ *Amitābha;* lottery; wearing a hat on the back of the head
仏陀 ぶっだ Buddha
曼×陀羅(=曼×荼×羅) まんだら mandala
阿蘭陀(=和蘭、和蘭陀) おらんだ Holland, the Netherlands
加奈陀 かなだ Canada
頭陀袋 ずだぶくろ sack, carry-all bag

SYNONYMS

● phonetic [d]

陀 PHONETIC [da] → 0409
達 phonetic [da] → 3893
提 phonetic [dai] → 0720
胴 phonetic [dō] → 1186

附

0410

1-3-5

▶**ATTACH**

フ つ(ける)▲ つ(く)▲

Ⓒ 附 fù

170	Jōyō	U9644
阝	S8-3-5	F1971

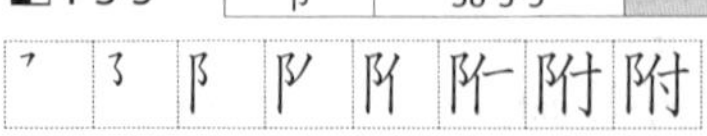

COMPOUNDS

[usu. 付]

❶ⓐ [original meaning] **ATTACH, append, add to, affix**
ⓑ ATTACHed, additional, supplementary
ⓒ ATTACH itself to, stick to, adhere to

a 添附する てんぷする attach, append, annex
b 附則 ふそく additional rules, bylaw
c 附着する ふちゃくする adhere [cling] to, agglutinate; cohere

❷ be **ATTACH**ed to, belong to, be affiliated with

附属する ふぞくする be attached to, belong to

❸ abbrev. of 附属校 ふぞくこう or 附属病院 ふぞくびょういん: **ATTACH**ed [affiliated] school, hospital in affiliation

赤十字附 せきじゅうじふ school attached to the Japan Red Cross Society

❹ⓐ deliver, hand over, grant
ⓑ entrust, commit to

a 交附する こうふする deliver, grant, hand (a ticket) to (a person)
寄附する きふする contribute, donate

❺ adjacent, near to

附近 ふきん neighborhood, environs, vicinity

INDEPENDENT

【ふ 附(=付)】 appendix; supplement
【ふする 附する(=付する)】 **ATTACH**, append, add to, affix; commit [submit] to, refer to; consign to, dispose of

KUN

【つける 附ける】 [usu. 付ける] same as 付ける つける 0035
【つく 附く】 [usu. 付く] same as 付く つく 0035

SYNONYMS

❶ⓐ & ❶ⓑ add to

付 ATTACH → 0035
附 ATTACH → 0410
加 ADD → 0042
追 add → 3840
添 ADD TO → 0641

ⓒ stick

着 STICK → 4110
貼 STICK → 1904
付 attach itself to → 0035
附 attach itself to → 0410

❹ⓐ transfer

譲 CEDE → 2080
渡 hand over → 0746
付 deliver → 0035
附 deliver → 0410

HOMOPHONES

つける

付 ATTACH →0035
着 PUT ON →4110
就 SET ABOUT →2129
即 IMMEDIATE →1439
点 POINT →2587
漬 PICKLE →0861

つく

付 ATTACH →0035
着 PUT ON →4110
就 SET ABOUT →2129
即 IMMEDIATE →1439
点 POINT →2587

NOTE

➡ see USAGE note at 付 0035

阻

▶OBSTRUCT

ソ　はば(む)

Ⓒ 阻 zǔ

0411

1-3-5

170	Jōyō	U963B
阝	S8-3-5	F1867

Stroke order: 1–8

COMPOUNDS

❶ [formerly also 沮 0399] (prevent the progress or passage of) **OBSTRUCT, impede, hinder, check**
阻害する そがいする obstruct, check, impede, hinder
阻止 そし obstruction, check, hindrance
❷ [formerly also 沮 0399] be dejected, lose heart
阻喪 そそう loss of spirit, dejection
❸ separate, isolate
阻隔 そかく separation, estrangement
❹ [formerly also 岨 0341] **steep**
険阻(=嶮岨)な けんそな steep (mountain pass), precipitous

KUN

【はばむ 阻む】[formerly also 沮む] **OBSTRUCT, impede, hinder, check, prevent**
道を阻む みちをはばむ obstruct one's way
成長を阻む せいちょうをはばむ hinder [check] the growth of (plants)

SPECIAL READINGS

悪阻▲ つわり(=おそ) morning sickness

SYNONYMS

❶ **obstruct and hinder**
遮 INTERRUPT →3916
塞 STOP UP →2924
阻 OBSTRUCT →0411
沮 OBSTRUCT →0399
奄 OBSTRUCT (by covering) →2757
妨 HINDER →0279
障 hinder →0875
碍 STAND IN THE WAY →1536
害 stand in the way →2826
梗 STOP UP →1204

USAGE

【はばむ】
阻む
[formerly also 沮む] obstruct, impede, hinder, check, prevent
沮む
[now replaced by 阻む] obstruct, impede, hinder, check, prevent

HOMOPHONES

はばむ 沮 OBSTRUCT →0399

咽

▶THROAT

イン　エツ▲　エン▲　のど▲　むせ(ぶ)▲

Ⓒ 咽 yàn yān yè

0412

1-3-6

30	Jōyō	U54BD
口	S9-3-6	F2199

Stroke order: 1–9

COMPOUNDS

❶ⓐ **THROAT**
ⓑ swallow
a 咽頭 いんとう pharynx; pharyngeal
耳鼻咽喉 じびいんこう nose, ear and throat
b 咽下 えんか(=えんげ) (act of) swallowing, deglutition
❷ⓐ be choked [stifled, smothered]
ⓑ sob
b 嗚×咽 おえつ sobbing, weeping, groaning, fit of crying

KUN

【のど 咽】[usu. 喉]
①ⓐ **THROAT**
ⓑ singing voice
a 咽から手が出る のどからてがでる want something desperately
② gutter (margin) (in printing)
【むせぶ 咽ぶ】
ⓐ be choked [stifled, smothered]
ⓑ sob
a 咽び泣く むせびなく sob, be choked with tears
b 暗涙に咽ぶ あんるいにむせぶ shed silent tears

SYNONYMS

❶ **throat**
咽 THROAT →0412

口 土 女 子 山 千 弓 彳 忄 扌 氵 犭 阝

喉 THROAT →0669

HOMOPHONES

のど 喉 THROAT →0669

NOTE

➡ see USAGE note at 喉 0669

咲

▶BLOOM

ショウ▲ さ(く) -ざき

Ⓝ 咲 Ⓒ 笑 xiào

0413

1-3-6

30	Jōyō	U54B2
口	S9-3-6	F1316

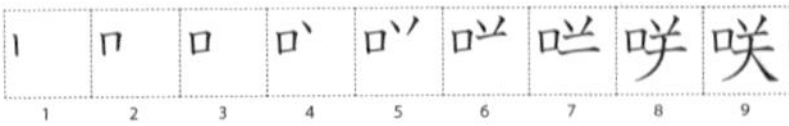

COMPOUNDS

● [original meaning, now obsolete] laugh, smile

KUN

【さく 咲く】**BLOOM, blossom, flower; effloresce**

咲き渡る さきわたる bloom over a wide area

早咲き はやざき early blooming, early flowering

狂い咲く くるいざく bloom out of season

文化が花と咲く ぶんかがはなとさく Fine arts effloresce

【-ざき -咲】**suffix indicating state of florescence**

五分咲き ごぶざき half-florescent

SYNONYMS

【さく】

○ **sprout and bloom**

萌 GERMINATE →2871

咲く BLOOM →0413

响

▶REVERBERATE

キョウ ひび(く)

0414

1-3-6

30	Nonstandard	U54CD
口	S9-3-6	F0000

traditional form →see 響 at 3573

咲

▶BLOOM

ショウ さ(く) -ざき

0415

1-3-6

30	Nonstandard	U54B2
口	S9-3-6	F0000

traditional form →see 咲 at 0413

垣

▶FENCE

エン▲ かき

Ⓒ 垣 yuán

0416

1-3-6

32	Jōyō	U57A3
土	S9-3-6	F1158

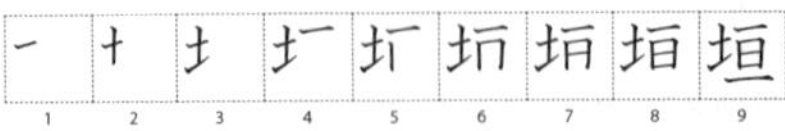

COMPOUNDS

● [original meaning, now archaic] **FENCE, wall**

垣牆 えんしょう fence, hedge

KUN

【かき 垣】[formerly also 牆] [also suffix] **FENCE, wall, hedge; barrier**

垣根 かきね fence, hedge

生け垣 いけがき hedge, quickset

石垣 いしがき stone wall

四つ目垣 よつめがき lattice fence

SYNONYMS

● **fences and walls**

壁 WALL →3601

塀 FENCE (for screening) →0677

垣 FENCE (for partitioning) →0416

牆 FENCE (for partitioning) →1393

柵 FENCE (with spaced pickets) →1116

堵 FENCE (made of earth) →0682

囲い enclosure →3807

欄 railing →1419

USAGE

【かき】

垣

[formerly also 牆] [also suffix] fence, wall, hedge; barrier

牆

[now replaced by 垣] [also suffix] fence, wall

HOMOPHONES

かき 牆 FENCE →1393

城

▶CASTLE

ジョウ しろ き* ㊔ ぐすく ぐしく なり くに

Ⓝ 城 Ⓒ 城 chéng

0417

1-3-6

32	Jōyō-6	U57CE
土	S9-3-6	F0323

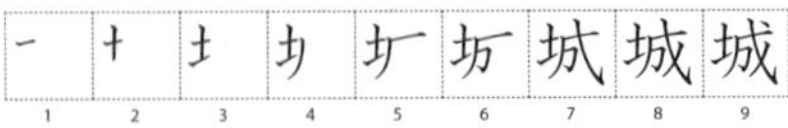

COMPOUNDS

❶ⓐ (fortified building) **CASTLE, fort, fortress, citadel, stronghold**

ⓑ (fortified stately residence) **CASTLE, palace**

ⓒ **suffix after names of CASTLEs**

a 城塞(=城砦) じょうさい fortress, stronghold, citadel

城壁 じょうへき castle wall, rampart

城下町 じょうかまち castle town, fief capital

城郭 じょうかく castle, fortress; castle walls, enclosure

籠城 ろうじょう confinement, keeping inside; holding a castle, sustaining a siege

牙城 がじょう stronghold, inner citadel
落城 らくじょう fall of a castle
築城 ちくじょう castle construction
b 城主 じょうしゅ lord of a castle
王城 おうじょう Imperial castle, royal palace
c 大阪城 おおさかじょう Osaka Castle

❷ [original meaning] **fortified town, city wall (in China)**
城市 じょうし fortified town, castle town
不夜城 ふやじょう red-light district, city that never sleeps
京城 けいじょう Seoul
万里の長城 ばんりのちょうじょう Great Wall of China

KUN

【しろ 城】**CASTLE, fort, citadel;** (place of privacy) **castle**
城跡 しろあと ruins of a castle
自分の城に閉じ籠もる じぶんのしろにとじこもる keep in one's own castle
根城 ねじろ stronghold, citadel; base of operations

【き 城】*hist* **CASTLE**
宮城県 みやぎけん Miyagi Prefecture
茨城県 いばらきけん Ibaraki Prefecture

SYNONYMS

❶ **strongholds**
城 CASTLE → 0417
塁 SMALL FORT → 3206
塞 FORT → 2924
砦 FORT → 3310
堡 FORT → 3500

垢

▶SURFACE DIRT
コウ ク あか
Ⓒ 垢 gòu

0418
1-3-6

32	Non-Jōyō	U57A2
土	S9-3-6	F2265

COMPOUNDS

ⓐ **SURFACE DIRT, grime, waste matter**
ⓑ **filth, impurity**
a 歯垢 しこう (dental) plaque
恥垢 ちこう smegma
耳垢 じこう(=みみあか) earwax, cerumen
蓬頭垢面 ほうとうこうめん unkempt hair and dirty face; being indifferent to one's appearance
b 無垢な むくな pure, innocent
白無垢 しろむく white kimono
三垢 さんく *Buddhism* the three defilements

KUN

【あか 垢】
ⓐ **SURFACE DIRT, grime, waste matter**
ⓑ **filth, impurity**
a 垢擦り あかすり scrubbing the skin (to remove grime)
垢染みる あかじみる become grimy [grubby]
垢抜ける あかぬける become refined [sophisticated]
手垢 てあか finger marks
水垢 みずあか (water) scale, mineral deposit
b 心の垢 こころのあか spiritual rust

SPECIAL READINGS

垢離 こり cold-water ablution

娃

▶BEAUTIFUL
アイ
Ⓒ 娃 wá

0419
1-3-6

38	Names	U5A03
女	S9-3-6	F0000

COMPOUNDS

ⓐ **BEAUTIFUL**
ⓑ **BEAUTIFUL woman**
a 娃鬟× あいかん beautiful woman
b 館娃 かんあい name of a palace in China

SYNONYMS

● **beautiful**
美 BEAUTIFUL → 2817
彪 MAGNIFICENT → 4115
綺 BEAUTIFUL → 1734
娃 BEAUTIFUL → 0419
佳 FINE → 0096
瑶 EXQUISITE → 1301
麗 OF GRACEFUL BEAUTY → 2672
艶 CHARMING → 2403
妙 of marvelous beauty → 0280
華 MAGNIFICENT → 2841
絢 GORGEOUS → 1705
斐 florid → 3449

姥

▶OLD WOMAN
ボ うば ㊔ とめ おけ
Ⓒ 姥 lǎo mǔ

0420
1-3-6

38	Names	U59E5
女	S9-3-6	F3173

KUN

【うば 姥】
① **OLD WOMAN**
姥捨て うばすて practice of abandoning old women
姥桜 うばざくら woman past her prime who is still attractive; cherry trees that blossom before putting forth leaves
姥貝 うばがい Sakhalin surf clam

山姥 やまんば(=やまうば) mountain witch

② **noh mask of an OLD WOMAN**

SYNONYMS

【うば】

① **old persons**

老 old person → 3963

爺 OLD MAN → 2656

翁 OLD MAN → 2611

婆 OLD WOMAN → 3433

姥 OLD WOMAN → 0420

USAGE

【うば】

姥

① old woman

② noh mask of an old woman

姆

[now always 乳母] wet nurse

HOMOPHONES

うば 姆 GOVERNESS → 0331

姻

▶MARRIAGE

イン

Ⓒ 姻 yīn

0421

1-3-6

38	Jōyō	U59FB
女	S9-3-6	F2517

Stroke order: 1–9

COMPOUNDS

ⓐ MARRIAGE

ⓑ relative by **MARRIAGE**

a 婚姻 こんいん marriage, matrimony

b 姻族 いんぞく relatives by marriage

姻戚 いんせき relatives by marriage, in-laws

SYNONYMS

ⓐ marrying and marriage

嫁 WED A MAN → 0780

婚 MARRY → 0566

姻 MARRIAGE → 0421

縁 marriage relation → 1754

ⓑ family and relations

族 FAMILY → 1195

家 FAMILY → 2827

門 family → 1100

氏 clan → 3669

縁 RELATION → 1754

姻 relative by marriage → 0421

親 RELATIVES → 2264

戚 RELATIVES → 4401

曽 GREAT- → 2632

姪

▶NIECE

テツ めい

Ⓒ 侄 zhí

0422

1-3-6

38	Names	U59EA
女	S9-3-6	F2763

COMPOUNDS

ⓐ NIECE, nephew

ⓑ child of a man's sister, child of a woman's brother

a 姪孫 てっそん grandniece, grandnephew

令姪 れいてつ your niece

KUN

【めい 姪】NIECE

姪っ子 めいっこ *colloq* niece

姪御 めいご your niece

又姪 まためい grandniece

SYNONYMS

ⓐ offspring of siblings

甥 NEPHEW → 1510

姪 NIECE → 0422

姫

▶DAUGHTER OF NOBLE BIRTH

キ ひめ ひめ-

0423

1-3-6

38	Nonstandard	U2F862
女	S9-3-6	F0000

traditional form → see 姬 at 0489

娭

▶GLAD

キ うれ(しい) ㊔ よし うれし

0424

1-3-6

38	Nonstandard	U5B09
女	S9-3-6	F0000

traditional form → see 嬉 at 0890

姙

▶BECOME PREGNANT

ニン はら(む)

0425

1-3-6

38	Nonstandard	U59D9
女	S9-3-6	F0000

alternative form → see 妊 at 0281

孤

▶SOLITARY

コ

Ⓝ 孤 Ⓒ 孤 gū

0426

1-3-6

39	Jōyō	U5B64
子	S9-3-6	F1417

Stroke order: 1–9

COMPOUNDS

❶ⓐ SOLITARY, lone, isolated

ⓑ lonely

a 孤独の こどくの solitary, lonely, alone

孤立 こりつ isolation
孤客 こかく lone traveler
孤島 ことう solitary island
孤軍 こぐん lone [isolated] force, forlorn force
孤城 こじょう solitary [isolated] castle
b 孤愁 こしゅう lonely contemplation

❷ [original meaning] orphan
孤児 こじ orphan

INDEPENDENT

【こ 孤】orphan; loneliness
幼にして孤となる ようにしてことなる be orphaned in one's babyhood
徳は孤ならず とくはこならず The good will not long remain lonely

SYNONYMS

❶ⓐ alone
独 ALONE → 0471
孤 SOLITARY → 0426

❷ offspring
子 CHILD → 4196
仔 OFFSPRING → 0038
孤 orphan → 0426
嫡 LEGITIMATE CHILD → 0839
息 son → 3278
男 son → 3147
惣 eldest son → 3452
娘 DAUGHTER → 0488
女 daughter → 4226
姫 DAUGHTER OF NOBLE BIRTH → 0489

NOTE

★ do not confuse with 弧 ARC → 0430

峡

0427
◧ 1-3-6

▶GORGE
キョウ ㊔ はざま
Ⓝ 峽 Ⓒ 峡 xiá

46	Jōyō	U5CE1
山	S9-3-6	F1840

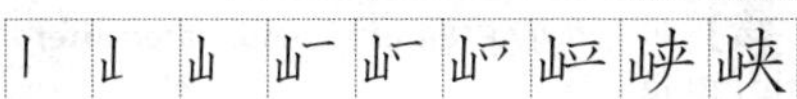
1 2 3 4 5 6 7 8 9

COMPOUNDS

❶ⓐ GORGE, ravine, glen
ⓑ suffix after names of GORGEs or valleys
a 峡谷 きょうこく gorge, ravine, canyon, valley
峡間 きょうかん between the mountains; ravine
山峡 さんきょう(=やまかい) gorge, ravine, glen
b 黒部峡 くろべきょう Kurobe Canyon

❷ narrows, strait
峡湾 きょうわん fjord
海峡 かいきょう straits, narrows, channel, sound
地峡 ちきょう isthmus

SYNONYMS

❶ valley
谷 VALLEY → 2536
渓 RAVINE → 0628
峡 GORGE → 0427

❷ inlets and bays
江 INLET → 0257
浦 coastal indentation → 0524
湾 BAY → 0748
峡 narrows → 0427

峠

0428
◧ 1-3-6

▶MOUNTAIN PASS
とうげ ㊔ たお
Ⓒ (国字)

46	Jōyō	U5CE0
山	S9-3-6	F1789

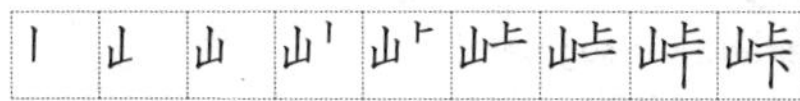
1 2 3 4 5 6 7 8 9

KUN

【とうげ 峠】
①ⓐ **MOUNTAIN PASS, ridge**
ⓑ **suffix after names of MOUNTAIN PASSes**
a 峠を越える とうげをこえる cross a pass, pass over the peak
峠道 とうげみち road over a mountain pass
b 碓氷峠 うすいとうげ Usui Pass
② crisis, climax, height, turning point
峠を越す とうげをこす the worst is over, pass the peak of (danger), turn the corner

SYNONYMS

【とうげ】
① **mountain parts**
頂 SUMMIT → 0164
峰 PEAK → 0494
嶺 RIDGE → 3013
峠 MOUNTAIN PASS → 0428
崖 CLIFF → 2862
壁 wall-like structure → 3601

形

0429
◧ 1-3-6

▶SHAPE
ケイ ギョウ かた -がた かたち なり

59	Nonstandard	U2F899
彡	S9-3-6	F0000

alternative form → see 形 at 1050

弧

0430
◧ 1-3-6

▶ARC
コ
Ⓝ 弧 Ⓒ 弧 hú

57	Jōyō	U5F27
弓	S9-3-6	F2714

口 土 女 子 山 干 弓 【彳】 忄 扌 氵 犭 阝

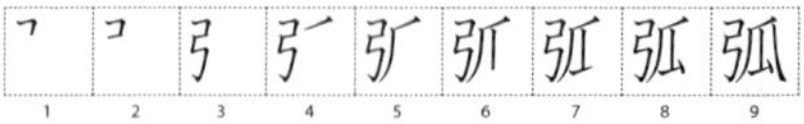

COMPOUNDS

❶ⓐ **ARC**
ⓑ *math* **ARC**

a 弧状の こじょうの arc-shaped
括弧 かっこ parentheses, brackets
b 弧線 こせん arc (of a circle)
弧形 こけい arc
円弧 えんこ circular arc; arc of a circle
劣弧 れっこ minor arc

❷ [original meaning, now archaic] **wooden bow**

INDEPENDENT

【こ 弧】 **ARC**; *math* arc
弧を描く こをえがく describe an arc

SYNONYMS

❶ **lines and line segments**
線 LINE →1760
弧 ARC →0430
弦 chord →0343
径 DIAMETER →0347
辺 side →3761

NOTE

★ do not confuse with 孤 SOLITARY →0426

後

0431

1-3-6

▶**AFTER**
ゴ コウ のち うし(ろ) うしろ あと おく(れる) ㊔ ごう
Ⓒ 后 hòu

60	Jōyō-2	U5F8C
彳	S9-3-6	F0038

COMPOUNDS

❶ [sometimes also 后 ご 3701] [also suffix] (subsequent in time) **AFTER, afterwards, later, subsequent**
後遺症 こういしょう sequela, aftereffect (of a disease)
後任 こうにん successor, replacement
後天的 こうてんてき acquired (immunity), learned
直後 ちょくご immediately after
生後 せいご after birth
今後 こんご after this, from now on
以後 いご after this, from now on, in future; after that, thereafter
午後 ごご afternoon
老後 ろうご one's old age
十年後 じゅうねんご ten years after [hence]
終戦後の しゅうせんごの postwar

❷ (subsequent in order) **AFTER, latter, second**
後者 こうしゃ the latter
後半 こうはん latter half, second half
後期 こうき latter period
後場 ごば afternoon session [market]
後半生 こうはんせい latter half of one's life
後手 ごて moving second (in a board game); rear guard
最後の さいごの last, final

❸ **AFTER**years, future generations, posterity
後世 こうせい future life, life to come
後事 こうじ future affairs, affairs after one's death
後裔× こうえい descendant, scion, offspring
後継者 こうけいしゃ successor, inheritor, heir
後続 こうぞく succession

❹ [also prefix] (behind in space) **AFTER-, rear, back, hind**
後部 こうぶ back part, rear
後援 こうえん support, backing
後退する こうたいする retreat, recede
後甲板 こうかんぱん afterdeck
後頭部 こうとうぶ back (part) of the head
後方 こうほう back, rear
前後 ぜんご before and after; order, sequence
背後 はいご back, rear
落後(=落伍)する らくごする straggle, drop out of line, fall out of the ranks

❺ [original meaning] fall behind, fall back, lag behind, be backwards
後進国 こうしんこく underdeveloped countries
後配株 こうはいかぶ deferred stock
後家 ごけ widow

INDEPENDENT

【ご 後】 **AFTER, afterward, later; since;** abbrev. of 午後 ごご: **afternoon**
後四時 ごよじ 4 p.m.
その後 そのご after that, afterward

KUN

【のち 後】 [also suffix] **AFTER, afterwards, later; after death; future**
後程 のちほど afterwards, later
後添い のちぞい one's second wife
後の世 のちのよ after ages, posterity; future life
その後 そののち since then, thereafter
二週間後に にしゅうかんのちに two weeks hence

【うしろ 後ろ, 後】 **back, rear**
後ろから うしろから from behind
後ろ足 うしろあし hind leg
後ろ姿 うしろすがた sight of one's back
後ろ楯 うしろだて backing, protection; supporter
後ろ向きに うしろむきに backwards, tail first

後ろめたく思う うしろめたくおもう have a guilty conscience
後ろ暗い事 うしろぐらいこと shady [questionable] matters

【あと 後】

①ⓐ [also suffix] (subsequent in time) **AFTER, afterward, later, subsequent**
ⓑ (subsequent in order) **AFTER, latter, next, following**
ⓒ **AFTER** death

a 後の あとの later, subsequent; the next [following]; back
後で あとで after, afterwards, later, later on
後片付け あとかたづけ cleaning up, clearing (the table); putting in order
後始末 あとしまつ settlement; cleaning up; putting in order
髭×剃×り後 ひげそりあと after shaving
三日後に みっかあとに three days after [later]

b 後払い あとばらい deferred payment
後書き あとがき postscript, afterword
後回し あとまわし deferment, postponement
後作 あとさく second crop

c 後を弔う あとをとむらう perform religious rites for the repose of a soul

② **back, rear**
後足 あとあし hind leg
後戻りする あともどりする go backward, move back, turn back; retrograde

③ⓐ descendant, posterity
ⓑ future

a 源氏の後 げんじのあと descendant of the Genji family

b 後後 あとあと distant future

④ⓐ **rest, remainder**
ⓑ and, and also

a 後金 あときん rest of the payment
後十分 あとじっぷん ten minutes more

b 鉛筆と後消しゴム えんぴつとあとけしごむ pencil and also eraser

⑤ consequences, results, conclusion
後を濁す あとをにごす leave a bad impression behind
後を引く あとをひく The effects linger [remain]

【おくれる 後れる】

ⓐ **fall behind, fall back, be outstripped, be backwards**
ⓑ outlive

a 後れ おくれ backwardness, lag; failure, defeat
後れを取る おくれをとる be beaten, be defeated
後れ毛 おくれげ straggling hair
手後れ ておくれ being too late

b 死に後れる しにおくれる outlive, survive

SYNONYMS

❶ **after**
後 AFTER →0431
余 after →2535

❷ **second**
乙 SECOND →4145
次 second →0058
後 AFTER (latter) →0431
中 MIDDLE →4262

❸ **future**
来 coming generations →4366
後 afteryears →0431

❹ **rear**
後 after- →0431
背 BACK →3182
裏 REAR →2652
尻 tail end →3766
尾 TAIL →3799

❺ **be late and delay**
遅 be late →3887
後 fall behind →0431
滞 fall into arrears →0815
延 POSTPONE →3812
猶 DELAY →0757

USAGE

❶【あと】

後
①ⓐ [also suffix] (subsequent in time) after, afterward, later, subsequent
ⓑ (subsequent in order) after, latter, next, following
ⓒ after death
② back, rear
③ⓐ descendant, posterity
ⓑ future
④ⓐ rest, remainder
ⓑ and, and also
⑤ consequences, results, conclusion

跡
①ⓐ (mark left by something) trace(s), track, mark, footprint, trail, sign; [also 痕] scar
ⓑ (sign of former presence) ruins, remains, aftermath
② succession
③ inheritance, headship of a family

蹟
[now replaced by 跡]
ⓐ (mark left by something) trace(s), track, mark, footprint, trail, sign
ⓑ (sign of former presence) ruins, remains, aftermath

痕
[also 跡] scar

❷【おくれる】
後れる
ⓐ fall behind, fall back, be outstripped, be backwards
ⓑ outlive
遅れる
ⓐ be late, be tardy, be delayed
ⓑ (of clocks) go slow, lose

❸【おくれ】
後れ
① backwardness, lag
② failure, defeat
遅れ
ⓐ being late
ⓑ (of clocks) going slow

HOMOPHONES

あと
跡 TRACE → 1937
蹟 TRACE → 2065
痕 SCAR → 4066
おくれる 遅 SLOW → 3887
おくれ 遅 SLOW → 3887

NOTE

➡ see COMPOUND FORMATION for 後釜 あとがま → 釜 2610

徊

▶MOVE TO AND FRO
カイ
Ⓒ 徊 huái huí

0432
1-3-6

60 彳	Non-Jōyō	U5F8A
	S9-3-6	F3179

COMPOUNDS

● [now also 回 3793] [original meaning] **MOVE TO AND FRO, walk around**
徘×徊する はいかいする loiter, wander about
低徊(=低回)する ていかいする linger, loiter, wander

SYNONYMS

● **wander**
浪 WANDER → 0527
遊 move about freely → 3896
漂 drift about → 0857
流 drift → 0529
低 WANDER ABOUT → 0350
徊 MOVE TO AND FRO → 0432

律

▶LAW
▶RHYTHM
リツ リチ レツ▲ ㊔ のり
Ⓒ 律 lǜ

0433
1-3-6

60 彳	Jōyō-6	U5F8B
	S9-3-6	F1040

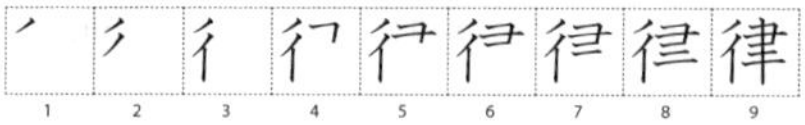

COMPOUNDS

❶ⓐ [also suffix] **LAW, rule, statute, regulation; commandment**
ⓑ [suffix] **LAW (of nature), principle**
ⓒ (bind by law) control, restrain
a 律令 りつりょう ancient laws
律儀 りちぎ honesty, faithfulness, loyalty
法律 ほうりつ law
規律 きりつ order, discipline; regulation, law
不文律 ふぶんりつ unwritten law [rule]
道徳律 どうとくりつ moral law
戒律 かいりつ commandments, precepts
黄金律 おうごんりつ golden rule
因果律 いんがりつ law of cause and effect, principle of causality
b 自然律 しぜんりつ natural law
c 自律 じりつ self-control, self-restraint

❷ **RHYTHM, tone, pitch**
律動 りつどう rhythm, rhythmic movement
一律 いちりつ uniformity, equality
旋律 せんりつ melody
調律 ちょうりつ tuning
韻律 いんりつ rhythm, meter, measure

❸ stanza of eight lines in Chinese poetry
律詩 りっし stanza of eight lines in Chinese poetry

❹ name of pentatonic music scale used in Japanese court music (D-E-G-A-B)
呂律 ろれつ articulation

INDEPENDENT

【りつ 律】**LAW**, rule, statute, regulation, commandment; poetic form (→❸); pentatonic scale (→❹)
【りっする 律する】apply a rule to, judge, measure

SYNONYMS

❶ⓐ **laws and rules**
法 LAW → 0391
律 LAW → 0433
典 CANON → 3253
憲 CONSTITUTION → 3001
令 ordinance → 2489
則 RULE → 1831
矩 RULE → 1475
規 REGULATION → 1231

紀 discipline → 1628

ⓑ **principle**

律 LAW → 0433

理 BASIC PRINCIPLE → 1220

❷ **musical elements**

韻 RHYME → 2279

律 RHYTHM → 0433

拍 BEAT → 0361

調 TONE → 1973

呂 ancient musical note → 2713

COMPOUND FORMATION

【一律 いちりつ】

一律 'uniformity, equality' originally referred to the same (一) or uniform tone (律 ❷).

待

0434

◧ 1-3-6

▶**WAIT**

タイ ま(つ) -ま(ち)

Ⓒ 待 dài dāi

60	Jōyō-3	U5F85
彳	S9-3-6	F0300

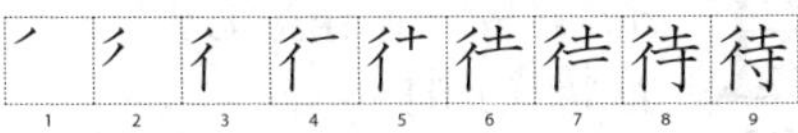

COMPOUNDS

❶ⓐ **WAIT**

ⓑ **WAIT for, await, expect, look forward to**

a 待機する たいきする wait for an opportunity, stand ready

待避する たいひする take shelter; shunt

b 待命 たいめい waiting for orders

待望の たいぼうの hoped-for, long-awaited

期待 きたい expectation, anticipation, hope

❷ **treat, entertain, receive**

待遇する たいぐうする treat, receive, entertain

接待する せったいする receive (guests), welcome; offer, serve, entertain

招待 しょうたい invitation

優待する ゆうたいする treat kindly, receive hospitably, give special consideration

歓待する かんたいする give a cordial [warm] reception, entertain

KUN

【まつ 待つ】

ⓐ **WAIT**

ⓑ **WAIT for, expect, look forward to**

a 待ち まち waiting, waiting time

待たせる またせる keep (a person) waiting

待ち合わせる まちあわせる wait, meet by appointment

待ち合わせ まちあわせ waiting (for an appointment or train)

待ちくたびれる まちくたびれる get tired of waiting

待ち伏せ まちぶせ ambush

待合室 まちあいしつ waiting room

待ち遠しい まちどうしい just can't wait for, long for

待ち兼ねる まちかねる wait impatiently [eagerly]

b 待ち望む まちのぞむ expect, look forward to

待ち受ける まちうける wait for, await, expect

【-まち -待ち】[suffix] **WAIT, waiting**

信号待ち しんごうまち waiting for a traffic light

キャンセル待ち きゃんせるまち waiting for a cancellation (on a flight)

SYNONYMS

❶ⓐ **wait**

待 WAIT → 0434

控える be in waiting → 0600

ⓑ **expect**

期 EXPECT → 2139

待 wait for → 0434

❷ **treat and welcome**

遇 TREAT → 3889

待 treat → 0434

扱う HANDLE → 0251

款 treat cordially → 2135

接 receive → 0607

迎 WELCOME → 3796

悔

0435

◧ 1-3-6

▶**REPENT**

カイ く(いる) く(やむ) くや(しい)

Ⓝ 悔 Ⓒ 悔 huǐ

61	Jōyō	U6094
忄	S9-3-6	F1426

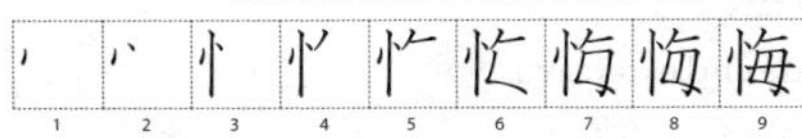

COMPOUNDS

● **REPENT, regret, be sorry**

悔悛× かいしゅん repentance, penitence

悔恨 かいこん regret, repentance

悔悟 かいご repentance, remorse

後悔する こうかいする be sorry, regret, repent

KUN

【くいる 悔いる】**REPENT, regret, be sorry**

悔い くい regret, repentance

悔い改める くいあらためる repent, be penitent

【くやむ 悔やむ】**REPENT, regret, lament; condole**

悔やまれる失策 くやまれるしっさく regrettable misstep

お悔やみ おくやみ condolence, visit of condolence

【くやしい 悔しい】[also 口惜しい] **vexing, mortifying, regrettable**

悔しさ くやしさ vexation, chagrin, regret

悔し泣き くやしなき crying from vexation, tears of regret

SYNONYMS

❶ **regret**
惜 REGRET → 0586
恨 regret → 0439
憾 STRONGLY REGRET → 0943
悔 REPENT → 0435

USAGE

【くやしい】
悔しい
[also 口惜しい] vexing, mortifying, regrettable
口惜しい
[also 悔しい] vexing, mortifying, regrettable

HOMOPHONES

くやしい 口惜しい → 4189, 0586

恢

0436
1-3-6

▶**EXTENSIVE**
カイ
Ⓝ 恢 Ⓒ 恢 huī

61	Names	U6062
忄	S9-3-6	F3212

COMPOUNDS

❶ [original meaning] **EXTENSIVE, great, vast**
天網恢恢疎にして漏らさず てんもうかいかいそにしてもらさず Heaven's net has large meshes, but nothing escapes

❷ [now replaced by 回 3793] recover, restore
恢復(=回復) かいふく recovery, restoration; rehabilitation

SYNONYMS

❶ **wide and extensive**
広 WIDE → 3769
紘 WIDE-RANGING → 1650
博 EXTENSIVE → 0170
恢 EXTENSIVE → 0436
浩 VAST → 0525
洸 VAST (expanse of water) → 0462
滉 DEEP AND VAST → 0811
曠 SPACIOUS → 1411
闊 BROAD → 4135

恰

0437
1-3-6

▶**JUST**
カッ– コウ あたか(も)
Ⓒ 恰 qià

61	Names	U6070
忄	S9-3-6	F1929

COMPOUNDS

❶ [original meaning] **JUST, exactly**
恰好(=格好) かっこう suitability, moderateness (in price); shape, form; appearance, manner
恰幅 かっぷく physique, bodily build
不恰好 ぶかっこう unshapely, misshapen; awkward, clumsy

KUN

【あたかも 恰も】[formerly also 宛も] **JUST like, as if**
恰も好し あたかもよし luckily, fortunately

SPECIAL READINGS

恰度 ちょうど [now usu. 丁度] just like, as if

SYNONYMS

❶ **exact**
確 CERTAIN → 1571
正 RIGHT → 4296
真- right → 2616
恰 JUST → 0437

HOMOPHONES

あたかも 宛 ADDRESS → 2762

NOTE

➡ see USAGE note at 宛 2762

恒

0438
1-3-6

▶**CONSTANT**
コウ ㊔ つね ひさ ひさし のぶ
Ⓝ 恆 Ⓒ 恒 héng

61	Jōyō	U6052
忄	S9-3-6	F1786

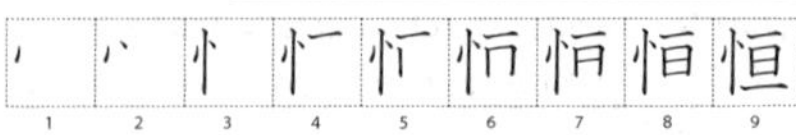

COMPOUNDS

❶ⓐ [original meaning] **CONSTANT, unchanging, fixed**
ⓑ **regular, established**
a 恒常 こうじょう constancy
恒産 こうさん fixed property
b 恒数 こうすう constant (in science)
恒星 こうせい fixed star
恒例 こうれい regular ceremony, established custom

❷ **permanent, lasting**
恒久 こうきゅう perpetuity, permanency

SYNONYMS

❶ **constant**
定 fixed → 2770
恒 CONSTANT → 0438
常 REGULAR → 3203
例 regular → 0099

❷ **of long duration**
長 LONG → 3163
永 ETERNAL → 2436
久 OF LONG DURATION → 4191
恒 permanent → 0438

口 土 女 子 山 干 弓 彳 【忄】 扌 氵 犭 阝

恨

0439

◧ 1-3-6

▶HOLD A GRUDGE

コン うら(む) うら(めしい)

Ⓒ 恨 hèn

61	Jōyō	U6068
忄	S9-3-6	F1617

Stroke order: 1 丶 2 丷 3 忄 4 忄 5 忄 6 忄 7 忄 8 恨 9 恨

COMPOUNDS

❶ⓐ HOLD A GRUDGE, hate, feel bitter against
ⓑ grudge, hatred

a 遺恨 いこん grudge, rancor, ill will
怨恨 えんこん grudge, enmity
b 多情多恨 たじょうたこん sensibility

❷ regret
恨事 こんじ regrettable matter
悔恨 かいこん regret, repentance
痛恨 つうこん deep regret, great sorrow

KUN

【うらむ 恨む】
ⓐ [formerly also 怨む] **HOLD A GRUDGE, feel resentment, feel bitter against**
ⓑ blame, reproach
a 恨み うらみ grudge, hatred, malice
逆恨み さかうらみ unjustified resentment through misunderstanding
ab 恨み言 うらみごと grudge; reproach
b 我が身を恨む わがみをうらむ blame oneself

【うらめしい 恨めしい】
ⓐ [formerly also 怨めしい] **resentful, reproachful, indignant**
ⓑ regrettable
a 恨めし気に うらめしげに reproachfully
彼が金を貸してくれないのが恨めしかった かれがかねをかしてくれないのがうらめしかった I thought it cruelly unkind of him not to lend me money

SYNONYMS

❶ hate and dislike
憎 HATE → 0845
悪 hate → 3413
忌む ABHOR → 2735
嫌 DISLIKE → 0781
恨 HOLD A GRUDGE → 0439
怨 HOLD A GRUDGE → 3179
厭 disagreeable → 3745

❷ regret
惜 REGRET → 0586
恨 regret → 0439
憾 STRONGLY REGRET → 0943
悔 REPENT → 0435

USAGE

❶【うらむ】
恨む
ⓐ [formerly also 怨む] hold a grudge, feel resentment, feel bitter against
ⓑ blame, reproach
怨む
[now usu. 恨む] hold a grudge, feel resentment, feel bitter against
憾む
be sorry for, regret

❷【うらみ】
恨み
[formerly also 怨み] grudge, hatred, malice
怨み
[now usu. 恨み] grudge, hatred, malice
憾み
regret, matter for regret

❸【うらめしい】
恨めしい
ⓐ [formerly also 怨めしい] resentful, reproachful, indignant
ⓑ regrettable
怨めしい
[now usu. 恨めしい] resentful, reproachful, indignant

HOMOPHONES

うらむ
怨 HOLD A GRUDGE → 3179
憾 STRONGLY REGRET → 0943
うらみ
怨 HOLD A GRUDGE → 3179
憾 STRONGLY REGRET → 0943
うらめしい 怨 HOLD A GRUDGE → 3179

恠

0440

◧ 1-3-6

▶MYSTERIOUS

カイ ケ あや(しい) あや(しむ)

61	Nonstandard	U6060
忄	S9-3-6	F0000

traditional form → see 怪 at 0354

恢

0441

◧ 1-3-6

▶EXTENSIVE

カイ

61	Nonstandard	U6062
忄	S9-3-6	F0000

traditional form → see 恢 at 0436

恆

0442

◧ 1-3-6

▶CONSTANT

コウ ㊔ つね ひさ ひさし のぶ

61	Names	U6046
忄	S9-3-6	F0000

traditional form → see 恒 at 0438

口 土 女 子 巾 干 弓 彳 【忄】 扌 氵 犭 阝

恊

0443
1-3-6

▶COOPERATE
キョウ ㊔ かの やす かなう

61	Nonstandard	U604A
忄	S9-3-6	F0000

traditional form → see 協 at 0103

悖

1-3-6

incorrect stroke-count
➡ see 1-3-7: 忄 at 0503

按

0444
1-3-6

▶HOLD DOWN
アン
Ⓒ 按 àn

64	Names	U6309
扌	S9-3-6	F2640

COMPOUNDS

❶ [original meaning] **HOLD DOWN with the hand, press down with the hand, rub with the hand**
按摩 あんま massage; massager, masseur, masseuse
按腹 あんぷく ventral massage
按手 あんしゅ ordination, laying on of hands

❷ [now also 案 2824] **according to**
按分する あんぶんする divide [distribute] proportionally
按配(=按排)する あんばいする arrange, distribute; adjust
按針 あんじん navigation by magnetic compass; pilot, navigator

❸ examine, consider

INDEPENDENT

【あんずる 按ずる】investigate, consider

SYNONYMS

❶ **push**
押 PUSH → 0371
突く THRUST → 2772
圧 apply pressure → 3688
挨 PUSH → 0510
按 HOLD DOWN → 0444

NOTE

➡ see USAGE note at 案 2824

挑

0445
1-3-6

▶PROVOKE
チョウ いど(む)
Ⓒ 挑 tiāo tiǎo

64	Jōyō	U6311
扌	S9-3-6	F1269

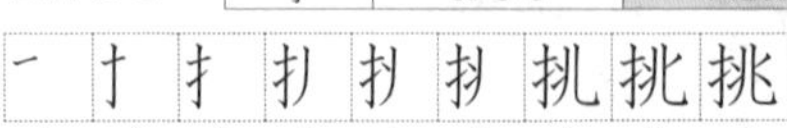

COMPOUNDS

● [original meaning] **PROVOKE, arouse, instigate, stir up, challenge**
挑戦 ちょうせん challenge, defiance
挑発する ちょうはつする provoke, incite, excite, stimulate

KUN

【いどむ 挑む】**challenge, defy, dare; make advances to**
戦いを挑む たたかいをいどむ challenge (a person) to a fight

SYNONYMS

● **incite**
挑 PROVOKE → 0445
唆 INSTIGATE → 0480
扇 FAN → 2449
煽 FAN → 1338
激 excite → 0955
奮 ROUSE UP → 3000
振 arouse to action → 0515
動 MOVE → 2232
起 rise to action → 4099

拷

0446
1-3-6

▶TORTURE
ゴウ
Ⓒ 拷 kǎo

64	Jōyō	U62F7
扌	S9-3-6	F2532

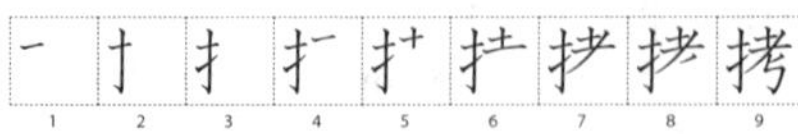

COMPOUNDS

● **TORTURE, flog, beat**
拷問 ごうもん torture; rack; third degree
拷問台 ごうもんだい rack, instrument of torture
拷器 ごうき [archaic] instruments of torture

SYNONYMS

● **torture and oppress**
拷 TORTURE → 0446
責める torture → 3115
虐 treat cruelly → 3989
迫 oppress → 3815

持

0447
1-3-6

▶HOLD
ジ も(つ) -も(ち) も(てる)
Ⓒ 持 chí

64	Jōyō-3	U6301
扌	S9-3-6	F0095

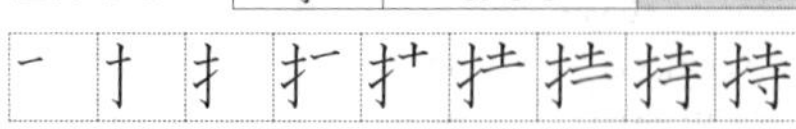

COMPOUNDS

❶ [original meaning] **HOLD, grasp, have; have with one**
持参する じさんする bring [take] with one, carry
把持 はじ grasp, hold, grip
棒持する ほうじする hold up, bear, present
支持する しじする support, maintain, back up
所持する しょじする have (money) about one; possess

❷ remain or cause to remain in a given condition:
ⓐ **HOLD out, hold up, last, endure**
ⓑ uphold, preserve, maintain, observe
a 持続する じぞくする continue, last; maintain
持久 じきゅう endurance, sustenance, persistence
持病 じびょう chronic illness
保持する ほじする maintain, preserve, retain
維持 いじ maintenance, upkeep, preservation
護持する ごじする defend, protect; uphold
b 持戒 じかい observance of the Buddhist commandments
矜×持 きょうじ(=きんじ) pride, dignity

❸ⓐ **HOLD in one's possession, possess, have**
ⓑ **HOLD on to one's opinion, adhere to**
a 持薬 じやく favorite medicine
享持する きょうじする secure rights and profits
住持 じゅうじ chief priest (of a temple)
b 持論 じろん pet theory
堅持する けんじする maintain firmly, hold fast to
固持する こじする persist in, adhere to

❹ draw, drawn game (of go)
持碁 じご drawn game of go

INDEPENDENT

【じ 持】 draw, drawn game (of go)

KUN

【もつ 持つ】

①ⓐ **HOLD, take, have**
ⓑ **have with one, carry**
a 持ち上げる もちあげる raise, lift up; flatter
持ち出す もちだす take out, carry out; run away with; advance (one's opinion); begin to have
持って行く もっていく take (with one)
持って来る もってくる bring (with one)
b 持ち越す もちこす carry forward, bring over, defer
持ち掛ける もちかける propose, offer (a suggestion)

②ⓐ **HOLD** in one's possession: **have, possess, own, bear**
ⓑ **HOLD (an opinion), have, harbor, cherish**
a 持ち主 もちぬし owner, proprietor
持ち物 もちもの one's property, one's possessions; one's baggage
持ち船 もちぶね one's own ship
手持ち てもち holdings
b 意見を持つ いけんをもつ hold an opinion

③ⓐ **HOLD (out), be supported, maintain, keep up**
ⓑ **HOLD up, last long, wear, endure**
a 持ち もち wear, durability, life; draw
持ち直す もちなおす improve, rally, recover
持堪える もちこたえる hold out, survive
身を持ち崩す みをもちくずす ruin oneself
b 長持ちする ながもちする last [keep] long, endure
この財布は五年持った このさいふはごねんもった This purse has lasted me five years

④ⓐ **take charge of**
ⓑ bear (expenses), stand, pay
a 受け持つ うけもつ have [take] charge of
掛け持ちする かけもちする hold two or more positions concurrently
b 持ち分 もちぶん quota, one's share; holdings
費用を持つ ひようをもつ bear the expenses

【-もち -持ち】

①ⓐ **person who has something, possessor**
ⓑ suitable for carrying on one's person, designed for
a 金持ち かねもち wealthy [rich] person
子持ち こもち motherhood, maternity
力持ち ちからもち man of great strength, muscleman
b 男持ちの時計 おとこもちのとけい gentlemen's watches

② [suffix] charge, expense
会社持ち かいしゃもち at company expense

③ **state (of a person's feeling)**
気持ち きもち feeling, sensation, mood
心持ち こころもち feeling, mood; slightly
面持ち おももち look, countenance, face

【もてる 持てる】 **be made much of, be welcomed, be popular**
持て成し もてなし hospitality, entertainment; treatment

SYNONYMS

❶ **take**
把 GRIP →0293
握 GRASP →0714
捉 GRASP →0518
執 SEIZE →2114
摑む GRASP →0848
捕 CATCH →0514
取 TAKE →1613
持 HOLD →0447

❶ **hold**
持 HOLD →0447
提 carry in hand →0720
携 CARRY IN HAND →0796

口 土 女 子 巾 干 弓 彳 忄 【扌】 氵 犭 阝

捧 hold up in both hands → 0594

❷ⓐ continue

続 CONTINUE → 1722
継 SUCCEED → 1720
連 IN SUCCESSION → 3849
持 HOLD → 0447

ⓑ preserve

留 KEEP → 3189
保 PRESERVE → 0107
持 uphold → 0447

❸ⓐ possess

有 HAVE → 3703
蔵 own → 2995
持 HOLD → 0447
属 BELONG TO → 3901
享 ENJOY → 2545
具 possess → 3159

ⓑ hold in the mind

持 HOLD → 0447
抱 HUG → 0363
懐 embosom → 0942

NOTE

➡ see COMPOUND FORMATION for 維持 いじ → 維 1733

挌

▶STRIKE

カク

Ⓒ 挌 gé

0448

1-3-6

64	Non-Jōyō	U630C
扌	S9-3-6	F0000

COMPOUNDS

● [now replaced by 格 1161] [original meaning] **STRIKE, hit, fight**

挌闘する かくとうする grapple, fight hand to hand

SYNONYMS

● strike

打 STRIKE → 0224
撲 DEAL A BLOW → 0903
殴 BEAT (strike a person) → 1099
蹴 KICK → 2074
撃 STRIKE → 3552
挌 STRIKE (a person) → 0448
撞 STRIKE (a ball or bell) → 0905
撥ねる strike (knock down) → 0907
当てる HIT → 2701
叩 KNOCK → 0208
拍 BEAT (strike repeatedly) → 0361
搏 BEAT (throb) → 0794

NOTE

★ do not confuse with 格 NORM → 1161

括

▶LUMP TOGETHER

カツ くく(る)▲

Ⓒ 括 kuò guā

0449

1-3-6

64	Jōyō	U62EC
扌	S9-3-6	F1706

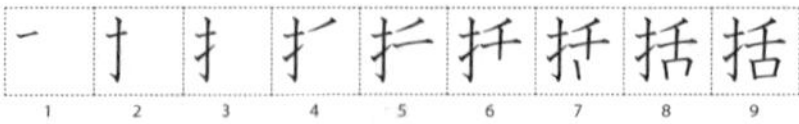

COMPOUNDS

● LUMP TOGETHER, lump, sum up, draw together

括弧 かっこ parentheses, brackets
括約筋 かつやくきん sphincter
一括する いっかつする lump together, sum up
総括的 そうかつてき all-inclusive, all-embracing
概括する がいかつする summarize, sum up, generalize
包括する ほうかつする include, comprehend, comprise
統括する とうかつする generalize

KUN

【くくる 括る】**fasten, make fast; bundle up, tie up; LUMP TOGETHER, sum up**

括り付ける くくりつける fasten (a person) to
引っ括る ひっくくる tie up
首を括る くびをくくる hang oneself
締め括り しめくくり completion, summing up; supervision

SYNONYMS

● combine

合 COMBINE → 2511
結 TIE → 1706
統 UNITE → 1710
括 LUMP TOGETHER → 0449
総 integrate → 1743
併 join together → 0092
綜 INTEGRATE → 1744
纏める PUT TOGETHER → 1814

挟

▶HOLD BETWEEN

キョウ はさ(む) はさ(まる) わきばさ(む)▲

Ⓝ 挾 Ⓒ 挟 xié

0450

1-3-6

64	Jōyō	U631F
扌	S9-3-6	F1741

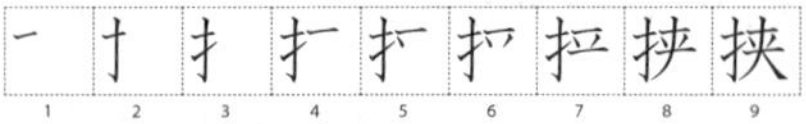

COMPOUNDS

❶ HOLD BETWEEN, pinch

挟瞼×器 きょうけんき entropion forceps
挟撃 きょうげき attack on both sides, pincer movement

挾殺 きょうさつ *baseball* rundown

❷ [original meaning, now archaic] hold under the arm

挾書 きょうしょ possession of books

KUN

【はさむ 挟む】

①ⓐ **HOLD BETWEEN, hold**

ⓑ **pinch, nip**

a テーブルを挟んで話し合う てーぶるをはさんではなしあう hold a conversation across the table

箸で漬け物を挟む はしでつけものをはさむ hold a pickle with chopsticks

紙挟み かみばさみ paper clip, paper holder

b ペンを唇に挟む ぺんをくちびるにはさむ nip a pen between one's lips

② [formerly also 挿む] **put (something) between, insert, interpose**

挟み込む はさみこむ insert

雑誌に挟む ざっしにはさむ place in a magazine

口を挟む くちをはさむ interject, cut into (a conversation)

【はさまる 挟まる】 get between, lie between, be caught in

指がドアに挟まる ゆびがどあにはさまる one's fingers are caught in a door

【わきばさむ 挟む】 hold under the arm

泰山を挟んで北海を超ゆ たいざんをわきばさんでほっかいをこゆ carry Taishan Mountain under one's arm and leap over the north sea

SYNONYMS

❶ **contain and include**

含 CONTAIN (have as a part) → 2534

容 CONTAIN (have within) → 2832

包 ENCOMPASS → 3684

挟 HOLD BETWEEN → 0450

USAGE

【はさむ】

挟む

①ⓐ hold between, hold

ⓑ pinch, nip

② [formerly also 挿む] put (something) between, insert, interpose

挿む

[now usu. 挟む] put (something) between, insert, interpose

鋏む

snip, clip

HOMOPHONES

はさむ

挿 INSERT → 0517

鋏 SCISSORS → 2173

拶

▶PRESS

サツ

Ⓒ 拶 zǎn zā

0451

1-3-6

64	Jōyō	U62F6
扌	S9-3-6	F1418

Stroke order: 一 十 扌 扌 扌 扌 拶 拶 拶 (1–9)

COMPOUNDS

● **PRESS on, draw near; be imminent**

挨拶 あいさつ greeting, salutation; speech, address; reply, response

挨拶状 あいさつじょう greeting card

SYNONYMS

● **approach**

寄る DRAW NEAR → 2856

迫 PRESS → 3815

近 NEAR → 3798

接 come close to → 0607

拶 PRESS → 0451

NOTE

➡ see COMPOUND FORMATION for 挨拶 あいさつ → 挨 0510

指

▶FINGER
▶POINT

シ ゆび さ(す) -さ(し) ㊔ いぶ

Ⓒ 指 zhǐ

0452

1-3-6

64	Jōyō-3	U6307
扌	S9-3-6	F0197

Stroke order: 一 十 扌 扌 扌 扌 指 指 指 (1–9)

COMPOUNDS

❶ⓐ [original meaning] **FINGER**

ⓑ counter for **FINGERs**

a 指紋 しもん fingerprint

指圧 しあつ *shiatsu*, acupressure

b 五指 ごし the five fingers

❷ⓐ **POINT (to), point out, indicate, show**

ⓑ **direct, instruct**

a 指定する していする designate, appoint

指示する しじする instruct, point out; indicate, point to

指摘する してきする point out

指数 しすう index (number); exponent

指名する しめいする nominate, designate, name

b 指南 しなん instruction, teaching; instructor, teacher

指導する しどうする guide, lead, instruct

指揮 しき command

指揮者 しきしゃ conductor; commander

指令 しれい order, instruction

❸ play or manipulate the pieces of board games, esp. shogi (Japanese chess)

指了図 しりょうず end game position

KUN

【ゆび 指】 **FINGER, toe**

指輪 ゆびわ (finger) ring
指差す ゆびさす point to
指切り ゆびきり pledge made by hooking each other's little fingers
人差し指 ひとさしゆび index finger
親指 おやゆび thumb
足の指 あしのゆび toe

【さす 指す】

①ⓐ **POINT to, point at, indicate**

ⓑ **aim at, have in view**

a 指し図 さしず directions
方向を指す ほうこうをさす point to a direction

b 目指す(=目差す) めざす aim for, have an eye on
頂上を目指す ちょうじょうをめざす set out for the summit

② **appoint, nominate; FINGER, accuse**

名指し なざし nomination, calling names

③ play board games (esp. shogi)

指し手 さして shogi move, shogi player
早指しチェス はやざしちぇす blitz chess

【-さし -指し】 [suffix] **player (of shogi)**

将棋指し しょうぎさし shogi player

SYNONYMS

❶ **hand and arm**

手 HAND → 4267
腕 ARM → 1269
肘 ELBOW → 1044
掌 PALM → 3215
指 FINGER → 0452
拇 THUMB → 0358
拳 FIST → 3295

❷ⓐ **indicate**

指 POINT → 0452
示 SHOW → 2435
標 MARK → 1347
宛てる ADDRESS → 2762

ⓑ **instruct**

訓 INSTRUCT → 1844
指 direct → 0452

HOMOPHONES

さす

差 DIFFERENCE → 4104
刺 STAB → 1625
挿 INSERT → 0517
注 POUR → 0383
射 SHOOT → 1850
止 STOP → 3659

-さし

差 DIFFERENCE → 4104
刺 STAB → 1625
止 STOP → 3659

NOTE

➡ see USAGE note at 差 4104

拭

0453

1-3-6

▶**WIPE**

ショク シキ▲ ふ(く) ぬぐ(う)

Ⓒ 拭 shì

64	Jōyō	U62ED
扌	S9-3-6	F1510

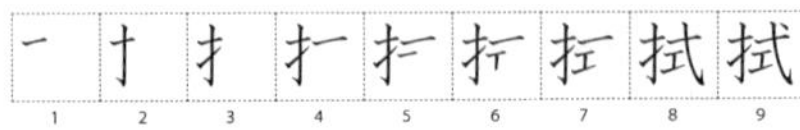

COMPOUNDS

● **WIPE (off, away), wipe clean, mop up**

払拭する ふっしょくする wipe out [away], dispel, cast aside (worries, etc.)

KUN

【ふく 拭く】 **WIPE (off, away), wipe clean, mop up**

拭き取る ふきとる wipe off [up]
拭き掃除 ふきそうじ cleaning, wiping
手拭き てふき (hand) towel
窓拭き まどふき window cleaning
乾拭き からぶき polishing with a dry cloth

【ぬぐう 拭う】

① **WIPE (off, away), mop up, brush away**

手拭い てぬぐい Japanese (hand) towel
口を拭う くちをぬぐう wipe one's mouth; feign innocence [ignorance]

② **expunge, blot out, erase**

尻拭い しりぬぐい bearing the consequences of someone else's error

SYNONYMS

● **clean and wash**

洗 WASH → 0465
漱 RINSE → 0865
拭 WIPE → 0453
滌 WASH → 0854
濯 RINSE → 0978
浴 BATHE → 0533
浄 cleanse → 0457
粛 PURGE → 4400
清 CLEAR → 0635
払 CLEAR AWAY → 0225
掃 SWEEP → 0611

拾

▶PICK UP

シュウ ジュウ ひろ(う) ㊔ おさむ

Ⓒ 拾 shí shè

0454

1-3-6

64	Jōyō-3	U62FE
扌	S9-3-6	F1488

一 十 扌 扌 扒 扴 拎 拾 拾

1 2 3 4 5 6 7 8 9

COMPOUNDS

❶ [original meaning] **PICK UP, gather**

拾得する しゅうとくする pick up, find

拾遺 しゅうい gleaning

収拾する しゅうしゅうする get under control, save (the situation)

❷ ten—used in legal documents and checks

金拾万円 きんじゅうまんえん 100,000 yen

INDEPENDENT

【じゅう 拾】ten (→❷)

KUN

【ひろう 拾う】**PICK UP, gather; find;** (acquire something hard to get) **get hold of, gain; pick out, select**

拾い上げる ひろいあげる pick up; pick out

拾い集める ひろいあつめる gather

拾い出す ひろいだす pick out, select

拾い物 ひろいもの thing picked up [found]; bargain

拾い読みする ひろいよみする read here and there, skim through

石を拾う いしをひろう pick up a stone

命拾い いのちびろい narrow escape (from death), close shave

SYNONYMS

❶ **get**

得 ACQUIRE →0577

拾 PICK UP →0454

獲 obtain →0959

収 TAKE IN →0031

取 TAKE →1613

❷ **ten**

十 TEN →4172

拾 ten (in legal documents) →0454

【ひろう】

◯ **raise**

揚 RAISE HIGH →0722

掲 PUT UP →0597

挙 RAISE →3106

上 raise →4212

起 raise up →4099

擡 RAISE (one's head) →0972

立てる STAND →2486

拾う PICK UP →0454

挺

incorrect stroke-count

➡ see 1-3-7: 扌 at 0512

1-3-6

洞

▶CAVE

ドウ ほら ㊔ とう ほこら

Ⓒ 洞 dòng

0455

1-3-6

85	Jōyō	U6D1E
氵	S9-3-6	F1688

丶 冫 氵 氵 汈 汌 泂 洞 洞

1 2 3 4 5 6 7 8 9

COMPOUNDS

❶ [also suffix] [original meaning] **CAVE, cavern, grotto; cavity, tunnel**

洞窟 どうくつ cavern, cave

洞穴 どうけつ cave, den, excavation

空洞 くうどう cave, cavern, hollow

風洞 ふうどう wind tunnel

鐘乳洞 しょうにゅうどう limestone cave [grotto]

❷ **see through, penetrate, have an insight into**

洞察 どうさつ insight, penetration

KUN

【ほら 洞】**CAVE, cavern, den**

洞穴 ほらあな cave, cavern, den

SYNONYMS

❶ **holes and cavities**

穴 HOLE →2682

洞 CAVE →0455

窟 CAVE →2923

窪 HOLLOW →2962

腔 BODY CAVITY →1267

孔 OPEN HOLE →0205

口 MOUTH →4189

坑 PIT →0277

堀 DITCH →0561

溝 CHANNEL →0810

壕 TRENCH →0966

濠 MOAT →0975

凹 concavity →4294

派

▶SECT

▶DISPATCH

ハ

Ⓝ 派 Ⓒ 派 pài pā

0456

1-3-6

85	Jōyō-6	U6D3E
氵	S9-3-6	F0453

丶 冫 氵 氵 汀 汀 沠 沠 派

1 2 3 4 5 6 7 8 9

口 土 女 子 山 千 弓 彳 忄 扌 【氵】 犭 阝

COMPOUNDS

❶ⓐ [also suffix] **SECT, faction, party; school; clique, group**

ⓑ **religious SECT, denomination**

a 派閥 はばつ clique, faction, coterie
一派 いっぱ sect, denomination; school; party
党派 とうは party, faction, clique
左派 さは left wing, left faction
流派 りゅうは school
学派 がくは school, sect
古典派 こてんは the classical school
田中派 たなかは Tanaka faction

b 宗派 しゅうは religious sect, denomination
真宗大谷派 しんしゅうおおたには Otani sect of Shinshu

❷ⓐ **branch off, diverge, derive**

ⓑ [original meaning] branch, offshoot

a 派生する はせいする derive from, stem from

b 分派 ぶんぱ branch, sect, denomination

❸ **DISPATCH, send**

派出する はしゅつする send out, dispatch
派米する はべいする dispatch to the U.S.
派遣する はけんする dispatch, send
派兵 はへい dispatch of troops
特派員 とくはいん special correspondent; delegate

❹ **unclassified compounds**

派手な はでな showy, flashy, gaudy
立派な りっぱな fine, excellent, admirable

INDEPENDENT

【は 派】 **SECT**, faction; group
彼の派 かれのは his sect [faction]

【はする 派する】 send, **DISPATCH**

SYNONYMS

❶ **parties and sects**

党 PARTY → 3190
閥 CLIQUE → 4126
流 school → 0529
派 SECT → 0456
翼 WING → 3379
系 faction → 2443
門 (religious) sect → 1100
宗 RELIGIOUS SECT (esp. Buddhist) → 2769

❸ **send**

送 SEND → 3837
投 SEND IN → 0300
回 send round → 3793
遣 DISPATCH → 3908
派 DISPATCH → 0456

浄

0457

1-3-6

▶**CLEAN**

ジョウ きよ(める)▲ ㊔ きよ きよし

Ⓝ 淨 Ⓒ 净 jìng

85	Jōyō	U6D44
氵	S9-3-6	F1550

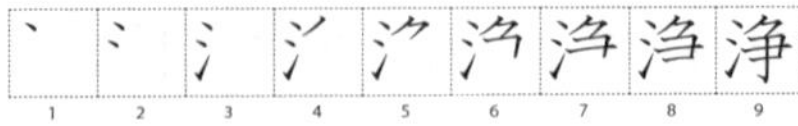

COMPOUNDS

❶ⓐ **CLEAN, pure, unstained**

ⓑ **CLEANse, purify**

ⓒ [formerly 滌 でき, じょう 0854] **wash, CLEANse**

a 清浄な せいじょうな pure, clean

b 浄化 じょうか purification, cleansing
浄書 じょうしょ clean copy
浄水場 じょうすいじょう water purification plant

c 洗浄 せんじょう washing, irrigation

❷ *Buddhism* pure, sacred

浄土 じょうど Pure Land, (Buddhist) paradise
浄土宗 じょうどしゅう *Jodo* sect (of Buddhism)
浄瑠璃 じょうるり *joruri*, ballad drama; clear lapis lazuli

KUN

【きよめる 浄める】

①ⓐ [usu. 清める] (rid of dirt or impurities) **CLEAN**se, purify

ⓑ [sometimes also 清める] (rid of moral taint) **purify, purge**

② [usu. 清める] exorcise

→ see 清 0635 for compounds

SYNONYMS

❶ⓐ **clean and purified**

浄 CLEAN → 0457
清 clean → 0635
純 PURE → 1649
潔 IMMACULATE → 0920
粋 REFINED (free from impurities) → 1645
精 refined (purified) → 1729
楚 NEAT AND TRIM → 3470

ⓑ & ❶ⓒ **clean and wash**

洗 WASH → 0465
漱 RINSE → 0865
拭 WIPE → 0453
滌 WASH → 0854
濯 RINSE → 0978
浴 BATHE → 0533
浄 cleanse → 0457
粛 PURGE → 4400
清 CLEAR → 0635
払 CLEAR AWAY → 0225
掃 SWEEP → 0611

HOMOPHONES

きよめる 清 CLEAR →0635

NOTE

➡ see USAGE note at 清 0635

洵

▶TRULY

ジュン ㊔ まこと ひとし

Ⓒ 洵 xún

0458

1-3-6

85	Names	U6D35
氵	S9-3-6	F0000

COMPOUNDS

● [archaic] **TRULY**, really, utterly

洵美 じゅんび truly beautiful, exquisite

SYNONYMS

● **true**

真 TRUE →2616
洵 TRULY →0458
実 REAL →2765
本 real →4314
正 genuine →4296
現 ACTUAL →1218

海

▶SEA

カイ うみ ㊔ あま ひろし み

Ⓝ 海 Ⓒ 海 hǎi

0459

1-3-6

85	Jōyō-2	U6D77
氵	S9-3-6	F0154

COMPOUNDS

❶ⓐ **SEA, ocean**
ⓑ (large landlocked body of water) **SEA**, large lake
ⓒ **suffix after names of SEAs**

a 海洋 かいよう ocean, sea
海外 かいがい overseas, abroad
海水浴 かいすいよく sea bathing
海岸 かいがん seashore, (sea) coast, beach
海産物 かいさんぶつ marine products
海軍 かいぐん navy
海面 かいめん surface of the sea
海里 かいり [also 浬] nautical mile
航海 こうかい voyage, ocean navigation
南海 なんかい southern sea; South Seas

c カスピ海 かすぴかい Caspian Sea
日本海 にほんかい Japan Sea

❷ⓐ a **SEA** of, a vast collection of
ⓑ as vast as the **SEA**

a 樹海 じゅかい (abundant) leafage ("sea of trees")
言海 げんかい dictionary, wordbook

b 海容 かいよう magnanimous forgiveness

❸ abbrev. of 海軍 かいぐん: navy

海相 かいしょう Navy Minister

INDEPENDENT

【かい 海】**SEA**; marine

KUN

【うみ 海】**SEA, ocean; lake**

海辺 うみべ seaside, beach, seashore
荒海 あらうみ rough sea, stormy sea

SPECIAL READINGS

海女 あま woman diver
海士 あま diver
海原 うなばら sea, ocean
海老▲ えび lobster, shrimp
海苔▲ のり laver
海螺▲ つぶ [usu. 螺] edible spiral-shelled gastropod

SYNONYMS

❶ **sea**

海 SEA →0459
洋 OCEAN →0468
沖 OFFING →0307
灘 OPEN SEA →1006

HOMOPHONES

かいり

浬 NAUTICAL MILE →0526
海里 →0459, 4356

つぶ

螺 SPIRAL-SHELLED GASTROPOD →1799
海螺 →0459, 1799

活

▶ACTIVE
▶LIVE

カツ い(きる)▲ い(かす)▲ い(ける)▲
㊔ いく

Ⓒ 活 huó

0460

1-3-6

85	Jōyō-2	U6D3B
氵	S9-3-6	F0190

COMPOUNDS

❶ⓐ **ACTIVE, lively, live, energetic, moving**
ⓑ activity, energy, vitality

a 活動 かつどう activity, action; function
活躍する かつやくする be active in, be actively engaged
活発な かっぱつな lively, active
活性 かっせい activity
活気 かっき vigor, spirit, animation
活況 かっきょう activity, briskness, prosperity

口 土 女 子 巾 干 弓 彳 忄 扌 【氵】 犭 阝

活写する かっしゃする describe vividly, paint a lively picture of
活火山 かっかざん active volcano
敏活 びんかつ quickness, alacrity
不活性化 ふかっせいか inactivation
b 部活 ぶかつ club activity

❷ abbrev. of 活動写真 かつどうしゃしん: motion picture
活弁 かつべん film interpreter, movie reciter
日活 にっかつ Nikkatsu Corporation

❸ⓐ (not fixed) **LIVE, movable**
ⓑ *elec* **LIVE**
a 活字 かつじ movable type, printing type
活版 かっぱん printing, typography
活軸 かつじく live axle
b 活線 かっせん live wire

❹ⓐ **LIVE, be alive**
ⓑ **let LIVE, keep alive**
ⓒ (having life) **LIVE**, living, alive
ⓓ life
a 活路 かつろ means of escape, way out
復活する ふっかつする revive, come to life again, be resurrected
b 活用する かつようする utilize, apply; conjugate, inflect
活殺 かっさつ life and death
c 活仏 かつぶつ living Buddha; grand Lama
d 死活 しかつ life and/or death

❺ (pass one's life) **LIVE, lead one's life**
生活 せいかつ life, existence; livelihood
自活 じかつ self-support

❻ [formerly 闊 4135] broad-minded, generous
快活(=快闊)な かいかつな cheerful, lively, light-hearted

INDEPENDENT

【かつ 活】 *judo* resuscitation; living, life
活を入れる かつをいれる apply the art of resuscitation
活を求める かつをもとめる try to find a way out

KUN

【いきる 活きる】 [now usu. 生きる] **be enlivened**
その一語で文章が活きる そのいちごでぶんしょうがいきる That single word gives life to the style

【いかす 活かす】 [now usu. 生かす]
① **make the most of**
学問を活かして使う がくもんをいかしてつかう put one's knowledge to practical use
② put life [vividness] into, vivify
絵を活かす えをいかす put life into a painting

【いける 活ける】 [now usu. 生ける] arrange (flowers)
活け花 いけばな flower arrangement

SYNONYMS

❶ⓐ **active**
活 ACTIVE →0460
動 dynamic →2232

❹ⓐ & ❹ⓑ & ❺ **live**
活 LIVE →0460
暮らす LIVE (pass one's life) →2971
生 live (be alive) →4309

HOMOPHONES

いきる 生 LIFE →4309
いかす 生 LIFE →4309
いける
生 LIFE →4309
埋 BURY →0484

NOTE

➡ see USAGE note at 生 4309

洪 0461

▸**FLOOD**
コウ ㊔ ひろ
Ⓒ 洪 hóng

1-3-6

85	Jōyō	U6D2A
氵	S9-3-6	F2196

Stroke order: 1–9

COMPOUNDS

❶ [original meaning] **FLOOD, inundation**
洪水 こうずい flood, inundation
洪積世 こうせきせい diluvial epoch

❷ great, grand, vast
洪大な こうだいな great, immense

❸ [rare] Hungary
日洪親善 にっこうしんぜん goodwill between Japan and Hungary

SYNONYMS

❶ **running water**
流 CURRENT →0529
潮 TIDE →0916
汐 TIDE →0259
瀬 rapids →0995
滝 WATERFALL →0813
洪 FLOOD →0461
渦 WHIRLPOOL →0735

洸 0462

▸**VAST**
コウ ㊔ ひかる あきら たけし ひろ ひろし
Ⓒ 洸 guāng

1-3-6

85	Names	U6D38
氵	S9-3-6	F0000

COMPOUNDS

[archaic]

ⓐ **VAST** and deep like an expanse of water
ⓑ glittering like water; surge of water

a 洸洋 こうよう great expanse of water; unfathomable, incoherent

b 洸洸 こうこう brave, valiant; surge (of water)

SYNONYMS

ⓐ **wide and extensive**

広 WIDE → 3769
紘 WIDE-RANGING → 1650
博 EXTENSIVE → 0170
恢 EXTENSIVE → 0436
浩 VAST → 0525
洸 VAST (expanse of water) → 0462
滉 DEEP AND VAST → 0811
曠 SPACIOUS → 1411
闊 BROAD → 4135

洛 0463

▶**KYOTO**
ラク
Ⓒ 洛 luò

◧ 1-3-6

85	Names	U6D1B
氵	S9-3-6	F1912

COMPOUNDS

❶ **KYOTO; capital**

洛中 らくちゅう inside Kyoto; inside the capital
洛外 らくがい outside Kyoto; outside the capital
京洛 けいらく(=きょうらく) capital; Kyoto
上洛する じょうらくする go to Kyoto
入洛する じゅらく(=にゅうらく)する enter Kyoto

❷ name of a river in China

SYNONYMS

❶ **Kansai cities**

阪 OSAKA → 0321
神 Kobe → 1143
京 KYOTO → 2546
洛 KYOTO → 0463

浅 0464

▶**SHALLOW**
セン あさ(い)
Ⓝ 淺 Ⓒ 浅 qiǎn

◧ 1-3-6

85	Jōyō-4	U6D45
氵	S9-3-6	F0847

1 2 3 4 5 6 7 8 9

COMPOUNDS

❶ [original meaning] (not deep) **SHALLOW**

浅海 せんかい shallow sea
深浅 しんせん depth

❷ (lacking profundity) **SHALLOW, superficial**

浅薄 せんぱく shallowness, superficiality, flimsiness
浅学 せんがく superficial knowledge
浅慮 せんりょ indiscretion, imprudence, thoughtlessness
浅才 せんさい lack of ability, incompetence

❸ light-colored, pale

浅紅 せんこう light red
浅緑 せんりょく(=あさみどり) light green

❹ slightly

浅酌低唱する せんしゃくていしょうする get slightly intoxicated and hum a tune

KUN

【あさい 浅い】**SHALLOW; superficial; light, pale; short (day); close (connection); slight (wound)**

浅瀬 あさせ shoal, shallows
浅はかな あさはかな frivolous, thoughtless
浅黒い あさぐろい dark-complexioned, tanned, swarthy
考えの浅い人 かんがえのあさいひと shallow-brained person
会社は創立以来日がまだ浅い かいしゃはそうりついらいひがまだあさい It is not long since the firm was established
春はまだ浅い はるはまだあさい It is still early spring

SYNONYMS

❷ **less in degree**

弱 WEAK → 1499
軽 LIGHT → 1909
微 SLIGHT → 0788
低 LOW → 0082
薄 THIN → 3004
浅 SHALLOW → 0464
仄 FAINT → 3664

❸ **light-colored**

淡 LIGHT → 0640
浅 light → 0464
薄い pale → 3004
鈍- DULL → 2123

洗 0465

▶**WASH**
セン あら(う)
Ⓒ 洗 xǐ xiǎn

◧ 1-3-6

85	Jōyō-6	U6D17
氵	S9-3-6	F1028

1 2 3 4 5 6 7 8 9

COMPOUNDS

● [original meaning] **WASH, clean**

洗浄 せんじょう washing, irrigation

口 土 女 子 山 干 弓 彳 忄 扌 【氵】 犭 阝

洗顔 せんがん washing one's face
洗剤 せんざい detergent, cleanser
洗礼 せんれい baptism
洗面所 せんめんじょ washroom; bathroom
洗面器 せんめんき washbowl, sink
洗濯 せんたく laundering, washing
洗練 せんれん refinement, polishing, elegance
水洗 すいせん flushing, washing

KUN

【あらう 洗う】**WASH, cleanse, bathe, rinse; inquire, probe**
洗い物 あらいもの washing, laundry; dishes to be washed
手洗い てあらい toilet; washstand

SYNONYMS

● **clean and wash**
洗 WASH → 0465
漱 RINSE → 0865
拭 WIPE → 0453
滌 WASH → 0854
濯 RINSE → 0978
浴 BATHE → 0533
浄 cleanse → 0457
粛 PURGE → 4400
清 CLEAR → 0635
払 CLEAR AWAY → 0225
掃 SWEEP → 0611

津 0466

▶**HARBOR**
シン つ
Ⓒ 津 jīn

1-3-6

85	Jōyō	U6D25
氵	S9-3-6	F0527

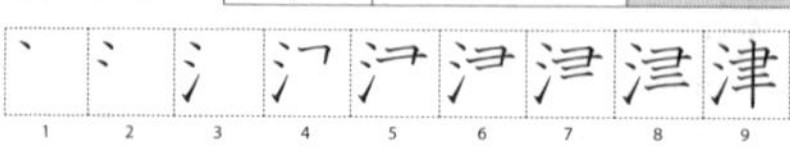

COMPOUNDS

● overflow, be replete
興味津津と きょうみしんしんと of absorbing [great] interest

KUN

【つ 津】*elegant* **HARBOR, ferry**
津津浦浦に つつうらうらに throughout the land, in every harbor and every bay
津波 つなみ tsunami, tidal wave

SYNONYMS

【つ】
○ **places for landing or stopping**
港 PORT → 0737
湊 PORT → 0743
津 HARBOR (*elegant*) → 0466
駅 STATION → 2292
停 stopping place → 0156

洲 0467

▶**SANDBAR**
シュウ す
Ⓒ 洲 zhōu

1-3-6

85	Names	U6D32
氵	S9-3-6	F1678

COMPOUNDS

❶ [original meaning] **SANDBAR**, shallows, shoal
❷ [now replaced by 州 しゅう 0064] continent, state
六大洲 ろくだいしゅう the Six Continents

KUN

【す 洲】[now usu. 州] **SANDBAR, shallows, shoal**
砂洲 さす sandbar, sandbank
座洲する ざすする strand, run aground

SYNONYMS

❶ & 【す】 **elevations in water**
島 ISLAND → 4103
州 sandbar → 0064
礁 REEF → 1588
洲 SANDBAR → 0467

HOMOPHONES

す 州 STATE → 0064

NOTE

➡ see USAGE note at 州 0064

洋 0468

▶**OCEAN**
▶**WESTERN**
ヨウ ㊔ ひろ ひろし
Ⓒ 洋 yáng

1-3-6

85	Jōyō-3	U6D0B
氵	S9-3-6	F0582

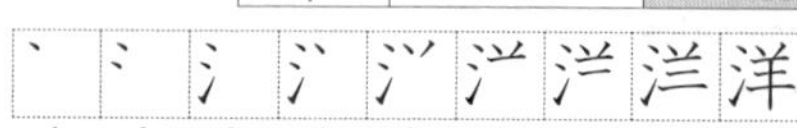

COMPOUNDS

❶ⓐ **OCEAN, sea**
ⓑ suffix after names of **OCEAN**s
ⓒ as wide or vast as the **OCEAN**
a 洋上 ようじょう in the ocean, on the sea
海洋 かいよう ocean, sea
大洋 たいよう ocean
b 太平洋 たいへいよう Pacific Ocean
インド洋 いんどよう Indian Ocean
c 洋洋たる ようようたる vast, boundless
❷ⓐ [also prefix] **WESTERN, European, foreign**
ⓑ **the West, the Occident**
a 洋風 ようふう Western [foreign] style
洋画 ようが foreign film; Western painting
洋服 ようふく (Western) clothes

洋品 ようひん haberdashery
洋裁 ようさい foreign-style dressmaking
洋酒 ようしゅ foreign wine [liquors]
洋式 ようしき Western style
洋室 ようしつ Western-style room
洋間 ようま Western-style room
洋食 ようしょく Western cooking, European dish
洋書 ようしょ foreign [Western] book
b 西洋 せいよう the West, the Occident
❸ abbrev. of 洋間 ようま: **WESTERN**-style room
和洋 わよう Japanese- and Western-style rooms

INDEPENDENT

【よう 洋】half of the world, eastern or **WESTERN** hemisphere
洋の東西を問わず ようのとうざいをとわず both in the Occident and the Orient, in all parts of the world

SYNONYMS

❶ⓐ & ❶ⓑ sea
海 SEA → 0459
洋 OCEAN → 0468
沖 OFFING → 0307
灘 OPEN SEA → 1006
❷ west
洋 WESTERN → 0468
西 the West → 4333

派

▶SECT
▶DISPATCH
ハ

0469
◧ 1-3-6

85	Nonstandard	U6D3E
氵	S9-3-6	F0000

traditional form → see 派 at 0456

流

▶FLOW
▶CURRENT
▶STYLE
リュウ ル なが(れる) なが(れ) なが(す) -なが(す)

0470
◧ 1-3-6

85	Nonstandard	U6D41
氵	S9-3-6	F0000

alternative form → see 流 at 0529

浮

◧ 1-3-6

incorrect stroke-count
➡ see ◧ 1-3-7: 氵 at 0522

独

▶ALONE
▶GERMANY
ドク ひと(り)

0471
◧ 1-3-6

Ⓝ 獨 Ⓒ 独 dú

94	Jōyō-5	U72EC
犭	S9-3-6	F0484

1 2 3 4 5 6 7 8 9

COMPOUNDS

❶ⓐ ALONE, by oneself, single, sole, solo
ⓑ act arbitrarily, act without the advice of others
a 独走 どくそう running alone; easy victory, walkover
独演 どくえん solo recital
独奏する どくそうする play solo, play alone
独立 どくりつ independence, self-reliance
独学 どくがく self-study, self-teaching
独身 どくしん single life; celibacy
独占 どくせん exclusive possession, monopoly
独裁 どくさい dictatorship, autocracy
単独の たんどくの single, independent, sole, lone
孤独の こどくの solitary, lonely, alone
b 独断 どくだん arbitrary decision, dogmatism
独善 どくぜん self-righteousness
❷ⓐ GERMANY
ⓑ German (language)
a 西独 せいどく West Germany
b 独文 どくぶん German literature
和独辞典 わどくじてん Japanese-German dictionary

INDEPENDENT

【どく 独】**GERMANY**

KUN

【ひとり 独り】
ⓐ **ALONE, solitary, by oneself**
ⓑ **single, unmarried**
a 独りぼっちの ひとりぼっちの solitary
独り旅 ひとりたび traveling alone, solitary journey
b 独り者 ひとりもの single [unmarried] man [woman]

SYNONYMS

❶ⓐ alone
独 ALONE → 0471
孤 SOLITARY → 0426
ⓑ acting arbitrarily
横 arbitrary → 1350
独 act arbitrarily → 0471
恣 SELF-INDULGENT → 3281
耽 INDULGE IN → 1665
擅 ARROGATE TO ONESELF → 0947
専 arrogate to oneself → 3272
逞 DO AS ONE PLEASES → 4004

口 土 女 子 巾 干 弓 彳 忄 扌 氵 【犭】 阝

❷ⓐ European countries

英 ENGLAND → 2782
独 GERMANY → 0471
仏 FRANCE → 0020
伊 ITALY → 0052
葡 PORTUGAL → 2902
西 Spain → 4333
蘭 the Netherlands → 3031
希 Greece → 2543
露 Russia → 3495
白 Belgium → 4305

USAGE

【ひとり】

独り
- ⓐ alone, solitary, by oneself
- ⓑ single, unmarried

一人
- ⓐ one person
- ⓑ only (child, son or daughter)

HOMOPHONES

ひとり 一人 → 4148, 4175

狐

▶FOX

コ きつね

N 狐 C 狐 hú

0472

1-3-6

94	Non-Jōyō	U72D0
犭	S9-3-6	F1999

COMPOUNDS

❶ [original meaning] **FOX**

狐狸× こり foxes and raccoon dogs; trickster, deceiver

白狐 びゃっこ spiritual white fox; Arctic fox

❷ distrustful, suspicious

狐疑 こぎ doubt, suspicion; hesitation, indecision

KUN

【きつね 狐】

① [also suffix] **FOX, esp. red fox**

狐狩り きつねがり fox hunting
狐の嫁入り きつねのよめいり sun shower
狐色 きつねいろ light brown
狐猿 きつねざる lemur
雌狐 めぎつね vixen
赤狐 あかぎつね red fox
北極狐 ほっきょくぎつね Arctic fox

② **FOX, sly person**

古狐 ふるぎつね sly old fox, old schemer

③ abbrev. of 狐うどん きつねうどん or 狐蕎麦 きつねそば: noodles in broth topped with fried bean curd

SYNONYMS

❶ undomesticated mammals

虎 TIGER → 3981
猿 MONKEY → 0824
鯨 WHALE → 2361
犀 RHINOCEROS → 3900
狼 WOLF → 0541
狐 FOX → 0472
羚 SEROW → 1695
鼠 RAT → 3340
獅 LION → 0825
豹 LEOPARD → 1847
熊 BEAR → 3530
象 ELEPHANT → 2647
麒 MALE CHINESE UNICORN → 2363
麟 FEMALE CHINESE UNICORN → 2376
猪 WILD BOAR → 0652
鹿 DEER → 3879

狭

▶NARROW

キョウ せま(い) せば(める) せば(まる)

N 狹 C 狭 xiá

0473

1-3-6

94	Jōyō	U72ED
犭	S9-3-6	F1259

1	2	3	4	5	6	7	8	9
ノ	犭	犭	犭	犭	犭	狂	狭	狭

COMPOUNDS

ⓐ [original meaning] **NARROW, constricted**

ⓑ (of limited scope) **NARROW, limited, restricted**

ⓒ **NARROW**, contract

a 狭小な きょうしょうな narrow, cramped, small-sized
狭窄 きょうさく stricture, stenosis
広狭 こうきょう width and narrowness, width

b 狭量な きょうりょうな narrow-minded
狭義 きょうぎ narrow meaning
偏狭な へんきょうな narrow-minded, intolerant; parochial

c 狭心症 きょうしんしょう angina pectoris

KUN

【せまい 狭い】 **NARROW, small, tight;** (of limited scope) **narrow (minded), limited, restricted**

狭苦しい せまくるしい narrow and close, cramped
狭き門 せまきもん narrow gate; school [position] hard to enter [get]
狭い部屋 せまいへや small room
視野の狭い しやのせまい narrow-minded, short-sighted

【せばめる 狭める】 *vt* **NARROW, contract, reduce**

範囲を狭める はんいをせばめる narrow down the range

【せばまる 狭まる】 *vi* **become NARROW, narrow, contract**

視界が狭まった しかいがせばまった Visibility became poor

SYNONYMS

● **narrow**

狭 NARROW → 0473
窄 NARROW → 2830

狩

0474

◧ 1-3-6

▸HUNT

シュ か(る) か(り) -が(り)

Ⓒ 狩 shòu

94	Jōyō	U72E9
犭	S9-3-6	F1690

COMPOUNDS

❶ [original meaning] **HUNT**

狩猟 しゅりょう hunting, hunt
狩猟期 しゅりょうき hunting season

❷ [archaic] Imperial visit to the countryside

巡狩 じゅんしゅ Imperial visit

KUN

【かる 狩る】 **HUNT**

狩人 かりゅうど hunter
狩り込み かりこみ roundup
狩り出す かりだす hunt out, round up
狩り集める かりあつめる muster, gather

【かり 狩り】 **HUNTing, hunt, chase**

狩りに行く かりにいく go hunting

【-がり -狩り】 [also suffix]

① **HUNTing; roundup**

熊狩り くまがり bear hunting
暴力団狩り ぼうりょくだんがり roundup of gangsters

② **gathering (fruits)**

葡萄狩り ぶどうがり grape picking
潮干狩り しおひがり shell gathering (at low tide)

③ viewing

紅葉狩り もみじがり viewing autumn leaves

SYNONYMS

❶ hunt and fish

猟 HUNTING → 0654
狩 HUNT → 0474
獲 CATCH GAME → 0959
漁 FISH → 0856
釣 ANGLE → 2108
弋 CATCH → 4230

HOMOPHONES

かる

刈 CLIP → 0032

駆 DRIVE → 2293

NOTE

➡ see USAGE note at 刈 0032

狐

◧ 1-3-6

incorrect stroke-count
➡ see ◧ 1-3-5: 犭 at 0407

限

0475

◧ 1-3-6

▸LIMIT

ゲン かぎ(る) かぎ(り) -かぎ(り)

Ⓒ 限 xiàn

170	Jōyō-5	U9650
阝	S9-3-6	F0523

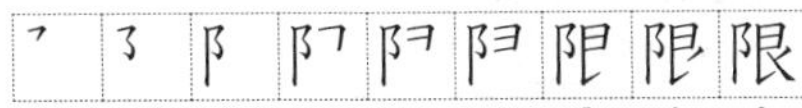

COMPOUNDS

❶ⓐ [original meaning] **LIMIT, set a limit, restrict**
ⓑ [also suffix] **LIMIT, bounds**

a 限定する げんていする limit, restrict, define
制限する せいげんする restrict, limit
局限する きょくげんする localize, limit, set limits to
時限爆弾 じげんばくだん time bomb

b 限度 げんど limit, bounds
限界 げんかい boundary, limit, bounds
期限 きげん time limit, term
上限 じょうげん upper limit, maximum
権限 けんげん power, authority; competence (of law)
門限 もんげん closing-time, lockup
無限の むげんの infinite, endless, unfathomable
最小限 さいしょうげん minimum

❷ [suffix] period, hour (in school)

第一限 だいいちげん first period

KUN

【かぎる 限る】 **LIMIT, restrict (to); be the best, be the only way**

日を限る ひをかぎる put a time-limit on
. . . とは限らない …とはかぎらない be not always [necessarily]…
その手に限る そのてにかぎる That's the best way

【かぎり 限り】 **LIMIT, limits, bound; as far (much) as possible**

限り無い かぎりない unlimited, limitless
限り有る かぎりある limited, finite
出来る限り できるかぎり as far as possible

【-かぎり -限り】 [suffix] **insofar as, this time only**

今度限り こんどかぎり for this once only

SYNONYMS

❶ⓐ restrain

制 CONTROL (restrain) → 1624

禁 PROHIBIT → 3469
限 LIMIT → 0475
抑 SUPPRESS → 0301
束 TIE UP → 4369
縛 BIND → 1779
控える HOLD BACK → 0600
扣える HOLD BACK → 0250
渋る hang [hold] back → 0625
ⓑ extreme
極 EXTREME → 1243
窮 extremity → 2983
限 LIMIT → 0475
涯 OUTER LIMITS → 0623
果て end → 4377

降

0476
1-3-6

▸DESCEND
コウ　ゴウ　お(りる)　お(ろす)　ふ(る)　ふ(り)　くだ(る)　くだ(す)

170	Nonstandard	U964D
阝	S9-3-6	F0000

traditional form → see 降 at 0548

唄

0477
1-3-7

▸DITTY
バイ▲　うた　うた(う)▲
Ⓒ 呗 bài bei

30	Jōyō	U5504
口	S10-3-7	F1950

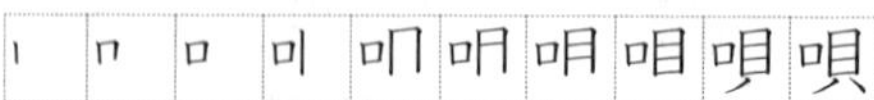
1 2 3 4 5 6 7 8 9 10

COMPOUNDS

● song in praise of Buddha's virtues
梵×唄 ぼんばい song in praise of Buddha's virtues

KUN

【うた 唄】[usu. 歌] [also suffix] **DITTY, song, ballad**—used esp. in reference to traditional Japanese songs
小唄 こうた ditty, ballad
子守唄 こもりうた lullaby
鼻唄 はなうた humming

【うたう 唄う】[usu. 歌う] **recite, sing**—used esp. in reference to traditional Japanese songs

SYNONYMS

【うた】
○ music and songs
楽 MUSIC → 3505
音 sound of music → 2570
節 tune → 3336
調べ melody → 1973
曲 MUSICAL COMPOSITION → 4340
歌 SONG → 2296
謡 POPULAR SONG → 2011
唄 DITTY → 0477

HOMOPHONES

うた 歌 SONG → 2296
うたう
歌 SONG → 2296
謡 POPULAR SONG → 2011
謳 EXTOL → 2061

NOTE

➡ see USAGE note at 歌 2296

哺

0478
1-3-7

▸NURSE
ホ
Ⓒ 哺 bǔ

30	Jōyō	U54FA
口	S10-3-7	F2945

1 2 3 4 5 6 7 8 9 10

COMPOUNDS

❶ [now also 保 0107] **NURSE, suckle**
哺乳類 ほにゅうるい Mammalia
哺乳瓶 ほにゅうびん baby bottle
哺育(=保育)する ほいくする nurture, bring up; suckle, nurse
反哺 はんぽ caring for one's parents in return
❷ food in one's mouth
握髪吐哺 あくはつとほ making extraordinary efforts to find and employ capable [wise] persons (said esp. of a statesman)

SYNONYMS

❶ raise and nourish
育 RAISE → 2544
飼 RAISE ANIMALS → 2149
養 FOSTER → 2998
滋 NOURISH → 0734
哺 NURSE → 0478
牧 PASTURE → 1083

哩

0479
1-3-7

▸MILE
リ　まいる
Ⓒ 哩 lī lǐ li

30	Names	U54E9
口	S10-3-7	F0000

COMPOUNDS

● used phonetically for *ri*
伽哩 かりー curry

KUN

【まいる 哩】**MILE**
海底二万哩 かいていにまんまいる 20000 Leagues Under the Sea

SYNONYMS

【まいる】
○ length units
寸 *sun* (3.03 cm) →3652
浬 NAUTICAL MILE (1852 m) →0526
反 *tan* (10.6 m) →3663
尺 *SHAKU* (30.3 cm) →4248
米 meter →4342
尋 fathom (1.8 m) →2918
間 *ken* (1.8 m) →4122
丈 *jo* (3.03 m) →4227
町 *cho* (109 m) →1430
里 LEAGUE, *ri* (3.9 km) →4356
哩 MILE (1609 m) →0479

唆 0480

▶INSTIGATE
サ そそのか(す)
Ⓒ 唆 suō
1-3-7

30	Jōyō	U5506
口	S10-3-7	F2260

Stroke order: 1–10

COMPOUNDS

● [original meaning] **INSTIGATE, incite, abet**
教唆 きょうさ instigation, incitement
示唆する しさする suggest, hint

KUN

【そそのかす 唆す】**INSTIGATE, egg on, abet, incite**
唆し そそのかし instigation
人に悪事を唆す ひとにあくじをそそのかす entice a person to do something wrong

SYNONYMS

● **incite**
挑 PROVOKE →0445
唆 INSTIGATE →0480
扇 FAN →2449
煽 FAN →1338
激 excite →0955
奮 ROUSE UP →3000
振 arouse to action →0515
動 MOVE →2232
起 rise to action →4099

哨 0481

▶SENTRY
ショウ
Ⓝ 哨 Ⓒ 哨 shào
1-3-7

30	Names	U54E8
口	S10-3-7	F2824

COMPOUNDS

● **SENTRY, watch, guard**
哨戒 しょうかい patrol, patrolling
哨戒機 しょうかいき patrol aircraft
哨兵 しょうへい sentry
哨舎 しょうしゃ sentry box
前哨 ぜんしょう outpost
前哨戦 ぜんしょうせん preliminary skirmish; prelude, run-up
歩哨 ほしょう sentry

SPECIAL READINGS

哨吶× さない *suona*, Chinese shawm
哨吶× ちゃるめら street vendor's flute

SYNONYMS

● **guard**
哨 SENTRY →0481
衛 GUARD →0938
守 guard →2697
警 guard →3595

啄 0482

▶PECK
タク トク ついば(む)
Ⓝ 啄 Ⓒ 啄 zhuó
1-3-7

30	Names	U5544
口	S10-3-7	F0000

COMPOUNDS

● **PECK, pick**
啄木 たくぼく *literary* woodpecker

KUN

【ついばむ 啄む】**PECK, pick**
虫を啄む むしをついばむ (of a bird) pick at a worm

SYNONYMS

● & 【ついばむ】 **ingest**
喫 INGEST →0668
服 take →1090
食 EAT →2578
喰う EAT →0670
飲 DRINK →2127
呑 SWALLOW →3059
啄 PECK →0482

● **bite**
噛 BITE →0988
啄 PECK →0482

哨 0483

▶SENTRY
ショウ
1-3-7

30	Nonstandard	U54E8
口	S10-3-7	F0000

traditional form →see 哨 at 0481

埋

▶BURY

マイ う(める) う(まる) う(もれる)
うず(める)▲ うず(まる)▲ い(ける)▲

0484

1-3-7

Ⓒ 埋 mái mán

32	Jōyō	U57CB
土	S10-3-7	F1194

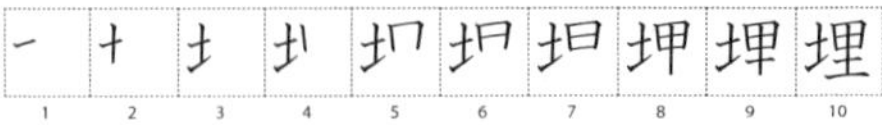

COMPOUNDS

● [original meaning] **BURY, embed**

埋葬 まいそう burial, interment
埋蔵物 まいぞうぶつ buried treasure
埋没する まいぼつする be buried; fall into oblivion
埋線 まいせん underground cable
埋設する まいせつする put [lay] underground

KUN

【うめる 埋める】*vt* **BURY, embed; fill up; make up for**

埋め立てる うめたてる reclaim, fill in
埋め立て うめたて reclamation (of land)
埋め合わせる うめあわせる make amends, compensate for
土に埋める つちにうめる bury in the ground
生き埋め いきうめ being buried alive
穴埋めする あなうめする fill a gap, make up a loss

【うまる 埋まる】*vi* **be filled up, be buried under, be embedded**

雪に埋まった小道 ゆきにうまったこみち lane buried deep in snow

【うもれる 埋もれる】*vi* **be buried, be buried in oblivion, live in obscurity**

埋もれ木 うもれぎ bogwood

【うずめる 埋める】*vt* **BURY**

骨を埋める ほねをうずめる die in (a foreign land)

【うずまる 埋まる】*vi* **be filled up (with)**

花で埋まる はなでうずまる be filled up with flowers

【いける 埋ける】**BURY**; bury coals in ashes

SYNONYMS

● **bury**

埋 BURY → 0484
葬 bury (a corpse) → 2910

HOMOPHONES

いける

生 LIFE → 4309
活 ACTIVE → 0460

NOTE

➡ see USAGE note at 生 4309

城

▶CASTLE

ジョウ しろ き* ㊔ ぐすく ぐしく なり くに

0485

1-3-7

32	Nonstandard	U2F852
土	S10-3-7	F0000

traditional form → see 城 at 0417

娩

▶GIVE BIRTH

ベン

0486

1-3-7

Ⓝ 娩 Ⓒ 娩 miǎn

38	Names	U5A29
女	S10-3-7	F3287

COMPOUNDS

● **GIVE BIRTH (to), deliver, bear**

娩出する べんしゅつする give birth, deliver
分娩 ぶんべん delivery, childbirth
擬娩 ぎべん couvade

SYNONYMS

● **give birth**

生 BE BORN → 4309
誕 BE BORN → 1987
産 GIVE BIRTH → 4089
娩 GIVE BIRTH → 0486
殖 MULTIPLY → 1253

娯

▶ENJOYMENT

ゴ

0487

1-3-7

Ⓝ 娯 Ⓒ 娱 yú

38	Jōyō	U5A2F
女	S10-3-7	F2390

COMPOUNDS

ⓐ **ENJOYMENT, amusement, merriment, pleasure**
ⓑ [original meaning] enjoy [amuse] oneself, be merry; amuse, give pleasure to

a 娯楽 ごらく amusement, pastime
娯楽街 ごらくがい amusement quarter
娯楽室 ごらくしつ recreation room

SYNONYMS

ⓐ **pleasure**

楽 PLEASURE → 3505
娯 ENJOYMENT → 0487
興 AMUSEMENT → 3622
玩 TAKE PLEASURE IN → 1085

娘

▶DAUGHTER
▶GIRL
ジョウ▲ むすめ こ▲

Ⓒ 娘 niáng

0488

◧1-3-7

38	Jōyō	U5A18
女	S10-3-7	F0612

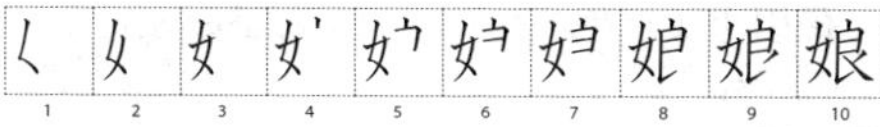

COMPOUNDS

● [original meaning] **GIRL,** beautiful maiden
娘子軍 じょうしぐん Amazons, Amazonian troops

KUN

【むすめ 娘】
① **DAUGHTER**
一人娘 ひとりむすめ only daughter
② [also suffix] **GIRL, maiden**
娘心 むすめごころ girlish innocence
小娘 こむすめ young girl, lass
箱入り娘 はこいりむすめ innocent [naive] girl of a good family
花売り娘 はなうりむすめ flower girl
【こ 娘】 [also 子 or コ] **GIRL,** gal
良い娘だ いいこだ She's a nice [good-looking] girl [gal]

SYNONYMS

【むすめ】
① **offspring**
子 CHILD → 4196
仔 OFFSPRING → 0038
孤 orphan → 0426
嫡 LEGITIMATE CHILD → 0839
息 son → 3278
男 son → 3147
惣 eldest son → 3452
娘 DAUGHTER → 0488
女 daughter → 4226
姫 DAUGHTER OF NOBLE BIRTH → 0489
② **woman**
女 WOMAN → 4226
婦 ADULT WOMAN → 0565
婆 OLD WOMAN → 3433
嬢 YOUNG LADY → 0936
娘 GIRL → 0488
雌 FEMALE → 1337
牝 FEMALE → 1020
媛 DAMSEL → 0688

HOMOPHONES

こ
子 CHILD → 4196
児 CHILD → 3153
仔 OFFSPRING → 0038
小 SMALL → 0007

NOTE

➡ see USAGE note at 子 4196

姫

▶DAUGHTER OF NOBLE BIRTH
キ▲ ひめ ひめ-

Ⓝ 姫 Ⓒ 姬 jī

0489

◧1-3-7

38	Jōyō	U59EB
女	S10-3-7	F1308

COMPOUNDS

❶ concubine, mistress (of a nobleman)
寵姫 ちょうき one's favorite mistress
❷ charming girl
美姫 びき beautiful maiden, beauty

KUN

【ひめ 姫】
①ⓐ **DAUGHTER [young lady] OF NOBLE [gentle] BIRTH, princess**
ⓑ [sometimes also 媛] **courtesy title after names of young ladies of noble birth**
a 姫君 ひめぎみ princess, highborn young lady
姫様 ひめさま daughter of a nobleman
姫宮 ひめみや princess
b 千姫 せんひめ Princess Sen
シンデレラ姫 しんでれらひめ Cinderella
② [sometimes also 媛] *elegant* **girl, charming girl**
歌姫 うたひめ songstress, chanteuse
舞姫 まいひめ dancing girl, dancer
【ひめ- 姫-】 [prefix] **small, little, pretty**
姫小松 ひめこまつ small pine

SYNONYMS

【ひめ】
① **offspring**
子 CHILD → 4196
仔 OFFSPRING → 0038
孤 orphan → 0426
嫡 LEGITIMATE CHILD → 0839
息 son → 3278
男 son → 3147
惣 eldest son → 3452
娘 DAUGHTER → 0488
女 daughter → 4226
姫 DAUGHTER OF NOBLE BIRTH → 0489

USAGE

【ひめ】

姫

①ⓐ daughter [young lady] of noble [gentle] birth, princess

ⓑ [sometimes also 媛] courtesy title after names of young ladies of noble birth

② [sometimes also 媛] *elegant* girl, charming girl

媛

[now usu. 姫]

① *elegant* damsel, beautiful young lady

② courtesy title after names of young ladies of noble birth

HOMOPHONES

ひめ 媛 DAMSEL → 0688

娠

0490

1-3-7

▶**CONCEIVE**

シン

Ⓒ 娠 shēn

38	Jōyō	U5A20
女	S10-3-7	F1961

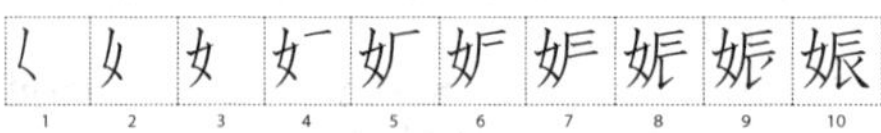

COMPOUNDS

● [original meaning] **CONCEIVE, become pregnant**

妊娠 にんしん pregnancy, conception

SYNONYMS

● **conceive**

妊 BECOME PREGNANT → 0281

娠 CONCEIVE → 0490

娯

0491

1-3-7

▶**ENJOYMENT**

ゴ

38	Nonstandard	U5A1B
女	S10-3-7	F0000

traditional form → see 娯 at 0487

孫

0492

1-3-7

▶**GRANDCHILD**

ソン まご

Ⓒ 孙 sūn

39	Jōyō-4	U5B6B
子	S10-3-7	F1000

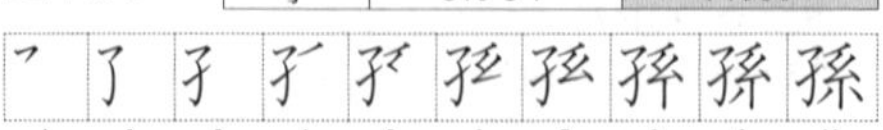

COMPOUNDS

❶ [original meaning] **GRANDCHILD**

皇孫 こうそん Imperial grandchild

嫡孫 ちゃくそん heir of the eldest son

王孫 おうそん royal grandson

❷ **descendant**

子孫 しそん descendant, offspring

天孫 てんそん descendant of a god

KUN

【まご 孫】 **GRANDCHILD;** [in compounds] **secondary**

孫娘 まごむすめ granddaughter

孫弟子 まごでし disciples of one's disciples

孫引き まごびき reference to secondary sources

SYNONYMS

❶ & ❷ **descendant**

孫 GRANDCHILD, descendant → 0492

胤 PROGENY → 0017

末 posterity → 4317

峨

0493

1-3-7

▶**HIGH AND RUGGED**

ガ

Ⓝ 峩 Ⓒ 峨 é

46	Names	U5CE8
山	S10-3-7	F2470

COMPOUNDS

● **HIGH AND RUGGED, precipitous**

峨峨たる ががたる rugged, precipitous

SYNONYMS

● **high**

高 HIGH → 2601

喬 TALL → 3129

峻 high and steep → 0495

峨 HIGH AND RUGGED → 0493

峰

0494

1-3-7

▶**PEAK**

ホウ みね ㊔ お

Ⓝ 峯 Ⓒ 峰 fēng

46	Jōyō	U5CF0
山	S10-3-7	F1368

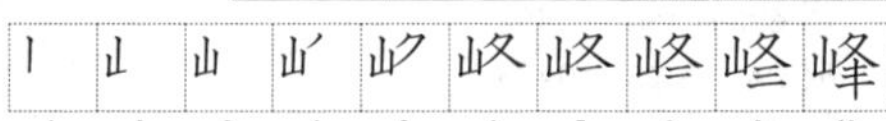

COMPOUNDS

ⓐ [also suffix] (mountain with pointed summit) **PEAK, high mountain**

ⓑ [original meaning] (pointed summit of a mountain) **PEAK, summit, mountaintop**

a 峰頭 ほうとう [rare] summit of a peak

主峰 しゅほう main peak

連峰 れんぽう mountain range, series of mountain peaks

未踏峰 みとうほう unclimbed mountain

b 高峰 こうほう lofty peak, high mountain

最高峰 さいこうほう highest peak; highest authority

KUN

【みね 峰】 [sometimes also 嶺]

①ⓐ (summit or vicinity of a summit) **PEAK, summit, ridge**
ⓑ **high mountain**
a 峰峰 みねみね peaks
峰伝いに みねづたいに along the ridges
ab 峰続き みねつづき succession of peaks
② **back of a sword**
峰打ち みねうち striking with the back of a sword

SYNONYMS

ⓐ mountains
峰 PEAK →0494
岳 HIGH MOUNTAIN →3164
山 MOUNTAIN →3658

ⓑ mountain parts
頂 SUMMIT →0164
峰 PEAK →0494
嶺 RIDGE →3013
峠 MOUNTAIN PASS →0428
崖 CLIFF →2862
壁 wall-like structure →3601

USAGE

【みね】
峰
[sometimes also 嶺]
①ⓐ (summit or vicinity of a summit) peak, summit, ridge
ⓑ high mountain
② back of a sword
嶺
[usu. 峰] same as 峰

HOMOPHONES

みね 嶺 RIDGE →3013

峻

0495
◧ 1-3-7

▶STERN
シュン ㊔ たかし たか とし たけし
Ⓒ 峻 jùn

46	Names	U5CFB
山	S10-3-7	F2708

COMPOUNDS

[rarely also 駿 2304]

❶ STERN, strict, severe, uncompromising
峻厳な しゅんげんな strict, stern, rigorous, severe
峻拒する しゅんきょする refuse flatly, reject sternly
峻別 しゅんべつ sharp distinction, strict discrimination
峻下剤 しゅんげざい drastic aperient

❷ (esp. of mountains) **high and steep, rising sharply, precipitous, towering, lofty**
峻険な しゅんけんな steep, precipitous
峻嶺 しゅんれい steep peak, high rugged mountain
急峻な きゅうしゅんな steep, sharp

SYNONYMS

❶ strict
厳 strict →4079
酷 SEVERE →1967
辣 SEVERE →1965
峻 STERN →0495

❷ high
高 HIGH →2601
喬 TALL →3129
峻 high and steep →0495
峨 HIGH AND RUGGED →0493

❷ steep
険 STEEP →0658
嶮 STEEP →0937
岨 STEEP →0341
急 steep →2595
峻 high and steep →0495

NOTE

★ do not confuse with 峻 LOFTY →0570

峽

0496
◧ 1-3-7

▶GORGE
キョウ ㊔ はざま

46	Names	U5CFD
山	S10-3-7	F0000

traditional form →see 峡 at 0427

徐

0497
◧ 1-3-7

▶SLOWLY
ジョ おもむ(ろに)▲ ㊔ しずか
Ⓒ 徐 xú

60	Jōyō	U5F90
彳	S10-3-7	F1738

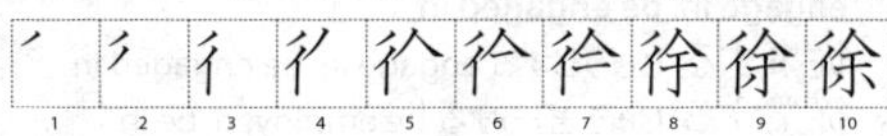

COMPOUNDS

● SLOWLY, gently, quietly
徐徐に じょじょに slowly, gradually
徐行する じょこうする go slowly
緩徐楽章 かんじょがくしょう adagio

KUN

【おもむろに 徐ろに】 **SLOWLY**, quietly; patiently
徐ろに時機を待つ おもむろにじきをまつ wait patiently for an opportunity

SYNONYMS

● slow
徐 SLOWLY →0497
遅 SLOW →3887
緩 SLACK →1757
慢 SLUGGISH →0844

1

従

▸FOLLOW

ジュウ ショウ ジュ したが(う) したが(える)

㊔ より つぐ

N 從 从 C 从 cóng

0498

1-3-7

60	Jōyō-6	U5F93
彳	S10-3-7	F0652

口 土 女 子 山 【彳】 忄 扌 氵 犭 阝 丬 亻 纟 歹

COMPOUNDS

❶ⓐ (go after) **FOLLOW, accompany, attend on**

ⓑ **FOLLOWer, attendant, servant, vassal**

a 従軍する じゅうぐんする follow [join] the army, go to the front

随従する ずいじゅうする follow the lead of, play second fiddle to

追従する ついじゅうする follow, be servile to; imitate

b 従者 じゅうしゃ follower, attendant, squire

従僕 じゅうぼく servant, attendant

主従 しゅじゅう(=しゅうじゅう) master and servant, lord and vassal

侍従 じじゅう chamberlain

❷ (act in accordance with) **FOLLOW (a person's instructions), comply with, obey, observe, submit to**

従順な じゅうじゅんな submissive, obedient, docile

服従する ふくじゅうする obey, submit to

盲従する もうじゅうする follow blindly

屈従 くつじゅう servile submission, subservience

追従 ついしょう flattery, sycophancy

❸ (take up as main work) **FOLLOW an occupation, engage in, be engaged in**

従事する じゅうじする engage in, be engaged in

従業する じゅうぎょうする be employed, be in service

専従者 せんじゅうしゃ full time worker

❹ⓐ [also prefix] **subordinate, second grade, secondary**

ⓑ accessory

a 従属する じゅうぞくする be subordinate, depend

従的な じゅうてきな subordinate, secondary

従節 じゅうせつ subordinate clause

従三位 じゅさんみ second grade of the third rank of honor

従因 じゅういん secondary cause

b 従犯 じゅうはん participation in crime, accessory

従物 じゅうぶつ accessory (thing)

❺ **next in kin**

従兄 じゅうけい(=いとこ) older cousin

❻ **since, from**

従来の じゅうらいの former, old, existing

従前の じゅうぜんの previous, former

❼ in proportion to, in accordance

従価税 じゅうかぜい *ad valorem* duty

❽ lax, easy

従容たる しょうようたる composed, calm, tranquil

❾ from north to south

合従 がっしょう alliance of states against a powerful enemy

INDEPENDENT

【じゅう 従】 subordinate, secondary; vassal, attendant

従たる じゅうたる secondary, subordinate, incidental, junior, accessory

KUN

【したがう 従う】

①ⓐ (go after) **FOLLOW, accompany, attend on**

ⓑ [in the form of 従って したがって] (result as a consequence) **FOLLOW, result in**

a 付き従う つきしたがう follow, accompany

b 従って したがって therefore, consequently, accordingly

②ⓐ **FOLLOW (a person's advice), obey, abide by, conform to; follow (a precedent)**

ⓑ **comply with, accede to**

a 忠告に従う ちゅうこくにしたがう follow [act upon] advice

b ...に従って …にしたがって in accordance with...; in proportion to...

③ **yield to, submit**

征服者に従う せいふくしゃにしたがう submit to a conqueror

【したがえる 従える】 **be attended by, take along; conquer, subjugate**

家来二人従えて けらいふたりしたがえて attended by two retainers

SYNONYMS

❶ⓐ **follow and pursue**

従 FOLLOW →0498

随 FOLLOW →0765

辿る FOLLOW (a path) →3968

追 CHASE →3840

❶ⓐ **accompany**

伴 ACCOMPANY →0068

添 accompany →0641

陪 ACCOMPANY A SUPERIOR →0655

侍 ATTEND UPON →0094

従 FOLLOW →0498

随 FOLLOW →0765

ⓑ **servants**

僕 MANSERVANT →0185

奴 SLAVE →0217

隷 UNDERLING →2201

臣 RETAINER →3806
従 follower →0498
供 attendant →0098

❷ **obey**
守 observe →2697
遵 OBEY →3929
順 OBEY →0018
隷 be subordinate to →2201
従 FOLLOW →0498

❹ⓐ **subordinate**
副 SECONDARY →2230
次 secondary →0058
従 subordinate →0498
亜 SUB- →4354
準 QUASI- →3541
半 semi- →4313
准 JUNIOR →0143
助 assistant →1440

NOTE
★ do not confuse with 徒 FOLLOWER →0499

徒 0499

◧ 1-3-7

▸**FOLLOWER**
ト いたずら▲ あだ▲
Ⓒ 徒 tú

60	Jōyō-4	U5F92
彳	S10-3-7	F1006

Stroke order: 1–10

COMPOUNDS
❶ [also suffix] (adherent) **FOLLOWER, believer, disciple, pupil**
信徒 しんと believer, devotee; the faithful
十二使徒 じゅうにしと the Twelve Apostles
学徒 がくと student, follower
生徒 せいと pupil, student
仏教徒 ぶっきょうと Buddhist

❷ⓐ **fellows, companions, gang, party**
ⓑ **fellow, person**
a 徒党 ととう clique, faction, conspirators
暴徒 ぼうと rioters, mobsters, insurgents
b 博徒 ばくと gambler

❸ⓐ vain, futile, wasted, worthless
ⓑ empty, empty-handed
a 徒労 とろう vain effort, lost labor
徒食 としょく idle life
b 徒手体操 としゅたいそう free-standing exercises

❹ [original meaning] **go on foot, walk, run**
徒歩 とほ walking, going on foot
徒競走 ときょうそう foot race

❺ punish, sentence to labor
徒刑 とけい penal servitude
囚徒 しゅうと prisoner, convict

INDEPENDENT
【と 徒】 party, gang, set; **FOLLOWER**, disciple
無頼の徒 ぶらいのと gang of rowdies
学問の徒 がくもんのと student, scholar

KUN
【いたずら 徒】 uselessness, idleness
徒に いたずらに in vain, uselessly, aimlessly, idly
【あだ 徒】 [in compounds] vain, empty, fruitless; ephemeral; fickle, frivolous
徒な あだな vain, futile
徒桜 あだざくら ephemeral cherry blossom
徒し心 あだしごころ fickle heart

SYNONYMS
❶ **students and followers**
生 STUDENT →4309
卒 graduate student →2549
学 scholar →3162
門 pupil →1100
弟 disciple →2537
徒 FOLLOWER →0499

❷ **fellow**
奴 GUY →0217
漢 FELLOW →0808
輩 FELLOW (*belittling*) →3482
徒 fellows →0499
棒 tough guy →1237
坊 COLLOQUIAL PERSON SUFFIX →0274
屋 colloquial person suffix →3842
物 character →1084

❸ⓐ **vain**
空 EMPTY →2767
虚 without substance →4017
徒 vain →0499

❹ **walk**
歩 WALK →3071
徒 go on foot →0499
脚 move on foot →1226
足 travel on foot →2714
踏 TREAD →1997

HOMOPHONES
いたずら 悪戯 →3413, 2351

NOTE
➡ see USAGE note at 戯 2351
★ do not confuse with 従 FOLLOW →0498

徑 0500

1-3-7

▶**PATH**
▶**DIAMETER**
ケイ ㊔ みち

60	Nonstandard	U5F91
彳	S10-3-7	F0000

traditional form → see 径 at 0347

悦 0501

1-3-7

▶**DELIGHTED**
エツ よろこ(ぶ)▲ **よろこ(ばす)**▲ ㊔ よし のぶ
Ⓝ 悅 Ⓒ 悦 yuè

61	Jōyō	U60A6
忄	S10-3-7	F1739

COMPOUNDS

ⓐ [original meaning] **DELIGHTED, pleased, happy**
ⓑ [archaic] please, delight, make happy

a 悦楽 えつらく pleasure, joy
喜悦 きえつ delight, rapture, joy
満悦 まんえつ great joy, rapture
愉悦 ゆえつ joy
法悦 ほうえつ religious exultation; ecstasy

INDEPENDENT

【えつ 悦】 delight, joy, rapture
一人悦に入る ひとりえつにいる chuckle with delight, be pleased with oneself

KUN

【よろこぶ 悦ぶ】 [now usu. 喜ぶ] *vi* be happy [glad], be **DELIGHTED**
悦び よろこび [now usu. 喜び] joy, delight
悦ばしい よろこばしい joyful, delightful, gratifying

【よろこばす 悦ばす】 [now usu. 喜ばす] *vt* please, gladden, make happy
親を悦ばす おやをよろこばす make one's parents happy
目を悦ばす めをよろこばす feast one's eyes (on)

SYNONYMS

ⓐ **pleased and pleasant**
楽 pleasurable → 3505
欣 JOYFUL → 1057
爽 REFRESHING → 4402
快 PLEASANT → 0289
朗 CHEERFUL → 1679
愉 PLEASED → 0710
悦 DELIGHTED → 0501
嬉しい GLAD → 0890
喜 HAPPY → 2889
歓 JOYOUS → 2342
驩 JOYOUS → 2333

HOMOPHONES

よろこぶ 喜 HAPPY → 2889
よろこび
喜 HAPPY → 2889
慶 FELICITATION → 3936
よろこばす 喜 HAPPY → 2889

NOTE

➡ see USAGE note at 喜 2889

悟 0502

1-3-7

▶**AWAKE TO**
ゴ さと(る) ㊔ さとし
Ⓒ 悟 wù

61	Jōyō	U609F
忄	S10-3-7	F1225

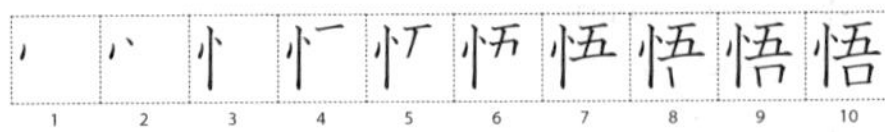

COMPOUNDS

❶ⓐ **AWAKE TO, become aware of, realize, comprehend**
ⓑ become aware of one's sins, repent

a 悟了 ごりょう complete comprehension
覚悟する かくごする be ready [prepared] for; be resigned; make up one's mind
b 悔悟 かいご repentance, remorse

❷ⓐ **AWAKE TO the Truth, become enlightened, attain satori**
ⓑ spiritual awakening, enlightenment, satori

a 悟道 ごどう spiritual enlightenment; philosophy; (Buddhist) enlightenment
b 悟入する ごにゅうする enter (Buddhist) enlightenment

❸ wisdom, intelligence, reason
悟性 ごせい wisdom, reason
大悟 たいご great wisdom

KUN

【さとる 悟る】
① **be spiritually awakened, attain (Buddhist) enlightenment [satori]**
悟り さとり satori, spiritual awakening
② [formerly 覚る] **AWAKE TO**, be aware of, perceive, discern, realize
悟り さとり satori, spiritual awakening; [formerly 覚り] comprehension, understanding
悟りが早い さとりがはやい be quick to understand

SYNONYMS

❶ⓐ **know and understand**
知 KNOW → 1446
通 know thoroughly → 3855
得 gain understanding of → 0577
分かる understand → 2466
解 understand → 1913

諒 UNDERSTAND → 1982
了 COMPREHEND → 4157
悟 AWAKE TO → 0502
惺 AWAKE TO → 0709

❶ⓐ & ❷ⓐ awake

悟 AWAKE TO → 0502
醒 AWAKE → 2033
覚 awake → 3217
惺 AWAKE TO → 0709

USAGE

❶【さとる】

悟る
① be spiritually awakened, attain (Buddhist) enlightenment [satori]
② [formerly 覚る] awake to, be aware of, perceive, discern, realize

覚る
[now usu. 悟る] awake to, be aware of, perceive, discern, realize

❷【さとり】

悟り
① satori, spiritual awakening
② [formerly 覚り] comprehension, understanding

覚り
[now usu. 悟り] comprehension, understanding

HOMOPHONES

さとる 覚 PERCEIVE → 3217
さとり 覚 PERCEIVE → 3217

悖

▶GO AGAINST

ハイ もと(る)

Ⓒ 悖 bèi

0503

◧ 1-3-7

61 忄	Non-Jōyō	U6096
	S10-3-7	F0000

COMPOUNDS

● [now replaced by 背 3182] **GO AGAINST**, be contrary to

悖徳 はいとく immorality, corruption, lapse from virtue

KUN

【もとる 悖る】**GO AGAINST, deviate from**

SYNONYMS

● violate

違 VIOLATE → 3907
破 BREAK → 1478
犯 offend against → 0229
反 act contrary to → 3663
悖 GO AGAINST → 0503
背 go against → 3182

悩

▶SUFFER

ノウ なや(む) なや(ます)

Ⓝ 惱 Ⓒ 恼 nǎo

0504

◧ 1-3-7

61 忄	Jōyō	U60A9
	S10-3-7	F1148

1	2	3	4	5	6	7	8	9	10
丶	忄	忄	忄	忄	忄	悩	悩	悩	悩

COMPOUNDS

ⓐ [original meaning] **SUFFER, be distressed**
ⓑ cause **SUFFER**ing, afflict
ⓒ SUFFERing, distress, pain, trouble, affliction

a 悩乱 のうらん worry, anguish
懊×悩 おうのう agony, anguish, trouble
b 悩殺する のうさつする fascinate, enchant
c 苦悩 くのう suffering, distress, anguish
煩悩 ぼんのう worldly desires, carnal desires

KUN

【なやむ 悩む】*vi* **be troubled, be worried; SUFFER, be distressed**

悩み なやみ troubles, worries, suffering, anguish
悩ましい なやましい distressful, full of cares and vexations; seductive, alluring
伸び悩む のびなやむ be held in check, fail to grow

【なやます 悩ます】*vt* **afflict, torment; trouble, annoy, harass**

頭を悩ます あたまをなやます rack one's brains

SYNONYMS

● trouble and suffering

困 BE IN TROUBLE → 3808
苛 torment → 2786
窮 BE IN EXTREMITY → 2983
悶 BE IN AGONY → 4119
悩 SUFFER → 0504
苦 SUFFERING → 2789
痛 PAIN → 4071
辛 HARD → 2531
煩 VEXED → 1295
難 DIFFICULT → 2310

悧

▶CLEVER

リ

Ⓒ 悧 lì

0505

◧ 1-3-7

61 忄	Non-Jōyō	U60A7
	S10-3-7	F3288

COMPOUNDS

● [now also 利 1431] **sharp, keen, CLEVER**

悧巧(=利口)な りこうな clever, bright, sharp, shrewd
怜悧(=伶俐) れいり cleverness, sagacity

SYNONYMS

● **intelligent and wise**

賢 WISE → 3518
俊 brilliant → 0117
鋭 SHARP → 2171
敏 NIMBLE → 1675
叡 PROFOUNDLY WISE → 2405
智 wise → 3458
慧 INTELLIGENT → 3485
怜 CLEVER → 0356
悧 CLEVER → 0505
俐 CLEVER → 0113
哲 SAGACIOUS → 3402
明 clear-sighted → 1060
聡 SHARP-WITTED → 1750

悄

0506

1-3-7

▶ **BECOME DISPIRITED**

ショウ

Ⓒ 悄 qiāo

61	Non-Jōyō	U6084
忄	S10-3-7	F3442

COMPOUNDS

● [now usu. 消 0531] **BECOME DISPIRITED, become disheartened; be worried**

悄然たる しょうぜんたる dejected, dispirited
悄悄と しょうしょうと dejectedly, dispiritedly

SPECIAL READINGS

悄気る しょげる be disheartened, be dispirited

SYNONYMS

● **grieve**

慨 DEPLORE → 0790
嘆 SIGH → 0773
悼 MOURN → 0587
傷 grieve → 0179
悲 feel sad → 3448
悄 BECOME DISPIRITED → 0506

● **sad and depressed**

悲 SAD → 3448
悄 BECOME DISPIRITED → 0506
哀 sorrowful → 2568
愁 MELANCHOLY → 3508
鬱 GLOOM → 3625
陰 gloomy → 0657
沈 depressed → 0306
寂 LONESOME → 2855
淋しい LONESOME → 0632
惨 MISERABLE → 0585

悌

0507

1-3-7

▶ **BROTHERLY LOVE**

テイ ダイ ㊔ やすし やす よし とも

Ⓒ 悌 tì

61	Names	U608C
忄	S10-3-7	F0000

COMPOUNDS

ⓐ [original meaning] **BROTHERLY LOVE, obedience to one's older brother**

ⓑ serving one's elders, obedience to one's seniors

ab 孝悌 こうてい filial piety and brotherly love
b 悌順 ていじゅん [archaic] obedience

SYNONYMS

ⓐ **fidelity**

忠 LOYALTY → 3087
義 faith → 2948
孝 FILIAL PIETY → 3973
悌 BROTHERLY LOVE → 0507
誠 SINCERITY → 1922
実 faithfulness → 2765
信 fidelity → 0115
操 constancy → 0948
節 moral integrity → 3336

悅

0508

1-3-7

▶ **DELIGHTED**

エツ よろこ(ぶ) よろこ(ばす) ㊔ よし のぶ

61	Nonstandard	U6085
忄	S10-3-7	F0000

traditional form → see 悦 at 0501

悔

0509

1-3-7

▶ **REPENT**

カイ く(いる) く(やむ) くや(しい)

61	Names	UFA3D
忄	S10-3-7	F0000

traditional form → see 悔 at 0435

悖

1-3-7

incorrect stroke-count
➡ see 1-3-8: 忄 at 0588

挨

0510

1-3-7

▶ **PUSH**

アイ

Ⓒ 挨 āi ái

64	Jōyō	U6328
扌	S10-3-7	F1416

1	2	3	4	5	6	7	8	9	10
一	十	扌	扌	扌	扌	扌	扌	挨	挨

COMPOUNDS

❶ **PUSH**

挨拶 あいさつ greeting, salutation; speech, address; reply, response

挨拶状 あいさつじょう greeting card

❷ [archaic] approach, come close, draw near

SYNONYMS

❶ **push**

押 PUSH →0371
突く THRUST →2772
圧 apply pressure →3688
挨 PUSH →0510
按 HOLD DOWN →0444

COMPOUND FORMATION

【挨拶 あいさつ】

挨拶 あいさつ 'greeting, salutation, etc.' derives from dialogues in which Zen practitioners present one another with riddle-like questions and push (挨 ❶) and press (拶) the other for answers to ascertain their level of enlightenment. From there, it came to refer broadly to exchanges of words between people.

挽

0511
1-3-7

▶**GRIND**
バン ひ(く)
Ⓝ 挽 Ⓒ 挽 wǎn

64	Names	U633D
扌	S10-3-7	F2565

COMPOUNDS

❶ [original meaning] **pull strongly, tug, draw**

挽回 ばんかい retrieval, recovery, restoration

❷ mourn

挽歌 ばんか elegy, funeral song

❸ turn (a potter's wheel)

KUN

【ひく 挽く】

① **GRIND (meat or coffee)**

挽き肉 ひきにく ground [minced] meat
挽き立てのコーヒー ひきたてのこーひー freshly ground coffee
粗挽き あらびき coarsely ground (coffee, grain), coarsely minced (meat)
合い挽き あいびき beef and pork ground together

② saw, cut with a saw

木挽き歌 こびきうた sawyer's song
縦挽き鋸 たてびきのこ ripsaw

SYNONYMS

【ひく】

① & ② **cut**

切 CUT →0030
薙ぐ MOW DOWN →3010
剪 PRUNE →2886
削 CUT BY CHIPPING →1837
挽く GRIND, saw →0511
断 CUT OFF →1885
截 CUT OFF →4092
裁 CUT OUT →4090
斬 CUT WITH A SWORD →1874
割 cut with a knife →2284
剖 DISSECT →2103
刈る CLIP →0032
伐 CUT DOWN →0046

HOMOPHONES

ひく

引 DRAW →0207
弾 PROJECTILE →0697
退 RETREAT →3838
惹 DRAW ATTENTION →2903
轢 RUN OVER →2095
牽 DRAW →2621
曳 DRAW →4348

NOTE

➡ see USAGE note at 引 0207

挺

0512
1-3-7

▶**COUNTER FOR LONG SOLID OBJECTS**
▶**VOLUNTEER BRAVELY**
チョウ テイ
Ⓒ 挺 tǐng

64	Names	U633A
扌	S10-3-7	F2477

COMPOUNDS

❶ [now also 丁 ちょう 4155]

ⓐ **COUNTER FOR LONG SOLID OBJECTS such as guns, oars, guitars or candles**

ⓑ counter for human-powered vehicles such as palanquins or rickshaws

a ピストル五挺 ぴすとるごちょう five pistols
ギター三挺 ぎたーさんちょう three guitars

❷ **VOLUNTEER BRAVELY**

挺身 ていしん volunteering
挺進する ていしんする go ahead of
空挺部隊 くうていぶたい airborne troops

INDEPENDENT

【ていする 挺する】 **VOLUNTEER BRAVELY**

SYNONYMS

❶ **counters for long objects**

本 counter for cylindrical objects →4314
筋 counter for slender objects →3319
竿 counter for poles or rods →3259
挺 COUNTER FOR LONG SOLID OBJECTS →0512

捗

▶MAKE PROGRESS

チョク　はかど(る)▲

Ⓝ 捗　Ⓒ 捗 bù

0513

1-3-7

64	Jōyō	U6357
扌	S10-3-7	F3418

一 十 扌 扌' 扌ト 扌卜 扌止 扌牛 扌步 捗
1 2 3 4 5 6 7 8 9 10

COMPOUNDS

● **MAKE PROGRESS**

進捗する しんちょくする progress, be under way

KUN

【はかどる　捗る】**MAKE** good **PROGRESS**

SYNONYMS

● **make progress**

進 ADVANCE →3873
亨 GO SMOOTHLY →2530
捗 MAKE PROGRESS →0513

捕

▶CATCH

**ホ　と(らえる)　と(らわれる)　と(る)
つか(まえる)　つか(まる)**

Ⓒ 捕 bǔ

0514

1-3-7

64	Jōyō	U6355
扌	S10-3-7	F0795

一 十 扌 扌一 扌厂 扌冂 扌円 扌肙 捕 捕
1 2 3 4 5 6 7 8 9 10

COMPOUNDS

❶ⓐ **CATCH, seize, grasp**
ⓑ (capture by force) **CATCH, capture, arrest**

a 捕獲する ほかくする catch (fish); capture (a ship), seize
捕捉する ほそくする catch, seize, capture; apprehend; understand
捕球 ほきゅう a catch (in baseball)
捕手 ほしゅ catcher
逮捕 たいほ arrest, capture
b 捕鯨 ほげい whaling
捕虜 ほりょ prisoner of war, captive

❷ *baseball* **CATCH**er

捕逸 ほいつ catcher-passed ball

INDEPENDENT

【ほ　捕】*baseball* **CATCH**er

KUN

【とらえる　捕らえる】

①ⓐ **CATCH, seize, grasp**
ⓑ (capture by force) **CATCH, capture, arrest**

a 袖を捕らえる そでをとらえる catch a person by the sleeve
b 泥棒を捕らえる どろぼうをとらえる arrest a thief
引っ捕らえる ひっとらえる capture, arrest, seize

② [also 捉える] (take hold as if with the hand) **grasp** (an idea), **seize** (an opportunity)

捕らえ所の無い とらえどころのない elusive, subtle, slippery

【とらわれる　捕らわれる】

①ⓐ **be caught, be arrested**
ⓑ [also 囚われる] **be imprisoned, be taken captive**

a 捕らわれ とらわれ captivity, imprisonment
敵に捕らわれる てきにとらわれる be caught by the enemy

② [also 囚われる] adhere to (tradition), be swayed by

捕らわれた考え とらわれたかんがえ conventional ideas, prejudiced opinion

【とる　捕る】**CATCH, take, seize**

捕り物 とりもの capture, arrest
魚を捕る さかなをとる catch fish
分捕る ぶんどる loot, grab

【つかまえる　捕まえる】**arrest, nab, capture, CATCH**

犯人を捕まえる はんにんをつかまえる arrest the culprit

【つかまる　捕まる】**be caught, be arrested**

取っ捕まる とっつかまる be caught

SYNONYMS

❶ⓐ **take**

把 GRIP →0293
握 GRASP →0714
捉 GRASP →0518
執 SEIZE →2114
摑む GRASP →0848
捕 CATCH →0514
取 TAKE →1613
持 HOLD →0447

ⓑ **catch a criminal**

捕 CATCH →0514
逮 CATCH A CRIMINAL →3875
拘 ARREST →0367
勾 ARREST →3660

USAGE

❶【とらえる】

捕らえる
①ⓐ catch, seize, grasp
ⓑ (capture by force) catch, capture, arrest
② [also 捉える] (take hold as if with the hand) **grasp** (an idea), **seize** (an opportunity)

捉える
[also 捕らえる] (take hold as if with the hand) **grasp** (an idea), **seize** (an opportunity)

❷【とらわれる】

捕らわれる
①ⓐ be caught, be arrested

ⓑ [also 囚われる] be imprisoned, be taken captive
② [also 囚われる] adhere to (tradition), be swayed by

囚われる
[also 捕らわれる]
① be imprisoned, be taken captive
② adhere to (tradition), be swayed by

❸【つかまえる】

捕まえる
arrest, nab, capture, catch

捉まえる
[usu. 摑まえる] grasp, grip, clutch

摑まえる
[sometimes also 捉まえる] catch, seize, grasp, get hold of

❹【つかまる】

捕まる
be caught, be arrested

捉まる
[usu. 摑まる] grasp, grip, clutch

摑まる
[sometimes also 捉まる] hold fast to, cling to

HOMOPHONES

とらえる 捉 GRASP →0518
とらわれる 囚 PRISONER →3776
とる
取 TAKE →1613
採 PICK →0606
撮 PHOTOGRAPH →0910
執 EXECUTE →2114
つかまえる
摑 GRASP →0848
捉 GRASP →0518
つかまる
摑 GRASP →0848
捉 GRASP →0518

NOTE

➡ see also USAGE note at 取 1613

振

0515

▮ 1-3-7

▸**SWING**

シン ふ(る) ぶ(る) ふ(り) -ぶ(り) ふ(るう) ふ(れる)

Ⓒ 振 zhèn

64	Jōyō	U632F
扌	S10-3-7	F0429

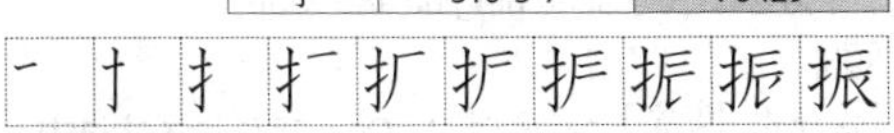

COMPOUNDS

❶ⓐ [original meaning] **SWING, oscillate, vibrate**
ⓑ *baseball* **SWING**
a 振動 しんどう vibration
振幅 しんぷく amplitude (of vibration)
b 強振する きょうしんする swing hard
三振 さんしん strikeout

❷ⓐ arouse to action, rouse up
ⓑ **rise, prosper, thrive**
a 振作する しんさくする promote, enhance, stimulate
b 振興 しんこう promotion, furtherance, rousing
不振 ふしん dullness, depression, stagnation, slump

INDEPENDENT

【しん 振】abbrev. of 三振 さんしん: strikeout

KUN

【ふる 振る】
①ⓐ *vt* **wave, shake; SWING, oscillate**
ⓑ **brandish, wield, flourish**
ⓒ **sprinkle, cast**
a 振り向く ふりむく turn around, look back
手を振る てをふる wave one's hand
b 振り子 ふりこ pendulum
c 振り袖 ふりそで long sleeved kimono
② yaw, wag
台風が進路を北に振った たいふうがしんろをきたにふった The typhoon changed course to the north
③ **reject, refuse; jilt, ditch**
振られる ふられる get the mitten, be kicked out
④ **give (a role), cast (a part)**
振り仮名 ふりがな small kana characters that indicate pronunciation
役を割り振る やくをわりふる assign a role to an actor
⑤ draw, issue, remit
振り替え ふりかえ change, transfer
振り込み ふりこみ bank transfer
⑥ **unclassified compounds**
振る舞う ふるまう behave oneself; entertain, treat

【ぶる 振る】**assume an air of, pretend, affect**
厭に振っている いやにぶっている reek of affectation
上品振る じょうひんぶる be prudish
学者振る がくしゃぶる assume the air of a scholar, be pedantic

【ふり 振り】**SWING, shake, wave; dress, personal appearance; show, make-believe, pretense; posture, gesture, action; counter for Japanese swords**
振り付け ふりつけ dance composition, choreography
身振り みぶり gesture, gesticulation
寝た振りをする ねたふりをする pretend to be asleep
人の振り見て我が振り直せ ひとのふりみてわがふりなおせ Correct your conduct by observing that of others

【-ぶり -振り】[also suffix]
① [sometimes also っ振り -っぷり] **manner, way, style**
枝振り えだぶり shape of a tree, ramifications
男っ振り おとこっぷり man's looks; public estimation
飲みっ振りが良いね のみっぷりがいいね You can really down it, eh!
② **after a lapse of**
久し振りに ひさしぶりに after a long time [interval]
三年振りに帰省する さんねんぶりにきせいする come home after three years' absence
③ size, amount
大振りの おおぶりの large, of a larger size

【ふるう 振るう】
①ⓐ [formerly also 揮う] **wield, brandish, manipulate, master**
ⓑ **wield (authority), exercise, exhibit (one's powers)**
ⓒ **shake**
a 槍を振るう やりをふるう wield a spear
b 腕を振るう うでをふるう display one's ability, exercise one's talent
c 振るい落とす ふるいおとす shake off
②ⓐ be in high spirits, be invigorated
ⓑ flourish, thrive, be prosperous
a 軍の士気が振るう ぐんのしきがふるう The morale of the army is high
b 振るわない ふるわない be dull, be in a bad way
振るった ふるった original, striking, extraordinary

【ふれる 振れる】
① *vi* **wave, shake; SWING, oscillate**
左右に振れる さゆうにふれる swing left and right
② **veer, deflect**
針が東に振れた はりがひがしにふれた The needle deflected to the east

SYNONYMS

❶ⓐ shake
振 SWING →0515
震 QUAKE →3481
揺 SHAKE →0723

❷ⓐ incite
挑 PROVOKE →0445
唆 INSTIGATE →0480
扇 FAN →2449
煽 FAN →1338
激 excite →0955
奮 ROUSE UP →3000
振 arouse to action →0515
動 MOVE →2232
起 rise to action →4099

ⓑ prospering and prosperity
隆 PROSPER →0661
振 rise →0515
興 RISE TO PROSPERITY →3622
盛 PROSPEROUS →3314
昌 PROSPERING →3069
栄 FLOURISH →3183
繁 THRIVE →3536
賑 BUSTLE →1959

USAGE

【ふるう】
振るう
①ⓐ [formerly also 揮う] wield, brandish, manipulate, master
ⓑ wield (authority), exercise, exhibit (one's powers)
ⓒ shake
②ⓐ be in high spirits, be invigorated
ⓑ flourish, thrive, be prosperous
揮う
[now usu. 振るう] wield, brandish, manipulate, master
震う
tremble, quiver, shudder
奮う
rouse up, rouse oneself, arouse

HOMOPHONES

ふるう
揮 WIELD →0717
震 QUAKE →3481
奮 ROUSE UP →3000

NOTE

➡ see COMPOUND FORMATION for 椀飯振舞 おうばんぶるまい →椀 1250

捜

0516

1-3-7

▸**LOOK FOR**
ソウ さが(す)
Ⓝ 搜 搜◇ Ⓒ 搜 sōu

64	Jōyō	U635C
扌	S10-3-7	F0932

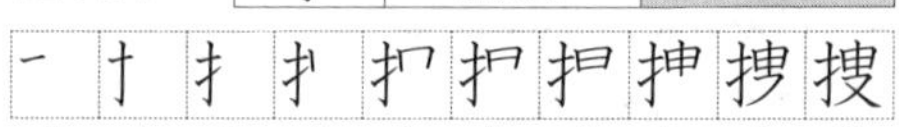

COMPOUNDS

● [original meaning] **LOOK FOR, search**
捜査 そうさ criminal investigation, search
捜索 そうさく search, investigation
博捜 はくそう searching far and wide

KUN

【さがす 捜す】[also 探す] **LOOK FOR (a lost object), search for, hunt for**
捜し物 さがしもの looking for something lost; thing to look for
宝捜し たからさがし treasure hunt

本を捜す ほんをさがす look for a book

SYNONYMS

● **seek**

探 SEARCH → 0613
索 SEARCH FOR → 3105
捜 LOOK FOR → 0516
求 SEEK → 4365
猟 hunt for → 0654

USAGE

【さがす】

捜す
[also 探す] look for (a lost object), search for, hunt for

探す
[also 捜す] search for (something desired), search about, look for

HOMOPHONES

さがす 探 PROBE → 0613

挿

▶INSERT
ソウ さ(す) はさ(む)▲
Ⓝ 插 揷◇ Ⓒ 插 chā

0517
◧ 1-3-7

64	Jōyō	U633F
扌	S10-3-7	F1717

1 2 3 4 5 6 7 8 9 10

COMPOUNDS

● [original meaning] **INSERT, put into, stick between**

挿入する そうにゅうする insert, put into
挿話 そうわ anecdote
挿画 そうが illustration (in a book)
挿花 そうか flower arrangement

KUN

【さす 挿す】

ⓐ **INSERT, put into, stick between**
ⓑ **INSERT seedlings, plant**

a 挿し絵 さしえ illustration (in a book)
挿し木 さしき cutting; cuttage
花瓶に花を挿す かびんにはなをさす put flowers in a vase

【はさむ 挿む】 [now usu. 挟む] put (something) between, **INSERT**, interpose

本に栞を挿む ほんにしおりをはさむ put a bookmark between the pages of a book

SYNONYMS

● **put in**

入 PUT IN → 4177
挿 INSERT → 0517
嵌 INLAY → 2897
-込む cause to move inward → 3762

HOMOPHONES

さす

指 FINGER → 0452
差 DIFFERENCE → 4104
刺 STAB → 1625
注 POUR → 0383
射 SHOOT → 1850
止 STOP → 3659

はさむ

挟 HOLD BETWEEN → 0450
鋏 SCISSORS → 2173

COMPOUND FORMATION

【挿話 そうわ】

挿話 'anecdote' refers to an inserted (挿) story (話).

NOTE

➡ see USAGE notes at 差 4104 and 挟 0450

捉

▶GRASP
ソク とら(える) つか(まえる)▲ つか(まる)▲
Ⓒ 捉 zhuō

0518
◧ 1-3-7

64	Jōyō	U6349
扌	S10-3-7	F1824

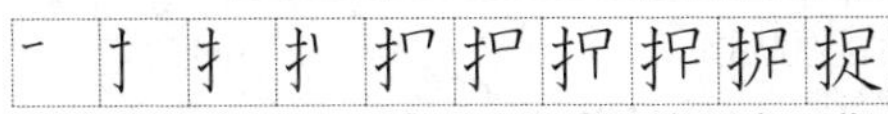
1 2 3 4 5 6 7 8 9 10

COMPOUNDS

❶ⓐ [original meaning, now archaic] **GRASP**, clutch, catch

ⓑ **capture, catch**

b 捕捉 ほそく seizure, capture; apprehension; understanding

❷ (take hold as if with the hand) **GRASP** (an idea), seize (an opportunity)

把捉する はそくする grasp (a meaning, etc.)

KUN

【とらえる 捉える】 [also 捕らえる] (take hold as if with the hand) **GRASP (an idea), seize (an opportunity)**

捉え所の無い とらえどころのない elusive, subtle
心を捉える こころをとらえる impress, charm
意味を捉える いみをとらえる grasp the meaning
言葉尻を捉える ことばじりをとらえる cavil at a person's words

【つかまえる 捉まえる】 [usu. 摑まえる] **GRASP**, grip, clutch

【つかまる 捉まる】 [usu. 摑まる] **GRASP**, grip, clutch

SYNONYMS

❷ **take**

把 GRIP → 0293
握 GRASP → 0714
捉 GRASP → 0518
執 SEIZE → 2114

1

掴む GRASP →0848
捕 CATCH →0514
取 TAKE →1613
持 HOLD →0447

HOMOPHONES

とらえる 捕 CATCH →0514
つかまえる
捕 CATCH →0514
掴 GRASP →0848
つかまる
捕 CATCH →0514
掴 GRASP →0848

NOTE

➡ see USAGE note at 捕 0514

挫 0519

▶**SPRAIN**
ザ くじ(く)▲ くじ(ける)▲
Ⓒ 挫 cuò

1-3-7

64	Jōyō	U632B
扌	S10-3-7	F2211

COMPOUNDS

❶ⓐ **SPRAIN, twist**
ⓑ **bruise, injure**
a 捻挫 ねんざ sprain
b 挫傷 ざしょう contusion
❷ **discourage, frustrate, dampen, crush**
挫折 ざせつ frustration, setback
頓挫する とんざする reach an impasse, fall through

KUN

【くじく 挫く】
① **SPRAIN**, twist
② discourage, frustrate, dampen, crush
鋭を挫く えいをくじく break the brunt
【くじける 挫ける】
① get **SPRAIN**ed, get twisted
② be discouraged, lose heart, be dampened

SYNONYMS

❶ **break**
破 BREAK →1478
拉ぐ crush →0372
崩 CRUMBLE →2863
挫 SPRAIN →0519
壊 BREAK DOWN →0934
毀す break down →2246
折 BREAK OFF →0297
割る crack →2284
裂 SPLIT →3331
砕 CRUSH UP →1458
摧 CRUSH UP →0849
潰す CRUSH →0919

挾 0520

▶**HOLD BETWEEN**
キョウ はさ(む) はさ(まる) わきばさ(む)

1-3-7

64	Nonstandard	U633E
扌	S10-3-7	F0000

traditional form →see 挟 at 0450

撈 0521

▶**DREDGE**
ロウ

1-3-7

64	Nonstandard	U22B50
扌	S10-3-7	F0000

traditional form →see 撈 at 0908

拷

1-3-7

incorrect stroke-count
➡ see 1-3-6: 扌 at 0446

浮 0522

▶**FLOAT**
フ う(く) う(かれる) う(かぶ) う(かべる)
Ⓝ 浮 Ⓒ 浮 fú

1-3-7

85	Jōyō	U6D6E
氵	S10-3-7	F0536

COMPOUNDS

❶ [original meaning] **FLOAT, rise to the surface**
浮沈 ふちん rise and fall, ebb and flow; ups and downs
浮上する ふじょうする surface, rise [float] to the surface
浮揚 ふよう floating
浮力 ふりょく buoyancy, lift
浮標 ふひょう (marker) buoy
浮遊 ふゆう floating, suspension
❷ **FLOATing, transient, insecure, insubstantial**
浮浪者 ふろうしゃ vagabond, loafer, hobo
浮動する ふどうする fluctuate; float, waft
浮説 ふせつ wild rumor, speculation
浮言 ふげん unfounded report, wild rumor
浮生 ふせい transient life
❸ thoughtless, flippant, fickle
浮薄な ふはくな frivolous, fickle, insincere
浮華 ふか empty show, frivolity, levity

KUN

【うく 浮く】 *vi* **FLOAT, rise to the surface; feel (one's teeth) loose, be set on edge; become buoyant; frivolous, flippant, insecure; be left over, be saved**
浮き うき float; buoy, life buoy
浮き彫り うきぼり relief, embossed carving

浮き上がる うきあがる float, rise to the surface
浮き草 うきくさ floating weed
浮き浮きと うきうきと buoyantly, cheerfully
浮き名を流す うきなをながす get a reputation as a philanderer
浮き世 うきよ transitory world, fleeting life
浮き足立つ うきあしだつ begin to waver [falter], lose confidence
歯の浮く様な音 はのうくようなおと noise that sets one's teeth on edge

【うかれる 浮かれる】*vi* **become buoyant, be gay, be in high spirits; be on the spree**
浮かれ男 うかれおとこ playboy
花に浮かれる はなにうかれる be intoxicated with the blossoms

【うかぶ 浮かぶ】**FLOAT, rise to the surface; loom up, appear; come across one's mind; rest in peace**
浮かばれない うかばれない cannot rest in peace, turn in one's grave
水に浮かぶ泡 みずにうかぶあわ bubbles on the water
微笑の浮かんだ唇 ほほえみのうかんだくちびる lips with a flickering smile
心に浮かぶ こころにうかぶ come across one's mind

【うかべる 浮かべる】*vt* **FLOAT, set afloat; express, show; call to mind**
ボートを浮かべる ぼーとをうかべる launch a boat
微笑を浮かべて びしょうをうかべて with a smile
思い浮かべる おもいうかべる call to mind

SPECIAL READINGS
浮気 うわき inconstancy; love affair; fickleness
浮つく うわつく be fickle, be flippant, be restless

SYNONYMS
❶ **float**
漂 DRIFT → 0857
浮 FLOAT → 0522

浜

▶BEACH
ヒン はま
Ⓝ 濱 濵 Ⓒ 滨 bīn

0523
1-3-7

85	Jōyō	U6D5C
氵	S10-3-7	F0913

Stroke order: 1–10

COMPOUNDS
❶ **BEACH, seashore, coast**
海浜 かいひん seashore, seaside, beach
❷ Yokohama
京浜 けいひん Tokyo and Yokohama

KUN
【はま 浜】**BEACH, seashore, coast;** *slang* **Yokohama; captured stone in the game of go**
浜辺 はまべ beach, seashore
浜風 はまかぜ beach wind
浜茄子 はまなす sweet brier
浜伝いに はまづたいに along the beach
浜っ子 はまっこ native of Yokohama
砂浜 すなはま sandy beach, sands

SYNONYMS
❶ **shores and watersides**
畔 WATERSIDE → 1472
-辺 -side → 3761
浜 BEACH → 0523
岸 SHORE → 2777
浦 SEASIDE → 0524
渚 STRAND → 0637
磯 ROCKY BEACH → 1587
汀 STRAND → 0228
❷ **Kanto region**
京 TOKYO → 2546
東 Tokyo → 4385
都 METROPOLIS OF TOKYO → 2120
浜 Yokohama → 0523
埼 SAITAMA → 0560
湘 SHONAN → 0742

浦

▶SEASIDE
ホ^ うら
Ⓒ 浦 pǔ

0524
1-3-7

85	Jōyō	U6D66
氵	S10-3-7	F1047

Stroke order: 1–10

COMPOUNDS
● [original meaning] **shore, coast, SEASIDE, water's edge**
曲浦 きょくほ winding coast [beach]

KUN
【うら 浦】
① *elegant* **SEASIDE, seashore**
浦風 うらかぜ sea breeze
浦人 うらびと seaside dweller
浦里 うらざと village by the sea
津津浦浦に つつうらうらに throughout the land, in every harbor and every bay
② **coastal indentation, inlet, small bay**
浦曲 うらわ coastal indentations

SYNONYMS
【うら】

① **shores and watersides**

畔 WATERSIDE → 1472
-辺 -side → 3761
浜 BEACH → 0523
岸 SHORE → 2777
浦 SEASIDE → 0524
渚 STRAND → 0637
磯 ROCKY BEACH → 1587
汀 STRAND → 0228

② **inlets and bays**

江 INLET → 0257
浦 coastal indentation → 0524
湾 BAY → 0748
峡 narrows → 0427

浩

0525

1-3-7

▶VAST

コウ ㊔ ひろ　ひろし　ひろむ　ごう　はる　ゆたか

Ⓝ 浩 Ⓒ 浩 hào

85	Names	U6D69
氵	S10-3-7	F1435

COMPOUNDS

ⓐ VAST (like an expanse of water), extensive, immense, great

ⓑ VAST (amount), huge (quantity); numerous

a 浩然たる こうぜんたる vast; magnanimous
b 浩瀚×な こうかんな bulky, voluminous

SYNONYMS

ⓐ wide and extensive

広 WIDE → 3769
紘 WIDE-RANGING → 1650
博 EXTENSIVE → 0170
恢 EXTENSIVE → 0436
浩 VAST → 0525
洸 VAST (expanse of water) → 0462
滉 DEEP AND VAST → 0811
曠 SPACIOUS → 1411
闊 BROAD → 4135

ⓑ big and huge

大 BIG → 4224
太 GREAT → 2673
浩 VAST → 0525
巨 HUGE → 3773
厖 BULKY → 3725

浬

0526

1-3-7

▶NAUTICAL MILE

リ　かいり　のっと

Ⓒ 浬 lǐ hǎilǐ

85	Names	U6D6C
氵	S10-3-7	F0000

KUN

【かいり　浬】 [also 海里] **NAUTICAL MILE**
【のっと　浬】 [also 節] **NAUTICAL MILE per hour, knot**

SYNONYMS

【かいり】

○ **length units**

寸 *sun* (3.03 cm) → 3652
浬 NAUTICAL MILE (1852 m) → 0526
反 *tan* (10.6 m) → 3663
尺 *SHAKU* (30.3 cm) → 4248
米 meter → 4342
尋 fathom (1.8 m) → 2918
間 *ken* (1.8 m) → 4122
丈 *jo* (3.03 m) → 4227
町 *cho* (109 m) → 1430
里 LEAGUE, *ri* (3.9 km) → 4356
哩 MILE (1609 m) → 0479

HOMOPHONES

かいり 海里 → 0459, 4356
のっと 節 JOINT → 3336

NOTE

➡ see USAGE note at 節 3336

浪

0527

1-3-7

▶BILLOW
▶WANDER

ロウ ㊔ なみ

Ⓒ 浪 làng

85	Jōyō	U6D6A
氵	S10-3-7	F1146

COMPOUNDS

❶ BILLOW, large wave, wave

波浪 はろう waves, billows
風浪 ふうろう wind and waves, heavy seas

❷ WANDER, roam, ramble, drift about

浪浪 ろうろう wandering
浪人 ろうにん lordless samurai, *ronin;* unsuccessful examinee; jobless person
放浪する ほうろうする wander about, roam
浮浪者 ふろうしゃ vagabond, loafer, hobo
流浪する るろうする wander [roam] about from place to place

❸ abbrev. of 浪人 ろうにん: student waiting for another chance to be enrolled in a university

三浪 さんろう unsuccessful examinee waiting for the third chance to be enrolled in a university

❹ wasteful, extravagant, unrestrained

浪費 ろうひ waste, extravagance

❺ abbrev. of 浪花 なにわ, old name of Osaka

浪曲 ろうきょく *naniwabushi,* form of traditional Japanese vaudeville

❻ used phonetically for *rō*

浪漫主義 ろうまんしゅぎ romanticism

SPECIAL READINGS

浪花▲ なにわ old name for Osaka

SYNONYMS

❶ **waves**

波 WAVE → 0388

浪 BILLOW → 0527

漣 RIPPLES → 0859

❷ **wander**

浪 WANDER → 0527

遊 move about freely → 3896

漂 drift about → 0857

流 drift → 0529

彽 WANDER ABOUT → 0350

徊 MOVE TO AND FRO → 0432

涙

0528

1-3-7

▶**TEAR**

ルイ なみだ

Ⓝ 涙 泪 Ⓒ 泪 lèi

85	Jōyō	U6D99
氵	S10-3-7	F1163

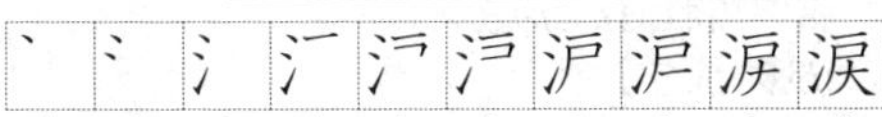

COMPOUNDS

● [original meaning] **TEAR, tears**

涙腺 るいせん lachrymal gland

涙嚢× るいのう lachrymal sac, dacryocyst

落涙する らくるいする shed tears

催涙ガス さいるいがす tear gas

暗涙に咽ぶ あんるいにむせぶ shed silent tears

KUN

【なみだ 涙】**TEAR, tears; sympathy; a mere particle of, a modicum of**

涙ぐむ なみだぐむ be moved to tears

涙を呑む なみだをのむ choke back one's tears, pocket an insult

涙雨 なみだあめ sprinkling rain

涙金 なみだきん small sum of consolation money

嬉し涙 うれしなみだ tears of joy

雀の涙程の補助金 すずめのなみだほどのほじょきん a mere particle of subsidy

SYNONYMS

● **bodily secretions**

乳 MILK → 1823

精 sperm → 1729

汗 SWEAT → 0256

涙 TEAR → 0528

唾 SALIVA → 0553

流

0529

1-3-7

▶**FLOW**
▶**CURRENT**
▶**STYLE**

リュウ ル なが(れる) なが(れ) なが(す) -なが(す)

Ⓝ 流◇ Ⓒ 流 liú

85	Jōyō-3	U6D41
氵	S10-3-7	F0204

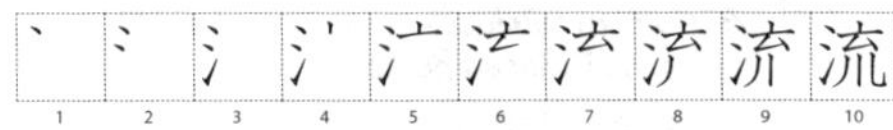

COMPOUNDS

❶ⓐ [original meaning] **FLOW, stream, run**

ⓑ **let FLOW, spill out, discharge, shed**

ⓒ be swept away by the **FLOW**, drift

a 流動する りゅうどうする flow, circulate, be liquid

流出 りゅうしゅつ outflow, effusion

漂流する ひょうりゅうする drift, be adrift

合流する ごうりゅうする flow together; join, unite

b 流血 りゅうけつ bloodshed

放流 ほうりゅう discharge; stocking (a river) with (fish)

c 流失する りゅうしつする be washed away

流木 りゅうぼく driftwood

浮流 ふりゅう floating, drifting

❷ **FLOWing, fluent**

流暢に りゅうちょうに fluently, flowingly, smoothly

流麗な りゅうれいな fluent, flowing

❸ⓐ (water or air flow) **CURRENT, stream, flow**

ⓑ (body of running water) **stream, river**

ⓒ (general tendency) **CURRENT, drift, trend**

a 海流 かいりゅう ocean current

気流 きりゅう air [atmospheric] current, air stream

暖流 だんりゅう warm current

上流 じょうりゅう upper stream (of a river); upper class

潮流 ちょうりゅう tide, current; tendency, trend

急流 きゅうりゅう rapid stream, swift current; swift-running river; rapids

b 本流 ほんりゅう main course (of a river), main stream

分流 ぶんりゅう distributary, river branch

c 時流 じりゅう fashion [current] of the times, general drift of affairs

主流 しゅりゅう main current, mainstream

底流 ていりゅう bottom current, undercurrent

❹ **electric CURRENT**

電流 でんりゅう electric current

交流 こうりゅう alternating current; interchange

整流 せいりゅう rectification

❺ⓐ **spread, be disseminated, be circulated, pervade**
ⓑ spreading of false rumors
a 流通 りゅうつう circulation of money or goods; flow of water; ventilation
流布 るふ circulation, dissemination, spread
流行する(=流行る) りゅうこうする(=はやる) be fashionable, be in vogue; prevail
b 流説 りゅうせつ groundless rumor, false report
❻ drift, wander
流民 るみん(=りゅうみん) roaming [wandering] people, displaced persons
流浪 るろう vagrancy
流離する りゅうりする wander alone in a strange country
❼ cast out, banish, exile
流罪 るざい banishment, exile
流刑 るけい deportation, banishment
❽ be abandoned before completion, prove abortive
流会 りゅうかい adjournment of a meeting, be called off (due to lack of attendance)
流産 りゅうざん miscarriage, abortion
❾ characteristic or institutionalized **STYLE**:
ⓐ [also suffix] **STYLE, way, mode, manner, form, fashion**
ⓑ [also suffix] **school, STYLE, system**
ⓒ counter for schools
a 自己流 じこりゅう one's own style, one's way of doing things
三島流の みしまりゅうの in the style of Mishima
b 流派 りゅうは school
流儀 りゅうぎ school, style, system, method
草月流 そうげつりゅう Sogetsu school of flower arrangement
❿ **class, order, rate, grade**
中流 ちゅうりゅう middle class
一流大学 いちりゅうだいがく first-rate university
二流 にりゅう second-rate
⓫ members of the same group or profession
女流文学者 じょりゅうぶんがくしゃ lady of letters
⓬ bloodline, descent
嫡流 ちゃくりゅう lineage of the eldest son; orthodox school
⓭ [also 旒 りゅう 1272] counter for flags
旗二流 はたにりゅう two flags

KUN

【ながれる 流れる】**FLOW, run; pass (time); drift away, float; wander, drift, stray; be called off; be forfeited**
流れ込む ながれこむ flow into, stream in; wander into (town)
流れ星 ながれぼし shooting star, meteor
流れ者 ながれもの vagrant
時が流れる ときがながれる Time flows
会が流れた かいがながれた The meeting was called off

【ながれ 流れ】
①ⓐ **FLOWing, flow, current, stream**
ⓑ (body of running water) **stream, river**
ⓒ **stream, FLOW (of things or people)**
a 川流れ かわながれ being carried away by a current
b 急な流れ きゅうなながれ rapid stream, swiftly running river
c 流れ作業 ながれさぎょう assembly-line system
車の流れ くるまのながれ flow of cars
音楽の流れ おんがくのながれ flow of music
②ⓐ descent, lineage
ⓑ school, **STYLE**
a 平家の流れ へいけのながれ the Heike line
b 三島の流れを汲む みしまのながれをくむ belong to Mishima's school (of literature)
③ suspension, postponement
会合をお流れにする かいごうをおながれにする postpone a meeting
④ forfeiture, foreclosure
質流れの時計 しちながれのとけい unredeemed (pawned) watch
⑤ counter for flags
旗二流れ はたふたながれ two flags

【ながす 流す】
①ⓐ **let FLOW, spill, drain**
ⓑ **set adrift, float**
ⓒ **wash, scrub (one's back)**
a 流し ながし sink; bath attendant; strolling musician; cruising taxi
流し込む ながしこむ pour into; wash down
涙を流す なみだをながす shed tears
b 流し網 ながしあみ drift net
c 背中を流す せなかをながす rinse one's back
② exile, banish
島流し しまながし exile
罪人を流す ざいにんをながす exile a criminal
③ forfeit, foreclose
質草を流す しちぐさをながす forfeit a pawned article
④ cruise along, stroll
タクシーが流す たくしーがながす Taxis cruise along
⑤ spread, broadcast
ラジオ番組で流す らじおばんぐみでながす broadcast on a radio program
噂を流す うわさをながす spread rumors
⑥ suspend, abort
総会を流す そうかいをながす call off a general meeting

【-ながす -流す】[verbal suffix] **ignore, do and disregard**
聞き流す ききながす let something go in one ear and out the other
受け流す うけながす ward off, elude; turn aside (a joke)

SPECIAL READINGS
流行▲ はやり(=りゅうこう) vogue, fashion; fad, craze
流石▲ さすが just as expected; like

SYNONYMS
❶ flow and drip
流 FLOW →0529
注 POUR →0383
濫 overflow →0990
溢 OVERFLOW →0807
漏 LEAK →0860
滴 DROP →0866
泌 SECRETE →0390
瀝 DRIP →0996
❷ smooth
流 flowing →0529
暢 FLUENT →1569
滑 SMOOTH →0809
❸ⓐ running water
流 CURRENT →0529
潮 TIDE →0916
汐 TIDE →0259
瀬 rapids →0995
滝 WATERFALL →0813
洪 FLOOD →0461
渦 WHIRLPOOL →0735
ⓑ rivers and streams
川 RIVER →0006
河 RIVER →0394
江 large river →0257
渓 mountain stream →0628
流 stream →0529
ⓒ tendency
向 tendency →3790
性 NATURE →0357
勢 trend →3542
傾 inclination →0174
潮 TIDE →0916
流 CURRENT →0529
❹ electricity and magnetism
電 ELECTRICITY →3465
流 electric current →0529
磁 MAGNETISM →1554
❺ⓐ make widely known
布 SPREAD →3691
流 spread →0529
伝 spread →0048
広 spread →3769
弘 DISSEMINATE (esp. Buddhism) →0223
及 REACH TO →4192
❻ wander
浪 WANDER →0527
遊 move about freely →3896
漂 drift about →0857
流 drift →0529
彽 WANDER ABOUT →0350
徊 MOVE TO AND FRO →0432
❾ⓐ way and style
風 MANNER →3730
様 MODE →1332
方 WAY →2459
途 WAY →3853
法 METHOD →0391
流 STYLE →0529
式 STYLE →3785
調 TONE →1973
ⓑ parties and sects
党 PARTY →3190
閥 CLIQUE →4126
流 school →0529
派 SECT →0456
翼 WING →3379
系 faction →2443
門 (religious) sect →1100
宗 RELIGIOUS SECT (esp. Buddhist) →2769
❿ class
級 GRADE →1630
段 grade →1471
位 RANK →0069
階 RANK →0761
身 social status →4368
格 STATUS →1161
等 CLASS →3321
流 class →0529
層 STRATUM →3920

浸
0530
1-3-7

▸SOAK
シン ひた(す) ひた(る)
Ⓝ 浸 Ⓒ 浸 jìn

85	Jōyō	U6D78
氵	S10-3-7	F1626

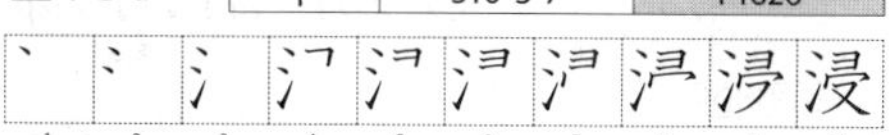

COMPOUNDS
❶ⓐ [original meaning] **SOAK, immerse**

b [formerly also 滲 0862] **permeate, infiltrate, penetrate; ooze, seep**

a 浸水 しんすい inundation, submergence

b 浸透 しんとう permeation, penetration

浸潤 しんじゅん permeation, infiltration

浸出 しんしゅつ percolation, exudation, effusion

2 gradual, gradually

浸食 しんしょく erosion, corrosion

KUN

【ひたす 浸す】*vt* **SOAK, dip, steep, immerse; drench, moisten**

浸し物 ひたしもの boiled greens flavored with soy

布を染料に浸す ぬのをせんりょうにひたす soak cloth in a dye

水浸し みずびたし submergence; being water-logged

牛乳に浸したパン ぎゅうにゅうにひたしたぱん bread dunked in milk

【ひたる 浸る】*vi* **be SOAKed in, dip in; be addicted to, be indulged in**

風呂の湯に浸る ふろのゆにひたる soak in a bath-tub, sink into a hot bath

幸福に浸る こうふくにひたる swim in bliss

入り浸り いりびたり frequenting; staying long

SYNONYMS

1 moisten

潤 moisten →0918

浸 SOAK →0530

漬ける immerse →0861

USAGE

【しんしょく】

浸食

erosion, corrosion

侵食

infringement, violation

NOTE

★ do not confuse with 侵 INVADE →0116

消

▸EXTINGUISH
▸SPEND

ショウ き(える) け(す)

0531

N 消 C 消 xiāo

1-3-7

85	Jōyō-3	U6D88
氵	S10-3-7	F0389

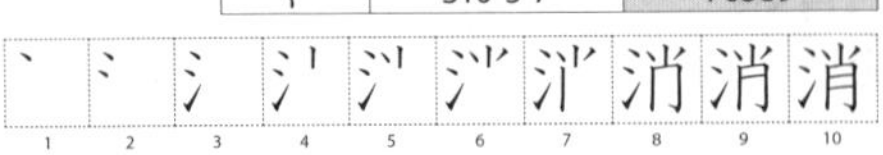

COMPOUNDS

1 (put out a light or fire) **EXTINGUISH, put out; switch off**

消防 しょうぼう fire fighting, prevention and extinction of fires

消防車 しょうぼうしゃ fire engine

消火 しょうか fire fighting

消灯する しょうとうする turn off the lights

2 a (wipe out of existence) **EXTINGUISH, eliminate, remove from, obliterate**

b disappear, vanish

a 消化 しょうか digestion; assimilation; consumption

消毒 しょうどく disinfection, sterilization

消音 しょうおん silencing (a machine)

消臭剤 しょうしゅうざい deodorant

消却する しょうきゃくする efface; erase

消磁 しょうじ demagnetization

解消する かいしょうする liquidate, annul, solve; be liquidated, be solved

抹消する まっしょうする erase, strike out

b 消息 しょうそく (personal) news, movements; letter

消失する しょうしつする disappear, vanish; die away

消滅する しょうめつする become extinct, disappear

3 a SPEND, use up, consume; become spent out

b [formerly also 銷 2174] **SPEND** (time), pass

a 消費する しょうひする consume, spend

消費者 しょうひしゃ consumer

消耗する しょうもうする consume, exhaust, use up

b 消夏 しょうか summering

消光する しょうこうする pass one's time

4 negative

消極的な しょうきょくてきな negative

5 [formerly also 銷 2174 or 悄 0506] become dispirited, become disheartened; be worried

消然(=悄然)たる しょうぜんたる dejected, dispirited

意気消沈(=意気銷沈)する いきしょうちんする be dispirited, be disheartened

KUN

【きえる 消える】*vi* **be EXTINGUISHed, go [die] out; disappear, vanish, melt away, wear out [away]**

消えた火 きえたひ dead fire

消え去る きえさる vanish, disappear

立ち消え たちぎえ going out; flickering out

【けす 消す】*vt* (put out a light or fire) **EXTINGUISH, put out; switch off;** (wipe out of existence) **extinguish, eliminate, remove from, obliterate; cancel, annul**

消し止める けしとめる put out, extinguish

消しゴム けしごむ eraser

消印 けしいん postmark, (postal) cancellation mark

インク消し いんくけし ink eraser

取り消す とりけす cancel, nullify, annul

SYNONYMS

1 extinguish

消 EXTINGUISH →0531

熄 GO OUT →1339

滅 go out →0812

❷ⓐ destroy

滅 DESTROY →0812
毀 DESTROY →2246
亡 perish →4210
消 EXTINGUISH →0531
剿 EXTERMINATE →2335

ⓑ disappear

消 disappear →0531
没 disappear →0305

❸ⓐ consume

消 SPEND →0531
費 expend →3221
尽 EXHAUST →3786
耗 WEAR AWAY →1660
銷 USE UP →2174

NOTE

➡ see COMPOUND FORMATION for 消息 しょうそく →息 3278

酒

▶ALCOHOLIC DRINK

シュ さけ さか-

Ⓒ 酒 jiǔ

0532

◧ 1-3-7

164	Jōyō-3	U9152
酉	S10-7-3	F0511

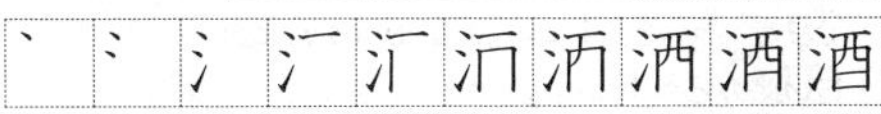

1 2 3 4 5 6 7 8 9 10

COMPOUNDS

ⓐ [also suffix] [original meaning] **ALCOHOLIC DRINK, wine, liquor, beer**

ⓑ **sake, rice wine**

a 酒造 しゅぞう sake brewing; distilling
酒家 しゅか wine shop, pub; heavy drinker
酒宴 しゅえん banquet, drinking bout
飲酒 いんしゅ drinking (alcoholic drinks)
洋酒 ようしゅ foreign wine [liquors]
醸造酒 じょうぞうしゅ brewage, liquor

b 清酒 せいしゅ (refined) sake

KUN

【さけ 酒, さか- 酒-】 **sake, rice wine; ALCOHOLIC DRINK, wine, liquor, beer**

お酒 おさけ sake, rice wine; alcoholic drink, wine, liquor, beer
酒癖が悪い さけぐせがわるい be a bad drunk
酒飲み さけのみ drinker
酒屋 さかや sake dealer, liquor store
酒場 さかば bar, barroom, pub, tavern
酒盛り さかもり drinking bout, merrymaking
甘酒 あまざけ sweet rice wine

SPECIAL READINGS

お神酒 おみき sacred wine [sake]; sake

SYNONYMS

● drinks

汁 JUICE, SOUP →0227
乳 MILK →1823
酒 ALCOHOLIC DRINK →0532
茶 TEA →2808
珈 COFFEE →1138
醇 UNDILUTED WINE →2001
酎 SHOCHU →1852

浴

▶BATHE

ヨク あ(びる) あ(びせる) ㊔ えき あみ

Ⓒ 浴 yù

0533

◧ 1-3-7

85	Jōyō-4	U6D74
氵	S10-3-7	F1145

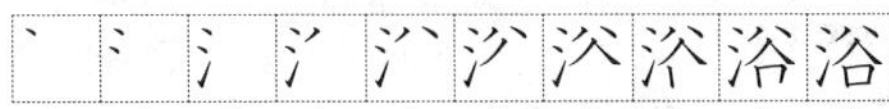

1 2 3 4 5 6 7 8 9 10

COMPOUNDS

❶ [original meaning] **BATHE**

浴場 よくじょう bath, bathhouse
浴槽 よくそう bathtub
浴室 よくしつ bathroom
入浴する にゅうよくする bathe, take a bath

❷ⓐ [suffix] **bath, bathing**

ⓑ (liquid or container for immersion) **bath**

a 海水浴 かいすいよく sea bathing
日光浴 にっこうよく sunbath
冷水浴 れいすいよく cold-water bath

b 塩浴 えんよく salt bath

INDEPENDENT

【よく 浴】 bath (→❷)
【よくする 浴する】 bask in, be favored with

KUN

【あびる 浴びる】 *vi* **BATHE, take a bath; be bathed (in sunlight); be washed (by the waves); be under fire; be charged with (a crime); be covered (with dust)**

水浴びする みずあびする bathe in cold water

【あびせる 浴びせる】 *vt* **pour (water) on; subject to, shower (abuse) upon, deluge with**

非難を浴びせる ひなんをあびせる heap abuse upon (a person)

SPECIAL READINGS

浴衣 ゆかた(=よくい) informal summer kimono, *yukata*

SYNONYMS

❶ clean and wash

洗 WASH →0465

漱 RINSE →0865
拭 WIPE →0453
滌 WASH →0854
濯 RINSE →0978
浴 BATHE →0533
浄 cleanse →0457
粛 PURGE →4400
清 CLEAR →0635
払 CLEAR AWAY →0225
掃 SWEEP →0611

❷ⓐ baths

浴 bath →0533
湯 hot bath →0747
泉 hot spring →3176

浮

0534

1-3-7

▸FLOAT

フ う(く) う(かれる) う(かぶ) う(かべる)

85	Nonstandard	U6D6E
氵	S10-3-7	F0000

traditional form → see 浮 at 0522

海

0535

1-3-7

▸SEA

カイ うみ ㊔ あま ひろし み

85	Names	UFA45
氵	S10-3-7	F0000

traditional form → see 海 at 0459

浩

0536

1-3-7

▸VAST

コウ ㊔ ひろ ひろし ひろむ ごう はる ゆたか

85	Nonstandard	U2F903
氵	S10-3-7	F0000

traditional form → see 浩 at 0525

浸

0537

1-3-7

▸SOAK

シン ひた(す) ひた(る)

85	Nonstandard	U6D78
氵	S10-3-7	F0000

traditional form → see 浸 at 0530

涉

0538

1-3-7

▸HAVE RELATIONS WITH

ショウ ㊔ わたる わたり

85	Names	U6D89
氵	S10-3-7	F0000

traditional form → see 渉 at 0638

消

0539

1-3-7

▸EXTINGUISH
▸SPEND

ショウ き(える) け(す)

85	Nonstandard	U6D88
氵	S10-3-7	F0000

traditional form → see 消 at 0531

涌

0540

1-3-7

▸WELL UP

ユウ ヨウ わ(く) ㊔ いさむ

85	Nonstandard	U6D8C
氵	S10-3-7	F0000

traditional form → see 湧 at 0749

淳

1-3-7

incorrect stroke-count
➡ see 1-3-8: 氵 at 0626

狼

0541

1-3-7

▸WOLF

ロウ おおかみ

Ⓒ 狼 láng

94	Names	U72FC
犭	S10-3-7	F1747

COMPOUNDS

● [original meaning] **WOLF**

狼藉 ろうぜき disorder; violence
狼瘡× ろうそう lupus, esp. lupus vulgaris
餓狼 がろう hungry wolf
虎狼 ころう tigers and wolves; greedy brute
天狼星 てんろうせい Sirius
周章狼狽×する しゅうしょうろうばいする be disconcerted, be confused

KUN

【おおかみ 狼】**WOLF**

狼男 おおかみおとこ werewolf
狼少年 おおかみしょうねん The Boy Who Cried Wolf; child reared by a wolf
一匹狼 いっぴきおおかみ lone wolf; loner, maverick
赤狼 あかおおかみ red wolf
袋狼 ふくろおおかみ Tasmanian tiger, Tasmanian wolf
送り狼 おくりおおかみ man who escorts a woman with lecherous motives

SPECIAL READINGS

狼狽×える うろたえる be flustered, lose one's presence of mind
狼煙(=烽×火) のろし beacon, signal fire [rocket]

SYNONYMS

● **undomesticated mammals**

虎 TIGER →3981
猿 MONKEY →0824
鯨 WHALE →2361

犀 RHINOCEROS → 3900
狼 WOLF → 0541
狐 FOX → 0472
羚 SEROW → 1695
鼠 RAT → 3340
獅 LION → 0825
豹 LEOPARD → 1847
熊 BEAR → 3530
象 ELEPHANT → 2647
麒 MALE CHINESE UNICORN → 2363
麟 FEMALE CHINESE UNICORN → 2376
猪 WILD BOAR → 0652
鹿 DEER → 3879

狹 0542

1-3-7

▶**NARROW**

キョウ　せま(い)　せば(める)　せば(まる)

94	Names	U72F9
犭	S10-3-7	F0000

traditional form → see 狭 at 0473

猛

1-3-7

incorrect stroke-count
➡ see 1-3-8: 犭 at 0653

陛 0543

1-3-7

▶**IMPERIAL PALACE STEPS**

ヘイ

Ⓒ 陛 bì

170	Jōyō-6	U965B
阝	S10-3-7	F1691

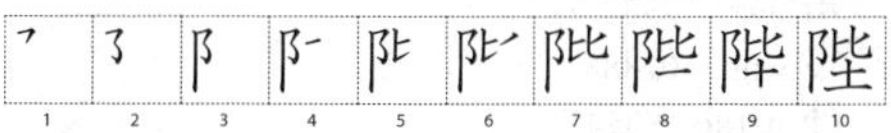

COMPOUNDS

● [original meaning] **IMPERIAL PALACE STEPS, steps leading to the imperial palace hall**

陛下 へいか His [Her, Your] Majesty; [original meaning] at the palace steps
陛衛 へいえい [archaic] Imperial guard
天皇陛下 てんのうへいか His Majesty the Emperor, His Imperial Majesty

SYNONYMS

● **steps**

段 STEP → 1471
階 stairs → 0761
陛 IMPERIAL PALACE STEPS → 0543
梯 LADDER → 1210

NOTE

★ do not confuse with 階 FLOOR → 0761

院 0544

1-3-7

▶**INSTITUTION**

イン

Ⓒ 院 yuàn

170	Jōyō-3	U9662
阝	S10-3-7	F0324

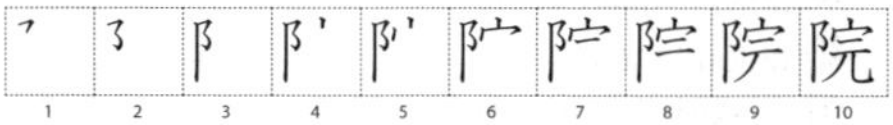

COMPOUNDS

❶ [also suffix] **INSTITUTION** or organization, esp.:
ⓐ medical **INSTITUTION**: **hospital, clinic, doctor's office**
ⓑ educational **INSTITUTION**: **academy, institute, school**

a 院長 いんちょう hospital director; academy president
病院 びょういん hospital
医院 いいん clinic
入院する にゅういんする be hospitalized
退院 たいいん discharge from a hospital
養老院 ようろういん institution for the aged

b 院生 いんせい graduate student
学院 がくいん institute, academy
孤児院 こじいん orphanage
大学院 だいがくいん graduate school
美容院 びよういん beauty shop [parlor]

❷ [also suffix] legislative **INSTITUTION** or body: **House, Diet, Congress, Parliament**

院内 いんない inside the House [Diet]
上院 じょういん Upper House
議院 ぎいん House, Diet Chamber
両院 りょういん both Houses
参議院 さんぎいん House of Councilors, Upper House
衆議院 しゅうぎいん House of Representatives, Lower House

❸ religious **INSTITUTION**: **monastery, (Buddhist) temple**

寺院 じいん temple
尼僧院 にそういん nunnery, convent
修道院 しゅうどういん monastery, convent

❹ⓐ ex-emperor, cloistered emperor; palace of ex-emperor
ⓑ honorific suffix after names of ex-emperors

a 院政 いんせい government by cloistered emperor
b 後鳥羽院 ごとばいん ex-Emperor Gotoba

❺ honorific suffix after posthumous Buddhist names

保善院 ほぜんいん Hozen of Blessed Memory

INDEPENDENT

【いん 院】**INSTITUTION**; House of Representatives, House of Councillors; palace of ex-emperor

院の内外 いんのないがい legislative circles

口 土 女 子 山 彳 忄 扌 氵 犭 【阝】 丬 饣 纟 歹

SYNONYMS

❶ organized bodies

会 SOCIETY → 2512
協 association → 0103
団 BODY → 3791
体 BODY → 0080
組 union → 1693
労 workers' union → 3155
連 federation → 3849
講 fraternity → 2046
院 INSTITUTION → 0544

ⓑ schools

校 SCHOOL → 1166
学 EDUCATIONAL INSTITUTION → 3162
院 INSTITUTION → 0544
塾 PRIVATE SCHOOL → 3546
大 UNIVERSITY → 4224
高 high school → 2601
中 junior high school → 4262
小 elementary school → 0007
園 kindergarten → 3914

❷ legislature

議 LEGISLATIVE BODY → 2078
会 assembly → 2512
院 House → 0544

❸ places of worship

堂 temple building → 3202
塔 pagoda → 0683
寺 BUDDHIST TEMPLE → 2687
刹 TEMPLE → 1620
社 Shinto shrine → 1042
宮 SHINTO SHRINE → 2828
院 monastery → 0544
教 church → 1887

陣

▶BATTLE FORMATION
▶CAMP

ジン

0545 Ⓒ 阵 zhèn

1-3-7

170	Jōyō	U9663
阝	S10-3-7	F0853

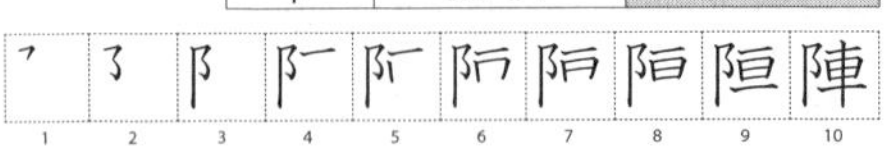

COMPOUNDS

❶ⓐ BATTLE FORMATION, battle array, troop deployment, battle position, battlefield
ⓑ battle, war
ⓒ battle troops, army

a 陣形 じんけい battle formation
陣容 じんよう battle formation; members of a group
陣立て じんだて battle array
円陣 えんじん circular formation, circle
西陣織 にしじんおり *Nishijin* brocade
b 陣没 じんぼつ death in battle
先陣 せんじん advance guard, vanguard
c 陣頭 じんとう head of an army

❷ army CAMP, encampment, position

陣営 じんえい camp, quarters
陣地 じんち encampment, position
退陣する たいじんする decamp, withdraw
論陣を張る ろんじんをはる argue about, take a firm stand

❸ [suffix] (group of persons performing a common action)
lineup, corps, CAMP, group

報道陣 ほうどうじん reportorial camp, press corps
教授陣 きょうじゅじん professorate, faculty, group of professors

❹ occurring in spells

陣痛 じんつう labor pains
一陣の風 いちじんのかぜ gust of wind

INDEPENDENT

【じん 陣】 **CAMP**, encampment; battle formation, battle position; battle

陣を張る じんをはる pitch camp
陣を立て直す じんをたてなおす redeploy troops
夏の陣 なつのじん summer battle

SYNONYMS

❶ⓑ warfare and rebellions

戦 WAR → 2242
軍 war → 2582
役 war → 0288
陣 battle → 0545
乱 rebellion → 1611
変 uprising → 2569
闘 FIGHT → 4136

❷ camps

陣 CAMP → 0545
営 BARRACKS → 3216

❸ groups

群 GROUP (of any kind) → 1942
班 SQUAD → 1182
軍 team → 2582
組 group (of people) → 1693
陣 lineup → 0545
連 set → 3849
族 common-interest group (*slang*) → 1195
党 PARTY → 3190
隊 PARTY (organized group) → 0762
団 BODY → 3791
伍 ranks → 0050

COMPOUND FORMATION

【西陣織 にしじんおり】

西陣 originally referred to the western (西) battlefield (陣 ❶ⓐ) in Kyoto. Since the area is well known as a textile district, 西陣織 '*Nishijin* brocade' refers to a type of brocade (織) from that area.

NOTE

★ do not confuse with 陳 SET FORTH → 0656

除

0546

◧ 1-3-7

▶RID OF

ジョ ジ のぞ(く) よ(ける)▲ -よ(け)▲

Ⓒ 除 chú

170	Jōyō-6	U9664
阝	S10-3-7	F0835

COMPOUNDS

❶ **RID OF, clear away, remove, eliminate**

除去する じょきょする rid of, remove, eliminate

除雪する じょせつする get rid of snow, remove snow

除外 じょがい exclusion, exception

解除する かいじょする remove [lift] (a ban), cancel; release, acquit

掃除 そうじ cleaning

排除 はいじょ exclusion, removal, elimination

削除する さくじょする delete, eliminate, cancel

控除 こうじょ (tax) deduction, subtraction

❷ get **RID OF** the old in favor of the new

除夜 じょや New Year's Eve

❸ *math* divide

除数 じょすう divisor

乗除 じょうじょ multiplication and division

INDEPENDENT

【じょ 除】*math* division

【じょする 除する】exclude; *math* divide

KUN

【のぞく 除く】**RID OF, remove; abolish, cancel; exclude, omit**

取り除く とりのぞく get rid of, remove, take away

月曜日を除いて げつようびをのぞいて excepting Mondays

【よける 除ける】[also 避ける] avoid, shun, evade; avert, ward off

【-よけ -除け】protection, keeping off; charm, amulet

霜除け しもよけ shelter against frost

弾除け たまよけ protection against bullets; charm against bullets

SYNONYMS

❶ **eliminate**

却 ELIMINATE → 1436

排 EXCLUDE → 0593

払う CLEAR AWAY → 0225

剥 PEEL OFF → 2105

耘 WEED → 1661

削 cross out → 1837

抹 wipe off → 0370

省 leave out → 3100

脱 REMOVE → 1225

去 take away → 2678

外す take off → 0215

除 RID OF → 0546

撤 WITHDRAW → 0912

❸ **divide**

除 divide → 0546

割る DIVIDE → 2284

陥

0547

◧ 1-3-7

▶FALL IN

カン おちい(る) おとしい(れる)

Ⓝ 陷 Ⓒ 陷 xiàn

170	Jōyō	U9665
阝	S10-3-7	F1448

COMPOUNDS

❶ⓐ [original meaning] **FALL IN, cave in, collapse, sink**

ⓑ cause to **FALL IN**to (a trap)

a 陥没する かんぼつする sink, fall, cave in

陥入する かんにゅうする subside, fall [cave] in, collapse

陥落する かんらくする fall in, cave in; surrender

b 陥穽× かんせい pitfall, trap; plot

❷ fall, surrender

失陥 しっかん fall, surrender of one's land

❸ **defect, fault**

欠陥 けっかん defect, fault, deficiency

KUN

【おちいる 陥る】*vi* **FALL INto, be led into, lapse into; fall (as of a castle), be reduced; fall in, sink**

誤りに陥る あやまりにおちいる fall into error

罪に陥る つみにおちいる slide into sin

穴に陥る あなにおちいる fall in a pit

【おとしいれる 陥れる】*vt* **entrap, entice, lead into; capture, carry (a castle)**

人を陥れる ひとをおとしいれる entrap a person

困難に陥れる こんなんにおとしいれる put (a person) in a fix

城を陥れる しろをおとしいれる carry a castle

SYNONYMS

❶ⓐ **collapse**

陥 FALL IN → 0547

落 FALL → 2907

崩 CRUMBLE → 2863
没 SINK → 0305

❸ **faults and flaws**
難 fault → 2310
短 shortcoming → 1515
疵 DEFECT → 4067
陥 defect → 0547
欠 incompleteness → 2481

降

▸DESCEND
コウ ゴウ▲ お(りる) お(ろす) ふ(る) ふ(り) くだ(る)▲ くだ(す)▲

0548
1-3-7

N 降 C 降 jiàng xiáng

170	Jōyō-6	U964D
阝	S10-3-7	F0530

COMPOUNDS

❶ move from a higher to a lower place:
ⓐ [original meaning] **DESCEND, fall, come down, drop**
ⓑ **DESCEND** from heaven: **fall, come down**—said of atmospheric moisture such as rain
ⓒ **alight, get off**

a 降下する こうかする descend, fall, drop
滑降 かっこう descent (in skiing)
昇降する しょうこうする ascend and descend, go up and down
沈降する ちんこうする precipitate, subside

b 降雨 こうう rainfall, rain
降水 こうすい precipitation
降雪 こうせつ snowfall, snow

c 降車する こうしゃする alight, get off, get down
乗降 じょうこう boarding and alighting, getting on and off

❷ⓐ **DESCEND** upon the earth, make an appearance
ⓑ cause to **DESCEND** upon, invoke (a divinity)

a 降誕 こうたん birth, nativity; advent
降臨 こうりん advent, descent

b 降神 こうしん spiritism, spiritualism

❸ⓐ cause to **DESCEND** to lower status, demote, reduce the rank or power of
ⓑ **DESCEND** to lower status, degrade oneself

a 降等 こうとう demotion
降給 こうきゅう reduction in pay

b 降嫁 こうか marriage of an Imperial princess to a subject

❹ⓐ **surrender, submit to**
ⓑ cause to surrender, conquer

a 降参する こうさんする surrender, submit, yield
降伏(=降服) こうふく surrender, submission

b 降魔 ごうま conquering the devil

❺ **onward, afterward**
以降 いこう on and after, hereafter

KUN

【おりる 降りる】
①ⓐ (dismount) **alight, get off, disembark**
ⓑ (come down from a high place) **alight, land, swoop**
ⓒ (of frost or rain) **fall, come down**

a 乗り降り のりおり boarding and alighting
b 飛び降りる(=飛び下りる) とびおりる jump off (a moving vehicle), jump down
c 舞い降りる まいおりる fly down, alight

② retire (from a position), withdraw, drop out (of a program), quit

【おろす 降ろす】
① **set (a passenger) down, discharge, unload**
乗客を降ろす じょうきゃくをおろす discharge passengers

② demote, deprive (someone) of (his) role
主役から降ろす しゅやくからおろす relieve someone of the leading role

【ふる 降る】 **fall, come down, rain**—said of atmospheric moisture such as rain or snow
降らす ふらす send (rain), shed
降り懸かる ふりかかる fall upon, come in one's way, impend upon

【ふり 降り】 **fall, rainfall, snowfall**
土砂降り どしゃぶり pouring rain, downpour
雪降り ゆきふり snowfall

【くだる 降る】 surrender, submit to
軍門に降る ぐんもんにくだる surrender, capitulate

【くだす 降す】 [usu. 下す] subjugate, subdue; defeat, beat

SYNONYMS

❶ⓐ **descend and fall**
落 FALL → 2907
墜 DROP DOWN → 3578
降 DESCEND → 0548
下 go down → 4186
倒 TOPPLE → 0139

ⓒ **get off**
降 alight → 0548
下 get down → 4186

❹ⓐ **submit and surrender**
服 SUBMIT → 1090
伏 submit → 0049
屈 bend in submission → 3821
降 surrender → 0548

HOMOPHONES

おりる 下 DOWN →4186

おろす

下 DOWN →4186

卸 WHOLESALE →1835

くだる 下 DOWN →4186

くだす 下 DOWN →4186

NOTE

➡ see USAGE note at 下 4186

陞

0549

◧ 1-3-7

▶ASCEND TO A HIGHER RANK

ショウ

Ⓒ 升 shēng

170	Non-Jōyō	U965E
阝	S10-3-7	F0000

COMPOUNDS

● [now replaced by 昇 3068] **ASCEND TO A HIGHER RANK, rise in rank, be promoted**

陞叙 しょうじょ promotion, advancement

陞進する しょうしんする be promoted, rise in rank

陞任 しょうにん promotion, advancement

SYNONYMS

● **rise in rank**

陞 ASCEND TO A HIGHER RANK →0549

昇 ascend to a higher rank →3068

進 advance in rank →3873

陦

0550

◧ 1-3-7

▶ISLAND

トウ しま

170	Nonstandard	U9666
阝	S10-3-7	F0000

traditional form →see 島 at 4103

陥

◧ 1-3-7

incorrect stroke-count

➡ see ◧ 1-3-8: 阝 at 0663

将

0551

◧ 1-3-7

▶GENERAL OFFICER

ショウ まさ(に)▲ ㊔ まさ まさし まさる ゆき はた

Ⓝ 將 Ⓒ 将 jiāng jiàng qiāng

41	Jōyō-6	U5C06
寸	S10-3-7	F0419

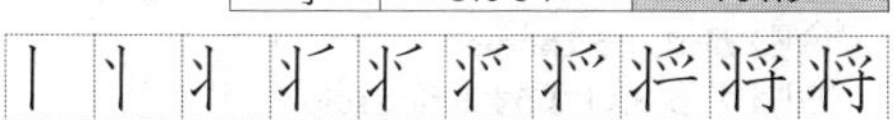

1 2 3 4 5 6 7 8 9 10

COMPOUNDS

❶ⓐ **GENERAL OFFICER, general, admiral, commander; leader**

ⓑ **leading person, superior**

a 将軍 しょうぐん commander, general

将校 しょうこう officer, commissioned officer

将兵 しょうへい officers and men

将官 しょうかん general, admiral

陸将 りくしょう lieutenant general, general officer

大将 たいしょう admiral, general; old chap

武将 ぶしょう commander, warlord

b 将棋 しょうぎ shogi, Japanese chess

王将 おうしょう king (in shogi)

主将 しゅしょう captain

女将 じょしょう(=おかみ) mistress, proprietress, landlady

❷ **on the verge of, be about to happen**

将来 しょうらい future; in the future

❸ take, bring

将来する しょうらいする invite, introduce; bring about, give rise to, cause

INDEPENDENT

【しょう 将】 commander, general, leader

将中に将たる しょうちゅうにしょうたる being a leader among leaders

KUN

【まさに 将に】 be about to, on the verge of

将に滅びんとしている まさにほろびんとしている be on the brink of ruin

SYNONYMS

❶ⓐ **military officers and ranks**

曹 SERGEANT →3414

尉 COMPANY OFFICER →2119

佐 FIELD OFFICER →0076

将 GENERAL OFFICER →0551

督 COMMANDER →3471

帥 COMMANDER IN CHIEF →1642

❷ **on the verge of**

-掛かる be on the verge of →0596

将 on the verge of →0551

-際 on the verge of →0874

臨 on the point of →2059

HOMOPHONES

まさに

正 RIGHT →4296

当 THE PRESENT →2701

NOTE

➡ see USAGE note at 正 4296

修候

◧ 1-3-7

incorrect classification

➡ see ◧ 1-2-8: 亻 at 0122

郷

◧ 1-3-7

incorrect stroke-count

➡ see ◧ 1-3-8: 阝 at 0664

卿 0552

▶**STATE MINISTER**

キョウ ケイ ㊔ あき のり あきら

26	Nonstandard	U537F
冂	S10-2-8	F0000

1-3-7

traditional form → see 卿 at 0769

唾 0553

▶**SALIVA**

ダ タ▲ つば つばき

Ⓒ 唾 tuò

30	Jōyō	U553E
口	S11-3-8	F1901

1-3-8

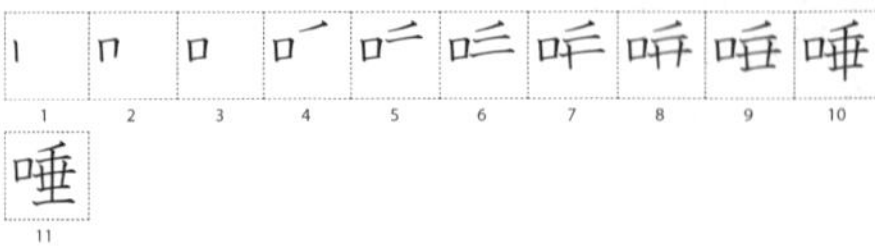

COMPOUNDS

ⓐ **SALIVA, spit, sputum**
ⓑ spit, expectorate

a 唾液 だえき saliva, sputum
唾壺 だこ spittoon
b 唾棄する だきする spit out; despise

KUN

【つば 唾】**spit, SALIVA, sputum**
唾する つばする spit
生唾 なまつば saliva (in one's mouth)
眉唾物 まゆつばもの fake, counterfeit

【つばき 唾】same as 唾 つば

SPECIAL READINGS

固唾 かたず saliva (in one's mouth at times of tension)

SYNONYMS

ⓐ **bodily secretions**
乳 MILK → 1823
精 sperm → 1729
汗 SWEAT → 0256
涙 TEAR → 0528
唾 SALIVA → 0553

喝 0554

▶**SHOUT AT**

カツ

Ⓝ 喝 Ⓒ 喝 hē hè

30	Jōyō	U559D
口	S11-3-8	F2076

1-3-8

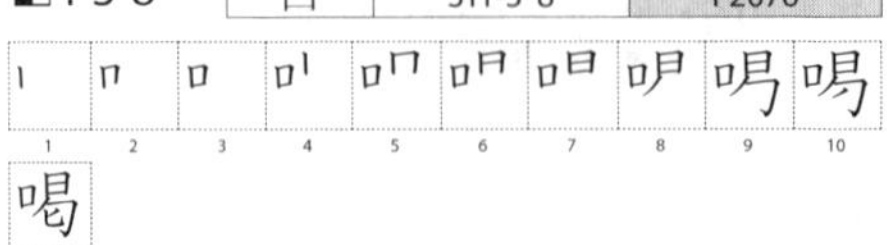

COMPOUNDS

❶ **SHOUT AT, roar, bark, bellow, bawl, bawl out**
喝采 かっさい applause, cheers
喝破する かっぱする shout someone down, declare, pronounce
一喝 いっかつ thundering cry, roar
大喝する だいかつする shout in a thunderous voice

❷ **SHOUT** threats **AT** someone, intimidate, threaten
恐喝する きょうかつする threaten, menace
恫×喝 どうかつ threat, intimidation

INDEPENDENT

【かつ 喝】shouting in Zen meditation to awaken trainees
【かっす 喝す】**SHOUT** threats **AT** someone

SYNONYMS

❶ **give out a call**
叫 SHOUT → 0233
号 holler → 2675
喝 SHOUT AT → 0554
喚 call out → 0666
呼 CALL → 0324
鳴 CRY → 0831
吠 BARK → 0269

❷ **threaten**
脅 THREATEN → 2614
劫 threaten → 1435
威 THREATEN BY FORCE → 4394
嚇 INTIMIDATE → 0964
喝 shout threats at → 0554

唱 0555

▶**SING**

ショウ とな(える) ㊔ うた

Ⓒ 唱 chàng

30	Jōyō-4	U5531
口	S11-3-8	F1320

1-3-8

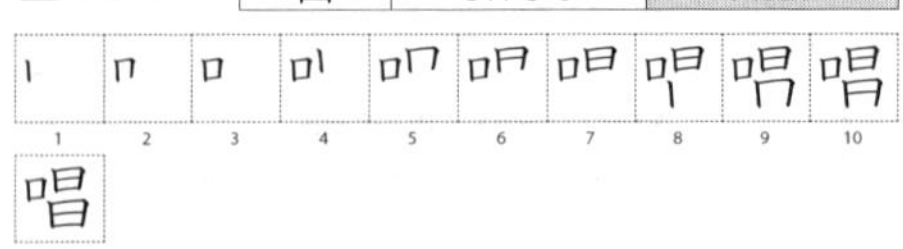

COMPOUNDS

❶ⓐ [original meaning] **SING, chant**
ⓑ song

a 合唱 がっしょう chorus
独唱する どくしょうする sing solo
b 唱歌 しょうか song

❷ [formerly also 誦 1951] **chant, recite, intone**
唱和する しょうわする chant [cheer] in chorus
吟唱する ぎんしょうする recite, chant
暗唱する あんしょうする recite from memory
詠唱する えいしょうする chant

三唱 さんしょう cheering (banzai) three times

❸ **advocate, preach**

唱導 しょうどう advocacy

提唱する ていしょうする advocate, propose

KUN

【となえる 唱える】**chant, recite, repeat; cry, cheer; advocate, set forth, preach; quote (prices)**

念仏を唱える ねんぶつをとなえる chant [repeat] the name of Buddha

主戦論を唱える しゅせんろんをとなえる advocate war

SYNONYMS

❶ⓐ **sing**

唱 SING →0555

歌 sing →2296

❷ **recite**

吟 RECITE →0271

誦 RECITE →1951

唱 chant →0555

読 READ →1943

詠 RECITE POETRY →1894

❸ **advocate**

唱 advocate →0555

説 preach →1949

唯

0556

◧ 1-3-8

▸**ONLY**

ユイ イ ただ▲ ㊔ ただし

Ⓒ 唯 wéi wěi

30	Jōyō	U552F
口	S11-3-8	F1439

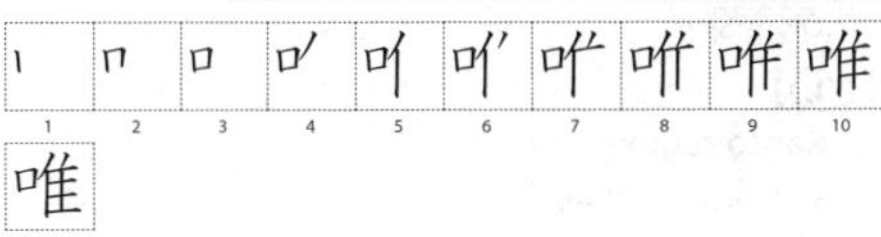

COMPOUNDS

❶ [rarely also 惟 ゆい 0582] **ONLY, sole, one and only**

唯一の ゆいいつの the only, the sole

唯一無二の ゆいいつむにの the one and only, unique

唯心論 ゆいしんろん idealism, spiritualism

唯美主義 ゆいびしゅぎ aestheticism

唯物主義 ゆいぶつしゅぎ materialism

❷ yes

唯唯諾諾として いいだくだくとして willingly, readily

KUN

【ただ 唯】[also 只] **ONLY, just, merely, solely**

唯一度 ただいちど only once

唯そこへ行きさえすれば良い ただそこへいきさえすればよい have [need] only to go there

SYNONYMS

❶ **only**

唯 ONLY →0556

一 one and only →4148

USAGE

【ただ】

唯

[also 只] only, just, merely, solely

只

① no charge

② ordinariness, plainness

③ doing nothing, being idle

只-

① free of charge, cost-free, for nothing

② ordinary, common, plain

③ [also 唯] only, just, merely, solely

HOMOPHONES

ただ 只 FREE OF CHARGE →2677

啄

0557

◧ 1-3-8

▸**PECK**

タク トク ついば(む)

30	Nonstandard	U5544
口	S11-3-8	F0000

traditional form →see 啄 at 0482

喋

◧ 1-3-8

incorrect stroke-count

➡ see ◧ 1-3-9: 口 at 0665

培

0558

◧ 1-3-8

▸**CULTIVATE**

バイ つちか(う) ㊔ ます

Ⓒ 培 péi

32	Jōyō	U57F9
土	S11-3-8	F1882

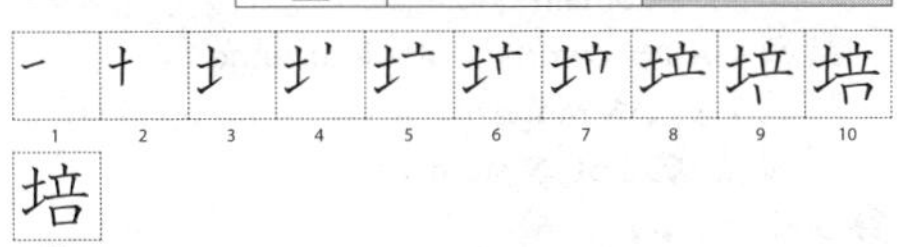

COMPOUNDS

ⓐ [original meaning] (work the earth to grow vegetation) **CULTIVATE, raise, grow**

ⓑ (grow microorganisms) **CULTIVATE**, culture

a 栽培 さいばい cultivation, raising, growing

b 培養 ばいよう cultivation, culture, incubation

培地 ばいち culture medium

KUN

【つちかう 培う】**raise, grow; CULTIVATE, foster**

異境に培われた花 いきょうにつちかわれたはな flower grown in a foreign land

愛国心を培う あいこくしんをつちかう foster a patriotic spirit

口 【土】 女 山 巾 弓 彳 忄 扌 氵 犭 阝 亻 彳 纟

SYNONYMS

ⓐ farm and plant

植 PLANT → 1247
栽 PLANT (saplings) → 4087
培 CULTIVATE → 0558
耕 TILL → 1659
作 raise crops → 0077
農 farm, FARMING → 3345
蒔 SOW → 2935
播 SOW → 0906
帯 BELT → 3191
圏 SPHERE → 3904

ⓑ range

程 EXTENT → 1524
範 range → 3360
域 area → 0559
圏 SPHERE → 3904
野 FIELD → 1877
界 field (*phys*) → 3172
場 field (*phys*, *psychol*) → 0678

域

▸BOUNDED AREA

イキ

Ⓒ 域 yù

0559

1-3-8

32	Jōyō-6	U57DF
土	S11-3-8	F0548

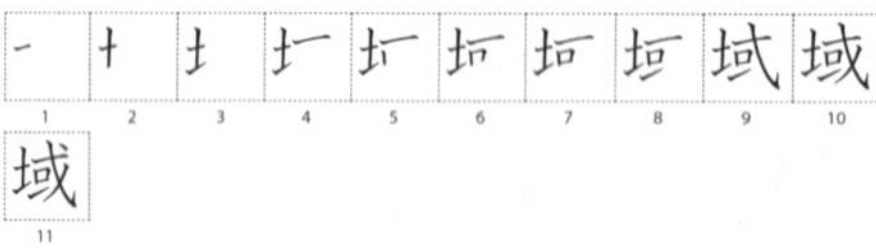

COMPOUNDS

❶ [also suffix]
ⓐ BOUNDED AREA, region, limits, zone, district
ⓑ (scope of something) **area, range**

a 域内の いきないの within the area
地域 ちいき region, area
水域 すいいき water area, waters
区域 くいき zone, area; limits
海域 かいいき sea area
全域 ぜんいき the whole area, entire region
b 聖域 せいいき holy [sacred] precincts, sanctuary
領域 りょういき territory, domain, sphere, province; *math* domain
音域 おんいき compass, (singing) range
職域 しょくいき range of one's work [occupation]
暴風域 ぼうふういき storm area

❷ land, country
異域 いいき foreign land

INDEPENDENT

【いき 域】 level, stage, confines
名人の域に達する めいじんのいきにたっする reach the stage of a master

SYNONYMS

❶ⓐ areas and localities

地 PLACE → 0236
方 locality → 2459
辺 VICINITY → 3761
域 BOUNDED AREA → 0559
区 DISTRICT → 3681
領 TERRITORY → 1567

埼

▸SAITAMA

キ▲ さい さき▲

Ⓒ 埼 qí

0560

1-3-8

32	Jōyō	U57FC
土	S11-3-8	F2090

KUN

【さい 埼】 SAITAMA Prefecture
埼玉県 さいたまけん Saitama Prefecture
埼京線 さいきょうせん Saikyo Line
埼北 さいほく Saihoku (northern Saitama)

【さき 埼】
ⓐ [now usu. 崎] **promontory, cape**
ⓑ **suffix after names of promontories or capes**
b 犬吠埼 いぬぼうさき Cape Inubo

SYNONYMS

【さい】

◯ Kanto region

京 TOKYO → 2546
東 Tokyo → 4385
都 METROPOLIS OF TOKYO → 2120
浜 Yokohama → 0523
埼 SAITAMA → 0560
湘 SHONAN → 0742

【さき】

◯ points of land

岬 CAPE → 0340
崎 PROMONTORY → 0569
埼 promontory → 0560

HOMOPHONES

さき 崎 PROMONTORY → 0569

NOTE

➡ see USAGE note at 崎 0569

堀

▶DITCH
クツ▴ ほり
Ⓒ 堀 kū

0561
1-3-8

32	Jōyō	U5800
土	S11-3-8	F0936

Stroke order: 1–11

COMPOUNDS

● [original meaning, now obsolete] **dig**

KUN

【ほり 堀】

① **DITCH, canal**
堀川 ほりかわ canal
堀割り ほりわり canal, ditch
用水堀 ようすいぼり irrigation ditch
釣り堀 つりぼり fishing pond, fishpond

② [sometimes also 濠 or 壕] **moat**
堀端 ほりばた edge of the moat
外堀 そとぼり outer moat

SYNONYMS

【ほり】

① **holes and cavities**
穴 HOLE →2682
洞 CAVE →0455
窟 CAVE →2923
窪 HOLLOW →2962
腔 BODY CAVITY →1267
孔 OPEN HOLE →0205
口 MOUTH →4189
坑 PIT →0277
堀 DITCH →0561
溝 CHANNEL →0810
壕 TRENCH →0966
濠 MOAT →0975
凹 concavity →4294

USAGE

【ほり】

堀
① ditch, canal
② [sometimes also 濠 or 壕] moat

濠
[usu. 堀, sometimes also 壕] moat

壕
① [usu. 堀] ditch, canal
② [usu. 堀, sometimes also 濠] moat

HOMOPHONES

ほり
濠 MOAT →0975
壕 TRENCH →0966

NOTE

★ do not confuse with 掘 DIG →0601

埴

▶CLAY
ショク はに
Ⓒ 埴 zhí

0562
1-3-8

32	Names	U57F4
土	S11-3-8	F3088

COMPOUNDS

● **CLAY**
埴土 しょくど soil with clay content of 50 percent or more

KUN

【はに 埴】**CLAY**
埴輪 はにわ unglazed earthen objects made in ancient Japan
埴土 はにつち clay
埴瓮× はにべ vessel made of clay

SPECIAL READINGS

埴生 はにゅう clay soil

SYNONYMS

● **land and soil**
土 SOIL →4211
地 GROUND →0236
壌 ARABLE SOIL →0933
泥 MUD →0384
陸 LAND →0659
埴 CLAY →0562

堆

▶PILED HIGH
タイ ツイ▴ うずたか(い)▴ ㊔ たか のぶ おか
Ⓒ 堆 duī

0563
1-3-8

32	Jōyō	U5806
土	S11-3-8	F2507

Stroke order: 1–11

COMPOUNDS

ⓐ **PILED HIGH, accumulated**
ⓑ **be piled up, accumulate**

a 堆石 たいせき pile of stones; moraine
堆朱 ついしゅ red lacquerware with patterns carved in relief

b 堆積 たいせき accumulation, pile, heap
堆肥 たいひ barnyard manure

KUN

【うずたかい 堆い】**PILED HIGH**, accumulated

堆く うずたかく in a heap [pile]

SYNONYMS

● **accumulate**

積 ACCUMULATE → 1579
溜 ACCUMULATE → 0814
累 CUMULATE → 3196
重 pile up → 4390
盛る heap up → 3314
堆 PILED HIGH → 0563

堵

0564

1-3-8

▶**FENCE**

ト

32	Nonstandard	U5835
土	S11-3-8	F0000

traditional form → see 堵 at 0682

婦

0565

1-3-8

▶**ADULT WOMAN**

フ

N 婦 C 妇 fù

38	Jōyō-5	U5A66
女	S11-3-8	F0655

COMPOUNDS

❶ⓐ **ADULT WOMAN, woman, lady**
ⓑ [original meaning] **married woman, wife, housewife**

a 婦人 ふじん woman, lady, female
婦警 ふけい policewoman
婦女 ふじょ woman, the fair sex
裸婦 らふ nude woman
b 主婦 しゅふ housewife
夫婦 ふうふ husband and wife, married couple
新婦 しんぷ bride

❷ⓐ [also suffix] **woman worker, working [career] woman**
ⓑ abbrev. of 看護婦 かんごふ nurse

a 娼×婦 しょうふ prostitute, harlot
看護婦 かんごふ nurse
掃除婦 そうじふ charwoman, cleaning woman
b 婦長 ふちょう chief nurse

INDEPENDENT

【ふ 婦】daughter-in-law

SYNONYMS

❶ⓐ **woman**

女 WOMAN → 4226
婦 ADULT WOMAN → 0565
婆 OLD WOMAN → 3433
嬢 YOUNG LADY → 0936
娘 GIRL → 0488
雌 FEMALE → 1337
牝 FEMALE → 1020
媛 DAMSEL → 0688

ⓑ **wives**

妻 WIFE → 3166
奥 wife → 3503
内 wife → 4277
室 wife (esp. of persons of rank) → 2802
嫡 legitimate wife → 0839
婦 married woman → 0565
嫁 BRIDE → 0780
寡 widow → 2957

❷ⓐ **workers and professionals**

家 professional → 2827
婦 woman worker → 0565
嬢 (unmarried) female worker → 0936
夫 MAN LABORER → 4271
匠 CRAFTSMAN → 3711
工 workman → 4190
客 skilled person → 2798
士 PROFESSION SUFFIX → 4213
師 profession suffix → 1680
者 person who → 3980
人 person of certain category → 4175
員 MEMBER (of a staff) → 2822
屋 colloquial occupation suffix → 3842
手 OCCUPATION SUFFIX → 4267

婚

0566

1-3-8

▶**MARRY**

コン

C 婚 hūn

38	Jōyō	U5A5A
女	S11-3-8	F0519

COMPOUNDS

ⓐ **MARRY, wed**
ⓑ [original meaning] **marriage, wedding**

a 婚姻 こんいん marriage, matrimony
婚礼 こんれい wedding ceremony
婚約 こんやく engagement, betrothal
結婚 けっこん marriage
求婚 きゅうこん proposal of marriage
再婚 さいこん remarriage, second marriage
離婚 りこん divorce
新婚の しんこんの newly wedded

b 婚儀 こんぎ wedding ceremony
金婚 きんこん golden wedding
近親婚 きんしんこん consanguineous marriage

SYNONYMS

● **marrying and marriage**
嫁 WED A MAN → 0780
婚 MARRY → 0566
姻 MARRIAGE → 0421
縁 marriage relation → 1754

娩

0567
◧ 1-3-8

▶**GIVE BIRTH**
ベン

38	Nonstandard	U5A29
女	S11-3-8	F0000

traditional form → see 娩 at 0486

婦

0568
◧ 1-3-8

▶**ADULT WOMAN**
フ

38	Nonstandard	U5A66
女	S11-3-8	F0000

traditional form → see 婦 at 0565

娩

◧ 1-3-8

incorrect stroke-count
➡ see ◧ 1-3-7: 女 at 0486

娯

◧ 1-3-8

incorrect stroke-count
➡ see ◧ 1-3-7: 女 at 0487

崎

0569
◧ 1-3-8

▶**PROMONTORY**
キ▲ さき
Ⓝ 﨑 嵜 嵜 Ⓒ 崎 qí

46	Jōyō	U5D0E
山	S11-3-8	F0590

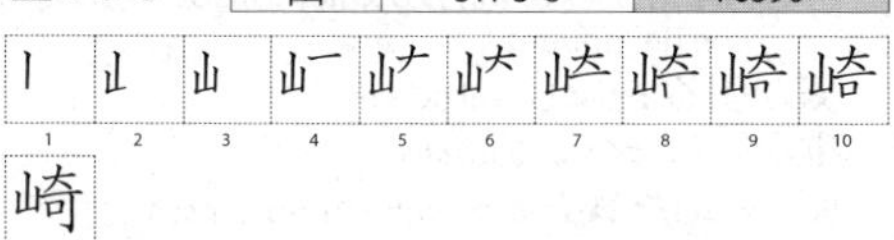

COMPOUNDS

❶ [archaic] **PROMONTORY**, cape
崎陽 きよう Nagasaki

❷ [rare] steep
崎崖 きがい steepness of a mountain

KUN

【さき 崎】
ⓐ [formerly also 埼] **PROMONTORY, cape**
ⓑ **suffix after names of promontories or capes**
a 州崎 すさき sandbar
b 御前崎 おまえざき Cape Omaezaki

SYNONYMS

❶ **points of land**
岬 CAPE → 0340
崎 PROMONTORY → 0569
埼 promontory → 0560

USAGE

【さき】
崎
ⓐ [formerly also 埼] promontory, cape
ⓑ suffix after names of promontories or capes
埼
same as 崎

HOMOPHONES

さき 埼 SAITAMA → 0560

崚

0570
◧ 1-3-8

▶**LOFTY**
リョウ
Ⓒ 崚 léng

46	Names	U5D1A
山	S11-3-8	F0000

COMPOUNDS

● [archaic] as **LOFTY** as a steep mountain range
崚層 りょうそう (of mountains) lofty, soaring

SYNONYMS

● **high**
高 HIGH → 2601
上 upper → 4212
崚 LOFTY → 0570

NOTE

★ do not confuse with 峻 STERN → 0495

崕

0571
◧ 1-3-8

▶**CLIFF**
ガイ がけ

46	Nonstandard	U5D15
山	S11-3-8	F0000

traditional form → see 崖 at 2862

帳

0572
◧ 1-3-8

▶**NOTEBOOK**
チョウ とばり▲
Ⓒ 帐 zhàng

50	Jōyō-3	U5E33
巾	S11-3-8	F1253

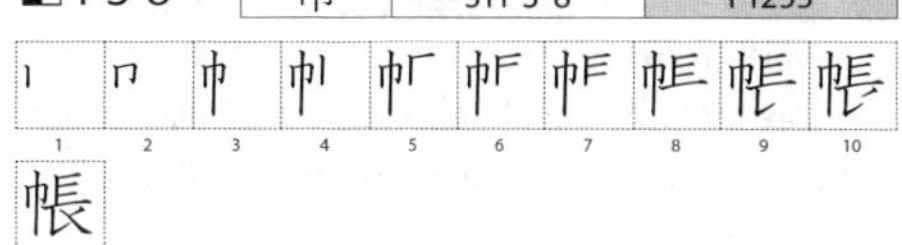

COMPOUNDS

❶ [formerly also 帖 0342] [also suffix] **NOTEBOOK, book, register, account book, album**

口 土 女 山 巾 【弓】 彳 忄 扌 氵 犭 阝 亻 彳 彡

帳面 ちょうめん notebook, account book, register
帳簿 ちょうぼ account book, ledger, register
帳尻 ちょうじり balance of accounts
手帳 てちょう pocketbook, memo
日記帳 にっきちょう diary
通帳 つうちょう bankbook, passbook

❷ [original meaning] **drapery, drop curtain, curtain**
几帳 きちょう screen
几帳面な きちょうめんな exact, precise, punctual
緞×帳 どんちょう thick curtain, drop curtain
開帳する かいちょうする unveil a Buddhist image; gamble

❸ net
蠅×帳 はいちょう fly-net cupboard

KUN

【とばり 帳】veil, curtain
夜の帳 よるのとばり veil of darkness

SPECIAL READINGS

蚊帳 かや mosquito net

SYNONYMS

❶ **notebook**
帳 NOTEBOOK → 0572
帖 NOTEBOOK → 0342
簿 RECORD BOOK → 3387
籍 REGISTER → 3394

❷ **curtain**
幕 CURTAIN → 2937
簾 BAMBOO SCREEN → 3388
帳 drapery → 0572

張

▸SPREAD
▸STRAIN
チョウ は(る) -は(り) -ば(り)

0573

Ⓒ 张 zhāng

1-3-8

57	Jōyō-5	U5F35
弓	S11-3-8	F0296

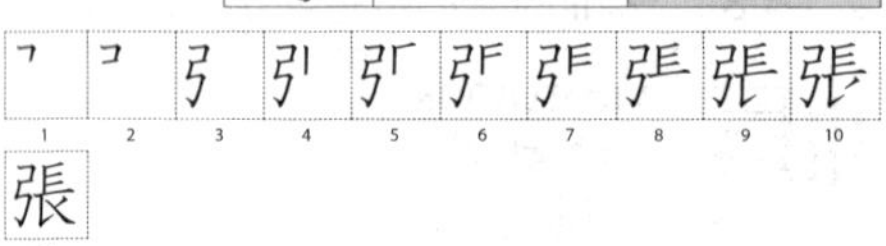

COMPOUNDS

❶ (open to the full extent) **SPREAD (out), extend (over), stretch**
拡張 かくちょう expansion, extension, enlargement
膨張(=膨脹) ぼうちょう expansion, swelling; growth, increase
伸張 しんちょう expansion, elongation
出張する しゅっちょうする travel on official business

❷ⓐ [original meaning] **STRAIN, stretch, be tense, tighten**
ⓑ tension
a 張力 ちょうりょく tension, tensile strength
緊張 きんちょう tension, strain
b 等張の とうちょうの isotonic

❸ **insist, persist**
主張する しゅちょうする insist on, assert, maintain
誇張 こちょう exaggeration, overstatement, magnification

❹ⓐ counter for bows or stringed instruments
ⓑ counter for curtains, screens or nets
a 琴一張 こといっちょう one koto (Japanese harp)
b 幕二張 まくにちょう two curtains
一張羅 いっちょうら one's Sunday best; only suit one has

❺ **unclassified compounds**
張本人 ちょうほんにん originator, perpetrator

KUN

【はる 張る】

① (open to the full extent) **SPREAD (out), extend over, stretch**
縄張り なわばり roping off; one's sphere of influence, one's territory
翼を張る つばさをはる spread the wings

②ⓐ **STRAIN, stretch, tighten**
ⓑ **be stretched [tightened], become taut**
ⓒ **be under STRAIN, be tense, be anxious; be enthusiastic**
a 張り はり tension; will power, pluck
引っ張る ひっぱる pull, draw; drag
糸を張る いとをはる stretch a string
b 張り裂ける はりさける burst (open), break, split
乳が張る ちちがはる The breasts swell
頬張る ほおばる cram one's mouth (with food)
突っ張る つっぱる become taut; thrust (one's opponent); stick to (one's opinion), insist on; *slang* be delinquent
気が張る きがはる feel nervous
欲を張る よくをはる lust for
c 張り詰めた はりつめた high-strung, tense
張り切る はりきる be in high spirits, be enthusiastic; stretch to the full
強張る(=硬ばる) こわばる become stiff, stiffen

③ [also 貼る]
ⓐ **stick, paste; apply to**
ⓑ **cover, line**
a 張り付ける はりつける stick on, paste
b タイルを張る たいるをはる tile a floor

④ **stick out, project**
張り出す はりだす project, jut out
角張った顔 かくばったかお squarish face

⑤ **keep watch, guard**
張り込む はりこむ look out for, ambush

見張る みはる watch, guard

⑥ⓐ **insist, persist**

ⓑ **display, demonstrate**

a 頑張る がんばる persist, be tenacious, hold out

意地を張る いじをはる be obstinate

b 威張る いばる put on airs, be haughty; boast, brag

見栄を張る みえをはる show off

⑦ hold, give (a banquet), run, manage

世帯を張る しょたいをはる keep [set up] house

⑧ *slang* slap, smack

張り倒す はりたおす knock down

⑨ rival, compete

張り合う はりあう compete, challenge

向こうを張る むこうをはる vie with one's opponent

【-はり -張り】counter for bows, stringed instruments or paper lanterns

弓三張り ゆみみはり three bows

【-ばり -張り】

① [suffix] **fashion, manner**

川端張りの小説 かわばたばりのしょうせつ novel written in imitation of Kawabata's

② [sometimes also -貼り] [also suffix] **covered with, lined with**

絹張り きぬばり lined with silk

③ unit for expressing the power of a bow in terms of number of persons

SYNONYMS

❶ **expand**

脹 SWELL → 1265

膨 EXPAND → 1380

張 SPREAD → 0573

氾 SPREAD OUT → 0226

広げる spread (out) → 3769

拡 ENLARGE → 0366

伸 STRETCH → 0079

延 EXTEND → 3812

❷ⓐ **tighten**

締める TIGHTEN → 1761

緊 TIGHTEN → 3517

張 STRAIN → 0573

USAGE

❶【はる】

張る

① (open to the full extent) spread (out), extend over, stretch

②ⓐ strain, stretch, tighten

ⓑ be stretched [tightened], become taut

ⓒ be under strain, be tense, be anxious; be enthusiastic

③ [also 貼る]

ⓐ stick, paste; apply to

ⓑ cover, line

④ stick out, project

⑤ keep watch, guard

⑥ⓐ insist, persist

ⓑ display, demonstrate

⑦ hold, give (a banquet), run, manage

⑧ *slang* slap, smack

⑨ rival, compete

貼る

[also 張る]

ⓐ stick, paste; apply to

ⓑ cover, line

❷【-ばり】

-張り

① [suffix] fashion, manner

② [sometimes also -貼り] [also suffix] covered with, lined with

③ unit for expressing the power of a bow in terms of number of persons

-貼り

[usu. -張り] [also suffix] covered with, lined with

HOMOPHONES

はる 貼 STICK → 1904

-ばり 貼 STICK → 1904

COMPOUND FORMATION

【出張 しゅっちょう】

出張する 'travel on official business' originally meant to go out (出) on a military expedition and pitch or set up (張 ❶) tents as a temporary battle position.

NOTE

➡ see COMPOUND FORMATION for

頑張る がんばる → 頑 1315

主張 しゅちょう → 主 2437

威張る いばる → 威 4394

強

▶STRONG

キョウ ゴウ つよ(い) つよ(まる) つよ(める) し(いる) こわ(い)▲ ㊔ つよし つとむ

0574

◧ 1-3-8

Ⓝ 強 Ⓒ 强 qiáng qiǎng jiàng

57	Jōyō-2	U5F37
弓	S11-3-8	F0179

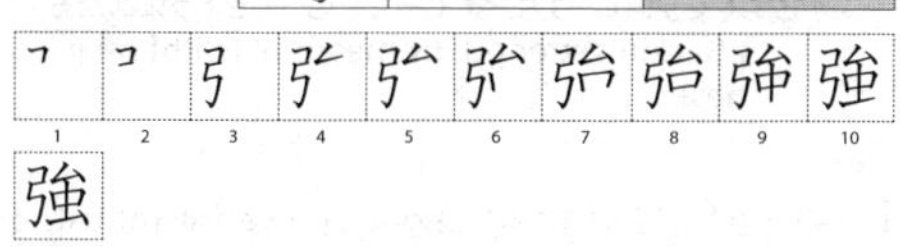

COMPOUNDS

❶ⓐ (having great strength) **STRONG, powerful; robust**

ⓑ [formerly also 鞏 きょう 3369] (capable of enduring) **STRONG, hard, solid, tough**

a 強力な きょうりょくな strong, powerful, mighty

強者 きょうしゃ strong man
強大な きょうだいな mighty, powerful, strong
強敵 きょうてき powerful enemy [rival]
強国 きょうこく powerful country
強力(=剛力) ごうりき Herculean strength; mountain carrier [guide]
屈強な くっきょうな strong, sturdy, robust
b 強壮な きょうそうな robust, strong, vigorous
強固な きょうこな firm, stable, solid, strong
強硬な きょうこうな firm (attitude), unbending; drastic (measure)
強情な ごうじょうな obstinate, headstrong
強膜 きょうまく sclera

❷ (of great intensity) **STRONG, severe, intense**
強度 きょうど intensity; strength
強風 きょうふう strong [high] wind
強震 きょうしん severe earthquake
強打 きょうだ heavy blow, slug; hitting (the ball) hard
強烈な きょうれつな intense, severe

❸ **strengthen, intensify**
強化 きょうか strengthening, intensification, build-up, reinforcement
強心剤 きょうしんざい cardiotonic drug
強調する きょうちょうする emphasize, stress
増強する ぞうきょうする reinforce, augment
補強する ほきょうする reinforce, strengthen

❹ **force, compel, coerce**
強制する きょうせいする compel, force
強行 きょうこう forcing, enforcement
強要 きょうよう coercion, extortion
強引な ごういんな overbearing, coercive
強訴 ごうそ direct petition
強姦× ごうかん rape
強盗 ごうとう robbery
勉強 べんきょう study; selling cheap; [rare] diligence

❺ [suffix] a little over
五キロ強 ごきろきょう a little over 5 kg [km]

INDEPENDENT

【きょう 強】strength, might; the **STRONG**
弱を以て強に当たる じゃくをもってきょうにあたる attacking strength by means of [with] weakness

KUN

【つよい 強い】**STRONG, mighty, powerful; robust; intense, violent, strong; hard, tough; be strong (in); brave, stout**
強さ つよさ strength, power, tenacity
強気 つよき strong feeling [market]
強味 つよみ one's strength, one's forte
強い心 つよいこころ stout heart [mind]
力強い ちからづよい powerful, vigorous, reassuring
粘り強い ねばりづよい tenacious, sticky; persistent

【つよまる 強まる】**become STRONG, gain strength**

【つよめる 強める】**strengthen, intensify; emphasize; lay stress on; reinforce**
語を強める ごをつよめる put stress on a word

【しいる 強いる】**force, compel, press**
強いて しいて against one's will, by force
無理強い むりじい forcing, compulsion, coercion

【こわい 強い】tough, hard, stiff
情が強い じょうがこわい be hardheaded, be stubborn

SYNONYMS

❶ⓐ **strong**
強 STRONG → 0574
壮 VIGOROUS → 0263
丈 STOUT → 4227
健 ROBUST (healthy) → 0152
逞しい ROBUST (sturdy) → 4004
康 HEALTHY → 3877
旺 ENERGETIC → 1061
潑 LIVELY → 0917

ⓑ **hard**
硬 HARD → 1518
堅 FIRM → 3502
鞏 TOUGH → 3369
固 SOLID → 3830
剛 TOUGH → 2107
強 STRONG → 0574
勁 STRONG → 1833

❷ **extreme in degree**
酷 SEVERE → 1967
強 STRONG → 0574
凄い tremendous → 0145
重 HEAVY → 4390
高 HIGH → 2601
深 DEEP → 0636
大 BIG → 4224
厳 SEVERE → 4079
激 intense → 0955
極 EXTREME → 1243
痛 bitter(ly) → 4071
切 keen → 0030
甚 EXTREMELY → 3271
祁 EXTREMELY → 1447
超 super- → 4107
頗る EXCEEDINGLY → 1552

❹ **compel and press**
圧 PRESSURE → 3688
迫 PRESS → 3815
強 force → 0574

押す PUSH →0371

HOMOPHONES

こわい

怖 FEARFUL →0353

恐 FEAR →3283

COMPOUND FORMATION

【勉強 べんきょう】

勉強 'study, etc.' is to force (強 ❹) oneself to make efforts (勉), that is, to work diligently or study hard.

NOTE

➡ see USAGE note at 怖 0353

術

0575

◧1-3-8

▶PRACTICAL ART

ジュツ すべ▲

Ⓝ 術 Ⓒ 术 shù zhú

144	Jōyō-5	U8853
行	S11-6-5	F0327

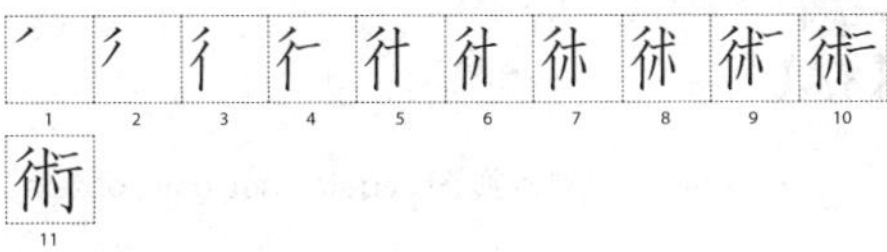

COMPOUNDS

❶ⓐ PRACTICAL ART, technique, skill

ⓑ technical art, technique, technology

a 美術 びじゅつ art, fine arts

芸術 げいじゅつ art, the arts

手術 しゅじゅつ surgical operation

戦術 せんじゅつ tactics, strategy

奇術 きじゅつ conjuring tricks, jugglery

医術 いじゅつ art of medicine

催眠術 さいみんじゅつ hypnotism, mesmerism

用兵術 ようへいじゅつ tactics, strategy

b 術語 じゅつご technical term, terminology

技術 ぎじゅつ technique, art, skill; technology

学術 がくじゅつ science, learning; arts and sciences

❷ magic, witchcraft

魔術 まじゅつ magic, sorcery, witchcraft

幻術 げんじゅつ magic, witchcraft

❸ artifice, stratagem, trick

術策 じゅっさく artifice, stratagem, trick

術中に じゅっちゅうに in the trap, entrapped

❹ [also suffix] abbrev. of 手術 しゅじゅつ: surgical operation

術後の じゅつごの postoperative

開腹術 かいふくじゅつ laparotomy

INDEPENDENT

【じゅつ 術】**PRACTICAL ART**, technique, skill; means, way; magic, witchcraft; artifice, stratagem, trick

術が尽きる じゅつがつきる be at one's wit's end

術を使う じゅつをつかう practice magic

術を授ける じゅつをさずける teach tricks to

護身の術 ごしんのじゅつ art of self-defense

KUN

【すべ 術】means, way

為す術も無く なすすべもなく at one's wit's end

SYNONYMS

❶ art

技 SKILL →0292

倆 SKILL →0136

術 PRACTICAL ART →0575

芸 ART →2738

道 the way of an art →3888

徠

0576

◧1-3-8

▶COME

ライ ㊔ き くる こ ゆき な きたる

Ⓒ 徕 lái lài

60	Names	U5FA0
彳	S11-3-8	F3470

COMPOUNDS

● COME, come to

徂×徠 そらい coming and going

SYNONYMS

● go and come

行 GO →0246

徠 COME →0576

往 GO ON →0348

出 go to →4310

参 go somewhere →2563

来 COME →4366

通 go to and from →3855

向 head toward →3790

赴 PROCEED TO →4095

嚮 GO TOWARD →3610

得

0577

◧1-3-8

▶ACQUIRE

▶GAIN

トク え(る) う(る) ㊔ のり

Ⓒ 得 dé de děi

60	Jōyō-4	U5F97
彳	S11-3-8	F0249

COMPOUNDS

❶ (obtain possession of) **ACQUIRE, obtain, gain**

獲得する かくとくする get, acquire, obtain

取得する しゅとくする acquire, gain; purchase

❷ⓐ (obtain as profit) **GAIN, earn, profit**

❺ (something earned) **GAIN, profit**

a 所得 しょとく income, earnings

b 損得 そんとく advantage and disadvantage; loss and gain

利得 りとく profit, benefit, gain

両得 りょうとく double gain

❸ⓐ GAIN understanding of, comprehend, realize

ⓑ GAIN one's end, attain one's goal, achieve satisfaction

a 習得する しゅうとくする learn, master, acquire (an art)

体得する たいとくする realize, learn (from experience), comprehend, master

納得 なっとく assent, consent, understanding

b 得意 とくい one's forte; pride; customer

得道する とくどうする attain salvation

得心する とくしんする consent to, be convinced of, be satisfied

説得する せっとくする persuade

❹ advantage, benefit

買い得品 かいどくひん good bargain

ごね得だ ごねどくだ It pays to make trouble

INDEPENDENT

【とく 得】 **GAIN, profit; advantage, benefit**

得な とくな profitable, advantageous, economical

得になる とくになる bring profit, do (a person) good

【とくする 得する】 **profit, GAIN, benefit**

KUN

【える 得る】

① [sometimes also 獲る] **ACQUIRE, get, gain, obtain, win**

得難い えがたい hard to get, rare

見得 みえ [sometimes also 見え] pose, posture

勝ち得る かちえる achieve, win, gain

心得る こころえる know, understand, give consent

② **can, be able to**

止むを得ない やむをえない unavoidable, cannot be helped

. . . せざるを得ない …せざるをえない cannot help (doing)

【うる 得る】

① literary form of 得る える

得る所が有る うるところがある get benefit from

② [verbal suffix] **can, be able to**

. . . し得る …しうる can, be able to

有り得る ありうる possible, likely

SYNONYMS

❶ **get**

得 ACQUIRE → 0577

拾 PICK UP → 0454

獲 obtain → 0959

収 TAKE IN → 0031

取 TAKE → 1613

❷ⓑ profit

利 PROFIT → 1431

益 PROFIT → 2849

儲ける PROFIT → 0202

得 GAIN → 0577

❸ⓐ know and understand

知 KNOW → 1446

通 know thoroughly → 3855

得 gain understanding of → 0577

分かる understand → 2466

解 understand → 1913

諒 UNDERSTAND → 1982

了 COMPREHEND → 4157

悟 AWAKE TO → 0502

惺 AWAKE TO → 0709

USAGE

【える】

得る

① [sometimes also 獲る] acquire, get, gain, obtain, win

② can, be able to

獲る

① catch game, hunt, fish

② [usu. 得る] acquire, get, gain, obtain, win

HOMOPHONES

える 獲 CATCH GAME → 0959

COMPOUND FORMATION

❶【得意 とくい】

得意 'one's forte, etc.' is to satisfactorily achieve (得 ❸ⓑ) one's desires (意) and take pride in one's achievements.

❷【説得 せっとく】

説得する 'persuade' is to persuade (説) a person so as to achieve (得 ❸ⓑ) one's ends.

NOTE

➡ see also USAGE note at 見 3151

御

0578

1-3-8

▸GENERAL HONORIFIC TERM

ギョ ゴ おん- お- み-

60	Nonstandard	U5FA1
彳	S11-3-8	F0000

traditional form → see 御 at 0703

從

0579

1-3-8

▸FOLLOW

ジュウ ショウ ジュ したが(う) したが(える)

㊔ より つぐ

60	Names	U5F9E
彳	S11-3-8	F0000

traditional form → see 従 at 0498

術 0580

1-3-8

▶PRACTICAL ART

ジュツ すべ

144	Nonstandard	U8853
行	S11-6-5	F0000

traditional form → see 術 at 0575

惧 0581

1-3-8

▶FEAR

グ ク゛

Ⓝ 惧 Ⓒ 惧 jù

61	Jōyō	U60E7
忄	S11-3-8	F2429

COMPOUNDS

❶ **FEAR, be afraid of, dread**

危惧 きぐ fear, misgivings

絶滅危惧種 ぜつめつきぐしゅ endangered species

疑惧 ぎぐ apprehension, misgivings

SYNONYMS

❶ **fear**

怖 FEARFUL → 0353

凄 UNCANNY → 0145

恐 FEAR → 3283

惧 FEAR → 0581

慄 TREMBLE WITH FEAR → 0791

兢 BE IN FEAR → 1971

惶 BE AFRAID → 0708

畏 BE OVERAWED → 3170

臆 FEEL TIMID → 1397

怯える BE FRIGHTENED → 0355

惟 0582

1-3-8

▶MEDITATE

イ ユイ おも(んみる) これ ㊔ ただ よし のぶ

Ⓒ 惟 wéi

61	Names	U60DF
忄	S11-3-8	F2595

COMPOUNDS

❶ **MEDITATE, ponder, think**

思惟 しい thinking, speculation

❷ [now always 唯 ゆい 0556] only

惟一の ゆいいつ(=ゆいつ)の the only, the sole

KUN

【おもんみる 惟んみる】 **reflect, MEDITATE**

つらつら惟んみるに つらつらおもんみるに on careful reflection, I find that…

【これ 惟】 [archaic] emphatic adverb

弁明惟努めたい べんめいこれつとめたい Well, I shall explain myself

SYNONYMS

❶ **think and consider**

思 THINK → 3173

惟 MEDITATE → 0582

省 INTROSPECT → 3100

稽 THINK → 1573

考 THINK → 3962

存 hold an opinion → 3702

案 think out → 2824

想 CONCEIVE → 3507

慮 CONSIDER → 4050

勘 take into consideration → 2231

銓 WEIGH → 2161

量 weigh → 3119

HOMOPHONES

これ

是 RIGHT → 3090

之 POSSESSIVE PARTICLE → 4228

此 THIS → 1017

NOTE

➡ see USAGE note at 是 3090

情 0583

1-3-8

▶EMOTION

▶ACTUAL CONDITIONS

ジョウ セイ なさ(け)

Ⓝ 情 Ⓒ 情 qíng

61	Jōyō-5	U60C5
忄	S11-3-8	F0116

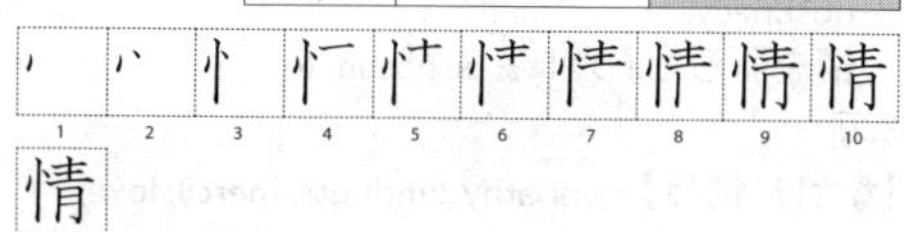

COMPOUNDS

❶ [original meaning] **EMOTION, feeling, sentiment, passion**

情緒 じょうちょ(=じょうしょ) emotion, feeling

情操 じょうそう sentiment

激情 げきじょう violent emotion, passion

感情 かんじょう feelings, emotion, sentiment

友情 ゆうじょう friendship, fellowship

表情 ひょうじょう expression, look

❷ **sympathy, compassion, kindness**

同情 どうじょう sympathy, compassion

人情 にんじょう human feelings, humanity, sympathy

❸ⓐ **love, affection**

ⓑ (illicit) love, love affair, lovemaking, sexual desire

a 愛情 あいじょう love, affection

b 情死 じょうし double love suicide
情事 じょうじ love affair, romance
情交 じょうこう sexual intercourse, illicit intercourse

❹ ACTUAL CONDITIONS, actual facts, real circumstances
情勢 じょうせい state of things, situation
情報 じょうほう information, intelligence, report, news
情況 じょうきょう conditions, circumstances
事情 じじょう circumstances, conditions, situation
実情 じつじょう actual circumstances, real state of affairs

❺ taste, elegance
情趣 じょうしゅ mood, sentiment, artistic effects, charms
風情 ふぜい appearance, air, taste, elegance

❻ obstinacy
強情な ごうじょうな obstinate, headstrong

INDEPENDENT

【じょう 情】
①ⓐ **EMOTION, feelings, sentiment, heart**
ⓑ **affection, love, passion, sexual desire**
ⓒ **sympathy, compassion, kindness**
ⓓ **faithfulness, good faith**
a 情の深い人 じょうのふかいひと kindhearted person
b 親の情 おやのじょう parental love
c 情の籠もった じょうのこもった sympathetic, warm-hearted

② actual facts, real circumstances
情を明かす じょうをあかす disclose the true facts

③ obstinacy
情を張る じょうをはる be obstinate

KUN

【なさけ 情け】**sympathy, kindness, mercy; love; taste**
情け深い なさけぶかい compassionate, kindhearted
情け無い なさけない unfeeling, cruel; pitiful, wretched; shameful
情けを交わす なさけをかわす have sexual intercourse

SYNONYMS

❶ feeling
感 SENSE (feeling) → 3514
情 EMOTION → 0583
心 HEART → 0011
気 spirits → 3960

❷ tender feelings for others
仁 BENEVOLENCE → 0021
慈 compassion → 2949
情 sympathy → 0583
悲 mercy → 3448
哀 PITY → 2568
憐 PITY → 0945

❸ⓐ love
愛 LOVE → 3133
情 love → 0583
恋 LOVE (for the opposite sex) → 2602
艶 ROMANCE → 2403
寵 AFFECTION → 3029

ⓑ sex
性 SEX → 0357
情 (illicit) love → 0583
春 love → 3184
色 lust → 2522
淫 LEWD → 0624

❹ states and situations
態 STATE → 3529
調 TONE → 1973
様 MODE → 1332
相 PHASE → 1120
状 CONDITION → 0322
況 CONDITIONS → 0395
景 business conditions → 3118
勢 course of events → 3542
境 SITUATION → 0835
局 current situation → 3800
情 ACTUAL CONDITIONS → 0583
訳 circumstances → 1865

惚

0584

1-3-8

▸FALL IN LOVE
▸GROW SENILE
コツ ほ(れる) ぼ(ける) ほう(ける)

Ⓒ 惚 hū

61	Names	U60DA
忄	S11-3-8	F1781

COMPOUNDS

● entranced, enchanted, enraptured
恍×惚 こうこつ ecstasy, trance

KUN

【ほれる 惚れる】
ⓐ **FALL IN LOVE**
ⓑ **admire, be impressed, be charmed**
ⓒ [suffix] be engrossed
a 惚れ薬 ほれぐすり love potion
一目惚れ ひとめぼれ love at first sight
b 惚れ惚れ ほれぼれ fondly, in fascination

【ぼける 惚ける】[also 呆ける]
①ⓐ **GROW SENILE**
ⓑ **be mentally slow, be befuddled**
a 惚け防止 ぼけぼうし dementia prevention
ab 惚け ぼけ being out of it, dementia, senility; idiot, fool; funny man (of a comedy duo)

b 寝惚ける ねぼける be half asleep, be half awake
時差惚け じさぼけ jet lag

② **be out of focus, become unclear [indistinct]**
古惚ける ふるぼける become old-looking, become worn out

【ほうける 惚ける】 [also 呆ける]
①ⓐ **GROW SENILE**
ⓑ **be mentally slow, be befuddled**
② [verbal suffix] **be engrossed in (doing something)**
遊び惚ける あそびほうける be absorbed in play; spend one's time in idle amusement

SPECIAL READINGS
惚気 のろけ speaking fondly of a loved one
自惚れ うぬぼれ self-conceit, vanity
見惚れる みとれる watch something in fascination

SYNONYMS
【ほれる】
ⓐ **love and like**
愛 LOVE → 3133
恋 LOVE (the opposite sex) → 2602
好 LIKE → 0240
慕 ADORE → 2970
惚れる FALL IN LOVE → 0584
玩 cherish → 1085

USAGE
❶ **【ぼける】**
惚ける
[also 呆ける]
①ⓐ grow senile
ⓑ be mentally slow, be befuddled
② be out of focus, become unclear [indistinct]
呆ける
[also 惚ける] same as 惚ける

❷ **【ほうける】**
惚ける
[also 呆ける]
①ⓐ grow senile
ⓑ be mentally slow, be befuddled
② [verbal suffix] be engrossed in (doing something)
呆ける
[also 惚ける] same as 惚ける

HOMOPHONES
ぼける 呆 DIM-WITTED → 2712
ほうける 呆 DIM-WITTED → 2712

惨

0585

1-3-8

▶**MISERABLE**
▶**CRUEL**
サン ザン みじ(め)
Ⓝ 慘 Ⓒ 惨 cǎn

61	Jōyō	U60E8
忄	S11-3-8	F1498

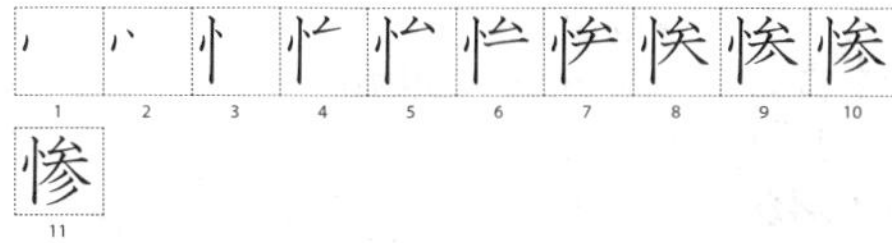

COMPOUNDS
❶ **MISERABLE, wretched, pitiable, tragic; terrible, horrible, disastrous**
惨事 さんじ disaster, tragic incident, catastrophe
惨状 さんじょう pitiful situation
惨禍 さんか terrible disaster, crushing calamity
惨劇 さんげき tragedy, tragic event
惨憺×たる さんたんたる pitiable, wretched, miserable, terrible, horrible
惨敗 ざんぱい miserable defeat
悲惨な ひさんな miserable, wretched, tragic, pitiable
凄惨な せいさんな ghastly, gruesome, lurid

❷ [usu. 残 ざん 1179] **CRUEL, ruthless, atrocious**
惨殺する ざんさつする murder cruelly, slaughter, butcher
惨酷 ざんこく cruelty, atrocity, brutality
無惨な むざんな cruel, atrocious; pitiful, tragic, miserable

INDEPENDENT
【さん 惨】 misery, wretchedness
惨たる光景 さんたるこうけい disastrous scene

KUN
【みじめ 惨め】
みじめな 惨めな **MISERABLE, pitiable, tragic**
惨めな思いをする みじめなおもいをする feel miserable

SYNONYMS
❶ **sad and depressed**
悲 SAD → 3448
悄 BECOME DISPIRITED → 0506
哀 sorrowful → 2568
愁 MELANCHOLY → 3508
鬱 GLOOM → 3625
陰 gloomy → 0657
沈 depressed → 0306
寂 LONESOME → 2855
淋しい LONESOME → 0632
惨 MISERABLE → 0585

❷ **cruel**
虐 CRUEL → 3989
惨 CRUEL → 0585
酷 SEVERE → 1967
辣 SEVERE → 1965
残 RUTHLESS → 1179
凶 ATROCIOUS → 3679
苛 HARSH → 2786

惜

0586

1-3-8

▶**REGRET**

セキ お(しい) お(しむ)

Ⓒ 惜 xī

61	Jōyō	U60DC
忄	S11-3-8	F1590

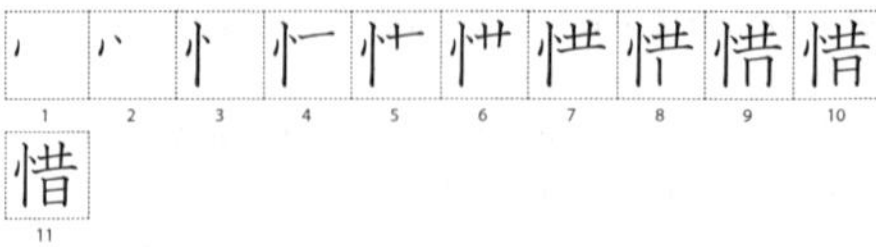

COMPOUNDS

❶ **REGRET, lament**

惜別 せきべつ parting regrets

惜敗 せきはい regrettable defeat

哀惜 あいせき lamentation, grief

❷ value highly, hold dear

愛惜 あいせき reluctance (to part)

KUN

【おしい 惜しい】**REGRETtable, disappointing; precious, valuable; too good (for)**

惜しさ おしさ unwillingness to lose [part with]

惜し気無く おしげなく unsparingly, generously, lavishly

それは惜しい それはおしい That's a pity!

命が惜しい いのちがおしい Life is dear

まだ捨てるには惜しい まだすてるにはおしい still too good to throw away

【おしむ 惜しむ】**grudge, be sparing of; REGRET; be reluctant; value**

惜しみ無く おしみなく freely, without stint

惜しむべき おしむべき regrettable, lamentable

出し惜しみする だしおしみする grudge, be stingy

別れを惜しむ わかれをおしむ loathe to part with

時間を惜しむ じかんをおしむ value time

SPECIAL READINGS

口惜しい▲(=悔しい) くやしい vexing, mortifying, regrettable

SYNONYMS

❶ **regret**

惜 REGRET → 0586

恨 regret → 0439

憾 STRONGLY REGRET → 0943

悔 REPENT → 0435

HOMOPHONES

くやしい

悔しい → 0435

口惜しい → 4189, 0586

NOTE

➡ see USAGE note at 悔 0435

悼

0587

1-3-8

▶**MOURN**

トウ いた(む)

Ⓒ 悼 dào

61	Jōyō	U60BC
忄	S11-3-8	F2262

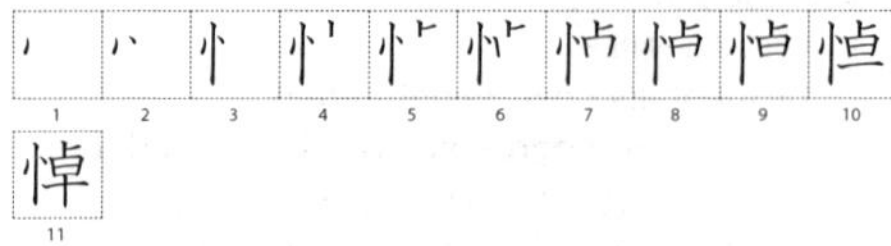

COMPOUNDS

● **MOURN, grieve, lament**

悼辞 とうじ message of condolence

哀悼する あいとうする condole, mourn, grieve

追悼 ついとう mourning

KUN

【いたむ 悼む】**MOURN, grieve over, be grieved at**

死を悼む しをいたむ mourn over the death of

SYNONYMS

● **grieve**

慨 DEPLORE → 0790

嘆 SIGH → 0773

悼 MOURN → 0587

傷 grieve → 0179

悲 feel sad → 3448

悄 BECOME DISPIRITED → 0506

● **mourn and mourning**

弔 CONDOLE → 4240

悼 MOURN → 0587

喪 MOURNING → 3504

忌 MOURNING → 2735

HOMOPHONES

いたむ

痛 PAIN → 4071

傷 WOUND → 0179

NOTE

➡ see USAGE note at 痛 4071

惇

0588

1-3-8

▶**SINCERE**

トン ジュン シュン ㊔ あつ あつし まこと すなお つとむ

Ⓒ 惇 dūn

61	Names	U60C7
忄	S11-3-8	F3128

COMPOUNDS

❶ [rare] **SINCERE**, honest, solid

惇厚な とんこうな sincere and kindhearted, honest and simple

惇朴(=惇樸×)な とんぼくな simple and honest

❷ [archaic] cordial, kind, warm, friendly

惇睦な とんぼくな cordial and friendly

SYNONYMS

❶ **purehearted**

純 PURE → 1649
淳 PUREHEARTED → 0626
清 clean → 0635
潔 IMMACULATE → 0920
廉 INCORRUPT → 3911
敦 HONEST → 2128
惇 SINCERE → 0588
直 straightforward → 3649
侃 FORTHRIGHT → 0097

惧

0589

◧ 1-3-8

▶**FEAR**

グ ク

61	Nonstandard	U60E7
忄	S11-3-8	F0000

traditional form → see 惧 at 0581

情

0590

◧ 1-3-8

▶**EMOTION**
▶**ACTUAL CONDITIONS**

ジョウ セイ なさ(け)

61	Nonstandard	U60C5
忄	S11-3-8	F0000

traditional form → see 情 at 0583

描

0591

◧ 1-3-8

▶**DEPICT**

ビョウ えが(く) か(く)

Ⓒ 描 miáo

64	Jōyō	U63CF
扌	S11-3-8	F0678

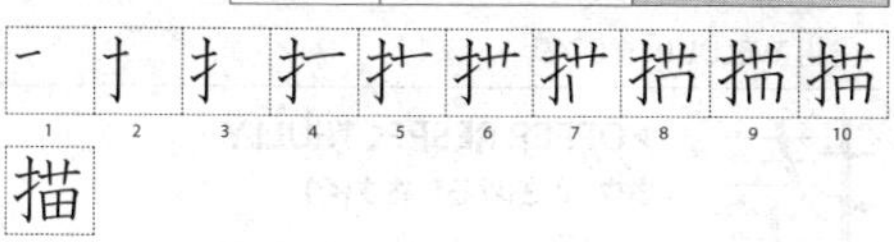

COMPOUNDS

❶ [original meaning] (represent in a picture) **DEPICT, draw, paint**

描画する びょうがする draw a picture, paint
素描 そびょう (rough) sketch
点描 てんびょう sketch
実物描写 じつぶつびょうしゃ model drawing

❷ (represent in words) **DEPICT, describe**

描写 びょうしゃ depiction, description; portrayal; drawing
描出 びょうしゅつ depiction, description; portrayal; drawing

KUN

【えがく 描く】

① [sometimes also 画く] (represent in a picture) **DEPICT, draw, paint**

油絵を描く あぶらえをえがく paint in oil

② (represent in words) **DEPICT, describe**

描き出す えがきだす delineate, depict, portray
思い描く おもいえがく imagine, figure, see

【かく 描く】 **draw, paint**

絵描き えかき painter, artist

SYNONYMS

❶ **draw**

描 DEPICT → 0591
画 draw → 3723

❷ **describe**

叙 DESCRIBE → 1834
抒 DESCRIBE → 0295
描 DEPICT → 0591
写 portray → 2493

USAGE

【えがく】

描く
① [sometimes also 画く] (represent in a picture) depict, draw, paint
② (represent in words) depict, describe

画く
[usu. 描く] draw, paint

HOMOPHONES

えがく 画 PICTURE → 3723
かく 書 WRITE → 3292

NOTE

➡ see also USAGE note at 書 3292

掩

0592

◧ 1-3-8

▶**COVER**

エン おお(う)

Ⓒ 掩 yǎn

64	Non-Jōyō	U63A9
扌	S11-3-8	F3218

COMPOUNDS

❶ [original meaning] **COVER, hide, conceal**

掩蔽 えんぺい cover, obscuration
掩蓋 えんがい cover; gun apron

❷ [now also 援 0715] **COVER, protect**

掩護する えんごする cover, protect, shelter
掩壕 えんごう cover trench

KUN

【おおう 掩う】 [now usu. 覆う]

ⓐ **COVER, veil**
ⓑ **hide, conceal, screen**

a 棺を掩う かんをおおう cover the coffin
顔を掩う かおをおおう cover one's face

SYNONYMS

❶ & ❷ **cover and wrap**

覆 COVER → 3386

掩 COVER →0592
被 cover →1495
包 WRAP →3684
蓋う COVER →2933
蔽 COVER →2991
葺く THATCH →2909

HOMOPHONES

おおう

覆 COVER →3386
被 BE SUBJECTED TO →1495
蓋 COVER →2933
蔽 COVER →2991

NOTE

➡ see USAGE note at 覆 3386

排

0593

1-3-8

▶**EXCLUDE**
▶**DISCHARGE**

ハイ

Ⓒ 排 pái pǎi

64	Jōyō	U6392
扌	S11-3-8	F1332

Stroke order: 1–11

COMPOUNDS

1a [original meaning] **EXCLUDE, expel, reject, drive out**

b anti-

a 排除 はいじょ exclusion, removal, elimination
排斥する はいせきする expel, reject, exclude, ostracize
排他的な はいたてきな exclusive, clannish
排他主義 はいたしゅぎ exclusivism

b 排外的 はいがいてき antiforeign, exclusive
排日 はいにち anti-Japanese

2 (put out, esp. undesirable substances) **DISCHARGE, exhaust, drain, excrete**

排出 はいしゅつ discharge, exhaust, evacuation
排水 はいすい drainage, draining; (of ships) displacement
排気 はいき exhaust, used steam; exhaustion, evacuation
排気ガス はいきがす exhaust gas
排尿 はいにょう urination

3 [usu. 配 1853] arrange, put in order

排列 はいれつ arrangement, disposition
按排する あんばいする arrange, distribute; adjust

INDEPENDENT

【はいする 排する】**EXCLUDE**, expel, reject, drive out; push open

SYNONYMS

1a drive out

斥 EXPEL →3690
排 EXCLUDE →0593
追 chase away →3840
退 cause to retreat →3838
駆 drive away →2293
逐 DRIVE OUT →3848
払う clear out →0225

1a eliminate

却 ELIMINATE →1436
排 EXCLUDE →0593
払う CLEAR AWAY →0225
剥 PEEL OFF →2105
耘 WEED →1661
削 cross out →1837
抹 wipe off →0370
省 leave out →3100
脱 REMOVE →1225
去 take away →2678
外す take off →0215
除 RID OF →0546
撤 WITHDRAW →0912

2 emit

出 PUT OUT →4310
発 EMIT →3174
放 radiate →1058
排 DISCHARGE →0593
射 SHOOT →1850
噴 SPOUT →0879
吐 SPEW →0235
湧 WELL UP →0749

捧

0594

1-3-8

▶**OFFER RESPECTFULLY**

ホウ ささ(げる) ささ(ぐ)

Ⓒ 捧 pěng

64	Names	U6367
扌	S11-3-8	F2134

COMPOUNDS

a OFFER RESPECTFULLY

b [now also 奉 3167 or 抱 0363] [original meaning] **hold up in both hands**

a 捧呈する ほうていする dedicate, present, offer (to a high personage)

b 捧持(=奉持)する ほうじする hold up, bear
捧腹絶倒(=抱腹絶倒)する ほうふくぜっとうする double up with laughter

KUN

【ささげる 捧げる】

①ⓐ **OFFER RESPECTFULLY, present**
ⓑ **hold up in both hands, lift up**

a 捧げ物 ささげもの offering, sacrifice
b 捧げ持つ ささげもつ hold (something) reverently with both hands

② **devote, sacrifice**
命を捧げる いのちをささげる give one's life, devote one's life (to a cause)

【ささぐ 捧ぐ】*elegant* same as 捧げる ささげる

SYNONYMS

ⓐ hold
持 HOLD → 0447
提 carry in hand → 0720
携 CARRY IN HAND → 0796
捧 hold up in both hands → 0594

ⓑ offer
供 OFFER (to a person or god) → 0098
献 OFFER (esp. to a superior) → 2240
納 offer (as to a god) → 1652
提 PRESENT → 0720
貢 offer tribute → 2838
奉 DEDICATE → 3167
捧 OFFER RESPECTFULLY → 0594

授

0595

1-3-8

▶CONFER

ジュ さず(ける) さず(かる)

Ⓒ 授 shòu

64	Jōyō-5	U6388
扌	S11-3-8	F0779

一 𠂇 扌 扌 扌 扌 扌 扌 扌 授 授 (strokes 1–11)

COMPOUNDS

❶ CONFER, grant, award; give, hand over
授与する じゅよする grant, give, confer
授賞 じゅしょう awarding a prize
授産 じゅさん providing with work, giving employment
授受 じゅじゅ giving and receiving
授乳 じゅにゅう breast-feeding

❷ teach, instruct, initiate
授業 じゅぎょう teaching, instruction; lesson
教授 きょうじゅ teaching; professor
伝授 でんじゅ instruction, initiation
口授 こうじゅ oral instruction

KUN

【さずける 授ける】**CONFER, grant, award; give, hand over**
学位を授ける がくいをさずける award a degree
. . . の秘伝を授ける …のひでんをさずける initiate into the secrets of

【さずかる 授かる】**be gifted with, be granted; be taught**
賞を授かる しょうをさずかる be awarded a prize

SYNONYMS

❶ give
与 GIVE → 4229
呈 PRESENT → 2715
進 present to a superior → 3873
上 give (to superior or others) → 4212
下 give (to inferior or speaker) → 4186
呉れる give (to speaker) → 3156
授 CONFER → 0595
賜 DEIGN TO GIVE → 1994
贈 PRESENT A GIFT → 2064
賄 BRIBE → 1931
賂 BRIBE → 1930

❷ teach
教 TEACH → 1887
啓 ENLIGHTEN → 3434
諄 TEACH WITH CARE → 1979
授 teach → 0595
育 educate → 2544
練 TRAIN → 1738
訓 INSTRUCT → 1844
誨 INSTRUCT → 1946
諭 ADMONISH → 2012
導 GUIDE → 3587
迪 EDIFY → 3817

掛

0596

1-3-8

▶SET
▶HANG

カイ^ ケイ^ か(ける) -か(ける) か(け) -か(け) -が(け) か(かる) -か(かる) -が(かる) か(かり) -が(かり) かかり -がかり

Ⓒ 挂 guà

64	Jōyō	U639B
扌	S11-3-8	F0754

一 𠂇 扌 扌 扌 扌 挂 挂 挂 掛 掛 (strokes 1–11)

COMPOUNDS

● [original meaning] **HANG, suspend**
掛留 けいりゅう *music* suspension

KUN

【かける 掛ける】
①ⓐ **SET, put on, put over, spread**
ⓑ **SET against, put up against, fasten**
ⓒ **SET on a scale, weigh**
ⓓ (set on one's head or shoulders) **wear, put on**

a 掛け布団 かけぶとん covering quilt
薦を掛ける こもをかける spread a mat
b 掛け小屋 かけごや lean-to; temporary theater
薬缶を掛ける やかんをかける put a kettle on (the stove)
梯子を掛ける はしごをかける set a ladder up against
c 計りに掛ける はかりにかける weigh on a scale
d 眼鏡を掛ける めがねをかける wear glasses
ショールを掛ける しょーるをかける put a shawl on

② **SET one's body down, sit, sit down**
掛け心地 かけごこち feel of a chair
腰掛け こしかけ chair, seat, bench, stool
腰を掛ける こしをかける sit down

③ **pour, sprinkle**
掛け汁 かけじる dressing, gravy
振り掛ける ふりかける sprinkle, spatter
水を掛ける みずをかける sprinkle water on (something)

④ **SET going, set in motion, turn on, start, operate; phone**
火を掛ける ひをかける set fire
レコードを掛ける れこーどをかける play a record
仕掛け しかけ device, mechanism
電話を掛ける でんわをかける make a phone call, telephone

⑤ ⓐ **SET before, present, pose**
ⓑ **SET** (a tax) on, lay, impose
a お目に掛ける おめにかける show to someone, present
舞台に掛ける ぶたいにかける put on stage
謎を掛ける なぞをかける pose a riddle
持ち掛ける もちかける propose, offer (a suggestion)
見せ掛け みせかけ outward appearance
b 掛け金 かけきん installment; premium
掛け値 かけね overcharge, inflated price; exaggeration
税金を掛ける ぜいきんをかける place a tax on
保険を掛ける ほけんをかける insure (something)

⑥ **exert influence on, impose**
迷惑を掛ける めいわくをかける impose trouble
心配を掛ける しんぱいをかける cause someone to worry
面倒を掛ける めんどうをかける put someone to trouble

⑦ **HANG, hang up, suspend**
掛け物 かけもの hanging scroll
掛け看板 かけかんばん hanging sign
カーテンを掛ける かーてんをかける hang up a curtain

⑧ **fasten onto, affix**
掛け時計 かけどけい wall clock
引っ掛ける ひっかける hang on, hook; throw on; trap, cheat; have a drink
フックに掛ける ふっくにかける hang on a hook

⑨ **fasten (one's mind) upon**
気に掛ける きにかける have one's mind upon, take to heart
願を掛ける がんをかける make a wish (to a god)

⑩ **lock, close**
掛け金 かけがね (window) latch
錠を掛ける じょうをかける fasten a lock

⑪ **speak, call out**
掛け声 かけごえ shout to mark time, shout of encouragement
掛け合い かけあい dialogue, duet; bargaining
気合いを掛ける きあいをかける raise a shout, cheer on
話し掛ける はなしかける call out to someone, accost

⑫ **entrust someone to (a physician), put under medical treatment**
医者に掛ける いしゃにかける entrust to a doctor (for treatment)

⑬ **spend (time or money)**
時間を掛ける じかんをかける spend time (on doing something)
お金を掛ける おかねをかける spend money (on something)

⑭ raise
帆を掛ける ほをかける raise a sail

⑮ **multiply**
掛け算 かけざん multiplication
八掛ける二 はちかけるに 2 times 8

⑯ mate (animals), cross (plants or animals)
二つの植物を掛け合わせて新種を作る ふたつのしょくぶつをかけあわせてしんしゅをつくる Make a new plant by crossing two others

⑰ pun, play on words
掛け詞 かけことば play on words (as a poetic device)
これは書名に掛けた謳い文句だ これはしょめいにかけたうたいもんくだ This slogan plays on the name [title] of the book

【-かける -掛ける】

① [verbal suffix]
ⓐ **start doing, begin to do; be about to do**
ⓑ **perform an action partway**
a 走り掛ける はしりかける start running
死に掛ける しにかける be dying
b 言い掛けて止める いいかけてやめる stop in the middle of a sentence

② **emphatic verbal suffix, somewhat vague in meaning, used to emphasize the action of the**

doer upon the object, e.g., latch on to, close in on, attach, etc.

詰め掛ける つめかける crowd (a house); throng to (a door)

押し掛ける おしかける force oneself upon (a person), go uninvited

追い掛ける(=追っ掛ける) おいかける(=おっかける) chase, run after

見掛ける みかける catch sight of

心掛ける こころがける bear in mind; try, endeavor, intend

出掛ける でかける go out, set off; be about to go out

【かけ 掛け】

① **noodles in broth**

掛けうどん かけうどん thick noodles in broth

② **credit, installment**

掛けにする かけにする give credit

掛け買い かけがい credit purchase

掛け売り かけうり credit sale

【-かけ -掛け】[also suffix]

① **rack, HANGer**

帽子掛け ぼうしかけ hat rack

タオル掛け たおるかけ towel rack

衣紋掛け えもんかけ coat hanger

② **garment, cover**

テーブル掛け てーぶるかけ tablecloth

肩掛け かたかけ shawl

前掛け まえかけ apron

③ dish prepared with broth or dressing on it

葛掛け くずかけ food dressed with liquid starch

④ **half-finished, in the process of**

食べ掛けのバナナ たべかけのばなな half-eaten banana

やり掛けの仕事 やりかけのしごと unfinished work

【-がけ -掛け】

① **half-done, in the process of, about to**

寝掛けに ねがけに when half-asleep

起き掛けに おきがけに when half-awake

帰り掛けに かえりがけに on the way home

② 10 percent

八掛け はちがけ 80%

③ multiple of, times as large

二つ掛け ふたつがけ two times

④ suffix indicating sitting capacity

三人掛けのベンチ さんにんがけのべんち bench for three persons

⑤ [suffix] vs., uneven match

五人掛け ごにんがけ five against one

⑥ [suffix] wearing, clad

浴衣掛けで ゆかたがけで wearing a *yukata*

【かかる 掛かる】

① **HANG, be suspended**

壁に掛かる かべにかかる hang on the wall

② **be SET over, cover**

そこに布団が掛かっている そこにふとんがかかっている The quilt is spread over there

霧が地面に掛かっている きりがじめんにかかっている Fog covers the ground

③ **splash**

掛かり湯 かかりゆ fresh bathwater to pour over oneself

私のズボンに水が掛かった わたくしのずぼんにみずがかかった My trousers were splashed with water

④ **lean against**

伸し掛かる のしかかる lean on (a person), bear down on

寄り掛かる よりかかる lean against something

梯子が壁に掛かっている はしごがかべにかかっている The ladder is leaning against the wall

⑤ ⓐ **be caught, be trapped**

ⓑ **be caught (on one's mind), weigh**

a 罠×に掛かる わなにかかる caught in a trap

引っ掛かる ひっかかる be caught, catch on; get entangled; be trapped

b 心に掛かる こころにかかる weigh on one's mind

気掛かり きがかり anxiety, concern, worry

⑥ **SET about, apply oneself to, be engaged in**

仕事に掛かる しごとにかかる get to work

用意に掛かる よういにかかる set about preparations

取り掛かる とりかかる commence, undertake

仕事に掛かり切りになる しごとにかかりきりになる give one's whole time to the job

⑦ ⓐ **depend upon, hinge upon**

ⓑ **involve, concern**

a 責任は彼に掛かる せきにんはかれにかかる Responsibility rests with him

金が有るか無いかに掛かる かねがあるかないかにかかる depend on whether or not there is money

子供に掛かる こどもにかかる depend on one's children

b 掛かり合い かかりあい involvement

手掛かり てがかり something to rely on, clue

⑧ consult (a doctor)

掛かり付けの医者 かかりつけのいしゃ family physician [doctor]

⑨ **start, start operating, work**

エンジンが掛かる えんじんがかかる The engine starts

電話が掛かって来る でんわがかかってくる get a phone call

⑩ appear (at a theater)

今映画が掛かっている いまえいががかかっている A film is now being shown
⑪ **require, cost; weigh**
時間が掛かる じかんがかかる take time
余り金が掛からない あまりかねがかからない It doesn't cost very much
目方はどの位掛かりますか めかたはどのくらいかかりますか How much does it weigh?
⑫ **attack, fall upon**
襲い掛かる おそいかかる assault, pounce upon, sweep down on (a person)
飛び掛かる とびかかる spring upon
敵に掛かる てきにかかる assail the enemy
⑬ approach, come near
山道に掛かる やまみちにかかる come to a mountain path
⑭ [formerly 繋る] anchor, moor
【-かかる -掛かる】 [verbal suffix]
① **be on the verge of**
死に掛かる しにかかる be dying
② **happen to (do something)**
来掛かる きかかる happen to come by
通り掛かる とおりかかる happen to pass by
【-がかる -掛かる】
① **resemble**
芝居掛かった しばいがかった theatrical, affected, pompous
② **tinged with**
藍色掛かった生地 あいいろがかったきじ cloth tinged with indigo
【かかり 掛かり】
① **expenses**
掛かりが嵩む かかりがかさむ Expenses get heavy
② **scale, scope**
大掛かりな おおがかりな large-scale, extensive
③ engagement, catching on
歯車の掛かりが悪い はぐるまのかかりがわるい The gears are improperly engaged
④ attack
【-がかり -掛かり】
① [suffix] **combined, in a group of**
一家掛かりで いっかがかりで with the whole family
五人掛かりで運ぶ ごにんがかりではこぶ be carried by five people
② [suffix] **requiring (a period of time)**
三年掛かりの仕事 さんねんがかりのしごと job requiring three years
③ [also suffix] resembling
能掛かり のうがかり resembling a noh performance
④ be entrusted to, depend on
親掛かりの おやがかりの dependent on one's parents

【かかり 掛】 [usu. 係]
ⓐ **person in charge (of a post, esp. in a government agency or railway company)**
ⓑ **charge, duty, post**
a 掛長 かかりちょう chief clerk
b 掛の人 かかりのひと official in charge
【-がかり -掛】 [usu. -係] [suffix] **person in charge (of a post, esp. in a government agency or railway company)**
出札掛 しゅっさつがかり ticket agent

SYNONYMS

【かける】
① **put**
据える INSTALL →0602
置 PLACE →3222
擱 LAY DOWN →0970
掛ける SET →0596
措 DISPOSE →0610
④ **set in motion**
動 MOVE →2232
駆 DRIVE →2293
掛ける set going →0596
⑦ **hang**
掛ける HANG →0596
垂 HANG DOWN →4382
懸 SUSPEND →3632
吊 SUSPEND →2686
釣り- suspended →2108
⑮ **multiply**
乗 multiply →4393
掛ける multiply →0596
①ⓐ **begin**
始 BEGIN →0335
-出す begin to do →4310
-掛ける start doing →0596
発 START →3174
起 start →4099
就 SET ABOUT →2129
開 OPEN →4121
創 initiate →2283
肇 ORIGINATE →3474
【-かかる】
① **on the verge of**
-掛かる be on the verge of →0596
将 on the verge of →0551
-際 on the verge of →0874
臨 on the point of →2059

USAGE

❶【かける】
掛ける
①ⓐ set, put on, put over, spread

ⓑ set against, put up against, fasten
ⓒ set on a scale, weigh
ⓓ (set on one's head or shoulders) wear, put on
② set one's body down, sit, sit down
③ pour, sprinkle
④ set going, set in motion, turn on, start, operate; phone
⑤ⓐ set before, present, pose
ⓑ set (a tax) on, lay, impose
⑥ exert influence on, impose
⑦ hang, hang up, suspend
⑧ fasten onto, affix
⑨ fasten (one's mind) upon
⑩ lock, close
⑪ speak, call out
⑫ entrust someone to (a physician), put under medical treatment
⑬ spend (time or money)
⑭ raise
⑮ multiply
⑯ mate (animals), cross (plants or animals)
⑰ pun, play on words

架ける
lay (a bridge or wire) across, build across, span (a river) with (a bridge), bridge
★かける in the sense of span or bridge is correctly written 架ける, not 掛ける. This is in spite of the fact that かけはし 'suspension bridge' is normally written 掛け橋.

懸ける
① [sometimes also 賭ける] stake (one's life), risk
② offer [set] a prize
③ [in compounds] be (greatly) different from, be far apart

賭ける
ⓐ wager, bet money
ⓑ [usu. 懸ける] stake (one's life), risk

駆ける
gallop, run quickly, dash

翔る
soar, fly

★掛ける is a complicated word with many meanings. Make a careful study of the equivalents and examples. In the sense of hang or suspend, 掛ける, *not* 懸ける, is correct. This is in spite of the fact that 懸 means to suspend or hang when used in compounds, as for example in 懸垂 けんすい 'suspension, etc.'.

❷【かけ】

掛け
① noodles in broth
② credit, installment

賭け
bet, wager

❸【かかる】

掛かる
① hang, be suspended
② be set over, cover
③ splash
④ lean against
⑤ⓐ be caught, be trapped
ⓑ be caught (on one's mind), weigh
⑥ set about, apply oneself to, be engaged in
⑦ⓐ depend upon, hinge upon
ⓑ involve, concern
⑧ consult (a doctor)
⑨ start, start operating, work
⑩ appear (at a theater)
⑪ require, cost; weigh
⑫ attack, fall upon
⑬ approach, come near
⑭ [formerly 繋る] anchor, moor

懸かる
① be suspended in midair (as of the moon), hang
② have a prize offered, have a reward (set on one's head)

架かる
span, (of cables) be laid across, be built across

係る
① affect, concern, involve
② *gram* modify
③ is the work of, is done by

繋る
[now usu. 掛かる] anchor, moor

罹る
ⓐ fall ill, contract (a disease)
ⓑ suffer (from a calamity)

★掛かる is the intransitive form of 掛ける and shares most of its meanings. Study the equivalents and examples under かかる above. Note that 掛かる is to hang in the sense of being snagged or caught on something, whereas 懸かる means to be suspended in midair.

❹【かかり】

掛かり
① expenses
② scale, scope
③ engagement, catching on
④ attack

掛
[usu. 係]
ⓐ person in charge (of a post, esp. in a government agency or railway company)
ⓑ charge, duty, post

係り
relation, connection (esp. in grammar)
★Note that 係り, *not* 係かり or 係, is the correct form here.

係
[sometimes also 掛]
ⓐ person in charge, official in charge, clerk
ⓑ charge, duty, post

❺【-がかり】
-掛かり
① [suffix] combined, in a group of
② [suffix] requiring (a period of time)
③ [also suffix] resembling
④ be entrusted to, depend on
-掛
[usu. -係] [suffix] person in charge (of a post, esp. in a government agency or railway company)
-係
[sometimes also -掛] [suffix] person in charge, official in charge, clerk

★Note how the meanings of かかり and -がかり vary in accordance with the different *okurigana* inflections.

HOMOPHONES

かける
架 LAY ACROSS →3178
懸 SUSPEND →3632
賭 WAGER →2021
駆 DRIVE →2293
翔 SOAR →1714

かけ 賭 WAGER →2021

かかる
懸 SUSPEND →3632
架 LAY ACROSS →3178
係 CONNECT →0108
繋 CONNECT →3612
罹 FALL ILL →3239

かかり 係 CONNECT →0108

-がかり 係 CONNECT →0108

掲 0597

▶PUT UP
ケイ かか(げる)
Ⓝ 掲 Ⓒ 揭 jiē
1-3-8

64	Jōyō	U63B2
扌	S11-3-8	F1136

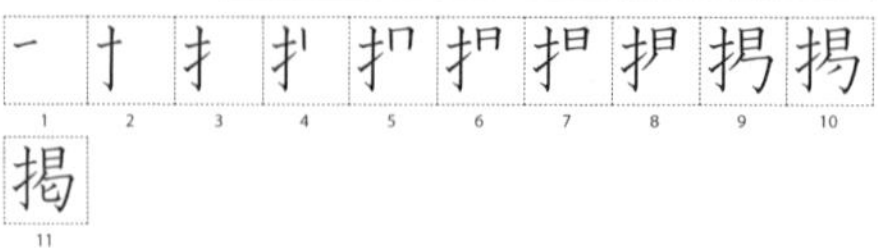

COMPOUNDS

❶ **PUT UP, display, hoist, raise**
掲揚する けいようする hoist, put up, fly (a flag)
掲示する けいじする put up a notice [bulletin]

❷ **display in writing, mention, show**
掲載する けいさいする publish, insert, print
前掲の ぜんけいの shown above, aforementioned

KUN

【かかげる 掲げる】**PUT UP, display, hoist, raise; display in writing, mention, carry, publish**
国旗を掲げる こっきをかかげる hoist the national flag
上に掲げた費用 うえにかかげたひよう the expenses mentioned above

SYNONYMS

❶ **raise**
揚 RAISE HIGH →0722
掲 PUT UP →0597
挙 RAISE →3106
上 raise →4212
起 raise up →4099
擡 RAISE (one's head) →0972
立てる STAND →2486
拾う PICK UP →0454

❶ **display**
展 DISPLAY →3862
陳 lay out (for exhibit) →0656
掲 PUT UP →0597

❷ **print and publish**
刷 PRINT →1623
印 print →1023
植 typeset →1247
刊 PUBLISH →0221
版 PUBLISHING →1082
載 PUT IN PRINT →4091
掲 display in writing →0597
幀 BOOKBINDING →0695

捲 0598

▶ROLL UP
ケン ま(く) まく(る) -まくる まくし-めく(る)
Ⓝ 捲 Ⓒ 卷 juǎn juàn
1-3-8

64	Names	U6372
扌	S11-3-8	F2545

COMPOUNDS

● **ROLL UP, wind, coil, whirl**
捲土重来 けんどちょうらい making another attempt with redoubled efforts
席捲(=席巻) せっけん sweeping conquest, sweeping over

KUN

【まく 捲く】[usu. 巻く] **ROLL UP, roll; wind, reel; wrap**
捲き上げる まきあげる roll up, hoist, heave up; take away; blow up (dust)
捲き線 まきせん coil, winding
高捲き たかまき detour (in gorge-climbing)

【まくる 捲る】**ROLL UP, tuck up**

腕捲り うでまくり rolling up one's sleeves

【-まくる -捲る】[verbal suffix] **do something incessantly**

押し捲くる おしまくる push and push

【まくし- 捲し-】verbal prefix implying that an action is done incessantly or with force

【めくる 捲る】**turn over (pages, etc.)**

雑誌をパラパラと捲る ざっしをぱらぱらとめくる flip through a magazine

SYNONYMS

● **wind and twine**

巻 ROLL UP → 3273

捲 ROLL UP → 0598

繰る REEL → 1806

絡 ENTWINE → 1709

纏 WIND AROUND → 1814

HOMOPHONES

まく 巻 ROLL UP → 3273

NOTE

➡ see USAGE note at 巻 3273

掬

0599

◧ 1-3-8

▶**SCOOP UP**

キク すく(う)

Ⓒ 掬 jū

64	Names	U63AC
扌	S11-3-8	F2701

COMPOUNDS

● **SCOOP UP**

一掬 いっきく scooping water in the hands; small amount

KUN

【すくう 掬う】

① **SCOOP UP, dip up, ladle out**

掬い上げる すくいあげる scoop up

掬い網 すくいあみ scoop net, insect net

金魚掬い きんぎょすくい festival game of catching goldfish in a paper ladle

② **trip (someone) up**

掬い投げ すくいなげ beltless arm throw (in sumo); scoop throw (in judo)

足を掬う あしをすくう trip someone up

SYNONYMS

● **take from water**

撈 DREDGE → 0908

掬 SCOOP UP → 0599

汲 DRAW WATER → 0310

控

0600

◧ 1-3-8

▶**HOLD BACK**

コウ ひか(える) ひか(え)

Ⓒ 控 kòng

64	Jōyō	U63A7
扌	S11-3-8	F1382

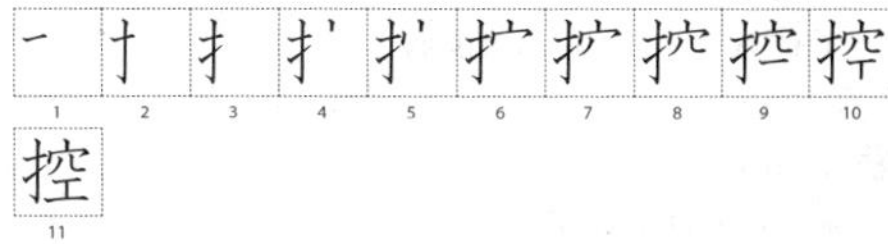

COMPOUNDS

❶ [formerly 扣 0250] **HOLD BACK part of something, deduct, subtract**

控除 こうじょ (tax) deduction, subtraction

❷ [original meaning, now rare] (keep in check) **HOLD BACK**, keep

控制する こうせいする hold back, keep

❸ **accuse in court, charge, sue**

控訴 こうそ (intermediate) appeal

KUN

【ひかえる 控える】[formerly also 扣える]

① (keep in check) **HOLD BACK, keep**

馬を控える うまをひかえる hold back a horse

②ⓐ (refrain from) **HOLD BACK** (from), restrain oneself, refrain

ⓑ **be moderate, be sparing**

a 差し控える さしひかえる be moderate in; withhold, desist from, refrain from

手控える てびかえる hang [hold] back, hold off, refrain

食べ物を控える たべものをひかえる be temperate in eating

b 控え目な ひかえめな modest, temperate, reserved

③ **be in waiting, wait**

別の間に控える べつのまにひかえる wait in another room

④ note down, write down, take notes

電話番号を控える でんわばんごうをひかえる jot down a phone number

⑤ have (something at hand)

選挙を控えて せんきょをひかえて with the election around the corner

【ひかえ 控え】[formerly also 扣え]

① **note, memo; counterfoil, stub**

控え書き ひかえがき notes, memo

捕り物控え とりものひかえ detective's memoirs

領収書の控え りょうしゅうしょのひかえ counterfoil of a receipt

② duplicate, copy

控えを取る ひかえをとる take a copy of

控え見本 ひかえみほん duplicate sample

③ **waiting; reserve, substitute, alternate**

口 土 女 山 巾 弓 彳 忄 【扌】 氵 犭 阝 亻 彳 纟

控えの間 ひかえのま antechamber, anteroom
控え室 ひかえしつ anteroom, waiting room
控えの力士 ひかえのりきし sumo wrestler waiting at the ringside
控え選手 ひかえせんしゅ reserve, substitute player

④ prop, stay
主控え しゅびかえ mainstay

SYNONYMS

❶ subtract
減 subtract → 0733
引く subtract → 0207
控 HOLD BACK → 0600
扣 HOLD BACK → 0250

❸ sue
訴 SUE → 1901
訟 LITIGATE → 1864
告 accuse of → 3062
控 accuse in court → 0600

【ひかえる】

① **pull**
引 DRAW → 0207
曳 DRAW → 4348
牽 DRAW → 2621
惹 DRAW ATTENTION → 2903
抽 DRAW OUT → 0359
抜 PULL OUT → 0290
控える HOLD BACK → 0600
扣える HOLD BACK → 0250
寄せる DRAW NEAR → 2856

② **restrain**
制 CONTROL (restrain) → 1624
禁 PROHIBIT → 3469
限 LIMIT → 0475
抑 SUPPRESS → 0301
束 TIE UP → 4369
縛 BIND → 1779
控える HOLD BACK → 0600
扣える HOLD BACK → 0250
渋る hang [hold] back → 0625

③ **wait**
待 WAIT → 0434
控える be in waiting → 0600

④ **write**
書 WRITE → 3292
筆 write → 3317
写 COPY → 2493
記 WRITE DOWN → 1843
紀 record in writing → 1628
控える note down → 0600
録 RECORD → 2186
登 register → 3208
註 ANNOTATE → 1893

USAGE

❶【ひかえる】

控える
[formerly also 扣える]
① (keep in check) hold back, keep
②ⓐ (refrain from) hold back (from), restrain oneself, refrain
ⓑ be moderate, be sparing
③ be in waiting, wait
④ note down, write down, take notes
⑤ have (something at hand)

扣える
[now replaced by 控える]
① (keep in check) hold back, keep
②ⓐ (refrain from) hold back (from), restrain oneself, refrain
ⓑ be moderate, be sparing
③ be in waiting, wait
④ note down, write down, take notes

❷【ひかえ】

控え
[formerly also 扣え]
① note, memo; counterfoil, stub
② duplicate, copy
③ waiting; reserve, substitute, alternate
④ prop, stay

扣え
[now replaced by 控え] same as 控え

HOMOPHONES

ひかえる 扣 HOLD BACK → 0250
ひかえ 扣 HOLD BACK → 0250

掘

0601
1-3-8

▶DIG
クツ ほ(る) -ほ(り)
Ⓒ 掘 jué

64	Jōyō	U6398
扌	S11-3-8	F1267

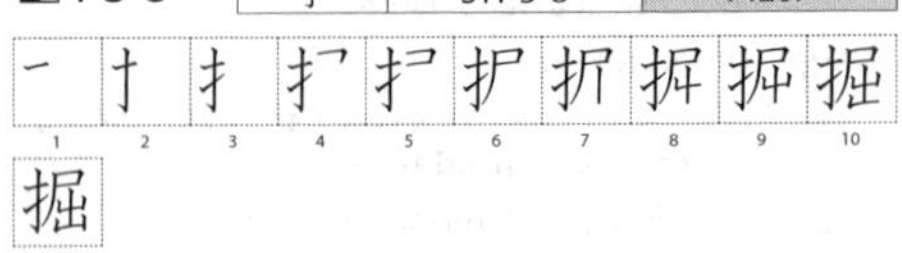

COMPOUNDS

ⓐ [original meaning] **DIG, excavate**
ⓑ DIG out, dig up, excavate

a 掘削する くっさくする dig out, excavate
採掘 さいくつ mining
試掘 しくつ prospecting, trial digging

b 掘進する くっしんする excavate, tunnel
発掘する はっくつする dig, excavate

KUN

【ほる 掘る】

ⓐ **DIG, bore, excavate**

ⓑ **DIG up, dig out, unearth**

a 掘り返す ほりかえす turn up (the soil), tear up (a road)

掘り下げる ほりさげる dig down; investigate, probe, delve into

【-ほり -掘り】**DIGging**

穴掘り あなほり digging a hole

露天掘り ろてんぼり open-air [strip] mining

SYNONYMS

● **dig**

掘 DIG → 0601

鑿 EXCAVATE → 3640

削 excavate → 1837

穿 DRILL → 2800

USAGE

【ほる】

掘る

ⓐ dig, bore, excavate

ⓑ dig up, dig out, unearth

彫る

ⓐ (cut so as to form designs or figures) engrave, carve, chisel

ⓑ tattoo

HOMOPHONES

ほる 彫 CARVE → 2117

NOTE

★ do not confuse with 堀 DITCH → 0561

据

▸INSTALL

キョ▲ す(える) す(わる)

Ⓒ 据 jù jū

0602

◧ 1-3-8

64	Jōyō	U636E
扌	S11-3-8	F1606

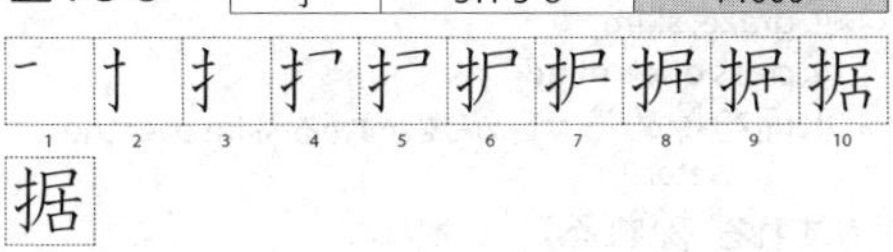

COMPOUNDS

❶ pinch, pick

拮×据 きっきょ assiduity, diligence, hard toil; [archaic] pinching

❷ [original meaning, now archaic] sit down

KUN

【すえる 据える】

① (set in position) **INSTALL, place in position, fix, mount, set up; set (a table); lay (a foundation)**

据え付ける すえつける install, equip, fit

据え置き すえおき leaving (a thing) as it stands; deferred savings

据え膳 すえぜん meal set before one; women's advances

見据える みすえる fix one's eyes, look hard

②ⓐ **INSTALL** a person in a post, place, appoint

ⓑ **INSTALL** a person in a seat, seat (a person)

a 後釜に据える あとがまにすえる install (a person) in (someone's) place

b 上座に据える かみざにすえる give (a guest) the seat of honor

腰を据える こしをすえる settle oneself (in a place)

【すわる 据わる】**be set**

目が据わって めがすわって with set eyes

腹の据わった男 はらのすわったおとこ man with plenty of guts

SYNONYMS

【すえる】

① **put**

据える INSTALL → 0602

置 PLACE → 3222

擱 LAY DOWN → 0970

掛ける SET → 0596

措 DISPOSE → 0610

① **equip and install**

据える INSTALL → 0602

敷 LAY → 2345

架 LAY ACROSS → 3178

装 FIT OUT → 3327

設 SET UP → 1863

備 PROVIDE → 0165

HOMOPHONES

すわる

座 SEAT → 3868

坐 SIT → 4361

NOTE

➡ see USAGE note at 座 3868

捺

▸AFFIX A SEAL

ナツ ダツ ナチ ナ お(す)

Ⓒ 捺 nà

0603

◧ 1-3-8

64	Names	U637A
扌	S11-3-8	F2999

COMPOUNDS

● **press heavily downwards; stamp**

捺印する なついんする affix a seal, stamp

指紋押捺 しもんおうなつ affixing one's fingerprint

KUN

【おす 捺す】[usu. 押す] **AFFIX A SEAL, stamp**

判を捺す はんをおす affix a seal

口 土 女 山 巾 弓 彳 忄 【扌】 氵 犭 阝 亻 彳 彡

SYNONYMS

● **mark**

印 imprint → 1023
押 seal → 0371
劃 MARK OFF → 2378
画 mark off → 3723
捺 AFFIX A SEAL → 0603

HOMOPHONES

おす

押 PUSH → 0371
推 INFER → 0612
圧 PRESSURE → 3688

NOTE

➡ see USAGE note at 押 0371

捻

0604

1-3-8

▶TWIST

ネン デン▲ ひね(る)▲ ねじ(る)▲ ねじ-▲

Ⓒ 捻 niǎn

64	Jōyō	U637B
扌	S11-3-8	F2389

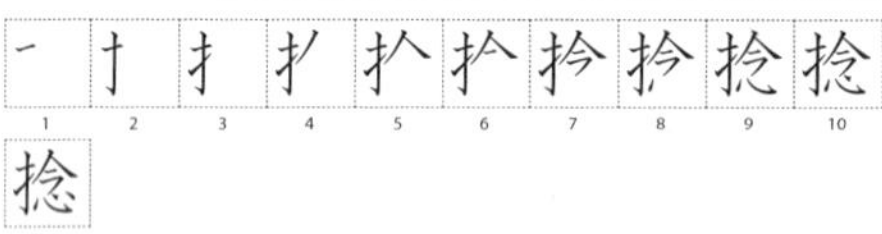

COMPOUNDS

● **TWIST, wrench, screw**

捻挫 ねんざ sprain
捻転 ねんてん twisting, torsion
捻出する ねんしゅつする manage to raise (funds), squeeze out (money, time), work out (a solution)

KUN

【ひねる 捻る】

ⓐ **TWIST**, wrench, turn (a switch), wring (a neck), pinch
ⓑ puzzle over, rack (one's brains), work out (an idea, poem, etc.)
ⓒ defeat easily

a 捻り ひねり twist, spin
捻り潰す ひねりつぶす crush (with one's fingers); easily defeat, crush
手捻り てびねり hand forming (of pottery), handwork
赤子の手を捻るよう あかごのてをひねるよう like taking candy from a baby
b 捻り出す ひねりだす work out, think up; manage to raise (funds)
首を捻る くびをひねる be puzzled; twist one's neck

【ねじる 捻る】 **TWIST**, wrench, screw, turn (a switch)

【ねじ- 捻じ-】

ⓐ verbal prefix indicating that an action is performed with a **TWIST**ing motion
ⓑ **TWIST**, writhe, squirm

a 捻じ伏せる ねじふせる hold down by force, twist one's arm

SPECIAL READINGS

捻子▲(=螺子) ねじ screw; spring, mainspring

SYNONYMS

● **turn**

旋 GYRATE → 1194
転 TURN → 1872
回 TURN ROUND → 3793
廻 TURN ROUND → 3833
巡 MAKE THE ROUNDS → 3781
循 CIRCULATE → 0704
斡 REVOLVE → 2168
捻 TWIST → 0604

掠

0605

1-3-8

▶PLUNDER

リャク かす(める) かす(れる) かす(る)

Ⓒ 掠 lüè

64	Names	U63A0
扌	S11-3-8	F2432

COMPOUNDS

● [now replaced by 略 1501] **PLUNDER, pillage, rob**

掠奪 りゃくだつ pillage, plunder, looting
侵掠する しんりゃくする invade, aggress (against)
劫掠 ごうりゃく extortion
奪掠 だつりゃく pillage, plunder, looting

KUN

【かすめる 掠める】

① **rob, cheat**

掠め取る かすめとる rob, cheat
人目を掠めて ひとめをかすめて by stealth, on the sly

②ⓐ **graze, skim**
ⓑ cross one's mind

a 水面を掠める すいめんをかすめる skim over the water

【かすれる 掠れる】 [also 擦れる]

ⓐ become blurred
ⓑ become hoarse [husky]

b 声が掠れる こえがかすれる become hoarse

【かする 掠る】 [also 擦る]

ⓐ **graze**
ⓑ **squeeze, exploit**

a 掠り傷 かすりきず scratch, graze, slight wound

SYNONYMS

● **steal and rob**

盗 STEAL → 3309
窃 STEAL → 2801

取 TAKE → 1613
奪 ROB → 2956
略 plunder → 1501
掠 PLUNDER → 0605
鹵 PLUNDER → 2634

USAGE

❶【かすれる】
掠れる
[also 擦れる]
ⓐ become blurred
ⓑ become hoarse [husky]
擦れる
[also 掠れる] same as 掠れる

❷【かする】
掠る
[also 擦る]
ⓐ graze
ⓑ squeeze, exploit
擦る
[also 掠る] same as 掠る

HOMOPHONES

かすれる 擦 RUB → 0971
かする 擦 RUB → 0971

採

▶PICK
▶GATHER
サイ と(る)

0606

Ⓝ 採 Ⓒ 采 cǎi cài

1-3-8

64	Jōyō-5	U63A1
扌	S11-3-8	F1012

一 十 扌 扩 扩 扩 扩 抨 抨 採 採 (strokes 1–11)

COMPOUNDS

❶ⓐ [original meaning] **PICK, pluck, gather**
ⓑ **GATHER (something useful), collect, mine, extract**

a 採取 さいしゅ picking, collecting, harvesting
採綿器 さいめんき cotton picker
伐採 ばっさい lumbering, lumber-felling, deforestation

b 採集 さいしゅう collecting, gathering
採掘 さいくつ mining
採炭 さいたん coal mining
採油 さいゆ drilling for oil, oil extraction
採血 さいけつ blood collecting [gathering]
採算 さいさん (commercial) profit
採点 さいてん marking, grading, rating
採録する さいろくする transcribe, record

❷ **PICK (out), select, adopt**

採用 さいよう adoption, acceptance; employment, appointment
採択する さいたくする adopt, select
採決 さいけつ ballot taking, vote, roll call

KUN

【とる 採る】

①ⓐ **GATHER, collect, extract (oil), produce (wine out of grapes)**
ⓑ admit (light)

a 山菜を採る さんさいをとる gather edible wild plants
葡萄からワインを採る ぶどうからわいんをとる make wine from grapes

b 明かり採り あかりとり skylight, dormer; transom

②ⓐ **PICK (out), choose, prefer**
ⓑ **adopt, take, engage**

a 採り上げる とりあげる adopt, accept, listen to
可否を採る かひをとる take the ayes and noes

b 新卒者を採る しんそつしゃをとる engage a new graduate

SYNONYMS

❶ⓐ **harvest**
採 PICK → 0606
摘 PICK → 0851
穫 HARVEST → 1598
刈る reap → 0032

ⓑ **gather**
集 COLLECT → 3445
蒐 COLLECT → 2942
聚 COLLECT → 3479
収 collect → 0031
採 GATHER → 0606
采 GATHER → 3077
萃 GATHER → 2882
湊 come together → 0743

❷ **choose**
選 CHOOSE → 3931
撰 choose → 0911
択 SELECT → 0299
採 PICK → 0606
摘 pick out → 0851
擢 SINGLE OUT → 0973
抜 single out → 0290
汰 SIFT OUT → 0312

HOMOPHONES

とる
取 TAKE → 1613
捕 CATCH → 0514
執 EXECUTE → 2114
撮 PHOTOGRAPH → 0910

NOTE

➡ see USAGE note at 取 1613

接

0607

1-3-8

▶**CONTACT**

セツ　つ(ぐ)

Ⓒ 接 jiē

64	Jōyō-5	U63A5
扌	S11-3-8	F0556

COMPOUNDS

❶ **CONTACT, touch, come in contact with**

接触 せっしょく contact, touch
接種 せっしゅ vaccination, inoculation
接点 せってん point of contact, contact
接線(=切線) せっせん tangent
接吻 せっぷん kiss
隣接 りんせつ contiguity, adjacency

❷ bring into **CONTACT**:
ⓐ **join, connect**
ⓑ weld, welding

a 接合 せつごう joining, union
接続 せつぞく connection, joining
接着 せっちゃく adhesion, gluing
b 溶接 ようせつ welding
融接 ゆうせつ fusion welding
鍛接 たんせつ forge welding

❸ **come close to, approach**

接近する せっきんする approach, draw near, come close
直接に ちょくせつに directly
間接的な かんせつてきな indirect, roundabout

❹ⓐ **receive (guests), welcome, meet**
ⓑ receive, accept

a 接待する せったいする receive (guests), welcome; offer, serve, entertain
面接 めんせつ interview
応接 おうせつ reception
b 接収する せっしゅうする requisition, take over, seize
接受する せつじゅする receive

INDEPENDENT

【せつ 接】(of electrical appliances) on, in **CONTACT**
【せっする 接する】**come in CONTACT, touch; adjoin, be contiguous; receive, see; receive, be in receipt of; meet with, encounter**

KUN

【つぐ 接ぐ】

ⓐ **join, piece together, set (a broken bone), splice (ropes)**
ⓑ graft (trees)

a 骨接ぎ ほねつぎ bonesetting
b 接ぎ木 つぎき grafting, grafted tree
木に竹を接ぐ きにたけをつぐ graft a bamboo shoot on a tree, sew a fox's skin to the lion's

SYNONYMS

❶ **touch**
触 TOUCH → 1914
接 CONTACT → 0607
撫 STROKE → 0904
当てる apply → 2701

❷ **join**
結 TIE → 1706
繫 CONNECT → 3612
縛 BIND → 1779
綴 BIND → 1746
繃 BIND UP → 1787
束 TIE UP → 4369
梱 PACK → 1205
連 LINK → 3849
係 CONNECT → 0108
接 join → 0607

❸ **approach**
寄る DRAW NEAR → 2856
迫 PRESS → 3815
近 NEAR → 3798
接 come close to → 0607
拶 PRESS → 0451

❹ⓐ **treat and welcome**
遇 TREAT → 3889
待 treat → 0434
扱う HANDLE → 0251
款 treat cordially → 2135
接 receive → 0607
迎 WELCOME → 3796

USAGE

【つぐ】

接ぐ
ⓐ join, piece together, set (a broken bone), splice (ropes)
ⓑ graft (trees)

継ぐ
① succeed (to), accede; inherit
② couple, link, relay
③ patch (up)
④ add to, replenish, feed

次ぐ
rank next to, come next [after]

注ぐ
pour out, pour in, fill

HOMOPHONES

つぐ

- 継 SUCCEED → 1720
- 次 NEXT → 0058
- 注 POUR → 0383

捨 0608

◧1-3-8

▶DISCARD

シャ　す(てる)

Ⓝ 捨 Ⓒ 舍 shě

64	Jōyō-6	U6368
扌	S11-3-8	F0877

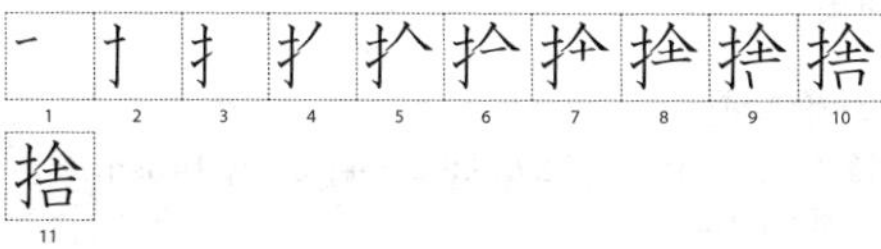

COMPOUNDS

❶ⓐ DISCARD, reject, cast away

ⓑ give up, abandon

a 取捨 しゅしゃ adoption or rejection, choice

用捨 ようしゃ adoption or rejection, choice

四捨五入 ししゃごにゅう rounding (to the nearest integer)

b 捨身 しゃしん becoming a priest; risking one's life for others

❷ give alms, dispense charity

喜捨する きしゃする give alms, donate

KUN

【すてる 捨てる】

① [sometimes also 棄てる]

ⓐ **DISCARD, throw away, cast aside**

ⓑ **abandon, desert, DISCARD, forsake, give up**

a ごみ捨て ごみすて dumping refuse; garbage pit, dumping ground

b 捨て子 すてご foundling, abandoned child; abandoning one's child

見捨てる みすてる forsake, desert

② leave unattended

捨てて置く すてておく leave something as it is

③ [in compounds] act as if getting rid of something

言い捨てる いいすてる say (something) over one's shoulder

SYNONYMS

❶ discard and abandon

- 捨 DISCARD → 0608
- 棄 ABANDON → 2651
- 諦 GIVE UP → 2010

USAGE

【すてる】

捨てる

① [sometimes also 棄てる]

ⓐ discard, throw away, cast aside

ⓑ abandon, desert, discard, forsake, give up

② leave unattended

③ [in compounds] act as if getting rid of something

棄てる

[usu. 捨てる]

ⓐ discard, throw away, cast aside

ⓑ abandon, desert, discard, forsake, give up

HOMOPHONES

すてる 棄 ABANDON → 2651

捷 0609

◧1-3-8

▶AGILE

ショウ　ジョウ ㊔ かつ　とし　はや　はやし　さとし　すぐる　かち　ちかし　まさる

Ⓒ 捷 jié

64	Names	U6377
扌	S11-3-8	F2761

COMPOUNDS

❶ AGILE, nimble, quick, alert; shrewd, keen

敏捷な びんしょうな agile, nimble, quick; shrewd, smart

❷ [rare] short (in distance)

捷路 しょうろ short-cut

❸ [original meaning] **victory**

捷報(=勝報) しょうほう report of a victory

SYNONYMS

❶ fast

- 速 QUICK → 3851
- 早 QUICK → 3042
- 疾 fast → 4064
- 快 fast → 0289
- 急 rapid → 2595
- 迅 SWIFT → 3780
- 敏 NIMBLE → 1675
- 即 IMMEDIATE → 1439
- 捷 AGILE → 0609

措 0610

◧1-3-8

▶DISPOSE

ソ　お(く)[▲]

Ⓒ 措 cuò

64	Jōyō	U63AA
扌	S11-3-8	F1591

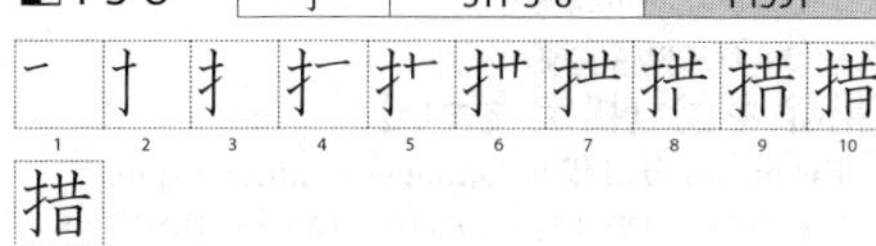

COMPOUNDS

❶ (put in the right position) **DISPOSE, place, arrange**

措定する そていする suppose, assume

措辞 そじ phraseology, wording

口 土 女 山 巾 弓 彳 忄 【扌】 氵 犭 阝 亻 彳 纟

措辞法 そじほう syntax

❷ (deal with) **DISPOSE of, take steps, manage**

措置 そち measure, step, action

❸ behavior, deportment

措止 そし demeanor, behavior

挙措 きょそ behavior, manner

❹ unclassified compounds

窮措大 きゅうそだい poor student [scholar]

KUN

【おく 措く】

① desist from, discontinue

賞賛して措かない しょうさんしておかない extol, applaud highly

② except, set apart, lay aside

措いて おいて except, no other

ここを措いて道は無い ここをおいてみちはない There is no other alternative

SYNONYMS

❶ **put**

据える INSTALL → 0602
置 PLACE → 3222
擱 LAY DOWN → 0970
掛ける SET → 0596
措 DISPOSE → 0610

❷ **deal with**

扱う HANDLE → 0251
処 DEAL WITH → 3764
辦 DISPOSE OF → 2028
措 dispose of → 0610
置 take proper steps → 3222

USAGE

【おいて】

措いて
except, no other

於て
① at, in, on
② as for, on one's part

HOMOPHONES

おく
置 PLACE → 3222
擱 LAY DOWN → 0970

おいて 於 AT → 1059

COMPOUND FORMATION

【措辞 そじ】【措定 そてい】

The meaning of 措 in Japanese is rather vague. 措 originally meant to put or arrange, which explains the formation of 措辞 'phraseology, wording', to place (措 ❶) words (辞) in the proper position. 措定する 'suppose, assume', a philosophical term, is, literally, to place (措 ❶) in a fixed (定) position.

NOTE

➡ see also USAGE note at 置 3222

掃

▸SWEEP

ソウ は(く)

Ⓝ 掃 Ⓒ 扫 sǎo sào

0611

1-3-8

64	Jōyō	U6383
扌	S11-3-8	F1449

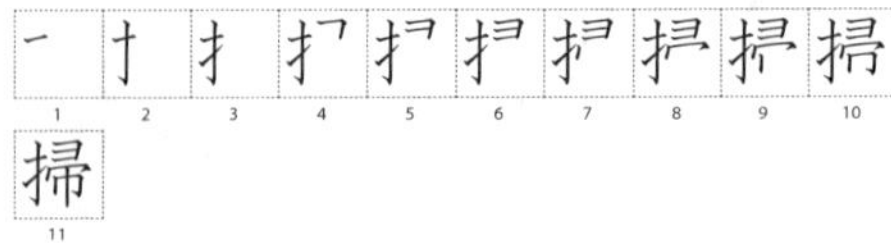

COMPOUNDS

❶ [original meaning] **SWEEP, sweep away, brush, clean up**

掃除 そうじ cleaning

掃除機 そうじき vacuum cleaner

掃射する そうしゃする sweep with fire, mow down

掃海 そうかい mine sweeping

清掃 せいそう cleaning

❷ [formerly also 勦 2335] exterminate, wipe out

掃滅する そうめつする wipe out, annihilate

掃討する そうとうする wipe out (the enemy), clear

一掃する いっそうする clean out, wipe out, dispel, eradicate

KUN

【はく 掃く】

① **SWEEP, brush, clean up**

掃き出す はきだす sweep out

掃き集める はきあつめる sweep up together

② [also 刷く] brush, apply with a brush

紅を掃く べにをはく give [have] a brush of rouge (to one's cheeks)

③ gather silkworms

掃き立て はきたて being newly swept; gathering silkworms from the egg paper

SYNONYMS

❶ **clean and wash**

洗 WASH → 0465
漱 RINSE → 0865
拭 WIPE → 0453
滌 WASH → 0854
濯 RINSE → 0978
浴 BATHE → 0533
浄 cleanse → 0457
粛 PURGE → 4400
清 CLEAR → 0635
払 CLEAR AWAY → 0225
掃 SWEEP → 0611

USAGE

【はく】

掃く

① sweep, brush, clean up

② [also 刷く] brush, apply with a brush

③ gather silkworms

刷く

[also 掃く] brush, apply with a brush

HOMOPHONES

はく 刷 PRINT → 1623

推

0612

1-3-8

▶INFER

スイ お(す)

Ⓒ 推 tuī

64	Jōyō-6	U63A8
扌	S11-3-8	F0787

COMPOUNDS

❶ **INFER, deduce, conjecture, surmise, guess**

推定する すいていする presume, infer

推理 すいり reasoning, inference

推測 すいそく conjecture, supposition

推察する すいさつする guess, conjecture, infer, imagine

推論 すいろん reasoning, inference, induction, deduction

類推 るいすい analogy

邪推する じゃすいする suspect without reason, mistrust

❷ **recommend, propose, nominate**

推薦する すいせんする recommend, nominate

推挙する すいきょする recommend, nominate

❸ **propel, drive, push**

推進する すいしんする propel, drive; promote

推力 すいりょく thrust, driving force

推薬 すいやく propellant

推敲×する すいこうする polish (a draft), refine

❹ change in succession

推移 すいい transition, change

KUN

【おす 推す】

① **INFER, deduce, conjecture, surmise, guess**

推して おして by conjecture [deduction]

推し量る おしはかる conjecture, surmise, guess

② **recommend, propose, nominate**

会長に推す かいちょうにおす recommend (a person) for the post of president

SYNONYMS

❶ **conjecture**

推 INFER → 0612

憶 SPECULATE → 0944

測 CONJECTURE → 0744

察 GUESS → 2961

❷ **recommend**

薦 RECOMMEND → 3008

推 recommend → 0612

❸ **force to move**

推 propel → 0612

駆 DRIVE → 2293

押す PUSH → 0371

HOMOPHONES

おす

押 PUSH → 0371

圧 PRESSURE → 3688

捺 AFFIX A SEAL → 0603

NOTE

➡ see USAGE note at 押 0371

探

0613

1-3-8

▶PROBE

▶SEARCH

タン さぐ(る) さが(す)

Ⓒ 探 tàn

64	Jōyō-6	U63A2
扌	S11-3-8	F0615

COMPOUNDS

❶ⓐ **PROBE, search into, explore, inquire**

ⓑ **SEARCH, look for**

a 探求 たんきゅう quest, search, pursuit

探究 たんきゅう investigation, search, inquiry

探査 たんさ inquiry, investigation

探測 たんそく sounding, probing

探訪 たんぼう (private) inquiry

探検(=探険) たんけん exploration, expedition

b 探索 たんさく search, quest; inquiry, investigation

探鉱 たんこう prospecting

探照灯 たんしょうとう searchlight

❷ⓐ spy on, trace, detect

ⓑ [rare] spy

a 探偵 たんてい detective work; detective, sleuth

探知 たんち detection

b 独探 どくたん German spy

❸ visit, view, appreciate

探勝 たんしょう sightseeing

探鳥 たんちょう bird-watching

KUN

【さぐる 探る】**PROBE, search into, explore**

探り さぐり sounding, probing; probe, stylet; spy
探り出す さぐりだす spy out
手探り てさぐり groping

【さがす 探す】[also 捜す] **SEARCH for (something desired), search about, look for**

探し回る さがしまわる search about for
職探し しょくさがし job hunting

SYNONYMS

❶ⓐ investigate and examine

閲 REVIEW →4132
審 EXAMINE CAREFULLY →2985
験 TEST →2306
勘 CHECK →2231
糾 INQUIRE INTO →1631
究 STUDY EXHAUSTIVELY →2729
察 INSPECT →2961
討 STUDY →1846
探 PROBE →0613
検 EXAMINE →1241
診 EXAMINE A PATIENT →1898
調 INVESTIGATE →1973
査 LOOK INTO →3092

ⓑ seek

探 SEARCH →0613
索 SEARCH FOR →3105
捜 LOOK FOR →0516
求 SEEK →4365
猟 hunt for →0654

❷ⓐ spy

偵 SPY →0157
探 spy on →0613

HOMOPHONES

さがす 捜 LOOK FOR →0516

NOTE

➡ see USAGE note at 捜 0516

挽

0614
1-3-8

▶GRIND
バン ひ(く)

64	Nonstandard	U633D
扌	S11-3-8	F0000

traditional form →see 挽 at 0511

捗

0615
1-3-8

▶MAKE PROGRESS
チョク はかど(る)

64	Nonstandard	U6357
扌	S11-3-8	F0000

traditional form →see 捗 at 0513

掴

0616
1-3-8

▶GRASP
カク つか(む) つか(まえる) つか(まる)

64	Nonstandard	U63B4
扌	S11-3-8	F0000

traditional form →see 摑 at 0848

採

0617
1-3-8

▶PICK
▶GATHER
サイ と(る)

64	Nonstandard	U63A1
扌	S11-3-8	F0000

traditional form →see 採 at 0606

捨

0618
1-3-8

▶DISCARD
シャ す(てる)

64	Nonstandard	U6368
扌	S11-3-8	F0000

traditional form →see 捨 at 0608

掻

0619
1-3-8

▶SCRATCH
ソウ か(く) かき- かい-

64	Nonstandard	U63BB
扌	S11-3-8	F0000

traditional form →see 搔 at 0800

掃

0620
1-3-8

▶SWEEP
ソウ は(く)

64	Nonstandard	U6383
扌	S11-3-8	F0000

traditional form →see 掃 at 0611

挽
1-3-8

incorrect stroke-count
➡ see 1-3-7: 扌 at 0511

插
1-3-8

incorrect stroke-count
➡ see 1-3-9: 扌 at 0730

捶
1-3-8

incorrect stroke-count
➡ see 1-3-9: 扌 at 0728

淀

0621
1-3-8

▶STAGNATE
デン よど(む) よど
Ⓒ 淀 diàn

85	Names	U6DC0
氵	S11-3-8	F2125

KUN

【よどむ 淀む】[also 澱む]
①ⓐ **STAGNATE, be stagnant**
ⓑ settle, precipitate

a 淀み よどみ pool (in river), backwater, stagnation; sedimentation, sediment, deposit; faltering, hesitation, pause

淀んだ空気 よどんだくうき stale air

b 川底の淀み かわぞこのよどみ sediment on the riverbed

② (of eyes) **become glazed, become glassy**

淀んだ目 よどんだめ glazed eyes

③ **hesitate, stammer, falter**

淀み無い よどみない (of speech) flowing, fluent

言い淀む いいよどむ hesitate to say

【よど 淀】

① [also 澱] pool, backwater, stagnation

② Yodo district (in Kyoto Prefecture)

淀川 よどがわ Yodo River

SYNONYMS

【よどむ】

①ⓐ **stagnate**

滞 STAGNATE →0815

淀む STAGNATE →0621

澱 SETTLE →0954

渋 NOT GO SMOOTHLY →0625

吃 STAMMER →0232

【よど】

① **stagnating water**

淵 DEEP WATER →0732

淀 pool →0621

澱 pool →0954

USAGE

【よどむ】

淀む

[also 澱む]

①ⓐ stagnate, be stagnant

ⓑ settle, precipitate

② (of eyes) become glazed, become glassy

③ hesitate, stammer, falter

澱む

[also 淀む] same as 淀む

HOMOPHONES

よどむ 澱 SETTLE →0954

よど 澱 SETTLE →0954

NOTE

➡ see also USAGE note at 澱 0954

液 0622

1-3-8

▶**LIQUID**

エキ

Ⓒ 液 yè

85 氵	Jōyō-5	U6DB2
	S11-3-8	F1104

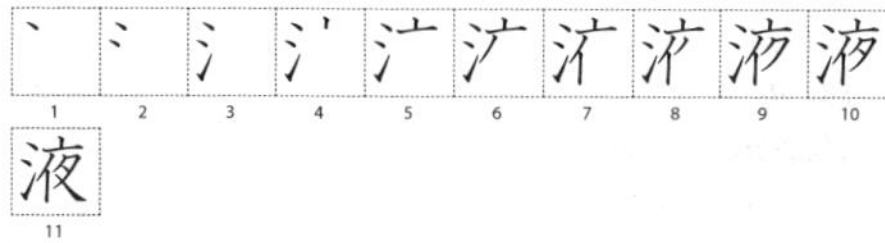

COMPOUNDS

[also suffix]

ⓐ [original meaning] **LIQUID, fluid**

ⓑ **solution**

ⓒ bodily secretion, juice

a 液体 えきたい liquid, fluid

廃液 はいえき waste fluid

血液 けつえき blood

乳液 にゅうえき milky lotion; latex

b 溶液 ようえき solution, solvent

消毒液 しょうどくえき antiseptic solution

c 胃液 いえき gastric juice

INDEPENDENT

【えき 液】**LIQUID, fluid; secretion; juice, sap**

液を絞る えきをしぼる squeeze the juice (from)

SYNONYMS

ⓐ **liquid**

液 LIQUID →0622

汁 fluid →0227

水 WATER →0010

涯 0623

1-3-8

▶**OUTER LIMITS**

ガイ

Ⓒ 涯 yá

85 氵	Jōyō	U6DAF
	S11-3-8	F1511

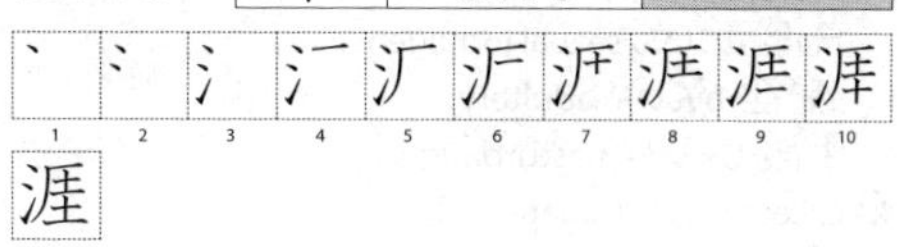

COMPOUNDS

❶ **OUTER LIMITS, end, bound**

生涯 しょうがい life, lifetime, career; for life

際涯 さいがい limits, end, extremity

天涯 てんがい far-off land (as remote as the horizon)

❷ [original meaning, now rare] water's edge, bank

水涯 すいがい water's edge

SYNONYMS

❶ **extreme**

極 EXTREME →1243

窮 extremity →2983

限 LIMIT →0475

涯 OUTER LIMITS →0623

果て end →4377

❶ **edges and boundaries**

縁 EDGE → 1754
端 edge → 1564
辺 border → 3761
境 BOUNDARY → 0835
疆 BOUNDARY → 1810
界 BOUNDS → 3172
際 VERGE → 0874
涯 OUTER LIMITS → 0623

COMPOUND FORMATION

【生涯 しょうがい】

生涯 'life, etc.' denotes the limits (涯 ❶) of one's life (生), i.e., the period from birth to death.

淫

0624

■ 1-3-8

▶**LEWD**

イン みだ(ら)

Ⓝ 淫 Ⓒ 淫 yín

85	Jōyō	U6DEB
氵	S11-3-8	F1960

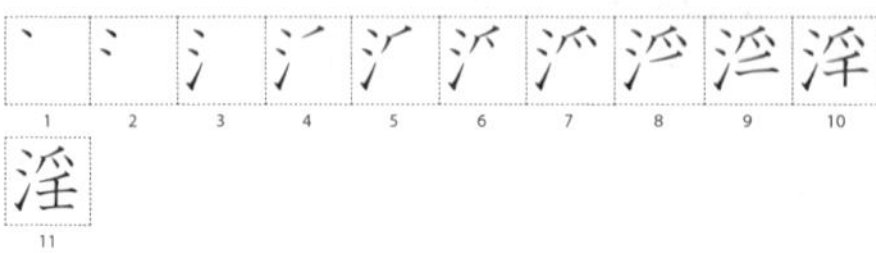

COMPOUNDS

❶ⓐ **LEWD, vulgar, lascivious**

ⓑ **LEWDness, vulgarity, sexuality**

a 淫乱 いんらん lewdness, lasciviousness
淫行 いんこう obscene [lewd] behavior
淫蕩× いんとう lewdness; sexual abandon
催淫剤 さいいんざい aphrodisiac

b 淫売 いんばい prostitution, prostitute
荒淫 こういん sexual indulgence
姦×淫 かんいん adultery
手淫 しゅいん masturbation

❷ excessive, inordinate
淫雨 いんう prolonged rain

INDEPENDENT

【いんする 淫する】go to excess, indulge in

KUN

【みだら 淫ら】**LEWD, bawdy, obscene**

SYNONYMS

❶ⓐ **sex**
性 SEX → 0357
情 (illicit) love → 0583
春 love → 3184
色 lust → 2522
淫 LEWD → 0624

渋

0625

■ 1-3-8

▶**NOT GO SMOOTHLY**
▶**ASTRINGENT**

ジュウ しぶ しぶ(い) しぶ(る)

Ⓝ 澁 澀 歮 Ⓒ 涩 sè

85	Jōyō	U6E0B
氵	S11-3-8	F1376

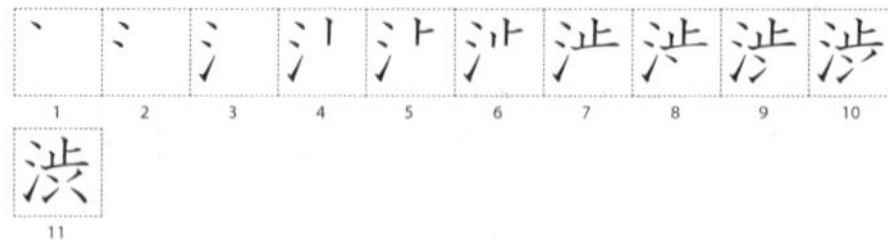

COMPOUNDS

❶ⓐ [original meaning] **NOT GO SMOOTHLY, make poor progress**

ⓑ difficult (to understand), abstruse

a 渋滞 じゅうたい delay, retardation, stagnation
苦渋 くじゅう distress, affliction

b 難渋 なんじゅう suffering, hardship
晦渋な かいじゅうな ambiguous, obscure, equivocal

❷ glum, sullen
渋面 じゅうめん sullen face

KUN

【しぶ 渋】**ASTRINGENT juice (of unripe persimmons), persimmon tannin**
渋紙 しぶがみ tanned paper
茶渋 ちゃしぶ tea incrustations

【しぶい 渋い】

① **ASTRINGENT, puckery, rough**—said esp. of the taste of unripe persimmons
渋柿 しぶがき puckery persimmon
渋い酒 しぶいさけ rough wine

② **glum, sullen, wry**
渋い顔をしている しぶいかおをしている look sullen, be grim-faced

③ **subdued, quiet, sober (color); refined, elegant**
渋い色 しぶいいろ sober [quiet] color
渋い着物 しぶいきもの tasteful dress

④ stingy, parsimonious
やり方が渋い やりかたがしぶい He has stingy ways

【しぶる 渋る】

① **hang [hold] back, hesitate, be reluctant**
渋渋 しぶしぶ reluctantly, grudgingly
言い渋る いいしぶる be reluctant [unwilling] to say
答えを渋る こたえをしぶる hesitate to answer, be reluctant to answer

② suffer from loose bowels with a gripping pain
渋り腹 しぶりばら painful loose bowels

SYNONYMS

❶ⓐ **stagnate**
滞 STAGNATE → 0815
淀む STAGNATE → 0621

澱 SETTLE → 0954
渋 NOT GO SMOOTHLY → 0625
吃 STAMMER → 0232

【しぶい】

① **tastes**

甘 SWEET → 4306
苦 BITTER → 2789
辛 PUNGENT → 2531
辣 PUNGENT → 1965
酸 sour → 1968
渋い ASTRINGENT → 0625
鹹 SALTY → 2366

【しぶる】

① **restrain**

制 CONTROL (restrain) → 1624
禁 PROHIBIT → 3469
限 LIMIT → 0475
抑 SUPPRESS → 0301
束 TIE UP → 4369
縛 BIND → 1779
控える HOLD BACK → 0600
扣える HOLD BACK → 0250
渋る hang [hold] back → 0625

淳

0626

1-3-8

▶**PUREHEARTED**

ジュン ㊔ あつ あつし きよし あき すなお きよ まこと

Ⓒ 淳 chún

85	Names	U6DF3
氵	S11-3-8	F1623

COMPOUNDS

● **PUREHEARTED, simple, innocent**

淳良な じゅんりょうな simple and kind, innocent
淳朴(=純朴) じゅんぼく simplicity and honesty

SYNONYMS

● **purehearted**

純 PURE → 1649
淳 PUREHEARTED → 0626
清 clean → 0635
潔 IMMACULATE → 0920
廉 INCORRUPT → 3911
敦 HONEST → 2128
惇 SINCERE → 0588
直 straightforward → 3649
侃 FORTHRIGHT → 0097

渇

0627

1-3-8

▶**RUN DRY**
▶**THIRST**

カツ かわ(く)

Ⓝ 渇 Ⓒ 渴 kě

85	Jōyō	U6E07
氵	S11-3-8	F2163

(stroke order 1–11)

COMPOUNDS

❶ [original meaning] **RUN DRY, dry up**

渇水 かっすい water shortage
枯渇する こかつする dry up, run dry; be exhausted, be depleted

❷ⓐ **THIRST, be thirsty; thirst**
ⓑ **THIRST** for, long for, crave

a 渇死する かっしする [archaic] die of thirst
飢渇 きかつ hunger and thirst
b 渇望する かつぼうする thirst for, long for, crave
渇仰 かつごう adoration

INDEPENDENT

【かつ 渇】**THIRST**

渇を癒やす かつをいやす quench one's thirst

【かっする 渇する】be **THIRST**y; dry up; thirst [long] for

KUN

【かわく 渇く】**be THIRSTy, thirst**

渇き かわき thirst
喉が渇く のどがかわく be thirsty

SYNONYMS

❶ **dry**

乾 DRY → 2113
干 DRY → 4187
燥 DRY UP (desiccate) → 1392
涸 DRY UP (run dry) → 0629
渇 RUN DRY → 0627
旱 DROUGHT → 3048

❷ⓐ **hunger and thirst**

渇 THIRST → 0627
餓 STARVED → 2176
飢 STARVE → 2101
饑 STARVE → 2281

ⓑ **wish and desire**

願 WISH → 2320
憧 YEARN AFTER → 0899
憬 YEARN AFTER → 0898
貪 COVET → 2630
望 HOPE → 3408

希 ASPIRE → 2543
懐 LONG FOR → 0942
慕 yearn for → 2970
渇 thirst for → 0627
欲 DESIRE → 1867
慾 DESIRE → 3551
求 SEEK → 4365

HOMOPHONES

かわく 乾 DRY → 2113
かわき 乾 DRY → 2113

NOTE

➡ see USAGE note at 乾 2113

渓

0628

1-3-8

▶RAVINE

ケイ ㊔ たに

Ⓝ 溪 谿 Ⓒ 溪 xī

85	Jōyō	U6E13
氵	S11-3-8	F2177

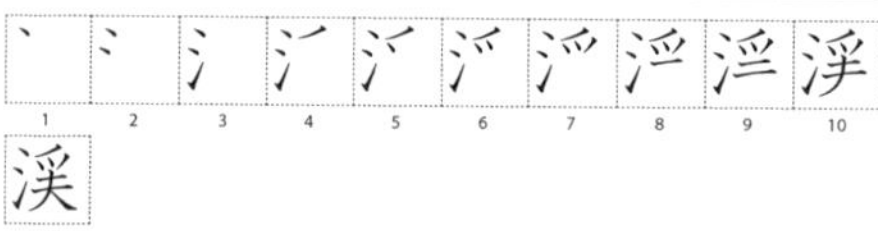

COMPOUNDS

ⓐ [also suffix] **RAVINE, valley**
ⓑ [original meaning] mountain stream, valley stream

a 渓谷 けいこく ravine, valley, canyon
渓間 けいかん ravine
雪渓 せっけい snowy valley [ravine]
耶馬渓 やばけい Yabakei Valley
b 渓流 けいりゅう mountain stream
渓声 けいせい sound of a valley stream

SYNONYMS

ⓐ **valley**
谷 VALLEY → 2536
渓 RAVINE → 0628
峡 GORGE → 0427

ⓑ **rivers and streams**
川 RIVER → 0006
河 RIVER → 0394
江 large river → 0257
渓 mountain stream → 0628
流 stream → 0529

涸

0629

1-3-8

▶DRY UP

コ か(れる) か(らす)

Ⓒ 涸 hé

85	Non-Jōyō	U6DB8
氵	S11-3-8	F3111

COMPOUNDS

● [now also 枯 1113] [original meaning] **DRY UP, run dry**
涸渇する こかつする dry up, run dry; be exhausted, be depleted

KUN

【かれる 涸れる】**DRY UP, run dry, be exhausted**
【からす 涸らす】**DRY UP, exhaust**
出涸らし でがらし used and insipid (as of tea or coffee)

SYNONYMS

● **dry**
乾 DRY → 2113
干 DRY → 4187
燥 DRY UP (desiccate) → 1392
涸 DRY UP (run dry) → 0629
渇 RUN DRY → 0627
旱 DROUGHT → 3048

HOMOPHONES

かれる 枯 WITHER → 1113
からす 枯 WITHER → 1113

NOTE

➡ see USAGE note at 枯 1113

淆

0630

1-3-8

▶INTERMINGLE

コウ

Ⓒ 淆 xiáo

85	Non-Jōyō	U6DC6
氵	S11-3-8	F0000

COMPOUNDS

● [now usu. 交 2508] [original meaning] **INTERMINGLE, mix, blend**
混淆する こんこうする mix up, jumble together

SYNONYMS

● **mix**
混 MIX → 0631
淆 INTERMINGLE → 0630
交 intermingle → 2508
雑 MIXED → 1752
錯 MIXED UP → 2187

混

0631

1-3-8

▶MIX

コン ま(じる) -ま(じり) ま(ざる) ま(ぜる) こ(む)

Ⓒ 混 hùn hún

85	Jōyō-5	U6DF7
氵	S11-3-8	F0960

[COMPOUNDS]

❶ⓐ (combine or cause to combine into an indistinguishable mass) **MIX, blend, mingle**

ⓑ suffix indicating fabric of MIXed composition

a 混血 こんけつ mixed-blood, racial mixture
混合 こんごう mixing, mixture
混声合唱 こんせいがっしょう mixed chorus
混紡 こんぼう mixed spinning
混浴 こんよく mixed bathing

b 二十パーセント麻混の綿 にじゅっぱーせんとあさこんのめん cotton mixed with 20% hemp

❷ **MIXed up, confused, disorderly, chaotic**
混雑 こんざつ confusion, disorder, congestion
混乱 こんらん disorder, confusion, chaos
混同 こんどう confusion; mixing
混迷 こんめい confusion, bewilderment; [formerly 昏迷] stupor, unconsciousness
混沌 こんとん [sometimes also 渾沌] chaos

❸ [also 渾 0738] (unified in an integrated whole) **entire, whole, complete**
混然一体となる こんぜんいったいとなる be joined together, form a complete whole

❹ [formerly 昏 3073] lose consciousness, faint
混迷 こんめい stupor, unconsciousness

[KUN]

【まじる 混じる】*vi* **be blended, get MIXed (with the constituents blending into each other)**
混じり合う まじりあう be blended, be mixed together
混じり気 まじりけ a dash of (something), impurity

【-まじり -混じり】[also suffix] **mingling of**
雨混じりの雪 あめまじりのゆき snow mingled with rain
鼻歌混じりで働く はなうたまじりではたらく work while humming a tune

【まざる 混ざる】same as 混じる まじる
混ざり物 まざりもの impurity

【まぜる 混ぜる】*vt*
ⓐ (combine together into a single mass) **blend, MIX, adulterate**
ⓑ **MIX by stirring, scramble, toss, churn**
a 混ぜ合わす まぜあわす mix together; blend, compound
b 混ぜ返す まぜかえす banter, make fun of (what a person says)
掻き混ぜる(=掻き交ぜる) かきまぜる mix by stirring, mix up, scramble, toss, churn

【こむ 混む】[usu. 込む] **be crowded, be congested, be packed**
混み合う こみあう be crowded, be packed, be jammed
人混み ひとごみ crowd [throng] (of people)

[SYNONYMS]

❶ⓐ **mix**
混 MIX →0631
淆 INTERMINGLE →0630
交 intermingle →2508
雑 MIXED →1752
錯 MIXED UP →2187

❷ **disordered**
紛 CONFUSED →1648
乱 DISORDERED →1611
錯 MIXED UP →2187
混 mixed up →0631
雑 mixed up →1752
沌 PRIMEVAL CHAOS →0314

[USAGE]

❶【まじる】
混じる
vi be blended, get mixed (with the constituents blending into each other)
交じる
vi be mingled, be mixed, intermingle (with the constituents remaining distinct)
★混じる and 交じる are often used interchangeably.

❷【まざる】
混ざる
same as 混じる まじる
交ざる
same as 交じる まじる

❸【まぜる】
混ぜる
vt
ⓐ (combine together into a single mass) blend, mix, adulterate
ⓑ mix by stirring, scramble, toss, churn
交ぜる
vt (combine together, with the constituents remaining distinct) mix, shuffle

[HOMOPHONES]

まじる 交 INTERCOURSE →2508
まざる 交 INTERCOURSE →2508
まぜる 交 INTERCOURSE →2508
こむ 込 MOVE INWARD →3762

[NOTE]

➡ see also USAGE note at 込 3762

淋

0632

◧1-3-8

▸**GONORRHEA**
▸**LONESOME**
リン さび(しい) さみ(しい)
Ⓒ 淋 lín lìn

85	Names	U6DCB
氵	S11-3-8	F2212

COMPOUNDS

❶ **GONORRHEA**

淋病 りんびょう gonorrhea

淋菌 りんきん gonococcus

❷ used phonetically for *rin*

淋巴 りんぱ lymph

❸ [original meaning] drip (with sweat), drench, pour

淋漓×たる りんりたる brimming, dripping

KUN

【さびしい　淋しい】[usu. 寂しい]

ⓐ **LONESOME, lonely, desolate, deserted**

ⓑ scarce, scanty

a 淋しがる さびしがる feel lonely, miss someone

物淋しい ものさびしい lonesome, desolate, dreary

心淋しい こころさびしい lonely, lonesome, forlorn

b 懐が淋しい ふところがさびしい have a scanty supply of money

【さみしい　淋しい】[usu. 寂しい] same as 淋しい さびしい

SYNONYMS

❶ **diseases and disease symptoms**

疱 SMALLPOX → 4070

淋 GONORRHEA → 0632

癌 CANCER → 4076

熱 fever → 3555

炎 INFLAMMATION → 3075

痢 DIARRHEA → 4068

下 diarrhea → 4186

【さびしい】

ⓐ **sad and depressed**

悲 SAD → 3448

悄 BECOME DISPIRITED → 0506

哀 sorrowful → 2568

愁 MELANCHOLY → 3508

鬱 GLOOM → 3625

陰 gloomy → 0657

沈 depressed → 0306

寂 LONESOME → 2855

淋しい LONESOME → 0632

惨 MISERABLE → 0585

HOMOPHONES

さびしい 寂 LONESOME → 2855

さみしい 寂 LONESOME → 2855

NOTE

➡ see USAGE note at 寂 2855

涼

0633

1-3-8

▶**COOL**

リョウ　すず(しい)　すず(む)

Ⓝ 涼 Ⓒ 凉 liáng liàng

85	Jōyō	U6DBC
氵	S11-3-8	F1614

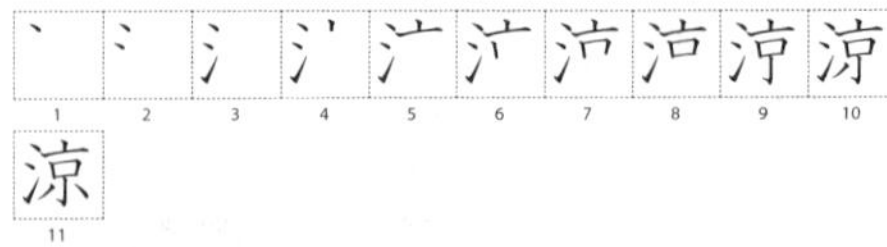

COMPOUNDS

❶ⓐ **COOL, refreshing**

ⓑ the **COOL**, cool evening air

a 涼気 りょうき cool air

涼風 りょうふう cool breeze

涼味 りょうみ coolness, cool

清涼な せいりょうな cool, refreshing

b 冷涼 れいりょう coolness

納涼 のうりょう enjoying the evening cool

❷ [also 寥 2960] desolate, deserted, empty

荒涼たる こうりょうたる desolate, dreary

INDEPENDENT

【りょう　涼】the **COOL**, the evening cool

涼を取る りょうをとる enjoy the cool breeze

KUN

【すずしい　涼しい】**COOL, refreshing**

涼しさ すずしさ coolness

涼しい顔 すずしいかお nonchalant (unruffled) air

【すずむ　涼む】**COOL oneself, enjoy the cool breeze**

涼み すずみ cooling oneself, enjoying the cool air

涼み台 すずみだい bench

SYNONYMS

❶ⓐ **cold**

冷 COLD → 0088

寒 COLD (weather) → 2894

涼 COOL → 0633

凜 SEVERELY COLD → 0195

済

0634

1-3-8

▶**SETTLE**

▶**RELIEVE**

サイ　セイ▲　す(む)　-ず(み)　-ずみ

す(まない)　す(ます)　-す(ます)　す(ませる)

㊔ わたる　いつき

Ⓝ 濟 Ⓒ 济 jì jǐ

85	Jōyō-6	U6E08
氵	S11-3-8	F0337

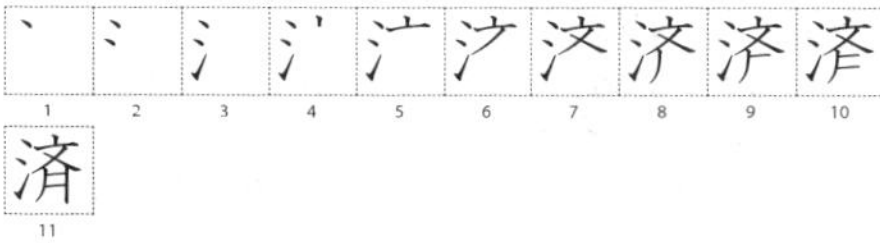

COMPOUNDS

❶ⓐ **SETTLE accounts, pay back, clear**
ⓑ **SETTLE, conclude, finish**

a 返済する へんさいする repay, reimburse
決済 けっさい settlement of accounts
弁済 べんさい repayment, payment, settlement
既済の きさいの paid up, already settled
b 完済 かんさい full payment, liquidation
未済の みさいの unsettled, unpaid, outstanding; unfinished

❷ **RELIEVE, aid, save, redeem**

済民 さいみん relieving the sufferings of the people
済度 さいど *Buddhism* salvation
経済 けいざい economy, economics
救済する きゅうさいする relieve, help, save, deliver
共済 きょうさい mutual aid

❸ numerous

多士済済 たしせいせい(=たしさいさい) galaxy of intellectuals

KUN

【すむ 済む】**be SETTLEd, end, be concluded; do [manage] (without), get off (with)**
済み すみ being settled
行かずに済む いかずにすむ need not go
少しの損で済む すこしのそんですむ get off with a little loss

【-ずみ -済み, -済】[suffix] **completed, finished, SETTLEd, concluded**
支払い済み しはらいずみ paid, settled
点検済み てんけんずみ inspection completed, checked up
使用済みの切手 しようずみのきって used stamps

【すまない 済まない】**inexcusable, unpardonable**
済みません すみません Excuse me/I am sorry

【すます 済ます】**SETTLE, finish, bring to a conclusion, get through with; make shift, manage (with), make (a thing) do [serve the purpose]**
勘定を済ます かんじょうをすます pay one's bill
仕事を済ます しごとをすます finish one's work
無しで済ます なしですます do without

【-すます -済ます】[also -澄ます] [verbal suffix] **perform an action well [perfectly]**
成り済ます なりすます successfully impersonate

【すませる 済ませる】same as 済ます すます

SYNONYMS

❶ⓐ **pay**

払う PAY → 0225
納 PAY (to the authorities) → 1652
済 settle accounts → 0634
支 pay out → 2473
賦 INSTALLMENT → 1992
償 RECOMPENSE → 0199

ⓑ **end**

終 END → 1692
絶 COME TO AN END → 1711
閉 CLOSE → 4116
了 FINISH → 4157
済 SETTLE → 0634
-上げる completion suffix → 4212
完 COMPLETE → 2727
結 CONCLUDE → 1706
竣 COMPLETE → 1528

❷ **rescue**

救 SAVE → 1891
済 RELIEVE → 0634

❷ **help**

助 HELP → 1440
佑 HELP (said esp. of God) → 0083
祐 DIVINE HELP → 1146
援 AID → 0715
佐 ASSIST → 0076
補 assist → 1529
輔 ASSIST → 1963
済 RELIEVE → 0634

HOMOPHONES

-すます 澄 LIMPID → 0915

NOTE

➡ see USAGE note at 澄 0915
➡ see COMPOUND FORMATION for 経済 けいざい → 経 1687

清

0635

◧ 1-3-8

▶**CLEAR**

セイ ショウ シン▲ きよ(い) きよ(まる) きよ(める) すが(やか)▲ ㊔ きよし すみ すが

Ⓝ 清 Ⓒ 清 qīng

85	Jōyō-4	U6E05
氵	S11-3-8	F0486

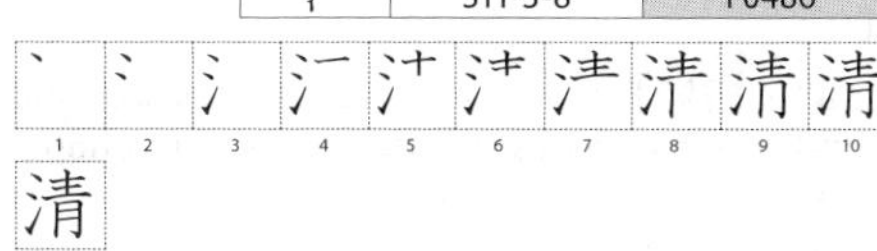

COMPOUNDS

❶ⓐ (of liquids) **CLEAR, unmixed**
ⓑ (of the weather) **CLEAR**

a 清水 せいすい pure [clear] water
清流 せいりゅう clear [limpid] stream

清酒 せいしゅ (refined) sake
血清 けっせい serum
河清 かせい clearing of the river water
b 清澄な せいちょうな clear, lucid; serene
清秋 せいしゅう clear fall (weather)

❷ (of sounds) **unvoiced, voiceless**
清音 せいおん unvoiced sound
清子音 せいしいん voiceless consonant

❸ⓐ (rid of impurities) **CLEAR, clean**
ⓑ **CLEAR up, settle (a debt)**
a 清掃 せいそう cleaning
六根清浄 ろっこんしょうじょう purification of one's self through detachment from the senses
b 清算 せいさん settlement, liquidation; clearing (off)
粛清 しゅくせい purge, purging, liquidation

❹ⓐ (free from dirt or impurities) **clean, pure, neat**
ⓑ (free from moral taint) **clean, honest, pure, honorable**
a 清潔 せいけつ cleanliness, neatness, purity
清浄 せいじょう purity, cleanness
清書 せいしょ fair [clean] copy
清純な せいじゅんな pure (and innocent)
清楚な せいそな neat and clean, tidy, trim
b 清濁 せいだく purity and impurity; good and evil
清廉 せいれん integrity, honesty, uprightness
清貧 せいひん honest [honorable] poverty
清教徒 せいきょうと Puritan

❺ cool, refreshing, clean
清新の せいしんの fresh, new
清涼な せいりょうな cool, refreshing
清風 せいふう cool [refreshing] breeze
清清する せいせいする feel refreshed, feel relieved

❻ quiet, tranquil
清閑 せいかん quiet, tranquility
清聴 せいちょう your kind attention (to my talk)

❼ Qing Dynasty, Manchu Dynasty (1644-1912 A.D.)
清国 しんこく China under the Manchus
日清戦争 にっしんせんそう the Sino-Japanese War (of 1894-95)

INDEPENDENT

【しん 清】 Qing Dynasty, Manchu Dynasty

KUN

【きよい 清い】 (free from dirt or impurities) **clean, pure, neat;** (free from moral taint) **clean, honest, pure, honorable**
清らかな きよらかな same as 清い きよい
清い月影 きよいつきかげ clear moon, beautiful moonlight
清い愛 きよいあい pure [platonic] love

【きよまる 清まる】 **be purified, be cleansed**
心が清まる こころがきよまる feel purified

【きよめる 清める】
①ⓐ [sometimes also 浄める] (rid of dirt or impurities) **cleanse, purify**
ⓑ [usu. 浄める] (rid of moral taint) **purify, purge**
a 清め きよめ purification, ablution
② [sometimes also 浄める] **exorcise**
身を清める みをきよめる cleanse oneself

【すがやか 清やか】
すがやかな 清やかな **refreshing; fresh; bracing**
清清しい すがすがしい refreshing; fresh; bracing

SPECIAL READINGS

清水 しみず spring water

SYNONYMS

❶ⓐ **clear**
透 TRANSPARENT → 3854
澄 LIMPID → 0915
清 CLEAR (liquid) → 0635
明 CLEAR (unclouded) → 1060
朗 CLEAR (sky) → 1679
冴える CRISP AND CLEAR → 0087

❸ **clean and wash**
洗 WASH → 0465
漱 RINSE → 0865
拭 WIPE → 0453
滌 WASH → 0854
濯 RINSE → 0978
浴 BATHE → 0533
浄 cleanse → 0457
粛 PURGE → 4400
清 CLEAR → 0635
払 CLEAR AWAY → 0225
掃 SWEEP → 0611

❹ⓐ **clean and purified**
浄 CLEAN → 0457
清 clean → 0635
純 PURE → 1649
潔 IMMACULATE → 0920
粋 REFINED (free from impurities) → 1645
精 refined (purified) → 1729
楚 NEAT AND TRIM → 3470

ⓑ **purehearted**
純 PURE → 1649
淳 PUREHEARTED → 0626
清 clean → 0635
潔 IMMACULATE → 0920
廉 INCORRUPT → 3911
敦 HONEST → 2128
惇 SINCERE → 0588
直 straightforward → 3649
侃 FORTHRIGHT → 0097

❼ **later Chinese dynasties**

唐 TANG DYNASTY → 3867
宋 SONG DYNASTY → 2730
元 Yuan Dynasty → 2428
明 Ming Dynasty → 1060
清 Qing Dynasty → 0635

USAGE

【きよめる】
清める
①ⓐ [sometimes also 浄める] (rid of dirt or impurities) **cleanse, purify**
ⓑ [usu. 浄める] (rid of moral taint) **purify, purge**
② [sometimes also 浄める] **exorcise**
浄める
①ⓐ [usu. 清める] (rid of dirt or impurities) **cleanse, purify**
ⓑ [sometimes also 清める] (rid of moral taint) **purify, purge**
② [usu. 清める] **exorcise**

HOMOPHONES

きよめる 浄 CLEAN → 0457

深 ▶DEEP

シン ふか(い) -ぶか(い) ふか(まる) ふか(める) み-▲ ㊔ ふかし

0636 Ⓒ 深 shēn

1-3-8

85	Jōyō-3	U6DF1
氵	S11-3-8	F0357

Stroke order: 1–11

COMPOUNDS

❶ⓐ [original meaning] (extending downward) **DEEP**
ⓑ (extending inward) **DEEP, distant, inmost, secluded**
ⓒ **depth**
a 深海 しんかい deep sea
深耕 しんこう deep plowing
深部 しんぶ deep part, depth
深呼吸 しんこきゅう deep breathing
b 深山幽谷に しんざんゆうこくに deep in the mountains
深窓 しんそう secluded inner room
c 水深 すいしん depth of water
❷ⓐ (difficult to fathom) **DEEP, profound, unfathomable, innermost**
ⓑ (of great intensity) **DEEP, intense, extreme, profound**
ⓒ [also prefix] **DEEP-colored, dark**
ⓓ **in the DEEP [dead] of night, late at night**
a 深遠 しんえん profundity, depth
深奥 しんおう esoteric doctrines, mysteries, depth
b 深刻な しんこくな serious, grave, keen, poignant
深甚なる しんじんなる deep, extreme
深謝 しんしゃ deep gratitude, sincere apology
c 深緑 しんりょく dark [deep] green
深紅色 しんこうしょく deep crimson, scarlet
d 深夜 しんや dead of night, midnight
深更 しんこう dead of night, midnight
❸ (characterized by deep friendship) **intimate, close, friendly, kind**
深交 しんこう close friendship
深切(=親切) しんせつ kindness

KUN

【ふかい 深い】 **DEEP, inmost, distant; profound, deep; intense, profound; deep-colored, dark; late (in the season); close, intimate; thick, dense**
深さ ふかさ depth; profundity
深み ふかみ depth, the deep; profundity
深い愛情 ふかいあいじょう deep affection
深い関係 ふかいかんけい close connection
深緑色 ふかみどりいろ dark [deep] green
深い霧 ふかいきり thick [dense] fog
奥深い おくぶかい(=おくふかい) deep, profound; esoteric
【-ぶかい -深い】 [also suffix] **DEEP, intense**
根深い ねぶかい deep-rooted, ingrained
興味深い きょうみぶかい of great interest
【ふかまる 深まる】 *vi* **DEEPen, become deeper**
秋が深まって冬になった あきがふかまってふゆになった Autumn deepened into winter
【ふかめる 深める】 *vt* **DEEPen, heighten, intensify, strengthen**
理解を深める りかいをふかめる cultivate a better understanding
【み- 深-】 [also prefix] indicates elegance or euphony
深山 みやま mountain recesses
深雪 みゆき deep snow

SYNONYMS

❶ⓑ **inner**
奥 inner → 3503
深 DEEP → 0636
幽 QUIET AND SECLUDED → 3731
❷ⓐ **profound**
玄 PROFOUND → 2485
幽 deep hidden → 3731
奥 inmost → 3503
深 DEEP → 0636
滉 DEEP AND VAST → 0811
ⓑ **extreme in degree**
酷 SEVERE → 1967
強 STRONG → 0574
凄い tremendous → 0145

重 HEAVY →4390
高 HIGH →2601
深 DEEP →0636
大 BIG →4224
厳 SEVERE →4079
激 intense →0955
極 EXTREME →1243
痛 bitter(ly) →4071
切 keen →0030
甚 EXTREMELY →3271
祁 EXTREMELY →1447
超 super- →4107
頗る EXCEEDINGLY →1552

❻ dark-colored

暗 DARK →1273
濃 dark →0956
深 DEEP →0636

渚 0637

1-3-8

▸STRAND

ショ なぎさ

Ⓝ 渚 Ⓒ 渚 zhǔ

85	Names	U6E1A
氵	S11-3-8	F2919

COMPOUNDS

❶ [archaic] **STRAND**, beach, waterside, shore

渚畔 しょはん waterside, shore

❷ [original meaning, now archaic] sandbar in a river

汀渚 ていしょ water's edge; sandbar

KUN

【なぎさ 渚】[sometimes also 汀] **STRAND, beach, waterside, shore**

渚伝い なぎさづたい along the shore

SYNONYMS

❶ shores and watersides

畔 WATERSIDE →1472
-辺 -side →3761
浜 BEACH →0523
岸 SHORE →2777
浦 SEASIDE →0524
渚 STRAND →0637
磯 ROCKY BEACH →1587
汀 STRAND →0228

USAGE

【なぎさ】

渚

[sometimes also 汀] strand, beach, waterside, shore

汀

[usu. 渚] strand, beach, waterside, shore

HOMOPHONES

なぎさ 汀 STRAND →0228

渉 0638

1-3-8

▸HAVE RELATIONS WITH

ショウ ㊔ わたる わたり

Ⓝ 渉 Ⓒ 涉 shè

85	Jōyō	U6E09
氵	S11-3-8	F1161

(stroke order 1–11)

COMPOUNDS

❶ HAVE RELATIONS [connections] WITH, relate, interrelate

渉外 しょうがい public relations
交渉 こうしょう negotiation, bargaining, discussion
干渉 かんしょう interference, intervention

❷ [original meaning] wade (across water), ford

渉禽類 しょうきんるい wading birds
徒渉 としょう wading, fording

❸ wander about in search for something

渉猟 しょうりょう searching far and wide (for); extensive reading

SYNONYMS

❶ relate

関 CONCERN →4129
係 CONNECT →0108
絡 INTERLINK →1709
渉 HAVE RELATIONS WITH →0638
連 LINK →3849
聯 LINK →1797

❷ cross

渡 CROSS →0746
渉 wade →0638
越 GO BEYOND →4108

❷ move through water

泳 SWIM →0385
游 SWIM →0750
渉 wade →0638
遡 GO UPSTREAM →4040
漕 ROW →0864

淑 0639

1-3-8

▸GRACEFUL

シュク しと(やか)▲ ㊔ よし とし ひで すみ

Ⓒ 淑 shū

85	Jōyō	U6DD1
氵	S11-3-8	F2442

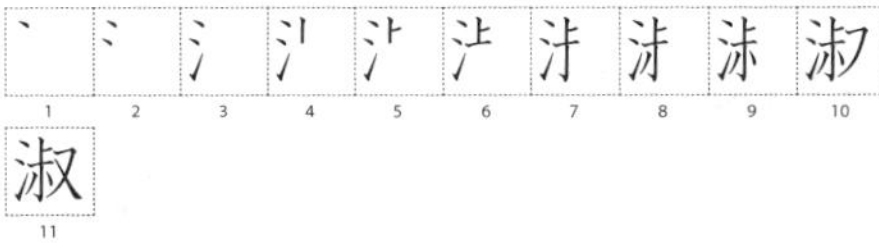

COMPOUNDS

❶ (of women) **GRACEFUL, gentle and kind, refined, fair**

淑徳 しゅくとく feminine grace, womanly virtues
淑女 しゅくじょ lady, gentlewoman
貞淑 ていしゅく chastity, female virtue

❷ adore, respect

私淑する ししゅくする adore, look up to

KUN

【しとやか 淑やか】

しとやかな 淑やかな **GRACEFUL**, gentle, modest
淑やかさ しとやかさ grace, gentleness, modesty

SYNONYMS

❶ **elegant**

雅 ELEGANT → 1532
淑 GRACEFUL → 0639
優 graceful → 0200
粋 REFINED → 1645
彬 REFINED AND GENTLE → 1201

淡

▶LIGHT

タン あわ(い) ㊔ あわし

Ⓒ 淡 dàn

0640

◧ 1-3-8

85	Jōyō	U6DE1
氵	S11-3-8	F1433

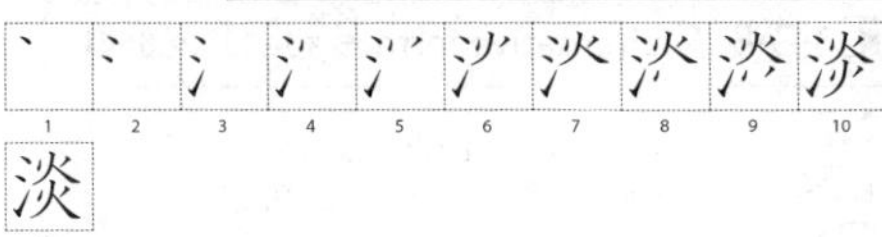

COMPOUNDS

❶ⓐ [also prefix] **LIGHT-colored, faint, pale**
ⓑ **LIGHT**-flavored, plain, not flavored

a 淡色 たんしょく light color
淡彩 たんさい light color
淡紅色 たんこうしょく pink, rose pink
濃淡 のうたん light and shade

b 淡白(=淡泊)な たんぱくな light (color, taste); plain, simple; indifferent

❷ **indifferent, unconcerned, disinterested**

淡淡たる たんたんたる indifferent, unconcerned
冷淡な れいたんな cool, indifferent

❸ (not saline) fresh (water)

淡水 たんすい fresh water
淡湖 たんこ freshwater lake

KUN

【あわい 淡い】**LIGHT (color, flavor), faint; fleeting, transitory**

淡さ あわさ faintness, lightness
淡雪 あわゆき light snow
淡い悲しみ あわいかなしみ fleeting sorrow

SYNONYMS

❶ⓐ **light-colored**

淡 LIGHT → 0640
浅 light → 0464
薄い pale → 3004
鈍- DULL → 2123

添

▶ADD TO

テン そ(える) そ(う)

Ⓝ 添◇ Ⓒ 添 tiān

0641

◧ 1-3-8

85	Jōyō	U6DFB
氵	S11-3-8	F1261

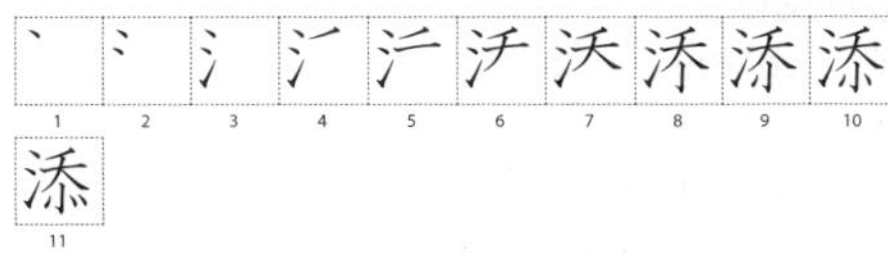

COMPOUNDS

❶ **ADD TO, append, affix, accompany**

添加する てんかする add, annex, append
添削 てんさく correction
添付する てんぷする attach, append, annex
添書 てんしょ accompanying letter

❷ **accompany, go along with, attend on**

添乗員 てんじょういん (escort) courier, tour conductor

KUN

【そえる 添える】**ADD TO, attach to, accompany; garnish**

添え物 そえもの addition, supplement; garnishing
添え書き そえがき postscript, additional writing
介添え かいぞえ assistance; helper, assistant, best man or bridesmaid
力添え ちからぞえ aid, help, assistance
手紙を添える てがみをそえる attach a letter to
パセリを添える ぱせりをそえる garnish (a dish) with parsley

【そう 添う】

① **accompany, go along with, stay with**

添い寝 そいね sleeping with (one's child)
付き添い つきそい attendance; attendant, escort

② marry

連れ添う つれそう be man and wife, be married to

③ meet (someone's wishes), suit

人の要求に添う ひとのようきゅうにそう meet one's demands

④ **ADD TO,** increase

趣が添う おもむきがそう add color to

SYNONYMS

❶ add to

付 ATTACH → 0035
附 ATTACH → 0410
加 ADD → 0042
追 add → 3840
添 ADD TO → 0641

❷ accompany

伴 ACCOMPANY → 0068
添 accompany → 0641
陪 ACCOMPANY A SUPERIOR → 0655
侍 ATTEND UPON → 0094
従 FOLLOW → 0498
随 FOLLOW → 0765

HOMOPHONES

そう 沿 ALONG → 0386

NOTE

➡ see USAGE note at 沿 0386

口 土 女 山 巾 弓 彳 忄 扌 【氵】 犭 阝 亻 亻 纟

渕
0642
◧ 1-3-8

▶**DEEP WATER**
エン ふち ㊔ のぶ ひろ ふか ふかし なみ すけ すえ しずか

85	Nonstandard	U6E15
氵	S11-3-8	F0000

traditional form → see 淵 at 0732

渊
0643
◧ 1-3-8

▶**DEEP WATER**
エン ふち ㊔ のぶ ひろ ふか ふかし なみ すけ すえ しずか

85	Nonstandard	U6E0A
氵	S11-3-8	F0000

traditional form → see 淵 at 0732

滛
0644
◧ 1-3-8

▶**LEWD**
イン みだ(ら)

85	Nonstandard	U6DEB
氵	S11-3-8	F0000

traditional form → see 淫 at 0624

淨
0645
◧ 1-3-8

▶**CLEAN**
ジョウ きよ(める) ㊔ きよ きよし

85	Names	U6DE8
氵	S11-3-8	F0000

traditional form → see 浄 at 0457

淚
0646
◧ 1-3-8

▶**TEAR**
ルイ なみだ

85	Names	U6DDA
氵	S11-3-8	F0000

traditional form → see 涙 at 0528

淸
0647
◧ 1-3-8

▶**CLEAR**
セイ ショウ シン きよ(い) きよ(まる) きよ(める) すが(やか) ㊔ きよし すみ すが

85	Nonstandard	U6DF8
氵	S11-3-8	F0000

traditional form → see 清 at 0635

淺
0648
◧ 1-3-8

▶**SHALLOW**
セン あさ(い)

85	Nonstandard	U6DFA
氵	S11-3-8	F0000

traditional form → see 浅 at 0464

渗
0649
◧ 1-3-8

▶**PERMEATE**
シン し(みる) にじ(む)

85	Nonstandard	U6E17
氵	S11-3-8	F0000

traditional form → see 滲 at 0862

添
0650
◧ 1-3-8

▶**ADD TO**
テン そ(える) そ(う)

85	Nonstandard	U6DFB
氵	S11-3-8	F0000

alternative form → see 添 at 0641

渡
◧ 1-3-8

incorrect stroke-count
➡ see ◧ 1-3-9: 氵 at 0746

游
◧ 1-3-8

incorrect stroke-count
➡ see ◧ 1-3-9: 氵 at 0750

猫
0651
◧ 1-3-8

▶**CAT**
ビョウ ねこ

Ⓝ 貓 Ⓒ 猫 māo máo

94	Jōyō	U732B
犭	S11-3-8	F1227

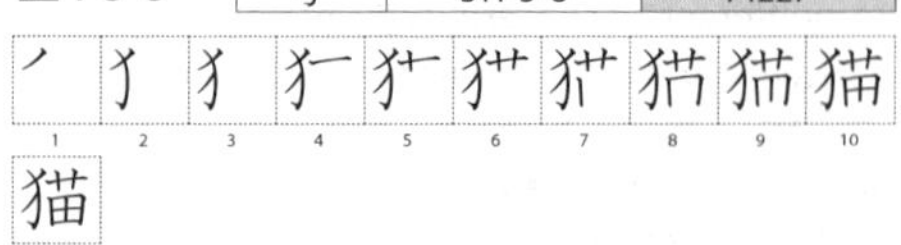

COMPOUNDS

● [original meaning] **CAT**

猫額大の土地 びょうがくだいのとち narrow strip of land
愛猫家 あいびょうか cat lover

KUN

【ねこ 猫】 [also suffix] **CAT; feline, catlike; clay foot warmer; wheelbarrow;** *slang* **geisha girl**
猫科 ねこか cat family, Felidae
猫背 ねこぜ stoop, bent back
猫被り ねこかぶり hypocrisy, false modesty; hypocrite, wolf in a lamb's skin
猫撫で声で ねこなでごえで in a soft coaxing voice
子猫 こねこ kitten
ペルシャ猫 ぺるしゃねこ Persian cat

SYNONYMS

● **domesticated mammals**
牛 CATTLE → 4263
馬 HORSE → 4086
豚 PIG → 1228
羊 SHEEP → 2708
犬 DOG → 4275
猫 CAT → 0651
兎 RABBIT → 4374

猪

▶WILD BOAR
チョ いのしし い ㊔ いの しし
Ⓝ 猪 豬 Ⓒ 猪 zhū

0652
◧1-3-8

94	Names	U732A
犭	S11-3-8	F1780

COMPOUNDS

ⓐ [original meaning] **WILD BOAR, boar**
ⓑ as daring and reckless as a **WILD BOAR**
a 野猪 やちょ wild boar
b 猪突 ちょとつ recklessness, foolhardiness

KUN

【いのしし 猪】 **WILD BOAR; reckless fellow, daredevil**
猪武者 いのししむしゃ foolhardy warrior; hotspur
【い 猪】 [in compounds] **WILD BOAR**
猪首 いくび bull neck

SYNONYMS

ⓐ **undomesticated mammals**
虎 TIGER → 3981
猿 MONKEY → 0824
鯨 WHALE → 2361
犀 RHINOCEROS → 3900
狼 WOLF → 0541
狐 FOX → 0472
羚 SEROW → 1695
鼠 RAT → 3340
獅 LION → 0825
豹 LEOPARD → 1847
熊 BEAR → 3530
象 ELEPHANT → 2647
麒 MALE CHINESE UNICORN → 2363
麟 FEMALE CHINESE UNICORN → 2376
猪 WILD BOAR → 0652
鹿 DEER → 3879

ⓐ **swine**
豚 PIG → 1228
豕 SWINE → 4357
猪 WILD BOAR → 0652
亥 THE BOAR → 2505

USAGE

【い】
猪
[in compounds] **wild boar**
亥
twelfth sign of the Oriental zodiac: **the Boar**

HOMOPHONES

い 亥 THE BOAR → 2505

猛

▶FIERCE
モウ ㊔ たけ たけし たける
Ⓒ 猛 měng

0653
◧1-3-8

94	Jōyō	U731B
犭	S11-3-8	F1467

COMPOUNDS

❶ⓐ [original meaning] (having a ferocious nature) **FIERCE, violent, savage, ferocious**
ⓑ [also prefix] (extremely severe) **FIERCE, violent; heavy, hard, intensive**
a 猛犬 もうけん fierce [ferocious] dog
猛獣 もうじゅう fierce [savage] animal [beast]
獰×猛な どうもうな fierce, ferocious
b 猛烈な もうれつな violent, vehement, fierce
猛然と もうぜんと fiercely
猛毒 もうどく deadly poison
猛爆 もうばく heavy bombing
猛襲 もうしゅう fierce attack
猛練習 もうれんしゅう hard training

❷ brave
猛将 もうしょう brave general, brave warrior
勇猛な ゆうもうな daring, brave, valiant

SPECIAL READINGS

猛者 もさ stalwart; veteran

SYNONYMS

❶ⓐ **violent**

暴 VIOLENT → 3138
猛 FIERCE → 0653
荒い WILD → 2810

ⓑ **extreme in power**

激 VIOLENT → 0955
荒 WILD → 2810
狂 raging → 0318
烈 VEHEMENT → 3286
猛 FIERCE → 0653

猟

0654

1-3-8

▸HUNTING

リョウ

Ⓝ 獵 Ⓒ 猎 liè

94	Jōyō	U731F
犭	S11-3-8	F1968

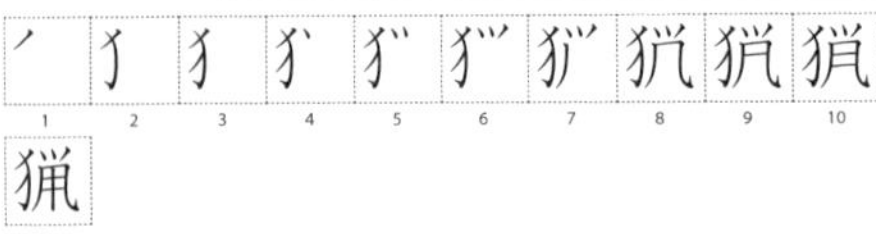

COMPOUNDS

❶ [original meaning] **HUNTING, shooting**

猟季 りょうき hunting season
猟銃 りょうじゅう hunting gun
猟犬 りょうけん hound, hunting dog
狩猟 しゅりょう hunting, hunt
銃猟 じゅうりょう shooting, hunting
禁猟 きんりょう prohibition of shooting [hunting]

❷ hunt for, search for, seek

猟奇 りょうき bizarrerie hunting
猟色 りょうしょく lewdness, debauchery
渉猟 しょうりょう searching far and wide (for); extensive reading

INDEPENDENT

【りょう 猟】**HUNTING, shooting; game**

猟をする りょうをする hunt, shoot

SYNONYMS

❶ **hunt and fish**

猟 HUNTING → 0654
狩 HUNT → 0474
獲 CATCH GAME → 0959
漁 FISH → 0856
釣 ANGLE → 2108
弋 CATCH → 4230

❷ **seek**

探 SEARCH → 0613
索 SEARCH FOR → 3105
捜 LOOK FOR → 0516
求 SEEK → 4365
猟 hunt for → 0654

陪

0655

1-3-8

▸ACCOMPANY A SUPERIOR

バイ

Ⓒ 陪 péi

170	Jōyō	U966A
阝	S11-3-8	F2466

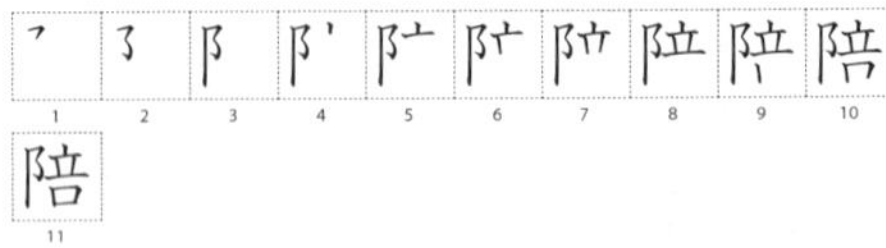

COMPOUNDS

❶ **ACCOMPANY A SUPERIOR, perform an action in the company of a superior, keep company with a person of rank, attend upon**

陪席 ばいせき sitting with one's superior
陪従する ばいじゅうする wait upon, attend on, accompany
陪食 ばいしょく dining with a superior
陪乗する ばいじょうする ride in the same carriage [car] (with a superior), attend on (one's superior) in the same carriage
陪審 ばいしん jury
陪侍 ばいじ attending on the nobility; retainer

❷ retainer's retainer, rear vassal

陪臣 ばいしん rear vassal, vassal's vassal, daimyo's retainer

SYNONYMS

❶ **accompany**

伴 ACCOMPANY → 0068
添 accompany → 0641
陪 ACCOMPANY A SUPERIOR → 0655
侍 ATTEND UPON → 0094
従 FOLLOW → 0498
随 FOLLOW → 0765

COMPOUND FORMATION

【陪審 ばいしん】

陪審 'jury' refers to a group of people attending on (陪 ❶) the judge and aiding him in trying (審).

NOTE

★ do not confuse with 部 SECTION → 2111

陳

0656

1-3-8

▸SET FORTH

チン ㊔ のぶ じん

Ⓒ 陈 chén

170	Jōyō	U9673
阝	S11-3-8	F1650

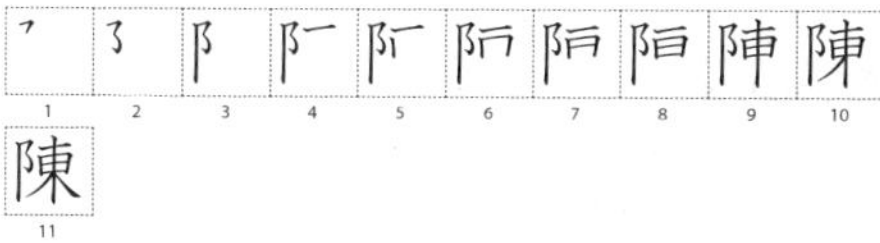

COMPONDS

❶ SET FORTH, state, explain, declare

陳情 ちんじょう petition, appeal

陳述する ちんじゅつする state, set forth, declare, expound

陳謝 ちんしゃ apology

開陳する かいちんする state, express (one's opinion)

❷ [original meaning] **lay out (for exhibit), put on display, spread out**

陳列する ちんれつする exhibit, display

出陳 しゅっちん submitting (something) to an exhibition

❸ old, stale

陳腐な ちんぷな old-fashioned, trite, worn-out

新陳代謝(=代謝) しんちんたいしゃ(=たいしゃ) metabolism; renewal, regeneration

❹ Chen Dynasty (557-589 A.D.)

INDEPENDENT

【ちん 陳】Chen Dynasty

【ちんずる 陳ずる】state, declare, expound

SYNONYMS

❶ speak and say

言 SAY → 2440

語る TELL → 1944

談 TALK → 1975

喋 TALK → 0665

諷 INSINUATE → 2005

謂う REFER TO → 2007

云 say → 2430

曰 SAY THAT → 3757

話 SPEAK → 1928

口 give mouth to → 4189

申す SPEAK HUMBLY → 4319

述 STATE → 3816

陳 SET FORTH → 0656

弁 SPEAK ELOQUENTLY → 2497

❷ display

展 DISPLAY → 3862

陳 lay out (for exhibit) → 0656

掲 PUT UP → 0597

❷ arrange

並 LINE UP → 2793

比 rank → 0029

列 arrange in a row → 1018

陳 lay out (for exhibit) → 0656

羅 spread out → 3244

揃える arrange properly → 0719

整 PUT IN ORDER → 3562

理 put in order → 1220

NOTE

➡ see COMPOUND FORMATION for 代謝(=新陳代謝) たいしゃ(=しんちんたいしゃ) → 謝 2048

★ do not confuse with 陣 BATTLE FORMATION → 0545

陰

0657

◧ 1-3-8

▸SHADE

イン かげ かげ(る)

Ⓝ 陰 Ⓒ 阴 yīn

170	Jōyō	U9670
阝	S11-3-8	F0983

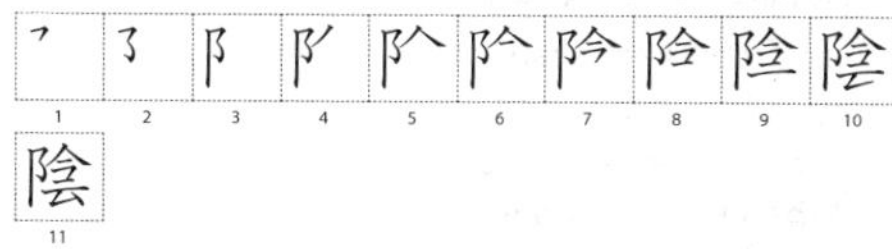

COMPOUNDS

❶ SHADE

陰影 いんえい shadow

緑陰 りょくいん shade of trees

樹陰 じゅいん [rare] shade of a tree

❷ [original meaning] **SHADE**d or north side of a mountain; south side of a stream

山陰 さんいん shaded or north side of a mountain; San'in district

❸ⓐ **SHADE**d, dark

ⓑ become cloudy, be overcast

a 陰湿な いんしつな dark and damp, dampish

夜陰 やいん darkness of the night, shades of night

b 陰晴 いんせい fine weather and cloudy weather

❹ in the **SHADE**s, hidden, secret, unseen

陰謀 いんぼう scheme, plot, conspiracy

陰徳 いんとく secret charity

❺ gloomy, melancholy, dejected

陰気 いんき gloominess, cheerlessness

陰鬱 いんうつ gloominess, melancholy

陰惨 いんさん sadness and gloom

❻ sex [reproductive] organ, esp. the female genital organ

陰部 いんぶ private parts, sex organ

陰唇 いんしん labium

陰茎 いんけい penis

❼ yin: the female and passive principle in Chinese dualistic philosophy representing negative concepts such as femininity, moon, darkness, earth, etc.

陰陽 いんよう yin and yang, positive and negative, active and passive

❽ⓐ **negative**

ⓑ *elec* **negative pole**

a 陰性 いんせい negative, dormant

b 陰電気 いんでんき negative electricity

❾ moon
陰暦 いんれき lunar calendar
太陰 たいいん moon
❿ time
光陰 こういん time, Father Time

INDEPENDENT

【いん 陰】yin (→❼); concealed, gloomy
陰に陽に いんにように openly and covertly, implicitly and explicitly

KUN

【かげ 陰】
① [formerly also 蔭] **SHADE**
日陰 ひかげ the shade
② [formerly also 蔭]
ⓐ **back side, reverse side**
ⓑ **behind the scenes**
a 戸の陰に隠れる とのかげにかくれる hide behind a door
b 陰で かげで behind one's back
陰口 かげぐち backbiting
③ [also 蔭] [in the form of お陰 おかげ] **grace, favor**
お陰で おかげで indebtedness; favor; help
お陰様で おかげさまで [polite] thanks to, due to
【かげる 陰る】[also 翳る] **darken, be clouded**
陰り かげり shade; gloom

SYNONYMS

❶ **shadow**
影 SHADOW →2381
翳 SHADOW →3567
陰 SHADE →0657
蔭 SHADE →2974
❸ⓐ **dark**
暗 DARK →1273
黒 BLACK →3406
陰 shaded →0657
闇 DARK →4134
晦 DARK →1196
昏 dark →3073
昧 DARK →1105
冥 DARK →2613
曖 SHADY →1383
❺ **sad and depressed**
悲 SAD →3448
悄 BECOME DISPIRITED →0506
哀 sorrowful →2568
愁 MELANCHOLY →3508
鬱 GLOOM →3625
陰 gloomy →0657
沈 depressed →0306
寂 LONESOME →2855
淋しい LONESOME →0632
惨 MISERABLE →0585
❻ **genitals**
陰 sex organ →0657
胎 WOMB →1149
恥 private parts →1664
❼ **yin and yang**
陰 yin →0657
陽 yang →0764
❽ⓐ **negative**
負 negative →2594
陰 negative →0657
❾ **moon**
月 MOON →3674
陰 moon →0657

USAGE

【かげり】
陰り
[formerly also 翳り] shade; gloom
翳り
[now usu. 陰り] shade; gloom
❶【かげる】
陰る
[also 翳る] darken, be clouded
翳る
[also 陰る] darken, be clouded

HOMOPHONES

かげ
蔭 SHADE →2974
影 SHADOW →2381
かげり 翳 SHADOW →3567
かげる 翳 SHADOW →3567

NOTE

➡ see also USAGE note at 影 2381

険

0658

▶**DANGER**
▶**STEEP**
ケン けわ(しい)
Ⓝ 險 Ⓒ 险 xiǎn

1-3-8

170	Jōyō-5	U967A
阝	S11-3-8	F0677

COMPOUNDS

❶ⓐ **DANGER, risk, hazard**
ⓑ **DANGERous, risky, hazardous**
a 危険な きけんな dangerous
保険 ほけん insurance
b 険悪な けんあくな dangerous, threatening, serious

冒険 ぼうけん adventure, risk
探険(=探検) たんけん exploration, expedition

❷ [formerly also 嶮 0937]
ⓐ **STEEP, precipitous**
ⓑ [original meaning] **STEEP** [inaccessible] place, steep pass, stronghold

a 険路 けんろ steep pass
険阻(=嶮岨) けんそ steepness, precipice
峻険な しゅんけんな steep, precipitous
b 天険 てんけん natural stronghold

❸ sinister, vicious
陰険な いんけんな sly, crafty, treacherous

❹ (figuratively) sharp (look), stern (expression)
険相 けんそう uncanny look

INDEPENDENT

【けん 険】 [formerly also 嶮 0937] **STEEP** place, impregnable pass, stronghold; stern expression
険の有る目 けんのあるめ sharp look
アルプスの険 あるぷすのけん steep pass in the Alps

KUN

【けわしい 険しい】 [sometimes also 嶮しい] (sharply inclined and difficult to climb) **STEEP, precipitous; craggy; severe, grim, fierce, angry**
険しさ けわしさ steepness; severity, grimness
険しい山 けわしいやま steep [craggy] mountain
険しい顔 けわしいかお grim face

SYNONYMS

❶ **danger**
危 DANGEROUS →3965
殆 dangerous →1130
険 DANGER →0658

❷ **steep**
険 STEEP →0658
嶮 STEEP →0937
岨 STEEP →0341
急 steep →2595
峻 high and steep →0495

USAGE

【けわしい】
険しい
[sometimes also 嶮しい] (sharply inclined and difficult to climb) steep, precipitous; craggy; severe, grim, fierce, angry
嶮しい
[usu. 険しい] (sharply inclined and difficult to climb) steep, precipitous; craggy; severe, grim, fierce, angry

HOMOPHONES

けわしい 嶮 STEEP →0937

COMPOUND FORMATION

【保険 ほけん】
保険 'insurance' means to guarantee (保) against hazards (険 ❶ⓐ).

陸

0659
▮1-3-8

▶**LAND**
リク ロク▲ おか▲ ㊔ くが みち むつ おく
Ⓒ 陆 lù liù

170	Jōyō-4	U9678
阝	S11-3-8	F0639

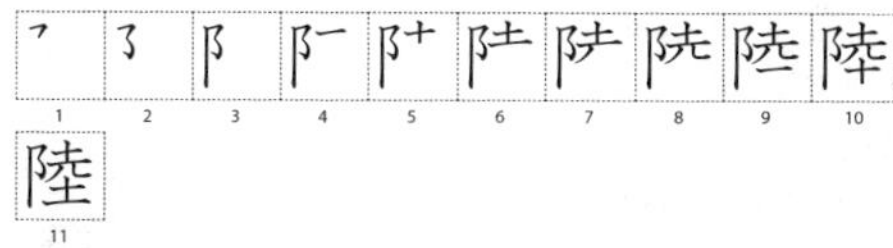

COMPOUNDS

❶ (solid ground of the earth, as distinguished from the sea) **LAND, shore**
陸地 りくち land
陸上 りくじょう land, ground; shore; track and field
陸橋 りっきょう overland bridge
陸兵 りくへい land troops
陸岸 りくがん shore, land
陸軍 りくぐん army
陸上自衛隊 りくじょうじえいたい Ground Self Defense Forces
大陸 たいりく continent
上陸 じょうりく landing, disembarkation
着陸 ちゃくりく landing, alighting

❷ abbrev. of 陸軍 りくぐん or 陸上自衛隊 りくじょうじえいたい army, Ground Self-Defense Forces
陸相(=陸軍大臣) りくしょう(=りくぐんだいじん) Minister of the Army
陸大 りくだい Military Staff College

❸ continuously
陸続と りくぞくと continuously, successively

❹ six—used in legal documents and checks
陸萬×円也 ろくまんえんなり sum of 60,000 yen

❺ abbrev. of 陸奥 むつ, old name for northeast Tohoku district
陸前 りくぜん Rikuzen (old name for Miyagi Prefecture)

❻ brilliant, vivid
光彩陸離たる こうさいりくりたる brilliant, dazzling

INDEPENDENT

【りく 陸】 **LAND, shore; six** (→❹)
陸を行く りくをいく go by land, travel overland

KUN

【おか 陸】 **LAND**, shore

陸釣り おかづり angling from the shore
陸稲 おかぼ(=りくとう) rice grown in a dry field

SYNONYMS

❶ **land and soil**
土 SOIL → 4211
地 GROUND → 0236
壌 ARABLE SOIL → 0933
泥 MUD → 0384
陸 LAND → 0659
埴 CLAY → 0562

❹ **six**
六 SIX → 2461
陸 six (in legal documents) → 0659

HOMOPHONES

おか
丘 HILL → 4307
岡 HILL → 3719
傍 BESIDE → 0166

NOTE

➡ see USAGE note at 丘 4307

陵 0660

▶**IMPERIAL MAUSOLEUM**
リョウ みささぎ
Ⓒ 陵 líng

1-3-8

170	Jōyō	U9675
阝	S11-3-8	F1895

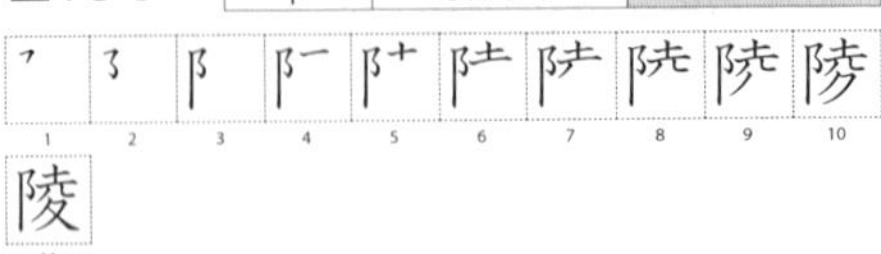

COMPOUNDS

❶ [also suffix] **IMPERIAL MAUSOLEUM, imperial tomb**
陵墓 りょうぼ imperial tomb
御陵 ごりょう imperial mausoleum
皇陵 こうりょう imperial mausoleum
仁徳陵 にんとくりょう Mausoleum of Emperor Nintoku

❷ [original meaning] **high mound, hillock**
丘陵 きゅうりょう hill, hillock
高陵土 こうりょうど kaolin, porcelain clay

❸ [also 凌 0144] surpass, outdo
陵駕する りょうがする excel, surpass, outdo

❹ [also 凌 0144] insult, offend
陵辱 りょうじょく insult; rape

INDEPENDENT

【りょう 陵】**IMPERIAL MAUSOLEUM**, imperial tomb

KUN

【みささぎ 陵】**IMPERIAL MAUSOLEUM, imperial tomb**

SYNONYMS

❶ **graves**
墓 GRAVE → 2930
墳 TUMULUS → 0887
陵 IMPERIAL MAUSOLEUM → 0660
廟 MAUSOLEUM → 3935
祢 FATHER'S MAUSOLEUM → 1142
塚 grave mound → 0675

❷ **hills**
丘 HILL → 4307
畝 RIDGE → 1857
岡 HILL → 3719
台 heights → 2498
坂 SLOPE → 0275
阪 slope → 0321
塚 MOUND → 0675
阜 MOUND → 3254
陵 high mound → 0660
稜 RIDGE → 1545

隆 0661

▶**PROSPER**
リュウ ㊔ たか たかし
Ⓝ 隆 Ⓒ 隆 lóng lōng

1-3-8

170	Jōyō	U9686
阝	S11-3-8	F1228

COMPOUNDS

❶ **PROSPER, rise to prosperity, flourish**
隆隆たる りゅうりゅうたる prosperous, thriving; brawny
隆盛 りゅうせい prosperity
隆昌 りゅうしょう prosperity
隆運 りゅううん prosperity, good fortune
興隆 こうりゅう prosperity, rise

❷ ⓐ **protuberant, elevated, bulging**
ⓑ elevate
a 隆起 りゅうき protuberance, elevation
b 隆鼻術 りゅうびじゅつ plastic surgery of the nose

SYNONYMS

❶ **prospering and prosperity**
隆 PROSPER → 0661
振 rise → 0515
興 RISE TO PROSPERITY → 3622
盛 PROSPEROUS → 3314
昌 PROSPERING → 3069
栄 FLOURISH → 3183
繁 THRIVE → 3536

賑 BUSTLE → 1959

❷ⓐ **protrude and protruding**

突 protruding → 2772
凸 CONVEX → 4298
隆 protuberant → 0661
起 RISE → 4099
出る stick out → 4310

陶

▸POTTERY

トウ ㊔ すえ

Ⓒ 陶 táo yáo

0662

1-3-8

170	Jōyō	U9676
阝	S11-3-8	F1648

1 2 3 4 5 6 7 8 9 10 11

COMPOUNDS

❶ **POTTERY, ceramics, earthenware**

陶器 とうき pottery, porcelain, chinaware
陶芸 とうげい ceramic art
陶磁器 とうじき porcelain, pottery, ceramics
陶工 とうこう potter, ceramist

❷ **contented, happy, entranced**

陶酔 とうすい intoxication; fascination, rapture
鬱陶しい うっとうしい gloomy, depressing; dull, cloudy

❸ influence a person, educate

陶冶 とうや training, education

INDEPENDENT

【とう 陶】**POTTERY, china, ceramics**

陶の人形 とうのにんぎょう ceramic figurine

SYNONYMS

❶ **ceramics ware**

陶 POTTERY → 0662
窯 ceramics → 2986
磁 porcelain → 1554

陷

▸FALL IN

カン おちい(る) おとしい(れる)

0663

1-3-8

170	Names	U9677
阝	S11-3-8	F0000

traditional form → see 陥 at 0547

隅

incorrect stroke-count
➡ see 1-3-9: 阝 at 0760

1-3-8

随

incorrect stroke-count
➡ see 1-3-9: 阝 at 0765

1-3-8

脩條

incorrect classification
➡ see 1-2-9: 亻 at 0149

1-3-8

悠

incorrect classification
➡ see 2-7-4: 攸 at 3407

1-3-8

郷

▸HOMETOWN

キョウ ゴウ さと▲ ㊔ こう みさと

Ⓝ 鄉 鄕◇ Ⓒ 乡 xiāng

0664

1-3-8

163	Jōyō-6	U90F7
阝	S11-3-8	F0914

1 2 3 4 5 6 7 8 9 10 11

COMPOUNDS

❶ **HOMETOWN, homeland, native place, birthplace**

郷里 きょうり one's old home, native place
郷土 きょうど one's birthplace
郷愁 きょうしゅう homesickness, nostalgia
故郷 こきょう hometown, birthplace
愛郷心 あいきょうしん love of one's hometown
同郷人 どうきょうじん person from the same province [town, village]
帰郷する ききょうする go [come] home

❷ⓐ the country, countryside, rural district

ⓑ village, hamlet

ⓒ *go*: former unit of administration smaller than 郡 ぐん and larger than 村 むら

a 郷士 ごうし country samurai
在郷者 ざいごうしゃ countryman, rustic
b 郷俗 きょうぞく village customs
郷村 ごうそん villages
郷邑 きょうゆう village, hamlet
c 白川郷 しらかわごう Shirakawa Village

❸ (figuratively) land, district

異郷 いきょう strange land, away from home
理想郷 りそうきょう ideal land, Utopia, earthly paradise
桃源郷 とうげんきょう Shangri-la

INDEPENDENT

【きょう 郷】**HOMETOWN**, homeland, birthplace
【ごう 郷】the country, countryside; village, hamlet

KUN

【さと 郷】[usu. 里] **HOMETOWN, one's birthplace**

故郷(=古里) ふるさと hometown, birthplace

SYNONYMS

❶ **villages and towns**

町 TOWN → 1430

村 VILLAGE → 1029
里 hamlet → 4356
郷 HOMETOWN → 0664
庄 FEUDAL VILLAGE → 3788
邑 VILLAGE → 2716

❷ⓐ **the country**

郊 SUBURB → 1638
里 COUNTRYSIDE → 4356
鄙 THE COUNTRY → 2338
郷 the country → 0664
辺 BORDERLAND → 3761

HOMOPHONES

さと 里 COUNTRYSIDE → 4356

NOTE

➡ see USAGE note at 里 4356
★ do not confuse with 卿 STATE MINISTER → 0769

喋

0665
1-3-9

▶**TALK**
チョウ しゃべ(る)
Ⓒ 喋 dié zhá

30	Names	U558B
口	S12-3-9	F1554

COMPOUNDS

● **TALK**, chat, chatter

喋喋喃×喃× ちょうちょうなんなん billing and cooing

KUN

【しゃべる 喋る】**TALK, chat, chatter**

喋りまくる しゃべりまくる chatter away
お喋り おしゃべり chattering, talk, chat; chatty, talkative; chatterbox, blabbermouth

SYNONYMS

● **speak and say**

言 SAY → 2440
語る TELL → 1944
談 TALK → 1975
喋 TALK → 0665
諷 INSINUATE → 2005
謂う REFER TO → 2007
云 say → 2430
曰 SAY THAT → 3757
話 SPEAK → 1928
口 give mouth to → 4189
申す SPEAK HUMBLY → 4319
述 STATE → 3816
陳 SET FORTH → 0656
弁 SPEAK ELOQUENTLY → 2497

喚

0666
1-3-9

▶**CALL**
カン わめ(く)▲
Ⓒ 唤 huàn

30	Jōyō	U559A
口	S12-3-9	F1979

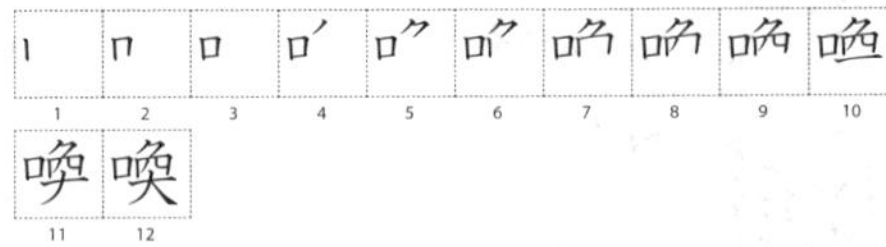

COMPOUNDS

❶ⓐ **CALL, call to, summon**
ⓑ (elicit) **CALL** out, arouse

a 喚問 かんもん summons
召喚する しょうかんする summon, cite, subpoena
b 喚起する かんきする awaken, rouse, arouse

❷ [original meaning] **CALL out, scream, shout, yell**

喚声 かんせい shout, yell, scream, clamor
叫喚 きょうかん shout, cry, scream

KUN

【わめく 喚く】cry, scream, shout

喚き声 わめきごえ shout, yell, outcry
喚き立てる わめきたてる bawl out, yell

SYNONYMS

❶ⓐ **call and invite**

呼ぶ CALL → 0324
喚 CALL → 0666
召 SUMMON → 2494
招 INVITE → 0374

❷ **give out a call**

叫 SHOUT → 0233
号 holler → 2675
喝 SHOUT AT → 0554
喚 call out → 0666
呼 CALL → 0324
鳴 CRY → 0831
吠 BARK → 0269

喧

0667
1-3-9

▶**BOISTEROUS**
ケン やかま(しい) かまびす(しい) かしま(しい) ㊔ はる あつ
Ⓒ 喧 xuān

30	Names	U55A7
口	S12-3-9	F1654

COMPOUNDS

● **BOISTEROUS, noisy, clamorous, vociferous**

喧嘩 けんか quarrel, fight, squabble
喧騒 けんそう clamor, din, noise
喧伝 けんでん widely talked about

喧喧囂×囂× けんけんごうごう state of uproar, pandemonium

KUN

【やかましい 喧しい】
ⓐ **BOISTEROUS, noisy**
ⓑ **faultfinding, fussy**
b 口喧しい くちやかましい nagging, critical; talkative

【かまびすしい 喧しい】
ⓐ **BOISTEROUS**, noisy, clamorous, vociferous
ⓑ faultfinding, fussy

【かしましい 喧しい】 noisy, deafening

SYNONYMS

● **loud**
高い loud → 2601
朗 CLEAR (voice) → 1679
騒 clamorous → 2308
喧 BOISTEROUS → 0667
嘩 BOISTEROUS → 0771

喫

▶**INGEST**
キツ
Ⓝ 喫 Ⓒ 吃 chī

0668
1-3-9

30	Jōyō	U55AB
口	S12-3-9	F1562

COMPOUNDS

❶ (introduce into one's body) **INGEST, eat, drink, inhale, swallow**
喫飯 きっぱん [rare] eating, taking a meal
喫茶店 きっさてん coffee shop, tea house
喫煙 きつえん smoking
満喫する まんきつする have enough, enjoy fully

❷ [formerly also 吃 0232] be subjected to, suffer, incur
喫驚する きっきょうする be astonished
喫水 きっすい draft, sea gauge

❸ [formerly also 吃 0232] urgent, pressing
喫緊事 きっきんじ urgent [pressing] matter

INDEPENDENT

【きっする 喫する】 suffer, sustain; take
惨敗を喫する ざんぱい(=さんぱい)をきっする sustain a crushing defeat

SYNONYMS

❶ **take in**
収 TAKE IN → 0031
摂 TAKE IN → 0799
喫 INGEST → 0668
吸 SUCK → 0234

❶ **ingest**
喫 INGEST → 0668
服 take → 1090
食 EAT → 2578
喰う EAT → 0670
飲 DRINK → 2127
呑 SWALLOW → 3059
啄 PECK → 0482

喉

▶**THROAT**
コウ のど
Ⓒ 喉 hóu

0669
1-3-9

30	Jōyō	U5589
口	S12-3-9	F1503

COMPOUNDS

● **THROAT**
喉頭 こうとう larynx
咽喉 いんこう throat
耳鼻咽喉科 じびいんこうか department of otolaryngology

KUN

【のど 喉】 [sometimes also 咽]
①ⓐ **THROAT**
ⓑ **singing voice**
a 喉元 のどもと throat
喉越し のどごし feeling of a drink going down one's throat
喉仏 のどぼとけ Adam's apple
喉笛 のどぶえ windpipe
喉ちんこ のどちんこ *colloq* uvula
b 喉自慢 のどじまん proud of one's voice
② gutter (margin) (in printing)
ページの喉側 ぺーじののどがわ gutter side of a page

SYNONYMS

● **throat**
咽 THROAT → 0412
喉 THROAT → 0669

USAGE

【のど】
喉
[sometimes also 咽]
①ⓐ throat
ⓑ singing voice
② gutter (margin) (in printing)

咽
[usu. 喉] same as 喉

HOMOPHONES

のど 咽 THROAT →0412

喰

▶EAT

サン く(う) く(らう)

Ⓒ 喰 cān

0670

1-3-9

30	Names	U55B0
口	S12-3-9	F1878

KUN

【くう 喰う】*colloq*

①ⓐ **EAT (greedily), devour**

ⓑ [now usu. 食う] get (as a slap in the face)

a 虫喰い むしくい worm-eaten; vermiculation, wormhole, moth hole; leaf warbler

一口喰う ひとくちくう take a bite, have a munch

飯を喰う めしをくう devour a meal

b びんたを喰う びんたをくう get slapped in the face

② unclassified compounds

漆喰 しっくい plaster, stucco

【くらう 喰らう】*vulgar*

ⓐ **EAT (greedily), devour**

ⓑ [now usu. 食らう] get (as a slap in the face)

b 面喰らう めんくらう be confused, be bewildered

一発喰らわす いっぱつくらわす give a blow

SPECIAL READINGS

馬喰 ばくろう cattle [horse] trader; good judge of horses [cattle]

SYNONYMS

【くう】

①ⓐ **ingest**

喫 INGEST →0668

服 take →1090

食 EAT →2578

喰う EAT →0670

飲 DRINK →2127

呑 SWALLOW →3059

啄 PECK →0482

HOMOPHONES

くう 食 EAT →2578

くらう 食 EAT →2578

NOTE

➡ see USAGE note at 食 2578

喩

▶METAPHOR

ユ たと(える)▲

Ⓝ 喻 Ⓒ 喻 yù

0671

1-3-9

30	Jōyō	U55A9
口	S12-3-9	F2394

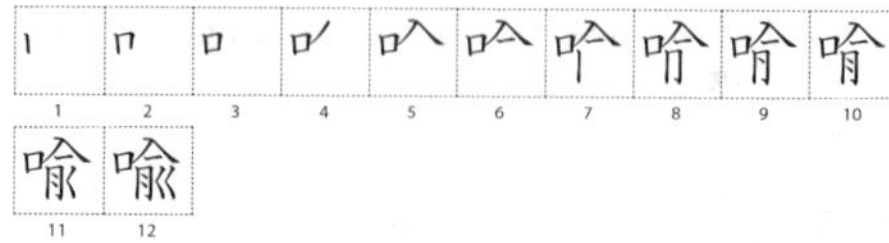

COMPOUNDS

● **METAPHOR, simile, allegory**

比喩(=譬喩) ひゆ simile, metaphor, allegory

直喩 ちょくゆ simile

暗喩 あんゆ metaphor

諷喩(=風喩) ふうゆ hint, insinuation, allegory

引喩 いんゆ allusion

KUN

【たとえる 喩える】[also 譬える] **compare to, liken, speak figuratively**

喩え たとえ metaphor, simile, allegory

死を眠りに喩える しをねむりにたとえる compare death to sleep

SYNONYMS

● **words and expressions**

語 WORD →1944

辞 WORD →1726

詞 WORDS →1897

句 PHRASE →3685

諺 PROVERB →2006

喩 METAPHOR →0671

HOMOPHONES

たとえる

例 EXAMPLE →0099

譬 COMPARE TO →3613

NOTE

➡ see USAGE note at 例 0099

喝

▶SHOUT AT

カツ

0672

1-3-9

30	Nonstandard	UFA36
口	S12-3-9	F0000

traditional form →see 喝 at 0554

喫

▶INGEST

キツ

0673

1-3-9

30	Nonstandard	U55AB
口	S12-3-9	F0000

traditional form →see 喫 at 0668

喻

▶METAPHOR

ユ たと(える)

0674

1-3-9

30	Nonstandard	U55BB
口	S12-3-9	F0000

traditional form →see 喩 at 0671

塚

▸MOUND

チョウ^ つか -づか

Ⓝ 塚 Ⓒ 冢 zhǒng

0675

1-3-9

32	Jōyō	U585A
土	S12-3-9	F1243

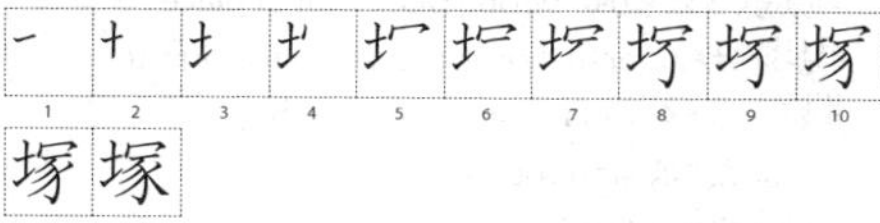

KUN

【つか 塚, -づか -塚】

① **MOUND, hillock, heap**

塚を築く つかをきずく pile up a mound

蟻×塚 ありづか anthill

貝塚 かいづか shell heap, shell mound; kitchen midden

一里塚 いちりづか milepost, milestone

② grave **MOUND**, tumulus; grave

塚穴 つかあな grave

SYNONYMS

【つか】

① **hills**

丘 HILL → 4307

畝 RIDGE → 1857

岡 HILL → 3719

台 heights → 2498

坂 SLOPE → 0275

阪 slope → 0321

塚 MOUND → 0675

阜 MOUND → 3254

陵 high mound → 0660

稜 RIDGE → 1545

② **graves**

墓 GRAVE → 2930

墳 TUMULUS → 0887

陵 IMPERIAL MAUSOLEUM → 0660

廟 MAUSOLEUM → 3935

祢 FATHER'S MAUSOLEUM → 1142

塚 grave mound → 0675

堰

▸DAM

エン せき せ(く)

Ⓒ 堰 yàn

0676

1-3-9

32	Names	U5830
土	S12-3-9	F2735

COMPOUNDS

ⓐ **DAM, sluice, weir**

ⓑ [original meaning, now archaic] **DAM**, stop up, check

a 堰堤 えんてい dike, weir

KUN

【せき 堰】**DAM, sluice**

堰板 せきいた sheeting, sheathing board, shuttering

井堰 いせき dam, sluice

可動堰 かどうぜき canal gates, river gates

【せく 堰く】[also 塞く]

ⓐ **DAM up**

ⓑ **check, prevent**

a 堰き止める(=塞き止める) せきとめる dam up, stop up; check

堰き止め湖 せきとめこ dammed lake

SYNONYMS

ⓐ **embankment**

堤 EMBANKMENT → 0681

防 dike → 0320

堰 DAM → 0676

USAGE

【せく】

堰く

[also 塞く]

ⓐ dam up

ⓑ check, prevent

塞く

[also 堰く] same as 堰く

HOMOPHONES

せく 塞 STOP UP → 2924

塀

▸FENCE

ヘイ

Ⓝ 塀 Ⓒ (国字)

0677

1-3-9

32	Jōyō	U5840
土	S12-3-9	F1904

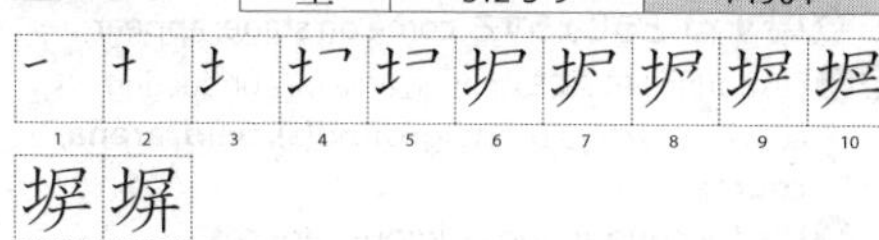

COMPOUNDS

● [also suffix] [original meaning] **FENCE (for screening), wall, board fence, enclosure**

土塀 どべい mud wall, plaster wall

板塀 いたべい board fence, wooden wall

煉瓦塀 れんがべい brick wall

ブロック塀 ぶろっくべい concrete (block) wall

INDEPENDENT

【へい 塀】**FENCE (for screening), wall, board fence, enclosure**

塀を巡らす へいをめぐらす surround with a wall, fence in

ロ【土】女山川工巾弓彡彳忄扌氵犭阝乡

SYNONYMS

❶ **fences and walls**

壁 WALL → 3601
塀 FENCE (for screening) → 0677
垣 FENCE (for partitioning) → 0416
牆 FENCE (for partitioning) → 1393
柵 FENCE (with spaced pickets) → 1116
堵 FENCE (made of earth) → 0682
囲い enclosure → 3807
欄 railing → 1419

場

▶PLACE
ジョウ ば
N 塲 C 场 chǎng cháng

0678
1-3-9

32	Jōyō-2	U5834
土	S12-3-9	F0041

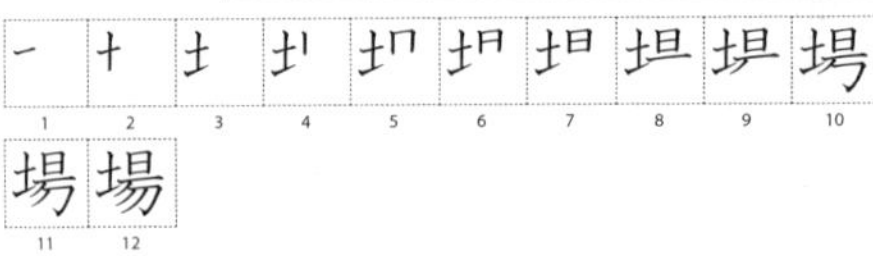

COMPOUNDS

❶ⓐ [also suffix] place or chamber for specific activity: **PLACE, hall, room, house; plant**
ⓑ **stage, scene**

a 会場 かいじょう place of meeting, site
式場 しきじょう hall of ceremony, stateroom
工場 こうじょう(=こうば) factory, plant, workshop
劇場 げきじょう theater
入場 にゅうじょう entrance, admission
出場する しゅつじょうする take part, participate
試験場 しけんじょう examination hall [room]; laboratory

b 登場する とうじょうする come on stage; appear

❷ⓐ [also suffix] **PLACE** or open area for conducting activities such as sports: **ground(s), field, arena, course**
ⓑ site for conducting religious services

a 球場 きゅうじょう baseball ground, ball park
戦場 せんじょう battlefield, front
運動場 うんどうじょう(うんどうば) playground, sports field
ゴルフ場 ごるふじょう golf links, golf course
競輪場 けいりんじょう cycle racing track [course]

b 斎場 さいじょう funeral hall; site of a religious service

❸ **market, exchange**

市場 しじょう market, mart
上場する じょうじょうする list (stocks)

INDEPENDENT

【じょう 場】**PLACE**, spot

KUN

【ば 場】

①ⓐ [also suffix] **PLACE, spot, site; ground**
ⓑ **space, room**

a 場所 ばしょ place, spot, site; space, room
場違い ばちがい wrong place; out of place
現場 げんば actual spot; job site, building site
職場 しょくば place of work, workshop
立場 たちば standpoint
酒場 さかば bar, barroom, pub, tavern
遊び場 あそびば playground
停車場 ていしゃば station
その場で そのばで then and there; on the spot, on that occasion

b 場を取る ばをとる occupy much space
広場 ひろば square, open space

② **occasion, moment; situation**

場合 ばあい occasion, situation, circumstances, case
夏場 なつば summertime

③ *theater* **scene**

場面 ばめん scene; situation
二幕三場 にまくさんば Act 2, Scene 3

④ **market, exchange; session; trading floor**

市場 いちば market, marketplace
相場 そうば market price; estimation

⑤ *phys, psychol* **field**

磁場 じば magnetic field
力の場 ちからのば field of force

SYNONYMS

❶ⓐ **places and positions**

所 PLACE → 1056
処 place → 3764
場 PLACE (for specific activity) → 0678
地 PLACE (particular location) → 0236
席 meeting place → 3865
位 POSITION → 0069
点 POINT → 2587
座 place → 3868

❷ⓐ **sports fields**

場 ground(s) → 0678
庭 COURT → 3866
野 baseball field → 1877

❸ **market**

市 MARKET → 2487
場 market → 0678

【ば】

③ **parts of plays**

幕 act → 2937
場 scene → 0678

⑤ **range**

程 EXTENT → 1524
範 range → 3360
域 area → 0559
圏 SPHERE → 3904
野 FIELD → 1877
界 field (*phys*) → 3172
場 field (*phys*, *psychol*) → 0678

NOTE

➡ see COMPOUND FORMATION for
相場 そうば → 相 1120
土壇場 どたんば → 土 4211

堺

0679

◧ 1-3-9

▶**SAKAI**

カイ さかい

Ⓒ 界 jiè

32	Names	U583A
土	S12-3-9	F1854

COMPOUNDS

❶ **SAKAI City (in Osaka Prefecture)**

阪堺線 はんかいせん Hankai Line (Osaka-Sakai Tramway)

❷ [usu. 界 3172] **bounds, boundary, border**

堺標 かいひょう boundary mark

KUN

【さかい 堺】**SAKAI**

堺市 さかいし Sakai city (in Osaka Prefecture)

HOMOPHONES

さかい 境 BOUNDARY → 0835

NOTE

➡ see USAGE note at 境 0835
★ 堺 and 界 were originally the same character.

堪

0680

◧ 1-3-9

▶**ENDURE**

カン タン▲ た(える) たま(る)▲ こら(える)▲ こた(える)▲

Ⓒ 堪 kān

32	Jōyō	U582A
土	S12-3-9	F1740

1	2	3	4	5	6	7	8	9	10	11	12
一	十	土	土一	圵	坩	坩	坩	堪	堪	堪	堪

COMPOUNDS

❶ **ENDURE, bear, tolerate**

堪忍(=勘忍)する かんにんする have patience, bear with; forgive, pardon

❷ **competent, fit for**

堪能 かんのう(=たんのう) skillful, proficient
不堪 ふかん [rare] incompetence

KUN

【たえる 堪える】

①ⓐ [sometimes also 耐える] **ENDURE, bear, stand, tolerate**

ⓑ **bear (a burden), hold out, stand**

a 堪え忍ぶ たえしのぶ endure, bear up, tolerate, put up with
堪え難い たえがたい unbearable
b 不幸に堪える ふこうにたえる bear up under misfortune
遺憾に堪えない いかんにたえない be really regrettable

② be fit for, be competent, be equal to

仕事に堪える しごとにたえる be fit for work

【たまる 堪る】[usu. in negative constructions] **can(not) stand, be (un)able to put up with**

堪らない たまらない cannot stand, be unbearable; cannot help (doing)

【こらえる 堪える】

ⓐ **ENDURE**, bear, stand, tolerate
ⓑ suppress, stifle, hold back

【こたえる 堪える】**ENDURE**, bear, stand; [also suffix] hold out [up], withstand

SYNONYMS

❶ **bear and endure**

堪 ENDURE → 0680
忍 BEAR → 2750
耐 WITHSTAND → 1634

USAGE

【たえる】

堪える
①ⓐ [sometimes also 耐える] endure, bear, stand, tolerate
ⓑ bear (a burden), hold out, stand
② be fit for, be competent, be equal to

耐える
ⓐ (resist physical forces) withstand, resist, be proof against
ⓑ [usu. 堪える] endure, bear, tolerate

HOMOPHONES

たえる 耐 WITHSTAND → 1634

NOTE

★ do not confuse with 勘 CHECK → 2231

堤

0681

◧ 1-3-9

▶**EMBANKMENT**

テイ つつみ

Ⓒ 堤 dī

32	Jōyō	U5824
土	S12-3-9	F1865

一 十 土 圹 圻 坦 垾 埕 埕 堤 堤 堤
1 2 3 4 5 6 7 8 9 10 11 12

COMPOUNDS

● [also suffix] [original meaning] **EMBANKMENT, dike, bank**
堤防 ていぼう bank, embankment, dike
突堤 とってい pier, breakwater
築堤 ちくてい embankment, bank; building an embankment
防潮堤 ぼうちょうてい tide embankment, seawall
防波堤 ぼうはてい breakwater

KUN

【つつみ 堤】**EMBANKMENT, dike, bank**
堤を築く つつみをきずく build an embankment

SYNONYMS

● **embankment**
堤 EMBANKMENT → 0681
防 dike → 0320
堰 DAM → 0676

堵

▶FENCE
ト
Ⓝ 堵 Ⓒ 堵 dǔ

0682
1-3-9

32	Names	U5835
土	S12-3-9	F2093

COMPOUNDS

● [original meaning] **FENCE (made of earth), enclosure**
安堵する あんどする feel relieved, feel a sense of peace [security]
本領安堵 ほんりょうあんど recognition by the shogunate of ownership of the inherited estate of a samurai in medieval Japan

SYNONYMS

● **fences and walls**
壁 WALL → 3601
塀 FENCE (for screening) → 0677
垣 FENCE (for partitioning) → 0416
牆 FENCE (for partitioning) → 1393
柵 FENCE (with spaced pickets) → 1116
堵 FENCE (made of earth) → 0682
囲い enclosure → 3807
欄 railing → 1419

COMPOUND FORMATION

【安堵する あんどする】
安堵する 'feel relieved, etc.' originally meant being at ease (安) within a walled enclosure (堵).

塔

▶TOWER
トウ
Ⓒ 塔 tǎ

0683
1-3-9

32	Jōyō	U5854
土	S12-3-9	F1486

一 十 土 圹 圹 塔 塔 塔 塔 塔 塔 塔
1 2 3 4 5 6 7 8 9 10 11 12

COMPOUNDS

❶ [also suffix] **TOWER**
鉄塔 てっとう steel tower; pylon
テレビ塔 てれびとう television tower
管制塔 かんせいとう control tower
エッフェル塔 えっふぇるとう Eiffel Tower

❷ⓐ [also suffix] **pagoda**
ⓑ [original meaning] dagoba, stupa
a 卒塔婆 そとば(=そとうば) wooden grave tablet; stupa, dagoba
仏塔 ぶっとう pagoda, Buddhist pagoda
堂塔 どうとう temple buildings, temple

INDEPENDENT

【とう 塔】**TOWER; pagoda**
五重の塔 ごじゅうのとう five-storied pagoda

SYNONYMS

❶ **tall buildings**
閣 TALL MAGNIFICENT BUILDING → 4128
楼 TALL BUILDING → 1284
塔 TOWER → 0683
台 observatory → 2498

❷ⓐ **places of worship**
堂 temple building → 3202
塔 pagoda → 0683
寺 BUDDHIST TEMPLE → 2687
刹 TEMPLE → 1620
社 Shinto shrine → 1042
宮 SHINTO SHRINE → 2828
院 monastery → 0544
教 church → 1887

NOTE

★ do not confuse with 搭 BOARD → 0721

堽

▶HILL
コウ おか

0684
1-3-9

32	Nonstandard	U583D
土	S12-3-9	F0000

traditional form → see 岡 at 3719

壻 0685

◧ 1-3-9

▶**SON-IN-LAW**

セイ むこ

33	Nonstandard	U58FB
士	S12-3-9	F0000

traditional form → see 婿 at 0689

媒 0686

◧ 1-3-9

▶**INTERMEDIATE**

バイ

Ⓒ 媒 méi

38	Jōyō	U5A92
女	S12-3-9	F1989

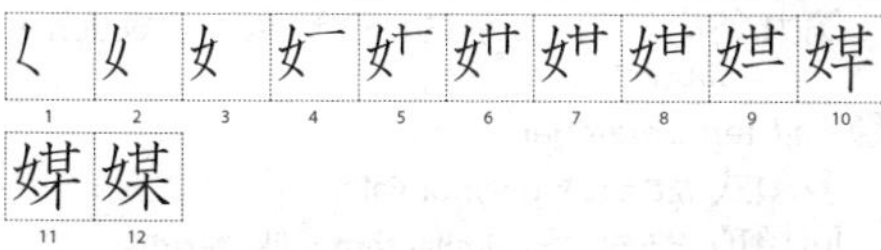

COMPOUNDS

ⓐ INTERMEDIATE, mediate, act as a go-between; act as a medium

ⓑ [original meaning] go-between, matchmaker

a 媒介 ばいかい mediation, intervention, intermediation

媒質 ばいしつ medium

媒体 ばいたい medium

媒染剤 ばいせんざい mordant

触媒 しょくばい catalyst, catalyzer

霊媒 れいばい (spiritualistic) medium

b 媒酌人 ばいしゃくにん go-between, matchmaker

SYNONYMS

ⓐ mediating and mediators

紹 INTRODUCE → 1691

介 MEDIATE → 2463

媒 INTERMEDIATE → 0686

仲 INTERMEDIARY → 0047

媚 0687

◧ 1-3-9

▶**FAWN UPON**

ビ こ(びる) こび

Ⓒ 媚 mèi

38	Non-Jōyō	U5A9A
女	S12-3-9	F2424

COMPOUNDS

❶ FAWN UPON; curry favor with

媚態 びたい coquetry

媚薬 びやく aphrodisiac, love potion

❷ [now also 美 2817] **beautiful, charming, fascinating**

風光明媚の地 ふうこうめいびのち place of scenic beauty

KUN

【こびる 媚びる】**FAWN UPON; curry favor with**

媚び諂ˣう こびへつらう fawn upon, toady, act obsequiously

権力に媚びる けんりょくにこびる be obsequious to power

【こび 媚】**flattery; coquetry**

SYNONYMS

❶ charm

魅 CHARM → 4131

幻 bewitch → 0206

媚 FAWN UPON → 0687

媛 0688

◧ 1-3-9

▶**DAMSEL**

エン オン▲ ひめ▲

Ⓝ 媛 Ⓒ 媛 yuàn yuán

38	Jōyō	U5A9B
女	S12-3-9	F2896

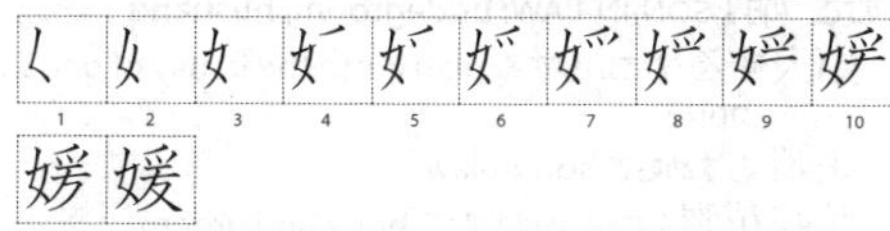

COMPOUNDS

❶ beautiful young lady

才媛 さいえん talented girl, accomplished woman, girl with scholastic ability

❷ beautiful, fascinating, attractive, charming

嬋ˣ媛たる せんえんたる beautiful and fascinating

KUN

【ひめ 媛】[now usu. 姫]

① *elegant* **DAMSEL, beautiful young lady**

② **courtesy title after names of young ladies of noble birth**

橘媛 たちばなひめ name of a woman in a Japanese myth

SYNONYMS

❶ woman

女 WOMAN → 4226

婦 ADULT WOMAN → 0565

婆 OLD WOMAN → 3433

嬢 YOUNG LADY → 0936

娘 GIRL → 0488

雌 FEMALE → 1337

牝 FEMALE → 1020

媛 DAMSEL → 0688

HOMOPHONES

ひめ 姫 DAUGHTER OF NOBLE BIRTH → 0489

NOTE

➡ see USAGE note at 姫 0489

婿

▶SON-IN-LAW

セイ むこ

Ⓝ 壻 聟◇ Ⓒ 婿 xù

0689

1-3-9

38 女	Jōyō	U5A7F
	S12-3-9	F2171

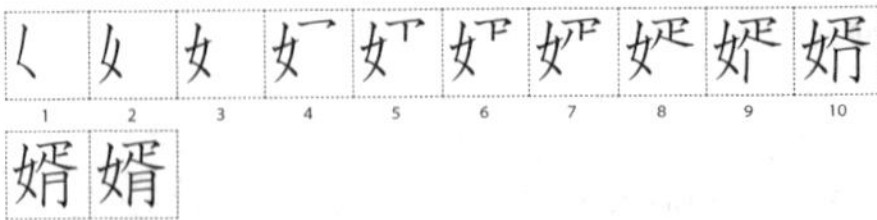

COMPOUNDS

● [original meaning] **SON-IN-LAW**

女婿 じょせい son-in-law

令婿 れいせい your son-in-law

KUN

【むこ 婿】**SON-IN-LAW; bridegroom, husband**

婿入する むこいりする marry into the family of one's bride

娘婿 むすめむこ son-in-law

花嫁花婿 はなよめはなむこ bride and groom

SYNONYMS

● **in-laws**

婿 SON-IN-LAW → 0689

嫁 daughter-in-law → 0780

姑 MOTHER-IN-LAW → 0332

媛

▶DAMSEL

エン オン ひめ

0690

1-3-9

38 女	Nonstandard	U5A9B
	S12-3-9	F0000

traditional form → see 媛 at 0688

崎

▶PROMONTORY

キ さき

0691

1-3-9

46 山	Nonstandard	UFA11
	S12-3-9	F0000

traditional form → see 崎 at 0569

順

1-3-9

incorrect classification

➡ see 1-1-11: 丿 at 0018

項

▶CLAUSE

コウ うなじ▲

Ⓒ 项 xiàng

0692

1-3-9

181 頁	Jōyō	U9805
	S12-9-3	F1154

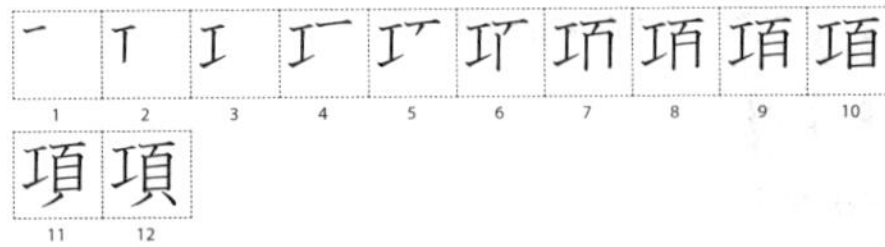

COMPOUNDS

❶ [also suffix] **CLAUSE, subsection, item, paragraph**

項目 こうもく clause, item, provision

事項 じこう matters, facts; articles, items

別項 べっこう separate paragraph, another clause

要項 ようこう important points; gist

条項 じょうこう articles (and clauses), terms

第九条第二項 だいきゅうじょうだいにこう Section 9, Subsection 2

❷ *math* term, member

多項式 たこうしき polynomial

同類項 どうるいこう similar terms, like terms

方程式の一項 ほうていしきのいっこう member of an equation

❸ [original meaning, now rare] nape

項領 こうりょう neck, collar

INDEPENDENT

【こう 項】**CLAUSE**, subsection, item, paragraph; *math* term, member

項に分かつ こうにわかつ itemize, paragraph

KUN

【うなじ 項】nape

SYNONYMS

❶ **parts of writing**

章 CHAPTER → 2624

段 passage → 1471

節 paragraph → 3336

款 ARTICLE → 2135

条 ARTICLE → 2726

項 CLAUSE → 0692

目 ITEM → 3777

箇 item → 3348

❸ **neck**

首 NECK → 2818

頸 NECK → 2035

項 nape → 0692

帽

▶HEADGEAR

ボウ

Ⓝ 帽 Ⓒ 帽 mào

0693

1-3-9

50 巾	Jōyō	U5E3D
	S12-3-9	F1601

丨	冂	巾	巾	巾	巾	帽	帽	帽	帽	帽	帽
1	2	3	4	5	6	7	8	9	10	11	12

COMPOUNDS

● [also suffix] [original meaning] **HEADGEAR, hat, cap**

帽子 ぼうし cap, hat
帽章 ぼうしょう badge on a cap
学帽 がくぼう school cap
制帽 せいぼう regulation [school] cap
脱帽 だつぼう taking off one's cap [hat]; submission
ベレー帽 べれーぼう beret (cap)
無帽の むぼうの hatless
登山帽 とざんぼう climber's hat

SYNONYMS

● **headgear**

帽 HEADGEAR → 0693
冠 CROWN → 2583
笠 SEDGE HAT → 3300
兜 HEADPIECE → 3499

幅 ▶WIDTH

フク はば

Ⓒ 幅 fú

0694

◧ 1-3-9

50	Jōyō	U5E45
巾	S12-3-9	F1184

丨	冂	巾	巾	巾	巾	巾	幅	幅	幅	幅	幅
1	2	3	4	5	6	7	8	9	10	11	12

COMPOUNDS

❶ [sometimes also 巾 4217] **WIDTH, breadth, range**

幅員 ふくいん width [extent] of roads or ships
増幅 ぞうふく amplification
振幅 しんぷく amplitude (of vibration)
全幅 ぜんぷく overall width, extreme breadth (of a ship), wing span

❷ⓐ scroll, scroll picture
ⓑ counter for scrolls or picture scrolls

a 画幅 がふく hanging picture, picture scroll
b 掛け軸二幅 かけじくにふく two scrolls

❸ border, exterior

辺幅 へんぷく outer appearance

INDEPENDENT

【ふく 幅】scroll, scroll picture

KUN

【はば 幅】[also suffix] **WIDTH, breadth, range; influence, power; difference (in price)**

幅広い はばひろい wide, broad
幅跳び はばとび broad jump
幅利き はばきき man of influence
大幅に おおはばに sharply, by a large margin
小幅 こはば single breadth, narrow range
横幅 よこはば breadth
値幅 ねはば difference (in price)

SYNONYMS

❶ **width**

幅 WIDTH → 0694
員 girth → 2822
径 DIAMETER → 0347

USAGE

【はば】

幅
[also suffix] width, breadth, range; influence, power; difference (in price)

巾
[usu. 幅] width, breadth, range

HOMOPHONES

はば 巾 CLOTH → 4217

COMPOUND FORMATION

【増幅 ぞうふく】

増幅 'amplification' is to increase (増) the range (幅 ❶).

NOTE

★ Though 幅 and 巾 are distinct characters, the latter is also used as an abbreviation of the former.

幀 ▶BOOKBINDING

テイ

Ⓒ 帧 zhēn

0695

◧ 1-3-9

50	Non-Jōyō	U5E40
巾	S12-3-9	F2695

COMPOUNDS

● [now usu. 丁 4155] **BOOKBINDING**

装幀する そうていする bind (a book)

SYNONYMS

● **print and publish**

刷 PRINT → 1623
印 print → 1023
植 typeset → 1247
刊 PUBLISH → 0221
版 PUBLISHING → 1082
載 PUT IN PRINT → 4091
掲 display in writing → 0597
幀 BOOKBINDING → 0695

帽

▶HEADGEAR

ボウ

0696

1-3-9

50	Nonstandard	U5E3D
巾	S12-3-9	F0000

traditional form →see 帽 at 0693

弾

▶PROJECTILE
▶SPRING BACK

ダン ひ(く) -ひ(き) はず(む) たま はじ(く)▲ はじ(ける)▲

0697

1-3-9

Ⓝ 彈 Ⓒ 弹 dàn tán

57	Jōyō	U5F3E
弓	S12-3-9	F0781

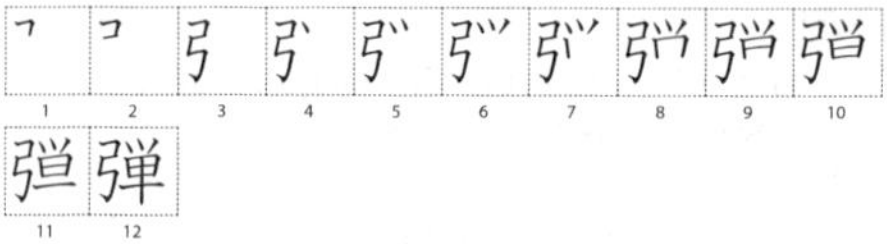

COMPOUNDS

❶ [also suffix] **PROJECTILE, bullet, shell, missile, (cannon) ball, bomb**

弾丸 だんがん shot, bullet, shell
弾薬 だんやく ammunition
弾頭 だんとう warhead
弾道弾 だんどうだん ballistic missile
爆弾 ばくだん bomb
砲弾 ほうだん cannonball, shell
銃弾 じゅうだん bullet, shot
散弾 さんだん shot
実弾 じつだん ball cartridge, live ammunition; money
不発弾 ふはつだん unexploded shell

❷ counter for steps, measures or stages

第一弾 だいいちだん first step

❸ **SPRING BACK (to the original shape), resile**

弾性 だんせい elasticity, resilience
弾力性 だんりょくせい elasticity, resilience; flexibility, adaptability
弾機 だんき(=ばね) spring

❹ⓐ impeach, censure
ⓑ **put down, suppress**

a 弾劾 だんがい impeachment, denunciation, accusation
糾弾 きゅうだん impeachment, censure
b 弾圧 だんあつ oppression, suppression
指弾 しだん rejection, disdain

❺ [original meaning] **play on (stringed instruments)**

弾奏 だんそう playing on stringed instruments
連弾 れんだん four-handed performance (on the piano)

INDEPENDENT

【だんずる(=だんじる) 弾ずる(=弾じる)】 play on stringed instruments

KUN

【ひく 弾く】 **play on (stringed instruments)**

弾き手 ひきて player, performer
弾き語り ひきがたり reciting to one's own accompaniment
爪弾く つまびく pluck the strings (of a guitar)

【-ひき -弾き】 [suffix] **player**

ベートーベン弾き べーとーべんひき Beethoven player
バイオリン弾き ばいおりんひき violinist

【はずむ 弾む】 **SPRING BACK (from a surface), bounce, rebound, bound; be animated, be spurred on; invest in, fork out (generously), treat oneself to; breathe hard**

弾み はずみ spring, bound; momentum, impulse, force; chance
気分が弾む きぶんがはずむ cheer up
チップを弾む ちっぷをはずむ tip generously
息を弾ませる いきをはずませる pant

【たま 弾】 **bullet, shot, shell**

鉄砲弾(=鉄砲玉) てっぽうだま gunshot, bullet; lost [truant] messenger; bull's-eye

【はじく 弾く】 *vt* **fillip, flip; repel, reject; use an abacus**

弾き はじき repellence; *slang* gun
弾き返す はじきかえす repel, reject
弾き出す はじきだす spring out; expel; calculate, estimate
爪弾き つまはじき fillip; ostracism; black sheep (of a family)

【はじける 弾ける】 *vi* burst [crack] open, spring off

弾け豆 はじけまめ pop beans
弾ける様に笑う はじけるようにわらう burst into laughter

SYNONYMS

❶ **projectiles and bombs**

弾 PROJECTILE →0697
丸 round projectile →4225
矢 ARROW →2502
槍 SPEAR →1329
爆 bomb →1415
雷 explosive device →3466

❸ **spring back**

弾 SPRING BACK →0697
反 return in original direction →3663

❹ⓐ **blame and accuse**

責 BLAME →3115
叱 SCOLD →0210

詰 REPRIMAND →1920
難 find fault with →2310
批 CRITICIZE →0294
劾 EXPOSE CRIMES →1618
弾 impeach →0697

❺ **play music**
奏 PLAY MUSIC →3185
弾 play on (stringed instruments) →0697
吹 BLOW →0272

HOMOPHONES

ひく
引 DRAW →0207
退 RETREAT →3838
惹 DRAW ATTENTION →2903
挽 GRIND →0511
轢 RUN OVER →2095
牽 DRAW →2621
曳 DRAW →4348

たま
玉 GEM →4289
珠 PEARL →1183
球 BALL →1219
璧 DISK-SHAPED JEWEL →3608

NOTE

➡ see USAGE notes at 玉 4289 and 引 0207

粥

0698
◧ 1-3-9

▶RICE GRUEL
シュク かゆ
Ⓝ 鬻 Ⓒ 粥 zhōu yù

119 米	Names S12-6-6	U7CA5 F2527

COMPOUNDS

● **RICE GRUEL**
粥腫 しゅくしゅ atheroma

INDEPENDENT

【しゅく 粥】**RICE GRUEL**; breakfast (at a Zen monastery)

KUN

【かゆ 粥】**RICE GRUEL**
七草粥 ななくさがゆ rice gruel containing the seven plants of spring
茶粥 ちゃがゆ tea gruel

SYNONYMS

● **rice**
米 RICE →4342
飯 COOKED RICE →2126
稲 RICE PLANT →1561
籾 UNHULLED RICE →1626
餅 RICE CAKE →2256
粥 RICE GRUEL →0698

强

0699
◧ 1-3-9

▶STRONG
キョウ ゴウ つよ(い) つよ(まる) つよ(める) し(いる) こわ(い) ㊔ つよし つとむ

57 弓	Nonstandard S12-3-9	U5F3A F0000

traditional form →see 強 at 0574

須

0700
◧ 1-3-9

▶MUST
ス シュ▲ ㊔ もとむ
Ⓒ 须 xū

181 頁	Jōyō S12-9-3	U9808 F1312

(stroke order 1–12)

COMPOUNDS

❶ **MUST, must have, absolutely necessary**
須要な しゅようなabsolutely necessary
必須の ひっすの indispensable, essential

❷ **moment, brief while**
須臾× しゅゆ short while, instant

❸ used phonetically for *shu* or *su*, esp. in the transliteration of Sanskrit Buddhist terms
須弥壇 しゅみだん dais for a Buddhist image

❹ [now always 鬚 しゅ 3539] [original meaning] beard
須髯× しゅぜん beard

SYNONYMS

❶ **need and necessity**
要 required →3263
必 must →0015
須 MUST →0700
需 DEMAND →3472
入 necessary →4177
用 needed for (a specific use) →3694

❸ **phonetic [s]/[sh]**
沙 phonetic [sha] →0311
刹 phonetic [setsu] →1620
遮 phonetic [sha] →3916
叉 phonetic [sha] →4194
世 phonetic [se] →4308
須 phonetic [shu] →0700
修 phonetic [shu] →0138
西 phonetic [su] →4333
相 phonetic [sō] →1120
薩 phonetic [satsu] →3016

復 0701

▸RETURN TO
フク また▲
Ⓒ 复 fù

1-3-9

60	Jōyō-5	U5FA9
彳	S12-3-9	F0672

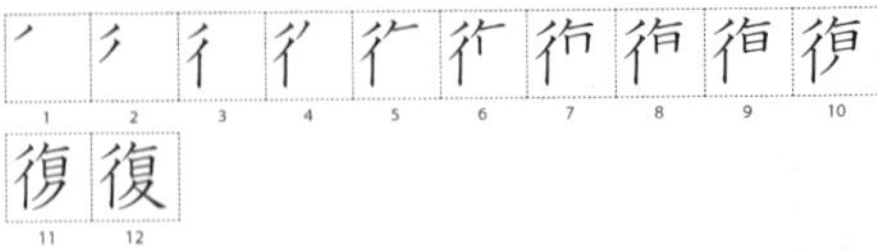

COMPOUNDS

❶ⓐ RETURN TO (a previous state or position), be restored, revert, reinstate
ⓑ [original meaning] **RETURN TO (a place), go back**

a 復活 ふっかつ revival, rebirth, resurrection
復旧 ふっきゅう restoration, recovery
復職 ふくしょく reinstatement, resumption of office
復元 ふくげん restoration to original state
回復 かいふく [formerly also 恢復] recovery, restoration; rehabilitation

b 復帰する ふっきする return, be restored, revert
復路 ふくろ return trip
往復 おうふく going and returning; round trip

❷ return a reply, reply
復命する ふくめいする report to, return (one's finding to a person)
復答 ふくとう reply, response
拝復 はいふく in reply to your letter; Dear Sir, Dear Madam

❸ repeat, redo
復習 ふくしゅう review
復誦(=復唱) ふくしょう recital, repetition, rehearsal
復刻する ふっこくする [sometimes also 覆刻する] republish, reissue
復文 ふくぶん retranslation (into the original language); reply letter
反復 はんぷく [sometimes also 反覆] repetition, reiteration

❹ revenge, take revenge
復讐× ふくしゅう revenge, vengeance
報復 ほうふく retaliation, reprisal, revenge

INDEPENDENT

【ふくする 復する】 **RETURN TO** (a previous state or position), be restored, revert to, resume

KUN

【また 復】 [now replaced by 又] again, once more [again], repeatedly
復いらっしゃい またいらっしゃい Call again!

SYNONYMS

❶ⓐ return and restore
返 RETURN →3797
戻 RETURN →2441
還 RETURN →3945
復 RETURN TO →0701
蘇 REVIVE →3032
甦 REVIVE →4109

ⓑ return
帰 RETURN →0148
還 RETURN →3945
回 turn back →3793
廻 turn back →3833
戻る RETURN →2441
復 RETURN TO →0701

❸ repeating and repetition
再 ANOTHER TIME →4332
又 AGAIN →4158
復 repeat →0701
重 DUPLICATE →4390
畳 reduplicate →3205
改 redo →0287
-換える redo →0716
-直す repetition suffix →3649
-返す do over →3797

HOMOPHONES

また
又 AGAIN →4158
亦 ALSO →2504

NOTE

➡ see USAGE note at 又 4158

街 0702

▸CITY QUARTER
ガイ カイ まち ㊔ ちまた
Ⓒ 街 jiē

1-3-9

144	Jōyō-4	U8857
行	S12-6-6	F0632

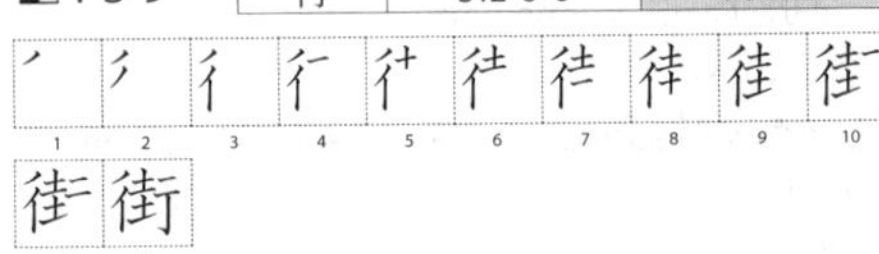

COMPOUNDS

❶ⓐ [also suffix] **CITY QUARTER(s), city center, busy street, shopping center, downtown**
ⓑ suffix after names of shopping centers and arcades

a 街路 がいろ street, road, avenue
ビル街 びるがい street of big business buildings
市街 しがい the streets, city, town
スラム街 すらむがい slum quarters
繁華街 はんかがい business [shopping] quarters; amusement quarters
商店街 しょうてんがい shopping center

中国人街 ちゅうごくじんがい Chinatown
住宅街 じゅうたくがい residential quarter
歓楽街 かんらくがい amusement center [quarter]
b 銀天街 ぎんてんがい Gintengai Shopping Center

❷ [original meaning] **city street, thoroughfare, crossroads**
街道 かいどう thoroughfare, highway
街頭 がいとう street
街灯 がいとう street lamp

KUN

【まち 街】**(busy) CITY QUARTER(s), city streets**
街の女 まちのおんな streetwalker
街角(=町角) まちかど street corner
街着 まちぎ street clothes
商人街 しょうにんまち business street
北野街 きたのまち Kitano shopping center

SYNONYMS

❶ **parts of towns**
区 WARD → 3681
街 CITY QUARTER → 0702
町 town section (*cho*) → 1430
丁 TOWN SUBSECTION (*chome*) → 4155
字 village or town section → 2696

❷ **ways and routes**
道 WAY (path) → 3888
径 PATH → 0347
軌 TRACK → 1832
線 LINE → 1760
澪 WATERWAY → 0957
途 WAY (route) → 3853
路 ROAD → 1936
筋 wayside → 3319
通り street → 3855
街 city street → 0702
辻 CROSSROADS → 3958
岐 forked road → 0285
巷 THE STREETS → 3097

HOMOPHONES

まち 町 TOWN → 1430

NOTE

➡ see USAGE note at 町 1430

御

0703

1-3-9

▶GENERAL HONORIFIC TERM

ギョ ゴ おん- お-▲ み-▲

Ⓝ 御 Ⓒ 御 yù

60	Jōyō	U5FA1
彳	S12-3-9	F0349

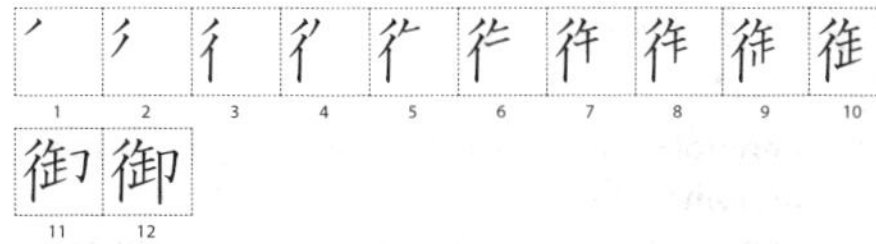

COMPOUNDS

❶ ⓐ [also prefix] **GENERAL HONORIFIC TERM for conveying respect**
ⓑ **general honorific prefix attached to Sino-Japanese compounds to convey humility**
ⓒ honorific suffix conveying respect for persons, esp. for members of another's family

a 御用 ごよう your order, your business
御飯 ごはん boiled rice; meal
御存じの方 ごぞんじのかた your acquaintance
御意 ぎょい your will, your pleasure
御馳走 ごちそう feast, treat
御成功 ごせいこう your success
御両親 ごりょうしん your (honorable) parents
御自身 ごじしん yourself; himself, herself
b 御案内申し上げます ごあんないもうしあげます I shall be pleased to show you the way
御説明致します ごせつめいいたします I beg to explain
c 母御 ははご your mother
嫁御 よめご bride
女御 にょうご court lady

❷ [also prefix] [honorific] imperial, emperor's
御所 ごしょ old imperial palace
御物 ぎょぶつ(=ごもつ) imperial property
御製 ぎょせい emperor's poem or song
御苑 ぎょえん Imperial garden
御用邸 ごようてい imperial villa
崩御 ほうぎょ demise [death] of an emperor

❸ [formerly also 馭 ぎょ 2282 or 禦 ぎょ 3561]
ⓐ **handle (affairs), control, manage**
ⓑ [original meaning] handle a horse well, train a horse

a 制御する せいぎょする control, govern, suppress
統御 とうぎょ rule, control, management
b 御者 ぎょしゃ coachman, driver

❹ [formerly also 禦 ぎょ 3561] **resist, keep out, ward off**
防御する ぼうぎょする defend, protect, safeguard

INDEPENDENT

【ぎょする 御する】handle, control, manage; [formerly also 馭する] handle a horse well, train a horse

KUN

【おん- 御-】**honorific prefix for conveying a greater degree of respect than お-**
御身 おんみ you [him]; your [his] honorable body
御大 おんたい boss, governor

御中 おんちゅう Messrs.

【お- 御-】

①ⓐ **general honorific prefix for conveying respect or politeness**

ⓑ **general honorific prefix for conveying humility**

a 御顔 おかお your (honorable) face

御日様 おひさま sun

御美しい事 おうつくしいこと How nice!

御玉 おたま ladle; egg

b 御会い出来て嬉しゅう御座います おあいできてうれしゅうございます I'm delighted to have the honor of seeing you

② [also 阿-] prefix for conveying intimacy, esp. before names of women

御花さん おはなさん Ohana

【み- 御-】 **honorific prefix**—used esp. in reference to religious matters or the emperor

主の御名 しゅのみな the Lord's name

明治天皇の御代 めいじてんのうのみよ reign of Emperor Meiji

SYNONYMS

❶ⓐ honorific prefixes

御 GENERAL HONORIFIC TERM → 0703

貴 YOUR HONORABLE → 3220

尊 your honorable → 2920

令 your honorable → 2489

USAGE

❶【お-】

御-

①ⓐ general honorific prefix for conveying respect or politeness

ⓑ general honorific prefix for conveying humility

② [also 阿-] prefix for conveying intimacy, esp. before names of women

阿-

[also 御-] prefix for conveying intimacy, esp. before names of women

❷【ぎょする】

御する

ⓐ handle, control, manage

ⓑ [formerly also 馭する] handle a horse well, train a horse

馭する

[now replaced by 御する] handle a horse well, train a horse

HOMOPHONES

お- 阿 PHONETIC [a] → 0408

NOTE

➡ see COMPOUND FORMATION for 御馳走 ごちそう → 走 2720

循 0704

1-3-9

▶CIRCULATE

ジュン

Ⓒ 循 xún

60	Jōyō	U5FAA
彳	S12-3-9	F1962

COMPOUNDS

❶ CIRCULATE, go round

循環 じゅんかん circulation, rotation; cycle

❷ [original meaning] follow (rules or customs), abide by

因循 いんじゅん conservatism; vacillation, indecision

SYNONYMS

❶ turn

旋 GYRATE → 1194

転 TURN → 1872

回 TURN ROUND → 3793

廻 TURN ROUND → 3833

巡 MAKE THE ROUNDS → 3781

循 CIRCULATE → 0704

斡 REVOLVE → 2168

捻 TWIST → 0604

衖 0705

1-3-9

▶THE STREETS

コウ ちまた ㊔ さと

144	Nonstandard	U8856
行	S12-6-6	F0000

traditional form → see 巷 at 3097

惰 0706

1-3-9

▶LAZY

ダ

Ⓒ 惰 duò

61	Jōyō	U60F0
忄	S12-3-9	F2839

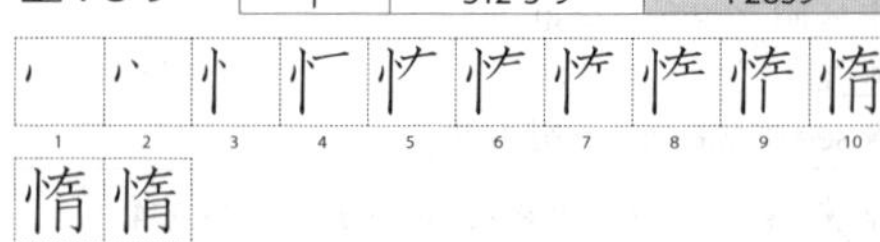

COMPOUNDS

❶ [original meaning] **LAZY, indolent, idle**

惰気 だき indolence, inactivity, laziness

惰眠 だみん indolence, idle slumber, inactivity

怠惰 たいだ laziness, idleness

❷ inertia; force of habit

惰性 だせい inertia, momentum; force of habit

惰力 だりょく inertia, momentum; force of habit

SYNONYMS

❶ **lazy**

惰 LAZY → 0706
怠 REMISS → 2588
慢 SLUGGISH → 0844

❷ **motion**

動 motion → 2232
惰 inertia → 0706

慌

0707

1-3-9

▶FLURRIED

コウ あわ(てる) あわ(ただしい)

Ⓝ 慌 Ⓒ 慌 huāng

61	Jōyō	U614C
忄	S12-3-9	F1581

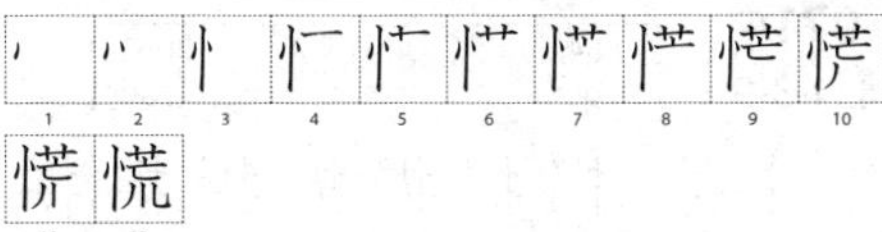

COMPOUNDS

● **frightened**

恐慌 きょうこう panic, scare, alarm

KUN

【あわてる 慌てる】 **be FLURRIED [fluttered], be confused, be in a hurry**

慌てふためく あわてふためく be all in a flurry, hurry-scurry, act helter-skelter
慌てて あわてて in confusion, in hot haste
慌て者 あわてもの flutterer, scatterbrain, bustling fellow
大慌て おおあわて total fluster, hot haste

【あわただしい 慌ただしい】 **FLURRIED, confused; busy, bustling, hurried**

慌ただしさ あわただしさ flurry, rush, restlessness
慌ただしい一生 あわただしいいっしょう fleeting life

SYNONYMS

【あわてる】

○ **busy**

忙 BUSY → 0248
繁 bustling → 3536
慌てる FLURRIED → 0707

NOTE

★ do not confuse with 荒 WILD → 2810

惶

0708

1-3-9

▶BE AFRAID

コウ

Ⓒ 惶 huáng

61	Non-Jōyō	U60F6
忄	S12-3-9	F0000

COMPOUNDS

● [now usu. 皇 3175] **BE AFRAID, be anxious; be flurried**

蒼惶(=倉皇)として そうこうとして in great haste
恐惶敬白 きょうこうけいはく Very truly yours

SYNONYMS

● **fear**

怖 FEARFUL → 0353
凄 UNCANNY → 0145
恐 FEAR → 3283
惧 FEAR → 0581
慄 TREMBLE WITH FEAR → 0791
兢 BE IN FEAR → 1971
惶 BE AFRAID → 0708
畏 BE OVERAWED → 3170
臆 FEEL TIMID → 1397
怯える BE FRIGHTENED → 0355

惺

0709

1-3-9

▶AWAKE TO

セイ ㊔ さとる さとし あきら しずか

Ⓒ 惺 xīng

61	Names	U60FA
忄	S12-3-9	F0000

COMPOUNDS

● [original meaning, now rare] **AWAKE TO**

惺悟する せいごする awaken to the Truth, become enlightened

SYNONYMS

● **know and understand**

知 KNOW → 1446
通 know thoroughly → 3855
得 gain understanding of → 0577
分かる understand → 2466
解 understand → 1913
諒 UNDERSTAND → 1982
了 COMPREHEND → 4157
悟 AWAKE TO → 0502
惺 AWAKE TO → 0709

● **awake**

悟 AWAKE TO → 0502
醒 AWAKE → 2033
覚 awake → 3217
惺 AWAKE TO → 0709

愉

0710

1-3-9

▶PLEASED

ユ たの(しい)▲ たの(しむ)▲

Ⓝ 愉 Ⓒ 愉 yú

61	Jōyō	U6109
忄	S12-3-9	F1744

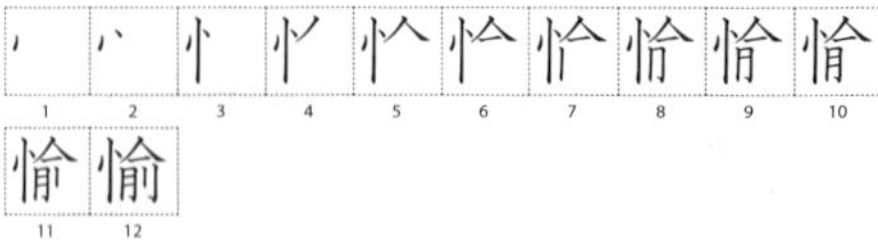

COMPOUNDS

● [original meaning] **PLEASED, delighted, happy, cheerful, joyful**

愉快な ゆかいな pleasant, delightful, joyful
愉悦 ゆえつ joy
愉色 ゆしょく pleased look, cheerful expression
愉楽 ゆらく pleasure, joy
不愉快な ふゆかいな unpleasant, disagreeable, cheerless

KUN

【たのしい 愉しい】[usu. 楽しい] pleasurable, pleasant, enjoyable, merry
愉しさ たのしさ pleasure, joy; pleasantness
愉しげな たのしげな joyous, merry, pleasant, happy, gay

【たのしむ 愉しむ】[usu. 楽しむ] take pleasure in, enjoy (oneself)
愉しみ たのしみ pleasure, enjoyment; amusement, diversion, hobby

SYNONYMS

● **pleased and pleasant**

楽 pleasurable → 3505
欣 JOYFUL → 1057
爽 REFRESHING → 4402
快 PLEASANT → 0289
朗 CHEERFUL → 1679
愉 PLEASED → 0710
悦 DELIGHTED → 0501
嬉しい GLAD → 0890
喜 HAPPY → 2889
歓 JOYOUS → 2342
驩 JOYOUS → 2333

HOMOPHONES

たのしい 楽 PLEASURE → 3505
たのしむ 楽 PLEASURE → 3505
たのしみ 楽 PLEASURE → 3505

NOTE

➡ see USAGE note at 楽 3505

慌

0711

1-3-9

▶**FLURRIED**

コウ あわ(てる) あわ(ただしい)

61	Nonstandard	U614C
忄	S12-3-9	F0000

traditional form → see 慌 at 0707

惱

0712

1-3-9

▶**SUFFER**

ノウ なや(む) なや(ます)

61	Nonstandard	U60F1
忄	S12-3-9	F0000

traditional form → see 悩 at 0504

愉

0713

1-3-9

▶**PLEASED**

ユ たの(しい) たの(しむ)

61	Nonstandard	U6109
忄	S12-3-9	F0000

traditional form → see 愉 at 0710

握

0714

1-3-9

▶**GRASP**

アク にぎ(る)

Ⓒ 握 wò

64	Jōyō	U63E1
扌	S12-3-9	F0951

COMPOUNDS

ⓐ **GRASP, seize, clasp, hold**
ⓑ **seize (power), hold (the reins of government)**

a 握力 あくりょく grasping power
握手 あくしゅ handshake, handshaking
一握 いちあく a handful (of sand)
b 把握する はあくする grip, grasp; understand, grasp
掌握する しょうあくする hold, seize, grasp, command

KUN

【にぎる 握る】

① ⓐ **GRASP, seize, clasp**
ⓑ seize (power), hold (the reins of government)
a 握り にぎり grasp, grip; handle; hand-rolled sushi
握り締める にぎりしめる squeeze, grip, clasp
b 権力を握る けんりょくをにぎる seize power

② **make hand-rolled sushi balls**
握り飯 にぎりめし rice ball
握り鮨× にぎりずし hand-rolled sushi
お握り おにぎり rice ball
寿司を握る すしをにぎる make hand-rolled sushi

SYNONYMS

ⓐ **take**

把 GRIP → 0293
握 GRASP → 0714
捉 GRASP → 0518
執 SEIZE → 2114
摑む GRASP → 0848

捕 CATCH → 0514
取 TAKE → 1613
持 HOLD → 0447

援

▸AID

エン ㊔ たすく

Ⓝ 援 Ⓒ 援 yuán

0715

◧ 1-3-9

64	Jōyō	U63F4
扌	S12-3-9	F0714

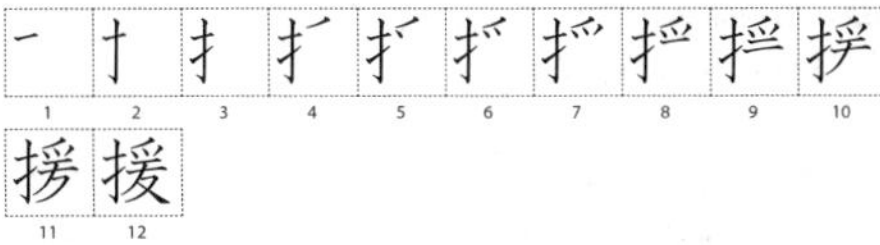

COMPOUNDS

1 a [original meaning] **AID, help out, give a hand, give support**

b [formerly 掩 0592] cover, protect

a 援助 えんじょ aid, assistance, help
援軍 えんぐん relieving force, reinforcements
支援 しえん support, backing, aid
応援 おうえん aid, reinforcement; support; cheering
後援する こうえんする give support [backing]
b 援護 えんご support, protection; covering

2 cite, quote, invoke (the law)
援用する えんようする quote, invoke

SYNONYMS

1 a help
助 HELP → 1440
佑 HELP (said esp. of God) → 0083
祐 DIVINE HELP → 1146
援 AID → 0715
佐 ASSIST → 0076
補 assist → 1529
輔 ASSIST → 1963
済 RELIEVE → 0634

換

▸EXCHANGE

カン か(える) -か(える) か(わる)

Ⓒ 换 huàn

0716

◧ 1-3-9

64	Jōyō	U63DB
扌	S12-3-9	F0924

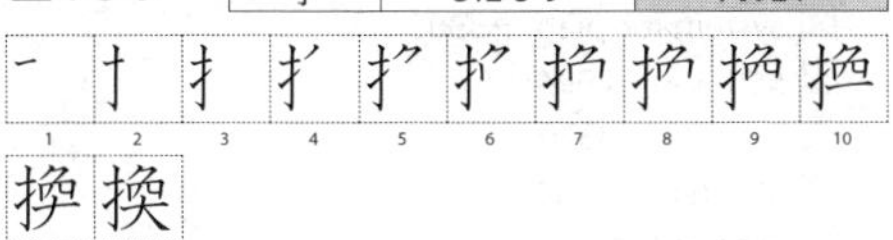

COMPOUNDS

● **EXCHANGE, interchange, change, turn, convert; take the place of, replace**
換気 かんき ventilation
換金する かんきんする cash (a check), turn into money
換算する かんざんする convert, change, exchange
変換 へんかん change, conversion, transformation
転換 てんかん conversion, switchover, turnabout
互換性 ごかんせい interchangeability, compatibility
交換する こうかんする exchange, interchange, barter, substitute

KUN

【かえる 換える】[sometimes also 替える] **EXCHANGE, interchange, trade, barter, change (money), convert**
換え かえ rate of exchange
本を金に換える ほんをかねにかえる exchange a book for money
ドルを円に換える どるをえんにかえる convert dollars into yen
十ドル札を換える じゅうどるさつをかえる get change for a ten-dollar bill
本と時計を換える ほんととけいをかえる swap a watch for a book
引き換える ひきかえる exchange, change, convert
一リットル百円換えで買う いちりっとるひゃくえんがえでかう purchase at 100 yen per liter

【-かえる -換える】[verbal suffix] **redo, renew, change**
書き換える かきかえる rewrite, renew (a bill), transfer
作り換える つくりかえる remake, reconstruct
乗り換える のりかえる change (trains), transfer

【かわる 換わる】**be EXCHANGEd, become interchanged, be converted, change**
換わり かわり exchange
段ボールがお金に換わる だんぼーるがおかねにかわる Cardboard can be traded in for money

SYNONYMS

● **change and replace**
変 CHANGE → 2569
替 REPLACE → 3457
代 SUBSTITUTE → 0034
迭 ALTERNATE → 3818
更 change → 4355
改 change → 0287
易 change → 3064
化 CHANGE INTO, -ize → 0022
遷 undergo transition → 3932
転 turn into → 1872
換 EXCHANGE → 0716
交 INTERCHANGE → 2508

【-かえる】
○ **repeating and repetition**
再 ANOTHER TIME → 4332

又 AGAIN →4158
復 repeat →0701
重 DUPLICATE →4390
畳 reduplicate →3205
改 redo →0287
-換える redo →0716
-直す repetition suffix →3649
-返す do over →3797

HOMOPHONES

かえる
替 REPLACE →3457
代 SUBSTITUTE →0034
変 CHANGE →2569

かえ
替 REPLACE →3457
代 SUBSTITUTE →0034
変 CHANGE →2569

かわる
替 REPLACE →3457
代 SUBSTITUTE →0034
変 CHANGE →2569

かわり
替 REPLACE →3457
代 SUBSTITUTE →0034
変 CHANGE →2569

NOTE

➡ see USAGE note at 変 2569

揮

▶**WIELD**
キ ふる(う)▲
Ⓒ 挥 huī

0717
1-3-9

64	Jōyō-6	U63EE
扌	S12-3-9	F1234

一 十 扌 扌 扌 扌 扌 扌 扌 揮 … 揮 (stroke order 1–12)

COMPOUNDS

❶ⓐ [original meaning] **WIELD, brandish, wave**
ⓑ **WIELD** the writing brush, write
a 指揮者 しきしゃ conductor; commander
b 揮毫×する きごうする write, draw, paint

❷ **WIELD (one's power), display (one's abilities)**
発揮する はっきする display, exhibit, demonstrate

❸ scatter, sprinkle, wipe away
揮発する きはつする volatilize
揮発油 きはつゆ gasoline

KUN

【ふるう 揮う】[now usu. 振るう] **WIELD**, brandish, manipulate, master
筆を揮う ふでをふるう drive a quill [pen], wield the writing brush

SYNONYMS

❶ **handle**
扱う HANDLE →0251
馭 HANDLE →2282
操 MANIPULATE →0948
揮 WIELD →0717
運 control movement skillfully →3894

❷ **express**
表 EXPRESS →3083
揮 WIELD →0717
寓 imply →2893

HOMOPHONES

ふるう
振 SWING →0515
震 QUAKE →3481
奮 ROUSE UP →3000

NOTE

➡ see USAGE note at 振 0515

揆

▶**PLOT**
キ
Ⓒ 揆 kuí

0718
1-3-9

64	Non-Jōyō	U63C6
扌	S12-3-9	F2239

COMPOUNDS

❶ **PLOT, plan**
一揆 いっき riot, uprising, revolt

❷ [also 軌 1832] **way of doing**

❸ [original meaning, now archaic] conjecture, estimate

INDEPENDENT

【き 揆(=軌)】**way of doing**
揆を一にする きをいつにする have the same way of doing

SYNONYMS

❶ **plans and planning**
計 PLAN →1828
画 DRAW UP A PLAN →3723
案 PROPOSAL →2824
企 PROJECT →2513
図 systematic plan →3809
謀 SCHEME →2004
策 SCHEME →3320
略 STRATEGY →1501
揆 PLOT →0718

NOTE

➡ see USAGE note at 軌 1832

揃 0719

◧1-3-9

▸MAKE UNIFORM

セン そろ(える) そろ(う) そろ(い) -ぞろ(い)

Ⓝ 揃 Ⓒ 揃 jiǎn

64	Names	U63C3
扌	S12-3-9	F1515

KUN

【そろえる 揃える】

① MAKE UNIFORM [even], act in line [concert]

高さを揃える たかさをそろえる make all of uniform height

歩調を揃える ほちょうをそろえる keep step with

口を揃えて くちをそろえて unanimously, in chorus

② arrange properly, put in order

靴を揃える くつをそろえる arrange the shoes

③ have a complete set of, assort

家具を揃える かぐをそろえる have a suite of furniture

取り揃える とりそろえる assort; gather, put together

一揃え ひとそろえ a set [suit]

品揃え しなぞろえ full stock of goods

④ collect, gather, put together

首を揃える くびをそろえる get together

数を揃える かずをそろえる have a complete set of, make up the number

【そろう 揃う】 be uniform [even], be in concert, match; become complete, make a pair [set]; get together, assemble, be all present

揃わない そろわない uneven, unequal, odd; incomplete

揃って そろって in a body, all together; all alike

揃った蔵書 そろったぞうしょ good collection of books

条件が揃う じょうけんがそろう satisfy the requirements

【そろい 揃い】

① uniformity, sameness

揃いの そろいの uniform, of the same pattern

②ⓐ counter for sets or suits

ⓑ set, pair

ⓒ [in compounds] assembly (of one sort), array

a 食器一揃い しょっきひとそろい a table service

b お揃いで おそろいで in a body, all together; hand in hand

c 揃い踏み そろいぶみ *sumo* stamping on the ring in unison

勢揃いする せいぞろいする assemble in full force, muster

【-ぞろい -揃い】 [suffix] assembly (of one sort), array

傑作揃い けっさくぞろい full array of masterpieces

SYNONYMS

【そろえる】

① fit

合 FIT → 2511

填まる fit → 0777

適 suit → 3918

揃える MAKE UNIFORM → 0719

② arrange

並 LINE UP → 2793

比 rank → 0029

列 arrange in a row → 1018

陳 lay out (for exhibit) → 0656

羅 spread out → 3244

揃える arrange properly → 0719

整 PUT IN ORDER → 3562

理 put in order → 1220

提 0720

◧1-3-9

▸PRESENT

テイ チョウ▲ ダイ▲ さ(げる) ㊔ つつみ

Ⓒ 提 tí dī

64	Jōyō-5	U63D0
扌	S12-3-9	F0543

1	2	3	4	5	6	7	8	9	10	11	12
一	十	扌	扌	扣	抇	押	担	捍	捍	提	提

COMPOUNDS

❶ (bring before a person, as for consideration) **PRESENT, bring forward, offer, tender, propose**

提案 ていあん proposition, proposal, suggestion

提出する ていしゅつする present, submit, turn in

提供する ていきょうする offer, tender; sponsor (a show)

提言 ていげん proposal, suggestion

提示する ていじする present, exhibit

提訴する ていそする present a case to (the court), file an action

提議 ていぎ proposition, proposal, motion

前提 ぜんてい premise, presupposition

❷ **carry in hand**

提琴 ていきん violin

提灯 ちょうちん paper lantern

❸ **help each other**

提携 ていけい cooperation, tie-up

❹ control, manage

提督 ていとく admiral

❺ used phonetically for *dai* in the transliteration of Sanskrit Buddhist terms

菩提 ぼだい *Bodhi*

1

KUN

【さげる 提げる】**carry in hand, take (a thing) with (a person)**

手提げ袋 てさげぶくろ handbag

SYNONYMS

❶ **offer**

供 OFFER (to a person or god) → 0098
献 OFFER (esp. to a superior) → 2240
納 offer (as to a god) → 1652
提 PRESENT → 0720
貢 offer tribute → 2838
奉 DEDICATE → 3167
捧 OFFER RESPECTFULLY → 0594

❷ **hold**

持 HOLD → 0447
提 carry in hand → 0720
携 CARRY IN HAND → 0796
捧 hold up in both hands → 0594

❺ **phonetic [d]**

陀 PHONETIC [da] → 0409
達 phonetic [da] → 3893
提 phonetic [dai] → 0720
胴 phonetic [dō] → 1186

HOMOPHONES

さげる 下 DOWN → 4186

NOTE

➡ see USAGE note at 下 4186

搭

▶**BOARD**

トウ

Ⓒ 搭 dā

0721

1-3-9

64	Jōyō	U642D
扌	S12-3-9	F2070

一 十 扌 扌 扌 扌 扌 扌 搭 搭 搭 搭 (1–12)

COMPOUNDS

❶ **BOARD, get on, embark**

搭乗する とうじょうする board, get on a plane, embark

❷ **load on BOARD (a ship or vehicle)**

搭載する とうさいする load, embark

SYNONYMS

❶ **get on**

乗 GET ON → 4393
搭 BOARD → 0721

❷ **load**

載 LOAD → 4091
積む load → 1579
搭 load on board → 0721

NOTE

★ do not confuse with 塔 TOWER → 0683

揚

▶**RAISE HIGH**
▶**EXALT**

ヨウ あ(げる) -あ(げ) あ(がる) ㊔ あき

Ⓒ 扬 yáng

0722

1-3-9

64	Jōyō	U63DA
扌	S12-3-9	F1303

一 十 扌 扌 扌 扌 扌 扌 扌 揚 揚 揚 (1–12)

COMPOUNDS

❶ⓐ (cause to rise high) **RAISE HIGH, lift, hoist, elevate, fly; rise, fly**

ⓑ **raise one's voice, declare in public**

a 揚力 ようりょく lift, lifting power
揚抗比 ようこうひ lift-drag ratio
揚炭機 ようたんき coal hoist
掲揚する けいようする hoist, put up, fly (a flag)
飛揚 ひよう flying, flight

b 揚言する ようげんする profess, declare in public, proclaim
抑揚 よくよう rising and falling (of tones), intonation

❷ⓐ (raise to a higher level of dignity) **EXALT, extol, praise, enhance, uplift**

ⓑ (raise one's spirits) **be EXALTed, be in high spirits**

a 称揚する しょうようする praise, admire, exalt, extol
発揚する はつようする exalt, raise, enhance
高揚(=昂揚)する こうようする exalt, enhance, uplift; surge up

b 意気揚揚と いきようようと exultantly, in exalted spirits, proudly

❸ land, unload, disembark

揚陸料 ようりくりょう landing charge

KUN

【あげる 揚げる】

① (cause to rise high or float in the air) **raise (a flag), send up, hoist, lift, fly (a kite), shoot up (fireworks)**

旗を揚げる はたをあげる raise [hoist] a flag
凧揚げ たこあげ kite flying

② **fry in deep fat**

揚げ あげ fried bean curd
揚げ物 あげもの fried food, a fry
魚を揚げる さかなをあげる fry fish

③ land, unload, disembark

陸揚げ りくあげ landing, unloading

引き揚げる ひきあげる withdraw, leave, return, repatriate

【-あげ -揚げ】

ⓐ [also suffix] **fried food, fry**

ⓑ fried bean curd

a 精進揚げ しょうじんあげ fried vegetables

b 油揚げ あぶらあげ fried bean curd

【あがる 揚がる】

① (rise high or float in the air) (of kites or flags) **be up, fly, be flying;** (of fireworks) **be shot up, be set off**

旗が揚がっている はたがあがっている The flag is up

② **be fried, fry**

③ (of appearance) stand out, improve

風采が揚がらない ふうさいがあがらない make a poor appearance

④ become elated, get into high spirits

意気が揚がっている いきがあがっている be in high spirits

SYNONYMS

❶ⓐ raise

揚 RAISE HIGH → 0722
掲 PUT UP → 0597
挙 RAISE → 3106
上 raise → 4212
起 raise up → 4099
擡 RAISE (one's head) → 0972
立てる STAND → 2486
拾う PICK UP → 0454

❷ⓐ praise

賛 PRAISE → 3484
頌 EULOGIZE → 1319
謳 EXTOL → 2061
讃 PRAISE → 2093
美 regard as beautiful → 2817
褒 COMMEND → 2662
嘉 commend (esp. an inferior) → 2953
彰 PROCLAIM MERITS → 2337
称 acclaim → 1491
賞 express admiration → 3237
揚 EXALT → 0722

ⓑ elated

亢 HIGH-SPIRITED → 2460
高 high-spirited → 2601
昂 high-spirited → 3065
揚 exalted → 0722
奮 roused up → 3000

【あげる】

② **cook**

煮 BOIL (cook by boiling) → 3460
沸 BOIL (undergo boiling) → 0387
炊 COOK → 1080
蒸 STEAM → 2936
焼く cook by fire → 1256
揚げる fry in deep fat → 0722
煎 ROAST, DECOCT → 2950

【-あげ】

ⓐ **cooked dishes**

-焼き roasted, baked or fried food → 1256
-揚げ fried food → 0722
-煮 boiled food → 3460

HOMOPHONES

あげる

上 UP → 4212
挙 NOMINATE → 3106

-あげ 上 UP → 4212

あがる

上 UP → 4212
挙 NOMINATE → 3106

NOTE

➡ see USAGE note at 上 4212

★ do not confuse with 楊 WILLOW → 1286

揺

0723

▶**SHAKE**

ヨウ ゆ(れる) ゆ(る) ゆ(らぐ) ゆ(るぐ) ゆ(する) ゆ(さぶる) ゆ(すぶる)

Ⓝ 搖 Ⓒ 摇 yáo

1-3-9

64	Jōyō	U63FA
扌	S12-3-9	F1044

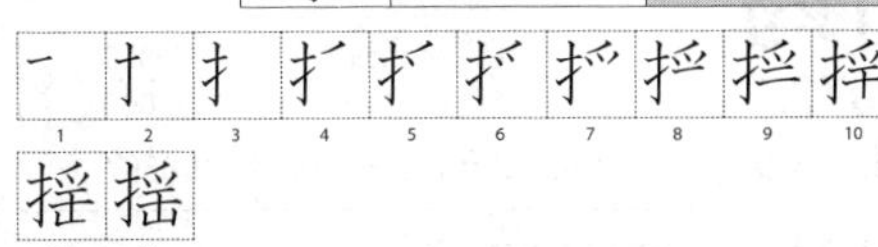

COMPOUNDS

● [original meaning] **SHAKE, sway, rock**

揺動 ようどう titubation; shaking, swinging
揺籃× ようらん cradle
動揺 どうよう shaking, trembling; restlessness, uneasiness, disquiet

KUN

【ゆれる 揺れる】**SHAKE, sway, vibrate, rock, swing**

揺れ ゆれ shaking, vibration, tremor
揺れ動く ゆれうごく rock; sway, vacillate
大揺れ おおゆれ severe quake; turbulence

【ゆる 揺る】**jolt, jog, be rocked**

揺り返し ゆりかえし aftershock, after quake
揺り起こす ゆりおこす shake up, wake by shaking
揺り籠 ゆりかご swinging cot, cradle
バスに揺られる ばすにゆられる be jolted along in a bus

【ゆらぐ 揺らぐ】*vi* **swing, sway, SHAKE, fluctuate**

揺らめく ゆらめく flicker, quiver, waver, sway

決心が揺らぐ けっしんがゆらぐ one's resolution wavers

【ゆるぐ 揺るぐ】**SHAKE, waver**

揺るぎ無い ゆるぎない firm, solid, steady

揺るがす ゆるがす shake, swing, sway, shock

【ゆする 揺する】**SHAKE, rock, joggle, swing, roll**

貧乏揺すり びんぼうゆすり nervous shaking of the body

【ゆさぶる 揺さぶる】**SHAKE, jolt, jerk**

揺さぶり ゆさぶり shaking; shaking up (one's adversary)

【ゆすぶる 揺すぶる】**SHAKE, swing, joggle, jolt**

木を揺すぶる きをゆすぶる shake a tree (for fruit)

SYNONYMS

● **shake**

振 SWING →0515

震 QUAKE →3481

揺 SHAKE →0723

援

0724

◧ 1-3-9

▶**AID**

エン ㊔ たすく

64	Nonstandard	U63F4
扌	S12-3-9	F0000

traditional form →see 援 at 0715

揭

0725

◧ 1-3-9

▶**PUT UP**

ケイ かか(げる)

64	Names	U63ED
扌	S12-3-9	F0000

traditional form →see 掲 at 0597

捲

0726

◧ 1-3-9

▶**ROLL UP**

ケン ま(く) まく(る) -まくる まくし-めく(る)

64	Nonstandard	U6372
扌	S12-3-9	F0000

traditional form →see 捲 at 0598

揃

0727

◧ 1-3-9

▶**MAKE UNIFORM**

セン そろ(える) そろ(う) そろ(い) -ぞろ(い)

64	Nonstandard	U63C3
扌	S12-3-9	F0000

traditional form →see 揃 at 0719

揷

0728

◧ 1-3-9

▶**INSERT**

ソウ さ(す) はさ(む)

64	Nonstandard	U63F7
扌	S12-3-9	F0000

alternative form →see 挿 at 0517

搜

0729

◧ 1-3-9

▶**LOOK FOR**

ソウ さが(す)

64	Names	U641C
扌	S12-3-9	F0000

traditional form →see 捜 at 0516

插

0730

◧ 1-3-9

▶**INSERT**

ソウ さ(す) はさ(む)

64	Nonstandard	U63D2
扌	S12-3-9	F0000

traditional form →see 挿 at 0517

搜

◧ 1-3-9

incorrect stroke-count

➡ see ◧ 1-3-10: 扌 at 0802

渥

0731

◧ 1-3-9

▶**GRACIOUS**

アク ㊔ あつ あつし

Ⓒ 渥 wò

85	Names	U6E25
氵	S12-3-9	F3029

COMPOUNDS

❶ **GRACIOUS, cordial, benevolent**

優渥な ゆうあくな gracious (words of the emperor)

❷ [archaic] glossy, shining with a beautiful luster

渥然たる あくぜんたる glossy

❸ [archaic] be moistened, soak wet; moisten

渥地 あくち marshland

SYNONYMS

❶ **kind**

厚 KIND →3726

篤 cordial →3371

懇 cordial →3606

慈 AFFECTIONATE →2949

温 warmhearted →0740

渥 GRACIOUS →0731

優 kindly →0200

淵

0732

◧ 1-3-9

▶**DEEP WATER**

エン ふち ㊔ のぶ ひろ ふか ふかし なみ すけ すえ しずか

Ⓝ 囦 渕 渊 Ⓒ 渊 yuān

85	Names	U6DF5
氵	S12-3-9	F1699

COMPOUNDS

❶ **DEEP WATER [pool], depths, abyss**

淵源 えんげん origin

海淵 かいえん ocean depths, deep

深淵 しんえん abyss, depths

❷ gathering spot

淵叢 えんそう gathering spot, center, hub

KUN

【ふち 淵】**DEEP WATER [pool], depths, abyss**

川の淵 かわのふち pool in a stream

絶望の淵 ぜつぼうのふち depths of despair

SYNONYMS

❶ & 【ふち】**kinds of water**

水 WATER → 0010

湯 HOT WATER → 0747

汽 STEAM → 0309

氷 ICE → 0043

淵 DEEP WATER → 0732

❶ **stagnating water**

淵 DEEP WATER → 0732

淀 pool → 0621

澱 pool → 0954

減

0733

1-3-9

▶**DECREASE**

ゲン へ(る) へ(らす)

Ⓒ 減 jiǎn

85 氵	Jōyō-5	U6E1B
	S12-3-9	F0717

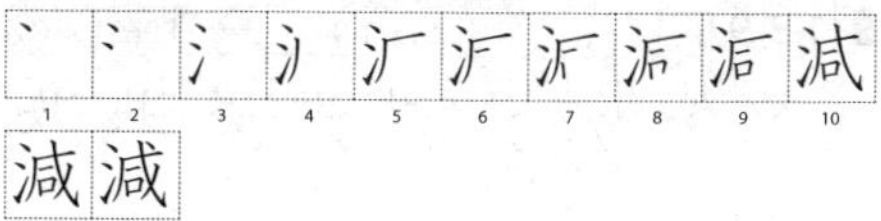

COMPOUNDS

❶ⓐ [original meaning] (grow or cause to grow less) **DECREASE, reduce, lessen**

ⓑ [also suffix] **DECREASE, reduction, fall**

a 減少する げんしょうする decrease, reduce, lessen

減税 げんぜい reduction of taxes, tax cut

減速 げんそく speed reduction

減配 げんぱい reduction in a dividend; smaller ration

減点 げんてん demerit mark

b 削減 さくげん curtailment, reduction

１０％減 じゅっぱーせんとげん decrease of 10 percent

❷ *math* **subtract**

減法 げんぽう subtraction

加減 かげん addition and subtraction; degree, extent; adjustment

INDEPENDENT

【げん 減】**DECREASE**, reduction, fall

【げんずる 減ずる】subtract, deduct; **DECREASE**, reduce

KUN

【へる 減る】*vi* **DECREASE, diminish, lessen, run low; wear**

減り へり decrease, reduction, fall

目減り めべり loss of weight

腹が減る はらがへる become hungry

【へらす 減らす】*vt* **DECREASE, reduce, lessen, shorten, cut**

磨り減らす すりへらす wear away [out]; exhaust

人減らし ひとべらし reduction of personnel

SYNONYMS

❶ **decrease**

減 DECREASE → 0733

耗 WEAR AWAY → 1660

削 cut down → 1837

縮 SHRINK → 1790

落 FALL → 2907

蝕 ERODE → 2258

❷ **subtract**

減 subtract → 0733

引く subtract → 0207

控 HOLD BACK → 0600

扣 HOLD BACK → 0250

滋

0734

1-3-9

▶**NOURISH**

ジ ㊔しげ しげる

Ⓝ 滋 Ⓒ 滋 zī

85 氵	Jōyō	U6ECB
	S12-3-9	F2023

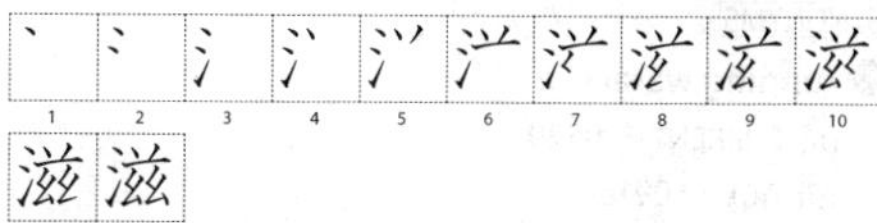

COMPOUNDS

❶ⓐ **NOURISH, moisten**

ⓑ **NOURISHing, nutritious, delicious**

a 滋養 じよう nourishment, nutrition

滋雨 じう beneficial rain

b 滋味に富む じみにとむ delicious, nutritious

滋強飲料 じきょういんりょう tonic drink

❷ [rare] grow luxuriantly, thrive, multiply

滋殖する じしょくする reproduce in large numbers, multiply

❸ abbrev. of 滋賀県 しがけん: Shiga Prefecture

京滋地方 けいじちほう Kyoto-Shiga district

SPECIAL READINGS

滋賀県 しがけん Shiga Prefecture

SYNONYMS

❶ⓐ **raise and nourish**

育 RAISE → 2544

飼 RAISE ANIMALS → 2149

養 FOSTER → 2998

滋 NOURISH → 0734

口 土 女 山 川 工 巾 弓 彡 彳 忄 扌 【氵】 犭 阝 乡 阝

哺 NURSE →0478
牧 PASTURE →1083

渦

▶WHIRLPOOL
カ うず
Ⓒ 涡 wō guō

0735
1-3-9

85 氵	Jōyō	U6E26
	S12-3-9	F1951

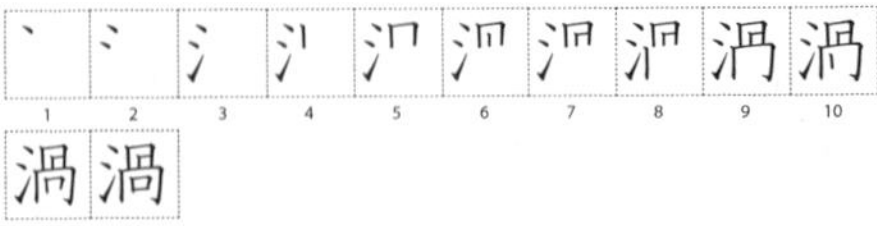

COMPOUNDS

● [original meaning] **WHIRLPOOL, eddy**
渦動 かどう vortex
渦紋 かもん whirlpool design
渦線 かせん spiral line
渦中 かちゅう maelstrom, vortex, whirlpool

KUN

【うず 渦】**WHIRLPOOL, eddy, vortex;** (tumultuous condition) **whirlpool, vortex**
渦巻く うずまく whirl, eddy, swirl
渦巻き うずまき eddy, whirlpool; coil
笑いの渦 わらいのうず clamor of laughter
政争の渦 せいそうのうず whirlpool of political strife

SYNONYMS

● **running water**
流 CURRENT →0529
潮 TIDE →0916
汐 TIDE →0259
瀬 rapids →0995
滝 WATERFALL →0813
洪 FLOOD →0461
渦 WHIRLPOOL →0735

湖

▶LAKE
コ みずうみ ㊔ うみ
Ⓒ 湖 hú

0736
1-3-9

85 氵	Jōyō-3	U6E56
	S12-3-9	F1216

COMPOUNDS

❶ⓐ [also suffix] [original meaning] **LAKE**
ⓑ **suffix after names of LAKEs**
a 湖上 こじょう on the lake
湖畔 こはん lake shore, lakeside
湖沼 こしょう lakes and marshes
淡水湖 たんすいこ freshwater lake
b 琵琶湖 びわこ Lake Biwa
❷ provinces of Hunan and Hubei in China
湖北 こほく Hubei

INDEPENDENT

【こ 湖】**LAKE**

KUN

【みずうみ 湖】**LAKE**
白鳥の湖 はくちょうのみずうみ Swan Lake

SYNONYMS

❶ **lakes and marshes**
沢 MARSH →0313
沼 MUDDY POND →0398
湖 LAKE →0736
池 POND →0253
潟 LAGOON →0921

港

▶PORT
コウ みなと
Ⓝ 港 Ⓒ 港 gǎng

0737
1-3-9

85 氵	Jōyō-3	U6E2F
	S12-3-9	F0831

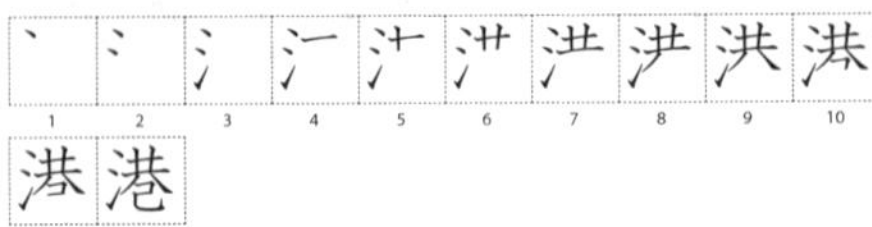

COMPOUNDS

ⓐ [also suffix] **PORT, harbor**
ⓑ suffix after names of **PORT**s or harbors
a 港湾 こうわん harbors
港口 こうこう harbor entrance
港内 こうない inside the harbor
寄港 きこう calling at a port
漁港 ぎょこう fishing port, fishery harbor
空港 くうこう airport
入港する にゅうこうする enter a port
貿易港 ぼうえきこう trade port
b 神戸港 こうべこう Kobe Harbor

KUN

【みなと 港】[sometimes also 湊] **PORT, harbor**
港町 みなとまち port town
港祭り みなとまつり port festival

SYNONYMS

● **places for landing or stopping**
港 PORT →0737
湊 PORT →0743
津 HARBOR (*elegant*) →0466
駅 STATION →2292

口 土 女 山 川 工 巾 弓 彡 彳 忄 扌 【氵】 犭 阝 纟 阝

停 stopping place →0156

USAGE

【みなと】

港

[sometimes also 湊] port, harbor

湊

[usu. 港] port, harbor

HOMOPHONES

みなと 湊 PORT →0743

渾

▸ENTIRE

コン

Ⓒ 浑 hún

0738

1-3-9

85	Non-Jōyō	U6E3E
氵	S12-3-9	F2587

COMPOUNDS

❶ [also 混 0631] (unified in an integrated whole) **ENTIRE, whole, complete**

渾身 こんしん whole body

渾然一体となる こんぜんいったいとなる be joined together, form a complete whole

❷ [now usu. 混 0631] **mixed up, confused, chaotic**

渾沌 こんとん chaos

❸ **large and powerful**

雄渾な ゆうこんな magnificent, sublime; vigorous, bold

SPECIAL READINGS

渾名 あだな nickname

SYNONYMS

❶ **all**

皆 ALL →3093

悉 THOROUGHLY →3405

総 TOTAL →1743

諸 VARIOUS →1984

毎 EVERY →2527

各 EACH →2692

都 all →2120

万 all →3653

全 WHOLE →2514

渾 ENTIRE →0738

一 all in one →4148

満 FULL →0739

丸 complete(ly) →4225

完 COMPLETE →2727

満

▸FULL

マン み(ちる) み(つ) み(たす) ㊔ みつる ま

Ⓝ 滿 Ⓒ 满 mǎn

0739

1-3-9

85	Jōyō-4	U6E80
氵	S12-3-9	F0388

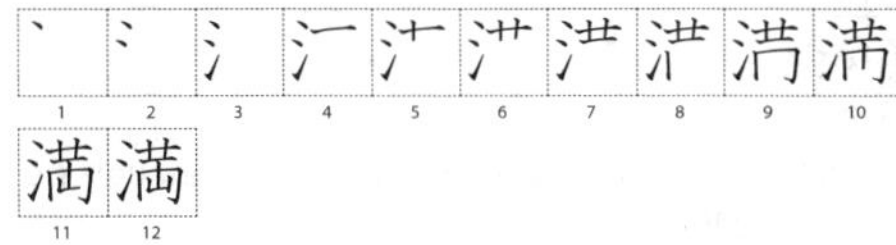

COMPOUNDS

❶ⓐ (filled to capacity) **FULL**

ⓑ (to the maximum extent) **FULL**

ⓒ (complete) **FULL, whole, entire, perfect**

ⓓ [prefix] **FULL, fully**—said of a person's age or period of time

a 満員 まんいん full to capacity

満塁 まんるい full bases

満満の まんまんの full of, brimming with

満腹の まんぷくの full, satiated

満場 まんじょう the whole house [assembly]

肥満した ひまんした fat, obese, corpulent

b 満月 まんげつ full moon

満開 まんかい full bloom

満潮 まんちょう high tide, high water

満載 まんさい full load

未満の みまんの less than

c 満点 まんてん full marks, perfect score

満面 まんめん whole face

満座 まんざ the whole assembly

d 満三歳だ まんさんさいだ be a full three years old

満二年 まんにねん a full two years

❷ⓐ [original meaning] **fill, fill up, be filled**

ⓑ **reach the FULL extent, expire**

ⓒ fulfill, carry out

a 充満する じゅうまんする be full, be filled with, overflow

金満家 きんまんか man of wealth, millionaire

b 満期 まんき expiration (of a term)

満了 まんりょう expiration, due

c 満願 まんがん completion [fulfillment] of a vow

❸ **satisfied**

満足 まんぞく satisfaction, contentment

満喫する まんきつする have enough, enjoy fully

不満 ふまん dissatisfaction, discontent

円満な えんまんな perfect, harmonious, well-rounded

❹ Manchuria

満州 まんしゅう Manchuria

満蒙 まんもう Manchuria and Mongolia

INDEPENDENT

【まん 満】**FULL**ness; age in full

満を持する まんをじする watch in readiness for a golden opportunity

年齢を満で数える ねんれいをまんでかぞえる count age in full

KUN

【みちる 満ちる】

① **be filled, be FULL of**

満ち足りる みちたりる be content, have enough, be happy

光に満ちた空 ひかりにみちたそら sky suffused with light

② reach the **FULL** extent:

ⓐ **expire, mature**

ⓑ (of tides) **rise,** (of the moon) **wax**

a 任期が満ちた にんきがみちた One's term of office has expired

b 満ち潮 みちしお high tide, high water

満ち欠け みちかけ waxing and waning (of the moon)

【みつ 満つ】[in negative constructions] **reach the limit (in numbers)**

. . . に満たない …にみたない less than…

【みたす 満たす】[sometimes also 充たす]

① **fill (up), pack**

水を満たす みずをみたす fill (a glass) with water

② **fill, fulfill, satisfy, meet (the demand)**

腹を満たす はらをみたす satisfy one's appetite

条件を満たす じょうけんをみたす answer the requirement

SYNONYMS

❶ⓐ & ❶ⓑ full

満 FULL → 0739

飽 SATIATED → 2148

ⓒ all

皆 ALL → 3093

悉 THOROUGHLY → 3405

総 TOTAL → 1743

諸 VARIOUS → 1984

毎 EVERY → 2527

各 EACH → 2692

都 all → 2120

万 all → 3653

全 WHOLE → 2514

渾 ENTIRE → 0738

一 all in one → 4148

満 FULL → 0739

丸 complete(ly) → 4225

完 COMPLETE → 2727

❷ⓐ & ❷ⓑ fill

充 FILL → 2507

湛 BE FULL OF → 0745

塡 FILL → 0777

満 fill → 0739

詰める STUFF → 1920

❸ suffice

足 SUFFICE → 2714

満 satisfied → 0739

USAGE

【みたす】

満たす

[sometimes also 充たす]

① fill (up), pack

② fill, fulfill, satisfy, meet (the demand)

充たす

[usu. 満たす] same as 満たす

HOMOPHONES

みたす 充 FILL → 2507

温

0740

◧ 1-3-9

▶WARM

オン あたた(か) あたた(かい) あたた(まる) あたた(める) ぬる(い)▲ ぬく(もる)▲ ㊔ あつ はる やす あつし ゆたか

Ⓝ 溫 Ⓒ 温 wēn

85	Jōyō-3	U6E29
氵	S12-3-9	F0683

COMPOUNDS

❶ [also prefix] **WARM, hot, temperate**

温暖な おんだんな warm, mild

温泉 おんせん hot spring

温水プール おんすいぷーる heated swimming pool

温室 おんしつ greenhouse

温度 おんど temperature

温和な おんわな (of the weather) mild, temperate

温湿布 おんしっぷ hot compress

温帯 おんたい temperate zone

❷ [also suffix] **temperature, heat, WARMth**

気温 きおん (atmospheric) temperature

低温 ていおん low temperature

保温 ほおん keeping warm, heat insulation

海水温 かいすいおん seawater temperature

❸ WARMhearted, kindly, gentle

温和(=穏和)な おんわな gentle, mild, genial

温厚な おんこうな gentle, courteous

温情 おんじょう warm feeling, kindliness, warmheartedness

❹ review

温古知新 おんこちしん learning from the past
❺ take good care of
温存する おんぞんする preserve, retain

INDEPENDENT

【おん 温】 **WARM** temper, gentle temper

KUN

【あたたか 温か】
あたたかな 温かな same as 温かい あたたかい
【あたたかい 温かい】
① **WARM (to the touch), lukewarm**
温かい御飯 あたたかいごはん warm rice
② **heartwarming, WARM (feeling or atmosphere)**
温かい歓迎 あたたかいかんげい warm reception
【あたたまる 温まる】
① (of objects or persons) **WARM oneself, take warmth, get warm, be heated**
日光に温まる にっこうにあたたまる bask in the sun, sun oneself
② **be heartwarming**
心温まる こころあたたまる heartwarming
【あたためる 温める】
① (raise the temperature of a thing) **WARM, heat**
コーヒーを温める こーひーをあたためる warm up coffee
② nurse (an idea), let (an idea) mellow
アイディアを温める あいでぃあをあたためる nurse an idea in one's mind
③ renew (an old friendship)
【ぬるい 温い】
① lukewarm, tepid; not hot [cold] enough
② lenient, indulgent, soft
【ぬくもる 温もる】 get **WARM**, warm [oneself]

SYNONYMS

❶ **hot**
熱 HOT → 3555
暑い HOT (weather) → 3121
炎 scorching → 3075
温 WARM → 0740
暖 WARM (esp. weather) → 1274
❸ **kind**
厚 KIND → 3726
篤 cordial → 3371
懇 cordial → 3606
慈 AFFECTIONATE → 2949
温 warmhearted → 0740
渥 GRACIOUS → 0731
優 kindly → 0200
【あたためる】
① **raise the temperature**
暖 WARM (the air) → 1274
煖 WARM (the air) → 1293
温める WARM (a thing) → 0740
熱 HEAT → 3555

HOMOPHONES

あたたか 暖 WARM → 1274
あたたかい 暖 WARM → 1274
あたたまる 暖 WARM → 1274
あたためる 暖 WARM → 1274

NOTE

➡ see USAGE note at 暖 1274

湿

0741
◧ 1-3-9

▶**DAMP**
シツ しめ(る) しめ(す)
Ⓝ 濕 Ⓒ 湿 shī

85	Jōyō	U6E7F
氵	S12-3-9	F1638

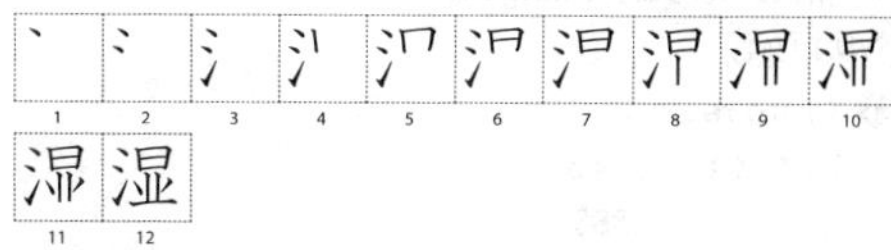

COMPOUNDS

❶ⓐ [original meaning] **DAMP, moist, wet, humid**
ⓑ **DAMPness, moisture, humidity**
a 湿地 しっち damp ground, swamp
湿布 しっぷ wet compress
湿気 しっけ(=しっき) moisture, dampness, humidity
湿電池 しつでんち wet cell
b 湿度 しつど humidity
乾湿 かんしつ dryness and moisture, humidity
防湿 ぼうしつ dampproofing, prevention of moisture
❷ itch
湿疹× しっしん eczema

KUN

【しめる 湿る】 **get DAMP, get wet**
湿り しめり dampness, moisture, humidity; rain
湿った しめった damp, moist, wet
湿っぽい しめっぽい damp, humid; gloomy, depressing
【しめす 湿す】 **DAMP, dampen, wet, moisten**
タオルを湿す たおるをしめす dampen a towel

SYNONYMS

❶ⓐ **wet**
湿 DAMP → 0741
潤 MOIST → 0918
濡れる GET WET → 0976

USAGE

【しめる】
湿る
get damp, get wet

口 土 女 山 川 工 巾 弓 彡 彳 忄 扌 【氵】 犭 阝 阝 飠

-染める
permeate with fluid or smoke

HOMOPHONES

しめる 染 DYE → 3181

湘 0742

▶SHONAN
ショウ
Ⓒ 湘 xiāng

1-3-9

85	Names	U6E58
氵	S12-3-9	F2967

COMPOUNDS

❶ abbrev. of 湘南 しょうなん: **SHONAN**
西湘 せいしょう west Shonan
❷ **Xiang River**
湘江 しょうこう Xiang River

SYNONYMS

❶ **Kanto region**
京 TOKYO → 2546
東 Tokyo → 4385
都 METROPOLIS OF TOKYO → 2120
浜 Yokohama → 0523
埼 SAITAMA → 0560
湘 SHONAN → 0742

湊 0743

▶PORT
ソウ みなと ㊔ み すすむ
Ⓒ 凑 còu

1-3-9

85	Names	U6E4A
氵	S12-3-9	F2413

COMPOUNDS

● come together, gather, collect
輻×湊 ふくそう congestion, overcrowding; convergence

KUN

【みなと 湊】[usu. 港] **PORT, harbor**

SYNONYMS

● **gather**
集 COLLECT → 3445
蒐 COLLECT → 2942
聚 COLLECT → 3479
収 collect → 0031
採 GATHER → 0606
采 GATHER → 3077
萃 GATHER → 2882
湊 come together → 0743

【みなと】
◯ **places for landing or stopping**
港 PORT → 0737
湊 PORT → 0743
津 HARBOR (*elegant*) → 0466
駅 STATION → 2292
停 stopping place → 0156

HOMOPHONES

みなと 港 PORT → 0737

NOTE

➡ see USAGE note at 港 0737

測 0744

▶MEASURE
▶CONJECTURE
ソク はか(る)
Ⓒ 测 cè

1-3-9

85	Jōyō-5	U6E2C
氵	S12-3-9	F0958

(stroke order 1–12)

COMPOUNDS

❶ⓐ [original meaning] **MEASURE, gauge, survey, fathom**
ⓑ **observe**
a 測定する そくていする measure, gauge
測量 そくりょう measurement, surveying
測深 そくしん sounding
b 測候所 そっこうじょ weather station
観測 かんそく observation
天測 てんそく astronomical observation
❷ **CONJECTURE, surmise, suppose, presume, presuppose; expect; estimate**
推測 すいそく conjecture, supposition
予測 よそく estimate, forecast, prediction
不測の ふそくの unexpected, unforeseen
憶測 おくそく conjecture, speculation, guess

KUN

【はかる 測る】(measure the physical dimensions of)
MEASURE, gauge (length, depth, distance or area)
標高を測る ひょうこうをはかる measure the height of (a mountain)

SYNONYMS

❶ⓐ **measure**
測 MEASURE → 0744
量 measure → 3119
❷ **conjecture**
推 INFER → 0612
憶 SPECULATE → 0944
測 CONJECTURE → 0744
察 GUESS → 2961

HOMOPHONES

はかる
量 QUANTITY → 3119

計 PLAN →1828
図 DRAWING →3809
謀 SCHEME →2004
諮 CONSULT →2009

NOTE

➡ see USAGE note at 計 1828

湛

0745

1-3-9

▸BE FULL OF

タン たた(える) ㊔ きよ よし やすし やす ふかし あつし

Ⓒ 湛 zhàn

85	Names	U6E5B
氵	S12-3-9	F2626

COMPOUNDS

● **BE FULL OF (liquid), fill with (liquid)**
湛水 たんすい filling (a paddy field) with water

KUN

【たたえる 湛える】
① **BE FULL OF (liquid), fill with (liquid)**
水を湛えた池 みずをたたえたいけ a pond full of water
② wear an expression
笑みを湛える えみをたたえる be all smiles

SYNONYMS

● **fill**
充 FILL →2507
湛 BE FULL OF →0745
塡 FILL →0777
満 fill →0739
詰める STUFF →1920

渡

0746

1-3-9

▸CROSS

ト わた(る) -わた(る) わた(す)

Ⓒ 渡 dù

85	Jōyō	U6E21
氵	S12-3-9	F0476

COMPOUNDS

❶ [original meaning] **CROSS (a body of water), ford, cross over, go overseas, go across**
渡航 とこう crossing, passage, voyage
渡米 とべい going to America
渡河 とか wading [fording] a river
渡来 とらい importation, influx

❷ **go through (life), pass**
渡世 とせい livelihood, subsistence
過渡期 かとき transitional period [stage]

❸ hand over, transfer, turn over
譲渡する じょうとする transfer, hand over

KUN

【わたる 渡る】
① **CROSS (a body of water), ford, cross over, go across**
渡り わたり passage, transit; migration; mutual arrangement, negotiation
綱渡り つなわたり tightrope walking [walker]
② migrate
渡り鳥 わたりどり migratory bird
渡り者 わたりもの migratory worker
③ go through (life), pass
世渡り よわたり living, subsistence
④ be transferred, be handed over, be supplied
人手に渡る ひとでにわたる fall into another's hands
不渡り ふわたり dishonor, nonpayment

【-わたる -渡る】 [verbal suffix] **reach all over, spread, extend**
晴れ渡る はれわたる clear up
染み渡る(=滲み渡る) しみわたる penetrate, pervade, spread

【わたす 渡す】 carry across (a river); hand over, deliver, transfer; build, span (a bridge)
渡し わたし ferry (crossing); ferry(boat); [also suffix] delivery
渡し船 わたしぶね ferryboat
言い渡す いいわたす announce, tell; sentence; order
手渡す てわたす hand over (to), give, deliver
引き渡す ひきわたす deliver, turn over, surrender

SYNONYMS

❶ **cross**
渡 CROSS →0746
渉 wade →0638
越 GO BEYOND →4108

❸ **transfer**
譲 CEDE →2080
渡 hand over →0746
付 deliver →0035
附 deliver →0410

USAGE

【わたる】
渡る
① cross (a body of water), ford, cross over, go across
② migrate
③ go through (life), pass
④ be transferred, be handed over, be supplied

亘る
extend over, extend for, range, span, last

HOMOPHONES

わたる 亘 EXTEND OVER →2438

湯

▸HOT WATER
トウ ゆ ㊔ ゆう
Ⓒ 汤 tāng shāng

0747
1-3-9

85	Jōyō-3	U6E6F
氵	S12-3-9	F0875

COMPOUNDS

❶ [original meaning] **HOT WATER, boiling water**
給湯 きゅうとう hot water supply
熱湯 ねっとう boiling water

❷ **hot bath, hot spring**
湯治 とうじ hot spring cure, taking healing baths
入湯 にゅうとう taking a hot bath
銭湯 せんとう public bath, bathhouse

❸ [also suffix] medical decoction, infusion
薬湯 やくとう infusion, decoction, medical bath
葛根湯 かっこんとう antifebrile infusion

KUN

【ゆ 湯】
① **HOT WATER**
湯気 ゆげ steam, vapor
湯飲み ゆのみ teacup
茶の湯 ちゃのゆ tea ceremony

② **hot bath, hot spring; bathhouse, public bath**
湯船 ゆぶね bathtub
湯殿 ゆどの bathroom
湯屋 ゆや public bath house

SYNONYMS

❶ **kinds of water**
水 WATER →0010
湯 HOT WATER →0747
汽 STEAM →0309
氷 ICE →0043
淵 DEEP WATER →0732

❷ **baths**
浴 bath →0533
湯 hot bath →0747
泉 hot spring →3176

湾

▸BAY
ワン
Ⓝ 灣 Ⓒ 湾 wān

0748
1-3-9

85	Jōyō	U6E7E
氵	S12-3-9	F1046

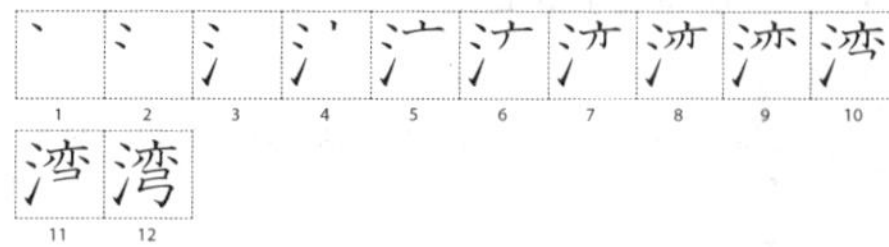

COMPOUNDS

❶ⓐ [original meaning] **BAY, gulf, inlet**
ⓑ **suffix after names of BAYs and gulfs**
a 湾口 わんこう bay entrance
湾内 わんない inside the bay
港湾局 こうわんきょく Port and Harbor Authority
b 東京湾 とうきょうわん Tokyo Bay
メキシコ湾 めきしこわん Gulf of Mexico

❷ [formerly also 彎 3634] curve
湾曲 わんきょく curve, crook, bend
湾入する わんにゅうする curve in

INDEPENDENT

【わん 湾】**BAY, gulf, inlet**

SYNONYMS

❶ **inlets and bays**
江 INLET →0257
浦 coastal indentation →0524
湾 BAY →0748
峡 narrows →0427

湧

▸WELL UP
ユウ ヨウ▲ わ(く) ㊔ いさむ
Ⓝ 涌 湧 Ⓒ 涌 yǒng

0749
1-3-9

85	Jōyō	U6E67
氵	S12-3-9	F1621

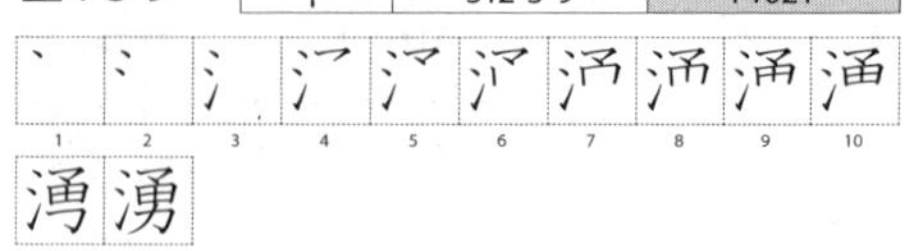

COMPOUNDS

● [original meaning] **WELL UP, spring forth, gush out**
湧出 ゆうしゅつ welling, gushing
湧水 ゆうすい welling of water

KUN

【わく 湧く】
①ⓐ **WELL UP, spring forth, gush out**
ⓑ (of emotions or ideas) **WELL UP, gush out, spring up, appear**
a 湧き水 わきみず spring water
湧き出る わきでる well up, spring forth

b 湧き上がる わきあがる arise
降って湧く ふってわく take place unexpectedly

② (of insects) **breed, be hatched**
ぼうふらが湧いた ぼうふらがわいた Mosquito larvae have hatched

SYNONYMS

● & 【わく】 ①ⓐ **emit**
出 PUT OUT → 4310
発 EMIT → 3174
放 radiate → 1058
排 DISCHARGE → 0593
射 SHOOT → 1850
噴 SPOUT → 0879
吐 SPEW → 0235
湧 WELL UP → 0749

HOMOPHONES

わく 沸 BOIL → 0387

NOTE

➡ see USAGE note at 沸 0387

游

0750
◧ 1-3-9

▶SWIM
ユウ およ(ぐ)
Ⓒ 游 yóu

85	Non-Jōyō	U6E38
氵	S12-3-9	F3344

COMPOUNDS

● [now usu. 遊 3896] [original meaning] **SWIM**
游泳 ゆうえい swimming
回游 かいゆう migration (of fish)
浮游する ふゆうする waft, float

KUN

【およぐ 游ぐ】 [usu. 泳ぐ] **SWIM;** (figuratively) **swim, get along**
游ぎ およぎ swimming

SYNONYMS

● **move through water**
泳 SWIM → 0385
游 SWIM → 0750
渉 wade → 0638
遡 GO UPSTREAM → 4040
漕 ROW → 0864

HOMOPHONES

およぐ 泳 SWIM → 0385

NOTE

➡ see USAGE note at 泳 0385

潑

0751
◧ 1-3-9

▶LIVELY
ハツ

85	Nonstandard	U6E8C
氵	S12-3-9	F0000

traditional form → see 潑 at 0917

滋

0752
◧ 1-3-9

▶NOURISH
ジ ㊔ しげ しげる

85	Nonstandard	U2F90B
氵	S12-3-9	F0000

traditional form → see 滋 at 0734

渴

0753
◧ 1-3-9

▶RUN DRY
▶THIRST
カツ かわ(く)

85	Names	U6E34
氵	S12-3-9	F0000

traditional form → see 渇 at 0627

港

0754
◧ 1-3-9

▶PORT
コウ みなと

85	Nonstandard	U6E2F
氵	S12-3-9	F0000

traditional form → see 港 at 0737

渚

0755
◧ 1-3-9

▶STRAND
ショ なぎさ

85	Names	UFA46
氵	S12-3-9	F0000

traditional form → see 渚 at 0637

湧

0756
◧ 1-3-9

▶WELL UP
ユウ ヨウ わ(く) ㊔ いさむ

85	Nonstandard	U6E67
氵	S12-3-9	F0000

traditional form → see 湧 at 0749

漣

◧ 1-3-9

incorrect stroke-count
➡ see ◧ 1-3-10: 氵 at 0822

猶

0757
◧ 1-3-9

▶DELAY
ユウ ユ▲ なお▲
Ⓝ 犹 猶 Ⓒ 犹 yóu

94	Jōyō	U7336
犭	S12-3-9	F2302

1	2	3	4	5	6	7	8	9	10	11	12
ノ	犭	犭	犭	犭'	犭"	犭𠂉	犭酉	犭酉	猶	猶	猶

口 土 女 山 川 工 巾 弓 彡 彳 忄 扌 氵 【犭】 阝 阝 阝

COMPOUNDS

❶ **DELAY, put off, postpone; waver, dally**

猶予する ゆうよする postpone, delay, extend; hesitate

執行猶予 しっこうゆうよ stay of execution, probation, suspended sentence

❷ just, like

猶子 ゆうし nephew ("like a son")

❸ Jew, Jewish

猶太 ゆだや Judea, Jewish people

日猶同祖論 にちゆうどうそろん hypothesis that Jews and Japanese are of common ancestry

KUN

【なお 猶】 [usu. 尚]

① ⓐ (in increasing degree) **still (more), all the more**

ⓑ **further, in addition, by the way**

a 猶の事 なおのこと all the more, still more

猶良い なおよい still better

b 猶一層悪い事は なおいっそうわるいことは what is worse still

② ⓐ **still, yet**

ⓑ **even, still**

a 春猶浅し はるなおあさし Spring is not yet far advanced

b 昼猶暗い ひるなおくらい be dark even in the daytime

③ *literary* **as, just like, no more...than**

鯨の魚にあらざるは猶馬の魚にあらざるが如し くじらのさかなにあらざるはなおうまのさかなにあらざるがごとし A whale is no more a fish than a horse is

SYNONYMS

❶ **be late and delay**

遅 be late → 3887

後 fall behind → 0431

滞 fall into arrears → 0815

延 POSTPONE → 3812

猶 DELAY → 0757

HOMOPHONES

なお 尚 STILL → 2774

NOTE

➡ see USAGE note at 尚 2774

猪

0758

1-3-9

▶**WILD BOAR**

チョ いのしし い ㊔ いの しし

94	Names	UFA16
犭	S12-3-9	F0000

traditional form → see 猪 at 0652

猶

0759

1-3-9

▶**DELAY**

ユウ ユ なお

94	Nonstandard	U7336
犭	S12-3-9	F0000

traditional form → see 猶 at 0757

隅

0760

1-3-9

▶**NOOK**

グウ すみ ㊔ くま

Ⓒ 隅 yú

170	Jōyō	U9685
阝	S12-3-9	F1375

COMPOUNDS

● [original meaning] **NOOK, corner**

一隅 いちぐう corner, nook

KUN

【すみ 隅】 **NOOK, corner; angle**

隅隅 すみずみ every nook and cranny

隅木 すみき angle rafter, angle [corner] block

隅から隅まで すみからすみまで every nook and cranny

隅に置けない すみにおけない be witty and knowing

片隅 かたすみ corner, nook

SYNONYMS

● **corners**

角 corner → 2541

圭 SHARP CORNER → 2688

隅 NOOK → 0760

隈 RECESS → 0763

NOTE

★ do not confuse with 隈 RECESS → 0763

階

0761

1-3-9

▶**FLOOR**
▶**RANK**

カイ きざはし▲ ㊔ しな はし

Ⓒ 阶 jiē

170	Jōyō-3	U968E
阝	S12-3-9	F0537

COMPOUNDS

❶ⓐ **FLOOR, story**

ⓑ **counter for FLOORs**

a 地階 ちかい basement, cellar
各階 かくかい every floor
b 三階 さんがい third floor

❷ **stairs, flight of stairs, steps, staircase**
階段 かいだん steps, flight of stairs
階下 かいか lower floor, downstairs
階梯 かいてい step, ladder; stepping-stone; guide

❸ **RANK, order, grade, class**
階級 かいきゅう class, estate; rank, grade
階層 かいそう social stratum, class; tier
位階 いかい court rank
段階 だんかい grade, rank, step, stage

INDEPENDENT

【かい 階】**FLOOR**; stairs, steps; *geol* stage
下の階 したのかい lower floor

KUN

【きざはし 階】stairs, steps

SYNONYMS

❶ **floor**
階 FLOOR → 0761
層 story → 3920

❷ **steps**
段 STEP → 1471
階 stairs → 0761
陛 IMPERIAL PALACE STEPS → 0543
梯 LADDER → 1210

❸ **class**
級 GRADE → 1630
段 grade → 1471
位 RANK → 0069
階 RANK → 0761
身 social status → 4368
格 STATUS → 1161
等 CLASS → 3321
流 class → 0529
層 STRATUM → 3920

NOTE

★ do not confuse with 陛 IMPERIAL PALACE STEPS → 0543

隊

0762

◧ 1-3-9

▶**PARTY**

タイ

Ⓝ 隊 Ⓒ 队 duì

170	Jōyō-4	U968A
阝	S12-3-9	F0410

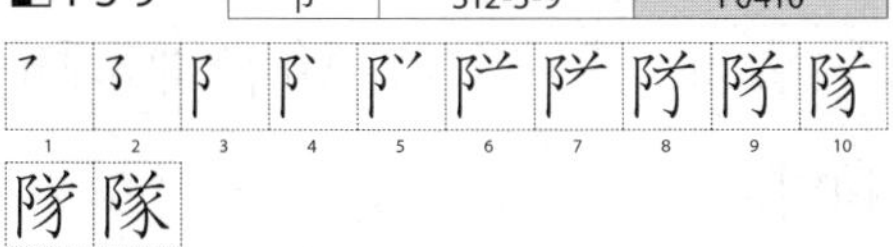

COMPOUNDS

❶ [also suffix] (organized group of people) **PARTY, group, troop, company, band**
隊員 たいいん member of the group
一隊 いったい party (of mountaineers), company (of soldiers), gang, troop, squad
楽隊 がくたい musical band
デモ隊 でもたい demonstrators
捜索隊 そうさくたい search party
親衛隊 しんえいたい bodyguards; groupies

❷ (organized group of troops) **PARTY, army unit, corps, body of troops**
隊長 たいちょう captain, leader, commander
隊形 たいけい battle formation, disposition of troops
軍隊 ぐんたい army, troops
部隊 ぶたい unit, corps, party, squad
連隊 れんたい regiment
中隊 ちゅうたい company, squadron
兵隊 へいたい soldier; troops
艦隊 かんたい squadron, fleet
自衛隊 じえいたい Self Defense Forces
警官隊 けいかんたい police force [squad]
分遣隊 ぶんけんたい detachment
別動隊 べつどうたい detached party [column]

INDEPENDENT

【たい 隊】**PARTY, company, corps**
隊を組む たいをくむ form a party, line up

SYNONYMS

❶ **groups**
群 GROUP (of any kind) → 1942
班 SQUAD → 1182
軍 team → 2582
組 group (of people) → 1693
陣 lineup → 0545
連 set → 3849
族 common-interest group (*slang*) → 1195
党 PARTY → 3190
隊 PARTY (organized group) → 0762
団 BODY → 3791
伍 ranks → 0050

❷ **armed forces**
軍 ARMY → 2582
兵 the military → 3158
勢 forces → 3542
隊 PARTY → 0762

口 土 女 山 川 工 巾 弓 彡 彳 忄 扌 氵 犭 【阝】 阝 阝

隈

▶**RECESS**
ワイ くま
Ⓒ 隈 wēi

0763
1-3-9

170	Names	U9688
阝	S12-3-9	F1990

COMPOUNDS

● **RECESS, nook, corner**
界隈 かいわい neighborhood, vicinity

KUN

【くま 隈】
① **RECESS, nook, corner**
隈なく くまなく in every nook and cranny
② **shadow, shade**
隈取り くまどり shading, gradation; kabuki makeup
隈笹 くまざさ *Sasa veitchii*

SYNONYMS

● **corners**
角 corner →2541
圭 SHARP CORNER →2688
隅 NOOK →0760
隈 RECESS →0763

NOTE

★ do not confuse with 隅 NOOK →0760

陽

▶**SUN**
ヨウ ひ˄ ㊔ はる あき あきら
Ⓒ 阳 yáng

0764
1-3-9

170	Jōyō-3	U967D
阝	S12-3-9	F0745

COMPOUNDS

❶ⓐ **SUN, sunlight**
ⓑ **SUNny, bright**
a 陽光 ようこう sunshine, sunlight, sun
陽暦 ようれき solar calendar
太陽 たいよう sun
落陽 らくよう setting sun
春陽 しゅんよう spring sunshine
b 陽気な ようきな cheerful, bright, sunny

❷ [original meaning] **SUNny or south side of a mountain; north side of a stream**
山陽 さんよう south side of a mountain; Sanyo district
漢陽 かんよう Hanyang (city in China)

❸ yang: the masculine and active principle in Chinese dualistic philosophy representing positive concepts such as masculinity, **SUN**, light, heaven, etc.
陰陽 いんよう yin and yang, positive and negative, active and passive

❹ⓐ **positive**
ⓑ *elec* **positive, positive pole**
a 陽性 ようせい positivity
陽画 ようが positive photographic print
陽子 ようし proton
b 陽極 ようきょく positive pole, anode
陽電気 ようでんき positive electricity

❺ male genitals
陽物 ようぶつ phallus, penis

❻ openly, ostensibly, explicitly
陽報 ようほう open reward, rewarding openly

INDEPENDENT

【よう 陽】yang (→❸); open, explicit
陰と陽 いんとよう the positive and the negative
陰に陽に いんにようにopenly and covertly, implicitly and explicitly

KUN

【ひ 陽】[usu. 日] **SUN, sunlight**
夕陽 ゆうひ setting sun

SYNONYMS

❶ⓐ **sun**
日 SUN →3759
陽 SUN →0764
旭 RISING SUN →3697

❸ **yin and yang**
陰 yin →0657
陽 yang →0764

❹ **positive**
陽 positive →0764
正 positive →4296

HOMOPHONES

ひ 日 DAY →3759

NOTE

➡ see USAGE note at 日 3759

随

▶**FOLLOW**
ズイ
Ⓝ 隨 Ⓒ 随 suí

0765
1-3-9

170	Jōyō	U968F
阝	S12-3-9	F1466

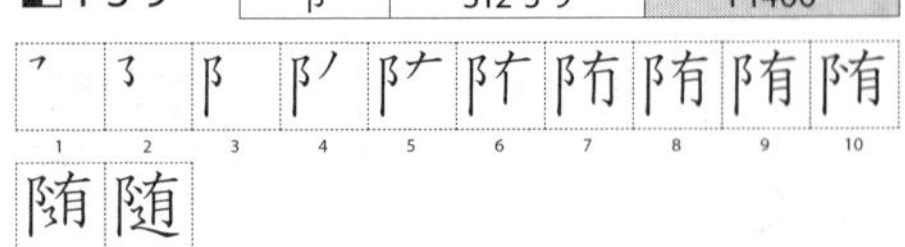

COMPOUNDS

❶ⓐ (go after) **FOLLOW, attend (on), accompany**
ⓑ (comply with) **FOLLOW**, obey

a 随行する ずいこうする attend on, accompany, follow
随員 ずいいん attendants, retinue
付随の ふずいの accompanying, incidental

b 随従する ずいじゅうする follow the lead of, play second fiddle to
随順する ずいじゅんする obey meekly, faithfully follow (one's master)
追随する ついずいする follow (in the wake of)

❷ **let (oneself) do (as one pleases), let things take their natural course**
随筆 ずいひつ essay; stray notes
随意に ずいいに voluntarily, at will
随想 ずいそう occasional thoughts
随分 ずいぶん extremely, considerably ("as much as one pleases")

❸ irrespective of time or place
随時に ずいじに anytime, as occasion calls
随所に ずいしょに everywhere

SYNONYMS

❶ⓐ **follow and pursue**
従 FOLLOW → 0498
随 FOLLOW → 0765
辿る FOLLOW (a path) → 3968
追 CHASE → 3840

❶ⓐ **accompany**
伴 ACCOMPANY → 0068
添 accompany → 0641
陪 ACCOMPANY A SUPERIOR → 0655
侍 ATTEND UPON → 0094
従 FOLLOW → 0498
随 FOLLOW → 0765

❷ **let do**
放 LET GO → 1058
随 let do → 0765

COMPOUND FORMATION

【随筆 ずいひつ】
随筆 'essay; stray notes' is, literally, something written (筆) in a manner that one pleases (随 ❷); that is, without following specific rules.

陰

0766

◧ 1-3-9

▶**SHADE**
イン かげ かげ(る)

170	Nonstandard	U9682
阝	S12-3-9	F0000

traditional form → see 陰 at 0657

隆

0767

◧ 1-3-9

▶**PROSPER**
リュウ ㊔ たか たかし

170	Nonstandard	U9686
阝	S12-3-9	F0000

traditional form → see 隆 at 0661

隊

0768

◧ 1-3-9

▶**PARTY**
タイ

170	Nonstandard	U968A
阝	S12-3-9	F0000

traditional form → see 隊 at 0762

郷

◧ 1-3-9

incorrect stroke-count
➡ see ◧ 1-3-10: 纟 at 0830

鄉

◧ 1-3-9

incorrect stroke-count
➡ see ◧ 1-3-10: 纟 at 0829

卿

0769

◧ 1-3-9

▶**STATE MINISTER**
キョウ ケイ ㊔ あき のり あきら
Ⓝ 卿 卿 Ⓒ 卿 qīng

26	Names	U537F
卩	S12-2-10	F1921

COMPOUNDS

❶ⓐ [also suffix] **STATE MINISTER, minister, peer, noble**
ⓑ courtesy title for noblemen and knighted persons of Britain: **Lord, Sir**

a 卿相 けいしょう top members of the imperial court
公卿 くぎょう(=こうけい, くげ) *hist* high-ranking court nobles
枢機卿 すうききょう(=すうきけい) (Catholic) cardinal

b ウィンストン卿 うぃんすとんきょう Sir Winston

❷ [archaic] [honorific]
ⓐ lord, sir
ⓑ you

❸ auspicious
卿雲 けいうん auspicious cloud

INDEPENDENT

【きょう 卿】
ⓐ **STATE MINISTER (in ancient Japan)**
ⓑ [archaic] [honorific] lord, sir

【けい 卿】 same as 卿 きょう

SYNONYMS

❶ **high officials**
相 MINISTER → 1120
宰 chief minister → 2829
卿 STATE MINISTER → 0769

❷ⓑ **second person pronouns**
君 YOU (*familiar*) → 3974

口 土 女 山 川 工 巾 弓 彡 彳 忄 扌 氵 犭 阝 阝 【卩】

汝 THOU → 0255
爾 thou → 4407
貴 you (*honorific*) → 3220
卿 you (*archaic*, *honorific*) → 0769

NOTE

★ do not confuse with 郷 HOMETOWN → 0664

卿 0770

1-3-9

▶**STATE MINISTER**

キョウ ケイ ㊔ あき のり あきら

26	Nonstandard	U2F833
卩	S12-2-10	F0000

traditional form → see 卿 at 0769

嘩 0771

1-3-10

▶**BOISTEROUS**

カ

Ⓝ 譁 Ⓒ 哗 huá huā

30	Names	U5629
口	S13-3-10	F1785

COMPOUNDS

● **BOISTEROUS, noisy, clamorous**
喧嘩 けんか quarrel, fight, squabble
喧嘩腰 けんかごし belligerent
口喧嘩 くちげんか quarrel

SYNONYMS

● **loud**
高い loud → 2601
朗 CLEAR (voice) → 1679
騒 clamorous → 2308
喧 BOISTEROUS → 0667
嘩 BOISTEROUS → 0771

嗅 0772

1-3-10

▶**SMELL**

キュウ か(ぐ)

Ⓒ 嗅 xiù

30	Jōyō	U55C5
口	S13-3-10	F2000

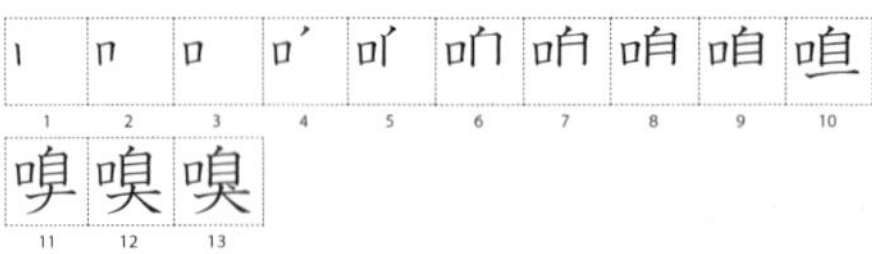

COMPOUNDS

● **SMELL, scent, sniff**
嗅覚 きゅうかく sense of smell
嗅神経 きゅうしんけい olfactory nerve

KUN

【かぐ 嗅ぐ】**SMELL, scent, sniff**
嗅ぎ分ける かぎわける scent out, discern
嗅ぎ当てる かぎあてる sniff out, scent out
嗅ぎ付ける かぎつける sniff out, get wind of
嗅ぎ回る かぎまわる sniff about [around], snoop
嗅ぎ煙草 かぎたばこ snuff

SYNONYMS

● **detect**
検 detect → 1241
感 SENSE → 3514
嗅 SMELL → 0772

嘆 0773

1-3-10

▶**SIGH**

タン なげ(く) なげ(かわしい)

Ⓝ 嘆 Ⓒ 叹 tàn

30	Jōyō	U5606
口	S13-3-10	F1547

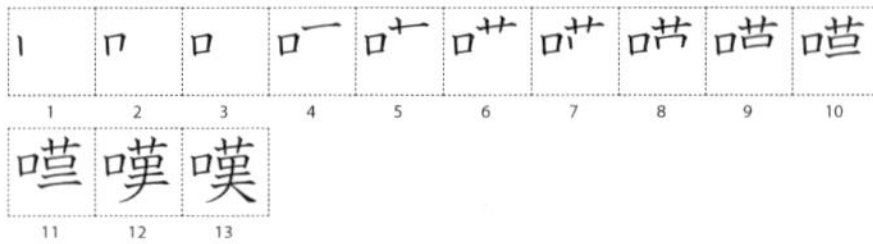

COMPOUNDS

[formerly also 歎 2344]

❶ [original meaning] **SIGH (in grief or despair), grieve, lament**
嘆息 たんそく sigh
嘆願 たんがん entreaty, appeal
悲嘆 ひたん grief, sorrow, lamentation
慨嘆 がいたん deploring, regret

❷ **SIGH in admiration, exclaim, admire, praise**
嘆声 たんせい sigh, lamentation; sigh of admiration
詠嘆 えいたん exclamation, admiration
賛嘆 さんたん praise, admiration
驚嘆 きょうたん admiration, wonder
感嘆する かんたんする admire, be struck with admiration

INDEPENDENT

【たん 嘆(=歎)】**SIGH**, grief, lamentation
髀×肉の嘆を託つ ひにくのたんをかこつ fret from forced idleness

【たんじる(=たんずる) 嘆じる(=歎じる、嘆ずる、歎ずる)】grieve, lament; **SIGH** in admiration

KUN

【なげく 嘆く】[formerly also 歎く] **SIGH (in grief or despair), grieve, lament; deplore**
嘆き なげき grief, lamentation
嘆き悲しむ なげきかなしむ grieve and moan
政治の腐敗を嘆く せいじのふはいをなげく deplore the corruption of politics

【なげかわしい 嘆かわしい】**lamentable, deplorable, regrettable**
嘆かわしい事態 なげかわしいじたい deplorable situation

SYNONYMS

❶ **cry and sigh**
泣 CRY → 0396
嘆 SIGH → 0773
歎 SIGH → 2344

❶ **grieve**
慨 DEPLORE → 0790
嘆 SIGH → 0773
悼 MOURN → 0587
傷 grieve → 0179
悲 feel sad → 3448
悄 BECOME DISPIRITED → 0506

❷ **feel deeply**
感 feel deeply → 3514
動 be moved → 2232
嘆 sigh in admiration → 0773

USAGE

❶【なげく】
嘆く
[formerly also 歎く] sigh (in grief or despair), grieve, lament; deplore
歎く
[now usu. 嘆く] same as 嘆く

❷【なげき】
嘆き
[formerly also 歎き] grief, lamentation
歎き
[now usu. 嘆き] grief, lamentation

HOMOPHONES

なげく 歎 SIGH → 2344
なげき 歎 SIGH → 2344

塩

▶**SALT**
エン しお
Ⓝ 鹽 Ⓒ 盐 yán

0774
◧ 1-3-10

32△ 土	Jōyō-4 / S13-3-10	U5869 / F1203

Stroke order: 一 十 土 ... 塩 (1–13)

COMPOUNDS

❶ [original meaning] **SALT**
塩分 えんぶん salt, salinity
塩水 えんすい salt water
食塩 しょくえん table salt
天然塩 てんねんえん natural salt

❷ [also suffix] chemical **SALT**, base, alkali
塩基 えんき base
炭酸塩 たんさんえん carbonate
中性塩 ちゅうせいえん neutral salt

❸ [also suffix] **chlorine, chloride compound**
塩酸 えんさん hydrochloric acid
塩素 えんそ chlorine
塩化 えんか chloridation, salification

INDEPENDENT

【えん 塩】chemical **SALT**, base, alkali

KUN

【しお 塩】**SALT**
塩味 しおあじ salty taste, seasoning
塩辛い しおからい salty
塩水 しおみず salt water
塩加減をする しおかげんをする season with salt

SPECIAL READINGS

塩梅▲ あんばい seasoning, flavoring; taste, flavor; condition, state

SYNONYMS

❶ **seasonings**
糖 SUGAR → 1777
塩 SALT → 0774
酢 VINEGAR → 1910
醋 VINEGAR → 2002
油 OIL → 0400
醬 FERMENTED SAUCE → 3569
噌 MISO → 0882
蜜 HONEY → 2958

❸ **lighter elements**
水 hydrogen → 0010
酸 OXYGEN → 1968
窒 NITROGEN → 2853
塩 chlorine → 0774
臭 bromine → 3261
硫 SULFUR → 1519
炭 carbon → 2806

塊

▶**LUMP**
カイ かたまり
Ⓒ 块 kuài

0775
◧ 1-3-10

32 土	Jōyō / S13-3-10	U584A / F1641

Stroke order: 一 十 土 ... 塊 (1–13)

COMPOUNDS

● **LUMP, mass; ingot; nugget**
塊土 かいど lump of earth
塊鉱 かいこう lump ore
地塊 ちかい block, landmass

金塊 きんかい nugget, gold ingot

KUN

【かたまり 塊】

① [usu. 固まり] **LUMP, mass, clod; ingot**

血の塊 ちのかたまり clot of blood

② [sometimes also 固まり] **group, crowd, cluster**

③ [usu. 固まり] devotee, worshiper; incarnation (of selfishness), personification

欲の塊 よくのかたまり lump of avarice, incarnation of selfishness

拝金主義の塊 はいきんしゅぎのかたまり money worshiper

SYNONYMS

● **bodies**

体 BODY → 0080

塊 LUMP → 0775

球 BALL → 1219

HOMOPHONES

かたまり 固 SOLID → 3830

NOTE

➡ see USAGE note at 固 3830

墝

0776

1-3-10

▶**HANAWA**

コウ はなわ

Ⓒ 墝 qiāo

32	Names	U5859
土	S13-3-10	F0000

COMPOUNDS

● [original meaning, now obsolete] hard, firm

KUN

【はなわ 墝】 Japanese surname: **HANAWA**

塡

0777

1-3-10

▶**FILL**

テン は(める)▲ は(まる)▲ ㊔ やす みつ ます さだ

Ⓝ 塡 Ⓒ 填 tián

32	Jōyō	U5861
土	S13-3-10	F2599

Stroke order: 1–13

COMPOUNDS

ⓐ FILL (in), stuff, load

ⓑ [original meaning] **stop up, plug**

a 塡料 てんりょう filler (for making paper)

充塡する じゅうてんする fill, fill up, plug; replenish

装塡する そうてんする load, charge

b 塡隙 てんげき caulking

補塡 ほてん compensating [making up] (for)

KUN

【はめる 塡める】 [usu. 嵌める]

①ⓐ put in, set in, insert, fit

ⓑ put on, slip on

a 塡め込み はめこみ insertion, inlaying

② entrap, ensnare; trick, deceive

旨く塡められた うまくはめられた I was cleverly taken in

【はまる 塡まる】 [usu. 嵌まる]

① fit, be fit for, suit

②ⓐ be trapped, be ensnared

ⓑ be addicted, be deep (into)

a 穴に塡まる あなにはまる fall in a pit

ab 塡まり込む はまりこむ get stuck [mired] in; be addicted to

SYNONYMS

ⓐ **fill**

充 FILL → 2507

湛 BE FULL OF → 0745

塡 FILL → 0777

満 fill → 0739

詰める STUFF → 1920

【はまる】

① **fit**

合 FIT → 2511

塡まる fit → 0777

適 suit → 3918

揃える MAKE UNIFORM → 0719

HOMOPHONES

はめる

嵌 INLAY → 2897

塡 FILL → 0777

はまる

嵌 INLAY → 2897

塡 FILL → 0777

NOTE

➡ see USAGE note at 嵌 2897

塚

0778

1-3-10

▶**MOUND**

チョウ つか -づか

32	Nonstandard	UFA10
土	S13-3-10	F0000

traditional form → see 塚 at 0675

填

0779

1-3-10

▶**FILL**

テン は(める) は(まる) ㊔ やす みつ ます さだ

32	Nonstandard	U586B
土	S13-3-10	F0000

traditional form → see 塡 at 0777

堰 incorrect stroke-count
➡ see ◧1-3-9: 土 at 0676
◧1-3-10

嫁

▶WED A MAN
▶BRIDE
カ よめ とつ(ぐ)
Ⓒ 嫁 jià

0780
◧1-3-10

38	Jōyō	U5AC1
女	S13-3-10	F1248

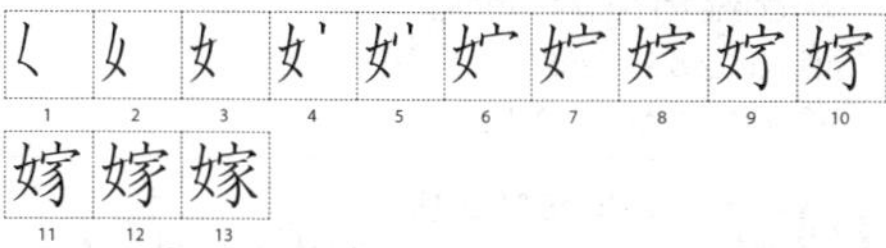

COMPOUNDS

❶ **WED A MAN, marry into a family**
降嫁 こうか marriage of an Imperial princess to a subject
再嫁 さいか second marriage
❷ **BRIDE**
惣嫁(=総嫁) そうか streetwalker (in the Edo period)
❸ **impute, blame (someone else)**
転嫁する てんかする impute, lay the blame on another

INDEPENDENT

【かする 嫁する】 **WED A MAN**; impute, blame (someone else)

KUN

【よめ 嫁】
ⓐ **BRIDE, (young) wife**
ⓑ **daughter-in-law**
a 嫁入る よめいる marry a man, wed
花嫁 はなよめ bride
兄嫁 あによめ sister-in-law, older brother's wife
b 嫁いびり よめいびり bullying a young wife
【とつぐ 嫁ぐ】 **WED [marry] A MAN, get married**
嫁ぎ先 とつぎさき family a woman has married into

SYNONYMS

❶ **marrying and marriage**
嫁 WED A MAN → 0780
婚 MARRY → 0566
姻 MARRIAGE → 0421
縁 marriage relation → 1754
❷ **wives**
妻 WIFE → 3166
奥 wife → 3503
内 wife → 4277
室 wife (esp. of persons of rank) → 2802
嫡 legitimate wife → 0839
婦 married woman → 0565
嫁 BRIDE → 0780
寡 widow → 2957
【よめ】
ⓑ **in-laws**
婿 SON-IN-LAW → 0689
嫁 daughter-in-law → 0780
姑 MOTHER-IN-LAW → 0332

NOTE

➡ see COMPOUND FORMATION for 惣嫁 そうか → 惣 3452

嫌

▶DISLIKE
ケン ゲン きら(う) きら(い) いや
Ⓝ 嫌 Ⓒ 嫌 xián

0781
◧1-3-10

38	Jōyō	U5ACC
女	S13-3-10	F0743

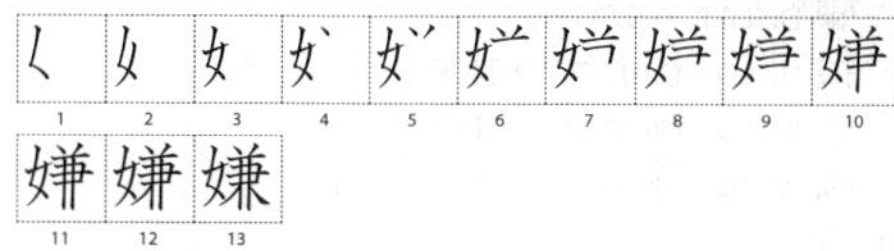

COMPOUNDS

❶ **DISLIKE, hate, detest**
嫌悪 けんお hatred, dislike, repugnance
嫌忌 けんき dislike, aversion
機嫌 きげん [sometimes also 譏嫌] mood, temper, disposition; health
❷ suspect
嫌疑 けんぎ suspicion

KUN

【きらう 嫌う】 **DISLIKE, have an aversion to**
交際を嫌う こうさいをきらう shun society
所嫌わず ところきらわず no matter where, indiscriminately
夫に嫌われる おっとにきらわれる lose one's husband's love
【きらい 嫌い】
①ⓐ **DISLIKE, aversion, antipathy**
ⓑ [suffix] **have a DISLIKE for; person having a dislike for something**
a 嫌いな きらいな distasteful, disagreeable, repugnant
嫌いだ きらいだ dislike, do not like
毛嫌い けぎらい prejudiced aversion
好き嫌い すききらい likes and dislikes, taste
雨が嫌い あめがきらい dislike rain
b 食わず嫌い くわずぎらい prejudice against (some food); aversion without even trying
人間嫌い にんげんぎらい misanthropist, man-hater; misanthropy, dislike for mankind
② undesirable tendency, tinge of (something to be criticized)

口 土 【女】 山 巾 彳 忄 扌 止 氵 犭 阝 阝

行き過ぎの嫌いが有る ゆきすぎのきらいがある
tend to go too far

【いや 嫌】

いやな 嫌な [formerly also 厭な] **disagreeable, repulsive**

嫌がる いやがる dislike, hate

嫌な気持 いやなきもち unpleasant feeling

嫌気が差す いやけがさす feel dislike for

嫌嫌(=厭厭) いやいや grudgingly, unwillingly; (of children) shaking of the head in refusal

SYNONYMS

❶ hate and dislike

憎 HATE → 0845

悪 hate → 3413

忌む ABHOR → 2735

嫌 DISLIKE → 0781

恨 HOLD A GRUDGE → 0439

怨 HOLD A GRUDGE → 3179

厭 disagreeable → 3745

USAGE

❶【いや】

嫌な

[formerly also 厭な] disagreeable, repulsive

厭な

[now usu. 嫌な] disagreeable, repulsive

否

ⓐ no

ⓑ being unwilling, wanting to say no

❷【いやいや】

嫌嫌

[also 厭厭]

ⓐ grudgingly, unwillingly

ⓑ (of children) shaking of the head in refusal

厭厭

[also 嫌嫌] same as 嫌嫌

否否

definitely [absolutely] not

HOMOPHONES

いや

厭 TIRE OF → 3745

否 SAY NO → 3058

NOTE

➡ see COMPOUND FORMATION for 機嫌 きげん → 機 1365

媾

▸MAKE PEACE

コウ

Ⓒ 媾 gòu

0782

1-3-10

38	Non-Jōyō	U5ABE
女	S13-3-10	F0000

COMPOUNDS

❶ [now replaced by 講 2046] **MAKE PEACE, come to terms**

媾和 こうわ peace, reconciliation

❷ [original meaning, now rare] have sexual intercourse

交媾 こうこう sexual union

媾合(=交合) こうごう sexual intercourse

SYNONYMS

❶ compromise

妥 COME TO TERMS → 3053

譲 concede → 2080

媾 MAKE PEACE → 0782

嫉

▸BE JEALOUS

シツ そね(む)▲ ねた(む)▲ ねた(ましい)▲

Ⓒ 嫉 jí

0783

1-3-10

38	Jōyō	U5AC9
女	S13-3-10	F2058

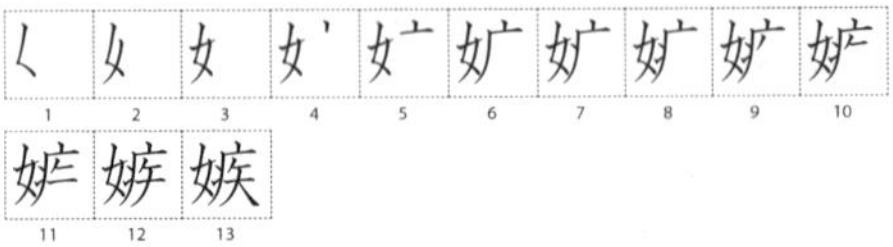

COMPOUNDS

ⓐ BE JEALOUS, be envious

ⓑ jealousy, envy

a 嫉視する しっしする regard with jealousy

b 嫉妬 しっと jealousy

KUN

【そねむ 嫉む】 [also 妬む] **BE JEALOUS**, be envious

【ねたむ 嫉む】 [also 妬む] **BE JEALOUS**, be envious

【ねたましい 嫉ましい】 [also 妬ましい]

ⓐ enviable

ⓑ jealous, envious

SYNONYMS

● jealous and envious

嫉 JEALOUS → 0783

妬 JEALOUS → 0337

羨 ENVIOUS → 2951

USAGE

【そねむ】

嫉む

[also 妬む] be jealous, be envious

妬む

[also 嫉む] be jealous, be envious

HOMOPHONES

ねたむ 妬 BE JEALOUS → 0337

ねたましい 妬 BE JEALOUS → 0337

そねむ 妬 BE JEALOUS → 0337

NOTE

➡ see also USAGE note at 妬 0337

嫌

0784

◧ 1-3-10

▶**DISLIKE**

ケン ゲン きら(う) きら(い) いや

38	Nonstandard	U5ACC
女	S13-3-10	F0000

traditional form → see 嫌 at 0781

媾

0785

◧ 1-3-10

▶**MAKE PEACE**

コウ

38	Nonstandard	U5ABE
女	S13-3-10	F0000

traditional form → see 媾 at 0782

嵯

0786

◧ 1-3-10

▶**RUGGED**

サ ザ シ

Ⓝ 嵯 Ⓒ 嵯 cuó

46	Names	U5D6F
山	S13-3-10	F2506

COMPOUNDS

● [rare] (of mountains) **RUGGED**, uneven; steep

嵯峨たる さがたる (of mountains) steep and high

SYNONYMS

● **bowed**

凹 CONCAVE → 4294

凸 CONVEX → 4298

嵯 RUGGED → 0786

幌

0787

◧ 1-3-10

▶**COVERING FOR VEHICLES**

コウ ほろ ㊔ あきら

Ⓒ 幌 huǎng

50	Names	U5E4C
巾	S13-3-10	F1836

KUN

【ほろ 幌】

① **COVERING FOR VEHICLES**: **canopy, hood, top**

幌馬車 ほろばしゃ covered wagon, prairie schooner

②ⓐ cloth used for tent-shaped mosquito nets

ⓑ *hist* cloth covering one's back to protect against arrows during battle

a 幌蚊帳 ほろがや tent-shaped mosquito net

③ used phonetically for *horo* or *poro*

札幌 さっぽろ Sapporo

SYNONYMS

【ほろ】

① **protective coverings**

盾 SHIELD → 3729

楯 SHIELD → 1281

鎧 ARMOR → 2211

甲 armor → 4293

縅 BRAID OF ARMOR → 1759

面 mask → 2590

兜 helmet → 3499

幌 COVERING FOR VEHICLES → 0787

微

0788

◧ 1-3-10

▶**SLIGHT**

ビ かす(か)▲

Ⓝ 微 Ⓒ 微 wēi

60	Jōyō	U5FAE
彳	S13-3-10	F0866

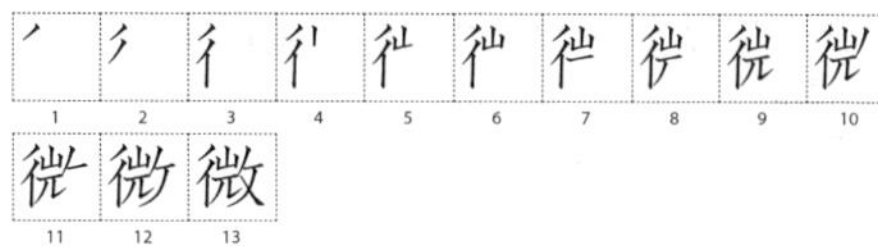

COMPOUNDS

❶ [also prefix]

ⓐ (of very small size) **SLIGHT, minute, small, tiny, microscopic, fine**

ⓑ (of very small quantity) **SLIGHT, very little**

a 微細な びさいな minute, fine; detailed, minute; delicate, subtle

微生物 びせいぶつ microorganism

微粒子 びりゅうし (minute) particle, corpuscle

微調整 びちょうせい minute adjustment; fine tuning

顕微鏡 けんびきょう microscope

b 微微たる びびたる slight, small, insignificant

微量 びりょう slight amount, extremely small quantity

微少 びしょう minute quantity

❷ⓐ (of low intensity) **SLIGHT, weak, faint**

ⓑ lose vigor, become weak

a 微笑 びしょう smile

微震 びしん slight earthquake

微温 びおん lukewarmness, tepidity

微光 びこう faint light

微弱な びじゃくな feeble, weak; faint, slight

微妙な びみょうな subtle, delicate

b 衰微 すいび decline, decay

❸ⓐ (of little importance or influence) **SLIGHT**, insignificant, beneath notice, mean, humble

ⓑ [humble] my humble, my poor

a 微賤 びせん low rank, humble station

軽微な けいびな slight, little, insignificant

b 微力 びりょく one's poor ability, the little one can do

微意 びい small token (of gratitude), my (humble) feelings

❹ unnoticed, concealed

微行 びこう traveling incognito

機微 きび niceties, delicate signs, inner workings

❺ [rare] 1/1,000,000

二微 にび 2/1,000,000

INDEPENDENT

【び 微】 minuteness; insignificance; [rare] 1/1,000,000

微に入り細を穿つ びにいりさいをうがつ go into the minutest details

KUN

【かすか 微か】

かすかな 微かな **faint, weak; dim, vague; scanty, SLIGHT**

微かな笑み かすかなえみ faint smile

微かに見える かすかにみえる be seen dimly

SYNONYMS

❶ⓐ small and tiny

小 SMALL → 0007
豆- miniature → 2442
微 SLIGHT → 0788
細 MINUTE → 1689
寸 A BIT OF → 3652

ⓑ few

少 LITTLE → 4278
寡 FEW → 2957
乏 SCANTY → 2432
薄 meager → 3004
微 SLIGHT → 0788
寸 A BIT OF → 3652
僅 A LITTLE → 0176
些 A BIT → 3251

❷ⓐ less in degree

弱 WEAK → 1499
軽 LIGHT → 1909
微 SLIGHT → 0788
低 LOW → 0082
薄 THIN → 3004
浅 SHALLOW → 0464
仄 FAINT → 3664

❸ⓐ unimportant

細 MINUTE → 1689
微 SLIGHT → 0788
小 SMALL → 0007
末 last in importance → 4317

NOTE

★ do not confuse with 徴 LEVY → 0841

微

0789

1-3-10

▶SLIGHT

ビ かす(か)

60	Nonstandard	U5FAE
彳	S13-3-10	F0000

traditional form → see 微 at 0788

慨

0790

1-3-10

▶DEPLORE

ガイ

Ⓝ 慨 慨 Ⓒ 慨 kǎi

61	Jōyō	U6168
忄	S13-3-10	F2174

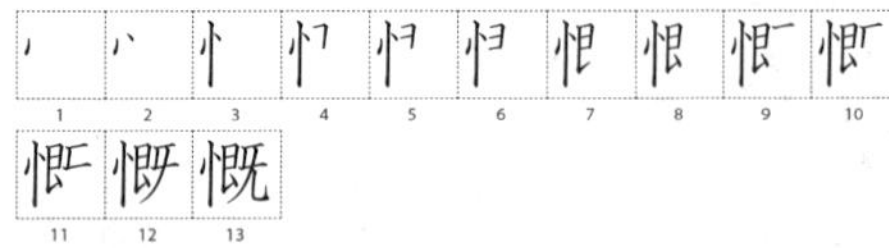

COMPOUNDS

ⓐ DEPLORE, lament, regret, grieve

ⓑ resent, be indignant, be angry

a 慨歎する がいたんする deplore, lament, regret
慨然と がいぜんと deploringly; indignantly
慨世 がいせい concern for the public welfare
感慨 かんがい deep [profound] emotion
ab 慷×慨 こうがい patriotic lamentation, deploration; righteous indignation
b 憤慨 ふんがい resentment, indignation

INDEPENDENT

【がいする 慨する】 DEPLORE, lament

SYNONYMS

ⓐ grieve

慨 DEPLORE → 0790
嘆 SIGH → 0773
悼 MOURN → 0587
傷 grieve → 0179
悲 feel sad → 3448
悄 BECOME DISPIRITED → 0506

ⓑ anger

怒 GET ANGRY → 3180
憤 INDIGNATION → 0897
慨 resent → 0790

NOTE

★ do not confuse with 概 GENERAL → 1322

慄

0791

1-3-10

▶TREMBLE WITH FEAR

リツ

Ⓒ 栗 lì

61	Jōyō	U6144
忄	S13-3-10	F2364

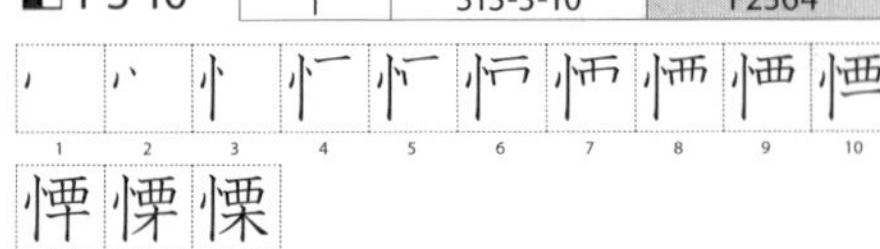

COMPOUNDS

● [rarely also 栗 3280] [original meaning] **TREMBLE WITH FEAR, shudder**

慄然として りつぜんとして with horror

戦慄する せんりつする shudder, shiver

SYNONYMS

● **fear**

怖 FEARFUL → 0353
凄 UNCANNY → 0145
恐 FEAR → 3283
惧 FEAR → 0581
慄 TREMBLE WITH FEAR → 0791
兢 BE IN FEAR → 1971
惶 BE AFRAID → 0708
畏 BE OVERAWED → 3170
臆 FEEL TIMID → 1397
怯える BE FRIGHTENED → 0355

慎

▶PRUDENT

シン つつし(む) ㊔ ちか

Ⓝ 愼 Ⓒ 慎 shèn

0792

1-3-10

61	Jōyō	U614E
忄	S13-3-10	F1407

1 2 3 4 5 6 7 8 9 10 11 12 13

COMPOUNDS

● **PRUDENT, discreet, careful**

慎重 しんちょう prudence, discretion, circumspection
謹慎 きんしん house arrest, domiciliary confinement; penitence
戒慎する かいしんする be cautious, be discreet

KUN

【つつしむ 慎む】

ⓐ **be PRUDENT, be discreet, be careful**
ⓑ restrain oneself, abstain from, be moderate

a 慎み つつしみ prudence, modesty, self-control
慎み深い つつしみぶかい discreet, prudent, modest
b 口を慎む くちをつつしむ be careful in speech
酒を慎む さけをつつしむ abstain from drinking

SYNONYMS

● **careful**

慎 PRUDENT → 0792
謹 carefully → 2045
精 meticulous → 1729

USAGE

【つつしむ】

慎む
ⓐ be prudent, be discreet, be careful
ⓑ restrain oneself, abstain from, be moderate

謹む
[usu. in TE-form] be respectful, be humble

HOMOPHONES

つつしむ 謹 RESPECTFULLY → 2045

愼

▶PRUDENT

シン つつし(む) ㊔ ちか

0793

1-3-10

61	Names	U613C
忄	S13-3-10	F0000

traditional form → see 慎 at 0792

慌

1-3-10

incorrect stroke-count
➡ see 1-3-9: 忄 at 0711

搏

▶BEAT

ハク

Ⓒ 搏 bó

0794

1-3-10

64	Non-Jōyō	U640F
扌	S13-3-10	F0000

COMPOUNDS

● [now also 拍 0361] [original meaning] **BEAT, clap, throb**

搏動 はくどう pulsation, pulsebeat
脈搏 みゃくはく pulse, pulsation

SPECIAL READINGS

羽搏く(=羽撃く) はばたく flap the wings, flutter

SYNONYMS

● **strike**

打 STRIKE → 0224
撲 DEAL A BLOW → 0903
殴 BEAT (strike a person) → 1099
蹴 KICK → 2074
撃 STRIKE → 3552
挌 STRIKE (a person) → 0448
撞 STRIKE (a ball or bell) → 0905
撥ねる strike (knock down) → 0907
当てる HIT → 2701
叩 KNOCK → 0208
拍 BEAT (strike repeatedly) → 0361
搏 BEAT (throb) → 0794

搬

▶CARRY

ハン

Ⓒ 搬 bān

0795

1-3-10

64	Jōyō	U642C
扌	S13-3-10	F2291

1 2 3 4 5 6 7 8 9 10 11 12 13

口 土 女 山 巾 彳 忄 【扌】 止 氵 犭 阝 纟

COMPOUNDS

● [original meaning] **CARRY, transport, convey**

搬送 はんそう conveyance
搬出する はんしゅつする carry out
搬入する はんにゅうする carry in
搬送波 はんそうは carrier wave
可搬式 かはんしき portable
運搬する うんぱんする carry, transport, convey, deliver

SYNONYMS

● **carry**

運 CARRY → 3894
搬 CARRY → 0795
輸 TRANSPORT → 2026

携

0796

1-3-10

▶**CARRY IN HAND**

ケイ たずさ(える) たずさ(わる)

Ⓝ 攜 擕 Ⓒ 携 xié

64	Jōyō	U643A
扌	S13-3-10	F0997

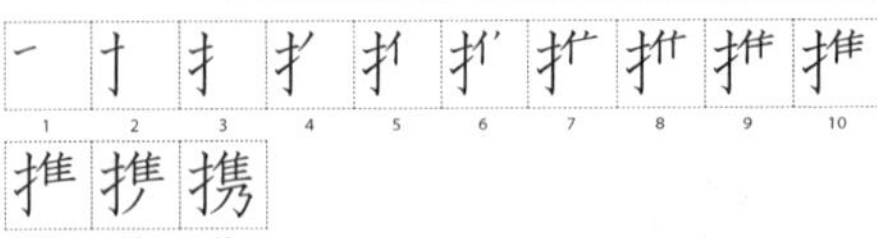

COMPOUNDS

❶ **CARRY IN HAND, carry (along) on one's person**

携帯する けいたいする carry, bring with one, equip oneself with
携行する けいこうする carry along, bring
携帯カメラ けいたいかめら hand camera
必携 ひっけい indispensableness; handbook, manual

❷ **join hands, work together, act in concert**

提携する ていけいする cooperate with, act in concert with, tie up with
連携 れんけい cooperation, league, concert

KUN

【たずさえる 携える】**CARRY IN one's HAND; take a thing [person] with one**

杖を携える つえをたずさえる carry a stick in one's hand
手を携えて てをたずさえて hand in hand
妻子を携える さいしをたずさえる be accompanied by one's family

【たずさわる 携わる】**participate in; concern oneself in**

教育に携わる人人 きょういくにたずさわるひとびと those who participate in education

SYNONYMS

❶ **hold**

持 HOLD → 0447
提 carry in hand → 0720
携 CARRY IN HAND → 0796
捧 hold up in both hands → 0594

❷ **cooperate**

協 COOPERATE → 0103
携 join hands → 0796
調 harmonize → 1973

摸

0797

1-3-10

▶**PATTERN AFTER**

モ モウ

Ⓒ 摸 mō mó

64	Non-Jōyō	U6478
扌	S13-3-10	F3166

COMPOUNDS

❶ [now replaced by 模 も 1326] **PATTERN AFTER, imitate, copy, model upon**

摸写する もしゃする copy, trace, reproduce
摸倣する もほうする imitate, copy
摸造 もぞう imitation, counterfeit
摸擬試験 もぎしけん sham [trial] examination

❷ [now usu. 模 も 1326] [original meaning] **grope, feel about [for], search**

摸牌×する もうぱいする identify a piece by touch in a mahjong game
暗中摸索 あんちゅうもさく groping in the dark

INDEPENDENT

【もする 摸する】copy, imitate

SPECIAL READINGS

掏×摸 すり pickpocket

SYNONYMS

❶ **imitate**

擬 IMITATE → 0969
倣 COPY AFTER → 0127
摸 PATTERN AFTER → 0797
模 pattern after → 1326
肖 MODEL → 2733
象 represent → 2647

搾

0798

1-3-10

▶**SQUEEZE**

サク しぼ(る)

Ⓒ 榨 zhà

64	Jōyō	U643E
扌	S13-3-10	F2498

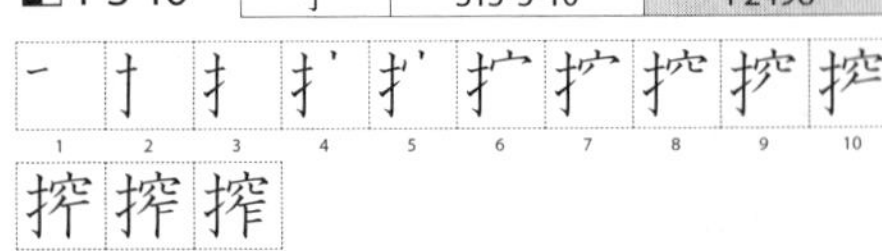

COMPOUNDS

ⓐ [original meaning] **SQUEEZE, extract, press**

ⓑ (obtain by force) **SQUEEZE, extort, exploit**

a 搾乳 さくにゅう milking
搾油 さくゆ oil expression [extraction]
圧搾する あっさくする press, compress
b 搾取する さくしゅする exploit, sweat, squeeze (money out of a person)

KUN

【しぼる 搾る】
①ⓐ **SQUEEZE, press, squash, extract**
ⓑ **SQUEEZE** (money from), sweat, screw
a 搾り しぼり squeezing
搾り滓× しぼりかす strained lees [draff]
搾り立てのオレンジジュース しぼりたてのおれんじじゅーす fresh orange juice
ab 搾り取る しぼりとる squeeze, extract; squeeze (money from), sweat
② scold, reprimand
油を搾る あぶらをしぼる press oil; give a sound scolding

SYNONYMS

ⓐ **squeeze**
搾 SQUEEZE → 0798
絞る WRING → 1707
圧 apply pressure → 3688

HOMOPHONES

しぼる 絞 STRANGLE → 1707
しぼり 絞 STRANGLE → 1707

NOTE

➡ see USAGE note at 絞 1707

摂

0799
◧ 1-3-10

▶**TAKE IN**
▶**ACT AS REGENT**
セツ ㊔ おさむ
Ⓝ 攝 Ⓒ 摄 shè

64	Jōyō	U6442
扌	S13-3-10	F1596

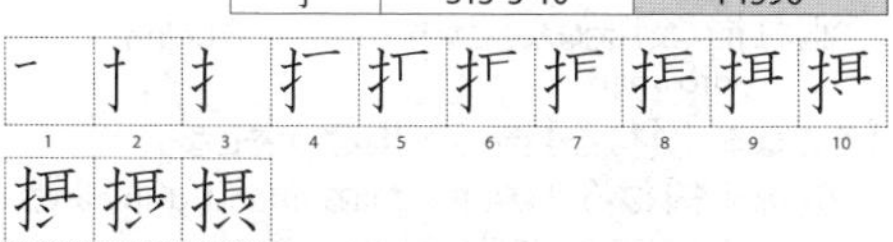

COMPOUNDS

❶ **TAKE IN, ingest, absorb, assimilate**
摂取する せっしゅする take (in), ingest, absorb
摂動 せつどう (gravitational) perturbation
包摂する ほうせつする connote, subsume
カロリーの摂取量 かろりーのせっしゅりょう caloric intake
❷ **ACT AS REGENT, represent, act as deputy; carry on in addition to**
摂政 せっしょう regency; regent
摂関家 せっかんけ line of regents
兼摂する けんせつする hold an additional post
❸ conserve one's health
摂生 せっせい preservation of one's health
❹ regulate
摂理 せつり providence
❺ **centigrade**
摂氏(=セ氏) せっし(=せし) centigrade

INDEPENDENT

【せっする 摂する】**ACT AS REGENT**; carry on in addition to

SYNONYMS

❶ **take in**
収 TAKE IN → 0031
摂 TAKE IN → 0799
喫 INGEST → 0668
吸 SUCK → 0234
❷ **substitute**
代 SUBSTITUTE → 0034
摂 ACT AS REGENT → 0799

掻

0800
◧ 1-3-10

▶**SCRATCH**
ソウ か(く) かき- かい-
Ⓝ 搔 Ⓒ 搔 sāo

64	Non-Jōyō	U6414
扌	S13-3-10	F1759

COMPOUNDS

● **SCRATCH, scrape**
掻爬× そうは curettage
掻器 そうき scraper
隔靴掻痒× かっかそうよう having an itch that one cannot scratch

KUN

【かく 掻く】
①ⓐ **SCRATCH, scrape**
ⓑ **shovel, rake**
ⓒ **paddle, stroke**
a 掻き毟×る かきむしる scratch, tear (at), rend
掻き傷 かききず scratch, abrasion
引っ掻く ひっかく scratch
足掻く あがく flounder, struggle; paw at the ground
b 掻き出す かきだす scrape out, rake out
掻き分ける かきわける push one's way through; shove aside
雪掻き ゆきかき snow shoveling; snow shovel, snowplow
耳掻き みみかき earpick
c 犬掻き いぬかき dog paddle
水掻き みずかき web (on feet); paddle
② thrum, strum, pluck
掻き鳴らす かきならす thrum, strum
③ shave (ice)

掻き氷 かきごおり shaved ice
笹掻きにする ささがきにする cut into long thin shavings

④ cut off (a person's head)
掻き切る かききる cut, slit
寝首を掻く ねくびをかく behead [kill] a sleeping person; take (someone) by surprise

⑤ expose an undesirable state, as in: sweat, cry, snore, experience (embarrassment)
汗を掻く あせをかく sweat, perspire
泣きべそを掻く なきべそをかく be close to tears, whimper
鼾×を掻く いびきをかく snore
恥を掻く はじをかく make a fool of oneself, be humiliated

⑥ unclassified compounds
藻掻く もがく struggle, make frantic efforts; writhe, wriggle, squirm
湯掻く ゆがく parboil, scald, blanch
裏を掻く うらをかく counterplot, outwit, defeat

【かき- 掻き-】 [sometimes 掻っ- かっ-] **emphatic verbal prefix**
掻き乱す かきみだす throw into disorder
掻っ払い かっぱらい pilferer; pilfering
掻き回す かきまわす stir (up); ransack, throw into confusion
掻き混ぜる(=掻き交ぜる) かきまぜる mix by stirring, mix up, scramble, toss, churn
掻き集める かきあつめる gather up, scrape up together
掻き消す かきけす wipe out, erase completely
掻っ穿じる かっぽじる dig up, peck at

【かい- 掻い-】 **emphatic verbal prefix**
掻い摘む かいつまむ sum up, summarize
掻い潜る かいくぐる slip through
掻い繰る かいぐる haul in hand over hand

損

▸LOSS
ソン そこ(なう) -そこ(なう) そこ(ねる) -そこ(ねる)
Ⓒ 损 sǔn

0801
1-3-10

64	Jōyō-5	U640D
扌	S13-3-10	F1224

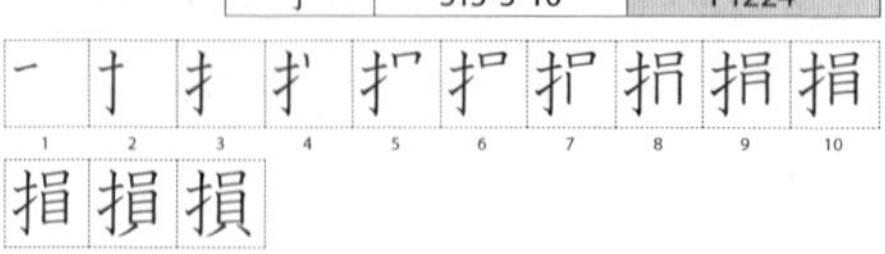

COMPOUNDS

❶ⓐ LOSS
ⓑ *elec* **LOSS**
ⓒ lose, suffer LOSS

a 損失 そんしつ loss
損益 そんえき profit and loss; advantage and disadvantage
損率 そんりつ loss factor
全損 ぜんそん total loss
駒損 こまそん(=こまぞん) loss of material (in shogi)

b 損流 そんりゅう loss current

c 欠損 けっそん deficit, deficiency; loss

❷ disadvantage
損得 そんとく advantage and disadvantage; loss and gain
骨折り損 ほねおりぞん waste of labor, vain efforts

❸ damage, harm
損害 そんがい damage, harm
損傷 そんしょう damage, injury
破損 はそん damage, breakdown
毀損(=棄損) きそん damage, injury, waste

❹ [original meaning] **decrease**
損耗 そんもう(=そんこう) wear, waste, loss

INDEPENDENT

【そん 損】 **LOSS; damage; disadvantage**
損になる そんになる do not pay
損な条件 そんなじょうけん unfavorable conditions

【そんする 損する】 **lose, suffer LOSS**

【そんじる(=そんずる) 損じる(=損ずる)】 lose; damage; [verbal suffix] fail to (do), fail in (doing)
読み損じる よみそんじる fail to read correctly

KUN

【そこなう 損なう】 **harm, hurt, injure, damage**
健康を損なう けんこうをそこなう lose one's health

【-そこなう -損なう】 [verbal suffix]

① **fail to (do), fail in (doing)**
見損なう みそこなう fail to see; make a mistake, misjudge

② come near (doing), make a narrow escape
溺れ損なう おぼれそこなう come near being drowned

【そこねる 損ねる】 same as 損なう そこなう
機嫌を損ねる きげんをそこねる offend, displease, hurt (a person's) feelings

【-そこねる -損ねる】 same as -損なう -そこなう

SYNONYMS

❶ losing and loss
失 LOSE →4325
喪 lose →3504
逸 LET SLIP →3872
損 LOSS, lose →0801
佚 LOST →0070

❸ harm and damage
害 HARM, damage →2826
損 damage →0801
傷 WOUND →0179

【-そこなう】
① **fail**
敗 fail →1868
落 fall through →2907
-損なう fail to (do) →0801

捜
0802
1-3-10

▶**LOOK FOR**
ソウ さが(す)

64	Nonstandard	U635C
扌	S13-3-10	F0000

alternative form →see 捜 at 0516

搖
0803
1-3-10

▶**SHAKE**
ヨウ ゆ(れる) ゆ(る) ゆ(らぐ) ゆ(るぐ) ゆ(する) ゆ(さぶる) ゆ(すぶる)

64	Names	U6416
扌	S13-3-10	F0000

traditional form →see 揺 at 0723

雌
1-3-10

incorrect stroke-count
➡ see 1-4-10: 止 at 1337

漠
0804
1-3-10

▶**DESERT**
▶**OBSCURE**
バク ㊔ ひろし
Ⓒ 漠 mò

85	Jōyō	U6F20
氵	S13-3-10	F1782

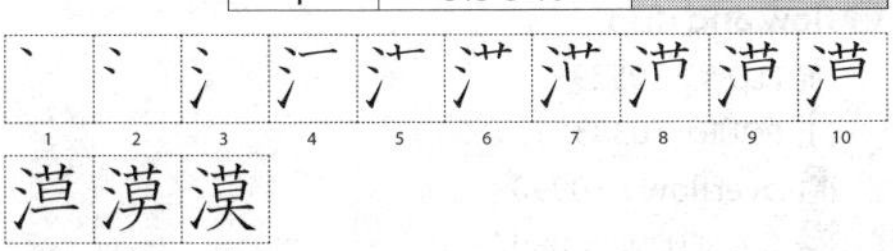

COMPOUNDS
❶ **DESERT**
漠北 ばくほく north of the Gobi Desert, Outer Mongolia
砂漠 さばく desert
❷ as vast or boundless as the **DESERT**
茫×漠たる ぼうばくたる vast, boundless; obscure, vague
広漠たる こうばくたる vast, wide, boundless
❸ **OBSCURE, vague**
漠然たる ばくぜんたる obscure, vague, hazy
空漠たる考え くうばくたるかんがえ vague [loose] ideas; idle thoughts
❹ lonesome, dreary
索漠たる さくばくたる dreary, bleak, desolate

INDEPENDENT
【ばくとした 漠とした】 *literary* **OBSCURE**; vast

SYNONYMS
❶ **uncultivated expanses of land**
野 FIELD →1877
原 PLAIN →3733
漠 DESERT →0804

溺
0805
1-3-10

▶**DROWN**
デキ ニョウ▲ ジョウ▲ おぼ(れる)
Ⓝ 溺 Ⓒ 溺 nì

85	Jōyō	U6EBA
氵	S13-3-10	F2220

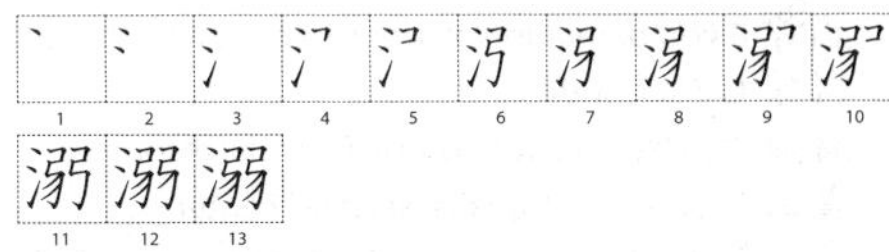

COMPOUNDS
ⓐ [original meaning] **DROWN**
ⓑ **indulge in, give oneself up [over] to, become addicted to**
a 溺死 できし death by drowning
溺水 できすい drowning
b 溺愛 できあい doting
耽溺 たんでき indulgence

KUN
【おぼれる 溺れる】
ⓐ **DROWN**
ⓑ **indulge in, give oneself up [over] to, become addicted to**
a 溺れ死ぬ おぼれじぬ die by drowning
溺れ損なう おぼれそこなう come near being drowned
溺れる者は藁をも摑む おぼれるものはわらをもつかむ A drowning man will catch at a straw
b 酒に溺れる さけにおぼれる become addicted to drinking

SYNONYMS
ⓐ **sink**
没 SINK →0305
沈 SINK →0306
潜 SUBMERGE →0922
溺 DROWN →0805

源
0806
1-3-10

▶**SOURCE**
ゲン みなもと ㊔ もと はじめ みなと
Ⓒ 源 yuán

85	Jōyō-6	U6E90
氵	S13-3-10	F0498

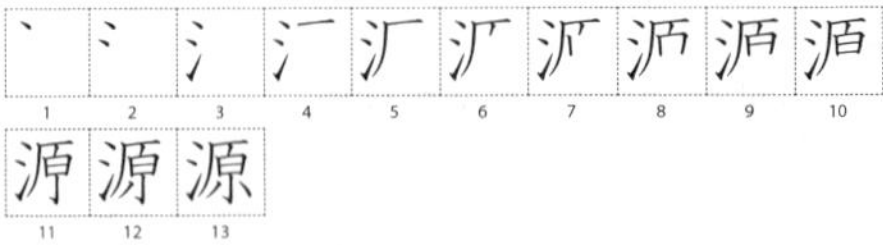

COMPOUNDS

❶ⓐ [also suffix] **SOURCE, origin, beginning, root**
ⓑ [original meaning] (place where water originates) SOURCE (of a river), fountainhead

a 源泉 げんせん fountainhead, source
根源 こんげん root, origin, source
起源 きげん origin, beginning
語源 ごげん derivation of a word, etymology
資源 しげん resources
財源 ざいげん revenue source, financial resources
震源 しんげん earthquake [seismic] center
栄養源 えいようげん source of nutrients
b 源流 げんりゅう source (of a stream)
水源 すいげん source [head] (of a stream), fountainhead

❷ abbrev. of 源氏 げんじ: the Genji Family, the Minamotos
源平 げんぺい Genji and Heike clans; two opposing sides

KUN

【みなもと 源】**SOURCE, fountainhead, origin**
河の源 かわのみなもと fountainhead
その源は明らかではない そのみなもとはあきらかではない It is of obscure origin

SYNONYMS

❶ⓐ beginnings
緒 OUTSET →1742
序 INTRODUCTORY PART →3803
端 start →1564
始 beginning →0335
初 beginning →1433
元 ORIGIN →2428
本 origin →4314
根 ROOT →1167
源 SOURCE →0806

ⓑ water sources
源 SOURCE →0806
泉 SPRING →3176
井 WELL →4265

溢

▸OVERFLOW
イツ あふ(れる) こぼ(す) こぼ(れる)
㊔ みつ みつる みつし
Ⓝ 溢 Ⓒ 溢 yì

0807
1-3-10

85	Names	U6EA2
氵	S13-3-10	F1806

COMPOUNDS

● OVERFLOW, inundate, spill
溢流する いつりゅうする overflow, spill
横溢する おういつする be filled with (vitality), overflow with
脳溢血 のういっけつ intracranial hemorrhage
充溢する じゅういつする overflow with, brim with

KUN

【あふれる 溢れる】**OVERFLOW, brim over, flood**
溢れかえる あふれかえる be awash with, teem with, be full of
溢れんばかり あふれんばかり overflowing, effusive, exuberant, bountiful
溢れ出す あふれだす begin to overflow, pour out
才能溢れる さいのうあふれる extremely talented, very gifted

【こぼす 溢す】
①ⓐ spill
ⓑ shed (tears)
a 目溢し めこぼし connivance, overlook
② grumble

【こぼれる 溢れる】
①ⓐ spill, fall out
ⓑ **OVERFLOW**
b 咲き溢れる さきこぼれる bloom all over
②ⓐ leak out (as of light)
ⓑ show (as of a smile)

SYNONYMS

● flow and drip
流 FLOW →0529
注 POUR →0383
濫 overflow →0990
溢 OVERFLOW →0807
漏 LEAK →0860
滴 DROP →0866
泌 SECRETE →0390
瀝 DRIP →0996

HOMOPHONES

こぼす 零 ZERO →3467
こぼれる 零 ZERO →3467

NOTE

➡ see USAGE note at 零 3467

漢

▸CHINESE
▸FELLOW
カン
Ⓝ 漢 Ⓒ 汉 hàn

0808
1-3-10

85	Jōyō-3	U6F22
氵	S13-3-10	F1063

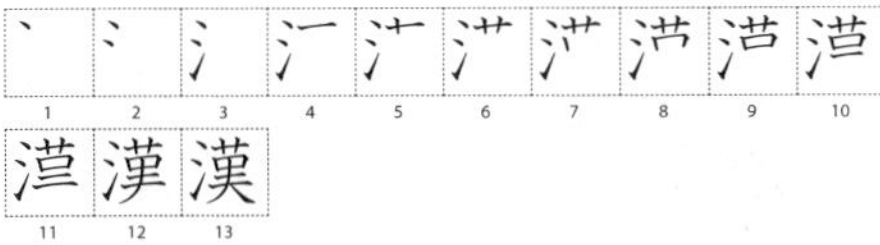

COMPOUNDS

❶ⓐ (of ancient China or its people) **CHINESE; old name for China, ancient China**
ⓑ Han Dynasty (206 B.C.-220 A.D.)

a 漢土 かんど China
漢方薬 かんぽうやく Chinese (herbal) medicine
漢民族 かんみんぞく Chinese people, Han race
b 漢朝 かんちょう Han Dynasty
前漢 ぜんかん Former Han

❷ⓐ CHINESE (language), classical Chinese
ⓑ kanji, CHINESE character, logograph

a 漢語 かんご Chinese-derived word, Chinese expression
漢文 かんぶん Chinese classics, Chinese writing
漢字 かんじ Chinese characters, kanji
漢詩 かんし classical Chinese poetry [poem]
b 漢和辞典 かんわじてん Chinese-Japanese character dictionary
漢英辞典(=漢英字典) かんえいじてん Japanese-English character dictionary, kanji dictionary
漢プリ かんぷり kanji printer
単漢選択キー たんかんせんたくきー single character selector button (in kanji word processors)

❸ [also suffix] **FELLOW, man**

好漢 こうかん nice fellow
痴漢 ちかん molester of women, masher
熱血漢 ねっけつかん hot-blooded man
大食漢 たいしょくかん great eater, glutton

❹ⓐ [original meaning] name of tributary of the Yangtze River: **Han River**
ⓑ Milky Way

a 漢水 かんすい Han River
b 銀漢 ぎんかん Milky Way

INDEPENDENT

【かん 漢】Han Dynasty

SYNONYMS

❶ⓐ China

華 CHINA → 2841
漢 CHINESE → 0808
支 China → 2473
中 People's Republic of China → 4262
胡 NATIVES OF ANCIENT CHINA → 1467
台 Taiwan → 2498
唐 Cathay → 3867
呉 KINGDOM OF WU → 3156

ⓑ earlier Chinese dynasties

夏 Xia Dynasty → 2619
商 Shang Dynasty → 2623
周 Zhou Dynasty → 3720
漢 Han Dynasty → 0808
晋 JIN DYNASTY → 3290
秦 QIN DYNASTY → 3192

❷ⓐ Chinese

漢 CHINESE (language) → 0808
中 Modern Chinese → 4262

ⓑ characters

字 CHARACTER → 2696
文 LETTER → 2458
漢 kanji → 0808
旁 RIGHT RADICAL → 2598

❸ fellow

奴 GUY → 0217
漢 FELLOW → 0808
輩 FELLOW (*belittling*) → 3482
徒 fellows → 0499
棒 tough guy → 1237
坊 COLLOQUIAL PERSON SUFFIX → 0274
屋 colloquial person suffix → 3842
物 character → 1084

滑

0809

◧ 1-3-10

▸SLIDE
▸SMOOTH

カツ コツ すべ(る) なめ(らか) ㊔ なめり

Ⓒ 滑 huá

85	Jōyō	U6ED1
氵	S13-3-10	F1294

COMPOUNDS

❶ SLIDE, glide, slip

滑走する かっそうする glide, volplane; slide
滑空機 かっくうき glider, sailplane
滑車 かっしゃ pulley, block, tackle

❷ SMOOTH

滑脱 かつだつ adaptation to circumstances
滑剤 かつざい lubricant
円滑な えんかつな smooth, harmonious
潤滑 じゅんかつ lubrication

❸ speak SMOOTHly and glibly, crack jokes

滑稽な こっけいな funny, jocular, humorous; laughable, ridiculous

KUN

【すべる 滑る】
① **SLIDE, glide, skate**

滑り すべり sliding, slipping
滑り台 すべりだい (playground) slide; launching platform
横滑り よこすべり skid, skidding
② [formerly also 辷る] **slip**
滑り落ちる すべりおちる slip off
口が滑る くちがすべる make a slip of the tongue
③ [formerly also 辷る] **flunk an (entrance) examination**
滑り止め すべりどめ tire chains; creepers; taking the entrance examination to a university as a safety measure in case one fails at other universities

【なめらか 滑らか】
なめらかな 滑らかな **SMOOTH, glassy**
滑らかに なめらかに smoothly

SYNONYMS
❶ **move**
動 MOVE → 2232
運 MOVE → 3894
滑 SLIDE → 0809
辷る SLIP → 3957
移 SHIFT → 1508
転 remove → 1872
遷 TRANSFER → 3932
繰る SHIFT ONWARD → 1806
❷ **smooth**
流 flowing → 0529
暢 FLUENT → 1569
滑 SMOOTH → 0809

USAGE
【すべる】
滑る
① slide, glide, skate
② [formerly also 辷る] slip
③ [formerly also 辷る] flunk an (entrance) examination
辷る
[now usu. 滑る]
① slip
② flunk an (entrance) examination

HOMOPHONES
すべる 辷 SLIP → 3957

溝
▶**CHANNEL**
コウ みぞ
Ⓝ 溝 Ⓒ 沟 gōu

0810
1-3-10

85	Jōyō	U6E9D
氵	S13-3-10	F1842

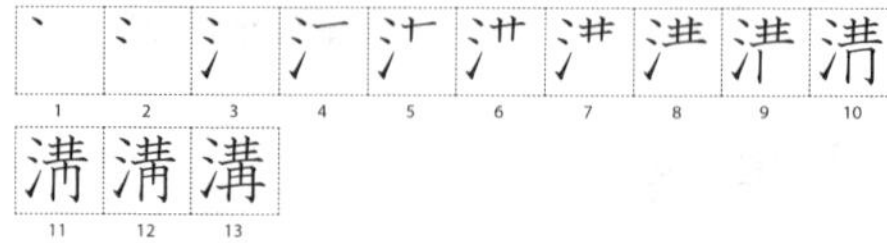

COMPOUNDS
❶ [original meaning] **CHANNEL, ditch, gutter, canal, trench**
溝渠× こうきょ ditch, sewer, canal
側溝 そっこう channel, ditch, gutter
排水溝 はいすいこう waterway, drainage, canal
下水溝 げすいこう ditch
海溝 かいこう sea trench
❷ [archaic] one hundred nonillion (10^{32})

KUN
【みぞ 溝】CHANNEL, ditch, drain, gutter; groove, slot; gap, gulf
溝掘り機 みぞほりき ditching machine
溝形鋼 みぞがたこう channel (type of section steel)
溝レール みぞれーる grooved rail
溝が有る みぞがある be estranged

SYNONYMS
❶ **holes and cavities**
穴 HOLE → 2682
洞 CAVE → 0455
窟 CAVE → 2923
窪 HOLLOW → 2962
腔 BODY CAVITY → 1267
孔 OPEN HOLE → 0205
口 MOUTH → 4189
坑 PIT → 0277
堀 DITCH → 0561
溝 CHANNEL → 0810
壕 TRENCH → 0966
濠 MOAT → 0975
凹 concavity → 4294

滉
▶**DEEP AND VAST**
コウ オウ ㊔ あきら ひろし ひろ ひかる
Ⓒ 滉 huàng

0811
1-3-10

85	Names	U6EC9
氵	S13-3-10	F0000

COMPOUNDS
[archaic]
❶ **DEEP AND VAST** like an expanse of water
滉瀁× こうよう vastness, great depth
❷ turbulence

SYNONYMS
❶ **wide and extensive**
広 WIDE → 3769
紘 WIDE-RANGING → 1650

博 EXTENSIVE → 0170
恢 EXTENSIVE → 0436
浩 VAST → 0525
洸 VAST (expanse of water) → 0462
溟 DEEP AND VAST → 0811
曠 SPACIOUS → 1411
闊 BROAD → 4135

❶ profound

玄 PROFOUND → 2485
幽 deep hidden → 3731
奥 inmost → 3503
深 DEEP → 0636
溟 DEEP AND VAST → 0811

滅

▶DESTROY

メツ ほろ(びる) ほろ(ぶ) ほろ(ぼす)

Ⓒ 灭 miè

0812

1-3-10

85	Jōyō	U6EC5
氵	S13-3-10	F1025

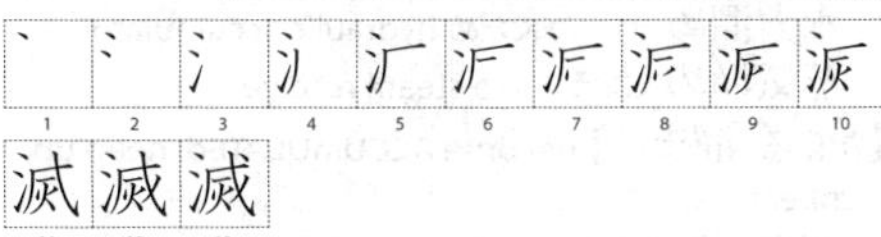

COMPOUNDS

❶ⓐ DESTROY, ruin, annihilate, wipe out
ⓑ meet with destruction, go to ruin, cease to exist

a 滅菌 めっきん sterilization
撃滅する げきめつする destroy, exterminate
絶滅 ぜつめつ extermination, eradication; extinction

b 滅亡 めつぼう ruin, downfall
消滅 しょうめつ extinction, disappearance
不滅 ふめつ immortality, indestructibility, imperishability
全滅 ぜんめつ annihilation, total destruction
潰滅(=壊滅) かいめつ destruction, annihilation
死滅 しめつ extinction, annihilation, destruction
自滅 じめつ natural decay; self-destruction, self-ruin
破滅 はめつ ruin, destruction, wreck, collapse, downfall

❷ go out, be extinguished

点滅する てんめつする (of light) go [come] on and off; turn [switch] on and off
明滅する めいめつする flicker, blink

❸ unreasonable, excessive, reckless, extreme

滅法 めっぽう extraordinarily, unreasonably
滅多な めったな reckless, careless
滅茶苦茶(=目茶苦茶)な めちゃくちゃな confused, incoherent; absurd, unreasonable
滅茶滅茶(=目茶目茶) めちゃめちゃ mess, wreck, ruin, shambles

❹ death of a priest or Buddha, entering Nirvana

滅度 めつど extinguishing illusion and passing over to Nirvana
入滅 にゅうめつ entering Nirvana, death of a saint
仏滅 ぶつめつ Buddha's death; most unlucky day

INDEPENDENT

【めつ 滅】 label on switches: OFF
【めっする 滅する】 be **DESTROY**ed, perish; destroy

KUN

【ほろびる 滅びる】 [sometimes also 亡びる] **go to ruin, meet with destruction, cease to exist; be overthrown**

滅びて行く民族 ほろびていくみんぞく dying race

【ほろぶ 滅ぶ】 [sometimes also 亡ぶ] literary form of 滅びる ほろびる
【ほろぼす 滅ぼす】 [sometimes also 亡ぼす] **DESTROY, ruin, annihilate; overthrow**

敵を滅ぼす てきをほろぼす destroy the enemy

SYNONYMS

❶ destroy

滅 DESTROY → 0812
毀 DESTROY → 2246
亡 perish → 4210
消 EXTINGUISH → 0531
剿 EXTERMINATE → 2335

❷ extinguish

消 EXTINGUISH → 0531
熄 GO OUT → 1339
滅 go out → 0812

❸ rash

滅 unreasonable → 0812
妄 RASH → 2509
盲 BLIND → 2547
暴 unrestrained → 3138
荒 WILD → 2810
濫 EXCESSIVE → 0990
乱 excessive → 1611

USAGE

❶【ほろびる】

滅びる
[sometimes also 亡びる] go to ruin, meet with destruction, cease to exist; be overthrown

亡びる
[usu. 滅びる] same as 滅びる

❷【ほろぶ】

滅ぶ
[sometimes also 亡ぶ] literary form of 滅びる ほろびる

亡ぶ
[usu. 滅ぶ] literary form of 亡びる ほろびる

❸【ほろぼす】

滅ぼす
[sometimes also 亡ぼす] destroy, ruin, annihilate; overthrow

亡ぼす
[usu. 滅ぼす] destroy, ruin, annihilate; overthrow

HOMOPHONES

ほろびる 亡 DECEASE →4210
ほろぶ 亡 DECEASE →4210
ほろぼす 亡 DECEASE →4210

滝

▶WATERFALL
ロウ▲ たき
Ⓝ 瀧 Ⓒ 泷 lóng shuāng

0813
1-3-10

85	Jōyō	U6EDD
氵	S13-3-10	F1669

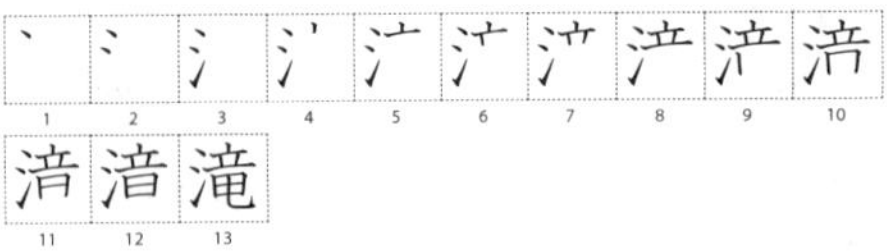

KUN

【たき 滝】**WATERFALL, falls, cascade**
滝壺 たきつぼ pool below a waterfall
滝川 たきがわ rapids
雄滝(=男滝) おだき the greater waterfall (of the two)

SYNONYMS

【たき】
◯ **running water**
流 CURRENT →0529
潮 TIDE →0916
汐 TIDE →0259
瀬 rapids →0995
滝 WATERFALL →0813
洪 FLOOD →0461
渦 WHIRLPOOL →0735

溜

▶ACCUMULATE
リュウ た(める) -ため た(まる)
Ⓝ 溜 Ⓒ 溜 liū liù

0814
1-3-10

85	Names	U6E9C
氵	S13-3-10	F1493

COMPOUNDS

❶ **ACCUMULATE (as of water)**
溜飲 りゅういん water brash, sour stomach
溜飲が下がる りゅういんがさがる be cured of water brash; have one's grudge satisfied
❷ [now usu. 留 りゅう 3189] **distill**
蒸溜 じょうりゅう distillation
分溜 ぶんりゅう fraction, fractional distillation
乾溜 かんりゅう dry distillation

KUN

【ためる 溜める】
①ⓐ **ACCUMULATE, heap up**
ⓑ **collect (stamps)**
ⓒ **store (esp. water)**
a 溜め ため sink, cesspool; manure sink
溜め息 ためいき sigh
b 切手を溜める きってをためる collect stamps
c 溜め池 ためいけ reservoir, irrigation pond, cistern
② **run up (a bill), leave undone**
家賃を溜める やちんをためる let the rent fall into arrears
③ [also 貯める] **save (money), lay up (one's income)**
溜め込む ためこむ save [store] up, hoard
【-ため -溜め】**receptacle [means] for accumulating, accumulator, receiver**
掃き溜め はきだめ garbage dump, trash heap
肥溜め こえだめ night soil vat
水力溜め すいりょくだめ hydraulic accumulator
蒸気溜め じょうきだめ steam receiver
【たまる 溜まる】**become ACCUMULATEd, heap up, collect**
溜まり場 たまりば gathering spot, haunt
吹き溜まり ふきだまり snowdrift, drift of dust [sand]
日溜まり ひだまり sunny spot
水溜まり みずたまり puddle, pool of water
一溜まりも無い ひとたまりもない stand no chance, be helpless

SYNONYMS

❶ **accumulate**
積 ACCUMULATE →1579
溜 ACCUMULATE →0814
累 CUMULATE →3196
重 pile up →4390
盛る heap up →3314
堆 PILED HIGH →0563

HOMOPHONES

ためる 貯 LAY UP →1903

NOTE

➡ see USAGE note at 貯 1903

滞

▶STAGNATE
▶STAY
タイ とどこお(る)
Ⓝ 滯 Ⓒ 滞 zhì

0815
1-3-10

85	Jōyō	U6EDE
氵	S13-3-10	F1429

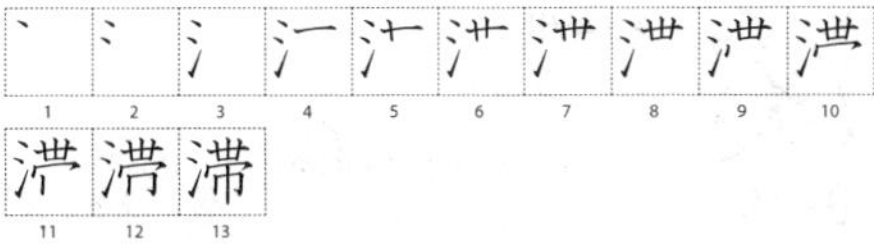

COMPOUNDS

❶ [original meaning] **STAGNATE, be at [in] a standstill, be blocked up, be retarded, congest**

滞貨 たいか freight congestion; accumulation of stocks
停滞 ていたい stagnation, accumulation; arrearage
渋滞 じゅうたい delay, retardation, stagnation
沈滞 ちんたい stagnation, dullness
遅滞 ちたい delay, retardation

❷ **fall into arrears, leave unpaid**

滞納 たいのう nonpayment, delinquency (in payment)
延滞 えんたい arrear, arrearage

❸ (remain in a given place) **STAY, remain, sojourn**

滞在 たいざい stay, sojourn
滞留 たいりゅう sojourn, stay
滞米 たいべい staying in America
滞欧 たいおう staying in Europe
滞空 たいくう staying [remaining] in the air

KUN

【とどこおる 滞る】**STAGNATE, be left undone; fall into arrears, be left unpaid**

滞り とどこおり hitch, hindrance; arrearage

SYNONYMS

❶ **stagnate**

滞 STAGNATE → 0815
淀む STAGNATE → 0621
澱 SETTLE → 0954
渋 NOT GO SMOOTHLY → 0625
吃 STAMMER → 0232

❷ **be late and delay**

遅 be late → 3887
後 fall behind → 0431
滞 fall into arrears → 0815
延 POSTPONE → 3812
猶 DELAY → 0757

❸ **stay**

滞 STAY → 0815
頓 STAY IN PLACE → 1320
留 STAY → 3189
逗 STAY → 4005
駐 STATIONED → 2297
屯 STATION TROOPS → 4268
在 reside temporarily → 3704
泊 STAY OVERNIGHT → 0389
宿 LODGE → 2858
寓 stay temporarily → 2893

❸ **remain**

残 REMAIN → 1179
余 REMAINING → 2535
留 STAY → 3189
滞 STAY → 0815

溶

0816

1-3-10

▶**DISSOLVE**
▶**MELT**

ヨウ と(ける) と(かす) と(く)

Ⓒ 溶 róng

85	Jōyō	U6EB6
氵	S13-3-10	F1545

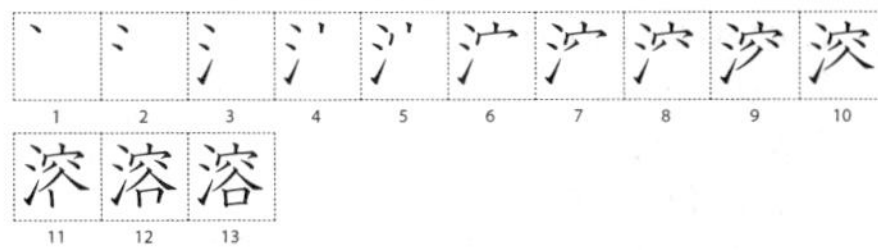

COMPOUNDS

❶ (pass or cause to pass into solution) **DISSOLVE**

溶解 ようかい dissolution, liquefaction; melting, fusion
溶液 ようえき solution, solvent
溶媒 ようばい solvent
溶血 ようけつ hemolysis
水溶性の すいようせいの water soluble

❷ [formerly 熔 1340 or 鎔 2214] (change or cause to change from solid to liquid, esp. by heat) **MELT**

溶融 ようゆう melting, fusion
溶接 ようせつ welding
溶岩 ようがん lava
溶鉱炉 ようこうろ smelting [blast] furnace

❸ [rare] having much water

溶溶たる ようようたる overflowing with water; vast, spacious

KUN

【とける 溶ける】*vi*

① (pass into solution) **DISSOLVE**

塩は水に溶ける しおはみずにとける Salt dissolves in water

②ⓐ [formerly 熔ける or 鎔ける] (of metals) **MELT (up), fuse, smelt**

ⓑ [also 解ける, formerly 融ける] (esp. of snow or ice) **MELT, thaw**

a 火で溶ける ひでとける melt in the fire
b 溶け込む とけこむ melt into, fuse into

【とかす 溶かす】*vt*

① (cause to pass into solution or to turn liquid) **DISSOLVE, melt, liquefy**

砂糖を水に溶かす さとうをみずにとかす dissolve sugar in water

②ⓐ [formerly 熔かす or 鎔かす] **MELT (up) (metals), fuse, smelt**

ⓑ [also 解かす, formerly also 融かす] **MELT (snow or ice), thaw (out)**

a 鉄を溶かす **てつをとかす** melt [fuse] iron

b 氷を溶かす **こおりをとかす** melt ice

【とく 溶く】 *vt*

① (cause to pass into solution) **DISSOLVE (paint)**

絵の具を溶く **えのぐをとく** dissolve colors

② whip an egg

溶きほぐす **ときほぐす** whip an egg

SYNONYMS

❶ & ❷ liquefy

溶 DISSOLVE, MELT → 0816

熔 MELT (metals) → 1340

鎔 MELT (metals) → 2214

解 DISSOLVE → 1913

融 FUSE → 2303

HOMOPHONES

とける

解 TAKE APART → 1913

融 FUSE → 2303

熔 MELT → 1340

鎔 MELT → 2214

とかす

解 TAKE APART → 1913

融 FUSE → 2303

熔 MELT → 1340

鎔 MELT → 2214

梳 COMB → 1209

とく

解 TAKE APART → 1913

説 EXPLAIN → 1949

梳 COMB → 1209

NOTE

➡ see USAGE note at 解 1913

溺

0817

1-3-10

▶DROWN

デキ ニョウ ジョウ おぼ(れる)

85	Nonstandard	U6EBA
氵	S13-3-10	F0000

traditional form → see 溺 at 0805

溢

0818

1-3-10

▶OVERFLOW

イツ あふ(れる) こぼ(す) こぼ(れる)

㊔ みつ みつる みつし

85	Nonstandard	U6EA2
氵	S13-3-10	F0000

traditional form → see 溢 at 0807

溪

0819

1-3-10

▶RAVINE

ケイ ㊔ たに

85	Nonstandard	U6EAA
氵	S13-3-10	F0000

traditional form → see 渓 at 0628

溝

0820

1-3-10

▶CHANNEL

コウ みぞ

85	Nonstandard	U6E9D
氵	S13-3-10	F0000

traditional form → see 溝 at 0810

溫

0821

1-3-10

▶WARM

オン あたた(か) あたた(かい) あたた(まる) あたた(める) ぬる(い) ぬく(もる) ㊔ あつ はる やす あつし ゆたか

85	Names	U6EAB
氵	S13-3-10	F0000

traditional form → see 温 at 0740

漣

0822

1-3-10

▶RIPPLES

レン さざなみ ㊔ なみ

85	Nonstandard	U6F23
氵	S13-3-10	F0000

traditional form → see 漣 at 0859

溯

0823

1-3-10

▶GO UPSTREAM

ソ さかのぼ(る)

85	Nonstandard	U6EAF
氵	S13-3-10	F0000

traditional form → see 遡 at 4040

漣

1-3-10

incorrect stroke-count

➡ see 1-3-11: 氵 at 0859

滿

1-3-10

incorrect stroke-count

➡ see 1-3-11: 氵 at 0869

猿

0824

1-3-10

▶MONKEY

エン さる

Ⓒ 猿 yuán

94	Jōyō	U733F
犭	S13-3-10	F1655

COMPOUNDS

● [original meaning] **MONKEY, ape**

猿人 えんじん ape-man
類人猿 るいじんえん anthropoid, troglodyte
犬猿 けんえん dog and monkey
犬猿の仲である けんえんのなかである lead a cat and dog life; be at enmity

KUN

【さる 猿】

① **MONKEY, ape**

猿真似 さるまね blind imitation
猿芝居 さるしばい monkey show; shallow-minded trick
猿回し さるまわし monkey showman, monkey show
日本猿 にほんざる Japan monkey
山猿 やまざる wild monkey; countryman, rustic

② sly person

猿知恵 さるぢえ shallow cunning

③ⓐ door bolt
ⓑ fastener

SYNONYMS

● **monkey**

猿 MONKEY → 0824
申 the Monkey → 4319

● **undomesticated mammals**

虎 TIGER → 3981
猿 MONKEY → 0824
鯨 WHALE → 2361
犀 RHINOCEROS → 3900
狼 WOLF → 0541
狐 FOX → 0472
羚 SEROW → 1695
鼠 RAT → 3340
獅 LION → 0825
豹 LEOPARD → 1847
熊 BEAR → 3530
象 ELEPHANT → 2647
麒 MALE CHINESE UNICORN → 2363
麟 FEMALE CHINESE UNICORN → 2376
猪 WILD BOAR → 0652
鹿 DEER → 3879

USAGE

【さる】

猿

① monkey, ape
② sly person
③ⓐ door bolt
ⓑ fastener

申

ninth sign of the Oriental zodiac: the Monkey

HOMOPHONES

さる 申 REPORT → 4319

獅

0825

◧ 1-3-10

▶**LION**

シ ㊔ たけ

Ⓒ 狮 shī

94	Names	U7345
犭	S13-3-10	F2248

COMPOUNDS

● **LION**

獅子 しし lion; left-hand guardian dog at a Shinto shrine
獅子座 ししざ Leo, the Lion (constellation)
獅子舞 ししまい lion dance

SYNONYMS

● **undomesticated mammals**

虎 TIGER → 3981
猿 MONKEY → 0824
鯨 WHALE → 2361
犀 RHINOCEROS → 3900
狼 WOLF → 0541
狐 FOX → 0472
羚 SEROW → 1695
鼠 RAT → 3340
獅 LION → 0825
豹 LEOPARD → 1847
熊 BEAR → 3530
象 ELEPHANT → 2647
麒 MALE CHINESE UNICORN → 2363
麟 FEMALE CHINESE UNICORN → 2376
猪 WILD BOAR → 0652
鹿 DEER → 3879

隙

0826

◧ 1-3-10

▶**GAP**

ゲキ ケキ˄ すき す(く)˄ す(かす)˄ ひま˄

Ⓝ 隟 隙 Ⓒ 隙 xì

170	Jōyō	U9699
阝	S13-3-10	F1959

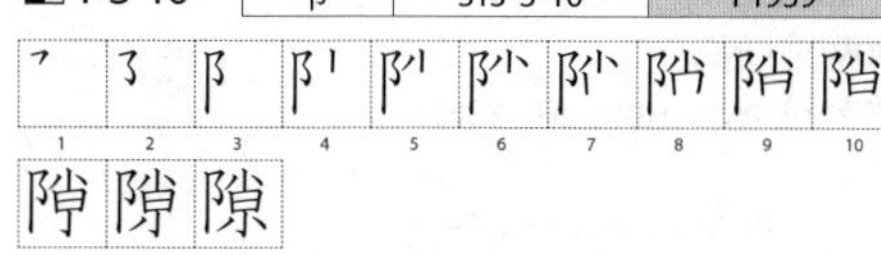

COMPOUNDS

● [original meaning] **GAP, interval, opening, space**

間隙 かんげき gap, interval
空隙 くうげき opening, crevice, gap, void
塡隙 てんげき caulking

INDEPENDENT

【げき 隙】 **GAP**, interval

KUN

【すき 隙】

① [also 透き] **GAP, interval**

隙間 すきま gap, opening; crack, crevice
手隙 てすき spare time, free time

② **chance, unguarded moment**
隙を見付ける すきをみつける seize an opportunity
隙を窺う すきをうかがう watch for an unguarded moment

【すく 隙く】[now usu. 透く] leave a **GAP**
隙いた枝 すいたえだ thinned branches

【すかす 隙かす】[now usu. 透かす] leave a space [opening], thin (out)
隙かさず すかさず without a moment's delay

【ひま 隙】
① [usu. 暇] time spent on doing something
手間隙 てまひま time and effort, trouble

② [archaic]
ⓐ **GAP**, space
ⓑ discord
ⓒ inattention, oversight

SYNONYMS

● **distance and interval**
距 DISTANCE → 1905
間 INTERVAL → 4122
程 EXTENT → 1524
隙 GAP → 0826

● **time periods**
時 TIME → 1155
季 SEASON (quarter) → 3161
候 SEASON (time of year) → 0133
頃 TIME → 0163
暇 FREE TIME → 1275
般 period of time → 1670
刻 POINT OF TIME → 1619
間 INTERVAL → 4122
隙 GAP → 0826
期 TERM → 2139
節 SEASON → 3336

HOMOPHONES

すき 透 PASS THROUGH → 3854
すく
透 PASS THROUGH → 3854
空 SKY → 2767
すかす
透 PASS THROUGH → 3854
空 SKY → 2767
ひま 暇 FREE TIME → 1275

NOTE

➡ see USAGE notes at 透 3854 and 暇 1275

口 土 女 山 巾 彳 忄 扌 止 氵 犭 【阝】 彡

隔

0827
1-3-10

▶**APART**
カク へだ(てる) へだ(たる)
Ⓝ 隔 Ⓒ 隔 gé

170	Jōyō	U9694
阝	S13-3-10	F1629

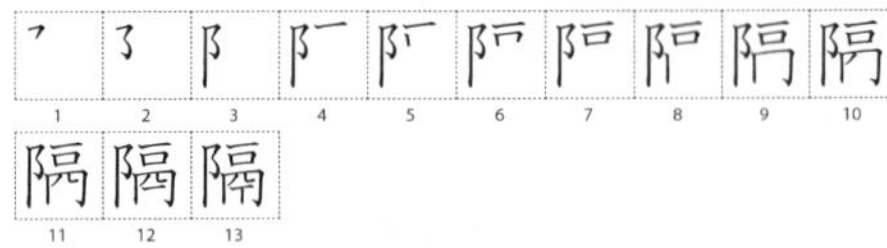

COMPOUNDS

❶ **APART, separated, distant**
隔世 かくせい distant age
隔絶する かくぜつする be separated, be isolated
遠隔の えんかくの distant, remote, far

❷ⓐ [original meaning] **partition, screen, interpose; separate, set APART**
ⓑ **partition; septum**

a 隔壁 かくへき partition, bulkhead; septum
隔膜 かくまく partition; diaphragm
隔離する かくりする isolate, segregate
横隔膜 おうかくまく diaphragm; midriff
b 間隔 かんかく interval, space
中隔 ちゅうかく septum
縦隔 じゅうかく mediastinum

❸ estrange, alienate
隔意 かくい reserve, alienation
疎隔 そかく estrangement, alienation

❹ **alternate, every other**
隔日 かくじつ alternate days
隔週に かくしゅうに biweekly
隔年の かくねんの every other year

KUN

【へだてる 隔てる】**separate, set APART; partition, screen, interpose; estrange, alienate**
隔て へだて partition; distinction, reserve, estrangement
別け隔て わけへだて discrimination, favoritism

【へだたる 隔たる】**be APART [separated], be distant; become estranged from**
隔たり へだたり distance, interval; gap, difference; estrangement
懸け隔たる かけへだたる be far apart; be different from

SYNONYMS

❶ **distant**
遠 DISTANT → 3906
遥 FAR → 3895
悠 far-off → 3407
遼 FARAWAY → 3930
隔 APART → 0827

離 separated → 2364
迂 ROUNDABOUT → 3969

❷ⓐ separate

割 DIVIDE → 2284
分 DIVIDE → 2466
解 TAKE APART → 1913
析 ANALYZE → 1072
別 SEPARATE → 1434
離 SEPARATE → 2364
隔 partition → 0827

隔

0828

▶APART

カク へだ(てる) へだ(たる)

170	Nonstandard	U9694
阝	S13-3-10	F0000

◧ 1-3-10 traditional form → see 隔 at 0827

鄕

0829

▶HOMETOWN

キョウ ゴウ さと ㊔ こう みさと

163	Nonstandard	U9115
阝	S13-3-10	F0000

◧ 1-3-10 traditional form → see 郷 at 0664

鄉

0830

▶HOMETOWN

キョウ ゴウ さと ㊔ こう みさと

163	Nonstandard	U90F7
阝	S13-3-10	F0000

◧ 1-3-10 alternative form → see 郷 at 0664

鳴

0831

▶CRY
▶SOUND

メイ な(く) な(る) な(らす)

Ⓒ 鸣 míng

196	Jōyō-2	U9CF4
鳥	S14-11-3	F0727

◧ 1-3-11

1	2	3	4	5	6	7	8	9	10	11	12	13	14
丨	ㄇ	口	口'	口ľ	叩	咱	咱	唣	鸣	鳴	鳴	鳴	鳴

COMPOUNDS

❶ⓐ [original meaning] (of birds and animals) **CRY, howl**
ⓑ CRY out, shout

a 鶏鳴 けいめい cockcrowing
b 悲鳴 ひめい shriek, scream

❷ SOUND, ring, roar

鳴動 めいどう rumbling
共鳴 きょうめい resonance
雷鳴 らいめい thunderclap
吹鳴 すいめい blowing (a whistle)
奏鳴曲 そうめいきょく sonata

KUN

【なく 鳴く】 (of animals, birds or insects) **CRY, chirp, ululate, howl, yelp, meow**

鳴き声 なきごえ cry, song, chirping
鳴き交わす なきかわす cry [howl] to each other, exchange wooing cries
長鳴き ながなき long crowing [warbling]

【なる 鳴る】 *vi* **SOUND, ring, roar, resound**

鳴り なり sound, ringing
鳴り響く なりひびく reverberate, echo, resound
鳴り渡る なりわたる resound [echo] far and wide
鳴り物 なりもの musical instruments; music, fanfare
高鳴る たかなる ring high, roar; (of one's heart) throb violently
耳鳴り みみなり buzzing in the ears, tinnitus

【ならす 鳴らす】 *vt* **ring, SOUND, chime; be famous; complain of, air one's grievances**

掻き鳴らす かきならす thrum, strum
作家として鳴らす さっかとしてならす be very popular as a writer
非を鳴らす ひをならす denounce publicly, cry against

SYNONYMS

❶ give out a call

叫 SHOUT → 0233
号 holler → 2675
喝 SHOUT AT → 0554
喚 call out → 0666
呼 CALL → 0324
鳴 CRY → 0831
吠 BARK → 0269

❷ make sound or noise

鳴 SOUND → 0831
響 REVERBERATE → 3573
騒 CLAMOR → 2308
轟 RESOUND → 3425

HOMOPHONES

なく 泣 CRY → 0396

NOTE

➡ see USAGE note at 泣 0396

噓

0832

▶LIE

キョ うそ

30	Nonstandard	U5618
口	S14-3-11	F0000

◧ 1-3-11 traditional form → see 嘘 at 0880

噌

0833

1-3-11

▶*MISO*

ソ ソウ

30	Nonstandard	U564C
口	S14-3-11	F0000

traditional form → see 噌 at 0882

嘆

0834

1-3-11

▶**SIGH**

タン なげ(く) なげ(かわしい)

30	Names	UFA37
口	S14-3-11	F0000

traditional form → see 嘆 at 0773

境

0835

1-3-11

▶**BOUNDARY**
▶**SITUATION**

キョウ ケイ さかい ㊔ さかえ

Ⓒ 境 jìng

32	Jōyō-5	U5883
土	S14-3-11	F0533

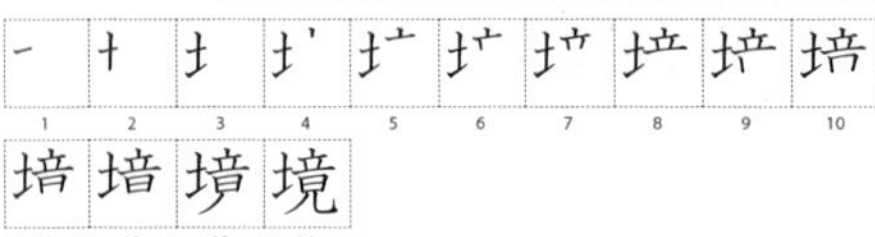

COMPOUNDS

❶ [formerly also 疆 きょう 1810] [original meaning]
BOUNDARY, border, frontier
- 境界 きょうかい boundary, border
- 境域 きょういき boundary; precincts, grounds
- 境内 けいだい grounds [premises] (of a shrine or temple)
- 国境 こっきょう (national) boundary [border]
- 越境 えっきょう border transgression, violation of the border
- 辺境 へんきょう frontier (district), remote region, border(land)
- 県境 けんきょう prefectural border

❷ region, place, country, land
- 秘境 ひきょう unexplored regions
- 異境 いきょう foreign country, strange land
- 仙境 せんきょう fairyland, enchanted land

❸ **SITUATION, condition(s), state**
- 境遇 きょうぐう one's lot, circumstances, situation in life
- 境地 きょうち state, stage; field, ground
- 環境 かんきょう environment, surroundings, circumstances
- 心境 しんきょう frame of mind, mental attitude [state]
- 逆境 ぎゃっきょう adversity, adverse [unfavorable] circumstances
- 進境 しんきょう progress, improvement

INDEPENDENT

【きょう 境】 region, place; state of mind
- 無人の境 むじんのきょう uninhabited land
- 無我の境 むがのきょう state of complete self-effacement

KUN

【さかい 境】 **BOUNDARY, border; place, region**
- 境目 さかいめ border, boundary line; crisis
- 境を異にする さかいをことにする live in different worlds
- 国境 くにざかい (national, state or provincial) boundary [border]
- 見境 みさかい distinction, discrimination
- 生死の境 せいしのさかい between life and death

SYNONYMS

❶ **edges and boundaries**
- 縁 EDGE → 1754
- 端 edge → 1564
- 辺 border → 3761
- 境 BOUNDARY → 0835
- 疆 BOUNDARY → 1810
- 界 BOUNDS → 3172
- 際 VERGE → 0874
- 涯 OUTER LIMITS → 0623

❸ **states and situations**
- 態 STATE → 3529
- 調 TONE → 1973
- 様 MODE → 1332
- 相 PHASE → 1120
- 状 CONDITION → 0322
- 況 CONDITIONS → 0395
- 景 business conditions → 3118
- 勢 course of events → 3542
- 境 SITUATION → 0835
- 局 current situation → 3800
- 情 ACTUAL CONDITIONS → 0583
- 訳 circumstances → 1865

USAGE

【さかい】

境
boundary, border; place, region

堺
Sakai

HOMOPHONES

さかい 堺 SAKAI → 0679

増

▶INCREASE

ゾウ ま(す) ま(し) ふ(える) ふ(やす)

Ⓝ 增 Ⓒ 增 zēng

0836

1-3-11

32	Jōyō-5	U5897
土	S14-3-11	F0460

COMPOUNDS

❶ⓐ [original meaning] (grow or cause to grow in quantity or number) **INCREASE, multiply, augment**

ⓑ [also suffix] **INCREASE, rise**

a 増加する ぞうかする increase, multiply, rise
増産 ぞうさん production increase
増税 ぞうぜい tax increase
増員する ぞういんする increase the staff [personnel]
増進する ぞうしんする promote, improve, advance
増幅 ぞうふく amplification
増大する ぞうだいする increase, enlarge, enhance

b 増減 ぞうげん increase and decrease, rise and fall
急増 きゅうぞう sudden [rapid] increase
自然増 しぜんぞう natural increase

❷ grow impudent, become arrogant
増長する ぞうちょうする grow presumptuous

INDEPENDENT

【ぞう 増】 INCREASE
五割の増 ごわりのぞう increase of 50%

KUN

【ます 増す】 [sometimes also 益す] *vi & vt* **INCREASE, augment, multiply**
増し刷り ましずり additional printing, reprinting
信用が増す しんようがます gain more confidence

【まし 増し】 [also suffix] **INCREASE, addition; one by one**
増しな ましな less objectionable, better, preferable
水増し みずまし watering; dilution
割増し料金 わりましりょうきん extra charge
日増しに ひましに day by day

【ふえる 増える】 *vi* (grow in number or in quantity) **INCREASE, accrue, multiply**
体重が増える たいじゅうがふえる gain weight
量が増える りょうがふえる gain in quantity

【ふやす 増やす】 *vt* (cause to grow in number or quantity) **INCREASE, add**
人手を増やす ひとでをふやす add to the staff

SYNONYMS

❶ increase
加 add to →0042
増 INCREASE →0836
殖 MULTIPLY →1253
倍 DOUBLE →0122

USAGE

❶【ます】
増す
[sometimes also 益す] *vi & vt* increase, augment, multiply
益す
[usu. 増す] *vi & vt* increase, augment, multiply

❷【ふえる】
増える
vi (grow in number or in quantity) increase, accrue, multiply
殖える
vi (increase of its own accord) multiply, increase, propagate

❸【ふやす】
増やす
vt (cause to grow in number or quantity) increase, add
殖やす
vt (cause to multiply of its own accord) multiply, increase, propagate, augment

HOMOPHONES

ます 益 BENEFIT →2849
ふえる 殖 MULTIPLY →1253
ふやす 殖 MULTIPLY →1253

NOTE

➡ see COMPOUND FORMATION for 増幅 ぞうふく →幅 0694

塀

▶FENCE

ヘイ

0837

1-3-11

32	Nonstandard	UFA39
土	S14-3-11	F0000

traditional form →see 塀 at 0677

塲

▶PLACE

ジョウ ば

0838

1-3-11

32	Nonstandard	U5872
土	S14-3-11	F0000

traditional form →see 場 at 0678

嫡

▶LEGITIMATE CHILD

チャク テキ▲

Ⓒ 嫡 dí

0839

1-3-11

38	Jōyō	U5AE1
女	S14-3-11	F2443

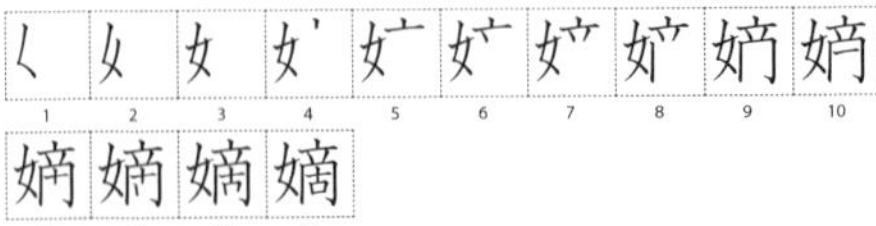

COMPOUNDS

❶ⓐ **LEGITIMATE CHILD, heir, successor**
ⓑ [original meaning] **legitimate wife, legal wife**

a 嫡子 ちゃくし legitimate child
廃嫡 はいちゃく disinheritance
b 嫡男 ちゃくなん heir, eldest son; legitimate son
嫡出 ちゃくしゅつ legitimacy (of birth)
嫡妻 ちゃくさい legitimate wife
嫡室 ちゃくしつ legitimate wife

❷ in direct line (of descent); orthodox
嫡流 ちゃくりゅう lineage of the eldest son; orthodox school

SYNONYMS

❶ⓐ **inheritors**
嫡 LEGITIMATE CHILD →0839
嗣 HEIR →2153

❶ⓐ **offspring**
子 CHILD →4196
仔 OFFSPRING →0038
孤 orphan →0426
嫡 LEGITIMATE CHILD →0839
息 son →3278
男 son →3147
惣 eldest son →3452
娘 DAUGHTER →0488
女 daughter →4226
姫 DAUGHTER OF NOBLE BIRTH →0489

ⓑ **wives**
妻 WIFE →3166
奥 wife →3503
内 wife →4277
室 wife (esp. of persons of rank) →2802
嫡 legitimate wife →0839
婦 married woman →0565
嫁 BRIDE →0780
寡 widow →2957

嶋

0840
1-3-11

▸**ISLAND**
トウ しま

46	Names	U5D8B
山	S14-3-11	F0000

traditional form →see 島 at 4103

徴

0841
1-3-11

▸**LEVY**
▸**SYMPTOM**
チョウ チ▲ しるし▲

Ⓝ 徵 Ⓒ 征 zhēng 徵 zhǐ

60	Jōyō	U5FB4
彳	S14-3-11	F0965

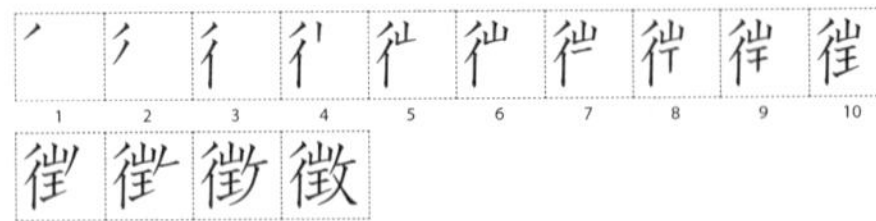

COMPOUNDS

❶ (collect taxes or payment) **LEVY, collect, impose**
徴収する ちょうしゅうする collect taxes [payment]
徴税 ちょうぜい tax collection
追徴する ついちょうする collect in addition
課徴金 かちょうきん surcharge (on imports)

❷ⓐ (enlist troops) **LEVY, conscript, recruit**
ⓑ (collect by force) requisition, commandeer

a 徴兵 ちょうへい conscription, enlistment, draft
徴募 ちょうぼ recruitment
徴集する ちょうしゅうする levy, recruit
b 徴発 ちょうはつ commandeering, requisition

❸ⓐ (evidence of a fact or event) **SYMPTOM, sign, indication, omen**
ⓑ evidence, proof

a 徴候 ちょうこう symptom, sign; omen
徴証 ちょうしょう token, sign
象徴 しょうちょう symbol
b 明徴 めいちょう clarification

❹ **characteristic, character, feature**
特徴 とくちょう distinctive feature, characteristic
標徴 ひょうちょう *biol* diagnostic character, distinguishing mark
性徴 せいちょう *biol* sexual character

❺ [rare] fourth note of the pentatonic scale (→see APPENDIX 8)

INDEPENDENT

【ちょう 徴】**SYMPTOM**, sign, indication
【ちょうする 徴する】judge by [from], refer to; solicit, seek
【ち 徴】[rare] fourth note of the pentatonic scale

KUN

【しるし 徴】
① effectiveness (of medicine)
② **SYMPTOM**, sign, indication
地震の徴 じしんのしるし signs of an earthquake

SYNONYMS

❶ **impose**
徴 LEVY →0841
課 impose →1980

口 土 女 【巾】 彳 忄 扌 氵 犭 阝

❷ enlist

徴 LEVY →0841
募 RAISE →2901

❸ⓐ signs

候 indication →0133
徴 SYMPTOM →0841
症 symptom (of a disease) →4065
気 sign →3960
兆 OMEN →0264

USAGE

【ちょうしゅうする】
徴収する
collect taxes [payment]
徴集する
levy, recruit

HOMOPHONES

しるし 印 MARK →1023

NOTE

➡ see also USAGE note at 印 1023
★ do not confuse with 徵 SLIGHT →0788

徳

0842

1-3-11

▸VIRTUE

トク ㊔ のり よし なる なり あつ

Ⓝ 德 悳 Ⓒ 德 dé

60	Jōyō-5	U5FB3
彳	S14-3-11	F0595

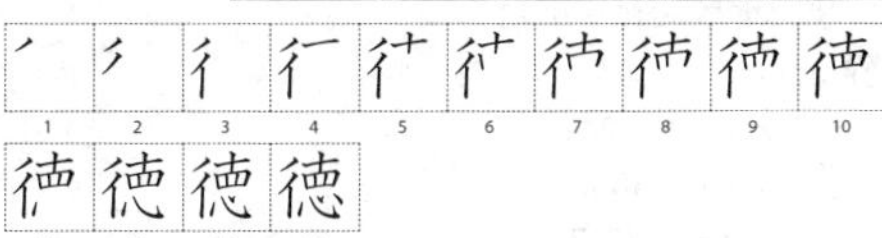

COMPOUNDS

❶ⓐ (moral excellence) **VIRTUE, morality**
ⓑ (act of moral excellence) **VIRTUE, virtuous deed**

a 徳行 とっこう virtuous deeds, goodness
徳義 とくぎ morality, sincerity
道徳 どうとく morality, morals
悪徳 あくとく vice, corruption, immorality
公徳 こうとく public morality
ab 美徳 びとく virtue, good deed

❷ act of kindness, favor

徳沢 とくたく grace, blessing
徳政 とくせい benevolent administration
報徳 ほうとく requital of a person's kindness

❸ⓐ profit, winnings
ⓑ benefits

a 徳用な とくような economical
徳分 とくぶん profits, winnings
b 余徳 よとく benefits (that descend to posterity of a man of great virtue)

INDEPENDENT

【とく 徳】 (moral excellence) **VIRTUE,** morality; (act of moral excellence) virtue, virtuous act; power of commanding respect; benefits
徳の高い とくのたかい virtuous, respectable
徳を行う とくをおこなう practice virtue

SYNONYMS

❶ moral goodness

徳 VIRTUE →0842
道 the way of moral conduct →3888
善 GOOD →2921
義 RIGHTEOUSNESS →2948

❷ favor

恵 FAVOR →3293
徳 act of kindness →0842
恩 GRACE →3289

慣

0843

1-3-11

▸HABITUAL PRACTICE

カン な(れる) な(らす)

Ⓒ 惯 guàn

61	Jōyō-5	U6163
忄	S14-3-11	F1081

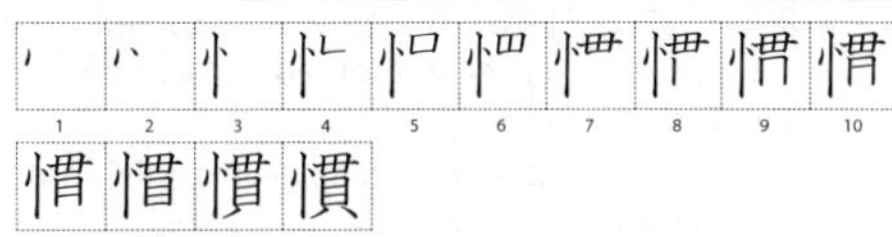

COMPOUNDS

❶ HABITUAL [usual, established] PRACTICE, custom, habit, usual way, convention

慣行 かんこう habitual [usual] practice
慣例 かんれい custom, usage, precedent
習慣 しゅうかん custom, habit

❷ grow accustomed to, get used to, become habituated

慣用 かんよう common use, usage

❸ remain in present state

慣性 かんせい inertia

KUN

【なれる 慣れる】 [sometimes also 馴れる] [also suffix] **grow accustomed to, get used to, become inured to, become experienced in**
慣れ なれ habituation, practice, experience
慣れた なれた practiced, experienced, familiar
慣れ親しむ なれしたしむ get used to, become familiar with
見慣れる みなれる get used to seeing
場慣れ ばなれ experience, poise in a critical situation

【ならす 慣らす】 [sometimes also 馴らす] **inure, habituate, accustom, make used to**

足慣らし(=足馴らし) あしならし walking exercise, warming up
使い慣らす つかいならす accustom oneself to using (a thing), train
体を寒さに慣らす からだをさむさにならす inure oneself to cold

SYNONYMS

❶ custom
慣 HABITUAL PRACTICE →0843
例 established practice →0099
習 CUSTOM →3306
風 manners →3730
俗 popular custom →0119
癖 HABIT →4080
弊 EVIL PRACTICE →3583

USAGE

❶【なれる】
慣れる
[sometimes also 馴れる] [also suffix] grow accustomed to, get used to, become inured to, become experienced in
馴れる
① become tame [domesticated]
② [usu. 慣れる] [also suffix] grow accustomed to, get used to, become inured to, become experienced in
③ [in compounds] become familiar [friendly] with; become overfamiliar with

❷【ならす】
慣らす
[sometimes also 馴らす] inure, habituate, accustom, make used to
馴らす
① tame, domesticate
② [usu. 慣らす] inure, habituate, accustom, make used to
均す
① level, make even, roll
② average

HOMOPHONES

なれる 馴 BECOME TAME →2290
ならす
馴 BECOME TAME →2290
均 EVEN →0276

慢

▸ARROGANT
▸SLUGGISH
マン

0844

Ⓒ 慢 màn

1-3-11

61	Jōyō	U6162
忄	S14-3-11	F1159

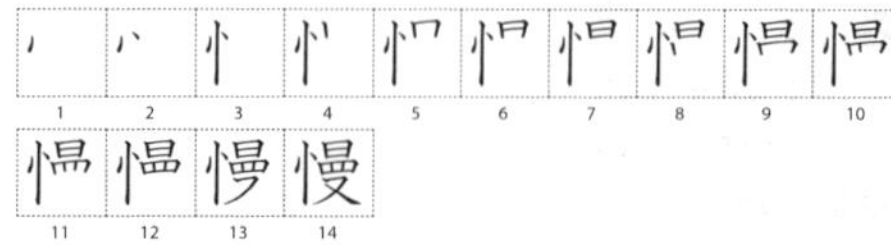

COMPOUNDS

❶ **ARROGANT, supercilious, haughty, conceited, proud**
慢心 まんしん self-conceit; pride
自慢 じまん pride, self-praise, vanity
高慢な こうまんな haughty, arrogant, proud
傲慢な ごうまんな arrogant, haughty, insolent
我慢 がまん patience, endurance; self-restraint

❷ (slow to act) **SLUGGISH, slow, dragging**
慢性の まんせいの chronic
緩慢な かんまんな slack, slow-moving, dull, inactive

❸ [original meaning] (lacking in vigor) **SLUGGISH**, lazy, idle
怠慢な たいまんな negligent, inattentive, remiss

INDEPENDENT

【まんじる(=まんずる) 慢じる(=慢ずる)】be self-conceited, swell with pride

SYNONYMS

❶ boasting and arrogance
誇 BOAST →1921
慢 ARROGANT →0844
傲 ARROGANT →0173

❷ slow
徐 SLOWLY →0497
遅 SLOW →3887
緩 SLACK →1757
慢 SLUGGISH →0844

❸ lazy
惰 LAZY →0706
怠 REMISS →2588
慢 SLUGGISH →0844

COMPOUND FORMATION

❶【我慢 がまん】
我慢 'patience, etc.' originally meant self (我) conceit (慢 ❶).

❷【慢性 まんせい】
慢性の 'chronic' refers to a disease that has the quality (性) of dragging on and on (慢 ❷).

NOTE

★ do not confuse with 漫 RAMBLING →0858

憎

0845

1-3-11

▶HATE

ゾウ にく(む) にく(い) にく(らしい) にく(しみ)

N 憎 C 憎 zēng

61	Jōyō	U618E
忄	S14-3-11	F1419

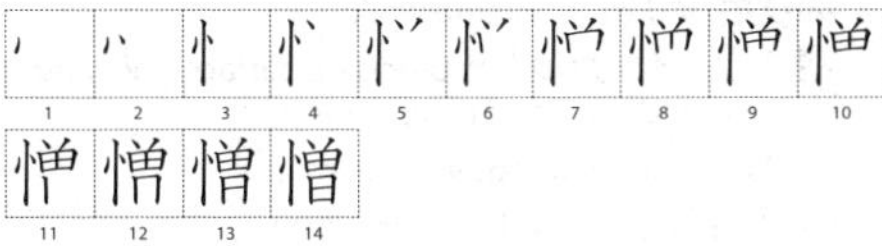

COMPOUNDS

a [original meaning] **HATE, detest**

b **HATE**, hatred

a 憎悪 ぞうお abhorrence, hatred

b 愛憎 あいぞう love and hate

KUN

【にくむ 憎む】**HATE, detest, abhor**

憎まれ口 にくまれぐち offensive [abusive] language

憎まれっ子 にくまれっこ bad [naughty] child

【にくい 憎い】**HATEful, abominable**

憎さ にくさ hatefulness, hatred

憎憎しい にくにくしい hateful, detestable

生憎 あいにく unfortunately, unluckily; I am sorry, but…

小面憎い こづらにくい saucy, cheeky, pert

【にくらしい 憎らしい】**HATEful, horrible, provoking**

小憎らしい こにくらしい saucy; provoking

【にくしみ 憎しみ】**hatred, enmity**

SYNONYMS

● **hate and dislike**

憎 HATE →0845

悪 hate →3413

忌む ABHOR →2735

嫌 DISLIKE →0781

恨 HOLD A GRUDGE →0439

怨 HOLD A GRUDGE →3179

厭 disagreeable →3745

慨

0846

1-3-11

▶DEPLORE

ガイ

61	Nonstandard	U6168
忄	S14-3-11	F0000

traditional form → see 慨 at 0790

慘

0847

1-3-11

▶MISERABLE

▶CRUEL

サン ザン みじ(め)

61	Nonstandard	U6158
忄	S14-3-11	F0000

traditional form → see 惨 at 0585

摑

0848

1-3-11

▶GRASP

カク つか(む) つか(まえる) つか(まる)

N 掴 C 掴 guāi guó

64	Names	U6451
扌	S14-3-11	F1542

KUN

【つかむ 摑む】

① **GRASP, grip, clutch, catch, seize**

摑み取り つかみどり taking (as much as one can hold) by the hand

摑み掛かる つかみかかる grab at

摑み所 つかみどころ hold, grip; point

鷲摑み わしづかみ grabbing hold

溺れる者は藁をも摑む おぼれるものはわらをもつかむ A drowning man will catch at a straw

② acquire, get, gain

証拠を摑む しょうこをつかむ obtain evidence

【つかまえる 摑まえる】[sometimes also 捉まえる] **catch, seize, GRASP, get hold of**

鳥を摑まえる とりをつかまえる catch a bird

【つかまる 摑まる】[sometimes also 捉まる] **hold fast to, cling to**

吊り革に摑まる つりかわにつかまる cling to a strap

SYNONYMS

【つかむ】

① **take**

把 GRIP →0293

握 GRASP →0714

捉 GRASP →0518

執 SEIZE →2114

摑む GRASP →0848

捕 CATCH →0514

取 TAKE →1613

持 HOLD →0447

HOMOPHONES

つかまえる

捕 CATCH →0514

捉 GRASP →0518

摑 GRASP →0848

つかまる

捕 CATCH →0514

捉 GRASP →0518

摑 GRASP →0848

口 土 女 山 彳 忄 【扌】 氵 犭 阝

NOTE

➡ see USAGE note at 捕 0514

摧

0849

1-3-11

▶CRUSH UP

サイ くだ(く) くだ(ける)

Ⓒ 摧 cuī

64	Non-Jōyō	U6467
扌	S14-3-11	F0000

COMPOUNDS

● [now replaced by 砕 1458] **CRUSH UP, break into pieces, smash**

破摧する はさいする crush, smash, crack to pieces

玉摧する ぎょくさいする die but never surrender

KUN

【くだく 摧く】 [now replaced by 砕く] *vt* **crush, smash, break into pieces, shatter; rack (one's brains); explain plainly**

【くだける 摧ける】 [now replaced by 砕ける] *vi* **be crushed, be broken, be smashed; break down, buckle, give way; become softened, become complaisant, get friendly; be easy [plain]**

SYNONYMS

● **break**

破 BREAK → 1478
拉ぐ crush → 0372
崩 CRUMBLE → 2863
挫 SPRAIN → 0519
壊 BREAK DOWN → 0934
毀す break down → 2246
折 BREAK OFF → 0297
割る crack → 2284
裂 SPLIT → 3331
砕 CRUSH UP → 1458
摧 CRUSH UP → 0849
潰す CRUSH → 0919

HOMOPHONES

くだく 砕 CRUSH UP → 1458
くだける 砕 CRUSH UP → 1458

NOTE

➡ see USAGE note at 砕 1458

摺

0850

1-3-11

▶RUB AGAINST

ショウ す(る)

Ⓝ 摺 Ⓒ 摺 zhé

64	Names	U647A
扌	S14-3-11	F2383

COMPOUNDS

❶ **RUB AGAINST**

摺動 しょうどう(=しゅうどう) moving along a smooth surface

❷ [original meaning] **fold**

摺曲 しょうきょく folding

KUN

【する 摺る】

ⓐ **RUB AGAINST**

ⓑ **print by rubbing**

a 摺り足 すりあし shuffling walk

摺り合わせ すりあわせ precision surface finishing; coordinating of ideas [opinions]

摺り鉢 すりばち (earthenware) mortar

引き摺る ひきずる drag along; trail

手摺り てすり handrail, railing

スプーン摺り切り一杯 すぷーんすりきりいっぱい level spoonful

b 摺り本 すりほん woodblock-printed book

石摺り いしずり print from stone, rubbing, rubbed copy

SYNONYMS

❶ **polish and rub**

磨 POLISH → 3946
擦 RUB → 0971
摩 RUB AGAINST → 3938
摺 RUB AGAINST → 0850
研 GRIND → 1456
削 CUT BY CHIPPING → 1837
瑳 POLISH → 1343

HOMOPHONES

する

擦 RUB → 0971
磨 POLISH → 3946
刷 PRINT → 1623

NOTE

➡ see USAGE note at 擦 0971

摘

0851

1-3-11

▶PICK

テキ つ(む) つ(まむ)▲

Ⓒ 摘 zhāi

64	Jōyō	U6458
扌	S14-3-11	F1152

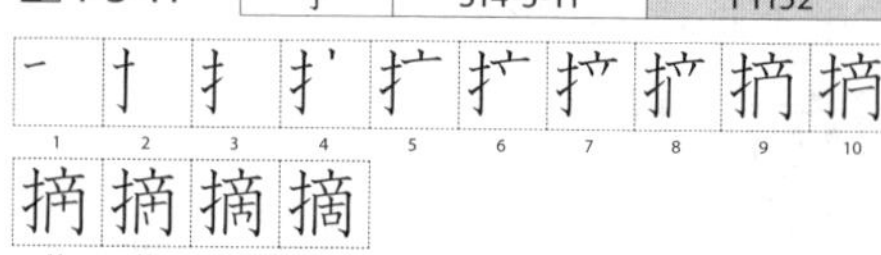

COMPOUNDS

❶ [original meaning] **PICK (flowers), pluck, gather**

摘果 てきか thinning out superfluous fruit

摘出する てきしゅつする extract, excise, remove; point out

❷ⓐ (choose the best part) **PICK out, select, make an extract**

ⓑ **point out (a person's mistakes), expose**

a 摘要 てきよう summary
摘記する てっきする summarize, epitomize
b 摘発する てきはつする expose, lay bare, disclose
指摘する してきする point out

KUN

【つむ 摘む】

① **PICK (flowers), pluck, gather**
摘み取る つみとる pick, pluck
摘み草 つみくさ gathering wild greens
茶摘み ちゃつみ tea-picking

②ⓐ nip
ⓑ [also 剪む] cut (one's hair), trim

a 芽を摘む めをつむ nip the buds; nip something in the bud
b 髪を摘む かみをつむ have one's hair cut [trimmed]

【つまむ 摘む】

①ⓐ **PICK**, pinch, take a pinch of; hold between one's fingers
ⓑ eat with one's fingers [chopsticks]; snack on
② sum up, summarize

SYNONYMS

❶ harvest
採 PICK →0606
摘 PICK →0851
穫 HARVEST →1598
刈る reap →0032

❷ⓐ choose
選 CHOOSE →3931
撰 choose →0911
択 SELECT →0299
採 PICK →0606
摘 pick out →0851
擢 SINGLE OUT →0973
抜 single out →0290
汰 SIFT OUT →0312

USAGE

【つむ】
摘む
① pick (flowers), pluck, gather
②ⓐ nip
ⓑ [also 剪む] cut (one's hair), trim
剪む
[also 摘む] cut (one's hair), trim

HOMOPHONES

つむ 剪 PRUNE →2886

摺

0852

1-3-11

▶RUB AGAINST
ショウ す(る)

64	Nonstandard	U647A
扌	S14-3-11	F0000

traditional form →see 摺 at 0850

摠

0853

1-3-11

▶TOTAL
▶GENERAL
ソウ す(べて) ㊔ ふさ さ

64	Nonstandard	U6460
扌	S14-3-11	F0000

traditional form →see 総 at 1743

擕

1-3-11

incorrect stroke-count
➡ see 1-3-10: 扌 at 0796

摸

1-3-11

incorrect stroke-count
➡ see 1-3-10: 扌 at 0797

滌

0854

1-3-11

▶WASH
デキ テキ ジョウ
Ⓒ 涤 dí

85	Non-Jōyō	U6ECC
氵	S14-3-11	F0000

COMPOUNDS

● [now replaced by 浄 0457] **WASH, cleanse**
洗滌する せんでき(=せんじょう)する wash, irrigate

SYNONYMS

● clean and wash
洗 WASH →0465
漱 RINSE →0865
拭 WIPE →0453
滌 WASH →0854
濯 RINSE →0978
浴 BATHE →0533
浄 cleanse →0457
粛 PURGE →4400
清 CLEAR →0635
払 CLEAR AWAY →0225
掃 SWEEP →0611

演

0855

1-3-11

▶PERFORM
エン ㊔ のぶ
Ⓒ 演 yǎn

85	Jōyō-5	U6F14
氵	S14-3-11	F0480

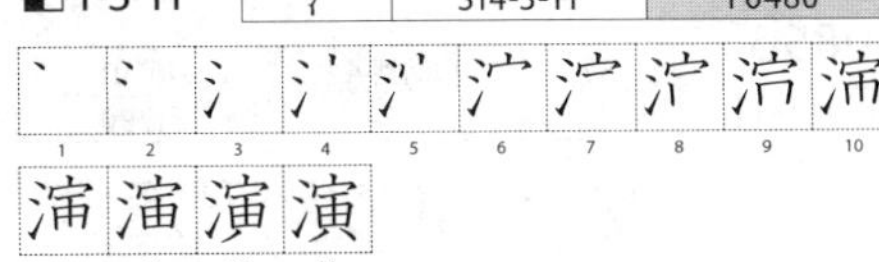

COMPOUNDS

❶ⓐ PERFORM, act, enact, play, entertain
ⓑ PERFORMance, acting, enactment, play

a 演劇 えんげき drama, play

口 土 女 山 彳 忄 扌 【氵】 犭 阝

口 土 女 山 彳 忄 扌 【氵】 犭 阝

演出 えんしゅつ production (of a play); representation
演技 えんぎ acting, performance
演奏 えんそう musical performance
演芸 えんげい performance, entertainments
主演する しゅえんする play the leading part
上演する じょうえんする put on stage
出演する しゅつえんする appear on stage, perform, play
b 開演 かいえん raising the curtain, commencing a performance
共演 きょうえん coacting, costarring
公演 こうえん public performance
初演 しょえん first performance, premier

❷ⓐ make a speech, lecture, expound
ⓑ speech, lecture

a 演説 えんぜつ (public) speech, address, oration
講演 こうえん lecture
b 演題 えんだい subject of a speech, speech title

❸ practice, exercise

演習 えんしゅう exercise, practice; military maneuvers; seminar
演算 えんざん mathematical operation

❹ deduce

演繹× えんえき deduction, deductive reasoning

INDEPENDENT

【えんじる(=えんずる) 演じる(=演ずる)】 **PERFORM, play, act**
ロミオを演じる ろみおをえんじる act the part of Romeo

SYNONYMS

❶ⓑ performance

劇 DRAMA →2399
演 performance →0855
芸 entertainment →2738

❷ speak in public

講 LECTURE →2046
演 make a speech →0855

漁

0856
◧1-3-11

▶FISH
ギョ リョウ あさ(る)▲ ㊔ いさり すなどり
Ⓒ 渔 yú

85	Jōyō-4	U6F01
氵	S14-3-11	F1290

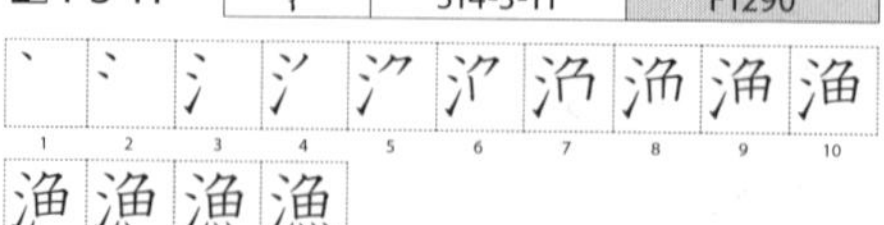

COMPOUNDS

❶ⓐ [original meaning] **FISH, angle**
ⓑ [also suffix] **FISHing, fishery**

a 漁業 ぎょぎょう fishing industry
漁船 ぎょせん fishing boat
漁獲 ぎょかく fishing; haul [catch] (of fish)
漁場 ぎょじょう fishing ground, fishery
漁師 りょうし fisherman
b 禁漁 きんりょう prohibition of fishing
出漁する しゅつりょうする go (off) fishing
鮭×漁 さけりょう salmon fishing
延縄漁 はえなわりょう longline fishing

❷ catch, haul

大漁 たいりょう large catch
不漁 ふりょう poor catch [haul]

❸ **FISH** for, search for, hunt for

漁色 ぎょしょく debauchery, philandering

INDEPENDENT

【りょう 漁】 **FISHing, fishery, fishing excursion; catch, haul**

KUN

【あさる 漁る】 [also verbal suffix] **FISH** for, search for, hunt for
漁り あさり search, rummaging search; fishing
掃き溜めを漁る はきだめをあさる pick a garbage dump, rummage a dustbin
買い漁る かいあさる hunt for, go round shopping

SYNONYMS

❶ hunt and fish

猟 HUNTING →0654
狩 HUNT →0474
獲 CATCH GAME →0959
漁 FISH →0856
釣 ANGLE →2108
弋 CATCH →4230

漂

0857
◧1-3-11

▶DRIFT
ヒョウ ただよ(う)
Ⓒ 漂 piāo piǎo piào

85	Jōyō	U6F02
氵	S14-3-11	F1543

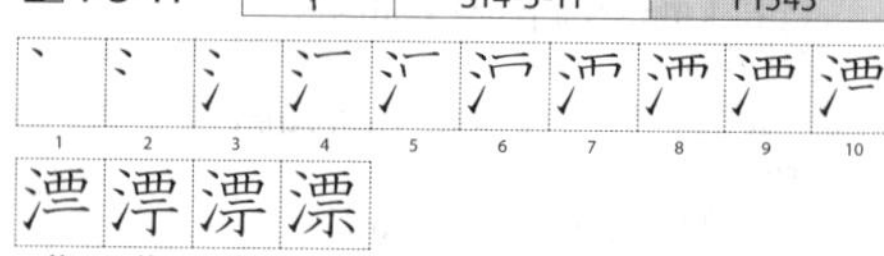

COMPOUNDS

❶ⓐ [original meaning] **DRIFT, float**
ⓑ DRIFT about, roam, wander

a 漂流する ひょうりゅうする drift, be adrift
漂着 ひょうちゃく drifting ashore
浮漂 ふひょう floating
b 漂泊 ひょうはく roaming, drifting about, wandering

漂浪 ひょうろう [rare] wandering
漂然(=飄×然)と ひょうぜんと aimlessly, unexpectedly

❷ bleach
漂白 ひょうはく bleaching, decolorization

KUN

【ただよう 漂う】**DRIFT, be adrift; float, waft; waver, flicker, play**
漂う小舟 ただようこぶね drifting boat
芳香が漂う ほうこうがただよう Fragrance floats in the air
唇に微笑を漂わせて くちびるにびしょうをただよわせて with a smile on one's lips

SYNONYMS

❶ⓐ **float**
漂 DRIFT →0857
浮 FLOAT →0522
ⓑ **wander**
浪 WANDER →0527
遊 move about freely →3896
漂 drift about →0857
流 drift →0529
徑 WANDER ABOUT →0350
徊 MOVE TO AND FRO →0432

漫 0858

▶**RAMBLING**
▶**COMIC**
マン
Ⓒ 漫 màn

1-3-11

85 氵	Jōyō	U6F2B
	S14-3-11	F1556

Stroke order: 1–14

COMPOUNDS

❶ **RAMBLING, random, discursive, desultory, aimless, unrestrained, casual**
漫遊する まんゆうする make a leisurely tour
漫文 まんぶん random notes
漫然たる まんぜんたる rambling, random, desultory
漫歩する まんぽする ramble, saunter
散漫な さんまんな desultory, vagrant, vague
放漫 ほうまん laxity, looseness, indiscretion
冗漫な じょうまんな diffuse, verbose, prolix

❷ **COMIC, idle**
漫画 まんが cartoon, comic strip
漫才 まんざい comic dialogue, comic backchat, *manzai*
漫談 まんだん idle talk, comic chat
漫楽 まんがく *manzai* accompanied by music
漫研(=漫画研究会) まんけん(=まんがけんきゅうかい) comic book [cartoon] research group

❸ [original meaning] vast, endless, boundless
漫漫たる まんまんたる vast, boundless
爛漫たる らんまんたる in full bloom; in profusion

❹ used phonetically for *man* in the transliteration of foreign words
浪漫主義 ろうまんしゅぎ romanticism

SYNONYMS

❶ **unrestrained**
漫 RAMBLING →0858
散 unrestrained →2137
宕 UNCONSTRAINED →2771

❷ **comic**
漫 COMIC →0858
戯 sportive →2351

NOTE

★ do not confuse with 慢 ARROGANT →0844

漣 0859

▶**RIPPLES**
レン さざなみ ㊔ なみ
Ⓝ 漣 Ⓒ 涟 lián

1-3-11

85 氵	Names	U6F23
	S14-3-11	F0000

COMPOUNDS

❶ [original meaning] **RIPPLES, wavelets**
漣音 れんおん mordent

❷ [rare] flow (as of tears)
漣漣たる涙 れんれんたるなみだ tears flowing incessantly

KUN

【さざなみ 漣】[also 小波 or 細波] **RIPPLES**, wavelets

SYNONYMS

❶ **waves**
波 WAVE →0388
浪 BILLOW →0527
漣 RIPPLES →0859

HOMOPHONES

さざなみ
小波 →0007, 0388
細波 →1689, 0388

漏 0860

▶**LEAK**
ロウ も(る) も(れる) も(らす)
Ⓒ 漏 lòu

1-3-11

85 氵	Jōyō	U6F0F
	S14-3-11	F1537

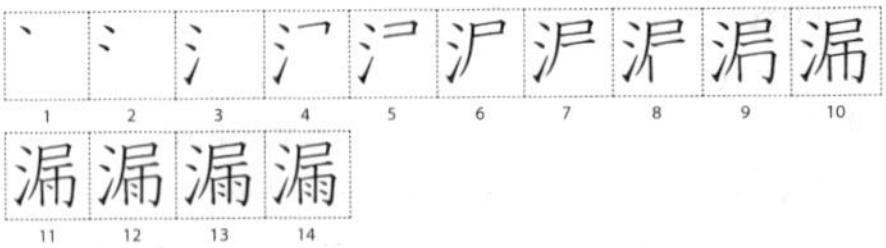

COMPOUNDS

❶ⓐ [original meaning] **LEAK**
ⓑ (of secrets) **LEAK (out), be disclosed, be divulged**

a 漏出 ろうしゅつ leak
漏水 ろうすい water leakage
漏電 ろうでん short circuit, leakage
歯槽膿×漏 しそうのうろう pyorrhea alveolaris
b 漏洩× ろうえい leakage, disclosure

❷ **omit, leave out**
遺漏 いろう omission, oversight, neglect
脱漏 だつろう omission
疎漏 そろう carelessness, inadvertence, oversight

❸ water clock
漏刻 ろうこく water clock

KUN

【もる 漏る】*vi* **LEAK, be leaky**
漏り もり leak, leakage
雨漏り あまもり leak in the roof, leaking of rain

【もれる 漏れる】*vi* **LEAK;** (of secrets) **leak, be disclosed, be divulged; find vent [expression]; be omitted, be left out**
漏れ もれ leak, leakage; omission, oversight
漏れ無く もれなく without omission, in full
ガス漏れ がすもれ gas leak
口から漏れる くちからもれる pass from one's lips
招待に漏れる しょうたいにもれる be left out of an invitation

【もらす 漏らす】*vt* **let LEAK; express, give vent to; reveal, disclose**
小便を漏らす しょうべんをもらす wet one's pants
秘密を漏らす ひみつをもらす betray [reveal] a secret

SYNONYMS

❶ⓐ **flow and drip**
流 FLOW →0529
注 POUR →0383
濫 overflow →0990
溢 OVERFLOW →0807
漏 LEAK →0860
滴 DROP →0866
泌 SECRETE →0390
瀝 DRIP →0996

❷ **omit**
漏 omit →0860
脱 leave out by mistake →1225
抜く leave out →0290
欠 missing →2481

漬

0861

1-3-11

▶**PICKLE**
シ* つ(ける) つ(かる) -づ(け) -づけ
Ⓒ 渍 zì

85	Jōyō	U6F2C
氵	S14-3-11	F1826

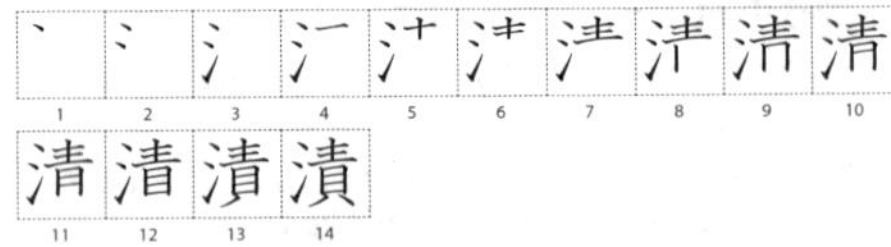

KUN

【つける 漬ける】*vt*
① **PICKLE (vegetables), salt, preserve**
漬け物 つけもの pickles, pickled vegetable
漬け菜 つけな pickled [salted] greens
菜を漬ける なをつける pickle greens
梅を塩に漬ける うめをしおにつける salt plums; preserve plums in salt

② **immerse, steep, soak, dip**
手を水に漬ける てをみずにつける immerse [dip] one's hand in water
衣服を良く漬けて置け いふくをよくつけておけ Give the clothes a thorough soak

【つかる 漬かる】*vi* **be immersed [steeped], soak, be soaked in, be submerged;** (of pickles) **be seasoned, be salted**
湯に漬かる ゆにつかる have a dip in the bath tub
白菜が良く漬かっている はくさいがよくつかっている The Chinese cabbage is well seasoned [salted]

【-づけ -漬け, -漬】[also suffix]
ⓐ **PICKLEs**
ⓑ **pickling with, preserving in**
a 千枚漬け せんまいづけ pickled sliced radishes
松前漬け まつまえづけ Matsumae pickles
b 塩漬け しおづけ salted [corned] food; pickling with salt
味噌漬け みそづけ vegetables preserved in *miso;* preserving in *miso*
ホルマリン漬け ほるまりんづけ specimen preserved in formalin

SYNONYMS

【つける】
① **preserve food**
漬ける PICKLE →0861
燻 SMOKE →1406
薫 smoke →3005

② **moisten**
潤 moisten →0918
浸 SOAK →0530

漬ける immerse →0861

【-づけ】

ⓐ **preserved foods**

-漬け pickles →0861

-干し dried food →4187

HOMOPHONES

つける

付 ATTACH →0035

附 ATTACH →0410

着 PUT ON →4110

就 SET ABOUT →2129

即 IMMEDIATE →1439

点 POINT →2587

-づけ 付 ATTACH →0035

NOTE

➡ see USAGE note at 付 0035

滲

0862

1-3-11

▶PERMEATE

シン し(みる) にじ(む)

Ⓝ 滲 Ⓒ 渗 shèn

85	Non-Jōyō	U6EF2
氵	S14-3-11	F2117

COMPOUNDS

● [now usu. 浸 0530] [original meaning] **PERMEATE,** infiltrate, penetrate; ooze, seep

滲透する しんとうする permeate, penetrate

滲出 しんしゅつ percolation, exudation, effusion

滲炭鋼 しんたんこう cement steel

KUN

【しみる 滲みる】[also 染みる]

ⓐ **PERMEATE, soak into**

ⓑ **penetrate (to the bone), come home to one's heart**

ⓒ **smart from irritation**

a 滲み込む しみこむ soak into, permeate

【にじむ 滲む】**blot, spread, run, blur; ooze, be saturated with (as of blood, tears or sweat)**

滲み易いインク にじみやすいいんく ink that runs easily

額に汗を滲ませて ひたいにあせをにじませて with a sweating brow

SYNONYMS

● **penetrate**

透 PASS THROUGH →3854

貫 PENETRATE →3112

破 break through →1478

滲 PERMEATE →0862

HOMOPHONES

しみる

染 DYE →3181

凍 FREEZE →0146

NOTE

➡ see USAGE note at 染 3181

漆

0863

1-3-11

▶LACQUER

シツ うるし 名 ぬり

Ⓒ 漆 qī

85	Jōyō	U6F06
氵	S14-3-11	F2158

COMPOUNDS

❶ [original meaning] **(Japanese or Chinese) LACQUER, varnish, japan, *urushi***

漆器 しっき lacquer ware

漆工 しっこう lacquer work, japanner

❷ (as black as lacquer) **pitch-black**

漆黒 しっこく pitch black

❸ **unclassified compounds**

漆喰 しっくい plaster, stucco

KUN

【うるし 漆】

① **Japanese LACQUER, varnish, japan, *urushi***

漆塗り うるしぬり lacquering, japanning; lacquer ware

② **Japanese LACQUER [varnish] tree**

漆かぶれ うるしかぶれ lacquer poisoning

SYNONYMS

❶ **pigments**

墨 INDIA INK →3423

漆 LACQUER →0863

藍 INDIGO →3024

堊 WHITEWASH →3442

❷ **black colors**

黒 BLACK →3406

漆 pitch-black →0863

黎 BLACK →3487

【うるし】

② **trees**

桜 CHERRY →1168

桐 PAULOWNIA →1173

桂 AROMATIC TREE, katsura tree →1163

梓 CATALPA →1207

桑 MULBERRY →2618

漆 Japanese lacquer tree →0863

樺 BIRCH →1324

椛 BIRCH →1202

梧 CHINESE PARASOL TREE →1200

檀 SPINDLE TREE →1385

椿 CAMELLIA → 1278
柳 WILLOW → 1115
柊 HOLLY → 1119
椋 *APHANANTHE ASPERA* → 1245
杠 spindle tree → 1114
槻 ZELKOVA → 1349
楢 OAK → 1287
樫 EVERGREEN OAK → 1364
柏 CYPRESS, JAPANESE EMPEROR OAK → 1110
榎 HACKBERRY → 1323
梶 PAPER MULBERRY → 1199
柘 JAPANESE BOXWOOD → 1117
楊 WILLOW → 1286
桧 JAPANESE CYPRESS → 1160
梛 *NAGEIA NAGI* → 1206
榊 SACRED SHINTO TREE → 1327
楓 MAPLE → 1280
松 PINE → 1075
杉 CRYPTOMERIA → 1027
槙 PODOCARPUS → 1330
楠 CAMPHOR TREE → 1283
樟 CAMPHOR TREE → 1351

漕

▶ROW
ソウ こ(ぐ)
Ⓒ 漕 cáo

0864
◧1-3-11

85	Names	U6F15
氵	S14-3-11	F2059

COMPOUNDS

❶ⓐ ROW, scull, paddle
ⓑ pedal
a 漕艇 そうてい rowing
競漕 きょうそう regatta, boat race
❷ (carry by ship or boat) ship
回漕業 かいそうぎょう shipping business

KUN

【こぐ 漕ぐ】
①ⓐ **ROW, scull, paddle**
ⓑ **pedal**
a 漕ぎ出す こぎだす begin rowing, row out
漕ぎ着ける こぎつける row up to (a destination); manage to attain, reach, make it (to)
漕ぎ手 こぎて rower, oarsman
船を漕ぐ ふねをこぐ row a boat; nod off
b 自転車を漕ぐ じてんしゃをこぐ pedal a bike
② unclassified compounds
阿漕 あこぎ greedy, ruthless

SYNONYMS

❶ move through water
泳 SWIM → 0385
游 SWIM → 0750
渉 wade → 0638
遡 GO UPSTREAM → 4040
漕 ROW → 0864

漱

▶RINSE
ソウ すす(ぐ) くちすす(ぐ)
Ⓒ 漱 shù

0865
◧1-3-11

85	Names	U6F31
氵	S14-3-11	F1902

COMPOUNDS

● RINSE (one's mouth), wash, gargle
漱石枕流 そうせきちんりゅう bad loser

KUN

【すすぐ 漱ぐ】**RINSE one's mouth, gargle**
口を漱ぐ くちをすすぐ rinse one's mouth, gargle
【くちすすぐ 漱ぐ】**RINSE one's mouth, gargle**
流れに漱ぐ ながれにくちすすぐ *literary* rinse one's mouth, gargle with river water

SYNONYMS

● clean and wash
洗 WASH → 0465
漱 RINSE → 0865
拭 WIPE → 0453
滌 WASH → 0854
濯 RINSE → 0978
浴 BATHE → 0533
浄 cleanse → 0457
粛 PURGE → 4400
清 CLEAR → 0635
払 CLEAR AWAY → 0225
掃 SWEEP → 0611

NOTE

★ do not confuse with 瀬 SHALLOWS → 0995

滴

▶DROP
テキ しずく したた(る)
Ⓒ 滴 dī

0866
◧1-3-11

85	Jōyō	U6EF4
氵	S14-3-11	F1913

1	2	3	4	5	6	7	8	9	10	11	12	13	14
丶	冫	氵	氵'	氵亠	氵亠	氵产	氵产	湳	滴	滴	滴	滴	滴

COMPOUNDS

❶ DROP, drip, trickle
滴下する てきかする drip, trickle
滴水 てきすい water dripping

点滴 てんてき falling drops of water; intravenous infusion

❷ⓐ [original meaning] (liquid globule) **DROP**
ⓑ counter for **DROPs**

a 水滴 すいてき water drop
雨滴 うてき raindrops
b 数滴 すうてき several drops
一滴 いってき a drop

KUN

【しずく 滴】[also 雫]
ⓐ (liquid globule) **DROP**
ⓑ counter for **DROPs**
a 露の滴 つゆのしずく dewdrop
b 一滴 ひとしずく a drop

【したたる 滴る】**drip, DROP, trickle**
滴り したたり dripping; drop, trickle
滴り落ちる したたりおちる trickle down

SYNONYMS

❶ **flow and drip**
流 FLOW →0529
注 POUR →0383
濫 overflow →0990
溢 OVERFLOW →0807
漏 LEAK →0860
滴 DROP →0866
泌 SECRETE →0390
瀝 DRIP →0996

❷ⓐ **small water masses**
滴 DROP →0866
雫 DROP →3430
泡 BUBBLE →0392
沫 BUBBLE →0397

USAGE

【しずく】
滴
[also 雫]
ⓐ (liquid globule) drop
ⓑ counter for drops
雫
[also 滴] same as 滴

HOMOPHONES

しずく 雫 DROP →3430

漸

0867
1-3-11

▶**GRADUALLY**
ゼン ようや(く)▲ ㊔ すすむ
Ⓒ 渐 jiàn jiān

85 氵	Jōyō	U6F38
	S14-3-11	F2697

Stroke order: 1–14

COMPOUNDS

ⓐ **GRADUALLY, gradual**
ⓑ advance **GRADUALLY**
a 漸次 ぜんじ gradually
漸進 ぜんしん gradual advance
漸減 ぜんげん gradual decrease
b 東漸 とうぜん eastward advance (as of culture)

INDEPENDENT

【ぜん 漸】gradual advance
漸を以て進歩する ぜんをもってしんぽする advance gradually

KUN

【ようやく 漸く】
① finally, at last, at length
② barely, narrowly, with difficulty
③ **GRADUALLY**

SYNONYMS

ⓐ **in succession**
連 IN SUCCESSION →3849
歴 successive →3748
逐 ONE BY ONE →3848
逓 progressively →3852
漸 GRADUALLY →0867

NOTE

★ do not confuse with 暫 SHORT WHILE →3553

漢

0868
1-3-11

▶**CHINESE**
▶**FELLOW**
カン

85 氵	Names	UFA47
	S14-3-11	F0000

traditional form →see 漢 at 0808

滿

0869
1-3-11

▶**FULL**
マン み(ちる) み(つ) み(たす) ㊔ みつる ま

85 氵	Nonstandard	U6EFF
	S14-3-11	F0000

traditional form →see 満 at 0739

滯

0870
1-3-11

▶**STAGNATE**
▶**STAY**
タイ とどこお(る)

85 氵	Names	U6EEF
	S14-3-11	F0000

traditional form →see 滞 at 0815

口 土 女 山 彳 忄 扌 【氵】 犭 阝

漥

0871

1-3-11

▶**HOLLOW**

ワ くぼ くぼ(む) くぼ(まる)

85	Nonstandard	U6F25
氵	S14-3-11	F0000

traditional form → see 窪 at 2962

淵

1-3-11

incorrect stroke-count
➡ see 1-3-9: 氵 at 0732

潟

1-3-11

incorrect stroke-count
➡ see 1-3-12: 氵 at 0921

獄

0872

1-3-11

▶**PRISON**

ゴク

Ⓒ 狱 yù

94	Jōyō	U7344
犬	S14-4-10	F1428

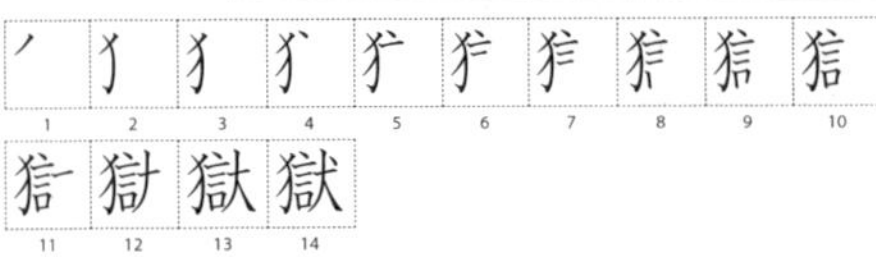

COMPOUNDS

❶ **PRISON, jail**
獄中記 ごくちゅうき diary written in prison
獄衣 ごくい prison uniform
獄死 ごくし death in prison
出獄 しゅつごく release from prison
牢×獄 ろうごく prison, jail
脱獄 だつごく prison break, jailbreak

❷ **hell**
地獄 じごく hell; inferno
煉獄 れんごく purgatory

❸ lawsuit, litigation
疑獄 ぎごく criminal case, scandal
大獄 たいごく wholesale arrest, roundup

INDEPENDENT

【ごく 獄】**PRISON**, jail
獄を破る ごくをやぶる break prison

SYNONYMS

❶ **prison**
獄 PRISON → 0872
監 prison → 3535

❷ **posthumous worlds**
天 HEAVEN → 4250
幽 world of the dead → 3731
獄 hell → 0872

隠

0873

1-3-11

▶**HIDE**

イン オン▲ かく(す) かく(し)- かく(れる)

Ⓝ 隱 乚 Ⓒ 隐 yǐn

170	Jōyō	U96A0
阝	S14-3-11	F0709

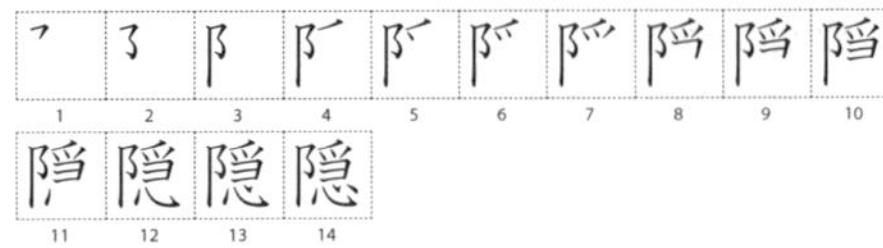

COMPOUNDS

❶ⓐ [original meaning] (conceal from sight) **HIDE, conceal**
ⓑ hidden from view, concealed, secret
ⓒ become hidden from view, disappear
a 隠蔽する いんぺいする conceal, cover up, hide
隠匿 いんとく concealment; misprision
b 隠語 いんご secret language, jargon
隠密 おんみつ secrecy, privacy; detective, spy
隠花植物 いんかしょくぶつ cryptogamic plant
c 隠滅する いんめつする extinction, destruction
隠見(=隠顕) いんけん appearance and disappearance

❷ retire from the world, live in seclusion
隠居 いんきょ retirement; person retired from active life
隠棲 いんせい secluded life

❸ feel pity, have compassion
惻×隠の情 そくいんのじょう pity, compassion

KUN

【かくす 隠す】*vt* **HIDE, conceal; hide (a matter from someone), keep secret**
隠し持つ かくしもつ carry (something) under cover
覆い隠す おおいかくす cover, mask

【かくし- 隠し-】[prefix] **hidden, concealed, secret**
隠し事 かくしごと secret
隠し芸 かくしげい hidden talent; parlor trick
隠しカメラ かくしかめら hidden [spy] camera
隠し財源 かくしざいげん secret resources
隠し場所 かくしばしょ place for concealment

【かくれる 隠れる】*vi* **HIDE, hide [conceal] oneself, disappear, be hidden from sight; be unknown [anonymous]; retire from the world;** [honorific] **pass away**
隠れ伏す かくれふす lie concealed
隠れん坊 かくれんぼう hide-and-seek
隠れ蓑 かくれみの invisibility cloak; pretext
隠れ道 かくれみち hidden path
隠れも無い かくれもない well-known
雲隠れする くもがくれする vanish behind the clouds; disappear, run away

野に隠れる のにかくれる retire from public service

SYNONYMS

❶ⓐ hide

隠 HIDE → 0873
蔽 COVER → 2991
伏 lie in concealment → 0049
潜 LURK → 0922
匿 CONCEAL → 3735
忍 perform by stealth → 2750

ⓑ secret and private

秘 SECRET → 1490
密 SECRET → 2857
暗 in the dark → 1273
私 PRIVATE → 1432
内 not public → 4277
隠 hidden from view → 0873

際

▸VERGE
▸OCCASION
サイ きわ -ぎわ

Ⓒ 际 jì

0874

1-3-11

170	Jōyō-5	U969B
阝	S14-3-11	F0267

(stroke order 1–14)

COMPOUNDS

❶ VERGE, brink, edge

際限 さいげん limits, end, bounds
際涯 さいがい limits, end, extremity
金輪際 こんりんざい never; *Buddhism* deepest bottom of the earth
天際 てんさい horizon

❷ OCCASION, time

実際の じっさいの true, real; actual; practical

❸ have relations, have social intercourse

交際 こうさい association, friendship, intercourse

❹ inter-, between, among

国際的な こくさいてきな international
学際的 がくさいてき interdisciplinary
州際通商委員会 しゅうさいつうしょういいんかい Interstate Commerce Commission

❺ occur unexpectedly

際会する さいかいする meet, face, confront

❻ degree, rank

分際 ぶんざい one's social position [standing]

INDEPENDENT

【さい 際】**OCCASION, time; when**

あの際に あのさいに on that occasion
食事の際に しょくじのさいに when eating

KUN

【きわ 際】**VERGE, edge, brink, side; occasion, time when something is about to happen, critical moment**

際立つ きわだつ be conspicuous, be prominent
際どい きわどい dangerous, risky, hairbreadth
際物 きわもの seasonal articles; temporary
水際 みずぎわ beach, waterside
窓際に まどぎわに at the window
. . . の際に …のきわに at the edge of; at the moment of

【-ぎわ -際】**on the VERGE of, on the point of**

間際 まぎわ on the verge of, just before, on the point of
死に際に しにぎわに on the verge of death

SYNONYMS

❶ edges and boundaries

縁 EDGE → 1754
端 edge → 1564
辺 border → 3761
境 BOUNDARY → 0835
疆 BOUNDARY → 1810
界 BOUNDS → 3172
際 VERGE → 0874
涯 OUTER LIMITS → 0623

❷ occasions

際 OCCASION → 0874
折 occasion → 0297
時 timely occasion → 1155
機 OPPORTUNITY → 1365
節 time → 3336

❹ between

中 MIDDLE → 4262
仲 intermediate → 0047
間 BETWEEN → 4122
際 inter- → 0874

【-ぎわ】

◯ on the verge of

-掛かる be on the verge of → 0596
将 on the verge of → 0551
-際 on the verge of → 0874
臨 on the point of → 2059

障

▸HINDRANCE
ショウ さわ(る)

Ⓒ 障 zhàng

0875

1-3-11

170	Jōyō-6	U969C
阝	S14-3-11	F0751

1	2	3	4	5	6	7	8	9	10	11	12	13	14

COMPOUNDS

❶ⓐ HINDRANCE, obstruction, obstacle, barrier
ⓑ [original meaning] **hinder, obstruct, block, screen**

a 障子 しょうじ paper sliding-door, *shoji*
故障 こしょう malfunction, breakdown; physical disorder; hindrance, obstacle, accident; objection, protest
支障 ししょう hindrance, obstacle, difficulty
万障 ばんしょう all hindrances, all obstacles
排障器 はいしょうき obstruction guard
罪障 ざいしょう sins
b 障壁 しょうへき barrier, obstacle; [formerly also 牆壁] wall, fence
障害 しょうがい obstacle, hindrance; (physical) disorder

❷ defend, protect; keep away, shut out
保障する ほしょうする (ensure that an undesirable condition does not occur) guarantee, secure, ensure

KUN

【さわる 障る】
① **hinder, interfere with**
障り さわり hindrance, obstacle; harm, bad effect; sickness
差し障り さしさわり obstacle, offense
月の障り つきのさわり menses
② affect, harm, jar on
体に障る からだにさわる affect one's health

SPECIAL READINGS

気障▲ きざ affectation

SYNONYMS

❶ⓐ obstacle
碍 HINDRANCE → 0875
関 BARRIER → 4129
ⓑ obstruct and hinder
遮 INTERRUPT → 3916
塞 STOP UP → 2924
阻 OBSTRUCT → 0411
沮 OBSTRUCT → 0399
奄 OBSTRUCT (by covering) → 2757
妨 HINDER → 0279
障 hinder → 0875
碍 STAND IN THE WAY → 1536
害 stand in the way → 2826
梗 STOP UP → 1204

HOMOPHONES

さわる 触 TOUCH → 1914
さわり 触 TOUCH → 1914

NOTE

➡ see USAGE notes at 保 0107 and 触 1914

隙 0876 ◧ 1-3-11

▶GAP
ゲキ ケキ すき す(く) す(かす) ひま

170	Nonstandard	U28EF6
阝	S14-3-11	F0000

traditional form → see 隙 at 0826

隟 0877 ◧ 1-3-11

▶GAP
ゲキ ケキ すき す(く) す(かす) ひま

170	Nonstandard	U969F
阝	S14-3-11	F0000

traditional form → see 隙 at 0826

嘲 0878 ◧ 1-3-12

▶SCOFF AT
チョウ トウ▲ あざけ(る)
Ⓝ 嘲 Ⓒ 嘲 cháo zhāo

30	Jōyō	U5632
口	S15-3-12	F2204

1	2	3	4	5	6	7	8	9	10	11	12	13	14	15

COMPOUNDS

● SCOFF AT, jeer at, ridicule, scorn, mock
嘲笑する ちょうしょうする laugh at, deride
嘲罵する ちょうばする taunt, insult, abuse
嘲弄 ちょうろう taunting, mockery, ridicule
自嘲 じちょう self-derision

KUN

【あざける 嘲る】**SCOFF AT, jeer at, ridicule, scorn, mock**
嘲り あざけり ridicule, scorn

SPECIAL READINGS

嘲笑う▲ あざわらう laugh at, deride

SYNONYMS

● disdain
侮 despise → 0091
軽 make light of → 1909
蔑 DESPISE → 2969
嘲 SCOFF AT → 0878

噴

▶SPOUT

フン ふ(く)

N 噴 C 喷 pēn pèn

0879

1-3-12

30	Jōyō	U5674
口	S15-3-12	F1526

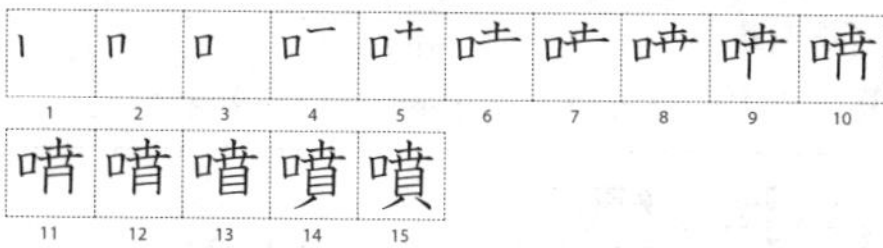

COMPOUNDS

● [original meaning] **SPOUT, emit, spurt, gush out**

噴出 ふんしゅつ spouting, gushing

噴水 ふんすい jet (of water), fountain

噴火 ふんか eruption, volcanic activity

噴火山 ふんかざん volcano

噴霧器 ふんむき sprayer, vaporizer, atomizer

噴射 ふんしゃ jet, jet propulsion

噴飯する ふんぱんする burst out laughing

KUN

【ふく 噴く】**SPOUT, emit, spurt, gush out**

噴き出す ふきだす spout, spurt, gush out; break into laughter

SYNONYMS

● **emit**

出 PUT OUT → 4310

発 EMIT → 3174

放 radiate → 1058

排 DISCHARGE → 0593

射 SHOOT → 1850

噴 SPOUT → 0879

吐 SPEW → 0235

湧 WELL UP → 0749

HOMOPHONES

ふく 吹 BLOW → 0272

NOTE

➡ see USAGE note at 吹 0272

嘘

▶LIE

キョ うそ

N 嘘 C 嘘 xū shī

0880

1-3-12

30	Non-Jōyō	U5653
口	S15-3-12	F1306

COMPOUNDS

❶ **LIE, falsehood**

嘘言 きょげん lie

❷ [original meaning, now rare] blow, breathe out

嘘吸 きょきゅう breathing, respiration

KUN

【うそ 嘘】

① [also prefix] **LIE, falsehood; fabrication, fiction**

嘘つき うそつき liar

嘘泣き うそなき fake crying

嘘の様 うそのよう unbelievable, incredible

嘘発見器 うそはっけんき lie detector, polygraph

嘘八百 うそはっぴゃく pack of lies

大嘘 おおうそ big lie

② **mistake, error**

嘘字 うそじ incorrect character

嘘の集合時間を教える うそのしゅうごうじかんをおしえる give someone a wrong meeting time

③ something inexpedient [objectionable]

ここで諦めるのは嘘だ ここであきらめるのはうそだ We can't give up now

SYNONYMS

❶ **falsehood**

偽 falsehood → 0149

嘘 LIE → 0880

嘱

▶CHARGE WITH

ショク

N 囑 C 嘱 zhǔ

0881

1-3-12

30	Jōyō	U5631
口	S15-3-12	F3044

COMPOUNDS

[sometimes also 属 3901]

❶ [original meaning] **CHARGE (a person) WITH (a job), ask someone to do something; entrust**

嘱託する しょくたくする entrust with

委嘱する いしょくする charge, commission [entrust] with

❷ fasten one's attention upon

嘱目する しょくもくする pay attention to

SYNONYMS

❶ **request**

請 REQUEST → 1983

訴 APPEAL TO → 1901

頼 ASK → 2041

嘱 CHARGE WITH → 0881

要 REQUIRE → 3263

願 ASK A FAVOR → 2320

求 SEEK → 4365

乞 BEG → 2457

❶ **commit**

託 ENTRUST → 1845
托 ENTRUST → 0252
預 DEPOSIT → 1317
委 COMMIT → 3160
任 LEAVE TO → 0057
嘱 CHARGE WITH → 0881

噌

▶*MISO*

ソ ソウ

Ⓝ 噌 Ⓒ 噌 chēng cēng

0882

1-3-12

30	Names	U564C
口	S15-3-12	F1947

COMPOUNDS

● ***MISO*, bean paste**

味噌 みそ *miso,* bean paste; flattery
蟹味噌 かにみそ crab guts
手前味噌 てまえみそ singing one's own praises
脳味噌 のうみそ brain, brains

SYNONYMS

● **seasonings**

糖 SUGAR → 1777
塩 SALT → 0774
酢 VINEGAR → 1910
醋 VINEGAR → 2002
油 OIL → 0400
醬 FERMENTED SAUCE → 3569
噌 MISO → 0882
蜜 HONEY → 2958

噂

▶RUMOR

ソン うわさ

Ⓝ 噂 Ⓒ 噂 zǔn

0883

1-3-12

30	Names	U5642
口	S15-3-12	F1326

KUN

【うわさ 噂】**RUMOR, hearsay, gossip**

噂話 うわさばなし gossip
噂通り うわさどおり as rumored
噂をすれば影 うわさをすればかげ Speak of the devil
根も葉も無い噂 ねもはもないうわさ groundless rumor
人の噂も七十五日 ひとのうわさもしちじゅうごにち A wonder lasts but nine days

SYNONYMS

【うわさ】

○ **stories**

話 story → 1928
談 account → 1975
語 tale → 1944
説 narrative → 1949
噂 RUMOR → 0883

嘲

▶SCOFF AT

チョウ トウ あざけ(る)

0884

1-3-12

30	Nonstandard	U5632
口	S15-3-12	F0000

traditional form → see 嘲 at 0878

噛

▶BITE

ゴウ か(む) か(ます) か(ませる)

0885

1-3-12

30	Nonstandard	U565B
口	S15-3-12	F0000

traditional form → see 噛 at 0988

噂

▶RUMOR

ソン うわさ

0886

1-3-12

30	Nonstandard	U5642
口	S15-3-12	F0000

traditional form → see 噂 at 0883

墳

▶TUMULUS

フン

Ⓝ 墳 Ⓒ 坟 fén

0887

1-3-12

32	Jōyō	U58B3
土	S15-3-12	F2014

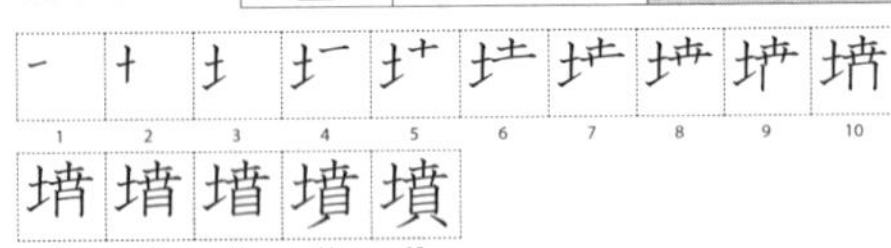

COMPOUNDS

● **TUMULUS, grave mound, tomb**

墳墓 ふんぼ grave, tomb
古墳 こふん tumulus, ancient tomb, old mound
円墳 えんぷん burial mound

SYNONYMS

● **graves**

墓 GRAVE → 2930
墳 TUMULUS → 0887
陵 IMPERIAL MAUSOLEUM → 0660
廟 MAUSOLEUM → 3935
祢 FATHER'S MAUSOLEUM → 1142
塚 grave mound → 0675

墟

▶RUINS

キョ

Ⓒ 墟 xū

0888

1-3-12

32	Non-Jōyō	U589F
土	S15-3-12	F2654

COMPOUNDS

● [now also 虚 4017] [original meaning] **RUINS**
廃墟 はいきょ ruins, remains

SYNONYMS

● **ruins**
墟 RUINS → 0888
虚 ruins → 4017

增

0889
◧ 1-3-12

▶**INCREASE**
ゾウ ま(す) ま(し) ふ(える) ふ(やす)

32	Names	U589E
土	S15-3-12	F0000

traditional form → see 増 at 0836

嬉

0890
◧ 1-3-12

▶**GLAD**
キ うれ(しい) ㊔ よし うれし
Ⓝ 娭 Ⓒ 嬉 xī

38	Names	U5B09
女	S15-3-12	F1385

COMPOUNDS

● [original meaning] be merry, play, sport
嬉嬉として ききとして merrily, joyfully
嬉戯する きぎする frisk, frolic

KUN

【うれしい 嬉しい】**GLAD, pleased, happy, delighted; joyful, delightful**
嬉しさ うれしさ joy, delight, gladness
嬉しそうな うれしそうな delightful, glad-looking

SYNONYMS

【うれしい】
○ **pleased and pleasant**
楽 pleasurable → 3505
欣 JOYFUL → 1057
爽 REFRESHING → 4402
快 PLEASANT → 0289
朗 CHEERFUL → 1679
愉 PLEASED → 0710
悦 DELIGHTED → 0501
嬉しい GLAD → 0890
喜 HAPPY → 2889
歓 JOYOUS → 2342
驩 JOYOUS → 2333

幡

0891
◧ 1-3-12

▶**LONG FLAG**
ハン バン マン はた
Ⓒ 幡 fān

50	Names	U5E61
巾	S15-3-12	F1639

COMPOUNDS

● **LONG FLAG, streamer, flag (esp. in Buddhism)**
幢×幡 どうばん hanging banner used as ornament in Buddhist temples
八幡船 ばはんせん Japanese pirate ship
八幡 はちまん God of War, *Hachiman*

INDEPENDENT

【ばん 幡】*patākā*: pendant streamer hung before a temple in honor of Buddha

KUN

【はた 幡】
① [usu. 旗] **flag, banner, standard, ensign**
幡幢× はたほこ(=はたぼこ) long-handled spear bearing a small flag used in Buddhist services and court ceremonies
② *patākā*: **pendant streamer hung before a temple in honor of Buddha**

SYNONYMS

● **flag**
旗 FLAG → 1321
幡 LONG FLAG → 0891
旒 COUNTER FOR FLAGS → 1272

HOMOPHONES

はた 旗 FLAG → 1321

NOTE

➡ see USAGE note at 旗 1321

彈

0892
◧ 1-3-12

▶**PROJECTILE**
▶**SPRING BACK**
ダン ひ(く) -ひ(き) はず(む) たま はじ(く) はじ(ける)

57	Names	U5F48
弓	S15-3-12	F0000

traditional form → see 弾 at 0697

衝

0893
◧ 1-3-12

▶**COLLIDE**
ショウ つ(く)▲
Ⓒ 冲 chōng chòng

144	Jōyō	U885D
行	S15-6-9	F1103

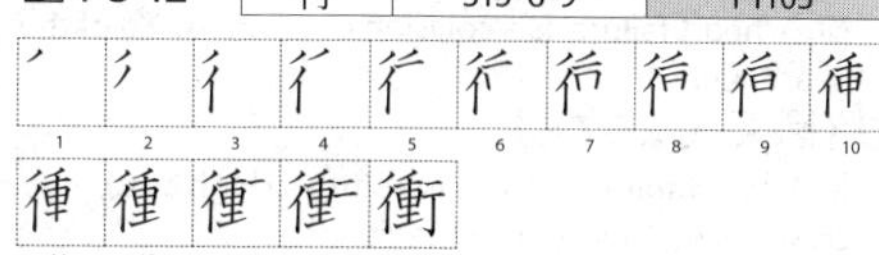

COMPOUNDS

❶ **COLLIDE, dash [run] against, crash**
衝突する しょうとつする collide (with), crash (into); conflict [clash] (with)
衝撃 しょうげき impact, shock, impulse
衝動 しょうどう impulse, urge
衝心 しょうしん heart failure

口 土 女 巾 弓 【彳】 忄 扌 氵 阝

衝天 しょうてん high spirits
緩衝 かんしょう buffer

❷ important position, strategic place, hub, focus
要衝 ようしょう key point, strategic position

❸ attack, strike
折衝 せっしょう negotiation, parley

❹ [original meaning, now archaic] thoroughfare, avenue

INDEPENDENT

【しょう 衝】important position, focus; *astron* opposition
攻撃の衝に当たる こうげきのしょうにあたる bear the brunt of an attack
世界交通の衝 せかいこうつうのしょう focus of the trade routes of the world

KUN

【つく 衝く】
① [usu. 突く] attack, strike at
中堅を衝く ちゅうけんをつく strike [attack] at the center [heart]
② [usu. 突く] brave, face courageously
嵐を衝いて進む あらしをついてすすむ proceed in the face of a storm
③ [usu. 突く] stimulate (the senses), be pungent
鼻を衝く はなをつく assail the nostrils
④ unclassified compounds
衝立て ついたて single-leaf screen

SYNONYMS

❶ collide
衝 COLLIDE →0893
牴 COLLIDE WITH →1134
觝 COLLIDE WITH →1892
突 DASH →2772
当たる HIT →2701

HOMOPHONES

つく
突 DASH →2772
撞 STRIKE →0905

COMPOUND FORMATION

❶【衝心 しょうしん】
衝心 'heart failure' is a collision or crash (衝 ❶) of the heart (心).

❷【衝天 しょうてん】
衝天 'high spirits' is to be in spirits so high as to crash (衝 ❶) or soar into the sky (天).

NOTE

➡ see USAGE note at 突 2772
➡ see COMPOUND FORMATION for 折衝 せっしょう →折 0297

口 土 女 巾 弓 【彳】 忄 扌 氵 阝

徹

0894
1-3-12

▶GO THROUGH
テツ ㊔ とおる あき
Ⓒ 彻 chè

60	Jōyō	U5FB9
彳	S15-3-12	F1092

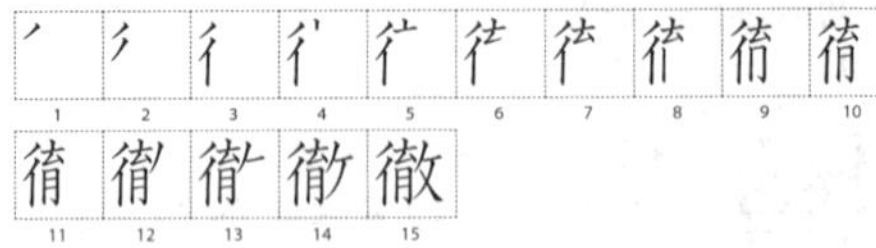

COMPOUNDS

❶ **GO THROUGH [with], be thorough, be exhaustive**
徹底的 てっていてき thorough, exhaustive
貫徹する かんてつする carry through, go through with, accomplish, attain
一徹な いってつな obstinate, stubborn
透徹した とうてつした lucid, clear, penetrating

❷ **all through, throughout**
徹夜 てつや all night vigil [sitting]
徹宵 てっしょう all night long, throughout the night

INDEPENDENT

【てっする 徹する】**GO THROUGH (with), be thorough, devote oneself to; penetrate, pierce**

SYNONYMS

❶ accomplish
達 ATTAIN →3893
遂 ACCOMPLISH →3892
成 ACHIEVE →4352
徹 GO THROUGH →0894
破 carry through with →1478
叶 BE FULFILLED →0209

❷ throughout
通 through →3855
徹 all through →0894
終 from beginning to end →1692
中 throughout →4262

NOTE

★ do not confuse with 撤 WITHDRAW →0912

徵

0895
1-3-12

▶LEVY
▶SYMPTOM
チョウ チ しるし

60	Names	U5FB5
彳	S15-3-12	F0000

traditional form →see 徴 at 0841

德

0896
1-3-12

▶VIRTUE
トク ㊔ のり よし なる なり あつ

60	Names	U5FB7
彳	S15-3-12	F0000

traditional form →see 徳 at 0842

憤 0897

◧ 1-3-12

▶INDIGNATION

フン いきどお(る)

Ⓝ 憤 Ⓒ 愤 fèn

61	Jōyō	U61A4
忄	S15-3-12	F1801

Stroke order: 1–15

COMPOUNDS

❶ⓐ **INDIGNATION, resentment, exasperation, rage**
ⓑ **be indignant, resent, be angry**

a 憤怒 ふんど(=ふんぬ) anger, rage, resentment
公憤 こうふん public indignation [resentment]
義憤 ぎふん righteous indignation
b 憤激する ふんげきする be inflamed by anger, flare up
憤慨 ふんがい resentment, indignation
憤然と ふんぜんと indignantly, in a rage
憤死する ふんしする die in a fit of anger
悲憤 ひふん indignation, resentment

❷ [also 奮 3000] rise to action, be stirred
発憤する はっぷんする be stimulated, be inspired, be roused

KUN

【いきどおる 憤る】**be indignant, resent, be angry**
憤り いきどおり indignation, resentment
時世を憤る じせいをいきどおる be indignant at the times

SYNONYMS

❶ **anger**
怒 GET ANGRY → 3180
憤 INDIGNATION → 0897
慨 resent → 0790

憬 0898

◧ 1-3-12

▶YEARN AFTER

ケイ あこが(れる)▲

Ⓒ 憬 jǐng

61	Jōyō	U61AC
忄	S15-3-12	F3278

Stroke order: 1–15

COMPOUNDS

● **YEARN AFTER**
憧憬する しょうけい(=どうけい)する yearn after

KUN

【あこがれる 憬れる】[usu. 憧れる] **YEARN AFTER; adore**
憬れ あこがれ yearning, longing

SYNONYMS

● **wish and desire**
願 WISH → 2320
憧 YEARN AFTER → 0899
憬 YEARN AFTER → 0898
貪 COVET → 2630
望 HOPE → 3408
希 ASPIRE → 2543
懐 LONG FOR → 0942
慕 yearn for → 2970
渇 thirst for → 0627
欲 DESIRE → 1867
慾 DESIRE → 3551
求 SEEK → 4365

HOMOPHONES

あこがれる 憧 YEARN AFTER → 0899

NOTE

➡ see USAGE note at 憧 0899

憧 0899

◧ 1-3-12

▶YEARN AFTER

ショウ ドウ▲ シュ▲ あこが(れる)

Ⓒ 憧 chōng

61	Jōyō	U61A7
忄	S15-3-12	F2155

Stroke order: 1–15

COMPOUNDS

● **YEARN AFTER**
憧憬する しょうけい(=どうけい)する yearn after

KUN

【あこがれる 憧れる】[sometimes also 憬れる] **YEARN AFTER; adore**
憧れ あこがれ yearning, longing
憧れの的 あこがれのまと object of envy; adored figure, idol
有名人に憧れる ゆうめいじんにあこがれる adore [be attracted to] a celebrity

SYNONYMS

● **wish and desire**
願 WISH → 2320
憧 YEARN AFTER → 0899
憬 YEARN AFTER → 0898
貪 COVET → 2630
望 HOPE → 3408

希 ASPIRE → 2543
懐 LONG FOR → 0942
慕 yearn for → 2970
渇 thirst for → 0627
欲 DESIRE → 1867
慾 DESIRE → 3551
求 SEEK → 4365

USAGE

【あこがれる】

憧れる
[sometimes also 憬れる] yearn after; adore

憬れる
[usu. 憧れる] yearn after; adore

HOMOPHONES

あこがれる 憬 YEARN AFTER → 0898

慨

0900

1-3-12

▶DEPLORE

ガイ

61	Nonstandard	UFA3E
忄	S15-3-12	F0000

traditional form → see 慨 at 0790

憐

0901

1-3-12

▶PITY

レン　あわ(れ)　あわ(れむ)

61	Nonstandard	U6190
忄	S15-3-12	F0000

traditional form → see 憐 at 0945

憎

0902

1-3-12

▶HATE

ゾウ　にく(む)　にく(い)　にく(らしい)　にく(しみ)

61	Names	UFA3F
忄	S15-3-12	F0000

traditional form → see 憎 at 0845

撲

0903

1-3-12

▶DEAL A BLOW

ボク

Ⓒ 扑 pū

64	Jōyō	U64B2
扌	S15-3-12	F1640

COMPOUNDS

● [original meaning] **DEAL [give] A BLOW, beat, strike forcefully, strike a blow**

撲殺 ぼくさつ clubbing to death
撲滅 ぼくめつ eradication, destruction
打撲 だぼく blow, stroke

SPECIAL READINGS

相撲 すもう sumo wrestling

SYNONYMS

● **strike**

打 STRIKE → 0224
撲 DEAL A BLOW → 0903
殴 BEAT (strike a person) → 1099
蹴 KICK → 2074
撃 STRIKE → 3552
挌 STRIKE (a person) → 0448
撞 STRIKE (a ball or bell) → 0905
撥ねる strike (knock down) → 0907
当てる HIT → 2701
叩 KNOCK → 0208
拍 BEAT (strike repeatedly) → 0361
搏 BEAT (throb) → 0794

NOTE

★ do not confuse with 僕 I → 0185

撫

0904

1-3-12

▶STROKE
▶PACIFY

ブ　な(でる)　㊔ よし　やす

Ⓒ 抚 fǔ

64	Names	U64AB
扌	S15-3-12	F1490

COMPOUNDS

❶ **STROKE, caress, fondle, rub, pat**

撫育する ぶいくする raise with love and care
愛撫する あいぶする caress, fondle, pet

❷ **PACIFY, appease, tame**

宣撫 せんぶ pacification [placation] (of an occupied people)
慰撫する いぶする soothe, console

KUN

【なでる 撫でる】

① **STROKE, caress, fondle, rub, pat**

撫で肩 なでがた sloping shoulders
犬の頭を撫でる いぬのあたまをなでる pat a dog on the head
逆撫でする さかなでする rub the wrong way, irritate
猫撫で声 ねこなでごえ coaxing [wheedling, ingratiating] voice
大和撫子 やまとなでしこ large pink, *Dianthus superbus* var. *longicalycinus;* woman who displays the feminine virtues of old Japan
胸を撫で下ろす むねをなでおろす be relieved, sigh with relief

② **comb (one's hair)**

撫で上げる なであげる comb back
撫で付ける なでつける comb down, smooth down

SYNONYMS

❶ **touch**
触 TOUCH → 1914
接 CONTACT → 0607
撫 STROKE → 0904
当てる apply → 2701

撞

▶STRIKE
ドウ シュ つ(く)
Ⓒ 撞 zhuàng

0905
◧ 1-3-12

64	Names	U649E
扌	S15-3-12	F3425

COMPOUNDS

● **STRIKE, thrust, hit**
撞球 どうきゅう billiards
撞着 どうちゃく contradiction
撞木 しゅもく wooden bell hammer

KUN

【つく 撞く】 [usu. 突く] poke, **STRIKE** (a bell)
鐘を撞く かねをつく strike a bell

SYNONYMS

● **strike**
打 STRIKE → 0224
撲 DEAL A BLOW → 0903
殴 BEAT (strike a person) → 1099
蹴 KICK → 2074
撃 STRIKE → 3552
挌 STRIKE (a person) → 0448
撞 STRIKE (a ball or bell) → 0905
撥ねる strike (knock down) → 0907
当てる HIT → 2701
叩 KNOCK → 0208
拍 BEAT (strike repeatedly) → 0361
搏 BEAT (throb) → 0794

HOMOPHONES

つく
突 DASH → 2772
衝 COLLIDE → 0893

NOTE

➡ see USAGE note at 突 2772

播

▶SOW
ハ バン ま(く) ㊔ ひろ すけ かし
Ⓒ 播 bō

0906
◧ 1-3-12

64	Names	U64AD
扌	S15-3-12	F2109

COMPOUNDS

❶ [original meaning] **SOW**
播種 はしゅ sowing, planting
点播 てんぱ sowing seeds at regular intervals

❷ **disseminate, spread**
伝播 でんぱ dissemination, transmission, propagation, spread

❸ abbrev. of 播磨 はりま, old name for southwest Hyogo Prefecture
播州 ばんしゅう old name for southwest Hyogo Prefecture
播但線 ばんたんせん Bantan Line (railway in Hyogo Prefecture)

KUN

【まく 播く】 [also 蒔く] **SOW**
種を播く たねをまく sow seeds
粗播き あらまき sparse sowing [seeding]

SYNONYMS

❶ **farm and plant**
植 PLANT → 1247
栽 PLANT (saplings) → 4087
培 CULTIVATE → 0558
耕 TILL → 1659
作 raise crops → 0077
農 farm, FARMING → 3345
蒔 SOW → 2935
播 SOW → 0906

HOMOPHONES

まく
蒔 SOW → 2935
撒 SCATTER → 0909

NOTE

➡ see USAGE note at 蒔 2935

撥

▶REPEL
ハツ バチ は(ねる)
Ⓒ 拨 bō

0907
◧ 1-3-12

64	Non-Jōyō	U64A5
扌	S15-3-12	F2460

COMPOUNDS

❶ [now usu. 発 はつ 3174] [original meaning] **REPEL, repulse, rebound**
撥水 はっすい water repellency
反撥 はんぱつ repulsion, repelling; rally (of the market); opposition

❷ [now replaced by 発 はつ 3174] stir, stir up
挑撥 ちょうはつ provocation, incitement, excitement, stimulation

❸ pluck (the strings); plectrum, pick
撥弦 はつげん plucking string instrument

❹ pronounce ん as a syllabic consonant
撥音 はつおん syllabic nasal in Japanese (ん)

INDEPENDENT

【ばち 撥】 plectrum, pick

1

口 土 女 巾 弓 彳 忄 【扌】 氵 阝

KUN

【はねる 撥ねる】

①ⓐ **flip, splash**

ⓑ **strike, knock down**

b 車に撥ねられる くるまにはねられる be struck by a car

② **reject, turn down**

突っ撥ねる つっぱねる reject [refuse] flatly

試験で撥ねられる しけんではねられる get flunked in an examination

③ **take a percentage for one's own**

上前を撥ねる うわまえをはねる take a cut, take a kickback

④ **sweep up (in brush stroke of kanji)**

⑤ **pronounce ん as a syllabic consonant**

SPECIAL READINGS

撥条(=発条) ぜんまい spring

撥条(=発条) ばね spring

SYNONYMS

❶ **resist**

抗 RESIST →0296

抵 RESIST →0377

耐 WITHSTAND →1634

対 OPPOSE →1025

反 COUNTER →3663

逆 rebel →3835

撥 REPEL →0907

叛 REBEL →1469

【はねる】

①ⓑ **strike**

打 STRIKE →0224

撲 DEAL A BLOW →0903

殴 BEAT (strike a person) →1099

蹴 KICK →2074

撃 STRIKE →3552

挌 STRIKE (a person) →0448

撞 STRIKE (a ball or bell) →0905

撥ねる strike (knock down) →0907

当てる HIT →2701

叩 KNOCK →0208

拍 BEAT (strike repeatedly) →0361

搏 BEAT (throb) →0794

HOMOPHONES

はねる 跳 JUMP →1934

NOTE

➡ see USAGE note at 跳 1934

撈

▶DREDGE

ロウ

Ⓝ 撈 Ⓒ 捞 lāo

0908

1-3-12

64	Non-Jōyō	U6488
扌	S15-3-12	F0000

COMPOUNDS

● [now usu. 労 3155] [original meaning] **DREDGE up, drag for, fish for**

漁撈 ぎょろう fishing, fishery

海底撈月 かいていろうげつ totally useless effort (like dredging for the reflected moon from the bottom of the sea)

SYNONYMS

● **take from water**

撈 DREDGE →0908

掬 SCOOP UP →0599

汲 DRAW WATER →0310

撒

▶SCATTER

サン サツ ま(く)

Ⓒ 撒 sǎ sā

0909

1-3-12

64	Names	U6492
扌	S15-3-12	F2399

COMPOUNDS

● [now replaced by 散 2137] [original meaning] **SCATTER, sprinkle, disperse**

撒水 さんすい(=さっすい) water sprinkling

撒布する さんぷ(=さっぷ)する scatter, sprinkle, spray

KUN

【まく 撒く】

① **SCATTER, sprinkle**

撒き散らす まきちらす scatter, spread

撒き餌 まきえ scattered animal feed, ground bait

ばら撒き ばらまき scattering; spending recklessly

水撒き みずまき watering, sprinkling

② give (someone) the slip

SYNONYMS

● **spread**

散 SCATTER →2137

布 SPREAD →3691

敷く LAY →2345

舗 PAVE →2177

塗 APPLY ON A SURFACE →3523

抹 wipe over →0370

撒 SCATTER →0909

HOMOPHONES

まく

蒔 SOW →2935

播 SOW →0906

NOTE

➡ see USAGE note at 蒔 2935

撮

▶PHOTOGRAPH

サツ と(る) -ど(り)

Ⓒ 撮 cuō zuǒ

0910

◧ 1-3-12

64	Jōyō	U64AE
扌	S15-3-12	F0996

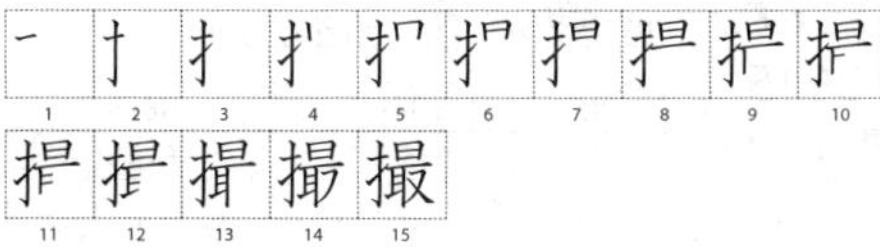

COMPOUNDS

❶ PHOTOGRAPH, take a picture, film

撮影 さつえい photographing, shooting (of a movie)
撮像管 さつぞうかん image pick-up [camera] tube
特撮 とくさつ trick work

❷ⓐ [original meaning] **pinch, take with fingers, gather**

ⓑ [archaic] **a pinch, a slight amount**

a 撮要 さつよう compendium, summary, outline
b 撮土 さつど a pinch of earth, small area

KUN

【とる 撮る】PHOTOGRAPH, shoot, film, videotape

写真を撮る しゃしんをとる take a picture
隠し撮り かくしどり sneaking a shot

【-どり -撮り】counter for number of shots [pictures] available in a film

十二枚撮りのフィルム じゅうにまいどりのふぃるむ film for 12 shots

SYNONYMS

❶ photograph

撮 PHOTOGRAPH → 0910
写 shoot → 2493

HOMOPHONES

とる

取 TAKE → 1613
採 PICK → 0606
執 EXECUTE → 2114
捕 CATCH → 0514

-どり 取 TAKE → 1613

NOTE

➡ see USAGE note at 取 1613

撰

▶COMPILE

セン サン えら(ぶ) ㊔ えらむ のぶ

Ⓝ 撰 Ⓒ 撰 zhuàn

0911

◧ 1-3-12

64	Names	U64B0
扌	S15-3-12	F2710

COMPOUNDS

❶ⓐ COMPILE, edit

ⓑ compilation, selection, anthology

a 撰者 せんじゃ author, compiler, editor
新撰 しんせん newly compiled [selected, edited]
修撰する しゅうせんする edit, compile
b 官撰 かんせん government compilation
勅撰集 ちょくせんしゅう imperial-commissioned poetry anthology

❷ [usu. 選 3931] **choose, select, elect**

特撰 とくせん special, select

❸ compose, write

撰述する せんじゅつする write
杜撰な ずさんな careless, slipshod, faulty

INDEPENDENT

【せん 撰】selection and compilation of an anthology

KUN

【えらぶ 撰ぶ】[sometimes also 選ぶ] **COMPILE, edit**

SYNONYMS

❶ compile

編 COMPILE → 1755
纂 COMPILE → 3393
撰 COMPILE → 0911
集 edit → 3445
輯 EDIT → 2025
著 AUTHOR → 2869

❷ choose

選 CHOOSE → 3931
撰 choose → 0911
択 SELECT → 0299
採 PICK → 0606
摘 pick out → 0851
擢 SINGLE OUT → 0973
抜 single out → 0290
汰 SIFT OUT → 0312

HOMOPHONES

えらぶ 選 CHOOSE → 3931

COMPOUND FORMATION

【杜撰 ずさん】

杜撰な 'careless, slipshod, faulty' evidently derives from an ancient Chinese legend about a poet named 杜黙 ともく who composed (撰 ❸) many poems that did not conform to the traditional stanza format.

1

口 土 女 巾 弓 彳 忄 【扌】 氵 阝

撤 0912

1-3-12

▶WITHDRAW

テツ

Ⓒ 撤 chè

64	Jōyō	U64A4
扌	S15-3-12	F1663

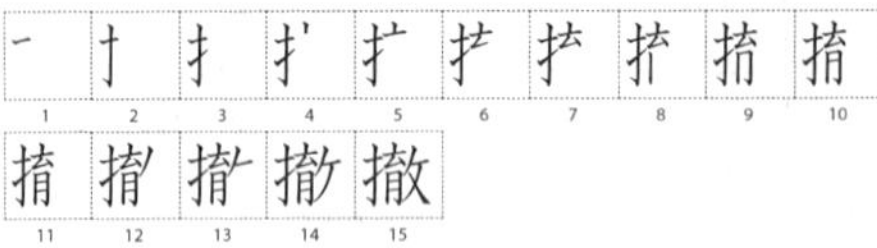

COMPOUNDS

❶ [original meaning] (take back) **WITHDRAW, remove, take away**

撤去 てっきょ removal, dismantlement (of a building); evacuation (of an army)

撤回 てっかい withdrawal, retraction

撤廃 てっぱい abolition, removal

❷ (move back) **WITHDRAW, retreat, evacuate**

撤退 てったい withdrawal, evacuation, pullout

撤兵する てっぺいする withdraw troops

撤収する てっしゅうする withdraw, pull out

SYNONYMS

❶ **eliminate**

却 ELIMINATE →1436

排 EXCLUDE →0593

払う CLEAR AWAY →0225

剥 PEEL OFF →2105

耘 WEED →1661

削 cross out →1837

抹 wipe off →0370

省 leave out →3100

脱 REMOVE →1225

去 take away →2678

外す take off →0215

除 RID OF →0546

撤 WITHDRAW →0912

❷ **leave and set forth**

去 GO AWAY →2678

離 leave →2364

発 START →3174

出 GO OUT →4310

退 RETREAT →3838

撤 WITHDRAW →0912

NOTE

★ do not confuse with 徹 GO THROUGH →0894

攜 0913

1-3-12

▶CARRY IN HAND

ケイ たずさ(える) たずさ(わる)

64	Nonstandard	U64D5
扌	S15-3-12	F0000

traditional form →see 携 at 0796

撰 0914

1-3-12

▶COMPILE

セン サン えら(ぶ) ㊔ えらむ のぶ

64	Nonstandard	U64B0
扌	S15-3-12	F0000

traditional form →see 撰 at 0911

澄 0915

1-3-12

▶LIMPID

チョウ す(む) す(ます) -す(ます) ㊔ きよし

Ⓝ 澂 Ⓒ 澄 chéng dèng

85	Jōyō	U6F84
氵	S15-3-12	F1481

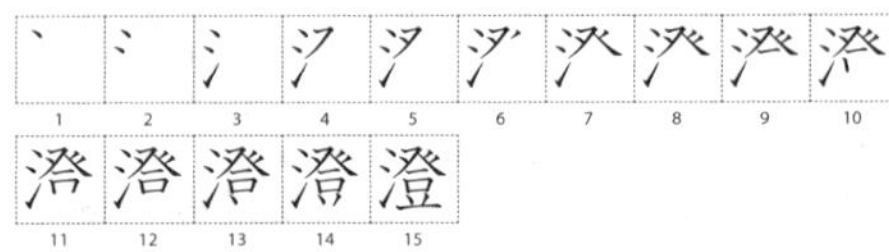

COMPOUNDS

● **LIMPID, clear, transparent, lucid, serene**

清澄な せいちょうな clear, lucid; serene

明澄な めいちょうな unclouded, clear, limpid

KUN

【すむ 澄む】*vi* **clear, become clear**

澄み切った すみきった perfectly clear

澄んだ水 すんだみず limpid water

【すます 澄ます】*vi* **look grave, look unconcerned; put on airs;** *vt* **strain (as one's ears); clear (water), make clear**

澄まし顔 すましがお smug face

澄まし汁 すましじる clear soup

耳を澄ます みみをすます strain one's ears

【-すます -澄ます】[also -済ます] [verbal suffix] **perform an action well [perfectly]**

研ぎ澄ます とぎすます sharpen [grind] well

見澄ます みすます observe carefully, watch intently

SYNONYMS

● **clear**

透 TRANSPARENT →3854

澄 LIMPID →0915

清 CLEAR (liquid) →0635

明 CLEAR (unclouded) →1060

朗 CLEAR (sky) →1679

冴える CRISP AND CLEAR →0087

USAGE

【-すます】

-澄ます

[also -済ます] [verbal suffix] perform an action well [perfectly]

-済ます

[also -澄ます] [verbal suffix] same as -澄ます

HOMOPHONES

-すます 済 SETTLE →0634

潮

0916

1-3-12

▶TIDE

チョウ しお うしお▲

Ⓝ 潮 Ⓒ 潮 cháo

85	Jōyō-6	U6F6E
氵	S15-3-12	F1111

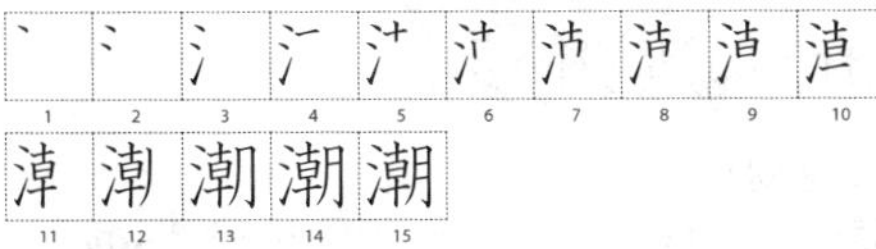

COMPOUNDS

❶ⓐ [original meaning] **TIDE, current**

ⓑ (ocean water in motion) **TIDE, seawater**

a 潮汐 ちょうせき ebb and flow, tide

干潮 かんちょう ebb tide

満潮 まんちょう high tide, high water

b 潮流 ちょうりゅう tide, current; tendency, trend

潮音 ちょうおん [rare] sound of waves

❷ⓐ (stream of events) **TIDE, tendency, trend, drift**

ⓑ (extreme condition) **TIDE, situation**

a 風潮 ふうちょう tide, trend, tendency

思潮 しちょう trend of thought

b 最高潮 さいこうちょう climax, acme

❸ menses

初潮 しょちょう beginning of menstrual function

KUN

【しお 潮】[sometimes also 汐]

①ⓐ **TIDE, current**

ⓑ seawater

a 潮干狩り しおひがり shell gathering (at low tide)

引き潮 ひきしお ebb tide, low water

血潮 ちしお blood

b 潮風 しおかぜ sea breeze, briny air

② **TIDE** (in the archaic sense of 'favorable occasion'), opportunity, chance

潮時 しおどき time of ebb and flow; good chance, favorable opportunity

【うしお 潮】**TIDE; seawater**

潮の如く押し寄せる うしおのごとくおしよせる surge, rush like a flood

SYNONYMS

❶ⓐ running water

流 CURRENT →0529

潮 TIDE →0916

汐 TIDE →0259

瀬 rapids →0995

滝 WATERFALL →0813

洪 FLOOD →0461

渦 WHIRLPOOL →0735

❷ⓐ tendency

向 tendency →3790

性 NATURE →0357

勢 trend →3542

傾 inclination →0174

潮 TIDE →0916

流 CURRENT →0529

USAGE

【しお】

潮

[sometimes also 汐]

①ⓐ tide, current

ⓑ seawater

② tide (in the archaic sense of 'favorable occasion'), opportunity, chance

汐

[usu. 潮] same as 潮

HOMOPHONES

しお 汐 TIDE →0259

潑

0917

1-3-12

▶LIVELY

ハツ

Ⓝ 溌 Ⓒ 泼 pō

85	Non-Jōyō	U6F51
氵	S15-3-12	F0000

COMPOUNDS

● [now also 発 3174] **LIVELY, energetic**

潑剌×たる はつらつたる lively, sprightly, vivid

活潑な かっぱつな lively, active

SYNONYMS

● strong

強 STRONG →0574

壮 VIGOROUS →0263

丈 STOUT →4227

健 ROBUST (healthy) →0152

逞しい ROBUST (sturdy) →4004

康 HEALTHY →3877

旺 ENERGETIC →1061

潑 LIVELY →0917

潤

0918

1-3-12

▶MOIST

ジュン うるお(う) うるお(す) うる(む)

㊔ まさる さかえ めぐみ しゅん

Ⓒ 润 rùn

85	Jōyō	U6F64
氵	S15-3-12	F1675

口 土 女 巾 弓 彳 忄 扌 【氵】 阝

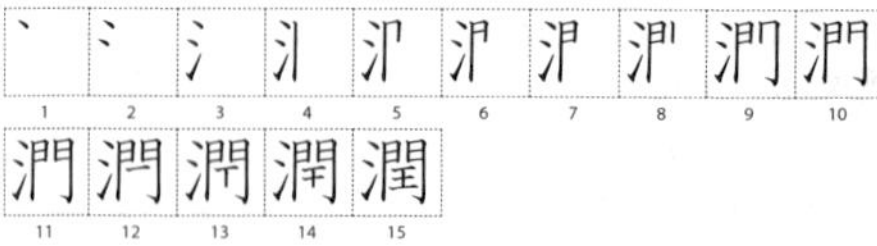

口 土 女 巾 弓 彳 忄 扌 【氵】 阝

COMPOUNDS

❶ⓐ **MOIST, wet**
ⓑ **MOISTen, be moistened, ooze, be wet**

a 湿潤な しつじゅんな moist, damp, wet
b 潤滑油 じゅんかつゆ lubricant, lubricating oil
潤筆料 じゅんぴつりょう fee for writing or painting
肺浸潤 はいしんじゅん infiltration of the lungs

❷ⓐ enrich, make prosperous; rich, abundant
ⓑ gain, profit; favor

a 潤沢 じゅんたく abundance, plenty
豊潤な ほうじゅんな rich and prosperous, luxurious
b 利潤 りじゅん profit, returns

❸ embellish

潤色 じゅんしょく rhetorical flourishes

KUN

【うるおう 潤う】**be MOISTened, be wet, be damp; receive benefits, profit, be made rich, become prosperous**

潤い うるおい moisture, dampness; gain, profit; tastefulness

【うるおす 潤す】**wet, MOISTen, dip. irrigate; profit, enrich, make prosperous**

喉を潤す のどをうるおす appease one's thirst

【うるむ 潤む】**be MOIST [wet] (with tears); be dimmed, become turbid, be clouded**

潤み うるみ moisture, blur, opacity
潤んだ目 うるんだめ eyes moist with tears; dim eyes

SYNONYMS

❶ⓐ **wet**

湿 DAMP →0741
潤 MOIST →0918
濡れる GET WET →0976

ⓑ **moisten**

潤 moisten →0918
浸 SOAK →0530
漬ける immerse →0861

COMPOUND FORMATION

【潤筆料 じゅんぴつりょう】

潤筆料 'fee for writing or painting' is a fee (料) for moistening (潤 ❶ⓑ) one's brush (筆).

潰

0919

1-3-12

▶**CRUSH**

カイ つぶ(す) -つぶす つぶ(れる) つい(える)▲

Ⓒ 溃 kuì huì

85	Jōyō	U6F70
氵	S15-3-12	F1575

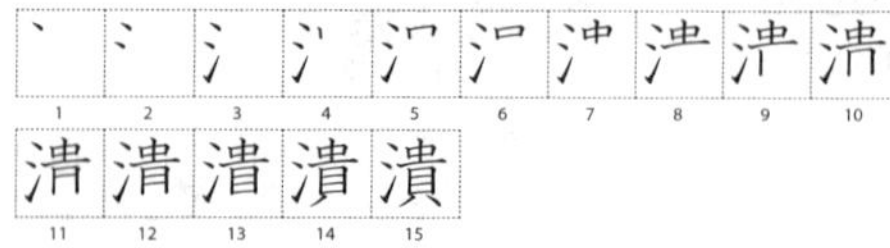

COMPOUNDS

❶ⓐ [usu. 壊 0934] [original meaning] **break down, destroy, collapse;** (of a dam) **burst**
ⓑ **fester, ulcerate**

a 潰滅する かいめつする be destroyed, be annihilated
崩潰する ほうかいする collapse, crumble, break down, cave in
倒潰 とうかい collapse, destruction, crumbling
全潰 ぜんかい complete collapse
決潰 けっかい rip, break
b 潰瘍 かいよう ulcer

❷ [also 壊 0934] be routed, be utterly defeated

潰走する かいそうする be routed, stampede

KUN

【つぶす 潰す】

①ⓐ **CRUSH, smash, batter, squash; scrap, junk**
ⓑ butcher, kill
ⓒ ruin, wreck

a 缶を潰す かんをつぶす crush a can

② humiliate, embarrass; discompose

顔を潰される かおをつぶされる be put out of countenance, lose face
肝を潰す きもをつぶす be frightened out of one's wits, be astounded

③ⓐ **pass, kill (time)**
ⓑ expend, use up

a 暇潰し ひまつぶし time killer; waste of time
b 穀潰し ごくつぶし good-for-nothing

【-つぶす -潰す】[verbal suffix]

ⓐ **CRUSH, smash, batter, squash**
ⓑ **wear down [away] beyond use, expend, use up**
ⓒ **blot out**

a 押し潰す おしつぶす squash, crush, flatten
叩き潰す たたきつぶす smash (up), defeat crushingly
磨り潰す すりつぶす pulverize, mash, grind
b 乗り潰す のりつぶす ride (a horse, vehicle) to death [beyond repair]
c 塗り潰す ぬりつぶす paint out

【つぶれる 潰れる】

①ⓐ **be CRUSHed [smashed], be battered, break**

ⓑ **be worn down, wear away**
ⓒ **collapse, be ruined**
c 酔い潰れる よいつぶれる drink oneself dead drunk
② be humiliated, be embarrassed; be discomposed
面目丸潰れ めんぼくまるつぶれ complete loss of face

【ついえる 潰える】
ⓐ be routed, be utterly defeated
ⓑ collapse

SYNONYMS

【つぶす】
①ⓐ **break**
破 BREAK → 1478
拉ぐ crush → 0372
崩 CRUMBLE → 2863
挫 SPRAIN → 0519
壊 BREAK DOWN → 0934
毀す break down → 2246
折 BREAK OFF → 0297
割る crack → 2284
裂 SPLIT → 3331
砕 CRUSH UP → 1458
摧 CRUSH UP → 0849
潰す CRUSH → 0919

HOMOPHONES

ついえる 費 EXPENSE → 3221

NOTE

➡ see USAGE note at 費 3221

潔

0920
◧ 1-3-12

▶**IMMACULATE**
ケツ いさぎよ(い) ㊔ きよし きよ いさお
Ⓝ 潔 Ⓒ 洁 jié

85	Jōyō-5	U6F54
氵	S15-3-12	F1694

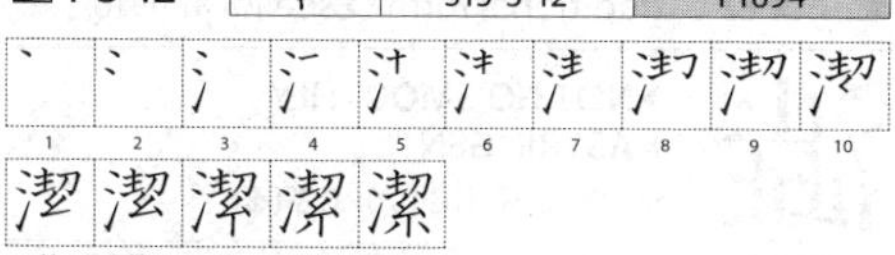

COMPOUNDS

❶ⓐ (free from stain) **IMMACULATE, clean, pure, spotless**
ⓑ (free from moral blemish) **IMMACULATE, pure, upright**
a 潔癖 けっぺき love of cleanliness, fastidiousness
清潔な せいけつな clean, neat, pure
不潔な ふけつな unclean, dirty, impure, maculate
b 潔白な けっぱくな innocent, pure, upright
純潔な じゅんけつな purehearted, immaculate, innocent
貞潔 ていけつ chastity and purity
❷ concise, brief
簡潔な かんけつな brief, concise

KUN

【いさぎよい 潔い】 **gallant, brave, manly, resolute**
潔さ いさぎよさ manliness, resolute composure
潔く いさぎよく bravely, manfully; frankly, with good grace
潔しとしない いさぎよしとしない be too proud (to do), find it against one's conscience (to do)

SYNONYMS

❶ⓐ **clean and purified**
浄 CLEAN → 0457
清 clean → 0635
純 PURE → 1649
潔 IMMACULATE → 0920
粋 REFINED (free from impurities) → 1645
精 refined (purified) → 1729
楚 NEAT AND TRIM → 3470
ⓑ **purehearted**
純 PURE → 1649
淳 PUREHEARTED → 0626
清 clean → 0635
潔 IMMACULATE → 0920
廉 INCORRUPT → 3911
敦 HONEST → 2128
惇 SINCERE → 0588
直 straightforward → 3649
侃 FORTHRIGHT → 0097

潟

0921
◧ 1-3-12

▶**LAGOON**
セキ▲ かた -がた
Ⓒ 舄 xì

85	Jōyō	U6F5F
氵	S15-3-12	F1637

COMPOUNDS

● tideland

KUN

【かた 潟, -がた -潟】
①ⓐ **LAGOON**
ⓑ **suffix after names of LAGOONs**
b 八郎潟 はちろうがた Lagoon Hachiro
② **beach at ebb tide**
干潟 ひがた beach at ebb tide
③ [also suffix] inlet, creek
難波潟 なにわがた Naniwa Bay (old name for Osaka Bay)

口
土
女
巾
弓
彳
忄
扌
【氵】
阝

SYNONYMS

【かた】

① lakes and marshes

沢 MARSH → 0313
沼 MUDDY POND → 0398
湖 LAKE → 0736
池 POND → 0253
潟 LAGOON → 0921

潜

0922

1-3-12

▶SUBMERGE
▶LURK

セン ひそ(む) もぐ(る) くぐ(る)▲ ㊔ ひそか

N 潛 潜 C 潜 qián

85 氵	Jōyō	U6F5C
	S15-3-12	F1205

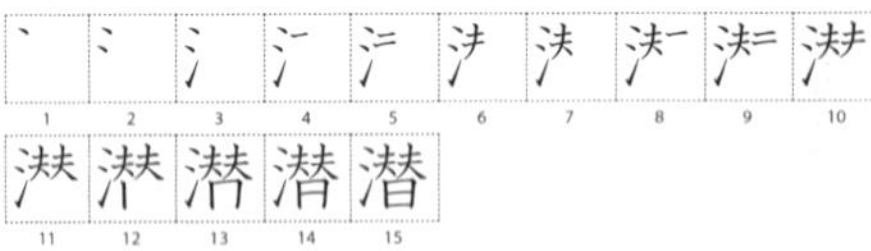

COMPOUNDS

❶ⓐ [original meaning] **SUBMERGE, dive**
ⓑ abbrev. of 潜水艦 **せんすいかん**: submarine

a 潜水 **せんすい** diving
潜水艦 **せんすいかん** submarine
潜航 **せんこう** submarine voyage, underwater navigation
b 原潜 **げんせん** nuclear submarine

❷ SUBMERGE oneself in thought, concentrate
潜心 **せんしん** meditation
沈潜する **ちんせんする** sink into deep thought; sink to the depths

❸ⓐ LURK, hide, lie concealed; be latent
ⓑ latent
a 潜伏 **せんぷく** concealment, hiding; latency
潜入 **せんにゅう** infiltration
潜行する **せんこうする** travel in disguise; move [travel] under water
潜在の **せんざいの** latent, potential
b 潜熱 **せんねつ** latent heat
潜像 **せんぞう** latent image

KUN

【ひそむ 潜む】**LURK in, lie concealed; be latent**
潜んでいる力 **ひそんでいるちから** latent power, potentiality

【もぐる 潜る】**dive into, SUBMERGE; get in, crawl in; lie low**
潜り **もぐり** diving; unlicensed (person)
潜り込む **もぐりこむ** get in, crawl into

【くぐる 潜る】
①ⓐ pass [duck] under; pass [go] through
ⓑ **dive, SUBMERGE**
② **get around, slip through, evade (the law)**

SYNONYMS

❶ⓐ sink
没 SINK → 0305
沈 SINK → 0306
潜 SUBMERGE → 0922
溺 DROWN → 0805

ⓑ boats and ships
船 SHIP → 1700
舶 OCEANGOING SHIP → 1699
艦 WARSHIP → 1817
潜 submarine → 0922
舟 SMALL BOAT → 4353
艇 BOAT → 1727
隻 COUNTER FOR SHIPS → 3426

❸ⓐ hide
隠 HIDE → 0873
蔽 COVER → 2991
伏 lie in concealment → 0049
潜 LURK → 0922
匿 CONCEAL → 3735
忍 perform by stealth → 2750

澂

0923

1-3-12

▶LIMPID

チョウ す(む) す(ます) -す(ます) ㊔ きよし

85 氵	Nonstandard	U6F82
	S15-3-12	F0000

traditional form → see 澄 at 0915

潮

0924

1-3-12

▶TIDE

チョウ しお うしお

85 氵	Nonstandard	U2F90F
	S15-3-12	F0000

traditional form → see 潮 at 0916

澁

0925

1-3-12

▶NOT GO SMOOTHLY
▶ASTRINGENT

ジュウ しぶ しぶ(い) しぶ(る)

85 氵	Names	U6F81
	S15-3-12	F0000

traditional form → see 渋 at 0625

潔

0926

1-3-12

▶IMMACULATE

ケツ いさぎよ(い) ㊔ きよし きよ いさお

85 氵	Nonstandard	U6F54
	S15-3-12	F0000

traditional form → see 潔 at 0920

澑

0927

◧ 1-3-12

▶**ACCUMULATE**

リュウ　た(める)　-ため　た(まる)

85	Nonstandard	U6F91
氵	S15-3-12	F0000

traditional form → see 溜 at 0814

潛

0928

◧ 1-3-12

▶**SUBMERGE**
▶**LURK**

セン　ひそ(む)　もぐ(る)　くぐ(る) ㊔ ひそか

85	Nonstandard	U6F5B
氵	S15-3-12	F0000

traditional form → see 潜 at 0922

隣

0929

◧ 1-3-12

▶**NEIGHBOR**

リン　とな(る)　となり

170	Nonstandard	U96A3
阝	S15-3-12	F0000

traditional form → see 隣 at 0961

隨

◧ 1-3-12

incorrect stroke-count
➡ see ◧1-3-13: 阝 at 0963

噸

0930

◧ 1-3-13

▶**TON**

トン

Ⓒ 吨 dūn

30	Non-Jōyō	U5678
口	S16-3-13	F0000

COMPOUNDS

[now also 屯 4268]

ⓐ [original meaning] **TON, tonnage**

ⓑ **shipping TON**

a 十六噸 じゅうろくとん 16 tons
英噸 えいとん British [long] ton

b 噸数 とんすう tonnage

SYNONYMS

ⓐ **weight units**

匁 MOMME (3.75 g) → 4276
斤 CATTY (600 g) → 3667
貫 *kan* (3.75 kg) → 3112
噸 TON → 0930
屯 ton → 4268

噴

0931

◧ 1-3-13

▶**SPOUT**

フン　ふ(く)

30	Nonstandard	U5674
口	S16-3-13	F0000

traditional form → see 噴 at 0879

壇

0932

◧ 1-3-13

▶**PLATFORM**

ダン　タン ㊔ まゆみ

Ⓒ 坛 tán

32	Jōyō	U58C7
土	S16-3-13	F1516

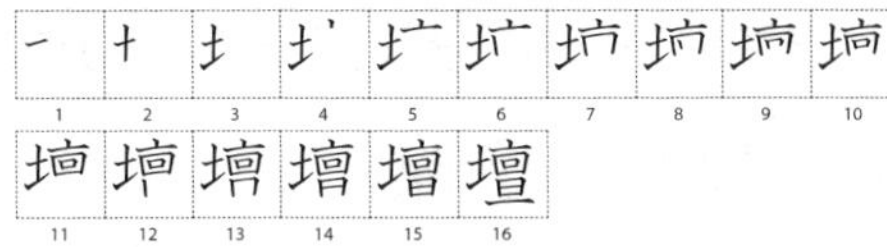

COMPOUNDS

❶ⓐ **PLATFORM, raised floor, stage, dais**

ⓑ [original meaning] **PLATFORM** for religious rites, altar

a 壇上 だんじょう on the platform, on the stage
壇場 だんじょう stage
演壇 えんだん platform, rostrum
花壇 かだん flower bed
教壇 きょうだん teacher's platform, rostrum

b 戒壇 かいだん ordination platform (in temples)
仏壇 ぶつだん family Buddhist altar
祭壇 さいだん altar

❷ **circles, world**

文壇 ぶんだん literary circles, world of literature
俳壇 はいだん haiku world
画壇 がだん artists' world, painting circles
詩壇 しだん poetical circles, world of poetry
劇壇 げきだん stage, theatrical world
土壇場 どたんば the last moment

INDEPENDENT

【だん　壇】 **PLATFORM, raised floor, stage, dais; altar**

壇に登る だんにのぼる get on the platform

SYNONYMS

❶ **flat supports**

台 STAND → 2498
座 SEAT → 3868
壇 PLATFORM → 0932
棚 SHELF → 1238
架 rack → 3178
床 BED → 3805

❷ **circles**

界 WORLD → 3172
壇 circles → 0932

NOTE

➡ see COMPOUND FORMATION for 土壇場 どたんば → 土 4211

口 【土】 女 山 彳 忄 扌 氵 犭 阝

壌 0933

▶**ARABLE SOIL**

ジョウ ㊔ みのる ゆたか

Ⓝ 壤 Ⓒ 壤 rǎng

1-3-13

32	Jōyō	U58CC
土	S16-3-13	F2002

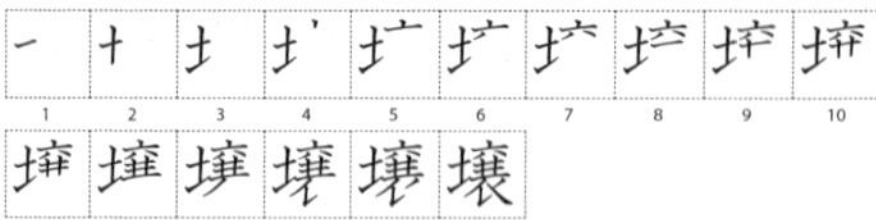

COMPOUNDS

ⓐ [original meaning] **ARABLE SOIL, (loose or loamy) soil, fertile soil, earth, loam**

ⓑ earth, land

a 土壌 どじょう soil, earth

b 天壌 てんじょう heaven and earth

SYNONYMS

● **land and soil**

土 SOIL →4211

地 GROUND →0236

壌 ARABLE SOIL →0933

泥 MUD →0384

陸 LAND →0659

埴 CLAY →0562

壊 0934

▶**BREAK DOWN**

カイ こわ(す) こわ(れる)

Ⓝ 壞 Ⓒ 坏 huài

1-3-13

32	Jōyō	U58CA
土	S16-3-13	F0923

COMPOUNDS

❶ [sometimes also 潰 0919] **BREAK DOWN, destroy, smash;** (of a dam) **burst**

壊滅 かいめつ destruction, annihilation

破壊する はかいする break (down), destroy, wreck

崩壊 ほうかい collapse, crumbling, breakdown, cave-in

全壊 ぜんかい complete collapse

決壊 けっかい rip, break

倒壊する とうかいする collapse, be destroyed, crumble

❷ [also 潰 0919] be routed, be utterly defeated

壊乱する かいらんする corrupt, demoralize

KUN

【こわす 壊す】 [sometimes also 毀す] *vt* **break (down), destroy, smash, take apart; spoil, mar, upset**

取り壊し とりこわし demolition, pulling down

ぶち壊す ぶちこわす destroy, demolish, smash; spoil, upset

【こわれる 壊れる】 [sometimes also 毀れる] *vi* **break (down), be broken; get out of order; be broken off, fall through, be upset**

壊れ物 こわれもの fragile article, breakables; broken article

壊れた時計 こわれたとけい broken clock

縁談が壊れた えんだんがこわれた The match was broken off

SYNONYMS

❶ **break**

破 BREAK →1478

拉ぐ crush →0372

崩 CRUMBLE →2863

挫 SPRAIN →0519

壊 BREAK DOWN →0934

毀す break down →2246

折 BREAK OFF →0297

割る crack →2284

裂 SPLIT →3331

砕 CRUSH UP →1458

摧 CRUSH UP →0849

潰す CRUSH →0919

USAGE

❶【こわす】

壊す

[sometimes also 毀す] *vt* break (down), destroy, smash, take apart; spoil, mar, upset

毀す

[usu. 壊す] *vt* break (down), destroy, smash, take apart; spoil, mar, upset

❷【こわれる】

壊れる

[sometimes also 毀れる] *vi* break (down), be broken; get out of order; be broken off, fall through, be upset

毀れる

[usu. 壊れる] *vi*

ⓐ break (down), be broken; get out of order

ⓑ be broken off, fall through, be upset

HOMOPHONES

こわす 毀 DESTROY →2246

こわれる 毀 DESTROY →2246

墳 0935

▶**TUMULUS**

フン

1-3-13

32	Nonstandard	U58B3
土	S16-3-13	F0000

traditional form →see 墳 at 0887

孃

▶YOUNG LADY

ジョウ

Ⓝ 孃 Ⓒ 娘 niáng

0936

1-3-13

38	Jōyō	U5B22
女	S16-3-13	F1447

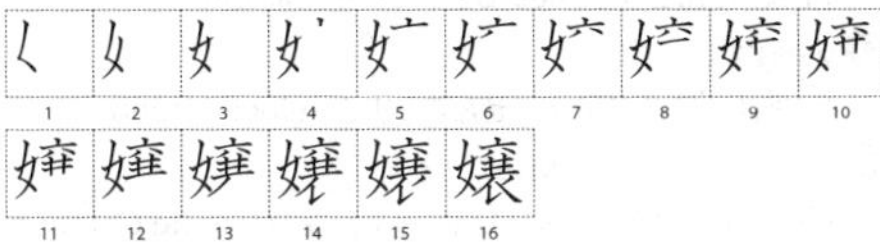

COMPOUNDS

❶ⓐ **unmarried YOUNG LADY, girl, mademoiselle**

ⓑ [also suffix] **(unmarried) female worker**

ⓒ daughter

a 令嬢 れいじょう daughter; young lady

老嬢 ろうじょう spinster

b 交換嬢 こうかんじょう telephone operator

案内嬢 あんないじょう usherette

c 愛嬢 あいじょう one's beloved daughter

❷ title after names of unmarried young ladies: Miss

良子嬢 よしこじょう Miss Yoshiko

INDEPENDENT

【じょう 嬢】 **YOUNG LADY; daughter**

お嬢さん おじょうさん young lady; your daughter

SYNONYMS

❶ⓐ **woman**

女 WOMAN → 4226

婦 ADULT WOMAN → 0565

婆 OLD WOMAN → 3433

嬢 YOUNG LADY → 0936

娘 GIRL → 0488

雌 FEMALE → 1337

牝 FEMALE → 1020

媛 DAMSEL → 0688

ⓑ **workers and professionals**

家 professional → 2827

婦 woman worker → 0565

嬢 (unmarried) female worker → 0936

夫 MAN LABORER → 4271

匠 CRAFTSMAN → 3711

工 workman → 4190

客 skilled person → 2798

士 PROFESSION SUFFIX → 4213

師 profession suffix → 1680

者 person who → 3980

人 person of certain category → 4175

員 MEMBER (of a staff) → 2822

屋 colloquial occupation suffix → 3842

手 OCCUPATION SUFFIX → 4267

❷ **titles of address**

氏 COURTESY TITLE → 3669

兄 familiar title (seniors) → 2676

君 FAMILIAR TITLE (peers) → 3974

嬢 Miss → 0936

様 FORMAL TITLE → 1332

殿 FORMAL HONORIFIC TITLE → 2247

師 honorific title (clergymen) → 1680

公 honorific title (noblemen) → 2468

嶮

▶STEEP

ケン けわ(しい)

Ⓒ 崄 xiǎn

0937

1-3-13

46	Non-Jōyō	U5DAE
山	S16-3-13	F3441

COMPOUNDS

[now replaced by 険 0658]

ⓐ [original meaning] **STEEP**, precipitous

ⓑ **STEEP** [inaccessible] place, steep pass, stronghold

a 嶮岨 けんそ steepness, precipice

峻嶮な しゅんけんな steep, precipitous

b 天嶮 てんけん natural stronghold

INDEPENDENT

【けん 嶮】 [now replaced by 険 0658] **STEEP** place, impregnable pass, stronghold; stern expression

アルプスの嶮 あるぷすのけん steep pass in the Alps

KUN

【けわしい 嶮しい】 [usu. 険しい] (sharply inclined and difficult to climb) **STEEP, precipitous; craggy; severe, grim, fierce, angry**

SYNONYMS

● **steep**

険 STEEP → 0658

嶮 STEEP → 0937

岨 STEEP → 0341

急 steep → 2595

峻 high and steep → 0495

HOMOPHONES

けわしい 険 DANGER → 0658

NOTE

➡ see USAGE note at 険 0658

衛

▶GUARD

エイ エ▲ ㊔ まもる もり

Ⓝ 衞 Ⓒ 卫 wèi

0938

1-3-13

144	Jōyō-5	U885B
行	S16-6-10	F0178

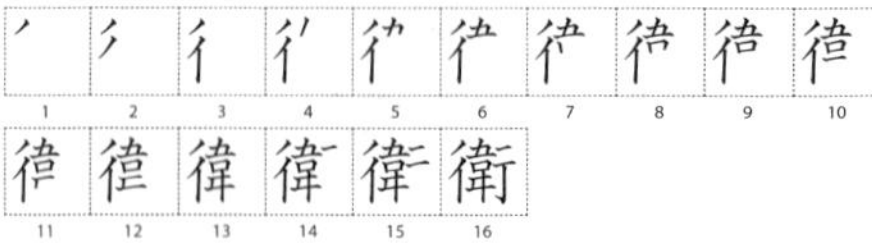

COMPOUNDS

❶ⓐ **GUARD, defend, escort, protect, preserve**
ⓑ **GUARD, keeper**

a 衛生 えいせい hygiene, sanitation, preservation of health
衛生的 えいせいてき sanitary, hygienic
護衛 ごえい guard, escort
自衛 じえい self-defense, self-protection
防衛 ぼうえい defense, protection
紅衛兵 こうえいへい Red Guards
近衛兵 このえへい personal guard

b 守衛 しゅえい guard, doorkeeper
前衛 ぜんえい advance guard, vanguard; forward player
警衛 けいえい guard, patrol, escort

❷ [original meaning] **revolve, go round, orbit**
衛星 えいせい satellite; moon

SYNONYMS

❶ⓐ **protect**
守 PROTECT (by watching over) → 2697
護 PROTECT (by safeguarding) → 2079
庇 PROTECT (by shielding) → 3802
衛 GUARD → 0938
警 GUARD AGAINST → 3595
防 defend → 0320
番 WATCH → 3416
保 PRESERVE → 0107
看 CARE FOR → 3992

ⓑ **guard**
哨 SENTRY → 0481
衛 GUARD → 0938
守 guard → 2697
警 guard → 3595

衡

0939
1-3-13

▶**BALANCE**
コウ ㊔ ひで
Ⓒ 衡 héng

144	Jōyō	U8861
行	S16-6-10	F1956

COMPOUNDS

❶ⓐ **BALANCE, equilibrium**
ⓑ **BALANCEd, stable**

a 平衡 へいこう equilibrium, balance

b 均衡 きんこう balance, equilibrium

❷ⓐ **scales, weighing machine**
ⓑ beam [arm] of a scale

a 度量衡 どりょうこう weights and measures
権衡 けんこう scales; balance, equilibrium

❸ weigh, consider
銓衡(=選考)する せんこうする select, screen

❹ horizontal, crosswise
連衡 れんこう lateral league of six states (in Chinese history); Japanese Confederation of Labor

SYNONYMS

❷ **measuring devices**
枡 MEASURE → 1070
尺 rule → 4248
計 meter → 1828
衡 scales → 0939
秤 BALANCE → 1488

衞

0940
1-3-13

▶**GUARD**
エイ エ ㊔ まもる もり

144	Names	U885E
行	S16-6-10	F0000

traditional form → see 衛 at 0938

徽

0941
1-3-13

▶**EMBLEM**
キ

120	Nonstandard	U5FBD
糸	S16-6-10	F0000

traditional form → see 徽 at 0968

懐

0942
1-3-13

▶**BOSOM**
▶**LONG FOR**
カイ ふところ なつ(かしい) なつ(かしむ) なつ(く) なつ(ける) ㊔ かね
Ⓝ 懷 Ⓒ 怀 huái

61	Jōyō	U61D0
忄	S16-3-13	F1178

COMPOUNDS

❶ (underside of garment covering chest) **BOSOM, pocket**
懐中 かいちゅう one's pocket

❷ⓐ [original meaning] (place in the bosom) **embosom, carry in the BOSOM**
ⓑ (harbor a thought) **embosom, cherish, harbor**

a 懐炉 かいろ pocket heater

懐胎 かいたい conception, becoming pregnant
懐妊 かいにん pregnancy, conception
b 懐疑 かいぎ doubt, skepticism, disbelief
抱懐する ほうかいする harbor, cherish, entertain

❸ (thoughts cherished in one's heart) **BOSOM, heart, feelings**
本懐 ほんかい one's long-cherished desire [object]
虚心坦懐 きょしんたんかい frankness, candidness
述懐 じゅっかい effusion of one's thoughts (and feelings), reminiscence

❹ **LONG FOR, miss, yearn, be attached to, be filled with nostalgia**
懐旧 かいきゅう longing for the old days
懐古 かいこ yearning for the old days
懐郷 かいきょう nostalgia, homesickness
追懐 ついかい recollection, reminiscence

KUN

【ふところ 懐】**BOSOM, breast; heart, mind; one's pocket, one's purse**
懐銭 ふところぜに pocket money
懐が寂しい ふところがさびしい have a scanty supply of money
自然の懐 しぜんのふところ bosom of Nature
内懐 うちぶところ inside pocket; bosom; one's real intention

【なつかしい 懐かしい】**dear, beloved, LONGed-FOR, old; long for, miss**
懐かしさ なつかしさ yearning, longing, nostalgia
人懐かしい ひとなつかしい miss people, long for others' presence

【なつかしむ 懐かしむ】**LONG [pine] FOR, yearn after, miss**
昔を懐かしむ むかしをなつかしむ view the past with nostalgia

【なつく 懐く】**become attached to; be tamed**
人懐っこい(=人懐こい) ひとなつっこい(=ひとなつこい) be affable, be sociable, love company; (of animals) take kindly to men

【なつける 懐ける】**make (another) attached to one, win a person's heart, win over; tame, domesticate**
手懐ける てなずける bring (a person or animal) round, gain over to one's side; influence with money

SYNONYMS

❶ **garment parts**
襟 COLLAR → 1599
袖 SLEEVE → 1496
懐 BOSOM → 0942
衿 COLLAR → 1465
裾 HEM → 1549

❷❻ **hold in the mind**
持 HOLD → 0447
抱 HUG → 0363
懐 embosom → 0942

❸ **psyche**
心 HEART → 0011
霊 SPIRIT (soul) → 3480
魂 SOUL, spirit → 1346
魄 SOUL → 1570
腹 heart → 1308
衷 INNER HEART → 2600
襟 inner mind → 1599
胸 breast → 1187
懐 BOSOM → 0942
神 MIND → 1143
気 SPIRIT (consciousness) → 3960
精 SPIRIT (mind) → 1729

❹ **wish and desire**
願 WISH → 2320
憧 YEARN AFTER → 0899
憬 YEARN AFTER → 0898
貪 COVET → 2630
望 HOPE → 3408
希 ASPIRE → 2543
懐 LONG FOR → 0942
慕 yearn for → 2970
渇 thirst for → 0627
欲 DESIRE → 1867
慾 DESIRE → 3551
求 SEEK → 4365

憾

0943

◧ 1-3-13

▶**STRONGLY REGRET**

カン うら(む)▲

Ⓒ 憾 hàn

61	Jōyō	U61BE
忄	S16-3-13	F2927

COMPOUNDS

● [original meaning] **STRONGLY REGRET, be sorry for, be dissatisfied**
遺憾な いかんな regrettable

KUN

【うらむ 憾む】be sorry for, regret
憾み うらみ regret, matter for regret
それは片手落ちの憾みが有る それはかたておちのうらみがある I'm sorry to say so, but it may not be quite fair

口 土 女 山 彳 【忄】 扌 氵 犭 阝

SYNONYMS

● **regret**

惜 REGRET → 0586
恨 regret → 0439
憾 STRONGLY REGRET → 0943
悔 REPENT → 0435

HOMOPHONES

うらむ

恨 HOLD A GRUDGE → 0439
怨 HOLD A GRUDGE → 3179

うらみ

恨 HOLD A GRUDGE → 0439
怨 HOLD A GRUDGE → 3179

NOTE

➡ see USAGE note at 恨 0439

憶

▸SPECULATE
▸REMEMBER
オク

0944
1-3-13

Ⓒ 忆 yì

61 忄	Jōyō	U61B6
	S16-3-13	F0944

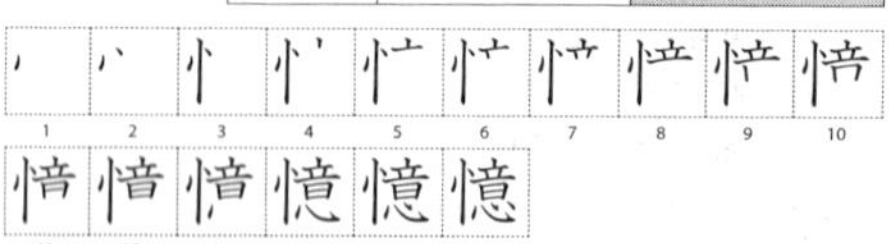

COMPOUNDS

❶ [formerly 臆 1397] (engage in conjectural thought) **SPECULATE, conjecture, guess, infer**

憶説 おくせつ hypothesis, speculation
憶測 おくそく conjecture, speculation, guess
憶断 おくだん jumping to hasty conclusions

❷ **REMEMBER, recall, recollect**

記憶 きおく memory, recollection
追憶 ついおく recollection, retrospection

❸ [usu. 臆 1397] fear, feel timid

憶病 おくびょう cowardice, timidity

SYNONYMS

❶ **conjecture**

推 INFER → 0612
憶 SPECULATE → 0944
測 CONJECTURE → 0744
察 GUESS → 2961

❷ **remember**

憶 REMEMBER → 0944
覚える COMMIT TO MEMORY → 3217
記 commit to memory → 1843
追 reminisce → 3840
顧 LOOK BACK → 2394
偲 RECOLLECT → 0153

憐

▸PITY
レン あわ(れ) あわ(れむ)

0945
1-3-13

Ⓝ 憐 Ⓒ 怜 lián

61 忄	Names	U6190
	S16-3-13	F2328

COMPOUNDS

● **PITY, sympathize, feel compassion**

憐憫×(=憐愍×) れんびん compassion, mercy
憐情 れんじょう pity, compassion
哀憐 あいれん pity, compassion
愛憐 あいれん tenderness, affection, sympathy
可憐な かれんな cute, sweet, pretty; tiny

KUN

【あわれ 憐れ】 [now usu. 哀れ] **PITY, sympathy**

憐れな あわれな pitiable; miserable

【あわれむ 憐れむ】 [now usu. 哀れむ] **PITY, sympathize, feel compassion**

憐れみ あわれみ pity, compassion
同病相憐れむ どうびょうあいあわれむ Fellow sufferers pity each other

SYNONYMS

● **tender feelings for others**

仁 BENEVOLENCE → 0021
慈 compassion → 2949
情 sympathy → 0583
悲 mercy → 3448
哀 PITY → 2568
憐 PITY → 0945

HOMOPHONES

あわれ 哀 SORROW → 2568
あわれむ 哀 SORROW → 2568

NOTE

➡ see USAGE note at 哀 2568

憤

▸INDIGNATION
フン いきどお(る)

0946
1-3-13

61 忄	Nonstandard	U61A4
	S16-3-13	F0000

traditional form → see 憤 at 0897

擅

▸ARROGATE TO ONESELF
セン ほしいまま

0947
1-3-13

Ⓒ 擅 shàn

64 扌	Non-Jōyō	U64C5
	S16-3-13	F0000

COMPOUNDS

● [now also 専 3272] [original meaning] **ARROGATE TO ONESELF, claim arbitrarily, do something on one's own authority**

擅断 せんだん arbitrary decision, arbitrariness
独擅場 どくせんじょう one's unrivaled sphere of activity, one's monopoly

KUN

【ほしいまま 擅】[usu. 恣] **self-indulgent, selfish; arbitrary**

SYNONYMS

● **acting arbitrarily**
横 arbitrary → 1350
独 act arbitrarily → 0471
恣 SELF-INDULGENT → 3281
耽 INDULGE IN → 1665
擅 ARROGATE TO ONESELF → 0947
専 arrogate to oneself → 3272
逞 DO AS ONE PLEASES → 4004

HOMOPHONES

ほしいまま 恣 SELF-INDULGENT → 3281

NOTE

➡ see USAGE note at 恣 3281

操

0948

◧ 1-3-13

▸MANIPULATE

ソウ みさお あやつ(る) ㊔ あや

Ⓒ 操 cāo

64	Jōyō-6	U64CD
扌	S16-3-13	F0988

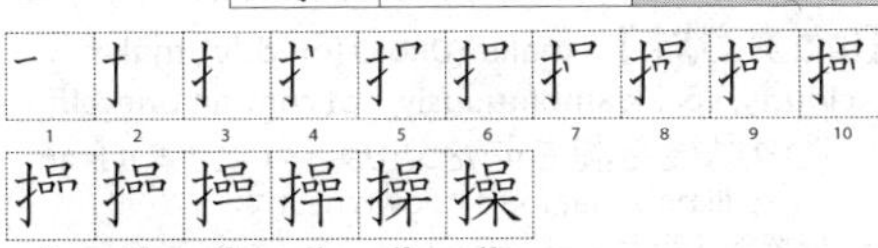

COMPOUNDS

❶ⓐ **MANIPULATE, handle, operate (a machine)**
ⓑ [original meaning] **hold in the hand**
a 操作 そうさ operation, manipulation, handling
操縦する そうじゅうする manage, control; steer; pilot, fly
操業 そうぎょう operation, work
操車 そうしゃ marshaling (in a classification yard)
b 操舵 そうだ steering

❷ **exercise, drill**
体操 たいそう gymnastics, physical exercise

❸ⓐ constancy, integrity, fidelity, moral principles
ⓑ chastity
a 情操 じょうそう sentiment
節操 せっそう constancy, fidelity, integrity, honor
b 操守 そうしゅ preserving one's chastity, adhering to moral principles
貞操 ていそう chastity, virginity

KUN

【みさお 操】**constancy, fidelity; chastity**
操を守る みさおをまもる preserve one's chastity; adhere to one's principles

【あやつる 操る】
ⓐ (operate skillfully with the hands) **MANIPULATE, handle, work, operate (a machine); steer (a ship)**
ⓑ (influence skillfully) **MANIPULATE, pull strings, mastermind**
a 操り あやつり manipulation; puppet
操り人形 あやつりにんぎょう puppet
巧みに操る たくみにあやつる manipulate, maneuver
英語を操る えいごをあやつる have a good command of English
b 世論を操る せろんをあやつる manipulate public opinion

SYNONYMS

❶ⓐ **handle**
扱う HANDLE → 0251
馭 HANDLE → 2282
操 MANIPULATE → 0948
揮 WIELD → 0717
運 control movement skillfully → 3894

❸ⓐ **fidelity**
忠 LOYALTY → 3087
義 faith → 2948
孝 FILIAL PIETY → 3973
悌 BROTHERLY LOVE → 0507
誠 SINCERITY → 1922
実 faithfulness → 2765
信 fidelity → 0115
操 constancy → 0948
節 moral integrity → 3336

ⓑ **chastity**
貞 CHASTE → 2586
操 chastity → 0948

擁

0949

◧ 1-3-13

▸SUPPORT

ヨウ

Ⓒ 拥 yōng

64	Jōyō	U64C1
扌	S16-3-13	F1883

COMPOUNDS

❶ **SUPPORT, protect**
擁立する ようりつする give backing to, support, help (to the throne)
擁護する ようごする protect, defend, support, safeguard

口 土 女 山 彳 忄 【扌】 氵 犭 阝

口 土 女 山 彳 忄 【扌】 氵 犭 阝

❷ [original meaning] **embrace, hold in one's arms, hug**
抱擁する ほうようする embrace, hug, hold in one's arms

INDEPENDENT

【ようする 擁する】 possess; have a person as the leader; embrace, hold in one's arms
巨富を擁する きょふをようする possess enormous wealth

SYNONYMS

❶ **support**
支 SUPPORT → 2473
擁 SUPPORT → 0949
扶 LEND SUPPORT TO → 0291
賛 back up → 3484

❷ **embrace**
抱 HUG → 0363
擁 embrace → 0949

據

0950
1-3-13

▸**GROUNDS**
キョ コ よ(る)

64	Nonstandard	U64DA
扌	S16-3-13	F0000

traditional form → see 拠 at 0369

擇

0951
1-3-13

▸**SELECT**
タク

64	Nonstandard	U64C7
扌	S16-3-13	F0000

traditional form → see 択 at 0299

擔

0952
1-3-13

▸**BEAR ON SHOULDER**
▸**UNDERTAKE**
タン かつ(ぐ) にな(う)

64	Nonstandard	U64D4
扌	S16-3-13	F0000

traditional form → see 担 at 0376

擕

1-3-13

incorrect stroke-count
➡ see 1-3-12: 扌 at 0913

濁

0953
1-3-13

▸**TURBID**
ダク ジョク▲ にご(る) にご(す)
Ⓒ 浊 zhuó

85	Jōyō	U6FC1
氵	S16-3-13	F1855

COMPOUNDS

❶ **TURBID, muddy, cloudy, impure**
濁流 だくりゅう muddy stream
濁度 だくど turbidity
濁酒 だくしゅ unrefined sake
混濁した こんだくした turbid, thick, muddy, cloudy
清濁 せいだく purity and impurity; good and evil
水質汚濁 すいしつおだく water pollution

❷ corrupt, depraved
濁世 じょくせ *Buddhism* corrupt world, the world of man
汚濁 おだく(=おじょく) corruption

❸ voiced, sonant
濁音 だくおん voiced sound, sonant
濁点 だくてん voiced consonant marks (as ゛ in だ)

KUN

【にごる 濁る】 *vi* **become TURBID [muddy, impure]; be vague; be in disorder; be voiced**
濁り にごり turbidity, muddiness; voiced sound; unrefined sake
濁り水 にごりみず muddy water
濁り酒 にごりざけ unrefined sake
濁った頭 にごったあたま vague head
濁った世の中 にごったよのなか this corrupt world
濁り点 にごりてん voiced consonant marks

【にごす 濁す】 *vt* **make TURBID [muddy], make cloudy; speak ambiguously, not commit oneself**
立つ鳥後を濁さず たつとりあとをにごさず It is an ill bird that fouls its own nest
お茶を濁す おちゃをにごす temporize, make do
言葉を濁す ことばをにごす not commit oneself

SYNONYMS

❶ **dirty**
汚 DIRTY → 0258
濁 TURBID → 0953

澱

0954
1-3-13

▸**SETTLE**
デン おり よど(む) よど
Ⓒ 淀 diàn

85	Non-Jōyō	U6FB1
氵	S16-3-13	F3036

COMPOUNDS

[now also 殿 2247]

ⓐ **SETTLE, precipitate**
ⓑ **settlings, sediment**
a 澱粉 でんぷん starch
沈澱 ちんでん precipitation, settlement

KUN

【おり 澱】 **settlings, sediment**
酒の澱 さけのおり sediment of wine, lees

【よどむ 澱む】[also 淀む]
① ⓐ **stagnate, be stagnant**
ⓑ **SETTLE, precipitate**
a 澱み よどみ pool, backwater, stagnation; sediment, deposit; faltering, hesitation
② (of eyes) **become glazed, become glassy**
③ **hesitate, stammer, falter**
【よど 澱】[also 淀] **pool, backwater, stagnation**

SYNONYMS

ⓐ stagnate
滞 STAGNATE →0815
淀む STAGNATE →0621
澱 SETTLE →0954
渋 NOT GO SMOOTHLY →0625
吃 STAMMER →0232

【よど】
◯ **stagnating water**
淵 DEEP WATER →0732
淀 pool →0621
澱 pool →0954

USAGE

【よど】
澱
[also 淀] pool, backwater, stagnation
淀
① [also 澱] pool, backwater, stagnation
② Yodo district (in Kyoto Prefecture)

HOMOPHONES

よどむ 淀 STAGNATE →0621
よど 淀 STAGNATE →0621

NOTE

➡ see also USAGE note at 淀 0621

激 ▸VIOLENT

ゲキ はげ(しい)
Ⓒ 激 jī

0955
◧ 1-3-13

85	Jōyō-6	U6FC0
氵	S16-3-13	F0594

COMPOUNDS

❶ⓐ (acting with extreme force) **VIOLENT, fierce, vehement**
ⓑ sudden, rapid
a 激烈な げきれつな vehement, furious, violent, severe
激戦 げきせん fierce [hard-fought] battle; hot contest
激突 げきとつ crash, collision
激情 げきじょう violent emotion, passion
b 激変(=劇変) げきへん sudden change, upheaval
激増 げきぞう sudden [rapid] increase
激動する げきどうする shake violently; be thrown into turmoil
急激な きゅうげきな sudden, abrupt
❷ [sometimes also 劇 2399] (of great intensity) **intense, VIOLENT, severe, strong**
激化 げきか(=げっか) intensification, aggravation
激賞 げきしょう high praise, unbounded admiration
激痛(=劇痛) げきつう violent [intense] pain
過激派 かげきは extreme radicals
❸ [formerly also 戟 2131] **excite, stimulate, stir up**
激励 げきれい encouragement
感激する かんげきする be deeply moved
憤激する ふんげきする be inflamed by anger, flare up
刺激する しげきする stimulate, excite

INDEPENDENT

【げきする 激する】get excited, be agitated, be enraged

KUN

【はげしい 激しい】[sometimes also 烈しい]
① (acting with extreme force) **VIOLENT, fierce, vehement**
激しさ はげしさ intensity, severity
激しい風 はげしいかぜ strong wind
② (of great intensity) **intense, VIOLENT, severe**
激しい競争 はげしいきょうそう hot competition

SYNONYMS

❶ⓐ extreme in power
激 VIOLENT →0955
荒 WILD →2810
狂 raging →0318
烈 VEHEMENT →3286
猛 FIERCE →0653
ⓑ sudden
急 SUDDEN →2595
激 sudden →0955
暴 sudden →3138
俄 SUDDEN →0106
頓 SUDDEN →1320
勃 SUDDENLY →1839
突 abruptly →2772
❷ extreme in degree
酷 SEVERE →1967
強 STRONG →0574
凄い tremendous →0145
重 HEAVY →4390
高 HIGH →2601
深 DEEP →0636

日 土 女 山 彳 忄 扌 【氵】 犭 阝

大 BIG →4224
厳 SEVERE →4079
激 intense →0955
極 EXTREME →1243
痛 bitter(ly) →4071
切 keen →0030
甚 EXTREMELY →3271
祁 EXTREMELY →1447
超 super- →4107
頗る EXCEEDINGLY →1552

❸ incite

挑 PROVOKE →0445
唆 INSTIGATE →0480
扇 FAN →2449
煽 FAN →1338
激 excite →0955
奮 ROUSE UP →3000
振 arouse to action →0515
動 MOVE →2232
起 rise to action →4099

USAGE

【はげしい】

激しい
[sometimes also 烈しい]
① (acting with extreme force) **violent, fierce, vehement**
② (of great intensity) **intense, violent, severe**

烈しい
[usu. 激しい] same as 激しい

HOMOPHONES

はげしい 烈 VEHEMENT →3286

濃

▶THICK
ノウ こ(い)
Ⓒ 浓 nóng

0956
1-3-13

85 氵	Jōyō	U6FC3
	S16-3-13	F0992

COMPOUNDS

❶ [also prefix] **THICK, concentrated, dense, heavy**
濃厚な のうこうな thick, dense, heavy, rich
濃度 のうど density
濃縮 のうしゅく concentration
濃霧 のうむ dense [thick] fog
濃密な のうみつな thick; crowded
濃硫酸 のうりゅうさん concentrated sulfuric acid

❷ [also prefix] **dark-colored, deep, rich**
濃紺 のうこん dark blue, navy blue
濃グレー のうぐれー dark gray
濃淡 のうたん light and shade
濃緑色 のうりょくしょく dark green

❸ abbrev. of 美濃 みの, old name for south Gifu Prefecture
濃尾平野 のうびへいや Nobi Plain

KUN

【こい 濃い】THICK, concentrated, dense; strong; thick-haired; intimate, thick; dark-colored, deep
濃さ こさ depth (of color); thickness, strength (as of coffee)
濃いスープ こいすーぷ thick soup
濃い仲である こいなかである bound by love, be thick (with)
濃紫 こむらさき dark purple

SYNONYMS

❶ dense
濃 THICK (concentrated) →0956
密 CLOSE →2857

❷ dark-colored
暗 DARK →1273
濃 dark →0956
深 DEEP →0636

澪

▶WATERWAY
レイ リョウ みお
Ⓒ 澪 líng

0957
1-3-13

85 氵	Names	U6FAA
	S16-3-13	F3082

COMPOUNDS

❶ WATERWAY, water route, channel, fairway
澪標 れいひょう *elegant* channel mark

❷ [original meaning, now archaic] **river name**

KUN

【みお 澪】WATERWAY, water route, channel, fairway for small boats
澪標 みおつくし channel mark
澪を引く みおをひく leave a wake behind

SYNONYMS

❶ &【みお】ways and routes
道 WAY (path) →3888
径 PATH →0347
軌 TRACK →1832
線 LINE →1760
澪 WATERWAY →0957
途 WAY (route) →3853
路 ROAD →1936
筋 wayside →3319
通り street →3855

街 city street → 0702
辻 CROSSROADS → 3958
岐 forked road → 0285
巷 THE STREETS → 3097

澤

0958

1-3-13

▶MARSH

タク さわ

85	Nonstandard	U6FA4
氵	S16-3-13	F0000

traditional form → see 沢 at 0313

獲

0959

1-3-13

▶CATCH GAME

カク え(る)

Ⓝ 獲 Ⓒ 获 huò

94	Jōyō	U7372
犭	S16-3-13	F1256

COMPOUNDS

❶ [original meaning] **CATCH GAME, fish, hunt, capture**

漁獲 ぎょかく fishing; haul [catch] (of fish)
捕獲する ほかくする catch (fish); capture (a ship), seize
乱獲 らんかく reckless fishing, excessive hunting
収獲 しゅうかく game; (good) result
鹵獲する ろかくする capture, seize, plunder

❷ **obtain, get, acquire**

獲得する かくとくする get, acquire, obtain

KUN

【える 獲る】

① **CATCH GAME, hunt, fish**

獲物 えもの game, spoils, catch, capture; good luck, prize

② [usu. 得る] acquire, get, gain, obtain, win

地位を獲る ちいをえる acquire a position

SYNONYMS

❶ **hunt and fish**

猟 HUNTING → 0654
狩 HUNT → 0474
獲 CATCH GAME → 0959
漁 FISH → 0856
釣 ANGLE → 2108
弋 CATCH → 4230

❷ **get**

得 ACQUIRE → 0577
拾 PICK UP → 0454
獲 obtain → 0959
収 TAKE IN → 0031
取 TAKE → 1613

HOMOPHONES

える 得 ACQUIRE → 0577

NOTE

➡ see USAGE note at 得 0577
★ do not confuse with 穫 HARVEST → 1598

獨

0960

1-3-13

▶ALONE
▶GERMANY

ドク ひと(り)

94	Nonstandard	U7368
犭	S16-3-13	F0000

traditional form → see 独 at 0471

隣

0961

1-3-13

▶NEIGHBOR

リン となる) となり

Ⓝ 厸 隣 鄰◇ Ⓒ 邻 lín

170	Jōyō	U96A3
阝	S16-3-13	F0999

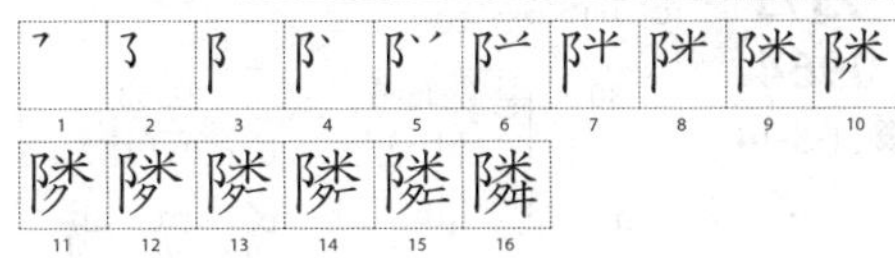

COMPOUNDS

❶ⓐ (live or be situated close by) **NEIGHBOR, adjoin**
ⓑ **NEIGHBORing, adjoining, adjacent**
ⓒ (houses or villages located near another) **NEIGHBOR**

a 隣接した りんせつした neighboring, adjoining, adjacent
b 隣国 りんこく neighboring country
隣家 りんか neighboring house
隣村 りんそん neighboring village
隣人 りんじん neighbor
近隣 きんりん neighborhood
c 善隣政策 ぜんりんせいさく Good Neighbor Policy

❷ [archaic] unit of administration in Zhou Dynasty China consisting of five households

KUN

【となる 隣る】 **NEIGHBOR, adjoin**

隣り合う となりあう adjoin, be next door to each other
隣り合わせの となりあわせの adjoining

【となり 隣】 **NEIGHBORing house, next door; next-door neighbor; next seat**

隣の となりの neighboring, adjacent
隣近所 となりきんじょ neighborhood
隣に住む となりにすむ live next door

SYNONYMS

❶ⓑ **near**

近 NEAR → 3798

隣 neighboring → 0961
傍 BESIDE → 0166
旁 BESIDE → 2598
沿 ALONG → 0386

險

0962
1-3-13

▶**DANGER**
▶**STEEP**
ケン けわ(しい)

170	Names	U96AA
阝	S16-3-13	F0000

traditional form → see 険 at 0658

隨

0963
1-3-13

▶**FOLLOW**
ズイ

170	Nonstandard	U96A8
阝	S16-3-13	F0000

traditional form → see 随 at 0765

嚇

0964
1-3-14

▶**INTIMIDATE**
カク おど(かす)▲
Ⓒ 吓 xià hè

30	Jōyō	U5687
口	S17-3-14	F2616

COMPOUNDS

❶ **INTIMIDATE, frighten, threaten, scare**
威嚇する いかくする intimidate, threaten, menace
恐嚇(=脅嚇) きょうかく [rare] intimidation, threat

❷ [also 赫 1960] [original meaning] explode with anger, be enraged
嚇怒する かくどする be greatly enraged, get furious

KUN

【おどかす 嚇かす】[now usu. 脅かす]
ⓐ threaten, menace, **INTIMIDATE**
ⓑ startle
a 嚇かして金を取る おどかしてかねをとる scare money out of (a person)

SYNONYMS

❶ **threaten**
脅 THREATEN → 2614
劫 threaten → 1435
威 THREATEN BY FORCE → 4394
嚇 INTIMIDATE → 0964
喝 shout threats at → 0554

HOMOPHONES

おどかす
脅 THREATEN → 2614
威 MIGHT → 4394

NOTE

➡ see USAGE note at 脅 2614

嚀

0965
1-3-14

▶**COURTEOUS**
ネイ
Ⓒ 宁 咛 níng

30	Non-Jōyō	U5680
口	S17-3-14	F0000

COMPOUNDS

❶ [now replaced by 寧 2959] **COURTEOUS, polite**
叮嚀(=丁寧)な ていねいな polite, courteous

SYNONYMS

❶ **courteous**
寧 COURTEOUS → 2959
鄭 COURTEOUS → 2379
叮 COURTEOUS → 0211
嚀 COURTEOUS → 0965
丁 courteous → 4155

壕

0966
1-3-14

▶**TRENCH**
ゴウ ほり
Ⓒ 壕 háo

32	Names	U58D5
土	S17-3-14	F2538

COMPOUNDS

❶ **TRENCH, dugout**
塹×壕 ざんごう trench, dugout
掩壕 えんごう cover trench
防空壕 ぼうくうごう air-raid shelter

❷ moat

INDEPENDENT

【ごう 壕】**TRENCH, dugout; moat**

KUN

【ほり 壕】
① [usu. 堀] **ditch, canal**
② [usu. 堀, sometimes also 濠] **moat**
外壕 そとぼり outer moat, castle moat

SYNONYMS

❶ **holes and cavities**
穴 HOLE → 2682
洞 CAVE → 0455
窟 CAVE → 2923
窪 HOLLOW → 2962
腔 BODY CAVITY → 1267
孔 OPEN HOLE → 0205
口 MOUTH → 4189
坑 PIT → 0277
堀 DITCH → 0561

溝 CHANNEL →0810
壕 TRENCH →0966
濠 MOAT →0975
凹 concavity →4294

HOMOPHONES

ほり
堀 DITCH →0561
濠 MOAT →0975

NOTE

➡ see USAGE note at 堀 0561

彌

0967
1-3-14

▶PHONETIC [mi]
ミ ビ や いや ㊔ わたる ひさ ひさし みつ ひろ

57	Names	U5F4C
弓	S17-3-14	F0000

traditional form → see 弥 at 0344

徽

0968
1-3-14

▶EMBLEM
キ
Ⓝ 徽 Ⓒ 徽 huī

60	Names	U5FBD
彳	S17-3-14	F3322

COMPOUNDS

● [now replaced by 記 1843] **EMBLEM, badge**
徽章 きしょう emblem, insignia

SYNONYMS

● **marks and signs**
標 MARK (identifying sign) →1347
徽 EMBLEM →0968
痕 SCAR →4066
印 MARK (visible sign) →1023
跡 TRACE →1937
蹟 TRACE →2065
踪 FOOTPRINTS →1996
紋 print →1651
符 SYMBOL →3299
号 SIGN →2675
栞 BOOKMARK →3285

擬

0969
1-3-14

▶IMITATE
ギ
Ⓒ 拟 nǐ

64	Jōyō	U64EC
扌	S17-3-14	F2327

Stroke order: 1–17

COMPOUNDS

❶ⓐ [original meaning] **IMITATE, copy, mimic, model after**
ⓑ [also prefix] imitation, dummy, pseudo
a 擬装 ぎそう camouflage, disguise
擬似 ぎじ false, dummy, pseudo
擬声語 ぎせいご onomatopoeic word
擬人 ぎじん personification, impersonation
擬製 ぎせい imitation, forgery
模擬の もぎの imitation, sham, mock, simulated
b 擬毛 ぎもう imitation wool
擬古典的な ぎこてんてきな pseudoclassic
擬爆弾 ぎばくだん dummy bomb
❷ feign, pretend
擬勢 ぎせい sham display of forces

INDEPENDENT

【ぎする 擬する】point (a gun) at, aim; nominate for office; **IMITATE**, mimic; liken, compare
後継内閣の首班に擬せられている こうけいないかくのしゅはんにぎせられている be considered as head of the incoming Cabinet

SYNONYMS

❶ⓐ **imitate**
擬 IMITATE →0969
倣 COPY AFTER →0127
摸 PATTERN AFTER →0797
模 pattern after →1326
肖 MODEL →2733
象 represent →2647
ⓑ **false**
虚 FALSE →4017
仮 fake →0053
偽 sham →0149
擬 imitation →0969
義 artificial →2948

COMPOUND FORMATION

【擬声語 ぎせいご】
擬声語 'onomatopoeic word' is a word (語) that imitates (擬 ❶ⓐ) a sound (声).

擱

0970
1-3-14

▶LAY DOWN
カク お(く)
Ⓒ 搁 gē gé

64	Non-Jōyō	U64F1
扌	S17-3-14	F0000

COMPOUNDS

❶ **LAY DOWN (one's pen)**
擱筆する かくひつする stop writing
❷ **run aground**
擱座する かくざする run aground; be stalled

KUN

【おく 擱く】**LAY DOWN (one's pen)**

筆を擱く ふでをおく lay down one's pen, stop writing

SYNONYMS

❶ put

据える INSTALL →0602
置 PLACE →3222
擱 LAY DOWN →0970
掛ける SET →0596
措 DISPOSE →0610

HOMOPHONES

おく

置 PLACE →3222
措 DISPOSE →0610

NOTE

➡ see USAGE note at 置 3222

擦

▶RUB

サツ す(る) す(れる) -ず(れ) こす(る)▲ こす(れる)▲ かす(る)▲ かす(れる)▲ さす(る)▲

0971

1-3-14

Ⓒ 擦 cā

64	Jōyō	U64E6
扌	S17-3-14	F1795

COMPOUNDS

● [original meaning] **RUB**

擦過傷 さっかしょう abrasion, scratch
摩擦する まさつする rub, chafe
摩擦 まさつ friction; rubbing, chafing
塗擦剤 とさつざい liniment

KUN

【する 擦る】*vt*

①ⓐ **RUB, chafe**
ⓑ **strike**

a 擦り傷 すりきず scratch, abrasion
頰擦り ほおずり nestling one's cheek to another's
b マッチを擦る まっちをする strike a match

② lose, forfeit

身代を擦る しんだいをする lose a person's fortune

【すれる 擦れる】*vi* **RUB, chafe, brush; wear, be worn; become sophisticated**

擦れ合う すれあう rub against each other, jostle with
擦れ違う すれちがう pass by each other, brush past
擦れて薄くなる すれてうすくなる wear thin
擦れっ枯らし すれっからし worldly-wise impudence, person dead to all sense of shame
衣擦れ きぬずれ rustling (of clothes)

【-ずれ -擦れ】[also suffix]

① **sore**

靴擦れ くつずれ shoe sore
床擦れ とこずれ bedsores

② sophistication

人擦れ ひとずれ sophistication
悪擦れ わるずれ over-sophistication

【こする 擦る】*vt* **RUB, scour, scrub, scrape**

擦り付ける こすりつける rub on, smear; nuzzle against
擦り落とす こすりおとす rub off, scrape off

【こすれる 擦れる】*vi* be **RUB**bed

木の葉の擦れる音 このはのこすれるおと rustling of leaves

【かする 擦る】[also 掠る]

ⓐ graze
ⓑ squeeze, exploit

【かすれる 擦れる】[also 掠れる]

ⓐ become blurred
ⓑ become hoarse [husky]

【さする 擦る】[also 摩る] **RUB** (with the hands), stroke

SYNONYMS

● polish and rub

磨 POLISH →3946
擦 RUB →0971
摩 RUB AGAINST →3938
摺 RUB AGAINST →0850
研 GRIND →1456
削 CUT BY CHIPPING →1837
瑳 POLISH →1343

【-ずれ】

① **injury**

傷 WOUND →0179
創 wound (cut) →2283
-擦れ sore →0971

USAGE

【する】

擦る
vt
①ⓐ rub, chafe
ⓑ strike
② lose, forfeit

磨る
polish, file, rub down

摺る
ⓐ rub against
ⓑ print by rubbing

刷る
print, put in print

HOMOPHONES

する
磨 POLISH →3946
擂 RUB AGAINST →0850
刷 PRINT →1623
かすれる 掠 PLUNDER →0605
かする 掠 PLUNDER →0605

NOTE

➡ see also USAGE note at 掠 0605

擡

0972

◧ 1-3-14

▶**RAISE**
タイ もた(げる)
Ⓒ 抬 tái

64	Non-Jōyō	U64E1
扌	S17-3-14	F3435

COMPOUNDS

● [now also 台 2498] [original meaning] **RAISE (one's head), lift**
擡頭する たいとうする raise one's head; come to the fore

KUN

【もたげる 擡げる】 **RAISE (one's head), lift**
頭を擡げる あたまをもたげる raise one's head; come to the fore

SYNONYMS

● **raise**
揚 RAISE HIGH →0722
掲 PUT UP →0597
挙 RAISE →3106
上 raise →4212
起 raise up →4099
擡 RAISE (one's head) →0972
立てる STAND →2486
拾う PICK UP →0454

擢

0973

◧ 1-3-14

▶**SINGLE OUT**
テキ ぬき(んでる)
Ⓝ 擢 Ⓒ 擢 zhuó

64	Names	U64E2
扌	S17-3-14	F2583

COMPOUNDS

● **SINGLE OUT, select**
抜擢 ばってき selection, choice

KUN

【ぬきんでる 擢んでる】 [usu. 抜きん出る] **stand out, excel, surpass**

SYNONYMS

● **choose**
選 CHOOSE →3931
撰 choose →0911
択 SELECT →0299
採 PICK →0606
摘 pick out →0851
擢 SINGLE OUT →0973
抜 single out →0290
汰 SIFT OUT →0312

【ぬきんでる】
◯ **excel**
勝 EXCEL →1268
抜 STAND OUT →0290
擢んでる stand out →0973
超 SURPASS →4107
越 GO BEYOND →4108
凌 SURPASS →0144
駕 outdo →3236

HOMOPHONES

ぬきんでる 抜きん出る →0290, 4310

擢

0974

◧ 1-3-14

▶**SINGLE OUT**
テキ ぬき(んでる)

64	Nonstandard	U64E2
扌	S17-3-14	F0000

traditional form →see 擢 at 0973

擴

◧ 1-3-14

incorrect stroke-count
➡ see ◧ 1-3-15: 扌 at 0989

濠

0975

◧ 1-3-14

▶**MOAT**
ゴウ ほり
Ⓒ 濠 háo

85	Non-Jōyō	U6FE0
氵	S17-3-14	F2400

COMPOUNDS

❶ [original meaning] **MOAT**
環濠集落 かんごうしゅうらく moated settlement

❷ [now replaced by 豪 2657] Australia
濠洲(=豪州) ごうしゅう Australia

INDEPENDENT

【ごう 濠】 MOAT

KUN

【ほり 濠】 [usu. 堀, sometimes also 壕] **MOAT**
内濠 うちぼり inner moat

SPECIAL READINGS

濠太剌×利 おーすとらりあ Australia

SYNONYMS

❶ **holes and cavities**
穴 HOLE →2682

洞 CAVE →0455
窟 CAVE →2923
窪 HOLLOW →2962
腔 BODY CAVITY →1267
孔 OPEN HOLE →0205
口 MOUTH →4189
坑 PIT →0277
堀 DITCH →0561
溝 CHANNEL →0810
壕 TRENCH →0966
濠 MOAT →0975
凹 concavity →4294

HOMOPHONES

ほり
堀 DITCH →0561
壕 TRENCH →0966

NOTE

➡ see USAGE note at 堀 0561

濡

0976
1-3-14

▶GET WET
ジュ ぬ(れる) ぬ(らす)
Ⓒ 濡 rú

85	Names	U6FE1
氵	S17-3-14	F1366

KUN

【ぬれる 濡れる】
① **GET WET, get moist, get damp**
濡れ縁 ぬれえん open veranda
濡れ衣 ぬれぎぬ false charge, unfounded suspicion
濡れ手で粟 ぬれてであわ easy profit ("Grabbing millet with wet hands")
びしょ濡れ びしょぬれ dripping wet, drenched [soaked] to the skin, wet through
泣き濡れる なきぬれる be tear-stained
露に濡れた つゆにぬれた dewy, wet with dew
② make love
濡れ場 ぬれば love scene (in a drama)
濡れ事 ぬれごと love affair
【ぬらす 濡らす】wet, moisten, dampen, soak

SYNONYMS

【ぬれる】
① **wet**
湿 DAMP →0741
潤 MOIST →0918
濡れる GET WET →0976

鴻

0977
1-3-14

▶LARGE WILD BIRD
コウ グ おおとり ひしくい ㊔ ひろし ひろ ひとし
Ⓒ 鸿 hóng

85	Names	U9D3B
氵	S17-3-14	F2559

COMPOUNDS

❶ **LARGE WILD BIRD such as a goose or swan**
鴻鵠[×] こうこく wild swan; symbol of a great man
❷ great, vast
鴻業 こうぎょう glorious achievement, great work

KUN

【おおとり 鴻】[also 大鳥 or 鳳] **LARGE WILD BIRD such as a crane or white stork**
【ひしくい 鴻】bean goose

SYNONYMS

❶ **&【おおとり】birds**
鷹 HAWK →3955
鷗 GULL →2370
烏 CROW →4088
雀 SPARROW →3117
燕 SWALLOW →3142
鴻 LARGE WILD BIRD →0977
鳳 MALE PHOENIX →3749
凰 FEMALE PHOENIX →3738
鵬 MYTHICAL HUGE BIRD →1416
鶏 CHICKEN →2221
酉 ROOSTER →4358
隼 FALCON →3427
鳩 PIGEON →0184
鷲 EAGLE →3598
鳶 BLACK KITE →3919
鶴 CRANE →2326
鷺 HERON →3621
鵜 CORMORANT →2067
鴨 DUCK →1582
雁 WILD GOOSE →3741

HOMOPHONES

おおとり
鳳 MALE PHOENIX →3749
鵬 MYTHICAL HUGE BIRD →1416
大鳥 →4224, 4105

NOTE

➡ see USAGE note at 鳳 3749

濯

0978
1-3-14

▶RINSE
タク
Ⓝ 濯 Ⓒ 濯 zhuó

85	Jōyō	U6FEF
氵	S17-3-14	F1977

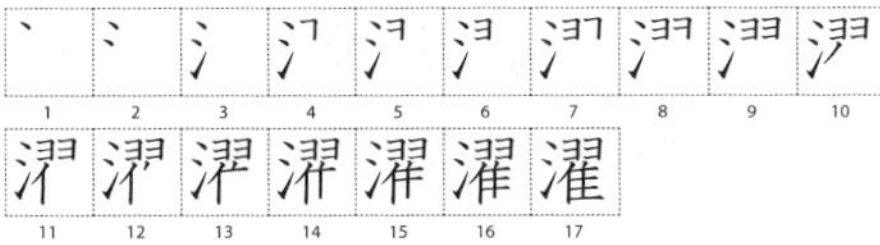

COMPOUNDS

● [original meaning] **RINSE, wash, wash out**

洗濯する せんたくする launder, wash

洗濯機 せんたくき washing machine

SYNONYMS

● **clean and wash**

洗 WASH → 0465

漱 RINSE → 0865

拭 WIPE → 0453

滌 WASH → 0854

濯 RINSE → 0978

浴 BATHE → 0533

浄 cleanse → 0457

粛 PURGE → 4400

清 CLEAR → 0635

払 CLEAR AWAY → 0225

掃 SWEEP → 0611

濵

0979

◧ 1-3-14

▶BEACH

ヒン はま

85	Nonstandard	U6FF5
氵	S17-3-14	F0000

traditional form → see 浜 at 0523

濱

0980

◧ 1-3-14

▶BEACH

ヒン はま

85	Nonstandard	U6FF1
氵	S17-3-14	F0000

traditional form → see 浜 at 0523

澀

0981

◧ 1-3-14

▶NOT GO SMOOTHLY
▶ASTRINGENT

ジュウ しぶ しぶ(い) しぶ(る)

85	Nonstandard	U6F80
氵	S17-3-14	F0000

traditional form → see 渋 at 0625

濶

0982

◧ 1-3-14

▶BROAD

カツ

85	Nonstandard	U6FF6
氵	S17-3-14	F0000

traditional form → see 闊 at 4135

濟

0983

◧ 1-3-14

▶SETTLE
▶RELIEVE

サイ セイ す(む) -ず(み) -ずみ す(まない) す(ます) -す(ます) す(ませる)

㊔ わたる いつき

85	Nonstandard	U6FDF
氵	S17-3-14	F0000

traditional form → see 済 at 0634

濕

0984

◧ 1-3-14

▶DAMP

シツ しめ(る) しめ(す)

85	Names	U6FD5
氵	S17-3-14	F0000

traditional form → see 湿 at 0741

濯

0985

◧ 1-3-14

▶RINSE

タク

85	Nonstandard	U6FEF
氵	S17-3-14	F0000

traditional form → see 濯 at 0978

濫

◧ 1-3-14

incorrect stroke-count

➡ see ◧ 1-3-15: 氵 at 0990

獲

0986

◧ 1-3-14

▶CATCH GAME

カク え(る)

94	Nonstandard	U7372
犭	S17-3-14	F0000

traditional form → see 獲 at 0959

隱

0987

◧ 1-3-14

▶HIDE

イン オン かく(す) かく(し)- かく(れる)

170	Nonstandard	U96B1
阝	S17-3-14	F0000

traditional form → see 隠 at 0873

噛

0988

◧ 1-3-15

▶BITE

ゴウ か(む) か(ます) か(ませる)

Ⓝ 噛 Ⓒ 啮 niè

30	Non-Jōyō	U5699
口	S18-3-15	F1558

COMPOUNDS

ⓐ **BITE**

ⓑ chew, gnaw

a 窮鼠噛猫 きゅうそごうびょう A cornered rat will bite the cat

b 噛砕 ごうさい grinding, crushing

KUN

【かむ 噛む】

①ⓐ **BITE**

ⓑ **chew, gnaw**

a 嚙み付く かみつく bite [snap] at

嚙み殺す かみころす bite to death; suppress (a smile), stifle (a yawn)

甘嚙み あまがみ play-biting

b 嚙み締める かみしめる chew well, bite hard; relish, savor; reflect upon, contemplate

嚙み砕く かみくだく crunch; simplify, explain plainly

嚙み煙草 かみたばこ chewing tobacco

爪を嚙む癖 つめをかむくせ habit of biting one's nails

② **gear [engage] with, be in gear [mesh]**

嚙み合う かみあう gear [engage] with, be in gear [mesh]; bite each other

③ **flub, blow (one's lines)**

台詞を嚙む せりふをかむ flub one's lines

④ **be [get] involved in, have a part [hand] in**

計画に一枚嚙む けいかくにいちまいかむ be involved in a plan

【かます 嚙ます】

①ⓐ **put something between someone's teeth, force someone to clamp with the teeth**

ⓑ **wedge something into a space (between two objects)**

a 猿ぐつわを嚙ます さるぐつわをかます gag (someone), put a gag (in someone's mouth)

b ドアにくさびを嚙ます どあにくさびをかます put a wedge under the door

② **give (as a slap in the face)**

ぶち嚙ます ぶちかます *sumo* bang into (an opponent) with full force; give a strong blow

パンチを嚙ます ぱんちをかます punch

【かませる 嚙ませる】 same as 嚙ます かます

紙を一枚嚙ませる かみをいちまいかませる wedge a piece of paper

SYNONYMS

ⓐ **bite**

嚙 BITE → 0988

啄 PECK → 0482

擴

0989

1-3-15

▶**ENLARGE**

カク ひろ(がる) ひろ(げる) ㊔ ひろ

64	Nonstandard	U64F4
扌	S18-3-15	F0000

traditional form → see 拡 at 0366

濫

0990

1-3-15

▶**EXCESSIVE**

ラン

Ⓒ 滥 làn

85	Jōyō	U6FEB
氵	S18-3-15	F2617

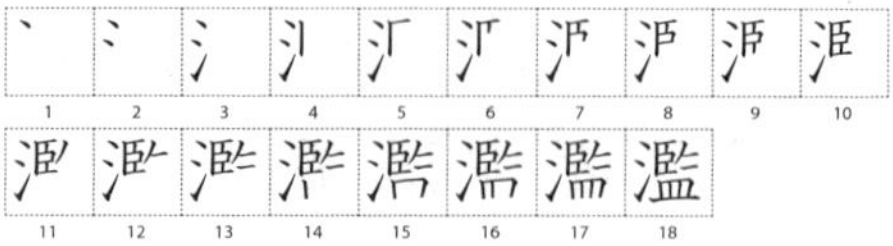

COMPOUNDS

❶ [also 乱 1611] **EXCESSIVE, indiscriminate, extravagant, inordinate, haphazard, reckless**

濫造 らんぞう excessive production, careless manufacture

濫伐 らんばつ indiscriminate deforestation, overcutting of forests

濫費 らんぴ extravagance, money wasting

濫用する らんようする abuse, use to excess

紙幣の濫発 しへいのらんぱつ excessive [reckless] issue of bank notes

❷ [original meaning] **overflow, flow over, inundate**

氾濫する はんらんする overflow, flood

❸ set afloat

濫觴× らんしょう genesis, origin

SYNONYMS

❶ **exceeding and excess**

過 EXCEED → 3891

超 SURPASS → 4107

越 GO BEYOND → 4108

濫 EXCESSIVE → 0990

余 EXCESS → 2535

剰 SURPLUS → 2233

冗 REDUNDANT → 2470

❶ **rash**

減 unreasonable → 0812

妄 RASH → 2509

盲 BLIND → 2547

暴 unrestrained → 3138

荒 WILD → 2810

濫 EXCESSIVE → 0990

乱 excessive → 1611

❷ **flow and drip**

流 FLOW → 0529

注 POUR → 0383

濫 overflow → 0990

溢 OVERFLOW → 0807

漏 LEAK → 0860

滴 DROP → 0866

泌 SECRETE → 0390

瀝 DRIP → 0996

獵

0991

1-3-15

▶**HUNTING**

リョウ

94	Nonstandard	U7375
犭	S18-3-15	F0000

traditional form → see 猟 at 0654

壞

▶BREAK DOWN
カイ こわ(す) こわ(れる)

0992
1-3-16

32	Names	U58DE
土	S19-3-16	F0000

traditional form → see 壊 at 0934

懷

▶BOSOM
▶LONG FOR
カイ ふところ なつ(かしい) なつ(かしむ) なつ(く) なつ(ける) ㊔ かね

0993
1-3-16

61	Names	U61F7
忄	S19-3-16	F0000

traditional form → see 懐 at 0942

瀕

▶ON THE VERGE OF
ヒン
Ⓝ 瀕 Ⓒ 濒 bīn

0994
1-3-16

85	Names	U7015
氵	S19-3-16	F2771

COMPOUNDS

❶ [rarely also 頻 2209] **ON THE VERGE OF**
瀕死 ひんし on the verge of death
❷ shore, bank
瀕海 ひんかい seaside, coastal

INDEPENDENT

【ひんする 瀕する】be ON THE VERGE OF

SYNONYMS

❶ **almost**
殆ど ALMOST → 1130
瀕 ON THE VERGE OF → 0994
甫めて BARELY → 4363
辛い bare → 2531

瀬

▶SHALLOWS
ライ* せ
Ⓝ 瀨 Ⓒ 濑 lài

0995
1-3-16

85	Jōyō	U702C
氵	S19-3-16	F1027

COMPOUNDS

● [original meaning, now archaic] **rapids**

KUN

【せ 瀬】
①ⓐ **SHALLOWS, shoal**
ⓑ **rapids, torrent, swift current**
a 瀬戸 せと strait, channel
瀬戸物 せともの pottery, china
浅瀬 あさせ shoal, shallows
早瀬 はやせ rapids, swift current
b 瀬を下る せをくだる descend the rapids
②ⓐ standpoint, one's ground
ⓑ occasion, opportunity
a 立つ瀬 たつせ one's ground, one's position
b 逢瀬 おうせ meeting, date
年の瀬 としのせ closing days of the year

SYNONYMS

【せ】
①ⓐ **shoals**
瀬 SHALLOWS → 0995
州 sandbar → 0064
礁 REEF → 1588
ⓑ **running water**
流 CURRENT → 0529
潮 TIDE → 0916
汐 TIDE → 0259
瀬 rapids → 0995
滝 WATERFALL → 0813
洪 FLOOD → 0461
渦 WHIRLPOOL → 0735

NOTE

★ do not confuse with 漱 RINSE → 0865

瀝

▶DRIP
レキ
Ⓒ 沥 lì

0996
1-3-16

85	Non-Jōyō	U701D
氵	S19-3-16	F0000

COMPOUNDS

[now also 歴 3748]
ⓐ [original meaning] **DRIP, trickle**
ⓑ **pour**
a 瀝青炭 れきせいたん bituminous coal
b 披瀝する ひれきする express (one's opinion), reveal (one's thoughts)

SYNONYMS

ⓐ **flow and drip**
流 FLOW → 0529
注 POUR → 0383
濫 overflow → 0990
溢 OVERFLOW → 0807
漏 LEAK → 0860
滴 DROP → 0866
泌 SECRETE → 0390
瀝 DRIP → 0996

瀨

0997

1-3-16

▶SHALLOWS

ライ せ

85	Names	U7028
氵	S19-3-16	F0000

traditional form → see 瀬 at 0995

瀧

0998

1-3-16

▶WATERFALL

ロウ たき

85	Names	U7027
氵	S19-3-16	F0000

traditional form → see 滝 at 0813

潛

0999

1-3-16

▶SUBMERGE
▶LURK

セン ひそ(む) もぐ(る) くぐ(る) ㊔ ひそか

85	Nonstandard	U6FF3
氵	S19-3-16	F0000

traditional form → see 潜 at 0922

壤

1000

1-3-17

▶ARABLE SOIL

ジョウ ㊔ みのる ゆたか

32	Nonstandard	U58E4
土	S20-3-17	F0000

traditional form → see 壌 at 0933

孃

1001

1-3-17

▶YOUNG LADY

ジョウ

38	Names	U5B43
女	S20-3-17	F0000

traditional form → see 嬢 at 0936

瀕

1002

1-3-17

▶ON THE VERGE OF

ヒン

85	Nonstandard	U7015
氵	S20-3-17	F0000

traditional form → see 瀕 at 0994

攜

1003

1-3-18

▶CARRY IN HAND

ケイ たずさ(える) たずさ(わる)

64	Nonstandard	U651C
扌	S21-3-18	F0000

traditional form → see 携 at 0796

攝

1004

1-3-18

▶TAKE IN
▶ACT AS REGENT

セツ ㊔ おさむ

64	Names	U651D
扌	S21-3-18	F0000

traditional form → see 摂 at 0799

灘

1005

1-3-18

▶OPEN SEA

タン なだ

85	Nonstandard	U7058
氵	S21-3-18	F0000

traditional form → see 灘 at 1006

灘

1-3-18

incorrect stroke-count
➡ see 1-3-19: 氵 at 1006

灘

1006

1-3-19

▶OPEN SEA

タン なだ

Ⓝ 灘 Ⓒ 滩 tān

85	Names	U7058
氵	S22-3-19	F2567

KUN

【なだ 灘】 **OPEN SEA; rough sea**

SYNONYMS

【なだ】

○ **sea**

海 SEA → 0459
洋 OCEAN → 0468
沖 OFFING → 0307
灘 OPEN SEA → 1006

巖

1007

1-3-20

▶CRAG

ガン いわお いわ ㊔ げん たけ いつく よし

46	Nonstandard	U5DD7
山	S23-3-20	F0000

traditional form → see 巌 at 3037

黴

1008

1-3-20

▶MOLD

バイ かび か(びる)

Ⓒ 霉 méi

203	Non-Jōyō	U9EF4
黑	S23-12-11	F3459

COMPOUNDS

● [now also 梅 1159] **MOLD, mildew, fungus**

黴毒 ばいどく syphilis
黴雨 ばいう rainy season (of early summer)
黴菌 ばいきん bacterium, germ

KUN

【かび 黴】 **MOLD, mildew, fungus**

黴臭い かびくさい (of smell) musty, fusty, stale

【かびる 黴びる】 **become musty, mildew**

SYNONYMS

● **fungus**

黴 MOLD → 1008
茸 MUSHROOM → 2809

菌 fungus → 2876

囑 1009

▶CHARGE WITH
ショク

30	Nonstandard	U56D1
口	S24-3-21	F0000

◧ 1-3-21 traditional form → see 嘱 at 0881

灣 1010

▶BAY
ワン

85	Nonstandard	U7063
氵	S25-3-22	F0000

◧ 1-3-22 traditional form → see 湾 at 0748

札 1011

▶TAG
サツ ふだ
Ⓒ 札 zhá

75	Jōyō-4	U672D
木	S5-4-1	F1125

◧ 1-4-1

一 十 才 木 札
1 2 3 4 5

COMPOUNDS

❶ⓐ TAG, plate, placard
ⓑ ticket
ⓒ [original meaning] thin wooden tablet used for writing in ancient China

a 標札(=表札) ひょうさつ nameplate, doorplate
門札 もんさつ doorplate, nameplate
鑑札 かんさつ license, certificate
b 検札 けんさつ examination of tickets
改札口 かいさつぐち ticket barrier [gate], wicket

❷ [also suffix] **bill, paper money, bank note**
札入れ さついれ billfold, wallet
札束 さつたば bundle of (bank) notes, wad of bills
贋×札 がんさつ(=にせさつ) counterfeit paper money, forged note
千円札 せんえんさつ 1000-yen bill

❸ tender, bid
入札する にゅうさつする tender, bid
落札 らくさつ successful bid

❹ document, certificate; letter
一札 いっさつ document, paper; bond

INDEPENDENT

【さつ 札】**bill, paper money, bank note**
札を崩す さつをくずす change a note

KUN

【ふだ 札】
① [also suffix] **TAG, tab, label, card, placard; billboard**
札を付ける ふだをつける put a tag on, label
値札 ねふだ price tag [mark, label]
手札 てふだ visiting card, card
守り札 まもりふだ paper charm
名札 なふだ nameplate
立て札 たてふだ bulletin board
質札 しちふだ pawn ticket

② **playing card**
切り札 きりふだ trump (card), last resort

③ tender, bill
入れ札 いれふだ tender, bid

SYNONYMS

❶ labels and slips
札 TAG → 1011
券 TICKET → 3256
票 SLIP → 3308
符 tally → 3299
節 token → 3336

❷ money
金 MONEY → 2552
銭 MONEY → 2159
貨 MONEY (legal tender), coin → 3113
幣 CURRENCY → 3582
銀 SILVER → 2156
財 finance → 1849
資 RESOURCES → 3342
-玉 coin suffix → 4289
札 bill → 1011

礼 1012

▶ETIQUETTE
▶RITE
レイ ライ ㊔ あや のり ひろ
Ⓝ 禮 祀 Ⓒ 礼 lǐ

113	Jōyō-3	U793C
礻	S5-4-1	F0769

◧ 1-4-1

丶 ラ 才 礻 礼
1 2 3 4 5

COMPOUNDS

❶ⓐ ETIQUETTE, courtesy, propriety, manners, ceremony
ⓑ [also suffix] **courtesy bow, salutation**

a 礼儀 れいぎ etiquette, courtesy, propriety, manners
礼節 れいせつ courtesy, etiquette
礼式 れいしき etiquette, manner
失礼 しつれい impoliteness, rudeness; bad manners; I beg your pardon/Goodbye
b 礼砲 れいほう salute gun
一礼 いちれい bow, greeting; courtesy
敬礼 けいれい salutation, salute, bow
栄誉礼 えいよれい salute of guards of honor

❷ [also suffix] [original meaning] **RITE, ceremony, ritual, religious service**

礼典 れいてん ceremony, ritual, rite
礼服 れいふく ceremonial dress
婚礼 こんれい wedding ceremony
洗礼 せんれい baptism
朝礼 ちょうれい morning gathering
立太子礼 りったいしれい ceremonial of instituting the Crown Prince

❸ **show respect to, treat politely**
礼拝 れいはい(=らいはい) worship; church service
礼遇 れいぐう honorable treatment
礼讃(=礼賛)する らいさんする worship, adore, glorify

❹ⓐ **thanks, gratitude, appreciation**
ⓑ **monetary gift, remuneration, reward**
a 礼状 れいじょう letter of thanks
礼金 れいきん reward, fee, honorarium
b 謝礼 しゃれい remuneration, reward; thanks
返礼 へんれい return present; return call

INDEPENDENT

【れい 礼】
① **bow, salutation**
礼をする れいをする salute, make a bow; reward, remunerate
② **ETIQUETTE, courtesy, propriety**
礼を失する れいをしっする be impolite [disrespectful]
③ⓐ **thanks, appreciation**
ⓑ reward, return present
a お礼 おれい thanks, appreciation; reward; gift, return present

SYNONYMS

❶ⓐ **etiquette**
礼 ETIQUETTE → 1012
儀 CEREMONY → 0191
ⓑ **bow**
礼 courtesy bow → 1012
拝 bow in veneration → 0360
❷ **ceremonies and festivities**
式 CEREMONY → 3785
儀 CEREMONY → 0191
典 formal ceremony → 3253
礼 RITE → 1012
斎 religious ritual → 2622
会 Buddhist ceremony → 2512
祭 FESTIVAL → 3311
❹ⓐ **thanking and gratitude**
謝 THANK → 2048
礼 thanks → 1012
恩 DEBT OF GRATITUDE → 3289
ⓑ **monetary gifts**
謝 monetary gift of thanks → 2048
礼 monetary gift → 1012

朴

1013
1-4-2

▶**SIMPLE**
ボク ほお▲
Ⓒ 朴 pǔ piáo

75	Jōyō	U6734
木	S6-4-2	F1844

一	十	才	木	朩	朴
1	2	3	4	5	6

COMPOUNDS

❶ **SIMPLE, unadorned, plain**
朴訥× ぼくとつ rugged honesty
朴直な ぼくちょくな simple and honest, artless, naive
素朴な そぼくな simple, naive, artless
質朴な しつぼくな simple, plain, unsophisticated
敦朴(=敦樸×)な とんぼくな [archaic] honest and simple
❷ unsociable
朴念仁 ぼくねんじん quiet unsociable person

KUN

【ほお 朴】*Magnolia hypoleuca* (tree used for the supports of clogs)
朴の木 ほおのき *Magnolia hypoleuca*

SYNONYMS

❶ **plain and simple**
素 PLAIN → 3108
朴 SIMPLE (unadorned) → 1013
単 simple (uncomplicated) → 2805

机

1014
1-4-2

▶**DESK**
キ つくえ
Ⓒ 机 jī

75	Jōyō-6	U673A
木	S6-4-2	F1568

一	十	才	木	札	机
1	2	3	4	5	6

COMPOUNDS

[?] **DESK, table**
机上 きじょう top of desk; academic, theoretical
机辺 きへん around the desk [table]
机下(=几下) きか under the desk

KUN

【つくえ 机】[also suffix] **DESK, table**
机でする仕事 つくえでするしごと desk work [job]
勉強机 べんきょうづくえ (writing) desk
事務机 じむづくえ office desk

SYNONYMS

[?] **tables and stands**

卓 TABLE → 2561
机 DESK → 1014
几 DESK → 4156
台 STAND → 2498

朽

▶DECAY
キュウ く(ちる)
Ⓒ 朽 xiǔ

1015
1-4-2

75	Jōyō	U673D
木	S6-4-2	F2320

1 2 3 4 5 6

COMPOUNDS

● [original meaning] **DECAY, rot**
朽廃する きゅうはいする decay, be dilapidated [ruined]
腐朽 ふきゅう deterioration, decay
老朽 ろうきゅう superannuation, decrepitude
不朽の ふきゅうの immortal, undecaying, eternal

KUN

【くちる 朽ちる】**DECAY, rot; remain in obscurity**
朽ち葉 くちば decayed leaves
朽ち果てる くちはてる decay completely, rot away; rust away; rusticate oneself

SYNONYMS

● **decay**
朽 DECAY → 1015
腐 ROT → 3921
枯 WITHER → 1113
萎 WITHER → 2872
銹 RUST → 2188

杈

▶RIGHT
▶POWER
ケン ゴン

1016
1-4-2

75	Nonstandard	U6743
木	S6-4-2	F0000

alternative form → see 権 at 1348

此

▶THIS
シ こ(れ) こ(の)
Ⓒ 此 cǐ

1017
1-4-2

77	Names	U6B64
止	S6-4-2	F1746

COMPOUNDS

● *demonstrative* **THIS**
此岸 しがん this world [life]

KUN

【これ 此れ】[also 是 or 之] *pronoun* **THIS**
此れから これから after this, from now on; the future
此れ位 これくらい(=これぐらい) (about) this much [amount]
此れ見よがしに これみよがしに ostentatiously
此れと言って これといって [in negative constructions] in particular, to speak of
彼此 あれこれ one thing or another, this and that

【この 此の】[sometimes also 斯の] *demonstrative* **THIS**
此の世界 このせかい this world
此度 このたび this occasion, now
此の頃 このごろ recently; these days
此の手 このて this way (of doing); this sort
此の方 このかた since; [polite] this person

SPECIAL READINGS

此処(=此所) ここ here, this place
此方 こちら this way [direction]; here; this (one); I, me, us, we; this person
此間 こないだ *colloq* the other day; recently
此奴 こいつ this fellow, this guy
彼方此方 あちこち(=あっちこっち) all over, many places; jumbled out of order

SYNONYMS

● **this and that**
本 THIS → 4314
爾 THAT → 4407
其れ THAT → 3255
彼 that → 0346
今 THIS (week, etc.) → 2464
当 THE PRESENT → 2701
該 the said → 1916
同 the same → 3707
之 this → 4228
是 this → 3090
此 THIS → 1017
斯 THIS → 2140

USAGE

【この】
此の
[sometimes also 斯の] *demonstrative* this
斯の
[usu. 此の] *demonstrative* this

HOMOPHONES

これ
之 POSSESSIVE PARTICLE → 4228
是 RIGHT → 3090
惟 MEDITATE → 0582
この 斯 THIS → 2140

NOTE

➡ see also USAGE note at 是 3090

1 木 止 【歹】 火 牙 牛 ネ 月 用 㐆 开 手 屯

列
▶ROW
レツ レ▲
Ⓒ 列 liè

1018
1-4-2

18	Jōyō-3	U5217
刂	S6-2-4	F0776

一 ア 歹 歹 歹 列 (stroke order 1–6)

COMPOUNDS

❶ⓐ [also suffix] **ROW, line, file, rank; series**
ⓑ counter for ROWs

a 行列 ぎょうれつ procession, queue; matrix
系列 けいれつ order, succession; series
戦列 せんれつ line of battle
序列 じょれつ rank, grade, order
等差数列 とうさすうれつ arithmetical progression [series]
パラフィン列 ぱらふぃんれつ paraffin series
b 三列 さんれつ three rows [lines]

❷ **arrange in a ROW, line up**
列車 れっしゃ (railway) train
列島 れっとう archipelago
列挙 れっきょ enumeration, listing
整列する せいれつする stand in a row, line up
陳列する ちんれつする exhibit, display

❸ attend, participate
列席 れっせき attendance, presence
参列する さんれつする attend, be present, participate

❹ many, numerous
列国 れっこく the powers, all nations
列強 れっきょう the great powers

❺ used phonetically for *re* or similar sounds in the transliteration of foreign words
列寧 れーにん Lenin

INDEPENDENT

【れつ 列】 **ROW, line, file, rank; column (of a matrix)**
列を作る れつをつくる form a line [row]

SYNONYMS

❶ⓐ **linear arrangements**
伍 RANK → 0050
列 ROW → 1018
行 LINE (esp. of print) → 0246
欄 COLUMN → 1419

❷ **arrange**
並 LINE UP → 2793
比 rank → 0029
列 arrange in a row → 1018
陳 lay out (for exhibit) → 0656
羅 spread out → 3244
揃える arrange properly → 0719
整 PUT IN ORDER → 3562
理 put in order → 1220

灯
▶LAMP
トウ ひ ほ-▲ ともしび▲ とも(す)▲
㊔ あかり
Ⓝ 燈 Ⓒ 灯 dēng

1019
1-4-2

86	Jōyō-4	U706F
火	S6-4-2	F1153

丶 丷 火 火 火 灯 (stroke order 1–6)

COMPOUNDS

ⓐ [also suffix] [original meaning] **LAMP, light, lantern**
ⓑ counter for LAMPs or lights

a 灯台 とうだい lighthouse; oil-lamp stand
灯火 とうか light, lamplight
灯油 とうゆ kerosene, lamp oil
電灯 でんとう lamp, electric light
街灯 がいとう street lamp
尾灯 びとう taillight
蛍光灯 けいこうとう fluorescent lamp [light]
b 五十灯 ごじっとう 50 lamps

INDEPENDENT

【とう 灯】 LAMP, light, lantern

KUN

【ひ 灯】 (source of illumination) **light, lantern, LAMP**
灯を付ける ひをつける turn on the light

【ほ- 灯-】 [also 火-] fire
灯影 ほかげ(=とうえい) firelight in the dark; shadows by the firelight

【ともしび 灯】 [also 灯火, sometimes also 燭] light, LAMP, flame
風前の灯 ふうぜんのともしび candle flickering before the wind; extremely precarious position

【ともす 灯す】 [usu. 点す] light (a lamp), set alight, turn on (a light)
灯火 ともしび [also 灯, sometimes also 燭] light, lamp, flame
松明を灯す たいまつをともす kindle a torch

SPECIAL READINGS

提灯▲ ちょうちん paper lantern
行灯▲ あんどん paper-enclosed oil lantern

SYNONYMS

ⓐ **light**
光 LIGHT → 3043
明 light → 1060
灯 LAMP → 1019
燭 CANDLE → 1391
照 sunlight → 3506

虹 RAINBOW → 1637

USAGE

【ともしび】

灯

[also 灯火, sometimes also 燭] light, lamp, flame

燭

[usu. 灯 or 灯火] light, lamp, flame

HOMOPHONES

ひ 火 FIRE → 4273
ほ- 火 FIRE → 4273
ともす 点 POINT → 2587
ともしび
燭 CANDLE → 1391
灯火 → 1019, 4273

NOTE

➡ see also USAGE notes at 火 4273 and 点 2587

邪

◧ 1-4-2

incorrect stroke-count
➡ see ◧ 1-4-3: 牙 at 1039

牝

1020
◧ 1-4-2

▶FEMALE
ヒン めす め- めん
Ⓒ 牝 pìn

93	Non-Jōyō	U725D
牛	S6-4-2	F2662

COMPOUNDS

● [original meaning] (of animals) **FEMALE**
牝馬 ひんば mare

KUN

【めす 牝】[usu. 雌] (of animals) **FEMALE**
牝犬 めすいぬ female dog, bitch
【め- 牝-】[usu. 雌] (of animals) **FEMALE**
牝牛 めうし cow
牝鹿 めじか doe
【めん 牝】[usu. 雌] (of animals) **FEMALE**
牝鳥(=牝鶏) めんどり hen

SYNONYMS

● **woman**
女 WOMAN → 4226
婦 ADULT WOMAN → 0565
婆 OLD WOMAN → 3433
嬢 YOUNG LADY → 0936
娘 GIRL → 0488
雌 FEMALE → 1337
牝 FEMALE → 1020
媛 DAMSEL → 0688

HOMOPHONES

めす 雌 FEMALE → 1337
め-
雌 FEMALE → 1337
女 WOMAN → 4226
めん 雌 FEMALE → 1337

NOTE

➡ see USAGE note at 雌 1337

祁

◧ 1-4-2

incorrect stroke-count
➡ see ◧ 1-4-3: 礻 at 1043

肌

1021
◧ 1-4-2

▶SKIN
キ[^] はだ
Ⓒ 肌 jī

130	Jōyō	U808C
月	S6-4-2	F1201

Stroke order: 1 2 3 4 5 6 (肌)

COMPOUNDS

● [original meaning] **SKIN** (of the human body)
肌膚 きふ skin
肌骨 きこつ skin and bones

KUN

【はだ 肌】[formerly also 膚]
①ⓐ **SKIN, body**
ⓑ **surface; grain (of wood)**
a 肌身 はだみ body
肌着 はだぎ underwear
肌を許す はだをゆるす surrender one's chastity to a man
肌色 はだいろ flesh-color
赤肌 あかはだ abraded skin
b 山肌 やまはだ surface of a mountain
美しい肌の材 うつくしいはだのざい wood of fine grain
②ⓐ disposition, temperament
ⓑ [suffix] **turn of mind**
a 肌が合わない はだがあわない cannot go together (with)
b 学者肌 がくしゃはだ scholarly bent of mind

SYNONYMS

● **kinds of skin**
皮 SKIN (of any kind) → 3771
膚 SKIN (of the human body) → 4049
肌 SKIN (of the human body) → 1021
革 LEATHER → 3099
韋 TANNED LEATHER → 2851
鱗 SCALES → 2375

朩 止 歹 火 牙 牛 ネ 【月】 ⺝ 𦣝 开 扌 㐄

USAGE

【はだ】

肌

[formerly also 膚]

①ⓐ skin, body

ⓑ surface; grain (of wood)

②ⓐ disposition, temperament

ⓑ [suffix] turn of mind

膚

[now replaced by 肌] same as 肌

HOMOPHONES

はだ 膚 SKIN →4049

肋

1022

◧1-4-2

▸**RIB**

ロク あばら ばら

Ⓒ 肋 lèi lē

130	Names	U808B
月	S6-4-2	F2912

COMPOUNDS

● [original meaning] **RIB, costa**

肋骨 ろっこつ rib, costa

肋膜 ろくまく pleura

肋間神経痛 ろっかんしんけいつう intercostal neuralgia

肋木 ろくぼく wall bars

中肋 ちゅうろく midrib, rachis (of a leaf)

KUN

【あばら 肋】**RIB, costa**

肋骨 あばらぼね rib, costa

【ばら 肋】**RIB**s (of beef or pork)

肋肉 ばらにく ribs (of beef or pork)

SYNONYMS

● **bone**

骨 BONE →3288

髄 MARROW →2316

椎 SPINE →1249

脊 SPINE →3297

肋 RIB →1022

骼 SKELETAL FRAME →2302

骸 skeleton →2301

那

◧1-4-2

incorrect stroke-count

➡ see ◧1-4-3: 那 at 1047

印

1023

◧1-4-2

▸**MARK**

▸**SEAL**

イン しるし -じるし しる(す)[▲] ㊔ かね

Ⓒ 印 yìn

26	Jōyō-4	U5370
卩	S6-2-4	F0742

Stroke order: 1 ㇒ 2 ⺁ 3 ⺊ 4 ⺋ 5 ⺍ 6 印

COMPOUNDS

❶ (visible sign) **MARK, imprint, sign**

烙[×]印 らくいん brand

❷ⓐ [original meaning] imprint, impress, make a **MARK**

ⓑ **imprint on the mind, make an impression**

a 印字 いんじ printing, typing

印刻 いんこく engraving

b 印象 いんしょう impression

❸ **print**

印刷 いんさつ printing

印行する いんこうする print and publish

影印 えいいん phototype process, photoengraving

❹ [also suffix] **SEAL, stamp; seal impression**

印鑑 いんかん personal seal

印税 いんぜい royalty (on a book)

印紙 いんし (revenue) stamp

調印 ちょういん signing, sealing; signature

消印 けしいん postmark, (postal) cancellation mark

封印 ふういん (stamped) seal

押印する おういんする seal, affix a seal

刻印 こくいん carved seal, stamp

ゴム印 ごむいん rubber stamp

偽造印 ぎぞういん forged seal

❺ India

印綿(=印棉) いんめん Indian raw cotton

日印関係 にちいんかんけい Japan-India relations

INDEPENDENT

【いん 印】**SEAL**, stamp; *Buddhism* hand signs; India

印を押す いんをおす affix one's seal

印を結ぶ いんをむすぶ make symbolic signs [gestures] with the fingers

【いんする 印する】print, impress

KUN

【しるし 印】

① **MARK, sign; symbol**

目印 めじるし mark, sign, landmark

矢印 やじるし arrow (mark)

② token (of appreciation)

感謝の印 かんしゃのしるし token of appreciation

③ proof

. . . の印として …のしるしとして as proof of...

【-じるし -印】**trademark, brand**

雪印 ゆきじるし Snow Brand

【しるす 印す】**MARK**, inscribe

SYNONYMS

❶ **marks and signs**

標 MARK (identifying sign) →1347

徽 EMBLEM → 0968
痕 SCAR → 4066
印 MARK (visible sign) → 1023
跡 TRACE → 1937
蹟 TRACE → 2065
踪 FOOTPRINTS → 1996
紋 print → 1651
符 SYMBOL → 3299
号 SIGN → 2675
栞 BOOKMARK → 3285

❷ mark
印 imprint → 1023
押 seal → 0371
劃 MARK OFF → 2378
画 mark off → 3723
捺 AFFIX A SEAL → 0603

❸ print and publish
刷 PRINT → 1623
印 print → 1023
植 typeset → 1247
刊 PUBLISH → 0221
版 PUBLISHING → 1082
載 PUT IN PRINT → 4091
掲 display in writing → 0597
幀 BOOKBINDING → 0695

❹ seals
印 SEAL → 1023
判 personal seal → 1441
璽 IMPERIAL SEAL → 3624

❺ Asian countries
日 JAPAN → 3759
緬 Myanmar → 1758
老 Laos → 3963
華 CHINA → 2841
蒙 Mongolia → 2938
鮮 Korea → 2355
泰 Thailand → 3193
越 Vietnam → 4108
印 India → 1023
竺 INDIA → 3248
比 Philippines → 0029

USAGE

【しるし】
印
① mark, sign; symbol
② token (of appreciation)
③ proof
徴
① effectiveness (of medicine)
② symptom, sign, indication

HOMOPHONES

しるし 徴 LEVY → 0841
しるす 記 WRITE DOWN → 1843

NOTE

➡ see also USAGE note at 記 1843

刑

1024

◧ 1-4-2

▶PENALTY

ケイ

Ⓒ 刑 xíng

18	Jōyō	U5211
刂	S6-2-4	F0841

一 二 チ 开 刑 刑
1 2 3 4 5 6

COMPOUNDS

ⓐ [also suffix] **PENALTY, punishment, sentence**
ⓑ [original meaning] punish, torture

a 刑罰 けいばつ penalty, punishment
刑期 けいき prison term
刑事 けいじ (police) detective
刑務所 けいむしょ prison
刑法 けいほう criminal law, penal code
処刑 しょけい execution, punishment
求刑する きゅうけいする demand a sentence (for the accused)
死刑 しけい capital punishment, death penalty
絞首刑 こうしゅけい death [execution] by hanging

INDEPENDENT

【けい 刑】**PENALTY, punishment, sentence**
刑に服する けいにふくする serve a sentence, endure a penalty
【けいする 刑する】sentence

SYNONYMS

ⓐ punishment
刑 PENALTY → 1024
罰 PUNISHMENT → 3228
懲 CHASTISE → 3623
処 DEAL WITH (lawbreakers) → 3764

NOTE

★ do not confuse with 刊 PUBLISH → 0221

邦

◧ 1-4-2

incorrect stroke-count
➡ see ◧ 1-4-3: 丰 at 1051

邨

◧ 1-4-2

incorrect stroke-count
➡ see ◧ 1-4-3: 屯 at 1053

対

▶OPPOSITE
▶OPPOSE

タイ ツイ

1025

1-4-3

Ⓝ 對 Ⓒ 对 duì

41	Jōyō-3	U5BFE
寸	S7-3-4	F0081

COMPOUNDS

❶ⓐ OPPOSITE, facing each other, opposed, opposing
ⓑ [original meaning] **face (each other), confront**

a 対談 たいだん talk, tête-à-tête, interview; personal negotiation
対話 たいわ dialogue, conversation
対岸 たいがん opposite bank [shore]
対座する たいざする sit opposite each other
対辺 たいへん opposite side
対局 たいきょく game of go [shogi]
b 対面する たいめんする meet, face
相対 そうたい relativity

❷ⓐ OPPOSE, confront (each other), counter
ⓑ [also prefix] **counter-, OPPOSITE, contra-, anti-**
ⓒ abbrev. of 対策 たいさく: countermeasure

a 対立 たいりつ opposition, antagonism
対抗 たいこう opposition, antagonism, rivalry; counteraction
対決 たいけつ confrontation, showdown
対戦 たいせん waging war; competition
反対する はんたいする oppose, object (to)
敵対 てきたい hostility, antagonism
b 対策 たいさく countermeasure, counterplan
対案 たいあん counterproposal
対語 ついご(=たいご) antonym
対潜水艦の たいせんすいかんの antisubmarine
c 失対 しったい measure against unemployment
選対本部 せんたいほんぶ election headquarters

❸ (place in opposition and compare) **OPPOSE, contrast**

対象 たいしょう object (of study), subject, target
対照 たいしょう contrast, comparison; control
対比する たいひする contrast, compare
対等 たいとう equality, parity
対称的な たいしょうてきな symmetrical
絶対の ぜったいの absolute
相対性理論 そうたいせいりろん theory of relativity

❹ [also prefix] **toward, to, in relation to, versus**

対米 たいべい toward [with] America
対日 たいにち toward [with] Japan
対外の たいがいの foreign; outside
対中国関係 たいちゅうごくかんけい relations with China

❺ⓐ cope with, treat, receive
ⓑ answer, reply

a 対処する たいしょする cope [deal] with, meet
対応する たいおうする correspond to, answer to; be equivalent; deal [cope] with
ab 応対 おうたい reception (of visitors); address

❻ⓐ (two things of the same kind) **pair, couple, set**
ⓑ counter for pairs

a 対偶 たいぐう pair; antithesis
対句 ついく couplet, antithesis
b 一対 いっつい a pair

❼ⓐ equal, even
ⓑ used phonetically for the transliteration of the English word *tie*

a 対価 たいか compensation, equivalent value
b 対スコア たいすこあ tie score

INDEPENDENT

【たい 対】

① the **OPPOSITE**, one of a pair
白の対は黒 しろのたいはくろ The opposite of white is black

②ⓐ versus, against, to (in competitions or transactions)
ⓑ *math* to (in ratios)

a 原告対被告 げんこくたいひこく plaintiff versus defendant
b 二対一 にたいいち two to one

③ⓐ *colloq* equal terms
ⓑ tie (→❼ⓑ)

a 対で勝負する たいでしょうぶする play a game on equal terms

④ annex building in old Japanese palace-style house

【たいする 対する】

① **face (each other), confront**
丘に対する部屋 おかにたいするへや room facing a hill

② **toward, to, in relation to**
彼は人に対して親切だ かれはひとにたいしてしんせつだ He is kind to others

③ⓐ **OPPOSE**, confront (each other), counter
ⓑ **as OPPOSEd to, in opposition to, against**

a 全力で敵に対する ぜんりょくでてきにたいする fight against the enemy with all one's might
b 口語体に対する文語体 こうごたいにたいするぶんごたい literary style as opposed to colloquial style

④ treat, receive, address
寛容を以て人に対する かんようをもってひとにたいする treat others with magnanimity

【つい 対】 (two things of the same kind) **pair, couple, set**

対になる ついになる form a pair

SYNONYMS

1a & 2b opposite

対 OPPOSITE → 1025
反 COUNTER → 3663
逆 REVERSE → 3835
倒 upside-down → 0139

b face

向 TURN TOWARD → 3790
面 FACE → 2590
対 face (each other) → 1025

2a resist

抗 RESIST → 0296
抵 RESIST → 0377
耐 WITHSTAND → 1634
対 OPPOSE → 1025
反 COUNTER → 3663
逆 rebel → 3835
撥 REPEL → 0907
叛 REBEL → 1469

3 compare

比 COMPARE → 0029
較 COMPARE → 1939
譬 COMPARE TO → 3613
校 COLLATE → 1166
照 check against → 3506
対 OPPOSE (contrast) → 1025
参 refer → 2563

6 two

二 TWO → 2421
弐 TWO (in legal documents) → 3961
双 SET OF TWO → 0028
対 pair → 1025
偶 COUPLE → 0150
両 BOTH → 4331

COMPOUND FORMATION

【絶対 ぜったい】

絶対の 'absolute' refers to something without match (絶); that is, to something that cannot compared in contrast (対 3) to something else.

NOTE

➡ see COMPOUND FORMATION for
相対 そうたい → 相 1120
対象 たいしょう → 象 2647

杖

1026

1-4-3

▶**STAFF**

ジョウ つえ ㊔ き もち てい

Ⓒ 杖 zhàng

75	Names	U6756
木	S7-4-3	F2001

COMPOUNDS

● STAFF, cane, walking stick

杖術 じょうじゅつ form of martial art using a cane staff
錫杖 しゃくじょう *khakkhara*, Buddhist priest's staff
金剛杖 こんごうじょう(=こんごうづえ) pilgrim's staff

INDEPENDENT

【じょう 杖】 severe caning; unit used for measuring agricultural land area in medieval Japan

KUN

【つえ 杖】

ⓐ **STAFF, cane, (walking) stick**
ⓑ **prop, support**

a 松葉杖 まつばづえ crutch(es)
仕込み杖 しこみづえ sword cane
転ばぬ先の杖 ころばぬさきのつえ A stitch in time saves nine ("Use a cane before you fall")

b 頬杖 ほおづえ resting one's chin in one's hands

SPECIAL READINGS

虎杖 いたどり Japanese knotweed

SYNONYMS

● long slender objects

棒 ROD → 1237
箸 CHOPSTICKS → 3359
桟 crosspiece → 1169
軸 AXLE → 1908
錘 SPINDLE → 2191
竿 POLE → 3259
杖 STAFF → 1026
錫 Buddhist priest's staff → 2189
軛 YOKE → 1873

杉

1027

1-4-3

▶**CRYPTOMERIA**

サン▲ すぎ

Ⓝ 杦 Ⓒ 杉 shān shā

75	Jōyō	U6749
木	S7-4-3	F1035

1	2	3	4	5	6	7
一	十	才	木	杉	杉	杉

COMPOUNDS

● [archaic] **CRYPTOMERIA**, Japanese [Japan] cedar, sugi

老杉 ろうさん old cryptomeria

KUN

【すぎ 杉】 **CRYPTOMERIA, Japanese [Japan] cedar, sugi**

杉林 すぎばやし cryptomeria forest
杉並木 すぎなみき avenue of cryptomerias
杉箸 すぎばし cryptomeria [sugi] chopsticks
杉垣 すぎがき cryptomeria hedge

SYNONYMS

● **trees**

桜 CHERRY → 1168
桐 PAULOWNIA → 1173
桂 AROMATIC TREE, katsura tree → 1163
梓 CATALPA → 1207
桑 MULBERRY → 2618
漆 Japanese lacquer tree → 0863
樺 BIRCH → 1324
椛 BIRCH → 1202
梧 CHINESE PARASOL TREE → 1200
檀 SPINDLE TREE → 1385
椿 CAMELLIA → 1278
柳 WILLOW → 1115
柊 HOLLY → 1119
椋 *APHANANTHE ASPERA* → 1245
柾 spindle tree → 1114
槻 ZELKOVA → 1349
楢 OAK → 1287
樫 EVERGREEN OAK → 1364
柏 CYPRESS, JAPANESE EMPEROR OAK → 1110
榎 HACKBERRY → 1323
梶 PAPER MULBERRY → 1199
柘 JAPANESE BOXWOOD → 1117
楊 WILLOW → 1286
桧 JAPANESE CYPRESS → 1160
梛 *NAGEIA NAGI* → 1206
榊 SACRED SHINTO TREE → 1327
楓 MAPLE → 1280
松 PINE → 1075
杉 CRYPTOMERIA → 1027
槙 PODOCARPUS → 1330
楠 CAMPHOR TREE → 1283
樟 CAMPHOR TREE → 1351

杓

1028

1-4-3

▶**DIPPER**

シャク

Ⓝ 杓 杓 Ⓒ 勺 sháo 杓 biāo

75	Non-Jōyō	U6753
木	S7-4-3	F3086

COMPOUNDS

● [rarely also 勺 3650] **DIPPER, ladle, spoon**

杓子 しゃくし dipper, (wooden) ladle
柄杓 ひしゃく ladle, dipper, scoop
茶杓 ちゃしゃく tea scoop

INDEPENDENT

【しゃく 杓】**DIPPER, ladle**

SPECIAL READINGS

杓文字 しゃもじ rice scoop

SYNONYMS

● **spoons**

斗 DIPPER → 3671
杓 DIPPER → 1028
匕 SPOON → 3641

村

1029

1-4-3

▶**VILLAGE**

ソン むら

Ⓝ 邨 Ⓒ 村 cūn

75	Jōyō-1	U6751
木	S7-4-3	F0189

1	2	3	4	5	6	7
一	十	才	木	木一	村	村

COMPOUNDS

ⓐ [also suffix] [original meaning] **VILLAGE, hamlet; rural district**
ⓑ (unit of local administration) **VILLAGE**
ⓒ counter for **VILLAGE**s

a 村落 そんらく village, hamlet
農村 のうそん farm village, agricultural community
漁村 ぎょそん fishing village
無医村 むいそん doctorless village
一宮村 いちのみやそん Ichinomiya Village
b 村長 そんちょう village mayor
市町村 しちょうそん cities, towns and villages; municipalities
c 六か村 ろっかそん six villages

INDEPENDENT

【そん 村】(unit of local administration) **VILLAGE**

KUN

【むら 村】

ⓐ [also suffix] **VILLAGE, hamlet**
ⓑ (unit of local administration) **VILLAGE**
ⓒ **suffix after names of VILLAGEs**

a 村人 むらびと villager
村里 むらざと village
村八分 むらはちぶ village ostracism
c 八木村 やぎむら Yagi Village

SYNONYMS

● **villages and towns**

町 TOWN → 1430
村 VILLAGE → 1029
里 hamlet → 4356
郷 HOMETOWN → 0664
庄 FEUDAL VILLAGE → 3788
邑 VILLAGE → 2716

杜

1030

◧ 1-4-3

▶GROVE

ト トウ ズ もり

Ⓒ 杜 dù

75	Names	U675C
木	S7-4-3	F2232

COMPOUNDS

❶ Chinese family name: **Du**

杜甫 とほ Du Fu (famous Chinese poet)

杜詩 とし poems of Du Fu

杜氏 とうじ chief brewer at a sake brewery (so called after the name of sake's alleged inventor)

杜撰な ずさんな careless, slipshod, faulty

杜漏な ずろうな careless, negligent

❷ [now replaced by 途 と 3853] shut out, stop, prevent

杜絶する とぜつする be stopped, be interrupted, cease

KUN

【もり 杜】[usu. 森] **GROVE, small woods (esp. surrounding temples or shrines)**

鎮守の杜 ちんじゅのもり grove of the village shrine

SYNONYMS

【もり】

○ **forest**

林 FOREST, small woods →1071

森 THICK WOODS →3123

杜 GROVE →1030

HOMOPHONES

もり 森 THICK WOODS →3123

NOTE

➡ see USAGE note at 森 3123

➡ see COMPOUND FORMATION for 杜撰 ずさん →撰 0911

材

1031

◧ 1-4-3

▶TIMBER

▶MATERIAL

ザイ

Ⓒ 材 cái

75	Jōyō-4	U6750
木	S7-4-3	F0566

Stroke order: 一 十 才 木 木一 村 材 (1 2 3 4 5 6 7)

COMPOUNDS

❶ [original meaning] **TIMBER, lumber, wood**

材木 ざいもく timber, lumber, wood, logs

木材 もくざい wood, timber, lumber

良材 りょうざい good timber

製材業 せいざいぎょう lumbering [sawing] industry

❷ⓐ [also suffix] **MATERIAL, raw material**

ⓑ **(written) MATERIALs, data**

a 材質 ざいしつ material properties; lumber quality

材料 ざいりょう material, matter, stuff; factor, element

素材 そざい material; subject matter

鋼材 こうざい steel materials, structural steel

資材 しざい materials

b 教材 きょうざい teaching materials [aids]

取材 しゅざい collection of data [materials], gathering of news

❸ⓐ **ability, talent**

ⓑ man of ability, capable person

a 材器 ざいき talent, ability

人材 じんざい (man of) talent, capable man

b 適材 てきざい man fit for the post

INDEPENDENT

【ざい 材】**TIMBER**, lumber; material; ability, talent

有為の材 ゆういのざい man of talent

SYNONYMS

❶ **kinds of wood**

木 WOOD →4261

材 TIMBER →1031

薪 FIREWOOD →3009

柴 BRUSHWOOD →3287

❷ⓐ **matter**

質 MATTER →3483

物 substance →1084

材 MATERIAL →1031

料 MATERIALS →1644

資 material resources →3342

杦

1032

◧ 1-4-3

▶CRYPTOMERIA

サン すぎ

75	Nonstandard	U6766
木	S7-4-3	F0000

traditional form →see 杉 at 1027

杓

1033

◧ 1-4-3

▶DIPPER

シャク

75	Nonstandard	U233D0
木	S7-4-3	F0000

traditional form →see 杓 at 1028

杓

1034

◧ 1-4-3

▶DIPPER

シャク

75	Nonstandard	U6753
木	S7-4-3	F0000

traditional form →see 杓 at 1028

栃 1035

◧1-4-3

▶JAPANESE HORSE CHESTNUT

とち　とちのき

75	Nonstandard	U6764
木	S7-4-3	F0000

traditional form → see 栃 at 1122

杤

◧1-4-3

incorrect stroke-count

➡ see ◧1-4-2: 木 at 1015

灼 1036

◧1-4-3

▶SCORCH

シャク　や(く)　あらた(か)

Ⓝ 灼 Ⓒ 灼 zhuó

86	Names	U707C
火	S7-4-3	F2632

COMPOUNDS

❶ⓐ SCORCH, burn

ⓑ cauterize

a 灼熱 しゃくねつ heat

b 焼灼 しょうしゃく cautery, cauterization

❷ shining brightly, vivid

赫灼たる かくしゃくたる brilliant, brightly shining

KUN

【やく 灼く】[usu. 焼く] SCORCH, burn; cauterize

【あらたか 灼か】miraculous

SYNONYMS

❶ burn

焼 BURN → 1256

燃 BURN (undergo combustion) → 1375

焚く BURN (build a fire) → 3450

焦 SCORCH → 3444

灼 SCORCH → 1036

炮 ROAST → 1132

燎 SET ON FIRE → 1376

HOMOPHONES

やく

焼 BURN → 1256

妬 BE JEALOUS → 0337

NOTE

➡ see USAGE note at 焼 1256

灼 1037

◧1-4-3

▶SCORCH

シャク　や(く)　あらた(か)

86	Nonstandard	U707C
火	S7-4-3	F0000

traditional form → see 灼 at 1036

壯 1038

◧1-4-3

▶VIGOROUS

▶GRAND

ソウ　㊔ たけ　たけし　まさ　つよし　もり

33	Names	U58EF
士	S7-3-4	F0000

traditional form → see 壮 at 0263

邪 1039

◧1-4-3

▶EVIL

ジャ　よこし(ま)

163	Nonstandard	U90AA
阝	S7-3-4	F0000

traditional form → see 邪 at 1443

牡 1040

◧1-4-3

▶MALE

ボ　おす　お-　おん

Ⓒ 牡 mǔ

93	Names	U7261
牛	S7-4-3	F1872

COMPOUNDS

● [original meaning] (of animals) MALE

牡丹 ぼたん peony, *Paeonia suffruticosa*

種牡馬 しゅぼば stallion, studhorse

KUN

【おす 牡】[usu. 雄] (of animals) MALE

牡猫 おすねこ tomcat

牡馬 おすうま stallion, male horse

【お- 牡-】[usu. 雄] (of animals) MALE

牡牛 おうし bull, steer

牡羊座 おひつじざ Aries, the Ram (constellation)

【おん 牡】[usu. 雄] (of animals) MALE

牡鳥(=牡鶏) おんどり rooster

SPECIAL READINGS

牡蠣× かき oyster

牡丹餅 ぼたもち rice cake covered with bean jam

棚牡丹 たなぼた windfall, godsend

SYNONYMS

● man

男 MAN → 3147

郎 YOUNG MAN → 1641

雄 MALE → 1271

牡 MALE → 1040

夫 male adult → 4271

翁 OLD MAN → 2611

爺 OLD MAN → 2656

HOMOPHONES

おす 雄 MALE → 1271

お-

雄 MALE → 1271

男 MAN → 3147

おん 雄 MALE →1271

NOTE

➡ see USAGE note at 雄 1271

玖 1041

▶NINE

キュウ ク ㊔ひさ たま

Ⓒ 玖 jiǔ

1-4-3

96	Names	U7396
王	S7-4-3	F2757

COMPOUNDS

❶ **NINE**—used in legal documents and checks

金玖萬参阡×弐百円也 きんきゅうまんさんぜんにひゃくえんなり the sum of ninety three thousand two hundred yen

❷ [original meaning, now archaic] **beautiful black jewel**

SYNONYMS

❶ **nine**

九 NINE →4176

玖 NINE →1041

❷ **precious stones**

玉 GEM →4289

珂 WHITE AGATE →1137

璧 DISK-SHAPED JEWEL →3608

琥 AMBER →1261

珀 AMBER →1136

珠 PEARL →1183

瑛 TRANSPARENT GEM →1259

瑠 LAPIS LAZULI →1342

璃 GLASSY SUBSTANCE →1358

晶 CRYSTAL →3122

玖 beautiful black jewel →1041

琉 LAPIS LAZULI →1221

琳 BEAUTIFUL GEM →1262

社 1042

▶COMPANY
▶SOCIETY

シャ やしろ ㊔もり こそ

Ⓝ 社 Ⓒ 社 shè

1-4-3

113	Jōyō-2	U793E
ネ	S7-4-3	F0057

Stroke order: 1–7

COMPOUNDS

❶ⓐ [also suffix] **COMPANY, firm, corporation; office**
ⓑ counter for companies

a 社員 しゃいん staff member, employee

社長 しゃちょう president (of a company)

社団 しゃだん corporation, association

会社 かいしゃ company, corporation, firm

公社 こうしゃ public corporation

入社 にゅうしゃ entering [joining] a company

本社 ほんしゃ head office, this office; head shrine, this shrine

新聞社 しんぶんしゃ newspaper office

出版社 しゅっぱんしゃ publishing company

b 二十二社 にじゅうにしゃ 22 companies

❷ⓐ **SOCIETY, community, the public, the world**
ⓑ **social, socialism; Socialist Party**
ⓒ abbrev. of 社会科 しゃかいか: social studies, civics

a 社会 しゃかい society, the world

社会人 しゃかいじん (full-fledged) member of society

社会科学 しゃかいかがく social sciences

社交 しゃこう social intercourse, society

社交的な しゃこうてきな sociable, friendly

b 民社党 みんしゃとう Democratic Socialist Party

c 倫社 りんしゃ ethics and civics

❸ **Shinto shrine**

社殿 しゃでん Shinto shrine

神社 じんじゃ Shinto shrine

総社(=惣社) そうじゃ shrine enshrining several gods

寺社 じしゃ shrines and temples

出雲大社 いずもたいしゃ The Grand Shrine of Izumo

❹ [original meaning] **tutelary deity**

社稷× しゃしょく the State (tutelary deity and god of grain)

❺ tribe

蕃社 ばんしゃ aborigines' village

INDEPENDENT

【しゃ 社】**COMPANY,** office; Socialist Party

社の方針 しゃのほうしん company policy

社・共 しゃきょう Social and Communist Parties

KUN

【やしろ 社】**Shinto shrine**

村のお社 むらのおやしろ village shrine

SYNONYMS

❶ **places of business**

店 SHOP (of any kind) →3828

舗 SHOP (esp. traditional) →2177

屋 SMALL SHOP →3842

社 COMPANY →1042

❷ⓐ **society**

社 SOCIETY →1042

世 WORLD →4308

公 PUBLIC →2468

❸ **places of worship**

堂 temple building →3202

塔 pagoda →0683

寺 BUDDHIST TEMPLE →2687

利 TEMPLE → 1620
社 Shinto shrine → 1042
宮 SHINTO SHRINE → 2828
院 monastery → 0544
教 church → 1887

NOTE

➡ see COMPOUND FORMATION for 惣社 そうじゃ → 惣 3452

祁

1043

1-4-3

▶**EXTREMELY**

キ

113	Nonstandard	U7941
ネ	S7-4-3	F0000

traditional form → see 祁 at 1447

肘

1044

1-4-3

▶**ELBOW**

チュウ▲ ひじ

Ⓒ 肘 zhǒu

130	Jōyō	U8098
月	S7-4-3	F2152

COMPOUNDS

● **ELBOW, area of arm around the elbow joint**

肘内障 ちゅうないしょう nursemaid's elbow, pulled elbow
掣×肘 せいちゅう restraint (by another person)

KUN

【ひじ 肘】**ELBOW**

肘打ち ひじうち elbow strike (in martial arts)
肘当て ひじあて elbow pad, elbow patch
肘鉄 ひじてつ abbrev. of 肘鉄砲 ひじでっぽう: elbow blow, elbow jab; rebuff, cold shoulder
肘掛け ひじかけ armrest
テニス肘 てにすひじ tennis elbow
肩肘張る かたひじはる swagger, put up a tough front, act pretentious

SYNONYMS

● **hand and arm**

手 HAND → 4267
腕 ARM → 1269
肘 ELBOW → 1044
掌 PALM → 3215
指 FINGER → 0452
拇 THUMB → 0358
拳 FIST → 3295

肝

1045

1-4-3

▶**LIVER**

カン きも

Ⓒ 肝 gān

130	Jōyō	U809D
月	S7-4-3	F1364

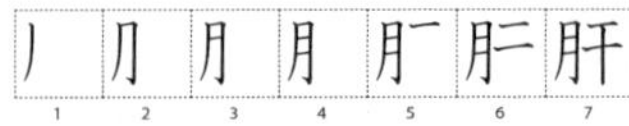

COMPOUNDS

❶ [original meaning] **LIVER**

肝臓 かんぞう liver
肝油 かんゆ liver oil
肝炎 かんえん hepatitis

❷ heart, mind

肝胆相照らす間柄である かんたんあいてらすあいだがらである be quite in sympathy with each other
肝銘(=感銘) かんめい deep impression
心肝 しんかん bottom of one's heart

❸ **main part, essence**

肝腎(=肝心)な かんじんな vital, essential, main
肝要な かんような important, vital, essential, necessary

INDEPENDENT

【かん 肝】**LIVER**

KUN

【きも 肝】**LIVER; inner heart; pluck, guts, courage, nerve**

肝に銘じる きもにめいじる be deeply impressed
肝っ玉 きもったま pluck, courage
肝を冷やす きもをひやす be struck with terror

SYNONYMS

❶ **internal organs**

心 HEART → 0011
肺 LUNG → 1147
胃 STOMACH → 3171
腸 INTESTINES → 1307
肝 LIVER → 1045
胆 GALLBLADDER → 1150
腎 KIDNEY → 3511

NOTE

➡ see COMPOUND FORMATION for 肝煎り きもいり → 煎 2950

肛

1046

1-4-3

▶**ANUS**

コウ

Ⓒ 肛 gāng

130	Non-Jōyō	U809B
月	S7-4-3	F2871

COMPOUNDS

● [original meaning] **ANUS**

肛門 こうもん anus

肛門科 こうもんか proctology; proctology clinic

脱肛 だっこう prolapse of the anus

SYNONYMS

● **buttocks**

尻 BUTTOCKS → 3766

肛 ANUS → 1046

那

1047

1-4-3

▶**PHONETIC [na]**

ナ ㊔ だ とも

Ⓝ 那 Ⓒ 那 nà nèi

163	Jōyō	U90A3
阝	S7-3-4	F0985

Stroke order: 1–7

COMPOUNDS

❶ **used PHONETICally for *na*, esp. in the translitera-tion of Sanskrit Buddhist terms or names**

旦那(=檀那) だんな master, husband, patron, protector; sir; [original meaning] donor

刹那 せつな moment, instant; *kṣaṇa* (1/75 of a second)

❷ [also 奈 2759] element for forming interrogative words

那辺 なへん where?

SYNONYMS

❶ **phonetic [na]**

那 PHONETIC [na] → 1047

奈 PHONETIC [na] → 2759

❷ **interrogatives**

奈 interrogative forming element → 2759

那 interrogative forming element → 1047

何 WHAT → 0073

誰 WHO → 1986

那

1048

1-4-3

▶**PHONETIC [na]**

ナ ㊔ だ とも

163	Nonstandard	U90A3
阝	S7-3-4	F0000

traditional form → see 那 at 1047

臼

1049

1-4-3

▶***USU***

134	Radical	U26951
臼	S7-7-0	F0000

radical variant → see 臼 at 4341

形

1050

1-4-3

▶**SHAPE**

ケイ ギョウ かた -がた かたち なり

Ⓝ 形◇ Ⓒ 形 xíng

59	Jōyō-2	U5F62
彡	S7-3-4	F0278

Stroke order: 1–7

COMPOUNDS

❶ⓐ [also suffix] [original meaning] **SHAPE, material form, figure**

ⓑ appearance, look, condition

a 形状 けいじょう shape, form, configuration

形態(=形体) けいたい shape, form, structure, morphology

形式 けいしき form, model, formality

形式的 けいしきてき formal

図形 ずけい figure, diagram

体形 たいけい form, figure

球形 きゅうけい globular shape

変形する へんけいする change shape, transform

人形 にんぎょう doll

長方形 ちょうほうけい rectangle

半月形の はんげつけいの semicircular, crescent-shaped

b 形勢 けいせい situation, state of affairs; prospects

形相 ぎょうそう features, look, aspect

❷ **appear in visible form, manifest**

形成する けいせいする form, make up, mold

形容する けいようする qualify, modify

形容詞 けいようし adjective

❸ body

形骸 けいがい ruin, wreck, mere skeleton

KUN

【かた 形】

①ⓐ **SHAPE, form; pattern, design**

ⓑ **marks, traces**

a 形どる かたどる [usu. 象る] model after, represent

形が崩れる かたがくずれる lose shape, get out of shape

花形 はながた floral pattern; star, lion; leading, popular, favorite

b 形見 かたみ keepsake, memento

② **security, pledge**

借金の形 しゃっきんのかた security for a loan

手形 てがた promissory note; hand print

【-がた -形】 [also suffix] **-SHAPEd**

卵形の たまごがたの egg-shaped

弓形の ゆみがたの arched, crescent-shaped

【かたち 形】

① **SHAPE, form**

形作る かたちづくる form, shape, make, mold

② [formerly also 貌] appearance, looks, figure

顔形 かおかたち features, looks

【なり 形】 **SHAPE**, form, figure; stature, size; appearance, dress, outfit, getup

弓形になる ゆみなりになる become bow-shaped, bend backward

大きな形をして おおきななりをして for all one's stoutness

身形 みなり dress, clothing; one's appearance

SYNONYMS

1a form

形 SHAPE → 1050

状 FORM (external) → 0322

体 FORM (characteristic) → 0080

姿 FIGURE → 3264

USAGE

【かたち】

形

① shape, form

② [formerly also 貌] appearance, looks, figure

貌

[now usu. 形]

ⓐ appearance, looks, figure

ⓑ aspect, condition

HOMOPHONES

かた 型 TYPE → 3266

かたどる 象 PHENOMENON → 2647

-がた 型 TYPE → 3266

かたち 貌 APPEARANCE → 1958

NOTE

➡ see also USAGE notes at 型 3266 and 象 2647

邦

▶STATE
▶JAPAN
ホウ ㊔ くに

1051

1-4-3

Ⓝ 邦 Ⓒ 邦 bāng

163	Jōyō	U90A6
阝	S7-3-4	F1302

一 = 三 丰 丰 ⺘ 邦 (strokes 1–7)

COMPOUNDS

1a STATE, country, nation

b [original meaning] domain, territory

a 邦家 ほうか one's country, the state

隣邦 りんぽう neighboring country

盟邦 めいほう ally, allied powers

東邦 とうほう eastern country, Oriental nation; the Orient

友邦 ゆうほう friendly nation, ally

連邦 れんぽう federation, confederation, union

本邦 ほんぽう this [our] country

異邦人 いほうじん foreigner, alien

b 邦土 ほうど realm, country

2a JAPAN, our country

b JAPANese (language)

a 邦人 ほうじん Japanese, fellow countryman

邦楽 ほうがく Japanese music

b 邦画 ほうが Japanese film [movie]; Japanese painting

邦訳 ほうやく translation into Japanese

邦字新聞 ほうじしんぶん Japanese-language newspaper

SYNONYMS

1a country

国 COUNTRY → 3831

邦 STATE → 1051

土 land → 4211

2a Japan

日 JAPAN → 3759

和 JAPAN → 1450

邦 JAPAN → 1051

国 Japanese → 3831

倭 ANCIENT NAME FOR JAPAN → 0140

邦

▶STATE
▶JAPAN
ホウ ㊔ くに

1052

1-4-3

163	Nonstandard	U90A6
阝	S7-3-4	F0000

traditional form → see 邦 at 1051

邨

▶VILLAGE
ソン むら

1053

1-4-3

163	Nonstandard	U90A8
阝	S7-3-4	F0000

traditional form → see 村 at 1029

卵

▶EGG
ラン たまご
Ⓒ 卵 luǎn

1054

1-4-3

26	Jōyō-6	U5375
卩	S7-2-5	F1507

(stroke order 1–7)

COMPOUNDS

a [original meaning] **EGG; spawn, roe**

b ovum

a 卵殻 らんかく eggshell

卵黄 らんおう yolk

鶏卵 けいらん (hen's) egg

産卵 さんらん egg-laying, spawning

b 卵子 らんし ovum, ovule, egg
卵巣 らんそう ovary
排卵 はいらん ovulation

INDEPENDENT

【らん 卵】ovum

KUN

【たまご 卵】

①ⓐ [also 玉子] **EGG**
ⓑ spawn, roe
a 卵焼き たまごやき fried egg, omelette
② (an expert) in the making
文士の卵 ぶんしのたまご hatching writer

SYNONYMS

ⓐ early states of animal life
胎 FETUS → 1149
卵 EGG → 1054
ⓑ reproductive cells
卵 ovum → 1054
精 sperm → 1729

USAGE

【たまご】
卵
①ⓐ [also 玉子] egg
ⓑ spawn, roe
② (an expert) in the making
玉子
[also 卵] egg

HOMOPHONES

たまご 玉子 → 4289, 4196

戸斤 1055

◧ 1-4-4

▶**PLACE**
▶**PARTICLE OF NOMINALIZATION**
ショ ところ -ところ どころ とこ

63	Nonstandard	U6240
戶	S8-4-4	F0000

traditional form → see 所 at 1056

所 1056

◧ 1-4-4

▶**PLACE**
▶**PARTICLE OF NOMINALIZATION**
ショ ところ -ところ どころ とこ▲
Ⓝ 所 Ⓒ 所 suǒ

63	Jōyō-3	U6240
戶	S8-4-4	F0099

1	2	3	4	5	6	7	8
一	ㄱ	ㅋ	戸	戸´	戸斤	所	所

COMPOUNDS

❶ⓐ [sometimes also 処 しょ 3764] (portion of space) **PLACE, spot, point, part**
ⓑ [also suffix] **PLACE for specific purpose, dwelling place, facilities, quarters**
a 場所 ばしょ place, spot, site; space, room
箇所(=個所) かしょ place, spot, point; part
住所 じゅうしょ one's dwelling, address
近所 きんじょ neighborhood
名所 めいしょ noted place, sights, scenic place
一所懸命(=一生懸命)に いっしょけんめい(=いっしょうけんめい)に for life, with all one's might
出所 しゅっしょ origin, source; release from prison
b 便所 べんじょ lavatory, bathroom
停留所 ていりゅうじょ (bus) stop, station
休憩所 きゅうけいじょ resting room [place], lounge

❷ [also suffix]
ⓐ PLACE for conducting specific activities: **office, bureau, organization, institution, institute, agency**
ⓑ PLACE equipped with facilities for specific task: **plant, station, factory, facilities**
a 所長 しょちょう head, chief, manager
役所 やくしょ public [government] office
入所する にゅうしょする enter (an institute); be put in prison
事務所 じむしょ office, one's place of business
研究所 けんきゅうじょ(=けんきゅうしょ) research laboratory [institute]
裁判所 さいばんしょ court of justice, courthouse
保健所 ほけんじょ public health center
b 発電所 はつでんしょ power plant, generating station
造船所 ぞうせんじょ dock yard, shipbuilding yard
製作所 せいさくしょ factory, works, plant

❸ⓐ PARTICLE OF NOMINALIZATION, function word for turning verbs into nouns
ⓑ function word indicating the passive voice
a 所以▲ ゆえん reason, grounds
所有する しょゆうする have, own, possess
所属する しょぞくする belong to, be attached to
所得 しょとく income, earnings
所望 しょもう desire, wish
所信 しょしん one's belief, one's opinion
所在 しょざい whereabouts, position, situation
所轄 しょかつ jurisdiction
b 所定の しょていの fixed, prescribed, stated

❹ point, feature
短所 たんしょ shortcoming, defect
急所 きゅうしょ vital part; vital point, tender spot

INDEPENDENT

【しょ 所】**PLACE** for specific activity or task (→❷): office, institution; plant, station
所の事情 しょのじじょう circumstances of the office

KUN

【ところ 所】

①ⓐ **PLACE, spot, site; part; room, space; district**

ⓑ **one's PLACE, one's house, one's address**

a 所所 ところどころ here and there, at places

所を替える ところをかえる change places, change sides

居所 いどころ one's address [residence], one's whereabouts

台所 だいどころ kitchen

b 所書き ところがき one's address

②ⓐ **time, moment**

ⓑ **occasion, case**

a 早い所 はやいところ promptly

今の所 いまのところ at present

書いている所だ かいているところだ I am writing now

彼は今来た所だ かれはいまきたところだ He has just arrived

b 所構わず ところかまわず irrespective of the occasion, indiscriminately

③ point, feature

詩人らしい所 しじんらしいところ something of a poet

強い所 つよいところ strong point

④ extent

...所では ...ところでは so far as...

倍でも安い所だ ばいでもやすいところだ It would be cheap even at twice the sum

⑤ passage, part

面白い所 おもしろいところ interesting passage

⑥ⓐ function word equiv. to relative pronoun: what, thing that, which, who

ⓑ [in the form of 所となる ところとなる] **function word indicating the passive voice**

a 彼の言う所 かれのいうところ what he says

私が愛する所の女性 わたくしがあいするところのじょせい the woman whom I love

b 人の好む所となる ひとのこのむところとなる be liked by people

⑦ⓐ when, upon, even if

ⓑ [in the form of 所が ところが] **but, however, on the contrary**

ⓒ [in the form of 所で ところで] **well, now, by the way, incidentally**

a 問い合わせた所、嘘だと分かった といあわせたところ, うそだとわかった On inquiry, the report proved false

損をした所で そんをしたところで even if one loses

b 所が失敗した ところがしっぱいした Nevertheless, I failed

c 所で猫は好きですか ところでねこはすきですか By the way, do you like cats?

【-ところ -所】

① **counter for PLACEs**

三所 みところ three places

② *literary* **counter for people**

宮様お二所 みやさまおふたところ two Imperial princes

【どころ 所】

① **anything but, far from; not to mention**

失望する所か しつぼうするどころか far from being disappointed

暑い所の騒ぎじゃない あついどころのさわぎじゃない "Hot" isn't the word

② [suffix] **PLACE**, point

摑み所 つかみどころ hold, grip; point

聞き所 ききどころ most important part, finest passage

拠り所 よりどころ grounds, foundation, authority

③ [suffix] producing center

お茶所 おちゃどころ tea-growing district, tea producing center

【とこ 所】 colloquial form of 所 ところ

僕ん所 ぼくんとこ at my place

早い所片付けよう はやいとこかたづけよう Let's finish up quickly

SPECIAL READINGS

所以▲ ゆえん reason, grounds

所謂▲ いわゆる what is called, so-called

所為▲ せい consequences, outcome; influence

余所(=他所)▲ よそ another place, strange parts

SYNONYMS

❶ **places and positions**

所 PLACE → 1056

処 place → 3764

場 PLACE (for specific activity) → 0678

地 PLACE (particular location) → 0236

席 meeting place → 3865

位 POSITION → 0069

点 POINT → 2587

座 place → 3868

❷ⓐ **public offices**

省 MINISTRY → 3100

庁 GOVERNMENT AGENCY → 3768

府 government office → 3824

公 public office → 2468

署 PUBLIC-SERVICE STATION → 3223

局 public service office → 3800

所 office → 1056

❸ⓐ **nominalizers**

所 PARTICLE OF NOMINALIZATION → 1056

事 nominalization word → 4384

子 NOUN SUFFIX → 4196

性 -ITY → 0357

USAGE

【ところ】

所

①ⓐ place, spot, site; part; room, space; district
ⓑ one's place, one's house, one's address
②ⓐ time, moment
ⓑ occasion, case
③ point, feature
④ extent
⑤ passage, part
⑥ⓐ function word equiv. to relative pronoun: what, thing that, which, who
ⓑ [in the form of 所となる ところとなる] function word indicating the passive voice
⑦ⓐ when, upon, even if
ⓑ [in the form of 所が ところが] but, however, on the contrary
ⓒ [in the form of 所で ところで] well, now, by the way, incidentally

処

[also suffix] place (for a specific purpose, as eating or resting)

HOMOPHONES

ところ 処 DEAL WITH →3764

COMPOUND FORMATION

【所以 ゆえん】

所以 'reason, grounds' is a combination of 以 and 所 ❸ⓐ, which functions as a particle of nominalization. 以 here is actually a verb turned into a noun by means of 所.

NOTE

➡ see COMPOUND FORMATION for
測候所 そっこじょ →測 0744
所詮 しょせん →詮 1923
一生懸命(=一所懸命) いっしょうけんめい (=いっしょけんめい) →生 4309

欣 1057

▶JOYFUL

キン ゴン ㊔ よし こん やすし

Ⓒ 欣 xīn

◧1-4-4

76	Names	U6B23
欠	S8-4-4	F2755

COMPOUNDS

ⓐ [original meaning] **JOYFUL, glad, happy**
ⓑ **JOYFUL**ly, gladly

a 欣悦 きんえつ gladness, joy
欣然と きんぜんと joyfully, gladly
欣喜雀躍する きんきじゃくやくする dance [jump] for joy
欣快 きんかい great pleasure
b 欣懐する きんかいする think happily of
欣求浄土 ごんぐじょうど seeking rebirth in the Pure Land

SYNONYMS

ⓐ **pleased and pleasant**
楽 pleasurable →3505
欣 JOYFUL →1057
爽 REFRESHING →4402
快 PLEASANT →0289
朗 CHEERFUL →1679
愉 PLEASED →0710
悦 DELIGHTED →0501
嬉しい GLAD →0890
喜 HAPPY →2889
歓 JOYOUS →2342
驩 JOYOUS →2333

放 1058

▶LET GO

ホウ はな(す) -(っ)ぱな(し) はな(つ) はな(れる) ほう(る)

Ⓒ 放 fàng

◧1-4-4

66	Jōyō-3	U653E
攵	S8-4-4	F0293

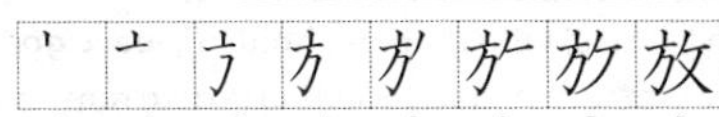
1 2 3 4 5 6 7 8

COMPOUNDS

❶ⓐ (set free) **LET GO, release, free**
ⓑ **send away, exile**

a 放流する ほうりゅうする discharge; stock (a river) with (fish)
放牧 ほうぼく pasturage, grazing
放課後 ほうかご after school
解放する かいほうする release, set free
釈放する しゃくほうする release, liberate, discharge, acquit
b 放逐する ほうちくする expel, banish, expatriate
放校 ほうこう expulsion from school
追放する ついほうする banish, purge, exile

❷ⓐ **LET things GO, let alone, leave as it is**
ⓑ **LET oneself GO, do as one pleases**

a 放任する ほうにんする leave (a matter) to take its own course, leave (a person) to himself
放置する ほうちする leave alone, neglect, leave as it is
放心 ほうしん absence of mind, abstraction
開放する かいほうする open, leave open
b 放談 ほうだん random [irresponsible] talk
放蕩×する ほうとうする live fast, throw one's money away
放浪 ほうろう wandering, roaming
奔放な ほんぽうな wild, extravagant; free-spirited
したい放題 したいほうだい as one pleases, at will

戶 戸 斤 【方】 日 木 歹 火 爿 片 牛 王 ネ 月 月 区 尸 ヨ

戶 戸 斤 【方】 日 木 歹 火 爿 片 牛 王 ネ 月 月 区 尸 ⺕

野放図な のほうずな unrestrained, unruly

❸ⓐ (give off in all directions) **radiate, emit, emanate, broadcast**

ⓑ **let out, discharge, excrete**

a 放射する ほうしゃする radiate, emit, emanate

放光 ほうこう emission of light

放映 ほうえい telecasting

放送 ほうそう broadcasting

民放 みんぽう commercial broadcast

b 放水 ほうすい discharge, drainage

放屁× ほうひ breaking wind

❹ [formerly 抛 0364]

ⓐ toss, throw, let fly

ⓑ **toss away, throw away, cast away**

a 放物線 ほうぶつせん parabola

b 放棄 ほうき abandonment, resignation

放擲×する ほうてきする abandon, give up, quit

❺ **set off, set fire to**

放火する ほうかする set fire to

KUN

【はなす 放す】

ⓐ (set free) **LET GO, release, free, turn loose**

ⓑ (release one's hold) **LET GO (one's hold of), leave go**

a 放し飼い はなしがい grazing; letting (a dog) run free

b 見放す みはなす desert, abandon, give up

手放す てばなす release [let go] one's hold

【-っぱなし -っ放し】 [sometimes also -放し -はなし] [verbal suffix] *colloq*

① **leaving something as it is**

やりっ放し やりっぱなし leaving alone, negligence

開けっ放す あけっぱなす leave open

掛けっ放しにする かけっぱなしにする leave (the radio) on

② performing successively

勝ちっ放し かちっぱなし winning straight victories, making a clean score

【はなつ 放つ】 **emit, give out, send forth; discharge, fire, let fly; set free, release; set fire**

芳香を放つ ほうこうをはなつ give out [off] fragrance

言い放つ いいはなつ declare, avow, venture to say

一発放つ いっぱつはなつ have a shot; break wind

【はなれる 放れる】 **free oneself of, get free**

狼が鎖を放れた おおかみがくさりをはなれた The wolf freed itself of its chain

【ほうる 放る】 [sometimes also 抛る] **throw, toss, fling, cast; throw up, neglect**

放り出す ほうりだす throw out; dismiss, expel

放って置く ほうっておく neglect, leave alone

放ったらかす ほったらかす neglect, let aside

SYNONYMS

❶ⓐ **release**

放 LET GO → 1058

釈 release → 1876

❷ **let do**

放 LET GO → 1058

随 let do → 0765

❸ **emit**

出 PUT OUT → 4310

発 EMIT → 3174

放 radiate → 1058

排 DISCHARGE → 0593

射 SHOOT → 1850

噴 SPOUT → 0879

吐 SPEW → 0235

湧 WELL UP → 0749

❹ⓐ **throw**

投 THROW → 0300

抛 TOSS → 0364

放 toss → 1058

USAGE

【ほうる】

放る

[sometimes also 抛る] throw, toss, fling, cast; throw up, neglect

抛る

[usu. 放る]

ⓐ toss, throw, fling, cast

ⓑ throw up, neglect

HOMOPHONES

はなす 離 SEPARATE → 2364

はなれる 離 SEPARATE → 2364

ほうる 抛 TOSS → 0364

NOTE

➡ see also USAGE note at 離 2364

於

1059

1-4-4

▶**AT**

オ おい(て) お(ける)

Ⓒ 于 yú 於 yū wū

70	Names	U65BC
方	S8-4-4	F1656

KUN

【おいて 於て】

① **AT, in, on**—in reference to time or place

東京に於て とうきょうにおいて in Tokyo

② **as for, on one's part**

その点に於て そのてんにおいて on that point, in that respect

【おける 於ける】 **in, AT**

日本に於ける外国人 にほんにおけるがいこくじん foreigner in Japan

HOMOPHONES

おいて 措 DISPOSE →0610

NOTE

➡ see USAGE note at 措 0610

明

1060

■ 1-4-4

▶**BRIGHT**
▶**CLEAR**

メイ ミョウ ミン▲ あ(かり) あか(るい) あか(るむ) あか(らむ) あき(らか) あ(ける) -あ(け) あ(く) あ(くる) あ(かす) ㊔ あきら とおる あけし はる とし

N 朙 明 C 明 míng

72	Jōyō-2	U660E
日	S8-4-4	F0074

1 2 3 4 5 6 7 8

COMPOUNDS

1 **a** [original meaning] **BRIGHT, brilliant, light**
b (of colors) **BRIGHT, light**
c (of cheerful disposition) **BRIGHT, cheerful**

a 明月 めいげつ bright moon, full moon; harvest moon
明星 みょうじょう Venus
明暗 めいあん light and dark; contrast
照明 しょうめい illumination, lighting
鮮明な せんめいな vivid, clear
b 明色 めいしょく bright [light] color
明度 めいど lightness, value of color
c 明朗な めいろうな cheerful, bright; clean (politics)

2 **a** light
b be lighted

a 灯明 とうみょう votive light offered (as to a god); stand for votive light; candlestand
b 明滅する めいめつする flicker, blink

3 **a** **CLEAR-sighted, bright, discerning, intelligent, wise**
b eyesight

a 明哲 めいてつ wisdom, sagacity; wise man
明察 めいさつ discernment, insight
賢明な けんめいな wise, intelligent; sensible
聡明な そうめいな sagacious, wise, sharp, mentally acute
不明 ふめい lack of sagacity [foresight], ignorance; missing persons
発明する はつめいする invent, devise
b 失明 しつめい loss of eyesight

4 **a** (free from doubt) **CLEAR, lucid, distinct, evident, obvious, explicit, manifest**
b **make CLEAR, clarify, throw light on, prove, demonstrate**

a 明確な めいかくな clear, precise, distinct
明治 めいじ Meiji era
明記する めいきする write clearly, specify
表明 ひょうめい manifestation, demonstration
不明な ふめいな obscure, unknown
自明の じめいの self-evident, obvious
公明正大な こうめいせいだいな fair, just
文明 ぶんめい civilization, culture
b 証明 しょうめい proof, evidence, verification
説明する せつめいする explain, illustrate

5 (unclouded) **CLEAR**, transparent, translucent
明澄な めいちょうな unclouded, clear, limpid
透明度 とうめいど transparency, degree of clearness

6 [also prefix] **next, the coming (day or year)**
明日 みょうにち(=あした, あす) tomorrow
明年 みょうねん next year
明朝 みょうちょう tomorrow morning
明晩 みょうばん tomorrow night
明年度 みょうねんど next (fiscal) year
明後日 みょうごにち(=あさって) day after tomorrow

7 Ming Dynasty (1368-1644 A.D.)
明朝 みんちょう Ming Dynasty
明朝体 みんちょうたい Ming-style typeface

8 **daybreak, dawn**
黎明 れいめい dawn, daybreak, beginning (of a new age)
未明 みめい early dawn, the gray of the morning

9 **a** abbrev. of 明治 めいじ: Meiji era
b abbrev. of 明治大学 めいじだいがく: Meiji University

a 明初 めいしょ first year of Meiji era
b 明大 めいだい Meiji University
早明戦 そうめいせん Waseda-Meiji (baseball) game

10 divinity, God
神明 しんめい deity, God

11 this world
幽明 ゆうめい this and the other world

INDEPENDENT

【めい 明】discernment, insight; eyesight
明を失う めいをうしなう lose one's eyesight
先見の明 せんけんのめい power of seeing into the future

【みん 明】Ming Dynasty

KUN

【あかり 明かり】**light, glimmer; lamp; proof**
明かり障子 あかりしょうじ paper screen door for admitting light
薄明かり うすあかり faint light, half-light of early morning

戸 戸 斤 方 【日】 木 歹 火 爿 片 牛 王 ネ 月 月 区 尸 ヨ

【あかるい 明るい】**BRIGHT, light; light (color); clear, uncorrupt;** (of cheerful disposition) **bright, cheerful;** (full of promise) **bright, promising; be well versed in**
明るさ あかるさ brightness; cheerfulness
明るい政治 あかるいせいじ clean politics
彼は文学に明るい かれはぶんがくにあかるい He is well-read in literature

【あかるむ 明るむ】**BRIGHTen; be cheered up**
明るみに出す あかるみにだす bring to light, make public
空が明るむ そらがあかるむ The sky brightens

【あからむ 明らむ】**BRIGHTen**

【あきらか 明らか】
あきらかな 明らかな **CLEAR, distinct, apparent, obvious, unquestionable; bright, cheerful**
明らかにする あきらかにする clarify; disclose, make public
明らかな事実 あきらかなじじつ obvious fact

【あける 明ける】
① **dawn, become light, break**
明け あけ dawn; expiration
夜明け よあけ dawn, daybreak
② (of the new year) **begin, open**
明けましておめでとうございます あけましておめでとうございます Happy New Year
年明け としあけ beginning of the year
③ expire, be over
冬が明けた ふゆがあけた Winter is over
④ [in compounds] **disclose, reveal**
打ち明ける うちあける confide in (someone), reveal, disclose

【-あけ -明け】[also suffix] **end, expiration**
忌み明け いみあけ end of mourning
連休明け れんきゅうあけ end of vacation

【あく 明く】
① **one's eyes open, regain sight**
目が明く めがあく regain sight
② be settled, be put in order
埒×が明かない らちがあかない remain unsettled, make no progress
③ (of clothing) **be opened (at the back)**
背の明いた服 せのあいたふく garment open at the back
④ [usu. 空く] have (a hole or aperture) in, (a gap) is open
明き あき gap, aperture space; vacancy; free time

【あくる 明くる】**next, following**
明くる日 あくるひ the following day

【あかす 明かす】
① [also suffix] **spend (the night), stay up all night (doing something)**
飲み明かす のみあかす drink the night away
夜を語り明かす よをかたりあかす talk the night away
② **disclose, reveal**
秘密を明かす ひみつをあかす disclose a secret

SPECIAL READINGS
明日 あす tomorrow
明日▲ あした tomorrow
明後日▲ あさって day after tomorrow
明太子▲ めんたいこ mentaiko

SYNONYMS
❶ⓐ bright
明 BRIGHT → 1060
昭 LUMINOUS → 1107
蛍 fluorescent → 3204
晃 DAZZLING → 3101
燦 BRILLIANT → 1390
赫 BLAZING → 1960
暉 radiant → 1276
熙 BRIGHT → 3559
晟 SUNNY → 3104
ⓑ vivid
明 BRIGHT → 1060
鮮 VIVID → 2355
❷ⓐ light
光 LIGHT → 3043
明 light → 1060
灯 LAMP → 1019
燭 CANDLE → 1391
照 sunlight → 3506
虹 RAINBOW → 1637
❸ⓐ intelligent and wise
賢 WISE → 3518
俊 brilliant → 0117
鋭 SHARP → 2171
敏 NIMBLE → 1675
叡 PROFOUNDLY WISE → 2405
智 wise → 3458
慧 INTELLIGENT → 3485
怜 CLEVER → 0356
悧 CLEVER → 0505
俐 CLEVER → 0113
哲 SAGACIOUS → 3402
明 clear-sighted → 1060
聡 SHARP-WITTED → 1750
❹ⓐ evident
明 CLEAR → 1060
鮮 VIVID → 2355
亮 LUCID → 2571
顕 MANIFEST → 2274
瞭 CLEAR → 1584
ⓑ explain

説 EXPLAIN → 1949
明 make clear → 1060
釈 ELUCIDATE → 1876
詮 EXPOUND → 1923
講 expound → 2046
解 CLARIFY → 1913
注 annotate → 0383

❺ clear
透 TRANSPARENT → 3854
澄 LIMPID → 0915
清 CLEAR (liquid) → 0635
明 CLEAR (unclouded) → 1060
朗 CLEAR (sky) → 1679
冴える CRISP AND CLEAR → 0087

❻ next
次 NEXT → 0058
明 next → 1060
翌 THE FOLLOWING → 3307
来 the coming → 4366

❼ later Chinese dynasties
唐 TANG DYNASTY → 3867
宋 SONG DYNASTY → 2730
元 Yuan Dynasty → 2428
明 Ming Dynasty → 1060
清 Qing Dynasty → 0635

USAGE

❶【あける】
明ける
① dawn, become light, break
② (of the new year) begin, open
③ expire, be over
④ [in compounds] disclose, reveal
空ける
① empty, clear, vacate, clear out
② leave space, make room
③ bore, make a hole
④ free oneself (to do), make spare time
開ける
open, unlock

❷【あく】
明く
① one's eyes open, regain sight
② be settled, be put in order
③ (of clothing) be opened (at the back)
④ [usu. 空く] have (a hole or aperture) in, (a gap) is open
空く
① become vacant, become vacated [empty]
② become available for use
③ become free [unoccupied]
④ [sometimes also 明く] have (a hole or aperture) in, (a gap) is open
開く
ⓐ open, become open
ⓑ (of a shop) open, begin

HOMOPHONES

あからむ 赤 RED → 2719
あける
空 SKY → 2767
開 OPEN → 4121
あく
空 SKY → 2767
開 OPEN → 4121
あき 空 SKY → 2767

COMPOUND FORMATION

❶【明治 めいじ】
明治 'Meiji era' literally means clear and impartial (明 ❹ⓐ) governing (治). It is the name of the Japanese era from 1868 to 1912.

❷【文明 ぶんめい】
文明 'civilization, culture' refers to the clear (明 ❹ⓐ) manifestation of learning or culture (文).

NOTE

➡ see also USAGE notes at 空 2767 and 赤 2719

旺

▶ENERGETIC
オウ さか(ん)▲ ㊔ あきら ひかる
Ⓒ 旺 wàng

1061
◧ 1-4-4

72	Jōyō	U65FA
日	S8-4-4	F2535

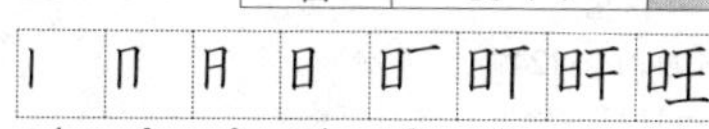

1 2 3 4 5 6 7 8

COMPOUNDS

❶ ENERGETIC, vigorous; flourishing
旺盛な おうせいな vigorous, in a flourishing condition

❷ [original meaning, now archaic] orb of the sun

KUN

【さかん 旺ん】
さかんな 旺んな [also 盛んな] **vigorous, ENERGETIC, lively**
精力が旺んだ せいりょくがさかんだ be full of energy [vigor]

SYNONYMS

❶ &【さかん】strong
強 STRONG → 0574
壮 VIGOROUS → 0263
丈 STOUT → 4227
健 ROBUST (healthy) → 0152
逞しい ROBUST (sturdy) → 4004
康 HEALTHY → 3877
旺 ENERGETIC → 1061
溌 LIVELY → 0917

HOMOPHONES

さかんな 盛 PROSPEROUS → 3314

NOTE

➡ see USAGE note at 盛 3314

明 1062

1-4-4

▶**BRIGHT**
▶**CLEAR**

メイ ミョウ ミン あ(かり) あか(るい) あか(るむ) あか(らむ) あき(らか) あ(ける) -あ(け) あ(く) あ(くる) あ(かす) ㊔ あきら とおる あけし はる とし

72	Nonstandard	U660E
日	S8-4-4	F0000

traditional form → see 明 at 1060

枇 1063

1-4-4

▶**LOQUAT**

ビ

Ⓒ 枇 pí

75	Names	U6787
木	S8-4-4	F3476

COMPOUNDS

❶ **LOQUAT**

枇杷 びわ loquat

❷ [archaic] spoon

SYNONYMS

❶ **fruits and fruit trees**

桃 PEACH → 1174
榛 HAZEL → 1328
椎 CHINQUAPIN → 1249
柚 YUZU → 1123
椰 COCONUT → 1285
柑 CITRUS → 1112
橙 BITTER ORANGE → 1369
葡 GRAPE → 2902
萄 GRAPE → 2870
柿 PERSIMMON → 1118
檎 APPLE → 1386
李 PLUM → 3050
枇 LOQUAT → 1063
杷 LOQUAT → 1065
苺 STRAWBERRY → 2780
菱 water chestnut → 2879
杏 APRICOT → 3049
梅 JAPANESE APRICOT → 1159
橘 MANDARIN → 1366
栗 CHESTNUT → 3280
栃 JAPANESE HORSE CHESTNUT → 1122
梨 PEAR → 3412
蕉 PLANTAIN → 2994

枕 1064

1-4-4

▶**PILLOW**

チン^ シン^ まくら

Ⓒ 枕 zhěn

75	Jōyō	U6795
木	S8-4-4	F1721

COMPOUNDS

● **PILLOW; pillow, use as a pillow**

枕頭 ちんとう one's bedside, head of one's bed
枕席 ちんせき bedding, bed; bedroom
漱石枕流 そうせきちんりゅう bad loser

KUN

【まくら 枕】

①ⓐ **PILLOW, headrest**
ⓑ (structural component) **bolster**

a 枕元 まくらもと near one's pillow, one's bedside
枕草子 まくらのそうし The Pillow Book
氷枕 こおりまくら ice pillow
手枕 てまくら using one's arm for a pillow
b 枕木 まくらぎ railroad tie [sleeper]

② orientation of one's head when lying down

北枕 きたまくら lying with one's head to the north; brown-lined puffer

③ preface, lead-in

枕詞 まくらことば epithet used in waka to modify certain words

杷 1065

1-4-4

▶**LOQUAT**

ハ ワ ㊔ え

Ⓒ 杷 pá

75	Names	U6777
木	S8-4-4	F3358

COMPOUNDS

❶ **LOQUAT**

枇杷 びわ loquat

❷ [original meaning, now archaic] (wooden or bamboo) rake

SYNONYMS

❶ **fruits and fruit trees**

桃 PEACH → 1174
榛 HAZEL → 1328
椎 CHINQUAPIN → 1249
柚 YUZU → 1123
椰 COCONUT → 1285
柑 CITRUS → 1112
橙 BITTER ORANGE → 1369
葡 GRAPE → 2902
萄 GRAPE → 2870
柿 PERSIMMON → 1118

檎 APPLE → 1386
李 PLUM → 3050
枇 LOQUAT → 1063
杷 LOQUAT → 1065
苺 STRAWBERRY → 2780
菱 water chestnut → 2879
杏 APRICOT → 3049
梅 JAPANESE APRICOT → 1159
橘 MANDARIN → 1366
栗 CHESTNUT → 3280
栃 JAPANESE HORSE CHESTNUT → 1122
梨 PEAR → 3412
蕉 PLANTAIN → 2994

杯

1066

◧1-4-4

▶CUP

ハイ さかずき

Ⓝ 盃 Ⓒ 杯 bēi

75	Jōyō	U676F
木	S8-4-4	F1121

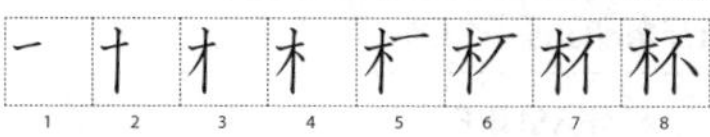

COMPOUNDS

❶ⓐ [original meaning] **wine CUP, cup, glass, goblet**
ⓑ **counter for CUPfuls, glassfuls, bowlfuls or spoonfuls**

a 杯盤 はいばん glasses and plates
金杯 きんぱい gold cup [goblet]
苦杯 くはい bitter ordeal
祝杯 しゅくはい a toast
乾杯 かんぱい a toast

b 一杯 いっぱい a cup (as of tea), a glass (as of beer)
茶二杯 ちゃにはい two cups of tea
砂糖三杯 さとうさんばい three spoons of sugar

❷ [also suffix] **prize CUP, trophy**
賞杯 しょうはい prize cup, trophy
賜杯 しはい trophy given by the emperor [prince]
デ杯 ではい Davis Cup
優勝杯 ゆうしょうはい championship cup, trophy

❸ **degree of fullness, capacity**
一杯 いっぱい fullness
満杯 まんぱい full to capacity

❹ⓐ counter for ships
ⓑ counter for octopi or cuttlefish

a 舟二杯 ふねにはい two boats

b 烏賊六杯 いかろっぱい six cuttlefish

INDEPENDENT

【はい 杯】 wine CUP, wine glass, sake cup
杯を重ねる はいをかさねる have one cup of sake after another

KUN

【さかずき 杯】 **wine CUP, sake cup**
杯を干す さかずきをほす drink the cup dry

SYNONYMS

❶ **vessels and receptacles**
盤 dish → 3533
鍋 POT → 2202
釜 IRON POT → 2610
鼎 TRIPOD CAULDRON → 4405
臼 MORTAR → 4341
碓 MORTAR → 1537
托 RECEPTACLE → 0252
皿 PLATE → 4286
盆 TRAY → 2581
膳 LEGGED TRAY → 1381
杯 CUP → 1066
鉢 BOWL → 2144
椀 WOODEN BOWL → 1250
碗 CERAMIC BOWL → 1539
丼 LARGE BOWL → 4323

❷ **prizes**
賞 PRIZE → 3237
杯 prize cup → 1066
章 decoration → 2624

板

1067

◧1-4-4

▶BOARD
▶PLATE

ハン バン いた

Ⓒ 板 bǎn

75	Jōyō-3	U677F
木	S8-4-4	F0755

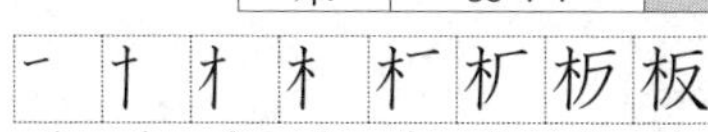

COMPOUNDS

❶ [original meaning] (sheet of wood) **BOARD, plank**
掲示板 けいじばん notice board
黒板 こくばん blackboard
看板 かんばん signboard, sign
甲板 かんぱん(=こうはん) deck

❷ⓐ [also suffix] (sheet of hard material, esp. metal) **PLATE, sheet, slab, tablet**
ⓑ [sometimes also 鈑 ばん 2122] sheet metal
ⓒ abbrev. of 投手板 とうしゅばん: pitcher's **PLATE**

a 鉄板 てっぱん iron [steel] plate
鋼板 こうはん steel plate
投手板 とうしゅばん pitcher's plate

b 板金 ばんきん sheet metal
ニッケル板 にっけるばん nickel plate

c 登板する とうばんする take the plate

❸ [usu. 版 はん 1082] printing block, wood block

板画 はんが woodcut print
板木 はんぎ (printing) block, woodcut

KUN

【いた 板】**BOARD, plank; panel, plate; the boards, stage; *kamaboko* (boiled fish paste); cook versed in Japanese cooking**
板切れ いたきれ piece of wood, scrap lumber
板に着く いたにつく be at home (on the stage)
戸板 といた wooden door [shutter]
俎×板 まないた chopping board

SYNONYMS

❶ & ❷ boards and plates
板 BOARD, PLATE → 1067
盤 BOARD → 3533

杭

▸STAKE
コウ くい
Ⓒ 杭 háng

1068
1-4-4

75	Names	U676D
木	S8-4-4	F2519

COMPOUNDS

● STAKE, post, pile, picket
支持杭 しじこう bearing pile

KUN

【くい 杭】**STAKE, post, pile, picket**
杭打ち くいうち pile-driving
橋杭 はしぐい bridge pillar
乱杭歯 らんぐいば uneven teeth
出る杭は打たれる でるくいはうたれる The stake that sticks out gets hammered in

SYNONYMS

● perforators
針 NEEDLE → 2099
串 SKEWER → 4364
杭 STAKE → 1068
釘 NAIL → 2100

枚

▸COUNTER FOR FLAT THINGS
マイ バイ▲ ㊔ ひら
Ⓒ 枚 méi

1069
1-4-4

75	Jōyō-6	U679A
木	S8-4-4	F0979

1	2	3	4	5	6	7	8
一	十	才	木	札	枚	枚	枚

COMPOUNDS

❶ⓐ COUNTER FOR thin FLAT THINGS, as sheets (of paper), boards, leaves (of a book), pages, articles of clothing, panes, etc.
ⓑ counter for order of precedence in sumo
a 枚数 まいすう number of flat things
紙五枚 かみごまい five sheets of paper
十円切手五枚 じゅうえんきってごまい five 10-yen stamps
b 二枚上がった にまいあがった be promoted by two ranks in sumo
❷ enumerate, count one by one
枚挙する まいきょする list, enumerate
大枚の金 たいまいのかね large sum of money

INDEPENDENT

【ばい 枚】*literary* gag
枚を銜×む ばいをふくむ (of a horse) be gagged

SYNONYMS

❶ⓐ counters for flat things
枚 COUNTER FOR FLAT THINGS → 1069
葉 counter for leaves → 2912
丁 counter for sheets → 4155
頁 counter for pages → 2589
通 counter for letters → 3855
竿 counter for flags → 3259

枡

▸MEASURE
ます
Ⓝ 桝 桝 Ⓒ (国字)

1070
1-4-4

75	Non-Jōyō	U67A1
木	S8-4-4	F3328

KUN

【ます 枡】[now usu. 升]
①ⓐ **MEASURE, measuring box**
ⓑ **box (seat)**
a 枡目 ますめ measure; square (of graph paper)
五升枡 ごしょうます 5-*sho* measure
② **square (as of graph paper)**
枡形 ますがた square (shape)

SYNONYMS

【ます】
①ⓐ **measuring devices**
枡 MEASURE → 1070
尺 rule → 4248
計 meter → 1828
衡 scales → 0939
秤 BALANCE → 1488

HOMOPHONES

ます 升 *SHO* → 4266

NOTE

➡ see USAGE note at 升 4266

林

▶FOREST

リン　はやし　㊔ しげ　しげる

Ⓒ 林 lín

1071

1-4-4

75	Jōyō-1	U6797
木	S8-4-4	F0624

一 十 才 木 朩 村 林 林

COMPOUNDS

❶ⓐ [also suffix] [original meaning] **FOREST, woods, grove**

ⓑ **FORESTry**

a 林業 りんぎょう forestry

林道 りんどう path through a forest, trail through the woods

林檎 りんご apple

森林 しんりん forest, woodland

山林 さんりん mountains and forests; forest on a mountain

杏林 きょうりん doctor

密林 みつりん close thicket, dense forest, jungle

営林 えいりん forest management

造林 ぞうりん afforestation, reforestation

原始林 げんしりん primeval forest

b 農林 のうりん agriculture and forestry

❷ something resembling a **FOREST** in profusion

林立する りんりつする stand close together, bristle (with)

辞林 じりん dictionary

酒池肉林 しゅちにくりん sumptuous feast

❸ circles, groups

芸林 げいりん artists' circles

KUN

【はやし 林】[also suffix] **small woods, grove, thicket**

松林 まつばやし pine forest

雑木林 ぞうきばやし thicket of assorted trees

SYNONYMS

❶ⓐ & 【はやし】 **forest**

林 FOREST, small woods → 1071

森 THICK WOODS → 3123

杜 GROVE → 1030

USAGE

【林 はやし 森 もり】

★The difference between the words 林 はやし and 森 もり is much like the difference between *woods* and *forest*. The latter is thicker and extends over a wide area. However, note that when 林 is used as a word element pronounced りん, it is closer to English *forest* than to *woods*.

NOTE

➡ see COMPOUND FORMATION for 杏林 きょうりん → 杏 3049

析

▶ANALYZE

セキ

Ⓒ 析 xī

1072

1-4-4

75	Jōyō	U6790
木	S8-4-4	F1276

一 十 才 木 朩 析 析 析

COMPOUNDS

ⓐ (separate an abstract entity into parts) **ANALYZE, dissect**

ⓑ (separate a material entity into parts) **ANALYZE**, separate, dissect, divide

a 分析 ぶんせき analysis

解析 かいせき analysis, analytical research

b 析出 せきしゅつ *chem* separating, eduction

開析台地 かいせきだいち dissected plateau

透析 とうせき *chem* dialysis

SYNONYMS

● **separate**

割 DIVIDE → 2284

分 DIVIDE → 2466

解 TAKE APART → 1913

析 ANALYZE → 1072

別 SEPARATE → 1434

離 SEPARATE → 2364

隔 partition → 0827

NOTE

★ do not confuse with 折 BREAK OFF → 0297

枝

▶BRANCH

シ　えだ　㊔ え

Ⓒ 枝 zhī

1073

1-4-4

75	Jōyō-5	U679D
木	S8-4-4	F1071

一 十 才 木 朩 朩 枝 枝

COMPOUNDS

❶ⓐ [original meaning] **BRANCH, twig**

ⓑ [usu. 支 2473] (something structurally analogous to a branch) **BRANCH**, offshoot

a 枝葉 しよう branches and leaves; minor details

枝垂れ桜 しだれざくら weeping cherry

楊枝 ようじ tooth pick

樹枝状の じゅしじょうの arborescent

b 枝族(=支族) しぞく tribe, branch family

枝折り しおり [usu. 栞] bookmark; guidebook

❷ [rare] counter for slender objects

長刀一枝 ちょうとういっし one long sword

KUN

【えだ 枝】**BRANCH, twig; branch, offshoot, ramification**

枝切り えだきり pruning
枝葉 えだは branches and leaves; minor details
枝分かれ えだわかれ branch, ramification
枝道 えだみち branch road, byway
枝毛 えだげ split hair

SYNONYMS

❶ⓐ branches and twigs

枝 BRANCH → 1073
梢 TIP OF A TWIG → 1208

HOMOPHONES

しおり

栞 BOOKMARK → 3285
枝折り → 1073, 0297

杵

▸WOODEN PESTLE

ショ きね ㊔ き

Ⓒ 杵 chǔ

1074

1-4-4

75	Names	U6775
木	S8-4-4	F2713

COMPOUNDS

● WOODEN PESTLE [mallet, pounder]

金剛杵 こんごうしょ *vajra* (mystical weapon in Hinduism and Buddhism)

KUN

【きね 杵】**WOODEN PESTLE [mallet, pounder]**

杵柄 きねづか mallet handle

SYNONYMS

● instruments for beating or pounding

槌 HAMMER → 1331
杵 WOODEN PESTLE → 1074
砧 BLOCK FOR BEATING CLOTH → 1477

松

▸PINE

ショウ まつ

Ⓝ 枀 枩 Ⓒ 松 sōng

1075

1-4-4

75	Jōyō-4	U677E
木	S8-4-4	F0334

1 2 3 4 5 6 7 8

COMPOUNDS

● PINE

松竹梅 しょうちくばい pine-bamboo-plum; congratulatory tree decorations
松根油 しょうこんゆ pine oil
青松 せいしょう green pine

KUN

【まつ 松】**PINE**

松林 まつばやし pine forest
松葉 まつば pine needle
松茸 まつたけ *matsutake* mushroom
門松 かどまつ pine decorations (for New Year's)

SYNONYMS

● trees

桜 CHERRY → 1168
桐 PAULOWNIA → 1173
桂 AROMATIC TREE, katsura tree → 1163
梓 CATALPA → 1207
桑 MULBERRY → 2618
漆 Japanese lacquer tree → 0863
樺 BIRCH → 1324
椛 BIRCH → 1202
梧 CHINESE PARASOL TREE → 1200
檀 SPINDLE TREE → 1385
椿 CAMELLIA → 1278
柳 WILLOW → 1115
柊 HOLLY → 1119
椋 *APHANANTHE ASPERA* → 1245
柾 spindle tree → 1114
槻 ZELKOVA → 1349
楢 OAK → 1287
樫 EVERGREEN OAK → 1364
柏 CYPRESS, JAPANESE EMPEROR OAK → 1110
榎 HACKBERRY → 1323
梶 PAPER MULBERRY → 1199
柘 JAPANESE BOXWOOD → 1117
楊 WILLOW → 1286
桧 JAPANESE CYPRESS → 1160
梛 *NAGEIA NAGI* → 1206
榊 SACRED SHINTO TREE → 1327
楓 MAPLE → 1280
松 PINE → 1075
杉 CRYPTOMERIA → 1027
槙 PODOCARPUS → 1330
楠 CAMPHOR TREE → 1283
樟 CAMPHOR TREE → 1351

枢

▸PIVOT

スウ

Ⓝ 樞 Ⓒ 枢 shū

1076

1-4-4

75	Jōyō	U67A2
木	S8-4-4	F2151

1 2 3 4 5 6 7 8

COMPOUNDS

ⓐ (central part) **PIVOT, center**

ⓑ [original meaning] **PIVOT**, hinged axis

a 枢要な すうような pivotal, cardinal
枢軸国 すうじくこく the Axis Powers
枢機 すうき most important affairs (of state)
枢密 すうみつ secret government affairs
中枢 ちゅうすう pivot, center

b 枢軸 すうじく central point, center; (mechanical) pivot, axis

SYNONYMS

ⓐ **essential part**
精 ESSENCE (essential part) → 1729
粋 essence (best part) → 1645
髄 essence (vital part) → 2316
枢 PIVOT → 1076
幹 TRUNK → 2152
綱 ESSENTIAL POINTS → 1735
旨 PURPORT → 2516
要 summary → 3263

枠

▶**FRAME**
わく
Ⓒ (国字)

1077
1-4-4

75	Jōyō	U67A0
木	S8-4-4	F1584

一 十 オ 木 木' 杁 枠 枠 (1–8)

KUN

【わく 枠】
①ⓐ **FRAME, framework**
ⓑ [original meaning] **spool, reel**

a 枠を付ける わくをつける frame, set a frame
枠組み わくぐみ framework, frame
窓枠 まどわく window frame, sash

b 糸枠 いとわく spool

② **FRAMEwork, limits, confines, bounds**
枠に嵌まった わくにはまった stereotyped
枠内 わくない within the limits [framework]

SYNONYMS

【わく】
① **frames**
枠 FRAME → 1077
骼 SKELETAL FRAME → 2302
格 framework → 1161
額 picture frame → 2273

柑

incorrect stroke-count
➡ see 1-4-5: 木 at 1112
1-4-4

柿

incorrect stroke-count
➡ see 1-4-5: 木 at 1118
1-4-4

柱

incorrect stroke-count
➡ see 1-4-5: 木 at 1124
1-4-4

歿

▶**DIE**
ボツ
Ⓒ 殁 没 mò

1078
1-4-4

78	Non-Jōyō	U6B7F
歹	S8-4-4	F2825

COMPOUNDS

● [now replaced by 没 0305] [original meaning] **DIE, perish**
歿後 ぼつご after one's death
戦歿する せんぼつする be killed in action
死歿 しぼつ death, demise
病歿 びょうぼつ death from sickness

INDEPENDENT

【ぼつ 歿】 [now replaced by 没 0305] indicates date of death
昭和三年歿 しょうわさんねんぼつ died 1928

【ぼっする 歿する】 [now replaced by 没する] **DIE**

SYNONYMS

● **die**
死 DIE → 4334
萎 WITHER → 2872
没 die → 0305
亡 DECEASE → 4210
殉 DIE A MARTYR → 1177
歿 DIE → 1078
去 pass away → 2678
逝 DEPART THIS LIFE → 3850
斃 FALL DOWN DEAD → 3593
枯 WITHER → 1113

炉

▶**FURNACE**
ロ
Ⓝ 爐 Ⓒ 炉 lú

1079
1-4-4

86	Jōyō	U7089
火	S8-4-4	F1686

丶 丷 少 火 火一 炉 炉 炉 (1–8)

COMPOUNDS

❶ [also suffix]
ⓐ **FURNACE, kiln**
ⓑ **reactor**

a 高炉 こうろ blast furnace

户 戸 斤 方 日 木 歹 【火】 爿 片 牛 王 ネ 月 月 区 戸 ヨ

転炉 てんろ rotary kiln
溶鉱炉 ようこうろ smelting [blast] furnace
電気炉 でんきろ electric furnace
反射炉 はんしゃろ reverberatory furnace
乾燥炉 かんそうろ drying kiln
燃焼炉 ねんしょうろ combustion furnace
b 炉心 ろしん reactor core
原子炉 げんしろ nuclear reactor
軽水炉 けいすいろ light-water reactor

❷ [original meaning] **hearth, fireplace**
炉端 ろばた fireside
炉床 ろしょう hearth
暖炉 だんろ fireplace, stove
懐炉 かいろ pocket heater
香炉 こうろ incense burner
囲炉裏 いろり hearth sunk in the floor

INDEPENDENT

【ろ 炉】 hearth, fireplace, fire; **FURNACE**, kiln
炉を囲む ろをかこむ sit around the fire

SYNONYMS

❶ⓐ **heating devices**
炉 FURNACE → 1079
窯 KILN → 2986
缶 steam boiler → 2526

炊

▶COOK
スイ た(く) -だ(き) ㊔ い
Ⓒ 炊 chuī

1080
1-4-4

86	Jōyō	U708A
火	S8-4-4	F2015

丶 丷 少 火 火' 炉 炒 炊
1 2 3 4 5 6 7 8

COMPOUNDS

● [original meaning] **COOK, boil**
炊事 すいじ cooking
炊婦 すいふ cook, kitchen maid
自炊 じすい cooking food for oneself

KUN

【たく 炊く】 **COOK, boil**
炊き込み御飯 たきこみごはん rice seasoned and cooked with various ingredients
炊き出し たきだし distribution of boiled rice (in emergency)
飯炊き めしたき cooking rice; kitchen maid, cook
煮炊き にたき cooking

【-だき -炊き】 **suffix indicating COOKing capacity**
一リットル炊きの いちりっとるだきの having a cooking capacity of one liter

SYNONYMS

● **cook**
煮 BOIL (cook by boiling) → 3460
沸 BOIL (undergo boiling) → 0387
炊 COOK → 1080
蒸 STEAM → 2936
焼く cook by fire → 1256
揚げる fry in deep fat → 0722
煎 ROAST, DECOCT → 2950

USAGE

【たく】
炊く
cook, boil
焚く
burn, kindle, build a fire

HOMOPHONES

たく 焚 BURN → 3450

状

▶FORM
▶CONDITION
▶LETTER
ジョウ

1081
1-4-4

94	Names	U72C0
犬	S8-4-4	F0000

traditional form → see 狀 at 0322

版

▶PRINTING PLATE
▶PUBLISHING
ハン
Ⓒ 版 bǎn

1082
1-4-4

91	Jōyō-5	U7248
片	S8-4-4	F0778

丿 丿' 𠂆 片 片一 片厂 版 版
1 2 3 4 5 6 7 8

COMPOUNDS

❶ [sometimes also 板 1067] [also suffix] **PRINTING PLATE, printing block, wood block**
版木 はんぎ (printing) block, woodcut
版画 はんが woodcut print
活版 かっぱん printing, typography
凸版 とっぱん letterpress, relief printing
木版 もくはん wood block printing, wood engraving
原色版 げんしょくばん heliotype
謄写版 とうしゃばん mimeograph

❷ **PUBLISHING, printing**
版行する はんこうする publish, print
版元 はんもと publisher
版権 はんけん copyright
出版 しゅっぱん publishing; publication
再版する さいはんする reprint

❸ⓐ [also suffix] **edition, impression, printing**

ⓑ counter for editions
a 初版 しょはん first edition
重版 じゅうはん second printing, reprint; second edition
地方版 ちほうばん local edition
決定版 けっていばん authoritative edition; last word
b 第二版 だいにはん second edition
❹ household or population register
版図 はんと territory

INDEPENDENT

【はん 版】 **printing block, plate; edition, impression, printing**
版を改める はんをあらためる revise an edition

SYNONYMS

❶ **printing plate**
版 PRINTING PLATE → 1082
梓 printing block → 1207
❷ **print and publish**
刷 PRINT → 1623
印 print → 1023
植 typeset → 1247
刊 PUBLISH → 0221
版 PUBLISHING → 1082
載 PUT IN PRINT → 4091
掲 display in writing → 0597
幀 BOOKBINDING → 0695
❸ **editions**
版 edition → 1082
刊 publication → 0221
訂 revision → 1829
刷 printing → 1623

牧

1083

◧ 1-4-4

▶**PASTURE**

ボク まき ㊔もく まい

Ⓒ 牧 mù

93	Jōyō-4	U7267
牛	S8-4-4	F1381

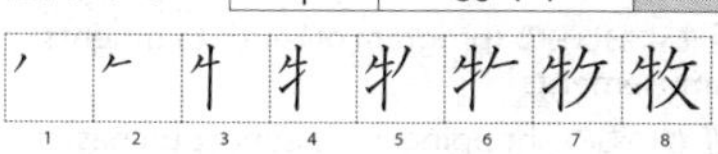

COMPOUNDS

❶ [original meaning] (put cattle to pasture) **PASTURE, tend cattle, herd, shepherd, raise cattle**
牧畜 ぼくちく livestock farming, cattle breeding
牧歌的な ぼっかてきな pastoral, idyllic
牧童 ぼくどう cowboy; shepherd
牧人 ぼくじん shepherd, herdsman
牧羊 ぼくよう sheep farming
放牧する ほうぼくする pasture, put to grass, graze
遊牧 ゆうぼく nomadism
❷ (give guidance to) **shepherd, lead, govern**
牧師 ぼくし pastor, minister, priest
牧民 ぼくみん [archaic] shepherding [governing] the people
❸ **PASTURE, grazing land, meadow**
牧場 ぼくじょう stock farm, pasture
牧草 ぼくそう pasture, grass
牧野 ぼくや pasture land, ranch
放牧地 ほうぼくち grazing land, pasture

KUN

【まき 牧】 **PASTURE**
牧場 まきば pasture, grazing land, meadow
牧を駆ける駒 まきをかけるこま horse galloping in the pasture

SYNONYMS

❶ **raise and nourish**
育 RAISE → 2544
飼 RAISE ANIMALS → 2149
養 FOSTER → 2998
滋 NOURISH → 0734
哺 NURSE → 0478
牧 PASTURE → 1083
❸ **cultivated fields**
畑 FIELD → 1131
畠 FIELD → 3186
牧 PASTURE → 1083
園 GARDEN → 3914
田 RICE FIELD → 3775
佃 CULTIVATED RICE FIELD → 0066
圃 VEGETABLE GARDEN → 3871

物

1084

◧ 1-4-4

▶**THING**

ブツ モツ もの もの-

Ⓒ 物 wù

93	Jōyō-3	U7269
牛	S8-4-4	F0048

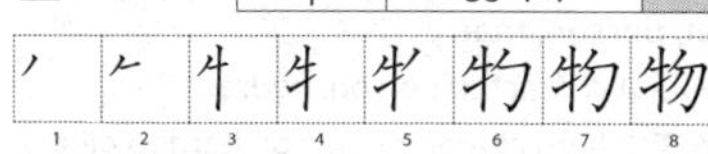

COMPOUNDS

❶ⓐ [also suffix] (inanimate material entity) **THING, object, article**
ⓑ (animate entity) **living THING, life**
ⓒ [also suffix] **commodity, goods, product**
a 物品 ぶっぴん goods, article, commodity
物体 ぶったい body, physical solid, object, substance
物的な ぶってきな material, physical
現物 げんぶつ (actual) thing; spot goods
見物 けんぶつ sightseeing, visit
実物 じつぶつ real thing, actual object, genuine article

風物 ふうぶつ natural objects [features], scenery; scenes and manners
荷物 にもつ baggage, load
書物 しょもつ book, volume
障害物 しょうがいぶつ obstacle, hurdle
b 動物 どうぶつ animal
植物 しょくぶつ plant, vegetation
生物 せいぶつ living thing, life, organism
c 物価 ぶっか prices (of commodities)
物資 ぶっし commodities, goods, resources
物産 ぶっさん product, produce
名物 めいぶつ specialty, noted product
産物 さんぶつ product, produce
貨物 かもつ freight, cargo, goods
穀物 こくもつ grain, cereals
出版物 しゅっぱんぶつ publication

❷ [also suffix] **substance, matter, material**
物質 ぶっしつ matter, substance
鉱物 こうぶつ mineral substance
毒物 どくぶつ poisonous substance, toxin
薬物 やくぶつ drugs, medicinal substances
化合物 かごうぶつ (chemical) compound
有機物 ゆうきぶつ organic matter
塩化物 えんかぶつ chloride

❸ⓐ (abstract entity) **THING(s), matter, affair, something**
ⓑ **physical phenomena, material world, reality**
a 物情 ぶつじょう public feeling
物騒な ぶっそうな dangerous, insecure, disturbed
禁物 きんもつ taboo, prohibited thing
b 物理 ぶつり physics; natural law
物象 ぶっしょう material phenomena; science of inanimate nature
博物学 はくぶつがく natural history

❹ (person distinguished by some characteristic) **character, person, man**
人物 じんぶつ character; person, figure
難物 なんぶつ hard character, person hard to please; hard nut to crack, difficulty
俗物 ぞくぶつ vulgar person, snob, Philistine
傑物 けつぶつ great man, outstanding figure

❺ select according to one's judgment, judge
物色する ぶっしょくする look for, pick out
物議 ぶつぎ public criticism [censure], public discussion

❻ die
物故 ぶっこ death

❼ [usu. 勿 もっ- 3661] **used phonetically for *motsu***
物体 もったい air of importance, superior airs
物体無い もったいない wasteful; be more than one deserves

物怪の幸い もっけのさいわい piece of good luck, windfall

INDEPENDENT

【ぶつ 物】 *slang* loot, hot goods; abbrev. of 物理学 ぶつりがく: physics
物を質入れする ぶつをしちいれする pawn hot goods

KUN

【もの 物】

①ⓐ [also suffix] (inanimate material entity) **THING, object, article, something**
ⓑ [also suffix] **commodity, goods, product**
ⓒ **possession, property**
a 物置き ものおき storeroom
物陰 ものかげ place behind something
建物 たてもの building, structure
品物 しなもの article, thing, goods
本物 ほんもの real thing [stuff], genuine article; expert performance
その物 そのもの the very thing, the thing itself
贈り物 おくりもの present, gift
織物 おりもの cloth, textile, fabric
読み物 よみもの reading matter, book
洗濯物 せんたくもの wash, washing, laundry
b 売り物 うりもの article for sale, offerings
近海物 きんかいもの shorefish, inshore catch
ハウス物 はうすもの vegetables grown in a hothouse
c 学校の物 がっこうのもの school property

② [also suffix] **THING(s), matter, something, act**
物語 ものがたり story, tale, legend
物語る ものがたる tell a story; demonstrate, prove
物事 ものごと things, matter; everything
物知り ものしり well-informed person, walking dictionary
物思い ものおもい reverie, meditation, anxiety
笑い物 わらいもの object of ridicule, subject of derision
催し物 もよおしもの (program of) entertainments, amusements
買い物 かいもの shopping, marketing; purchase
捕り物 とりもの capture, arrest
噴飯物 ふんぱんもの something that makes one laugh, quite absurd thing

③ something, somebody, a success
物に成る ものになる come to good, prove successful
物の数に入らない もののかずにはいらない be insignificant, be off the map
物ともせずに ものともせずに in defiance of, in the face of
大物 おおもの great man, big shot

④ reason, sense

物の分かった もののわかった sensible, fair-minded
物心 ものごころ judgment, discretion

【もの- 物-】 somehow, in some way or other
物凄い ものすごい ghastly, weird; terrible, tremendous
物足りない ものたりない be somehow unsatisfied, feel something wanting; be unsatisfactory
物悲しい ものがなしい sad, melancholy

SYNONYMS

❶ⓐ object
物 THING → 1084
品 ARTICLE → 2795
体 BODY → 0080

ⓑ animal
獣 BEAST → 2384
畜 LIVESTOCK → 2599
生 LIFE → 4309
物 living thing → 1084

ⓒ merchandise
産 product → 4089
品 ARTICLE (of merchandise) → 2795
貨 GOODS → 3113
物 commodity → 1084

❷ matter
質 MATTER → 3483
物 substance → 1084
材 MATERIAL → 1031
料 MATERIALS → 1644
資 material resources → 3342

❸ⓐ abstract thing
事 ABSTRACT THING → 4384
物 THING → 1084

ⓑ phenomenon
象 PHENOMENON → 2647
気 natural phenomenon → 3960
物 physical phenomena → 1084

❹ fellow
奴 GUY → 0217
漢 FELLOW → 0808
輩 FELLOW (*belittling*) → 3482
徒 fellows → 0499
棒 tough guy → 1237
坊 COLLOQUIAL PERSON SUFFIX → 0274
屋 colloquial person suffix → 3842
物 character → 1084

USAGE

【もの】
物
①ⓐ [also suffix] (inanimate material entity) thing, object, article, something
ⓑ [also suffix] commodity, goods, product
ⓒ possession, property
② [also suffix] thing(s), matter, something, act
③ something, somebody, a success
④ reason, sense

者
person, fellow, somebody

HOMOPHONES

もの 者 PERSON → 3980

玩 1085

1-4-4

▸TAKE PLEASURE IN
ガン もてあそ(ぶ)▲ ㊔ よし
ⓒ 玩 wán

96	Jōyō	U73A9
王	S8-4-4	F2417

1	2	3	4	5	6	7	8
一	T	千	王	王一	王二	玩	玩

COMPOUNDS

❶ (play with) **TAKE PLEASURE IN, toy with, trifle with**
玩弄する がんろうする make sport of, toy with, play with
玩具 がんぐ(=おもちゃ) toy, plaything
食玩(=食品玩具) しょくがん(=しょくひんがんぐ) small toy sold with food

❷ (appreciate) **TAKE PLEASURE IN, relish, cherish**
玩味 がんみ relishing, appreciation
愛玩動物 あいがんどうぶつ pet animal

KUN

【もてあそぶ 玩ぶ】 [usu. 弄ぶ]
①ⓐ **toy [fiddle] with (something) with one's hands**
ⓑ **toy [trifle] with; do (with something) as one pleases**
a 髪を玩ぶ かみをもてあそぶ fiddle with one's hair
b 人の気持ちを玩ぶ ひとのきもちをもてあそぶ toy with people's feelings
② **TAKE PLEASURE IN**, appreciate, enjoy as a diversion
詩歌を玩ぶ しいかをもてあそぶ enjoy poetry

SPECIAL READINGS

玩具▲ おもちゃ(=がんぐ) toy, plaything

SYNONYMS

❶ pleasure
楽 PLEASURE → 3505
娯 ENJOYMENT → 0487
興 AMUSEMENT → 3622
玩 TAKE PLEASURE IN → 1085

❷ love and like
愛 LOVE → 3133
恋 LOVE (the opposite sex) → 2602
好 LIKE → 0240
慕 ADORE → 2970
惚れる FALL IN LOVE → 0584

玩 cherish → 1085

HOMOPHONES

もてあそぶ 弄 TOY WITH → 3057

NOTE

➡ see USAGE note at 弄 3057

祈 1086

1-4-4

▶PRAY

キ いの(る)

Ⓝ 祈 Ⓒ 祈 qí

113	Jōyō	U7948
ネ	S8-4-4	F1529

COMPOUNDS

● [original meaning] **PRAY**

祈祷 きとう prayer

祈願する きがんする pray, implore

祈念 きねん prayer

KUN

【いのる 祈る】[formerly also 祷る] **PRAY, wish for**

祈り いのり prayer

祈り求める いのりもとめる pray for

SYNONYMS

● **pray and worship**

祈 PRAY → 1086

祷 PRAY → 1224

願 pray → 2320

拝 WORSHIP → 0360

祀 WORSHIP AS GOD → 1448

崇 REVERENCE → 2864

斎 OBSERVE RELIGIOUS ABSTINENCE → 2622

呪 SPELL → 0323

USAGE

❶【いのる】

祈る

[formerly also 祷る] pray, wish for

祷る

[now usu. 祈る] pray, wish for

❷【いのり】

祈り

[formerly also 祷り] prayer

祷り

[now usu. 祈り] prayer

HOMOPHONES

いのる 祷 PRAY → 1224

いのり 祷 PRAY → 1224

祉 1087

1-4-4

▶BLESSEDNESS

シ

Ⓝ 祉 Ⓒ 祉 zhǐ

113	Jōyō	U7949
ネ	S8-4-4	F1633

COMPOUNDS

● [original meaning] **BLESSEDNESS, happiness**

祉福 しふく [archaic] happiness, prosperity; blessedness and joy

福祉 ふくし welfare

SYNONYMS

● **happiness**

幸 HAPPINESS → 2755

祉 BLESSEDNESS → 1087

福 FORTUNE → 1303

祇 1088

1-4-4

▶EARTHLY GOD

ギ シ ㊔ まさ のり けさ つみ もと ひろ

113	Nonstandard	U7947
ネ	S8-4-4	F0000

traditional form → see 祇 at 1459

肪 1089

1-4-4

▶ANIMAL FAT

ボウ

Ⓒ 肪 fáng

130	Jōyō	U80AA
月	S8-4-4	F1903

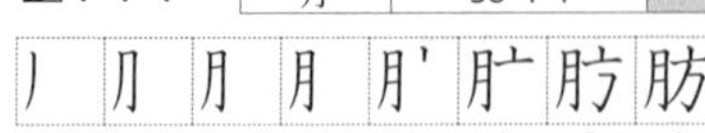

COMPOUNDS

● [original meaning] **ANIMAL FAT, fat**

脂肪 しぼう fat, grease

SYNONYMS

● **fats and oils**

油 OIL → 0400

脂 FAT → 1190

肪 ANIMAL FAT → 1089

膏 FAT → 2658

蠟 WAX → 1818

服 1090

1-4-4

▶CLOTHES

▶SUBMIT

フク ㊔ はとり

Ⓝ 服 Ⓒ 服 fú fù

74	Jōyō-3	U670D
月	S8-4-4	F0555

丿 月 月 月 月⁷ 肌 服 服

1 2 3 4 5 6 7 8

COMPOUNDS

❶ⓐ [also suffix] **CLOTHES, clothing, dress, costume**
ⓑ put on **CLOTHES**, don
a 服装 ふくそう dress, garments, attire
服飾 ふくしょく dress and its ornaments
洋服 ようふく (Western) clothes
呉服 ごふく dry goods; drapery
制服 せいふく uniform, regulation uniform
衣服 いふく clothes, dress, clothing
紳士服 しんしふく men's suit
宇宙服 うちゅうふく spacesuit
b 元服 げんぷく ceremony of attaining manhood

❷ⓐ [also 伏 0049] **SUBMIT to, yield to, surrender; obey, observe**
ⓑ **cause to SUBMIT**
a 服罪 ふくざい submitting to a sentence
服従 ふくじゅう obedience, submission
屈服する くっぷくする bend in submission, submit to, surrender, yield to
承服 しょうふく consent, acceptance
感服 かんぷく admiration, wonder
不服 ふふく dissatisfaction, discontent; disagreement; objection; complaint
b 征服 せいふく conquest, subjugation
克服する こくふくする conquer, overcome, subjugate

❸ serve, discharge one's duties
服役 ふくえき penal servitude; military service
服務 ふくむ duty, public service

❹ⓐ **take (medicine or tea)**
ⓑ counter for packets of medicine, sips (of tea) or puffs (of smoke)
a 服用する ふくようする take (medicine)
服毒する ふくどくする take poison
内服薬 ないふくやく medicine for internal use
b 一服 いっぷく a dose (of medicine); a puff [whiff] (of a cigarette); a sip (of tea); rest; lull, calm market

❺ appropriate, embezzle
着服する ちゃくふくする embezzle, misappropriate

❻ mourning
服喪する ふくもする go into mourning
除服する じょふくする come out of mourning

INDEPENDENT

【ふく 服】**CLOTHES, clothing, dress, costume**
【ふくする 服する】**SUBMIT** to, yield; obey, observe; admit; serve, discharge one's duties; take, drink

SYNONYMS

❶ⓐ **clothing**
服 CLOTHES → 1090
袴 FORMAL DIVIDED SKIRT → 1509
蓑 STRAW RAINCOAT → 2941
-着 wear → 4110
衣 GARMENT → 2506
装 DRESS → 3327
裳 DRESS → 3231
襤 RAGS → 1607
袈 BUDDHIST SURPLICE → 3200
裟 BUDDHIST CASSOCK → 3420
襖 overgarment → 1600

❷ **submit and surrender**
服 SUBMIT → 1090
伏 submit → 0049
屈 bend in submission → 3821
降 surrender → 0548

❹ⓐ **ingest**
喫 INGEST → 0668
服 take → 1090
食 EAT → 2578
喰う EAT → 0670
飲 DRINK → 2127
呑 SWALLOW → 3059
啄 PECK → 0482

NOTE

➡ see COMPOUND FORMATION for 元服 げんぷく → 元 2428

肥 1091

▶**FATTEN**

ヒ こ(える) こえ こ(やす) こ(やし) ふと(る)▲
㊔ ゆたか
Ⓒ 肥 féi

◧ 1-4-4

130	Jōyō-5	U80A5
月	S8-4-4	F1404

丿 月 月 月 月⁷ 肌 肥 肥

1 2 3 4 5 6 7 8

COMPOUNDS

❶ **FATTEN, fat up, grow fat, make fat**
肥大した ひだいした fat, enlarged
肥満する ひまんする become obese
肥馬 ひば fat horse
肥育 ひいく fattening

❷ⓐ **FATTEN the soil, fertilize, enrich**
ⓑ (of land) fat, fertile, rich
ⓒ **fertilizer**
a 施肥 せひ fertilization, manuring
b 肥沃な ひよくな fertile, productive
c 肥料 ひりょう fertilizer, manure
堆肥 たいひ barnyard manure
金肥 きんぴ chemical fertilizer

❸ old name for Nagasaki, Saga and Kumamoto prefectures
豊肥本線 ほうひほんせん Hohi Main Line (Oita-Kumamoto Railway)

KUN

【こえる 肥える】 **FATTEN, grow fat, grow fertile; have a trained (eye or ear)**
肥え太る こえふとる grow fat
耳が肥えている みみがこえている have an ear for music

【こえ 肥】 **manure, fertilizer; night soil**
肥汲み こえくみ carrying night soil; night soil man
肥溜め こえだめ night soil vat

【こやす 肥やす】 **manure, fertilize; FATTEN; enrich oneself**
馬を肥やす うまをこやす fatten a horse
私腹を肥やす しふくをこやす fill [stuff] one's own pocket by taking advantage of a position

【こやし 肥やし】 **manure; night soil**
肥やし桶 こやしおけ night soil pail

【ふとる 肥る】 [usu. 太る] grow fat, **FATTEN**, gain weight
肥った ふとった fat, stout, plump

SYNONYMS

❶ **fatten**
肥 FATTEN → 1091
太る grow fat → 2673

HOMOPHONES

ふとる 太 GREAT → 2673

NOTE

➡ see USAGE note at 太 2673

朋

1092

1-4-4

▶**COMRADE**

ホウ とも

Ⓝ 朋 Ⓒ 朋 péng

74	Names	U670B
月	S8-4-4	F1427

COMPOUNDS

❶ **COMRADE, friend, companion, mate, fellow**
朋友 ほうゆう friend, companion
朋輩 ほうばい comrade, friend, associate

❷ clique, group
朋党 ほうとう faction, clique

KUN

【とも 朋】 [usu. 友] **friend, companion, pal**

SYNONYMS

❶ **friends and associates**
僚 COLLEAGUE → 0186
輩 FELLOW → 3482
朋 COMRADE → 1092
友 FRIEND → 3670
侶 COMPANION → 0114

HOMOPHONES

とも
友 FRIEND → 3670
共 JOINT → 3045
供 OFFER → 0098

NOTE

➡ see USAGE note at 友 3670

股

1093

1-4-4

▶**CROTCH**

コ また もも▲

Ⓒ 股 gǔ

130	Jōyō	U80A1
月	S8-4-4	F1393

丿 1 | 𠂊 2 | 月 3 | 月 4 | 月' 5 | 肌 6 | 肞 7 | 股 8

COMPOUNDS

● [original meaning] **CROTCH (of the human body), inner thigh**
股関節 こかんせつ coxa
股間 こかん crotch
股肱× ここう one's right-hand man, one's trusted henchman
四股 しこ stamping on the sumo ring

KUN

【また 股】
ⓐ **CROTCH (of the human body), inner thigh**
ⓑ [sometimes also 叉 or 俣] (place of furcation) **CROTCH (of a tree), fork (of a road)**
a 股下 またした length of the legs, inseam
股旅 まただび wandering life of a gambler
股に掛ける またにかける travel all over, be active in places widely apart
内股 うちまた inside of a thigh; pigeon-toe; throwing down the opponent with one's leg between his [her] legs (in judo)
大股 おおまた straddle; long stride; thigh-scooping body drop (in sumo)
b 二股 ふたまた bifurcation; *slang* two-timing
三股 さんまた forked stick

【もも 股】 **thigh**
股引 ももひき long underpants; working trousers
太股 ふともも thigh

SYNONYMS

● **trunk parts**
胸 CHEST → 1187
腹 BELLY → 1308
胴 TRUNK → 1186
腰 WAIST → 1311
背 BACK → 3182

肩 SHOULDER → 2446
股 CROTCH → 1093
脇 ARMPIT → 1188
腋 ARMPIT → 1266

【また】

ⓑ **furcation**

叉 FORK → 4194
俣 BIFURCATION → 0111
股 CROTCH → 1093
岐 forked road → 0285

USAGE

【また】

股

ⓐ crotch (of the human body), inner thigh
ⓑ [sometimes also 叉 or 俣] (place of furcation) crotch (of a tree), fork (of a road)

俣

[usu. 股, sometimes also 叉] [in compounds] bifurcation, fork (as of a body of water)

叉

[usu. 股, sometimes also 俣] (place of furcation) crotch (of a tree), fork (of a road)

HOMOPHONES

また

叉 FORK → 4194
俣 BIFURCATION → 0111

肢

1094

◧ 1-4-4

▶**LIMB**

シ

Ⓒ 肢 zhī

130	Jōyō	U80A2
月	S8-4-4	F2005

1	2	3	4	5	6	7	8
丿	月	月	月	月一	月十	肢	肢

COMPOUNDS

ⓐ [original meaning] (human or animal appendage) **LIMB, member, arm or leg**

ⓑ (subdivision) **LIMB**, branch

a 肢体 したい limbs, members
下肢 かし lower limbs, legs
四肢 しし limbs, legs and arms
前肢 ぜんし forelimb, front leg

b 多肢選択式試問 たしせんたくしきしもん multiple-choice question
選択肢 せんたくし choices (of a multiple-choice test)

SYNONYMS

ⓐ **limbs**

肢 LIMB → 1094
腕 ARM → 1269
脚 LEG → 1226

胏

1095

◧ 1-4-4

▶**LUNG**

ハイ

130	Nonstandard	U80BA
月	S8-4-4	F0000

traditional form → see 肺 at 1147

服

1096

◧ 1-4-4

▶**CLOTHES**
▶**SUBMIT**

フク ㊔ はとり

74	Nonstandard	U670D
月	S8-4-4	F0000

traditional form → see 服 at 1090

朋

1097

◧ 1-4-4

▶**COMRADE**

ホウ とも

74	Nonstandard	U670B
月	S8-4-4	F0000

traditional form → see 朋 at 1092

欧

1098

◧ 1-4-4

▶**EUROPE**

オウ

Ⓝ 歐 Ⓒ 欧 ōu

76	Jōyō	U6B27
欠	S8-4-4	F1054

1	2	3	4	5	6	7	8
一	フ	ヌ	区	区′	区⺈	欧	欧

COMPOUNDS

● **EUROPE**

欧州 おうしゅう Europe
欧米 おうべい Europe and America
欧亜 おうあ Europe and Asia
欧文 おうぶん foreign text
全欧 ぜんおう the whole of Europe
西欧 せいおう West Europe, the Occident
東欧 とうおう East Europe

INDEPENDENT

【おう 欧】**EUROPE**

SYNONYMS

● **continents**

亜 Asia → 4354
阿 Africa → 0408
欧 EUROPE → 1098
米 AMERICA → 4342
豪 Australia → 2657

1
戶 戸 斤 方 日 木 歹 火 爿 片 牛 王 ネ 月 月 【区】 尸 扌

殴

▶BEAT

オウ　なぐ(る)

Ⓝ 毆 Ⓒ 殴 ōu

1099

1-4-4

79	Jōyō	U6BB4
殳	S8-4-4	F1664

Stroke order: 一 ア ヌ 区 区 区 殴 殴 (1–8)

COMPOUNDS

● [original meaning] (strike a person) **BEAT (up), hit, strike, thrash**

殴打 おうだ blow, beating

殴殺する おうさつする beat to death

KUN

【なぐる　殴る】**BEAT up, beat, hit, strike, thrash**

殴り倒す なぐりたおす knock down

殴り合う なぐりあう fight, exchange blows

殴り込み なぐりこみ attack, raid

横殴り よこなぐり side sweep, side blow

書き殴る かきなぐる write [scribble] off

SYNONYMS

● **strike**

打 STRIKE →0224

撲 DEAL A BLOW →0903

殴 BEAT (strike a person) →1099

蹴 KICK →2074

撃 STRIKE →3552

挌 STRIKE (a person) →0448

撞 STRIKE (a ball or bell) →0905

撥ねる strike (knock down) →0907

当てる HIT →2701

叩 KNOCK →0208

拍 BEAT (strike repeatedly) →0361

搏 BEAT (throb) →0794

門

▶GATE

モン　かど　㊔ と

Ⓝ 门◆ Ⓒ 门 mén

1100

1-4-4

169	Jōyō-2	U9580
門	S8-8-0	F0210

Stroke order: 丨 ㄏ 尸 尸 尸 門 門 門 (1–8)

RADICAL

mon or ***mongamae*** 'gate' (間 開 関), used in characters related to gates, doors or outer enclosures

COMPOUNDS

❶ⓐ [also suffix] [original meaning] **GATE, gateway, entrance, door**

ⓑ narrow orifice, esp. in the human body

a 門戸 もんこ door, entrance; school

門番 もんばん gatekeeper, janitor

正門 せいもん main gate, main entrance

校門 こうもん school gate

通用門 つうようもん side door

b 門脈 もんみゃく portal vein

肛門 こうもん anus

噴門 ふんもん cardia

❷ⓐ **field, branch, division**

ⓑ *biol* phylum, division, subkingdom

a 門外漢 もんがいかん layman, outsider

専門 せんもん specialty, profession

部門 ぶもん class, group, division, department, section; genus

仏門 ぶつもん Buddhism; priesthood

b 節足動物門 せっそくどうぶつもん Arthropoda

❸ (from the idea of people gathering under the same gateway)

ⓐ (persons under same teacher) **pupil, disciple**

ⓑ **(religious) sect, branch, school**

a 門下生 もんかせい disciple, pupil

門弟 もんてい pupil, disciple

入門する にゅうもんする become a pupil of, enter a private school

同門 どうもん fellow pupil

b 門徒 もんと sectarian, follower, believer

破門 はもん excommunication, expulsion

宗門 しゅうもん religious sect

禅門 ぜんもん Zen sect

稲門 とうもん Waseda University

❹ **family, clan**

門閥 もんばつ (renowned) lineage, pedigree

名門 めいもん distinguished [noted] family; prestigious establishment

一門 いちもん family, the whole clan

❺ counter for cannons

大砲三門 たいほうさんもん three cannons

INDEPENDENT

【もん　門】

① **GATE, entrance, door**

門を開ける もんをあける open the gate

② (religious) sect, branch, school

Ａ氏の門に入る えーしのもんにはいる study under Mr. A

③ *biol* phylum, division, subkingdom

KUN

【かど　門】**door, GATE, gateway**

門出 かどで departure, setting out

門口 かどぐち front door, entrance, gateway

笑う門には福来たる わらうかどにはふくきたる Fortune comes to a merry home

SYNONYMS

❶ⓐ **doors**
戸 DOOR → 2429
扉 HINGED DOOR → 2453
門 GATE → 1100
口 entrance (or exit) → 4189
襖 OPAQUE SLIDING DOOR → 1600

❷ⓐ **branch of study**
科 SUBJECT OF STUDY → 1463
学 branch of study → 3162
門 field → 1100

❸ⓐ **students and followers**
生 STUDENT → 4309
卒 graduate student → 2549
学 scholar → 3162
門 pupil → 1100
弟 disciple → 2537
徒 FOLLOWER → 0499

ⓑ **parties and sects**
党 PARTY → 3190
閥 CLIQUE → 4126
流 school → 0529
派 SECT → 0456
翼 WING → 3379
系 faction → 2443
門 (religious) sect → 1100
宗 RELIGIOUS SECT (esp. Buddhist) → 2769

❹ **family and relations**
族 FAMILY → 1195
家 FAMILY → 2827
門 family → 1100
氏 clan → 3669
縁 RELATION → 1754
姻 relative by marriage → 0421
親 RELATIVES → 2264
戚 RELATIVES → 4401
曽 GREAT- → 2632

非

1101

◧ 1-4-4

▸**IS NOT**
ヒ あら(ず)▲
Ⓒ 非 fēi

175	Jōyō-5	U975E
非	S8-8-0	F0603

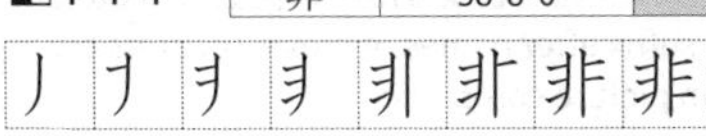

RADICAL

arazu 'not' (靠× 靡×), used for character classification

COMPOUNDS

❶ⓐ [also prefix] **IS NOT, not, non-, un-, in-**—element of contrariety usu. placed before nouns

ⓑ unfavorable, unlucky

a 非常 ひじょう emergency, calamity
非常に ひじょうに very, extremely, greatly
非鉄金属 ひてつきんぞく nonferrous metals
非番 ひばん off duty
非情の ひじょうの coldhearted; inanimate
非礼 ひれい impoliteness
非売品 ひばいひん articles not for sale
非公式の ひこうしきの informal, unofficial
非金属 ひきんぞく nonmetal
非科学的な ひかがくてきな unscientific
非常識 ひじょうしき lack of common sense

b 非運 ひうん bad luck, misfortune

❷ⓐ **wrong, wrongdoing, mistake**
ⓑ **wrong, not right**

a 是非 ぜひ right and/or wrong; by all means, at any cost
前非 ぜんぴ one's past folly [sin]

b 非行 ひこう delinquency, misdeed, misdemeanor
非道い ひどい [also 酷い] cruel, harsh, rough; severe, intense, heavy

❸ [sometimes also 誹 1978] **slander, calumniate, defame**
非難(=批難) ひなん criticism, blame
非毀 ひき defamation
非議する ひぎする criticize, censure

INDEPENDENT

【ひ 非】 **wrong, wrongdoing, mistake**
非とする ひとする condemn, denounce

KUN

【あらず 非ず】 *literary* not
然に非ず さにあらず Not so

SYNONYMS

❶ⓐ **terms of negation**
不 NOT (negation) → 4242
非 IS NOT (contrariety) → 1101
無 WITHOUT (nonexistence) → 2648
没 lacking in → 0305
欠 LACK → 2481
否 OR NOT → 3058
未 NOT YET → 4318
莫 NOT → 2839
勿 DO NOT → 3661

❷ⓐ **wrongdoing and evil**
罪 sin → 3224
非 wrong(doing) → 1101
邪 wrong → 1443
悪 evil (something bad) → 3413
弊 evil(s) (something undesirable) → 3583

HOMOPHONES

ひどい

酷い →1967

非道い →1101, 3888

NOTE

➡ see USAGE notes at 不 4242 and 酷 1967

【手】方 日 木 歹 火 牛 王 ネ 月

拝

1102

1-4-5

▶WORSHIP
▶HUMBLY

ハイ おが(む)

64	Names	U62DC
手	S9-4-5	F0000

traditional form → see 拜 at 0360

施

1103

1-4-5

▶CARRY OUT

シ セ ほどこ(す)

Ⓒ 施 shī

70	Jōyō	U65BD
方	S9-4-5	F0730

COMPOUNDS

❶ CARRY OUT, put into practice, enforce, execute, conduct

施行する しこうする enforce, execute, carry out

施工する せこう(=しこう)する execute (a building contract), carry out

施術 しじゅつ surgical operation

施策 しさく enforcement of a policy

施政 しせい administration, government

実施する じっしする carry out, enforce, execute

❷ give alms, give charity, dispense gratis, render services (to the needy)

施薬 せやく free medicine

施行する せぎょうする give alms

施主 せしゅ chief mourner; donor, benefactor

施餓鬼 せがき service for the unmourned dead

布施 ふせ alms

❸ make, construct, equip

施設 しせつ equipment, facilities; institution, establishment

施条 しじょう making lines; rifling a gun barrel

❹ apply, spread

施肥 せひ fertilization, manuring

KUN

【ほどこす 施す】

① **conduct, perform, take (measures), CARRY OUT; apply**

応急手当を施す おうきゅうてあてをほどこす give (a person) first aid

策を施す さくをほどこす take measures

面目を施す めんぼくをほどこす win honor, get credit

② **give alms [charity], dispense (medicine) gratis, render services**

施し ほどこし alms, almsgiving

SYNONYMS

❶ execute

執 EXECUTE →2114

行 ACT →0246

履 FULFILL →3933

施 CARRY OUT →1103

践 IMPLEMENT →1938

果たす effect →4377

遂 ACCOMPLISH →3892

❷ donate

施 give alms →1103

恵む give charity →3293

寄 CONTRIBUTE →2856

醵 CONTRIBUTE MONEY →2087

献 donate →2240

映

1104

1-4-5

▶REFLECT
▶PROJECT

エイ うつ(る) うつ(す) は(える) -ば(え)

㊔ てる あき

Ⓝ 暎 Ⓒ 映 yìng

72	Jōyō-6	U6620
日	S9-4-5	F0335

COMPOUNDS

❶ REFLECT, mirror, shine

映射する えいしゃする [rare] reflect, shine

反映 はんえい reflection

❷ PROJECT (an image), screen (a film), show

映像 えいぞう (TV) picture, image; reflection

映写 えいしゃ projection

映画 えいが cinema, film, movie

上映する じょうえいする screen, show, project

放映する ほうえいする televise, telecast

❸ⓐ abbrev. of 映画 えいが: motion picture, movie, film

ⓑ abbrev. of 映画館 えいがかん or 映画会社 えいががいしゃ: suffix after names of movie theaters or motion picture companies

a 映倫 えいりん Motion Picture Code of Ethics Committee

映配 えいはい film distributing company

b 銀映 ぎんえい The Ginei Movie Theater

大映 だいえい Daiei Motion Picture Company

INDEPENDENT

【えいじる(=えいずる) 映じる(=映ずる)】 be **REFLECT**ed, shine on; impress, appear (to)

水に映じる みずにえいじる be reflected in the water

KUN

【うつる 映る】

① ⓐ **be REFLECTed, be imaged, be mirrored**

ⓑ **be PROJECTed, be on (TV)**

a 映り うつり reflection; quality of a picture [film]; match, harmony

鏡に映る かがみにうつる be reflected in a mirror

② match, suit, be becoming

この色は良く映る このいろはよくうつる The colors match well

【うつす 映す】

① **REFLECT, mirror**

鏡に自分の姿を映す かがみにじぶんのすがたをうつす reflect oneself in a mirror

② **PROJECT (a motion picture)**

映画をスクリーンに映す えいがをすくりーんにうつす project a motion picture on a screen

障子に影を映す しょうじにかげをうつす project a shadow on a *shoji* (paper sliding door)

【はえる 映える】

① **shine, excel in brilliance**

照り映える てりはえる glow (in the sun), be lighted up

面映ゆい おもはゆい abashed, made self-conscious

② [also 栄える] look better [to advantage], go well with

映えない色 はえないいろ dull color

映え はえ glory, splendor

【-ばえ -映え】

① **glow**

夕映え ゆうばえ evening [sunset] glow

② [also -栄え] looking better

代わり映えがしない かわりばえがしない It's none the better for the change

③ [usu. -栄え] result, effect

出来映え できばえ result, effect, workmanship

SYNONYMS

❶ **shine and reflect**

輝 SHINE BRILLIANTLY → 1775

光 shine → 3043

照 ILLUMINATE → 3506

映 REFLECT → 1104

耀 SHINE BRILLIANTLY → 1812

燿 SHINE → 1407

閃 FLASH → 4114

煌 GLITTER → 1296

❷ **project**

映 PROJECT → 1104

写 project → 2493

❸ⓐ **motion picture**

映 motion picture → 1104

画 film → 3723

USAGE

❶【うつり】

映り

① ⓐ reflection

ⓑ quality of a picture [film]

② match, harmony

写り

print, impression

移り

① change, transition

② return present

❷【はえる】

映える

① shine, excel in brilliance

② [also 栄える] look better [to advantage], go well with

栄える

[also 映える] look better [to advantage], go well with

❸【-ばえ】

-映え

① glow

② [also -栄え] looking better

③ [usu. -栄え] result, effect

-栄え

① [also -映え] looking better

② [sometimes also -映え] result, effect

HOMOPHONES

うつる

写 COPY → 2493

移 SHIFT → 1508

うつり

写 COPY → 2493

移 SHIFT → 1508

うつす

写 COPY → 2493

移 SHIFT → 1508

はえる 栄 FLOURISH → 3183

-ばえ 栄 FLOURISH → 3183

はえ 栄 FLOURISH → 3183

NOTE

➡ see also USAGE note at 写 2493

昧

1105

1-4-5

▸**DARK**

マイ バイ▴

Ⓒ 昧 mèi

72	Jōyō	U6627
日	S9-4-5	F1898

手 方 【日】 木 歹 火 牛 王 ネ 月

1	2	3	4	5	6	7	8	9
丨	冂	月	日	日一	日二	日+	昧	昧

COMPOUNDS

❶ **DARK, dim**

曖昧 あいまい vague, unclear, ambiguous, fuzzy

❷ **DARK**, ignorant, foolish

愚昧 ぐまい stupid and ignorant

蒙昧 もうまい ignorance

❸ used phonetically for *mai* in the transliteration of Sanskrit Buddhist terms

三昧 さんまい *Buddhism* spiritual concentration, *samādhi;* [suffix] absorption in, indulgence in, spree

贅×沢三昧 ぜいたくざんまい indulging in every possible luxury

SYNONYMS

❶ **dark**

暗 DARK → 1273
黒 BLACK → 3406
陰 shaded → 0657
闇 DARK → 4134
晦 DARK → 1196
昏 dark → 3073
昧 DARK → 1105
冥 DARK → 2613
曖 SHADY → 1383

❸ **phonetic [m]**

弥 PHONETIC [mi] → 0344
摩 phonetic [ma] → 3938
昧 phonetic [mai] → 1105
蜜 phonetic [mitsu] → 2958
勿 phonetic [mot] → 3661
牟 PHONETIC [mu] → 2518

NOTE

★ do not confuse with 味 TASTE → 0325

昨

1106

1-4-5

▶**YESTERDAY**
▶**LAST**

サク

Ⓒ 昨 zuó

72	Jōyō-4	U6628
日	S9-4-5	F0756

1	2	3	4	5	6	7	8	9
丨	冂	月	日	日'	日⺈	昨	昨	昨

COMPOUNDS

❶ⓐ [also prefix] **YESTERDAY, yesterday's**

ⓑ yesteryear

a 昨日 さくじつ yesterday

昨晩 さくばん last night, last evening

昨夜 さくや last night

昨紙 さくし yesterday's paper

昨五月二日 さくごがつふつか yesterday, May 2

昨今 さっこん these days

❷ⓐ (most recent) **LAST (year, etc.)**

ⓑ [prefix] **LAST** year's, of last year

a 昨年 さくねん last year

昨春 さくしゅん last spring

一昨昨日 いっさくさくじつ three days ago

b 昨昭和五十五年 さくしょうわごじゅうごねん last year, 1980

SPECIAL READINGS

昨日 きのう yesterday

昨夜▲ ゆうべ last night, last evening

一昨日▲ おととい(=いっさくじつ) day before yesterday

SYNONYMS

❶ⓐ **yesterday and today**

今 today → 2464
昨 YESTERDAY → 1106

❷ⓐ **most recent**

昨 LAST → 1106
去 last → 2678
先 last → 3046

昭

1107

1-4-5

▶**LUMINOUS**

ショウ ㊔ あき　あきら　てる

Ⓒ 昭 zhāo

72	Jōyō-3	U662D
日	S9-4-5	F0553

1	2	3	4	5	6	7	8	9
丨	冂	月	日	日⺈	日刀	昭	昭	昭

COMPOUNDS

❶ⓐ [original meaning, now rare] (emitting light) **LUMINOUS**, bright, shining

ⓑ (enjoying the glory of enlightened rule) **enlightened, glorious, illustrious**

a 昭昭たる しょうしょうたる [rare] bright, clear; obvious, plain

b 昭代 しょうだい enlightened era, glorious reign

昭和 しょうわ Showa era

❷ [archaic] (clearly intelligible) **LUMINOUS**, clear, obvious, evident

昭然たる しょうぜんたる clear, manifest

❸ abbrev. of 昭和 しょうわ: **Showa era**

昭電 しょうでん Showa Denko (name of a company)

INDEPENDENT

【しょう 昭】abbrev. of 昭和 しょうわ: Showa era

昭五十六年 しょうごじゅうろくねん fifty-sixth year of the Showa era (1981)

SYNONYMS

❶ **bright**

明 BRIGHT → 1060

昭 LUMINOUS → 1107
蛍 fluorescent → 3204
晃 DAZZLING → 3101
燦 BRILLIANT → 1390
赫 BLAZING → 1960
暉 radiant → 1276
熙 BRIGHT → 3559
晟 SUNNY → 3104

COMPOUND FORMATION

【昭和 しょうわ】

昭和 'Showa era' refers to the era of enlightenment (昭 ❶❻) and peace (和). It is the name of the Japanese era beginning in 1926.

旺

1108

1-4-5

▶**DAY OF THE WEEK**

ヨウ ㊔ てる

72	Nonstandard	U2B782
日	S9-4-5	F0000

handwritten form → see 曜 at 1402

柱

1109

1-4-5

▶**PILLAR**

チュウ はしら

Ⓝ 柱 Ⓒ 柱 zhù

75	Jōyō-3	U67F1
木	S9-4-5	F1331

Stroke order: 1 一 2 十 3 才 4 木 5 木' 6 木' 7 杧 8 杧 9 柱

COMPOUNDS

❶ⓐ [original meaning] **PILLAR, post, column, pole**
ⓑ something shaped like a **PILLAR**
ⓒ *mining* **PILLAR**, post

a 石柱 せきちゅう stone pillar
円柱 えんちゅう column, shaft, cylinder
電柱 でんちゅう telegraph [telephone, electric] pole
門柱 もんちゅう gate post, pier
b 氷柱 ひょうちゅう icicle; block [square pillar] of ice
c 炭柱 たんちゅう coal pillar
鉱柱 こうちゅう pillar, rib
残柱 ざんちゅう pillar

❷ [also suffix] *math* cylinder
柱面 ちゅうめん cylindrical surface
直円柱 ちょくえんちゅう right cylinder

❸ something that supports like a **PILLAR**; mainstay, prop
支柱 しちゅう prop, stay, support
国家の柱石 こっかのちゅうせき pillar of state

INDEPENDENT

【ちゅう 柱】 *math* cylinder

KUN

【はしら 柱】 [also suffix] **PILLAR, post, column; prop, mainstay; adductor (of bivalves); counter for gods**
柱時計 はしらどけい grandfather's clock
大黒柱 だいこくばしら principal post, central pillar (of a house); prop, mainstay
貝柱 かいばしら adductor muscle
三柱の神 みはしらのかみ three gods

SYNONYMS

❶ **supporting structures**
柱 PILLAR → 1109
礎 FOUNDATION STONE → 1595
桁 BEAM → 1165
梁 BEAM → 3410

柏

1110

1-4-5

▶**CYPRESS**
▶**JAPANESE EMPEROR OAK**

ハク ヒャク かしわ

Ⓒ 柏 bó bǎi bò

75	Names	U67CF
木	S9-4-5	F2017

COMPOUNDS

● **CYPRESS, tree of the cypress family**
柏槙 びゃくしん juniper
松柏 しょうはく pine and cypress, evergreen; dutiful

KUN

【かしわ 柏】

① **JAPANESE EMPEROR OAK, daimyo oak**
柏木 かしわぎ Japanese emperor oak tree
柏餅 かしわもち rice cakes wrapped in oak leaves
赤芽柏 あかめがしわ Japanese mallotus, *Mallotus japonicus*

② unclassified compounds
柏手(=拍手) かしわで clapping one's hands in prayer (at a shrine)

SYNONYMS

● & 【かしわ】 **trees**
桜 CHERRY → 1168
桐 PAULOWNIA → 1173
桂 AROMATIC TREE, katsura tree → 1163
梓 CATALPA → 1207
桑 MULBERRY → 2618
漆 Japanese lacquer tree → 0863
樺 BIRCH → 1324
椛 BIRCH → 1202
梧 CHINESE PARASOL TREE → 1200
檀 SPINDLE TREE → 1385
椿 CAMELLIA → 1278
柳 WILLOW → 1115
柊 HOLLY → 1119

手 方 日 【木】 歹 火 牛 王 ネ 月

椋 *APHANANTHE ASPERA* → 1245
柾 spindle tree → 1114
槻 ZELKOVA → 1349
楢 OAK → 1287
樫 EVERGREEN OAK → 1364
柏 CYPRESS, JAPANESE EMPEROR OAK → 1110
榎 HACKBERRY → 1323
梶 PAPER MULBERRY → 1199
柘 JAPANESE BOXWOOD → 1117
楊 WILLOW → 1286
桧 JAPANESE CYPRESS → 1160
梛 *NAGEIA NAGI* → 1206
榊 SACRED SHINTO TREE → 1327
楓 MAPLE → 1280
松 PINE → 1075
杉 CRYPTOMERIA → 1027
槇 PODOCARPUS → 1330
楠 CAMPHOR TREE → 1283
樟 CAMPHOR TREE → 1351

柄

1111

1-4-5

▸**CHARACTER**
▸**HANDLE**
ヘイ がら¹ がら² え つか▲ ㊔ から
Ⓝ 柄 Ⓒ 柄 bǐng

75	Jōyō	U67C4
木	S9-4-5	F0840

COMPOUNDS

❶ [original meaning] **HANDLE, handhold, grip**
葉柄 ようへい leafstalk, stipe

❷ (ability to handle) **authority, power**
権柄 けんぺい power, authority
横柄な おうへいな overbearing, arrogant

❸ (handling of a specific subject) **topic**
話柄 わへい subject, topic (of conversation)

KUN

【がら¹ 柄】

①ⓐ [in compounds] [also suffix] **CHARACTER, nature, quality, fineness, grade; social standing, status**
ⓑ [suffix] considering the **CHARACTER** of (the matter in question), in view of; in character, appropriate to

a 人柄 ひとがら character, personality
役柄 やくがら nature [quality] of one's office, one's position
作柄 さくがら harvest, crop; quality (of an artistic production)
事柄 ことがら matter, affair, circumstances
身柄 みがら one's person; social standing
間柄 あいだがら relation, terms
家柄 いえがら social standing of a family; lineage, descent; good family
身分柄 みぶんがら social standing, status
仕事柄 しごとがら character of work; because of [in connection with] one's work

b 時局柄 じきょくがら in view of the present situation
時節柄の贈り物 じせつがらのおくりもの seasonable gift

② [in compounds] **pattern (on cloth), design, figure**
柄物 がらもの patterned cloth
花柄 はながら flower pattern

③ [in compounds] **physique, build**
小柄 こがら small build, short stature

④ [in compounds] shaft
矢柄 やがら shaft of an arrow

【がら² 柄】

①ⓐ **CHARACTER (of a person), nature, breeding**
ⓑ in **CHARACTER**, becoming

a 柄の悪い がらのわるい ill-bred
柄にも無く がらにもなく unlike one, out of one's way
彼はそんな事を言う柄じゃない かれはそんなことをいうがらじゃない It's out of character of him to say such a thing

② **pattern (on cloth), design, figure**
流行の柄 りゅうこうのがら pattern now in fashion

【え 柄】**HANDLE, crank, grip, haft; shaft**
柄の長い柄杓 えのながいひしゃく long-handled ladle
長柄 ながえ long handle, long shaft
取り柄 とりえ merit, worth, recommendable feature

【つか 柄】hilt, **HANDLE**
柄頭 つかがしら pommel

SPECIAL READINGS

柄杓▲ ひしゃく ladle, dipper, scoop

SYNONYMS

❶ & 【え】 **handles**
柄 HANDLE → 1111
手 handle → 4267
把 GRIP → 0293

【がら¹】

①ⓐ **nature and character**
性 NATURE → 0357
気 temperament → 3960
質 QUALITY → 3483
品 grade of excellence → 2795
柄 CHARACTER → 1111
格 (good) character → 1161
ⓑ **aspect**
面 side → 2590

上 from the viewpoint of → 4212
柄 considering the character of → 1111

② **pattern**
模 PATTERN (decorative design) → 1326
文 decorative pattern → 2458
柄 pattern (on cloth) → 1111
様 pattern → 1332
紋 figure → 1651

USAGE

【つか】
柄
hilt, handle
束
① hand breadth
② short support
③ bulk (of a book)

HOMOPHONES

つか 束 TIE UP → 4369

COMPOUND FORMATION

❶【事柄 ことがら】
事柄 'matter, affair, circumstances' refers to the nature (柄 がら¹ ①ⓐ) of a matter (事).

❷【取り柄 とりえ】
取り柄 'merit, worth, recommendable feature' probably comes from the idea of something (柄 え) worthwhile holding on to (取).

柑

1112
◧ 1-4-5

▶**CITRUS**
カン
Ⓒ 柑 gān

75	Names	U67D1
木	S9-4-5	F2636

COMPOUNDS

● **CITRUS, orange**
柑橘類 かんきつるい citrus fruits, oranges
金柑 きんかん kumquat
伊予柑 いよかん Iyo orange, *Citrus iyo*

SPECIAL READINGS

蜜柑 みかん mandarin orange, esp. Satsuma mandarin, *Citrus unshiu*

SYNONYMS

● **fruits and fruit trees**
桃 PEACH → 1174
榛 HAZEL → 1328
椎 CHINQUAPIN → 1249
柚 YUZU → 1123
椰 COCONUT → 1285
柑 CITRUS → 1112
橙 BITTER ORANGE → 1369
葡 GRAPE → 2902
萄 GRAPE → 2870
柿 PERSIMMON → 1118
檎 APPLE → 1386
李 PLUM → 3050
枇 LOQUAT → 1063
杷 LOQUAT → 1065
苺 STRAWBERRY → 2780
菱 water chestnut → 2879
杏 APRICOT → 3049
梅 JAPANESE APRICOT → 1159
橘 MANDARIN → 1366
栗 CHESTNUT → 3280
栃 JAPANESE HORSE CHESTNUT → 1122
梨 PEAR → 3412
蕉 PLANTAIN → 2994

枯

1113
◧ 1-4-5

▶**WITHER**
コ か(れる) か(らす)
Ⓒ 枯 kū

75	Jōyō	U67AF
木	S9-4-5	F1858

1	2	3	4	5	6	7	8	9
一	十	オ	木	木一	木十	村	枯	枯

COMPOUNDS

❶ⓐ (of plants) (dry up and die) **WITHER, die**
ⓑ (loss vigor) **WITHER, decline**
a 枯死 こし withering, dying
b 栄枯盛衰 えいこせいすい prosperity and decline, rise and fall

❷ [formerly also 涸 0629] **dry up, run dry**
枯渇 こかつ drying up, running dry; exhaustion, depletion

❸ seasoned, refined
枯淡 こたん seasoned [refined] simplicity

KUN

【かれる 枯れる】
① **WITHER, die**
枯れ葉 かれは dead [withered] leaf
枯れ木 かれき dead [withered] tree
枯れ野 かれの desolate [dreary] field
立ち枯れの たちがれの blighted, withered
夏枯れ なつがれ summer inactivity, summer slump
② be seasoned
枯れた演技 かれたえんぎ well-seasoned acting

【からす 枯らす】
① **let WITHER, blight, kill**
木枯らし こがらし cold wintry wind
② season

SYNONYMS

❶ⓐ **decay**
朽 DECAY → 1015

腐 ROT → 3921
枯 WITHER → 1113
萎 WITHER → 2872
錆 RUST → 2188

❶ⓐ die

死 DIE → 4334
萎 WITHER → 2872
没 die → 0305
亡 DECEASE → 4210
殉 DIE A MARTYR → 1177
歿 DIE → 1078
去 pass away → 2678
逝 DEPART THIS LIFE → 3850
斃 FALL DOWN DEAD → 3593
枯 WITHER → 1113

USAGE

❶【かれる】

枯れる
① wither, die
② be seasoned

涸れる
dry up, run dry, be exhausted

❷【からす】

枯らす
① let wither, blight, kill
② season

涸らす
dry up, exhaust

HOMOPHONES

かれる 涸 DRY UP → 0629
からす 涸 DRY UP → 0629

柾 1114

◧1-4-5

▸STRAIGHT GRAIN

キュウ まさ まさき ㊔ まさし

Ⓒ (国字)

75	Names	U67FE
木	S9-4-5	F3403

KUN

【まさ 柾】**STRAIGHT [regular] GRAIN of wood**

柾目(=正目) まさめ straight [regular] grain of wood

【まさき 柾】[also 正木] **spindle tree**

SYNONYMS

【まさき】

◯ **trees**

桜 CHERRY → 1168
桐 PAULOWNIA → 1173
桂 AROMATIC TREE, katsura tree → 1163
梓 CATALPA → 1207
桑 MULBERRY → 2618
漆 Japanese lacquer tree → 0863
樺 BIRCH → 1324
椛 BIRCH → 1202
梧 CHINESE PARASOL TREE → 1200
檀 SPINDLE TREE → 1385
椿 CAMELLIA → 1278
柳 WILLOW → 1115
柊 HOLLY → 1119
椋 *APHANANTHE ASPERA* → 1245
柾 spindle tree → 1114
槻 ZELKOVA → 1349
楢 OAK → 1287
樫 EVERGREEN OAK → 1364
柏 CYPRESS, JAPANESE EMPEROR OAK → 1110
榎 HACKBERRY → 1323
梶 PAPER MULBERRY → 1199
柘 JAPANESE BOXWOOD → 1117
楊 WILLOW → 1286
桧 JAPANESE CYPRESS → 1160
梛 *NAGEIA NAGI* → 1206
榊 SACRED SHINTO TREE → 1327
楓 MAPLE → 1280
松 PINE → 1075
杉 CRYPTOMERIA → 1027
槙 PODOCARPUS → 1330
楠 CAMPHOR TREE → 1283
樟 CAMPHOR TREE → 1351

HOMOPHONES

まさき 正木 → 4296, 4261

柳 1115

◧1-4-5

▸WILLOW

リュウ やなぎ ㊔ やぎ やなき

Ⓝ 栁 桺 Ⓒ 柳 liǔ

75	Jōyō	U67F3
木	S9-4-5	F0919

一 十 才 木 木′ 杉 杉 柳 柳
1 2 3 4 5 6 7 8 9

COMPOUNDS

❶ [original meaning] **WILLOW**

蒲柳 ほりゅう purple willow; infirmity, delicate constitution

花柳 かりゅう geisha girls, courtesans; red-light district

花柳界 かりゅうかい red-light district

❷ as slender or graceful as a **WILLOW**

柳眉 りゅうび beautiful eyebrows

❸ unclassified compounds

川柳 せんりゅう short humorous verse, satirical poem

KUN

【やなぎ 柳】**WILLOW**

柳腰 やなぎごし slim waist

SYNONYMS

❶ trees

桜 CHERRY → 1168
桐 PAULOWNIA → 1173
桂 AROMATIC TREE, katsura tree → 1163
梓 CATALPA → 1207
桑 MULBERRY → 2618
漆 Japanese lacquer tree → 0863
樺 BIRCH → 1324
椛 BIRCH → 1202
梧 CHINESE PARASOL TREE → 1200
檀 SPINDLE TREE → 1385
椿 CAMELLIA → 1278
柳 WILLOW → 1115
柊 HOLLY → 1119
椋 *APHANANTHE ASPERA* → 1245
柾 spindle tree → 1114
槻 ZELKOVA → 1349
楢 OAK → 1287
樫 EVERGREEN OAK → 1364
柏 CYPRESS, JAPANESE EMPEROR OAK → 1110
榎 HACKBERRY → 1323
梶 PAPER MULBERRY → 1199
柘 JAPANESE BOXWOOD → 1117
楊 WILLOW → 1286
桧 JAPANESE CYPRESS → 1160
梛 *NAGEIA NAGI* → 1206
榊 SACRED SHINTO TREE → 1327
楓 MAPLE → 1280
松 PINE → 1075
杉 CRYPTOMERIA → 1027
槙 PODOCARPUS → 1330
楠 CAMPHOR TREE → 1283
樟 CAMPHOR TREE → 1351

COMPOUND FORMATION

❶【花柳 かりゅう】

花柳 'geisha girls, etc.' literally "blossoms (花) and willows (柳 ❶)," is a poetic term for courtesan.

❷【川柳 せんりゅう】

川柳 'short humorous verse, satirical poem' derives from its originator's name and is unrelated to its constituent components 柳 'willow' and 川 'river'.

柵

1116

◧ 1-4-5

▸FENCE

サク しがらみ▲

Ⓒ 栅 zhà shān

75	Jōyō	U67F5
木	S9-4-5	F2253

Stroke order: 1 一 2 † 3 オ 4 木 5 木 6 杤 7 柵 8 柵 9 柵

COMPOUNDS

● **FENCE, palisade, stockade, paling**

柵状組織 さくじょうそしき palisade layer
鉄柵 てっさく iron fence

INDEPENDENT

【さく 柵】[also suffix] **FENCE with spaced posts, railing**

KUN

【しがらみ 柵】weir; bonds, fetters

SYNONYMS

● **fences and walls**

壁 WALL → 3601
塀 FENCE (for screening) → 0677
垣 FENCE (for partitioning) → 0416
牆 FENCE (for partitioning) → 1393
柵 FENCE (with spaced pickets) → 1116
堵 FENCE (made of earth) → 0682
囲い enclosure → 3807
欄 railing → 1419

柘

1117

◧ 1-4-5

▸JAPANESE BOXWOOD

シャ つげ ㊔ つく

Ⓒ 柘 zhè

75	Names	U67D8
木	S9-4-5	F0000

KUN

【つげ 柘】[usu. 柘植 or 黄楊] **JAPANESE BOXWOOD**

SPECIAL READINGS

柘榴× (=石榴×) ざくろ pomegranate
柘植 つげ [also 黄楊, sometimes also 柘] Japanese boxwood

SYNONYMS

【つげ】

○ **trees**

桜 CHERRY → 1168
桐 PAULOWNIA → 1173
桂 AROMATIC TREE, katsura tree → 1163
梓 CATALPA → 1207
桑 MULBERRY → 2618
漆 Japanese lacquer tree → 0863
樺 BIRCH → 1324
椛 BIRCH → 1202
梧 CHINESE PARASOL TREE → 1200
檀 SPINDLE TREE → 1385
椿 CAMELLIA → 1278
柳 WILLOW → 1115
柊 HOLLY → 1119
椋 *APHANANTHE ASPERA* → 1245
柾 spindle tree → 1114
槻 ZELKOVA → 1349

楢 OAK → 1287
樫 EVERGREEN OAK → 1364
柏 CYPRESS, JAPANESE EMPEROR OAK → 1110
榎 HACKBERRY → 1323
梶 PAPER MULBERRY → 1199
柘 JAPANESE BOXWOOD → 1117
楊 WILLOW → 1286
桧 JAPANESE CYPRESS → 1160
梛 *NAGEIA NAGI* → 1206
榊 SACRED SHINTO TREE → 1327
楓 MAPLE → 1280
松 PINE → 1075
杉 CRYPTOMERIA → 1027
槙 PODOCARPUS → 1330
楠 CAMPHOR TREE → 1283
樟 CAMPHOR TREE → 1351

HOMOPHONES

つげ
黄楊 → 3116, 1286
柘植 → 1117, 1247

柿

1118

1-4-5

▶**PERSIMMON**

シ˄ かき ㊔ かつ かげ

Ⓒ 柿 shì

75	Jōyō	U67FF
木	S9-4-5	F2122

COMPOUNDS

● **PERSIMMON**
熟柿 じゅくし ripe persimmon

KUN

【かき 柿】**kaki, Japanese PERSIMMON**
柿渋 かきしぶ astringent persimmon juice
柿色 かきいろ reddish-brown; yellowish-brown
干し柿 ほしがき dried persimmons
渋柿 しぶがき puckery persimmon

SYNONYMS

● **fruits and fruit trees**
桃 PEACH → 1174
榛 HAZEL → 1328
椎 CHINQUAPIN → 1249
柚 YUZU → 1123
椰 COCONUT → 1285
柑 CITRUS → 1112
橙 BITTER ORANGE → 1369
葡 GRAPE → 2902
萄 GRAPE → 2870
柿 PERSIMMON → 1118
檎 APPLE → 1386
李 PLUM → 3050
枇 LOQUAT → 1063
杷 LOQUAT → 1065
苺 STRAWBERRY → 2780
菱 water chestnut → 2879
杏 APRICOT → 3049
梅 JAPANESE APRICOT → 1159
橘 MANDARIN → 1366
栗 CHESTNUT → 3280
栃 JAPANESE HORSE CHESTNUT → 1122
梨 PEAR → 3412
蕉 PLANTAIN → 2994

NOTE

★ In print, 柿 is almost indistinguishable from another character, 柹× こけら 'wood shavings' (which is not listed in this dictionary). The right-hand element of 柿 かき is 市 いち (亠 + 巾), whereas in 柹× こけら it is 巾 with an intersecting 一.

柊

1119

1-4-5

▶**HOLLY**

シュウ シュ ひいらぎ ㊔ ひらぎ くき

Ⓝ 柊 Ⓒ 柊 zhōng

75	Names	U67CA
木	S9-4-5	F0000

KUN

【ひいらぎ 柊】**HOLLY, *Osumanthus ilicifolius***

SYNONYMS

【ひいらぎ】

○ **trees**
桜 CHERRY → 1168
桐 PAULOWNIA → 1173
桂 AROMATIC TREE, katsura tree → 1163
梓 CATALPA → 1207
桑 MULBERRY → 2618
漆 Japanese lacquer tree → 0863
樺 BIRCH → 1324
椛 BIRCH → 1202
梧 CHINESE PARASOL TREE → 1200
檀 SPINDLE TREE → 1385
椿 CAMELLIA → 1278
柳 WILLOW → 1115
柊 HOLLY → 1119
椋 *APHANANTHE ASPERA* → 1245
柾 spindle tree → 1114
槻 ZELKOVA → 1349
楢 OAK → 1287
樫 EVERGREEN OAK → 1364
柏 CYPRESS, JAPANESE EMPEROR OAK → 1110
榎 HACKBERRY → 1323
梶 PAPER MULBERRY → 1199
柘 JAPANESE BOXWOOD → 1117

楊 WILLOW → 1286
桧 JAPANESE CYPRESS → 1160
梛 *NAGEIA NAGI* → 1206
榊 SACRED SHINTO TREE → 1327
楓 MAPLE → 1280
松 PINE → 1075
杉 CRYPTOMERIA → 1027
槙 PODOCARPUS → 1330
楠 CAMPHOR TREE → 1283
樟 CAMPHOR TREE → 1351

相

1120
◧ 1-4-5

▶**PHASE**
▶**MUTUAL**
▶**MINISTER**

ソウ ショウ あい- ㊔ すけ
Ⓒ 相 xiāng xiàng

109	Jōyō-3	U76F8
目	S9-5-4	F0111

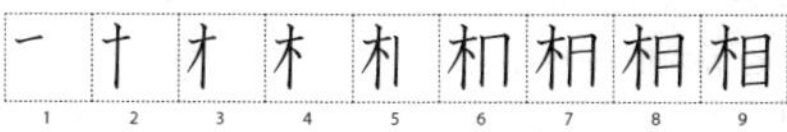

COMPOUNDS

❶ⓐ (outer appearance or state, esp. as indication of characteristic essence) **PHASE, looks, appearance, aspect, state, condition**
ⓑ *chem, astron, phys* **PHASE**
ⓒ *elec* **PHASE**; counter for phases
ⓓ *geol* facies
ⓔ [also suffix] *gram* aspect (of verbs)

a 様相 ようそう aspect, phase, condition
時代相 じだいそう phases of the times
貧相な ひんそうな poor-looking
寝相 ねぞう one's sleeping posture
色相 しきそう color phase
世相 せそう phases [aspect] of life, social conditions
真相 しんそう truth, facts, real situation
諸相 しょそう various aspects, various phases
実相 じっそう real state of affairs

b 位相 いそう phase, topology
気相 きそう gaseous phase
月相 げっそう phase of the moon

c 分相機 ぶんそうき phase splitter
三相電動機 さんそうでんどうき three-phase motor

d 層相 そうそう facies

e 進行相 しんこうそう progressive aspect

❷ⓐ **physiognomy**
ⓑ read a person's physiognomy; [original meaning] observe carefully

a 人相 にんそう looks, physiognomy
手相 てそう palmistry, lines of palm
骨相 こっそう physique
家相 かそう physiognomy of a house

b 観相学 かんそうがく physiognomy

❸ **MUTUAL, reciprocal; mutually**
相互の そうごの mutual, reciprocal
相談 そうだん consultation
相当する そうとうする correspond to, be proportionate; be suitable for, become
相違 そうい difference, disparity
相対的な そうたいてきな relative
相応な そうおうな suitable, fit; becoming; adequate
相殺 そうさい offset, cancellation
相関 そうかん mutual relationship, correlation
相似 そうじ similarity, resemblance
相思相愛 そうしそうあい mutual love

❹ [also suffix] **MINISTER (of state), councilor**
首相 しゅしょう prime minister
蔵相 ぞうしょう Minister of Finance
文相 ぶんしょう Minister of Education, Science and Culture
外相 がいしょう Minister of Foreign Affairs
労働相 ろうどうしょう Minister of Labor

❺ **succeed to, inherit**
相続 そうぞく succession; inheritance
相伝 そうでん inheritance

❻ⓐ **used phonetically for *sō***
ⓑ **function word indicating appearance**

a 相場 そうば market price; estimation

b 可哀相な かわいそうな poor, pitiable, pathetic
悲し相な顔 かなしそうなかお sad-looking face

❼ abbrev. of 相模 さがみ, old name for Kanagawa Prefecture
相鉄 そうてつ Sagami Railway

INDEPENDENT

【そう 相】 aspect, **PHASE**; features; physiognomy; phase (→ ❶ⓑ & ❶ⓒ); *geol* facies; aspect (of verbs)
相を見る そうをみる read (a person's) physiognomy
険悪の相 けんあくのそう a wild look

KUN

【あい- 相-】 [also prefix]
①ⓐ **each other, MUTUALly**
ⓑ **together**

a 相性 あいしょう affinity, congeniality
相槌を打つ あいづちをうつ make (agreeable) responses (in a conversation)
相手 あいて partner; opponent

b 相乗り あいのり riding together
相合傘で あいあいがさで sharing the same umbrella
相棒 あいぼう pal, mate, companion

② **emphatic verbal prefix**
相変わらず あいかわらず as usual, as before
相次いで あいついで in succession

手 方 日 【木】 歹 火 牛 王 ネ 月

SPECIAL READINGS

相撲 すもう sumo wrestling
相応しい▲ ふさわしい suitable, appropriate

SYNONYMS

❶ⓐ appearance
容 APPEARANCE →2832
貌 APPEARANCE →1958
姿 FIGURE →3264
相 PHASE →1120
体 FORM (outer appearance) →0080
色 COLOR →2522
風 air →3730

❶ⓐ states and situations
態 STATE →3529
調 TONE →1973
様 MODE →1332
相 PHASE →1120
状 CONDITION →0322
況 CONDITIONS →0395
景 business conditions →3118
勢 course of events →3542
境 SITUATION →0835
局 current situation →3800
情 ACTUAL CONDITIONS →0583
訳 circumstances →1865

❸ mutual
相 MUTUAL →1120
互 RECIPROCAL →4245

❹ high officials
相 MINISTER →1120
宰 chief minister →2829
卿 STATE MINISTER →0769

❻ⓐ phonetic [s]/[sh]
沙 phonetic [sha] →0311
刹 phonetic [setsu] →1620
遮 phonetic [sha] →3916
叉 phonetic [sha] →4194
世 phonetic [se] →4308
須 phonetic [shu] →0700
修 phonetic [shu] →0138
西 phonetic [su] →4333
相 phonetic [sō] →1120
薩 phonetic [satsu] →3016

USAGE

【あい】

相-
[also prefix]
①ⓐ each other, mutually
ⓑ together
② emphatic verbal prefix

合い
① [in compounds]
ⓐ fitting
ⓑ prearranged, agreed upon
② [also 間] (space between) interval, space, opening
③ [also 間]
ⓐ (time between) interval, intermission
ⓑ between seasons
④ [also 間] [in compounds] mixed (blood)

間
[also 合い or 合]
① (space between) interval, space, opening
②ⓐ [also prefix] (time between) interval, intermission
ⓑ between seasons
③ [in compounds] mixed (blood)

HOMOPHONES

あい-
合 COMBINE →2511
間 INTERVAL →4122

COMPOUND FORMATION

❶【相当 そうとう】
相当する 'correspond to, etc.' means to correspond to (当) each other (相 ❸).

❷【相対 そうたい】
相対 'relativity' originally meant to face (対) each other (相 ❸).

❸【相場 そうば】
相場 'market price; estimation' consists of 相 ❻ⓐ, apparently used phonetically without relation to its meaning, and 場, in this case used in the sense of market.

柢

1121

◧ 1-4-5

▶BOTTOM
テイ
Ⓒ 柢 dǐ

75	Non-Jōyō	U67E2
木	S9-4-5	F0000

COMPOUNDS

ⓐ [now replaced by 底 3827] **BOTTOM, basis, origin**
ⓑ [original meaning, now archaic] root
ab 根柢 こんてい root, basis, foundation

SYNONYMS

ⓐ bottoms and bases
底 BOTTOM →3827
柢 BOTTOM →1121
下 lower part →4186
基 BASE →3312
礎 FOUNDATION STONE →1595
麓 FOOT OF MOUNTAIN →3494
磐 BEDROCK →3534

盤 bedrock → 3533
床 BED → 3805

栃

1122
◧ 1-4-5

▶**JAPANESE HORSE CHESTNUT**
とち とちのき▲
Ⓝ 橡 杤 Ⓒ (国字)

75	Jōyō	U6803
木	S9-4-5	F2347

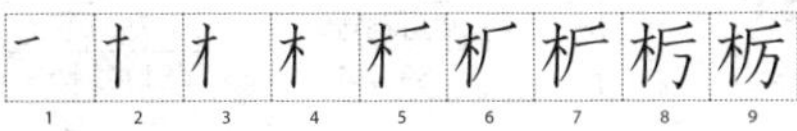

KUN

【とち 栃】JAPANESE HORSE CHESTNUT
栃の木 とちのき Japanese horse chestnut
栃木県 とちぎけん Tochigi Prefecture
栃栗毛 とちくりげ dark chestnut color (said of horses)

【とちのき 栃】JAPANESE HORSE CHESTNUT

SYNONYMS

【とち】
○ **fruits and fruit trees**
桃 PEACH → 1174
榛 HAZEL → 1328
椎 CHINQUAPIN → 1249
柚 YUZU → 1123
椰 COCONUT → 1285
柑 CITRUS → 1112
橙 BITTER ORANGE → 1369
葡 GRAPE → 2902
萄 GRAPE → 2870
柿 PERSIMMON → 1118
檎 APPLE → 1386
李 PLUM → 3050
枇 LOQUAT → 1063
杷 LOQUAT → 1065
苺 STRAWBERRY → 2780
菱 water chestnut → 2879
杏 APRICOT → 3049
梅 JAPANESE APRICOT → 1159
橘 MANDARIN → 1366
栗 CHESTNUT → 3280
栃 JAPANESE HORSE CHESTNUT → 1122
梨 PEAR → 3412
蕉 PLANTAIN → 2994

柚

1123
◧ 1-4-5

▶**YUZU**
ユウ ユ ゆず
Ⓒ 柚 yòu yóu

75	Names	U67DA
木	S9-4-5	F3038

COMPOUNDS

● (aromatic Japanese citron) **YUZU**
柚子 ゆず [also 柚] yuzu
柚餅子 ゆべし sweet yuzu dumpling
晩白柚 ばんぺいゆ pomelo

KUN

【ゆず 柚】[also 柚子] (aromatic Japanese citron) **YUZU**
柚湯 ゆずゆ yuzu hot bath

SYNONYMS

● & 【ゆず】 **fruits and fruit trees**
桃 PEACH → 1174
榛 HAZEL → 1328
椎 CHINQUAPIN → 1249
柚 YUZU → 1123
椰 COCONUT → 1285
柑 CITRUS → 1112
橙 BITTER ORANGE → 1369
葡 GRAPE → 2902
萄 GRAPE → 2870
柿 PERSIMMON → 1118
檎 APPLE → 1386
李 PLUM → 3050
枇 LOQUAT → 1063
杷 LOQUAT → 1065
苺 STRAWBERRY → 2780
菱 water chestnut → 2879
杏 APRICOT → 3049
梅 JAPANESE APRICOT → 1159
橘 MANDARIN → 1366
栗 CHESTNUT → 3280
栃 JAPANESE HORSE CHESTNUT → 1122
梨 PEAR → 3412
蕉 PLANTAIN → 2994

HOMOPHONES

ゆず 柚子 → 1123, 4196

柱

1124
◧ 1-4-5

▶**PILLAR**
チュウ はしら

75	Nonstandard	U67F1
木	S9-4-5	F0000

traditional form → see 柱 at 1109

柄

1125
◧ 1-4-5

▶**CHARACTER**
▶**HANDLE**
ヘイ がら[1] がら[2] え つか ㊔ から

75	Nonstandard	U67C4
木	S9-4-5	F0000

traditional form → see 柄 at 1111

1

手 方 日 【木】 歹 火 牛 王 ネ 月

栁

▸WILLOW

リュウ やなぎ ㊔ やぎ やなき

1126

1-4-5

75	Nonstandard	U6801
木	S9-4-5	F0000

traditional form → see 柳 at 1115

枩

▸PINE

ショウ まつ

1127

1-4-5

75	Nonstandard	U67D7
木	S9-4-5	F0000

traditional form → see 松 at 1075

柊

▸HOLLY

シュウ シュ ひいらぎ ㊔ ひらぎ くき

1128

1-4-5

75	Nonstandard	U67CA
木	S9-4-5	F0000

traditional form → see 柊 at 1119

様

▸MODE
▸FORMAL TITLE

ヨウ さま ざま

1129

1-4-5

75	Nonstandard	U69D8
木	S9-4-5	F0000

handwritten form → see 様 at 1332

枇

incorrect stroke-count
➡ see 1-4-4: 木 at 1063

1-4-5

殆

▸ALMOST

タイ ほとん(ど) ㊔ ちか

ⓒ 殆 dài

1130

1-4-5

78	Names	U6B86
歹	S9-4-5	F2324

COMPOUNDS

● **dangerous, precarious**

危殆 きたい danger, jeopardy, peril

KUN

【ほとんど 殆ど】

ⓐ **ALMOST, nearly, mostly**

ⓑ [in negative constructions] **hardly, barely**

a 殆どの人 ほとんどのひと most people

b 殆ど知らない ほとんどしらない hardly [barely] know, know next to nothing

SYNONYMS

● **danger**

危 DANGEROUS → 3965
殆 dangerous → 1130
険 DANGER → 0658

【ほとんど】

ⓐ **almost**

殆ど ALMOST → 1130
瀕 ON THE VERGE OF → 0994
甫めて BARELY → 4363
辛い bare → 2531

畑

▸FIELD

はた はたけ -ばたけ

ⓒ 畑 tián (国字)

1131

1-4-5

102	Jōyō-3	U7551
田	S9-5-4	F1365

1	2	3	4	5	6	7	8	9
丶	丷	少	火	灯	灯	畑	畑	畑

KUN

【はた 畑】 [formerly also 畠] **(plowed or cultivated) FIELD, farm, vegetable garden, plantation**

畑地 はたち farmland
畑作 はたさく dry field farming, dry field crop
田畑 たはた(=でんぱた) fields and rice paddies

【はたけ 畑】 [formerly also 畠]

① **(plowed or cultivated) FIELD, farm, vegetable garden, plantation**

畑を作る はたけをつくる cultivate a field, farm

② one's **FIELD**, one's specialty

畑違いだ はたけちがいだ be out of one's field

【-ばたけ -畑】

① [also suffix] **FIELD, farm, vegetable garden, plantation**

花畑 はなばたけ flower garden
段段畑 だんだんばたけ terraced fields, terraced farm
コーヒー畑 こーひーばたけ coffee plantation

② [suffix] one's **FIELD**, one's specialty

技術畑の人 ぎじゅつばたけのひと man in the technical line, career technician

SYNONYMS

【はた】

○ & 【はたけ】 ① **cultivated fields**

畑 FIELD → 1131
畠 FIELD → 3186
牧 PASTURE → 1083
園 GARDEN → 3914
田 RICE FIELD → 3775
佃 CULTIVATED RICE FIELD → 0066
圃 VEGETABLE GARDEN → 3871

USAGE

❶ 【はた】

畑

[formerly also 畠] (plowed or cultivated) field, farm, vegetable garden, plantation

畠

[now usu. 畑] same as 畑

❷【はたけ】

畑

[formerly also 畠]

① (plowed or cultivated) field, farm, vegetable garden, plantation

② one's field, one's specialty

畠

[now usu. 畑] same as 畑

❸【-ばたけ】

-畑

① [also suffix] field, farm, vegetable garden, plantation

② [suffix] one's field, one's specialty

-畠

[now usu. 畑]

① [also suffix] field, farm, vegetable garden, plantation

② [suffix] one's field, one's specialty

HOMOPHONES

はた 畠 FIELD → 3186

はたけ 畠 FIELD → 3186

-ばたけ 畠 FIELD → 3186

炮

1132

◧ 1-4-5

▶**ROAST**

ホウ

Ⓒ 炮 pào páo bāo

86	Non-Jōyō	U70AE
火	S9-4-5	F0000

COMPOUNDS

❶ [original meaning] **ROAST, bake**

炮烙×(=焙×烙×) ほうろく parching pan, baking pan

❷ [now always 砲 1479] cannon

鉄炮 てっぽう firearm

SYNONYMS

❶ **burn**

焼 BURN → 1256

燃 BURN (undergo combustion) → 1375

焚く BURN (build a fire) → 3450

焦 SCORCH → 3444

灼 SCORCH → 1036

炮 ROAST → 1132

燎 SET ON FIRE → 1376

牲

1133

◧ 1-4-5

▶**SACRIFICE**

セイ

Ⓒ 牲 shēng

93	Jōyō	U7272
牛	S9-4-5	F1715

1	2	3	4	5	6	7	8	9
ノ	𠂉	牛	牛	牜	牜	牪	牲	牲

COMPOUNDS

❶ **SACRIFICE**

犠牲 ぎせい sacrifice

❷ [original meaning, now archaic] **sacrificial animal, SACRIFICE**

SYNONYMS

❶ **sacrifice**

犠 SACRIFICE → 1394

牲 SACRIFICE → 1133

牴

1134

◧ 1-4-5

▶**COLLIDE WITH**

テイ

Ⓒ 抵 dǐ

93	Non-Jōyō	U7274
牛	S9-4-5	F0000

COMPOUNDS

● [now replaced by 抵 0377] **COLLIDE WITH, touch**

牴触 ていしょく conflict; contradiction; incompatibility

SYNONYMS

● **collide**

衝 COLLIDE → 0893

牴 COLLIDE WITH → 1134

觝 COLLIDE WITH → 1892

突 DASH → 2772

当たる HIT → 2701

珍

1135

◧ 1-4-5

▶**RARE**

チン めずら(しい) ㊔ うず よし

Ⓝ 珎 Ⓒ 珍 zhēn

96	Jōyō	U73CD
王	S9-4-5	F1274

1	2	3	4	5	6	7	8	9
一	T	干	王	玐	玠	玪	珍	珍

COMPOUNDS

❶ⓐ [original meaning] (of infrequent occurrence or unusual excellence) **RARE, infrequent, precious**

ⓑ [also prefix] **curious, strange, queer, odd, funny**

a 珍味 ちんみ food of delicate flavor, delicacy

珍品 ちんぴん rare article, curio

珍客 ちんきゃく unexpected (but welcome) visitor

b 珍妙な ちんみょうな queer, odd, fantastic

珍奇な ちんきな novel, curious; rare; strange

珍現象 ちんげんしょう strange phenomenon

珍紛漢紛 ちんぷんかんぷん gibberish, unintelligible speech

❷ value highly, treasure

珍重する ちんちょうする value highly, treasure

INDEPENDENT

【ちん 珍】**RARE** phenomenon

珍中の珍 ちんちゅうのちん black swan; rarity
珍な ちんな curious, strange, marvelous, queer; rare

KUN

【めずらしい 珍しい】**RARE, infrequent, unusual; uncommon, new, novel; precious (due to the rarity of the thing)**
珍しさ めずらしさ rarity; novelty
珍しがる めずらしがる think (it) a curiosity
物珍しげに ものめずらしげに curiously, with curious eyes

SYNONYMS

❶ⓐ **rare**
珍 RARE → 1135
希 RARE → 2543
稀 RARE → 1523
ⓑ **abnormal**
変 ABNORMAL → 2569
奇 UNUSUAL → 2756
畸 UNUSUAL → 1533
怪 MYSTERIOUS → 0354
妖 MYSTERIOUS → 0282
妙 strange → 0280
異 not ordinary → 3195
珍 curious → 1135

珀

▶**AMBER**
ハク
Ⓒ 珀 pò

1136
1-4-5

96	Names	U73C0
王	S9-4-5	F3410

COMPOUNDS

● **AMBER**
琥珀 こはく amber

SYNONYMS

● **precious stones**
玉 GEM → 4289
珂 WHITE AGATE → 1137
璧 DISK-SHAPED JEWEL → 3608
琥 AMBER → 1261
珀 AMBER → 1136
珠 PEARL → 1183
瑛 TRANSPARENT GEM → 1259
瑠 LAPIS LAZULI → 1342
璃 GLASSY SUBSTANCE → 1358
晶 CRYSTAL → 3122
玖 beautiful black jewel → 1041
琉 LAPIS LAZULI → 1221
琳 BEAUTIFUL GEM → 1262

珂

▶**WHITE AGATE**
カ
Ⓒ 珂 kē

1137
1-4-5

96	Names	U73C2
王	S9-4-5	F2989

COMPOUNDS

❶ [original meaning, now archaic] **WHITE AGATE**, jewel
❷ **Chinese mactra, *Mactra chinensis***
馬珂貝(=馬鹿貝) ばかがい Chinese mactra, *Mactra chinensis*

SYNONYMS

❶ **precious stones**
玉 GEM → 4289
珂 WHITE AGATE → 1137
璧 DISK-SHAPED JEWEL → 3608
琥 AMBER → 1261
珀 AMBER → 1136
珠 PEARL → 1183
瑛 TRANSPARENT GEM → 1259
瑠 LAPIS LAZULI → 1342
璃 GLASSY SUBSTANCE → 1358
晶 CRYSTAL → 3122
玖 beautiful black jewel → 1041
琉 LAPIS LAZULI → 1221
琳 BEAUTIFUL GEM → 1262

珈

▶**COFFEE**
カ
Ⓒ 珈 jiā

1138
1-4-5

96	Names	U73C8
王	S9-4-5	F3293

COMPOUNDS

❶ **used phonetically for *ka, kō* or *ko*, esp. in the sense of COFFEE**
珈琲× こーひー coffee
❷ [original meaning, now obsolete] ornamental hairpin

SYNONYMS

❶ **drinks**
汁 JUICE, SOUP → 0227
乳 MILK → 1823
酒 ALCOHOLIC DRINK → 0532
茶 TEA → 2808
珈 COFFEE → 1138
醇 UNDILUTED WINE → 2001
酎 SHOCHU → 1852
❶ **phonetic [k]/[g]**
迦 PHONETIC [ka] → 3982
珈 phonetic [kō] → 1138
伽 PHONETIC [ga] → 0074
瓦 phonetic [ga] → 4288

手 方 日 木 歹 火 牛 【王】 ネ 月

祇 phonetic [gi] → 1459

玲

▶TINKLING OF JADES
レイ ㊔ あきら りょう たま すず
Ⓒ 玲 líng

1139
1-4-5

96	Names	U73B2
王	S9-4-5	F2270

COMPOUNDS

❶ [archaic] **TINKLING OF JADES**, sound of jewels
玲玲 れいれい tinkling of jades

❷ brilliant, translucent, clear and bright
玲瓏×たる れいろうたる brilliant, translucent, clear; sweetly ringing (as tinklings of jades)

SYNONYMS

❶ **kinds of sound**
音 SOUND → 2570
声 VOICE → 2724
響 reverberation → 3573
韻 melodious tone → 2279
玲 TINKLING OF JADES → 1139

珊

▶CORAL
サン
Ⓒ 珊 shān

1140
1-4-5

96	Names	U73CA
王	S9-4-5	F2355

COMPOUNDS

● CORAL
珊瑚 さんご coral

珎

▶RARE
チン めずら(しい) ㊔ うず よし

1141
1-4-5

96	Nonstandard	U73CE
王	S9-4-5	F0000

traditional form → see 珍 at 1135

祢

▶FATHER'S MAUSOLEUM
デイ ネ ㊔ や
Ⓝ 禰 禰 Ⓒ 祢 mí

1142
1-4-5

113	Names	U7962
ネ	S9-4-5	F0000

COMPOUNDS

❶ [original meaning, now rare] **FATHER'S MAUSOLEUM**
祢廟 でいびょう father's mausoleum
祢祖 でいそ mausoleums of one's father and grandfather; one's late father and late grandfather

❷ **unclassified compounds**
祢宜 ねぎ Shinto priest, esp. senior priest
宿祢 すくね courtesy title after names of nobility: Lord; third highest of eight hereditary titles in ancient Japan

SYNONYMS

❶ **graves**
墓 GRAVE → 2930
墳 TUMULUS → 0887
陵 IMPERIAL MAUSOLEUM → 0660
廟 MAUSOLEUM → 3935
祢 FATHER'S MAUSOLEUM → 1142
塚 grave mound → 0675

神

▶GOD
▶MIND
シン ジン かみ かん- こう- ㊔ かむ か みわ
Ⓝ 神 Ⓒ 神 shén

1143
1-4-5

113	Jōyō-3	U795E
ネ	S9-4-5	F0160

1	2	3	4	5	6	7	8	9
丶	ラ	ネ	ネ	ネ	祁	神	神	神

COMPOUNDS

❶ⓐ **GOD, God, deity, spirit**
ⓑ **Shinto deity, *kami***
a 神学 しんがく theology
神父 しんぷ priest, Father
神仏 しんぶつ gods and Buddha; Shinto and Buddhism
多神教 たしんきょう polytheism
b 神宮 じんぐう Shinto shrine; Grand Shrine at Ise
神道 しんとう Shinto, the Way of the Gods
神社 じんじゃ Shinto shrine

❷ **divine, sacred, GODly, supernatural, mysterious**
神聖な しんせいな holy, sacred, divine
神話 しんわ myth, mythology
神木 しんぼく sacred tree
神童 しんどう child prodigy
神秘的な しんぴてきな mysterious

❸ **MIND, consciousness, spirit, soul**
神経 しんけい nerve; sensitivity; worry
神髄(=真髄) しんずい essence, quintessence, soul
精神 せいしん mind, soul, heart; intention, motive; the spirit (of something)
失神する しっしんする lose consciousness, faint
色神 しきしん color sense (ability of color discrimination)

❹ Kobe
阪神 はんしん Hanshin, Osaka and Kobe

INDEPENDENT

【しん 神】**MIND**, spirit; divine power; abbrev. of 神道 しんとう: Shinto

妙技神に入る みょうぎしんにいる be divinely skilled

KUN

【かみ 神】**GOD, God, the Lord; deity; Shinto deity, *kami;*** [in compounds] **divine**

神様 かみさま god, God
神業 かみわざ providence, superhuman feat
神風 かみかぜ providential [divine] wind; suicide plane, kamikaze
死に神 しにがみ god of death

【かん- 神-】**GOD**

神主 かんぬし Shinto priest

【こう- 神-】**GOD**

神神しい こうごうしい divine, solemn

SPECIAL READINGS

お神酒 おみき sacred wine [sake]; sake
神楽 かぐら sacred (Shinto) music and dancing
神輿(=御輿)▲ みこし portable shrine, sacred palanquin
神奈川県 かながわけん Kanagawa Prefecture

SYNONYMS

❶ god

神 GOD → 1143
帝 the Supreme Being → 2573
天 HEAVEN → 4250
主 Lord → 2437
祇 EARTHLY GOD → 1459

❷ holy

聖 HOLY → 3509
神 divine → 1143
霊 miraculous → 3480

❸ psyche

心 HEART → 0011
霊 SPIRIT (soul) → 3480
魂 SOUL, spirit → 1346
魄 SOUL → 1570
腹 heart → 1308
衷 INNER HEART → 2600
襟 inner mind → 1599
胸 breast → 1187
懐 BOSOM → 0942
神 MIND → 1143
気 SPIRIT (consciousness) → 3960
精 SPIRIT (mind) → 1729

❹ Kansai cities

阪 OSAKA → 0321
神 Kobe → 1143
京 KYOTO → 2546
洛 KYOTO → 0463

手 方 日 木 歹 火 牛 王 【ネ】 月

COMPOUND FORMATION

【神経 しんけい】

神経 'nerve, etc.' is that which passes through (経) the body and mind (神 ❸).

祝

1144

1-4-5

▶CELEBRATE

シュク シュウ いわ(う) ㊔ はじめ ほうり のり とき

Ⓝ 祝 Ⓒ 祝 zhù

113	Jōyō-4	U795D
ネ	S9-4-5	F1339

Stroke order: 1–9

COMPOUNDS

❶ⓐ CELEBRATE
ⓑ congratulate, felicitate

a 祝賀 しゅくが celebration; congratulation
祝日 しゅくじつ holiday, festival day
慶祝 けいしゅく celebration, congratulation
b 祝言 しゅうげん wedding
祝儀 しゅうぎ celebration; congratulatory gift; tip
祝電 しゅくでん congratulatory telegram

❷ⓐ bless, pray, express good wishes
ⓑ prayer

a 祝福 しゅくふく blessing
b 祝祷 しゅくとう benediction, blessing (in Christianity)

❸ [original meaning] **priest** (in ancient religions)

巫×祝 ふしゅく ancient priest; shrine maiden

INDEPENDENT

【しゅく 祝】celebration; congratulation
【しゅくする 祝する】**CELEBRATE**; congratulate; wish good luck

KUN

【いわう 祝う】**CELEBRATE, commemorate; congratulate, felicitate**

祝い いわい celebration; congratulation
祝い酒 いわいざけ celebratory drink
人の成功を祝う ひとのせいこうをいわう congratulate a person on his [her] success

SPECIAL READINGS

祝詞 のりと Shinto ritual prayer

SYNONYMS

❶ celebrating and congratulating

祝 CELEBRATE → 1144
慶 FELICITATION → 3936
賀 CONGRATULATE → 3212
寿 CONGRATULATIONS → 4372

祖

▶ANCESTOR

ソ

Ⓝ 祖 Ⓒ 祖 zǔ

1145

◧1-4-5

113	Jōyō-5	U7956
ネ	S9-4-5	F0901

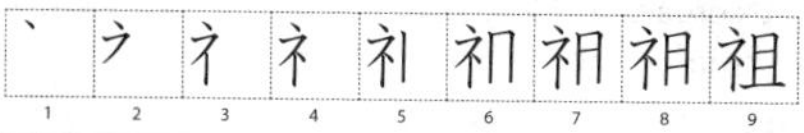

COMPOUNDS

❶ⓐ ANCESTOR, forefather

ⓑ grandparent

a 祖先 そせん ancestor, forefather

祖国 そこく one's native country

b 祖父母 そふぼ grandparents

先祖 せんぞ forefather, ancestor

❷ founder, originator

開祖 かいそ founder, originator

元祖 がんそ originator, pioneer

教祖 きょうそ founder of a religion, head of a sect

INDEPENDENT

【そ 祖】forefather, **ANCESTOR**; founder, originator, father

医学の祖 いがくのそ founder of medical science

SPECIAL READINGS

お祖父さん▲ おじいさん grandfather

お祖母さん▲ おばあさん grandmother

祐

▶DIVINE HELP

ユウ ウ ㊔ すけ さち ひろし ゆたか たすく まさ ひろ よし

Ⓝ 祐 Ⓒ 祐 yòu

1146

◧1-4-5

113	Names	U7950
ネ	S9-4-5	F1611

COMPOUNDS

ⓐ [also 佑 ゆう 0083] [original meaning] **DIVINE HELP, heavenly assistance [protection]**

ⓑ [also 右 ゆう 3693] help, assist

a 天祐 てんゆう grace of Heaven, providential help

神祐 しんゆう [rare] divine help, heavenly protection

b 祐筆 ゆうひつ amanuensis, private secretary

SYNONYMS

● help

助 HELP → 1440

佑 HELP (said esp. of God) → 0083

祐 DIVINE HELP → 1146

援 AID → 0715

佐 ASSIST → 0076

補 assist → 1529

輔 ASSIST → 1963

済 RELIEVE → 0634

肺

▶LUNG

ハイ

Ⓝ 肺 Ⓒ 肺 fèi

1147

◧1-4-5

130	Jōyō-6	U80BA
月	S9-4-5	F1809

COMPOUNDS

❶ⓐ [original meaning] **LUNG, lungs**

ⓑ [also prefix] pulmonary

a 肺臓 はいぞう lungs

肺活量 はいかつりょう lung breathing capacity

肺癌 はいがん lung cancer

肺炎 はいえん pneumonia, inflammation of the lungs

b 肺結核 はいけっかく pulmonary tuberculosis

❷ innermost heart

肺肝 はいかん [rare] innermost heart; lungs and liver

肺腑× はいふ lungs; one's innermost heart

❸ aircraft engine

片肺飛行 かたはいひこう one-engine flight

INDEPENDENT

【はい 肺】LUNG, lungs; pulmonary disease, phthisis, tuberculosis

肺が弱い はいがよわい have a weak chest

肺を病んでいる はいをやんでいる suffer from tuberculosis

SYNONYMS

❶ internal organs

心 HEART → 0011

肺 LUNG → 1147

胃 STOMACH → 3171

腸 INTESTINES → 1307

肝 LIVER → 1045

胆 GALLBLADDER → 1150

腎 KIDNEY → 3511

胞

▶MEMBRANOUS SAC

ホウ

Ⓝ 胞 Ⓒ 胞 bāo

1148

◧1-4-5

130	Jōyō	U80DE
月	S9-4-5	F1239

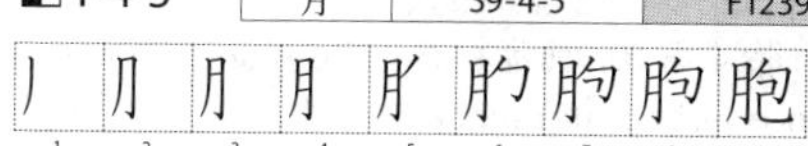

COMPOUNDS

❶ any small MEMBRANOUS SAC such as a vesicle, theca, sac, sheath, capsule or cell

胞子 ほうし spore

細胞 さいぼう cell

芽胞 がほう spore
小胞 しょうほう vesicle
肺胞 はいほう alveolus

❷ⓐ [original meaning] afterbirth, amnion
ⓑ womb

a 胞衣 ほうい afterbirth
b 同胞 どうほう brothers; brethren, fellow countrymen

SPECIAL READINGS

同胞▲ はらから brothers; brethren, fellow countrymen

SYNONYMS

❶ **bags**
俵 STRAW SACK → 0129
袋 BAG → 3201
鞄 BAG (for carrying) → 2248
包 wrapper → 3684
胞 MEMBRANOUS SAC → 1148

COMPOUND FORMATION

【同胞 どうほう】
同胞 'brothers, etc.' refers to persons of the same (同) womb (胞 ❷ⓑ) or mother.

胎

▶FETUS
▶WOMB
タイ

Ⓒ 胎 tāi

1149

1-4-5

130	Jōyō	U80CE
月	S9-4-5	F2049

Stroke order: 丿 1, 月 2, 月 3, 月 4, 月 5, 胎 6, 胎 7, 胎 8, 胎 9

COMPOUNDS

❶ [original meaning] **FETUS, embryo**
胎児 たいじ embryo, fetus
胎動 たいどう quickening, fetal movement; indication
堕胎 だたい abortion

❷ⓐ **WOMB, uterus**
ⓑ (figuratively) **WOMB, origin, beginning**

a 胎内 たいない interior of the womb
胎生 たいせい viviparity
胎教 たいきょう prenatal care
母胎 ぼたい mother's womb
b 胚×胎する はいたいする originate in, arise from

❸ conceive, become pregnant
懐胎 かいたい conception, becoming pregnant
受胎 じゅたい conception, fertilization

INDEPENDENT

【たい 胎】 WOMB

SYNONYMS

❶ **early states of animal life**
胎 FETUS → 1149
卵 EGG → 1054

❷ⓐ **genitals**
陰 sex organ → 0657
胎 WOMB → 1149
恥 private parts → 1664

胆

▶GALLBLADDER
タン

Ⓝ 膽 Ⓒ 胆 dǎn

1150

1-4-5

130	Jōyō	U80C6
月	S9-4-5	F1607

Stroke order: 丿 1, 月 2, 月 3, 月 4, 月 5, 胆 6, 胆 7, 胆 8, 胆 9

COMPOUNDS

❶ **GALLBLADDER, gall**
胆嚢× たんのう gall, gallbladder
胆汁 たんじゅう bile, gall
胆石 たんせき gallstone

❷ **pluck, guts, courage, nerve, gall**
胆力 たんりょく pluck, courage, nerve
大胆 だいたん boldness, daring
豪胆 ごうたん boldness, iron nerves
落胆 らくたん disappointment, discouragement

❸ one's inner heart, feelings
魂胆 こんたん secret intention, ulterior motive
肝胆相照らす間柄である かんたんあいてらすあいだがらである be quite in sympathy with each other

INDEPENDENT

【たん 胆】 pluck, guts, courage

SYNONYMS

❶ **internal organs**
心 HEART → 0011
肺 LUNG → 1147
胃 STOMACH → 3171
腸 INTESTINES → 1307
肝 LIVER → 1045
胆 GALLBLADDER → 1150
腎 KIDNEY → 3511

❷ **courage**
勇 bravery → 2592
胆 pluck → 1150

胞

▶MEMBRANOUS SAC
ホウ

1151
◧ 1-4-5

130	Nonstandard	U80DE
月	S9-4-5	F0000

traditional form → see 胞 at 1148

脉

▶VEIN
▶PULSE
ミャク

1152
◧ 1-4-5

130	Nonstandard	U8109
月	S9-4-5	F0000

alternative form → see 脈 at 1189

旅

▶TRAVEL
リョ たび
Ⓝ 旅 Ⓒ 旅 lǚ

1153
◧ 1-4-6

70	Jōyō-3	U65C5
方	S10-4-6	F0509

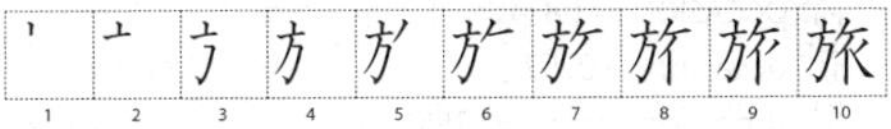

COMPOUNDS

❶ⓐ **TRAVEL, traveling, journey, trip**
ⓑ **TRAVEL, take a trip**
ⓒ **TRAVELer**

a 旅行 りょこう travel, trip
旅券 りょけん passport
b 旅装 りょそう traveling outfit
旅費 りょひ traveling expenses
旅客 りょかく traveler, passenger, tourist
旅客機 りょかっき passenger plane
c 旅館 りょかん Japanese inn
逆旅 げきりょ inn

❷ [original meaning] brigade, troops
旅団 りょだん brigade

KUN

【たび 旅】**journey, TRAVELing, travel, trip**
旅する たびする travel, take a trip
旅立つ たびだつ go on a journey, set off
旅人 たびびと traveler
旅路 たびじ journey
船旅 ふなたび voyage

SYNONYMS

❶ⓐ & ❶ⓑ **journey**
旅 TRAVEL → 1153
行 trip → 0246
遊 tour → 3896
巡 tour around → 3781

NOTE

★ do not confuse with 旋 GYRATE → 1194

旅

▶TRAVEL
リョ たび

1154
◧ 1-4-6

70	Nonstandard	UF983
方	S10-4-6	F0000

traditional form → see 旅 at 1153

時

▶TIME
ジ とき -どき
Ⓒ 时 shí

1155
◧ 1-4-6

72	Jōyō-2	U6642
日	S10-4-6	F0024

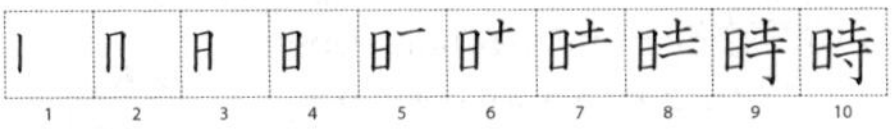

COMPOUNDS

❶ⓐ [original meaning] (continuous duration) **TIME, duration, interval**
ⓑ (specific time) **the TIME, o'clock, hour**
ⓒ [suffix] **TIME, at the time of, when**

a 時間 じかん time, period; hour
時刻 じこく time; hour
時効 じこう prescription, limitation (of action)
同時の どうじの simultaneous
臨時の りんじの temporary, provisional, special
一時 いちじ for a time, temporarily; once; one o'clock
b 時限 じげん time limit, closing time; period, hour
八時 はちじ eight o'clock
何時ですか なんじですか What time is it?
日時 にちじ date, time
c 昼食時 ちゅうしょくじ lunch time
出願時 しゅつがんじ (at the) time of application

❷ⓐ **TIME(s), age, period, season**
ⓑ (opportune moment) **TIMEly occasion, right time, opportunity**
ⓒ current TIMEs, currently, present

a 時代 じだい age, era, period; antiquity
時勢 じせい trend of the times, spirit of the age
時期 じき time, season
当時 とうじ at that time, in those days; at the present time
b 時機 じき opportunity, chance
時宜 じぎ right time [occasion], proper time
時節 じせつ season, times; occasion
c 時事 じじ current events
時価 じか current price

❸ at TIMEs, periodically
時習 じしゅう periodic reviewing

❹ⓐ **hour**
ⓑ counter for hours

a 時速 じそく speed per hour

時給 じきゅう payment by the hour
一時間 いちじかん one hour
b 五十時 ごじゅうじ 50 hours

❺ *gram* tense
時制 じせい tense
現在完了時 げんざいかんりょうじ present perfect tense

KUN

【とき 時】

①ⓐ **TIME, hour, moment**
ⓑ **TIMEs, age, the day**
ⓒ (former unit of time) two-hour period

a 時が移る ときがうつる Time elapses
一時 ひととき time, while, moment
引け時 ひけどき closing time (of school)
b 時の ときの then, of the day
戦争の時 せんそうのとき times of war
c 子の時 ねのとき midnight

②ⓐ **right TIME, opportunity, occasion, case; season**
ⓑ [also 秋] critical moment

a 時には ときには occasionally
時時 ときどき sometimes, occasionally; each occasion
時を待つ ときをまつ wait for a favorable chance
時と場合によって ときとばあいによって should time and circumstances permit
丁度良い時に ちょうどよいときに just at the right moment
b 危急存亡の時 ききゅうそんぼうのとき crisis, critical moment

③ⓐ **when**
ⓑ **in case of, if, in the event of**

a 家に帰る時 いえにかえるとき when returning home
b 五時迄に帰らない時は ごじまでにかえらないときは if I don't come back till five o'clock

④ *gram* tense
法と時 ほうととき mood and tense

【-どき -時】[suffix]

① **TIME, proper time, season**
食事時 しょくじどき mealtime
花見時 はなみどき (cherry) blossom season

② suffix indicating **TIME** in former system of measuring time
九つ時 ここのつどき midnight, noon

SPECIAL READINGS

時計 とけい clock, watch
時雨 しぐれ late fall or early winter rain

SYNONYMS

❶ **time periods**
時 TIME → 1155
季 SEASON (quarter) → 3161
候 SEASON (time of year) → 0133
頃 TIME → 0163
暇 FREE TIME → 1275
般 period of time → 1670
刻 POINT OF TIME → 1619
間 INTERVAL → 4122
隙 GAP → 0826
期 TERM → 2139
節 SEASON → 3336

❷ⓐ **long time periods**
時 TIME → 1155
代 age → 0034
紀 ERA → 1628
世 AGE → 4308
朝 dynastic period → 2130
期 period → 2139
劫 KALPA → 1435

ⓑ **occasions**
際 OCCASION → 0874
折 occasion → 0297
時 timely occasion → 1155
機 OPPORTUNITY → 1365
節 time → 3336

❹ⓐ **short time periods**
頃 moment → 0163
瞬 INSTANT → 1594
秒 SECOND → 1462
分 MINUTE → 2466
時 hour → 1155
暫 SHORT WHILE → 3553

USAGE

【とき】

時
①ⓐ time, hour, moment
ⓑ times, age, the day
ⓒ (former unit of time) two-hour period
②ⓐ right time, opportunity, occasion, case; season
ⓑ [also 秋] critical moment
③ⓐ when
ⓑ in case of, if, in the event of
④ *gram* tense

秋
[also 時] critical moment

HOMOPHONES

とき 秋 AUTUMN → 1464

晒

▶BLEACH
▶EXPOSE
サイ さら(す)

1156
◧1-4-6

Ⓒ 晒 shài

72	Names	U6652
日	S10-4-6	F2376

KUN

【さらす 晒す】

① **BLEACH, refine**

晒し さらし bleaching; bleached cotton
晒木綿 さらしもめん bleached cotton cloth
洗い晒し あらいざらし faded from washing

② [also 曝す] **EXPOSE (to view, to the elements)**

晒し者 さらしもの pilloried criminal exposed to public view; someone subjected to public scorn [humiliation]
恥晒し はじさらし disgrace, shame
野晒し のざらし weather-beaten

③ **soak**

水に晒す みずにさらす soak in water

SYNONYMS

【さらす】

① **discolor**

褪 FADE → 1577
晒す BLEACH → 1156

② **reveal**

発 reveal → 3174
露 EXPOSE → 3495
曝 EXPOSE → 1410
晒す EXPOSE → 1156
暴 disclose → 3138
披 OPEN OUT → 0362
顕 MANIFEST → 2274
現 cause to appear → 1218

USAGE

【さらす】

晒す
① bleach, refine
② [also 曝す] expose (to view, to the elements)
③ soak

曝す
[also 晒す] expose (to view, to the elements)

HOMOPHONES

さらす 曝 EXPOSE → 1410

晦

▶DARK
▶LAST DAY OF THE LUNAR MONTH
カイ くら(ます) つごもり

1157
◧1-4-6

72	Nonstandard	U6666
日	S10-4-6	F0000

traditional form → see 晦 at 1196

晄

▶DAZZLING
コウ ㊔ てる あき あきら ひかる のぼる あつし

1158
◧1-4-6

72	Names	U6644
日	S10-4-6	F0000

traditional form → see 晃 at 3101

晠

◧1-4-6

incorrect stroke-count
➡ see ◧1-4-7: 日 at 1198

梅

▶JAPANESE APRICOT
バイ うめ

1159
◧1-4-6

Ⓝ 梅 楳 Ⓒ 梅 méi

75	Jōyō-4	U6885
木	S10-4-6	F1147

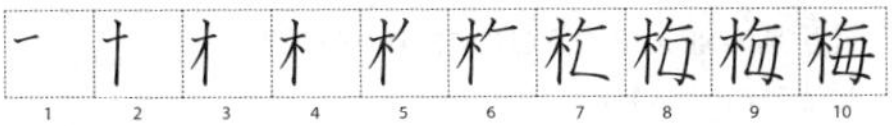

COMPOUNDS

❶ⓐ **JAPANESE APRICOT tree, *ume* tree; Japanese apricot, *ume***
ⓑ ***ume* blossom**

a 梅林 ばいりん *ume* grove
梅花 ばいか *ume* blossoms
梅雨(=黴雨) ばいう rainy season (of early summer)
b 紅梅 こうばい red-blossomed Japanese apricot
観梅 かんばい *ume* blossom viewing
塩梅 あんばい seasoning, flavoring; taste, flavor; condition, state

❷ **rainy season (when the *ume* blossoms in Japan)**

入梅 にゅうばい beginning of the rainy season

❸ [formerly 黴 1008] mold, mildew, fungus

梅毒 ばいどく syphilis

KUN

【うめ 梅】 **JAPANESE APRICOT tree, *ume* tree; *ume* blossom; Japanese apricot (the fruit), *ume***

梅の実 うめのみ Japanese apricot, *ume*
梅見 うめみ *ume* blossom viewing
梅干し うめぼし pickled *ume*
梅酒 うめしゅ *ume* [apricot] brandy

SPECIAL READINGS

梅雨 つゆ rainy season (of early summer)
梅雨入り つゆいり setting in of the rainy season
梅雨明け つゆあけ end of the rainy season

SYNONYMS

❶ⓐ **fruits and fruit trees**

桃 PEACH → 1174
榛 HAZEL → 1328
椎 CHINQUAPIN → 1249
柚 YUZU → 1123

椰 COCONUT → 1285
柑 CITRUS → 1112
橙 BITTER ORANGE → 1369
葡 GRAPE → 2902
萄 GRAPE → 2870
柿 PERSIMMON → 1118
檎 APPLE → 1386
李 PLUM → 3050
枇 LOQUAT → 1063
杷 LOQUAT → 1065
苺 STRAWBERRY → 2780
菱 water chestnut → 2879
杏 APRICOT → 3049
梅 JAPANESE APRICOT → 1159
橘 MANDARIN → 1366
栗 CHESTNUT → 3280
栃 JAPANESE HORSE CHESTNUT → 1122
梨 PEAR → 3412
蕉 PLANTAIN → 2994

ⓑ flowering plants

菊 CHRYSANTHEMUM → 2875
菖 IRIS → 2881
菫 VIOLET → 2877
蓮 LOTUS → 2940
葛 KUDZU → 2905
蓬 JAPANESE MUGWORT → 2973
葵 MALLOW → 2906
蓉 COTTON ROSE → 2944
芙 LOTUS → 2737
蘭 ORCHID → 3031
萩 *HAGI* → 2908
藤 WISTERIA → 3025
桜 cherry blossom → 1168
梅 *ume* blossom → 1159

桧

1160

◧ 1-4-6

▸JAPANESE CYPRESS

カイ ひのき ひ

Ⓝ 檜 Ⓒ 桧 huì guì

75	Names	U6867
木	S10-4-6	F3491

KUN

【ひのき 桧】 [also 桧木] **JAPANESE CYPRESS, *hinoki***

桧林 ひのきばやし Japanese cypress forest

【ひ 桧】 **cypress, esp. JAPANESE CYPRESS**

桧皮 ひわだ(=ひはだ) cypress bark

桧葉 ひば cypress leaf; *hiba, Thujopsis dolabrata;* garden variety of Japanese cypress

桧扇 ひおうぎ formal folding fan made of Japanese cypress; leopard lily

唐桧 とうひ spruce, esp. *Picea jezoensis* var. *hondoensis*

SPECIAL READINGS

桧木 ひのき [also 桧] Japanese cypress, *hinoki*

翌桧 あすなろ *hiba, Thujopsis dolabrata*

SYNONYMS

【ひのき】

◯ trees

桜 CHERRY → 1168
桐 PAULOWNIA → 1173
桂 AROMATIC TREE, katsura tree → 1163
梓 CATALPA → 1207
桑 MULBERRY → 2618
漆 Japanese lacquer tree → 0863
樺 BIRCH → 1324
椛 BIRCH → 1202
梧 CHINESE PARASOL TREE → 1200
檀 SPINDLE TREE → 1385
椿 CAMELLIA → 1278
柳 WILLOW → 1115
柊 HOLLY → 1119
椋 *APHANANTHE ASPERA* → 1245
柾 spindle tree → 1114
槻 ZELKOVA → 1349
楢 OAK → 1287
樫 EVERGREEN OAK → 1364
柏 CYPRESS, JAPANESE EMPEROR OAK → 1110
榎 HACKBERRY → 1323
梶 PAPER MULBERRY → 1199
柘 JAPANESE BOXWOOD → 1117
楊 WILLOW → 1286
桧 JAPANESE CYPRESS → 1160
梛 *NAGEIA NAGI* → 1206
榊 SACRED SHINTO TREE → 1327
楓 MAPLE → 1280
松 PINE → 1075
杉 CRYPTOMERIA → 1027
槙 PODOCARPUS → 1330
楠 CAMPHOR TREE → 1283
樟 CAMPHOR TREE → 1351

HOMOPHONES

ひのき 桧木 → 1160, 4261

格

1161

◧ 1-4-6

▸NORM
▸STATUS

カク コウ キャク▲ ゴウ▲ ㊔ いたる ただ のり

Ⓒ 格 gé gē

75	Jōyō-5	U683C
木	S10-4-6	F0343

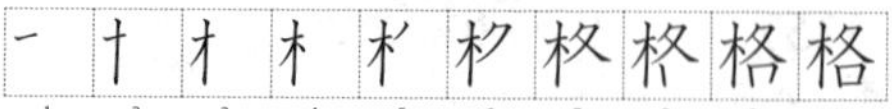
1 2 3 4 5 6 7 8 9 10

COMPOUNDS

❶ⓐ **NORM, standard, model, pattern, rule, regulation**
ⓑ **ability to meet the NORM, qualification, eligibility, competency, capacity**
ⓒ (make conform to the norm) rectify, correct, show the right way to

a 格外の かくがいの nonstandard, extraordinary, special
格別な かくべつな particular, exceptional
格式 かくしき established form, formalities
規格 きかく standard, norm
本格 ほんかく fundamental rules, propriety
本格的な ほんかくてきな full-scale, full-fledged; standard
語格 ごかく rules of grammar, usage

b 資格 しかく qualifications, competence, capacity
合格する ごうかくする pass (an examination), be found eligible [qualified]
失格する しっかくする be disqualified

c 格言 かくげん maxim, proverb

❷ **STATUS, rank, capacity, standing, class, grade**
格上げする かくあげする raise to higher status, promote to a higher rank
格式 かくしき status, social standing
格付けする かくづけする grade, rate, classify
昇格 しょうかく promotion in status
同格 どうかく same status, equality; apposition
寺格 じかく status of a Buddhist temple
リーダー格 りーだーかく capacity as a leader
価格 かかく price, cost

❸ (degree of excellence) **(good) character, personality; (high) quality, distinction, style**
格差 かくさ difference in quality [price]
格安な かくやすな inexpensive, reasonable in price
格調 かくちょう tone, strain, style
人格 じんかく character, personality
性格 せいかく character, personality
品格 ひんかく dignity, grace
風格の有る人物 ふうかくのあるじんぶつ man of distinctive character
厳格な げんかくな strict, stern, severe, rigorous

❹ⓐ **framework, latticework, grid**
ⓑ [formerly also 骼 かく 2302] **frame, build, physique**

a 格子 こうし latticework, lattice, grid
格天井 ごうてんじょう coffered ceiling

b 体格 たいかく physique, build
骨格 こっかく frame, physique; framework, skeletal structure

❺ [also suffix] *gram* case
主格 しゅかく nominative case
目的格 もくてきかく objective case

❻ [also 恰 かっ- 0437] **just, exactly**
格好 かっこう suitability, moderateness (in price); shape, form; appearance, manner

❼ [formerly 挌 かく 0448] **strike, hit, fight**
格闘する かくとうする grapple, fight hand to hand

❽ put away, store
格納 かくのう housing, hangar

❾ [also suffix] Imperial ordinance in Nara and Heian periods
弘仁格 こうにんきゃく Ordinance of the Konin Era

❿ *logic* figure, schema
第二格 だいにかく second figure

⓫ investigate thoroughly, search to the very source
格物致知 かくぶつちち gaining a perfect knowledge of natural laws

⓬ [usu. 角 かく 2541] unit of type size equiv. to one em quad
半格 はんかく en quad

INDEPENDENT

【かく 格】**NORM, standard, rule; status, rank, capacity, class;** *gram* **case;** *logic* **figure, schema**
格を上げる かくをあげる raise the standard
格を守る かくをまもる observe the rules
格が上がる かくがあがる be promoted to a higher rank
. . . の格で …のかくで in the capacity of, as
名詞の格 めいしのかく case of a noun

SYNONYMS

❶ⓐ **model**
範 MODEL → 3360
典 CANON → 3253
模 PATTERN → 1326
程 ESTABLISHED FORM → 1524
式 form → 3785
準 STANDARD → 3541
格 NORM → 1161

❷ **class**
級 GRADE → 1630
段 grade → 1471
位 RANK → 0069
階 RANK → 0761
身 social status → 4368
格 STATUS → 1161
等 CLASS → 3321
流 class → 0529
層 STRATUM → 3920

❸ **nature and character**
性 NATURE → 0357
気 temperament → 3960
質 QUALITY → 3483

方 日 【木】 歹 火 牛 王 ネ 月 月

方 日 【木】 歹 火 牛 王 ネ 月 月

品 grade of excellence → 2795
柄 CHARACTER → 1111
格 (good) character → 1161
❹ⓐ **frames**
枠 FRAME → 1077
骼 SKELETAL FRAME → 2302
格 framework → 1161
額 picture frame → 2273

COMPOUND FORMATION

❶【格言 かくげん】
格言 'maxim, proverb' is a saying (言) that shows one the right way (格 ❶ⓒ).

❷【厳格 げんかく】
厳格な 'strict, etc.' refers to the strictness (厳) of a person's character (格 ❸).

NOTE

★ do not confuse with 格 STRIKE → 0448

核 1162

▸**NUCLEUS**
カク
Ⓒ 核 hé hú
1-4-6

75	Jōyō	U6838
木	S10-4-6	F1016

Stroke order: 一 十 才 木 木' 朩 朩 杉 核 核 (1–10)

COMPOUNDS

[also prefix and suffix]

❶ⓐ (central part) **NUCLEUS, core**
ⓑ *biol, chem* **NUCLEUS**
ⓒ [original meaning] kernel (of a fruit), putamen

a 核仁 かくじん nucleus
核家族 かくかぞく nucleus family
中核 ちゅうかく core, nucleus; kernel
b 核崩壊 かくほうかい disintegration of a cell nucleus
核酸 かくさん nucleic acid
細胞核 さいぼうかく nucleus (of a cell)
神経核 しんけいかく neuron
結核 けっかく tuberculosis
痔×核 じかく hemorrhoids
c 果核 かかく putamen

❷ⓐ (central part of an atom) **NUCLEUS**
ⓑ **nuclear, atomic**
ⓒ abbrev. of 核兵器 かくへいき: nuclear weapons

a 核反応 かくはんのう nuclear reaction
核融合 かくゆうごう nuclear fusion
原子核 げんしかく atomic nucleus
b 核エネルギー かくえねるぎー nuclear energy
核兵器 かくへいき nuclear weapons
c 核防衛力 かくぼうえいりょく nuclear defenses
核戦争 かくせんそう nuclear war

INDEPENDENT

【かく 核】**NUCLEUS, kernel, core; nucleus (of a cell); atomic nucleus**
核の傘 かくのかさ nuclear umbrella

SYNONYMS

❶ **central parts**
核 NUCLEUS → 1162
仁 kernel → 0021
心 core → 0011
芯 CORE → 2744
ⓐ **middle**
中 MIDDLE → 4262
央 CENTER → 4322
心 HEART → 0011
核 NUCLEUS → 1162
❷ⓐ & ❷ⓑ **particle**
粒 GRAIN → 1682
子 particle suffix → 4196
核 NUCLEUS → 1162

桂 1163

▸**AROMATIC TREE**
ケイ かつら ㊔ よし
Ⓒ 桂 guì
1-4-6

75	Names	U6842
木	S10-4-6	F1535

COMPOUNDS

❶ **general term for AROMATIC TREEs, esp. cinnamon or cassia**
桂冠 けいかん crown of laurel
肉桂 にっけい cinnamon tree
月桂樹 げっけいじゅ laurel
カシア桂皮 かしあけいひ cassia

❷ [rare] tree in the moon (according to ancient Chinese legend); moon
桂月 けいげつ [archaic] moon
月桂 げっけい laurel in the moon; moonlight

❸ name of chess piece in shogi (Japanese chess): *keima*, knight
桂馬 けいま *keima*, knight
桂成り けいなり knight promotion

INDEPENDENT

【けい 桂】*keima* (→❸)
桂を落とす けいをおとす lose a knight

KUN

【かつら 桂】**katsura tree, katsura**
桂男 かつらおとこ man in the moon

SYNONYMS

❶ & 【かつら】 **trees**
桜 CHERRY → 1168

桐 PAULOWNIA → 1173
桂 AROMATIC TREE, katsura tree → 1163
梓 CATALPA → 1207
桑 MULBERRY → 2618
漆 Japanese lacquer tree → 0863
樺 BIRCH → 1324
椛 BIRCH → 1202
梧 CHINESE PARASOL TREE → 1200
檀 SPINDLE TREE → 1385
椿 CAMELLIA → 1278
柳 WILLOW → 1115
柊 HOLLY → 1119
椋 *APHANANTHE ASPERA* → 1245
柾 spindle tree → 1114
槻 ZELKOVA → 1349
楢 OAK → 1287
樫 EVERGREEN OAK → 1364
柏 CYPRESS, JAPANESE EMPEROR OAK → 1110
榎 HACKBERRY → 1323
梶 PAPER MULBERRY → 1199
柘 JAPANESE BOXWOOD → 1117
楊 WILLOW → 1286
桧 JAPANESE CYPRESS → 1160
梛 *NAGEIA NAGI* → 1206
榊 SACRED SHINTO TREE → 1327
楓 MAPLE → 1280
松 PINE → 1075
杉 CRYPTOMERIA → 1027
槙 PODOCARPUS → 1330
楠 CAMPHOR TREE → 1283
樟 CAMPHOR TREE → 1351

桔

▶PLANT NAME ELEMENT

キツ ケツ キ

Ⓒ 桔 jú jié

1164

1-4-6

75	Names	U6854
木	S10-4-6	F3023

COMPOUNDS

❶ **PLANT NAME ELEMENT**

桔梗 ききょう Chinese bellflower, balloon flower

❷ unclassified compounds

桔抗(=拮×抗)する きっこうする vie [compete] with, rival; compare with (桔抗 is an incorrect spelling for 拮×抗)

❸ [original meaning, now rare] well sweep

桔槹× きっこう(=けっこう) well sweep

SYNONYMS

❶ **plants**

菜 VEGETABLE → 2880
植 PLANT → 1247
栽 garden plant → 4087
茨 thorny shrub → 2812
苔 MOSS → 2792
蔓 VINE → 2975
桔 PLANT NAME ELEMENT → 1164

桁

▶BEAM
▶DIGIT

コウ▲ けた

Ⓒ 桁 héng

1165

1-4-6

75	Jōyō	U6841
木	S10-4-6	F2416

COMPOUNDS

❶ **BEAM**, girder, spar

❷ kimono rack

衣桁 いこう kimono rack

KUN

【けた 桁】

① **BEAM, girder, spar**

井桁 いげた well crib; parallel crosses
橋桁 はしげた bridge girder
主桁 しゅげた main girder

② **DIGIT, figure, unit, place, order of magnitude**

桁違い けたちがい different order of magnitude; exceptional, incomparable, in a different league
桁外れ けたはずれ exceptional, incomparable, in a different league
桁数 けたすう number of digits [places]
一桁 ひとけた one digit; single-digit
下二桁 しもふたけた last two figures of a number

③ rod of an abacus

SYNONYMS

❶ **supporting structures**

柱 PILLAR → 1109
礎 FOUNDATION STONE → 1595
桁 BEAM → 1165
梁 BEAM → 3410

【けた】

② **kinds of numbers**

数 NUMBER (mathematical unit) → 2245
員 fixed number → 2822
号 NUMBER (numerical designation) → 2675
番 No. → 3416
第 ORDINAL NUMBER PREFIX → 3298
-目 ordinal number suffix → 3777
次 numerical order suffix → 0058
桁 DIGIT → 1165

校 1166

▶SCHOOL
▶COLLATE
コウ キョウ▲
Ⓒ 校 xiào jiào

1-4-6

75	Jōyō-1	U6821
木	S10-4-6	F0316

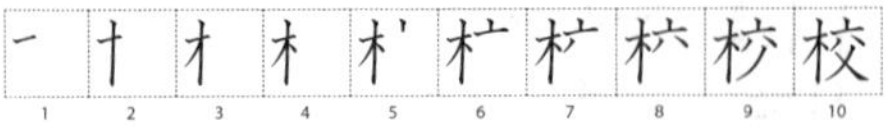

COMPOUNDS

❶ⓐ [also suffix] **SCHOOL**
ⓑ counter for **SCHOOL**s
a 校長 こうちょう principal, schoolmaster, rector
校舎 こうしゃ school building
校内 こうない school grounds
校友 こうゆう schoolmate, alumnus
校則 こうそく school regulations
学校 がっこう school, college
母校 ぼこう one's alma mater, one's old school
登校 とうこう attending school
高校 こうこう senior high school
予備校 よびこう preparatory school
b 二十五校 にじゅうごこう 25 schools

❷ⓐ **COLLATE, proofread, check, examine, revise**
ⓑ proof
ⓒ counter for proofs
a 校合する きょうごう(=こうごう)する collate, examine and compare
校正 こうせい proofreading
校訂 こうてい revision
校正刷り こうせいずり galley proofs
校閲 こうえつ revision, reviewing, editing
校了 こうりょう final proof
b 初校 しょこう first proof
c 三校目 さんこうめ third proof

❸ commanding officer
将校 しょうこう officer, commissioned officer

INDEPENDENT

【こう 校】proofreading
校を重ねる こうをかさねる proofread again and again

SYNONYMS

❶ **schools**
校 SCHOOL → 1166
学 EDUCATIONAL INSTITUTION → 3162
院 INSTITUTION → 0544
塾 PRIVATE SCHOOL → 3546
大 UNIVERSITY → 4224
高 high school → 2601
中 junior high school → 4262
小 elementary school → 0007
園 kindergarten → 3914

❷ⓐ **revise**
訂 REVISE → 1829
閲 REVIEW → 4132
校 COLLATE → 1166

❷ⓐ **compare**
比 COMPARE → 0029
較 COMPARE → 1939
譬 COMPARE TO → 3613
校 COLLATE → 1166
照 check against → 3506
対 OPPOSE (contrast) → 1025
参 refer → 2563

根 1167

▶ROOT
コン ね -ね
Ⓒ 根 gēn

1-4-6

75	Jōyō-3	U6839
木	S10-4-6	F0397

COMPOUNDS

❶ [original meaning] **ROOT (of a plant)**
根菜 こんさい root crops
毛根 もうこん root of a hair
大根 だいこん Japanese radish
球根 きゅうこん bulb

❷ⓐ (primary source) **ROOT, source, origin**
ⓑ (essential part) **ROOT, basis, foundation**
ⓒ radically, completely
a 根源 こんげん root, origin, source
語根 ごこん root [origin] of a word
b 根本 こんぽん basis, foundation; origin, source
根底 こんてい root, basis, foundation
根拠 こんきょ grounds, basis, authority
c 根絶する こんぜつする eradicate, exterminate, root out
根治する こんじ(=こんち)する cure radically, be completely cured

❸ⓐ *math* **ROOT**, radical
ⓑ *chem* radical
a 根号 こんごう radical sign
平方根 へいほうこん square root
b 水酸根 すいさんこん hydroxyl radical

❹ **perseverance, stamina, mental energy**
根気 こんき perseverance, patience, energy
根性 こんじょう nature, spirit, temper; will power; guts
精根 せいこん energy, vitality

❺ organ; sense organ (esp. in Buddhism)
男根 だんこん penis

六根清浄 ろっこんしょうじょう purification of one's self through detachment from the senses

❻ *Buddhism*

ⓐ *indriya* (Sanskrit): powerful act capable of producing something

ⓑ character [nature] of man

a 機根 きこん capacity of the common people to understand the teachings of Buddhism

INDEPENDENT

【こん 根】 *math* **ROOT**; radical; *chem* **radical**; perseverance, stamina, mental energy

根の良い こんのよい persevering, enduring

KUN

【ね 根】 **ROOT; source, origin; basis, foundation; nature**

根っ子 ねっこ root; stump, stub

根元 ねもと root; base

根強い ねづよい deep-rooted

根付く ねづく take root

根回し ねまわし maneuvering behind the scenes; digging around the roots

根掘り葉掘り ねほりはほり inquisitively, in great detail

根も葉も無い噂 ねもはもないうわさ groundless rumor

根深い ねぶかい deep-rooted, ingrained

根はおとなしい ねはおとなしい be tenderhearted by nature

性根 しょうね nature, disposition

【-ね -根】 **used phonetically for *ne*, esp. for euphony**

屋根 やね roof

羽根 はね fan, blade

垣根 かきね fence, hedge

SYNONYMS

❶ **supporting parts of plants**

根 ROOT → 1167

株 stump → 1172

幹 TRUNK → 2152

茎 STEM → 2788

❷ⓐ **beginnings**

緒 OUTSET → 1742

序 INTRODUCTORY PART → 3803

端 start → 1564

始 beginning → 0335

初 beginning → 1433

元 ORIGIN → 2428

本 origin → 4314

根 ROOT → 1167

源 SOURCE → 0806

ⓑ **basis**

基 BASE → 3312

本 BASIS → 4314

素 ELEMENT → 3108

礎 foundation → 1595

底 BOTTOM → 3827

根 ROOT → 1167

拠 GROUNDS → 0369

桜

▶CHERRY

オウ さくら

Ⓝ 櫻 Ⓒ 樱 yīng

1168

◧ 1-4-6

75	Jōyō-5	U685C
木	S10-4-6	F1329

COMPOUNDS

ⓐ **CHERRY tree, (Japanese) flowering cherry, *sakura***

ⓑ **CHERRY blossom**

a 桜花 おうか cherry blossoms

桜桃 おうとう cherry

b 観桜 かんおう cherry-blossom viewing

KUN

【さくら 桜】 **CHERRY tree, (Japanese) flowering cherry, *sakura*; cherry blossom; pink; horse meat**

桜ん坊(=桜桃) さくらんぼ cherry

桜色 さくらいろ pink

桜貝 さくらがい carpenter's tellin, pink shell

桜肉 さくらにく horse meat

山桜 やまざくら wild cherry tree

葉桜 はざくら cherry tree in leaf

SYNONYMS

ⓐ **trees**

桜 CHERRY → 1168

桐 PAULOWNIA → 1173

桂 AROMATIC TREE, katsura tree → 1163

梓 CATALPA → 1207

桑 MULBERRY → 2618

漆 Japanese lacquer tree → 0863

樺 BIRCH → 1324

椛 BIRCH → 1202

梧 CHINESE PARASOL TREE → 1200

檀 SPINDLE TREE → 1385

椿 CAMELLIA → 1278

柳 WILLOW → 1115

柊 HOLLY → 1119

椋 *APHANANTHE ASPERA* → 1245

柾 spindle tree → 1114

槻 ZELKOVA → 1349

楢 OAK → 1287

樫 EVERGREEN OAK → 1364

柏 CYPRESS, JAPANESE EMPEROR OAK → 1110

榎 HACKBERRY → 1323
梶 PAPER MULBERRY → 1199
柘 JAPANESE BOXWOOD → 1117
楊 WILLOW → 1286
桧 JAPANESE CYPRESS → 1160
梛 *NAGEIA NAGI* → 1206
榊 SACRED SHINTO TREE → 1327
楓 MAPLE → 1280
松 PINE → 1075
杉 CRYPTOMERIA → 1027
槙 PODOCARPUS → 1330
楠 CAMPHOR TREE → 1283
樟 CAMPHOR TREE → 1351

ⓑ **flowering plants**
菊 CHRYSANTHEMUM → 2875
菖 IRIS → 2881
菫 VIOLET → 2877
蓮 LOTUS → 2940
葛 KUDZU → 2905
蓬 JAPANESE MUGWORT → 2973
葵 MALLOW → 2906
蓉 COTTON ROSE → 2944
芙 LOTUS → 2737
蘭 ORCHID → 3031
萩 *HAGI* → 2908
藤 WISTERIA → 3025
桜 cherry blossom → 1168
梅 *ume* blossom → 1159

桟

1169

1-4-6

▶**PLANK BRIDGE**

サン ㊔ かけはし

Ⓝ 棧 Ⓒ 栈 zhàn

75	Jōyō	U685F
木	S10-4-6	F2217

Stroke order: 1–10

COMPOUNDS

● **PLANK BRIDGE, suspension bridge, plank passageway**
桟道 さんどう plank road, plank bridge, suspension bridge
桟橋 さんばし (landing) pier, jetty, wharf
桟梯子 さんばしご gangway ladder

INDEPENDENT

【さん 桟】crosspiece; frame; bolt (of a door)
桟を打ち付ける さんをうちつける nail a crosspiece (to)
障子の桟 しょうじのさん frame of a *shoji* (paper sliding door)
戸の桟を外す とのさんをはずす unbolt the door

SPECIAL READINGS

桟敷 さじき reviewing stand, box, gallery

SYNONYMS

● **bridges**
橋 BRIDGE → 1367
桟 PLANK BRIDGE → 1169

【さん】
○ **long slender objects**
棒 ROD → 1237
箸 CHOPSTICKS → 3359
桟 crosspiece → 1169
軸 AXLE → 1908
錘 SPINDLE → 2191
竿 POLE → 3259
杖 STAFF → 1026
錫 Buddhist priest's staff → 2189
軛 YOKE → 1873

栖

1170

1-4-6

▶**INHABIT**

セイ す す(む) すみか

Ⓒ 栖 qī xī

75	Names	U6816
木	S10-4-6	F2700

COMPOUNDS

ⓐ [now replaced by 生 4309] (of animals) **INHABIT, live**
ⓑ (of people) **live, dwell, reside**
a 栖息する せいそくする inhabit, live
b 隠栖 いんせい secluded life
幽栖する ゆうせいする live a quiet life in seclusion away from the masses

KUN

【す 栖】[usu. 巣]
ⓐ (structure for birds, insects or animals) **nest, beehive; web; lair, den**
ⓑ (place favoring the growth of something dangerous) **nest, den, hangout (for bandits)**

【すむ 栖む】[usu. 棲む] (of animals) **INHABIT**, live

【すみか 栖】[usu. 住み処, sometimes also 住み家] dwelling, abode
終の栖 ついのすみか one's final abode

SYNONYMS

● **reside**
住 LIVE → 0072
居 RESIDE → 3822
棲 INHABIT (said of animals), live → 1246
栖 INHABIT (said of animals), live → 1170
生 inhabit → 4309
植 colonize → 1247

HOMOPHONES

すむ
住 LIVE → 0072
棲 INHABIT → 1246
す 巣 NEST → 2861

NOTE

➡ see USAGE notes at 住 0072 and 巣 2861

栓

1171

1-4-6

▶STOPPER

セン

Ⓝ 栓 Ⓒ 栓 shuān

75	Jōyō	U6813
木	S10-4-6	F2425

Stroke order: 1–10

COMPOUNDS

❶ⓐ [original meaning] **STOPPER, plug, cork, peg; door bolt**
ⓑ **STOPPER**, block up
a 栓抜き せんぬき bottle opener, corkscrew
コルク栓 こるくせん cork
脳血栓 のうけっせん cerebral thrombosis
b 密栓する みっせんする stopper tightly, seal hermetically
❷ [also suffix] stopcock, tap, faucet, spigot
水栓 すいせん water tap, faucet
消火栓 しょうかせん fire hydrant, fireplug

INDEPENDENT

【せん 栓】**STOPPER, cork, plug; stopcock, faucet, tap**
栓を抜く せんをぬく uncork a bottle
瓶の栓 びんのせん bottle stopper
水道の栓 すいどうのせん water spigot

SYNONYMS

❶ⓐ & ❷ **stoppers**
栓 STOPPER → 1171
弁 VALVE → 2497

株

1172

1-4-6

▶STOCK

シュ▲ かぶ

Ⓒ 株 zhū

75	Jōyō-6	U682A
木	S10-4-6	F0648

Stroke order: 1–10

COMPOUNDS

● [original meaning] stump, stub
守株 しゅしゅ stupidity, lack of innovation

KUN

【かぶ 株】
①ⓐ [also suffix] **STOCK, stocks, shares**
ⓑ **counter for STOCKs or shares**
ⓒ abbrev. of 株式会社 かぶしきがいしゃ: joint **STOCK** corporation, Ltd., Inc.
a 株を買う かぶをかう buy stock
株式 かぶしき stocks, shares
株価 かぶか price of stocks
株券 かぶけん share [stock] certificate
株主 かぶぬし stockholder
株式会社 かぶしきがいしゃ joint stock corporation
新株 しんかぶ new stock
優先株 ゆうせんかぶ preference shares
b 二百株 にひゃっかぶ 200 shares
c 山田製紙株 やまだせいしかぶ Yamada Paper Manufacturing Company Ltd.
②ⓐ **stump, stub**
ⓑ **root, plant**
ⓒ counter for plants with roots
a 切り株 きりかぶ stump
b 株分け かぶわけ root division
c レタス五株 れたすごかぶ five heads of lettuce
③ assets, business practice, goodwill
商売の株 しょうばいのかぶ goodwill of a business
④ position, reputation
親分株 おやぶんかぶ position of boss [big shot]
⑤ one's forte, one's specialty
お株を取られる おかぶをとられる be outdone, be beaten in one's own field

SYNONYMS

● & 【かぶ】②ⓐ **supporting parts of plants**
根 ROOT → 1167
株 stump → 1172
幹 TRUNK → 2152
茎 STEM → 2788
【かぶ】
①ⓐ **securities**
株 STOCK → 1172
債 BOND → 0177

COMPOUND FORMATION

【守株 しゅしゅ】
守株 is a classical Chinese allusion that originally meant to stay and keep watch (守) by a stump (株) in the hope of catching a hare. The reasoning behind this strange behavior is that since a hare had once accidentally dashed against the stump and died there, maybe another one would come by. This gave rise to the current meaning of 'stupidity, lack of innovation'.

NOTE

➡ see COMPOUND FORMATION for 株式 かぶしき →式 3785

方 日 【木】 歹 火 牛 王 ネ 月 月

桐

1173

1-4-6

▶**PAULOWNIA**

トウ ドウ きり ㊔ ひさ

Ⓒ 桐 tóng

75	Names	U6850
木	S10-4-6	F1702

COMPOUNDS

● **PAULOWNIA**

桐油 とうゆ tung oil, (Chinese) wood oil

梧桐 ごとう Chinese parasol (tree), phoenix tree, *Firmiana platanifolia*

KUN

【きり 桐】**PAULOWNIA**

桐材 きりざい paulownia wood

SYNONYMS

● **trees**

桜 CHERRY → 1168
桐 PAULOWNIA → 1173
桂 AROMATIC TREE, katsura tree → 1163
梓 CATALPA → 1207
桑 MULBERRY → 2618
漆 Japanese lacquer tree → 0863
樺 BIRCH → 1324
椛 BIRCH → 1202
梧 CHINESE PARASOL TREE → 1200
檀 SPINDLE TREE → 1385
椿 CAMELLIA → 1278
柳 WILLOW → 1115
柊 HOLLY → 1119
椋 *APHANANTHE ASPERA* → 1245
柾 spindle tree → 1114
槻 ZELKOVA → 1349
楢 OAK → 1287
樫 EVERGREEN OAK → 1364
柏 CYPRESS, JAPANESE EMPEROR OAK → 1110
榎 HACKBERRY → 1323
梶 PAPER MULBERRY → 1199
柘 JAPANESE BOXWOOD → 1117
楊 WILLOW → 1286
桧 JAPANESE CYPRESS → 1160
梛 *NAGEIA NAGI* → 1206
榊 SACRED SHINTO TREE → 1327
楓 MAPLE → 1280
松 PINE → 1075
杉 CRYPTOMERIA → 1027
槙 PODOCARPUS → 1330
楠 CAMPHOR TREE → 1283
樟 CAMPHOR TREE → 1351

桃

1174

1-4-6

▶**PEACH**

トウ もも

Ⓒ 桃 táo

75	Jōyō	U6843
木	S10-4-6	F1628

1	2	3	4	5	6	7	8	9	10
一	十	才	木	杊	杊	杊	桃	桃	桃

COMPOUNDS

● [original meaning] **PEACH tree; peach**

桃花 とうか [rare] peach blossom

桃李 とうり peach and plum

桜桃 おうとう cherry

黄桃 おうとう yellow peach

扁桃腺 へんとうせん tonsils

KUN

【もも 桃】**PEACH; peach tree**

桃色 ももいろ rose, pink

桃園 ももぞの peach orchard

桃割れ ももわれ *momoware* coiffure

SYNONYMS

● **fruits and fruit trees**

桃 PEACH → 1174
榛 HAZEL → 1328
椎 CHINQUAPIN → 1249
柚 YUZU → 1123
椰 COCONUT → 1285
柑 CITRUS → 1112
橙 BITTER ORANGE → 1369
葡 GRAPE → 2902
萄 GRAPE → 2870
柿 PERSIMMON → 1118
檎 APPLE → 1386
李 PLUM → 3050
枇 LOQUAT → 1063
杷 LOQUAT → 1065
苺 STRAWBERRY → 2780
菱 water chestnut → 2879
杏 APRICOT → 3049
梅 JAPANESE APRICOT → 1159
橘 MANDARIN → 1366
栗 CHESTNUT → 3280
栃 JAPANESE HORSE CHESTNUT → 1122
梨 PEAR → 3412
蕉 PLANTAIN → 2994

桝

1175

◧1-4-6

▶**MEASURE**

ます

75	Nonstandard	U67A1
木	S10-4-6	F0000

traditional form → see 枡 at 1070

栓

1176

◧1-4-6

▶**STOPPER**

セン

75	Nonstandard	U6813
木	S10-4-6	F0000

traditional form → see 栓 at 1171

梛

◧1-4-6

incorrect stroke-count

➡ see ◧1-4-7: 木 at 1206

殉

1177

◧1-4-6

▶**DIE A MARTYR**

ジュン

Ⓒ 殉 xùn

78	Jōyō	U6B89
歹	S10-4-6	F2483

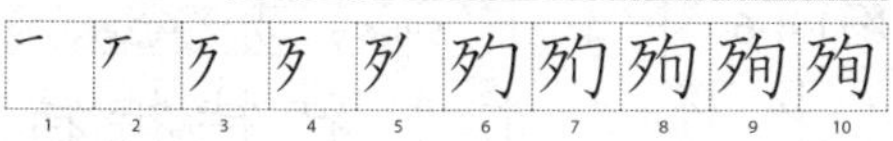

COMPOUNDS

ⓐ **DIE A MARTYR, sacrifice oneself, die for a cause**

ⓑ follow (one's master) to the grave

a 殉教 じゅんきょう martyrdom

殉職 じゅんしょく dying at one's post

殉国 じゅんこく dying for one's country

殉難者 じゅんなんしゃ martyr, victim

b 殉死する じゅんしする follow (one's master) by committing suicide

INDEPENDENT

【じゅんじる 殉じる】**DIE A MARTYR**

SYNONYMS

ⓐ **die**

死 DIE → 4334

萎 WITHER → 2872

没 die → 0305

亡 DECEASE → 4210

殉 DIE A MARTYR → 1177

歿 DIE → 1078

去 pass away → 2678

逝 DEPART THIS LIFE → 3850

斃 FALL DOWN DEAD → 3593

枯 WITHER → 1113

殊

1178

◧1-4-6

▶**SPECIAL**

シュ こと

Ⓒ 殊 shū

78	Jōyō	U6B8A
歹	S10-4-6	F1482

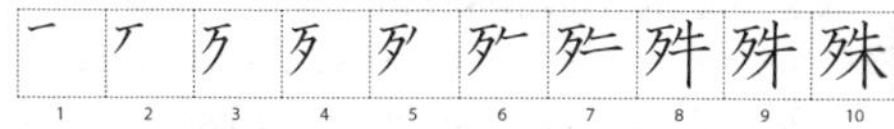

COMPOUNDS

● (exceptional) **SPECIAL, distinguished, unusual, above others**

殊勲 しゅくん meritorious deeds, distinguished service

殊勝な しゅしょうな laudable, praiseworthy

殊遇 しゅぐう special favor

特殊な とくしゅな special, unique

KUN

【こと 殊】[in compounds] **SPECIALness, distinctiveness**

殊に ことに especially, distinctly, exceptionally, above all

殊の外 ことのほか exceedingly, beyond measure; unexpectedly

殊更に ことさらに especially; intentionally, deliberately

SYNONYMS

● **special**

特 SPECIAL (distinct) → 1181

別 special (distinct) → 1434

殊 SPECIAL (exceptional) → 1178

専 EXCLUSIVE → 3272

USAGE

【こと】

殊

[in compounds] specialness, distinctiveness

異

difference

HOMOPHONES

こと 異 DIFFERENT → 3195

残

1179

◧1-4-6

▶**REMAIN**

▶**RUTHLESS**

ザン のこ(る) のこ(す)

Ⓝ 殘 Ⓒ 残 cán

78	Jōyō-4	U6B8B
歹	S10-4-6	F0320

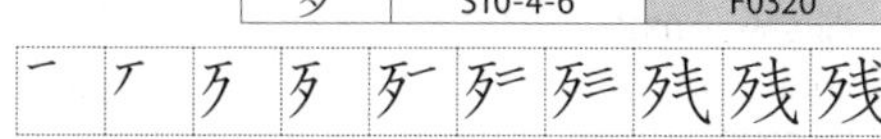

COMPOUNDS

❶ **REMAIN, linger, stay**

残余 ざんよ remainder, residue, remnant

方 日 木 歹 【火】 牛 王 ネ 月 月

残高 ざんだか balance, remainder
残額 ざんがく balance (of an account)
残業 ざんぎょう overtime
残飯 ざんぱん leftover food [rice]
残雪 ざんせつ lingering snow
残念 ざんねん regret, disappointment, chagrin

❷ [sometimes also 惨 0585] **RUTHLESS, cruel, brutal**
残酷な ざんこくな cruel, ruthless, atrocious
残虐な ざんぎゃくな cruel, atrocious, brutal, inhuman
残忍 ざんにん cruelty, atrocity, brutality
無残な むざんな cruel, atrocious; pitiful, tragic, miserable

❸ injure, destroy
廃残 はいざん ruin, decline

INDEPENDENT

【ざん 残】**REMAIN**der, balance
百円の残 ひゃくえんのざん balance of 100 yen

KUN

【のこる 残る】**REMAIN, linger, stay; be left over; survive;** *sumo* **remain in competition, stay in the ring**
残り のこり remainder, remnant, residue, leavings
残らず のこらず entirely, without exception
残り物 のこりもの leftovers, remains, scraps
残った のこった Not yet!
生き残る いきのこる survive, outlive

【のこす 残す】**leave (behind), keep back; reserve, save; bequeath, hand down (to posterity);** *sumo* **REMAIN in competition, stay in the ring;** [in compounds] **leave undone**
食べ残し たべのこし leftover food
取り残す とりのこす leave (behind)
言い残す いいのこす leave word with, state in one's will; leave (something) unsaid, forget to mention

SPECIAL READINGS

名残 なごり parting; memory; remains
名残惜しい なごりおしい be sorry to part, be sad to leave

SYNONYMS

❶ **remain**
残 REMAIN → 1179
余 REMAINING → 2535
留 STAY → 3189
滞 STAY → 0815

❷ **cruel**
虐 CRUEL → 3989
惨 CRUEL → 0585
酷 SEVERE → 1967
辣 SEVERE → 1965
残 RUTHLESS → 1179
凶 ATROCIOUS → 3679
苛 HARSH → 2786

【のこす】
◯ **leave**
遺 LEAVE BEHIND → 3928
残す leave → 1179

NOTE

➡ see COMPOUND FORMATION for 残念 ざんねん → 念 2554

烟

1180
1-4-6

▶**SMOKE**
エン けむ(る) けむり けむ(い)

86	Nonstandard	U70DF
火	S10-4-6	F0000

alternative form → see 煙 at 1294

特

1181
1-4-6

▶**SPECIAL**
トク
Ⓒ 特 tè

93	Jōyō-4	U7279
牛	S10-4-6	F0225

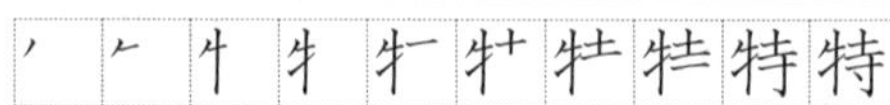

COMPOUNDS

ⓐ (distinct among others) **SPECIAL, peculiar, unique, exclusive**

ⓑ (surpassing what is common) **SPECIAL**, extraordinary

a 特別の とくべつの special, particular; extraordinary
特色 とくしょく characteristic
特徴 とくちょう distinctive feature, characteristic
特価 とっか special price, bargain price
特集 とくしゅう special edition
特許 とっきょ patent; special permission; concession
特権 とっけん privilege, exclusive right
特使 とくし special envoy [messenger]
特定の とくていの specific, particular
特殊な とくしゅな special, unique
特急 とっきゅう super-express
特大 とくだい extra large, oversize
特有の とくゆうの characteristic (of); special, peculiar
特異な とくいな peculiar, unique
特産 とくさん special product, specialty
特訓 とっくん special [intensive] training, crash course
独特 どくとく peculiarity, uniqueness

b 特等 とくとう special class [grade]
奇特な きとくな praiseworthy; benevolent

INDEPENDENT

【とく 特】 **SPECIAL grade (of a product)**

特に とくに specially, particularly, especially

SYNONYMS

ⓐ **special**

特 SPECIAL (distinct) → 1181
別 special (distinct) → 1434
殊 SPECIAL (exceptional) → 1178
専 EXCLUSIVE → 3272

班

1182

1-4-6

▶SQUAD

ハン

Ⓒ 班 bān

96	Jōyō-6	U73ED
王	S10-4-6	F1630

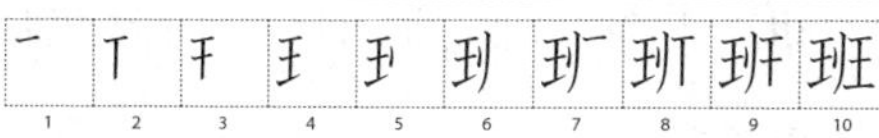

COMPOUNDS

❶ [also suffix] small group of individuals engaged in a common effort:

ⓐ **SQUAD, group, party, team, crew**
ⓑ (military unit) **SQUAD, corps**

a 班長 はんちょう squad [group] leader
班員 はんいん member of a group
取材班 しゅざいはん data collecting party
三班 さんぱん group 3
救護班 きゅうごはん relief squad [party]
作業班 さぎょうはん work party

b 第四中隊第二班 だいよんちゅうたいだいにはん second squad of the fourth company

❷ [usu. 斑 1260] spot, speck

班点 はんてん spot, speck

❸ order, seating order, precedence, ranking

班次 はんじ precedence, ranking
首班 しゅはん head (of state or of a cabinet), prime minister

❹ allot, distribute

班田 はんでん *hist* ancient farmland allotment

INDEPENDENT

【はん 班】 **SQUAD, group**

三つの班に分ける みっつのはんにわける divide into three groups

SYNONYMS

❶ⓐ **groups**

群 GROUP (of any kind) → 1942
班 SQUAD → 1182
軍 team → 2582
組 group (of people) → 1693
陣 lineup → 0545
連 set → 3849
族 common-interest group (*slang*) → 1195
党 PARTY → 3190
隊 PARTY (organized group) → 0762
団 BODY → 3791
伍 ranks → 0050

COMPOUND FORMATION

【首班 しゅはん】

首班 'head, etc.' is the man who occupies the top or leading (首) seat or rank (班 ❸).

珠

1183

1-4-6

▶PEARL

シュ たま▲ ㊔ み

Ⓒ 珠 zhū

96	Jōyō	U73E0
王	S10-4-6	F1725

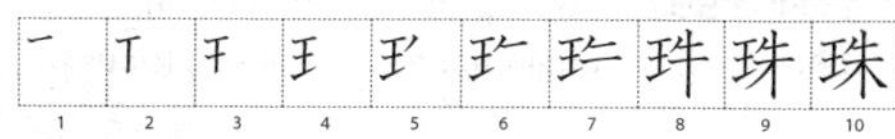

COMPOUNDS

ⓐ **PEARL**
ⓑ **something round like a PEARL, bead**

a 珠玉 しゅぎょく jewel, gem
真珠 しんじゅ pearl

b 珠算 しゅざん calculation on the abacus

KUN

【たま 珠】 [now usu. 玉, formerly also 璧] **gem, jewel, precious stone, PEARL; bead**

珠暖簾 たまのれん bead curtain

SPECIAL READINGS

数珠 じゅず (Buddhist) rosary

SYNONYMS

ⓐ **precious stones**

玉 GEM → 4289
珂 WHITE AGATE → 1137
璧 DISK-SHAPED JEWEL → 3608
琥 AMBER → 1261
珀 AMBER → 1136
珠 PEARL → 1183
瑛 TRANSPARENT GEM → 1259
瑠 LAPIS LAZULI → 1342
璃 GLASSY SUBSTANCE → 1358
晶 CRYSTAL → 3122
玖 beautiful black jewel → 1041
琉 LAPIS LAZULI → 1221
琳 BEAUTIFUL GEM → 1262

HOMOPHONES

たま

玉 GEM → 4289
球 BALL → 1219
弾 PROJECTILE → 0697
璧 DISK-SHAPED JEWEL → 3608

NOTE

➡ see USAGE note at 玉 4289

方 日 木 歹 火 牛 王 【ネ】 月 月

祥

1184

1-4-6

▶**AUSPICIOUS**

ショウ ㊔ さち よし やす ただ

Ⓝ 祥 Ⓒ 祥 xiáng

113	Jōyō	U7965
ネ	S10-4-6	F1697

COMPOUNDS

❶ⓐ **AUSPICIOUS, propitious, favorable**

ⓑ **AUSPICIOUS omen, lucky sign**

a 不祥事 ふしょうじ scandal, inauspicious event

b 吉祥 きちじょう(=きっしょう) auspicious omen

発祥 はっしょう origin; appearance of auspicious omen

瑞祥 ずいしょう auspicious sign, good omen

❷ death or mourning anniversary

祥月 しょうつき death month

SYNONYMS

❶ **good fortune**

吉 LUCKY → 2691

嘉 HAPPY → 2953

祥 AUSPICIOUS → 1184

瑞 AUSPICIOUS OMEN → 1302

禎 PROPITIOUS OMEN → 1305

幸 GOOD FORTUNE → 2755

福 FORTUNE → 1303

倖 GOOD FORTUNE → 0134

朕

1185

1-4-6

▶**IMPERIAL WE**

チン

Ⓝ 朕 Ⓒ 朕 zhèn

74	Jōyō	U6715
月	S10-4-6	F3286

INDEPENDENT

【ちん 朕】**IMPERIAL WE**—formal first person pronoun used chiefly by the emperor of Japan

朕の ちんの Our

朕が意 ちんがい Our will

SYNONYMS

【ちん】

○ **first person pronouns**

私 I (*polite*) → 1432

我 SELF → 4362

己 ONESELF → 4188

身 ONE'S PERSON → 4368

僕 I (*familiar*) → 0185

俺 I (*intimate*) → 0124

吾 I (*elegant*) → 3060

予 I (*pompous*) → 2477

余 I (*pompous*) → 2535

麿 I (*archaic*) → 3949

朕 IMPERIAL WE → 1185

自 SELF → 4338

胴

1186

1-4-6

▶**TRUNK**

ドウ

Ⓒ 胴 dòng

130	Jōyō	U80F4
月	S10-4-6	F1916

COMPOUNDS

❶ [original meaning] **TRUNK (of the body), torso, abdomen**

胴体 どうたい trunk, body, torso, hull

胴巻き どうまき bellyband

胴衣 どうい jacket, vest

胴上げ どうあげ tossing (a person in triumph)

❷ (main body of anything) **TRUNK**, body, main part

胴乱 どうらん collecting [botanical] case

双胴機 そうどうき twin-fuselage plane

❸ used phonetically for *dō*

胴欲 どうよく avarice, greed

胴元 どうもと bookmaker (in gambling)

INDEPENDENT

【どう 胴】**TRUNK; main body of anything**

胴が長い どうがながい have a long trunk

胴を着ける どうをつける put on body armor

SYNONYMS

❶ **trunk parts**

胸 CHEST → 1187

腹 BELLY → 1308

胴 TRUNK → 1186

腰 WAIST → 1311

背 BACK → 3182

肩 SHOULDER → 2446

股 CROTCH → 1093

脇 ARMPIT → 1188

腋 ARMPIT → 1266

❸ **phonetic [d]**

陀 PHONETIC [da] → 0409

達 phonetic [da] → 3893

提 phonetic [dai] → 0720

胴 phonetic [dō] → 1186

胸

▸**CHEST**
キョウ　むね　むな-
Ⓒ 胸 xiōng

1187
◧ 1-4-6

130	Jōyō-6	U80F8
月	S10-4-6	F0638

COMPOUNDS

❶ⓐ [original meaning] **CHEST, breast, thorax**
ⓑ breast height

a 胸囲 きょうい chest measurement
胸部 きょうぶ breast, chest
胸骨 きょうこつ breastbone
胸郭 きょうかく thorax, chest
気胸 ききょう pneumothorax
b 胸壁 きょうへき chest wall; breast work
胸像 きょうぞう bust

❷ (seat of emotions) **breast, (inmost) heart, mind, feelings**
胸裏 きょうり one's bosom, one's heart, one's feelings
胸中 きょうちゅう mind, heart, one's feelings, thoughts
度胸 どきょう courage, pluck, heart

KUN

【むね 胸, むな- 胸-】 **CHEST, breast, thorax; heart, lungs;** (seat of emotions) **breast, bosom, heart**
胸飾り むねかざり brooch
胸板 むないた breast
胸毛 むなげ chest hair
胸焼け むねやけ heartburn, sour stomach
胸を病む むねをやむ become consumptive
胸騒ぎ むなさわぎ uneasiness, (heart) flutter, emotional upset
胸を痛める むねをいためる worry oneself (about)
鳩胸 はとむね chicken [pigeon] breast

SYNONYMS

❶ⓐ trunk parts
胸 CHEST → 1187
腹 BELLY → 1308
胴 TRUNK → 1186
腰 WAIST → 1311
背 BACK → 3182
肩 SHOULDER → 2446
股 CROTCH → 1093
脇 ARMPIT → 1188
腋 ARMPIT → 1266

❶ⓐ chest
胸 CHEST → 1187
乳 breast → 1823

❷ psyche
心 HEART → 0011
霊 SPIRIT (soul) → 3480
魂 SOUL, spirit → 1346
魄 SOUL → 1570
腹 heart → 1308
衷 INNER HEART → 2600
襟 inner mind → 1599
胸 breast → 1187
懐 BOSOM → 0942
神 MIND → 1143
気 SPIRIT (consciousness) → 3960
精 SPIRIT (mind) → 1729

脇

▸**SIDE**
▸**ARMPIT**
キョウ▲　わき
Ⓒ 胁 xié

1188
◧ 1-4-6

130	Jōyō	U8107
月	S10-4-6	F1131

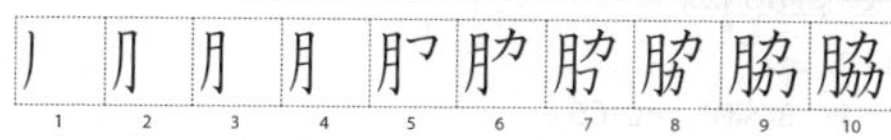

COMPOUNDS

ⓐ SIDE, flank
ⓑ [original meaning] **ARMPIT**

a 脇侍(=脇士、夾×侍、挟侍) きょうじ flanking attendants to principal image of Buddha in a temple
脇息 きょうそく (portable) armrest

KUN

【わき 脇】
① [formerly also 傍]
ⓐ **SIDE**
ⓑ **the other way, another place**
a 脇腹 わきばら one's side, flank; illegitimate birth
脇差 わきざし short sword
関脇 せきわけ second champion sumo wrestler
両脇 りょうわき both sides
b 脇見 わきみ looking aside
脇道 わきみち side road; digression
脇目 わきめ looking aside; eyes of an onlooker

② [formerly also 傍] **supporting actor [role]**
脇役 わきやく supporting actor [role]
脇能 わきのう minor piece in noh plays

③ [also 腋]
ⓐ **ARMPIT**
ⓑ armhole
a 脇毛 わきげ hair of the armpit
脇の下 わきのした armpit, axilla
小脇 こわき under one's arm

方 日 木 歹 火 牛 王 ネ 【月】 月

SYNONYMS

ⓐ side
- 側 SIDE →0155
- 脇 SIDE →1188
- 方 side →2459
- 辺 -side →3761
- 面 side →2590
- 傍 BESIDE →0166
- 横 SIDEWAYS →1350

ⓑ trunk parts
- 胸 CHEST →1187
- 腹 BELLY →1308
- 胴 TRUNK →1186
- 腰 WAIST →1311
- 背 BACK →3182
- 肩 SHOULDER →2446
- 股 CROTCH →1093
- 脇 ARMPIT →1188
- 腋 ARMPIT →1266

HOMOPHONES

わき
- 傍 BESIDE →0166
- 腋 ARMPIT →1266

NOTE

➡ see USAGE note at 傍 0166

脈

1189

1-4-6

▶**VEIN**
▶**PULSE**

ミャク

Ⓝ 脈 脉◇ Ⓒ 脉 mài mò

130	Jōyō-4	U8108
月	S10-4-6	F1315

COMPOUNDS

❶ [original meaning] (any blood vessel) **VEIN, artery, blood vessel**
- 脈管 みゃっかん blood vessel; duct
- 動脈 どうみゃく artery
- 静脈 じょうみゃく vein

❷ⓐ something resembling a VEIN in shape or structure
ⓑ *geol* **VEIN**, seam
- *a* 脈脈たる みゃくみゃくたる continuous, unbroken; pulsating forcefully
- 山脈 さんみゃく mountain range
- 葉脈 ようみゃく veins of a leaf
- *b* 鉱脈 こうみゃく (mineral) vein, deposit, lode
- 水脈 すいみゃく water vein; waterway

❸ (distinctive thread) **VEIN, thread, line**
- 脈絡 みゃくらく logical connection, chain of reasoning
- 文脈 ぶんみゃく context
- 乱脈 らんみゃく disorder, confusion, chaos
- 人脈 じんみゃく line of connections
- 金脈 きんみゃく (questionable) financial connections; vein of gold

❹ PULSE, pulsation
- 脈拍 みゃくはく pulse, pulsation
- 徐脈 じょみゃく bradycardia
- 平脈 へいみゃく regular pulse
- 不整脈 ふせいみゃく arrhythmia

INDEPENDENT

【みゃく 脈】**PULSE, pulsation; hope**
- 脈を取る みゃくをとる take a pulse
- まだ脈が有る まだみゃくがある be not altogether hopeless

SYNONYMS

❶ tubular passages
- 管 PIPE →3349
- 筒 TUBE →3323
- 道 passage →3888
- 脈 VEIN →1189
- 樋 WATER PIPE →1353

❷ line
- 線 LINE →1760
- 筋 THREADLIKE STRUCTURE →3319
- 条 strip →2726
- 脈 VEIN →1189
- 棒 straight line →1237
- 縞 STRIPE →1784
- 軸 AXIS →1908

❸ reasoning
- 理 REASON →1220
- 筋 thread →3319
- 脈 VEIN →1189

脂

1190

1-4-6

▶**FAT**

シ あぶら

Ⓒ 脂 zhī

130	Jōyō	U8102
月	S10-4-6	F1430

COMPOUNDS

❶ [original meaning] **FAT, grease, animal fat**
- 脂肪 しぼう fat, grease
- 脂質 ししつ lipid, fats
- 油脂 ゆし fats and oils
- 脱脂粉乳 だっしふんにゅう skim milk

❷ resin

樹脂 じゅし resin

❸ rouge, lipstick

脂粉 しふん cosmetics, rouge and powder

KUN

【あぶら 脂】[formerly also 膏] **FAT, grease, lard, blubber; greasy substance**

脂ぎった あぶらぎった greasy, oily

脂が乗る あぶらがのる be in good table quality; get into the swing of (as one's work)

脂性 あぶらしょう fatty constitution

SYNONYMS

❶ **fats and oils**

油 OIL → 0400

脂 FAT → 1190

肪 ANIMAL FAT → 1089

膏 FAT → 2658

蠟 WAX → 1818

HOMOPHONES

あぶら

油 OIL → 0400

膏 FAT → 2658

NOTE

➡ see USAGE note at 油 0400

脆

1191

◧ 1-4-6

▶ **FRAGILE**

ゼイ もろ(い)

Ⓒ 脆 cuì

130	Non-Jōyō	U8106
月	S10-4-6	F2688

COMPOUNDS

● **FRAGILE, brittle, flimsy, weak**

脆弱な ぜいじゃくな fragile, frail, weak

脆弱性 ぜいじゃくせい vulnerability, fragility

脆性 ぜいせい brittleness, fragility

KUN

【もろい 脆い】

① **FRAGILE, brittle, flimsy, weak**

脆い関係 もろいかんけい fragile relationship

脆いガラス もろいがらす brittle glass

脆くも敗れる もろくもやぶれる be easily defeated

② **tenderhearted, easily moved**

涙脆い なみだもろい easily moved to tears

情に脆い じょうにもろい tenderhearted, sentimental, emotional

SYNONYMS

● **weak**

弱 WEAK → 1499

柔 SOFT → 2591

脆 FRAGILE → 1191

癈 DISABLED → 4077

脈

1192

◧ 1-4-6

▶ **VEIN**

▶ **PULSE**

ミャク

130	Nonstandard	U8108
月	S10-4-6	F0000

traditional form → see 脈 at 1189

朕

1193

◧ 1-4-6

▶ **IMPERIAL WE**

チン

74	Nonstandard	U6715
月	S10-4-6	F0000

traditional form → see 朕 at 1185

旋

1194

◧ 1-4-7

▶ **GYRATE**

セン

Ⓒ 旋 xuán xuàn

70	Jōyō	U65CB
方	S11-4-7	F1832

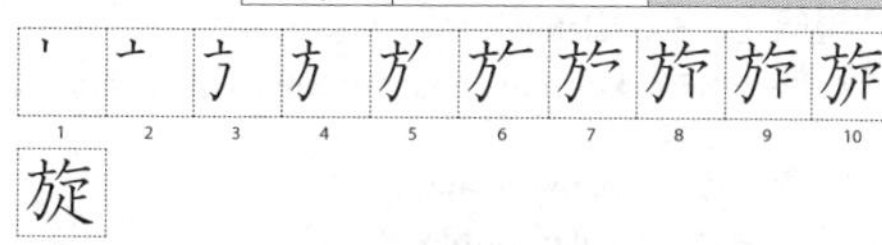

COMPOUNDS

❶ **GYRATE, whirl, revolve, spiral, go around**

旋回 せんかい revolution, rotation, circling, swiveling

旋転 せんてん gyration, whirling, revolution, rotation

旋盤 せんばん lathe

旋削 せんさく turning (on a lathe)

旋風 せんぷう whirlwind

旋律 せんりつ melody

螺旋 らせん spiral, helix; screw

❷ **render a service to, mediate**

斡旋 あっせん good offices, services; mediation

周旋業 しゅうせんぎょう brokerage

❸ return, turn back

凱旋 がいせん triumphal return

SYNONYMS

❶ **turn**

旋 GYRATE → 1194

転 TURN → 1872

回 TURN ROUND → 3793

廻 TURN ROUND → 3833

巡 MAKE THE ROUNDS → 3781

循 CIRCULATE → 0704

斡 REVOLVE → 2168

捻 TWIST → 0604

【方】日 木 火 爿 王 正 ネ 月 夫

NOTE

★ do not confuse with 旅 TRAVEL → 1153

族

1195

1-4-7

▶FAMILY

ゾク

Ⓒ 族 zú

70	Jōyō-3	U65CF
方	S11-4-7	F0330

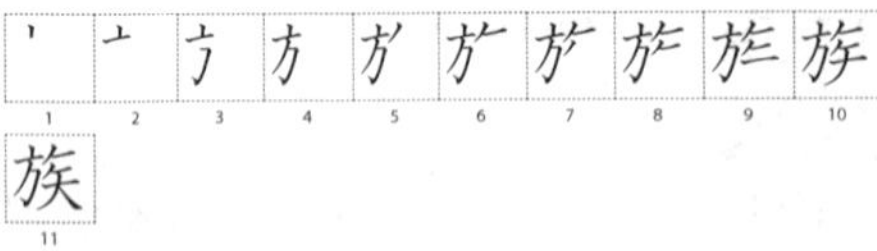

COMPOUNDS

❶ⓐ FAMILY, kinsman; relatives

ⓑ FAMILY of rank, nobility

ⓒ [rare] death penalty (in ancient China) imposed on an offender and his whole **FAMILY**

a 家族 かぞく family, household

遺族 いぞく bereaved family

親族 しんぞく relative

一族 いちぞく kinsman, relative, one's (whole) family; race

血族 けつぞく blood relative

b 貴族 きぞく nobility, noble

皇族 こうぞく imperial family, royalty

c 族滅 ぞくめつ putting an entire family to death

❷ race, clan, tribe

民族 みんぞく race, people, nation

部族 ぶぞく tribe

種族 しゅぞく race, tribe; family, genus; species

蛮族 ばんぞく savage tribe

アリアン族 ありあんぞく Aryan family

アイヌ族 あいぬぞく the Ainu race

❸ⓐ [also suffix] **class of things with common features, as a FAMILY of languages**

ⓑ *math* **FAMILY**

ⓒ *chem* group (of elements)

a 語族 ごぞく family of languages

水族館 すいぞくかん aquarium

b 関数族 かんすうぞく family of functions

亜族 あぞく subgroup (of the periodic table)

c 白金族 はっきんぞく platinum group

❹ [also suffix] *slang* (group of persons who share a common interest or engage in a common activity) **tribe, herd, clan, gang, set, clique**

雷族 かみなりぞく Thunder Herd, hot-rodders

暴走族 ぼうそうぞく motorcycle gang, hot-rodders

深夜族 しんやぞく the night owls

社用族 しゃようぞく expense-account spenders

ながら族 ながらぞく persons who do two things at the same time (as studying while watching TV)

団地族 だんちぞく housing project dwellers

❺ [formerly also 簇 3377] form a cluster

族生する ぞくせいする (of plants) grow in clusters

SYNONYMS

❶ⓐ family and relations

族 FAMILY → 1195

家 FAMILY → 2827

門 family → 1100

氏 clan → 3669

縁 RELATION → 1754

姻 relative by marriage → 0421

親 RELATIVES → 2264

戚 RELATIVES → 4401

曽 GREAT- → 2632

❷ people

民 PEOPLE → 3770

族 race → 1195

❹ groups

群 GROUP (of any kind) → 1942

班 SQUAD → 1182

軍 team → 2582

組 group (of people) → 1693

陣 lineup → 0545

連 set → 3849

族 common-interest group (*slang*) → 1195

党 PARTY → 3190

隊 PARTY (organized group) → 0762

団 BODY → 3791

伍 ranks → 0050

晦

1196

1-4-7

▶DARK

▶LAST DAY OF THE LUNAR MONTH

カイ くら(ます) つごもり

Ⓝ 晦 Ⓒ 晦 huì

72	Names	U6666
日	S11-4-7	F2665

COMPOUNDS

ⓐ DARK, obscure

ⓑ abscond, conceal oneself

a 晦冥 かいめい darkness

晦渋な かいじゅうな ambiguous, obscure, equivocal

b 韜×晦する とうかいする conceal one's talents [position, intentions]; conceal oneself

KUN

【くらます 晦ます】 [also 暗ます]

① **abscond, conceal oneself**

② **deceive, fool, dissemble**

【つごもり 晦】[also 晦日] **LAST DAY OF THE LUNAR MONTH**

SPECIAL READINGS

晦日 つごもり [also 晦] last day of the month
大晦日 おおみそか(=おおつごもり) last day of the year, December 31

SYNONYMS

ⓐ dark
暗 DARK → 1273
黒 BLACK → 3406
陰 shaded → 0657
闇 DARK → 4134
晦 DARK → 1196
昏 dark → 3073
昧 DARK → 1105
冥 DARK → 2613
曖 SHADY → 1383

【つごもり】
◯ days
日 DAY → 3759
曜 DAY OF THE WEEK → 1402
昼 DAYTIME → 3841
旦 first day → 3041
朔 FIRST DAY OF THE LUNAR MONTH → 1678
晦 LAST DAY OF THE LUNAR MONTH → 1196

HOMOPHONES

つごもり 晦日 → 1196, 3759
くらます 暗 DARK → 1273

晩

1197
◧ 1-4-7

▸EVENING
バン

72	Names	U665A
日	S11-4-7	F0000

traditional form → see 晩 at 1232

晟

1198
◧ 1-4-7

▸SUNNY
セイ ジョウ ㊔ あきら のぼる あき てる なり ひかる

72	Nonstandard	U6660
日	S11-4-7	F0000

traditional form → see 晟 at 3104

梶

1199
◧ 1-4-7

▸PAPER MULBERRY
ビ かじ
Ⓒ 梶 wěi

75	Names	U68B6
木	S11-4-7	F1973

KUN

【かじ 梶】
① **PAPER MULBERRY**
梶の木 かじのき paper mulberry
② steering device:
ⓐ [usu. 舵] **rudder**
ⓑ [usu. 舵] **helm, tiller, wheel**
ⓒ oar
ⓓ shafts (of a rickshaw)
a 梶木(=梶木鮪×) かじき(=かじきまぐろ) marlin, swordfish
d 梶棒 かじぼう shafts (of a rickshaw or similar vehicle), thills

SYNONYMS

【かじ】
① **trees**
桜 CHERRY → 1168
桐 PAULOWNIA → 1173
桂 AROMATIC TREE, katsura tree → 1163
梓 CATALPA → 1207
桑 MULBERRY → 2618
漆 Japanese lacquer tree → 0863
樺 BIRCH → 1324
椛 BIRCH → 1202
梧 CHINESE PARASOL TREE → 1200
檀 SPINDLE TREE → 1385
椿 CAMELLIA → 1278
柳 WILLOW → 1115
柊 HOLLY → 1119
椋 *APHANANTHE ASPERA* → 1245
柾 spindle tree → 1114
槻 ZELKOVA → 1349
楢 OAK → 1287
樫 EVERGREEN OAK → 1364
柏 CYPRESS, JAPANESE EMPEROR OAK → 1110
榎 HACKBERRY → 1323
梶 PAPER MULBERRY → 1199
柘 JAPANESE BOXWOOD → 1117
楊 WILLOW → 1286
桧 JAPANESE CYPRESS → 1160
梛 *NAGEIA NAGI* → 1206
榊 SACRED SHINTO TREE → 1327
楓 MAPLE → 1280
松 PINE → 1075
杉 CRYPTOMERIA → 1027
槙 PODOCARPUS → 1330
楠 CAMPHOR TREE → 1283
樟 CAMPHOR TREE → 1351
② **parts of boats and ships**
舵 STEERING DEVICE → 1697
梶 steering device → 1199
櫓 SCULL → 1412
櫂 OAR → 1405
舷 GUNWALE → 1698
艙 SHIP'S HOLD → 1786

HOMOPHONES

かじ 舵 STEERING DEVICE → 1697

NOTE

➡ see USAGE note at 舵 1697

梧

1200

1-4-7

▶**CHINESE PARASOL TREE**

ゴ ギョ 名 きり さとし

C 梧 wú

75	Names	U68A7
木	S11-4-7	F3440

COMPOUNDS

● [rare] **CHINESE PARASOL TREE**, phoenix tree

梧桐 ごとう Chinese parasol (tree), phoenix tree, *Firmiana platanifolia*

SYNONYMS

● **trees**

桜 CHERRY → 1168
桐 PAULOWNIA → 1173
桂 AROMATIC TREE, katsura tree → 1163
梓 CATALPA → 1207
桑 MULBERRY → 2618
漆 Japanese lacquer tree → 0863
樺 BIRCH → 1324
椛 BIRCH → 1202
梧 CHINESE PARASOL TREE → 1200
檀 SPINDLE TREE → 1385
椿 CAMELLIA → 1278
柳 WILLOW → 1115
柊 HOLLY → 1119
椋 *APHANANTHE ASPERA* → 1245
柾 spindle tree → 1114
槻 ZELKOVA → 1349
楢 OAK → 1287
樫 EVERGREEN OAK → 1364
柏 CYPRESS, JAPANESE EMPEROR OAK → 1110
榎 HACKBERRY → 1323
梶 PAPER MULBERRY → 1199
柘 JAPANESE BOXWOOD → 1117
楊 WILLOW → 1286
桧 JAPANESE CYPRESS → 1160
梛 *NAGEIA NAGI* → 1206
榊 SACRED SHINTO TREE → 1327
楓 MAPLE → 1280
松 PINE → 1075
杉 CRYPTOMERIA → 1027
槙 PODOCARPUS → 1330
楠 CAMPHOR TREE → 1283
樟 CAMPHOR TREE → 1351

彬

1201

1-4-7

▶**REFINED AND GENTLE**

ヒン 名 あき あきら あや よし

C 彬 bīn

59	Names	U5F6C
彡	S11-3-8	F2769

COMPOUNDS

● [rare] (having both appearance and substance)
REFINED AND GENTLE, handsome and solid in character, having a due combination of plainness and ornament

彬蔚× ひんうつ handsome, erudite and refined

文質彬彬 ぶんしつひんぴん refined, handsome and solid in character

SYNONYMS

● **elegant**

雅 ELEGANT → 1532
淑 GRACEFUL → 0639
優 graceful → 0200
粋 REFINED → 1645
彬 REFINED AND GENTLE → 1201

椛

1202

1-4-7

▶**BIRCH**

かば 名 なぎ

C (国字)

75	Names	U691B
木	S11-4-7	F0000

KUN

【かば 椛】BIRCH

SYNONYMS

【かば】

○ **trees**

桜 CHERRY → 1168
桐 PAULOWNIA → 1173
桂 AROMATIC TREE, katsura tree → 1163
梓 CATALPA → 1207
桑 MULBERRY → 2618
漆 Japanese lacquer tree → 0863
樺 BIRCH → 1324
椛 BIRCH → 1202
梧 CHINESE PARASOL TREE → 1200
檀 SPINDLE TREE → 1385
椿 CAMELLIA → 1278
柳 WILLOW → 1115
柊 HOLLY → 1119
椋 *APHANANTHE ASPERA* → 1245
柾 spindle tree → 1114
槻 ZELKOVA → 1349
楢 OAK → 1287
樫 EVERGREEN OAK → 1364
柏 CYPRESS, JAPANESE EMPEROR OAK → 1110

榎 HACKBERRY → 1323
梶 PAPER MULBERRY → 1199
柘 JAPANESE BOXWOOD → 1117
楊 WILLOW → 1286
桧 JAPANESE CYPRESS → 1160
梛 *NAGEIA NAGI* → 1206
榊 SACRED SHINTO TREE → 1327
楓 MAPLE → 1280
松 PINE → 1075
杉 CRYPTOMERIA → 1027
槙 PODOCARPUS → 1330
楠 CAMPHOR TREE → 1283
樟 CAMPHOR TREE → 1351

HOMOPHONES

かば 樺 BIRCH → 1324

NOTE

➡ see USAGE note at 樺 1324

械

1203

■ 1-4-7

▶MECHANICAL CONTRIVANCE

カイ かせ▲

Ⓒ 械 xiè

75	Jōyō-4	U68B0
木	S11-4-7	F1519

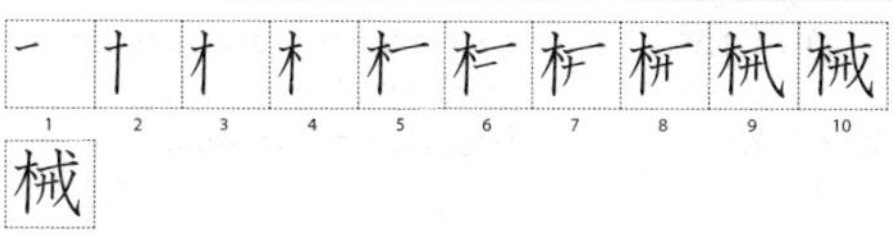

COMPOUNDS

● **MECHANICAL CONTRIVANCE, device, instrument, tool**

機械 きかい machine, mechanism
器械 きかい instrument, apparatus, appliance

KUN

【かせ 械】[original meaning] fetters, shackles
足械 あしかせ fetters, shackles, hobbles

SYNONYMS

● **machines and tools**

機 MACHINE → 1365
械 MECHANICAL CONTRIVANCE → 1203
具 IMPLEMENT → 3159
器 INSTRUMENT → 3367
儀 measuring instrument → 0191
鏡 OPTICAL INSTRUMENT → 2219
董 OLD TOOL → 2911

梗

1204

■ 1-4-7

▶STOP UP

コウ キョウ▲

Ⓒ 梗 gěng

75	Jōyō	U6897
木	S11-4-7	F2278

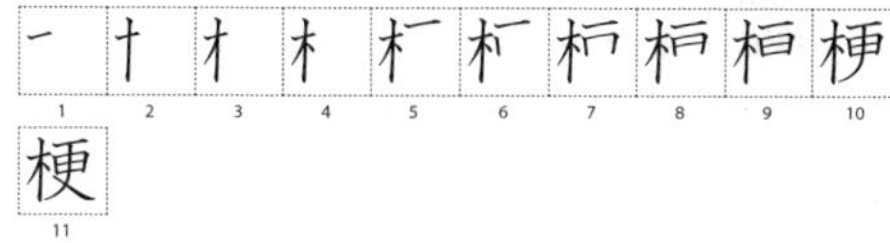

COMPOUNDS

❶ **STOP UP, close up, clog**

梗塞 こうそく stoppage; tightness; infarction
脳梗塞 のうこうそく stroke, cerebral infarction

❷ outline, summary, general idea

梗概 こうがい outline, summary

❸ **branch, stem**

桔梗 ききょう Chinese bellflower, balloon flower
花梗 かこう flower stalk, peduncle
青梗菜 ちんげんさい bok choy

❹ plant name element

SYNONYMS

❶ **obstruct and hinder**

遮 INTERRUPT → 3916
塞 STOP UP → 2924
阻 OBSTRUCT → 0411
沮 OBSTRUCT → 0399
奄 OBSTRUCT (by covering) → 2757
妨 HINDER → 0279
障 hinder → 0875
碍 STAND IN THE WAY → 1536
害 stand in the way → 2826
梗 STOP UP → 1204

❶ **close**

閉 CLOSE → 4116
鎖 lock up → 2213
封 SEAL → 1639
梗 STOP UP → 1204
塞 STOP UP → 2924

梱

1205

■ 1-4-7

▶PACK

コン こり

Ⓒ 梱 捆 kǔn

75	Non-Jōyō	U68B1
木	S11-4-7	F3429

COMPOUNDS

❶ **PACK, (tie in a) bundle**

梱包 こんぽう packing, packaging; package
同梱する どうこんする include (something) in a package

方 日 【木】 火 月 王 正 ネ 月 夫

開梱する かいこんする open (a pack), unpack

❷ [original meaning, now obsolete] **doorsill, threshold**

KUN

【こり 梱】

①ⓐ **bale, PACK, package**

ⓑ **counter for bales**

ab 一梱の生糸 ひとこりのきいと a bale of raw silk

② **wicker trunk, wicker suitcase**

SYNONYMS

❶ **join**

結 TIE → 1706
繋 CONNECT → 3612
縛 BIND → 1779
綴 BIND → 1746
緘 BIND UP → 1787
束 TIE UP → 4369
梱 PACK → 1205
連 LINK → 3849
係 CONNECT → 0108
接 join → 0607

梛

1206

1-4-7

▶*NAGEIA NAGI*

ナ なぎ

Ⓒ 梛 nuó

75	Names	U689B
木	S11-4-7	F0000

KUN

【なぎ 梛】 ***NAGEIA NAGI***

梛筏× なぎいかだ butcher's broom, *Ruscus aculeatus*

SYNONYMS

【なぎ】

◯ **trees**

桜 CHERRY → 1168
桐 PAULOWNIA → 1173
桂 AROMATIC TREE, katsura tree → 1163
梓 CATALPA → 1207
桑 MULBERRY → 2618
漆 Japanese lacquer tree → 0863
樺 BIRCH → 1324
椛 BIRCH → 1202
梧 CHINESE PARASOL TREE → 1200
檀 SPINDLE TREE → 1385
椿 CAMELLIA → 1278
柳 WILLOW → 1115
柊 HOLLY → 1119
椋 *APHANANTHE ASPERA* → 1245
柾 spindle tree → 1114
槻 ZELKOVA → 1349
楢 OAK → 1287
樫 EVERGREEN OAK → 1364
柏 CYPRESS, JAPANESE EMPEROR OAK → 1110
榎 HACKBERRY → 1323
梶 PAPER MULBERRY → 1199
柘 JAPANESE BOXWOOD → 1117
楊 WILLOW → 1286
桧 JAPANESE CYPRESS → 1160
梛 *NAGEIA NAGI* → 1206
榊 SACRED SHINTO TREE → 1327
楓 MAPLE → 1280
松 PINE → 1075
杉 CRYPTOMERIA → 1027
槙 PODOCARPUS → 1330
楠 CAMPHOR TREE → 1283
樟 CAMPHOR TREE → 1351

梓

1207

1-4-7

▶**CATALPA**

シ あずさ

Ⓒ 梓 zǐ

75	Names	U6893
木	S11-4-7	F2489

COMPOUNDS

❶ [archaic] **CATALPA**, catalpa tree, Japanese catalpa tree

梓宮 しきゅう emperor's coffin (so called because it was made of catalpa wood)

❷ **printing block, woodcut; wood printing**

上梓 じょうし publishing

❸ [archaic] carpentry, woodwork; cabinetmaker

梓匠 ししょう woodworker, cabinetmaker

INDEPENDENT

【し 梓】 printing block

梓に上せる しにのぼせる publish, bring (a book) into the world

KUN

【あずさ 梓】 **CATALPA, Japanese catalpa tree**

梓弓 あずさゆみ catalpa bow

SYNONYMS

❶ **trees**

桜 CHERRY → 1168
桐 PAULOWNIA → 1173
桂 AROMATIC TREE, katsura tree → 1163
梓 CATALPA → 1207
桑 MULBERRY → 2618
漆 Japanese lacquer tree → 0863
樺 BIRCH → 1324
椛 BIRCH → 1202
梧 CHINESE PARASOL TREE → 1200
檀 SPINDLE TREE → 1385
椿 CAMELLIA → 1278
柳 WILLOW → 1115

柊 HOLLY → 1119
椋 *APHANANTHE ASPERA* → 1245
柾 spindle tree → 1114
槻 ZELKOVA → 1349
楢 OAK → 1287
樫 EVERGREEN OAK → 1364
柏 CYPRESS, JAPANESE EMPEROR OAK → 1110
榎 HACKBERRY → 1323
梶 PAPER MULBERRY → 1199
柘 JAPANESE BOXWOOD → 1117
楊 WILLOW → 1286
桧 JAPANESE CYPRESS → 1160
梛 *NAGEIA NAGI* → 1206
榊 SACRED SHINTO TREE → 1327
楓 MAPLE → 1280
松 PINE → 1075
杉 CRYPTOMERIA → 1027
槙 PODOCARPUS → 1330
楠 CAMPHOR TREE → 1283
樟 CAMPHOR TREE → 1351

❷ **printing plate**
版 PRINTING PLATE → 1082
梓 printing block → 1207

梢

▸TIP OF A TWIG
ショウ こずえ
Ⓝ 梢 Ⓒ 梢 shāo sào

1208
◧ 1-4-7

75	Names	U68A2
木	S11-4-7	F2629

COMPOUNDS

❶ⓐ [original meaning] **TIP OF A TWIG or branch**
ⓑ **tip, end**
ab 末梢 まっしょう tip, end; tip of a twig; *anat* periphery
b 末梢神経 まっしょうしんけい peripheral nerve

❷ [archaic] **rudder**
梢子 しょうし boatman

KUN

【こずえ 梢】**treetop, TIP OF A TWIG**
松の梢 まつのこずえ top of a pine tree

SYNONYMS

❶ⓐ **branches and twigs**
枝 BRANCH → 1073
梢 TIP OF A TWIG → 1208
ⓑ **extremity**
端 END → 1564
末 end → 4317
梢 tip → 1208
先 point → 3046
尖 POINT → 2700
鋒 POINT OF A BLADE → 2172

梳

▸COMB
ソ と(く) と(かす) す(く) けず(る) くしけず(る)
Ⓒ 梳 shū

1209
◧ 1-4-7

75	Non-Jōyō	U68B3
木	S11-4-7	F3389

COMPOUNDS

● [original meaning] **COMB (one's hair)**
梳毛 そもう combed wool [yarn]
梳綿機 そめんき carding machine

KUN

【とく 梳く】[also 解く] **COMB (one's hair)**
【とかす 梳かす】[sometimes also 解かす] **COMB (one's hair)**
髪を梳かす かみをとかす comb one's hair
【すく 梳く】**COMB (one's hair)**
羊毛を梳く ようもうをすく card wool
【けずる 梳る】**COMB (one's hair)**
【くしけずる 梳る】**COMB (one's hair)**

SYNONYMS

● **comb**
櫛 COMB → 1413
梳 COMB → 1209

HOMOPHONES

とく
解 TAKE APART → 1913
溶 DISSOLVE → 0816
説 EXPLAIN → 1949

とかす
解 TAKE APART → 1913
融 FUSE → 2303
溶 DISSOLVE → 0816
熔 MELT → 1340
鎔 MELT → 2214

NOTE

➡ see USAGE note at 解 1913

梯

▸LADDER
テイ はし はしご ㊔ かけはし
Ⓒ 梯 tī

1210
◧ 1-4-7

75	Names	U68AF
木	S11-4-7	F2339

COMPOUNDS

❶ [original meaning] **LADDER, stairs, bridge**
梯形 ていけい trapezoid
階梯 かいてい step, ladder; stepping-stone; guide
雲梯 うんてい monkey bars; scaling ladder used in ancient China
舷梯 げんてい gangway (ladder)

❷ unclassified compounds
梯梧(=梯姑) でいご Indian coral tree

KUN

【はし 梯】[in compounds] LADDER
梯子 はしご [sometimes also 梯] ladder
梯子車 はしごしゃ hook-and-ladder truck
梯子酒 はしござけ barhopping
縄梯子 なわばしご rope ladder
【はしご 梯】[usu. 梯子] LADDER

SYNONYMS

❶ steps
段 STEP → 1471
階 stairs → 0761
陛 IMPERIAL PALACE STEPS → 0543
梯 LADDER → 1210

HOMOPHONES

はしご 梯子 → 1210, 4196
はし
橋 BRIDGE → 1367
端 END → 1564
箸 CHOPSTICKS → 3359

NOTE

➡ see USAGE note at 橋 1367

桶
1211
1-4-7

▶BUCKET
トウ おけ
Ⓒ 桶 tǒng

75	Names	U6876
木	S11-4-7	F2068

COMPOUNDS

● BUCKET, tub, pail; wooden vessel
湯桶読み ゆとうよみ reading of a compound in which *kun* and *on* are mixed (in that order)

KUN

【おけ 桶】BUCKET, tub, pail; wooden vessel
手桶 ておけ pail, bucket
風呂桶 ふろおけ bath pail; bathtub
洗い桶 あらいおけ washtub, dishpan
棺桶 かんおけ coffin, casket
火桶 ひおけ wooden brazier
飼い葉桶 かいばおけ manger, crib

SYNONYMS

● containers
箱 BOX → 3362
壺 JAR → 2890
槽 TANK → 1352
樽 BARREL → 1368
棺 COFFIN → 1240
桶 BUCKET → 1211
笈 BOX CARRIED ON THE BACK → 3274
鞘 SHEATH → 2259
箪 BAMBOO BOX → 3381
函 BOX → 3724
籠 BASKET → 3398
袋 BAG → 3201
鞄 BAG (for carrying) → 2248
器 VESSEL → 3367
瓶 BOTTLE → 1702
缶 CAN → 2526
缶 EARTHENWARE JAR → 2525

梅
1212
1-4-7

▶JAPANESE APRICOT
バイ うめ

75	Names	UFA44
木	S11-4-7	F0000

traditional form → see 梅 at 1159

桝
1213
1-4-7

▶MEASURE
ます

75	Nonstandard	U685D
木	S11-4-7	F0000

traditional form → see 枡 at 1070

栁
1214
1-4-7

▶WILLOW
リュウ やなぎ ㊔ やぎ やなき

75	Nonstandard	U687A
木	S11-4-7	F0000

traditional form → see 柳 at 1115

梢
1215
1-4-7

▶TIP OF A TWIG
ショウ こずえ

75	Nonstandard	U68A2
木	S11-4-7	F0000

traditional form → see 梢 at 1208

焔
1216
1-4-7

▶FLAME
エン ほのお

86	Nonstandard	U7114
火	S11-4-7	F0000

traditional form → see 焰 at 1255

焔
1-4-7

incorrect stroke-count
➡ see 1-4-8: 火 at 1255

將
1217
1-4-7

▶GENERAL OFFICER
ショウ まさ(に) ㊔ まさ まさし まさる ゆき はた

41	Names	U5C07
寸	S11-3-8	F0000

traditional form → see 将 at 0551

現

1218

1-4-7

▶ACTUAL
▶APPEAR

ゲン あらわ(れる) あらわ(す) ㊔ あきら

Ⓒ 现 xiàn

96	Jōyō-5	U73FE
王	S11-4-7	F0100

Stroke order: 1–11

COMPOUNDS

❶ⓐ [also prefix] (occurring at the present moment) **ACTUAL, present, current, existing, now**
ⓑ *Buddhism* present life, life in this world

a 現在 げんざい present time, now; present tense; actually
現代 げんだい present age, modern times, today
現行の げんこうの present, existing, current, actual
現職 げんしょく present post [office]; incumbent
現住所 げんじゅうしょ present address
現内閣 げんないかく present cabinet
b 現世 げんせ this world, this life
過現未 かげんみ past, present and future, three temporal states of existence

❷ⓐ (existing in fact) **ACTUAL, real**
ⓑ **on hand**—said esp. of money

a 現実 げんじつ actuality, reality
現状 げんじょう present condition
現地 げんち actual place [locale]
現役 げんえき active service
現場 げんば actual spot; job site, building site
b 現金 げんきん cash

❸ⓐ **APPEAR, become visible, come into view, be revealed, materialize**
ⓑ **cause to APPEAR, show, reveal**

a 現象 げんしょう phenomenon
出現する しゅつげんする appear, make an appearance, emerge
実現する じつげんする realize, materialize
表現する ひょうげんする express, represent, manifest; give expression to
b 現像 げんぞう developing (a film)
再現する さいげんする reenact, reproduce
顕現 けんげん manifestation

INDEPENDENT

【げん 現】**ACTUALity;** abbrev. of 現在形 げんざいけい: **present tense;** abbrev. of 現職 げんしょく: **incumbent**
現に げんに actually, really, as a matter of fact
無所属・現 むしょぞくげん incumbent member (of the House of Representatives) without party affiliation

KUN

【あらわれる 現れる】
① **APPEAR, emerge, come out, become visible, materialize**
現れ あらわれ embodiment, materialization
雲間に現れた月 くもまにあらわれたつき moon peeping from behind the clouds
② become known, attain distinction; be exposed [found out]
悪事が現れた あくじがあらわれた The evil deed was discovered

【あらわす 現す】
① **cause to APPEAR, show, display, reveal**
姿を現す すがたをあらわす make an appearance
② attain distinction, become famous
名を現す なをあらわす distinguish oneself

SYNONYMS

❶ⓐ **present**
今 PRESENT →2464
当 THE PRESENT →2701
現 ACTUAL →1218

❷ⓐ **true**
真 TRUE →2616
洵 TRULY →0458
実 REAL →2765
本 real →4314
正 genuine →4296
現 ACTUAL →1218

❸ⓐ **appear**
現 APPEAR →1218
出 come out →4310
顕 MANIFEST →2274
ⓑ **reveal**
発 reveal →3174
露 EXPOSE →3495
曝 EXPOSE →1410
晒す EXPOSE →1156
暴 disclose →3138
披 OPEN OUT →0362
顕 MANIFEST →2274
現 cause to appear →1218

HOMOPHONES

あらわれる 表 EXPRESS →3083
あらわれ 表 EXPRESS →3083
あらわす
表 EXPRESS →3083
著 AUTHOR →2869

NOTE

➡ see USAGE note at 表 3083

1 方 日 木 火 爿 【王】 𤣩 礻 月 夫

球

▶BALL
キュウ　たま
Ⓒ 球 qiú

1219
1-4-7

96	Jōyō-3	U7403
王	S11-4-7	F0510

COMPOUNDS

❶ⓐ [original meaning] (spherical body) **BALL, globe, sphere**
ⓑ [suffix] **light bulb**

a 球体 きゅうたい sphere, globe
球形 きゅうけい globular shape
球根 きゅうこん bulb
地球 ちきゅう the Earth
眼球 がんきゅう eyeball
b 電球 でんきゅう light bulb

❷ⓐ **BALL (in a sports game)**
ⓑ [also suffix] **manner of delivering a BALL, esp. in baseball; ball**
ⓒ counter for number of pitches

a 球技 きゅうぎ ball game
硬球 こうきゅう regulation ball
b 投球 とうきゅう throwing a ball, pitching
好球 こうきゅう good pitch
速球 そっきゅう fast ball
内角球 ないかっきゅう inside ball, insider
c 四球 しきゅう base on balls
第一球 だいいっきゅう first pitch

❸ⓐ **BALL game, -ball**
ⓑ abbrev. of 野球 やきゅう: **baseball**

a 野球 やきゅう baseball
卓球 たっきゅう table tennis, ping-pong
庭球 ていきゅう tennis
b 球団 きゅうだん baseball team
球場 きゅうじょう baseball ground, ball park

INDEPENDENT

【きゅう　球】**globe, sphere, BALL**

KUN

【たま　球】
ⓐ **BALL (in a sports game)**
ⓑ light bulb

a 球拾い たまひろい picking up balls; poor (ball) player
釣り球 つりだま deceptive pitch
b 電気の球 でんきのたま electric [light] bulb

SYNONYMS

❶ⓐ **spherical object**
玉 spherical object → 4289
球 BALL → 1219
丸 round body → 4225
鞠 BALL → 2268
毬 BALL → 4001

❶ⓐ **bodies**
体 BODY → 0080
塊 LUMP → 0775
球 BALL → 1219

❶ⓐ **three-dimensional shapes**
錐 CONE → 2190
筒 cylinder → 3323
角 cube → 2541
球 sphere → 1219

HOMOPHONES

たま
玉 GEM → 4289
珠 PEARL → 1183
弾 PROJECTILE → 0697
璧 DISK-SHAPED JEWEL → 3608

NOTE

➡ see USAGE note at 玉 4289

理

▶REASON
▶BASIC PRINCIPLE
リ　ことわり▲　㊔ まさ　みち　さと　ただ　のり　おさむ
Ⓒ 理 lǐ

1220
1-4-7

96	Jōyō-2	U7406
王	S11-4-7	F0059

COMPOUNDS

❶ⓐ **REASON, what is right and proper**
ⓑ (rational thought) **REASON, logic, line of thought**

a 理想 りそう ideal
理由 りゆう reason, cause, ground
理念 りねん concept, idea
道理 どうり reason, right, justice, truth
合理的な ごうりてきな rational, logical, reasonable
無理な むりな unreasonable, unjustifiable; impossible; forced; excessive; irrational (equation)
b 理性 りせい reason, reasoning power
理屈 りくつ reason, logic; argument; pretext; theory
理不尽な りふじんな unreasonable, unjust, absurd
論理 ろんり logic
条理 じょうり reason, logic

❷ **realize, appreciate, understand**

理解する りかいする understand, comprehend

❸ BASIC PRINCIPLE(s) (as of a science), rationale of things, law, theory, doctrine

理論 りろん theory
原理 げんり principle, theory
真理 しんり truth
定理 ていり theorem, proposition
心理 しんり mental state, mentality; psychology
生理 せいり physiological functions, physiology; menstruation
地理 ちり geographical features, topography; geography
哲理 てつり philosophy (of something)

❹ⓐ natural science, physics
ⓑ abbrev. of 物理学 ぶつりがく: physics
ⓒ abbrev. of 理科 りか: **science**

a 理学 りがく (physical) science
理科 りか science; science department
物理学 ぶつりがく physics, physical science
b 理化学 りかがく physics and chemistry
c 理工学部 りこうがくぶ department [school] of science and engineering
理系 りけい science (department)

❺ⓐ manage, run
ⓑ abbrev. of 理事会 りじかい: board of trustees

a 理事 りじ director, trustee
管理する かんりする administer, supervise, manage, exercise control [jurisdiction] over
処理する しょりする manage, deal with, dispose of; process, treat
総理大臣 そうりだいじん prime minister
代理 だいり representation; agency; proxy, deputy
料理する りょうりする cook; handle, manage
受理する じゅりする accept (a report)
b 安保理 あんぽり Security Council

❻ⓐ put in order, arrange
ⓑ cut (one's hair), dress

a 修理する しゅうりする repair, mend
整理する せいりする put in order, arrange; liquidate, disorganize; retrench; cut, dispose of
b 理容 りよう hairdressing
理髪 りはつ haircut, hairdressing

❼ [original meaning] grain, texture, line, stripe

木理 もくり grain of wood
大理石 だいりせき marble

INDEPENDENT

【り 理】
①ⓐ **REASON**, what is right and proper
ⓑ (rational thought) **REASON**, logic, line of thought

a 理が非でも りがひでも right or wrong, by fair means or foul
理外の理 りがいのり transcendental reason
b 理の有る りのある justifiable

② principle, law, philosophy
陰陽の理 おんみょうのり principle of duality

③ **truth**
不変の理 ふへんのり eternal truth
自明の理 じめいのり self-evident truth, axiom

KUN

【ことわり 理】 *literary* **REASON**, right, justice
彼がそう云うのも理だ かれがそういうのもことわりだ He may well say so

SYNONYMS

❶ⓐ reason
理 REASON → 1220
訳 SENSE → 1865
ⓑ reasoning
理 REASON → 1220
筋 thread → 3319
脈 VEIN → 1189

❸ principle
律 LAW → 0433
理 BASIC PRINCIPLE → 1220

❺ⓐ direct and supervise
制 CONTROL → 1624
理 manage → 1220
経 MANAGE → 1687
管 EXERCISE CONTROL → 3349
轄 EXERCISE JURISDICTION OVER → 2056
掌 TAKE CHARGE OF → 3215
監 OVERSEE → 3535
督 SUPERVISE → 3471
司 OFFICIATE → 3648
宰 PRESIDE → 2829
営 MANAGE → 3216

❻ⓐ arrange
並 LINE UP → 2793
比 rank → 0029
列 arrange in a row → 1018
陳 lay out (for exhibit) → 0656
羅 spread out → 3244
揃える arrange properly → 0719
整 PUT IN ORDER → 3562
理 put in order → 1220

NOTE

➡ see COMPOUND FORMATION for
論理 ろんり → 論 1981
理不尽 りふじん → 尽 3786
理屈 りくつ → 屈 3821

方 日 木 火 片 【王】 正 ネ 月 夫

方 日 木 火 爿 【王】 𤣩 ネ 月 夫

琉

1221

1-4-7

▶**LAPIS LAZULI**

リュウ ル

Ⓒ 琉 liú

96	Names	U7409
王	S11-4-7	F2218

COMPOUNDS

ⓐ (kind of gemstone) **LAPIS LAZULI**

ⓑ abbrev. of 琉球 りゅうきゅう: **Okinawa**

a 琉璃(=瑠璃) るり lapis lazuli, lapis lazuli blue; [archaic] glass

b 琉歌 りゅうか Okinawan tanka, *ryuka*

SYNONYMS

ⓐ **precious stones**

玉 GEM → 4289
珂 WHITE AGATE → 1137
璧 DISK-SHAPED JEWEL → 3608
琥 AMBER → 1261
珀 AMBER → 1136
珠 PEARL → 1183
瑛 TRANSPARENT GEM → 1259
瑠 LAPIS LAZULI → 1342
璃 GLASSY SUBSTANCE → 1358
晶 CRYSTAL → 3122
玖 beautiful black jewel → 1041
琉 LAPIS LAZULI → 1221
琳 BEAUTIFUL GEM → 1262

NOTE

➡ see NOTE at 瑠 1342

琢

1222

1-4-7

▶**POLISH**

タク ㊔ たか みがく

Ⓝ 琢 Ⓒ 琢 zhuó zuó

96	Names	U7422
王	S11-4-7	F3393

COMPOUNDS

❶ **POLISH [improve] one's skills, cultivate one's mind**

切磋[×]琢磨 せっさたくま working hard together, assiduity in friendly rivalry

❷ [original meaning] **POLISH** (jade or jewels), carve

彫琢する ちょうたくする carve and polish; elaborate

SYNONYMS

❶ **cultivate**

修 CULTIVATE → 0138
養 FOSTER (one's intellect) → 2998
練 TRAIN → 1738
錬 REFINE → 2185
鍛 train → 2206
磨 POLISH → 3946
琢 POLISH → 1222

疎疏

incorrect stroke-count
➡ see 1-5-7: 疋 at 1511

1-4-7

視

1223

1-4-7

▶**REGARD**

シ み(る)[▲]

Ⓝ 視 Ⓒ 视 shì

147	Jōyō-6	U8996
見	S11-7-4	F0346

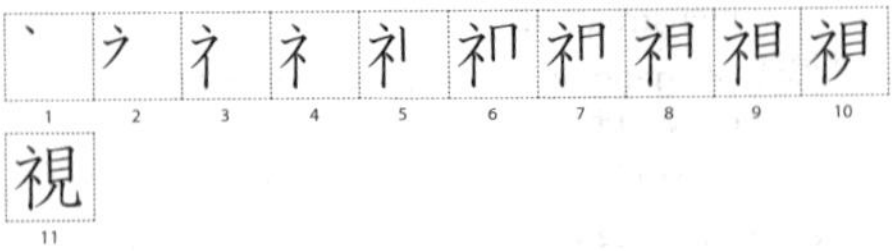

COMPOUNDS

❶ⓐ [original meaning] (look at attentively) **REGARD, look at, gaze**

ⓑ **inspect, watch over**

a 視聴者 しちょうしゃ viewer, audience
視界 しかい field of vision, visibility
視野 しや field of vision; one's mental horizon
視力 しりょく eyesight
視覚 しかく sense of sight
視点 してん viewpoint, point of view
凝視する ぎょうしする stare, gaze at
注視する ちゅうしする gaze steadily at, observe (a person) closely

b 視察 しさつ inspection, observation
監視する かんしする watch, keep under observation, exercise surveillance
巡視 じゅんし inspection tour
警視庁 けいしちょう Metropolitan Police Office

❷ **eyesight, vision**

近視 きんし nearsightedness, shortsightedness
乱視 らんし astigmatism

❸ [also suffix] **REGARD as, consider**

軽視する けいしする make light of, despise; neglect
敵視する てきしする regard as an enemy
無視する むしする ignore, disregard
重要視する じゅうようしする regard as important, think much of

❹ [prefix] *astron* apparent

視地平 しちへい apparent horizon

KUN

【みる 視る】 [usu. 見る] **look over, examine; look up, refer to**

SYNONYMS

❶ **see and look**

見 SEE → 3151
看 WATCH → 3992
察 INSPECT → 2961

窺 WATCH FURTIVELY → 3002
瞥 GLANCE AT → 3592
目 look → 3777
観 VIEW → 2359
覧 LOOK OVER → 3538
眺 LOOK OUT OVER → 1503
望 LOOK AFAR → 3408
仰 LOOK UP → 0051
顧 LOOK BACK → 2394
視 REGARD → 1223

❸ judge
判 JUDGE → 1441
裁 JUDGE → 4090
鑑 APPRAISE → 2226
評 evaluate → 1895
審 TRY → 2985
決 DECIDE → 0308
視 REGARD → 1223

HOMOPHONES

みる
見 SEE → 3151
診 EXAMINE A PATIENT → 1898
観 VIEW → 2359
看 WATCH → 3992

NOTE

➡ see USAGE note at 見 3151

祷

1224

1-4-7

▶PRAY
トウ いの(る)
Ⓝ 禱 Ⓒ 祷 dǎo

113	Names	U7977
ネ	S11-4-7	F0000

COMPOUNDS

ⓐ [original meaning] **PRAY, wish for**
ⓑ PRAYer
a 祈祷 きとう prayer
主祷文 しゅとうぶん The Lord's Prayer
b 黙祷 もくとう silent prayer
祝祷 しゅくとう benediction, blessing (in Christianity)

KUN

【いのる 祷る】[now usu. 祈る] **PRAY, wish for**
祷り いのり prayer

SYNONYMS

● pray and worship
祈 PRAY → 1086
祷 PRAY → 1224
願 pray → 2320
拝 WORSHIP → 0360
祀 WORSHIP AS GOD → 1448

崇 REVERENCE → 2864
斎 OBSERVE RELIGIOUS ABSTINENCE → 2622
呪 SPELL → 0323

HOMOPHONES

いのる 祈 PRAY → 1086
いのり 祈 PRAY → 1086

NOTE

➡ see USAGE note at 祈 1086

脱

1225

1-4-7

▶REMOVE
▶ESCAPE FROM
ダツ ぬ(ぐ) ぬ(げる)
Ⓝ 脫 Ⓒ 脱 tuō

130	Jōyō	U8131
月	S11-4-7	F0846

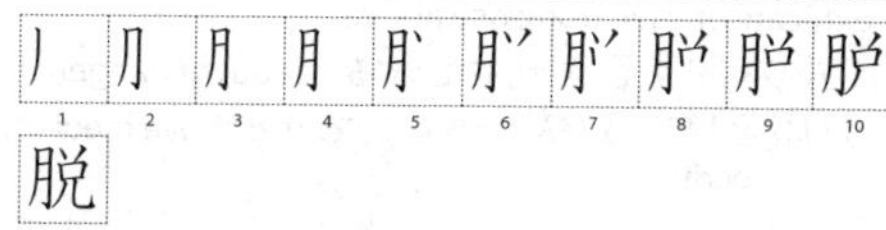

COMPOUNDS

❶ⓐ [also prefix] **REMOVE, eliminate, de- (as in *decarbonate*)**
ⓑ REMOVE (one's) clothes, take off, undress
a 脱脂 だっし fat removal
脱毛 だつもう removal of hair; falling out of hair
脱色 だっしょく decolorization
脱水 だっすい dehydration
脱炭酸 だつたんさん decarbonation
b 脱帽 だつぼう taking off one's cap [hat]; submission
脱衣 だつい undressing
脱皮 だっぴ ecdysis; self-renewal

❷ⓐ get out of place, come off
ⓑ leave out by mistake, omit; be left out, be omitted
a 脱線 だっせん derailment; deviation, aberration
脱肛 だっこう prolapse of the anus
脱臼 だっきゅう dislocation
b 脱落する だつらくする be omitted; fall away [behind], drop out
脱漏 だつろう omission
逸脱 いつだつ deviation, departure from the norm

❸ⓐ [also prefix] **ESCAPE FROM (an undesirable situation), get away from, extricate oneself from, withdraw from**
ⓑ extricate oneself from worldly affairs
a 脱税 だつぜい tax evasion
脱退 だったい withdrawal, secession
脱出 だっしゅつ escape, extrication
脱走 だっそう desertion, escape
脱獄 だつごく prison break, jailbreak
脱却する だっきゃくする get rid of; slough off

方 日 木 火 爿 王 疋 ネ 【月】 夫

方 日 木 火 月 王 正 ネ 【月】 夫

脱会 だっかい withdrawal (from an organization)
脱石油 だつせきゆ extrication from dependence on oil
離脱 りだつ breakaway, separation, secession
b 脱俗 だつぞく unworldliness
洒×脱な しゃだつな free and easy, unconstrained
超脱 ちょうだつ transcendency, detachment
解脱 げだつ *Buddhism* deliverance (of one's soul), salvation

❹ lose one's strength
脱力感 だつりょくかん feeling of exhaustion
虚脱 きょだつ (physical) collapse, prostration; absentmindedness

INDEPENDENT

【だっする 脱する】**ESCAPE FROM**, get away from, extricate oneself from; rise above
危険を脱する きけんをだっする get out of danger
凡庸を脱する ぼんようをだっする rise above mediocrity

KUN

【ぬぐ 脱ぐ】*vt* **REMOVE (one's) clothes, take off, undress**
脱ぎ捨てる ぬぎすてる throw off (clothes), kick off (boots)

【ぬげる 脱げる】*vi* (of clothes or footwear) **come off, slip off**
靴が脱げない くつがぬげない My shoes will not come off

SYNONYMS

❶ⓐ eliminate
却 ELIMINATE → 1436
排 EXCLUDE → 0593
払う CLEAR AWAY → 0225
剥 PEEL OFF → 2105
耘 WEED → 1661
削 cross out → 1837
抹 wipe off → 0370
省 leave out → 3100
脱 REMOVE → 1225
去 take away → 2678
外す take off → 0215
除 RID OF → 0546
撤 WITHDRAW → 0912

❷ⓐ come off
脱 get out of place → 1225
外れる come off → 0215
剥 PEEL OFF → 2105

ⓑ omit
漏 omit → 0860
脱 leave out by mistake → 1225
抜く leave out → 0290
欠 missing → 2481

❸ⓐ escape
逃 ESCAPE → 3839
遁 FLEE → 4027
亡 flee → 4210
走 run away → 2720
脱 ESCAPE FROM → 1225

脚

1226

1-4-7

▶LEG

キャク キャ あし

Ⓝ 脚◇ Ⓒ 脚 jiǎo jué

130	Jōyō	U811A
月	S11-4-7	F1108

Stroke order: 1–11

COMPOUNDS

❶ⓐ [original meaning] **LEG, foot**
ⓑ move on foot, walk, run
a 脚力 きゃくりょく strength of one's legs; walking ability
脚線美 きゃくせんび beauty of leg lines
馬脚 ばきゃく horse's legs; one's true character
健脚の けんきゃくの strong in walking
b 行脚 あんぎゃ pilgrimage; walking tour; tour
飛脚 ひきゃく express messenger; postman (in former times)

❷ⓐ (leg-shaped support) **LEG, base**
ⓑ counter for **LEG**ged furniture
ⓒ foot, lower part, bottom
a 脚部 きゃくぶ leg (as of a table)
脚立 きゃたつ footstool; stepladder
三脚 さんきゃく tripod
橋脚 きょうきゃく bridge pier
b 机二脚 つくえにきゃく two desks
c 脚注 きゃくちゅう footnote
立脚する りっきゃくする be based on

❸ bottom radical of Chinese characters, **LEG** radical
偏旁冠脚 へんぼうかんきゃく the radicals

❹ plot of a play, script
脚本 きゃくほん script, playbook, drama, scenario
脚色 きゃくしょく dramatization

❺ social standing
失脚する しっきゃくする lose one's social standing

INDEPENDENT

【きゃく 脚】undercarriage (of an aircraft)

KUN

【あし 脚】
① [also 足] (leg-shaped support) **LEG**

三本脚の机 さんぼんあしのつくえ three-legged table

② [also 足] movement, pace

雨脚 あまあし density of the falling rain; pace (of the approaching shower)

③ bottom radical of Chinese characters, **LEG** radical

人脚 ひとあし *hitoashi*, 'bottom legs' radical (儿)

SYNONYMS

❶ⓐ limbs

肢 LIMB → 1094
腕 ARM → 1269
脚 LEG → 1226

❶ⓐ leg

足 FOOT → 2714
脚 LEG → 1226
膝 KNEE → 1359

ⓑ walk

歩 WALK → 3071
徒 go on foot → 0499
脚 move on foot → 1226
足 travel on foot → 2714
踏 TREAD → 1997

HOMOPHONES

あし 足 FOOT → 2714

NOTE

➡ see USAGE note at 足 2714

脳

1227

◧ 1-4-7

▶BRAIN

ノウ

Ⓝ 腦 Ⓒ 脑 nǎo

130	Jōyō-6	U8133
月	S11-4-7	F0906

Stroke order: 1–11

COMPOUNDS

❶ⓐ [also prefix] [original meaning] **BRAIN**

ⓑ (intellectual capacity) **BRAIN(s), intellect, mind**

a 脳髄 のうずい brain

脳炎 のうえん brain inflammation, encephalitis

脳細胞 のうさいぼう brain cells

脳死 のうし brain death

大脳 だいのう cerebrum

b 脳裏 のうり brain, mind, memory

頭脳 ずのう brain; brains, head

首脳 しゅのう head, leader

❷ xylem, woody tissue

樟脳 しょうのう camphor

INDEPENDENT

【のう 脳】**BRAIN; brains**

脳の損傷 のうのそんしょう brain damage

SYNONYMS

❶ⓐ head

頭 HEAD → 2019
首 HEAD → 2818
脳 BRAIN → 1227

COMPOUND FORMATION

【樟脳 しょうのう】

樟脳 'camphor' refers to the woody substance (脳 ❷) obtained from the camphor tree (樟).

豚

1228

◧ 1-4-7

▶PIG

トン ぶた

Ⓒ 豚 tún

152	Jōyō	U8C5A
豖	S11-7-4	F1815

Stroke order: 1–11

COMPOUNDS

ⓐ [original meaning] **PIG, hog, swine**

ⓑ **PIG [hog] meat, pork**

ⓒ [humble] as worthless as a **PIG**

a 豚舎 とんしゃ pigsty, pigpen

養豚 ようとん swine keeping

b 豚カツ とんかつ pork cutlet

c 豚児 とんじ my (foolish) son

INDEPENDENT

【とん 豚】**PIG; pork**

KUN

【ぶた 豚】**PIG, hog, swine, boar; pig [hog] meat, pork**

豚小屋 ぶたごや hogpen

豚肉 ぶたにく pork, hog meat

豚箱 ぶたばこ *slang* police cell, jug

子豚 こぶた piglet

SPECIAL READINGS

河豚▲ ふぐ *fugu*, globefish, swellfish

SYNONYMS

ⓐ swine

豚 PIG → 1228
豕 SWINE → 4357
猪 WILD BOAR → 0652
亥 THE BOAR → 2505

ⓐ domesticated mammals

牛 CATTLE → 4263

馬 HORSE → 4086
豚 PIG → 1228
羊 SHEEP → 2708
犬 DOG → 4275
猫 CAT → 0651
兎 RABBIT → 4374

方 日 木 火 爿 王 正 ネ 【月】 夫

脱

1229

1-4-7

▶REMOVE
▶ESCAPE FROM

ダツ ぬ(ぐ) ぬ(げる)

130	Nonstandard	U812B
月	S11-4-7	F0000

traditional form → see 脫 at 1225

朖

1230

1-4-7

▶CHEERFUL
▶CLEAR

ロウ ほが(らか) ㊔ あき あきら お

74	Nonstandard	U6716
月	S11-4-7	F0000

traditional form → see 朗 at 1679

規

1231

1-4-7

▶REGULATION

キ ㊔ のり ただし

Ⓝ 規 Ⓒ 规 guī

147	Jōyō-5	U898F
見	S11-7-4	F0575

COMPOUNDS

❶ⓐ REGULATION, rule, standard
ⓑ regulate, control

a 規定 きてい regulations, rules; provisions
規則 きそく rule, regulation
規約 きやく agreement, rules, bylaws
規律 きりつ order, discipline; regulation, law
規範 きはん standard, norm, criterion
規格 きかく standard, norm
規準 きじゅん standard, criterion
法規 ほうき laws and regulations
内規 ないき private rules [regulations], bylaws
校規 こうき school regulations
b 規制する きせいする regulate, control
新規に しんきに newly

❷ [original meaning] **compass**

規矩 きく standard, rule; compass and ruler
規模 きぼ scale, scope
定規 じょうぎ ruler, rule, square

SYNONYMS

❶ⓐ laws and rules

法 LAW → 0391
律 LAW → 0433
典 CANON → 3253
憲 CONSTITUTION → 3001
令 ordinance → 2489
則 RULE → 1831
矩 RULE → 1475
規 REGULATION → 1231
紀 discipline → 1628

NOTE

➡ see COMPOUND FORMATION for 規模 きぼ → 模 1326

晩

1232

1-4-8

▶EVENING

バン

Ⓝ 晩 Ⓒ 晚 wǎn

72	Jōyō-6	U6669
日	S12-4-8	F1083

COMPOUNDS

❶ EVENING, night

晩方 ばんがた toward evening
晩鐘 ばんしょう evening bell, curfew (bell)
晩御飯 ばんごはん supper
毎晩 まいばん every evening [night]
今晩 こんばん this evening, tonight
今晩は こんばんは good evening

❷ⓐ (advanced) late, drawing toward the end, in the latter part
ⓑ late in life

a 晩春 ばんしゅん late spring
早晩 そうばん sooner or later
b 晩学 ばんがく late education
晩年 ばんねん late in life
晩婚 ばんこん late marriage

INDEPENDENT

【ばん 晩】**EVENING, night**

晩に ばんに in the evening

SYNONYMS

❶ evening and night

夜 NIGHT → 2550
晩 EVENING → 1232
夕 EVENING → 4195
宵 EARLY EVENING → 2831
暮 DUSK → 2971

❷ **late**

遅 LATE (delayed) → 3887

晩 late (advanced) → 1232

晏 LATE → 3103

暁

1233

◧ 1-4-8

▸DAWN

ギョウ あかつき ㊔ あき あけ さとし きょう さとる あきら

Ⓝ 曉 Ⓒ 晓 xiǎo

72	Jōyō	U6681
日	S12-4-8	F1915

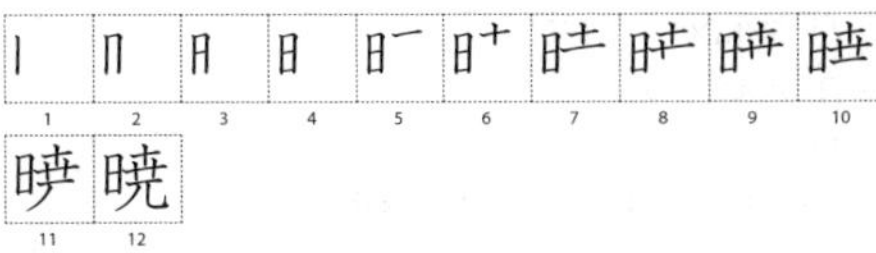

COMPOUNDS

❶ [original meaning] **DAWN, daybreak**

暁天 ぎょうてん dawn

暁星 ぎょうせい morning star, Venus

今暁 こんぎょう at daybreak today

❷ be as clear as **DAWN**, understand thoroughly

通暁する つうぎょうする have a thorough knowledge of

KUN

【あかつき 暁】**DAWN, daybreak; in the event of**

暁の空 あかつきのそら dawning sky

成功の暁には せいこうのあかつきには when one has succeeded

SYNONYMS

❶ **morning and dawn**

朝 MORNING → 2130

暁 DAWN → 1233

旦 DAYBREAK → 3041

曙 DAWN → 1384

晨 EARLY MORNING → 3110

晴

1234

◧ 1-4-8

▸FINE WEATHER

セイ は(れる) は(れ) は(れ)- -ば(れ) は(らす) ㊔ はる

Ⓝ 晴 Ⓒ 晴 qíng

72	Jōyō-2	U6674
日	S12-4-8	F0819

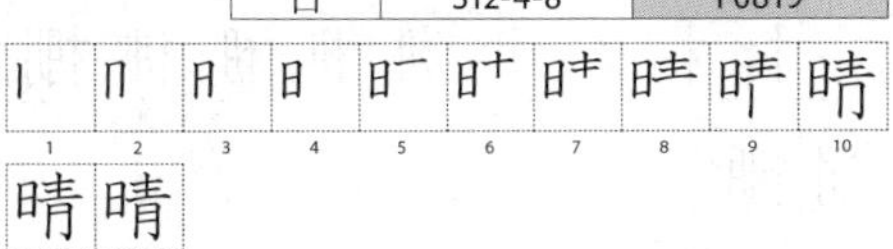

COMPOUNDS

● [original meaning] **FINE WEATHER, fair weather, clear [cloudless] sky, bright sky**

晴天 せいてん fine [fair] weather, cloudless sky

晴雨計 せいうけい barometer

晴耕雨読 せいこううどく working in the field in fine weather and reading at home in rainy weather

晴曇 せいどん fine and cloudy weather

KUN

【はれる 晴れる】**clear up, become fine; cease to rain; be dispelled, be dissipated; be refreshed, be enlivened**

晴れた空 はれたそら clear [cloudless] sky

晴れ上がる はれあがる clear up

晴れやかな笑顔 はれやかなえがお beaming smile

疑いが晴れる うたがいがはれる be cleared of a charge

【はれ 晴れ】**FINE WEATHER, clear sky; ceremonial [formal] occasion, gala**

晴れの日 はれのひ fine day; formal occasion

【はれ- 晴れ-】**formal, ceremonial, gala**

晴れ着 はれぎ one's best (clothes), gala [holiday] dress

晴れ舞台 はれぶたい gala occasion

【-ばれ -晴れ】[suffix] **FINE WEATHER, bright sky**

五月晴れ さつきばれ fine weather in early summer [during the rainy season]

梅雨晴れ つゆばれ sunny spell during the rainy season

【はらす 晴らす】

① **dispel (doubts or gloom), clear away**

気晴らし きばらし diversion, relaxation

疑いを晴らす うたがいをはらす dispel doubts

② **unclassified compounds**

素晴らしい すばらしい splendid, magnificent, wonderful, excellent

見晴らし みはらし view, outlook

SYNONYMS

● **weather**

候 SEASONAL WEATHER → 0133

天 weather → 4250

晴 FINE WEATHER → 1234

暎

1235

◧ 1-4-8

▸REFLECT

▸PROJECT

エイ うつ(る) うつ(す) は(える) -ば(え)

㊔ てる あき

72	Nonstandard	U668E
日	S12-4-8	F0000

traditional form → see 映 at 1104

【日】 木 歹 火 片 牙 王 ネ 月 月 厷

晴

1236
1-4-8

▶FINE WEATHER
セイ は(れる) は(れ) は(れ)- -ば(れ)
は(らす) ㊔ はる

72	Nonstandard	UFA12
日	S12-4-8	F0000

traditional form → see 晴 at 1234

棒

1237
1-4-8

▶ROD
ボウ ㊔ ささげ
Ⓒ 棒 bàng

75	Jōyō-6	U68D2
木	S12-4-8	F1198

COMPOUNDS

❶ⓐ [original meaning] **ROD, stick, bar, pole, staff, club**
ⓑ RODlike, rod-shaped; bar of, stick of
ⓒ strike with a ROD, hit with a club

a 棒状 ぼうじょう cylinder or rod-shaped
棒高跳び ぼうたかとび pole vault [jump]
棒術 ぼうじゅつ *bojutsu* (art of using a stick as a weapon), cudgels
警棒 けいぼう policeman's club, nightstick
編み棒 あみぼう knitting needle
棍×棒 こんぼう cudgel, club
鉄棒 てつぼう iron rod; horizontal bars
心棒 しんぼう axle, shaft, arbor
延べ棒 のべぼう ingot
b 棒温度計 ぼうおんどけい bar thermometer
c 痛棒 つうぼう severe attack, bitter criticism

❷ⓐ straight line, thick straight line
ⓑ **in a straight line, straight**

a 棒グラフ ぼうぐらふ bar graph
b 棒立ち ぼうだち standing erect
棒読み ぼうよみ reading without expression; reading a Chinese classical text without translating it into Japanese
棒暗記 ぼうあんき memorization word by word

❸ **tough guy, fellow, chum**
泥棒 どろぼう thief, crook
用心棒 ようじんぼう bodyguard, bouncer; bar, bolt
相棒 あいぼう pal, mate, companion

❹ unclassified compounds
箆×棒な べらぼうな absurd, unreasonable, awful

INDEPENDENT

【ぼう 棒】**ROD, stick, bar, pole, staff, club, baton; straight line, dash; waste, futility; *bojutsu***
棒で殴る ぼうでなぐる hit with a club
棒を引く ぼうをひく draw a line
棒に振る ぼうにふる sacrifice, waste
チョコレートの棒 ちょこれーとのぼう bar of chocolate

SYNONYMS

❶ⓐ & ❶ⓑ **long slender objects**
棒 ROD → 1237
箸 CHOPSTICKS → 3359
桟 crosspiece → 1169
軸 AXLE → 1908
錘 SPINDLE → 2191
竿 POLE → 3259
杖 STAFF → 1026
錫 Buddhist priest's staff → 2189
軛 YOKE → 1873

❷ⓐ **line**
線 LINE → 1760
筋 THREADLIKE STRUCTURE → 3319
条 strip → 2726
脈 VEIN → 1189
棒 straight line → 1237
縞 STRIPE → 1784
軸 AXIS → 1908

ⓑ **straight**
直 STRAIGHT → 3649
棒 straight → 1237

❸ **fellow**
奴 GUY → 0217
漢 FELLOW → 0808
輩 FELLOW (*belittling*) → 3482
徒 fellows → 0499
棒 tough guy → 1237
坊 COLLOQUIAL PERSON SUFFIX → 0274
屋 colloquial person suffix → 3842
物 character → 1084

棚

1238
1-4-8

▶SHELF
ホウ▲ たな -だな
Ⓝ 棚 Ⓒ 棚 péng

75	Jōyō	U68DA
木	S12-4-8	F1563

COMPOUNDS

❶ [original meaning] **SHELF**
陸棚 りくほう continental shelf
❷ [archaic] suspension bridge

KUN

【たな 棚, -だな -棚】
ⓐ [also suffix] **SHELF, rack, ledge, mantelpiece**
ⓑ (natural shelflike structure) **SHELF, ledge (of rock)**
ⓒ continental **SHELF**
a 棚卸し(=店卸し) たなおろし inventory
棚牡丹 たなぼた windfall, godsend
棚上げする たなあげする shelve (up), pigeonhole
棚引く たなびく trail, hang [lie] over
書棚 しょだな bookshelf
本棚 ほんだな bookshelf
食器棚 しょっきだな cupboard, sideboard
b 岩棚 いわだな ledge
c 大陸棚 たいりくだな continental shelf
陸棚 りくだな continental shelf

SYNONYMS

❶ **flat supports**
台 STAND → 2498
座 SEAT → 3868
壇 PLATFORM → 0932
棚 SHELF → 1238
架 rack → 3178
床 BED → 3805

HOMOPHONES

たな 店 SHOP → 3828

NOTE

➡ see USAGE note at 店 3828

椅

1239
◧ 1-4-8

▶**CHAIR**
イ
Ⓒ 椅 yǐ yī

75	Jōyō	U6905
木	S12-4-8	F1345

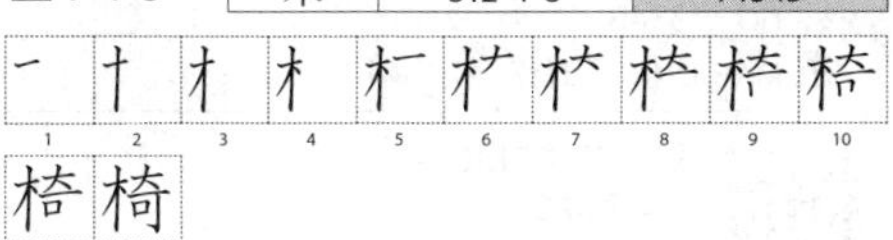

COMPOUNDS

● **CHAIR**
椅子 いす chair
車椅子 くるまいす wheelchair
長椅子 ながいす couch, bench

SYNONYMS

● **seat**
席 SEAT → 3865
座 SEAT → 3868
椅 CHAIR → 1239
鞍 SADDLE → 2255

棺

1240
◧ 1-4-8

▶**COFFIN**
カン
Ⓒ 棺 guān

75	Jōyō	U68FA
木	S12-4-8	F2360

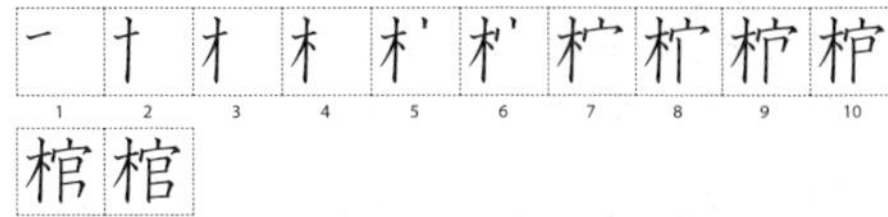

COMPOUNDS

● [original meaning] **COFFIN, casket**
棺桶 かんおけ coffin, casket
石棺 せっかん sarcophagus
納棺する のうかんする place a body in a coffin
出棺 しゅっかん carrying the coffin out of the house

INDEPENDENT

【かん 棺】 **COFFIN**, casket
棺に納める かんにおさめる lay in a coffin

SYNONYMS

● **containers**
箱 BOX → 3362
壺 JAR → 2890
槽 TANK → 1352
樽 BARREL → 1368
棺 COFFIN → 1240
桶 BUCKET → 1211
笈 BOX CARRIED ON THE BACK → 3274
鞘 SHEATH → 2259
簞 BAMBOO BOX → 3381
函 BOX → 3724
籠 BASKET → 3398
袋 BAG → 3201
鞄 BAG (for carrying) → 2248
器 VESSEL → 3367
瓶 BOTTLE → 1702
缶 CAN → 2526
缶 EARTHENWARE JAR → 2525

検

1241
◧ 1-4-8

▶**EXAMINE**
ケン
Ⓝ 檢 Ⓒ 检 jiǎn

75	Jōyō-5	U691C
木	S12-4-8	F0564

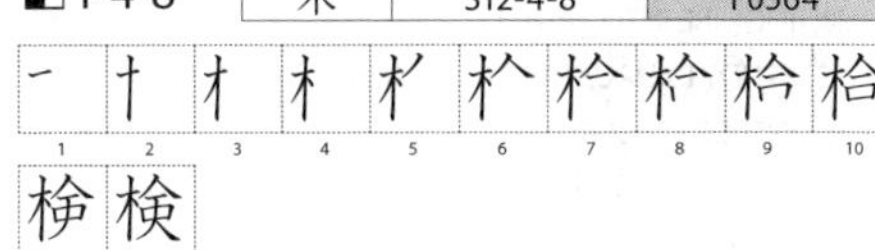

COMPOUNDS

❶ⓐ **EXAMINE, inspect, investigate, verify, test, check**
ⓑ **examination, inspection, test, -opsy**

a 検査 けんさ inspection, examination, test
検討する けんとうする examine, study, investigate
検診 けんしん medical examination
検証 けんしょう verification, identification; inspection
検察 けんさつ criminal investigation; prosecution
検事 けんじ public prosecutor
検閲 けんえつ censorship; inspection, review
検便 けんべん stool examination
検定 けんてい examination; official approval
探検(=探険) たんけん exploration, expedition
点検 てんけん inspection, examination

b 車検 しゃけん automobile inspection
三等検 さんとうけん test for third-grade articles
生検 せいけん biopsy

❷ **detect, search, measure**
検索する けんさくする look up (a word in a dictionary), search for, refer to
検出する けんしゅつする detect, find
検温 けんおん thermometry
検波 けんぱ detection, demodulation
検流計 けんりゅうけい galvanometer

❸ abbrev. of 検察庁 けんさつちょう: public prosecutors office
地検 ちけん district public prosecutors office
送検する そうけんする commit for trial, send to the prosecutors office

❹ restrict, restrain, regulate
検挙 けんきょ arrest, roundup
検束 けんそく arrest, custody

❺ [original meaning] put a seal on
検印 けんいん seal of approval

INDEPENDENT

【けんする 検する】**EXAMINE**, investigate; regulate

SYNONYMS

❶ⓐ **investigate and examine**
閲 REVIEW → 4132
審 EXAMINE CAREFULLY → 2985
験 TEST → 2306
勘 CHECK → 2231
糾 INQUIRE INTO → 1631
究 STUDY EXHAUSTIVELY → 2729
察 INSPECT → 2961
討 STUDY → 1846
探 PROBE → 0613
検 EXAMINE → 1241
診 EXAMINE A PATIENT → 1898
調 INVESTIGATE → 1973
査 LOOK INTO → 3092

ⓑ **examination**
検 examination → 1241
試 examination (school test) → 1925

❷ **detect**
検 detect → 1241
感 SENSE → 3514
嗅 SMELL → 0772

棋

1242
1-4-8

▸**SHOGI**
キ
Ⓝ 碁◇ Ⓒ 棋 qí

75	Jōyō	U68CB
木	S12-4-8	F1622

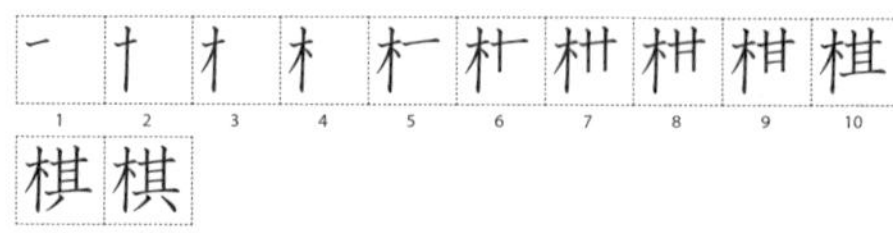

COMPOUNDS

ⓐ **SHOGI, Japanese chess; chess**
ⓑ go, Chinese checkers

ab 棋士 きし professional go [shogi] player
棋界 きかい go circles; shogi circles
棋譜 きふ record of a game of shogi [go]
棋道 きどう art of shogi [go]
将棋 しょうぎ shogi, Japanese chess
西洋将棋 せいようしょうぎ chess

SYNONYMS

ⓐ **board games**
局 board game → 3800
棋 SHOGI → 1242
碁 GO → 3346
雀 MAHJONG → 3117

極

1243
1-4-8

▸**EXTREME**
▸**POLE**
キョク ゴク きわ(める) きわ(まる) きわ(まり) きわ(み) き(める)▲ -ぎ(め)▲ き(まる)▲
Ⓒ 极 jí

75	Jōyō-4	U6975
木	S12-4-8	F0616

COMPOUNDS

❶ⓐ [also suffix] (utmost or exceedingly great) **EXTREME, utmost, maximum, ultimate, highest, ultra-, hyper-**
ⓑ **EXTREME, utmost point, extremity, limit**
ⓒ **reach the EXTREME, go to extremes**

a 極端な きょくたんな extreme; radical
極限 きょくげん utmost limits, limit
極楽 ごくらく *Buddhism* paradise
b 極右 きょくう extreme right
極東 きょくとう Far East
極度 きょくど highest degree, extreme
c 極超短波 ごくちょうたんぱ ultrashort waves
極刑 きょっけい capital punishment, extreme penalty
極力 きょくりょく to the utmost, to the best of one's power
窮極の きゅうきょくの ultimate, extreme
至極 しごく very, most, exceedingly, extremely
積極的な せっきょくてきな positive, active

❷ⓐ **geographical POLE**
ⓑ **magnetic POLE, electrical pole, electrode**

a 極光 きょっこう aurora
極地 きょくち polar regions, pole
極距離 きょくきょり polar distance
北極 ほっきょく North Pole
b エヌ極 えぬきょく magnetic north pole
多極化 たきょくか multipolarization
陽極 ようきょく positive pole, anode

❸ Imperial throne [rank]
大極殿 だいごくでん Council Hall in the Imperial Palace

❹ discern, ascertain
極印 ごくいん hallmark; brand of villainy

❺ [archaic] quindecillion (10^{48})

INDEPENDENT

【きょく 極】**EXTREME, extremity, height, climax, zenith;** (magnetic or geographical) **pole**
混乱の極に達する こんらんのきょくにたっする come to extreme disorder

【ごく 極(=極く)】**EXTREMEly, very, most**
極小さい ごくちいさい very small
極希な ごくまれな extremely rare

KUN

【きわめる 極める】[also 窮める]
ⓐ **carry to extremity, go to EXTREMEs, be extremely (cruel)**
ⓑ **go to the EXTREME [end], reach an extreme, go to the highest point**

a 極めて きわめて extremely, very
口を極めて誉める くちをきわめてほめる be lavish in another's praise
暴虐を極める ぼうぎゃくをきわめる act with extreme violence
惨状を極める さんじょうをきわめる present a very terrible [miserable] sight
貧困を極める ひんこんをきわめる be reduced to extreme poverty, be extremely poor
b 極め付きの品 きわめつきのしな article of certified genuineness
見極める みきわめる see through, discern; ascertain, grasp
山頂を極める さんちょうをきわめる reach the summit

【きわまる 極まる】[also suffix] **reach an EXTREME (state or point), be extremely (dangerous)**
感極まる かんきわまる be overcome with emotion
危険極まる きけんきわまる extremely dangerous

【きわまり 極まり】[sometimes also 窮まり] **extremity, limit**
極まり無い きわまりない extremely, in the extreme
痛快極まり無い つうかいきわまりない be extremely thrilling

【きわみ 極み】**height, apex, utmost**
栄華の極み えいがのきわみ apex of prosperity

【きめる 極める】[usu. 決める]
① decide, determine, fix
② agree upon, arrange
③ (bring to a conclusion) settle, conclude
→see 決 0308 for compounds

【-ぎめ -極め】[sometimes also -決め] indicates periods of time (esp. months)
月極め駐車場 つきぎめちゅうしゃじょう parking lot rented on a monthly basis

【きまる 極まる】[usu. 決まる]
① be decided [fixed], be settled, be arranged
② be certain [sure], be a matter of course
→see 決 0308 for compounds

SYNONYMS

❶ⓐ **most**
最 MOST →3120
至 utmost →2707
極 EXTREME →1243

❶ⓐ **extreme in degree**
酷 SEVERE →1967
強 STRONG →0574
凄い tremendous →0145
重 HEAVY →4390
高 HIGH →2601
深 DEEP →0636
大 BIG →4224
厳 SEVERE →4079
激 intense →0955
極 EXTREME →1243

日【木】歹火片牙王ネ月月厶

痛 bitter(ly) →4071
切 keen →0030
甚 EXTREMELY →3271
祁 EXTREMELY →1447
超 super- →4107
頗る EXCEEDINGLY →1552
ⓑ extreme
極 EXTREME →1243
窮 extremity →2983
限 LIMIT →0475
涯 OUTER LIMITS →0623
果て end →4377

USAGE

❶【きわめる】

極める
[also 窮める]
ⓐ carry to extremity, go to extremes, be extremely (cruel)
ⓑ go to the extreme [end], reach an extreme, go to the highest point

窮める
① [also 極める]
ⓐ carry to extremity, go to extremes, be extremely (cruel)
ⓑ go to the extreme [end], reach an extreme, go to the highest point
② [usu. 究める] investigate thoroughly, study exhaustively, master

究める
[sometimes also 窮める] investigate thoroughly, study exhaustively, master

❷【きわまる】

極まる
[also suffix] reach an extreme (state or point), be extremely (dangerous)

窮まる
[sometimes also 谷まる]
ⓐ come to an end, terminate
ⓑ come to the end of one's tether, be at a loss

谷まる
[usu. 窮まる] same as 窮まる

❸【きわまり】

極まり
[sometimes also 窮まり] extremity, limit

窮まり
[now usu. 極まり] extremity, limit

❹【きわみ】

極み
height, apex, utmost

窮み
extremity, end, limit

HOMOPHONES

きわめる
窮 BE IN EXTREMITY →2983
究 STUDY EXHAUSTIVELY →2729
きわまる
窮 BE IN EXTREMITY →2983
谷 VALLEY →2536
きわまり 窮 BE IN EXTREMITY →2983
きわみ 窮 BE IN EXTREMITY →2983
きめる 決 DECIDE →0308
-ぎめ 決 DECIDE →0308
きまる 決 DECIDE →0308

NOTE

➡ see also USAGE note at 決 0308

棉

1244

1-4-8

▸COTTON
メン わた
Ⓒ 棉 mián

75	Non-Jōyō	U68C9
木	S12-4-8	F0000

COMPOUNDS

[now replaced by 綿 1736]
ⓐ COTTON plant
ⓑ COTTON fiber, cotton cloth, cotton wool
a 棉花 めんか raw cotton, cotton wool
棉実油 めんじつゆ cottonseed oil
b 印棉 いんめん Indian raw cotton

KUN

【わた 棉】 [now replaced by 綿]
ⓐ **COTTON plant**
ⓑ **COTTON fiber, cotton cloth, cotton wool**
b 木棉 きわた cotton fiber; ceiba

SYNONYMS

ⓑ fabrics
織 woven fabric →1801
紬 PONGEE →1684
紗 GAUZE →1653
絹 SILK →1721
綾 TWILL →1740
綿 COTTON →1736
棉 COTTON →1244
麻 HEMP →3878
毛 wool →4264
錦 BROCADE →2181

HOMOPHONES

わた 綿 COTTON →1736

NOTE

➡ see USAGE note at 綿 1736

椋

1245

1-4-8

▶*APHANANTHE ASPERA*

リョウ むく ㊔ むくのき くら

Ⓒ 椋 liáng

75	Names	U690B
木	S12-4-8	F3119

COMPOUNDS

● *APHANANTHE ASPERA*

椋木 りょうぼく *Aphananthe aspera*

KUN

【むく 椋】

① *APHANANTHE ASPERA*

椋の木 むくのき *Aphananthe aspera*

② gray starling

椋鳥 むくどり gray starling, *Sturnus cineraceus*

SYNONYMS

● & 【むく】① **trees**

桜 CHERRY → 1168
桐 PAULOWNIA → 1173
桂 AROMATIC TREE, katsura tree → 1163
梓 CATALPA → 1207
桑 MULBERRY → 2618
漆 Japanese lacquer tree → 0863
樺 BIRCH → 1324
椛 BIRCH → 1202
梧 CHINESE PARASOL TREE → 1200
檀 SPINDLE TREE → 1385
椿 CAMELLIA → 1278
柳 WILLOW → 1115
柊 HOLLY → 1119
椋 *APHANANTHE ASPERA* → 1245
柾 spindle tree → 1114
槻 ZELKOVA → 1349
楢 OAK → 1287
樫 EVERGREEN OAK → 1364
柏 CYPRESS, JAPANESE EMPEROR OAK → 1110
榎 HACKBERRY → 1323
梶 PAPER MULBERRY → 1199
柘 JAPANESE BOXWOOD → 1117
楊 WILLOW → 1286
桧 JAPANESE CYPRESS → 1160
梛 *NAGEIA NAGI* → 1206
榊 SACRED SHINTO TREE → 1327
楓 MAPLE → 1280
松 PINE → 1075
杉 CRYPTOMERIA → 1027
槙 PODOCARPUS → 1330
楠 CAMPHOR TREE → 1283
樟 CAMPHOR TREE → 1351

棲

1246

1-4-8

▶**INHABIT**

セイ す(む)

Ⓒ 栖 qī xī

75	Names	U68F2
木	S12-4-8	F1966

COMPOUNDS

ⓐ [now usu. 生 4309] (of animals) **INHABIT, live**

ⓑ (of people) **live, dwell, reside**

a 棲息する せいそくする inhabit, live
水棲の すいせいの aquatic, living in the water
両棲類 りょうせいるい Amphibia, amphibian

b 同棲する どうせいする live together, cohabit with
隠棲 いんせい secluded life
幽棲する ゆうせいする live a quiet life in seclusion away from the masses

KUN

【すむ 棲む】[sometimes also 栖む] (of animals) **INHABIT, live**

棲み分け すみわけ *biol* habitat isolation; compartmentalization, segregation

鳥が棲む森 とりがすむもり woods inhabited by birds

SYNONYMS

● **reside**

住 LIVE → 0072
居 RESIDE → 3822
棲 INHABIT (said of animals), live → 1246
栖 INHABIT (said of animals), live → 1170
生 inhabit → 4309
植 colonize → 1247

HOMOPHONES

すむ

住 LIVE → 0072
栖 INHABIT → 1170

NOTE

➡ see USAGE note at 住 0072

植

1247

1-4-8

▶**PLANT**

ショク う(える) う(わる) ㊔ たね

Ⓒ 植 zhí

75	Jōyō-3	U690D
木	S12-4-8	F0805

1	2	3	4	5	6	7	8	9	10	11	12
一	十	才	木	木	杧	杧	枯	柿	植	植	植

COMPOUNDS

❶ [original meaning] **PLANT**

植樹 しょくじゅ tree planting

植栽 しょくさい raising trees and plants
移植 いしょく transplanting

❷ **PLANT, plants, vegetation**
植物 しょくぶつ plant, vegetation
植物園 しょくぶつえん botanical garden
植生 しょくせい vegetation
動植物 どうしょくぶつ animals and plants

❸ [sometimes also 殖 1253] **colonize, settle**
植民地 しょくみんち colony, settlement
入植 にゅうしょく settlement, immigration

❹ typeset, set in type
植字 しょくじ typesetting, composition
誤植 ごしょく typographical error, misprint
写植 しゃしょく phototypesetting

KUN

【うえる 植える】 **PLANT, raise, grow; typeset, set in type**
植木 うえき garden plant, shrub, pot plant
田植え たうえ rice planting

【うわる 植わる】 **be PLANTed**

SPECIAL READINGS

柘植▲ つげ [also 黄楊, sometimes also 柘] Japanese boxwood

SYNONYMS

❶ **farm and plant**
植 PLANT → 1247
栽 PLANT (saplings) → 4087
培 CULTIVATE → 0558
耕 TILL → 1659
作 raise crops → 0077
農 farm, FARMING → 3345
蒔 SOW → 2935
播 SOW → 0906

❷ **plants**
菜 VEGETABLE → 2880
植 PLANT → 1247
栽 garden plant → 4087
茨 thorny shrub → 2812
苔 MOSS → 2792
蔓 VINE → 2975
桔 PLANT NAME ELEMENT → 1164

❸ **reside**
住 LIVE → 0072
居 RESIDE → 3822
棲 INHABIT (said of animals), live → 1246
栖 INHABIT (said of animals), live → 1170
生 inhabit → 4309
植 colonize → 1247

❹ **print and publish**
刷 PRINT → 1623
印 print → 1023
植 typeset → 1247
刊 PUBLISH → 0221
版 PUBLISHING → 1082
載 PUT IN PRINT → 4091
掲 display in writing → 0597
幀 BOOKBINDING → 0695

HOMOPHONES

つげ
柘 JAPANESE BOXWOOD → 1117
黄楊 → 3116, 1286
柘植 → 1117, 1247

棟

1248

1-4-8

▶BLOCK
トウ むね むな- ㊔ みね
Ⓒ 栋 dòng

75	Jōyō	U68DF
木	S12-4-8	F1687

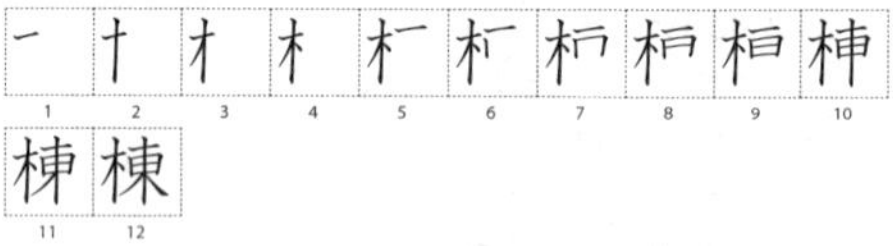

COMPOUNDS

❶ⓐ [also suffix] (long building or part thereof) **BLOCK, building, ward**
ⓑ **counter for BLOCKs of flats or buildings**
a 病棟 びょうとう (hospital) ward
翼棟 よくとう wing (of a building)
研究室棟 けんきゅうしつとう research laboratory building, laboratory block
b 第三棟 だいさんとう Block No. 3

❷ [original meaning] **ridge, edge of a roof**
上棟式 じょうとうしき ceremony of raising the ridgepole

❸ chief, head, leader
棟梁 とうりょう chief support, pillar (of a nation), chief, leader, foreman

KUN

【むね 棟】
① **ridge, ridgepole**
棟上げ むねあげ ridgepole raising
②ⓐ **building, house**
ⓑ counter for buildings or houses
a 別棟 べつむね another building, outhouse
b 一棟四戸建て ひとむねよんこだて tenement house divided into four apartments
三棟 みむね three buildings [houses]

【むな- 棟-】 **ridge, ridgepole**
棟瓦 むながわら ridge tile
棟木 むなぎ ridgepole

SYNONYMS

❶ **buildings**

閣 TALL MAGNIFICENT BUILDING → 4128
宇 large building → 2699
殿 PALACE → 2247
堂 HALL → 3202
館 PUBLIC BUILDING → 2196
舎 BUILDING → 2555
棟 BLOCK → 1248
厩 HORSE STABLE → 3746

❷ **roof parts**

軒 EAVES → 1851
庇 EAVES → 3802
棟 ridge → 1248
瓦 roof tile → 4288

【むね】

②ⓑ **counters for houses**

軒 COUNTER FOR HOUSES → 1851
戸 counter for households → 2429
棟 counter for buildings → 1248

椎

1249

◧1-4-8

▶**SPINE**
▶**CHINQUAPIN**

ツイ ズイ▲ スイ▲ しい▲

Ⓒ 椎 zhuī

75	Jōyō	U690E
木	S12-4-8	F1948

一 十 才 木 村 村 村 村 村 村 椎 椎 (1–12)

COMPOUNDS

❶ **SPINE, backbone**

椎骨 ついこつ vertebra
脊椎 せきつい spine, backbone

❷ [original meaning, now archaic] mallet, hammer

KUN

【しい 椎】**CHINQUAPIN**

椎茸 しいたけ shiitake (mushroom), *Lentinula edodes*
椎の実 しいのみ sweet acorn

SYNONYMS

❶ **bone**

骨 BONE → 3288
髄 MARROW → 2316
椎 SPINE → 1249
脊 SPINE → 3297
肋 RIB → 1022
骼 SKELETAL FRAME → 2302
骸 skeleton → 2301

【しい】

◯ **fruits and fruit trees**

桃 PEACH → 1174
榛 HAZEL → 1328
椎 CHINQUAPIN → 1249
柚 YUZU → 1123
椰 COCONUT → 1285
柑 CITRUS → 1112
橙 BITTER ORANGE → 1369
葡 GRAPE → 2902
萄 GRAPE → 2870
柿 PERSIMMON → 1118
檎 APPLE → 1386
李 PLUM → 3050
枇 LOQUAT → 1063
杷 LOQUAT → 1065
苺 STRAWBERRY → 2780
菱 water chestnut → 2879
杏 APRICOT → 3049
梅 JAPANESE APRICOT → 1159
橘 MANDARIN → 1366
栗 CHESTNUT → 3280
栃 JAPANESE HORSE CHESTNUT → 1122
梨 PEAR → 3412
蕉 PLANTAIN → 2994

椀

1250

◧1-4-8

▶**WOODEN BOWL**

ワン ㊔ まり

Ⓒ 碗 wǎn

75	Names	U6900
木	S12-4-8	F2635

COMPOUNDS

❶ⓐ **WOODEN BOWL, bowl**
ⓑ food served in a bowl

a 椀盛 わんもり dish consisting of cooked food served in a bowl with clear soup
椀子蕎麦 わんこそば style of serving *soba* in which small portions are continuously added to the bowl until the eater is full
汁椀 しるわん soup bowl

b 止め椀 とめわん soup served at the end of a formal dinner

❷ counter for food or drink served in a bowl

INDEPENDENT

【わん 椀】**WOODEN BOWL, bowl**

SPECIAL READINGS

椀飯振舞(=大盤振舞) おうばんぶるまい(=おおばんぶるまい) lavishly treating others, lavishing gifts on others

SYNONYMS

❶ⓐ **vessels and receptacles**

盤 dish → 3533

鍋 POT → 2202
釜 IRON POT → 2610
鼎 TRIPOD CAULDRON → 4405
臼 MORTAR → 4341
碓 MORTAR → 1537
托 RECEPTACLE → 0252
皿 PLATE → 4286
盆 TRAY → 2581
膳 LEGGED TRAY → 1381
杯 CUP → 1066
鉢 BOWL → 2144
椀 WOODEN BOWL → 1250
碗 CERAMIC BOWL → 1539
丼 LARGE BOWL → 4323

COMPOUND FORMATION

【椀飯振舞 おうばんぶるまい】

椀飯振舞 'lavishly treating others, etc.', is entertaining (振舞) others with plenty of food (椀飯). 椀飯, the pronunciation of which shifted from わんばん to わうばん to おうばん, originally meant rice (飯) served in a bowl (椀). By extension, it came to refer to the food served at a banquet. 椀飯 was mistakenly replaced by 大盤, which is far more common today.

棚

1251

◧ 1-4-8

▶**SHELF**

ホウ たな -だな

75	Nonstandard	U68DA
木	S12-4-8	F0000

traditional form → see 棚 at 1238

棧

1252

◧ 1-4-8

▶**PLANK BRIDGE**

サン ㊔ かけはし

75	Nonstandard	U68E7
木	S12-4-8	F0000

traditional form → see 栈 at 1169

椰

◧ 1-4-8

incorrect stroke-count
➡ see ◧ 1-4-9: 木 at 1285

楳

◧ 1-4-8

incorrect stroke-count
➡ see ◧ 1-4-9: 木 at 1288

槌

◧ 1-4-8

incorrect stroke-count
➡ see ◧ 1-4-9: 木 at 1290

殖

1253

◧ 1-4-8

▶**MULTIPLY**

ショク ふ(える) ふ(やす)

Ⓒ 殖 zhí

78	Jōyō	U6B96
歹	S12-4-8	F1619

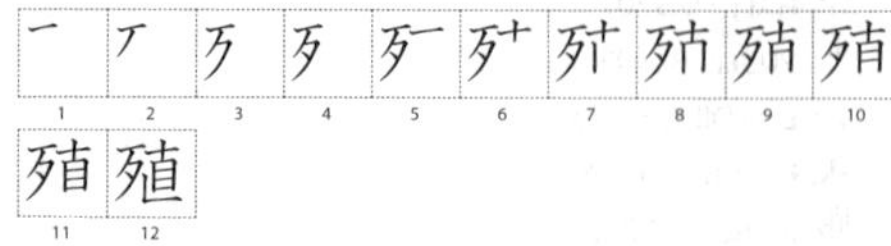

COMPOUNDS

❶ⓐ [original meaning] (produce offspring) **MULTIPLY, propagate, breed**

ⓑ (increase the quantity of, esp. wealth) **MULTIPLY, increase, make (money)**

a 増殖する ぞうしょくする multiply, propagate, increase

繁殖する はんしょくする breed, propagate, increase, multiply

生殖 せいしょく reproduction, procreation, generation

b 殖産 しょくさん increase of production; enhancement of one's fortune

利殖 りしょく moneymaking

❷ multitude, great deal

学殖 がくしょく scholarship, learning, knowledge

❸ [usu. 植 1247] colonize, settle

殖民 しょくみん colonization

拓殖 たくしょく colonization, exploitation

KUN

【ふえる 殖える】 *vi* (increase of its own accord) **MULTIPLY, increase, propagate**—said esp. of wealth or living things

蠅[×]が殖える はえがふえる Flies multiply

財産が殖える ざいさんがふえる become rich

【ふやす 殖やす】 *vt* (cause to multiply of its own accord) **MULTIPLY, increase, propagate, augment**—said esp. of wealth or living things

貯金を殖やす ちょきんをふやす increase one's savings

家畜を殖やす かちくをふやす breed cattle

SYNONYMS

❶ⓐ **give birth**

生 BE BORN → 4309
誕 BE BORN → 1987
産 GIVE BIRTH → 4089
娩 GIVE BIRTH → 0486
殖 MULTIPLY → 1253

ⓑ **increase**

加 add to → 0042
増 INCREASE → 0836
殖 MULTIPLY → 1253

倍 DOUBLE →0122

HOMOPHONES

ふえる 増 INCREASE →0836

ふやす 増 INCREASE →0836

NOTE

➡ see USAGE note at 増 0836

殘

1254

1-4-8

▶**REMAIN**
▶**RUTHLESS**

ザン のこ(る) のこ(す)

78 歹	Nonstandard	U6B98
	S12-4-8	F0000

traditional form → see 残 at 1179

焰

1255

1-4-8

▶**FLAME**

エン ほのお

Ⓝ 燄 焰 Ⓒ 焰 yàn

86 火	Names	U7130
	S12-4-8	F0000

COMPOUNDS

[now usu. 炎 3075]

a [original meaning] **FLAME, blaze**

b (figuratively) **FLAMEs (as of passion)**

a 焰硝(=煙硝) えんしょう gunpowder
火焰 かえん flames, blaze
光焰 こうえん light and flame

b 情焰 じょうえん flaming desires, burning passions
気焰を吐く きえんをはく talk big, talk a lot of hot air

KUN

【ほのお 焰】

ⓐ [now replaced by 炎] **FLAME, blaze**

ⓑ [now usu. 炎] (figuratively) **FLAMEs (as of passion)**

b 嫉妬の焰 しっとのほのお The Flames of Jealousy (movie title)

SYNONYMS

a fire
火 FIRE →4273
炎 FLAME →3075
焰 FLAME →1255

HOMOPHONES

ほのお 炎 FLAME →3075

NOTE

➡ see USAGE note at 炎 3075

焼

1256

1-4-8

▶**BURN**

ショウ や(く) や(き) や(き)- -や(き) や(ける)

Ⓝ 燒 Ⓒ 烧 shāo

86 火	Jōyō-4	U713C
	S12-4-8	F0731

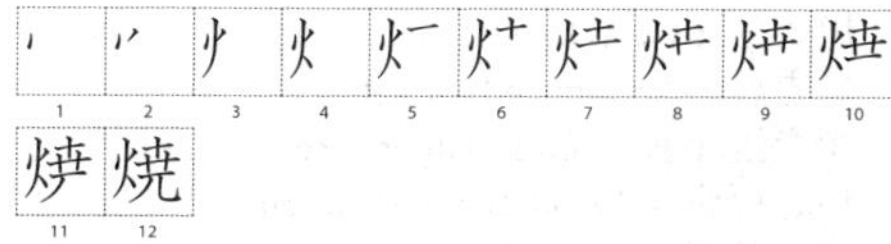

COMPOUNDS

a [original meaning] (set or be set on fire) **BURN, incinerate**

b be BURNt (down), be destroyed by fire

a 焼却する しょうきゃくする destroy by fire, incinerate
焼身自殺 しょうしんじさつ suicide by fire, burning oneself to death
焼香する しょうこうする burn [offer] incense
焼夷弾 しょういだん incendiary bomb
焼死 しょうし death by fire
焼酎 しょうちゅう *shochu*

b 全焼する ぜんしょうする be burnt down
半焼 はんしょう partial destruction by fire
類焼する るいしょうする catch fire from next door

KUN

【やく 焼く】*vt*

①ⓐ [sometimes also 灼く] **BURN, set on fire, incinerate; scorch; cauterize**
ⓑ **bake (pottery), fire**
ⓒ **cremate**

a 炭焼き すみやき charcoal making

b 焼き物 やきもの pottery, porcelain, earthenware

c 焼き場 やきば crematory

② cook by fire: **bake, roast, broil, grill, toast**
焼き網 やきあみ toasting grill, broiling grill

③ [sometimes also 妬く] **BURN with jealousy, be envious**
焼き餅 やきもち roasted rice cake; jealousy

④ print (photos)
焼き付け やきつけ printing (photos)
焼き増し やきまし extra prints

⑤ take the trouble to do something
余計な世話を焼く よけいなせわをやく poke one's nose (in) where one is not wanted

【やき 焼き】

① **roasting, broiling; baking, toasting**
焼きの足りない やきのたりない underfired

② annealing
焼き戻し やきもどし tempering
焼き入れ やきいれ quenching, hardening
焼きを入れる やきをいれる harden, temper; discipline; torture

③ figurative meaning
焼きが回る やきがまわる become decrepit, become dull

【やき- 焼き-】[also prefix] **roasted, broiled, baked, parched**

焼き芋 やきいも baked sweet potato
焼き鳥 やきとり grilled chicken
焼き飯 やきめし frizzled [fried] rice
焼き豆腐 やきどうふ broiled bean curd
焼き蕎麦 やきそば chow mein
焼き肉 やきにく roast meat, *yakiniku*

【-やき -焼き】[also suffix]
① **roasted, baked or fried food**
鋤×焼き すきやき sukiyaki
鉄板焼き てっぱんやき meat and vegetables roasted on hot plate
目玉焼き めだまやき fried eggs, sunny side up
カルメ焼き かるめやき brittle
② **ware, pottery, porcelain**
有田焼き ありたやき Arita ware [porcelain]

【やける 焼ける】*vi*
①ⓐ **BURN, be burnt, be destroyed by fire; be scorched**
ⓑ (of the sky) **glow, BURN**
a 焼け跡 やけあと ruins of fire
日焼け ひやけ suntan
b 夕焼け ゆうやけ sunset glow
② be cooked by fire: **be baked, be roasted, be broiled, be toasted**
良く焼けた よくやけた well done, done brown
③ [sometimes also 妬ける] be jealous, **BURN** with jealousy
焼けて堪まらない やけてたまらない How I envy him!
④ have heartburn
胸焼け むねやけ heartburn, sour stomach
⑤ be subjected to (the trouble of doing something for someone)
世話の焼ける せわのやける troublesome, annoying

SYNONYMS

● **burn**
焼 BURN → 1256
燃 BURN (undergo combustion) → 1375
焚く BURN (build a fire) → 3450
焦 SCORCH → 3444
灼 SCORCH → 1036
炮 ROAST → 1132
燎 SET ON FIRE → 1376

【やく】
② **cook**
煮 BOIL (cook by boiling) → 3460
沸 BOIL (undergo boiling) → 0387
炊 COOK → 1080
蒸 STEAM → 2936
焼く cook by fire → 1256
揚げる fry in deep fat → 0722
煎 ROAST, DECOCT → 2950
② **work metals**
錬 REFINE (crude metals) → 2185
煉 REFINE (crude metals) → 1297
鍛 FORGE → 2206
鋳 CAST → 2170
焼き annealing → 1256
冶 WORK METALS → 0089

【-やき】
① **cooked dishes**
-焼き roasted, baked or fried food → 1256
-揚げ fried food → 0722
-煮 boiled food → 3460

USAGE

❶【やく】
焼く
vt
①ⓐ [sometimes also 灼く] burn, set on fire, incinerate; scorch; cauterize
ⓑ bake (pottery), fire
ⓒ cremate
② cook by fire: bake, roast, broil, grill, toast
③ [sometimes also 妬く] burn with jealousy, be envious
④ print (photos)
⑤ take the trouble to do something
妬く
[usu. 焼く] burn with jealousy, be envious
灼く
[usu. 焼く] scorch, burn; cauterize

❷【やける】
焼ける
vi
①ⓐ burn, be burnt, be destroyed by fire; be scorched
ⓑ (of the sky) glow, burn
② be cooked by fire: be baked, be roasted, be broiled, be toasted
③ [sometimes also 妬ける] be jealous, burn with jealousy
④ have heartburn
⑤ be subjected to (the trouble of doing something for someone)
妬ける
[usu. 焼ける] be jealous, burn with jealousy

HOMOPHONES

やく
妬 BE JEALOUS → 0337
灼 SCORCH → 1036
やける 妬 BE JEALOUS → 0337

煉

1257

1-4-8

▸REFINE

レン ね(る)

86	Nonstandard	U7149
火	S12-4-8	F0000

traditional form → see 煉 at 1297

煤

1-4-8

incorrect stroke-count
➡ see 1-4-9: 火 at 1292

牃

1-4-8

incorrect stroke-count
➡ see 1-4-9: 片 at 1299

雅

1258

1-4-8

▸ELEGANT

ガ みや(び) ㊔ まさ まさし つね

172	Nonstandard	U96C5
隹	S12-8-4	F0000

traditional form → see 雅 at 1532

瑛

1259

1-4-8

▸TRANSPARENT GEM

エイ ㊔ よう あきら てる あき

Ⓒ 瑛 yīng

96	Names	U745B
王	S12-4-8	F2744

COMPOUNDS

● [original meaning, now archaic] **TRANSPARENT GEM**, jewel

玉瑛 ぎょくえい transparent gem, crystal

SYNONYMS

● **precious stones**

玉 GEM → 4289
珂 WHITE AGATE → 1137
璧 DISK-SHAPED JEWEL → 3608
琥 AMBER → 1261
珀 AMBER → 1136
珠 PEARL → 1183
瑛 TRANSPARENT GEM → 1259
瑠 LAPIS LAZULI → 1342
璃 GLASSY SUBSTANCE → 1358
晶 CRYSTAL → 3122
玖 beautiful black jewel → 1041
琉 LAPIS LAZULI → 1221
琳 BEAUTIFUL GEM → 1262

斑

1260

1-4-8

▸SPOT

ハン まだら▲ ふ▲ ぶち▲ むら▲

Ⓒ 斑 bān

67	Jōyō	U6591
文	S12-4-8	F2523

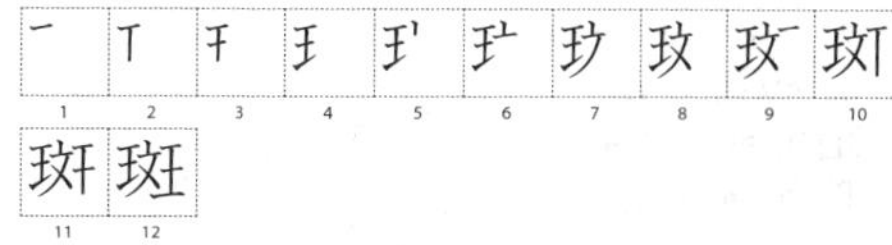

COMPOUNDS

ⓐ [sometimes also 班 1182] [also suffix] **SPOT, speck**
ⓑ SPOTted, streaked, variegated

a 斑点 はんてん spot, speck
斑状組織 はんじょうそしき porphyritic structure
大赤斑 だいせきはん Jupiter's Great Red Spot
紫斑病 しはんびょう purpura
蒙古斑 もうこはん Mongolian spot
b 斑条 はんじょう variegated streaks

KUN

【まだら 斑】
ⓐ **SPOT**, speck
ⓑ **SPOT**ted, streaked, variegated
b 斑牛 まだらうし brindled ox
羽斑蚊(=翅×斑蚊) はまだらか *Anopheles* (mosquito)

【ふ 斑】**SPOT**, speck
斑入りの ふいりの variegated, spotted
虎斑 とらふ tiger stripes
胡麻斑海豹 ごまふあざらし spotted seal

【ぶち 斑】dapple, mottle; dappled, mottled
斑毛 ぶちげ leopard (horse coat pattern)
黒斑 くろぶち black spots

【むら 斑】
ⓐ unevenness, streakiness, streak
ⓑ inconsistency, irregularity, erraticness
a 色斑 いろむら color unevenness
b 斑気な むらきな moody, capricious, whimsical

SPECIAL READINGS

斑鳩▲ いかる Japanese grosbeak
雀斑▲ そばかす freckles
石斑魚▲ うぐい Japanese dace, *Tribolodon hakonensis*

琥

1261

1-4-8

▸AMBER

コ

Ⓒ 琥 hǔ

96	Names	U7425
王	S12-4-8	F3345

COMPOUNDS

● **AMBER**

琥珀 こはく amber

SYNONYMS

● **precious stones**

玉 GEM → 4289
珂 WHITE AGATE → 1137

璧 DISK-SHAPED JEWEL → 3608
琥 AMBER → 1261
珀 AMBER → 1136
珠 PEARL → 1183
瑛 TRANSPARENT GEM → 1259
瑠 LAPIS LAZULI → 1342
璃 GLASSY SUBSTANCE → 1358
晶 CRYSTAL → 3122
玖 beautiful black jewel → 1041
琉 LAPIS LAZULI → 1221
琳 BEAUTIFUL GEM → 1262

琳

1262
1-4-8

▶BEAUTIFUL GEM
リン ㊔ たま
Ⓒ 琳 lín

96	Names	U7433
王	S12-4-8	F3136

COMPOUNDS

● [rare] **BEAUTIFUL GEM**
琳瑯× りんろう beautiful gem
琳瑯×たる りんろうたる like the tinkling sound of a jade

SYNONYMS

● **precious stones**
玉 GEM → 4289
珂 WHITE AGATE → 1137
璧 DISK-SHAPED JEWEL → 3608
琥 AMBER → 1261
珀 AMBER → 1136
珠 PEARL → 1183
瑛 TRANSPARENT GEM → 1259
瑠 LAPIS LAZULI → 1342
璃 GLASSY SUBSTANCE → 1358
晶 CRYSTAL → 3122
玖 beautiful black jewel → 1041
琉 LAPIS LAZULI → 1221
琳 BEAUTIFUL GEM → 1262

琢

1263
1-4-8

▶POLISH
タク ㊔ たか みがく

96	Names	UFA4A
王	S12-4-8	F0000

traditional form → see 琢 at 1222

祿

1264
1-4-8

▶RETAINER'S STIPEND
ロク ㊔ よし
Ⓝ 祿 Ⓒ 禄 lù

113	Names	U7984
ネ	S12-4-8	F1660

COMPOUNDS

❶ (ration of rice paid to samurai in feudal Japan) **RETAINER'S STIPEND, official pay, fief**
禄高 ろくだか amount of one's fief [stipend]
俸禄 ほうろく retainer's stipend, official pay [salary]
微禄 びろく small stipend

❷ happiness, prosperity, wealth
禄命 ろくめい one's lot
福禄寿 ふくろくじゅ God of Wealth and Longevity

INDEPENDENT

【ろく 禄】**RETAINER'S STIPEND**, fief (→❶)
四百石の禄 よんひゃっこくのろく fief of 400 *koku*

SYNONYMS

❶ **pay and earnings**
給 PAY → 1708
賃 WAGE → 3341
料 FEE → 1644
俸 SALARY → 0128
禄 RETAINER'S STIPEND → 1264
収 income → 0031

脹

1265
1-4-8

▶SWELL
チョウ は(れる) ふく(らむ) ふく(れる)
Ⓒ 胀 zhàng

130	Names	U8139
月	S12-4-8	F3048

COMPOUNDS

❶ **SWELL, expand, bulge**
膨脹(=膨張) ぼうちょう expansion, swelling; growth, increase
腫脹 しゅちょう swelling, puffiness

❷ [original meaning] have a **SWELL**ed [full] stomach
脹満 ちょうまん tympanites

KUN

【はれる 脹れる】[usu. 腫れる] **SWELL**, become swollen; tumefy
脹れ はれ swelling, boil
脹れぼったい はれぼったい somewhat swollen, puffy
みみず脹れ みみずばれ wale, welt

【ふくらむ 脹らむ】[usu. 膨らむ] **expand, SWELL (out), get big, become inflated**
脹らみ ふくらみ swelling, bulge, puff
脹ら脛× ふくらはぎ calf

【ふくれる 脹れる】[usu. 膨れる]
① **expand, SWELL (out), get big, become inflated**
脹れ上がる ふくれあがる swell up
下脹れの しもぶくれの full-cheeked, round-faced
② **get sulky, sulk, fret, get peevish**
脹れっ面 ふくれっつら sulky look [face], sullen look

SYNONYMS

❶ expand

脹 SWELL → 1265
膨 EXPAND → 1380
張 SPREAD → 0573
氾 SPREAD OUT → 0226
広げる spread (out) → 3769
拡 ENLARGE → 0366
伸 STRETCH → 0079
延 EXTEND → 3812

❶ swell and swelling

脹 SWELL → 1265
腫 SWELLING → 1310
瘍 SWELLING → 4073
爛 break out in sores → 1427

HOMOPHONES

ふくらむ 膨 EXPAND → 1380
ふくれる 膨 EXPAND → 1380
はれる 腫 SWELLING → 1310

NOTE

➡ see USAGE notes at 膨 1380 and 腫 1310

腋

1266

◧1-4-8

▸ARMPIT

エキ わき

Ⓒ 腋 yè

130	Non-Jōyō	U814B
月	S12-4-8	F2841

COMPOUNDS

● ARMPIT

腋窩×腺 えきかせん axillary gland
腋芽 えきが(=わきめ) axillary bud

KUN

【わき 腋】[also 脇]

ⓐ **ARMPIT**

ⓑ **armhole**

a 腋毛 わきげ hair of the armpit
腋の下 わきのした armpit, axilla

SYNONYMS

● trunk parts

胸 CHEST → 1187
腹 BELLY → 1308
胴 TRUNK → 1186
腰 WAIST → 1311
背 BACK → 3182
肩 SHOULDER → 2446
股 CROTCH → 1093
脇 ARMPIT → 1188
腋 ARMPIT → 1266

HOMOPHONES

わき

傍 BESIDE → 0166
脇 SIDE → 1188

NOTE

➡ see USAGE note at 傍 0166

腔

1267

◧1-4-8

▸BODY CAVITY

コウ クウ

Ⓒ 腔 qiāng

130	Names	U8154
月	S12-4-8	F2445

COMPOUNDS

ⓐ BODY CAVITY

ⓑ body

a 腔腸動物 こうちょうどうぶつ coelenterate
口腔 こうくう(=こうこう) mouth, oral cavity
腹腔 ふくくう(=ふくこう, ふっこう) abdominal cavity
腹腔鏡 ふくくうきょう laparoscope
滑腔砲 かっこうほう smoothbore

b 満腔 まんこう heartfelt, wholehearted

SYNONYMS

● holes and cavities

穴 HOLE → 2682
洞 CAVE → 0455
窟 CAVE → 2923
窪 HOLLOW → 2962
腔 BODY CAVITY → 1267
孔 OPEN HOLE → 0205
口 MOUTH → 4189
坑 PIT → 0277
堀 DITCH → 0561
溝 CHANNEL → 0810
壕 TRENCH → 0966
濠 MOAT → 0975
凹 concavity → 4294

勝

1268

◧1-4-8

▸WIN

▸EXCEL

ショウ か(つ) -が(ち) まさ(る) すぐ(れる)▲

㊔ よし すぐる すぐり

Ⓝ 勝 Ⓒ 胜 shèng shēng

19	Jōyō-3	U52DD
力	S12-2-10	F0282

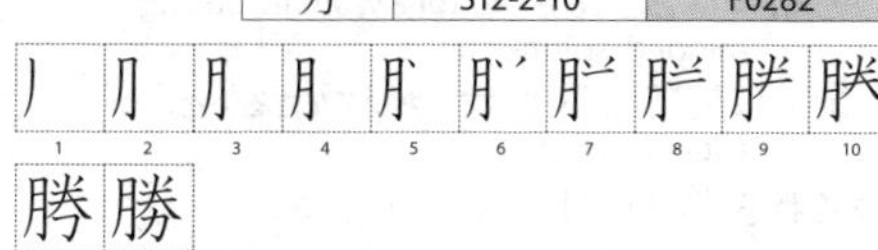

COMPOUNDS

❶ⓐ WIN, defeat

ⓑ **WIN, victory**
ⓒ **counter for WINs (in sports)**

a 勝者 しょうしゃ winner
全勝する ぜんしょうする win all the games, make a clean sweep
優勝 ゆうしょう victory, championship
b 勝利 しょうり victory, triumph, win
勝敗 しょうはい victory or defeat
勝負 しょうぶ victory or defeat; match, game
決勝戦 けっしょうせん final round match, finals
大勝 たいしょう great [sweeping] victory
連勝 れんしょう straight victories
c 二勝三敗 にしょうさんぱい two wins and three defeats

❷ **EXCEL, surpass, outdo**
殊勝な しゅしょうな laudable, praiseworthy

❸ place of natural beauty
勝地 しょうち beauty spot
景勝 けいしょう picturesque scenery
名勝 めいしょう place of scenic beauty

INDEPENDENT

【しょう 勝】 place of natural beauty
天下の勝 てんかのしょう beautiful scenery

KUN

【かつ 勝つ】
①ⓐ **WIN, defeat, triumph**
ⓑ [formerly 克つ] **control (oneself), overcome**
a 勝ち かち win, victory
勝ち取る かちとる gain, win
b 赤が勝っている あかがかっている predominated by red
② **unclassified compounds**
勝手 かって one's own way; convenience; circumstances; kitchen

【-がち -勝ち】 [suffix]
① **apt to, prone to; predominated by**
病気勝ちだ びょうきがちだ be prone to diseases
極端に走り勝ちだ きょくたんにはしりがちだ be apt to go to extremes
② **WIN, victory**
逆転勝ちする ぎゃくてんがちする win after defeat seems certain

【まさる 勝る】 [sometimes also 優る] **EXCEL, be better than, surpass**
男勝りの おとこまさりの (of a woman) strong-minded, spirited
全てに於て勝る すべてにおいてまさる excel in every respect

【すぐれる 勝れる】 [now usu. 優れる]
① be superior to, be **EXCEL**lent, be better than, surpass
勝れた業績 すぐれたぎょうせき outstanding achievement
② [usu. in negative constructions] be fine, feel well
気分が勝れない きぶんがすぐれない not feel well

SYNONYMS

❶ **win**
勝 WIN → 1268
克 OVERCOME → 2540
剋 OVERCOME → 4097
征 CONQUER → 0349
破 BREAK → 1478
凱 TRIUMPH → 2286

❷ **excel**
勝 EXCEL → 1268
抜 STAND OUT → 0290
擢んでる stand out → 0973
超 SURPASS → 4107
越 GO BEYOND → 4108
凌 SURPASS → 0144
駕 outdo → 3236

USAGE

❶【かつ】
勝つ
①ⓐ win, defeat, triumph
ⓑ [formerly 克つ] control (oneself), overcome
② unclassified compounds
克つ
[now usu. 勝つ] control (oneself), overcome

❷【まさる】
勝る
[sometimes also 優る] excel, be better than, surpass
優る
[usu. 勝る] excel, be better than, surpass

HOMOPHONES

かつ 克 OVERCOME → 2540
まさる 優 SUPERIOR → 0200
すぐれる 優 SUPERIOR → 0200

NOTE

➡ see also USAGE note at 優 0200

腕

1269
1-4-8

▶**ARM**
ワン うで
Ⓒ 腕 wàn

130	Jōyō	U8155
月	S12-4-8	F0765

COMPOUNDS

❶ **ARM**

腕章 わんしょう armband, arm badge
腕力 わんりょく muscular strength
上腕 じょうわん upper arm
左腕投手 さわんとうしゅ left-handed pitcher

❷ **skill, ability**

手腕 しゅわん ability, skill
才腕 さいわん ability, skill
敏腕 びんわん ability, capability

❸ **unclassified compounds**

腕白 わんぱく naughtiness, mischief

KUN

【うで 腕】**ARM; skill, ability**

腕時計 うでどけい wrist watch
腕首 うでくび wrist
腕が良い うでがいい be skilled, be able
腕前 うでまえ skill, ability, capacity
腕利き うできき man of ability

SYNONYMS

❶ **hand and arm**

手 HAND → 4267
腕 ARM → 1269
肘 ELBOW → 1044
掌 PALM → 3215
指 FINGER → 0452
拇 THUMB → 0358
拳 FIST → 3295

❶ **limbs**

肢 LIMB → 1094
腕 ARM → 1269
脚 LEG → 1226

❷ **skill**

力 POWER → 4178
能 ABILITY → 1676
技 SKILL → 0292
倆 SKILL → 0136
腕 skill → 1269
才 TALENT → 4218

NOTE

➡ see COMPOUND FORMATION for 腕前 うでまえ → 前 2819

勝

1270
◧ 1-4-8

▶**WIN**
▶**EXCEL**

ショウ か(つ) -が(ち) まさ(る) すぐ(れる)
㊔ よし すぐる すぐり

19	Nonstandard	U52DD
力	S12-2-10	F0000

traditional form → see 勝 at 1268

雄

1271
◧ 1-4-8

▶**MALE**
▶**HEROIC**

ユウ お- おす おん▲ ㊔ かつ たけ たけし かず たか
Ⓒ 雄 xióng

172	Jōyō	U96C4
隹	S12-8-4	F0794

一 ナ 厷 厷 厷 厷 厷' 厷' 厷 雄 雄 雄
1 2 3 4 5 6 7 8 9 10 11 12

COMPOUNDS

❶ [original meaning] (of plants or animals) **MALE**

雄性 ゆうせい male characteristics, manliness
雄蕊× ゆうずい(=おしべ) stamen
雌雄 しゆう male and female; victory or defeat

❷ⓐ **HEROIC, manly, brave, bold**
ⓑ (impressive in scale) **HEROIC, grand, magnificent**

a 雄壮な ゆうそうな brave, heroic, gallant
雄姿 ゆうし brave [imposing] figure
雄武 ゆうぶ bravery
雄断 ゆうだん manly decision

b 雄弁な ゆうべんな eloquent, fluent
雄渾な ゆうこんな magnificent, sublime; vigorous, bold
雄図 ゆうと ambitious enterprise, grand project
雄飛する ゆうひする launch out, embark upon (a career)
雄大な ゆうだいな grand, magnificent, heroic

❸ **hero, great man, great leader, master**

英雄 えいゆう hero
両雄 りょうゆう two great men
群雄 ぐんゆう rival leaders [barons]

❹ victory

雌雄を決する しゆうをけっする fight a decisive battle

INDEPENDENT

【ゆう 雄】hero, great leader, master

一世の雄 いっせいのゆう greatest hero [mastermind] of the age
私学の雄 しがくのゆう one of the leading private schools

KUN

【お- 雄-】

ⓐ (of plants) **MALE**
ⓑ **manly, masculine**
ⓒ [sometimes also 牡-] (of animals) **MALE**
ⓓ [also 男] the larger or stronger of two

a 雄花 おばな male flower
b 雄雄しい おおしい manly, brave, heroic
c 雄牛 おうし bull, steer

日 木 歹 火 片 牙 王 ネ 月 月 【厷】

d 雄滝 おだき the greater waterfall (of the two)

【おす 雄】[sometimes also 牡] (of animals) **MALE**

雄犬 おすいぬ male dog

【おん 雄】[sometimes also 牡] (of animals) **MALE**

雄鳥(=雄鶏) おんどり rooster

SYNONYMS

❶ **man**

男 MAN → 3147
郎 YOUNG MAN → 1641
雄 MALE → 1271
牡 MALE → 1040
夫 male adult → 4271
翁 OLD MAN → 2611
爺 OLD MAN → 2656

❷ⓐ **brave**

勇 BRAVE → 2592
侠 chivalrous → 0110
赳 VALIANT → 4100
驍 VALIANT → 2327
敢 bold → 2142
豪 bold and unrestrained → 2657
雄 HEROIC → 1271
壮 heroic → 0263
義 chivalrous → 2948
凜 gallant → 0195

ⓑ **great**

偉 GREAT (of superior character) → 0167
大 BIG → 4224
宏 GRAND (large in scale) → 2728
壮 GRAND (having grandeur) → 0263
豪 MAGNIFICENT → 2657
雄 HEROIC → 1271
碩 EMINENT → 1555

❸ **great persons**

豪 GREAT MAN → 2657
傑 OUTSTANDING PERSON → 0175
雄 hero → 1271
匠 CRAFTSMAN → 3711
聖 great master → 3509

USAGE

❶【お】

雄-

ⓐ (of plants) male
ⓑ manly, masculine
ⓒ [sometimes also 牡-] (of animals) male
ⓓ [also 男] the larger or stronger of two

牡-

[usu. 雄-] (of animals) male

男

① *elegant* man, male
② [in compounds] the larger or stronger of two

❷【おす】

雄

[sometimes also 牡] (of animals) male

牡

[usu. 雄] (of animals) male

❸【おん】

雄

[sometimes also 牡] (of animals) male

牡

[usu. 雄] (of animals) male

HOMOPHONES

お-

牡 MALE → 1040
男 MAN → 3147

おす 牡 MALE → 1040

おん 牡 MALE → 1040

旒

1272

1-4-9

▶**COUNTER FOR FLAGS**

リュウ

Ⓒ 旒 liú

70	Non-Jōyō	U65D2
方	S13-4-9	F0000

COMPOUNDS

ⓐ [now also 流 0529] **COUNTER FOR FLAGS**

ⓑ [original meaning] **flying end of a long flag; flag, pennant**

a 旗二旒 はたにりゅう two flags

b 旗旒信号 きりゅうしんごう flag signaling

SYNONYMS

ⓐ **flag**

旗 FLAG → 1321
幡 LONG FLAG → 0891
旒 COUNTER FOR FLAGS → 1272

暗

1273

1-4-9

▶**DARK**

アン くら(い) くら(ます)▲

Ⓒ 暗 àn

72	Jōyō-3	U6697
日	S13-4-9	F0701

1	2	3	4	5	6	7	8	9	10	11	12	13
丨	冂	巾	日	日'	旷	旷	昈	昈	暗	暗	暗	暗

COMPOUNDS

❶ⓐ [formerly also 闇 4134] [original meaning] **DARK, dim**

ⓑ [formerly also 闇 4134] **DARKness**

ⓒ [also prefix] **DARK-colored**

a 暗黒 あんこく darkness

暗室 あんしつ dark room

暗雲 あんうん dark clouds
暗夜 あんや dark night
b 暗中模索 あんちゅうもさく groping in the dark
明暗 めいあん light and dark; contrast
c 暗色 あんしょく dark color
暗赤色 あんせきしょく dark red

❷ in the DARK, hidden, secret
暗殺 あんさつ assassination
暗号 あんごう code, password
暗礁 あんしょう sunken rock, unknown reef; deadlock
暗黙の あんもくの tacit
暗示 あんじ hint, suggestion

❸ [formerly also 闇 4134] (lacking wisdom) **DARK,** ignorant, foolish
暗愚な人人 あんぐなひとびと dark souls
暗黒時代 あんこくじだい the Dark Ages
暗君 あんくん foolish ruler

❹ from memory, by heart, by rote
暗記する あんきする learn by heart, memorize
暗誦(=暗唱)する あんしょうする recite from memory
暗算 あんざん mental arithmetic [calculation]

INDEPENDENT

【あん 暗】DARKness
【あんに 暗に】tacitly, by implication

KUN

【くらい 暗い】
ⓐ [sometimes also 昏い, 闇い, or 冥い] **DARK, dim;** (of colors) **dark;** (producing gloom) **dark, dreary, dismal;** (concealed) **dark, shadowy, shady**
ⓑ be ignorant, be a stranger to
a 暗さ くらさ darkness; gloom
暗闇 くらやみ in darkness
暗い色 くらいいろ dark color
暗い過去 くらいかこ shadowy past
暗い気持になる くらいきもちになる feel gloomy
薄暗い うすぐらい gloomy, dim
b 世事に暗い せじにくらい know little of the world

【くらます 暗ます】[also 晦ます]
① abscond, conceal oneself
② deceive, fool, dissemble

SYNONYMS

❶ⓐ dark
暗 DARK → 1273
黒 BLACK → 3406
陰 shaded → 0657
闇 DARK → 4134
晦 DARK → 1196
昏 dark → 3073
昧 DARK → 1105
冥 DARK → 2613
曖 SHADY → 1383

ⓒ dark-colored
暗 DARK → 1273
濃 dark → 0956
深 DEEP → 0636

❷ secret and private
秘 SECRET → 1490
密 SECRET → 2857
暗 in the dark → 1273
私 PRIVATE → 1432
内 not public → 4277
隠 hidden from view → 0873

❸ foolish
愚 FOOLISH → 3513
暗 DARK → 1273
痴 STUPID → 4072
鈍 DULL → 2123
呆 DIM-WITTED → 2712
魯 DULL → 2665
闇 DARK → 4134
蒙 IGNORANCE → 2938

USAGE

【くらい】
暗い
ⓐ [sometimes also 昏い, 闇い, or 冥い] dark, dim; (of colors) dark; (producing gloom) dark, dreary, dismal; (concealed) dark, shadowy, shady
ⓑ be ignorant, be a stranger to

冥い
[usu. 暗い, sometimes also 昏い or 闇い] dark, dim; (of colors) dark; (producing gloom) dark, dreary, dismal; (concealed) dark, shadowy, shady

昏い
[usu. 暗い, sometimes also 闇い or 冥い] dark, dim; (of colors) dark; (producing gloom) dark, dreary, dismal; (concealed) dark, shadowy, shady

闇い
[usu. 暗い, sometimes also 昏い or 冥い] dark, dim; (of colors) dark; (producing gloom) dark, dreary, dismal; (concealed) dark, shadowy, shady

【くらます】
暗ます
[also 晦ます]
① abscond, conceal oneself
② deceive, fool, dissemble

晦ます
[also 暗ます] same as 暗ます

HOMOPHONES

くらい
冥 DARK → 2613
昏 LOSE CONSCIOUSNESS → 3073
闇 DARK → 4134

くらます 晦 DARK →1196

暖

1274

1-4-9

▶WARM

ダン ノン▲ あたた(か) あたた(かい) あたた(まる) あたた(める) ㊔ はる

Ⓝ 暖 Ⓒ 暖 nuǎn

72	Jōyō-6	U6696
日	S13-4-9	F1359

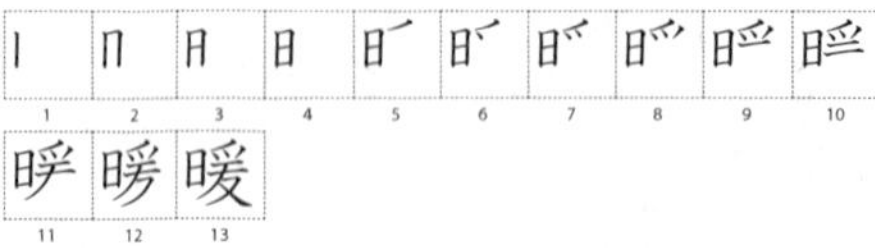

COMPOUNDS

ⓐ WARM (esp. weather), mild, genial, temperate

ⓑ [formerly also 煖 だん 1293] **WARM (the surrounding air), warm up, heat**

a 暖流 だんりゅう warm current
暖地 だんち warm district, region of mild climate
暖冬 だんとう mild winter
暖衣飽食 だんいほうしょく warm clothes and plenty to eat
温暖な おんだんな warm, mild

b 暖房 だんぼう heating
暖炉 だんろ fireplace, stove
暖気 だんき warmth, warm weather
暖簾 のれん shop curtain, *noren;* credit, reputation

INDEPENDENT

【だん 暖】**WARM**th, heat
暖を取る だんをとる warm oneself

KUN

【あたたか 暖か】
あたたかな 暖かな same as 暖かい あたたかい
暖かみ あたたかみ warmth
暖かな毛布 あたたかなもうふ warm blanket

【あたたかい 暖かい】
①ⓐ (of weather) **WARM, mild, genial, temperate**
ⓑ **WARM (color)**
a 暖かさ あたたかさ warmth
今日は暖かい きょうはあたたかい It is warm today
b 暖かい色 あたたかいいろ warm color
② **WARMhearted, kindhearted, sympathetic**
暖かい人 あたたかいひと warmhearted person

【あたたまる 暖まる】(surrounding air rises in temperature) **get WARM, be warmed, warm**
暖まった空気 あたたまったくうき warmed air

【あたためる 暖める】(warm up the surrounding air) **WARM, warm up, heat**
部屋を暖める へやをあたためる heat the room

SYNONYMS

ⓐ hot
熱 HOT →3555
暑い HOT (weather) →3121
炎 scorching →3075
温 WARM →0740
暖 WARM (esp. weather) →1274

ⓑ &【あたためる】raise the temperature
暖 WARM (the air) →1274
煖 WARM (the air) →1293
温める WARM (a thing) →0740
熱 HEAT →3555

USAGE

❶【あたたかい】
暖かい
①ⓐ (of weather) warm, mild, genial, temperate
ⓑ warm (color)
② warmhearted, kindhearted, sympathetic
温かい
① warm (to the touch), lukewarm
② heartwarming, warm (feeling or atmosphere)

★Note the difference between sense ② of 暖かい and 温かい, roughly equivalent to the difference between *warmhearted* and *heartwarming*. Study the equivalents and examples carefully, as these words are easily confused by Japanese and foreigners alike. There is no difference between the forms あたたかい and あたたかな, except that the former is an adjective and the latter a noun adjective.

❷【あたたまる】
暖まる
(surrounding air rises in temperature) get warm, be warmed, warm
温まる
① (of objects or persons) warm oneself, take warmth, get warm, be heated
② be heartwarming

❸【あたためる】
暖める
(warm up the surrounding air) warm, warm up, heat
温める
① (raise the temperature of a thing) warm, heat
② nurse (an idea), let (an idea) mellow
③ renew (an old friendship)

❹【あたたか】
暖か
same as 暖かい あたたかい
温か
same as 温かい あたたかい

HOMOPHONES

あたたか 温 WARM →0740
あたたかい 温 WARM →0740

あたたまる 温 WARM →0740
あたためる 温 WARM →0740

COMPOUND FORMATION

【暖簾 のれん】

暖簾 'shop curtain, etc.' originally referred to a reed screen (簾) used in warming (暖 ⓑ) taverns or restaurants. の is a corrupt form of the reading のん.

NOTE

➡ see COMPOUND FORMATION for 暖房 だんぼう →房 2445

暇

1275

1-4-9

▶FREE TIME

カ ひま いとま▲

Ⓒ 暇 xiá 假 jià

72	Jōyō	U6687
日	S13-4-9	F1520

(stroke order 1–13)

COMPOUNDS

ⓐ **FREE TIME, spare time, leisure**
ⓑ **leave of absence, vacation**

a 余暇 よか leisure, spare time
寸暇 すんか moment's leisure
休暇 きゅうか holiday, vacation
b 賜暇 しか leave of absence, furlough
請暇 せいか request for leave of absence; leave of absence

KUN

【ひま 暇】

① **FREE TIME, spare time, leisure; dullness, slackness; dismissal, discharge**
暇潰し ひまつぶし time killer; waste of time
暇が無い ひまがない have no (free) time, be busy
暇な商売 ひまなしょうばい dull business
暇が出る ひまがでる be discharged
② [sometimes also 隙] **time spent on doing something**
手間暇 てまひま time and effort, trouble

【いとま 暇】 time to spare; dismissal; farewell
暇も無く いとまもなく without losing time (to do)
暇乞い いとまごい leave-taking, farewell visit
永のお暇になる ながのおいとまになる be dismissed

SYNONYMS

ⓐ **time periods**
時 TIME →1155
季 SEASON (quarter) →3161
候 SEASON (time of year) →0133
頃 TIME →0163
暇 FREE TIME →1275
般 period of time →1670
刻 POINT OF TIME →1619
間 INTERVAL →4122
隙 GAP →0826
期 TERM →2139
節 SEASON →3336

ⓐ **leisure**
暇 FREE TIME →1275
閑 LEISURE →4123

ⓑ **holiday**
休 holiday →0056
暇 leave of absence →1275

USAGE

【ひま】

暇
① free time, spare time, leisure; dullness, slackness; dismissal, discharge
② [sometimes also 隙] time spent on doing something

隙
① [usu. 暇] time spent on doing something
② [archaic]
ⓐ gap, space
ⓑ discord
ⓒ inattention, oversight

HOMOPHONES

ひま 隙 GAP →0826

暉

1276

1-4-9

▶SUNLIGHT

キ ㊔ てる あきら あき ひかる ひかり

Ⓒ 晖 huī

72	Names	U6689
日	S13-4-9	F0000

COMPOUNDS

ⓐ [rare] **SUNLIGHT**, sunshine, rays of the sun
ⓑ [archaic] as bright as **SUNLIGHT**, radiant, luminous

a 落暉 らっき the setting sun

SYNONYMS

ⓑ **bright**
明 BRIGHT →1060
昭 LUMINOUS →1107
蛍 fluorescent →3204
晃 DAZZLING →3101
燦 BRILLIANT →1390
赫 BLAZING →1960
暉 radiant →1276
熙 BRIGHT →3559
晟 SUNNY →3104

暖

▶WARM

ダン ノン あたた(か) あたた(かい)
あたた(まる) あたた(める) ㊔ はる

1277

1-4-9

72	Nonstandard	U6696
日	S13-4-9	F0000

traditional form → see 暖 at 1274

暎

incorrect stroke-count
➡ see 1-4-8: 日 at 1235

1-4-9

椿

▶CAMELLIA

チン チュン つばき

Ⓒ 椿 chūn

1278

1-4-9

75	Names	U693F
木	S13-4-9	F2499

COMPOUNDS

❶ⓐ [original meaning, now archaic] fragrant cedar, *Cedrela chinensis*
ⓑ name of mythical holly tree that symbolizes longevity
a 香椿 ちゃんちん *Cedrela chinensis*
b 椿寿 ちんじゅ long life
❷ [honorific] father
椿庭 ちんてい father
❸ **unexpected occurrence**
椿事 ちんじ accident, mishap; disaster

KUN

【つばき 椿】**CAMELLIA**
椿油 つばきあぶら camellia oil

SYNONYMS

❶ⓐ & 【つばき】 **trees**
桜 CHERRY → 1168
桐 PAULOWNIA → 1173
桂 AROMATIC TREE, katsura tree → 1163
梓 CATALPA → 1207
桑 MULBERRY → 2618
漆 Japanese lacquer tree → 0863
樺 BIRCH → 1324
椛 BIRCH → 1202
梧 CHINESE PARASOL TREE → 1200
檀 SPINDLE TREE → 1385
椿 CAMELLIA → 1278
柳 WILLOW → 1115
柊 HOLLY → 1119
椋 *APHANANTHE ASPERA* → 1245
枉 spindle tree → 1114
槻 ZELKOVA → 1349
楢 OAK → 1287
樫 EVERGREEN OAK → 1364
柏 CYPRESS, JAPANESE EMPEROR OAK → 1110
榎 HACKBERRY → 1323
梶 PAPER MULBERRY → 1199
柘 JAPANESE BOXWOOD → 1117
楊 WILLOW → 1286
桧 JAPANESE CYPRESS → 1160
梛 *NAGEIA NAGI* → 1206
榊 SACRED SHINTO TREE → 1327
楓 MAPLE → 1280
松 PINE → 1075
杉 CRYPTOMERIA → 1027
槙 PODOCARPUS → 1330
楠 CAMPHOR TREE → 1283
樟 CAMPHOR TREE → 1351

楕

▶ELLIPSE

ダ

Ⓝ 橢 Ⓒ 椭 tuǒ

1279

1-4-9

75	Names	U6955
木	S13-4-9	F2959

COMPOUNDS

● **ELLIPSE, oval**
楕円 だえん ellipse, oval
楕円体 だえんたい ellipsoid

SYNONYMS

● **circle**
円 CIRCLE → 3673
圏 circle → 3904
丸 round or spherical shape → 4225
楕 ELLIPSE → 1279

楓

▶MAPLE

フウ かえで

Ⓒ 枫 fēng

1280

1-4-9

75	Names	U6953
木	S13-4-9	F2773

COMPOUNDS

❶ **MAPLE, maple tree**
楓林 ふうりん maple grove
観楓会 かんぷうかい maple-leaf viewing
❷ [rare] liquidambar (kind of tree)
楓属 ふうぞく genus *Liquidambar*
楓子香 ふうしこう galbanum

INDEPENDENT

【ふう 楓】[rare] liquidambar, *Liquidambar formosana*

KUN

【かえで 楓】**MAPLE, maple tree**
楓糖 ふうとう maple sugar

SYNONYMS

❶ **trees**

桜 CHERRY → 1168
桐 PAULOWNIA → 1173
桂 AROMATIC TREE, katsura tree → 1163
梓 CATALPA → 1207
桑 MULBERRY → 2618
漆 Japanese lacquer tree → 0863
樺 BIRCH → 1324
椛 BIRCH → 1202
梧 CHINESE PARASOL TREE → 1200
檀 SPINDLE TREE → 1385
椿 CAMELLIA → 1278
柳 WILLOW → 1115
柊 HOLLY → 1119
椋 *APHANANTHE ASPERA* → 1245
柾 spindle tree → 1114
槻 ZELKOVA → 1349
楢 OAK → 1287
樫 EVERGREEN OAK → 1364
柏 CYPRESS, JAPANESE EMPEROR OAK → 1110
榎 HACKBERRY → 1323
梶 PAPER MULBERRY → 1199
柘 JAPANESE BOXWOOD → 1117
楊 WILLOW → 1286
桧 JAPANESE CYPRESS → 1160
梛 *NAGEIA NAGI* → 1206
榊 SACRED SHINTO TREE → 1327
楓 MAPLE → 1280
松 PINE → 1075
杉 CRYPTOMERIA → 1027
槙 PODOCARPUS → 1330
楠 CAMPHOR TREE → 1283
樟 CAMPHOR TREE → 1351

楯

1281

◧ 1-4-9

▸SHIELD

ジュン たて

Ⓒ 盾 dùn 楯 dùn shǔn

75	Names	U696F
木	S13-4-9	F2670

COMPOUNDS

● **SHIELD, escutcheon**

楯鱗 じゅんりん placoid scale
防楯 ぼうじゅん gun shield, gun mantlet

KUN

【たて 楯】[usu. 盾] **SHIELD, escutcheon**

楯突く たてつく oppose, defy; rebel
楯籠る(=立て籠る) たてこもる barricade [shut] oneself in, hold (a fort)
後ろ楯 うしろだて backing, protection; supporter
小楯 こだて small shield, screen
法律を楯に取って ほうりつをたてにとって on the authority of law

SYNONYMS

● **protective coverings**

盾 SHIELD → 3729
楯 SHIELD → 1281
鎧 ARMOR → 2211
甲 armor → 4293
縅 BRAID OF ARMOR → 1759
面 mask → 2590
兜 helmet → 3499
幌 COVERING FOR VEHICLES → 0787

HOMOPHONES

たて 盾 SHIELD → 3729

NOTE

➡ see USAGE note at 盾 3729

楷

1282

◧ 1-4-9

▸SQUARE STYLE

カイ

Ⓒ 楷 kǎi jiē

75	Jōyō	U6977
木	S13-4-9	F0000

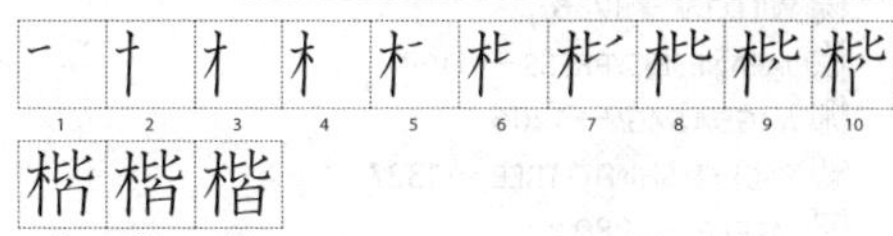

COMPOUNDS

● **SQUARE STYLE of Chinese characters, *kaisho***

楷書 かいしょ square style of Chinese characters

INDEPENDENT

【かい 楷】*kaisho* (→ ●)

SYNONYMS

● **styles of Chinese characters**

楷 SQUARE STYLE → 1282
行 *gyosho* → 0246
草 *sosho* → 2813

楠

1283

◧ 1-4-9

▸CAMPHOR TREE

ナン くす くすのき

Ⓒ 楠 nán

75	Names	U6960
木	S13-4-9	F2206

KUN

【くす 楠】[sometimes also 樟] **CAMPHOR TREE**

楠の木 くすのき camphor tree

【くすのき 楠】[sometimes also 樟] **CAMPHOR TREE**

SYNONYMS

【くす】

○ **trees**

桜 CHERRY → 1168
桐 PAULOWNIA → 1173

桂 AROMATIC TREE, katsura tree → 1163
梓 CATALPA → 1207
桑 MULBERRY → 2618
漆 Japanese lacquer tree → 0863
樺 BIRCH → 1324
椛 BIRCH → 1202
梧 CHINESE PARASOL TREE → 1200
檀 SPINDLE TREE → 1385
椿 CAMELLIA → 1278
柳 WILLOW → 1115
柊 HOLLY → 1119
椋 *APHANANTHE ASPERA* → 1245
柾 spindle tree → 1114
槻 ZELKOVA → 1349
楢 OAK → 1287
樫 EVERGREEN OAK → 1364
柏 CYPRESS, JAPANESE EMPEROR OAK → 1110
榎 HACKBERRY → 1323
梶 PAPER MULBERRY → 1199
柘 JAPANESE BOXWOOD → 1117
楊 WILLOW → 1286
桧 JAPANESE CYPRESS → 1160
梛 *NAGEIA NAGI* → 1206
榊 SACRED SHINTO TREE → 1327
楓 MAPLE → 1280
松 PINE → 1075
杉 CRYPTOMERIA → 1027
槙 PODOCARPUS → 1330
楠 CAMPHOR TREE → 1283
樟 CAMPHOR TREE → 1351

USAGE

❶【くす】
楠
[sometimes also 樟] camphor tree
樟
[usu. 楠] camphor tree

❷【くすのき】
楠
[sometimes also 樟] camphor tree
樟
[usu. 楠] camphor tree

HOMOPHONES

くす 樟 CAMPHOR TREE → 1351
くすのき 樟 CAMPHOR TREE → 1351

楼 ▸TALL BUILDING

1284
1-4-9

ロウ
Ⓝ 樓 Ⓒ 楼 lóu

75	Jōyō	U697C
木	S13-4-9	F1823

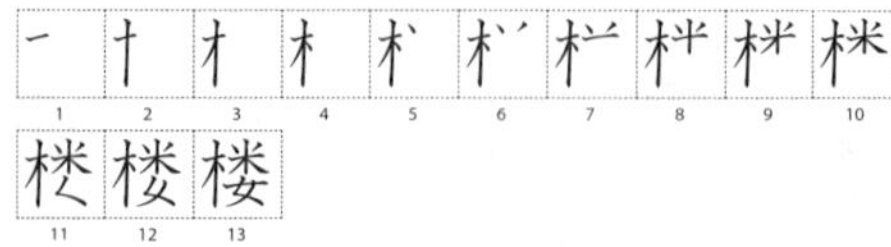

COMPOUNDS

❶ [original meaning] **TALL BUILDING, tower, storied building; watchtower, lookout**
楼閣 ろうかく multistoried building
鐘楼 しょうろう bell tower, belfry
望楼 ぼうろう watchtower, observation tower, lookout
五層楼 ごそうろう five-storied building [tower]
高楼 こうろう lofty [high] building; skyscraper
登楼する とうろうする go into a tall building; visit a brothel
摩天楼 まてんろう skyscraper

❷ suffix after names of **TALL BUILDING**s, inns, restaurants, etc.
山水楼 さんすいろう Sansuiro (name of an exclusive restaurant)

INDEPENDENT

【ろう 楼】**TALL BUILDING**, tower; lookout, belvedere
楼に登る ろうにのぼる go up a tower

SYNONYMS

❶ **tall buildings**
閣 TALL MAGNIFICENT BUILDING → 4128
楼 TALL BUILDING → 1284
塔 TOWER → 0683
台 observatory → 2498

椰 ▸COCONUT

1285
1-4-9

ヤ ㊔ やし
Ⓒ 椰 yē

75	Names	U6930
木	S13-4-9	F3264

COMPOUNDS

● **COCONUT tree; coconut**
椰子 やし coconut tree; coconut

SYNONYMS

● **fruits and fruit trees**
桃 PEACH → 1174
榛 HAZEL → 1328
椎 CHINQUAPIN → 1249
柚 YUZU → 1123
椰 COCONUT → 1285
柑 CITRUS → 1112
橙 BITTER ORANGE → 1369
葡 GRAPE → 2902
萄 GRAPE → 2870
柿 PERSIMMON → 1118

檎 APPLE → 1386
李 PLUM → 3050
枇 LOQUAT → 1063
杷 LOQUAT → 1065
苺 STRAWBERRY → 2780
菱 water chestnut → 2879
杏 APRICOT → 3049
梅 JAPANESE APRICOT → 1159
橘 MANDARIN → 1366
栗 CHESTNUT → 3280
栃 JAPANESE HORSE CHESTNUT → 1122
梨 PEAR → 3412
蕉 PLANTAIN → 2994

楊

1286

◧1-4-9

▸**WILLOW**

ヨウ ㊔ やな やなぎ

Ⓒ 杨 yáng

75	Names	U694A
木	S13-4-9	F2214

COMPOUNDS

● **WILLOW**

爪楊枝(=爪楊子) つまようじ toothpick; [rare] willow-made toothbrush

SPECIAL READINGS

黄楊 つげ [also 柘植, sometimes also 柘] Japanese boxwood

SYNONYMS

● **trees**

桜 CHERRY → 1168
桐 PAULOWNIA → 1173
桂 AROMATIC TREE, katsura tree → 1163
梓 CATALPA → 1207
桑 MULBERRY → 2618
漆 Japanese lacquer tree → 0863
樺 BIRCH → 1324
椛 BIRCH → 1202
梧 CHINESE PARASOL TREE → 1200
檀 SPINDLE TREE → 1385
椿 CAMELLIA → 1278
柳 WILLOW → 1115
柊 HOLLY → 1119
椋 *APHANANTHE ASPERA* → 1245
柾 spindle tree → 1114
槻 ZELKOVA → 1349
楢 OAK → 1287
樫 EVERGREEN OAK → 1364
柏 CYPRESS, JAPANESE EMPEROR OAK → 1110
榎 HACKBERRY → 1323
梶 PAPER MULBERRY → 1199
柘 JAPANESE BOXWOOD → 1117
楊 WILLOW → 1286
桧 JAPANESE CYPRESS → 1160
梛 *NAGEIA NAGI* → 1206
榊 SACRED SHINTO TREE → 1327
楓 MAPLE → 1280
松 PINE → 1075
杉 CRYPTOMERIA → 1027
槙 PODOCARPUS → 1330
楠 CAMPHOR TREE → 1283
樟 CAMPHOR TREE → 1351

HOMOPHONES

つげ

柘 JAPANESE BOXWOOD → 1117
黄楊 → 3116, 1286
柘植 → 1117, 1247

NOTE

★ do not confuse with 揚 RAISE HIGH → 0722

楢

1287

◧1-4-9

▸**OAK**

ユウ なら

Ⓝ 楢 Ⓒ 楢 yóu

75	Names	U6962
木	S13-4-9	F3434

KUN

【なら 楢】**OAK, esp. konara oak**

小楢 こなら konara oak, *Quercus serrata*
水楢 みずなら mizunara oak, *Quercus mongolica* var. *grosseserrata*

SYNONYMS

【なら】

○ **trees**

桜 CHERRY → 1168
桐 PAULOWNIA → 1173
桂 AROMATIC TREE, katsura tree → 1163
梓 CATALPA → 1207
桑 MULBERRY → 2618
漆 Japanese lacquer tree → 0863
樺 BIRCH → 1324
椛 BIRCH → 1202
梧 CHINESE PARASOL TREE → 1200
檀 SPINDLE TREE → 1385
椿 CAMELLIA → 1278
柳 WILLOW → 1115
柊 HOLLY → 1119
椋 *APHANANTHE ASPERA* → 1245
柾 spindle tree → 1114
槻 ZELKOVA → 1349
楢 OAK → 1287
樫 EVERGREEN OAK → 1364
柏 CYPRESS, JAPANESE EMPEROR OAK → 1110
榎 HACKBERRY → 1323

梶 PAPER MULBERRY → 1199
柘 JAPANESE BOXWOOD → 1117
楊 WILLOW → 1286
桧 JAPANESE CYPRESS → 1160
梛 *NAGEIA NAGI* → 1206
榊 SACRED SHINTO TREE → 1327
楓 MAPLE → 1280
松 PINE → 1075
杉 CRYPTOMERIA → 1027
槙 PODOCARPUS → 1330
楠 CAMPHOR TREE → 1283
樟 CAMPHOR TREE → 1351

楳 1288

1-4-9

▸**JAPANESE APRICOT**
バイ うめ

75	Nonstandard	U6973
木	S13-4-9	F0000

traditional form → see 梅 at 1159

榊 1289

1-4-9

▸**SACRED SHINTO TREE**
さかき

75	Nonstandard	U698A
木	S13-4-9	F0000

traditional form → see 榊 at 1327

槌 1290

1-4-9

▸**HAMMER**
ツイ つち ㊔ てつ

75	Nonstandard	U69CC
木	S13-4-9	F0000

traditional form → see 槌 at 1331

楢 1291

1-4-9

▸**OAK**
ユウ なら

75	Nonstandard	U6962
木	S13-4-9	F0000

traditional form → see 楢 at 1287

極 1-4-9
incorrect stroke-count
➡ see 1-4-8: 木 at 1243

槌 1-4-9
incorrect stroke-count
➡ see 1-4-10: 木 at 1331

樋 1-4-9
incorrect stroke-count
➡ see 1-4-10: 木 at 1336

煤 1292

1-4-9

▸**SOOT**
バイ すす すす(ける)
Ⓒ 煤 méi

86	Names	U7164
火	S13-4-9	F3049

COMPOUNDS

● **SOOT**
煤煙 ばいえん soot and smoke
煤塵 ばいじん dust and soot, particulate matter

KUN

【すす 煤】**SOOT**
煤色 すすいろ color of soot, gray
煤竹 すすたけ(=すすだけ) smoked bamboo; bamboo duster used for housecleaning
煤払い すすはらい (traditional Japanese end-of-the-year) housecleaning

【すすける 煤ける】**become SOOTy [soot-stained]; become dirty with age**

SYNONYMS

● **products of combustion**
灰 ASH → 3699
殻 cinders → 1883
炭 CHARCOAL → 2806
煤 SOOT → 1292
煙 SMOKE → 1294

煖 1293

1-4-9

▸**WARM**
ダン
Ⓒ 暖 nuǎn

86	Non-Jōyō	U7156
火	S13-4-9	F0000

COMPOUNDS

● [now replaced by 暖 1274] [original meaning] **WARM, warm up, heat**
煖房 だんぼう heating
煖炉 だんろ fireplace, stove
煖気 だんき warmth, warm weather

SYNONYMS

● **raise the temperature**
暖 WARM (the air) → 1274
煖 WARM (the air) → 1293
温める WARM (a thing) → 0740
熱 HEAT → 3555

煙 1294

1-4-9

▸**SMOKE**
エン けむ(る) けむり けむ(い)
Ⓝ 煙 烟◇ Ⓒ 烟 yān

86	Jōyō	U7159
火	S13-4-9	F1002

丶	丷	火	火	灬	炉	炉	烟	烟	烟
1	2	3	4	5	6	7	8	9	10

煙	煙	煙
11	12	13

COMPOUNDS

❶ⓐ **SMOKE**
ⓑ **SMOKE**like substance such as soot
a 煙突 えんとつ chimney, smokestack
煙幕 えんまく smoke screen
b 煤煙 ばいえん soot and smoke
油煙 ゆえん lamp soot [smoke]

❷ **smoking, cigarettes**
禁煙 きんえん NO SMOKING; giving up smoking
喫煙 きつえん smoking
嫌煙権 けんえんけん right to dislike smoking
節煙 せつえん moderation in smoking

KUN

【けむる 煙る】 **SMOKE; be hazy**
【けむり 煙】 **SMOKE, fumes**
煙になる けむりになる vanish in thin air
雪煙 ゆきけむり smoky snow flakes
【けむい 煙い】 **smoky**
煙たい けむたい smoky; feeling awkward

SPECIAL READINGS

煙草▲ たばこ tobacco; cigarette
煙草屋▲ たばこや tobacco shop

SYNONYMS

❶ⓐ **products of combustion**
灰 ASH → 3699
殻 cinders → 1883
炭 CHARCOAL → 2806
煤 SOOT → 1292
煙 SMOKE → 1294

煩

1295
◧1-4-9

▶VEXED
ハン ボン わずら(う) わずら(わす)
Ⓒ 烦 fán

86	Jōyō	U7169
火	S13-4-9	F2335

丶	丷	火	火	灬	灬	炉	炉	烦	烦
1	2	3	4	5	6	7	8	9	10

煩	煩	煩
11	12	13

COMPOUNDS

❶ [original meaning] **VEXED, annoyed, irritated, troubled, worried**
煩悶 はんもん anguish, worry
煩悩 ぼんのう worldly desires, carnal desires

❷ **vexatious, intricate, confused, entangled**
煩雑な はんざつな vexatious, troublesome, intricate
煩瑣×な はんさな vexatious, troublesome, complicated
煩労 はんろう trouble, pains

INDEPENDENT

【はん 煩】 trouble
煩を避ける はんをさける spare the trouble (of doing)

KUN

【わずらう 煩う】 **worry about, feel anxious, be VEXED**
煩い わずらい worry, agony, vexation
煩わしい わずらわしい vexatious, troublesome, complicated
思い煩う おもいわずらう worry about, be vexed
【わずらわす 煩わす】 **trouble, bother, give trouble; annoy, pester, vex**
人手を煩わす ひとでをわずらわす trouble a person
心を煩わす こころをわずらわす worry oneself over

SYNONYMS

❶ **trouble and suffering**
困 BE IN TROUBLE → 3808
苛 torment → 2786
窮 BE IN EXTREMITY → 2983
悶 BE IN AGONY → 4119
悩 SUFFER → 0504
苦 SUFFERING → 2789
痛 PAIN → 4071
辛 HARD → 2531
煩 VEXED → 1295
難 DIFFICULT → 2310

❷ **complex**
繁 complicated → 3536
煩 vexatious → 1295

HOMOPHONES

わずらう 患 AFFECTED BY DISEASE → 3415
わずらい 患 AFFECTED BY DISEASE → 3415

NOTE

➡ see USAGE note at 患 3415

煌

1296
◧1-4-9

▶GLITTER
コウ きら(めく) Ⓝ あき てる あけ
Ⓒ 煌 huáng

86	Names	U714C
火	S13-4-9	F2613

COMPOUNDS

● [original meaning] **GLITTER, twinkle, sparkle, glisten, gleam**
煌煌と こうこうと brilliantly, dazzlingly, brightly

KUN

【きらめく 煌めく】**GLITTER, twinkle, sparkle, glisten, gleam**
煌めき きらめき glitter, twinkle, sparkle, glisten, gleam

SYNONYMS

❶ **shine and reflect**
輝 SHINE BRILLIANTLY → 1775
光 shine → 3043
照 ILLUMINATE → 3506
映 REFLECT → 1104
耀 SHINE BRILLIANTLY → 1812
燿 SHINE → 1407
閃 FLASH → 4114
煌 GLITTER → 1296

煉

1297
◧ 1-4-9

▶**REFINE**
レン ね(る)
Ⓝ 煉 Ⓒ 炼 liàn

86	Names	U7149
火	S13-4-9	F2684

COMPOUNDS

❶ⓐ [now also 錬 2185] [original meaning] **REFINE (crude metals), smelt; work metals, temper**
ⓑ [now also 練 1738] **REFINE** (one's skills), purify
a 煉丹術 れんたんじゅつ art of making elixirs, alchemy
精煉する せいれんする refine (metals), smelt (copper); temper
b 煉獄 れんごく purgatory
洗煉された せんれんされた refined, polished
試煉 しれん trial, test, probation
修煉 しゅうれん training, practice
❷ [now also 練 1738] knead
煉乳 れんにゅう condensed milk
煉炭 れんたん (charcoal or coal) briquette
煉瓦 れんが brick

KUN

【ねる 煉る】[now also 練る] knead

SYNONYMS

❶ⓐ **work metals**
錬 REFINE (crude metals) → 2185
煉 REFINE (crude metals) → 1297
鍛 FORGE → 2206
鋳 CAST → 2170
焼き annealing → 1256
冶 WORK METALS → 0089

HOMOPHONES

ねる
練 TRAIN → 1738
錬 REFINE → 2185

NOTE

➡ see USAGE note at 練 1738

煙

1298
◧ 1-4-9

▶**SMOKE**
エン けむ(る) けむり けむ(い)

86	Nonstandard	U7159
火	S13-4-9	F0000

traditional form → see 煙 at 1294

牒

1299
◧ 1-4-9

▶**OFFICIAL NOTICE**
チョウ
Ⓒ 牒 dié

91	Names	U7252
片	S13-4-9	F3301

COMPOUNDS

❶ **OFFICIAL NOTICE**
通牒 つうちょう notification, circular
最後通牒 さいごつうちょう ultimatum
❷ [now usu. 丁 4155] [original meaning] wooden placard, label, tag
符牒 ふちょう sign; secret price tag; password

INDEPENDENT

【ちょう 牒】*hist* thin wooden tablet for writing; type of official document in ancient Japan

SYNONYMS

❶ **written communications**
状 LETTER → 0322
文 LETTER → 2458
翰 LETTER → 2198
書 letter → 3292
信 written communication → 0115
電 telegram → 3465
牒 OFFICIAL NOTICE → 1299

瑚

1300
◧ 1-4-9

▶**CORAL**
ゴ コ
Ⓒ 瑚 hú

96	Names	U745A
王	S13-4-9	F2809

COMPOUNDS

❶ **CORAL**
珊瑚 さんご coral
❷ [original meaning, now archaic] receptacle for ancestral offerings

SYNONYMS

❶ **shells**
殻 SHELL (of any kind) → 1883
甲 SHELL (of animals) → 4293
貝 seashell → 3150
螺 SPIRAL-SHELLED GASTROPOD → 1799

瑚 CORAL → 1300

瑶

1301

1-4-9

▸EXQUISITE

ヨウ 名 たま

N 瑤 C 瑶 yáo

96 王	Names S13-4-9	U7476 F0000

COMPOUNDS

❶ⓐ [rare] **EXQUISITE, beautiful like a gem, glittering, splendid; ornamented with gems**

ⓑ [original meaning, now archaic] **beautiful white gem**

a 瑶台 ようだい beautiful building ornamented with gems; fairyland

瑶顔 ようがん exquisite countenance, beautiful face

❷ [archaic] **fairyland, place where immortal wizards live**

瑶池 ようち place where immortals live; beautiful pond

❸ [archaic] [honorific] **your** (esp. in reference to letters)

瑶緘× ようかん your letter

SYNONYMS

❶ⓐ **beautiful**

美 BEAUTIFUL → 2817
彪 MAGNIFICENT → 4115
綺 BEAUTIFUL → 1734
娃 BEAUTIFUL → 0419
佳 FINE → 0096
瑶 EXQUISITE → 1301
麗 OF GRACEFUL BEAUTY → 2672
艶 CHARMING → 2403
妙 of marvelous beauty → 0280
華 MAGNIFICENT → 2841
絢 GORGEOUS → 1705
斐 florid → 3449

瑞

1302

1-4-9

▸AUSPICIOUS OMEN

ズイ スイ みず- 名 しるし みつ たま

C 瑞 ruì

96 王	Names S13-4-9	U745E F2188

COMPOUNDS

❶ⓐ **AUSPICIOUS [good] OMEN, luck sign**

ⓑ **auspicious, propitious, good**

a 奇瑞 きずい auspicious [good] omen

b 瑞祥 ずいしょう auspicious sign, good omen

瑞兆 ずいちょう auspicious sign, good omen

瑞雲 ずいうん auspicious clouds

❷ [rare]

ⓐ Switzerland

ⓑ Sweden

a 瑞西 すいす Switzerland

b 瑞典 すうぇーでん Sweden

❸ [original meaning, now obsolete] **jade tablet used as a token of authority in ancient China**

KUN

【みず- 瑞-】 **young and fresh, vigorous**

瑞瑞しい みずみずしい young and fresh, fresh-looking, juicy

瑞穂の国 みずほのくに Land of Vigorous Rice Plants, Japan

SYNONYMS

❶ **good fortune**

吉 LUCKY → 2691
嘉 HAPPY → 2953
祥 AUSPICIOUS → 1184
瑞 AUSPICIOUS OMEN → 1302
禎 PROPITIOUS OMEN → 1305
幸 GOOD FORTUNE → 2755
福 FORTUNE → 1303
倖 GOOD FORTUNE → 0134

HOMOPHONES

みず- 水 WATER → 0010

NOTE

➡ see USAGE note at 水 0010

福

1303

1-4-9

▸FORTUNE

フク 名 とみ よし

N 福 C 福 fú

113 ネ	Jōyō-3 S13-4-9	U798F F0507

1	2	3	4	5	6	7	8	9	10	11	12	13
丶	㇇	ネ	ネ	ネ一	礻𠃍	礻冂	礻口	礻日	福	福	福	福

COMPOUNDS

ⓐ **(good) FORTUNE, blessing, good luck, prosperity, happiness**

ⓑ (riches) **FORTUNE, wealth**

a 福徳 ふくとく fortune, happiness and prosperity

福利 ふくり public welfare, well-being, prosperity

福祉 ふくし welfare

福音 ふくいん gospel, good news

祝福 しゅくふく blessing

大福 だいふく great fortune, good luck; rice cake stuffed with bean jam

禍福 かふく fortune and misfortune

幸福な こうふくな happy; blessed, fortunate

b 裕福な ゆうふくな rich, wealthy

INDEPENDENT

【ふく 福】(good) **FORTUNE**, blessing, good luck, prosperity, happiness

福は内鬼は外 ふくはうち,おにはそと Fortune in, Devils out!

SYNONYMS

a happiness

幸 HAPPINESS → 2755
祉 BLESSEDNESS → 1087
福 FORTUNE → 1303

a good fortune

吉 LUCKY → 2691
嘉 HAPPY → 2953
祥 AUSPICIOUS → 1184
瑞 AUSPICIOUS OMEN → 1302
禎 PROPITIOUS OMEN → 1305
幸 GOOD FORTUNE → 2755
福 FORTUNE → 1303
倖 GOOD FORTUNE → 0134

禍 1304

▶**CALAMITY**

カ わざわい▲

Ⓝ 禍 Ⓒ 祸 huò

1-4-9

113	Jōyō	U798D
ネ	S13-4-9	F2508

COMPOUNDS

a [original meaning] **CALAMITY, misfortune, disaster, evil**

b slip, accident

a 禍福 かふく fortune and misfortune
禍根 かこん root of evil
災禍 さいか accident, natural calamity, disaster, misfortune
黄禍 こうか Yellow Peril
水禍 すいか flood disaster; drowning
惨禍 さんか terrible disaster, crushing calamity

b 舌禍 ぜっか unfortunate slip of the tongue
交通禍 こうつうか traffic accident

INDEPENDENT

【か 禍】**CALAMITY**, misfortune, disaster

風雨の禍 ふううのか disaster caused by wind and rain

KUN

【わざわい 禍】[now usu. 災い] **CALAMITY**, misfortune, disaster, evil, serious trouble

禍する わざわいする be the ruin of

口は禍の元 くちはわざわいのもと Out of the mouth comes evil

SYNONYMS

a misfortune and disaster

災 NATURAL CALAMITY → 2734
難 DISASTER → 2310
禍 CALAMITY → 1304
厄 MISFORTUNE → 3665
凶 BAD LUCK → 3679

HOMOPHONES

わざわい 災 NATURAL CALAMITY → 2734

NOTE

➡ see USAGE note at 災 2734

禎 1305

▶**PROPITIOUS OMEN**

テイ ㊔ さだ よし ただし さち ただ とも

Ⓝ 禎 Ⓒ 祯 zhēn

1-4-9

113	Names	U798E
ネ	S13-4-9	F2840

COMPOUNDS

[archaic]

a PROPITIOUS OMEN

b happiness

a 禎祥 ていしょう good omen

SYNONYMS

a good fortune

吉 LUCKY → 2691
嘉 HAPPY → 2953
祥 AUSPICIOUS → 1184
瑞 AUSPICIOUS OMEN → 1302
禎 PROPITIOUS OMEN → 1305
幸 GOOD FORTUNE → 2755
福 FORTUNE → 1303
倖 GOOD FORTUNE → 0134

禅 1306

▶**ZEN**

ゼン

Ⓝ 禪 Ⓒ 禅 chán shàn

1-4-9

113	Jōyō	U7985
ネ	S13-4-9	F1549

COMPOUNDS

1 a ZEN Buddhism, Chan

b ZEN meditation, dhyana

a 禅宗 ぜんしゅう Zen sect
禅僧 ぜんそう Zen priest [monk]
禅寺 ぜんでら Zen temple

b 禅定 ぜんじょう Samadhi, meditative concentration
座禅 ざぜん Zen meditation

❷ abdicate (the throne)
禅譲 ぜんじょう abdication

❸ [original meaning, now archaic] ancient Chinese sacrificial ritual
封禅 ほうぜん ancient Chinese sacrificial ritual

INDEPENDENT

【ぜん 禅】**ZEN Buddhism; Zen meditation**

SYNONYMS

❶ **religions and sects**
仏 Buddhism →0020
法 Buddha's teachings →0391
禅 ZEN →1306
儒 CONFUCIANISM →0197
道 Taoism →3888

腸

▶INTESTINES
チョウ はらわた▲
Ⓝ 膓 Ⓒ 肠 cháng

1307
◧ 1-4-9

130	Jōyō-4	U8178
月	S13-4-9	F1680

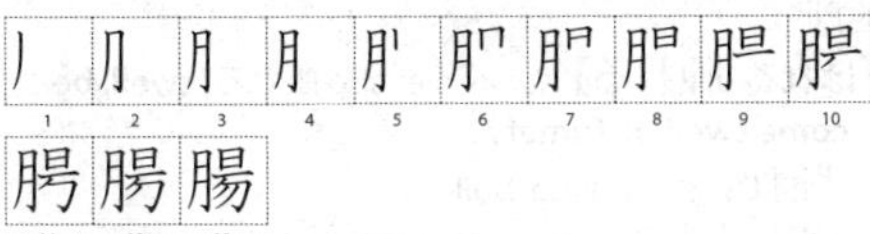

COMPOUNDS

❶ⓐ [original meaning] **INTESTINES, entrails, bowels**
ⓑ [prefix] intestinal, enteric

a 腸炎 ちょうえん enteritis
胃腸 いちょう stomach and intestines [bowels]
小腸 しょうちょう small intestine
脱腸 だっちょう enterocele
盲腸 もうちょう cecum, appendix
灌×腸(=浣×腸)する かんちょうする give an enema

b 腸結核 ちょうけっかく intestinal tuberculosis
腸チフス ちょうちふす typhoid fever

❷ mind, heart
断腸 だんちょう heartbreak

INDEPENDENT

【ちょう 腸】**INTESTINES, entrails, bowels**
腸の病気 ちょうのびょうき bowel disease

KUN

【はらわた 腸】entrails, bowels, guts; placenta (of a melon); mind, heart
腸の腐った男 はらわたのくさったおとこ man with a corrupt heart

SYNONYMS

❶ **internal organs**
心 HEART →0011
肺 LUNG →1147
胃 STOMACH →3171
腸 INTESTINES →1307
肝 LIVER →1045
胆 GALLBLADDER →1150
腎 KIDNEY →3511

腹

▶BELLY
フク はら
Ⓒ 腹 fù

1308
◧ 1-4-9

130	Jōyō-6	U8179
月	S13-4-9	F0666

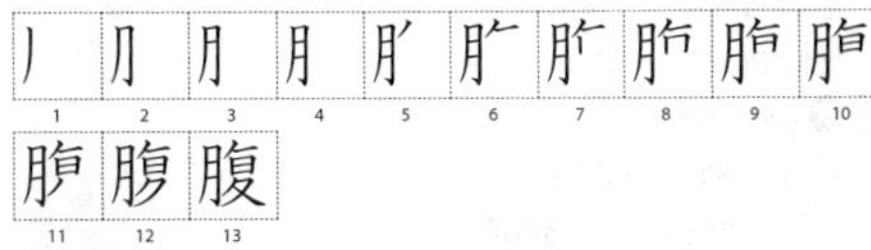

COMPOUNDS

❶ⓐ [original meaning] **BELLY, abdomen, stomach, bowels**
ⓑ (uterus) **BELLY**, womb

a 腹部 ふくぶ abdomen, belly
腹痛 ふくつう stomachache, abdominal pain
満腹 まんぷく full belly, satiety
切腹 せっぷく harakiri, suicide by disembowelment
空腹 くうふく empty stomach, hunger

b 同腹の どうふくの uterine (brothers)

❷ something shaped like a **BELLY**, thickest or widest part
船腹 せんぷく bottoms; shipping, tonnage; freight space
中腹に ちゅうふくに halfway up the mountain

❸ⓐ **heart, mind, intention**
ⓑ **guts, courage**

a 腹案 ふくあん plan, scheme, idea
腹心 ふくしん trusted friend, trusted retainer

b 剛腹 ごうふく magnanimity
立腹する りっぷくする get angry, lose one's temper

KUN

【はら 腹】**BELLY, abdomen; bowels; stomach; womb;** (counter for the young) **litter (of animals); roe (of fish);** (thickest part) **belly; heart, mind, *hara*; intention, guts; temper**
腹一杯 はらいっぱい full stomach
腹違い はらちがい (born) of a different mother, half-blooded
腹黒い はらぐろい blackhearted, malicious
腹を立てる はらをたてる get angry, take offense
下腹 したはら abdomen
船の腹 ふねのはら belly of a boat

方 日 木 火 片 王 ネ 【月】 元 扌 予 分 公 屯

方 日 木 火 片 王 ネ 【月】 元 扌 予 分 公 屯

樽の腹 たるのはら belly of a cask; midsection of a barrel
太っ腹な ふとっぱらな generous, large-minded, big-hearted

SYNONYMS

❶ⓐ trunk parts
胸 CHEST → 1187
腹 BELLY → 1308
胴 TRUNK → 1186
腰 WAIST → 1311
背 BACK → 3182
肩 SHOULDER → 2446
股 CROTCH → 1093
脇 ARMPIT → 1188
腋 ARMPIT → 1266

❸ⓐ psyche
心 HEART → 0011
霊 SPIRIT (soul) → 3480
魂 SOUL, spirit → 1346
魄 SOUL → 1570
腹 heart → 1308
衷 INNER HEART → 2600
襟 inner mind → 1599
胸 breast → 1187
懐 BOSOM → 0942
神 MIND → 1143
気 SPIRIT (consciousness) → 3960
精 SPIRIT (mind) → 1729

NOTE

➡ see COMPOUND FORMATION for 立腹 りっぷく → 立 2486

腺

▶GLAND
セン
ⓒ 腺 xiàn (国字)

1309
1-4-9

130	Jōyō	U817A
月	S13-4-9	F2415

COMPOUNDS

● [also suffix] [original meaning] **GLAND**
腺熱 せんねつ glandular fever
腺病質 せんびょうしつ lymphatic temperament, scrofulousness
甲状腺 こうじょうせん thyroid gland
乳腺 にゅうせん mammary gland
唾液腺 だえきせん salivary gland
内分泌腺 ないぶんぴせん endocrine gland
リンパ腺 りんぱせん lymphatic gland

INDEPENDENT

【せん 腺】GLAND

腫

▶SWELLING
シュ ショウ▲ は(れる) は(らす)
ⓒ 肿 zhǒng

1310
1-4-9

130	Jōyō	U816B
月	S13-4-9	F1788

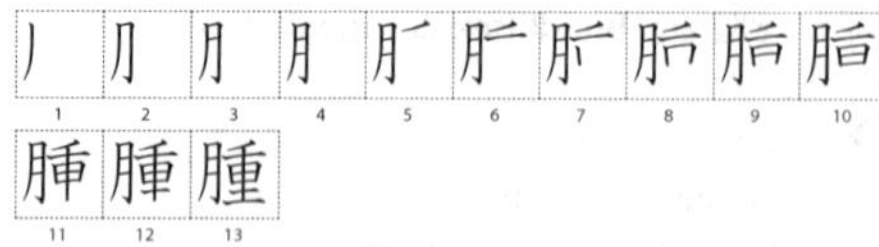

COMPOUNDS

● [also suffix] **SWELLING; tumor, neoplasm**
腫脹 しゅちょう swelling, puffiness
腫瘍 しゅよう tumor, neoplasm, growth
腫瘤× しゅりゅう lump, mass, tumor
筋腫 きんしゅ myoma
肉腫 にくしゅ sarcoma
浮腫 ふしゅ(=むくみ) swelling, edema
リンパ腫 りんぱしゅ lymphoma

KUN

【はれる 腫れる】 [sometimes also 脹れる] **swell, become swollen; tumefy**
腫れ はれ swelling, boil
腫れ上がる はれあがる swell up
腫れ物に触るように はれものにさわるように with great caution, gingerly
惚れた腫れた ほれたはれた head over heels in love

【はらす 腫らす】cause to swell; tumefy, inflame
泣き腫らす なきはらす cry one's eyes out

SPECIAL READINGS

浮腫む▲ むくむ become swollen

SYNONYMS

● swell and swelling
脹 SWELL → 1265
腫 SWELLING → 1310
瘍 SWELLING → 4073
爛 break out in sores → 1427

USAGE

【はれる】
腫れる
[sometimes also 脹れる] swell, become swollen; tumefy
脹れる
[usu. 腫れる] swell, become swollen; tumefy

HOMOPHONES

はれる 脹 SWELL → 1265

腰 1311

▶WAIST

ヨウ こし

Ⓝ 腰 Ⓒ 腰 yāo

1-4-9

130	Jōyō	U8170
月	S13-4-9	F0686

丿 月 月 月 肝 肝 肟 胛 脝 腰 腰 腰 腰
1 2 3 4 5 6 7 8 9 10 11 12 13

COMPOUNDS

● [original meaning] **WAIST, hips, loin, pelvic region**

腰部 ようぶ waist, hips
腰間 ようかん hips
腰痛 ようつう lumbago, pain in the hips
腰囲 ようい hip measurement
細腰 さいよう slender hips

KUN

【こし 腰】

①ⓐ **WAIST, hips, loin, pelvic region**
ⓑ (middle part) **WAIST;** (of garments) **waist, hips**
ⓒ lower part (of a wall)

a 腰骨 こしぼね hipbone, innominate bone
腰掛ける こしかける sit down
足腰 あしこし legs and loins
b 腰巻 こしまき loincloth
腰上げ こしあげ tuck at the waist
c 腰張りをする こしばりをする paper the lower part (of a wall)
障子の腰 しょうじのこし lower part of a *shoji* (paper sliding door)

② [also suffix] stick-to-itiveness, tenacity, perseverance
腰が強い こしがつよい take a firm stand, be firm
弱腰 よわごし weak attitude
物腰 ものごし movements, (polite) bearing, mien
話の腰を折る はなしのこしをおる butt in, interfere
本腰を入れる ほんごしをいれる set about in earnest

③ sticky, glutinous; stiff, retaining shape (of clothes)
この餅は腰が有る このもちはこしがある This *mochi* is glutinous
布地の腰が強い ぬのじのこしがつよい The cloth is stiff

④ counter for objects attached to the **WAIST**, as swords, *hakama* (divided skirt), etc.
太刀二腰 たちふたこし two swords

⑤ third verse of a waka poem
腰折れ こしおれ poor poem; stooped over (old people)

SYNONYMS

● **trunk parts**

胸 CHEST → 1187
腹 BELLY → 1308
胴 TRUNK → 1186
腰 WAIST → 1311
背 BACK → 3182
肩 SHOULDER → 2446
股 CROTCH → 1093
脇 ARMPIT → 1188
腋 ARMPIT → 1266

腳 1312

▶LEG

キャク キャ あし

1-4-9

130	Nonstandard	U8173
月	S13-4-9	F0000

alternative form → see 脚 at 1226

腦 1313

▶BRAIN

ノウ

1-4-9

130	Nonstandard	U8166
月	S13-4-9	F0000

traditional form → see 脳 at 1227

腰 1314

▶WAIST

ヨウ こし

1-4-9

130	Nonstandard	U8170
月	S13-4-9	F0000

traditional form → see 腰 at 1311

頑 1315

▶STUBBORN

ガン

Ⓒ 顽 wán

1-4-9

181	Jōyō	U9811
頁	S13-9-4	F1484

一 二 テ 元 元 元 元 頑 頑 頑 頑 頑 頑
1 2 3 4 5 6 7 8 9 10 11 12 13

COMPOUNDS

ⓐ **STUBBORN, obstinate; hardheaded, thickheaded**
ⓑ (unyielding) **STUBBORN, firm, tenacious**

a 頑固な がんこな stubborn, obstinate, bigoted
頑強な がんきょうな stubborn, unyielding
頑丈な がんじょうな solid, firm; strong
頑健 がんけん robust health
b 頑張る がんばる persist, be tenacious, hold out

INDEPENDENT

【がんとして 頑として】**STUBBORN**ly, firmly

SYNONYMS

● **firm and obstinate**

堅 FIRM → 3502
固 FIRM, stiff → 3830
確 firm → 1571
毅 RESOLUTE → 2341
剛 TOUGH → 2107
頑 STUBBORN → 1315
硬 hard-line → 1518

COMPOUND FORMATION

【頑張る がんばる】
頑張る 'persist, etc.' derives from, and is a new way of writing, the expression 我に張る がにはる 'to insist on one's way'.

瓶

1316
1-4-9

▶BOTTLE
ビン かめ

98	Nonstandard	U7501
瓦	S13-5-8	F0000

traditional form → see 甁 at 1702

預

1317
1-4-9

▶DEPOSIT
ヨ あず(ける) あず(かる)
ⓒ 预 yù

181	Jōyō-5	U9810
頁	S13-9-4	F1278

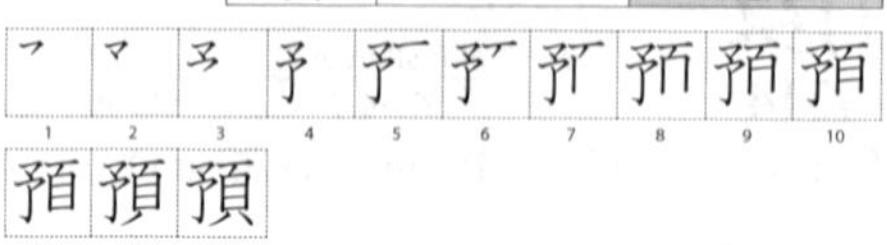

COMPOUNDS

❶ **DEPOSIT**
預金 よきん deposit, bank account
預託する よたくする deposit
預貸率 よたいりつ loan-deposit ratio
預貯金 よちょきん deposits and savings, bank account
預血する よけつする deposit blood (in a blood bank)

❷ [usu. 予 2477] previously, in advance
預言 よげん prophecy (in Christianity)

KUN

【あずける 預ける】 **DEPOSIT, entrust, leave with; leave (a child) in the care of**
預け あずけ custody, keeping
預け金 あずけきん key money
預け入れる あずけいれる make a deposit

【あずかる 預かる】
① **receive on DEPOSIT, take charge of, keep**
預かり あずかり custody; undecided match, draw, tie
保護預かり ほごあずかり safe deposit

② refrain from (doing something)
批評は暫く預かる ひひょうはしばらくあずかる I refrain from commenting on it now

③ leave (a game) undecided
預かりにする あずかりにする call off (a game) as a draw

SYNONYMS

❶ **commit**
託 ENTRUST → 1845
托 ENTRUST → 0252
預 DEPOSIT → 1317
委 COMMIT → 3160
任 LEAVE TO → 0057
嘱 CHARGE WITH → 0881

USAGE

【あずかる】
預かる
① receive on deposit, take charge of, keep
② refrain from (doing something)
③ leave (a game) undecided
与る
① participate in, take part in, share in
② enjoy, receive

HOMOPHONES

あずかる 与 GIVE → 4229

NOTE

➡ see also USAGE note at 予 2477

頒

1318
1-4-9

▶DISTRIBUTE WIDELY
ハン わか(つ)▲
ⓒ 颁 bān

181	Jōyō	U9812
頁	S13-9-4	F4345

COMPOUNDS

❶ **DISTRIBUTE WIDELY, circulate, promulgate**
頒布 はんぷ distribution, circulation
頒価 はんか distribution price
頒行 はんこう [rare] distribution, circulation, promulgation

❷ [archaic] mottled, streaked
頒白 はんぱく grayish hair

KUN

【わかつ 頒つ】 [usu. 分かつ] distribute (things among people)
実費でお頒ちします じっぴでおわかちします It will be offered at actual cost

SYNONYMS

❶ **distribute**

配 DISTRIBUTE → 1853
頒 DISTRIBUTE WIDELY → 1318
分 DIVIDE → 2466

HOMOPHONES

わかつ 分 DIVIDE → 2466

NOTE

➡ see USAGE note at 分 2466

頌

▸EULOGIZE
ショウ ジュ ㊔ のぶ
ⓒ 颂 sòng

1319
◧ 1-4-9

181	Names	U980C
頁	S13-9-4	F0000

COMPOUNDS

❶ⓐ **EULOGIZE, extol, praise highly**
ⓑ poem of eulogy, hymn of praise
a 頌徳 しょうとく eulogy
b 頌歌 しょうか anthem, carol, hymn of praise
❷ celebrate, congratulate
頌春 しょうしゅん Happy New Year
❸ [now always 誦 しょう 1951] [original meaning] recite

INDEPENDENT

【しょう 頌】eulogy, panegyric
【しょうする 頌する】**EULOGIZE**, extol, praise highly

SYNONYMS

❶ⓐ **praise**

賛 PRAISE → 3484
頌 EULOGIZE → 1319
謳 EXTOL → 2061
讃 PRAISE → 2093
美 regard as beautiful → 2817
褒 COMMEND → 2662
嘉 commend (esp. an inferior) → 2953
彰 PROCLAIM MERITS → 2337
称 acclaim → 1491
賞 express admiration → 3237
揚 EXALT → 0722

頓

▸SUDDEN
▸STAY IN PLACE
トン トツ▲ とみ▲ ㊔ はや
ⓒ 顿 dùn dú

1320
◧ 1-4-9

181	Jōyō	U9813
頁	S13-9-4	F2161

Stroke order: 1–13

COMPOUNDS

❶ⓐ **SUDDEN**
ⓑ at once [one time]
a 頓智(=頓知) とんち (quick or ready) wit
頓死 とんし sudden death
頓悟 とんご *Buddhism* sudden enlightenment
素っ頓狂 すっとんきょう harum-scarum, hysteric
b 頓服 とんぷく dose of medicine
❷ **STAY [keep] IN PLACE, stop**
頓挫する とんざする reach an impasse, fall through
整頓 せいとん proper arrangement
無頓着 むとんちゃく(=むとんじゃく) indifferent (to), careless (about)
停頓 ていとん deadlock, standstill
❸ unclassified compounds
頓珍漢 とんちんかん absurd, incoherent, irrelevant
頓馬 とんま idiot, fool

KUN

【とみ 頓】**SUDDEN**
頓に とみに suddenly, all at once, rapidly

SYNONYMS

❶ **stay**

滞 STAY → 0815
頓 STAY IN PLACE → 1320
留 STAY → 3189
逗 STAY → 4005
駐 STATIONED → 2297
屯 STATION TROOPS → 4268
在 reside temporarily → 3704
泊 STAY OVERNIGHT → 0389
宿 LODGE → 2858
寓 stay temporarily → 2893

❶ **sudden**

急 SUDDEN → 2595
激 sudden → 0955
暴 sudden → 3138
俄 SUDDEN → 0106
頓 SUDDEN → 1320
勃 SUDDENLY → 1839
突 abruptly → 2772

旗

▸FLAG
キ はた
ⓒ 旗 qí

1321
◧ 1-4-10

70	Jōyō-4	U65D7
方	S14-4-10	F1232

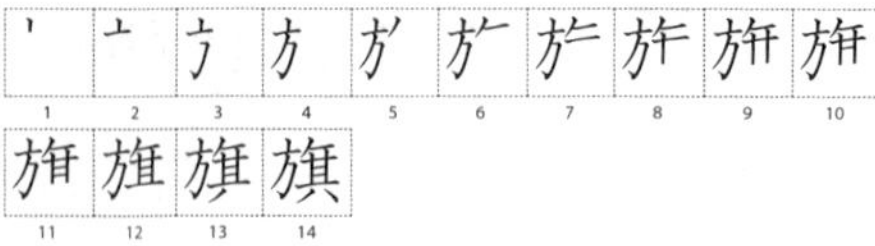

COMPOUNDS

❶ⓐ **FLAG, banner, standard, ensign**

ⓑ [suffix] **FLAG, emblem**

a 旗艦 きかん flagship

旗手 きしゅ standard bearer

国旗 こっき national flag

反旗を翻す はんきをひるがえす rise the standard of revolt, raise in revolt

b 星条旗 せいじょうき the Stars and Stripes

国連旗 こくれんき United Nations Emblem

日章旗 にっしょうき Rising Sun flag

❷ [also 麾 3937] command

旗下の きかの under one's command, under the banner (of)

KUN

【はた 旗】[sometimes also 幡] **FLAG, banner, standard, ensign**

旗揚げ はたあげ raising an army; launching business

手旗 てばた semaphore [hand] flag

SYNONYMS

❶ **flag**

旗 FLAG → 1321

幡 LONG FLAG → 0891

旒 COUNTER FOR FLAGS → 1272

USAGE

【はた】

旗

[sometimes also 幡] flag, banner, standard, ensign

幡

① [usu. 旗] flag, banner, standard, ensign

② *patākā*: pendant streamer hung before a temple in honor of Buddha

HOMOPHONES

はた 幡 LONG FLAG → 0891

概

1322

1-4-10

▶**GENERAL**

ガイ おおむ(ね)▲

Ⓝ 概 槪 Ⓒ 概 gài

75	Jōyō	U6982
木	S14-4-10	F1411

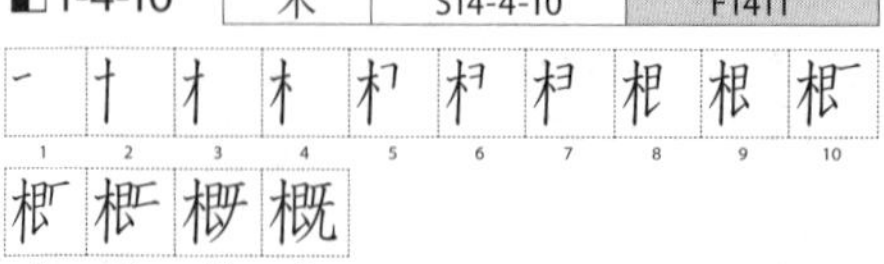

COMPOUNDS

❶ⓐ **GENERAL, on the whole, approximate, rough**

ⓑ **GENERAL outline**

ⓒ **GENERALize**

a 概論 がいろん outline, general remarks

概算 がいさん approximation, rough estimate [calculation]

概況 がいきょう general condition [situation], outlook

概念 がいねん general idea, concept

b 概略 がいりゃく outline, summary; roughly, approximately

概要 がいよう outline, summary, synopsis

一概に いちがいに unconditionally; wholly, indiscriminately

大概 たいがい generally, mostly; probably, maybe

c 概括する がいかつする summarize, sum up, generalize

❷ manner of carrying [conducting] oneself, looks

気概 きがい spirit, pluck

INDEPENDENT

【がい 概】manner of carrying [conducting] oneself

将軍の概が有る しょうぐんのがいがある look like a commander

【がいして 概して】**GENERAL**ly, on the whole, as a rule

KUN

【おおむね 概ね】**GENERAL**ly, on the whole, approximately, roughly

SYNONYMS

❶ⓐ **approximately**

約 APPROXIMATELY → 1632

概 GENERAL → 1322

大 in substance → 4224

-頃 ABOUT → 0163

位 about → 0069

-方 about → 2459

-程 ...or thereabouts → 1524

辺り thereabouts → 3761

NOTE

★ do not confuse with 慨 DEPLORE → 0790

榎

1323

1-4-10

▶**HACKBERRY**

カ えのき え

Ⓒ 榎 jiă

75	Names	U698E
木	S14-4-10	F2548

KUN

【えのき 榎】**Chinese HACKBERRY**

榎茸 えのきたけ enokitake, enoki mushroom

【え 榎】[archaic] Chinese **HACKBERRY**

榎葉 えのは *dialect* landlocked masu salmon

SYNONYMS

【えのき】

◯ **trees**

桜 CHERRY → 1168
桐 PAULOWNIA → 1173
桂 AROMATIC TREE, katsura tree → 1163
梓 CATALPA → 1207
桑 MULBERRY → 2618
漆 Japanese lacquer tree → 0863
樺 BIRCH → 1324
椛 BIRCH → 1202
梧 CHINESE PARASOL TREE → 1200
檀 SPINDLE TREE → 1385
椿 CAMELLIA → 1278
柳 WILLOW → 1115
柊 HOLLY → 1119
椋 *APHANANTHE ASPERA* → 1245
枉 spindle tree → 1114
槻 ZELKOVA → 1349
楢 OAK → 1287
樫 EVERGREEN OAK → 1364
柏 CYPRESS, JAPANESE EMPEROR OAK → 1110
榎 HACKBERRY → 1323
梶 PAPER MULBERRY → 1199
柘 JAPANESE BOXWOOD → 1117
楊 WILLOW → 1286
桧 JAPANESE CYPRESS → 1160
梛 *NAGEIA NAGI* → 1206
榊 SACRED SHINTO TREE → 1327
楓 MAPLE → 1280
松 PINE → 1075
杉 CRYPTOMERIA → 1027
槙 PODOCARPUS → 1330
楠 CAMPHOR TREE → 1283
樟 CAMPHOR TREE → 1351

樺

1324

1-4-10

▶**BIRCH**

カ ゲ かば ㊔ かんば

Ⓒ 桦 huà

75	Names	U6A3A
木	S14-4-10	F2219

COMPOUNDS

● [original meaning, now archaic] **BIRCH**

KUN

【かば 樺】

① **BIRCH**

白樺 しらかば white birch, Betula tauschii

② **reddish yellow**

樺色 かばいろ reddish yellow

SYNONYMS

● & 【かば】 ① **trees**

桜 CHERRY → 1168
桐 PAULOWNIA → 1173
桂 AROMATIC TREE, katsura tree → 1163
梓 CATALPA → 1207
桑 MULBERRY → 2618
漆 Japanese lacquer tree → 0863
樺 BIRCH → 1324
椛 BIRCH → 1202
梧 CHINESE PARASOL TREE → 1200
檀 SPINDLE TREE → 1385
椿 CAMELLIA → 1278
柳 WILLOW → 1115
柊 HOLLY → 1119
椋 *APHANANTHE ASPERA* → 1245
枉 spindle tree → 1114
槻 ZELKOVA → 1349
楢 OAK → 1287
樫 EVERGREEN OAK → 1364
柏 CYPRESS, JAPANESE EMPEROR OAK → 1110
榎 HACKBERRY → 1323
梶 PAPER MULBERRY → 1199
柘 JAPANESE BOXWOOD → 1117
楊 WILLOW → 1286
桧 JAPANESE CYPRESS → 1160
梛 *NAGEIA NAGI* → 1206
榊 SACRED SHINTO TREE → 1327
楓 MAPLE → 1280
松 PINE → 1075
杉 CRYPTOMERIA → 1027
槙 PODOCARPUS → 1330
楠 CAMPHOR TREE → 1283
樟 CAMPHOR TREE → 1351

USAGE

【かば】

樺
① birch
② reddish yellow

椛
birch

HOMOPHONES

かば 椛 BIRCH → 1202

構

1325

1-4-10

▶**CONSTRUCT**
▶**MIND**

コウ かま(える) かま(う)

Ⓝ 構 Ⓒ 构 gòu

75	Jōyō-5	U69CB
木	S14-4-10	F0379

方 【木】 止 火 王 月 云

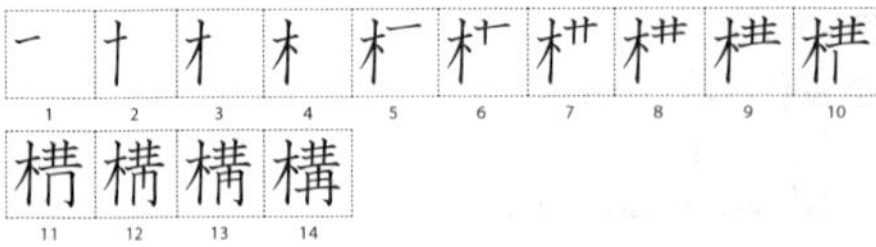

COMPOUNDS

❶ⓐ [original meaning] (build by assembling parts) **CONSTRUCT, frame, assemble, form, compose**
ⓑ **structure, framework, CONSTRUCTion, fabrication**

a 構成 こうせい composition, construction, formation, organization
構造 こうぞう structure, construction, framework
構築する こうちくする construct, build
構文 こうぶん sentence construction, syntax

b 機構 きこう mechanism, structure; system, organization; frame, framework
結構 けっこう structure, construction; quite, well enough, fairly well; all right; no thank you
虚構 きょこう fabrication, fiction

❷ **plan CONSTRUCTively, frame, contrive, devise**
構想する こうそうする conceive, contrive; plan
構図 こうず design, plot, plan

❸ premises, enclosure
構内 こうない premises, compound, grounds
構外 こうがい out of the premises

KUN

【かまえる 構える】**set up (a house), take up, keep; assume a posture, make ready**
構え かまえ structure, construction, style; posture, attitude; enclosure radical (of Chinese characters), embracing radical
居を構える きょをかまえる take up one's residence
銃を構えて じゅうをかまえて ready with a rifle leveled
待ち構える まちかまえる wait eagerly for, be on the watch for
心構え こころがまえ mental attitude; preparation
二段構え にだんがまえ two-stage preparation

【かまう 構う】
① **MIND, care about, be concerned about**
構わない かまわない do not care [mind], be indifferent (to)
人が何と言おうと構わない ひとがなんといおうとかまわない I don't care what people say about me

② **care for; entertain**
どうぞお構い無く どうぞおかまいなく Please don't trouble yourself (on my account)

③ meddle in, butt in
私の事を構わないでくれ わたしのことをかまわないでくれ Leave me [let me be] alone!

④ tease, molest
犬を構う いぬをかまう tease a dog

SYNONYMS

❶ⓐ **make**
作 MAKE → 0077
造 MAKE → 3856
成 FORM → 4352
工 MANUFACTURE → 4190
製 MANUFACTURE → 3478
産 PRODUCE → 4089
調 PREPARE → 1973
組む ASSEMBLE → 1693
構 CONSTRUCT → 1325

ⓑ **structure**
構 structure → 1325
造り MAKE → 3856

【かまう】
① **worry**
憂 BE ANXIOUS → 2664
配 concern oneself → 1853
構う MIND → 1325
虞 FEARS (of undesirable event) → 4037

模

1326

1-4-10

▸**PATTERN**

モ ボ

Ⓒ 模 mó mú

75	Jōyō-6	U6A21
木	S14-4-10	F0807

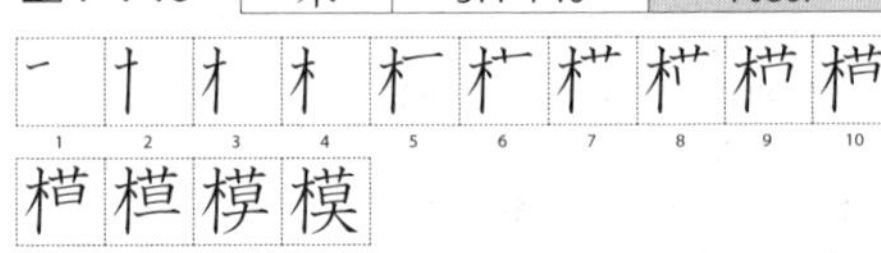

COMPOUNDS

❶ (something worthy of imitation) **PATTERN, model, norm, exemplar**
模範 もはん model, pattern, example
模型 もけい model, pattern, mold
模式標本 もしきひょうほん type specimen

❷ [formerly also 摸 も 0797] **PATTERN after, imitate, copy, model upon**
模造 もぞう imitation, counterfeit
模擬の もぎの imitation, sham, mock, simulated
模擬試験 もぎしけん mock examination
模倣する もほうする imitate, copy
模写する もしゃする copy, trace, reproduce

❸ (decorative design) **PATTERN, design, figure**
模様 もよう pattern, design; appearance, circumstances
規模 きぼ scale, scope

❹ [formerly also 摸 も 0797] grope, feel about [for], search
模索 もさく groping

❺ vague, dim, indistinct
模糊 もこ dimness, vagueness

INDEPENDENT

【もする 模する(=摸する)】copy, imitate

SYNONYMS

❶ model
範 MODEL → 3360
典 CANON → 3253
模 PATTERN → 1326
程 ESTABLISHED FORM → 1524
式 form → 3785
準 STANDARD → 3541
格 NORM → 1161

❷ imitate
擬 IMITATE → 0969
倣 COPY AFTER → 0127
摸 PATTERN AFTER → 0797
模 pattern after → 1326
肖 MODEL → 2733
象 represent → 2647

❸ pattern
模 PATTERN (decorative design) → 1326
文 decorative pattern → 2458
柄 pattern (on cloth) → 1111
様 pattern → 1332
紋 figure → 1651

COMPOUND FORMATION

【規模 きぼ】
規模 'scale, scope' originally referred to the shape or pattern (模 ❸) of an object drawn with the aid of a compass (規). This came to signify the overall structure or scale of things.

榊

1327

◧ 1-4-10

▸SACRED SHINTO TREE

さかき

Ⓝ 榊 Ⓒ (国字)

75	Names	U698A
木	S14-4-10	F2486

KUN

【さかき 榊】SACRED SHINTO TREE:
ⓐ ***Cleyera japonica***
ⓑ **evergreen tree planted or used at a shrine**

SYNONYMS

【さかき】

◯ **trees**
桜 CHERRY → 1168
桐 PAULOWNIA → 1173
桂 AROMATIC TREE, katsura tree → 1163
梓 CATALPA → 1207
桑 MULBERRY → 2618
漆 Japanese lacquer tree → 0863
樺 BIRCH → 1324
椛 BIRCH → 1202
梧 CHINESE PARASOL TREE → 1200
檀 SPINDLE TREE → 1385
椿 CAMELLIA → 1278
柳 WILLOW → 1115
柊 HOLLY → 1119
椋 *APHANANTHE ASPERA* → 1245
柾 spindle tree → 1114
槻 ZELKOVA → 1349
楢 OAK → 1287
樫 EVERGREEN OAK → 1364
柏 CYPRESS, JAPANESE EMPEROR OAK → 1110
榎 HACKBERRY → 1323
梶 PAPER MULBERRY → 1199
柘 JAPANESE BOXWOOD → 1117
楊 WILLOW → 1286
桧 JAPANESE CYPRESS → 1160
梛 *NAGEIA NAGI* → 1206
榊 SACRED SHINTO TREE → 1327
楓 MAPLE → 1280
松 PINE → 1075
杉 CRYPTOMERIA → 1027
槙 PODOCARPUS → 1330
楠 CAMPHOR TREE → 1283
樟 CAMPHOR TREE → 1351

榛

1328

◧ 1-4-10

▸HAZEL

シン はしばみ はり はん-

Ⓒ 榛 zhēn

75	Names	U699B
木	S14-4-10	F3174

COMPOUNDS

❶ [original meaning, now archaic] **HAZEL, filbert**
❷ [archaic] bush, thicket of assorted trees, coppice

KUN

【はしばみ 榛】**HAZEL, *Corylus heterophylla var. Thunbergii***
【はり 榛】**alder, black alder, *Alnus japonica***
【はん- 榛-】[in compounds] **alder, black alder, *Alnus japonica***
榛の木 はん(=はり)のき alder, black alder, *Alnus japonica*

SYNONYMS

【はしばみ】

◯ **fruits and fruit trees**
桃 PEACH → 1174
榛 HAZEL → 1328
椎 CHINQUAPIN → 1249
柚 YUZU → 1123

椰 COCONUT → 1285
柑 CITRUS → 1112
橙 BITTER ORANGE → 1369
葡 GRAPE → 2902
萄 GRAPE → 2870
柿 PERSIMMON → 1118
檎 APPLE → 1386
李 PLUM → 3050
枇 LOQUAT → 1063
杷 LOQUAT → 1065
苺 STRAWBERRY → 2780
菱 water chestnut → 2879
杏 APRICOT → 3049
梅 JAPANESE APRICOT → 1159
橘 MANDARIN → 1366
栗 CHESTNUT → 3280
栃 JAPANESE HORSE CHESTNUT → 1122
梨 PEAR → 3412
蕉 PLANTAIN → 2994

槍 1329

▶SPEAR
ソウ やり ㊔ ほこ
Ⓒ 枪 qiāng

1-4-10

75	Names	U69CD
木	S14-4-10	F1642

COMPOUNDS

● SPEAR, lance
槍術 そうじゅつ spearmanship
槍騎兵 そうきへい lancer
聖槍 せいそう holy lance
竹槍 ちくそう bamboo spear

KUN

【やり 槍】
①ⓐ SPEAR, lance
ⓑ javelin (in athletics)
a 槍先 やりさき spearhead
槍玉に挙げる やりだまにあげる single out for criticism
長槍 ながやり long spear, pike
横槍 よこやり interruption
一本槍 いっぽんやり single-minded policy; one's sole talent
雨が降ろうが槍が降ろうが あめがふろうがやりがふろうが Come hell or high water
b 槍投げ やりなげ javelin (throw)
② name of chess piece in shogi (Japanese chess)

SYNONYMS

● projectiles and bombs
弾 PROJECTILE → 0697
丸 round projectile → 4225
矢 ARROW → 2502
槍 SPEAR → 1329
爆 bomb → 1415
雷 explosive device → 3466

槙 1330

▶PODOCARPUS
テン シン まき
Ⓝ 槇 Ⓒ 槙 diān

1-4-10

75	Names	U69D9
木	S14-4-10	F2908

COMPOUNDS

● cedar or related trees
柏槙 びゃくしん juniper

KUN

【まき 槙】 PODOCARPUS; cedar, white cedar
犬槙 いぬまき podocarpus, *Podocarpus macrophyllus*

SYNONYMS

【まき】
○ trees
桜 CHERRY → 1168
桐 PAULOWNIA → 1173
桂 AROMATIC TREE, katsura tree → 1163
梓 CATALPA → 1207
桑 MULBERRY → 2618
漆 Japanese lacquer tree → 0863
樺 BIRCH → 1324
椛 BIRCH → 1202
梧 CHINESE PARASOL TREE → 1200
檀 SPINDLE TREE → 1385
椿 CAMELLIA → 1278
柳 WILLOW → 1115
柊 HOLLY → 1119
椋 *APHANANTHE ASPERA* → 1245
柾 spindle tree → 1114
槻 ZELKOVA → 1349
楢 OAK → 1287
樫 EVERGREEN OAK → 1364
柏 CYPRESS, JAPANESE EMPEROR OAK → 1110
榎 HACKBERRY → 1323
梶 PAPER MULBERRY → 1199
柘 JAPANESE BOXWOOD → 1117
楊 WILLOW → 1286
桧 JAPANESE CYPRESS → 1160
梛 *NAGEIA NAGI* → 1206
榊 SACRED SHINTO TREE → 1327
楓 MAPLE → 1280
松 PINE → 1075
杉 CRYPTOMERIA → 1027
槙 PODOCARPUS → 1330
楠 CAMPHOR TREE → 1283

樟 CAMPHOR TREE → 1351

槌

▶HAMMER

ツイ つち ㊔ てつ

Ⓝ 槌 Ⓒ 槌 chuí

1331

◧ 1-4-10

75	Names	U69CC
木	S14-4-10	F2309

COMPOUNDS

● **HAMMER, mallet**

槌骨 ついこつ malleus

鉄槌 てっつい (iron) hammer

KUN

【つち 槌】**HAMMER, mallet**

槌鯨 つちくじら Baird's beaked whale

金槌 かなづち hammer; someone who cannot swim

木槌 きづち wooden hammer

小槌 こづち (small) mallet, gavel

相槌を打つ あいづちをうつ make (agreeable) responses (in a conversation)

SYNONYMS

● **instruments for beating or pounding**

槌 HAMMER → 1331

杵 WOODEN PESTLE → 1074

砧 BLOCK FOR BEATING CLOTH → 1477

様

▶MODE

▶FORMAL TITLE

ヨウ さま ざま▲

Ⓝ 様 样◆ Ⓒ 样 yàng

1332

◧ 1-4-10

75	Jōyō-3	U69D8
木	S14-4-10	F0188

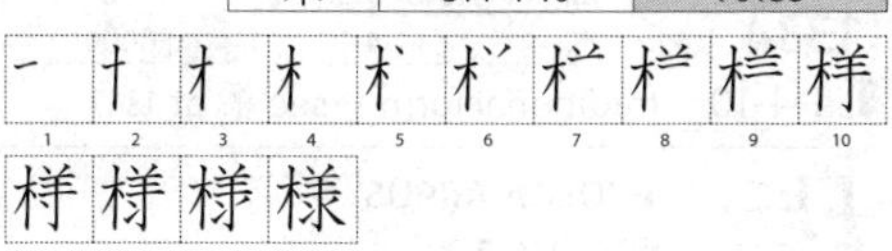

COMPOUNDS

❶ⓐ (manner of doing) **MODE, method, way, manner, style**

ⓑ [verbal suffix] **way of doing**

a 様式 ようしき mode, manner; style, order

今様の いまようの modern, up to date

各人各様 かくじんかくよう So many men, so many ways

唐様 からよう Chinese style [design]

同様に どうように similarly

b 泳ぎ様 およぎよう way of swimming

仕様が無い しようがない have no choice; it is no use; cannot bear

❷ (manner of being) **MODE, state, aspect, appearance**

様相 ようそう aspect, phase, condition

様子 ようす situation, aspect, circumstances; appearance, looks; sign, indication

様態 ようたい mode

異様な いような strange, odd, singular

❸ⓐ **variety, sort, kind**

ⓑ [suffix] **like, such as**

a 一様 いちよう uniformity, equality

多様な たような various, manifold

左様 さよう such; yes; let me see

b 歯ブラシ様の物 はぶらしようのもの something resembling a toothbrush

❹ **pattern, figure**

模様 もよう pattern, design; appearance, circumstances

文様 もんよう pattern, design

INDEPENDENT

【よう 様】

① **way, manner, MODE, method**

この様に このように in this way

② **like, as**

天使の様な少女 てんしのようなしょうじょ angel of a girl

雪の様に白い ゆきのようにしろい white as snow

③ **kind, sort, the like (of something)**

彼はどの様な人ですか かれはどのようなひとですか What sort of person is he?

④ⓐ **appearance, looks**

ⓑ **it appears that, it seems**

b 雨の様だ あめのようだ It looks like rain

⑤ **in order to, so that**

風邪を引かない様にセーターを着た かぜをひかないようにせーたーをきた I put on a sweater so as not to catch a cold

⑥ **that, thus**

彼に電話する様に言った かれにでんわするようにいった I told him to telephone

邪魔をしない様に じゃまをしないように Leave me alone!

長生きなさいます様に ながいきなさいますように May you live long!

最近煙草を吸う様になった さいきんたばこをすうようになった I started smoking recently

KUN

【さま 様】

① **state, situation; appearance**

有り様 ありさま condition, state of affairs; sight

② **kind, sort**

様様な さまざまな various, manifold

③ **FORMAL TITLE: Mr., Miss, Mrs., Ms., Esq.**

山本様 やまもとさま Mr. Yamamoto

貴様 きさま [belittling] you; [original meaning] sir, madam

方 【木】 止 火 王 月 云

④ [often preceded by お- or 御- ご-] **suffix for forming polite phrases**
お気の毒様 おきのどくさま I am sorry
御苦労様 ごくろうさま I thank you for your kind efforts
お陰様で おかげさまで thanks to you

【ざま 様】
① state, plight, appearance, spectacle
様を見ろ ざまをみろ Serves you right!
② [suffix]
ⓐ when, as soon as
ⓑ way of doing
ⓒ direction
a 妻の方を振り向き様、彼は黙れと叫んだ つまのほうをふりむきざま, かれはだまれとさけんだ "Shut up!" cried he, turning to his wife
b 生き様 いきざま way of life, form of existence
c 後ろ様に倒れる うしろざまにたおれる fall backward

SYNONYMS

❶ **way and style**
風 MANNER → 3730
様 MODE → 1332
方 WAY → 2459
途 WAY → 3853
法 METHOD → 0391
流 STYLE → 0529
式 STYLE → 3785
調 TONE → 1973

❷ **states and situations**
態 STATE → 3529
調 TONE → 1973
様 MODE → 1332
相 PHASE → 1120
状 CONDITION → 0322
況 CONDITIONS → 0395
景 business conditions → 3118
勢 course of events → 3542
境 SITUATION → 0835
局 current situation → 3800
情 ACTUAL CONDITIONS → 0583
訳 circumstances → 1865

❸ⓐ **kinds and types**
型 TYPE → 3266
類 KIND → 2275
色 kind → 2522
般 SORT → 1670
属 genus → 3901
品 category → 2795
種 VARIETY → 1560
様 variety → 1332

ⓑ **similar**
類 similar → 2275
様 like → 1332
如 AS → 0239
-通り as → 3855
云 SUCH → 2430

❹ **pattern**
模 PATTERN (decorative design) → 1326
文 decorative pattern → 2458
柄 pattern (on cloth) → 1111
様 pattern → 1332
紋 figure → 1651

【さま】
③ **titles of address**
氏 COURTESY TITLE → 3669
兄 familiar title (seniors) → 2676
君 FAMILIAR TITLE (peers) → 3974
嬢 Miss → 0936
様 FORMAL TITLE → 1332
殿 FORMAL HONORIFIC TITLE → 2247
師 honorific title (clergymen) → 1680
公 honorific title (noblemen) → 2468

構

1333
1-4-10

▶**CONSTRUCT**
▶**MIND**
コウ かま(える) かま(う)

75	Nonstandard	U69CB
木	S14-4-10	F0000

traditional form → see 構 at 1325

槗

1334
1-4-10

▶**BRIDGE**
キョウ はし

75	Nonstandard	U69D7
木	S14-4-10	F0000

traditional form → see 橋 at 1367

槇

1335
1-4-10

▶**PODOCARPUS**
テン シン まき

75	Names	U69C7
木	S14-4-10	F0000

traditional form → see 槙 at 1330

樋

1336
1-4-10

▶**WATER PIPE**
トウ とい ひ

75	Nonstandard	U6A0B
木	S14-4-10	F0000

traditional form → see 樋 at 1353

雌

1337

1-4-10

▶FEMALE

シ め- めす めん▲

Ⓒ 雌 cí

172	Jōyō	U96CC
隹	S14-8-6	F2469

COMPONENTS

❶ [original meaning] (of plants or animals) **FEMALE**

雌雄 しゆう male and female; victory or defeat

雌蕊× しずい pistil

❷ weak, retiring, inferior

雌伏する しふくする remain in obscurity, lie low, bide one's time

KUN

【め- 雌-】

ⓐ (of plants) **FEMALE**

ⓑ [sometimes also 牝-] (of animals) **FEMALE**

ⓒ [also 女] the weaker or smaller of two

a 雌花 めばな female flower

雌蕊× めしべ pistil

b 雌捻子(=雌螺子) めねじ female screw

雌牛 めうし cow

c 雌滝 めだき the smaller waterfall (of the two)

【めす 雌】 [sometimes also 牝] (of animals) **FEMALE**

雌の狐 めすのきつね vixen, bitch fox

雌犬 めすいぬ female dog, bitch

【めん 雌】 [sometimes also 牝] (of animals) **FEMALE**

雌鳥(=雌鶏) めんどり hen

SYNONYMS

❶ **woman**

女 WOMAN → 4226

婦 ADULT WOMAN → 0565

婆 OLD WOMAN → 3433

嬢 YOUNG LADY → 0936

娘 GIRL → 0488

雌 FEMALE → 1337

牝 FEMALE → 1020

媛 DAMSEL → 0688

USAGE

❶【め】

雌-

ⓐ (of plants) female

ⓑ [sometimes also 牝-] (of animals) female

ⓒ [also 女] the weaker or smaller of two

牝-

[usu. 雌] (of animals) female

女

① *elegant* the fair sex, woman, female

② [in compounds] the weaker or smaller of two

❷【めす】

雌

[sometimes also 牝] (of animals) female

牝

[usu. 雌] (of animals) female

❸【めん】

雌

[sometimes also 牝] (of animals) female

牝

[usu. 雌] (of animals) female

HOMOPHONES

め-

牝 FEMALE → 1020

女 WOMAN → 4226

めす 牝 FEMALE → 1020

めん 牝 FEMALE → 1020

煽

1338

1-4-10

▶FAN

セン あお(る) おだ(てる) あお(ぐ)

Ⓝ 煽 Ⓒ 煽 扇 shān

86	Non-Jōyō	U717D
火	S14-4-10	F2286

COMPOUNDS

● [now usu. 扇 2449] (move to action) **FAN, stir up, instigate**

煽動する せんどうする instigate, agitate

煽情的な せんじょうてきな inflammatory, lascivious

KUN

【あおる 煽る】

ⓐ **FAN, flap**

ⓑ **FAN, stir up, instigate**

ab 煽り あおり influence; gust (of wind)

【おだてる 煽てる】

ⓐ **stir up, instigate, incite**

ⓑ **flatter**

ab 煽て おだて instigation, flattery

【あおぐ 煽ぐ】 [usu. 扇ぐ] **FAN**

煽ぎ立てる あおぎたてる fan incessantly; agitate, instigate

SYNONYMS

● **incite**

挑 PROVOKE → 0445

唆 INSTIGATE → 0480

扇 FAN → 2449

煽 FAN → 1338

激 excite → 0955

奮 ROUSE UP → 3000

振 arouse to action → 0515

動 MOVE → 2232
起 rise to action → 4099

HOMOPHONES

あおぐ 扇 FAN → 2449

NOTE

➡ see USAGE note at 扇 2449

熄

1339

1-4-10

▶**GO OUT**

ソク

Ⓒ 熄 xī

86	Non-Jōyō	U7184
火	S14-4-10	F3209

COMPOUNDS

● [now replaced by 息 3278] [original meaning] **GO OUT, die out**

終熄する しゅうそくする cease, come to an end

SYNONYMS

● **extinguish**

消 EXTINGUISH → 0531
熄 GO OUT → 1339
滅 go out → 0812

熔

1340

1-4-10

▶**MELT**

ヨウ と(ける) と(かす)

Ⓒ 熔 róng

86	Non-Jōyō	U7194
火	S14-4-10	F0000

COMPOUNDS

● [now replaced by 溶 0816] (change or cause to change from solid to liquid, esp. by heat) **MELT**

熔解する ようかいする melt, fuse
熔融 ようゆう melting, fusion
熔接する ようせつする weld
熔鉱炉 ようこうろ smelting [blast] furnace
熔銑 ようせん molten iron
熔岩 ようがん lava

KUN

【とける 熔ける】[now usu. 溶ける] *vi* (of metals) **MELT (up), fuse, smelt**

【とかす 熔かす】[now usu. 溶かす] *vt* **MELT (up) (metals), fuse, smelt**

鉄を熔かす てつをとかす melt [fuse] iron

SYNONYMS

● **liquefy**

溶 DISSOLVE, MELT → 0816
熔 MELT (metals) → 1340
鎔 MELT (metals) → 2214
解 DISSOLVE → 1913
融 FUSE → 2303

HOMOPHONES

とける

解 TAKE APART → 1913
融 FUSE → 2303
溶 DISSOLVE → 0816
鎔 MELT → 2214

とかす

解 TAKE APART → 1913
融 FUSE → 2303
溶 DISSOLVE → 0816
鎔 MELT → 2214
梳 COMB → 1209

NOTE

➡ see USAGE note at 解 1913

煽

1341

1-4-10

▶**FAN**

セン あお(る) おだ(てる) あお(ぐ)

86	Nonstandard	U717D
火	S14-4-10	F0000

traditional form → see 煽 at 1338

瑠

1342

1-4-10

▶**LAPIS LAZULI**

ル リュウ▲

Ⓝ 瑠◇ Ⓒ 琉 liú

96	Jōyō	U7460
王	S14-4-10	F2280

1	2	3	4	5	6	7	8	9	10	11	12	13	14
一	T	干	王	王´	王᷄	王᷄	王𠃌	王𠃌	王𠃌	瑠	瑠	瑠	瑠

COMPOUNDS

ⓐ (kind of gemstone) **LAPIS LAZULI**
ⓑ (variant of blue) **LAPIS LAZULI**, lapis lazuli blue

a 瑠璃(=琉璃) るり lapis lazuli, lapis lazuli blue; [archaic] glass
b 瑠璃色 るりいろ lapis lazuli blue, bright blue
瑠璃唐草 るりからくさ baby blue-eyes (name of plant)
浄瑠璃 じょうるり *joruri*, ballad drama; clear lapis lazuli

SYNONYMS

ⓐ **precious stones**

玉 GEM → 4289
珂 WHITE AGATE → 1137
璧 DISK-SHAPED JEWEL → 3608
琥 AMBER → 1261
珀 AMBER → 1136
珠 PEARL → 1183
瑛 TRANSPARENT GEM → 1259
瑠 LAPIS LAZULI → 1342

璃 GLASSY SUBSTANCE → 1358
晶 CRYSTAL → 3122
玖 beautiful black jewel → 1041
琉 LAPIS LAZULI → 1221
琳 BEAUTIFUL GEM → 1262

ⓑ blue and purple colors

青 BLUE → 3084
碧 DEEP BLUE → 3515
瑠 LAPIS LAZULI (bright blue) → 1342
紺 DARK BLUE → 1688
藍 INDIGO → 3024
紫 PURPLE → 3332
蒼 PALE BLUE → 2943

NOTE

★ Though 瑠 and 琉 are distinct characters, they have the same meanings and may be used interchangeably. However, りゅうきゅう, another name for Okinawa, is usu. written 琉球.

瑳

1343

1-4-10

▸POLISH

サ

Ⓒ 瑳 cuō

96	Names	U7473
王	S14-4-10	F0000

COMPOUNDS

● POLISH, grind

切瑳(=切磋×)する せっさする work [study] hard, cultivate one's own character
切瑳琢磨 せっさたくま working hard together, assiduity in friendly rivalry

SYNONYMS

● polish and rub

磨 POLISH → 3946
擦 RUB → 0971
摩 RUB AGAINST → 3938
摺 RUB AGAINST → 0850
研 GRIND → 1456
削 CUT BY CHIPPING → 1837
瑳 POLISH → 1343

瑤

1344

1-4-10

▸EXQUISITE

ヨウ ㊔ たま

96	Nonstandard	U7464
王	S14-4-10	F0000

traditional form → see 瑶 at 1301

璃

1-4-10

incorrect stroke-count
➡ see 1-4-11: 王 at 1358

膜

1345

1-4-10

▸MEMBRANE

マク

Ⓒ 膜 mó

130	Jōyō	U819C
月	S14-4-10	F1695

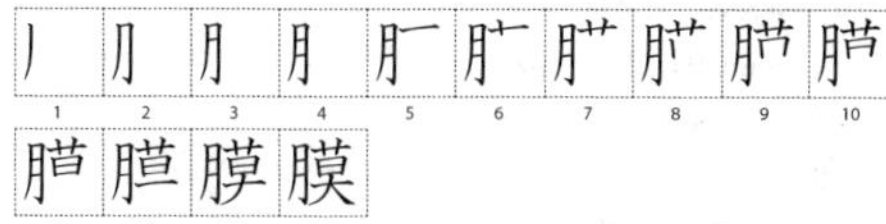

COMPOUNDS

● [also suffix] [original meaning] **MEMBRANE, film**

膜状の まくじょうの membranous, filmy
粘膜 ねんまく mucous membrane
角膜 かくまく cornea
腹膜 ふくまく peritoneum
鼓膜 こまく eardrum
細胞膜 さいぼうまく cellular membrane
イオン交換膜 いおんこうかんまく ion exchange membrane

INDEPENDENT

【まく 膜】**MEMBRANE**, film
膜が張る まくがはる A film is formed

魂

1346

1-4-10

▸SOUL

コン たましい たま▲

Ⓒ 魂 hún

194	Jōyō	U9B42
鬼	S14-10-4	F1380

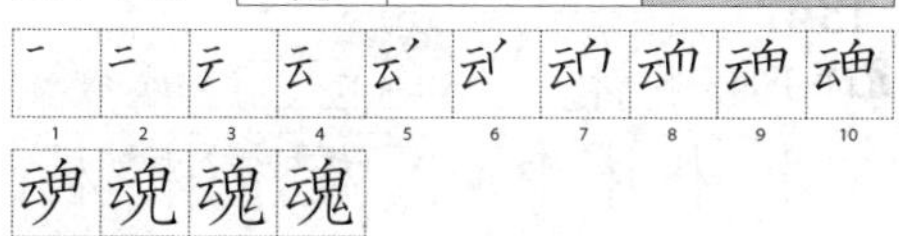

COMPOUNDS

❶ [original meaning] **SOUL, spirit**

魂魄 こんぱく soul, spirit, ghost
霊魂 れいこん spirit, soul
英魂 えいこん departed spirit

❷ spirit, heart

魂胆 こんたん secret intention, ulterior motive
闘魂 とうこん fighting spirit
心魂 しんこん one's soul [heart]
商魂 しょうこん commercial enthusiasm, salesmanship

KUN

【たましい 魂】**SOUL, spirit**
魂を入れ替える たましいをいれかえる reform (oneself), turn over a new leaf
面魂 つらだましい determined expression, plucky countenance

【たま 魂】[also 霊] **SOUL**, spirit, ghost
魂送り たまおくり sending off the spirits of the dead
人魂 ひとだま spirit of a dead person

SYNONYMS

❶ & ❷ psyche
心 HEART → 0011
霊 SPIRIT (soul) → 3480
魂 SOUL, spirit → 1346
魄 SOUL → 1570
腹 heart → 1308
衷 INNER HEART → 2600
襟 inner mind → 1599
胸 breast → 1187
懐 BOSOM → 0942
神 MIND → 1143
気 SPIRIT (consciousness) → 3960
精 SPIRIT (mind) → 1729

USAGE

【たま】
魂
[also 霊] soul, spirit, ghost
霊
[also 魂] soul, spirit, ghost

HOMOPHONES

たま 霊 SPIRIT → 3480

標

1347

1-4-11

▸MARK
ヒョウ ㊔ しめぎ しめ すえ
Ⓒ 标 biāo

75	Jōyō-4	U6A19
木	S15-4-11	F0868

COMPOUNDS

❶ⓐ (identifying sign) **MARK, sign, symbol, label, inscription**
ⓑ (something serving as a guide) **MARK, landmark, signpost, indication**
a 標章 ひょうしょう ensign, emblem, mark
標札(=表札) ひょうさつ nameplate, doorplate
商標 しょうひょう trademark
墓標 ぼひょう grave post, grave marker, gravestone
音標 おんぴょう phonetic sign
b 標識 ひょうしき sign, mark; beacon
指標 しひょう index, indication
浮標 ふひょう (marker) buoy
座標 ざひょう coordinates
里程標 りていひょう milestone, milepost
境界標 きょうかいひょう boundary mark

❷ (something aimed at) **MARK, target, standard**
標的 ひょうてき target, mark
標準 ひょうじゅん standard, norm, criterion
目標 もくひょう mark, target, goal, object

❸ MARK, indicate, designate
標示する ひょうじする post up, declare, demonstrate
標語 ひょうご slogan, motto, catch word
標本 ひょうほん specimen, sample
標高 ひょうこう elevation, (height) above the sea
標記する ひょうきする mark; write a title
標題 ひょうだい title, headline, caption

INDEPENDENT

【ひょう 標】post, sign post; **MARK**, target

SYNONYMS

❶ⓐ marks and signs
標 MARK (identifying sign) → 1347
徽 EMBLEM → 0968
痕 SCAR → 4066
印 MARK (visible sign) → 1023
跡 TRACE → 1937
蹟 TRACE → 2065
踪 FOOTPRINTS → 1996
紋 print → 1651
符 SYMBOL → 3299
号 SIGN → 2675
栞 BOOKMARK → 3285

❷ target
的 TARGET → 1444
標 MARK → 1347
狙 AIM → 0406
目 aim → 3777

❸ indicate
指 POINT → 0452
示 SHOW → 2435
標 MARK → 1347
宛てる ADDRESS → 2762

NOTE

➡ see USAGE note at 表 3083

権

1348

1-4-11

▸RIGHT
▸POWER
ケン ゴン
Ⓝ 權 权◇ Ⓒ 权 quán

75	Jōyō-6	U6A29
木	S15-4-11	F0224

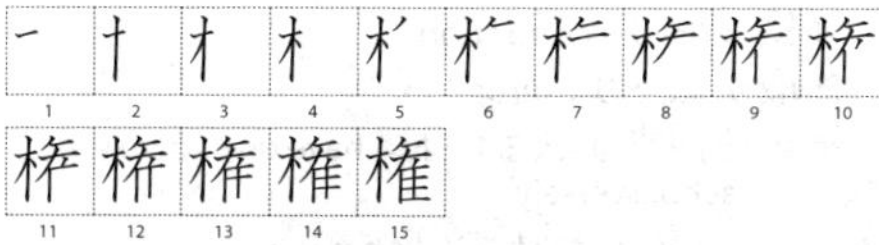

COMPOUNDS

❶ [also suffix] **RIGHT, privilege, claim**

権利 けんり right; authority; privilege
権限 けんげん power, authority; competence (of law)
債権 さいけん credit, claim
職権 しょっけん official [legal] authority
特権 とっけん privilege, exclusive right
有権者 ゆうけんしゃ elector, voter; holder of a right
棄権 きけん abstention from voting, abandoning one's right
人権 じんけん human rights
男女同権 だんじょどうけん equal rights for men and women
所有権 しょゆうけん ownership, proprietary rights
参政権 さんせいけん suffrage, right to vote

❷ **POWER to control, ability to exact obedience, authority**

権威 けんい authority, power
権力 けんりょく power, authority, influence
権勢 けんせい power, influence, authority
政権 せいけん political power, administrative power
実権 じっけん real power
制海権 せいかいけん command of the sea, naval supremacy

❸ temporary, transient—said esp. of Buddhist incarnation

権現 ごんげん incarnation of Buddha; Tokugawa Ieyasu
権化 ごんげ incarnation, embodiment

❹ scheme, expediency

権謀 けんぼう artifice, wiles, trick

❺ [original meaning] balance weight

権衡 けんこう scales; balance, equilibrium

INDEPENDENT

【けん 権】**POWER**, authority
兵馬の権 へいばのけん military power

SYNONYMS

❷ **power and authority**

力 POWER → 4178
威 MIGHT → 4394
勢 POWER (to influence) → 3542
権 POWER (to control) → 1348
覇 SUPREMACY → 3392

槻

1349

◧ 1-4-11

▶ZELKOVA

キ つき

Ⓒ 槻 guī

75	Names	U69FB
木	S15-4-11	F2401

KUN

【つき 槻】***tsuki*: ZELKOVA *serrata var. tsuki*; old name for *keyaki* (Zelkova)**

SYNONYMS

【つき】

◯ **trees**

桜 CHERRY → 1168
桐 PAULOWNIA → 1173
桂 AROMATIC TREE, katsura tree → 1163
梓 CATALPA → 1207
桑 MULBERRY → 2618
漆 Japanese lacquer tree → 0863
樺 BIRCH → 1324
椛 BIRCH → 1202
梧 CHINESE PARASOL TREE → 1200
檀 SPINDLE TREE → 1385
椿 CAMELLIA → 1278
柳 WILLOW → 1115
柊 HOLLY → 1119
椋 *APHANANTHE ASPERA* → 1245
柾 spindle tree → 1114
槻 ZELKOVA → 1349
楢 OAK → 1287
樫 EVERGREEN OAK → 1364
柏 CYPRESS, JAPANESE EMPEROR OAK → 1110
榎 HACKBERRY → 1323
梶 PAPER MULBERRY → 1199
柘 JAPANESE BOXWOOD → 1117
楊 WILLOW → 1286
桧 JAPANESE CYPRESS → 1160
梛 *NAGEIA NAGI* → 1206
榊 SACRED SHINTO TREE → 1327
楓 MAPLE → 1280
松 PINE → 1075
杉 CRYPTOMERIA → 1027
槙 PODOCARPUS → 1330
楠 CAMPHOR TREE → 1283
樟 CAMPHOR TREE → 1351

横

1350

◧ 1-4-11

▶SIDEWAYS

オウ よこ

Ⓝ 横 Ⓒ 横 héng hèng

75	Jōyō-3	U6A2A
木	S15-4-11	F0457

1

一 十 才 木 木 朩 栱 栱 栱 栱 横 横 横 横 横

【木】王 月 区

COMPOUNDS

❶ⓐ **SIDEWAYS, horizontal, across, crosswise, transverse, lateral, latitudinal**

ⓑ place **SIDEWAYS**, lay across, lay down

a 横転する おうてんする roll, fall down sidelong; barrel roll

横断する おうだんする cross, traverse

横断歩道 おうだんほどう pedestrian crossing; crosswalk

横隔膜 おうかくまく diaphragm; midriff

縦横に じゅうおうに vertically and horizontally, in all directions; freely

b 横臥する おうがする lie on one's side, repose

❷ **arbitrary, perverse, despotic, tyrannical, overbearing**

横暴な おうぼうな arbitrary, tyrannical, despotic

横着な おうちゃくな impudent, brazen; idle, lazy

横領 おうりょう seizure, embezzlement, usurpation

横行する おうこうする be rampant, overrun, swagger, strut

横柄な おうへいな overbearing, arrogant

専横 せんおう arbitrariness, despotism

❸ unnatural

横死 おうし unnatural [violent] death

❹ overflow

横溢する おういつする be filled with (vitality), overflow with

KUN

【よこ 横】

①ⓐ **side, flank, width; transverse direction**

ⓑ [in compounds] **side(ways), (a)cross, horizontal, lateral**

a 横から よこから from one's side

横書きする よこがきする write laterally, write from left to right

横文字 よこもじ letters written in lateral lines; European [Western] language

横顔 よこがお profile, face seen from side

横道 よこみち side street

横綱 よこづな (grand) champion sumo wrestler

b 横たわる よこたわる lie (down)

横這い よこばい crawling sideways; remain at the same level

横風 よこかぜ side wind

横糸 よこいと [also 緯糸 or 緯] woof

横投げ よこなげ throwing sideways

横切る よこぎる cross, go across

② [in compounds] **arbitrary, perverse, wrong**

横槍 よこやり interruption

横取り よこどり usurpation

横車を押す よこぐるまをおす have one's own way, act perversely

③ abbrev. of 横浜 よこはま: Yokohama

東横線 とうよこせん Toyoko Line (between Tokyo and Yokohama)

SYNONYMS

❶ⓐ **side**

側 SIDE → 0155

脇 SIDE → 1188

方 side → 2459

辺 -side → 3761

面 side → 2590

傍 BESIDE → 0166

横 SIDEWAYS → 1350

❷ **acting arbitrarily**

横 arbitrary → 1350

独 act arbitrarily → 0471

恣 SELF-INDULGENT → 3281

耽 INDULGE IN → 1665

擅 ARROGATE TO ONESELF → 0947

専 arrogate to oneself → 3272

逞 DO AS ONE PLEASES → 4004

HOMOPHONES

よこいと

緯 LATITUDE → 1782

横糸 → 1350, 2703

緯糸 → 1782, 2703

NOTE

➡ see USAGE note at 緯 1782

樟

1351

1-4-11

▶**CAMPHOR TREE**

ショウ くす くすのき

Ⓒ 樟 zhāng

75	Names	U6A1F
木	S15-4-11	F0000

COMPOUNDS

● **CAMPHOR TREE**

樟脳 しょうのう camphor

KUN

【くす 樟】[usu. 楠] **CAMPHOR TREE**

樟の木 くすのき camphor tree

【くすのき 樟】[usu. 楠] **CAMPHOR TREE**

SYNONYMS

● **trees**

桜 CHERRY → 1168

桐 PAULOWNIA → 1173

桂 AROMATIC TREE, katsura tree → 1163

梓 CATALPA → 1207

桑 MULBERRY → 2618
漆 Japanese lacquer tree → 0863
樺 BIRCH → 1324
椛 BIRCH → 1202
梧 CHINESE PARASOL TREE → 1200
檀 SPINDLE TREE → 1385
椿 CAMELLIA → 1278
柳 WILLOW → 1115
柊 HOLLY → 1119
椋 *APHANANTHE ASPERA* → 1245
柾 spindle tree → 1114
槻 ZELKOVA → 1349
楢 OAK → 1287
樫 EVERGREEN OAK → 1364
柏 CYPRESS, JAPANESE EMPEROR OAK → 1110
榎 HACKBERRY → 1323
梶 PAPER MULBERRY → 1199
柘 JAPANESE BOXWOOD → 1117
楊 WILLOW → 1286
桧 JAPANESE CYPRESS → 1160
梛 *NAGEIA NAGI* → 1206
榊 SACRED SHINTO TREE → 1327
楓 MAPLE → 1280
松 PINE → 1075
杉 CRYPTOMERIA → 1027
槙 PODOCARPUS → 1330
楠 CAMPHOR TREE → 1283
樟 CAMPHOR TREE → 1351

HOMOPHONES

くす 楠 CAMPHOR TREE → 1283
くすのき 楠 CAMPHOR TREE → 1283

NOTE

➡ see USAGE note at 楠 1283
➡ see COMPOUND FORMATION for 樟脳 しょうのう → 脳 1227

槽

1352

1-4-11

▶**TANK**

ソウ ふね▲

Ⓒ 槽 cáo

75	Jōyō	U69FD
木	S15-4-11	F2243

Stroke order: 1–15

COMPOUNDS

ⓐ [also suffix] **TANK, vat, tub**
ⓑ **TANK** or tub-shaped cavity

a 油槽 ゆそう oil tank
浴槽 よくそう bathtub
貯水槽 ちょすいそう water tank
水槽 すいそう water tank
浄化槽 じょうかそう tank for purifying water
b 歯槽 しそう alveolus, socket of a tooth

KUN

【ふね 槽】[also 船] tub, **TANK**, vessel
湯槽 ゆぶね bathtub

SYNONYMS

ⓐ **containers**
箱 BOX → 3362
壺 JAR → 2890
槽 TANK → 1352
樽 BARREL → 1368
棺 COFFIN → 1240
桶 BUCKET → 1211
笈 BOX CARRIED ON THE BACK → 3274
鞘 SHEATH → 2259
箪 BAMBOO BOX → 3381
函 BOX → 3724
籠 BASKET → 3398
袋 BAG → 3201
鞄 BAG (for carrying) → 2248
器 VESSEL → 3367
瓶 BOTTLE → 1702
缶 CAN → 2526
缶 EARTHENWARE JAR → 2525

HOMOPHONES

ふね
船 SHIP → 1700
舟 SMALL BOAT → 4353

NOTE

➡ see USAGE note at 船 1700

樋

1353

1-4-11

▶**WATER PIPE**

トウ とい ひ

Ⓝ 樋 Ⓒ 桶 tōng

75	Names	U6A0B
木	S15-4-11	F2502

KUN

【とい 樋】**WATER [rainwater] PIPE, gutter, (eaves) trough, downspout**
雨樋 あまどい rainwater pipe, rain gutter, eaves trough
竪樋(=縦樋) たてどい downspout
鎖樋 くさりとい rain chain

【ひ 樋】
ⓐ **WATER PIPE, drainpipe, gutter, trough**
ⓑ sluice gate, water gate
ⓒ groove

a 懸け樋(=筧×) かけひ bamboo [wooden] water pipe
b 樋門 ひもん sluice

SYNONYMS

【とい】
○ tubular passages
管 PIPE →3349
筒 TUBE →3323
道 passage →3888
脈 VEIN →1189
樋 WATER PIPE →1353

槪

1354
1-4-11

▶GENERAL
ガイ おおむ(ね)

75	Nonstandard	U2F8EA
木	S15-4-11	F0000

traditional form → see 概 at 1322

樓

1355
1-4-11

▶TALL BUILDING
ロウ

75	Nonstandard	U6A13
木	S15-4-11	F0000

traditional form → see 楼 at 1284

樞

1356
1-4-11

▶PIVOT
スウ

75	Nonstandard	U6A1E
木	S15-4-11	F0000

traditional form → see 枢 at 1076

樣

1357
1-4-11

▶MODE
▶FORMAL TITLE
ヨウ さま ざま

75	Names	U6A23
木	S15-4-11	F0000

traditional form → see 様 at 1332

樫

1-4-11

incorrect stroke-count
➡ see 1-4-12: 木 at 1364

楕

1-4-11

incorrect stroke-count
➡ see 1-4-12: 木 at 1370

璃

1358
1-4-11

▶GLASSY SUBSTANCE
リ ㊔ あき
Ⓒ 璃 lí

96	Jōyō	U7483
王	S15-4-11	F2580

COMPOUNDS

● GLASSY SUBSTANCE, glass; crystal
瑠璃(=琉璃) るり lapis lazuli, lapis lazuli blue; [archaic] glass
玻×璃 はり crystal; glass
浄瑠璃 じょうるり *joruri*, ballad drama; clear lapis lazuli

SYNONYMS

● precious stones
玉 GEM →4289
珂 WHITE AGATE →1137
璧 DISK-SHAPED JEWEL →3608
琥 AMBER →1261
珀 AMBER →1136
珠 PEARL →1183
瑛 TRANSPARENT GEM →1259
瑠 LAPIS LAZULI →1342
璃 GLASSY SUBSTANCE →1358
晶 CRYSTAL →3122
玖 beautiful black jewel →1041
琉 LAPIS LAZULI →1221
琳 BEAUTIFUL GEM →1262

膝

1359
1-4-11

▶KNEE
シツ▲ ひざ
Ⓒ 膝 xī

130	Jōyō	U819D
月	S15-4-11	F1226

COMPOUNDS

● [original meaning] KNEE
膝下 しっか near one's knee; near a parent [guardian]
膝関節 しつかんせつ knee joint
膝蓋骨 しつがいこつ kneecap, patella
膝行 しっこう moving forward [backward] by sliding on one's knees (in the presence of high-ranking individuals)

KUN

【ひざ 膝】
ⓐ KNEE
ⓑ lap
a 膝元 ひざもと near one's knee; near someone (esp. a parent or guardian)

膝の皿 ひざのさら kneecap
膝を交えて ひざをまじえて sitting knee to knee; intimately
膝を崩す ひざをくずす sit at ease
立て膝 たてひざ sitting with one knee drawn up
b 膝掛け ひざかけ lap blanket
膝枕 ひざまくら lying with one's head in another's lap

SYNONYMS

● **leg**
足 FOOT → 2714
脚 LEG → 1226
膝 KNEE → 1359

腸

1360
1-4-11

▸INTESTINES
チョウ はらわた

130	Nonstandard	U8193
月	S15-4-11	F0000

traditional form → see 腸 at 1307

鴎

1361
1-4-11

▸GULL
オウ かもめ

196	Nonstandard	U9D0E
鳥	S15-11-4	F0000

traditional form → see 鷗 at 2370

曉

1362
1-4-12

▸DAWN
ギョウ あかつき ㊔ あき あけ さとし きょう さとる あきら

72	Names	U66C9
日	S16-4-12	F0000

traditional form → see 暁 at 1233

樹

1363
1-4-12

▸STANDING TREE
ジュ き^ ㊔ いつき みき たつ しげ
Ⓒ 树 shù

75	Jōyō-6	U6A39
木	S16-4-12	F0790

1	2	3	4	5	6	7	8	9	10	11	12	13	14	15	16
一	十	才	木	木	杧	杧	桔	桔	桔	桔	桔	桔	桔	樹	樹

COMPOUNDS

❶ [also suffix] [original meaning] **STANDING TREE, tree**
樹木 じゅもく tree; trees and shrubs
樹脂 じゅし resin
樹氷 じゅひょう trees covered with ice
植樹 しょくじゅ tree planting
街路樹 がいろじゅ roadside trees

❷ set up, establish
樹立 じゅりつ establishment, founding

KUN

【き 樹】[usu. 木] **STANDING TREE, tree**

SYNONYMS

❶ **tree**
木 TREE → 4261
樹 STANDING TREE → 1363

HOMOPHONES

き 木 TREE → 4261

NOTE

➡ see USAGE note at 木 4261

樫

1364
1-4-12

▸EVERGREEN OAK
かし
Ⓒ 樫 jiān

75	Names	U6A2B
木	S16-4-12	F2563

KUN

【かし 樫】**EVERGREEN OAK**
樫粉 かしこ(=かしご) oak flour, acorn flour
白樫 しらかし Chinese evergreen oak, bamboo-leaf oak

SYNONYMS

【かし】

○ **trees**
桜 CHERRY → 1168
桐 PAULOWNIA → 1173
桂 AROMATIC TREE, katsura tree → 1163
梓 CATALPA → 1207
桑 MULBERRY → 2618
漆 Japanese lacquer tree → 0863
樺 BIRCH → 1324
椛 BIRCH → 1202
梧 CHINESE PARASOL TREE → 1200
檀 SPINDLE TREE → 1385
椿 CAMELLIA → 1278
柳 WILLOW → 1115
柊 HOLLY → 1119
椋 *APHANANTHE ASPERA* → 1245
柾 spindle tree → 1114
槻 ZELKOVA → 1349
楢 OAK → 1287
樫 EVERGREEN OAK → 1364
柏 CYPRESS, JAPANESE EMPEROR OAK → 1110
榎 HACKBERRY → 1323
梶 PAPER MULBERRY → 1199
柘 JAPANESE BOXWOOD → 1117
楊 WILLOW → 1286
桧 JAPANESE CYPRESS → 1160
梛 *NAGEIA NAGI* → 1206

榊 SACRED SHINTO TREE → 1327
楓 MAPLE → 1280
松 PINE → 1075
杉 CRYPTOMERIA → 1027
槙 PODOCARPUS → 1330
楠 CAMPHOR TREE → 1283
樟 CAMPHOR TREE → 1351

機

▸MACHINE
▸AIRCRAFT
▸OPPORTUNITY

キ はた

1365

1-4-12

Ⓒ 机 jī

75	Jōyō-4	U6A5F
木	S16-4-12	F0136

一 十 才 木 木 朩 朩 朩 朩 朩 朩 朩 朩 朩 機 機
1 2 3 4 5 6 7 8 9 10 11 12 13 14 15 16

COMPOUNDS

❶ⓐ [also suffix] **MACHINE, machinery, apparatus**
ⓑ counter for heavy **MACHINE**ry
ⓒ [also suffix] (electronic device for processing data) **MACHINE**, computer

a 機械 きかい machine, mechanism
機器 きき machinery and tools, apparatus
機構 きこう mechanism, structure; system, organization; frame, framework
機関 きかん engine, machine; agency, facilities, institution
機動性 きどうせい mobility, maneuverability
機動隊 きどうたい riot police
電機 でんき electrical machinery and appliances
洗濯機 せんたくき washing machine
電算機 でんさんき electronic computer
原動機 げんどうき motor, prime mover
b 発電機三機 はつでんきさんき three dynamos
８ビット機 はちびっとき 8-bit machine
ＩＢＭ互換機 あいびーえむごかんき IBM compatible computer

❷ [original meaning] loom
機業 きぎょう textile industry
織機 しょっき loom

❸ⓐ [also suffix] **AIRCRAFT, airplane**
ⓑ counter for **AIRCRAFT** or airplanes

a 機種 きしゅ type of airplane [machine], model
機首 きしゅ nose (of an airplane)
機体 きたい fuselage, body (of an airplane); machine
機長 きちょう plane captain
日航機 にっこうき JAL airplane
ジェット機 じぇっとき jet airplane
b 五機 ごき five airplanes

❹ **OPPORTUNITY, occasion, chance, time, crucial point**
機会 きかい opportunity, occasion
機運 きうん opportunity, chance
時機 じき opportunity, chance
好機 こうき favorable opportunity, good chance
契機 けいき opportunity, chance; *philosophy* moment
危機 きき crisis, emergency
転機 てんき turning point
待機する たいきする wait for an opportunity, stand ready
投機 とうき speculation, venture

❺ⓐ **function (as of the mind), action**
ⓑ **wit, keen perception**

a 機能 きのう function, faculty
動機 どうき motive, incentive
b 機敏な きびんな smart, shrewd, quick-witted; quick, prompt
機智 きち wit, resources, tact
機転 きてん tact, ready wit

❻ important part, crucial point
枢機 すうき most important affairs (of state)

❼ **organic, organic matter**
有機物 ゆうきぶつ organic matter
無機化学 むきかがく inorganic chemistry

❽ something kept secret or difficult to fathom
機密 きみつ secrecy, secret

❾ [formerly 譏 2069] **slander, censure, criticize**
機嫌 きげん mood, temper, disposition; health

INDEPENDENT

【き 機】**OPPORTUNITY**, chance, occasion; aircraft, airplane
機を逸する きをいっする miss an opportunity [chance]
機に乗じる きにじょうじる take advantage of an opportunity
他の機 ほかのき another airplane

KUN

【はた 機】**loom**
機織り はたおり weaving; weaver; grasshopper
機屋 はたや weaver
手機 てばた handloom

SYNONYMS

❶ **machines and tools**
機 MACHINE → 1365
械 MECHANICAL CONTRIVANCE → 1203
具 IMPLEMENT → 3159
器 INSTRUMENT → 3367

儀 measuring instrument →0191
鏡 OPTICAL INSTRUMENT →2219
董 OLD TOOL →2911

❸ⓐ **aircraft and spacecraft**

機 AIRCRAFT →1365
空 aircraft →2767
船 spaceship →1700

❹ **occasions**

際 OCCASION →0874
折 occasion →0297
時 timely occasion →1155
機 OPPORTUNITY →1365
節 time →3336

❺ⓐ **potency**

効 EFFECT →1617
験 efficacy →2306
能 action →1676
機 function →1365

COMPOUND FORMATION

❶【機動性　きどうせい】

機動性 'mobility, maneuverability' originally referred to the capacity (性) of a machine (機 ❶ⓐ) in action (動)

❷【機嫌　きげん】

機嫌 'mood, etc.' was formerly written 譏嫌, meaning slander (譏 or 機 ❾) and dislike (嫌).

橘

1366

◧1-4-12

▶**MANDARIN**

キツ　たちばな ㊔ きち

Ⓒ 橘 jú 桔 jú jié

75	Names	U6A58
木	S16-4-12	F2313

COMPOUNDS

● **MANDARIN orange, tangerine; citrus fruit; mandarin tree**

柑橘類 かんきつるい citrus fruits, oranges

KUN

【たちばな　橘】**MANDARIN tree; kind of mandarin orange**

SYNONYMS

● **fruits and fruit trees**

桃 PEACH →1174
榛 HAZEL →1328
椎 CHINQUAPIN →1249
柚 YUZU →1123
椰 COCONUT →1285
柑 CITRUS →1112
橙 BITTER ORANGE →1369
葡 GRAPE →2902
萄 GRAPE →2870
柿 PERSIMMON →1118
檎 APPLE →1386
李 PLUM →3050
枇 LOQUAT →1063
杷 LOQUAT →1065
苺 STRAWBERRY →2780
菱 water chestnut →2879
杏 APRICOT →3049
梅 JAPANESE APRICOT →1159
橘 MANDARIN →1366
栗 CHESTNUT →3280
栃 JAPANESE HORSE CHESTNUT →1122
梨 PEAR →3412
蕉 PLANTAIN →2994

橋

1367

◧1-4-12

▶**BRIDGE**

キョウ　はし

Ⓝ 橋 Ⓒ 桥 qiáo

75	Jōyō-3	U6A4B
木	S16-4-12	F0497

1	2	3	4	5	6	7	8	9	10	11	12	13	14	15	16
一	十	才	木	木	木	杧	杧	杧	桥	桥	桥	橋	橋	橋	橋

COMPOUNDS

ⓐ [also suffix] [original meaning] **BRIDGE**

ⓑ *anat* pons

a 橋梁 きょうりょう bridge
橋脚 きょうきゃく bridge pier
架橋 かきょう bridge building
鉄橋 てっきょう iron bridge
歩道橋 ほどうきょう pedestrian bridge

b 脳橋 のうきょう pons

INDEPENDENT

【きょう　橋】*anat* pons

KUN

【はし　橋】[also suffix] **BRIDGE**

橋渡し はしわたし mediation, good offices
釣り橋 つりばし suspension bridge
丸木橋 まるきばし log bridge
吉野川橋 よしのがわばし Yoshinogawa Bridge

SYNONYMS

ⓐ **bridges**

橋 BRIDGE →1367
桟 PLANK BRIDGE →1169

USAGE

【はし】

橋
[also suffix] bridge

梯
[in compounds] ladder

端
①end, extremity, tip
②edge, margin, brink, border; side
③beginning
④unwanted piece, scrap, fragment

箸
chopsticks

HOMOPHONES

はし
端 END →1564
箸 CHOPSTICKS →3359
梯 LADDER →1210

樽
▶BARREL
ソン たる
Ⓝ 樽 Ⓒ 樽 zūn
1368
1-4-12

75	Names	U6A3D
木	S16-4-12	F1873

COMPOUNDS

● **BARREL, cask, keg**
樽俎× そんそ party (with food and drink)
樽酒 そんしゅ(=たるざけ) barreled sake

KUN

【たる 樽】**BARREL, cask, keg**
酒樽 さかだる wine [sake] cask [barrel]
角樽 つのだる two-handled keg

SYNONYMS

● **containers**
箱 BOX →3362
壺 JAR →2890
槽 TANK →1352
樽 BARREL →1368
棺 COFFIN →1240
桶 BUCKET →1211
笈 BOX CARRIED ON THE BACK →3274
鞘 SHEATH →2259
箪 BAMBOO BOX →3381
函 BOX →3724
籠 BASKET →3398
袋 BAG →3201
鞄 BAG (for carrying) →2248
器 VESSEL →3367
瓶 BOTTLE →1702
缶 CAN →2526
缶 EARTHENWARE JAR →2525

橙
▶BITTER ORANGE
トウ だいだい ㊔ と
Ⓒ 橙 chéng
1369
1-4-12

75	Names	U6A59
木	S16-4-12	F3400

COMPOUNDS

● **BITTER ORANGE, *Citrus aurantium***
橙皮油 とうひゆ orange-peel oil

KUN

【だいだい 橙】**BITTER ORANGE, *Citrus aurantium***
橙色 だいだいいろ orange (color)

SYNONYMS

● **fruits and fruit trees**
桃 PEACH →1174
榛 HAZEL →1328
椎 CHINQUAPIN →1249
柚 YUZU →1123
椰 COCONUT →1285
柑 CITRUS →1112
橙 BITTER ORANGE →1369
葡 GRAPE →2902
萄 GRAPE →2870
柿 PERSIMMON →1118
檎 APPLE →1386
李 PLUM →3050
枇 LOQUAT →1063
杷 LOQUAT →1065
苺 STRAWBERRY →2780
菱 water chestnut →2879
杏 APRICOT →3049
梅 JAPANESE APRICOT →1159
橘 MANDARIN →1366
栗 CHESTNUT →3280
栃 JAPANESE HORSE CHESTNUT →1122
梨 PEAR →3412
蕉 PLANTAIN →2994

橢
▶ELLIPSE
ダ
1370
1-4-12

75	Nonstandard	U6A62
木	S16-4-12	F0000

traditional form →see 楕 at 1279

槪
▶GENERAL
ガイ おおむ(ね)
1371
1-4-12

75	Nonstandard	U69EA
木	S16-4-12	F0000

traditional form →see 概 at 1322

横
1372
◧ 1-4-12

▶**SIDEWAYS**
オウ よこ

75	Names	U6A6B
木	S16-4-12	F0000

traditional form → see 横 at 1350

樽
1373
◧ 1-4-12

▶**BARREL**
ソン たる

75	Nonstandard	U6A3D
木	S16-4-12	F0000

traditional form → see 樽 at 1368

櫔
1374
◧ 1-4-12

▶**JAPANESE HORSE CHESTNUT**
とち とちのき

75	Nonstandard	U2371C
木	S16-4-12	F0000

traditional form → see 栃 at 1122

檎
◧ 1-4-12

incorrect stroke-count
➡ see ◧ 1-4-13: 木 at 1386

燃
1375
◧ 1-4-12

▶**BURN**
ネン も(える) も(やす) も(す)
Ⓒ 燃 rán

86	Jōyō-5	U71C3
火	S16-4-12	F1116

COMPOUNDS

● **BURN, undergo combustion**
燃焼 ねんしょう combustion, burning
燃料 ねんりょう fuel
燃費 ねんぴ mileage
可燃性 かねんせい combustibility
内燃機関 ないねんきかん internal combustion engine
再燃する さいねんする revive, come to the fore again

KUN

【もえる 燃える】*vi*
ⓐ **BURN, undergo combustion, blaze**
ⓑ **BURN** with emotion
a 燃え尽きる もえつきる burn out [away], be burned up
燃え付く もえつく catch fire

【もやす 燃やす】*vt* **BURN**
闘志を燃やす とうしをもやす burn with combativeness

【もす 燃す】colloquial equiv. of 燃やす もやす

SYNONYMS

● **burn**
焼 BURN → 1256
燃 BURN (undergo combustion) → 1375
焚く BURN (build a fire) → 3450
焦 SCORCH → 3444
灼 SCORCH → 1036
炮 ROAST → 1132
燎 SET ON FIRE → 1376

USAGE

【もえる】
燃える
vi
ⓐ burn, undergo combustion, blaze
ⓑ burn with emotion
萌える
sprout, bud, burst into bud

HOMOPHONES

もえる 萌 GERMINATE → 2871

燎
1376
◧ 1-4-12

▶**SET ON FIRE**
リョウ ㊔ あきら
Ⓒ 燎 liáo liǎo

86	Names	U71CE
火	S16-4-12	F0000

COMPOUNDS

❶ **SET ON FIRE, burn**
燎原の火 りょうげんのひ prairie fire, wild fire; fast-spreading disaster [rumor]

❷ **bonfire**
燎火 りょうか bonfire

SYNONYMS

❶ **burn**
焼 BURN → 1256
燃 BURN (undergo combustion) → 1375
焚く BURN (build a fire) → 3450
焦 SCORCH → 3444
灼 SCORCH → 1036
炮 ROAST → 1132
燎 SET ON FIRE → 1376

燒
1377
◧ 1-4-12

▶**BURN**
ショウ や(く) や(き) や(き)- -や(き) や(ける)

86	Names	U71D2
火	S16-4-12	F0000

traditional form → see 焼 at 1256

燈 1378

▶LAMP

トウ ひ ほ- ともしび とも(す) ㊔ あかり

86	Names	U71C8
火	S16-4-12	F0000

1-4-12

traditional form → see 灯 at 1019

瑠 1379

▶LAPIS LAZULI

ル リュウ

96	Nonstandard	U74A2
王	S16-4-12	F0000

1-4-12

alternative form → see 瑠 at 1342

膨 1380

▶EXPAND

ボウ ふく(らむ) ふく(れる)

Ⓒ 膨 péng

130	Jōyō	U81A8
月	S16-4-12	F1457

1-4-12

COMPOUNDS

❶ [original meaning] **EXPAND, swell, bulge, inflate**

膨大 ぼうだい swelling, expansion

膨脹(=膨張) ぼうちょう expansion, swelling; growth, increase

膨隆する ぼうりゅうする swell up

膨満する ぼうまんする be inflated

❷ [formerly 厖 3725] bulky, extensive

膨大な ぼうだいな bulky, massive, extensive

KUN

【ふくらむ 膨らむ】[sometimes also 脹らむ] **EXPAND, swell (out), get big, become inflated**

膨らみ ふくらみ swelling, bulge, puff

膨らます ふくらます cause to bulge, expand, dilate; raise

膨らし粉 ふくらしこ baking powder

【ふくれる 膨れる】[sometimes also 脹れる]

① **EXPAND, swell (out), get big, become inflated**

青膨れ あおぶくれ dropsical swelling

着膨れる きぶくれる be thickly clad

② **get sulky, sulk, fret, get peevish**

膨れっ面 ふくれっつら sulky look [face], sullen look

SYNONYMS

❶ **expand**

脹 SWELL → 1265

膨 EXPAND → 1380

張 SPREAD → 0573

氾 SPREAD OUT → 0226

広げる spread (out) → 3769

拡 ENLARGE → 0366

伸 STRETCH → 0079

延 EXTEND → 3812

USAGE

❶【ふくらむ】

膨らむ

[sometimes also 脹らむ] expand, swell (out), get big, become inflated

脹らむ

[usu. 膨らむ] same as 膨らむ

❷【ふくれる】

膨れる

[sometimes also 脹れる]

① expand, swell (out), get big, become inflated

② get sulky, sulk, fret, get peevish

脹れる

[usu. 膨れる] same as 膨れる

HOMOPHONES

ふくらむ 脹 SWELL → 1265

ふくれる 脹 SWELL → 1265

膳 1381

▶LEGGED TRAY

▶MEAL

ゼン セン▲ かしわで▲ ㊔ よし

Ⓒ 膳 shàn

130	Jōyō	U81B3
月	S16-4-12	F1533

1-4-12

COMPOUNDS

❶ **LEGGED TRAY, low table**

お膳立て おぜんだて setting the table; preparation

配膳 はいぜん setting the table; serving a meal

食膳 しょくぜん dining tray, food on a tray

会席膳 かいせきぜん elaborate legless dinner tray; legless tray for formal dinners

❷ **MEAL, meal served on a tray, cooked food**

据え膳 すえぜん meal set before one; women's advances

❸ **counter for bowls of rice, counter for pairs of chopsticks**

一膳 いちぜん a bowl (of rice); a pair (of chopsticks)

INDEPENDENT

【ぜん 膳】**LEGGED TRAY**; meal

一の膳 いちのぜん first course at a banquet

KUN

【かしわで 膳】[also 膳夫] [archaic] cooks for the imperial court in ancient Japan; serving of **MEAL**s on trays

SPECIAL READINGS

膳夫▲ かしわで [also 膳] [archaic] cooks for the imperial court in ancient Japan; serving of meals on trays

SYNONYMS

❶ vessels and receptacles
- 盤 dish → 3533
- 鍋 POT → 2202
- 釜 IRON POT → 2610
- 鼎 TRIPOD CAULDRON → 4405
- 臼 MORTAR → 4341
- 碓 MORTAR → 1537
- 托 RECEPTACLE → 0252
- 皿 PLATE → 4286
- 盆 TRAY → 2581
- 膳 LEGGED TRAY → 1381
- 杯 CUP → 1066
- 鉢 BOWL → 2144
- 椀 WOODEN BOWL → 1250
- 碗 CERAMIC BOWL → 1539
- 丼 LARGE BOWL → 4323

❷ food
- 飯 MEAL → 2126
- 膳 MEAL → 1381
- 食 FOOD, meal → 2578
- 糧 FOOD PROVISIONS → 1800
- 餌 ANIMAL FEED → 2257
- 肴 ACCOMPANIMENT FOR DRINKS → 2567

HOMOPHONES

かしわで 膳夫 → 1381, 4271

膸

◧1-4-12

incorrect stroke-count
➡ see ◧1-4-13: 月 at 1400

豫

1382
◧1-4-12

▶IN ADVANCE
ヨ あらかじ(め) かね(て) ㊔ やすし

152	Nonstandard	U8C6B
豕	S16-7-9	F0000

traditional form → see 予 at 2477

曖

1383
◧1-4-13

▶SHADY
アイ
Ⓒ 暧 ài

72	Jōyō	U66D6
日	S17-4-13	F2094

COMPOUNDS

● SHADY, indistinct, unclear

曖昧 あいまい vague, unclear, ambiguous, fuzzy

SYNONYMS

● dark
- 暗 DARK → 1273
- 黒 BLACK → 3406
- 陰 shaded → 0657
- 闇 DARK → 4134
- 晦 DARK → 1196
- 昏 dark → 3073
- 昧 DARK → 1105
- 冥 DARK → 2613
- 曖 SHADY → 1383

曙

1384
◧1-4-13

▶DAWN
ショ ジョ あけぼの ㊔ あけ あきら
Ⓝ 曙 Ⓒ 曙 shǔ

72	Names	U66D9
日	S17-4-13	F3473

COMPOUNDS

● DAWN, daybreak

曙光 しょこう first streak of daylight, dawn

KUN

【あけぼの 曙】

① *elegant* **DAWN, daybreak**

曙色 あけぼのいろ yellowish pink

② **beginning, sign (of something new [good])**

時代の曙 じだいのあけぼの dawn of a new era

SYNONYMS

● morning and dawn
- 朝 MORNING → 2130
- 暁 DAWN → 1233
- 旦 DAYBREAK → 3041
- 曙 DAWN → 1384
- 晨 EARLY MORNING → 3110

檀

1385
◧1-4-13

▶SPINDLE TREE
ダン タン まゆみ
Ⓒ 檀 tán

75	Names	U6A80
木	S17-4-13	F2512

COMPOUNDS

❶ SPINDLE TREE, *Euonymus Sieboldiana*

檀紙 だんし spindle-tree paper

❷ sandalwood

白檀 びゃくだん sandalwood, *Santalum album*

❸ used phonetically for *dan* in the transliteration of Sanskrit Buddhist terms

檀家 だんか family which supports a Buddhist temple, parishioner
檀那(=旦那) だんな master, husband, patron, protector; sir; [original meaning] donor
檀那寺 だんなでら one's family temples, parish temple

KUN

【まゆみ 檀】[also 真弓] **SPINDLE TREE, *Euronymus Sieboldiana***

SYNONYMS

❶ & ❷ trees
桜 CHERRY → 1168
桐 PAULOWNIA → 1173
桂 AROMATIC TREE, katsura tree → 1163
梓 CATALPA → 1207
桑 MULBERRY → 2618
漆 Japanese lacquer tree → 0863
樺 BIRCH → 1324
椛 BIRCH → 1202
梧 CHINESE PARASOL TREE → 1200
檀 SPINDLE TREE → 1385
椿 CAMELLIA → 1278
柳 WILLOW → 1115
柊 HOLLY → 1119
椋 *APHANANTHE ASPERA* → 1245
柾 spindle tree → 1114
槻 ZELKOVA → 1349
楢 OAK → 1287
樫 EVERGREEN OAK → 1364
柏 CYPRESS, JAPANESE EMPEROR OAK → 1110
榎 HACKBERRY → 1323
梶 PAPER MULBERRY → 1199
柘 JAPANESE BOXWOOD → 1117
楊 WILLOW → 1286
桧 JAPANESE CYPRESS → 1160
梛 *NAGEIA NAGI* → 1206
榊 SACRED SHINTO TREE → 1327
楓 MAPLE → 1280
松 PINE → 1075
杉 CRYPTOMERIA → 1027
槙 PODOCARPUS → 1330
楠 CAMPHOR TREE → 1283
樟 CAMPHOR TREE → 1351

HOMOPHONES

まゆみ 真弓 → 2616, 4193

檎 1386

▸APPLE
ゴ
Ⓒ 檎 qín

◧1-4-13

75	Names	U6A8E
木	S17-4-13	F2921

COMPOUNDS

● APPLE
林檎 りんご apple
林檎病 りんごびょう fifth disease, *Erythema infectiosum*

SYNONYMS

● fruits and fruit trees
桃 PEACH → 1174
榛 HAZEL → 1328
椎 CHINQUAPIN → 1249
柚 YUZU → 1123
椰 COCONUT → 1285
柑 CITRUS → 1112
橙 BITTER ORANGE → 1369
葡 GRAPE → 2902
萄 GRAPE → 2870
柿 PERSIMMON → 1118
檎 APPLE → 1386
李 PLUM → 3050
枇 LOQUAT → 1063
杷 LOQUAT → 1065
苺 STRAWBERRY → 2780
菱 water chestnut → 2879
杏 APRICOT → 3049
梅 JAPANESE APRICOT → 1159
橘 MANDARIN → 1366
栗 CHESTNUT → 3280
栃 JAPANESE HORSE CHESTNUT → 1122
梨 PEAR → 3412
蕉 PLANTAIN → 2994

檜 1387

▸JAPANESE CYPRESS
カイ ひのき ひ

75	Names	U6A9C
木	S17-4-13	F0000

◧1-4-13 traditional form → see 桧 at 1160

檢 1388

▸EXAMINE
ケン

75	Names	U6AA2
木	S17-4-13	F0000

◧1-4-13 traditional form → see 検 at 1241

櫛 1389

▸COMB
シツ くし ㊔ きよ

75	Nonstandard	U6ADB
木	S17-4-13	F0000

◧1-4-13 traditional form → see 櫛 at 1413

構

◧ 1-4-13

incorrect stroke-count
➡ see ◧ 1-4-12: 木 at 1374

燦

1390

◧ 1-4-13

▶BRILLIANT

サン ㊔ あきら

Ⓒ 灿 càn

86	Names	U71E6
火	S17-4-13	F2986

COMPOUNDS

● **BRILLIANT, bright, glittering, shining**

燦然たる さんぜんたる brilliant, glorious
燦燦と降り注ぐ さんさんとふりそそぐ (of the sun) shine brilliantly

INDEPENDENT

【さんたる 燦たる】**BRILLIANT**, resplendent

SYNONYMS

● **bright**

明 BRIGHT → 1060
昭 LUMINOUS → 1107
蛍 fluorescent → 3204
晃 DAZZLING → 3101
燦 BRILLIANT → 1390
赫 BLAZING → 1960
暉 radiant → 1276
熙 BRIGHT → 3559
晟 SUNNY → 3104

燭

1391

◧ 1-4-13

▶CANDLE

ショク ソク ともしび

Ⓒ 烛 zhú

86	Names	U71ED
火	S17-4-13	F2114

COMPOUNDS

ⓐ **CANDLE**
ⓑ **lamp, light, lantern, flame**

a 燭台 しょくだい candlestick, candlestand
燭光 しょっこう candlepower
手燭 しゅしょく(=てしょく) portable candlestick
国際燭 こくさいしょく international candlepower
メートル燭 めーとるしょく meter candle
b 蠟燭 ろうそく candle
華燭 かしょく bright light

INDEPENDENT

【しょく 燭】light, lamp, flame; **CANDLE**power

KUN

【ともしび 燭】[usu. 灯 or 灯火] light, lamp, flame

SYNONYMS

● **light**

光 LIGHT → 3043
明 light → 1060
灯 LAMP → 1019
燭 CANDLE → 1391
照 sunlight → 3506
虹 RAINBOW → 1637

HOMOPHONES

ともしび

灯 LAMP → 1019
灯火 → 1019, 4273

NOTE

➡ see USAGE note at 灯 1019

燥

1392

◧ 1-4-13

▶DRY UP

ソウ

Ⓒ 燥 zào

86	Jōyō	U71E5
火	S17-4-13	F2069

COMPOUNDS

❶ [original meaning] (become very dry, esp. by the action of heat) **DRY UP, parch, desiccate**

乾燥する かんそうする dry up, desiccate, become parched [dry]
枯燥する こそうする dry up, parch
高燥地 こうそうち high and dry ground
無味乾燥な むみかんそうな dry as dust, insipid

❷ [formerly 躁 2083] restless, impatient, rash, impetuous

焦燥 しょうそう fretfulness, impatience

SYNONYMS

❶ **dry**

乾 DRY → 2113
干 DRY → 4187
燥 DRY UP (desiccate) → 1392
涸 DRY UP (run dry) → 0629
渇 RUN DRY → 0627
旱 DROUGHT → 3048

❷ **impatient**

焦 BE IMPATIENT → 3444
躁 RESTLESS → 2083
燥 restless → 1392

牆

1393

◧ 1-4-13

▶FENCE

ショウ かき

Ⓒ 墙 qiáng

90	Non-Jōyō	U7246
爿	S17-4-13	F0000

日 木 火 爿 【牛】 王 月 月

COMPOUNDS

● [now replaced by 障 0875] [original meaning] **FENCE, wall**

牆壁 しょうへき fence, wall; barrier

KUN

【かき 牆】 [now replaced by 垣] [also suffix] **FENCE, wall**

SYNONYMS

● **fences and walls**

壁 WALL → 3601
塀 FENCE (for screening) → 0677
垣 FENCE (for partitioning) → 0416
牆 FENCE (for partitioning) → 1393
柵 FENCE (with spaced pickets) → 1116
堵 FENCE (made of earth) → 0682
囲い enclosure → 3807
欄 railing → 1419

HOMOPHONES

かき 垣 FENCE → 0416

NOTE

➡ see USAGE note at 垣 0416

犠

▶**SACRIFICE**

ギ

Ⓝ 犧 Ⓒ 牺 xī

1394

1-4-13

93	Jōyō	U72A0
牛	S17-4-13	F1708

(stroke order 1–17)

COMPOUNDS

❶ⓐ **SACRIFICE**

ⓑ *baseball* **SACRIFICE**

a 犠牲 ぎせい sacrifice

b 犠打 ぎだ sacrifice, sacrifice batting

犠飛 ぎひ sacrifice fly

❷ [original meaning, now archaic] (sacrificial animal offered to a deity) **SACRIFICE**

犠牛 ぎぎゅう sacrificial bullock

供犠 くぎ(=きょうぎ) sacrificial animal, sacrifice

SYNONYMS

❶ **sacrifice**

犠 SACRIFICE → 1394
牲 SACRIFICE → 1133

環

▶**RING**
▶**SURROUND**

カン わ▲ ㊔ たまき たま

Ⓝ 環 Ⓒ 环 huán

1395

1-4-13

96	Jōyō	U74B0
王	S17-4-13	F0713

(stroke order 1–17)

COMPOUNDS

❶ⓐ **RING, circle, loop**

ⓑ *chem* **RING**, cycle

ⓒ cycle

a 環状の かんじょうの ring-shaped, circular

環状線 かんじょうせん belt line

環指 かんし ring finger

環礁 かんしょう atoll

一環 いっかん link; part

金環食 きんかんしょく annular eclipse

b 環化 かんか cyclization

ベンゼン環 べんぜんかん benzene ring

c 生活環 せいかつかん life cycle

❷ **SURROUND, encircle; around**

環境 かんきょう environment, surroundings, circumstances

環海 かんかい surrounding seas

循環 じゅんかん circulation, rotation; cycle

❸ abbrev. of 環状線 かんじょうせん: belt line

環七 かんなな Loop 7 (name of a Tokyo road)

INDEPENDENT

【かん 環】 *chem* **RING**; cycle

KUN

【わ 環】 [usu. 輪] **RING**, circle, link

指環 ゆびわ (finger) ring

SYNONYMS

❶ⓐ **circular objects**

環 RING → 1395
輪 WHEEL, RING → 1999
車 WHEEL → 4367
盤 DISK → 3533
釧 ARMLET → 2109

❷ **surround**

囲む ENCLOSE → 3807
環 SURROUND → 1395
包 ENCOMPASS → 3684

HOMOPHONES

わ 輪 WHEEL → 1999

NOTE

➡ see USAGE note at 輪 1999

環

1396

1-4-13

▶RING
▶SURROUND

カン わ ㊔ たまき たま

96	Nonstandard	U74B0
王	S17-4-13	F0000

traditional form → see 環 at 1395

臆

1397

1-4-13

▶FEEL TIMID

オク

Ⓒ 臆 yì

130	Jōyō	U81C6
月	S17-4-13	F2209

COMPOUNDS

❶ [sometimes also 憶 0944] **FEEL TIMID, fear**

臆病 おくびょう cowardice, timidity

臆面もなく おくめんもなく audaciously, impudently, unabashedly

❷ⓐ [now usu. 憶 0944] (engage in conjectural thought) **speculate, conjecture, guess, infer**

ⓑ [original meaning] thoughts, feelings

a 臆説 おくせつ hypothesis, speculation

臆測 おくそく conjecture, speculation, guess

臆断 おくだん jumping to hasty conclusions

b 胸臆 きょうおく one's inmost thoughts [feelings]

INDEPENDENT

【おくする 臆する】**fear, FEEL TIMID**

SYNONYMS

❶ **fear**

怖 FEARFUL → 0353

凄 UNCANNY → 0145

恐 FEAR → 3283

惧 FEAR → 0581

慄 TREMBLE WITH FEAR → 0791

兢 BE IN FEAR → 1971

惶 BE AFRAID → 0708

畏 BE OVERAWED → 3170

臆 FEEL TIMID → 1397

怯える BE FRIGHTENED → 0355

謄

1398

1-4-13

▶TRANSCRIBE

トウ

Ⓝ 謄 Ⓒ 誊 téng

149	Jōyō	U8B04
言	S17-7-10	F3500

COMPOUNDS

❶ [original meaning] (make an exact copy of an original text) **TRANSCRIBE, copy, duplicate (a document)**

謄本 とうほん certified copy, transcript; copy of the domiciliary register

謄写 とうしゃ copy, reproduction, mimeograph

謄写版 とうしゃばん mimeograph

SYNONYMS

❶ **copy**

写 COPY → 2493

謄 TRANSCRIBE → 1398

複 duplicate → 1565

拓 copy by rubbing → 0375

NOTE

★ do not confuse with 騰 RISE → 1422

膽

1399

1-4-13

▶GALLBLADDER

タン

130	Nonstandard	U81BD
月	S17-4-13	F0000

traditional form → see 胆 at 1150

髓

1400

1-4-13

▶MARROW

ズイ

130	Nonstandard	U81B8
月	S17-4-13	F0000

traditional form → see 髄 at 2316

謄

1401

1-4-13

▶TRANSCRIBE

トウ

149	Nonstandard	U8B04
言	S17-7-10	F0000

traditional form → see 謄 at 1398

曜

1402

1-4-14

▶DAY OF THE WEEK

ヨウ ㊔ てる

Ⓝ 曜 旺◆ Ⓒ 曜 yào

72	Jōyō-2	U66DC
日	S18-4-14	F1004

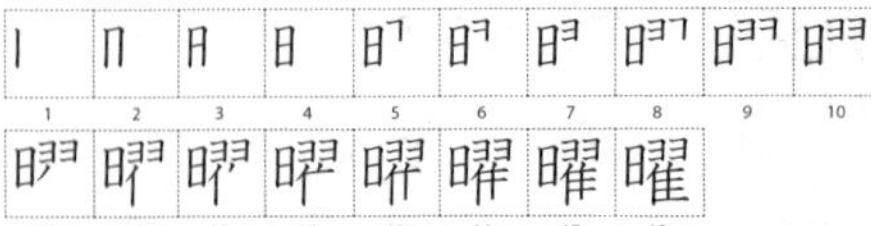

COMPOUNDS

❶ DAY OF THE WEEK, **-day**
曜日 ようび day of the week
七曜 しちよう seven days of the week; [archaic] sun, moon and five planets
日曜日 にちようび Sunday
木曜日 もくようび Thursday
水曜日 すいようび Wednesday
七曜表 しちようひょう calendar

❷ⓐ [original meaning] luminous, bright
ⓑ [archaic] luminous heavenly body
a 黒曜石 こくようせき obsidian, volcanic glass
b 曜霊 ようれい literary term for the sun

SYNONYMS

❶ **days**
日 DAY → 3759
曜 DAY OF THE WEEK → 1402
昼 DAYTIME → 3841
旦 first day → 3041
朔 FIRST DAY OF THE LUNAR MONTH → 1678
晦 LAST DAY OF THE LUNAR MONTH → 1196

曙

▶**DAWN**
ショ ジョ **あけぼの** ㊔ あけ あきら

1403
1-4-14

72	Nonstandard	U66D9
日	S18-4-14	F0000

traditional form → see 曙 at 1384

曜

▶**DAY OF THE WEEK**
ヨウ ㊔ てる

1404
1-4-14

72	Nonstandard	U66DC
日	S18-4-14	F0000

traditional form → see 曜 at 1402

曠

incorrect stroke-count
➡ see 1-4-15: 日 at 1411

1-4-14

櫂

▶**OAR**
トウ **かい**
Ⓒ 棹 zhào

1405
1-4-14

75	Names	U6AC2
木	S18-4-14	F3354

COMPOUNDS

● OAR, paddle
櫂歌(=棹×歌) とうか boat song, barcarole

KUN

【かい 櫂】 **OAR, paddle**
櫓櫂(=艪×櫂) ろかい sculls and paddles

SYNONYMS

● **parts of boats and ships**
舵 STEERING DEVICE → 1697
梶 steering device → 1199
櫓 SCULL → 1412
櫂 OAR → 1405
舷 GUNWALE → 1698
艙 SHIP'S HOLD → 1786

燻

▶**SMOKE**
クン いぶ(す) いぶ(る) くす(ぶる) くゆ(らす)
Ⓒ 熏 xūn xùn

1406
1-4-14

86	Non-Jōyō	U71FB
火	S18-4-14	F2985

COMPOUNDS

● [now also 薫 3005] [original meaning] **SMOKE, fumigate, fume**
燻製 くんせい smoking (fish or meat)
燻蒸する くんじょうする fumigate, smoke

KUN

【いぶす 燻す】 **SMOKE, fumigate, fume**
燻し いぶし fumigation; oxidization (of metal)
【いぶる 燻る】 **SMOKE, smolder**
燻り出す いぶりだす smoke (an animal) out (of its den)
【くすぶる 燻ぶる】 **SMOKE, smolder**
【くゆらす 燻らす】 **SMOKE [puff] (a cigar [cigarette]), burn (incense), cause to emit light smoke**

SYNONYMS

● **preserve food**
漬ける PICKLE → 0861
燻 SMOKE → 1406
薫 smoke → 3005

燿

▶**SHINE**
ヨウ シャク ㊔ てる あきら
Ⓝ 燿 Ⓒ 耀 yào

1407
1-4-14

86	Names	U71FF
火	S18-4-14	F3078

COMPOUNDS

● [original meaning, now rare] **SHINE**, illuminate
燿燿 ようよう shining brightly

SYNONYMS

● **shine and reflect**
輝 SHINE BRILLIANTLY → 1775

光 shine → 3043
照 ILLUMINATE → 3506
映 REFLECT → 1104
耀 SHINE BRILLIANTLY → 1812
燿 SHINE → 1407
閃 FLASH → 4114
煌 GLITTER → 1296

NOTE

★ do not confuse with 耀 SHINE BRILLIANTLY → 1812

燿
1408
◧ 1-4-14

▶SHINE
ヨウ シャク ㊔ てる あきら

86	Nonstandard	U71FF
火	S18-4-14	F0000

traditional form → see 燿 at 1407

禰
1409
◧ 1-4-14

▶FATHER'S MAUSOLEUM
デイ ネ ㊔ や

113	Nonstandard	U7962
ネ	S18-4-14	F0000

traditional form → see 祢 at 1142

臟
◧ 1-4-14

incorrect stroke-count
➡ see ◧ 1-4-15: 月 at 1417

曝
1410
◧ 1-4-15

▶EXPOSE
バク さら(す) さら(ける)
Ⓒ 曝 pù 暴 bào

72	Names	U66DD
日	S19-4-15	F2691

COMPOUNDS

ⓐ [original meaning] **EXPOSE to the sun**
ⓑ [now also 暴 3138] **EXPOSE; disclose, divulge**
a 曝書 ばくしょ airing of books
b 曝露 ばくろ exposure, disclosure
被曝 ひばく exposure to radiation

KUN

【さらす 曝す】[also 晒す] **EXPOSE (to view, to the elements)**
恥曝し はじさらし disgrace, shame
雨曝し あまざらし weather-beaten, exposed to the rain
吹き曝し ふきさらし windswept, exposed to the wind
【さらける 曝ける】**EXPOSE, disclose, reveal, lay bare**
曝け出す さらけだす expose, disclose, lay bare

SYNONYMS

ⓐ **reveal**
発 reveal → 3174
露 EXPOSE → 3495
曝 EXPOSE → 1410
晒す EXPOSE → 1156
暴 disclose → 3138
披 OPEN OUT → 0362
顕 MANIFEST → 2274
現 cause to appear → 1218

HOMOPHONES

さらす 晒 BLEACH → 1156

NOTE

➡ see USAGE note at 晒 1156

曠
1411
◧ 1-4-15

▶SPACIOUS
コウ
Ⓒ 旷 kuàng

72	Non-Jōyō	U66E0
日	S19-4-15	F0000

COMPOUNDS

❶ [now usu. 広 3769] [original meaning] **SPACIOUS, vast, open**
曠野 こうや vast plain, prairie
曠然とした こうぜんとした spacious, wide open
❷ unexcelled, unrivaled, unprecedented
曠古の こうこの historic, unprecedented
曠世の こうせいの unparalleled, matchless
❸ neglect
曠職 こうしょく neglect of official duty

SYNONYMS

❶ **wide and extensive**
広 WIDE → 3769
紘 WIDE-RANGING → 1650
博 EXTENSIVE → 0170
恢 EXTENSIVE → 0436
浩 VAST → 0525
洸 VAST (expanse of water) → 0462
滉 DEEP AND VAST → 0811
曠 SPACIOUS → 1411
闊 BROAD → 4135

櫓
1412
◧ 1-4-15

▶SCULL
▶WATCHTOWER
ロ やぐら
Ⓒ 橹 lǔ

75	Names	U6AD3
木	S19-4-15	F2435

COMPOUNDS

● **SCULL**
櫓櫂 ろかい sculls and paddles
櫓杭 ろぐい fulcrum peg (in a traditional oarlock)

INDEPENDENT

【ろ 櫓】**Japanese SCULL**

KUN

【やぐら 櫓】

ⓐ **WATCHTOWER, (lookout) tower, turret**

ⓑ **high wooden stage [scaffolding]**

ⓒ wooden frame (of a kotatsu)

ⓓ *archaic* weapons storehouse

a 物見櫓 ものみやぐら watchtower

火の見櫓 ひのみやぐら fire lookout [watchtower]

b 櫓太鼓 やぐらだいこ drums announcing the start of a stage performance [sumo bouts]

SYNONYMS

● **parts of boats and ships**

舵 STEERING DEVICE → 1697

梶 steering device → 1199

櫓 SCULL → 1412

櫂 OAR → 1405

舷 GUNWALE → 1698

艙 SHIP'S HOLD → 1786

櫛

1413

1-4-15

▶COMB

シツ くし ㊔ きよ

Ⓝ 櫛 櫛 Ⓒ 栉 zhì

75	Names	U6ADB
木	S19-4-15	F2677

COMPOUNDS

● **COMB**

櫛鱗 しつりん ctenoid scales

櫛比する しっぴする line up in a closely packed row

櫛風沐×雨 しっぷうもくう struggling through wind and rain, undergoing hardships

KUN

【くし 櫛】**COMB**

櫛笥× くしげ [archaic] toiletries case

解き櫛 ときぐし wide-toothed comb

SYNONYMS

● **comb**

櫛 COMB → 1413

梳 COMB → 1209

櫛

1414

1-4-15

▶COMB

シツ くし ㊔ きよ

75	Nonstandard	U6ADB
木	S19-4-15	F0000

traditional form → see 櫛 at 1413

爆

1415

1-4-15

▶EXPLODE

バク

Ⓒ 爆 bào

86	Jōyō	U7206
火	S19-4-15	F0930

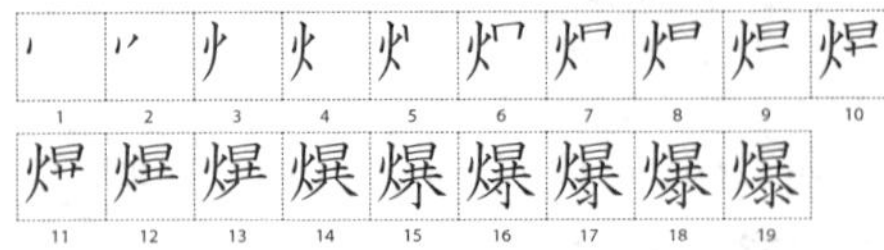

COMPOUNDS

❶ⓐ [original meaning] **EXPLODE, detonate, burst**

ⓑ bomb, raid

a 爆発 ばくはつ explosion, blast; eruption

爆弾 ばくだん bomb

爆破する ばくはする blast, blow up, explode

爆風 ばくふう (bomb or explosion) blast

爆笑する ばくしょうする roar with laughter, burst into laughter

爆撃 ばくげき bombing, bombardment

b 空爆 くうばく aerial bombing

被爆者 ひばくしゃ victim of atomic air raid

❷ abbrev. of 爆弾 ばくだん: **bomb**

原爆 げんばく atomic bomb

水爆 すいばく hydrogen bomb

SYNONYMS

❶ⓐ **explode**

爆 EXPLODE → 1415

発 discharge → 3174

ⓑ **attack**

攻 ATTACK → 0286

撃 STRIKE → 3552

襲 RAID → 3633

侵 INVADE → 0116

爆 bomb → 1415

❷ **projectiles and bombs**

弾 PROJECTILE → 0697

丸 round projectile → 4225

矢 ARROW → 2502

槍 SPEAR → 1329

爆 bomb → 1415

雷 explosive device → 3466

鵬

1416

1-4-15

▶MYTHICAL HUGE BIRD

ホウ ボウ おおとり ㊔ とも

Ⓝ 鵬 Ⓒ 鹏 péng

196	Names	U9D6C
鳥	S19-11-8	F2856

COMPOUNDS

ⓐ [original meaning] **MYTHICAL HUGE BIRD, phoenix**

ⓑ as huge or great as a Chinese mythical bird

a 大鵬 たいほう mythical huge bird; sage

KUN

【おおとり 鵬】[also 大鳥 or 鳳] **huge bird such as a mythical Chinese phoenix**

SYNONYMS

ⓐ & 【おおとり】 **mythical animals**

竜 DRAGON → 2603
辰 THE DRAGON → 3713
麒 MALE CHINESE UNICORN → 2363
麟 FEMALE CHINESE UNICORN → 2376
鵬 MYTHICAL HUGE BIRD → 1416
鳳 MALE PHOENIX → 3749
凰 FEMALE PHOENIX → 3738

ⓑ & 【おおとり】 **birds**

鷹 HAWK → 3955
鴎 GULL → 2370
烏 CROW → 4088
雀 SPARROW → 3117
燕 SWALLOW → 3142
鴻 LARGE WILD BIRD → 0977
鳳 MALE PHOENIX → 3749
凰 FEMALE PHOENIX → 3738
鵬 MYTHICAL HUGE BIRD → 1416
鶏 CHICKEN → 2221
酉 ROOSTER → 4358
隼 FALCON → 3427
鳩 PIGEON → 0184
鷲 EAGLE → 3598
鳶 BLACK KITE → 3919
鶴 CRANE → 2326
鷺 HERON → 3621
鵜 CORMORANT → 2067
鴨 DUCK → 1582
雁 WILD GOOSE → 3741

HOMOPHONES

おおとり

鳳 MALE PHOENIX → 3749
鴻 LARGE WILD BIRD → 0977
大鳥 → 4224, 4105

NOTE

➡ see USAGE note at 鳳 3749

臓

1417

◧ 1-4-15

▶INTERNAL ORGAN

ゾウ

Ⓝ 臟 Ⓒ 脏 zàng zāng

130	Jōyō-6	U81D3
月	S19-4-15	F1202

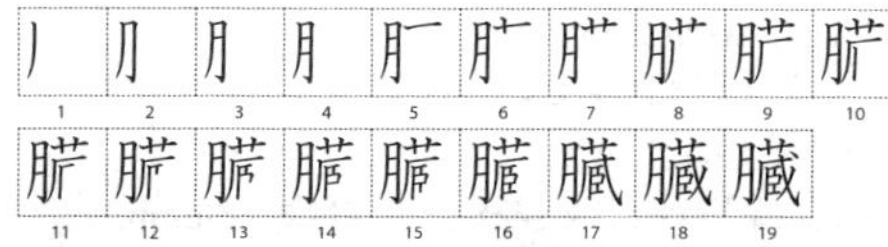

COMPOUNDS

● [original meaning] **INTERNAL ORGAN, viscus**

臓器 ぞうき internal organs, viscera
臓物 ぞうもつ entrails, giblets
内臓 ないぞう viscera, internal organs
心臓 しんぞう heart
肝臓 かんぞう liver
五臓 ごぞう the five viscera (liver, lungs, heart, kidneys and spleen)

SYNONYMS

● **organ**

臓 INTERNAL ORGAN → 1417
器 organ → 3367
官 organ → 2766

鵬

1418

◧ 1-4-15

▶MYTHICAL HUGE BIRD

ホウ ボウ おおとり ㊔ とも

196	Nonstandard	U9D6C
鳥	S19-11-8	F0000

traditional form → see 鵬 at 1416

欄

1419

◧ 1-4-16

▶COLUMN

ラン

Ⓝ 欄 Ⓒ 栏 lán

75	Jōyō	U6B04
木	S20-4-16	F1924

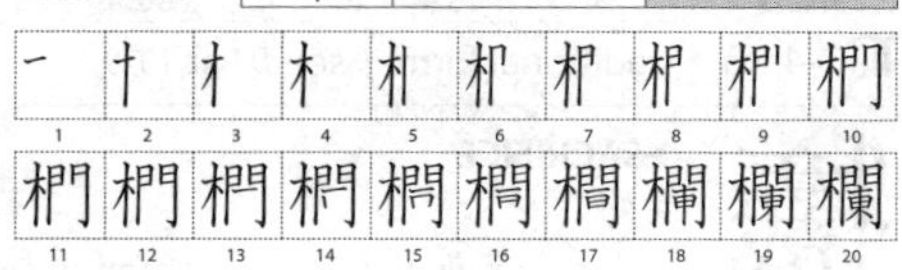

COMPOUNDS

❶ [also suffix]

ⓐ **COLUMN (as of a newspaper or periodical), section, page**

ⓑ (section of written material) **COLUMN, blank column, blank, space**

a 本欄 ほんらん this column
広告欄 こうこくらん advertisement column
スポーツ欄 すぽーつらん sports section [page]

b 欄外 らんがい margin
空欄 くうらん blank column, blank
登記番号欄 とうきばんごうらん registry number column

❷ railing, balustrade, handrail

欄干 らんかん railing, handrail, balustrade
高欄 こうらん balustrade, handrail

❸ file (of a chessboard)
　ビショップ欄 びしょっぷらん bishop file

INDEPENDENT

【らん 欄】COLUMN, section (→❶ⓐ); column, blank column (→❶ⓑ); railing, balustrade; file (of a chessboard)
　欄に記入する らんにきにゅうする fill in the blank (column)

SYNONYMS

❶ⓐ parts of periodicals
　欄 COLUMN → 1419
　面 page (of a newspaper) → 2590
ⓑ linear arrangements
　伍 RANK → 0050
　列 ROW → 1018
　行 LINE (esp. of print) → 0246
　欄 COLUMN → 1419
❷ fences and walls
　壁 WALL → 3601
　塀 FENCE (for screening) → 0677
　垣 FENCE (for partitioning) → 0416
　牆 FENCE (for partitioning) → 1393
　柵 FENCE (with spaced pickets) → 1116
　堵 FENCE (made of earth) → 0682
　囲い enclosure → 3807
　欄 railing → 1419

爐

1420

1-4-16

▶FURNACE

ロ

86	Nonstandard	U7210
火	S20-4-16	F0000

traditional form → see 炉 at 1079

犧

1421

1-4-16

▶SACRIFICE

ギ

93	Nonstandard	U72A7
牛	S20-4-16	F0000

traditional form → see 犠 at 1394

騰

1422

1-4-16

▶RISE

トウ ㊔ のぼる

Ⓝ 騰 Ⓒ 腾 téng

187	Jōyō	U9A30
馬	S20-10-10	F2080

COMPOUNDS

● [original meaning] **RISE, jump up, advance**—said esp. of prices
　騰貴 とうき rise (in prices)
　騰落 とうらく rise and fall, fluctuations
　高騰(=昂騰) こうとう steep rise (in prices), jump
　暴騰 ぼうとう sudden (price) rise
　沸騰 ふっとう boiling, seething, bubbling

SYNONYMS

● ascend
　昇 ASCEND → 3068
　上 go up → 4212
　騰 RISE (esp. in price) → 1422
　登 CLIMB → 3208

NOTE

★ do not confuse with 謄 TRANSCRIBE → 1398

騰

1423

1-4-16

▶RISE

トウ ㊔ のぼる

187	Nonstandard	U9A30
馬	S20-10-10	F0000

traditional form → see 騰 at 1422

權

1424

1-4-17

▶RIGHT
▶POWER

ケン ゴン

75	Nonstandard	U6B0A
木	S21-4-17	F0000

traditional form → see 権 at 1348

櫻

1425

1-4-17

▶CHERRY

オウ さくら

75	Names	U6AFB
木	S21-4-17	F0000

traditional form → see 桜 at 1168

欄

1426

1-4-17

▶COLUMN

ラン

75	Names	UF91D
木	S21-4-17	F0000

traditional form → see 欄 at 1419

爛

1427

1-4-17

▶OVERRIPE

ラン ただ(れる)

Ⓒ 烂 làn

86	Non-Jōyō	U721B
火	S21-4-17	F2705

COMPOUNDS

❶ [now also 乱 1611] **OVERRIPE, rotten**

爛熟する らんじゅくする become overripe; attain full maturity
腐爛する ふらんする ulcerate, decompose

❷ **bright, brilliant**
爛爛たる らんらんたる glaring, flaming, blazing
絢爛たる けんらんたる gorgeous, dazzling; flowery (speech)
桜花爛漫 おうからんまん The cherry blossoms are in full glory

❸ **break out in sores, be inflamed, be ulcerated**
靡×爛 びらん sore, inflammation, ulceration

INDEPENDENT

【らんたる 爛たる】**bright, brilliant**

KUN

【ただれる 爛れる】**break out in sores, be inflamed, be ulcerated**
爛れた皮膚 ただれたひふ inflamed skin
爛れ目 ただれめ sore eyes

SYNONYMS

❶ **mature**
熟 MATURE → 3558
成 grow up → 4352
稔 RIPEN → 1544
爛 OVERRIPE → 1427
実る bear fruit → 2765

❸ **swell and swelling**
脹 SWELL → 1265
腫 SWELLING → 1310
瘍 SWELLING → 4073
爛 break out in sores → 1427

欟

◧ 1-4-18

incorrect stroke-count
➡ see ◧ 1-4-17: 木 at 1424

臓

1428
◧ 1-4-18

▶**INTERNAL ORGAN**
ゾウ

130	Names	U81DF
月	S22-4-18	F0000

traditional form → see 臓 at 1417

禮

1429
◧ 1-5-1

▶**ETIQUETTE**
▶**RITE**
レイ ライ ㊔ あや のり ひろ

113	Nonstandard	UFA18
示	S6-5-1	F0000

traditional form → see 礼 at 1012

邪

◧ 1-5-2

incorrect stroke-count
➡ see ◧ 1-5-3: 牙 at 1443

町

1430
◧ 1-5-2

▶**TOWN**
チョウ まち
Ⓝ 甼 Ⓒ 町 tǐng

102	Jōyō-1	U753A
田	S7-5-2	F0277

1	2	3	4	5	6	7
丨	冂	罒	用	田	田一	町

COMPOUNDS

❶ⓐ **TOWN, city**
ⓑ (unit of local administration) **TOWN**
ⓒ **suffix after names of TOWNs**
a 町人 ちょうにん tradesman (in Edo period), townsman, townsfolk
町家 ちょうか town house; tradesman's house
町長 ちょうちょう town headman [manager]
町名 ちょうめい town name
b 町立の ちょうりつの established by the town
市町村 しちょうそん cities, towns and villages; municipalities
c 小山町 おやまちょう town of Oyama

❷ⓐ (subdivision in the Japanese addressing system) **TOWN section, *cho***
ⓑ **suffix after names of TOWN sections (*cho*)**
a 町会 ちょうかい town block association
b 一宮町 いちのみやちょう Ichinomiya-cho

❸ street, lane
横町 よこちょう bystreet, sideway

❹ *cho*:
ⓐ unit of sq. measure equiv. to approx. 99.2 ares or 10 *tan* (反)
ⓑ [sometimes also 丁 4155] former unit of length equiv. to approx. 109 m or 60 *ken* (間)
a 町歩 ちょうぶ hectare
b 二町 にちょう two *cho*

INDEPENDENT

【ちょう 町】TOWN (→ ❶ⓑ); **town section, *cho*** (→ ❷ⓐ); *cho* (→ ❹)
町の方針 ちょうのほうしん policies of the town [*cho*]

KUN

【まち 町】
① [also suffix]
ⓐ **TOWN**
ⓑ (unit of local administration) **TOWN**
ⓒ **suffix after names of TOWNs**
a 町へ行く まちへいく go to town
町工場 まちこうば town factory
町外れ まちはずれ outskirts of a town
港町 みなとまち port town
温泉町 おんせんまち spa town, hot spring resort
b 町役場 まちやくば town office

c 水上町 みなかみまち town of Minakami
②ⓐ (subdivision in the Japanese addressing system) ***machi*, TOWN section**
ⓑ **suffix after names of TOWN sections (*machi*)**
b 信濃町 しなのまち Shinanomachi
③ [usu. 街] **(busy) city quarter(s), city streets**
町筋 まちすじ street
町並み まちなみ rows of stores and houses on a street
下町 したまち (downtown) business quarters, old part of Tokyo

SYNONYMS

❶ **cities and towns**
都 METROPOLIS → 2120
京 CAPITAL → 2546
畿 CAPITAL → 4408
市 CITY → 2487
町 TOWN → 1430
❶ **villages and towns**
町 TOWN → 1430
村 VILLAGE → 1029
里 hamlet → 4356
郷 HOMETOWN → 0664
庄 FEUDAL VILLAGE → 3788
邑 VILLAGE → 2716
❷ **parts of towns**
区 WARD → 3681
街 CITY QUARTER → 0702
町 town section (*cho*) → 1430
丁 TOWN SUBSECTION (*chome*) → 4155
字 village or town section → 2696
❹ⓐ **area units**
坪 *TSUBO* (3.3 sq. m) → 0328
歩 *bu* (3.3 sq. m) → 3071
畝 *se* (0.99 ares) → 1857
反 *tan* (9.9 ares) → 3663
町 *cho* (99.2 ares) → 1430
ⓑ **length units**
寸 *sun* (3.03 cm) → 3652
浬 NAUTICAL MILE (1852 m) → 0526
反 *tan* (10.6 m) → 3663
尺 *SHAKU* (30.3 cm) → 4248
米 meter → 4342
尋 fathom (1.8 m) → 2918
間 *ken* (1.8 m) → 4122
丈 *jo* (3.03 m) → 4227
町 *cho* (109 m) → 1430
里 LEAGUE, *ri* (3.9 km) → 4356
哩 MILE (1609 m) → 0479

USAGE

【まち】
町
① [also suffix]
ⓐ town
ⓑ (unit of local administration) town
ⓒ suffix after names of towns
②ⓐ (subdivision in the Japanese addressing system) *machi*, town section
ⓑ suffix after names of town sections (*machi*)
③ [usu. 街] (busy) city quarter(s), city streets
街
(busy) city quarter(s), city streets

HOMOPHONES

まち 街 CITY QUARTER → 0702

祁 incorrect stroke-count
➡ see 1-5-3: 礻 at 1447
1-5-2

利

▶**ADVANTAGE**
▶**PROFIT**
リ き(く) ㊔ とし と かが かず よし
ⓒ 利 lì

1431
1-5-2

18	Jōyō-4	U5229
刂	S7-2-5	F0228

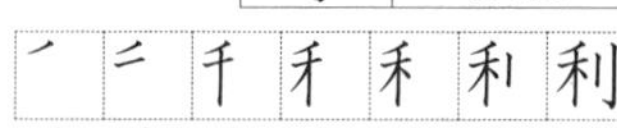

COMPOUNDS

❶ⓐ **ADVANTAGE, benefit, superiority, convenience, expediency**
ⓑ **be of ADVANTAGE to, benefit**
a 利点 りてん advantage, point in favor
有利な ゆうりな advantageous, favorable; profitable
権利 けんり right; authority; privilege
便利 べんり convenience, handiness, usefulness
b 利用する りようする utilize, make use of, avail oneself of
❷ⓐ **PROFIT, gains, advantage, benefit**
ⓑ [also suffix] **interest (on money)**
a 利益 りえき profit, gains; benefit
利害 りがい interests
利食い りぐい profit taking
利得 りとく profit, benefit, gain
営利 えいり profit, gain
b 利子 りし interest
利息 りそく interest
複利 ふくり compound interest
六分半利 ろくぶはんり 6.5% bonds
❸ⓐ sharp(-edged), keen
ⓑ [formerly also 悧 0505] **sharp, keen, clever**

牙 田 【礻】 禾 ネ 另 去 氏 历 艮 且 半 牛

a 利刀 りとう sharp sword
鋭利な えいりな sharp, keen; acute, sharp, clever
b 利口(=悧巧)な りこうな clever, bright, sharp, shrewd

❹ **victory**
勝利 しょうり victory, triumph, win

❺ used phonetically for *ri*
砂利 じゃり gravel, fine gravel, ballast
仏舎利 ぶっしゃり Buddha's ashes
伊太利 いたりー Italy

INDEPENDENT

【り 利】 **ADVANTAGE**, profit; interest; victory
地の利 ちのり vantage ground, advantageous position

【りする 利する】 **PROFIT**, benefit (by)

KUN

【きく 利く】

① **work (well), function (properly)**
利き きき function, efficacy
耳が利く みみがきく have a sharp ear
左利き ひだりきき left-handedness; left-hander; drinker, wine lover

② speak (esp. as a mediator)
口利き くちきき mediation; mediator, mouthpiece

SYNONYMS

❶ **benefit**
利 ADVANTAGE → 1431
益 BENEFIT → 2849
為 SAKE → 4395
用 use(ful) → 3694
役 SERVICE → 0288

❷ⓐ **profit**
利 PROFIT → 1431
益 PROFIT → 2849
儲ける PROFIT → 0202
得 GAIN → 0577

ⓑ **interest and dividend**
利 interest → 1431
子 interest → 4196
配 dividend → 1853

HOMOPHONES

きく 効 EFFECT → 1617
きき 効 EFFECT → 1617

NOTE

➡ see USAGE note at 効 1617

私

1432

◧ 1-5-2

▶**PRIVATE**
▶**I**
シ わたくし わたし
Ⓒ 私 sī

115	Jōyō-6	U79C1
禾	S7-5-2	F0043

COMPOUNDS

❶ⓐ [also suffix] [original meaning] (pertaining to a particular person) **PRIVATE, personal**
ⓑ (intimate) **PRIVATE**, clandestine, secret, confidential
ⓒ illicit, illegal

a 私的な してきな private, personal
私学 しがく private [nongovernmental] school [college, university]
私鉄 してつ nongovernmental [private] railroad line
私物 しぶつ private property
私立の しりつ(=わたくしりつ)の private, nongovernmental
私書箱 ししょばこ post office box (P.O.B.)
私生活 しせいかつ one's private life
私費 しひ private expense
公私 こうし public and private
b 私語 しご secret talk, whispering
c 私生児 しせいじ illegitimate child, bastard child
私通 しつう illicit intercourse

❷ selfish
私腹を肥やす しふくをこやす fill [stuff] one's own pocket by taking advantage of a position
公平無私な こうへいむしな fair and disinterested, impartial

KUN

【わたくし 私】

① **I, myself**—polite first person pronoun
私達 わたくしたち we
私小説 わたくししょうせつ(=ししょうせつ) first person novel, private [real] life novel

② **PRIVATE**ness, privacy; partiality
私事 わたくしごと personal affairs
私する わたくしする think only of oneself, possess oneself

【わたし 私】 **I, myself**—polite first person pronoun (formerly used esp. by women)
私の わたしの my
私達 わたしたち we

SYNONYMS

❶ⓐ & ❶ⓑ **secret and private**
秘 SECRET → 1490
密 SECRET → 2857

牙 田 示 禾 【ネ】 另 去 氏 历 艮 且 半 半

暗 in the dark → 1273
私 PRIVATE → 1432
内 not public → 4277
隠 hidden from view → 0873

【わたくし】
① **first person pronouns**
私 I (*polite*) → 1432
我 SELF → 4362
己 ONESELF → 4188
身 ONE'S PERSON → 4368
僕 I (*familiar*) → 0185
俺 I (*intimate*) → 0124
吾 I (*elegant*) → 3060
予 I (*pompous*) → 2477
余 I (*pompous*) → 2535
麿 I (*archaic*) → 3949
朕 IMPERIAL WE → 1185
自 SELF → 4338

初

1433

1-5-2

▶**FIRST**

ショ　はじ(め)　はじ(めて)　はつ　はつ-　うい-　-そ(める)　-ぞ(め) ㊔ もと

Ⓒ 初 chū

18	Jōyō-4	U521D
刀	S7-2-5	F0206

COMPOUNDS

❶ⓐ FIRST, initial, original
ⓑ [prefix] **FIRST**
a 初回 しょかい first time; first inning
初日 しょにち first day, opening day
初版 しょはん first edition
初代 しょだい first generation, founder
初任給 しょにんきゅう initial salary
初志 しょし original aim [intention]
b 初対面 しょたいめん first meeting

❷ⓐ [also suffix] **beginning, origin, early stages**
ⓑ beginning stages, FIRST steps
a 最初 さいしょ first, outset, beginning
当初の とうしょの original, initial, first
b 初期 しょき early days, early stage, beginning; early, initial
初夏 しょか early summer
初歩 しょほ first steps, rudiments, the ABCs (of)
初級 しょきゅう beginner's class, junior course
初心者 しょしんしゃ beginner

KUN

【はじめ 初め】
① (initial period) **beginning (of the month), outset, FIRST stage, early period**
初めは はじめは at first; originally
年度初め ねんどはじめ beginning of the (fiscal) year
② **including, as well as, not to speak of**
田中氏初め六人 たなかしはじめろくにん Mr. Tanaka and five others

【はじめて 初めて】 **for the FIRST time; not…until**
初めての はじめての first, first-time
初めまして はじめまして I am glad to meet you
健康は失って初めてその価値が分かる けんこうはうしなってはじめてそのかちがわかる We don't know the value of health till we lose it

【はつ 初】 **the FIRST, first time**
初に はつに for the first time
初の成功 はつのせいこう the first success

【はつ- 初-】 [also prefix] **FIRST, early, new, inaugural; first (of the new year or season)**
初恋 はつこい first love
初舞台 はつぶたい one's first appearance on stage, debut
初日の出 はつひので first sunrise of the year
初詣で はつもうで first visit to a shrine [temple] during the New Year

【うい- 初-】 **FIRST**
初陣 ういじん one's first battle
初孫 ういまご(=はつまご) first grandchild
初初しい ういういしい innocent, naive, fresh

【-そめる -初める】 [verbal suffix] **begin to (occur); for the FIRST time**
咲き初める さきそめる begin to bloom

【-ぞめ -初め】 [verbal suffix] **performing an action for the FIRST time (of the year)**
書き初め かきぞめ New Year's writing

SYNONYMS

❶ original
素 primary → 3108
原 ORIGINAL → 3733
本 original → 4314
初 FIRST → 1433

❶ first
甲 FIRST → 4293
初 FIRST → 1433

❷ beginnings
緒 OUTSET → 1742
序 INTRODUCTORY PART → 3803
端 start → 1564
始 beginning → 0335
初 beginning → 1433
元 ORIGIN → 2428
本 origin → 4314
根 ROOT → 1167

源 SOURCE → 0806

USAGE

❶【はじめ】

初め

① (initial period) **beginning (of the month), outset, first stage, early period**

② **including, as well as, not to speak of**

始め

① (act or point of commencement) **beginning, start**

② (source) **beginning, origin**

❷【はじめて】

初めて

for the first time; not…until

始めて

begin and… (TE-form of 始める はじめる)

甫めて

literary barely, just

HOMOPHONES

はじめ 始 BEGIN → 0335

はじめて

始 BEGIN → 0335

甫 BARELY → 4363

-そめる 染 DYE → 3181

-ぞめ 染 DYE → 3181

NOTE

➡ see also USAGE note at 染 3181

別

1434

▶**SEPARATE**
▶**ANOTHER**

ベツ わか(れる) わ(ける)▲ ㊔ わけ

Ⓒ 别 bié biè

1-5-2

18	Jōyō-4	U5225
刂	S7-2-5	F0219

Stroke order: 1–7

COMPOUNDS

❶ⓐ [original meaning] (part company) **SEPARATE, part from, be separated**
ⓑ **parting company**
ⓒ (be apart) **SEPARATE, separated**

a 別離 べつり separation, parting
別居 べっきょ separation, limited divorce
別辞 べつじ farewell address, parting words

b 離別 りべつ parting, separation; divorce
告別 こくべつ leave taking, farewell

c 別荘 べっそう villa, country cottage
別冊 べっさつ separate volume, extra issue
別館 べっかん annex, extension, outbuilding
別巻 べっかん separate volume, extra issue
別間 べつま separate room, special room
別別に べつべつに separately, individually, respectively
別送 べっそう separate post

❷ⓐ (divide by differences) **SEPARATE (into groups), sort, classify, distinguish**
ⓑ [suffix] **classified by**

a 差別 さべつ discrimination
個別的に こべつてきに individually, severally, singly
区別する くべつする distinguish; classify, divide
分別する ぶんべつする classify, distinguish; divide, separate
分別 ふんべつ discretion, prudence, judgment, good sense
判別する はんべつする distinguish, discriminate
類別 るいべつ classification
戸別 こべつ each house
大別する たいべつする divide into major classes

b 職業別電話帳 しょくぎょうべつでんわちょう classified telephone directory
府県別人口 ふけんべつじんこう population classified by prefectures

❸ⓐ [also prefix] **ANOTHER, different, distinct**
ⓑ (distinct among others) **special, particular**

a 別個の べっこの another, different; separate
別種 べっしゅ another kind, distinct species
別人 べつじん another [different] person
別名 べつめい alias, another name
別世界 べっせかい another world [planet]
別問題 べつもんだい another question [problem]

b 別段の べつだんの particular, special
別格 べっかく extra status
特別の とくべつの special, particular; extraordinary
格別な かくべつな particular, exceptional

INDEPENDENT

【べつ 別】

① **distinction, difference**
男女の別 だんじょのべつ distinction of sex

② **ANOTHER thing, an extra**
別の本 べつのほん another [different] book

③ **exception**
別にする べつにする set aside [apart]

【べつに 別に】**SEPARATEly, apart; in addition; particularly**

【べっして 別して】especially, particularly

KUN

【わかれる 別れる】

ⓐ **SEPARATE, part from, bid farewell**

ⓑ **SEPARATE** (from one's spouse), divorce

a 別れ わかれ separation, parting, leave-taking, farewell
別れ別れに わかれわかれに separately, apart

b 別れ話 わかればなし talk about divorce

死に別れる しにわかれる be separated from (one's spouse) by death

【わける 別ける】[usu. 分ける] (cause to separate) part, **SEPARATE**, set aside

別けて(も) わけて(も) above all, in particular

SYNONYMS

❶ⓐ part company

別 SEPARATE → 1434
離 SEPARATE → 2364
訣 SEPARATE → 1861

❷ⓐ separate

割 DIVIDE → 2284
分 DIVIDE → 2466
解 TAKE APART → 1913
析 ANALYZE → 1072
別 SEPARATE → 1434
離 SEPARATE → 2364
隔 partition → 0827

❸ⓐ other

他 OTHER → 0039
余 other → 2535
別 ANOTHER → 1434

ⓑ special

特 SPECIAL (distinct) → 1181
別 special (distinct) → 1434
殊 SPECIAL (exceptional) → 1178
専 EXCLUSIVE → 3272

HOMOPHONES

わかれる 分 DIVIDE → 2466
わかれ 分 DIVIDE → 2466
わける 分 DIVIDE → 2466

NOTE

➡ see USAGE note at 分 2466

劫

1435

1-5-2

▶KALPA

コウ ゴウ おびや(かす)

N 刧 C 劫 jié

19	Names	U52AB
力	S7-2-5	F2748

COMPOUNDS

❶ *Buddhism* **KALPA, aeon**

永劫 えいごう eternity
億劫 おっくう(=おっこう) bothersome, a hassle

❷ [original meaning] threaten, menace, endanger

劫火 ごうか world-destroying conflagration
劫掠 ごうりゃく(=きょうりゃく) pillage, plunder

INDEPENDENT

【こう 劫】*Buddhism* **KALPA**, aeon; *ko*, fight in the game of go

KUN

【おびやかす 劫かす】[now always 脅かす] threaten, menace, endanger; intimidate, scare; coerce

SYNONYMS

❶ threaten

脅 THREATEN → 2614
劫 threaten → 1435
威 THREATEN BY FORCE → 4394
嚇 INTIMIDATE → 0964
喝 shout threats at → 0554

❷ long time periods

時 TIME → 1155
代 age → 0034
紀 ERA → 1628
世 AGE → 4308
朝 dynastic period → 2130
期 period → 2139
劫 KALPA → 1435

HOMOPHONES

おびやかす 脅 THREATEN → 2614

COMPOUND FORMATION

【億劫 おっくう, おっこう】

億劫 'bothersome, a hassle' originally was a Buddhist word literally meaning a hundred million (億) kalpa (劫 ❶), or an extremely long time. As anything that takes a very long time is a bothersome hassle, the compound came to be used in this sense.

NOTE

➡ see USAGE note at 脅 2614

却

1436

1-5-2

▶ELIMINATE

キャク かえ(って)▲

N 卻◇ C 却 què

26	Jōyō	U5374
卩	S7-2-5	F1420

一	十	土	去	去	去	却
1	2	3	4	5	6	7

COMPOUNDS

❶ **ELIMINATE, exclude, remove, get rid of**—used as the second element in verbal compounds similar to *off* in *kill off*

除却する じょきゃくする exclude, eliminate
脱却する だっきゃくする get rid of; slough off
消却する しょうきゃくする efface; erase
忘却する ぼうきゃくする forget
焼却する しょうきゃくする destroy by fire, incinerate
売却する ばいきゃくする sell off, dispose of by sale
償却する しょうきゃくする repay, refund

❷ **reject, turn down, decline**

却下する きゃっかする reject, dismiss, turn down

棄却する ききゃくする turn down, reject, renounce

❸ retreat, step back

退却する たいきゃくする retreat

❹ **return**

返却する へんきゃくする return

KUN

【かえって 却って】 on the contrary, rather

SYNONYMS

❶ **eliminate**

却 ELIMINATE → 1436
排 EXCLUDE → 0593
払う CLEAR AWAY → 0225
剝 PEEL OFF → 2105
耘 WEED → 1661
削 cross out → 1837
抹 wipe off → 0370
省 leave out → 3100
脱 REMOVE → 1225
去 take away → 2678
外す take off → 0215
除 RID OF → 0546
撤 WITHDRAW → 0912

❷ **refuse and reject**

拒 REFUSE → 0368
断る refuse → 1885
否 SAY NO → 3058
却 reject → 1436

刧

1437

◧ 1-5-2

▸KALPA

コウ ゴウ おびや(かす)

18	Nonstandard	U5227
刀	S7-2-5	F0000

traditional form → see 劫 at 1435

邸

◧ 1-5-2

incorrect stroke-count

➡ see ◧1-5-3: 氐 at 1451

励

1438

◧ 1-5-2

▸ENCOURAGE

レイ はげ(む) はげ(ます) ㊔ つとむ

Ⓝ 勵 Ⓒ 励 lì

19	Jōyō	U52B1
力	S7-2-5	F1649

1	2	3	4	5	6	7
一	厂	厂	厅	厉	厉	励

COMPOUNDS

❶ (impart confidence or spirit) **ENCOURAGE, cheer up, inspire**

奨励 しょうれい encouragement, promotion, stimulation, incitement

激励する げきれいする encourage, urge, cheer up

督励 とくれい urging (one's subordinates)

❷ *elec* excite

励磁電流 れいじでんりゅう exciting current

励振管 れいしんかん exciter tube

他励 たれい separate excitation

❸ [original meaning] **make efforts, work hard at, be diligent**

励行する れいこうする observe strictly, carry out

励声 れいせい straining one's voice

精励 せいれい diligence, industry

勉励 べんれい diligence, industry

奮励 ふんれい strenuous efforts [exertions]

KUN

【はげむ 励む】 **strive for, make efforts, be diligent**

励み はげみ encouragement, incentive

勉強に励む べんきょうにはげむ work hard at one's lessons

【はげます 励ます】 **ENCOURAGE, urge, cheer up; raise [strain] (one's voice)**

励まし はげまし encouragement, stimulation

病人を励ます びょうにんをはげます cheer up an invalid

声を励ます こえをはげます raise one's voice

SYNONYMS

❶ **urge**

勧 URGE → 2334
催 PRESS FOR → 0178
促 HASTEN → 0118
誘 INDUCE → 1952
励 ENCOURAGE → 1438
侑 URGE TO EAT → 0101

❸ **exert oneself**

努 EXERT → 3154
勉 ENDEAVOR → 4113
励 make efforts → 1438
勤 work diligently → 2287
尽 use all one's strength → 3786
精 put one's heart into → 1729
孜 MAKE DILIGENT EFFORTS → 0284

即

1439

◧ 1-5-2

▸IMMEDIATE

ソク つ(く)▲ つ(ける)▲ すなわ(ち)▲

Ⓝ 卽 Ⓒ 即 jí

26	Jōyō	U5373
卩	S7-2-5	F1250

1	2	3	4	5	6	7
㇕	㇕	ヨ	艮	艮	即	即

COMPOUNDS

❶ⓐ **IMMEDIATE, prompt, instant, on the spot**

牙 田 示 禾 ネ 另 去 氏 历 艮 【且】 半 半

❶ⓑ [original meaning] be in **IMMEDIATE** [close] contact

a 即死 そくし instant death, death on the spot
即売 そくばい sale on the spot, spot sale
即時 そくじ immediately, promptly
即刻 そっこく immediately, instantly
即座に そくざに immediately, promptly, at once
即効 そっこう immediate effect
即答 そくとう prompt answer
即金 そっきん immediate cash, ready cash
一触即発 いっしょくそくはつ touch-and-go situation, hair-trigger crisis

b 即応する そくおうする meet, adopt oneself to, conform to
不即不離の ふそくふりの neutral, middle-of-the-road

❷ same (day, etc.)
即日 そくじつ same day

❸ **namely, that is**
色即是空 しきそくぜくう Matter is void/Form [Matter] is nonsubstantial

❹ ascend (the throne)
即位する そくいする ascend the throne

INDEPENDENT

【そく 即】 namely, that is, i.e.; **IMMEDIATE**ly, on the spot
即実行せよ そくじっこうせよ Do it immediately
生即死 せいそくし Life is death

【そくする 即する】 conform to, agree with; be in **IMMEDIATE** [close] contact, be based on

KUN

【つく 即く】
① [now usu. 就く] ascend to (the throne)
位に即く くらいにつく ascend to the throne
② be in **IMMEDIATE** [close] contact, be based on
即かず離れずの態度 つかずはなれずのたいど neutral attitude

【つける 即ける】 [now usu. 就ける] enthrone
王位に即ける おういにつける place on the throne

【すなわち 即ち】
ⓐ **namely, that is, i.e.**
ⓑ **nothing but, precisely**
a 救世主即ちキリスト きゅうせいしゅすなわちきりすと the Savior, that is, Christ

SYNONYMS

❶ⓐ **fast**
速 QUICK → 3851
早 QUICK → 3042
疾 fast → 4064
快 fast → 0289
急 rapid → 2595
迅 SWIFT → 3780
敏 NIMBLE → 1675
即 IMMEDIATE → 1439
捷 AGILE → 0609

❶ⓐ **immediate**
即 IMMEDIATE → 1439
直 straight away → 3649
忽 IN AN INSTANT → 3080

USAGE

❶【すなわち】
即ち
ⓐ namely, that is, i.e.
ⓑ nothing but, precisely
乃ち
ⓐ thereupon, whereupon, accordingly
ⓑ and then

❷【そくする】
即する
ⓐ conform to, agree with
ⓑ be in immediate [close] contact, be based on
則する
conform to the rules, follow precedent

HOMOPHONES

つく
就 SET ABOUT → 2129
着 PUT ON → 4110
付 ATTACH → 0035
附 ATTACH → 0410
点 POINT → 2587

つける
就 SET ABOUT → 2129
着 PUT ON → 4110
付 ATTACH → 0035
附 ATTACH → 0410
点 POINT → 2587
漬 PICKLE → 0861

すなわち 乃 POSSESSIVE PARTICLE → 3643

NOTE

➡ see also USAGE notes at 付 0035 and 速 3851
➡ see COMPOUND FORMATION for 即座 そくざ → 座 3868

助

1440

1-5-2

▸**HELP**
ジョ たす(ける) たす(かる) すけ ㊔ たすく
Ⓒ 助 zhù

19	Jōyō-3	U52A9
力	S7-2-5	F0240

COMPOUNDS

❶ⓐ [original meaning] **HELP, aid, assist**
ⓑ (act of helping) **HELP, aid**

❸ **save, rescue, relieve**

a 助手 じょしゅ assistant, helper
助成 じょせい fostering; aid, assistance
助言 じょげん advice
援助 えんじょ aid, assistance, help
補助 ほじょ assistance, support, aid
b 一助 いちじょ help, aid
天助 てんじょ Heaven's help
c 助命 じょめい sparing a person's life
救助 きゅうじょ rescue, relief

❷ [also prefix] **assistant, auxiliary**
助詞 じょし *gram* postpositional particle
助役 じょやく assistant official; deputy mayor; deputy station-master
助教授 じょきょうじゅ assistant [associate] professor
助監督 じょかんとく assistant director [manager]
助動詞 じょどうし auxiliary verb

KUN

【たすける 助ける】
① [formerly also 扶ける] **HELP, aid, assist**
助け たすけ aid, rescue, relief
助け合う たすけあう help each other
手助け てだすけ help, assistance
② **save, rescue, relieve**
助け出す たすけだす rescue (a person) from [out of], deliver [extricate] (a person) from

【たすかる 助かる】**be HELPed, be rescued, be spared**
大助かり おおだすかり big help

【すけ 助】
① **HELPing, assisting; assistant vaudevillian**
助太刀する すけだちする help (a person in a fight), back up
助っ人 すけっと *colloq* helper, backer, supporter
② *colloq* suffix for derisive nicknames
飲み助 のみすけ drunkard
雲助 くもすけ reckless and dishonest cabdriver or palanquin bearer
③ *slang* broad, chick
助番 すけばん leader of a group of delinquent girls
助平 すけべい lewd person; Peeping Tom

SYNONYMS

❶ **help**
助 HELP → 1440
佑 HELP (said esp. of God) → 0083
祐 DIVINE HELP → 1146
援 AID → 0715
佐 ASSIST → 0076
補 assist → 1529
輔 ASSIST → 1963
済 RELIEVE → 0634

❷ **subordinate**
副 SECONDARY → 2230
次 secondary → 0058
従 subordinate → 0498
亜 SUB- → 4354
準 QUASI- → 3541
半 semi- → 4313
准 JUNIOR → 0143
助 assistant → 1440

USAGE

【たすける】
助ける
① [formerly also 扶ける] help, aid, assist
② save, rescue, relieve
扶ける
[now usu. 助ける] help, aid, assist

HOMOPHONES

たすける 扶 LEND SUPPORT TO → 0291

判

1441

1-5-2

▶**JUDGE**
ハン バン わか(る)▲ ㊔ さだ
N 判 C 判 pàn

18	Jōyō-5	U5224
刂	S7-2-5	F0321

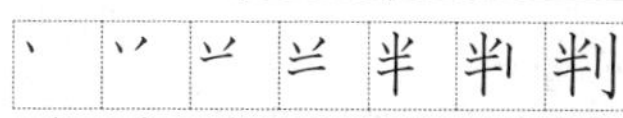

COMPOUNDS

❶ⓐ (pass legal judgment) **JUDGE, hand down a decision, pronounce sentence**
ⓑ (decide upon critically) **JUDGE, decide, distinguish, differentiate**
a 判決 はんけつ judicial decision, judgment, sentence
判事 はんじ judge
判例 はんれい (judicial) precedent
裁判 さいばん trial, judgment, decision
公判 こうはん (public) trial [hearing]
b 判断する はんだんする judge, decide; interpret, foretell, read
判定する はんていする judge, decide
批判する ひはんする criticize, comment
評判 ひょうばん fame, reputation
審判 しんぱん(=しんばん) refereeing, judgment; referee, umpire

❷ puzzle out, solve, decipher
判読 はんどく decipherment, interpretation

❸ **obvious, clear**
判明する はんめいする become clear, be confirmed
判然と はんぜんと clearly, distinctly, plainly

❹ **personal seal, seal, stamp, chop; seal impression**
判子 はんこ handstamp, seal; seal impression
盲判 めくらばん undeliberated endorsement

血判 けっぱん seal of blood

❺ [also suffix] format, size (of books or paper)

菊判 きくばん small octavo, medium octavo

二つ折り判 ふたつおりばん folio

❻ [in compounds] former oval Japanese gold coin

大判 おおばん large oval Japanese gold coin

小判 こばん smaller-sized oval Japanese gold coin

INDEPENDENT

【はん 判】personal seal, seal, chop; stamp, seal impression; format, size (of books or paper)

判を押す はんをおす affix a seal

【はんじる 判じる】**JUDGE**, decide; puzzle out, decipher; guess, interpret

【ばん 判】format, size

KUN

【わかる 判る】[usu. 分かる, sometimes also 解る]

①ⓐ (grasp the meaning of) understand, comprehend, see

ⓑ (be sympathetic toward) understand, show understanding for (another's feelings)

a 判り わかり understanding

判り難い わかりにくい hard to understand, incomprehensible, unintelligible

b 物判りの良い ものわかりのよい understanding; sensible

②ⓐ know, tell, recognize

ⓑ be made known, be brought to light

a 先の事は判らない さきのことはわからない cannot tell what will happen in the future

b 身元が判る みもとがわかる be identified

③ appreciate

音楽が判る おんがくがわかる have an ear [appreciation] for music

SYNONYMS

❶ judge

判 JUDGE → 1441

裁 JUDGE → 4090

鑑 APPRAISE → 2226

評 evaluate → 1895

審 TRY → 2985

決 DECIDE → 0308

視 REGARD → 1223

❹ seals

印 SEAL → 1023

判 personal seal → 1441

璽 IMPERIAL SEAL → 3624

HOMOPHONES

わかる

分 DIVIDE → 2466

解 TAKE APART → 1913

NOTE

➡ see USAGE note at 分 2466

刋 1442

▶JUDGE

ハン バン わか(る) ㊔ さだ

1-5-2

18	Nonstandard	U5224
刂	S7-2-5	F0000

traditional form → see 判 at 1441

邪 1443

▶EVIL

ジャ よこし(ま)▲

Ⓝ 邪 Ⓒ 邪 xié

1-5-3

163	Jōyō	U90AA
阝	S8-3-5	F1268

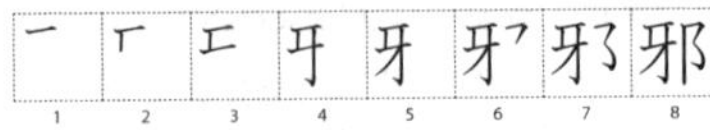

COMPOUNDS

❶ⓐ (morally bad) **EVIL, wicked, bad, unjust, heretical, wrong**

ⓑ (causing harm) **EVIL**

ⓒ wrong, EVIL

a 邪悪 じゃあく wickedness, vice

邪心 じゃしん wicked heart, evil design

邪道 じゃどう evil course; heresy

b 邪魔 じゃま hindrance, obstruction, impediment

c 無邪気 むじゃき innocence, simplicity

正邪の区別 せいじゃのくべつ discrimination between right and wrong

❷ *baseball* foul

邪飛 じゃひ foul fly

INDEPENDENT

【じゃ 邪】wrong, injustice, unrighteousness

邪は正に勝たず じゃはせいにかたず Virtue triumphs over vice

KUN

【よこしま 邪ま】

よこしまな 邪まな **EVIL**, wicked, vicious; unjust; dishonest

邪まな心 よこしまなこころ evil heart

SPECIAL READINGS

風邪 かぜ(=ふうじゃ) (common) cold

SYNONYMS

❶ⓐ evil

邪 EVIL → 1443

兇 ATROCIOUS → 3044

凶 ATROCIOUS → 3679

悪 BAD → 3413

ⓒ wrongdoing and evil

罪 sin → 3224

非 wrong(doing) → 1101

邪 wrong → 1443
悪 evil (something bad) → 3413
弊 evil(s) (something undesirable) → 3583

NOTE

➡ see COMPOUND FORMATION for 邪魔 じゃま → 魔 3953

的 1444

▶TARGET
▶ADJECTIVAL SUFFIX
テキ まと
Ⓝ 的 Ⓒ 的 de dí dì

1-5-3

106	Jōyō-4	U7684
白	S8-5-3	F0032

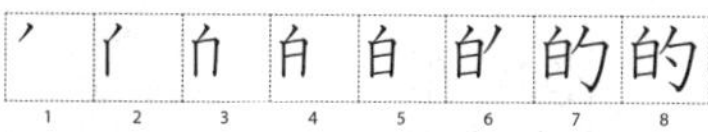

COMPOUNDS

❶ⓐ TARGET, mark, bull's eye
ⓑ right on TARGET, accurate

a 標的 ひょうてき target, mark
射的 しゃてき target practice, shooting
目的 もくてき object, purpose
b 的中する てきちゅうする hit the mark, hit (on) it
的確な てきかくな precise, accurate, exact

❷ SUFFIX for forming ADJECTIVEs from nouns or word elements—used to express resemblance, relation or the like (similar to English *-tic* or *-al*)

劇的な げきてきな dramatic
歴史的 れきしてき historical
合理的な ごうりてきな rational, logical, reasonable
法的 ほうてき legal, legalistic
私的な してきな private, personal
規則的 きそくてき systematic, regular
知的 ちてき intellectual, mental
国際的な こくさいてきな international

❸ suffix indicating endearment or derision—often attached to a person's name (similar to *boy* in *Jimmy Boy*)

権的 ごんてき nickname for 権兵衛 ごんべえ

KUN

【まと 的】**TARGET, mark; object, target**
的外れの まとはずれの out of focus; off the point
的に達しない まとにたっしない fall short of the mark

SYNONYMS

❶ⓐ target
的 TARGET → 1444
標 MARK → 1347
狙 AIM → 0406
目 aim → 3777

❷ modifier suffixes
然 MODIFIER FORMING SUFFIX → 3456
乎 MODIFIER FORMING SUFFIX → 4316
如 modifier suffix → 0239
爾 adjective suffix → 4407
的 ADJECTIVAL SUFFIX → 1444

的 1445

▶TARGET
▶ADJECTIVAL SUFFIX
テキ まと

1-5-3

106	Nonstandard	U7684
白	S8-5-3	F0000

traditional form → see 的 at 1444

知 1446

▶KNOW
チ し(る) し(らせる) し(れる) ㊔ とも さとし かず さと のり さとる
Ⓒ 知 zhī

1-5-3

111	Jōyō-2	U77E5
矢	S8-5-3	F0058

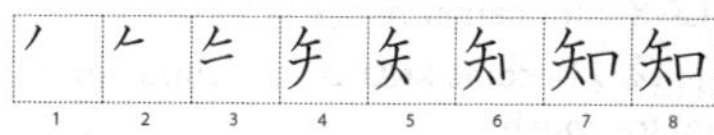

COMPOUNDS

❶ⓐ KNOW, be aware of, understand; perceive, recognize
ⓑ [formerly also 智 3458] **KNOWledge, wisdom, intelligence, intellect**
ⓒ [formerly 智 3458] wise, clever, resourceful

a 知識 ちしき knowledge
知覚 ちかく perception, sensation
周知の しゅうちの known to all, universally known
承知する しょうちする consent [agree] to; permit; forgive; know, understand
探知 たんち detection
b 知恵 ちえ wisdom, intelligence, sagacity
知能 ちのう intelligence, mental capacity
知性 ちせい intellect, intelligence
知覚知 ちかくち knowledge by acquaintance
知情意 ちじょうい intellect, emotion and volition
c 知将 ちしょう resourceful general

❷ let KNOW, inform
通知する つうちする notify, inform, let know
告知する こくちする notify, announce

❸ⓐ come to KNOW, become acquainted with
ⓑ acquaintance, friend

a 知人 ちじん acquaintance, friend
b 旧知 きゅうち old friend

❹ govern, rule
県知事 けんちじ prefectural governor

INDEPENDENT

【ち 知(=智)】wisdom, intellect, intelligence, sense; stratagem
知余って勇足らず ちあまってゆうたらず be too sagacious to be bold

牙 白 矢 【礻】 禾 氏

KUN

【しる 知る】**KNOW, be aware of, understand; perceive, recognize, feel; infer; become acquainted with; be concerned with; reign, govern**

知れない しれない maybe, perhaps; there is no way to know

知らん顔 しらんかお feigned ignorance, unconcerned air

知り合い しりあい acquaintance

知らず知らず しらずしらず unawares, without knowing it

知ろし召す しろしめす reign

物知り ものしり well-informed person, walking dictionary

それは僕の知った事じゃない それはぼくのしったことじゃない It's no concern of mine

【しらせる 知らせる】**let KNOW, inform, tell, report**

知らせ しらせ information, notice, report

【しれる 知れる】**become KNOWn; be found out; not amount too much**

知れた しれた trifling, negligible; obvious

知れ渡る しれわたる become widely known

高が知れている たかがしれている not amount to much

SYNONYMS

❶ⓐ perceive

覚 PERCEIVE → 3217
知 KNOW → 1446
感 FEEL → 3514
認 RECOGNIZE → 1948

❶ⓐ know and understand

知 KNOW → 1446
通 know thoroughly → 3855
得 gain understanding of → 0577
分かる understand → 2466
解 understand → 1913
諒 UNDERSTAND → 1982
了 COMPREHEND → 4157
悟 AWAKE TO → 0502
惺 AWAKE TO → 0709

ⓑ wisdom

識 KNOWLEDGE → 2070
知 knowledge → 1446
智 WISDOM → 3458
慧 prajna (transcendental wisdom) → 3485
哲 PHILOSOPHY → 3402

❶ⓑ learning and knowledge

業 studies → 3227
学 learning → 3162
文 culture → 2458
識 KNOWLEDGE → 2070
知 knowledge → 1446

❷ inform and communicate

報 INFORM → 2133
通 COMMUNICATE → 3855
告 NOTIFY → 3062
届ける give notice → 3820
達 issue a notice → 3893
知 let know → 1446
申 REPORT → 4319
稟 REPORT TO → 2649
宣 PROCLAIM → 2799

祁

1447

1-5-3

▶EXTREMELY

キ

N 祁 C 祁 qí

113	Names	U7941
示	S8-5-3	F3361

COMPOUNDS

● EXTREMELY, intensely, exceedingly

祁寒 きかん severe cold

SYNONYMS

● extreme in degree

酷 SEVERE → 1967
強 STRONG → 0574
凄い tremendous → 0145
重 HEAVY → 4390
高 HIGH → 2601
深 DEEP → 0636
大 BIG → 4224
厳 SEVERE → 4079
激 intense → 0955
極 EXTREME → 1243
痛 bitter(ly) → 4071
切 keen → 0030
甚 EXTREMELY → 3271
祁 EXTREMELY → 1447
超 super- → 4107
頗る EXCEEDINGLY → 1552

祀

1448

1-5-3

▶WORSHIP AS GOD

シ まつ(る)

C 祀 sì

113	Non-Jōyō	U7940
示	S8-5-3	F1910

COMPOUNDS

ⓐ WORSHIP AS GOD, deify

ⓑ enshrine

a 祭祀 さいし religious service; festival

b 奉祀する ほうしする enshrine

KUN

【まつる 祀る】[now usu. 祭る]

ⓐ **WORSHIP AS GOD, deify**
ⓑ **enshrine**
a 先祖を祀る せんぞをまつる worship one's ancestors

SYNONYMS

ⓐ pray and worship
祈 PRAY → 1086
祷 PRAY → 1224
願 pray → 2320
拝 WORSHIP → 0360
祀 WORSHIP AS GOD → 1448
崇 REVERENCE → 2864
斎 OBSERVE RELIGIOUS ABSTINENCE → 2622
呪 SPELL → 0323

HOMOPHONES

まつる 祭 FESTIVAL → 3311

NOTE

➡ see USAGE note at 祭 3311

社

1449

◧ 1-5-3

▶**COMPANY**
▶**SOCIETY**
シャ やしろ ㊔ もり こそ

113	Names	UFA4C
示	S8-5-3	F0000

traditional form → see 社 at 1042

和

1450

◧ 1-5-3

▶**HARMONIOUS**
▶**PEACE**
▶**JAPAN**
ワ オ やわ(らぐ) やわ(らげる) なご(む) なご(やか) ㊔ かず より やす やわら やまと たか よし かつ とも

Ⓝ 咊 龢

Ⓒ 和 hé hè huó huò hú

30	Jōyō-3	U548C
口	S8-3-5	F0164

1	2	3	4	5	6	7	8
㇒	二	千	禾	禾	和	和	和

COMPOUNDS

❶ⓐ HARMONIOUS, in accord, peaceful, friendly
ⓑ [original meaning] **harmonize, sing in harmony**
a 和気 わき harmonious atmosphere
和合 わごう harmony, concord; union
調和 ちょうわ harmony, accord, agreement, symmetry
共和制 きょうわせい republicanism
b 和声 わせい harmony, concord, consonance
昭和 しょうわ Showa era

❷ PEACE
和平 わへい peace
和解する わかいする make peace, come to terms
平和 へいわ peace, harmony
講和 こうわ peace, reconciliation

❸ gentle, mild, soft
緩和する かんわする ease, relieve, alleviate
温和(=穏和)な おんわな gentle, mild, genial
柔和な にゅうわな gentle, mild, tender, meek

❹ⓐ JAPAN, Japanese
ⓑ JAPANese (language)
a 和服 わふく Japanese clothes, kimono
和歌 わか Japanese poem, tanka
和食 わしょく Japanese-style food
和風 わふう Japanese style; gentle breeze
和語 わご native Japanese word (not derived from Chinese)
b 和訳 わやく Japanese translation
和英 わえい Japanese-English
漢和辞典 かんわじてん Chinese-Japanese character dictionary

❺ sum, total
総和 そうわ sum total, lump sum
代数的和 だいすうてきわ algebraic sum

❻ mix
混和 こんわ mixture, mingling
中和 ちゅうわ neutralization; counteraction (of poison)

❼ used phonetically for *o*
和尚 おしょう Buddhist priest [abbot] in charge of a temple

INDEPENDENT

【わ 和】 **harmony, accord; PEACE; sum**
和を結ぶ わをむすぶ make peace
夫婦の和 ふうふのわ concord between husband and wife, conjugal harmony
二と三の和は五 にとさんのわはご The sum of two and three is five

KUN

【やわらぐ 和らぐ】 *vi* **soften; abate, lessen; calm down**
和らぎ やわらぎ abatement, alleviation; peacefulness
寒さが和らいだ さむさがやわらいだ The cold has decreased its severity

【やわらげる 和らげる】 *vt* **soften, tone down, calm; lessen, mitigate, relieve**
苦痛を和らげる くつうをやわらげる relieve a person's pain

【なごむ 和む】 **be softened, become lukewarm**
心が和む こころがなごむ feel relaxed

【なごやか 和やか】
なごやかな 和やかな **PEACEful, mild, gentle**
和やかな家庭 なごやかなかてい harmonious [happy] family

SPECIAL READINGS

大和 やまと [also 倭] Yamato (old name for Japan)
大和魂 やまとだましい the Japanese spirit
日和 ひより weather

SYNONYMS

❶ⓐ familiar and friendly
親 INTIMATE → 2264
密 CLOSE → 2857
近 NEAR → 3798
睦 FRIENDLY → 1534
懇 FAMILIAR → 3606
和 HARMONIOUS → 1450

❷ peace
和 PEACE → 1450
安 public peace → 2695
治 public order → 0393

❹ⓐ Japan
日 JAPAN → 3759
和 JAPAN → 1450
邦 JAPAN → 1051
国 Japanese → 3831
倭 ANCIENT NAME FOR JAPAN → 0140

❺ total
総 TOTAL → 1743
計 total → 1828
和 sum → 1450

HOMOPHONES

やまと
倭 ANCIENT NAME FOR JAPAN → 0140
大和 → 4224, 1450

NOTE

➡ see COMPOUND FORMATION for 昭和 しょうわ → 昭 1107

邸

1451
◧1-5-3

▶STATELY RESIDENCE
テイ やしき▲
Ⓒ 邸 dǐ

163	Jōyō	U90B8
阝	S8-3-5	F1299

Stroke order: 1–8

COMPOUNDS

ⓐ STATELY RESIDENCE, mansion, official residence, villa, house
ⓑ suffix for forming names of residences or mansions
ⓒ [original meaning, now obsolete] residence where feudal lords used to lodge when in the capital

a 邸宅 ていたく residence, mansion
公邸 こうてい official residence
官邸 かんてい official residence
私邸 してい one's private residence
別邸 べってい villa, country residence
b 徳川公爵邸 とくがわこうしゃくてい mansion of Prince Tokugawa
山本氏邸 やまもとしてい Mr. Yamamoto's residence

KUN

【やしき 邸】 [now usu. 屋敷] mansion, residence

SYNONYMS

● houses
家 HOUSE → 2827
屋 HOUSE → 3842
軒 house → 1851
戸 HOUSEHOLD → 2429
宅 DWELLING HOUSE → 2698
居 residence → 3822
邸 STATELY RESIDENCE → 1451
住 housing → 0072
庵 HERMITAGE → 3876

● mansions
邸 STATELY RESIDENCE → 1451
館 stately mansion → 2196
荘 VILLA → 2814

USAGE

【やしき】
邸
[now usu. 屋敷] mansion, residence
屋敷
① [sometimes also 邸] mansion, residence
② residential lot

HOMOPHONES

やしき 屋敷 → 3842, 2345

毗

1452
◧1-5-4

▶PHONETIC [bi]
ヒ ビ ㊔ のぶ よし やす まさ とも てる ひで たる すけ

102	Nonstandard	U6BD7
田	S9-5-4	F0000

traditional form → see 毘 at 3169

畍

1453
◧1-5-4

▶WORLD
▶BOUNDS
カイ ㊔ さかい

102	Nonstandard	U754D
田	S9-5-4	F0000

traditional form → see 界 at 3172

畊

1454

◧1-5-4

▶TILL

コウ たがや(す) ㊔ おさむ やす つとむ

102	Nonstandard	U754A
田	S9-5-4	F0000

traditional form → see 耕 at 1659

皈

1455

◧1-5-4

▶RETURN

キ かえ(る) かえ(す)

106	Nonstandard	U7688
白	S9-5-4	F0000

traditional form → see 帰 at 0148

矩

◧1-5-4

incorrect stroke-count

➡ see ◧1-5-5: 矢 at 1475

研

1456

◧1-5-4

▶GRIND

▶RESEARCH

ケン と(ぐ)

Ⓝ 硏 Ⓒ 研 yán yàn

112	Jōyō-3	U7814
石	S9-5-4	F0546

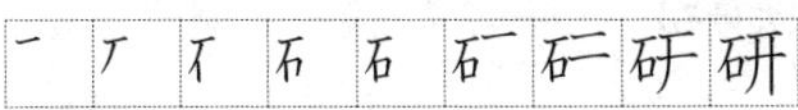

1 2 3 4 5 6 7 8 9

COMPOUNDS

❶ [original meaning] **GRIND, polish**

研磨する けんまする grind, polish; study hard, brush up

研削 けんさく grinding

研米機 けんまいき rice polisher

❷ⓐ **RESEARCH, study (hard), investigate**

ⓑ abbrev. of 研究所 けんきゅうしょ or 研究会 けんきゅうかい: **RESEARCH** institute, laboratory, research society

a 研究 けんきゅう research, study

研修 けんしゅう study and training

研鑽× けんさん study

b 技研 ぎけん technical research institute

癌研 がんけん Cancer Research Institute

KUN

【とぐ 研ぐ】[rarely also 砥ぐ] **sharpen, GRIND, whet, polish; wash (rice)**

研ぎ とぎ grinding, polish, sharpening

研ぎ石 とぎいし whetstone, knife sharpener

研ぎ澄ます とぎすます sharpen [grind] well

SYNONYMS

❶ **polish and rub**

磨 POLISH → 3946

擦 RUB → 0971

摩 RUB AGAINST → 3938

摺 RUB AGAINST → 0850

研 GRIND → 1456

削 CUT BY CHIPPING → 1837

瑳 POLISH → 1343

❷ⓐ **learn and study**

学 STUDY → 3162

考 study → 3962

習 LEARN → 3306

研 RESEARCH → 1456

究 STUDY EXHAUSTIVELY → 2729

攻 specialize → 0286

USAGE

【とぐ】

研ぐ

[rarely also 砥ぐ] sharpen, grind, whet, polish; wash (rice)

砥ぐ

[now always 研ぐ] sharpen, grind, whet, polish

HOMOPHONES

とぐ 砥 WHETSTONE → 1480

砂

1457

◧1-5-4

▶SAND

サ シャ すな ㊔ さご いさご まさご

Ⓒ 砂 shā

112	Jōyō-6	U7802
石	S9-5-4	F1059

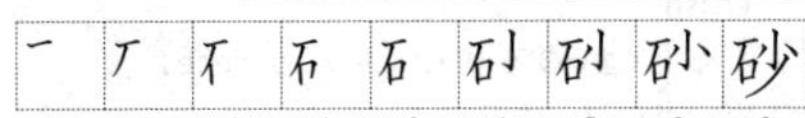

1 2 3 4 5 6 7 8 9

COMPOUNDS

[sometimes also 沙 さ 0311]

ⓐ **SAND (of fine constitution)**

ⓑ **SANDy, granular**

a 砂漠 さばく desert

砂丘 さきゅう sand dune, sand hill

砂岩 さがん sandstone

砂州(=砂洲) さす sandbar, sandbank

土砂 どしゃ earth and sand

b 砂糖 さとう sugar

砂金 さきん gold dust

砂鉄 さてつ iron sand

KUN

【すな 砂】[sometimes also 沙] **SAND, grit**

砂地 すなじ sandy place

砂浜 すなはま sandy beach, sands

砂場 すなば sandbox

SPECIAL READINGS

砂利 じゃり gravel, fine gravel, ballast

SYNONYMS

ⓐ **sand**

砂 SAND (fine) → 1457

沙 SAND (granular) → 0311

USAGE

【すな】

砂

[sometimes also 沙] sand, grit

沙

[usu. 砂] same as 砂

HOMOPHONES

すな 沙 SAND → 0311

砕

1458

1-5-4

▶CRUSH UP

サイ くだ(く) くだ(ける)

Ⓝ 碎 Ⓒ 碎 suì

112	Jōyō	U7815
石	S9-5-4	F1887

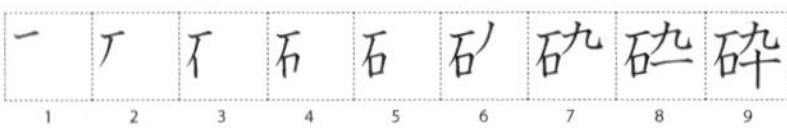

COMPOUNDS

❶ [formerly also 摧 0849] [original meaning] **CRUSH UP, break into pieces, smash**

砕岩機 さいがんき rock crusher

砕氷船 さいひょうせん ice breaker

砕石 さいせき quarrying

破砕する はさいする crush, smash, crack to pieces

粉砕する ふんさいする pulverize, shatter, smash, crush

爆砕する ばくさいする blast, blow to pieces

玉砕 ぎょくさい death for honor

❷ exert oneself to the utmost, rack one's brain

粉骨砕身する ふんこつさいしんする do one's best, exert oneself

KUN

【くだく 砕く】 [formerly also 摧く] *vt* **crush, smash, break into pieces, shatter; rack (one's brains); explain plainly**

打ち砕く うちくだく break to pieces, smash, crush; baffle, frustrate

噛み砕く かみくだく crunch; simplify, explain plainly

【くだける 砕ける】 [formerly also 摧ける] *vi* **be crushed, be broken, be smashed; break down, buckle, give way; become softened, become complaisant, get friendly; be easy [plain]**

砕け散る くだけちる be smashed up

砕けた態度 くだけたたいど friendly attitude

砕けた文章 くだけたぶんしょう plain [informal] writing

腰砕け こしくだけ breaking down in the middle of a bout; weakening of one's attitude

SYNONYMS

❶ **break**

破 BREAK → 1478

拉ぐ crush → 0372

崩 CRUMBLE → 2863

挫 SPRAIN → 0519

壊 BREAK DOWN → 0934

毀す break down → 2246

折 BREAK OFF → 0297

割る crack → 2284

裂 SPLIT → 3331

砕 CRUSH UP → 1458

摧 CRUSH UP → 0849

潰す CRUSH → 0919

❶ **break into small pieces**

砕 CRUSH UP → 1458

抹 pulverize → 0370

USAGE

❶【くだく】

砕く

[formerly also 摧く] *vt* crush, smash, break into pieces, shatter; rack (one's brains); explain plainly

摧く

[now replaced by 砕く] *vt* crush, smash, break into pieces, shatter; rack (one's brains); explain plainly

❷【くだける】

砕ける

[formerly also 摧ける] *vi* be crushed, be broken, be smashed; break down, buckle, give way; become softened, become complaisant, get friendly; be easy [plain]

摧ける

[now replaced by 砕ける] *vi* be crushed, be broken, be smashed; break down, buckle, give way; become softened, become complaisant, get friendly; be easy [plain]

HOMOPHONES

くだく 摧 CRUSH UP → 0849

くだける 摧 CRUSH UP → 0849

祇

1459

1-5-4

▶EARTHLY GOD

ギ シ ㊔ まさ のり けさ つみ もと ひろ

Ⓝ 祇 Ⓒ 祇 qí

113	Names	U7947
示	S9-5-4	F2510

COMPOUNDS

❶ **EARTHLY GOD, local god, god**

神祇 じんぎ gods of heaven and earth

地祇 ちぎ earthly deities

❷ **used phonetically for *gi* in the transliteration of Sanskrit Buddhist terms**

祇園 ぎおん name of an entertainment district in Kyoto; Jetavana (name of an ancient garden and monastery in India)

阿僧祇 あそうぎ 10^{56}, 10^{64}; *Buddhism* a number too great to count, *asaṃkhyeya*

SPECIAL READINGS

神祇官 かみづかさ(=かんづかさ, じんぎかん) Department of Worship (in ancient Japan); Department of Divinities (1868-1871)

地祇(=国つ神) くにつかみ earthly deities

SYNONYMS

❶ **god**

神 GOD → 1143

帝 the Supreme Being → 2573

天 HEAVEN → 4250

主 Lord → 2437

祇 EARTHLY GOD → 1459

❷ **phonetic [k]/[g]**

迦 PHONETIC [ka] → 3982

珈 phonetic [kō] → 1138

伽 PHONETIC [ga] → 0074

瓦 phonetic [ga] → 4288

祇 phonetic [gi] → 1459

祈

1460

1-5-4

▸PRAY

キ いの(る)

113	Names	UFA4E
示	S9-5-4	F0000

traditional form → see 祈 at 1086

祉

1461

1-5-4

▸BLESSEDNESS

シ

113	Names	UFA4D
示	S9-5-4	F0000

traditional form → see 祉 at 1087

秒

1462

1-5-4

▸SECOND

ビョウ

Ⓒ 秒 miǎo

115	Jōyō-3	U79D2
禾	S9-5-4	F1627

Stroke order: 1–9

COMPOUNDS

❶ⓐ (unit of time) **SECOND**

ⓑ (unit of angular measure) **SECOND**

ⓒ **counter for SECONDs**

ⓓ (brief while) **SECOND, moment**

a 秒速 びょうそく speed per second

秒針 びょうしん second hand

秒時計 びょうどけい stop watch

秒読み びょうよみ counting the seconds; countdown

c 三十五秒 さんじゅうごびょう 35 seconds

二分三十秒 にふんさんじゅうびょう 2′30″

d 寸秒 すんびょう a moment, a second

❷ [original meaning, now archaic] beard of grain

INDEPENDENT

【びょう 秒】SECOND

SYNONYMS

❶ⓐ **short time periods**

頃 moment → 0163

瞬 INSTANT → 1594

秒 SECOND → 1462

分 MINUTE → 2466

時 hour → 1155

暫 SHORT WHILE → 3553

科

1463

1-5-4

▸SUBJECT OF STUDY

カ ㊔ しな

Ⓒ 科 kē

115	Jōyō-2	U79D1
禾	S9-5-4	F0525

Stroke order: 1–9

COMPOUNDS

❶ [also suffix] **SUBJECT OF STUDY, branch of academic study, subdivision of a discipline**

科目 かもく school subject; subdivision, items

教科 きょうか school subject; course of study, curriculum

学科 がっか school subject; course of study

理科 りか science; science department

分科会 ぶんかかい sectional subcommittee

百科事典 ひゃっかじてん encyclopedia

社会科 しゃかいか social studies

❷ [also suffix] **course (of study), department (of a university or hospital)**

内科 ないか (department of) internal medicine

外科 げか (department of) surgery

歯科 しか dentistry

本科 ほんか regular course [department]

文科 ぶんか literary department

小児科 しょうにか (department of) pediatrics

❸ **study systematically**

科学 かがく science

❹ *biol* family

科名 かめい family name

猫科 ねこか cat family, Felidae

❺ⓐ punishment, sentence

ⓑ **offense, criminal record**

a 科料 かりょう police fine, minor fine

b 前科 ぜんか previous offense, criminal record

罪科 ざいか offense, crime, guilt; punishment

田 白 矢 石 示 【禾】 ネ 古 正 疋 手

❻ rule, law

金科玉条 きんかぎょくじょう golden rule

❼ acting, performance

科白 かはく(=せりふ) speech, words (in a play); one's remarks

❽ civil examinations in ancient China

科挙 かきょ ancient Chinese higher civil service examinations

INDEPENDENT

【か 科】 course (of study), department (of a university or hospital); *biol* family

彼とは科が違う かれとはかがちがう He is not in the same department

この科の植物 このかのしょくぶつ plant of this family

【かする 科する】 inflict (a punishment), impose (a penalty)

SYNONYMS

❶ **branch of study**

科 SUBJECT OF STUDY → 1463

学 branch of study → 3162

門 field → 1100

❷ **units of learning**

課 LESSON → 1980

科 course → 1463

講 LECTURE → 2046

秋 1464

▶**AUTUMN**

シュウ あき とき▲ Ⓝ みのる

Ⓝ 穐 龝 Ⓒ 秋 qiū

1-5-4

115	Jōyō-2	U79CB
禾	S9-5-4	F0650

Stroke order: 1–9

COMPOUNDS

❶ [original meaning] **AUTUMN, fall**

秋分 しゅうぶん autumnal equinox

秋思 しゅうし lonely feeling of fall

晩秋 ばんしゅう late fall

今秋 こんしゅう this [next] autumn

春秋 しゅんじゅう spring and autumn; years, age; Chronicles of Lu

春夏秋冬 しゅんかしゅうとう four seasons, all (the) year round

❷ years, time

千秋 せんしゅう a thousand years, many years

KUN

【あき 秋】 **AUTUMN, fall**

秋風 あきかぜ autumn breeze

【とき 秋】 [also 時] critical moment

危急存亡の秋 ききゅうそんぼうのとき crisis, critical moment

SYNONYMS

❶ **cold seasons**

冬 WINTER → 2679

寒 coldest season → 2894

秋 AUTUMN → 1464

HOMOPHONES

とき 時 TIME → 1155

NOTE

➡ see USAGE note at 時 1155

衿 1465

▶**COLLAR**

キン えり

Ⓒ 衿 jīn

1-5-4

145	Names	U887F
ネ	S9-5-4	F2464

COMPOUNDS

● **COLLAR, lapel, neck**

開衿(=開襟)シャツ かいきんしゃつ wing-collared [open-neck] shirt

KUN

【えり 衿】 [also 襟]

ⓐ [original meaning] **COLLAR, lapel, neck**

ⓑ nape

a 衿裏 えりうら lining of the collar

半衿 はんえり neckpiece (on a kimono)

SYNONYMS

● & 【えり】 ⓐ **garment parts**

襟 COLLAR → 1599

袖 SLEEVE → 1496

懐 BOSOM → 0942

衿 COLLAR → 1465

裾 HEM → 1549

HOMOPHONES

えり 襟 COLLAR → 1599

NOTE

➡ see USAGE note at 襟 1599

故 1466

▶**OLD**

▶**THE LATE**

コ ゆえ

Ⓒ 故 gù

1-5-4

66	Jōyō-5	U6545
攵	S9-4-5	F0715

Stroke order: 1–9

COMPOUNDS

❶ⓐ (of an earlier time) **OLD, former**

ⓑ (of the past) **OLD, of old, ancient**

❸ things of **OLD**, tradition
a 故郷 こきょう hometown, birthplace
故国 ここく one's native land [country]
故旧 こきゅう old acquaintance
b 故事 こじ tradition; historical fact, origin
故実 こじつ ancient customs
故老(=古老) ころう elder, old man; old-timer
c 温故知新 おんこちしん Exploring the old [past] one comes to understand the new [present]
典故 てんこ authentic precedent
❷ⓐ [prefix] **THE LATE, deceased**
ⓑ die
a 故川田氏 こかわだし the late Mr. Kawada
故人 こじん the deceased
b 物故する ぶっこする die
❸ **incident, affair, event, occurrence**
故障 こしょう malfunction, breakdown; physical disorder; hindrance, obstacle, accident; objection, protest
事故 じこ accident, incident, trouble
世故 せこ worldly affairs
❹ **intentional, on purpose**
故意 こい intention, purpose, bad faith
故買 こばい buying stolen goods
❺ reason, cause, grounds
縁故 えんこ relation, connection; relative

KUN

【ゆえ 故】
ⓐ **reason, cause, grounds**
ⓑ circumstances
a 故に ゆえに therefore, accordingly
...の故に …のゆえに on account of..., by reason of...
ab 故有って ゆえあって for a certain reason; owing to unavoidable circumstances

SPECIAL READINGS

何故▲ なぜ why, for what reason

SYNONYMS

❶ⓐ **former**
旧 FORMER → 0014
元 former → 2428
故 OLD (earlier time) → 1466
前 previous → 2819
嘗て previously → 3230
曽 previously → 2632
先 former → 3046
既 ALREADY → 1498
ⓑ **old**
古 OLD (not new) → 2495
老 OLD (not young) → 3963
故 OLD (of the past) → 1466
旧 old → 0014
❷ⓐ **dead**
故 THE LATE → 1466
亡 deceased → 4210
❸ **incident**
事 AFFAIR → 4384
故 incident → 1466
変 unexpected event → 2569

【ゆえ】
ⓐ **cause and reason**
因 CAUSE → 3792
由 REASON → 4311
為 because → 4395
故 reason → 1466
訳 reason → 1865

胡

1467

1-5-4

▶**NATIVES OF ANCIENT CHINA**

コ ゴ ウ ㊔えび えびす ひさ

Ⓒ 胡 hú

74	Names	U80E1
月	S9-4-5	F1719

COMPOUNDS

❶ **NATIVES living in the north or west OF ANCIENT CHINA**
胡国 ここく ancient countries in the north or west of China; barbarous country
胡服 こふく Mongol [Tatar] dress
胡弓 こきゅう Chinese fiddle
❷ **foreign**
胡麻 ごま sesame
胡椒× こしょう pepper
❸ **suspicious; absurd**
胡散臭い うさんくさい suspicious-looking, questionable, shady
胡乱な うろんな suspicious-looking, questionable; in disorder
❹ [original meaning, now rare] loose flesh around the throat of cows or hens
胡髯× こぜん beard

INDEPENDENT

【こ 胡】*Hu*: generic term for the **NATIVES** of north or west **OF ANCIENT CHINA**

SPECIAL READINGS

胡瓜 きゅうり cucumber
胡坐 あぐら sitting cross-legged

SYNONYMS

❶ **China**
華 CHINA → 2841
漢 CHINESE → 0808
支 China → 2473
中 People's Republic of China → 4262

胡 NATIVES OF ANCIENT CHINA → 1467
台 Taiwan → 2498
唐 Cathay → 3867
呉 KINGDOM OF WU → 3156

政

1468

1-5-4

▶**POLITICAL ADMINISTRATION**

セイ ショウ まつりごと まん▲ ㊔ まさ まさる

Ⓒ 政 zhèng

66	Jōyō-5	U653F
攵	S9-4-5	F0094

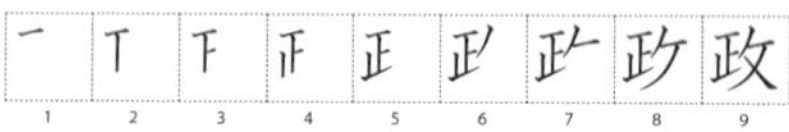

COMPOUNDS

❶ⓐ [also suffix] **POLITICAL ADMINISTRATION, government**
ⓑ form of government, government system

a 政府 せいふ government, administration
政治 せいじ government, administration, politics
政権 せいけん political power, administrative power
政策 せいさく policy, political measures
政令 せいれい government ordinance, cabinet order
行政 ぎょうせい administration
内政 ないせい domestic administration, internal affairs
郵政 ゆうせい postal system
国政 こくせい (national) administration, government
施政 しせい administration, government
民政 みんせい civil administration [government]
摂政 せっしょう regency; regent
東京都政 とうきょうとせい government of Tokyo Metropolis

b 共和政 きょうわせい republicanism

❷ **politics, political affairs**
政党 せいとう political party
政界 せいかい political world
政局 せいきょく political situation
政経 せいけい politics and economics

❸ **management (of one's affairs), administration**
家政 かせい household management
財政 ざいせい public finance, financial affairs

KUN

【まつりごと 政】 **administration, government, affairs of state**
政を執る まつりごとをとる administer the affairs of state

【まん 政】 [in compounds] **POLITICAL ADMINISTRATION, government**
政所 まんどころ administrative office (in the shogunate government); titled lady

SYNONYMS

❶ⓐ **government**
政 POLITICAL ADMINISTRATION → 1468
治 government → 0393

叛

1469

1-5-4

▶**REBEL**

ハン ホン そむ(く)

Ⓝ 叛 Ⓒ 叛 pàn

29	Non-Jōyō	U53DB
又	S9-2-7	F2276

COMPOUNDS

● [now replaced by 反 はん, ほん 3663] [original meaning] **REBEL, revolt**
叛乱 はんらん rebellion, revolt
叛逆 はんぎゃく revolt, rebellion, mutiny
叛旗 はんき flag [standard] of revolt
叛徒 はんと rebels, insurgents
謀叛 むほん rebellion, revolt, treason

KUN

【そむく 叛く】 [usu. 背く] **REBEL against, go against, disobey, violate**
親に叛く おやにそむく disobey one's parent(s)

SYNONYMS

● **resist**
抗 RESIST → 0296
抵 RESIST → 0377
耐 WITHSTAND → 1634
対 OPPOSE → 1025
反 COUNTER → 3663
逆 rebel → 3835
撥 REPEL → 0907
叛 REBEL → 1469

HOMOPHONES

そむく 背 BACK → 3182

NOTE

➡ see USAGE note at 背 3182

叛

1470

1-5-4

▶**REBEL**

ハン ホン そむ(く)

29	Nonstandard	U53DB
又	S9-2-7	F0000

traditional form → see 叛 at 1469

段

1471

1-5-4

▶**STEP**

ダン タン▲

Ⓒ 段 duàn

79	Jōyō-6	U6BB5
殳	S9-4-5	F0469

COMPOUNDS

❶ⓐ **STEP, stair, rung**
ⓑ **counter for STEPs**
a 段丘 だんきゅう terrace, bench (in geography)
階段 かいだん steps, flight of stairs
石段 いしだん stone steps
b 百段 ひゃくだん 100 steps

❷ⓐ (division or level) **STEP, stage, level**
ⓑ counter for **STEP**s or stages
a 段階 だんかい grade, rank, step, stage
段段 だんだん gradually, little by little; one after another
値段 ねだん price
一段と いちだんと greater, more, further
格段の相違 かくだんのそうい marked difference
多段式ロケット ただんしきろけっと multistage rocket
b 二段ベッド にだんべっど double bunk

❸ (step in a ranking system) **grade, degree or rank in go, karate, judo or various martial arts (higher than 級 きゅう)**
段違い だんちがい different class, different level; widely apart
初段 しょだん first degree black belt (as in karate)
有段者 ゆうだんしゃ grade holder
五段 ごだん fifth grade (as in karate)

❹ (means to an end) **STEP, measure**
段取り だんどり program, plan, step, course of action
手段 しゅだん means, way, step
算段 さんだん contrivance, management

❺ subdivision of a literary or artistic work:
ⓐ **passage (of a text or music), paragraph**
ⓑ act, scene (of a play)
a 段落 だんらく end of paragraph; conclusion
b 段物 だんもの musical [dramatic] piece in several acts
忠臣蔵六段目 ちゅうしんぐらろくだんめ Sixth Act of "Chushingura"

❻ⓐ column (of print), rank
ⓑ counter for columns (of print)
a 全段 ぜんだん whole page (of a newspaper)
b 二段組 にだんぐみ double column setting

❼ **case, occasion**
普段(=不断)の ふだんの usual, ordinary, everyday, habitual
別段の べつだんの particular, special

❽ [now usu. 反 たん 3663] *tan*: unit of sq. measure equiv. to approx. 9.9 ares or 300 *bu* (歩)

INDEPENDENT

【だん 段】
① **STEP, stair, rung**
梯子の段 はしごのだん rung of a ladder
② (division or level) **STEP**, stage, level
五の段の九九 ごのだんのくく the five times table
③ **grade, degree** (→❸)
段を取る だんをとる obtain a degree (in judo); get a black belt
④ subdivision of a literary or artistic work:
ⓐ passage (of a text or music), paragraph
ⓑ act, scene
a 物語の最後の段 ものがたりのさいごのだん last part of a story
⑤ column (of print)
⑥ case, occasion
いざと云う段になると いざというだんになると when the matter comes to a crisis

【たん 段】 *tan* (→❽)

SYNONYMS

❶ **steps**
段 STEP →1471
階 stairs →0761
陛 IMPERIAL PALACE STEPS →0543
梯 LADDER →1210

❸ **class**
級 GRADE →1630
段 grade →1471
位 RANK →0069
階 RANK →0761
身 social status →4368
格 STATUS →1161
等 CLASS →3321
流 class →0529
層 STRATUM →3920

❹ **means**
策 MEASURE →3320
段 STEP →1471
手 means →4267

❺ⓐ **parts of writing**
章 CHAPTER →2624
段 passage →1471
節 paragraph →3336
款 ARTICLE →2135
条 ARTICLE →2726
項 CLAUSE →0692
目 ITEM →3777
箇 item →3348

畔

▶WATERSIDE
ハン あぜ▲ ㊔ くろ
Ⓝ 畔 Ⓒ 畔 pàn

1472
1-5-5

102	Jōyō	U7554
田	S10-5-5	F2256

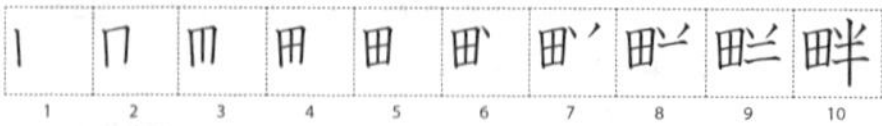

COMPOUNDS

❶ **WATERSIDE, water's edge, bank, shore**
湖畔 こはん lake shore, lakeside
河畔 かはん riverside, banks of a river
池畔 ちはん edge of a pond
橋畔 きょうはん approach to a bridge
吉野川畔 よしのがわはん the banks of Yoshino River

❷ [original meaning] ridge between rice fields

KUN

【あぜ 畔】ridge between rice fields
畔道 あぜみち footpath between rice fields

SYNONYMS

❶ **shores and watersides**
畔 WATERSIDE → 1472
-辺 -side → 3761
浜 BEACH → 0523
岸 SHORE → 2777
浦 SEASIDE → 0524
渚 STRAND → 0637
磯 ROCKY BEACH → 1587
汀 STRAND → 0228

畔

▶WATERSIDE
ハン あぜ ㊔ くろ

1473
1-5-5

102	Nonstandard	U7554
田	S10-5-5	F0000

traditional form → see 畔 at 1472

毗

incorrect stroke-count
➡ see 1-5-4: 田 at 1452

1-5-5

眠

▶SLEEP
ミン ねむ(る) ねむ(い)
Ⓒ 眠 mián

1474
1-5-5

109	Jōyō	U7720
目	S10-5-5	F0871

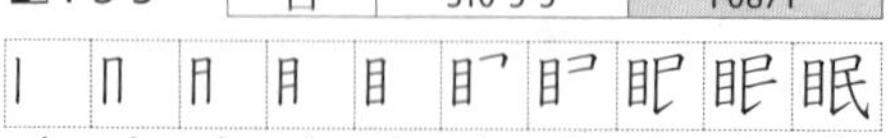

COMPOUNDS

● [original meaning] **SLEEP**
睡眠 すいみん sleep, slumber
催眠術 さいみんじゅつ hypnotism, mesmerism
不眠 ふみん sleeplessness, insomnia
冬眠 とうみん hibernation ("winter sleep")
安眠 あんみん quiet sleep, peaceful slumber
永眠 えいみん eternal sleep, death

KUN

【ねむる 眠る】**SLEEP; die; lie idle**
眠り ねむり sleep, slumber, nap
眠り込む ねむりこむ fall asleep
眠っている金 ねむっているかね money lying idle
安らかに眠れ やすらかにねむれ May rest in peace the deceased

【ねむい 眠い】**SLEEPy**
眠たい ねむたい sleepy
眠気 ねむけ sleepiness

SYNONYMS

● **sleep**
眠 SLEEP → 1474
睡 SLEEP → 1535
寝 GO TO SLEEP → 2925

矩

▶RULE
ク かね ㊔ のり つね ただす ただし
Ⓝ 矩 Ⓒ 矩 jǔ

1475
1-5-5

111	Names	U77E9
矢	S10-5-5	F1963

COMPOUNDS

❶ⓐ (established standard) **RULE, standard, criterion**
ⓑ (measuring tool) carpenter's square, **RULE**, ruler
a 矩則 くそく rule, standard
b 規矩 きく standard, rule; compass and ruler

❷ square, rectangle
矩形 くけい rectangle

❸ *astron* quadrature
矩象 くしょう quadrature

INDEPENDENT

【く 矩】*astron* quadrature

KUN

【かね 矩】**carpenter's square, metal measure; regular *shaku* (尺) (approx. 12 in.)**
矩尺(=曲尺) かねじゃく carpenter's square; regular *shaku* (尺) (approx. 12 in.)

SYNONYMS

❶ⓐ **laws and rules**
法 LAW → 0391
律 LAW → 0433
典 CANON → 3253
憲 CONSTITUTION → 3001
令 ordinance → 2489
則 RULE → 1831

矩 RULE → 1475
規 REGULATION → 1231
紀 discipline → 1628

NOTE

★ do not confuse with 短 SHORT → 1515

矩
1476
1-5-5

▶RULE
ク かね 名 のり つね ただす ただし

111	Nonstandard	U77E9
矢	S10-5-5	F0000

traditional form → see 矩 at 1475

砧
1477
1-5-5

▶BLOCK FOR BEATING CLOTH
チン きぬた 名 きぬ
C 砧 zhēn

112	Names	U7827
石	S10-5-5	F0000

COMPOUNDS

● stone **BLOCK FOR BEATING CLOTH**
鉄砧 てっちん anvil

KUN

【きぬた 砧】stone **BLOCK FOR BEATING CLOTH**
砧骨 きぬたこつ(=ちんこつ) incus

SYNONYMS

● **instruments for beating or pounding**
槌 HAMMER → 1331
杵 WOODEN PESTLE → 1074
砧 BLOCK FOR BEATING CLOTH → 1477

破
1478
1-5-5

▶BREAK
ハ やぶ(る) やぶ(れる)
C 破 pò

112	Jōyō-5	U7834
石	S10-5-5	F0649

1	2	3	4	5	6	7	8	9	10
一	ｱ	𠂇	石	石	石	矿	矿	破	破

COMPOUNDS

❶ⓐ [original meaning] **BREAK, smash**
ⓑ **BREAK through, penetrate**
ⓒ **BREAK** out (of jail), escape

a 破壊する はかいする break (down), destroy, wreck
破片 はへん fragment, broken piece, scrap
破損 はそん damage, breakdown
破砕する はさいする crush, smash, crack to pieces
破滅 はめつ ruin, destruction, wreck, collapse, downfall
爆破 ばくは blasting, blowing up, explosion
難破 なんぱ shipwreck
打破する だはする break down, overthrow, abolish

b 突破する とっぱする break [smash] through; surmount; exceed
看破する かんぱする see through, penetrate, read (another's thoughts)

c 破牢× はろう jailbreak
破獄 はごく jailbreak

❷ **BREAK the enemy, defeat**
撃破する げきはする defeat, rout; destroy
論破する ろんぱする refute, defeat in argument
連破する れんぱする defeat one's enemy in succession

❸ⓐ (act contrary to) **BREAK (as a promise), breach, violate**
ⓑ **BREAK with (the moral conventions), be exceptional**

a 破棄 はき breaking (a treaty), annulment
破談 はだん cancellation, breaking off
破約 はやく breach of contract

b 破格の はかくの exceptional, unconventional; irregular, contrary to usage
破廉恥 はれんち shamelessness, infamy, impudence
破門 はもん excommunication, expulsion

❹ **BREAK down, go to pieces, go broke**
破局 はきょく collapse, catastrophe
破綻 はたん failure, rupture; bankruptcy
破産する はさんする go bankrupt, go broke

❺ **carry through with, perform an action to the end**
読破する どくはする read through
走破する そうはする run [cover] the whole distance
描破する びょうはする depict thoroughly

❻ second part of a traditional Japanese performance
序破急 じょはきゅう artistic modulations in traditional Japanese performances; opening, middle and climax [end]

INDEPENDENT

【は 破】second part of a traditional Japanese performance

KUN

【やぶる 破る】
①ⓐ **BREAK, smash, destroy**
ⓑ **tear, rip**

a 戸を破る とをやぶる break a door
b 紙を破る かみをやぶる tear (up) paper

② (force one's way) **BREAK through, penetrate, break out (of jail)**
囲みを破る かこみをやぶる break through a siege
見破る みやぶる see through, penetrate, read (another's thoughts)
金庫破り きんこやぶり safecracking; safecracker

③ **BREAK the enemy, defeat**
敵を破る てきをやぶる defeat one's enemy

④ (surpass) **BREAK (a record)**
記録を破る きろくをやぶる break the record
⑤ⓐ (act contrary to) **BREAK (a promise), breach, violate**
ⓑ **BREAK** with (the moral conventions), be exceptional
a 規則を破る きそくをやぶる violate the rules
b 型破りの かたやぶりの extraordinary, uncommon
⑥ baffle, thwart, frustrate
スト破り すとやぶり strikebreaker, scab; strikebreaking

【やぶれる 破れる】
① **tear, be torn, rip open**
破れ目 やぶれめ rent, tear, split
② **be ruined**
国破れて くにやぶれて with one's country in ruins
③ be baffled, be frustrated
破れた夢 やぶれたゆめ shattered dream

SYNONYMS

❶ⓐ **break**
破 BREAK → 1478
拉ぐ crush → 0372
崩 CRUMBLE → 2863
挫 SPRAIN → 0519
壊 BREAK DOWN → 0934
毀す break down → 2246
折 BREAK OFF → 0297
割る crack → 2284
裂 SPLIT → 3331
砕 CRUSH UP → 1458
摧 CRUSH UP → 0849
潰す CRUSH → 0919
ⓑ **penetrate**
透 PASS THROUGH → 3854
貫 PENETRATE → 3112
破 break through → 1478
滲 PERMEATE → 0862
❷ **win**
勝 WIN → 1268
克 OVERCOME → 2540
剋 OVERCOME → 4097
征 CONQUER → 0349
破 BREAK → 1478
凱 TRIUMPH → 2286
❸ⓐ **violate**
違 VIOLATE → 3907
破 BREAK → 1478
犯 offend against → 0229
反 act contrary to → 3663
悖 GO AGAINST → 0503
背 go against → 3182
❹ **degenerate**
落 FALL → 2907
衰 DECLINE → 2604
頽 DECLINE → 2039
堕 DEGENERATE → 3501
綻 UNRAVEL → 1745
破 break down → 1478
❺ **accomplish**
達 ATTAIN → 3893
遂 ACCOMPLISH → 3892
成 ACHIEVE → 4352
徹 GO THROUGH → 0894
破 carry through with → 1478
叶 BE FULFILLED → 0209

USAGE

【やぶれる】
破れる
① tear, be torn, rip open
② be ruined
③ be baffled, be frustrated
敗れる
be defeated, be beaten, lose

HOMOPHONES

やぶれる 敗 BE DEFEATED → 1868

NOTE

➡ see COMPOUND FORMATION for 破瓜 はか → 瓜 3789

砲

1479

1-5-5

▶**HEAVY GUN**
ホウ
Ⓝ 砲 Ⓒ 炮 pào

112	Jōyō	U7832
石	S10-5-5	F1176

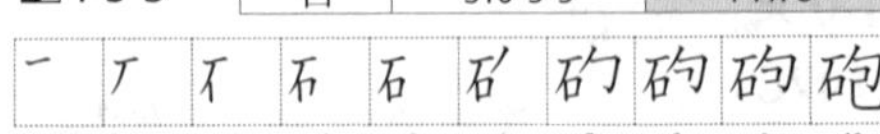

COMPOUNDS

❶ [rarely also 炮 1132]
ⓐ [also suffix] **HEAVY GUN, gun, artillery, ordnance**
ⓑ **cannon**
a 砲火 ほうか gunfire
砲声 ほうせい sound of firing, roar of cannon
砲術 ほうじゅつ gunnery, artillery
祝砲 しゅくほう feu de joie, artillery [gun] salute
鉄砲 てっぽう gun, firearm
銃砲 じゅうほう firearm
重砲 じゅうほう heavy gun
発砲する はっぽうする fire, discharge (a gun)
対戦車砲 たいせんしゃほう antitank gun
b 砲丸 ほうがん cannonball
大砲 たいほう gun, cannon, artillery
❷ suffix after names of main batters

田 目 矢 【石】 示 禾 立 衤 疋 艮 弓 弓

ＯＮ砲 おーえぬほう Oh and Nagashima (famous baseball stars)

❸ [original meaning, now obsolete] catapult

INDEPENDENT

【ほう 砲】 cannon; artillery, guns

SYNONYMS

❶ **weapons for shooting**

銃 GUN (portable firearm) → 2157
砲 HEAVY GUN → 1479
火 firearms → 4273
弓 BOW → 4193

砥

1480
◧ 1-5-5

▶**WHETSTONE**
シ と と(ぐ)
Ⓒ 砥 dǐ

112	Names	U7825
石	S10-5-5	F2440

COMPOUNDS

❶ **WHETSTONE, grindstone**

砥礪× しれい whetstone; diligent study, self-disciplinary efforts

❷ⓐ sharpen, grind, whet, polish
ⓑ strive for, make efforts

KUN

【と 砥】 **WHETSTONE, grindstone**

砥石 といし whetstone, grindstone
砥草(=木賊) とくさ scouring rush
中砥 なかと(=ちゅうど) medium-grade whetstone
革砥 かわと leather strop

【とぐ 砥ぐ】 [now always 研ぐ] sharpen, grind, whet, polish

SYNONYMS

❶ **kinds of stone**

硯 INKSTONE → 1517
砥 WHETSTONE → 1480

HOMOPHONES

とぐ 研 GRIND → 1456

NOTE

➡ see USAGE note at 研 1456

砲

1481
◧ 1-5-5

▶**HEAVY GUN**
ホウ

112	Nonstandard	U7832
石	S10-5-5	F0000

traditional form → see 砲 at 1479

砿

1482
◧ 1-5-5

▶**ORE**
▶**MINE**
コウ

112	Nonstandard	U783F
石	S10-5-5	F0000

traditional form → see 礦 at 1606

祕

1483
◧ 1-5-5

▶**SECRET**
ヒ ひ(める)

113	Names	U7955
示	S10-5-5	F0000

traditional form → see 秘 at 1490

神

1484
◧ 1-5-5

▶**GOD**
▶**MIND**
シン ジン かみ かん- こう- ㊔ かむ か みわ

113	Names	UFA19
示	S10-5-5	F0000

traditional form → see 神 at 1143

祝

1485
◧ 1-5-5

▶**CELEBRATE**
シュク シュウ いわ(う) ㊔ はじめ ほうり のり とき

113	Names	UFA51
示	S10-5-5	F0000

traditional form → see 祝 at 1144

祖

1486
◧ 1-5-5

▶**ANCESTOR**
ソ

113	Names	UFA50
示	S10-5-5	F0000

traditional form → see 祖 at 1145

祐

1487
◧ 1-5-5

▶**DIVINE HELP**
ユウ ウ ㊔ すけ さち ひろし ゆたか たすく まさ ひろ よし

113	Names	UFA4F
示	S10-5-5	F0000

traditional form → see 祐 at 1146

秤

1488
◧ 1-5-5

▶**BALANCE**
ビン ショウ ヒョウ はかり
Ⓝ 秤 Ⓒ 秤 chèng

115	Names	U79E4
禾	S10-5-5	F2459

COMPOUNDS

● **BALANCE, scale(s)**

秤量(=称量) しょうりょう weighing on a balance
秤量 ひょうりょう weighing on a balance; maximum weight capacity

秤動 ひょうどう libration (of a heavenly body)
天秤 てんびん balance, scale(s)
天秤座 てんびんざ Libra, the Scales

KUN

【はかり 秤】**BALANCE, scale(s), weighing machine**
秤に掛ける はかりにかける weigh on a scale; weigh the pros and cons
皿秤 さらばかり balance
台秤 だいばかり platform scale
水秤 みずばかり water level

SYNONYMS

● measuring devices
枡 MEASURE → 1070
尺 rule → 4248
計 meter → 1828
衡 scales → 0939
秤 BALANCE → 1488

秩

▶ORDER
チツ ㊔ ちち
Ⓒ 秩 zhì

1489
1-5-5

115	Jōyō	U79E9
禾	S10-5-5	F1776

COMPOUNDS

❶ ORDER, methodical arrangement
秩序 ちつじょ order, discipline; method, system
❷ [rare] fief, retainer's stipend, salary
秩禄 ちつろく official salary

SYNONYMS

❶ order
序 ORDER (sequence/arrangement) → 3803
順 ORDER (sequence) → 0018
次 order (sequence) → 0058
番 NUMERICAL ORDER → 3416
秩 ORDER (methodical arrangement) → 1489

秘

▶SECRET
ヒ ひ(める)
Ⓝ 祕 Ⓒ 秘 mì bì

1490
1-5-5

115	Jōyō-6	U79D8
禾	S10-5-5	F0695

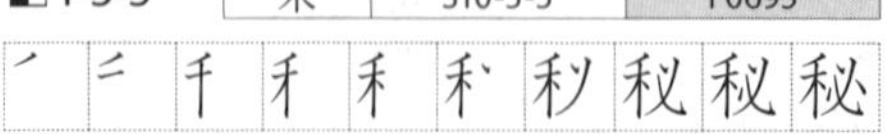

COMPOUNDS

❶ⓐ [original meaning] (without the knowledge of others) **SECRET, private, clandestine, hidden**
ⓑ (something kept secret) **SECRET, secrecy**
ⓒ [original meaning] (beyond human understanding) **SECRET, mysterious, abstruse**
a 秘密 ひみつ secret, mystery; privacy
秘術 ひじゅつ secret (art); the best of one's skill
秘訣 ひけつ secret, key
秘伝 ひでん secret, mystery
秘宝 ひほう (hidden) treasure
秘書 ひしょ secretary; treasured book
黙秘する もくひする keep silent, keep secret
b 極秘 ごくひ strict secrecy, top secret
部外秘の ぶがいひの restricted
c 神秘 しんぴ mystery
❷ constipated
秘結 ひけつ constipation, costiveness
便秘 べんぴ constipation

INDEPENDENT

【ひ 秘】**SECRET**
秘中の秘 ひちゅうのひ top secret, secret of secrets
【ひする 秘する】keep **SECRET**, conceal, hide

KUN

【ひめる 秘める】**keep SECRET, conceal, hide**
秘め事 ひめごと secret
心に秘める こころにひめる keep to oneself

SYNONYMS

❶ⓐ & ❶ⓑ secret and private
秘 SECRET → 1490
密 SECRET → 2857
暗 in the dark → 1273
私 PRIVATE → 1432
内 not public → 4277
隠 hidden from view → 0873

NOTE

➡ see COMPOUND FORMATION for 秘書 ひしょ → 書 3292

称

▶APPELLATION
ショウ たた(える)▲
Ⓝ 稱 Ⓒ 称 chēng chèn chèng

1491
1-5-5

115	Jōyō	U79F0
禾	S10-5-5	F0815

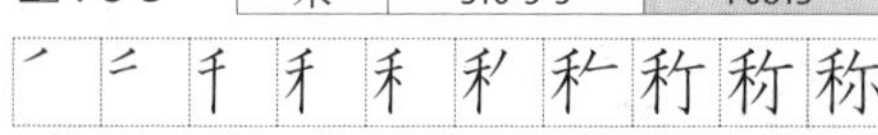

COMPOUNDS

❶ⓐ APPELLATION, name, title
ⓑ name, call, designate, entitle
a 称号 しょうごう title, degree
名称 めいしょう appellation, name, title
通称 つうしょう popular [common] name
俗称 ぞくしょう popular [common] name
愛称 あいしょう nickname, pet name

総称 そうしょう generic name, general term
b 呼称する こしょうする call, name
誇称する こしょうする boast, exaggerate
自称する じしょうする profess oneself (to be someone), call [style] oneself

❷ acclaim, commend, praise, admire
称賛(=賞賛) しょうさん laudation, praise, admiration, commendation
称揚 しょうよう praise, admiration, exaltation

❸ **symmetrical, matching**
対称 たいしょう symmetry

❹ *gram* person
一人称 いちにんしょう first person
他称 たしょう third person

INDEPENDENT

【しょう 称】name, title, designation; fame
【しょうする 称する】name, designate; pretend, claim; acclaim, praise
病と称する やまいとしょうする feign illness, pretend to be ill

KUN

【たたえる 称える】praise, extol
誉め称える ほめたたえる admire, applaud, praise

SYNONYMS

❶ⓐ **name**
名 NAME → 2693
銘 name (inscribed by maker) → 2158
姓 SURNAME → 0334
氏 FAMILY NAME → 3669
称 APPELLATION → 1491
題 TITLE → 4139
号 DESIGNATION → 2675

ⓑ **name**
呼 CALL → 0324
言う call → 2440
称 name → 1491

❷ **praise**
賛 PRAISE → 3484
頌 EULOGIZE → 1319
謳 EXTOL → 2061
讃 PRAISE → 2093
美 regard as beautiful → 2817
褒 COMMEND → 2662
嘉 commend (esp. an inferior) → 2953
彰 PROCLAIM MERITS → 2337
称 acclaim → 1491
賞 express admiration → 3237
揚 EXALT → 0722

HOMOPHONES

たたえる 讃 PRAISE → 2093

NOTE

➡ see USAGE note at 讃 2093

租 1492 ◧ 1-5-5

▶LAND TAX
ソ
Ⓒ 租 zū

115	Jōyō	U79DF
禾	S10-5-5	F2381

COMPOUNDS

❶ **LAND TAX, crop tax, taxes**
租税 そぜい taxes, taxation
租庸調 そようちょう taxes in kind or service (former tax system), corvée
田租 でんそ rice field tax
地租 ちそ land tax
免租 めんそ tax exemption
貢租 こうそ tribute, annual tax

❷ rent, lease (land or a house)
租借する そしゃくする lease
租界 そかい concession, settlement

SYNONYMS

❶ **tax**
税 TAX → 1525
租 LAND TAX → 1492
貢 TRIBUTE → 2838
賦 levy → 1992

秤 1493 ◧ 1-5-5

▶BALANCE
ビン ショウ ヒョウ はかり

115	Nonstandard	U79E4
禾	S10-5-5	F0000

traditional form → see 秤 at 1488

竝 1494 ◧ 1-5-5

▶LINE UP
ヘイ なみ な(み) なら(べる) なら(ぶ) なら(びに)

117	Nonstandard	U7ADD
立	S10-5-5	F0000

traditional form → see 並 at 2793

被 1495 ◧ 1-5-5

▶BE SUBJECTED TO
ヒ こうむ(る) おお(う)▲ かぶ(る)▲ かぶ(せる)▲
Ⓒ 被 bèi

145	Jōyō	U88AB
衤	S10-5-5	F0797

`	ラ	ネ	ネ	ネ	衤	衤	衤	被	被
1	2	3	4	5	6	7	8	9	10

COMPOUNDS

❶ⓐ BE SUBJECTED TO, undergo, suffer
ⓑ auxiliary verb for forming the passive voice similar to the English *be*

a 被害 ひがい damage, harm
被弾 ひだん being bombed
被災 ひさい suffering, affection
b 被傭者(=被用者) ひようしゃ employee
被爆者 ひばくしゃ victim of atomic air raid
被告人 ひこくにん defendant
被保険者 ひほけんしゃ insured person
被選挙権 ひせんきょけん eligibility for election

❷ⓐ cover, envelope; wear
ⓑ cover(ing), clothing

a 被覆 ひふく covering, coating
被膜 ひまく tunic, capsule
b 被服 ひふく clothing
外被 がいひ outer cover
法被 はっぴ (workman's) livery coat
花被 かひ perianth, floral envelope

KUN

【こうむる 被る】[also 蒙る] **BE SUBJECTED TO, undergo, receive, sustain**
損害を被る そんがいをこうむる suffer a loss
恩恵を被る おんけいをこうむる share in the benefit

【おおう 被う】[usu. 覆う] cover, veil
被い おおい cover, mantle
雪で被われる ゆきでおおわれる be covered with snow

【かぶる 被る】put on headgear, wear; pour (as water) on oneself, be covered with; take upon oneself; *photography* be fogged
猫被り ねこかぶり hypocrisy, false modesty; hypocrite, wolf in a lamb's skin
引っ被る ひっかぶる pull (a thing) over one's head
泥を被る どろをかぶる be covered with mud; take another's fault upon oneself

【かぶせる 被せる】cover, put (a thing) on, plate (a thing) with, pour, dash (water) on; pin (a crime) on, frame
土を被せる つちをかぶせる cover with earth
歯に金を被せる はにきんをかぶせる crown a tooth with gold
押っ被せる おっかぶせる put a thing on top of another

SYNONYMS

❶ⓐ be subjected to
被 BE SUBJECTED TO → 1495
受 be subjected to → 3076

❷ⓐ cover and wrap
覆 COVER → 3386
掩 COVER → 0592
被 cover → 1495
包 WRAP → 3684
蓋う COVER → 2933
蔽 COVER → 2991
葺く THATCH → 2909

【かぶる】
◯ **wear and put on**
着 PUT ON → 4110
装 DRESS → 3327
帯 WEAR (esp. at the belt) → 3191
穿く PUT ON → 2800
纏 put on → 1814
履く put on footwear → 3933
被る put on headgear → 1495

USAGE

【こうむる】
被る
[also 蒙る] be subjected to, undergo, receive, sustain
蒙る
[also 被る] same as 被る

HOMOPHONES

こうむる 蒙 IGNORANCE → 2938
おおう
覆 COVER → 3386
蓋 COVER → 2933
掩 COVER → 0592
蔽 COVER → 2991

NOTE

➡ see also USAGE note at 覆 3386

袖

1496
◨ 1-5-5

▸SLEEVE
シュウ そで
Ⓒ 袖 xiù

145	Jōyō	U8896
ネ	S10-5-5	F1564

`	ラ	ネ	ネ	ネ	衤	衤	衤	袖	袖
1	2	3	4	5	6	7	8	9	10

COMPOUNDS

● [original meaning] **SLEEVE**
袖手傍観する しゅうしゅぼうかんする look on with folded arms [with one's hands in one's sleeves], remain a passive onlooker
袖珍本 しゅうちんぼん pocket-size book
袖状移植片 しゅうじょういしょくへん sleeve graft
領袖 りょうしゅう leader, chief

KUN

【そで 袖】 [also suffix] **SLEEVE; wing (as of a building)**

袖口 そでぐち edge of a sleeve; cuff, sleeve band, wristband

長袖の ながそでの long-sleeved

七分袖 しちぶそで three-quarter sleeves

元禄袖 げんろくそで short and round sleeves of a kimono

舞台の左右の袖 ぶたいのさゆうのそで wings of a stage

片袖机 かたそでづくえ desk with a wing

SYNONYMS

● **garment parts**

襟 COLLAR → 1599

袖 SLEEVE → 1496

懐 BOSOM → 0942

衿 COLLAR → 1465

裾 HEM → 1549

COMPOUND FORMATION

【領袖 りょうしゅう】

領袖 'leader, chief' refers to the collar (領) and sleeve (袖), which are the most prominent parts of one's garment.

鬥 ▸*TŌGAMAE*

1497

◧ 1-5-5

191	Radical	U9B25
鬥	S10-10-0	F0000

RADICAL

tōgamae 'fight' (鬩× 鬪 鬧×), used in characters related to fighting

---

既 ▸**ALREADY**

キ すで(に)

Ⓝ 旣 既 Ⓒ 既 jì

1498

◧ 1-5-5

71	Jōyō	U65E2
旡	S10-5-5	F1392

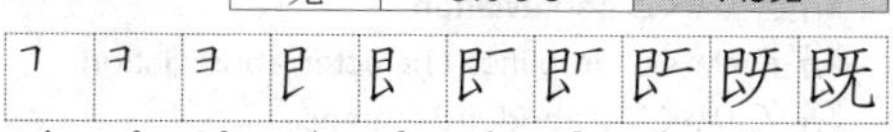

COMPOUNDS

❶ [also prefix] **ALREADY, previous**

既刊の きかんの already published

既婚の きこんの already married

既存の きそんの existing

既定の きていの fixed, prearranged

既往症 きおうしょう previous illness, medical history

既知数 きちすう known quantity

既報 きほう previous report

既製の きせいの ready-made, ready-to-wear

既製品 きせいひん ready-made goods

既発表の きはっぴょうの already published

❷ finish

皆既日食 かいきにっしょく total solar eclipse

KUN

【すでに 既に】

①ⓐ [formerly also 已に] **ALREADY**

ⓑ **previously**

a 彼は既に出発していた かれはすでにしゅっぱつしていた He had already started

b 既に申した様に すでにもうしたように as I have previously stated

② itself, in itself

その事が既に そのことがすでに the fact itself, the very fact

SYNONYMS

❶ **former**

旧 FORMER → 0014

元 former → 2428

故 OLD (earlier time) → 1466

前 previous → 2819

嘗て previously → 3230

曽 previously → 2632

先 former → 3046

既 ALREADY → 1498

USAGE

【すでに】

既に

①ⓐ [formerly also 已に] already

ⓑ previously

② itself, in itself

已に

[now usu. 既に] already

HOMOPHONES

すでに 已 CEASE → 4185

弱 ▸**WEAK**

ジャク よわ(い) よわ(る) よわ(まる) よわ(める)

Ⓝ 弱 Ⓒ 弱 ruò

1499

◧ 1-5-5

57	Jōyō-2	U5F31
弓	S10-3-7	F0895

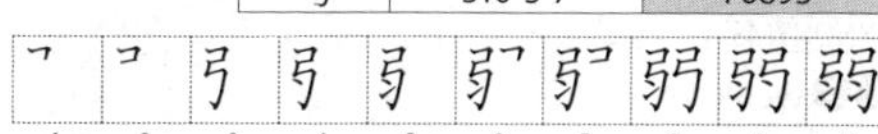

COMPOUNDS

❶ⓐ [also prefix] [original meaning] (lacking strength) **WEAK, feeble**

ⓑ [also prefix] (lacking force) **WEAK**

ⓒ **WEAK**en

a 弱点 じゃくてん weak point

弱肉強食 じゃくにくきょうしょく law of the jungle (the strong prey on the weak)
虚弱な きょじゃくな weak, feeble, sickly
b 弱震 じゃくしん weak earthquake, minor tremor
弱毒 じゃくどく weak poison
弱電器 じゃくでんき light electrical appliance
弱酸性 じゃくさんせい slight acidity
c 衰弱する すいじゃくする weaken, lose vigor
❷ [also 若 2785] young
弱年 じゃくねん youth, early age
弱冠 じゃっかん 20 years old; youth
❸ [suffix] a little less than
一マイル弱 いちまいるじゃく a little less than a mile

INDEPENDENT

【じゃく 弱】**WEAK**ness, feebleness; the weak
弱を以て強に当たる じゃくをもってきょうにあたる attacking strength by means of [with] weakness

KUN

【よわい 弱い】**WEAK, feeble; fragile, frail, invalid;** (lacking competence) **weak, poor, unskilled**
弱さ よわさ weakness
弱み よわみ weakness; shortcoming
弱火 よわび low fire, gentle heating
弱味 よわみ weak point, sore spot
弱気な よわきな timid; weak-spirited; bearish (stock market)
弱音 よわね complaints
ひ弱な ひよわな weak, delicate, sickly
か弱い かよわい weak, frail, tender
数字に弱い すうじによわい not good with figures

【よわる 弱る】*vi* **WEAKen, wane; be debilitated [emaciated]; be embarrassed, be in a fix**
弱り果てる よわりはてる be worn out; be helpless
大弱りの おおよわりの very much annoyed

【よわまる 弱まる】*vi* **WEAKen, abate, wane**
弱まり よわまり weakening, abatement
風が弱まった かぜがよわまった The wind has fallen

【よわめる 弱める】*vt* **WEAKen, attenuate, lower, soften, tone down, dilute**
ガスを弱める がすをよわめる turn down the gas
語気を弱める ごきをよわめる soften one's voice

SYNONYMS

❶ⓐ weak
弱 WEAK → 1499
柔 SOFT → 2591
脆 FRAGILE → 1191
癈 DISABLED → 4077
ⓑ less in degree
弱 WEAK → 1499
軽 LIGHT → 1909
微 SLIGHT → 0788
低 LOW → 0082
薄 THIN → 3004
浅 SHALLOW → 0464
仄 FAINT → 3664
ⓒ weaken
衰 DECLINE → 2604
弱 weaken → 1499
❷ young
若 YOUNG → 2785
弱 young → 1499
少 young → 4278
青 youthful → 3084
幼 VERY YOUNG → 0222
稚 CHILDISH → 1543

弱

1500

1-5-5

▸WEAK
ジャク よわ(い) よわ(る) よわ(まる) よわ(める)

57	Nonstandard	U5F31
弓	S10-3-7	F0000

traditional form → see 弱 at 1499

略

1501

1-5-6

▸ABRIDGED
▸STRATEGY
リャク ほぼ▲
Ⓝ 畧◇ Ⓒ 略 lüè

102	Jōyō-5	U7565
田	S11-5-6	F0718

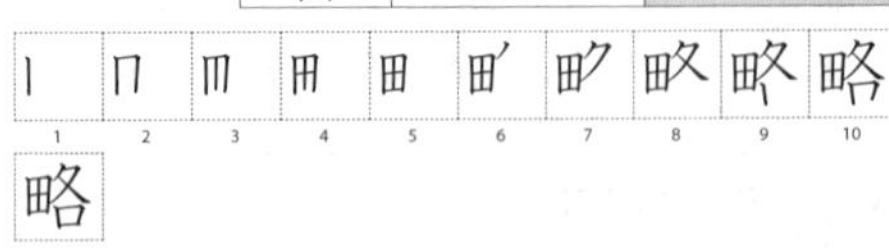

COMPOUNDS

❶ⓐ ABRIDGED, brief, concise
ⓑ essentials, gist
a 略語 りゃくご abbreviation
略字 りゃくじ simplified character; abbreviation
略文 りゃくぶん abridged sentence
略歴 りゃくれき brief personal history
簡略な かんりゃくな simple, brief, concise; informal
b 要略 ようりゃく epitome, summary, outline
概略 がいりゃく outline, summary; roughly, approximately
❷ⓐ omit, leave out
ⓑ informal
a 省略する しょうりゃくする omit, abbreviate, abridge
中略 ちゅうりゃく ellipsis, omission (of interior parts)
b 略式の りゃくしきの informal, summary
略服 りゃくふく informal clothes [dress]

❸ **STRATEGY, plan, tactics, scheme, stratagem**
計略 けいりゃく stratagem, plan, scheme
戦略 せんりゃく strategy, stratagem
政略 せいりゃく political tactics [maneuver], politicking
策略 さくりゃく artifice, stratagem, scheme
謀略 ぼうりゃく stratagem, scheme, plot
党略 とうりゃく party politics [tactics]

❹ [formerly also 掠 0605] **plunder, pillage**
略奪 りゃくだつ pillage, plunder, looting
略取 りゃくしゅ capture, occupation, plunder
侵略する しんりゃくする invade, aggress (against)
攻略 こうりゃく capture, conquest; invasion

❺ supervise, plan
経略する けいりゃくする administer, rule

INDEPENDENT

【りゃく 略】**abbreviation, abridgment; omission; outline, summary**
ＥはＥＡＳＴの略である いーはいーすとのりゃくである "E" is an abbreviation of "East"

【りゃくす 略す】**abbreviate, shorten; omit, leave out**
略して りゃくして for short

KUN

【ほぼ 略】
ⓐ nearly, almost, just about, practically
ⓑ approximately, roughly, about, more or less

SYNONYMS

❶ⓐ **short and shortened**
短 SHORT → 1515
簡 simplified → 3380
略 ABRIDGED → 1501

❷ⓐ **abridge**
要 SUMMARIZE → 3263
抄 EXCERPT → 0298
約 CONTRACT → 1632
略 omit → 1501

❸ **plans and planning**
計 PLAN → 1828
画 DRAW UP A PLAN → 3723
案 PROPOSAL → 2824
企 PROJECT → 2513
図 systematic plan → 3809
謀 SCHEME → 2004
策 SCHEME → 3320
略 STRATEGY → 1501
揆 PLOT → 0718

❹ **steal and rob**
盗 STEAL → 3309
窃 STEAL → 2801
取 TAKE → 1613
奪 ROB → 2956
略 plunder → 1501
掠 PLUNDER → 0605
鹵 PLUNDER → 2634

眸

1502
1-5-6

▶**EYE**
ボウ ひとみ
Ⓒ 眸 móu

109	Names	U7738
目	S11-5-6	F2178

COMPOUNDS

ⓐ [original meaning] **EYE, eyes**
ⓑ pupil (of the eye)
a 眸子 ぼうし eye; pupil
双眸 そうぼう both eyes
明眸 めいぼう bright eyes, beautiful eyes
一眸(=一望) いちぼう sweep of the eye

KUN

【ひとみ 眸】[usu. 瞳]
ⓐ **pupil, the apple of one's EYE**
ⓑ **one's EYEs**
b 黒い眸 くろいひとみ (beautiful) dark eyes

SYNONYMS

● **eye**
目 EYE → 3777
眼 EYE → 1504
眸 EYE → 1502
瞳 PUPIL → 1583

HOMOPHONES

ひとみ 瞳 PUPIL → 1583

NOTE

➡ see USAGE note at 瞳 1583

眺

1503
1-5-6

▶**LOOK OUT OVER**
チョウ なが(める)
Ⓒ 眺 tiào

109	Jōyō	U773A
目	S11-5-6	F1084

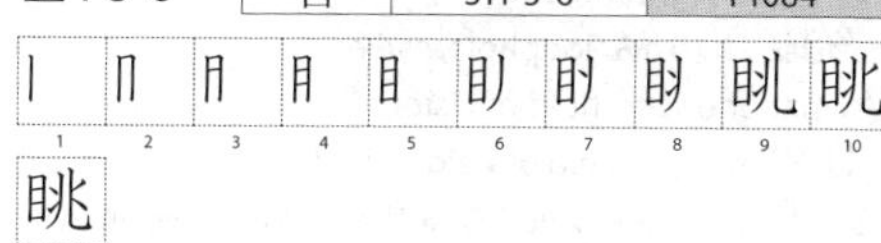

COMPOUNDS

● [original meaning] **LOOK OUT OVER, look far and wide, look afar, gaze**
眺望 ちょうぼう view, prospect, outlook

KUN

【ながめる 眺める】**LOOK OUT OVER, look afar, gaze, look at, watch**

眺め ながめ view, scene; prospect, outlook
海を眺める うみをながめる look out over the sea
月を眺める つきをながめる gaze at the moon

SYNONYMS

● **see and look**
見 SEE → 3151
看 WATCH → 3992
察 INSPECT → 2961
窺 WATCH FURTIVELY → 3002
瞥 GLANCE AT → 3592
目 look → 3777
観 VIEW → 2359
覧 LOOK OVER → 3538
眺 LOOK OUT OVER → 1503
望 LOOK AFAR → 3408
仰 LOOK UP → 0051
顧 LOOK BACK → 2394
視 REGARD → 1223

眼

1504
1-5-6

▶EYE
ガン ゲン まなこ まな-▲ め▲ ㊔ さっか
Ⓒ 眼 yǎn

109	Jōyō-5	U773C
目	S11-5-6	F0504

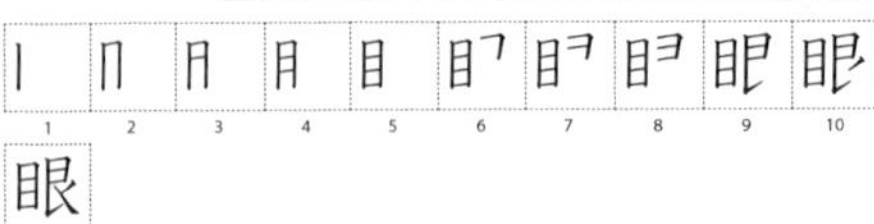

COMPOUNDS

❶ⓐ [original meaning] **EYE**
ⓑ (small hole) **EYE, eyelet, loop**
a 眼球 がんきゅう eyeball
眼科 がんか ophthalmology
碧眼 へきがん blue eyes
近眼 きんがん nearsightedness
双眼鏡 そうがんきょう binoculars
開眼 かいげん opening one's eyes to the truth, enlightenment
b 銃眼 じゅうがん loophole, eyelet
❷ what one sees, field of vision
眼界 がんかい field of vision, sight
着眼する ちゃくがんする notice, aim at, have an eye to
❸ [also suffix] (power of discrimination) **EYE, discernment, insight**
眼力 がんりき insight, power of observation
眼識 がんしき insight, discrimination
審美眼 しんびがん an eye for the beautiful, aesthetic sense
❹ key point, gist
眼目 がんもく main object [point], gist, essence
主眼 しゅがん prime object, central aim, gist
❺ [formerly 嵌 がん 2897] inlay, set in
象眼 ぞうがん inlaid work, inlaying

INDEPENDENT

【がん 眼】**EYE**
眼を付ける がんをつける fasten one's eye on (a person)

KUN

【まなこ 眼】**EYE**
寝惚け眼 ねぼけまなこ sleepy eyes; drowsy look
団栗眼 どんぐりまなこ goggle eyes, round eyes
【まな- 眼】[in compounds] **EYE**
眼差し まなざし look, expression
【め 眼】[usu. 目] **EYE**
眼鏡 めがね(=がんきょう) glasses, spectacles; judgment, insight

SYNONYMS

❶ **eye**
目 EYE → 3777
眼 EYE → 1504
眸 EYE → 1502
瞳 PUPIL → 1583
❸ **discernment**
識 power of discrimination → 2070
眼 EYE → 1504

HOMOPHONES

め
目 EYE → 3777
芽 BUD → 2784

NOTE

➡ see USAGE note at 目 3777

務

1505
1-5-6

▶DUTY
ム つと(める) つと(まる) ㊔ つかさ つとむ ちか かね
Ⓒ 务 wù

19	Jōyō-5	U52D9
力	S11-2-9	F0243

COMPOUNDS

❶ (task required by one's occupation) **DUTY, task, office, function**
任務 にんむ duty, part, function; mission
勤務 きんむ duty, service, work
職務 しょくむ duty, duties, function
業務 ぎょうむ business, affairs, work, service

❷ (moral or legal obligations) **DUTY, responsibility, obligation**
義務 ぎむ duty, obligation
責務 せきむ responsibility and obligation, responsibility to do one's duty
債務 さいむ debt, obligation, liabilities
❸ **affairs, business**
国務 こくむ duties of state, national affairs
外務 がいむ foreign affairs
事務 じむ business, clerical work, duties of an office
総務 そうむ general affairs; manager, director
公務 こうむ public service, official affairs
専務 せんむ managing [executive] director
法務 ほうむ judicial affairs; clerical duty

KUN

【つとめる 務める】
ⓐ **discharge [perform] one's duties**
ⓑ **play [act, perform] (a part or role)**
a 務め つとめ duty, task, responsibility
b 議長を務める ぎちょうをつとめる act as chairman
【つとまる 務まる】**be fit [qualified] for**
後任が務まる こうにんがつとまる be fit to succeed

SYNONYMS

❶ **work and employment**
務 DUTY → 1505
任 OFFICE → 0057
役 SERVICE (esp. public) → 0288
勤 SERVICE (employment) → 2287
業 WORK → 3227
職 EMPLOYMENT → 1803
労 LABOR → 3155
❷ **responsibility**
務 DUTY → 1505
任 duty → 0057
責 RESPONSIBILITY → 3115
分 one's part → 2466
❸ **affairs**
用 THINGS TO DO → 3694
事 affairs → 4384
務 affairs → 1505

USAGE

【つとまる】
務まる
be fit [qualified] for
勤まる
be fit for, be equal to (the task)

HOMOPHONES

つとめる
勤 SERVICE → 2287
努 EXERT → 3154
勉 ENDEAVOR → 4113
つとめ 勤 SERVICE → 2287
つとまる 勤 SERVICE → 2287

NOTE

➡ see also USAGE note at 勤 2287

研 ▶**GRIND** ▶**RESEARCH**
ケン と(ぐ)

1506
◧ 1-5-6

112	Nonstandard	U784F
石	S11-5-6	F0000

traditional form → see 研 at 1456

祥 ▶**AUSPICIOUS**
ショウ ㊔ さち よし やす ただ

1507
◧ 1-5-6

113	Names	UFA1A
示	S11-5-6	F0000

traditional form → see 祥 at 1184

移 ▶**SHIFT**
イ うつ(る) うつ(す)
Ⓒ 移 yí

1508
◧ 1-5-6

115	Jōyō-5	U79FB
禾	S11-5-6	F0547

(stroke order 1–11)

COMPOUNDS

ⓐ (change in position, time or state) **SHIFT, move, change**
ⓑ **cause to SHIFT, transfer, remove, move**
a 移行する いこうする shift [switch] over
移動する いどうする move, shift, transfer
移転 いてん transfer, removal; change of address
移植 いしょく transplanting
推移 すいい transition, change
b 移住 いじゅう migration, immigration; move
移籍 いせき transfer of one's name in the register
移民 いみん immigration, emigration; immigrant, emigrant

KUN

【うつる 移る】*vi*
① **move (to a new house)**
移り うつり change, transition; return present
東京に移る とうきょうにうつる move to Tokyo
② **SHIFT, change, pass**
移り変わり うつりかわり change, transition
③ **be infected with; be contagious**
燃え移る もえうつる (of fire) spread, extend itself
下痢が移った げりがうつった be infected with diarrhea

④ (of odors) soak in

移り香 うつりが lingering [absorbed] scent

【うつす 移す】*vt*

①ⓐ **SHIFT, move, transfer**

ⓑ **transfuse (liquids or colors)**

ⓒ divert, turn, direct

a 移し替える うつしかえる shift [move] (an object) to [into]

都会に移す とかいにうつす move (an object or person) to the city

口移し くちうつし mouth-to-mouth feeding; conveying by word of mouth

計画を実行に移す けいかくをじっこうにうつす carry a plan into practice

② **transmit (a disease)**

風邪を移す かぜをうつす give [transmit] a cold (to someone)

SYNONYMS

● **move**

動 MOVE → 2232
運 MOVE → 3894
滑 SLIDE → 0809
辷る SLIP → 3957
移 SHIFT → 1508
転 remove → 1872
遷 TRANSFER → 3932
繰る SHIFT ONWARD → 1806

HOMOPHONES

うつる

写 COPY → 2493
映 REFLECT → 1104

うつり

映 REFLECT → 1104
写 COPY → 2493

うつす

写 COPY → 2493
映 REFLECT → 1104

NOTE

➡ see USAGE notes at 写 2493 and 映 1104

袴

1509

◧ 1-5-6

▸**FORMAL DIVIDED SKIRT**

コ はかま

Ⓒ 袴 kù

145	Names	U88B4
衤	S11-5-6	F2230

COMPOUNDS

● **Japanese FORMAL DIVIDED SKIRT**

着袴の儀 ちゃっこのぎ ceremony of fitting a child with a *hakama*

KUN

【はかま 袴】**Japanese FORMAL DIVIDED SKIRT**

お袴料 おはかまりょう betrothal money given from woman to man

羽織袴 はおりはかま Japanese male formal attire

藤袴 ふじばかま thoroughwort, *Eupatorium fortunei*

SYNONYMS

● **clothing**

服 CLOTHES → 1090
袴 FORMAL DIVIDED SKIRT → 1509
蓑 STRAW RAINCOAT → 2941
-着 wear → 4110
衣 GARMENT → 2506
装 DRESS → 3327
裳 DRESS → 3231
襤 RAGS → 1607
袈 BUDDHIST SURPLICE → 3200
裟 BUDDHIST CASSOCK → 3420
褸 overgarment → 1600

甥

1510

◧ 1-5-7

▸**NEPHEW**

セイ おい

Ⓒ 甥 shēng

100	Names	U7525
生	S12-5-7	F2325

COMPOUNDS

● **NEPHEW**

令甥 れいせい [honorific] your nephew

KUN

【おい 甥】**NEPHEW**

甥っ子 おいっこ nephew

甥御 おいご [honorific] (another person's) nephew

又甥 またおい grandnephew

SYNONYMS

● **offspring of siblings**

甥 NEPHEW → 1510
姪 NIECE → 0422

疏

1511

◧ 1-5-7

▸**LET PASS**

ソ ショ

Ⓒ 疏 shū

103	Names	U758F
疋	S12-5-7	F0000

COMPOUNDS

❶ [now usu. 疎 1512]

ⓐ **LET PASS, pass**

ⓑ (cause water to pass) **clear, dredge (a watercourse)**

a 意志の疏通 いしのそつう mutual understanding

b 疏水 そすい canal

❷ [sometimes also 疎 1512] **commentary on earlier commentary, sub-commentary, annotation**

注疏(=註疏) ちゅうそ detailed commentary
上疏 じょうそ reporting in writing to the emperor
義疏 ぎしょ commentary (on a scripture)

INDEPENDENT

【しょ 疏】scripture notes

SYNONYMS

❶ⓐ **pass**
通 PASS → 3855
過 PASS BY → 3891
経 PASS THROUGH → 1687
疏 LET PASS → 1511

疎

1512

◧ 1-5-7

▶SPARSE
▶ESTRANGE
ソ うと(い) うと(む) まば(ら)▲ おろそ(か)▲
Ⓝ 踈 Ⓒ 疏 shū

103	Jōyō	U758E
疋	S12-5-7	F1804

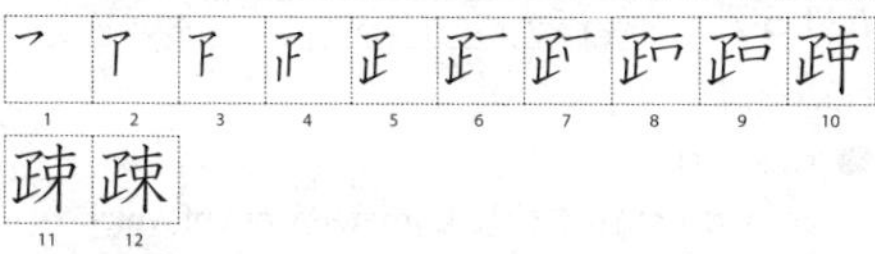

COMPOUNDS

❶ **SPARSE, thin, scattered, sporadic**
疎開 そかい dispersal, evacuation
疎密 そみつ sparseness and luxuriant growth
疎林 そりん sparse woods
過疎 かそ depopulation
空疎な くうそな empty, unsubstantial

❷ⓐ **ESTRANGE, alienate, neglect**
ⓑ **ESTRANGEd, alienated, distant**
a 疎外 そがい estrangement, alienation
疎隔 そかく estrangement, alienation
b 疎水性の そすいせいの hydrophobic
疎遠 そえん estrangement, alienation, neglect

❸ negligent, careless
疎漏 そろう carelessness, inadvertence, oversight

❹ [formerly also 疏 1511]
ⓐ let pass, pass
ⓑ (cause water to pass) clear, dredge (a watercourse)
a 疎通 そつう mutual understanding
b 疎水 そすい canal

❺ [usu. 疏 1511] commentary on earlier commentary, sub-commentary, annotation
注疎 ちゅうそ detailed commentary

INDEPENDENT

【そ 疎】**SPARSE**ness; estrangement
人口が疎である じんこうがそである be sparsely populated

KUN

【うとい 疎い】**ESTRANGEd, distant; ignorant of**
去る者は日日に疎し さるものはひびにうとし Out of sight, out of mind
世事に疎い せじにうとい know but little of the world

【うとむ 疎む】**neglect, shun, ESTRANGE, alienate**
疎ましい うとましい disagreeable, offensive
疎んじる うとんじる neglect, shun, alienate
友達に疎んじられる ともだちにうとんじられる be treated distantly by one's friends

【まばら 疎ら】
まばらな 疎らな **SPARSE**, thin, scattered, sporadic

【おろそか 疎か】
おろそかな 疎かな negligent, careless

SYNONYMS

❶ **rare and sparse**
薄い THIN → 3004
希 RARE → 2543
疎 SPARSE → 1512
粗 COARSE → 1683
稀 RARE → 1523

❷ **estrange**
疎 ESTRANGE → 1512
離 separate from → 2364
遠 DISTANT → 3906

皓

1513

◧ 1-5-7

▶BRIGHT WHITE
コウ ㊔ あき あきら ひかる ひろし てる ひろ
Ⓝ 皓 Ⓒ 皓 hào

106	Names	U7693
白	S12-5-7	F3196

COMPOUNDS

● [original meaning] **BRIGHT WHITE, sparkling white, beautifully white, pure white**
皓月 こうげつ [archaic] bright white moon
皓礬× こうばん white vitriol, zinc sulfate heptahydrate
明眸皓歯 めいぼうこうし starry eyes and beautiful white teeth (said of beautiful women)

SYNONYMS

● **white colors**
白 WHITE → 4305
皓 BRIGHT WHITE → 1513
銀 SILVER → 2156

皓

1514
1-5-7

▶BRIGHT WHITE

コウ ㊔ あき あきら ひかる ひろし てる ひろ

106	Nonstandard	U7693
白	S12-5-7	F0000

traditional form → see 皓 at 1513

短

1515
1-5-7

▶SHORT

タン みじか(い)

Ⓒ 短 duǎn

111	Jōyō-3	U77ED
矢	S12-5-7	F0770

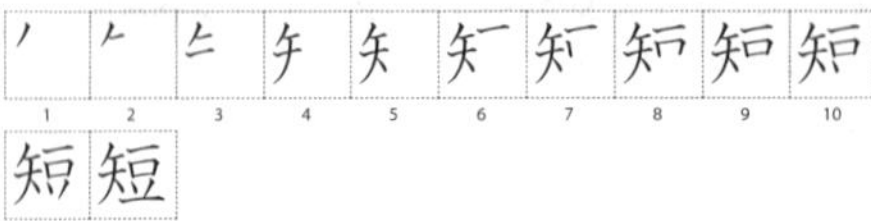

COMPOUNDS

❶ⓐ [also prefix] [original meaning] (not long) **SHORT**
ⓑ (of short duration) **SHORT, brief**
ⓒ SHORTen

a 短波 たんぱ shortwave
短気 たんき short [hot] temper
短歌 たんか tanka, Japanese verse
b 短期 たんき short term
短期大学 たんきだいがく junior college
短期間 たんきかん short term, short time
c 短縮 たんしゅく shortening, contraction, reduction

❷ SHORTcoming, defect
短所 たんしょ shortcoming, defect
一長一短 いっちょういったん merits and demerits, strong and weak points

❸ abbrev. of 短期大学 たんきだいがく: junior college
栄養短 えいようたん Junior College of Nutrition

❹ *music* minor
短調 たんちょう minor key
ハ短調 はたんちょう C minor

INDEPENDENT

【たん 短】 **SHORTcoming, defect**
短を補う たんをおぎなう remedy one's defects

KUN

【みじかい 短い】 **SHORT, brief**
短過ぎる みじかすぎる too short
手短に てみじかに shortly, briefly

SYNONYMS

❶ⓐ short and shortened
短 SHORT → 1515
簡 simplified → 3380
略 ABRIDGED → 1501

❷ faults and flaws
難 fault → 2310
短 shortcoming → 1515
疵 DEFECT → 4067
陥 defect → 0547
欠 incompleteness → 2481

NOTE

★ do not confuse with 矩 RULE → 1475

規

1516
1-5-7

▶REGULATION

キ ㊔ のり ただし

111	Nonstandard	U4093
矢	S12-5-7	F0000

traditional form → see 規 at 1231

硯

1517
1-5-7

▶INKSTONE

ケン すずり

Ⓒ 砚 yàn

112	Names	U786F
石	S12-5-7	F3104

COMPOUNDS

● INKSTONE
硯石 けんせき(=すずりいし) material out of which inkstones are made

KUN

【すずり 硯】 **INKSTONE**

SYNONYMS

● kinds of stone
硯 INKSTONE → 1517
砥 WHETSTONE → 1480

硬

1518
1-5-7

▶HARD

コウ かた(い)

Ⓒ 硬 yìng

112	Jōyō	U786C
石	S12-5-7	F1413

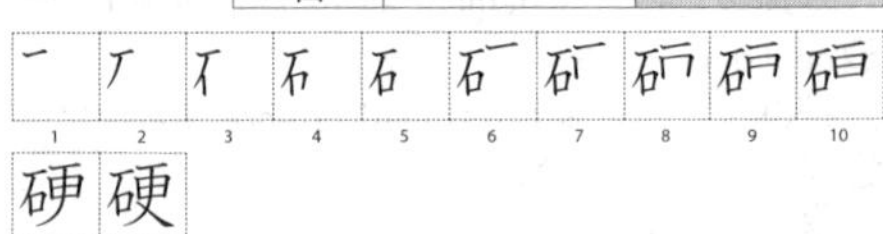

COMPOUNDS

❶ [original meaning] **HARD, firm, tough, solid**
硬度 こうど hardness
硬化する こうかする harden, stiffen
硬貨 こうか coin, metallic currency
硬式 こうしき hardball (baseball)
硬直 こうちょく stiffness, rigidity
硬骨 こうこつ hard bone; firmness

❷ [formerly also 鯁 2357] **HARD-line, stiff, unyielding, obdurate**

硬派 こうは hard-line elements, stalwart
硬軟両派 こうなんりょうは stalwart and insurgent factions
強硬な きょうこうな firm (attitude), unbending; drastic (measure)

❸ immature, unrefined
生硬な せいこうな crude, immature, unpolished

INDEPENDENT

【こう 硬】**HARD**
硬の芯 こうのしん hard pencil lead

KUN

【かたい 硬い】
① (resisting pressure) **HARD, tough, strong (esp. metals or stone)**
硬さ かたさ hardness
硬い石 かたいいし hard stone
②ⓐ stiff (style), uninteresting
ⓑ **stiff (facial expression)**
a 硬い文章 かたいぶんしょう stiff style
b 硬い表情 かたいひょうじょう stiff expression

SYNONYMS

❶ **hard**
硬 HARD → 1518
堅 FIRM → 3502
鞏 TOUGH → 3369
固 SOLID → 3830
剛 TOUGH → 2107
強 STRONG → 0574
勁 STRONG → 1833

❷ **firm and obstinate**
堅 FIRM → 3502
固 FIRM, stiff → 3830
確 firm → 1571
毅 RESOLUTE → 2341
剛 TOUGH → 2107
頑 STUBBORN → 1315
硬 hard-line → 1518

HOMOPHONES

かたい
堅 FIRM → 3502
固 SOLID → 3830
難 DIFFICULT → 2310

NOTE

➡ see USAGE note at 固 3830

硫

1519

1-5-7

▶**SULFUR**
リュウ
Ⓒ 硫 liú

112	Jōyō	U786B
石	S12-5-7	F2321

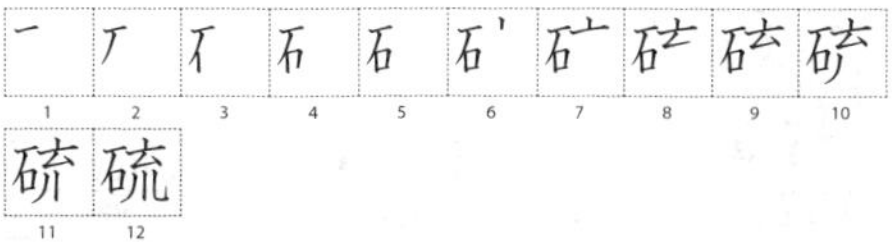

COMPOUNDS

● [original meaning] **SULFUR**
硫酸 りゅうさん sulfuric acid
硫安 りゅうあん ammonium sulfate
硫化する りゅうかする sulfurize
加硫 かりゅう vulcanization
脱硫 だつりゅう desulfurization

SPECIAL READINGS

硫黄 いおう sulfur

SYNONYMS

● **lighter elements**
水 hydrogen → 0010
酸 OXYGEN → 1968
窒 NITROGEN → 2853
塩 chlorine → 0774
臭 bromine → 3261
硫 SULFUR → 1519
炭 carbon → 2806

硝

1520

1-5-7

▶**NITER**
ショウ
Ⓝ 硝 Ⓒ 硝 xiāo

112	Jōyō	U785D
石	S12-5-7	F2375

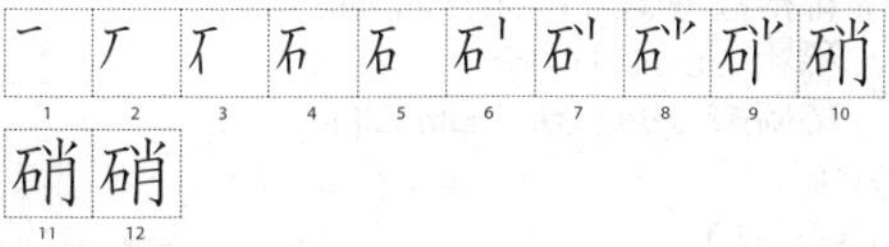

COMPOUNDS

● **NITER, saltpeter, potassium nitrate**
硝石 しょうせき saltpeter
硝酸 しょうさん nitric acid
硝薬 しょうやく gunpowder
硝煙 しょうえん gunpowder smoke
硝化 しょうか nitrification

SPECIAL READINGS

硝子▲ がらす glass

SYNONYMS

● **nitrogen**
窒 NITROGEN → 2853
硝 NITER → 1520

硝 1521

▶NITER
ショウ

112	Nonstandard	U785D
石	S12-5-7	F0000

1-5-7

traditional form → see 硝 at 1520

視 1522

▶REGARD
シ み(る)

113	Names	UFA61
示	S12-5-7	F0000

1-5-7

traditional form → see 視 at 1223

稀 1523

▶RARE
キ ケ まれ
Ⓒ 稀 xī

115	Names	U7A00
禾	S12-5-7	F2102

1-5-7

COMPOUNDS

❶ [also 希 き,け 2543] (not frequent) **RARE, uncommon, unusual, scarce**
稀代の きたい(=きだい)の uncommon, rare
稀有な けう(=きゆう)な rare, unusual, uncommon
稀少な きしょうな scarce, rare
古稀 こき three score and ten, seventy years of age

❷ [now usu. 希 き 2543]
ⓐ [original meaning] (thin in density) **RARE, rarefied, dilute, thin**
ⓑ [also prefix] *chem* dilute
a 稀薄な きはくな dilute, thin, rare, sparse
稀釈 きしゃく dilution
b 稀硫酸 きりゅうさん dilute sulfuric acid

KUN

【まれ 稀】
まれな 稀な [sometimes also 希な] **RARE, uncommon, scarce, unique**

SYNONYMS

❶ & 【まれ】 rare
珍 RARE → 1135
希 RARE → 2543
稀 RARE → 1523
❷ rare and sparse
薄い THIN → 3004
希 RARE → 2543
疎 SPARSE → 1512
粗 COARSE → 1683
稀 RARE → 1523

HOMOPHONES

まれ 希 RARE → 2543

NOTE

➡ see USAGE note at 希 2543

➡ see COMPOUND FORMATION for 古希 こき → 希 2543

程 1524

▶EXTENT
▶ESTABLISHED FORM
テイ ほど -ほど
Ⓝ 程 Ⓒ 程 chéng

1-5-7

115	Jōyō-5	U7A0B
禾	S12-5-7	F0636

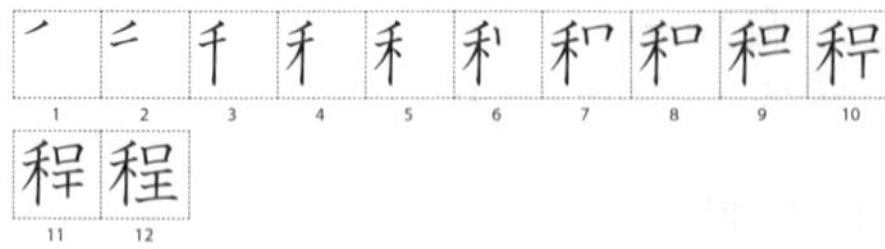

COMPOUNDS

❶ⓐ **EXTENT, degree, range, limit**
ⓑ (range of distance) **EXTENT, distance, range, mileage, journey**
a 程度 ていど degree, extent, standard
b 射程 しゃてい shooting range
旅程 りょてい distance to be covered; plan of one's trip
航程 こうてい run (of a ship), sail; flight
マイル程 まいるてい mileage
音程 おんてい (musical) interval, distance (between tones)

❷ⓐ **ESTABLISHED FORM** or mode of behavior: **rule, regulation, standard procedure, pattern**
ⓑ established order of doing things: **process, course**
ⓒ preestablished program of events: **schedule, program, plan, agenda, course of study**
a 規程 きてい official regulations, inner rules
方程式 ほうていしき equation
b 工程 こうてい process of manufacture, amount of work
過程 かてい process, course
課程 かてい course, curriculum
c 日程 にってい a day's program, order of the day
上程する じょうていする introduce on the agenda, lay [introduce] a bill before the Diet

KUN

【ほど 程】
①ⓐ **EXTENT, degree, measure; limit**
ⓑ **EXTENT [degree] of distance, time or quality**
a 程良く ほどよく properly, rightly, moderately
程を過ごす ほどをすごす break bounds, go too far
どれ程 どれほど how far; how long; how many [much]
左程 さほど (not) much, (not) very
成程 なるほど I see, really, indeed
b 程遠い ほどとおい far (from), distant, fall far short of
程無く ほどなく soon (afterward); shortly; before long
先程 さきほど some time ago, a little while ago

② one's position, one's social status

身の程 みのほど one's social position, one's own place

③ state of affairs

真偽の程 しんぎのほど whether it is true or not

④ *particle*

ⓐ **as, as…as, (not) so…as**

ⓑ **the more [less]…the more [less]**

a 僕は奴にそんな質問をする程馬鹿じゃない ぼくはやつにそんなしつもんをするほどばかじゃない I'm not so stupid as to ask him such a question

b 早ければ早い程良い はやければはやいほどよい The sooner, the better

【-ほど -程】…or thereabouts, about, approximately

三週間程 さんしゅうかんほど three weeks or thereabouts

SYNONYMS

❶ⓐ degree

程 EXTENT → 1524

度 DEGREE → 3844

分 relative degree → 2466

ⓑ distance and interval

距 DISTANCE → 1905

間 INTERVAL → 4122

程 EXTENT → 1524

隙 GAP → 0826

❶ⓑ range

程 EXTENT → 1524

範 range → 3360

域 area → 0559

圏 SPHERE → 3904

野 FIELD → 1877

界 field (*phys*) → 3172

場 field (*phys, psychol*) → 0678

❷ⓐ model

範 MODEL → 3360

典 CANON → 3253

模 PATTERN → 1326

程 ESTABLISHED FORM → 1524

式 form → 3785

準 STANDARD → 3541

格 NORM → 1161

【-ほど】

○ approximately

約 APPROXIMATELY → 1632

概 GENERAL → 1322

大 in substance → 4224

-頃 ABOUT → 0163

位 about → 0069

-方 about → 2459

-程 …or thereabouts → 1524

辺り thereabouts → 3761

COMPOUND FORMATION

【成程 なるほど】

成程 'I see, etc.' originally meant attaining (成) the greatest possible extent (程 ほど ①ⓐ), i.e., as much as possible. What this has to do with "I see" is quite a mystery.

税

1525

◧ 1-5-7

▸TAX

ゼイ ㊔ おさむ ちから えつ

Ⓝ 税 Ⓒ 税 shuì

115	Jōyō-5	U7A0E
禾	S12-5-7	F0593

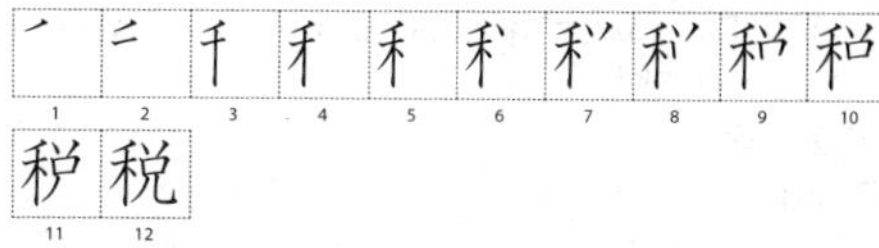

COMPOUNDS

❶ [also suffix] **TAX, duty**

税金 ぜいきん tax, duty; rates

税関 ぜいかん customhouse

租税 そぜい taxes, taxation

課税 かぜい taxation

脱税 だつぜい tax evasion

減税 げんぜい reduction of taxes, tax cut

納税 のうぜい tax payment

所得税 しょとくぜい income tax

間接税 かんせつぜい indirect tax

❷ dues, rates, fee

郵税 ゆうぜい postage, postal rates

印税 いんぜい royalty (on a book)

入港税 にゅうこうぜい port dues [fees]

INDEPENDENT

【ぜい 税】TAX, duty

税を納める ぜいをおさめる pay a tax

税を課する ぜいをかする impose a tax

SYNONYMS

❶ tax

税 TAX → 1525

租 LAND TAX → 1492

貢 TRIBUTE → 2838

賦 levy → 1992

程

1526

◧ 1-5-7

▸EXTENT
▸ESTABLISHED FORM

テイ ほど -ほど

115	Nonstandard	U7A0B
禾	S12-5-7	F0000

traditional form → see 程 at 1524

税 1527

▶TAX
ゼイ ㊔ おさむ ちから えつ

115	Nonstandard	U7A05
禾	S12-5-7	F0000

1-5-7

traditional form → see 税 at 1525

竣 1528

▶COMPLETE
シュン
Ⓒ 竣 jùn

117	Names	U7AE3
立	S12-5-7	F3475

1-5-7

COMPOUNDS

● COMPLETE, finish (a project or task)

竣工する しゅんこうする (of construction work) be completed

SYNONYMS

● end

終 END → 1692
絶 COME TO AN END → 1711
閉 CLOSE → 4116
了 FINISH → 4157
済 SETTLE → 0634
-上げる completion suffix → 4212
完 COMPLETE → 2727
結 CONCLUDE → 1706
竣 COMPLETE → 1528

補 1529

▶SUPPLEMENT
ホ おぎな(う) ㊔ すけ たすく
Ⓒ 补 bǔ

145	Jōyō-6	U88DC
衤	S12-5-7	F0808

1-5-7

COMPOUNDS

❶ⓐ SUPPLEMENT, make up for, compensate; replenish, supply
ⓑ SUPPLEMENTary, extra

a 補足 ほそく supplement, replenishment
補遺 ほい supplement
補償する ほしょうする compensate, indemnify
補充する ほじゅうする supplement, replenish, recruit
補給 ほきゅう supply, replenishment
補欠 ほけつ filling a vacancy; substitute, alternate
補正する ほせいする revise, correct

b 補習 ほしゅう supplementary lessons
補則 ほそく supplementary rules

❷ (fill a vacancy) appoint, assign, select

補任する ほにんする appoint to office
候補者 こうほしゃ candidate, applicant

❸ repair, mend

補修する ほしゅうする repair, mend

❹ⓐ [formerly also 輔 1963] assist, aid; give guidance
ⓑ [suffix] assistant, aid, apprentice

a 補佐(=輔佐)する ほさする assist, help
補助する ほじょする assist, support, aid
補導する ほどうする guide, direct, lead; take into custody

b 書記補 しょきほ assistant clerk
警部補 けいぶほ assistant inspector
外交官補 がいこうかんほ probationary diplomat

INDEPENDENT

【ほする 補する】 be appointed

KUN

【おぎなう 補う】 SUPPLEMENT, make up for, compensate; replenish, supply

補い おぎない supplement, replenishment, reparation
欠陥を補う けっかんをおぎなう make up for a fault
不足を補う ふそくをおぎなう make up for a shortage

SYNONYMS

❶ⓐ supplement

補 SUPPLEMENT → 1529
足 supplement → 2714
給 SUPPLY → 1708
充 fill up (a vacancy) → 2507

ⓑ additional

追 additional → 3840
補 supplementary → 1529
副 accessory → 2230

❷ appoint

任 appoint → 0057
補 appoint → 1529
挙 NOMINATE → 3106

❹ⓐ help

助 HELP → 1440
佑 HELP (said esp. of God) → 0083
祐 DIVINE HELP → 1146
援 AID → 0715
佐 ASSIST → 0076
補 assist → 1529
輔 ASSIST → 1963
済 RELIEVE → 0634

ⓑ assistant

補 assistant → 1529
丞 AIDE → 3146

COMPOUND FORMATION

【候補者 こうほしゃ】

候補者 'candidate, applicant' is a person (者) waiting (候) to be appointed (補 ❷).

裕 1530

◧ 1-5-7

▶**ABUNDANT**

ユウ ㊔ ひろ ひろし ゆたか やす みち

Ⓒ 裕 yù

145	Jōyō	U88D5
ネ	S12-5-7	F1051

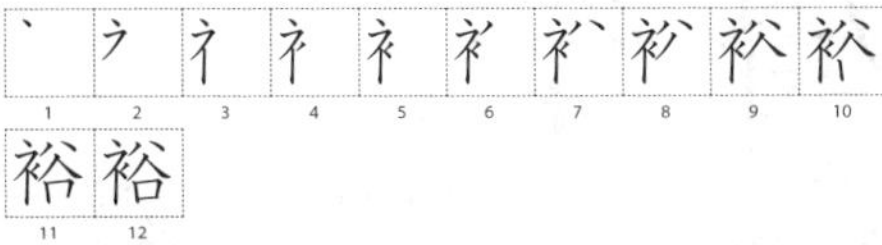

COMPOUNDS

❶ **ABUNDANT, plentiful, ample**

裕福な ゆうふくな rich, wealthy

余裕 よゆう surplus, margin, room; composure

富裕な ふゆうな wealthy, rich

❷ **tolerant, big-hearted**

裕度 ゆうど *elec* tolerance

SYNONYMS

❶ **plentiful**

百 numerous → 2519

沃 FERTILE → 0315

万 myriad → 3653

多 MANY → 2694

豊 PLENTIFUL → 3344

沢 plentiful → 0313

穣 YIELDING ABUNDANTLY → 1597

裕 ABUNDANT → 1530

饒 ABUNDANT → 2280

富 RICH → 2892

裡 1531

◧ 1-5-7

▶**REAR**

リ うら

145	Names	U88E1
ネ	S12-5-7	F0000

traditional form → see 裏 at 2652

雅 1532

◧ 1-5-8

▶**ELEGANT**

ガ みや(び)▲ ㊔ まさ まさし つね

Ⓝ 雅 Ⓒ 雅 yǎ yā

172	Jōyō	U96C5
隹	S13-8-5	F1175

COMPOUNDS

❶ⓐ **ELEGANT, refined, graceful, artistic, sophisticated**

ⓑ proper and **ELEGANT**, standard, classical

a 雅趣 がしゅ elegance, artistry, taste

雅号 がごう pen name, pseudonym

優雅な ゆうがな elegant, graceful, refined

風雅 ふうが elegance, refinement, daintiness

b 雅楽 ががく ceremonial court music

高雅な こうがな refined, elegant, chaste

❷ honorific prefix

雅兄 がけい polite word used in addressing a friend in a letter

INDEPENDENT

【が 雅】 elegance, good taste

KUN

【みやび 雅び】 **elegance, gracefulness; refined taste**

雅びやかな みやびやかな elegant, graceful, refined

SYNONYMS

❶ **elegant**

雅 ELEGANT → 1532

淑 GRACEFUL → 0639

優 graceful → 0200

粋 REFINED → 1645

彬 REFINED AND GENTLE → 1201

畸 1533

◧ 1-5-8

▶**UNUSUAL**

キ

Ⓒ 畸 jī

102	Non-Jōyō	U7578
田	S13-5-8	F0000

COMPOUNDS

[now replaced by 奇 2756]

❶ **UNUSUAL, strange, odd, extraordinary, queer, eccentric**

畸人 きじん eccentric (person), queer [odd] fellow

❷ **deformity, malformation**

畸形 きけい deformity, malformation

SYNONYMS

❶ **abnormal**

変 ABNORMAL → 2569

奇 UNUSUAL → 2756

畸 UNUSUAL → 1533

怪 MYSTERIOUS → 0354

妖 MYSTERIOUS → 0282

妙 strange → 0280

異 not ordinary → 3195

珍 curious → 1135

牙 田 【目】 石 示 禾 立 ネ 号 此

睦

▶FRIENDLY

ボク むつ(まじい)▲ むつ(む)▲ ㊔ ちか よし もく む あつ のぶ とも あつし とき ちかし まこと よしみ

Ⓒ 睦 mù

1534

1-5-8

109	Jōyō	U7766
目	S13-5-8	F2258

Stroke order: 1–13

COMPOUNDS

ⓐ **FRIENDLY, harmonious, peaceful**

ⓑ [original meaning] live together in harmony

a 親睦 しんぼく friendliness, amity, intimacy

和睦 わぼく reconciliation, peace

敦睦な とんぼくな [archaic] cordial and friendly, affectionate

KUN

【むつまじい 睦まじい】 **FRIENDLY, intimate, harmonious**

【むつむ 睦む】 **get along well together**

睦言 むつごと lover's talk, whispered intimacies

SYNONYMS

ⓐ **familiar and friendly**

親 INTIMATE → 2264

密 CLOSE → 2857

近 NEAR → 3798

睦 FRIENDLY → 1534

懇 FAMILIAR → 3606

和 HARMONIOUS → 1450

睡

▶SLEEP

スイ

Ⓒ 睡 shuì

1535

1-5-8

109	Jōyō	U7761
目	S13-5-8	F1704

Stroke order: 1–13

COMPOUNDS

ⓐ [original meaning] **SLEEP, doze**

ⓑ **SLEEP**, nap

a 睡眠 すいみん sleep, slumber

睡魔 すいま sleepiness, drowsiness

睡蓮 すいれん water lily

熟睡 じゅくすい sound sleep

昏睡状態 こんすいじょうたい comatose state

ab 仮睡 かすい nap, doze

午睡 ごすい nap, afternoon sleep

一睡もしなかった いっすいもしなかった had a sleepless night

SYNONYMS

● **sleep**

眠 SLEEP → 1474

睡 SLEEP → 1535

寝 GO TO SLEEP → 2925

碍

▶STAND IN THE WAY

ガイ ゲ

Ⓝ 礙 Ⓒ 碍 ài

1536

1-5-8

112	Non-Jōyō	U788D
石	S13-5-8	F3461

COMPOUNDS

● [now also 害 2826] **STAND IN THE WAY, hinder, obstruct, interfere with**

碍子 がいし insulator

妨碍する ぼうがいする disturb, hinder, obstruct, hamper, impede, interfere

障碍 しょうがい obstacle, hindrance; (physical) disorder

無碍 むげ free from obstacles

SYNONYMS

● **obstruct and hinder**

遮 INTERRUPT → 3916

塞 STOP UP → 2924

阻 OBSTRUCT → 0411

沮 OBSTRUCT → 0399

奄 OBSTRUCT (by covering) → 2757

妨 HINDER → 0279

障 hinder → 0875

碍 STAND IN THE WAY → 1536

害 stand in the way → 2826

梗 STOP UP → 1204

碓

▶MORTAR

タイ うす

Ⓒ 碓 duì

1537

1-5-8

112	Names	U7893
石	S13-5-8	F0000

KUN

【うす 碓】 [usu. 臼] **MORTAR; trip-hammer mill**

碓氷峠 うすいとうげ Usui Pass

SYNONYMS

【うす】

○ **vessels and receptacles**

盤 dish → 3533

鍋 POT → 2202

釜 IRON POT → 2610
鼎 TRIPOD CAULDRON → 4405
臼 MORTAR → 4341
碓 MORTAR → 1537
托 RECEPTACLE → 0252
皿 PLATE → 4286
盆 TRAY → 2581
膳 LEGGED TRAY → 1381
杯 CUP → 1066
鉢 BOWL → 2144
椀 WOODEN BOWL → 1250
碗 CERAMIC BOWL → 1539
丼 LARGE BOWL → 4323

HOMOPHONES

うす 臼 MORTAR → 4341

NOTE

➡ see USAGE note at 臼 4341

碇 1538 ◧1-5-8

▶ANCHOR
テイ いかり
Ⓒ 碇 dìng

112	Non-Jōyō	U7887
石	S13-5-8	F3147

COMPOUNDS

● [now usu. 停 0156] ANCHOR
碇泊する ていはくする anchor, moor
碇置 ていち anchorage

KUN

【いかり 碇】ANCHOR
碇綱(=錨×綱) いかりづな anchor cable

SYNONYMS

● weight
錘 weight → 2191
鎮 weight → 2210
碇 ANCHOR → 1538

碗 1539 ◧1-5-8

▶CERAMIC BOWL
ワン
Ⓒ 碗 wǎn

112	Names	U7897
石	S13-5-8	F2142

COMPOUNDS

❶ CERAMIC BOWL, bowl
茶碗 ちゃわん teacup; rice bowl
茶碗蒸し ちゃわんむし savory egg custard
夫婦茶碗 めおとぢゃわん pair of matching teacups

❷ counter for servings of food or drink in a bowl

INDEPENDENT

【わん 碗】CERAMIC BOWL, bowl

SYNONYMS

❶ vessels and receptacles
盤 dish → 3533
鍋 POT → 2202
釜 IRON POT → 2610
鼎 TRIPOD CAULDRON → 4405
臼 MORTAR → 4341
碓 MORTAR → 1537
托 RECEPTACLE → 0252
皿 PLATE → 4286
盆 TRAY → 2581
膳 LEGGED TRAY → 1381
杯 CUP → 1066
鉢 BOWL → 2144
椀 WOODEN BOWL → 1250
碗 CERAMIC BOWL → 1539
丼 LARGE BOWL → 4323

碑 1540 ◧1-5-8

▶MONUMENT
ヒ いしぶみ

112	Names	UFA4B
石	S13-5-8	F0000

traditional form → see 碑 at 1553

碎 1541 ◧1-5-8

▶CRUSH UP
サイ くだ(く) くだ(ける)

112	Names	U788E
石	S13-5-8	F0000

traditional form → see 砕 at 1458

祿 1542 ◧1-5-8

▶RETAINER'S STIPEND
ロク ㊔ よし

113	Names	U797F
示	S13-5-8	F0000

traditional form → see 禄 at 1264

稚 1543 ◧1-5-8

▶CHILDISH
チ ㊔ わか
Ⓝ 穉 Ⓒ 稚 zhì

115	Jōyō	U7A1A
禾	S13-5-8	F1797

1	2	3	4	5	6	7	8	9	10	11	12	13
ノ	二	千	禾	禾	禾	利	秆	秆	稚	稚	稚	稚

COMPOUNDS

❶ CHILDISH, infantile, immature; very young
稚気 ちき childishness
稚拙な ちせつな childish, unskillful
稚児 ちご infant, child

牙 田 目 石 示 【禾】 立 ネ 号 此

幼稚な ようちな childish, infantile, crude
幼稚園 ようちえん kindergarten

❷ young person
丁稚 でっち apprentice

SYNONYMS

❶ **young**
若 YOUNG → 2785
弱 young → 1499
少 young → 4278
青 youthful → 3084
幼 VERY YOUNG → 0222
稚 CHILDISH → 1543

稔

1544
1-5-8

▶RIPEN
ネン ジン みの(る) ㊔ とし なる のり なり
Ⓒ 稔 rěn

115	Names	U7A14
禾	S13-5-8	F2318

COMPOUNDS

● [original meaning] **RIPEN**—said esp. of rice
稔実不良 ねんじつふりょう poor crop (of rice)
豊稔 ほうねん(=ほうじん) [archaic] bumper harvest

KUN

【みのる 稔る】 [usu. 実る] **bear fruit, RIPEN**
稔り みのり crop, ripening

SYNONYMS

● **mature**
熟 MATURE → 3558
成 grow up → 4352
稔 RIPEN → 1544
爛 OVERRIPE → 1427
実る bear fruit → 2765

HOMOPHONES

みのる 実 REAL → 2765
みのり 実 REAL → 2765

NOTE

➡ see USAGE note at 実 2765

稜

1545
1-5-8

▶RIDGE
リョウ ロウ ㊔ たか たかし いつ いず
Ⓒ 棱 léng líng lēng

115	Names	U7A1C
禾	S13-5-8	F2592

COMPOUNDS

❶ RIDGE
稜線 りょうせん ridgeline

❷ authority, power
稜威 りょうい the august virtue of His Majesty the Emperor

SYNONYMS

❶ **hills**
丘 HILL → 4307
畝 RIDGE → 1857
岡 HILL → 3719
台 heights → 2498
坂 SLOPE → 0275
阪 slope → 0321
塚 MOUND → 0675
阜 MOUND → 3254
陵 high mound → 0660
稜 RIDGE → 1545

靖

1546
1-5-8

▶PACIFY
セイ ㊔ やす やすし のぶ おさむ はる しず
Ⓝ 靖 Ⓒ 靖 jìng

174	Names	U9756
青	S13-8-5	F1395

COMPOUNDS

ⓐ [archaic] **PACIFY, quell, put down**
ⓑ [original meaning, now archaic] **peaceful, tranquil, quiet**
a 靖国 せいこく pacifying the nation
b 閑靖 かんせい quiet, tranquil

SYNONYMS

ⓐ **conquer and suppress**
征 CONQUER → 0349
討 SUPPRESS BY ARMED FORCE → 1846
伐 CUT DOWN → 0046
鎮 QUELL → 2210
靖 PACIFY → 1546

靖

1547
1-5-8

▶PACIFY
セイ ㊔ やす やすし のぶ おさむ はる しず

174	Nonstandard	UFA1C
青	S13-8-5	F0000

traditional form → see 靖 at 1546

褐

1548
1-5-8

▶BROWN
カツ
Ⓝ 褐 Ⓒ 褐 hè

145	Jōyō	U8910
ネ	S13-5-8	F2719

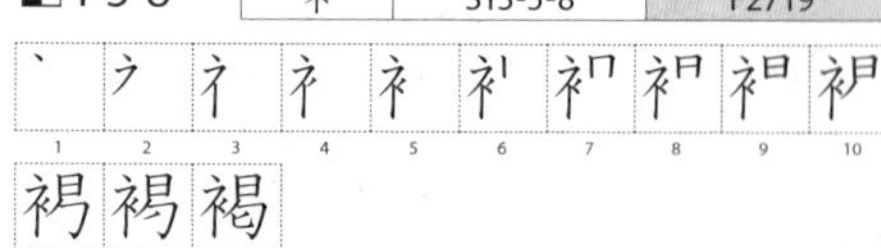

COMPOUNDS

❶ **BROWN, dirty brown**

褐色 かっしょく brown
褐炭 かったん brown coal, lignite
褐藻 かっそう brown algae
茶褐色 ちゃかっしょく brown, liver brown

❷ [original meaning, now archaic] coarse cloth or garment

SYNONYMS

❶ **brown colors**

褐 BROWN → 1548
茶 light brown → 2808

裾

1549

◧1-5-8

▶**HEM**

キョ▲ すそ

Ⓒ 裾 jū

145	Jōyō	U88FE
衤	S13-5-8	F1777

Stroke order: 1–13

COMPOUNDS

ⓐ **HEM**, cuff, skirt, train
ⓑ edge, fringe

b 裾礁 きょしょう fringing reef

INDEPENDENT

【きょ 裾】train of an old ceremonial court dress

KUN

【すそ 裾】

ⓐ **HEM, cuff, skirt, train**
ⓑ **end, edge, fringe**
ⓒ cut edge of a hairdo
ⓓ foot (of a mountain)

a 裾除け すそよけ underskirt
裳裾 もすそ hem [cuff, train] of clothing
b お裾分け おすそわけ sharing
d 裾野 すその foot of a mountain

SYNONYMS

● **garment parts**

襟 COLLAR → 1599
袖 SLEEVE → 1496
懐 BOSOM → 0942
衿 COLLAR → 1465
裾 HEM → 1549

裸

1550

◧1-5-8

▶**NAKED**

ラ はだか

Ⓒ 裸 luǒ

145	Jōyō	U88F8
衤	S13-5-8	F1296

Stroke order: 1–13

COMPOUNDS

ⓐ [original meaning] (without clothing) **NAKED, nude, bare**
ⓑ (without covering) **NAKED**, uncovered, bare

a 裸婦 らふ nude woman
裸体 らたい naked [nude] body, nudity
全裸の ぜんらの stark naked, nude
b 裸出 らしゅつ exposure
裸眼 らがん naked eye
赤裸裸 せきらら nakedness, frankness

KUN

【はだか 裸】**NAKED body; being uncovered [bare]; being penniless**

裸の はだかの naked, nude, bare, undressed
裸馬 はだかうま barebacked horse
裸虫 はだかむし caterpillar; person with scanty supply of clothes
裸線 はだかせん bare wire
裸一貫の人 はだかいっかんのひと person with no property but his [her] own body
素っ裸の すっぱだかの stark naked, in one's bare skin

SPECIAL READINGS

裸足▲ はだし barefoot, bare feet

SYNONYMS

● **naked**

裸 NAKED → 1550
素 bare → 3108

號

1551

◧1-5-8

▶**NUMBER**
▶**DESIGNATION**
▶**SIGN**

ゴウ

141	Nonstandard	U865F
虍	S13-6-7	F0000

traditional form → see 号 at 2675

雌

◧1-5-8

incorrect classification/ stroke-count

➡ see ◧1-4-10: 止 at 1337

【皮】石示禾立衤令圣申

頗
1552
1-5-9

▶**EXCEEDINGLY**
ハ すこぶ(る)
Ⓒ 颇 pō

181	Names	U9817
頁	S14-9-5	F0000

COMPOUNDS

● **one-sided, biased, partial, unfair, prejudiced**
偏頗 へんぱ favoritism, discrimination

KUN

【すこぶる 頗る】**EXCEEDINGLY, extremely, very much**

SYNONYMS

● **one side**
片- one side → 4272
偏 ONE-SIDED → 0151
頗 one-sided → 1552

【すこぶる】
○ **extreme in degree**
酷 SEVERE → 1967
強 STRONG → 0574
凄い tremendous → 0145
重 HEAVY → 4390
高 HIGH → 2601
深 DEEP → 0636
大 BIG → 4224
厳 SEVERE → 4079
激 intense → 0955
極 EXTREME → 1243
痛 bitter(ly) → 4071
切 keen → 0030
甚 EXTREMELY → 3271
祁 EXTREMELY → 1447
超 super- → 4107
頗る EXCEEDINGLY → 1552

碑
1553
1-5-9

▶**MONUMENT**
ヒ いしぶみ▲
Ⓝ 碑 Ⓒ 碑 bēi

112	Jōyō	U7891
石	S14-5-9	F2016

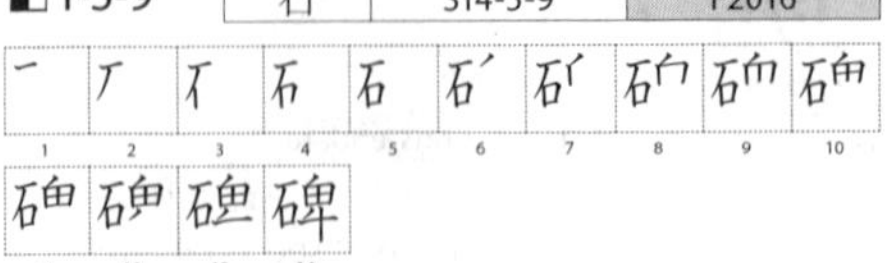

COMPOUNDS

ⓐ **MONUMENT, stone monument**
ⓑ suffix after names of **MONUMENT**s
a 碑文 ひぶん epitaph, inscription
石碑 せきひ stone monument, tombstone
墓碑 ぼひ tombstone, gravestone
歌碑 かひ monument inscribed with a tanka poem
記念碑 きねんひ monument

INDEPENDENT

【ひ 碑】**MONUMENT**
新田義貞の碑 にったよしさだのひ monument in memory of Yoshisada Nitta

KUN

【いしぶみ 碑】stone **MONUMENT**

磁
1554
1-5-9

▶**MAGNETISM**
ジ
Ⓝ 磁 Ⓒ 磁 cí

112	Jōyō-6	U78C1
石	S14-5-9	F1693

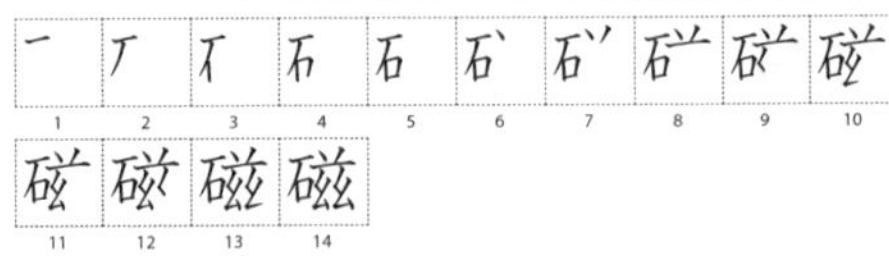

COMPOUNDS

❶ⓐ **MAGNETISM**
ⓑ [also prefix] **magnetic**
ⓒ [original meaning] **magnet**
a 磁気 じき magnetism
磁力線 じりょくせん line of magnetic force
磁場 じば magnetic field
磁極 じきょく magnetic pole
電磁波 でんじは electromagnetic waves
b 磁方位 じほうい magnetic bearing
c 磁石 じしゃく magnet; compass
❷ porcelain, chinaware
陶磁器 とうじき porcelain, pottery, ceramics
青磁 せいじ celadon porcelain
白磁 はくじ white porcelain

SYNONYMS

❶ⓐ & ❶ⓑ **electricity and magnetism**
電 ELECTRICITY → 3465
流 electric current → 0529
磁 MAGNETISM → 1554
❷ **ceramics ware**
陶 POTTERY → 0662
窯 ceramics → 2986
磁 porcelain → 1554

碩
1555
1-5-9

▶**EMINENT**
セキ ジャク ㊔ ひろ ひろし みつる
Ⓒ 硕 shuò

112	Names	U78A9
石	S14-5-9	F3133

COMPOUNDS

● EMINENT, great

碩学 せきがく *literary* eminent scholar, man of erudition

SYNONYMS

● great

偉 GREAT (of superior character) → 0167
大 BIG → 4224
宏 GRAND (large in scale) → 2728
壮 GRAND (having grandeur) → 0263
豪 MAGNIFICENT → 2657
雄 HEROIC → 1271
碩 EMINENT → 1555

磁 1556

▶MAGNETISM

ジ

1-5-9

112	Nonstandard	U25535
石	S14-5-9	F0000

traditional form → see 磁 at 1554

福 1557

▶FORTUNE

フク ㊔ とみ よし

1-5-9

113	Names	UFA1B
示	S14-5-9	F0000

traditional form → see 福 at 1303

禍 1558

▶CALAMITY

カ わざわい

1-5-9

113	Names	UFA52
示	S14-5-9	F0000

traditional form → see 禍 at 1304

禎 1559

▶PROPITIOUS OMEN

テイ ㊔ さだ よし ただし さち ただ とも

1-5-9

113	Names	UFA53
示	S14-5-9	F0000

traditional form → see 禎 at 1305

種 1560

▶VARIETY
▶SEED

シュ たね -ぐさ▲ ㊔ くさ かず

Ⓒ 种 zhǒng zhòng

1-5-9

115	Jōyō-4	U7A2E
禾	S14-5-9	F0443

1	2	3	4	5	6	7	8	9	10	11	12	13	14
丿	二	千	禾	禾	禾	禾	秆	秆	秆	秆	種	種	種

COMPOUNDS

❶ⓐ VARIETY, kind, type, sort, breed, race
ⓑ counter for kinds, varieties or events (in sport programs)

a 種目 しゅもく item; event (as a race)
種種の しゅじゅの various, diverse
各種の かくしゅの each [every] kind, various
一種の いっしゅの a kind of, of a sort
機種 きしゅ type of airplane [machine], model
業種 ぎょうしゅ type of industry, category of business
職種 しょくしゅ type of occupation, occupational category
品種 ひんしゅ kind, variety, description, brand
人種 じんしゅ (human) race

b 第三種郵便物 だいさんしゅゆうびんぶつ third-class mail matter
五種競技 ごしゅきょうぎ pentathlon, five events

❷ⓐ [also suffix] *biol* **species, VARIETY**
ⓑ *logic* species

a 亜種 あしゅ subspecies
変種 へんしゅ variety; mutation
ホルスタイン種 ほるすたいんしゅ Holstein, Holstein-Friesian

b 種概念 しゅがいねん *logic* species

❸ **SEED**

種子 しゅし seed, pit, stone
種皮 しゅひ seed coat, testa

❹ [original meaning] sow, plant

播種 はしゅ sowing, planting

❺ vaccinate

種痘 しゅとう vaccination against smallpox
予防接種 よぼうせっしゅ protective inoculation, vaccination

❻ breeding, reproduction

種畜 しゅちく breeding stock
断種 だんしゅ castration, sterilization

INDEPENDENT

【しゅ 種】 **kind, sort;** *biol* **species, VARIETY;** *logic* **species**

種の起源 しゅのきげん Origin of Species
この種の このしゅの this kind of

KUN

【たね 種】

① **SEED, stone, kernel, pip**

菜種 なたね rapeseed, coleseed

②ⓐ kind, species, **VARIETY**; quality
ⓑ breed, stock

a 変わり種 かわりだね novelty, exception, freak

b 種馬 たねうま stud horse, stallion
一粒種 ひとつぶだね one's only child

③ [formerly also 胤] paternal blood, offspring

種違い たねちがい half brother, half sister

皮 石 示【禾】立 衤 令 圣 申

④ⓐ material, matter
ⓑ **subject, topic, matter, news**
a 料理の種を仕込む りょうりのたねをしこむ prepare for cooking
b 特種 とくだね exclusive news, scoop
⑤ **cause, source, origin**
悩みの種 なやみのたね cause of annoyance
⑥ trick, secret, gimmick
種明かし たねあかし exposure of a trick
【-ぐさ -種】[usu. -草] **material, stuff**
質種 しちぐさ article for pawning
笑い種 わらいぐさ laughingstock

SYNONYMS

❶ⓐ kinds and types
型 TYPE →3266
類 KIND →2275
色 kind →2522
般 SORT →1670
属 genus →3901
品 category →2795
種 VARIETY →1560
様 variety →1332
❸ early states of plant life
芽 BUD →2784
蕾 BUD (of a flower) →3006
苗 SEEDLING →2781
種 SEED →1560

USAGE

【たね】
種
① seed, stone, kernel, pip
②ⓐ kind, species, variety; quality
ⓑ breed, stock
③ [formerly also 胤] paternal blood, offspring
④ⓐ material, matter
ⓑ subject, topic, matter, news
⑤ cause, source, origin
⑥ trick, secret, gimmick
胤
[now usu. 種] paternal blood, offspring

HOMOPHONES

たね 胤 PROGENY →0017
-ぐさ 草 GRASS →2813

NOTE

➡ see also USAGE note at 草 2813

稲

1561
1-5-9

▸RICE PLANT
トウ いね いな- ㊔ しね
Ⓝ 稲 Ⓒ 稻 dào

115	Jōyō	U7A32
禾	S14-5-9	F1238

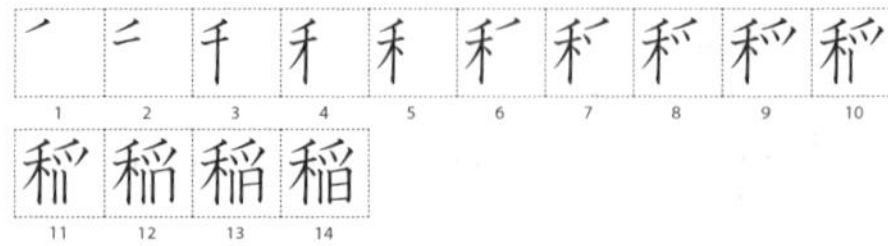

COMPOUNDS

● RICE PLANT, rice
水稲 すいとう paddy-rice plant, aquatic rice
陸稲 りくとう(=おかぼ) rice grown in a dry field
晩稲 ばんとう late growing rice

KUN

【いね 稲】**RICE PLANT**
稲刈り いねかり rice reaping
【いな- 稲-】
① **RICE PLANT, rice**
稲作 いなさく rice crop; raising rice plants
稲穂 いなほ ear of rice
稲田 いなだ rice field
② **lightning**
稲妻 いなずま lightning
稲光 いなびかり lightning

SYNONYMS

● rice
米 RICE →4342
飯 COOKED RICE →2126
稲 RICE PLANT →1561
籾 UNHULLED RICE →1626
餅 RICE CAKE →2256
粥 RICE GRUEL →0698

COMPOUND FORMATION

【稲妻 いなずま】
稲妻 'lightning' consist of 稲 'rice plants' and 妻 'wife', which in this case means 'husband'. It originates from the belief that ears of rice are produced as a result of a spiritual union between lightning and rice plants.

稱

1562
1-5-9

▸APPELLATION
ショウ たた(える)

115	Nonstandard	U7A31
禾	S14-5-9	F0000

traditional form → see 称 at 1491

稲

1-5-9

incorrect stroke-count
➡ see 1-5-10: 禾 at 1576

颯

1563
1-5-9

▸SOUND OF GUSTING WIND
サツ ソウ
Ⓒ 飒 sà

182	Names	U98AF
風	S14-9-5	F2800

COMPOUNDS

a [archaic] **SOUND OF GUSTING WIND**s; gust of wind

b like a gust of wind

a 颯然たる さつぜんたる (of a gust of wind) blowing suddenly

b 颯爽と さっそうと smart, brisk, dashing

SYNONYMS

a wind

風 WIND → 3730

嵐 STORM → 2898

颱 TYPHOON → 4138

台 typhoon → 2498

凪 CALM → 3709

颯 SOUND OF GUSTING WIND → 1563

端

1564

◧ 1-5-9

▸**END**

タン はし は[1] は[2] はた -ばた はな▲ はし(た)▲ ㊔ ただし

Ⓒ 端 duān

117	Jōyō	U7AEF
立	S14-5-9	F0613

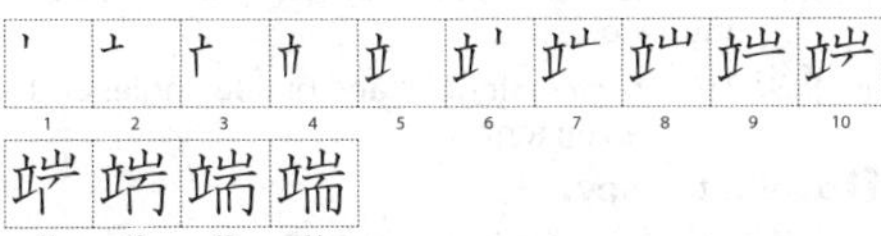

COMPOUNDS

1 END, extremity, tip

端子 たんし terminal

突端 とったん tip, point

両端 りょうたん both ends

先端(=尖端) せんたん pointed end, tip; spearhead; vanguard

末端 まったん end, tip, termination

一端 いったん one end, edge, side; a part

極端 きょくたん extreme, extremity, pole

異端 いたん heresy, paganism, heterodoxy

2 start, beginning, starting point, origin

端緒 たんしょ(=たんちょ) beginning, start, first step; clue

端午 たんご festival on the 5th of May (of the lunar calendar)

発端 ほったん origin, beginning, outset

戦端を開く せんたんをひらく take up arms (against), open hostilities

途端に とたんに just as, just at the moment

3 [original meaning] correct, proper, upright

端正な たんせいな correct, just, proper

端然と たんぜんと properly

端座(=端坐)する たんざする sit upright [properly]

端麗な たんれいな graceful, elegant, handsome

4 straight, direct

端的に たんてきに directly, straightforwardly, frankly

5 matter, event

多端 たたん many items; pressure of business

万端 ばんたん everything, all

INDEPENDENT

【たん 端】 start, beginning, origin

. . . に端を発する …にたんをはっする have its origin in…

KUN

【はし 端】

① **END, extremity, tip**

紐の端 ひものはし end of a string

両端 りょうはし both ends

② **edge, margin, brink, border; side**

端端に はしばしに here and there, in some parts

道の端 みちのはし edge of a street

右端 みぎはし right side, right margin

③ beginning

端書き はしがき preface, introduction

④ unwanted piece, scrap, fragment

端くれ はしくれ fag end

木の端 きのはし fragment of wood

【は[1] 端】 **edge, border**

山の端 やまのは edge [brow] of mountain

【は[2] 端】 [in compounds] **odd thing, fragment, piece**—historically sometimes interchangeable with 葉, as in the word はがき, which is now always written 葉書

端数 はすう fraction, odd sum

端役 はやく minor role [part]

半端 はんぱ fragment, odd item; incompleteness

下っ端 したっぱ underling, subordinate

【はた 端, -ばた -端】 [also suffix] **edge, side**

池の端で いけのはたで near [by] the pond

道端 みちばた roadside, wayside

海岸端 かいがんばた seaside

【はな 端】 [also 鼻]

① outset, beginning

寝入り端に ねいりばなに just when one has fallen asleep

② **END**, protruded point

【はした 端た, 端】 fraction, odd sum; small change, small sum

端たない はしたない vulgar, disgraceful, shameful

SYNONYMS

1 & 【はし】 ① **extremity**

端 END → 1564

末 end → 4317

梢 tip → 1208

先 point → 3046

尖 POINT →2700
鋒 POINT OF A BLADE →2172

❷ **beginnings**

緒 OUTSET →1742
序 INTRODUCTORY PART →3803
端 start →1564
始 beginning →0335
初 beginning →1433
元 ORIGIN →2428
本 origin →4314
根 ROOT →1167
源 SOURCE →0806

❸ **right**

正 RIGHT →4296
是 RIGHT →3090
尤 RIGHT →3755
端 correct →1564

【はし】

② &【はた】edges and boundaries

縁 EDGE →1754
端 edge →1564
辺 border →3761
境 BOUNDARY →0835
疆 BOUNDARY →1810
界 BOUNDS →3172
際 VERGE →0874
涯 OUTER LIMITS →0623

USAGE

❶【は²】

端

[in compounds] **odd thing, fragment, piece**—historically sometimes interchangeable with 葉, as in the word はがき, which is now always written 葉書

葉

[in compounds] **fragment, piece**—historically sometimes interchangeable with 端, as in the word はがき, which is now always written 葉書

❷【はた】

端

[also suffix] **edge, side**

傍

bystander, outsider

HOMOPHONES

はし

橋 BRIDGE →1367
箸 CHOPSTICKS →3359
梯 LADDER →1210

は² 葉 LEAF →2912
はた 傍 BESIDE →0166
はな 鼻 NOSE →3357

NOTE

➡ see also USAGE notes at 橋 1367 and 鼻 3357

複

1565

1-5-9

▸COMPOUND

フク ㊔ はら

Ⓒ 复 fù

145	Jōyō-5	U8907
ネ	S14-5-9	F1064

Stroke order: 1–14

COMPOUNDS

❶ⓐ **COMPOUND, double, multiple, complex, composite**

ⓑ doubles (as in tennis)

a 複合 ふくごう compound, composite, complex
複利 ふくり compound interest
複視 ふくし polyopia
複葉機 ふくようき biplane
複星 ふくせい multiple star
複数 ふくすう plural
複雑な ふくざつな complicated, complex, involved, intricate

b 単複 たんぷく *gram* singular and plural; singles and doubles (in tennis)

❷ **duplicate, copy**

複本(=副本) ふくほん duplicate, copy
複製 ふくせい duplication, reproduction
複写 ふくしゃ copy, duplication

❸ [original meaning, now archaic] **lined garment**

複衣 ふくい lined garment

INDEPENDENT

【ふく 複】plural; doubles (in tennis); place ticket (in horse racing)

SYNONYMS

❶ⓐ **compound**

複 COMPOUND →1565
倍 DOUBLE →0122
重 DUPLICATE →4390

❷ **copy**

写 COPY →2493
謄 TRANSCRIBE →1398
複 duplicate →1565
拓 copy by rubbing →0375

褐

1566

1-5-9

▸BROWN

カツ

145	Nonstandard	UFA60
ネ	S14-5-9	F0000

traditional form → see 褐 at 1548

褪

incorrect stroke-count
➡ see ◧1-5-10: 衤 at 1577

◧1-5-9

領

▸TERRITORY
リョウ ㊔ みね
Ⓒ 领 lǐng

1567
◧1-5-9

181	Jōyō-5	U9818
頁	S14-9-5	F0493

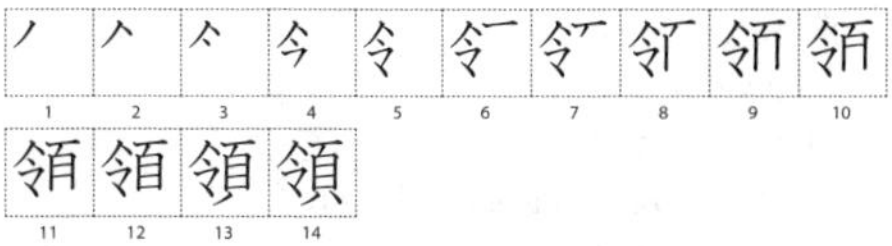

COMPOUNDS

❶ⓐ [also suffix] **TERRITORY, domain, possession, estate**
ⓑ fief, feudal estate, feudal manor

a 領土 りょうど territory, domain
領内 りょうない domains, territory
領海 りょうかい territorial water
領地 りょうち territory, possession, dominion, domain; fief, feud
領空 りょうくう airspace
天領 てんりょう imperial demesne; shogunal demesne
日本領 にほんりょう Japanese territory
カンボジア領 かんぼじありょう Cambodian possession

b 領主 りょうしゅ lord of a fief [manor]
領民 りょうみん population of a fief

❷ⓐ (sphere of action) **TERRITORY, domain, area**
ⓑ area of the cerebral cortex

a 領域 りょういき territory, domain, sphere, province; *math* domain
領分 りょうぶん territory, domain; sphere of action
本領 ほんりょう characteristic, one's specialty; one's line

b 運動領 うんどうりょう motor area

❸ **take possession of, occupy, have jurisdiction over**
領有 りょうゆう possession
占領する せんりょうする capture, occupy, take possession of
横領する おうりょうする seize upon, embezzle, usurp

❹ **receive**
領収書 りょうしゅうしょ receipt, voucher
受領 じゅりょう receipt
拝領する はいりょうする receive (from a superior), be bestowed

❺ **leader, chief, head, administrator**
領事 りょうじ consul, consular representative
領事館 りょうじかん consulate
大統領 だいとうりょう president
首領 しゅりょう leader, head, chief

❻ **main point, essentials, outline**
要領 ようりょう gist, essentials; outline; procedure
綱領 こうりょう essential [main] points, gist, outline; summary

❼ [usu. 了 4157] understand, comprehend
領承する りょうしょうする acknowledge, understand, note

❽ [original meaning] nape (of the neck), collar
領袖 りょうしゅう leader, chief

❾ counter for suits of armor or Japanese clothing
具足二領 ぐそくにりょう two suits of armor

INDEPENDENT

【りょう 領】TERRITORY, domain
【りょうする 領する】govern, rule over, possess, prevail

SYNONYMS

❶ⓐ **areas and localities**
地 PLACE → 0236
方 locality → 2459
辺 VICINITY → 3761
域 BOUNDED AREA → 0559
区 DISTRICT → 3681
領 TERRITORY → 1567
帯 BELT → 3191
圏 SPHERE → 3904

ⓑ **feudal territorial divisions**
藩 FEUDAL DOMAIN → 3022
国 province (in former Japan) → 3831
領 fief → 1567
封 daimiate → 1639
荘 manor (in feudal Japan) → 2814

❸ **occupy**
占 OCCUPY → 2496
拠 occupy → 0369
領 take possession of → 1567
専 take exclusive possession of → 3272

❹ **receive**
受 RECEIVE → 3076
享 ENJOY → 2545
領 receive → 1567
収 TAKE IN → 0031
納 ACCEPT → 1652
貰 GET → 3219
戴 RECEIVE HUMBLY → 4093
頂 RECEIVE HUMBLY → 0164
拝 have the honor to receive → 0360

❺ **leaders**
主 MASTER → 2437

皮 石 示 禾 立 衤 令 【圣】 申

王 KING → 4247
長 CHIEF → 3163
頭 HEAD → 2019
首 LEADER → 2818
領 leader → 1567
魁 LEADER → 4125

NOTE

➡ see COMPOUND FORMATION for 領袖 りょうしゅう → 袖 1496

頚

1568

1-5-9

▶NECK

ケイ くび

181	Nonstandard	U981A
頁	S14-9-5	F0000

traditional form → see 頸 at 2035

暢

1569

1-5-9

▶FLUENT

チョウ ㊔ のぶ のぼる とおる よう まさ いたる なが

Ⓒ 畅 chàng

72	Names	U66A2
日	S14-4-10	F2641

COMPOUNDS

● **FLUENT(ly), smooth(ly), free(ly), with ease**

暢達 ちょうたつ fluency, facileness

流暢な りゅうちょうな fluent, flowing, smooth

SPECIAL READINGS

暢気な のんきな easygoing, happy-go-lucky; free from care

SYNONYMS

● **smooth**

流 flowing → 0529
暢 FLUENT → 1569
滑 SMOOTH → 0809

魄

1570

1-5-10

▶SOUL

ハク

Ⓒ 魄 pò tuò bó

194	Non-Jōyō	U9B44
鬼	S15-10-5	F3163

COMPOUNDS

❶ⓐ [now also 迫 3815] **SOUL, spirit**

ⓑ **baser animal spirit of man**

a 気魄 きはく spirit, soul, vigor

魂魄 こんぱく soul, spirit, ghost

❷ **out of luck**

落魄する らくはくする be reduced to poverty

❸ [archaic] dark portion of the moon

死魄 しはく waning moon

SYNONYMS

❶ⓐ **psyche**

心 HEART → 0011
霊 SPIRIT (soul) → 3480
魂 SOUL, spirit → 1346
魄 SOUL → 1570
腹 heart → 1308
衷 INNER HEART → 2600
襟 inner mind → 1599
胸 breast → 1187
懐 BOSOM → 0942
神 MIND → 1143
気 SPIRIT (consciousness) → 3960
精 SPIRIT (mind) → 1729

確

1571

1-5-10

▶CERTAIN

カク たし(か) たし(かめる) しっか(り)▲

㊔ あきら

Ⓒ 确 què

112	Jōyō-5	U78BA
石	S15-5-10	F0294

COMPOUNDS

ⓐ **CERTAIN, definite, positive, sure, reliable, accurate**

ⓑ (not easily moved) **firm, solid, steadfast, sound**

a 確認 かくにん confirmation, ascertainment

確実な かくじつな certain, sure, reliable; sound, solid

確証 かくしょう certain [definite] proof, positive evidence, corroboration

確率 かくりつ probability

確答 かくとう definite answer [reply]

正確な せいかくな accurate, precise, exact

明確な めいかくな clear, precise, distinct

的確な てきかくな precise, accurate, exact

b 確保する かくほする secure, make sure of, ensure

確立する かくりつする establish, build up

確信する かくしんする believe firmly, be convinced

確執 かくしつ(=かくしゅう) discord, strife

確定 かくてい decision, settlement; confirmation

確固たる かっこたる firm, sure, resolute

INDEPENDENT

【かくたる 確たる】**CERTAIN**, definite, positive, sure, reliable

確たる証拠 かくたるしょうこ certain [definite] evidence

KUN

【たしか 確か】**perhaps, probably, I suppose, if I remember correctly**

確かな たしかな certain, definite, positive, sure, reliable, trustworthy; able, competent, sober, sane

確かそうだ たしかそうだ probably so

確かな事実 たしかなじじつ established [certain] fact

確かな筋 たしかなすじ reliable source

気は確かだ きはたしかだ be sane, be in one's senses

【たしかめる 確かめる】**ascertain, make sure of, confirm, corroborate**

確かめ たしかめ confirmation, certification, ascertainment

真偽を確かめる しんぎをたしかめる make sure of the truth

【しっかり 確り】

しっかりと 確りと

ⓐ tightly, fast, securely, firmly, steadily

ⓑ properly, well

SYNONYMS

ⓐ exact

確 CERTAIN → 1571

正 RIGHT → 4296

真- right → 2616

恰 JUST → 0437

ⓐ certain

必 WITHOUT FAIL → 0015

確 CERTAIN → 1571

筈 OUGHT TO → 3318

ⓑ firm and obstinate

堅 FIRM → 3502

固 FIRM, stiff → 3830

確 firm → 1571

毅 RESOLUTE → 2341

剛 TOUGH → 2107

頑 STUBBORN → 1315

硬 hard-line → 1518

NOTE

➡ see COMPOUND FORMATION for 確執 かくしつ(=かくしゅう) → 執 2114

磁

◧ 1-5-10

incorrect stroke-count

➡ see ◧ 1-5-9: 石 at 1556

稼

1572

◧ 1-5-10

▶**WORK**

カ かせ(ぐ)

Ⓒ 稼 jià

115	Jōyō	U7A3C
禾	S15-5-10	F1463

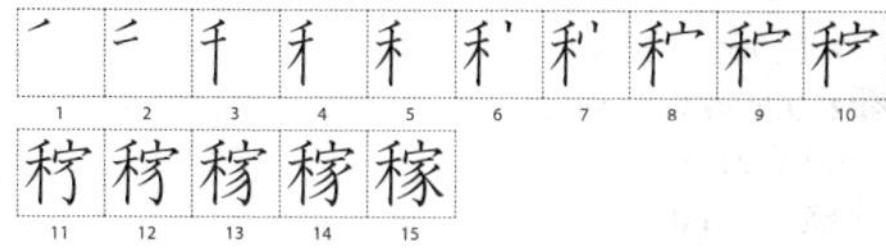

COMPOUNDS

● WORK, work for a living, earn

稼働(=稼動) かどう working, work; operation (of a machine)

稼業 かぎょう trade, business; work; occupation

KUN

【かせぐ 稼ぐ】**WORK, work for a living, earn; gain a profitable situation**

稼ぎ かせぎ labor, work; earnings, income

稼ぎ手 かせぎて breadwinner, supporter; good [hard] worker

稼ぎ取る かせぎとる earn by working

出稼ぎ でかせぎ working away from home

共稼ぎ ともかせぎ working together (for a living), working in double harness

点数を稼ぐ てんすうをかせぐ score points with (a person)

時間を稼ぐ じかんをかせぐ gain time

SYNONYMS

● work

働 WORK → 0172

稼 WORK (for a living) → 1572

労 LABOR → 3155

勤める serve (in an office) → 2287

仕 SERVE → 0037

稽

1573

◧ 1-5-10

▶**THINK**

ケイ ㊔ よし のり とき

Ⓝ 稽 Ⓒ 稽 jī qǐ

115	Jōyō	U7A3D
禾	S15-5-10	F1598

COMPOUNDS

❶ THINK about, consider, contemplate

稽古 けいこ practice, rehearsal; learning

荒唐無稽 こうとうむけい absurdity, nonsense

❷ⓐ detain, keep

ⓑ remain, stay

a 稽留流産 けいりゅうりゅうざん missed abortion

b 滑稽な こっけいな funny, jocular, humorous; laughable, ridiculous

❸ bow to the floor

稽首 けいしゅ bowing to the floor

SYNONYMS

❶ think and consider

思 THINK → 3173
惟 MEDITATE → 0582
省 INTROSPECT → 3100
稽 THINK → 1573
考 THINK → 3962
存 hold an opinion → 3702
案 think out → 2824
想 CONCEIVE → 3507
慮 CONSIDER → 4050
勘 take into consideration → 2231
銓 WEIGH → 2161
量 weigh → 3119

稿

1574

◧1-5-10

▶MANUSCRIPT

コウ

Ⓝ 槀 Ⓒ 稿 gǎo

115	Jōyō	U7A3F
禾	S15-5-10	F1242

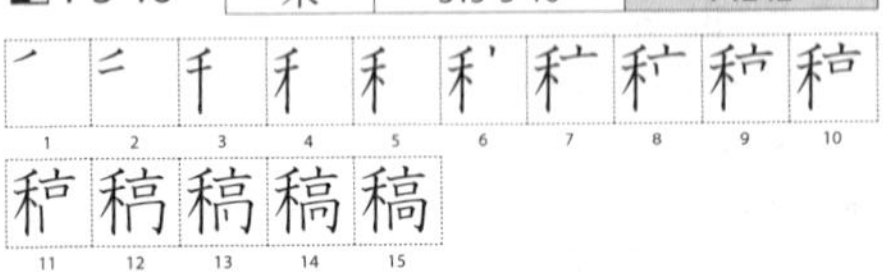

COMPOUNDS

❶ [also suffix] **MANUSCRIPT, draft, copy**

稿料 こうりょう payment for a manuscript
原稿 げんこう manuscript, draft, copy
寄稿 きこう contribution (to a newspaper)
草稿 そうこう outline, draft
遺稿 いこう posthumous work [manuscript]
投稿する とうこうする contribute (an article)
脱稿する だっこうする finish writing, complete (a novel)
決定稿 けっていこう final manuscript

❷ [original meaning, now archaic] straw, stalk of grain

稿人 こうじん straw figure

INDEPENDENT

【こう 稿】**MANUSCRIPT**, copy, draft

稿を改める こうをあらためる rewrite a manuscript

SYNONYMS

❶ manuscript

稿 MANUSCRIPT → 1574
草 draft → 2813
案 draft → 2824

穂

1575

◧1-5-10

▶SPIKE

スイ ほ ㊔ みのる みのり

Ⓝ 穗 Ⓒ 穗 suì

115	Jōyō	U7A42
禾	S15-5-10	F1348

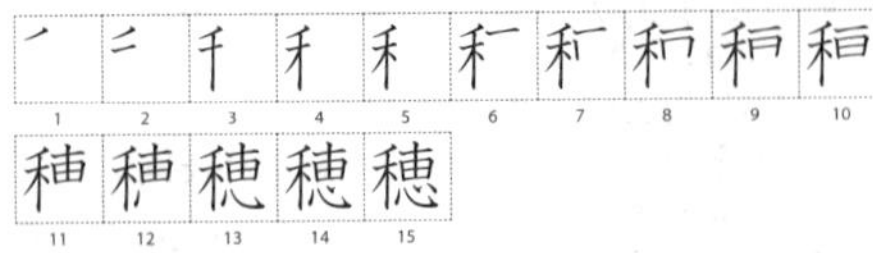

COMPOUNDS

● [original meaning] **SPIKE, ear [head] of grain**

穂状の すいじょうの shaped like an ear of grain
出穂期 しゅっすいき sprouting season (of ears of grain)
花穂 かすい spike

KUN

【ほ 穂】**SPIKE, ear [head] of grain; something shaped like a spike, as the tip of a writing brush**

穂波 ほなみ waving heads (of grain)
穂先 ほさき spike [ear] of grain; spike of a spear; tip of a writing brush
稲穂 いなほ ear of rice
落ち穂 おちぼ gleanings

SYNONYMS

● inflorescences

穂 SPIKE → 1575
穎 GLUME → 2036

稲

1576

◧1-5-10

▶RICE PLANT

トウ いね いな- ㊔ しね

115	Names	U7A3B
禾	S15-5-10	F0000

traditional form → see 稲 at 1561

褪

1577

◧1-5-10

▶FADE

タイ トン あ(せる)

Ⓒ 褪 tuì tùn

145	Non-Jōyō	U892A
ネ	S15-5-10	F2976

COMPOUNDS

● [now usu. 退 3838] **FADE, discolor**

褪色する たいしょくする fade, grow dull in color
褪紅色 たいこうしょく pink

KUN

【あせる 褪せる】**FADE, discolor**

色褪せる いろあせる fade, grow dull in color

SYNONYMS

● **discolor**

褪 FADE → 1577

晒す BLEACH → 1156

穏

1578

1-5-11

▶**CALM**
▶**MILD**

オン おだ(やか) ㊔ やす

Ⓝ 穩 Ⓒ 稳 wěn

115	Jōyō	U7A4F
禾	S16-5-11	F1582

COMPOUNDS

❶ **CALM, peaceful, quiet, tranquil, placid**

平穏な へいおんな calm, quiet, tranquil

安穏 あんのん peace, quiet, tranquility

不穏な ふおんな disquieting, restless

❷ **MILD, gentle, moderate, temperate**

穏健な おんけんな moderate, temperate, sound

穏和(=温和)な おんわな gentle, mild, genial

穏当な おんとうな proper, reasonable, moderate

穏便な おんびんな gentle, quiet, peaceable; private

KUN

【おだやか 穏やか】

おだやかな 穏やかな **CALM, tranquil, peaceful; mild, gentle; moderate, reasonable**

穏やかな海 おだやかなうみ calm sea

穏やかな人 おだやかなひと mild [gentle] person

穏やかさ おだやかさ mildness, gentleness

穏やかな風 おだやかなかぜ gentle breeze

穏やかに話す おだやかにはなす talk quietly

穏やかな処置 おだやかなしょち moderate measure, reasonable step

SYNONYMS

❶ **calm and peaceful**

安 PEACEFUL → 2695

康 peaceful → 3877

寧 peaceful → 2959

泰 TRANQUIL → 3193

静 QUIET → 2164

平 CALM → 4291

穏 CALM → 1578

❷ **gentle**

優しい gentle → 0200

穏 MILD → 1578

柔 SOFT → 2591

積

1579

1-5-11

▶**ACCUMULATE**

セキ つ(む) -づ(み) つ(もる) つ(もり)

㊔ もり

Ⓒ 积 jī

115	Jōyō-4	U7A4D
禾	S16-5-11	F0705

COMPOUNDS

❶ⓐ [original meaning] **ACCUMULATE, pile up, heap up**

ⓑ **ACCUMULATEd, many**

a 積載 せきさい loading, carrying

積極的に せっきょくてきに positively, actively

堆積 たいせき accumulation, pile, heap

蓄積 ちくせき accumulation, stockpiling

山積する さんせきする form a (huge) pile

累積 るいせき accumulation

b 積雪 せきせつ (fallen) snow

積年 せきねん many years

❷ **size, volume, capacity, area**

面積 めんせき area, square measure

体積 たいせき (cubic) volume, capacity

容積 ようせき capacity, volume, bulk

❸ *math* **product**

積算法 せきさんほう integration

相乗積 そうじょうせき product (of A multiplied by B)

INDEPENDENT

【せき 積】*math* product

ＡとＢの積 えーとびーのせき product of A and B

KUN

【つむ 積む】*vt*

① **pile up, heap (up), stack**

積み上げる つみあげる pile [heap] up, accumulate

上積み うわづみ upper load, deck cargo; loading on top, overlaying

② **load, ship, stow aboard**

積み込む つみこむ load (up), put on board, stow aboard

船積み ふなづみ shipment, shipping

③ **ACCUMULATE, lay by, save, amass**

積み立て つみたて laying by, reserving, accumulation

【-づみ -積み】[suffix]

① **shipment**

汽船積み きせんづみ shipment by steamer

② **capacity**

【禾】甲

九トン積み貨車 きゅうとんづみかしゃ 9-ton freight car

【つもる 積もる】 *vi* **ACCUMULATE, get accumulated, be piled up; estimate, calculate, measure**

降り積もる ふりつもる (of snow) pile up

見積もる みつもる estimate

【つもり 積もり】intention, purpose

行く積もりだ いくつもりだ intend to go

SYNONYMS

❶ⓐ accumulate

積 ACCUMULATE → 1579
溜 ACCUMULATE → 0814
累 CUMULATE → 3196
重 pile up → 4390
盛る heap up → 3314
堆 PILED HIGH → 0563

❷ quantity and number

量 QUANTITY → 3119
嵩 BULK → 2927
積 size → 1579
額 AMOUNT → 2273
分 content → 2466
数 NUMBER → 2245
勢 strength → 3542

【つむ】

② load

載 LOAD → 4091
積む load → 1579
搭 load on board → 0721

USAGE

【つむ】

積む
① pile up, heap (up), stack
② load, ship, stow aboard
③ accumulate, lay by, save, amass

詰む
① be packed, become fine [close]
② be checkmated

HOMOPHONES

つむ 詰 REPRIMAND → 1920

稽

1580

1-5-11

▶THINK

ケイ ㊔ よし のり とき

115	Nonstandard	U25874
禾	S16-5-11	F0000

traditional form → see 稽 at 1573

穐

1581

1-5-11

▶AUTUMN

シュウ あき とき ㊔ みのる

115	Nonstandard	U7A50
禾	S16-5-11	F0000

traditional form → see 秋 at 1464

鴨

1582

1-5-11

▶WILD DUCK

オウ かも ㊔ まさ

Ⓒ 鸭 yā

196	Names	U9D28
鳥	S16-11-5	F1692

COMPOUNDS

● WILD DUCK, duck

鴨脚 おうきゃく [rare] ginkgo

KUN

【かも 鴨】

① WILD DUCK

鴨嘴× かものはし platypus

鴨茅 かもがや orchard grass

合鴨(=間鴨) あいがも cross between a mallard and domestic duck

② easy mark, sucker

鴨葱× かもねぎ abbrev. of 鴨が葱×を背負って来る かもがねぎをしょってくる: Along comes a sucker just begging to be parted from his money

③ unclassified compounds

鴨居 かもい lintel (over sliding doors)

SPECIAL READINGS

家鴨 あひる domestic duck

SYNONYMS

● birds

鷹 HAWK → 3955
鷗 GULL → 2370
烏 CROW → 4088
雀 SPARROW → 3117
燕 SWALLOW → 3142
鴻 LARGE WILD BIRD → 0977
鳳 MALE PHOENIX → 3749
凰 FEMALE PHOENIX → 3738
鵬 MYTHICAL HUGE BIRD → 1416
鶏 CHICKEN → 2221
酉 ROOSTER → 4358
隼 FALCON → 3427
鳩 PIGEON → 0184
鷲 EAGLE → 3598
鳶 BLACK KITE → 3919
鶴 CRANE → 2326
鷺 HERON → 3621
鵜 CORMORANT → 2067

鴨 DUCK → 1582
雁 WILD GOOSE → 3741

瞳

▶PUPIL
ドウ トウ▲ ひとみ
Ⓒ 瞳 tóng

1583
◧ 1-5-12

109	Jōyō	U77B3
目	S17-5-12	F1944

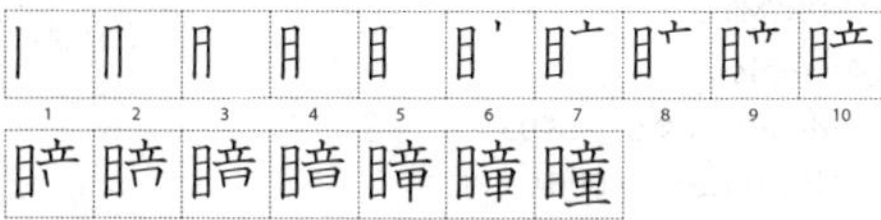

COMPOUNDS

● [original meaning] **PUPIL (of the eye)**
瞳孔 どうこう pupil
瞳子 どうし pupil

KUN

【ひとみ 瞳】[sometimes also 眸]
ⓐ **PUPIL**
ⓑ **one's eyes**
a 瞳の ひとみの pupilary
b 瞳を凝らす ひとみをこらす strain one's eyes

SYNONYMS

● **eye**
目 EYE → 3777
眼 EYE → 1504
眸 EYE → 1502
瞳 PUPIL → 1583

USAGE

【ひとみ】
瞳
[sometimes also 眸]
ⓐ pupil
ⓑ one's eyes
眸
[usu. 瞳]
ⓐ pupil, the apple of one's eye
ⓑ one's eyes

★Both these characters have the same meaning, but the latter has a more literary flavor.

HOMOPHONES

ひとみ 眸 EYE → 1502

瞭

▶CLEAR
リョウ ㊔ あきら
Ⓒ 了 liǎo

1584
◧ 1-5-12

109	Jōyō	U77AD
目	S17-5-12	F2323

COMPOUNDS

ⓐ [rarely also 亮 2571] **CLEAR, obvious**
ⓑ [original meaning] **CLEARly visible**
a 明瞭な めいりょうな clear, plain, lucid
b 一目瞭然の いちもくりょうぜんの quite obvious, as clear as day

SYNONYMS

ⓐ **evident**
明 CLEAR → 1060
鮮 VIVID → 2355
亮 LUCID → 2571
顕 MANIFEST → 2274
瞭 CLEAR → 1584

瞬

▶INSTANT
シュン またた(く)

1585
◧ 1-5-12

109	Nonstandard	U77AC
目	S17-5-12	F0000

traditional form → see 瞬 at 1594

矯

▶RECTIFY
キョウ た(める) ㊔ たかし
Ⓒ 矫 jiǎo jiáo

1586
◧ 1-5-12

111	Jōyō	U77EF
矢	S17-5-12	F2783

COMPOUNDS

❶ **RECTIFY, reform, correct, straighten out**
矯正 きょうせい correction, rectification
矯風 きょうふう moral reform
❷ extreme, eccentric
矯激な きょうげきな radical, extreme, eccentric
奇矯 ききょう eccentricity
❸ pretend, feign, falsify
矯飾 きょうしょく pretense, affectation

KUN

【ためる 矯める】
① **straighten; correct, redress, remedy**
枝を矯める えだをためる straighten a branch
不正を矯める ふせいをためる redress injustice
② aim with one eye

矯めつ眇×めつする ためつすがめつする scrutinize, scan

SYNONYMS

❶ **correct**

正 RIGHT → 4296
直す correct → 3649
訂 REVISE → 1829
改 REFORM → 0287
矯 RECTIFY → 1586
匡 RECTIFY → 3710

磯

1587

1-5-12

▶**ROCKY BEACH**

キ いそ

Ⓒ 矶 jī

112	Names	U78EF
石	S17-5-12	F2032

KUN

【いそ 磯】

① **ROCKY BEACH, beach, seashore**

磯辺 いそべ rocky beach, beach
磯巾着 いそぎんちゃく sea anemone, seaflower
磯釣り いそづり fishing from rocks near the shore
磯伝いに いそづたいに along the beach
荒磯 あらいそ reefy coast, windswept and wave-beaten shore

② flank of a koto

SYNONYMS

【いそ】

① **shores and watersides**

畔 WATERSIDE → 1472
-辺 -side → 3761
浜 BEACH → 0523
岸 SHORE → 2777
浦 SEASIDE → 0524
渚 STRAND → 0637
磯 ROCKY BEACH → 1587
汀 STRAND → 0228

礁

1588

1-5-12

▶**REEF**

ショウ

Ⓒ 礁 jiāo

112	Jōyō	U7901
石	S17-5-12	F2552

COMPOUNDS

● [original meaning] **REEF, sunken rock**

岩礁 がんしょう reef
珊瑚礁 さんごしょう coral reef
座礁(=坐礁)する ざしょうする run aground, be stranded
環礁 かんしょう atoll
暗礁 あんしょう sunken rock, unknown reef; deadlock

INDEPENDENT

【しょう 礁】 **REEF**

SYNONYMS

● **shoals**

瀬 SHALLOWS → 0995
州 sandbar → 0064
礁 REEF → 1588

● **elevations in water**

島 ISLAND → 4103
州 sandbar → 0064
礁 REEF → 1588
洲 SANDBAR → 0467

禪

1589

1-5-12

▶**ZEN**

ゼン

113	Names	U79AA
示	S17-5-12	F0000

traditional form → see 禅 at 1306

穉

1590

1-5-12

▶**CHILDISH**

チ ㊔ わか

115	Nonstandard	U7A49
禾	S17-5-12	F0000

traditional form → see 稚 at 1543

穗

1591

1-5-12

▶**SPIKE**

スイ ほ ㊔ みのる みのり

115	Names	U7A57
禾	S17-5-12	F0000

traditional form → see 穂 at 1575

襖

1592

1-5-12

▶**OPAQUE SLIDING DOOR**

オウ ふすま あお

145	Nonstandard	U8956
ネ	S17-5-12	F0000

traditional form → see 襖 at 1600

襍

1593

1-5-12

▶**MISCELLANEOUS**
▶**MIXED**

ザツ ゾウ ㊔ さい くさ

145	Nonstandard	U894D
ネ	S17-5-12	F0000

traditional form → see 雑 at 1752

瞬

1594

1-5-13

▶INSTANT

シュン　またた(く)

Ⓝ 瞬 Ⓒ 瞬 shùn

109	Jōyō	U77AC
目	S18-5-13	F0814

COMPOUNDS

❶ **INSTANT, moment; in the twinkling of an eye**

瞬間 しゅんかん instant, moment, second

瞬時 しゅんじ instant, moment; minute

一瞬 いっしゅん instant, moment

❷ [original meaning] blink, wink

KUN

【またたく　瞬く】**wink, blink; twinkle, flicker**

瞬き またたき wink; twinkle (of stars)

瞬く間に またたくまに in the twinkling of an eye

SYNONYMS

❶ **short time periods**

頃 moment → 0163

瞬 INSTANT → 1594

秒 SECOND → 1462

分 MINUTE → 2466

時 hour → 1155

暫 SHORT WHILE → 3553

礎

1595

1-5-13

▶FOUNDATION STONE

ソ　いしずえ　㊔ もとい　いそ

Ⓒ 础 chǔ

112	Jōyō	U790E
石	S18-5-13	F1599

COMPOUNDS

ⓐ **FOUNDATION STONE, cornerstone, foundation**

ⓑ (nonphysical support) **foundation, basis**

a 礎石 そせき foundation stone, cornerstone

礎材 そざい foundation materials

柱礎 ちゅうそ plinth

定礎 ていそ laying of a foundation stone

b 基礎 きそ basis, foundation

国礎 こくそ pillar of state

KUN

【いしずえ　礎】**FOUNDATION STONE, cornerstone; foundation, basis, base**

礎を築く いしずえをきずく lay the foundation (for)

SYNONYMS

ⓐ **supporting structures**

柱 PILLAR → 1109

礎 FOUNDATION STONE → 1595

桁 BEAM → 1165

梁 BEAM → 3410

ⓐ **bottoms and bases**

底 BOTTOM → 3827

柢 BOTTOM → 1121

下 lower part → 4186

基 BASE → 3312

礎 FOUNDATION STONE → 1595

麓 FOOT OF MOUNTAIN → 3494

磐 BEDROCK → 3534

盤 bedrock → 3533

床 BED → 3805

ⓑ **basis**

基 BASE → 3312

本 BASIS → 4314

素 ELEMENT → 3108

礎 foundation → 1595

底 BOTTOM → 3827

根 ROOT → 1167

拠 GROUNDS → 0369

禮

1596

1-5-13

▶ETIQUETTE

▶RITE

レイ　ライ　㊔ あや　のり　ひろ

113	Names	U79AE
示	S18-5-13	F0000

traditional form → see 礼 at 1012

穰

1597

1-5-13

▶YIELDING ABUNDANTLY

ジョウ　㊔ みのる　ゆたか　みのり　ゆずる　しげ

Ⓝ 穰 Ⓒ 穰 ráng

115	Names	U7A63
禾	S18-5-13	F3368

COMPOUNDS

❶ **YIELDING ABUNDANTLY, abundant (harvest), luxuriant, plentiful**

豊穣 ほうじょう abundant crop, rich harvest

❷ [original meaning, now archaic] stalk of grain

❸ [archaic] ten octillion (10^{28})

SYNONYMS

❶ **plentiful**

百 numerous → 2519

沃 FERTILE → 0315
万 myriad → 3653
多 MANY → 2694
豊 PLENTIFUL → 3344
沢 plentiful → 0313
穣 YIELDING ABUNDANTLY → 1597
裕 ABUNDANT → 1530
饒 ABUNDANT → 2280
富 RICH → 2892

穫 1598

▶**HARVEST**

カク

Ⓝ 穫 Ⓒ 获 huò

1-5-13

115	Jōyō	U7A6B
禾	S18-5-13	F2267

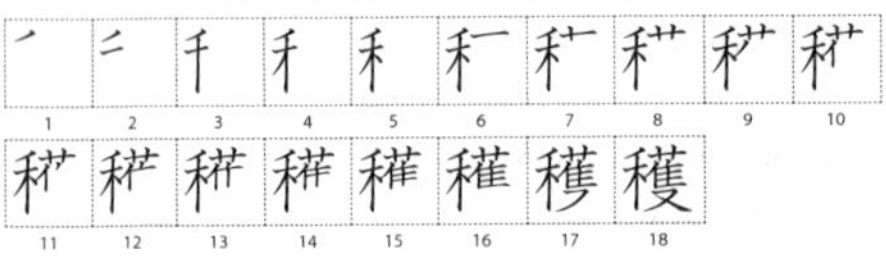

COMPOUNDS

● [original meaning] **HARVEST, reap, gather**
収穫する しゅうかくする harvest, gather in, reap

SYNONYMS

● **harvest**
採 PICK → 0606
摘 PICK → 0851
穫 HARVEST → 1598
刈る reap → 0032

NOTE

★ do not confuse with 獲 CATCH GAME → 0959

襟 1599

▶**COLLAR**

キン えり

Ⓒ 襟 jīn

1-5-13

145	Jōyō	U895F
ネ	S18-5-13	F1952

COMPOUNDS

❶ **COLLAR, lapel**
開襟シャツ かいきんしゃつ wing-collared [open-neck] shirt

❷ inner mind, heart, bosom, thoughts
襟懐 きんかい inner thoughts, feelings
胸襟 きょうきん bosom, heart

KUN

【えり 襟】[also 衿]
ⓐ **COLLAR, lapel, neck**
ⓑ nape
a 襟巻き えりまき scarf, muffler
襟を正す えりをただす straighten oneself
詰め襟 つめえり stand-up collar
b 襟首 えりくび neck, back of neck

SYNONYMS

❶ **garment parts**
襟 COLLAR → 1599
袖 SLEEVE → 1496
懐 BOSOM → 0942
衿 COLLAR → 1465
裾 HEM → 1549

❷ **psyche**
心 HEART → 0011
霊 SPIRIT (soul) → 3480
魂 SOUL, spirit → 1346
魄 SOUL → 1570
腹 heart → 1308
衷 INNER HEART → 2600
襟 inner mind → 1599
胸 breast → 1187
懐 BOSOM → 0942
神 MIND → 1143
気 SPIRIT (consciousness) → 3960
精 SPIRIT (mind) → 1729

USAGE

【えり】
襟
[also 衿]
ⓐ collar, lapel, neck
ⓑ nape
衿
[also 襟] same as 襟

HOMOPHONES

えり 衿 COLLAR → 1465

襖 1600

▶**OPAQUE SLIDING DOOR**

オウ ふすま あお

Ⓝ 襖 Ⓒ 袄 ǎo

1-5-13

145	Names	U8956
ネ	S18-5-13	F2085

COMPOUNDS

● **overgarment**
素襖 すおう *hist* ceremonial dress of lower-class samurai

KUN

【ふすま 襖】**OPAQUE SLIDING DOOR**
襖絵 ふすまえ images drawn or painted on fusuma

【あお 襖】*hist* formal garment worn by military officers in ancient Japan

SYNONYMS

● clothing

服 CLOTHES → 1090
袴 FORMAL DIVIDED SKIRT → 1509
蓑 STRAW RAINCOAT → 2941
-着 wear → 4110
衣 GARMENT → 2506
装 DRESS → 3327
裳 DRESS → 3231
襤 RAGS → 1607
袈 BUDDHIST SURPLICE → 3200
裟 BUDDHIST CASSOCK → 3420
襖 overgarment → 1600

【ふすま】

○ doors

戸 DOOR → 2429
扉 HINGED DOOR → 2453
門 GATE → 1100
口 entrance (or exit) → 4189
襖 OPAQUE SLIDING DOOR → 1600

礙 1601 1-5-14

▶STAND IN THE WAY
ガイ ゲ

112	Nonstandard	U7919
石	S19-5-14	F0000

traditional form → see 碍 at 1536

礦 1-5-14

incorrect stroke-count
➡ see 1-5-15: 石 at 1606

禰 1602 1-5-14

▶FATHER'S MAUSOLEUM
デイ ネ ㊔ や

113	Names	U79B0
示	S19-5-14	F0000

traditional form → see 祢 at 1142

禱 1603 1-5-14

▶PRAY
トウ いの(る)

113	Names	U79B1
示	S19-5-14	F0000

traditional form → see 祷 at 1224

穫 1604 1-5-14

▶HARVEST
カク

115	Nonstandard	U7A6B
禾	S19-5-14	F0000

traditional form → see 穫 at 1598

穩 1605 1-5-14

▶CALM
▶MILD
オン おだ(やか) ㊔ やす

115	Nonstandard	U7A69
禾	S19-5-14	F0000

traditional form → see 穏 at 1578

襤 1-5-14

incorrect stroke-count
➡ see 1-5-15: 衤 at 1607

礦 1606 1-5-15

▶ORE
▶MINE
コウ

Ⓝ 砿 Ⓒ 矿 kuàng

112	Non-Jōyō	U7926
石	S20-5-15	F0000

COMPOUNDS

[now replaced by 鉱 2145]

❶ [original meaning] **ORE**

礦石 こうせき ore, mineral
礦業 こうぎょう mining (industry)

❷ⓐ **MINE**

ⓑ suffix after names of **MINE**s

a 炭礦 たんこう coal mine
b 夕張礦 ゆうばりこう Yubari Mine

SYNONYMS

❶ **metal**

金 METAL → 2552
鉱 ORE → 2145
礦 ORE → 1606
鈑 SHEET METAL → 2122

❷ **mine**

坑 PIT → 0277
鉱 MINE → 2145
礦 MINE → 1606
山 mine → 3658

襤 1607 1-5-15

▶RAGS
ラン

Ⓒ 褴 lán

145	Non-Jōyō	U8964
衤	S20-5-15	F0000

COMPOUNDS

● [rarely also 藍 3024] [original meaning] **RAGS, tattered clothes**

襤褸× らんる(=ぼろ) rags, tattered clothes

SYNONYMS

● **clothing**

服 CLOTHES → 1090
袴 FORMAL DIVIDED SKIRT → 1509

蓑 STRAW RAINCOAT →2941
-着 wear →4110
衣 GARMENT →2506
装 DRESS →3327
裳 DRESS →3231
襤 RAGS →1607
袈 BUDDHIST SURPLICE →3200
裟 BUDDHIST CASSOCK →3420
襖 overgarment →1600

龝

1608

1-5-16

▶AUTUMN

シュウ あき とき ㊔ みのる

115	Nonstandard	U9F9D
禾	S21-5-16	F0000

traditional form →see 秋 at 1464

穰

1609

1-5-17

▶YIELDING ABUNDANTLY

ジョウ ㊔ みのる ゆたか みのり ゆずる しげ

115	Names	U7A70
禾	S22-5-17	F0000

traditional form →see 穣 at 1597

糺

1610

1-6-1

▶INQUIRE INTO

キュウ ただ(す) ㊔ ただし

120	Nonstandard	U7CFA
糸	S7-6-1	F0000

alternative form →see 糾 at 1631

乱

1611

1-6-1

▶DISORDERED

ラン みだ(れる) みだ(る) みだ(す)

Ⓝ 亂 Ⓒ 乱 luàn

5	Jōyō-6	U4E71
乚	S7-1-6	F0689

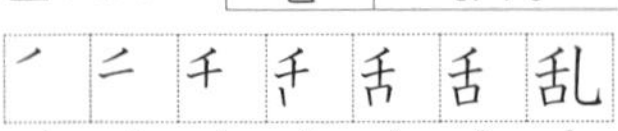

COMPOUNDS

❶ [also prefix]
ⓐ **DISORDERED, confused, chaotic, boisterous, abusive, reckless**
ⓑ random
ⓒ [also 濫 0990] **excessive, indiscriminate, extravagant, inordinate, haphazard, reckless**

a 乱雑 らんざつ disorder, confusion
乱暴 らんぼう violence, roughness; rape
乱闘 らんとう free-for-all [confused] fight, melee
乱気流 らんきりゅう turbulent air, turbulence
波乱(=波瀾×) はらん disturbance, troubles; fluctuation
混乱 こんらん disorder, confusion, chaos

b 乱数 らんすう random number
乱編成ファイル らんへんせいふぁいる random file

c 乱読 らんどく indiscriminate reading
乱用 らんよう abuse, misuse, misappropriation
乱造 らんぞう excessive production, careless manufacture
乱開発 らんかいはつ indiscriminate development

❷ⓐ **social disorder, disturbance**
ⓑ **rebellion, civil war, war, riot, revolt**

a 動乱 どうらん upheaval, disturbance, agitation
戦乱 せんらん disturbances of war

b 反乱 はんらん rebellion, revolt

❸ be corrupt, be demoralized
乱行 らんぎょう profligacy, debauchery, misconduct
淫乱 いんらん lewdness, lasciviousness

❹ [formerly 爛 1427] overripe, rotten
腐乱 ふらん ulceration, decomposition

INDEPENDENT

【らん 乱】rebellion, civil war, war, riot, revolt, disturbance
乱を起こす らんをおこす rise in rebellion
応仁の乱 おうにんのらん Onin War (1467-1477)

KUN

【みだれる 乱れる】**be DISORDERED, go out of order, be confused; be disturbed, be chaotic; be disheveled; be demoralized**
乱れ みだれ disorder, disturbance, unrest
乱れ髪 みだれがみ disheveled hair
心が乱れる こころがみだれる lose one's composure

【みだる 乱る】*elegant* become DISORDERED; put into disorder

【みだす 乱す】**put into disorder, throw into confusion, disturb; dishevel**
掻き乱す かきみだす throw into disorder

SYNONYMS

❶ⓐ **disordered**
紛 CONFUSED →1648
乱 DISORDERED →1611
錯 MIXED UP →2187
混 mixed up →0631
雑 mixed up →1752
沌 PRIMEVAL CHAOS →0314

ⓒ **rash**
滅 unreasonable →0812
妄 RASH →2509
盲 BLIND →2547
暴 unrestrained →3138
荒 WILD →2810
濫 EXCESSIVE →0990
乱 excessive →1611

❷ⓑ **warfare and rebellions**

戦 WAR → 2242
軍 war → 2582
役 war → 0288
陣 battle → 0545
乱 rebellion → 1611
変 uprising → 2569
闘 FIGHT → 4136

乱 1-6-1

incorrect stroke-count
➡ see 1-7-1: 孚 at 1823

糾 1612 1-6-2

▶INQUIRE INTO
キュウ ただ(す) ㊔ ただし

120	Nonstandard	U7CFE
糸	S8-6-2	F0000

traditional form → see 糾 at 1631

取 1613 1-6-2

▶TAKE
シュ と(る) と(り) と(り)- とり- -ど(り)
Ⓒ 取 qǔ

29	Jōyō-3	U53D6
又	S8-2-6	F0098

一 1 丅 2 F 3 F 4 E 5 耳 6 取 7 取 8

COMPOUNDS

❶ⓐ [original meaning] (grasp with the hands) **TAKE, pick, gather**
ⓑ (bring into one's possession) **TAKE, obtain, acquire, get, gather**
ⓒ **TAKE** one of several, pick out, choose
ⓓ **TAKE away from, steal**

a 採取 さいしゅ picking, collecting, harvesting
摘取する てきしゅする pick, pluck up
b 取材する しゅざいする collect data [materials], gather news
取得する しゅとくする acquire, gain; purchase
摂取する せっしゅする take (in), ingest, absorb
二点先取する にてんせんしゅする take [score] the first two points of the game
聴取する ちょうしゅする listen to, give a hearing to
c 取捨する しゅしゃする take or leave, choose
d 詐取 さしゅ fraud, swindle
搾取 さくしゅ exploitation, sweating, squeezing

❷ face a challenge, come to grips with
進取の精神 しんしゅのせいしん progressive [enterprising] spirit

KUN

【とる 取る】

①ⓐ **TAKE, take hold of, seize**
ⓑ **TAKE off, take away, remove, delete, leave out**
ⓒ **TAKE** (a life) away, kill
ⓓ (ingest food) **TAKE, have, eat**
ⓔ (secure by payment) **TAKE** (in) (a newspaper), subscribe to; buy, order
ⓕ (take in crops) **harvest, reap, gather**
ⓖ (take money for) charge, ask

a 取れる とれる can be held; come off, fall off; be removed; be produced; be understood; be interpreted
取り柄 とりえ merit, worth, recommendable feature
取り上げる とりあげる take [pick] up; take away, confiscate; deliver a baby; accept, listen to; adopt (a proposal)
取り分け とりわけ especially, above all
塵取り ちりとり dustpan
遣り取り やりとり giving and taking, exchanges
手に取る てにとる take in one's hand
色取る いろどる [also 彩る] color, paint, dye; make up
b 取り外す とりはずす remove, dismantle
汲み取る くみとる draw [dip] up, drain; take into consideration
帽子を取る ぼうしをとる take off one's hat
c 蚊取り線香 かとりせんこう mosquito-repellent incense
d 朝食を取る ちょうしょくをとる take breakfast
e 朝日新聞を取る あさひしんぶんをとる take in [subscribe to] the *Asahi* (newspaper)
f 取り入れる とりいれる take in; harvest; accept, adopt, introduce
g 食費を取る しょくひをとる charge for one's meal

② get or cause to come into one's possession:
ⓐ **TAKE, receive, get, obtain, accept, acquire**
ⓑ **TAKE possession of (a castle), seize, capture, conquer**
ⓒ **TAKE** away from, deprive, steal
ⓓ (reserve) **TAKE**, book, engage

a 取り戻す とりもどす take back, regain, restore
取り込む とりこむ take in, introduce, incorporate; be in confusion
関取 せきとり ranking sumo wrestler
受け取る うけとる receive, accept; understand
満点を取る まんてんをとる get full marks
連絡を取る れんらくをとる get in touch with
b 城を取る しろをとる take a castle
c 寝取る ねとる steal another's wife [husband, lover]
d 席を取って置く せきをとっておく book [take] a seat

③ cause an abstract thing or action to shift towards oneself or elsewhere:
ⓐ **TAKE down (notes), write, record**
ⓑ **TAKE on (responsibility), assume**
ⓒ **TAKE** (the meaning of a passage), make out, interpret
ⓓ **TAKE** count, measure
ⓔ undergo, suffer

a 書き取る かきとる write down, note down
　ノートを取る のーとをとる note down, take notes
b 責任を取る せきにんをとる take responsibility for
　気取る きどる make an affected pose, assume airs
c 意味を取る いみをとる understand the meaning of, follow the sense
d 脈を取る みゃくをとる take a pulse
e 不覚を取る ふかくをとる suffer a defeat

④ **TAKE (time), take up (space), require**
　手間を取る てまをとる take time, be detained
　場所を取る ばしょをとる take up [occupy] space

【とり 取り】star performer; active partner in judo performances
　頭取 とうどり (bank) president; greenroom manager

【とり- 取り-, 取-】
① **emphatic verbal prefix implying that the action is performed with thoroughness and care**
　取り扱う とりあつかう handle, deal with, treat; deal in; handle, manipulate, operate; conduct; accept, take in
　取り決める とりきめる make arrangements, agree upon
　取り組む とりくむ grapple, tackle (a problem)
　取り消し とりけし cancellation, annulment
　取り調べ とりしらべ investigation, inquiry
　取り締まり とりしまり management, control, regulation; director, supervisor
　取り止めの無い とりとめのない wandering, incoherent, vague
　取り立てて とりたてて particularly
　取り巻く とりまく surround, encircle
② **transaction, dealings**
　取り引き とりひき transaction, dealings
　公取委(=公正取引委員会) こうとりい(=こうせいとりひきいいんかい) Fair Trade Commission
　証取法(=証券取引法) しょうとりほう(=しょうけんとりひきほう) Securities and Exchange Act
③ abbrev. of 取り扱い とりあつかい: handling, operating
　取説(=取り扱い説明書) とりせつ(=とりあつかいせつめいしょ) instruction manual

【-どり -取り】
① **arrangement, placement**
　間取り まどり room arrangement
　日取り ひどり schedule
② **manner, style**
　足取り あしどり one's manner of walking; trace (of a culprit's movement); (price) movement

SYNONYMS

❶ⓐ &【とる】①ⓐ take
把 GRIP →0293
握 GRASP →0714
捉 GRASP →0518
執 SEIZE →2114
摑む GRASP →0848
捕 CATCH →0514
取 TAKE →1613
持 HOLD →0447

ⓑ get
得 ACQUIRE →0577
拾 PICK UP →0454
獲 obtain →0959
収 TAKE IN →0031
取 TAKE →1613

ⓓ steal and rob
盗 STEAL →3309
窃 STEAL →2801
取 TAKE →1613
奪 ROB →2956
略 plunder →1501
掠 PLUNDER →0605
鹵 PLUNDER →2634

USAGE

❶【とる】
取る
①ⓐ take, take hold of, seize
　ⓑ take off, take away, remove, delete, leave out
　ⓒ take (a life) away, kill
　ⓓ (ingest food) take, have, eat
　ⓔ (secure by payment) take (in) (a newspaper), subscribe to; buy, order
　ⓕ (take in crops) harvest, reap, gather
　ⓖ (take money for) charge, ask
② get or cause to come into one's possession:
　ⓐ take, receive, get, obtain, accept, acquire
　ⓑ take possession of (a castle), seize, capture, conquer
　ⓒ take away from, deprive, steal
　ⓓ (reserve) take, book, engage
③ cause an abstract thing or action to shift towards oneself or elsewhere:
　ⓐ take down (notes), write, record
　ⓑ take on (responsibility), assume
　ⓒ take (the meaning of a passage), make out, interpret
　ⓓ take count, measure
　ⓔ undergo, suffer
④ take (time), take up (space), require

採る
①ⓐ gather, collect, extract (oil), produce (wine out of grapes)
　ⓑ admit (light)
②ⓐ pick (out), choose, prefer
　ⓑ adopt, take, engage

執る

① perform (duties), conduct, transact, take (trouble)

② perform an action while holding an object (such as a pen)

③ persist in, insist on

捕る

catch, take, seize

撮る

photograph, shoot, film, videotape

❷【-どり】

-取り

① arrangement, placement

② manner, style

-撮り

counter for number of shots [pictures] available in a film

HOMOPHONES

とる

採 PICK →0606

執 EXECUTE →2114

捕 CATCH →0514

撮 PHOTOGRAPH →0910

-どり 撮 PHOTOGRAPH →0910

いろどる

彩る →2115

色取る →2522, 1613

COMPOUND FORMATION

【関取 せきとり】

関取 'ranking sumo wrestler' is a sumo wrestler (関) who acquired (取る ②ⓐ) a high rank.

NOTE

➡ see COMPOUND FORMATION for 取り柄 とりえ →柄 1111

耺

1614

◧ 1-6-2

▶**EMPLOYMENT**

ショク ソク

128	Nonstandard	U2B7C9
耳	S8-6-2	F0000

handwritten form →see 職 at 1803

耶

◧ 1-6-2

incorrect stroke-count

➡ see ◧ 1-6-3: 耳 at 1635

臥

◧ 1-6-2

incorrect stroke-count

➡ see ◧ 1-7-2: 臣 at 1825

卧

◧ 1-6-2

incorrect stroke-count

➡ see ◧ 1-7-2: 臣 at 1826

到

1615

◧ 1-6-2

▶**ARRIVE**

トウ いた(る)▲

Ⓒ 到 dào

18	Jōyō	U5230
刂	S8-2-6	F1106

COMPOUNDS

❶ **ARRIVE (at), reach, come to**

到着 とうちゃく arrival

到達 とうたつ arrival; attainment

到来 とうらい arrival, advent

殺到する さっとうする rush in, pour in; descend on

❷ **reach [go to] the limit of**

到底 とうてい after all, in the long run

到頭 とうとう at last, after all

❸ scrupulous, attentive

周到な しゅうとうな scrupulous, cautious, circumspect

精到な せいとうな meticulous

KUN

【いたる 到る】[usu. 至る] **ARRIVE at, reach, come to**

目的地に到る もくてきちにいたる arrive at one's destination

SYNONYMS

❶ **arrive**

着 ARRIVE →4110

到 ARRIVE →1615

至 COME TO →2707

及 REACH TO →4192

届く REACH →3820

達 ATTAIN →3893

HOMOPHONES

いたる 至 COME TO →2707

NOTE

➡ see USAGE note at 至 2707

剆

1616

◧ 1-6-2

▶**DRAMA**

ゲキ

18	Nonstandard	U5287
刂	S8-2-6	F0000

handwritten form →see 劇 at 2399

効

1617

◧ 1-6-2

▶**EFFECT**

コウ き(く)

Ⓝ 效 Ⓒ 效 xiào

19	Jōyō-5	U52B9
力	S8-2-6	F0664

COMPOUNDS

ⓐ EFFECT, efficacy (esp. of drugs), virtue
ⓑ (state of being operative or in force) **EFFECT, effectiveness, validity**

a 効果 こうか effect, efficacy; result
効率 こうりつ efficiency
効能 こうのう effect, efficacy
即効 そっこう immediate effect
薬効 やっこう effect of a medicine
特効薬 とっこうやく specific medicine
ab 効力 こうりょく effect, efficacy; effect (as of a law), validity
有効な ゆうこうな effective, valid
無効 むこう invalidity, ineffectiveness
b 発効する はっこうする become effective, take effect, come into force

INDEPENDENT

【こう 効】**EFFECT**, efficacy, virtue
効が有る こうがある be efficacious, be beneficial to

KUN

【きく 効く】**be EFFECTive, have an effect, produce a desired effect**
効き きき effectiveness (esp. of drugs)
効き目 ききめ effect, efficacy
良く効く薬 よくきくくすり very efficacious medicine

SYNONYMS

ⓐ potency
効 EFFECT → 1617
験 efficacy → 2306
能 action → 1676
機 function → 1365

USAGE

❶【きく】
効く
be effective, have an effect, produce a desired effect
利く
① work (well), function (properly)
② speak (esp. as a mediator)

❷【きき】
効き
effectiveness (esp. of drugs)
利き
function, efficacy

HOMOPHONES

きく 利 ADVANTAGE → 1431
きき 利 ADVANTAGE → 1431

郊

1-6-2

incorrect stroke-count
➡ see 1-6-3: 交 at 1638

劾

1618

1-6-2

▶EXPOSE CRIMES
ガイ
Ⓒ 劾 hé

19	Jōyō	U52BE
力	S8-2-6	F3202

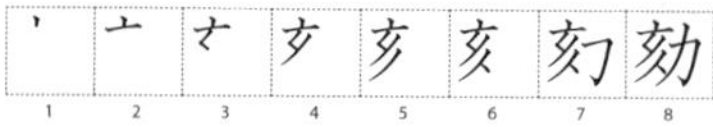

COMPOUNDS

● EXPOSE (a person's) CRIMES or misdeeds, impeach, accuse; investigate crime
劾奏する がいそうする report an official's offense to the emperor
弾劾する だんがいする impeach, denounce, accuse

SYNONYMS

● blame and accuse
責 BLAME → 3115
叱 SCOLD → 0210
詰 REPRIMAND → 1920
難 find fault with → 2310
批 CRITICIZE → 0294
劾 EXPOSE CRIMES → 1618
弾 impeach → 0697

刻

1619

1-6-2

▶ENGRAVE
▶POINT OF TIME
コク　きざ(む)　きざ(み)　㊔とき
Ⓒ 刻 kè

18	Jōyō-6	U523B
刂	S8-2-6	F0726

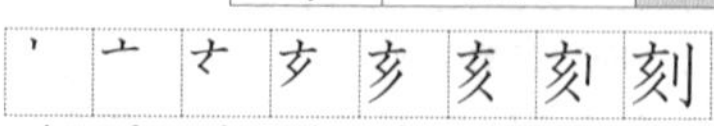

COMPOUNDS

❶ [original meaning] (cut letters or designs on a surface) **ENGRAVE, carve, chisel**
刻印 こくいん carved seal, stamp
刻字 こくじ carving characters; carved characters
彫刻する ちょうこくする sculpt, carve, engrave
陰刻 いんこく white line

❷ⓐ POINT OF TIME, time, moment, hour
ⓑ (period of time) time, interval
ⓒ two-hour period in former system of measuring time

a 刻限 こくげん time, appointed time
刻一刻 こくいっこく moment by moment, hour by hour
時刻 じこく time; hour
遅刻 ちこく tardiness, lateness

定刻 ていこく regular [appointed] time
即刻 そっこく immediately, instantly
b 夕刻 ゆうこく evening
c 上刻 じょうこく first third of a two-hour period
❸ division of a water clock
漏刻 ろうこく water clock
❹ **cruel, severe**
刻薄(=酷薄) こくはく cruelty, inhumanity
深刻な しんこくな serious, grave, keen, poignant

INDEPENDENT

【こく 刻】 two-hour period (→❷ⓒ)
子の刻 ねのこく midnight
【こくする 刻する】 ENGRAVE

KUN

【きざむ 刻む】 **cut fine, chop up; ENGRAVE, carve; notch;** (of a clock) **tick (away)**
刻み きざみ notch, nick; shredded tobacco
刻み付ける きざみつける engrave, inscribe
刻み出す きざみだす carve out
小刻みに こきざみに little by little, piecemeal
切り刻む きりきざむ cut, chop, mince
【きざみ 刻み】 [in compounds]
ⓐ **minced, shredded**
ⓑ **at equal intervals**
a 刻み煙草 きざみたばこ pipe tobacco; shredded tobacco
b 五分刻みで ごふんきざみで every five minutes

SYNONYMS

❶ **form and carve**
刻 ENGRAVE → 1619
彫 CARVE → 2117
塑 MODEL → 3525
鋳 CAST → 2170
❷ **time periods**
時 TIME → 1155
季 SEASON (quarter) → 3161
候 SEASON (time of year) → 0133
頃 TIME → 0163
暇 FREE TIME → 1275
般 period of time → 1670
刻 POINT OF TIME → 1619
間 INTERVAL → 4122
隙 GAP → 0826
期 TERM → 2139
節 SEASON → 3336

刹 ▸BUDDHIST TEMPLE

1620
◧1-6-2

サツ セツ
ⓒ 刹 chà shā

18	Jōyō	U5239
刂	S8-2-6	F2503

Stroke order: ノ ㄨ 㐅 ⺗ 杀 杀 刹 刹 (1–8)

COMPOUNDS

❶ **BUDDHIST TEMPLE**
名刹 めいさつ famous temple
古刹 こさつ ancient temple
巨刹 きょさつ large temple
梵×刹 ぼんさつ(=ぼんせつ) Buddhist temple
❷ **used phonetically for *setsu* in the transliteration of Sanskrit Buddhist terms**
刹那 せつな moment, instant; *kṣaṇa* (1/75 of a second)
刹那的 せつなてき ephemeral, transitory
羅刹 らせつ *rākṣasa*, evil spirit

INDEPENDENT

【さつ 刹】 central pillar of a pagoda
【せつ 刹】 *ksetra*: realm, country (in Buddhism); pagoda, temple

SYNONYMS

❶ **places of worship**
堂 temple building → 3202
塔 pagoda → 0683
寺 BUDDHIST TEMPLE → 2687
刹 TEMPLE → 1620
社 Shinto shrine → 1042
宮 SHINTO SHRINE → 2828
院 monastery → 0544
教 church → 1887
❷ **phonetic [s]/[sh]**
沙 phonetic [sha] → 0311
刹 phonetic [setsu] → 1620
遮 phonetic [sha] → 3916
叉 phonetic [sha] → 4194
世 phonetic [se] → 4308
須 phonetic [shu] → 0700
修 phonetic [shu] → 0138
西 phonetic [su] → 4333
相 phonetic [sō] → 1120
薩 phonetic [satsu] → 3016

NOTE

★ do not confuse with 殺 KILL → 1677

糸 耳 臣 至 虍 交 亥 豕 【年】 赤 有 帚 自 帯 束 孛

卸 1621

◧1-6-2

▸WHOLESALE

シャ おろ(す) おろし おろ(し)

26	Nonstandard	U5378
卩	S8-2-6	F0000

traditional form → see 卸 at 1835

叔 1622

◧1-6-2

▸YOUNGER SIBLING OF PARENT

シュク ㊔ よし とし

Ⓒ 叔 shū

29	Jōyō	U53D4
又	S8-2-6	F1401

丨 1 ⺊ 2 上 3 丰 4 丰 5 尗 6 叔 7 叔 8

COMPOUNDS

❶ **YOUNGER SIBLING OF one's PARENT, uncle, aunt**

叔父 しゅくふ(=おじ) uncle (younger than one's parent)

叔母 しゅくぼ(=おば) aunt (younger than one's parent)

❷ [archaic] third-born brother, younger brother

伯叔 はくしゅく brothers

❸ [rare] declining, terminal

叔世 しゅくせい age of decline (said of a nation)

SPECIAL READINGS

叔父 おじ uncle (younger than one's parent)

叔母 おば aunt (younger than one's parent)

SYNONYMS

❶ **siblings of parents**

叔 YOUNGER SIBLING OF PARENT → 1622

伯 OLDER SIBLING OF PARENT → 0067

郁

◧1-6-2

incorrect stroke-count

➡ see ◧1-6-3: 有 at 1640

刷 1623

◧1-6-2

▸PRINT

サツ す(る) -ず(り) -ずり は(く)▲

Ⓒ 刷 shuā shuà

18	Jōyō-4	U5237
刂	S8-2-6	F1497

フ 1 コ 2 尸 3 尸 4 吊 5 帚 6 刷 7 刷 8

COMPOUNDS

❶ⓐ **PRINT, put in print**

ⓑ **counter for PRINTings**

a 印刷 いんさつ printing

縮刷する しゅくさつする print in reduced size

増刷 ぞうさつ additional printing, reprinting

b 第四版三刷 だいよんはんさんさつ fourth edition, third printing

❷ⓐ [original meaning] brush, scrub

ⓑ brush

a 刷新する さっしんする reform, renovate, clean up

b 刷子 さっし brush, commutator brush

KUN

【する 刷る】 **PRINT, put in print**

刷り すり printing

刷り上げる すりあげる finish printing, print off

【-ずり -刷り, -刷】

ⓐ [suffix] **PRINTing**

ⓑ counter for **PRINT**ings

a 校正刷り こうせいずり galley proofs

多色刷り たしょくずり polychrome printing

b 第四刷 だいよんずり fourth printing

【はく 刷く】 [also 掃く] brush, apply with a brush

刷毛 はけ brush

紅を刷く べにをはく give [have] a brush of rouge (to one's cheeks)

SYNONYMS

❶ⓐ **print and publish**

刷 PRINT → 1623

印 print → 1023

植 typeset → 1247

刊 PUBLISH → 0221

版 PUBLISHING → 1082

載 PUT IN PRINT → 4091

掲 display in writing → 0597

幀 BOOKBINDING → 0695

ⓑ **editions**

版 edition → 1082

刊 publication → 0221

訂 revision → 1829

刷 printing → 1623

HOMOPHONES

する

摺 RUB AGAINST → 0850

擦 RUB → 0971

磨 POLISH → 3946

はく 掃 SWEEP → 0611

NOTE

➡ see USAGE notes at 擦 0971 and 掃 0611

郎

◧1-6-2

incorrect stroke-count

➡ see ◧1-6-3: 良 at 1641

制

▶SYSTEM
▶CONTROL

セイ ㊔ のり おさむ

Ⓒ 制 zhì

1624

◧ 1-6-2

18	Jōyō-5	U5236
刂	S8-2-6	F0229

ノ ⺊ 𠂉 𠂉 𠂔 朱 𫝀 制 (1 2 3 4 5 6 7 8)

COMPOUNDS

❶ⓐ (organizational form) **SYSTEM, organization, institution**
ⓑ [suffix] **SYSTEM**

a 制度 せいど system, organization, institution
体制 たいせい system, structure, organization
市制 しせい city organization
税制 ぜいせい tax system

b 天皇制 てんのうせい emperor system of Japan
六・三制 ろくさんせい the 6-3 school year system

❷ **establish rules, enact, institute**
制定する せいていする establish, enact
制憲する せいけんする establish a constitution
制服 せいふく uniform, regulation uniform

❸ⓐ (hold in restraint) **CONTROL, restrain, restrict, suppress, inhibit**
ⓑ [prefix] anti-, -inhibiting

a 制止する せいしする control, check, stop (a person) from (doing)
制限 せいげん restriction, limit
制御する せいぎょする control, govern, suppress
抑制する よくせいする control, suppress, inhibit
強制する きょうせいする compel, force

b 制癌剤 せいがんざい cancer-inhibiting drug
制酸薬 せいさんやく gastric antacid

❹ⓐ (exercise authority) **CONTROL, regulate, dominate, command**
ⓑ have the upper hand, get the better of

a 制海権 せいかいけん command of the sea, naval supremacy
管制塔 かんせいとう control tower
統制する とうせいする control, regulate
規制する きせいする regulate, control

b 制勝する せいしょうする win, chalk up a win
先制する せんせいする get a head start on

❺ make, produce (films)
制作 せいさく production (of a film), (literary) work
編制する へんせいする organize, form

INDEPENDENT

【せい 制】SYSTEM
【せいする 制する】CONTROL, govern; suppress, restrain; have the upper hand, get the better of

SYNONYMS

❶ **system**
系 SYSTEM → 2443
制 SYSTEM → 1624
統 INTERCONNECTED SYSTEM → 1710
網 network → 1737

❸ⓐ **restrain**
制 CONTROL (restrain) → 1624
禁 PROHIBIT → 3469
限 LIMIT → 0475
抑 SUPPRESS → 0301
束 TIE UP → 4369
縛 BIND → 1779
控える HOLD BACK → 0600
扣える HOLD BACK → 0250
渋る hang [hold] back → 0625

❹ⓐ **direct and supervise**
制 CONTROL → 1624
理 manage → 1220
経 MANAGE → 1687
管 EXERCISE CONTROL → 3349
轄 EXERCISE JURISDICTION OVER → 2056
掌 TAKE CHARGE OF → 3215
監 OVERSEE → 3535
督 SUPERVISE → 3471
司 OFFICIATE → 3648
宰 PRESIDE → 2829
営 MANAGE → 3216

NOTE

➡ see USAGE note at 製 3478

刺

▶STAB

シ さ(す) さ(さる) さ(し) さし とげ▲

Ⓒ 刺 cì cī

1625

◧ 1-6-2

18	Jōyō	U523A
刂	S8-2-6	F0838

一 𠃌 冂 市 朿 朿 朿刂 刺 (1 2 3 4 5 6 7 8)

COMPOUNDS

❶ⓐ [original meaning] **STAB, pierce, prick, thrust**
ⓑ **STAB to death, assassinate**
ⓒ **irritate**

a 刺傷 ししょう stab, pierced wound
刺繡 ししゅう embroidery
刺殺する しさつする stab to death

b 刺客 しかく assassin

c 刺激 しげき stimulus; stimulation, excitation

❷ prickle, thorn, needle
刺状突起 しじょうとっき prickle (of plants)
有刺鉄線 ゆうしてっせん barbed wire

❸ **satirize, criticize**
風刺 ふうし satire, sarcasm

❹ **calling card**
名刺 めいし calling [business] card

INDEPENDENT

【し 刺】 calling card
刺を通じる しをつうじる present one's card

KUN

【さす 刺す】
①ⓐ **STAB, pierce, prick, thrust**
ⓑ **sting, bite**
a 突き刺す つきさす stab, pierce, thrust
b 蜂に刺される はちにさされる be stung by a bee
② sew, stitch
雑巾を刺す ぞうきんをさす quilt a dustcloth
③ *baseball* catch (a runner) out
三塁で刺される さんるいでさされる be put [thrown] out at third base

【ささる 刺さる】 **stick, be stuck**
喉に刺さった骨 のどにささったほね bone stuck in one's throat

【さし 刺し, 刺】
① **STABbing, piercing, pricking**
② stitch
刺し子 さしこ quilting
③ ***sashimi*, sliced raw flesh (esp. of fish)**
刺身 さしみ *sashimi*, sliced raw flesh (esp. of fish)
牛刺 ぎゅうさし sliced raw beef

【とげ 刺】 thorn, prickle, barb; harshness, sarcasm
刺を抜く とげをぬく pull out a thorn
刺の有る言葉 とげのあることば harsh language, stinging [barbed] words

SPECIAL READINGS

刺青▲ いれずみ tattooing

SYNONYMS

❶ⓐ **stab**
刺 STAB → 1625
突く THRUST → 2772

ⓑ **kill**
殺 KILL → 1677
劉 KILL → 2398
刺 stab to death → 1625
絞 STRANGLE → 1707
窒 CHOKE → 2853

❷ **needle**
針 NEEDLE → 2099
刺 prickle → 1625
茨 THORN → 2812

HOMOPHONES

さす
差 DIFFERENCE → 4104
指 FINGER → 0452
挿 INSERT → 0517
注 POUR → 0383
射 SHOOT → 1850
止 STOP → 3659

さし
差 DIFFERENCE → 4104
指 FINGER → 0452
止 STOP → 3659

NOTE

➡ see USAGE note at 差 4104

勃
◧ 1-6-2

incorrect stroke-count
➡ see ◧ 1-7-2: 孛 at 1839

籾
1626
◧ 1-6-3

▸**UNHULLED RICE**
もみ
Ⓝ 籾 Ⓒ 籾 ní

119	Names	U7C7E
米	S9-6-3	F3477

KUN

【もみ 籾】
ⓐ **UNHULLED RICE**
ⓑ **rice husk**
a 籾摺り もみすり rice hulling
種籾 たねもみ seed rice
b 籾殻 もみがら rice husks

SYNONYMS

【もみ】
ⓐ **rice**
米 RICE → 4342
飯 COOKED RICE → 2126
稲 RICE PLANT → 1561
籾 UNHULLED RICE → 1626
餅 RICE CAKE → 2256
粥 RICE GRUEL → 0698

粈
1627
◧ 1-6-3

▸**UNHULLED RICE**
もみ

119	Nonstandard	U7C7E
米	S9-6-3	F0000

traditional form → see 籾 at 1626

紀

1628

◧1-6-3

▶ERA

キ ㊔ のり きの あき おさむ とし もと よし すみ ただ

Ⓒ 纪 jì jǐ

120	Jōyō-4	U7D00
糸	S9-6-3	F0461

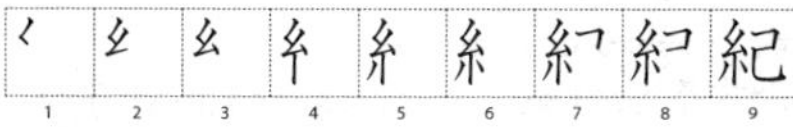

COMPOUNDS

❶ⓐ ERA, epoch, period of years, age
ⓑ [suffix] *geol* period
ⓒ age of a person

a 紀元 きげん era
世紀 せいき century
西紀 せいき Christian era
皇紀 こうき Imperial era
千年紀 せんねんき millennium
b デボン紀 でぼんき Devonian period
c 芳紀 ほうき age (of a young lady)

❷ⓐ record [put down] in writing, record systematically, chronicle
ⓑ chronicle(s), annals, historical record
ⓒ abbrev. of 日本書紀 にほんしょき: Nihonshoki (Chronicles of Japan)

a 紀要 きよう bulletin, proceedings
紀行 きこう travelogue
b 日本書紀 にほんしょき Nihonshoki (Chronicles of Japan)
c 記紀 きき Kojiki and Nihonshoki

❸ discipline, morals, order, code of behavior
校紀 こうき school discipline
風紀 ふうき public morals
綱紀 こうき law and order, official discipline
軍紀 ぐんき military discipline, troop morals
党紀 とうき party discipline

❹ abbrev. of 紀伊 きい, old name for Wakayama and south Mie prefectures
紀勢本線 きせいほんせん Kisei Main Line (Wakayama-Mie Railway)

INDEPENDENT

【き 紀】*geol* period

SYNONYMS

❶ⓐ long time periods
時 TIME → 1155
代 age → 0034
紀 ERA → 1628
世 AGE → 4308
朝 dynastic period → 2130
期 period → 2139
劫 KALPA → 1435

❷ⓐ write
書 WRITE → 3292
筆 write → 3317
写 COPY → 2493
記 WRITE DOWN → 1843
紀 record in writing → 1628
控える note down → 0600
録 RECORD → 2186
登 register → 3208
註 ANNOTATE → 1893

❸ laws and rules
法 LAW → 0391
律 LAW → 0433
典 CANON → 3253
憲 CONSTITUTION → 3001
令 ordinance → 2489
則 RULE → 1831
矩 RULE → 1475
規 REGULATION → 1231
紀 discipline → 1628

NOTE

★ do not confuse with 記 WRITE DOWN → 1843

紅

1629

◧1-6-3

▶CRIMSON

コウ ク べに くれない あか(い)▲ ㊔ くれ あか もみ

Ⓒ 红 hóng gōng

120	Jōyō-6	U7D05
糸	S9-6-3	F1062

COMPOUNDS

❶ CRIMSON, deep red, red
紅白 こうはく red and white
紅海 こうかい Red Sea
紅葉 こうよう(=もみじ) red leaves, crimson foliage, autumn tints
紅旗 こうき Red Flag
紅茶 こうちゃ black tea
紅衛兵 こうえいへい Red Guards
深紅色 しんこうしょく deep crimson, scarlet
深紅 しんく crimson

❷ of a woman
紅涙 こうるい tears of a beautiful woman; tears of blood

KUN

【べに 紅】**rouge, lipstick; CRIMSON, red**
紅花 べにばな safflower
紅色 べにいろ red, crimson
口紅 くちべに lipstick, rouge

米【糸】而耳至虫开交圭有良自

頬紅 ほおべに blusher

【くれない 紅】**CRIMSON, deep red, scarlet**

薄紅 うすくれない light crimson, pink

【あかい 紅い】[usu. 赤い] **CRIMSON**, deep red

紅組 あかぐみ red team

SPECIAL READINGS

紅葉 もみじ red leaves, crimson foliage, autumn tints; Japanese maple

SYNONYMS

❶ **red colors**

赤 RED → 2719
紅 CRIMSON → 1629
緋 SCARLET → 1732
朱 VERMILION → 4344
丹 CINNABAR → 4249
茜 MADDER → 2811

【べに】

◯ **cosmetics**

紅 rouge → 1629
粉 face powder → 1643
黛 EYEBROW INK → 3240

HOMOPHONES

あかい 赤 RED → 2719

NOTE

➡ see USAGE note at 赤 2719

級

1630

1-6-3

▶**GRADE**

キュウ

Ⓝ 級 Ⓒ 级 jí

120	Jōyō-3	U7D1A
糸	S9-6-3	F0810

Stroke order: く 幺 幺 幺 糸 糸 糹 紉 級 (1–9)

COMPOUNDS

❶ⓐ [also suffix] [original meaning] **GRADE, class, rank, degree, rating, level**

ⓑ **GRADE or rank in go, judo or various martial arts (lower than 段 だん)**

a 等級 とうきゅう class, grade, rank, magnitude

特級品 とっきゅうひん special grade article

階級 かいきゅう class, estate; rank, grade

b ライト級選手 らいときゅうせんしゅ lightweight boxer

初級 しょきゅう beginner's class, junior course

上級 じょうきゅう higher grade, advanced class, high class

高級 こうきゅう high rank, high class [grade]

昇級 しょうきゅう promotion to a higher grade, advancement

第一級殺人 だいいっきゅうさつじん first degree murder

大使級会談 たいしきゅうかいだん ambassador-level conference

囲碁三級 いごさんきゅう third rank in the game of go

❷ (school) **GRADE, class, school year**

級友 きゅうゆう classmate

級長 きゅうちょう class president

学級 がっきゅう class, grade

進級する しんきゅうする be promoted (to a higher grade)

同級 どうきゅう same class [grade]

三年級 さんねんきゅう third year class

❸ decapitated head

首級 しゅきゅう decapitated head

INDEPENDENT

【きゅう 級】**GRADE, class**

上の級に進む うえのきゅうにすすむ move up to a higher grade

SYNONYMS

❶ⓐ **class**

級 GRADE → 1630
段 grade → 1471
位 RANK → 0069
階 RANK → 0761
身 social status → 4368
格 STATUS → 1161
等 CLASS → 3321
流 class → 0529
層 STRATUM → 3920

❷ **class in school**

組 class → 1693
級 GRADE → 1630

糾

1631

1-6-3

▶**INQUIRE INTO**

キュウ ただ(す)▲ ㊔ ただし

Ⓝ 糾 糺◇ Ⓒ 纠 jiū

120	Jōyō	U7CFE
糸	S9-6-3	F2447

Stroke order: く 幺 幺 幺 糸 糸 糹 糾 糾 (1–9)

COMPOUNDS

❶ **INQUIRE INTO (esp. a crime), investigate into, examine**

糾明 きゅうめい searching examination

糾弾 きゅうだん impeachment, censure

糾問 きゅうもん cross-examination, arraignment

❷ gather together

糾合する きゅうごうする gather together, muster, rally

❸ entangle

紛糾 ふんきゅう complication, disorder, entanglement

KUN

【ただす 糾す】**INQUIRE INTO**, investigate into, examine

元を糾す もとをただす inquire into the origin, go to the bottom of an affair

SYNONYMS

❶ **investigate and examine**

閲 REVIEW → 4132
審 EXAMINE CAREFULLY → 2985
験 TEST → 2306
勘 CHECK → 2231
糾 INQUIRE INTO → 1631
究 STUDY EXHAUSTIVELY → 2729
察 INSPECT → 2961
討 STUDY → 1846
探 PROBE → 0613
検 EXAMINE → 1241
診 EXAMINE A PATIENT → 1898
調 INVESTIGATE → 1973
査 LOOK INTO → 3092

HOMOPHONES

ただす

正 RIGHT → 4296
質 QUALITY → 3483

NOTE

➡ see USAGE note at 正 4296

約

1632

◧ 1-6-3

▶**PROMISE**
▶**CONTRACT**
▶**APPROXIMATELY**

ヤク

Ⓝ 約 Ⓒ 约 yuē yāo

120	Jōyō-4	U7D04
糸	S9-6-3	F0297

𠃋	𠃋	幺	糸	糸	糸	糹	約	約
1	2	3	4	5	6	7	8	9

COMPOUNDS

❶ⓐ **PROMISE, make an agreement, conclude a treaty**

ⓑ **PROMISE, agreement, contract, treaty**

a 約束 やくそく promise, vow, pledge
契約 けいやく contract, agreement
予約 よやく reservation, preengagement; subscription
公約 こうやく public pledge [promise]
誓約 せいやく vow, pledge, oath, swearing

b 約款 やっかん article, stipulation, provision, clause
条約 じょうやく treaty
婚約 こんやく engagement, betrothal
解約 かいやく dissolution [cancellation] of a contract

❷ⓐ [original meaning] **CONTRACT, abridge, summarize, shorten**

ⓑ *math* reduce

a 括約筋 かつやくきん sphincter
制約 せいやく restriction, limitation; condition
集約的な しゅうやくてきな intensive
要約 ようやく summary, abridged statement

b 約分 やくぶん reduction of a fraction to lowest terms
公約数 こうやくすう common divisor

❸ **economical, frugal**

節約する せつやくする economize, save
倹約する けんやくする economize, be frugal [thrifty]

INDEPENDENT

【やく 約】

① **PROMISE**, vow

約を交わす やくをかわす exchange promises

② **APPROXIMATELY, about**

約百万円 やくひゃくまんえん approximately one million yen
約三年 やくさんねん about three years

③ abridgment, abbreviation

【やくす 約す】**PROMISE**, vow, pledge; abridge, abbreviate, contract; *math* reduce

SYNONYMS

❶ **promise**

約 PROMISE → 1632
締 CONCLUDE (a treaty) → 1761
協 reach an agreement → 0103
契 MAKE AN AGREEMENT → 3267
盟 ALLIANCE → 3468
誓 VOW → 3424

❷ⓐ **contract and shrink**

縮 SHRINK → 1790
約 CONTRACT → 1632
攣 CRAMP → 3635

❷ⓐ **abridge**

要 SUMMARIZE → 3263
抄 EXCERPT → 0298
約 CONTRACT → 1632
略 omit → 1501

【やく】

② **approximately**

約 APPROXIMATELY → 1632
概 GENERAL → 1322
大 in substance → 4224
-頃 ABOUT → 0163
位 about → 0069
-方 about → 2459

-程 ...or thereabouts → 1524
辺り thereabouts → 3761

約 **1633** 1-6-3

▶**PROMISE**
▶**CONTRACT**
▶**APPROXIMATELY**
ヤク

120	Nonstandard	U7D04
糸	S9-6-3	F0000

traditional form → see 約 at 1632

耐 **1634** 1-6-3

▶**WITHSTAND**
タイ た(える)
Ⓒ 耐 nài

126	Jōyō	U8010
而	S9-6-3	F1311

Stroke order: 1–9

COMPOUNDS

❶ⓐ (resist physical forces) **WITHSTAND, resist**
ⓑ [also prefix] **-proof, -resistant, -resisting**
ab 耐火 たいか fireproof
耐震 たいしん earthquake-proof
耐熱 たいねつ heat-resisting
耐水 たいすい waterproof
耐アルカリ性 たいあるかりせい alkali resistance
❷ **endure, bear, last**
耐久 たいきゅう endurance, persistence; durability, life
耐乏 たいぼう austerity, voluntary privation
忍耐 にんたい perseverance, patience, endurance

KUN

【たえる 耐える】
ⓐ (resist physical forces) **WITHSTAND, resist, be proof against**
ⓑ [usu. 堪える] **endure, bear, tolerate**
a 火に耐える ひにたえる be fireproof
b 重圧に耐える じゅうあつにたえる withstand pressures

SYNONYMS

❶ **resist**
抗 RESIST → 0296
抵 RESIST → 0377
耐 WITHSTAND → 1634
対 OPPOSE → 1025
反 COUNTER → 3663
逆 rebel → 3835
撥 REPEL → 0907
叛 REBEL → 1469
ⓐ & ❷ **bear and endure**
堪 ENDURE → 0680
忍 BEAR → 2750
耐 WITHSTAND → 1634

HOMOPHONES

たえる 堪 ENDURE → 0680

NOTE

➡ see USAGE note at 堪 0680

耶 **1635** 1-6-3

▶**INTERROGATIVE PARTICLE**
ヤ か や
Ⓒ 耶 yē yé

128	Names	U8036
耳	S9-6-3	F2540

COMPOUNDS

❶ used phonetically for *Jesus*
耶蘇 やそ Jesus
❷ [archaic] father
耶嬢 やじょう father and mother

KUN

【か 耶】 [formerly also 乎, now always か] **INTERROGATIVE PARTICLE**
女子有り問うて曰く誰耶と じょしありとうていわくたれかと A woman asked, "Who art thou?"
【や 耶】 [also 哉 or 也] classical rhetorical or exclamatory particle
安ぞ敢えて毒とせん耶 いずくんぞあえてどくとせんや How dare you regard it as poison?

SYNONYMS

【か】
◯ **classical particles**
耶 INTERROGATIVE PARTICLE → 1635
也 rhetorical particle → 4214
哉 EXCLAMATORY PARTICLE → 4084

USAGE

【か】
耶
[formerly also 乎, now always か] interrogative particle
乎
[formerly also 耶, now always か] interrogative particle

HOMOPHONES

や
也 CLASSICAL COPULA → 4214
哉 EXCLAMATORY PARTICLE → 4084
か 乎 MODIFIER FORMING SUFFIX → 4316

NOTE

➡ see also USAGE note at 也 4214

致

1636

◧1-6-3

▶**BRING ABOUT**
▶**DO HUMBLY**

チ いた(す) ㊔ むね のり

133	Nonstandard	U26936
至	S9-6-3	F0000

traditional form → see 致 at 1668

虹

1637

◧1-6-3

▶**RAINBOW**

コウ▲ にじ

Ⓒ 虹 hóng jiàng

142	Jōyō	U8679
虫	S9-6-3	F2388

1	2	3	4	5	6	7	8	9
丨	口	口	中	虫	虫	虫一	虫T	虹

COMPOUNDS

● **RAINBOW**

虹蜺× こうげい *literary* rainbow
虹彩 こうさい iris
白虹 はっこう [rare] white rainbow

KUN

【にじ 虹】**RAINBOW**

虹色 にじいろ rainbow colors

SYNONYMS

● **light**

光 LIGHT → 3043
明 light → 1060
灯 LAMP → 1019
燭 CANDLE → 1391
照 sunlight → 3506
虹 RAINBOW → 1637

COMPOUND FORMATION

【虹彩 こうさい】

虹彩 'iris' literally refers to the colors (彩) of the rainbow (虹). The meaning of iris probably derives from the idea that the iris represents a rainbowlike display of eye colors. It may be an abbreviation of 虹彩膜 こうさいまく 'rainbow-colored membrane', the Chinese term for iris.

形

◧1-6-3

incorrect classification
➡ see ◧1-3-6: 干 at 0429

郊

1638

◧1-6-3

▶**SUBURB**

コウ

Ⓒ 郊 jiāo

163	Jōyō	U90CA
阝	S9-3-6	F1743

1	2	3	4	5	6	7	8	9
丶	亠	𠆢	六	交	交	交ㇹ	交阝	郊

COMPOUNDS

● [original meaning] **SUBURB, outskirts, country**

郊外 こうがい suburbs, outskirts
郊野 こうや suburban fields
近郊 きんこう suburbs, outskirts
断郊競争 だんこうきょうそう cross-country race
西郊 せいこう [rare] western suburb

SYNONYMS

● **the country**

郊 SUBURB → 1638
里 COUNTRYSIDE → 4356
鄙 THE COUNTRY → 2338
郷 the country → 0664
辺 BORDERLAND → 3761

封

1639

◧1-6-3

▶**SEAL**

フウ ホウ

Ⓒ 封 fēng

41	Jōyō	U5C01
寸	S9-3-6	F1321

1	2	3	4	5	6	7	8	9
一	十	土	圭	圭	圭	圭一	封	封

COMPOUNDS

❶ **SEAL, seal off, block, enclose**

封印 ふういん (stamped) seal
封鎖 ふうさ blockade
封書 ふうしょ sealed letter
封殺 ふうさつ *baseball* force-out
密封する みっぷうする seal hermetically, seal up
同封する どうふうする enclose (in a letter)

❷ⓐ (invest with a fief or feudal estate) **enfeoff**

ⓑ (territory of a daimyo) daimiate, fief

a 封建的な ほうけんてきな feudal, feudalistic; old-fashioned
封建主義 ほうけんしゅぎ feudalism
封建制度 ほうけんせいど feudalism

b 封地 ほうち daimiate, fief
封土 ほうど daimiate, fief

❸ *baseball* abbrev. of 封殺 ふうさつ: force-out, force play

二封 にふう two force-outs

INDEPENDENT

【ふう 封】**SEAL, sealing, closing;** abbrev. of 封殺 ふうさつ: *baseball* **force-out**

封を切る ふうをきる break the seal

【ふうじる(=ふうずる) 封じる(=封ずる)】**SEAL,** glue up, fasten; enclose, block, seal off; shut up by incantation; bar, ban, prohibit

私は口を封じられている わたくしはくちをふうじられている My lips are sealed

【ほう 封】daimiate, fief

SYNONYMS

❶ **close**

閉 CLOSE → 4116
鎖 lock up → 2213
封 SEAL → 1639
梗 STOP UP → 1204
塞 STOP UP → 2924

❷ⓑ **feudal territorial divisions**

藩 FEUDAL DOMAIN → 3022
国 province (in former Japan) → 3831
領 fief → 1567
封 daimiate → 1639
荘 manor (in feudal Japan) → 2814

郁

1640
1-6-3

▶AROMATIC
イク ㊔ かおる あや ふみ ゆう くに
Ⓒ 郁 yù

163	Names	U90C1
阝	S9-3-6	F1784

COMPOUNDS

❶ **AROMATIC, rich in aroma, fragrant, sweet-smelling**
馥×郁たる ふくいくたる sweet-smelling, fragrant

❷ teeming with culture, flourishing
郁郁たる いくいくたる teeming with culture, flourishing; diffusing of aroma, aromatic

SYNONYMS

❶ **smell and fragrance**

気 smell → 3960
匂い SMELL → 3662
臭 BAD SMELL → 3261
香 SWEET SMELL → 3177
馨 PERFUME → 3575
芳 FRAGRANT → 2739
薫 BALMY → 3005
郁 AROMATIC → 1640

郎

1641
1-6-3

▶YOUNG MAN
▶MALE NAME SUFFIX
ロウ ㊔ お
Ⓝ 郞 Ⓒ 郎 láng làng

163	Jōyō	U90CE
阝	S9-3-6	F0091

COMPOUNDS

❶ *elegant* **YOUNG MAN, man; husband**
郎君 ろうくん [rare] young nobleman, young lord
野郎 やろう guy, fellow, man, rascal
遊冶郎 ゆうやろう man of pleasure, libertine
新郎新婦 しんろうしんぷ bride and bridegroom

❷ **SUFFIX for forming MALE NAMEs, usu. indicating order of birth**
一郎 いちろう Ichiro (name of eldest son)
次郎 じろう Jiro (name of second son)
太郎 たろう Taro

❸ retainer, vassal, manservant
郎等(=郎党) ろうどう retainers, vassals, followers
下郎 げろう servant; menial
女郎 じょろう prostitute, courtesan

SYNONYMS

❶ **man**

男 MAN → 3147
郎 YOUNG MAN → 1641
雄 MALE → 1271
牡 MALE → 1040
夫 male adult → 4271
翁 OLD MAN → 2611
爺 OLD MAN → 2656

❷ **name suffixes**

郎 MALE NAME SUFFIX → 1641
麿 CLASSICAL MALE NAME SUFFIX → 3949
彦 MALE NAME ELEMENT → 4085
-子 female name element → 4196

帥

1642
1-6-3

▶COMMANDER IN CHIEF
スイ
Ⓒ 帅 shuài

50	Jōyō	U5E25
巾	S9-3-6	F2157

COMPOUNDS

ⓐ **COMMANDER IN CHIEF, leader, general**
ⓑ [original meaning] command, lead troops

a 元帥 げんすい marshal, general
将帥 しょうすい commander
総帥 そうすい commander in chief
b 統帥 とうすい supreme command

SYNONYMS

ⓐ **military officers and ranks**

曹 SERGEANT → 3414
尉 COMPANY OFFICER → 2119
佐 FIELD OFFICER → 0076
将 GENERAL OFFICER → 0551
督 COMMANDER → 3471
帥 COMMANDER IN CHIEF → 1642

NOTE

★ do not confuse with 師 MASTER → 1680

粉

1643

◧1-6-4

▶**POWDER**

フン こ こな でしめーとる▲

Ⓒ 粉 fěn

119	Jōyō-4	U7C89
米	S10-6-4	F1431

1	2	3	4	5	6	7	8	9	10
									粉

COMPOUNDS

❶ⓐ [original meaning] **POWDER, dust**
ⓑ (grind to a powder) **POWDER**, pulverize

a 粉末 ふんまつ powder
粉乳 ふんにゅう powdered milk
鉄粉 てっぷん iron powder
精粉 せいふん fine powder

b 粉砕 ふんさい pulverization

❷ (powdered meal) **flour, meal**
穀粉 こくふん grain [rice] flour
澱粉 でんぷん starch
米粉 べいふん rice flour
製粉 せいふん flour milling

❸ⓐ face **POWDER**, cosmetics
ⓑ apply face **POWDER**, make up

a 脂粉 しふん cosmetics, rouge and powder
紅粉 こうふん rouge and powder

b 粉飾 ふんしょく embellishment, makeup

❹ (color of powdered meal) white, whitewashed
粉壁 ふんぺき white wall

KUN

【こ 粉】[also suffix] **POWDER, dust; flour, meal**
洗濯粉 せんたくこ detergent
小麦粉 こむぎこ (wheat) flour

【こな 粉】**POWDER, dust; flour, meal**
粉薬 こなぐすり powdered medicine
粉粉になる こなごなになる go to pieces, break into fragments

【でしめーとる 粉】decimeter

SYNONYMS

❶ⓐ **powder**
粉 POWDER → 1643
末 powder → 4317

❷ **cereal**
穀 CEREAL → 2294
禾 CEREAL → 4315
粉 flour → 1643

❸ⓐ **cosmetics**
紅 rouge → 1629
粉 face powder → 1643
黛 EYEBROW INK → 3240

ⓑ **decorate**
飾 DECORATE → 2150
粧 APPLY MAKEUP → 1703
粉 apply face powder → 1643
装 DRESS → 3327

料

1644

◧1-6-4

▶**FEE**
▶**MATERIALS**

リョウ

Ⓒ 料 liào

68	Jōyō-4	U6599
斗	S10-4-6	F0261

1	2	3	4	5	6	7	8	9	10
									料

COMPOUNDS

❶ [also suffix]
ⓐ (charge for services) **FEE, charge, rate, allowance**
ⓑ (payment received for services) **FEE, remuneration**

a 料金 りょうきん charge, rate, fee, fare
無料 むりょう no charge, free
送料 そうりょう postage, carriage
手数料 てすうりょう commission, (handling) fee, charge
使用料 しようりょう rental fee
入場料 にゅうじょうりょう admission fee

b 診察料 しんさつりょう consultation fee
給料 きゅうりょう salary, pay, wages

❷ⓐ **MATERIALS, material, stuff, matter**
ⓑ [also suffix] **MATERIALS** for cooking: **ingredients, foodstuff, cuisine**
ⓒ **(written) MATERIALS, data**

a 材料 ざいりょう material, matter, stuff; factor, element
原料 げんりょう raw material
燃料 ねんりょう fuel
食料 しょくりょう food, foodstuffs
清涼飲料水 せいりょういんりょうすい cooling drink

b 料理 りょうり cooking, cuisine; handling
料亭 りょうてい high-class restaurant, Japanese restaurant
調味料 ちょうみりょう seasoning, flavoring

c 資料 しりょう materials, data
史料 しりょう historical materials [records]

❸ conjecture, infer, consider
料簡 りょうけん idea, thought, intention, discretion
思料(=思量)する しりょうする consider carefully, think

INDEPENDENT

【りょう 料】**MATERIALS**; fee, charge
研究の料 けんきゅうのりょう research materials

SYNONYMS

❶ⓐ **fee and price**

【米】糸缶耒耒耳至舌舟虫交毎育殺逆良𦣻孝

料 FEE →1644
代 CHARGE →0034
賃 CHARGES →3341
銭 money paid →2159
費 EXPENSE →3221
価 PRICE →0095
値 price →0123
ⓑ **pay and earnings**
給 PAY →1708
賃 WAGE →3341
料 FEE →1644
俸 SALARY →0128
禄 RETAINER'S STIPEND →1264
収 income →0031
❷ **matter**
質 MATTER →3483
物 substance →1084
材 MATERIAL →1031
料 MATERIALS →1644
資 material resources →3342

NOTE

➡ see COMPOUND FORMATION for 潤筆料 じゅんぴつりょう →潤 0918

粋

1645

1-6-4

▶**REFINED**

スイ いき

Ⓝ 粹 Ⓒ 粹 cuì

119	Jōyō	U7C8B
米	S10-6-4	F1732

Stroke order: 1–10

COMPOUNDS

❶ⓐ (free from impurities) **REFINED, pure, unmixed**
ⓑ (best part) **essence, quintessence**

a 純粋な じゅんすいな pure, genuine; unalloyed, unmixed
生粋の きっすいの trueborn, pure, genuine
b 精粋 せいすい essence, purity
国粋 こくすい national characteristics

❷ (free from coarseness) **REFINED, sophisticated, polished, elegant, cultivated, tasteful**
粋人 すいじん refined [romantic] man
粋狂(=酔狂) すいきょう vagary, whim
無粋(=不粋)な ぶすいな lacking in polish, inelegant; unromantic

❸ [formerly 萃 2882] **gather, assemble**
抜粋 ばっすい extract, excerpt, selection

INDEPENDENT

【すい 粋】essence, pith, quintessence; refinement, cultivation; delicacy, considerateness
粋な人 すいなひと man of well-cultivated tastes
粋な裁き すいなさばき delicate judgment
流行の粋 りゅうこうのすい the cream [pink] of fashion

KUN

【いき 粋】**smartness, stylishness, chic**
粋な いきな stylish, smart, chic
粋がる いきがる try to appear smart

SYNONYMS

❶ⓐ **clean and purified**
浄 CLEAN →0457
清 clean →0635
純 PURE →1649
潔 IMMACULATE →0920
粋 REFINED (free from impurities) →1645
精 refined (purified) →1729
楚 NEAT AND TRIM →3470
ⓑ **essential part**
精 ESSENCE (essential part) →1729
粋 essence (best part) →1645
髄 essence (vital part) →2316
枢 PIVOT →1076
幹 TRUNK →2152
綱 ESSENTIAL POINTS →1735
旨 PURPORT →2516
要 summary →3263
❷ **elegant**
雅 ELEGANT →1532
淑 GRACEFUL →0639
優 graceful →0200
粋 REFINED →1645
彬 REFINED AND GENTLE →1201

紡

1646

1-6-4

▶**SPIN**

ボウ つむ(ぐ)

Ⓒ 纺 fǎng

120	Jōyō	U7D21
糸	S10-6-4	F2485

Stroke order: 1–10

COMPOUNDS

● [original meaning] **SPIN, make yarn**
紡糸 ぼうし spinning; spun cotton [wool]
紡績 ぼうせき spinning
紡織 ぼうしょく spinning and weaving
紡錘 ぼうすい spindle
紡毛 ぼうもう carded wool
混紡 こんぼう mixed spinning
綿紡 めんぼう cotton spinning

KUN

【つむぐ 紡ぐ】**SPIN, make yarn**

綿を糸に紡ぐ めんをいとにつむぐ spin cotton into yarn

SYNONYMS

● **weave and sew**

織 WEAVE → 1801
紡 SPIN → 1646
績 spin → 1788
縫 SEW → 1781
編 KNIT → 1755
辮 PLAIT → 2085
組 braid → 1693
繡 EMBROIDER → 1805

紐

▸STRING

チュウ ひも ㊔ くみ

ⓒ 纽 niǔ

1647

1-6-4

120	Names	U7D10
糸	S10-6-4	F1920

COMPOUNDS

● [original meaning] **STRING**

紐帯 ちゅうたい cords and belts; bond, ties; important social ties [foundations]

KUN

【ひも 紐】

① **STRING, cord**

紐解く ひもとく open (a book), untie (a scroll), read [peruse] (a book)
紐を結ぶ ひもをむすぶ tie a string
靴紐 くつひも shoelace
組み紐 くみひも plaited cord (used with kimonos)
腰紐 こしひも sash used to secure a kimono at the waist
財布の紐を握る さいふのひもをにぎる hold the purse strings

② conditions, restrictions, **STRING**s

紐付き ひもつき conditional; with strings attached

③ man who is financially dependent on a woman, pimp

④ mantle (of a mollusk)

SYNONYMS

● **ropes and lines**

綱 ROPE (esp. of fiber) → 1735
絃 STRING → 1685
縄 ROPE (esp. of straw) → 1756
緒 cord → 1742
組 braid → 1693
索 cable → 3105
鎖 CHAIN → 2213
線 LINE → 1760
紐 STRING → 1647
弦 STRING → 0343

紛

▸CONFUSED

フン まぎ(れる) -まぎ(れ) まぎ(らす) まぎ(らわす) まぎ(らわしい)

ⓒ 纷 fēn

1648

1-6-4

120	Jōyō	U7D1B
糸	S10-6-4	F1384

COMPOUNDS

ⓐ [original meaning] (in a jumbled state) **CONFUSED, tangled, disorderly**

ⓑ confusion, trouble

a 紛争 ふんそう conflict, strife
紛失 ふんしつ loss
紛紛と ふんぷんと confusedly; in profusion
紛乱 ふんらん confusion, disorder
紛糾 ふんきゅう complication, disorder, entanglement

b 内紛 ないふん internal trouble [strife]; storm in a teacup

KUN

【まぎれる 紛れる】 be CONFUSED with, get mixed with, be mistaken for; be diverted from

紛れ まぎれ confusion
紛れ込む まぎれこむ get lost among, disappear in (the crowd)
闇に紛れて やみにまぎれて under cover of night
気が紛れる きがまぎれる be diverted [distracted] from

【-まぎれ -紛れ】 [suffix] **in a fit of, out of, taking advantage of**

腹立ち紛れに はらだちまぎれに in a fit of anger
どさくさ紛れに どさくさまぎれに taking advantage of the confusion

【まぎらす 紛らす】 divert, distract; beguile, evade, conceal

悲しみを紛らす かなしみをまぎらす divert one's mind from sorrow
冗談に紛らす じょうだんにまぎらす turn it off as a joke

【まぎらわす 紛らわす】 same as 紛らす まぎらす

【まぎらわしい 紛らわしい】 confusing, misleading, ambiguous

紛らわしい名前 まぎらわしいなまえ confusing [misleading] name

SYNONYMS

ⓐ **disordered**

紛 CONFUSED → 1648
乱 DISORDERED → 1611
錯 MIXED UP → 2187
混 mixed up → 0631

雑 mixed up → 1752
沌 PRIMEVAL CHAOS → 0314

純 1649

◧ 1-6-4

▶PURE

ジュン ㊔ すみ よし ますみ

Ⓒ 纯 chún

120	Jōyō-6	U7D14
糸	S10-6-4	F0850

Stroke order: 1–10

COMPOUNDS

❶ⓐ [also prefix] **PURE, genuine, unalloyed**
ⓑ **PUREly, entirely**

a 純粋な じゅんすいな pure, genuine; unalloyed, unmixed
純良な じゅんりょうな pure (and good), genuine
純金 じゅんきん pure gold, solid gold
純毛 じゅんもう pure wool, all wool
純正な じゅんせいな pure, genuine
純文学 じゅんぶんがく pure literature
単純な たんじゅんな simple, uncomplicated, plain

b 純日本式 じゅんにほんしき purely Japanese style

❷ **PUREhearted, innocent, chaste**
純潔な じゅんけつな purehearted, immaculate, innocent
純真な じゅんしんな naive, pure, genuine, sincere
純情 じゅんじょう pure heart; self-sacrificing devotion
純朴(=醇朴) じゅんぼく simplicity and honesty
清純な せいじゅんな pure (and innocent)

❸ [also suffix] net, clear
純益 じゅんえき net profit
純トン数 じゅんとんすう net tonnage
純増 じゅんぞう net increase
純収入 じゅんしゅうにゅう net revenue

INDEPENDENT

【じゅん 純】 purity
純な じゅんな pure, innocent, chaste
純な少女 じゅんなしょうじょ maiden pure in heart, virgin

SYNONYMS

❶ⓐ **clean and purified**
浄 CLEAN → 0457
清 clean → 0635
純 PURE → 1649
潔 IMMACULATE → 0920
粋 REFINED (free from impurities) → 1645
精 refined (purified) → 1729
楚 NEAT AND TRIM → 3470

❷ **purehearted**
純 PURE → 1649
淳 PUREHEARTED → 0626
清 clean → 0635
潔 IMMACULATE → 0920
廉 INCORRUPT → 3911
敦 HONEST → 2128
惇 SINCERE → 0588
直 straightforward → 3649
侃 FORTHRIGHT → 0097

紘 1650

◧ 1-6-4

▶WIDE-RANGING

コウ ㊔ ひろ ひろし ひろむ

Ⓝ 綋 Ⓒ 纮 hóng

120	Names	U7D18
糸	S10-6-4	F2781

COMPOUNDS

❶ **WIDE-RANGING, throughout the breadth and length of the land, vast, spacious**
八紘 はっこう eight directions; the whole world
八紘一宇 はっこういちう the whole world under one roof

❷ [archaic] hat string fastened under the chin

❸ [original meaning, now obsolete] stretched rope, thick rope

SYNONYMS

❶ **wide and extensive**
広 WIDE → 3769
紘 WIDE-RANGING → 1650
博 EXTENSIVE → 0170
恢 EXTENSIVE → 0436
浩 VAST → 0525
洸 VAST (expanse of water) → 0462
滉 DEEP AND VAST → 0811
曠 SPACIOUS → 1411
闊 BROAD → 4135

紋 1651

◧ 1-6-4

▶CREST

モン ㊔ あや

Ⓒ 纹 wén wèn

120	Jōyō	U7D0B
糸	S10-6-4	F1489

Stroke order: 1–10

COMPOUNDS

❶ [also suffix] **CREST, family crest, coat of arms**
紋章 もんしょう crest, family insignia, coat of arms
紋付き もんつき crested kimono
紋様 もんよう crest pattern
家紋 かもん family crest [badge]

❷ⓐ [original meaning] **figure (on a surface), design, pattern, lines on a surface**
ⓑ **print**
a 紋織り もんおり figured textiles
波紋 はもん ripple; stir, sensation
風紋 ふうもん wind-wrought pattern on the sands
b 指紋 しもん fingerprint
声紋 せいもん voiceprint
掌紋 しょうもん palm print

INDEPENDENT

【もん 紋】**CREST**, family crest, coat of arms; figure on textiles
五つ紋の着物 いつつもんのきもの kimono with five crests

SYNONYMS

❶ **insignia**
紋 CREST → 1651
章 BADGE → 2624
❷ⓐ **pattern**
模 PATTERN (decorative design) → 1326
文 decorative pattern → 2458
柄 pattern (on cloth) → 1111
様 pattern → 1332
紋 figure → 1651
ⓑ **marks and signs**
標 MARK (identifying sign) → 1347
徽 EMBLEM → 0968
痕 SCAR → 4066
印 MARK (visible sign) → 1023
跡 TRACE → 1937
蹟 TRACE → 2065
踪 FOOTPRINTS → 1996
紋 print → 1651
符 SYMBOL → 3299
号 SIGN → 2675
栞 BOOKMARK → 3285

NOTE

➡ see USAGE note at 文 2458

納

1652
1-6-4

▶**PAY**
▶**ACCEPT**
▶**PUT AWAY**

ノウ ナッ- ナ ナン トウ おさ(める) -おさ(める) おさ(まる) ㊔ おさむ いり のり

Ⓝ 納 Ⓒ 纳 nà

120	Jōyō-6	U7D0D
糸	S10-6-4	F0903

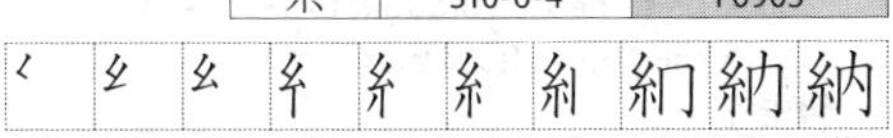

COMPOUNDS

❶ hand over payment or goods:
ⓐ **PAY to the authorities, make payment**
ⓑ **deliver goods to a customer, supply goods**
a 納税 のうぜい tax payment
納入 のうにゅう payment; delivery
納付 のうふ payment; delivery
納期 のうき payment date; delivery date
滞納 たいのう nonpayment, delinquency (in payment)
未納の みのうの unpaid, in arrears
分納 ぶんのう payment in installments; installment delivery
返納する へんのうする return (to the authorities), restore
b 納品 のうひん delivery of goods; delivered goods
❷ offer (as to a god), dedicate, present
納采 のうさい presenting [exchanging] betrothal presents between royal families
奉納 ほうのう dedication (to a deity), offering
献納 けんのう offering, presentation, donation
結納 ゆいのう ceremonial exchange of betrothal gifts; betrothal present [gift]
❸ⓐ **ACCEPT, receive, enjoy**
ⓑ **ACCEPT what a person says, agree with**
a 納涼 のうりょう enjoying the evening cool
納受する のうじゅする accept, receive
受納 じゅのう acceptance, receipt
出納 すいとう receipts and expenses, incomings and outgoings
御笑納下さい ごしょうのうください Please accept this small present
b 納得 なっとく assent, consent, understanding
❹ [original meaning] **PUT AWAY, put in, store, put in place, consign**
納棺 のうかん placing in the coffin
納屋 なや outhouse, shed, barn
納戸 なんど back room, closet
納豆 なっとう fermented soybeans
収納 しゅうのう storing; harvesting; receipt
格納する かくのうする house
❺ last, end
納会 のうかい last meeting of the year, closing session of the month
❻ former councilor of state
大納言 だいなごん chief councilor of state

KUN

【おさめる 納める】
① hand over payment or goods:
ⓐ **PAY to the authorities, make payment**
ⓑ **deliver to a customer, supply goods**
a 月謝を納める げっしゃをおさめる pay a school fee

1

b 品物を納める しなものをおさめる deliver goods

② offer (as to a god), dedicate, present

絵馬を納める えまをおさめる offer a votive picture (of a horse) to a shrine

③ⓐ **PUT AWAY, store, consign**

ⓑ [also 収める] **put (back) in place, replace**

a 倉庫に納める そうこにおさめる store in a warehouse

b 元の所に納める もとのところにおさめる put (a thing) back in its place

④ [also 収める] **ACCEPT**

どうぞお納め下さい どうぞおおさめください Please accept it

【-おさめる -納める】 [verbal suffix] **finish, conclude**

舞い納める まいおさめる conclude a dance

見納め みおさめ last [farewell] look

【おさまる 納まる】

①ⓐ **be paid**

ⓑ **be delivered**

a 国庫に納まった金 こっこにおさまったかね money paid to the (National) Treasury

b 品物が納まった しなものがおさまった Commodities have been delivered

②ⓐ be placed (in a position or post), be installed

ⓑ stay (in the stomach)

a 学長に納まる がくちょうにおさまる take one's position as rector

b 食べ物が胃に納まらない たべものがいにおさまらない No food I eat stays in my stomach

③ be satisfied

納まらない おさまらない be unsatisfied, feel grieved

SYNONYMS

❶ⓐ pay

払う PAY →0225

納 PAY (to the authorities) →1652

済 settle accounts →0634

支 pay out →2473

賦 INSTALLMENT →1992

償 RECOMPENSE →0199

ⓑ supply

供 supply →0098

給 SUPPLY →1708

納 deliver goods to a customer →1652

❷ offer

供 OFFER (to a person or god) →0098

献 OFFER (esp. to a superior) →2240

納 offer (as to a god) →1652

提 PRESENT →0720

貢 offer tribute →2838

奉 DEDICATE →3167

捧 OFFER RESPECTFULLY →0594

❸ⓐ receive

受 RECEIVE →3076

享 ENJOY →2545

領 receive →1567

収 TAKE IN →0031

納 ACCEPT →1652

貰 GET →3219

戴 RECEIVE HUMBLY →4093

頂 RECEIVE HUMBLY →0164

拝 have the honor to receive →0360

❹ store

蔵 STORE →2995

蓄 STORE UP →2931

貯 LAY UP →1903

納 PUT AWAY →1652

USAGE

❶【おさめる】

納める

① hand over payment or goods:

ⓐ pay to the authorities, make payment

ⓑ deliver to a customer, supply goods

② offer (as to a god), dedicate, present

③ⓐ put away, store, consign

ⓑ [also 収める] put (back) in place, replace

④ [also 収める] accept

収める

①ⓐ gain, obtain, reap

ⓑ achieve, attain

② collect materials and record [write down]

③ [also 納める] put (back) in place, replace

④ [also 納める] accept

治める

ⓐ govern, rule over, reign over, manage

ⓑ bring under control, put down, suppress, pacify, quell

修める

① cultivate, pursue, practice, study; master, complete

② order (one's life)

❷【おさまる】

納まる

①ⓐ be paid

ⓑ be delivered

②ⓐ be placed (in a position or post), be installed

ⓑ stay (in the stomach)

③ be satisfied

収まる

① be put (back) in place, be restored

②ⓐ be settled, be brought to a settlement

ⓑ calm down (as of the wind)

治まる

① be in peace, be governed well

② be cured, be relieved (of pain)
修まる
govern oneself, conduct oneself well

HOMOPHONES

おさめる
収 TAKE IN →0031
治 GOVERN →0393
修 CULTIVATE →0138

おさまる
収 TAKE IN →0031
治 GOVERN →0393
修 CULTIVATE →0138

COMPOUND FORMATION

【納豆 なっとう】
納豆 'fermented soybeans' refers to soybeans (豆) put away (納 ❹) in straw wrappers until they ferment.

紗

1653

1-6-4

▶**GAUZE**

サ シャ

Ⓒ 纱 shā

120	Names	U7D17
糸	S10-6-4	F1771

COMPOUNDS

● [original meaning] **GAUZE, silk gauze, gossamer, thin silk [cloth]**
薄紗 はくさ gossamer, delicate gauze
羅紗 らしゃ woolen cloth
袱×紗 ふくさ (small) crepe wrapper

INDEPENDENT

【しゃ 紗】**GAUZE**, gossamer
紗の様な しゃのような gauzy

SYNONYMS

● **fabrics**
織 woven fabric →1801
紬 PONGEE →1684
紗 GAUZE →1653
絹 SILK →1721
綾 TWILL →1740
綿 COTTON →1736
棉 COTTON →1244
麻 HEMP →3878
毛 wool →4264
錦 BROCADE →2181

紙

1654

1-6-4

▶**PAPER**

シ かみ

Ⓝ 帋 Ⓒ 纸 zhǐ

120	Jōyō-2	U7D19
糸	S10-6-4	F0473

COMPOUNDS

❶ⓐ [also suffix] [original meaning] **PAPER**
ⓑ **PAPER bearing writing**
a 紙幣 しへい paper currency, bank note, bill
白紙 はくし blank sheet, flyleaf; clean slate
用紙 ようし blank form, stationery
製紙 せいし paper manufacture
表紙 ひょうし cover, binding
包装紙 ほうそうし wrapping paper
b 紙面 しめん space (on a printed page)
紙上計画 しじょうけいかく paper plan

❷ [also suffix] **newspaper, periodical, publication**
本紙 ほんし this newspaper
日刊紙 にっかんし daily newspaper
地方紙 ちほうし local newspaper

❸ **stamp**
印紙 いんし (revenue) stamp
証紙 しょうし certificate stamp

KUN

【かみ 紙】**PAPER**
紙袋 かみぶくろ paper bag
紙切れ かみきれ scrap [piece] of paper
紙屑 かみくず waste paper
張り紙 はりがみ patch of paper; sticker
手紙 てがみ letter
塵紙 ちりがみ tissue paper, toilet paper

SYNONYMS

❶ **paper**
紙 PAPER →1654
葉 LEAF →2912
丁 sheet →4155
箋 PIECE OF PAPER →3352
頁 PAGE →2589
面 page (of a newspaper) →2590

❷ **periodicals**
誌 MAGAZINE →1950
紙 newspaper →1654
報 bulletin →2133

級

1655

1-6-4

▶**GRADE**

キュウ

120	Nonstandard	U7D1A
糸	S10-6-4	F0000

traditional form →see 級 at 1630

納
1656
1-6-4

▶PAY
▶ACCEPT
▶PUT AWAY

ノウ ナッ- ナ ナン トウ おさ(める) -おさ(める) おさ(まる) ㊔ おさむ いり のり

120	Nonstandard	U7D0D
糸	S10-6-4	F0000

traditional form → see 納 at 1652

級
1-6-4

incorrect stroke-count
➡ see 1-6-3: 糸 at 1630

缼
1657
1-6-4

▶LACK

ケツ ケン か(ける) か(く) か(かす)

121	Nonstandard	U7F3C
缶	S10-6-4	F0000

traditional form → see 欠 at 2481

缺
1658
1-6-4

▶LACK

ケツ ケン か(ける) か(く) か(かす)

121	Nonstandard	U7F3A
缶	S10-6-4	F0000

traditional form → see 欠 at 2481

耕
1659
1-6-4

▶TILL

コウ たがや(す) ㊔ おさむ やす つとむ

Ⓝ 畊 耕 Ⓒ 耕 gēng

127	Jōyō-5	U8015
耒	S10-6-4	F1685

COMPOUNDS

❶ [original meaning] **TILL, plow**

耕作する こうさくする cultivate, plow, till
耕地 こうち arable land, farm land
耕具 こうぐ farm implements
耕運機 こううんき cultivator, tiller
農耕 のうこう farming
深耕 しんこう deep plowing
晴耕雨読 せいこううどく working in the field in fine weather and reading at home in rainy weather

❷ earn one's livelihood by writing [copying]

筆耕料 ひっこうりょう copying fee

KUN

【たがやす 耕す】**TILL, plow, cultivate**

耕し得る土地 たがやしうるとち arable land

SYNONYMS

❶ **farm and plant**

植 PLANT → 1247
栽 PLANT (saplings) → 4087
培 CULTIVATE → 0558
耕 TILL → 1659
作 raise crops → 0077
農 farm, FARMING → 3345
蒔 SOW → 2935
播 SOW → 0906

耗
1660
1-6-4

▶WEAR AWAY

モウ コウ

Ⓝ 耗 Ⓒ 耗 hào

127	Jōyō	U8017
耒	S10-6-4	F2574

COMPOUNDS

ⓐ **WEAR AWAY, wear out, use up, consume**
ⓑ become worn out, become exhausted

a 摩耗する まもうする wear away, wear out
減耗 げんもう natural decrease
消耗する しょうもうする consume, exhaust, use up
損耗する そんもう(=そんこう)する wear out, be wasted, be worn out

b 心神耗弱 しんしんこうじゃく diminished mental capacity

SYNONYMS

ⓐ **decrease**

減 DECREASE → 0733
耗 WEAR AWAY → 1660
削 cut down → 1837
縮 SHRINK → 1790
落 FALL → 2907
蝕 ERODE → 2258

ⓐ **consume**

消 SPEND → 0531
費 expend → 3221
尽 EXHAUST → 3786
耗 WEAR AWAY → 1660
銷 USE UP → 2174

耘
1661
1-6-4

▶WEED

ウン

Ⓒ 耘 yún

127	Non-Jōyō	U8018
耒	S10-6-4	F0000

COMPOUNDS

● [now also 運 3894] [original meaning] **WEED, remove weeds**

耕耘機 こううんき cultivator, tiller

SYNONYMS

● **eliminate**

却 ELIMINATE → 1436
排 EXCLUDE → 0593
払う CLEAR AWAY → 0225
剝 PEEL OFF → 2105
耘 WEED → 1661
削 cross out → 1837
抹 wipe off → 0370
省 leave out → 3100
脱 REMOVE → 1225
去 take away → 2678
外す take off → 0215
除 RID OF → 0546
撤 WITHDRAW → 0912

耕

1662

1-6-4

▶TILL

コウ たがや(す) ㊔ おさむ やす つとむ

127	Nonstandard	U8015
耒	S10-6-4	F0000

traditional form → see 耕 at 1659

耗

1663

1-6-4

▶WEAR AWAY

モウ コウ

127	Nonstandard	U8017
耒	S10-6-4	F0000

traditional form → see 耗 at 1660

恥

1664

1-6-4

▶SHAME

チ は(じる) はじ は(じらう) は(ずかしい)

Ⓝ 耻◇ Ⓒ 耻 chǐ

61	Jōyō	U6065
心	S10-4-6	F1173

Stroke order: 一 丁 F F E 耳 耳 耴 恥 恥 (1–10)

COMPOUNDS

❶ⓐ **SHAME, disgrace, dishonor, humiliation**
ⓑ **feel [be] ashamed**

a 恥辱 ちじょく disgrace, dishonor, shame
羞恥 しゅうち shyness; sense of shame
b 厚顔無恥な こうがんむちな shameless, unscrupulous
破廉恥 はれんち shamelessness, infamy, impudence

❷ private parts, pubic region
恥骨 ちこつ pubic bone, pubis
恥丘 ちきゅう mons pubis, mons veneris
恥部 ちぶ private parts; something to be ashamed of

KUN

【はじる 恥じる】 [sometimes also 羞じる] **feel ashamed**
恥じ入る はじいる feel quite ashamed

【はじ 恥】 [sometimes also 羞] **SHAME, disgrace, humiliation**
恥知らず はじしらず shameless person
恥曝し はじさらし disgrace, shame

【はじらう 恥じらう】 [sometimes also 羞じらう] **be shy [coy], look abashed**
恥じらい はじらい shyness

【はずかしい 恥ずかしい】 [sometimes also 羞ずかしい] **shy; ashamed; SHAMEful, disgraceful**
恥ずかしがる はずかしがる be shy [coy], be abashed
気恥ずかしい きはずかしい feel ashamed, feel awkward

SYNONYMS

❶ **disgrace**
恥 SHAME → 1664
羞 shame → 4106
辱 HUMILIATE → 3400
侮 INSULT → 0091
罵 ABUSE → 3233
汚 defile → 0258
誹 SLANDER → 1978
譏 SLANDER → 2069

❷ **genitals**
陰 sex organ → 0657
胎 WOMB → 1149
恥 private parts → 1664

USAGE

❶【はじる】
恥じる
[sometimes also 羞じる] feel ashamed
羞じる
[usu. 恥じる] feel ashamed

❷【はじ】
恥
[sometimes also 羞] shame, disgrace, humiliation
羞
[usu. 恥] shame, disgrace, humiliation

❸【はじらう】
恥じらう
[sometimes also 羞じらう] be shy [coy], look abashed
羞じらう
[usu. 恥じらう] be shy, be coy, look abashed

❹【はずかしい】
恥ずかしい
[sometimes also 羞ずかしい] shy; ashamed; shameful, disgraceful

羞ずかしい
[usu. 恥ずかしい] shy; ashamed; shameful, disgraceful

HOMOPHONES

はじる 羞 SHY →4106
はじ 羞 SHY →4106
はじらう 羞 SHY →4106
はずかしい 羞 SHY →4106

耽

1665
1-6-4

▶INDULGE IN
タン ふけ(る)
Ⓒ 耽 dān

128	Names	U803D
耳	S10-6-4	F2607

COMPOUNDS

● INDULGE IN, be absorbed in
耽溺する たんできする indulge in (pleasure)
耽美派 たんびは the aesthetic school

KUN

【ふける 耽る】 INDULGE IN, be absorbed in
読み耽る よみふける be absorbed in reading

SYNONYMS

● & 【ふける】 acting arbitrarily
横 arbitrary →1350
独 act arbitrarily →0471
恣 SELF-INDULGENT →3281
耽 INDULGE IN →1665
擅 ARROGATE TO ONESELF →0947
専 arrogate to oneself →3272
逞 DO AS ONE PLEASES →4004

耻

1666
1-6-4

▶SHAME
チ は(じる) はじ は(じらう) は(ずかしい)

128	Nonstandard	U803B
耳	S10-6-4	F0000

alternative form →see 恥 at 1664

聀

1667
1-6-4

▶EMPLOYMENT
ショク ソク

128	Nonstandard	U803A
耳	S10-6-4	F0000

handwritten form →see 職 at 1803

致

1668
1-6-4

▶BRING ABOUT
▶DO HUMBLY
チ いた(す) ㊔ むね のり
Ⓝ 致 Ⓒ 致 zhì

133	Jōyō	U81F4
至	S10-6-4	F1031

COMPOUNDS

❶ⓐ **BRING ABOUT, cause to, lead to, incur**
ⓑ cause to reach an extreme
a 致死の ちしの lethal, fatal
致命的 ちめいてき fatal
一致 いっち accord, agreement
合致 がっち agreement, concurrence
b 極致 きょくち culmination, acme

❷ⓐ [original meaning] **cause to come, invite, lure**
ⓑ cause to reach, send, forward
a 誘致 ゆうち lure, enticement, attraction; bringing about
招致 しょうち summons, invitation
拉致する らちする take (a person) away, kidnap
b 送致 そうち sending, forwarding

❸ good taste, elegance, grace
風致 ふうち taste, elegance
筆致 ひっち literary style; stroke of the brush, touch

❹ resign, retire
致仕 ちし resignation; 70 years of age

KUN

【いたす 致す】
① **DO HUMBLY, perform an action (with humility)**
致し方 いたしかた way, method
これは如何致しましょうか これはいかがいたしましょうか What shall I do with this?
どう致しまして どういたしまして You are welcome

②ⓐ **BRING ABOUT**, lead to, cause
ⓑ forward, send
a 人を死に致す ひとをしにいたす cause the death of a person
不才の致す所 ふさいのいたすところ be due to my incompetence
b 思いを致す おもいをいたす give one's thought to, think of

③ render (assistance), exert (oneself)
力を致す ちからをいたす make an effort, render assistance

SYNONYMS

❶ⓐ **cause**
致 BRING ABOUT →1668
誘 INDUCE →1952

【いたす】
① **do and act**
為 DO →4395
仕 DO →0037
致す DO HUMBLY →1668
行 ACT →0246
作 WORK →0077

舐

▶TASTE

シ な(める) な(めずる)

Ⓝ 舐 Ⓒ 舐 shì

1669

1-6-4

135	Non-Jōyō	U8210
舌	S10-6-4	F1754

COMPOUNDS

● lick, lap, suck

舐犢×の愛 しとくのあい doting by parents

KUN

【なめる 舐める】[also 嘗める]

①ⓐ **TASTE, have a taste**

ⓑ **TASTE, undergo, experience (hardship, etc.)**

a 塩を舐める しおをなめる taste the salt

b 辛酸を舐める しんさんをなめる experience hardships

② **lick, lap, suck**

舐め尽くす なめつくす lick thoroughly; burn to the ground

べろべろ舐める べろべろなめる lick up with one's tongue

③ burn down, consume, devour

総舐め そうなめ annihilation; a sweeping victory

④ make light of, treat with contempt

【なめずる 舐めずる】[also 嘗めずる] lick around (one's lips)

舌舐めずりする したなめずりする lick one's lips; await eagerly

SYNONYMS

【なめる】

①ⓐ **taste**

味 TASTE (savor) → 0325

嘗める TASTE (have a taste) → 3230

舐める TASTE (have a taste) → 1669

HOMOPHONES

なめる 嘗 TASTE → 3230

なめずる 嘗 TASTE → 3230

NOTE

➡ see USAGE note at 嘗 3230

般

▶SORT

ハン

Ⓒ 般 bān bō pán

1670

1-6-4

137	Jōyō	U822C
舟	S10-6-4	F0874

COMPOUNDS

❶ (things of the same category) **SORT, kind, way**

一般の いっぱんの general, universal, widespread

全般の ぜんぱんの whole, general, overall

万般 ばんぱん all things, all affairs, all sorts of matters

百般の ひゃっぱんの all, every, all sorts of

諸般の しょはんの various, several, all, every

❷ **period of time**

先般 せんぱん the other day, some time ago

今般 こんぱん now, recently

過般 かはん some time ago, recently

❸ used phonetically for *han* in the transliteration of

般若 はんにゃ *Prajñā*

般若 はんにゃ wisdom, *Prajñā*

SYNONYMS

❶ **kinds and types**

型 TYPE → 3266

類 KIND → 2275

色 kind → 2522

般 SORT → 1670

属 genus → 3901

品 category → 2795

種 VARIETY → 1560

様 variety → 1332

❷ **time periods**

時 TIME → 1155

季 SEASON (quarter) → 3161

候 SEASON (time of year) → 0133

頃 TIME → 0163

暇 FREE TIME → 1275

般 period of time → 1670

刻 POINT OF TIME → 1619

間 INTERVAL → 4122

隙 GAP → 0826

期 TERM → 2139

節 SEASON → 3336

航

▶NAVIGATE

コウ ㊔ わたる

Ⓒ 航 háng

1671

1-6-4

137	Jōyō-4	U822A
舟	S10-6-4	F0911

COMPOUNDS

❶ⓐ (travel over water) **NAVIGATE, sail, cruise**

ⓑ navigation, voyage

a 航行 こうこう navigation, cruise

航法 こうほう navigation

航海 こうかい voyage, ocean navigation

航路 こうろ sea route, course

潜航 せんこう submarine voyage, underwater navigation

運航 うんこう navigation; (airline or shipping) service
難航 なんこう hard passage, rough going
b 欠航 けっこう suspension of (ferry or aircraft) service
密航 みっこう secret passage, stowing away

❷ⓐ (travel through the air) **NAVIGATE, fly**
ⓑ abbrev. of 航空 こうくう: flying, aviation

a 航空 こうくう aviation, aerial navigation
航空機 こうくうき aircraft, airplane
航空券 こうくうけん plane ticket
航宙 こうちゅう space flight
b 日航 にっこう Japan Airlines

INDEPENDENT

【こうする 航する】**NAVIGATE**, sail, cruise

SYNONYMS

❶ⓐ **travel by vehicle**
乗 RIDE → 4393
走 travel by vehicle → 2720
航 NAVIGATE → 1671
騎 RIDE ON HORSEBACK → 2307

❷ⓐ **fly**
飛 FLY → 4389
蜚 FLY → 3473
翔 SOAR → 1714
航 NAVIGATE → 1671

舩 1672

▸SHIP
セン ふね ふな- -ぶね

137	Nonstandard	U8229
舟	S10-6-4	F0000

1-6-4 alternative form → see 船 at 1700

蚊 1673

▸MOSQUITO
ブン▲ か
Ⓒ 蚊 wén

142	Jōyō	U868A
虫	S10-6-4	F2344

1-6-4

Stroke order: 1–10

COMPOUNDS

● [original meaning] **MOSQUITO**
飛蚊症 ひぶんしょう myodesopsia

KUN

【か 蚊】[also suffix] **MOSQUITO**
蚊の鳴く様な声 かのなくようなこえ very thin [faint] voice
蚊取り線香 かとりせんこう mosquito-repellent incense
蚊帳 かや mosquito net
藪×蚊 やぶか striped mosquito
小型赤家蚊 こがたあかいえか *Culex tritaeniorhynchus*

SYNONYMS

● **insects**
蚊 MOSQUITO → 1673
蛍 FIREFLY → 3204
蝶 BUTTERFLY → 1772
蚕 SILKWORM → 3107
蟬 CICADA → 1804
蜂 BEE → 1728
蛔 ROUNDWORM → 1717

效 1674

▸EFFECT
コウ き(く)

66	Nonstandard	U6548
攵	S10-4-6	F0000

1-6-4 traditional form → see 効 at 1617

敏 1675

▸NIMBLE
ビン ㊔ とし さとし さとる さと
Ⓝ 敏 Ⓒ 敏 mǐn

66	Jōyō	U654F
攵	S10-4-6	F1280

1-6-4

Stroke order: 1–10

COMPOUNDS

❶ (physically agile) **NIMBLE, agile, quick, alert**
敏速 びんそく quickness, agility, activity
敏捷な びんしょうな agile, nimble, quick; shrewd, smart
機敏 きびん smartness, shrewdness, sharpness; quickness, promptness

❷ (mentally agile) **NIMBLE, clever, shrewd; keen, sharp**
敏感な びんかんな sensitive
敏腕 びんわん ability, capability
鋭敏な えいびんな sharp, keen, sensitive

INDEPENDENT

【びん 敏】agility, alacrity, quickness
機を見るに敏なり きをみるにびんなり be quick at seizing an opportunity

SYNONYMS

❶ **fast**
速 QUICK → 3851
早 QUICK → 3042
疾 fast → 4064
快 fast → 0289
急 rapid → 2595
迅 SWIFT → 3780
敏 NIMBLE → 1675

即 IMMEDIATE → 1439
捷 AGILE → 0609

❷ **intelligent and wise**
賢 WISE → 3518
俊 brilliant → 0117
鋭 SHARP → 2171
敏 NIMBLE → 1675
叡 PROFOUNDLY WISE → 2405
智 wise → 3458
慧 INTELLIGENT → 3485
怜 CLEVER → 0356
悧 CLEVER → 0505
俐 CLEVER → 0113
哲 SAGACIOUS → 3402
明 clear-sighted → 1060
聡 SHARP-WITTED → 1750

能

1676
1-6-4

▶ABILITY
ノウ ㊔ よし のり たか
Ⓒ 能 néng

130	Jōyō-5	U80FD
月	S10-4-6	F0200

COMPOUNDS

❶ⓐ **ABILITY, capability**
ⓑ **able, skilled, skillful**
a 能力 のうりょく ability, capacity, faculty
技能 ぎのう skill, ability, capacity
芸能 げいのう public entertainment
才能 さいのう talent, ability
万能 ばんのう omnipotence
有能な ゆうのうな able, competent
知能 ちのう intelligence, mental capacity
本能 ほんのう instinct
b 能筆 のうひつ skillful penmanship
能弁 のうべん eloquence, oratory
能吏 のうり able official

❷ **possible, can**
可能性 かのうせい possibility
不能な ふのうな impossible; impotent

❸ⓐ **action, function, effect, efficiency**
ⓑ **act upon, affect**
a 能率 のうりつ efficiency
機能 きのう function, faculty
性能 せいのう performance, capacity, efficiency
効能 こうのう effect, efficacy
b 能動的 のうどうてき active

❹ *phys* **energy, power**
放射能 ほうしゃのう radioactivity

❺ noh play
能面 のうめん noh mask
脇能 わきのう minor piece in noh plays

INDEPENDENT

【のう 能】**ABILITY, capability; noh play**
能が無い のうがない have no merit
能を演ずる のうをえんずる play a noh drama

SYNONYMS

❶ⓐ **skill**
力 POWER → 4178
能 ABILITY → 1676
技 SKILL → 0292
倆 SKILL → 0136
腕 skill → 1269
才 TALENT → 4218
ⓑ **skillful**
巧 SKILLFUL → 0219
能 able → 1676

❷ **possible**
可 -ABLE → 3687
能 possible → 1676

❸ⓐ **potency**
効 EFFECT → 1617
験 efficacy → 2306
能 action → 1676
機 function → 1365

殺

1677
1-6-4

▶KILL
サツ サイ セツ ころ(す) -ごろ(し) そ(ぐ)▲
Ⓝ 殺 Ⓒ 杀 shā

79	Jōyō-4	U6BBA
殳	S10-4-6	F0257

COMPOUNDS

❶ **KILL, murder**
殺人 さつじん murder, homicide
殺生する せっしょうする destroy life, kill animals
殺害 さつがい(=せつがい) murder, killing, assassination
殺菌 さっきん sterilization, pasteurization
暗殺 あんさつ assassination
自殺 じさつ suicide
謀殺 ぼうさつ premeditated murder
射殺する しゃさつする shoot to death
銃殺する じゅうさつする shoot to death, execute by firing squad

❷ obliterate, wipe out
殺風景 さっぷうけい inelegance; lack of refinement

抹殺する まっさつする erase, strike out; deny, ignore; do away with, liquidate

❸ **dampen, reduce, cut down**

減殺する げんさいする lessen, diminish, reduce

相殺する そうさいする offset, cancel each other

❹ [emphatic auxiliary] **entirely, utterly, completely**

殺到する さっとうする rush in, pour in; descend on

悩殺する のうさつする fascinate, enchant

KUN

【ころす 殺す】 **KILL, murder; bump off; massacre; pawn, waste; hold back (tears);** *baseball* **strike out**

殺し ころし killing, murder

殺し屋 ころしや hired killer

締め殺す しめころす strangle to death

轢き殺す ひきころす kill by running over

感情を殺す かんじょうをころす suppress one's emotions

【-ごろし -殺し】 [also suffix] **KILLing, murder, -cide**

人殺し ひとごろし murder; murderer

幼児殺し ようじごろし infanticide

二人殺し ふたりごろし double murder

【そぐ 殺ぐ】 [also 削ぐ]

① chip, cut off

殺がれた耳 そがれたみみ mutilated ear

②ⓐ diminish, reduce, dampen

ⓑ spoil

b 興を殺ぐ きょうをそぐ spoil the fun of

SYNONYMS

❶ **kill**

殺 KILL → 1677

剄 KILL → 2398

刺 stab to death → 1625

絞 STRANGLE → 1707

窒 CHOKE → 2853

HOMOPHONES

そぐ 削 CUT BY CHIPPING → 1837

NOTE

➡ see USAGE note at 削 1837

★ do not confuse with 刹 BUDDHIST TEMPLE → 1620

朔

1678

1-6-4

▶**FIRST DAY OF THE LUNAR MONTH**

サク ついたち ㊔ はじめ はじむ もと

Ⓒ 朔 shuò

74	Names	U6714
月	S10-4-6	F3113

COMPOUNDS

❶ **FIRST DAY OF THE LUNAR MONTH**

朔日 さくじつ(=ついたち) [usu. 一日] first day of the lunar month

❷ **north**

朔風 さくふう north wind

INDEPENDENT

【さく 朔】 conjunction; **FIRST DAY OF THE LUNAR MONTH**

KUN

【ついたち 朔】 [usu. 一日] **FIRST DAY OF THE (LUNAR) MONTH**

SYNONYMS

❶ **days**

日 DAY → 3759

曜 DAY OF THE WEEK → 1402

昼 DAYTIME → 3841

旦 first day → 3041

朔 FIRST DAY OF THE LUNAR MONTH → 1678

晦 LAST DAY OF THE LUNAR MONTH → 1196

USAGE

【ついたち】

朔

[usu. 一日] first day of the (lunar) month

一日

[sometimes also 朔] 1st of the month

HOMOPHONES

ついたち 一日 → 4148, 3759

朗

1679

1-6-4

▶**CHEERFUL**

▶**CLEAR**

ロウ ほが(らか) ㊔ あき あきら お

Ⓝ 朗 朖 Ⓒ 朗 lǎng

74	Jōyō-6	U6717
月	S10-4-6	F1405

Stroke order: 1–10

COMPOUNDS

❶ (marked by or conductive to cheer) **CHEERFUL, bright, cheery**

朗報 ろうほう cheering [good] news

明朗な めいろうな cheerful, bright; clean (politics)

❷ⓐ **CLEAR (voice), loud and clear, sonorous, loud, resonant**

ⓑ [original meaning] **CLEAR (sky), bright (moon)**

a 朗詠 ろうえい reciting, chanting

朗吟する ろうぎんする recite, sing

朗読 ろうどく reading aloud

朗朗たる ろうろうたる clear (and ringing), sonorous, resonant; bright (moon)

b 晴朗な せいろうな clear, fair, serene

KUN

【ほがらか 朗らか】

ほがらかな 朗らかな **CHEERFUL, bright; clear (sky)**

朗らかに笑う ほがらかにわらう laugh merrily, smile brightly

SYNONYMS

❶ **pleased and pleasant**
楽 pleasurable → 3505
欣 JOYFUL → 1057
爽 REFRESHING → 4402
快 PLEASANT → 0289
朗 CHEERFUL → 1679
愉 PLEASED → 0710
悦 DELIGHTED → 0501
嬉しい GLAD → 0890
喜 HAPPY → 2889
歓 JOYOUS → 2342
驩 JOYOUS → 2333

❷ⓐ **loud**
高い loud → 2601
朗 CLEAR (voice) → 1679
騒 clamorous → 2308
喧 BOISTEROUS → 0667
嘩 BOISTEROUS → 0771

ⓑ **clear**
透 TRANSPARENT → 3854
澄 LIMPID → 0915
清 CLEAR (liquid) → 0635
明 CLEAR (unclouded) → 1060
朗 CLEAR (sky) → 1679
冴える CRISP AND CLEAR → 0087

師

1680
◧ 1-6-4

▶**MASTER**
シ ㊔ もろ かず のり
Ⓒ 师 shī

50	Jōyō-5	U5E2B
巾	S10-3-7	F0353

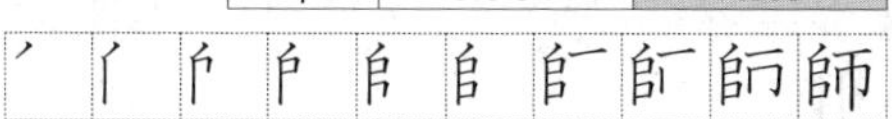
1 2 3 4 5 6 7 8 9 10

COMPOUNDS

❶ **MASTER, teacher, instructor**
師範 しはん teacher, master, coach
師匠 ししょう master, teacher
師事する しじする study under, look up to (a person) as one's teacher
師走 しわす December
教師 きょうし teacher, instructor
講師 こうし speaker, lecturer
恩師 おんし one's respected teacher, one's former teacher

❷ honorific title, esp. after names of clergymen or traditional artists
ホメイニ師 ほめいにし the Ayatollah Khomeini
宝井馬琴師 たからいばきんし Master Bakin Takarai

❸ [also suffix] **member of a profession or performer of an action**
医師 いし doctor, physician, surgeon
技師 ぎし engineer, technician
牧師 ぼくし pastor, minister, priest
絵師 えし painter, artist
美容師 びようし beauty artist
ペテン師 ぺてんし swindler, finagler

❹ [original meaning] army
師団 しだん army division

❺ [rare] god (of natural phenomena)
風師 ふうし wind god

❻ [archaic] capital city
京師 けいし old city of Kyoto

INDEPENDENT

【し 師】 **MASTER**, teacher, instructor
師と仰ぐ しとあおぐ look up to (a person) as one's preceptor

SYNONYMS

❷ **titles of address**
氏 COURTESY TITLE → 3669
兄 familiar title (seniors) → 2676
君 FAMILIAR TITLE (peers) → 3974
嬢 Miss → 0936
様 FORMAL TITLE → 1332
殿 FORMAL HONORIFIC TITLE → 2247
師 honorific title (clergymen) → 1680
公 honorific title (noblemen) → 2468

❸ **workers and professionals**
家 professional → 2827
婦 woman worker → 0565
嬢 (unmarried) female worker → 0936
夫 MAN LABORER → 4271
匠 CRAFTSMAN → 3711
工 workman → 4190
客 skilled person → 2798
士 PROFESSION SUFFIX → 4213
師 profession suffix → 1680
者 person who → 3980
人 person of certain category → 4175
員 MEMBER (of a staff) → 2822
屋 colloquial occupation suffix → 3842
手 OCCUPATION SUFFIX → 4267

COMPOUND FORMATION

【師走 しわす】
According to one theory, 師走 'December' originally referred to a Buddhist monk (師 ❶) running around (走) at the end of the year.

NOTE

★ do not confuse with 帥 COMMANDER IN CHIEF → 1642

米糸缶耒耒耳至舌舟虫交毎育柔並良皀【孝】

教 incorrect stroke-count
➡ see 1-7-4: 孝 at 1887
1-6-4

粘 ▶STICKY

ネン ねば(る)

N 黏 C 黏 nián 粘 zhān

1681
1-6-5

119	Jōyō	U7C98
米	S11-6-5	F1736

COMPOUNDS

● [original meaning] **STICKY, glutinous, viscous, adhesive**
粘着性 ねんちゃくせい stickiness, adhesion, viscosity
粘土 ねんど clay
粘板岩 ねんばんがん clay rock, slate
粘膜 ねんまく mucous membrane
粘度 ねんど viscosity
粘液 ねんえき mucus
粘性 ねんせい stickiness, viscidity

KUN

【ねばる 粘る】**be STICKY, be glutinous; persevere**
粘い ねばい sticky
粘り ねばり stickiness; tenacity
粘り強い ねばりづよい tenacious, sticky; persistent
粘つく ねばつく be sticky, be glutinous
粘っこい ねばっこい sticky; stiff, tenacious

粒 ▶GRAIN

リュウ つぶ

C 粒 lì

1682
1-6-5

119	Jōyō	U7C92
米	S11-6-5	F1561

COMPOUNDS

❶ⓐ (small particulate mass) **GRAIN, granule**
ⓑ *phys* **GRAIN**, particle
ⓒ counter for **GRAIN**s
a 粒子 りゅうし particle, grain
粒状の りゅうじょうの granular
顆×粒 かりゅう granule
b 粒度 りゅうど particle size, grain size
粒径 りゅうけい grain [particle] diameter
粒界 りゅうかい grain boundary
素粒子 そりゅうし elementary particle
c 米十粒 こめじゅうりゅう ten grains of rice

❷ [original meaning] **GRAIN** (of rice), grain (of cereal)
粒粒辛苦 りゅうりゅうしんく assiduously, painstakingly
穀粒 こくりゅう grain

KUN

【つぶ 粒】**GRAIN, particle; drop; counter for grains or drops; each person or thing**
粒粒の つぶつぶの granulated, lumpy
粒揃い つぶぞろい uniform excellence
粒選りの つぶよりの the pick, the choice
米粒 こめつぶ grain of rice
雨粒 あまつぶ raindrop
一粒の涙 ひとつぶのなみだ one tear

SYNONYMS

❶ **particle**
粒 GRAIN → 1682
子 particle suffix → 4196
核 NUCLEUS → 1162

COMPOUND FORMATION

【粒粒辛苦 りゅうりゅうしんく】
粒粒辛苦 'assiduously, painstakingly' originally referred to working as strenuously (辛苦) as peasants did at growing rice grain (粒 ❷) by grain (粒 ❷).

粗 ▶COARSE

ソ あら(い) あら-

C 粗 cū

1683
1-6-5

119	Jōyō	U7C97
米	S11-6-5	F1709

COMPOUNDS

❶ (not fine) **COARSE, rough, rugged**
粗密 そみつ roughness and fineness
粗大な そだいな coarse, rough, unpolished
粗布 そふ coarse cloth
精粗 せいそ fineness or coarseness; minuteness or roughness

❷ⓐ (of inferior quality) **COARSE, crude, inferior, poor, humble, shabby**—used esp. as a term of humility before items presented as gifts
ⓑ (of unrefined manner) **COARSE**, crude, rude, rough, harsh
a 粗悪な そあくな coarse, crude, bad, inferior
粗品 そしな trifling gift, inferior goods

粗茶 そちゃ coarse tea
粗末な そまつな coarse, crude, inferior, humble
お粗末様 おそまつさま [humble] It was nothing at all/The pleasure was all mine
b 粗雑な そざつな coarse, rough, crude
粗暴な そぼうな wild, rude

❸ (in the natural state) **crude, raw, unrefined, unprocessed**
粗製 そせい crude manufacture
粗鉱 そこう unprocessed ore
粗鋼 そこう crude steel

❹ **careless, negligent**
粗相 そそう carelessness, careless mistake, blunder
粗忽な そこつな careless, thoughtless, rash

INDEPENDENT

【そ 粗】 COARSEness, roughness
粗に過ぎる そにすぎる be too rough

KUN

【あらい 粗い】
①ⓐ (not fine) **COARSE, rough, gross**
ⓑ (not smooth) **COARSE, rough, rugged**
ⓒ (not elaborate) **COARSE, rough, crude, gross**
a 粗 あら fault, defect; bony parts (of a fish)
粗い網 あらいあみ coarse net
b 粗い肌 あらいはだ rough skin
c 粗い細工 あらいさいく rough workmanship
② **sparse, scattered**
種を粗く播く たねをあらくまく sow sparsely

【あら- 粗-】
①ⓐ [also 荒-] (not elaborate) **COARSE, rough, crude, gross**
ⓑ (in the natural state) **crude, raw, unrefined, unprocessed**
a 粗筋 あらすじ outline, summary
粗造り あらづくり rough work
b 粗金 あらがね ore
② **sparse, scattered**
粗播き あらまき sparse sowing [seeding]

SYNONYMS

❶ **rare and sparse**
薄い THIN → 3004
希 RARE → 2543
疎 SPARSE → 1512
粗 COARSE → 1683
稀 RARE → 1523

❷ⓐ **bad**
悪 BAD → 3413
劣 INFERIOR → 3047
下 of low grade → 4186
弊 shabby → 3583
粗 COARSE → 1683
駄 GOOD FOR NOTHING → 2291
廃 WASTE → 3902

ⓑ **vulgar and unrefined**
俗 vulgar → 0119
卑 MEAN → 3270
賤 MEAN → 1993
鄙 MEAN → 2338
俚 RURAL → 0112
里 rural → 4356
粗 COARSE → 1683
野 rustic → 1877
蛮 barbaric → 2638

❸ **natural**
地 natural → 0236
野 wild → 1877
粗 crude → 1683
原 in the original state → 3733

HOMOPHONES

あらい 荒 WILD → 2810
あら- 荒 WILD → 2810

NOTE

➡ see USAGE note at 荒 2810

紬

1684

1-6-5

▶PONGEE
チュウ つむぎ
Ⓒ 䌷 chōu chóu

120	Names	U7D2C
糸	S11-6-5	F3307

KUN

【つむぎ 紬】 PONGEE, coarse silk [cotton] cloth
紬糸 つむぎいと silk thread spun from either waste cocoons or cotton

SYNONYMS

【つむぎ】
◯ **fabrics**
織 woven fabric → 1801
紬 PONGEE → 1684
紗 GAUZE → 1653
絹 SILK → 1721
綾 TWILL → 1740
綿 COTTON → 1736
棉 COTTON → 1244
麻 HEMP → 3878
毛 wool → 4264
錦 BROCADE → 2181

絃 1685

▶STRING

ゲン ㊔ つる お

Ⓒ 弦 xián

1-6-5

120	Names	U7D43
糸	S11-6-5	F2951

COMPOUNDS

[now usu. 弦 0343]

❶ [original meaning]

ⓐ STRING or chord of a musical instrument

ⓑ counter for STRINGs [chords]

a 絃楽器 げんがっき stringed instruments

b 三絃 さんげん three-stringed instrument, shamisen

❷ STRINGed instrument, the strings

絃歌 げんか singing and (string) music

管絃楽 かんげんがく orchestral music

SYNONYMS

❶ⓐ ropes and lines

綱 ROPE (esp. of fiber) → 1735

絃 STRING → 1685

縄 ROPE (esp. of straw) → 1756

緒 cord → 1742

組 braid → 1693

索 cable → 3105

鎖 CHAIN → 2213

線 LINE → 1760

紐 STRING → 1647

弦 STRING → 0343

絆 1686

▶BONDS

ハン きずな ほだ(す)

Ⓒ 绊 bàn

1-6-5

120	Names	U7D46
糸	S11-6-5	F2304

COMPOUNDS

❶ BONDS, fetters, tether

脚絆 きゃはん gaiters, leggings

羈×絆 きはん fetters, shackles, bonds

❷ bind, tie, fetter, tether, shackle

絆創膏 ばんそうこう adhesive plaster [tape]

KUN

【きずな 絆】

ⓐ (interpersonal connection) BONDS, ties

ⓑ (rope to fasten domestic animals) tether

a 固い絆 かたいきずな strong bond, close ties

【ほだす 絆す】

ⓐ restrain, restrict, bind, fetter

ⓑ tether with rope

b 絆される ほだされる be moved [swayed, fettered] by (affection, kindness, etc.)

SYNONYMS

❶ personal relations

縁 RELATION → 1754

交 INTERCOURSE → 2508

好 friendship → 0240

仲 PERSONAL RELATIONS → 0047

誼 FRIENDSHIP → 1977

絆 BONDS → 1686

経 1687

▶PASS THROUGH

▶MANAGE

ケイ キョウ へ(る) た(つ)▲ たていと▲

㊔ つね のぶ のり

Ⓝ 經 圣◇ Ⓒ 经 jīng

1-6-5

120	Jōyō-5	U7D4C
糸	S11-6-5	F0125

COMPOUNDS

❶ⓐ (go through without stopping) PASS THROUGH, go through

ⓑ PASS THROUGH an experience, experience

ⓒ (of time) pass, elapse

a 経由する けいゆする go via, pass through

神経 しんけい nerve; sensitivity; worry

b 経験 けいけん experience

経歴 けいれき personal history

c 経過する けいかする pass, elapse

❷ MANAGE (the affairs of an organization or a state), administer

経世 けいせい administration, government, conduct of state affairs

経理 けいり accounting

経済 けいざい economy, economics

経済的 けいざいてき economical, economic

経営 けいえい management

❸ abbrev. of 経済 けいざい: economics

経企庁(=経済企画庁) けいきちょう(=けいざいきかくちょう) Economic Planning Agency

経団連(=経済団体連合会) けいだんれん(=けいざいだんたいれんごうかい) Federation of Economic Organizations

政経 せいけい politics and economics

❹ⓐ religious classic, Buddhist scriptures, sutra

ⓑ classical works; Chinese classics

a 経典 きょうてん sacred books, scripture, sutras; Bible

経文 きょうもん sutras

阿弥陀経 あみだきょう the Sukhavati sutra

仏経 ぶっきょう sutras

b 経史 きょうし Chinese classics

❺ⓐ **periodic, regular, ordinary**

ⓑ period, menstruation

a 経常費 けいじょうひ ordinary expenditure

経費 けいひ expense(s), cost(s), expenditure, upkeep

b 月経 げっけい menstruation

閉経 へいけい menopause

❻ [original meaning] warp

整経機 せいけいき warping machine

❼ **longitude**

経度 けいど longitude

西経 せいけい west longitude

❽ *Chinese medicine* meridian; blood vessels

INDEPENDENT

【けい 経】main plot (of a story)

【きょう 経】sutra

KUN

【へる 経る】**pass, elapse, go by; PASS [go] THROUGH; pass [go] through, experience**

十年を経て じゅうねんをへて after ten years

手続きを経る てつづきをへる go through formalities

【たつ 経つ】**pass, elapse, go by**

時間が経つ じかんがたつ Time goes by

【たていと 経】[also 縦糸 or 経糸] warp

SYNONYMS

❶ⓐ **pass**

通 PASS → 3855

過 PASS BY → 3891

経 PASS THROUGH → 1687

疏 LET PASS → 1511

ⓒ **elapse**

過 PASS BY → 3891

経 pass → 1687

歴 pass → 3748

去 pass away → 2678

❷ **direct and supervise**

制 CONTROL → 1624

理 manage → 1220

経 MANAGE → 1687

管 EXERCISE CONTROL → 3349

轄 EXERCISE JURISDICTION OVER → 2056

掌 TAKE CHARGE OF → 3215

監 OVERSEE → 3535

督 SUPERVISE → 3471

司 OFFICIATE → 3648

宰 PRESIDE → 2829

営 MANAGE → 3216

❹ⓐ **books**

本 BOOK → 4314

典 STANDARD WORK → 3253

経 religious classic → 1687

書 BOOK → 3292

冊 bound book → 4295

籍 books → 3394

著 literary work → 2869

巻 VOLUME → 3273

編 piece of writing → 1755

篇 PIECE OF WRITING → 3361

鑑 REFERENCE VOLUME → 2226

❻ **threads and fibers**

糸 THREAD → 2703

緯 woof → 1782

経 warp → 1687

繊 FIBER → 1789

維 FIBER → 1733

綸 THREAD → 1739

緬 FINE THREAD → 1758

❼ **latitude and longitude**

緯 LATITUDE → 1782

経 longitude → 1687

USAGE

【たていと】

経

[also 縦糸 or 経糸] warp

縦糸

[also 経糸 or 経] warp

経糸

[also 経 or 縦糸] warp

HOMOPHONES

たつ

立 STAND → 2486

建 BUILD → 3834

起 RISE → 4099

発 START → 3174

たていと

縦糸 → 1783, 2703

経糸 → 1687, 2703

COMPOUND FORMATION

【経済 けいざい】

経済 'economy, economics' is an abbreviation of 経国済民 けいこくさいみん 'administration and statesmanship', that is, administrating (経 ❷) the country (国) and relieving (済) the sufferings of the people (民). 経済 was coined in Japan by means of characters imported from China and then "exported" back to China.

NOTE

➡ see also USAGE note at 立 2486

➡ see COMPOUND FORMATION for 神経 しんけい → 神 1143

1

米 【糸】 羊 舌 舟 虫 幷

紺

▶DARK BLUE

コン

Ⓒ 绀 gàn

1688

1-6-5

120	Jōyō	U7D3A
糸	S11-6-5	F1981

COMPOUNDS

● [original meaning] **DARK BLUE, navy blue**

紺色 こんいろ dark blue, navy blue
紺地 こんじ dark blue ground; dark blue cloth
紺青 こんじょう Prussian blue, deep blue
紺屋 こうや(=こんや) dyer; dyer's shop
紫紺 しこん purplish blue
濃紺 のうこん dark blue, navy blue

INDEPENDENT

【こん 紺】**DARK BLUE, navy blue**
紺の背広 こんのせびろ blue business suit

SYNONYMS

● **blue and purple colors**
青 BLUE →3084
碧 DEEP BLUE →3515
瑠 LAPIS LAZULI (bright blue) →1342
紺 DARK BLUE →1688
藍 INDIGO →3024
紫 PURPLE →3332
蒼 PALE BLUE →2943

細

▶SLENDER
▶MINUTE

サイ ほそ(い) ほそ(る) こま(か) こま(かい) ささ(やか)▲ ㊔ ささ

1689

1-6-5

Ⓒ 细 xì

120	Jōyō-2	U7D30
糸	S11-6-5	F0440

COMPOUNDS

❶ [also prefix] [original meaning] **SLENDER, fine, thin, narrow**
細流 さいりゅう streamlet, brooklet, rivulet
細腰 さいよう slender hips
細動脈 さいどうみゃく arteriole
毛細血管 もうさいけっかん capillary vessel
繊細な せんさいな delicate, fine, subtle

❷ⓐ (very small) **MINUTE, fine, small, microscopic**
ⓑ (detailed) **MINUTE, detailed, close, elaborate**

a 細胞 さいぼう cell
細菌 さいきん bacteria, germ, microbe
細分する さいぶんする subdivide, fractionate
微細な びさいな minute, fine; detailed, minute; delicate, subtle

b 細部 さいぶ details, particulars
細心 さいしん carefulness, discretion
細工 さいく work, craftsmanship; artifice, tactics
詳細 しょうさい details, particulars
明細 めいさい particulars, details, specifics
精細な せいさいな detailed, minute, exact

❸ (beneath notice) **MINUTE, minor, trifling, insignificant**
細事 さいじ minor details
細君 さいくん wife
零細な れいさいな small, trifling, petty
些細な さざいな trifling, slight, insignificant

INDEPENDENT

【さい 細】**MINUTE** details
微に入り細を穿つ びにいりさいをうがつ go into the minutest details

KUN

【ほそい 細い】**SLENDER; fine, thin; narrow; small, slight; sensitive, delicate**
細い糸 ほそいいと fine thread
細長い ほそながい slender, linear, long and narrow
細面 ほそおもて slender face
心細い こころぼそい helpless, forlorn; lonely
神経が細い しんけいがほそい be oversensitive

【ほそる 細る】**get thin, taper off; dwindle, be reduced**
身が細る みがほそる become thin, lose weight
先細り さきぼそり tapering off [away]
食が細る しょくがほそる lose one's appetite

【こまか 細か】
こまかな 細かな (very small) **MINUTE, fine, small;** (detailed) **minute, elaborate, close; thrifty, frugal, stingy**
事細かに ことこまかに minutely, in detail

【こまかい 細かい】same as 細かな こまかな
細かく こまかく finely, minutely
細かい金 こまかいかね small change
細細した こまごました sundry
細かい指示 こまかいしじ detailed instructions
神経が細かい しんけいがこまかい be sensitive, have delicate feeling
金銭に細かい きんせんにこまかい be scrimpy about money

【ささやか 細やか】

ささやかな 細やかな small, modest

SPECIAL READINGS

細波▲ さざなみ [also. 漣 or 小波] ripples, wavelets

SYNONYMS

❶ **thin**

薄 THIN → 3004
細 SLENDER → 1689
繊 FINE → 1789
痩 GET THIN → 4069

❷ⓐ **small and tiny**

小 SMALL → 0007
豆- miniature → 2442
微 SLIGHT → 0788
細 MINUTE → 1689
寸 A BIT OF → 3652

ⓑ **detailed**

詳 DETAILED → 1926
細 MINUTE → 1689
緻 MINUTE → 1780
密 CLOSE → 2857
精 meticulous → 1729

❸ **unimportant**

細 MINUTE → 1689
微 SLIGHT → 0788
小 SMALL → 0007
末 last in importance → 4317

HOMOPHONES

さざなみ

漣 RIPPLES → 0859
小波 → 0007, 0388
細波 → 1689, 0388

紳

1690

1-6-5

▶GENTLEMAN

シン

Ⓒ 绅 shēn

120	Jōyō	U7D33
糸	S11-6-5	F1828

Stroke order: 1–11

COMPOUNDS

❶ **GENTLEMAN, gentry; men of rank**

紳士 しんし gentleman
紳商 しんしょう merchant prince, rich merchant
貴紳 きしん men of rank, notables

❷ [original meaning, now archaic] ornamental sash worn by ancient Chinese noblemen

SYNONYMS

❶ **gentleman**

紳 GENTLEMAN → 1690
子 gentleman → 4196
士 man of learning and virtue → 4213

紹

1691

1-6-5

▶INTRODUCE

ショウ ㊔ つぐ あき

Ⓒ 绍 shào

120	Jōyō	U7D39
糸	S11-6-5	F0954

Stroke order: 1–11

COMPOUNDS

● **INTRODUCE, bring together**

紹介する しょうかいする introduce, present
紹介状 しょうかいじょう letter of introduction

SYNONYMS

● **mediating and mediators**

紹 INTRODUCE → 1691
介 MEDIATE → 2463
媒 INTERMEDIATE → 0686
仲 INTERMEDIARY → 0047

終

1692

1-6-5

▶END

シュウ お(わる) -お(わる) お(える) つい▲ つい(に)▲

Ⓝ 終 Ⓒ 终 zhōng

120	Jōyō-3	U7D42
糸	S11-6-5	F0311

Stroke order: 1–11

COMPOUNDS

❶ⓐ **END, come to an end, finish, terminate**
ⓑ **bring to an END, finish, complete**
ⓒ **END one's life, die**

a 終了する しゅうりょうする end, conclude, complete; expire
終結 しゅうけつ end, conclusion, termination
終戦 しゅうせん end of the war
終極の しゅうきょくの ultimate, final
b 終業時間 しゅうぎょうじかん closing hour
c 臨終 りんじゅう hour of death, one's last moment

❷ⓐ **END, ending, finish**
ⓑ [also prefix] **last, final, terminal**

a 最終 さいしゅう last, the end; final
b 終始 しゅうし from beginning to end, always

米 【糸】 羊 舌 舟 虫 并

終点 しゅうてん last stop, terminus
終盤戦 しゅうばんせん end game
終列車 しゅうれっしゃ last train
終刊号 しゅうかんごう final issue
終着駅 しゅうちゃくえき terminal station, railroad terminal

❸ from beginning to **END**, all through, all
終日 しゅうじつ all [throughout] the day
終身 しゅうしん all through life
終夜 しゅうや all night

KUN

【おわる 終わる】[rarely also 畢る] *vi* **END, come to an end, finish, terminate; end one's life, die**
終わり おわり end(ing), conclusion
終わり頃 おわりごろ toward the end

【-おわる -終わる】[verbal suffix] **bring an action to an END, finish**
読み終わる よみおわる read through, finish reading

【おえる 終える】*vt* **END, finish, complete**
し終える しおえる finish doing something

【つい 終】*elegant* the **END**

【ついに 終に】[usu. 遂に] at last, at length, in the **END**, finally

SYNONYMS

❶ **end**
終 END → 1692
絶 COME TO AN END → 1711
閉 CLOSE → 4116
了 FINISH → 4157
済 SETTLE → 0634
-上げる completion suffix → 4212
完 COMPLETE → 2727
結 CONCLUDE → 1706
竣 COMPLETE → 1528

❷ⓐ **ends**
末 LAST PART → 4317
終 END → 1692
畢 END → 3194
尾 end → 3799
局 close → 3800

ⓑ **last**
末 last in time → 4317
終 last → 1692

❸ **throughout**
通 through → 3855
徹 all through → 0894
終 from beginning to end → 1692
中 throughout → 4262

USAGE

【おわる】
終わる
[rarely also 畢る] *vi* end, come to an end, finish, terminate; end one's life, die
畢る
[now always 終わる] end, come to an end, finish, terminate; end one's life, die

HOMOPHONES

ついに 遂 ACCOMPLISH → 3892
おわる 畢 END → 3194

NOTE

➡ see also USAGE note at 遂 3892

組

1693

▸**ORGANIZE**
▸**ASSEMBLE**
ソ く(む) くみ -ぐみ
Ⓒ 組 zǔ

1-6-5

120	Jōyō-2	U7D44
糸	S11-6-5	F0194

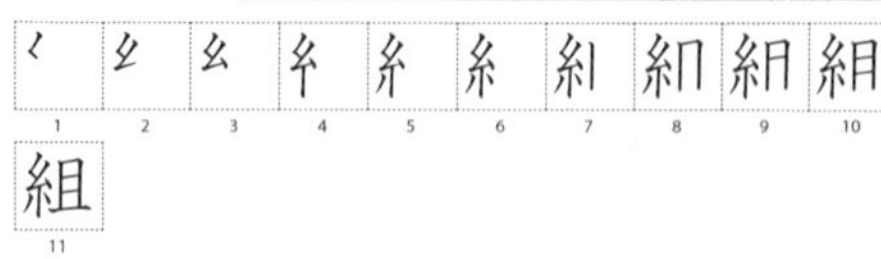

COMPOUNDS

❶ⓐ **ORGANIZE, form, arrange, unite**
ⓑ organization
a 組織する そしきする organize, form, set up; constitute, construct
組成 そせい composition, formation, construction
組閣する そかくする form a cabinet, organize a ministry
b 改組 かいそ reorganization (of a union)

❷ abbrev. of 組合 くみあい: **union**
日教組 にっきょうそ Japan Teachers Union
労組 ろうそ labor union
職組 しょくそ employees' union

❸ⓐ [original meaning] braid, plait
ⓑ to braid
a 編組機械 へんそきかい knitting machinery

KUN

【くむ 組む】
①ⓐ **ASSEMBLE, construct, put together, fit together**
ⓑ **unite, associate oneself with, ORGANIZE**
a 組み立てる くみたてる assemble, construct, erect
組み込む くみこむ incorporate, integrate, put in
組み合わせる くみあわせる combine, assort, join together, match
組み合わせ くみあわせ combination; assortment

仕組み しくみ construction; arrangement; plan, plot
番組 ばんぐみ (TV) program
団体を組む だんたいをくむ form an organization
b 組んで事業をする くんでじぎょうをする join forces [tie up] (with others) in business
縁組 えんぐみ marriage, (conjugal) union
② **cross (one's legs); fold (one's arms)**
足を組む あしをくむ cross one's legs
手を組む てをくむ join hands together
③ **grapple with**
取り組む とりくむ grapple, tackle (a problem)
④ **typeset, compose**
組み くみ typesetting, composition
組み版 くみはん typesetting, composition
活字を組む かつじをくむ set type
⑤ braid
組み紐 くみひも plaited cord (used with kimonos)
糸を組む いとをくむ braid string
【くみ 組】
①ⓐ **group (of people), team, company, party, gang**
ⓑ set (of tea cups), suit
a 組合 くみあい union, guild, association
組合頭 くみあいがしら group leader
組を作る くみをつくる make up a party
赤組 あかぐみ red team
b 茶器組 ちゃきぐみ tea set
② [also suffix] (school) **class**
会話の組 かいわのくみ conversation class
一年三組 いちねんさんくみ first-grade, class three
【-ぐみ -組】[suffix]
① **group, gang**
三人組の強盗 さんにんぐみのごうとう gang of three robbers
四人組 よにんぐみ the Gang of Four
② **company**
大林組 おおばやしぐみ Obayashi & Company

SYNONYMS

❶ⓐ **organize**
組 ORGANIZE → 1693
結 form → 1706
編 put together → 1755
❷ **organized bodies**
会 SOCIETY → 2512
協 association → 0103
団 BODY → 3791
体 BODY → 0080
組 union → 1693
労 workers' union → 3155
連 federation → 3849
講 fraternity → 2046
院 INSTITUTION → 0544
❸ⓐ **ropes and lines**
綱 ROPE (esp. of fiber) → 1735
絃 STRING → 1685
縄 ROPE (esp. of straw) → 1756
緒 cord → 1742
組 braid → 1693
索 cable → 3105
鎖 CHAIN → 2213
線 LINE → 1760
紐 STRING → 1647
弦 STRING → 0343
ⓑ **weave and sew**
織 WEAVE → 1801
紡 SPIN → 1646
績 spin → 1788
縫 SEW → 1781
編 KNIT → 1755
辮 PLAIT → 2085
組 braid → 1693
繡 EMBROIDER → 1805
【くむ】
①ⓐ **make**
作 MAKE → 0077
造 MAKE → 3856
成 FORM → 4352
工 MANUFACTURE → 4190
製 MANUFACTURE → 3478
産 PRODUCE → 4089
調 PREPARE → 1973
組む ASSEMBLE → 1693
構 CONSTRUCT → 1325
【くみ】
① **groups**
群 GROUP (of any kind) → 1942
班 SQUAD → 1182
軍 team → 2582
組 group (of people) → 1693
陣 lineup → 0545
連 set → 3849
族 common-interest group (*slang*) → 1195
党 PARTY → 3190
隊 PARTY (organized group) → 0762
団 BODY → 3791
伍 ranks → 0050
② **class in school**
組 class → 1693
級 GRADE → 1630

NOTE

➡ see COMPOUND FORMATION for 番組 ばんぐみ → 番 3416

終 1694

▶END
シュウ お(わる) -お(わる) お(える) つい つい(に)

1-6-5

120	Nonstandard	U7D42
糸	S11-6-5	F0000

traditional form → see 終 at 1692

羚 1695

▶SEROW
レイ
Ⓒ 羚 líng

1-6-5

123	Names	U7F9A
羊	S11-6-5	F0000

COMPOUNDS

● [original meaning] **SEROW**
羚羊 れいよう antelope

SPECIAL READINGS

羚羊(=氈×鹿) かもしか serow

SYNONYMS

● **undomesticated mammals**
虎 TIGER → 3981
猿 MONKEY → 0824
鯨 WHALE → 2361
犀 RHINOCEROS → 3900
狼 WOLF → 0541
狐 FOX → 0472
羚 SEROW → 1695
鼠 RAT → 3340
獅 LION → 0825
豹 LEOPARD → 1847
熊 BEAR → 3530
象 ELEPHANT → 2647
麒 MALE CHINESE UNICORN → 2363
麟 FEMALE CHINESE UNICORN → 2376
猪 WILD BOAR → 0652
鹿 DEER → 3879

舐 1696

▶TASTE
シ な(める) な(めずる)

1-6-5

135	Nonstandard	U445B
舌	S11-6-5	F0000

traditional form → see 舐 at 1669

舵 1697

▶STEERING DEVICE
ダ かじ
Ⓒ 舵 duò

1-6-5

137	Names	U8235
舟	S11-6-5	F2363

COMPOUNDS

STEERING DEVICE:
ⓐ rudder
ⓑ helm, tiller, wheel
a 方向舵 ほうこうだ rudder
昇降舵 しょうこうだ *aeronautics* elevator
b 舵手 だしゅ helmsman, coxswain
操舵 そうだ steering

KUN

【かじ 舵】[sometimes also 梶] **STEERING DEVICE**:
ⓐ **rudder**
ⓑ **helm, tiller, wheel**
a 舵板 かじいた rudder blade
b 舵取り かじとり helmsman, coxswain; steering, guidance
舵を取る かじをとる steer; manage
面舵 おもかじ starboarding the helm
取り舵 とりかじ porting the helm

SYNONYMS

● **parts of boats and ships**
舵 STEERING DEVICE → 1697
梶 steering device → 1199
櫓 SCULL → 1412
櫂 OAR → 1405
舷 GUNWALE → 1698
艙 SHIP'S HOLD → 1786

USAGE

【かじ】
舵
[sometimes also 梶] steering device:
ⓐ rudder
ⓑ helm, tiller, wheel
梶
① paper mulberry
② steering device:
ⓐ [usu. 舵] rudder
ⓑ [usu. 舵] helm, tiller, wheel
ⓒ oar
ⓓ shafts (of a rickshaw)

HOMOPHONES

かじ 梶 PAPER MULBERRY → 1199

舷

1698

1-6-5

▸GUNWALE

ゲン ふなばた▲ ふなべり▲

Ⓒ 舷 xián

137	Jōyō	U8237
舟	S11-6-5	F2473

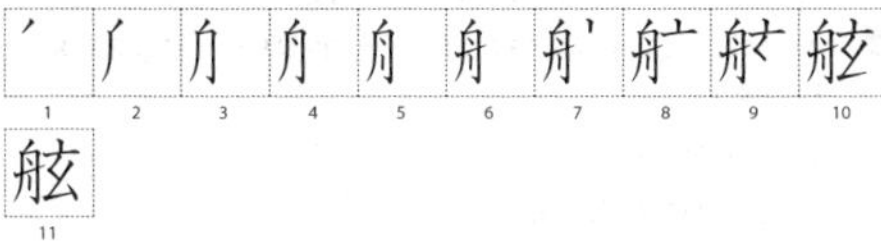

COMPOUNDS

● **GUNWALE**

舷窓 げんそう porthole
舷側 げんそく ship's side, broadside
舷梯 げんてい gangway (ladder)
右舷 うげん starboard
乾舷 かんげん freeboard (of a ship)
登舷礼 とうげんれい ceremonial assembling of a ship's crew on deck

INDEPENDENT

【げん 舷】**GUNWALE**

KUN

【ふなばた 舷】**GUNWALE**
【ふなべり 舷】same as 舷 ふなばた

SYNONYMS

● **parts of boats and ships**

舵 STEERING DEVICE → 1697
梶 steering device → 1199
櫓 SCULL → 1412
櫂 OAR → 1405
舷 GUNWALE → 1698
艙 SHIP'S HOLD → 1786

舶

1699

1-6-5

▸OCEANGOING SHIP

ハク

Ⓒ 舶 bó

137	Jōyō	U8236
舟	S11-6-5	F2377

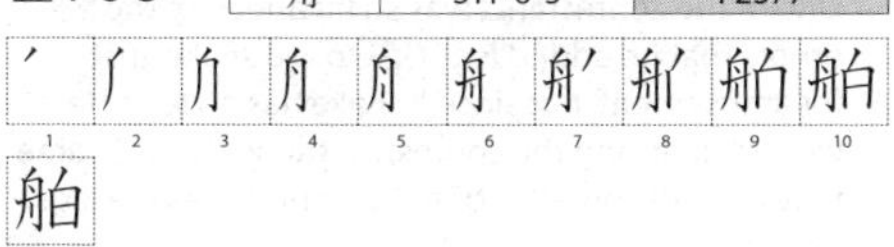

COMPOUNDS

❶ [original meaning] **OCEANGOING SHIP, ship, vessel**

舶用機関 はくようきかん marine engine
船舶 せんぱく ship, vessel; craft

❷ **import, ship**

舶来 はくらい imported goods, foreign-made articles
舶載 はくさい ocean transportation; importation, imported goods

SYNONYMS

❶ **boats and ships**

船 SHIP → 1700
舶 OCEANGOING SHIP → 1699
艦 WARSHIP → 1817
潜 submarine → 0922
舟 SMALL BOAT → 4353
艇 BOAT → 1727
隻 COUNTER FOR SHIPS → 3426

船

1700

1-6-5

▸SHIP

セン ふね ふな- -ぶね

Ⓝ 舩◇ Ⓒ 船 chuán

137	Jōyō-2	U8239
舟	S11-6-5	F0407

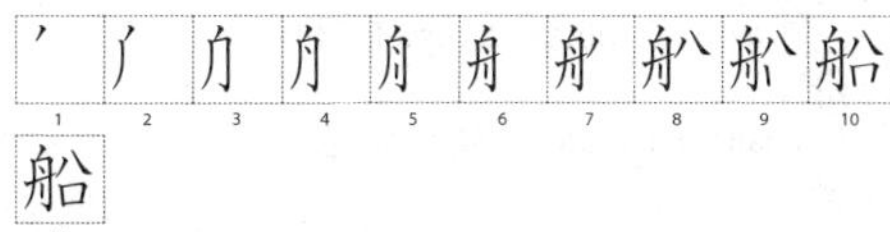

COMPOUNDS

[also suffix]

ⓐ [original meaning] **SHIP, boat, vessel, seacraft**
ⓑ **spaceship, airship**

a 船舶 せんぱく ship, vessel; craft
船長 せんちょう (ship) captain
汽船 きせん steamship
風船 ふうせん balloon
造船 ぞうせん shipbuilding
商船 しょうせん merchant ship, trading vessel
貨物船 かもつせん freighter, cargo ship
b 宇宙船 うちゅうせん spaceship
軌道船 きどうせん orbiter
飛行船 ひこうせん ship, airship

KUN

【ふね 船】

① **SHIP, boat, vessel, seacraft**
船に乗る ふねにのる board a ship
② [also 槽] tub, tank, vessel
湯船 ゆぶね bathtub

【ふな- 船-】[also 舟-] [also prefix] **SHIP**

船乗り ふなのり sailor, seaman
船旅 ふなたび voyage
船便 ふなびん surface [sea] mail; shipping service
船火事 ふなかじ fire on a ship

【-ぶね -船】[also -舟] [also suffix] **SHIP, vessel**

助け船 たすけぶね lifeboat; help
乗り合い船 のりあいぶね ferryboat

SYNONYMS

ⓐ boats and ships

船 SHIP → 1700
舶 OCEANGOING SHIP → 1699
艦 WARSHIP → 1817
潜 submarine → 0922
舟 SMALL BOAT → 4353
艇 BOAT → 1727
隻 COUNTER FOR SHIPS → 3426

ⓑ aircraft and spacecraft

機 AIRCRAFT → 1365
空 aircraft → 2767
船 spaceship → 1700

USAGE

❶【ふね】

船
① ship, boat, vessel, seacraft
② [also 槽] tub, tank, vessel

舟
small boat [craft], (row)boat

槽
[also 船] tub, tank, vessel

❷【ふな-】

船-
[also 舟-] [also prefix] ship

舟-
[also 船-] [also prefix] small boat

❸【-ぶね】

-船
[also -舟] [also suffix] ship, vessel

-舟
[also -船] [also suffix] small boat

HOMOPHONES

ふね
舟 SMALL BOAT → 4353
槽 TANK → 1352

ふな- 舟 SMALL BOAT → 4353
-ぶね 舟 SMALL BOAT → 4353

蛇

▶SNAKE
ジャ ダ へび
Ⓒ 蛇 shé yí

1701
1-6-5

142	Jōyō	U86C7
虫	S11-6-5	F1672

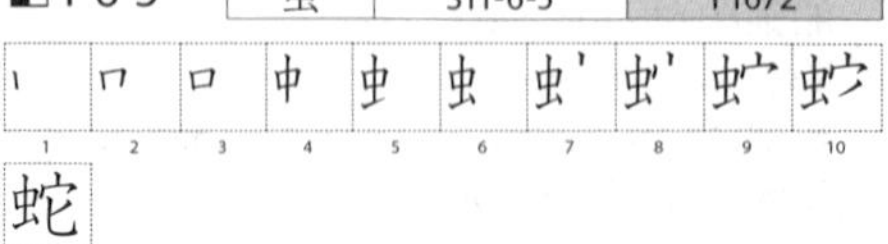

COMPOUNDS

❶ [original meaning] **SNAKE, serpent**

蛇蝎× だかつ snake and scorpion, viper
蛇行する だこうする meander, zigzag
蛇足 だそく superfluity, redundancy
蛇の目 じゃのめ umbrella with a snake's eye pattern; double circle pattern
大蛇 だいじゃ big snake, serpent

❷ objects shaped like a SNAKE, as tubes, pipes or the like

蛇口 じゃぐち faucet
蛇管 じゃかん hose
蛇腹 じゃばら bellows; cornice

INDEPENDENT

【じゃ 蛇】**SNAKE**, serpent

蛇の道は蛇 じゃのみちはへび One devil knows another

KUN

【へび 蛇】[also suffix] **SNAKE, serpent**

蛇の様な へびのような snakelike, snaky, serpentine
蛇座 へびざ the Serpent (constellation)
毒蛇 どくへび poisonous snake
がらがら蛇 がらがらへび rattlesnake

SYNONYMS

❶ snake

蛇 SNAKE → 1701
巳 THE SERPENT → 4197

❶ reptiles and amphibians

亀 TURTLE → 2637
蛇 SNAKE → 1701
竜 DRAGON → 2603
蛙 FROG → 1716
黽 FROG → 4404

COMPOUND FORMATION

【蛇足 だそく】

蛇足 'superfluity, redundancy' derives from an ancient Chinese tale of a group of servants that competed for getting a drink from their master. They held a contest in which the fastest one to draw a picture of a snake (蛇 ❶) was to be the winner. One of the contestants was so far ahead of the others that he added legs (足) to the snake, just for amusement. But since a snake has no legs, he wound up losing the contest. In this way, 蛇足 came to represent something "as superfluous as the legs on a snake."

瓶

▶BOTTLE
ビン かめ▲
Ⓝ 甁 Ⓒ 瓶 píng

1702
1-6-5

98	Jōyō	U74F6
瓦	S11-5-6	F1593

COMPOUNDS

❶ⓐ [also suffix] **BOTTLE, flask, decanter, vase, jar**
ⓑ counter for **BOTTLE**s

a 瓶詰め びんづめ bottling
広口瓶 ひろくちびん widemouthed bottle, jar
花瓶 かびん flower vase
魔法瓶 まほうびん thermos bottle
徳用瓶 とくようびん economy bottle

b 二瓶 ふたびん two bottles

❷ kettle, teapot
鉄瓶 てつびん iron kettle

INDEPENDENT

【びん 瓶】 **BOTTLE, flask, decanter**

KUN

【かめ 瓶】 earthenware pot, jar, vase

SYNONYMS

❶ⓐ **containers**
箱 BOX → 3362
壺 JAR → 2890
槽 TANK → 1352
樽 BARREL → 1368
棺 COFFIN → 1240
桶 BUCKET → 1211
笈 BOX CARRIED ON THE BACK → 3274
鞘 SHEATH → 2259
箪 BAMBOO BOX → 3381
函 BOX → 3724
籠 BASKET → 3398
袋 BAG → 3201
鞄 BAG (for carrying) → 2248
器 VESSEL → 3367
瓶 BOTTLE → 1702
缶 CAN → 2526
缶 EARTHENWARE JAR → 2525

NOTE

➡ see COMPOUND FORMATION for 魔法瓶 まほうびん → 魔 3953

粧

1703
◧ 1-6-6

▶ **APPLY MAKEUP**
ショウ
Ⓒ 妝 zhuāng

119	Jōyō	U7CA7
米	S12-6-6	F1579

COMPOUNDS

● [original meaning] **APPLY MAKEUP [cosmetics], make up, adorn oneself**
化粧する けしょうする make up, put on makeup
美粧院 びしょういん beauty shop

SYNONYMS

● **decorate**
飾 DECORATE → 2150
粧 APPLY MAKEUP → 1703
粉 apply face powder → 1643
装 DRESS → 3327

絵

1704
◧ 1-6-6

▶ **PICTURE**
カイ エ
Ⓝ 繪 Ⓒ 绘 huì

120	Jōyō-2	U7D75
糸	S12-6-6	F0645

COMPOUNDS

● [sometimes also 画 え 3723] [also prefix and suffix] [original meaning] **PICTURE, painting, drawing, sketch, illustration**
絵画 かいが pictures, paintings, drawings
絵本 えほん picture book
絵描き えかき painter, artist
絵の具 えのぐ coloring materials, colors, oils, paint
絵葉書 えはがき picture postcard
絵日記 えにっき diary with illustrations
油絵 あぶらえ oil painting
浮世絵 うきよえ *ukiyoe*, color print of everyday life in old Japan

INDEPENDENT

【え 絵】
ⓐ [sometimes also 画 え 3723] **PICTURE, painting, drawing, sketch, illustration, cut, (woodcut) print**
ⓑ [usu. 画 え 3723] television field

a 絵の展覧会 えのてんらんかい art exhibition

SYNONYMS

● **picture**
絵 PICTURE → 1704
画 PICTURE → 3723
図 DRAWING → 3809

USAGE

【え】

絵

ⓐ [sometimes also 画] picture, painting, drawing, sketch, illustration, cut, (woodcut) print

ⓑ [usu. 画] television field

画

ⓐ [usu. 絵] [also suffix] picture, painting, drawing, sketch, illustration, cut, (woodcut) print

ⓑ [sometimes also 絵] television field

HOMOPHONES

え 画 PICTURE → 3723

絢

1705

1-6-6

▶**GORGEOUS**

ケン ㊔ あや じゅん

ⓒ 绚 xuàn

120	Names	U7D62
糸	S12-6-6	F2923

COMPOUNDS

ⓐ GORGEOUS, resplendent, brilliant, florid

ⓑ [original meaning, now archaic] **GORGEOUS** pattern, beautiful design

a 絢爛たる けんらんたる gorgeous, dazzling; flowery (speech)

b 絢文 けんぶん colorful pattern

SYNONYMS

ⓐ beautiful

美 BEAUTIFUL → 2817
彪 MAGNIFICENT → 4115
綺 BEAUTIFUL → 1734
娃 BEAUTIFUL → 0419
佳 FINE → 0096
瑶 EXQUISITE → 1301
麗 OF GRACEFUL BEAUTY → 2672
艶 CHARMING → 2403
妙 of marvelous beauty → 0280
華 MAGNIFICENT → 2841
絢 GORGEOUS → 1705
斐 florid → 3449

結

1706

1-6-6

▶**TIE**
▶**CONCLUDE**

ケツ ケチ▲ むす(ぶ) ゆ(う) ゆ(わえる)

ⓒ 结 jié jiē

120	Jōyō-4	U7D50
糸	S12-6-6	F0156

COMPOUNDS

❶ⓐ [original meaning] **TIE (up), bind, knot**

ⓑ (bring or come together closely) **TIE, unite, join**

a 結髪 けっぱつ hairdressing, hairdo
結縄 けつじょう knotting a rope
結束 けっそく unity, union
連結する れんけつする connect, couple, link
直結する ちょっけつする connect directly with

b 結合する けつごうする unite, combine, join together
結婚 けっこん marriage
結縁 けちえん making a connection (with Buddha)
締結する ていけつする conclude, contract
妥結 だけつ compromise, agreement, understanding

❷ⓐ form into a mass, congeal, coagulate

ⓑ form (an organization), organize, set up

a 結晶 けっしょう crystallization, crystal; grain; fruit(s)
結核 けっかく tuberculosis
結集 けっしゅう concentration, regimentation
凍結 とうけつ freezing
凝結する ぎょうけつする congeal, coagulate, solidify

b 結成する けっせいする form, organize
結構 けっこう structure, construction; quite, well enough, fairly well; all right; no thank you
結社 けっしゃ association, society, fraternity
結団する けつだんする form into an organization

❸ⓐ (bring to an end) **CONCLUDE, close, finish, settle**

ⓑ concluding stanza in a Chinese quatrain

a 結論 けつろん conclusion
結局 けっきょく after all, finally, in conclusion
結末 けつまつ termination, end, close, conclusion
結語 けつご conclusion, concluding remarks
結願 けちがん expiration of one's vow term
終結する しゅうけつする end, close, terminate
完結する かんけつする complete, conclude, finish; be complete, be concluded, be finished

b 起承転結 きしょうてんけつ introduction, development, turn and conclusion (of a Chinese quatrain)

❹ bear fruit, result in

結実する けつじつする bear fruit; be successful, achieve success
結果 けっか result, outcome, consequence

KUN

【むすぶ 結ぶ】

①ⓐ **TIE (up), bind, knot**

ⓑ (connect as if by tying) **TIE, join, link**

a 紐を結ぶ ひもをむすぶ tie a string

b 結び付ける むすびつける tie up, join together, link together

東京と大阪を結ぶ とうきょうとおおさかをむすぶ link Tokyo with Osaka
手を結ぶ てをむすぶ join hands

② (settle a transaction) **CONCLUDE**, close, make (a contract)
国交を結ぶ こっこうをむすぶ enter into diplomatic relations

③ take form, result in
実を結ぶ みをむすぶ bear fruit
夢を結ぶ ゆめをむすぶ fall asleep, sleep

④ (bring to an end) **CONCLUDE, close, finish**
結び むすび end, close, conclusion; [also suffix] knot, tie; uniting; *Japanese grammar* relation, connection; rice ball
小結び こむすび third ranking sumo wrestler

⑤ set up, build
庵を結ぶ いおりをむすぶ build oneself a hermitage

【ゆう 結う】dress (the hair), do up (one's hair); TIE (up), bind, fasten
結納 ゆいのう ceremonial exchange of betrothal gifts; betrothal present [gift]
髪結い かみゆい hairdresser; hairdressing
帯を結い上げる おびをゆいあげる do up a sash

【ゆわえる 結わえる】TIE (up), bind, fasten
縄を杭に結わえる なわをくいにゆわえる tie [fasten] a rope to a post

SYNONYMS

❶ⓐ join
結 TIE → 1706
繋 CONNECT → 3612
縛 BIND → 1779
綴 BIND → 1746
繃 BIND UP → 1787
束 TIE UP → 4369
梱 PACK → 1205
連 LINK → 3849
係 CONNECT → 0108
接 join → 0607

ⓑ combine
合 COMBINE → 2511
結 TIE → 1706
統 UNITE → 1710
括 LUMP TOGETHER → 0449
総 integrate → 1743
併 join together → 0092
綜 INTEGRATE → 1744
纏める PUT TOGETHER → 1814

❷ⓐ solidify and coagulate
固 solidify → 3830
凝 CONGEAL → 0198
結 form into a mass → 1706
凍 FREEZE → 0146

ⓑ organize
組 ORGANIZE → 1693
結 form → 1706
編 put together → 1755

❸ⓐ end
終 END → 1692
絶 COME TO AN END → 1711
閉 CLOSE → 4116
了 FINISH → 4157
済 SETTLE → 0634
-上げる completion suffix → 4212
完 COMPLETE → 2727
結 CONCLUDE → 1706
竣 COMPLETE → 1528

絞

▸STRANGLE
▸WRING
コウ しぼ(る) し(める) し(まる)

1707

Ⓒ 绞 jiǎo

1-6-6

120	Jōyō	U7D5E
糸	S12-6-6	F1643

COMPOUNDS

● STRANGLE, strangulate, hang
絞殺する こうさつする strangle, hang
絞首刑 こうしゅけい death [execution] by hanging
絞罪 こうざい hanging, execution by hanging

KUN

【しぼる 絞る】
①ⓐ **WRING, wring out**
ⓑ strain, rack (one's brains)
a 絞り しぼり iris diaphragm; white spots on a dyed ground, tie-dyed fabrics; variegation, spots (in flowers)
お絞り おしぼり wet towel, steamed towel
雑巾を絞る ぞうきんをしぼる wring a floorcloth
b 知恵を絞る ちえをしぼる rack one's brains, think hard

② tighten, close tight, press
袋の口を絞る ふくろのくちをしぼる close a bag tight by pulling the drawstring

③ⓐ make narrow, focus; lower (the volume)
ⓑ narrow down to, focus on
b 議論を要点だけに絞る ぎろんをようてんだけにしぼる narrow an argument down

【しめる 絞める】
① **STRANGLE, strangulate, wring**
絞め殺す しめころす strangle to death

首を絞める くびをしめる strangle, wring the neck

② squeeze

羽交い絞め はがいじめ pinioning

【しまる 絞まる】 be **STRANGLEd**

首が絞まる くびがしまる have one's neck wrung

SYNONYMS

● **kill**

殺 KILL → 1677

劉 KILL → 2398

刺 stab to death → 1625

絞 STRANGLE → 1707

窒 CHOKE → 2853

【しぼる】

①ⓐ **squeeze**

搾 SQUEEZE → 0798

絞る WRING → 1707

圧 apply pressure → 3688

USAGE

❶【しぼる】

絞る

①ⓐ wring, wring out

ⓑ strain, rack (one's brains)

② tighten, close tight, press

③ⓐ make narrow, focus; lower (the volume)

ⓑ narrow down to, focus on

搾る

①ⓐ squeeze, press, squash, extract

ⓑ squeeze (money from), sweat, screw

② scold, reprimand

❷【しぼり】

絞り

① iris diaphragm

②ⓐ white spots on a dyed ground, tie-dyed fabrics

ⓑ variegation, spots (in flowers)

搾り

squeezing

HOMOPHONES

しぼる 搾 SQUEEZE → 0798

しぼり 搾 SQUEEZE → 0798

しめる

締 CONCLUDE → 1761

〆 SUM → 4179

閉 CLOSE → 4116

しまる

締 CONCLUDE → 1761

閉 CLOSE → 4116

NOTE

➡ see also USAGE note at 締 1761

給

1708

1-6-6

▶**SUPPLY**

▶**PAY**

キュウ たま(う)▲ たも(う)▲ -たま(え)▲

Ⓒ 给 gěi jǐ

120	Jōyō-4	U7D66
糸	S12-6-6	F0788

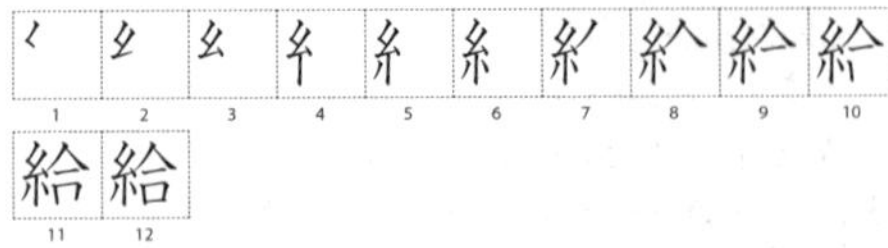

COMPOUNDS

❶ⓐ (provide with something requisite) **SUPPLY, provide**

ⓑ [original meaning] (make up for a deficiency) **SUPPLY, supplement**

ⓒ *economics* **SUPPLY**

a 給水 きゅうすい water supply

給油 きゅうゆ supply of oil

給食 きゅうしょく (provision of) meals

支給 しきゅう provision, supply; allowance, grant; payment

配給 はいきゅう distribution, supply; rationing

供給する きょうきゅうする supply, furnish, provide

b 補給 ほきゅう supply, replenishment

自給 じきゅう self-supply, self-support

c 需給 じゅきゅう supply and demand

❷ give, donate, grant

給血 きゅうけつ donation of blood

❸ [also suffix] **PAY, salary, wages**

給料 きゅうりょう salary, pay, wages

給与 きゅうよ allowance, grant; pay, salary

給付する きゅうふする make a presentation, grant, pay

月給 げっきゅう monthly pay [salary]

俸給 ほうきゅう salary, pay

時間給 じかんきゅう payment by the hour

固定給 こていきゅう regular pay, fixed salary

初任給 しょにんきゅう initial salary

❹ serve; servant

給仕 きゅうじ office boy, page (boy), waiter; service at table

女給 じょきゅう waitress, barmaid, hostess

INDEPENDENT

【きゅうする 給する】 allow, grant; **SUPPLY**, provide

KUN

【たまう, たもう 給う】

① [sometimes also 賜う] [suffix] *literary* deign to (perform an action for an inferior)

天皇が立ち給う てんのうがたちたまう His Majesty deigns to stand up

② [usu. 賜う] *literary* deign to give, bestow, grant, award

拝謁を給う はいえつをたまう deign to grant an audience

お言葉を給う おことばをたまう deign to give a message

【-たまえ -給え】 verbal suffix for forming polite imperatives

行き給え いきたまえ(=ゆきたまえ) Please go

SYNONYMS

❶ⓐ supply

供 supply → 0098
給 SUPPLY → 1708
納 deliver goods to a customer → 1652

ⓑ supplement

補 SUPPLEMENT → 1529
足 supplement → 2714
給 SUPPLY → 1708
充 fill up (a vacancy) → 2507

❸ pay and earnings

給 PAY → 1708
賃 WAGE → 3341
料 FEE → 1644
俸 SALARY → 0128
禄 RETAINER'S STIPEND → 1264
収 income → 0031

USAGE

【たまう】

給う

① [sometimes also 賜う] [suffix] *literary* deign to (perform an action for an inferior)

② [usu. 賜う] *literary* deign to give, bestow, grant, award

賜う

① [sometimes also 給う] *literary* deign to give, bestow, grant, award

② [usu. 給う] [suffix] *literary* (perform an action for an inferior) deign to

HOMOPHONES

たまう 賜 DEIGN TO GIVE → 1994

絡

1709

1-6-6

▶INTERLINK
▶ENTWINE

ラク から(む) から(まる) から(める)

Ⓒ 络 luò lào

120	Jōyō	U7D61
糸	S12-6-6	F1010

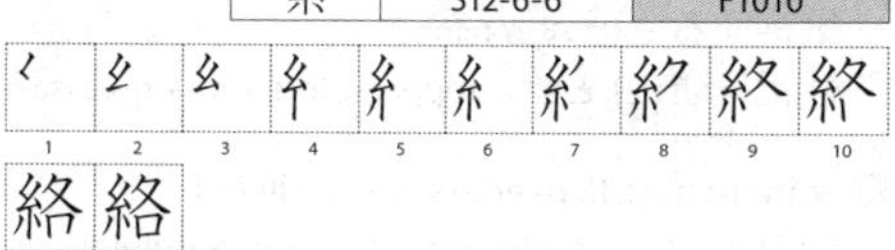

COMPOUNDS

❶ INTERLINK, link, connect, join

連絡 れんらく connection, contact; communication

脈絡 みゃくらく logical connection, chain of reasoning

短絡 たんらく short circuit

❷ [original meaning] **ENTWINE, twine, intertwine**

籠絡する ろうらくする inveigle, ensnare, entice

交絡 こうらく *statistics* confounding, interrelationship

❸ *Chinese medicine* subsidiary meridians in the human body through which vital energy, blood and nutriments flow

KUN

【からむ 絡む】 **ENTWINE, twine around, get caught; be involved; pick a fight**

絡み からみ entanglement; involvement, relationship

絡み合う からみあう intertwine, entwine, interlock

痰×が絡む たんがからむ Phlegm sticks in the throat

金が絡んだ問題 かねがからんだもんだい matter involving money

【からまる 絡まる】 **ENTWINE, twine around, get caught [entangled]**

絡まり からまり entanglement

木に絡まる植物 きにからまるしょくぶつ creeping plant on trees

【からめる 絡める】 **ENTWINE, twine around, entangle; coat, cover, baste; link, involve**

指を絡め合う ゆびをからめあう entangle (each other's) fingers

魚にたれを絡める さかなにたれをからめる baste fish with sauce

SYNONYMS

❶ relate

関 CONCERN → 4129
係 CONNECT → 0108
絡 INTERLINK → 1709
渉 HAVE RELATIONS WITH → 0638
連 LINK → 3849
聯 LINK → 1797

❷ wind and twine

巻 ROLL UP → 3273
捲 ROLL UP → 0598
繰る REEL → 1806
絡 ENTWINE → 1709
纏 WIND AROUND → 1814

米【糸】羊舟虫吉

統 1710

1-6-6

▸UNITE
▸INTERCONNECTED SYSTEM

トウ す(べる) ㊔ おさむ のり むね もと つな

Ⓒ 统 tǒng

120	Jōyō-5	U7D71
糸	S12-6-6	F0462

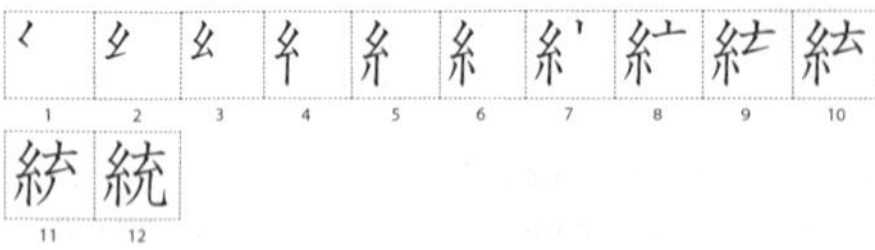

COMPOUNDS

❶ **UNITE, unify, gather into one**

統一 とういつ unity, coordination, standardization
統合する とうごうする integrate, combine, unify
統計 とうけい statistics
統轄 とうかつ general control, control and jurisdiction

❷ (unite under one rule) **rule, govern, command**

統治する とうちする rule, govern, reign over
統制 とうせい control, regulation
統率 とうそつ leadership, command
総統 そうとう sovereign, highest post of the government
大統領 だいとうりょう president

❸ **INTERCONNECTED SYSTEM, lineage**

系統 けいとう system; geological formation; lineage, ancestry
血統 けっとう lineage, blood, bloodline
正統派 せいとうは orthodox school
伝統 でんとう tradition, convention

❹ [rare] counter for set nets

二統 にとう two set nets

❺ *geol* series

沖積統 ちゅうせきとう alluvial series

INDEPENDENT

【とう 統】 *geol* series

KUN

【すべる 統べる】 **UNITE, unify, gather into one;** (unite under one rule) **rule, govern, command**

統べ合わせる すべあわせる unite, bring together
三軍を統べる さんぐんをすべる command three forces

SYNONYMS

❶ **combine**

合 COMBINE → 2511
結 TIE → 1706
統 UNITE → 1710
括 LUMP TOGETHER → 0449
総 integrate → 1743
併 join together → 0092
綜 INTEGRATE → 1744
纏める PUT TOGETHER → 1814

❷ **govern**

治 GOVERN → 0393
統 rule → 1710

❸ **system**

系 SYSTEM → 2443
制 SYSTEM → 1624
統 INTERCONNECTED SYSTEM → 1710
網 network → 1737

NOTE

➡ see COMPOUND FORMATION for 伝統 でんとう → 伝 0048

絶 1711

1-6-6

▸BREAK OFF
▸COME TO AN END

ゼツ た(える) た(やす) た(つ)

Ⓝ 絕 Ⓒ 绝 jué

120	Jōyō-5	U7D76
糸	S12-6-6	F0502

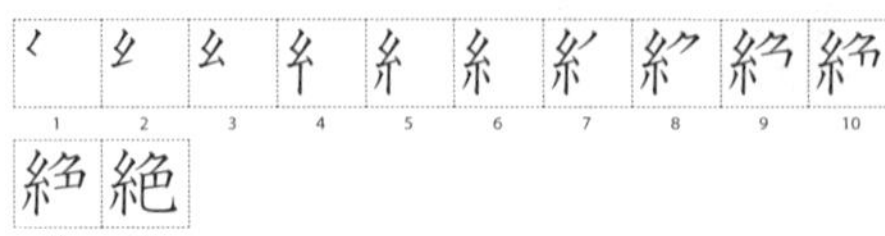

COMPOUNDS

❶ⓐ **BREAK OFF, discontinue, cut off, sever**
ⓑ cutoff, isolated

a 絶交 ぜっこう breaking off friendship [diplomatic relations]
絶縁 ぜつえん breaking off relations; insulation, isolation
絶版になる ぜっぱんになる go out of print
絶食 ぜっしょく fasting
断絶 だんぜつ severance, rupture; discontinuation
中絶 ちゅうぜつ interruption, discontinuance; abortion
根絶する こんぜつする eradicate, exterminate, root out

b 絶海 ぜっかい distant seas
絶島 ぜっとう lonely island

❷ **COME TO AN END, cease to exist**

絶望 ぜつぼう despair, hopelessness
絶滅 ぜつめつ extermination, eradication; extinction
絶息する ぜっそくする expire, die
気絶する きぜつする faint
杜絶(=途絶) とぜつ stoppage, interruption, cessation

❸ **without match, peerless, unparalleled**

絶対 ぜったい absoluteness; absolute; absolutely, unconditionally

絶対に ぜったいに absolutely, unconditionally
絶賛 ぜっさん great admiration
絶好の ぜっこうの splendid, grand, best, golden
絶妙な ぜつみょうな miraculous, exquisite, superb
絶世の ぜっせいの peerless, unequaled
絶景 ぜっけい superb view, picturesque scenery
絶唱 ぜっしょう superb song [poem]
空前絶後 くうぜんぜつご the first and probably the last

❹ reject, decline, refuse
拒絶する きょぜつする refuse, reject, deny
謝絶 しゃぜつ declination, refusal

❺ Chinese quatrain poetry
絶句 ぜっく Chinese quatrain poetry; breaking off in one's speech

INDEPENDENT

【ぜっする 絶する】be beyond (as words or imagination)
想像を絶する そうぞうをぜっする be beyond imagination, be unimaginable

KUN

【たえる 絶える】**COME TO AN END, cease to exist; become extinct**
絶えず たえず constantly, always
絶え間 たえま interval, gap
絶え間無く たえまなく incessantly, without a break
絶えてしまった種 たえてしまったしゅ extinct species
途絶える とだえる come to an end
通信が絶える つうしんがたえる Correspondence has ceased
死に絶える しにたえる die out, become extinct

【たやす 絶やす】**exterminate, extirpate, eradicate; allow to run out, run out of**
鼠を絶やす ねずみをたやす exterminate rats
酒を絶やす さけをたやす run out of wine

【たつ 絶つ】
① **BREAK OFF, discontinue, cut off, sever**
連絡を絶つ れんらくをたつ sever the connection
② exterminate, extirpate, eradicate
禍根を絶つ かこんをたつ strike at the root of an evil

SYNONYMS

❶ⓐ discontinue
絶 BREAK OFF → 1711
廃 ABOLISH → 3902
断 CUT OFF → 1885
止 STOP → 3659
休 suspend → 0056
停 suspend → 0156
已む CEASE → 4185

❷ end
終 END → 1692
絶 COME TO AN END → 1711
閉 CLOSE → 4116
了 FINISH → 4157
済 SETTLE → 0634
-上げる completion suffix → 4212
完 COMPLETE → 2727
結 CONCLUDE → 1706
竣 COMPLETE → 1528

❷ come to an end
尽 be exhausted → 3786
絶 COME TO AN END → 1711

❸ excellent and superior
優 SUPERIOR → 0200
絶 without match → 1711
卓 PROMINENT → 2561
快 splendid → 0289
妙 MARVELOUS → 0280
秀 EXCELLENT → 3152
英 DISTINGUISHED → 2782
尤 outstanding → 3755
傑 outstanding → 0175
穎 TALENTED → 2036
逸 exceptional → 3872
名 first-rate → 2693
上 of upper grade → 4212

HOMOPHONES

たつ
断 CUT OFF → 1885
裁 CUT OUT → 4090

NOTE

➡ see USAGE note at 断 1885
➡ see COMPOUND FORMATION for 絶対 ぜったい → 対 1025

絲

1712
◧ 1-6-6

▶THREAD
シ いと

120	Nonstandard	U7D72
糸	S12-6-6	F0000

traditional form → see 糸 at 2703

絕

1713
◧ 1-6-6

▶BREAK OFF
▶COME TO AN END
ゼツ た(える) た(やす) た(つ)

120	Nonstandard	U7D55
糸	S12-6-6	F0000

traditional form → see 絶 at 1711

1 米 糸 【羊】 舟 虫 吉 舌

翔

1714

1-6-6

▶SOAR

ショウ かけ(る) と(ぶ) ㊔ か が

Ⓝ 翔 Ⓒ 翔 xiáng

124	Names	U7FD4
羽	S12-6-6	F1552

COMPOUNDS

● **SOAR, fly**

翔破する しょうはする complete a flight
飛翔 ひしょう flight, soaring
滑翔機 かっしょうき sailplane, glider
競翔 きょうしょう flying race (between pigeons)

KUN

【かける 翔る】**SOAR, fly**

天翔る あまがける ride the skies
飛び翔る とびかける soar, fly

【とぶ 翔ぶ】**SOAR, fly**

翔んでる とんでる groovy, far-out, flipped out

SYNONYMS

● **fly**

飛 FLY → 4389
蜚 FLY → 3473
翔 SOAR → 1714
航 NAVIGATE → 1671

HOMOPHONES

かける

駆 DRIVE → 2293
掛 SET → 0596
懸 SUSPEND → 3632
架 LAY ACROSS → 3178
賭 WAGER → 2021

とぶ

飛 FLY → 4389
跳 JUMP → 1934

NOTE

➡ see USAGE notes at 掛 0596 and 飛 4389

翔

1715

1-6-6

▶SOAR

ショウ かけ(る) と(ぶ) ㊔ か が

124	Nonstandard	U7FD4
羽	S12-6-6	F0000

traditional form → see 翔 at 1714

艇

1-6-6

incorrect stroke-count

➡ see 1-6-7: 舟 at 1727

蛙

1716

1-6-6

▶FROG

ア ワ かえる かわず

Ⓒ 蛙 wā

142	Non-Jōyō	U86D9
虫	S12-6-6	F2550

COMPOUNDS

● [original meaning] **FROG, toad**

蛙鳴蟬噪× あめいせんそう annoying noise, loud buzz; fruitless argument
蛙声 あせい croak of a frog [toad]
蛙黽 あぼう [archaic] tree frog [toad]

KUN

【かえる 蛙】**FROG, toad**

蛙跳び かえるとび leapfrog
蛙泳ぎ かえるおよぎ breaststroke
蛙の子は蛙 かえるのこはかえる Like father, like son
雨蛙 あまがえる tree frog, esp. Japanese tree frog
蟇×蛙 ひきがえる toad, esp. Japanese toad
牛蛙 うしがえる American bullfrog
河鹿蛙 かじかがえる kajika frog, *Buergeria buergeri*

【かわず 蛙】

ⓐ **FROG**, toad
ⓑ kajika **FROG**, *Buergeria buergeri*

a 井の中の蛙大海を知らず いのなかのかわずたいかいをしらず A frog in the well knows nothing of the great ocean/have limited views [opinions]

SYNONYMS

● **reptiles and amphibians**

亀 TURTLE → 2637
蛇 SNAKE → 1701
竜 DRAGON → 2603
蛙 FROG → 1716
黽 FROG → 4404

蛔

1717

1-6-6

▶ROUNDWORM

カイ

Ⓒ 蛔 huí

142	Non-Jōyō	U86D4
虫	S12-6-6	F0000

COMPOUNDS

● [now replaced by 回 3793] [original meaning] **ROUNDWORM, ascarid**

蛔虫 かいちゅう roundworm, ascarid

SYNONYMS

● **insects**

蚊 MOSQUITO → 1673
蛍 FIREFLY → 3204
蝶 BUTTERFLY → 1772
蚕 SILKWORM → 3107

蟬 CICADA → 1804
蜂 BEE → 1728
蛔 ROUNDWORM → 1717

喆 1718

◧ 1-6-6

▸SAGACIOUS
▸PHILOSOPHY

テツ ㊔ さと さとし さとる あき あきら のり

30	Nonstandard	U5586
口	S12-3-9	F0000

traditional form → see 哲 at 3402

琵

◧ 1-6-6

incorrect classification
➡ see ⬒2-8-4: 琵 at 3453

粮 1719

◧ 1-6-7

▸FOOD PROVISIONS

リョウ ロウ かて

119	Nonstandard	U7CAE
米	S13-6-7	F0000

traditional form → see 糧 at 1800

継 1720

◧ 1-6-7

▸SUCCEED

ケイ つ(ぐ) まま-▲

Ⓝ 繼 Ⓒ 继 jì

120	Jōyō	U7D99
糸	S13-6-7	F0748

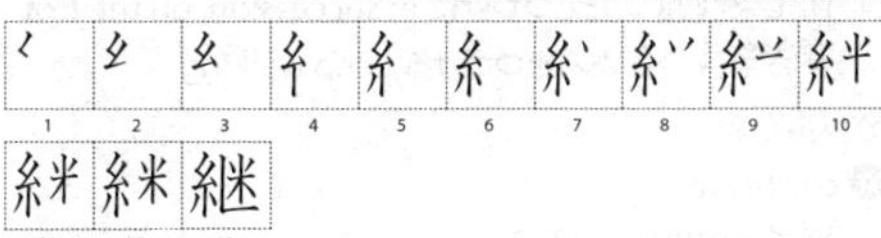

COMPOUNDS

❶ⓐ (come after and take the place of) **SUCCEED (to), accede, inherit**
ⓑ (come next or after) **SUCCEED, continue, follow**
ⓒ **execute (a race) by relay**

a 継承する けいしょうする succeed to, accede to, inherit
継嗣 けいし successor, heir, heiress
継投 けいとう relieving the (starting) pitcher
後継 こうけい succession; successor, inheritor, heir
b 継続する けいぞくする continue, last, maintain
継起する けいきする occur in succession
c 継走 けいそう relay race
継泳 けいえい relay swimming
継電器 けいでんき (electric) relay
中継 ちゅうけい relay, rebroadcasting

❷ step-; second (wife or husband)
継母 けいぼ stepmother
継夫 けいふ second husband

KUN

【つぐ 継ぐ】

① **SUCCEED (to), accede; inherit**
家を継ぐ いえをつぐ succeed to a house
受け継ぐ うけつぐ inherit, succeed to
跡継ぎ あとつぎ successor, heir
引き継ぐ ひきつぐ take over, hand over; succeed to, inherit

② couple, link, relay
継ぎ足す つぎたす add to; extend, piece out
言葉を継ぐ ことばをつぐ continue (to say)

③ **patch (up)**
継ぎ つぎ a patch
継ぎ接ぎ つぎはぎ patching (and darning)

④ add to, replenish, feed

【まま- 継-】 step-
継母 ままはは stepmother
継子 ままこ stepchild

SYNONYMS

❶ⓐ **succeed**
継 SUCCEED → 1720
承 succeed to → 0016
嗣 inherit → 2153

ⓑ **continue**
続 CONTINUE → 1722
継 SUCCEED → 1720
連 IN SUCCESSION → 3849
持 HOLD → 0447

❷ **related by marriage**
義 -in-law → 2948
継 step- → 1720

HOMOPHONES

つぐ
接 CONTACT → 0607
次 NEXT → 0058
注 POUR → 0383
つぎ 次 NEXT → 0058

NOTE

➡ see USAGE notes at 接 0607 and 次 0058

絹 1721

◧ 1-6-7

▸SILK

ケン きぬ

Ⓒ 绢 juàn

120	Jōyō-6	U7D79
糸	S13-6-7	F1892

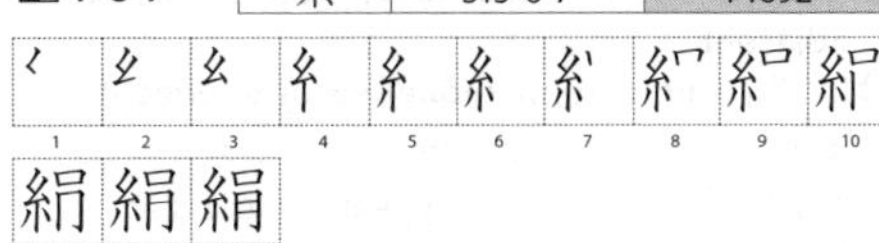

COMPOUNDS

● [original meaning] **SILK**

絹布 けんぷ silk, silk cloth
絹糸 けんし(=きぬいと) silk thread
人絹 じんけん artificial silk; rayon
正絹 しょうけん (pure) silk

KUN

【きぬ 絹】**SILK, silk fabrics**

絹織物 きぬおりもの silk fabrics [goods]
絹地 きぬじ silk fabrics
絹糸 きぬいと silk thread
薄絹 うすぎぬ sheer silk

SYNONYMS

● **fabrics**

織 woven fabric → 1801
紬 PONGEE → 1684
紗 GAUZE → 1653
絹 SILK → 1721
綾 TWILL → 1740
綿 COTTON → 1736
棉 COTTON → 1244
麻 HEMP → 3878
毛 wool → 4264
錦 BROCADE → 2181

USAGE

【きぬ】

絹
silk, silk fabrics

衣
elegant garment

HOMOPHONES

きぬ 衣 GARMENT → 2506

続

1722

1-6-7

▶**CONTINUE**

ゾク　つづ(く)　つづ(ける) ㊔ つぎ　つぐ

Ⓝ 續 Ⓒ 续 xù

120	Jōyō-4	U7D9A
糸	S13-6-7	F0230

COMPOUNDS

ⓐ [original meaning] **CONTINUE, follow, ensue, be adjacent**

ⓑ [prefix] **continuation, sequel, second series**

a 続行 ぞっこう continuation
続出する ぞくしゅつする appear in succession
続落 ぞくらく continuous drop (of stocks)
続続 ぞくぞく in rapid succession, one after another
継続する けいぞくする continue, last, maintain
連続 れんぞく continuation, succession, series
接続する せつぞくする connect, join
持続力 じぞくりょく tenacity

b 続近代文明論 ぞくきんだいぶんめいろん Later Thoughts on Modern Civilization

INDEPENDENT

【ぞく 続】continuation, sequel, second series

正と続 せいとぞく first and second series

KUN

【つづく 続く】*vi* **CONTINUE, go on, follow, ensue; be adjacent, lead to**

続き つづき continuation, sequel, second series; [also suffix] continuation (in time and space), succession, spell
続き物 つづきもの serial story
晴天続き せいてんつづき spell of fine weather
引き続く ひきつづく continue, last; occur in succession, ensue
寝室に続く廊下 しんしつにつづくろうか corridor leading to the bedroom
手続き てつづき procedure, formalities

【つづける 続ける】*vt* [also verbal suffix] **CONTINUE, keep up, go ahead**

続け様に つづけざまに successively, in a row
立て続けに たてつづけに in succession, on the trot
歩き続ける あるきつづける keep walking

SYNONYMS

ⓐ **continue**

続 CONTINUE → 1722
継 SUCCEED → 1720
連 IN SUCCESSION → 3849
持 HOLD → 0447

經

1723

1-6-7

▶**PASS THROUGH**
▶**MANAGE**

ケイ　キョウ　へ(る)　た(つ)　たていと
㊔ つね　のぶ　のり

120	Nonstandard	U7D93
糸	S13-6-7	F0000

traditional form → see 経 at 1687

紘

1724

1-6-7

▶**WIDE-RANGING**

コウ ㊔ ひろ　ひろし　ひろむ

120	Nonstandard	U7D8B
糸	S13-6-7	F0000

traditional form → see 紘 at 1650

綀

1725

◧ 1-6-7

▶**WEAVE**

ショク シキ お(る) お(り) おり -おり -お(り)

120	Nonstandard	U26017
糸	S13-6-7	F0000

traditional form → see 織 at 1801

辞

1726

◧ 1-6-7

▶**WORD**
▶**RESIGN**

ジ や(める)

Ⓝ 辭 Ⓒ 辞 cí

160	Jōyō-4	U8F9E
辛	S13-7-6	F0942

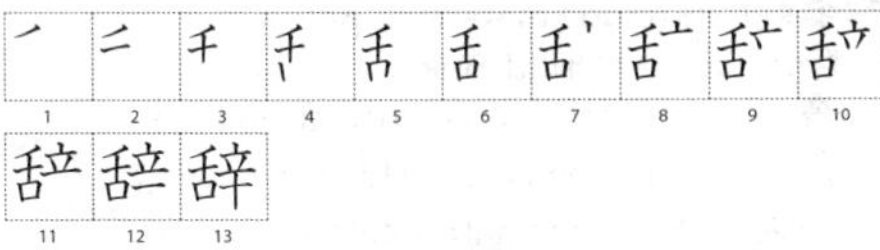

COMPOUNDS

❶ⓐ **WORD, term, phrase, expression, sentence**
ⓑ *gram* function **WORD**, particle

a 辞典 じてん dictionary
辞書 じしょ dictionary
世辞 せじ compliment
式辞 しきじ address
措辞 そじ phraseology, wording
b 接辞 せつじ affix

❷ **RESIGN, retire, quit**
辞職 じしょく resignation
辞表 じひょう (letter of) resignation
辞意 じい intention to resign

❸ **decline, refuse**
辞退 じたい declining, refusal

❹ leave, depart
辞去する じきょする leave, quit, retire
辞世 じせい passing away; death poem

❺ **express one's gratitude**
辞儀 じぎ bow, polite bow

❻ form of poetic prose in ancient China
楚辞 そじ collection of poems by Qu Yuan and others, Chuci

INDEPENDENT

【じ 辞】formal message; **WORD**, expression; function word; form of poetic prose in ancient China
告別の辞 こくべつのじ parting [farewell] address

【じする 辞する】**RESIGN**; decline; take one's leave
職を辞する しょくをじする resign one's post

KUN

【やめる 辞める】**RESIGN, retire, quit**
会社を辞める かいしゃをやめる leave the company

SYNONYMS

❶ **words and expressions**
語 WORD → 1944
辞 WORD → 1726
詞 WORDS → 1897
句 PHRASE → 3685
諺 PROVERB → 2006
喩 METAPHOR → 0671

❷ **resign**
辞 RESIGN → 1726
退 retire → 3838

USAGE

【やめる】
辞める
resign, retire, quit
罷める
[in the form of 罷めさせる やめさせる] fire, discharge
止める
[sometimes also 已める]
①ⓐ stop (performing an action), cease, discontinue
ⓑ give up, abandon, quit
② abolish, do away with
已める
[usu. 止める] same as 止める

HOMOPHONES

やめる
罷 DISMISS → 3234
止 STOP → 3659
已 CEASE → 4185

NOTE

➡ see COMPOUND FORMATION for 措辞 そじ → 措 0610

艇

1727

◧ 1-6-7

▶**BOAT**

テイ

Ⓒ 艇 tǐng

137	Jōyō	U8247
舟	S13-6-7	F2231

COMPOUNDS

● [also suffix] [original meaning] **BOAT, small boat, light craft**
艇長 ていちょう coxswain, captain (of a submarine)
舟艇 しゅうてい boat, craft
短艇 たんてい boat
競艇 きょうてい boat race
艦艇 かんてい war vessels

警備艇 けいびてい guardship
救命艇 きゅうめいてい lifeboat

INDEPENDENT

【てい 艇】small **BOAT**, boat

SYNONYMS

❶ **boats and ships**
船 SHIP → 1700
舶 OCEANGOING SHIP → 1699
艦 WARSHIP → 1817
潜 submarine → 0922
舟 SMALL BOAT → 4353
艇 BOAT → 1727
隻 COUNTER FOR SHIPS → 3426

蜂

▶BEE
ホウ はち
Ⓒ 蜂 fēng

1728
1-6-7

142	Jōyō	U8702
虫	S13-6-7	F2052

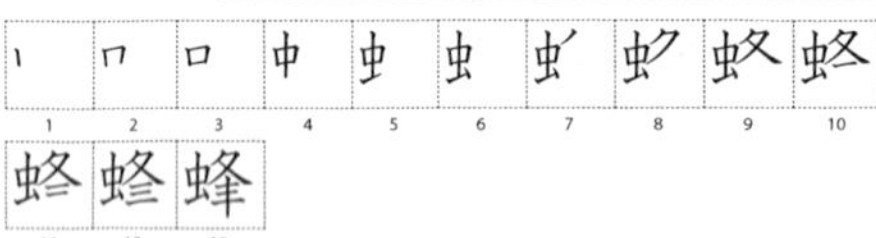

COMPOUNDS

❶ **BEE, wasp, hornet**
蜂巣 ほうそう beehive, hive
養蜂 ようほう beekeeping, apiculture
❷ swarm, crowd together
蜂起 ほうき uprising, revolt

KUN

【はち 蜂】**BEE, wasp, hornet**
蜂蜜 はちみつ honey
蜂鳥 はちどり hummingbird
蜂の巣 はちのす beehive, honeycomb
蜜蜂 みつばち honeybee, hive bee
熊蜂 くまばち hornet
女王蜂 じょおうばち queen bee

SYNONYMS

❶ **insects**
蚊 MOSQUITO → 1673
蛍 FIREFLY → 3204
蝶 BUTTERFLY → 1772
蚕 SILKWORM → 3107
蟬 CICADA → 1804
蜂 BEE → 1728
蛔 ROUNDWORM → 1717

精

▶REFINE
▶ESSENCE
▶SPIRIT
セイ ショウ ㊔ すぐる きよし きよ
Ⓝ 精 Ⓒ 精 jīng

1729
1-6-8

119	Jōyō-5	U7CBE
米	S14-6-8	F0581

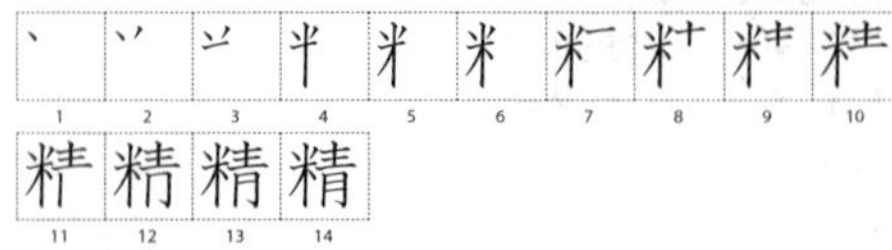

COMPOUNDS

❶ⓐ **REFINE (crude materials), polish**
ⓑ (purified) **REFINEd, fine**
ⓒ [original meaning] polish rice, clean
a 精錬 せいれん refining, smelting; tempering
精製 せいせい refining; careful manufacture
b 精糖 せいとう refined sugar, sugar refining
精油 せいゆ refined oil; essential oil, essence
c 精白 せいはく refining, polishing
精米 せいまい rice polishing; polished [white] rice
❷ⓐ (essential part of a substance) **ESSENCE**, extract, spirit
ⓑ (essential substance of life) **sperm, semen**
a 酒精 しゅせい spirit of wine, alcohol
木精 もくせい wood alcohol; spirit of wood
糊精 こせい dextrin(e)
薄荷精 はっかせい essence of mint
b 精子 せいし sperm
精液 せいえき semen, sperm
受精 じゅせい fertilization, impregnation; pollination
夢精 むせい nocturnal emission, wet dream
❸ⓐ (essential part) **ESSENCE, quintessence, spirit**
ⓑ choice, picked, best
a 精髄 せいずい essence, soul, spirit, pith
精華 せいか flower, essence, glory
b 精肉 せいにく choice meat
精鋭 せいえい best [pick] (of the aviators), choice (of an army)
精兵 せいへい picked troops
❹ **meticulous, careful, elaborate, precise, exact, detailed, fine**
精査 せいさ minute investigation, close inspection, careful examination
精選 せいせん careful selection
精緻な せいちな minute, subtle, delicate, exquisite
精巧な せいこうな elaborate, exquisite, ingenious
精密 せいみつ precision, accuracy, minuteness
精度 せいど precision, accuracy

精算 せいさん exact calculation; settlement of accounts
精通する せいつうする be well versed in, have thorough knowledge of

❺ⓐ (source of vital energy) **SPIRIT, energy, vitality, vigor**
ⓑ (spiritual part of man) **SPIRIT, mind, soul**

a 精力 せいりょく energy, vitality, vigor
精気 せいき spirit, energy, essence
精根 せいこん energy, vitality
精精 せいぜい with all one's might; at most, at best
精一杯 せいいっぱい with all one's might
b 精神 せいしん mind, soul, heart; intention, motive; the spirit (of something)
精魂 せいこん spirit, soul; vitality

❻ put one's heart into, be diligent
精励 せいれい diligence, industry
精勤 せいきん diligence, good attendance
精進 しょうじん diligence, concentration, devotion; religious purification; abstinence from (eating) fish and meat
丹精(=丹誠) たんせい efforts, pains
無精 ぶしょう indolence, laziness

❼ (supernatural being) **SPIRIT**, sprite, fairy
精霊 せいれい spirit of a dead person; spirit, sprite
妖精 ようせい fairy, elf, sprite

INDEPENDENT

【せい 精】

①ⓐ (essential part of a substance) **ESSENCE**, extract, spirit
ⓑ (essential substance of life) sperm, semen

a バニラの精 ばにらのせい vanilla extract
b 精を漏らす せいをもらす have an involuntary emission of semen

② (source of vital energy) **SPIRIT**, energy, vitality, vigor
精が尽きる せいがつきる one's energy is gone, be exhausted
精を出す せいをだす work hard [diligently]

③ (supernatural being) **SPIRIT**, sprite, fairy
花の精 はなのせい spirit of a flower

SYNONYMS

❶ⓐ refine
錬 REFINE (crude metals) → 2185
精 REFINE (crude materials) → 1729
留 distill → 3189

ⓑ clean and purified
浄 CLEAN → 0457
清 clean → 0635
純 PURE → 1649
潔 IMMACULATE → 0920
粋 REFINED (free from impurities) → 1645
精 refined (purified) → 1729
楚 NEAT AND TRIM → 3470

❷ⓑ bodily secretions
乳 MILK → 1823
精 sperm → 1729
汗 SWEAT → 0256
涙 TEAR → 0528
唾 SALIVA → 0553

❷ⓑ reproductive cells
卵 ovum → 1054
精 sperm → 1729

❸ⓐ essential part
精 ESSENCE (essential part) → 1729
粋 essence (best part) → 1645
髄 essence (vital part) → 2316
枢 PIVOT → 1076
幹 TRUNK → 2152
綱 ESSENTIAL POINTS → 1735
旨 PURPORT → 2516
要 summary → 3263

❹ careful
慎 PRUDENT → 0792
謹 carefully → 2045
精 meticulous → 1729

❹ detailed
詳 DETAILED → 1926
細 MINUTE → 1689
緻 MINUTE → 1780
密 CLOSE → 2857
精 meticulous → 1729

❺ⓐ life energy
精 SPIRIT → 1729
気 vital energy → 3960

ⓑ psyche
心 HEART → 0011
霊 SPIRIT (soul) → 3480
魂 SOUL, spirit → 1346
魄 SOUL → 1570
腹 heart → 1308
衷 INNER HEART → 2600
襟 inner mind → 1599
胸 breast → 1187
懐 BOSOM → 0942
神 MIND → 1143
気 SPIRIT (consciousness) → 3960
精 SPIRIT (mind) → 1729

❻ exert oneself
努 EXERT → 3154
勉 ENDEAVOR → 4113
励 make efforts → 1438
勤 work diligently → 2287
尽 use all one's strength → 3786

精 put one's heart into → 1729
孜 MAKE DILIGENT EFFORTS → 0284

❼ **supernatural and evil beings**

鬼 DEVIL → 3291
魔 DEMON → 3953
怪 monster → 0354
霊 SPIRIT → 3480
精 SPIRIT → 1729

精

1730

1-6-8

▶**REFINE**
▶**ESSENCE**
▶**SPIRIT**

セイ ショウ ㊔ すぐる きよし きよ

119	Nonstandard	UFA1D
米	S14-6-8	F0000

traditional form → see 精 at 1729

粹

1731

1-6-8

▶**REFINED**

スイ いき

119	Names	U7CB9
米	S14-6-8	F0000

traditional form → see 粋 at 1645

緋

1732

1-6-8

▶**SCARLET**

ヒ あけ

Ⓒ 绯 fēi

120	Names	U7DCB
糸	S14-6-8	F2406

COMPOUNDS

● **SCARLET**

緋縅し ひおどし scarlet-threaded suit of armor
緋鯉 ひごい red carp, golden carp

INDEPENDENT

【ひ 緋】SCARLET, cardinal

緋の衣 ひのころも scarlet robe

KUN

【あけ 緋】[usu. 朱] **red, blood red**

SYNONYMS

● **red colors**

赤 RED → 2719
紅 CRIMSON → 1629
緋 SCARLET → 1732
朱 VERMILION → 4344
丹 CINNABAR → 4249
茜 MADDER → 2811

HOMOPHONES

あけ 朱 VERMILION → 4344

NOTE

➡ see USAGE note at 朱 4344

維

1733

1-6-8

▶**FIBER**

イ ㊔ これ まさ ただ しげ つな

Ⓒ 维 wéi

120	Jōyō	U7DAD
糸	S14-6-8	F1069

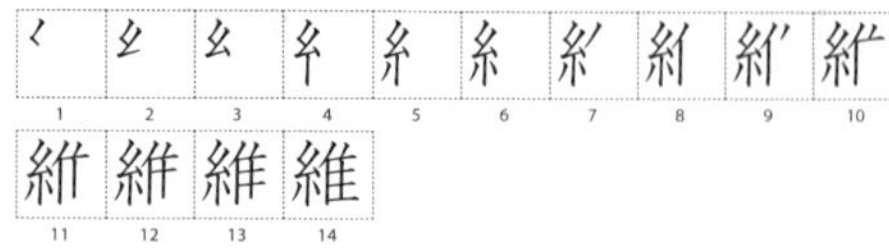

COMPOUNDS

❶ⓐ **FIBER**

ⓑ [original meaning, now archaic] rope

a 繊維 せんい fiber, textile
線維束 せんいそく fascicle

b 維管束 いかんそく vascular bundle

❷ **tie up, hold together, maintain**

維持する いじする maintain, keep (up), preserve

❸ **emphatic prefix**

維新 いしん renovation, restoration; Imperial Restoration of 1868

SYNONYMS

❶ⓐ **threads and fibers**

糸 THREAD → 2703
緯 woof → 1782
経 warp → 1687
繊 FIBER → 1789
維 FIBER → 1733
綸 THREAD → 1739
緬 FINE THREAD → 1758

COMPOUND FORMATION

❶【維持 いじ】

維持する 'maintain, etc.' literally means to secure (維 ❷) something so as to hold (持) it in place.

❷【維新 いしん】

維新 'renovation, etc.' is to totally (維 ❸) reform or make new (新).

綺

1734

1-6-8

▶**BEAUTIFUL**

キ ㊔ あや

Ⓒ 绮 qǐ

120	Names	U7DBA
糸	S14-6-8	F1871

COMPOUNDS

❶ [now also 奇 2756] **BEAUTIFUL, gorgeous, elegant, decorative**

綺麗な きれいな beautiful, pretty; clean; fair
綺想曲 きそうきょく caprice, capriccio

❷ fine thin silk with slanting weave

綺羅 きら fine clothes, gorgeous dress

❸ clever, amusing
綺談 きだん colorful story

SYNONYMS

❶ **beautiful**
美 BEAUTIFUL →2817
彪 MAGNIFICENT →4115
綺 BEAUTIFUL →1734
娃 BEAUTIFUL →0419
佳 FINE →0096
瑶 EXQUISITE →1301
麗 OF GRACEFUL BEAUTY →2672
艶 CHARMING →2403
妙 of marvelous beauty →0280
華 MAGNIFICENT →2841
絢 GORGEOUS →1705
斐 florid →3449

綱

▸ESSENTIAL POINTS
▸ROPE
コウ つな
Ⓒ 纲 gāng

1735
1-6-8

120	Jōyō	U7DB1
糸	S14-6-8	F1298

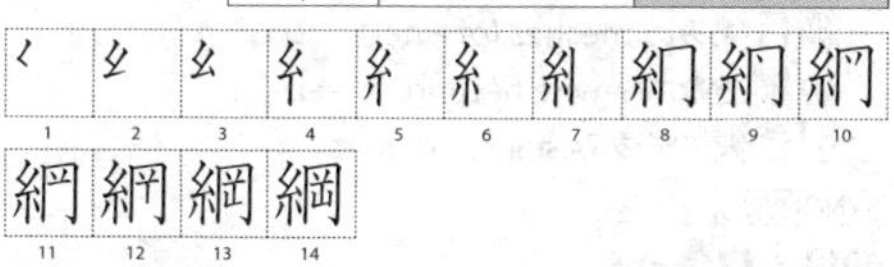

COMPOUNDS

❶ **ESSENTIAL [main] POINTS, essence, gist, outline**
綱領 こうりょう essential [main] points, gist, outline; summary
綱要 こうよう elements, essentials; outline
要綱 ようこう outline, gist; general plan
大綱 たいこう outline, general features
❷ guiding principle, discipline, morals
綱紀 こうき law and order, official discipline
政綱 せいこう political principle, policy
❸ *biol* class, -acea
亜綱 あこう subclass
甲殻綱 こうかくこう Crustacea
❹ [original meaning] **ROPE** (esp. headrope on a net)

INDEPENDENT

【こう 綱】 *biol* class

KUN

【つな 綱】 **ROPE (esp. of fiber), line, cord, cable; sumo grand championship**
綱渡り つなわたり tightrope walking [walker]
綱引き つなひき tug of war; forward puller (of a rickshaw)
綱を張る つなをはる be a grand champion
手綱 たづな bridle, reins
頼みの綱 たのみのつな last ray of hope
横綱 よこづな (grand) champion sumo wrestler

SYNONYMS

❶ **essential part**
精 ESSENCE (essential part) →1729
粋 essence (best part) →1645
髄 essence (vital part) →2316
枢 PIVOT →1076
幹 TRUNK →2152
綱 ESSENTIAL POINTS →1735
旨 PURPORT →2516
要 summary →3263
❷ **policy**
策 policy →3320
是 policy →3090
綱 guiding principle →1735
【つな】
◯ **ropes and lines**
綱 ROPE (esp. of fiber) →1735
絃 STRING →1685
縄 ROPE (esp. of straw) →1756
緒 cord →1742
組 braid →1693
索 cable →3105
鎖 CHAIN →2213
線 LINE →1760
紐 STRING →1647
弦 STRING →0343

NOTE

★ do not confuse with 網 NET →1737

綿

▸COTTON
メン わた
Ⓝ 緜 Ⓒ 绵 mián

1736
1-6-8

120	Jōyō-5	U7DBF
糸	S14-6-8	F1580

COMPOUNDS

❶ [formerly also 棉 1244]
ⓐ **COTTON plant**
ⓑ **COTTON fiber, cotton cloth, cotton wool**
a 綿花 めんか raw cotton, cotton wool
b 綿糸 めんし cotton yarn [thread]
綿羊(=緬羊) めんよう sheep
綿紡 めんぼう cotton spinning
綿織物 めんおりもの cotton goods

原綿 げんめん raw cotton
木綿 もめん cotton, cotton cloth
梳綿機 そめんき carding machine
印綿 いんめん Indian raw cotton

❷ minute, fine
綿密な めんみつな close, minute, detailed

❸ everlasting
綿綿たる めんめんたる endless, continuous

INDEPENDENT

【めん 綿】COTTON

KUN

【わた 綿】[formerly also 棉]
ⓐ COTTON plant
ⓑ COTTON fiber, cotton cloth, cotton wool
a 綿の実 わたのみ cotton seed
b 綿繰り わたくり cotton ginning
綿菓子 わたがし cotton candy

SYNONYMS

❶ⓐ fiber-producing plants
麻 HEMP → 3878
綿 COTTON → 1736

ⓑ fabrics
織 woven fabric → 1801
紬 PONGEE → 1684
紗 GAUZE → 1653
絹 SILK → 1721
綾 TWILL → 1740
綿 COTTON → 1736
棉 COTTON → 1244
麻 HEMP → 3878
毛 wool → 4264
錦 BROCADE → 2181

USAGE

【わた】
綿
[formerly also 棉]
ⓐ cotton plant
ⓑ cotton fiber, cotton cloth, cotton wool
棉
[now replaced by 綿] same as 綿

HOMOPHONES

わた 棉 COTTON → 1244

網

▸**NET**
モウ あみ
Ⓝ 網 Ⓒ 网 wǎng

1737
1-6-8

120	Jōyō	U7DB2
糸	S14-6-8	F1374

Stroke order: 1–14

COMPOUNDS

❶ⓐ [original meaning] **NET (for catching animals)**
ⓑ (reticulated fabric) **NET, netting**
ⓒ catch with a **NET**, capture everything
a 漁網 ぎょもう fishing net
鉄条網 てつじょうもう barbed wire entanglements
b 網状組織 もうじょうそしき network, reticulum
網膜 もうまく retina
c 網羅する もうらする encompass, comprehend

❷ (something that entraps) **NET**
天網 てんもう Heaven's net, Heaven's vengeance
法網 ほうもう net of the law, justice

❸ [suffix] **NETwork**
通信網 つうしんもう communications network
鉄道網 てつどうもう railway network
放送網 ほうそうもう broadcasting network

KUN

【あみ 網】**NET, netting**
網目 あみめ meshes (of a net)
金網 かなあみ wire netting, screen
引き網 ひきあみ seine, dragnet

SYNONYMS

❶ⓐ & ❶ⓑ net
網 NET → 1737
羅 bird net → 3244

❸ system
系 SYSTEM → 2443
制 SYSTEM → 1624
統 INTERCONNECTED SYSTEM → 1710
網 network → 1737

NOTE

★ do not confuse with 綱 ESSENTIAL POINTS → 1735

練

▸**TRAIN**
レン ね(る) ね(り)-
Ⓝ 練 Ⓒ 练 liàn

1738
1-6-8

120	Jōyō-3	U7DF4
糸	S14-6-8	F0952

Stroke order: 1–14

COMPOUNDS

❶ⓐ [sometimes also 錬 2185] **TRAIN, practice, exercise, drill, discipline; refine**

❻ (make proficient) **TRAIN, drill**
❻ **TRAINed, experienced, skilled**

ab 練成 れんせい training, drilling
練習 れんしゅう practice, training
習練する しゅうれんする train, discipline
b 訓練 くんれん training, drill
教練 きょうれん military drill
c 練達 れんたつ skill, dexterity
未練 みれん lingering affection, reluctance to give up
熟練した じゅくれんした skilled, experienced, proficient

❷ [formerly 煉 1297]
ⓐ refine (one's skills), purify
ⓑ knead

a 洗練された せんれんされた refined, polished
試練 しれん trial, test, probation
b 練乳 れんにゅう condensed milk
練炭 れんたん (charcoal or coal) briquette

❸ [original meaning] (soften and whiten raw silk by boiling) gloss, boil off, soften
精練 せいれん scouring; training

KUN

【ねる 練る】
①ⓐ **TRAIN, drill, exercise**
ⓑ polish (one's style), refine
a 練り上げる ねりあげる train up, discipline
b 文を練る ぶんをねる polish one's style
② gloss, boil off, soften
練り絹 ねりぎぬ glossed silk
③ walk in procession
練り歩く ねりあるく parade, march
④ [formerly 煉る] knead
練り ねり kneading; gloss; tempering
⑤ [formerly 錬る] temper (metals), forge, refine, smelt

【ねり- 練り-】 [also prefix] **paste**
練り薬 ねりぐすり medicated paste
練り製品 ねりせいひん fish paste

SYNONYMS

❶ⓐ **cultivate**
修 CULTIVATE →0138
養 FOSTER (one's intellect) →2998
練 TRAIN →1738
錬 REFINE →2185
鍛 train →2206
磨 POLISH →3946
琢 POLISH →1222

ⓑ **teach**
教 TEACH →1887
啓 ENLIGHTEN →3434
諄 TEACH WITH CARE →1979
授 teach →0595
育 educate →2544
練 TRAIN →1738
訓 INSTRUCT →1844
誨 INSTRUCT →1946
諭 ADMONISH →2012
導 GUIDE →3587
迪 EDIFY →3817

USAGE

❶【ねる】
練る
①ⓐ train, drill, exercise
ⓑ polish (one's style), refine
② gloss, boil off, soften
③ walk in procession
④ [formerly 煉る] knead
⑤ [formerly 錬る] temper (metals), forge, refine, smelt

錬る
[now usu. 練る] temper (metals), forge, refine, smelt

煉る
[now also 練る] knead

❷【れん 練 錬】
★These two characters are often interchangeable in the sense of training or cultivating one's character, but 練 is usually preferred. In compounds related to metalworking, such as 鍛錬 たんれん 'forging', only 錬 is used.

HOMOPHONES

ねる
錬 REFINE →2185
煉 REFINE →1297

COMPOUND FORMATION

❶【未練 みれん】
未練 'lingering affection, reluctance to give up' originally meant unskilled or inexperienced; that is, a person who is not yet (未) sufficiently experienced or skilled (練 ❶ⓒ).

❷【試練 しれん】
試練 'trial, test, probation' is to have one's faith purified (練 ❷ⓐ) by being tried (試).

綸

1739

1-6-8

▶**THREAD**
リン カン ケン
Ⓒ 纶 lún guān

120	Names	U7DB8
糸	S14-6-8	F2725

COMPOUNDS

❶ [original meaning] **THREAD, thick thread, cord**
綸子(=綾子) りんず figured satin

経綸する けいりんする govern, administer (state affairs)

❷ words spoken by a son of Heaven, imperial edict

綸言 りんげん the emperor's word, imperial message

SYNONYMS

❶ threads and fibers

糸 THREAD → 2703
緯 woof → 1782
経 warp → 1687
繊 FIBER → 1789
維 FIBER → 1733
綸 THREAD → 1739
緬 FINE THREAD → 1758

綾

1740

1-6-8

▸TWILL

リョウ あや

Ⓒ 绫 líng

120	Names	U7DBE
糸	S14-6-8	F1625

COMPOUNDS

● [original meaning] **TWILLed silk**

綾羅 りょうら figured silk and thin silk; elaborated cloth

KUN

【あや 綾】

①ⓐ [in compounds] **TWILL, twilled fabric**

ⓑ **TWILLed silk**

ⓒ [in compounds] as beautiful or intricate as TWILLed silk

a 綾織り あやおり twill
綾錦 あやにしき twill damask and brocade
b 綾取り あやとり cat's cradle
c 目も綾な めもあやな dazzlingly beautiful, brilliant

② [also 文] figure, design, pattern (as of cloth)

綾を成して あやをなして in beautiful patterns

③ [also 文]

ⓐ **figure of speech, rhetorical flourish**

ⓑ intricate and subtle details, intricacies

a 言葉の綾 ことばのあや figure of speech
b 事件の綾 じけんのあや web of the case

SYNONYMS

【あや】

①ⓐ **fabrics**

織 woven fabric → 1801
紬 PONGEE → 1684
紗 GAUZE → 1653
絹 SILK → 1721
綾 TWILL → 1740
綿 COTTON → 1736
棉 COTTON → 1244
麻 HEMP → 3878
毛 wool → 4264
錦 BROCADE → 2181

USAGE

【あや】

綾

①ⓐ [in compounds] twill, twilled fabric

ⓑ twilled silk

ⓒ [in compounds] as beautiful or intricate as twilled silk

② [also 文] figure, design, pattern (as of cloth)

③ [also 文]

ⓐ figure of speech, rhetorical flourish

ⓑ intricate and subtle details, intricacies

文

[also 綾]

① figure, design, pattern (as of cloth)

②ⓐ figure of speech, rhetorical flourish

ⓑ intricate and subtle details, intricacies

HOMOPHONES

あや 文 LETTER → 2458

緑

1741

1-6-8

▸GREEN

リョク ロク みどり ㊔ えん

Ⓝ 綠 Ⓒ 绿 lǜ lù

120	Jōyō-3	U7DD1
糸	S14-6-8	F1293

Stroke order: 1–14

COMPOUNDS

❶ⓐ [original meaning] **GREEN, emerald**

ⓑ [prefix] **GREENish**

a 緑色 りょくしょく green, verdure
緑茶 りょくちゃ green tea, Japanese tea
緑青 ろくしょう verdigris, copper [green] rust
葉緑素 ようりょくそ chlorophyll
b 緑白色 りょくはくしょく greenish white

❷ (abounding in growth) **GREEN**, verdant

緑地帯 りょくちたい green belt
緑化 りょっか tree planting, afforestation
緑土 りょくど verdant area

KUN

【みどり 緑】 [sometimes also 翠]

① **GREEN; verdure**

緑色 みどりいろ green
緑に覆われた山 みどりにおおわれたやま mountain robed in verdure
緑の黒髪 みどりのくろかみ glossy black hair (of a young woman)

浅緑 あさみどり(=せんりょく) light green

② *elegant* young leaves

SYNONYMS

❶ **green colors**

緑 GREEN → 1741

青 GREEN → 3084

翠 JADE GREEN → 3356

USAGE

【みどり】

緑

[sometimes also 翠]

① green; verdure

② *elegant* young leaves

翠

[usu. 緑] same as 緑

HOMOPHONES

みどり 翠 JADE GREEN → 3356

NOTE

★ do not confuse with 縁 RELATION → 1754

緒

1742

◧ 1-6-8

▶OUTSET

ショ チョ お いとぐち▲

Ⓝ 緒 Ⓒ 绪 xù

120	Jōyō	U7DD2
糸	S14-6-8	F0626

COMPOUNDS

❶ **OUTSET, beginning, inception, first step, early stage**

緒戦 しょせん(=ちょせん) beginning of hostilities, early stage of a war

緒論 しょろん introduction, preface

緒言 しょげん(=ちょげん) foreword, preface

端緒 たんしょ(=たんちょ) beginning, start, first step; clue

❷ **mental or emotional state**

情緒 じょうちょ(=じょうしょ) emotion, feeling

心緒 しんしょ(=しんちょ) emotion; mind

❸ⓐ **thread of events, line, lineage**

ⓑ [original meaning, now archaic] end of a thread

a 由緒 ゆいしょ history, lineage

一緒に いっしょに together; at the same time; in a lump

❹ **used phonetically for *sho***

内緒(=内証) ないしょ(=ないしょう) secrecy, privacy

INDEPENDENT

【しょ(=ちょ) 緒】 beginning, inception

緒に就く しょ(=ちょ)につく get underway, be started

KUN

【お 緒】 cord, strap, thong; string

緒締め おじめ string-fastener

臍×の緒 へそのお umbilical cord

鼻緒 はなお clog thong, strap

【いとぐち 緒】 [now usu. 糸口] beginning, first step; clue

緒を開く いとぐちをひらく make a beginning; find a clue

SYNONYMS

❶ **beginnings**

緒 OUTSET → 1742

序 INTRODUCTORY PART → 3803

端 start → 1564

始 beginning → 0335

初 beginning → 1433

元 ORIGIN → 2428

本 origin → 4314

根 ROOT → 1167

源 SOURCE → 0806

【お】

◯ **ropes and lines**

綱 ROPE (esp. of fiber) → 1735

絃 STRING → 1685

縄 ROPE (esp. of straw) → 1756

緒 cord → 1742

組 braid → 1693

索 cable → 3105

鎖 CHAIN → 2213

線 LINE → 1760

紐 STRING → 1647

弦 STRING → 0343

USAGE

【いとぐち】

緒

[now usu. 糸口] beginning, first step; clue

糸口

[formerly also 緒] beginning, first step; clue

HOMOPHONES

いとぐち 糸口 → 2703, 4189

COMPOUND FORMATION

【一緒 いっしょ】

一緒に 'together, etc.' is "correctly" (but not actually) written 一所に 'in one place' and can probably be explained as one (一) thread or line (緒 ❸ⓐ) of events.

1 米【糸】耳虫号此杂

総

1743

1-6-8

▶TOTAL
▶GENERAL

ソウ す(べて)▲ ㊔ ふさ さ

Ⓝ 總 緫 揔 Ⓒ 总 zǒng

120	Jōyō-5	U7DCF
糸	S14-6-8	F0326

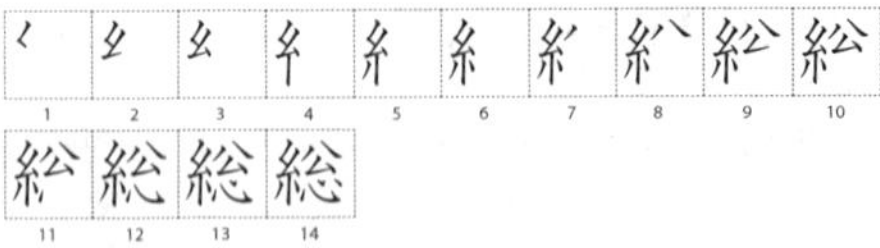

COMPOUNDS

❶ⓐ [also prefix] **TOTAL, whole, combined, full, complete, gross**
ⓑ [sometimes also 綜 1744] **integrate, unify, TOTAL**

a 総額 そうがく total amount, sum total
総数 そうすう total (number)
総点 そうてん sum total of one's marks
総体 そうたい the whole, all; on the whole, generally
総掛かり そうがかり combined efforts
総二階 そうにかい full two-story house
総予算 そうよさん complete budget
総量 そうりょう gross weight [volume]

b 総計する そうけいする total, sum up
総合する そうごうする synthesize, integrate, put together
総括する そうかつする generalize, summarize
総論 そうろん introduction, outline

❷ [formerly also 惣 3452] [also suffix] (applicable to the whole) **GENERAL, overall; ordinary**
総会 そうかい general meeting
総務 そうむ general affairs; manager, director
総選挙 そうせんきょ general election
総辞職 そうじしょく resignation en masse
総評(=日本労働組合総評議会) そうひょう(=にほんろうどうくみあいそうひょうぎかい) General Council of Trade Unions of Japan
総菜 そうざい daily [household] dish, side dish
総社 そうじゃ shrine enshrining several gods
総嫁 そうか streetwalker (in the Edo period)

❸ [formerly also 惣 3452]
ⓐ [also prefix] (of highest or supreme rank) **GENERAL, -general, supreme, head, -in-chief**
ⓑ exercise **GENERAL** control, supervise, manage

a 総長 そうちょう president of a university, chancellor
総監 そうかん governor-general, inspector general
総裁 そうさい president, governor
総理 そうり president, prime minister
総統 そうとう sovereign, highest post of the government
総監督 そうかんとく general manager
総本山 そうほんざん sectarian headquarters temple
総領息子 そうりょうむすこ eldest son

❹ [original meaning] tuft, fringe
総状花序 そうじょうかじょ racemous inflorescence, raceme

❺ old name for Chiba Prefecture
総武線 そうぶせん Sobu Line (Chiba-Tokyo Railway)
房総半島 ぼうそうはんとう Boso Peninsula

INDEPENDENT

【そうじて 総じて】**GENERAL**ly, in general, as a rule

KUN

【すべて 総べて】[also 凡て or 全て]
①ⓐ all, everything, the whole
ⓑ entirely, wholly
a 総べての すべての all, entire, whole
② **GENERAL**ly, as a rule

SYNONYMS

❶ⓐ **total**
総 TOTAL → 1743
計 total → 1828
和 sum → 1450

❶ⓐ **all**
皆 ALL → 3093
悉 THOROUGHLY → 3405
総 TOTAL → 1743
諸 VARIOUS → 1984
毎 EVERY → 2527
各 EACH → 2692
都 all → 2120
万 all → 3653
全 WHOLE → 2514
渾 ENTIRE → 0738
一 all in one → 4148
満 FULL → 0739
丸 complete(ly) → 4225
完 COMPLETE → 2727

ⓑ **combine**
合 COMBINE → 2511
結 TIE → 1706
統 UNITE → 1710
括 LUMP TOGETHER → 0449
総 integrate → 1743
併 join together → 0092
綜 INTEGRATE → 1744
纏める PUT TOGETHER → 1814

❷ **general**
総 GENERAL → 1743
惣 GENERAL → 3452
汎 OVERALL → 0254

❸ⓐ **high-ranking**
貴 NOBLE → 3220
上 upper → 4212

高 HIGH → 2601
総 GENERAL → 1743
太 of highest rank → 2673

HOMOPHONES

すべて

凡 COMMONPLACE → 3656
全 WHOLE → 2514

NOTE

➡ see USAGE notes at 惣 3452 and 凡 3656
➡ see COMPOUND FORMATION for
惣菜 そうざい → 惣 3452
惣社 そうじゃ → 惣 3452
惣嫁 そうか → 惣 3452

綜

1744

◧ 1-6-8

▶**INTEGRATE**

ソウ ㊔ おさむ

Ⓒ 综 zōng zèng

120	Names	U7D9C
糸	S14-6-8	F2982

COMPOUNDS

❶ [now usu. 総 1743] **INTEGRATE, unify, total**

綜合する そうごうする synthesize, integrate, put together
綜覧 そうらん general survey; comprehensive bibliography

❷ **intertwine**

錯綜した さくそうした complicated, intricate

SYNONYMS

❶ **combine**

合 COMBINE → 2511
結 TIE → 1706
統 UNITE → 1710
括 LUMP TOGETHER → 0449
総 integrate → 1743
併 join together → 0092
綜 INTEGRATE → 1744
纏める PUT TOGETHER → 1814

綻

1745

◧ 1-6-8

▶**UNRAVEL**

タン ほころ(びる) ほころ(ぶ)

Ⓒ 绽 zhàn

120	Jōyō	U7DBB
糸	S14-6-8	F2128

1	2	3	4	5	6	7	8	9	10	11	12	13	14
㇛	纟	幺	糸	糸	糸	糸'	糸'	綻	綻	綻	綻	綻	綻

COMPOUNDS

● **UNRAVEL, come apart, fall apart**

破綻 はたん failure, rupture; bankruptcy

KUN

【ほころびる 綻びる】

ⓐ **UNRAVEL, come apart at the seams**
ⓑ **begin to open [bloom]**
ⓒ (of facial expressions) **relax, break into (a smile)**

a 綻び ほころび open seam, tear

【ほころぶ 綻ぶ】 same as 綻びる ほころびる

SYNONYMS

● **degenerate**

落 FALL → 2907
衰 DECLINE → 2604
頽 DECLINE → 2039
堕 DEGENERATE → 3501
綻 UNRAVEL → 1745
破 break down → 1478

綴

1746

◧ 1-6-8

▶**BIND**
▶**COMPOSE**

テイ テツ つづ(る) と(じる)

Ⓒ 缀 zhuì

120	Names	U7DB4
糸	S14-6-8	F2100

COMPOUNDS

❶ⓐ **BIND, file**

ⓑ [original meaning] **sew up, stitch together; mend**

ab 点綴する てんてい(=てんてつ)する intersperse; dot
補綴 ほてい(=ほてつ) mending; composing (poetry)

❷ⓐ (put words together correctly) **COMPOSE, write**

ⓑ **spell**

a 綴文 ていぶん(=てつぶん) compose, write
b 綴字 ていじ(=つづりじ) spelling
原綴 げんてつ spelling in the original language

KUN

【つづる 綴る】

ⓐ (put words together correctly) **COMPOSE, write**
ⓑ **spell**

a 詩歌を綴る しいかをつづる compose poetry
ab 綴り方 つづりかた composition; spelling
b 綴り つづり spelling, orthography; binding, patching

【とじる 綴じる】

ⓐ **BIND, file**
ⓑ **sew up, stitch together; mend**

a 綴じて とじて in bound form
綴じ込み とじこみ file
綴じ本 とじほん bound book
和綴じ わとじ Japanese-style bookbinding
袋綴じ ふくろとじ dual page
b 綴じ針 とじばり large sewing needle
綴じ蓋 とじぶた mended lid

SYNONYMS

❶ⓐ join

結 TIE → 1706
繫 CONNECT → 3612
縛 BIND → 1779
綴 BIND → 1746
緘 BIND UP → 1787
束 TIE UP → 4369
梱 PACK → 1205
連 LINK → 3849
係 CONNECT → 0108
接 join → 0607

❷ⓐ create

創 CREATE → 2283
作 compose → 0077
綴 COMPOSE → 1746
生 produce → 4309
発 START → 3174
起 generate → 4099

HOMOPHONES

とじる 閉 CLOSE → 4116

NOTE

➡ see USAGE note at 閉 4116

網

1747

1-6-8

▶NET

モウ あみ

120	Nonstandard	U7DB2
糸	S14-6-8	F0000

traditional form → see 網 at 1737

綠

1748

1-6-8

▶GREEN

リョク ロク みどり ㊔ えん

120	Names	U7DA0
糸	S14-6-8	F0000

traditional form → see 緑 at 1741

綫

1749

1-6-8

▶LINE

セン

120	Nonstandard	U7DAB
糸	S14-6-8	F0000

traditional form → see 線 at 1760

聡

1750

1-6-8

▶SHARP-WITTED

ソウ さと(い) ㊔ さとし さとる あき あきら とし

Ⓝ 聰 聽 Ⓒ 聪 cōng

128	Names	U8061
耳	S14-6-8	F2181

COMPOUNDS

ⓐ SHARP-WITTED, quick-witted, clever, bright, astute, perceptive

ⓑ [original meaning] sharp-eared, quick of hearing

a 聡明な そうめいな sagacious, wise, sharp, mentally acute

KUN

【さとい 聡い】**SHARP-WITTED, quick-witted, clever**

利に聡い りにさとい be wide-awake to one's interests

耳聡い みみざとい sharp-[keen-]eared

SYNONYMS

ⓐ intelligent and wise

賢 WISE → 3518
俊 brilliant → 0117
鋭 SHARP → 2171
敏 NIMBLE → 1675
叡 PROFOUNDLY WISE → 2405
智 wise → 3458
慧 INTELLIGENT → 3485
怜 CLEVER → 0356
悧 CLEVER → 0505
俐 CLEVER → 0113
哲 SAGACIOUS → 3402
明 clear-sighted → 1060
聡 SHARP-WITTED → 1750

蝋

1751

1-6-8

▶WAX

ロウ

142	Nonstandard	U874B
虫	S14-6-8	F0000

traditional form → see 蠟 at 1818

蝶

1-6-8

incorrect stroke-count

➡ see 1-6-9: 虫 at 1772

號

1-6-8

incorrect stroke-count

➡ see 1-5-8: 号 at 1551

雌

1-6-8

incorrect classification

➡ see 1-4-10: 止 at 1337

雑

1752

1-6-8

▶MISCELLANEOUS
▶MIXED

ザツ ゾウ ㊔ さい くさ

Ⓝ 雜 襍 Ⓒ 杂 zá

172	Jōyō-5	U96D1
隹	S14-8-6	F0691

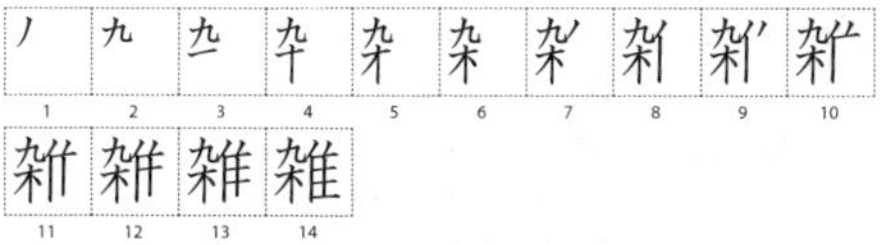

COMPOUNDS

❶ [also prefix] **MISCELLANEOUS, various, sundry, motley**
雑多 ざった miscellaneous, various
雑誌 ざっし magazine, journal
雑用 ざつよう miscellaneous business
雑費 ざっぴ miscellaneous expenses
雑貨 ざっか sundries, general cargo; miscellaneous goods
雑文家 ざつぶんか miscellaneous writer, miscellanist
雑木 ぞうき miscellaneous trees
雑歌 ぞうか miscellaneous poems
雑所得 ざつしょとく miscellaneous [sundry] incomes
雑談 ざつだん chat, idle talk
雑煮 ぞうに rice cakes boiled with vegetables

❷ⓐ [original meaning] **MIXED, blended**
ⓑ **MIXED up, disorderly, confused, intricate**
a 雑種 ざっしゅ mixed breed, hybrid
雑居地 ざっきょち mixed residential quarter
b 雑然とした ざつぜんとした promiscuous, disorderly
複雑な ふくざつな complicated, complex, involved, intricate
混雑した こんざつした confused, disorderly; congested
乱雑な らんざつな disorderly, confused
繁雑な はんざつな complicated, intricate, confused
煩雑な はんざつな vexatious, troublesome, intricate
錯雑 さくざつ complication, intricacy

❸ **coarse, rough, low class, ordinary**
雑草 ざっそう weed
雑音 ざつおん noise, jarring and grating; jamming; interference
雑巾 ぞうきん rag; mop
雑言 ぞうごん foul language, abuse
雑兵 ぞうひょう ordinary soldiers, rank and file
雑人 ぞうにん low-call people
粗雑な そざつな coarse, rough, crude

INDEPENDENT

【ざつ 雑】**miscellany**
雑な ざつな coarse, rough, crude
雑の部 ざつのぶ(=ぞうのぶ) miscellany

SPECIAL READINGS

雑魚 ざこ small fish, small fry; lesser fry

SYNONYMS

❶ **various**
諸 VARIOUS → 1984
庶 MANIFOLD → 3880
雑 MISCELLANEOUS → 1752

❷ⓐ **mix**
混 MIX → 0631
淆 INTERMINGLE → 0630
交 intermingle → 2508
雑 MIXED → 1752
錯 MIXED UP → 2187

ⓑ **disordered**
紛 CONFUSED → 1648
乱 DISORDERED → 1611
錯 MIXED UP → 2187
混 mixed up → 0631
雑 mixed up → 1752
沌 PRIMEVAL CHAOS → 0314

糊

1753

◧ 1-6-9

▶**PASTE**
コ のり
Ⓒ 糊 hú hū hù

119	Names	U7CCA
米	S15-6-9	F2717

COMPOUNDS

❶ⓐ [also suffix] **PASTE, glue**
ⓑ starch
ⓒ size, sizing
a 糊化 こか gelatinization
糊着する こちゃくする glue on, paste [glue] together, become glued together
電極糊 でんきょくこ electrode paste
b 糊精 こせい dextrin(e)
c 糊剤 こざい sizing agent, paste

❷ eat rice gruel; eke out a living
糊口 ここう bare livelihood, subsistence

❸ⓐ **vague, unclear**
ⓑ make vague [unclear]
a 模糊 もこ dimness, vagueness
b 糊塗 こと covering up, glossing over

KUN

【のり 糊】
ⓐ **PASTE, glue**
ⓑ **starch (for clothes)**
a 糊付け のりづけ pasting
糊代 のりしろ overlap width; margin to paste up
血糊 ちのり sticky (clots of) blood
b 洗濯糊 せんたくのり laundry starch

米
【糸】
耳
虫
光
夹

縁

1754
1-6-9

▸RELATION
▸EDGE
エン -ネン▲ ふち へり▲ えにし▲ ㊔ ゆかり より

Ⓝ 縁 Ⓒ 缘 yuán

120	Jōyō	U7E01
糸	S15-6-9	F0870

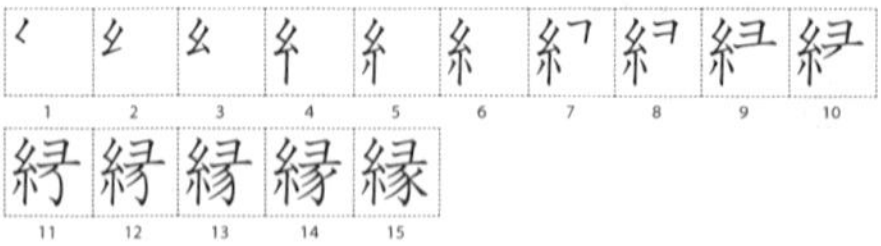

COMPOUNDS

❶ⓐ RELATION (between persons), affinity, personal relations, connection, relationship
ⓑ family RELATION, relations, relative, kinsman

a 縁故 えんこ relation, connection; relative
腐れ縁 くされえん unhappy yet inseparable relation; fatal bonds
因縁 いんねん connection, affinity; pretext; origin
絶縁 ぜつえん breaking off relations; insulation, isolation
無縁の むえんの unrelated; without relatives, having no surviving relatives

b 血縁 けつえん blood relation
遠縁 とおえん distant relation

❷ marriage RELATION, marriage

縁談 えんだん marriage proposal
縁組 えんぐみ marriage, (conjugal) union
内縁の妻 ないえんのつま common-law wife

❸ *Buddhism*
ⓐ karma RELATION, predestination, fate, destiny
ⓑ indirect cause, contributory cause

a 宿縁 しゅくえん karma, destiny, fate
ab 縁起 えんぎ origin, history; omen, luck
b 因縁 いんねん karma, fate; direct and indirect causes

❹ⓐ EDGE, margin
ⓑ [original meaning] **fringe, hem**

a 縁辺 えんぺん border, edge; relations
b 外縁 がいえん outer edge, brink

❺ (edge of building) **veranda, porch, balcony**

縁側 えんがわ veranda
縁先 えんさき edge of a veranda

INDEPENDENT

【えん 縁】

①ⓐ RELATION, affinity, connection
ⓑ family RELATION, relative

a 縁が無い えんがない have no relation to
縁を切る えんをきる sever connections; get a divorce
b 縁が遠い えんがとおい distantly related

② marriage RELATION, marriage

夫婦の縁を結ぶ ふうふのえんをむすぶ get married

③ⓐ karma RELATION, fate, destiny, chance
ⓑ *Buddhism* indirect cause, contributory cause

a 不思議な縁で ふしぎなえんで by happy chance

④ veranda, porch, balcony

縁の下 えんのした space under the floor
縁の下の力持ち えんのしたのちからもち thankless task; person who does a thankless task

KUN

【ふち 縁】**EDGE, verge, brink, border, side; frame; hem, fringe**

縁取り ふちどり bordering, hemming
盆の縁 ぼんのふち edge of a tray
額縁 がくぶち (picture) frame

【へり 縁】**EDGE**, verge; hem

【えにし 縁】**RELATION** (between man and woman), affinity

SYNONYMS

❶ⓐ personal relations

縁 RELATION → 1754
交 INTERCOURSE → 2508
好 friendship → 0240
仲 PERSONAL RELATIONS → 0047
誼 FRIENDSHIP → 1977
絆 BONDS → 1686

ⓑ family and relations

族 FAMILY → 1195
家 FAMILY → 2827
門 family → 1100
氏 clan → 3669
縁 RELATION → 1754
姻 relative by marriage → 0421
親 RELATIVES → 2264
戚 RELATIVES → 4401
曽 GREAT- → 2632

❷ marrying and marriage

嫁 WED A MAN → 0780
婚 MARRY → 0566
姻 MARRIAGE → 0421
縁 marriage relation → 1754

❸ⓐ fate and fortune

運 FORTUNE → 3894
命 fate → 2553
業 karma → 3227
縁 karma relation → 1754
籤 LOT → 3399

❹ⓐ edges and boundaries

縁 EDGE → 1754
端 edge → 1564
辺 border → 3761

境 BOUNDARY → 0835
疆 BOUNDARY → 1810
界 BOUNDS → 3172
際 VERGE → 0874
涯 OUTER LIMITS → 0623

NOTE

★ do not confuse with 緑 GREEN → 1741

編

▶COMPILE
▶KNIT
ヘン あ(む) -あ(み)
Ⓝ 編 Ⓒ 编 biān

1755
◧ 1-6-9

120	Jōyō-5	U7DE8
糸	S15-6-9	F0578

COMPOUNDS

❶ⓐ COMPILE, edit, compose
ⓑ COMPILEd by, edited by

a 編集 へんしゅう editing, compilation
編纂 へんさん compilation, editing
編者 へんしゃ(=へんじゃ) editor, compiler
編成する へんせいする form, compose, compile
b 浅田先生編 あさだせんせいへん edited by Prof. Asada

❷ (bring together and arrange) **put together, COMPILE, organize, form, arrange**
編制する へんせいする organize, form
編曲 へんきょく arrangement (of a melody)
編入する へんにゅうする include, incorporate; admit
改編する かいへんする reorganize, remodel

❸ [formerly also 篇 3361]
ⓐ [also suffix] **piece of writing, literary work; film**
ⓑ **volume, book**
ⓒ chapter, section, part, canto

a 巨編 きょへん great literary work
長編 ちょうへん long piece, full-length work (as of a novel or a film)
予告編 よこくへん preview, trailer
詩編 しへん book of poetry; Psalms
b 続編 ぞくへん sequel, supplementary volume
c 後編 こうへん latter part, latter volume

❹ [formerly also 篇 3361] counter for pieces of writing such as volumes, chapters, parts, or poems
一編の詩 いっぺんのし one poem
第一編 だいいっぺん Chapter 1, Canto 1

❺ [original meaning] **KNIT**
編組機械 へんそきかい knitting machinery

❻ string for binding books of bamboo tablets
韋編 いへん leather cord

INDEPENDENT

【へん 編】chapter, section, part; compilation, editing
二の編 にのへん Part 2

KUN

【あむ 編む】**KNIT, braid; compile, edit**
編み機 あみき knitting machine
編み物 あみもの knitting, knitted goods
本を編む ほんをあむ compile a book

【-あみ -編み】[also suffix] **KNITting, knitted**
機械編み きかいあみ machine knitted
レース編み れーすあみ lace knitting

SYNONYMS

❶ compile
編 COMPILE → 1755
纂 COMPILE → 3393
撰 COMPILE → 0911
集 edit → 3445
輯 EDIT → 2025
著 AUTHOR → 2869

❷ organize
組 ORGANIZE → 1693
結 form → 1706
編 put together → 1755

❸ⓐ books
本 BOOK → 4314
典 STANDARD WORK → 3253
経 religious classic → 1687
書 BOOK → 3292
冊 bound book → 4295
籍 books → 3394
著 literary work → 2869
巻 VOLUME → 3273
編 piece of writing → 1755
篇 PIECE OF WRITING → 3361
鑑 REFERENCE VOLUME → 2226

❺ weave and sew
織 WEAVE → 1801
紡 SPIN → 1646
績 spin → 1788
縫 SEW → 1781
編 KNIT → 1755
辮 PLAIT → 2085
組 braid → 1693
繍 EMBROIDER → 1805

NOTE

★ Note the difference between the words 編成 and 編制, both へんせい, under meanings ❶ and ❷ above.

縄

▶ROPE

ジョウ なわ ㊔ つな

Ⓝ 縄 Ⓒ 绳 shéng

1756

1-6-9

120	Jōyō	U7E04
糸	S15-6-9	F1072

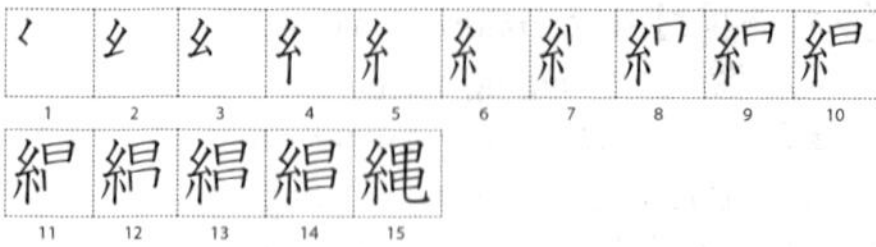

COMPOUNDS

❶ⓐ [original meaning] **ROPE, straw rope, cord, spun yarn**

ⓑ inking line, inked string

a 縄文 じょうもん straw-rope pattern

捕縄 ほじょう rope for binding criminals

自縄自縛に陥る じじょうじばくにおちいる be caught in one's own trap

b 縄墨 じょうぼく inked timber-marking string; standard

❷ standard, norm

準縄 じゅんじょう level and inked string; rule, standard

KUN

【なわ 縄】(straw) **ROPE, cord, bonds**

縄跳び なわとび rope skipping, rope jumping

縄張り なわばり roping off; one's sphere of influence, one's territory

泥縄 どろなわ expediency coming too late (like making a rope after finding the thief)

SYNONYMS

❶ⓐ **ropes and lines**

綱 ROPE (esp. of fiber) → 1735

紘 STRING → 1685

縄 ROPE (esp. of straw) → 1756

緒 cord → 1742

組 braid → 1693

索 cable → 3105

鎖 CHAIN → 2213

線 LINE → 1760

紐 STRING → 1647

弦 STRING → 0343

緩

▶SLACK

カン ゆる(い) ゆる(やか) ゆる(む) ゆる(める)

Ⓝ 緩 Ⓒ 缓 huǎn

1757

1-6-9

120	Jōyō	U7DE9
糸	S15-6-9	F1483

COMPOUNDS

❶ (reduce tension) **SLACK, slacken, loosen**

緩和 かんわ easing, relief, alleviation

緩衝弁 かんしょうべん cushion valve

弛緩 しかん relaxation; atony

❷ (not fast or lively) **SLACK, slow, sluggish**

緩慢な かんまんな slack, slow-moving, dull, inactive

緩球 かんきゅう slow ball

緩行 かんこう going slowly

緩急 かんきゅう fast and slow motion, high and low speed; emergency

緩下剤 かんげざい laxative

KUN

【ゆるい 緩い】**SLACK, loose; lenient, easy; gentle, slow; loose, watery (bowels)**

緩さ ゆるさ slackness, looseness, lenience, gentleness

緩目の ゆるめの somewhat loose

緩い規則 ゆるいきそく lenient regulations

緩いカーブ ゆるいかーぶ gentle curve

腹が緩い はらがゆるい have loose bowels

【ゆるやか 緩やか】

ゆるやかな 緩やかな **SLACK, loose; lenient, easy; gentle, slow**

緩やかさ ゆるやかさ slackness, looseness, lenience, gentleness

緩やかな衣服 ゆるやかないふく loose garment

緩やかに進む ゆるやかにすすむ proceed slowly

【ゆるむ 緩む】[sometimes also 弛む] *vi* **SLACK(en), loosen, relax; be assuaged, abate, moderate, ease off**

緩み ゆるみ slackness, looseness; slack

結び目が緩む むすびめがゆるむ A knot comes loose

気が緩んで きがゆるんで in lack of vigilance

【ゆるめる 緩める】[sometimes also 弛める] *vt* **loosen, unloose, unfasten; ease (up), mitigate, moderate**

手綱を緩める たづなをゆるめる slack the reins

速度を緩める そくどをゆるめる ease up the speed

SYNONYMS

❶ **loosen**

弛 SLACKEN → 0245

緩 SLACK → 1757

❷ **slow**

徐 SLOWLY → 0497

遅 SLOW → 3887

緩 SLACK → 1757

慢 SLUGGISH →0844

USAGE

❶【ゆるむ】

緩む

[sometimes also 弛む] *vi* slack(en), loosen, relax; be assuaged, abate, moderate, ease off

弛む

[usu. 緩む] *vi*

ⓐ slacken, slack, loosen, relax

ⓑ be assuaged, abate, moderate, ease off

❷【ゆるめる】

緩める

[sometimes also 弛める] *vt* loosen, unloose, unfasten; ease (up), mitigate, moderate

弛める

[usu. 緩める] *vt*

ⓐ loosen, unloose, unfasten

ⓑ ease (up), mitigate, moderate

HOMOPHONES

ゆるむ 弛 SLACKEN →0245

ゆるめる 弛 SLACKEN →0245

緬 1758

◧1-6-9

▶FINE THREAD

メン

Ⓒ 缅 miǎn

120	Non-Jōyō	U7DEC
糸	S15-6-9	F3139

COMPOUNDS

❶ FINE THREAD

緬羊(=綿羊) めんよう sheep

縮緬 ちりめん crepe, silk crepe

❷ [rare] Burma, Myanmar

緬甸× めんでん(=びるま) Burma

英緬戦争 えいめんせんそう Anglo-Burmese Wars

SYNONYMS

❶ threads and fibers

糸 THREAD →2703

緯 woof →1782

経 warp →1687

繊 FIBER →1789

維 FIBER →1733

綸 THREAD →1739

緬 FINE THREAD →1758

❷ Asian countries

日 JAPAN →3759

緬 Myanmar →1758

老 Laos →3963

華 CHINA →2841

蒙 Mongolia →2938

鮮 Korea →2355

泰 Thailand →3193

越 Vietnam →4108

印 India →1023

竺 INDIA →3248

比 Philippines →0029

縅 1759

◧1-6-9

▶BRAID OF ARMOR

おど(し)

Ⓒ (国字)

120	Non-Jōyō	U7E05
糸	S15-6-9	F0000

KUN

【おどし 縅し】[sometimes also 威し] **BRAID or thread OF Japanese ARMOR**

緋縅し鎧 ひおどしよろい scarlet-threaded suit of armor

SYNONYMS

【おどし】

◯ **protective coverings**

盾 SHIELD →3729

楯 SHIELD →1281

鎧 ARMOR →2211

甲 armor →4293

縅 BRAID OF ARMOR →1759

面 mask →2590

兜 helmet →3499

幌 COVERING FOR VEHICLES →0787

HOMOPHONES

おどし

脅 THREATEN →2614

威 MIGHT →4394

NOTE

➡ see USAGE note at 脅 2614

線 1760

◧1-6-9

▶LINE

セン

Ⓝ 綫 Ⓒ 线 xiàn

120	Jōyō-2	U7DDA
糸	S15-6-9	F0338

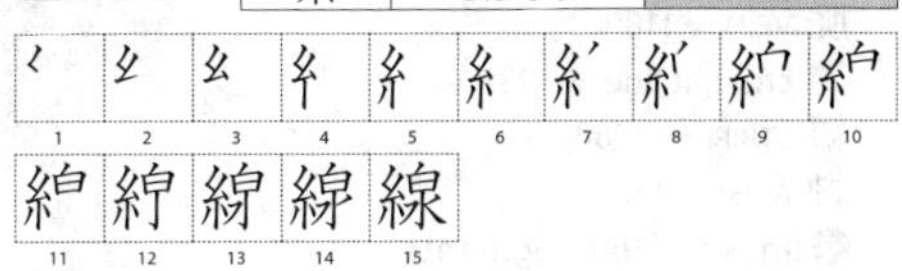

COMPOUNDS

❶ⓐ (continuous lengthwise mark) **LINE**

ⓑ (border, esp. between two surfaces) **LINE**

ⓒ *geometry* **LINE**

a 線画 せんが line drawing

線審 せんしん linesman

直線 ちょくせん straight line

下線 かせん underline

戦線 せんせん (war) front, battle line
前線 ぜんせん front line, fighting front; *meteorology* front
b 水平線 すいへいせん horizon
c 放物線 ほうぶつせん parabola

❷ **something resembling a LINE, as a ray or beam**
線香 せんこう stick of incense, joss stick
光線 こうせん ray (of light), beam
三味線 しゃみせん shamisen (Japanese three-stringed musical instrument)
打線 だせん batting line-up
伏線 ふくせん preparation, foreshadow
放射線 ほうしゃせん radiation, radioactive rays

❸ *elec* **LINE, wire, cable**
無線 むせん radio, wireless
電線 でんせん electric wire
内線 ないせん telephone extension; inner line
回線 かいせん circuit
電話線 でんわせん telephone line

❹ (public transportation route) **LINE, track, route**
線路 せんろ (railway) line, track
路線 ろせん route, way, line
沿線の えんせんの along a railway line
脱線 だっせん derailment; deviation, aberration
東海道線 とうかいどうせん Tokaido Line
二番線 にばんせん Track No. 2

INDEPENDENT

【せん 線】LINE (→❶); *elec* **line, wire, cable; something resembling a line;** (course of action) **line**
線を引く せんをひく draw a line
線の太い人 せんのふといひと strong-nerved person
良い線を行く いいせんをいく be on the right track

SYNONYMS

❶ⓐ & ❶ⓑ line
線 LINE → 1760
筋 THREADLIKE STRUCTURE → 3319
条 strip → 2726
脈 VEIN → 1189
棒 straight line → 1237
縞 STRIPE → 1784
軸 AXIS → 1908

ⓒ lines and line segments
線 LINE → 1760
弧 ARC → 0430
弦 chord → 0343
径 DIAMETER → 0347
辺 side → 3761

❸ ropes and lines
綱 ROPE (esp. of fiber) → 1735
絃 STRING → 1685
縄 ROPE (esp. of straw) → 1756
緒 cord → 1742
組 braid → 1693
索 cable → 3105
鎖 CHAIN → 2213
線 LINE → 1760
紐 STRING → 1647
弦 STRING → 0343

❹ ways and routes
道 WAY (path) → 3888
径 PATH → 0347
軌 TRACK → 1832
線 LINE → 1760
澪 WATERWAY → 0957
途 WAY (route) → 3853
路 ROAD → 1936
筋 wayside → 3319
通り street → 3855
街 city street → 0702
辻 CROSSROADS → 3958
岐 forked road → 0285
巷 THE STREETS → 3097

NOTE

➡ see COMPOUND FORMATION for 子午線 しごせん → 子 4196

締

1761

1-6-9

▶CONCLUDE
▶TIGHTEN

テイ し(まる) し(まり) し(める) -し(め) -じ(め)

Ⓒ 缔 dì

120	Jōyō	U7DE0
糸	S15-6-9	F1020

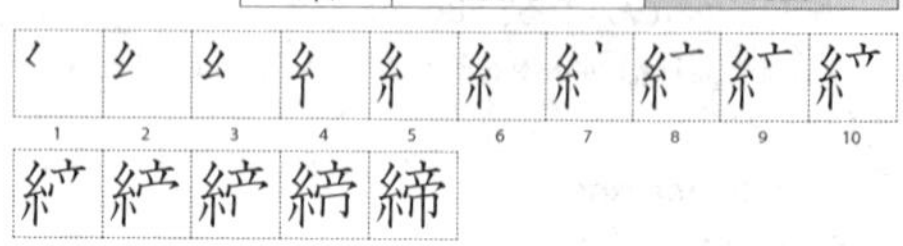

COMPOUNDS

❶ⓐ unite two nations by reaching an agreement: **CONCLUDE (a treaty), contract, form (an alliance)**
ⓑ [archaic] unite in wedlock, marry
a 締結する ていけつする conclude, contract
締約 ていやく conclusion of a treaty
締盟 ていめい conclusion of a treaty of alliance

❷ [original meaning] tie together with a string, bind, connect
結締組織 けっていそしき connective tissue

INDEPENDENT

【ていする 締する】CONCLUDE (a treaty), contract (a friendship)

KUN

【しまる 締まる】*vi*

①ⓐ **TIGHTEN, become taut; be compact, be firm**
ⓑ **TIGHTEN one's belt, be frugal**

a 締まった体格 しまったたいかく well-knit frame, firm build

b 締まり屋 しまりや thrifty person, tightfisted person

② **brace oneself up, become steady**

引き締まる ひきしまる tighten, become tight; be braced up

③ (of the market) **become firm**

小締まり こじまり firmer tendency

④ [in compounds] **exercise (tight) control over, regulate**

取り締まる とりしまる manage, control, superintend

【しまり 締まり】

① **tightness, firmness, steadiness**

締まりの無い しまりのない loose, slack, lax

② **fastening [locking] of a door**

戸締まり とじまり fastening the doors

【しめる 締める】*vt*

①ⓐ **TIGHTEN, tauten**
ⓑ **fasten, tie up, bind**

a ベルトを締める べるとをしめる tighten one's belt

b 締め括る しめくくる bind fast; settle, round off (a passage)

締め金 しめがね buckle, clasp, clamp

② exercise tight [rigid] control over, exercise close supervision; reprimand

締め上げる しめあげる screw up; put the screws on

元締め もとじめ manager, controller

③ [also 〆る] sum, sum [add] up; close the account

締め しめ summing up; *judo* choking [strangling] techniques

締めて しめて in all, all told

締め切り日 しめきりび closing day, time limit, deadline

④ economize, save

家計を締める かけいをしめる economize in the household

⑤ [also 〆る] [in compounds] **fasten, lock (a door or window), shut**

締め出す しめだす shut the door on (a person), shut out

締め切る しめきる close (up); fix a deadline

締め切り(=〆切) しめきり closing day, deadline; Closed, No Entrance

⑥ [also 〆る] **finish off a bout of eating and drinking (with a closing dish)**

⑦ [also 〆る] **pickle, marinate (fish) (with vinegar)**

【-しめ, -じめ -締め】

① [also 〆] **counter for reams or bundles of paper**

紙二締め かみふたしめ two reams of paper

② *judo* **choke, choking [strangling] techniques**

片十字締め かたじゅうじじめ cross choke

SYNONYMS

❶ⓐ **promise**

約 PROMISE → 1632

締 CONCLUDE (a treaty) → 1761

協 reach an agreement → 0103

契 MAKE AN AGREEMENT → 3267

盟 ALLIANCE → 3468

誓 VOW → 3424

【しめる】

①ⓐ **tighten**

締める TIGHTEN → 1761

緊 TIGHTEN → 3517

張 STRAIN → 0573

USAGE

❶【しまる】

締まる

vi

①ⓐ tighten, become taut; be compact, be firm
ⓑ tighten one's belt, be frugal
② brace oneself up, become steady
③ (of the market) become firm
④ [in compounds] exercise (tight) control over, regulate

閉まる

vi be shut, be closed, shut, close

絞まる

be strangled

★Note that when used independently the words 閉める and 閉まる mean to shut in the sense of moving into a closed position. 締 in that sense, appears in such compounds as 締め切る しめきる 'fasten, shut up' and 戸締まり とじまり 'fastening the doors', and means to fasten or secure with a lock.

❷【しめる】

締める

vt

①ⓐ tighten, tauten
ⓑ fasten, tie up, bind
② exercise tight [rigid] control over, exercise close supervision; reprimand
③ [also 〆る] sum, sum [add] up; close the account
④ economize, save
⑤ [also 〆る] [in compounds] fasten, lock (a door or window), shut
⑥ [also 〆る] finish off a bout of eating and drinking (with a closing dish)
⑦ [also 〆る] pickle, marinate (fish) (with vinegar)

〆る

[also 締める]

① add up, sum [add] up; close the account

② [in compounds] fasten, lock (a door or window), shut
③ finish off a bout of eating or drinking (with a closing dish)
④ pickle, marinate (fish) (with vinegar)

閉める
vt (move into closed position) shut, close

絞める
① strangle, strangulate, wring
② squeeze

HOMOPHONES

しまる
閉 CLOSE → 4116
絞 STRANGLE → 1707

しめる
〆 SUM → 4179
閉 CLOSE → 4116
絞 STRANGLE → 1707

緻
1762
◧ 1-6-9

▶**MINUTE**
チ

120	Nonstandard	U7DFB
糸	S15-6-9	F0000

traditional form → see 緻 at 1780

緣
1763
◧ 1-6-9

▶**RELATION**
▶**EDGE**
エン -ネン ふち へり えにし ㊔ ゆかり より

120	Names	U7DE3
糸	S15-6-9	F0000

traditional form → see 縁 at 1754

編
1764
◧ 1-6-9

▶**COMPILE**
▶**KNIT**
ヘン あ(む) -あ(み)

120	Nonstandard	U7DE8
糸	S15-6-9	F0000

traditional form → see 編 at 1755

緯
1765
◧ 1-6-9

▶**LATITUDE**
イ よこいと ぬき

120	Nonstandard	U7DEF
糸	S15-6-9	F0000

traditional form → see 緯 at 1782

緩
1766
◧ 1-6-9

▶**SLACK**
カン ゆる(い) ゆる(やか) ゆる(む) ゆる(める)

120	Nonstandard	U7DE9
糸	S15-6-9	F0000

traditional form → see 緩 at 1757

練
1767
◧ 1-6-9

▶**TRAIN**
レン ね(る) ね(り)-

120	Names	UFA57
糸	S15-6-9	F0000

traditional form → see 練 at 1738

緖
1768
◧ 1-6-9

▶**OUTSET**
ショ チョ お いとぐち

120	Names	U7DD6
糸	S15-6-9	F0000

traditional form → see 緒 at 1742

總
1769
◧ 1-6-9

▶**TOTAL**
▶**GENERAL**
ソウ す(べて) ㊔ ふさ さ

120	Nonstandard	U7DEB
糸	S15-6-9	F0000

traditional form → see 総 at 1743

縫
◧ 1-6-9

incorrect stroke-count
➡ see ◧ 1-6-10: 糸 at 1781

聯
1770
◧ 1-6-9

▶**LINK**
レン

128	Nonstandard	U8068
耳	S15-6-9	F0000

traditional form → see 聯 at 1797

聰
1771
◧ 1-6-9

▶**SHARP-WITTED**
ソウ さと(い) ㊔ さとし さとる あき あきら とし

128	Nonstandard	U8066
耳	S15-6-9	F0000

traditional form → see 聡 at 1750

蝶
1772
◧ 1-6-9

▶**BUTTERFLY**
チョウ
Ⓒ 蝶 dié

142	Names	U8776
虫	S15-6-9	F1750

COMPOUNDS

● [also suffix] [original meaning] **BUTTERFLY**
蝶蝶 ちょうちょう butterfly
胡蝶 こちょう butterfly
高山蝶 こうざんちょう alpine butterfly
紋白蝶 もんしろちょう cabbage butterfly

INDEPENDENT

【ちょう 蝶】**BUTTERFLY**

SYNONYMS

● **insects**

蚊 MOSQUITO → 1673
蛍 FIREFLY → 3204
蝶 BUTTERFLY → 1772
蚕 SILKWORM → 3107
蟬 CICADA → 1804
蜂 BEE → 1728
蛔 ROUNDWORM → 1717

蝦 1773

▶SHRIMP
カ えび
Ⓒ 虾 xiā

142	Names	U8766
虫	S15-6-9	F2259

1-6-9

KUN

【えび 蝦】SHRIMP, prawn, lobster, crayfish
蝦蟹 えびがに crayfish
蝦尾 えびお goldfish with a shrimp-like tail; head of a shamisen or lute
小蝦 こえび small shrimp

SPECIAL READINGS

蝦夷 えぞ peoples formerly of northern Japan with distinct language and culture; Ezo, Yezo
蝦夷 えみし old name of 蝦夷 えぞ
蝦蟇× がま toad, esp. Japanese toad
蝦蛄×(=青竜蝦) しゃこ mantis shrimp, esp. *Oratosquilla oratoria*

SYNONYMS

【えび】
○ crustaceans
蝦 SHRIMP → 1773
蟹 CRAB → 3611

蝉 1774

▶CICADA
セン せみ

142	Nonstandard	U8749
虫	S15-6-9	F0000

1-6-9 traditional form → see 蟬 at 1804

輝 1775

▶SHINE BRILLIANTLY
キ かがや(く) ㊔ てる あきら
Ⓒ 辉 huī

159	Jōyō	U8F1D
車	S15-7-8	F1117

1-6-9

(stroke order 1–15)

COMPOUNDS

● SHINE BRILLIANTLY, glitter, sparkle, radiate
輝線 きせん bright line
輝石 きせき pyroxene, augite
輝度 きど brightness
輝輝 きき brilliance
光輝有る こうきある shining, brilliant, glorious, splendid

KUN

【かがやく 輝く】[sometimes also 耀く or 赫く] SHINE BRILLIANTLY, glitter, gleam, sparkle, light up, brighten
輝き かがやき brilliancy
輝かしい かがやかしい bright (future), brilliant (achievement)
輝き渡る かがやきわたる shine out far and wide
輝かしい業績 かがやかしいぎょうせき brilliant achievements, bright future
喜びに輝く目 よろこびにかがやくめ eyes sparkling with joy

SYNONYMS

● shine and reflect
輝 SHINE BRILLIANTLY → 1775
光 shine → 3043
照 ILLUMINATE → 3506
映 REFLECT → 1104
耀 SHINE BRILLIANTLY → 1812
燿 SHINE → 1407
閃 FLASH → 4114
煌 GLITTER → 1296

USAGE

【かがやく】
輝く
[sometimes also 耀く or 赫く] shine brilliantly, glitter, gleam, sparkle, light up, brighten
耀く
[usu. 輝く, sometimes also 赫く] shine brilliantly, glitter, gleam, sparkle, light up, brighten
赫く
[usu. 輝く, sometimes also 耀く] shine brilliantly, glitter, gleam, sparkle, light up, brighten

HOMOPHONES

かがやく
耀 SHINE BRILLIANTLY → 1812
赫 BLAZING → 1960

頬 1776

▶CHEEK
キョウ ほお ほほ ㊔ ほ つら

181	Nonstandard	U982C
頁	S15-9-6	F0000

1-6-9 traditional form → see 頰 at 2043

【米】 糸 舟

糖 1777

▶SUGAR
トウ
Ⓝ 糖 Ⓒ 糖 táng

1-6-10

119	Jōyō-6	U7CD6
米	S16-6-10	F1494

COMPOUNDS

❶ⓐ (sweet substance derived from sugar cane or beets) SUGAR
ⓑ [also suffix] (water-soluble sweet carbohydrate) SUGAR
ⓒ abbrev. of 製糖 せいとう: SUGAR manufacturing

a 砂糖 さとう sugar
グラニュー糖 ぐらにゅーとう granulated sugar
精糖 せいとう refined sugar, sugar refining
製糖業 せいとうぎょう sugar manufacturing industry

b 糖分 とうぶん sugar content
糖尿病 とうにょうびょう diabetes
果糖 かとう fruit sugar, fructose
蔗×糖 しょとう sucrose
葡萄糖 ぶどうとう grape sugar, dextrose

c 日糖 にっとう Dai-Nippon Sugar, Inc.

❷ sweets
金平糖 こんぺいとう confetti
有平糖 あるへいとう toffee

INDEPENDENT

【とう 糖】 SUGAR (→❶ⓑ)
血液中の糖 けつえきちゅうのとう blood sugar

SYNONYMS

❶ⓐ seasonings
糖 SUGAR →1777
塩 SALT →0774
酢 VINEGAR →1910
醋 VINEGAR →2002
油 OIL →0400
醤 FERMENTED SAUCE →3569
噌 MISO →0882
蜜 HONEY →2958

糖 1778

▶SUGAR
トウ

1-6-10

119	Nonstandard	UFA03
米	S16-6-10	F0000

traditional form →see 糖 at 1777

縛 1779

▶BIND
バク しば(る)
Ⓝ 縛 Ⓒ 缚 fù

1-6-10

120	Jōyō	U7E1B
糸	S16-6-10	F1609

COMPOUNDS

❶ⓐ [original meaning] BIND, tie up
ⓑ apprehension by BINDing, arrest

a 緊縛 きんばく tight binding
就縛する しゅうばくする be put in bonds, come under arrest

b 捕縛する ほばくする put in bonds, arrest

❷ (restrain as if with bonds) BIND, restrict, restrain
束縛する そくばくする restrain, restrict, bind, fetter
呪縛 じゅばく spell
自縄自縛に陥る じじょうじばくにおちいる be caught in one's own trap

INDEPENDENT

【ばく 縛】 apprehension, arrest
縛に就く ばくにつく be put in bonds, come under arrest

KUN

【しばる 縛る】 BIND, tie, fasten; (restrain as if with bonds) bind, restrict, restrain
縛り上げる しばりあげる bind [tie] up
きつく縛る きつくしばる fasten tightly
規則で縛る きそくでしばる restrict (a person) by rule
金縛りになっている かなしばりになっている be bound hand and foot; be tied down with money

SYNONYMS

❶ⓐ join
結 TIE →1706
繋 CONNECT →3612
縛 BIND →1779
綴 BIND →1746
繃 BIND UP →1787
束 TIE UP →4369
梱 PACK →1205
連 LINK →3849
係 CONNECT →0108
接 join →0607

❷ restrain
制 CONTROL (restrain) →1624
禁 PROHIBIT →3469

限 LIMIT →0475
抑 SUPPRESS →0301
束 TIE UP →4369
縛 BIND →1779
控える HOLD BACK →0600
扣える HOLD BACK →0250
渋る hang [hold] back →0625

緻 1780

▶MINUTE
チ
N 緻 C 致 zhì

1-6-10

120	Jōyō	U7DFB
糸	S16-6-10	F2661

COMPOUNDS

● **MINUTE, detailed, elaborate, careful, fine**
緻密な ちみつな minute, close, elaborate, exact
精緻な せいちな minute, subtle, delicate, exquisite
細緻な さいちな minute, delicate, meticulous
巧緻な こうちな elaborate, exquisite, detailed

SYNONYMS

● **detailed**
詳 DETAILED →1926
細 MINUTE →1689
緻 MINUTE →1780
密 CLOSE →2857
精 meticulous →1729

縫 1781

▶SEW
ホウ ぬ(う)
N 縫 C 缝 féng fèng

1-6-10

120	Jōyō	U7E2B
糸	S16-6-10	F1821

COMPOUNDS

❶ [original meaning] **SEW, stitch**
縫合する ほうごうする suture, stitch (a wound)
縫工 ほうこう seamstress, tailor
裁縫 さいほう sewing, needlework, dressmaking
天衣無縫 てんいむほう perfect beauty with no trace of artifice

❷ mend, patch up
弥縫する びほうする patch up, make shift

KUN

【ぬう 縫う】**SEW, stitch**
縫い合わせる ぬいあわせる sew up [together]
手縫いの てぬいの hand-tailored[-sewed]
傷口を縫う きずぐちをぬう sew up [suture] a wound

SYNONYMS

❶ **weave and sew**
織 WEAVE →1801
紡 SPIN →1646
績 spin →1788
縫 SEW →1781
編 KNIT →1755
辮 PLAIT →2085
組 braid →1693
繡 EMBROIDER →1805

COMPOUND FORMATION

【天衣無縫 てんいむほう】
天衣無縫 'perfect beauty with no trace of artifice' is being like a robe (衣) from heaven (天) without (無) the slightest trace of sewing (縫 ❶).

緯 1782

▶LATITUDE
イ よこいと▲ ぬき▲
N 緯 C 纬 wěi

1-6-10

120	Jōyō	U7DEF
糸	S16-6-10	F1813

COMPOUNDS

❶ **LATITUDE, lines of latitude**
緯度 いど latitude
緯線 いせん parallels of latitude
経緯 けいい latitude and longitude
北緯 ほくい north latitude

❷ [original meaning] woof, weft
経緯 けいい warp and woof; circumstances, details

❸ [rare] books about charms and omens circulated as appendixes to the Chinese classics
緯書 いしょ book of omens appended to Confucian Chinese classics

INDEPENDENT

【い 緯】main plot (of a story)

KUN

【よこいと 緯】[also 横糸 or 緯糸] woof
【ぬき 緯】woof

SYNONYMS

❶ **latitude and longitude**

緯 LATITUDE → 1782
経 longitude → 1687

❷ **threads and fibers**
糸 THREAD → 2703
緯 woof → 1782
経 warp → 1687
繊 FIBER → 1789
維 FIBER → 1733
綸 THREAD → 1739
緬 FINE THREAD → 1758

USAGE

【よこいと】
緯
[also 横糸 or 緯糸] woof
横糸
[also 緯糸 or 緯] woof
緯糸
[also 横糸 or 緯] woof

HOMOPHONES

よこいと
横糸 → 1350, 2703
緯糸 → 1782, 2703

米 【糸】 舟

縦

1783
1-6-10

▶VERTICAL
ジュウ たて
Ⓝ 縱 Ⓒ 纵 zòng

120	Jōyō-6	U7E26
糸	S16-6-10	F1578

1 2 3 4 5 6 7 8 9 10 11 12 13 14 15 16

COMPOUNDS

❶ **VERTICAL, lengthwise, perpendicular, longitudinal**
縦断 じゅうだん cutting vertically
縦横に じゅうおうに vertically and horizontally, in all directions; freely
縦貫する じゅうかんする run through, traverse
縦走 じゅうそう running lengthwise; mountain range traversing
縦線 じゅうせん vertical line, bar (in music)

❷ **self-indulgent, wayward, selfish, as one pleases**
放縦 ほうじゅう self-indulgence
操縦 そうじゅう management, controlling; steering; piloting, flying

KUN

【たて 縦】
①ⓐ **length, height**
ⓑ [sometimes also 竪-] **VERTICAL, upright**
a 縦の たての vertical, longitudinal
b 縦書き たてがき vertical writing
縦縞 たてじま vertical stripes
② warp
縦糸 たていと [also 経糸 or 経] warp

SYNONYMS

❶ **vertical**
縦 VERTICAL → 1783
竪- VERTICAL → 3516
垂 perpendicular → 4382
立て- standing → 2486
直 STRAIGHT → 3649

HOMOPHONES

たて
立 STAND → 2486
建 BUILD → 3834
竪 VERTICAL → 3516

たていと
経 PASS THROUGH → 1687
縦糸 → 1783, 2703
経糸 → 1687, 2703

NOTE

➡ see USAGE notes at 立 2486 and 経 1687

縞

1784
1-6-10

▶STRIPE
コウ しま
Ⓒ 缟 gǎo

120	Names	U7E1E
糸	S16-6-10	F2556

COMPOUNDS

● **STRIPE, streak**
氷縞粘土 ひょうこうねんど varve

KUN

【しま 縞】**STRIPE, streak**
縞模様 しまもよう striped pattern
縞瑪×瑙× しまめのう onyx
縞馬 しまうま zebra
縦縞 たてじま vertical stripes
格子縞 こうしじま check pattern
干渉縞 かんしょうじま interference fringe

SYNONYMS

● **line**
線 LINE → 1760
筋 THREADLIKE STRUCTURE → 3319
条 strip → 2726
脈 VEIN → 1189
棒 straight line → 1237
縞 STRIPE → 1784
軸 AXIS → 1908

HOMOPHONES

しま 島 ISLAND → 4103

NOTE

➡ see USAGE note at 島 4103

縛

▶BIND

バク しば(る)

1785

◧1-6-10

120	Nonstandard	U7E1B
糸	S16-6-10	F0000

traditional form → see 縛 at 1779

緻

incorrect stroke-count

➡ see ◧1-6-9: 緻 at 1762

◧1-6-10

艙

▶SHIP'S HOLD

ソウ

Ⓒ 舱 cāng

1786

◧1-6-10

137	Non-Jōyō	U8259
舟	S16-6-10	F0000

COMPOUNDS

● [now replaced by 倉 2607] **SHIP'S HOLD, cabin**

艙口 そうこう hatch, hatchway

船艙 せんそう hold (of a ship), hatch

SYNONYMS

● **parts of boats and ships**

舵 STEERING DEVICE → 1697

梶 steering device → 1199

櫓 SCULL → 1412

櫂 OAR → 1405

舷 GUNWALE → 1698

艙 SHIP'S HOLD → 1786

繃

▶BIND UP

ホウ

Ⓒ 绷 bēng

1787

◧1-6-11

120	Non-Jōyō	U7E43
糸	S17-6-11	F0000

COMPOUNDS

● [now replaced by 包 3684] **BIND UP, strap up**

繃帯 ほうたい bandage, dressing

SYNONYMS

● **join**

結 TIE → 1706

繋 CONNECT → 3612

縛 BIND → 1779

綴 BIND → 1746

繃 BIND UP → 1787

束 TIE UP → 4369

梱 PACK → 1205

連 LINK → 3849

係 CONNECT → 0108

接 join → 0607

績

▶ACHIEVEMENTS

セキ ㊔ いさお

Ⓒ 绩 jì

1788

◧1-6-11

120	Jōyō-5	U7E3E
糸	S17-6-11	F1252

COMPOUNDS

❶ **ACHIEVEMENTS, accomplishments, merit, results, record**

成績 せいせき results, record, achievement

実績 じっせき (actual) result, positive achievements

業績 ぎょうせき achievements; business results

功績 こうせき meritorious deed, achievement

戦績 せんせき war record, military achievements; results, score

不成績 ふせいせき poor result, underachievement

❷ [original meaning] **spin thread, make yarn**

紡績 ぼうせき spinning

SYNONYMS

❶ **accomplishment**

績 ACHIEVEMENTS → 1788

功 MERIT → 0218

勲 MERITORIOUS SERVICE → 3560

❷ **weave and sew**

織 WEAVE → 1801

紡 SPIN → 1646

績 spin → 1788

縫 SEW → 1781

編 KNIT → 1755

辮 PLAIT → 2085

組 braid → 1693

繡 EMBROIDER → 1805

纖

▶FINE

▶FIBER

セン

Ⓝ 纖 繊◇ Ⓒ 纤 xiān qiàn

1789

◧1-6-11

120	Jōyō	U7E4A
糸	S17-6-11	F1820

COMPOUNDS

❶ⓐ **FINE, slender**

ⓑ **FINE** and delicate, slender and graceful

a 繊細な せんさいな delicate, fine, subtle

繊毛 せんもう cilia, fine hair

繊切り(=千切り) せんぎり long thin strips (of a vegetable)

b 繊指 せんし woman's slender fingers

繊手 せんしゅ delicate hands

❷ [original meaning] **FIBER, filament**

繊維 せんい fiber, textile

繊条 せんじょう filament

化繊 かせん synthetic fiber

合繊 ごうせん synthetic fiber

❸ [rare] 1/10,000,000

三繊 さんせん 3/10,000,000

INDEPENDENT

【せん 繊】long thin strips (of a vegetable); [rare] 1/10,000,000

大根を繊に切る だいこんをせんにきる cut a radish into fine strips

SYNONYMS

❶ⓐ **thin**

薄 THIN → 3004

細 SLENDER → 1689

繊 FINE → 1789

痩 GET THIN → 4069

❷ **threads and fibers**

糸 THREAD → 2703

緯 woof → 1782

経 warp → 1687

繊 FIBER → 1789

維 FIBER → 1733

綸 THREAD → 1739

緬 FINE THREAD → 1758

縮

1790

1-6-11

▶SHRINK

シュク ちぢ(む) ちぢ(まる) ちぢ(める) ちぢ(れる) ちぢ(らす) ㊔ おさむ

Ⓒ 缩 suō sù

120	Jōyō-6	U7E2E
糸	S17-6-11	F1169

COMPOUNDS

❶ⓐ [original meaning] (draw together) **SHRINK, contract**

ⓑ (make or become smaller) **SHRINK, reduce, shorten**

a 収縮 しゅうしゅく contraction, shrinking

伸縮 しんしゅく expansion and contraction

短縮 たんしゅく shortening, contraction, reduction

b 縮小 しゅくしょう reduction, curtailment, cut

縮減する しゅくげんする reduce, diminish

軍縮 ぐんしゅく reduction of armaments

濃縮する のうしゅくする concentrate

❷ (draw back) **SHRINK (as with fear), curl up, recoil, wince**

畏縮する いしゅくする shrink, flinch, wince

恐縮する きょうしゅくする feel much obliged, deeply appreciate; regret; feel embarrassed

KUN

【ちぢむ 縮む】*vi* **SHRINK, contract; cringe**

縮み ちぢみ shrinkage; cotton crepe

縮み織り ちぢみおり cotton crepe, preshrunk cloth

縮み上がる ちぢみあがる cringe, wince, flinch

伸び縮み のびちぢみ expansion and contraction, flexibility

【ちぢまる 縮まる】*vi* **be shortened, be contracted**

【ちぢめる 縮める】*vt* **contract, shorten, SHRINK**

【ちぢれる 縮れる】*vi* **be wavy, curl; SHRINK, be wrinkled**

縮れ毛 ちぢれげ curly, wavy, or fuzzy hair

【ちぢらす 縮らす】*vt* **curl, crinkle, crimp**

SYNONYMS

❶ⓐ **contract and shrink**

縮 SHRINK → 1790

約 CONTRACT → 1632

攣 CRAMP → 3635

ⓑ **decrease**

減 DECREASE → 0733

耗 WEAR AWAY → 1660

削 cut down → 1837

縮 SHRINK → 1790

落 FALL → 2907

蝕 ERODE → 2258

繃

1791

1-6-11

▶BIND UP

ホウ

120	Nonstandard	U7E43
糸	S17-6-11	F0000

traditional form → see 绷 at 1787

縫

1792

1-6-11

▶SEW

ホウ ぬ(う)

120	Nonstandard	U7E2B
糸	S17-6-11	F0000

traditional form → see 縫 at 1781

【糸】耳 臣 虫

縱

1793

1-6-11

▶VERTICAL

ジュウ たて

120	Names	U7E31
糸	S17-6-11	F0000

traditional form → see 縦 at 1783

繡

1794

1-6-11

▶EMBROIDER

シュウ ㊔ ぬい

120	Nonstandard	U7E4D
糸	S17-6-11	F0000

traditional form → see 繍 at 1805

總

1795

1-6-11

▶TOTAL

▶GENERAL

ソウ す(べて) ㊔ ふさ さ

120	Nonstandard	U7E3D
糸	S17-6-11	F0000

traditional form → see 総 at 1743

聴

1796

1-6-11

▶LISTEN

チョウ き(く)

Ⓝ 聽 Ⓒ 听 tīng

128	Jōyō	U8074
耳	S17-6-11	F0955

COMPOUNDS

❶ⓐ [original meaning] **LISTEN, hear**

ⓑ sense [capacity] of hearing

a 聴取する ちょうしゅする listen to, give a hearing to

聴衆 ちょうしゅう audience

聴講 ちょうこう lecture attendance

聴聞会 ちょうもんかい hearing

聴覚 ちょうかく sense of hearing

傍聴する ぼうちょうする hear, listen to; attend

視聴者 しちょうしゃ viewer, audience

公聴会 こうちょうかい public [open] hearing

傾聴 けいちょう listening closely

b 聴力 ちょうりょく power [sense] of hearing

難聴 なんちょう hardness of hearing

❷ⓐ LISTEN to (instructions), obey

ⓑ comply with, grant (permission)

a 聴従する ちょうじゅうする follow advice

b 聴許 ちょうきょ permission

KUN

【きく 聴く】LISTEN (to), give an ear to

民の声を聴く たみのこえをきく listen to the voice of the people

SYNONYMS

❶ⓐ **hear**

聞 HEAR → 4127

聴 LISTEN → 1796

HOMOPHONES

きく

聞 HEAR → 4127

訊 INQUIRE → 1842

NOTE

➡ see USAGE note at 聞 4127

聯

1797

1-6-11

▶LINK

レン

Ⓝ 聯 Ⓒ 联 lián

128	Non-Jōyō	U806F
耳	S17-6-11	F2868

COMPOUNDS

❶ [now replaced by 連 3849]

ⓐ (join together) **LINK, join**

ⓑ (connect as if by linking) **LINK, connect, join, unite**

a 聯立 れんりつ alliance, coalition

聯句 れんく linked verse

聯珠 れんじゅ *gobang*

b 聯絡 れんらく connection, contact; communication

聯想 れんそう association (of ideas)

聯合 れんごう combination, union, alliance; association

聯邦 れんぽう federation, confederation, union

聯盟 れんめい union, federation, league

聯隊 れんたい regiment

関聯 かんれん connection, relation, association

❷ⓐ **couplet**

ⓑ **counter for stanzas [verses]**

a 対聯 たいれん distich, couplet

b 五聯の詩 ごれんのし five-verse poem

SYNONYMS

❶ **relate**

関 CONCERN → 4129

係 CONNECT → 0108

絡 INTERLINK → 1709

渉 HAVE RELATIONS WITH → 0638

連 LINK → 3849

聯 LINK → 1797

聰

1798

1-6-11

▶SHARP-WITTED

ソウ さと(い) ㊔ さとし さとる あき あきら とし

128	Nonstandard	U8070
耳	S17-6-11	F0000

traditional form → see 聡 at 1750

臨 incorrect stroke-count
➡ see ■1-7-11: 臣 at 2059
■1-6-11

螺 1799

▶SPIRAL-SHELLED GASTROPOD
ラ つぶ にし
Ⓒ 螺 luó
■1-6-11

142	Names	U87BA
虫	S17-6-11	F2549

COMPOUNDS

❶ **SPIRAL-SHELLED GASTROPOD, conch, snail**
螺鈿× らでん mother-of-pearl
法螺 ほら conch; boasting, bragging, big talk
❷ **spiral, helix; screw**
螺旋 らせん spiral, helix; screw

KUN

【つぶ 螺】 [sometimes also 海螺] edible **SPIRAL-SHELLED GASTROPOD**
螺貝 つぶがい edible spiral-shelled gastropod
【にし 螺】 [sometimes also 辛螺] *nishi* shell
田螺 たにし viviparid (snail)

SPECIAL READINGS

螺子(=捻子) ねじ screw; spring, mainspring
栄螺(=拳螺) さざえ turban shell, esp. horned turban, *Turbo cornutus*
海螺 つぶ [usu. 螺] edible spiral-shelled gastropod
辛螺 にし [usu. 螺] *nishi* shell

SYNONYMS

❶ **shells**
殻 SHELL (of any kind) → 1883
甲 SHELL (of animals) → 4293
貝 seashell → 3150
螺 SPIRAL-SHELLED GASTROPOD → 1799
瑚 CORAL → 1300

HOMOPHONES

つぶ 海螺 → 0459, 1799
にし 辛螺 → 2531, 1799

糧 1800

▶FOOD PROVISIONS
リョウ ロウ かて
Ⓝ 粮 Ⓒ 粮 liáng
■1-6-12

119	Jōyō	U7CE7
米	S18-6-12	F1758

COMPOUNDS

● **FOOD PROVISIONS, food, foodstuffs**
糧食 りょうしょく provisions, food, rations
糧道 りょうどう supply of provisions
食糧 しょくりょう provisions, food, foodstuffs
衣糧 いりょう clothing and food
兵糧 ひょうろう army provisions, food

KUN

【かて 糧】 **provisions, food;** (figuratively) **food, bread, pabulum**
日日の糧 ひびのかて daily food
心の糧 こころのかて mental pabulum for thought

SYNONYMS

● **food**
飯 MEAL → 2126
膳 MEAL → 1381
食 FOOD, meal → 2578
糧 FOOD PROVISIONS → 1800
餌 ANIMAL FEED → 2257
肴 ACCOMPANIMENT FOR DRINKS → 2567

織 1801

▶WEAVE
ショク シキ お(る) お(り) おり -おり -お(り)
Ⓝ 綩 Ⓒ 织 zhī
■1-6-12

120	Jōyō-5	U7E54
糸	S18-6-12	F0610

COMPOUNDS

❶ⓐ [original meaning] **WEAVE**
ⓑ woven fabric, textile
a 織工 しょっこう weaver
織機 しょっき loom
織女星 しょくじょせい Vega
紡織 ぼうしょく spinning and weaving
染織 せんしょく dyeing and weaving
製織 せいしょく weaving
b 織布 しょくふ woven fabric
❷ **organize**
組織 そしき organization, system; constitution, construction; tissue

KUN

【おる 織る】 **WEAVE**
織り込む おりこむ interweave
織物 おりもの cloth, textile, fabric
機織り はたおり weaving; weaver; grasshopper
【おり 織り, 織】 **texture, WEAVE; weaving**
織り目 おりめ texture

目の細かな織り めのこまかなおり fine texture
羽織 はおり Japanese half coat, *haori*

【-おり -織, -織り】[also suffix] **woven fabric, brocade**
毛織 けおり woolen fabric, woolen cloth
西陣織 にしじんおり *Nishijin* brocade

SYNONYMS

❶ⓐ weave and sew
織 WEAVE →1801
紡 SPIN →1646
績 spin →1788
縫 SEW →1781
編 KNIT →1755
辮 PLAIT →2085
組 braid →1693
繡 EMBROIDER →1805

ⓑ fabrics
織 woven fabric →1801
紬 PONGEE →1684
紗 GAUZE →1653
絹 SILK →1721
綾 TWILL →1740
綿 COTTON →1736
棉 COTTON →1244
麻 HEMP →3878
毛 wool →4264
錦 BROCADE →2181

HOMOPHONES

おる 折 BREAK OFF →0297

COMPOUND FORMATION

【織女星 しょくじょせい】
織女星 'Vega' is the star (星) of the weaver (織 ❶ⓐ) girl (女) in Chinese mythology.

NOTE

➡ see USAGE note at 折 0297
➡ see COMPOUND FORMATION for 西陣織 にしじんおり →陣 0545

繕

▸MEND
ゼン つくろ(う)
Ⓒ 缮 shàn

1802
◧1-6-12

120	Jōyō	U7E55
糸	S18-6-12	F2497

Stroke order: 1–18

COMPOUNDS

● [original meaning] (fix and/or make whole) **MEND, repair**
修繕する しゅうぜんする mend, repair
営繕 えいぜん building and repairs, maintenance

KUN

【つくろう 繕う】**MEND, repair, darn; trim, tidy, adjust; cover up, smooth over, save**
繕い つくろい mending, darning
繕い立てる つくろいたてる put up a good front
身繕い みづくろい tidying up oneself, grooming oneself
見繕う みつくろう choose (a thing) at one's own discretion
取り繕う とりつくろう smooth over, temporize

SYNONYMS

● repair
直す FIX →3649
修 REPAIR →0138
繕 MEND →1802

繩

◧1-6-12

incorrect stroke-count
➡ see ◧1-6-13: 糸 at 1807

職

▸EMPLOYMENT
ショク ソク▲
Ⓝ 聀◆ 耺◆ Ⓒ 职 zhí

1803
◧1-6-12

128	Jōyō-5	U8077
耳	S18-6-12	F0432

Stroke order: 1–18

COMPOUNDS

❶ [also suffix]
ⓐ EMPLOYMENT, occupation, work, job
ⓑ abbrev. of 職業 しょくぎょう or 職務 しょくむ: **EMPLOYMENT, duty**
ⓒ post, office

a 職業 しょくぎょう occupation, vocation, profession
職務 しょくむ duty, duties, function
職場 しょくば place of work, workshop
職種 しょくしゅ type of occupation, occupational category
職員 しょくいん staff, employee, personnel
職歴 しょくれき one's professional [work] experience, one's business career
就職 しゅうしょく finding employment
退職 たいしょく retirement, resignation
無職の むしょくの without occupation, unemployed
内職 ないしょく side job
専門職 せんもんしょく profession, professional job

b 職安 しょくあん Public Employment Security Office
c 公職 こうしょく public office
現職 げんしょく present post [office]; incumbent
管理職 かんりしょく administrative [managerial] position
汚職 おしょく (official) corruption, bribery
❷ [also suffix] **craftsman, artisan**
職人 しょくにん craftsman, artisan
畳職 たたみしょく tatami maker
❸ knowledge
有職 ゆうそく knowledge of ancient court practices

INDEPENDENT

【しょく 職】**EMPLOYMENT, occupation, work, job; post, office; (professional) skill**
職を探す しょくをさがす seek employment, hunt for a job
職を辞する しょくをじする resign one's post

SYNONYMS

❶ **work and employment**
務 DUTY → 1505
任 OFFICE → 0057
役 SERVICE (esp. public) → 0288
勤 SERVICE (employment) → 2287
業 WORK → 3227
職 EMPLOYMENT → 1803
労 LABOR → 3155

蝉

▶CICADA
セン せみ
N 蟬 C 蝉 chán

1804
1-6-12

142	Names	U87EC
虫	S18-6-12	F2521

COMPOUNDS

● **CICADA**
蛙鳴蝉噪× あめいせんそう annoying noise, loud buzz; fruitless argument

KUN

【せみ 蝉】
① **CICADA**
蝉時雨 せみしぐれ outburst of cicadas singing
油蝉 あぶらぜみ large brown cicada, *Graptopsaltria nigrofuscata*
夏蝉 なつぜみ summer cicadas
空蝉 うつせみ cast-off cicada shell, cicada; person of this world, the real world
② unclassified compounds
川蝉(=翡×翠) かわせみ kingfisher, esp. common kingfisher

SYNONYMS

● **insects**
蚊 MOSQUITO → 1673
蛍 FIREFLY → 3204
蝶 BUTTERFLY → 1772
蚕 SILKWORM → 3107
蝉 CICADA → 1804
蜂 BEE → 1728
蛔 ROUNDWORM → 1717

繍

▶EMBROIDER
シュウ ㊔ ぬい
N 繡 C 绣 xiù

1805
1-6-13

120	Names	U7E61
糸	S19-6-13	F2660

COMPOUNDS

● **EMBROIDER; embroidery**
繍花 しゅうか flower-pattern embroidery
刺繍 ししゅう embroidery
錦繍 きんしゅう brocades and embroidered textiles; beautiful textile, beautiful clothes

SYNONYMS

● **weave and sew**
織 WEAVE → 1801
紡 SPIN → 1646
績 spin → 1788
縫 SEW → 1781
編 KNIT → 1755
辮 PLAIT → 2085
組 braid → 1693
繍 EMBROIDER → 1805

繰

▶REEL
▶SHIFT ONWARD
ソウ▲ く(る)[1] く(る)[2]
C 缫 sāo 缲 qiāo

1806
1-6-13

120	Jōyō	U7E70
糸	S19-6-13	F0984

COMPOUNDS

● **REEL**, wind
繰糸機 そうしき silk reeling machine

KUN

【くる[1] 繰る】
①ⓐ **REEL (silk off a cocoon); gin (cotton); spin**
ⓑ **REEL** in, reel up, wind, roll out
a 繰り綿 くりわた ginned cotton
繰り取る くりとる reel off
b 繰り出す くりだす draw out; call out (troops), sally forth

手繰る たぐる pull in hand over hand, draw in, reel in; retrace
掻い繰る かいぐる haul in hand over hand
雨戸を繰る あまどをくる roll open the shutters

② shift one by one, transfer in succession, perform repeatedly:
ⓐ turn over (the pages of a book), look up [consult] (a dictionary or calendar)
ⓑ count one by one, reckon
a 辞書を繰る じしょをくる consult a dictionary
b 指で日を繰る ゆびでひをくる count the days on one's fingers

【くる² 繰る】[in compounds]
①ⓐ **SHIFT ONWARD to the next stage, move up, carry over**
ⓑ **shift (a plan) to the next phase**
a 繰り上げる くりあげる advance, move up
繰り込み理論 くりこみりろん renormalization theory
b 繰り入れ金 くりいれきん transfer balance
繰り替える くりかえる exchange; appropriate (money to some other purpose)
繰り延べる くりのべる postpone, put off
繰り合わせる くりあわせる make time, arrange matters

② **shift for, make shift, get along, manage**
やり繰り やりくり tiding over, makeshift, management
資金繰り しきんぐり raising funds
臍×繰り へそくり secret savings, pin money

③ⓐ **perform an action repeatedly**
ⓑ move [roll] back and forth (between the fingers)
a 繰り返す くりかえす repeat, do over again
繰り言 くりごと same story told over and over again; grumble
b 爪繰る つまぐる finger, roll between the thumb and the fingers
乳繰り合う ちちくりあう have a love intrigue, flirt

④ unclassified compounds
勘繰る かんぐる guess at someone's true intentions, doubt

SYNONYMS

【くる¹】
① **wind and twine**
巻 ROLL UP →3273
捲 ROLL UP →0598
繰る REEL →1806
絡 ENTWINE →1709
纏 WIND AROUND →1814

【くる²】
① **move**
動 MOVE →2232
運 MOVE →3894
滑 SLIDE →0809
辷る SLIP →3957
移 SHIFT →1508
転 remove →1872
遷 TRANSFER →3932
繰る SHIFT ONWARD →1806

COMPOUND FORMATION

【乳繰り合う ちちくりあう】
乳繰り合う 'have a love intrigue, flirt' is, literally, to roll (繰る くる² ③ⓑ) a woman's breasts (乳) between one's fingers.

縄
1807
◧1-6-13

▶**ROPE**
ジョウ なわ ㊔ つな

120	Nonstandard	U7E69
糸	S19-6-13	F0000

traditional form →see 縄 at 1756

繪
1808
◧1-6-13

▶**PICTURE**
カイ エ

120	Nonstandard	U7E6A
糸	S19-6-13	F0000

traditional form →see 絵 at 1704

蠏
1809
◧1-6-13

▶**CRAB**
カイ かに

142	Nonstandard	U880F
虫	S19-6-13	F0000

traditional form →see 蟹 at 3611

疆
1810
◧1-6-13

▶**BOUNDARY**
キョウ
Ⓒ 疆 jiāng

102	Non-Jōyō	U7586
田	S19-5-14	F3201

COMPOUNDS

● [now usu. 境 0835] [original meaning] **BOUNDARY, border, frontier**
辺疆 へんきょう frontier (district), remote region, border(land)
新疆 しんきょう Xinjiang

SYNONYMS

● **edges and boundaries**
縁 EDGE →1754
端 edge →1564
辺 border →3761
境 BOUNDARY →0835
疆 BOUNDARY →1810
界 BOUNDS →3172
際 VERGE →0874
涯 OUTER LIMITS →0623

【糸】 舟 光

繼

1811

◧ 1-6-14

▶**SUCCEED**

ケイ つ(ぐ) まま-

120	Nonstandard	U7E7C
糸	S20-6-14	F0000

traditional form → see 継 at 1720

艦

◧ 1-6-14

incorrect stroke-count

➡ see ◧ 1-6-15: 舟 at 1817

耀

1812

◧ 1-6-14

▶**SHINE BRILLIANTLY**

ヨウ かがや(く) ㊔ あき あきら てる

Ⓝ 耀 Ⓒ 耀 yào

124	Names	U8000
羽	S20-6-14	F3061

COMPOUNDS

ⓐ [original meaning] **SHINE BRILLIANTLY**

ⓑ **brilliant, bright; glorious**

a 眩×耀する げんようする shine dazzlingly

b 栄耀 えいよう luxurious and glorious life

KUN

【かがやく 耀く】[usu. 輝く, sometimes also 赫く]

SHINE BRILLIANTLY, glitter, gleam, sparkle, light up, brighten

耀く太陽 かがやくたいよう the shining sun

目が耀く めがかがやく one's eyes sparkle

栄誉に耀く えいよにかがやく shine in the glory

SYNONYMS

ⓐ **shine and reflect**

輝 SHINE BRILLIANTLY → 1775

光 shine → 3043

照 ILLUMINATE → 3506

映 REFLECT → 1104

耀 SHINE BRILLIANTLY → 1812

燿 SHINE → 1407

閃 FLASH → 4114

煌 GLITTER → 1296

HOMOPHONES

かがやく

輝 SHINE BRILLIANTLY → 1775

赫 BLAZING → 1960

NOTE

➡ see USAGE note at 輝 1775

★ do not confuse with 燿 SHINE → 1407

燿

1813

◧ 1-6-14

▶**SHINE BRILLIANTLY**

ヨウ かがや(く) ㊔ あき あきら てる

124	Nonstandard	U8000
羽	S20-6-14	F0000

traditional form → see 耀 at 1812

纏

1814

◧ 1-6-15

▶**PUT TOGETHER**

▶**WIND AROUND**

テン まと(める) まと(う) まと(まる) まつ(わる)

Ⓝ 纏 Ⓒ 缠 chán

120	Names	U7E8F
糸	S21-6-15	F2450

COMPOUNDS

❶ⓐ [original meaning] **WIND AROUND, bind, tangle**

ⓑ twine round, hang about; be related to

a 纏足 てんそく foot-binding

纏綿 てんめん entanglement, involvement

❷ [now also 天 4250] **put on, be wrapped in**

半纏 はんてん short coat, workman's livery coat

KUN

【まとめる 纏める】

ⓐ **PUT TOGETHER, bring together, collect**

ⓑ **summarize, organize**

ⓒ **settle, conclude**

a 纏め買い まとめがい bulk buying, stocking up

纏め役 まとめやく mediator, facilitator, organizer

一纏め ひとまとめ one bundle [pack, bunch]

b 纏め まとめ summary, conclusion

考えを文章に纏める かんがえをぶんしょうにまとめる put one's ideas in writing

【まとう 纏う】

① **WIND AROUND**

付き纏う つきまとう follow (around), shadow

足手纏い あしでまとい burden, drag

② **put on, wear**

一糸纏わず いっしまとわず stark naked

【まとまる 纏まる】

ⓐ be collected, come together

ⓑ be settled, be in order

b 纏まり まとまり settlement, conclusion; unity, coherence

【まつわる 纏わる】

① be related to, concern

それに纏わる話 それにまつわるはなし story related to it

② coil (about); follow (about)

SYNONYMS

❶ⓐ **wind and twine**

巻 ROLL UP → 3273

捲 ROLL UP → 0598

繰る REEL → 1806

絡 ENTWINE → 1709

纏 WIND AROUND → 1814

❷ **wear and put on**

着 PUT ON → 4110

装 DRESS → 3327

帯 WEAR (esp. at the belt) → 3191
穿く PUT ON → 2800
纏 put on → 1814
履く put on footwear → 3933
被る put on headgear → 1495

【まとめる】

ⓐ **combine**

合 COMBINE → 2511
結 TIE → 1706
統 UNITE → 1710
括 LUMP TOGETHER → 0449
総 integrate → 1743
併 join together → 0092
綜 INTEGRATE → 1744
纏める PUT TOGETHER → 1814

纎

1815

◧ 1-6-15

▶**FINE**
▶**FIBER**
セン

120	Nonstandard	U7E8E
糸	S21-6-15	F0000

alternative form → see 纖 at 1789

續

1816

◧ 1-6-15

▶**CONTINUE**
ゾク　つづ(く)　つづ(ける) ㊔ つぎ　つぐ

120	Nonstandard	U7E8C
糸	S21-6-15	F0000

traditional form → see 続 at 1722

繡

◧ 1-6-15

incorrect stroke-count
➡ see ◧1-6-13: 糹 at 1805

艦

1817

◧ 1-6-15

▶**WARSHIP**
カン
Ⓒ 舰 jiàn

137	Jōyō	U8266
舟	S21-6-15	F1096

COMPOUNDS

● **WARSHIP, battleship**

艦船 かんせん ships and warships
艦隊 かんたい squadron, fleet
艦艇 かんてい war vessels
艦長 かんちょう captain of a warship
軍艦 ぐんかん warship

INDEPENDENT

【かん 艦】 **WARSHIP**, battleship
艦と運命を共にする かんとうんめいをともにする go down with the ship

SYNONYMS

● **boats and ships**

船 SHIP → 1700
舶 OCEANGOING SHIP → 1699
艦 WARSHIP → 1817
潜 submarine → 0922
舟 SMALL BOAT → 4353
艇 BOAT → 1727
隻 COUNTER FOR SHIPS → 3426

蠟

1818

◧ 1-6-15

▶**WAX**
ロウ
Ⓝ 蝋 Ⓒ 蜡 là

142	Names	U881F
虫	S21-6-15	F2169

COMPOUNDS

● [original meaning] **WAX, beeswax**

蠟燭 ろうそく candle
蠟人形 ろうにんぎょう wax figure
蠟石 ろうせき agalmatolite
蜜蠟 みつろう beeswax
封蠟 ふうろう sealing wax
屍蠟 しろう adipocere
生蠟 きろう crude Japan wax

INDEPENDENT

【ろう 蠟】 **WAX**

SYNONYMS

● **fats and oils**

油 OIL → 0400
脂 FAT → 1190
肪 ANIMAL FAT → 1089
膏 FAT → 2658
蠟 WAX → 1818

纏

1819

◧ 1-6-16

▶**PUT TOGETHER**
▶**WIND AROUND**
テン　まと(める)　まと(う)　まと(まる)　まつ(わる)

120	Nonstandard	U7E92
糸	S22-6-16	F0000

traditional form → see 纏 at 1814

纖

1820

1-6-17

▶**FINE**
▶**FIBER**
セン

120	Names	U7E96
糸	S23-6-17	F0000

traditional form → see 繊 at 1789

罐

1821

1-6-17

▶**CAN**
カン かま

121	Nonstandard	U7F50
缶	S23-6-17	F0000

traditional form → see 缶 at 2526

罐

1822

1-6-18

▶**CAN**
カン かま

121	Nonstandard	U7F36
缶	S24-6-18	F0000

alternative form → see 缶 at 2526

乳

1823

1-7-1

▶**MILK**
ニュウ ちち ち
Ⓝ 乳 Ⓒ 乳 rǔ

5	Jōyō-6	U4E73
乚	S8-1-7	F0962

Stroke order: 1 2 3 4 5 6 7 8 (乳)

COMPOUNDS

1a (mammalian secretion) **MILK**
b (food product) **MILK**
c MILKlike substance

a 母乳 ぼにゅう mother's milk
牛乳 ぎゅうにゅう (cow's) milk
b 乳業 にゅうぎょう dairy industry
乳価 にゅうか price of milk
粉乳 ふんにゅう powdered milk
脱脂乳 だっしにゅう nonfat milk
c 乳液 にゅうえき milky lotion; latex
豆乳 とうにゅう soybean milk

2 breast, breasts
乳房 にゅうぼう(=ちぶさ) breast, nipple
乳癌 にゅうがん breast cancer
乳頭 にゅうとう nipple

3 infancy
乳児 にゅうじ infant, baby, suckling
乳歯 にゅうし milk teeth

KUN

【ちち 乳】**MILK; breast, breasts**
乳牛 ちちうし(=にゅうぎゅう) milch cow, dairy cattle
乳首 ちちくび(=ちくび) teat, nipple
乳繰り合う ちちくりあう have a love intrigue, flirt

【ち 乳】**loop;** [in compounds] **MILK; breast**
乳飲み子 ちのみご baby, suckling
旗に乳を付ける はたにちをつける sew loops on a flag

SPECIAL READINGS

乳母 うば [rarely also 姆] wet nurse

SYNONYMS

1a bodily secretions
乳 MILK → 1823
精 sperm → 1729
汗 SWEAT → 0256
涙 TEAR → 0528
唾 SALIVA → 0553

b drinks
汁 JUICE, SOUP → 0227
乳 MILK → 1823
酒 ALCOHOLIC DRINK → 0532
茶 TEA → 2808
珈 COFFEE → 1138
醇 UNDILUTED WINE → 2001
酎 SHOCHU → 1852

1b dairy products
酪 DAIRY PRODUCTS → 1940
乳 MILK → 1823
醍 CREAM → 2031
醐 CREAM → 2032

2 chest
胸 CHEST → 1187
乳 breast → 1823

HOMOPHONES

うば
姆 GOVERNESS → 0331
乳母 → 1823, 4287

NOTE

➡ see COMPOUND FORMATION for 乳繰り合う ちちくりあう → 繰 1806

乳

1824

1-7-1

▶**MILK**
ニュウ ちち ち

5	Nonstandard	U4E73
乚	S8-1-7	F0000

traditional form → see 乳 at 1823

臥

1825

1-7-2

▶**LIE DOWN**
ガ ふ(せる) ふ(す)
Ⓝ 臥 Ⓒ 卧 wò

131	Names	U81E5
臣	S9-7-2	F2194

COMPOUNDS

1 [original meaning] **LIE DOWN**

臥薪嘗胆 がしんしょうたん perseverance; enduring hardships for the sake of vengeance
仰臥 ぎょうが lying face up
行住坐臥(=行住座臥) ぎょうじゅうざが the four cardinal behaviors (walking, stopping [standing], sitting and lying); daily life

❷ **be confined to one's bed, be sick in bed**
臥床 がしょう being confined to bed
病臥 びょうが being sick in bed

INDEPENDENT

【がする 臥する】LIE DOWN

KUN

【ふせる 臥せる】
① LIE DOWN
② **be confined to one's bed, be sick in bed**
風邪で臥っている かぜでふせっている be laid up with a cold

【ふす 臥す】same as 臥せる ふせる
臥し所 ふしど bed

SPECIAL READINGS

草臥れる くたびれる get tired, wear out

SYNONYMS

❶ **lie down**
伏 PROSTRATE → 0049
臥 LIE DOWN → 1825
寝る lie down → 2925

❷ **disease**
病 ILLNESS → 4062
疾 DISEASE → 4064
風 (infectious) disease → 3730
症 PATHOLOGICAL CONDITION → 4065
患 AFFECTED BY DISEASE → 3415
疫 EPIDEMIC → 4061
罹 FALL ILL → 3239
臥 be sick in bed → 1825

HOMOPHONES

ふせる 伏 PROSTRATE → 0049
ふす 伏 PROSTRATE → 0049

NOTE

➡ see USAGE note at 伏 0049

卧

1826

1-7-2

▶**LIE DOWN**

ガ ふ(せる) ふ(す)

131	Nonstandard	U5367
臣	S9-7-2	F0000

traditional form → see 臥 at 1825

訃

1827

1-7-2

▶**NEWS OF DEATH**

フ

Ⓒ 讣 fù

149	Jōyō	U8A03
言	S9-7-2	F3497

Stroke order: 1–9

COMPOUNDS

● **NEWS OF a person's DEATH**
訃報 ふほう news of a person's death, obituary
訃音 ふいん(=ふおん) news of a person's death

INDEPENDENT

【ふ 訃】NEWS OF a person's DEATH

SYNONYMS

● **information**
報 information → 2133
信 MESSAGE → 0115
訃 NEWS OF DEATH → 1827

計

1828

1-7-2

▶**PLAN**
▶**COMPUTE**

ケイ はか(る) はか(らう) ㊔ かず

Ⓒ 计 jì

149	Jōyō-2	U8A08
言	S9-7-2	F0319

Stroke order: 1–9

COMPOUNDS

❶ⓐ **PLAN, design, devise, scheme**
ⓑ **PLAN, stratagem**
a 計画 けいかく plan, project
設計 せっけい design, plan
b 計略 けいりゃく stratagem, plan, scheme
妙計 みょうけい ingenious trick, clever scheme
奸×計 かんけい vicious plan, crafty design

❷ **COMPUTE, calculate, reckon, count, estimate**
計算 けいさん computation, calculation
計上する けいじょうする sum up, appropriate (a sum for some purpose)
計量 けいりょう measuring, weighing
推計する すいけいする estimate
統計 とうけい statistics
会計 かいけい account, finance; bill
集計 しゅうけい totalization, classified total

❸ [also suffix] **meter, gauge, measuring instrument**
計器 けいき meter, gauge; instrument
時計 とけい clock, watch
速度計 そくどけい speedometer
地震計 じしんけい seismometer

温度計 おんどけい thermometer

❹ **total, sum total**

合計 ごうけい sum total, total
総計 そうけい total, total amount
小計 しょうけい subtotal

INDEPENDENT

【けい 計】**PLAN, scheme, plot, stratagem; total, sum total**

計五万円 けいごまんえん total 50,000 yen
国家百年の計 こっかひゃくねんのけい permanent national policy

KUN

【はかる 計る】

① **COMPUTE, calculate, estimate**

所要時間を計る しょようじかんをはかる calculate the time required

② **guess, surmise, fathom**

計り知れない はかりしれない unfathomable, inestimable

③ **PLAN**, design, scheme

国の将来を計る くにのしょうらいをはかる plan [provide] for the future of the country

④ deceive, play upon, take in

計られる はかられる be taken in

【はからう 計らう】**see to, arrange, manage, dispose; talk together, discuss**

計らい はからい discretion, arrangement, disposition, good offices
見計らう みはからう choose at one's own discretion; time (one's visit)

SYNONYMS

❶ **plans and planning**

計 PLAN → 1828
画 DRAW UP A PLAN → 3723
案 PROPOSAL → 2824
企 PROJECT → 2513
図 systematic plan → 3809
謀 SCHEME → 2004
策 SCHEME → 3320
略 STRATEGY → 1501
揆 PLOT → 0718

❷ **calculate and count**

算 CALCULATE → 3351
計 COMPUTE → 1828
数 count → 2245

❸ **measuring devices**

枡 MEASURE → 1070
尺 rule → 4248
計 meter → 1828
衡 scales → 0939
秤 BALANCE → 1488

❹ **total**

総 TOTAL → 1743
計 total → 1828
和 sum → 1450

USAGE

【はかる】

計る
① compute, calculate, estimate
② guess, surmise, fathom
③ plan, design, scheme
④ deceive, play upon, take in

測る
(measure the physical dimensions of) measure, gauge (length, depth, distance or area)

量る
① (determine the weight or volume of) measure, weigh
② [in compounds] guess, surmise, fathom

図る
① strive for, work for, promote, look to, provide for, seek
② bring about, attempt
③ [in negative constructions] expect, look forward to

謀る
scheme, plot, conspire, contrive

諮る
consult, confer, ask (a person's) opinion

HOMOPHONES

はかる

測 MEASURE → 0744
量 QUANTITY → 3119
図 DRAWING → 3809
謀 SCHEME → 2004
諮 CONSULT → 2009

訂

1829

1-7-2

▶REVISE

テイ

Ⓒ 订 dìng

149	Jōyō	U8A02
言	S9-7-2	F2131

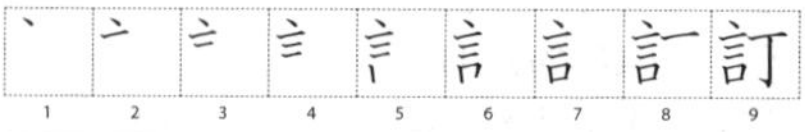

COMPOUNDS

ⓐ **REVISE, correct, edit**
ⓑ revision, edition
ⓒ counter for **REVISE**d editions

a 訂正する ていせいする correct, amend, revise
改訂する かいていする revise, edit
校訂する こうていする revise

b 新訂 しんてい new revision

c 三訂版 さんていばん third revised edition

INDEPENDENT

【ていする 訂する】**REVISE**, correct, amend

SYNONYMS

ⓐ **revise**

訂 REVISE → 1829
閲 REVIEW → 4132
校 COLLATE → 1166

ⓐ **correct**

正 RIGHT → 4296
直す correct → 3649
訂 REVISE → 1829
改 REFORM → 0287
矯 RECTIFY → 1586
匡 RECTIFY → 3710

ⓑ **editions**

版 edition → 1082
刊 publication → 0221
訂 revision → 1829
刷 printing → 1623

卻

1830

◧ 1-7-2

▶ELIMINATE

キャク かえ(って)

26	Nonstandard	U537B
卩	S9-2-7	F0000

alternative form → see 却 at 1436

則

1831

◧ 1-7-2

▶RULE

ソク のっと(る)▲ のり▲ ㊔ とき つね

Ⓒ 则 zé

18	Jōyō-5	U5247
刂	S9-2-7	F0973

Stroke order: 1–9

COMPOUNDS

ⓐ [also suffix] **RULE, regulation, principle, law**
ⓑ counter for **RULE**s or items

a 規則 きそく rule, regulation
法則 ほうそく law, rule
鉄則 てっそく ironclad rule, immutable law
原則 げんそく principle, general rule
学則 がくそく school regulations
教則 きょうそく rules for teaching
反則 はんそく violation of rules, infringement, foul
罰則 ばっそく penal regulations, punitive provisions
付則 ふそく additional rules, bylaw
自民党則 じみんとうそく rules of the Liberal Democratic Party

b 五則 ごそく five rules

INDEPENDENT

【そくする 則する】conform to the **RULE**s, follow precedent

KUN

【のっとる 則る】conform to the **RULE**s, follow, model

【のり 則】[usu. 法] **law, RULE, regulation; model, pattern; religious doctrine; sacred teachings of Buddha**

則を越える のりをこえる violate the laws of nature

SYNONYMS

ⓐ **laws and rules**

法 LAW → 0391
律 LAW → 0433
典 CANON → 3253
憲 CONSTITUTION → 3001
令 ordinance → 2489
則 RULE → 1831
矩 RULE → 1475
規 REGULATION → 1231
紀 discipline → 1628

HOMOPHONES

のり 法 LAW → 0391

NOTE

➡ see USAGE notes at 即 1439 and 法 0391

軌

1832

◧ 1-7-2

▶TRACK

キ

Ⓒ 轨 guǐ

159	Jōyō	U8ECC
車	S9-7-2	F1845

Stroke order: 1–9

COMPOUNDS

❶ⓐ **(wheel) TRACK, rut, path**
ⓑ **railway TRACK**

a 軌跡 きせき locus; tracks
軌道 きどう track, railway; planetary orbit; beaten track

b 軌条 きじょう rails

❷ beaten **TRACK**; model, paragon

常軌 じょうき beaten track, proper course

❸ⓐ gauge of a railway **TRACK**
ⓑ [original meaning] distance between the wheels of a carriage

a 広軌 こうき broad gauge

INDEPENDENT

【き 軌(=揆)】way of doing

軌を一にする きをいつにする have the same way of doing

臣 言 谷 貝 車 【巠】 余 缶 亩 肖 肖 孛 皀 君 良 束 享

SYNONYMS

❶ **ways and routes**

道 WAY (path) → 3888
径 PATH → 0347
軌 TRACK → 1832
線 LINE → 1760
澪 WATERWAY → 0957
途 WAY (route) → 3853
路 ROAD → 1936
筋 wayside → 3319
通り street → 3855
街 city street → 0702
辻 CROSSROADS → 3958
岐 forked road → 0285
巷 THE STREETS → 3097

❶ **trace**

軌 TRACK → 1832
跡 TRACE → 1937

USAGE

【き】

軌
[also 揆] way of doing
揆
[also 軌] way of doing

勁

▸STRONG
ケイ キョウ ㊔ つよし
Ⓒ 劲 jìn jìng

1833
1-7-2

19	Names	U52C1
力	S9-2-7	F2971

COMPOUNDS

● **STRONG, stiff, hard**

勁草 けいそう strong man with sense of fidelity
勁弓 けいきゅう stiff bow

SYNONYMS

● **hard**

硬 HARD → 1518
堅 FIRM → 3502
鞏 TOUGH → 3369
固 SOLID → 3830
剛 TOUGH → 2107
強 STRONG → 0574
勁 STRONG → 1833

叙

▸DESCRIBE
ジョ ㊔ のぶ
Ⓝ 敍 敘 Ⓒ 叙 xù

1834
1-7-2

29△	Jōyō	U53D9
又	S9-2-7	F2330

1	2	3	4	5	6	7	8	9
丿	𠆢	亼	亽	全	伞	余	叙	叙

COMPOUNDS

❶ [formerly also 抒 0295] **DESCRIBE, narrate, depict, explain**

叙述 じょじゅつ description, depiction
叙説 じょせつ explanation, interpretation
叙情詩 じょじょうし lyric poem [poetry]
叙事 じょじ narration, description
自叙伝 じじょでん autobiography
平叙文 へいじょぶん declarative sentence

❷ confer (a rank) upon, bestow

叙位 じょい conferment of a rank
叙勲 じょくん decoration, bestowal of an order

INDEPENDENT

【じょする 叙する】**DESCRIBE**, depict; confer

男爵に叙せられる だんしゃくにじょせられる be conferred (a) baron

SYNONYMS

❶ **describe**

叙 DESCRIBE → 1834
抒 DESCRIBE → 0295
描 DEPICT → 0591
写 portray → 2493

卸

▸WHOLESALE
シャ▲ おろ(す) おろし おろ(し)
Ⓝ 卸 Ⓒ 卸 xiè

1835
1-7-2

26	Jōyō	U5378
卩	S9-2-7	F2570

1	2	3	4	5	6	7	8	9
丿	𠂉	𠂉	午	午	𢀖	缶	卸	卸

KUN

【おろす 卸す】**WHOLESALE, sell wholesale**

小売りに卸す こうりにおろす sell wholesale to a retailer

【おろし 卸, 卸し】[also prefix and suffix] **WHOLESALE, wholesale trade; wholesaler**

卸商 おろししょう wholesaler
卸売り おろしうり wholesale
卸値 おろしね wholesale price
卸相場 おろしそうば wholesale price [market]
野菜を卸しで買う やさいをおろしでかう buy vegetables wholesale
貴金属卸 ききんぞくおろし wholesale [wholesaler] in precious metals
棚卸し(=店卸し) たなおろし inventory

SYNONYMS

【おろす】

◯ **sell and trade**

売 SELL → 2722
卸す WHOLESALE → 1835
販 ENGAGE IN SALES → 1869
商 TRADE → 2623
貿 TRADE → 3214
易 EXCHANGE → 3064

USAGE

【おろし】

卸
[also prefix and suffix] **wholesale, wholesale trade; wholesaler**

卸し
see comment below

下ろし
grated radish; vegetable grater

★卸し is a verbal gerund while 卸 is a noun. Both these forms are used in the sense of wholesaling. In the sense of grating vegetables, only 下ろし should be used. In the latter sense, おろし is sometimes mistakenly written 卸し.

HOMOPHONES

おろす
下 DOWN → 4186
降 DESCEND → 0548
おろし 下 DOWN → 4186

NOTE

➡ see also USAGE note at 下 4186

畆

1836

◧ 1-7-2

▶RIDGE

ボウ うね せ ㊔ あぜ

102	Nonstandard	U7546
田	S9-5-4	F0000

traditional form → see 畝 at 1857

削

1837

◧ 1-7-2

▶CUT BY CHIPPING

サク けず(る) そ(ぐ)▲

Ⓝ 削 Ⓒ 削 xiāo xuē

18	Jōyō	U524A
刂	S9-2-7	F1336

1	2	3	4	5	6	7	8	9
丨	丷	䒑	𬺷	肖	肖	肖	肖	削

COMPOUNDS

❶ⓐ **CUT BY CHIPPING, whittle, cut metal (with a cutting tool), machine**
ⓑ [formerly 鑿 3640] (cut a hole in) **excavate, drill**

a 切削 せっさく cutting, machining
研削 けんさく grinding
旋削 せんさく turning (on a lathe)
b 削岩機 さくがんき rock drill
削井 さくせい well drilling
掘削する くっさくする dig out, excavate
開削 かいさく excavation, cutting, digging

❷ⓐ **cut down, whittle down, curtail**
ⓑ **cross out, strike off, delete, cancel**

a 削減 さくげん curtailment, reduction
b 削除 さくじょ deletion, elimination, cancellation
添削する てんさくする correct, touch up ("add and delete")

KUN

【けずる 削る】**whittle, shave, sharpen, CUT BY CHIPPING; cut down, whittle down, curtail; cross out, strike off, delete, cancel**

削り屑 けずりくず shavings, chips
鉛筆削り えんぴつけずり pencil sharpener
荒削り あらけずり rough planing, roughing, machining
予算を削る よさんをけずる curtail a budget
一字削る いちじけずる delete a letter

【そぐ 削ぐ】[also 殺ぐ]

① chip, cut off
鼻を削がれる はなをそがれる have one's nose mutilated [cut off]

②ⓐ diminish, reduce, dampen
ⓑ spoil

a 気勢を削ぐ きせいをそぐ diminish [dampen] the spirit
b 興を削ぐ きょうをそぐ spoil the fun of

SYNONYMS

❶ⓐ **polish and rub**
磨 POLISH → 3946
擦 RUB → 0971
摩 RUB AGAINST → 3938
摺 RUB AGAINST → 0850
研 GRIND → 1456
削 CUT BY CHIPPING → 1837
瑳 POLISH → 1343

❶ⓐ **cut**
切 CUT → 0030
薙ぐ MOW DOWN → 3010
剪 PRUNE → 2886
削 CUT BY CHIPPING → 1837
挽く GRIND, saw → 0511
断 CUT OFF → 1885
截 CUT OFF → 4092
裁 CUT OUT → 4090
斬 CUT WITH A SWORD → 1874
割 cut with a knife → 2284
剖 DISSECT → 2103
刈る CLIP → 0032
伐 CUT DOWN → 0046

ⓑ **dig**
掘 DIG → 0601

鑿 EXCAVATE → 3640
削 excavate → 1837
穿 DRILL → 2800

❷ⓐ **decrease**

減 DECREASE → 0733
耗 WEAR AWAY → 1660
削 cut down → 1837
縮 SHRINK → 1790
落 FALL → 2907
蝕 ERODE → 2258

ⓑ **eliminate**

却 ELIMINATE → 1436
排 EXCLUDE → 0593
払う CLEAR AWAY → 0225
剝 PEEL OFF → 2105
耘 WEED → 1661
削 cross out → 1837
抹 wipe off → 0370
省 leave out → 3100
脱 REMOVE → 1225
去 take away → 2678
外す take off → 0215
除 RID OF → 0546
撤 WITHDRAW → 0912

USAGE

【そぐ】

削ぐ
[also 殺ぐ]
① chip, cut off
②ⓐ diminish, reduce, dampen
ⓑ spoil

殺ぐ
[also 削ぐ] same as 削ぐ

HOMOPHONES

そぐ 殺 KILL → 1677

剕 1838

▸**CUT BY CHIPPING**
サク けず(る) そ(ぐ)

18	Nonstandard	U524A
刂	S9-2-7	F0000

◧1-7-2

traditional form → see 削 at 1837

勃 1839

▸**SUDDENLY**
ボツ ホツ▲ ㊔ ひろ ひら
Ⓒ 勃 bó

19	Jōyō	U52C3
力	S9-2-7	F1890

◧1-7-2

COMPOUNDS

❶ **SUDDENLY, abruptly**

勃発 ぼっぱつ outbreak, sudden occurrence
勃然として ぼつぜんとして suddenly, with sudden force; in a fit of anger
勃興 ぼっこう sudden rise, sudden increase in power
勃起 ぼっき (male) erection

❷ well up with force, erupt, rush

勃勃たる ぼつぼつたる spirited, rising, energetic
鬱勃たる うつぼつたる irresistible, pent-up, burning

SYNONYMS

❶ **sudden**

急 SUDDEN → 2595
激 sudden → 0955
暴 sudden → 3138
俄 SUDDEN → 0106
頓 SUDDEN → 1320
勃 SUDDENLY → 1839
突 abruptly → 2772

卽 1840

▸**IMMEDIATE**
ソク つ(く) つ(ける) すなわ(ち)

26	Names	U537D
卩	S9-2-7	F0000

◧1-7-2

traditional form → see 即 at 1439

郡 ◧1-7-2

incorrect stroke-count
➡ see ◧1-7-3: 君 at 1858

郎 ◧1-7-2

incorrect stroke-count
➡ see ◧1-7-3: 良 at 1859

勅 1841

▸**IMPERIAL DECREE**
チョク ㊔ とき
Ⓝ 敕 Ⓒ 敕 chì

19	Jōyō	U52C5
力	S9-2-7	F2084

◧1-7-2

COMPOUNDS

ⓐ **IMPERIAL [royal] DECREE, imperial order [edict]**
ⓑ imperial

a 勅宣 ちょくせん imperial decree
勅語 ちょくご imperial rescript
詔勅 しょうちょく imperial edict
神勅 しんちょく oracle

b 勅使 ちょくし imperial messenger
勅選 ちょくせん imperial nomination

INDEPENDENT

【ちょく 勅】**IMPERIAL DECREE** [order]

SYNONYMS

ⓐ **imperial decree**
- 勅 IMPERIAL DECREE → 1841
- 詔 IMPERIAL EDICT → 1900
- 宣 imperial proclamation → 2799

郭 1-7-2

incorrect stroke-count
➡ see 1-8-3: 享 at 2112

訊 1842 1-7-3

▶**INQUIRE**

ジン き(く) たず(ねる)

Ⓒ 讯 xùn

149	Names	U8A0A
言	S10-7-3	F0876

COMPOUNDS

● [usu. 尋 2918] **interrogate, question**
- 訊問する じんもんする question, examine, interrogate

KUN

【きく 訊く】[now usu. 聞く] **ask, INQUIRE**
- 訊き返す ききかえす ask again; ask in return
- 道を訊く みちをきく ask the way

【たずねる 訊ねる】[usu. 尋ねる]

ⓐ **question, interrogate**

ⓑ **INQUIRE (about, after), ask, question**

SYNONYMS

【きく】

○ **inquire**
- 問 QUESTION → 4117
- 詰 question closely → 1920
- 聞く ask → 4127
- 質 query → 3483
- 尋ねる INQUIRE → 2918
- 訊 INQUIRE → 1842
- 伺う INQUIRE (*humble*) → 0078
- 諮 CONSULT → 2009
- 詢 ASK FOR ADVICE → 1917

HOMOPHONES

きく
- 聞 HEAR → 4127
- 聴 LISTEN → 1796

たずねる
- 尋 INQUIRE → 2918
- 訪 VISIT → 1860

NOTE

➡ see USAGE notes at 聞 4127 and 尋 2918

記 1843 1-7-3

▶**WRITE DOWN**

キ しる(す) ㊔ のり

Ⓒ 记 jì

149	Jōyō-2	U8A18
言	S10-7-3	F0161

Stroke order: 1–10

COMPOUNDS

❶ⓐ [original meaning] **WRITE DOWN, record, put down in writing**

ⓑ [also suffix] **written account, record, description**

a
- 記録 きろく record, document, chronicle; (new) record
- 記者 きしゃ journalist, reporter; editor
- 記事 きじ news, article; account
- 記入 きにゅう entry, record
- 記名する きめいする sign one's name, register
- 明記する めいきする write clearly, specify
- 登記 とうき registration, registry
- 下記の かきの following, undermentioned
- 表記する ひょうきする write, express in writing; write on a surface
- 標記する ひょうきする mark; write a title

b
- 日記 にっき diary
- 手記 しゅき note, memorandum; memoirs
- 伝記 でんき biography
- 旅行記 りょこうき travel record, travel book
- 古事記 こじき Kojiki (Ancient Chronicles)

❷ **commit to memory, memorize, remember, bear in mind**
- 記憶 きおく memory, recollection
- 記念日 きねんび memorial day, anniversary
- 暗記 あんき learning by heart, memorizing
- 銘記する めいきする bear in mind, remember; inscribe, engrave
- 強記 きょうき good memory

❸ **officer managing records and documents**
- 書記 しょき clerk, secretary

❹ [formerly also 徽 0968] **sign, mark, emblem**
- 記号 きごう symbol, mark, sign
- 記章 きしょう medal, badge; emblem, insignia

❺ abbrev. of 古事記 こじき: Kojiki (Ancient Chronicles)
- 記紀 きき Kojiki and Nihonshoki

INDEPENDENT

【き 記】**written account, description; record; used at the beginning of official records**
- 思い出の記 おもいでのき one's memoirs
- 二月二十八日記 にがつにじゅうはちにちき recorded on February 28

【きする 記する】**record, WRITE DOWN**

KUN

【しるす 記す】**WRITE DOWN, record, put down in writing**

書き記す かきしるす write down, record, register

SYNONYMS

❶ⓐ write

書 WRITE → 3292
筆 write → 3317
写 COPY → 2493
記 WRITE DOWN → 1843
紀 record in writing → 1628
控える note down → 0600
録 RECORD → 2186
登 register → 3208
註 ANNOTATE → 1893

ⓑ records

記 written account → 1843
録 RECORD → 2186
譜 SYSTEMATIC RECORD → 2068
誌 records → 1950
史 HISTORY → 4324
伝 biography → 0048

❷ remember

憶 REMEMBER → 0944
覚える COMMIT TO MEMORY → 3217
記 commit to memory → 1843
追 reminisce → 3840
顧 LOOK BACK → 2394
偲 RECOLLECT → 0153

USAGE

【しるす】

記す
write down, record, put down in writing

印す
mark, inscribe

HOMOPHONES

しるす 印 MARK → 1023

NOTE

➡ see also USAGE note at 表 3083
★ do not confuse with 紀 ERA → 1628

訓

1844

1-7-3

▸INSTRUCT

クン ㊔ さとし のり くに

Ⓒ 训 xùn

149	Jōyō-4	U8A13
言	S10-7-3	F1277

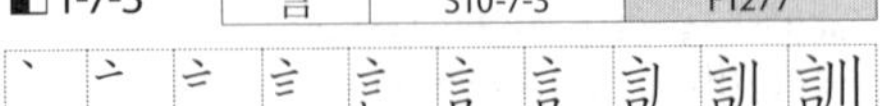
1 2 3 4 5 6 7 8 9 10

COMPOUNDS

❶ INSTRUCT, teach, admonish

訓練 くんれん training, drill
訓辞 くんじ admonitory speech
訓戒 くんかい admonition, warning
訓導 くんどう old word for licensed elementary school teacher; instruction

❷ (give orders) **INSTRUCT, advise, order**

訓示 くんじ instruction
訓令 くんれい instructions, (official) orders, directive

❸ precept, lesson, admonition, INSTRUCTion, teachings

家訓 かくん family precepts
教訓 きょうくん lesson, precept, teachings
処生訓 しょせいくん guiding motto for one's life

❹ Japanese-derived pronunciation of kanji, *kun* reading

訓読 くんどく(=くんよみ) Japanese-derived pronunciation of kanji, *kun* reading
和訓 わくん Japanese reading of a Chinese character

❺ decipher, interpret, explain

訓解 くんかい explanation, interpretation
訓釈する くんしゃくする explain the meanings of old words

INDEPENDENT

【くん 訓】***kun* reading; precept, lesson, one's teachings**

【くんずる 訓ずる】read in the *kun*

SYNONYMS

❶ teach

教 TEACH → 1887
啓 ENLIGHTEN → 3434
諄 TEACH WITH CARE → 1979
授 teach → 0595
育 educate → 2544
練 TRAIN → 1738
訓 INSTRUCT → 1844
誨 INSTRUCT → 1946
諭 ADMONISH → 2012
導 GUIDE → 3587
迪 EDIFY → 3817

❷ instruct

訓 INSTRUCT → 1844
指 direct → 0452

❸ precept

戒 commandment → 3972
訓 precept → 1844

託

1845

▌1-7-3

▶**ENTRUST**

タク かこつ(ける)▲ かこ(つ)▲

Ⓒ 托 tuō

149	Jōyō	U8A17
言	S10-7-3	F1402

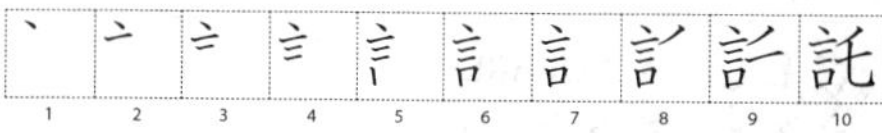

COMPOUNDS

❶ [also 托 0252] [original meaning] **ENTRUST (a person with a thing), place (a thing) in someone's charge, commit, ask**

託児所 たくじしょ day nursery

委託する いたくする entrust with, charge with, consign

嘱託 しょくたく part-time employee

寄託する きたくする deposit, entrust

信託 しんたく trust

結託する けったくする conspire with, be in collusion with

供託金 きょうたくきん deposit money

屈託の無い くったくのない free from worry, carefree

❷ express oneself indirectly; oracle

託宣 たくせん (Buddhist or Shinto) oracle

御託 ごたく repetitious talk; saucy speech, pretentious statement

神託 しんたく oracle

❸ make a pretext of, give pretext

託言 たくげん excuse, pretext, plea

仮託 かたく pretext, pretense, plea

INDEPENDENT

【たくす 託す】 [sometimes also 托す] **ENTRUST (a person with a thing); anchor (one's hope); convey (one's feelings) in (verse)**

KUN

【かこつける 託ける】 make a pretext of, use (a thing) as pretext

病気に託けて びょうきにかこつけて under the pretext of ill health

【かこつ 託つ】 complain of, rail [repine] at

不遇を託つ ふぐうをかこつ repine at one's hard lot

SYNONYMS

❶ **commit**

託 ENTRUST → 1845

托 ENTRUST → 0252

預 DEPOSIT → 1317

委 COMMIT → 3160

任 LEAVE TO → 0057

嘱 CHARGE WITH → 0881

討

1846

▌1-7-3

▶**STUDY**

▶**SUPPRESS BY ARMED FORCE**

トウ う(つ)

Ⓒ 讨 tǎo

149	Jōyō-6	U8A0E
言	S10-7-3	F0896

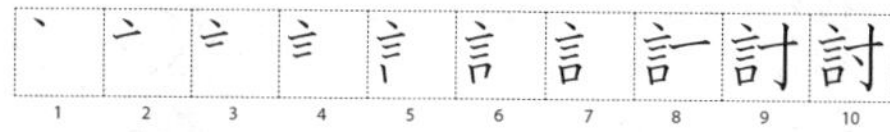

COMPOUNDS

❶ (inquire into and examine closely) **STUDY, scrutinize, examine, discuss**

討議 とうぎ discussion, debate, deliberation

討論 とうろん debate, discussion, argument

討究 とうきゅう investigation, study

検討する けんとうする examine, study, investigate

❷ **SUPPRESS BY ARMED FORCE, put down [attack] the enemy, send a punitive expedition**

討伐 とうばつ suppression (of a rebellion), punitive expedition

討幕する とうばくする attack the shogunate

討匪× とうひ suppression of bandits

掃討する そうとうする wipe out (the enemy), clear

追討する ついとうする hunt down and kill

征討 せいとう subjugation, conquest

KUN

【うつ 討つ】

① **kill (with a sword or spear)**

敵討ち かたきうち vendetta, revenge

②ⓐ **SUPPRESS BY ARMED FORCE, put down [attack] the enemy, send a punitive expedition**

ⓑ [usu. 撃つ, sometimes also 打つ] **attack, strike, assault**

a 敵を討つ てきをうつ quell the enemy

b 討ち入る うちいる break into (a house to kill the master), raid

手討ち てうち capital punishment given personally by a feudal lord

不意討ち ふいうち surprise attack

夜討ち ようち night attack

SYNONYMS

❶ **investigate and examine**

閲 REVIEW → 4132

審 EXAMINE CAREFULLY → 2985

験 TEST → 2306

勘 CHECK → 2231

糾 INQUIRE INTO → 1631

究 STUDY EXHAUSTIVELY → 2729

察 INSPECT → 2961

討 STUDY → 1846

探 PROBE → 0613

検 EXAMINE → 1241

診 EXAMINE A PATIENT → 1898
調 INVESTIGATE → 1973
査 LOOK INTO → 3092

❷ **conquer and suppress**
征 CONQUER → 0349
討 SUPPRESS BY ARMED FORCE → 1846
伐 CUT DOWN → 0046
鎮 QUELL → 2210
靖 PACIFY → 1546

HOMOPHONES

うつ
撃 STRIKE → 3552
打 STRIKE → 0224

NOTE

➡ see USAGE note at 打 0224

豹 1847

▶**LEOPARD**
ヒョウ ㊔ はだら
Ⓝ 豹 Ⓒ 豹 bào

1-7-3

153	Names	U8C79
豸	S10-7-3	F2964

COMPOUNDS

● [original meaning] **LEOPARD, panther**
豹柄 ひょうがら leopard print, leopard pattern
豹変 ひょうへん sudden drastic change (in behavior)
黒豹 くろひょう black panther
アメリカ豹 あめりかひょう jaguar
全豹 ぜんぴょう whole picture, entirety

INDEPENDENT

【ひょう 豹】**LEOPARD, panther**

SPECIAL READINGS

海豹 あざらし earless seal, true seal

SYNONYMS

● **undomesticated mammals**
虎 TIGER → 3981
猿 MONKEY → 0824
鯨 WHALE → 2361
犀 RHINOCEROS → 3900
狼 WOLF → 0541
狐 FOX → 0472
羚 SEROW → 1695
鼠 RAT → 3340
獅 LION → 0825
豹 LEOPARD → 1847
熊 BEAR → 3530
象 ELEPHANT → 2647
麒 MALE CHINESE UNICORN → 2363
麟 FEMALE CHINESE UNICORN → 2376
猪 WILD BOAR → 0652
鹿 DEER → 3879

COMPOUND FORMATION

【全豹 ぜんぴょう】
全豹 'whole picture, entirety' derives from 全豹一斑 ぜんぴょういっぱん, an ancient Chinese saying meaning to guess the appearance of the entire (全) leopard (豹) by looking at a single (一) spot (斑).

豹 1848

▶**LEOPARD**
ヒョウ ㊔ はだら

1-7-3

153	Nonstandard	U8C79
豸	S10-7-3	F0000

traditional form → see 豹 at 1847

財 1849

▶**WEALTH**
ザイ サイ ㊔ たから
Ⓒ 财 cái

1-7-3

154	Jōyō-5	U8CA1
貝	S10-7-3	F0681

1	2	3	4	5	6	7	8	9	10
丨	冂	月	目	目	貝	貝	貝一	貝†	財

COMPOUNDS

❶ⓐ **WEALTH, fortune, money; property, assets, goods, commodities**
ⓑ [suffix] **goods, assets, property**
a 財貨 ざいか wealth, money and property; goods
財産 ざいさん property, fortune, wealth
財布 さいふ purse, wallet
私財 しざい private funds, private property
蓄財 ちくざい accumulation of wealth
資財 しざい property, fortune, assets
b 家財 かざい household effects [goods]
耐久消費財 たいきゅうしょうひざい durable consumer goods
文化財 ぶんかざい cultural assets [properties]

❷ **finance, funds, revenue**
財界 ざいかい business world, economic circles
財源 ざいげん revenue source, financial resources
財政 ざいせい public finance, financial affairs
財団法人 ざいだんほうじん juridical foundation, juridical person
財務 ざいむ financial affairs

INDEPENDENT

【ざい 財】**WEALTH, fortune, money; property, goods**
財を成す ざいをなす build a fortune

SYNONYMS

❶ⓐ **wealth**
財 WEALTH → 1849
産 property → 4089
富 riches → 2892

宝 TREASURE →2764
❷ **money**
金 MONEY →2552
銭 MONEY →2159
貨 MONEY (legal tender), coin →3113
幣 CURRENCY →3582
銀 SILVER →2156
財 finance →1849
資 RESOURCES →3342
-玉 coin suffix →4289
札 bill →1011

射

1850
1-7-3

▶**SHOOT**
シャ い(る) さ(す)▲
Ⓒ 射 shè

41	Jōyō-6	U5C04
寸	S10-3-7	F0836

COMPOUNDS
❶ⓐ **SHOOT, fire**
ⓑ [original meaning] **SHOOT** an arrow
a 射撃 しゃげき shooting, gunshot, firing
射的 しゃてき target practice, shooting
射程 しゃてい shooting range
射殺する しゃさつする shoot to death
発射する はっしゃする discharge, shoot, launch
高射砲 こうしゃほう antiaircraft gun, high-angle gun
❷ (emit forcefully) **SHOOT (out) (radiation or liquids), emit, radiate, discharge, eject**
射精 しゃせい ejaculation, seminal emission
放射する ほうしゃする radiate, emit, emanate
日射 にっしゃ insolation, solar radiation
反射 はんしゃ reflection
直射日光 ちょくしゃにっこう direct rays of the sun
注射 ちゅうしゃ injection, shot
❸ archery
射手 しゃしゅ archer
騎射 きしゃ shooting on horseback, equestrian archery

INDEPENDENT
【しゃ 射】 **archery**
射を学ぶ しゃをまなぶ learn archery

KUN
【いる 射る】 **SHOOT (an arrow), let off (an arrow)**
射止める いとめる shoot to death; win, acquire
射抜く いぬく shoot through
【さす 射す】 [also 差す] **shine on**
障子に影が射す しょうじにかげがさす A shadow is cast on the *shoji* (paper sliding-door)

SYNONYMS
❶ **shoot**
射 SHOOT →1850
撃 fire →3552
発 discharge →3174
❷ **emit**
出 PUT OUT →4310
発 EMIT →3174
放 radiate →1058
排 DISCHARGE →0593
射 SHOOT →1850
噴 SPOUT →0879
吐 SPEW →0235
湧 WELL UP →0749

HOMOPHONES
さす
差 DIFFERENCE →4104
指 FINGER →0452
刺 STAB →1625
挿 INSERT →0517
注 POUR →0383
止 STOP →3659

NOTE
➡ see USAGE note at 差 4104

軒

1851
1-7-3

▶**EAVES**
▶**COUNTER FOR HOUSES**
ケン のき
Ⓒ 轩 xuān

159	Jōyō	U8ED2
車	S10-7-3	F1251

COMPOUNDS
❶ **EAVES**, canopy
軒灯 けんとう eaves lantern, door light
❷ⓐ **COUNTER FOR HOUSES**
ⓑ house
a 四軒 よんけん four houses
一軒家 いっけんや solitary house; private home
数軒 すうけん several houses
b 軒別に けんべつに house to house
❸ suffix after names of restaurants or shops
来来軒 らいらいけん The Rairai (name of a Chinese restaurant)
東海軒 とうかいけん Tokai Restaurant
❹ rise high
意気軒高(=意気軒昂)として いきけんこうとして in high spirits

❺ [original meaning, now archaic] chariot used by noblemen in ancient China

KUN

【のき 軒】**EAVES**

軒下 のきした under the eaves

軒先 のきさき edge of the eaves, house frontage

軒並み のきなみ row of houses; all round, across the board

SYNONYMS

❶ **roof parts**

軒 EAVES → 1851

庇 EAVES → 3802

棟 ridge → 1248

瓦 roof tile → 4288

❷ⓐ **counters for houses**

軒 COUNTER FOR HOUSES → 1851

戸 counter for households → 2429

棟 counter for buildings → 1248

ⓑ **houses**

家 HOUSE → 2827

屋 HOUSE → 3842

軒 house → 1851

戸 HOUSEHOLD → 2429

宅 DWELLING HOUSE → 2698

居 residence → 3822

邸 STATELY RESIDENCE → 1451

住 housing → 0072

庵 HERMITAGE → 3876

酎

▸*SHOCHU*

チュウ

Ⓒ 酎 zhòu

1852

1-7-3

164	Jōyō	U914E
酉	S10-7-3	F2294

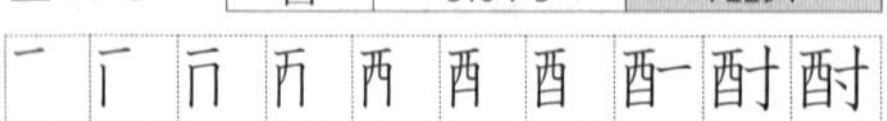

1 2 3 4 5 6 7 8 9 10

COMPOUNDS

❶ (low-class distilled spirits) ***SHOCHU***

酎ハイ ちゅうはい *shochu* with tonic water

焼酎 しょうちゅう *shochu*

❷ [original meaning, now obsolete] triple-brewed thick alcoholic drink

SYNONYMS

❶ **drinks**

汁 JUICE, SOUP → 0227

乳 MILK → 1823

酒 ALCOHOLIC DRINK → 0532

茶 TEA → 2808

珈 COFFEE → 1138

醇 UNDILUTED WINE → 2001

酎 SHOCHU → 1852

配

▸DISTRIBUTE

ハイ くば(る)

Ⓒ 配 pèi

1853

1-7-3

164	Jōyō-3	U914D
酉	S10-7-3	F0309

1 2 3 4 5 6 7 8 9 10

COMPOUNDS

❶ **DISTRIBUTE, apportion, allot, allocate**

配達 はいたつ delivery

配給 はいきゅう distribution, supply; rationing

配本 はいほん distribution of books

配付 はいふ distribution, apportionment

配当する はいとうする allot

配役 はいやく cast (of a play)

分配 ぶんぱい division, distribution, allotment

勾配 こうばい slope, incline; gradient

❷ [sometimes also 排 0593] **match, put in order, arrange**

配置 はいち arrangement; posting (of troops)

配合 はいごう combination, distribution, arrangement; harmony

配列 はいれつ arrangement, disposition

配色 はいしょく color arrangement [scheme]

按配する あんばいする arrange, distribute; adjust

❸ⓐ **match [join] in marriage, get married**

ⓑ mate (animals), breed

a 配偶者 はいぐうしゃ spouse, mate

b 交配 こうはい mating

❹ **concern oneself with (a person's welfare), be concerned about**

配慮 はいりょ consideration, care, concern

心配 しんぱい anxiety, concern, worry, uneasiness; good offices

高配 こうはい your trouble, your good offices

手配 てはい arrangement, preparation; search instruction (by police)

❺ abbrev. of 配当 はいとう: dividend

減配 げんぱい reduction in a dividend; smaller ration

無配の むはいの without dividend

❻ **place under, subordinate**

配下 はいか subordinates, followers

支配する しはいする control, manage, govern

采配 さいはい baton (of command)

軍配 ぐんばい sumo umpire's fan; commander's fan (in old Japan); stratagem

❼ send a criminal to exile, banish

配流 はいる exile, banishment

配所 はいしょ place of exile

❽ **used phonetically for *hai***

気配 けはい sign, indication

INDEPENDENT

【はいする 配する】 allot, arrange; match; [archaic] exile

KUN

【くばる 配る】 DISTRIBUTE, apportion, allot, allocate; concern oneself with, attend to

トランプを配る とらんぷをくばる deal cards

心配り こころくばり exerting care, attention

SYNONYMS

❶ **distribute**

配 DISTRIBUTE → 1853

頒 DISTRIBUTE WIDELY → 1318

分 DIVIDE → 2466

❹ **worry**

憂 BE ANXIOUS → 2664

配 concern oneself → 1853

構う MIND → 1325

虞 FEARS (of undesirable event) → 4037

❺ **interest and dividend**

利 interest → 1431

子 interest → 4196

配 dividend → 1853

酌

1854

◧ 1-7-3

▶POUR WINE

シャク く(む)

Ⓝ 酌 Ⓒ 酌 zhuó

164	Jōyō	U914C
酉	S10-7-3	F2159

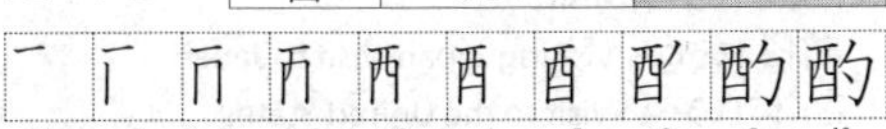

COMPOUNDS

❶ [original meaning] **POUR [serve] WINE or sake, fill a person's cup; drink wine**

酌婦 しゃくふ barmaid, waitress

晩酌 ばんしゃく evening drink

手酌 てじゃく self-service in sake drinking

❷ weigh and consider, take into consideration

酌量 しゃくりょう consideration, extenuation

参酌する さんしゃくする take into consideration, make allowances for

媒酌 ばいしゃく matchmaking

INDEPENDENT

【しゃく 酌】 serving wine

お酌 おしゃく serving wine

酌をする しゃくをする serve wine or sake; fill a person's cup

KUN

【くむ 酌む】 drink, have a drink

酒を酌み交わす さけをくみかわす drink together, help one another to sake

SYNONYMS

❶ **offer wine**

酌 POUR WINE → 1854

献 offer wine → 2240

酬 reciprocate wineglasses → 1941

USAGE

【くむ】

酌む

drink, have a drink

汲む

①ⓐ draw water, ladle, scoop up, pump

ⓑ pour (a drink) into a cup [glass]

② consider, sympathize with

HOMOPHONES

くむ 汲 DRAW WATER → 0310

酌

1855

◧ 1-7-3

▶POUR WINE

シャク く(む)

164	Nonstandard	U914C
酉	S10-7-3	F0000

traditional form → see 酌 at 1854

髟

1856

◧ 1-7-3

▶*KAMIKANMURI*

190	Radical	U9ADF
髟	S10-10-0	F0000

RADICAL

kamikanmuri 'hair' (髪 鬚 髭ˣ), used in characters related to human hair

---

畝

1857

◧ 1-7-3

▶RIDGE

ボウ▲ うね せ▲ ㊔ あぜ

Ⓝ 畂 畆 Ⓒ 亩 mǔ

102	Jōyō	U755D
田	S10-5-5	F2441

KUN

【うね 畝】 [original meaning] **RIDGE, furrow; rib, cord (of textiles)**

畝溝 うねみぞ furrow ridges

畝織 うねおり rep, ribbed fabric

【せ 畝】*se*, are: unit of sq. measure equiv. to approx. 0.99 ares or 30 *bu* (歩), used esp. for measuring fields or farms
十畝 じっせ approx. 10 ares
町段畝歩 ちょうたんせぶ units of sq. measure (for rice fields, forests, etc.)

SYNONYMS

【うね】
◯ hills
丘 HILL → 4307
畝 RIDGE → 1857
岡 HILL → 3719
台 heights → 2498
坂 SLOPE → 0275
阪 slope → 0321
塚 MOUND → 0675
阜 MOUND → 3254
陵 high mound → 0660
稜 RIDGE → 1545
◯ area units
坪 *TSUBO* (3.3 sq. m) → 0328
歩 *bu* (3.3 sq. m) → 3071
畝 *se* (0.99 ares) → 1857
反 *tan* (9.9 ares) → 3663
町 *cho* (99.2 ares) → 1430

郡

▶COUNTY
グン こおり▲ ㊔ くに
Ⓒ 郡 jùn

1858
1-7-3

163	Jōyō-4	U90E1
阝	S10-3-7	F1398

Stroke order: 1–10

COMPOUNDS

❶ⓐ COUNTY (of a Japanese prefecture or U.S. state), district, subprefecture
ⓑ suffix after names of counties
a 郡部 ぐんぶ counties; rural districts
郡長 ぐんちょう head county official, district headman
郡制 ぐんせい county system
郡県 ぐんけん counties and prefectures
b 名西郡 みょうざいぐん Myozai District
❷ prefecture in ancient China

INDEPENDENT

【ぐん 郡】COUNTY, district

KUN

【こおり 郡】unit of administration in former Japan

SYNONYMS

❶ territorial divisions
州 STATE → 0064
県 PREFECTURE → 3269
府 URBAN PREFECTURE → 3824
道 district of Hokkaido → 3888
都 METROPOLIS OF TOKYO → 2120
省 province in China → 3100
郡 COUNTY → 1858

郎

▶YOUNG MAN
▶MALE NAME SUFFIX
ロウ ㊔ お

1859
1-7-3

163	Names	U90DE
阝	S10-3-7	F0000

traditional form → see 郎 at 1641

郭

1-7-3

incorrect stroke-count
➡ see 1-8-3: 享 at 2112

訪

▶VISIT
ホウ おとず(れる) たず(ねる) と(う)▲
Ⓒ 访 fǎng

1860
1-7-4

149	Jōyō-6	U8A2A
言	S11-7-4	F0661

Stroke order: 1–11

COMPOUNDS

❶ⓐ VISIT, call on
ⓑ VISIT, call
a 訪問 ほうもん visit
訪日 ほうにち visiting Japan, visit to Japan
訪米 ほうべい visit to the United States
訪客 ほうきゃく visitor
来訪する らいほうする visit, call
b 歴訪 れきほう round of calls
❷ inquire into, investigate
探訪する たんぼうする make inquiries, inquire into

KUN

【おとずれる 訪れる】VISIT, call on, pay a visit
訪れ おとずれ visit, call; advent, arrival
病院を訪れる びょういんをおとずれる visit at a hospital

【たずねる 訪ねる】VISIT, call on, pay a visit
友人を訪ねる ゆうじんをたずねる call on a friend

【とう 訪う】call on, VISIT

SYNONYMS

❶ visit
訪 VISIT → 1860
参 VISIT A HOLY PLACE → 2563

詣 VISIT A HOLY PLACE → 1918
寄 call at → 2856
伺 call on → 0078

HOMOPHONES

たずねる
尋 INQUIRE → 2918
訊 INQUIRE → 1842
とう 問 QUESTION → 4117

NOTE

➡ see USAGE notes at 尋 2918 and 問 4117

訣 1861

1-7-4

▶**SEPARATE**
ケツ
Ⓒ 诀 jué

149	Names	U8A23
言	S11-7-4	F2702

COMPOUNDS

[now also 決 0308]

❶ **SEPARATE, part, bid farewell**
訣別 けつべつ separation, farewell
永訣 えいけつ last farewell

❷ **secrets (as of an art), knack**
秘訣 ひけつ secret, key
要訣 ようけつ main point

SYNONYMS

❶ **part company**
別 SEPARATE → 1434
離 SEPARATE → 2364
訣 SEPARATE → 1861

許 1862

1-7-4

▶**PERMIT**
キョ ゆる(す) もと▲ ㊔ こ
Ⓒ 许 xǔ

149	Jōyō-5	U8A31
言	S11-7-4	F0671

(stroke order 1–11)

COMPOUNDS

ⓐ [original meaning] **PERMIT, allow, approve, sanction**
ⓑ **permission, license, authorization**
a 許可 きょか permission, approval, authorization
許容する きょようする tolerate, allow, permit
許諾する きょだくする consent, approve, permit
b 黙許 もっきょ tacit permission
免許 めんきょ license, permit
特許 とっきょ patent; special permission; concession
公許 こうきょ official permission, license

KUN

【ゆるす 許す】
①ⓐ **PERMIT, allow, approve**
ⓑ **license, authorize**
a 許し ゆるし permission
結婚を許す けっこんをゆるす give permission to marry
時間の許す限り じかんのゆるすかぎり as long as time allows
b 開業を許す かいぎょうをゆるす license to practice (law)
②ⓐ **forgive, pardon, excuse**
ⓑ **exempt, exonerate, excuse from**
a 過失を許す かしつをゆるす forgive (a person) for his [her] fault
b そればかりはお許し下さい そればかりはおゆるしください Please let me be excused from that
③ relax one's caution, let in on, yield to
心を許せる人 こころをゆるせるひと confidant, one's trusted friend
肌を許す はだをゆるす surrender one's chastity to a man
④ (let something unfavorable happen) allow, suffer, sustain
ヒットを許す ひっとをゆるす allow a hit
⑤ admit, acknowledge
自他共に許す じたともにゆるす be acknowledged by oneself and others

【もと 許】 [now usu. 元] in the vicinity of, near (a person), with (someone), under (someone's roof)
手許 てもと at hand, within reach; cash at hand
国許 くにもと one's home, one's birthplace
父母の許 ふぼのもと under one's parents' roof

SPECIAL READINGS

許嫁▲(=許婚▲) いいなずけ one's fiancé [fiancée], one's betrothed

SYNONYMS

ⓐ **permit**
許 PERMIT → 1862
免 license → 2565
准 grant permission → 0143
允 GIVE CONSENT → 2476

【ゆるす】
②ⓐ **forgive**
赦 AMNESTY → 1870
免 EXEMPT → 2565
許す forgive → 1862
恕 FORGIVE WITH COMPASSION → 3282
宥 PARDON → 2803

HOMOPHONES

もと

元 ORIGIN → 2428
下 DOWN → 4186
本 BASIS → 4314
基 BASE → 3312
素 ELEMENT → 3108

NOTE

➡ see USAGE note at 元 2428

設

1863
1-7-4

▶**SET UP**
セツ もう(ける)
Ⓒ 设 shè

149	Jōyō-5	U8A2D
言	S11-7-4	F0340

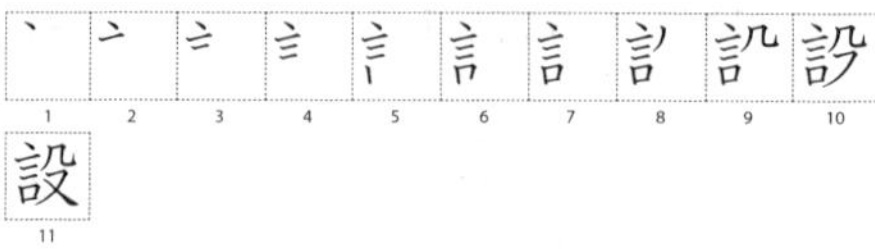

COMPOUNDS

❶ⓐ (assemble and/or erect) **SET UP, install, erect, construct**
ⓑ (found) **SET UP (as an institution), establish, found**

a 設備 せつび equipment, facilities
建設 けんせつ construction, building, erection
埋設する まいせつする put [lay] underground
施設 しせつ equipment, facilities; institution, establishment

b 設立する せつりつする establish, found, set up
設置する せっちする establish, found, set up
設定 せってい establishment, creation, fixation, setting up
開設 かいせつ establishment, inauguration
創設 そうせつ establishment, founding
特設する とくせつする set up specially
私設の しせつの private

❷ (put forth) **SET UP (plans), pose (a question)**
設計 せっけい design, plan
設問する せつもんする pose a question

KUN

【もうける 設ける】**SET UP, establish, found; organize; prepare (seats), provide**
設け もうけ preparation, provision; establishment
工場を設ける こうじょうをもうける set up a factory
席を設ける せきをもうける give a banquet

SYNONYMS

❶ⓐ **build**
建 BUILD (a building) → 3834
造 build (various structures) → 3856
築 CONSTRUCT → 3370
設 SET UP → 1863

❶ⓐ **equip and install**
据える INSTALL → 0602
敷 LAY → 2345
架 LAY ACROSS → 3178
装 FIT OUT → 3327
設 SET UP → 1863
備 PROVIDE → 0165

ⓑ **found**
立 ESTABLISH → 2486
設 SET UP → 1863
置 found → 3222

訟

1864
1-7-4

▶**LITIGATE**
ショウ
Ⓒ 讼 sòng

149	Jōyō	U8A1F
言	S11-7-4	F1899

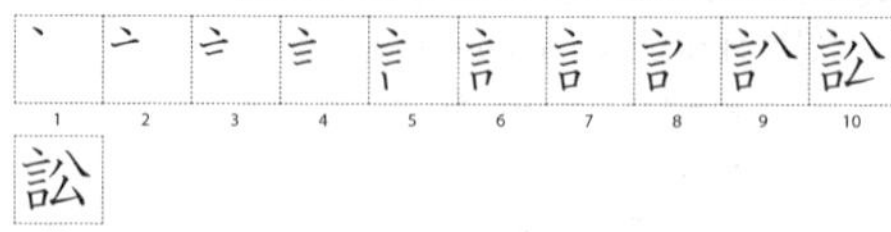

COMPOUNDS

ⓐ **LITIGATE, bring a case to court, sue**
ⓑ [rare] **dispute, argue**

a 訟務部 しょうむぶ Litigation Department (of the Ministry of Justice)
訴訟 そしょう lawsuit, litigation

b 争訟 そうしょう dispute

SYNONYMS

ⓐ **sue**
訴 SUE → 1901
訟 LITIGATE → 1864
告 accuse of → 3062
控 accuse in court → 0600

訳

1865
1-7-4

▶**TRANSLATE**
▶**SENSE**
ヤク わけ
Ⓝ 譯 Ⓒ 译 yì

149	Jōyō-6	U8A33
言	S11-7-4	F0834

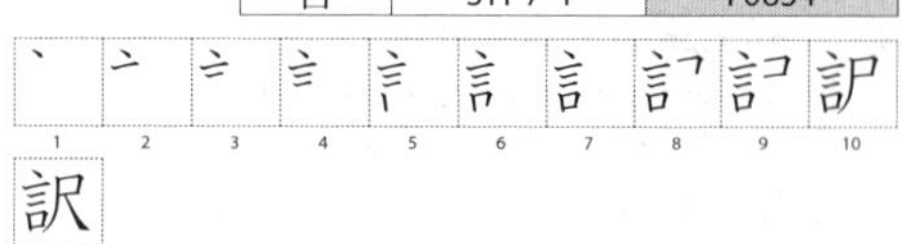

COMPOUNDS

ⓐ [original meaning] **TRANSLATE, interpret, render**

b [also suffix] **translation, rendering, version, interpretation**

c [suffix] **TRANSLATEd by**

a 訳者 やくしゃ translator
 通訳 つうやく interpreting; interpreter
 翻訳 ほんやく translation, rendering

b 直訳 ちょくやく literal translation
 新訳 しんやく new translation
 和文英訳 わぶんえいやく Japanese-English translation
 日本語訳 にほんごやく Japanese translation [version]

c 米川正夫訳 よねかわまさおやく translated by Masao Yonekawa

INDEPENDENT

【やく 訳】**translation, rendering**
 巧い訳 うまいやく good translation

【やくす 訳す】**TRANSLATE**
 訳し難い やくしがたい difficult to translate

KUN

【わけ 訳】

① **SENSE, meaning**
 訳の分からない言葉 わけのわからないことば words that make no sense, meaningless words

② **(good) SENSE, reason**
 訳の分かった人 わけのわかったひと sensible man
 訳知り わけしり person who knows the world; possessing an understanding about love affairs

③ **reason, cause, ground(s)**
 訳も無く わけもなく without reason, without cause
 言い訳 いいわけ apology, excuse, explanation
 申し訳 もうしわけ excuse, apology, explanation

④ circumstances, matter, case
 訳を説明する わけをせつめいする explain the circumstances
 どう云う訳だ どういうわけだ What's the matter?
 内訳 うちわけ items (of an account), details, breakdown

⑤ natural consequence
 彼女が怒る訳だ かのじょがおこるわけだ No wonder she got angry

⑥ [in negative constructions] trouble
 訳無く わけなく without difficulty, easily

SYNONYMS

a translate
 訳 TRANSLATE → 1865
 翻 RENDER → 2391

【わけ】

① **meaning**
 義 MEANING → 2948
 意 MEANING → 2650
 訳 SENSE → 1865
 旨 PURPORT → 2516
 趣 PURPOSE → 4111

② **reason**
 理 REASON → 1220
 訳 SENSE → 1865

③ **cause and reason**
 因 CAUSE → 3792
 由 REASON → 4311
 為 because → 4395
 故 reason → 1466
 訳 reason → 1865

④ **states and situations**
 態 STATE → 3529
 調 TONE → 1973
 様 MODE → 1332
 相 PHASE → 1120
 状 CONDITION → 0322
 況 CONDITIONS → 0395
 景 business conditions → 3118
 勢 course of events → 3542
 境 SITUATION → 0835
 局 current situation → 3800
 情 ACTUAL CONDITIONS → 0583
 訳 circumstances → 1865

𧦅

1866

◧ 1-7-4

▶**EXTOL**

オウ うた(う)

149	Nonstandard	U27985
言	S11-7-4	F0000

traditional form → see 謳 at 2061

註

◧ 1-7-4

incorrect stroke-count
➡ see ◧ 1-7-5: 言 at 1893

欲

1867

◧ 1-7-4

▶**DESIRE**

ヨク ほっ(する) ほ(しい)

Ⓒ 欲 yù

76	Jōyō-6	U6B32
欠	S11-4-7	F0732

COMPOUNDS

a [formerly also 慾 3551] [original meaning] **DESIRE, craving; avarice, greed**

b DESIRE, wish, want, crave for

a 欲情 よくじょう sexual desire, craving, passion

欲深 よくふか(=よくぶか) greed, avarice; miser, greedy person
欲深い よくぶかい greed, avaricious
欲張り よくばり greed; greedy
食欲 しょくよく appetite (for food)
物欲 ぶつよく worldly desires
性欲 せいよく sexual desire, lust
意欲 いよく volition, will, desire
知識欲 ちしきよく intellectual thirst
b 欲念 よくねん desire, wish; passion
欲求 よっきゅう want(s), desire, wish
欲望 よくぼう desire, craving
貪欲 どんよく greed, avarice

INDEPENDENT

【よく 欲(=慾)】**DESIRE, craving; avarice, greed**
欲の奴隷 よくのどれい slave to avarice

KUN

【ほっする 欲する】**DESIRE, wish, want, crave for**
平和を欲する へいわをほっする desire [wish for] peace

【ほしい 欲しい】**want, DESIRE, wish for**
欲しがる ほしがる desire, want, wish for, covet
来て欲しくない きてほしくない I don't want you to come

SYNONYMS

ⓐ will and intention
志 AMBITION → 2725
意 MIND → 2650
図 intention → 3809
気 mind to do something → 3960
念 thought of doing something → 2554
趣 PURPOSE → 4111
欲 DESIRE → 1867

ⓑ wish and desire
願 WISH → 2320
憧 YEARN AFTER → 0899
憬 YEARN AFTER → 0898
貪 COVET → 2630
望 HOPE → 3408
希 ASPIRE → 2543
懐 LONG FOR → 0942
慕 yearn for → 2970
渇 thirst for → 0627
欲 DESIRE → 1867
慾 DESIRE → 3551
求 SEEK → 4365

敗

▸BE DEFEATED
ハイ やぶ(れる)
Ⓒ 败 bài

1868
1-7-4

66	Jōyō-4	U6557
攵	S11-4-7	F0793

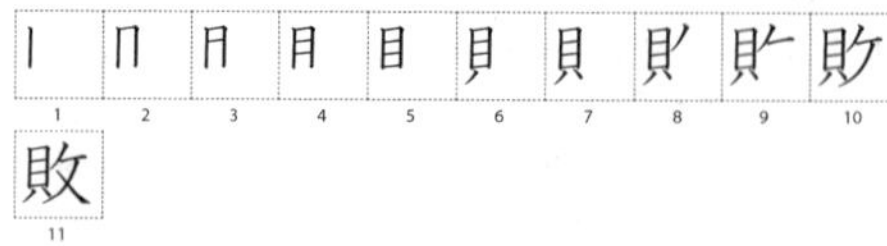

COMPOUNDS

❶ⓐ BE DEFEATED, lose
ⓑ defeat
ⓒ counter for number of defeats
a 敗北 はいぼく defeat, setback
敗軍 はいぐん defeated army
敗戦 はいせん lost battle, defeat
勝敗 しょうはい victory or defeat
b 連敗 れんぱい successive defeats
完敗 かんぱい crushing defeat; complete failure
c 一勝二敗 いっしょうにはい one victory and two defeats

❷ fail
失敗 しっぱい failure, mistake
成敗 せいはい success or failure
成敗 せいばい punishment

❸ spoil, rot, be ruined
腐敗する ふはいする rot, decay; become corrupt

INDEPENDENT

【はい 敗】defeat
敗を取る はいをとる suffer a defeat

KUN

【やぶれる 敗れる】**BE DEFEATED, be beaten, lose**
試合に敗れる しあいにやぶれる lose a game

SYNONYMS

❶ lose
負 LOSE → 2594
敗 BE DEFEATED → 1868

❷ fail
敗 fail → 1868
落 fall through → 2907
-損なう fail to (do) → 0801

HOMOPHONES

やぶれる 破 BREAK → 1478

NOTE

➡ see USAGE note at 破 1478

販

▸ENGAGE IN SALES

ハン

Ⓒ 贩 fàn

1869

◧1-7-4

154	Jōyō	U8CA9
貝	S11-7-4	F1050

COMPOUNDS

ⓐ **ENGAGE IN SALES, deal in, sell, trade, market**

ⓑ abbrev. of 販売 はんばい **sales**

a 販売する はんばいする engage in sales, sell, market
販路 はんろ market, outlet
市販 しはん marketing
再販 さいはん resale

b 信販 しんぱん sales on credit
自販 じはん automobile sales

SYNONYMS

● **sell and trade**

売 SELL → 2722
卸す WHOLESALE → 1835
販 ENGAGE IN SALES → 1869
商 TRADE → 2623
貿 TRADE → 3214
易 EXCHANGE → 3064

赦

▸AMNESTY

シャ

Ⓒ 赦 shè

1870

◧1-7-4

155	Jōyō	U8D66
赤	S11-7-4	F2006

COMPOUNDS

ⓐ (forgive a crime or error) **AMNESTY, pardon, forgive, excuse**

ⓑ **AMNESTY, general pardon**

a 赦免 しゃめん pardon, amnesty, clemency
容赦 ようしゃ pardon, forgiveness, mercy

b 恩赦 おんしゃ amnesty, general pardon
特赦 とくしゃ amnesty, special pardon
大赦 たいしゃ amnesty, general amnesty

SYNONYMS

● **forgive**

赦 AMNESTY → 1870
免 EXEMPT → 2565
許す forgive → 1862
恕 FORGIVE WITH COMPASSION → 3282
宥 PARDON → 2803

距

◧1-7-4

incorrect stroke-count
➡ see ◧1-7-5: 𧾷 at 1905

軟

▸SOFT

ナン やわ(らか) やわ(らかい)

Ⓒ 软 ruǎn

1871

◧1-7-4

159	Jōyō	U8EDF
車	S11-7-4	F1975

COMPOUNDS

❶ⓐ [original meaning] (not hard) **SOFT**

ⓑ (lacking vigor) **SOFT, weak**

a 軟化 なんか softening; weakening (of the market)
軟骨 なんこつ cartilage
柔軟な じゅうなんな soft, pliable, flexible
硬軟 こうなん hardness

b 軟弱 なんじゃく weakness; effeminacy
軟調 なんちょう weakness; bearish tone
軟着陸 なんちゃくりく soft landing

❷ erotic, sexually wanton

軟文学 なんぶんがく erotic literature
軟派 なんぱ a flirt; moderate party

INDEPENDENT

【なん 軟】**SOFT**ness

KUN

【やわらか 軟らか】

やわらかな 軟らかな [also 柔らかな]

① **SOFT, tender**
軟らかな土 やわらかなつち soft earth

② **SOFT**, subdued (color or light)
軟らかな光 やわらかなひかり soft light

③ gentle, meek, mild
軟らかな風 やわらかなかぜ gentle breeze

【やわらかい 軟らかい】[also 柔らかい]

① **SOFT, tender**
軟らかい若葉 やわらかいわかば soft young leaf

② **gentle, meek**
軟らかく話す やわらかくはなす speak gently

③ informal
軟らかい文章 やわらかいぶんしょう informal style

SYNONYMS

❶ⓐ **soft**

柔 SOFT (supple and yielding) → 2591
軟 SOFT (not hard) → 1871
塑 plastic → 3525

HOMOPHONES

やわらか 柔 SOFT → 2591
やわらかい 柔 SOFT → 2591

NOTE

➡ see USAGE note at 柔 2591

転

1872

1-7-4

▶**TURN**

テン ころ(がる) ころ(げる) ころ(がす) ころ(ぶ) ㊔ うたた

Ⓝ 轉 Ⓒ 转 zhuǎn zhuàn zhuǎi

159	Jōyō-3	U8EE2
車	S11-7-4	F0383

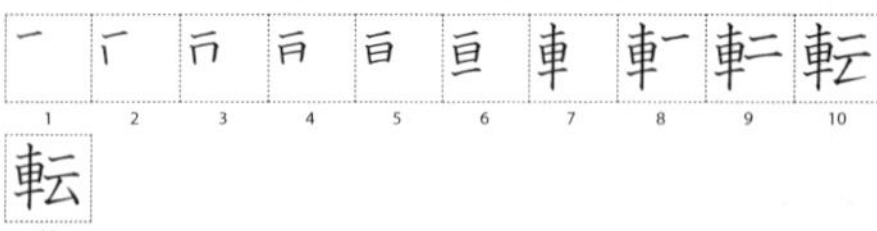

COMPOUNDS

❶ [original meaning] **TURN, revolve, rotate**
回転する かいてんする revolve, rotate, turn
自転 じてん rotation (of the earth)
運転する うんてんする operate, drive, run

❷ [formerly also 顛 2317] **TURN over, roll over, tumble down, fall over**
転倒する てんとうする tumble, fall down; invert, reverse; upset
転落する てんらくする fall off, tumble down
転覆する てんぷくする overturn, turn over, upset; overthrow
七転八倒する しちてんばっとう(しってんばっとう)する toss oneself about in great pain

❸ⓐ (undergo change) **TURN into, turn, change, convert**
ⓑ **remove, move, change, transfer**
a 転化 てんか change, transformation, inversion
転換 てんかん conversion, switchover, turnabout
転向 てんこう turn, conversion, about-face
転義 てんぎ figurative meaning
変転 へんてん change, transition
好転 こうてん take a turn for the better
一転 いってん complete change; turn
逆転 ぎゃくてん reversal, turnabout, inversion; reverse rotation
b 転居する てんきょする move, change one's residence
転職 てんしょく change of occupation
転転とする てんてんとする wander about; change hands; roll
移転する いてんする transfer, remove; move

❹ third stanza in a Chinese quatrain; the **TURN**
起承転結 きしょうてんけつ introduction, development, turn and conclusion (of a Chinese quatrain)

INDEPENDENT

【てん 転】 corruption (of a word's meaning)
【てんじる 転じる】 **TURN** round, turn; turn, shift; turn into, change; remove, be transferred

KUN

【ころがる 転がる】 *vi* **roll over, tumble over**
転がり込む ころがりこむ role in; fall in one's way
【ころげる 転げる】 same as 転がる ころがる
転げ落ちる ころげおちる fall off, tumble down
【ころがす 転がす】 *vt* **roll; roll over, tumble over**
車を転がす くるまをころがす drive a car
【ころぶ 転ぶ】 *vi* **tumble down, fall over**
寝転ぶ ねころぶ lie down

SYNONYMS

❶ **turn**
旋 GYRATE → 1194
転 TURN → 1872
回 TURN ROUND → 3793
廻 TURN ROUND → 3833
巡 MAKE THE ROUNDS → 3781
循 CIRCULATE → 0704
斡 REVOLVE → 2168
捻 TWIST → 0604

❷ **overturn**
覆 OVERTURN → 3386
翻 TURN OVER → 2391
反 turn over → 3663
顛 TURN [roll] OVER → 2317
転 turn [roll] over → 1872
倒 TOPPLE → 0139
轢 RUN OVER → 2095

❸ⓐ **change and replace**
変 CHANGE → 2569
替 REPLACE → 3457
代 SUBSTITUTE → 0034
迭 ALTERNATE → 3818
更 change → 4355
改 change → 0287
易 change → 3064
化 CHANGE INTO, -ize → 0022
遷 undergo transition → 3932
転 turn into → 1872
換 EXCHANGE → 0716
交 INTERCHANGE → 2508

ⓑ **move**
動 MOVE → 2232

運 MOVE → 3894
滑 SLIDE → 0809
辷る SLIP → 3957
移 SHIFT → 1508
転 remove → 1872
遷 TRANSFER → 3932
繰る SHIFT ONWARD → 1806

COMPOUND FORMATION

【運転 うんてん】

運転する 'operate, drive, run' is to put something in motion (運) and keep it rolling or moving (転 ❶).

軛

1873

1-7-4

▶**YOKE**

ヤク くびき

Ⓒ 轭 è

159	Non-Jōyō	U8EDB
車	S11-7-4	F0000

COMPOUNDS

● [now also 役 0288] [original meaning] **YOKE**

共軛 きょうやく *math* conjugation

KUN

【くびき 軛】[also 頸木] **YOKE**

SYNONYMS

● **long slender objects**

棒 ROD → 1237
箸 CHOPSTICKS → 3359
桟 crosspiece → 1169
軸 AXLE → 1908
錘 SPINDLE → 2191
竿 POLE → 3259
杖 STAFF → 1026
錫 Buddhist priest's staff → 2189
軛 YOKE → 1873

HOMOPHONES

くびき 頸木 → 2035, 4261

斬

1874

1-7-4

▶**CUT WITH A SWORD**

ザン サン▲ き(る)

Ⓒ 斩 zhǎn

69	Jōyō	U65AC
斤	S11-4-7	F1086

COMPOUNDS

❶ **CUT (a person) WITH A SWORD, cut down, kill**

斬首 ざんしゅ decapitation
斬罪 ざんざい decapitation

❷ conspicuous, prominent

斬新な ざんしんな new, novel, original

INDEPENDENT

【ざん 斬】beheading, decapitation

KUN

【きる 斬る】

① [also 切る] **CUT (a person) WITH A SWORD, cut down, kill**

斬り死に きりじに fighting (with a sword) to death
斬り掛かる きりかかる slash at, assault with a sword
斬り捨てる きりすてる cut down, slay; truncate, round down; discard, cast away
首斬り くびきり decapitation; firing, layoff; *hist* small sword for decapitation

② criticize severely, attack

SYNONYMS

❶ **cut**

切 CUT → 0030
薙ぐ MOW DOWN → 3010
剪 PRUNE → 2886
削 CUT BY CHIPPING → 1837
挽く GRIND, saw → 0511
断 CUT OFF → 1885
截 CUT OFF → 4092
裁 CUT OUT → 4090
斬 CUT WITH A SWORD → 1874
割 cut with a knife → 2284
剖 DISSECT → 2103
刈る CLIP → 0032
伐 CUT DOWN → 0046

HOMOPHONES

きる

切 CUT → 0030
伐 CUT DOWN → 0046
剪 PRUNE → 2886
截 CUT OFF → 4092

NOTE

➡ see USAGE note at 切 0030

酔

1875

1-7-4

▶**BECOME INTOXICATED**

スイ よ(う) よ(い)

Ⓝ 醉 Ⓒ 醉 zuì

164	Jōyō	U9154
酉	S11-7-4	F1206

言 谷 貝 赤 足 車 酉 【釆】 里 余 豸 每 売 皀 坐 四 孝 夆 良 束 求 亨

COMPOUNDS

❶ **BECOME INTOXICATED (with alcohol), get drunk**
酔態 すいたい drunkenness, intoxication
酔漢 すいかん drunkard, drunken fellow
泥酔した でいすいした dead-drunk
麻酔 ますい anesthesia

❷ **be intoxicated (with strong emotion), be infatuated, be fascinated**
心酔 しんすい infatuation
陶酔 とうすい intoxication; fascination, rapture

KUN

【よう 酔う】 **get drunk [high], BECOME INTOXICATED; be intoxicated (with delight), be in rapture; feel sick (as from riding in a vehicle)**
酔っ払う よっぱらう get drunk
酔っ払い よっぱらい drunkard, boozer
酔い痴れる よいしれる be fuddled [drunk] (with)

【よい 酔い】 [also suffix] **drunkenness, intoxication; motion sickness**
二日酔い ふつかよい hangover, morning after
船酔い ふなよい seasickness
乗り物酔い のりものよい motion sickness

SYNONYMS

❶ **become stupefied**
酔 BECOME INTOXICATED → 1875
麻 BECOME NUMB → 3878

釈

1876

1-7-4

▶**ELUCIDATE**

シャク ㊔ せき

Ⓝ 釋 Ⓒ 释 shì

165	Jōyō	U91C8
釆	S11-7-4	F1220

COMPOUNDS

❶ⓐ **ELUCIDATE, explain, interpret, explicate**
ⓑ elucidation, explanation, interpretation, commentary
ⓒ explain oneself, make an excuse, vindicate
a 解釈 かいしゃく interpretation, explanation
注釈 ちゅうしゃく annotation, note, comment
会釈する えしゃくする salute, greet, bow slightly
b 語釈 ごしゃく definition of words
c 釈明する しゃくめいする explain, vindicate; apologize

❷ **release, free**
釈放 しゃくほう release, liberation, discharge, acquittal
保釈する ほしゃくする bail, let (a prisoner) out on bail

❸ⓐ clear up, dispel
ⓑ dissolve (in water)
a 釈然として しゃくぜんとして with sudden illumination
b 希釈 きしゃく dilution

❹ⓐ ***Śākyamuni,* Buddha**
ⓑ prefix preceding the name or posthumous name of a Buddhist
a 釈迦 しゃか *Śākyamuni, Gautama*
釈典 しゃくてん Buddhist literature, Buddhist sutras
b 釈空海 しゃくくうかい Kukai (name of a Buddhist priest)

INDEPENDENT

【しゃく 釈】 explanation, elucidation, interpretation
難解文の釈 なんかいぶんのしゃく elucidation of a difficult passage

SYNONYMS

❶ⓐ **explain**
説 EXPLAIN → 1949
明 make clear → 1060
釈 ELUCIDATE → 1876
詮 EXPOUND → 1923
講 expound → 2046
解 CLARIFY → 1913
注 annotate → 0383

❷ **release**
放 LET GO → 1058
釈 release → 1876

❹ⓐ **Buddha**
仏 BUDDHA → 0020
釈 Sakyamuni → 1876

NOTE

➡ see COMPOUND FORMATION for 会釈 えしゃく → 会 2512

野

1877

1-7-4

▶**FIELD**

ヤ の の- ㊔ のう ぬ

Ⓝ 埜 壄 Ⓒ 野 yě

166	Jōyō-2	U91CE
里	S11-7-4	F0117

COMPOUNDS

❶ⓐ [original meaning] **(uncultivated) FIELD, open country, wilderness**
ⓑ **cultivated FIELD**
a 野外 やがい field, fields, open air

平野 へいや plain(s), open field
原野 げんや vast plain, wilderness, field
荒野 こうや wilderness, the wilds, wasteland
b 野菜 やさい vegetables, greens
❷ (sphere of action) **FIELD, range, area**
分野 ぶんや field, sphere, area
視野 しや field of vision; one's mental horizon
照射野 しょうしゃや irradiation field (of x rays)
❸ⓐ **baseball FIELD**
ⓑ abbrev. of 野手 やしゅ: **FIELD**er
a 野球 やきゅう baseball
内野 ないや infield
外野 がいや outfield; outsiders
b 野選 やせん fielder's choice
❹ⓐ (growing or occurring in the field) **wild, undomesticated, savage**
ⓑ **rustic, unrefined, coarse, vulgar, savage**
a 野犬 やけん stray dog
野鳥 やちょう wild fowl, wild bird
野性 やせい wild nature, uncouthness
野獣 やじゅう wild animal, wild game
b 野蛮な やばんな savage, barbarous, uncivilized
野趣 やしゅ charms of the countryside, rural beauty
野暮な やぼな unrefined, rustic, boorish
粗野な そやな rustic, rude, vulgar
❺ **nongovernmental, (party or people) outside the government**
野党 やとう opposition party
朝野 ちょうや government and people
在野の ざいやの out of office [power], in opposition
❻ **audacious, inordinate**
野心 やしん ambition, inordinate aspiration
野望 やぼう ambition, designs, treason

INDEPENDENT

【や 野】 (uncultivated) **FIELD**, open country, wilderness; the opposition
野に在る やにある be in private life; be in opposition
虎を野に放つ とらをやにはなつ let loose a tiger in the field

KUN

【の 野】 [also suffix] **(uncultivated) FIELD, open country, plain**
野の花 ののはな wild flowers
野原 のはら field, plain
野良 のら the fields
枯れ野 かれの desolate [dreary] field
武蔵野 むさしの Musashi Plain

【の- 野-】
ⓐ [also prefix] **wild, undomesticated**
ⓑ (lacking restraint) **wild, unruly**
a 野菊 のぎく wild chrysanthemum; aster
野兎 のうさぎ hare
野葡萄 のぶどう wild grape
b 野放しの のばなしの untethered, loose, at grass, at large
野放図な のほうずな unrestrained, unruly

SYNONYMS

❶ⓐ **uncultivated expanses of land**
野 FIELD → 1877
原 PLAIN → 3733
漠 DESERT → 0804
❷ **range**
程 EXTENT → 1524
範 range → 3360
域 area → 0559
圏 SPHERE → 3904
野 FIELD → 1877
界 field (*phys*) → 3172
場 field (*phys*, *psychol*) → 0678
❸ⓐ **sports fields**
場 ground(s) → 0678
庭 COURT → 3866
野 baseball field → 1877
❹ⓐ **natural**
地 natural → 0236
野 wild → 1877
粗 crude → 1683
原 in the original state → 3733
ⓑ **vulgar and unrefined**
俗 vulgar → 0119
卑 MEAN → 3270
賤 MEAN → 1993
鄙 MEAN → 2338
俚 RURAL → 0112
里 rural → 4356
粗 COARSE → 1683
野 rustic → 1877
蛮 barbaric → 2638

斜

1878

◧ 1-7-4

▸**OBLIQUE**

シャ なな(め) はす▴

Ⓒ 斜 xié

68	Jōyō	U659C
斗	S11-4-7	F1446

Stroke order: ノ 𠆢 亼 亼 仐 全 余 余 余 斜 斜 (1–11)

COMPOUNDS

● [also prefix] [original meaning] **OBLIQUE, diagonal, slanting, inclined, sloping, leaning, tilting**

斜線 しゃせん oblique line, slanting line, slash mark
斜面 しゃめん slope, slanting surface
斜影 しゃえい slanting shadow
斜滑降 しゃかっこう traversing (in skiing)
斜投影 しゃとうえい oblique projection
傾斜 けいしゃ inclination, slant, tilt
ピサの斜塔 ぴさのしゃとう Leaning Tower of Pisa

INDEPENDENT

【しゃ 斜】**OBLIQUE**ness, slant, inclination

斜に構える しゃにかまえる couch (a sword); stand ready (to do)

KUN

【ななめ 斜め】[also prefix] **OBLIQUEness, slant, inclination; displeasure**

斜めな ななめな oblique, diagonal, slanting; displeased, cross
斜め応力 ななめおうりょく oblique stress
斜め入射 ななめにゅうしゃ oblique incidence
御機嫌斜めだ ごきげんななめだ be in a bad temper

【はす 斜】slant, bias, obliquity

斜交いに はすかいに obliquely, diagonally

SYNONYMS

● **obliqueness and inclining**

斜 OBLIQUE → 1878
傾 INCLINE → 0174

敍

1879

1-7-4

▶**DESCRIBE**

ジョ ㊔ のぶ

66	Names	U654D
支	S11-4-7	F0000

traditional form → see 叙 at 1834

敘

1880

1-7-4

▶**DESCRIBE**

ジョ ㊔ のぶ

66	Nonstandard	U6558
攵	S11-4-7	F0000

traditional form → see 叙 at 1834

殺

1881

1-7-4

▶**KILL**

サツ サイ セツ ころ(す) -ごろ(し) そ(ぐ)

79	Nonstandard	UF970
殳	S11-4-7	F0000

traditional form → see 殺 at 1677

敏

1882

1-7-4

▶**NIMBLE**

ビン ㊔ とし さとし さとる さと

66	Names	UFA41
攵	S11-4-7	F0000

traditional form → see 敏 at 1675

殼

1883

1-7-4

▶**SHELL**

カク から がら

Ⓝ 殻 Ⓒ 壳 ké qiào

79	Jōyō	U6BBB
殳	S11-4-7	F2013

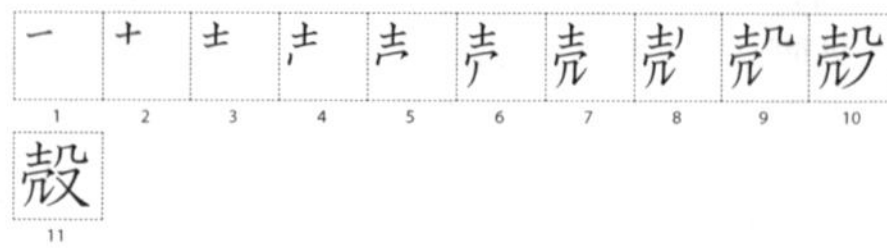

COMPOUNDS

ⓐ **SHELL (of any kind), crust**
ⓑ electron **SHELL**

a 殻頂 かくちょう umbo, apex of a shell
甲殻類 こうかくるい Crustacea
地殻 ちかく crust (of the earth)
卵殻 らんかく eggshell
b 原子のＭ殻 げんしのえむかく M shell

INDEPENDENT

【かく 殻】**SHELL**, crust; electron shell

殻の内部 かくのないぶ inside of a shell

KUN

【から 殻】

①ⓐ **SHELL, crust**
ⓑ **husk, hull**

a 殻を閉ざす からをとざす retire into one's shell, close up like an oyster
卵の殻 たまごのから eggshell
貝殻 かいがら shell
b 豆殻 まめがら bean husk

② **castoff skin, refuse**

抜け殻 ぬけがら castoff skin; mere shadow of one's true self

【がら 殻】**cinders, ashes**

燃え殻 もえがら cinders
石炭殻 せきたんがら coal cinders
吸い殻 すいがら cigarette butt

SYNONYMS

ⓐ **shells**

殻 SHELL (of any kind) → 1883
甲 SHELL (of animals) → 4293
貝 seashell → 3150
螺 SPIRAL-SHELLED GASTROPOD → 1799
瑚 CORAL → 1300

【がら】

◯ **products of combustion**

灰 ASH → 3699

殻 cinders → 1883

炭 CHARCOAL → 2806

煤 SOOT → 1292

煙 SMOKE → 1294

HOMOPHONES

から 空 SKY → 2767

NOTE

➡ see USAGE note at 空 2767

★ do not confuse with 穀 CEREAL → 2294

既

1884

▶**ALREADY**

キ すで(に)

71	Nonstandard	U65E2
旡	S11-4-7	F0000

1-7-4

traditional form → see 既 at 1498

断

1885

▶**CUT OFF**
▶**RESOLVE**

ダン た(つ) ことわ(る)

Ⓝ 斷 Ⓒ 断 duàn

1-7-4

69	Jōyō-5	U65AD
斤	S11-4-7	F0350

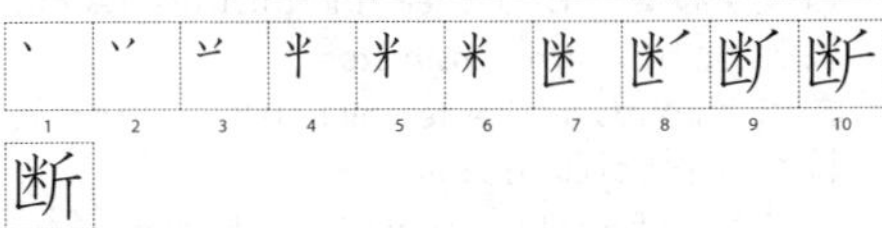

COMPOUNDS

❶ⓐ [original meaning] (detach by severing) **CUT OFF, sever, cut apart**

ⓑ cut across, go through

a 断片 だんぺん fragment, piece

断面 だんめん (cross) section, profile

断頭台 だんとうだい guillotine

断裁機 だんさいき paper cutter

切断する せつだんする cut (off), sever

b 横断 おうだん crossing, traversing

❷ⓐ (cause to discontinue) **CUT OFF (the water supply), sever (a connection), break off (relations), discontinue**

ⓑ abstain from, give up

a 断絶 だんぜつ severance, rupture; discontinuation

断交 だんこう severing [breaking off] relations

断続的に だんぞくてきに intermittently, off and on

断水 だんすい suspension of water supply

中断する ちゅうだんする interrupt, discontinue, suspend

遮断 しゃだん interception, interruption, blockade, isolation

油断 ゆだん negligence, carelessness, inattentiveness

b 断食 だんじき fasting

断念 だんねん abandonment, relinquishment

禁断の木の実 きんだんのこのみ the forbidden fruit

❸ (make a firm decision or judgment) **RESOLVE, decide, conclude**

断定 だんてい decision, conclusion

断言 だんげん (positive) assertion, declaration

断罪 だんざい judgment of a crime

決断 けつだん decision, determination, resolution

判断 はんだん judgment, decision

診断 しんだん diagnosis

予断 よだん prediction, foregone conclusion

❹ resolutely, decisively, absolutely

断固たる だんこたる firm, conclusive, determined

断行する だんこうする carry out resolutely

断然 だんぜん resolutely, decisively

❺ permission, prior notice

無断で むだんで without permission; without notice [warning]

INDEPENDENT

【だん 断】decision, judgment, ruling; OFF (marking for circuits)

断を下す だんをくだす make a decision, pass judgment

【だんずる(=だんじる) 断ずる(=断じる)】**conclude; judge**

断じて だんじて decidedly, absolutely

KUN

【たつ 断つ】

① (detach by severing) **CUT OFF, sever, cut apart**

断ち切る たちきる cut off, disconnect

② (stop or interrupt the intended course) **CUT OFF, intercept**

退路を断つ たいろをたつ cut off the retreat

③ abstain from, give up

塩断ち しおだち abstinence from salt as a vow

【ことわる 断る】**refuse, reject, decline; give notice beforehand, call attention to; obtain consent, ask for permission**

断り ことわり refusal, declining; prohibition; notice, warning; permission; excuse, apology

断る迄も無く ことわるまでもなく needless to say

断らずに ことわらずに without permission

申し出を断る もうしでをことわる turn down an offer

SYNONYMS

❶ⓐ cut

切 CUT → 0030

薙ぐ MOW DOWN → 3010

剪 PRUNE → 2886
削 CUT BY CHIPPING → 1837
挽く GRIND, saw → 0511
断 CUT OFF → 1885
截 CUT OFF → 4092
裁 CUT OUT → 4090
斬 CUT WITH A SWORD → 1874
割 cut with a knife → 2284
剖 DISSECT → 2103
刈る CLIP → 0032
伐 CUT DOWN → 0046

❷ⓐ discontinue
絶 BREAK OFF → 1711
廃 ABOLISH → 3902
断 CUT OFF → 1885
止 STOP → 3659
休 suspend → 0056
停 suspend → 0156
已む CEASE → 4185

❸ decide
決 DECIDE → 0308
断 RESOLVE → 1885
定 FIX → 2770

❹ resolutely
敢 BOLDLY → 2142
断 resolutely → 1885
決 decisively → 0308

【ことわる】
◯ refuse and reject
拒 REFUSE → 0368
断る refuse → 1885
否 SAY NO → 3058
却 reject → 1436

USAGE

【たつ】
断つ
① (detach by severing) cut off, sever, cut apart
② (stop or interrupt the intended course) cut off, intercept
③ abstain from, give up

絶つ
① break off, discontinue, cut off, sever
② exterminate, extirpate, eradicate

裁つ
cut out (a garment), cut (paper)

HOMOPHONES

たつ
絶 BREAK OFF → 1711
裁 CUT OUT → 4090

NOTE

➡ see COMPOUND FORMATION for 油断 ゆだん → 油 0400

朙 1886

1-7-4

▶**BRIGHT**
▶**CLEAR**

メイ ミョウ ミン あ(かり) あか(るい) あか(るむ) あか(らむ) あき(らか) あ(ける) -あ(け) あ(く) あ(くる) あ(かす) ㊔ あきら とおる あけし はる とし

74	Nonstandard	U6719
月	S11-4-7	F0000

traditional form → see 明 at 1060

教 1887

1-7-4

▶**TEACH**
▶**RELIGION**

キョウ おし(える) おそ(わる) ㊔ のり みち かず たか

Ⓝ 教 Ⓒ 教 jiāo jiào

66	Jōyō-2	U6559
攵	S11-4-7	F0124

1	2	3	4	5	6	7	8	9	10	11
一	十	土	耂	耂	考	孝	孝	教	教	教

COMPOUNDS

❶ [original meaning] **TEACH, instruct, educate**
教育 きょういく education, teaching
教授する きょうじゅする teach, instruct, give lessons
教師 きょうし teacher, instructor
教員 きょういん teacher, teaching staff
教室 きょうしつ classroom, class
教養 きょうよう culture, education, cultivation
教科 きょうか school subject; course of study, curriculum
教材 きょうざい teaching materials [aids]
教訓 きょうくん lesson, precept, teachings
文教 ぶんきょう education, culture

❷ abbrev. of 教育 きょういく or 教職員 きょうしょくいん: education, school personnel
教委 きょうい Board of Education
日教組 にっきょうそ Japan Teachers Union

❸ⓐ **RELIGION, religious teachings, religious sect**
ⓑ **suffix after names of RELIGIONs**
a 教会 きょうかい church
教祖 きょうそ founder of a religion, head of a sect
宗教 しゅうきょう religion, faith, creed
殉教 じゅんきょう martyrdom
布教する ふきょうする propagate (a religion)
b 仏教 ぶっきょう Buddhism
キリスト教 きりすときょう Christianity
ユダヤ教 ゆだやきょう Judaism
イスラム教 いすらむきょう Islam

❹ church
教区 きょうく parish

教籍 きょうせき church membership

KUN

【おしえる 教える】**TEACH, instruct, educate; tell, show, inform; reveal, suggest**

教え おしえ teaching, education; lesson; teachings, religious teachings

教え込む おしえこむ inculcate, instill, train

教え子 おしえご one's (former) pupil

【おそわる 教わる】**be taught, learn, take lessons in, receive lessons**

英語を教わる えいごをおそわる be taught English

SYNONYMS

❶ teach

教 TEACH → 1887
啓 ENLIGHTEN → 3434
諄 TEACH WITH CARE → 1979
授 teach → 0595
育 educate → 2544
練 TRAIN → 1738
訓 INSTRUCT → 1844
誨 INSTRUCT → 1946
諭 ADMONISH → 2012
導 GUIDE → 3587
迪 EDIFY → 3817

❸ religion

教 RELIGION → 1887
宗 religion → 2769
道 the Way → 3888

❹ places of worship

堂 temple building → 3202
塔 pagoda → 0683
寺 BUDDHIST TEMPLE → 2687
刹 TEMPLE → 1620
社 Shinto shrine → 1042
宮 SHINTO SHRINE → 2828
院 monastery → 0544
教 church → 1887

敎

1888

1-7-4

▶TEACH
▶RELIGION

キョウ おし(える) おそ(わる) ㊔ のり みち かず たか

66 攵	Nonstandard	U654E
	S11-4-7	F0000

traditional form → see 教 at 1887

朗

1889

1-7-4

▶CHEERFUL
▶CLEAR

ロウ ほが(らか) ㊔ あき あきら お

74 月	Names	UF929
	S11-4-7	F0000

traditional form → see 朗 at 1679

敕

1890

1-7-4

▶IMPERIAL DECREE

チョク ㊔ とき

66 攵	Nonstandard	U6555
	S11-4-7	F0000

traditional form → see 勅 at 1841

救

1891

1-7-4

▶SAVE

キュウ すく(う)

Ⓒ 救 jiù

66 攵	Jōyō-4	U6551
	S11-4-7	F0980

1	2	3	4	5	6	7	8	9	10	11
一	十	才	才	求	求	求	求	救	救	救

COMPOUNDS

● [original meaning] **SAVE, rescue, deliver, help**

救済する きゅうさいする relieve, help, save, deliver
救命 きゅうめい lifesaving
救出 きゅうしゅつ rescue, relief, deliverance
救世主 きゅうせいしゅ the Savior, the Messiah
救援 きゅうえん relief, rescue, help
救助 きゅうじょ rescue, relief
救難 きゅうなん rescue, salvage
救急車 きゅうきゅうしゃ ambulance

KUN

【すくう 救う】**SAVE, rescue, deliver, help, relieve**

救い すくい rescue, relief, help, salvation
救い出す すくいだす help out, rescue from
救い主 すくいぬし rescuer, Savior

SYNONYMS

● rescue

救 SAVE → 1891
済 RELIEVE → 0634

敦

1-7-4

incorrect stroke-count
➡ see 1-8-4: 享 at 2128

觝

1892

1-7-5

▶COLLIDE WITH

テイ

Ⓒ 抵 dǐ

148 角	Non-Jōyō	U89DD
	S12-7-5	F0000

COMPOUNDS

● [now replaced by 抵 0377] [original meaning] **COLLIDE WITH, touch**

觝触する ていしょくする conflict with; be contrary to; be incompatible with

SYNONYMS

❶ **collide**

衝 COLLIDE → 0893
牴 COLLIDE WITH → 1134
觝 COLLIDE WITH → 1892
突 DASH → 2772
当たる HIT → 2701

註

▸ANNOTATE
チュウ
Ⓒ 注 zhù

1893
1-7-5

149	Names	U8A3B
言	S12-7-5	F2361

COMPOUNDS

[now replaced by 注 0383]

❶ⓐ **ANNOTATE, explain with notes**
ⓑ **annotation, explanatory notes, comment**

a 註釈 ちゅうしゃく annotation, note, comment
註解 ちゅうかい annotation, explanatory notes
註記 ちゅうき annotation, commentary
評註 ひょうちゅう commentary, notes and comments
脚註 きゃくちゅう footnote
b 標註 ひょうちゅう marginal notations

❷ write down, take notes of, record
註文する ちゅうもんする order, place an order; request

❸ abbrev. of 註文 ちゅうもん: order
発註する はっちゅうする place an order
受註する じゅちゅうする receive an order

INDEPENDENT

【ちゅう 註】**annotation, explanatory notes, comment**
【ちゅうする 註する】**ANNOTATE**, comment

SYNONYMS

❶ **write**

書 WRITE → 3292
筆 write → 3317
写 COPY → 2493
記 WRITE DOWN → 1843
紀 record in writing → 1628
控える note down → 0600
録 RECORD → 2186
登 register → 3208
註 ANNOTATE → 1893

NOTE

➡ see COMPOUND FORMATION for 注文 ちゅうもん → 文 2458

詠

▸RECITE POETRY
エイ よ(む) ㊔ うた なが
Ⓝ 咏 Ⓒ 咏 yǒng

1894
1-7-5

149	Jōyō	U8A60
言	S12-7-5	F2009

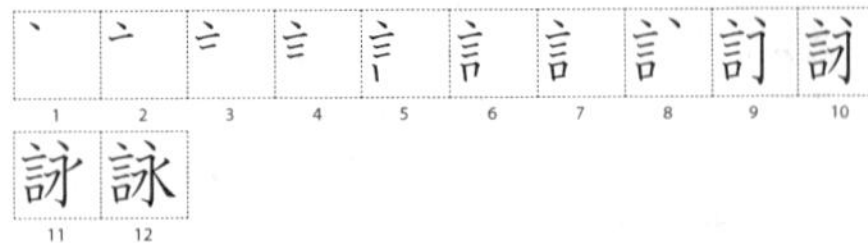

COMPOUNDS

❶ [original meaning] **RECITE POETRY, chant, sing**
詠唱 えいしょう chanting; aria
吟詠 ぎんえい reciting [chanting] a poem; poem
朗詠 ろうえい reciting, chanting

❷ **write poetry, compose waka or haiku**
詠歌 えいか composing poetry; Buddhist hymn
題詠 だいえい poetry composed on a set theme

❸ poem, ode
詠草 えいそう draft of a poem

❹ exclaim in admiration, praise
詠嘆(=詠歎) えいたん exclamation, admiration

INDEPENDENT

【えい 詠】poem
. . . の詠 …のえい poem written by…
【えいじる(=えいずる) 詠じる(=詠ずる)】**RECITE POETRY**; write poetry, compose waka or haiku
. . . を詠じた詩 …をえいじたし a poem about…

KUN

【よむ 詠む】**compose (waka or haiku poems)**
詠み人知らず よみびとしらず waka-composer unknown; author unknown
和歌を詠む わかをよむ compose a waka

SYNONYMS

❶ **recite**

吟 RECITE → 0271
誦 RECITE → 1951
唱 chant → 0555
読 READ → 1943
詠 RECITE POETRY → 1894

HOMOPHONES

よむ 読 READ → 1943

NOTE

➡ see USAGE note at 読 1943

評

▸COMMENT
ヒョウ
Ⓝ 評 Ⓒ 评 píng

1895
1-7-5

149	Jōyō-5	U8A55
言	S12-7-5	F0587

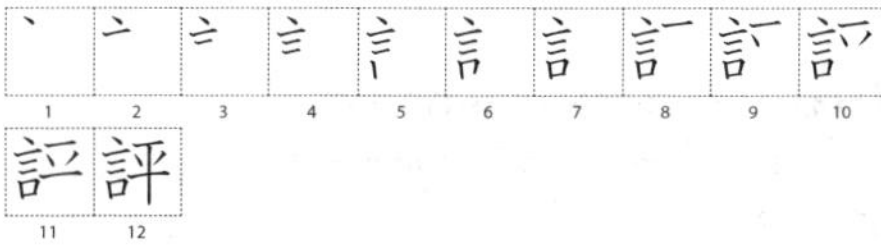

COMPOUNDS

❶ⓐ COMMENT, criticize, review

ⓑ [also suffix] **COMMENT, criticism**

a 評論 ひょうろん comment, criticism, review

評判 ひょうばん fame, reputation

評釈 ひょうしゃく annotation, commentary

評者 ひょうしゃ critic, reviewer

論評 ろんぴょう comment, criticism, review

批評する ひひょうする criticize, comment

b 好評 こうひょう favorable criticism [comment], public favor

定評 ていひょう established reputation

書評 しょひょう book reviews

下馬評 げばひょう gossip, advance rumor

映画評 えいがひょう film review

❷ⓐ evaluate, appraise, judge, decide by consultation

ⓑ reputation

a 評価 ひょうか evaluation, appraisal

評点 ひょうてん examination marks, rating

評定 ひょうてい rating, evaluation

評議 ひょうぎ conference, consultation

評定 ひょうじょう conference, consultation

評決 ひょうけつ decision, verdict

b 世評 せひょう public opinion; reputation

❸ abbrev. of 評議会 ひょうぎかい council

総評(=日本労働組合総評議会) そうひょう(=にほんろうどうくみあいそうひょうぎかい) General Council of Trade Unions of Japan

INDEPENDENT

【ひょう 評】**COMMENT, criticism; reputation**

大方の評では おおかたのひょうでは according to public opinion

【ひょうする 評する】COMMENT, criticize

SYNONYMS

❶ⓐ comment upon

批 CRITICIZE → 0294

評 COMMENT → 1895

ⓑ explanatory remarks

注 annotation → 0383

評 COMMENT → 1895

❷ⓐ judge

判 JUDGE → 1441

裁 JUDGE → 4090

鑑 APPRAISE → 2226

評 evaluate → 1895

審 TRY → 2985

決 DECIDE → 0308

視 REGARD → 1223

詐

1896

◧ 1-7-5

▶SWINDLE

サ いつわ(る)▲

Ⓒ 诈 zhà

149	Jōyō	U8A50
言	S12-7-5	F2097

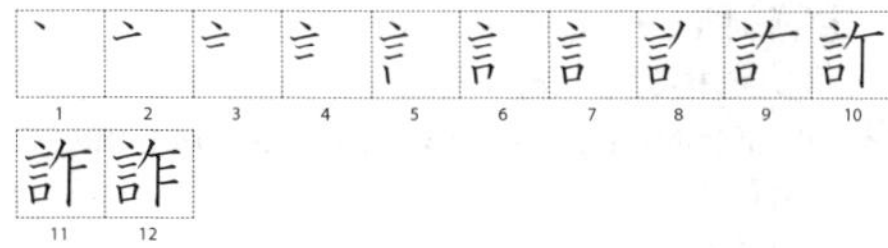

COMPOUNDS

● SWINDLE, defraud, falsify, deceive; feign, pretend

詐欺 さぎ swindle, fraud

詐取 さしゅ fraud, swindle

詐称 さしょう misrepresentation, false statement

KUN

【いつわる 詐る】[now usu. 偽る] (cause to believe a falsehood) **falsify, deceive, cheat**

詐って金を取る いつわってかねをとる obtain money by fraud

SYNONYMS

● deceive

欺 DECEIVE → 2138

騙 DECEIVE → 2314

詐 SWINDLE → 1896

惑 mislead → 3461

拐 defraud → 0365

偽 FALSIFY → 0149

詭 TRICK → 1919

HOMOPHONES

いつわる 偽 FALSIFY → 0149

NOTE

➡ see USAGE note at 偽 0149

詞

1897

◧ 1-7-5

▶WORDS

シ ㊔ のり

Ⓒ 词 cí

149	Jōyō-6	U8A5E
言	S12-7-5	F1442

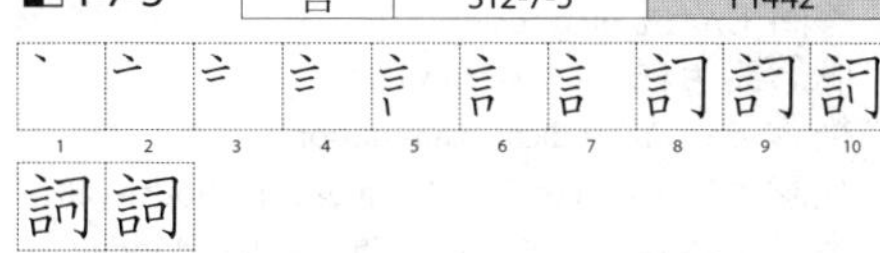

COMPOUNDS

❶ⓐ WORDS, wording, lyrics, expressions

ⓑ [also suffix] **part of speech**

角【言】貝足身車酉釆自

a 歌詞 かし words [lyrics] of a song
祝詞 しゅくし congratulations
賞詞(=頌詞) しょうし (words of) praise, eulogy
誓詞 せいし oath, pledge
作詞 さくし writing lyrics

b 品詞 ひんし part of speech
動詞 どうし verb
名詞 めいし noun
定冠詞 ていかんし definite article
前置詞 ぜんちし preposition

❷ style of Chinese poetry usu. associated with the Song Dynasty
宋詞 そうし Song poetry

INDEPENDENT

【し 詞】 lyrics (of a popular song)

SPECIAL READINGS

祝詞 のりと Shinto ritual prayer
台詞▲ せりふ one's lines, words

SYNONYMS

❶ words and expressions
語 WORD → 1944
辞 WORD → 1726
詞 WORDS → 1897
句 PHRASE → 3685
諺 PROVERB → 2006
喩 METAPHOR → 0671

診

▶EXAMINE A PATIENT

シン み(る)

Ⓒ 诊 zhěn

1898

1-7-5

149	Jōyō	U8A3A
言	S12-7-5	F1129

COMPOUNDS

● EXAMINE A PATIENT, diagnose
診察する しんさつする examine (a patient)
診療 しんりょう diagnosis and treatment
診療所 しんりょうじょ clinic
診断 しんだん diagnosis
聴診器 ちょうしんき stethoscope
検診 けんしん medical examination
往診 おうしん doctor's visit to a patient, house call
本日休診 ほんじつきゅうしん Office Closed Today (sign at doctor's office)
打診する だしんする sound out, tap (a person's views); examine by percussion

KUN

【みる 診る】 EXAMINE (A PATIENT)
脈を診る みゃくをみる examine one's pulse

SYNONYMS

● investigate and examine
閲 REVIEW → 4132
審 EXAMINE CAREFULLY → 2985
験 TEST → 2306
勘 CHECK → 2231
糾 INQUIRE INTO → 1631
究 STUDY EXHAUSTIVELY → 2729
察 INSPECT → 2961
討 STUDY → 1846
探 PROBE → 0613
検 EXAMINE → 1241
診 EXAMINE A PATIENT → 1898
調 INVESTIGATE → 1973
査 LOOK INTO → 3092

HOMOPHONES

みる
見 SEE → 3151
観 VIEW → 2359
看 WATCH → 3992
視 REGARD → 1223

NOTE

➡ see USAGE note at 見 3151

証

▶PROVE
▶CERTIFICATE

ショウ あかし▲

Ⓝ 證 Ⓒ 证 zhèng

1899

1-7-5

149	Jōyō-5	U8A3C
言	S12-7-5	F0444

COMPOUNDS

❶ⓐ [original meaning] **PROVE, testify, bear witness; guarantee**
ⓑ proof, evidence, testimony

a 証明 しょうめい proof, evidence, verification
証言 しょうげん testimony, verbal evidence
証人 しょうにん witness, attestor
保証する ほしょうする (assume responsibility for) guarantee, vouch for, certify
実証 じっしょう actual proof

b 証書 しょうしょ bond, deed; certificate
証拠 しょうこ proof, evidence
検証する けんしょうする verify, identify; inspect

確証する かくしょうする prove positively [definitely], corroborate

❷ⓐ [also suffix] **CERTIFICATE, card, license**
ⓑ abbrev. of 証券 しょうけん: **CERTIFICATE of stock, securities, bond**

a 免許証 めんきょしょう license
会員証 かいいんしょう membership card
b 証券 しょうけん bill, bond, securities
証取り法 しょうとりほう Securities and Exchange Act

INDEPENDENT

【しょう 証】proof, evidence, testimony
証として しょうとして in proof of, in sign of
【しょうする 証する】**PROVE**, give evidence; bear witness

KUN

【あかし 証】proof, evidence, vindication
身の証を立てる みのあかしをたてる vindicate one's innocence

SYNONYMS

❷ⓐ **certificates**
証 CERTIFICATE → 1899
券 CERTIFICATE → 3256
状 official document → 0322
免 license → 2565

NOTE

➡ see USAGE note at 保 0107

詔

1900

◧ 1-7-5

▶**IMPERIAL EDICT**
ショウ みことのり
Ⓒ 诏 zhào

149	Jōyō	U8A54
言	S12-7-5	F2658

Stroke order: 1–12

COMPOUNDS

● [original meaning] **IMPERIAL EDICT, imperial rescript**
詔令 しょうれい imperial edict
詔勅 しょうちょく imperial edict
詔書 しょうしょ imperial edict
大詔 たいしょう imperial rescript [mandate]

KUN

【みことのり 詔】**IMPERIAL EDICT**

SYNONYMS

● **imperial decree**
勅 IMPERIAL DECREE → 1841
詔 IMPERIAL EDICT → 1900

宣 imperial proclamation → 2799

訴

1901

◧ 1-7-5

▶**APPEAL TO**
▶**SUE**
ソ うった(える)
Ⓒ 诉 sù

149	Jōyō	U8A34
言	S12-7-5	F1009

Stroke order: 1–12

COMPOUNDS

❶ⓐ **APPEAL TO a higher court**
ⓑ **SUE, litigate, take legal action**

a 控訴 こうそ (intermediate) appeal
上訴する じょうそする appeal to a higher court
b 訴訟 そしょう lawsuit, litigation
訴願 そがん appeal, petition
訴状 そじょう written complaint
起訴 きそ prosecution, indictment, litigation
告訴 こくそ legal action, complaint, accusation
公訴 こうそ arraignment, prosecution
敗訴 はいそ losing a suit [case]

❷ (try to deal with one's grievances by asking for sympathy) **APPEAL TO,** entreat, implore
哀訴 あいそ entreaty, complaint
愁訴する しゅうそする entreat, implore, appeal

KUN

【うったえる 訴える】**SUE, appeal to the law, litigate; complain; appeal to (a sense of justice), resort to (violence); appeal to (the heart or the eye)**
訴え うったえ lawsuit, action, appeal, complaint
隣人を訴える りんじんをうったえる sue one's neighbor
理性に訴える りせいにうったえる appeal to one's reason
暴力に訴える ぼうりょくにうったえる resort to violence
貧者への援助を訴える ひんじゃへのえんじょをうったえる appeal to people to help the poor
人に訴える力が無い ひとにうったえるちからがない be of little appeal to people

SYNONYMS

❶ⓑ **sue**
訴 SUE → 1901
訟 LITIGATE → 1864
告 accuse of → 3062
控 accuse in court → 0600

❷ **request**
請 REQUEST → 1983

訴 APPEAL TO → 1901
頼 ASK → 2041
嘱 CHARGE WITH → 0881
要 REQUIRE → 3263
願 ASK A FAVOR → 2320
求 SEEK → 4365
乞 BEG → 2457

評

1902

1-7-5

▶COMMENT

ヒョウ

149	Nonstandard	U8A55
言	S12-7-5	F0000

traditional form → see 評 at 1895

貯

1903

1-7-5

▶LAY UP

チョ た(める)▲ たくわ(える)▲

Ⓒ 贮 zhù

154	Jōyō-4	U8CAF
貝	S12-7-5	F1576

(stroke order 1–12)

COMPOUNDS

● [original meaning] **LAY UP (money or supplies), lay by, save, store up, lay in, stock**

貯金 ちょきん savings, deposit
貯蓄 ちょちく savings
貯蔵する ちょぞうする store, preserve, set aside
貯水池 ちょすいち reservoir
貯炭 ちょたん storing coal; stored coal
預貯金 よちょきん deposits and savings, bank account
郵貯(=郵便貯金) ゆうちょ(=ゆうびんちょきん) postal [post-office] savings [deposit]

KUN

【ためる 貯める】[also 溜める] save (money), **LAY UP** (one's income)

金を貯める かねをためる save money

【たくわえる 貯える】[usu. 蓄える] store up, lay in stock, save, lay aside

貯え たくわえ store, reserve, stock; savings

SYNONYMS

● **store**

蔵 STORE → 2995
蓄 STORE UP → 2931
貯 LAY UP → 1903
納 PUT AWAY → 1652

USAGE

【ためる】

貯める
[also 溜める] save (money), lay up (one's income)

溜める
①ⓐ accumulate, heap up
ⓑ collect (stamps)
ⓒ store (esp. water)
② run up (a bill), leave undone
③ [also 貯める] save (money), lay up (one's income)

HOMOPHONES

ためる 溜 ACCUMULATE → 0814
たくわえる 蓄 STORE UP → 2931
たくわえ 蓄 STORE UP → 2931

NOTE

➡ see also USAGE note at 蓄 2931

貼

1904

1-7-5

▶STICK

チョウ テン▲ は(る) -ばり

Ⓒ 贴 tiē

154	Jōyō	U8CBC
貝	S12-7-5	F1712

(stroke order 1–12)

COMPOUNDS

● [original meaning] **STICK, paste; apply to**

貼付する ちょうふ(=てんぷ)する stick, paste, append

KUN

【はる 貼る】[also 張る]

ⓐ **STICK, paste; apply to**
ⓑ **cover, line**

a 貼り付ける はりつける stick on, paste
貼り合わせる はりあわせる paste together
貼り紙 はりがみ sticker, label, poster
切り貼り きりばり cutting and pasting, patching (up)

b 下貼り したばり undercoat, first coat
床にタイルを貼る ゆかにたいるをはる tile a floor

【-ばり -貼り】[usu. -張り] [also suffix] **covered with, lined with**

絹貼り きぬばり lined with silk
紙貼り かみばり lined with paper

SYNONYMS

● **stick**

着 STICK → 4110
貼 STICK → 1904
付 attach itself to → 0035

附 attach itself to →0410

HOMOPHONES

はる 張 SPREAD →0573

-ばり 張 SPREAD →0573

NOTE

➡ see USAGE note at 張 0573

距

▶DISTANCE

キョ

Ⓝ 距 Ⓒ 距 jù

1905

1-7-5

157	Jōyō	U8DDD
足	S12-7-5	F1219

COMPOUNDS

1a DISTANCE, range, spacing

b be at a DISTANCE from, be apart

a 角距 かっきょ angular distance

測距儀 そっきょぎ range finder

輪距 りんきょ wheel track

高距 こうきょ elevation (above sea level)

b 距離 きょり distance, range; interval

2a *anat* ankle

b [original meaning, now archaic] cockspur

a 距骨 きょこつ anklebone, talus

b 距爪 きょそう cockspur

SYNONYMS

1a distance and interval

距 DISTANCE →1905

間 INTERVAL →4122

程 EXTENT →1524

隙 GAP →0826

距

▶DISTANCE

キョ

1906

1-7-5

157	Nonstandard	U8DDD
足	S12-7-5	F0000

traditional form →see 距 at 1905

躰

▶BODY

▶FORM

タイ テイ からだ

1907

1-7-5

158	Nonstandard	U8EB0
身	S12-7-5	F0000

alternative form →see 体 at 0080

軸

▶AXLE

▶AXIS

ジク

Ⓒ 轴 zhóu zhòu

1908

1-7-5

159	Jōyō	U8EF8
車	S12-7-5	F1763

COMPOUNDS

1a [original meaning] **AXLE, shaft, spindle**

b something resembling an **AXLE** in shape or function, as a scroll roller or penholder

a 軸箱 じくばこ axle box

車軸 しゃじく wheel axle, axle

動軸 どうじく driving axle

死軸 しじく dead axle

b 軸木 じくぎ splint; scroll roller

巻軸 まきじく scroll; scroll roller

ペン軸 ぺんじく penholder

2 [also suffix]

a (line about which rotation occurs) **AXIS**

b *math* **AXIS**

c *optics* **AXIS**

d *anat* **AXIS**

a 軸線 じくせん axis, shaft line

地軸 ちじく axis of the earth

回転軸 かいてんじく axis of revolution

左右軸 さゆうじく lateral axis

主軸 しゅじく principal axis; main spindle [shaft]

b 座標軸 ざひょうじく coordinate axis

c 屈折軸 くっせつじく axis of refraction

d 軸索 じくさく axon, axis cylinder

3 (central part) **AXIS, center, pivot**

枢軸 すうじく central point, center; (mechanical) pivot, axis

新機軸 しんきじく new departure, milestone, breakthrough

4a scroll, scroll picture, *kakemono*

b counter for scrolls

a 軸物 じくもの scroll picture

掛け軸 かけじく scroll

b 巻き物二軸 まきものにじく two scrolls

INDEPENDENT

【じく 軸】**AXLE, shaft; holder; axis;** *math* **axis;** *bot* **axis, stem; scroll;** ***kakemono;*** **matchwood, matchstick**

軸の じくの axial

軸を掛ける じくをかける hang a scroll picture

ペンの軸 ぺんのじく penholder

角 言 貝 足 身 【車】 酉 釆 臼

茸の軸 きのこのじく stem of a mushroom

SYNONYMS

❶ **long slender objects**

棒 ROD → 1237
箸 CHOPSTICKS → 3359
桟 crosspiece → 1169
軸 AXLE → 1908
錘 SPINDLE → 2191
竿 POLE → 3259
杖 STAFF → 1026
錫 Buddhist priest's staff → 2189
軛 YOKE → 1873

❷ **line**

線 LINE → 1760
筋 THREADLIKE STRUCTURE → 3319
条 strip → 2726
脈 VEIN → 1189
棒 straight line → 1237
縞 STRIPE → 1784
軸 AXIS → 1908

軽

1909
1-7-5

▶**LIGHT**
ケイ かる(い) かろ(やか)
Ⓝ 輕 Ⓒ 轻 qīng

159	Jōyō-3	U8EFD
車	S12-7-5	F0684

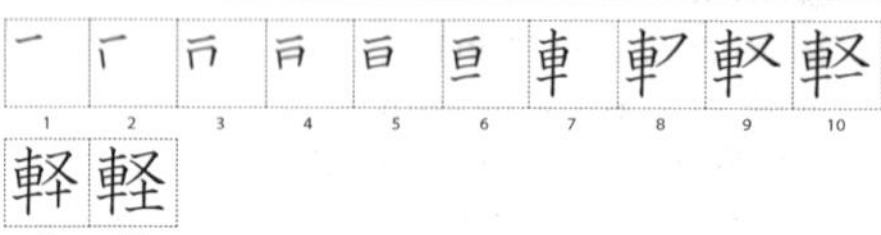

COMPOUNDS

❶ [also prefix] [original meaning] (not heavy) **LIGHT**
軽量 けいりょう light weight
軽油 けいゆ gas oil, light oil
軽金属 けいきんぞく light metals

❷ⓐ (not intense) **LIGHT, slight**
ⓑ [also prefix] (not difficult or serious) **LIGHT, easy, simple**

a 軽震 けいしん weak earthquake
軽傷 けいしょう slight injury
軽減する けいげんする reduce, lighten, mitigate
軽便 けいべん convenience, simplicity
軽食 けいしょく light meal, snack

b 軽易な けいいな easy, light, simple
軽労働 けいろうどう light labor
軽犯罪 けいはんざい minor offense
軽音楽 けいおんがく light music

❸ⓐ **LIGHT-headed, frivolous, thoughtless, rash**
ⓑ (moving quickly) **LIGHT-footed, nimble, agile, simple**

a 軽率な けいそつな rash, light-headed, careless
軽薄な けいはくな insincere, frivolous, flippant, fickle

b 軽快な けいかいな light, nimble, quick; cheerful

❹ **make LIGHT of, think little of**
軽視する けいしする make light of, despise; neglect
軽蔑 けいべつ contempt, disdain

KUN

【かるい 軽い】 (not heavy) **LIGHT, lightweight;** (not intense) **light, slight;** (not difficult or serious) **light, easy, simple; light (taste);** (not important) **light, insignificant**

軽さ かるさ lightness
軽軽と かるがると easily
軽はずみ かるはずみ rashness, hastiness
軽い犯罪 かるいはんざい minor offense
身軽な みがるな light, agile, nimble
気軽な きがるな lighthearted, cheerful; ready
手軽な てがるな easy, light, plain
尻軽な女 しりがるなおんな wanton girl

【かろやか 軽やか】
かろやかな 軽やかな **LIGHT, nimble, airy**

SYNONYMS

❷ⓐ **less in degree**

弱 WEAK → 1499
軽 LIGHT → 1909
微 SLIGHT → 0788
低 LOW → 0082
薄 THIN → 3004
浅 SHALLOW → 0464
仄 FAINT → 3664

ⓑ **easy**

易 EASY (without difficulty) → 3064
安 easy (without effort) → 2695
簡 SIMPLE → 3380
軽 LIGHT → 1909

❹ **disdain**

侮 despise → 0091
軽 make light of → 1909
蔑 DESPISE → 2969
嘲 SCOFF AT → 0878

酢

1910
1-7-5

▶**VINEGAR**
サク す
Ⓒ 酢 zuò cù

164	Jōyō	U9162
酉	S12-7-5	F2268

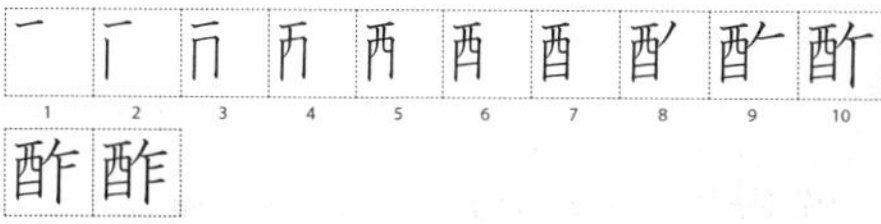

COMPOUNDS

● [formerly also 醋 2002] [original meaning] **VINEGAR**
酢酸 さくさん acetic acid

KUN

【す 酢】[formerly also 醋] [also suffix] **VINEGAR**
酢の物 すのもの pickled dish
酢蛸× すだこ (sliced and) pickled octopus
酢料理 すりょうり pickled dish
醸造酢 じょうぞうす brewed vinegar

SYNONYMS

● **seasonings**
糖 SUGAR → 1777
塩 SALT → 0774
酢 VINEGAR → 1910
醋 VINEGAR → 2002
油 OIL → 0400
醤 FERMENTED SAUCE → 3569
噌 MISO → 0882
蜜 HONEY → 2958

● **sour substances**
酢 VINEGAR → 1910
酸 ACID → 1968

USAGE

【す】
酢
[formerly also 醋] [also suffix] vinegar
醋
[now replaced by 酢] [also suffix] vinegar

HOMOPHONES

す 醋 VINEGAR → 2002

釉

1911

◧ 1-7-5

▶**GLAZE**

ユウ うわぐすり くすり ㊔ ゆ つや

Ⓒ 釉 yòu

165	Names	U91C9
釆	S12-7-5	F3191

COMPOUNDS

● **GLAZE, enamel**
釉薬 ゆうやく glaze, enamel

INDEPENDENT

【ゆう 釉】**GLAZE, enamel**

KUN

【うわぐすり 釉】[also 釉薬, 上薬] **GLAZE, enamel**
釉を掛けた皿 うわぐすりをかけたさら glazed plate

【くすり 釉】**GLAZE**, enamel
釉掛け(=薬掛け) くすりがけ glazing, enameling
灰釉 はいぐすり ash glaze

SPECIAL READINGS

釉薬 うわぐすり [also 釉, 上薬] glaze, enamel

HOMOPHONES

うわぐすり
釉薬 → 1911, 3011
上薬 → 4212, 3011
くすり 薬 DRUG → 3011

NOTE

➡ see USAGE note at 薬 3011

旣

1912

◧ 1-7-5

▶**ALREADY**

キ すで(に)

71	Nonstandard	UFA42
旡	S12-5-7	F0000

traditional form → see 既 at 1498

解

1913

◧ 1-7-6

▶**TAKE APART**
▶**DISSOLVE**
▶**CLARIFY**

カイ ゲ と(く) と(かす) と(ける) ほど(く)▲ ほど(ける)▲ わか(る)▲ ㊔ さとる

Ⓝ 觧 Ⓒ 解 jiě jiè xiè

148	Jōyō-5	U89E3
角	S13-7-6	F0185

COMPOUNDS

❶ [original meaning] (break into component parts) **TAKE APART, resolve, dissolve, separate, dissect**
解体 かいたい dismantling (a machine), scrapping; dissolution, disorganization; dissection
解剖 かいぼう dissection, autopsy; analysis
解像力 かいぞうりょく resolving power (of a lens)
解析 かいせき analysis, analytical research
分解する ぶんかいする take apart [to pieces]; analyze, decompose; be decomposed, break down
瓦解 がかい collapse, breakup, downfall
電解 でんかい electrolysis

❷ **DISSOLVE, melt, liquefy**
解凍 かいとう thawing, defrosting
溶解する ようかいする dissolve, liquefy; melt, fuse
潮解 ちょうかい deliquescence
融解 ゆうかい fusion, melting
氷解する ひょうかいする melt away, be cleared [dispelled]

❸ⓐ (cause to disperse) **DISSOLVE (a meeting), break up (an organization), dispel**
ⓑ (take away the binding power) **DISSOLVE, cancel (a contract), release, lift (a ban)**

a 解散 かいさん breakup, dispersion; dissolution
解組する かいそする break up an organization
解放する かいほうする release, set free
解消 かいしょう liquidation, annulment, solution
b 解除 かいじょ removal [lifting] (of a ban), cancellation; release, acquittal
解約 かいやく dissolution [cancellation] of a contract
解禁 かいきん removal of a ban; opening of the fishing [hunting] season

❹ untie, undo, unfasten
解纜× かいらん unmooring, sailing off

❺ⓐ **release from office, discharge, dismiss**
ⓑ (release from pain) **relieve, alleviate**

a 解任する かいにんする release from office, dismiss, discharge
解雇する かいこする discharge, dismiss, fire
b 解毒剤 げどくざい antidote
解熱 げねつ alleviation of fever
解脱 げだつ *Buddhism* deliverance (of one's soul), salvation
緩解 かんかい relief [remission] (of pain)

❻ⓐ **CLARIFY, explain, elucidate, interpret**
ⓑ **explanation, commentary**

a 解説 かいせつ explanation, commentary
解釈 かいしゃく interpretation, explanation
解明する かいめいする explain, elucidate
弁解 べんかい explanation, vindication, justification, excuse
図解 ずかい explanatory diagram, illustration
b 詳解 しょうかい detailed [minute] explanation, full commentary
注解 ちゅうかい annotation, explanatory notes

❼ⓐ **solve, find a solution, settle**
ⓑ **solution, answer**

a 解決 かいけつ solution, settlement
解答する かいとうする solve, answer
解法 かいほう solution, key to solution
和解 わかい reconciliation, amicable settlement
b 正解 せいかい right answer, correct solution

❽ **understand, comprehend**
理解する りかいする understand, comprehend
見解 けんかい opinion, view
了解 りょうかい understanding, comprehension; consent
誤解 ごかい misunderstanding, misconception
難解な なんかいな difficult, hard to understand
不可解な ふかかいな incomprehensible, inexplicable, baffling

INDEPENDENT

【かい 解】explanation, commentary; solution; *math* root (of an equation)
解を示す かいをしめす show the solution
解と係数の関係 かいとけいすうのかんけい relation between the roots and coefficients

【かいする 解する】understand, comprehend; interpret
人語を解する じんごをかいする understand human speech
善意に解する ぜんいにかいする take it in a favorable sense

【げせない 解せない】be beyond understanding

KUN

【とく 解く】
① **undo, unfasten, unloosen, unsew**
解き放す ときはなす set free
髪を解く かみをとく undo one's hair
② **DISSOLVE**, cancel, release, lift
禁を解く きんをとく lift [remove] a ban
③ **solve, work out**
謎解き なぞとき solution of a riddle
④ [also 梳く] comb (one's hair)
髪を解く かみをとく comb one's hair
⑤ *literary* relieve (a person) of a post
任を解かれる にんをとかれる be relieved of one's post

【とかす 解かす】
① [also 溶かす, formerly also 融かす] *vt* **melt (snow or ice), thaw (out)**
氷を解かす こおりをとかす melt ice
② [usu. 梳かす] **comb (one's hair)**
髪を解かす かみをとかす comb one's hair

【とける 解ける】*vi*
① **come loose, come undone**
靴紐が解けた くつひもがとけた The shoestrings came untied
② be allayed, relent
③ **be solved, be resolved, be cleared**
解けない問題 とけないもんだい insoluble problem
④ [also 溶ける, formerly 融ける] (esp. of snow or ice) **melt, thaw**
雪解け ゆきどけ thawing of snow

【ほどく 解く】*vt* undo, untie, unfasten, loosen; unravel, unknit
結び目を解く むすびめをほどく undo a knot

【ほどける 解ける】*vi* come undone, come loose; unravel

【わかる 解る】[usu. 分かる, sometimes also 判る]
①ⓐ (grasp the meaning of) understand, comprehend, see

1913

ⓑ (be sympathetic toward) understand, show understanding for (another's feelings)

a 解り わかり understanding

解り難い わかりにくい hard to understand, incomprehensible, unintelligible

b 物解りの良い ものわかりのいい understanding; sensible

②ⓐ know, tell, recognize

ⓑ be made known, be brought to light

a 先の事は解らない さきのことはわからない cannot tell what will happen in the future

b 身元が解る みもとがわかる be identified

③ appreciate

音楽が解る おんがくがわかる have an ear [appreciation] for music

SYNONYMS

❶ **separate**

割 DIVIDE → 2284
分 DIVIDE → 2466
解 TAKE APART → 1913
析 ANALYZE → 1072
別 SEPARATE → 1434
離 SEPARATE → 2364
隔 partition → 0827

❷ **liquefy**

溶 DISSOLVE, MELT → 0816
熔 MELT (metals) → 1340
鎔 MELT (metals) → 2214
解 DISSOLVE → 1913
融 FUSE → 2303

❸ⓐ **disperse**

解 DISSOLVE → 1913
散 SCATTER → 2137

❺ⓐ **dismiss**

罷 DISMISS → 3234
免 discharge → 2565
解 release from office → 1913

❻ **explain**

説 EXPLAIN → 1949
明 make clear → 1060
釈 ELUCIDATE → 1876
詮 EXPOUND → 1923
講 expound → 2046
解 CLARIFY → 1913
注 annotate → 0383

❼ **answer**

答 ANSWER → 3322
解 solve → 1913
返 reply → 3797
応 RESPOND → 3804

❽ **know and understand**

知 KNOW → 1446
通 know thoroughly → 3855
得 gain understanding of → 0577
分かる understand → 2466
解 understand → 1913
諒 UNDERSTAND → 1982
了 COMPREHEND → 4157
悟 AWAKE TO → 0502
惺 AWAKE TO → 0709

USAGE

❶【とく】

解く

① undo, unfasten, unloosen, unsew
② dissolve, cancel, release, lift
③ solve, work out
④ [also 梳く] comb (one's hair)
⑤ *literary* relieve (a person) of a post

説く

① explain
② preach, advocate; persuade

溶く

vt

① (cause to pass into solution) dissolve (paint)
② whip an egg

梳く

[also 解く] comb (one's hair)

❷【とかす】

解かす

① [also 溶かす, formerly also 融かす] *vt* melt (snow or ice), thaw (out)
② [usu. 梳かす] comb (one's hair)

融かす

[now usu. 解かす or 溶かす] *vt* melt (snow or ice), thaw (out)

溶かす

vt

① (cause to pass into solution or to turn liquid) dissolve, melt, liquefy
②ⓐ [formerly 熔かす or 鎔かす] melt (up) (metals), fuse, smelt
ⓑ [also 解かす, formerly also 融かす] melt (snow or ice), thaw (out)

熔かす

[now usu. 溶かす] *vt* melt (up) (metals), fuse, smelt

鎔かす

[now usu. 溶かす] *vt* melt (up) (metals), fuse, smelt

梳かす

[sometimes also 解かす] comb (one's hair)

❸【とける】

解ける

vi

① come loose, come undone
② be allayed, relent
③ be solved, be resolved, be cleared

④ [also 溶ける, formerly 融ける] (esp. of snow or ice) **melt, thaw**

融ける

[now usu. 解ける or 溶ける] *vi* (esp. of snow or ice) **melt, thaw**

溶ける

vi

① (pass into solution) **dissolve**

②ⓐ [formerly 熔ける or 鎔ける] (of metals) **melt (up), fuse, smelt**

ⓑ [also 解ける, formerly 融ける] (esp. of snow or ice) **melt, thaw**

熔ける

[now usu. 溶ける] *vi* (of metals) **melt (up), fuse, smelt**

鎔ける

[now usu. 溶ける] *vi* (of metals) **melt (up), fuse, smelt**

HOMOPHONES

とく

説 EXPLAIN →1949
溶 DISSOLVE →0816
梳 COMB →1209

とかす

融 FUSE →2303
溶 DISSOLVE →0816
熔 MELT →1340
鎔 MELT →2214
梳 COMB →1209

とける

融 FUSE →2303
溶 DISSOLVE →0816
熔 MELT →1340
鎔 MELT →2214

わかる

分 DIVIDE →2466
判 JUDGE →1441

NOTE

➡ see also USAGE note at 分 2466

触

1914

1-7-6

▶TOUCH

ショク ふ(れる) さわ(る)

Ⓝ 觸 Ⓒ 触 chù

148	Jōyō	U89E6
角	S13-7-6	F0817

COMPOUNDS

❶ⓐ TOUCH, contact

ⓑ perceive by TOUCHing, feel

a 接触 せっしょく contact, touch
一触即発 いっしょくそくはつ touch-and-go situation, hair-trigger crisis
感触 かんしょく (sense of) touch, feeling

b 触角 しょっかく feeler, antenna
触覚 しょっかく sense of touch
触媒 しょくばい catalyst, catalyzer

❷ conflict with, violate

抵触する ていしょくする conflict with; be contrary to; be incompatible with

KUN

【ふれる 触れる】**TOUCH, feel; come in contact with, meet; touch on, mention; conflict with, violate; announce, hawk**

触れ ふれ proclamation, official notice; touch
触れ合う ふれあう come in contact
触れ合い ふれあい contact, touch
触れ込み ふれこみ (exaggerated) introduction
手を触れるな てをふれるな Hands off!
目に触れる めにふれる catch the eye, attract attention
要点に触れる ようてんにふれる come to [touch on] the point
法に触れる ほうにふれる violate the law

【さわる 触る】

① **TOUCH, feel**

触り さわり touch, feel; impression (of a person); most impressive passage, punch line
肌触り はだざわり touch, feel

② become involved in

触らぬ神に祟り無し さわらぬかみにたたりなし Let sleeping dogs lie
寄ると触ると よるとさわると whenever they come together

SYNONYMS

❶ touch

触 TOUCH →1914
接 CONTACT →0607
撫 STROKE →0904
当てる apply →2701

USAGE

❶【さわる】

触る

① touch, feel

② become involved in

障る

① hinder, interfere with

② affect, harm, jar on

❷【さわり】

触り

① touch, feel

② impression (of a person)

③ most impressive passage, punch line

障り

① hindrance, obstacle

②ⓐ harm, bad effect

ⓑ sickness

HOMOPHONES

さわる 障 HINDRANCE → 0875

さわり 障 HINDRANCE → 0875

1915 解

▶TAKE APART
▶DISSOLVE
▶CLARIFY

カイ ゲ と(く) と(かす) と(ける) ほど(く) ほど(ける) わか(る) ㊔ さとる

1-7-6

148 角	Nonstandard	U89E7
	S13-7-6	F0000

traditional form → see 解 at 1913

1916 該

▶CORRESPOND TO

ガイ

Ⓒ 该 gāi

1-7-6

149 言	Jōyō	U8A72
	S13-7-6	F2201

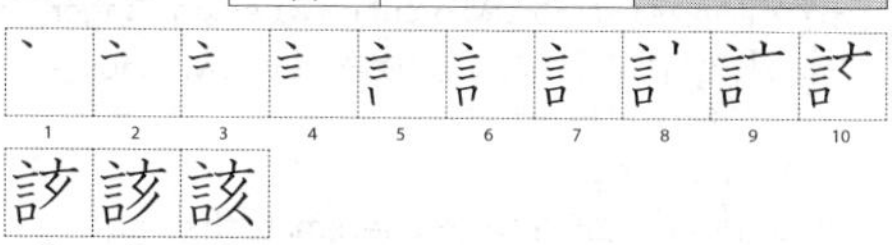

COMPOUNDS

❶ⓐ **CORRESPOND TO, conform to, apply to, fall under**

ⓑ [also prefix] **the said, the one in question, that**

a 該当する がいとうする come under, be applicable to

当該 とうがい the said, the concerned

b 該案 がいあん the said proposal

該問題 がいもんだい the said problem, the matter in question

❷ inclusive, extensive

該博な がいはくな extensive (knowledge), profound (learning)

SYNONYMS

❶ⓐ **correspond to**

該 CORRESPOND TO → 1916

準 apply correspondingly → 3541

当 be equivalent → 2701

ⓑ **this and that**

本 THIS → 4314

爾 THAT → 4407

其れ THAT → 3255

彼 that → 0346

今 THIS (week, etc.) → 2464

当 THE PRESENT → 2701

該 the said → 1916

同 the same → 3707

之 this → 4228

是 this → 3090

此 THIS → 1017

斯 THIS → 2140

1917 詢

▶ASK FOR ADVICE

ジュン シュン ㊔ まこと

Ⓒ 询 xún

1-7-6

149 言	Names	U8A62
	S13-7-6	F0000

COMPOUNDS

● [rare] **ASK FOR ADVICE**, consult, inquire

諮詢(=咨×詢)する しじゅんする consult, inquire

SYNONYMS

● **inquire**

問 QUESTION → 4117

詰 question closely → 1920

聞く ask → 4127

質 query → 3483

尋ねる INQUIRE → 2918

訊 INQUIRE → 1842

伺う INQUIRE (*humble*) → 0078

諮 CONSULT → 2009

詢 ASK FOR ADVICE → 1917

1918 詣

▶VISIT A HOLY PLACE

ケイ もう(でる) ㊔ ゆき

Ⓒ 诣 yì

1-7-6

149 言	Jōyō	U8A63
	S13-7-6	F2048

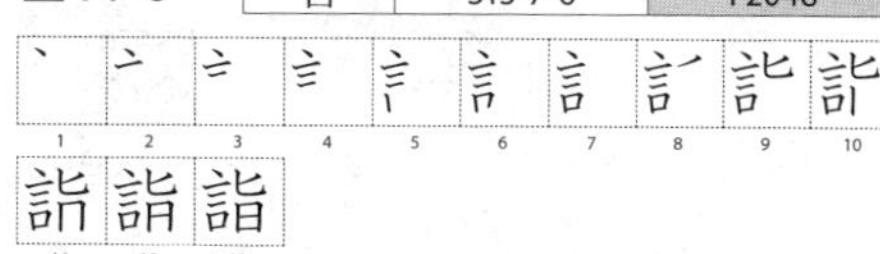

COMPOUNDS

❶ **VISIT A HOLY PLACE (as a temple, shrine or the Imperial Palace), make a pilgrimage**

参詣 さんけい visit to a temple [shrine], worship, pilgrimage

❷ **attain an elevated state**

造詣 ぞうけい attainments, scholarship

KUN

【もうでる 詣でる】**VISIT A HOLY PLACE (as a temple, shrine or the Imperial Palace), make a pilgrimage**

詣で もうで pilgrimage, visit

初詣で はつもうで first visit to a shrine [temple] during the New Year

SYNONYMS

❶ visit
訪 VISIT → 1860
参 VISIT A HOLY PLACE → 2563
詣 VISIT A HOLY PLACE → 1918
寄 call at → 2856
伺 call on → 0078

詭

1919
1-7-6

▶**TRICK**
キ
ⓒ 诡 guǐ

149	Non-Jōyō	U8A6D
言	S13-7-6	F0000

COMPOUNDS

● [now also 奇 2756] [original meaning] **TRICK, cheat, deceive, defraud**
詭計 きけい artifice, trick
詭弁 きべん sophism, sophistry

SYNONYMS

● **deceive**
欺 DECEIVE → 2138
騙 DECEIVE → 2314
詐 SWINDLE → 1896
惑 mislead → 3461
拐 defraud → 0365
偽 FALSIFY → 0149
詭 TRICK → 1919

詰

1920
1-7-6

▶**REPRIMAND**
▶**STUFF**
キツ つ(める) つ(め) -づ(め) つ(まる) つ(む)
ⓒ 诘 jié jí

149	Jōyō	U8A70
言	S13-7-6	F0967

1	2	3	4	5	6	7	8	9	10	11	12	13
丶	亠	亠	言	言	言	言	訁	訁	訁	詁	詰	詰

COMPOUNDS

❶ [original meaning] **REPRIMAND, reprove, censure, rebuke**
詰責する きっせきする [rare] reproach, reprove, reprimand
面詰する めんきつする reprimand (a person) personally
難詰する なんきつする blame, censure, reproach

❷ **question closely, press a person hard with questions, interrogate**
詰問する きつもんする cross-examine, cross-question, question closely

❸ [rare] cramped, confined
詰屈した きっくつした rugged

KUN

【つめる 詰める】

①ⓐ (fill by packing closely) **STUFF, fill, pack into, cram; charge**
ⓑ (fill an aperture) **STUFF** (up), stop up, block up
a 瓶に詰める びんにつめる fill a bottle
b 詰め合わせ つめあわせ combination, assortment
詰め込む つめこむ cram, stuff, pack
詰め物 つめもの stuffing
息を詰める いきをつめる hold one's breath

② place close together; sit close; write close
詰め掛ける つめかける crowd (a house); throng to (a door)
行間を詰める ぎょうかんをつめる crowd the lines

③ be stationed at, be on duty, attend office
詰めている つめている be in attendance [on duty]
詰め所 つめしょ station, office, guardroom

④ shorten; cut down, reduce, economize
指を詰める ゆびをつめる cut off a person's finger
暮らしを詰める くらしをつめる cut down housekeeping expenses

⑤ checkmate, mate
王を詰める おうをつめる checkmate the king

⑥ keep doing, keep up, go on with
詰めて通う つめてかよう frequent tirelessly
根を詰める こんをつめる strain one's nerve

⑦ finalize
問題を詰める もんだいをつめる work toward a solution to a problem

【つめ 詰め】

① **STUFFing, packing, stopper**
②ⓐ final stage [move]
ⓑ checkmating
a 大詰め おおづめ finale, end
b 詰め将棋 つめしょうぎ chess problem
③ edge, approach (of a bridge)
橋の西詰め はしのにしづめ western edge of a bridge

【-づめ -詰め】

① [also suffix]
ⓐ **packed in, bottled in, boxed in**
ⓑ filled with
a 缶詰め かんづめ canned goods, canning; cooping-up, confining
箱詰めの はこづめの packed in a case; boxed (candies)
b 四百字詰め よんひゃくじづめ with 400 characters
② persisting in doing something

立ち詰めでいる たちづめでいる keep standing
理詰め りづめ reasoning, cogent argument

③ [suffix] on duty at
本省詰め ほんしょうづめ service at the Head Office

【つまる 詰まる】

①ⓐ **be STUFFed, be full, be packed**
ⓑ **be stopped [plugged] up, be [get] blocked, get clogged**

a ぎっしり詰まっている ぎっしりつまっている be crammed, be packed full
鼻詰まり はなづまり nasal congestion
b 声を詰まらせて こえをつまらせて in a chocked voice

② **be shortened, become shorter; contract**
詰まり つまり in short, after all; blockade; stuffing; ultimate
それは洗うと詰まる それはあらうとつまる It shrinks when washed

③ [also suffix] **be driven to a corner, be cornered; be hard up**
言葉に詰まる ことばにつまる be at a loss for words
返答に詰まる へんとうにつまる be embarrassed for a reply
行き詰まる いきづまる reach the limits, come to the end of one's tether
金詰まり かねづまり money distress, shortage of money

【つむ 詰む】

① **be packed, become fine [close]**
目の詰んだ めのつんだ fine(-grained), close

② be checkmated
詰み つみ checkmate

SYNONYMS

❶ **blame and accuse**
責 BLAME → 3115
叱 SCOLD → 0210
詰 REPRIMAND → 1920
難 find fault with → 2310
批 CRITICIZE → 0294
劾 EXPOSE CRIMES → 1618
弾 impeach → 0697

❷ **inquire**
問 QUESTION → 4117
詰 question closely → 1920
聞く ask → 4127
質 query → 3483
尋ねる INQUIRE → 2918
訊 INQUIRE → 1842
伺う INQUIRE (*humble*) → 0078
諮 CONSULT → 2009
詢 ASK FOR ADVICE → 1917

【つめる】

① **fill**
充 FILL → 2507
湛 BE FULL OF → 0745
塡 FILL → 0777
満 fill → 0739
詰める STUFF → 1920

HOMOPHONES

つむ 積 ACCUMULATE → 1579

NOTE

➡ see USAGE note at 積 1579

誇

1921

1-7-6

▶**BOAST**

コ ほこ(る)

Ⓒ 夸 kuā

149	Jōyō	U8A87
言	S13-7-6	F1373

(Stroke order 1–13)

COMPOUNDS

ⓐ [original meaning] **BOAST, brag, be proud**

ⓑ **exaggerate, overstate**

a 誇称 こしょう boasting, exaggeration
誇示 こじ ostentation, display, showing off
誇色 こしょく proud countenance
b 誇張する こちょうする exaggerate, overstate, magnify
誇大 こだい exaggeration, magnification

KUN

【ほこる 誇る】 **BOAST, brag, take pride in, peacock oneself**
誇り ほこり pride
誇らしい ほこらしい proud
誇り顔 ほこりがお triumphant look
勝ち誇る かちほこる be triumphant
咲き誇る さきほこる be in all glory

SYNONYMS

ⓐ **boasting and arrogance**
誇 BOAST → 1921
慢 ARROGANT → 0844
傲 ARROGANT → 0173

誠

1922

1-7-6

▶**SINCERITY**

セイ まこと ㊔ まさ のぶ たかし しげ よし とも あき なり

Ⓝ 誠 Ⓒ 诚 chéng

149	Jōyō-6	U8AA0
言	S13-7-6	F1342

丶	亠	亡	言	言	言	言	訁	訢	訢
1	2	3	4	5	6	7	8	9	10
訧	誠	誠							
11	12	13							

COMPOUNDS

● **SINCERITY, true heart, honesty, fidelity**

誠実 せいじつ sincerity, honesty, faith
誠意 せいい sincerity, good faith
忠誠 ちゅうせい faithfulness, fidelity
至誠 しせい sincerity, devotion

KUN

【まこと 誠】

① **SINCERITY, true heart, honesty, fidelity**

誠を尽くす まことをつくす do with sincerity

② [sometimes also 実 or 真] **truth, reality**

誠の まことの true, genuine
誠に まことに truly, really; very, extremely
誠しやかに まことしやかに plausibly, with seeming truth
嘘か誠か うそかまことか true or false

SYNONYMS

● **fidelity**

忠 LOYALTY → 3087
義 faith → 2948
孝 FILIAL PIETY → 3973
悌 BROTHERLY LOVE → 0507
誠 SINCERITY → 1922
実 faithfulness → 2765
信 fidelity → 0115
操 constancy → 0948
節 moral integrity → 3336

USAGE

【まこと】

誠
① sincerity, true heart, honesty, fidelity
② [sometimes also 実 or 真] truth, reality

実
[usu. 誠, sometimes also 真] truth, reality

真
[usu. 誠, sometimes also 実] truth, reality

HOMOPHONES

まこと

実 REAL → 2765
真 TRUE → 2616

詮

1923

1-7-6

▸**EXPOUND**

セン かい▲ ㊔ のり さと とし あきら はる さとる とも さとし

Ⓝ 詮 Ⓒ 诠 quán

149	Jōyō	U8A6E
言	S13-7-6	F2118

丶	亠	亡	言	言	言	言	訁	訁	訁
1	2	3	4	5	6	7	8	9	10
訡	詮	詮							
11	12	13							

COMPOUNDS

❶ **EXPOUND, elucidate, explain**

詮議 せんぎ discussion, examination; interrogation
詮索 せんさく scrutiny, prying, inquiry
所詮 しょせん after all

❷ avail, use, worth, effect, result

❸ required means, methods called for

INDEPENDENT

【せん 詮】avail, use, worth, effect, result; required means, methods called for

詮無い せんない no use, no avail, no help for

【せんずる 詮ずる】contemplate deeply, meditate on

詮ずる所 せんずるところ after all, after all due consideration

KUN

【かい 詮】avail, use, worth, effect, result

詮(=甲斐)が有る かいがある fruitful, effective, worth, worthwhile

SYNONYMS

❶ **explain**

説 EXPLAIN → 1949
明 make clear → 1060
釈 ELUCIDATE → 1876
詮 EXPOUND → 1923
講 expound → 2046
解 CLARIFY → 1913
注 annotate → 0383

COMPOUND FORMATION

【所詮 しょせん】

所詮 'after all' is Buddhist in origin and combines 詮 'expound' with 所, which indicates the passive voice, yielding the meaning 'that which is expounded' (i.e., the substance of Buddhist scriptures). By extension, it came to mean 'after all is said and done' or 'after all', for reasons that are not clear.

詩 ▸POETRY

シ ㊔ うた

Ⓒ 诗 shī

1924

◧ 1-7-6

149	Jōyō-3	U8A69
言	S13-7-6	F1073

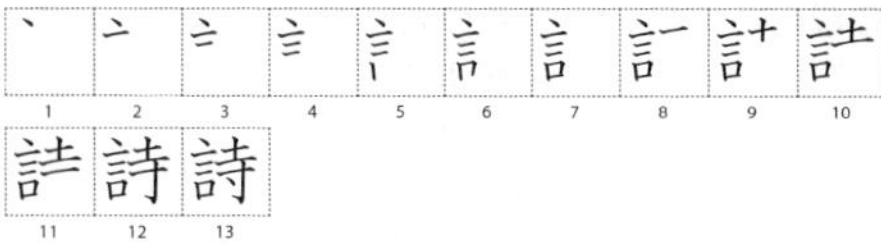

COMPOUNDS

ⓐ [also suffix] [original meaning] **POETRY, poem, verse**

ⓑ **Chinese POETRY [poem]**

a 詩人 しじん poet
詩情 しじょう poetic sentiment, poetical interest
詩集 ししゅう anthology of poems
詩的な してきな poetic
叙事詩 じょじし epic (poem), epic poetry

b 詩吟 しぎん reciting Chinese poems
詩歌 しいか(=しか) Chinese and Japanese poetry; poems
唐詩 とうし Tang poetry

INDEPENDENT

【し 詩】**POETRY, poem, lines, verse, rhyme; Chinese poetry [poem]**
詩を作る しをつくる compose a poem

SYNONYMS

ⓐ **poetry**
詩 POETRY → 1924
歌 Japanese poetry → 2296
俳 HAIKU → 0126
句 HAIKU → 3685

試 ▸TRY

シ こころ(みる) ため(す)

Ⓒ 试 shì

1925

◧ 1-7-6

149	Jōyō-4	U8A66
言	S13-7-6	F0707

COMPOUNDS

❶ⓐ [original meaning] (attempt to do) **TRY, attempt**
ⓑ (test the quality of) **TRY, test, sample**

a 試案 しあん tentative plan, draft
試作 しさく trial manufacture
試算する しさんする make a trial calculation
試写 ししゃ preview, private showing
試行錯誤 しこうさくご trial and error

b 試食 ししょく sampling (of food)
試験 しけん test, examination
試練 しれん trial, test, probation
試運転 しうんてん test run

❷ abbrev. of 試験 しけん: **examination, school test**
入試 にゅうし entrance examination
追試 ついし supplementary examination
模試 もし sham examination

❸ **used phonetically for *shi***
試合 しあい match, game

KUN

【こころみる 試みる】**TRY, attempt, test**
試み こころみ trial, attempt, test
抵抗を試みる ていこうをこころみる offer [put up] resistance

【ためす 試す】**TRY, test, experiment**
試し ためし trial, test, try
力を試す ちからをためす try one's strength

SYNONYMS

❶ **try**
試 TRY → 1925
験 TEST → 2306

❷ **examination**
検 examination → 1241
試 examination (school test) → 1925

COMPOUND FORMATION

【試合 しあい】

試合 'match, game' consists of 試 ❸, used phonetically for 為 し, the verb stem of 為る する 'to do'. It derives from 為合う しあう 'do something to each other'.

NOTE

➡ see COMPOUND FORMATION for 試練 しれん → 練 1738

詳 ▸DETAILED

ショウ くわ(しい) つまび(らか)▲ ㊔ よし

Ⓒ 详 xiáng

1926

◧ 1-7-6

149	Jōyō	U8A73
言	S13-7-6	F1170

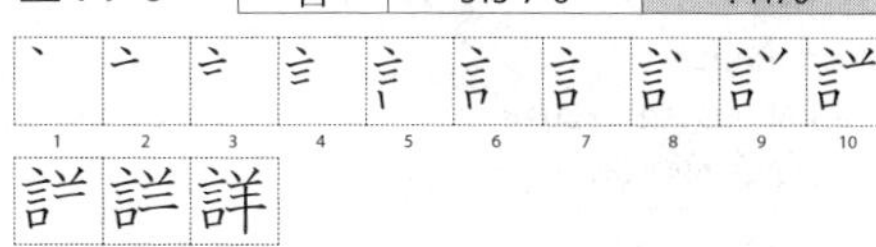

COMPOUNDS

ⓐ **DETAILED, minute, full**

ⓑ [original meaning] explain [investigate] in detail

ⓒ know in detail

a 詳細 しょうさい details, particulars
詳密な しょうみつな minute, detailed, elaborate
詳察 しょうさつ careful observation

b 詳報 しょうほう detailed report
詳論する しょうろんする explain in detail
c 未詳の みしょうの unknown
不詳 ふしょう unknown, unidentified

KUN

【くわしい 詳しい】**DETAILED, minute; complete, full; exact, accurate; know well (about), be (well) versed in**
詳しさ くわしさ detailedness; completeness; knowledge
詳しい話 くわしいはなし detailed account
この辺の地理に詳しい このへんのちりにくわしい know every inch of this neighborhood

【つまびらか 詳らか】
つまびらかな 詳らかな **DETAILED**; accurate; clearly known
詳らかでない つまびらかでない be unknown
事情を詳らかにする じじょうをつまびらかにする reveal the circumstances

SYNONYMS

ⓐ **detailed**
詳 DETAILED → 1926
細 MINUTE → 1689
緻 MINUTE → 1780
密 CLOSE → 2857
精 meticulous → 1729

詫

1927
1-7-6

▶**APOLOGIZE**
タ わ(びる)
Ⓒ 诧 chà

149	Names	U8A6B
言	S13-7-6	F2129

KUN

【わびる 詫びる】**APOLOGIZE**
詫び状 わびじょう letter of apology
詫びを入れる わびをいれる make an apology
お詫び おわび apology

SYNONYMS

【わびる】
◯ **apologize**
謝 APOLOGIZE → 2048
詫びる APOLOGIZE → 1927

話

1928
1-7-6

▶**SPEAK**
ワ はな(す) はなし
Ⓒ 话 huà

149	Jōyō-2	U8A71
言	S13-7-6	F0054

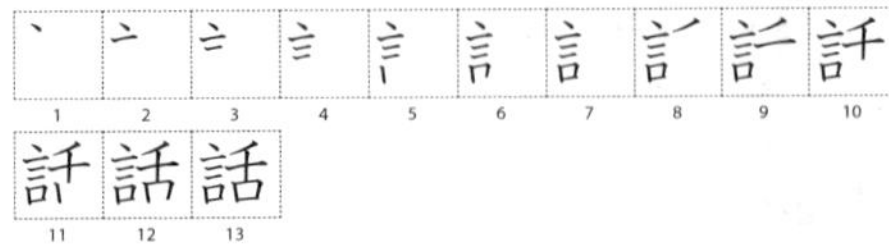

COMPOUNDS

❶ⓐ [original meaning] **SPEAK, talk, converse**
ⓑ **conversation, speech, talk**
a 話者 わしゃ speaker, narrator
会話 かいわ conversation
対話 たいわ dialogue, conversation
電話 でんわ telephone; phone call
談話 だんわ talk, conversation
b 話題 わだい topic [subject] of conversation
世話 せわ help, aid, good offices; care; everyday affairs
閑話休題 かんわきゅうだい to return to the subject

❷ⓐ **story, tale, fable**
ⓑ counter for stories
a 神話 しんわ myth, mythology
童話 どうわ nursery tale, fairy tale
民話 みんわ folk tale, folk story
実話 じつわ true story
挿話 そうわ anecdote
b 第五話 だいごわ story No. 5

KUN

【はなす 話す】**SPEAK, talk; tell; consult with**
話し合う はなしあう discuss, talk over, consult with
話し声 はなしごえ voice; whisper
話し言葉 はなしことば spoken language
話し込む はなしこむ have a long talk (with)
事情を話す じじょうをはなす explain the situation

【はなし 話】[also suffix] **talk, conversation, speech; chat; rumor, report; consultation, agreement**
話の種 はなしのたね topic of conversation
笑い話 わらいばなし funny [humorous] story
昔話 むかしばなし legend, old tale
思い出話 おもいでばなし reminiscent talk

SYNONYMS

❶ⓐ **speak and say**
言 SAY → 2440
語る TELL → 1944
談 TALK → 1975
喋 TALK → 0665
諷 INSINUATE → 2005
謂う REFER TO → 2007
云 say → 2430
曰 SAY THAT → 3757
話 SPEAK → 1928
口 give mouth to → 4189
申す SPEAK HUMBLY → 4319

述 STATE → 3816
陳 SET FORTH → 0656
弁 SPEAK ELOQUENTLY → 2497

❷ⓐ stories

話 story → 1928
談 account → 1975
語 tale → 1944
説 narrative → 1949
噂 RUMOR → 0883

COMPOUND FORMATION

【世話 せわ】

世話 'help, aid, etc.' originally meant society (世) chat (話 ❶ⓑ) or daily gossip. It is not clear how this is related to its current meaning of helping or taking care.

NOTE

➡ see COMPOUND FORMATION for
挿話 そうわ → 挿 0517
閑話休題 かんわきゅうだい → 閑 4123

詮

1929

◧ 1-7-6

▶EXPOUND

セン かい ㊔ のり さと とし あきら はる さとる とも さとし

149 言	Nonstandard	U8A6E
	S13-7-6	F0000

traditional form → see 詮 at 1923

誕

◧ 1-7-6

incorrect stroke-count
➡ see ◧ 1-7-8: 言 at 1987

賂

1930

◧ 1-7-6

▶BRIBE

ロ まいない▲

ⓒ 赂 lù

154 貝	Jōyō	U8CC2
	S13-7-6	F2836

COMPOUNDS

● BRIBE; bribery

賄賂 わいろ bribe, bribery

KUN

【まいない 賂】[also 賄]
ⓐ **BRIBE**; bribery
ⓑ [archaic] offering, gift of gratitude

SYNONYMS

● give

与 GIVE → 4229
呈 PRESENT → 2715
進 present to a superior → 3873
上 give (to superior or others) → 4212
下 give (to inferior or speaker) → 4186
呉れる give (to speaker) → 3156
授 CONFER → 0595
賜 DEIGN TO GIVE → 1994
贈 PRESENT A GIFT → 2064
賄 BRIBE → 1931
賂 BRIBE → 1930

HOMOPHONES

まいない 賄 BRIBE → 1931

NOTE

➡ see USAGE note at 賄 1931

賄

1931

◧ 1-7-6

▶BRIBE

ワイ まかな(う) まいない▲

ⓒ 贿 huì

154 貝	Jōyō	U8CC4
	S13-7-6	F2221

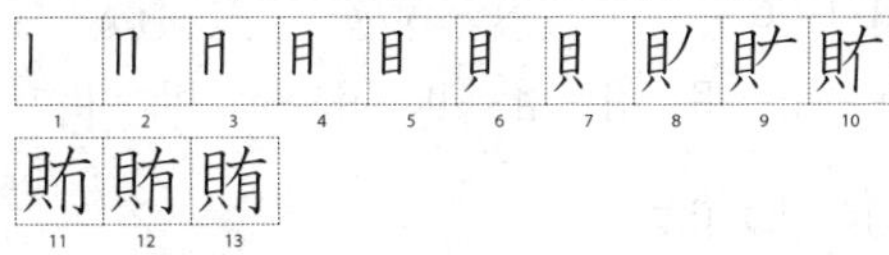

COMPOUNDS

● BRIBE

賄賂 わいろ bribe, bribery
収賄 しゅうわい acceptance of a bribe, corruption
贈賄する ぞうわいする bribe, corrupt
贈収賄 ぞうしゅうわい corruption, bribery

KUN

【まかなう 賄う】**manage to cover (expenses), meet (the demand); provide meals [board], cater**

賄い まかない board, meals; boarding, catering; cook
賄い婦 まかないふ female cook
千円で賄う せんえんでまかなう manage to cover the expenses with 1000 yen
需要を賄う じゅようをまかなう meet the demand

【まいない 賄】[also 賂]
ⓐ **BRIBE**; bribery
ⓑ [archaic] offering, gift of gratitude

SYNONYMS

● give

与 GIVE → 4229
呈 PRESENT → 2715
進 present to a superior → 3873
上 give (to superior or others) → 4212
下 give (to inferior or speaker) → 4186
呉れる give (to speaker) → 3156
授 CONFER → 0595

角 言【貝】足 車 酉 釆 君

賜 DEIGN TO GIVE → 1994
贈 PRESENT A GIFT → 2064
賄 BRIBE → 1931
賂 BRIBE → 1930

USAGE

【まいない】

賄
[also 賂]
ⓐ bribe; bribery
ⓑ [archaic] offering, gift of gratitude

賂
[also 賄] same as 賄

HOMOPHONES

まいない 賂 BRIBE → 1930

賊

▶BANDIT

ゾク

Ⓝ 賊 Ⓒ 贼 zéi

1932

1-7-6

154	Jōyō	U8CCA
貝	S13-7-6	F1422

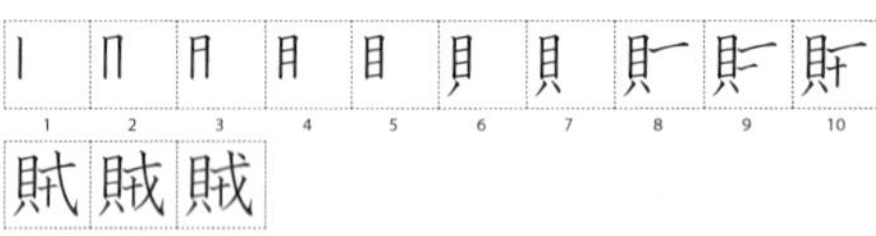

COMPOUNDS

❶ⓐ BANDIT, robber, pirate, thief
ⓑ rebel, traitor, insurgent

a 賊徒 ぞくと bandit, robber; rebels, traitors
盗賊 とうぞく thief, robber, bandit
海賊 かいぞく pirate
山賊 さんぞく bandit, mountain robber
匪×賊 ひぞく bandit

b 賊軍 ぞくぐん insurgents, rebel army
逆賊 ぎゃくぞく rebel, traitor, insurgent
国賊 こくぞく traitor (to the country)

❷ [original meaning] harm, injure, kill
賊虐 ぞくぎゃく damage and ill treatment

INDEPENDENT

【ぞく 賊】 thief, burglar; rebel, insurgent
賊を捕らえる ぞくをとらえる arrest [catch] a thief
【ぞくする 賊する】 harm, hurt, kill

SPECIAL READINGS

烏賊▲ いか squid, cuttlefish

SYNONYMS

❶ⓐ thieves
盗 thief → 3309
泥 petty thief → 0384
賊 BANDIT → 1932

NOTE

★ do not confuse with 賦 INSTALLMENT → 1992

賊

▶BANDIT

ゾク

1933

1-7-6

154	Nonstandard	U8CCA
貝	S13-7-6	F0000

traditional form → see 賊 at 1932

跳

▶JUMP

チョウ は(ねる) と(ぶ) -と(び)

Ⓒ 跳 tiào

1934

1-7-6

157	Jōyō	U8DF3
足	S13-7-6	F1608

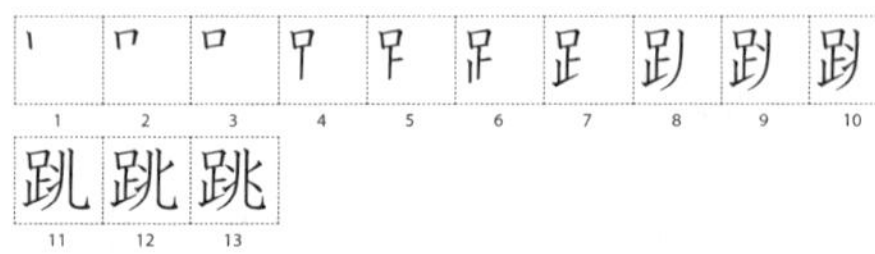

COMPOUNDS

❶ [original meaning] **JUMP, leap, spring**
跳躍する ちょうやくする jump, leap, spring
跳馬 ちょうば long horse (vault)
反跳 はんちょう *phys* recoil

❷ be rampant
跳梁 ちょうりょう rampancy, domination; [original meaning] jumping about

KUN

【はねる 跳ねる】

①ⓐ **leap, spring, JUMP, hop**
ⓑ **bound, rebound, recoil**
ⓒ (of the market) **JUMP** (to)

a 跳ね起きる はねおきる jump up, spring up
b 跳び跳ねる とびはねる jump up and down, hop
bc 跳ね返る はねかえる rebound, bounce; (of the market) recover

② (of the theater) be over, close

【とぶ 跳ぶ】

ⓐ **JUMP, leap, spring**
ⓑ **JUMP** [leap] over, vault

a 縄跳び なわとび rope skipping, rope jumping
b 跳び過ぎる とびすぎる overleap, overjump

【-とび -跳び】 [also suffix] **JUMP**
棒高跳び ぼうたかとび pole vault [jump]
背面跳び はいめんとび backward jump, Fosbury flop

SYNONYMS

❶ jump
跳 JUMP → 1934
躍 LEAP → 2090
蹶 SPRING TO ONE'S FEET → 2073

USAGE

【はねる】

跳ねる

①ⓐ leap, spring, jump, hop

ⓑ bound, rebound, recoil

ⓒ (of the market) **jump (to)**

② (of the theater) **be over, close**

撥ねる

①ⓐ flip, splash

ⓑ strike, knock down

② reject, turn down

③ take a percentage for one's own

④ sweep up (in brush stroke of kanji)

⑤ pronounce ん as a syllabic consonant

HOMOPHONES

はねる 撥 REPEL → 0907

とぶ

飛 FLY → 4389

翔 SOAR → 1714

NOTE

➡ see also USAGE note at 飛 4389

跨

1935

◧ 1-7-6

▶STRADDLE

コ また(ぐ) また(がる)

ⓒ 跨 kuà

157	Names	U8DE8
足	S13-7-6	F2679

COMPOUNDS

❶ⓐ (be astride) **STRADDLE, sit [stand] astride**

ⓑ (extend across) **STRADDLE, stretch across [over]**

a 跨座式鉄道 こざしきてつどう straddle-beam monorail

b 跨線橋 こせんきょう overpass

❷ crotch, inner thigh

跨下 こか under one's crotch, between one's thighs

KUN

【またぐ 跨ぐ】

ⓐ (step over) **STRADDLE, stride over [across], cross**

ⓑ (extend across) **STRADDLE, stretch across [over]**

ⓒ (be astride) **STRADDLE, sit [stand] astride**

a 一跨ぎ ひとまたぎ a single stride; a short distance

b 川を跨ぐ橋 かわをまたぐはし bridge extending over the river

【またがる 跨がる】

ⓐ (be astride) **STRADDLE, sit [stand] astride**

ⓑ (extend across) **STRADDLE, stretch across [over]**

a 馬に跨がる うまにまたがる mount [sit astride] a horse

SYNONYMS

❶ **extend over**

亘 EXTEND OVER → 2438

及 REACH TO → 4192

跨 STRADDLE → 1935

路

1936

◧ 1-7-6

▶ROAD

ロ ル▲ -じ みち▲ ㊔ おうじ

ⓒ 路 lù

157	Jōyō-3	U8DEF
足	S13-7-6	F0399

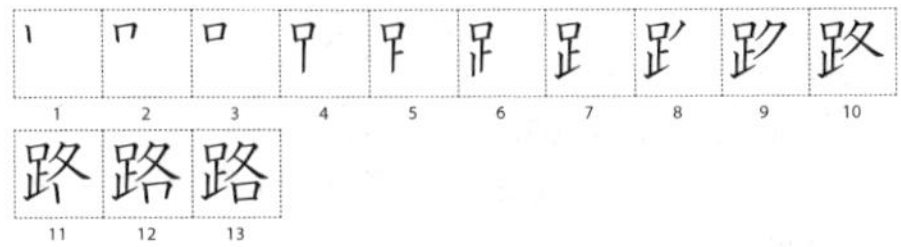

COMPOUNDS

❶ⓐ [also suffix] **ROAD, route, way**

ⓑ journey, traveling

a 路上 ろじょう on the road, road

路面 ろめん road surface

路線 ろせん route, way, line

路地 ろじ alley, lane

道路 どうろ road, street, way

空路 くうろ air route, airway

線路 せんろ (railway) line, track

通路 つうろ passage, pathway, alley, aisle

悪路 あくろ bad road

滑走路 かっそうろ runway

b 路用 ろよう traveling expenses

路銀 ろぎん traveling expenses

❷ *elec* **circuit, wire**

回路 かいろ (electric) circuit

短路 たんろ short circuit

閉路 へいろ closed circuit

断路 だんろ disconnection (of a wire)

❸ line of reasoning, logic

理路 りろ reasoning, argument

❹ important position, high rank

要路 ようろ important position, the authorities; important road

当路 とうろ the authorities

❺ used phonetically for *ru,* esp. in the transliteration of foreign names

路加 るか St. Luke

KUN

【-じ -路】

①ⓐ **way (to), route**—often used as suffix after names of provinces in old Japan

ⓑ suffix indicating number of days of a journey

a 旅路 たびじ journey

伊勢路 いせじ way to Ise

b 五日路 いつかじ five days' journey

② suffix indicating age in tens of years

五十路 いそじ 50 years old

【みち 路】[now usu. 道] **ROAD, avenue, boulevard**

町を貫く路 まちをつらぬくみち road passing through the town

SYNONYMS

❶ⓐ ways and routes

道 WAY (path) → 3888
径 PATH → 0347
軌 TRACK → 1832
線 LINE → 1760
澪 WATERWAY → 0957
途 WAY (route) → 3853
路 ROAD → 1936
筋 wayside → 3319
通り street → 3855
街 city street → 0702
辻 CROSSROADS → 3958
岐 forked road → 0285
巷 THE STREETS → 3097

❺ phonetic [r]

呂 PHONETIC [ro] → 2713
路 phonetic [ru] → 1936
羅 PHONETIC [ra] → 3244

HOMOPHONES

みち 道 WAY → 3888

NOTE

➡ see USAGE note at 道 3888

跡

1937

1-7-6

▶TRACE

セキ あと

Ⓝ 迹◇ Ⓒ 迹 jì

157	Jōyō	U8DE1
足	S13-7-6	F0816

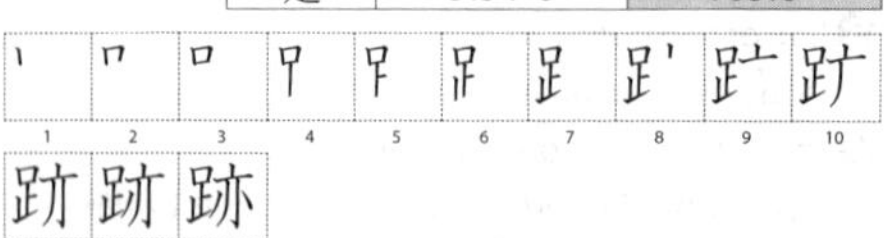

1 2 3 4 5 6 7 8 9 10 11 12 13

COMPOUNDS

❶ [formerly also 蹟 2065]

ⓐ (mark left by something) **TRACE(s), track, mark, footprint, trail**

ⓑ (sign of former presence) **TRACEs, ruins, remains**

a 足跡 そくせき footprint, footmark; the course of one's life, one's achievements
追跡 ついせき pursuit, chase, follow-up
軌跡 きせき locus; tracks
航跡 こうせき wake, track; flight path, vapor trail
人跡 じんせき human traces
筆跡 ひっせき handwriting, holograph

b 遺跡 いせき ruins, remains
史跡 しせき historic spot [remains]
古跡 こせき historic remains, ruins

❷ sign, indication, phenomenon

奇跡 きせき miracle, wonder

❸ traditional family name, status or property

門跡 もんぜき status of a temple leading a Buddhist sect, esp. Honganji Temple; priest-prince
名跡 みょうせき family name

KUN

【あと 跡】

①ⓐ (mark left by something) **TRACE(s), track, mark, footprint, trail, sign;** [also 痕] **scar**

ⓑ (sign of former presence) **ruins, remains, aftermath**

a 跡形も無く あとかたもなく without leaving any trace
傷跡 きずあと scar, cicatrix
足跡 あしあと footprint, footmark

b 跡始末(=後始末)する あとしまつする settle, take remedial measures
城跡 しろあと ruins of a castle

② succession

跡を絶たない あとをたたない (there) be no end to
跡を絶つ あとをたつ put an end to, wipe out

③ inheritance, headship of a family

跡継ぎ あとつぎ successor, heir
跡目 あとめ headship of a family, family property

SYNONYMS

❶ⓐ marks and signs

標 MARK (identifying sign) → 1347
徽 EMBLEM → 0968
痕 SCAR → 4066
印 MARK (visible sign) → 1023
跡 TRACE → 1937
蹟 TRACE → 2065
踪 FOOTPRINTS → 1996
紋 print → 1651
符 SYMBOL → 3299
号 SIGN → 2675
栞 BOOKMARK → 3285

❶ⓐ trace

軌 TRACK → 1832
跡 TRACE → 1937

HOMOPHONES

あと

後 AFTER → 0431
蹟 TRACE → 2065
痕 SCAR → 4066

NOTE

➡ see USAGE note at 後 0431

践 ▶IMPLEMENT

1938

◧ 1-7-6

セン

Ⓝ 踐 Ⓒ 践 jiàn

157	Jōyō	U8DF5
足	S13-7-6	F2022

COMPOUNDS

❶ (give practical effect to and ensure actual fulfillment) **IMPLEMENT, carry through, put in practice, carry out**

践言する せんげんする keep one's word
実践する じっせんする put in practice, implement

❷ accession (to the throne)

践祚× せんそ accession (to the throne)

❸ [archaic] step (upon), tread upon

践踏する せんとうする trample down

SYNONYMS

❶ **execute**

執 EXECUTE → 2114
行 ACT → 0246
履 FULFILL → 3933
施 CARRY OUT → 1103
践 IMPLEMENT → 1938
果たす effect → 4377
遂 ACCOMPLISH → 3892

較 ▶COMPARE

1939

◧ 1-7-6

カク コウ▲ くら(べる)▲

Ⓒ 较 jiào

159	Jōyō	U8F03
車	S13-7-6	F1361

COMPOUNDS

● **COMPARE**

較量 こうりょう [rare] comparison
較差 かくさ(=こうさ) range
比較する ひかくする compare with, draw a comparison

KUN

【くらべる 較べる】[usu. 比べる] **COMPARE,** contrast

大きさを較べる おおきさをくらべる compare the size

SYNONYMS

● **compare**

比 COMPARE → 0029
較 COMPARE → 1939
譬 COMPARE TO → 3613
校 COLLATE → 1166
照 check against → 3506
対 OPPOSE (contrast) → 1025
参 refer → 2563

HOMOPHONES

くらべる 比 COMPARE → 0029

NOTE

➡ see USAGE note at 比 0029

酪 ▶DAIRY PRODUCTS

1940

◧ 1-7-6

ラク

Ⓒ 酪 lào

164	Jōyō	U916A
酉	S13-7-6	F3229

COMPOUNDS

● **DAIRY PRODUCTS**

酪農 らくのう dairy farming
酪農家 らくのうか dairy farmer, dairyman
酪製品 らくせいひん dairy products
酪酸 らくさん butyric acid
乳酪 にゅうらく dairy products
牛酪 ぎゅうらく butter
乾酪 かんらく cheese

SYNONYMS

● **dairy products**

酪 DAIRY PRODUCTS → 1940
乳 MILK → 1823
醍 CREAM → 2031
醐 CREAM → 2032

酬 ▶RECIPROCATE

1941

◧ 1-7-6

シュウ むく(いる)▲

Ⓒ 酬 chóu

164	Jōyō	U916C
酉	S13-7-6	F2007

角 言 貝 足 車 【酉】 𤣩 君

COMPOUNDS

❶ⓐ RECIPROCATE, requite, recompense; respond
ⓑ remuneration, reward

a 応酬 おうしゅう response, reply; exchange
b 報酬 ほうしゅう remuneration, reward; pay

❷ [original meaning] **RECIPROCATE** [exchange] wine-glasses, offer wine in return
献酬 けんしゅう exchange of sake cups

KUN

【むくいる 酬いる】[now usu. 報いる]
ⓐ requite, repay
ⓑ recompense, reward
a 酬い むくい recompense, return
b 労に酬いる ろうにむくいる recompense a person for his [her] labor

SYNONYMS

❶ⓐ compensate
償 RECOMPENSE →0199
賠 COMPENSATE →1991
酬 RECIPROCATE →1941
報 REQUITE →2133

❷ offer wine
酌 POUR WINE →1854
献 offer wine →2240
酬 reciprocate wineglasses →1941

HOMOPHONES

むくいる 報 INFORM →2133
むくい 報 INFORM →2133

NOTE

➡ see USAGE note at 報 2133

酵
◧1-7-6

incorrect stroke-count
➡ see ◧1-7-7: 酉 at 1966

琵
◧1-7-6

incorrect classification/stroke-count
➡ see ⬒2-8-4: 𤣩𤣩 at 3453

群
1942
◧1-7-6

▶**GROUP**
グン　む(れる)　む(れ)　むら　むら(がる)
Ⓝ 羣◇　Ⓒ 群 qún

123 羊	Jōyō-5	U7FA4
	S13-6-7	F0926

Stroke order: ㇇ ⺕ ヨ 尹 尹 君 君 君 君' 君⺷ 君⺷ 群 群 (1–13)

COMPOUNDS

❶ⓐ [also suffix] **GROUP (of any kind), crowd, flock, cluster, swarm**
ⓑ GROUP (in U.S. Army or Air Force)
ⓒ *chem* **GROUP**

a 群衆 ぐんしゅう crowd of people, multitude
群像 ぐんぞう *art* group
魚群 ぎょぐん school of fish
一群の羊 いちぐんのひつじ flock of sheep
抜群の ばつぐんの preeminent, outstanding
層群 そうぐん *geol* group
子音群 しいんぐん consonant cluster
流星群 りゅうせいぐん meteoric swarm

❷ⓐ form a GROUP, cluster
ⓑ in GROUPs, many

a 群生する ぐんせいする grow gregariously [in crowds]
群集 ぐんしゅう crowd, mob; forming a large group (of people)
b 群島 ぐんとう group of islands, archipelago
群落 ぐんらく many communities; cluster of plants
群発地震 ぐんぱつじしん earthquake swarm

INDEPENDENT

【ぐん 群】**GROUP, crowd** (→❶)
群を成して ぐんをなして in a group, in crowds, in swarms

KUN

【むれる 群れる】**crowd together, throng, flock together, swarm**
人が群れる ひとがむれる be crowded with people

【むれ 群れ】**GROUP, crowd, flock, swarm, herd**
群れを成す むれをなす form groups
羊の群れ ひつじのむれ flock of sheep

【むら 群】[sometimes also 叢]
ⓐ [in compounds] **GROUP, crowd, flock**
ⓑ counter for **GROUPs** or flocks
a 群雀 むらすずめ flock of sparrows
b 一群 ひとむら a flock, a bunch

【むらがる 群がる】[sometimes also 叢がる] **crowd together, throng, flock together, swarm**
蜂が群がる はちがむらがる be swarmed with bees

SYNONYMS

❶ groups
群 GROUP (of any kind) →1942
班 SQUAD →1182
軍 team →2582
組 group (of people) →1693
陣 lineup →0545
連 set →3849
族 common-interest group (*slang*) →1195
党 PARTY →3190
隊 PARTY (organized group) →0762
団 BODY →3791
伍 ranks →0050

ⓐ **crowd**
群 GROUP → 1942
衆 MULTITUDE → 3325
叢 CROWD TOGETHER → 3243
簇 FORM A CLUSTER → 3377

USAGE

❶【むら】
群
[sometimes also 叢]
ⓐ [in compounds] group, crowd, flock
ⓑ counter for groups or flocks
叢
[usu. 群] same as 群

❷【むらがる】
群がる
[sometimes also 叢がる] crowd together, throng, flock together, swarm
叢がる
[usu. 群がる] same as 群がる

HOMOPHONES

むら 叢 CROWD TOGETHER → 3243
むらがる 叢 CROWD TOGETHER → 3243

COMPOUND FORMATION

【抜群 ばつぐん】
抜群の 'preeminent, outstanding' is rising above (抜) the crowds (群 ❶ⓐ), i.e., to be extraordinary or outstanding.

読 1943

▶READ
ドク トク トウ よ(む) -よ(み)
Ⓝ 讀 Ⓒ 读 dú dòu

◧ 1-7-7

149	Jōyō-2	U8AAD
言	S14-7-7	F0306

Stroke order: 1 丶 2 亠 3 亠 4 言 5 言 6 言 7 言 8 訁 9 訁 10 訁 11 訁 12 訁 13 訁 14 読

COMPOUNDS

❶ⓐ **READ**
ⓑ **READ (aloud), recite, chant**
a 読者 どくしゃ reader, subscriber
読本 とくほん reader, reading book
読書 どくしょ reading a book, reading
読解力 どっかいりょく ability to read and understand
愛読書 あいどくしょ one's favorite book
熟読 じゅくどく careful reading
b 朗読 ろうどく reading aloud
音読する おんどくする read aloud

❷ **READing or pronunciation of Chinese characters**
音読 おんどく(=おんよみ) Chinese-derived pronunciation of kanji, *on* reading
訓読 くんどく(=くんよみ) Japanese-derived pronunciation of kanji, *kun* reading

❸ division of text
読点 とうてん comma
句読 くとう punctuation, pointing

KUN

【よむ 読む】
①ⓐ **READ**
ⓑ **READ** (aloud), recite, chant
a 読み よみ reading; reading (of Chinese characters); judgment, foresight, insight
読み物 よみもの reading matter, book
読み手 よみて reader, subscriber; reciter
読み方 よみかた way of reading; reading (of a Chinese character)
楽譜を読む がくふをよむ read music
立ち読み たちよみ browsing (in a bookstore)
b 読み上げる よみあげる read aloud, read off
経を読む きょうをよむ chant a sutra

② (interpret the meaning of) **READ**, comprehend, divine, guess, estimate
読み取る よみとる read (someone's) mind; read (the calibration)
人の心を読む ひとのこころをよむ guess what a person is thinking, read a person's thoughts
票読み ひょうよみ estimation of the number of possible votes a person will get

【-よみ -読み】[suffix] **READing (of Chinese characters)**
重箱読み じゅうばこよみ reading of a compound in which *on* and *kun* are mixed (in that order)
湯桶読み ゆとうよみ reading of a compound in which *kun* and *on* are mixed (in that order)

SPECIAL READINGS

読経 どきょう sutra chanting

SYNONYMS

❶ⓑ **recite**
吟 RECITE → 0271
誦 RECITE → 1951
唱 chant → 0555
読 READ → 1943
詠 RECITE POETRY → 1894

USAGE

【よむ】
読む
①ⓐ read
ⓑ read (aloud), recite, chant
② (interpret the meaning of) read, comprehend, divine, guess, estimate

【言】豸貝赤足車辛酉豸克每

詠む
compose (waka or haiku poems)

★Note that although 詠 means to recite poetry as an element in the formation of *on* compounds, the word 詠む よむ is only used in the sense of composing (not reciting) poetry. Reciting poetry is expressed by 読む よむ.

HOMOPHONES

よむ 詠 RECITE POETRY → 1894

語

1944

1-7-7

▶LANGUAGE
▶WORD
▶TELL

ゴ かた(る) かた(らう)

Ⓒ 语 yǔ yù

149	Jōyō-2	U8A9E
言	S14-7-7	F0129

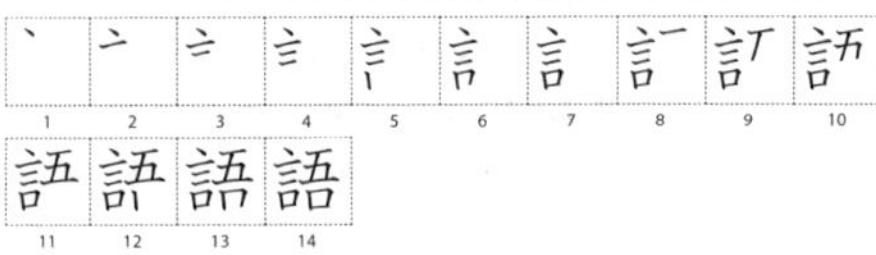

COMPOUNDS

❶ⓐ [also suffix] **LANGUAGE, speech**
ⓑ suffix for forming names of LANGUAGEs

a 語学 ごがく language study, linguistics
言語 げんご language, speech, words
国語 こくご national language; Japanese
文語 ぶんご literary [written] language
敬語 けいご honorific language, polite speech
標準語 ひょうじゅんご standard language [speech]
外国語 がいこくご foreign language
b 英語 えいご English
日本語 にほんご Japanese

❷ [also suffix] **WORD, term, phrase**
語意 ごい meaning of a word
語句 ごく words and phrases
語彙 ごい vocabulary
単語 たんご word
用語 ようご terminology; diction, wording; vocabulary
主語 しゅご subject (word)
流行語 りゅうこうご word [phrase] in fashion, word [phrase] on everybody's lips

❸ [original meaning] **talk, speak**
語気 ごき manner of speaking
語調 ごちょう tone (of voice), note, accent
私語 しご secret talk, whispering

❹ tale, story, narrative, legend
落語 らくご *rakugo*, Japanese-style comic story

INDEPENDENT

【ご 語】**WORD, term; speech, manner of speaking**
語の意味 ごのいみ meaning of a word
語を結ぶ ごをむすぶ conclude one's speech
ゲーテの語に曰く げーてのごにいわく according to Goethe

KUN

【かたる 語る】
①ⓐ (express in words) **TELL, talk, speak**
ⓑ **TELL (a story), narrate, relate**
a 真実を語る しんじつをかたる speak the truth
b 語り手 かたりて narrator, storyteller
語り伝える かたりつたえる pass on (a story or tradition)
語り合う かたりあう talk together, have a chat with
語り かたり narrative
語り草(=語り種) かたりぐさ story, topic
物語 ものがたり story, tale, legend
② recite, chant
義太夫語り ぎだゆうかたり *gidayu* reciter

【かたらう 語らう】**talk together, chat; invite (to); conspire, plot together**
語らい かたらい talk, chat; lover's vow
語らうに友無く かたらうにともなく with no friend to talk to
仲間を語らって なかまをかたらって together with one's lot

SYNONYMS

❶ language
語 LANGUAGE → 1944
弁 dialect → 2497

❷ words and expressions
語 WORD → 1944
辞 WORD → 1726
詞 WORDS → 1897
句 PHRASE → 3685
諺 PROVERB → 2006
喩 METAPHOR → 0671

❹ stories
話 story → 1928
談 account → 1975
語 tale → 1944
説 narrative → 1949
噂 RUMOR → 0883

【かたる】
① **speak and say**
言 SAY → 2440
語る TELL → 1944
談 TALK → 1975
喋 TALK → 0665
諷 INSINUATE → 2005
謂う REFER TO → 2007
云 say → 2430

曰 SAY THAT →3757
話 SPEAK →1928
口 give mouth to →4189
申す SPEAK HUMBLY →4319
述 STATE →3816
陳 SET FORTH →0656
弁 SPEAK ELOQUENTLY →2497

USAGE

❶【かたる】

語る
①ⓐ (express in words) **tell, talk, speak**
ⓑ tell (a story), narrate, relate
② recite, chant

騙る
① swindle, defraud
② assume (another's) name

❷【かたり】

語り
narrative

騙り
fraud, swindle

HOMOPHONES

かたる 騙 DECEIVE →2314
かたり 騙 DECEIVE →2314

NOTE

➡ see COMPOUND FORMATION for 擬声語 ぎせいご →擬 0969

誤 1945

▶MISTAKE
ゴ あやま(る) -あやま(る)
Ⓝ 誤 Ⓒ 误 wù

◧ 1-7-7

149 言	Jōyō-6 S14-7-7	U8AA4 F1264

COMPOUNDS

ⓐ **MISTAKE, err, make a mistake**
ⓑ [also prefix] **MISTAKEn, mis-, incorrect, wrong**
ⓒ **MISTAKE, error**

a 誤解 ごかい misunderstanding, misconception
b 誤字 ごじ wrong character, misprint
誤報 ごほう misinformation, incorrect report
誤算 ごさん miscalculation; misjudgment
誤写 ごしゃ error in copying
誤投下 ごとうか accidental bombing
誤謬 ごびゅう mistake, error, fallacy
誤差 ごさ error, aberration
c 誤魔化す ごまかす deceive, cheat; evade; pretend
錯誤 さくご mistake, error
正誤 せいご correction of errors

KUN

【あやまる 誤る】

① [formerly also 謬る] **MISTAKE, make a mistake, err**
誤り あやまり mistake, error, slip
誤って あやまって by mistake, accidentally
② mislead, lead astray
人を誤る ひとをあやまる mislead a person

【-あやまる -誤る】 [verbal suffix] **make a MISTAKE in performing an action**
言い誤る いいあやまる mistake, make a mistake in speaking
見誤る みあやまる fail to recognize [see], mistake

SYNONYMS

● **mistakes and mistaking**
過 error →3891
失 SLIP →4325
誤 MISTAKE →1945
謬 MISTAKE →2060
錯 mistaken →2187
-違える mis- →3907

HOMOPHONES

あやまる
謬 MISTAKE →2060
謝 THANK →2048

NOTE

➡ see USAGE note at 謝 2048

誨 1946

▶INSTRUCT
カイ
Ⓒ 诲 huì

◧ 1-7-7

149 言	Non-Jōyō S14-7-7	U8AA8 F0000

COMPOUNDS

● [now replaced by 戒 3972] [original meaning] **INSTRUCT, teach**
教誨 きょうかい exhortation, preaching

SYNONYMS

● **teach**
教 TEACH →1887
啓 ENLIGHTEN →3434
諄 TEACH WITH CARE →1979
授 teach →0595
育 educate →2544
練 TRAIN →1738
訓 INSTRUCT →1844
誨 INSTRUCT →1946
諭 ADMONISH →2012
導 GUIDE →3587
迪 EDIFY →3817

【言】豸 貝 赤 足 車 辛 酉 镸 克 每

誡

▸CAUTION AGAINST
カイ いまし(める)
Ⓒ 诫 jiè

1947
◧ 1-7-7

149	Non-Jōyō	U8AA1
言	S14-7-7	F0000

COMPOUNDS

[now replaced by 戒 かい 3972]

❶ **CAUTION AGAINST, admonish, warn, give warning**
誡告 かいこく caution, warning, reprimand
訓誡する くんかいする admonish, warn

❷ commandment, *śīla,* precept
十誡 じっかい the Ten Commandments (of Moses)

❸ instruct, teach

KUN

【いましめる 誡める】[usu. 戒める, sometimes also 警める] **CAUTION AGAINST, admonish, warn**

SYNONYMS

❶ **warn**
警 WARN → 3595
戒 CAUTION → 3972
誡 CAUTION AGAINST → 1947
諭 ADMONISH → 2012
告 advise → 3062

HOMOPHONES

いましめる
戒 CAUTION → 3972
警 GUARD AGAINST → 3595

NOTE

➡ see USAGE note at 戒 3972

認

▸RECOGNIZE
ニン みと(める)
Ⓝ 認 Ⓒ 认 rèn

1948
◧ 1-7-7

149	Jōyō-6	U8A8D
言	S14-7-7	F0380

COMPOUNDS

❶ [original meaning] (be aware of something perceived) **RECOGNIZE, perceive, identify**
認識 にんしき cognition, perception; understanding
誤認 ごにん mistake, misconception, misunderstanding
確認 かくにん confirmation, ascertainment

❷ (approve or give permission for) **RECOGNIZE, acknowledge, approve, admit**
認可する にんかする approve, authorize, give permission
認定 にんてい authorization, recognition, acknowledgment
認知 にんち recognition, acknowledgment
承認 しょうにん approval, recognition
公認 こうにん official recognition [approval], authorization, certification
黙認 もくにん tacit [silent] approval, toleration

KUN

【みとめる 認める】**RECOGNIZE, acknowledge, approve, admit; judge, conclude; see, witness**
認め みとめ approval; private seal
認め難い みとめがたい unapprovable
認め印 みとめいん informal seal
誤りを認める あやまりをみとめる admit to a mistake
必要と認める ひつようとみとめる judge as necessary
人影を認める ひとかげをみとめる make out someone's figure

SYNONYMS

❶ **perceive**
覚 PERCEIVE → 3217
知 KNOW → 1446
感 FEEL → 3514
認 RECOGNIZE → 1948

❷ **agree and approve**
賛 APPROVE OF → 3484
可 APPROVE → 3687
認 RECOGNIZE → 1948
諾 CONSENT → 1974
承 AGREE TO → 0016
肯 ASSENT → 3072
容 tolerate → 2832

説

▸EXPLAIN
▸THEORY
セツ ゼイ と(く) ㊔ さとし
Ⓝ 說 Ⓒ 说 shuō shuì yuè

1949
◧ 1-7-7

149	Jōyō-4	U8AAC
言	S14-7-7	F0198

COMPOUNDS

❶ⓐ [original meaning] **EXPLAIN**
ⓑ explanation, statement
a 説明 せつめい explanation, description
解説 かいせつ explanation, commentary

演説 えんぜつ (public) speech, address, oration
論説 ろんせつ discourse, dissertation; editorial
力説する りきせつする emphasize, lay stress on, insist upon
b 概説 がいせつ general statement, outline
序説 じょせつ introduction
言説 げんせつ remark, statement

❷ preach, advocate; persuade
説教 せっきょう preaching, scolding
説法 せっぽう (Buddhist) sermon, preaching, moralizing
説得 せっとく persuasion
遊説 ゆうぜい electioneering tour; campaign speech

❸ⓐ [also suffix] (proposed explanation) **THEORY, doctrine**
ⓑ opinion, view
a 学説 がくせつ theory
仮説 かせつ hypothesis
新説 しんせつ new theory [doctrine]; new opinion
地動説 ちどうせつ heliocentric [Copernican] theory
原子説 げんしせつ atomic theory
b 社説 しゃせつ editorial (article)
自説 じせつ one's own view
通説 つうせつ common opinion, popular view

❹ narrative, story
説話 せつわ narrative, tale
小説 しょうせつ novel, story, fiction
伝説 でんせつ legend, folk tale

❺ [also suffix] **rumor**
風説 ふうせつ rumor, hearsay
解散説 かいさんせつ rumor of dissolution

❻ style of Chinese poetry

INDEPENDENT

【せつ 説】**THEORY, doctrine; opinion, view; rumor**
説を立てる せつをたてる put forward a theory
お説の通りです おせつのとおりです I agree with you
. . . との説が有る …とのせつがある Rumors hold that…

KUN

【とく 説く】
① **EXPLAIN**
説き明かす ときあかす explain, solve; make clear
② **preach, advocate; persuade**
口説く くどく persuade; seduce

SYNONYMS

❶ explain
説 EXPLAIN → 1949
明 make clear → 1060
釈 ELUCIDATE → 1876
詮 EXPOUND → 1923
講 expound → 2046
解 CLARIFY → 1913
注 annotate → 0383

❷ advocate
唱 advocate → 0555
説 preach → 1949

❸ⓐ theory
論 THEORY (systematic knowledge) → 1981
説 THEORY (proposed explanation) → 1949
ⓑ opinion
見 view (personal opinion) → 3151
観 VIEW (conception) → 2359
説 opinion → 1949
論 opinion → 1981

❹ stories
話 story → 1928
談 account → 1975
語 tale → 1944
説 narrative → 1949
噂 RUMOR → 0883

HOMOPHONES

とく
解 TAKE APART → 1913
溶 DISSOLVE → 0816
梳 COMB → 1209

NOTE

➡ see USAGE note at 解 1913
➡ see COMPOUND FORMATION for 説得 せっとく →得 0577

誌 ▸MAGAZINE

シ

Ⓒ 志 zhì

1950

◧ 1-7-7

149	Jōyō-6	U8A8C
言	S14-7-7	F0711

COMPOUNDS

❶ⓐ [also suffix] **MAGAZINE, periodical**
ⓑ suffix after names of MAGAZINEs or periodicals
a 誌面 しめん page of a magazine
誌上で しじょうで in a magazine
雑誌 ざっし magazine, journal
週刊誌 しゅうかんし weekly magazine
b ニューズウィーク誌 にゅーずうぃーくし Newsweek

❷ⓐ [also suffix] **records, document**

❺ record, write down
a 日誌 にっし diary
植物誌 しょくぶつし flora
地誌 ちし topography, geographical description
b 墓誌 ぼし epitaph, inscription on a tomb

SYNONYMS

❶ periodicals
誌 MAGAZINE → 1950
紙 newspaper → 1654
報 bulletin → 2133

❷ⓐ records
記 written account → 1843
録 RECORD → 2186
譜 SYSTEMATIC RECORD → 2068
誌 records → 1950
史 HISTORY → 4324
伝 biography → 0048

誦

1951
1-7-7

▶RECITE
ショウ ジュ ズ
Ⓒ 诵 sòng

149	Non-Jōyō	U8AA6
言	S14-7-7	F2942

COMPOUNDS

● [now also 唱 しょう 0555, rarely also 頌 しょう 1319]
RECITE, read aloud, chant, intone
誦経 ずきょう reciting [chanting] a sutra
暗誦する あんしょうする recite from memory
吟誦 ぎんしょう reciting (poetry), chanting
愛誦する あいしょうする love to recite (a poem), read with pleasure
読誦する どくじゅする read aloud, recite, intone

INDEPENDENT

【しょうする 誦する】**RECITE, chant, read aloud**
【じゅする 誦する】**RECITE, chant, read aloud**

SYNONYMS

● recite
吟 RECITE → 0271
誦 RECITE → 1951
唱 chant → 0555
読 READ → 1943
詠 RECITE POETRY → 1894

誘

1952
1-7-7

▶INDUCE
ユウ さそ(う) いざな(う)▲
Ⓒ 诱 yòu

149	Jōyō	U8A98
言	S14-7-7	F1015

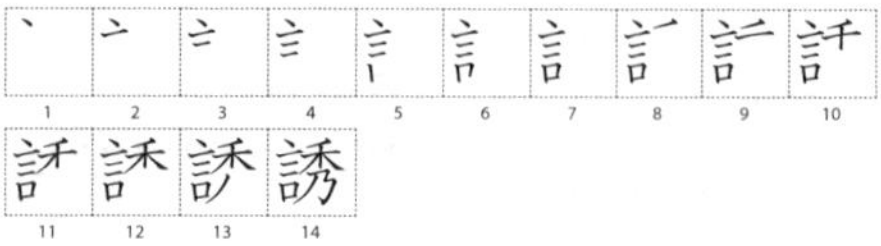

COMPOUNDS

❶ⓐ (move by persuasion) **INDUCE, lure, tempt, entice, seduce; lead, guide**
ⓑ (produce by induction) **INDUCE**
a 誘致する ゆうちする lure, entice, invite; bring about, cause
誘惑 ゆうわく temptation, seduction
誘引する ゆういんする entice, induce, attract
誘導する ゆうどうする induce, incite; guide, lead
誘拐 ゆうかい kidnapping, abduction
誘蛾×灯 ゆうがとう luring lamp
誘殺する ゆうさつする seduce and kill
勧誘する かんゆうする induce, invite, canvass, persuade
b 誘電子 ゆうでんし (electrical) inductor
誘爆 ゆうばく induced explosion

❷ (stimulate the occurrence of) **INDUCE, bring about, cause**
誘発する ゆうはつする cause, induce, lead up to
誘起する ゆうきする give rise to, lead to
誘因 ゆういん immediate cause, incentive

KUN

【さそう 誘う】**invite, ask; INDUCE, provoke, cause; allure, tempt, entice, seduce**
誘い さそい temptation, allurement, enticement; invitation
誘い水 さそいみず pump priming
誘い出す さそいだす decoy, entice, lure away
芝居に誘う しばいにさそう invite a person to the theater

【いざなう 誘う】*elegant* invite, ask; lure, entice
悪の道へ誘う あくのみちへいざなう lead astray, lure a person to evil ways

SYNONYMS

❶ⓐ urge
勧 URGE → 2334
催 PRESS FOR → 0178
促 HASTEN → 0118
誘 INDUCE → 1952
励 ENCOURAGE → 1438
侑 URGE TO EAT → 0101

❷ cause
致 BRING ABOUT → 1668
誘 INDUCE → 1952

誤
1953
◧ 1-7-7

▶**MISTAKE**
ゴ あやま(る) -あやま(る)

149	Nonstandard	U8AA4
言	S14-7-7	F0000

traditional form → see 誤 at 1945

認
1954
◧ 1-7-7

▶**RECOGNIZE**
ニン みと(める)

149	Nonstandard	U8A8D
言	S14-7-7	F0000

traditional form → see 認 at 1948

誠
1955
◧ 1-7-7

▶**SINCERITY**
セイ まこと ㊔ まさ のぶ たかし しげ よし とも あき なり

149	Nonstandard	U8AA0
言	S14-7-7	F0000

traditional form → see 誠 at 1922

說
1956
◧ 1-7-7

▶**EXPLAIN**
▶**THEORY**
セツ ゼイ と(く) ㊔ さとし

149	Nonstandard	U8AAA
言	S14-7-7	F0000

traditional form → see 説 at 1949

誕
1957
◧ 1-7-7

▶**BE BORN**
タン

149	Nonstandard	U8A95
言	S14-7-7	F0000

traditional form → see 誕 at 1987

諄
◧ 1-7-7

incorrect stroke-count
➡ see ◧1-7-8: 言 at 1979

誇
◧ 1-7-7

incorrect stroke-count
➡ see ◧1-7-6: 言 at 1921

貌
1958
◧ 1-7-7

▶**APPEARANCE**
ボウ かたち▲
Ⓝ 皃 Ⓒ 貌 mào

153	Jōyō	U8C8C
豸	S14-7-7	F1524

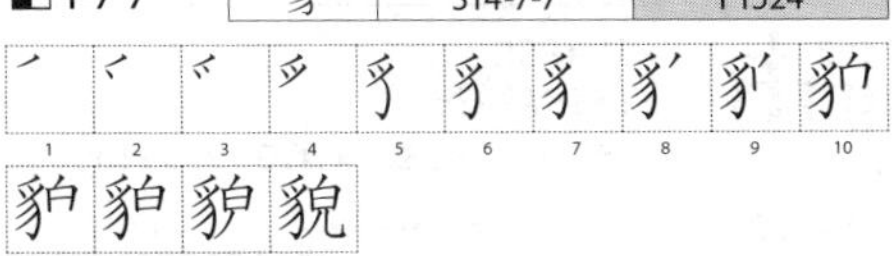

COMPOUNDS

ⓐ [original meaning] **APPEARANCE, looks, figure**

ⓑ aspect, condition

a 容貌 ようぼう looks, personal appearance
美貌 びぼう good looks, pretty features
体貌 たいぼう appearance
変貌 へんぼう transfiguration, metamorphosis
b 全貌 ぜんぼう full view, whole aspect

KUN

【かたち 貌】[now usu. 形]
ⓐ **APPEARANCE**, looks, figure
ⓑ aspect, condition
a 顔貌 かおかたち features, looks

SYNONYMS

ⓐ appearance
容 APPEARANCE → 2832
貌 APPEARANCE → 1958
姿 FIGURE → 3264
相 PHASE → 1120
体 FORM (outer appearance) → 0080
色 COLOR → 2522
風 air → 3730

HOMOPHONES

かたち 形 SHAPE → 1050

NOTE

➡ see USAGE note at 形 1050

賑
1959
◧ 1-7-7

▶**BUSTLE**
シン にぎ(わう) にぎ(わす) にぎ(やか)
㊔ とも とみ
Ⓒ 赈 zhèn

154	Names	U8CD1
貝	S14-7-7	F2055

COMPOUNDS

❶ BUSTLE, be lively, prosper, flourish, thrive
殷×賑 いんしん prosperity, bustle

❷ [archaic] give alms [charity]
賑給 しんごう(=しんきゅう) almsgiving to the poor and refugees by the Imperial Court in ancient Japan

KUN

【にぎわう 賑わう】
ⓐ **BUSTLE, be busy, be crowded**
ⓑ prosper, flourish, thrive
a 賑わい にぎわい bustle, activity, crowd

【にぎわす 賑わす】
ⓐ **enliven**
ⓑ make prosperous

【にぎやか 賑やか】
ⓐ **bustling, busy, crowded**
ⓑ **cheerful, lively**
a 賑やかさ にぎやかさ liveliness, busyness

SYNONYMS

❶ **prospering and prosperity**
隆 PROSPER → 0661
振 rise → 0515
興 RISE TO PROSPERITY → 3622
盛 PROSPEROUS → 3314
昌 PROSPERING → 3069
栄 FLOURISH → 3183
繁 THRIVE → 3536
賑 BUSTLE → 1959

賦 1-7-7
incorrect stroke-count
➡ see 1-7-8: 貝 at 1992

赫
1960
1-7-7
▶BLAZING
カク かがや(く)
Ⓒ 赫 hè

155	Non-Jōyō	U8D6B
赤	S14-7-7	F3489

COMPOUNDS

❶ⓐ (shining intensely) **BLAZING, resplendent, brilliant**
ⓑ (magnificent) **BLAZING, resplendent, brilliant, glorious**
ab 赫赫たる かっかくたる(=かくかくたる) splendid, brilliant, glorious
赫奕×たる かくえき(=かくやく)たる bright, brilliant, glowing; vigorous, energetic, thriving
❷ [now also 嚇 0964] **BLAZING [exploding] with anger, be enraged**
赫怒する かくどする be greatly enraged, get furious

KUN

【かがやく 赫く】 [usu. 輝く, sometimes also 耀く] **shine brilliantly, glitter, gleam, sparkle, light up, brighten**

SYNONYMS

❶ **bright**
明 BRIGHT → 1060
昭 LUMINOUS → 1107
蛍 fluorescent → 3204
晃 DAZZLING → 3101
燦 BRILLIANT → 1390
赫 BLAZING → 1960
暉 radiant → 1276
熙 BRIGHT → 3559
晟 SUNNY → 3104

HOMOPHONES

かがやく
輝 SHINE BRILLIANTLY → 1775
耀 SHINE BRILLIANTLY → 1812

NOTE

➡ see USAGE note at 輝 1775

踊
1961
1-7-7
▶DANCE
ヨウ おど(る) おどり)
Ⓝ 踴 Ⓒ 踊 yǒng

157	Jōyō	U8E0A
足	S14-7-7	F1319

(stroke order 1–14)

COMPOUNDS

❶ **DANCE**
舞踊 ぶよう dancing, dance
民踊 みんよう folk dance
❷ [original meaning] leap up, jump up and down
踊躍する ようやくする leap with joy, jump about

KUN

【おどる 踊る】 **DANCE (energetically)**
踊り手 おどりて dancer
【おどり 踊り】 [also suffix] **DANCE, dancing**
盆踊り ぼんおどり Bon Festival dance

SYNONYMS

❶ & 【おどる】 **dance**
踊 DANCE (energetically) → 1961
舞 DANCE (gracefully) → 2666

USAGE

❶ 【おどる】
踊る
dance (energetically)
躍る
ⓐ leap, jump, bound
ⓑ (of one's heart) throb, leap
❷ 【おどり】
踊り
[also suffix] dance, dancing
躍り
leaping, jumping

HOMOPHONES

おどる 躍 LEAP → 2090
おどり 躍 LEAP → 2090

踈
1962
1-7-7
▶SPARSE
▶ESTRANGE
ソ うと(い) うと(む) まば(ら) おろそ(か)

157	Nonstandard	U8E08
足	S14-7-7	F0000

traditional form → see 疎 at 1512

輔

1963

1-7-7

▶**ASSIST**

ホ フ ㊔ すけ たすく

Ⓒ 辅 fǔ

159	Names	U8F14
車	S14-7-7	F1764

COMPOUNDS

❶ [now usu. 補 1529] **ASSIST, aid; give guidance**

輔佐 ほさ assistance, aid; assistant; counselor, adviser

輔弼× ほひつ assistance, council

輔導 ほどう guidance; custody

❷ [original meaning] wheel guard

唇歯輔車 しんしほしゃ mutual dependence

SYNONYMS

❶ **help**

助 HELP → 1440
佑 HELP (said esp. of God) → 0083
祐 DIVINE HELP → 1146
援 AID → 0715
佐 ASSIST → 0076
補 assist → 1529
輔 ASSIST → 1963
済 RELIEVE → 0634

COMPOUND FORMATION

【唇歯輔車 しんしほしゃ】

唇歯輔車 'mutual dependence' is relying on one another like lips (唇) and teeth (歯) or as wheel guard (輔 ❷) and cart (車).

輕

1964

1-7-7

▶**LIGHT**

ケイ かる(い) かろ(やか)

159	Nonstandard	U8F15
車	S14-7-7	F0000

traditional form → see 軽 at 1909

辣

1965

1-7-7

▶**PUNGENT**
▶**SEVERE**

ラツ

Ⓒ 辣 là

160	Jōyō	U8FA3
辛	S14-7-7	F2729

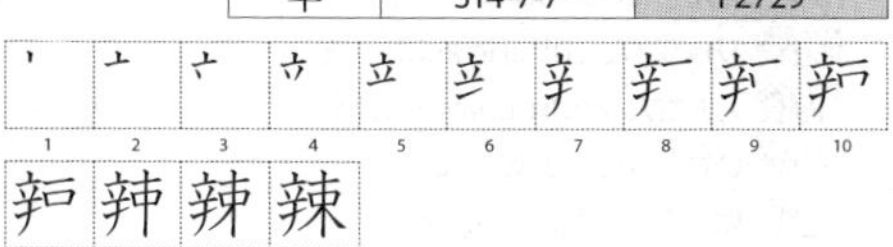

COMPOUNDS

❶ **PUNGENT, hot, spicy**

辣韮×(=薤×、辣韭) らっきょう Japanese shallot, *Allium chinense*

辣油 らーゆ Chinese red chili oil

❷ⓐ (strict) **SEVERE, exacting, harsh**

ⓑ (cruel) **SEVERE, harsh, brutal**

a 辣腕 らつわん shrewdness, acumen, tact

辛辣な しんらつな bitter, pungent, acrid, poignant, severe

b 悪辣 あくらつ unscrupulous, crafty, wily, foul

SYNONYMS

❶ **tastes**

甘 SWEET → 4306
苦 BITTER → 2789
辛 PUNGENT → 2531
辣 PUNGENT → 1965
酸 sour → 1968
渋い ASTRINGENT → 0625
鹹 SALTY → 2366

❷ⓐ **strict**

厳 strict → 4079
酷 SEVERE → 1967
辣 SEVERE → 1965
峻 STERN → 0495

ⓑ **cruel**

虐 CRUEL → 3989
惨 CRUEL → 0585
酷 SEVERE → 1967
辣 SEVERE → 1965
残 RUTHLESS → 1179
凶 ATROCIOUS → 3679
苛 HARSH → 2786

酵

1966

1-7-7

▶**FERMENT**

コウ

Ⓒ 酵 jiào

164	Jōyō	U9175
酉	S14-7-7	F1862

COMPOUNDS

ⓐ (something that causes fermentation) **FERMENT**

ⓑ (undergo fermentation) **FERMENT**

a 酵素 こうそ ferment; enzyme

酵母 こうぼ yeast; ferment

酵母菌 こうぼきん yeast fungus

b 発酵 はっこう fermentation, zymosis

SYNONYMS

ⓑ **brew and ferment**

醸 BREW → 2086
醗 BREW → 2076
酵 FERMENT → 1966

酷

1967

1-7-7

▶SEVERE

コク ひど(い)▲

Ⓝ 酷 Ⓒ 酷 kù

164	Jōyō	U9177
酉	S14-7-7	F1553

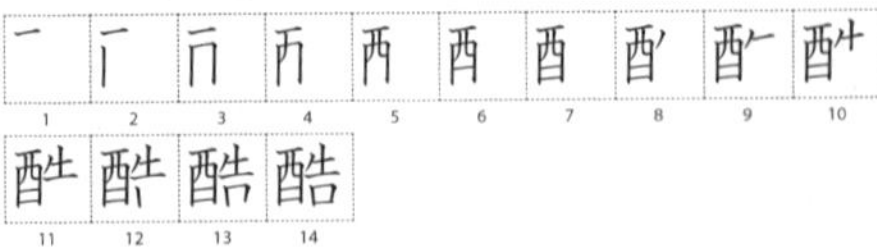

COMPOUNDS

❶ **SEVERE, harsh, cruel, brutal, merciless**

酷刑 こっけい severe punishment
酷評 こくひょう severe criticism
酷薄(=刻薄)な こくはくな cruel, inhumane
酷使する こくしする drive (a person) hard, abuse, sweat (one's workers), overwork
残酷な ざんこくな cruel, ruthless, atrocious
苛酷(=過酷)な かこくな severe, harsh, cruel

❷ (of great intensity) **SEVERE, intense**

酷寒 こっかん severe [intense] cold; depth of winter
酷暑 こくしょ severe heat
酷似 こくじ close resemblance

INDEPENDENT

【こく 酷】severity, harshness, cruelty

酷な こくな severe, harsh, stringent, rigorous, strict; unfair
酷なやり方 こくなやりかた cruel act

KUN

【ひどい 酷い】[also 非道い]

① cruel, harsh, rough

酷さ ひどさ harshness, severity
酷い仕打ち ひどいしうち cruel treatment

② **SEVERE**, intense, heavy

酷く暑い ひどくあつい It's awfully hot

SYNONYMS

❶ **strict**

厳 strict →4079
酷 SEVERE →1967
辣 SEVERE →1965
峻 STERN →0495

❶ **cruel**

虐 CRUEL →3989
惨 CRUEL →0585
酷 SEVERE →1967
辣 SEVERE →1965
残 RUTHLESS →1179
凶 ATROCIOUS →3679
苛 HARSH →2786

❷ **extreme in degree**

酷 SEVERE →1967
強 STRONG →0574
凄い tremendous →0145
重 HEAVY →4390
高 HIGH →2601
深 DEEP →0636
大 BIG →4224
厳 SEVERE →4079
激 intense →0955
極 EXTREME →1243
痛 bitter(ly) →4071
切 keen →0030
甚 EXTREMELY →3271
祁 EXTREMELY →1447
超 super- →4107
頗る EXCEEDINGLY →1552

USAGE

【ひどい】

酷い
[also 非道い]
① cruel, harsh, rough
② severe, intense, heavy

非道い
[also 酷い] same as 酷い

HOMOPHONES

ひどい 非道い →1101, 3888

酸

1968

1-7-7

▶ACID
▶OXYGEN

サン す(い)

Ⓒ 酸 suān

164	Jōyō-5	U9178
酉	S14-7-7	F1058

COMPOUNDS

❶ [also suffix] **ACID, acidity**

酸性 さんせい acidity
酸基 さんき acid radical
硫酸 りゅうさん sulfuric acid
塩酸 えんさん hydrochloric acid
胃酸 いさん stomach acid
乳酸 にゅうさん lactic acid
アミノ酸 あみのさん amino acid

❷ sour, **ACID**, tart

酸味 さんみ sourness

❸ **OXYGEN**

酸素 さんそ oxygen

酸化 さんか oxidation

❹ sick at heart, grieved, distressed

酸鼻 さんび extreme pain, deep sorrow

INDEPENDENT

【さん 酸】**ACID; sourness**

酸とアルカリ さんとあるかり acid and alkali

KUN

【すい 酸い】**sour, ACID**

酸っぱい すっぱい sour

SYNONYMS

❶ **sour substances**

酢 VINEGAR → 1910

酸 ACID → 1968

❷ **tastes**

甘 SWEET → 4306

苦 BITTER → 2789

辛 PUNGENT → 2531

辣 PUNGENT → 1965

酸 sour → 1968

渋い ASTRINGENT → 0625

鹹 SALTY → 2366

❸ **lighter elements**

水 hydrogen → 0010

酸 OXYGEN → 1968

窒 NITROGEN → 2853

塩 chlorine → 0774

臭 bromine → 3261

硫 SULFUR → 1519

炭 carbon → 2806

酷

1969

▌1-7-7

▸SEVERE

コク ひど(い)

164	Nonstandard	U9177
酉	S14-7-7	F0000

traditional form → see 酷 at 1967

醇

▌1-7-7

incorrect stroke-count

➡ see ▌1-7-8: 醇 at 2001

疑

1970

▌1-7-7

▸DOUBT

ギ うたが(う)

Ⓒ 疑 yí

103	Jōyō-6	U7591
疋	S14-5-9	F0623

COMPOUNDS

❶ **DOUBT, suspect**

疑惑 ぎわく doubt, suspicion

疑問 ぎもん question, problem, doubt

疑心 ぎしん doubt, suspicion, fear

半信半疑の はんしんはんぎの dubious, incredulous

懐疑 かいぎ doubt, skepticism, disbelief

容疑 ようぎ suspicion

❷ hesitate

遅疑する ちぎする hesitate, vacillate

INDEPENDENT

【ぎ 疑】**DOUBT**, suspicion

KUN

【うたがう 疑う】**DOUBT, be suspicious, distrust**

疑い うたがい doubt, suspicion; question

疑わしい うたがわしい doubtful, suspicious

SYNONYMS

❶ **doubt**

疑 DOUBT → 1970

怪しむ suspect → 0354

兢

1971

▌1-7-7

▸BE IN FEAR

キョウ

Ⓒ 兢 jīng

10	Non-Jōyō	U5162
儿	S14-2-12	F0000

COMPOUNDS

● [now replaced by 恐 3283] **BE IN FEAR, tremble**

戦戦兢兢として せんせんきょうきょうとして with fear and trembling

SYNONYMS

● **fear**

怖 FEARFUL → 0353

凄 UNCANNY → 0145

恐 FEAR → 3283

惧 FEAR → 0581

慄 TREMBLE WITH FEAR → 0791

兢 BE IN FEAR → 1971

惶 BE AFRAID → 0708

畏 BE OVERAWED → 3170

臆 FEEL TIMID → 1397

怯える BE FRIGHTENED → 0355

毓

1972

▌1-7-7

▸RAISE

イク そだ(つ) そだ(ち) そだ(てる)

はぐく(む) ㊔ やす なる

80	Nonstandard	U6BD3
毋	S14-5-9	F0000

traditional form → see 育 at 2544

調

1973

1-7-8

▶TONE
▶INVESTIGATE
▶PREPARE

チョウ しら(べる) しら(べ) ととの(う) ととの(える) ㊔ まもる つき つぎ

Ⓝ 調 Ⓒ 调 diào tiáo

149	Jōyō-3	U8ABF
言	S15-7-8	F0211

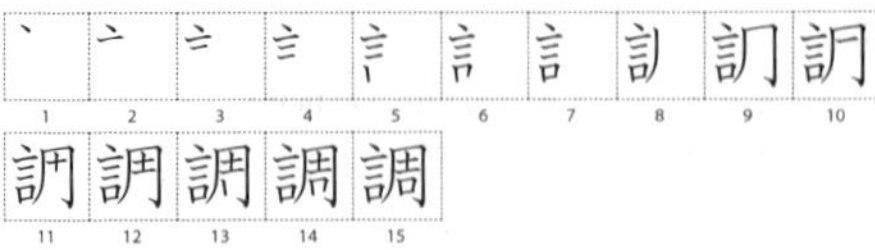

COMPOUNDS

❶ⓐ (characteristic quality, as of music, poetry or color) **TONE, tune, key, note, pitch, rhythm, meter**
ⓑ (characteristic quality of speech) **TONE, strain, note, accent**

a 調子 ちょうし tone, tune; key, note; condition, state (of health); manner, way
音調 おんちょう tune, tone, rhythm, melody, harmony
短調 たんちょう minor key
正調 せいちょう orthodox tune
七五調で しちごちょうで in seven-and-five syllable meter
色調 しきちょう tone (of color)
強調 きょうちょう emphasis, stress
b 口調 くちょう tone, expression
語調 ごちょう tone (of voice), note, accent
声調 せいちょう tone of voice, style; tone (in Chinese phonetics)

❷ (general quality or well-balanced condition) **TONE, condition, state (of health)**
好調 こうちょう favorable [good] condition
順調に じゅんちょうに favorably, smoothly
基調 きちょう keynote, underlying tone, basis
歩調 ほちょう pace, step, cadence
単調な たんちょうな monotonous, dull
体調 たいちょう health condition

❸ [suffix] (characteristic style or general trend) **TONE,** style, form, manner, atmosphere
軍国調 ぐんこくちょう wartime atmosphere
文語調 ぶんごちょう flavor of literary style
である調 であるちょう *de aru* style

❹ⓐ **INVESTIGATE, look into, examine, inquire, check**
ⓑ abbrev. of 調査会 ちょうさかい: board of investigation [inquiry], commission

a 調査 ちょうさ investigation, examination, inquiry, survey
調書 ちょうしょ protocol, written evidence, record
再調する さいちょうする reexamine, reinvestigate
b 税調 ぜいちょう Tax Commission

❺ⓐ **PREPARE, make ready, make to order**
ⓑ **PREPARE (medicines or food), compound, mix, blend**

a 調製 ちょうせい preparation, manufacture, execution (of an order)
調達 ちょうたつ supply, procurement; execution (of an order); raising (money)
調度 ちょうど personal effects, furnishings, supplies
新調する しんちょうする make (a new suit), have (new shoes) made
b 調理する ちょうりする cook, prepare (food)
調味 ちょうみ seasoning, flavoring
調合 ちょうごう compounding, mixing, preparation
調剤 ちょうざい preparation [compounding] of medicines
調色 ちょうしょく mixing colors

❻ⓐ [original meaning] **harmonize, bring into accord [harmony], mediate**
ⓑ **act in harmony, cooperate**

a 調印 ちょういん signing, sealing; signature
調停する ちょうていする mediate, arbitrate, make peace
調和 ちょうわ harmony, accord, agreement, symmetry
b 協調する きょうちょうする cooperate, act harmoniously
同調する どうちょうする align oneself, act in concert with

❼ **adjust, regulate, tune**
調整する ちょうせいする regulate, adjust
調節する ちょうせつする regulate, adjust; modulate, tune
調律 ちょうりつ tuning
空調 くうちょう air conditioning

❽ play (a tune) on (the koto)
調琴 ちょうきん playing the koto

❾ tame, break in, train, drill
調教 ちょうきょう breaking, training (animals)
調馬 ちょうば horsebreaking, horse training
調練 ちょうれん military drill

❿ local product used for paying taxes in ancient Japan
租庸調 そようちょう taxes in kind or service (former tax system), corvée

⓫ curse
調伏 ちょうぶく curse; exorcism

INDEPENDENT

【ちょう 調】local product used for paying taxes in ancient Japan

KUN

【しらべる 調べる】**INVESTIGATE, look into, examine, inquire, check; play (a tune) on (the koto)**

調べ直す しらべなおす reexamine, review
調べ合わす しらべあわす tune to; check against
事実を調べる じじつをしらべる investigate the facts

【しらべ 調べ】
① **investigation, examination**
取り調べ とりしらべ investigation, inquiry
下調べ したしらべ preliminary examination [inquiry], preparation
② melody, tune
妙なる調べ たえなるしらべ sweet tune, enchanting melody
六段の調べ ろくだんのしらべ Rokudan (name of a koto composition)

【ととのう 調う】
① **be PREPARED [ready], be fully equipped**
調度が調う ちょうどがととのう get fully furnished
② be arranged [settled], be agreed upon
協議が調った きょうぎがととのった An agreement has been arrived at

【ととのえる 調える】
① **PREPARE, make ready, procure, raise (money)**
夕食を調える ゆうしょくをととのえる get supper ready
旅装を調える りょそうをととのえる prepare for a journey
金を調える かねをととのえる raise money
② season, flavor
味を調える あじをととのえる season, flavor
③ (bring to a conclusion) arrange, settle, conclude
縁談を調える えんだんをととのえる arrange a marriage

SYNONYMS

❶ **musical elements**
韻 RHYME → 2279
律 RHYTHM → 0433
拍 BEAT → 0361
調 TONE → 1973
呂 ancient musical note → 2713

❷ **states and situations**
態 STATE → 3529
調 TONE → 1973
様 MODE → 1332
相 PHASE → 1120
状 CONDITION → 0322
況 CONDITIONS → 0395
景 business conditions → 3118
勢 course of events → 3542
境 SITUATION → 0835
局 current situation → 3800
情 ACTUAL CONDITIONS → 0583
訳 circumstances → 1865

❸ **way and style**
風 MANNER → 3730
様 MODE → 1332
方 WAY → 2459
途 WAY → 3853
法 METHOD → 0391
流 STYLE → 0529
式 STYLE → 3785
調 TONE → 1973

❹ⓐ **investigate and examine**
閲 REVIEW → 4132
審 EXAMINE CAREFULLY → 2985
験 TEST → 2306
勘 CHECK → 2231
糾 INQUIRE INTO → 1631
究 STUDY EXHAUSTIVELY → 2729
察 INSPECT → 2961
討 STUDY → 1846
探 PROBE → 0613
検 EXAMINE → 1241
診 EXAMINE A PATIENT → 1898
調 INVESTIGATE → 1973
査 LOOK INTO → 3092

❺ **make**
作 MAKE → 0077
造 MAKE → 3856
成 FORM → 4352
工 MANUFACTURE → 4190
製 MANUFACTURE → 3478
産 PRODUCE → 4089
調 PREPARE → 1973
組む ASSEMBLE → 1693
構 CONSTRUCT → 1325

ⓐ **prepare**
備 PROVIDE → 0165
調 PREPARE → 1973

❻ **cooperate**
協 COOPERATE → 0103
携 join hands → 0796
調 harmonize → 1973

【しらべ】
② **music and songs**
楽 MUSIC → 3505
音 sound of music → 2570
節 tune → 3336
調べ melody → 1973
曲 MUSICAL COMPOSITION → 4340
歌 SONG → 2296
謡 POPULAR SONG → 2011
唄 DITTY → 0477

USAGE

❶【ととのう】

調う

① be prepared [ready], be fully equipped

② be arranged [settled], be agreed upon

整う

be in order, be adjusted [regulated], be made up properly

❷【ととのえる】

調える

① prepare, make ready, procure, raise (money)

② season, flavor

③ (bring to a conclusion) arrange, settle, conclude

整える

(put in order) arrange, tidy up, adjust (clothes), regulate

HOMOPHONES

ととのう 整 PUT IN ORDER → 3562

ととのえる 整 PUT IN ORDER → 3562

諾

▶CONSENT

ダク

Ⓒ 诺 nuò

1974

1-7-8

149	Jōyō	U8AFE
言	S15-7-8	F2120

COMPOUNDS

❶ⓐ CONSENT (to), say yes, agree to, assent

ⓑ yes, aye

a 受諾 じゅだく acceptance

承諾 しょうだく consent, assent, agreement, acceptation

応諾 おうだく consent, assent

快諾 かいだく ready consent

内諾 ないだく informal [private] consent

b 諾否 だくひ definitive answer, yes or no

諾諾 だくだく yes, yes

❷ Norway

日諾 にちだく Japan and Norway

INDEPENDENT

【だく 諾】*literary* CONSENT

【だくする 諾する】CONSENT, say yes

SYNONYMS

❶ⓐ agree and approve

賛 APPROVE OF → 3484

可 APPROVE → 3687

認 RECOGNIZE → 1948

諾 CONSENT → 1974

承 AGREE TO → 0016

肯 ASSENT → 3072

容 tolerate → 2832

ⓑ terms of assent

然 SO → 3456

諾 yes → 1974

談

▶TALK

ダン

Ⓒ 谈 tán

1975

1-7-8

149	Jōyō-3	U8AC7
言	S15-7-8	F0529

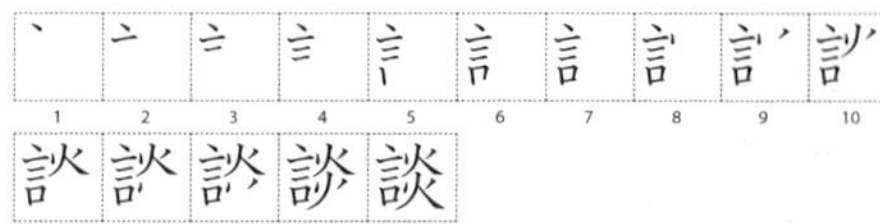

COMPOUNDS

❶ⓐ [original meaning] **TALK, converse, speak, confer, discuss**

ⓑ [also suffix] **TALK, conversation**

a 談合 だんごう consultation, negotiation

談話 だんわ talk, conversation

会談 かいだん conversation, talk, conference

相談する そうだんする consult, talk over, confer

対談する たいだんする talk with, converse; negotiate in person with

b 懇談 こんだん familiar talk [chat]

座談会 ざだんかい round-table talk, symposium

冗談 じょうだん joke

政談 せいだん political talk

車中談 しゃちゅうだん informal talk given (as by a politician) aboard a train

❷ account, story, tale

怪談 かいだん ghost story

講談 こうだん storytelling, narration; historical narrative

冒険談 ぼうけんだん account of an adventure; adventure story

INDEPENDENT

【だん 談】*literary* TALK, conversation; account

同日の談ではない どうじつのだんではない not to be mentioned in the same breath

【だんじる(=だんずる) 談じる(=談ずる)】TALK about, discuss; negotiate with

SYNONYMS

❶ⓐ speak and say

言 SAY → 2440

語る TELL → 1944

談 TALK → 1975

喋 TALK → 0665

諷 INSINUATE → 2005
謂う REFER TO → 2007
云 say → 2430
曰 SAY THAT → 3757
話 SPEAK → 1928
口 give mouth to → 4189
申す SPEAK HUMBLY → 4319
述 STATE → 3816
陳 SET FORTH → 0656
弁 SPEAK ELOQUENTLY → 2497

ⓑ speech

言 SPEECH → 2440
談 TALK → 1975
舌 TONGUE → 2711
口 MOUTH → 4189

❷ stories

話 story → 1928
談 account → 1975
語 tale → 1944
説 narrative → 1949
噂 RUMOR → 0883

NOTE

➡ see COMPOUND FORMATION for 冗談 じょうだん → 冗 2470

謁 ▶BE GRANTED AN AUDIENCE

エツ

Ⓝ 謁 Ⓒ 谒 yè

1976

◧ 1-7-8

149	Jōyō	U8B01
言	S15-7-8	F2579

COMPOUNDS

❶ BE GRANTED [have] AN AUDIENCE with a superior, esp. a ruler or the emperor

謁見 えっけん audience
拝謁 はいえつ audience with the emperor

❷ [original meaning, now archaic] **beseech, beg, request**

請謁する せいえつする request, beseech; request an audience

INDEPENDENT

【えつ 謁】 audience (with the emperor)
謁を賜わる えつをたまわる be granted an audience
【えっする 謁する】 be received in audience

SYNONYMS

❶ meet

会 MEET → 2512
遇 ENCOUNTER → 3889
遭 MEET WITH → 3917
見 SEE → 3151
謁 BE GRANTED AN AUDIENCE → 1976
逢 MEET → 4002

誼 ▶FRIENDSHIP

ギ よしみ ㊔ よし

Ⓒ 谊 yì

1977

◧ 1-7-8

149	Names	U8ABC
言	S15-7-8	F3062

COMPOUNDS

● [also 宜 2763 or 義 2948] **FRIENDSHIP; favor, kindness**

友誼(=友宜) ゆうぎ friendship, fellowship
交誼(=交宜) こうぎ friendship, amity
好誼(=好宜) こうぎ warm friendship
高誼(=高宜) こうぎ your kindness [favor]
恩誼(=恩義) おんぎ obligation, debt of gratitude
情誼(=情宜、情義)を尽くす じょうぎをつくす do (a person) a kindness

KUN

【よしみ 誼】 **FRIENDSHIP; favor, kindness**

SYNONYMS

● personal relations

縁 RELATION → 1754
交 INTERCOURSE → 2508
好 friendship → 0240
仲 PERSONAL RELATIONS → 0047
誼 FRIENDSHIP → 1977
絆 BONDS → 1686

誹 ▶SLANDER

ヒ ハイ そし(る)

Ⓒ 诽 fěi

1978

◧ 1-7-8

149	Non-Jōyō	U8AB9
言	S15-7-8	F3214

COMPOUNDS

● [now also 非 ひ 1101] [original meaning] **SLANDER, calumniate, defame**

誹諧(=俳諧) はいかい *haikai*, (humorous) haiku
誹謗× ひぼう slander, abuse
誹議する ひぎする criticize, censure

KUN

【そしる 誹る】 [sometimes also 譏る] **SLANDER, libel, criticize**

誹り そしり criticism

SYNONYMS

● disgrace

恥 SHAME → 1664

羞 shame →4106
辱 HUMILIATE →3400
侮 INSULT →0091
罵 ABUSE →3233
汚 defile →0258
誹 SLANDER →1978
譏 SLANDER →2069

HOMOPHONES

そしる 譏 SLANDER →2069

諄 1979

▶TEACH WITH CARE

ジュン シュン くど(い) ㊔ あつ あつし まこと いたる しげ とも

ⓒ 谆 zhūn

◧1-7-8

149	Names	U8AC4
言	S15-7-8	F0000

COMPOUNDS

ⓐ TEACH WITH CARE
ⓑ [rare] with care, tenderly, earnestly
a 諄諄たる じゅんじゅんたる teaching with care

KUN

【くどい 諄い】**tedious, diffuse, prolix, wordy; importunate, inquisitive**
諄い話 くどいはなし old wives' tale

SYNONYMS

ⓐ **teach**
教 TEACH →1887
啓 ENLIGHTEN →3434
諄 TEACH WITH CARE →1979
授 teach →0595
育 educate →2544
練 TRAIN →1738
訓 INSTRUCT →1844
誨 INSTRUCT →1946
諭 ADMONISH →2012
導 GUIDE →3587
迪 EDIFY →3817

課 1980

▶SECTION
▶LESSON

カ

ⓒ 课 kè

◧1-7-8

149	Jōyō-4	U8AB2
言	S15-7-8	F0813

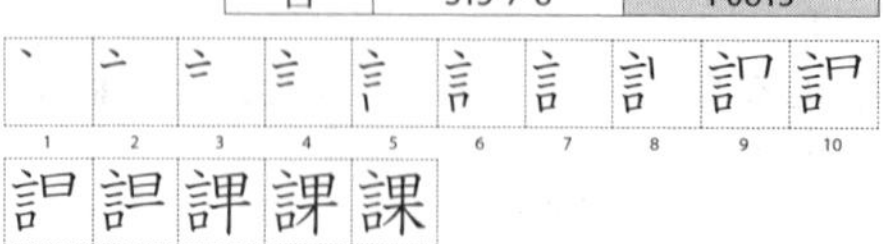

COMPOUNDS

❶ [also suffix] **SECTION, department (of a company or government office)**
課長 かちょう section chief [head]
分課 ぶんか section, subdivision; dividing into sections
人事課 じんじか personnel section
会計課 かいけいか accounts [accounting] section

❷ⓐ **LESSON, task**
ⓑ counter for **LESSON**s
a 課程 かてい course, curriculum
課目(=科目) かもく school subject, course, curriculum
学課 がっか lesson, school work
日課 にっか daily lesson, daily task
放課後 ほうかご after school
b 二課勉強する にかべんきょうする study two lessons

❸ **impose, levy**
課題 かだい task, assignment; problem
課税 かぜい taxation
課徴金 かちょうきん surcharge (on imports)
賦課 ふか levy, imposition, assessment

❹ [original meaning] **evaluate, rate**
考課 こうか evaluation, rating

INDEPENDENT

【か 課】**SECTION, department (of a company or government office); lesson, task**
課の仕事 かのしごと job [responsibility] of a section
次の課 つぎのか next lesson
【かする 課する】**impose, levy**

SYNONYMS

❶ **divisions of organizations**
課 SECTION →1980
部 department →2111
局 BUREAU →3800

❷ **units of learning**
課 LESSON →1980
科 course →1463
講 LECTURE →2046

❸ **impose**
徴 LEVY →0841
課 impose →1980

論 1981

▶ARGUE
▶THEORY

ロン ㊔ さとし

ⓒ 论 lùn lún

◧1-7-8

149	Jōyō-6	U8AD6
言	S15-7-8	F0265

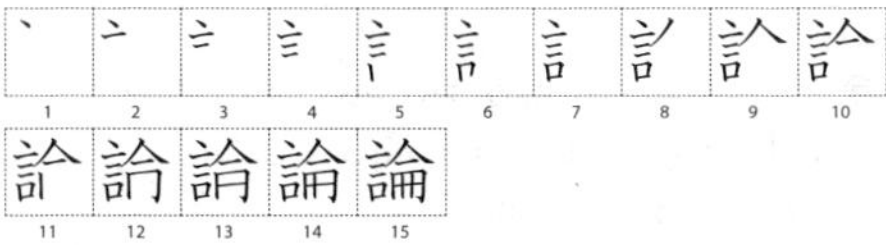

COMPOUNDS

❶ⓐ [original meaning] (put forth reasons) **ARGUE, discuss, discourse, reason**
ⓑ (contend in argument) **ARGUE, dispute**
ⓒ **argument, argumentation, debate**

a 論評 ろんぴょう comment, criticism, review
論説 ろんせつ discourse, dissertation; editorial
論理 ろんり logic
論理的 ろんりてき logical
評論 ひょうろん comment, criticism, review
理論 りろん theory
言論 げんろん speech, discussion
推論 すいろん reasoning, inference, induction, deduction

b 論議 ろんぎ discussion, argument, debate
論争する ろんそうする dispute, argue

c 討論 とうろん debate, discussion, argument
議論 ぎろん argument, discussion
結論 けつろん conclusion
反論 はんろん counterargument, refutation
勿論 もちろん of course, no doubt, naturally

❷ [also suffix]
ⓐ (systematically organized knowledge) **THEORY, doctrine, system of thought**
ⓑ **opinion, view**
ⓒ **essay, treatise, comments**

a 進化論 しんかろん theory of evolution
音韻論 おんいんろん phonology

b 世論 せろん(=よろん) public opinion
異論 いろん different [dissenting] opinion; objection, dissent, protest
持論 じろん pet theory
時論 じろん current view, contemporary opinion; comments on current events
強硬論 きょうこうろん hard line

c 論文 ろんぶん thesis, paper, treatise, dissertation
芸術論 げいじゅつろん essay on art
時事論 じじろん comments on current events

❸ [also suffix] **question, issue, problem**
論外な ろんがいな out of the question, beside the point
国防論 こくぼうろん the question of national defense
漢字制限論 かんじせいげんろん the question of limiting the use of Chinese characters

❹ abbrev. of 論文 ろんぶん thesis
卒論 そつろん graduation thesis, dissertation

❺ The Analects of Confucius
論孟 ろんもう The Confucian Analects and the Discourses of Mencius

INDEPENDENT

【ろん 論】**argument, argumentation, debate; opinion, view**
論より証拠 ろんよりしょうこ Proof is better than argument
論が分かれている ろんがわかれている Opinion is divided

【ろんじる(=ろんずる) 論じる(=論ずる)】
① (contend in argument) **ARGUE, dispute**
声高に論じる こわだかにろんじる argue loudly
② (set forth one's opinion systematically) **discuss, discourse, comment on, treat**
文学を論じる ぶんがくをろんじる discuss literature
③ consider, take into account
同列に論じる どうれつにろんじる consider (something) in the same bracket

SYNONYMS

❶ **argue and discuss**
議 DISCUSS → 2078
争 CONTEND → 2523
論 ARGUE → 1981
弁 argue (for) → 2497
諏 CONSULT → 1985

❷ⓐ **theory**
論 THEORY (systematic knowledge) → 1981
説 THEORY (proposed explanation) → 1949

ⓑ **opinion**
見 view (personal opinion) → 3151
観 VIEW (conception) → 2359
説 opinion → 1949
論 opinion → 1981

❸ **question**
題 PROBLEM → 4139
問 QUESTION (inquiry) → 4117
論 question (issue) → 1981
謎 RIDDLE → 2047

COMPOUND FORMATION

❶【論理 ろんり】
論理 'logic' is the thread or chain of reasoning (理) of an argument (論 ❶ⓒ).

❷【勿論 もちろん】
勿論 'of course, etc.' is a state without (勿) argument (論 ❶ⓒ).

NOTE

★ do not confuse with 諭 ADMONISH → 2012

【言】豸貝足車酉名

諒

▶UNDERSTAND
リョウ ㊔ まこと あき あきら まさ
Ⓒ 谅 liàng

1982
1-7-8

149	Names	U8AD2
言	S15-7-8	F2682

COMPOUNDS

❶ [now usu. 了 4157]
ⓐ **UNDERSTAND, comprehend, know clearly**
ⓑ [rarely also 亮 2571] show **UNDERSTAND**ing, be sympathetic, acknowledge, forgive

a 諒解 りょうかい understanding, comprehension; consent
諒承する りょうしょうする acknowledge, understand, note
b 諒察する りょうさつする consider, take into account, sympathize with

❷ really, truly
諒闇 りょうあん court [national] mourning

INDEPENDENT

【りょう 諒】[sometimes also 了 4157] **UNDERSTAND**ing, comprehension
諒とする(=了とする) りょうとする understand, appreciate; excuse

【りょうする 諒する】**UNDERSTAND**, appreciate, excuse

SYNONYMS

❶ **know and understand**
知 KNOW → 1446
通 know thoroughly → 3855
得 gain understanding of → 0577
分かる understand → 2466
解 understand → 1913
諒 UNDERSTAND → 1982
了 COMPREHEND → 4157
悟 AWAKE TO → 0502
惺 AWAKE TO → 0709

COMPOUND FORMATION

【諒闇 りょうあん】
諒闇 'court [national] mourning' originates from the idea of being truly (諒 ❷) dark (闇).

請

▶REQUEST
セイ シン ショウ▲ こ(う) う(ける)
Ⓝ 請 Ⓒ 请 qǐng

1983
1-7-8

149	Jōyō	U8ACB
言	S15-7-8	F1082

(stroke order diagram, strokes 1–15)

COMPOUNDS

❶ [original meaning] **REQUEST, ask, beg, solicit**
請求 せいきゅう demand, request, claim
請願 せいがん petition
請訓 せいくん request for instructions
申請 しんせい application, petition, request
要請する ようせいする request, demand
懇請する こんせいする request earnestly, solicit, entreat
普請 ふしん building, construction

❷ (request a person's presence) invite
招請 しょうせい invitation

INDEPENDENT

【しょうじる(=しょうずる) 請じる(=招じる、請ずる、招ずる)】invite; usher in

KUN

【こう 請う】
ⓐ **ask, REQUEST, solicit**
ⓑ [also 乞う] beg
a 寄付を請う きふをこう solicit donations

【うける 請ける】
① **undertake, take upon oneself**
請け合う うけあう assure, guarantee; undertake
請け負う うけおう contract for, undertake
下請け したうけ subcontract
② redeem (pawned goods), ransom
請け出す うけだす redeem, pay off, take out of pawn

SYNONYMS

❶ **request**
請 REQUEST → 1983
訴 APPEAL TO → 1901
頼 ASK → 2041
嘱 CHARGE WITH → 0881
要 REQUIRE → 3263
願 ASK A FAVOR → 2320
求 SEEK → 4365
乞 BEG → 2457

USAGE

【こう】
請う
ⓐ ask, request, solicit
ⓑ [also 乞う] beg
乞う
ⓐ [also 請う] beg
ⓑ [in compounds] solicit, pray for

HOMOPHONES

こう 乞 BEG → 2457
うける
受 RECEIVE → 3076
享 ENJOY → 2545

承 AGREE TO →0016

COMPOUND FORMATION

【普請 ふしん】

普請 'building, construction' originally meant to solicit (請 ❶) donations and voluntary labor from the public at large (普) for building Buddhist temples.

NOTE

➡ see also USAGE note at 受 3076

諸

▶VARIOUS

ショ もろ▲

Ⓝ 諸 Ⓒ 诸 zhū

1984

1-7-8

149	Jōyō-6	U8AF8
言	S15-7-8	F0646

COMPOUNDS

● [also prefix] **VARIOUS, all kinds of; many, all**

諸説 しょせつ various views [theories]

諸島 しょとう archipelago

諸派 しょは minor parties

諸君 しょくん Ladies and Gentlemen, my friends, you

諸国 しょこく various [all] countries

諸般の しょはんの various, several, all, every

諸問題 しょもんだい various [all] questions [problems]

諸行無常 しょぎょうむじょう All things flow and nothing is permanent (a Buddhist concept)

KUN

【もろ 諸】[in compounds] **togetherness, being all in one piece; both**

諸に もろに altogether, completely, bodily

諸共に もろともに altogether, one and all

諸諸の もろもろの various, diverse

諸手(=両手) もろて both hands

SYNONYMS

● **all**

皆 ALL →3093

悉 THOROUGHLY →3405

総 TOTAL →1743

諸 VARIOUS →1984

毎 EVERY →2527

各 EACH →2692

都 all →2120

万 all →3653

全 WHOLE →2514

渾 ENTIRE →0738

一 all in one →4148

満 FULL →0739

丸 complete(ly) →4225

完 COMPLETE →2727

● **various**

諸 VARIOUS →1984

庶 MANIFOLD →3880

雑 MISCELLANEOUS →1752

諏

▶CONSULT

シュ ス

Ⓒ 诹 zōu

1985

1-7-8

149	Names	U8ACF
言	S15-7-8	F2064

COMPOUNDS

● **CONSULT**

諏訪湖 すわこ Lake Suwa

諮諏 ししゅ [rare] consult, refer (a matter) to

SYNONYMS

● **argue and discuss**

議 DISCUSS →2078

争 CONTEND →2523

論 ARGUE →1981

弁 argue (for) →2497

諏 CONSULT →1985

誰

▶WHO

スイ▲ だれ たれ▲ た▲

Ⓒ 谁 shuí shéi

1986

1-7-8

149	Jōyō	U8AB0
言	S15-7-8	F0414

COMPOUNDS

● [original meaning] **WHO**

誰何する すいかする challenge (an unknown person), ask a person's identity

KUN

【だれ 誰】**WHO; someone, somebody; anyone, anybody**

誰の だれの whose

誰か だれか someone, somebody

誰でも だれでも anyone, anybody

誰一人 だれひとり no one, nobody, none

彼は誰ですか かれはだれですか Who is he?

【たれ 誰】literary form of 誰 だれ

誰彼 たれかれ this or that person

【た 誰】*literary* **WHO**
誰が為に たがために for whom

SYNONYMS

● **interrogatives**
奈 interrogative forming element → 2759
那 interrogative forming element → 1047
何 WHAT → 0073
誰 WHO → 1986

誕

1987
1-7-8

▸**BE BORN**
タン
Ⓝ 誕 Ⓒ 诞 dàn

149	Jōyō-6	U8A95
言	S15-7-8	F1323

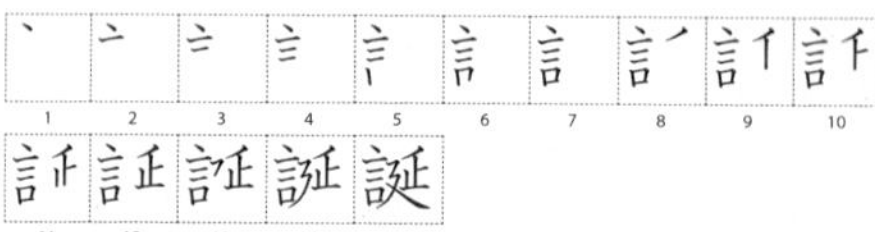

COMPOUNDS

❶ ⓐ **BE BORN**
ⓑ **birth**
a 誕生 たんじょう birth, nativity
誕生日 たんじょうび birthday
b 誕辰 たんしん birthday
生誕 せいたん birth, nativity
キリストの降誕 きりすとのこうたん the Nativity, the Advent

❷ [original meaning] absurd, fantastic, deceitful
荒誕 こうたん wild talk, nonsense, lies

SYNONYMS

❶ **give birth**
生 BE BORN → 4309
誕 BE BORN → 1987
産 GIVE BIRTH → 4089
娩 GIVE BIRTH → 0486
殖 MULTIPLY → 1253

諷

1988
1-7-8

▸**TONE**
▸**INVESTIGATE**
▸**PREPARE**
チョウ しら(べる) しら(べ) ととの(う) ととの(える) ㊔ まもる つき つぎ

149	Nonstandard	U8ABF
言	S15-7-8	F0000

traditional form → see 調 at 1973

請

1989
1-7-8

▸**REQUEST**
セイ シン ショウ こ(う) う(ける)

149	Nonstandard	U8ACB
言	S15-7-8	F0000

traditional form → see 請 at 1983

謀

1-7-8

incorrect stroke-count
➡ see 1-7-9: 言 at 2004

誤

1-7-8

incorrect stroke-count
➡ see 1-7-7: 言 at 1945

誘

1-7-8

incorrect stroke-count
➡ see 1-7-7: 言 at 1952

謎

1-7-8

incorrect stroke-count
➡ see 1-7-9: 言 at 2015

貓

1990
1-7-8

▸**CAT**
ビョウ ねこ

153	Nonstandard	U8C93
豸	S15-7-8	F0000

traditional form → see 猫 at 0651

賠

1991
1-7-8

▸**COMPENSATE**
バイ
Ⓒ 赔 péi

154	Jōyō	U8CE0
貝	S15-7-8	F2162

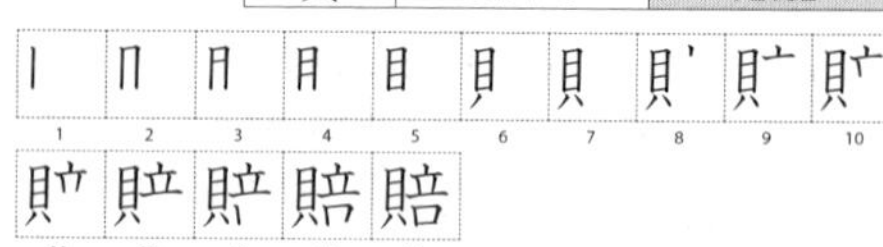

COMPOUNDS

● [original meaning] **COMPENSATE, indemnify**
賠償する ばいしょうする indemnify, compensate, recompense
賠償金 ばいしょうきん indemnity, reparation
賠責 ばいせき liability insurance
自賠法 じばいほう Automobile Accident Compensation Act

SYNONYMS

● **compensate**
償 RECOMPENSE → 0199
賠 COMPENSATE → 1991
酬 RECIPROCATE → 1941
報 REQUITE → 2133

賦

1992
1-7-8

▸**INSTALLMENT**
フ ブ▲
Ⓒ 赋 fù

154	Jōyō	U8CE6
貝	S15-7-8	F2712

【言】豸 貝 足 車 酉 谷

1	2	3	4	5	6	7	8	9	10
丨	冂	月	月	目	目	貝	貝	貝	貝

11	12	13	14	15
貝	貝	貝	賦	賦

COMPOUNDS

❶ **INSTALLMENT, payment by installment**
賦払い ぶばらい installment system, easy payment plan
月賦 げっぷ monthly installments
割賦 かっぷ(=わっぷ) payment by installments

❷ levy, levying, tax; exacted service
賦課する ふかする levy, impose, assess
賦役 ふえき slave labor, corvée, levy of labor

❸ⓐ natural endowment [gift]
ⓑ endow, give
a 天賦 てんぷ natural gift
b 賦与 ふよ endowment

❹ ode, prose poem; descriptive prose interspersed with verse
詞賦 しふ Chinese poetry
早春賦 そうしゅんふ Ode to Early Spring

INDEPENDENT

【ふ 賦】ode, prose poem; descriptive prose interspersed with verse
【ふする 賦する】levy, allot; compose, write (a poem)

SYNONYMS

❶ **pay**
払う PAY → 0225
納 PAY (to the authorities) → 1652
済 settle accounts → 0634
支 pay out → 2473
賦 INSTALLMENT → 1992
償 RECOMPENSE → 0199

❷ **tax**
税 TAX → 1525
租 LAND TAX → 1492
貢 TRIBUTE → 2838
賦 levy → 1992

NOTE

★ do not confuse with 賊 BANDIT → 1932

賤

1993

◧ 1-7-8

▶**MEAN**
セン いや(しい) いや(しむ) いや(しめる) しず
Ⓒ 贱 jiàn

154	Non-Jōyō	U8CE4
貝	S15-7-8	F2639

COMPOUNDS

❶ (low in social status) **MEAN, lowly, humble, inferior in position**
賤民 せんみん lowly people, outcasts
貴賤 きせん high and low, all ranks
下賤の げせんの of low birth, vulgar
卑賤 ひせん lowly position, humble condition

❷ⓐ (of poor appearance) **MEAN, shabby, seedy**
ⓑ (lacking elevating human qualities) **MEAN, base, vulgar, despicable**
b 賤業婦 せんぎょうふ prostitute

❸ **despise, disdain, look down on, regard with contempt**
賤称 せんしょう [rare] depreciatory name

❹ [original meaning, now archaic] inexpensive, cheap

KUN

【いやしい 賤しい】[now usu. 卑しい]
① (low in social status) **MEAN**, lowly, humble, inferior in position
賤しい稼業 いやしいかぎょう mean occupation
②ⓐ (of poor appearance) **MEAN**, shabby, seedy
ⓑ (lacking elevating human qualities) **MEAN**, base, vulgar, despicable
a 賤しい身形 いやしいみなり shabby appearance
b 賤しい笑い いやしいわらい mean smirk
【いやしむ 賤しむ】[now usu. 卑しむ] **despise, disdain, look down on, regard with contempt**
賤しむべき いやしむべき despicable
労働を賤しむ ろうどうをいやしむ despise labor
【いやしめる 賤しめる】[now usu. 卑しめる] same as 賤しむ いやしむ
【しず 賤】(low in social status) **MEAN, lowly, humble, inferior in position**
賤の女 しずのめ woman of lowly birth

SYNONYMS

❶ **vulgar and unrefined**
俗 vulgar → 0119
卑 MEAN → 3270
賤 MEAN → 1993
鄙 MEAN → 2338
俚 RURAL → 0112
里 rural → 4356
粗 COARSE → 1683
野 rustic → 1877
蛮 barbaric → 2638

HOMOPHONES

いやしい 卑 MEAN → 3270
いやしむ 卑 MEAN → 3270
いやしめる 卑 MEAN → 3270

NOTE

➡ see USAGE note at 卑 3270

賜

1994

1-7-8

▶**DEIGN TO GIVE**

シ たまわ(る) たま(う)▲ たも(う)▲

Ⓒ 赐 cì

154 貝	Jōyō	U8CDC
	S15-7-8	F2274

COMPOUNDS

ⓐ [original meaning] **DEIGN TO GIVE, bestow, grant, award; be awarded, have the honor to receive**

ⓑ gift, boon

a 賜金 しきん money grant
賜杯 しはい trophy given by the emperor [prince]
賜暇 しか leave of absence, furlough
下賜する かしする grant, deign to give

b 恩賜 おんし Imperial gift

KUN

【たまわる 賜る】**DEIGN TO GIVE, bestow, grant, award; be awarded, have the honor to receive**
賜り物 たまわりもの gift, boon

【たまう, たもう 賜う】

① [sometimes also 給う] *literary* **DEIGN TO GIVE**, bestow, grant, award
賜物 たまもの gift, boon; result, fruit
拝謁を賜う はいえつをたまう deign to grant an audience

② [usu. 給う] [suffix] *literary* (perform an action for an inferior) deign to
天皇が立ち賜う てんのうがたちたもう His Majesty deigns to stand up

SYNONYMS

ⓐ **give**
与 GIVE → 4229
呈 PRESENT → 2715
進 present to a superior → 3873
上 give (to superior or others) → 4212
下 give (to inferior or speaker) → 4186
呉れる give (to speaker) → 3156
授 CONFER → 0595
賜 DEIGN TO GIVE → 1994
贈 PRESENT A GIFT → 2064
賄 BRIBE → 1931
賂 BRIBE → 1930

HOMOPHONES

たまう 給 SUPPLY → 1708

NOTE

➡ see USAGE note at 給 1708

賭

1995

1-7-8

▶**WAGER**

ト か(ける)

154 貝	Nonstandard	U8CED
	S15-7-8	F0000

traditional form → see 賭 at 2021

踪

1996

1-7-8

▶**FOOTPRINTS**

ソウ シュウ▲

Ⓒ 踪 zōng

157 足	Jōyō	U8E2A
	S15-7-8	F2336

COMPOUNDS

● [original meaning] **FOOTPRINTS; traces, remains; whereabouts**
踪跡 そうせき traces, tracks; whereabouts
失踪 しっそう absconding, disappearance

SYNONYMS

● **marks and signs**
標 MARK (identifying sign) → 1347
徽 EMBLEM → 0968
痕 SCAR → 4066
印 MARK (visible sign) → 1023
跡 TRACE → 1937
蹟 TRACE → 2065
踪 FOOTPRINTS → 1996
紋 print → 1651
符 SYMBOL → 3299
号 SIGN → 2675
栞 BOOKMARK → 3285

踏

1997

1-7-8

▶**TREAD**

トウ ふ(む) ふ(まえる)

Ⓒ 踏 tà tā

157 足	Jōyō	U8E0F
	S15-7-8	F0893

COMPOUNDS

❶ [original meaning] **TREAD (on), step on, stamp, trample**
踏破する とうはする crush underfoot; travel on foot
未踏の みとうの untrodden, unexplored
舞踏(=舞蹈) ぶとう dancing

❷ go to the spot (to investigate something)
踏査 とうさ survey, investigation
❸ [formerly also 蹈 2055] follow, pursue
踏襲する とうしゅうする follow, follow suit
❹ [formerly 沓 3074] **crowded, confused**
雑踏 ざっとう hustle and bustle, traffic jam

KUN

【ふむ 踏む】 **step on, TREAD on, stamp; go through, finish; estimate, value; rhyme**
踏み入れる ふみいれる walk in on, tread upon
踏み切る ふみきる make a bold start, take a plunge; take off; *sumo* step out of the ring
踏ん張る ふんばる keep one's footing, stand firm; hold out; make an effort
踏切 ふみきり railroad crossing
足踏み あしぶみ stepping, step, tread

【ふまえる 踏まえる】 **step on, stand on; be based on**
政府の方針を踏まえて せいふのほうしんをふまえて based on government policy

SYNONYMS

❶ **walk**
歩 WALK → 3071
徒 go on foot → 0499
脚 move on foot → 1226
足 travel on foot → 2714
踏 TREAD → 1997
❶ **step on**
踏 TREAD → 1997
蹈 STEP ON → 2055
藉 TRAMPLE ON → 3017

踐
1998
◧ 1-7-8

▸**IMPLEMENT**
セン

157	Nonstandard	U8E10
足	S15-7-8	F0000

traditional form → see 践 at 1938

輪
1999
◧ 1-7-8

▸**WHEEL**
▸**RING**
リン わ
Ⓒ 轮 lún

159	Jōyō-4	U8F2A
車	S15-7-8	F0844

1	2	3	4	5	6	7	8	9	10	11	12	13	14	15
一	𠃊	戸	戸	百	亘	車	車	軜	軜	軩	輪	輪	輪	輪

COMPOUNDS

❶ⓐ [original meaning] **WHEEL**
ⓑ **counter for WHEELs**
a 車輪 しゃりん wheel
前輪 ぜんりん front wheel
b 二輪車 にりんしゃ two-wheeled vehicle, bicycle
一輪車 いちりんしゃ unicycle; wheelbarrow
❷ **WHEELed vehicle, cycle, bicycle, automobile**
輪業 りんぎょう bicycle industry
輪禍 りんか automobile accident, traffic accident
輪タク りんたく pedicab, trishaw
競輪 けいりん bicycle race
駐輪場 ちゅうりんじょう bicycle parking lot
❸ **RING, circle**
輪状の りんじょうの ring-shaped, annular
輪形の りんけいの ring-shaped, circular
年輪 ねんりん annual ring, growth ring
五輪のマーク ごりんのまーく the five-ring Olympic emblem
❹ⓐ corolla, flower
ⓑ counter for flowers
a 大輪の たいりんの large-flowered
b 一輪の花 いちりんのはな a (single) flower
❺ take turns, rotate, alternate
輪転 りんてん rotation
輪番 りんばん turn, rotation
輪唱する りんしょうする troll, sing in a circular canon
輪読 りんどく reading by turns
❻ **periphery, outline**
輪郭 りんかく contour, outline, profile

KUN

【わ 輪】
① [sometimes also 環] **RING, circle, link**
輪投げ わなげ quoits, ringtoss
輪ゴム わごむ rubber band
輪になって踊る わになっておどる dance in a circle [ring]
指輪 ゆびわ (finger) ring
② **WHEEL**

SYNONYMS

❶ & ❸ **circular objects**
環 RING → 1395
輪 WHEEL, RING → 1999
車 WHEEL → 4367
盤 DISK → 3533
釧 ARMLET → 2109
❷ **vehicle**
車 VEHICLE → 4367
輌 VEHICLE → 2000
乗 vehicle → 4393
輪 wheeled vehicle → 1999
駕 CARRIAGE → 3236

輿 PALANQUIN → 3626
台 COUNTER FOR VEHICLES → 2498

❺ **alternate**
迭 ALTERNATE → 3818
交 INTERCHANGE → 2508
輪 take turns → 1999

USAGE

【わ】
輪
① [sometimes also 環] ring, circle, link
② wheel
環
[usu. 輪] ring, circle, link

HOMOPHONES

わ 環 RING → 1395

NOTE

★ do not confuse with 輸 TRANSPORT → 2026

輛

▸VEHICLE
リョウ
Ⓒ 辆 liàng

2000
1-7-8

159	Non-Jōyō	U8F1B
車	S15-7-8	F2649

COMPOUNDS

[now usu. 両 4331]
ⓐ **VEHICLE, railway car**
ⓑ counter for railway cars
a 車輛 しゃりょう vehicle, car; rolling stock
b 三輛 さんりょう three cars, three coaches

SYNONYMS

ⓐ **vehicle**
車 VEHICLE → 4367
輛 VEHICLE → 2000
乗 vehicle → 4393
輪 wheeled vehicle → 1999
駕 CARRIAGE → 3236
輿 PALANQUIN → 3626
台 COUNTER FOR VEHICLES → 2498

ⓑ **kinds of railway**
鉄 railway → 2147
電 electric railway → 3465
車 railway car → 4367
両 counter for railway cars → 4331
輛 counter for railway cars → 2000

醇

▸UNDILUTED WINE
ジュン シュン ㊔ あつし あつ
Ⓒ 醇 chún

2001
1-7-8

164	Names	U9187
酉	S15-7-8	F0000

COMPOUNDS

❶ **UNDILUTED WINE [liquor]**
醇酒 じゅんしゅ mellow wine
醇味 じゅんみ (of liquor) rich [mellow] taste
芳醇(=芳純)な ほうじゅんな (of liquor) mellow, rich

❷ [now usu. 純 1649] **pure; purehearted**
醇乎(=純乎)たる じゅんこたる sheer, pure
醇朴(=純朴) じゅんぼく simplicity and honesty

❸ humane, sympathetic
醇厚(=純厚)な じゅんこうな warmhearted, kind-hearted

INDEPENDENT

【じゅんなる 醇なる】undiluted liquor; pure

SYNONYMS

❶ **drinks**
汁 JUICE, SOUP → 0227
乳 MILK → 1823
酒 ALCOHOLIC DRINK → 0532
茶 TEA → 2808
珈 COFFEE → 1138
醇 UNDILUTED WINE → 2001
酎 SHOCHU → 1852

醋

▸VINEGAR
サク す
Ⓒ 醋 cù

2002
1-7-8

164	Non-Jōyō	U918B
酉	S15-7-8	F0000

COMPOUNDS

● [now replaced by 酢 1910] [original meaning] **VINEGAR**
醋酸 さくさん acetic acid

KUN

【す 醋】[now replaced by 酢] [also suffix] **VINEGAR**
醋蛸× すだこ (sliced and) pickled octopus

SYNONYMS

● **seasonings**
糖 SUGAR → 1777
塩 SALT → 0774
酢 VINEGAR → 1910
醋 VINEGAR → 2002
油 OIL → 0400
醤 FERMENTED SAUCE → 3569
噌 MISO → 0882
蜜 HONEY → 2958

HOMOPHONES

す 酢 VINEGAR → 1910

NOTE

➡ see USAGE note at 酢 1910

醉 2003 ◧1-7-8

▶**BECOME INTOXICATED**
スイ よ(う) よ(い)

164	Names	U9189
酉	S15-7-8	F0000

traditional form → see 酔 at 1875

欿 ◧1-7-8

incorrect stroke-count
➡ see ◧1-8-8: 臽 at 2200

謀 2004 ◧1-7-9

▶**SCHEME**
ボウ ム はか(る) はかりごと▲
Ⓒ 谋 móu

149	Jōyō	U8B00
言	S16-7-9	F1177

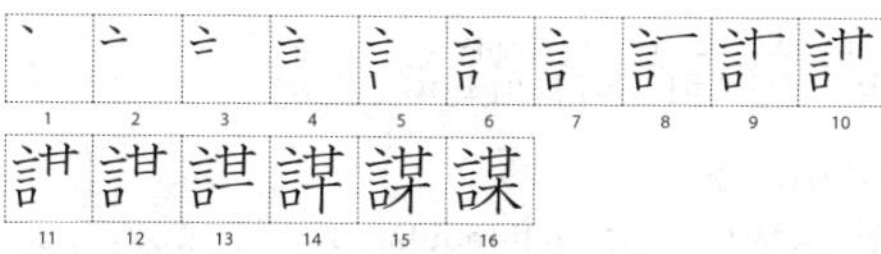

COMPOUNDS

❶ⓐ **SCHEME, plot, conspire, contrive**
ⓑ **SCHEME, plot, conspiracy, intrigue**
a 謀殺 ぼうさつ premeditated murder
首謀者 しゅぼうしゃ ringleader, mastermind
b 謀略 ぼうりゃく stratagem, scheme, plot
謀反 むほん rebellion, revolt, treason
共謀 きょうぼう conspiracy, collusion
陰謀 いんぼう scheme, plot, conspiracy
❷ⓐ plan, think ahead
ⓑ **plan, strategy**
a 謀臣 ぼうしん strategist, tactician; schemer
b 深謀 しんぼう deeply laid plan
無謀 むぼう recklessness, imprudence
参謀 さんぼう staff officer, the staff; adviser, counselor

KUN

【はかる 謀る】**SCHEME, plot, conspire, contrive**
暗殺を謀る あんさつをはかる plot an assassination
【はかりごと 謀】**SCHEME**, plot, stratagem, conspiracy

SYNONYMS

❶ **plans and planning**
計 PLAN → 1828
画 DRAW UP A PLAN → 3723
案 PROPOSAL → 2824
企 PROJECT → 2513
図 systematic plan → 3809
謀 SCHEME → 2004
策 SCHEME → 3320
略 STRATEGY → 1501
揆 PLOT → 0718

HOMOPHONES

はかる
計 PLAN → 1828
図 DRAWING → 3809
諮 CONSULT → 2009
量 QUANTITY → 3119
測 MEASURE → 0744

NOTE

➡ see USAGE note at 計 1828

諷 2005 ◧1-7-9

▶**INSINUATE**
フウ
Ⓒ 讽 fěng

149	Non-Jōyō	U8AF7
言	S16-7-9	F3415

COMPOUNDS

❶ [now usu. 風 3730] **INSINUATE, hint, satirize**
諷刺 ふうし satire, sarcasm
諷喩 ふうゆ hint, insinuation, allegory
❷ [archaic] recite, chant
諷誦 ふうじゅ reciting
諷詠 ふうえい composition and recitation of poems

INDEPENDENT

【ふうする 諷する】**INSINUATE, hint, satirize**

SYNONYMS

❶ **speak and say**
言 SAY → 2440
語る TELL → 1944
談 TALK → 1975
喋 TALK → 0665
諷 INSINUATE → 2005
謂う REFER TO → 2007
云 say → 2430
曰 SAY THAT → 3757
話 SPEAK → 1928
口 give mouth to → 4189
申す SPEAK HUMBLY → 4319
述 STATE → 3816
陳 SET FORTH → 0656
弁 SPEAK ELOQUENTLY → 2497

諺 2006 ◧1-7-9

▶**PROVERB**
ゲン ことわざ ㊔ たけし こと おう
Ⓝ 諺 Ⓒ 谚 yàn

149	Names	U8AFA
言	S16-7-9	F3297

COMPOUNDS

● **PROVERB, maxim, saying**

【言】豆 豕 貝 足 車 辛 酉 巠 𠂤 𠂤 步 禿 東 夾

諺文 げんぶん(=おんもん, うんむん) old name for Hangul
俗諺 ぞくげん popular saying, proverb
俚諺 りげん traditional [folk] saying, proverb

KUN

【ことわざ 諺】 **PROVERB, maxim, saying**

SYNONYMS

● **words and expressions**
語 WORD → 1944
辞 WORD → 1726
詞 WORDS → 1897
句 PHRASE → 3685
諺 PROVERB → 2006
喩 METAPHOR → 0671

謂

2007
1-7-9

▸**REFER TO**
イ い(う) いわ(れ)
Ⓒ 谓 wèi

149	Names	U8B02
言	S16-7-9	F2753

KUN

【いう 謂う】 [usu. 言う] **REFER TO, call**—used chiefly in certain set expressions
謂わば いわば as it were, so to call it
これを音素と謂う これをおんそという To this is given the term "phoneme"
ここで船とは宇宙船を謂う ここでふねとはうちゅうせんをいう By "ship" here is meant a spaceship

【いわれ 謂れ】 **reason, origin, history**

SPECIAL READINGS

所謂 いわゆる what is called, so-called

SYNONYMS

【いう】
○ **speak and say**
言 SAY → 2440
語る TELL → 1944
談 TALK → 1975
喋 TALK → 0665
諷 INSINUATE → 2005
謂う REFER TO → 2007
云 say → 2430
曰 SAY THAT → 3757
話 SPEAK → 1928
口 give mouth to → 4189
申す SPEAK HUMBLY → 4319
述 STATE → 3816
陳 SET FORTH → 0656
弁 SPEAK ELOQUENTLY → 2497

HOMOPHONES

いう
言 SAY → 2440
云 SUCH → 2430

NOTE

➡ see USAGE note at 言 2440

諧

2008
1-7-9

▸**HARMONIOUS**
▸**JEST**
カイ
Ⓒ 谐 xié

149	Jōyō	U8AE7
言	S16-7-9	F2875

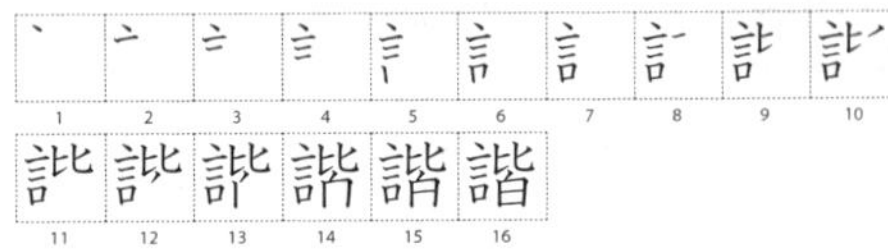

COMPOUNDS

❶ **HARMONIOUS, well-regulated**
諧調 かいちょう harmony (of sound or rhythm), euphony
諧声 かいせい vocal harmony, harmonious voices

❷ **JEST, joke**
諧謔× かいぎゃく humor, joke, jest, banter
誹諧(=俳諧) はいかい *haikai*, (humorous) haiku

諮

2009
1-7-9

▸**CONSULT**
シ はか(る)
Ⓝ 諮 Ⓒ 谘 zī

149	Jōyō	U8AEE
言	S16-7-9	F2305

COMPOUNDS

● **CONSULT, confer, ask for advice, inquire**
諮問する しもんする consult, inquire
諮議する しぎする consult, confer

KUN

【はかる 諮る】 **CONSULT, confer, ask (a person's) opinion**
委員会に諮る いいんかいにはかる submit (a plan) to a committee for deliberation

SYNONYMS

● **inquire**
問 QUESTION → 4117
詰 question closely → 1920
聞く ask → 4127

質 query → 3483
尋ねる INQUIRE → 2918
訊 INQUIRE → 1842
伺う INQUIRE (*humble*) → 0078
諮 CONSULT → 2009
詢 ASK FOR ADVICE → 1917

HOMOPHONES

はかる
謀 SCHEME → 2004
図 DRAWING → 3809
計 PLAN → 1828
量 QUANTITY → 3119
測 MEASURE → 0744

NOTE

➡ see USAGE note at 計 1828

諦

2010

1-7-9

▶GIVE UP

テイ タイ▲ あきら(める)

Ⓒ 谛 dì

149	Jōyō	U8AE6
言	S16-7-9	F1934

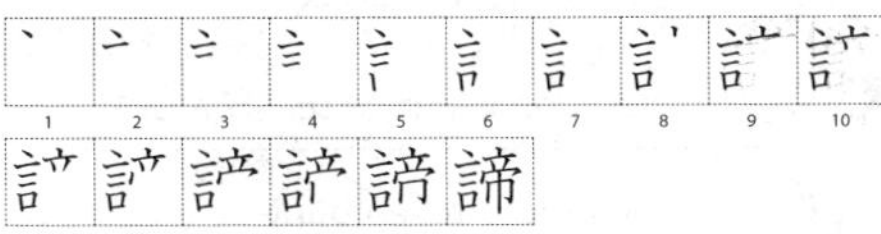

COMPOUNDS

❶ GIVE UP, abandon, resign oneself
諦念 ていねん feeling of resignation; a heart that understands truth

❷ [original meaning] **detail, make clear; detailed, clear**
諦観 ていかん clear vision; resignation

❸ *Buddhism* **truth**
真諦 しんたい *Buddhism* ultimate truth, essence
要諦 ようてい secret, cardinal point

KUN

【あきらめる 諦める】GIVE UP, abandon, resign oneself
諦め あきらめ resignation, acceptance

SYNONYMS

❶ discard and abandon
捨 DISCARD → 0608
棄 ABANDON → 2651
諦 GIVE UP → 2010

謡

2011

1-7-9

▶POPULAR SONG

ヨウ うたい うた(う)

Ⓝ 謠 Ⓒ 谣 yáo

149	Jōyō	U8B21
言	S16-7-9	F1918

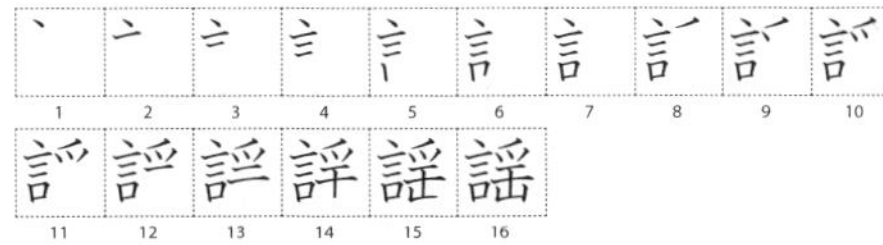

COMPOUNDS

❶ⓐ POPULAR SONG, ballad, folk song
ⓑ chant in a noh drama
a 俗謡 ぞくよう popular song, ballad
民謡 みんよう folk song [ballad]
歌謡曲 かようきょく popular song
童謡 どうよう children's song, nursery rhyme
里謡 りよう ballad, folk song
b 謡曲 ようきょく noh chant

❷ [original meaning, now archaic] **sing**

KUN

【うたい 謡】*utai*, chanting of a noh text
謡物 うたいもの an *utai* piece for recitation

【うたう 謡う】recite, chant (esp. from a noh drama text)
謡を謡う うたいをうたう recite an *utai*

SYNONYMS

❶ⓐ music and songs
楽 MUSIC → 3505
音 sound of music → 2570
節 tune → 3336
調べ melody → 1973
曲 MUSICAL COMPOSITION → 4340
歌 SONG → 2296
謡 POPULAR SONG → 2011
唄 DITTY → 0477

HOMOPHONES

うたう
歌 SONG → 2296
唄 DITTY → 0477
謳 EXTOL → 2061

NOTE

➡ see USAGE note at 歌 2296

諭

2012

1-7-9

▶ADMONISH

ユ さと(す) ㊔ さとし ゆう さとる

Ⓝ 諭 Ⓒ 谕 yù

149	Jōyō	U8AED
言	S16-7-9	F2071

【言】豆豕貝足車辛酉巠 歩禿束夾

COMPOUNDS

ⓐ ADMONISH, give guidance, instruct, advise, persuade
ⓑ official guidance, Imperial instructions, edict
a 諭旨 ゆし official suggestion or instruction (to a subordinate)
教諭 きょうゆ teacher, instructor
説諭 せつゆ admonition, reproof
訓諭 くんゆ [rare] admonition, caution, warning
b 勅諭 ちょくゆ Imperial instructions, Imperial mandate

KUN

【さとす 諭す】ADMONISH, give guidance, instruct, advise; persuade, reason (with)
諭し さとし guidance, admonition
教え諭す おしえさとす give guidance

SYNONYMS

ⓐ warn
警 WARN → 3595
戒 CAUTION → 3972
誡 CAUTION AGAINST → 1947
諭 ADMONISH → 2012
告 advise → 3062
ⓐ teach
教 TEACH → 1887
啓 ENLIGHTEN → 3434
諄 TEACH WITH CARE → 1979
授 teach → 0595
育 educate → 2544
練 TRAIN → 1738
訓 INSTRUCT → 1844
誨 INSTRUCT → 1946
諭 ADMONISH → 2012
導 GUIDE → 3587
迪 EDIFY → 3817

NOTE

★ do not confuse with 論 ARGUE → 1981

【言】豆 豕 貝 足 車 辛 酉 巠 㚇 㠯 步 秃 束 夾

謁

2013
1-7-9

▶BE GRANTED AN AUDIENCE
エツ

149	Names	UFA62
言	S16-7-9	F0000

traditional form → see 謁 at 1976

諺

2014
1-7-9

▶PROVERB
ゲン ことわざ ㊔ たけし こと おう

149	Nonstandard	U8AFA
言	S16-7-9	F0000

traditional form → see 諺 at 2006

謎

2015
1-7-9

▶RIDDLE
メイ なぞ

149	Nonstandard	U8B0E
言	S16-7-9	F0000

alternative form → see 謎 at 2047

諮

2016
1-7-9

▶CONSULT
シ はか(る)

149	Nonstandard	U8AEE
言	S16-7-9	F0000

traditional form → see 諮 at 2009

諸

2017
1-7-9

▶VARIOUS
ショ もろ

149	Names	UFA22
言	S16-7-9	F0000

traditional form → see 諸 at 1984

諭

2018
1-7-9

▶ADMONISH
ユ さと(す) ㊔ さとし ゆう さとる

149	Nonstandard	U2F9D0
言	S16-7-9	F0000

traditional form → see 諭 at 2012

謎

1-7-9

incorrect stroke-count
➡ see 1-7-10: 言 at 2047

頭

2019
1-7-9

▶HEAD
トウ ズ ト あたま かしら -がしら かぶり*
㊔ かみ つむり
Ⓒ 头 tóu

181	Jōyō-2	U982D
頁	S16-9-7	F0191

(stroke order 1–16)

COMPOUNDS

❶ [original meaning] HEAD
頭骨 とうこつ skull
頭部 とうぶ head
頭囲 とうい head measurement
頭痛 ずつう headache
頭脳 ずのう brain; brains, head
羊頭狗肉 ようとうくにく using a better name to sell inferior goods, crying wine and selling vinegar
没頭する ぼっとうする be absorbed in
出頭する しゅっとうする attend, present oneself

❷ (person in a leading position) **HEAD, chief, leader**
頭目 とうもく chief, head, boss
頭取 とうどり (bank) president; greenroom manager
頭領 とうりょう head, chief, boss
教頭 きょうとう head teacher, vice principal

❸ⓐ (upper end) **HEAD, top**
ⓑ **beginning**
a 喉頭 こうとう larynx
弾頭 だんとう warhead
先頭 せんとう forefront, head, top
毛頭 もうとう (not) in the least, (not) a bit
b 頭注 とうちゅう headnote
冒頭 ぼうとう beginning, opening
年頭 ねんとう beginning of the year
音頭 おんど leading (in singing); folk song

❹ **vicinity, front**
店頭 てんとう shop [store] front
街頭で がいとうで in the streets
念頭 ねんとう mind, thoughts

❺ⓐ counter for large animals, esp. cattle; **HEAD** (of cattle)
ⓑ number of persons
a 頭数 とうすう number of heads
牛五頭 うしごとう five head of cattle
b 人頭税 じんとうぜい(=にんとうぜい) poll tax, capitation (tax)

INDEPENDENT

【ず 頭】**HEAD**
頭が高い ずがたかい hold one's head high, be haughty

KUN

【あたま 頭】
①ⓐ **HEAD**
ⓑ **hair of the HEAD**
ⓒ (intellectual faculty) **HEAD, brains, intelligence**
a 頭が痛い あたまがいたい have a headache
b 頭を刈る あたまをかる cut one's hair
c 頭の良い子 あたまのいいこ bright [intelligent] child

② **consideration, mind**
頭に入れる あたまにいれる keep in mind

③ⓐ (upper end) **HEAD, top**
ⓑ beginning
a 頭打ち あたまうち (of stocks) hit the top [ceiling]
b 頭金 あたまきん down payment
頭から あたまから from the beginning

④ (person in a leading position) **HEAD**, chief, leader
頭株 あたまかぶ chief, leader

⑤ **number of persons**
頭数 あたまかず number of persons, head count

頭割り あたまわり sharing, capitation

【かしら 頭】**HEAD; chief, leader, master; top, first place; head of a puppet used in *bunraku;* top radical of a Chinese character, crown radical**
頭文字 かしらもじ capital letter, initials
頭遣い かしらつかい puppeteer for the head
尾頭付き おかしらつき fish served whole [complete with head and tail]
旗頭 はたがしら leader, boss
人の頭に立つ ひとのかしらにたつ stand at the head of others
網頭 あみがしら *amigashira,* 'net' radical (⺫)

【-がしら -頭】
① **HEAD, top, end**
波頭 なみがしら wave crest
目頭 めがしら eyes

② [also suffix] person in the leading position
稼ぎ頭 かせぎがしら biggest earner
出世頭 しゅっせがしら the most successful

③ the moment
出会い頭に であいがしらに upon meeting suddenly, as one passes by

【かぶり 頭】**HEAD**
頭を振る かぶりをふる shake one's head (in denial)

SYNONYMS

❶ **head**
頭 HEAD → 2019
首 HEAD → 2818
脳 BRAIN → 1227

❷ **leaders**
主 MASTER → 2437
王 KING → 4247
長 CHIEF → 3163
頭 HEAD → 2019
首 LEADER → 2818
領 leader → 1567
魁 LEADER → 4125

❸ⓐ **tops**
上 upper part → 4212
頂 SUMMIT → 0164
頭 HEAD → 2019

❺ⓐ **counters for animals**
匹 COUNTER FOR ANIMALS → 3680
頭 counter for large animals → 2019
羽 counter for birds → 0265
疋 counter for animals → 4292

NOTE

➡ see COMPOUND FORMATION for 羊頭狗肉 ようとうくにく → 羊 2708

豬

2020

1-7-9

▶**WILD BOAR**

チョ いのしし い ㊔ いの しし

152	Nonstandard	U8C6C
豕	S16-7-9	F0000

traditional form → see 猪 at 0652

賭

2021

1-7-9

▶**WAGER**

ト か(ける)

Ⓝ 賭 Ⓒ 赌 dǔ

154	Jōyō	U8CED
貝	S16-7-9	F1705

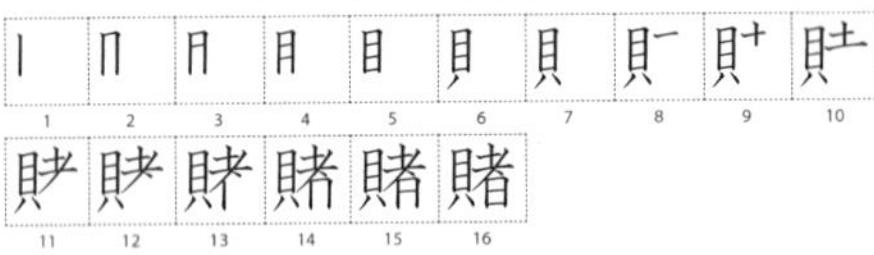

COMPOUNDS

ⓐ **WAGER, bet money**
ⓑ stake (one's life), risk

a 賭博 とばく gambling
賭場 とば gambling den
b 賭する とする stake, risk; bet, wager

KUN

【かける 賭ける】
ⓐ **WAGER, bet money**
ⓑ [usu. 懸ける] **stake (one's life), risk**

a 賭け かけ bet, wager
賭け金 かけきん stakes, bet
賭け事 かけごと betting, gambling
賭け碁 かけご playing go for stakes
金を賭ける かねをかける bet money
b 命を賭ける いのちをかける risk one's life

SYNONYMS

ⓐ **risk**
冒 RISK → 3088
賭 WAGER → 2021
懸 stake → 3632

HOMOPHONES

かける
懸 SUSPEND → 3632
掛 SET → 0596
架 LAY ACROSS → 3178
駆 DRIVE → 2293
翔 SOAR → 1714
かけ 掛 SET → 0596

NOTE

➡ see USAGE note at 掛 0596

蹄

2022

1-7-9

▶**HOOF**

テイ ひづめ

Ⓒ 蹄 tí

157	Names	U8E44
足	S16-7-9	F2739

COMPOUNDS

● [original meaning] **HOOF**
蹄鉄 ていてつ horseshoe
蹄叉 ていさ fourchette
装蹄 そうてい shoeing a horse, horseshoeing
馬蹄 ばてい horse's hooves
口蹄疫 こうていえき foot-and-mouth disease
偶蹄類 ぐうているい artiodactyls

KUN

【ひづめ 蹄】 **HOOF**

SPECIAL READINGS

羊蹄 ぎしぎし Japanese dock, *Rumex japonicus*

SYNONYMS

● **ungual**
爪 NAIL → 3756
蹄 HOOF → 2022

蹈

2023

1-7-9

▶**STEP ON**

トウ

157	Nonstandard	U280BB
足	S16-7-9	F0000

traditional form → see 蹈 at 2055

踴

2024

1-7-9

▶**DANCE**

ヨウ おど(る) おど(り)

157	Nonstandard	U8E34
足	S16-7-9	F0000

traditional form → see 踊 at 1961

蹈

1-7-9

incorrect stroke-count
➡ see 1-7-10: 𧾷 at 2055

輯

2025

1-7-9

▶**EDIT**

シュウ

Ⓒ 辑 jí

159	Names	U8F2F
車	S16-7-9	F3066

COMPOUNDS

[now replaced by 集 3445]
ⓐ (collect written materials) **EDIT, compile**
ⓑ **EDITion, series**

a 輯録 しゅうろく compilation, editing
編輯する へんしゅうする edit, compile
集輯 しゅうしゅう gather together and compile

b 特輯 とくしゅう special edition
第一輯 だいいっしゅう first series

SYNONYMS

● **compile**
編 COMPILE → 1755
纂 COMPILE → 3393
撰 COMPILE → 0911
集 edit → 3445
輯 EDIT → 2025
著 AUTHOR → 2869

輸

2026
◧ 1-7-9

▶**TRANSPORT**
ユ シュ▲
Ⓝ 輸 Ⓒ 输 shū

159	Jōyō-5	U8F38
車	S16-7-9	F0987

COMPOUNDS

❶ⓐ [original meaning] (transfer by vehicle) **TRANSPORT, ship, carry, convey**
ⓑ **transfer**
a 輸送する ゆそうする transport, convey
運輸 うんゆ transport(ation), conveyance
空輸 くうゆ air transportation
b 輸出 ゆしゅつ export
輸入 ゆにゅう import, importation
輸血 ゆけつ blood transfusion
❷ abbrev. of 輸入 ゆにゅう or 輸出 ゆしゅつ: **import, export**
輸銀 ゆぎん import-export bank
禁輸 きんゆ embargo
直輸 ちょくゆ direct import [export]
密輸 みつゆ smuggling, contraband trade
❸ [rare] lose, be defeated
輸贏× ゆえい(=しゅえい) gain or loss

INDEPENDENT

【ゆする 輸する】**TRANSPORT**, carry; give, yield; be defeated

SYNONYMS

❶ⓐ **carry**
運 CARRY → 3894
搬 CARRY → 0795
輸 TRANSPORT → 2026

NOTE

★ do not confuse with 輪 WHEEL → 1999

輸

2027
◧ 1-7-9

▶**TRANSPORT**
ユ シュ

159	Nonstandard	U2F9DF
車	S16-7-9	F0000

traditional form → see 輸 at 2026

辦

2028
◧ 1-7-9

▶**DISPOSE OF**
ベン
Ⓒ 办 bàn

160	Non-Jōyō	U8FA6
辛	S16-7-9	F0000

COMPOUNDS

● [now replaced by 弁 2497] [original meaning] **DISPOSE OF, manage, attend to**
合辦 ごうべん joint management [venture]

SYNONYMS

● **deal with**
扱う HANDLE → 0251
処 DEAL WITH → 3764
辦 DISPOSE OF → 2028
措 dispose of → 0610
置 take proper steps → 3222

辯

2029
◧ 1-7-9

▶**SPEAK ELOQUENTLY**
▶**VALVE**
ベン わきま(える)

160	Nonstandard	U8FA8
辛	S16-7-9	F0000

traditional form → see 弁 at 2497

辧

2030
◧ 1-7-9

▶**SPEAK ELOQUENTLY**
▶**VALVE**
ベン わきま(える)

18	Nonstandard	U8FA7
刀	S16-2-14	F0000

traditional form → see 弁 at 2497

醍

2031
◧ 1-7-9

▶**CREAM**
ダイ
Ⓒ 醍 tí

164	Names	U918D
酉	S16-7-9	F2511

COMPOUNDS

● [archaic] **CREAM** made from butter—now used only in 醍醐 だいご
醍醐 だいご cream made from butter; *Buddhism* the best taste, the finest thing in this world
醍醐味 だいごみ the best, the epitome

SYNONYMS

● **dairy products**

酪 DAIRY PRODUCTS → 1940
乳 MILK → 1823
醍 CREAM → 2031
醐 CREAM → 2032

醐

2032
1-7-9

▶**CREAM**
ゴ
Ⓒ 醐 hú

164	Names	U9190
酉	S16-7-9	F2518

COMPOUNDS

● [archaic] **CREAM** made from butter—now used only in 醍醐 だいご

醍醐 だいご cream made from butter; *Buddhism* the best taste, the finest thing in this world
醍醐味 だいごみ the best, the epitome

SYNONYMS

● **dairy products**
酪 DAIRY PRODUCTS → 1940
乳 MILK → 1823
醍 CREAM → 2031
醐 CREAM → 2032

醒

2033
1-7-9

▶**AWAKE**
セイ さ(ます)▲ さ(める)▲ ㊔ さめ さむる
Ⓒ 醒 xǐng

164	Jōyō	U9192
酉	S16-7-9	F2047

Stroke order: 1–16

COMPOUNDS

❶ⓐ **AWAKE, wake up**
ⓑ be disillusioned

a 覚醒する かくせいする awake, wake up; be awakened, be disillusioned
半睡半醒 はんすいはんせい half asleep and half awake
警醒 けいせい warning; waking up

❷ **AWAKE** to the Truth, become enlightened

KUN

【さます 醒ます】[also 覚ます] *vt*
① **AWAKE**, wake up
② disillusion
③ make sober

【さめる 醒める】[also 覚める] *vi*
① **AWAKE**, wake up
醒め遣らぬ さめやらぬ lingering (excitement, etc.), not entirely awake
② be disillusioned, come to one's senses
興醒め きょうざめ wet blanket, turnoff
③ become sober
酔い醒め よいざめ sobering up

SYNONYMS

❶ **awake**
悟 AWAKE TO → 0502
醒 AWAKE → 2033
覚 awake → 3217
惺 AWAKE TO → 0709

HOMOPHONES

さめる
覚 PERCEIVE → 3217
冷 COLD → 0088

さます
覚 PERCEIVE → 3217
冷 COLD → 0088

NOTE

➡ see USAGE note at 覚 3217

醗

2034
1-7-9

▶**BREW**
ハツ

164	Nonstandard	U9197
酉	S16-7-9	F0000

traditional form → see 醱 at 2076

頸

2035
1-7-9

▶**NECK**
ケイ くび
Ⓝ 頚 Ⓒ 颈 jǐng gěng

181	Non-Jōyō	U9838
頁	S16-9-7	F2319

COMPOUNDS

ⓐ [original meaning] **NECK**
ⓑ **narrow part, NECK (of a bottle)**

a 頸部 けいぶ neck (region)
頸椎 けいつい cervical vertebrae

KUN

【くび 頸】[now usu. 首]
ⓐ [original meaning] **NECK**
ⓑ **narrow part, NECK (of a bottle)**

a 頸飾り くびかざり necklace
頸木 くびき [also 軛] yoke
b 手頸 てくび wrist
バイオリンの頸 ばいおりんのくび neck of a violin

SYNONYMS

ⓐ **neck**
首 NECK → 2818
頸 NECK → 2035
項 nape → 0692

HOMOPHONES

くび 首 HEAD → 2818

くびき

軛 YOKE → 1873

頸木 → 2035, 4261

NOTE

➡ see USAGE note at 首 2818

穎

2036

◧ 1-7-9

▶GLUME

▶TALENTED

エイ

Ⓝ 頴 Ⓒ 颖 yǐng

115	Non-Jōyō	U7A4E
禾	S16-5-11	F0000

COMPOUNDS

❶ⓐ [original meaning] **GLUME, awn**

ⓑ **tip of a pointed object**

a 穎果 えいか caryopsis

b 穎脱する えいだつする gain recognition, rise above one's fellows

❷ **TALENTED, intelligent, distinguished, outstanding**

穎才 えいさい [now usu. 英才] talent, genius; gifted person, talented person

穎悟 えいご intelligent, shrewd

INDEPENDENT

【えい 穎】**GLUME, awn**

SYNONYMS

❶ **inflorescences**

穂 SPIKE → 1575

穎 GLUME → 2036

❷ **excellent and superior**

優 SUPERIOR → 0200

絶 without match → 1711

卓 PROMINENT → 2561

快 splendid → 0289

妙 MARVELOUS → 0280

秀 EXCELLENT → 3152

英 DISTINGUISHED → 2782

尤 outstanding → 3755

傑 outstanding → 0175

穎 TALENTED → 2036

逸 exceptional → 3872

名 first-rate → 2693

上 of upper grade → 4212

頴

2037

◧ 1-7-9

▶GLUME

▶TALENTED

エイ

181	Nonstandard	U9834
頁	S16-9-7	F0000

traditional form → see 穎 at 2036

頻

2038

◧ 1-7-9

▶FREQUENTLY

ヒン しき(りに)

181	Nonstandard	UFA6A
頁	S16-9-7	F0000

traditional form → see 頻 at 2209

頹

2039

◧ 1-7-9

▶DECLINE

タイ

Ⓝ 頽 Ⓒ 颓 tuí

181	Non-Jōyō	U983D
頁	S16-9-7	F3376

COMPOUNDS

● [now also 退 3838] **DECLINE, decay**

頽勢 たいせい one's declining fortunes, decay

頽廃 たいはい degeneration, decadence, deterioration

頽唐 たいとう decadence, decline

頽齢 たいれい declining years

衰頽 すいたい decline, decay, degeneration

SYNONYMS

● **degenerate**

落 FALL → 2907

衰 DECLINE → 2604

頽 DECLINE → 2039

堕 DEGENERATE → 3501

綻 UNRAVEL → 1745

破 break down → 1478

頹

2040

◧ 1-7-9

▶DECLINE

タイ

181	Nonstandard	U9839
頁	S16-9-7	F0000

traditional form → see 頽 at 2039

頼

2041

◧ 1-7-9

▶RELY ON

▶ASK

ライ たの(む) たの(もしい) たよ(る)

㊔ より

Ⓝ 賴 Ⓒ 赖 lài

154	Jōyō	U983C
貝	S16-7-9	F0456

言 豆 豕 貝 足 車 辛 酉 臣 𠂤 𠂤 歩 秃 【束】 夾

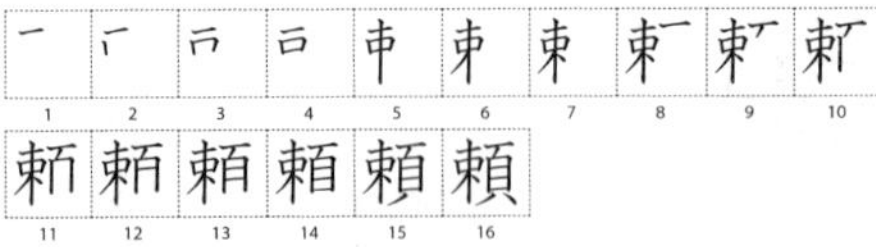

COMPOUNDS

❶ **RELY ON, depend on, trust**

信頼する しんらいする rely on, have confidence, trust in

無頼漢 ぶらいかん villain, scoundrel

❷ **ASK, request**

頼信紙 らいしんし telegraph (application) blank

依頼する いらいする request, make a request; entrust, commission; rely on, depend on

KUN

【たのむ 頼む】 **ASK, request**

頼み たのみ request, favor; reliance, dependence

頼み込む たのみこむ request earnestly

【たのもしい 頼もしい】 **reliable, trustworthy; hopeful**

【たよる 頼る】 **RELY ON, depend on, trust**

頼り たより reliance, dependence, trust; help, support

頼り無い たよりない unreliable, undependable; vague; helpless, forlorn

SYNONYMS

❶ **rely on**

頼 RELY ON → 2041

依 DEPEND ON → 0093

❷ **request**

請 REQUEST → 1983

訴 APPEAL TO → 1901

頼 ASK → 2041

嘱 CHARGE WITH → 0881

要 REQUIRE → 3263

願 ASK A FAVOR → 2320

求 SEEK → 4365

乞 BEG → 2457

賴

2042

1-7-9

▸**RELY ON**
▸**ASK**

ライ たの(む) たの(もしい) たよ(る)

㊔ より

154	Names	U8CF4
貝	S16-7-9	F0000

traditional form → see 頼 at 2041

頬

2043

1-7-9

▸**CHEEK**

キョウ▴ ほお ほほ ㊔ ほ つら

Ⓝ 頰 Ⓒ 颊 jiá

181	Jōyō	U9830
頁	S16-9-7	F1214

COMPOUNDS

● **CHEEK**

頬骨 きょうこつ cheekbone, zygomatic bone

頬筋 きょうきん buccinator (muscle)

KUN

【ほお 頬】 **CHEEK (of the face)**

頬っぺた ほっぺた *colloq* cheek

頬擦り ほおずり nestling one's cheek to another's

頬紅 ほおべに blusher

頬張る ほおばる cram one's mouth (with food)

頬を染める ほおをそめる blush

面頬 めんぽう(=めんぼう) visor, face guard

【ほほ 頬】 same as 頬 ほお

SYNONYMS

● **front parts of head**

顔 FACE → 2277

面 FACE → 2590

額 forehead → 2273

顎 chin → 2276

頬 CHEEK → 2043

吻 PROBOSCIS → 0270

謙

2044

1-7-10

▸**HUMBLE**

ケン へりくだ(る)▴ ㊔ かね

Ⓝ 謙 Ⓒ 谦 qiān

149	Jōyō	U8B19
言	S17-7-10	F1723

COMPOUNDS

● **HUMBLE, modest**

謙遜 けんそん humility, modesty

謙虚な けんきょな humble, modest

謙譲 けんじょう modesty, humility

KUN

【へりくだる 謙る】 [also 遜る] be **HUMBLE**, be modest

SYNONYMS

● **humble**

謙 HUMBLE → 2044

遜 HUMBLE → 4041

拝 HUMBLY → 0360

HOMOPHONES

へりくだる 遜 HUMBLE →4041

NOTE

➡ see USAGE note at 遜 4041

謹

2045

1-7-10

▶RESPECTFULLY

キン つつし(む) ㊔ のり

Ⓝ 謹 Ⓒ 谨 jǐn

149	Jōyō	U8B39
言	S17-7-10	F2385

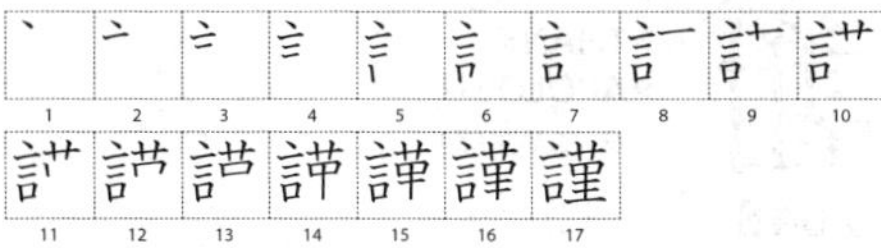

COMPOUNDS

❶ RESPECTFULLY, with respect, reverently; respectful

謹賀新年 きんがしんねん Happy New Year
謹呈する きんていする present, make a present
謹厳な きんげんな stern, grave, solemn
謹告する きんこくする inform with respect, announce respectfully
謹啓 きんけい Dear Sirs, Gentlemen
謹書 きんしょ written respectfully

❷ carefully, attentively, cautiously

謹製 きんせい careful production
謹聴する きんちょうする listen attentively
謹慎 きんしん house arrest, domiciliary confinement; penitence

KUN

【つつしむ 謹む】 [usu. in TE-form] **be respectful, be humble**

謹んで つつしんで respectfully, reverently, humbly

SYNONYMS

❶ respectful

恭 RESPECTFUL →3109
謹 RESPECTFULLY →2045
奉 reverentially →3167
拝 HUMBLY →0360

❷ careful

慎 PRUDENT →0792
謹 carefully →2045
精 meticulous →1729

HOMOPHONES

つつしむ 慎 PRUDENT →0792

NOTE

➡ see USAGE note at 慎 0792

講

2046

1-7-10

▶LECTURE

コウ

Ⓝ 講 Ⓒ 讲 jiǎng

149	Jōyō-5	U8B1B
言	S17-7-10	F0865

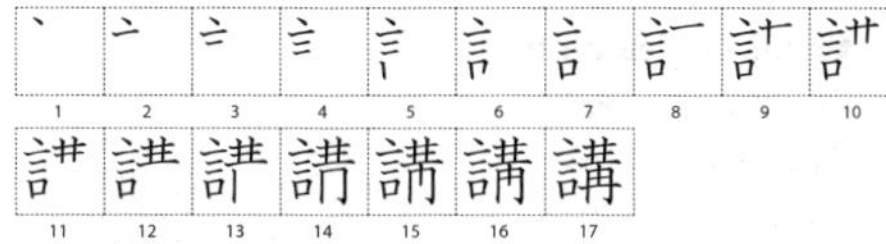

COMPOUNDS

❶ⓐ LECTURE, speak in public
ⓑ LECTURE
ⓒ counter for LECTUREs

a 講演 こうえん lecture
講師 こうし speaker, lecturer
講堂 こうどう lecture hall, auditorium
講座 こうざ lectureship, (professor's) chair; course of study
講壇 こうだん lecture platform
講読する こうどくする read and explain

b 開講する かいこうする begin a series of one's lectures
受講する じゅこうする attend lectures

c 近代文学十講 きんだいぶんがくじっこう Ten Lectures on Modern Literature
第二講 だいにこう second lecture

❷ⓐ expound, explain, interpret
ⓑ speak, tell

a 講義 こうぎ lecture
講話 こうわ lecture, discourse

b 講談 こうだん storytelling, narration; historical narrative

❸ study, practice

講習 こうしゅう short training course
講武 こうぶ military training

❹ [formerly also 媾 0782] **make peace, come to terms**

講和する こうわする make peace with, reconcile

❺ⓐ fraternity, religious association
ⓑ mutual financing association

a 講社 こうしゃ religious association, fraternity
講中 こうじゅう religious association (of non-Christians); club

b 恵比須講 えびすこう fête in honor of *Ebisu*
頼母子講 たのもしこう mutual financing association

INDEPENDENT

【こう 講】 mutual financing association

無尽の講 むじんのこう mutual financing association

【こうじる(=こうずる) 講じる(=講ずる)】 LECTURE, give a lecture; devise, think out

手段を講じる しゅだんをこうじる take steps [measures]

SYNONYMS

❶ⓐ **speak in public**
講 LECTURE →2046
演 make a speech →0855
ⓑ **units of learning**
課 LESSON →1980
科 course →1463
講 LECTURE →2046
❷ **explain**
説 EXPLAIN →1949
明 make clear →1060
釈 ELUCIDATE →1876
詮 EXPOUND →1923
講 expound →2046
解 CLARIFY →1913
注 annotate →0383
❺ **organized bodies**
会 SOCIETY →2512
協 association →0103
団 BODY →3791
体 BODY →0080
組 union →1693
労 workers' union →3155
連 federation →3849
講 fraternity →2046
院 INSTITUTION →0544

謎 2047

▸RIDDLE
メイ▲ なぞ
Ⓝ 謎◈ Ⓒ 谜 mí mèi
1-7-10

149	Jōyō	U8B0E
言	S17-7-10	F1585

COMPOUNDS

● **RIDDLE, puzzle, enigma**
謎語 めいご mysterious words, enigma

KUN

【なぞ 謎】
ⓐ **RIDDLE, puzzle**
ⓑ **enigma, mystery**
a 謎謎 なぞなぞ riddle, puzzle
謎解き なぞとき solution of a riddle
謎掛け なぞかけ a word play in which a pun is played to connect two seemingly unrelated things or statements
b 謎めく なぞめく be enigmatic or puzzling, be wrapped in mystery
謎を解く なぞをとく solve a mystery

SYNONYMS

【なぞ】
ⓐ **question**
題 PROBLEM →4139
問 QUESTION (inquiry) →4117
論 question (issue) →1981
謎 RIDDLE →2047

謝 2048

▸THANK
▸APOLOGIZE
シャ あやま(る)
Ⓒ 谢 xiè
1-7-10

149	Jōyō-5	U8B1D
言	S17-7-10	F1094

COMPOUNDS

❶ⓐ **THANK, be grateful**
ⓑ **monetary gift of THANKs, remuneration, reward, fee**
a 謝恩 しゃおん expression of gratitude
感謝 かんしゃ gratitude, thanks
b 謝礼 しゃれい remuneration, reward; thanks
月謝 げっしゃ monthly fee
薄謝 はくしゃ small remuneration, small token of gratitude
❷ **APOLOGIZE**
謝罪 しゃざい apology
陳謝 ちんしゃ apology
❸ decline, refuse
謝絶する しゃぜつする decline, refuse
❹ fade, wither, atrophy
代謝(=新陳代謝) たいしゃ(=しんちんたいしゃ) metabolism; renewal, regeneration
❺ [formerly 藉 3017] console, solace
慰謝料 いしゃりょう consolation money

INDEPENDENT

【しゃする 謝する】THANK; apologize; decline

KUN

【あやまる 謝る】APOLOGIZE
謝り あやまり apology, excuse
平謝り ひらあやまり humble apology

SYNONYMS

❶ⓐ **thanking and gratitude**
謝 THANK →2048

礼 thanks → 1012
恩 DEBT OF GRATITUDE → 3289
❻ **monetary gifts**
謝 monetary gift of thanks → 2048
礼 monetary gift → 1012
❷ **apologize**
謝 APOLOGIZE → 2048
詫びる APOLOGIZE → 1927

USAGE

【あやまる】
謝る
apologize
誤る
① [formerly also 謬る] mistake, make a mistake, err
② mislead, lead astray
謬る
[now usu. 誤る] mistake, make a mistake, err

HOMOPHONES

あやまる
誤 MISTAKE → 1945
謬 MISTAKE → 2060

COMPOUND FORMATION

【代謝(=新陳代謝) たいしゃ(=しんちんたいしゃ)】
代謝 'metabolism, etc.' is the replacing (代) of what has atrophied (謝 ❹).

譁

▶BOISTEROUS
カ

149	Nonstandard	U8B41
言	S17-7-10	F0000

2049
◧ 1-7-10 traditional form → see 嘩 at 0771

謙

▶HUMBLE
ケン へりくだ(る) ㊔ かね

149	Nonstandard	U8B19
言	S17-7-10	F0000

2050
◧ 1-7-10 traditional form → see 謙 at 2044

講

▶LECTURE
コウ

149	Nonstandard	U8B1B
言	S17-7-10	F0000

2051
◧ 1-7-10 traditional form → see 講 at 2046

謠

▶POPULAR SONG
ヨウ うたい うた(う)

149	Names	U8B20
言	S17-7-10	F0000

2052
◧ 1-7-10 traditional form → see 謡 at 2011

購

▶PURCHASE
コウ
Ⓝ 購 Ⓒ 购 gòu

2053
◧ 1-7-10

154	Jōyō	U8CFC
貝	S17-7-10	F1436

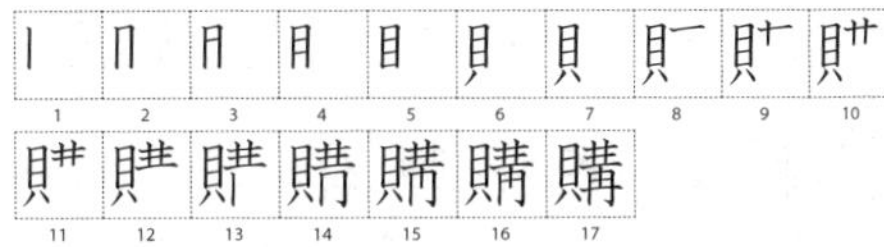

COMPOUNDS

● [original meaning] **PURCHASE, buy**
購買 こうばい purchase, buying
購読 こうどく subscription
購入 こうにゅう purchase, buying
購書 こうしょ purchasing books; purchased books

SYNONYMS

● **buy**
買 BUY → 3211
購 PURCHASE → 2053

購

▶PURCHASE
コウ

154	Nonstandard	U8CFC
貝	S17-7-10	F0000

2054
◧ 1-7-10 traditional form → see 購 at 2053

蹈

▶STEP ON
トウ
Ⓝ 蹈 Ⓒ 蹈 dǎo

2055
◧ 1-7-10

157	Non-Jōyō	U8E48
足	S17-7-10	F0000

COMPOUNDS

❶ [original meaning] **STEP ON, tread**
舞蹈(=舞踏) ぶとう dancing
❷ [now usu. 踏 1997] follow, pursue
蹈襲する とうしゅうする follow, follow suit

SPECIAL READINGS

蹈鞴× たたら foot bellows
蹈鞴×を踏む たたらをふむ totter

SYNONYMS

❶ **step on**
踏 TREAD → 1997
蹈 STEP ON → 2055
藉 TRAMPLE ON → 3017

轄

2056

1-7-10

▶EXERCISE JURISDICTION OVER

カツ

Ⓝ 轄 Ⓒ 辖 xiá

159	Jōyō	U8F44
車	S17-7-10	F2193

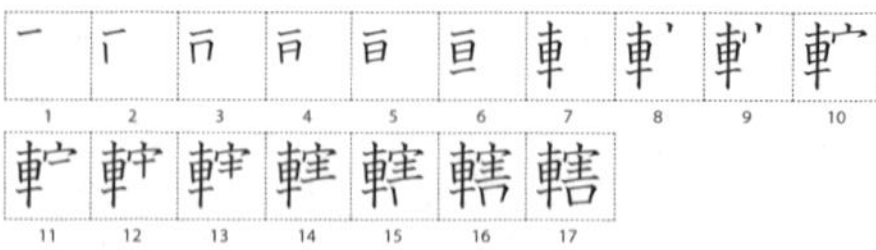

COMPOUNDS

❶ **EXERCISE [have] JURISDICTION OVER, control, supervise, administer**

統轄 とうかつ general control, control and jurisdiction

管轄 かんかつ jurisdiction, control

直轄 ちょっかつ direct jurisdiction [control], immediate supervision

分轄 ぶんかつ separate control [jurisdiction]

所轄 しょかつ jurisdiction

❷ [original meaning, now archaic] wedge

車轄 しゃかつ linchpin

SYNONYMS

❶ **direct and supervise**

制 CONTROL →1624

理 manage →1220

経 MANAGE →1687

管 EXERCISE CONTROL →3349

轄 EXERCISE JURISDICTION OVER →2056

掌 TAKE CHARGE OF →3215

監 OVERSEE →3535

督 SUPERVISE →3471

司 OFFICIATE →3648

宰 PRESIDE →2829

営 MANAGE →3216

轄

2057

1-7-10

▶EXERCISE JURISDICTION OVER

カツ

159	Nonstandard	U8F44
車	S17-7-10	F0000

traditional form →see 轄 at 2056

醜

2058

1-7-10

▶UGLY

シュウ みにく(い) しこ▲

Ⓒ 丑 chǒu

164	Jōyō	U919C
酉	S17-7-10	F1974

COMPOUNDS

❶ **UGLY, bad-looking, unsightly**

醜悪な しゅうあくな ugly, repulsive

醜女 しゅうじょ ugly woman

美醜 びしゅう beauty or ugliness

❷ disgraceful, dishonorable, indecent

醜行 しゅうこう disgraceful [scandalous] conduct

醜聞 しゅうぶん scandal, ill fame

醜態 しゅうたい disgraceful behavior, shameful conduct

INDEPENDENT

【しゅう 醜】 ugliness; disgrace

醜と美 しゅうとび ugliness and beauty

KUN

【みにくい 醜い】 **UGLY, bad-looking; ignoble, disgraceful, mean**

醜さ みにくさ ugliness

醜い女 みにくいおんな ugly [homely] woman

醜い争い みにくいあらそい scandalous dispute

【しこ 醜】 [in compounds] *elegant*

ⓐ ugliness

ⓑ term of humility

a 醜女 しこめ ugly woman

b 醜の御楯 しこのみたて the humble shield of our Sovereign Lord

臨

2059

1-7-11

▶BE PRESENT AT

リン のぞ(む)

Ⓝ 臨◆ Ⓒ 临 lín

131	Jōyō-6	U81E8
臣	S18-7-11	F1313

COMPOUNDS

❶ⓐ **BE PRESENT AT, be on the spot, attend, come to, visit**

ⓑ (of a ruler or superior) descend upon, come down upon, arrive

a 臨床医 りんしょうい clinician

臨席 りんせき presence, attendance

臨場 りんじょう presence, attendance; visit

臨検 りんけん spot inspection, raid

臨在 りんざい presence

来臨 らいりん attendance, presence; visit

b 君臨する くんりんする reign, rule over, dominate

❷ⓐ on the point of, on the verge of, face to face with

ⓑ abbrev. of 臨時 りんじ: temporary, provisional

a 臨時の りんじの temporary, provisional, special

臨終 りんじゅう hour of death, one's last moment

臨界点 りんかいてん critical point [temperature]

臨機応変 りんきおうへん adaptation to circumstances

b 臨休 りんきゅう extra [special] holiday

❸ [original meaning] overlook, look down on, face

臨海学校 りんかいがっこう seaside school

臨港の りんこうの facing [along] the harbor

❹ copy, imitate

臨写 りんしゃ copying

KUN

【のぞむ 臨む】

① **BE PRESENT AT, be on the spot, attend, come to, visit**

会合に臨む かいごうにのぞむ be present at a meeting

② come face to face, meet, be confronted with

別れに臨んで わかれにのぞんで at parting (with)

③ overlook, face, border on

海に臨んだホテル うみにのぞんだほてる hotel on the sea

SYNONYMS

❶ⓐ attend

臨 BE PRESENT AT → 2059

登 attend → 3208

出 appear → 4310

❶ⓐ exist and be

在 BE → 3704

存 EXIST → 3702

有 exist → 3703

居 be present → 3822

臨 BE PRESENT AT → 2059

也 CLASSICAL COPULA → 4214

❷ⓐ on the verge of

-掛かる be on the verge of → 0596

将 on the verge of → 0551

-際 on the verge of → 0874

臨 on the point of → 2059

HOMOPHONES

のぞむ 望 HOPE → 3408

NOTE

➡ see USAGE note at 望 3408

謬

▶MISTAKE

ビュウ あやま(る)

Ⓝ 謬 Ⓒ 谬 miù

2060

1-7-11

149	Non-Jōyō	U8B2C
言	S18-7-11	F0000

COMPOUNDS

ⓐ MISTAKE, make a mistake, err

ⓑ wrong, MISTAKEn, false

ab 謬説 びゅうせつ fallacy, mistaken opinion

謬見 びゅうけん wrong view, mistaken notion

謬伝 びゅうでん false report [rumor]

誤謬 ごびゅう mistake, error, fallacy

KUN

【あやまる 謬る】[now usu. 誤る] **MISTAKE, make a mistake, err**

謬り あやまり mistake, error, slip

SYNONYMS

ⓐ mistakes and mistaking

過 error → 3891

失 SLIP → 4325

誤 MISTAKE → 1945

謬 MISTAKE → 2060

錯 mistaken → 2187

-違える mis- → 3907

HOMOPHONES

あやまる

誤 MISTAKE → 1945

謝 THANK → 2048

NOTE

➡ see USAGE note at 謝 2048

謳

▶EXTOL

オウ うた(う)

Ⓝ 謳 Ⓒ 讴 ōu

2061

1-7-11

149	Non-Jōyō	U8B33
言	S18-7-11	F2467

COMPOUNDS

● [original meaning] **sing (a tune)**

謳歌する おうかする glorify, eulogize, applaud

KUN

【うたう 謳う】

ⓐ (sing the joys of) **EXTOL, eulogize**

ⓑ **declare, state, express**

ab 謳われる うたわれる be famous for

b 謳い文句 うたいもんく catchphrase, promotional line

SYNONYMS

● praise

賛 PRAISE → 3484

頌 EULOGIZE →1319
謳 EXTOL →2061
讃 PRAISE →2093
美 regard as beautiful →2817
褒 COMMEND →2662
嘉 commend (esp. an inferior) →2953
彰 PROCLAIM MERITS →2337
称 acclaim →1491
賞 express admiration →3237
揚 EXALT →0722

HOMOPHONES

うたう
歌 SONG →2296
謡 POPULAR SONG →2011
唄 DITTY →0477

NOTE

➡ see USAGE note at 歌 2296

謬 2062

1-7-11

▶**MISTAKE**

ビュウ　あやま(る)

149	Nonstandard	U8B2C
言	S18-7-11	F0000

traditional form →see 謬 at 2060

謹 2063

1-7-11

▶**RESPECTFULLY**

キン　つつし(む) ㊔ のり

149	Names	UFA63
言	S18-7-11	F0000

traditional form →see 謹 at 2045

贈 2064

1-7-11

▶**PRESENT A GIFT**

ゾウ　ソウ　おく(る)

Ⓝ 贈 Ⓒ 赠 zèng

154	Jōyō	U8D08
貝	S18-7-11	F1583

COMPOUNDS

❶ **PRESENT A GIFT, give a present**
贈答品 ぞうとうひん present, gift
贈呈 ぞうてい presentation
贈与 ぞうよ donation, presentation
贈賄 ぞうわい bribery, corruption
寄贈 きぞう(=きそう) donation, presentation

❷ confer a rank posthumously
贈位する ぞういする confer a posthumous rank
遺贈 いぞう testation, bequest

INDEPENDENT

【ぞう 贈】presentation; conferment
贈中村先生 ぞうなかむらせんせい presented to Prof. Nakamura

KUN

【おくる 贈る】

① **present (a gift), give (a present)**
贈り物 おくりもの present, gift
花を贈る はなをおくる give flowers as a gift

② bestow on, confer upon
死後に位を贈る しごにくらいをおくる confer a posthumous rank

SYNONYMS

❶ **give**
与 GIVE →4229
呈 PRESENT →2715
進 present to a superior →3873
上 give (to superior or others) →4212
下 give (to inferior or speaker) →4186
呉れる give (to speaker) →3156
授 CONFER →0595
賜 DEIGN TO GIVE →1994
贈 PRESENT A GIFT →2064
賄 BRIBE →1931
賂 BRIBE →1930

HOMOPHONES

おくる 送 SEND →3837

NOTE

➡ see USAGE note at 送 3837

蹟 2065

1-7-11

▶**TRACE**

セキ　あと

Ⓒ 迹 jì

157	Names	U8E5F
足	S18-7-11	F2351

COMPOUNDS

[now usu. 跡 1937]

❶ⓐ [original meaning] (mark left by something) **TRACE(s), track, mark, footprint, trail**
ⓑ (sign of former presence) **TRACEs, ruins, remains**

a 筆蹟 ひっせき handwriting, holograph
手蹟 しゅせき holograph, calligraphic specimen
真蹟 しんせき genuine handwriting

b 遺蹟 いせき ruins, remains
古蹟 こせき historic remains; ruins
史蹟 しせき historic spot [remains]
旧蹟 きゅうせき historic spot

❷ **sign, indication, phenomenon**
奇蹟 きせき miracle, wonder

KUN

【あと 蹟】[now replaced by 跡]
ⓐ (mark left by something) **TRACE**(s), track, mark, footprint, trail, sign
ⓑ (sign of former presence) ruins, remains, aftermath

SYNONYMS

❶ⓐ marks and signs
標 MARK (identifying sign) → 1347
徽 EMBLEM → 0968
痕 SCAR → 4066
印 MARK (visible sign) → 1023
跡 TRACE → 1937
蹟 TRACE → 2065
踪 FOOTPRINTS → 1996
紋 print → 1651
符 SYMBOL → 3299
号 SIGN → 2675
栞 BOOKMARK → 3285

HOMOPHONES

あと
後 AFTER → 0431
跡 TRACE → 1937
痕 SCAR → 4066

NOTE

➡ see USAGE note at 後 0431

轉

2066
1-7-11

▶**TURN**
テン ころ(がる) ころ(げる) ころ(がす) ころ(ぶ) ㊔ うたた

159	Names	U8F49
車	S18-7-11	F0000

traditional form → see 転 at 1872

鵜

2067
1-7-11

▶**CORMORANT**
テイ う
Ⓒ 鹈 tí

196	Names	U9D5C
鳥	S18-11-7	F2082

KUN

【う 鵜】CORMORANT
鵜呑み うのみ accepting (a story) unthinkingly; swallowing whole
鵜飼い うかい cormorant fishing; cormorant fisherman
鵜匠 うしょう cormorant fisherman
鵜の目鷹の目 うのめたかのめ eyes of a predator, keen eyes
川鵜(=河鵜) かわう great cormorant

SYNONYMS

【う】
◯ **birds**
鷹 HAWK → 3955
鷗 GULL → 2370
烏 CROW → 4088
雀 SPARROW → 3117
燕 SWALLOW → 3142
鴻 LARGE WILD BIRD → 0977
鳳 MALE PHOENIX → 3749
凰 FEMALE PHOENIX → 3738
鵬 MYTHICAL HUGE BIRD → 1416
鶏 CHICKEN → 2221
酉 ROOSTER → 4358
隼 FALCON → 3427
鳩 PIGEON → 0184
鷲 EAGLE → 3598
鳶 BLACK KITE → 3919
鶴 CRANE → 2326
鷺 HERON → 3621
鵜 CORMORANT → 2067
鴨 DUCK → 1582
雁 WILD GOOSE → 3741

NOTE

➡ see COMPOUND FORMATION for 鵜呑み うのみ → 呑 3059

譜

2068
1-7-12

▶**SYSTEMATIC RECORD**
フ
Ⓝ 譜 Ⓒ 谱 pǔ

149	Jōyō	U8B5C
言	S19-7-12	F1894

COMPOUNDS

❶ [also suffix] **SYSTEMATIC RECORD**, as:
ⓐ record, chronology, chart
ⓑ record of shogi, chess or go
ⓒ family record, genealogy
a 年譜 ねんぷ chronological record
b 棋譜 きふ record of a game of shogi [go]
c 譜代 ふだい successive generations; hereditary Tokugawa daimyo
系譜 けいふ genealogy, family tree
家譜 かふ genealogy, pedigree
皇統譜 こうとうふ Imperial family record
❷ (musical record) **sheet music, musical score, notes**
楽譜 がくふ (sheet of) music, musical score
採譜 さいふ recording a tune in musical notes
暗譜 あんぷ memorizing musical scores
五線譜 ごせんふ staff notation
❸ [also suffix] album

花譜 かふ flower album

INDEPENDENT

【ふ 譜】sheet music, musical score
譜を読む ふをよむ read music

SYNONYMS

❶ **records**
記 written account → 1843
録 RECORD → 2186
譜 SYSTEMATIC RECORD → 2068
誌 records → 1950
史 HISTORY → 4324
伝 biography → 0048

譏

▶**SLANDER**
キ そし(る)
Ⓒ 讥 jī

2069
1-7-12

149	Non-Jōyō	U8B4F
言	S19-7-12	F0000

COMPOUNDS

● [original meaning] **SLANDER, censure, criticize**
譏誹 きひ [archaic] slander, abuse
譏嫌 きげん [now usu. 機嫌] mood, temper, disposition; health

KUN

【そしる 譏る】[usu. 誹る] **SLANDER, libel, criticize**
譏り そしり criticism

SYNONYMS

● **disgrace**
恥 SHAME → 1664
羞 shame → 4106
辱 HUMILIATE → 3400
侮 INSULT → 0091
罵 ABUSE → 3233
汚 defile → 0258
誹 SLANDER → 1978
譏 SLANDER → 2069

HOMOPHONES

そしる 誹 SLANDER → 1978

NOTE

➡ see COMPOUND FORMATION for 機嫌 きげん → 機 1365

識

▶**DISCRIMINATE**
▶**KNOWLEDGE**
シキ ㊔ さとる のり
Ⓒ 识 shí zhì

2070
1-7-12

149	Jōyō-5	U8B58
言	S19-7-12	F0434

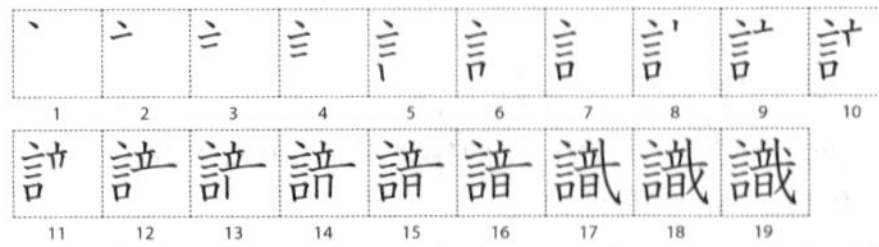

COMPOUNDS

❶ⓐ **DISCRIMINATE, discern, recognize**
ⓑ **power of discrimination, discernment**
ⓒ *Buddhism* consciousness
a 識別する しきべつする discriminate, discern, recognize
認識 にんしき cognition, perception; understanding
鑑識する かんしきする identify, judge; discern
眼識 がんしき insight, discrimination
b 意識する いしきする be conscious of, be aware of
c 六識 ろくしき six consciousnesses

❷ **(acquired) KNOWLEDGE, sense, wisdom, learning**
識見 しきけん knowledge, judgment, discernment
知識 ちしき knowledge
常識 じょうしき common sense, common knowledge
良識 りょうしき good sense
有識者 ゆうしきしゃ learned [informed, intellectual] people, the wise
学識 がくしき learning, scholarship

❸ⓐ know, be acquainted with
ⓑ acquaintance
a 識字 しきじ teaching illiterate people how to read
b 面識 めんしき acquaintance
相識の そうしきの mutually acquainted

❹ write down, record
識語 しきご editor's note; preface; postscript

❺ landmark, sign
道路標識 どうろひょうしき signpost

SYNONYMS

❶ⓐ **discriminate**
識 DISCRIMINATE → 2070
弁 distinguish → 2497
分 tell apart → 2466
ⓑ **discernment**
識 power of discrimination → 2070
眼 EYE → 1504

❷ **wisdom**
識 KNOWLEDGE → 2070
知 knowledge → 1446
智 WISDOM → 3458
慧 prajna (transcendental wisdom) → 3485
哲 PHILOSOPHY → 3402

❷ **learning and knowledge**
業 studies → 3227
学 learning → 3162
文 culture → 2458

識 KNOWLEDGE → 2070
知 knowledge → 1446

證

2071
◧ 1-7-12

▶**PROVE**
▶**CERTIFICATE**
ショウ　あかし

149	Nonstandard	U8B49
言	S19-7-12	F0000

traditional form → see 証 at 1899

贈

2072
◧ 1-7-12

▶**PRESENT A GIFT**
ゾウ　ソウ　おく(る)

154	Names	UFA65
貝	S19-7-12	F0000

traditional form → see 贈 at 2064

蹶

2073
◧ 1-7-12

▶**SPRING TO ONE'S FEET**
ケツ
Ⓒ 蹶 jué juě

157	Non-Jōyō	U8E76
足	S19-7-12	F0000

COMPOUNDS

❶ [now also 決 0308] **SPRING TO ONE'S FEET, rouse oneself**
蹶起する けっきする rise to action
蹶然と けつぜんと with a spring; resolutely
❷ [original meaning, now archaic] stumble, fall over
顛蹶する てんけつする stumble and fall

SYNONYMS

❶ **jump**
跳 JUMP → 1934
躍 LEAP → 2090
蹶 SPRING TO ONE'S FEET → 2073

蹴

2074
◧ 1-7-12

▶**KICK**
シュウ　シュク▲　け(る)　け-
Ⓒ 蹴 cù jiù

157	Jōyō	U8E74
足	S19-7-12	F1531

COMPOUNDS

● **KICK**
蹴球 しゅうきゅう soccer
一蹴する いっしゅうする kick; defeat easily; reject [turn down] flatly

KUN

【ける 蹴る】
ⓐ **KICK**
ⓑ **reject**
a 蹴り けり kick
蹴り上げる けりあげる kick up
飛び蹴り とびげり flying kick
缶蹴り かんけり kick the can (game)
踏んだり蹴ったり ふんだりけったり It never rains but it pours
b 縁談を蹴る えんだんをける reject a marriage proposal

【け- 蹴-】[in compounds] **KICK**
蹴散らす けちらす kick about; defeat
蹴飛ばす けとばす kick (away); refuse, reject
蹴落とす けおとす kick down, defeat
蹴鞠 けまり ancient football game
蹴爪 けづめ cockspur
足蹴にする あしげにする kick; treat (someone) badly

SYNONYMS

● **strike**
打 STRIKE → 0224
撲 DEAL A BLOW → 0903
殴 BEAT (strike a person) → 1099
蹴 KICK → 2074
撃 STRIKE → 3552
挌 STRIKE (a person) → 0448
撞 STRIKE (a ball or bell) → 0905
撥ねる strike (knock down) → 0907
当てる HIT → 2701
叩 KNOCK → 0208
拍 BEAT (strike repeatedly) → 0361
搏 BEAT (throb) → 0794

辯

2075
◧ 1-7-12

▶**SPEAK ELOQUENTLY**
▶**VALVE**
ベン　わきま(える)

97	Nonstandard	U74E3
瓜	S19-5-14	F0000

traditional form → see 弁 at 2497

醱

2076
◧ 1-7-12

▶**BREW**
ハツ
Ⓝ 醗 Ⓒ 酦 pō

164	Non-Jōyō	U91B1
酉	S19-7-12	F0000

COMPOUNDS

● [now usu. 発 3174] **BREW, ferment**
醱酵 はっこう fermentation, zymosis

SYNONYMS

● **brew and ferment**
醸 BREW → 2086

醱 BREW → 2076
酵 FERMENT → 1966

觸 2077

▶TOUCH
ショク ふ(れる) さわ(る)

1-7-13

148	Nonstandard	U89F8
角	S20-7-13	F0000

traditional form → see 触 at 1914

議 2078

▶DISCUSS
▶LEGISLATIVE BODY
ギ
Ⓒ 议 yì

1-7-13

149	Jōyō-4	U8B70
言	S20-7-13	F0215

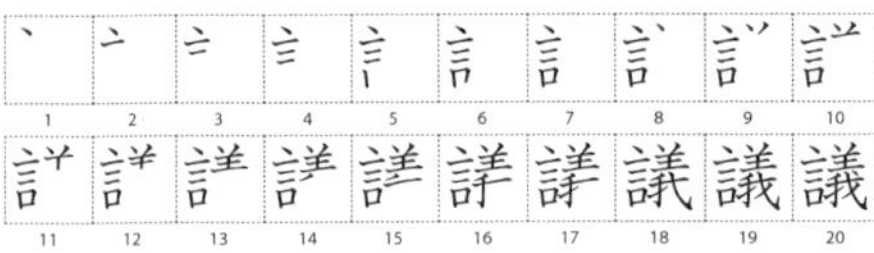

COMPOUNDS

❶ⓐ [original meaning] (talk together) **DISCUSS, consult**
ⓑ (conduct a formal discussion) **DISCUSS, debate, deliberate, argue, propose**

a 議題 ぎだい topic for discussion
議決 ぎけつ decision, resolution
議事 ぎじ proceedings, business
会議 かいぎ conference, meeting, council
審議する しんぎする deliberate, consider, discuss
閣議 かくぎ cabinet conference

b 議論 ぎろん argument, discussion
討議する とうぎする discuss, debate on, deliberate upon
論議する ろんぎする discuss, argue, debate
不思議な ふしぎな strange, mysterious, wonderful
衆議院 しゅうぎいん House of Representatives, Lower House

❷ⓐ [also suffix] **LEGISLATIVE BODY, legislature**
ⓑ abbrev. of 議員 ぎいん: **member of an assembly, assemblyman**

a 議会 ぎかい assembly, national assembly
議員 ぎいん member of an assembly, assemblyman
議長 ぎちょう chairman, president (of the senate)
議場 ぎじょう assembly hall; the House
議院 ぎいん House, Diet Chamber

b 区議 くぎ ward assemblyman
都議 とぎ Metropolitan assemblyman

❸ **proposal, proposition, opinion**
議案 ぎあん bill, measure
決議 けつぎ resolution, decision
異議 いぎ objection, complaint
建議 けんぎ proposal, suggestion

❹ criticize
誹議(=非議)する ひぎする criticize, censure

INDEPENDENT

【ぎ 議】**DISCUSS**ion, debate, deliberation, consultation; proposal
議に上る ぎにのぼる come up for discussion

【ぎする 議する】**DISCUSS**, examine, deliberate; consult, consider

SYNONYMS

❶ **argue and discuss**
議 DISCUSS → 2078
争 CONTEND → 2523
論 ARGUE → 1981
弁 argue (for) → 2497
諏 CONSULT → 1985

❷ⓐ **legislature**
議 LEGISLATIVE BODY → 2078
会 assembly → 2512
院 House → 0544

護 2079

▶PROTECT
ゴ まも(る)▲ ㊔ もり
Ⓝ 護 Ⓒ 护 hù

1-7-13

149	Jōyō-5	U8B77
言	S20-7-13	F0472

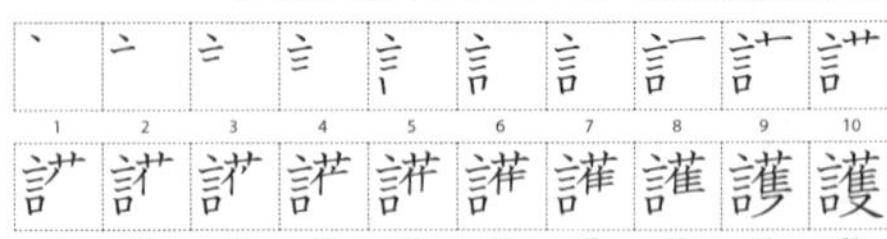

COMPOUNDS

❶ [original meaning] **PROTECT, safeguard, shield, defend**
護衛 ごえい guard, escort
護憲 ごけん safeguarding the constitution
護送 ごそう safeguard, convoy, escort
護身術 ごしんじゅつ art of self-defense
護符 ごふ charm, amulet
守護 しゅご protection, guard, defense, safeguard
保護する ほごする protect, safeguard, preserve, look after
援護 えんご support, protection; covering
弁護する べんごする defend, speak in defense of (another)
看護する かんごする nurse, attend on
擁護する ようごする protect, defend, support, safeguard

❷ used phonetically for *go*
護摩 ごま *homa*, Buddhist rite of cedar-stick burning

KUN

【まもる 護る】[now usu. 守る] **PROTECT, defend, guard, watch over**
身を護る みをまもる defend oneself

SYNONYMS

❶ **protect**
守 PROTECT (by watching over) → 2697
護 PROTECT (by safeguarding) → 2079
庇 PROTECT (by shielding) → 3802
衛 GUARD → 0938
警 GUARD AGAINST → 3595
防 defend → 0320
番 WATCH → 3416
保 PRESERVE → 0107
看 CARE FOR → 3992

HOMOPHONES

まもる 守 PROTECT → 2697

NOTE

➡ see USAGE note at 守 2697

讓

2080
1-7-13

▶**CEDE**
ジョウ ゆず(る) ㊔ まもる
Ⓝ 讓 Ⓒ 让 ràng

149	Jōyō	U8B72
言	S20-7-13	F1465

COMPOUNDS

❶ⓐ **CEDE, transfer, assign, give up, yield**
ⓑ sell, dispose of
a 讓渡 じょうと transfer, conveyance
讓与 じょうよ transfer
讓位 じょうい abdication
委讓 いじょう transfer, assignment
b 分讓 ぶんじょう sale (of land) in lots, lotting-out
❷ **concede, yield to, relinquish**
讓歩 じょうほ concession, compromise
互讓 ごじょう mutual concessions, compromise
❸ modesty, humility
謙讓 けんじょう modesty, humility

KUN

【ゆずる 讓る】**transfer, assign, give up, yield; sell, dispose of; concede, yield to, relinquish; leave, defer, postpone**
讓り渡す ゆずりわたす turn over, convey
讓り合う ゆずりあう compromise, concede
親讓りの おやゆずりの hereditary
安く讓る やすくゆずる sell (a thing) cheap
後日に讓る ごじつにゆずる keep (the matter) for another occasion

SYNONYMS

❶ⓐ **transfer**
讓 CEDE → 2080
渡 hand over → 0746
付 deliver → 0035
附 deliver → 0410
❷ **compromise**
妥 COME TO TERMS → 3053
讓 concede → 2080
媾 MAKE PEACE → 0782

譜

2081
1-7-13

▶**SYSTEMATIC RECORD**
フ

149	Nonstandard	U8B5C
言	S20-7-13	F0000

traditional form → see 譜 at 2068

譯

2082
1-7-13

▶**TRANSLATE**
▶**SENSE**
ヤク わけ

149	Nonstandard	U8B6F
言	S20-7-13	F0000

traditional form → see 訳 at 1865

躁

2083
1-7-13

▶**RESTLESS**
ソウ
Ⓒ 躁 zào

157	Non-Jōyō	U8E81
足	S20-7-13	F3222

COMPOUNDS

● [now also 燥 1392] [original meaning] **RESTLESS, impatient, rash, impetuous**
躁病 そうびょう mania
躁鬱病 そううつびょう manic-depressive psychosis
狂躁(=狂騒) きょうそう wild excitement
焦躁 しょうそう fretfulness, impatience

SYNONYMS

● **impatient**
焦 BE IMPATIENT → 3444
躁 RESTLESS → 2083
燥 restless → 1392

軆

2084
1-7-13

▶**BODY**
▶**FORM**
タイ テイ からだ

158	Nonstandard	U8EC6
身	S20-7-13	F0000

traditional form → see 体 at 0080

辮 2085

▶PLAIT

ベン

Ⓒ 辫 biàn

◧1-7-13

120	Non-Jōyō	U8FAE
糸	S20-6-14	F0000

COMPOUNDS

● [now usu. 弁 2497] **PLAIT, braid**

辮髪 べんぱつ pigtail, queue

SYNONYMS

● **hair**

毛 HAIR (of any kind) → 4264
髪 HAIR (on the head) → 3528
辮 PLAIT → 2085
羽 FEATHER → 0265
眉 EYEBROW → 3991
鬚 BEARD → 3539

● **weave and sew**

織 WEAVE → 1801
紡 SPIN → 1646
績 spin → 1788
縫 SEW → 1781
編 KNIT → 1755
辮 PLAIT → 2085
組 braid → 1693
繡 EMBROIDER → 1805

釀 2086

▶BREW

ジョウ かも(す)

Ⓝ 醸 Ⓒ 酿 niàng

◧1-7-13

164	Jōyō	U91B8
酉	S20-7-13	F2299

COMPOUNDS

● **BREW, make alcoholic beverages**

醸造 じょうぞう brewing; distilling
醸母 じょうぼ yeast, leaven
醸成する じょうせいする brew; bring about

KUN

【かもす 醸す】**BREW; distill; cause, bring about**

醸し出す かもしだす engender, bring about
酒を醸す さけをかもす brew sake
物議を醸す ぶつぎをかもす give rise to hostile comment

SYNONYMS

● **brew and ferment**

醸 BREW → 2086
醱 BREW → 2076
酵 FERMENT → 1966

醵 2087

▶CONTRIBUTE MONEY

キョ

Ⓒ 醵 jù

◧1-7-13

164	Non-Jōyō	U91B5
酉	S20-7-13	F0000

COMPOUNDS

● [now also 拠 0369] **CONTRIBUTE MONEY to a common purpose**

醵出 きょしゅつ donation, contribution
醵金 きょきん contribution, subscription

SYNONYMS

● **donate**

施 give alms → 1103
恵む give charity → 3293
寄 CONTRIBUTE → 2856
醵 CONTRIBUTE MONEY → 2087
献 donate → 2240

釋 2088

▶ELUCIDATE

シャク ㊔ せき

◧1-7-13

165	Nonstandard	U91CB
釆	S20-7-13	F0000

traditional form → see 釈 at 1876

護 2089

▶PROTECT

ゴ まも(る) ㊔ もり

◧1-7-14

149	Nonstandard	U8B77
言	S21-7-14	F0000

traditional form → see 護 at 2079

躍 2090

▶LEAP

ヤク おど(る)

Ⓝ 躍 Ⓒ 跃 yuè

◧1-7-14

157	Jōyō	U8E8D
足	S21-7-14	F1087

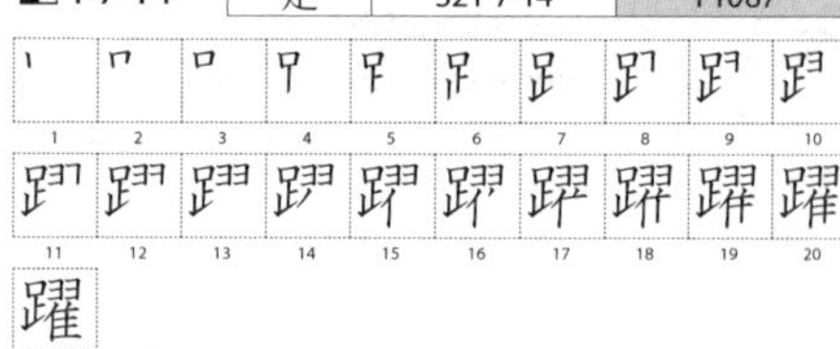

COMPOUNDS

❶ [original meaning] **LEAP, jump up, spring**

躍進する やくしんする make rapid progress, advance by leaps and bounds
飛躍 ひやく leap, jump

一躍 いちやく at a bound, with a jump
跳躍する ちょうやくする jump, leap, spring

❷ **move as if LEAPing with excitement, stir, be active**
躍動する やくどうする move lively, throb
躍如たる やくじょたる vivid, graphic, lifelike
躍起 やっき excitement, enthusiasm, desperation
活躍 かつやく (great) activity, action
暗躍 あんやく secret maneuvers

KUN

【おどる 躍る】
ⓐ **LEAP, jump, bound**
ⓑ (of one's heart) throb, **LEAP**
a 躍り おどり leaping, jumping
躍り上がる おどりあがる spring up, leap to one's feet
躍り込む おどりこむ jump into; rush into

SYNONYMS

❶ **jump**
跳 JUMP → 1934
躍 LEAP → 2090
蹶 SPRING TO ONE'S FEET → 2073

HOMOPHONES

おどる 踊 DANCE → 1961
おどり 踊 DANCE → 1961

NOTE

➡ see USAGE note at 踊 1961

躍 2091

◨ 1-7-14

▶**LEAP**
ヤク おど(る)

157 足	Nonstandard S21-7-14	U8E8D F0000

traditional form → see 躍 at 2090

辯 2092

◨ 1-7-14

▶**SPEAK ELOQUENTLY**
▶**VALVE**
ベン わきま(える)

160 辛	Nonstandard S21-7-14	U8FAF F0000

traditional form → see 弁 at 2497

讃 2093

◨ 1-7-15

▶**PRAISE**
サン たた(える) ㊔ ささ
N 讃 C 赞 zàn

149 言	Names S22-7-15	U8B83 F2110

COMPOUNDS

❶ [now usu. 賛 3484] [original meaning] **PRAISE, laud, admire, commend**
讃嘆 さんたん praise, admiration
讃辞 さんじ eulogy, praise, compliment
讃美歌 さんびか hymn, psalm
和讃 わさん Japanese translation of Buddhist hymns of praise
賞讃(=称讃)する しょうさんする praise, laud, admire

❷ [now replaced by 賛 3484] legend or inscription on a picture
画讃 がさん legend [writing] on a picture
自画自讃 じがじさん painting with the eulogy written in by the artist himself; self-praise

❸ abbrev. of 讃岐 さぬき, old name for Kagawa Prefecture
土讃線 どさんせん Dosan Line (Kochi-Kagawa Railway)

INDEPENDENT

【さん 讃】 legend or inscription on a picture; a style of Chinese poetry

KUN

【たたえる 讃える】 **PRAISE, laud, admire, commend**

SYNONYMS

❶ **praise**
賛 PRAISE → 3484
頌 EULOGIZE → 1319
謳 EXTOL → 2061
讃 PRAISE → 2093
美 regard as beautiful → 2817
褒 COMMEND → 2662
嘉 commend (esp. an inferior) → 2953
彰 PROCLAIM MERITS → 2337
称 acclaim → 1491
賞 express admiration → 3237
揚 EXALT → 0722

USAGE

【たたえる】
讃える
praise, laud, admire, commend
称える
praise, extol

HOMOPHONES

たたえる 称 APPELLATION → 1491

讀 2094

◨ 1-7-15

▶**READ**
ドク トク トウ よ(む) -よ(み)

149 言	Nonstandard S22-7-15	U8B80 F0000

traditional form → see 読 at 1943

轢 2095

▶RUN OVER

レキ ひ(く)

Ⓒ 轹 lì

1-7-15

159	Non-Jōyō	U8F62
車	S22-7-15	F2609

COMPOUNDS

❶ [original meaning] **RUN OVER (with a vehicle), knock down**

轢死 れきし being killed by a train or automobile

轢断する れきだんする cut in two under train wheels

❷ **creak, squeak; grate**

軋×轢 あつれき friction, discord, strife

KUN

【ひく 轢く】**RUN OVER (with a vehicle), knock down**

轢き逃げ ひきにげ hit-and-run

轢き殺す ひきころす kill by running over

SYNONYMS

❶ **overturn**

覆 OVERTURN →3386

翻 TURN OVER →2391

反 turn over →3663

顛 TURN [roll] OVER →2317

転 turn [roll] over →1872

倒 TOPPLE →0139

轢 RUN OVER →2095

HOMOPHONES

ひく

引 DRAW →0207

弾 PROJECTILE →0697

退 RETREAT →3838

惹 DRAW ATTENTION →2903

挽 GRIND →0511

牽 DRAW →2621

曳 DRAW →4348

NOTE

➡ see USAGE note at 引 0207

讓 2096

▶CEDE

ジョウ ゆず(る) ㊔ まもる

1-7-17

149	Names	U8B93
言	S24-7-17	F0000

traditional form → see 譲 at 2080

釀 2097

▶BREW

ジョウ かも(す)

1-7-17

164	Names	U91C0
酉	S24-7-17	F0000

traditional form → see 醸 at 2086

讚 2098

▶PRAISE

サン たた(える) ㊔ ささ

1-7-19

149	Nonstandard	U8B9A
言	S26-7-19	F0000

traditional form → see 讃 at 2093

針 2099

▶NEEDLE

シン はり

Ⓒ 针 zhēn

1-8-2

167	Jōyō-6	U91DD
金	S10-8-2	F1142

1	2	3	4	5	6	7	8	9	10
ノ	𠆢	亼	今	全	令	余	金	金一	針

COMPOUNDS

❶ⓐ [original meaning] **NEEDLE**

ⓑ **NEEDLE-shaped object as the hand of clock or pointer of an instrument**

a 運針 うんしん handling of a needle

b 針葉樹 しんようじゅ conifer

長針 ちょうしん long [minute] hand

秒針 びょうしん second hand

指針 ししん compass needle; indicator, pointer; hand; guiding principle

磁針 じしん magnetic needle

検針 けんしん inspection of a meter

羅針盤 らしんばん compass

避雷針 ひらいしん lightning rod

❷ [formerly also 鍼 2204] **acupuncture**

針術 しんじゅつ acupuncture

針灸 しんきゅう acupuncture and moxibustion

❸ **direction, bearing**

針路 しんろ course, direction

方針 ほうしん course, policy, plan

KUN

【はり 針】

①ⓐ [also suffix] **NEEDLE**

ⓑ **NEEDLE-shaped object as the hand of a clock or pointer of an instrument**

a 針仕事 はりしごと needlework, sewing

針山 はりやま pincushion

針箱 はりばこ needlecase, sewing box

針状の はりじょうの needle-shaped, pointed

針で刺す はりでさす prick with a needle

縫い針 ぬいばり needle

木綿針 もめんばり needle for cotton thread

鉤×針 かぎばり hook, crochet needle

b 針金 はりがね wire

釣り針 つりばり (fish)hook

② sting, sarcasm

針を含んだ言葉 はりをふくんだことば stinging [scathing] words

SYNONYMS

❶ **needle**

針 NEEDLE →2099
刺 prickle →1625
茨 THORN →2812

❶ **perforators**

針 NEEDLE →2099
串 SKEWER →4364
杭 STAKE →1068
釘 NAIL →2100

USAGE

【はり】

針
①ⓐ [also suffix] needle
ⓑ needle-shaped object as the hand of a clock or pointer of an instrument
② sting, sarcasm

鍼
[now also 針]
ⓐ acupuncture
ⓑ acupuncture needle

HOMOPHONES

はり 鍼 ACUPUNCTURE →2204

NOTE

➡ see COMPOUND FORMATION for 羅針盤 らしんばん →羅 3244

釘

2100
1-8-2

▶**NAIL**
テイ くぎ
Ⓒ 钉 dīng dìng

167	Names	U91D8
金	S10-8-2	F2205

COMPOUNDS

❶ **NAIL**

釘頭 ていとう nailhead

❷ [now replaced by 丁 4155] book binding

装釘する そうていする bind (a book)

KUN

【くぎ 釘】NAIL

釘抜き くぎぬき pincers, nail puller
釘付け くぎづけ nailing; pegging; being stationary
釘を差す くぎをさす remind (a person) of, give a warning
五寸釘 ごすんくぎ long nail, spike
木釘 きくぎ wooden peg
目釘 めくぎ rivet on a sword hilt

SYNONYMS

❶ **perforators**

針 NEEDLE →2099
串 SKEWER →4364
杭 STAKE →1068
釘 NAIL →2100

飢

2101
1-8-2

▶**STARVE**
キ う(える)
Ⓝ 飢 Ⓒ 饥 jī

184	Jōyō	U98E2
食	S10-8-2	F1922

1	2	3	4	5	6	7	8	9	10
ノ	𠆢	𠆢	今	今	今	食	食	飣	飢

COMPOUNDS

[formerly also 饑 2281]

ⓐ [original meaning] **STARVE, be hungry, famish**

ⓑ **year of famine**

a 飢餓 きが starvation, hunger, famine
飢民 きみん starving people
飢渇 きかつ hunger and thirst

b 飢饉× ききん famine, failure of crops; shortage

KUN

【うえる 飢える】[formerly also 餓える]

ⓐ **STARVE, be hungry, famish**
ⓑ **hunger [STARVE] for (love), thirst for (knowledge)**

a 飢え うえ hunger, starvation
飢え死に うえじに (death by) starvation

b 愛に飢える あいにうえる hunger [starve] for love

SYNONYMS

ⓐ **hunger and thirst**

渇 THIRST →0627
餓 STARVED →2176
飢 STARVE →2101
饑 STARVE →2281

USAGE

【うえる】

飢える
[formerly also 餓える]
ⓐ starve, be hungry, famish
ⓑ hunger [starve] for (love), thirst for (knowledge)

餓える
[now usu. 飢える] same as 飢える

HOMOPHONES

うえる 餓 STARVED →2176

剤

2102
1-8-2

▶**PREPARATION**
ザイ
Ⓝ 劑 Ⓒ 剂 jì

18	Jōyō	U5264
刂	S10-2-8	F1262

鈫 食 【斉】 音 享 奐 彔 录 罔 者 垂

COMPOUNDS

❶ⓐ [also suffix] [original meaning] **pharmaceutical PREPARATION, drug, medicine**
ⓑ [also suffix] **chemical PREPARATION, chemical**

a 薬剤 やくざい medicine, drugs
調剤する ちょうざいする prepare [compound] medicines
錠剤 じょうざい pill, tablet
ビタミン剤 びたみんざい vitamin preparation
調合剤 ちょうごうざい preparation, mixture
消化剤 しょうかざい digestive, peptic
鎮痛剤 ちんつうざい anodyne, painkiller
b 洗剤 せんざい detergent, cleanser
殺虫剤 さっちゅうざい insecticide, vermicide
酸化防止剤 さんかぼうしざい antioxidant

❷ counter for doses
下剤二剤 げざいにざい two doses of a purgative preparation

SYNONYMS

❶ⓐ **medicines**
薬 DRUG → 3011
剤 PREPARATION → 2102
錠 PILL → 2180
丸 pill suffix → 4225
鍼 ACUPUNCTURE → 2204
灸 MOXIBUSTION → 2752

剖

▶**DISSECT**
ボウ
Ⓒ 剖 pōu

2103
◧1-8-2

18	Jōyō	U5256
刂	S10-2-8	F2293

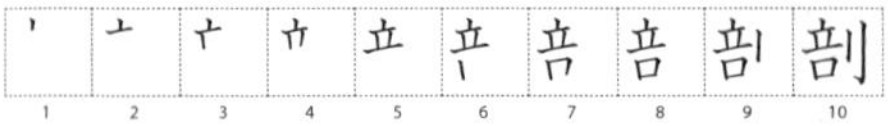

COMPOUNDS

● [original meaning] **DISSECT, cut open, split in two**
剖検 ぼうけん autopsy, necropsy
解剖する かいぼうする dissect, anatomize, hold an autopsy; analyze
解剖学 かいぼうがく anatomy

SYNONYMS

● **cut**
切 CUT → 0030
薙ぐ MOW DOWN → 3010
剪 PRUNE → 2886
削 CUT BY CHIPPING → 1837
挽く GRIND, saw → 0511
断 CUT OFF → 1885
截 CUT OFF → 4092
裁 CUT OUT → 4090
斬 CUT WITH A SWORD → 1874
割 cut with a knife → 2284
剖 DISSECT → 2103
刈る CLIP → 0032
伐 CUT DOWN → 0046

部
◧1-8-2

incorrect stroke-count
➡ see ◧1-8-3: 音 at 2111

郭
◧1-8-2

incorrect stroke-count
➡ see ◧1-8-3: 享 at 2112

剣

▶**SWORD**
ケン つるぎ
Ⓝ 劍 劎◇ 劔◇ Ⓒ 剑 jiàn

2104
◧1-8-2

18	Jōyō	U5263
刂	S10-2-8	F0899

COMPOUNDS

ⓐ [original meaning] **(double-edged) SWORD, sword, blade**
ⓑ **SWORDsmanship, fencing, *kendo***

a 刀剣 とうけん sword
銃剣 じゅうけん bayonet
真剣 しんけん real sword; seriousness
手裏剣 しゅりけん throwing knife
b 剣道 けんどう fencing, swordsmanship, *kendo*
剣客 けんきゃく swordsman, fencer

INDEPENDENT

【けん 剣】**SWORD** (esp. double-edged), blade; bayonet; swordsmanship; sting (of a bee)
剣を抜く けんをぬく draw a sword

KUN

【つるぎ 剣】**SWORD (esp. double-edged)**
剣の山を登る つるぎのやまをのぼる perform a hazardous deed

SYNONYMS

ⓐ **cutting weapons**
刀 SWORD (single-edged) → 3642
剣 SWORD (double-edged) → 2104
矛 HALBERD → 2501
戟 HALBERD → 2131
鉾 DECORATIVE HALBERD → 2154
戈 DAGGER-AX → 4274

剥

2105

1-8-2

▶PEEL OFF

ハク　ホク▲　は(がす)　は(ぐ)　は(がれる)　は(げる)　む(く)▲

Ⓝ 剥　Ⓒ 剥 bō bāo

18	Jōyō	U525D
刂	S10-2-8	F1592

COMPOUNDS

ⓐ **PEEL OFF (as of skin), tear [rip] off, strip (off), flay**
ⓑ (come off of a surface) **PEEL OFF, wear off**
ⓒ **disrobe, strip (someone) of, deprive (someone) of**

a 剥製 はくせい stuffing, mounting; stuffed animal
b 剥離 はくり exfoliation, peeling off
剥落 はくらく coming off, peeling off
剥片 はくへん flake, chip
c 剥奪 はくだつ deprivation, forfeiture, revocation

KUN

【はがす　剥がす】*vt* (remove from a surface) **PEEL OFF, tear [rip] off, strip (off); skin, flay**
引き剥がす ひきはがす tear off, pull off
貸し剥がし かしはがし withdrawal of loan credit, insistence on loan repayment

【はぐ　剥ぐ】*vt*
ⓐ (remove from a surface) **PEEL OFF, tear [rip] off, strip (off); skin, flay**
ⓑ **disrobe, strip (someone) of, deprive (someone) of**
a 剥ぎ取る はぎとる tear off, strip off, rip off; rob, strip
皮剥 かわはぎ thread-sail filefish
b 追い剥ぎ おいはぎ highway robbery; highway robber

【はがれる　剥がれる】*vi* (come off of a surface) **PEEL OFF, come unstuck**

【はげる　剥げる】*vi*
ⓐ **PEEL OFF, come off, wear off**
ⓑ **fade, discolor**
a 剥げ落ちる はげおちる peel off, come off

【むく　剥く】*vt*
ⓐ (remove the surface layer) peel, strip, hull, pare, skin
ⓑ bare
a 引ん剥く ひんむく peel, strip
擦り剥く すりむく (of skin) scrape, skin, graze, chafe
b 剥き出しの むきだしの bare, naked, unwrapped; blunt, open, undisguised
白目を剥く しろめをむく open one's eyes wide; show the whites of one's eyes

SYNONYMS

ⓐ **come off**
脱 get out of place →1225
外れる come off →0215
剥 PEEL OFF →2105

ⓑ **eliminate**
却 ELIMINATE →1436
排 EXCLUDE →0593
払う CLEAR AWAY →0225
剥 PEEL OFF →2105
耘 WEED →1661
削 cross out →1837
抹 wipe off →0370
省 leave out →3100
脱 REMOVE →1225
去 take away →2678
外す take off →0215
除 RID OF →0546
撤 WITHDRAW →0912

剝

2106

1-8-2

▶PEEL OFF

ハク　ホク　は(がす)　は(ぐ)　は(がれる)　は(げる)　む(く)

18	Nonstandard	U5265
刂	S10-2-8	F0000

traditional form →see 剥 at 2105

剛

2107

1-8-2

▶TOUGH

ゴウ　㊔ つよし　たけし　たけ　たか　つよ　たける　よし　こう　かた

Ⓒ 刚 gāng

18	Jōyō	U525B
刂	S10-2-8	F1456

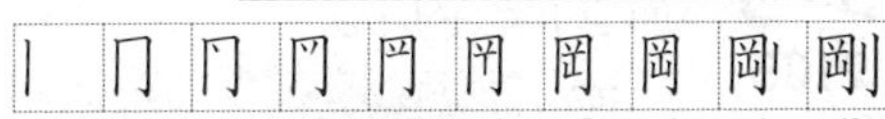

COMPOUNDS

❶ [original meaning] (hard and strong) **TOUGH, strong, rigid, hard**
剛性 ごうせい rigidity
剛体 ごうたい rigid body
剛力(=強力) ごうりき Herculean strength; mountain carrier [guide]
剛球 ごうきゅう *baseball* fast ball
金剛石 こんごうせき diamond

❷ (of strong spirit) **TOUGH, stout, resolute, brave**
剛毅な ごうきな hardy, sturdy
剛健 ごうけん fortitude and vigor, sturdiness, virility; manliness
剛直 ごうちょく moral courage, integrity
剛勇 ごうゆう bravery, prowess

INDEPENDENT

【ごう　剛】*literary* **TOUGH**ness, strength, hardiness

柔能く剛を制す じゅうよくごうをせいす Softness overcomes hardness/Soft words win hard hearts

SYNONYMS

❶ hard

硬 HARD → 1518
堅 FIRM → 3502
鞏 TOUGH → 3369
固 SOLID → 3830
剛 TOUGH → 2107
強 STRONG → 0574
勁 STRONG → 1833

❷ firm and obstinate

堅 FIRM → 3502
固 FIRM, stiff → 3830
確 firm → 1571
毅 RESOLUTE → 2341
剛 TOUGH → 2107
頑 STUBBORN → 1315
硬 hard-line → 1518

都

1-8-2

incorrect stroke-count
➡ see 1-8-3: 者 at 2120

郵

1-8-2

incorrect stroke-count
➡ see 1-8-3: 垂 at 2121

釣

2108

1-8-3

▸**ANGLE**

チョウ つ(る) つ(り) つ(り)-

N 釣 C 钓 diào

167	Jōyō	U91E3
金	S11-8-3	F1013

COMPOUNDS

● [original meaning] **ANGLE**, fish

釣魚 ちょうぎょ fishing, angling
釣果 ちょうか catch, haul

KUN

【つる 釣る】

① **ANGLE, fish**

釣り上げる つりあげる fish up, land

② decoy, allure, take in

釣り出す つりだす fish out, draw out, decoy

【つり 釣り】

① [also suffix] **angling, rod fishing**

釣り糸 つりいと fishing line
釣り師 つりし angler
魚釣り さかなつり angling, fishing
鮪×釣り まぐろつり tuna fishing
一本釣り いっぽんづり pole-and-line fishing

② **change (for money)**

お釣り おつり change
釣り銭 つりせん change

【つり- 釣り-】 [also 吊り] **suspended, hanging**

釣り橋 つりばし suspension bridge
釣鐘 つりがね hanging bell, temple bell
釣り合う つりあう balance; match, be in harmony
釣り合い つりあい balance, equilibrium; proportion
釣り下げる つりさげる suspend from

SYNONYMS

● &【つる】① hunt and fish

猟 HUNTING → 0654
狩 HUNT → 0474
獲 CATCH GAME → 0959
漁 FISH → 0856
釣 ANGLE → 2108
弋 CATCH → 4230

【つり-】

○ hang

掛ける HANG → 0596
垂 HANG DOWN → 4382
懸 SUSPEND → 3632
吊 SUSPEND → 2686
釣り- suspended → 2108

USAGE

❶【つる】

釣る
① angle, fish
② decoy, allure, take in

吊る
① [also 釣る] suspend, hang, swing, sling
② lift by the loins (in sumo wrestling)
③ [formerly 攣る] cramp, have a cramp
④ [formerly 攣る] turn up, slant upward

攣る
[now usu. 吊る]
① cramp, have a cramp
② turn up, slant upward

❷【つり】

釣り
① [also suffix] angling, rod fishing
② change (for money)

釣り-
[also 吊り] suspended, hanging

吊り
① ⓐ suspension, hanging; suspender(s)
ⓑ [also 釣り-] suspended, hanging

②lifting by the loins (in sumo wrestling)

HOMOPHONES

つる

吊 SUSPEND →2686

攣 CRAMP →3635

つり 吊 SUSPEND →2686

釧

▶ARMLET

セン くしろ

Ⓒ 钏 chuàn

2109

◧1-8-3

167	Names	U91E7
金	S11-8-3	F3144

KUN

【くしろ 釧】[archaic] **ARMLET** worn around the elbow

SYNONYMS

【くしろ】

◯ **circular objects**

環 RING →1395

輪 WHEEL, RING →1999

車 WHEEL →4367

盤 DISK →3533

釧 ARMLET →2109

釣

▶ANGLE

チョウ つ(る) つ(り) つ(り)-

2110

◧1-8-3

167	Nonstandard	U91E3
金	S11-8-3	F0000

traditional form →see 釣 at 2108

彬

◧1-8-3

incorrect classification

➡ see ◧1-4-7: 木 at 1201

部

▶SECTION

ブ -べ▲

Ⓒ 部 bù

2111

◧1-8-3

163	Jōyō-3	U90E8
阝	S11-3-8	F0046

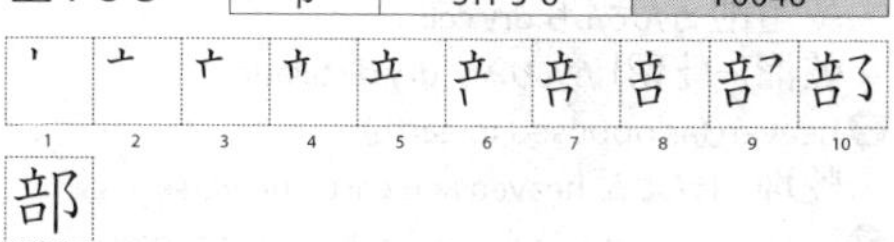

1 2 3 4 5 6 7 8 9 10 11

COMPOUNDS

❶ⓐ [also suffix] **SECTION, part, category, division, region**

ⓑ [original meaning, now archaic] divide in **SECTIONs**, divide in half

a 部分 ぶぶん part, section, portion

部品 ぶひん parts, accessories

部門 ぶもん class, group, division, department, section; genus

部類 ぶるい class, category, division

一部 いちぶ part, portion, section; a copy (of a book)

北部 ほくぶ north, northern part

全部 ぜんぶ all, the whole; wholly, entirely

内部 ないぶ interior, inner parts

上部 じょうぶ upper part [section], top; surface

中央部 ちゅうおうぶ central part

心臓部 しんぞうぶ region of the heart

第三部 だいさんぶ Section 3

❷ⓐ **SECTION** of Chinese character dictionary, radical of Chinese character

ⓑ counter for **SECTIONs** of Chinese character dictionaries

a 部首 ぶしゅ radical (of Chinese characters)

水部 みずのぶ 'water' radical

❸ⓐ [also suffix] section or major subdivision of an organization: **department, division, SECTION, faculty; military unit**

ⓑ club, group

a 部属 ぶぞく section, division

部長 ぶちょう section chief, department head

部会 ぶかい section meeting

部下 ぶか subordinate

部隊 ぶたい unit, corps, party, squad

幹部 かんぶ executive, (managing) staff

学部 がくぶ faculty, department

編集部 へんしゅうぶ editorial department [staff]

文学部 ぶんがくぶ department [faculty] of literature

営業部 えいぎょうぶ business department, sales department

文化事業部 ぶんかじぎょうぶ Cultural Affairs Department

b 野球部 やきゅうぶ baseball club

❹ **counter for copies of printed matter**

部数 ぶすう number of copies, circulation

一部二百円 いちぶにひゃくえん 200 yen per copy

❺ community

部落 ぶらく community, village, hamlet

部族 ぶぞく tribe

INDEPENDENT

【ぶ 部】**SECTION, division, head; section (of a company), department, division; class, category**

. . . の部に入る …のぶにはいる fall under the heading of; be classed among

KUN

【-べ -部】**hereditary clan engaged in specific profession in ancient Japan**

語部 かたりべ clan of professional reciters

SPECIAL READINGS

部屋 へや room, chamber

SYNONYMS

❶ⓐ **part**

分 PART →2466
部 SECTION →2111
局 LIMITED PART →3800
片 FRAGMENT →4272

❸ⓐ **divisions of organizations**

課 SECTION →1980
部 department →2111
局 BUREAU →3800

❹ **counters for books**

冊 COUNTER FOR BOOKS →4295
巻 counter for volumes →3273
部 counter for copies →2111

NOTE

★ do not confuse with 陪 ACCOMPANY A SUPERIOR →0655

郭

2112

1-8-3

▶OUTER ENCLOSURE

カク くるわ▲ 名 ひろ

Ⓒ 郭 guō

163	Jōyō	U90ED
阝	S11-3-8	F1884

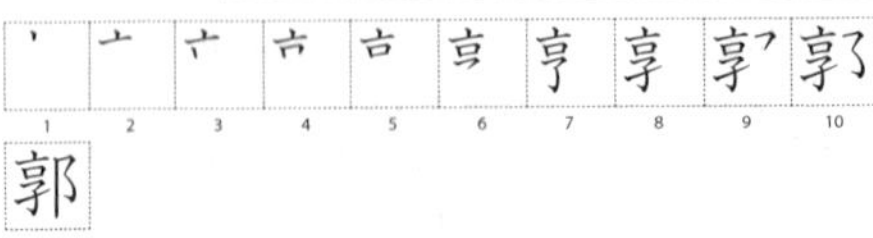

COMPOUNDS

[formerly also 廓 3923]

❶ [original meaning] **OUTER ENCLOSURE [walls], outline, contour**

外郭 がいかく outer block [enclosure]; outline, contour
城郭 じょうかく castle, fortress; castle walls, enclosure
輪郭 りんかく contour, outline, profile
胸郭 きょうかく thorax, chest

❷ district, red-light district

遊郭 ゆうかく licensed quarters, red-light district
一郭 いっかく a block

❸ open, wide, empty

郭清する かくせいする purify, clean up, purge

KUN

【くるわ 郭】[formerly also 廓]

① red-light district

郭通いをする くるわがよいをする frequent a house of ill fame

② area enclosed by earthwork

SYNONYMS

❶ **periphery**

周 PERIPHERY →3720
囲 circumference →3807
郭 OUTER ENCLOSURE →2112
廓 OUTER ENCLOSURE →3923

USAGE

【くるわ】

郭

[formerly also 廓]

① red-light district
② area enclosed by earthwork

廓

[now usu. 郭] same as 郭

HOMOPHONES

くるわ 廓 OUTER ENCLOSURE →3923

乾

2113

1-8-3

▶DRY

カン ケン▲ かわ(く) かわ(かす) ほ(す)▲ ひ(る)▲ いぬい▲

Ⓒ 干 gān 乾 qián

5	Jōyō	U4E7E
乙	S11-1-10	F1355

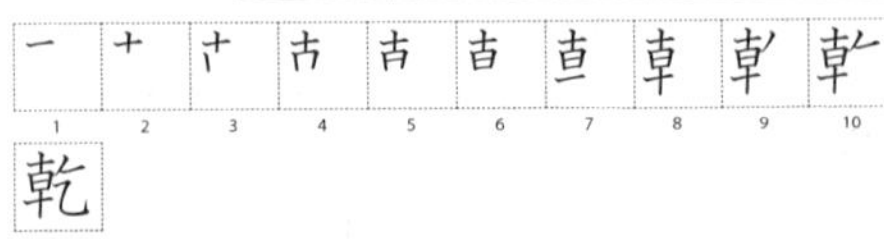

COMPOUNDS

❶ⓐ [original meaning] **DRY, dry up, desiccate**
ⓑ **DRY, dried**

a 乾燥する かんそうする dry up, desiccate, become parched [dry]
乾杯する かんぱいする drink a toast, toast
乾季 かんき dry season

b 乾枯する かんこする completely dry up
乾物 かんぶつ dry provisions, groceries
乾パン かんぱん cracker, hard biscuit
乾電池 かんでんち dry cell
乾溜(=乾留) かんりゅう dry distillation

❷ heaven (as opposed to earth)

乾坤× けんこん heaven and earth, universe

❸ first of the eight trigrams in the Book of Changes: northwest

❹ one of the four supplementary signs of the Oriental zodiac: northwest

乾位 けんい [rare] northwest

KUN

【かわく 乾く】*vi* **DRY (up), run dry**

乾き かわき drying, dryness
乾きの早い かわきのはやい fast drying (clothes)

【かわかす 乾かす】*vt* **DRY, desiccate**
着物を乾かす きものをかわかす dry clothes
【ほす 乾す】[now usu. 干す] *vt*
ⓐ draw off (liquids), drain off
ⓑ drink up, drain **DRY**
a 池を乾す いけをほす drain off a pond
干乾し ひぼし starving
b 飲み乾す のみほす drink up
【ひる 乾る】[now usu. 干る] *vi* get **DRY**, parch
乾物 ひもの dried fish
【いぬい 乾】one of the four supplementary signs of the Oriental zodiac: **northwest**

SYNONYMS

❶ **dry**
乾 DRY → 2113
干 DRY → 4187
燥 DRY UP (desiccate) → 1392
涸 DRY UP (run dry) → 0629
渇 RUN DRY → 0627
旱 DROUGHT → 3048

USAGE

❶【かわく】
乾く
vi dry (up), run dry
渇く
be thirsty, thirst
❷【かわき】
乾き
drying, dryness
渇き
thirst

HOMOPHONES

かわく 渇 RUN DRY → 0627
かわき 渇 RUN DRY → 0627
ほす 干 DRY → 4187
ひる 干 DRY → 4187

NOTE

➡ see also USAGE note at 干 4187

執 2114

▸**EXECUTE**
▸**SEIZE**
シツ シュウ と(る)
Ⓒ 执 zhí

▌1-8-3

32	Jōyō	U57F7
土	S11-3-8	F1055

1	2	3	4	5	6	7	8	9	10	11
一	十	土	圥	圭	幸	幸	幸	㚔	執	執

COMPOUNDS

❶ (perform a specific task with care) **EXECUTE, carry out, perform, conduct**
執行する しっこうする execute, perform, carry out
執務 しつむ performance of one's official duties
執事 しつじ steward, butler
中執(=中央執行委員会) ちゅうしつ(=ちゅうおうしっこういいんかい) Central Executive Committee
❷ⓐ **SEIZE**, hold in hands; seize power
ⓑ **SEIZE [hold] an object (such as a pen) and perform an action with**
ⓒ [original meaning] **SEIZE** a criminal
a 執金鋼 しっこんごう Diamond Holder (name of a Buddhist celestial being)
執権 しっけん regent
b 執筆 しっぴつ writing
執刀する しっとうする perform an operation
❸ **adhere to, stick fast to, hold fast to, persist in**
執念 しゅうねん tenacity of purpose, vindictiveness, spite
執着する しゅうちゃく(=しゅうじゃく)する be attached to; adhere to, hold fast to
執拗×な しつような obstinate; tenacious, persistent
固執する こしつ(=こしゅう)する adhere to, persist in
確執 かくしつ(=かくしゅう) discord, strife
偏執狂 へんしつきょう(=へんしゅうきょう) monomaniac

KUN

【とる 執る】
① **perform (duties), conduct, transact, take (trouble)**
執り行う とりおこなう carry out, perform
事務を執る じむをとる do [attend to] business
② perform an action while holding an object (such as a pen)
筆を執る ふでをとる write, pen, draw
③ persist in, insist on
固く自説を執る かたくじせつをとる persist in one's views

SYNONYMS

❶ **execute**
執 EXECUTE → 2114
行 ACT → 0246
履 FULFILL → 3933
施 CARRY OUT → 1103
践 IMPLEMENT → 1938
果たす effect → 4377
遂 ACCOMPLISH → 3892
❷ⓑ **take**
把 GRIP → 0293
握 GRASP → 0714

金林音享章幸【采】采周周尿者垂

捉 GRASP →0518
執 SEIZE →2114
摑む GRASP →0848
捕 CATCH →0514
取 TAKE →1613
持 HOLD →0447

❸ **adhere to**

執 adhere to →2114
着 stick to →4110

HOMOPHONES

とる

取 TAKE →1613
採 PICK →0606
捕 CATCH →0514
撮 PHOTOGRAPH →0910

COMPOUND FORMATION

❶【確執 かくしつ(=かくしゅう)】

確執 'discord, strife' originally meant firm (確) adherence (執 ❸) to one's own views. Since insisting on one's own opinion leads to an argument, 確執 came to denote discord or strife.

❷【偏執狂 へんしつきょう(=へんしゅうきょう)】

偏執狂 'monomaniac' is a maniac (狂) who sticks to (執 ❸) only one thing (偏).

NOTE

➡ see USAGE note at 取 1613

彩

2115

▶**BEAUTIFUL COLORING**

サイ いろど(る) ㊔ あや

Ⓝ 彩 Ⓒ 彩 cǎi

◧1-8-3

59	Jōyō	U5F69
彡	S11-3-8	F1357

COMPOUNDS

❶ⓐ **BEAUTIFUL [brilliant] COLORING, coloration, color, variegated colors**

ⓑ [original meaning] **color, paint**

a 色彩 しきさい color, coloring, hue, tinge
多彩な たさいな colorful, varicolored; variegated, diversified
五彩 ごさい five beautiful colors
虹彩 こうさい iris
光彩 こうさい luster, brilliancy

b 彩色 さいしょく coloring, painting
彩画 さいが painting, colored picture
彩管 さいかん paintbrush

❷ (outward appearance) color, appearance

生彩 せいさい life, vividness
異彩 いさい conspicuousness

KUN

【いろどる 彩る】[also 色取る] **color, paint, dye; make up**

彩り いろどり coloring, coloration, color scheme; makeup
夕日に彩られた空 ゆうひにいろどられたそら sky colored by the setting sun

SYNONYMS

❶ⓐ **color**

色 COLOR →2522
彩 BEAUTIFUL COLORING →2115

ⓑ **color**

彩 color →2115
染 DYE →3181

HOMOPHONES

いろどる 色取る →2522, 1613

NOTE

➡ see COMPOUND FORMATION for 虹彩 こうさい →虹 1637

彩

2116

▶**BEAUTIFUL COLORING**

サイ いろど(る) ㊔ あや

◧1-8-3

59	Nonstandard	U5F69
彡	S11-3-8	F0000

traditional form →see 彩 at 2115

彫

2117

▶**CARVE**

チョウ ほ(る) -ぼ(り)

Ⓝ 彫 Ⓒ 雕 diāo

◧1-8-3

59	Jōyō	U5F6B
彡	S11-3-8	F1569

COMPOUNDS

● [original meaning] (cut so as to form a desired shape or design) **CARVE, sculpt, engrave**

彫刻 ちょうこく sculpture, carving, engraving
彫像 ちょうぞう carved statue
彫金 ちょうきん metal carving, chasing
彫塑 ちょうそ carving and modeling, plastic arts; clay model

KUN

【ほる 彫る】

ⓐ (cut so as to form designs or figures) **engrave, CARVE, chisel**

ⓑ tattoo

a 彫り物 ほりもの carving; tattoo

木彫り きぼり woodcarving
浮き彫り うきぼり relief, embossed carving
【-ぼり -彫り】[suffix] **carving, sculpture**
鎌倉彫り かまくらぼり carvings of the Kamakura style

SYNONYMS

● form and carve
刻 ENGRAVE → 1619
彫 CARVE → 2117
塑 MODEL → 3525
鋳 CAST → 2170

HOMOPHONES

ほる 掘 DIG → 0601

NOTE

➡ see USAGE note at 掘 0601

彫

2118

1-8-3

▶CARVE

チョウ ほ(る) -ぼ(り)

59	Nonstandard	U2F89A
彡	S11-3-8	F0000

traditional form → see 彫 at 2117

尉

2119

1-8-3

▶COMPANY OFFICER

イ ジョウ▲ ㊔ やす

Ⓒ 尉 wèi yù

41	Jōyō	U5C09
寸	S11-3-8	F1733

1	2	3	4	5	6	7	8	9	10	11
㇕	コ	尸	尸	尸	尸	尸	尉	尉	尉	尉

COMPOUNDS

❶ (military officer or rank such as captain or lieutenant) **COMPANY OFFICER**
尉官 いかん company officer
空軍大尉 くうぐんたいい air force captain
中尉 ちゅうい first lieutenant (U.S. Army)
少尉 しょうい second lieutenant

❷ (white-haired) old man (in a noh drama)
黒色尉 こくしきじょう Old Black Joe (a noh mask)

INDEPENDENT

【じょう 尉】(white-haired) old man (in a noh drama)

SYNONYMS

❶ military officers and ranks
曹 SERGEANT → 3414
尉 COMPANY OFFICER → 2119
佐 FIELD OFFICER → 0076
将 GENERAL OFFICER → 0551
督 COMMANDER → 3471

帥 COMMANDER IN CHIEF → 1642

都

2120

1-8-3

▶METROPOLIS
▶METROPOLIS OF TOKYO

ト ツ みやこ ㊔ くに みや つぎ さと

Ⓝ 都 Ⓒ 都 dū dōu

163	Jōyō-3	U90FD
阝	S11-3-8	F0288

1	2	3	4	5	6	7	8	9	10	11
一	十	土	耂	耂	者	者	者	者	都	都

COMPOUNDS

❶ METROPOLIS, capital
都会 とかい city, town
都市 とし cities, urban communities
都市ガス としがす town gas
都心 としん heart [center] of a city
東京都 とうきょうと Metropolis of Tokyo
首都 しゅと capital (city)
遷都 せんと transfer of the capital

❷ⓐ METROPOLIS OF TOKYO, Tokyo
ⓑ (of the Metropolis of Tokyo) **Metropolitan, Tokyo**
a 都立の とりつの metropolitan, under control of the Tokyo Metropolitan government
都内で とないで in Tokyo Metropolis
都営 とえい run by the metropolitan government
東都 とうと Tokyo Metropolis
b 都庁 とちょう Tokyo Metropolitan Government Office
都電 とでん Metropolitan Electric Railway
都議選 とぎせん Tokyo Assembly elections

❸ all, every, everything
都度 つど each time, whenever
都合 つごう convenience, circumstances; in all, altogether, totally

❹ beautiful, elegant
都雅 とが elegance

❺ exercise control
都督 ととく governor general

INDEPENDENT

【と 都】**METROPOLIS OF TOKYO**
都の との Metropolitan, municipal

KUN

【みやこ 都】**capital; city**
都落ち みやこおち rustication

SYNONYMS

❶ cities and towns
都 METROPOLIS → 2120
京 CAPITAL → 2546

畿 CAPITAL → 4408
市 CITY → 2487
町 TOWN → 1430

❷ **Kanto region**
京 TOKYO → 2546
東 Tokyo → 4385
都 METROPOLIS OF TOKYO → 2120
浜 Yokohama → 0523
埼 SAITAMA → 0560
湘 SHONAN → 0742

❷ **territorial divisions**
州 STATE → 0064
県 PREFECTURE → 3269
府 URBAN PREFECTURE → 3824
道 district of Hokkaido → 3888
都 METROPOLIS OF TOKYO → 2120
省 province in China → 3100
郡 COUNTY → 1858

❸ **all**
皆 ALL → 3093
悉 THOROUGHLY → 3405
総 TOTAL → 1743
諸 VARIOUS → 1984
毎 EVERY → 2527
各 EACH → 2692
都 all → 2120
万 all → 3653
全 WHOLE → 2514
渾 ENTIRE → 0738
一 all in one → 4148
満 FULL → 0739
丸 complete(ly) → 4225
完 COMPLETE → 2727

COMPOUND FORMATION

【都合 つごう】
都合 'convenience, circumstances; in all, altogether, totally' refers to combining (合) everything (都 ❸) together.

郵

2121
1-8-3

▶**MAIL**
ユウ
Ⓒ 邮 yóu

163	Jōyō-6	U90F5
阝	S11-3-8	F1180

Stroke order: 1–11

COMPOUNDS

● (postal delivery system) **MAIL, post**
郵便 ゆうびん mail service, mail, postal matter
郵便局 ゆうびんきょく post office
郵便屋さん ゆうびんやさん mailman
郵政 ゆうせい postal system
郵送 ゆうそう mailing
郵税 ゆうぜい postage, postal rates
郵船 ゆうせん mail steamer
郵貯(=郵便貯金) ゆうちょ(=ゆうびんちょきん) postal [post-office] savings [deposit]
郵袋 ゆうたい mailbag

INDEPENDENT

【ゆう 郵】 abbrev. of 郵便番号 ゆうびんばんごう: postal code, zip code
郵１００ ゆうひゃく zip code 100

SYNONYMS

● **mail**
郵 MAIL → 2121
便 POST → 0105

鈑

2122
1-8-4

▶**SHEET METAL**
バン
Ⓒ 钣 bǎn

167	Non-Jōyō	U9211
金	S12-8-4	F0000

COMPOUNDS

● [now usu. 板 1067] **SHEET METAL**
鈑金 ばんきん sheet metal

SYNONYMS

● **metal**
金 METAL → 2552
鉱 ORE → 2145
礦 ORE → 1606
鈑 SHEET METAL → 2122

鈍

2123
1-8-4

▶**DULL**
ドン にぶ(い) にぶ(る) にぶ- なま(る)▲ なまく(ら)▲
Ⓒ 钝 dùn

167	Jōyō	U920D
金	S12-8-4	F1839

Stroke order: 1–12

COMPOUNDS

❶ⓐ [original meaning] (not sharp) **DULL, blunt**
ⓑ (not intense) **DULL, slow**
a 鈍器 どんき dull weapon, blunt sword
鈍角 どんかく obtuse angle

b 鈍痛 どんつう dull pain
鈍行 どんこう ordinary [slow] train

❷ (not agile) **DULL, dull-witted, slow, stupid**
鈍才 どんさい dullness, stupidity
鈍感 どんかん thickheadedness
鈍重な どんじゅうな dull-witted, phlegmatic
愚鈍 ぐどん stupidity, silliness

INDEPENDENT

【どん 鈍】 **DULL**ness, slowness
鈍な どんな dull, slow, stupid, dull-brained

KUN

【にぶい 鈍い】 **DULL, slow-witted, thickheaded; slow, sluggish; dull, blunt (sword); dim (light); dull (color)**
鈍さ にぶさ dullness, sluggishness
鈍い音 にぶいおと thick sound
鈍い男 にぶいおとこ dolt, dullard

【にぶる 鈍る】 *vi* **become DULL; weaken**
鈍らす にぶらす *vt* dull, blunt; weaken
決心が鈍る けっしんがにぶる waver in one's resolution
腕が鈍る うでがにぶる become less capable

【にぶ- 鈍-】 [prefix] (of colors) **DULL**
鈍黄色 にぶきいろ dull yellow

【なまる 鈍る】 (of cutlery) become **DULL**, get blunted; be weakened, become less capable
体が鈍った からだがなまった The body has lost its former agility

【なまくら 鈍ら】 **DULL** blade; lazy fellow; good-for-nothing, useless (thing)

SYNONYMS

❷ **foolish**
愚 FOOLISH → 3513
暗 DARK → 1273
痴 STUPID → 4072
鈍 DULL → 2123
呆 DIM-WITTED → 2712
魯 DULL → 2665
闇 DARK → 4134
蒙 IGNORANCE → 2938

【にぶ-】
◯ **light-colored**
淡 LIGHT → 0640
浅 light → 0464
薄い pale → 3004
鈍- DULL → 2123

欽

2124
◧ 1-8-4

▸**REVERE**
キン ㊔ よし まこと ひとし
Ⓒ 钦 qīn

76 欠	Names	U6B3D
	S12-4-8	F2727

COMPOUNDS

❶ **REVERE, respect, adore, admire**
欽慕 きんぼ admiration, adoration, reverence

❷ imperial, authorized by the emperor
欽定憲法 きんていけんぽう constitution granted by the emperor

SYNONYMS

❶ **respect**
敬 RESPECT → 2136
尊 HONOR → 2920
畏 respect → 3170
欽 REVERE → 2124
仰 look up to → 0051
崇 REVERENCE → 2864
尚 VALUE HIGHLY → 2774
重 set value on → 4390
拝 WORSHIP → 0360
慕 ADORE → 2970

鉛

2125
◧ 1-8-4

▸**LEAD**
エン なまり

167 金	Nonstandard	U9206
	S12-8-4	F0000

traditional form → see 鉛 at 2143

靴

◧ 1-8-4

incorrect stroke-count
➡ see ◧ 1-9-4: 靴 at 2235

飯

2126
◧ 1-8-4

▸**COOKED RICE**
▸**MEAL**
ハン めし ㊔ いい
Ⓝ 飯 Ⓒ 饭 fàn

184 飠	Jōyō-4	U98EF
	S12-8-4	F0968

COMPOUNDS

❶ **COOKED RICE, boiled rice**
御飯 ごはん boiled rice; meal
炊飯器 すいはんき rice cooker
赤飯 せきはん cooked rice and red beans

❷ⓐ **MEAL**

b food

a 飯店 はんてん (high-class) Chinese restaurant; hotel (in Chinese)
飯場 はんば bunkhouse, workers' living quarters
夕飯 ゆうはん evening meal, supper
b 飯台 はんだい dining table
残飯 ざんぱん leftover food [rice]

KUN

【めし 飯】 **COOKED RICE, boiled rice; meal; livelihood**
飯炊き めしたき cooking rice; kitchen maid, cook
飯粒 めしつぶ grain of boiled rice
飯が食えない めしがくえない cannot make a living
焼き飯 やきめし frizzled [fried] rice
昼飯 ひるめし lunch, midday meal

SYNONYMS

1 rice
米 RICE → 4342
飯 COOKED RICE → 2126
稲 RICE PLANT → 1561
籾 UNHULLED RICE → 1626
餅 RICE CAKE → 2256
粥 RICE GRUEL → 0698

2 food
飯 MEAL → 2126
膳 MEAL → 1381
食 FOOD, meal → 2578
糧 FOOD PROVISIONS → 1800
餌 ANIMAL FEED → 2257
肴 ACCOMPANIMENT FOR DRINKS → 2567

NOTE

➡ see COMPOUND FORMATION for 椀飯振舞 おうばんぶるまい → 椀 1250

飲

2127
1-8-4

▸DRINK
イン の(む) -の(み)
N 飮 C 饮 yǐn yìn

184	Jōyō-3	U98F2
食	S12-8-4	F0549

COMPOUNDS

a DRINK
b [original meaning] **DRINK alcoholic beverages**
c **DRINK, beverage**

a 飲食 いんしょく eating and drinking
飲食店 いんしょくてん eating place, restaurant
飲酒 いんしゅ drinking (alcoholic drinks)
b 愛飲する あいいんする be fond of drinking
c 飲料 いんりょう drink, beverage
飲料水 いんりょうすい drinking [potable] water
溜飲 りゅういん water brash, sour stomach

INDEPENDENT

【いん 飲】 [rare] **DRINK** (of sake); drinking (sake)

KUN

【のむ 飲む】
① *a* **DRINK**
b [also 呑む] **DRINK alcoholic beverages**
a 飲み込む のみこむ swallow, gulp down; grasp, take in
飲み物 のみもの beverage
飲み水 のみみず drinking [potable] water
b 飲み屋 のみや bar, tavern
② smoke
一服飲む いっぷくのむ have a smoke

【-のみ -飲み】 [suffix] **DRINKer**
大酒飲み おおざけのみ guzzler, boozer

SYNONYMS

ingest
喫 INGEST → 0668
服 take → 1090
食 EAT → 2578
喰う EAT → 0670
飲 DRINK → 2127
呑 SWALLOW → 3059
啄 PECK → 0482

USAGE

【のむ】
飲む
① *a* drink
b [also 呑む] drink alcoholic beverages
② smoke
呑む
① *a* swallow, gulp
b swallow (one's feelings), hold back
② [also 飲む] drink (esp. alcoholic beverages)
③ accept
④ look down on, make light of
⑤ conceal

HOMOPHONES

のむ 呑 SWALLOW → 3059

敦

2128
1-8-4

▸HONEST
トン 名 あつ あつし つる つとむ のぶ あつむ
C 敦 dūn duì

66	Names	U6566
攵	S12-4-8	F1935

COMPOUNDS

❶ [rare] **HONEST**, staunch, sincere, simple

敦厚な とんこうな sincere and kindhearted, honest and simple

敦朴(=敦樸×)な とんぼくな [archaic] honest and simple

❷ [archaic] cordial, warm, kind, kindhearted

敦睦な とんぼくな cordial and friendly, affectionate

❸ used phonetically for *ton*

倫敦 ろんどん London

SYNONYMS

❶ **purehearted**

純 PURE → 1649
淳 PUREHEARTED → 0626
清 clean → 0635
潔 IMMACULATE → 0920
廉 INCORRUPT → 3911
敦 HONEST → 2128
惇 SINCERE → 0588
直 straightforward → 3649
侃 FORTHRIGHT → 0097

就

2129

◧ 1-8-4

▶**SET ABOUT**

シュウ ジュ つ(く) つ(ける) ㊔ なり

Ⓒ 就 jiù

43	Jōyō-6	U5C31
尢	S12-3-9	F1023

COMPOUNDS

❶ⓐ **SET ABOUT a task, set out, proceed to do, set to, enter upon, launch into, take up (a position)**

ⓑ set out, go to

a 就職 しゅうしょく finding employment

就任 しゅうにん assumption of office, inauguration

就学する しゅうがくする enter school

就労する しゅうろうする set to work, find employment

就航 しゅうこう (of ships) going into commission

就業 しゅうぎょう employment, starting work

b 就寝する しゅうしんする go to bed

就眠する しゅうみんする go to sleep

去就 きょしゅう one's course of action

❷ **accomplish, achieve**

成就 じょうじゅ accomplishment, achievement, attainment

KUN

【つく 就く】

①ⓐ **SET ABOUT a task, set out, enter upon, take up (a position), assume (office), enter (a business)**

ⓑ set out, start, leave

a 就いて ついて about, concerning

職に就く しょくにつく take up employment

b 帰途に就く きとにつく leave for home

② [formerly 即く] ascend to (the throne)

位に就く くらいにつく ascend to the throne

③ study under (a teacher)

先生に就く せんせいにつく study under (a teacher)

【つける 就ける】

① **install [place] a person in a position**

役に就ける やくにつける place someone in a position

② [formerly 即ける] enthrone

王位に就ける おういにつける place on the throne

③ make (a person) study under (a teacher)

良い先生に就ける よいせんせいにつける have one study under a good teacher

SYNONYMS

❶ⓐ **begin**

始 BEGIN → 0335
-出す begin to do → 4310
-掛ける start doing → 0596
発 START → 3174
起 start → 4099
就 SET ABOUT → 2129
開 OPEN → 4121
創 initiate → 2283
肇 ORIGINATE → 3474

HOMOPHONES

つく

付 ATTACH → 0035
着 PUT ON → 4110
附 ATTACH → 0410
即 IMMEDIATE → 1439
点 POINT → 2587

つける

付 ATTACH → 0035
附 ATTACH → 0410
着 PUT ON → 4110
即 IMMEDIATE → 1439
点 POINT → 2587
漬 PICKLE → 0861

NOTE

➡ see USAGE note at 付 0035

朝

2130

1-8-4

▶**MORNING**
▶**DYNASTY**

チョウ あさ ㊔ とも あした はじめ

Ⓝ 朝 Ⓒ 朝 zhāo cháo

74	Jōyō-2	U671D
月	S12-4-8	F0182

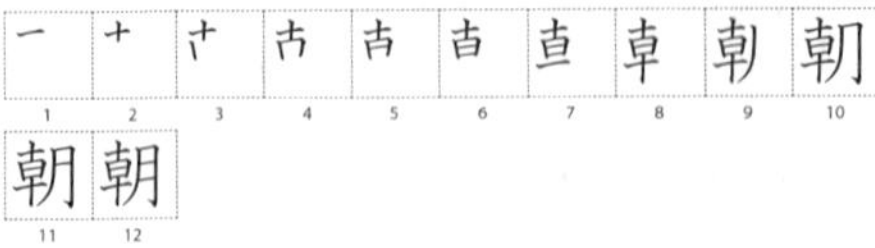

COMPOUNDS

❶ **MORNING, forenoon, morn**
朝刊 ちょうかん morning edition [paper]
朝食 ちょうしょく breakfast
早朝 そうちょう early morning
一朝一夕に いっちょういっせきに in one day, in a short time

❷ [also suffix]
ⓐ **DYNASTY, reign, rule**
ⓑ **dynastic period, age**
a 王朝 おうちょう dynasty, Imperial regime
b 清朝 しんちょう Qing Dynasty, Manchu Dynasty
平安朝 へいあんちょう Heian Period

❸ court, government
朝廷 ちょうてい Imperial Court
朝野 ちょうや government and people
朝貢する ちょうこうする bring tribute

❹ⓐ North Korea, Korea
ⓑ Korean (language)
a 朝鮮 ちょうせん (North) Korea
b 日朝辞典 にっちょうじてん Japanese-Korean dictionary

❺ country ruled by emperor (esp. Japan)
帰朝する きちょうする come back to one's country (Japan)
来朝する らいちょうする come to Japan

INDEPENDENT

【ちょう 朝】**DYNASTY**, reign; dynastic period; in office, in power
桓×武天皇の朝 かんむてんのうのちょう in the reign of Emperor Kanmu

【ちょうする 朝する】proceed to the court

KUN

【あさ 朝】**MORNING, forenoon, morn**
朝方 あさがた toward morning
朝日 あさひ [sometimes also 旭] rising sun, morning sun; rays of the morning sun
朝顔 あさがお morning glory; bell (of a trombone)
朝飯 あさめし breakfast
朝早く あさはやく early in the morning
朝御飯 あさごはん breakfast
毎朝 まいあさ every morning

SPECIAL READINGS

今朝 けさ this morning

SYNONYMS

❶ **morning and dawn**
朝 MORNING → 2130
暁 DAWN → 1233
旦 DAYBREAK → 3041
曙 DAWN → 1384
晨 EARLY MORNING → 3110

❷ⓑ **long time periods**
時 TIME → 1155
代 age → 0034
紀 ERA → 1628
世 AGE → 4308
朝 dynastic period → 2130
期 period → 2139
劫 KALPA → 1435

❸ **governments**
官 GOVERNMENT → 2766
幕 SHOGUNATE → 2937
廷 COURT → 3795
朝 court → 2130
宮 Imperial Court → 2828

❹ⓐ **Korea**
鮮 Korea → 2355
朝 North Korea → 2130
韓 SOUTH KOREA → 2218

HOMOPHONES

あさひ
旭 RISING SUN → 3697
朝日 → 2130, 3759

NOTE

➡ see USAGE note at 旭 3697

戟

2131

1-8-4

▶**HALBERD**

ゲキ ほこ

Ⓒ 戟 jǐ

62	Names	U621F
戈	S12-4-8	F2801

COMPOUNDS

❶ [original meaning] **HALBERD, two-pronged lance**
剣戟 けんげき weapons, arms

❷ [now replaced by 激 0955] stir up, stimulate, excite
刺戟する しげきする stimulate, excite

INDEPENDENT

【げき 戟】**HALBERD, two-pronged lance**

KUN

【ほこ 戟】[usu. 矛, sometimes also 鋒] **HALBERD**

SYNONYMS

❶ **cutting weapons**

刀 SWORD (single-edged) →3642
剣 SWORD (double-edged) →2104
矛 HALBERD →2501
戟 HALBERD →2131
鉾 DECORATIVE HALBERD →2154
戈 DAGGER-AX →4274

HOMOPHONES

ほこ

矛 HALBERD →2501
鉾 DECORATIVE HALBERD →2154
鋒 POINT OF A BLADE →2172
戈 DAGGER-AX →4274

NOTE

➡ see USAGE note at 矛 2501

朝

▸MORNING
▸DYNASTY
チョウ あさ ㊔ とも あした はじめ

2132
◧1-8-4

74	Nonstandard	U671D
月	S12-4-8	F0000

traditional form →see 朝 at 2130

乾

◧1-8-4

incorrect stroke-count
➡ see ◧1-8-3: 卓 at 2113

報

▸INFORM
▸REQUITE
ホウ むく(いる) むく(う)

2133
◧1-8-4

Ⓒ 报 bào

32	Jōyō-5	U5831
土	S12-3-9	F0147

1	2	3	4	5	6	7	8	9	10	11	12
一	十	土	士	幸	幸	幸	幸	幸	郣	郣	報

COMPOUNDS

❶ⓐ **INFORM, report, announce, convey**
ⓑ **INFORMation, report, news**
ⓒ [also suffix] **bulletin, newspaper, magazine**

a 報道 ほうどう news, report, information
報告する ほうこくする report, inform
通報する つうほうする report, send information
b 一報 いっぽう information, notification
予報 よほう forecast, prediction
情報 じょうほう information, intelligence, report, news
電報 でんぽう telegram
広報(=弘報) こうほう (public) information, public relations
公報 こうほう public [official] report [bulletin]
日報 にっぽう daily report, daily news
速報 そくほう prompt report, news flash
c 官報 かんぽう official gazette, official telegram
画報 がほう illustrated magazine
研究所報 けんきゅうしょほう research institute bulletin

❷ **signal, warning**

時報 じほう time signal; review
警報 けいほう warning signal, alarm
大雨注意報 おおあめちゅういほう storm warning

❸ⓐ (make return for) **REQUITE, return, repay; reward, recompense**
ⓑ (take revenge) **REQUITE**, avenge, retaliate

a 報奨 ほうしょう reward, compensation
報恩 ほうおん repaying a kindness, gratitude
報酬 ほうしゅう remuneration, reward; pay
返報 へんぽう requital, retaliation, revenge
b 報復 ほうふく retaliation, reprisal, revenge

INDEPENDENT

【ほう 報】**INFORM**ation, news
報に接する ほうにせっする get information, be informed of

【ほうじる(=ほうずる) 報じる(=報ずる)】**report, INFORM; return, requite**

KUN

【むくいる 報いる】
① [formerly also 酬いる]
ⓐ **REQUITE, repay**
ⓑ **recompense, reward**

a 報い むくい recompense, return; punishment, retribution
b 労に報いる ろうにむくいる recompense a person for his [her] labor

② revenge oneself on, retaliate

【むくう 報う】same as 報いる むくいる
報われる むくわれる be rewarded

SYNONYMS

❶ⓐ **inform and communicate**

報 INFORM →2133
通 COMMUNICATE →3855
告 NOTIFY →3062
届ける give notice →3820
達 issue a notice →3893
知 let know →1446
申 REPORT →4319
稟 REPORT TO →2649
宣 PROCLAIM →2799

釒 革 食 享 京 章 幸 【壳】 𡕒 荷 背 其 頁 皇

ⓑ **information**
報 information → 2133
信 MESSAGE → 0115
訃 NEWS OF DEATH → 1827
ⓒ **periodicals**
誌 MAGAZINE → 1950
紙 newspaper → 1654
報 bulletin → 2133
❷ **signal**
号 signal → 2675
報 signal → 2133
❸ⓐ **compensate**
償 RECOMPENSE → 0199
賠 COMPENSATE → 1991
酬 RECIPROCATE → 1941
報 REQUITE → 2133

USAGE

❶【むくいる】
報いる
① [formerly also 酬いる]
ⓐ requite, repay
ⓑ recompense, reward
② revenge oneself on, retaliate
酬いる
[now usu. 報いる]
ⓐ requite, repay
ⓑ recompense, reward
❷【むくい】
報い
ⓐ [formerly also 酬い] recompense, return
ⓑ punishment, retribution
酬い
[now usu. 報い] recompense, return

HOMOPHONES

むくいる 酬 RECIPROCATE → 1941
むくい 酬 RECIPROCATE → 1941

NOTE

➡ see also USAGE note at 広 3769

殼
2134
◧1-8-4

▶**SHELL**
カク から がら

79	Nonstandard	U6BBC
殳	S12-4-8	F0000

traditional form → see 殻 at 1883

款
2135
◧1-8-4

▶**ARTICLE**
カン
Ⓒ 款 kuǎn

76	Jōyō	U6B3E
欠	S12-4-8	F2884

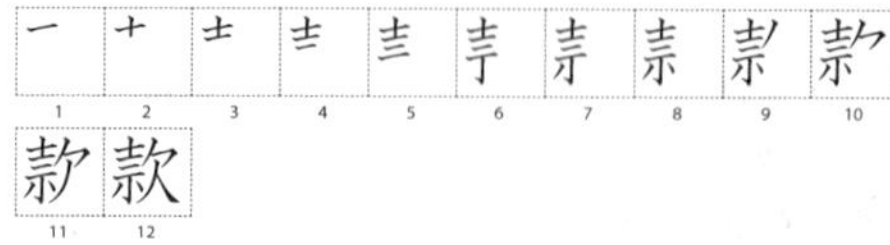

COMPOUNDS

❶ⓐ **ARTICLE, item, subsection**
ⓑ counter for **ARTICLE**s or subsections
a 定款 ていかん articles of association, company contract
約款 やっかん article, stipulation, provision, clause
条款 じょうかん article, stipulation, provision, clause
b 第二款 だいにかん Article 2
❷ **sum of money, funds**
借款 しゃっかん loan
❸ [usu. 歓 2342] **treat cordially, have friendly relations with**
款待 かんたい cordial [warm] reception
交款 こうかん exchange of cordialities
❹ inscription, seal
落款 らっかん sign and seal, signature

INDEPENDENT

【かん 款】goodwill, cordiality; **ARTICLE**, item, subsection
款を通ずる かんをつうずる form a close friendship; communicate secretly

SYNONYMS

❶ **parts of writing**
章 CHAPTER → 2624
段 passage → 1471
節 paragraph → 3336
款 ARTICLE → 2135
条 ARTICLE → 2726
項 CLAUSE → 0692
目 ITEM → 3777
箇 item → 3348
❸ **treat and welcome**
遇 TREAT → 3889
待 treat → 0434
扱う HANDLE → 0251
款 treat cordially → 2135
接 receive → 0607
迎 WELCOME → 3796

敬
2136
◧1-8-4

▶**RESPECT**
ケイ キョウ▲ うやま(う) ㊔ たか たかし よし ゆき ひろ のり とし あき
Ⓝ 敬 Ⓒ 敬 jìng

66	Jōyō-6	U656C
攵	S12-4-8	F1140

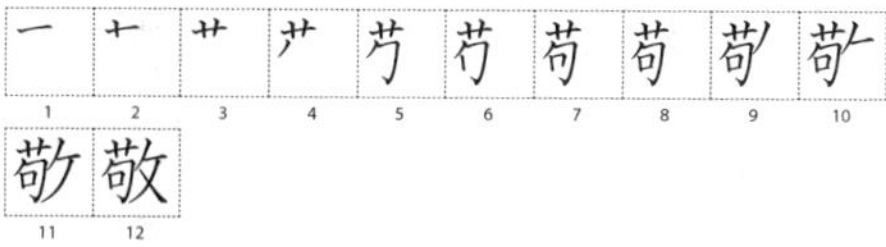

COMPOUNDS

● **RESPECT, revere, honor**

敬意 けいい respect, regard, honor
敬称 けいしょう honorific title, term of respect
敬老 けいろう respect for the aged
敬語 けいご honorific language, polite speech
敬遠する けいえんする keep at a respectful distance; avoid
敬具 けいぐ Yours truly [respectfully]
敬服する けいふくする have great admiration for
敬愛 けいあい respect and affection, veneration
尊敬する そんけいする respect, esteem, honor, revere
失敬な しっけいな disrespectful, rude, impolite
愛敬 あいきょう (personal) charm, winsomeness, courtesy

INDEPENDENT

【けいする 敬する】 **RESPECT**, esteem, honor

KUN

【うやまう 敬う】 **RESPECT, revere, reverence, honor, venerate**

敬い うやまい respect, reverence, veneration, honor, esteem
神を敬う かみをうやまう revere God

SYNONYMS

● **respect**

敬 RESPECT → 2136
尊 HONOR → 2920
畏 respect → 3170
欽 REVERE → 2124
仰 look up to → 0051
崇 REVERENCE → 2864
尚 VALUE HIGHLY → 2774
重 set value on → 4390
拝 WORSHIP → 0360
慕 ADORE → 2970

散

▶SCATTER

サン ち(る) ち(らす) -ち(らす) ち(らかす) ち(らかる) ち(らばる)

2137

◧1-8-4

Ⓒ 散 sàn sǎn

66	Jōyō-4	U6563
攵	S12-4-8	F0750

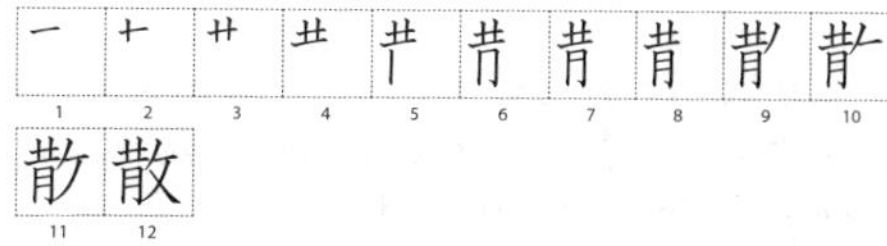

COMPOUNDS

❶ⓐ **SCATTER, disperse, break up**

ⓑ [formerly also 撒 さん, さつ 0909] [original meaning] **(cause to) SCATTER, sprinkle, adjourn (a meeting), disperse**

a 散乱 さんらん dispersion, scattering
散発的な さんぱつてきな sporadic
解散 かいさん breakup, dispersion; dissolution
拡散 かくさん scattering, diffusion
分散 ぶんさん dispersion, breakup, divergence; variance
四散する しさんする scatter (in all directions)
一目散に いちもくさんに at full [top] speed

b 散髪 さんぱつ haircut
散布 さんぷ(=さっぷ) scattering, sprinkling, spraying
散水 さんすい water sprinkling
散会する さんかいする break up, adjourn, disperse

❷ⓐ **unrestrained, free, carefree, relaxed, loose**

ⓑ **random, haphazard**

a 散歩 さんぽ walk, (leisurely) stroll
散文 さんぶん prose
閑散 かんさん leisure, inactivity

b 散散に さんざんに severely, terribly, unsparingly
散漫な さんまんな desultory, vagrant, vague

❸ powdered medicine

散剤 さんざい powdered medicine
胃散 いさん powder for the stomach

INDEPENDENT

【さんじる(=さんずる) 散じる(=散ずる)】 spend, squander; dispel, dissipate

家財を散じる かざいをさんじる squander one's fortune
鬱を散じる うつをさんじる chase one's gloom away

KUN

【ちる 散る】 *vi*

① **SCATTER, disperse, break up, dissipate**

散り散りに ちりぢりに scatteredly, separately
飛び散る とびちる fly off, fly apart, scatter

② **fall, be SCATTERed [shed]; die**

散る落葉 ちるおちば falling leaves
南海に散る なんかいにちる die in the south sea

③ run, spread, blur

この紙はインクが散る このかみはいんくがちる Ink runs [spreads] on this paper

④ resolve, be resolved

腫れ物が散った はれものがちった The tumor has resolved

⑤ be distracted
気が散った きがちった My attention was distracted

【ちらす 散らす】 *vt* **SCATTER, disperse, strew, break up, dissipate; resolve; distract**
散らし ちらし leaflet, handbill, flyer; uncaked *sushi*
追い散らす おいちらす drive away, scatter, rout
盲腸を散らす もうちょうをちらす resolve appendicitis
気を散らす きをちらす distract a person's attention

【-ちらす -散らす】 verbal suffix indicating disorder or indiscretion
食い散らす くいちらす eat untidily, eat a bit of everything
当たり散らす あたりちらす find fault with everybody, make oneself disagreeable

【ちらかす 散らかす】 *vt* **SCATTER (around), disarrange, leave untidy**
部屋を散らかす へやをちらかす litter a room (with things)

【ちらかる 散らかる】 *vi* **lie SCATTERed about, be in disorder**
散らかった紙屑 ちらかったかみくず scattered [littered] paper scraps

【ちらばる 散らばる】 be SCATTERed; be in disorder
ユダヤ人は世界各国に散らばっている ゆだやじんはせかいかっこくにちらばっている The Jews are dispersed all over the world

SYNONYMS

❶ⓐ spread
散 SCATTER → 2137
布 SPREAD → 3691
敷く LAY → 2345
舗 PAVE → 2177
塗 APPLY ON A SURFACE → 3523
抹 wipe over → 0370
撒 SCATTER → 0909

ⓑ disperse
解 DISSOLVE → 1913
散 SCATTER → 2137

❷ unrestrained
漫 RAMBLING → 0858
散 unrestrained → 2137
宕 UNCONSTRAINED → 2771

欺

2138
1-8-4

▶DECEIVE
ギ あざむ(く)
Ⓒ 欺 qī

76	Jōyō	U6B3A
欠	S12-4-8	F1930

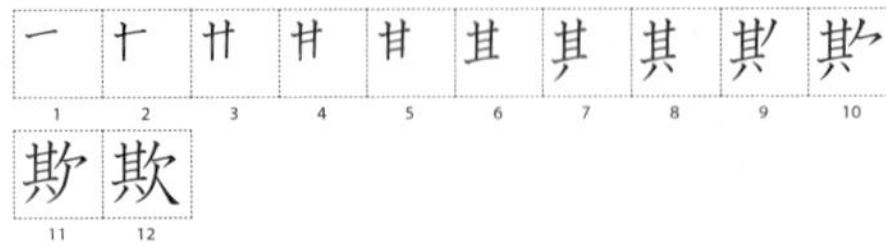

COMPOUNDS

● [original meaning] **DECEIVE, cheat, swindle**
欺瞞× ぎまん deception, imposition
詐欺 さぎ swindle, fraud

KUN

【あざむく 欺く】 DECEIVE, cheat, delude; be comparable to; outshine
欺き惑わす あざむきまどわす deceive and lead astray
花を欺く美人 はなをあざむくびじん woman as pretty as a flower

SYNONYMS

● deceive
欺 DECEIVE → 2138
騙 DECEIVE → 2314
詐 SWINDLE → 1896
惑 mislead → 3461
拐 defraud → 0365
偽 FALSIFY → 0149
詭 TRICK → 1919

期

2139
1-8-4

▶TERM
▶EXPECT
キ ゴ
Ⓝ 朞 朞 Ⓒ 期 qī jī

74	Jōyō-3	U671F
月	S12-4-8	F0187

COMPOUNDS

❶ⓐ [also suffix] **TERM, school term, period, season, quarter; stage, phase; session**
ⓑ (deadline) **TERM, time limit, appointed day**
ⓒ inevitable moment

a 期間 きかん term, period
期末試験 きまつしけん term-end examination
学期 がっき school term
時期 じき time, season
第一期計画 だいいっきけいかく first phase of a plan
初期 しょき early days, early stage, beginning; early, initial
上半期 かみはんき first half of the (fiscal) year
定期 ていき fixed term; fixed deposit; commuter's pass; regular, periodic

b 期限 きげん time limit, term
延期する えんきする postpone, defer
任期 にんき one's term of office
満期 まんき expiration (of a term)
c 最期 さいご one's last moments, death
❷ⓐ [also suffix] **period, age, time, occasion**
ⓑ geological age
a 青年期 せいねんき adolescence
幼児期 ようじき babyhood
平安後期 へいあんこうき late Heian period
画期的な かっきてきな epoch-making, epochal
b 氷河期 ひょうがき ice age
❸ **EXPECT, look forward to, anticipate, hope for**
期待する きたいする expect, look forward to, anticipate, hope for
予期する よきする expect, anticipate, hope for
所期の しょきの expected, anticipated, hoped-for
❹ determine, decide; promise, pledge
期成 きせい resolution to carry out (a plan)

INDEPENDENT

【き 期】 time, date, occasion
【きする 期する】 fix a date, determine; resolve; promise; **EXPECT**, hope for
【ご 期】 inevitable moment
【ごする 期する】 wait **EXPECT**antly for

SYNONYMS

❶ⓐ **time periods**
時 TIME → 1155
季 SEASON (quarter) → 3161
候 SEASON (time of year) → 0133
頃 TIME → 0163
暇 FREE TIME → 1275
般 period of time → 1670
刻 POINT OF TIME → 1619
間 INTERVAL → 4122
隙 GAP → 0826
期 TERM → 2139
節 SEASON → 3336
❷ⓐ **long time periods**
時 TIME → 1155
代 age → 0034
紀 ERA → 1628
世 AGE → 4308
朝 dynastic period → 2130
期 period → 2139
劫 KALPA → 1435
❸ **expect**
期 EXPECT → 2139
待 wait for → 0434

斯

2140

◧ 1-8-4

▶THIS

シ か(く) か(かる) こ(の) こ(う) ㊔ のり つな

Ⓒ 斯 sī

69	Names	U65AF
斤	S12-4-8	F2750

COMPOUNDS

ⓐ *demonstrative* **THIS**
ⓑ *pronoun* **THIS**
a 斯文 しぶん this field of study; Confucian studies
斯界 しかい this world [circle, field]

KUN

【かく 斯く】 like **THIS**, thus, such
斯くして かくして in this way, thus
【かかる 斯かる】 like **THIS** [these], such, this kind of
【この 斯の】 [usu. 此の] *demonstrative* **THIS**
【こう 斯う】
ⓐ like **THIS**, thus, such
ⓑ uh
a 斯うした こうした such, like this [these], this kind of

SPECIAL READINGS

瓦斯 がす gas

SYNONYMS

● **this and that**
本 THIS → 4314
爾 THAT → 4407
其れ THAT → 3255
彼 that → 0346
今 THIS (week, etc.) → 2464
当 THE PRESENT → 2701
該 the said → 1916
同 the same → 3707
之 this → 4228
是 this → 3090
此 THIS → 1017
斯 THIS → 2140

HOMOPHONES

この 此 THIS → 1017

NOTE

➡ see USAGE note at 此 1017

朞

2141

◧ 1-8-4

▶TERM
▶EXPECT

キ ゴ

74	Nonstandard	U671F
月	S12-4-8	F0000

traditional form → see 期 at 2139

金 革 食 享 京 卓 幸 壳 隶 苟 肯 其 【耳】 皇

敢

2142
1-8-4

▸BOLDLY
カン あ(えて)▲ あ(えない)▲ あ(えず)▲
Ⓒ 敢 gǎn

66	Jōyō	U6562
攵	S12-4-8	F1909

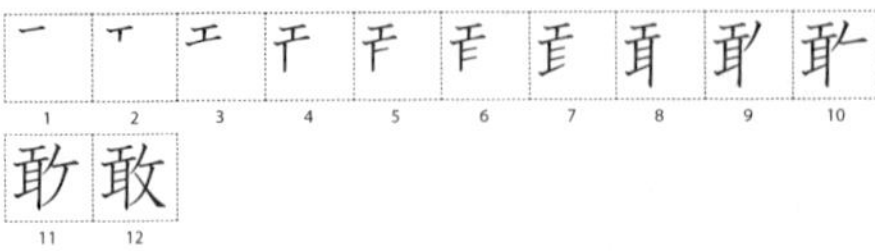

COMPOUNDS

ⓐ BOLDLY, daringly, bravely, fearlessly, resolutely
ⓑ bold, daring, brave, fearless, resolute

a 敢闘する かんとうする fight bravely
敢然(と) かんぜん(と) boldly, bravely
b 敢行 かんこう decisive [daring] action
果敢な かかんな bold, daring; resolute
勇敢な ゆうかんな brave, courageous, daring, heroic

KUN

【あえて 敢えて】**BOLDLY, daringly;** [in negative constructions] **(not) at all**
敢えてする あえてする dare [venture] to do
敢えて驚くには当たらない あえておどろくにはあたらない There is nothing strange about it

【あえない 敢えない】sad, tragic
敢えない最期 あえないさいご tragic death
敢え無く あえなく sadly, tragically

【あえず 敢えず】*literary* **hardly finishing (doing), unable to do sufficiently**
涙塞き敢えず なみだせきあえず unable to fight back tears
取り敢えず とりあえず as a temporary measure, for the present, in a hurry; first of all

SYNONYMS

ⓐ resolutely
敢 BOLDLY → 2142
断 resolutely → 1885
決 decisively → 0308

ⓑ brave
勇 BRAVE → 2592
侠 chivalrous → 0110
赳 VALIANT → 4100
驍 VALIANT → 2327
敢 bold → 2142
豪 bold and unrestrained → 2657
雄 HEROIC → 1271
壮 heroic → 0263
義 chivalrous → 2948
凜 gallant → 0195

毀

1-8-4

incorrect stroke-count
➡ see 1-9-4: 皇 at 2246

鉛

2143
1-8-5

▸LEAD
エン なまり
Ⓝ 鉛 Ⓒ 铅 qiān yán

167	Jōyō	U925B
金	S13-8-5	F2066

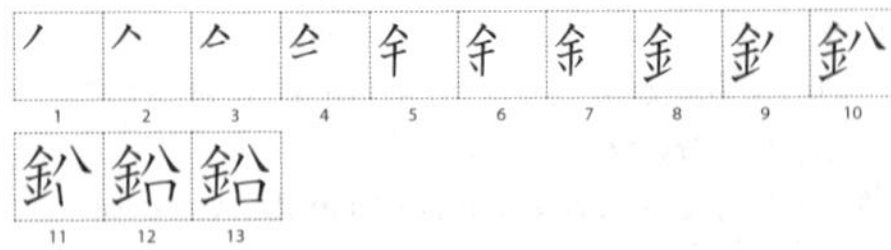

COMPOUNDS

● [original meaning] **LEAD**
鉛毒 えんどく lead poisoning
鉛筆 えんぴつ pencil
鉛管 えんかん lead pipe
加鉛ガソリン かえんがそりん leaded gasoline
亜鉛 あえん zinc

KUN

【なまり 鉛】**LEAD**
鉛色 なまりいろ lead color; livid

SYNONYMS

● **metals**
金 GOLD → 2552
銀 SILVER → 2156
銅 COPPER → 2155
鉄 IRON → 2147
鉛 LEAD → 2143
錫 TIN → 2189

鉢

2144
1-8-5

▸BOWL
ハチ ハツ
Ⓒ 钵 bō

167	Jōyō	U9262
金	S13-8-5	F1677

COMPOUNDS

❶ⓐ BOWL, pot, basin
ⓑ Buddhist priest's rice BOWL

a 鉢物 はちもの food served in bowls; bonsai
菓子鉢 かしばち bowl for confectioneries
鉄鉢 てっぱち mendicant priest's begging bowl
托鉢 たくはつ religious mendicancy, begging bonze

衣鉢 いはつ(=えはつ) mysteries (of Buddhism or an art)

❷ⓐ flowerpot

ⓑ counter for potted plants

a 鉢植え はちうえ potted plant

植木鉢 うえきばち flowerpot

b 菊二鉢 きくふたはち two flowerpots of chrysanthemums

❸ crown (of the head), brainpan, skull

鉢巻き はちまき headband

鉢合わせ はちあわせ bumping of heads; running into someone

INDEPENDENT

【はち 鉢】basin; flowerpot; crown (of the head), brainpan, skull

お鉢 おはち rice tub; one's turn

鉢の花 はちのはな flower in a pot

鉢の開いた頭 はちのひらいたあたま flat-crowned head

SYNONYMS

❶ⓐ vessels and receptacles

盤 dish → 3533
鍋 POT → 2202
釜 IRON POT → 2610
鼎 TRIPOD CAULDRON → 4405
臼 MORTAR → 4341
碓 MORTAR → 1537
托 RECEPTACLE → 0252
皿 PLATE → 4286
盆 TRAY → 2581
膳 LEGGED TRAY → 1381
杯 CUP → 1066
鉢 BOWL → 2144
椀 WOODEN BOWL → 1250
碗 CERAMIC BOWL → 1539
丼 LARGE BOWL → 4323

COMPOUND FORMATION

❶【托鉢 たくはつ】

托鉢 'religious mendicancy, begging bonze' represents a Buddhist bonze making rounds from house to house chanting sutra and holding out (托) his begging bowl (鉢 ❶ⓑ) for rice.

❷【衣鉢 いはつ(=えはつ)】

衣鉢 'mysteries (of Buddhism or an art)' represents the surplice (衣) and bowl (鉢 ❶ⓑ) that a Buddhist master would hand his disciple to symbolize initiation into the secrets of Buddhism. It is chiefly used in the expression 衣鉢を継ぐ いはつをつぐ 'have the mysteries of one master's art imparted to one'.

鉱

2145

1-8-5

▶**ORE**
▶**MINE**
コウ

Ⓝ 鑛 Ⓒ 矿 kuàng

167	Jōyō-5	U9271
金	S13-8-5	F1724

COMPOUNDS

❶ [formerly also 礦 1606] [also suffix] [original meaning] **ORE**

鉱石 こうせき ore, mineral
鉱床 こうしょう ore deposit
鉱山 こうざん mine
鉱坑 こうこう mine, shaft, pit
金鉱 きんこう gold ore; gold mine
鉄鉱 てっこう iron ore
磁鉄鉱 じてっこう magnetite, loadstone

❷ⓐ MINE

ⓑ suffix after names of **MINE**s

a 鉱業 こうぎょう mining (industry)

炭鉱 たんこう coal mine

b 夕張鉱 ゆうばりこう Yubari Mine

SYNONYMS

❶ metal

金 METAL → 2552
鉱 ORE → 2145
礦 ORE → 1606
鈑 SHEET METAL → 2122

❷ mine

坑 PIT → 0277
鉱 MINE → 2145
礦 MINE → 1606
山 mine → 3658

鈴

2146

1-8-5

▶**BELL**
レイ リン すず

Ⓒ 铃 líng

167	Jōyō	U9234
金	S13-8-5	F1133

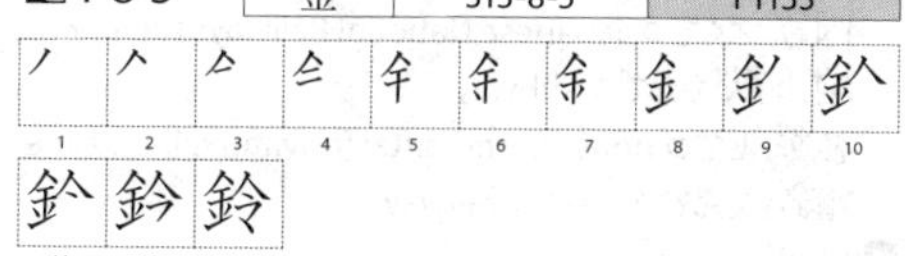

COMPOUNDS

● [original meaning] **BELL (that jingles or rings)**

電鈴 でんれい electric bell

振鈴 しんれい ringing bell, hand bell
予鈴 よれい the first bell
銀鈴 ぎんれい silver bell
風鈴 ふうりん wind-bell
呼び鈴 よびりん (call) bell, doorbell

INDEPENDENT

【りん 鈴】**BELL**, doorbell
鈴を鳴らす りんをならす ring a bell

KUN

【すず 鈴】**BELL (that jingles)**
鈴蘭 すずらん lily of the valley
鈴虫 すずむし "bell ring" insect (a kind of cricket)

SYNONYMS

● **bells**
鈴 BELL (that jingles or rings) →2146
鐘 BELL (that tolls) →2222

鉄

2147
◧ 1-8-5

▸**IRON**
テツ くろがね▲ ㊔ かね くろかね
Ⓝ 鐵 鐡 銕 Ⓒ 铁 tiě

167	Jōyō-3	U9244
金	S13-8-5	F0557

ノ 𠆢 亼 亼 午 伞 乐 金 金 釒 (strokes 1–13)

COMPOUNDS

❶ⓐ [original meaning] **IRON**
ⓑ as hard or rigid as **IRON**
a 鉄鋼 てっこう iron and steel
鉄板 てっぱん iron [steel] plate
鉄筋 てっきん ferro-(concrete)
鉄砲 てっぽう gun, firearm
鉄道 てつどう railway
鉄骨 てっこつ steel [iron] frame
製鉄 せいてつ iron manufacture
非鉄金属 ひてつきんぞく nonferrous metals
b 鉄則 てっそく ironclad rule, immutable law

❷ **IRON** blue, reddish black
鉄色 てついろ iron blue, reddish black

❸ abbrev. of 鉄道 てつどう: **railway, railroad line**
国鉄 こくてつ Japanese National Railways (defunct)
地下鉄 ちかてつ subway
私鉄 してつ nongovernmental [private] railroad line
電鉄 でんてつ electric railway

❹ blade, weapon
寸鉄 すんてつ short blade, small weapon; epigram, pithy saying

INDEPENDENT

【てつ 鉄】**IRON; iron blue, reddish black**
鉄の てつの ferrous, ferric
鉄のカーテン てつのかーてん iron curtain

KUN

【くろがね 鉄】*elegant* **IRON**

SYNONYMS

❶ⓐ **metals**
金 GOLD →2552
銀 SILVER →2156
銅 COPPER →2155
鉄 IRON →2147
鉛 LEAD →2143
錫 TIN →2189

❶ⓐ **iron and steel**
鉄 IRON →2147
銑 PIG IRON →2160
鋼 STEEL →2183

❸ **kinds of railway**
鉄 railway →2147
電 electric railway →3465
車 railway car →4367
両 counter for railway cars →4331
輛 counter for railway cars →2000

鞄

◧ 1-8-5

incorrect stroke-count
➡ see ◧ 1-9-5: 革 at 2248

鞄

◧ 1-8-5

incorrect stroke-count
➡ see ◧ 1-9-5: 革 at 2249

飽

2148
◧ 1-8-5

▸**SATIATED**
ホウ あ(きる) あ(かす) あ(く)
Ⓝ 飽 Ⓒ 饱 bǎo

184	Jōyō	U98FD
食	S13-8-5	F1829

ノ 𠆢 亽 今 今 今 食 食 食 飣 飣 飽 飽 (strokes 1–13)

COMPOUNDS

● [original meaning] (have a full stomach) **SATIATED, sated, satisfied, surfeited**
飽食する ほうしょくする satiate oneself, surfeit, eat one's fill
飽満 ほうまん satiety, surfeit
飽食暖衣 ほうしょくだんい being well fed and well clad
飽和 ほうわ saturation

KUN

【あきる 飽きる】

ⓐ [also suffix] **be SATIATED, be surfeited, be fed up**

ⓑ [sometimes also 厭きる or 倦きる] **grow tired of, lose interest in**

a 聞き飽きる ききあきる be fed up listening to
快楽に飽きる かいらくにあきる be satiated with pleasures

b 飽き あき weariness, tiresomeness
飽きっぽい あきっぽい be fickle [capricious], get soon wearied of
飽き飽きする あきあきする be sick (of), be bored (with), be fed up

【あかす 飽かす】**surfeit, satiate, spend unsparingly; tire, bore (a reader)**
金に飽かして かねにあかして regardless of expense, sparing no money
聴衆を飽かさない ちょうしゅうをあかさない hold the attention of the audience

【あく 飽く】*elegant* same as 飽きる あきる
飽かず あかず insatiably, without being bored
飽く迄 あくまで to the last, stubbornly

SYNONYMS

● **full**
満 FULL →0739
飽 SATIATED →2148

USAGE

【あきる】
飽きる
ⓐ [also suffix] be satiated, be surfeited, be fed up
ⓑ [sometimes also 厭きる or 倦きる] grow tired of, lose interest in
倦きる
[usu. 飽きる, sometimes also 厭きる] grow tired of, lose interest in
厭きる
[usu. 飽きる, sometimes also 倦きる] grow tired of, lose interest in

HOMOPHONES

あきる
厭 TIRE OF →3745
倦 TIRE OF →0131

飼 2149

◧1-8-5

▸**RAISE ANIMALS**

シ か(う)

Ⓝ 飼 Ⓒ 饲 sì

184	Jōyō-5	U98FC
食	S13-8-5	F1352

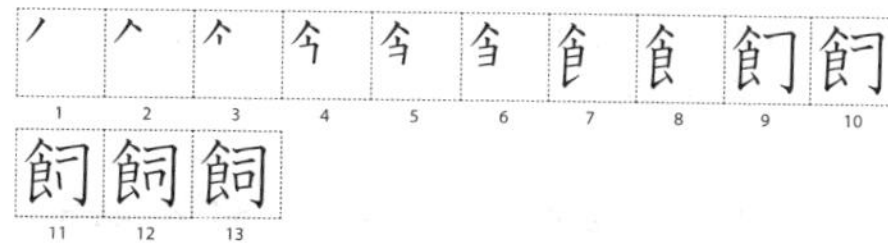

COMPOUNDS

● [original meaning] **RAISE ANIMALS, rear, breed, keep**
飼育する しいくする raise animals, breed, rear
飼養 しよう breeding, raising
飼料 しりょう fodder

KUN

【かう 飼う】**raise (animals), rear; keep (a dog), feed (cattle)**
飼い犬 かいいぬ house dog
飼い殺し かいごろし keeping (an employee) in service for life
羊飼い ひつじかい shepherd
放し飼い はなしがい grazing; letting (a dog) run free

SYNONYMS

● **raise and nourish**
育 RAISE →2544
飼 RAISE ANIMALS →2149
養 FOSTER →2998
滋 NOURISH →0734
哺 NURSE →0478
牧 PASTURE →1083

飾 2150

◧1-8-5

▸**DECORATE**

ショク かざ(る) かざ(り)

Ⓝ 餝 飾 Ⓒ 饰 shì

184	Jōyō	U98FE
食	S13-8-5	F1254

COMPOUNDS

❶ⓐ [original meaning] **DECORATE, adorn, ornament, embellish**
ⓑ **decoration, ornament**
ⓒ **hair ornament; hair**

a 装飾する そうしょくする ornament, adorn, decorate
修飾する しゅうしょくする decorate, ornament; *gram* modify
電飾 でんしょく decorative illumination
満艦飾の船 まんかんしょくのふね full dress ship

b 服飾 ふくしょく dress and its ornaments

c 落飾 らくしょく tonsure

❷ affect, be ostentatious, embellish

虚飾 きょしょく ostentation, affectation, show
粉飾する ふんしょくする embellish, color, rig

KUN

【かざる 飾る】 **DECORATE, ornament, adorn, embellish; affect, be affected; exhibit, display; gloss over (one's defects)**
飾り立てる かざりたてる decorate gaudily, deck out
着飾る きかざる dress up

【かざり 飾り】 **ornament, decoration; embellishment, display, ostentation**
飾り気の無い かざりけのない unaffected, plain
飾り窓 かざりまど show window, display window
首飾り くびかざり necklace

金 革 【食】 幷 卓 𠕋

SYNONYMS

❶ⓐ & ❶ⓑ decorate
飾 DECORATE → 2150
粧 APPLY MAKEUP → 1703
粉 apply face powder → 1643
装 DRESS → 3327

飴

▶CANDY
あめ

2151
1-8-5

184	Nonstandard	U98F4
飠	S13-8-5	F0000

traditional form → see 飴 at 2250

瓶

1-8-5

incorrect classification
➡ see 1-4-9: 扌 at 1316

幹

▶TRUNK
カン みき ㊔ もと
Ⓝ 榦 Ⓒ 干 gàn

2152
1-8-5

51	Jōyō-5	U5E79
干	S13-3-10	F0945

COMPOUNDS

❶ [original meaning] **tree TRUNK**
樹幹 じゅかん trunk, shaft
根幹 こんかん basis, root; keynote; [original meaning] root and trunk
躯×幹 くかん body, trunk, physique

❷ (main part of something) **TRUNK, main part**
幹線 かんせん trunk line, main line
幹部 かんぶ executive, (managing) staff
幹事 かんじ manager, secretary; organizer
基幹 きかん mainstay, nucleus
主幹 しゅかん editor in chief

❸ ability, talent (in performing office work)
才幹 さいかん ability, capability

KUN

【みき 幹】 **tree TRUNK**

SYNONYMS

❶ supporting parts of plants
根 ROOT → 1167
株 stump → 1172
幹 TRUNK → 2152
茎 STEM → 2788

❷ essential part
精 ESSENCE (essential part) → 1729
粋 essence (best part) → 1645
髄 essence (vital part) → 2316
枢 PIVOT → 1076
幹 TRUNK → 2152
綱 ESSENTIAL POINTS → 1735
旨 PURPORT → 2516
要 summary → 3263

嗣

▶HEIR
シ ㊔ つぐ つぎ
Ⓒ 嗣 sì

2153
1-8-5

30	Jōyō	U55E3
口	S13-3-10	F2081

COMPOUNDS

❶ HEIR, successor
嗣子 しし heir, successor
後嗣 こうし heir, successor
令嗣 れいし your [his] heir
皇嗣 こうし Imperial Heir, Crown Prince

❷ inherit, succeed
継嗣 けいし successor, heir, heiress

INDEPENDENT

【し 嗣】 **HEIR,** successor
皇帝の嗣 こうていのし emperor's heir

SYNONYMS

❶ inheritors
嫡 LEGITIMATE CHILD → 0839
嗣 HEIR → 2153

❷ succeed
継 SUCCEED → 1720
承 succeed to → 0016
嗣 inherit → 2153

鉾

2154

1-8-6

▶DECORATIVE HALBERD

ボウ ほこ

Ⓒ 鉾 móu

167	Non-Jōyō	U927E
金	S14-8-6	F3250

KUN

【ほこ 鉾】**DECORATIVE HALBERD**

山鉾 やまぼこ festival float mounted with a decorative halberd

蒲鉾 かまぼこ steamed fish paste

SYNONYMS

【ほこ】

○ **cutting weapons**

刀 SWORD (single-edged) →3642
剣 SWORD (double-edged) →2104
矛 HALBERD →2501
戟 HALBERD →2131
鉾 DECORATIVE HALBERD →2154
戈 DAGGER-AX →4274

HOMOPHONES

ほこ

矛 HALBERD →2501
戈 DAGGER-AX →4274
戟 HALBERD →2131
鋒 POINT OF A BLADE →2172

NOTE

➡ see USAGE note at 矛 2501

銅

2155

1-8-6

▶COPPER

ドウ あかがね▲

Ⓒ 铜 tóng

167	Jōyō-5	U9285
金	S14-8-6	F1768

COMPOUNDS

❶ [also prefix] [original meaning] **COPPER**

銅鉱 どうこう copper ore
銅線 どうせん copper wire
銅山 どうざん copper mine
銅貨 どうか copper coin, copper
銅相場 どうそうば market price of copper
青銅 せいどう bronze

❷ **bronze**

銅像 どうぞう bronze statue [image]
銅鐸× どうたく bronze bell

INDEPENDENT

【どう 銅】**COPPER;** abbrev. of 銅メダル どうめだる: **copper medal**

銅の どうの copper

KUN

【あかがね 銅】[also 赤金] **COPPER**

銅の器 あかがねのうつわ copper vessel

SYNONYMS

❶ **metals**

金 GOLD →2552
銀 SILVER →2156
銅 COPPER →2155
鉄 IRON →2147
鉛 LEAD →2143
錫 TIN →2189

USAGE

【あかがね】

銅
[also 赤金] copper

赤金
[also 銅] copper

HOMOPHONES

あかがね 赤金 →2719, 2552

銀

2156

1-8-6

▶SILVER

ギン しろがね▲ ㊔ かね しろかね

Ⓒ 银 yín

167	Jōyō-3	U9280
金	S14-8-6	F0562

COMPOUNDS

❶ⓐ **SILVER**

ⓑ (of silvery color) **SILVER**

a 銀貨 ぎんか silver coin
水銀 すいぎん mercury, quicksilver
純銀 じゅんぎん pure silver
硝酸銀 しょうさんぎん silver nitrate
金銀 きんぎん gold and silver; money

b 銀色 ぎんいろ silver color, silveriness
銀婚式 ぎんこんしき silver wedding
銀河 ぎんが Milky Way; galaxy
銀髪 ぎんぱつ silver hair
銀紙 ぎんがみ aluminum [tin] foil, silver paper

❷ (medium of exchange) **SILVER, silver coin, money, wages**

銀行 ぎんこう bank

銀座 ぎんざ the Ginza; mint (during Edo period)
銀本位制 ぎんほんいせい silver standard
賃銀(=賃金) ちんぎん wages, pay
労銀 ろうぎん wages (for labor)
❸ abbrev. of 銀行 ぎんこう: **bank**
日銀 にちぎん Bank of Japan
勧銀 かんぎん hypothecary bank
開銀 かいぎん development bank
❹ name of chess piece in shogi (Japanese chess): *gin*, the **SILVER**
銀将 ぎんしょう *gin*
銀交換 ぎんこうかん exchange of *gins*
❺ *astron* galactic
銀経 ぎんけい galactic longitude

INDEPENDENT

【ぎん 銀】**SILVER;** abbrev. of 銀メダル ぎんめだる: **silver medal; *gin*** (→ ❹)
銀を取る ぎんをとる desilverize; capture a *gin*

KUN

【しろがね 銀】[sometimes also 白金]
ⓐ **SILVER**
ⓑ **SILVER** coin

SYNONYMS

❶ⓐ metals
金 GOLD → 2552
銀 SILVER → 2156
銅 COPPER → 2155
鉄 IRON → 2147
鉛 LEAD → 2143
錫 TIN → 2189
ⓑ white colors
白 WHITE → 4305
皓 BRIGHT WHITE → 1513
銀 SILVER → 2156
❷ money
金 MONEY → 2552
銭 MONEY → 2159
貨 MONEY (legal tender), coin → 3113
幣 CURRENCY → 3582
銀 SILVER → 2156
財 finance → 1849
資 RESOURCES → 3342
-玉 coin suffix → 4289
札 bill → 1011
❸ bank
銀 bank → 2156
行 bank → 0246

HOMOPHONES

しろがね 白金 → 4305, 2552

NOTE

➡ see USAGE note at 金 2552
➡ see COMPOUND FORMATION for 銀座 ぎんざ → 座 3868

銃

2157
1-8-6

▶GUN
ジュウ
Ⓒ 铳 chòng

167	Jōyō	U9283
金	S14-8-6	F1067

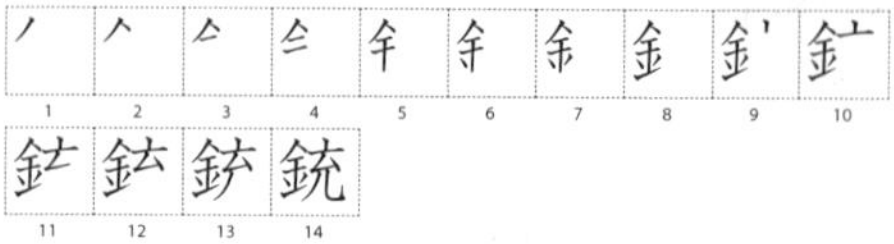

COMPOUNDS

[also suffix]
ⓐ (portable firearm) **GUN, rifle, firearm**
ⓑ (something resembling a gun in shape or function) **GUN**
a 銃声 じゅうせい sound of gunfire
銃撃 じゅうげき shooting, gunning (down)
銃砲 じゅうほう firearm
拳銃 けんじゅう pistol, handgun
猟銃 りょうじゅう hunting gun
短銃 たんじゅう pistol
ライフル銃 らいふるじゅう rifle
機関銃 きかんじゅう machine gun
b 鋲×打ち銃 びょううちじゅう rivet gun

INDEPENDENT

【じゅう 銃】**GUN, rifle**
銃の筒 じゅうのつつ barrel of a gun

SYNONYMS

ⓐ weapons for shooting
銃 GUN (portable firearm) → 2157
砲 HEAVY GUN → 1479
火 firearms → 4273
弓 BOW → 4193

銘

2158
1-8-6

▶INSCRIPTION
メイ
Ⓒ 铭 míng

167	Jōyō	U9298
金	S14-8-6	F1460

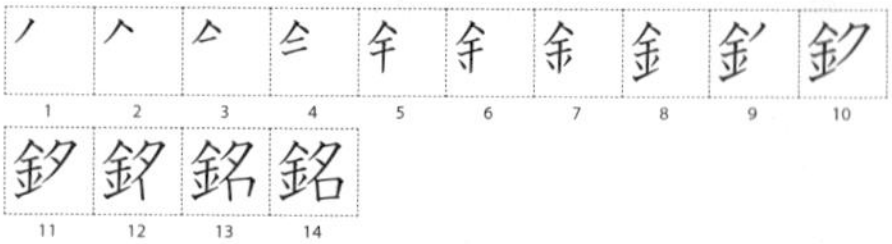

COMPOUNDS

❶ [original meaning] (name or words inscribed on metal or stone) **INSCRIPTION, epitaph (usu. written in classical Chinese)**

銘文 めいぶん inscription

碑銘 ひめい inscription, epitaph

墓碑銘 ぼひめい epitaph, inscription on a tombstone

❷ **engrave on one's mind, bear in mind**

銘記する めいきする bear in mind, remember; inscribe, engrave

感銘 かんめい deep impression

❸ **name (inscribed by maker on finished product), appellation, signature**

銘刀 めいとう sword inscribed by the sword smith

銘板 めいばん nameplate (of machines)

銘柄 めいがら brand name, brand, name

銘打つ めいうつ engrave an inscription; call [designate] itself

無銘の むめいの anonymous

❹ of well-known name, of noted brand, choice, superior

銘茶 めいちゃ refined tea

銘酒 めいしゅ choice [superior] sake

❺ motto

座右銘 ざゆうめい motto

❻ **unclassified compounds**

銘銘 めいめい each, severally

INDEPENDENT

【めい 銘】**INSCRIPTION**, epitaph, signature; name, brand name, appellation; precept, motto, maxim

銘を刻む めいをきざむ engrave an inscription

座右の銘 ざゆうのめい (one's) motto

【めいずる 銘ずる】impress, stamp, engrave

SYNONYMS

❶ **writing**

文 WRITINGS → 2458

筆 WRITING → 3317

書 writing(s) → 3292

銘 INSCRIPTION → 2158

❸ **name**

名 NAME → 2693

銘 name (inscribed by maker) → 2158

姓 SURNAME → 0334

氏 FAMILY NAME → 3669

称 APPELLATION → 1491

題 TITLE → 4139

号 DESIGNATION → 2675

銭

2159

◧ 1-8-6

▸**MONEY**

セン ぜに

Ⓝ 錢 Ⓒ 钱 qián

167 金	Jōyō-5 S14-8-6	U92AD F1188

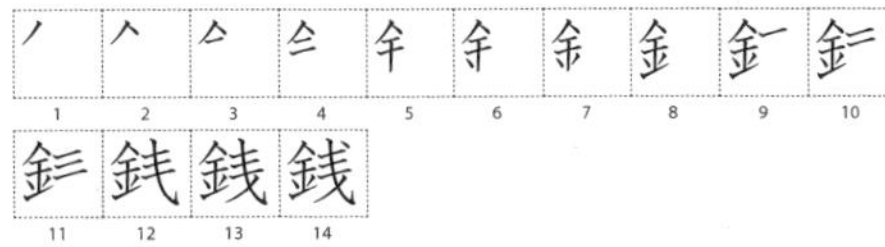

COMPOUNDS

❶ⓐ **MONEY, cash**

ⓑ **coin, copper coin**

a 金銭 きんせん money, cash

釣り銭 つりせん change

無銭の むせんの penniless, moneyless

守銭奴 しゅせんど miser, slave of money

賽×銭 さいせん money offering

b バラ銭 ばらせん (small) change, loose coins

銅銭 どうせん copper coin

穴明き銭 あなあきせん perforated coin

❷ **MONEY paid, charges, fee**

銭湯 せんとう public bath, bathhouse

木戸銭 きどせん gate money, admission fee

煙草銭 たばこせん tobacco money

❸ sen:

ⓐ **monetary unit equiv. to 1/100 of a yen (円)**

ⓑ former monetary unit equiv. to 1/1000 of a *kan* (貫)

a 二円五十銭 にえんごじゅっせん 2 yen 50 sen

INDEPENDENT

【せん 銭】sen (→❸)

KUN

【ぜに 銭】**MONEY, cash; coin, copper coin**

銭の取れる ぜにのとれる worth the money

銭箱 ぜにばこ cashbox

銭入れ ぜにいれ purse, till

銭亀 ぜにがめ baby spotted turtle, young Japanese terrapin

小銭 こぜに small money, small coin [change]

日銭 ひぜに daily income in cash

身銭 みぜに one's own money

SYNONYMS

❶ⓐ **money**

金 MONEY → 2552

銭 MONEY → 2159

貨 MONEY (legal tender), coin → 3113

幣 CURRENCY → 3582

銀 SILVER → 2156

財 finance → 1849

資 RESOURCES → 3342
-玉 coin suffix → 4289
札 bill → 1011

❷ **fee and price**
料 FEE → 1644
代 CHARGE → 0034
賃 CHARGES → 3341
銭 money paid → 2159
費 EXPENSE → 3221
価 PRICE → 0095
値 price → 0123

❸ **Japanese money denominations**
文 *mon* → 2458
両 *ryo* → 4331
厘 *RIN* → 3727
銭 sen → 2159
円 YEN → 3673

銑

2160
1-8-6

▸PIG IRON
セン
Ⓒ 铣 xiǎn xǐ

167	Names	U9291
金	S14-8-6	F4004

COMPOUNDS

● **PIG IRON**
銑鉄 せんてつ pig iron
溶銑 ようせん molten iron
白銑 はくせん white pig iron

SYNONYMS

● **iron and steel**
鉄 IRON → 2147
銑 PIG IRON → 2160
鋼 STEEL → 2183

銓

2161
1-8-6

▸WEIGH
セン
Ⓒ 铨 quán

167	Non-Jōyō	U9293
金	S14-8-6	F0000

COMPOUNDS

● [now replaced by 選 3931] [original meaning] **WEIGH, evaluate**
銓衡(=選考)する せんこうする select, screen

SYNONYMS

● **think and consider**
思 THINK → 3173
惟 MEDITATE → 0582
省 INTROSPECT → 3100
稽 THINK → 1573
考 THINK → 3962
存 hold an opinion → 3702
案 think out → 2824
想 CONCEIVE → 3507
慮 CONSIDER → 4050
勘 take into consideration → 2231
銓 WEIGH → 2161
量 weigh → 3119

鋏

2162
1-8-6

▸SCISSORS
キョウ はさみ はさ(む)

167	Nonstandard	U28987
金	S14-8-6	F0000

traditional form → see 鋏 at 2173

銕

2163
1-8-6

▸IRON
テツ くろがね ㊔ かね くろかね

167	Nonstandard	U9295
金	S14-8-6	F0000

traditional form → see 鉄 at 2147

静

2164
1-8-6

▸QUIET
セイ ジョウ しず- しず(か) しず(まる) しず(める) ㊔ やすし
Ⓝ 靜 Ⓒ 静 jìng

174	Jōyō-4	U9759
青	S14-8-6	F0627

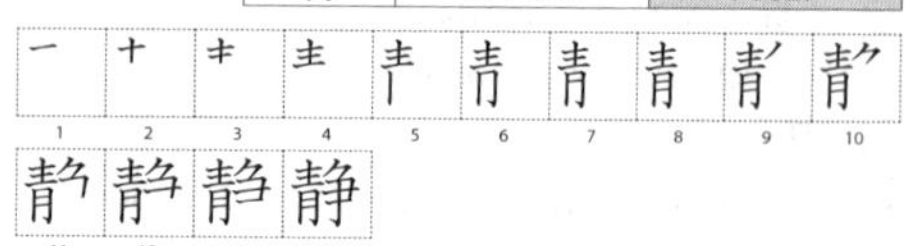

COMPOUNDS

❶ⓐ [original meaning] (free from noise) **QUIET, still, silent**
ⓑ (free of agitation) **QUIET, calm, serene, tranquil**
ⓒ (make quiet) **QUIET, calm, still**
a 静寂 せいじゃく silence, quietness, stillness
静聴する せいちょうする listen quietly
b 沈静 ちんせい stillness, tranquility, slackness
平静な へいせいな calm, serene
冷静な れいせいな cool, calm, cool-headed, dispassionate
c 鎮静する ちんせいする calm down, be tranquilized, subside; calm, tranquilize

❷ (motionless)
ⓐ **still, QUIET, static, inactive**
ⓑ [prefix] static, statical
a 静止する せいしする stand still, come to a standstill
静脈 じょうみゃく vein
静座 せいざ sitting quietly, meditation
b 静圧比 せいあつひ static pressure ratio
静電気 せいでんき static electricity

INDEPENDENT

【せい 静】QUIET, calm, stillness
静と動 せいとどう stillness and motion

KUN

【しず- 静-】**QUIET, calm**
静けさ しずけさ stillness, silence, tranquility
静静と しずしずと quietly, gently, calmly, slowly

【しずか 静か】
しずかな 静かな **QUIET, silent, still; calm, tranquil, gentle, quiet**
静かさ しずかさ quiet, calm
静かにしなさい しずかにしなさい Be quiet!
物静かな ものしずかな quiet, still, calm

【しずまる 静まる】
ⓐ **become QUIET, grow still**
ⓑ **calm down, become tranquil, be lulled**
a 静まり返る しずまりかえる become still as death
寝静まる ねしずまる fall fast asleep
b 嵐が静まった あらしがしずまった The storm has abated

【しずめる 静める】
ⓐ (make quiet) **QUIET, calm, still**
ⓑ (make calm) **appease, calm, pacify**
b 気を静める きをしずめる compose oneself, becalm one's feelings

SYNONYMS

❶ⓐ **quiet**
静 QUIET →2164
閑 QUIET →4123
寂 quiet →2855
幽 QUIET AND SECLUDED →3731
粛 still →4400
黙 SILENT →3554
ⓑ **calm and peaceful**
安 PEACEFUL →2695
康 peaceful →3877
寧 peaceful →2959
泰 TRANQUIL →3193
静 QUIET →2164
平 CALM →4291
穏 CALM →1578
❷ⓐ **not moving**
固 FIRM →3830
定 fixed →2770
静 still →2164
止 still →3659

USAGE

❶【しずまる】
静まる
ⓐ become quiet, grow still
ⓑ calm down, become tranquil, be lulled
鎮まる
① be quelled, be suppressed, subside, be put down
② be alleviated, be relieved, be soothed
③ be enshrined
❷【しずめる】
静める
ⓐ (make quiet) quiet, calm, still
ⓑ (make calm) appease, calm, pacify
鎮める
① quell, suppress, put down, subdue, pacify
② alleviate (pain), relieve, allay, soothe
沈める
ⓐ sink, send to the bottom, submerge
ⓑ sink oneself into (a chair), lower oneself
ⓒ sink down in the world, go to ruin

HOMOPHONES

しずまる 鎮 QUELL →2210
しずめる
鎮 QUELL →2210
沈 SINK →0306

鞍
◧1-8-6
incorrect stroke-count
➡ see ◧1-9-6: 鞍 at 2255

餅
2165
◧1-8-6
▶**RICE CAKE**
ヘイ もち

184	Nonstandard	U9905
食	S14-8-6	F0000

alternative form →see 餠 at 2256

餌
2166
◧1-8-6
▶**ANIMAL FEED**
ジ えさ え

184	Nonstandard	U990C
食	S14-8-6	F0000

alternative form →see 餌 at 2257

蝕
2167
◧1-8-6
▶**ERODE**
ショク むしば(む)

142	Nonstandard	U8755
虫	S14-6-8	F0000

traditional form →see 蝕 at 2258

斡
2168
◧1-8-6
▶**REVOLVE**
アツ ㊔ まる
Ⓒ 斡 wò

68	Names	U65A1
斗	S14-4-10	F2891

COMPOUNDS

● **REVOLVE, go around**

斡旋 あっせん good offices, services; mediation

SYNONYMS

● turn

旋 GYRATE → 1194
転 TURN → 1872
回 TURN ROUND → 3793
廻 TURN ROUND → 3833
巡 MAKE THE ROUNDS → 3781
循 CIRCULATE → 0704
斡 REVOLVE → 2168
捻 TWIST → 0604

榦 2169

▶TRUNK
カン みき ㊔ もと

75 木	Nonstandard	U69A6
	S14-4-10	F0000

1-8-6
traditional form → see 幹 at 2152

鋳 2170

▶CAST
チュウ い(る)
N 鑄 C 铸 zhù

167 金	Jōyō	U92F3
	S15-8-7	F2352

1-8-7

COMPOUNDS

● [original meaning] **CAST, mint, coin**

鋳鉄 ちゅうてつ iron casting
鋳造 ちゅうぞう casting, minting, coining
鋳金 ちゅうきん casting
鋳鋼 ちゅうこう cast steel
改鋳 かいちゅう recoinage, recasting

KUN

【いる 鋳る】**CAST, mint, coin**

鋳物 いもの cast metal, casting
鋳型 いがた mold, cast, matrix, die
鋳直し いなおし recasting

SYNONYMS

● work metals

錬 REFINE (crude metals) → 2185
煉 REFINE (crude metals) → 1297
鍛 FORGE → 2206
鋳 CAST → 2170
焼き annealing → 1256
冶 WORK METALS → 0089

● form and carve

刻 ENGRAVE → 1619
彫 CARVE → 2117
塑 MODEL → 3525
鋳 CAST → 2170

鋭 2171

▶SHARP
エイ するど(い) ㊔ とし さとし
N 鋭 C 锐 ruì

167 金	Jōyō	U92ED
	S15-8-7	F1358

1-8-7

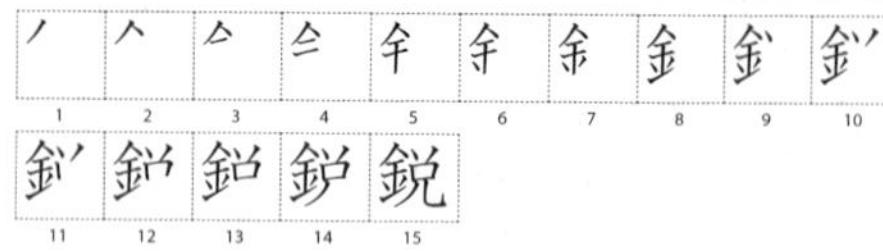

COMPOUNDS

❶ⓐ [original meaning] (having an acute point) **SHARP, pointed**

ⓑ (having an acute edge) **SHARP, acute**

a 鋭鋒 えいほう brunt (of an attack); incisive reasoning
先鋭(=尖鋭)な せんえいな radical; acute, sharp
b 鋭利な えいりな sharp, keen; acute, sharp, clever
鋭角 えいかく acute angle

❷ **SHARP-witted, quick, trenchant**

鋭敏な えいびんな sharp, keen, sensitive

❸ **vigorous, energetic, stinging**

鋭気有る えいきある spirited, dashing
鋭意 えいい zeal

❹ **the choice, the best (esp. troops)**

鋭兵 えいへい picked troops
新鋭な しんえいな fresh picked
精鋭 せいえい best [pick] (of the aviators), choice (of an army)

INDEPENDENT

【えい 鋭】**SHARP**ness; vigor; (sharp) weapon

鋭を挫く えいをくじく break the brunt
鋭を取る えいをとる take up a weapon

KUN

【するどい 鋭い】**pointed, acute; SHARP-witted, quick-witted, shrewd, keen, acute; violent, stinging, pungent**

鋭さ するどさ sharpness, acuteness, poignancy
鋭いナイフ するどいないふ sharp knife
鋭い批判 するどいひはん sharp criticism
頭の鋭い男 あたまのするどいおとこ man of keen intelligence

SYNONYMS

❶ sharp

鋭 SHARP → 2171
先 pointed → 3046
尖 pointed → 2700

❷ **intelligent and wise**

賢 WISE → 3518
俊 brilliant → 0117
鋭 SHARP → 2171
敏 NIMBLE → 1675
叡 PROFOUNDLY WISE → 2405
智 wise → 3458
慧 INTELLIGENT → 3485
怜 CLEVER → 0356
悧 CLEVER → 0505
俐 CLEVER → 0113
哲 SAGACIOUS → 3402
明 clear-sighted → 1060
聡 SHARP-WITTED → 1750

鋒

2172

◧1-8-7

▶POINT OF A BLADE

ホウ　きっさき　ほこ　ほこさき　㊔ さき

Ⓒ 锋 fēng

167	Names	U92D2
金	S15-8-7	F2402

COMPOUNDS

❶ [original meaning] **POINT OF A BLADE [sword]; spearhead**

鋒鋩[×] ほうぼう point of a blade; sharp words, vicious character
機鋒 きほう sword point, spearhead; brunt

❷ **brunt, sharp force**

鋭鋒 えいほう brunt (of an attack); incisive reasoning
舌鋒 ぜっぽう (sharp) tongue
筆鋒 ひっぽう power of the pen, sharp pen; tip of a writing brush

❸ van(guard) (of an army)

先鋒 せんぽう van(guard); first player in a team match (in kendo or judo)

INDEPENDENT

【ほう　鋒】**POINT OF A BLADE** [sword]; sword

KUN

【きっさき　鋒】[usu. 切っ先]
ⓐ **POINT OF A BLADE** [sword]
ⓑ tone of argument, force of an attack
【ほこ　鋒】[usu. 矛, sometimes also 戟] **halberd**
【ほこさき　鋒】[usu. 矛先] spearhead; the aim (of an attack); the brunt (of an argument)

SYNONYMS

❶ **extremity**

端 END → 1564
末 end → 4317
梢 tip → 1208
先 point → 3046
尖 POINT → 2700
鋒 POINT OF A BLADE → 2172

❷ **energy and force**

力 POWER, force → 4178
勢 physical power → 3542
気 energy → 3960
圧 PRESSURE → 3688
鋒 brunt → 2172

HOMOPHONES

きっさき 切っ先 → 0030, 3046

ほこ

矛 HALBERD → 2501
戟 HALBERD → 2131
鉾 DECORATIVE HALBERD → 2154
戈 DAGGER-AX → 4274

NOTE

➡ see USAGE note at 矛 2501

鋏

2173

◧1-8-7

▶SCISSORS

キョウ　はさみ　はさ(む)

Ⓝ 鋏 Ⓒ 铗 jiá

167	Non-Jōyō	U92CF
金	S15-8-7	F3127

COMPOUNDS

❶ⓐ **SCISSORS, shears**
ⓑ **punch**

b 入鋏 にゅうきょう (ticket) punching

❷ **snip, clip**

KUN

【はさみ　鋏】
ⓐ **SCISSORS, shears**
ⓑ **punch**

a 花鋏 はなばさみ flower scissors
剪定鋏 せんていばさみ pruning shears

【はさむ　鋏む】**snip, clip**

枝を鋏む えだをはさむ trim [prune] a tree

SYNONYMS

❶ⓐ **cutting instruments**

刀 cutting tool → 3642
鎌 SICKLE → 2212
刃 BLADE → 3646
鋏 SCISSORS → 2173
鋸 SAW → 2184
斧 AXE → 2558
鍬 HOE → 2205
錐 DRILL → 2190
鑿 CHISEL → 3640

HOMOPHONES

はさむ

挟 HOLD BETWEEN → 0450
挿 INSERT → 0517

NOTE

➡ see USAGE note at 挟 0450

銷

2174

1-8-7

▶**USE UP**

ショウ

Ⓒ 销 xiāo

167	Non-Jōyō	U92B7
金	S15-8-7	F0000

COMPOUNDS

[now replaced by 消 0531]

❶ **USE UP, consume, spend**

銷夏 しょうか summering

意気銷沈する いきしょうちんする be dispirited, be disheartened

❷ⓐ eliminate, obliterate

ⓑ disappear, vanish

a 銷却する しょうきゃくする efface; erase

❸ [original meaning, now archaic] melt (metals), be melted

SYNONYMS

❶ **consume**

消 SPEND → 0531

費 expend → 3221

尽 EXHAUST → 3786

耗 WEAR AWAY → 1660

銷 USE UP → 2174

鋭

2175

1-8-7

▶**SHARP**

エイ するど(い) ㊔ とし さとし

167	Nonstandard	U92B3
金	S15-8-7	F0000

traditional form → see 鋭 at 2171

鞘

1-8-7

incorrect stroke-count

➡ see 1-9-7: 革 at 2259

鞘

1-8-7

incorrect stroke-count

➡ see 1-9-7: 革 at 2260

餓

2176

1-8-7

▶**STARVED**

ガ う(える)▲

Ⓝ 餓 Ⓒ 饿 è

184	Jōyō	U9913
食	S15-8-7	F2210

1	2	3	4	5	6	7	8	9	10	11	12	13	14	15
ノ	𠆢	亽	今	今	今	食	食	食	食	飦	飳	餓	餓	餓

COMPOUNDS

● [original meaning] **STARVED, hungry**

餓死 がし death from starvation

餓鬼 がき hungry ghost; *slang* kid

飢餓 きが starvation, hunger, famine

KUN

【うえる 餓える】 [now usu. 飢える]

ⓐ starve, be hungry, famish

ⓑ hunger [starve] for (love), thirst for (knowledge)

a 餓え死に うえじに (death by) starvation

SYNONYMS

● **hunger and thirst**

渇 THIRST → 0627

餓 STARVED → 2176

飢 STARVE → 2101

饑 STARVE → 2281

HOMOPHONES

うえる 飢 STARVE → 2101

NOTE

➡ see USAGE note at 飢 2101

舗

2177

1-8-7

▶**PAVE**

▶**SHOP**

ホ ㊔ しき

Ⓝ 舖 Ⓒ 铺 pū pù

9△	Jōyō	U8217
人	S15-2-13	F1700

1	2	3	4	5	6	7	8	9	10	11	12	13	14	15
ノ	𠆢	亼	今	全	全	舎	舎	舎	舎	舎	舗	舗	舗	舗

COMPOUNDS

❶ **PAVE, lay**

舗装 ほそう paving

舗道 ほどう pavement, paved street

❷ [also suffix] **SHOP, store**—said esp. of shops having a long tradition

店舗 てんぽ shop, store

老舗 ろうほ(=しにせ) old [long-established] shop

名舗 めいほ famous store, quality shop

本舗 ほんぽ head office, main shop

薬舗 やくほ pharmacy, drugstore

新聞舗 しんぶんほ newspaper distributor

❸ counter for sheets

地図二舗 ちずにほ two maps

SYNONYMS

❶ **spread**

散 SCATTER → 2137

布 SPREAD → 3691

敷く LAY → 2345
舗 PAVE → 2177
塗 APPLY ON A SURFACE → 3523
抹 wipe over → 0370
撒 SCATTER → 0909

❷ **places of business**
店 SHOP (of any kind) → 3828
舗 SHOP (esp. traditional) → 2177
屋 SMALL SHOP → 3842
社 COMPANY → 1042

舖

2178
◧ 1-8-7

▶**PAVE**
▶**SHOP**
ホ ㊔ しき

135	Nonstandard	U8216
舌	S15-6-9	F0000

traditional form → see 舗 at 2177

緜

2179
◧ 1-8-7

▶**COTTON**
メン わた

120	Nonstandard	U7DDC
糸	S15-6-9	F0000

traditional form → see 綿 at 1736

錠

2180
◧ 1-8-8

▶**LOCK**
▶**PILL**
ジョウ
Ⓒ 锭 dìng

167	Jōyō	U9320
金	S16-8-8	F2039

COMPOUNDS

❶ [also suffix] **LOCK, padlock**
錠前 じょうまえ lock
手錠 てじょう handcuffs
文字合わせ錠 もじあわせじょう combination lock

❷ⓐ [also suffix] **PILL, tablet**
ⓑ counter for **PILL**s
a 錠剤 じょうざい pill, tablet
糖衣錠 とういじょう sugar-coated pill
ビタミン錠 びたみんじょう vitamin tablet [pill]
モヒ錠 もひじょう tablet of morphine
b 二錠 にじょう two pills

INDEPENDENT

【じょう 錠】LOCK
錠を掛ける じょうをかける fasten a lock

SYNONYMS

❶ **locks and keys**
鍵 KEY → 2203
錠 LOCK → 2180

❷ **medicines**
薬 DRUG → 3011
剤 PREPARATION → 2102
錠 PILL → 2180
丸 pill suffix → 4225
鍼 ACUPUNCTURE → 2204
灸 MOXIBUSTION → 2752

錦

2181
◧ 1-8-8

▶**BROCADE**
キン にしき ㊔ かね にし
Ⓒ 锦 jǐn

167	Jōyō	U9326
金	S16-8-8	F1965

COMPOUNDS

❶ [original meaning] **BROCADE**
錦旗 きんき gold-brocade flag; pennant

❷ term of respect
錦地 きんち your place of residence

KUN

【にしき 錦】(Japanese) **BROCADE; fine dress**
錦絵 にしきえ color print
錦鯉 にしきごい colored carp
毛織錦 けおりにしき woolen brocade

SYNONYMS

❶ **fabrics**
織 woven fabric → 1801
紬 PONGEE → 1684
紗 GAUZE → 1653
絹 SILK → 1721
綾 TWILL → 1740
綿 COTTON → 1736
棉 COTTON → 1244
麻 HEMP → 3878
毛 wool → 4264
錦 BROCADE → 2181

錮

2182
◧ 1-8-8

▶**IMPRISON**
コ
Ⓒ 锢 gù

167	Jōyō	U932E
金	S16-8-8	F0000

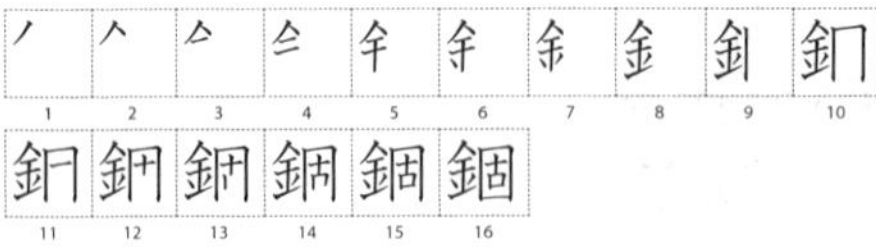

COMPOUNDS

❶ [now also 固 3830] **IMPRISON, hold in custody**
禁錮 きんこ imprisonment

❷ [original meaning, now obsolete] plug with molten metal

SYNONYMS

❶ **imprison and confine**
拘 ARREST → 0367
禁 confine → 3469
留 keep in custody → 3189
置 place in custody → 3222
錮 IMPRISON → 2182

鋼

▸STEEL
コウ はがね
Ⓒ 钢 gāng gàng

2183
1-8-8

167	Jōyō-6	U92FC
金	S16-8-8	F1983

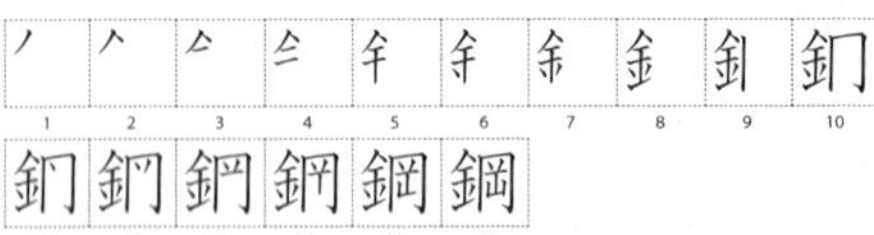

COMPOUNDS

ⓐ [also suffix] [original meaning] **STEEL**
ⓑ hard like **STEEL**
a 鋼材 こうざい steel materials, structural steel
鋼板 こうはん steel plate
鋼管 こうかん steel pipe [tubing]
鋼線 こうせん steel wire
製鋼 せいこう steel manufacture
鉄鋼 てっこう iron and steel
ステンレス鋼 すてんれすこう stainless steel
b 鋼玉 こうぎょく corundum

INDEPENDENT

【こう 鋼】**STEEL**

KUN

【はがね 鋼】**STEEL**
鋼色 はがねいろ steel blue

SYNONYMS

ⓐ **iron and steel**
鉄 IRON → 2147
銑 PIG IRON → 2160
鋼 STEEL → 2183

鋸

▸SAW
キョ のこぎり のこ
Ⓒ 锯 jù jū

2184
1-8-8

167	Names	U92F8
金	S16-8-8	F3055

COMPOUNDS

● **SAW**
鋸歯 きょし saw tooth

KUN

【のこぎり 鋸】**SAW**
鋸鎌 のこぎりがま toothed sickle
鋸草 のこぎりそう Siberian yarrow, *Achillea sibirica;* achillea
鋸鮫 のこぎりざめ sawshark, esp. Japanese sawshark

【のこ 鋸】**SAW**
丸鋸 まるのこ circular [buzz] saw
糸鋸 いとのこ coping saw, fretsaw
帯鋸 おびのこ(=おびのこぎり) band saw

SPECIAL READINGS

大鋸屑 おがくず sawdust

SYNONYMS

● **cutting instruments**
刀 cutting tool → 3642
鎌 SICKLE → 2212
刃 BLADE → 3646
鋏 SCISSORS → 2173
鋸 SAW → 2184
斧 AXE → 2558
鍬 HOE → 2205
錐 DRILL → 2190
鑿 CHISEL → 3640

錬

▸REFINE
レン ね(る)▲
Ⓝ 鍊 Ⓒ 炼 liàn

2185
1-8-8

167	Jōyō	U932C
金	S16-8-8	F2216

COMPOUNDS

❶ [formerly also 煉 1297] [original meaning] **REFINE (crude metals), smelt; work metals, temper**
錬金術 れんきんじゅつ alchemy
錬鉄 れんてつ wrought iron
錬鋼 れんこう wrought steel
精錬 せいれん refining, smelting; tempering
製錬 せいれん smelting

鍛錬する たんれんする temper, forge; train, discipline

❷ [usu. 練 1738] **REFINE one's mental and physical skills, train, cultivate, improve one's character**

錬成 れんせい training, drilling

錬磨する れんまする train, practice, cultivate

修錬する しゅうれんする train, discipline

KUN

【ねる 錬る】[now usu. 練る] temper (metals), forge, **REFINE**, smelt

SYNONYMS

❶ **work metals**

錬 REFINE (crude metals) → 2185

煉 REFINE (crude metals) → 1297

鍛 FORGE → 2206

鋳 CAST → 2170

焼き annealing → 1256

冶 WORK METALS → 0089

❶ **refine**

錬 REFINE (crude metals) → 2185

精 REFINE (crude materials) → 1729

留 distill → 3189

❷ **cultivate**

修 CULTIVATE → 0138

養 FOSTER (one's intellect) → 2998

練 TRAIN → 1738

錬 REFINE → 2185

鍛 train → 2206

磨 POLISH → 3946

琢 POLISH → 1222

HOMOPHONES

ねる

練 TRAIN → 1738

煉 REFINE → 1297

NOTE

➡ see USAGE note at 練 1738

録

▶RECORD

ロク

Ⓝ 錄 Ⓒ 录 lù

2186

◧ 1-8-8

167	Jōyō-4	U9332
金	S16-8-8	F0685

COMPOUNDS

❶ⓐ [original meaning] **RECORD, write down, register**

ⓑ **RECORD on tape**

a 記録する きろくする record, register, write down; set a record

収録する しゅうろくする collect, record, write down

登録 とうろく registration

b 録音 ろくおん sound recording

録音テープ ろくおんてーぷ tape (for recording)

録画 ろくが videotaping

❷ [also suffix] **RECORD, records; proceedings, annals**

目録 もくろく catalog

付録 ふろく appendix, supplement

会議録 かいぎろく minutes, proceedings

語録 ごろく analects, sayings

SYNONYMS

❶ **write**

書 WRITE → 3292

筆 write → 3317

写 COPY → 2493

記 WRITE DOWN → 1843

紀 record in writing → 1628

控える note down → 0600

録 RECORD → 2186

登 register → 3208

註 ANNOTATE → 1893

❷ **records**

記 written account → 1843

録 RECORD → 2186

譜 SYSTEMATIC RECORD → 2068

誌 records → 1950

史 HISTORY → 4324

伝 biography → 0048

錯

▶MIXED UP

サク シャク[▲]

Ⓒ 错 cuò

2187

◧ 1-8-8

167	Jōyō	U932F
金	S16-8-8	F1722

COMPOUNDS

❶ⓐ **MIXED UP, intricate, confused, disordered, complicated**

ⓑ *chem* complex

a 錯雑 さくざつ complication, intricacy

錯綜 さくそう complication, intricacy

交錯した こうさくした mingled, entangled, complicated, intricate

b 錯イオン さくいおん complex ion

❷ⓐ **mistaken, erroneous, wrong**

❻ put in the wrong place, invert

a 錯誤 さくご mistake, error

錯覚 さっかく false perception, mistaken idea, (optical) illusion

錯乱 さくらん distraction, derangement, confusion

b 錯角 さっかく alternate interior angles

錯字症 さくじしょう paragraphia

倒錯 とうさく perversion, inversion

❸ unclassified compounds

介錯する かいしゃくする assist a person in committing hara-kiri

SYNONYMS

❶❶ mix

混 MIX → 0631

淆 INTERMINGLE → 0630

交 intermingle → 2508

雑 MIXED → 1752

錯 MIXED UP → 2187

❶❶ disordered

紛 CONFUSED → 1648

乱 DISORDERED → 1611

錯 MIXED UP → 2187

混 mixed up → 0631

雑 mixed up → 1752

沌 PRIMEVAL CHAOS → 0314

❷❶ mistakes and mistaking

過 error → 3891

失 SLIP → 4325

誤 MISTAKE → 1945

謬 MISTAKE → 2060

錯 mistaken → 2187

-違える mis- → 3907

錆

2188

1-8-8

▶RUST

セイ さび さ(びる)

Ⓝ 錆 Ⓒ 锖 qiāng

167	Names	U9306
金	S16-8-8	F2673

COMPOUNDS

● RUST; patina

防錆 ぼうせい anti-rust

不錆鋼 ふせいこう stainless steel

KUN

【さび 錆】

① **RUST; patina**

錆止め さびどめ anticorrosive, rust preventive

赤錆 あかさび rust

② bad karma, retribution

身から出た錆 みからでたさび Suffering the consequences of one's own actions

【さびる 錆びる】**RUST, get rusty**

錆び付く さびつく rust together; get rusty

SYNONYMS

● decay

朽 DECAY → 1015

腐 ROT → 3921

枯 WITHER → 1113

萎 WITHER → 2872

錆 RUST → 2188

錫

2189

1-8-8

▶TIN

シャク すず ㊔ やす ます たまう ゆたか あとう

Ⓒ 锡 xī

167	Names	U932B
金	S16-8-8	F2876

COMPOUNDS

● *khakkhara*, Buddhist priest's staff

錫杖 しゃくじょう *khakkhara*, Buddhist priest's staff

巡錫 じゅんしゃく preaching tour

INDEPENDENT

【しゃく 錫】*khakkhara*, Buddhist priest's staff

KUN

【すず 錫】**TIN**

錫製品 すずせいひん tinware

錫婚式 すずこんしき tin wedding (anniversary)

錫石 すずいし cassiterite

酸化錫 さんかすず stannous oxide; stannic oxide

SYNONYMS

● long slender objects

棒 ROD → 1237

箸 CHOPSTICKS → 3359

桟 crosspiece → 1169

軸 AXLE → 1908

錘 SPINDLE → 2191

竿 POLE → 3259

杖 STAFF → 1026

錫 Buddhist priest's staff → 2189

軛 YOKE → 1873

【すず】

○ metals

金 GOLD → 2552

銀 SILVER → 2156

銅 COPPER → 2155

鉄 IRON → 2147

鉛 LEAD → 2143

錫 TIN → 2189

錐

▶CONE
▶DRILL
スイ きり
Ⓒ 锥 zhuī

2190
◧1-8-8

167	Names	U9310
金	S16-8-8	F2981

COMPOUNDS

❶ **CONE or conelike object (such as a pyramid)**
錐体 すいたい cone, pyramid
円錐 えんすい cone
三角錐 さんかくすい triangular pyramid

❷ **DRILL, auger, awl**
錐刀 すいとう stiletto, dagger
試錐 しすい (test) boring
立錐の余地もない りっすいのよちもない tightly packed (with people) ("no space to set a drill")

KUN

【きり 錐】**DRILL, auger**
錐揉×み きりもみ (tail)spin
円錐(=丸錐) まるぎり awl

SYNONYMS

❶ **three-dimensional shapes**
錐 CONE → 2190
筒 cylinder → 3323
角 cube → 2541
球 sphere → 1219

❷ **cutting instruments**
刀 cutting tool → 3642
鎌 SICKLE → 2212
刃 BLADE → 3646
鋏 SCISSORS → 2173
鋸 SAW → 2184
斧 AXE → 2558
鍬 HOE → 2205
錐 DRILL → 2190
鑿 CHISEL → 3640

錘

▶SPINDLE
スイ つむ おもり
Ⓒ 锤 chuí

2191
◧1-8-8

167	Names	U9318
金	S16-8-8	F3781

COMPOUNDS

❶ⓐ **SPINDLE (for spinning)**
ⓑ counter for **SPINDLEs**
a 紡錘 ぼうすい spindle
休錘 きゅうすい idle spindles
b 十万錘 じゅうまんすい 100,000 spindles

❷ [original meaning] **weight, counterweight, plumb**
鉛錘 えんすい plumb
平衡錘 へいこうすい counterpoise, counterweight

KUN

【つむ 錘】**SPINDLE**
錘形の つむがたの spindle-shaped, fusiform

【おもり 錘】[also 重り] **weight, plumb, sinker, plummet**
糸に錘を付ける いとにおもりをつける weight a line

SYNONYMS

❶ **long slender objects**
棒 ROD → 1237
箸 CHOPSTICKS → 3359
桟 crosspiece → 1169
軸 AXLE → 1908
錘 SPINDLE → 2191
竿 POLE → 3259
杖 STAFF → 1026
錫 Buddhist priest's staff → 2189
軛 YOKE → 1873

❷ **weight**
錘 weight → 2191
鎮 weight → 2210
碇 ANCHOR → 1538

HOMOPHONES

おもり 重 HEAVY → 4390

NOTE

➡ see USAGE note at 重 4390

録

▶RECORD
ロク

2192
◧1-8-8

167	Names	U9304
金	S16-8-8	F0000

traditional form → see 録 at 2186

錆

▶RUST
セイ さび さ(びる)

2193
◧1-8-8

167	Nonstandard	U9306
金	S16-8-8	F0000

traditional form → see 錆 at 2188

錢

▶MONEY
セン ぜに

2194
◧1-8-8

167	Nonstandard	U9322
金	S16-8-8	F0000

traditional form → see 銭 at 2159

鍵

◧1-8-8

incorrect stroke-count
➡ see ◧1-8-9: 釒 at 2203

靜

2195

1-8-8

▸**QUIET**

セイ ジョウ しず- しず(か) しず(まる) しず(める) ㊔ やすし

174	Names	U975C
青	S16-8-8	F0000

traditional form → see 静 at 2164

鞠

1-8-8

incorrect stroke-count
➡ see 1-9-8: 革 at 2268

館

2196

1-8-8

▸**PUBLIC BUILDING**

カン やかた たて▴ ㊔ だて たち しろ

Ⓝ 館 舘◇ Ⓒ 馆 guǎn

184	Jōyō-3	U9928
食	S16-8-8	F0503

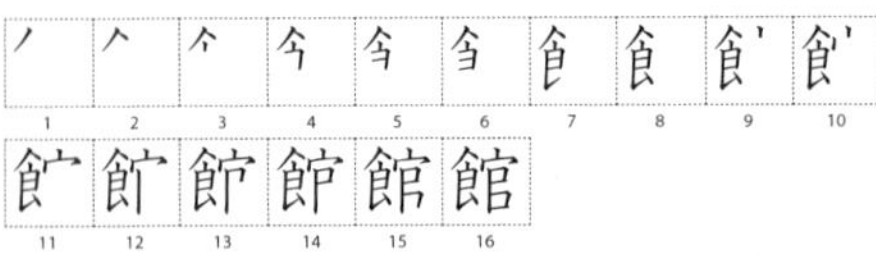

COMPOUNDS

❶ⓐ [also suffix] **PUBLIC BUILDING (esp. a large building for cultural activities), hall, edifice, pavilion**
ⓑ **building**

a 館長 かんちょう director, superintendent
会館 かいかん hall, assembly hall
図書館 としょかん library
大使館 たいしかん embassy
公民館 こうみんかん public hall, citizen's hall
体育館 たいいくかん gymnasium, gym
映画館 えいがかん cinema house, movie theater
文明館 ぶんめいかん The Bunmeikan Theater
カナダ館 かなだかん The Canada Pavilion

b 館内 かんない in the building
本館 ほんかん this building; main building
別館 べっかん annex, extension, outbuilding

❷ⓐ [original meaning] **inn, lodge**
ⓑ **suffix after names of inns, hotels, restaurants or movie theaters**

a 旅館 りょかん Japanese inn
b 風月館 ふうげつかん The Fugetsukan Inn

INDEPENDENT

【かん 館】cinema house, movie theater

KUN

【やかた 館】**stately mansion, palace, manor house**
【たて 館】**fort**
衣川の館 ころもがわのたて Fort of Koromogawa

SYNONYMS

❶ **buildings**
閣 TALL MAGNIFICENT BUILDING → 4128
宇 large building → 2699
殿 PALACE → 2247
堂 HALL → 3202
館 PUBLIC BUILDING → 2196
舎 BUILDING → 2555
棟 BLOCK → 1248
厩 HORSE STABLE → 3746

❷ **temporary quarters**
舎 temporary quarters → 2555
寮 DORMITORY → 2984
宿 lodging → 2858
館 inn → 2196
亭 INN → 2572
寓 TEMPORARY ABODE → 2893

【やかた】
◯ **mansions**
邸 STATELY RESIDENCE → 1451
館 stately mansion → 2196
荘 VILLA → 2814

舘

2197

1-8-8

▸**PUBLIC BUILDING**

カン やかた たて ㊔ だて たち しろ

135	Nonstandard	U8218
舌	S16-6-10	F0000

alternative form → see 館 at 2196

翰

2198

1-8-8

▸**LETTER**

カン

Ⓝ 翰 Ⓒ 翰 hàn

124	Non-Jōyō	U7FF0
羽	S16-6-10	F3151

COMPOUNDS

❶ [now also 簡 3380] **LETTER, note**
書翰 しょかん letter, correspondence
手翰 しゅかん letter
宸×翰 しんかん imperial letter

❷ **the pen, literary work**
翰林院 かんりんいん academy

❸ [original meaning] brush, writing brush, paintbrush
翰墨 かんぼく brush and ink; writing, drawing

SYNONYMS

❶ **written communications**
状 LETTER → 0322
文 LETTER → 2458
翰 LETTER → 2198
書 letter → 3292
信 written communication → 0115
電 telegram → 3465
牒 OFFICIAL NOTICE → 1299

翰
2199
◧1-8-8

▶LETTER
カン

124	Nonstandard	U7FF0
羽	S16-6-10	F0000

traditional form → see 翰 at 2198

燄
2200
◧1-8-8

▶FLAME
エン ほのお

86	Nonstandard	U71C4
火	S16-4-12	F0000

traditional form → see 焔 at 1255

隷
2201
◧1-8-8

▶UNDERLING
レイ
Ⓝ 隸 Ⓒ 隶 lì

171	Jōyō	U96B7
隶	S16-8-8	F2141

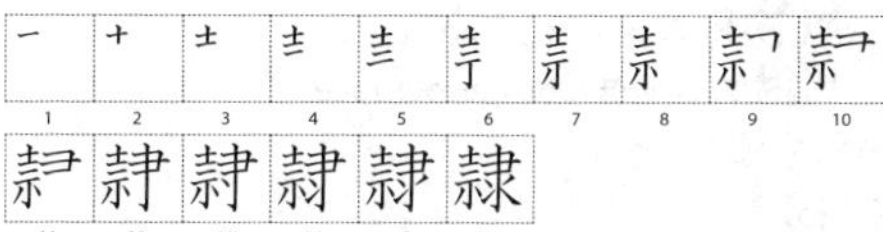

COMPOUNDS

❶ (lowly person in servitude) **UNDERLING, subordinate, servant, lackey**
隷下 れいか followers, subordinates
奴隷 どれい slave, servant

❷ [original meaning] **be subordinate [subject] to, be under, be attached to**
隷従 れいじゅう slavery, servitude; servile obedience
隷属 れいぞく subordination

❸ *reisho,* ancient square style of Chinese characters
隷書 れいしょ *reisho,* ancient square style of Chinese characters
篆×隷 てんれい seal style and ancient square style

INDEPENDENT

【れい 隷】*reisho* (→❸)

SYNONYMS

❶ **servants**
僕 MANSERVANT → 0185
奴 SLAVE → 0217
隷 UNDERLING → 2201
臣 RETAINER → 3806
従 follower → 0498
供 attendant → 0098

❷ **obey**
守 observe → 2697
遵 OBEY → 3929
順 OBEY → 0018
隷 be subordinate to → 2201
従 FOLLOW → 0498

鍋
2202
◧1-8-9

▶POT
カ▲ なべ
Ⓒ 锅 guō

167	Jōyō	U934B
金	S17-8-9	F1603

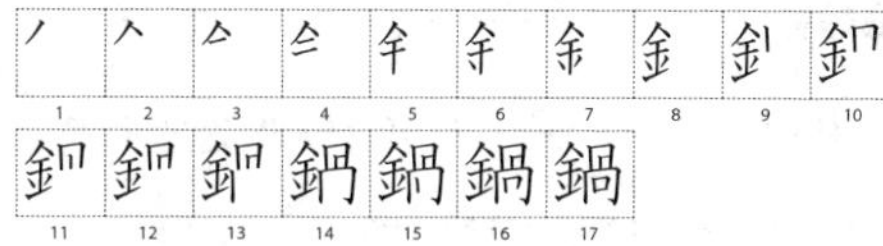

COMPOUNDS

● [original meaning] **POT, pan**

KUN

【なべ 鍋】
ⓐ [also suffix] **POT, pan**
ⓑ **food served in POTs**
a 鍋蓋 なべぶた pot lid; *nabebuta,* "lid" radical (亠)
鍋焼き なべやき scalloped; scalloped noodles
土鍋 どなべ earthen pot
大鍋 おおなべ cauldron
片手鍋 かたてなべ single-handled pot
シチュー鍋 しちゅーなべ stew pot [pan], skillet
b 鍋物 なべもの food served in a pot
寄せ鍋 よせなべ chowder

SYNONYMS

【なべ】
ⓐ **vessels and receptacles**
盤 dish → 3533
鍋 POT → 2202
釜 IRON POT → 2610
鼎 TRIPOD CAULDRON → 4405
臼 MORTAR → 4341
碓 MORTAR → 1537
托 RECEPTACLE → 0252
皿 PLATE → 4286
盆 TRAY → 2581
膳 LEGGED TRAY → 1381
杯 CUP → 1066
鉢 BOWL → 2144
椀 WOODEN BOWL → 1250
碗 CERAMIC BOWL → 1539
丼 LARGE BOWL → 4323

鍵
2203
◧1-8-9

▶KEY
ケン かぎ
Ⓒ 键 jiàn

167	Jōyō	U9375
金	S17-8-9	F1532

1	2	3	4	5	6	7	8	9	10
11	12	13	14	15	16	17			

【金】革 卓 歩

COMPOUNDS

❶ⓐ [original meaning, now rare] (implement for opening) **KEY**

ⓑ (control button or lever on musical instruments or machines) **KEY**

ⓒ counter for **KEY**s (of a piano)

a 関鍵 かんけん [rare] lock and key; locking doors; vital point

b 鍵盤 けんばん keyboard
黒鍵 こっけん chromatic key
継電鍵 けいでんけん relay key

c 八十八鍵 はちじゅうはちけん 88 keys

❷ **KEY** to secret knowledge
秘鍵 ひけん secret principle, hidden mysteries

INDEPENDENT

【けん 鍵】**KEY (of a piano or typewriter)**

KUN

【かぎ 鍵】**KEY; lock;** (vital information) **key, solution**
鍵穴 かぎあな keyhole
勝敗の鍵を握る しょうはいのかぎをにぎる hold the key to victory, have the game in one's hands

SYNONYMS

❶ⓐ &【かぎ】**locks and keys**
鍵 KEY → 2203
錠 LOCK → 2180

鍼

2204

1-8-9

▶**ACUPUNCTURE**

シン はり

Ⓒ 针 zhēn

167	Non-Jōyō	U937C
金	S17-8-9	F3433

COMPOUNDS

ⓐ [now also 針 2099] **ACUPUNCTURE**

ⓑ [original meaning] **ACUPUNCTURE needle**

a 鍼術 しんじゅつ acupuncture
鍼灸 しんきゅう acupuncture and moxibustion

KUN

【はり 鍼】[now also 針]

ⓐ **ACUPUNCTURE**

ⓑ **ACUPUNCTURE needle**

a 鍼医 はりい acupuncturist
鍼治療 はりちりょう acupuncture

SYNONYMS

ⓐ **medicines**
薬 DRUG → 3011
剤 PREPARATION → 2102
錠 PILL → 2180
丸 pill suffix → 4225
鍼 ACUPUNCTURE → 2204
灸 MOXIBUSTION → 2752

HOMOPHONES

はり 針 NEEDLE → 2099

NOTE

➡ see USAGE note at 針 2099

鍬

2205

1-8-9

▶**HOE**

シュウ くわ

Ⓝ 鍫 Ⓒ 锹 qiāo

167	Names	U936C
金	S17-8-9	F2681

KUN

【くわ 鍬】**HOE**
鍬入れ くわいれ ground breaking
鍬形虫 くわがたむし stag beetle
馬鍬 まぐわ(=まんが) harrow, rake

SYNONYMS

【くわ】

◯ **cutting instruments**
刀 cutting tool → 3642
鎌 SICKLE → 2212
刃 BLADE → 3646
鋏 SCISSORS → 2173
鋸 SAW → 2184
斧 AXE → 2558
鍬 HOE → 2205
錐 DRILL → 2190
鑿 CHISEL → 3640

鍛

2206

1-8-9

▶**FORGE**

タン きた(える) ㊔ かじ

Ⓒ 锻 duàn

167	Jōyō	U935B
金	S17-8-9	F1819

1	2	3	4	5	6	7	8	9	10
11	12	13	14	15	16	17			

COMPOUNDS

❶ [original meaning] **FORGE, work metal, temper**
鍛練(=鍛錬)する たんれんする temper, forge; train, discipline
鍛造 たんぞう forging
鍛接 たんせつ forge welding
鍛鋼 たんこう forged steel
鍛工 たんこう metalworker

鍛鉄 たんてつ tempering iron, wrought iron

❷ train, cultivate one's physical and mental skills, attain proficiency

鍛成 たんせい training, cultivation

KUN

【きたえる 鍛える】**FORGE, temper; train, drill, discipline, attain proficiency**

鍛え上げた腕 きたえあげたうで highly-trained skill

SPECIAL READINGS

鍛冶 かじ (=たんや) forging; smith

SYNONYMS

❶ **work metals**

錬 REFINE (crude metals) → 2185
煉 REFINE (crude metals) → 1297
鍛 FORGE → 2206
鋳 CAST → 2170
焼き annealing → 1256
冶 WORK METALS → 0089

❷ **cultivate**

修 CULTIVATE → 0138
養 FOSTER (one's intellect) → 2998
練 TRAIN → 1738
錬 REFINE → 2185
鍛 train → 2206
磨 POLISH → 3946
琢 POLISH → 1222

鍊

2207

1-8-9

▶REFINE

レン ね(る)

167	Names	U934A
金	S17-8-9	F0000

traditional form → see 錬 at 2185

鞕

1-8-9

incorrect stroke-count
➡ see 1-9-9: 韋 at 2272

韓

2208

1-8-9

▶SOUTH KOREA

カン から

178	Nonstandard	U97D3
韋	S17-9-8	F0000

traditional form → see 韓 at 2218

頻

2209

1-8-9

▶FREQUENTLY

ヒン しき(りに)▲

Ⓝ 頻 Ⓒ 频 pín

181	Jōyō	U983B
頁	S17-9-8	F1812

COMPOUNDS

❶ **FREQUENTLY, repeatedly, often; frequent**

頻発する ひんぱつする occur frequently
頻度 ひんど frequency
頻繁に ひんぱんに frequently, very often
頻出 ひんしゅつ frequent appearance
頻数 ひんすう frequency
頻尿 ひんにょう pollakiuria

❷ [now always 瀕 0994] on the verge of

頻死 ひんし on the verge of death

KUN

【しきりに 頻りに】**FREQUENTLY, repeatedly, often; incessantly; earnestly**

鎮

2210

1-8-10

▶QUELL

チン しず(める) しず(まる) ㊔ しん しげ まもる

Ⓝ 鎭 Ⓒ 镇 zhèn

167	Jōyō	U93AE
金	S18-8-10	F1612

COMPOUNDS

❶ⓐ (put down by force) **QUELL, pacify, suppress, subdue, put down**

ⓑ (make calm) **QUELL, pacify, appease, soothe**

a 鎮圧する ちんあつする quell, suppress
鎮定 ちんてい suppression, subdual
鎮火する ちんかする be extinguished

b 鎮守の神 ちんじゅのかみ guardian god, local deity
鎮痛剤 ちんつうざい anodyne, painkiller
鎮静する ちんせいする calm down, be tranquilized, subside; calm, tranquilize
鎮魂曲 ちんこんきょく requiem

❷ⓐ [original meaning] weight (for pressing down)

ⓑ weighty, important, central

a 文鎮 ぶんちん paperweight

b 重鎮 じゅうちん man of influence, prominent figure

❸ be enshrined

鎮座する ちんざする be enshrined

❹ peace-keeping centers in ancient China, peace-keeping force

鎮台 ちんだい garrison (in Meiji era)

❺ Chinese town or township (with a population of over 50,000)
景徳鎮 けいとくちん Jingdezhen

INDEPENDENT

【ちん 鎮】 Chinese town or township

KUN

【しずめる 鎮める】
① **QUELL, suppress, put down, subdue, pacify**
反乱を鎮める はんらんをしずめる quell a rebellion
② alleviate (pain), relieve, allay, soothe
痛みを鎮める いたみをしずめる alleviate pain

【しずまる 鎮まる】
① **be QUELLed, be suppressed, subside, be put down**
暴動が鎮まった ぼうどうがしずまった The riot was put down
② be alleviated, be relieved, be soothed
③ be enshrined

SYNONYMS

❶ **conquer and suppress**
征 CONQUER → 0349
討 SUPPRESS BY ARMED FORCE → 1846
伐 CUT DOWN → 0046
鎮 QUELL → 2210
靖 PACIFY → 1546

❷ⓐ **weight**
錘 weight → 2191
鎮 weight → 2210
碇 ANCHOR → 1538

HOMOPHONES

しずめる
静 QUIET → 2164
沈 SINK → 0306
しずまる 静 QUIET → 2164

NOTE

➡ see USAGE note at 静 2164

鎧

2211
1-8-10

▶**ARMOR**
ガイ よろい
Ⓒ 铠 kǎi

167	Names	U93A7
金	S18-8-10	F2457

COMPOUNDS

● **ARMOR**
鎧竜 がいりゅう ankylosaur
鎧球 がいきゅう American football
鎧袖一触 がいしゅういっしょく beating someone hands down

KUN

【よろい 鎧】 **ARMOR**
鎧戸 よろいど louver door [window]; shutter
鎧一具 よろいいちぐ a suit of armor

SYNONYMS

● **protective coverings**
盾 SHIELD → 3729
楯 SHIELD → 1281
鎧 ARMOR → 2211
甲 armor → 4293
縅 BRAID OF ARMOR → 1759
面 mask → 2590
兜 helmet → 3499
幌 COVERING FOR VEHICLES → 0787

鎌

2212
1-8-10

▶**SICKLE**
レン▲ かま ㊔ けん かね
Ⓝ 鎌 Ⓒ 镰 lián

167	Jōyō	U938C
金	S18-8-10	F1461

COMPOUNDS

❶ [original meaning] **SICKLE**, scythe
❷ [archaic] abbrev. of 鎌倉 かまくら: Kamakura
鎌府 れんぷ Kamakura

KUN

【かま 鎌】 **SICKLE, scythe; trick, artifice**
鎌入れ かまいれ harvesting
鎌形の かまがたの sickle-shaped, falciform
鎌鼬× かまいたち "weasel-cut" (cut in the skin from exposure to a vacuum formed by a cyclone)
鎌を掛ける かまをかける ask a leading question
大鎌 おおがま scythe

SYNONYMS

❶ **cutting instruments**
刀 cutting tool → 3642
鎌 SICKLE → 2212
刃 BLADE → 3646
鋏 SCISSORS → 2173
鋸 SAW → 2184
斧 AXE → 2558
鍬 HOE → 2205
錐 DRILL → 2190
鑿 CHISEL → 3640

鎖

2213

1-8-10

▶**CHAIN**

サ くさり

Ⓝ 鏁 鎻 Ⓒ 锁 suǒ

167	Jōyō	U9396
金	S18-8-10	F1574

COMPOUNDS

❶ⓐ [original meaning] **CHAIN**

ⓑ **linked as if with a CHAIN**

a 鎖状 さじょう chainlike

測鎖 そくさ measuring chain

側鎖 そくさ *chem* side chain

b 鎖骨 さこつ collar bone, clavicle

連鎖 れんさ chain (as of reasoning), link, series; connection

❷ⓐ (from the idea of binding with a chain) **lock up, shut, confine**

ⓑ [archaic] lock, latch

a 鎖国 さこく national isolation, exclusion of foreigners

閉鎖する へいさする lock, close, shut

封鎖 ふうさ blockade

KUN

【くさり 鎖】**CHAIN; tether; connection; passage (of a story), snatch (of a song)**

鎖伝動 くさりでんどう chain drive

鎖編み くさりあみ chain stitch

金鎖 きんぐさり gold chain

一鎖 ひとくさり one passage

SYNONYMS

❶ⓐ **ropes and lines**

綱 ROPE (esp. of fiber) → 1735

絃 STRING → 1685

縄 ROPE (esp. of straw) → 1756

緒 cord → 1742

組 braid → 1693

索 cable → 3105

鎖 CHAIN → 2213

線 LINE → 1760

紐 STRING → 1647

弦 STRING → 0343

❷ⓐ **close**

閉 CLOSE → 4116

鎖 lock up → 2213

封 SEAL → 1639

梗 STOP UP → 1204

塞 STOP UP → 2924

鎔

2214

1-8-10

▶**MELT**

ヨウ と(ける) と(かす)

Ⓒ 熔 róng

167	Non-Jōyō	U9394
金	S18-8-10	F0000

COMPOUNDS

● [now replaced by 溶 0816] [original meaning] **MELT (up) metals, fuse, smelt**

鎔解する ようかいする melt, fuse

鎔接する ようせつする weld

鎔鉱炉 ようこうろ smelting [blast] furnace

鎔銑 ようせん molten iron

KUN

【とける 鎔ける】[now usu. 溶ける] *vi* (of metals) **MELT (up), fuse, smelt**

【とかす 鎔かす】[now usu. 溶かす] *vt* **MELT (up) (metals), fuse, smelt**

鉄を鎔かす てつをとかす melt [fuse] iron

SYNONYMS

● **liquefy**

溶 DISSOLVE, MELT → 0816

熔 MELT (metals) → 1340

鎔 MELT (metals) → 2214

解 DISSOLVE → 1913

融 FUSE → 2303

HOMOPHONES

とける

解 TAKE APART → 1913

融 FUSE → 2303

溶 DISSOLVE → 0816

熔 MELT → 1340

とかす

解 TAKE APART → 1913

融 FUSE → 2303

溶 DISSOLVE → 0816

熔 MELT → 1340

梳 COMB → 1209

NOTE

➡ see USAGE note at 解 1913

鎮

2215

1-8-10

▶**QUELL**

チン しず(める) しず(まる) ㊔ しん しげ まもる

167	Names	U93AD
金	S18-8-10	F0000

traditional form → see 鎮 at 2210

鎌

2216

1-8-10

▶SICKLE

レン かま ㊔ けん かね

167	Nonstandard	U938C
金	S18-8-10	F0000

traditional form → see 鎌 at 2212

鎖

2217

1-8-10

▶CHAIN

サ くさり

167	Nonstandard	U9396
金	S18-8-10	F0000

traditional form → see 鎖 at 2213

韓

2218

1-8-10

▶SOUTH KOREA

カン から▲

Ⓝ 韓 Ⓒ 韩 hán

178	Jōyō	U97D3
韋	S18-10-8	F0860

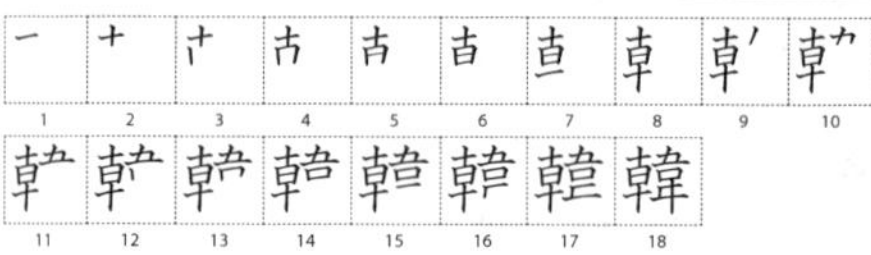

COMPOUNDS

❶ⓐ **SOUTH KOREA, Republic of Korea**

ⓑ name of state in late Zhou Dynasty

ⓒ **SOUTH**ern part of **KOREA**n Peninsula in ancient times

a 韓国 かんこく South Korea

大韓民国 だいかんみんこく Republic of Korea

日韓 にっかん Japan and (South) Korea

訪韓 ほうかん visit to Korea

bc 三韓 さんかん the Three Han States; the Three Countries of Korea

❷ Chinese family name

韓非子 かんぴし Han Feizi, famous legalist in the Period of Warring Kingdoms; title of 20-volume work by Han Feizi

INDEPENDENT

【かん 韓】 **SOUTH KOREA**

KUN

【から 韓】

ⓐ elegant term for Korea

ⓑ [also 唐] foreign countries

a 韓人 からびと Korean

SYNONYMS

❶ **Korea**

鮮 Korea → 2355

朝 North Korea → 2130

韓 SOUTH KOREA → 2218

HOMOPHONES

から 唐 TANG DYNASTY → 3867

NOTE

➡ see USAGE note at 唐 3867

鏡

2219

1-8-11

▶MIRROR

▶OPTICAL INSTRUMENT

キョウ かがみ

Ⓒ 镜 jìng

167	Jōyō-4	U93E1
金	S19-8-11	F1077

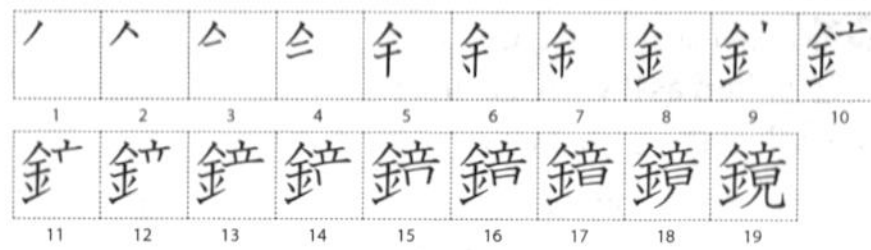

COMPOUNDS

[also suffix]

❶ [original meaning] **MIRROR**

鏡台 きょうだい dressing table

鏡高 きょうこう height of a mirror stand

鏡面 きょうめん surface of a mirror

鏡鑑 きょうかん mirror; paragon, mirror

反射鏡 はんしゃきょう reflex mirror, reflector

三面鏡 さんめんきょう vanity [dresser] with three mirrors

❷ **OPTICAL INSTRUMENT, viewing instrument, -scope, lens**

検鏡 けんきょう microscopic examination, microscopy

望遠鏡 ぼうえんきょう telescope

顕微鏡 けんびきょう microscope

潜望鏡 せんぼうきょう periscope

老眼鏡 ろうがんきょう spectacles for the aged, reading glasses

KUN

【かがみ 鏡】

① **MIRROR**

鏡板 かがみいた panel, scene-panel

手鏡 てかがみ hand glass

② round **MIRROR**-shaped rice cake

鏡開き かがみびらき cutting of New Year's rice cakes

③ barrelhead

鏡を抜く かがみをぬく open a barrel

SPECIAL READINGS

眼鏡 めがね(=がんきょう) glasses, spectacles; judgment, insight

SYNONYMS

❷ **machines and tools**

機 MACHINE → 1365

械 MECHANICAL CONTRIVANCE → 1203

具 IMPLEMENT → 3159
器 INSTRUMENT → 3367
儀 measuring instrument → 0191
鏡 OPTICAL INSTRUMENT → 2219
董 OLD TOOL → 2911

USAGE

【かがみ】

鏡
① mirror
② round mirror-shaped rice cake
③ barrelhead

鑑
(something worthy of being copied) mirror, model, paragon

HOMOPHONES

かがみ 鑑 APPRAISE → 2226

鏁

2220

◧ 1-8-11

▶**CHAIN**

サ くさり

167	Nonstandard	U93C1
金	S19-8-11	F0000

traditional form → see 鎖 at 2213

鵬

◧ 1-8-11

incorrect classification
➡ see ◧ 1-4-15: 月 at 1416

鵬

◧ 1-8-11

incorrect classification
➡ see ◧ 1-4-15: 月 at 1418

鶏

2221

◧ 1-8-11

▶**CHICKEN**

ケイ にわとり とり▲

Ⓝ 鷄 雞◇ Ⓒ 鸡 jī

196	Jōyō	U9D8F
鳥	S19-11-8	F1838

1	2	3	4	5	6	7	8	9	10
11	12	13	14	15	16	17	18	19	

COMPOUNDS

● [original meaning] **CHICKEN, hen, cock; poultry**
鶏肉 けいにく chicken (meat)
鶏卵 けいらん (hen's) egg
鶏舎 けいしゃ henhouse
養鶏 ようけい chicken raising
闘鶏 とうけい cockfight, fighting cock

KUN

【にわとり 鶏】 **CHICKEN, hen, cock**
【とり 鶏】 [also 鳥] **CHICKEN**; fowl, poultry
若鶏 わかどり spring chicken

SPECIAL READINGS

鶏冠▲ とさか cockscomb, crest
軍鶏▲ しゃも game fowl, gamecock
矮×鶏▲ ちゃぼ (Japanese) bantam

SYNONYMS

● **birds**
鷹 HAWK → 3955
鷗 GULL → 2370
烏 CROW → 4088
雀 SPARROW → 3117
燕 SWALLOW → 3142
鴻 LARGE WILD BIRD → 0977
鳳 MALE PHOENIX → 3749
凰 FEMALE PHOENIX → 3738
鵬 MYTHICAL HUGE BIRD → 1416
鶏 CHICKEN → 2221
酉 ROOSTER → 4358
隼 FALCON → 3427
鳩 PIGEON → 0184
鷲 EAGLE → 3598
鳶 BLACK KITE → 3919
鶴 CRANE → 2326
鷺 HERON → 3621
鵜 CORMORANT → 2067
鴨 DUCK → 1582
雁 WILD GOOSE → 3741

HOMOPHONES

とり
鳥 BIRD → 4105
酉 THE ROOSTER → 4358
禽 BIRD → 2654

NOTE

➡ see USAGE note at 鳥 4105

鐘

2222

◧ 1-8-12

▶**BELL**

ショウ かね

Ⓒ 钟 zhōng

167	Jōyō	U9418
金	S20-8-12	F1877

1	2	3	4	5	6	7	8	9	10
11	12	13	14	15	16	17	18	19	20

COMPOUNDS

ⓐ [original meaning] **BELL (that tolls)**
ⓑ **BELL or sound of a bell (as for announcing), alarm**
a 鐘楼 しょうろう bell tower, belfry
梵×鐘 ぼんしょう temple bell
b 警鐘 けいしょう alarm bell, warning
時鐘 じしょう time bell

半鐘 はんしょう fire bell [alarm]

KUN

【かね 鐘】**BELL (that tolls), gong**

釣鐘 つりがね hanging bell, temple bell

【釒】

SYNONYMS

❶ **bells**

鈴 BELL (that jingles or rings) → 2146

鐘 BELL (that tolls) → 2222

鐡

2223

◧1-8-12

▶**IRON**

テツ くろがね ㊔ かね くろかね

167	Nonstandard	U9421
金	S20-8-12	F0000

traditional form → see 鉄 at 2147

鐵

2224

◧1-8-13

▶**IRON**

テツ くろがね ㊔ かね くろかね

167	Nonstandard	U9435
金	S21-8-13	F0000

traditional form → see 鉄 at 2147

鑄

2225

◧1-8-14

▶**CAST**

チュウ い(る)

167	Names	U9444
金	S22-8-14	F0000

traditional form → see 鋳 at 2170

鑑

◧1-8-14

incorrect stroke-count

➡ see ◧1-8-15: 釒 at 2226

鑛

◧1-8-14

incorrect stroke-count

➡ see ◧1-8-15: 釒 at 2227

鑑

2226

◧1-8-15

▶**APPRAISE**

▶**REFERENCE VOLUME**

カン かんが(みる) かがみ▲

Ⓝ 鑒 Ⓒ 鉴 jiàn

167	Jōyō	U9451
金	S23-8-15	F1451

COMPOUNDS

❶ **APPRAISE, judge, appreciate, discern, identify**

鑑賞 かんしょう appreciation

鑑定する かんていする appraise, judge, estimate, identify

鑑識する かんしきする identify, judge; discern

鑑別 かんべつ discrimination, judgment

無鑑査の むかんさの not submitted to the selecting committee

❷ **REFERENCE VOLUME, directory, handbook, book**

図鑑 ずかん picture [illustrated] book

年鑑 ねんかん yearbook

名鑑 めいかん list, directory

宝鑑 ほうかん handbook, thesaurus

❸ **mark of identification, sign**

鑑札 かんさつ license, certificate

印鑑 いんかん personal seal

❹ⓐ [original meaning, now archaic] **ancient bronze mirror**

ⓑ (something worthy of being copied) **mirror, paragon, model**

b 亀鑑 きかん pattern, paragon, mirror

KUN

【かんがみる 鑑みる】**take into consideration, take warning by**

. . . に鑑みて …にかんがみて in view of…

【かがみ 鑑】(something worthy of being copied) **mirror, model, paragon**

武士の鑑 ぶしのかがみ paragon of knighthood

SYNONYMS

❶ **judge**

判 JUDGE → 1441

裁 JUDGE → 4090

鑑 APPRAISE → 2226

評 evaluate → 1895

審 TRY → 2985

決 DECIDE → 0308

視 REGARD → 1223

❷ **books**

本 BOOK → 4314

典 STANDARD WORK → 3253

経 religious classic → 1687

書 BOOK → 3292

冊 bound book → 4295

籍 books → 3394

著 literary work → 2869

巻 VOLUME → 3273

編 piece of writing → 1755

篇 PIECE OF WRITING → 3361

鑑 REFERENCE VOLUME → 2226

HOMOPHONES

かがみ 鏡 MIRROR → 2219

NOTE

➡ see USAGE note at 鏡 2219

鑛

▶**ORE**
▶**MINE**
コウ

2227
◧1-8-15

167	Nonstandard	U945B
金	S23-8-15	F0000

traditional form →see 鉱 at 2145

罐

▶**CAN**
カン かま

2228
◧1-8-17

167	Nonstandard	U9475
金	S25-8-17	F0000

traditional form →see 缶 at 2526

飢

▶**STARVE**
キ う(える)

2229
◧1-9-2

184	Nonstandard	U98E2
飠	S11-9-2	F0000

traditional form →see 飢 at 2101

副

▶**SECONDARY**
フク ㊔ **そえ そい**
Ⓒ 副 fù

2230
◧1-9-2

18	Jōyō-4	U526F
刂	S11-2-9	F1138

COMPOUNDS

❶ [also prefix]
ⓐ **SECONDARY, sub-, subordinate, vice-, deputy, assistant**
ⓑ (in addition to the main thing) **accessory, side-, extra, supplementary, additional**

a 副作用 ふくさよう secondary effect, reaction
副次的な ふくじてきな secondary
副大統領 ふくだいとうりょう vice-president
副総理 ふくそうり deputy prime minister
正副 せいふく principal and vice [assistant]; original and copy

b 副詞 ふくし adverb
副神経 ふくしんけい accessory nerves
副賞 ふくしょう supplementary [extra] prize
副業 ふくぎょう subsidiary business
副収入 ふくしゅうにゅう additional income
副産物 ふくさんぶつ by-product, side line

❷ duplicate, copy
副本 ふくほん duplicate, copy

INDEPENDENT

【ふく 副】**SECONDARY**, assistant; duplicate, copy

副二名 ふくにめい two assistants

SYNONYMS

❶ⓐ **subordinate**
副 SECONDARY →2230
次 secondary →0058
従 subordinate →0498
亜 SUB- →4354
準 QUASI- →3541
半 semi- →4313
准 JUNIOR →0143
助 assistant →1440

ⓑ **additional**
追 additional →3840
補 supplementary →1529
副 accessory →2230

勘

▶**CHECK**
▶**INTUITIVE PERCEPTION**
カン
Ⓒ 勘 kān

2231
◧1-9-2

19	Jōyō	U52D8
力	S11-2-9	F1091

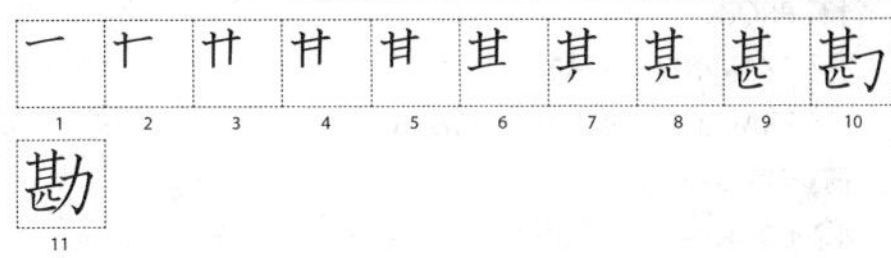

COMPOUNDS

❶ⓐ **CHECK, examine, collate, compare**
ⓑ **take into consideration, give consideration to, think about**

a 勘定 かんじょう calculation; account, settlement of accounts
勘校する かんこうする examine and correct, collate
勘合 かんごう [rare] checking and verifying

b 勘考 かんこう consideration, deliberation
勘案する かんあんする take into consideration, give consideration (to)
勘弁する かんべんする pardon, forgive; tolerate

❷ **CHECK** into a crime, examine officially (and pass judgment), interrogate, find fault with
勘当 かんどう disinheritance
勘気 かんき disfavor, disgrace
勅勘 ちょっかん Imperial imputation

❸ abbrev. of 勘定 かんじょう: **CHECK**, bill, account
割り勘 わりかん equal split, Dutch treat

❹ **INTUITIVE PERCEPTION**: **sense, perception; horse sense, intuition, sixth sense**
勘違い かんちがい wrong guess [impression]
勘付く かんづく sense (a danger)
山勘で やまかんで by guesswork

❺ vital point

勘所 かんどころ vital point

❻ endure

勘忍(=堪忍) かんにん patience, forbearance; forgiveness, pardon

INDEPENDENT

【かん 勘】 **sense, perception; horse sense, intuition**

勘の良い人 かんのいいひと person of quick perception

勘を働かせる かんをはたらかせる use one's head, think quickly

音楽に対する勘 おんがくにたいするかん musical sense

SYNONYMS

❶ⓐ investigate and examine

閲 REVIEW → 4132
審 EXAMINE CAREFULLY → 2985
験 TEST → 2306
勘 CHECK → 2231
糾 INQUIRE INTO → 1631
究 STUDY EXHAUSTIVELY → 2729
察 INSPECT → 2961
討 STUDY → 1846
探 PROBE → 0613
検 EXAMINE → 1241
診 EXAMINE A PATIENT → 1898
調 INVESTIGATE → 1973
査 LOOK INTO → 3092

ⓑ think and consider

思 THINK → 3173
惟 MEDITATE → 0582
省 INTROSPECT → 3100
稽 THINK → 1573
考 THINK → 3962
存 hold an opinion → 3702
案 think out → 2824
想 CONCEIVE → 3507
慮 CONSIDER → 4050
勘 take into consideration → 2231
銓 WEIGH → 2161
量 weigh → 3119

❹ sense

感 SENSE → 3514
覚 sense → 3217
勘 INTUITIVE PERCEPTION → 2231

NOTE

➡ see COMPOUND FORMATION for
勘弁 かんべん → 弁 2497
勘当 かんどう → 当 2701

★ do not confuse with 堪 ENDURE → 0680

都
1-9-2

incorrect stroke-count
➡ see 1-9-3: 者 at 2234

動
2232
1-9-2

▸**MOVE**

ドウ うご(く) うご(かす) やや(もすれば)▲

Ⓒ 动 dòng

19	Jōyō-3	U52D5
力	S11-2-9	F0056

Stroke order: 1–11

COMPOUNDS

❶ⓐ [original meaning] **MOVE, be in action, vibrate, pulsate**

ⓑ [also prefix] dynamic, moving, kinetic

ⓒ [also suffix] *phys* **motion, vibration, action**

a 動物 どうぶつ animal
動揺する どうようする shake, tremble; be disturbed, waver
運動 うんどう motion, movement; exercise; campaign
自動 じどう automatic operation; automatic
移動する いどうする move, shift, transfer
不動産 ふどうさん immovable property, real estate
機動性 きどうせい mobility, maneuverability

b 動安定 どうあんてい dynamic stability
動摩擦 どうまさつ kinetic friction

c 動静 どうせい movements, state of affairs, conditions
波動 はどう wave motion, undulation
反動 はんどう backlash, recoil, reaction
上下動 じょうげどう vertical motion [shock]

❷ⓐ (set in motion, esp. machines) **MOVE, drive, operate**

ⓑ MOVE (personnel) to another position; make a motion

ⓒ (be active) **MOVE, change, vary**

a 動力 どうりょく power
駆動 くどう drive (of a machine)
始動 しどう starting (machines)
原動力 げんどうりょく motive force
伝動 でんどう transmission, drive, gearing
電動の でんどうの electric powered

b 動議 どうぎ a motion
人事異動 じんじいどう personnel changes, reshuffle

c 動向 どうこう trend, tendency, movement
活動 かつどう activity, action; function
変動 へんどう change, fluctuation

❸ⓐ **MOVE to action, arouse, stir**
ⓑ **be MOVEd with emotion, be excited, be startled**

a 動員する どういんする mobilize (an army)
動機 どうき motive, incentive
出動する しゅつどうする take the field, be dispatched, turn out
扇動する せんどうする instigate, agitate
発動する はつどうする exercise, invoke; move, put in motion

b 動転する どうてんする be frightened, be stunned
感動する かんどうする be moved, be impressed

❹ⓐ **behave, act**
ⓑ **behavior, conduct**

ab 動作 どうさ action, movement; bearing, behavior
行動 こうどう action, conduct, behavior
挙動 きょどう deportment, conduct, behavior, action
言動 げんどう speech and behavior [conduct]

❺ **fall into disorder, be disturbed**

動乱 どうらん upheaval, disturbance, agitation
騒動 そうどう disturbance, uproar; strife; confusion
暴動 ぼうどう riot, disturbance, uprising

❻ abbrev. of 動物 どうぶつ: animal

動植物 どうしょくぶつ animals and plants

❼ abbrev. of 動詞 どうし: verb

動名詞 どうめいし gerund
他動 たどう transitive verb

❽ abbrev. of 動力車 どうりょくしゃ: railway motive power

動労 どうろう National Railway Motive Power Union

INDEPENDENT

【どう 動】motion, vibration; *phys* action

動と反動 どうとはんどう action and reaction

【どうじる(=どうずる) 動じる(=動ずる)】**be MOVEd with emotion**

KUN

【うごく 動く】*vi* **MOVE, shift, stir, shake; work, run, operate; change, vary;** (take action) **move, act, be active; be moved, be touched**

動き うごき movement, motion, activity; trend, development
動き回る うごきまわる move about; get about; be busily engaged
身動きする みうごきする move (about), stir
電気で動く でんきでうごく run by electricity
値動き ねうごき fluctuation [movement] in prices
陰で動く かげでうごく act behind the scenes
心が動く こころがうごく feel inclined to

【うごかす 動かす】*vt* **MOVE, shift, remove; set in motion, drive, operate; change, alter;** (exert influence) **move, affect, touch**

動かし難い うごかしがたい immovable; unshakable, undeniable
机を動かす つくえをうごかす move [shift] a desk
揺り動かす ゆりうごかす shake, swing; shock
心を動かされる こころをうごかされる be moved

【ややもすれば 動もすれば】be apt to, be prone to, be liable to

SYNONYMS

❶ⓐ **move**

動 MOVE → 2232
運 MOVE → 3894
滑 SLIDE → 0809
辷る SLIP → 3957
移 SHIFT → 1508
転 remove → 1872
遷 TRANSFER → 3932
繰る SHIFT ONWARD → 1806

ⓑ **active**

活 ACTIVE → 0460
動 dynamic → 2232

ⓒ **motion**

動 motion → 2232
惰 inertia → 0706

❷ⓐ **set in motion**

動 MOVE → 2232
駆 DRIVE → 2293
掛ける set going → 0596

❸ⓐ **incite**

挑 PROVOKE → 0445
唆 INSTIGATE → 0480
扇 FAN → 2449
煽 FAN → 1338
激 excite → 0955
奮 ROUSE UP → 3000
振 arouse to action → 0515
動 MOVE → 2232
起 rise to action → 4099

ⓑ **feel deeply**

感 feel deeply → 3514
動 be moved → 2232
嘆 sigh in admiration → 0773

❹ⓑ **behavior**

行 conduct → 0246
挙 deportment → 3106
動 behavior → 2232

NOTE

➡ see COMPOUND FORMATION for 機動性 きどうせい → 機 1365

剰

2233
1-9-2

▶**SURPLUS**
ジョウ
Ⓝ 剰 Ⓒ 剩 shèng

18	Jōyō	U5270
刂	S11-2-9	F1879

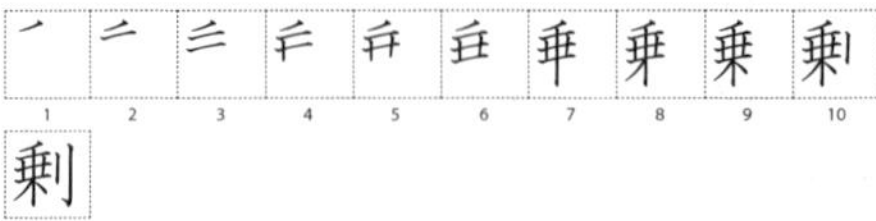

COMPOUNDS

● [original meaning] **SURPLUS, excessive, redundant**
剰余 じょうよ surplus, remainder, balance
剰員 じょういん superfluous member
過剰 かじょう surplus, excess
余剰 よじょう surplus, remainder, residue

SYNONYMS

● **exceeding and excess**
過 EXCEED → 3891
超 SURPASS → 4107
越 GO BEYOND → 4108
濫 EXCESSIVE → 0990
余 EXCESS → 2535
剰 SURPLUS → 2233
冗 REDUNDANT → 2470

都

2234
1-9-3

▶**METROPOLIS**
▶**METROPOLIS OF TOKYO**
ト ツ みやこ ㊔ くに みや つぎ さと

163	Names	UFA26
阝	S12-3-9	F0000

traditional form → see 都 at 2120

靴

2235
1-9-4

▶**SHOES**
カ くつ
Ⓒ 靴 xuē

177	Jōyō	U9774
革	S13-9-4	F1570

COMPOUNDS

● [original meaning] **SHOES, boots**
製靴 せいか shoemaking
軍靴 ぐんか military shoes, combat boots
隔靴掻痒× かっかそうよう having an itch that one cannot scratch

KUN

【くつ 靴】 [sometimes also 沓] [also suffix] **SHOES, boots**
靴下 くつした socks, stockings
靴墨 くつずみ shoe polish
靴音 くつおと sound of a person's footsteps
靴直し くつなおし shoe mending
靴ブラシ くつぶらし shoe brush
皮靴 かわぐつ leather shoes
長靴 ながぐつ boots, top boots
運動靴 うんどうぐつ sneakers
紳士靴 しんしぐつ men's shoes
スケート靴 すけーとぐつ skates

SYNONYMS

● **footwear**
靴 SHOES → 2235
沓 FOOTWEAR → 3074
駄 clogs → 2291
履 footwear → 3933
足 counter for footwear → 2714

USAGE

【くつ】
靴
[sometimes also 沓] [also suffix] shoes, boots
沓
[usu. 靴] footwear, sandals, clogs

HOMOPHONES

くつ 沓 FOOTWEAR → 3074

韵

2236
1-9-4

▶**RHYME**
イン

180	Nonstandard	U97F5
音	S13-9-4	F0000

traditional form → see 韻 at 2279

飯

2237
1-9-4

▶**COOKED RICE**
▶**MEAL**
ハン めし ㊔ いい

184	Nonstandard	UFA2A
食	S13-9-4	F0000

traditional form → see 飯 at 2126

飲

2238
1-9-4

▶**DRINK**
イン の(む) -の(み)

184	Nonstandard	U98EE
食	S13-9-4	F0000

traditional form → see 飲 at 2127

新 2239

◧1-9-4

▸**NEW**

シン あたら(しい) あら(た) あら- にい-

㊔ あたらし よし ちか

Ⓒ 新 xīn

69	Jōyō-2	U65B0
斤	S13-4-9	F0069

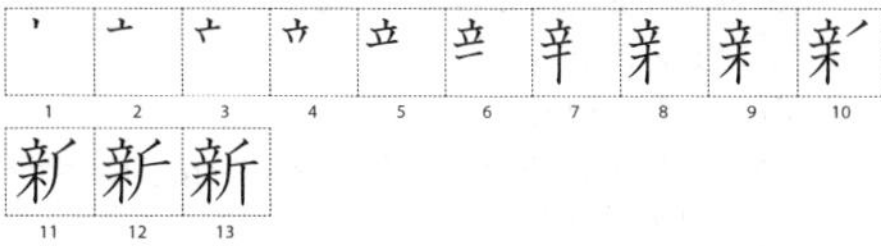

COMPOUNDS

❶ⓐ [also prefix] **NEW, novel, fresh**
ⓑ (close in time) **NEW, recent; newly**

a 新旧 しんきゅう old and new
新聞 しんぶん newspaper
新鮮な しんせんな fresh
新年 しんねん New Year
新製品 しんせいひん new products
新発明 しんはつめい new invention [discovery]
新世界 しんせかい new world, the New World
新設する しんせつする establish newly, create
新人 しんじん new talent, rookie; newcomer
新刊 しんかん new publication
新幹線 しんかんせん Shinkansen, Bullet Train
新学期 しんがっき new term
ab 最新の さいしんの newest, latest
b 新興の しんこうの rising, newly-established
新入生 しんにゅうせい new student [pupil], freshman
新米 しんまい new rice; new hand, novice

❷ **make NEW, renew, renovate**
一新する いっしんする renovate, change completely; be renovated
革新 かくしん innovation, reform, renovation
更新する こうしんする renew, renovate, innovate
維新 いしん renovation, restoration; Imperial Restoration of 1868

❸ abbrev. of 新暦 しんれき: **NEW** [Gregorian] calendar
新正月 しんしょうがつ January (according to the new calendar)

❹ abbrev. of 新記録 しんきろく: **NEW** record
世界新 せかいしん new world record

INDEPENDENT

【しん 新】**NEW**ness, novelty; new [Gregorian] calendar
新の七月七日 しんのしちがつなのか 7th of July, New Style

KUN

【あたらしい 新しい】**NEW, novel, fresh; recent, latest; modern**
新しく あたらしく new, newly, anew
真新しい まあたらしい brand-new
目新しい めあたらしい novel, new, original

【あらた 新た】
あらたな 新たな **NEW, fresh**
新たに あらたに newly, afresh; again

【あら- 新-】**NEW, fresh**
新手 あらて fresh supply of troops; newcomer; new method

【にい- 新-】**NEW; first**
新妻 にいづま new wife
新枕 にいまくら bridal bed

SYNONYMS

❶ⓐ **new**
新 NEW → 2239
鮮 FRESH → 2355
生 raw → 4309
ⓑ **recent**
近 RECENT → 3798
新 NEW → 2239

❷ **reform**
改 REFORM → 0287
革 REFORM → 3099
更 RENEW → 4355
新 make new → 2239

❸ **calendars**
暦 CALENDAR → 3747
新 new calendar → 2239
旧 old calendar → 0014

NOTE

➡ see COMPOUND FORMATION for
維新 いしん → 維 1733
代謝(=新陳代謝) たいしゃ(=しんちんたいしゃ) → 謝 2048

献 2240

◧1-9-4

▸**OFFER**

ケン コン

Ⓝ 獻 Ⓒ 献 xiàn

94	Jōyō	U732E
犬	S13-4-9	F1314

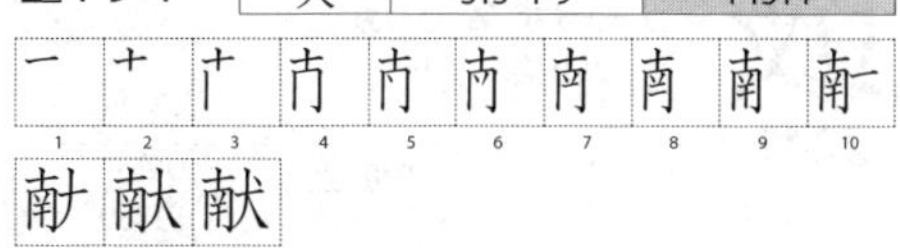

COMPOUNDS

❶ⓐ **OFFER (esp. to a superior), present, dedicate**
ⓑ **donate, contribute**

a 献納する けんのうする offer, present, donate
献上する けんじょうする present (a gift to a superior)

献身 けんしん self-sacrifice, devotion
献呈 けんてい presentation
b 献木 けんぼく donating lumber to a shrine
献金する けんきんする donate [contribute] money
献血 けんけつ blood donation
貢献 こうけん contribution, services

❷ⓐ OFFER wine to a guest
ⓑ counter for **OFFER**ings [drinks] of wine
a 献酬 けんしゅう exchange of sake cups
献酌 けんしゃく offering a drink
献立 こんだて menu, preparations
b 一献 いっこん a cup of sake

❸ literature, records
文献 ぶんけん literature, documentary records

INDEPENDENT

【けんずる 献ずる】present, dedicate, **OFFER**

SYNONYMS

❶ⓐ offer
供 OFFER (to a person or god) →0098
献 OFFER (esp. to a superior) →2240
納 offer (as to a god) →1652
提 PRESENT →0720
貢 offer tribute →2838
奉 DEDICATE →3167
捧 OFFER RESPECTFULLY →0594

ⓑ donate
施 give alms →1103
恵む give charity →3293
寄 CONTRIBUTE →2856
醵 CONTRIBUTE MONEY →2087
献 donate →2240

❷ⓐ offer wine
酌 POUR WINE →1854
献 offer wine →2240
酬 reciprocate wineglasses →1941

NOTE

➡ see COMPOUND FORMATION for 献立 こんだて →立 2486

鼓

2241
◧1-9-4

▸DRUM
コ つづみ ㊔ つつみ
Ⓝ 皷 Ⓒ 鼓 gǔ

207	Jōyō	U9F13
鼓	S13-13-0	F1730

Stroke order: 一 十 士 吉 吉 吉 吉 壴 壴 壴 鼓 鼓 鼓 (1–13)

RADICAL

tsuzumi 'drum' (鼕×), used in characters related to drums or their sound

COMPOUNDS

❶ⓐ DRUM
ⓑ DRUM, beat, tap
a 鼓笛隊 こてきたい drum and fife band
鼓手 こしゅ drummer
鼓膜 こまく eardrum
太鼓 たいこ (big) drum; professional jester; flatterer; big obi bow
b 鼓動 こどう beat, palpitation
鼓腹する こふくする drum the belly; be happy and contented

❷ rouse, stir up, encourage
鼓舞 こぶ encouragement, stimulation
鼓吹 こすい inspiration, inculcation, advocacy

INDEPENDENT

【こする 鼓する】beat; rouse up
勇を鼓する ゆうをこする summon up one's courage

KUN

【つづみ 鼓】**hand DRUM, tabor**
大鼓 おおつづみ large hand drum
腹鼓を打つ はらつづみをうつ drum the belly; eat to one's heart's content
舌鼓を打つ したつづみをうつ smack at, eat with relish

SYNONYMS

❶ⓐ musical instruments
琴 KOTO →3455
箏 KOTO →3353
鼓 DRUM →2241
笛 FLUTE →3303
琵 LUTE →3453
琶 LUTE →3454
笙 *SHO* →3302

NOTE

➡ see COMPOUND FORMATION for 鼓吹 こすい →吹 0272

戦

2242
◧1-9-4

▸WAR
セン いくさ たたか(う)
Ⓝ 戰 Ⓒ 战 zhàn

62	Jōyō-4	U6226
戈	S13-4-9	F0076

Stroke order: 丶 丷 ⺍ ⺍ 当 当 単 単 単 単 戦 戦 戦 (1–13)

COMPOUNDS

❶ⓐ [original meaning] **WAR, wage war, fight**
ⓑ [also suffix] **WAR, battle, combat, warfare**
ⓒ [also suffix] (active hostility) **WAR, battle**

a 戦争 せんそう war, battle
戦闘 せんとう battle, fight, combat
戦場 せんじょう battlefield, front
b 戦前 せんぜん prewar period, period before Second World War
戦後 せんご postwar period, period after Second World War
戦線 せんせん (war) front, battle line
作戦 さくせん tactics, strategy; (military) operations, maneuvers
敗戦 はいせん lost battle, defeat
挑戦 ちょうせん challenge, defiance
空中戦 くうちゅうせん air battle, dogfight
生物戦 せいぶつせん biological warfare
c 論戦 ろんせん verbal battle, controversy
経済戦 けいざいせん economic war

❷ [also suffix] **match, game, contest**
観戦する かんせんする watch (a ball game); observe (military operations)
早明戦 そうめいせん Waseda-Meiji (baseball) game
決勝戦 けっしょうせん final round match, finals

❸ tremble, shudder
戦慄 せんりつ shuddering, shivering
戦戦兢兢(=戦戦恐恐)として せんせんきょうきょうとして with fear and trembling

KUN

【いくさ 戦】WAR, fight, battle
【たたかう 戦う】
① **wage WAR, fight**
戦い たたかい war, fight, battle; match, game, contest
戦い抜く たたかいぬく fight to a finish
敵と戦う てきとたたかう fight one's enemy
議論を戦わす ぎろんをたたかわす have a discussion
② **contest, contend, play a match [game]**
正正堂堂と戦おう せいせいどうどうとたたかおう Let's play the game fairly

SYNONYMS

❶ⓐ **fight and war**
闘 FIGHT → 4136
戦 WAR → 2242
征 go on a military expedition → 0349
ⓑ **warfare and rebellions**
戦 WAR → 2242
軍 war → 2582
役 war → 0288
陣 battle → 0545
乱 rebellion → 1611
変 uprising → 2569
闘 FIGHT → 4136
❷ **game**
技 game → 0292
戦 match → 2242
【たたかう】
② **compete**
競 COMPETE → 2322
戦う contest → 2242
闘 FIGHT → 4136
争 CONTEND → 2523

USAGE

❶【たたかう】
戦う
① wage war, fight
② contest, contend, play a match [game]
闘う
(struggle with) fight (against), contend with, strive against
❷【たたかい】
戦い
① war, fight, battle
② match, game, contest
闘い
struggle, conflict

HOMOPHONES

たたかう 闘 FIGHT → 4136
たたかい 闘 FIGHT → 4136

歇
2243
◧ 1-9-4

▶TAKE A REST
ケツ
Ⓒ 歇 xiē

76	Non-Jōyō	U6B47
欠	S13-4-9	F0000

COMPOUNDS

● [now replaced by 欠 2481] [original meaning] **TAKE A REST**
間歇 かんけつ intermittence

SYNONYMS

● **rest**
休 REST → 0056
息 rest → 3278
憩 TAKE A REST → 3590
歇 TAKE A REST → 2243

敬

2244
1-9-4

▶**RESPECT**
ケイ キョウ うやま(う) ㊔ たか たかし よし ゆき ひろ のり とし あき

66	Nonstandard	U656C
攵	S13-4-9	F0000

traditional form → see 敬 at 2136

数

2245
1-9-4

▶**NUMBER**
スウ ス かず かぞ(える)
Ⓝ 數 Ⓒ 数 shù shǔ

66	Jōyō-2	U6570
攵	S13-4-9	F0139

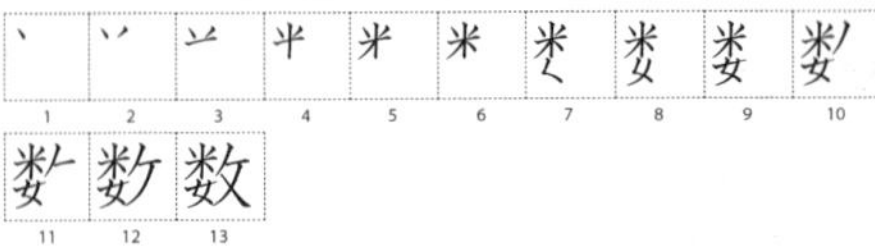

COMPOUNDS

❶ⓐ [also suffix] (amount) **NUMBER, quantity**
ⓑ *gram* **NUMBER**
a 数量 すうりょう quantity, volume
総数 そうすう total (number)
多数の たすうの a number of, many
手数 てすう(=てかず) trouble, bother, pains
トン数 とんすう tonnage
人数 にんずう(=にんず) number of people
回数 かいすう frequency, number of times
生徒数 せいとすう number of pupils
b 複数形 ふくすうけい plural form
❷ [prefix] (a small number, esp. between three and five) **several**
数回 すうかい several times
数年間 すうねんかん several years
十数頁 じゅうすうページ ten odd pages
❸ [also suffix] (abstract mathematical unit) **NUMBER, numbers**
数字 すうじ figure, numeral
対数 たいすう logarithm
指数 しすう index (number); exponent
関数(=函数) かんすう *math* function
自然数 しぜんすう natural number
無理数 むりすう irrational number
❹ **count, enumerate, reckon**
数詞 すうし *gram* numeral
算数 さんすう arithmetic; calculation
❺ **mathematics**
数学 すうがく mathematics
英数 えいすう English and mathematics
❻ fate, destiny
数奇な すうきな unlucky
❼ scheme, plot
権謀術数 けんぼうじゅっすう trickery, wiles, finesse
❽ used phonetically for *su*
数寄屋(=数奇屋) すきや tea-ceremony arbor
手数入り でずいり display of a sumo champion in the ring

INDEPENDENT

【すう 数】**NUMBER**; fate, destiny
勝敗の数 しょうはいのすう issue of the battle

KUN

【かず 数】**NUMBER**
数多く かずおおく in large numbers
数数の かずかずの numerous, many
頭数 あたまかず number of persons, head count
【かぞえる 数える】**count, reckon, calculate, NUMBER, enumerate**
数えで二十 かぞえではたち 20 years old by Japanese count
大作曲家の一人に数えられる だいさっきょくかのひとりにかぞえられる be reckoned among the greatest composers

SPECIAL READINGS

数珠 じゅず (Buddhist) rosary

SYNONYMS

❶ⓐ **quantity and number**
量 QUANTITY → 3119
嵩 BULK → 2927
積 size → 1579
額 AMOUNT → 2273
分 content → 2466
数 NUMBER → 2245
勢 strength → 3542
❷ **some**
幾- SOME → 4403
何- several → 0073
数 several → 2245
或る A CERTAIN → 3978
❸ **kinds of numbers**
数 NUMBER (mathematical unit) → 2245
員 fixed number → 2822
号 NUMBER (numerical designation) → 2675
番 No. → 3416
第 ORDINAL NUMBER PREFIX → 3298
-目 ordinal number suffix → 3777
次 numerical order suffix → 0058
桁 DIGIT → 1165
❹ **calculate and count**
算 CALCULATE → 3351
計 COMPUTE → 1828
数 count → 2245

COMPOUND FORMATION

【手数 てすう(=てかず)】

手数 'trouble, bother, pains' refers to a great deal (数 ❶ⓐ) of trouble (手).

毀

2246

◧ 1-9-4

▸**DESTROY**

キ こぼ(つ)▴ こぼ(れる)▴ こわ(す)▴ こわ(れる)▴

Ⓒ 毀 huǐ

79	Jōyō	U6BC0
殳	S13-4-9	F2790

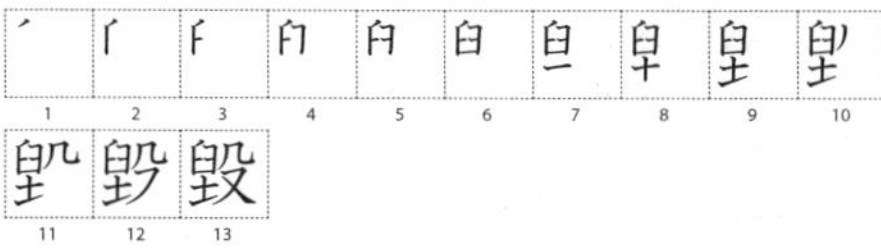

COMPOUNDS

❶ [now also 棄 2651] [original meaning] **DESTROY, ruin, damage**

毀棄する ききする destroy, demolish, damage

毀傷 きしょう injury, damage

名誉毀損 めいよきそん libel, defamation, slander

破毀する はきする reverse (the original judgment)

❷ defame, slander

毀誉褒貶× きよほうへん praise and censure, criticisms

非毀(=誹毀) ひき defamation

KUN

【こぼつ 毀つ】 *elegant* break, **DESTROY**, damage

【こぼれる 毀れる】 be chipped, be nicked—said of blades

【こわす 毀す】 [usu. 壊す] *vt* break (down), **DESTROY**, smash, take apart; spoil, mar, upset

取り毀す とりこわす demolish, pull down

【こわれる 毀れる】 [usu. 壊れる] *vi*

ⓐ break (down), be broken; get out of order

ⓑ be broken off, fall through, be upset

SYNONYMS

❶ **destroy**

滅 DESTROY → 0812

毀 DESTROY → 2246

亡 perish → 4210

消 EXTINGUISH → 0531

剿 EXTERMINATE → 2335

【こわす】

◯ **break**

破 BREAK → 1478

拉ぐ crush → 0372

崩 CRUMBLE → 2863

挫 SPRAIN → 0519

壊 BREAK DOWN → 0934

毀す break down → 2246

折 BREAK OFF → 0297

割る crack → 2284

裂 SPLIT → 3331

砕 CRUSH UP → 1458

摧 CRUSH UP → 0849

潰す CRUSH → 0919

HOMOPHONES

こわす 壊 BREAK DOWN → 0934

こわれる 壊 BREAK DOWN → 0934

NOTE

➡ see USAGE note at 壊 0934

殿

2247

◧ 1-9-4

▸**PALACE**

▸**FORMAL HONORIFIC TITLE**

デン テン との -どの

Ⓒ 殿 diàn

79	Jōyō	U6BBF
殳	S13-4-9	F0692

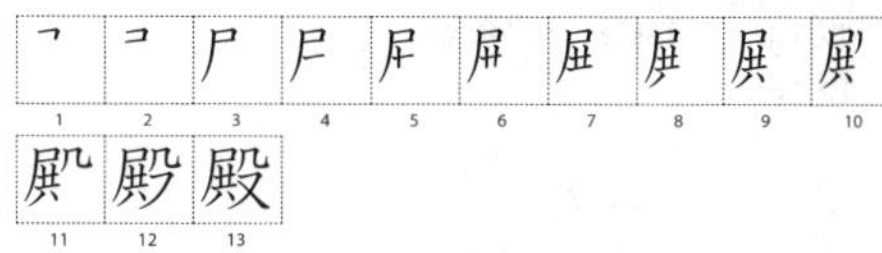

COMPOUNDS

❶ⓐ (large stately building) **PALACE, hall, mansion**

ⓑ (residence of nobility) **PALACE, shrine, temple**

ⓒ suffix after names of large buildings, esp. within the court or shrine grounds

a 殿堂 でんどう hall, palace, shrine; sanctuary

寝殿 しんでん main house

b 殿中で でんちゅうで in the palace

御殿 ごてん palace

宮殿 きゅうでん palace (of a royal person)

神殿 しんでん shrine, sanctuary

c 紫宸×殿 ししんでん Hall for State Ceremonies

❷ [also suffix] **FORMAL HONORIFIC TITLE**

殿下 でんか His Imperial Highness

貴殿 きでん you

保善院殿 ほぜんいんでん His Lordship Hozen of Blessed Memory

❸ [formerly 澱 でん 0954] settle, precipitate

沈殿 ちんでん precipitation, settlement

❹ the rear, the rear guard

殿軍 でんぐん rear guard

KUN

【との 殿】

①ⓐ **lord; my lord, his lordship**

ⓑ gentleman

a 殿様 とのさま feudal lord

若殿 わかとの young lord

b 殿方 とのがた men, gentlemen

② part of a building, stately building

高殿 たかどの stately mansion; two-[three-]storied house
湯殿 ゆどの bathroom

【-どの -殿】**FORMAL HONORIFIC TITLE: Esquire, Esq., Mister**
山田太郎殿 やまだたろうどの Taro Yamada, Esq.
議長殿 ぎちょうどの Mr. Chairman

【革】 飠 壴

SYNONYMS

❶ⓐ **buildings**
閣 TALL MAGNIFICENT BUILDING → 4128
宇 large building → 2699
殿 PALACE → 2247
堂 HALL → 3202
館 PUBLIC BUILDING → 2196
舎 BUILDING → 2555
棟 BLOCK → 1248
厩 HORSE STABLE → 3746

ⓑ **palace**
宮 ROYAL PALACE → 2828
殿 PALACE → 2247
閣 FEUDAL PALACE → 4130

❷ & 【-どの】 **titles of address**
氏 COURTESY TITLE → 3669
兄 familiar title (seniors) → 2676
君 FAMILIAR TITLE (peers) → 3974
嬢 Miss → 0936
様 FORMAL TITLE → 1332
殿 FORMAL HONORIFIC TITLE → 2247
師 honorific title (clergymen) → 1680
公 honorific title (noblemen) → 2468

鞄 2248

1-9-5

▶**BAG**
ホウ かばん
Ⓝ 鞄 Ⓒ 鞄 páo

177	Names	U9784
革	S14-9-5	F2396

KUN

【かばん 鞄】**BAG, briefcase, suitcase**
鞄持ち かばんもち private secretary; flunky
旅行鞄 りょこうかばん traveling bag, suitcase
通学鞄 つうがくかばん school bag

SYNONYMS

【かばん】
◯ **containers**
箱 BOX → 3362
壺 JAR → 2890
槽 TANK → 1352
樽 BARREL → 1368
棺 COFFIN → 1240
桶 BUCKET → 1211
笈 BOX CARRIED ON THE BACK → 3274
鞘 SHEATH → 2259
簞 BAMBOO BOX → 3381
函 BOX → 3724
籠 BASKET → 3398
袋 BAG → 3201
鞄 BAG (for carrying) → 2248
器 VESSEL → 3367
瓶 BOTTLE → 1702
缶 CAN → 2526
缶 EARTHENWARE JAR → 2525

◯ **bags**
俵 STRAW SACK → 0129
袋 BAG → 3201
鞄 BAG (for carrying) → 2248
包 wrapper → 3684
胞 MEMBRANOUS SAC → 1148

鞄 2249

1-9-5

▶**BAG**
ホウ かばん

177	Nonstandard	U9784
革	S14-9-5	F0000

traditional form → see 鞄 at 2248

飴 2250

1-9-5

▶**CANDY**
あめ
Ⓝ 飴 Ⓒ 饴 yí

184	Non-Jōyō	U98F4
飠	S14-9-5	F2736

KUN

【あめ 飴】**CANDY, sweets; syrup**
飴玉 あめだま candy
飴色 あめいろ translucent amber (color)
飴煮 あめに sweet boiled food
飴と鞭 あめとむち carrot and stick (policy)
喉飴 のどあめ throat lozenge, cough drop
水飴 みずあめ starch syrup
綿飴 わたあめ cotton candy
林檎飴 りんごあめ candied apple, toffee apple

SYNONYMS

【あめ】
◯ **confectionery**
菓 CONFECTIONERY → 2873
飴 CANDY → 2250

飽 2251

1-9-5

▶**SATIATED**
ホウ あ(きる) あ(かす) あ(く)

184	Nonstandard	U98FD
飠	S14-9-5	F0000

traditional form → see 飽 at 2148

飼

▶**RAISE ANIMALS**

シ か(う)

2252

◧1-9-5

184	Nonstandard	UFA2B
飠	S14-9-5	F0000

traditional form → see 飼 at 2149

飾

▶**DECORATE**

ショク かざ(る) かざ(り)

2253

◧1-9-5

184	Nonstandard	U98FE
飠	S14-9-5	F0000

traditional form → see 飾 at 2150

皷

▶**DRUM**

コ つづみ ㊔ つつみ

2254

◧1-9-5

107	Nonstandard	U76B7
皮	S14-5-9	F0000

traditional form → see 鼓 at 2241

鞍

▶**SADDLE**

アン くら

Ⓒ 鞍 ān

2255

◧1-9-6

177	Names	U978D
革	S15-9-6	F2439

COMPOUNDS

● **SADDLE**

鞍馬 あんば pommel horse, side horse; saddled horse

鞍上 あんじょう on top of a saddle

鞍部 あんぶ col, saddle between mountains

KUN

【くら 鞍】**SADDLE**

鞍替え くらがえ changing jobs [quarters, loyalties]

荷鞍 にぐら packsaddle

SYNONYMS

● **seat**

席 SEAT → 3865

座 SEAT → 3868

椅 CHAIR → 1239

鞍 SADDLE → 2255

餅

▶**RICE CAKE**

ヘイ もち

Ⓝ 餠 餅◈ Ⓒ 饼 bǐng

2256

◧1-9-6

184	Jōyō	U9905
飠	S15-9-6	F1937

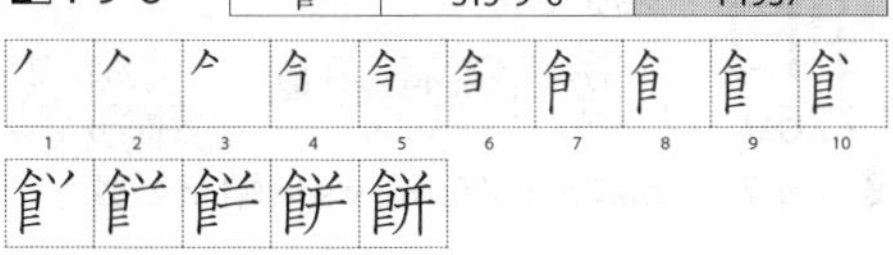

COMPOUNDS

● **RICE CAKE; food made from cereal dough**

餅餤× へいだん Heian-period confection made of boiled duck [goose] eggs and vegetables wrapped in rice cake and cut in squares

煎餅 せんべい rice cracker, wafer

血餅 けっぺい (blood) clot

画餅に帰す がべいにきす come to naught, fall through

KUN

【もち 餅】**RICE CAKE**

餅搗×き もちつき pounding mochi

餅米 もちごめ glutinous rice

餅肌 もちはだ soft, smooth skin

焼き餅 やきもち roasted rice cake; jealousy

鏡餅 かがみもち pair of stacked round rice cakes offered to the gods

桜餅 さくらもち rice cake filled with bean jam and wrapped in a preserved cherry leaf

絵に描いた餅 えにかいたもち pie in the sky

SYNONYMS

● **rice**

米 RICE → 4342

飯 COOKED RICE → 2126

稲 RICE PLANT → 1561

籾 UNHULLED RICE → 1626

餅 RICE CAKE → 2256

粥 RICE GRUEL → 0698

餌

▶**ANIMAL FEED**

ジ えさ え

Ⓝ 餌◈ Ⓒ 饵 ěr

2257

◧1-9-6

184	Jōyō	U990C
飠	S15-9-6	F2101

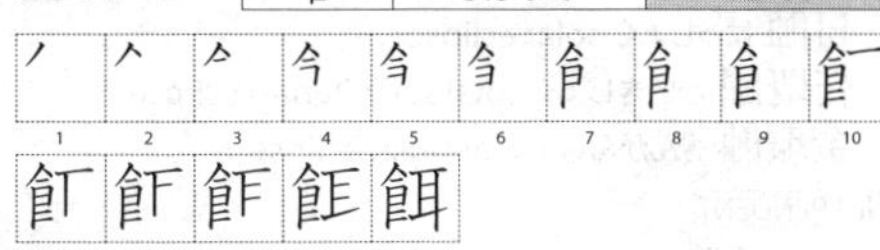

COMPOUNDS

ⓐ **ANIMAL FEED**

ⓑ **bait, prey**

a 給餌 きゅうじ feeding (animals)

食餌療法 しょくじりょうほう dietary cure

b 擬餌 ぎじ artificial bait

好餌 こうじ bait, decoy, lure

KUN

【えさ 餌】

ⓐ **ANIMAL FEED**

ⓑ **bait, prey**

ⓒ *slang* meal

a 餌場 えさば feeding grounds
ab 餌箱 えさばこ feed tray [trough, box, bowl]; bait box

【え 餌】
ⓐ **food, feed**
ⓑ **bait, prey**
a 餌付け えづけ artificial feeding
b 餌食 えじき prey, victim
撒き餌 まきえ scattered animal feed, ground bait
生餌 いきえ live bait

SYNONYMS

ⓐ **food**
飯 MEAL → 2126
膳 MEAL → 1381
食 FOOD, meal → 2578
糧 FOOD PROVISIONS → 1800
餌 ANIMAL FEED → 2257
肴 ACCOMPANIMENT FOR DRINKS → 2567

蝕

2258
1-9-6

▶**ERODE**
ショク むしば(む)
N 蝕 C 蚀 shí

142	Non-Jōyō	U8755
虫	S15-6-9	F2965

COMPOUNDS

[now usu. 食 2578]
❶ [original meaning] (be eaten as if by worms) **ERODE, corrode**
浸蝕 しんしょく erosion, corrosion
腐蝕 ふしょく corrosion
侵蝕 しんしょく infringement, violation
❷ [also suffix] **eclipse, occultation**
蝕甚(=食尽) しょくじん maximum eclipse
月蝕 げっしょく lunar eclipse
日蝕 にっしょく solar eclipse
皆既蝕 かいきしょく total solar [lunar] eclipse
金環蝕 きんかんしょく annular eclipse

INDEPENDENT

【しょく 蝕】[now usu. 食 2578] **eclipse**

KUN

【むしばむ 蝕む】[also 虫食む]
① (of worms) **eat in**
② **undermine, affect**

SYNONYMS

❶ **decrease**
減 DECREASE → 0733
耗 WEAR AWAY → 1660
削 cut down → 1837
縮 SHRINK → 1790
落 FALL → 2907
蝕 ERODE → 2258

HOMOPHONES

むしばむ 虫食む → 4343, 2578

鞘

2259
1-9-7

▶**SHEATH**
ショウ さや
N 鞘 C 鞘 qiào shāo

177	Names	U9798
革	S16-9-7	F2251

COMPOUNDS

● **SHEATH, scabbard, casing**
鞘翅×類 しょうしるい beetles
腱×鞘 けんしょう sheath of tendon
髄鞘 ずいしょう myelin sheath

KUN

【さや 鞘】
① **SHEATH, scabbard, casing**
鞘当て さやあて rivalry ("touching of sheaths")
元の鞘に収まる もとのさやにおさまる make up (after a conflict)
② margin, difference
鞘取り さやとり arbitrage
利鞘 りざや profit margin

SPECIAL READINGS

海鞘 ほや sea squirt

SYNONYMS

● **containers**
箱 BOX → 3362
壺 JAR → 2890
槽 TANK → 1352
樽 BARREL → 1368
棺 COFFIN → 1240
桶 BUCKET → 1211
笈 BOX CARRIED ON THE BACK → 3274
鞘 SHEATH → 2259
簞 BAMBOO BOX → 3381
函 BOX → 3724
籠 BASKET → 3398
袋 BAG → 3201
鞄 BAG (for carrying) → 2248
器 VESSEL → 3367
瓶 BOTTLE → 1702
缶 CAN → 2526
缶 EARTHENWARE JAR → 2525

鞘

2260
1-9-7

▶**SHEATH**
ショウ さや

177	Nonstandard	U9798
革	S16-9-7	F0000

traditional form → see 鞘 at 2259

餓

2261

◧ 1-9-7

▶**STARVED**

ガ う(える)

184	Nonstandard	U9913
飠	S16-9-7	F0000

traditional form → see 餓 at 2176

餝

2262

◧ 1-9-7

▶**DECORATE**

ショク かざ(る) かざ(り)

184	Nonstandard	U991D
飠	S16-9-7	F0000

traditional form → see 飾 at 2150

餘

2263

◧ 1-9-7

▶**REMAINING**
▶**EXCESS**

ヨ あま(る) あま(り) あま(す)

184	Nonstandard	U9918
飠	S16-9-7	F0000

traditional form → see 余 at 2535

親

2264

◧ 1-9-7

▶**PARENT**
▶**RELATIVES**
▶**INTIMATE**

シン おや おや- した(しい) した(しむ)

㊔ ちか ちかし

Ⓒ 亲 qīn qìng

147	Jōyō-2	U89AA
見	S16-7-9	F0172

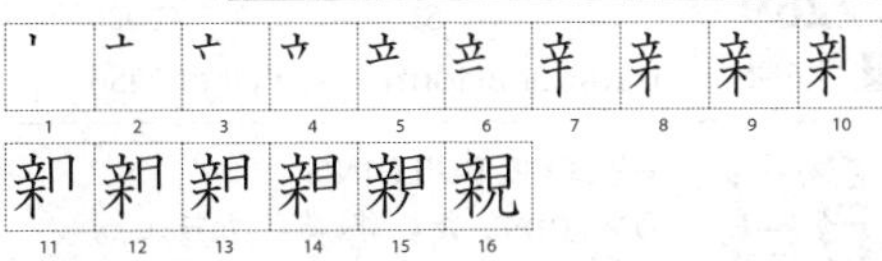

COMPOUNDS

❶ PARENT

親権 しんけん parental authority
親子 しんし(=おやこ) parent and child
両親 りょうしん parents

❷ **RELATIVES, kin, relations (by marriage)**

親族 しんぞく relative
親類 しんるい relatives, relations
親戚 しんせき relative
三親等 さんしんとう kinsman of the third degree (of consanguinity)
肉親 にくしん blood relation

❸ **INTIMATE, familiar, close, friendly**

親友 しんゆう close [intimate] friend
親密な しんみつな intimate, close
親愛 しんあい love, affection
親切な しんせつな kind, friendly, obliging
日イ親善 にちいしんぜん friendly relations between Japan and Israel

❹ [prefix] **pro- (some country)**

親日 しんにち pro-Japan
親米 しんべい pro-American

❺ **oneself, in person**—said esp. of actions performed by the emperor

親展書 しんてんしょ confidential letter
親政 しんせい direct Imperial rule

INDEPENDENT

【しん 親】**RELATIVES**

親は泣き寄る しんはなきよる Relatives come and mourn together

KUN

【おや 親】**PARENT, father, mother; card dealer; (gambling) banker**

親指 おやゆび thumb
親分 おやぶん boss, big shot
親孝行 おやこうこう filial piety [duty]
親不孝 おやふこう lack of filial piety
父親 ちちおや father

【おや- 親-】[also prefix] **PARENT, mother; master**

親船 おやぶね mother ship
親会社 おやがいしゃ parent company

【したしい 親しい】**INTIMATE, familiar, close, friendly**

親しさ したしさ intimacy
親しい友達 したしいともだち close [intimate] friend
親しく したしく intimately; personally, in person

【したしむ 親しむ】**be INTIMATE with, commune with; form a liking for, take to**

親しみ したしみ intimacy, familiarity

SYNONYMS

❶ **parents**

親 PARENT → 2264
父 FATHER → 2467
母 MOTHER → 4287

❷ **family and relations**

族 FAMILY → 1195
家 FAMILY → 2827
門 family → 1100
氏 clan → 3669
縁 RELATION → 1754
姻 relative by marriage → 0421
親 RELATIVES → 2264
戚 RELATIVES → 4401
曽 GREAT- → 2632

❸ **familiar and friendly**

親 INTIMATE → 2264
密 CLOSE → 2857
近 NEAR → 3798
睦 FRIENDLY → 1534

懇 FAMILIAR → 3606
和 HARMONIOUS → 1450

【おや-】

◯ **main**

主 MAIN → 2437
正 chief → 4296
本 head → 4314
親- PARENT → 2264
首 leading → 2818

NOTE

➡ see COMPOUND FORMATION for 親展書 しんてんしょ → 展 3862

龍

2265

1-9-7

▶DRAGON

リュウ リョウ たつ

212	Names	U9F8D
龍	S16-16-0	F0000

traditional form → see 竜 at 2603
radical variant → see 龍 at 2266

龍

2266

1-9-7

▶DRAGON

リュウ リョウ たつ

212	Nonstandard	U7ADC
龍	S16-16-0	F0000

traditional form → see 竜 at 2603

RADICAL

ryū 'dragon' (龕×), used in characters related to dragons

縣

2267

1-9-7

▶PREFECTURE

ケン ㊔ がた あがた

109	Names	U7E23
目	S16-5-10	F0000

traditional form → see 県 at 3269

鞠

2268

1-9-8

▶BALL

キク キュウ クウ まり

Ⓒ 鞠 jū

177	Names	U97A0
革	S17-9-8	F3210

COMPOUNDS

❶ [rare] **BALL**

蹴鞠 しゅうきく ancient football game

❷ inquire, examine

鞠訊する きくじんする inquire into (a crime), examine

❸ bring [rear] up

鞠育する きくいくする bring [rear] up

❹ bend oneself

鞠躬×如たる きっきゅうじょたる in a humble or respectful manner

INDEPENDENT

【きくする 鞠する】 inquire into (a crime), examine

KUN

【まり 鞠】 [also 毬] **BALL**

鞠靴 まりぐつ ancient football shoes
鞠突き まりつき ball-bouncing game
蹴鞠 けまり ancient football game

SYNONYMS

❶ & 【まり】 **spherical object**

玉 spherical object → 4289
球 BALL → 1219
丸 round body → 4225
鞠 BALL → 2268
毬 BALL → 4001

USAGE

【まり】

鞠
[also 毬] ball

毬
[also 鞠] ball

HOMOPHONES

まり 毬 BALL → 4001

餅

2269

1-9-8

▶RICE CAKE

ヘイ もち

184	Nonstandard	U9920
食	S17-9-8	F0000

traditional form → see 餅 at 2256

館

2270

1-9-8

▶PUBLIC BUILDING

カン やかた たて ㊔ だて たち しろ

184	Nonstandard	UFA2C
食	S17-9-8	F0000

traditional form → see 館 at 2196

隸

2271

1-9-8

▶UNDERLING

レイ

171	Nonstandard	U96B8
隶	S17-8-9	F0000

traditional form → see 隷 at 2201

鞭

2272

1-9-9

▶WHIP

ベン むち

Ⓒ 鞭 biān

177	Names	U97AD
革	S18-9-9	F2254

COMPOUNDS

❶ **WHIP, lash, rod, cane**

鞭毛 べんもう flagellum

教鞭を執る きょうべんをとる teach ("take a teacher's whip")

❷ⓐ WHIP, lash, give the rod

ⓑ spur on

a 先鞭を着ける せんべんをつける pioneer, blaze a trail, have a head start

b 鞭撻× べんたつ encouragement, urging

KUN

【むち 鞭】**WHIP, lash, rod, cane**

鞭打つ むちうつ whip, lash, give the rod; spur on

鞭打ち症 むちうちしょう whiplash (injury)

飴と鞭 あめとむち carrot and stick (policy)

額

▸AMOUNT

ガク ひたい ㊔ ぬか

Ⓒ 额 é

2273

◧ 1-9-9

181	Jōyō-5	U984D
頁	S18-9-9	F0741

COMPOUNDS

❶ [also suffix] **AMOUNT (of money), sum, volume, quantity**

額面 がくめん face value; denomination

金額 きんがく amount of money, sum

多額 たがく large amount [sum]

総額 そうがく total amount, sum total

全額 ぜんがく sum total, total amount

月額 げつがく monthly amount [sum]

生産額 せいさんがく amount of production

❷ **picture frame, frame, framed picture**

額縁 がくぶち (picture) frame

扁額 へんがく tablet, framed picture

❸ [original meaning] **forehead, brow**

前額部 ぜんがくぶ forehead; frontlet

INDEPENDENT

【がく 額】**AMOUNT (of money), sum, volume; picture frame, framed picture, tablet**

額にする がくにする set in a frame

巨大な額 きょだいながく colossal amount

KUN

【ひたい 額】**forehead, brow**

広い額 ひろいひたい broad forehead, high brow

SYNONYMS

❶ **quantity and number**

量 QUANTITY → 3119

嵩 BULK → 2927

積 size → 1579

額 AMOUNT → 2273

分 content → 2466

数 NUMBER → 2245

勢 strength → 3542

❷ **frames**

枠 FRAME → 1077

骼 SKELETAL FRAME → 2302

格 framework → 1161

額 picture frame → 2273

❸ **front parts of head**

顔 FACE → 2277

面 FACE → 2590

額 forehead → 2273

顎 chin → 2276

頬 CHEEK → 2043

吻 PROBOSCIS → 0270

顕

▸MANIFEST

ケン ㊔ あき あきら

Ⓝ 顯 Ⓒ 显 xiǎn

2274

◧ 1-9-9

181	Jōyō	U9855
頁	S18-9-9	F1618

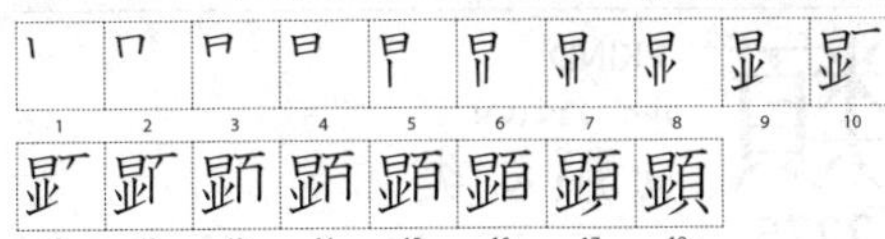

COMPOUNDS

❶ⓐ (readily perceived) **MANIFEST, apparent, noticeable, obvious**

ⓑ [original meaning] (show plainly) **MANIFEST, reveal, expose**

a 顕著な けんちょな notable, conspicuous; clear, obvious

顕示する けんじする reveal

顕在化する けんざいかする be actualized

顕現 けんげん manifestation

露顕(=露見) ろけん discovery, detection, exposure

b 顕微鏡 けんびきょう microscope

❷ⓐ make (a person's virtues) known

ⓑ well-known, prominent, high ranking

a 顕彰する けんしょうする give recognition, exalt, honor

顕揚する けんようする extol, exalt

b 顕職 けんしょく prominent post

貴顕 きけん distinguished person

❸ *Buddhism* exoteric

顕教 けんきょう Exoteric Buddhism

SYNONYMS

❶ⓐ **evident**

明 CLEAR →1060
鮮 VIVID →2355
亮 LUCID →2571
顕 MANIFEST →2274
瞭 CLEAR →1584

❶ⓐ conspicuous
著 CONSPICUOUS →2869
顕 MANIFEST →2274
卓 PROMINENT →2561
傑 outstanding →0175

ⓑ appear
現 APPEAR →1218
出 come out →4310
顕 MANIFEST →2274

❶ⓑ reveal
発 reveal →3174
露 EXPOSE →3495
曝 EXPOSE →1410
晒す EXPOSE →1156
暴 disclose →3138
披 OPEN OUT →0362
顕 MANIFEST →2274
現 cause to appear →1218

類

▸KIND
ルイ たぐ(い)
Ⓝ 類 Ⓒ 类 lèi

2275
1-9-9

181	Jōyō-4	U985E
頁	S18-9-9	F0563

COMPOUNDS

❶ⓐ KIND, class, sort, category, genus, species
ⓑ [suffix] **things of the same KIND, group**
ⓒ separate by KIND, classify
ⓓ [also suffix] **idiomatic term for biological class or order**

a 種類 しゅるい kind, sort, species, type
人類 じんるい mankind, humankind
同類 どうるい same kind, same class
衣類 いるい clothes, garments
b 下着類 したぎるい underclothes
辞書類 じしょるい dictionaries (and similar books)
c 分類 ぶんるい classification
d 哺乳類 ほにゅうるい Mammalia
食肉類 しょくにくるい carnivorous animals, Carnivora

❷ of the same **KIND**:
ⓐ similar, resembling, synonymous
ⓑ be similar, resemble, be alike
ⓒ similar example, parallel, precedent

a 類書 るいしょ books of the same kind, similar books
類型 るいけい similar type, prototype, pattern
類語 るいご synonym, correlated word
b 類似 るいじ resemblance, similarity
c 類例 るいれい similar example, parallel
比類 ひるい parallel, equal, match

❸ be affected by someone else's disaster (spreading flames)
類焼 るいしょう catching fire from next door

❹ blood relation, kin
類縁 るいえん affinity, family relationship
親類 しんるい relatives, relations

INDEPENDENT

【るい 類】**KIND**, sort, class, genus, species; similar example, parallel; *logic* genus
類の無い るいのない unparalleled, unprecedented
この類の このるいの this kind
同じ類に属する おなじるいにぞくする belong to the same class

【るいする 類する】be similar, be like

KUN

【たぐい 類い】**KIND, sort, class; peer, equal**
類い希な たぐいまれな unique, rare
同じ類いの物 おなじたぐいのもの things of the same kind

SYNONYMS

❶ⓐ kinds and types
型 TYPE →3266
類 KIND →2275
色 kind →2522
般 SORT →1670
属 genus →3901
品 category →2795
種 VARIETY →1560
様 variety →1332

❷ⓐ similar
類 similar →2275
様 like →1332
如 AS →0239
-通り as →3855
云 SUCH →2430

ⓑ resemble
似 RESEMBLE →0071
類 be similar →2275

顎

▶**JAW**

ガク あご

Ⓒ 颚 è

2276

◧ 1-9-9

181 頁	Jōyō	U984E
	S18-9-9	F1749

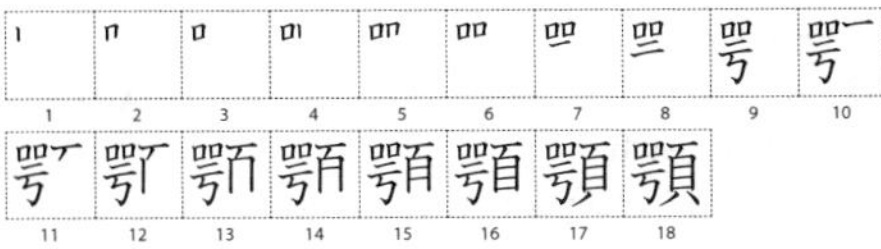

COMPOUNDS

● **JAW**

顎関節 がくかんせつ jaw joint

顎骨 がっこつ(=がくこつ) jawbone

KUN

【あご 顎】

ⓐ **JAW**

ⓑ **chin**

a 下顎 したあご lower jaw

b 顎鬚 あごひげ beard

顎で使う あごでつかう order someone about

二重顎 にじゅうあご double chin

SYNONYMS

【あご】

ⓑ **front parts of head**

顔 FACE →2277

面 FACE →2590

額 forehead →2273

顎 chin →2276

頬 CHEEK →2043

吻 PROBOSCIS →0270

顔

▶**FACE**

ガン かお

Ⓝ 顏 Ⓒ 颜 yán

2277

◧ 1-9-9

181 頁	Jōyō-2	U9854
	S18-9-9	F0134

COMPOUNDS

❶ⓐ **FACE, countenance**

ⓑ (facial expression) **FACE, looks, features**

a 顔面 がんめん face

洗顔 せんがん washing one's face

紅顔 こうがん rosy face, peachy cheeks

b 顔色 がんしょく(=かおいろ) complexion, countenance, expression

童顔の どうがんの boyish looking, baby-faced

厚顔な こうがんな impudent, shameless, brazen

破顔 はがん broad smile

❷ color, coloring

顔料 がんりょう cosmetics; color, pigment

❸ [original meaning, now archaic] forehead

竜顔 りゅうがん(=りょうがん) emperor's face

KUN

【かお 顔】

①ⓐ **FACE**

ⓑ [also suffix] (facial expression) **FACE, looks, expression**

a 顔付き かおつき face, countenance; expression, look

顔触れ かおぶれ personnel

顔合わせ かおあわせ meeting, introduction; being matched against each other

顔馴染み かおなじみ familiar face, friend

素顔 すがお face without makeup

b 笑顔 えがお smiling face, smile

知らん顔 しらんかお feigned ignorance, unconcerned air

怒った顔 おこったかお angry face [countenance]

② **FACE,** prestige, honor

顔を潰される かおをつぶされる be put out of countenance, lose face

顔が立つ かおがたつ save one's face

③ reputation, influence

顔の広い人 かおのひろいひと person with many contacts

SYNONYMS

❶ⓐ **front parts of head**

顔 FACE →2277

面 FACE →2590

額 forehead →2273

顎 chin →2276

頬 CHEEK →2043

吻 PROBOSCIS →0270

ⓑ **expression**

顔 FACE →2277

色 COLOR →2522

顏

▶**FACE**

ガン かお

2278

◧ 1-9-9

181 頁	Nonstandard	U984F
	S18-9-9	F0000

traditional form →see 顔 at 2277

1

韻

▶RHYME

イン

Ⓝ 韵 Ⓒ 韵 yùn

2279

1-9-10

【音】 韻

180	Jōyō	U97FB
音	S19-9-10	F2495

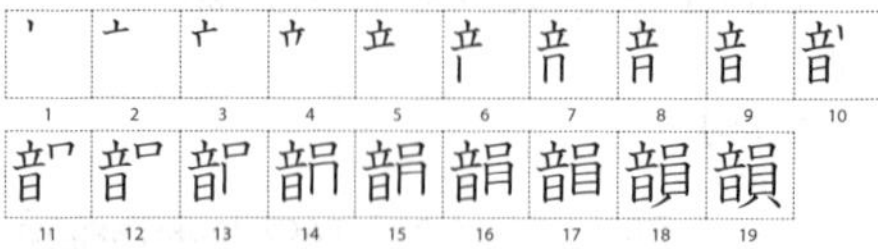

COMPOUNDS

❶ⓐ [original meaning] **RHYME, rhyming**

ⓑ **RHYME**d poetry, verse

a 韻律 いんりつ rhythm, meter, measure

押韻 おういん rhyme, rhyming

頭韻 とういん alliteration, head rhyme

脚韻 きゃくいん rhyme, end rhyme

b 韻文 いんぶん poetry, verse

❷ **melodious tone, agreeable sound, resonance**

余韻 よいん lingering tone, resonance, reverberation; aftertaste, impregnated elegance

松韻 しょういん music of the pines

❸ simple or compound vowel, final (of a Chinese syllable or character)

韻母 いんぼ final

韻書 いんしょ Chinese dictionary arranged by finals

音韻組織 おんいんそしき sound system

❹ charm, grace, elegance

風韻 ふういん taste, grace

INDEPENDENT

【いん 韻】 **RHYME**

韻を踏む いんをふむ rhyme (with)

SYNONYMS

❶ⓐ **musical elements**

韻 RHYME → 2279

律 RHYTHM → 0433

拍 BEAT → 0361

調 TONE → 1973

呂 ancient musical note → 2713

❷ **kinds of sound**

音 SOUND → 2570

声 VOICE → 2724

響 reverberation → 3573

韻 melodious tone → 2279

玲 TINKLING OF JADES → 1139

闕

1-9-10

incorrect classification

➡ see ◻3-8-11: 門 at 4137

饒

▶ABUNDANT

ジョウ

Ⓒ 饶 ráo

2280

1-9-12

184	Non-Jōyō	U9952
飠	S21-9-12	F2716

COMPOUNDS

● [now also 冗 2470] [original meaning] **ABUNDANT, plentiful, rich**

饒舌 じょうぜつ garrulity, loquacity

豊饒 ほうじょう fertility, fruitfulness

SYNONYMS

● **plentiful**

百 numerous → 2519

沃 FERTILE → 0315

万 myriad → 3653

多 MANY → 2694

豊 PLENTIFUL → 3344

沢 plentiful → 0313

穣 YIELDING ABUNDANTLY → 1597

裕 ABUNDANT → 1530

饒 ABUNDANT → 2280

富 RICH → 2892

饑

▶STARVE

キ

Ⓒ 饥 jī

2281

1-9-12

184	Non-Jōyō	U9951
飠	S21-9-12	F0000

COMPOUNDS

[now replaced by 飢 2101]

ⓐ [original meaning] **STARVE, be hungry, famish**

ⓑ **crop failure, famine**

a 饑餓 きが starvation, hunger, famine

饑渇 きかつ hunger and thirst

b 饑饉[×] ききん famine, failure of crops; shortage

SYNONYMS

ⓐ **hunger and thirst**

渇 THIRST → 0627

餓 STARVED → 2176

飢 STARVE → 2101

饑 STARVE → 2281

馭

▶HANDLE

ギョ

Ⓒ 驭 御 yù

2282

1-10-2

187	Non-Jōyō	U99AD
馬	S12-10-2	F3449

COMPOUNDS

[now replaced by 御 0703]

ⓐ HANDLE, control, manage
ⓑ [original meaning] **HANDLE a horse well, train a horse**
a 制馭する せいぎょする control, govern, suppress
b 馭者 ぎょしゃ coachman, driver

INDEPENDENT

【ぎょする 馭する】**HANDLE** a horse well, train a horse

SYNONYMS

ⓐ handle
扱う HANDLE →0251
馭 HANDLE →2282
操 MANIPULATE →0948
揮 WIELD →0717
運 control movement skillfully →3894

NOTE

➡ see USAGE note at 御 0703

創

2283

◧ 1-10-2

▶CREATE
ソウ つく(る) ㊔ はじめ
Ⓒ 创 chuàng chuāng

18	Jōyō-6	U5275
刂	S12-2-10	F0941

COMPOUNDS

❶ⓐ CREATE, bring into being, invent
ⓑ initiate, originate, start
a 創造 そうぞう creation
創作する そうさくする create, produce; write a story
創意 そうい original idea, ingenuity
創世記 そうせいき Genesis
独創的 どくそうてき original, creative
b 創立する そうりつする establish, organize, start
創始 そうし initiating, creation, foundation
創刊 そうかん launching a magazine; first issue
創業 そうぎょう inauguration of an enterprise
創設 そうせつ establishment, founding

❷ [original meaning] wound, cut, laceration
創傷 そうしょう wound
銃創 じゅうそう gunshot wound
絆創膏 ばんそうこう adhesive plaster [tape]

KUN

【つくる 創る】[usu. 作る] **CREATE, bring into being**
天地を創る てんちをつくる create the heavens and the earth

SYNONYMS

❶ⓐ create
創 CREATE →2283
作 compose →0077
綴 COMPOSE →1746
生 produce →4309
発 START →3174
起 generate →4099
ⓑ begin
始 BEGIN →0335
-出す begin to do →4310
-掛ける start doing →0596
発 START →3174
起 start →4099
就 SET ABOUT →2129
開 OPEN →4121
創 initiate →2283
肇 ORIGINATE →3474
❷ injury
傷 WOUND →0179
創 wound (cut) →2283
-擦れ sore →0971

HOMOPHONES

つくる
作 MAKE →0077
造 MAKE →3856

NOTE

➡ see USAGE note at 作 0077

割

2284

◧ 1-10-2

▶DIVIDE
カツ わ(る) わり わ(り) わ(れる) さ(く)
Ⓝ 割 Ⓒ 割 gē

18	Jōyō-6	U5272
刂	S12-2-10	F0522

COMPOUNDS

❶ (separate into parts) **DIVIDE (up), split; cede**
割賦 かっぷ(=わっぷ) payment by installments
割拠する かっきょする hold one's own ground
割愛する かつあいする part with (something), give up; omit (reluctantly)
割譲 かつじょう cession of territory
分割する ぶんかつする divide up, partition, split

❷ [original meaning] **cut with a knife, cut in two**
割腹 かっぷく disembowelment, harakiri
割礼 かつれい circumcision
割線 かっせん secant

KUN

【わる 割る】*vi*

① ⓐ **DIVIDE (up), cut (in half), allot**
ⓑ *math* **DIVIDE**
a 割り当て わりあて assignment, allotment
割り勘 わりかん equal split, Dutch treat
割り前 わりまえ share, one's lot, quota
b 割り算 わりざん division
割り切る わりきる divide; give a clear-cut solution
② ⓐ **crack, break**
ⓑ **split, chop (wood)**
a コップを割る こっぷをわる crack [break] a glass
b 割り印 わりいん tally impression
割り箸 わりばし half-split (disposable) chopsticks
二つ割り ふたつわり cutting in two; one half
③ **push open, separate, part**
割り込む わりこむ wedge (oneself) in, squeeze oneself into
④ **open up, disclose**
割り出す わりだす deduce, infer; calculate, compute
口を割る くちをわる speak out, confess
腹を割って はらをわって frankly
⑤ drop below (a price level)
原価を割って げんかをわって below cost
⑥ *sumo* step out (of the ring)
⑦ dilute
炭酸で割る たんさんでわる dilute with soda

【わり 割】
① ⓐ **rate, proportion, ratio**
ⓑ **counter for units of 10%**
ⓒ abbrev. of 割引 わりびき: **discount**
a 割に わりに comparatively, rather
割引く わりびく give a discount, make a reduction
割引 わりびき discount, reduction
割合 わりあい rate, proportion, ratio; comparatively
割合に わりあいに relatively; a little, rather
一日百円の割で いちにちひゃくえんのわりで at the rate of 100 yen a day
b 一割 いちわり 10%
三割五分 さんわりごぶ 35%
c 割興 わりこう discount industrial bank bond
学割 がくわり student discount
② profit, gain
割の良い わりのいい remunerative, paying, profitable, advantageous

【わり 割り】**dilution; equal split, Dutch treat;** [in compounds] **allotment, assignment**
割りで払う わりではらう split the account
水割り みずわり whisky and water
役割 やくわり assigning [allotment of] parts; part, role, duty
時間割り じかんわり hour assignment, time table

【われる 割れる】*vi* **crack, break, be smashed; be DIVIDEd [forked], be separated;** (lose unity) **split (into);** *math* **be divisible; drop below (a price level);** *colloq* **be disclosed**
割れ目 われめ crevice, crack; cleft
割れた卵 われたたまご broken egg
ひび割れ ひびわれ crack, fissure
前割れの まえわれの open in front
仲間割れ なかまわれ split among friends, division in the camp
二で割れる にでわれる be divisible by two
コスト割れ こすとわれ cutting into cost
身元が割れる みもとがわれる be identified

【さく 割く】
① **spare (time), set [put] aside**
時間を割く じかんをさく spare time (for)
② cede, alienate
領土を割く りょうどをさく cede a territory

SYNONYMS

❶ **separate**
割 DIVIDE → 2284
分 DIVIDE → 2466
解 TAKE APART → 1913
析 ANALYZE → 1072
別 SEPARATE → 1434
離 SEPARATE → 2364
隔 partition → 0827

❷ **cut**
切 CUT → 0030
薙ぐ MOW DOWN → 3010
剪 PRUNE → 2886
削 CUT BY CHIPPING → 1837
挽く GRIND, saw → 0511
断 CUT OFF → 1885
截 CUT OFF → 4092
裁 CUT OUT → 4090
斬 CUT WITH A SWORD → 1874
割 cut with a knife → 2284
剖 DISSECT → 2103
刈る CLIP → 0032
伐 CUT DOWN → 0046

【わる】
① ⓑ **divide**
除 divide → 0546
割る DIVIDE → 2284
② **break**
破 BREAK → 1478
拉ぐ crush → 0372
崩 CRUMBLE → 2863
挫 SPRAIN → 0519
壊 BREAK DOWN → 0934

毀す break down →2246
折 BREAK OFF →0297
割る crack →2284
裂 SPLIT →3331
砕 CRUSH UP →1458
摧 CRUSH UP →0849
潰す CRUSH →0919

【わり】

①ⓐ **rate**

率 RATE →2625
割 rate →2284
比 ratio →0029
歩 percentage →3071

HOMOPHONES

さく 裂 SPLIT →3331

NOTE

➡ see USAGE note at 裂 3331

剳

2285

◧ 1-10-2

▶**DIVIDE**

カツ わ(る) わり わ(り) わ(れる) さ(く)

18	Nonstandard	U2F822
刂	S12-2-10	F0000

traditional form →see 割 at 2284

凱

2286

◧ 1-10-2

▶**TRIUMPH**

ガイ カイ ㊔ よし とき たのし

Ⓒ 凯 kǎi

16	Names	U51F1
几	S12-2-10	F2676

COMPOUNDS

❶ **TRIUMPH, victory**

凱旋する がいせんする return from a victorious campaign
凱旋門 がいせんもん arch of triumph
凱歌 がいか triumphal song

❷ enjoy, take pleasure

凱風 がいふう south wind; summer breeze

SYNONYMS

❶ **win**

勝 WIN →1268
克 OVERCOME →2540
剋 OVERCOME →4097
征 CONQUER →0349
破 BREAK →1478
凱 TRIUMPH →2286

勤

2287

◧ 1-10-2

▶**SERVICE**

キン ゴン つと(める) -づと(め) つと(まる) いそ(しむ)▲ ㊔ つとむ いそ

Ⓝ 勤 Ⓒ 勤 qín

19	Jōyō-6	U52E4
力	S12-2-10	F0904

COMPOUNDS

❶ (employment in general) **SERVICE, duty, work, employment**

勤続 きんぞく continuous service, continuance in service
通勤する つうきんする commute, go to one's office
転勤する てんきんする be transferred (to another office)
欠勤 けっきん absence (from work)
夜勤 やきん night duty

❷ **work diligently [hard], labor, strive; work faithfully**

勤勉 きんべん diligence, assiduity, industry
勤務する きんむする do duty, serve, be on duty, work
勤労 きんろう labor, work, service
勤倹 きんけん diligence and thrift
勤行 ごんぎょう Buddhistic service, sutra chanting
忠勤 ちゅうきん loyal [faithful] service

KUN

【つとめる 勤める】 **serve (in an office), hold a job, be in the SERVICE of**

勤め つとめ service, employment, duties; Buddhistic service, sutra chanting; prostitute service
勤め先 つとめさき (one's place of) employment
勤め上げる つとめあげる serve out one's time, perform one's service

【-づとめ -勤め】 [suffix] **serving in, being in the SERVICE of**

会社勤め かいしゃづとめ serving in a company

【つとまる 勤まる】 **be fit for, be equal to (the task)**

勤まらない つとまらない be unfit [incompetent] for

【いそしむ 勤しむ】 work diligently, strive, make efforts

仕事に勤しむ しごとにいそしむ be assiduous in one's business

SYNONYMS

❶ **work and employment**

務 DUTY →1505
任 OFFICE →0057
役 SERVICE (esp. public) →0288

勤 SERVICE (employment) → 2287
業 WORK → 3227
職 EMPLOYMENT → 1803
労 LABOR → 3155
❷ **exert oneself**
努 EXERT → 3154
勉 ENDEAVOR → 4113
励 make efforts → 1438
勤 work diligently → 2287
尽 use all one's strength → 3786
精 put one's heart into → 1729
孜 MAKE DILIGENT EFFORTS → 0284
【つとめる】
◯ **work**
働 WORK → 0172
稼 WORK (for a living) → 1572
労 LABOR → 3155
勤める serve (in an office) → 2287
仕 SERVE → 0037

USAGE

❶ **【つとめる】**
勤める
serve (in an office), hold a job, be in the service of
務める
ⓐ discharge [perform] one's duties
ⓑ play [act, perform] (a part or role)
努める
[sometimes also 勉める] endeavor, make efforts, try hard, work diligently
勉める
[usu. 努める] same as 努める
❷ **【つとめ】**
勤め
① service, employment, duties
② Buddhistic service, sutra chanting
③ prostitute service
務め
duty, task, responsibility

HOMOPHONES

つとめる
務 DUTY → 1505
努 EXERT → 3154
勉 ENDEAVOR → 4113
つとめ 務 DUTY → 1505
つとまる 務 DUTY → 1505

NOTE

➡ see also USAGE note at 務 1505

剰 2288

▶**SURPLUS**
ジョウ

18	Names	U5269
刂	S12-2-10	F0000

1-10-2
traditional form → see 剩 at 2233

馳 2289

▶**RUN QUICKLY**
チ **は(せる)** ㊔ はやし とし
Ⓒ 驰 chí

187	Names	U99B3
馬	S13-10-3	F1864

1-10-3

COMPOUNDS

ⓐ [original meaning] **RUN QUICKLY; gallop**
ⓑ drive a horse [car]
a 御馳走 ごちそう feast, treat
御馳走様 ごちそうさま Thank you (for the meal)/I've enjoyed the meal
背馳 はいち inconsistency, contradiction
b 馳駆 ちく dashing on a horse; running around, exerting oneself

KUN

【はせる 馳せる】
①ⓐ **RUN QUICKLY; gallop**
ⓑ **drive (a car); gallop (a horse)**
a 馳せ参じる はせさんじる hasten to join
遅れ馳せ(=後れ馳せ) おくればせ belated, eleventh hour
② think about [of], direct one's thoughts to
思いを馳せる おもいをはせる think about [of], direct one's thoughts to
③ make renowned, win (fame)
名を馳せる なをはせる win fame, make a name for oneself

SYNONYMS

ⓐ **run**
走 RUN → 2720
奔 RUSH → 2758
馳 RUN QUICKLY → 2289
駆 gallop → 2293

NOTE

➡ see COMPOUND FORMATION for 御馳走 ごちそう → 走 2720

馴 2290

▶**BECOME TAME**
ジュン **な(れる) な(らす)**
Ⓒ 驯 xùn

187	Names	U99B4
馬	S13-10-3	F1671

1-10-3

COMPOUNDS

ⓐ [original meaning] **BECOME TAME [domesticated], get used to humans**

b [now also 順 0018] **tame, domesticate**
a 馴致する じゅんちする tame, habituate; lead to
b 馴化 じゅんか acclimation

KUN

【なれる 馴れる】
① **BECOME TAME [domesticated]**
馴れた なれた tame, domesticated
馴染む なじむ become familiar; grow accustomed; get (clothing) to fit
人馴れ ひとなれ being used to people, being tame
② [usu. 慣れる] [also suffix] grow accustomed to, get used to, become inured to, become experienced in
不馴れ ふなれ inexperienced, unfamiliar (with)
場馴れ ばなれ experience, poise in a critical situation
見馴れる みなれる become used to seeing
③ [in compounds] **become familiar [friendly] with; become overfamiliar with**
馴れ合う なれあう collude, conspire; establish clandestine liaisons
馴れ馴れしい なれなれしい overfamiliar, unceremonial
馴れ初め なれそめ start of a romance, beginning of love

【ならす 馴らす】
① **tame, domesticate**
馴らし手 ならして tamer
飼い馴らす かいならす tame (an animal), domesticate
② [usu. 慣らす] inure, habituate, accustom, make used to
足馴らし あしならし walking practice, warming up

SPECIAL READINGS

馴鹿 となかい reindeer

HOMOPHONES

なれる 慣 HABITUAL PRACTICE → 0843
ならす
慣 HABITUAL PRACTICE → 0843
均 EVEN → 0276

NOTE

➡ see USAGE note at 慣 0843

駄

2291
1-10-4

▶**GOOD FOR NOTHING**
ダ タ▲
C 驮 tuó duò

187	Jōyō	U99C4
馬	S14-10-4	F1182

1 2 3 4 5 6 7 8 9 10 11 12 13 14 (stroke order)

COMPOUNDS

1 [also prefix] **GOOD FOR NOTHING, no good, poor, shabby, useless, worthless**
駄目 だめ *go* cross that does not constitute a territory; no good, useless; No!
駄作 ださく poor piece of writing
駄菓子 だがし cheap sweets
駄洒×落 だじゃれ poor joke, pun
駄駄を捏×ねる だだをこねる be unreasonable
無駄な むだな no good, fruitless, wasteful
2 **clogs, sandals**
下駄 げた geta, wooden clogs
足駄 あしだ high clogs, rain clogs
雪駄 せった leather-soled sandals
3 **a** carry by packhorse
b horse load, pack
c counter for horse loads
a 駄賃 だちん packhorse charge; tip
駄馬 だば packhorse, workhorse, hack
b 荷駄 にだ horse load, pack
c 薪二駄 たきぎにだ two horse loads of firewood

SYNONYMS

1 **bad**
悪 BAD → 3413
劣 INFERIOR → 3047
下 of low grade → 4186
弊 shabby → 3583
粗 COARSE → 1683
駄 GOOD FOR NOTHING → 2291
廃 WASTE → 3902
2 **footwear**
靴 SHOES → 2235
沓 FOOTWEAR → 3074
駄 clogs → 2291
履 footwear → 3933
足 counter for footwear → 2714

駅

2292
1-10-4

▶**STATION**
エキ
N 驛 C 驿 yì

187	Jōyō-3	U99C5
馬	S14-10-4	F0976

1 2 3 4 5 6 7 8 9 10 11 12 13 14 (stroke order)

COMPOUNDS

❶ⓐ [also prefix and suffix] **STATION, railway station, railroad depot**
ⓑ **suffix after names of STATIONs**

a 駅前の えきまえの in front of the station
駅長 えきちょう stationmaster
駅員 えきいん station employee
駅ビル えきびる station building
駅弁 えきべん station lunch
各駅 かくえき every station; local train
貨物駅 かもつえき freight depot
b 神戸駅 こうべえき Kobe Station

❷ⓐ [original meaning] relay **STATION**, post station, stage
ⓑ relay, transmit by stages

a 宿駅 しゅくえき post town, relay station
b 駅伝 えきでん post-horse, stagecoach; long-distance relay race
駅逓 えきてい transportation from post to post; postal service in Meiji era

INDEPENDENT

【えき 駅】 **railway STATION; relay station**
駅迄歩く えきまであるく walk to the station
立派な駅 りっぱなえき beautiful station

SYNONYMS

❶ **places for landing or stopping**
港 PORT →0737
湊 PORT →0743
津 HARBOR (*elegant*) →0466
駅 STATION →2292
停 stopping place →0156

❷ⓐ **post station**
駅 relay station →2292
逓 RELAY →3852
宿 post station →2858

駆

2293
1-10-4

▶**DRIVE**
ク か(ける) か(る)
Ⓝ 驅 駈 敺 Ⓒ 驱 qū

187	Jōyō	U99C6
馬	S14-10-4	F0878

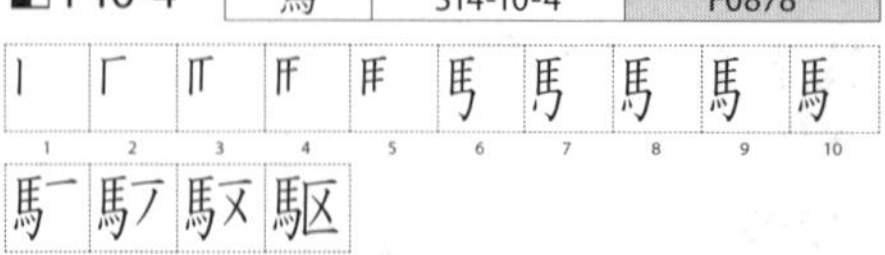

COMPOUNDS

❶ⓐ **DRIVE (a machine), set in motion, handle**
ⓑ [original meaning] **DRIVE** a horse

a 駆動 くどう drive (of a machine)
駆使する くしする use freely, have good command of
b 馳駆する ちくする dash around on a horse, run around; exert oneself (for another)

❷ **DRIVE away, drive out, expel**
駆除する くじょする exterminate, destroy, drive away
駆逐する くちくする drive away, drive out, expel
駆虫剤 くちゅうざい insecticide, vermicide

❸ **gallop, run quickly**
疾駆する しっくする ride fast, drive a horse fast
長駆 ちょうく long march, expedition to a distant region
先駆者 せんくしゃ pioneer, forerunner
前駆する ぜんくする ride in advance, lead the way

KUN

【かける 駆ける】 **gallop, run quickly, dash**
駆けっこ かけっこ race, foot race, running match
駆け回る かけまわる bustle about, run about
駆け落ち かけおち elopement
駆け引き かけひき bargaining; tactics
駆け足 かけあし gallop, run
先駆け さきがけ [sometimes also 魁] the first to charge; lead, pioneer

【かる 駆る】
① **DRIVE (a car), urge (a horse) on, spur on**
駆り立てる かりたてる drive, spur on; stir up
駆り集める かりあつめる mobilize, round up
② prompt, inspire
駆られる かられる be driven by (one's feelings), succumb to

SYNONYMS

❶ⓐ **set in motion**
動 MOVE →2232
駆 DRIVE →2293
掛ける set going →0596

❶ⓐ **force to move**
推 propel →0612
駆 DRIVE →2293
押す PUSH →0371

❷ **drive out**
斥 EXPEL →3690
排 EXCLUDE →0593
追 chase away →3840
退 cause to retreat →3838
駆 drive away →2293
逐 DRIVE OUT →3848
払う clear out →0225

❸ **run**
走 RUN →2720
奔 RUSH →2758

駞 RUN QUICKLY → 2289
駆 gallop → 2293

HOMOPHONES

かける
掛 SET → 0596
懸 SUSPEND → 3632
架 LAY ACROSS → 3178
賭 WAGER → 2021
翔 SOAR → 1714

かる
狩 HUNT → 0474
刈 CLIP → 0032

さきがけ
魁 LEADER → 4125
先駆け → 3046, 2293

COMPOUND FORMATION

【駆け引き　かけひき】
駆け引き 'bargaining; tactics' originally referred to advance (駆ける) and retreat (引く) in battle.

NOTE

➡ see USAGE notes at 掛 0596 and 刈 0032

駐
◧ 1-10-4

incorrect stroke-count
➡ see ◧ 1-10-5: 駐 at 2299

穀
2294
◧ 1-10-4

▶**CEREAL**
コク
Ⓝ 穀 Ⓒ 谷 穀 gǔ

115	Jōyō-6	U7A40
禾	S14-5-9	F2186

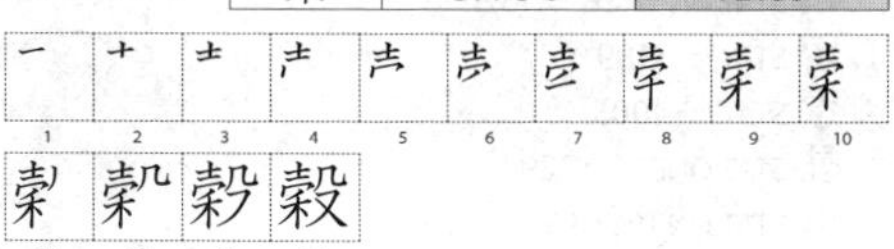

COMPOUNDS

❶ **CEREAL, grain, corn**
穀物 こくもつ grain, cereals
穀類 こくるい grains
穀粒 こくりゅう grain
穀倉 こくそう granary, grain elevator
穀粉 こくふん grain [rice] flour
穀食 こくしょく cereal diet, grain-eating
五穀 ごこく the five cereals, (staple) grains

❷ [original meaning] husk, hull
脱穀する だっこくする thresh

SYNONYMS

❶ **cereal**
穀 CEREAL → 2294
禾 CEREAL → 4315
粉 flour → 1643

NOTE

★ do not confuse with 殻 SHELL → 1883

歎
2295
◧ 1-10-4

▶**SIGH**
タン　なげ(く)

76	Nonstandard	U6B4E
欠	S14-4-10	F0000

traditional form → see 嘆 at 2344

歌
2296
◧ 1-10-4

▶**SONG**
カ　うた　うた(う)
Ⓒ 歌 gē

76	Jōyō-2	U6B4C
欠	S14-4-10	F0475

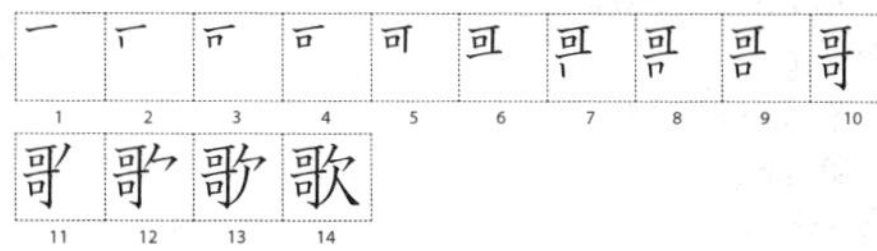

COMPOUNDS

❶ [also suffix] **SONG**
歌謡 かよう song, ballad
歌曲 かきょく song (in the classical style)
歌詞 かし words [lyrics] of a song
国歌 こっか national anthem
校歌 こうか school song, alma mater song
流行歌 りゅうこうか popular song

❷ [original meaning] **sing**
歌手 かしゅ singer
歌劇 かげき opera
歌舞伎 かぶき kabuki

❸ **Japanese poetry, waka, tanka, poem**
詩歌 しいか(=しか) Chinese and Japanese poetry; poems
短歌 たんか tanka, Japanese verse
和歌 わか Japanese poem, tanka
連歌 れんが verse linking, poetic dialogue

KUN

【うた　歌】[also suffix]
① [sometimes also 唄] **SONG, ballad**
歌声 うたごえ singing (voice)
歌合戦 うたがっせん singing matches
替え歌 かえうた parody on a song
子守歌 こもりうた lullaby

② Japanese poem, waka, tanka, ode, verse
歌詠み うたよみ tanka composer
召し歌 めしうた tanka dedicated to the emperor in response to His Majesty's public invitation

【うたう　歌う】
① [sometimes also 唄う] **sing, recite**

歌い手 うたいて singer
歌い上げる うたいあげる sing at the top of one's voice; express one's feelings fully in a poem

② express in a poem
神の徳を歌った歌 かみのとくをうたったうた poem in praise of God

SYNONYMS

❶ **music and songs**
楽 MUSIC → 3505
音 sound of music → 2570
節 tune → 3336
調べ melody → 1973
曲 MUSICAL COMPOSITION → 4340
歌 SONG → 2296
謡 POPULAR SONG → 2011
唄 DITTY → 0477

❷ **sing**
唱 SING → 0555
歌 sing → 2296

❸ **poetry**
詩 POETRY → 1924
歌 Japanese poetry → 2296
俳 HAIKU → 0126
句 HAIKU → 3685

USAGE

❶【うた】
歌
[also suffix]
① [sometimes also 唄] song, ballad
② Japanese poem, waka, tanka, ode, verse
唄
[usu. 歌] [also suffix] ditty, song, ballad

❷【うたう】
歌う
① [sometimes also 唄う] sing, recite
② express in a poem
謡う
recite, chant (esp. from a noh drama text)
唄う
[usu. 歌う] recite, sing
謳う
ⓐ (sing the joys of) extol, eulogize
ⓑ declare, state, express

HOMOPHONES

うた 唄 DITTY → 0477
うたう
謡 POPULAR SONG → 2011
唄 DITTY → 0477
謳 EXTOL → 2061

歎

◧ 1-10-4

incorrect stroke-count
➡ see ◧ 1-11-4: 歎 at 2344

駐

2297
◧ 1-10-5

▶**STATIONED**
チュウ
Ⓝ 駐 Ⓒ 驻 zhù

187	Jōyō	U99D0
馬	S15-10-5	F1335

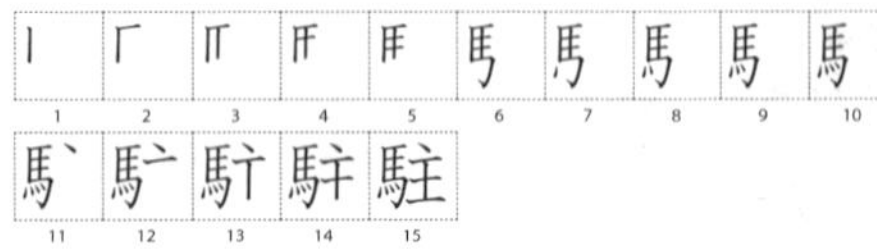

COMPOUNDS

❶ [also prefix] **STATIONED (at, in), resident in**
駐留する ちゅうりゅうする be stationed at, stay
駐在 ちゅうざい residence, stay
駐屯する ちゅうとんする be stationed, occupy
駐日大使 ちゅうにちたいし ambassador to Japan
駐英 ちゅうえい stationed in England
駐独 ちゅうどく stationed in Germany

❷ **park**
駐車場 ちゅうしゃじょう parking area
駐輪場 ちゅうりんじょう bicycle parking lot
駐停車する ちゅうていしゃする park or stop a vehicle

SYNONYMS

❶ **stay**
滞 STAY → 0815
頓 STAY IN PLACE → 1320
留 STAY → 3189
逗 STAY → 4005
駐 STATIONED → 2297
屯 STATION TROOPS → 4268
在 reside temporarily → 3704
泊 STAY OVERNIGHT → 0389
宿 LODGE → 2858
寓 stay temporarily → 2893

❷ **stop**
止 STOP → 3659
停 HALT → 0156
駐 park → 2297

駒

2298
◧ 1-10-5

▶**HORSE**
▶**CHESSMAN**
ク゚ こま
Ⓒ 驹 jū

187	Jōyō	U99D2
馬	S15-10-5	F1588

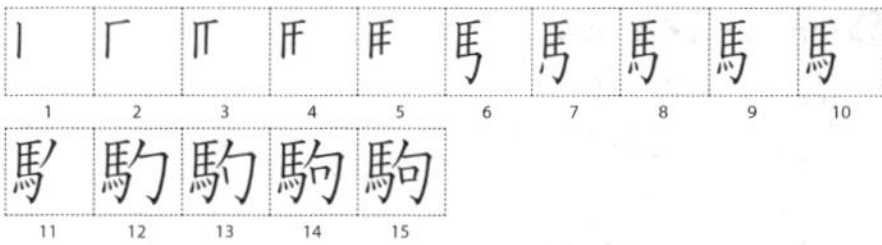

KUN

【こま 駒】

①ⓐ *elegant* **HORSE, colt**

ⓑ [original meaning] **pony, small HORSE**

a 駒座 こまざ Equuleus

駒鳥 こまどり robin

当歳駒 とうさいごま one year-old colt, yearling

② **CHESSMAN, shogi piece, piece used in various board games**

駒損 こまそん(=こまぞん) loss of material (in shogi)

将棋の駒 しょうぎのこま shogi pieces, chessmen

持ち駒 もちごま captured piece

③ bridge (of musical instruments)

三味線の駒 しゃみせんのこま bridge of shamisen

④ wood piece

SYNONYMS

【こま】

① **horse**

馬 HORSE → 4086

駒 HORSE (*elegant*) → 2298

駿 FLEET STEED → 2304

午 the Horse → 2478

駐

2299

◧ 1-10-5

▶STATIONED

チュウ

187	Nonstandard	U99D0
馬	S15-10-5	F0000

traditional form → see 駐 at 2297

駈

2300

◧ 1-10-5

▶DRIVE

ク か(ける) か(る)

187	Names	U99C8
馬	S15-10-5	F0000

traditional form → see 駆 at 2293

骸

2301

◧ 1-10-6

▶DEAD BODY

ガイ カイ▲ むくろ▲ から▲

Ⓒ 骸 hái

188	Jōyō	U9AB8
骨	S16-10-6	F2056

COMPOUNDS

❶ **DEAD BODY, corpse**

死骸(=屍骸) しがい corpse, body, remains

遺骸 いがい remains, corpse, body

残骸 ざんがい ruins, wreckage

形骸化する けいがいかする become a mere shell [dead letter]

❷ **bones, skeleton**

骸骨 がいこつ skeleton

KUN

【むくろ 骸】 **DEAD BODY**, corpse

【から 骸】 **DEAD BODY**, corpse

亡骸 なきがら remains, corpse, body

SYNONYMS

❶ **body**

体 BODY → 0080

身 BODY (esp. vs. mind) → 4368

肉 FLESH → 3966

屍 CORPSE → 3843

尸 CORPSE → 4198

骸 DEAD BODY → 2301

❷ **bone**

骨 BONE → 3288

髄 MARROW → 2316

椎 SPINE → 1249

脊 SPINE → 3297

肋 RIB → 1022

骼 SKELETAL FRAME → 2302

骸 skeleton → 2301

骼

2302

◧ 1-10-6

▶SKELETAL FRAME

カク

Ⓒ 骼 gé

188	Non-Jōyō	U9ABC
骨	S16-10-6	F0000

COMPOUNDS

● [now replaced by 格 1161] **SKELETAL FRAME, skeleton, build**

骨骼 こっかく frame, physique; framework, skeletal structure

SYNONYMS

● **bone**

骨 BONE → 3288

髄 MARROW → 2316

椎 SPINE → 1249

脊 SPINE → 3297

肋 RIB → 1022

骼 SKELETAL FRAME → 2302

骸 skeleton → 2301

● **frames**

枠 FRAME → 1077
骼 SKELETAL FRAME → 2302
格 framework → 1161
額 picture frame → 2273

融 ▶FUSE

2303

1-10-6

ユウ と(ける)▲ と(かす)▲ ㊔ とおる

Ⓒ 融 róng

142	Jōyō	U878D
虫	S16-6-10	F0910

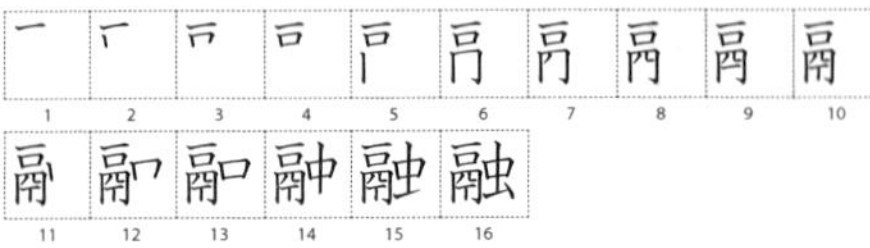

COMPOUNDS

❶ (become liquefied by heat, esp. in the joining of metals) **FUSE**
融解 ゆうかい fusion, melting
融点 ゆうてん fusion point
融熱 ゆうねつ heat of fusion
融接 ゆうせつ fusion welding
溶融 ようゆう melting, fusion
核融合 かくゆうごう nuclear fusion

❷ (be united as if by melting) **FUSE**, blend, melt together
融合 ゆうごう fusion, merger; harmony
融和 ゆうわ harmony, reconciliation

❸ (from the idea of passing smoothly) **finance, accommodate with a loan**
融資 ゆうし financing, advance of funds, loan
融通 ゆうずう financing, accommodation; flexibility
金融 きんゆう circulation of money, money market, finance
特融 とくゆう special loan [finance]

❹ [archaic] bright, glowing
融朗 ゆうろう clearness, brightness

KUN

【とける 融ける】[now usu. 解ける or 溶ける] *vi* (esp. of snow or ice) melt, thaw
雪融け ゆきどけ thawing of snow

【とかす 融かす】[now usu. 解かす or 溶かす] *vt* melt (snow or ice), thaw (out)
氷を融かす こおりをとかす melt ice

SYNONYMS

❶ **liquefy**
溶 DISSOLVE, MELT → 0816
熔 MELT (metals) → 1340
鎔 MELT (metals) → 2214
解 DISSOLVE → 1913
融 FUSE → 2303

❸ **lend and borrow**
借 BORROW → 0137
債 DEBT → 0177
貸 LEND → 3213
融 finance → 2303

HOMOPHONES

とける
解 TAKE APART → 1913
溶 DISSOLVE → 0816
熔 MELT → 1340
鎔 MELT → 2214

とかす
解 TAKE APART → 1913
溶 DISSOLVE → 0816
熔 MELT → 1340
鎔 MELT → 2214
梳 COMB → 1209

NOTE

➡ see USAGE note at 解 1913

駿 ▶FLEET STEED

2304

1-10-7

シュン スン ㊔ する はやお はやし とし たかし すすむ

Ⓒ 骏 jùn

187	Names	U99FF
馬	S17-10-7	F1703

COMPOUNDS

❶ⓐ [original meaning] **FLEET STEED, swift horse, fine horse**
ⓑ [also 俊 しゅん 0117] **swift-footed, fleet-footed**
a 駿馬 しゅんば(=しゅんめ) fleet steed, fine horse
b 駿足 しゅんそく swift horse, fleet steed; fleet speed; fast runner; brilliant person

❷ [now usu. 俊 しゅん 0117] brilliant, talented, bright
駿才 しゅんさい genius, person of exceptional talent

❸ abbrev. of 駿河 するが, old name for eastern Shizuoka Prefecture
駿府 すんぷ old name for Shizuoka City

❹ [now always 峻 0495]
ⓐ stern, strict
ⓑ high and steep, precipitous
→ see 峻 0495 for compounds

INDEPENDENT

【しゅん 駿】talent; talented person, genius
関東の駿 かんとうのしゅん genius of Kanto

SYNONYMS

❶ⓐ **horse**
馬 HORSE → 4086
駒 HORSE (*elegant*) → 2298
駿 FLEET STEED → 2304
午 the Horse → 2478

谿

2305

1-10-7

▶**RAVINE**

ケイ ㊔ たに

150	Nonstandard	U8C3F
谷	S17-7-10	F0000

traditional form → see 渓 at 0628

豃

1-10-7

incorrect classification

➡ see 2-11-6: 豃 at 3567

験

2306

1-10-8

▶**TEST**

ケン ゲン

Ⓝ 驗 Ⓒ 验 yàn

187	Jōyō-4	U9A13
馬	S18-10-8	F0513

COMPOUNDS

❶ [original meaning] **TEST, try, attempt, examine, verify**

験算(=検算) けんざん verification of accounts, checking figures

試験する しけんする test, examine

実験 じっけん experiment

体験する たいけんする experience, go through, (actually) feel

受験する じゅけんする take an examination

❷ⓐ efficacy (as of medicine), effectiveness

ⓑ efficacy of a Buddhist prayer or ascetic practices

a 効験 こうけん effect, efficacy, virtue

b 修験者 しゅげんじゃ ascetic (living in the mountains)

霊験 れいげん(=れいけん) miracle, miraculous virtue

INDEPENDENT

【けんする 験する】 **TEST**, examine

【げん 験】 omen

験が良い げんがいい The omen is good

SYNONYMS

❶ **investigate and examine**

閲 REVIEW → 4132

審 EXAMINE CAREFULLY → 2985

験 TEST → 2306

勘 CHECK → 2231

糾 INQUIRE INTO → 1631

究 STUDY EXHAUSTIVELY → 2729

察 INSPECT → 2961

討 STUDY → 1846

探 PROBE → 0613

検 EXAMINE → 1241

診 EXAMINE A PATIENT → 1898

調 INVESTIGATE → 1973

査 LOOK INTO → 3092

❶ **try**

試 TRY → 1925

験 TEST → 2306

❷ⓐ **potency**

効 EFFECT → 1617

験 efficacy → 2306

能 action → 1676

機 function → 1365

騎

2307

1-10-8

▶**RIDE ON HORSEBACK**

キ

Ⓒ 骑 qí

187	Jōyō	U9A0E
馬	S18-10-8	F1305

COMPOUNDS

❶ [original meaning] **RIDE ON HORSEBACK**

騎馬 きば horse riding

騎手 きしゅ rider, horseman, jockey

騎乗の きじょうの mounted, on horseback

騎兵 きへい cavalry soldier, cavalry

騎士 きし knight

❷ⓐ horseman, knight

ⓑ counter for horsemen

a 単騎 たんき single horseman, lone rider

一騎打ち いっきうち single combat; straight fight

b 侍八騎 さむらいはっき eight samurai on horseback, eight mounted warriors

SYNONYMS

❶ **travel by vehicle**

乗 RIDE → 4393

走 travel by vehicle → 2720

航 NAVIGATE → 1671

騎 RIDE ON HORSEBACK → 2307

騒

2308

1-10-8

▶**CLAMOR**

ソウ さわ(ぐ)

Ⓝ 騷 Ⓒ 骚 sāo

187	Jōyō	U9A12
馬	S18-10-8	F0990

COMPOUNDS

❶ⓐ [original meaning] **CLAMOR, raise a clamor, be uproarious, make a noise, bustle**
ⓑ **CLAMORous, uproarious, noisy**

ab 騒音 そうおん noise
騒騒しい そうぞうしい clamorous, uproarious, noisy, boisterous
騒動 そうどう disturbance, uproar; strife; confusion
騒然たる そうぜんたる noisy, confused
騒乱 そうらん commotion, riot
喧騒 けんそう clamor, din, noise
物騒な ぶっそうな dangerous, insecure, disturbed

❷ sentimental, poetic
騒人 そうじん poet, literary man

KUN

【さわぐ 騒ぐ】**CLAMOR, raise a clamor, be uproarious, make a noise, bustle; make merry, have a spree; clamor against, kick up a row; get agitated, make a fuss; noise about**
騒ぎ さわぎ clamor, uproar; tumult, agitation; [in negative constructions] matter (of)
騒がしい さわがしい noisy, boisterous; troubled
騒ぎ立てる さわぎたてる make a great fuss
大騒ぎ おおさわぎ uproar, racket, row

SYNONYMS

❶ⓐ **make sound or noise**
鳴 SOUND → 0831
響 REVERBERATE → 3573
騒 CLAMOR → 2308
轟 RESOUND → 3425

ⓑ **loud**
高い loud → 2601
朗 CLEAR (voice) → 1679
騒 clamorous → 2308
喧 BOISTEROUS → 0667
嘩 BOISTEROUS → 0771

髄 incorrect stroke-count
➡ see ◧1-10-9: 骨 at 2316
◧1-10-8

離 incorrect stroke-count
➡ see ◧1-11-8: 离 at 2364
◧1-10-8

雜
2309
◧1-10-8

▶**MISCELLANEOUS**
▶**MIXED**
ザツ ゾウ ㊔ さい くさ

172	Names	U96DC
隹	S18-8-10	F0000

traditional form → see 雑 at 1752

難
2310
◧1-10-8

▶**DIFFICULT**
▶**DISASTER**
ナン かた(い) -がた(い) むずか(しい) むつか(しい) -にく(い)▲
Ⓝ 難 Ⓒ 难 nán nàn

172	Jōyō-6	U96E3
隹	S18-8-10	F0442

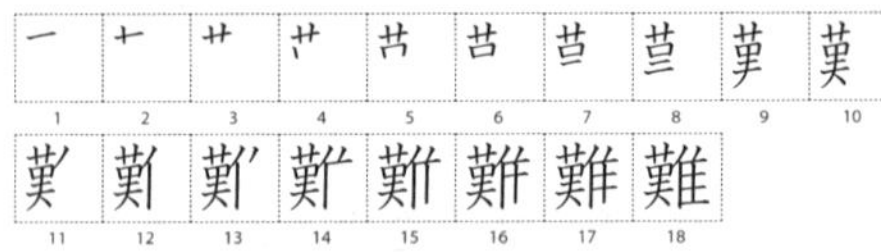

COMPOUNDS

❶ⓐ [also prefix] **DIFFICULT, hard, troublesome**
ⓑ [also suffix] **DIFFICULTy, trouble, hardship, distress**

a 難航 なんこう hard passage, rough going
難問 なんもん difficult problem [question]
難解な なんかいな difficult, hard to understand
難易 なんい (relative) difficulty, hardness (or ease)
難事業 なんじぎょう difficult undertaking [project], uphill task
難儀 なんぎ hardship, trouble
至難の しなんの most difficult
困難 こんなん difficulty, trouble, distress, hardship
万難 ばんなん thousand and one difficulties, innumerable difficulties

b 難無く なんなく easily, without difficulty
生活難 せいかつなん living difficulties, economic distress
就職難 しゅうしょくなん difficulty of finding employment, job shortage

❷ **DISASTER, calamity, accident, misfortune**
難民 なんみん refugee, displaced person
遭難する そうなんする meet with disaster
避難 ひなん refuge, shelter, evacuation
海難 かいなん disaster at sea, shipwreck
災難 さいなん calamity, disaster, accident, misfortune

❸ⓐ **fault, defect, blemish**
ⓑ **find fault with, criticize, blame, reproach**

a 難点 なんてん weakness, fault, flaw; difficult point
無難 ぶなん safety, security; faultlessness

b 難色 なんしょく disapproval, reluctance
難詰する なんきつする blame, censure, reproach

非難(=批難) ひなん criticism, blame

INDEPENDENT

【なん 難】 **DISASTER**, accident, danger; fault, flaw; difficulty, trouble

難に遭う なんにあう meet with disaster

難を言えば... なんをいえば… To be critical…

難中の難 なんちゅうのなん hardest of all

【なんじる(=なんずる) 難じる(=難ずる)】 criticize unfavorably, blame, reproach

KUN

【かたい 難い】 **DIFFICULT, hard**

言うは易く行うは難し いうはやすくおこなうはかたし Easier said than done

【-がたい -難い】 [verbal suffix] **DIFFICULT to do**

し難い しがたい difficult to do, impossible

有り難う ありがとう thank you

【むずかしい 難しい】 **DIFFICULT, hard, troublesome; doubtful, unpromising; sullen, glum, hard to please**

難しさ むずかしさ difficulty, complexity

難しい病気 むずかしいびょうき serious disease

気難しい きむずかしい moody, hard to please

【むつかしい 難しい】 same as 難しい むずかしい

【-にくい -難い】 [verbal suffix] **DIFFICULT**, hard, troublesome, awkward

扱い難い あつかいにくい hard to handle

答え難い質問 こたえにくいしつもん awkward [difficult] question

SYNONYMS

❶ trouble and suffering

困 BE IN TROUBLE →3808

苛 torment →2786

窮 BE IN EXTREMITY →2983

悶 BE IN AGONY →4119

悩 SUFFER →0504

苦 SUFFERING →2789

痛 PAIN →4071

辛 HARD →2531

煩 VEXED →1295

難 DIFFICULT →2310

❷ misfortune and disaster

災 NATURAL CALAMITY →2734

難 DISASTER →2310

禍 CALAMITY →1304

厄 MISFORTUNE →3665

凶 BAD LUCK →3679

❸ⓐ faults and flaws

難 fault →2310

短 shortcoming →1515

疵 DEFECT →4067

陥 defect →0547

欠 incompleteness →2481

ⓑ blame and accuse

責 BLAME →3115

叱 SCOLD →0210

詰 REPRIMAND →1920

難 find fault with →2310

批 CRITICIZE →0294

劾 EXPOSE CRIMES →1618

弾 impeach →0697

HOMOPHONES

かたい

硬 HARD →1518

堅 FIRM →3502

固 SOLID →3830

NOTE

➡ see USAGE note at 固 3830

➡ see COMPOUND FORMATION for 有り難う ありがとう →有 3703

雞

2311

◧ 1-10-8

▶**CHICKEN**

ケイ にわとり とり

172	Nonstandard	U96DE
隹	S18-8-10	F0000

alternative form →see 鶏 at 2221

雛

2312

◧ 1-10-8

▶**CHICK**

スウ ジュ ひな ひよこ

Ⓝ 鶵 Ⓒ 雏 chú

172	Names	U96DB
隹	S18-8-10	F2357

COMPOUNDS

● [original meaning, now archaic] **CHICK**, youngling

雛僧 すうそう young Buddhist priest

KUN

【ひな 雛】

① **CHICK(en), fledgling, poultry**

雛鳥 ひなどり fledgling (esp. chicken)

雛げし ひなげし red poppy, corn poppy, ponceau

② **doll**

雛祭り ひなまつり Doll Festival (March 3)

雛人形 ひなにんぎょう dolls (usu. displayed in tiers)

③ [in compounds] **tiny, little, cute**

雛形 ひながた pattern, model, sample, prototype

【ひよこ 雛】 **CHICK, chicken; fledgling, greenhorn**

あいつはまだ雛だ あいつはまだひよこだ He is still a greenhorn

SYNONYMS

【ひな】

① **bird**

鳥 BIRD →4105

禽 BIRD → 2654
雛 CHICK → 2312

歸

2313
1-10-8

▶RETURN
キ かえ(る) かえ(す)

77	Nonstandard	U6B78
止	S18-4-14	F0000

traditional form → see 帰 at 0148

騙

2314
1-10-9

▶DECEIVE
ヘン だま(す) かた(る)
Ⓝ 騙 Ⓒ 骗 piàn

187	Non-Jōyō	U9A19
馬	S19-10-9	F2030

COMPOUNDS

● **DECEIVE, cheat, swindle, defraud**
騙取 へんしゅ swindling
欺騙 ぎへん deception

KUN

【だます 騙す】**DECEIVE, cheat, swindle, defraud**
騙し討ち だましうち sneak attack, foul play
騙し絵 だましえ trompe l'oeil
子供騙し こどもだまし mere child's play, kid stuff

【かたる 騙る】
① **swindle, defraud**
騙り かたり fraud, swindle
② **assume (another's) name**
他人の名を騙って たにんのなをかたって under a false name

SYNONYMS

● **deceive**
欺 DECEIVE → 2138
騙 DECEIVE → 2314
詐 SWINDLE → 1896
惑 mislead → 3461
拐 defraud → 0365
偽 FALSIFY → 0149
詭 TRICK → 1919

HOMOPHONES

かたる 語 LANGUAGE → 1944
かたり 語 LANGUAGE → 1944

NOTE

➡ see USAGE note at 語 1944

騙

2315
1-10-9

▶DECEIVE
ヘン だま(す) かた(る)

187	Nonstandard	U9A19
馬	S19-10-9	F0000

traditional form → see 騙 at 2314

髄

2316
1-10-9

▶MARROW
ズイ
Ⓝ 髓 髄 Ⓒ 髓 suǐ

188	Jōyō	U9AC4
骨	S19-10-9	F2184

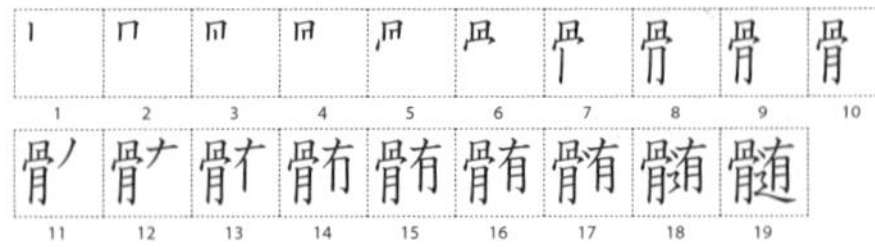

COMPOUNDS

❶ [original meaning] **MARROW, pith**
髄液 ずいえき spinal fluid
髄虫 ずいむし rice borer, pearl moth
骨髄 こつずい bone marrow
脊髄 せきずい spinal cord

❷ (vital part) **essence, core, heart**
真髄(=神髄) しんずい essence, quintessence, soul
精髄 せいずい essence, soul, spirit, pith

INDEPENDENT

【ずい 髄】**MARROW**, pith
葦の髄 あしのずい pith of a ditch reed

SYNONYMS

❶ **bone**
骨 BONE → 3288
髄 MARROW → 2316
椎 SPINE → 1249
脊 SPINE → 3297
肋 RIB → 1022
骼 SKELETAL FRAME → 2302
骸 skeleton → 2301

❷ **essential part**
精 ESSENCE (essential part) → 1729
粋 essence (best part) → 1645
髄 essence (vital part) → 2316
枢 PIVOT → 1076
幹 TRUNK → 2152
綱 ESSENTIAL POINTS → 1735
旨 PURPORT → 2516
要 summary → 3263

顚

2317
1-10-9

▶TURN OVER
テン
Ⓝ 顛 Ⓒ 颠 diān

181	Names	U985A
頁	S19-9-10	F2650

COMPOUNDS

❶ [now usu. 転 1872] [original meaning] **TURN OVER, roll over, tumble down, fall over**

顚倒する てんとうする tumble, fall down; invert, reverse; upset

顚落 てんらく fall, spill; degradation

顚覆する てんぷくする overturn, turn over, upset; overthrow

七顚八倒する しちてんばっとう(=しってんばっとう)する toss oneself about in great pain

❷ⓐ top, summit

ⓑ top, beginning

a 山顚 さんてん top of a mountain

b 顚末 てんまつ circumstances, details, course of events

SYNONYMS

❶ overturn

覆 OVERTURN → 3386

翻 TURN OVER → 2391

反 turn over → 3663

顚 TURN [roll] OVER → 2317

転 turn [roll] over → 1872

倒 TOPPLE → 0139

轢 RUN OVER → 2095

顛

2318

1-10-9

▸TURN OVER

テン

181	Nonstandard	U985B
頁	S19-9-10	F0000

traditional form → see 顚 at 2317

類

2319

1-10-9

▸KIND

ルイ たぐ(い)

181	Names	UF9D0
頁	S19-9-10	F0000

traditional form → see 類 at 2275

願

2320

1-10-9

▸WISH

▸ASK A FAVOR

ガン ねが(う) -ねがい▲

Ⓒ 愿 yuàn

181	Jōyō-4	U9858
頁	S19-9-10	F0738

一	厂	厂	厂	历	盾	盾	戶	原	原
1	2	3	4	5	6	7	8	9	10
原	原	原	原	願	願	願	願	願	
11	12	13	14	15	16	17	18	19	

COMPOUNDS

❶ⓐ WISH, desire, hope for

ⓑ one's WISH, one's desire

a 願望 がんぼう wish, desire, aspiration

念願する ねんがんする desire, wish (for), pray (for)

b 宿願 しゅくがん long-cherished desire

悲願 ひがん one's pathetic wish; vows resulting from the compassion of the Buddhas

❷ⓐ pray, prayer

ⓑ vow

a 願文 がんもん written petition read before a god

祈願する きがんする pray, implore

b 満願 まんがん completion [fulfillment] of a vow

結願 けちがん expiration of one's vow term

❸ ASK A FAVOR, petition, apply for, request, beg

願書 がんしょ written application

出願 しゅつがん application

志願する しがんする volunteer, apply for

請願 せいがん petition

懇願する こんがんする beg earnestly, implore, entreat

依願退職 いがんたいしょく retirement at one's own request

INDEPENDENT

【がん 願】 vow to some particular end

願を掛ける がんをかける make a wish (to a god)

KUN

【ねがう 願う】 WISH, desire, hope for; pray; ask a favor, petition, apply for, request, beg

願い ねがい wish, desire; prayer; request, petition; application

願わくは ねがわくは I pray/I wish

願い出る ねがいでる make an application

宜しくお願いします よろしくおねがいします Please be so kind as to.../I am glad to make your acquaintance

【-ねがい -願】 [suffix] written application

辞職願 じしょくねがい (written) resignation

SYNONYMS

❶ wish and desire

願 WISH → 2320

憧 YEARN AFTER → 0899

憬 YEARN AFTER → 0898

貪 COVET → 2630

望 HOPE → 3408

希 ASPIRE → 2543

懐 LONG FOR → 0942

慕 yearn for → 2970

渇 thirst for → 0627

欲 DESIRE → 1867

慾 DESIRE → 3551

求 SEEK → 4365

❷ⓐ pray and worship

祈 PRAY → 1086

祷 PRAY → 1224

願 pray → 2320

拝 WORSHIP → 0360

祀 WORSHIP AS GOD → 1448
崇 REVERENCE → 2864
斎 OBSERVE RELIGIOUS ABSTINENCE → 2622
呪 SPELL → 0323

❸ **request**

請 REQUEST → 1983
訴 APPEAL TO → 1901
頼 ASK → 2041
嘱 CHARGE WITH → 0881
要 REQUIRE → 3263
願 ASK A FAVOR → 2320
求 SEEK → 4365
乞 BEG → 2457

騷

2321

▶**CLAMOR**

ソウ さわ(ぐ)

187	Names	U9A37
馬	S20-10-10	F0000

1-10-10 traditional form → see 騒 at 2308

競

2322

1-10-10

▶**COMPETE**

キョウ ケイ きそ(う) せ(る)

Ⓝ 競 竞◆ Ⓒ 竞 jìng

117	Jōyō-4	U7AF6
立	S20-5-15	F0599

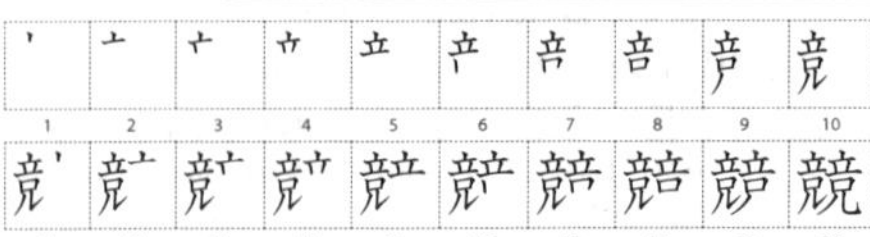

COMPOUNDS

❶ [original meaning] **COMPETE, contend, vie**

競争する きょうそうする compete, contend, vie
競技 きょうぎ match, contest, game; sporting event
競泳 きょうえい swimming race
競演 きょうえん recital contest
競走 きょうそう race, sprint
競輪 けいりん bicycle race
競馬 けいば horse racing

❷ bid, bid for

競売 きょうばい auction

KUN

【きそう 競う】**COMPETE with, contend, rival, vie**

競い合う きそいあう compete with, vie for

【せる 競る】**bid, make a bid for; COMPETE, vie**

競り市 せりいち auction sale

SYNONYMS

❶ **compete**

競 COMPETE → 2322
戦う contest → 2242
鬪 FIGHT → 4136
争 CONTEND → 2523

驅

2323

▶**DRIVE**

ク か(ける) か(る)

187	Nonstandard	U9A45
馬	S21-10-11	F0000

1-10-11 traditional form → see 駆 at 2293

鷄

2324

▶**CHICKEN**

ケイ にわとり とり

196	Names	U9DC4
鳥	S21-11-10	F0000

1-10-11 traditional form → see 鶏 at 2221

鶵

2325

▶**CHICK**

スウ ジュ ひな ひよこ

196	Nonstandard	U9DB5
鳥	S21-11-10	F0000

1-10-11 traditional form → see 雛 at 2312

鶴

2326

1-10-11

▶**CRANE**

カク▲ つる ㊔ づ たず

Ⓒ 鹤 hè

196	Jōyō	U9DB4
鳥	S21-11-10	F1282

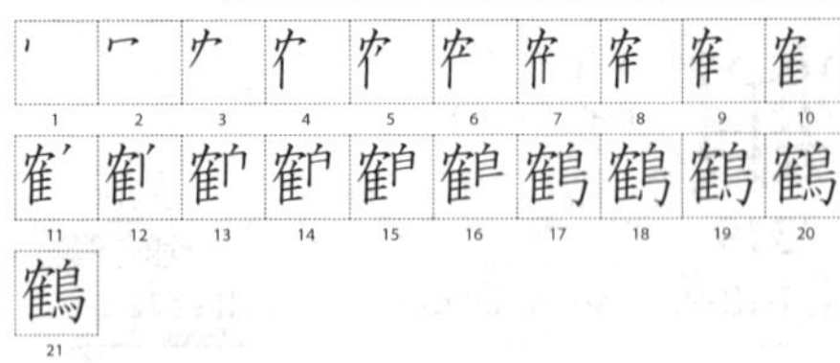

COMPOUNDS

❶ [original meaning, now archaic] **CRANE**, stork

❷ await with a **CRANE**d neck, await expectantly

鶴首して待つ かくしゅしてまつ wait with a craned [an outstretched] neck, wait expectantly

KUN

【つる 鶴】[also suffix] **CRANE, stork**

鶴科 つるか Gruidae
鶴嘴× つるはし pickax, hack; mandrel
丹頂鶴 たんちょうづる Japanese crane
千羽鶴 せんばづる string of a thousand folded-paper cranes

SYNONYMS

❶ **birds**

鷹 HAWK → 3955
鷗 GULL → 2370
烏 CROW → 4088
雀 SPARROW → 3117

燕 SWALLOW → 3142
鴻 LARGE WILD BIRD → 0977
鳳 MALE PHOENIX → 3749
凰 FEMALE PHOENIX → 3738
鵬 MYTHICAL HUGE BIRD → 1416
鶏 CHICKEN → 2221
酉 ROOSTER → 4358
隼 FALCON → 3427
鳩 PIGEON → 0184
鷲 EAGLE → 3598
鳶 BLACK KITE → 3919
鶴 CRANE → 2326
鷺 HERON → 3621
鵜 CORMORANT → 2067
鴨 DUCK → 1582
雁 WILD GOOSE → 3741

驍 2327 ◧1-10-12

▶VALIANT

ギョウ ㊔ いさ つよし たかし すぐる

Ⓒ 骁 xiāo

187	Names	U9A4D
馬	S22-10-12	F0000

COMPOUNDS

❶ **VALIANT, brave and strong, gallant**
驍将 ぎょうしょう valiant general [leader]
驍勇 ぎょうゆう bravery, courage, gallantry

❷ [original meaning] fine horse

SYNONYMS

❶ **brave**
勇 BRAVE → 2592
俠 chivalrous → 0110
赳 VALIANT → 4100
驍 VALIANT → 2327
敢 bold → 2142
豪 bold and unrestrained → 2657
雄 HEROIC → 1271
壮 heroic → 0263
義 chivalrous → 2948
凜 gallant → 0195

髄 ◧1-10-12

incorrect stroke-count
➡ see ◧1-10-13: 髓 at 2332

鬚 ◧1-10-12

incorrect classification
➡ see ⬒2-10-12: 髟 at 3539

聽 2328 ◧1-10-12

▶LISTEN

チョウ き(く)

128	Names	U807D
耳	S22-6-16	F0000

traditional form → see 聴 at 1796

驛 2329 ◧1-10-13

▶STATION

エキ

187	Nonstandard	U9A5B
馬	S23-10-13	F0000

traditional form → see 駅 at 2292

驗 2330 ◧1-10-13

▶TEST

ケン ゲン

187	Names	U9A57
馬	S23-10-13	F0000

traditional form → see 験 at 2306

體 2331 ◧1-10-13

▶BODY
▶FORM

タイ テイ からだ

188	Nonstandard	U9AD4
骨	S23-10-13	F0000

traditional form → see 体 at 0080

髓 2332 ◧1-10-13

▶MARROW

ズイ

188	Nonstandard	U9AD3
骨	S23-10-13	F0000

traditional form → see 髄 at 2316

驩 2333 ◧1-10-17

▶JOYOUS

カン

Ⓒ 欢 huān

187	Non-Jōyō	U9A69
馬	S27-10-17	F0000

COMPOUNDS

[now replaced by 歓 2342]

ⓐ **be JOYOUS, be happy, be merry, rejoice**

ⓑ joy, pleasure

b 交驩する こうかんする exchange cordialities

SYNONYMS

ⓐ **pleased and pleasant**
楽 pleasurable → 3505
欣 JOYFUL → 1057
爽 REFRESHING → 4402
快 PLEASANT → 0289
朗 CHEERFUL → 1679
愉 PLEASED → 0710
悦 DELIGHTED → 0501

【馬】

嬉しい GLAD →0890
喜 HAPPY →2889
歓 JOYOUS →2342
驩 JOYOUS →2333

勧

▸URGE

カン すす(める) ㊔ すすむ

Ⓝ 勸 勸 Ⓒ 劝 quàn

2334

◧1-11-2

19	Jōyō	U52E7
力	S13-2-11	F1452

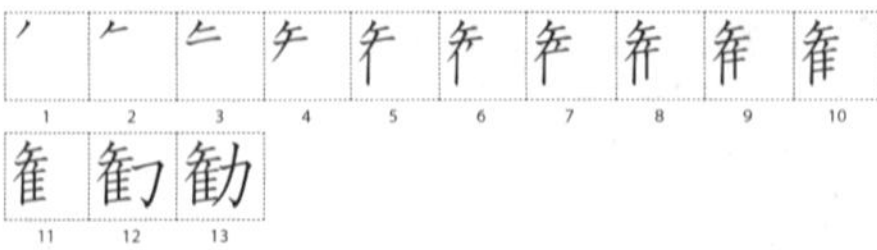

COMPOUNDS

ⓐ [original meaning] (persuade to act) **URGE, persuade, advise**

ⓑ encourage, promote

a 勧告 かんこく advice, counsel, recommendation
勧誘する かんゆうする induce, invite, canvass, persuade

b 勧業 かんぎょう encouragement of industry
勧奨する かんしょうする encourage, promote, stimulate
勧善懲悪 かんぜんちょうあく rewarding good and punishing evil, political justice
勧銀 かんぎん hypothecary bank

KUN

【すすめる 勧める】

①ⓐ **URGE, persuade, advise**

ⓑ [sometimes also 奨める] **encourage, promote, stimulate**

a 勧め すすめ exhortation, encouragement
切に勧める せつにすすめる urge strongly

b 行く様に勧める いくようにすすめる encourage someone to go

② **offer, present**

酒を勧める さけをすすめる offer wine; press wine on

SYNONYMS

ⓐ urge

勧 URGE →2334
催 PRESS FOR →0178
促 HASTEN →0118
誘 INDUCE →1952
励 ENCOURAGE →1438
侑 URGE TO EAT →0101

ⓑ advance

進 ADVANCE →3873
興 cause to rise →3622
奨 ENCOURAGE →3524
勧 encourage →2334

HOMOPHONES

すすめる

奨 ENCOURAGE →3524
薦 RECOMMEND →3008
進 ADVANCE →3873

NOTE

➡ see USAGE note at 進 3873

畐

◧1-11-2

incorrect stroke-count

➡ see ◧1-11-3: 畐 at 2338

剿

▸EXTERMINATE

ソウ ショウ

Ⓒ 剿 jiǎo chāo

2335

◧1-11-2

18	Non-Jōyō	U527F
刂	S13-2-11	F0000

COMPOUNDS

● [now replaced by 掃 0611] **EXTERMINATE, wipe out**

剿滅する そうめつする wipe out, annihilate

SYNONYMS

● **destroy**

滅 DESTROY →0812
毀 DESTROY →2246
亡 perish →4210
消 EXTINGUISH →0531
剿 EXTERMINATE →2335

勤

▸SERVICE

キン ゴン つと(める) -づと(め) つと(まる) いそ(しむ) ㊔ つとむ いそ

2336

◧1-11-2

19	Names	UFA34
力	S13-2-11	F0000

traditional form →see 勤 at 2287

彰

▸PROCLAIM MERITS

ショウ ㊔ あき あきら てる あや

Ⓒ 彰 zhāng

2337

◧1-11-3

59	Jōyō	U5F70
彡	S14-3-11	F1807

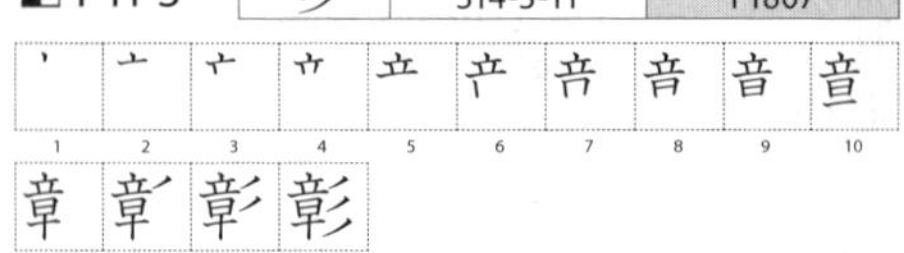

COMPOUNDS

❶ [sometimes also 章 2624] **PROCLAIM the MERITS of a person (to the public), make (a person's virtues) well known, give public recognition**

彰徳する しょうとくする [rare] praise publicly, make another's virtues well known

顕彰する けんしょうする give recognition, exalt, honor

表彰する ひょうしょうする commend (officially), give public recognition

❷ [archaic]

ⓐ manifest, show clearly, reveal

ⓑ manifest, clear, obvious

a 彰明する しょうめいする manifest, exhibit clearly

SYNONYMS

❶ **praise**

賛 PRAISE → 3484
頌 EULOGIZE → 1319
謳 EXTOL → 2061
讃 PRAISE → 2093
美 regard as beautiful → 2817
褒 COMMEND → 2662
嘉 commend (esp. an inferior) → 2953
彰 PROCLAIM MERITS → 2337
称 acclaim → 1491
賞 express admiration → 3237
揚 EXALT → 0722

鄙

2338

◧ 1-11-3

▶**MEAN**
▶**THE COUNTRY**

ヒ ひな ひな(びる)

Ⓒ 鄙 bǐ

163	Non-Jōyō	U9119
阝	S14-3-11	F3004

COMPOUNDS

❶ [now replaced by 卑 3270] (lacking in elevating human qualities) **MEAN, vulgar, despicable**

鄙劣な ひれつな mean, base, cowardly

鄙猥×な ひわいな indecent, obscene

野鄙な やひな vulgar, base, mean

❷ [now replaced by 卑 3270] [humble] my humble

鄙見 ひけん my humble opinion

❸ [original meaning] **THE COUNTRY, countryside, out-of-the-way place**

都鄙 とひ town and country

辺鄙な へんぴな out-of-the-way, unfrequented, remote

KUN

【ひな 鄙】 THE COUNTRY

鄙歌 ひなうた country [rural] song

【ひなびる 鄙びる】 **be countrified**

SYNONYMS

❶ **vulgar and unrefined**

俗 vulgar → 0119
卑 MEAN → 3270
賤 MEAN → 1993
鄙 MEAN → 2338

俚 RURAL → 0112
里 rural → 4356
粗 COARSE → 1683
野 rustic → 1877
蛮 barbaric → 2638

❸ **the country**

郊 SUBURB → 1638
里 COUNTRYSIDE → 4356
鄙 THE COUNTRY → 2338
郷 the country → 0664
辺 BORDERLAND → 3761

對

2339

◧ 1-11-3

▶**OPPOSITE**
▶**OPPOSE**

タイ ツイ

41	Nonstandard	U5C0D
寸	S14-3-11	F0000

traditional form → see 対 at 1025

敵

2340

◧ 1-11-4

▶**ENEMY**

テキ かたき かな(う)▲

Ⓒ 敌 dí

66	Jōyō-5	U6575
攵	S15-4-11	F0659

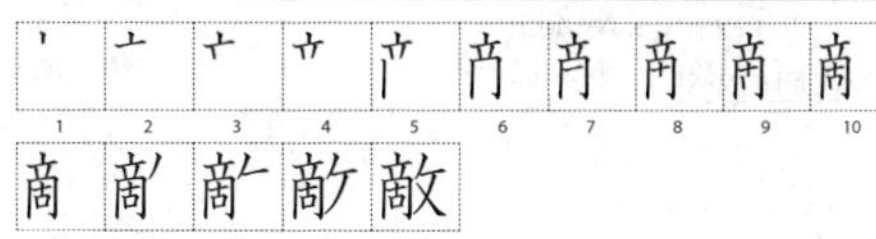

COMPOUNDS

❶ⓐ [also prefix] **ENEMY, foe**

ⓑ **opponent, rival**

a 敵国 てきこく enemy country

敵意 てきい hostility, enmity

強敵 きょうてき powerful enemy [rival]

b 敵王 てきおう opponent's king (in shogi)

敵艦隊 てきかんたい enemy fleet

❷ⓐ **confront the ENEMY, oppose, resist**

ⓑ match, equal

a 敵対する てきたいする oppose, fight against

不敵な ふてきな daring, dauntless

b 無敵の むてきの matchless, invincible

❸ **unclassified compounds**

素敵な すてきな grand, cute, fine

INDEPENDENT

【てき 敵】 **ENEMY, foe; opponent, rival**

【てきする 敵する】 oppose, fight against, match, equal

KUN

【かたき 敵】

ⓐ [also 仇] **ENEMY, foe**

ⓑ **opponent, rival**
ⓒ [also 仇] **revenge, retaliation**
b 商売敵 しょうばいがたき business rival
c 敵討ち かたきうち vendetta, revenge

【かなう 敵う】
① be a match for, compare with
君には敵わない きみにはかなわない I am no match for you
② stand, bear
こう暑くては敵わない こうあつくてはかなわない I can't stand the heat

SYNONYMS

❶ⓐ & ❶ⓑ enemy
敵 ENEMY → 2340
仇 FOE → 0023

USAGE

【かたき】
敵
ⓐ [also 仇] enemy, foe
ⓑ opponent, rival
ⓒ [also 仇] revenge, retaliation
仇
[also 敵]
ⓐ enemy, foe
ⓑ revenge, retaliation

HOMOPHONES

かなう
適 SUITABLE → 3918
叶 BE FULFILLED → 0209
かたき 仇 FOE → 0023

NOTE

➡ see also USAGE note at 適 3918

毅

2341
1-11-4

▶**RESOLUTE**
キ ㊔ つよし たけ たけし たか たかし はたす つよ よし こわし たける
Ⓒ 毅 yì

79	Names	U6BC5
殳	S15-4-11	F2024

COMPOUNDS

● **RESOLUTE, determined, firm, dauntless**
毅然として きぜんとして resolutely, firmly, bravely
剛毅な ごうきな hardy, sturdy

SYNONYMS

● **firm and obstinate**
堅 FIRM → 3502
固 FIRM, stiff → 3830
確 firm → 1571
毅 RESOLUTE → 2341
剛 TOUGH → 2107
頑 STUBBORN → 1315

硬 hard-line → 1518

歡

2342
1-11-4

▶**JOYOUS**
カン ㊔ よし
Ⓝ 歡 歡 Ⓒ 欢 huān

76	Jōyō	U6B53
欠	S15-4-11	F1499

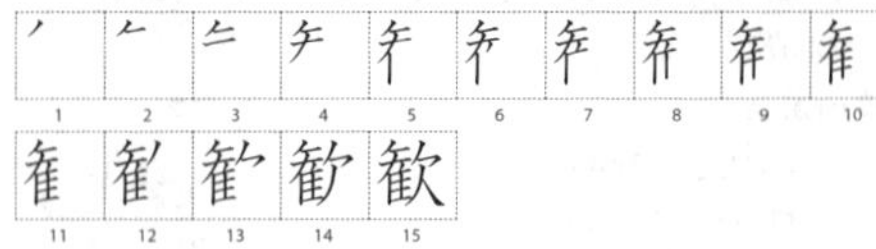

COMPOUNDS

[formerly also 驩 2333]
ⓐ [original meaning] **be JOYOUS, be happy, be merry, rejoice**
ⓑ joy, pleasure
ⓒ [sometimes also 款 2135] treat cordially, have friendly relations with
a 歓喜 かんき joy, delight
歓楽 かんらく pleasure, merriment
歓談 かんだん pleasant chat [talk]
歓迎 かんげい welcome
歓送 かんそう sending off
歓声 かんせい cheers, shout of joy
b 哀歓 あいかん joys and sorrows
c 歓待 かんたい cordial [warm] reception, hospitality
交歓 こうかん exchange of cordialities

INDEPENDENT

【かん 歓】 joy, delight, pleasure
歓を尽くす かんをつくす enjoy oneself to one's heart's content

SYNONYMS

ⓐ **pleased and pleasant**
楽 pleasurable → 3505
欣 JOYFUL → 1057
爽 REFRESHING → 4402
快 PLEASANT → 0289
朗 CHEERFUL → 1679
愉 PLEASED → 0710
悦 DELIGHTED → 0501
嬉しい GLAD → 0890
喜 HAPPY → 2889
歓 JOYOUS → 2342
驩 JOYOUS → 2333

穀

2343
1-11-4

▶**CEREAL**
コク

115	Names	UFA54
禾	S15-5-10	F0000

traditional form → see 穀 at 2294

歎

2344

◧1-11-4

▶SIGH

タン なげ(く)

Ⓝ 歎 Ⓒ 叹 tàn

76	Names	U6B4E
欠	S15-4-11	F2715

COMPOUNDS

[now usu. 嘆 0773]

❶ [original meaning] **SIGH (in grief or despair), grieve, lament; deplore**

歎声 たんせい sigh, lamentation; sigh of admiration

歎息する たんそくする sigh; sigh in grief

歎願する たんがんする entreat, petition, appeal

悲歎 ひたん grief, sorrow, lamentation

慨歎する がいたんする deplore, lament, regret

嗟×歎 さたん lamentation, deploration; admiration

❷ **SIGH in admiration, exclaim, admire, praise**

驚歎する きょうたんする admire, wonder, be struck with admiration

感歎符 かんたんふ exclamation mark

詠歎 えいたん exclamation, admiration

INDEPENDENT

【たん 歎】 **SIGH**, grief, lamentation

歎じる(=歎ずる) たんじる(=たんずる) grieve, lament; sigh in admiration

KUN

【なげく 歎く】 [now usu. 嘆く]

① **SIGH** (in grief or despair), grieve, lament; deplore

歎き なげき grief, lamentation

② **SIGH** in admiration, exclaim, admire, praise

SYNONYMS

❶ **cry and sigh**

泣 CRY → 0396

嘆 SIGH → 0773

歎 SIGH → 2344

HOMOPHONES

なげく 嘆 SIGH → 0773

なげき 嘆 SIGH → 0773

NOTE

➡ see USAGE note at 嘆 0773

敷

2345

◧1-11-4

▶LAY

フ し(く) -し(き) ㊔ のぶ

Ⓝ 敷 Ⓒ 敷 fū

66	Jōyō	U6577
攵	S15-4-11	F0607

1	2	3	4	5	6	7	8	9	10	11	12	13	14	15
一	𠂆	冂	冃	甴	由	甶	亩	亩	㫗	旉	旉	旉	敷	敷

COMPOUNDS

● [also 布 3691] [original meaning] (dispose over a surface) **LAY (as a railroad track), spread**

敷設 ふせつ construction, laying

敷衍× ふえん expatiation, amplification, elaboration

KUN

【しく 敷く】

①ⓐ (spread over a surface) **LAY, spread, lay under**

ⓑ (dispose over a surface) **LAY (as a railroad track), construct, pave**

ⓒ **LAY** out, arrange

a 敷き詰める しきつめる spread all over

敷物 しきもの carpet, rug

敷布 しきふ sheet

敷布団 しきぶとん (Japanese style) mattress

布団を敷く ふとんをしく make a bed

b 敷石 しきいし paving stone, pavement

敷地 しきち (building) site, (plot of) ground, lot

敷居 しきい threshold, doorsill; windowsill

屋敷 やしき [sometimes also 邸] mansion, residence; residential lot

c 陣を敷く じんをしく take up a position, encamp

② **promulgate**

法令を敷く ほうれいをしく promulgate a law

③ [in compounds] **make a deposit**

敷金 しききん deposit money

【-しき -敷き】

① [also suffix] **underlay, mat**

下敷き したじき underlay; being buried; model

土瓶敷き どびんしき teapot mat [rest], tea cloth

② **bed, foundation**

板敷き いたじき wooden floor

SPECIAL READINGS

桟敷 さじき reviewing stand, box, gallery

SYNONYMS

● **equip and install**

据える INSTALL → 0602

敷 LAY → 2345

架 LAY ACROSS → 3178

装 FIT OUT → 3327

設 SET UP → 1863

備 PROVIDE → 0165

【しく】

①ⓐ **spread**

散 SCATTER → 2137

布 SPREAD → 3691

敷く LAY → 2345

舗 PAVE → 2177

塗 APPLY ON A SURFACE → 3523

抹 wipe over → 0370

撒 SCATTER →0909

【-しき】

① mats

畳 TATAMI →3205

薦 straw mat →3008

-敷き underlay →2345

HOMOPHONES

やしき

邸 STATELY RESIDENCE →1451

屋敷 →3842, 2345

NOTE

➡ see USAGE note at 邸 1451

敷 2346

▶LAY

フ し(く) -し(き) ㊔ のぶ

66	Nonstandard	U6577
攵	S15-4-11	F0000

1-11-4 traditional form →see 敷 at 2345

數 2347

▶NUMBER

スウ ス かず かぞ(える)

66	Nonstandard	U6578
攵	S15-4-11	F0000

1-11-4 traditional form →see 数 at 2245

敺 2348

▶DRIVE

ク か(ける) か(る)

66	Nonstandard	U657A
攴	S15-4-11	F0000

1-11-4 traditional form →see 駆 at 2293

歐 2349

▶EUROPE

オウ

76	Nonstandard	U6B50
欠	S15-4-11	F0000

1-11-4 traditional form →see 欧 at 1098

毆 2350

▶BEAT

オウ なぐ(る)

79	Nonstandard	U6BC6
殳	S15-4-11	F0000

1-11-4 traditional form →see 殴 at 1099

戯 2351

▶SPORT

ギ ゲ▲ たわむ(れる)

Ⓝ 戲 戱 Ⓒ 戏 xì

62	Jōyō	U622F
戈	S15-4-11	F1679

1-11-4

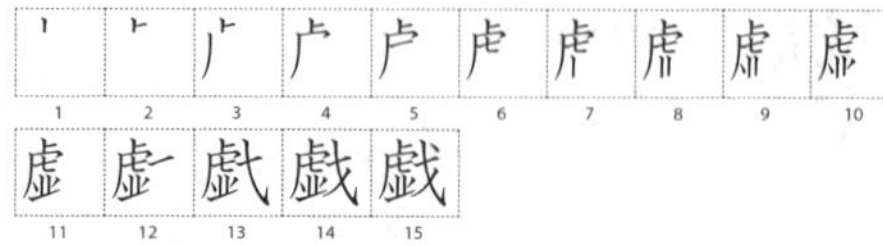

COMPOUNDS

❶ⓐ SPORT, frolic, play

ⓑ SPORT, fun, play, jest, joke

ⓒ play with (a woman), dally, flirt

a 遊戯 ゆうぎ game, pastime, amusement

嬉戯する きぎする frisk, frolic

b 児戯 じぎ child's play, kid stuff

球戯 きゅうぎ ball game

c 前戯 ぜんぎ foreplay

❷ SPORTive, frolicsome, humorous

戯評 ぎひょう humorous [sarcastic] comments, cartoon, caricature

戯画 ぎが cartoon, comics

戯文 ぎぶん nonsense literature, burlesque, literary parody

戯作者 げさくしゃ fiction writer, author of popular stories

❸ theatrical play, performance, drama

戯曲 ぎきょく drama, play

KUN

【たわむれる 戯れる】**SPORT, play, frolic; joke, jest; dally, flirt**

戯れ たわむれ play, sport, fun, caprice; joke, jest; flirtation

子猫がボールに戯れている こねこがぼーるにたわむれている The kitten is playing with a ball

女と戯れる おんなとたわむれる flirt with a woman

SPECIAL READINGS

悪戯▲ いたずら mischief, prank, practical joke

SYNONYMS

❶ⓐ & ❶ⓒ play

遊 PLAY →3896

戯 SPORT →2351

弄 TOY WITH →3057

❷ comic

漫 COMIC →0858

戯 sportive →2351

USAGE

【いたずら】

悪戯

mischief, prank, practical joke

徒

uselessness, idleness

HOMOPHONES

いたずら

悪戯 →3413, 2351

徒 FOLLOWER →0499

鮎 2352

◧1-11-5

▶**AYU**
デン ネン あゆ
Ⓒ 鲇 nián

195	Names	U9B8E
魚	S16-11-5	F1851

KUN

【あゆ 鮎】**AYU, sweetfish**
鮎並 あいなめ rock trout
稚鮎 ちあゆ young ayu

SYNONYMS

【あゆ】
○ **fishes**
鯉 CARP → 2358
鮎 AYU → 2352
鯛 TAI → 2360
鰯 SARDINE → 2367
鱒 TROUT → 2371
鮫 SHARK → 2354

瓢 2353

◧1-11-5

▶**BOTTLE GOURD**
ヒョウ ひさご ふくべ

97	Nonstandard	U74E2
瓜	S16-5-11	F0000

traditional form → see 瓢 at 2356

瓢

◧1-11-5

incorrect stroke-count
➡ see ◧1-11-6: 票 at 2356

鮫 2354

◧1-11-6

▶**SHARK**
コウ さめ
Ⓒ 鲛 jiāo

195	Non-Jōyō	U9BAB
魚	S17-11-6	F2887

COMPOUNDS

● **SHARK**
鮫人 こうじん Chinese mermaid [merman]

KUN

【さめ 鮫】[also suffix] **SHARK**
鮫皮 さめがわ sharkskin
鮫鞘 さめざや sharkskin scabbard
鮫肌 さめはだ dry scaly skin
甚平鮫 じんべいざめ whale shark
頬白鮫 ほおじろざめ great white shark
撞木鮫 しゅもくざめ hammerhead shark

SYNONYMS

● **fishes**
鯉 CARP → 2358
鮎 AYU → 2352
鯛 TAI → 2360
鰯 SARDINE → 2367
鱒 TROUT → 2371
鮫 SHARK → 2354

鮮 2355

◧1-11-6

▶**FRESH**
▶**VIVID**
セン あざ(やか)
Ⓒ 鲜 xiān xiǎn

195	Jōyō	U9BAE
魚	S17-11-6	F0592

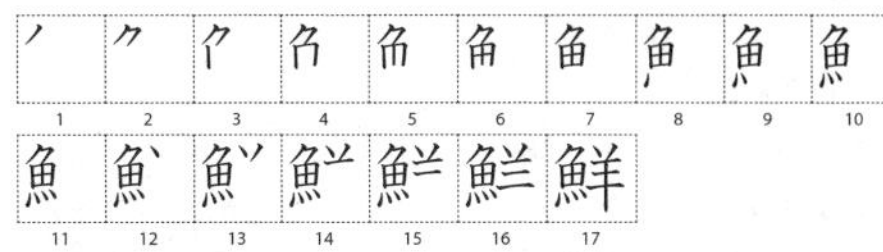

COMPOUNDS

❶ **FRESH**
鮮魚 せんぎょ fresh fish
鮮度 せんど (degree of) freshness
新鮮な しんせんな fresh
生鮮な せいせんな fresh

❷ⓐ **VIVID, brilliant, clean**
ⓑ (of colors) **VIVID, brightly-colored**
a 鮮麗な せんれいな vivid, gorgeous
鮮烈な せんれつな glaringly vivid, striking
鮮明な せんめいな vivid, clear
b 鮮紅 せんこう scarlet, bright red

❸ **Korea**
朝鮮 ちょうせん (North) Korea
南鮮 なんせん South Korea
北鮮 ほくせん North Korea

❹ little, few
鮮少な せんしょうな very little

KUN

【あざやか 鮮やか】
あざやかな 鮮やかな **VIVID, clear;** (of colors) **vivid, bright; neat, graceful**
鮮やかさ あざやかさ vividness, brightness
鮮やかな飛行振り あざやかなひこうぶり skillful piloting

SYNONYMS

❶ **new**
新 NEW → 2239
鮮 FRESH → 2355
生 raw → 4309

❷ⓐ **evident**
明 CLEAR → 1060
鮮 VIVID → 2355
亮 LUCID → 2571
顕 MANIFEST → 2274

【魚】 票

瞭 CLEAR → 1584

ⓑ **vivid**

明 BRIGHT → 1060

鮮 VIVID → 2355

❸ **Korea**

鮮 Korea → 2355

朝 North Korea → 2130

韓 SOUTH KOREA → 2218

❸ **Asian countries**

日 JAPAN → 3759

緬 Myanmar → 1758

老 Laos → 3963

華 CHINA → 2841

蒙 Mongolia → 2938

鮮 Korea → 2355

泰 Thailand → 3193

越 Vietnam → 4108

印 India → 1023

竺 INDIA → 3248

比 Philippines → 0029

瓢

2356

1-11-6

▶**BOTTLE GOURD**

ヒョウ ひさご ふくべ

Ⓝ 瓢 Ⓒ 瓢 piáo

97	Names	U74E2
瓜	S17-6-11	F3057

COMPOUNDS

❶ [original meaning] **BOTTLE GOURD, calabash**

瓢箪 ひょうたん bottle gourd, calabash

干瓢(=乾瓢) かんぴょう strips of dried gourd

青瓢箪 あおびょうたん green [unripe] calabash; weakling

❷ ladle, dipper, scoop

INDEPENDENT

【ひょう 瓢】**BOTTLE GOURD**, calabash

KUN

【ひさご 瓢】

①ⓐ gourd, calabash

ⓑ (container) calabash

② ladle, dipper, scoop

【ふくべ 瓢】

ⓐ **BOTTLE GOURD**, calabash

ⓑ (container) calabash

ⓒ round **BOTTLE GOURD** [calabash]

SPECIAL READINGS

瓢虫(=天道虫、紅娘) てんとうむし ladybug

SYNONYMS

❶ **vegetables**

菜 greens → 2880

蕪 TURNIP → 2990

芋 POTATO → 2706

豆 BEAN → 2442

蕗 BUTTERBUR → 3007

茄 EGGPLANT → 2787

芹 JAPANESE PARSLEY → 2742

瓜 GOURD → 3789

瓢 BOTTLE GOURD → 2356

芥 mustard → 2741

鯁

2357

1-11-7

▶**UPRIGHT**

コウ

Ⓒ 鲠 gěng

195	Non-Jōyō	U9BC1
魚	S18-11-7	F0000

COMPOUNDS

❶ [now replaced by 硬 1518] **UPRIGHT, firm, staunch, unyielding**

鯁骨の こうこつの firm, uncompromising

鯁骨漢 こうこつかん man of firm character

❷ [original meaning, now obsolete] fishbone

SYNONYMS

❶ **virtuous**

正 RIGHT → 4296

義 righteous → 2948

善 GOOD → 2921

良 GOOD → 4373

鯁 UPRIGHT → 2357

鯉

2358

1-11-7

▶**CARP**

リ こい

Ⓒ 鲤 lǐ

195	Names	U9BC9
魚	S18-11-7	F2428

COMPOUNDS

● [original meaning, now rare] **CARP**

養鯉 ようり carp breeding

KUN

【こい 鯉】**CARP**

鯉幟× こいのぼり carp streamer

錦鯉 にしきごい colored carp

SYNONYMS

● **fishes**

鯉 CARP → 2358

鮎 AYU → 2352

鯛 TAI → 2360

鰯 SARDINE → 2367

鱒 TROUT → 2371

鮫 SHARK → 2354

観

▸VIEW

カン み(る)▲ ㊔ み

Ⓝ 觀 觀 Ⓒ 观 guān guàn

2359

◧ 1-11-7

147 見	Jōyō-4	U89B3
	S18-7-11	F0413

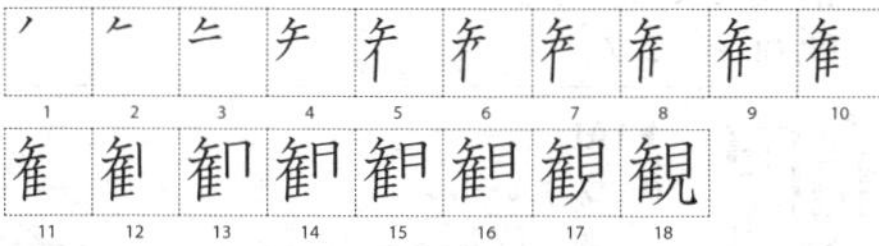

COMPOUNDS

❶ [original meaning] **VIEW, behold, look; observe, inspect**

観光 かんこう sightseeing
観客 かんきゃく audience, spectators
観劇 かんげき theatergoing
観察 かんさつ observation, supervision
観賞 かんしょう admiration, enjoyment
傍観する ぼうかんする look on, sit as a spectator
楽観 らっかん optimism, hopeful view

❷ⓐ **VIEW, spectacle, sight**
ⓑ **appearance, look, condition**

a 景観 けいかん scene, spectacle, view, sight
美観 びかん fine view, beautiful sight
壮観 そうかん grand sight, magnificent view
b 外観 がいかん external appearance, outward show

❸ [also suffix] **VIEW, conception, outlook, theory**

観点 かんてん point of view
観念 かんねん idea, conception, notion
主観 しゅかん subjectivity; subject
先入観 せんにゅうかん preconception, bias, prejudice
人生観 じんせいかん one's view [theory] of life, outlook on life
世界観 せかいかん world view, outlook on the world

❹ Taoist temple

道観 どうかん Taoist temple

❺ [rare] watchtower, turret

楼観 ろうかん watchtower

❻ unclassified compounds

観音 かんのん *Avalokiteśvara*, Buddhist Goddess of Mercy

INDEPENDENT

【かん 観】appearance, look, condition; Taoist temple
. . . の観が有る …のかんがある appear, look like
【かんじる(=かんずる) 観じる(=観ずる)】grasp the truth after thinking it over

KUN

【みる 観る】[usu. 見る] **VIEW** (flowers), watch (a movie), see, observe, appreciate

花を観る はなをみる view (cherry) blossoms

SYNONYMS

❶ **see and look**

見 SEE → 3151
看 WATCH → 3992
察 INSPECT → 2961
窺 WATCH FURTIVELY → 3002
瞥 GLANCE AT → 3592
目 look → 3777
観 VIEW → 2359
覧 LOOK OVER → 3538
眺 LOOK OUT OVER → 1503
望 LOOK AFAR → 3408
仰 LOOK UP → 0051
顧 LOOK BACK → 2394
視 REGARD → 1223

❷ⓐ **view**

景 SCENE → 3118
風 (beautiful) scenery → 3730
光 scenery → 3043
観 VIEW → 2359

❸ **opinion**

見 view (personal opinion) → 3151
観 VIEW (conception) → 2359
説 opinion → 1949
論 opinion → 1981

HOMOPHONES

みる

見 SEE → 3151
看 WATCH → 3992
診 EXAMINE A PATIENT → 1898
視 REGARD → 1223

NOTE

➡ see USAGE note at 見 3151

鬪

◧ 1-11-7

incorrect classification
➡ see ◻3-8-10: 門 at 4136

鯛

▸TAI

チョウ たい

Ⓝ 鯛 Ⓒ 鲷 diāo

2360

◧ 1-11-8

195 魚	Names	U9BDB
	S19-11-8	F2651

KUN

【たい 鯛】**TAI, sea bream, porgy**

鯛飯 たいめし rice and minced tai
鯛焼き たいやき fish-shaped pancake filled with bean jam
真鯛 まだい red tai, red sea bream

SYNONYMS

【たい】

○ **fishes**

鯉 CARP → 2358
鮎 AYU → 2352
鯛 TAI → 2360
鰯 SARDINE → 2367
鱒 TROUT → 2371
鮫 SHARK → 2354

鯨

2361

1-11-8

▶WHALE

ゲイ くじら

Ⓒ 鲸 jīng

195	Jōyō	U9BE8
魚	S19-11-8	F2223

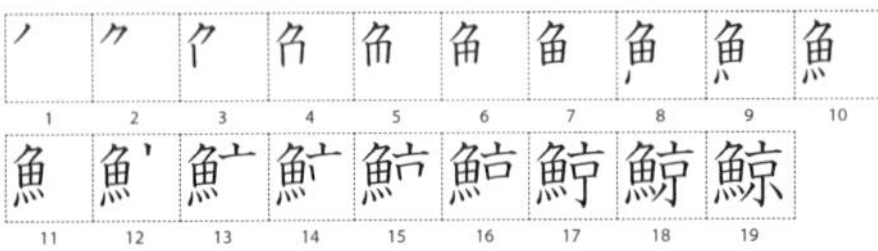

COMPOUNDS

a [original meaning] **WHALE**

b huge like a **WHALE**

a 鯨肉 げいにく whale meat
鯨油 げいゆ whale oil
鯨骨 げいこつ whale bone
巨鯨 きょげい huge whale
捕鯨 ほげい whaling

b 鯨飲馬食する げいいんばしょくする drink like a fish and eat like a horse, eat mountains of food and drink oceans of liquor
鯨波 げいは huge waves; battle cry

KUN

【くじら 鯨】 [also suffix] **WHALE**

鯨幕 くじらまく black and white curtain (spread at a funeral service)
鯨座 くじらざ the Whale, Cetus
鯨尺 くじらじゃく long foot
抹香鯨 まっこうくじら sperm whale
白長須鯨 しろながすくじら blue whale

SYNONYMS

a **undomesticated mammals**

虎 TIGER → 3981
猿 MONKEY → 0824
鯨 WHALE → 2361
犀 RHINOCEROS → 3900
狼 WOLF → 0541
狐 FOX → 0472
羚 SEROW → 1695
鼠 RAT → 3340
獅 LION → 0825
豹 LEOPARD → 1847
熊 BEAR → 3530
象 ELEPHANT → 2647
麒 MALE CHINESE UNICORN → 2363
麟 FEMALE CHINESE UNICORN → 2376
猪 WILD BOAR → 0652
鹿 DEER → 3879

鯛

2362

1-11-8

▶TAI

チョウ たい

195	Nonstandard	U9BDB
魚	S19-11-8	F0000

traditional form → see 鯛 at 2360

麒

2363

1-11-8

▶MALE CHINESE UNICORN

キ

Ⓒ 麒 qí

198	Names	U9E92
鹿	S19-11-8	F3292

COMPOUNDS

● **MALE CHINESE UNICORN**

麒麟 きりん giraffe; male and female Chinese unicorns
麒麟草 きりんそう orange stonecrop, *Sedum kamtschaticum*
麒麟児 きりんじ child prodigy, genius
麒麟血(麒麟竭×) きりんけつ dragon's blood

SYNONYMS

● **undomesticated mammals**

虎 TIGER → 3981
猿 MONKEY → 0824
鯨 WHALE → 2361
犀 RHINOCEROS → 3900
狼 WOLF → 0541
狐 FOX → 0472
羚 SEROW → 1695
鼠 RAT → 3340
獅 LION → 0825
豹 LEOPARD → 1847
熊 BEAR → 3530
象 ELEPHANT → 2647
麒 MALE CHINESE UNICORN → 2363
麟 FEMALE CHINESE UNICORN → 2376
猪 WILD BOAR → 0652
鹿 DEER → 3879

● **mythical animals**

竜 DRAGON → 2603
辰 THE DRAGON → 3713
麒 MALE CHINESE UNICORN → 2363
麟 FEMALE CHINESE UNICORN → 2376
鵬 MYTHICAL HUGE BIRD → 1416

鳳 MALE PHOENIX → 3749
凰 FEMALE PHOENIX → 3738

離

▸**SEPARATE**
リ　はな(れる)　はな(す)
Ⓝ 离◆ Ⓒ 离 lí

2364
1-11-8

172	Jōyō	U96E2
隹	S19-8-11	F0396

COMPOUNDS

1a (be or become disconnected) **SEPARATE (from), be separated, be detached, disjoin, scatter**
b (be apart) **SEPARATEd, distant**
a 離散する りさんする scatter, disperse, be broken up
分離する ぶんりする separate, split; be separated
電離 でんり electrolytic dissociation, ionization
剥離 はくり exfoliation, peeling off
支離滅裂な しりめつれつな incoherent, inconsistent, disconnected
隔離 かくり isolation, segregation
b 離島 りとう outlying island
離心率 りしんりつ eccentricity
距離 きょり distance, range; interval

2 (sever relations) **SEPARATE from, withdraw, be estranged, be alienated**
離婚 りこん divorce
離縁する りえんする divorce; cancel adoption
離反 りはん estrangement, alienation, desertion
背離する はいりする be estranged, be alienated
乖×離 かいり estrangement, alienation; detachment

3a (part company) **SEPARATE**, part from, be separated
b leave, depart, go away, quit, secede
a 離別する りべつする part from, be separated from; divorce
会者定離 えしゃじょうり Those who meet must part
b 離合 りごう meeting and parting
離脱する りだつする break away, leave, secede
離陸 りりく takeoff
離日 りにち departure from Japan
離村する りそんする desert one's village
離党 りとう secession from a party
離農 りのう giving up farming

4 third of the eight trigrams in the Book of Changes: south, the fire

KUN

【はなれる 離れる】*vi*
①ⓐ **SEPARATE, be separated, become disjointed**
ⓑ **be (a long time or distance) away**
a 離れ離れになる はなればなれになる get separated, be dispersed
b 遠く離れて とおくはなれて at a long distance
現実離れする げんじつばなれする become disconnected from reality
② be estranged from, cut oneself off
③ **leave, quit, go away**
都会を離れる とかいをはなれる leave town

【はなす 離す】*vt*
①ⓐ **SEPARATE, part, divide**
ⓑ **detach, keep apart, isolate**
a 切り離す きりはなす cut [chop] off, sever, detach
b 引き離す ひきはなす draw apart, separate; get a lead on
② estrange

SYNONYMS

1a separate
割 DIVIDE → 2284
分 DIVIDE → 2466
解 TAKE APART → 1913
析 ANALYZE → 1072
別 SEPARATE → 1434
離 SEPARATE → 2364
隔 partition → 0827
b distant
遠 DISTANT → 3906
遥 FAR → 3895
悠 far-off → 3407
遼 FARAWAY → 3930
隔 APART → 0827
離 separated → 2364
迂 ROUNDABOUT → 3969

2 estrange
疎 ESTRANGE → 1512
離 separate from → 2364
遠 DISTANT → 3906

3a part company
別 SEPARATE → 1434
離 SEPARATE → 2364
訣 SEPARATE → 1861
b leave and set forth
去 GO AWAY → 2678
離 leave → 2364
発 START → 3174
出 GO OUT → 4310
退 RETREAT → 3838
撤 WITHDRAW → 0912

魚 鹿 【离】 莫

USAGE

❶【はなれる】

離れる

①ⓐ separate, be separated, become disjointed

ⓑ be (a long time or distance) away

② be estranged from, cut oneself off

③ leave, quit, go away

放れる

free oneself of, get free

❷【はなす】

離す

①ⓐ separate, part, divide

ⓑ detach, keep apart, isolate

② estrange

放す

ⓐ (set free) let go, release, free, turn loose

ⓑ (release one's hold) let go (one's hold of), leave go

HOMOPHONES

はなれる 放 LET GO → 1058

はなす 放 LET GO → 1058

難

▶DIFFICULT
▶DISASTER

ナン かた(い) -がた(い) むずか(しい) むつか(しい) -にく(い)

2365

1-11-8

172	Names	UFA68
隹	S19-8-11	F0000

traditional form → see 難 at 2310

鹹

▶SALTY

カン から(い)

Ⓒ 咸 xián

2366

1-11-9

197	Non-Jōyō	U9E79
鹵	S20-11-9	F0000

COMPOUNDS

● [original meaning] **SALTY, briny, saline**

鹹水湖 かんすいこ saltwater lake

鹹味 かんみ saltiness

KUN

【からい 鹹い】[now usu. 辛い] **SALTY, briny, saline**

海の水は鹹い うみのみずはからい Seawater tastes salty

SYNONYMS

● **tastes**

甘 SWEET → 4306

苦 BITTER → 2789

辛 PUNGENT → 2531

辣 PUNGENT → 1965

酸 sour → 1968

渋い ASTRINGENT → 0625

鹹 SALTY → 2366

HOMOPHONES

からい 辛 PUNGENT → 2531

NOTE

➡ see USAGE note at 辛 2531

鰯

▶SARDINE

いわし

Ⓝ 鰯 Ⓒ 鰯 ruò

2367

1-11-10

195	Names	U9C2F
魚	S21-11-10	F3160

KUN

【いわし 鰯】**SARDINE**

鰯雲 いわしぐも cirrocumulus

鰯鯨 いわしくじら sei whale

真鰯 まいわし Japanese pilchard, Japanese sardine

片口鰯 かたくちいわし Japanese anchovy

畳鰯 たたみいわし sheet of dried sardines

鯛の尾より鰯の頭 たいのおよりいわしのあたま Better be the head of a dog than the tail of a lion

SPECIAL READINGS

干鰯 ほしか dried sardine

SYNONYMS

【いわし】

○ **fishes**

鯉 CARP → 2358

鮎 AYU → 2352

鯛 TAI → 2360

鰯 SARDINE → 2367

鱒 TROUT → 2371

鮫 SHARK → 2354

鰯

▶SARDINE

いわし

2368

1-11-10

195	Nonstandard	U9C2F
魚	S21-11-10	F0000

traditional form → see 鰯 at 2367

競

▶COMPETE

キョウ ケイ きそ(う) せ(る)

2369

1-11-11

117	Nonstandard	U7AF8
立	S22-5-17	F0000

traditional form → see 競 at 2322

鷗

▶GULL

オウ かもめ

Ⓝ 鴎 Ⓒ 鸥 ōu

2370

1-11-11

196	Names	U9DD7
鳥	S22-11-11	F2362

COMPOUNDS

● **GULL, seagull**

白鷗 はくおう white gull

KUN

【かもめ 鷗】**GULL, seagull**

百合鷗 ゆりかもめ black-headed gull

黒盗賊鷗 くろとうぞくかもめ parasitic jaeger, Arctic skua

フルマ鷗 ふるまかもめ fulmar, northern fulmar

SYNONYMS

● **birds**

鷹 HAWK → 3955

鷗 GULL → 2370

烏 CROW → 4088

雀 SPARROW → 3117

燕 SWALLOW → 3142

鴻 LARGE WILD BIRD → 0977

鳳 MALE PHOENIX → 3749

凰 FEMALE PHOENIX → 3738

鵬 MYTHICAL HUGE BIRD → 1416

鶏 CHICKEN → 2221

酉 ROOSTER → 4358

隼 FALCON → 3427

鳩 PIGEON → 0184

鷲 EAGLE → 3598

鳶 BLACK KITE → 3919

鶴 CRANE → 2326

鷺 HERON → 3621

鵜 CORMORANT → 2067

鴨 DUCK → 1582

雁 WILD GOOSE → 3741

鱒 2371

▶**TROUT**

ソン ます

Ⓝ 鱒 Ⓒ 鳟 zūn

◧ 1-11-12

195	Names	U9C52
魚	S23-11-12	F3248

COMPOUNDS

● **TROUT**

鮭×鱒 けいそん salmon and trout

養鱒 ようそん trout farming

KUN

【ます 鱒】**TROUT**

虹鱒 にじます rainbow trout

桜鱒 さくらます masu salmon

紅鱒 べにます sockeye salmon

SYNONYMS

● **fishes**

鯉 CARP → 2358

鮎 AYU → 2352

鯛 TAI → 2360

鰯 SARDINE → 2367

鱒 TROUT → 2371

鮫 SHARK → 2354

鱗 2372

▶**SCALES**

リン うろこ

195	Nonstandard	U9C57
魚	S23-11-12	F0000

◧ 1-11-12 traditional form → see 鱗 at 2375

鱒 2373

▶**TROUT**

ソン ます

195	Nonstandard	U9C52
魚	S23-11-12	F0000

◧ 1-11-12 traditional form → see 鱒 at 2371

麟 2374

▶**FEMALE CHINESE UNICORN**

リン

198	Nonstandard	U9E9F
鹿	S23-11-12	F0000

◧ 1-11-12 traditional form → see 麟 at 2376

鱗 2375

▶**SCALES**

リン うろこ

Ⓝ 鱗 Ⓒ 鳞 lín

◧ 1-11-13

195	Names	U9C57
魚	S24-11-13	F2721

COMPOUNDS

● **SCALES (of animals or plants)**

鱗粉 りんぷん scales (of an insect)

鱗状 りんじょう scaly, scale-like

鱗片葉 りんぺんよう scale leaf

片鱗 へんりん a scale; part, glimpse, hint

逆鱗 げきりん wrath of one's superior, imperial wrath

銀鱗 ぎんりん silvery scales; fish

KUN

【うろこ 鱗】**SCALES (of fish or reptiles)**

鱗雲 うろこぐも cirrocumulus clouds

目から鱗が落ちる めからうろこがおちる Be awakened to the truth (have the scales fall from one's eyes)

SYNONYMS

● **kinds of skin**

皮 SKIN (of any kind) → 3771

膚 SKIN (of the human body) → 4049

肌 SKIN (of the human body) → 1021

革 LEATHER → 3099

韋 TANNED LEATHER → 2851

鱗 SCALES → 2375

COMPOUND FORMATION

【逆鱗 げきりん】

逆鱗 'imperial wrath, etc.', used in the phrase 逆鱗に触れる げきりんにふれる, refers to a single scale (鱗) on a dragon's chin growing in the opposite (逆) direction to its other scales. According to Chinese myth, the dragon would kill anyone who dared to touch the scale.

麟 2376 1-11-13

▸**FEMALE CHINESE UNICORN**

リン

N 麟 C 麟 lín

198	Names	U9E9F
鹿	S24-11-13	F2821

COMPOUNDS

● [original meaning] **FEMALE CHINESE UNICORN**

麒麟 きりん giraffe; male and female Chinese unicorns

SYNONYMS

● **undomesticated mammals**

虎 TIGER → 3981
猿 MONKEY → 0824
鯨 WHALE → 2361
犀 RHINOCEROS → 3900
狼 WOLF → 0541
狐 FOX → 0472
羚 SEROW → 1695
鼠 RAT → 3340
獅 LION → 0825
豹 LEOPARD → 1847
熊 BEAR → 3530
象 ELEPHANT → 2647
麒 MALE CHINESE UNICORN → 2363
麟 FEMALE CHINESE UNICORN → 2376
猪 WILD BOAR → 0652
鹿 DEER → 3879

● **mythical animals**

竜 DRAGON → 2603
辰 THE DRAGON → 3713
麒 MALE CHINESE UNICORN → 2363
麟 FEMALE CHINESE UNICORN → 2376
鵬 MYTHICAL HUGE BIRD → 1416
鳳 MALE PHOENIX → 3749
凰 FEMALE PHOENIX → 3738

亂 2377 1-12-1

▸**DISORDERED**

ラン みだ(れる) みだ(る) みだ(す)

5	Nonstandard	U4E82
乚	S13-1-12	F0000

traditional form → see 乱 at 1611

鄭 1-12-2

incorrect stroke-count
➡ see 1-12-3: 奠 at 2379

鄭 1-12-2

incorrect stroke-count
➡ see 1-12-3: 奠 at 2380

鄰 1-12-2

incorrect stroke-count
➡ see 1-12-3: 粦 at 2382

劃 2378 1-12-2

▸**MARK OFF**

カク

C 划 huà huá

18	Non-Jōyō	U5283
刂	S14-2-12	F0000

COMPOUNDS

[now replaced by 画 3723]

❶ [original meaning] **MARK OFF, draw a line, demarcate, partition**

劃期的 かっきてき epoch-making, epochal
劃一化 かくいつか standardization
劃定する かくていする demarcate
劃然と かくぜんと distinctly, clearly
区劃 くかく division, section; boundary

❷ draw up a plan, plan, design

劃策する かくさくする plan, scheme
企劃 きかく plan, project

INDEPENDENT

【かくする 劃する(=画する)】**MARK OFF**; plan

SYNONYMS

❶ **mark**

印 imprint → 1023
押 seal → 0371
劃 MARK OFF → 2378
画 mark off → 3723
捺 AFFIX A SEAL → 0603

鄭 2379 1-12-3

▸**COURTEOUS**

テイ ジョウ

N 鄭 C 郑 zhèng

163	Names	U912D
阝	S15-3-12	F2011

COMPOUNDS

❶ [now replaced by 丁 4155] **COURTEOUS**

鄭重な ていちょうな polite, courteous

❷ [rare]

ⓐ Chinese family name: Zheng
ⓑ name of a state in ancient China: Zheng

a 鄭箋 ていせん commentary on the Book of Odes by Zheng Xuan

b 鄭声 ていせい (decadent) music of the state of Zheng

SYNONYMS

❶ **courteous**

甯 COURTEOUS → 2959
鄭 COURTEOUS → 2379
町 COURTEOUS → 0211
嚀 COURTEOUS → 0965
丁 courteous → 4155

鄭

2380

◧ 1-12-3

▸COURTEOUS

テイ ジョウ

163	Nonstandard	U912D
阝	S15-3-12	F0000

traditional form → see 鄭 at 2379

影

2381

◧ 1-12-3

▸SHADOW

エイ かげ

Ⓒ 影 yǐng

59	Jōyō	U5F71
彡	S15-3-12	F0500

1 2 3 4 5 6 7 8 9 10 11 12 13 14 15

COMPOUNDS

❶ⓐ [formerly also 翳 3567] [original meaning] (partial darkness) **SHADOW, silhouette**

ⓑ (reflected image) **SHADOW, image, reflection**

a 影響 えいきょう influence, effect
暗影 あんえい shadow, gloom
陰影 いんえい shadow

b 影像 えいぞう image; shadow, phantom
人影 じんえい human figure; shadow of a person
投影 とうえい cast shadow; projection
倒影 とうえい inverted image
撮影 さつえい photographing, shooting (of a movie)

❷ⓐ (faint indication) **SHADOW** (of), traces (of), signs (of)

ⓑ (apparition) **SHADOW**, phantom, vision

a 機影 きえい sight [signs] of an airplane
船影 せんえい signs of a ship

b 幻影 げんえい vision, phantom, illusion

❸ light
月影 げつえい(=つきかげ) moonlight; moon
灯影 とうえい(=ほかげ) firelight in the dark; shadows by the firelight

❹ picture, portrait
近影 きんえい one's recent photograph

KUN

【かげ 影】

①ⓐ (partial darkness) **SHADOW, silhouette**

ⓑ (reflected image) **SHADOW, image, reflection**

a 淡い影 あわいかげ light shadow

b 影武者 かげむしゃ dummy general, general's double
影を映す かげをうつす mirror the image (of)

②ⓐ (faint indication) **SHADOW (of), traces (of), signs (of)**

ⓑ [in compounds] **figure, appearance**

a 影も形も無い かげもかたちもない nowhere to be seen
面影 おもかげ face; traces

b 人影 ひとかげ human figure; shadow of a person

③ [in compounds] **light**
日影 ひかげ sunshine; shadow
火影(=灯影) ほかげ shadows from firelight
月影 つきかげ moonlight; moonshine

SYNONYMS

❶ⓐ **shadow**
影 SHADOW → 2381
翳 SHADOW → 3567
陰 SHADE → 0657
蔭 SHADE → 2974

ⓑ **image**
像 IMAGE → 0187
影 SHADOW → 2381

USAGE

❶【かげ】

影
①ⓐ (partial darkness) shadow, silhouette
ⓑ (reflected image) shadow, image, reflection
②ⓐ (faint indication) shadow (of), traces (of), signs (of)
ⓑ [in compounds] figure, appearance
③ [in compounds] light

陰
① [formerly also 蔭] shade
② [formerly also 蔭]
ⓐ back side, reverse side
ⓑ behind the scenes
③ [also 蔭] [in the form of お陰 おかげ] grace, favor

蔭
① [also 陰] [in the form of お蔭 おかげ] grace, favor
② [now usu. 陰] shade
③ [now usu. 陰]
ⓐ back side, reverse side
ⓑ behind the scenes

★Though 影 has the basic meaning of shadow, in compounds it is used in the more or less the opposite sense, i.e., light. 陰 specifically refers to shade;

奐 奠【景】粦

it also signifies the reverse side of something, or, figuratively, behind the scenes.

❷【ひかげ】

日影
① sunshine
② shadow

日陰
the shade

HOMOPHONES

かげ
陰 SHADE → 0657
蔭 SHADE → 2974

COMPOUND FORMATION

【影響 えいきょう】

影響 'influence, effect' consists of 影 ❶ⓐ 'shadow' and 響 'echo'. "Just as the presence of a shape casts a shadow and the presence of a sound produces an echo, the presence of a cause must lead to an effect." By this strange logic, 影響 came to mean influence.

箕
奠
景
【粦】

鄰 2382

▶**NEIGHBOR**

リン となる(る) となり

163	Nonstandard	U9130
阝	S15-3-12	F0000

1-12-3

alternative form → see 隣 at 0961

默 2383

▶**SILENT**

モク だま(る) もだ(す)

203	Names	U9ED8
黑	S16-12-4	F0000

1-12-4

traditional form → see 黙 at 3554

獸 2384

▶**BEAST**

ジュウ けもの けだもの▲

Ⓝ 獸 Ⓒ 兽 shòu

94	Jōyō	U7363
犬	S16-4-12	F1634

1-12-4

COMPOUNDS

ⓐ [original meaning] **BEAST, animal**
ⓑ bestial, brutal

a 獸医 じゅうい veterinarian
野獸 やじゅう wild animal, wild game
猛獸 もうじゅう fierce [savage] animal [beast]
怪獸 かいじゅう monster; beast
珍獸 ちんじゅう rare animal
b 獸心 じゅうしん brutal heart

INDEPENDENT

【じゅう 獸】**BEAST**; brute

KUN

【けもの 獸】**BEAST; brute**
獸道 けものみち animal trail
獸偏 けものへん *kemonohen*, "dog" radical (犭)

【けだもの 獸】**BEAST**; brute

SYNONYMS

ⓐ **animal**
獸 BEAST → 2384
畜 LIVESTOCK → 2599
生 LIFE → 4309
物 living thing → 1084

歖 2385

▶**HAPPY**

キ よろこ(ぶ) よろこ(ばす) ㊔ よし のぶ

76	Nonstandard	U6B56
欠	S16-4-12	F0000

1-12-4

traditional form → see 喜 at 2889

戰 2386

▶**WAR**

セン いくさ たたか(う)

62	Names	U6230
戈	S16-4-12	F0000

1-12-4

traditional form → see 戦 at 2242

戲 2387

▶**SPORT**

ギ ゲ たわむ(れる)

62	Nonstandard	U6231
戈	S16-4-12	F0000

1-12-4

traditional form → see 戯 at 2351

黏 2388

▶**STICKY**

ネン ねば(る)

202	Nonstandard	U9ECF
黍	S17-12-5	F0000

1-12-5

traditional form → see 粘 at 1681

點 2389

▶**POINT**

テン つ(ける) つ(く) た(てる) とも(す)

203	Nonstandard	U9EDE
黑	S17-12-5	F0000

1-12-5

traditional form → see 点 at 2587

齡 2390

▶**AGE**

レイ よわい▲ とし▲

Ⓝ 齢 令◇ Ⓒ 龄 líng

211	Jōyō	U9F62
歯	S17-12-5	F0887

1-12-5

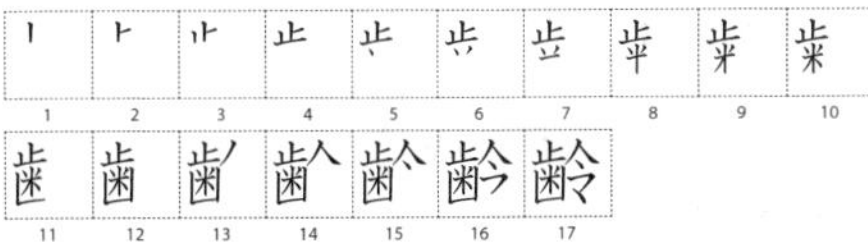

COMPOUNDS

● [also 令 2489] **AGE, years**

年齢 ねんれい age, years
樹齢 じゅれい age of a tree
高齢 こうれい advanced age
老齢 ろうれい old age
学齢 がくれい school age
月齢 げつれい moon's age

KUN

【よわい 齢】**AGE**

七十の齢を重ねる ななじゅうのよわいをかさねる live to be 70 years old

【とし 齢】[usu. 年 or 歳] one's years, **AGE**

SYNONYMS

● **age**

齢 AGE → 2390
令 age → 2489
年 years → 2528
歳 AGE SUFFIX → 3131
才 AGE SUFFIX → 4218
寿 life span → 4372

HOMOPHONES

とし

年 YEAR → 2528
歳 YEAR → 3131

NOTE

➡ see USAGE note at 年 2528
★ Though 齢 and 令 are distinct characters, the latter is also used as an abbreviated form of the former.

翻 2391

◧ 1-12-6

▶TURN OVER
▶RENDER
ホン ファン▲ ひるがえ(る) ひるがえ(す)
Ⓝ 飜 翻◇ Ⓒ 翻 fān

124	Jōyō	U7FFB
羽	S18-6-12	F1718

COMPOUNDS

❶ⓐ **TURN OVER, reverse**
ⓑ turn (a person) round one's little finger, make sport of

a 翻倒する ほんとうする [rare] turn upside-down
翻意する ほんいする change one's mind
翻然と ほんぜんと suddenly
b 翻弄する ほんろうする trifle with, make sport of, toss about (as of a boat)

❷ⓐ **RENDER (written texts) in another form, translate, adapt, transcribe**
ⓑ remake, reproduce

a 翻訳する ほんやくする translate, render
翻字 ほんじ transliteration
翻案 ほんあん adaptation
b 翻刻 ほんこく reprint

❸ [original meaning] flutter, wave, fly

翩×翻たる へんぽんたる fluttering, waving

❹ grade of a winning hand in mahjong

二翻役 りゃんふぁんやく winning hand which redoubles the score

KUN

【ひるがえる 翻る】*vi* **TURN OVER; wave, flutter**

翻って考えると ひるがえってかんがえると on (further) reflection, on second thought
風に翻る かぜにひるがえる flutter [wave] in the wind

【ひるがえす 翻す】*vt* **change (one's mind), reverse (a decision); wave, flutter; dodge**

前説を翻す ぜんせつをひるがえす change one's former opinion
身を翻す みをひるがえす dodge, turn aside adroitly

SYNONYMS

❶ⓐ **overturn**

覆 OVERTURN → 3386
翻 TURN OVER → 2391
反 turn over → 3663
顛 TURN [roll] OVER → 2317
転 turn [roll] over → 1872
倒 TOPPLE → 0139
轢 RUN OVER → 2095

❷ⓐ **translate**

訳 TRANSLATE → 1865
翻 RENDER → 2391

飜 2392

◧ 1-12-6

▶TURN OVER
▶RENDER
ホン ファン ひるがえ(る) ひるがえ(す)

124	Nonstandard	U7FFB
羽	S18-6-12	F0000

alternative form → see 翻 at 2391

辭 2393

◧ 1-12-7

▶WORD
▶RESIGN
ジ や(める)

160	Nonstandard	U8FAD
辛	S19-7-12	F0000

traditional form → see 辞 at 1726

【翻】

1

麒

incorrect stroke-count
➡ see 1-11-8: 鹿 at 2363

1-12-8

【鹿】

顧

▸**LOOK BACK**

コ かえり(みる) ㊔ み

Ⓝ 顧 Ⓒ 顾 gù

2394

1-12-9

181	Jōyō	U9867
頁	S21-9-12	F1412

COMPOUNDS

❶ⓐ [original meaning] **LOOK BACK, turn around**
ⓑ **LOOK BACK upon (the past), retrospect**

a 顧問 こもん adviser, consultant
一顧もしない いっこもしない take no notice of, not give a damn
右顧左眄×する うこさべんする look to the right and left, hesitate

b 後顧 こうこ looking back, worry
回顧する かいこする look back on, retrospect

❷ have regard for, be concerned about
顧慮する こりょする have regard, take into consideration

❸ **show favor to, patronize, take care of**
顧客 こきゃく customer, patron, client
恩顧 おんこ favors, patronage
愛顧 あいこ patronage, favor

KUN

【かえりみる 顧みる】

①ⓐ **LOOK BACK, turn around**
ⓑ **LOOK BACK upon the past, review, retrospect**

a 顧みて他を言う かえりみてたをいう give an evasive answer

b 昔を顧みる むかしをかえりみる look back upon the past

② have regard for, consider
家庭を顧みない かていをかえりみない think little of one's family

SYNONYMS

❶ⓐ **see and look**
見 SEE → 3151
看 WATCH → 3992
察 INSPECT → 2961
窺 WATCH FURTIVELY → 3002
瞥 GLANCE AT → 3592
目 look → 3777
観 VIEW → 2359
覧 LOOK OVER → 3538
眺 LOOK OUT OVER → 1503
望 LOOK AFAR → 3408
仰 LOOK UP → 0051
顧 LOOK BACK → 2394
視 REGARD → 1223

ⓑ **remember**
憶 REMEMBER → 0944
覚える COMMIT TO MEMORY → 3217
記 commit to memory → 1843
追 reminisce → 3840
顧 LOOK BACK → 2394
偲 RECOLLECT → 0153

USAGE

【かえりみる】

顧みる
①ⓐ look back, turn around
ⓑ look back upon the past, review, retrospect
② have regard for, consider

省みる
introspect, examine oneself, reflect upon oneself

HOMOPHONES

かえりみる 省 MINISTRY → 3100

COMPOUND FORMATION

【顧問 こもん】

顧問 'adviser, consultant' originally referred to the emperor turning to (顧 ❶ⓐ) his subjects to ask (問) for advice.

顧

▸**LOOK BACK**

コ かえり(みる) ㊔ み

2395

181	Nonstandard	U9867
頁	S21-9-12	F0000

1-12-9

traditional form → see 顧 at 2394

飜

▸**TURN OVER**
▸**RENDER**

ホン ファン ひるがえ(る) ひるがえ(す)

2396

183	Names	U98DC
飛	S21-9-12	F0000

1-12-9

traditional form → see 翻 at 2391

劍

▸**SWORD**

ケン つるぎ

2397

18	Names	U528D
刂	S15-2-13	F0000

1-13-2

traditional form → see 剣 at 2104

劉

2398

◧ 1-13-2

▶KILL

リュウ ㊔ のぶ みずち

Ⓒ 刘 liú

18	Names	U5289
刂	S15-2-13	F1440

COMPOUNDS

● [original meaning, now obsolete] **KILL**—now used only in names

SYNONYMS

● **kill**

殺 KILL → 1677
劉 KILL → 2398
刺 stab to death → 1625
絞 STRANGLE → 1707
窒 CHOKE → 2853

劇

2399

◧ 1-13-2

▶DRAMA

ゲキ

Ⓝ 𠞊◆ Ⓒ 剧 jù

18	Jōyō-6	U5287
刂	S15-2-13	F0826

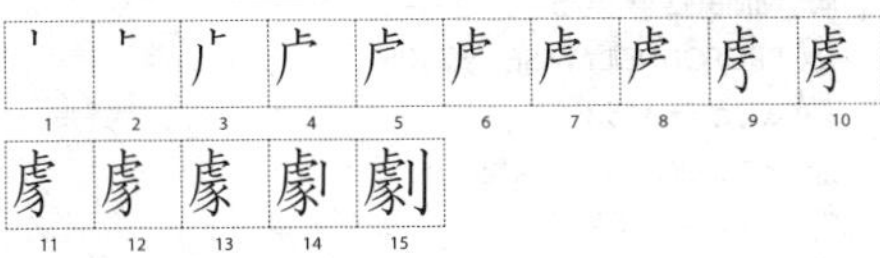

COMPOUNDS

❶ⓐ [also suffix] **DRAMA, play, theatrical performance**

ⓑ abbrev. of 劇場 げきじょう: theater

a 劇場 げきじょう theater
劇団 げきだん dramatic company, theatrical troupe
劇映画 げきえいが film drama
劇的な げきてきな dramatic
演劇 えんげき drama, play
歌劇 かげき opera
喜劇 きげき comedy
悲劇 ひげき tragedy, tragic drama
時代劇 じだいげき period adventure drama, period film

b 帝劇 ていげき The Imperial Theatre

❷ [usu. 激 0955] [original meaning] intense, severe

劇薬 げきやく powerful medicine
劇痛(=激痛) げきつう violent [intense] pain
劇変(=激変) げきへん sudden change, upheaval

❸ busy

劇務(=激務) げきむ busy [hard] work, severe duty

INDEPENDENT

【げき 劇】**DRAMA, play, theatrical performance**

劇を演じる げきをえんじる perform a play

SYNONYMS

❶ⓐ **performance**

劇 DRAMA → 2399
演 performance → 0855
芸 entertainment → 2738

劔

2400

◧ 1-13-3

▶SWORD

ケン つるぎ

18	Nonstandard	U5294
刀	S16-2-14	F0000

alternative form → see 剣 at 2104

劒

2401

◧ 1-13-3

▶SWORD

ケン つるぎ

18	Nonstandard	U5292
刀	S16-2-14	F0000

alternative form → see 剣 at 2104

戲

2402

◧ 1-13-4

▶SPORT

ギ ゲ たわむ(れる)

62	Names	U6232
戈	S17-4-13	F0000

traditional form → see 戯 at 2351

艶

2403

◧ 1-13-6

▶CHARMING
▶ROMANCE

エン つや なま(めかしい)▲ あで(やか)▲
㊔ よし

Ⓝ 豔 Ⓒ 艳 yàn

139	Jōyō	U8276
色	S19-6-13	F1925

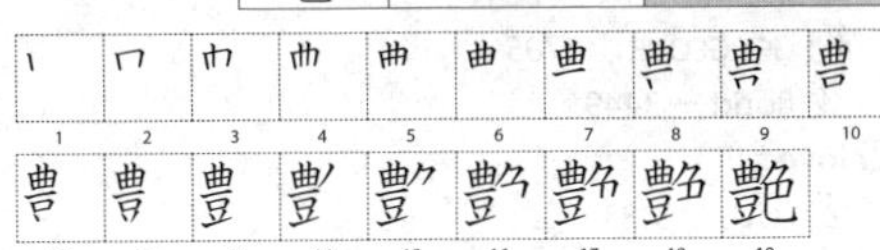

COMPOUNDS

❶ [original meaning] **CHARMING, beautiful, fascinating, voluptuous**

艶容 えんよう fascinating figure, charming look
艶美 えんび beauty, charm
濃艶な のうえんな charming, bewitching, enchanting
妖艶な ようえんな fascinating, voluptuous

❷ **ROMANCE, love, love affair**

艶聞 えんぶん love affair, romance, one's love story
艶書 えんしょ love letter
艶福 えんぷく good fortune in love

INDEPENDENT

【えん 艶】CHARMING beauty

艶な えんな charming, fascinating, voluptuous

KUN

【つや 艶】

① **gloss, luster, glaze**

艶艶した つやつやした glossy, bright

艶消し つやけし grinding, frosting; disillusionment

② **charm, color**

艶の有る声 つやのあるこえ charming voice

③ [in compounds] love, **ROMANCE**

艶っぽい つやっぽい romantic, spicy, coquettish

艶事 つやごと love affair, romance

【なまめかしい 艶めかしい】**CHARMING**, fascinating; coquettish, voluptuous

艶めかしい姿 なまめかしいすがた bewitching figure

艶めかしい目付きで なまめかしいめつきで with coquettish eyes

【あでやか 艶やか】

あでやかな 艶やかな **CHARMING**, fascinating, fair

艶姿 あですがた charming figure

SYNONYMS

❶ **beautiful**

美 BEAUTIFUL → 2817
彪 MAGNIFICENT → 4115
綺 BEAUTIFUL → 1734
娃 BEAUTIFUL → 0419
佳 FINE → 0096
瑶 EXQUISITE → 1301
麗 OF GRACEFUL BEAUTY → 2672
艶 CHARMING → 2403
妙 of marvelous beauty → 0280
華 MAGNIFICENT → 2841
絢 GORGEOUS → 1705
斐 florid → 3449

❷ **love**

愛 LOVE → 3133
情 love → 0583
恋 LOVE (for the opposite sex) → 2602
艶 ROMANCE → 2403
寵 AFFECTION → 3029

【つや】

① **luster**

艶 gloss → 2403
沢 luster → 0313

劑

2404

1-14-2

▶**PREPARATION**

ザイ

18	Nonstandard	U5291
刂	S16-2-14	F0000

traditional form → see 剤 at 2102

叡

2405

1-14-2

▶**PROFOUNDLY WISE**

エイ ㊔ さとし さとる あきら とおる まさ よし ただ とし

Ⓝ 睿 Ⓒ 睿 ruì

29	Names	U53E1
又	S16-2-14	F1967

COMPOUNDS

❶ [now usu. 英 2782] [original meaning] **PROFOUNDLY WISE, intelligent, farsighted, wise**

叡智 えいち sagacity, wisdom

❷ emperor's, imperial

叡覧 えいらん [archaic] emperor's personal inspection

叡慮 えいりょ [archaic] emperor's mind

叡聞に達する えいぶんにたっする reach the emperor's ears

SYNONYMS

❶ **intelligent and wise**

賢 WISE → 3518
俊 brilliant → 0117
鋭 SHARP → 2171
敏 NIMBLE → 1675
叡 PROFOUNDLY WISE → 2405
智 wise → 3458
慧 INTELLIGENT → 3485
怜 CLEVER → 0356
悧 CLEVER → 0505
俐 CLEVER → 0113
哲 SAGACIOUS → 3402
明 clear-sighted → 1060
聡 SHARP-WITTED → 1750

勳

2406

1-14-2

▶**MERITORIOUS SERVICE**

クン いさお ㊔ いさ いさむ

19	Names	U52F3
力	S16-2-14	F0000

traditional form → see 勲 at 3560

勵

2407

1-14-2

▶**ENCOURAGE**

レイ はげ(む) はげ(ます) ㊔ つとむ

19	Nonstandard	U52F5
力	S16-2-14	F0000

traditional form → see 励 at 1438

斷

2408

1-14-4

▶**CUT OFF**
▶**RESOLVE**

ダン た(つ) ことわ(る)

69	Nonstandard	U65B7
斤	S18-4-14	F0000

traditional form → see 断 at 1885

顯

2409

◧ 1-14-9

▶MANIFEST

ケン ㊔ あき あきら

181	Names	U986F
頁	S23-9-14	F0000

traditional form → see 顕 at 2274

獸

2410

◧ 1-15-4

▶BEAST

ジュウ けもの けだもの

94	Names	U7378
犬	S19-4-15	F0000

traditional form → see 獣 at 2384

齡

2411

◧ 1-15-5

▶AGE

レイ よわい とし

211	Nonstandard	U9F61
歯	S20-15-5	F0000

traditional form → see 齢 at 2390

獻

2412

◧ 1-16-4

▶OFFER

ケン コン

94	Nonstandard	U737B
犬	S20-4-16	F0000

traditional form → see 献 at 2240

勸

2413

◧ 1-17-2

▶URGE

カン すす(める) ㊔ すすむ

19	Nonstandard	U52F8
力	S19-2-17	F0000

traditional form → see 勧 at 2334

歡

2414

◧ 1-17-4

▶JOYOUS

カン ㊔ よし

76	Nonstandard	U6B61
欠	S21-4-17	F0000

traditional form → see 歓 at 2342

龢

2415

◧ 1-17-5

▶HARMONIOUS
▶PEACE
▶JAPAN

ワ オ やわ(らぐ) やわ(らげる) なご(む) なご(やか) ㊔ かず より やす やわら やまと たか よし かつ とも

214	Nonstandard	U9FA2
龠	S22-17-5	F0000

traditional form → see 和 at 1450

觀

2416

◧ 1-17-7

▶VIEW

カン み(る) ㊔ み

147	Nonstandard	U89C0
見	S24-7-17	F0000

traditional form → see 観 at 2359

勸

2417

◧ 1-18-2

▶URGE

カン すす(める) ㊔ すすむ

19	Nonstandard	U52E7
力	S20-2-18	F0000

traditional form → see 勧 at 2334

歡

2418

◧ 1-18-4

▶JOYOUS

カン ㊔ よし

76	Nonstandard	U6B53
欠	S22-4-18	F0000

traditional form → see 歓 at 2342

艷

2419

◧ 1-18-6

▶CHARMING
▶ROMANCE

エン つや なま(めかしい) あで(やか) ㊔ よし

139	Nonstandard	U8277
色	S24-6-18	F0000

traditional form → see 艶 at 2403

觀

2420

◧ 1-18-7

▶VIEW

カン み(る) ㊔ み

147	Nonstandard	U89B3
見	S25-7-18	F0000

traditional form → see 観 at 2359

2

UP-DOWN
上下型

二

2421

2-1-1

一 二

1 2

▸**TWO**

ニ ふた ふた(つ) ㊔ つぎ つぐ かず

Ⓝ 弍 Ⓒ 二 èr

7	Jōyō-1	U4E8C
二	S2-2-0	F0020

RADICAL

ni 'two' (五 互 井), used for character classification

COMPOUNDS

❶ⓐ [original meaning] **TWO, second**

ⓑ TWO times, twice

ⓒ divide in **TWO**

a 二百 にひゃく 200

二月 にがつ February

二次 にじ second, secondary

二塁 にるい second base

二階 にかい second floor; upstairs

b 二番目 にばんめ second

二度と にどと never, never again

二十 にじゅう [sometimes also 廿] 20

c 二分する にぶんする halve, bisect

❷ *baseball* second base, second baseman

二遊間 にゆうかん between second baseman and shortstop

❸ rank with, equal

無二の むにの peerless

INDEPENDENT

【に 二】 **TWO, second**

KUN

【ふた 二】 [in compounds] **TWO**

二言 ふたこと two words; repetition

二人 ふたり two persons

二心 ふたごころ(=にしん) duplicity, double dealing; divided loyalty

【ふたつ 二つ】 **TWO; two years old**

二つ目 ふたつめ second

SPECIAL READINGS

二十歳(=二十) はたち 20 years old

二十日 はつか 20 days; 20th of the month

二日 ふつか two days; 2nd of the month

十重二十重 とえはたえ manifold, multitude

SYNONYMS

❶ⓐ small numbers

一 ONE → 4148

十 TEN → 4172

廿 TWENTY → 4258

二 TWO → 2421

三 THREE → 2423

四 FOUR → 3778

五 FIVE → 4244

六 SIX → 2461

七 SEVEN → 4169

八 EIGHT → 3644

九 NINE → 4176

❶ⓐ two

二 TWO → 2421

弍 TWO (in legal documents) → 3961

双 SET OF TWO → 0028

対 pair → 1025

偶 COUPLE → 0150

両 BOTH → 4331

USAGE

【ふた】

二

[in compounds] two

双

[in compounds] set of two, pair

HOMOPHONES

ふた 双 SET OF TWO →0028

にじゅう

廿 TWENTY →4258

二十 →2421, 4172

丫

▶*NISUI*

2422

2-1-1

15	Radical	U51AB
冫	S2-2-0	F0000

RADICAL

nisui 'ice' (冷 冴 凍), used in characters related to freezing or cold

辶

2-1-1

incorrect stroke-count
➡ see 2-1-2: 丶 at 2425

三

▶THREE

サン み み(つ) みっ(つ) ㊔ ぞう さぶ そ そう かず さむ

Ⓒ 三 sān

2423

2-1-2

1	Jōyō-1	U4E09
一	S3-1-2	F0030

一 二 三
1 2 3

COMPOUNDS

❶ⓐ [original meaning] **THREE, third**

ⓑ **THREE times**

a 三千 さんぜん 3000

三角 さんかく triangle

三角形 さんかくけい triangle

三人称 さんにんしょう *gram* third person

三塁 さんるい third base

三分する さんぶんする trisect

三脚 さんきゃく tripod

三流の さんりゅうの third-rate

七五三 しちごさん the lucky numbers; gala day for children of three, five and seven

第三 だいさん third

b 三回 さんかい three times

❷ *baseball* third base, third baseman

三本間 さんぼんかん between third and home base

❸ many, several

三拝九拝 さんぱいきゅうはい kowtowing, bowing repeatedly

INDEPENDENT

【さん 三】 **THREE, third**

KUN

【み 三】 [in compounds] **THREE**

三日月 みかづき new moon

【みつ 三つ】 **THREE; three years old**

三つ折 みつおり threefold, folded in three

三日 みっか three days; 3rd of the month

【みっつ 三つ】 **THREE; three years old**

SPECIAL READINGS

三味線 しゃみせん shamisen (Japanese three-stringed musical instrument)

SYNONYMS

❶ⓐ **small numbers**

一 ONE →4148

十 TEN →4172

廿 TWENTY →4258

二 TWO →2421

三 THREE →2423

四 FOUR →3778

五 FIVE →4244

六 SIX →2461

七 SEVEN →4169

八 EIGHT →3644

九 NINE →4176

❶ⓐ **three**

三 THREE →2423

参 three (in legal documents) →2563

鼎 triangular →4405

氵

▶*SANZUI*

2424

2-1-2

85	Radical	U6C35
氵	S3-3-0	F0000

radical variant →see 水 at 0010

辶

▶*SHINNYŌ, SHINNYŪ*

2425

2-1-2

162	Radical	UFA66
辶	S3-3-0	F0000

radical variant →see 辵 at 2444

彡

▶*SANZUKURI*

2426

2-1-2

59	Radical	U5F61
彡	S3-3-0	F0000

RADICAL

sanzukuri 'decoration' (形 影 彦), used in characters related to decorating or brilliance

彳 ▸GYŌNINBEN

一 **2427**
丶 2-1-2

60	Radical	U5F73
彳	S3-3-0	F0000

RADICAL

gyōninben 'locomotion' (後 得 彼), used in characters related to locomotion or roads

---

乏 2-1-2

incorrect stroke-count
➡ see 2-1-3: ノ at 2432

亢 2-1-2

incorrect classification
➡ see 4-3-4 at 4237

元 ▸ORIGIN

2428
2-1-3

ゲン ガン もと ㊔ はじめ もとむ つかさ もとい はる ゆき まさ

Ⓒ 元 yuán

10	Jōyō-2	U5143
儿	S4-2-2	F0223

一 二 テ 元
1 2 3 4

COMPOUNDS

❶ⓐ ORIGIN, beginning, original state
ⓑ ORIGINal, first, basic
ⓒ beginning of a new period, first year of a new era

a 元日 がんじつ New Year's Day
根元 こんげん root; base
還元 かんげん restoration; reduction, deoxidization
b 元来 がんらい originally, primarily, essentially
元祖 がんそ originator, pioneer
元価(=原価) げんか cost price
c 紀元二千年 きげんにせんねん year 2000 of the Christian era
中元 ちゅうげん midyear gift; July 15th (lunar calendar)

❷ primordial energy of the universe
元気 げんき vigor, energy; spirits; health

❸ (original amount) **principal, capital**
元利 がんり principal and interest
元金 がんきん principal, capital

❹ⓐ element, unit, basic element, essence, entity
ⓑ *math* **element, dimension**

a 元素 げんそ element, chemical element
二元論 にげんろん dualism
単元制度 たんげんせいど unit credit system
b 単位元 たんいげん unit element
三次元 さんじげん three dimensions

❺ *math* unknown quantity
多元方程式 たげんほうていしき plural equation

❻ (Chinese monetary unit) **yuan**
百元 ひゃくげん 100 yuan

❼ Yuan Dynasty (1271-1368 A.D.) (Chinese dynasty ruled by the Mongols)
元寇× げんこう the Mongolian Invasions

❽ era
元号 げんごう era name

❾ⓐ [original meaning] head
ⓑ (leading figure) **head, leader, chief, eldest**

a 元服 げんぷく ceremony of attaining manhood
b 元首 げんしゅ ruler, sovereign
元老 げんろう elder [senior] statesman; senior member

INDEPENDENT

【げん 元】yuan; Yuan Dynasty; *math* element

KUN

【もと 元】

①ⓐ **ORIGIN, beginning, genesis**
ⓑ [also suffix] **place of ORIGIN, source**
ⓒ **one's ORIGIN, one's antecedents, one's past**
ⓓ (something that brings about a result) **ORIGIN, cause**

a 元は もとは originally
元元 もともと originally, from the first [outset]; by nature
火の元 ひのもと origin of a fire
b 製造元 せいぞうもと manufacturer
ガスの元栓を切る がすのもとせんをきる turn the gas off at the main
c 地元民 じもとみん local people
身元(=身許) みもと one's birth, one's identity, one's background
d 元を糾す もとをただす inquire into the origin, go to the bottom of an affair

② [also prefix] **former, ex-, one-time, past**
元首相 もとしゅしょう ex-Prime Minister
元の通り もとのとおり as it was before

③ **capital, principal; prime cost**
元手 もとで capital, fund
元が掛かる もとがかかる cost much, be expensive
元を切って売る もとをきってうる sell at a loss, sell under prime cost

④ [formerly also 許] in the vicinity of, near (a person), with (someone), under (someone's roof)
→see 許 1862 for compounds

⑤ [sometimes also 素] **raw material, base**
→see 素 3108 for compounds

SYNONYMS

❶ⓐ beginnings
緒 OUTSET → 1742

序 INTRODUCTORY PART → 3803
端 start → 1564
始 beginning → 0335
初 beginning → 1433
元 ORIGIN → 2428
本 origin → 4314
根 ROOT → 1167
源 SOURCE → 0806

❹ element
素 ELEMENT → 3108
元 element → 2428
単 unit → 2805

❼ later Chinese dynasties
唐 TANG DYNASTY → 3867
宋 SONG DYNASTY → 2730
元 Yuan Dynasty → 2428
明 Ming Dynasty → 1060
清 Qing Dynasty → 0635

【もと】
② former
旧 FORMER → 0014
元 former → 2428
故 OLD (earlier time) → 1466
前 previous → 2819
嘗て previously → 3230
曽 previously → 2632
先 former → 3046
既 ALREADY → 1498

USAGE

【もと】
元
①ⓐ origin, beginning, genesis
ⓑ [also suffix] place of origin, source
ⓒ one's origin, one's antecedents, one's past
ⓓ (something that brings about a result) origin, cause
② [also prefix] former, ex-, one-time, past
③ capital, principal; prime cost
④ [formerly also 許] in the vicinity of, near (a person), with (someone), under (someone's roof)
⑤ [sometimes also 素] raw material, base

本
① (the most important thing) basis, essential thing, principle
②ⓐ root (of a tree)
ⓑ counter for plants with roots
③ first half of a tanka poem

基
(underlying support) basis, foundation, grounds, authority

下
① lower part, bottom
② [in the form of 下に もとに] (subject to the influence of) under (the supervision of)

許
[now usu. 元] in the vicinity of, near (a person), with (someone), under (someone's roof)

素
[now usu. 元] raw material, base

HOMOPHONES

もと
本 BASIS → 4314
基 BASE → 3312
下 DOWN → 4186
許 PERMIT → 1862
素 ELEMENT → 3108

COMPOUND FORMATION

❶【元気 げんき】
元気 'vigor, energy; spirits; health' originally referred to the primordial energy (気) of the universe (元 ❷).

❷【元服 げんぷく】
元服 'ceremony of attaining manhood' originally referred to the ceremonial hat that was donned (服) on the head (元 ❾ⓐ).

戸

2429

2-1-3

▶DOOR
▶HOUSEHOLD

コ と¹ と² ㊔べ ど へ

Ⓝ 戶 户◇ Ⓒ 户 hù

63	Jōyō-2	U6238
戸	S4-4-0	F0251

radical variant → see 戸 at 3668

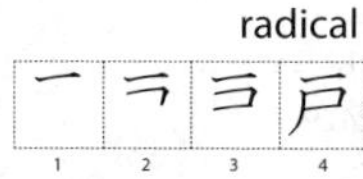

COMPOUNDS

❶ [original meaning] **DOOR**
戸外 こがい open-air, outdoors
門戸 もんこ door, entrance; school

❷ⓐ (house as a social unit) **HOUSEHOLD, house, family**
ⓑ **counter for HOUSEHOLDs or houses**

a 戸別に こべつに from house to house
戸戸 ここ every [each] house
戸籍 こせき family register
戸主 こしゅ head of a family, master of a house
戸数 こすう number of households [houses]

b 五戸 ごこ five houses

❸ one's capacity for alcohol
下戸 げこ nondrinker, poor drinker
泣き上戸 なきじょうご maudlin drinker

KUN

【と¹ 戸】**DOOR, sliding door; shutter**

- 戸口 とぐち door, doorway
- 戸棚 とだな closet, cupboard, wardrobe
- 戸袋 とぶくろ built-in box for shutters
- 戸締まり とじまり fastening the doors
- 雨戸 あまど shutter
- ガラス戸 がらすど glass door

【と² 戸】[in compounds] **used phonetically for *to***

- 戸惑う とまどう be puzzled, be perplexed
- 井戸 いど (water) well
- 瀬戸際 せとぎわ critical moment

SYNONYMS

❶ doors

- 戸 DOOR → 2429
- 扉 HINGED DOOR → 2453
- 門 GATE → 1100
- 口 entrance (or exit) → 4189
- 襖 OPAQUE SLIDING DOOR → 1600

❷ⓐ houses

- 家 HOUSE → 2827
- 屋 HOUSE → 3842
- 軒 house → 1851
- 戸 HOUSEHOLD → 2429
- 宅 DWELLING HOUSE → 2698
- 居 residence → 3822
- 邸 STATELY RESIDENCE → 1451
- 住 housing → 0072
- 庵 HERMITAGE → 3876

ⓑ counters for houses

- 軒 COUNTER FOR HOUSES → 1851
- 戸 counter for households → 2429
- 棟 counter for buildings → 1248

云

2430

2-1-3

▶SUCH

ウン い(う) ㊔ とも ひと これ おき

Ⓒ 云 yún

7	Names	U4E91
二	S4-2-2	F0890

COMPOUNDS

❶ SUCH, so

- 云云 うんぬん so and so, such and such, and so forth, et cetera
- 云云する うんぬんする say something or other, comment, criticize
- 云爾 うんじ(=しかいう) [archaic] such as

❷ say, speak

- 云為 うんい words and deeds, sayings and doings

KUN

【いう 云う】**SUCH, such as, like, of this kind**

- そう云う物 そういうもの thing such as this
- こう云った話 こういったはなし this kind of story

SYNONYMS

❶ similar

- 類 similar → 2275
- 様 like → 1332
- 如 AS → 0239
- -通り as → 3855
- 云 SUCH → 2430

❷ speak and say

- 言 SAY → 2440
- 語る TELL → 1944
- 談 TALK → 1975
- 喋 TALK → 0665
- 諷 INSINUATE → 2005
- 謂う REFER TO → 2007
- 云 say → 2430
- 曰 SAY THAT → 3757
- 話 SPEAK → 1928
- 口 give mouth to → 4189
- 申す SPEAK HUMBLY → 4319
- 述 STATE → 3816
- 陳 SET FORTH → 0656
- 弁 SPEAK ELOQUENTLY → 2497

HOMOPHONES

いう

- 言 SAY → 2440
- 謂 REFER TO → 2007

NOTE

➡ see USAGE note at 言 2440

辶

2431

2-1-3

▶SHINNYŌ, SHINNYŪ

162	Radical	U8FB6
辶	S4-4-0	F0000

radical variant → see 辵 at 2444

乏

2432

2-1-3

▶SCANTY

ボウ とぼ(しい)

Ⓒ 乏 fá

4	Jōyō	U4E4F
ノ	S4-1-3	F1696

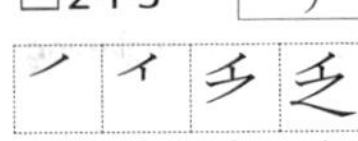

COMPOUNDS

ⓐ (insufficient) **SCANTY, scarce, lacking, deficient**

ⓑ (lacking in resources) **poor, destitute**

- *a* 欠乏 けつぼう lack, shortage, scarcity
- *b* 窮乏 きゅうぼう destitution, poverty
- 貧乏な びんぼうな poor, destitute

耐乏 たいぼう austerity, voluntary privation

KUN

【とぼしい 乏しい】 **SCANTY, scarce, meager, short of; poor, destitute**

乏しさ とぼしさ scarcity
乏しくなる とぼしくなる run short, get scarce
乏しきを分かつ とぼしきをわかつ share poverty
金が乏しい かねがとぼしい be short of money

SYNONYMS

ⓐ **few**

少 LITTLE → 4278
寡 FEW → 2957
乏 SCANTY → 2432
薄 meager → 3004
微 SLIGHT → 0788
寸 A BIT OF → 3652
僅 A LITTLE → 0176
些 A BIT → 3251

ⓑ **poor**

貧 POOR → 2631
乏 poor → 2432
窮 destitute → 2983

爫 2433

▸ ***TSUMEKANMURI***

2-1-3

87	Radical	U722B
爫	S4-4-0	F0000

radical variant → see 爪 at 3756

爫 2434

▸ ***NOTSU***

2-1-3

87	Radical	UFA49
爫	S4-4-0	F0000

radical variant → see 爪 at 3756

壬 2-1-3

incorrect classification
➡ see 4-4-2 at 4257

毛 2-1-3

incorrect classification
➡ see 4-4-3 at 4264

手 2-1-3

incorrect classification
➡ see 4-4-3 at 4267

示 2435

▸ **SHOW**

ジ シ しめ(す)

Ⓒ 示 shì

2-1-4

113	Jōyō-5	U793A
示	S5-5-0	F0428

一 二 亍 亓 示
1 2 3 4 5

RADICAL

shimesu 'deity' (禁 票 祭), used in characters related to deities, worship or religion
Left variant: 礻 ***nehen*** or ***shimesuhen*** (福 神)
Left variant: 示 × ***shimesuhen*** (祀)

COMPOUNDS

❶ (cause to be seen) **SHOW, display, present**

示圧計 しあつけい pressure gauge
展示 てんじ display, exhibition
表示する ひょうじする indicate, show, express, manifest
標示する ひょうじする post up, declare, demonstrate
掲示 けいじ notice, bulletin
提示する ていじする present, exhibit
告示 こくじ notification, bulletin

❷ (point out) **SHOW, indicate, suggest, instruct**

示唆 しさ suggestion, hint
示談 じだん out-of-court [private] settlement
示威 じい show of force
示達 じたつ(=したつ) instructions, directions
指示 しじ instruction; indication
暗示 あんじ hint, suggestion
誇示する こじする make a display of, show off
啓示 けいじ revelation
訓示 くんじ instruction
教示 きょうじ instruction, teaching

KUN

【しめす 示す】 (cause to be seen) **SHOW, display, present;** (point out) **show, indicate, suggest, instruct**

示し しめし discipline; revelation
示し合わす しめしあわす prearrange, conspire (with)
指し示す さししめす indicate, show, point to

SYNONYMS

❶ **show**

示 SHOW → 2435
見せる show → 3151
呈 PRESENT → 2715

❷ **indicate**

指 POINT → 0452
示 SHOW → 2435
標 MARK → 1347
宛てる ADDRESS → 2762

NOTE

➡ see USAGE note at 表 3083

永

▸ETERNAL

エイ なが(い) ㊔ ひさ ひさし のり

Ⓒ 永 yǒng

2436

2-1-4

85	Jōyō-5	U6C38
水	S5-4-1	F0710

COMPOUNDS

● **ETERNAL, everlasting, permanent, long, perpetual**

永遠 えいえん eternity
永久 えいきゅう permanence, eternity
永住 えいじゅう permanent residence
永続する えいぞくする last long, remain permanently
永眠 えいみん eternal sleep, death
永寿 えいじゅ long life
永小作 えいこさく perpetual land lease

KUN

【ながい 永い】(lasting forever) **ETERNAL, everlasting, long**

永年(=長年) ながねん many years, long time
末永く すえながく forever
日永 ひなが a long day

SYNONYMS

● **of long duration**

長 LONG →3163
永 ETERNAL →2436
久 OF LONG DURATION →4191
恒 permanent →0438

HOMOPHONES

ながい 長 LONG →3163

NOTE

➡ see USAGE note at 長 3163
★ do not confuse with 氷 ICE →0043

主

▸MAIN
▸MASTER

シュ ス シュウ▲ ぬし おも あるじ▲

㊔ かず つかさ ちから

Ⓝ 主 Ⓒ 主 zhǔ

2437

2-1-4

3	Jōyō-3	U4E3B
丶	S5-1-4	F0085

COMPOUNDS

❶ [also prefix] **MAIN, principal, head, leading, chief**

主要な しゅような main, principal, essential
主義 しゅぎ principle, -ism
主力 しゅりょく main force, main body
主流 しゅりゅう main current, mainstream
主演する しゅえんする play the leading part
主役 しゅやく leading part, starring role
主翼 しゅよく wing (of an aircraft)
主成分 しゅせいぶん principal ingredient, main component

❷ⓐ **be the MAIN performer of a function, preside over, sponsor, officiate**
ⓑ **regard as MAIN or central, hold in high regard**

a 主催する しゅさいする sponsor, promote
主導権 しゅどうけん leadership, initiative
主宰する しゅさいする preside (over), superintend, supervise

b 主知主義 しゅちしゅぎ intellectualism
主張する しゅちょうする insist on, assert, maintain

❸ⓐ [also suffix] **MASTER, lord, chief, host, head, owner, proprietor, employer**
ⓑ **MASTER of the house, head of a family, husband**
ⓒ **MASTER of a religious rite, chief priest; presiding officer, superintendent, manager**
ⓓ **MASTER of a state, ruler**

a 主人 しゅじん master, head, host, proprietor; husband
主将 しゅしょう captain
主従 しゅじゅう(=しゅうじゅう) master and servant, lord and vassal
喪主 もしゅ chief mourner
船主 せんしゅ shipowner
商店主 しょうてんしゅ proprietor of a shop, storekeeper

b 主客 しゅきゃく host and guest; principal and auxiliary; main guest
主婦 しゅふ housewife
戸主 こしゅ head of a family, master of a house
亭主 ていしゅ husband; master, host

c 主事 しゅじ manager, director, superintendent
主任 しゅにん person in charge, head, chief
坊主 ぼうず Buddhist priest [monk], bonze; shaven head; sonny, sonny boy, boy
法主 ほっす(=ほうしゅ, ほっしゅ) high priest (of a Buddhist sect)
祭主 さいしゅ master of a religious rite

d 主権 しゅけん sovereignty
毛沢東主席 もうたくとうしゅせき Chairman Mao Zedong
自主 じしゅ independence, autonomy
民主主義 みんしゅしゅぎ democracy
君主 くんしゅ monarch, sovereign

❹ [also suffix] Lord, our Lord, Jesus Christ

天主 てんしゅ Lord of Heaven, God
救世主 きゅうせいしゅ the Savior, the Messiah

造物主 ぞうぶつしゅ Creator, Maker

❺ⓐ **subject (opposite of object)**

ⓑ *gram* subject

a 主体 しゅたい main part; subject

主観 しゅかん subjectivity; subject

主観的 しゅかんてき subjective

主題 しゅだい subject, theme

b 主語 しゅご subject (word)

INDEPENDENT

【しゅ 主】

① **MASTER**, lord, chief; one's lord, ruler

主が主なら家来も家来 しゅがしゅならけらいもけらい Like master, like man

② Lord, our Lord

主の祈り しゅのいのり the Lord's Prayer

万軍の主 ばんぐんのしゅ Lord of hosts

③ **MAIN thing, primary object, first consideration**

主たる しゅたる main, chief, principal

主として しゅとして mainly, chiefly

④ subject (opposite of object)

【しゅう 主】 one's **MASTER**, one's lord

KUN

【ぬし 主】

① [also suffix]

ⓐ **owner, proprietor**

ⓑ **MASTER, chief, head**

a 主の無い傘 ぬしのないかさ ownerless umbrella

家主 やぬし house owner, landlord, landlady

株主 かぶぬし stockholder

持ち主 もちぬし owner, proprietor

雇い主 やといぬし employer, master

飼い主 かいぬし pet owner

b 所帯主 しょたいぬし head of a family, householder

② [also suffix] **performer of an action**

落とし主 おとしぬし owner of a lost article, loser

買い主 かいぬし buyer, purchaser

③ guardian spirit; great old-timer

会社の主 かいしゃのぬし great old-timer of the firm

④ *slang* you

御主 おぬし you

【おも 主】

おもな 主な [sometimes also 重な] **chief, principal, MAIN, foremost**

主に おもに mainly, chiefly; mostly

主立った おもだった principal, leading, chief, main

【あるじ 主】 **MASTER, landlord; husband, mistress**

一家の主 いっかのあるじ master of the household

SYNONYMS

❶ **main**

主 MAIN → 2437

正 chief → 4296

本 head → 4314

親- PARENT → 2264

首 leading → 2818

❸ⓐ **leaders**

主 MASTER → 2437

王 KING → 4247

長 CHIEF → 3163

頭 HEAD → 2019

首 LEADER → 2818

領 leader → 1567

魁 LEADER → 4125

ⓑ **husband**

夫 HUSBAND → 4271

主 master of the house → 2437

❹ **god**

神 GOD → 1143

帝 the Supreme Being → 2573

天 HEAVEN → 4250

主 Lord → 2437

祇 EARTHLY GOD → 1459

USAGE

【おもな】

主な

[sometimes also 重な] chief, principal, main, foremost

重な

[usu. 主な] chief, principal, main, foremost

HOMOPHONES

おも 重 HEAVY → 4390

COMPOUND FORMATION

【主張 しゅちょう】

主張する 'insist on, assert, maintain' is to have a high regard (主 ❷ⓑ) for one's own opinion and persist (張) in it.

禾

2-1-4

incorrect classification

➡ see 4-5-3 at 4315

乎

2-1-4

incorrect classification

➡ see 4-5-3 at 4316

亘

2438

2-1-5

▶**EXTEND OVER**

コウ わた(る) ㊔ のぶ せん つね

Ⓝ 亙◇ Ⓒ 亘 gèn

7	Names	U4E98
二	S6-2-4	F2892

COMPOUNDS

● [archaic] **EXTEND OVER**, extend across, extend for, range

亘古 こうこ from ancient times, for ever
連亘 れんこう extending in a row

KUN

【わたる 亘る】**EXTEND OVER, extend for, range, span, last**
幾年にも亘る いくねんにもわたる extend over so many years
数キロに亘る すうきろにわたる extend over several kilometers

SYNONYMS

● **extend over**
亘 EXTEND OVER → 2438
及 REACH TO → 4192
跨 STRADDLE → 1935

HOMOPHONES

わたる 渡 CROSS → 0746

NOTE

➡ see USAGE note at 渡 0746

亥

2439
2-1-5

▶**THE BOAR**
ガイ い

8	Nonstandard	U4EA5
亠	S6-2-4	F0000

traditional form → see 亥 at 2505

舌

2-1-5

incorrect classification
➡ see 2-3-3: 千 at 2711

言

2440
2-1-6

▶**SAY**
▶**SPEECH**
ゲン ゴン い(う) こと ㊔ とき のぶ
Ⓒ 言 yán

149	Jōyō-2	U8A00
言	S7-7-0	F0012

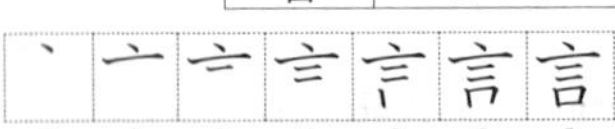

RADICAL

kotoba 'speech' (誉 誓 謄), used in characters related to speech, words or expressions
Left variant: 訁× ***gonben*** (訓 詠 調)

COMPOUNDS

❶ [original meaning] **SAY, speak, talk**
言明 げんめい declaration, announcement
言及する げんきゅうする refer to, mention, touch upon
発言する はつげんする speak, utter
宣言 せんげん declaration, proclamation
予言する よげんする predict, forecast
断言する だんげんする assert, declare
提言 ていげん proposal, suggestion
過言 かごん saying too much, exaggeration
他言する たごんする tell to others, divulge

❷ⓐ **SPEECH, words, saying**
ⓑ counter for words or letters

a 言語 げんご language, speech, words
言論 げんろん speech, discussion
言語道断な ごんごどうだんな inexcusable, outrageous, absurd
証言 しょうげん testimony, verbal evidence
格言 かくげん maxim, proverb
方言 ほうげん dialect
狂言 きょうげん noh farce, comic interlude in a noh drama; kabuki play; sham, put-up job
無言 むごん silence, muteness

b 五言絶句 ごごんぜっく Chinese quatrain with five letters in each line

INDEPENDENT

【げん 言】word, **SPEECH**, remark, statement
言を左右にする げんをさゆうにする equivocate, be noncommittal
言を守る げんをまもる keep one's word

KUN

【いう 言う】

①ⓐ **SAY, speak, talk (about)**
ⓑ **tell, relate**

a 言わば いわば so to speak, in a sense; in short
言い回し いいまわし expression, manner [turn] of expression
言い方 いいかた way of speaking, expression
言い表わす いいあらわす express, say
言い換える いいかえる express in different words
言い出す いいだす begin to speak; suggest, propose

b 物言い ものいい manner of speaking; objection

② **state, declare, affirm**
言い分 いいぶん one's say [claim]; objection, complaint
言い渡す いいわたす announce, tell; sentence; order
言いなり いいなり doing as one is told
言い掛かり いいがかり false accusation [charge]
言い付ける いいつける tell, order
意見を言う いけんをいう state one's opinion

③ⓐ **call, name; express (in a foreign language)**
ⓑ [sometimes also 謂う] **refer to, call**—used chiefly in certain set expressions

a 典子と言う人 のりこというひと person called Noriko
これを音素と言う これをおんそという To this is given the term "phoneme"

b 言うに言われぬ いうにいわれぬ inexpressible, indescribable

④ **sound, be heard**

ガタガタ言う音 がたがたいうおと rattling sound

【こと 言】[in compounds] **word**

言の葉 ことのは *literary* word

言葉 ことば word, term; wording; language

言葉遣い ことばづかい wording, usage

言付ける ことづける leave a message

一言 ひとこと single word

独り言 ひとりごと soliloquy, monologue

寝言 ねごと talking in one's sleep

SYNONYMS

❶ **speak and say**

言 SAY → 2440

語る TELL → 1944

談 TALK → 1975

喋 TALK → 0665

諷 INSINUATE → 2005

謂う REFER TO → 2007

云 say → 2430

曰 SAY THAT → 3757

話 SPEAK → 1928

口 give mouth to → 4189

申す SPEAK HUMBLY → 4319

述 STATE → 3816

陳 SET FORTH → 0656

弁 SPEAK ELOQUENTLY → 2497

❷ⓐ **speech**

言 SPEECH → 2440

談 TALK → 1975

舌 TONGUE → 2711

口 MOUTH → 4189

【いう】

③ⓐ **name**

呼 CALL → 0324

言う call → 2440

称 name → 1491

USAGE

【いう】

言う

①ⓐ say, speak, talk (about)

ⓑ tell, relate

② state, declare, affirm

③ⓐ call, name; express (in a foreign language)

ⓑ [sometimes also 謂う] refer to, call

④ sound, be heard

謂う

[usu. 言う] refer to, call

云う

such, such as, like, of this kind

HOMOPHONES

いう

謂 REFER TO → 2007

云 SUCH → 2430

NOTE

➡ see COMPOUND FORMATION for

格言 かくげん → 格 1161

言葉 ことば → 葉 2912

戻

2441

2-1-6

▶**RETURN**

レイ もど(す) もど(る)

Ⓝ 戻 Ⓒ 戾

63	Jōyō	U623B
戸	S7-4-3	F0524

COMPOUNDS

❶ **RETURN, give back**

返戻する へんれいする return, give back

❷ [original meaning] go against, disobey

背戻する はいれいする disobey, infringe, run counter to

暴戻 ぼうれい tyranny, atrocity

KUN

【もどす 戻す】**RETURN, give back, send back; throw up, vomit**

戻し もどし returning, giving back

払い戻し はらいもどし refund, repayment

取り戻す とりもどす take back, regain, restore

買い戻し かいもどし redemption, repurchase

【もどる 戻る】**RETURN, come [go] back; turn back; return to, revert to, unwind itself**

戻り もどり return; reaction, recovery

戻り道 もどりみち the way back

立ち戻る たちもどる return, come back

SYNONYMS

❶ & 【もどす】 **return and restore**

返 RETURN → 3797

戻 RETURN → 2441

還 RETURN → 3945

復 RETURN TO → 0701

蘇 REVIVE → 3032

甦 REVIVE → 4109

【もどる】

◯ **return**

帰 RETURN → 0148

還 RETURN → 3945

回 turn back → 3793

廻 turn back → 3833

戻る RETURN → 2441

復 RETURN TO → 0701

豆

2442

2-1-6

▶BEAN

トウ ズ まめ まめ-

Ⓒ 豆 dòu

151	Jōyō-3	U8C46
豆	S7-7-0	F1185

RADICAL

mame 'ritual vessel' (豊 豎 豈[×]), used in characters related to sacrificial vessels or pedestals

Left variant: 𧯞[×] *mamehen* (豌[×])

COMPOUNDS

❶ⓐ BEAN, pea

ⓑ soybean

a 豆腐 とうふ tofu (Japanese bean curd)

大豆 だいず soybean

b 豆乳 とうにゅう soybean milk

納豆 なっとう fermented soybeans

❷ [original meaning, now archaic] ancient sacrificial vessel

俎[×]豆 そとう ancient altar of sacrifice

KUN

【まめ 豆】

①ⓐ [also suffix] **BEAN, pea**

ⓑ **soybean**

a 豌[×]豆豆 えんどうまめ peas

b 黒豆 くろまめ black soybean

② blister, corn

血豆 ちまめ blood blister

【まめ- 豆-】 [prefix] **miniature, midget, mini-, small**

豆電球 まめでんきゅう miniature light bulb

豆台風 まめたいふう small typhoon

SPECIAL READINGS

小豆 あずき adzuki bean

SYNONYMS

❶ cereals

米 RICE →4342

麦 WHEAT →3061

豆 BEAN →2442

粟 FOXTAIL MILLET →3326

黍 PROSO MILLET →3210

蕎 BUCKWHEAT →2993

蒋 WILD RICE →2976

❶ vegetables

菜 greens →2880

蕪 TURNIP →2990

芋 POTATO →2706

豆 BEAN →2442

蕗 BUTTERBUR →3007

茄 EGGPLANT →2787

芹 JAPANESE PARSLEY →2742

瓜 GOURD →3789

瓢 BOTTLE GOURD →2356

芥 mustard →2741

【まめ-】

◯ **small and tiny**

小 SMALL →0007

豆- miniature →2442

微 SLIGHT →0788

細 MINUTE →1689

寸 A BIT OF →3652

NOTE

➡ see COMPOUND FORMATION for 納豆 なっとう →納 1652

系

2443

2-1-6

▶SYSTEM

▶LINEAGE

ケイ ㊔ いと

Ⓒ 系 xì jì

120	Jōyō-6	U7CFB
糸	S7-6-1	F0608

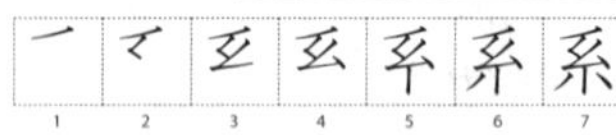

COMPOUNDS

❶ⓐ [also suffix] (group of interrelated elements) **SYSTEM, interrelated group**

ⓑ *chem, phys, biol* **SYSTEM**

ⓒ *geol* **SYSTEM**

a 系統 けいとう system; geological formation; lineage, ancestry

系列 けいれつ order, succession; series

体系 たいけい system, organization

b 太陽系 たいようけい solar system

結晶系 けっしょうけい system of crystallization

二成文系 にせいぶんけい binary system

神経系 しんけいけい nervous system

消化系 しょうかけい digestive system

c デボン系 でぼんけい Devonian system

❷ [also suffix] **LINEAGE, family line, descent, ancestry**

系図 けいず genealogy, pedigree

直系 ちょっけい direct descent line

家系 かけい family line, lineage, ancestry

日系米人 にっけいべいじん American of Japanese descent, Japanese-American

❸ [suffix] faction, clique, group

左派系 さはけい left faction

田中系の政治家 たなかけいのせいじか politician of the Tanaka faction [clique]

INDEPENDENT

【けい 系】 **SYSTEM;** *math* corollary

SYNONYMS

❶ⓐ system

系 SYSTEM → 2443
制 SYSTEM → 1624
統 INTERCONNECTED SYSTEM → 1710
網 network → 1737

❷ lineage

系 LINEAGE → 2443
血 BLOOD → 4339

❸ parties and sects

党 PARTY → 3190
閥 CLIQUE → 4126
流 school → 0529
派 SECT → 0456
翼 WING → 3379
系 faction → 2443
門 (religious) sect → 1100
宗 RELIGIOUS SECT (esp. Buddhist) → 2769

辵

2444

▀2-1-6

▶***SHINNYŌ, SHINNYŪ***

162	Radical	U8FB5
辵	S7-7-0	F0000

RADICAL

shinnyō or ***shinnyū*** 'advance', used in characters related to advancing or going
Enclosures: 辶 辶 ***shinnyō*** or ***shinnyū*** (込 辺 迄)

秀 ▀2-1-6 incorrect classification
➡ see ▀2-5-2: 禾 at 3152

兎 ▀2-1-6 incorrect classification
➡ see ■4-7-4 at 4374

釆 ▀2-1-6 incorrect classification
➡ see ■4-7-3 at 4370

呑 ▀2-1-6 incorrect classification
➡ see ▀2-4-3: 夭 at 3063

妥 豸 ▀2-1-6 incorrect classification
➡ see ▀2-4-3: ⺥ at 3053

房

2445

▀2-1-7

▶**CHAMBER**

ボウ ふさ ㊔ のぶ

Ⓝ 房 Ⓒ 房 fáng

63	Jōyō	U623F
戸	S8-4-4	F0630

COMPOUNDS

❶ⓐ [original meaning] **CHAMBER, (small) room, cell**
ⓑ CHAMBER for sleeping, bedroom
ⓒ enclosed space resembling a **CHAMBER**

a 暖房 だんぼう heating
冷房 れいぼう air conditioning
監房 かんぼう cell, ward
官房 かんぼう secretariat
書房 しょぼう bookstore, publishing company
文房具 ぶんぼうぐ stationery, writing materials
b 房事 ぼうじ sex, lovemaking
女房 にょうぼう wife; court lady
c 心房 しんぼう atrium, chamber of the heart
子房 しぼう ovary (of plants)

❷ house, residence; living quarters of a priest
僧房(=僧坊) そうぼう priest's living quarters in a Buddhist temple

❸ suffix after names of publishing companies or bookstores
富山房 ふざんぼう name of a publisher

❹ tuft, tassel
乳房 にゅうぼう(=ちぶさ) breast, nipple

❺ abbrev. of 安房 あわ, old name for south Chiba Prefecture
房総半島 ぼうそうはんとう Boso Peninsula

INDEPENDENT

【ぼう 房】**CHAMBER**, room, cell; priest's lodge; cell
房の内 ぼうのうち inside of a chamber

KUN

【ふさ 房】**tuft, tassel, fringe; cluster, bunch**
房房した ふさふさした tufty, fringy
一房の髪 ひとふさのかみ a tuft of hair
バナナ一房 ばななひとふさ a bunch [cluster] of bananas

SYNONYMS

❶ rooms

室 ROOM → 2802
間 room → 4122
房 CHAMBER → 2445
斎 study → 2622
堂 HALL → 3202

❹ bundles and clusters

束 BUNDLE → 4369
房 tuft → 2445

COMPOUND FORMATION

❶【暖房 だんぼう】
暖房 'heating' is to warm (暖) a room (房 **❶ⓐ**).

❷【官房 かんぼう】

官房 'secretariat' originally referred to a secretary's (官) chamber (房 ❶ⓐ).

❸【文房具 ぶんぼうぐ】

文房具 'stationery, writing materials' is an implement or implements (具) used in a chamber (房 ❶ⓐ) for writing (文).

❹【房事 ぼうじ】

房事 'sex, lovemaking' refers to the affairs (事) of the bedroom (房 ❶ⓑ).

❺【女房 にょうぼう】

女房 'wife; court lady' originally denoted the chamber (房 ❶ⓑ) of a court lady (女). It is now used in referring to one's wife.

肩

2446

2-1-7

▶**SHOULDER**

ケン かた

Ⓝ 肩 Ⓒ 肩 jiān

130	Jōyō	U80A9
月	S8-4-4	F0825

Stroke order: 1–8

COMPOUNDS

ⓐ [original meaning] **SHOULDER**

ⓑ something resembling a **SHOULDER**

a 肩甲骨 けんこうこつ shoulder blade, scapula

肩章 けんしょう shoulder strap

双肩 そうけん both shoulders

比肩する ひけんする equal, rank with, compare favorably

強肩 きょうけん *baseball* strong arm

b 路肩 ろけん(=ろかた) shoulder of a road

KUN

【かた 肩】**SHOULDER; upper right**

肩に担ぐ かたにかつぐ shoulder, bear

肩凝り かたこり stiff shoulders

肩書き かたがき title, degree

SYNONYMS

ⓐ **trunk parts**

胸 CHEST → 1187

腹 BELLY → 1308

胴 TRUNK → 1186

腰 WAIST → 1311

背 BACK → 3182

肩 SHOULDER → 2446

股 CROTCH → 1093

脇 ARMPIT → 1188

腋 ARMPIT → 1266

秀 2-1-7

incorrect classification/stroke-count

➡ see 2-5-2: 禾 at 3152

垂 2-1-7

incorrect classification

➡ see 4-8-2 at 4382

兎 2-1-7

incorrect classification

➡ see 2-5-3: 襾 at 3165

委季 2-1-7

incorrect classification

➡ see 2-5-3: 禾 at 3160

受采 2-1-7

incorrect classification

➡ see 2-4-4: 爫 at 3076

争桀 2-1-7

incorrect classification

➡ see 2-4-4: ⺤ at 3078

扁

2447

2-1-8

▶**FLAT**

ヘン

63	Nonstandard	U6241
戸	S9-4-5	F0000

traditional form → see 扁 at 3728

音

2448

2-1-8

▶**SOUND**

オン イン -ノン おと ね

180	Nonstandard	U97F3
音	S9-9-0	F0000

traditional form → see 音 at 2570

RADICAL

oto 'sound' (韶×), used in characters related to sound or music

Variant: 音 ***oto*** (韻 響)

重 2-1-8

incorrect classification

➡ see 4-9-2 at 4390

香 2-1-8

incorrect classification

➡ see 2-5-4: 禾 at 3177

扇

2449

2-1-9

▶**FAN**

セン おうぎ あお(ぐ)▲

Ⓝ 扇 Ⓒ 扇 shàn shān

63	Jōyō	U6247
戸	S10-4-6	F1857

Stroke order: 1–10

COMPOUNDS

❶ⓐ (implement for creating a current) **FAN, folding fan**

ⓑ (machine for creating a current) **FAN**

a 扇子 せんす folding fan
扇状地 せんじょうち alluvial delta
白扇 はくせん white fan
b 換気扇 かんきせん ventilation fan
❷ⓐ (create a current) **FAN, blow**
ⓑ [formerly also 煽 1338] (move to action) **FAN, stir up, instigate**
a 扇風機 せんぷうき electric fan
b 扇動する せんどうする instigate, agitate
扇情的な せんじょうてきな inflammatory, lascivious

KUN

【おうぎ 扇】**FAN, folding fan**
舞扇 まいおうぎ dancer's fan
【あおぐ 扇ぐ】[sometimes also 煽ぐ] **FAN**

SYNONYMS

❷ⓑ **incite**
挑 PROVOKE → 0445
唆 INSTIGATE → 0480
扇 FAN → 2449
煽 FAN → 1338
激 excite → 0955
奮 ROUSE UP → 3000
振 arouse to action → 0515
動 MOVE → 2232
起 rise to action → 4099

USAGE

【あおぐ】
扇ぐ
[sometimes also 煽ぐ] fan
煽ぐ
[usu. 扇ぐ] fan

HOMOPHONES

あおぐ 煽 FAN → 1338

鬲
2450
2-1-9

▶*KAKU*

193	Radical	U9B32
鬲	S10-10-0	F0000

RADICAL

kaku 'ritual tripod' (鬻), used in characters related to ritual tripod vessels or their use
Variant: 鬲× *kaku* (鬴×)

晉
2451
2-1-9

▶JIN DYNASTY
シン ㊔ すすむ くに ゆき

72	Nonstandard	U6649
日	S10-4-6	F0000

traditional form → see 晋 at 3290

垂
2-1-9

incorrect classification
➡ see 4-10-2 at 4396

啇
2452
2-1-10

▶TRADE
ショウ あきな(う) ㊔ あき

30	Nonstandard	U5546
口	S11-3-8	F0000

traditional form → see 商 at 2623

悉
2-1-10

incorrect classification
➡ see 2-7-4: 釆 at 3405

扉
2453
2-1-11

▶HINGED DOOR
ヒ とびら
Ⓝ 扉 Ⓒ 扉 fēi

63	Jōyō	U6249
戸	S12-4-8	F1476

COMPOUNDS

● [also suffix] [original meaning] **HINGED DOOR, door, door leaf**
開扉する かいひする open the door
門扉 もんぴ leaves [doors] of a gate
鉄扉 てっぴ iron door
防水扉 ぼうすいひ watertight door

KUN

【とびら 扉】
① [also suffix] **HINGED DOOR, door; door leaf**
扉を排する とびらをはいする push open the door
扉は開かれた とびらはひらかれた The door is open (to the public)
自動扉 じどうとびら automatic door
防火扉 ぼうかとびら fire door
② title page [leaf], front page
扉絵 とびらえ frontispiece
裏扉 うらとびら back leaf

SYNONYMS

● **doors**
戸 DOOR → 2429
扉 HINGED DOOR → 2453
門 GATE → 1100
口 entrance (or exit) → 4189
襖 OPAQUE SLIDING DOOR → 1600

雇

▶EMPLOY

コ やと(う)

Ⓝ 僱 雇 Ⓒ 雇 gù

2454

2-1-11

172	Jōyō	U96C7
隹	S12-8-4	F1354

COMPOUNDS

● **EMPLOY, engage**

雇用(=雇傭)する こようする employ, hire
雇主 こしゅ employer
雇員 こいん employee
解雇 かいこ discharge, dismissal

KUN

【やとう 雇う】[formerly also 傭う]
ⓐ **EMPLOY, engage**
ⓑ **hire (as a boat), charter**

a 雇い やとい employee; employment
雇 やとい government employee
雇い入れる やといいれる employ, engage
雇い口 やといぐち employment, job
日雇い ひやとい daily employment; day laborer
b 船を雇う ふねをやとう hire a boat

SYNONYMS

● **employ**

雇 EMPLOY → 2454
用 EMPLOY → 3694
使う employ → 0100
傭 HIRE → 0181
役 press into service → 0288

USAGE

❶【やとう】
雇う
[formerly also 傭う]
ⓐ employ, engage
ⓑ hire (as a boat), charter
傭う
[now usu. 雇う]
ⓐ hire, employ
ⓑ hire (as a boat), charter

❷【やとい】
雇い
[also 傭い] employee; employment
傭い
[also 雇い] employee; employment

HOMOPHONES

やとう 傭 HIRE → 0181
やとい 傭 HIRE → 0181

番 2-1-11
incorrect classification
➡ see 2-7-5: 釆 at 3416

黍 2-1-11
incorrect classification
➡ see 2-5-7: 禾 at 3210

爲 2-1-11
incorrect classification
➡ see 2-4-8: 爫 at 3127

愛舜 2-1-12
incorrect classification
➡ see 2-4-9: ⺤ at 3133

爵 2-1-16
incorrect classification
➡ see 2-4-13: ⺤ at 3143

亡 2-2-1
incorrect classification
➡ see 4-3-2 at 4210

个

▶COUNTER FOR ITEMS

カ コ

2455

2-2-1

2	Nonstandard	U4E2A
丨	S3-1-2	F0000

alternative form → see 箇 at 3348

个

▶INDIVIDUAL
▶GENERAL COUNTER

コ カ

2456

2-2-1

2	Nonstandard	U4E2A
丨	S3-1-2	F0000

alternative form → see 個 at 0132

乞

▶BEG

コツ▲ コ▲ キツ▲ キ▲ こ(う)

Ⓒ 乞 qǐ

2457

2-2-1

5	Jōyō	U4E5E
乙	S3-1-2	F1875

COMPOUNDS

ⓐ [original meaning] **BEG**
ⓑ [in compounds] solicit, pray for

a 乞食 こじき beggar
乞丐× こつがい(=きっかい) begging; beggar
乞士 こっし *bhikkhu*, fully ordained Buddhist monk

KUN

【こう 乞う】

ⓐ [also 請う] **BEG**

ⓑ [in compounds] **solicit, pray for**

a 物乞い ものごい beggar; begging

命乞い いのちごい begging for one's life

b 乞い願わくは(=希くは) こいねがわくは I pray in earnest that, I beg that, I yearn that

雨乞い あまごい ritual prayer for rain

暇乞い いとまごい leave-taking, farewell visit

SYNONYMS

● **request**

請 REQUEST → 1983

訴 APPEAL TO → 1901

頼 ASK → 2041

嘱 CHARGE WITH → 0881

要 REQUIRE → 3263

願 ASK A FAVOR → 2320

求 SEEK → 4365

乞 BEG → 2457

HOMOPHONES

こう 請 REQUEST → 1983

NOTE

➡ see USAGE note at 請 1983

ケ

▀2-2-1

incorrect classification
➡ see ■4-3-4 at 4238

乏

▀2-2-1

incorrect classification/stroke-count
➡ see ▀2-1-3: ノ at 2432

文

2458

▀2-2-2

▶**LETTER**
▶**WRITINGS**

ブン モン ふみ あや▲ ㊔ ゆき のり

Ⓝ 文 Ⓒ 文 wén

67	Jōyō-1	U6587
文	S4-4-0	F0088

radical variant → see 文 at 2462

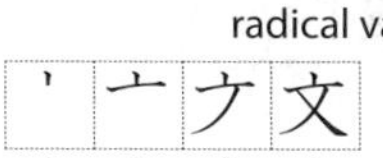

COMPOUNDS

❶ⓐ (written symbol) **LETTER, character, script, inscription**

ⓑ style of writing, calligraphic style

a 文字 もじ(=もんじ) character, letter

文字通り もじどおり literally

文字 もんじ character, letter; writings

文盲 もんもう illiteracy

金石文 きんせきぶん ancient inscriptions on monuments

b 古文 こぶん classics, ancient writings, paleography

❷ⓐ [also suffix] **WRITINGS, composition, text, document**

ⓑ **written or spoken language**

ⓒ **written work, book**

ⓓ **LETTER, note**

a 文章 ぶんしょう writing, composition, essay; prose

文書 ぶんしょ(=もんじょ) document, letter, note

文献 ぶんけん literature, documentary records

文体 ぶんたい (literary) style

文房具 ぶんぼうぐ stationery, writing materials

論文 ろんぶん thesis, paper, treatise, dissertation

作文 さくぶん composition, essay; writing

原文 げんぶん text, original text

全文 ぜんぶん whole text

不文律 ふぶんりつ unwritten law [rule]

注文 ちゅうもん order, ordering; request

判決文 はんけつぶん judgment paper

起請文 きしょうもん written pledge

b 文法 ぶんぽう grammar

文句 もんく phrase, expression; complaint

和文 わぶん Japanese text

c 文庫 ぶんこ library; collection of literary works; box for stationery

d 文通 ぶんつう correspondence, exchange of letters

文面 ぶんめん contents of a letter

❸ [also suffix]

ⓐ **sentence**

ⓑ *computer science* **statement**

a 文脈 ぶんみゃく context

文化的 ぶんかてき cultural

単文 たんぶん simple sentence

疑問文 ぎもんぶん interrogative sentence

b 条件文 じょうけんぶん conditional statement

❹ⓐ **LETTERs, literature, the pen**

ⓑ abbrev. of 文学 ぶんがく: literature

a 文学 ぶんがく literature, letters

文学者 ぶんがくしゃ literary man; man of letters

文芸 ぶんげい literature, literary art, art and literature

文豪 ぶんごう great man of letters, literary master

文語 ぶんご literary [written] language

b 文博 ぶんはく doctor of literature

英文科 えいぶんか department of English literature

❺ⓐ **culture, learning, the arts**

ⓑ abbrev. of 文化 ぶんか: **culture**

ⓒ abbrev. of 文部省 もんぶしょう: Ministry of Education, Science and Culture

a 文化 ぶんか culture

文明 ぶんめい civilization, culture

文教 ぶんきょう education, culture

文部省 もんぶしょう Ministry of Education, Science and Culture

人文科学 じんぶんかがく cultural sciences, humanities

b 文革 ぶんかく Cultural Revolution

文系 ぶんけい liberal arts (department)

重文(=重要文化財) じゅうぶん(=じゅうようぶんかざい) important cultural property; compound sentence

c 文相 ぶんしょう Minister of Education, Science and Culture

❻ civil, civil affairs

文民 ぶんみん civilian

文官 ぶんかん civil official

❼ [also suffix] [original meaning] decorative pattern, figure, design

文様 もんよう pattern, design

縄文 じょうもん straw-rope pattern

渦状文 かじょうもん spiral pattern

❽ phenomenon, feature

天文学 てんもんがく astronomy

地文 ちもん physiographical features

❾ *mon*:

ⓐ former monetary unit equiv. to 1/1000 of a *kan* (貫)

ⓑ unit of footwear size equiv. to 2.4 cm

a 文無しの もんなしの penniless

b 十文の足袋 ともんのたび size 10 *tabi*, digitated socks of about 24 cm sole

❿ unclassified compounds

文楽 ぶんらく Japanese puppet show, *bunraku*

INDEPENDENT

【ぶん 文】

① WRITINGS, composition; (literary) style

文を練る ぶんをねる polish one's style

文は人なり ぶんはひとなり The style is the man

②ⓐ sentence

ⓑ *computer science* statement

a 文を組み立てる ぶんをくみたてる construct a sentence

③ literary culture or learning, literary attainments, culture

文は武に優る ぶんはぶにまさる The pen is mightier than the sword

④ abbrev. of 文学部 ぶんがくぶ: faculty [department] of LETTERs [literature]

東大文 とうだいぶん Faculty of Letters, University of Tokyo

【もん 文】 *mon* (→❾)

KUN

【ふみ 文】 **LETTER, love letter; book**

文読む月日 ふみよむつきひ days of reading

恋文 こいぶみ love letter

【あや 文】 [also 綾]

① **figure, design, pattern (as of cloth)**

美しい文 うつくしいあや beautiful design

②ⓐ **figure of speech, rhetorical flourish**

ⓑ **intricate and subtle details, intricacies**

a 文の無い文体 あやのないぶんたい plain style

SYNONYMS

❶ **characters**

字 CHARACTER → 2696

文 LETTER → 2458

漢 kanji → 0808

旁 RIGHT RADICAL → 2598

❷ⓐ & ❷ⓑ **writing**

文 WRITINGS → 2458

筆 WRITING → 3317

書 writing(s) → 3292

銘 INSCRIPTION → 2158

ⓓ **written communications**

状 LETTER → 0322

文 LETTER → 2458

翰 LETTER → 2198

書 letter → 3292

信 written communication → 0115

電 telegram → 3465

牒 OFFICIAL NOTICE → 1299

❸ **sentence and sentence parts**

句 PHRASE → 3685

文 sentence → 2458

節 clause → 3336

❺ⓐ **learning and knowledge**

業 studies → 3227

学 learning → 3162

文 culture → 2458

識 KNOWLEDGE → 2070

知 knowledge → 1446

❼ **pattern**

模 PATTERN (decorative design) → 1326

文 decorative pattern → 2458

柄 pattern (on cloth) → 1111

様 pattern → 1332

紋 figure → 1651

❾ⓐ **Japanese money denominations**

文 *mon* → 2458

両 *ryo* → 4331

厘 *RIN* → 3727

銭 sen → 2159

円 YEN → 3673

USAGE

【もんよう】

文様
pattern, design

紋様
crest pattern

HOMOPHONES

あや 綾 TWILL → 1740

COMPOUND FORMATION

【注文 ちゅうもん】

注文 'order, etc.' consists of 文 ❷ⓐ 'document' and 注 'write down'. It can be explained as a document or record (文書 ぶんしょ) for submitting information (注進 ちゅうしん). Now it usu. refers to a document or a request specifying one's wishes, i.e., an order.

NOTE

➡ see also USAGE note at 綾 1740

➡ see COMPOUND FORMATION for
- 文化 ぶんか → 化 0022
- 文明 ぶんめい → 明 1060
- 文房具 ぶんぼうぐ → 房 2445
- 表意文字 ひょういもじ → 表 3083
- 文楽 ぶんらく → 楽 3505

★ The symbol 文 is used in maps and signboards: school—in this sense it has no reading and usu. appears in the form ⊗ or 㓞.

方

2459

2-2-2

▶**DIRECTION**
▶**WAY**
▶**SQUARE**

ホウ かた -かた -がた -なた▲ ㊔ まさ みち

Ⓒ 方 fāng

70	Jōyō-2	U65B9
方	S4-4-0	F0033

Stroke order: 1 丶 2 亠 3 方 4 方

RADICAL

kata 'square' (旁 施 族), used for character classification

COMPOUNDS

❶ [original meaning] **DIRECTION, bearing, orientation**
- 方向 ほうこう direction, bearing; course
- 方位 ほうい direction, bearing
- 四方 しほう all directions, cardinal points
- 前方 ぜんぽう front
- 左方に さほうに to the left, on the left side
- 北方 ほっぽう north, northward; northern district
- 快方に向かう かいほうにむかう get better, improve, convalesce
- 途方に暮れる とほうにくれる be at a loss, be puzzled

❷ **locality, place, district, region, area, countryside**
- 方面 ほうめん direction, district; field, sphere
- 方言 ほうげん dialect
- 方方に ほうぼうに in several places; everywhere, all over
- 遠方 えんぽう great distance; distant place
- 地方 ちほう locality, district, region

❸ⓐ (one part of) **side, one side**
ⓑ (one of concerned persons) **side, party, part**
- *a* 一方 いっぽう one side, one hand; a party, the other party; in the meantime; only
- 片方 かたほう one side, the other side
- 両方 りょうほう both
- 他方 たほう other side [hand]
- *b* 双方 そうほう both sides [parties]
- 当方 とうほう I, we, our part
- 先方 せんぽう the other party, they; one's destination

❹ⓐ **WAY of doing, method, means, procedure**
ⓑ **prescription, recipe**
- *a* 方法 ほうほう method, way; system; scheme, means; process, procedure; plan
- 方針 ほうしん course, policy, plan
- 方策 ほうさく plan, policy, scheme
- 方式 ほうしき formula, mode; method
- 方程式 ほうていしき equation
- *b* 処方 しょほう prescription; recipe
- 漢方 かんぽう Chinese medicine
- 秘方 ひほう secret method, secret recipe

❺ⓐ (equal-sided rectangle) **SQUARE**
ⓑ (second power) **SQUARE**
- *a* 方円 ほうえん squares and circles
- 方眼紙 ほうがんし graph paper
- 正方形 せいほうけい square
- *b* 方丈 ほうじょう 10 sq. feet; abbot's chamber; chief priest
- 平方 へいほう square (measure); square (of a number)
- 立方 りっぽう cube

❻ upright, honest
- 品行方正な人 ひんこうほうせいなひと person of good conduct

❼ just, just now
- 方今 ほうこん present time

❽ occultism
- 方術 ほうじゅつ method; art; magic

INDEPENDENT

【ほう 方】

① **DIRECTION, side, way**
- . . . の方に …のほうに in the direction of, towards
- 右の方に みぎのほうに on the right side, to the right

どちらの方へ どちらのほうへ which way
② (one of concerned persons) side, part
私の方では わたくしのほうでは on [for] my part [side]
③ **SQUARE**
方二十マイル ほうにじゅうまいる 20 sq. miles
④ function word used for comparison
彼は働くよりも遊ぶ方だ かれははたらくよりもあそぶほうだ He is more given to idling than to work
彼は怠ける方だ かれはなまけるほうだ He is rather idle
君は帰った方が良い きみはかえったほうがよい You had better go home
侮辱を受けて生きるより死んだ方がましだ ぶじょくをうけていきるよりしんだほうがましだ I would rather die than live in dishonor

KUN

【かた 方】
①ⓐ **DIRECTION**
ⓑ place, area
a 東の方に ひがしのかたに in an easterly direction
b 上方 かみがた Kyoto and its neighborhood
②ⓐ [honorific] **person, gentleman, lady**
ⓑ [archaic] honorific title
a 方方 かたがた all gentlemen, all people
あの方 あのかた that gentleman [lady], he, she
b お万の方 おまんのかた Lady Oman
③ time
来し方 きしかた(=こしかた) past, days gone by
久方振りに ひさかたぶりに after a long time
今し方 いましがた just now, a moment ago

【-かた -方】
① [verbal suffix]
ⓐ **WAY of doing, manner, style, method; how to (do)**
ⓑ **suffix of nominalization**
a 仕方 しかた way, method, means
話し方 はなしかた one's way of speaking
教え方 おしえかた method of teaching
綴り方 つづりかた composition; spelling
出方 でかた one's attitude, move; theater attendant, usher
やり方 やりかた way of doing, method, procedure; step, measure
b 撃ち方止め うちかたやめ Cease fire!
② [also suffix] **side, party**
味方 みかた friend, ally, one's side
相手方 あいてかた other [opposite] party
父方の ちちかたの on the paternal side
売り方 うりかた seller, selling side; art of selling
③ [also suffix] person in charge
賄い方 まかないかた kitchen manager, chef
裏方 うらかた property man, sceneshifter
親方 おやかた boss, chief, master
土方 どかた construction laborer, navvy
④ [honorific] counter for persons
お二方 おふたかた two persons
⑤ [suffix] care of, c/o
足立様方高木様 あだちさまかたたかぎさま Mr. Takagi, c/o Mr. Adachi
⑥ **about, approximately, roughly**
大方 おおかた almost, nearly; probably
粗方 あらかた mostly, roughly, almost, on the whole
一方ならず ひとかたならず unusually, exceedingly, not a little
目方 めかた weight

【-がた -方】
① [also suffix]
ⓐ about; by
ⓑ (of time) **toward**
a 二割方減 にわりがたげん decrease of about 20 percent
利子を二分方引き下げる りしをにぶがたひきさげる lower the rate of interest by 2 percent
b 夕方 ゆうがた evening
明け方 あけがた toward daylight
② **polite plural suffix**
お偉方 おえらがた dignitary, exalted personalities
奥方 おくがた wife of a nobleman
殿方 とのがた men, gentlemen
貴方方 あなたがた you (plural)
先生方 せんせいがた teachers; doctors
③ [also suffix] the side of
敵方 てきがた hostile party
徳川方 とくがわがた Tokugawa's side

【-なた -方】 **DIRECTION; place**
貴方 あなた you
其方 そなた there, your place; thou, you
彼方 かなた other side, there

SPECIAL READINGS

行方 ゆくえ one's whereabouts

SYNONYMS

❶ **direction**
方 DIRECTION →2459
向 direction →3790
❷ **areas and localities**
地 PLACE →0236
方 locality →2459
辺 VICINITY →3761
域 BOUNDED AREA →0559
区 DISTRICT →3681
領 TERRITORY →1567

帯 BELT → 3191
圏 SPHERE → 3904

❸ side

側 SIDE → 0155
脇 SIDE → 1188
方 side → 2459
辺 -side → 3761
面 side → 2590
傍 BESIDE → 0166
横 SIDEWAYS → 1350

❹ⓐ & 【-かた】 ①ⓐ way and style

風 MANNER → 3730
様 MODE → 1332
方 WAY → 2459
途 WAY → 3853
法 METHOD → 0391
流 STYLE → 0529
式 STYLE → 3785
調 TONE → 1973

❺ⓐ square

方 SQUARE → 2459
角 square → 2541

ⓑ mathematical power

乗 power → 4393
方 SQUARE → 2459
平 square (measure) → 4291

【かた】

②ⓐ person

人 HUMAN BEING → 4175
者 PERSON → 3980
方 person (*honorific*) → 2459
氏 person (*polite*) → 3669

【-かた】

③ person in charge

係 PERSON IN CHARGE → 0108
-方 person in charge → 2459
員 MEMBER (of a staff) → 2822

【-がた】

①ⓐ approximately

約 APPROXIMATELY → 1632
概 GENERAL → 1322
大 in substance → 4224
-頃 ABOUT → 0163
位 about → 0069
-方 about → 2459
-程 ...or thereabouts → 1524
辺り thereabouts → 3761

② plural suffixes

-達 plural suffix → 3893
-等 plural suffix → 3321
衆 somewhat polite plural suffix → 3325
-共 belittling plural suffix → 3045
-方 polite plural suffix → 2459

亢

2460

2-2-2

▶HIGH-SPIRITED

コウ

Ⓒ 亢 kàng

8 亠	Non-Jōyō	U4EA2
	S4-2-2	F0000

COMPOUNDS

❶ [now replaced by 興 3622 or 高 2601] **HIGH-SPIRITED, excited, elated**

亢奮(=興奮)する こうふんする get excited, be agitated, be aroused

亢進(=高進、昂進)する こうしんする rise, exasperate, accelerate

❷ [archaic] ascend

亢竜 こうりょう(=こうりゅう) dragon which has already ascended to the heavens

SYNONYMS

❶ elated

亢 HIGH-SPIRITED → 2460
高 high-spirited → 2601
昂 high-spirited → 3065
揚 exalted → 0722
奮 roused up → 3000

六

2461

2-2-2

▶SIX

ロク リク▲ む む(つ) むっ(つ) むい

Ⓒ 六 liù

12 八	Jōyō-1	U516D
	S4-2-2	F0173

Stroke order: 1 2 3 4

COMPOUNDS

● SIX, sixth

六百 ろっぴゃく 600
六時 ろくじ six o'clock
六月 ろくがつ June
六角 ろっかく hexagon
六法 ろっぽう the six codes (of law), statute book
六書 りくしょ the six classes of Chinese characters; Hexateuch
第六感 だいろっかん the sixth sense, intuition

INDEPENDENT

【ろく 六】 SIX

KUN

【む 六】 [in compounds] **SIX**

六月目 むつきめ the sixth month

【むつ 六つ】 SIX; six years old, 6 o'clock (in former time system)

明け六つ あけむつ the sixth hour of the morning

【むっつ 六つ】SIX; six years old

六つ目 むっつめ sixth

【むい 六】[in compounds] SIX

六日 むいか six days; 6th of the month

SYNONYMS

● small numbers

一 ONE →4148
十 TEN →4172
廿 TWENTY →4258
二 TWO →2421
三 THREE →2423
四 FOUR →3778
五 FIVE →4244
六 SIX →2461
七 SEVEN →4169
八 EIGHT →3644
九 NINE →4176

● six

六 SIX →2461
陸 six (in legal documents) →0659

文

2462

2-2-2

▶LETTER
▶WRITINGS

ブン モン ふみ あや ㊔ ゆき のり

67	Nonstandard	U6587
文	S4-4-0	F0000

traditional form →see 文 at 2458

RADICAL

bun or *bunnyō* 'pattern' (斐×), used in characters related to patterns or designs

Variant: 文 *bun* or *bunnyō* (斑)

介

2463

2-2-2

▶MEDIATE

カイ ㊔ すけ たすく ゆき よし

Ⓒ 介 jiè

9	Jōyō	U4ECB
人	S4-2-2	F0376

COMPOUNDS

❶ MEDIATE, intervene, go between; lie between

介入 かいにゅう intervention
介在する かいざいする lie between
媒介 ばいかい mediation, intervention, intermediation
紹介 しょうかい introduction, presentation
仲介 ちゅうかい mediation

❷ give a helping hand, lend support to, protect

介抱する かいほうする nurse, care for
介錯する かいしゃくする assist a person in committing hara-kiri
厄介 やっかい trouble, annoyance

❸ [usu. 貝 3150] shellfish

魚介 ぎょかい marine products

❹ take to heart, mind

介意する かいいする care about

❺ little, trifling

一介の学生 いっかいのがくせい a mere student

INDEPENDENT

【かいする 介する】MEDIATE; take to heart, mind

意に介する いにかいする mind, take (something) to heart
仲人を介して なこうどをかいして through a matchmaker

SYNONYMS

❶ mediating and mediators

紹 INTRODUCE →1691
介 MEDIATE →2463
媒 INTERMEDIATE →0686
仲 INTERMEDIARY →0047

HOMOPHONES

かい 貝 SHELLFISH →3150

COMPOUND FORMATION

【厄介 やっかい】

厄介 'trouble, annoyance' formerly meant to help (介 ❷) someone who is in trouble (厄).

今

2464

2-2-2

▶PRESENT
▶THIS

コン キン いま

Ⓒ 今 jīn

9	Jōyō-2	U4ECA
人	S4-2-2	F0071

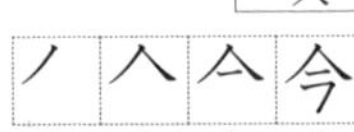

COMPOUNDS

❶ⓐ PRESENT, now
ⓑ of the PRESENT, current

a 今後 こんご after this, from now on
今日 こんにち today, these days
今昔 こんじゃく past and present, yesterday and today
今日は こんにちは Hello/Good morning [afternoon, day]
昨今 さっこん these days

b 今上陛下 きんじょうへいか the reigning emperor

❷ⓐ [also prefix] THIS (week, etc.), the present (term)
ⓑ today, today's

a 今回 こんかい this time; lately
今月 こんげつ this month

今週 こんしゅう this week
今期 こんき present term
b 今夜 こんや tonight, this evening

❸ **next, following**
今度 こんど this time; next time, another time; recently

KUN

【いま 今】**now, THIS moment;** [also prefix] **present day, modern; just now, a moment ago; soon, at once; further, another**
今頃 いまごろ about this time
今迄 いままで till now, so far, up to the present
今時 いまどき recently, these days
今風 いまふう modern style
今浦島 いまうらしま Urashima [Rip Van Winkle] of today
今言った事 いまいったこと what you said just now
今にも いまにも at any moment
今行きます いまいきます I'll come at once
今に いまに before long, someday, one of these days
今一度 いまいちど once more
今少し いますこし a little more
只今 ただいま at present, now; just now; soon; Hello (used by person returning home)

SPECIAL READINGS

今日 きょう today
今朝 けさ this morning
今年 ことし this year
今宵▲ こよい this evening, tonight

SYNONYMS

❶ⓐ **present**
今 PRESENT → 2464
当 THE PRESENT → 2701
現 ACTUAL → 1218

❷ⓐ **this and that**
本 THIS → 4314
爾 THAT → 4407
其れ THAT → 3255
彼 that → 0346
今 THIS (week, etc.) → 2464
当 THE PRESENT → 2701
該 the said → 1916
同 the same → 3707
之 this → 4228
是 this → 3090
此 THIS → 1017
斯 THIS → 2140

ⓑ **yesterday and today**
今 today → 2464
昨 YESTERDAY → 1106

仐 2465

2-2-2

▶**UMBRELLA**
サン かさ

9	Nonstandard	U4ED0
人	S4-2-2	F0000

handwritten form → see 傘 at 2640

分 2466

2-2-2

▶**DIVIDE**
▶**PART**
▶**MINUTE**
ブン フン ブ わ(ける) わ(け) わ(かれる) わ(かる) わ(かつ)
Ⓒ 分 fēn fèn

18	Jōyō-2	U5206
刀	S4-2-2	F0014

ノ	八	分	分
1	2	3	4

COMPOUNDS

❶ⓐ [original meaning] **DIVIDE into parts, part, separate, sever**
ⓑ (become separated into parts) **DIVIDE, be divided, come apart**
ⓒ (group according to kind) **DIVIDE, separate, sort, classify**
a 分割する ぶんかつする divide up, partition, split
分譲 ぶんじょう sale (of land) in lots, lotting-out
分析 ぶんせき analysis
分離 ぶんり separation, split
分担 ぶんたん partial charge, allotment
分解 ぶんかい disintegration, disassembly; analysis, decomposition
分数 ぶんすう fraction
処分する しょぶんする dispose of, deal [do] with; punish
区分する くぶんする divide, section, subdivide
b 分野 ぶんや field, sphere, area
分裂する ぶんれつする be divided, split, break up, be disrupted
分科会 ぶんかかい sectional subcommittee
分散 ぶんさん dispersion, breakup, divergence; variance
分立 ぶんりつ separation, segregation
分泌 ぶんぴつ(=ぶんぴ) secretion
分布 ぶんぷ distribution
c 分類する ぶんるいする classify, divide into classes
分別する ぶんべつする classify, distinguish; divide, separate

❷ (parcel out) **DIVIDE (up), distribute, apportion, share**
分配する ぶんぱいする divide, distribute, allot
配分 はいぶん distribution, division, allocation
按分(=案分)する あんぶんする divide [distribute] proportionally

❸ⓐ **branch off, branch out, diverge**
ⓑ [also prefix] **branch, offshoot**

a 分岐する ぶんきする diverge, branch off
分身 ぶんしん the other self, one's alter ego; branch, offshoot
b 分家 ぶんけ branch family, offshoot; setting up a branch family
分派 ぶんぱ branch, sect, denomination
分工場 ぶんこうじょう branch factory

❹ **tell apart, distinguish**

分別 ふんべつ discretion, prudence, judgment, good sense
不分明な ふぶんめいな obscure, vague
検分する けんぶんする inspect, examine, survey

❺ⓐ (segment of a whole) **PART, division, section, piece**
ⓑ [also suffix] (equal portion of a whole) **PART, fraction**
ⓒ (constituent element) **PART, component**
ⓓ [also suffix] (allotted portion) **PART, share, portion, ration, helping**

a 分量 ぶんりょう quantity
部分 ぶぶん part, section, portion
半分 はんぶん half
積分 せきぶん integral calculus, integration
自分 じぶん self, oneself
b 三分の一 さんぶんのいち one third, a third part
c 分子 ぶんし molecule; numerator
成分 せいぶん ingredient, component, constituent
d 言い分 いいぶん one's say [claim]; objection, complaint
余分 よぶん excess, extra, surplus
取り分 とりぶん one's share, portion
四人分 よにんぶん four helpings [servings]
一年分 いちねんぶん a year's supply

❻ [also suffix] **content, percentage; quantity, amount**

水分 すいぶん water, moisture, humidity
糖分 とうぶん sugar content
アルコール分 あるこーるぶん percentage of alcohol
栄養分 えいようぶん nutritious substance, nourishment
増加分 ぞうかぶん increment

❼ⓐ **relative degree, extent, rate**
ⓑ **condition, state**

a 十分(=充分)な じゅうぶんな full, enough, sufficient; plentiful
多分 たぶん probably, perhaps, maybe
幾分 いくぶん partially, somewhat, in a way
随分 ずいぶん extremely, considerably ("as much as one pleases")
存分に ぞんぶんに to one's heart's content, freely
b 何分 なにぶん anyway, anyhow; please
気分 きぶん feeling, mood; atmosphere

❽ⓐ (one's share in something) **one's PART, one's duty**
ⓑ **one's lot, one's place, one's station in life, social position**
ⓒ [also suffix] **assumed relation between one person and another**

a 本分 ほんぶん one's duty, one's part
職分 しょくぶん duty, vocation
名分 めいぶん justification, just cause
b 身分 みぶん social position [standing]; circumstances; rank, identity
性分 しょうぶん nature, temperament
天分 てんぶん one's natural gift [endowment]
応分の おうぶんの appropriate, reasonable (in view of one's position), within one's power [means]
c 親分 おやぶん boss, big shot
兄弟分 きょうだいぶん sworn brother, pal

❾ⓐ (unit of time) **MINUTE**
ⓑ (unit of angular measure) **MINUTE**
ⓒ **counter for MINUTEs**

a 分速 ふんそく speed per minute
毎分 まいふん every minute
bc 二十分 にじっぷん 20 minutes
北緯五度十分 ほくいごどじっぷん 5°10′ north latitude

❿ **time, short period of time**

当分 とうぶん for some time, for a while, for the present, temporarily
時分 じぶん time, hour; season, time of the year
夜分 やぶん nighttime, night, evening

⓫ **equinox**

分点 ぶんてん equinox
春分 しゅんぶん vernal equinox

⓬ⓐ **tenth PART of an equally divided whole**
ⓑ 1/10 of 10%: **0.01**

a 四分六 しぶろく ratio of four to six
砂糖三分に水七分 さとうさんぶにみずしちぶ three parts of sugar to seven of water
b 三割五分 さんわりごぶ 35%
百分率 ひゃくぶんりつ percentage

⓭ *bu*: unit equiv. to one-tenth of other units:
ⓐ 1/10 of a degree of temperature
ⓑ former unit of length equiv. to approx. 3 mm or 1/10 of a *sun* (寸)
ⓒ unit of footwear size equiv. to 2.4 mm or 1/10 of a *mon* (文)

a 三十七度五分 さんじゅうななどごぶ 37.5°C (said of bodily temperature)
b 一寸五分 いっすんごぶ 1 *sun* 5 *bu*
五分刈り ごぶがり short cropping, closely cropped hair

c 九文三分の足袋 くもんさんぶのたび *tabi* (digitated socks) of 9 *mon* 3 *bu* (in size)

⓮ *fun*: former unit of weight equiv. to 0.375 g or 1/10 of a momme (匁)

八匁五分 はちもんめごふん 8 momme 5 *fun*

⓯ *bu*: former monetary unit equiv. to 1/4 of a *ryo* (両)

一分銀 いちぶぎん silver coin worth 1 *bu*

⓰ thickness

分厚い ぶあつい bulky, massive

INDEPENDENT

【ぶん 分】

① **amount, quantity**

残った分 のこったぶん amount left over

② (allotted portion) **PART, share, portion, ration, helping**

自分の分 じぶんのぶん one's share [own]

③ⓐ (one's share in something) one's **PART**, one's duty

ⓑ one's lot, one's place, one's station in life, social position

a 己の分を尽くす おのれのぶんをつくす do one's part [duty]

b 分に過ぎた ぶんにすぎた undue, above one's means [station]

④ⓐ relative degree, extent, rate

ⓑ condition, state

a この分で行けば このぶんでいけば if things go on at this rate

b この分では このぶんでは as things are

⑤ kind, lot

前に買った分 まえにかったぶん the lot I bought earlier

【ふん 分】**MINUTE** (→ ❾ⓐ & ❾ⓑ); *fun* (→ ⓮)

分に直す ふんになおす convert into minutes

【ぶ 分】

①ⓐ degree of advantage

ⓑ [usu. 歩 ぶ 3071] degree of profit

a 分が悪い ぶがわるい be at a disadvantage, have no edge

b 分の良い仕事 ぶのいいしごと profitable job

② 0.01 (→ ⓬ⓑ)

③ *bu* (→ ⓭)

分迄読む ぶまでよむ read to the order of 1/10

④ thickness

分が薄い ぶがうすい be thin

⑤ *bu* (→ ⓯)

KUN

【わける 分ける】

①ⓐ **DIVIDE into parts, part, separate, sever**

ⓑ (group according to kind) **DIVIDE, separate, sort, classify**

ⓒ [sometimes also 別ける] (cause to separate) **PART, separate, set aside**

a 二つに分ける ふたつにわける divide into two

切り分ける きりわける cut and divide

b 項目別に分ける こうもくべつにわける classify by subject

見分ける みわける discriminate, distinguish

選り分ける よりわける sort out, classify

c 喧嘩を分ける けんかをわける separate quarreling persons

② (parcel out) **DIVIDE (up), distribute, apportion, share**

分け前 わけまえ share, portion

分け合う わけあう share (with a person)

③ **draw (with), end in a tie**

引き分け ひきわけ draw; drawn game [match]

【わけ 分け】[also suffix] **draw, drawn game**

一勝二敗一分け いっしょうにはいいちわけ one victory, two defeats, one draw

【わかれる 分かれる】

ⓐ (become separated into parts) **DIVIDE, be divided, come apart; disperse**

ⓑ **branch off, branch out, diverge**

a 分かれ わかれ branch, offshoot, fork

左右に分かれる さゆうにわかれる part right and left

b 分かれ道 わかれみち branch road, fork

【わかる 分かる】[sometimes also 判る or 解る]

①ⓐ (grasp the meaning of) **understand, comprehend, see**

ⓑ (be sympathetic toward) **understand, show understanding for (another's feelings)**

a 分かり わかり understanding

分かり難い わかりにくい hard to understand, incomprehensible, unintelligible

b 分からず屋 わからずや obstinate person, hardhead

物分かりの良い ものわかりのよい understanding, sensible

②ⓐ **know, tell, recognize**

ⓑ **be made known, be brought to light**

a 先の事は分からない さきのことはわからない cannot tell what will happen in the future

b 身元が分かる みもとがわかる be identified

③ appreciate

音楽が分かる おんがくがわかる have an ear [appreciation] for music

【わかつ 分かつ】

① **DIVIDE, separate**

分かち難い わかちがたい inseparable

② **distinguish, discriminate**

昼夜を分かたず ちゅうやをわかたず day and night, by day and night

③ [sometimes also 頒つ] **distribute (things among people)**

分かち合う わかちあう share (with others)

SPECIAL READINGS

大分県 おおいたけん Oita Prefecture

SYNONYMS

❶ separate

割 DIVIDE → 2284
分 DIVIDE → 2466
解 TAKE APART → 1913
析 ANALYZE → 1072
別 SEPARATE → 1434
離 SEPARATE → 2364
隔 partition → 0827

❷ distribute

配 DISTRIBUTE → 1853
頒 DISTRIBUTE WIDELY → 1318
分 DIVIDE → 2466

❸ⓐ diverge

岐 DIVERGE → 0285
分 branch off → 2466

ⓑ branch

支 BRANCH → 2473
分 branch → 2466

❹ discriminate

識 DISCRIMINATE → 2070
弁 distinguish → 2497
分 tell apart → 2466

❺ part

分 PART → 2466
部 SECTION → 2111
局 LIMITED PART → 3800
片 FRAGMENT → 4272

❻ quantity and number

量 QUANTITY → 3119
嵩 BULK → 2927
積 size → 1579
額 AMOUNT → 2273
分 content → 2466
数 NUMBER → 2245
勢 strength → 3542

❼ⓐ degree

程 EXTENT → 1524
度 DEGREE → 3844
分 relative degree → 2466

❽ⓐ responsibility

務 DUTY → 1505
任 duty → 0057
責 RESPONSIBILITY → 3115
分 one's part → 2466

❾ⓐ short time periods

頃 moment → 0163
瞬 INSTANT → 1594
秒 SECOND → 1462
分 MINUTE → 2466
時 hour → 1155
暫 SHORT WHILE → 3553

【わかる】

① know and understand

知 KNOW → 1446
通 know thoroughly → 3855
得 gain understanding of → 0577
分かる understand → 2466
解 understand → 1913
諒 UNDERSTAND → 1982
了 COMPREHEND → 4157
悟 AWAKE TO → 0502
惺 AWAKE TO → 0709

USAGE

❶【わける】

分ける

①ⓐ divide into parts, part, separate, sever
ⓑ (group according to kind) divide, separate, sort, classify
ⓒ [sometimes also 別ける] (cause to separate) part, separate, set aside
② (parcel out) divide (up), distribute, apportion, share
③ draw (with), end in a tie

別ける

[usu. 分ける] (cause to separate) part, separate, set aside

❷【わかれる】

分かれる

ⓐ (become separated into parts) divide, be divided, come apart; disperse
ⓑ branch off, branch out, diverge

別れる

ⓐ separate, part from, bid farewell
ⓑ separate (from one's spouse), divorce

❸【わかれ】

分かれ

branch, offshoot, fork

別れ

separation, parting, leave-taking, farewell

❹【わかる】

分かる

[sometimes also 判る or 解る]

①ⓐ (grasp the meaning of) understand, comprehend, see
ⓑ (be sympathetic toward) understand, show understanding for (another's feelings)
②ⓐ know, tell, recognize
ⓑ be made known, be brought to light
③ appreciate

判る
[usu. 分かる, sometimes also 解る] same as 分かる
解る
[usu. 分かる, sometimes also 判る] same as 分かる

❺【わかつ】
分かつ
① divide, separate
② distinguish, discriminate
③ [sometimes also 頒つ] distribute (things among people)
頒つ
[usu. 分かつ] distribute (things among people)

❻【ぶ】
分
①ⓐ degree of advantage
ⓑ [usu. 歩] degree of profit
② 1/10 of 10%: 0.01
③ *bu*: unit equiv. to one-tenth of other units:
ⓐ 1/10 of a degree of temperature
ⓑ former unit of length equiv. to approx. 3 mm or 1/10 of a *sun* (寸)
ⓒ unit of footwear size equiv. to 2.4 mm or 1/10 of a *mon* (文)
④ thickness
⑤ *bu*: former monetary unit equiv. to 1/4 of a *ryo* (両)
歩
① [sometimes also 分] percentage, commission
② *bu*: unit of sq. measure equiv. to approx. 3.3 sq. m or 36 sq. *shaku* (尺), used esp. for measuring fields or farms

HOMOPHONES
わける 別 SEPARATE → 1434
わかれる 別 SEPARATE → 1434
わかれ 別 SEPARATE → 1434
わかる
判 JUDGE → 1441
解 TAKE APART → 1913
わかつ 頒 DISTRIBUTE WIDELY → 1318

NOTE
➡ see COMPOUND FORMATION for 案分 あんぶん → 案 2824

父 2467

▶**FATHER**
フ ちち
Ⓝ 父 Ⓒ 父 fù fǔ
2-2-2

88	Jōyō-2	U7236
父	S4-4-0	F0227

radical variant → see 父 at 2469

ノ ハ 父 父
1 2 3 4

COMPOUNDS
❶ⓐ (male parent) **FATHER**
ⓑ **FATHER-in-law**
ⓒ (term of respect for old man) **FATHER**, elder
a 父母 ふぼ father and mother, parents
父兄 ふけい one's father and older brothers; guardians
父子 ふし father and child
祖父 そふ grandfather
b 義父 ぎふ father-in-law; foster father, stepfather
岳父 がくふ one's wife's father
c 父老 ふろう elder
❷ (title of respect for priests) **FATHER**
神父 しんぷ priest, Father
教父 きょうふ Father (of the Church); godfather

KUN
【ちち 父】 (male parent) **FATHER; founder, originator;** *Christianity* **Father, Lord**
父親 ちちおや father
原子物理学の父 げんしぶつりがくのちち father of atomic physics
在天の父 ざいてんのちち our Father in heaven

SPECIAL READINGS
お父さん おとうさん daddy, papa
伯父 おじ uncle (older than one's parent)
叔父 おじ uncle (younger than one's parent)
お祖父さん▲ おじいさん grandfather

SYNONYMS
❶ⓐ **parents**
親 PARENT → 2264
父 FATHER → 2467
母 MOTHER → 4287
❷ **clergymen**
僧 BONZE → 0180
坊 Buddhist priest → 0274
尼 BUDDHIST NUN → 3767
父 FATHER → 2467

公 2468

▶**PUBLIC**
コウ ク▲ おおやけ ㊔ きみ ひろ ただし あきら まさ ただ とも きん たか
Ⓒ 公 gōng
2-2-2

12	Jōyō-2	U516C
八	S4-2-2	F0167

ノ 八 公 公
1 2 3 4

COMPOUNDS
❶ⓐ [original meaning] (relating to the public) **PUBLIC, open**
ⓑ the **PUBLIC, society, community**

a 公演 こうえん public performance
公園 こうえん park, public garden
公開 こうかい opening to the public
公害 こうがい environmental pollution
公表 こうひょう public [official] announcement, proclamation
公判 こうはん (public) trial [hearing]
公聴会 こうちょうかい public [open] hearing
公選 こうせん public election, election by popular vote
公募 こうぼ appeal for public subscription
公論 こうろん public opinion, consensus
公言する こうげんする declare in public; profess
b 公共 こうきょう public society, community
公会堂 こうかいどう town [public] hall
公衆 こうしゅう the public

❷ⓐ [also prefix] (relating to the government) **PUBLIC, formal, official, governmental, state-managed**
ⓑ **PUBLIC office, government office**
a 公務員 こうむいん public service personnel, government worker
公社 こうしゃ public corporation
公団 こうだん public corporation
公式の こうしきの formal, official
公認 こうにん official recognition [approval], authorization, certification
公営 こうえい public management
公立の こうりつの public (institution)
公約 こうやく public pledge [promise]
公定 こうてい official, officially fixed
b 公邸 こうてい official residence
公文書 こうぶんしょ official document
公報 こうほう public [official] report [bulletin]
奉公 ほうこう public duty [service]; domestic service, apprenticeship

❸ [also prefix] *math* **common, general**
公式 こうしき formula; formality
公算 こうさん probability
公約数 こうやくすう common divisor
公倍数 こうばいすう common multiple

❹ **impartial, fair, unbiased, just**
公明 こうめい fairness, justice
公正 こうせい justice, fairness, impartiality
公平 こうへい impartiality, fairness

❺ⓐ nobleman, lord, prince
ⓑ honorific title after names of noblemen
a 公子 こうし young nobleman
公家(=公卿) くげ court noble
公方 くぼう Imperial Court; shogun, tycoon
b 徳川公 とくがわこう Prince Tokugawa

❻ⓐ duke
ⓑ title after names of dukes
a 公爵 こうしゃく duke, prince
b ヨーク公 よーくこう Duke of York

❼ⓐ term of respect used in addressing one's elders or peers
ⓑ suffix expressing intimacy or derision
a 貴公 きこう you
尊公 そんこう you
主人公 しゅじんこう head, master; hero, heroine
b 熊公八公 くまこうはちこう Tom, Dick and Harry

❽ abbrev. of 公明党 こうめいとう: Komeito (Clean Government Party)
社公連合 しゃこうれんごう coalition of the Socialist Party and the Komeito

INDEPENDENT

【こう 公】state, government; **PUBLIC**, society; you (used on very formal occasions)

KUN

【おおやけ 公】**the PUBLIC, the government; Imperial Court; public affairs**
公の おおやけの public, formal, official, governmental
公にする おおやけにする publish, announce officially

SYNONYMS

❶ⓐ **public**
公 PUBLIC → 2468
俗 POPULAR → 0119
巷 the public → 3097
ⓑ **the people**
民 PEOPLE → 3770
衆 the multitude(s) → 3325
庶 the masses → 3880
公 PUBLIC → 2468

❶ⓑ **society**
社 SOCIETY → 1042
世 WORLD → 4308
公 PUBLIC → 2468

❷ⓑ **public offices**
省 MINISTRY → 3100
庁 GOVERNMENT AGENCY → 3768
府 government office → 3824
公 public office → 2468
署 PUBLIC-SERVICE STATION → 3223
局 public service office → 3800
所 office → 1056

❸ **widespread**
普 WIDESPREAD → 2919
遍 ALL OVER → 3890
通 common → 3855
公 common (math) → 2468

❹ impartial

公 impartial → 2468
平 equal → 4291

❺ⓐ nobility

爵 RANK OF NOBILITY → 3143
公 nobleman → 2468
侯 FEUDAL LORD → 0109

ⓑ titles of address

氏 COURTESY TITLE → 3669
兄 familiar title (seniors) → 2676
君 FAMILIAR TITLE (peers) → 3974
嬢 Miss → 0936
様 FORMAL TITLE → 1332
殿 FORMAL HONORIFIC TITLE → 2247
師 honorific title (clergymen) → 1680
公 honorific title (noblemen) → 2468

❻ noblemen

公 duke → 2468
侯 marquis → 0109
伯 COUNT → 0067
子 viscount → 4196
男 baron → 3147

NOTE

➡ see USAGE note at 広 3769

父

2469

2-2-2

▸FATHER

フ ちち

88	Nonstandard	U7236
父	S4-4-0	F0000

traditional form → see 父 at 2467

RADICAL

chichi 'father' (爺), used in characters related to fathers or someone like a father

---

冗

2470

2-2-2

▸REDUNDANT

ジョウ

Ⓒ 冗 rǒng

14	Jōyō	U5197
冖	S4-2-2	F1647

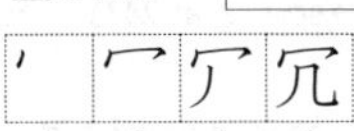

COMPOUNDS

❶ⓐ (exceeding what is necessary) **REDUNDANT, superfluous, useless, unnecessary**

ⓑ (needlessly repetitive) **REDUNDANT,** verbose, diffuse, tedious

a 冗長な じょうちょうな verbose, redundant, prolix
冗費 じょうひ unnecessary expenses
冗員 じょういん useless member of the staff
冗談 じょうだん joke

b 冗漫な じょうまんな diffuse, verbose, prolix
冗語 じょうご redundant word, verbiage, superfluity

❷ [also 饒 2280] abundant, plentiful, rich

冗舌 じょうぜつ garrulity, loquacity

SYNONYMS

❶ⓐ exceeding and excess

過 EXCEED → 3891
超 SURPASS → 4107
越 GO BEYOND → 4108
濫 EXCESSIVE → 0990
余 EXCESS → 2535
剰 SURPLUS → 2233
冗 REDUNDANT → 2470

COMPOUND FORMATION

【冗談 じょうだん】

冗談 'joke' refers to useless or redundant (冗 ❶ⓐ) talk (談).

冗

2471

2-2-2

▸YONKASHIRA

122	Radical	U34C1
网	S4-4-0	F0000

radical variant → see 网 at 3708

殳

2472

2-2-2

▸RUMATA, HOKOZUKURI

79	Radical	U6BB3
殳	S4-4-0	F0000

RADICAL

rumata or ***hokozukuri*** 'club' (段 殺 殿), used in characters related to beating or killing

---

支

2473

2-2-2

▸BRANCH
▸SUPPORT

シ ささ(える) つか(える)▴ ㊔ はせ

Ⓝ 支 Ⓒ 支 zhī

65	Jōyō-5	U652F
支	S4-4-0	F0328

radical variant → see 支 at 2474

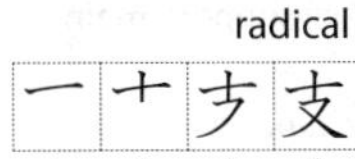

COMPOUNDS

❶ⓐ [sometimes also 枝 1073] (something structurally analogous to a branch) **BRANCH, offshoot**

ⓑ BRANCH off, diverge

ⓒ [original meaning, now archaic] **BRANCH,** twig

a 支店 してん branch (office), branch (store)
支局 しきょく branch office
支部 しぶ branch office
支社 ししゃ branch office

b 支流 しりゅう tributary, branch
支線 しせん branch line; spur
支離滅裂 しりめつれつ incoherence, inconsistency, disruption

❷ⓐ (bear the weight of) **SUPPORT, prop up, hold up**
ⓑ (provide with aid) **SUPPORT, maintain**

a 支柱 しちゅう prop, stay, support
支点 してん fulcrum, point of support
支索 しさく stay
b 支持 しじ support, maintenance, backing
支援 しえん support, backing, aid

❸ⓐ **pay out, disburse, defray**
ⓑ **allocate, distribute, provide**

a 支出 ししゅつ expenditure, disbursement, outgo
支払う しはらう pay
収支 しゅうし incomings and outgoings, earnings and expenses
b 支給 しきゅう provision, supply; allowance, grant; payment
支度する したくする arrange, prepare; [original meaning, now archaic] measure, estimate

❹ **control, regulate**

支配する しはいする control, manage, govern

❺ China

支那 しな China
南支 なんし South China
駐支の ちゅうしの resident in China

❻ used phonetically for *shi,* esp. in the transliteration of foreign words

切支丹 きりしたん early Christianity in Japan; Jesuitism

❼ sign of the Oriental zodiac

十二支 じゅうにし the twelve signs of the Oriental zodiac
干支 かんし sexagenary cycle

❽ obstruction, hindrance

支障 ししょう hindrance, obstacle, difficulty

KUN

【ささえる 支える】(bear the weight of) **SUPPORT, prop up, hold up;** (provide with aid) **support, maintain; check**

支え ささえ prop, fulcrum, stay, support
屋根を支える やねをささえる hold up the roof
一家を支える いっかをささえる support one's family

【つかえる 支える】

ⓐ **get clogged, get blocked, get caught [stuck]; be occupied**
ⓑ (of words) **be at a loss for, stumble over**

a 差し支える さしつかえる be hindered [impeded]

SYNONYMS

❶ⓐ **branch**

支 BRANCH → 2473
分 branch → 2466

❷ⓐ **bear**

負 BEAR (on the back) → 2594
荷 carry on shoulder → 2840
担 BEAR ON SHOULDER → 0376
支 SUPPORT → 2473

ⓑ **support**

支 SUPPORT → 2473
擁 SUPPORT → 0949
扶 LEND SUPPORT TO → 0291
賛 back up → 3484

❸ⓐ **pay**

払う PAY → 0225
納 PAY (to the authorities) → 1652
済 settle accounts → 0634
支 pay out → 2473
賦 INSTALLMENT → 1992
償 RECOMPENSE → 0199

❺ **China**

華 CHINA → 2841
漢 CHINESE → 0808
支 China → 2473
中 People's Republic of China → 4262
胡 NATIVES OF ANCIENT CHINA → 1467
台 Taiwan → 2498
唐 Cathay → 3867
呉 KINGDOM OF WU → 3156

COMPOUND FORMATION

【支度 したく】

支度する 'arrange, prepare, etc.', which consists of 支 ❸ⓑ 'allocate' and 度 'measure', originally meant to measure but this meaning is now archaic.

攴

2474
2-2-2

▶**BRANCH**
▶**SUPPORT**
シ ささ(える) つか(える) ㊔ はせ

65	Nonstandard	U652F
支	S4-4-0	F0000

traditional form → see 支 at 2473

RADICAL

shinyō or ***jūmata*** 'branch', used in characters related to branching out or holding between
Right variant: 支 ***shinyō*** or ***jūmata***

攴

2475
2-2-2

▶***BOKUZUKURI, TOMATA***

66	Radical	U6534
支	S4-4-0	F0000

RADICAL

bokuzukuri or ***tomata*** 'strike' (敲×), used in characters related to striking, forcing or other actions

Right variant: 攵 ***nobun*** (政 放 整)

允

▸GIVE CONSENT

イン ㊔ まさ みつ のぶ まこと みつる ただし よし すけ ちか

Ⓒ 允 yǔn

2476

2-2-2

10	Names	U5141
儿	S4-2-2	F2480

COMPOUNDS

❶ **GIVE CONSENT, comply, accede to, permit**

允可 いんか compliance, permission, assent

允許 いんきょ compliance, permission, assent

❷ [archaic] truly, greatly

允文允武 いんぶんいんぶ be versed in the literary and military arts

❸ [archaic] sincerity

允恭 いんきょう sincerity, courtesy

SYNONYMS

❶ **permit**

許 PERMIT → 1862

免 license → 2565

准 grant permission → 0143

允 GIVE CONSENT → 2476

予

▸IN ADVANCE

ヨ あらかじ(め)▲ かね(て)▲ ㊔ やすし

Ⓝ 豫 Ⓒ 予 yǔ yú

2477

2-2-2

6△	Jōyō-3	U4E88
亅	S4-1-3	F0398

1	2	3	4
㇇	マ	予 (stroke 3)	予

COMPOUNDS

❶ [sometimes also 預 1317] **IN ADVANCE, pre-, fore-, beforehand, previously, prior to, preliminary**

予言 よげん prediction, forecast

予知 よち premonition, foreknowledge

予報 よほう forecast, prediction

予測 よそく estimate, forecast, prediction

予算 よさん budget; estimate, calculation

予期 よき expectation, anticipation, hope

予価 よか probable [predetermined] price

予約 よやく reservation, preengagement; subscription

予定 よてい schedule, plan, prearrangement; expectation; estimate

予備 よび reserve, spare; preparation, preliminaries

予科 よか preparatory course

予防 よぼう prevention, protection, precaution

予習 よしゅう preparation (of one's lessons)

予感 よかん premonition, hunch

❷ **waver, vacillate; delay, dally**

猶予する ゆうよする postpone, delay, extend; hesitate

❸ abbrev. of 伊予 いよ, old name for Ehime Prefecture

予讃線 よさんせん Yosan Line (Ehime-Kagawa Railway)

INDEPENDENT

【よ 予】

① [also 余 2535] I, myself, the present writer—historically used as a formal first person pronoun but now only used pompously

予の辞書に不可能の文字は無い よのじしょにふかのうのもじはない In my dictionary, there's no such word as impossible

② abbrev. of 予価 よか: probable [predetermined] price

予五百円 よごひゃくえん probable price 500 yen

KUN

【あらかじめ 予め】**IN ADVANCE**, beforehand, previously, ahead of time

予め計画を立てる あらかじめけいかくをたてる plan ahead

【かねて 予て】previously, already, before; for a long time, (from) before

SYNONYMS

❶ **before**

前 BEFORE → 2819

先 AHEAD → 3046

予 IN ADVANCE → 2477

【よ】

① **first person pronouns**

私 I (*polite*) → 1432

我 SELF → 4362

己 ONESELF → 4188

身 ONE'S PERSON → 4368

僕 I (*familiar*) → 0185

俺 I (*intimate*) → 0124

吾 I (*elegant*) → 3060

予 I (*pompous*) → 2477

余 I (*pompous*) → 2535

麿 I (*archaic*) → 3949

朕 IMPERIAL WE → 1185

自 SELF → 4338

USAGE

【よげん】

予言

prediction, forecast

預言
prophecy (in Christianity)

NOTE

➡ see NOTE at 余 2535

亠 𠆢 八 冂 几 十 ⺊ 厶 マ 【𠂉】 𠂉 亻 メ 九

午 2478 2-2-2

▶NOON

ゴ うま▲

Ⓒ 午 wǔ

24	Jōyō-2	U5348
十	S4-2-2	F0873

ノ 𠂉 𠂉 午 (1 2 3 4)

COMPOUNDS

❶ **NOON, noontime**

午睡 ごすい nap, afternoon sleep
午前 ごぜん morning, forenoon
午後 ごご afternoon
正午 しょうご noon, noontime

❷ seventh sign of the Oriental zodiac: the Horse—(time) 11 a.m.-1 p.m., (direction) south, (season) May (of the lunar calendar) (→see APPENDIX 8)

子午線 しごせん meridian
端午 たんご festival on the 5th of May (of the lunar calendar)

KUN

【うま 午】 seventh sign of the Oriental zodiac: the Horse (→❷)

SYNONYMS

❶ **noon**

午 NOON →2478
昼 midday →3841

❷ **horse**

馬 HORSE →4086
駒 HORSE (*elegant*) →2298
駿 FLEET STEED →2304
午 the Horse →2478

HOMOPHONES

うま 馬 HORSE →4086

NOTE

➡ see USAGE note at 馬 4086
➡ see COMPOUND FORMATION for 子午線 しごせん →子 4196

攵 2479 2-2-2

▶*NOBUN*

66	Radical	U6535
攵	S4-4-0	F0000

radical variant →see 攴 at 2475

气 2480 2-2-2

▶*KIGAMAE*

84	Radical	U6C14
气	S4-4-0	F0000

RADICAL

kigamae 'vapor' (気 氣 氛×), used in characters related to vapor or gas

乞 2-2-2

incorrect stroke-count
➡ see 2-2-1: 𠂉 at 2457

欠 2481 2-2-2

▶**LACK**

ケツ ケン▲ か(ける) か(く) か(かす)

Ⓝ 缺 欿 Ⓒ 缺 quē 欠 qiàn

76	Jōyō-4	U6B20
欠	S4-4-0	F1021

ノ 𠂊 ケ 欠 (1 2 3 4)

RADICAL

akubi 'yawn' (次 欧 歌), used in characters related to opening or closing of the mouth

COMPOUNDS

❶ⓐ **LACK, be short of, be deficient**
ⓑ **LACK, shortage, deficiency**

a 欠乏 けつぼう lack, shortage, scarcity
欠如 けつじょ lack, shortage
欠員 けついん vacant position
不可欠な ふかけつな indispensable
b 欠損 けっそん deficit, deficiency; loss
ガス欠 がすけつ running out of gas

❷ⓐ **incompleteness, imperfection, defect**
ⓑ **incomplete, imperfect, defective**

a 欠点 けってん weak point, defect
完全無欠 かんぜんむけつ absolute perfection
b 欠陥 けっかん defect, fault, deficiency

❸ⓐ **be absent from**
ⓑ missing, omitted

a 欠席 けっせき absence, nonattendance
欠勤 けっきん absence (from work)
b 欠字 けつじ omitted word, blank type

❹ **vacancy, vacant post, absence**

補欠 ほけつ filling a vacancy; substitute, alternate
出欠 しゅっけつ attendance

❺ neglect, fail in

欠礼 けつれい failure to pay one's compliments

❻ [formerly also 歇 2243] take a rest

間欠 かんけつ intermittence

❼ [archaic] yawn

欠伸 けんしん yawning and stretching

INDEPENDENT

【けつ 欠】**LACK**, shortage, deficiency; absence; vacancy, vacant post

欠を補う けつをおぎなう supply a lack, bridge a gap

KUN

【かける 欠ける】**LACK, be short of, be deficient; be vacant [missing]; wane; be broken off**

欠けてゆく月 かけてゆくつき waning moon

欠けら かけら fragment, chip

欠けたコップ かけたこっぷ chipped cup

常識に欠ける じょうしきにかける lack in common sense

一人欠けている ひとりかけている one person missing

【かく 欠く】**LACK, want, be short of; neglect, omit; break off, chip**

事欠く ことかく lack, be in need of

義理を欠く ぎりをかく fail in one's social duties

コップの縁を欠く こっぷのふちをかく chip the rim of a glass

【かかす 欠かす】**miss, fail to attend**

欠かせない かかせない indispensable

SPECIAL READINGS

欠伸▲ あくび yawn

SYNONYMS

❶ⓐ terms of negation

不 NOT (negation) → 4242

非 IS NOT (contrariety) → 1101

無 WITHOUT (nonexistence) → 2648

没 lacking in → 0305

欠 LACK → 2481

否 OR NOT → 3058

未 NOT YET → 4318

莫 NOT → 2839

勿 DO NOT → 3661

❷ⓐ faults and flaws

難 fault → 2310

短 shortcoming → 1515

疵 DEFECT → 4067

陥 defect → 0547

欠 incompleteness → 2481

❸ⓑ omit

漏 omit → 0860

脱 leave out by mistake → 1225

抜く leave out → 0290

欠 missing → 2481

NOTE

➡ see USAGE note at 不 4242

★ 欠 けん 'yawn' was originally a different character from 缺 けつ 'lack, etc.'. 欠 now replaces 缺, the latter which is considered a variant form of 欠.

乏 2-2-2

incorrect classification

➡ see 2-1-3: ⼃ at 2432

爻 **2482** 2-2-2

▶*MEME*

89	Radical	U723B
爻	S4-4-0	F0000

RADICAL

meme 'crisscross', used for character classification

Variant: 爻 *meme* (俎× 爽 爾)

爻 **2483** 2-2-2

▶*MEME*

89	Radical	U723B
爻	S4-4-0	F0000

radical variant → see 爻 at 2482

卆 **2484** 2-2-2

▶**GRADUATE**

ソツ

24	Nonstandard	U5346
十	S4-2-2	F0000

handwritten form → see 卒 at 2549

玄 **2485** 2-2-3

▶**PROFOUND**

ゲン ㊔もと はるか はる

Ⓒ 玄 xuán

95	Jōyō	U7384
玄	S5-5-0	F0767

1	2	3	4	5
丶	亠	𠫓	玄	玄

RADICAL

gen 'dark' (率), used in characters related to darkness

COMPOUNDS

❶ PROFOUND, abstruse, mystic, occult, mysterious, esoteric

玄妙な げんみょうな abstruse, occult, mysterious

玄関 げんかん entrance, (front) door

幽玄な ゆうげんな subtle and profound, quiet and beautiful, occult

❷ unpolished

玄米 げんまい unpolished rice

玄麦 げんばく unpolished barley

❸ black tinged with red or yellow

玄武岩 げんぶがん basalt, whin(stone)

玄黄 げんこう [rare] heaven and earth; black and yellow silk (offered to gods)

❹ great-great-grandchild

玄孫 げんそん great-great-grandchild

INDEPENDENT

【げん 玄】profundity, occultness

SPECIAL READINGS

玄人 くろうと expert, master hand; prostitute

SYNONYMS

❶ **profound**

玄 PROFOUND → 2485

幽 deep hidden → 3731

奥 inmost → 3503

深 DEEP → 0636

淵 DEEP AND VAST → 0811

COMPOUND FORMATION

【玄関 げんかん】

玄関 'entrance, (front) door' originally referred to the gateway (関) to the esoteric (玄 ❶) teachings of Buddhism.

立

2486

2-2-3

▶**STAND**
▶**ESTABLISH**

リツ リュウ た(つ) -た(つ) た(ち)- た(てる) -た(てる) た(て)- たて- -た(て) -だ(て) -だ(てる) りっとる▲

Ⓒ 立 𥫗

117	Jōyō-1	U7ACB
立	S5-5-0	F0045

1 2 3 4 5

RADICAL

tatsu 'stand' (競 章 竪), used in characters related to standing

Left variant: 𧺆× *tatsuhen* (端 竦× 竭×)

COMPOUNDS

❶ⓐ [original meaning] **STAND, stand up, stand erect**

ⓑ **STAND on one's own legs, be independent**

a 立像 りつぞう standing image, statue

立腹する りっぷくする get angry, lose one's temper

立身する りっしんする establish oneself in life

立候補 りっこうほ candidacy

起立 きりつ standing up, rising

直立する ちょくりつする stand erect [upright], rise perpendicularly

b 自立する じりつする become independent, establish oneself

独立する どくりつする become independent, stand on one's own legs [feet]

❷ **STANDpoint, stand, position**

対立 たいりつ opposition, antagonism

中立 ちゅうりつ neutrality; neutralization

孤立する こりつする be isolated, stand alone

❸ⓐ **ESTABLISH, set up, erect, found, institute**

ⓑ **ESTABLISHed by (the nation, municipality, etc.)**

a 設立 せつりつ establishment, foundation, setting up

樹立する じゅりつする establish, found

創立する そうりつする establish, organize, start

確立 かくりつ establishment

建立 こんりゅう erection, building (as a temple)

b 市立の しりつ(=いちりつ)の municipal, city

私立の しりつ(=わたくしりつ)の private, nongovernmental

会社立の かいしゃりつの established by the company

❹ **ESTABLISH regulations, enact, lay down**

立証 りっしょう proof, demonstration, substantiation

立法 りっぽう legislation, lawmaking

立案する りつあんする make a plan, devise, draft

立志 りっし fixing one's aim in life

❺ **exist, come into existence**

成立 せいりつ coming into existence, materialization; formation, organization; conclusion

両立 りょうりつ coexistence, compatibility

存立 そんりつ existence, subsistence

❻ begin

立春 りっしゅん first day of spring

立冬 りっとう first day of winter

❼ **cubic, three-dimensional**

立体 りったい solid (body), cube

立方体 りっぽうたい cube

立米 りゅうべい cubic meter

❽ (help someone) ascend the throne

立太子 りったいし official investiture of the Crown Prince

擁立する ようりつする give backing to, support, help (to the throne)

❾ abbrev. of 立教大学 りっきょうだいがく: Rikkyo University

立明戦 りつめいせん Rikkyo-Meiji (baseball) game

❿ **unclassified compounds**

立派な りっぱな fine, excellent, admirable

KUN

【たつ 立つ】

①ⓐ **STAND, stand up, rise**

ⓑ **STAND out, be conspicuous**

ⓒ (stand on one's own legs) **ESTABLISH** oneself, begin life

ⓓ **STAND** up to (criticism)

a 立場 たちば standpoint

立ち上がる たちあがる stand up, rise to one's feet; take action
立ち直る たちなおる regain one's footing, recover; (of the market) improve
b 目立つ めだつ stand out, be conspicuous
引き立つ ひきたつ be set off, improve in appearance, contrast well
c 文を以て立つ ぶんをもってたつ live by the pen
d 面目が立つ めんもく(=めんぼく)がたつ save one's face
② [formerly 起つ] **rise (to action), rouse oneself**
祖国の為に立つ そこくのためにたつ rise to the rescue of one's country
③ begin an action:
ⓐ [sometimes also 発つ] **start (on a journey), leave, depart**
ⓑ (of seasons) begin, come
ⓒ (of the market) open
a 先立つ さきだつ precede, go before; die before
旅立ち たびだち departure
b 秋立つ日 あきたつひ first day [beginning] of autumn
c 市が立つ日 いちがたつひ market day
④ (of birds) **take wing, rise in the air**
飛び立つ とびたつ rise in the air, take flight
⑤ evaporate, rise (in vapor), (of smoke) go up
立ち上る たちのぼる go up, rise, ascend
⑥ (of waves) run high
波立つ海 なみだつうみ choppy sea
⑦ (of plans or policies) be formed, be **ESTABLISH**ed; be decided; make sense, hold water
言い訳が立たない いいわけがたたない admit no excuse
⑧ be proficient in
筆が立つ ふでがたつ wield a facile pen
⑨ **STAND in good stead, be useful**
役立つ やくだつ be of use, serve a purpose
⑩ (of rumors) spread
噂が立っている うわさがたっている A rumor is about
⑪ get excited
苛立つ いらだつ be irritated, be nettled, be impatient
浮き立つ うきたつ be enlivened, be exhilarated
腹が立つ はらがたつ get angry, take offense
⑫ *math* give, make (an integral quotient)
十六を五で割ると三が立って一が余る じゅうろくをごでわるとさんがたっていちがあまる Sixteen divided by five gives three with a remainder of one
⑬ (of arrows or thorns) stick into, run into
喉に骨が立った のどにほねがたった A bone got caught in the throat

【-たつ -立つ】
① **verbal suffix indicating intensity of action or beginning**
煮立つ にたつ boil up, begin to boil
② **take form, be formed**
成り立つ なりたつ consist of; be realized, be concluded, materialize
生い立ち おいたち one's upbringing, one's childhood
③ **unclassified compounds**
夕立ち ゆうだち sudden evening shower
顔立ち かおだち looks, features

【たち- 立ち-】
① [also prefix] **STANDing**
立ち読みする たちよみする browse (in a bookstore)
立ち小便 たちしょうべん urinating outdoors (while standing)
立ち話 たちばなし chatting while standing up
② **emphatic verbal prefix**
立ち戻る たちもどる return, come back
立ち入る たちいる enter, trespass
立ち会う たちあう attend, take part in, witness
立ち去る たちさる leave, depart; quit
立入禁止 たちいりきんし no trespassing [entry]
立ち退く たちのく leave, depart, evacuate; take refuge; vacate, leave, quit

【たてる 立てる】
① **STAND, make stand, erect, raise, set**
立て掛ける たてかける lean against, set against
旗を立てる はたをたてる hoist a flag
候補者を立てる こうほしゃをたてる put up a candidate
②ⓐ **ESTABLISH, set up, form**
ⓑ **ESTABLISH (laws), enact, lay (plans), develop (a theory)**
a 計画を立てる けいかくをたてる make plans
b 立て直す たてなおす rally, make over; reorganize
献立 こんだて menu, preparations
仮説を立てる かせつをたてる build up a hypothesis
③ **ESTABLISH** oneself, support oneself
身を立てる みをたてる make a success in life
生計を立てる せいけいをたてる make a living
④ look up to, respect
夫を立てる おっとをたてる treat one's husband with due respect
引き立てる ひきたてる favor; set off; march (a prisoner) off
⑤ⓐ do one's duty, be loyal
ⓑ save face
a 義理を立てる ぎりをたてる do one's duty, be faithful
b 顔を立てる かおをたてる save (a person's) face

⑥ raise (one's voice)
音を立てるな おとをたてるな Don't make a noise
⑦ set (a rumor) afloat
噂を立てられる うわさをたてられる be gossiped about
⑧ make an oath
誓いを立てている ちかいをたてている be under a vow
⑨ **render (distinguished services)**
手柄を立てる てがらをたてる do a meritorious deed
⑩ sharpen (a saw)
目立をする めたてをする set the teeth of a saw
⑪ [usu. 閉てる] shut (as a paper sliding door)
戸を立てる とをたてる shut a door
⑫ [also 点てる] make tea
抹茶を立てる まっちゃをたてる prepare powdered tea
⑬ **make use of**
役立てる やくだてる put to use, make use of, turn to account
⑭ become angry
腹を立てる はらをたてる get angry, take offense

【-たてる -立てる】
① emphatic verbal suffix:
ⓐ **repeatedly, incessantly; intensely**
ⓑ up, about (as in *stir up* and *noise about*)
a 攻め立てる せめたてる make an incessant onslaught
b 見立てる みたてる diagnose, judge; select
騒ぎ立てる さわぎたてる make a great fuss
書き立てる かきたてる write up
② **assemble, make**
組み立てる くみたてる assemble, construct, erect
仕立てる したてる tailor; prepare

【たて- 立て-, 立-】
①ⓐ **STANDing**
ⓑ [formerly also 竪] **vertical, upright**
a 立て看板 たてかんばん standing signboard
b 立て型ピアノ たてがたぴあの upright piano
② leading
立て役者 たてやくしゃ leading actor; leader
③ **unclassified compounds**
立て替える たてかえる pay for another; pay in advance

【-たて -立て】
① [also suffix] **STAND, standing object**
傘立て かさたて umbrella stand
衝立て ついたて single-leaf screen
② [verbal suffix] fresh from, hot from, wet from
外国から帰り立ての人 がいこくからかえりたてのひと a man just returned from overseas
焼き立ての魚 やきたてのさかな fish hot from the oven
③ counter for successive victories [defeats]
三立てを食う さんたてをくう lose three games straight

【-だて -立て】
① **counter for:**
ⓐ **number of carriage horses or boat oars**
ⓑ **number of films in a multifeature movie**
a 四頭立ての馬車 よんとうだてのばしゃ carriage and four
b 二本立ての映画 にほんだてのえいが double feature movie
② doing on purpose, doing something uncalled for
隠し立て かくしだて keeping secret, concealment

【-だてる -立てる】 **suffix for forming verbs from nouns**
荒立てる あらだてる aggravate, make serious
証拠立てる しょうこだてる prove, substantiate

【りっとる 立】 liter
五十立 ごじゅうりっとる 50 liters

SYNONYMS

❶ **assume upright position**
立 STAND → 2486
起 RISE → 4099
❷ **standpoint**
地 one's ground → 0236
立 standpoint → 2486
❸ **found**
立 ESTABLISH → 2486
設 SET UP → 1863
置 found → 3222
❿ **capacity units**
勺 *SHAKU* (0.018 liters) → 3650
合 *go* (0.18 liters) → 2511
立 liter → 2486
升 *SHO* (1.8 liters) → 4266
斗 *TO* (18 liters) → 3671
石 *koku* (180 liters) → 3689

【たてる】
① **raise**
揚 RAISE HIGH → 0722
掲 PUT UP → 0597
挙 RAISE → 3106
上 raise → 4212
起 raise up → 4099
擡 RAISE (one's head) → 0972
立てる STAND → 2486
拾う PICK UP → 0454

【たて-】
① **vertical**

縦 VERTICAL → 1783
竪- VERTICAL → 3516
垂 perpendicular → 4382
立て- standing → 2486
直 STRAIGHT → 3649

USAGE

❶【たつ】

立つ

①ⓐ stand, stand up, rise
ⓑ stand out, be conspicuous
ⓒ (stand on one's own legs) establish oneself, begin life
ⓓ stand up to (criticism)
② [formerly 起つ] rise (to action), rouse oneself
③ begin an action:
ⓐ [sometimes also 発つ] start (on a journey), leave, depart
ⓑ (of seasons) begin, come
ⓒ (of the market) open
④ (of birds) take wing, rise in the air
⑤ evaporate, rise (in vapor), (of smoke) go up
⑥ (of waves) run high
⑦ (of plans or policies) be formed, be established; be decided; make sense, hold water
⑧ be proficient in
⑨ stand in good stead, be useful
⑩ (of rumors) spread
⑪ get excited
⑫ *math* give, make (an integral quotient)
⑬ (of arrows or thorns) stick into, run into

建つ

be built, be erected, be established

起つ

[now usu. 立つ] rise (to action), rouse oneself

発つ

[now usu. 立つ] start (on a journey), leave, depart

経つ

pass, elapse, go by

❷【たてる】

立てる

① stand, make stand, erect, raise, set
②ⓐ establish, set up, form
ⓑ establish (laws), enact, lay (plans), develop (a theory)
③ establish oneself, support oneself
④ look up to, respect
⑤ⓐ do one's duty, be loyal
ⓑ save face
⑥ raise (one's voice)
⑦ set (a rumor) afloat
⑧ make an oath
⑨ render (distinguished services)
⑩ sharpen (a saw)
⑪ [usu. 閉てる] shut (as a paper sliding door)
⑫ [also 点てる] make tea
⑬ make use of
⑭ become angry

建てる

ⓐ build, construct, erect, put up
ⓑ establish (a nation)

点てる

[also 立てる] make tea

閉てる

[sometimes also 立てる] shut (as a paper sliding door)

❸【たて】

立て-

①ⓐ standing
ⓑ [formerly also 竪] vertical, upright
② leading
③ unclassified compounds

縦

①ⓐ length, height
ⓑ [sometimes also 竪-] vertical, upright
② warp

竪

① [now usu. 立て-] vertical, upright
② [now usu. 縦] length, height

建て

[in compounds] business commitment, sales contract

❹【-だて】

-立て

① counter for:
ⓐ number of carriage horses or boat oars
ⓑ number of films in a multifeature movie
② doing on purpose, doing something uncalled for

-建て

[also suffix]
① way of building, method of construction
② currency of exchange
③ average number of pages (of a newspaper or magazine)

HOMOPHONES

たつ

建 BUILD → 3834
起 RISE → 4099
発 START → 3174
経 PASS THROUGH → 1687

たてる

建 BUILD → 3834
点 POINT → 2587
閉 CLOSE → 4116

たて-

縦 VERTICAL → 1783

竪 VERTICAL →3516
建 BUILD →3834
-だて 建 BUILD →3834

COMPOUND FORMATION

❶【立腹 りっぷく】
立腹する 'get angry, etc.', literally to have one's bowels (腹) stand up (立 ❶ⓐ), derives from 腹が立つ はらがたつ 'get angry'.

❷【献立 こんだて】
献立 'menu, preparations' originally referred to making plans (立てる ②ⓑ) for offering wine (献) to guests.

市 2487

▶CITY
▶MARKET
シ いち

Ⓒ 市 shì

2-2-3

50	Jōyō-2	U5E02
巾	S5-3-2	F0186

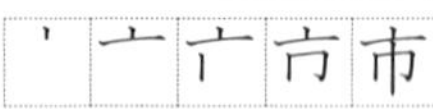
1 2 3 4 5

COMPOUNDS

❶ⓐ CITY, town
ⓑ [also prefix] (unit of local administration) **CITY, municipality**
ⓒ **suffix after names of cities**

a 市井の出来事 しせいのできごと events on the street
市内 しない city
市民 しみん citizens, townsmen
市外 しがい city outskirts, suburbs
b 市長 しちょう mayor
市営 しえい municipal management
市役所 しやくしょ municipal office, city hall
都市 とし cities, urban communities
同市 どうし same city
c 大阪市 おおさかし Osaka city
高松市 たかまつし Takamatsu city

❷ⓐ [original meaning] **MARKET, fair**
ⓑ *economics* **MARKET**

a 市場 しじょう market, mart
市販 しはん marketing
b 市況 しきょう market conditions, tone of the market
市価 しか market price

INDEPENDENT

【し 市】CITY (→❶ⓐ & ❶ⓑ)

KUN

【いち 市】**MARKET, fair; crowded quarters**
市場 いちば market, marketplace
市を成す いちをなす have a crowd of people
競り市 せりいち auction sale
闇市 やみいち black market
我楽多市 がらくたいち rummage sale

SYNONYMS

❶ **cities and towns**
都 METROPOLIS →2120
京 CAPITAL →2546
畿 CAPITAL →4408
市 CITY →2487
町 TOWN →1430

❷ **market**
市 MARKET →2487
場 market →0678

主 2488

▶MAIN
▶MASTER
シュ ス シュウ ぬし おも あるじ ㊔ かず つかさ ちから

2-2-3

3	Nonstandard	U4E3B
丶	S5-1-4	F0000

traditional form →see 主 at 2437

令 2489

▶COMMAND
レイ ㊔ よし りょう のり

Ⓒ 令 lìng lǐng

2-2-3

9	Jōyō-4	U4EE4
人	S5-2-3	F0728

1 2 3 4 5

COMPOUNDS

❶ [also suffix] [original meaning] **COMMAND, order, decree**
命令 めいれい command, orders; edict, decree
司令 しれい commanding; commander, commandant
軍令 ぐんれい military command
辞令 じれい written appointment; wording, phraseology
指令 しれい order, instruction
訓令 くんれい instructions, (official) orders, directive
号令する ごうれいする give an order, command
動員令 どういんれい mobilization order(s)

❷ [also suffix] **ordinance, law, act**
政令 せいれい government ordinance, cabinet order
法令 ほうれい laws and ordinances, statute
戒厳令 かいげんれい martial law

❸ⓐ [also prefix] [honorific] your honorable
ⓑ good, fair

a 令嬢 れいじょう daughter; young lady
令夫人 れいふじん Mrs., madam, your wife
b 令名 れいめい fair name, good repute

巧言令色 こうげんれいしょく flattery, honeyed words

❹ *hist* administrator, governor, chief

県令 けんれい (former) prefectural governor

❺ [also 齢 2390] age, years

年令 ねんれい age, years

→ see 齢 2390 for other compounds

INDEPENDENT

【れい 令】COMMAND, order

【れいする 令する】COMMAND, order, dictate

SYNONYMS

❶ **command**

令 COMMAND → 2489

麾 COMMAND → 3937

命 ORDER → 2553

❷ **laws and rules**

法 LAW → 0391

律 LAW → 0433

典 CANON → 3253

憲 CONSTITUTION → 3001

令 ordinance → 2489

則 RULE → 1831

矩 RULE → 1475

規 REGULATION → 1231

紀 discipline → 1628

❸ⓐ **honorific prefixes**

御 GENERAL HONORIFIC TERM → 0703

貴 YOUR HONORABLE → 3220

尊 your honorable → 2920

令 your honorable → 2489

❺ **age**

齢 AGE → 2390

令 age → 2489

年 years → 2528

歳 AGE SUFFIX → 3131

才 AGE SUFFIX → 4218

寿 life span → 4372

仝

2490

2-2-3

▶**SAME**

ドウ　おな(じ)

9	Nonstandard	U4EDD
人	S5-2-3	F0000

alternative form → see 同 at 3707

尒

2491

2-2-3

▶**THAT**

ジ　ニ　なんじ　㊔ ちか　しか　みつる　あきら

42	Nonstandard	U5C12
小	S5-3-2	F0000

traditional form → see 爾 at 4407

令

2492

2-2-3

▶**AGE**

レイ　よわい　とし

9	Nonstandard	U4EE4
人	S5-2-3	F0000

alternative form → see 齢 at 2390

写

2493

2-2-3

▶**COPY**

シャ　うつ(す)　うつ(る)

Ⓝ 寫 冩 Ⓒ 写 xiě

14△	Jōyō-3	U5199
冖	S5-2-3	F0516

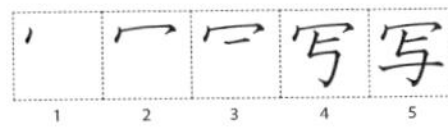

COMPOUNDS

❶ (reproduce an original, esp. by writing) **COPY, make a copy, transcribe, reproduce, imitate**

写経 しゃきょう copying of a sutra, copied sutra

写生 しゃせい sketching [drawing] from nature; portrayal

写本 しゃほん manuscript, written copy

謄写 とうしゃ copy, reproduction, mimeograph

複写 ふくしゃ copy, duplication

書写 しょしゃ transcription, copying, handwriting

模写(=摸写) もしゃ copying, tracing, reproduction

❷ (depict in pictures or words) **portray, picture, depict, describe**

写真 しゃしん photograph

写実 しゃじつ objective description; realism

描写 びょうしゃ depiction, description; portrayal; drawing

❸ⓐ **shoot, photograph, take pictures**

ⓑ project (an image), show (a film), screen

a 写植 しゃしょく phototypesetting

特写 とくしゃ exclusive shooting [photographing] (for a magazine)

接写 せっしゃ close-up photograph

b 映写 えいしゃ projection

試写 ししゃ preview, private showing

KUN

【うつす 写す】*vt*

① **COPY, make a copy, transcribe, reproduce, imitate**

写し うつし copy, transcript, duplicate, imitation

生き写し いきうつし close resemblance

② portray, picture, depict, describe, express

山水を写した絵 さんすいをうつしたえ picture representing a landscape

③ **take a picture, photograph, shoot**

写真を写す しゃしんをうつす take a picture, photograph

【うつる 写る】*vi*

亠 人 冂 冖 刀 十 卜 厶 又 亠 マ 𠂉

① (of pictures) **be taken, come out**
写り うつり print, impression
この写真に写っている人 このしゃしんにうつっているひと the man in this photograph
② **be seen through**
透けて写る すけてうつる be seen through
③ appear upon, be impressed upon (a surface in the original form)
紙の裏に写った字 かみのうらにうつったじ letter imprinted from the next page (by chance)

SYNONYMS

❶ **copy**
写 COPY → 2493
謄 TRANSCRIBE → 1398
複 duplicate → 1565
拓 copy by rubbing → 0375

❶ **write**
書 WRITE → 3292
筆 write → 3317
写 COPY → 2493
記 WRITE DOWN → 1843
紀 record in writing → 1628
控える note down → 0600
録 RECORD → 2186
登 register → 3208
註 ANNOTATE → 1893

❷ **describe**
叙 DESCRIBE → 1834
抒 DESCRIBE → 0295
描 DEPICT → 0591
写 portray → 2493

❸ⓐ **photograph**
撮 PHOTOGRAPH → 0910
写 shoot → 2493

ⓑ **project**
映 PROJECT → 1104
写 project → 2493

USAGE

❶【うつす】
写す
vt
① copy, make a copy, transcribe, reproduce, imitate
② portray, picture, depict, describe, express
③ take a picture, photograph, shoot
映す
① reflect, mirror
② project (a motion picture)
移す
vt
①ⓐ shift, move, transfer
ⓑ transfuse (liquids or colors)
ⓒ divert, turn, direct
② transmit (a disease)

❷【うつる】
写る
vi
① (of pictures) be taken, come out
② be seen through
③ appear upon, be impressed upon (a surface in the original form)
映る
①ⓐ be reflected, be imaged, be mirrored
ⓑ be projected, be on (TV)
② match, suit, be becoming
移る
vi
① move (to a new house)
② shift, change, pass
③ be infected with; be contagious
④ (of odors) soak in

HOMOPHONES

うつす
映 REFLECT → 1104
移 SHIFT → 1508
うつる
映 REFLECT → 1104
移 SHIFT → 1508
うつり
映 REFLECT → 1104
移 SHIFT → 1508

NOTE

➡ see also USAGE note at 映 1104

召

2494
2-2-3

▶**SUMMON**
ショウ め(す)
Ⓒ 召 zhào shào

30	Jōyō	U53EC
口	S5-3-2	F1540

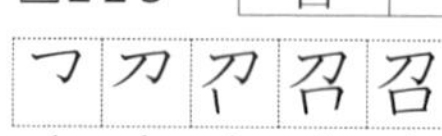

COMPOUNDS

● [original meaning] **SUMMON (esp. one's inferior), call together, convene**
召集する しょうしゅうする call together
召還する しょうかんする recall, call back
召喚 しょうかん summons, citation
応召者 おうしょうしゃ draftee

KUN

【めす 召す】[honorific] **SUMMON, call, send for; wear, put on; take (as a bath, vehicle or food); be pleased with**
召使 めしつかい servant

お召し物 おめしもの dress, clothes
召し上がる めしあがる eat, drink
思し召し おぼしめし your (honorable) wishes
お気に召しましたか おきにめしましたか Is it pleasing to you, sir [madam]?

SYNONYMS

● **call and invite**
呼ぶ CALL → 0324
喚 CALL → 0666
召 SUMMON → 2494
招 INVITE → 0374

古

2495
2-2-3

▶OLD
コ　ふる(い)　ふる-　-ふる(す)
Ⓒ 古 gǔ

30	Jōyō-2	U53E4
口	S5-3-2	F0301

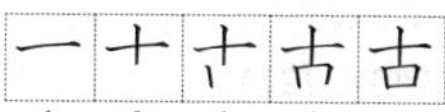
1 2 3 4 5

COMPOUNDS

ⓐ [original meaning] (not new) **OLD**
ⓑ [also prefix] (of the remote past) **OLD, ancient, obsolete**
ⓒ **OLD** times, ancient times

a 古書 こしょ old book, rare book
古風 こふう old style; old customs
稽古 けいこ practice, rehearsal; learning
b 古典 こてん classics; old book
古跡 こせき historic remains, ruins
古代 こだい ancient times, antiquity, remote ages
古語 こご obsolete word; old proverb
古文書 こもんじょ ancient documents; paleography
古今 ここん ancient and modern times
古希 こき three score and ten, seventy years of age
考古学 こうこがく archaeology
復古 ふっこ revival (of the ancient regime), restoration
c 中古 ちゅうこ Middle Ages; secondhand [used] goods

KUN

【ふるい　古い】**OLD, antiquated, outdated, ancient**
古 ふる old thing, used article
古さ ふるさ oldness, antiqueness
古びる ふるびる grow old; look old
古臭い ふるくさい antiquated, old-fashioned; obsolete
古本 ふるほん old book, secondhand book
中古 ちゅうぶる(=ちゅうこ) secondhand [used] goods

【ふる-　古-】[prefix] **OLD, secondhand**
古新聞 ふるしんぶん old newspapers

【-ふるす　-古す】[verbal suffix] **become or cause to become OLD**
使い古す つかいふるす wear out (a thing) by use
言い古した言葉 いいふるしたことば hackneyed saying

SYNONYMS

● **old**
古 OLD (not new) → 2495
老 OLD (not young) → 3963
故 OLD (of the past) → 1466
旧 old → 0014

NOTE

➡ see COMPOUND FORMATION for 古希 こき → 希 2543

古

2-2-3

incorrect stroke-count
➡ see 2-2-4: 十 at 2517

占

2496
2-2-3

▶OCCUPY
▶DIVINE
セン　し(める)　うらな(う)　㊔ うら
Ⓒ 占 zhān zhàn

25	Jōyō	U5360
卜	S5-2-3	F0959

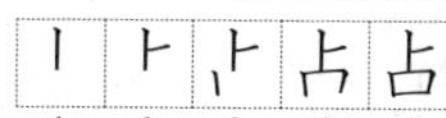
1 2 3 4 5

COMPOUNDS

❶ **OCCUPY, hold, seize, take (up)**
占拠 せんきょ occupation, exclusive possession
占有する せんゆうする occupy, take possession of
占領地 せんりょうち occupied area
独占 どくせん exclusive possession, monopoly

❷ [original meaning] **DIVINE, tell fortune, augur**
占星術 せんせいじゅつ astrology

KUN

【しめる　占める】**OCCUPY, hold, take (up); account for, amount to**
独り占め ひとりじめ monopoly, exclusive possession
買い占める かいしめる buy up
三割を占める さんわりをしめる account for [amount to] 30%

【うらなう　占う】[formerly also トう] **DIVINE, tell (a person's) fortune, augur**
占い うらない divination, fortunetelling
占い師 うらないし diviner, fortuneteller
星占い ほしうらない astrology

SYNONYMS

❶ **occupy**
占 OCCUPY → 2496
拠 occupy → 0369

領 take possession of → 1567
専 take exclusive possession of → 3272

❷ **divine**
占 DIVINE → 2496
卜 DIVINE → 4174
易 divination → 3064

USAGE

❶【うらなう】
占う
[formerly also 卜う] divine, tell (a person's) fortune, augur
卜う
[now usu. 占う] divine, tell (a person's) fortune, augur

❷【うらない】
占い
[formerly also 卜] divination, fortunetelling
卜
[now usu. 占い] divination, fortunetelling

HOMOPHONES

うらなう 卜 DIVINE → 4174
うらない 卜 DIVINE → 4174

弁

▶**SPEAK ELOQUENTLY**
▶**VALVE**

ベン わきま(える)▲

2497

2-2-3

N 辨 瓣 辯 辦
C 辨 辩 辫 弁 biàn
办 瓣 bàn

55	Jōyō-5	U5F01
廾	S5-3-2	F0804

ム ム 厶 弁 弁
1 2 3 4 5

COMPOUNDS

❶ [formerly 辯 2092]
ⓐ **SPEAK ELOQUENTLY, orate, talk**
ⓑ **speech, talk**

a 弁士 べんし speaker, talker; film interpreter
雄弁 ゆうべん eloquence, fluency
熱弁 ねつべん fervent speech, passionate eloquence
能弁家 のうべんか eloquent speaker, orator
答弁する とうべんする reply, answer; defend oneself

b 弁舌 べんぜつ speech
多弁な たべんな talkative
訥×弁 とつべん slowness of speech

❷ [suffix] (regional speech) **dialect, accent**
東北弁 とうほくべん Tohoku dialect [accent]
関西弁 かんさいべん Kansai dialect [accent]

❸ [formerly 辯 2092]
ⓐ **argue, debate, dispute**
ⓑ **argue for [in favor of], speak (up) for, defend, explain, justify**

a 弁論 べんろん discussion, argument; oral proceedings
弁護士 べんごし lawyer, attorney
詭弁 きべん sophism, sophistry
代弁する だいべんする speak [act] for another; pay by proxy

b 弁明 べんめい vindication, explanation, defense
弁解 べんかい explanation, vindication, justification, excuse
抗弁する こうべんする make a plea, demur, defend oneself

❹ [formerly 瓣 2075] [also suffix]
ⓐ (machine part) **VALVE**
ⓑ *anat* **VALVE**

a 安全弁 あんぜんべん safety valve
排気弁 はいきべん exhaust valve

b 弁膜 べんまく valve (in internal organs)
半月弁 はんげつべん semilunar valve

❺ [formerly 辨 2029 or 辦 2028] **distinguish, discriminate, differentiate, discern**
弁別する べんべつする discriminate, distinguish
弁証法 べんしょうほう dialectic
思弁 しべん speculation
勘弁する かんべんする pardon, forgive; tolerate

❻ [formerly 辨 2029 or 辦 2028]
ⓐ [formerly 辦 2028] **dispose of, manage, attend to**
ⓑ **pay, defray**

a 弁務官 べんむかん commissioner
弁理士 べんりし patent attorney
弁当 べんとう box lunch, lunch, picnic lunch
合弁 ごうべん joint management [venture]

b 弁済 べんさい repayment, payment, settlement
弁償する べんしょうする compensate, indemnify
自弁する じべんする pay one's own expenses
支弁する しべんする pay, defray, disburse

❼ [formerly also 辨 2029 or 辦 1609] abbrev. of 弁当 べんとう: **box lunch, lunch**
駅弁 えきべん station lunch
腰弁で こしべんで carrying lunch with one

❽ [formerly 辮 2085] plait, braid
弁髪 べんぱつ pigtail, queue

❾ [formerly 瓣 2075] **petal (of a flower)**
花弁 かべん(=はなびら) petal
離弁花 りべんか schizopetalus flower

❿ⓐ [original meaning, now archaic] conical cap worn by military officers in ancient times
ⓑ [archaic] military officer of low rank

b 武弁 ぶべん soldier

INDEPENDENT

【べん 弁】speech, tongue; **VALVE** (→❹); *bot* petal, valve

【べんじる(=べんずる) 弁じる(=弁ずる)】speak, make a speech; argue for [in favor of]

弁じ立てる べんじたてる speak eloquently, talk volubly

KUN

【わきまえる 弁える】discern, discriminate; know, bear in mind

弁えの無い わきまえのない undiscerning, indiscreet

SYNONYMS

❶ⓐ **speak and say**

言 SAY → 2440
語る TELL → 1944
談 TALK → 1975
喋 TALK → 0665
諷 INSINUATE → 2005
謂う REFER TO → 2007
云 say → 2430
曰 SAY THAT → 3757
話 SPEAK → 1928
口 give mouth to → 4189
申す SPEAK HUMBLY → 4319
述 STATE → 3816
陳 SET FORTH → 0656
弁 SPEAK ELOQUENTLY → 2497

❷ **language**

語 LANGUAGE → 1944
弁 dialect → 2497

❸ **argue and discuss**

議 DISCUSS → 2078
争 CONTEND → 2523
論 ARGUE → 1981
弁 argue (for) → 2497
諏 CONSULT → 1985

❹ⓐ **stoppers**

栓 STOPPER → 1171
弁 VALVE → 2497

❺ **discriminate**

識 DISCRIMINATE → 2070
弁 distinguish → 2497
分 tell apart → 2466

COMPOUND FORMATION

【勘弁 かんべん】

勘弁する 'pardon, forgive; tolerate' originally meant to give careful thought to a matter (勘) and distinguish (弁 ❺) between good and bad. How this is related to the current meaning 'pardon, etc.' is not clear.

NOTE

➡ see COMPOUND FORMATION for 弁当 べんとう → 当 2701

台 2498

2-2-3

▶**STAND**
▶**COUNTER FOR VEHICLES**

ダイ タイ

Ⓝ 臺 Ⓒ 台 tái tāi

30△	Jōyō-2	U53F0
口	S5-3-2	F0354

COMPOUNDS

❶ [also suffix]

ⓐ (structure for placing on) **STAND, pedestal, rack, table, support, mount**

ⓑ (elevated structure) **STAND, platform**

a 台座 だいざ pedestal, base, stand
燭台 しょくだい candlestick, candlestand
楽譜台 がくふだい music stand
鏡台 きょうだい dressing table
荷台 にだい carrier, bed (of a truck)
寝台 しんだい bed, sleeping berth
流し台 ながしだい sink, washstand
実験台 じっけんだい testing bench; subject of an experiment

b 閲兵台 えっぺいだい reviewing stand
証人台 しょうにんだい witness stand
滑り台 すべりだい (playground) slide; launching platform

❷ [also suffix] [original meaning] (elevated structure commanding a wide view) **observatory, lookout, tower, tall building**

天文台 てんもんだい astronomical observatory
気象台 きしょうだい meteorological observatory
灯台 とうだい lighthouse; oil-lamp stand
露台 ろだい balcony
見張り台 みはりだい lookout

❸ⓐ (elevated land structure) **heights, hill, terrace, tableland**

ⓑ suffix after names of elevated places such as heights or hills

a 台地 だいち plateau, tableland
高台 たかだい high ground, hill, height

b 駿河台 するがだい Surugadai Hill

❹ⓐ **COUNTER FOR VEHICLES (as automobiles or bicycles)**

ⓑ **counter for machines or mechanical devices (as sewing machines, televisions, telephones, etc.)**

a 台数 だいすう number of vehicles [machines]
自動車十台 じどうしゃじゅうだい ten cars

b ミシン六台 みしんろくだい six sewing machines

❺ suffix indicating numerical range: **level, mark**

千円台 せんえんだい the 1000-yen level (between 1000 and 2000 yen)

五十点台の成績 ごじゅってんだいのせいせき school mark in the 50's (between 50 and 60)

大台 おおだい (stock) 100-yen unit, high level (of stock prices)

❻ⓐ (physical) **base, framework, base material**

ⓑ (nonphysical) **basis, foundation**

a 台紙 だいし paste board, ground paper

車台 しゃだい car body, chassis

土台 どだい foundation, base, basis; utterly

b 台帳 だいちょう ledger, register

台無しになる だいなしになる be spoiled, come to nothing

❼ **stage; the STAND, the theater**

台本 だいほん playbook, script, scenario

台辞 だいじ one's lines, words

舞台 ぶたい stage, the boards

❽ **Taiwan, Formosa**

台湾 たいわん Taiwan

台中関係 たいちゅうかんけい relations between Taiwan and China

台北 たいほく Taipei

❾ [formerly 颱 たい 4138] **typhoon**

台風 たいふう typhoon

❿ **kitchen**

台所 だいどころ kitchen

御台 みだい wife of a shogun or a highest-ranking nobleman

⓫ⓐ [honorific] you, your

ⓑ honorific term referring to the emperor or the gods

a 台顔 だいがん your face

尊台 そんだい you

b 台覧 たいらん inspection by the emperor or extremely noble persons

⓬ trapezoid

台形 だいけい trapezoid

円錐台 えんすいだい circular truncated cone

⓭ office or official of the central government

台閣 たいかく(=だいかく) Cabinet; tall building

鎮台 ちんだい garrison (in Meiji era)

⓮ [also 擡 たい 0972] raise (one's head), lift

台頭する たいとうする raise one's head; come to the fore

⓯ counter for 16-page units in printing

二台 にだい two 16-page units

INDEPENDENT

【だい 台】 **STAND, pedestal, rack, table, mount; platform**

台に載せる だいにのせる set on a stand

【たい 台】 Taiwan; abbrev. of 台風 たいふう: typhoon

SPECIAL READINGS

台詞▲ せりふ one's lines, words

SYNONYMS

❶ **flat supports**

台 STAND → 2498

座 SEAT → 3868

壇 PLATFORM → 0932

棚 SHELF → 1238

架 rack → 3178

床 BED → 3805

❶ **tables and stands**

卓 TABLE → 2561

机 DESK → 1014

几 DESK → 4156

台 STAND → 2498

❷ **tall buildings**

閣 TALL MAGNIFICENT BUILDING → 4128

楼 TALL BUILDING → 1284

塔 TOWER → 0683

台 observatory → 2498

❸ⓐ **hills**

丘 HILL → 4307

畝 RIDGE → 1857

岡 HILL → 3719

台 heights → 2498

坂 SLOPE → 0275

阪 slope → 0321

塚 MOUND → 0675

阜 MOUND → 3254

陵 high mound → 0660

稜 RIDGE → 1545

❹ⓐ **vehicle**

車 VEHICLE → 4367

輌 VEHICLE → 2000

乗 vehicle → 4393

輪 wheeled vehicle → 1999

駕 CARRIAGE → 3236

輿 PALANQUIN → 3626

台 COUNTER FOR VEHICLES → 2498

❽ **China**

華 CHINA → 2841

漢 CHINESE → 0808

支 China → 2473

中 People's Republic of China → 4262

胡 NATIVES OF ANCIENT CHINA → 1467

台 Taiwan → 2498

唐 Cathay → 3867

呉 KINGDOM OF WU → 3156

❾ **wind**

風 WIND →3730
嵐 STORM →2898
颱 TYPHOON →4138
台 typhoon →2498
凪 CALM →3709
颯 SOUND OF GUSTING WIND →1563

USAGE

【-だい】

-台

suffix indicating numerical range: **level, mark**

千円台 せんえんだい the 1000-yen level (between 1000 and 2000 yen)

五十点台の成績 ごじゅってんだいのせいせき school mark in the 50's (between 50 and 60)

-代

ⓐ suffix for range of a person's age in ten-year periods: **-ies**

ⓑ suffix indicating years spanning a specific period: **-ies, the…-hundreds**

二十代の男 にじゅうだいのおとこ a man in his twenties

千九百年代 せんきゅうひゃくねんだい the 1900's

★The above two suffixes are very similar in meaning and are easily confused. Study the equivalents and examples carefully.

圣

2499

2-2-3

▸PASS THROUGH
▸MANAGE

ケイ キョウ へ(る) た(つ) たていと
㊔ つね のぶ のり

32	Nonstandard	U5723
土	S5-3-2	F0000

alternative form →see 経 at 1687

圣

2500

2-2-3

▸PATH
▸DIAMETER

ケイ ㊔ みち

32	Nonstandard	U5723
土	S5-3-2	F0000

alternative form →see 径 at 0347

主

2-2-3

incorrect classification
➡ see 2-1-4: 丶 at 2437

矛

2501

2-2-3

▸HALBERD

ム ボウ* ほこ
Ⓒ 矛 máo

110	Jōyō	U77DB
矛	S5-5-0	F1818

1	2	3	4	5
フ	マ	予	予	矛

RADICAL

hoko 'lance' (矜×), used in characters related to lances, halberds or spears

COMPOUNDS

● [original meaning] **ancient Chinese weapon resembling a HALBERD or spear**

矛盾 むじゅん contradiction

KUN

【ほこ 矛】

ⓐ [sometimes also 鉾 or 戟] **ancient HALBERD or spear consisting of a long shaft and a double-edged blade**

ⓑ [formerly 戈] **arms**

a 矛先 ほこさき [sometimes also 鉾] spearhead; the aim (of an attack); the brunt (of an argument)

SYNONYMS

● **cutting weapons**

刀 SWORD (single-edged) →3642
剣 SWORD (double-edged) →2104
矛 HALBERD →2501
戟 HALBERD →2131
鉾 DECORATIVE HALBERD →2154
戈 DAGGER-AX →4274

USAGE

【ほこ】

矛

ⓐ [sometimes also 鉾 or 戟] **ancient halberd or spear consisting of a long shaft and a double-edged blade**

ⓑ [formerly 戈] **arms**

戟

[usu. 矛, sometimes also 鉾] **halberd**

鉾

decorative halberd

鋒

[usu. 矛, sometimes also 戟] **halberd**

戈

[now usu. 矛] **arms**

HOMOPHONES

ほこ

鉾 DECORATIVE HALBERD →2154
戈 DAGGER-AX →4274
戟 HALBERD →2131
鋒 POINT OF A BLADE →2172

COMPOUND FORMATION

【矛盾 むじゅん】

矛盾 'contradiction' derives from an ancient Chinese legend. Once upon a time there was a proud merchant who claimed that his halberd (矛) was so powerful that it could pierce any shield, and that his shield (盾) was so strong that it could repel any halberd in the world. Then came along a wise man and queried: "What happens if your irresistible halberd strikes against your impenetrable shield?" The merchant considered this dilemma at great length. At last he exclaimed: "Golly! That must be a contradiction!" In this way, 矛盾 came to mean contradiction for all ages to come.

矢

▸ARROW

シ や

Ⓒ 矢 shǐ

2502

2-2-3

111	Jōyō-2	U77E2
矢	S5-5-0	F0948

丿 𠂉 𠂊 午 矢
1 2 3 4 5

RADICAL

ya 'arrow' (矦×), used in characters related to arrows or handling of arrows

Left variant: 矢× *yahen* (知 短 矯)

COMPOUNDS

● [original meaning] **ARROW**

弓矢 きゅうし(=ゆみや) bow and arrow

一矢を報いる いっしをむくいる return a blow, retaliate

KUN

【や 矢】

①ⓐ **ARROW, dart**

ⓑ **wedge**

a 矢印 やじるし arrow (mark)

矢先 やさき arrowhead

毒矢 どくや poisoned arrow [dart]

② **used phonetically for *ya***

矢鱈×に やたらに indiscriminately; recklessly; thoughtlessly

矢張り(=矢っ張り) やはり(=やっぱり) as I thought, as expected; also; still; after all (is said and done)

SYNONYMS

● **projectiles and bombs**

弾 PROJECTILE → 0697

丸 round projectile → 4225

矢 ARROW → 2502

槍 SPEAR → 1329

爆 bomb → 1415

雷 explosive device → 3466

尓

▸THAT

ジ ニ なんじ ㊔ ちか しか みつる あきら

2503

2-2-3

42	Nonstandard	U5C13
小	S5-3-2	F0000

alternative form → see 爾 at 4407

亦

▸ALSO

エキ また

Ⓒ 亦 yì

2504

2-2-4

8	Names	U4EA6
亠	S6-2-4	F2775

KUN

【また 亦】[now usu. 又] [often preceded by も] **ALSO, too, as well**

彼も亦良い人だ かれもまたいいひとだ He is a nice man, too

私も亦 わたしもまた I also, me too

SYNONYMS

【また】

○ **additionally**

亦 ALSO → 2504

兼 CONCURRENTLY → 2850

又 also, and → 4158

而うして and → 2520

及び and → 4192

並びに and also → 2793

傍ら besides → 0166

尚 STILL → 2774

更に furthermore → 4355

且つ AS WELL → 4297

HOMOPHONES

また

又 AGAIN → 4158

復 RETURN TO → 0701

NOTE

➡ see USAGE note at 又 4158

亥

▸THE BOAR

ガイ い

Ⓝ 亥 Ⓒ 亥 hài

2505

2-2-4

8	Names	U4EA5
亠	S6-2-4	F3020

COMPOUNDS

● twelfth sign of the Oriental zodiac: **THE BOAR**—(time) 9-11 p.m., (direction) NNW, (season) October (of the lunar calendar) (→ see APPENDIX 8)

亥月 がいげつ October (of the lunar calendar)

KUN

【い 亥】twelfth sign of the Oriental zodiac: **THE BOAR** (→●)

亥の刻 いのこく 10 o'clock in the evening

SYNONYMS

● **swine**

豚 PIG → 1228

豕 SWINE → 4357

猪 WILD BOAR → 0652

亥 THE BOAR → 2505

HOMOPHONES

い 猪 WILD BOAR → 0652

NOTE

➡ see USAGE note at 猪 0652

衣

2506

2-2-4

▶GARMENT

イ エ▲ ころも きぬ▲ -ぎ▲

Ⓒ 衣 yī yì

145	Jōyō-4	U8863
衣	S6-6-0	F0879

Stroke order: 1–6

RADICAL

koromo 'clothes' (裁 袋 製), used in characters related to clothes or their qualities

Left variant: 衤 ***koromohen*** (補 被 袖)

Variant: 𧘇 ***koromo*** (裏 哀 衷)

COMPOUNDS

❶ⓐ **GARMENT, garments, clothing, clothes**

ⓑ **outer GARMENT, gown, (priestly) robe, surplice**

a 衣装(=衣裳) いしょう clothes, garment, dress, costume

衣類 いるい clothes, garments

衣服 いふく clothes, dress, clothing

衣料 いりょう clothing, garments

衣食住 いしょくじゅう food, clothing and shelter, the necessities of life

着衣 ちゃくい one's clothes [clothing]

b 衣鉢 いはつ(=えはつ) mysteries (of Buddhism or an art)

白衣 はくい(=びゃくえ) white robe [dress]; white coat

法衣 ほうい(=ほうえ) sacerdotal robe

僧衣 そうい priestly robe

天衣無縫 てんいむほう perfect beauty with no trace of artifice

胴衣 どうい jacket, vest

外衣 がいい outer garment

❷ outer coating

糖衣 とうい sugar coating

地衣 ちい lichen

INDEPENDENT

【い 衣】clothing, clothes

衣・食・住 いしょくじゅう food, clothing and shelter, the necessities of life

KUN

【ころも 衣】**outer GARMENT, gown, (priestly) robe; garments, clothing, clothes;** (outer covering) **garment, coating (as of tempura), frosting**

衣替え ころもがえ seasonal change of clothes

羽衣 はごろも robe of feathers

墨染めの衣 すみぞめのころも black robe (of a priest)

緑の衣で覆われた山 みどりのころもでおおわれたやま mountain covered with a garment of green

砂糖の衣 さとうのころも icing

【きぬ 衣】*elegant* **GARMENT**

衣擦れ きぬずれ rustling (of clothes)

濡れ衣 ぬれぎぬ false charge, unfounded suspicion

歯に衣を着せない はにきぬをきせない not mince matters

【-ぎ -衣】[usu. -着] outer **GARMENT**, clothes, wear

上衣 うわぎ outer garment, coat, jacket

SPECIAL READINGS

浴衣 ゆかた(=よくい) informal summer kimono, *yukata*

SYNONYMS

❶ **clothing**

服 CLOTHES → 1090

袴 FORMAL DIVIDED SKIRT → 1509

蓑 STRAW RAINCOAT → 2941

-着 wear → 4110

衣 GARMENT → 2506

装 DRESS → 3327

裳 DRESS → 3231

襤 RAGS → 1607

袈 BUDDHIST SURPLICE → 3200

裟 BUDDHIST CASSOCK → 3420

襖 overgarment → 1600

HOMOPHONES

きぬ 絹 SILK → 1721

-ぎ 着 PUT ON → 4110

NOTE

➡ see USAGE notes at 絹 1721 and 着 4110

➡ see COMPOUND FORMATION for

天衣無縫 てんいむほう → 縫 1781

衣鉢 いはつ(=えはつ) → 鉢 2144

充

2507

2-2-4

▶**FILL**

ジュウ あ(てる) み(たす)▲ ㊔ みつ みつる あつ まこと よし みち

Ⓝ 充 Ⓒ 充 chōng

10	Jōyō	U5145
儿	S6-2-4	F1075

Stroke order: 1–6

COMPOUNDS

❶ⓐ **FILL, become full**
ⓑ **FILL, fill up, stop up**

a 充填する じゅうてんする fill, fill up, plug; replenish
充満する じゅうまんする be full, be filled with, overflow
充分(=十分)な じゅうぶんな full, enough, sufficient; plentiful
拡充 かくじゅう expansion, amplification

b 充足 じゅうそく sufficiency
充実した じゅうじつした full, complete, rich

❷ **FILL up (a vacancy), make up for (a deficiency)**
充員 じゅういん reserves
補充する ほじゅうする supplement, replenish, recruit

❸ allot, assign, appropriate
充当する じゅうとうする allot, appropriate, earmark
充用する じゅうようする appropriate, earmark

KUN

【あてる 充てる】[sometimes also 当てる, but in compounds always 当てる] **allot, assign, appropriate**
金を借金の返済に充てる かねをしゃっきんのへんさいにあてる allot money to the payment of debts

【みたす 充たす】[usu. 満たす]
① **FILL** (up), pack
コップを充たす こっぷをみたす fill a glass
② **FILL**, fulfill, satisfy, meet (the demand)
条件を充たす じょうけんをみたす answer the requirement

SYNONYMS

❶ **fill**
充 FILL → 2507
湛 BE FULL OF → 0745
塡 FILL → 0777
満 fill → 0739
詰める STUFF → 1920

❷ **supplement**
補 SUPPLEMENT → 1529
足 supplement → 2714
給 SUPPLY → 1708
充 fill up (a vacancy) → 2507

❸ **allot**
充 allot → 2507
当 assign → 2701

HOMOPHONES

あてる
当 THE PRESENT → 2701
宛 ADDRESS → 2762

みたす 満 FULL → 0739

NOTE

➡ see USAGE notes at 当 2701 and 満 0739

交

2508

2-2-4

▶**INTERCOURSE**
▶**INTERCHANGE**

コウ まじ(わる) まじ(える) ま(じる) ま(ざる) ま(ぜる) -か(う) か(わす) こもごも▲
㊔ かた

Ⓒ 交 jiāo

8	Jōyō-2	U4EA4
亠	S6-2-4	F0305

Stroke order: 1–6

COMPOUNDS

❶ⓐ **INTERCOURSE, friendly relations, association, friendship**
ⓑ **have friendly relations with, associate**

a 交際 こうさい association, friendship, intercourse
国交 こっこう diplomatic relations, national friendship

b 外交 がいこう diplomacy, foreign relations
断交 だんこう severing [breaking off] relations

❷ unite in sexual **INTERCOURSE**
性交 せいこう sexual intercourse
情交 じょうこう sexual intercourse, illicit intercourse

❸ⓐ (give and receive mutually) **INTERCHANGE, exchange**
ⓑ (succeed each other) **INTERCHANGE, alternate, go back and forth**

a 交換する こうかんする exchange, interchange, barter, substitute
交易 こうえき trade, commerce
文化交流 ぶんかこうりゅう cultural exchange

b 交代(=交替)する こうたいする relieve (a person), take turns, alternate
交番 こうばん police box
交互に こうごに mutually, reciprocally, alternately
交流 こうりゅう alternating current; interchange
交通 こうつう traffic, transport; communications
交通費 こうつうひ transportation expenses, carfare
交通事故 こうつうじこ traffic accident
交渉 こうしょう negotiation, bargaining, discussion

❹ [original meaning] **intercross, intersect, cross**
交差する こうさする cross, intersect (each other)

交差点 こうさてん crossing, intersection, crossroads; junction
交戦 こうせん war, battle
❺ [formerly also 淆 0630] **intermingle, mix, blend**
交織 こうしょく mixed weave
交錯 こうさく mixture, blending, complication
混交する こんこうする mix up, jumble together
❻ **hand over, deliver**
交付する こうふする deliver, grant, hand (a ticket) to (a person)
手交する しゅこうする hand, deliver
❼ abbrev. of 交通 こうつう: traffic
道交法(=道路交通法) どうこうほう(=どうろこうつうほう) Road Traffic Act
❽ abbrev. of 交渉 こうしょう: negotiation, bargaining
団交 だんこう collective bargaining

INDEPENDENT

【こう 交】change (of season), turn
春夏の交 しゅんかのこう change from spring to summer

KUN

【まじわる 交わる】*vi* **cross, intersect; associate with, keep company with, mingle with, mix with; have friendly relations with, associate; have sexual relations with**
交わり まじわり acquaintance, relations; sexual intercourse
二線の交わる点 にせんのまじわるてん junction of two lines
女と交わる おんなとまじわる sleep with a woman
【まじえる 交える】*vt* **mix; cross; exchange**
ユーモアを交える ゆーもあをまじえる intersperse with humor
膝を交えて ひざをまじえて sitting knee to knee; intimately
言葉を交える ことばをまじえる exchange words
【まじる 交じる】*vi* **be mingled, be mixed, intermingle (with the constituents remaining distinct)**
白髪交じりの髪 しらがまじりのかみ grizzly hair
子供に交じって遊ぶ こどもにまじってあそぶ join children at play
【まざる 交ざる】same as 交じる まじる
英語が交ざった文 えいごがまざったぶん writing interspersed with English
【まぜる 交ぜる】*vt* (combine together, with the constituents remaining distinct) **mix, shuffle**
交ぜ織り まぜおり mixed weave
ない交ぜ ないまぜ intertwinement, blend
【-かう -交う】[verbal suffix] **act reciprocally**
飛び交う とびかう fly about
行き交う いきかう come and go, go back and forth
【かわす 交わす】**exchange; lay across**
取り交わす とりかわす exchange, interchange
見交わす みかわす exchange glances
枝を交わして えだをかわして with branches crossing each other
【こもごも 交(=交交)】alternately; in succession
悲喜交交 ひきこもごも joy and sorrow in succession

SYNONYMS

❶ **personal relations**
縁 RELATION → 1754
交 INTERCOURSE → 2508
好 friendship → 0240
仲 PERSONAL RELATIONS → 0047
誼 FRIENDSHIP → 1977
絆 BONDS → 1686
❸ⓐ **change and replace**
変 CHANGE → 2569
替 REPLACE → 3457
代 SUBSTITUTE → 0034
迭 ALTERNATE → 3818
更 change → 4355
改 change → 0287
易 change → 3064
化 CHANGE INTO, -ize → 0022
遷 undergo transition → 3932
転 turn into → 1872
換 EXCHANGE → 0716
交 INTERCHANGE → 2508
ⓑ **alternate**
迭 ALTERNATE → 3818
交 INTERCHANGE → 2508
輪 take turns → 1999
❹ **intercross**
交 intercross → 2508
差 cross → 4104
❺ **mix**
混 MIX → 0631
淆 INTERMINGLE → 0630
交 intermingle → 2508
雑 MIXED → 1752
錯 MIXED UP → 2187

HOMOPHONES

まじる 混 MIX → 0631
まざる 混 MIX → 0631
まぜる 混 MIX → 0631

NOTE

➡ see USAGE note at 混 0631

妄

▸RASH

モウ ボウ みだ(りに)▲

Ⓝ 妄 Ⓒ 妄 wàng

2509
2-2-4

38	Jōyō	U5984
女	S6-3-3	F2172

COMPOUNDS

❶ [also 盲 2547] [original meaning] **RASH, reckless, wild, outrageous, thoughtless, indiscriminate**

妄言 ぼうげん(=もうげん) rash remark, thoughtless words
妄想 もうそう wild idea [fancy], paranoiac delusion
妄信 もうしん blind belief, credulity
妄評 ぼうひょう(=もうひょう) unjust [unfair] criticism
軽挙妄動する けいきょもうどうする act rashly

❷ false, untrue, absurd, preposterous

妄語 もうご lie, falsehood
迷妄 めいもう illusion, fallacy
虚妄 きょもう falsehood, untruth

KUN

【みだりに 妄りに】without permission; without cause, unreasonably; indiscriminately, at random

妄りに入るべからず みだりにはいるべからず No entry without permission

SYNONYMS

❶ **rash**

濊 unreasonable →0812
妄 RASH →2509
盲 BLIND →2547
暴 unrestrained →3138
荒 WILD →2810
濫 EXCESSIVE →0990
乱 excessive →1611

衣

▸KOROMO

2510
2-2-4

145	Radical	U8863
衣	S6-6-0	F0000

radical variant →see 衣 at 2506

亨

2-2-4

incorrect stroke-count
➡ see 2-2-5: 亠 at 2530

孛

2-2-4

incorrect stroke-count
➡ see 2-2-5: 亠 at 2532

合

▸COMBINE
▸FIT

ゴウ ガッ- カッ- あ(う) -あ(う) あ(い) あい- -あ(い) -あい あ(わす) あ(わせる) -あ(わせる)

Ⓒ 合 hé

2511
2-2-4

30	Jōyō-2	U5408
口	S6-3-3	F0037

COMPOUNDS

❶ [original meaning] **COMBINE, unite, join together, meet**

合同の ごうどうの combined, united, joint; congruent
合計する ごうけいする add up, total
合成 ごうせい composition, synthesis
合弁 ごうべん joint management [venture]
合併する がっぺいする combine, unite, merge
合衆国 がっしゅうこく the United States (of America)
合唱 がっしょう chorus
合宿する がっしゅくする lodge together, stay in a camp for training
合戦 かっせん battle, encounter
合点 がってん(=がてん) understand, comprehend, grasp
集合する しゅうごうする gather, meet, assemble; summon, call together
都合 つごう convenience, circumstances; in all, altogether, totally
総合 そうごう synthesis, integration
結合する けつごうする unite, combine, join together
連合 れんごう combination, union, alliance; association
統合する とうごうする integrate, combine, unify
化合物 かごうぶつ (chemical) compound
混合する こんごうする mix, mingle

❷ **juxtapose, put side by side**

照合する しょうごうする verify, compare, collate
校合する きょうごう(=こうごう)する collate, examine and compare

❸ **FIT, suit, agree, accord, coincide**

合格 ごうかく passing an examination, eligibility
合理 ごうり rationality
合理化 ごうりか rationalization, streamlining
合法 ごうほう legality, legitimacy
合意 ごうい mutual agreement [consent]
合致 がっち agreement, concurrence
適合する てきごうする suit, be fit, conform (to)

❹ *go*:

ⓐ unit of capacity equiv. to approx. 0.18 liters or 1/10 of a *sho* (升)
ⓑ former unit of sq. measure equiv. to approx. 0.33 sq. m or 1/10 of a *tsubo* (坪)

a 五合升 ごごうます 5-*go* measure

❺ 1/10 of the height of a given mountain

八合目 はちごうめ eighth station (of Mt. Fuji)

❻ counter for engagements, esp. in fencing matches

合戦数合で かっせんすうごうで after crossing swords several times

❼ counter for lidded utensils or receptacles

❽ *astron* conjunction

内合 ないごう inferior conjunction

❾ abbrev. of 合成 ごうせい: synthetic

合繊 ごうせん synthetic fiber

INDEPENDENT

【ごう 合】*go* (→❹); *astron* conjunction; sum, total

KUN

【あう 合う】*vi*

①ⓐ **FIT, suit**
ⓑ **harmonize, agree with, coincide**

a 体に良く合う からだによくあう fit (a person) well

b 似合う にあう befit, suit; match well

② **come together, meet**

噛み合う かみあう gear [engage] with, be in gear [mesh]; bite each other

③ⓐ **be right [correct]**
ⓑ (of a clock) indicate the right time

a 合わない答え あわないこたえ incorrect answer

④ pay, be profitable

引き合う ひきあう pay (off), be profitable; pull against each other

【-あう -合う】[verbal suffix] **act upon each other, act reciprocally**

知り合う しりあう get acquainted with each other

折れ合う おれあう make concessions, come to an agreement

殴り合う なぐりあう fight, exchange blows

【あい 合い, あい- 合-】

① [in compounds]
ⓐ **FITting**
ⓑ **prearranged, agreed upon**

a 合い鍵 あいかぎ duplicate key, passkey

b 合図 あいず signal, sign

合い言葉 あいことば password

② [also 間] (space between) **interval, space, opening**

合いの戸 あいのと door between the rooms

③ [also 間]
ⓐ (time between) **interval, intermission**
ⓑ between seasons

a 合の手 あいのて interlude

合間 あいま interval

b 合い服 あいふく between-season wear

④ [also 間] [in compounds] **mixed (blood)**

合いの子 あいのこ *derogatory* person of mixed parentage; crossbreed

合い挽き あいびき beef and pork ground together

【-あい -合い, -合】

① element after verbs:
ⓐ **for forming nouns**
ⓑ **indicating reciprocality**

a 組合 くみあい union, guild, association

試合 しあい match, game

b 話し合い はなしあい talk, discussion, negotiation, consultation

見合い みあい meeting with a view to marriage; looking at each other

②ⓐ **appearance, general impression**
ⓑ **situation, condition, occasion**

a 色合い いろあい tone [shade] of color, coloring, tint

b 具合(=工合) ぐあい condition, state; health; manner, way

場合 ばあい occasion, situation, circumstances, case

③ **degree, extent**

度合 どあい degree, extent, rate

歩合 ぶあい rate, percentage; commission

割合 わりあい rate, proportion, ratio; comparatively

④ suffix used to indicate general concepts

意味合い いみあい meaning

筋合い すじあい reason

【あわす 合わす】same as 合わせる あわせる

合わせ鏡 あわせかがみ mirrors set against each other

混ぜ合わす まぜあわす mix together; blend, compound

仕合わせ しあわせ [also 幸せ, formerly also 倖せ] happiness, blessing; good fortune

【あわせる 合わせる】*vt*

①ⓐ (make into one) **COMBINE, unite, join**
ⓑ [usu. 併せる] (bring two or more things together) **join together, COMBINE, merge**

a 組み合わせる くみあわせる combine, assort, join together, match

b 合わせ技 あわせわざ *judo* combined trick

②ⓐ juxtapose, put side by side [on top]
ⓑ make (persons) confront each other

a 背中合わせに せなかあわせに back to back

詰め合わせ つめあわせ combination, assortment

b 顔合わせ かおあわせ meeting, introduction; being matched against each other

③ **mix, compound**

薬を合わせる くすりをあわせる compound a medicine

④ⓐ **make FIT, adjust, tune**
ⓑ **harmonize, match**

a ラジオを合わせる らじおをあわせる tune in the radio

b 音楽に合わせて踊る おんがくにあわせておどる dance to the music

⑤ **sum [add] up**

合わせて百個 あわせてひゃっこ a hundred in total

⑥ **collate, tally with**

照らし合わせる てらしあわせる check by comparison, collate, verify

問い合わせ といあわせ reference, request for information

打ち合わせ うちあわせ preliminary [previous] arrangement, preliminaries

申し合わせる もうしあわせる make arrangement, mutually agree

【-あわせる -合わせる】 [verbal suffix]

① **act upon each other, act reciprocally**

見合わせる みあわせる look at each other; put off, give up

待ち合わせる まちあわせる wait, meet by appointment

② **happen to**

居合わせる いあわせる happen to be present

有り合わせの ありあわせの available, in [on] hand

SYNONYMS

❶ **combine**

合 COMBINE → 2511
結 TIE → 1706
統 UNITE → 1710
括 LUMP TOGETHER → 0449
総 integrate → 1743
併 join together → 0092
綜 INTEGRATE → 1744
纏める PUT TOGETHER → 1814

❸ **fit**

合 FIT → 2511
填まる fit → 0777
適 suit → 3918
揃える MAKE UNIFORM → 0719

❹ⓐ **capacity units**

勺 *SHAKU* (0.018 liters) → 3650
合 *go* (0.18 liters) → 2511
立 liter → 2486
升 *SHO* (1.8 liters) → 4266
斗 *TO* (18 liters) → 3671
石 *koku* (180 liters) → 3689

USAGE

【あわせる】

合わせる

①ⓐ (make into one) combine, unite, join

ⓑ [usu. 併せる] (bring two or more things together) join together, combine, merge

②ⓐ juxtapose, put side by side [on top]

ⓑ make (persons) confront each other

③ mix, compound

④ⓐ make fit, adjust, tune

ⓑ harmonize, match

⑤ sum [add] up

⑥ collate, tally with

併せる

[sometimes also 合わせる] (bring two or more things together) join together, combine, merge

会わせる

have (a person) meet (another), allow (a person) to see (someone)

遭わせる

subject to (an unfavorable experience), expose to

HOMOPHONES

あう

会 MEET → 2512
遭 MEET WITH → 3917
遇 TREAT → 3889
逢 MEET → 4002

あい

間 INTERVAL → 4122
相 PHASE → 1120

あわせる

併 TOGETHER → 0092
会 MEET → 2512
遭 MEET WITH → 3917

しあわせ

幸せ → 2755
倖せ → 0134
仕合わせ → 0037, 2511

COMPOUND FORMATION

【仕合わせ しあわせ】

仕合わせ 'happiness, blessing; good fortune' consists of 仕 'do' and 合わす. It is a variant of 幸せ and derives from the verb 仕合わす しあわす 'make shift'.

NOTE

➡ see also USAGE notes at 会 2512 and 相 1120 and 幸 2755

➡ see COMPOUND FORMATION for

乳繰り合う ちちくりあう → 繰 1806
試合 しあい → 試 1925
都合 つごう → 都 2120
合図 あいず → 図 3809

会 2512

▶**MEET**
▶**SOCIETY**

カイ エ あ(う) あ(わせる)

Ⓝ 會 Ⓒ 会 huì kuài

2-2-4

9△	Jōyō-2	U4F1A
人	S6-2-4	F0026

ノ 人 𠆢 亼 会 会
1 2 3 4 5 6

COMPOUNDS

❶ [original meaning] (encounter by chance or arrangement) **MEET, see, encounter, interview**
会話 かいわ conversation
会談 かいだん conversation, talk, conference
会見 かいけん interview, audience
会食する かいしょくする dine together, have [take] a meal together
再会する さいかいする meet again
密会する みっかいする meet secretly
面会 めんかい seeing, interview

❷ⓐ [also suffix] **MEETing, gathering; assembly, conference**
ⓑ [also suffix] **party**
ⓒ **session (of a legislative body, esp. the Japanese Diet)**
a 会合 かいごう meeting, gathering
会館 かいかん hall, assembly hall
会場 かいじょう place of meeting, site
会議 かいぎ conference, meeting, council
集会 しゅうかい gathering, meeting, assembly
総会 そうかい general meeting
開会 かいかい opening a meeting
大会 たいかい mass meeting, rally; meet, tournament
座談会 ざだんかい round-table talk, symposium
b 忘年会 ぼうねんかい year-end party ("forget the year party")
晩餐×会 ばんさんかい dinner party
c 会期 かいき session (of the Diet)
休会 きゅうかい adjournment, recess (of the Diet)

❸ (legislative) **assembly, council**
議会 ぎかい assembly, national assembly
国会 こっかい National Diet; national assembly, congress
県会 けんかい prefectural assembly

❹ⓐ [also suffix] **SOCIETY, association, club, circle, guild**
ⓑ **suffix after names of societies or clubs**
a 会社 かいしゃ company, corporation, firm
会員 かいいん member
協会 きょうかい association, society
社会 しゃかい society, the world
同好会 どうこうかい association of like-minded persons; club
b イエズス会 いえずすかい Society of Jesus

❺ **comprehend, understand, realize**
会得 えとく understanding, comprehension, perception
会釈 えしゃく salutation, greeting, bow
会心の かいしんの congenial, satisfying, after one's heart

❻ **opportunity, occasion**
機会 きかい opportunity, occasion

❼ **accounting**
会計 かいけい account, finance; bill

❽ Buddhist ceremony
法会 ほうえ Buddhist mass
放生会 ほうじょうえ ceremony of releasing captive animals

❾ **chief city, capital**
都会 とかい city, town

❿ **verify**
照会する しょうかいする inquire, apply for information

INDEPENDENT

【かい 会】**MEETing, gathering, party; society, association**
会に出席する かいにしゅっせきする attend a meeting
会の創立者 かいのそうりつしゃ founder of a society
【かいする 会する】**MEET**, assemble; join
【え 会】Buddhist ceremony

KUN

【あう 会う】(encounter by chance or arrangement) **MEET, see, encounter, interview**
人に会う ひとにあう meet [see] a person
立ち会う たちあう attend, take part in, witness
出会い であい meeting, encounter
【あわせる 会わせる】**have (a person) MEET (another), allow (a person) to see (someone)**
社長に会わせる しゃちょうにあわせる arrange a meeting with the company president

SYNONYMS

❶ **meet**
会 MEET → 2512
遇 ENCOUNTER → 3889
遭 MEET WITH → 3917
見 SEE → 3151
謁 BE GRANTED AN AUDIENCE → 1976
逢 MEET → 4002

❷ⓐ **assembly**
会 meeting → 2512
集 gathering → 3445
ⓑ **social gatherings**
宴 BANQUET → 2825
饗 BANQUET → 3616
会 party → 2512

❸ **legislature**
議 LEGISLATIVE BODY → 2078
会 assembly → 2512

2512

院 House → 0544

❹ **organized bodies**

会 SOCIETY → 2512
協 association → 0103
団 BODY → 3791
体 BODY → 0080
組 union → 1693
労 workers' union → 3155
連 federation → 3849
講 fraternity → 2046
院 INSTITUTION → 0544

❽ **ceremonies and festivities**

式 CEREMONY → 3785
儀 CEREMONY → 0191
典 formal ceremony → 3253
礼 RITE → 1012
斎 religious ritual → 2622
会 Buddhist ceremony → 2512
祭 FESTIVAL → 3311

USAGE

【あう】

会う
(encounter by chance or arrangement) **meet, see, encounter, interview**

合う
vi
①ⓐ fit, suit
ⓑ harmonize, agree with, coincide
② come together, meet
③ⓐ be right [correct]
ⓑ (of a clock) indicate the right time
④ pay, be profitable

遇う
[also 遭う] (come upon, esp. by accident) **meet with, encounter, be confronted**

遭う
[also 遇う] (come upon, esp. by accident) **meet with, encounter, be confronted**

逢う
(encounter by chance or arrangement) **meet, see, encounter**—used esp. in reference to romantic encounters

HOMOPHONES

あう
遭 MEET WITH → 3917
遇 TREAT → 3889
合 COMBINE → 2511
逢 MEET → 4002

あわせる
合 COMBINE → 2511
併 TOGETHER → 0092
遭 MEET WITH → 3917

COMPOUND FORMATION

【会釈 えしゃく】

会釈 'salutation, greeting, bow' originally meant to comprehend (会 ❺) and interpret (釈) the precepts of Buddhism. What this has to do with bowing is not clear.

NOTE

➡ see also USAGE note at 合 2511

企

2513

2-2-4

▸**PROJECT**

キ くわだ(てる) たくら(む)▴

Ⓒ 企 qǐ

9	Jōyō	U4F01
人	S6-2-4	F0508

COMPOUNDS

❶ⓐ (form a plan or intention for) **PROJECT, draw up [organize] a project, lay plans, undertake a project**
ⓑ **PROJECT, plan, program**

a 企図 きと plan, scheme, intention
企業 きぎょう undertaking, enterprise; business enterprise, company
企及する ききゅうする try to attain (something)

b 企画 きかく plan, project

❷ⓐ [original meaning, now obsolete] stand on tiptoe
ⓑ [rare] expect anxiously (as if standing on tiptoe)

b 企望する きぼうする look forward to, hope for

KUN

【くわだてる 企てる】**plan, contrive, design, plot, scheme, PROJECT; attempt, try, undertake**

企て くわだて plan, scheme, project, enterprise; attempt
陰謀を企てる いんぼうをくわだてる plot against
殺害を企てる さつがいをくわだてる make an attempt on a person's life

【たくらむ 企む】**plot, scheme, conspire**

SYNONYMS

❶ **plans and planning**

計 PLAN → 1828
画 DRAW UP A PLAN → 3723
案 PROPOSAL → 2824
企 PROJECT → 2513
図 systematic plan → 3809
謀 SCHEME → 2004
策 SCHEME → 3320
略 STRATEGY → 1501
揆 PLOT → 0718

全

2514

2-2-4

▶**WHOLE**

ゼン まった(く) すべ(て) ㊔ また まさ たけ

Ⓝ 全 Ⓒ 全 quán

9△	Jōyō-3	U5168
人	S6-2-4	F0114

ノ 人 亼 仝 全 全 (1 2 3 4 5 6)

COMPOUNDS

❶ⓐ [also prefix] (including everything) **WHOLE, all, complete, total, entire**

ⓑ wholly, completely; at the height of

ⓒ in all, a total of

a 全部 ぜんぶ all, the whole; wholly, entirely
全体の ぜんたいの whole, entire; general
全力 ぜんりょく all one's might, full capacity
全焼 ぜんしょう total destruction by fire
全般の ぜんぱんの whole, general, overall
全集 ぜんしゅう complete works
全員 ぜんいん all members, entire staff
全額 ぜんがく sum total, total amount
全速力 ぜんそくりょく full [top] speed, full steam

b 全勝する ぜんしょうする win all the games, make a clean sweep
全廃する ぜんぱいする abolish wholly, do away with
全国民 ぜんこくみん the whole nation

c 全然 ぜんぜん wholly, totally, completely; (not) at all
全六巻 ぜんろっかん complete in six volumes, six volumes in all

❷ (extending over the full range) **WHOLE, all, pan-**

全国 ぜんこく the whole country
全校 ぜんこう the whole school
全米 ぜんべい all America, pan-America
全世界 ぜんせかい the whole world
全アジア会議 ぜんあじあかいぎ Pan-Asiatic Conference

❸ⓐ (free from flaws or damage) **WHOLE, complete, perfect, intact**

ⓑ (free from impurities) **WHOLE**, pure

a 完全な かんぜんな perfect, complete, whole
万全の ばんぜんの perfect, infallible, absolutely secure
安全 あんぜん safety, security
健全な けんぜんな healthy, sound

b 全乳 ぜんにゅう whole milk, pure milk
全麦の ぜんばくの whole-wheat

❹ keep **WHOLE**, keep intact

保全する ほぜんする preserve the integrity of, keep intact

INDEPENDENT

【ぜん 全】**WHOLE**ness

KUN

【まったく 全く】**entirely, completely, wholly, utterly; truly, indeed**

全くの浪費 まったくのろうひ sheer waste
全うする まっとうする accomplish, fulfill, carry out

【すべて 全て】[also 凡て or 総べて]

①ⓐ **all, everything, the WHOLE**

ⓑ **entirely, wholly**

a 全ての すべての all, entire, whole

② **generally, as a rule**

SYNONYMS

❶ & ❷ & ❸ all

皆 ALL →3093
悉 THOROUGHLY →3405
総 TOTAL →1743
諸 VARIOUS →1984
毎 EVERY →2527
各 EACH →2692
都 all →2120
万 all →3653
全 WHOLE →2514
渾 ENTIRE →0738
一 all in one →4148
満 FULL →0739
丸 complete(ly) →4225
完 COMPLETE →2727

HOMOPHONES

すべて

凡 COMMONPLACE →3656
総 TOTAL →1743

NOTE

➡ see USAGE note at 凡 3656

➡ see COMPOUND FORMATION for 全豹 ぜんぴょう →豹 1847

全

2515

2-2-4

▶**WHOLE**

ゼン まった(く) すべ(て) ㊔ また まさ たけ

11	Nonstandard	U5168
入	S6-2-4	F0000

traditional form →see 全 at 2514

羊 羊

2-2-4

incorrect classification

➡ see 2-3-3: 䒑 at 2708

写

2-2-4

incorrect stroke-count

➡ see 2-2-3: 冖 at 2493

亠 八 入 ソ 冖 【匕】 十 ム 亠 七 ケ ク 𠂉

旨

2516

2-2-4

▶**PURPORT**

シ むね うま(い)▲

Ⓒ 旨 zhǐ

72	Jōyō	U65E8
日	S6-4-2	F1504

Stroke order: 1 2 3 4 5 6

COMPOUNDS

❶ⓐ (main idea) **PURPORT, meaning, tenet, substance, gist, point**

ⓑ (reason for an action) **PURPORT, purpose, aim**

a 要旨 ようし gist, point, essentials, summary; purport

主旨 しゅし gist, main point, substance

論旨 ろんし point of an argument

b 趣旨 しゅし purpose, aim; purport, meaning

宗旨 しゅうし tenets of a religious sect; (religious) sect

本旨 ほんし main object, true aim

❷ Imperial decree, orders, instructions; Imperial wish

聖旨 せいし Imperial will [wish]

❸ [original meaning] tasty, excellent

旨酒 ししゅ [archaic] good wine

KUN

【むね 旨】

① **effect, PURPORT**

その旨を書き送る そのむねをかきおくる write to (a person) to that effect

② order

③ [formerly also 宗] principle, aim

正確を旨とする せいかくをむねとする aim at accuracy

【うまい 旨い】

① [also 甘い] delicious, tasty; sweet

旨い料理 うまいりょうり tasty dish

② successful, satisfactory; profitable

旨い仕事 うまいしごと profitable business

③ [also 巧い or 上手い] skillful, clever; splendid, excellent

旨く うまく skillfully, cleverly; successfully; luckily

旨い絵 うまいえ excellent picture [painting]

英語が旨い えいごがうまい speak English well

SYNONYMS

❶ⓐ essential part

精 ESSENCE (essential part) → 1729

粋 essence (best part) → 1645

髄 essence (vital part) → 2316

枢 PIVOT → 1076

幹 TRUNK → 2152

綱 ESSENTIAL POINTS → 1735

旨 PURPORT → 2516

要 summary → 3263

ⓑ meaning

義 MEANING → 2948

意 MEANING → 2650

訳 SENSE → 1865

旨 PURPORT → 2516

趣 PURPOSE → 4111

USAGE

❶【むね】

旨

① effect, purport

② order

③ [formerly also 宗] principle, aim

宗

[now usu. 旨] principle, aim

❷【うまい】

旨い

① [also 甘い] delicious, tasty; sweet

② successful, satisfactory; profitable

③ [also 巧い or 上手い] skillful, clever; splendid, excellent

甘い

[also 旨い] delicious, tasty; sweet

巧い

[also 上手い or 旨い] skillful, clever; splendid, excellent

上手い

[also 巧い or 旨い] skillful, clever; splendid, excellent

❸【しゅし】

趣旨

purpose, aim; purport, meaning; opinion

主旨

gist, main point, substance

HOMOPHONES

むね 宗 RELIGIOUS SECT → 2769

うまい

甘い → 4306

巧い → 0219

上手い → 4212, 4267

丗

2517

2-2-4

▶**WORLD**

▶**AGE**

セイ セ よ

24	Nonstandard	U534B
十	S6-2-4	F0000

alternative form → see 世 at 4308

牟

2518
2-2-4

▶**PHONETIC [mu]**
ム ㊔もと ます
Ⓒ 牟 móu mù

93	Names	U725F
牛	S6-4-2	F2703

COMPOUNDS

❶ **used PHONETICally for *mu*, esp. in the transliteration of Sanskrit Buddhist terms**
牟尼 むに *muni,* Indian ascetic [sage]; Buddha
釈迦牟尼 しゃかむに *Śākyamuni,* Buddha

❷ [original meaning, now archaic] moo, lowing of a cow

SYNONYMS

❶ **phonetic [m]**
弥 PHONETIC [mi] →0344
摩 phonetic [ma] →3938
昧 phonetic [mai] →1105
蜜 phonetic [mitsu] →2958
勿 phonetic [mot] →3661
牟 PHONETIC [mu] →2518

百

2519
2-2-4

▶**HUNDRED**
ヒャク もも▲ ㊔どう お と
Ⓒ 百 bǎi

106	Jōyō-1	U767E
白	S6-5-1	F0279

1	2	3	4	5	6
一	丆	𠂀	百	百	百

COMPOUNDS

❶ **HUNDRED**
百円 ひゃくえん 100 yen
百分率 ひゃくぶんりつ percentage
百倍 ひゃくばい hundredfold, hundred times
五百七十 ごひゃくななじゅう 570

❷ **numerous, various**
百姓 ひゃくしょう farmer, peasant
百貨店 ひゃっかてん department store
百科事典 ひゃっかじてん encyclopedia
百計 ひゃっけい all means

INDEPENDENT

【ひゃく 百】**HUNDRED**

KUN

【もも 百】*elegant* **HUNDRED; many**
百夜 ももよ a hundred nights
百千鳥 ももちどり hundreds (and thousands) of birds, all sorts of birds

SPECIAL READINGS

百舌▲ もず shrike
八百長 やおちょう rigged affair, fixed game
八百屋 やおや greengrocer; jack-of-all-trades

SYNONYMS

❶ **large numbers**
百 HUNDRED →2519
千 THOUSAND →4219
万 TEN THOUSAND →3653
億 HUNDRED MILLION →0192
兆 TRILLION →0264
京 ten quadrillion →2546

❷ **plentiful**
百 numerous →2519
沃 FERTILE →0315
万 myriad →3653
多 MANY →2694
豊 PLENTIFUL →3344
沢 plentiful →0313
穣 YIELDING ABUNDANTLY →1597
裕 ABUNDANT →1530
饒 ABUNDANT →2280
富 RICH →2892

NOTE

➡ see COMPOUND FORMATION for 百姓 ひゃくしょう →姓 0334

而

2520
2-2-4

▶**DIRECTION WORD**
ジ しこ(うして) しか(して) しか(も)
Ⓒ 而 ér

126	Names	U800C
而	S6-6-0	F2453

RADICAL

shikashite 'beard' (耐), used for character classification

COMPOUNDS

❶ **DIRECTION WORD indicating direction in space or time**
而来 じらい since then, after that
而後 じご from now on, hereafter
而立 じりつ age 30
形而上学 けいじじょうがく metaphysics
形而下 けいじか physical, material

❷ [original meaning, now obsolete] beard

KUN

【しこうして 而うして】and
然り而うして しかりしこうして Aye, and...

【しかして 而して】[sometimes also 然して] and, and then

【しかも 而も】[now usu. 然も]
ⓐ moreover, furthermore
ⓑ and yet, nevertheless
b 道の常は無為にして而も為さざるは無 みちのつねはむいにしてしかもなさざるはなし Tao abides in nonaction, yet nothing is left undone (Laozi)

SPECIAL READINGS

似而非 えせ false, pseudo-; would-be

SYNONYMS

❶ **direction indicators**

至 to →2707
-行き bound for →0246
-向け (bound) for →3790
迄 UP TO →3967
以 TO THE…OF →0045
自 from →4338
来 since →4366
而 DIRECTION WORD →2520

【しこうして】

◯ **additionally**

亦 ALSO →2504
兼 CONCURRENTLY →2850
又 also, and →4158
而うして and →2520
及び and →4192
並びに and also →2793
傍ら besides →0166
尚 STILL →2774
更に furthermore →4355
且つ AS WELL →4297

USAGE

【しかして】

而して
[sometimes also 然して] and, and then

然して
[usu. 而して] and, and then

HOMOPHONES

しかも 然 MODIFIER FORMING SUFFIX →3456
しかして 然 MODIFIER FORMING SUFFIX →3456

NOTE

➡ see also USAGE note at 然 3456

㐂

2521

2-2-4

▶**HAPPY**

キ よろこ(ぶ) よろこ(ばす) ㊔ よし のぶ

1	Nonstandard	U3402
一	S6-1-5	F0000

handwritten form →see 喜 at 2889

色

2522

2-2-4

▶**COLOR**

ショク シキ いろ

Ⓒ 色 sè shǎi

139	Jōyō-2	U8272
色	S6-6-0	F0269

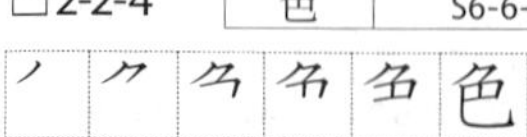

1 2 3 4 5 6

RADICAL

iro 'color', used in characters related to facial expressions or colors

Right variant: 色 ✕ ***irozukuri*** (艶 艷)

COMPOUNDS

❶ⓐ [also suffix] **COLOR, coloring**
ⓑ counter for **COLOR**s

a 色彩 しきさい color, coloring, hue, tinge
色素 しきそ pigment, coloring matter
青色 せいしょく(=あおいろ) blue
原色 げんしょく primary color
天然色 てんねんしょく natural color; technicolor

b 三色写真 さんしょくしゃしん three color photography

❷ⓐ (facial expression) **COLOR, complexion, countenance, look**
ⓑ good looks (of a woman), beauty

a 顔色 がんしょく(=かおいろ) complexion, countenance, expression
血色 けっしょく complexion
気色 きしょく(=けしき) mood, feeling; looks, countenance

b 容色 ようしょく looks, features
才色 さいしょく wit and beauty

❸ [also suffix]
ⓐ (characteristic feature) **COLOR, character, feature**
ⓑ (political tendency) **COLOR**ing

a 特色 とくしょく characteristic
地方色 ちほうしょく local color
異色の いしょくの novel, unique
物色する ぶっしょくする look for, pick out

b 政治色 せいじしょく political coloring

❹ **scenery, scene**

景色 けしき scenery, landscape
春色 しゅんしょく spring scenery

❺ⓐ **lust, sensual pleasure, sexual passion, love**
ⓑ [original meaning] sexual intercourse, sexual love

a 色情 しきじょう lust
色欲 しきよく lust, carnal desire, sexual passion
色魔 しきま woman hunter, sex fiend
女色 じょしょく woman's charms, lust
好色家 こうしょくか lecher, Don Juan
酒色 しゅしょく wine and women, sensual pleasures

b 男色 だんしょく sodomy, unnatural act

❻ *Buddhism* things of this world directly perceptible by the senses; matter

色即是空 しきそくぜくう Matter is void/Form [Matter] is nonsubstantial

KUN

【いろ 色】

①ⓐ [also suffix] **COLOR, hue, tint, shade**
ⓑ **counter for COLOR**s

ⓒ (substance that imparts color) **COLOR, dye, pigment**

a 色取る いろどる [also 彩る] color, paint, dye; make up
黄色 きいろ yellow
橙色 だいだいいろ orange (color)
小麦色 こむぎいろ light brown, suntan
薔×薇×色 ばらいろ rose color
b 三色 みいろ three colors
c 色を塗る いろをぬる paint, daub

②ⓐ (skin tone) **COLOR, complexion**
ⓑ (facial expression) **COLOR, look, expression; indication, tone**

a 色を失う いろをうしなう lose color, turn pale
色香 いろか beauty, loveliness, feminine charms; color and scent
b 秋の色 あきのいろ autumnal tints

③ⓐ sensuality, lust, sexual passion; love affair
ⓑ lover, mistress

a 色気 いろけ sex appeal, sensuality; fancifulness; inclination, interest; shade of color
b 色男 いろおとこ beau, dandy, gallant

④ something extra, action to gratify another person
色を付ける いろをつける add something extra; shade an account

⑤ⓐ **kind, sort**
ⓑ counter for kinds

a 色んな いろんな various kinds of
色色な いろいろな various kinds of
十人十色 じゅうにんといろ So many men, so many minds
b 二色 ふたいろ two kinds

SYNONYMS

❶ color
色 COLOR → 2522
彩 BEAUTIFUL COLORING → 2115

❷ⓐ expression
顔 FACE → 2277
色 COLOR → 2522

❸ⓐ appearance
容 APPEARANCE → 2832
貌 APPEARANCE → 1958
姿 FIGURE → 3264
相 PHASE → 1120
体 FORM (outer appearance) → 0080
色 COLOR → 2522
風 air → 3730

❺ⓐ sex
性 SEX → 0357
情 (illicit) love → 0583
春 love → 3184
色 lust → 2522
淫 LEWD → 0624

【いろ】

⑤ kinds and types
型 TYPE → 3266
類 KIND → 2275
色 kind → 2522
般 SORT → 1670
属 genus → 3901
品 category → 2795
種 VARIETY → 1560
様 variety → 1332

HOMOPHONES

いろどる
彩る → 2115
色取る → 2522, 1613

争

2523
2-2-4

▶CONTEND
ソウ あらそ(う)
Ⓝ 爭 Ⓒ 争 zhēng

6△	Jōyō-4	U4E89
亅	S6-1-5	F0359

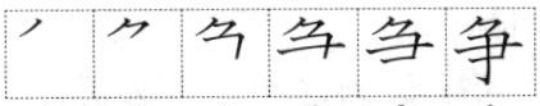

COMPOUNDS

ⓐ [original meaning] (struggle in opposition) **CONTEND, contest, compete, struggle for**
ⓑ (strive in debate) **CONTEND, dispute, argue**

a 争奪 そうだつ scramble, contest, struggle
戦争 せんそう war, battle
競争する きょうそうする compete, contend, vie
紛争 ふんそう conflict, strife
闘争 とうそう fight, conflict
b 争議 そうぎ dispute, strike
争点 そうてん point of contention, issue
論争 ろんそう dispute, argument

KUN

【あらそう 争う】 (struggle in opposition) **CONTEND, contest, compete, struggle for;** (strive in debate) **contend, dispute, argue**
争い あらそい dissension, feud, discord, quarrel; competition; dispute
争われない あらそわれない indisputable
優勝を争う ゆうしょうをあらそう contend for victory
一刻を争う いっこくをあらそう race against time
政権争い せいけんあらそい struggle for political power
言い争い いいあらそい dispute, quarrel

SYNONYMS

ⓐ compete
競 COMPETE → 2322

戦う contest → 2242
闘 FIGHT → 4136
争 CONTEND → 2523

ⓑ **argue and discuss**
議 DISCUSS → 2078
争 CONTEND → 2523
論 ARGUE → 1981
弁 argue (for) → 2497
諏 CONSULT → 1985

危
2-2-4

incorrect classification
➡ see ☐3-4-2: 产 at 3965

危
2524
2-2-4

▶**DANGEROUS**
キ あぶ(ない) あや(うい) あや(ぶむ)

26	Nonstandard	U5371
㔾	S6-2-4	F0000

traditional form → see 危 at 3965

缶
2525
2-2-4

▶**EARTHENWARE JAR**
フ
Ⓒ 缶 fǒu

121	Non-Jōyō	U7F36
缶	S6-6-0	F0000

RADICAL

hotogi 'earthenware' (罐 罎× 罍×), used in characters related to earthenware or pottery

COMPOUNDS

● [original meaning, now rare] **EARTHENWARE JAR**
撃缶 げきふ beating the vase for marking time

SYNONYMS

● **containers**
箱 BOX → 3362
壺 JAR → 2890
槽 TANK → 1352
樽 BARREL → 1368
棺 COFFIN → 1240
桶 BUCKET → 1211
笈 BOX CARRIED ON THE BACK → 3274
鞘 SHEATH → 2259
箪 BAMBOO BOX → 3381
函 BOX → 3724
籠 BASKET → 3398
袋 BAG → 3201
鞄 BAG (for carrying) → 2248
器 VESSEL → 3367
瓶 BOTTLE → 1702
缶 CAN → 2526
缶 EARTHENWARE JAR → 2525

NOTE

★ do not confuse with 缶 CAN → 2526

缶
2526
2-2-4

▶**CAN**
カン かま▲
Ⓝ 罐 鑵 鑵◇ Ⓒ 罐 guàn

121	Jōyō	U7F36
缶	S6-6-0	F1856

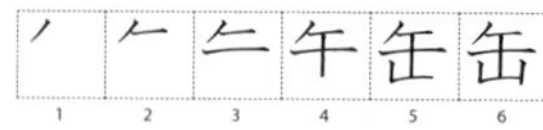

COMPOUNDS

❶ⓐ **CAN, tin**
ⓑ [suffix] **CANned [tinned] food**
a 缶切り かんきり can opener
缶詰め かんづめ canned goods, canning; cooping-up, confining
b ビスケット缶 びすけっとかん can of biscuits
蟹缶 かにかん canned crab

❷ⓐ [usu. 罐 1821] **steam boiler**
ⓑ **kettle**
a 汽缶室 きかんしつ boiler room; stokehold, fire room
b 薬缶 やかん kettle

INDEPENDENT

【かん 缶】**CAN, tin**

KUN

【かま 缶】[usu. 罐 1821] boiler
缶焚き かまたき fireman, stoker

SYNONYMS

❶ **containers**
箱 BOX → 3362
壺 JAR → 2890
槽 TANK → 1352
樽 BARREL → 1368
棺 COFFIN → 1240
桶 BUCKET → 1211
笈 BOX CARRIED ON THE BACK → 3274
鞘 SHEATH → 2259
箪 BAMBOO BOX → 3381
函 BOX → 3724
籠 BASKET → 3398
袋 BAG → 3201
鞄 BAG (for carrying) → 2248
器 VESSEL → 3367
瓶 BOTTLE → 1702
缶 CAN → 2526
缶 EARTHENWARE JAR → 2525

❷ⓐ **heating devices**
炉 FURNACE → 1079
窯 KILN → 2986
缶 steam boiler → 2526

HOMOPHONES

かま

窯 KILN →2986

釜 IRON POT →2610

NOTE

➡ see USAGE note at 窯 2986

★ do not confuse with 缶 EARTHENWARE JAR →2525

毎 2527

▶EVERY

マイ ごと▲ -ごと(に)▲ ㊔ つね

Ⓝ 毎 Ⓒ 毎 měi

2-2-4

80	Jōyō-2	U6BCE
毋	S6-4-2	F0669

COMPOUNDS

❶ [also prefix] **EVERY, each**

毎日 まいにち every day

毎朝 まいあさ every morning

毎回 まいかい every time

毎年 まいねん(=まいとし) every year

毎号 まいごう each [every] issue

毎度 まいど every [each] time, always

毎週 まいしゅう every week

毎土曜日 まいどようび every Saturday

❷ abbrev. of 毎日 まいにち—used in proper names

東毎 とうまい abbrev. of 東京毎日新聞社 とうきょうまいにちしんぶんしゃ (name of a newspaper publisher)

KUN

【ごと 毎】 **EVERY**, each

夜毎 よごと every night

【-ごとに -毎に】 **EVERY, each, at an interval of**

二日目毎に ふつかめごとに every other day

SYNONYMS

❶ **all**

皆 ALL →3093

悉 THOROUGHLY →3405

総 TOTAL →1743

諸 VARIOUS →1984

毎 EVERY →2527

各 EACH →2692

都 all →2120

万 all →3653

全 WHOLE →2514

渾 ENTIRE →0738

一 all in one →4148

満 FULL →0739

丸 complete(ly) →4225

完 COMPLETE →2727

年 2528

▶YEAR

ネン とし ㊔ とせ ね みのる

Ⓒ 年 nián

2-2-4

51	Jōyō-1	U5E74
干	S6-3-3	F0005

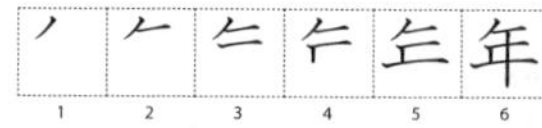

COMPOUNDS

❶ⓐ [also suffix] (period of revolution around the sun) **YEAR, solar year**

ⓑ [also suffix] (period from January 1 to December 31 or equiv.) **YEAR, calendar year**

ⓒ **YEARly, annual**

ⓓ **counter for YEARs**

ⓔ **suffix indicating the chronological order of YEARs in a given era**

a 年年 ねんねん year by year, annually

太陽年 たいようねん solar year

火星年 かせいねん Martian year

b 年度 ねんど year, fiscal year; school year; term

年間 ねんかん period of one year

年月 ねんげつ years (and months), time

年月日 ねんがっぴ date

毎年 まいねん every year

去年 きょねん last year

新年 しんねん New Year

一昨年 いっさくねん(=おととし) the year before last

c 年金 ねんきん annuity, pension

年産 ねんさん yearly output, annual production

年収 ねんしゅう annual income

d 五十年 ごじゅうねん 50 years

e 千九百五十八年 せんきゅうひゃくごじゅうはちねん 1958

昭和六十年 しょうわろくじゅうねん sixtieth year of the Showa era (1985)

❷ **YEARs, one's age**

年齢(=年令) ねんれい age, years

年輩(=年配) ねんぱい age, years; elderly age

少年 しょうねん boy

定年 ていねん mandatory retirement age

中年 ちゅうねん middle age

晩年 ばんねん late in life

❸ **age, era, epoch**

年代 ねんだい age, era, period; date

年号 ねんごう name of era, reign title

❹ term of service

年季(=年期) ねんき one's term of service

❺ [original meaning, now rare] **period of crop bearing, harvest**

祈年祭 きねんさい(=としごいまつり) prayer service for a good crop

INDEPENDENT

【ねん 年】**YEAR**; term of service

年に一度 ねんにいちど once a year

年が明けた ねんがあけた My term of service is up

KUN

【とし 年】

① [formerly also 歳] **YEAR**

お年玉 おとしだま New Year's (money) gift

今年 ことし this year

毎年 まいとし every year

半年 はんとし(=はんねん) half a year

閏年 うるうどし leap year

② [also 歳, sometimes also 齢] **one's YEARs, age**

年寄り としより old [aged] person, the aged; older councilor

年上の としうえの older, senior

年取った としとった old, aged

年頃 としごろ age; marriageable age; adolescence, puberty

SYNONYMS

❶ **year**

年 YEAR → 2528

歳 YEAR → 3131

❷ **age**

齢 AGE → 2390

令 age → 2489

年 years → 2528

歳 AGE SUFFIX → 3131

才 AGE SUFFIX → 4218

寿 life span → 4372

USAGE

【とし】

年

① [formerly also 歳] year

② [also 歳, sometimes also 齢] one's years, age

歳

ⓐ [now usu. 年] year

ⓑ [also 年, sometimes also 齢] one's years, age

齢

[usu. 年 or 歳] one's years, age

HOMOPHONES

とし

歳 YEAR → 3131

齢 AGE → 2390

気

2-2-4

incorrect classification

➡ see ☐3-4-2: 气 at 3960

忘

2529

2-2-5

▶**FORGET**

ボウ わす(れる)

Ⓝ 忘 Ⓒ 忘 wàng

61	Jōyō-6	U5FD8
心	S7-4-3	F0802

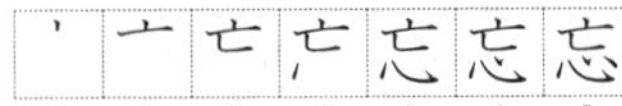

1 2 3 4 5 6 7

COMPOUNDS

● [original meaning] **FORGET**

忘却する ぼうきゃくする forget

忘恩 ぼうおん ingratitude

忘年会 ぼうねんかい year-end party ("forget the year party")

健忘 けんぼう forgetfulness, short memory

備忘 びぼう reminder

INDEPENDENT

【ぼうずる 忘ずる】**FORGET**

KUN

【わすれる 忘れる】**FORGET; leave behind; dismiss from one's mind**

忘れ物 わすれもの something left (behind), lost item

忘れっぽい わすれっぽい forgetful, have a bad memory

忘れられる わすれられる be forgotten, slip into obscurity

見忘れる みわすれる forget, not recognize

SYNONYMS

● **forget**

忘 FORGET → 2529

遺 LEAVE BEHIND → 3928

亨

2530

2-2-5

▶**GO SMOOTHLY**

コウ キョウ ㊔ とおる あきら りょう みち ゆき

Ⓒ 亨 hēng

8	Names	U4EA8
亠	S7-2-5	F2544

COMPOUNDS

● [archaic] **GO SMOOTHLY**, proceed well

亨通 こうつう prosperous, doing well

亨運 こううん prosperity

SYNONYMS

● **make progress**

進 ADVANCE → 3873

亨 GO SMOOTHLY → 2530

捗 MAKE PROGRESS → 0513

NOTE

★ do not confuse with 享 ENJOY → 2545

辛

2531

2-2-5

▸**PUNGENT**
▸**HARD**

シン から(い) つら(い)▲ -づら(い)▲ かのと▲

Ⓝ 辛 Ⓒ 辛 xīn

160	Jōyō	U8F9B
辛	S7-7-0	F1235

Stroke order: 1 2 3 4 5 6 7

RADICAL

karai 'acrid' (辜× 辟× 辞), used for character classification

Left variant: 𧾷× ***karai*** (辦 辣)

COMPOUNDS

❶ **PUNGENT, hot, spicy**

辛辣な しんらつな bitter, pungent, acrid, poignant, severe

香辛料 こうしんりょう spices, seasoning

❷ (difficult to bear) **HARD, trying, bitter, painful, toilsome**

辛苦 しんく hardships, trials; labor, trouble

辛酸 しんさん hardships, privations

辛抱 しんぼう patience, endurance, forbearance

辛労 しんろう toil, trouble

❸ barely, narrowly

辛勝 しんしょう narrow victory

❹ eighth calendar sign (→see APPENDIX 8)

辛亥 しんがい 48th of the sexagenary cycle

KUN

【からい 辛い】

①ⓐ **PUNGENT, hot**

ⓑ [formerly also 鹹い] **salty, briny, saline**

ⓒ **dry (wine)**

a 辛い味 からいあじ pungent taste

辛子(=芥子) からし mustard

唐辛子 とうがらし red pepper

b 塩辛い しおからい salty

c 辛口の からくちの salty; hot; dry (sake)

② **strict, severe**

点が辛い てんがからい be severe in marking

世知辛い せちがらい hard to live, exigent

③ [in compounds] bare, narrow

辛うじて かろうじて barely, narrowly

辛くも からくも barely, narrowly, with difficulty

【つらい 辛い】

ⓐ (difficult to bear) **HARD, trying, bitter**

ⓑ (harsh in treatment) **HARD, harsh, heartbreaking**

a 辛い目に会う つらいめにあう have a hard time of it

b 辛く当たる つらくあたる treat badly

【-づらい -辛い】 [verbal suffix] **HARD**, difficult (to do something)

読み辛い よみづらい hard to read

【かのと 辛】 eighth calendar sign

SPECIAL READINGS

辛螺▲ にし [usu. 螺] *nishi* shell

SYNONYMS

❶ **tastes**

甘 SWEET → 4306

苦 BITTER → 2789

辛 PUNGENT → 2531

辣 PUNGENT → 1965

酸 sour → 1968

渋い ASTRINGENT → 0625

鹹 SALTY → 2366

❷ **trouble and suffering**

困 BE IN TROUBLE → 3808

苛 torment → 2786

窮 BE IN EXTREMITY → 2983

悶 BE IN AGONY → 4119

悩 SUFFER → 0504

苦 SUFFERING → 2789

痛 PAIN → 4071

辛 HARD → 2531

煩 VEXED → 1295

難 DIFFICULT → 2310

【からい】

③ **almost**

殆ど ALMOST → 1130

瀕 ON THE VERGE OF → 0994

甫めて BARELY → 4363

辛い bare → 2531

USAGE

【からい】

辛い

①ⓐ pungent, hot

ⓑ [formerly also 鹹い] salty, briny, saline

ⓒ dry (wine)

② strict, severe

③ [in compounds] bare, narrow

鹹い

[now usu. 辛い] salty, briny, saline

HOMOPHONES

からい 鹹 SALTY → 2366

にし

螺 SPIRAL-SHELLED GASTROPOD → 1799

辛螺 → 2531, 1799

NOTE

➡ see COMPOUND FORMATION for 粒粒辛苦 りゅうりゅうしんく → 粒 1682

【工】亠 八 丷 冖 刀 十 子 ⺈ 𠂉 乂

斈
2532
■2-2-5

▶**STUDY**
▶**EDUCATIONAL INSTITUTION**
ガク まな(ぶ)

39	Nonstandard	U6588
子	S7-3-4	F0000

alternative form → see 学 at 3162

弃
2533
■2-2-5

▶**ABANDON**
キ す(てる)

55	Nonstandard	U5F03
廾	S7-3-4	F0000

traditional form → see 棄 at 2651

享
■2-2-5

incorrect stroke-count
➡ see ■2-2-6: 亠 at 2545

含
2534
■2-2-5

▶**CONTAIN**
ガン ふく(む) ふく(める)
Ⓒ 含 hán

30	Jōyō	U542B
口	S7-3-4	F0803

COMPOUNDS

❶ (have as a part) **CONTAIN, include, comprise**
含有する がんゆうする contain, have, hold
含糖量 がんとうりょう sugar content
含水炭素 がんすいたんそ carbohydrate
包含する ほうがんする include, encompass, cover; imply

❷ [original meaning] hold [keep] in one's mouth
含味する がんみする taste, relish; appreciate

❸ imply, involve, **CONTAIN**, be pregnant with
含蓄の有る がんちくのある significant, pregnant, suggestive

KUN

【ふくむ 含む】**CONTAIN, include, comprise; hold [keep] in one's mouth; bear in mind, cherish; imply, involve**
含み ふくみ implication, hidden meaning; atmosphere, tone (of the market)
含まれる ふくまれる be included [comprised] in
含ませる ふくませる soak (in water), saturate
含み笑い ふくみわらい suppressed laugh [smile]
...と云う事を含んで …ということをふくんで with the understanding that...
強含み つよふくみ strengthening, strong tone

【ふくめる 含める】**include; give instructions**
含め煮 ふくめに food boiled in sugar syrup
...を含めて をふくめて including, inclusive of
言い含める いいふくめる instruct carefully

SYNONYMS

❶ **contain and include**
含 CONTAIN (have as a part) → 2534
容 CONTAIN (have within) → 2832
包 ENCOMPASS → 3684
挟 HOLD BETWEEN → 0450

余
2535
■2-2-5

▶**REMAINING**
▶**EXCESS**
ヨ あま(る) あま(り) あま(す)
Ⓝ 餘 Ⓒ 余 yú

9	Jōyō-5	U4F59
人	S7-2-5	F0658

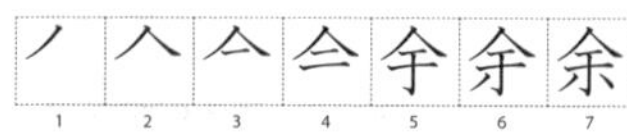

COMPOUNDS

❶ⓐ **REMAINING, lingering, secondary**
ⓑ **after**
a 余地 よち room, space, margin
余暇 よか leisure, spare time
余生 よせい one's remaining years
余波 よは secondary effect, aftereffect
余韻 よいん lingering tone, resonance, reverberation; aftertaste, impregnated elegance
刑余の人 けいよのひと ex-convict
b 余震 よしん aftershock

❷ⓐ **EXCESS, surplus, remainder, overplus**
ⓑ [suffix] **in EXCESS of, over, more than**
a 余剰 よじょう surplus, remainder, residue
余裕 よゆう surplus, margin, room; composure
余分 よぶん excess, extra, surplus
余計な よけいな excess, surplus; needless
余程 よほど very, greatly, highly, considerably; by far
残余 ざんよ remainder, residue, remnant
b 千円余 せんえんよ over 1000 yen

❸ **other, another, additional**
余所 よそ another place, strange parts
余罪 よざい other crimes [charges]
余儀無い よぎない unavoidable, inevitable
余録 よろく additional gain
余談 よだん digression

❹ complementary, co-
余角 よかく complementary angle
余弦 よげん cosine
余色 よしょく complementary color

❺ [also 予 2477] I, myself, the present writer
余輩 よはい we

INDEPENDENT

【よ 余】

① **EXCESS**, surplus, remainder

二月の余も ふたつきのよも even longer than two months

② [also 予 2477] I, myself, the present writer—historically used as a formal first person pronoun but now only used pompously

余の辞書に不可能の文字は無い よのじしょにふかのうのもじはない In my dictionary, there's no such word as impossible

KUN

【あまる 余る】**remain over, be in EXCESS, be more than enough; exceed (one's powers), be beyond one**

余った金 あまったかね surplus money

思い余る おもいあまる be at a loss

有り余っている ありあまっている be in excess

手に余る課題 てにあまるかだい task beyond one's powers

【あまり 余り】

① **remainder, residual; surplus, EXCESS**

余りの あまりの remaining, residual; excessive, too much

② [colloquially also あんまり] **EXCESSively, too, too much; (not) very, (not) much**

余りに(も) あまりに(も) too, excessively

余り面白くない あまりおもしろくない not very interesting

それは余りだ それはあんまりだ That's too much

③ [suffix] over, more than

一月余り ひとつきあまり over a month

【あます 余す】**leave over, let remain; save**

余す所無く あますところなく exhaustively, thoroughly

持て余す もてあます do not know what to do with, find unmanageable

SYNONYMS

❶ⓐ remain

残 REMAIN → 1179
余 REMAINING → 2535
留 STAY → 3189
滞 STAY → 0815

ⓑ after

後 AFTER → 0431
余 after → 2535

❷ⓐ exceeding and excess

過 EXCEED → 3891
超 SURPASS → 4107
越 GO BEYOND → 4108
濫 EXCESSIVE → 0990
余 EXCESS → 2535
剰 SURPLUS → 2233
冗 REDUNDANT → 2470

❸ other

他 OTHER → 0039
余 other → 2535
別 ANOTHER → 1434

【よ】

② **first person pronouns**

私 I (*polite*) → 1432
我 SELF → 4362
己 ONESELF → 4188
身 ONE'S PERSON → 4368
僕 I (*familiar*) → 0185
俺 I (*intimate*) → 0124
吾 I (*elegant*) → 3060
予 I (*pompous*) → 2477
余 I (*pompous*) → 2535
麿 I (*archaic*) → 3949
朕 IMPERIAL WE → 1185
自 SELF → 4338

NOTE

➡ see COMPOUND FORMATION for 余弦 よげん → 正 4296

★ The old form of 余 in senses ❶ to ❹ is 餘. In sense ❺, 余 itself is the original form, which is interchangeable with 予.

谷

2536

2-2-5

▸**VALLEY**

コク たに きわ(まる)▲ ㊔ や やつ はざま

Ⓒ 谷 gǔ

150	Jōyō-2	U8C37
谷	S7-7-0	F0450

Stroke order: 1 ノ, 2 ハ, 3 ク, 4 穴, 5 仌, 6 谷, 7 谷

RADICAL

tani 'valley' (豁× 谿), used in characters related to valleys

Left variant: 谷× ***tanihen*** (谺×)

COMPOUNDS

● [original meaning] **VALLEY, gorge, ravine**

渓谷 けいこく ravine, valley, canyon

峡谷 きょうこく gorge, ravine, canyon, valley

幽谷 ゆうこく deep ravine, secluded valley

KUN

【たに 谷】**VALLEY, ravine, gorge; trough**

谷川 たにがわ valley stream, mountain stream

谷水 たにみず valley water, rill

谷底 たにそこ bottom of a ravine, valley bottom

谷間 たにま valley, gorge

【きわまる 谷まる】[usu. 窮まる]

ⓐ come to an end, terminate

ⓑ come to the end of one's tether, be at a loss

→see 窮 2983 for compounds

SYNONYMS

❶ valley

谷 VALLEY →2536
渓 RAVINE →0628
峡 GORGE →0427

HOMOPHONES

きわまる

極 EXTREME →1243
窮 BE IN EXTREMITY →2983

NOTE

➡ see USAGE note at 極 1243

弟

2537

2-2-5

▶**YOUNGER BROTHER**

テイ ダイ デ おとうと ㊔ おと

Ⓒ 弟 dì

57	Jōyō-2	U5F1F
弓	S7-3-4	F0725

Stroke order: 1–7

COMPOUNDS

❶ⓐ YOUNGER BROTHER
ⓑ child

a 弟妹 ていまい younger brothers and sisters
兄弟 きょうだい(=けいてい) brother
義弟 ぎてい brother-in-law
愚弟 ぐてい my foolish younger brother
b 子弟 してい son, child

❷ (someone who follows a master) **disciple, pupil, apprentice**

弟子 でし disciple, pupil, apprentice
弟子入りする でしいりする become a disciple [pupil, apprentice]
徒弟 とてい apprentice
門弟 もんてい pupil, disciple
師弟 してい master and pupil

❸ follower

孝弟(=孝悌) こうてい filial piety and brotherly love

❹ [humble] I

小弟 しょうてい my foolish brother; I

INDEPENDENT

【てい 弟】YOUNGER BROTHER

兄たり難く弟たり難し けいたりがたくていたりがたし There is little to choose between the two

KUN

【おとうと 弟】YOUNGER BROTHER

SYNONYMS

❶ⓐ siblings

妹 YOUNGER SISTER →0333
姉 OLDER SISTER →0336
兄 OLDER BROTHER →2676
弟 YOUNGER BROTHER →2537

❷ **students and followers**

生 STUDENT →4309
卒 graduate student →2549
学 scholar →3162
門 pupil →1100
弟 disciple →2537
徒 FOLLOWER →0499

宜

2538

2-2-5

▶**RIGHT**

ギ よろ(しい) よろ(しく) ㊔ よし のぶ のり

14	Nonstandard	U519D
冖	S7-2-5	F0000

traditional form →see 宜 at 2763

免

2539

2-2-5

▶**EXEMPT**

メン まぬか(れる) まぬが(れる)

10	Nonstandard	UFA32
儿	S7-2-5	F0000

traditional form →see 免 at 2565

克

2540

2-2-5

▶**OVERCOME**

コク か(つ)▲ ㊔ よし まさる

Ⓒ 克 kè

10	Jōyō	U514B
儿	S7-2-5	F1605

Stroke order: 1–7

COMPOUNDS

❶ [formerly also 剋 4097] **OVERCOME, conquer, win**

克服 こくふく conquest, subjugation
克復 こくふく restoration
克己 こっき self-denial, self-control
超克する ちょうこくする overcome, conquer, surmount, get over
相克する そうこくする struggle with each other, conflict
下克上 げこくじょう the lower dominating the upper

❷ **be able to do something well**

克明 こくめい scrupulousness, diligence

KUN

【かつ 克つ】[now usu. 勝つ] **control (oneself), OVERCOME**

己に克つ おのれにかつ control oneself

SYNONYMS

❶ **win**

勝 WIN →1268
克 OVERCOME →2540

剋 OVERCOME → 4097
征 CONQUER → 0349
破 BREAK → 1478
凱 TRIUMPH → 2286

HOMOPHONES

かつ 勝 WIN → 1268

NOTE

➡ see USAGE note at 勝 1268

孟 incorrect stroke-count
➡ see 2-3-5: 子 at 2760
2-2-5

角

▶**ANGLE**
▶**HORN**
カク かど つの 名 すみ
Ⓒ 角 jiǎo jué

2541
2-2-5

148	Jōyō-2	U89D2
角	S7-7-0	F0700

ノ ク 𠂊 ⺈ 角 角 角 (strokes 1–7)

RADICAL

tsuno 'horn' (觜×), used in characters related to horns or horn products
Left variant: 角× *tsunohen* (解 触 觝)

COMPOUNDS

1 **a** [also suffix] **ANGLE**
b [prefix] *phys* **angular**
a 角度 かくど angle, angular measure, degree
多角的な たかくてきな multilateral, many-sided, diversified
三角 さんかく triangle
直角 ちょっかく right angle
方角 ほうがく direction
迎え角 むかえかく angle of attack
前進角 ぜんしんかく angle of advance
b 角速度 かくそくど angular velocity
角分散 かくぶんさん angular dispersion

2 **a** **corner, ANGLE, edge**
b *baseball* **corner**
a 天の一角 てんのいっかく corner of the sky, point of heaven
折角 せっかく with much trouble; specially
b 内角 ないかく inside corner; inner angle

3 **a** [original meaning] **HORN, antler, antenna**
b **HORNy**, keratinous
a 牛角 ぎゅうかく horns
触角 しょっかく feeler, antenna
b 角膜 かくまく cornea
角質 かくしつ horny substance, keratin

4 **a** [also prefix and suffix] **square, squared**
b cube, block
a 角瓶 かくびん square [shoulder] bottle
角材 かくざい squared timber
角行灯 かくあんどん square paper lantern
五センチ角 ごせんちかく 5 cm sq.
b 角砂糖 かくざとう cube sugar

5 name of chess piece in shogi (Japanese chess): ***kaku***, bishop
角取り かくとり capturing a bishop
成り角 なりかく *narikaku*, promoted bishop

6 compete, vie, fight, wrestle
角逐する かくちくする compete with, vie with
角牛 かくぎゅう bullfight

7 sumo wrestling
角界 かくかい sumo circles
好角家 こうかくか sumo fan, wrestling enthusiast

8 [sometimes also 格 1161] unit of type size equiv. to one em quad
半角 はんかく en quad

9 [rare] third note of the pentatonic scale (→ see APPENDIX 8)

INDEPENDENT

【かく 角】
① square; squared timber; **ANGLE**; *kaku* (→ **5**)
角に切る かくにきる cut into squares [cubes]
角を捨てる かくをすてる sacrifice a bishop
二つの角 ふたつのかく two angles
② [rare] third note of the pentatonic scale

KUN

【かど 角】**corner, edge; ANGLE; stiffness, angularity, harshness**
角の有る かどのある angular, angled
角を取る かどをとる round off the corners
四つ角 よつかど street corner, intersection

【つの 角】**HORN, antler; tentacle, antenna; wing (of a building)**
角笛 つのぶえ bugle, horn
鹿の角 しかのつの antler

SYNONYMS

1 **angle and angular measure**
角 ANGLE → 2541
度 DEGREE → 3844

2 **corners**
角 corner → 2541
圭 SHARP CORNER → 2688
隅 NOOK → 0760
隈 RECESS → 0763

3 **a** **body projections**
角 HORN → 2541
尾 TAIL → 3799

4 **a** **square**

方 SQUARE → 2459
角 square → 2541
ⓑ **three-dimensional shapes**
錐 CONE → 2190
筒 cylinder → 3323
角 cube → 2541
球 sphere → 1219

NOTE

➡ see COMPOUND FORMATION for 折角 せっかく → 折 0297

毎

2542

2-2-5

▶**EVERY**

マイ ごと -ごと(に) ㊔ つね

80	Names	U6BCF
毋	S7-5-2	F0000

traditional form → see 每 at 2527

希

2543

2-2-5

▶**RARE**
▶**ASPIRE**

キ ケ▲ まれ▲ ㊔ のぞみ

Ⓒ 希 xī

50	Jōyō-4	U5E0C
巾	S7-3-4	F1041

Stroke order: 1 2 3 4 5 6 7

COMPOUNDS

❶ [also 稀 き,け 1523] (not frequent) **RARE, uncommon, unusual, scarce**
希書 きしょ rare book
希元素 きげんそ rare element
希少な きしょうな scarce, rare
希有な けう(=きゆう)な rare, unusual, uncommon
古希 こき three score and ten, seventy years of age

❷ [formerly also 稀 き 1523]
ⓐ (thin in density) **RARE, rarefied, dilute, thin**
ⓑ [also prefix] *chem* dilute
a 希薄な きはくな dilute, thin, rare, sparse
希釈 きしゃく dilution
b 希硫酸 きりゅうさん dilute sulfuric acid

❸ **ASPIRE, hope, desire, long for**
希望 きぼう hope, wish, aspiration
希求する ききゅうする aspire to, seek, demand

❹ Greece, Greek
希臘× ぎりしゃ Greece

KUN

【まれ 希】
まれな 希な [usu. 稀な] **RARE, uncommon, scarce, unique**

SYNONYMS

❶ **rare**
珍 RARE → 1135
希 RARE → 2543
稀 RARE → 1523

❷ **rare and sparse**
薄い THIN → 3004
希 RARE → 2543
疎 SPARSE → 1512
粗 COARSE → 1683
稀 RARE → 1523

❸ **wish and desire**
願 WISH → 2320
憧 YEARN AFTER → 0899
憬 YEARN AFTER → 0898
貪 COVET → 2630
望 HOPE → 3408
希 ASPIRE → 2543
懐 LONG FOR → 0942
慕 yearn for → 2970
渇 thirst for → 0627
欲 DESIRE → 1867
慾 DESIRE → 3551
求 SEEK → 4365

❹ **European countries**
英 ENGLAND → 2782
独 GERMANY → 0471
仏 FRANCE → 0020
伊 ITALY → 0052
葡 PORTUGAL → 2902
西 Spain → 4333
蘭 the Netherlands → 3031
希 Greece → 2543
露 Russia → 3495
白 Belgium → 4305

USAGE

【まれな】
希な
[formerly also 稀な] rare, uncommon, scarce, unique
稀な
[now replaced by 希な] same as 希な

HOMOPHONES

まれ 稀 RARE → 1523

COMPOUND FORMATION

【古希 こき】
古希 'three score and ten, etc.' derives from the passage 人生七十古来希なり じんせいしちじゅうこらいまれなり meaning that since ancient times (古) a life of seventy years has been a rare (希 ❶) phenomenon.

育

2544

2-2-6

▶**RAISE**

イク そだ(つ) そだ(ち) そだ(てる)
はぐく(む) ㊔ やす なる

Ⓝ 毓 育 Ⓒ 育 yù yō

130	Jōyō-3	U80B2
月	S8-4-4	F0374

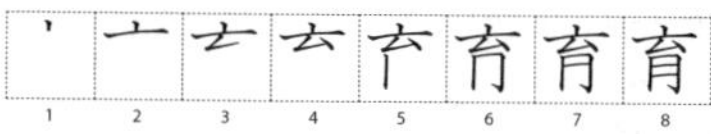

COMPOUNDS

❶ (care for the growth of children, animals or plants)
RAISE, bring up, rear, breed, cultivate
育成する いくせいする bring up, rear
育児 いくじ infant rearing, nursing of children
育種 いくしゅ plant breeding
保育 ほいく nurture, upbringing; lactation, nursing
養育 よういく fostering, bringing up, education
飼育する しいくする raise animals, breed, rear

❷ [original meaning] **grow, grow up, be brought up**
発育する はついくする grow, develop
成育する せいいくする grow (up), be brought up

❸ **educate, teach, train**
育英 いくえい education of the gifted or promising
教育 きょういく education, teaching
体育 たいいく physical training [education]

KUN

【そだつ 育つ】**be brought up, grow up; grow, be bred**
育ち過ぎる そだちすぎる be overgrown

【そだち 育ち】
① **breeding, upbringing**
育ちが良い そだちがよい be well-bred
② [suffix] **RAISEd in**
神戸育ち こうべそだち raised in Kobe

【そだてる 育てる】**bring up, rear, RAISE; breed, cultivate; educate, train**
育て上げる そだてあげる bring up, rear, educate
育ての親 そだてのおや foster parent

【はぐくむ 育む】**bring up, nurse; foster, cultivate; cover, sit over**
自由の育まれた所 じゆうのはぐくまれたところ cradle of liberty

SYNONYMS

❶ **raise and nourish**
育 RAISE →2544
飼 RAISE ANIMALS →2149
養 FOSTER →2998
滋 NOURISH →0734
哺 NURSE →0478
牧 PASTURE →1083

❷ **grow**
成 grow up →4352
長 grow (up) →3163
生 grow →4309
育 grow →2544
発 develop →3174
伸 expand →0079
展 UNFOLD →3862

❸ **teach**
教 TEACH →1887
啓 ENLIGHTEN →3434
諄 TEACH WITH CARE →1979
授 teach →0595
育 educate →2544
練 TRAIN →1738
訓 INSTRUCT →1844
誨 INSTRUCT →1946
諭 ADMONISH →2012
導 GUIDE →3587
迪 EDIFY →3817

享

2545

2-2-6

▶**ENJOY**

キョウ う(ける)▲ ㊔ とおる たか あきら みち ゆき

Ⓒ 享 xiǎng

8	Jōyō	U4EAB
亠	S8-2-6	F2078

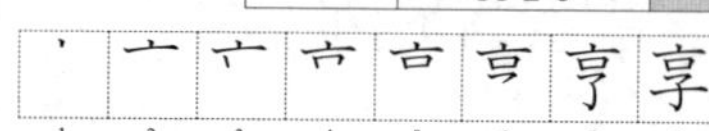

COMPOUNDS

● (benefit from something given) **ENJOY, receive, be given, possess**
享受する きょうじゅする enjoy, receive, be given
享有する きょうゆうする enjoy, possess, participate in
享楽 きょうらく enjoyment
享年 きょうねん age at death

KUN

【うける 享ける】[usu. 受ける] **ENJOY,** be granted
生を享ける せいをうける be born, live
恩寵を享ける おんちょうをうける enjoy (a person's) favor

SYNONYMS

● **receive**
受 RECEIVE →3076
享 ENJOY →2545
領 receive →1567
収 TAKE IN →0031
納 ACCEPT →1652
貰 GET →3219
戴 RECEIVE HUMBLY →4093

頂 RECEIVE HUMBLY →0164
拝 have the honor to receive →0360

● **possess**
有 HAVE →3703
蔵 own →2995
持 HOLD →0447
属 BELONG TO →3901
享 ENJOY →2545
具 possess →3159

HOMOPHONES

うける
受 RECEIVE →3076
承 AGREE TO →0016
請 REQUEST →1983

NOTE

➡ see USAGE note at 受 3076
★ do not confuse with 亨 GO SMOOTHLY →2530

京

2546
2-2-6

▶**CAPITAL**
▶**TOKYO**
▶**KYOTO**

キョウ ケイ キン▲ ㊔ みやこ あつ

Ⓝ 京 Ⓒ 京 jīng

8 亠	Jōyō-2	U4EAC
	S8-2-6	F0201

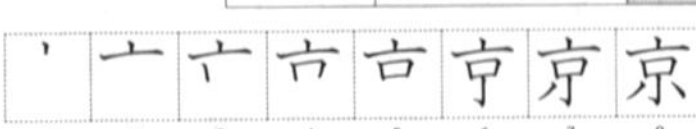

COMPOUNDS

❶ **CAPITAL, metropolis**
京洛 けいらく(=きょうらく) capital; Kyoto
京都 きょうと Kyoto
英京 えいきょう capital of England, London
東京 とうきょう Tokyo
北京 ぺきん Beijing, Peking

❷ **TOKYO**
京浜 けいひん Tokyo and Yokohama
上京する じょうきょうする go to Tokyo
帰京する ききょうする return to Tokyo
滞京する たいきょうする stay in Tokyo [the capital]
在京中 ざいきょうちゅう during one's stay in Tokyo

❸ **KYOTO**
京女 きょうおんな Kyoto woman
京人形 きょうにんぎょう Kyoto doll
京阪神 けいはんしん Kyoto-Osaka-Kobe
京大 きょうだい University of Kyoto

❹ ten quadrillion (10^{16})
二京 にけい 20 quadrillion

INDEPENDENT

【きょう 京】**CAPITAL**, metropolis; Kyoto; ten quadrillion (10^{16})
京の都 きょうのみやこ Kyoto
【けい 京】**CAPITAL**, metropolis; ten quadrillion (10^{16})

SYNONYMS

❶ **cities and towns**
都 METROPOLIS →2120
京 CAPITAL →2546
畿 CAPITAL →4408
市 CITY →2487
町 TOWN →1430

❷ **Kanto region**
京 TOKYO →2546
東 Tokyo →4385
都 METROPOLIS OF TOKYO →2120
浜 Yokohama →0523
埼 SAITAMA →0560
湘 SHONAN →0742

❸ **Kansai cities**
阪 OSAKA →0321
神 Kobe →1143
京 KYOTO →2546
洛 KYOTO →0463

❹ **large numbers**
百 HUNDRED →2519
千 THOUSAND →4219
万 TEN THOUSAND →3653
億 HUNDRED MILLION →0192
兆 TRILLION →0264
京 ten quadrillion →2546

盲

2547
2-2-6

▶**BLIND**

モウ めくら▲

Ⓝ 盲 Ⓒ 盲 máng

109 目	Jōyō	U76F2
	S8-5-3	F2222

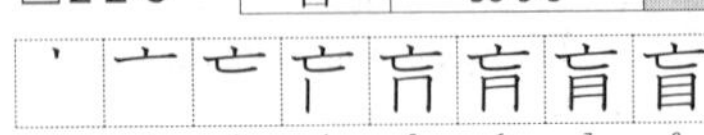

COMPOUNDS

❶ⓐ [original meaning] **BLIND, blindness**
ⓑ [also prefix] **BLIND person**
ⓒ (closed at one end) **BLIND**

a 盲人 もうじん blind person
盲目 もうもく blindness
盲点 もうてん blind spot; scotoma
色盲 しきもう color blindness

b 盲導犬 もうどうけん guide dog, Seeing Eye dog
盲学校 もうがっこう school for the blind

c 盲管 もうかん cul-de-sac
盲腸 もうちょう cecum, appendix

❷ [also 妄 2509] (not based on reason) **BLIND, reckless, aimless**

盲従 もうじゅう blind obedience
盲動 もうどう acting blindly
盲信 もうしん blind belief
盲想 もうそう wild idea [fancy], paranoiac delusion
盲爆 もうばく blind [unscrupulous] bombing

❸ ignorant, illiterate
文盲 もんもう illiteracy

KUN

【めくら 盲】**BLIND**ness, blind person; ignorance, illiteracy
盲穴 めくらあな blind hole
盲判 めくらばん undeliberated endorsement
明き盲 あきめくら person blind to the outer world (due to carelessness or ignorance); illiterate person; amaurosis

SYNONYMS

❷ rash
減 unreasonable → 0812
妄 RASH → 2509
盲 BLIND → 2547
暴 unrestrained → 3138
荒 WILD → 2810
濫 EXCESSIVE → 0990
乱 excessive → 1611

斉

▶UNIFORM
セイ サイ▲ ㊔ ひとし ひさし いつき なり
Ⓝ 齊 亝 Ⓒ 齐 qí

2548
2-2-6

210	Jōyō	U6589
斉	S8-8-0	F1347

radical variant → see 齊 at 2659

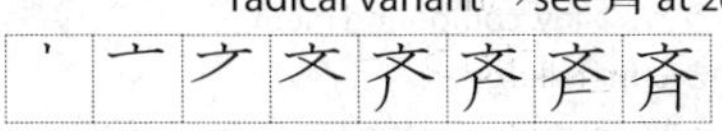

COMPOUNDS

❶ⓐ UNIFORM, equal, even, symmetrical
ⓑ put in order, arrange
a 斉一 せいいつ uniformity, good order
均斉(=均整) きんせい symmetry
整斉の せいせいの symmetrical
不斉地用タイヤ ふせいちようたいや off-the-road tire
b 斉家 せいか governing one's family

❷ in unison, simultaneously
斉唱する せいしょうする sing in unison
斉射 せいしゃ volley, fusillade
一斉に いっせいに all together, all at once, simultaneously

❸ⓐ name of an ancient Chinese kingdom now in Shandong Province
ⓑ Southern Qi Dynasty (479-502 A.D.)

❹ [now always 斎 さい 2622] observe religious abstinence, abstain, purify oneself, fast
斉戒 さいかい religious purification

INDEPENDENT

【さい 斉】Southern Qi Dynasty

SYNONYMS

❶ⓐ same and uniform
等 EQUAL → 3321
平 equal → 4291
均 EVEN → 0276
斉 UNIFORM → 2548
同 SAME → 3707
一 same → 4148

NOTE

★ do not confuse with 斎 OBSERVE RELIGIOUS ABSTINENCE → 2622

卒

▶GRADUATE
ソツ
Ⓝ 卆◆ Ⓒ 卒 zú cù

2549
2-2-6

24	Jōyō-4	U5352
十	S8-2-6	F1135

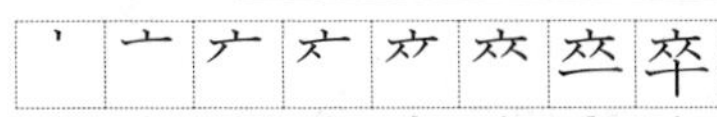

COMPOUNDS

❶ⓐ GRADUATE, complete one's studies
ⓑ [also suffix] **GRADUATE student, graduate**
a 卒業 そつぎょう graduation
卒論 そつろん graduation thesis, dissertation
b 学卒 がくそつ (university or school) graduate
中卒 ちゅうそつ junior high graduate
東大卒 とうだいそつ graduate from Tokyo University

❷ⓐ [original meaning] **private, common soldier; pawn (in Chinese chess)**
ⓑ underling
a 兵卒 へいそつ private, common soldier
b 従卒 じゅうそつ underling

❸ [also 率 2625] suddenly, unexpectedly
卒然(=率然) そつぜん suddenly, unexpectedly
卒中 そっちゅう apoplexy

❹ die, pass away
卒去 そっきょ death

INDEPENDENT

【そつ 卒】**GRADUATE**(d); private
昨年度の卒 さくねんどのそつ graduated last year
千九百七十九年卒 せんきゅうひゃくななじゅうくねんそつ graduated in 1979

【そっする 卒する】die, pass away

SYNONYMS

❶ⓑ students and followers

生 STUDENT → 4309
卒 graduate student → 2549
学 scholar → 3162
門 pupil → 1100
弟 disciple → 2537
徒 FOLLOWER → 0499

❷ⓐ soldiers and warriors

兵 SOLDIER → 3158
卒 private → 2549
士 MILITARY MAN → 4213
武 warrior → 3979
侍 SAMURAI → 0094

夜

2550
2-2-6

▶**NIGHT**

ヤ よ よる

Ⓒ 夜 yè

36	Jōyō-2	U591C
夕	S8-3-5	F0236

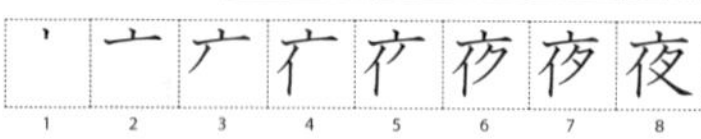

COMPOUNDS

❶ [original meaning] **NIGHT, evening**

夜間 やかん night, nighttime
夜分 やぶん nighttime, night, evening
夜半 やはん midnight
夜学 やがく evening class, night school
夜具 やぐ bedclothes, bedding; quilt
昼夜 ちゅうや day and night
今夜 こんや tonight, this evening
徹夜 てつや all night vigil [sitting]
深夜 しんや dead of night, midnight
前夜 ぜんや previous night; eve

❷ used phonetically for *ya* in the transliteration of Sanskrit Buddhist terms

夜叉 やしゃ *yakṣa,* demon

KUN

【よ 夜】 **NIGHT, evening**

夜中 よなか midnight, dead of night
夜明け よあけ dawn, daybreak
夜空 よぞら night sky
夜更け よふけ late at night; in the dead of night
月夜 つきよ moonlit night

【よる 夜】 **NIGHT, evening**

夜昼 よるひる day and night

SYNONYMS

❶ evening and night

夜 NIGHT → 2550
晩 EVENING → 1232
夕 EVENING → 4195
宵 EARLY EVENING → 2831
暮 DUSK → 2971

辛

2551
2-2-6

▶**PUNGENT**
▶**HARD**

シン から(い) つら(い) -づら(い) かのと

160	Nonstandard	U2840C
辛	S8-7-1	F0000

traditional form → see 辛 at 2531

金

2552
2-2-6

▶**METAL**
▶**GOLD**
▶**MONEY**

キン コン ゴン▲ かね かな- -がね

Ⓒ 金 jīn

167	Jōyō-1	U91D1
金	S8-8-0	F0079

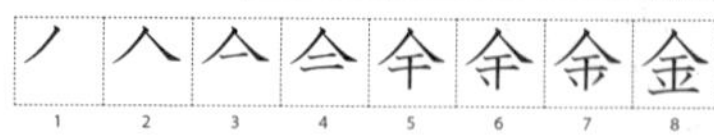

RADICAL

kane 'metal' (釜 鑿), used in characters related to metals or metal products

Left variant: 釒× ***kanehen*** (鉄 録 針)

COMPOUNDS

❶ⓐ [original meaning] **METAL**
ⓑ the fourth of the five elements: **METAL** (→ see APPENDIX 8)

a 金属 きんぞく metal
金鉄 きんてつ metal; firmness
合金 ごうきん alloy, compound metal
冶金 やきん metallurgy
白金 はっきん platinum, platina

❷ⓐ [also prefix] **GOLD**
ⓑ [suffix] carats (of gold)

a 金貨 きんか gold coin
金鉱 きんこう gold ore; gold mine
金時計 きんどけい gold watch
純金 じゅんきん pure gold, solid gold
黄金 おうごん gold; money
b 十八金 じゅうはちきん 18-carat gold

❸ⓐ **GOLDen, yellow**
ⓑ as precious as **GOLD**, excellent

a 金色 きんいろ(=こんじき) golden color
金髪 きんぱつ blonde, golden hair
b 金婚式 きんこんしき golden wedding
金言 きんげん golden rule, golden saying, maxim
金剛力 こんごうりき Herculean strength
金堂 こんどう main temple structure

❹ **MONEY, cash, coin**

金額 きんがく amount of money, sum
金融 きんゆう circulation of money, money market, finance
金利 きんり interest (on money); rate of interest
現金 げんきん cash
預金 よきん deposit, bank account
資金 しきん funds, capital
料金 りょうきん charge, rate, fee, fare
退職金 たいしょくきん retirement allowance [pay]

❺ **Friday**
金曜(日) きんよう(び) Friday
月金 げつきん(=げっきん) Mondays and Fridays

❻ Venus
金星 きんせい Venus

❼ name of chess piece in shogi (Japanese chess): *kin*, the GOLD
金将 きんしょう *kin*
金取り きんとり capturing a *kin*

❽ abbrev. of **金庫 きんこ**: depository, cash office
信金 しんきん credit union [guild]

INDEPENDENT

【きん 金】GOLD; sum of money; Friday; abbrev. of 金メダル きんめだる: **gold medal; *kin* (→❼)**
金の指輪 きんのゆびわ gold ring
金千円 きんせんえん one thousand yen
水泳で金を取る すいえいできんをとる win the gold medal in a swimming race

【ごん 金】 the fourth of the five elements: **METAL**

KUN

【かね 金】MONEY, cash, coin; metal, iron
金持ち かねもち wealthy [rich] person
金貸し かねかし moneylender, moneylending
金儲け かねもうけ making money
金を払う かねをはらう pay money
金鋸 かなのこ(=かねのこ) hacksaw
お金 おかね money
有り金 ありがね money on hand, ready cash

【かな- 金-】METAL
金物 かなもの hardware
金網 かなあみ wire netting, screen
金具 かなぐ metal fittings or fixtures
金槌 かなづち hammer; someone who cannot swim

【-がね -金】something made of METAL
引き金 ひきがね trigger
口金 くちがね metal clasp, snap; metal cap
針金 はりがね wire
白金 しろがね [usu. 銀] silver; silver coin
赤金 あかがね [also 銅] copper

SYNONYMS

❶ⓐ metal
金 METAL → 2552
鉱 ORE → 2145
礦 ORE → 1606
鈑 SHEET METAL → 2122

❷ⓐ metals
金 GOLD → 2552
銀 SILVER → 2156
銅 COPPER → 2155
鉄 IRON → 2147
鉛 LEAD → 2143
錫 TIN → 2189

❸ⓐ yellow colors
黄 YELLOW → 3116
金 golden → 2552

❹ money
金 MONEY → 2552
銭 MONEY → 2159
貨 MONEY (legal tender), coin → 3113
幣 CURRENCY → 3582
銀 SILVER → 2156
財 finance → 1849
資 RESOURCES → 3342
-玉 coin suffix → 4289
札 bill → 1011

❺ days of the week
日 Sunday → 3759
月 Monday → 3674
火 Tuesday → 4273
水 Wednesday → 0010
木 Thursday → 4261
金 Friday → 2552
土 Saturday → 4211

USAGE

【しろがね】
白金
[usu. 銀]
ⓐ silver
ⓑ silver coin
銀
[sometimes also 白金] same as 白金

HOMOPHONES

しろがね
銀 SILVER → 2156
白金 → 4305, 2552

あかがね
銅 COPPER → 2155
赤金 → 2719, 2552

かりがね
雁 WILD GOOSE → 3741
雁が音 → 3741, 2570
雁金 → 3741, 2552

NOTE

➡ see also USAGE note at 銅 2155
➡ see COMPOUND FORMATION for 金木犀 きんもくせい →犀 3900

命

▶ORDER
▶LIFE
メイ ミョウ いのち ㊔ まこと のぶ
Ⓒ 命 mìng

2553
2-2-6

30	Jōyō-3	U547D
口	S8-3-5	F0245

ノ 人 亼 亽 合 合 命 命
1 2 3 4 5 6 7 8

COMPOUNDS

❶ [original meaning] **ORDER, command, instruction**
命令 めいれい command, orders; edict, decree
使命 しめい mission, appointed task
勅命 ちょくめい Imperial order [command]

❷ **LIFE**
生命 せいめい life
一生懸命(=一所懸命)に いっしょうけんめい (=いっしょけんめい)に for life, with all one's might
寿命 じゅみょう life span
長命 ちょうめい long life
人命 じんめい (human) life
亡命 ぼうめい exile
致命傷 ちめいしょう fatal wound

❸ **fate, god's will, destiny, luck**
命運 めいうん one's fate [doom]
革命 かくめい revolution
運命 うんめい fate, fortune, destiny
宿命 しゅくめい fate, destiny
本命 ほんめい probable [prospective] winner, most likely candidate

❹ⓐ **assign a name [title], name**
ⓑ **appoint to a post**
a 命題 めいだい proposition, thesis
命中 めいちゅう hit, on-target impact
命名 めいめい naming, christening
b 任命する にんめいする appoint, nominate

INDEPENDENT

【めい 命】**ORDER**, command, instruction; life; fate, destiny
命に依り めいにより by order [command], under the orders of
命旦夕に迫る めいたんせきにせまる be on the brink of death
死生命有り しせいめいあり Life and death are providential

【めいずる(=めいじる) 命ずる(=命じる)】**ORDER, command; appoint, nominate**

KUN

【いのち 命】**LIFE**
命懸けで いのちがけで at the risk of one's life
命取りの いのちとりの fatal, deadly

SYNONYMS

❶ **command**
令 COMMAND →2489
麾 COMMAND →3937
命 ORDER →2553

❷ **life**
生 LIFE →4309
命 LIFE →2553
寿 LONGEVITY →4372

❸ **fate and fortune**
運 FORTUNE →3894
命 fate →2553
業 karma →3227
縁 karma relation →1754
籤 LOT →3399

COMPOUND FORMATION

【革命 かくめい】
革命 'revolution' is a change (革) in God's will or fate (命 ❸).

NOTE

➡ see COMPOUND FORMATION for
使命 しめい →使 0100
一生懸命(=一所懸命) いっしょうけんめい (=いっしょけんめい) →生 4309

念

▶THOUGHTS
ネン
Ⓒ 念 niàn

2554
2-2-6

61	Jōyō-4	U5FF5
心	S8-4-4	F0446

ノ 人 亼 今 今 念 念 念
1 2 3 4 5 6 7 8

COMPOUNDS

❶ⓐ **THOUGHTS, inner thoughts, mind, idea, conception**
ⓑ **thought of doing something, intention, desire, wish**
a 念頭に置く ねんとうにおく give thought to, bear in mind
観念 かんねん idea, conception, notion
概念 がいねん general idea, concept
残念 ざんねん regret, disappointment, chagrin
信念 しんねん belief, faith
懸念する けねんする be anxious, feel concern, fear

断念する だんねんする give up (an idea), abandon, relinquish
専念する せんねんする give undivided attention to, concentrate (on), devote oneself to
邪念 じゃねん vicious mind, evil thoughts
b 念願 ねんがん one's heart's desire, one's heartiest wish
執念 しゅうねん tenacity of purpose, vindictiveness, spite
一念 いちねん wholehearted wish, determined soul

❷ attention, care, precaution
念入りな ねんいりな careful, elaborate
入念に にゅうねんに carefully, scrupulously
丹念 たんねん application, assiduity, diligence

❸ keep one's THOUGHTS on, bear in mind, remember
記念 きねん commemoration, memory
失念 しつねん lapse of memory, oblivion

❹ chant, intone, invoke
念仏 ねんぶつ Buddhist invocation, prayer to Amitabha
念珠 ねんじゅ rosary
祈念する きねんする pray, offer a prayer

❺ twenty
念五日 ねんごにち 25 days; 25th of the month

❻ *Buddhism* extremely short interval, moment, instant
一念 いちねん brief instant

INDEPENDENT

【ねん 念】
① **THOUGHTS**, feeling, sense
感謝の念 かんしゃのねん feelings of gratitude
② desire, wish, concern
復讐ˣの念 ふくしゅうのねん desire for vengeance
③ attention, care, precaution
念の為 ねんのため by way of precaution, to make sure
念を入れる ねんをいれる pay attention to
念を押す ねんをおす call attention to, make sure of, emphasize

【ねんじる(=ねんずる) 念じる(=念ずる)】pray, invoke, chant (a sutra); have (something) at heart, wish
必勝を念じる ひっしょうをねんじる pray for one's victory
経を念じる きょうをねんじる chant a sutra
良かれと念じる よかれとねんじる wish a person well

SYNONYMS

❶ⓐ thought
念 THOUGHTS →2554
考え thought →3962
意 MIND →2650
想 conception →3507

ⓑ will and intention
志 AMBITION →2725
意 MIND →2650
図 intention →3809
気 mind to do something →3960
念 thought of doing something →2554
趣 PURPOSE →4111
欲 DESIRE →1867

❷ attention
気 care →3960
念 attention →2554

COMPOUND FORMATION

【残念 ざんねん】
残念 'regret, disappointment, chagrin' literally refers to one's lingering (残) thoughts (念 ❶ⓐ), i.e., the misgivings one feels when certain events fail to transpire.

舎

2555

▀ 2-2-6

▸BUILDING

シャ ㊔ や

Ⓝ 舎 Ⓒ 舍 shè

9△	Jōyō-5	U820E
人	S8-2-6	F1099

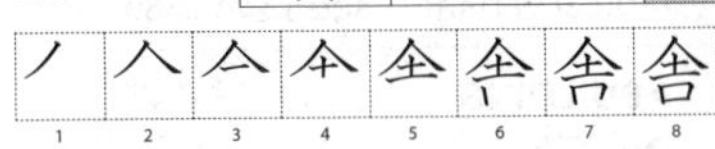

COMPOUNDS

❶ BUILDING, house, quarter, hut
駅舎 えきしゃ station building
校舎 こうしゃ school building
庁舎 ちょうしゃ government building
鶏舎 けいしゃ henhouse

❷ temporary quarters, dormitory, lodging house, inn
舎監 しゃかん dormitory inspector [superintendent]
兵舎 へいしゃ barracks
宿舎 しゅくしゃ lodgings, quarters
客舎 きゃくしゃ hotel, inn
寄宿舎 きしゅくしゃ dormitory, boarding house; hostel

❸ [humble] my
舎弟 しゃてい my younger brother

❹ unit of distance in ancient China equiv. to 30 *ri* (里)
三舎を避ける さんしゃをさける be put to shame, be outshone

❺ used phonetically for *sha* or *sei*
舎利 しゃり Buddha's bones, *sarira;* remains, ashes

INDEPENDENT

【しゃ 舎】dormitory, boarding house

SPECIAL READINGS

田舎 いなか country, rural district

SYNONYMS

❶ **buildings**

閣 TALL MAGNIFICENT BUILDING → 4128
宇 large building → 2699
殿 PALACE → 2247
堂 HALL → 3202
館 PUBLIC BUILDING → 2196
舎 BUILDING → 2555
棟 BLOCK → 1248
厩 HORSE STABLE → 3746

❷ **temporary quarters**

舎 temporary quarters → 2555
寮 DORMITORY → 2984
宿 lodging → 2858
館 inn → 2196
亭 INN → 2572
寓 TEMPORARY ABODE → 2893

亠 【𠆢】 八 ᐯ 刀 十 ⺊ 厶 ⺈ メ

𩙿 2556

▶ *SHOKUHEN*

184	Radical	U98E0
食	S8-8-0	F0000

2-2-6

radical variant → see 食 at 2580

舍 2557

▶ **BUILDING**

シャ ㊔ や

135	Nonstandard	U820D
舌	S8-6-2	F0000

2-2-6

traditional form → see 舎 at 2555

斧 2558

▶ **AXE**

フ おの ㊔ はじめ

Ⓒ 斧 fǔ

69	Names	U65A7
斤	S8-4-4	F2812

2-2-6

COMPOUNDS

● [original meaning] **AXE, hatchet**

斧斤 ふきん axe
斧鑿 ふさく [archaic] elaboration; lucubration; chisel and axe
斧正 ふせい forthright correction [revision]
石斧 せきふ stone axe

KUN

【おの 斧】 **AXE, hatchet**

斧足類 おのあしるい(=ふそくるい) bivalves, bivalvia
蟷×螂×の斧 とうろうのおの courageous but doomed resistance

SPECIAL READINGS

手斧 ちょうな adze

SYNONYMS

● **cutting instruments**

刀 cutting tool → 3642
鎌 SICKLE → 2212
刃 BLADE → 3646
鋏 SCISSORS → 2173
鋸 SAW → 2184
斧 AXE → 2558
鍬 HOE → 2205
錐 DRILL → 2190
鑿 CHISEL → 3640

卷券

2-2-6

incorrect classification
➡ see 2-6-2: 龹 at 3257

並

2-2-6

incorrect classification
➡ see 2-3-5: 䒑 at 2793

兎 2559

▶ **RABBIT**

ト うさぎ ㊔ う うさ

10	Nonstandard	U2F80F
儿	S8-2-6	F0000

2-2-6

traditional form → see 兎 at 4374

尭 2560

▶ **YAO**

ギョウ ㊔ たか たかし あき あきら

Ⓝ 堯 Ⓒ 尧 yáo

32	Names	U5C2D
土	S8-3-5	F0000

2-2-6

COMPOUNDS

❶ name of a legendary sage monarch in ancient China: **YAO**

尭舜 ぎょうしゅん Yao and Shun (two of the most celebrated monarchs in ancient China)

❷ [archaic] high, noble

尭尭たる ぎょうぎょうたる high (as of a mountain)

INDEPENDENT

【ぎょう 尭】 YAO (→ ❶)

SYNONYMS

❶ **rulers**

君 RULER → 3974
王 KING → 4247
帝 EMPEROR → 2573
天 Heaven's messenger on earth → 4250
皇 EMPEROR → 3175
尭 YAO → 2560
舜 SHUN → 3134

直

incorrect classification
➡ see □3-1-7: ⺃ at 3649

2-2-6

卓

2561

2-2-6

▶**TABLE**
▶**PROMINENT**

タク ㊔ すぐる たか たかし まさる つな

Ⓝ 桌 Ⓒ 卓 zhuó 桌 zhuō

24	Jōyō	U5353
十	S8-2-6	F1304

COMPOUNDS

❶ **TABLE, desk**

卓球 たっきゅう table tennis, ping-pong
卓上電話 たくじょうでんわ desk phone
食卓 しょくたく dining table
円卓 えんたく round table
電卓 でんたく pocket calculator

❷ [original meaning] **PROMINENT, eminent, outstanding, unexcelled, superior**

卓効 たっこう remarkable efficacy
卓見 たっけん farsightedness, penetration, excellent views
卓越 たくえつ excellence, superiority
卓説 たくせつ excellent opinion
卓立する たくりつする be prominent, stand out
卓抜 たくばつ prominence, excellence, superiority

INDEPENDENT

【たく 卓】**TABLE**, desk

卓を囲む たくをかこむ sit at table, have a meal together

SYNONYMS

❶ **tables and stands**

卓 TABLE → 2561
机 DESK → 1014
几 DESK → 4156
台 STAND → 2498

❷ **conspicuous**

著 CONSPICUOUS → 2869
顕 MANIFEST → 2274
卓 PROMINENT → 2561
傑 outstanding → 0175

❷ **excellent and superior**

優 SUPERIOR → 0200
絶 without match → 1711
卓 PROMINENT → 2561
快 splendid → 0289
妙 MARVELOUS → 0280
秀 EXCELLENT → 3152
英 DISTINGUISHED → 2782
尤 outstanding → 3755
傑 outstanding → 0175
穎 TALENTED → 2036
逸 exceptional → 3872
名 first-rate → 2693
上 of upper grade → 4212

奌

2562

2-2-6

▶**POINT**

テン つ(ける) つ(く) た(てる) とも(す)

37△	Nonstandard	U70B9
大	S8-3-5	F0000

alternative form → see 点 at 2587

参

2563

2-2-6

▶**PARTICIPATE**
▶**VISIT A HOLY PLACE**

サン シン▲ まい(る) ㊔ み

Ⓝ 參 叅 Ⓒ 参 cān shēn cēn

28	Jōyō-4	U53C2
厶	S8-2-6	F0365

COMPOUNDS

❶ **PARTICIPATE, take part in, join in**

参加する さんかする participate, join, take part in
参謀 さんぼう staff officer, the staff; adviser, counselor
参事 さんじ councilor, secretary
参議院 さんぎいん House of Councilors, Upper House
参戦 さんせん participation in a war
参与 さんよ participation (in public affairs); counselor, consultant

❷ abbrev. of 参議院 さんぎいん: House of Councillors, Upper House

衆参両院 しゅうさんりょういん both Houses (of the Diet)

❸ **VISIT A HOLY PLACE (as a temple, shrine or the Imperial Palace), make a pilgrimage; visit (a superior) in order to pay one's respects**

参拝 さんぱい worship, visit to a shrine [temple]
参詣 さんけい visit to a temple [shrine], worship, pilgrimage
参上する さんじょうする go to see, call on, pay one's respects
参内 さんだい attendance at the Imperial Court
墓参 ぼさん visit to a grave
日参 にっさん daily visit (of worship); frequent visit

❹ **go somewhere, go (to), come**

参観 さんかん visit, inspection
参集する さんしゅうする gather, meet, congregate
持参する じさんする bring [take] with one, carry
古参 こさん senior, old-timer, veteran; seniority

新参 しんざん newcomer, greenhorn

❺ **refer, consult, collate**

参考 さんこう reference, consultation

参考書 さんこうしょ reference book [work]

参照 さんしょう reference, comparison

❻ **be stumped, be beaten**

降参する こうさんする surrender, submit, yield

❼ three—used in legal documents and checks

金参千円也 きんさんぜんえんなり 3000 yen

❽ **unclassified compounds**

人参 にんじん carrot

INDEPENDENT

【さん 参】 three (→❼)

【さんずる(=さんじる) 参ずる(=参じる)】 [humble] go, come

KUN

【まいる 参る】

①ⓐ [humble] **go, come**

ⓑ [humble verb following the TE-form of other verbs] **go and do, perform an action and return to the point of departure**

a 今参ります いままいります I'm coming

そちらへは参りません そちらへはまいりません I won't go there

b 取って参ります とってまいります I'll fetch it

車を呼んで参りましょうか くるまをよんでまいりましょうか Shall I send for a cab?

② VISIT A HOLY PLACE (as a temple, shrine or grave), make a pilgrimage

お参り おまいり worshipping at a shrine; visiting a temple

寺参り てらまいり visit to a temple

お礼参り おれいまいり visiting a shrine or temple to offer thanks; calling on a person to settle old scores

③ be stumped, be beaten; die

参った まいった That licks me!/I'm done for!/You got me there

④ be captivated by (a woman's beauty), be infatuated

彼女にすっかり参っている かのじょにすっかりまいっている be dead gone on her

SYNONYMS

❶ **participate and join**

参 PARTICIPATE → 2563

与 take part in → 4229

加 join → 0042

入 ENTER → 4177

❸ **visit**

訪 VISIT → 1860

参 VISIT A HOLY PLACE → 2563

詣 VISIT A HOLY PLACE → 1918

寄 call at → 2856

伺 call on → 0078

❹ **go and come**

行 GO → 0246

徠 COME → 0576

往 GO ON → 0348

出 go to → 4310

参 go somewhere → 2563

来 COME → 4366

通 go to and from → 3855

向 head toward → 3790

赴 PROCEED TO → 4095

嚮 GO TOWARD → 3610

❺ **compare**

比 COMPARE → 0029

較 COMPARE → 1939

譬 COMPARE TO → 3613

校 COLLATE → 1166

照 check against → 3506

対 OPPOSE (contrast) → 1025

参 refer → 2563

❼ **three**

三 THREE → 2423

参 three (in legal documents) → 2563

鼎 triangular → 4405

亝 2564

2-2-6

▶**UNIFORM**

セイ サイ ㊔ ひとし ひさし いつき なり

7	Nonstandard	U4E9D
二	S8-2-6	F0000

traditional form → see 斉 at 2548

免 2565

2-2-6

▶**EXEMPT**

メン まぬか(れる) まぬが(れる)

Ⓝ 兔 Ⓒ 免 miǎn

10	Jōyō	U514D
儿	S8-2-6	F1270

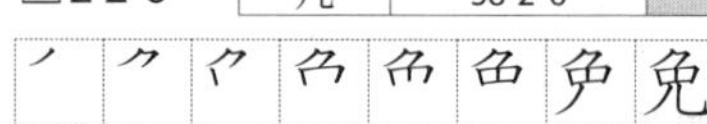

1 2 3 4 5 6 7 8

COMPOUNDS

❶ⓐ **EXEMPT from, free from, release, excuse, forgive**

ⓑ **be EXEMPTed, be immune**

ⓒ **EXEMPTion, remission**

a 免除 めんじょ exemption, exoneration, dismissal

免税 めんぜい tax exemption

御免 ごめん (your) pardon; decline, refusal; permission

御免なさい ごめんなさい I'm sorry/Excuse me

御免下さい ごめんください Excuse me/Pardon me

赦免 しゃめん pardon, amnesty, clemency

b 免疫 めんえき immunity (from a disease)
c 減免 げんめん reduction and exemption

❷ⓐ license, permit, grant a request
ⓑ abbrev. of 免許 めんきょ: **license**

a 免許 めんきょ license, permit
免状 めんじょう license, diploma
b 特免 とくめん special exemption; special license

❸ discharge, dismiss, remove from office
免職 めんしょく dismissal, discharge
懲戒免職 ちょうかいめんしょく disciplinary discharge
罷免 ひめん dismissal, discharge
任免 にんめん appointment and dismissal [removal]

INDEPENDENT

【めんじる 免じる】**EXEMPT**, release; dismiss, discharge
...に免じて ...にめんじて out of respect for...

KUN

【まぬかれる, まぬがれる 免れる】**be EXEMPTed from, be released from; escape, be saved from, avoid**
焼失を免れる しょうしつをまぬかれる be saved from the fire

SYNONYMS

❶ forgive
赦 AMNESTY → 1870
免 EXEMPT → 2565
許す forgive → 1862
恕 FORGIVE WITH COMPASSION → 3282
宥 PARDON → 2803

❷ⓐ permit
許 PERMIT → 1862
免 license → 2565
准 grant permission → 0143
允 GIVE CONSENT → 2476

ⓑ certificates
証 CERTIFICATE → 1899
券 CERTIFICATE → 3256
状 official document → 0322
免 license → 2565

❸ dismiss
罷 DISMISS → 3234
免 discharge → 2565
解 release from office → 1913

兔

2566
2-2-6

▶RABBIT
ト うさぎ ㊔ う うさ

10	Nonstandard	U5154
儿	S8-2-6	F0000

alternative form → see 兎 at 4374

肴

2567
2-2-6

▶ACCOMPANIMENT FOR DRINKS
コウ さかな
Ⓒ 肴 yáo

130	Names	U80B4
月	S8-4-4	F2463

COMPOUNDS

ACCOMPANIMENT FOR DRINKS:
❶ side dish to go with drinks
酒肴 しゅこう(=さけさかな) food and drink
佳肴(=嘉肴) かこう delicacy, rare treat
❷ [original meaning] cooked fish, cooked meat

KUN

【さかな 肴】ACCOMPANIMENT FOR DRINKS:
ⓐ side dish to go with drinks
ⓑ entertainment [conversation] to liven up a drinking party
b 肴舞 さかなまい dance performed at a feast

SYNONYMS

❶ food
飯 MEAL → 2126
膳 MEAL → 1381
食 FOOD, meal → 2578
糧 FOOD PROVISIONS → 1800
餌 ANIMAL FEED → 2257
肴 ACCOMPANIMENT FOR DRINKS → 2567

HOMOPHONES

さかな 魚 FISH → 2636

NOTE

➡ see USAGE note at 魚 2636

哀

2568
2-2-7

▶SORROW
▶PITY
アイ あわ(れ) あわ(れむ) かな(しい)▲
Ⓒ 哀 āi

30	Jōyō	U54C0
口	S9-3-6	F1403

(stroke order 1–9)

COMPOUNDS

❶ⓐ SORROW, grief, sadness, pathos
ⓑ SORROWful, sad, pathetic
ⓒ feel **SORROW** for, grieve, mourn

a 哀歓 あいかん joys and sorrows
喜怒哀楽 きどあいらく joy and anger; emotion
b 哀感 あいかん pathos
哀愁 あいしゅう sadness, sorrow, pensiveness
哀話 あいわ sad story, tragic tale
哀切な あいせつな pathetic, plaintive
悲哀 ひあい sorrow, sadness
c 哀悼 あいとう condolence, mourning, grieving

哀哭×する あいこくする mourn, lament, wail
❷ⓐ **PITY, sympathy**
ⓑ **feel PITY for, pity**
ⓒ pitifully
a 哀憐 あいれん pity, compassion
b 可哀相な かわいそうな poor, pitiable, pathetic
c 哀願 あいがん entreaty, supplication

KUN

【あわれ 哀れ】
ⓐ [formerly also 憐れ] **PITY, sympathy**
ⓑ **pathos**
ⓒ Alas! (in aesthetic sense)
a 哀れな あわれな pitiable; miserable
【あわれむ 哀れむ】
① [formerly also 憐れむ] **PITY, sympathize, feel compassion**
哀れみ あわれみ pity, compassion
② feel the pathos of things, appreciate the beauties (of nature)
月を哀れむ つきをあわれむ enjoy the beauty of the moon
【かなしい 哀しい】[now usu. 悲しい] (causing sorrow) **sad, SORROWful, pathetic**
哀しい歌 かなしいうた sad song, doleful song
哀しい出来事 かなしいできごと sad event

SYNONYMS

❶ⓐ **sorrow**
哀 SORROW →2568
憂 grief →2664
ⓑ **sad and depressed**
悲 SAD →3448
悄 BECOME DISPIRITED →0506
哀 sorrowful →2568
愁 MELANCHOLY →3508
鬱 GLOOM →3625
陰 gloomy →0657
沈 depressed →0306
寂 LONESOME →2855
淋しい LONESOME →0632
惨 MISERABLE →0585
❷ⓐ **tender feelings for others**
仁 BENEVOLENCE →0021
慈 compassion →2949
情 sympathy →0583
悲 mercy →3448
哀 PITY →2568
憐 PITY →0945

USAGE

❶【あわれ】
哀れ
ⓐ [formerly also 憐れ] pity, sympathy
ⓑ pathos
ⓒ Alas! (in aesthetic sense)
憐れ
[now usu. 哀れ] pity, sympathy

HOMOPHONES

あわれ 憐 PITY →0945
あわれむ 憐 PITY →0945
かなしい 悲 SAD →3448

NOTE

➡ see also USAGE note at 悲 3448
★ do not confuse with 衷 INNER HEART →2600

変

▶**CHANGE**
▶**ABNORMAL**
ヘン か(わる) か(わり) か(える)

2569
2-2-7

Ⓝ 變 Ⓒ 变 biàn

34△	Jōyō-4	U5909
夊	S9-3-6	F0155

Stroke order: 1–9 (変)

COMPOUNDS

❶ⓐ [original meaning] **CHANGE, alter, transform, vary, shift**
ⓑ **CHANGE, variation, mutation**
a 変化 へんか change, transformation, variety; declension
変質 へんしつ change in quality, degeneration
変更 へんこう alteration, change, modification
変動 へんどう change, fluctuation
変形 へんけい transformation
変電所 へんでんしょ transformer substation
変革 へんかく change, reform, revolution
変貌 へんぼう transfiguration, metamorphosis
b 一変する いっぺんする change completely
激変(=劇変) げきへん sudden change, upheaval
❷ **ABNORMAL, extraordinary, unusual, irregular, eccentric, odd**
変則の へんそくの irregular, abnormal
変態性欲 へんたいせいよく abnormal sexuality, perversion
変人 へんじん eccentric person, crank
変化 へんげ goblin, ghost
❸ extraordinary event:
ⓐ **unexpected event [incident], extraordinary phenomenon, accident, disaster, emergency**
ⓑ **uprising, upheaval, disturbance**
a 変事 へんじ accident, emergency
変死 へんし accidental [unnatural] death
異変 いへん accident, extraordinary event
天変地異 てんぺんちい extraordinary natural phenomenon

大変な たいへんな awful, terrible; serious, grave

b 事変 じへん incident, upheaval; accident

政変 せいへん coup d'état

❹ *music* flat

変ホ長調 へんほちょうちょう E flat major

重変 じゅうへん double flat

❺ *Buddhism* picture of paradise or hell

地獄変 じごくへん Picture of Hell

INDEPENDENT

【へん 変】**uprising, disturbance, incident; emergency, accident**

承久の変 じょうきゅうのへん Jokyu Uprising

【へんな 変な】**strange, extraordinary, odd, weird, eccentric, funny-looking; suspicious-looking**

変な外人 へんながいじん weird foreigner

【へんじる(=へんずる) 変じる(=変ずる)】**CHANGE,** turn into, transmute

KUN

【かわる 変わる】

①ⓐ **CHANGE, undergo change, be altered, be transformed**

ⓑ **CHANGE** addresses, move, be transferred

a 変わり目 かわりめ turning point

移り変わる うつりかわる change, shift

生まれ変わる うまれかわる be born again; start one's life afresh

天気が変わった てんきがかわった The weather changed

相変わらず あいかわらず as usual, as before

b 新しい家に変わる あたらしいいえにかわる move to a new house

② **be different, differ; be extraordinary, be odd**

変わり者 かわりもの eccentric person, queer fish

変わった かわった different; unusual, extraordinary, odd

【かわり 変わり】

① **CHANGE**

変わり無く かわりなく without change, uniformly; peacefully, well

② **difference**

どっちでも変わりは無い どっちでもかわりはない Whichever you choose, it makes no difference

③ something wrong, accident

④ **eccentricity**

風変わり ふうがわり eccentricity, extraordinariness

【かえる 変える】

ⓐ **CHANGE, alter, convert, transform, turn into**

ⓑ **CHANGE to a different time or place**

ⓒ **reform, revise, amend**

a 変え かえ change, changing

形と色を変える かたちといろをかえる change the shape and color of

鉛を金に変える なまりをきんにかえる convert lead into gold

観点を変える かんてんをかえる change one's point of view

b 予定を変える よていをかえる change the schedule

位置を変える いちをかえる change the position of

c 法律を変える ほうりつをかえる revise [amend] the law

SYNONYMS

❶ **change and replace**

変 CHANGE → 2569
替 REPLACE → 3457
代 SUBSTITUTE → 0034
迭 ALTERNATE → 3818
更 change → 4355
改 change → 0287
易 change → 3064
化 CHANGE INTO, -ize → 0022
遷 undergo transition → 3932
転 turn into → 1872
換 EXCHANGE → 0716
交 INTERCHANGE → 2508

❷ **abnormal**

変 ABNORMAL → 2569
奇 UNUSUAL → 2756
畸 UNUSUAL → 1533
怪 MYSTERIOUS → 0354
妖 MYSTERIOUS → 0282
妙 strange → 0280
異 not ordinary → 3195
珍 curious → 1135

❸ⓐ **incident**

事 AFFAIR → 4384
故 incident → 1466
変 unexpected event → 2569

ⓑ **warfare and rebellions**

戦 WAR → 2242
軍 war → 2582
役 war → 0288
陣 battle → 0545
乱 rebellion → 1611
変 uprising → 2569
闘 FIGHT → 4136

USAGE

❶【かわる】

変わる

①ⓐ change, undergo change, be altered, be transformed

ⓑ change addresses, move, be transferred

② be different, differ; be extraordinary, be odd

[ユ] ∧ 八 ソ 冖 十 ト ム 亠 マ ク ク

機械の機構が変わった きかいのきこうがかわった The machine's mechanism has undergone changes. [altered]

代わる
substitute, be substituted for (a person), take the place of
機械が人力に代わる きかいがじんりょくにかわる Machines take the place of human labor

換わる
be exchanged, become interchanged, be converted, change
この機械は金に換わる このきかいはかねにかわる This machine can be traded in for money

替わる
be replaced, change places with, replace, take turns, relieve, change
機械が替わった きかいがかわった The (old) machine was replaced (by a new one)

❷【かわり】
変わり
① change
② difference
③ something wrong, accident
④ eccentricity

代わり
①ⓐ substitution, substitute
ⓑ substitute, deputy, proxy
② compensation, exchange
③ though…on the other hand

換わり
exchange

替わり
① turn, shift
② replacement (for a maid)
③ substitute program (of a kabuki play)

❸【かえる】
変える
ⓐ change, alter, convert, transform, turn into
ⓑ change to a different time or place
ⓒ reform, revise, amend
馬を牛に変える うまをうしにかえる Change a horse into a cow (by magic)

代える
substitute, use in place of, replace (something) with (another)
馬を牛に代える うまをうしにかえる Substitute a horse for a cow/Use a horse in place of a cow

換える
[sometimes also 替える] exchange, interchange, trade, barter, change (money), convert
馬を牛と換える うまをうしとかえる Exchange a horse for a cow

替える
①ⓐ replace (one thing or person by another), renew, change
ⓑ change to something new (as a job or set of clothes), change over to
馬を替える うまをかえる Replace an old horse with a new one
② [usu. 換える] exchange, interchange, trade, barter, change (money), convert

❹【かえ】
変え
change, changing

代え
substitute, proxy

換え
rate of exchange

替え-
substitute, spare, extra

★The above words are easily confused. Study the examples above in addition to the examples under each entry. Note that the distinction between these words as independent *kun* words does not necessarily apply to their meanings in the formation of compounds. For example, though 両替 りょうがえ 'changing money, exchange of money' is written with 替, かえる in the sense of changing money is written 換える.

HOMOPHONES

かわる
代 SUBSTITUTE →0034
換 EXCHANGE →0716
替 REPLACE →3457

かわり
代 SUBSTITUTE →0034
換 EXCHANGE →0716
替 REPLACE →3457

かえる
代 SUBSTITUTE →0034
換 EXCHANGE →0716
替 REPLACE →3457

かえ
代 SUBSTITUTE →0034
換 EXCHANGE →0716
替 REPLACE →3457

COMPOUND FORMATION

【大変 たいへん】
大変な 'awful, terrible, etc.' formerly referred to a great (大) calamity (変 ❸ⓐ).

音

2570

2-2-7

▸SOUND

オン イン -ノン▲ おと ね

Ⓝ 音 Ⓒ 音 yīn

180	Jōyō-1	U97F3
音	S9-9-0	F0221

radical variant → see 音 at 2448

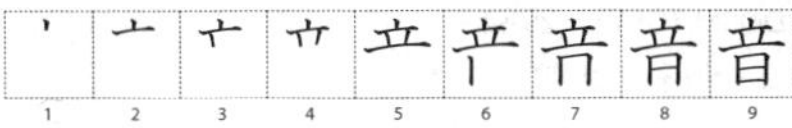

COMPOUNDS

❶ [also suffix]

ⓐ (vibratory disturbance) **SOUND, noise, roar**

ⓑ (auditory sensation) **SOUND**

ⓒ [original meaning] **speech SOUND, voice, pronunciation**

a 音響 おんきょう sound
騒音 そうおん noise
録音 ろくおん sound recording
b 音質 おんしつ sound [tone] quality
音声 おんせい voice, sound
c 音韻論 おんいんろん phonology
音節 おんせつ syllable
発音 はつおん pronunciation
英音 えいおん English pronunciation
子音 しいん(=しおん) consonant ("child sound")
母音 ぼいん vowel ("mother sound")
五十音 ごじゅうおん Japanese syllabary
破裂音 はれつおん plosive, stop

❷ⓐ **SOUND of music, music, note, tune, melody**

ⓑ abbrev. of 音楽 おんがく: music

a 音楽 おんがく music
音痴 おんち tone deafness
音符 おんぷ note; phonetic element of kanji
低音 ていおん low-pitched sound, bass
不協和音 ふきょうわおん discord, dissonance
b 音大 おんだい music college
労音 ろうおん Workers' Music Council

❸ **Chinese-derived pronunciation of kanji, *on* reading**

音読み おんよみ Chinese-derived pronunciation of kanji, *on* reading
音訓 おんくん *on* and *kun* readings
漢音 かんおん Han reading of Chinese characters

❹ news, report, information

音信 おんしん(=いんしん) correspondence, communication
福音 ふくいん gospel, good news

❺ unclassified compounds

観音 かんのん *Avalokiteśvara,* Buddhist Goddess of Mercy

INDEPENDENT

【おん 音】 **SOUND; speech sound; *on* reading;** abbrev. of 音楽 おんがく: **music**

音で読む おんでよむ read kanji in the *on* reading
Ｓの音 えすのおん *s* sound

KUN

【おと 音】 **SOUND, noise, roar; fame**

音を出す おとをだす produce a sound
音に聞く おとにきく famous, widely known
足音 あしおと sound of footsteps
物音 ものおと noise, sound
波の音 なみのおと roar of waves

【ね 音】 **SOUND, note, tone**

音色 ねいろ tone, quality of a sound
鐘の音 かねのね toll of a bell, chimes
本音 ほんね one's real intentions
雁が音 かりがね [also 雁, 雁金] *elegant* cry of the wild goose; wild goose

SYNONYMS

❶ **kinds of sound**

音 SOUND → 2570
声 VOICE → 2724
響 reverberation → 3573
韻 melodious tone → 2279
玲 TINKLING OF JADES → 1139

❷ **music and songs**

楽 MUSIC → 3505
音 sound of music → 2570
節 tune → 3336
調べ melody → 1973
曲 MUSICAL COMPOSITION → 4340
歌 SONG → 2296
謡 POPULAR SONG → 2011
唄 DITTY → 0477

HOMOPHONES

かりがね

雁 WILD GOOSE → 3741
雁が音 → 3741, 2570
雁金 → 3741, 2552

亮

2571

2-2-7

▸LUCID

リョウ ㊔ あきら あき まこと すけ とおる よし かつ

Ⓒ 亮 liàng

8	Names	U4EAE
亠	S9-2-7	F1946

COMPOUNDS

❶ⓐ [now always 瞭 1584] (easily understood) **LUCID**, clear

ⓑ [now always 諒 1982] **show LUCID understanding**

a 亮然たる りょうぜんたる obvious, clear
明亮な めいりょうな lucid, clear, plain
b 亮察する りょうさつする consider, take into account, sympathize with

❷ [archaic] (suffused with light) **bright, LUCID, brilliant**
亮月 りょうげつ bright moonlight
亮直 りょうちょく rightfulness

SYNONYMS

❶ⓐ **evident**
明 CLEAR →1060
鮮 VIVID →2355
亮 LUCID →2571
顕 MANIFEST →2274
瞭 CLEAR →1584

NOTE

★ do not confuse with 亭 INN →2572

亭

2572
2-2-7

▶**INN**
▶**PSEUDONYM SUFFIX**
テイ チン▲
Ⓒ 亭 tíng

8	Jōyō	U4EAD
亠	S9-2-7	F1322

COMPOUNDS

❶ⓐ **INN, hostelry**
ⓑ **suffix after names of INNs**
a 亭主 ていしゅ husband; master, host
旅亭 りょてい inn, hotel
b 石亭 せきてい The Sekitei (name of an inn)

❷ⓐ **restaurant, Japanese restaurant**
ⓑ **suffix after names of quality restaurants**
a 料亭 りょうてい high-class restaurant, Japanese restaurant
b 夕月亭 ゆうづきてい The Yuzukitei (name of a Japanese restaurant)

❸ [original meaning] arbor, bower, pavilion
池亭 ちてい arbor [bower] by a lake

❹ suffix after names of vaudeville houses or variety theaters
若竹亭 わかたけてい The Wakatake Variety Theater

❺ **SUFFIX for forming PSEUDONYMs or stage names**
二葉亭 ふたばてい Futabatei (name of a writer)
三遊亭円歌 さんゆうていえんか Enka Sanyutei (name of a comic story teller)

❻ lofty
亭亭たる大木 ていていたるたいぼく lofty tree

INDEPENDENT

【てい 亭】 arbor, bower
【ちん 亭】 arbor, bower

SYNONYMS

❶ **temporary quarters**
舎 temporary quarters →2555
寮 DORMITORY →2984
宿 lodging →2858
館 inn →2196
亭 INN →2572
寓 TEMPORARY ABODE →2893

❷ⓑ **restaurant suffixes**
亭 quality restaurant suffix →2572
閣 high-class restaurant suffix →4128
園 restaurant suffix →3914
苑 restaurant suffix →2783

❺ **pseudonym suffixes**
亭 PSEUDONYM SUFFIX →2572
屋 stage name suffix →3842

NOTE

★ do not confuse with 亮 LUCID →2571

帝

2573
2-2-7

▶**EMPEROR**
テイ みかど▲
Ⓒ 帝 dì

50	Jōyō	U5E1D
巾	S9-3-6	F0933

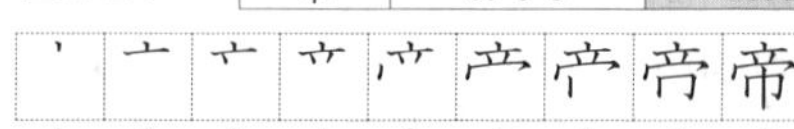

COMPOUNDS

❶ⓐ **EMPEROR, empress**
ⓑ **imperial**
a 帝王 ていおう monarch, emperor
皇帝 こうてい emperor
女帝 じょてい empress, queen
露帝 ろてい Czar, Russian emperor
b 帝国 ていこく empire, imperial
帝政 ていせい imperial government
帝劇 ていげき The Imperial Theatre

❷ abbrev. of 帝国主義 ていこくしゅぎ: imperialism
反帝 はんてい anti-imperialism
米帝 べいてい U.S. imperialism

❸ [original meaning] the Supreme Being, Lord of Heaven
天帝 てんてい Lord of Heaven, the Creator
上帝 じょうてい God, the Lord

INDEPENDENT

【てい 帝】 **EMPEROR**, empress

KUN

【みかど 帝】*literary* **EMPEROR** of Japan

時の帝 ときのみかど emperor of the time

SYNONYMS

❶ **rulers**

君 RULER → 3974
王 KING → 4247
帝 EMPEROR → 2573
天 Heaven's messenger on earth → 4250
皇 EMPEROR → 3175
尭 YAO → 2560
舜 SHUN → 3134

❸ **god**

神 GOD → 1143
帝 the Supreme Being → 2573
天 HEAVEN → 4250
主 Lord → 2437
祇 EARTHLY GOD → 1459

彦

2574

2-2-7

▶**MALE NAME ELEMENT**

ゲン ひこ ㊔ ひろ よし やす

59	Nonstandard	U5F65
彡	S9-3-6	F0000

traditional form → see 彥 at 4085

竒

2575

2-2-7

▶**UNUSUAL**

キ く(しき)

8	Nonstandard	U7AD2
亠	S9-2-7	F0000

traditional form → see 奇 at 2756

亰

2576

2-2-7

▶**CAPITAL**
▶**TOKYO**
▶**KYOTO**

キョウ ケイ キン ㊔ みやこ あつ

8	Nonstandard	U4EB0
亠	S9-2-7	F0000

traditional form → see 京 at 2546

弯

2577

2-2-7

▶**CURVE**

ワン

57	Nonstandard	U5F2F
弓	S9-3-6	F0000

traditional form → see 彎 at 3634

彦

2-2-7

incorrect classification
➡ see ☐3-6-3: 产 at 4085

食

2578

2-2-7

▶**EAT**
▶**FOOD**

ショク ジキ く(う) く(らう) た(べる)

Ⓝ 食 Ⓒ 食 shí sì

184	Jōyō-2	U98DF
食	S9-9-0	F0142

radical variant → see 飠 at 2580

COMPOUNDS

❶ ⓐ [original meaning] **EAT**
ⓑ feed

a 食事 しょくじ meal, dinner, board
食欲 しょくよく appetite (for food)
食卓 しょくたく dining table
食堂 しょくどう dining hall [room]; restaurant
飲食 いんしょく eating and drinking
寝食 しんしょく eating and sleeping
断食 だんじき fasting
蚕食する さんしょくする encroach on, make an inroad into
菜食主義者 さいしょくしゅぎしゃ vegetarian

b 食客 しょっかく hanger-on, parasite

❷ [also prefix and suffix] **FOOD, dish**

食糧 しょくりょう provisions, food, foodstuffs
食中毒 しょくちゅうどく food poisoning
食パン しょくぱん plain bread
食物 しょくもつ food, provisions
主食 しゅしょく staple food
和食 わしょく Japanese-style food
乞食 こじき beggar
流動食 りゅうどうしょく liquid food [diet]

❸ ⓐ **meal**
ⓑ counter for meals

a 食後に しょくごに after meals
朝食 ちょうしょく breakfast
給食 きゅうしょく (provision of) meals

b 三食賄い付きの さんしょくまかないつきの with three meals served

❹ [formerly also 蝕 しょく 2258] [also suffix] **eclipse, occultation**

食連星 しょくれんせい eclipsing variable
日食 にっしょく solar eclipse
星食 せいしょく occultation
皆既食 かいきしょく total solar [lunar] eclipse
金環食 きんかんしょく annular eclipse

❺ [formerly also 蝕 しょく 2258] erode, corrode

腐食 ふしょく corrosion; erosion
浸食 しんしょく erosion, corrosion

INDEPENDENT

【しょく 食】
ⓐ **EATing; appetite; food**
ⓑ [formerly also 蝕 2258] eclipse
a 食を断つ しょくをたつ fast
食が進む しょくがすすむ have a good appetite

KUN

【くう 食う】 *colloq*
①ⓐ **EAT, have a meal**
ⓑ **live on, subsist on, feed on**
a 食い物 くいもの food; victim
食い違う くいちがう cross; be in discord (with)
飯を食う めしをくう have a meal
b 食い詰める くいつめる go broke
翻訳で食って行く ほんやくでくっていく live on translation
② **hold on to (in one's mouth), not let go**
食い下がる くいさがる hang on (to one's opponent); persist
食い込む くいこむ eat (one's way) into, encroach; cause a deficit
食い止める くいとめる check, hold back
③ consume, spend
ガソリンを食う車 がそりんをくうくるま gas-guzzling car
④ beat, excel
横綱を食う よこづなをくう beat a grand champion
⑤ [formerly also 喰う] get (as a slap in the face)

【くらう 食らう】 *vulgar*
① **EAT, drink**
大食らい おおぐらい glutton
② [formerly also 喰らう] get (as a slap in the face)
食らい込む くらいこむ be sent up, be imprisoned

【たべる 食べる】 **EAT, have a meal; live on, subsist on, feed on**
食べ過ぎ たべすぎ overeating
食べ物 たべもの food
食べ頃の たべごろの good for eating, ripe enough for eating

SPECIAL READINGS

虫食む▲ むしばむ [also 蝕む] (of worms) eat in; undermine, affect

SYNONYMS

❶ⓐ ingest
喫 INGEST → 0668
服 take → 1090
食 EAT → 2578
喰う EAT → 0670
飲 DRINK → 2127
呑 SWALLOW → 3059
啄 PECK → 0482

❷ & ❸ⓐ food
飯 MEAL → 2126
膳 MEAL → 1381
食 FOOD, meal → 2578
糧 FOOD PROVISIONS → 1800
餌 ANIMAL FEED → 2257
肴 ACCOMPANIMENT FOR DRINKS → 2567

USAGE

❶【くう】
食う
colloq
①ⓐ eat, have a meal
ⓑ live on, subsist on, feed on
② hold on to (in one's mouth), not let go
③ consume, spend
④ beat, excel
⑤ [formerly also 喰う] get (as a slap in the face)
喰う
colloq
① eat (greedily), devour
ⓑ [now usu. 食う] get (as a slap in the face)
② unclassified compounds

❷【くらう】
食らう
vulgar
① eat, drink
② [formerly also 喰らう] get (as a slap in the face)
喰らう
vulgar
①ⓐ eat (greedily), devour
ⓑ [now usu. 食らう] get (as a slap in the face)

HOMOPHONES

くう 喰 EAT → 0670
くらう 喰 EAT → 0670
むしばむ
蝕 ERODE → 2258
虫食む → 4343, 2578

NOTE

➡ see COMPOUND FORMATION for 蚕食 さんしょく → 蚕 3107

飠

▸ ***SHOKUHEN***

2579

2-2-7

184	Radical	U2967F
食	S9-9-0	F0000

radical variant → see 食 at 2580

食

2580

2-2-7

▸**EAT**
▸**FOOD**
ショク ジキ く(う) く(らう) た(べる)

184	Nonstandard	U2EDD
食	S9-9-0	F0000

traditional form → see 食 at 2578

RADICAL

shoku 'food' (饗 餐×), used in characters related to food or eating

Left variants: 𩙿 飠 *shokuhen* (館 飲 饑)

Variant: 食 *shoku* (養)

盆

2581

2-2-7

▸**TRAY**
▸**BON FESTIVAL**
ボン

Ⓒ 盆 pén

108	Jōyō	U76C6
皿	S9-5-4	F1770

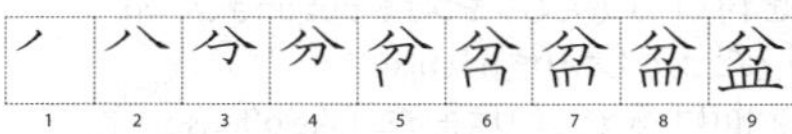

COMPOUNDS

❶ⓐ **TRAY, dish**
ⓑ [original meaning] **basin, pot**

a 茶盆 ちゃぼん tea tray
菓子盆 かしぼん cake tray [dish]
b 盆景 ぼんけい tray landscape, miniature garden
盆栽 ぼんさい bonsai (potted dwarf tree)
盆地 ぼんち basin, valley

❷ **BON FESTIVAL, Feast of Lanterns** (Japanese festival held in July)
盆祭り ぼんまつり Bon Festival
盆踊り ぼんおどり Bon Festival dance
旧盆 きゅうぼん Bon Festival by the lunar calendar

INDEPENDENT

【ぼん 盆】 **TRAY; Bon Festival**
お盆 おぼん Bon Festival

SYNONYMS

❶ **vessels and receptacles**
盤 dish → 3533
鍋 POT → 2202
釜 IRON POT → 2610
鼎 TRIPOD CAULDRON → 4405
臼 MORTAR → 4341
碓 MORTAR → 1537
托 RECEPTACLE → 0252
皿 PLATE → 4286
盆 TRAY → 2581
膳 LEGGED TRAY → 1381
杯 CUP → 1066
鉢 BOWL → 2144
椀 WOODEN BOWL → 1250
碗 CERAMIC BOWL → 1539
丼 LARGE BOWL → 4323

前 首 etc.

incorrect classification
➡ see 2-3-6: 䒑 at 2817

2-2-7

軍

2582

2-2-7

▸**ARMY**
グン ㊔ すすむ

Ⓒ 军 jūn

159	Jōyō-4	U8ECD
車	S9-7-2	F0122

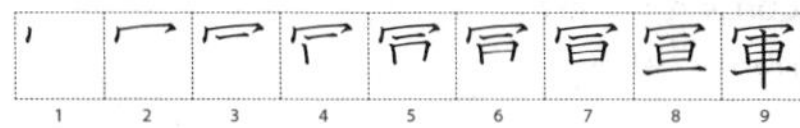

COMPOUNDS

❶ⓐ [also prefix and suffix] **ARMY, the military, armed forces, troops**
ⓑ suffix after names of armies
ⓒ **military**
ⓓ organization resembling an **ARMY**

a 軍隊 ぐんたい army, troops
軍人 ぐんじん soldier, military man
軍事力 ぐんじりょく military force
軍縮 ぐんしゅく reduction of armaments
軍部 ぐんぶ military authorities, the military
軍当局 ぐんとうきょく military authorities
空軍 くうぐん air force
敵軍 てきぐん hostile army force, enemy troops
b 連合軍 れんごうぐん allied forces, the Allies
アメリカ軍 あめりかぐん U.S. Army
c 軍服 ぐんぷく military uniform
軍医 ぐんい military doctor
軍政 ぐんせい military administration
軍国主義 ぐんこくしゅぎ militarism
d 救世軍 きゅうせいぐん Salvation Army

❷ war, battle
軍陣 ぐんじん camp, battlefield
軍船 ぐんせん warship
軍歌 ぐんか war song
軍記 ぐんき war chronicle

❸ [also suffix] **team**
巨人軍 きょじんぐん Giants (Japanese baseball team)
一軍 いちぐん major league team
女性軍 じょせいぐん women's team

INDEPENDENT

【ぐん 軍】 **ARMY, troops; war, battle**
軍を駐屯させる ぐんをちゅうとんさせる post military forces in

SYNONYMS

❶ armed forces
軍 ARMY → 2582
兵 the military → 3158
勢 forces → 3542
隊 PARTY → 0762

❷ warfare and rebellions
戦 WAR → 2242
軍 war → 2582
役 war → 0288
陣 battle → 0545
乱 rebellion → 1611
変 uprising → 2569
闘 FIGHT → 4136

❸ groups
群 GROUP (of any kind) → 1942
班 SQUAD → 1182
軍 team → 2582
組 group (of people) → 1693
陣 lineup → 0545
連 set → 3849
族 common-interest group (*slang*) → 1195
党 PARTY → 3190
隊 PARTY (organized group) → 0762
団 BODY → 3791
伍 ranks → 0050

冠 2583

▶**CROWN**
カン　かんむり　㊔ かむり
Ⓒ 冠 guān guàn
2-2-7

14	Jōyō	U51A0
冖	S9-2-7	F1742

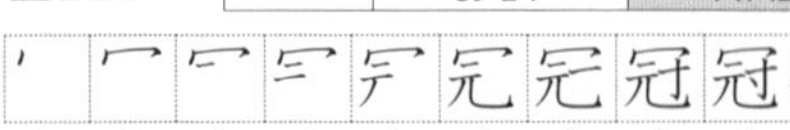

COMPOUNDS

❶ⓐ [original meaning] **CROWN, coronet; cap, headgear**
ⓑ wear a CROWN as a symbol of coming of age
a 王冠 おうかん crown, diadem, cap
戴冠式 たいかんしき coronation (ceremony)
b 冠婚葬祭 かんこんそうさい ceremonial occasions (coming of age, marriage, funeral and ancestral worship)
冠者 かんじゃ young man (come of age)

❷ⓐ something resembling a **CROWN**, top part
ⓑ (be at the highest part) **CROWN**, be on top
a 冠動脈 かんどうみゃく coronary artery
極冠 きょっかん polar cap
金冠 きんかん (gold) crown (for a tooth); gold coronet
b 冠水 かんすい submersion under water
冠詞 かんし *gram* article

❸ (honorary distinction) **CROWN**, honor
冠絶する かんぜつする be unique, be unsurpassed, rank foremost
栄冠 えいかん honor, glory; garland, laurels
三冠王 さんかんおう winner of a triple crown

❹ top radical of a Chinese character, **CROWN** radical
偏旁冠脚 へんぼうかんきゃく the radicals

INDEPENDENT

【かん 冠】**CROWN**, coronet, diadem; the first, the best
冠たる かんたる the first, the best

【かんする 冠する】invest (with), **CROWN**; name, designate, entitle

KUN

【かんむり 冠】**CROWN, coronet, diadem; top radical (→❹); (bad) temper**
冠を付ける かんむりをつける put on a crown
お冠だ おかんむりだ be sulky
冠を曲げる かんむりをまげる take offense
李下に冠を正さず りかにかんむりをたださず Refrain from doing anything that may incur suspicion
草冠 くさかんむり *kusakanmuri*, 'grass' radical (艹)

SPECIAL READINGS

鶏冠▲ とさか cockscomb, crest

SYNONYMS

❶ⓐ headgear
帽 HEADGEAR → 0693
冠 CROWN → 2583
笠 SEDGE HAT → 3300
兜 HEADPIECE → 3499

NOTE

➡ see COMPOUND FORMATION for 李下に冠を正さず りかにかんむりをたださず → 李 3050

南 2584

▶**SOUTH**
ナン　ナ　みなみ　㊔ なみ　みな
Ⓒ 南 nán nā
2-2-7

24	Jōyō-2	U5357
十	S9-2-7	F0378

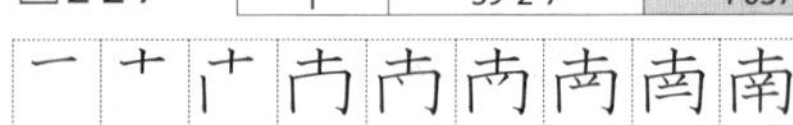

COMPOUNDS

❶ SOUTH, southern
南北 なんぼく north and south
南西 なんせい southwest
南阿 なんあ Republic of South Africa
南海 なんかい southern sea; South Seas
南極 なんきょく South Pole

南下する なんかする go down south
南蛮人 なんばんじん early Europeans (in Japan); southern barbarians
南東 なんとう southeast
南部 なんぶ south(ern) part; South
東南 とうなん southeast

❷ used phonetically for *na,* esp. in the transliteration of Sanskrit Buddhist terms or foreign place names
南無 なむ Amen, hail (in Buddhist prayers)
南無阿弥陀仏 なむあみだぶつ Hail *Amitābha*!/I devote myself entirely to *Amitābha*
越南 えつなん Vietnam

KUN

【みなみ 南】[also prefix] **SOUTH**
南アメリカ みなみあめりか South America
南風 みなみかぜ south wind
南口 みなみぐち south exit

SPECIAL READINGS

南瓜▲ かぼちゃ pumpkin

SYNONYMS

❶ & 【みなみ】 **cardinal points**
東 EAST →4385
西 WEST →4333
北 NORTH →0230
南 SOUTH →2584
巽 SOUTHEAST →3329
艮 NORTHEAST →4330

桒

2585

2-2-7

▸MULBERRY

ソウ くわ

75	Nonstandard	U6852
木	S9-4-5	F0000

traditional form →see 桑 at 2618

貞

2586

2-2-7

▸CHASTE

テイ ㊔ さだ ただ ただし

Ⓒ 贞 zhēn

154	Jōyō	U8C9E
貝	S9-7-2	F1512

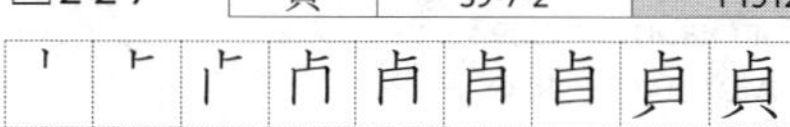

COMPOUNDS

❶ **CHASTE, faithful**
貞女 ていじょ chaste woman, faithful wife
貞操 ていそう chastity, virginity
貞節 ていせつ chastity, virtue; constancy, principle
貞淑 ていしゅく chastity, female virtue
貞潔な ていけつな chaste and pure
不貞な ふていな unchaste
童貞 どうてい male virgin, virginity

❷ [original meaning, now archaic] **divination in ancient China**

SYNONYMS

❶ **chastity**
貞 CHASTE →2586
操 chastity →0948

点

2587

2-2-7

▸POINT

テン つ(ける)▲ つ(く)▲ た(てる)▲ とも(す)▲

Ⓝ 點 奌◇ Ⓒ 点 diǎn

86△	Jōyō-2	U70B9
灬	S9-4-5	F0241

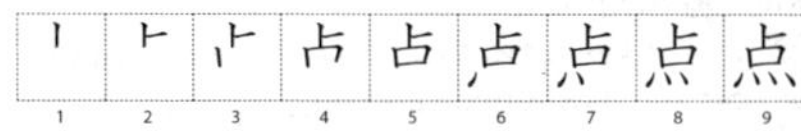

COMPOUNDS

❶ⓐ (small spot) **POINT, dot, spot**
ⓑ *math* **POINT**
ⓒ mark with a **POINT** [dot], punctuate
a 点在する てんざいする be dotted [studded] with
点線 てんせん dotted [perforated] line
b 交点 こうてん intersecting point
c 画竜点睛× がりょうてんせい completing the eyes of a painted dragon, giving a finishing touch

❷ⓐ (any dotlike mark or symbol) **POINT, decimal point, dot, period**
ⓑ dot (as opposed to a stroke) of Chinese characters
a 点字 てんじ Braille
小数点 しょうすうてん decimal point
句読点 くとうてん punctuation marks
b 点画 てんかく dots and strokes of Chinese characters

❸ [also suffix]
ⓐ (definite place) **POINT**
ⓑ (definite position) **POINT**
a 地点 ちてん spot, point, place
焦点 しょうてん focus, focal point; (photographic) focus
拠点 きょてん strongpoint, base
終点 しゅうてん last stop, terminus
出発点 しゅっぱつてん starting point
b 沸点 ふってん boiling point
死点 してん dead point
凝固点 ぎょうこてん freezing point

❹ [also suffix] (unit of scoring) **POINT, mark**
点数 てんすう points, score
得点 とくてん the marks obtained, the points made, score
同点 どうてん tie, draw
採点 さいてん marking, grading, rating

❺ⓐ [also suffix] (specific matter) **POINT, detail, particular**
ⓑ **POINT** of view
a 重点 じゅうてん important point; importance, emphasis, stress; priority
欠点 けってん weak point, defect
争点 そうてん point of contention, issue
問題点 もんだいてん controversial point
b 観点 かんてん point of view
❻ **counter for various articles**
三点セット さんてんせっと set of three pieces (of furniture)
❼ **kindle, light, ignite**
点滅する てんめつする (of light) go [come] on and off; turn [switch] on and off
❽ⓐ drop (of liquid)
ⓑ drip, pour (tea)
a 点点と てんてんと in drops; here and there
点滴 てんてき falling drops of water; intravenous infusion
点眼器 てんがんき eye dropper
b 点茶 てんちゃ making tea (in a tea ceremony)

INDEPENDENT

【てん 点】
①ⓐ (small spot) **POINT, dot, spot**
ⓑ *math* **POINT**
ab 点と線 てんとせん points and lines
②ⓐ (any dotlike mark or symbol) **POINT, decimal point, dot, period**
ⓑ **dot (as opposed to a stroke) of Chinese characters**
ab 点を打つ てんをうつ mark with a dot [point]
③ (definite place) **POINT**
どの点迄 どのてんまで to what extent
④ (unit of scoring) **POINT, mark**
点が良い てんがよい have good marks
⑤ (specific matter) **POINT, detail, particular**
問題の点 もんだいのてん point in dispute
その点に於て そのてんにおいて on that point, in that respect
⑥ fault, defect
点の打ち所が無い てんのうちどころがない be above reproach
【てんじる(=てんずる) 点じる(=点ずる)】 drop, drip; kindle, light; make tea

KUN

【つける 点ける】 light, turn [switch] on
電灯を点ける でんとうをつける turn [switch] on an electric lamp
【つく 点く】 be lighted, be switched on, go on
ガスが点いている がすがついている The gas is on
【たてる 点てる】 [also 立てる] make tea
野点 のだて open-air tea ceremony
【ともす 点す】 [sometimes also 灯す] light (a lamp), set alight, turn on (a light)
松明を点す たいまつをともす kindle a torch

SYNONYMS

❸ **places and positions**
所 PLACE → 1056
処 place → 3764
場 PLACE (for specific activity) → 0678
地 PLACE (particular location) → 0236
席 meeting place → 3865
位 POSITION → 0069
点 POINT → 2587
座 place → 3868
❻ **general counters**
丁 MISCELLANEOUS COUNTER → 4155
個 GENERAL COUNTER → 0132
箇 COUNTER FOR ITEMS → 3348
点 counter for articles → 2587
件 counter for cases → 0054

USAGE

【ともす】
点す
[sometimes also 灯す] light (a lamp), set alight, turn on (a light)
灯す
[usu. 点す] same as 点す

HOMOPHONES

つける
付 ATTACH → 0035
附 ATTACH → 0410
着 PUT ON → 4110
就 SET ABOUT → 2129
即 IMMEDIATE → 1439
漬 PICKLE → 0861
つく
付 ATTACH → 0035
附 ATTACH → 0410
着 PUT ON → 4110
就 SET ABOUT → 2129
即 IMMEDIATE → 1439
たてる
立 STAND → 2486
建 BUILD → 3834
閉 CLOSE → 4116
ともす 灯 LAMP → 1019

NOTE

➡ see also USAGE notes at 付 0035 and 立 2486
➡ see COMPOUND FORMATION for 焦点 しょうてん → 焦 3444

怠

▸REMISS

タイ おこた(る) なま(ける)

Ⓒ 怠 dài

2588

2-2-7

61	Jōyō	U6020
心	S9-4-5	F1928

COMPOUNDS

ⓐ [original meaning] (inclined to idleness) **REMISS, idle, lazy, sluggish**

ⓑ (neglectful) **REMISS, negligent, careless**

a 怠惰な たいだな lazy, idle

倦怠 けんたい fatigue, languor, weariness

b 怠慢な たいまんな negligent, inattentive, remiss

怠業 たいぎょう slowdown strike, deliberate idleness

KUN

【おこたる 怠る】**be REMISS, neglect; be off one's guard; get better**

怠り おこたり negligence, carelessness

注意を怠る ちゅういをおこたる be off one's guard

病が怠る やまいがおこたる The patient has gotten better

【なまける 怠ける】**be lazy, be idle; neglect**

怠け者 なまけもの idle [lazy] fellow

勉強を怠ける べんきょうをなまける neglect one's studies

SYNONYMS

● **lazy**

惰 LAZY → 0706

怠 REMISS → 2588

慢 SLUGGISH → 0844

頁

▸PAGE

ケツ ぺーじ

Ⓒ 页 yè

2589

2-2-7

181	Names	U9801
頁	S9-9-0	F1615

RADICAL

ōgai 'head' (題 領 順), used in characters related to the head

COMPOUNDS

❶ **PAGE**

頁岩 けつがん shale

❷ [original meaning, now obsolete] **head**

KUN

【ぺーじ 頁】

ⓐ [also suffix] **PAGE, leaf**

ⓑ **counter for PAGEs; page no.**

a 頁数 ぺーじすう number of pages

頁付け ぺーじづけ pagination

余白頁 よはくぺーじ blank page

b 九十頁 きゅうじゅっぺーじ page 90

五百頁の本 ごひゃくぺーじのほん book of 500 pages

SYNONYMS

【ぺーじ】

ⓐ **paper**

紙 PAPER → 1654

葉 LEAF → 2912

丁 sheet → 4155

箋 PIECE OF PAPER → 3352

頁 PAGE → 2589

面 page (of a newspaper) → 2590

ⓑ **counters for flat things**

枚 COUNTER FOR FLAT THINGS → 1069

葉 counter for leaves → 2912

丁 counter for sheets → 4155

頁 counter for pages → 2589

通 counter for letters → 3855

竿 counter for flags → 3259

面

▸FACE

メン おも おもて つら

Ⓒ 面 miàn

2590

2-2-7

176	Jōyō-3	U9762
面	S9-9-0	F0130

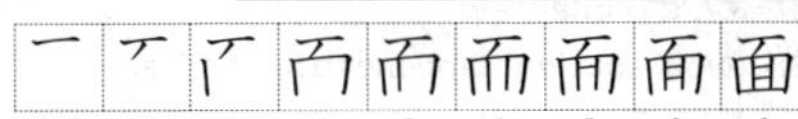

RADICAL

men 'face' (靨× 靤× 靦×), used in characters related to the face or its qualities

COMPOUNDS

❶ⓐ [original meaning] (front of head) **FACE, countenance**

ⓑ (value in the eyes of others) **FACE, dignity, honor**

a 面相 めんそう countenance, features, looks

面通し めんとおし identification parade

面食い めんくい person who puts much store by good looks (in choosing his [her] lover)

面面 めんめん everyone, all

顔面 がんめん face

洗面 せんめん washing one's face

七面鳥 しちめんちょう turkey

b 面目 めんぼく(=めんもく) face, honor, prestige

面子 めんつ face, honor

体面 たいめん honor, dignity, reputation

❷ⓐ (front or significant surface) **FACE, front**

ⓑ (outer surface) **FACE, surface, side**

ⓒ counter for flat surfaces such as tennis courts, mirrors or go boards

a 表面 ひょうめん surface, face, outside; appearance

全面 ぜんめん front, facade
正面衝突 しょうめんしょうとつ head-on collision, front crash
画面 がめん picture; television field; screen
印面 いんめん face of a seal
額面 がくめん face value; denomination
書面 しょめん letter, document
図面 ずめん drawing, plan, map, sketch
b 地面 じめん surface, ground, land
月面 げつめん lunar surface
斜面 しゃめん slope, slanting surface
c テニスコート三面 てにすこーとさんめん three tennis courts
❸ [also suffix] *math* **FACE, surface, plane**
面積 めんせき area, square measure
曲面 きょくめん curved surface
七面体 しちめんたい heptahedron
線織面 せんしきめん ruled surface
❹ⓐ (have the front toward) **FACE, front on, look toward**
ⓑ **meet FACE to face, confront in person**
a 面壁 めんぺき meditation facing the wall
直面する ちょくめんする face, confront
当面の とうめんの present, immediate; urgent, pressing
b 面会する めんかいする see, have an interview
面接 めんせつ interview
面罵 めんば abusing someone to his [her] face
面識 めんしき acquaintance
面談 めんだん interview
❺ⓐ **side, quarter, direction**
ⓑ [also suffix] (distinct aspect) **side, aspect, phase, plane**
a 側面 そくめん side, flank
両面 りょうめん both sides
方面 ほうめん direction, district; field, sphere
一面 いちめん one side; on the other hand; whole surface
反面 はんめん the other side
全面的 ぜんめんてき all-out, overall, general
b 局面 きょくめん situation, aspect of an affair; position (in a chess game)
場面 ばめん scene; situation
技術面 ぎじゅつめん technical side
軍事面 ぐんじめん military plane
❻ⓐ [also suffix] **mask**
ⓑ (protective covering for the face) **mask, FACE guard, protector, headgear**
a 仮面 かめん mask, disguise
舞楽面 ぶがくめん mask worn by a *bugaku* dancer
b 面頬 めんぽう(=めんぼう) visor, face guard
防毒面 ぼうどくめん gas mask
❼ [also suffix] **page (of a newspaper)**
紙面 しめん space (on a printed page)
社会面 しゃかいめん local news page, city news page
二面 にめん second page (of a newspaper)
❽ counter for kotos (Japanese harps)
琴二面 ことにめん two kotos
❾ corner
面取り めんとり chamfering, beveling
❿ **unclassified compounds**
面倒な めんどうな troublesome, worrisome; difficult
面倒臭い めんどうくさい troublesome, tiresome, annoying
面妖な めんような strange, mysterious, weird
面食らう めんくらう be confused, be bewildered
工面する くめんする contrive, manage, make shift; raise (money)

INDEPENDENT

【めん 面】
① **FACE**
面と向かって めんとむかって face to face
②ⓐ **mask**
ⓑ **FACE** guard, headgear
a 狐の面 きつねのめん mask of the fox
③ⓐ **surface, FACE, side**
ⓑ *math* **FACE**
a 滑らかな面 なめらかなめん smooth surface
b 立方体は六つの面を持つ りっぽうたいはむっつのめんをもつ A cube has six faces
④ (distinct aspect) **side, aspect, phase**
財政の面 ざいせいのめん the financial aspect
⑤ corner
面を取る めんをとる plane off the corners
【めんする 面する】**FACE, front on**

KUN

【おも 面】
①ⓐ [in compounds] (front of head) **FACE**
ⓑ *elegant* surface of the water
a 面影 おもかげ face; traces
面持ち おももち look, countenance, face
面白い おもしろい interesting, amusing, pleasant
b 水の面 みずのおも surface of the water
② unclassified compounds
面舵 おもかじ starboarding the helm
【おもて 面】
①ⓐ (front of head) **FACE**
ⓑ (outer surface) **FACE, surface (as of water)**
a 細面 ほそおもて slender face
b 水の面 みずのおもて face of the water
② mask

【つら 面】*colloq* (front of head) **FACE, surface;** [suffix] **(facial expression) face, look**
痘痕面 あばたづら pockmarked face
仏頂面 ぶっちょうづら sulky look, sour face
横っ面 よこっつら side face
字面 じづら appearance of written words, face
川面 かわづら(=かわも) surface of a river

SPECIAL READINGS

面皰×▲ にきび pimple, acne
真面目な まじめな serious, sober, earnest, steady

SYNONYMS

❶ⓐ front parts of head
顔 FACE → 2277
面 FACE → 2590
額 forehead → 2273
顎 chin → 2276
頬 CHEEK → 2043
吻 PROBOSCIS → 0270

❷ⓐ front
前 front → 2819
面 FACE → 2590
首 HEAD → 2818

ⓑ outside
外 OUTSIDE → 0215
表 SURFACE → 3083
面 FACE → 2590

❹ face
向 TURN TOWARD → 3790
面 FACE → 2590
対 face (each other) → 1025

❺ⓐ side
側 SIDE → 0155
脇 SIDE → 1188
方 side → 2459
辺 -side → 3761
面 side → 2590
傍 BESIDE → 0166
横 SIDEWAYS → 1350

ⓑ aspect
面 side → 2590
上 from the viewpoint of → 4212
柄 considering the character of → 1111

❻ⓑ protective coverings
盾 SHIELD → 3729
楯 SHIELD → 1281
鎧 ARMOR → 2211
甲 armor → 4293
縅 BRAID OF ARMOR → 1759
面 mask → 2590
兜 helmet → 3499
幌 COVERING FOR VEHICLES → 0787

❼ paper
紙 PAPER → 1654
葉 LEAF → 2912
丁 sheet → 4155
箋 PIECE OF PAPER → 3352
頁 PAGE → 2589
面 page (of a newspaper) → 2590

❼ parts of periodicals
欄 COLUMN → 1419
面 page (of a newspaper) → 2590

HOMOPHONES

おもて 表 EXPRESS → 3083

NOTE

➡ see USAGE note at 表 3083
➡ see COMPOUND FORMATION for 面白い おもしろい → 白 4305

柔

2591

2-2-7

▶SOFT
ジュウ ニュウ やわ(らか) やわ(らかい) やわ▲ やわ(ら)▲
Ⓒ 柔 róu

75	Jōyō	U67D4
木	S9-4-5	F1349

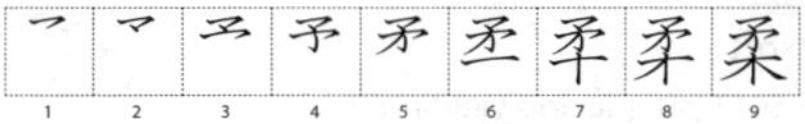

COMPOUNDS

❶ⓐ [original meaning] (supple and yielding) **SOFT, tender, pliant**
ⓑ SOFTen, appease, conciliate
a 柔毛 じゅうもう soft hair
柔軟な じゅうなんな soft, pliable, flexible
b 懐柔する かいじゅうする appease, win over

❷ⓐ (of gentle disposition) **SOFT, softhearted, gentle, mild**
ⓑ (weakly) **SOFT**, weak-looking, frail
a 柔順な じゅうじゅんな obedient, gentle
柔和 にゅうわ gentleness, mildness, tenderness, meekness
b 柔弱な にゅうじゃくな weak, effeminate
優柔不断の ゆうじゅうふだんの indecisive, vacillating

❸ judo
柔道 じゅうどう judo
柔術 じゅうじゅつ jujitsu, jujutsu

INDEPENDENT

【じゅう 柔】 **SOFT**ness, gentleness
柔能く剛を制す じゅうよくごうをせいす Softness overcomes hardness/Soft words win hard hearts
剛と柔 ごうとじゅう hardness and softness

KUN

【やわらか 柔らか】
やわらかな 柔らかな [also 軟らかな]
① **SOFT, tender**
柔らかみ やわらかみ (touch of) softness
② **SOFT**, subdued (color or light)
柔らかな光 やわらかなひかり soft light
③ **gentle, meek, mild**
柔らかな風 やわらかなかぜ gentle breeze
お手柔らかに おてやわらかに gently, mildly; Don't be hard on me!
【やわらかい 柔らかい】[also 軟らかい]
① **SOFT, tender**
柔らかい毛布 やわらかいもうふ soft blanket
② **gentle, meek**
物腰の柔らかい ものごしのやわらかい gentle-mannered
③ informal
柔らかい文章 やわらかいぶんしょう informal style
【やわ 柔】
やわな 柔な frail, fragile
柔肌 やわはだ soft fair skin
【やわら 柔ら】**old term for judo or jujutsu**

SYNONYMS

❶ⓐ soft
柔 SOFT (supple and yielding) → 2591
軟 SOFT (not hard) → 1871
塑 plastic → 3525
❷ⓐ gentle
優しい gentle → 0200
穏 MILD → 1578
柔 SOFT → 2591
ⓑ weak
弱 WEAK → 1499
柔 SOFT → 2591
脆 FRAGILE → 1191
癈 DISABLED → 4077

USAGE

❶【やわらかな】
柔らかな
[also 軟らかな]
① soft, tender
② soft, subdued (color or light)
③ gentle, meek, mild
軟らかな
[also 柔らかな] same as 柔らかな
❷【やわらかい】
柔らかい
[also 軟らかい]
① soft, tender
② gentle, meek
③ informal
軟らかい
[also 柔らかい] same as 柔らかい

HOMOPHONES

やわらか 軟 SOFT → 1871
やわらかい 軟 SOFT → 1871

勇

2592
2-2-7

▶BRAVE
ユウ いさ(む) ㊔ はや とし
Ⓝ 勇 Ⓒ 勇 yǒng

19	Jōyō-4	U52C7
力	S9-2-7	F1089

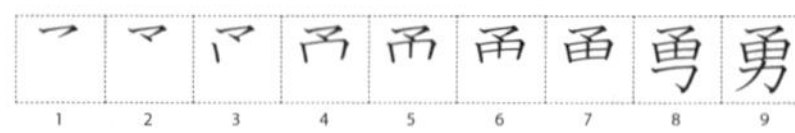

COMPOUNDS

ⓐ [original meaning] **BRAVE, courageous, bold, valiant**
ⓑ BRAVEry, courage, valor, heroism
a 勇敢な ゆうかんな brave, courageous, daring, heroic
勇気 ゆうき courage, valor, bravery, nerve
勇将 ゆうしょう brave general
勇猛 ゆうもう daring, bravery, valor
勇士 ゆうし brave warrior
勇退する ゆうたいする retire voluntarily
b 武勇 ぶゆう bravery, valor
豪勇 ごうゆう bravery, valor, daring
蛮勇 ばんゆう brute courage, reckless valor

INDEPENDENT

【ゆう 勇】**BRAVE**ry, courage, valor, heroism
勇を鼓す ゆうをこす take heart, screw up one's courage

KUN

【いさむ 勇む】**be encouraged, be in high spirits; prance**
勇ましい いさましい brave, courageous, bold, valiant

SYNONYMS

ⓐ brave
勇 BRAVE → 2592
侠 chivalrous → 0110
赳 VALIANT → 4100
驍 VALIANT → 2327
敢 bold → 2142
豪 bold and unrestrained → 2657
雄 HEROIC → 1271
壮 heroic → 0263
義 chivalrous → 2948
凜 gallant → 0195
ⓑ courage

勇 bravery → 2592
胆 pluck → 1150

勇

▶BRAVE

ユウ いさ(む) ㊔ はや とし

2593

2-2-7

19	Nonstandard	U52C7
力	S9-2-7	F0000

traditional form → see 勇 at 2592

負

▶BEAR
▶LOSE

フ ま(ける) ま(かす) お(う)

Ⓝ 負 Ⓒ 负 fù

2594

2-2-7

154	Jōyō-3	U8CA0
貝	S9-7-2	F0506

COMPOUNDS

❶ [original meaning] **BEAR [carry] on the back**
負荷 ふか load, burden

❷ⓐ **BEAR (responsibility), take upon oneself, sustain**
ⓑ **BEAR a debt, owe**

a 負担 ふたん burden, charge, responsibility
負託する ふたくする charge (someone) with responsibility
負傷する ふしょうする be injured [wounded], get hurt

b 負債 ふさい debt, liabilities

❸ be proud
抱負 ほうふ aspiration, ambition
自負する じふする be conceited, be self-confident

❹ **LOSE, be defeated**
勝負 しょうぶ victory or defeat; match, game

❺ⓐ *math* negative
ⓑ *elec* negative

a 負数 ふすう negative number
正負 せいふ positive and negative, plus and minus

b 負極 ふきょく cathode, negative pole; south magnetic pole

INDEPENDENT

【ふ 負】 *math, elec* negativeness
負の ふの negative
負の電荷 ふのでんか negative charge

KUN

【まける 負ける】 **LOSE (a game), be defeated [beaten]; yield to, be overcome; reduce (the price); be poisoned (with lacquer)**
負け まけ defeat, loss, losing (a game)
負け惜しみ まけおしみ unwillingness to admit oneself beaten
誘惑に負ける ゆうわくにまける yield [succumb] to temptation
百円負ける ひゃくえんまける take off 100 yen
漆に負ける うるしにまける be poisoned with lacquer

【まかす 負かす】 **defeat, beat, vanquish, outdo, outplay**
相手を負かす あいてをまかす defeat the opponent
言い負かす いいまかす talk (a person) down, confute

【おう 負う】 **BEAR [carry] on the back; bear (responsibility), take upon oneself; sustain; be proud; bear a debt, owe**
負い目 おいめ debt, unfulfilled promise
背負う せおう carry on one's back, shoulder, bear
請け負い うけおい contract (for work), contracted work
傷を負う きずをおう sustain a wound, be injured
気負う きおう be eager [enthusiastic]

SYNONYMS

❶ **bear**
負 BEAR (on the back) → 2594
荷 carry on shoulder → 2840
担 BEAR ON SHOULDER → 0376
支 SUPPORT → 2473

❷ **undertake**
負 BEAR → 2594
担 UNDERTAKE → 0376

❹ **lose**
負 LOSE → 2594
敗 BE DEFEATED → 1868

❺ **negative**
負 negative → 2594
陰 negative → 0657

急

▶URGENT
▶HURRY
▶SUDDEN

キュウ いそ(ぐ) いそ(ぎ) せ(く)▲ せ(かす)▲

Ⓝ 急 Ⓒ 急 jí

2595

2-2-7

61	Jōyō-3	U6025
心	S9-4-5	F0406

COMPOUNDS

❶ⓐ **URGENT, imminent, pressing**
ⓑ emergency, exigency, crisis

a 急務 きゅうむ urgent business, pressing need
急迫 きゅうはく urgency, imminence
急用 きゅうよう urgent business
緊急な きんきゅうな urgent, pressing, emergent

早急な さっきゅう(=そうきゅう)な urgent, pressing
至急に しきゅうに urgently, with all haste, at once
b 急場 きゅうば emergency, exigency, crisis
救急 きゅうきゅう first aid
応急 おうきゅう emergency, makeshift

❷ⓐ HURRY, hasten
ⓑ rapid, fast, swift, speedy, express
a 急造 きゅうぞう hurried construction
急派する きゅうはする dispatch, expedite, rush
急行 きゅうこう express train [bus]; going in a hurry
b 急速な きゅうそくな rapid, swift, prompt
急ピッチ きゅうぴっち quick [fast] pace
急性の きゅうせいの acute
急進する きゅうしんする advance rapidly, make rapid progress
急流 きゅうりゅう rapid stream, swift current; swift-running river; rapids
急遽× きゅうきょ in a hurry, in haste
緩急 かんきゅう fast and slow motion, high and low speed; emergency

❸ abbrev. of 急行 きゅうこう: **express train [bus]**
特急 とっきゅう super-express
準急 じゅんきゅう local express, semi-express (train)
東急 とうきゅう Tokyu Corporation

❹ [also prefix] **SUDDEN, unexpected**
急激な きゅうげきな sudden, abrupt
急増 きゅうぞう sudden [rapid] increase
急落 きゅうらく sudden drop [fall], steep decline
急変 きゅうへん sudden change [turn]; accident
急死 きゅうし sudden death
急病 きゅうびょう sudden (attack of) illness
急カーブ きゅうかーぶ sharp curve [turn]
急停車 きゅうていしゃ sudden stop

❺ [also prefix] (sharply inclined) **steep**
急坂 きゅうはん steep hill [slope]
急傾斜 きゅうけいしゃ steep slope [incline]

❻ **vital**
急所 きゅうしょ vital part; vital point, tender spot

❼ climax in a traditional Japanese performance (as court music)
序破急 じょはきゅう artistic modulations in traditional Japanese performances; opening, middle and climax [end]

INDEPENDENT

【きゅう 急】
① urgency
焦眉の急 しょうびのきゅう urgent need
② **emergency, crisis**
急を救う きゅうをすくう help (a person) out of danger
急な きゅうな urgent; hasty; rapid, sudden; steep, sharp
③ rapidity, swiftness
④ **SUDDEN**ness
⑤ steepness, sharpness
⑥ climax

KUN

【いそぐ 急ぐ】 *vi* [also verbal suffix] **HURRY (up), hasten**
道を急ぐ みちをいそぐ hurry on one's way
売り急ぐ うりいそぐ sell in haste, be eager to sell

【いそぎ 急ぎ】 **HURRY, haste**
急ぎの いそぎの hurried, hasty; pressing, urgent
急ぎ足 いそぎあし quick pace
大急ぎで おおいそぎで in a great [urgent] hurry, against time

【せく 急く】 *vi* be in a **HURRY**, be hasty, be impatient
【せかす 急かす】 *vt* **HURRY**, rush, press, urge

SYNONYMS

❶ⓐ urgent
急 URGENT → 2595
緊 EXIGENT → 3517
迫 pressing → 3815

❷ⓐ hurry
急 HURRY → 2595
促 HASTEN → 0118
ⓑ fast
速 QUICK → 3851
早 QUICK → 3042
疾 fast → 4064
快 fast → 0289
急 rapid → 2595
迅 SWIFT → 3780
敏 NIMBLE → 1675
即 IMMEDIATE → 1439
捷 AGILE → 0609

❹ sudden
急 SUDDEN → 2595
激 sudden → 0955
暴 sudden → 3138
俄 SUDDEN → 0106
頓 SUDDEN → 1320
勃 SUDDENLY → 1839
突 abruptly → 2772

❺ steep
険 STEEP → 0658
嶮 STEEP → 0937
峭 STEEP → 0341
急 steep → 2595
峻 high and steep → 0495

急

2596

2-2-7

▶URGENT
▶HURRY
▶SUDDEN

キュウ いそ(ぐ) いそ(ぎ) せ(く) せ(かす)

61	Nonstandard	U6025
心	S9-4-5	F0000

traditional form → see 急 at 2595

兔

2-2-7

incorrect stroke-count
➡ see 2-2-6: ⺈ at 2566

負

2597

2-2-7

▶BEAR
▶LOSE

フ ま(ける) ま(かす) お(う)

154	Nonstandard	U8CA0
貝	S9-7-2	F0000

traditional form → see 負 at 2594

旁

2598

2-2-8

▶RIGHT RADICAL
▶BESIDE

ボウ つくり かたがた

Ⓒ 旁 páng

70	Non-Jōyō	U65C1
方	S10-4-6	F0000

COMPOUNDS

❶ **RIGHT RADICAL of a Chinese characters**
偏旁 へんぼう left and right radicals

❷ [now usu. 傍 0166] **BESIDE, side**
旁註(=傍注) ぼうちゅう side notes, gloss

KUN

【つくり 旁】**RIGHT RADICAL of a Chinese characters**
筆旁 ふでづくり *fudezukuri*, 'brush' radical (聿)
節旁 ふしづくり *fushizukuri*, 'seal' radical (卩, 㔾)

【かたがた 旁】**by way of, at the same time**
散歩旁 さんぽかたがた while taking a walk

SYNONYMS

❶ **characters**
字 CHARACTER → 2696
文 LETTER → 2458
漢 kanji → 0808
旁 RIGHT RADICAL → 2598

❷ **near**
近 NEAR → 3798
隣 neighboring → 0961
傍 BESIDE → 0166
旁 BESIDE → 2598
沿 ALONG → 0386

畜

2599

2-2-8

▶LIVESTOCK

チク

Ⓒ 畜 chù xù

102	Jōyō	U755C
田	S10-5-5	F1957

COMPOUNDS

❶ⓐ **LIVESTOCK, domestic animals or fowls**
ⓑ **beast, animal**

a 畜類 ちくるい livestock, domestic animals
畜産業 ちくさんぎょう stockraising
畜舎 ちくしゃ barns and poultry sheds
家畜 かちく domestic animal, livestock
有畜農業 ゆうちくのうぎょう agriculture with livestock raising as a major side line

b 畜力 ちくりょく animal power
畜生 ちくしょう beast; Damn it!
人畜無害な じんちくむがいな harmless to man and beast

❷ **raise LIVESTOCK, rear, domesticate**
畜犬税 ちくけんぜい dog tax
牧畜 ぼくちく livestock farming, cattle breeding

SYNONYMS

❶ **animal**
獣 BEAST → 2384
畜 LIVESTOCK → 2599
生 LIFE → 4309
物 living thing → 1084

NOTE

★ do not confuse with 蓄 STORE UP → 2931

衷

2600

2-2-8

▶INNER HEART

チュウ ㊔ まこと

Ⓒ 衷 zhōng

145	Jōyō	U8877
衣	S10-6-4	F3007

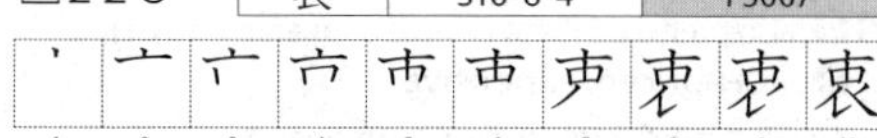

COMPOUNDS

❶ **INNER HEART, true heart, inner feelings; sincerity**
衷心 ちゅうしん inner heart, inmost feelings
衷情 ちゅうじょう inmost feeling, true heart
苦衷 くちゅう mental suffering, dilemma
微衷 びちゅう one's innermost thoughts [feelings]

❷ **happy mean, moderation, propriety**
折衷 せっちゅう compromise, eclecticism

SYNONYMS

❶ **psyche**

【亠】 亠 八 ハ ソ 冖 力 匕 十 ⺊ 又 ⼹ ⺈ 𠂉

心 HEART → 0011
霊 SPIRIT (soul) → 3480
魂 SOUL, spirit → 1346
魄 SOUL → 1570
腹 heart → 1308
衷 INNER HEART → 2600
襟 inner mind → 1599
胸 breast → 1187
懐 BOSOM → 0942
神 MIND → 1143
気 SPIRIT (consciousness) → 3960
精 SPIRIT (mind) → 1729

NOTE

★ do not confuse with 哀 SORROW → 2568

高 2601

▸**HIGH**

コウ たか(い) たか -だか たか(まる) たか(める) (名) たかし たけ

Ⓝ 高◇ Ⓒ 高 gāo

2-2-8

189	Jōyō-2	U9AD8
高	S10-10-0	F0065

RADICAL

takai 'high', used for character classification

COMPOUNDS

❶ⓐ (extending upward) **HIGH, tall, lofty**
ⓑ **height; HIGH place**

a 高度 こうど altitude, height; high degree
高山 こうざん high mountain, lofty peak
高地 こうち high ground, plateau, heights
高原 こうげん plateau, tableland, heights
高架線 こうかせん elevated railway; overhead wires
最高峰 さいこうほう highest peak; highest authority

b 標高 ひょうこう elevation, (height) above the sea
座高 ざこう one's sitting height
登高 とうこう climbing a height

❷ⓐ [also prefix] (of great degree or quantity) **HIGH**
ⓑ **HIGH-priced, expensive**

a 高速 こうそく high speed, high gear
高熱 こうねつ intense heat; high fever
高級 こうきゅう high rank, high class [grade]
高等な こうとうな higher, high-grade, advanced
高等学校 こうとうがっこう senior high school
高校 こうこう senior high school
高裁 こうさい high court
高齢 こうれい advanced age
高給 こうきゅう high salary
高血圧 こうけつあつ high blood pressure
高温 こうおん high temperature
高音 こうおん high-pitched sound [tone], high key
高気圧 こうきあつ high (atmospheric) pressure
高速道路 こうそくどうろ freeway, expressway; highway, turnpike
高炭素鋼 こうたんそこう high-carbon steel
最高の さいこうの maximum, supreme, highest

b 高価な こうかな expensive, high-priced
高騰(=昂騰) こうとう steep rise (in prices), jump

❸ (elevated in rank or character) **HIGH, noble, eminent, lofty**

高位 こうい high rank, honors
高官 こうかん high office, high official, dignitary
高貴な こうきな high and noble
高名 こうめい fame, high reputation; your name
高尚な こうしょうな high, noble, elegant
高潔な こうけつな noble, high-minded, upright

❹ⓐ (showing pride or arrogance) **HIGH**, high-hatted, proud, haughty
ⓑ [formerly also 昂 3065 or 亢 2460] **HIGH**-spirited, excited, elated

a 高慢な こうまんな haughty, arrogant, proud

b 高揚(=昂揚)する こうようする exalt, enhance, uplift; surge up
意気軒高(=意気軒昂)として いきけんこうとして in high spirits

❺ⓐ abbrev. of 高等学校 こうとうがっこう: **HIGH** school
ⓑ suffix after names of **HIGH** schools

a 高卒 こうそつ high school graduate

b 城北高 じょうほくこう Johoku High School

❻ [honorific] your, your honorable

高評 こうひょう your esteemed opinion
高堂 こうどう your beautiful home; you

❼ great-great-grand

高祖父 こうそふ great-great-grandfather

INDEPENDENT

【こう 高】abbrev. of 高気圧 こうきあつ: anticyclone

【こうじる(=こうずる) 高じる(=昂じる、高ずる、昂ずる)】grow worse, grow in intensity

KUN

【たかい 高い】

① (extending upward) **HIGH, tall, lofty**

高さ たかさ height, altitude; pitch
高み たかみ height, elevated place
高跳び たかとび high jump
高台 たかだい high ground, hill, height
高波 たかなみ high waves
小高い こだかい slightly elevated

②ⓐ (of great degree) **HIGH, elevated, superior**
ⓑ **HIGH-priced, expensive**
ⓒ **loud (voice)**

a 高高 たかだか at most, at the highest

高い濃度 たかいのうど high concentration
甲高い かんだかい high-pitched, shrill
名高い なだかい famous, well-known
b 高値 たかね high price
c 高らかな たからかな loud, sonorous, ringing
高笑い たかわらい loud laughter
③ (elevated in rank or character) **HIGH, lofty, noble**
気高い けだかい noble, lofty, high-minded
身分の高い人 みぶんのたかいひと man of high position
④ **HIGH**, proud, haughty
高ぶる たかぶる be highly strung, get excited; be proud, be haughty
お高く留まる おたかくとまる assume an air of importance, put on airs

【たか 高】**quantity, amount, sum**
高が たかが at most, at best, only
高を括る たかをくくる make light of, underrate
高が知れている たかがしれている not amount to much

【-だか -高】[suffix]
①ⓐ **amount of money, total (proceeds)**
ⓑ **amount, quantity, yield**
a 売上高 うりあげだか sales, proceeds
b 生産高 せいさんだか output, yield
② **indicates a rise in prices**
物価高 ぶっかだか high prices of commodities
五円高 ごえんだか (be quoted) 5 yen higher

【たかまる 高まる】**rise (in degree or rank), be raised; increase; build**
高まり たかまり rise, swell, elevation
関心が高まる かんしんがたかまる take a growing interest in

【たかめる 高める】**raise, elevate, enhance, improve**
婦人の地位を高める ふじんのちいをたかめる raise the position of women

SYNONYMS

❶ⓐ high
高 HIGH → 2601
喬 TALL → 3129
峻 high and steep → 0495
峨 HIGH AND RUGGED → 0493

❶ⓐ high
高 HIGH → 2601
上 upper → 4212
峨 LOFTY → 0570

ⓑ height
高 height → 2601
丈 STATURE → 4227
背 stature → 3182

❷ⓐ extreme in degree
酷 SEVERE → 1967
強 STRONG → 0574
凄い tremendous → 0145
重 HEAVY → 4390
高 HIGH → 2601
深 DEEP → 0636
大 BIG → 4224
厳 SEVERE → 4079
激 intense → 0955
極 EXTREME → 1243
痛 bitter(ly) → 4071
切 keen → 0030
甚 EXTREMELY → 3271
祁 EXTREMELY → 1447
超 super- → 4107
頗る EXCEEDINGLY → 1552

ⓑ expensive
貴 precious → 3220
高 high-priced → 2601

❸ high-ranking
貴 NOBLE → 3220
上 upper → 4212
高 HIGH → 2601
総 GENERAL → 1743
太 of highest rank → 2673

❹ⓑ elated
亢 HIGH-SPIRITED → 2460
高 high-spirited → 2601
昂 high-spirited → 3065
揚 exalted → 0722
奮 roused up → 3000

❺ schools
校 SCHOOL → 1166
学 EDUCATIONAL INSTITUTION → 3162
院 INSTITUTION → 0544
塾 PRIVATE SCHOOL → 3546
大 UNIVERSITY → 4224
高 high school → 2601
中 junior high school → 4262
小 elementary school → 0007
園 kindergarten → 3914

【たかい】
②ⓒ **loud**
高い loud → 2601
朗 CLEAR (voice) → 1679
騒 clamorous → 2308
喧 BOISTEROUS → 0667
嘩 BOISTEROUS → 0771

恋 2602

▶**LOVE**

レン こ(う) こい こい(しい)

Ⓝ 戀 Ⓒ 恋 liàn

2-2-8

61	Jōyō	U604B
心	S10-4-6	F0760

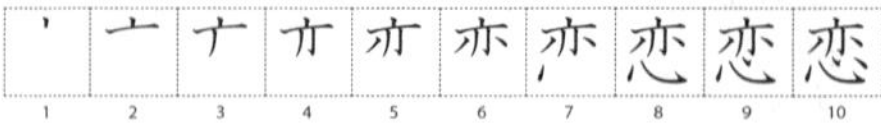

COMPOUNDS

❶ⓐ [original meaning] **LOVE (the opposite sex)**
ⓑ **LOVE (for the opposite sex)**

a 恋愛 れんあい love (for the opposite sex)
恋情 れんじょう love, attachment
恋慕する れんぼする love, fall in love with
b 失恋 しつれん unrequited love
悲恋 ひれん blighted love

❷ beloved, dearest
恋恋とする れんれんとする be ardently attached to (a girl)

KUN

【こう 恋う】**LOVE**
恋い慕う こいしたう miss, yearn for

【こい 恋】**LOVE (for the opposite sex), tender passion**
恋する こいする love, fall in love with
恋人 こいびと lover, sweetheart
恋文 こいぶみ love letter
初恋 はつこい first love

【こいしい 恋しい】**beloved, dear, darling**

SYNONYMS

❶ⓐ **love and like**
愛 LOVE → 3133
恋 LOVE (the opposite sex) → 2602
好 LIKE → 0240
慕 ADORE → 2970
惚れる FALL IN LOVE → 0584
玩 cherish → 1085

ⓑ **love**
愛 LOVE → 3133
情 love → 0583
恋 LOVE (for the opposite sex) → 2602
艶 ROMANCE → 2403
寵 AFFECTION → 3029

NOTE

➡ see USAGE note at 愛 3133

竜 2603

▶**DRAGON**

リュウ リョウ▲ たつ

Ⓝ 龍 龍 Ⓒ 龙 lóng

2-2-8

212	Jōyō	U7ADC
竜	S10-10-0	F1130

radical variant → see 龍 at 2266

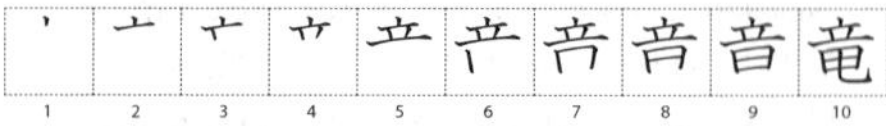

COMPOUNDS

❶ⓐ **DRAGON**
ⓑ suffix for forming names of extinct animals

a 竜神 りゅうじん dragon god, dragon king
竜宮 りゅうぐう Palace of the Dragon King
竜虎 りゅうこ(=りょうこ) dragon and tiger; hero
b 恐竜 きょうりゅう dinosaur, titanosaur
魚竜 ぎょりゅう ichthyosaur

❷ imperial
竜顔 りゅうがん(=りょうがん) emperor's face

❸ name of chess piece in shogi (Japanese chess): *naribisha*, promoted rook
竜王 りゅうおう *naribisha;* dragon king [god]

INDEPENDENT

【りゅう 竜】**DRAGON**; fossil reptile; *naribisha* (→❸)

KUN

【たつ 竜】**DRAGON**

SYNONYMS

❶ⓐ **reptiles and amphibians**
亀 TURTLE → 2637
蛇 SNAKE → 1701
竜 DRAGON → 2603
蛙 FROG → 1716
黽 FROG → 4404

❶ⓐ **mythical animals**
竜 DRAGON → 2603
辰 THE DRAGON → 3713
麒 MALE CHINESE UNICORN → 2363
麟 FEMALE CHINESE UNICORN → 2376
鵬 MYTHICAL HUGE BIRD → 1416
鳳 MALE PHOENIX → 3749
凰 FEMALE PHOENIX → 3738

❶ⓐ **dragon**
竜 DRAGON → 2603
辰 THE DRAGON → 3713

USAGE

【たつ】
竜
dragon
辰
fifth sign of the Oriental zodiac: the Dragon

HOMOPHONES

たつ 辰 THE DRAGON →3713

衰

▶DECLINE

スイ おとろ(える)

Ⓝ 衰 Ⓒ 衰 shuāi cuī

2604

2-2-8

145	Jōyō	U8870
衣	S10-6-4	F1667

1 2 3 4 5 6 7 8 9 10

COMPOUNDS

ⓐ DECLINE, fall into decay, degenerate, weaken, emaciate

ⓑ DECLINE, downfall

a 衰退 すいたい decline, decay, degeneration

衰弱する すいじゃくする weaken, lose vigor

減衰する げんすいする damp, be attenuated

老衰 ろうすい senility

盛衰 せいすい ups and downs, rise and fall, prosperity and decline

b 衰運 すいうん declining fortune

衰亡 すいぼう ruin, fall, collapse

KUN

【おとろえる 衰える】**weaken, lose vigor, become emaciated; wither, fade; DECLINE, decay, go downhill**

衰え おとろえ weakening, emaciation, decline

痩せ衰える やせおとろえる become emaciated, grow thin and worn out

SYNONYMS

ⓐ degenerate

落 FALL →2907

衰 DECLINE →2604

頽 DECLINE →2039

堕 DEGENERATE →3501

綻 UNRAVEL →1745

破 break down →1478

ⓐ weaken

衰 DECLINE →2604

弱 weaken →1499

竟

▶COMPETE

キョウ ケイ きそ(う) せ(る)

2605

2-2-8

117	Nonstandard	U7AF6
立	S10-5-5	F0000

handwritten form →see 競 at 2322

衰

▶DECLINE

スイ おとろ(える)

2606

2-2-8

145	Nonstandard	U8870
衣	S10-6-4	F0000

traditional form →see 衰 at 2604

禼

2-2-8

incorrect stroke-count

➡ see 2-2-9: 亠 at 2627

倉

▶STOREHOUSE

ソウ くら

Ⓒ 仓 cāng

2607

2-2-8

9	Jōyō-4	U5009
人	S10-2-8	F0724

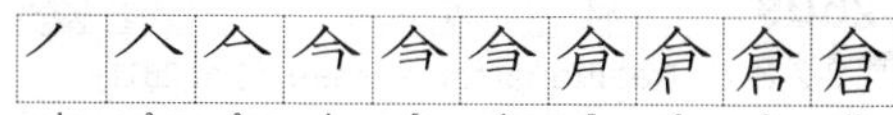

1 2 3 4 5 6 7 8 9 10

COMPOUNDS

❶ⓐ STOREHOUSE, warehouse, granary

ⓑ [formerly 艙 1786] ship's hold, cabin

a 倉庫 そうこ warehouse, storehouse

穀倉 こくそう granary, grain elevator

弾倉 だんそう magazine (of a rifle)

b 船倉 せんそう hold (of a ship), hatch

❷ [formerly also 蒼 2943] hurried, flurried

倉卒な そうそつな hurried, sudden

倉皇(=蒼惶)として そうこうとして in great haste

KUN

【くら 倉】[also 蔵, sometimes also 庫] **STOREHOUSE (esp. for grains or goods), warehouse, granary**

倉荷 くらに warehouse goods

倉渡し くらわたし ex warehouse

SYNONYMS

❶ⓐ storehouse

倉 STOREHOUSE →2607

蔵 storehouse →2995

庫 STORAGE CHAMBER →3864

USAGE

【くら】

倉

[also 蔵, sometimes also 庫] storehouse (esp. for grains or goods), warehouse, granary

蔵

[also 倉, sometimes also 庫] storehouse (for temporary preservation), storeroom, godown

庫

[usu. 倉, sometimes also 蔵] warehouse (for merchandise), storeroom

HOMOPHONES

くら

蔵 STORE → 2995
庫 STORAGE CHAMBER → 3864

益

▶BENEFIT
▶PROFIT

エキ ヤク ま(す) ㊔ よし やす

2608
2-2-8

108	Nonstandard	UFA17
皿	S10-5-5	F0000

traditional form → see 益 at 2849

翁

▶OLD MAN

オウ おきな ㊔ おき

2609
2-2-8

124	Nonstandard	U7FC1
羽	S10-6-4	F0000

traditional form → see 翁 at 2611

釜

▶IRON POT

フ▲ かま

Ⓝ 釜 Ⓒ 釜 fǔ

2610
2-2-8

167	Jōyō	U91DC
金	S10-8-2	F1996

COMPOUNDS

● [original meaning] **IRON POT, kettle, cauldron**

釜中 ふちゅう inside of a pot

KUN

【かま 釜】

①ⓐ **IRON POT, kettle, cauldron**
ⓑ **boiler**

a 釜茹×で かまゆで boiling in a cauldron
電気釜 でんきがま electric rice-cooker
鍋釜 なべかま pots and pans; kitchen utensils
後釜 あとがま successor, replacement
b 風呂釜 ふろがま bath heater

② *slang* buttocks

お釜 おかま (male) homosexual

SYNONYMS

● **vessels and receptacles**

盤 dish → 3533
鍋 POT → 2202
釜 IRON POT → 2610
鼎 TRIPOD CAULDRON → 4405
臼 MORTAR → 4341
碓 MORTAR → 1537
托 RECEPTACLE → 0252
皿 PLATE → 4286
盆 TRAY → 2581
膳 LEGGED TRAY → 1381
杯 CUP → 1066
鉢 BOWL → 2144
椀 WOODEN BOWL → 1250
碗 CERAMIC BOWL → 1539
丼 LARGE BOWL → 4323

HOMOPHONES

かま

窯 KILN → 2986
缶 CAN → 2526

COMPOUND FORMATION

【後釜 あとがま】

後釜 'successor, replacement' originally referred to a pot (釜) placed on a still-burning stove after (後) the first pot has been removed.

NOTE

➡ see USAGE note at 窯 2986

翁

▶OLD MAN

オウ おきな▲ ㊔ おき

Ⓝ 翁 Ⓒ 翁 wēng

2611
2-2-8

124	Jōyō	U7FC1
羽	S10-6-4	F1891

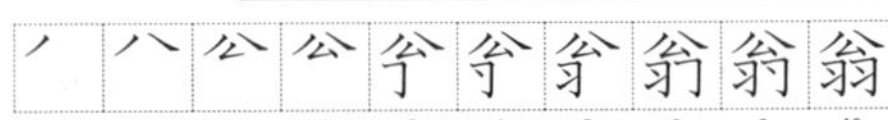

COMPOUNDS

ⓐ **OLD MAN, aged man, elder**
ⓑ honorific suffix after names of venerable old men

a 老翁 ろうおう old man
村翁 そんおう village elder
白頭翁 はくとうおう white-haired old man; wind-flower
b 吉田翁 よしだおう the venerable Mr. Yoshida, old Mr. Yoshida

INDEPENDENT

【おう 翁】**OLD MAN**, aged man

KUN

【おきな 翁】**OLD MAN**, aged man

翁の面 おきなのめん old man's mask
翁貝 おきながい lantern shell

SYNONYMS

ⓐ **old persons**

老 old person → 3963
爺 OLD MAN → 2656
翁 OLD MAN → 2611
婆 OLD WOMAN → 3433
姥 OLD WOMAN → 0420

ⓐ **man**

男 MAN → 3147
郎 YOUNG MAN → 1641

雄 MALE → 1271
牡 MALE → 1040
夫 male adult → 4271
翁 OLD MAN → 2611
爺 OLD MAN → 2656

ⓑ honorific suffixes
翁 honorific suffix → 2611
老 honorific suffix → 3963

釜 2612

▶**IRON POT**
フ かま

167	Nonstandard	U91E1
金	S10-8-2	F0000

2-2-8

traditional form → see 釜 at 2610

差

2-2-8

incorrect classification
➡ see 3-7-3: 羊 at 4104

益兼

2-2-8

incorrect classification
➡ see 2-3-7: 䒑 at 2849

冥 2613

▶**DARK**
▶**WORLD OF THE DEAD**
メイ ミョウ くら(い)▲
Ⓒ 冥 míng

14	Jōyō	U51A5
冖	S10-2-8	F2524

2-2-8

COMPOUNDS

❶ⓐ [original meaning] **DARK, dim**
ⓑ DARKness
a 冥冥 めいめい dark, invisible, obscure
冥闇(=冥暗) めいあん gloom, shade
b 晦冥 かいめい darkness

❷ DARK, ignorant, foolish
頑冥 がんめい stubbornness

❸ WORLD OF THE DEAD, the other world, Hades
冥土(=冥途) めいど *Buddhism* the other world, realm of the dead
冥福 めいふく happiness in the other world
冥王星 めいおうせい Pluto
幽冥 ゆうめい Hades, realm of the dead

❹ miraculous, divine
冥加 みょうが divine protection [blessing], providence
冥利 みょうり providence, luck, (divine) favor
冥罰 めいばつ retribution, divine punishment

❺ meditate, contemplate
冥想 めいそう meditation, contemplation

KUN

【くらい 冥い】[usu. 暗い, sometimes also 昏い or 闇い] **DARK**, dim; (of colors) dark; (producing gloom) dark, dreary, dismal; (concealed) dark, shadowy, shady

SYNONYMS

❶ dark
暗 DARK → 1273
黒 BLACK → 3406
陰 shaded → 0657
闇 DARK → 4134
晦 DARK → 1196
昏 dark → 3073
昧 DARK → 1105
冥 DARK → 2613
曖 SHADY → 1383

HOMOPHONES

くらい
暗 DARK → 1273
昏 LOSE CONSCIOUSNESS → 3073
闇 DARK → 4134

NOTE

➡ see USAGE note at 暗 1273

脅 2614

▶**THREATEN**
キョウ おびや(かす) おど(す) おど(かす)
Ⓒ 胁 xié

130	Jōyō	U8105
月	S10-4-6	F1394

2-2-8

COMPOUNDS

❶ THREATEN (with force), intimidate, menace, coerce
脅迫する きょうはくする threaten, intimidate, menace
脅威 きょうい threat, menace
脅迫状 きょうはくじょう intimidating letter

❷ [original meaning, now archaic] ribs, sides, flanks

KUN

【おびやかす 脅かす】[rarely also 劫かす] **THREATEN, menace, endanger; intimidate, scare; coerce**
平和が脅かされている へいわがおびやかされている Peace is at stake

【おどす 脅す】[formerly also 威す] **THREATEN, menace, intimidate**
脅し おどし threat, menace, intimidation
脅し文句 おどしもんく threatening language, bluff

【おどかす 脅かす】[formerly also 威かす or 嚇かす]
ⓐ **THREATEN, menace, intimidate**
ⓑ **startle**

a 脅かして金を取る おどかしてかねをとる scare money out of (a person)
b 脅かすなよ おどかすなよ What a start you gave me!

SYNONYMS

❶ threaten
脅 THREATEN → 2614
劫 threaten → 1435
威 THREATEN BY FORCE → 4394
嚇 INTIMIDATE → 0964
喝 shout threats at → 0554

USAGE

❶【おどす】
脅す
[formerly also 威す] threaten, menace, intimidate
威す
[now usu. 脅す] same as 脅す

❷【おどし】
脅し
[formerly also 威し] threat, menace, intimidation
威し
①ⓐ [now usu. 脅し] threat, menace, intimidation
ⓑ [in compounds] something that scares or startles
② [usu. 縅し] braid or thread of Japanese armor
縅し
[sometimes also 威し] braid or thread of Japanese armor

❸【おどかす】
脅かす
[formerly also 威かす or 嚇かす]
ⓐ threaten, menace, intimidate
ⓑ startle
威かす
[now usu. 脅かす] same as 脅かす
嚇かす
[now usu. 脅かす] same as 脅かす

❹【おびやかす】
脅かす
[rarely also 劫かす] threaten, menace, endanger; intimidate, scare; coerce
劫かす
[now always 脅かす] threaten, menace, endanger; intimidate, scare; coerce

HOMOPHONES

おどす 威 MIGHT → 4394
おどし
威 MIGHT → 4394
縅 BRAID OF ARMOR → 1759
おどかす
威 MIGHT → 4394
嚇 INTIMIDATE → 0964
おびやかす 劫 KALPA → 1435

眞

2615
2-2-8

▶TRUE
シン ま ま- まこと ㊔ さな まさ まな まこ さね ちか さだ なお

109	Names	U771E
目	S10-5-5	F0000

traditional form → see 真 at 2616

真

2616
2-2-8

▶TRUE
シン ま ま- まこと▲ ㊔ さな まさ まな まこ さね ちか さだ なお
Ⓝ 眞 Ⓒ 真 zhēn

109	Jōyō-3	U771F
目	S10-5-5	F0148

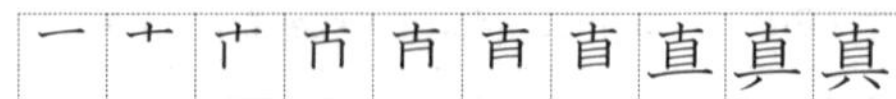
1 2 3 4 5 6 7 8 9 10

COMPOUNDS

❶ⓐ [also prefix] **TRUE, real, actual, genuine**
ⓑ truth, reality, genuineness
ⓒ TRUE nature, essence
a 真価 しんか true value
真意 しんい true meaning [signification]; real intention
真剣 しんけん real sword; seriousness
真相 しんそう truth, facts, real situation
真犯人 しんはんにん the real criminal
b 真実 しんじつ truth, reality
真偽 しんぎ truth or falsehood; authenticity
写真 しゃしん photograph
c 真如 しんにょ the absolute, absolute reality
❷ natural, inborn, pure
純真な じゅんしんな naive, pure, genuine, sincere
天真 てんしん naïveté, simplicity, innocence
❸ square style of Chinese characters
真書 しんしょ square style

INDEPENDENT

【しん 真】truth, reality, genuineness; square style of Chinese characters; star performer
真の しんの true, real, genuine; utter
真に しんに truly, indeed, really
真の友 しんのとも true friend
真に迫る しんにせまる be true to nature [life], be lifelike
真で書く しんでかく write in the square style

KUN

【ま 真】truth
真に受ける まにうける take seriously, believe
【ま- 真-】 [also prefix]
① **TRUE, genuine, pure**
真心 まごころ sincerity, true heart
真ん中 まんなか center, middle

真似をする まねをする imitate, mimic, mock
真似る まねる imitate, mimic

② **right, just, exactly, due (north)**
真上 まうえ right above
真北 まきた due north
真正面 ましょうめん right in front
真弓 まゆみ [also 檀] spindle tree, *Euonymus sieboldiana*

③ **complete, full**
真帆 まほ full sail
真四角 ましかく regular square
真っ裸の まっぱだかの stark naked
真ん丸 まんまる perfect circle
真っ暗な まっくらな pitch-dark

④ honest, serious
真顔 まがお serious face
真人間 まにんげん honest man

⑤ **in the midst of**
真夏 まなつ midsummer
真っ最中 まっさいちゅう midst, height
真夜中 まよなか middle [dead] of the night

【まこと 真】 [usu. 誠, sometimes also 実] **truth, reality**
真に まことに truly, really; very, extremely
嘘か真か うそかまことか true or false

SPECIAL READINGS
真面な▲ まともな decent, self-respecting; honest; right-minded

SYNONYMS
❶ⓐ & ❶ⓑ true
真 TRUE → 2616
洵 TRULY → 0458
実 REAL → 2765
本 real → 4314
正 genuine → 4296
現 ACTUAL → 1218

【ま-】
② **exact**
確 CERTAIN → 1571
正 RIGHT → 4296
真- right → 2616
恰 JUST → 0437

HOMOPHONES
まこと
誠 SINCERITY → 1922
実 REAL → 2765
まゆみ
檀 SPINDLE TREE → 1385
真弓 → 2616, 4193

NOTE
➡ see USAGE note at 誠 1922

索
2-2-8
incorrect classification
➡ see 2-4-6: 𡗗 at 3105

桌
2617
2-2-8
▶**TABLE**
▶**PROMINENT**
タク ㊔ すぐる たか たかし まさる つな

75	Nonstandard	U684C
木	S10-4-6	F0000

traditional form → see 卓 at 2561

桑
2618
2-2-8
▶**MULBERRY**
ソウ くわ
Ⓝ 桒 Ⓒ 桑 sāng

75	Jōyō	U6851
木	S10-4-6	F1868

COMPOUNDS
❶ MULBERRY; mulberry tree
桑園 そうえん mulberry farm [plantation]
桑田 そうでん mulberry plantation
❷ used phonetically for *sō*
桑門 そうもん priesthood, Buddhism

KUN
【くわ 桑】 **MULBERRY; mulberry tree**
桑畑 くわばたけ mulberry field
桑摘み くわつみ picking mulberry leaves
桑原桑原 くわばらくわばら Heaven forbid that thunder strike us!

SYNONYMS
❶ trees
桜 CHERRY → 1168
桐 PAULOWNIA → 1173
桂 AROMATIC TREE, katsura tree → 1163
梓 CATALPA → 1207
桑 MULBERRY → 2618
漆 Japanese lacquer tree → 0863
樺 BIRCH → 1324
椛 BIRCH → 1202
梧 CHINESE PARASOL TREE → 1200
檀 SPINDLE TREE → 1385
椿 CAMELLIA → 1278
柳 WILLOW → 1115
柊 HOLLY → 1119
椋 *APHANANTHE ASPERA* → 1245
柾 spindle tree → 1114
槻 ZELKOVA → 1349
楢 OAK → 1287
樫 EVERGREEN OAK → 1364

柏 CYPRESS, JAPANESE EMPEROR OAK → 1110
榎 HACKBERRY → 1323
梶 PAPER MULBERRY → 1199
柘 JAPANESE BOXWOOD → 1117
楊 WILLOW → 1286
桧 JAPANESE CYPRESS → 1160
梛 *NAGEIA NAGI* → 1206
榊 SACRED SHINTO TREE → 1327
楓 MAPLE → 1280
松 PINE → 1075
杉 CRYPTOMERIA → 1027
槙 PODOCARPUS → 1330
楠 CAMPHOR TREE → 1283
樟 CAMPHOR TREE → 1351

夏

2619
2-2-8

▶**SUMMER**
カ ゲ なつ
Ⓒ 夏 xià

35	Jōyō-2	U590F
夊	S10-3-7	F0708

Stroke order: 1 2 3 4 5 6 7 8 9 10

COMPOUNDS

❶ **SUMMER**
夏季 かき summer, summer season
夏期 かき summer, summertime
夏至 げし summer solstice
春夏秋冬 しゅんかしゅうとう four seasons, all (the) year round
初夏 しょか early summer
盛夏 せいか midsummer

❷ Xia Dynasty (c. 2205-c. 1782 B.C.) (the first Chinese dynasty)
夏朝 かちょう Xia Dynasty

INDEPENDENT

【か 夏】Xia Dynasty

KUN

【なつ 夏】SUMMER
夏休み なつやすみ summer vacation
夏ばて(=夏負け)する なつばて(=なつまけ)する suffer from the summer heat
真夏 まなつ midsummer
常夏 とこなつ everlasting summer

SYNONYMS

❶ **warm seasons**
春 SPRING → 3184
夏 SUMMER → 2619
暑 SUMMER HEAT → 3121

❷ **earlier Chinese dynasties**
夏 Xia Dynasty → 2619
商 Shang Dynasty → 2623
周 Zhou Dynasty → 3720
漢 Han Dynasty → 0808
晋 JIN DYNASTY → 3290
秦 QIN DYNASTY → 3192

奐

2620
2-2-8

▶**FISH**
ギョ うお さかな -ざかな ㊔ お

195	Nonstandard	U29D4B
魚	S10-10-0	F0000

alternative form → see 魚 at 2636

氣

2-2-8

incorrect classification
➡ see ☐3-4-6: 气 at 4000

牽

2621
2-2-9

▶**DRAW**
ケン ひ(く) ㊔ ひた とし とき くる
Ⓒ 牵 qiān

93	Names	U727D
牛	S11-4-7	F2345

COMPOUNDS

● **DRAW, pull, haul, tug**
牽引 けんいん hauling, towing, pulling
牽制する けんせいする check, restrain; divert, feint
牽連する けんれんする be connected
牽強 けんきょう distortion of facts
牽牛星 けんぎゅうせい Altair

KUN

【ひく 牽く】[now usu. 引く, sometimes also 曳く]
DRAW, pull, haul, tug
一頭牽き いっとうびき one-horse (carriage)

SYNONYMS

● **pull**
引 DRAW → 0207
曳 DRAW → 4348
牽 DRAW → 2621
惹 DRAW ATTENTION → 2903
抽 DRAW OUT → 0359
抜 PULL OUT → 0290
控える HOLD BACK → 0600
扣える HOLD BACK → 0250
寄せる DRAW NEAR → 2856

HOMOPHONES

ひく
引 DRAW → 0207
挽 GRIND → 0511
弾 PROJECTILE → 0697
轢 RUN OVER → 2095
惹 DRAW ATTENTION → 2903

退 RETREAT → 3838
曳 DRAW → 4348

NOTE

➡ see USAGE note at 引 0207

斎 2622

▶OBSERVE RELIGIOUS ABSTINENCE

サイ とき▲ ㊔ ひとし いつき

Ⓝ 齋 Ⓒ 斋 zhāi

2-2-9

210	Jōyō	U658E
斉	S11-8-3	F1093

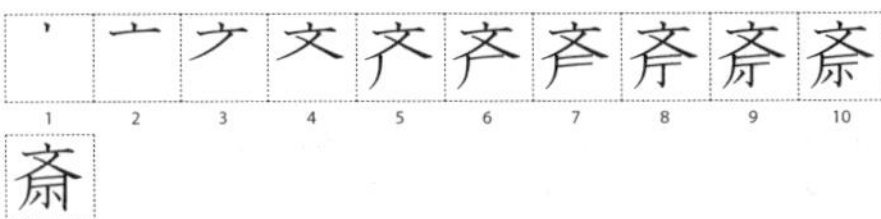

COMPOUNDS

❶ⓐ [rarely also 斉 2548] **OBSERVE RELIGIOUS ABSTINENCE, abstain, purify oneself, fast**
ⓑ religious abstinence, purification
a 斎戒 さいかい religious purification
潔斎 けっさい religious abstinence, purification
b 斎日 さいじつ [rare] days of abstinence, fast day
小斎 しょうさい abstinence (in Catholicism)

❷ⓐ religious ritual [service], Shinto ritual (esp. at Ise Shrine)
ⓑ Buddhist ritual [service]
a 斎主 さいしゅ Chief Priest of the Great Shrine of Ise
b 斎場 さいじょう funeral hall; site of a religious service

❸ⓐ **study, room for study**
ⓑ suffix after names of studies
a 書斎 しょさい study, library

❹ suffix after pen names or pseudonyms
北斎 ほくさい Hokusai (name of a famous artist)

KUN

【とき 斎】meal served to a Buddhist priest; meal served after a Buddhist service

SYNONYMS

❶ⓐ **pray and worship**
祈 PRAY → 1086
祷 PRAY → 1224
願 pray → 2320
拝 WORSHIP → 0360
祀 WORSHIP AS GOD → 1448
崇 REVERENCE → 2864
斎 OBSERVE RELIGIOUS ABSTINENCE → 2622
呪 SPELL → 0323

❷ **ceremonies and festivities**
式 CEREMONY → 3785
儀 CEREMONY → 0191
典 formal ceremony → 3253
礼 RITE → 1012
斎 religious ritual → 2622
会 Buddhist ceremony → 2512
祭 FESTIVAL → 3311

❸ **rooms**
室 ROOM → 2802
間 room → 4122
房 CHAMBER → 2445
斎 study → 2622
堂 HALL → 3202

NOTE

★ do not confuse with 斉 UNIFORM → 2548

商 2623

▶TRADE

ショウ あきな(う) ㊔ あき

Ⓝ 商 Ⓒ 商 shāng

2-2-9

30	Jōyō-3	U5546
口	S11-3-8	F0448

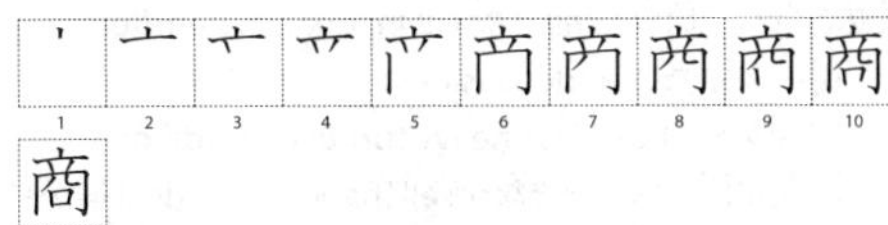

COMPOUNDS

❶ⓐ **TRADE, trade in, deal in**
ⓑ **TRADE, commerce, business; sales**
a 商品 しょうひん goods, commodities
商店 しょうてん shop, store
商業 しょうぎょう commerce, trade, business
商社 しょうしゃ company, firm
商売 しょうばい trade, business, commerce
商法 しょうほう trade, business, commerce; commercial law
商人 しょうにん merchant, trader, tradesman
商船 しょうせん merchant ship, trading vessel
商標 しょうひょう trademark
b 商談 しょうだん business talk; negotiations
通商 つうしょう commerce, trade, commercial relation [intercourse]
行商 ぎょうしょう itinerant trade, peddling
月商 げっしょう monthly sales

❷ [also suffix] **merchant, TRADEr, dealer, businessman, shopkeeper**
画商 がしょう picture dealer
豪商 ごうしょう wealthy merchant
貿易商 ぼうえきしょう trading merchant, importer, exporter
士農工商 しのうこうしょう warriors, farmers, artisans and tradesmen (the four classes of Tokugawa Japan)

❸ abbrev. of 商業高校 しょうぎょうこうこう or 商学部 しょうがくぶ: commercial high school, faculty of commerce
徳商 とくしょう Tokushima Commercial High School
❹ confer, discuss
商量 しょうりょう consideration, deliberation
協商 きょうしょう entente, agreement
❺ *math* quotient
微分商 びぶんしょう differential quotient
❻ Shang [Yin] Dynasty (16th-11th centuries B.C.)
商王朝 しょうおうちょう Shang Dynasty
❼ [rare] second note of the pentatonic scale (→ see APPENDIX 8)

INDEPENDENT

【しょう 商】abbrev. of 商業 しょうぎょう: **TRADE;** *math* quotient; Shang [Yin] Dynasty; [rare] second note of the pentatonic scale

KUN

【あきなう 商う】**sell, TRADE in, deal in, handle**
商い あきない trade, business
大商い おおあきない heavy turnover [trading]
茶を商う ちゃをあきなう sell [handle] tea, deal in tea

SYNONYMS

❶ⓐ **sell and trade**
売 SELL → 2722
卸す WHOLESALE → 1835
販 ENGAGE IN SALES → 1869
商 TRADE → 2623
貿 TRADE → 3214
易 EXCHANGE → 3064
ⓑ **industry and business**
業 BUSINESS, INDUSTRY → 3227
商 TRADE → 2623
産 industry → 4089
工 manufacturing industry → 4190
❷ **merchant**
屋 shopkeeper → 3842
商 merchant → 2623
❻ **earlier Chinese dynasties**
夏 Xia Dynasty → 2619
商 Shang Dynasty → 2623
周 Zhou Dynasty → 3720
漢 Han Dynasty → 0808
晋 JIN DYNASTY → 3290
秦 QIN DYNASTY → 3192

章

2624
2-2-9

▶**CHAPTER**
▶**BADGE**

ショウ ㊔ あき あきら あや ふみ のり ゆき たか

Ⓒ 章 zhāng

117	Jōyō-3	U7AE0
立	S11-5-6	F0690

COMPOUNDS

❶ⓐ [also suffix] (division of text) **CHAPTER**
ⓑ [original meaning] (section of musical composition) movement
a 章句 しょうく passage, chapter and verse
章節 しょうせつ chapter and verse
第一章 だいいっしょう Chapter 1
b 楽章 がくしょう (music) movement
❷ **writing, letter**
文章 ぶんしょう writing, composition, essay; prose
玉章 ぎょくしょう excellent composition; your letter
❸ⓐ [also suffix] (device serving as insignia) **BADGE, emblem, medal, insignia**
ⓑ (distinctive mark) **BADGE, emblem**
a 帽章 ぼうしょう badge on a cap
腕章 わんしょう armband, arm badge
会員章 かいいんしょう membership badge
紋章 もんしょう crest, family insignia, coat of arms
校章 こうしょう school emblem
b 印章 いんしょう seal, stamp
❹ [also suffix] **decoration, medal, order**
勲章 くんしょう decoration, order, medal
褒章 ほうしょう medal of merit
瑞宝章 ずいほうしょう Order of the Sacred Treasure
❺ regulations, constitution
憲章 けんしょう constitution, charter
❻ be confused, be scared
周章狼狽×する しゅうしょうろうばいする be disconcerted, be confused
❼ [usu. 彰 2337] [archaic] make known (someone's virtues to the public)
表章する ひょうしょうする express, make clear (someone's virtues)

INDEPENDENT

【しょう 章】**CHAPTER**
章を改める しょうをあらためる begin a new chapter

SPECIAL READINGS

章魚▲ たこ octopus

SYNONYMS

❶ⓐ **parts of writing**
章 CHAPTER → 2624
段 passage → 1471
節 paragraph → 3336
款 ARTICLE → 2135
条 ARTICLE → 2726
項 CLAUSE → 0692
目 ITEM → 3777
箇 item → 3348

❸ **insignia**
紋 CREST → 1651
章 BADGE → 2624

❹ **prizes**
賞 PRIZE → 3237
杯 prize cup → 1066
章 decoration → 2624

率

2625

2-2-9

▶**RATE**
▶**LEAD**
ソツ リツ ひき(いる)
Ⓝ 率 Ⓒ 率 shuài lǜ

95	Jōyō-5	U7387
玄	S11-5-6	F0583

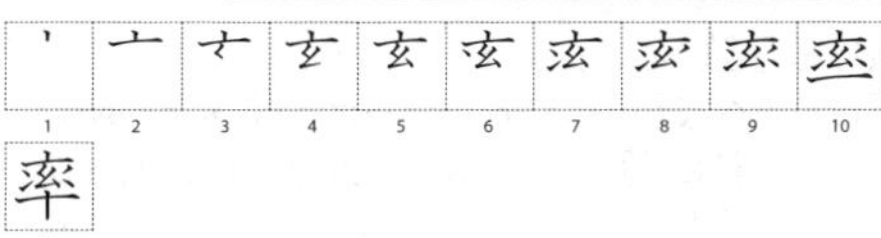

COMPOUNDS

❶ [also suffix] **RATE, proportion; index, coefficient; modulus**
比率 ひりつ ratio, percentage
効率 こうりつ efficiency
百分率 ひゃくぶんりつ percentage
能率 のうりつ efficiency
伸び率 のびりつ growth rate; coefficient of extension
利率 りりつ interest rate, interest
打率 だりつ batting average
確率 かくりつ probability
保険料率 ほけんりょうりつ premium rate
弾性率 だんせいりつ modulus of elasticity

❷ **LEAD, head, command (troops)**
率先 そっせん taking the lead [initiative]
統率する とうそつする lead, command
引率者 いんそつしゃ leader, commander

❸ **frank, straightforward**
率直な そっちょくな frank, openhearted

❹ **rash, hasty**
軽率な けいそつな rash, light-headed, careless

❺ [also 卒 そつ 2549] suddenly, unexpectedly
率然 そつぜん suddenly, unexpectedly

INDEPENDENT

【りつ 率】 **RATE, proportion, percentage; index, coefficient; modulus**
率を定める りつをさだめる fix the rate

KUN

【ひきいる 率いる】 **LEAD, head, command (troops)**
一軍を率いて いちぐんをひきいて at the head of an army

SYNONYMS

❶ **rate**
率 RATE → 2625
割 rate → 2284
比 ratio → 0029
歩 percentage → 3071

❷ **lead and escort**
率 LEAD → 2625
引 lead → 0207
導 GUIDE → 3587
連 take along → 3849

髙

2626

2-2-9

▶**HIGH**
コウ たか(い) たか -だか たか(まる) たか(める) ㊔ たかし たけ

189	Nonstandard	U9AD9
高	S11-10-1	F0000

alternative form → see 高 at 2601

离

2627

2-2-9

▶**SEPARATE**
リ はな(れる) はな(す)

114	Nonstandard	U79BB
禸	S11-5-6	F0000

handwritten form → see 離 at 2364

產

2628

2-2-9

▶**GIVE BIRTH**
▶**PRODUCE**
サン う(む) う(まれる) うぶ- む(す)

100	Nonstandard	U7522
生	S11-5-6	F0000

traditional form → see 産 at 4089

率

2629

2-2-9

▶**RATE**
▶**LEAD**
ソツ リツ ひき(いる)

8	Nonstandard	U7387
亠	S11-2-9	F0000

traditional form → see 率 at 2625

産

2-2-9

incorrect classification
➡ see ☐3-6-5: 产 at 4089

[亠] 𠆢 八 丷 冖 ⺊ 厶 ⺈

畩
incorrect classification
➡ see 4-10-3 at 4397
2-2-9

貪

▶COVET
ドン タン▲ トン▲ むさぼ(る)
Ⓒ 贪 tān

2630
2-2-9

154	Jōyō	U8CAA
貝	S11-7-4	F2487

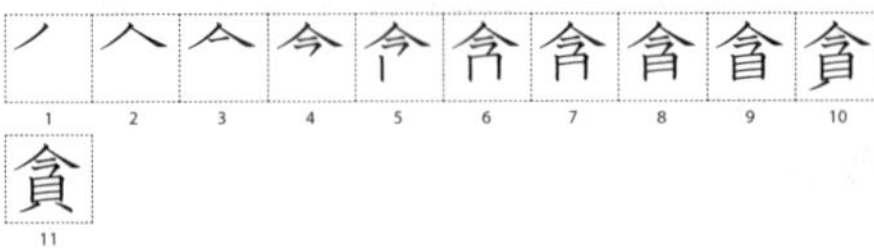

COMPOUNDS

ⓐ **COVET, lust insatiably for, be greedy for; devour**
ⓑ **COVET**ous, greedy

a 貪欲 どんよく greed, avarice
貪婪× どんらん(=とんらん, たんらん) covetousness, greed
貪食 どんしょく voracity, ravenousness
貪愛 とんあい(=どんあい) insatiable lust; *Buddhism* attachment, craving
貪汚 たんお filthy greed
b 突っ慳×貪 つっけんどん blunt, curt, brusque

KUN

【むさぼる 貪る】
ⓐ **COVET, lust insatiably for, be greedy for**
ⓑ indulge in
a 貪り食う むさぼりくう devour greedily
貪り読む むさぼりよむ read avidly
b 快を貪る かいをむさぼる enjoy oneself to the full

SYNONYMS

ⓐ **wish and desire**
願 WISH → 2320
憧 YEARN AFTER → 0899
憬 YEARN AFTER → 0898
貪 COVET → 2630
望 HOPE → 3408
希 ASPIRE → 2543
懐 LONG FOR → 0942
慕 yearn for → 2970
渇 thirst for → 0627
欲 DESIRE → 1867
慾 DESIRE → 3551
求 SEEK → 4365

貧

▶POOR
ヒン ビン まず(しい)
Ⓒ 贫 pín

2631
2-2-9

154	Jōyō-5	U8CA7
貝	S11-7-4	F1223

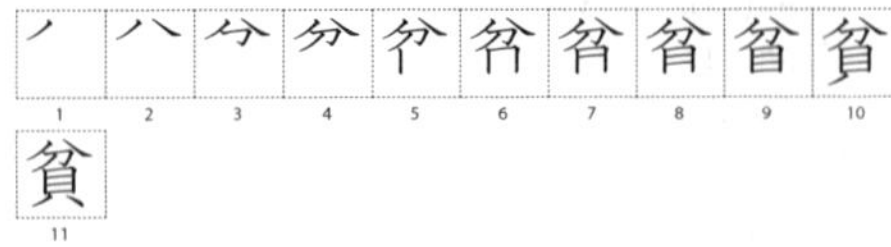

COMPOUNDS

❶ [original meaning] (lacking in wealth) **POOR, destitute**
貧乏 びんぼう poverty, destitution
貧乏人 びんぼうにん poor person, the poor
貧困 ひんこん poverty, indigence, destitution; lack, shortage
貧富 ひんぷ rich and poor
貧窮 ひんきゅう poverty
貧農 ひんのう needy peasant
素寒貧 すかんぴん dire poverty; pauper

❷ (lacking in) **POOR (in), scanty**
貧弱な ひんじゃくな poor, meager, scanty
貧血 ひんけつ anemia

INDEPENDENT

【ひん 貧】 *literary* poverty
【ひんする 貧する】 become **POOR**, live in poverty
貧すれば鈍する ひんすればどんする Poverty dulls the wit

KUN

【まずしい 貧しい】 **POOR, needy, destitute;** (lacking in) **poor (in), meager, scanty**
貧しさ まずしさ poverty
貧しく暮らす まずしくくらす live in poverty
才能が貧しい さいのうがまずしい poor in ability

SYNONYMS

❶ **poor**
貧 POOR → 2631
乏 poor → 2432
窮 destitute → 2983

曽

▶GREAT-
ソウ ゾ ソ▲ ゾウ▲ ひ▲ ひい▲ かつ(て)▲
㊔ ます つね なり
Ⓝ 曾 Ⓒ 曾 zēng céng

2632
2-2-9

73	Jōyō	U66FD
日	S11-4-7	F2105

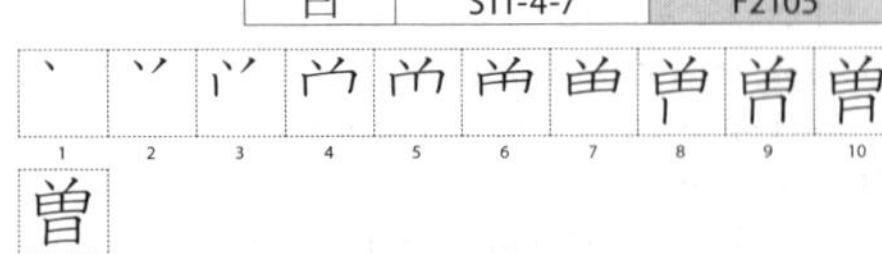

COMPOUNDS

❶ (three generations removed) **GREAT-**
曽孫 そうそん great-grandchild
曽祖父母 そうそふぼ great-grandparents

❷ **previously, formerly, once, before**
曽遊 そうゆう previous visit
未曽有 みぞう unprecedented, unheard of

❸ used phonetically for *so*
伊曽保物語 いそほものがたり Aesop's Fables

KUN

【ひ 曽】[prefix] (three generations removed) **GREAT-**
曽孫 ひまご(=ひいまご,ひひこ,ひこ,ひこまご) great-grandchild

【ひい 曽】[prefix] (three generations removed) **GREAT-**
曽祖母 ひいばば(=ひばば,ひおおば) great-grandmother
曽祖父 ひいじじ(=ひじじ,ひおおじ) great-grandfather

【かつて 曽て】[also 嘗て]
ⓐ previously, formerly, once, before
ⓑ [in negative constructions] (not) ever
b 未だ曽て いまだかつて [in negative constructions] (not) until now, (not) ever before, (not) yet

SYNONYMS

❶ **family and relations**
族 FAMILY →1195
家 FAMILY →2827
門 family →1100
氏 clan →3669
縁 RELATION →1754
姻 relative by marriage →0421
親 RELATIVES →2264
戚 RELATIVES →4401
曽 GREAT- →2632

❷ **former**
旧 FORMER →0014
元 former →2428
故 OLD (earlier time) →1466
前 previous →2819
嘗て previously →3230
曽 previously →2632
先 former →3046
既 ALREADY →1498

HOMOPHONES

かつて 嘗 TASTE →3230

NOTE

➡ see USAGE note at 嘗 3230

盖 剪 incorrect classification
➡ see ▀2-3-8: 䒑 at 2887
▀2-2-9

冨
2633
▀2-2-9

▶**RICH**
フ フウ フッ- と(む) とみ ㊔ ひさ

14	Names	U51A8
冖	S11-2-9	F0000

traditional form → see 富 at 2892

鹵
2634
▀2-2-9

▶**PLUNDER**
ロ
Ⓒ 卤 lǔ

197	Non-Jōyō	U9E75
鹵	S11-11-0	F0000

RADICAL

ro 'salt' (鹹 鹸×), used in characters related to salt

COMPOUNDS

❶ **PLUNDER, rob, capture**
鹵獲する ろかくする capture, seize, plunder

❷ **big shield**
鹵簿 ろぼ imperial cortege [procession]

❸ [archaic] salt, rock salt

SYNONYMS

❶ **steal and rob**
盗 STEAL →3309
窃 STEAL →2801
取 TAKE →1613
奪 ROB →2956
略 plunder →1501
掠 PLUNDER →0605
鹵 PLUNDER →2634

叅
2635
▀2-2-9

▶**PARTICIPATE**
▶**VISIT A HOLY PLACE**
サン シン まい(る) ㊔ み

28	Nonstandard	U53C3
ム	S11-2-9	F0000

traditional form → see 参 at 2563

魚
2636
▀2-2-9

▶**FISH**
ギョ うお さかな -ざかな ㊔ お
Ⓝ 奐◇ Ⓒ 鱼 yú

195	Jōyō-2	U9B5A
魚	S11-11-0	F0935

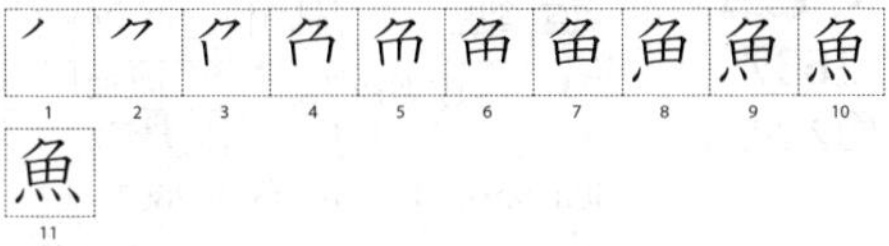

RADICAL

uo 'fish' (魯 鯊×), used in characters related to fish names or marine animals

Left variant: 魚× *uohen* (鮮 鯛 鯨)

亠 へ 八 ソ 冖 ト 厶 【⺈】

COMPOUNDS

ⓐ [also suffix] [original meaning] **FISH**
ⓑ something shaped like a **FISH**

a 魚類 ぎょるい fishes
魚介類 ぎょかいるい marine products
金魚 きんぎょ goldfish
鮮魚 せんぎょ fresh fish
人魚 にんぎょ mermaid, merman
深海魚 しんかいぎょ deep-sea fish
熱帯魚 ねったいぎょ tropical fish
b 魚雷 ぎょらい torpedo

KUN

【うお 魚】**FISH**
魚市場 うおいちば fish market
川魚 かわうお(=かわざかな) river fish, freshwater fish
飛び魚 とびうお flying fish

【さかな 魚, -ざかな -魚】[also suffix] **FISH**
魚屋 さかなや fish shop; fish dealer
小魚 こざかな small fish, fry
干し魚 ほしざかな dried fish, stockfish
焼き魚 やきざかな broiled fish

SPECIAL READINGS

雑魚 ざこ small fish, small fry; lesser fry

SYNONYMS

ⓐ **fish**
魚 FISH → 2636
貝 SHELLFISH → 3150

USAGE

【さかな】
魚
[also suffix] fish
肴
accompaniment for drinks:
ⓐ side dish to go with drinks
ⓑ entertainment [conversation] to liven up a drinking party

HOMOPHONES

さかな 肴 ACCOMPANIMENT FOR DRINKS → 2567

亀

2637
2-2-9

▶**TURTLE**
キ かめ ㊔ ひさし すすむ ひさ
Ⓝ 龜 龜◇ Ⓒ 龟 guī jūn qiū

213	Jōyō	U4E80
亀	S11-11-0	F1211

radical variant → see 龜 at 2667

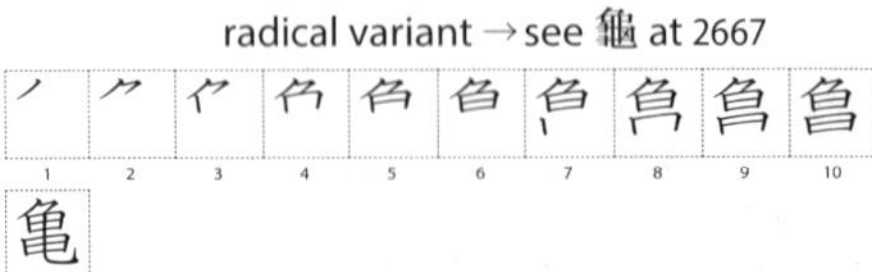

COMPOUNDS

ⓐ [original meaning] **TURTLE, tortoise**
ⓑ shaped like a **TURTLE**

a 亀甲 きっこう carapace of a turtle, tortoiseshell
亀卜 きぼく divination by tortoiseshells
b 亀裂 きれつ crack, fissure
亀頭 きとう glans

KUN

【かめ 亀】**TURTLE, tortoise**
海亀 うみがめ (sea) turtle

SYNONYMS

ⓐ **reptiles and amphibians**
亀 TURTLE → 2637
蛇 SNAKE → 1701
竜 DRAGON → 2603
蛙 FROG → 1716
黽 FROG → 4404

蛮

2638
2-2-10

▶**BARBARIAN**
バン
Ⓝ 蠻 Ⓒ 蛮 mán

142	Jōyō	U86EE
虫	S12-6-6	F1793

COMPOUNDS

❶ⓐ [formerly also 蕃 2989] **BARBARIAN, savage, uncivilized tribe**
ⓑ foreigner, foreign country
ⓒ [original meaning] ancient name for tribes south of China

a 蛮人 ばんじん savage, barbarian; aboriginal
蛮語 ばんご language of the barbarians
蛮族 ばんぞく savage tribe
野蛮な やばんな savage, barbarous, uncivilized
南蛮 なんばん southern barbarians, Europeans from the South (from 16th to 18th centuries); meat cooked with onions; red pepper

❷ barbaric, barbarous, coarse, wild
蛮声 ばんせい rough voice
蛮カラ ばんから rough and uncouth vigor
蛮勇 ばんゆう brute courage, reckless valor

SYNONYMS

❶ⓐ **savage**
蛮 BARBARIAN → 2638
夷 BARBARIAN → 4349
蕃 BARBARIAN → 2989
❷ **vulgar and unrefined**

俗 vulgar →0119
卑 MEAN →3270
賤 MEAN →1993
鄙 MEAN →2338
俚 RURAL →0112
里 rural →4356
粗 COARSE →1683
野 rustic →1877
蛮 barbaric →2638

童

▸CHILD
ドウ わらべ
Ⓒ 童 tóng

2639
2-2-10

117	Jōyō-3	U7AE5
立	S12-5-7	F1186

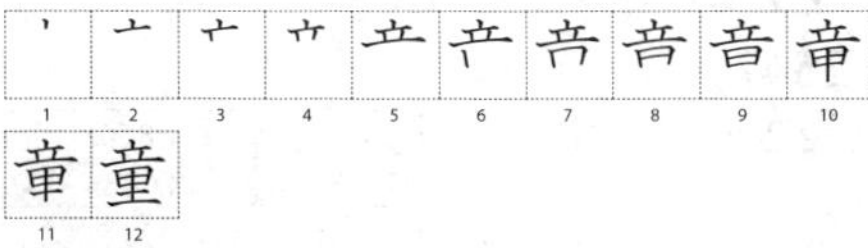

COMPOUNDS

● (young person) **CHILD, youngster**
童心 どうしん child's mind [heart]
童顔 どうがん boyish face, baby face
童謡 どうよう children's song, nursery rhyme
童話 どうわ nursery tale, fairy tale
児童 じどう child, juvenile
学童 がくどう schoolchild

KUN

【わらべ 童】CHILD
童歌 わらべうた children's folk songs

SPECIAL READINGS

河童▲ かっぱ water sprite, *kappa;* excellent swimmer

SYNONYMS

● **child**
児 CHILD (of any age) →3153
子 CHILD →4196
童 CHILD (young person) →2639
幼 young child →0222
坊 SONNY →0274

棄

2-2-10
incorrect stroke-count
➡ see 2-2-11: 亠 at 2651

傘

▸UMBRELLA
サン かさ
Ⓝ 仐◆ Ⓒ 伞 sǎn

2640
2-2-10

9	Jōyō	U5098
人	S12-2-10	F1658

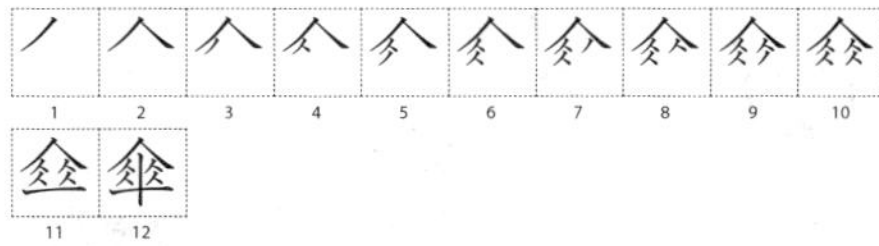

COMPOUNDS

❶ⓐ **something shaped like an UMBRELLA**
ⓑ **something that protects like an UMBRELLA**
a 傘形器官 さんけいきかん *bot* umbraculum
鉄傘 てっさん iron dome
b 傘伐林 さんばつりん shelterwood forest
傘下の さんかの under the influence or jurisdiction of, subsidiary
落下傘 らっかさん parachute
❷ abbrev. of 落下傘 らっかさん: parachute
主傘 しゅさん main parachute
開傘 かいさん opening of a parachute
❸ unclassified compounds
傘寿 さんじゅ 80 years old, one's 80th birthday

KUN

【かさ 傘】
ⓐ **UMBRELLA, parasol**
ⓑ something that protects like an **UMBRELLA**
a 傘を差す かさをさす hold an umbrella
雨傘 あまがさ umbrella
日傘 ひがさ parasol
洋傘 ようがさ umbrella, parasol
b 核の傘 かくのかさ nuclear umbrella

USAGE

【かさ】
傘
ⓐ umbrella, parasol
ⓑ something that protects like an umbrella
笠
①ⓐ sedge hat, bamboo hat, conical hat
ⓑ something that protects like a hat
② shade (of a lamp), hood, something shaped like a sedge hat

HOMOPHONES

かさ 笠 SEDGE HAT →3300

COMPOUND FORMATION

【傘寿 さんじゅ】
傘 is sometimes abbreviated to 仐, which consists of 八 'eight' and 十 'ten', i.e., 80. This gave rise to the word 傘寿, '80 years old, etc.', which means celebrating one's long life (寿) of 80 years (傘 ❸).

禽

2-2-10
incorrect stroke-count
➡ see 2-2-11: 𠆢 at 2654

奠

▶OFFERING

テン デン

Ⓝ 奠 Ⓒ 奠 diàn

2641

2-2-10

37	Non-Jōyō	U5960
大	S12-3-9	F0000

COMPOUNDS

❶ [now replaced by 典 でん 3253] **OFFERING**

香奠 こうでん obituary [condolence] gift, incense money

❷ **establish, settle**

奠都 てんと transfer of the capital

SYNONYMS

❶ **offering**

奠 OFFERING → 2641

幣 offering → 3582

貢 TRIBUTE → 2838

曾

▶GREAT-

ソウ ゾ ソ ゾウ ひ ひい かつ(て)

㊔ ます つね なり

2642

2-2-10

73	Names	U66FE
日	S12-4-8	F0000

traditional form → see 曽 at 2632

尊

▶HONOR

ソン たっと(い) とうと(い) たっと(ぶ) とうと(ぶ) ㊔ たか たかし みこと

2643

2-2-10

41	Nonstandard	U5C0A
寸	S12-3-9	F0000

traditional form → see 尊 at 2920

奠

▶OFFERING

テン デン

2644

2-2-10

37	Nonstandard	U5960
大	S12-3-9	F0000

traditional form → see 奠 at 2641

爺

2-2-10

incorrect stroke-count

➡ see 2-2-11: 八 at 2656

着

2-2-10

incorrect classification

➡ see 3-7-5: 羊 at 4110

善 普 etc.

2-2-10

incorrect classification

➡ see 2-3-9: 䒑 at 2919

悳

▶VIRTUE

トク ㊔ のり よし なる なり あつ

2645

2-2-10

61	Nonstandard	U60B3
心	S12-4-8	F0000

traditional form → see 德 at 0842

叅

▶PARTICIPATE

▶VISIT A HOLY PLACE

サン シン まい(る) ㊔ み

2646

2-2-10

28	Nonstandard	U53C5
ム	S12-2-10	F0000

traditional form → see 参 at 2563

象

▶PHENOMENON

▶ELEPHANT

ショウ ゾウ かたど(る)▲ ㊔ きさ

Ⓒ 象 xiàng

2647

2-2-10

152	Jōyō-4	U8C61
豕	S12-7-5	F0485

COMPOUNDS

❶ (outward manifestation of things) **PHENOMENON, outer appearance, material form; things, object**

現象 げんしょう phenomenon

気象 きしょう atmospheric phenomena, weather conditions

天象 てんしょう astronomical phenomena

万象 ばんしょう all things [manifestations] in the universe

対象 たいしょう object (of study), subject, target

抽象 ちゅうしょう abstraction

❷ **represent, symbolize**

象徴する しょうちょうする symbolize

象形文字 しょうけいもじ hieroglyph, pictograph

❸ (mental representation) **image, mental image**

印象 いんしょう impression

心象 しんしょう image, mental picture

表象 ひょうしょう representation, image, idea

❹ [original meaning] **ELEPHANT**

象さん ぞうさん elephant

象牙 ぞうげ ivory

巨象 きょぞう gigantic elephant

アフリカ象 あふりかぞう African elephant

INDEPENDENT

【ぞう 象】**ELEPHANT**

象の鼻 ぞうのはな trunk of an elephant

KUN

【かたどる 象る】[sometimes also 形どる] model after, represent

手を象った字 てをかたどったじ character representing a hand

SYNONYMS

❶ **phenomenon**

象 PHENOMENON → 2647

気 natural phenomenon → 3960

物 physical phenomena → 1084

❷ **imitate**

擬 IMITATE → 0969

倣 COPY AFTER → 0127

摸 PATTERN AFTER → 0797

模 pattern after → 1326

肖 MODEL → 2733

象 represent → 2647

❹ **undomesticated mammals**

虎 TIGER → 3981

猿 MONKEY → 0824

鯨 WHALE → 2361

犀 RHINOCEROS → 3900

狼 WOLF → 0541

狐 FOX → 0472

羚 SEROW → 1695

鼠 RAT → 3340

獅 LION → 0825

豹 LEOPARD → 1847

熊 BEAR → 3530

象 ELEPHANT → 2647

麒 MALE CHINESE UNICORN → 2363

麟 FEMALE CHINESE UNICORN → 2376

猪 WILD BOAR → 0652

鹿 DEER → 3879

USAGE

【かたどる】

象る

[sometimes also 形どる] model after, represent

形どる

[usu. 象る] model after, represent

HOMOPHONES

かたどる 形 SHAPE → 1050

COMPOUND FORMATION

❶【対象 たいしょう】

対象 'object, etc.' (German *Gegenstand*) is the object or phenomenon (象 ❶) that stands in contradistinction (対) to oneself.

❷【抽象 ちゅうしょう】

抽象 'abstraction' is the process of separating or extracting (抽) the inherent properties of a physical phenomenon or object (象 ❶).

NOTE

➡ see also USAGE note at 像 0187

無 2648

▶**WITHOUT**
▶**NOTHING**

ム ブ な(い)

Ⓒ 无 wú mó

2-2-10

86	Jōyō-4	U7121
灬	S12-4-8	F0151

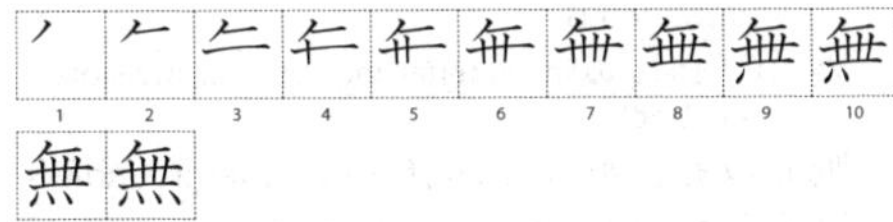

COMPOUNDS

❶ [also prefix] **WITHOUT, -less, non-, un-, in-, no**—element indicating nonexistence or lack

無給で むきゅうで without pay [salary]

無用の むようの useless; unnecessary; forbidden

無限の むげんの infinite, endless, unfathomable

無断で むだんで without permission; without notice [warning]

無料 むりょう no charge, free

無理な むりな unreasonable, unjustifiable; impossible; forced; excessive; irrational (equation)

無理やりに むりやりに by force, against one's will

無死 むし *baseball* with no outs

無礼 ぶれい discourtesy, rudeness

無能 むのう inefficiency, incompetence

無毒の むどくの nonpoisonous

無休で むきゅうで without leave [holiday]

無関係の むかんけいの irrelevant, unrelated

無責任 むせきにん irresponsibility

無事故 むじこ no accident, no trouble

無職の むしょくの without occupation, unemployed

無期限の むきげんの indefinite

無条件の むじょうけんの unconditional, unqualified

無意識に むいしきに unconsciously, without thinking

無人の むじんの uninhabited; unmanned

無神経な むしんけいな insensitive, inconsiderate

無造作に むぞうさに easily; casually

無恥 むち shamelessness, impudence

無名の むめいの nameless, obscure

無闇に むやみに rashly, thoughtlessly; excessively; needlessly

無意味な むいみな meaningless; absurd

無害な むがいな harmless

無関心 むかんしん apathy, indifference

無制限の むせいげんの unlimited, free, unrestricted

無生物 むせいぶつ inanimate object

【工 亠 𠆢 八 丷 冖】

無知 むち ignorance
無用心 ぶようじん insecurity, carelessness
無色の むしょくの colorless; neutral
無力 むりょく powerlessness, helplessness, impotence
無数の むすうの countless, innumerable
無論 むろん of course, no doubt, naturally
無益な むえきな useless; futile
無法な むほうな lawless, unlawful; unreasonable; outrageous
無形の むけいの immaterial, incorporeal; invisible; abstract
無実の むじつの innocent; false, untrue; groundless
無情な むじょうな heartless, coldhearted
無性に むしょうに very much, extremely
無心 むしん innocence; request
無風の むふうの calm, windless
無機物 むきぶつ inorganic substance
無欲な むよくな unselfish; disinterested

❷ **NOTHING, nothingness, nonexistence**
皆無 かいむ nothing
有無 うむ existence, presence; yes or no
絶無 ぜつむ nothing, nil, naught

❸ **set at naught, disregard**
無視する むしする ignore, disregard

❹ abbrev. of 無所属 むしょぞく: independent, affiliated with no party
無現(=無所属現) むげん(=むしょぞくげん) incumbent candidate unaffiliated with a party

INDEPENDENT

【む 無】 **NOTHING, naught**
無から有は生じない むからゆうはしょうじない Nothing comes from nothing
無にする むにする bring to naught
無に帰する むにきする come to naught [nothing]

KUN

【ない 無い】
①ⓐ **there is no, do not exist, have not**
ⓑ **be missing, lack**
a 無しで なしで without
金が無い かねがない have no money
資本無しで しほんなしで without capital
子が無い こがない have no children
ab 無くす なくす lose, be deprived of; get rid of, remove, do away with
無くなる なくなる disappear, be gone; run short; get lost, be missing
b 財布が無い さいふがない My purse is missing
② **not, do not**
行きたく無い いきたくない do not want to go
寒くも無いし暑くも無い さむくもないしあつくもない It is neither hot nor cold

SYNONYMS

❶ **terms of negation**
不 NOT (negation) → 4242
非 IS NOT (contrariety) → 1101
無 WITHOUT (nonexistence) → 2648
没 lacking in → 0305
欠 LACK → 2481
否 OR NOT → 3058
未 NOT YET → 4318
莫 NOT → 2839
勿 DO NOT → 3661

❷ **emptiness and nothing**
空 EMPTY → 2767
白 WHITE (blank) → 4305
虚 VOID → 4017
無 NOTHING → 2648

USAGE

❶【ない】
無い
①ⓐ there is no, do not exist, have not
ⓑ be missing, lack
② not, do not
亡い
not in this world, dead

❷【なくす】
無くす
ⓐ lose, be deprived of
ⓑ get rid of, remove, do away with
亡くす
lose (a parent), be bereft of

❸【なくなる】
無くなる
ⓐ disappear, be gone; run short
ⓑ get lost, be missing
亡くなる
die, be dead

HOMOPHONES

ない 亡 DECEASE → 4210
なくす 亡 DECEASE → 4210
なくなる 亡 DECEASE → 4210

NOTE

➡ see also USAGE note at 不 4242
➡ see COMPOUND FORMATION for 天衣無縫 てんいむほう → 縫 1781

稟

2649
2-2-11

▶**REPORT TO**
ヒン リン ㊔ うくる
Ⓝ 稟◇ Ⓒ 禀 bǐng

115	Names	U7A1F
禾	S13-5-8	F3298

COMPOUNDS

❶ **REPORT TO (a superior), petition**

稟議 りんぎ(=ひんぎ) reaching a decision via circular
稟告 りんこく petition, application

❷ **inborn, innate, natural**

稟質 ひんしつ one's nature
稟性 ひんせい one's nature
天稟 てんぴん(=てんりん) natural gift

❸ [archaic] receive orders

SYNONYMS

❶ **inform and communicate**

報 INFORM →2133
通 COMMUNICATE →3855
告 NOTIFY →3062
届ける give notice →3820
達 issue a notice →3893
知 let know →1446
申 REPORT →4319
稟 REPORT TO →2649
宣 PROCLAIM →2799

意

2650

▶**MIND**
▶**MEANING**

イ ㊔ おき

Ⓒ 意 yì

2-2-11

61	Jōyō-3	U610F
心	S13-4-9	F0082

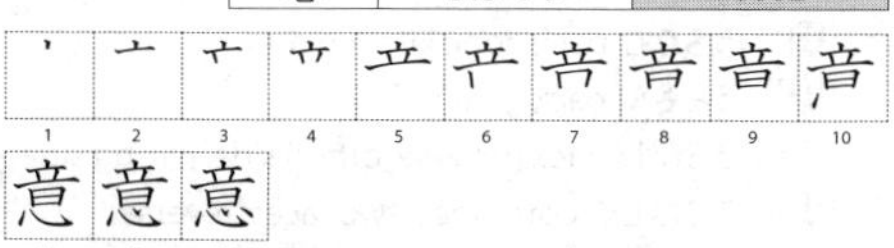

COMPOUNDS

❶ **MIND, heart, thoughts, feelings; opinion**

意識 いしき consciousness, awareness
意見 いけん opinion, view; admonition
意気 いき heart, mind, (high) spirits
意外な いがいな unexpected, unforeseen, surprising
意地 いじ nature, disposition; will power, backbone
意地悪 いじわる nastiness; ill-natured person
注意 ちゅうい attention, care, advice
用意する よういする prepare, ready oneself, make arrangements
好意 こうい goodwill, favor, kindness
誠意 せいい sincerity, good faith
合意 ごうい mutual agreement [consent]

❷ **MIND (to do something), intention, will, inclination, desire**

意向 いこう intention, inclination
意志 いし will, volition
意欲 いよく volition, will, desire
意図 いと intention, aim
決意する けついする make up one's mind, resolve, determine
得意 とくい one's forte; pride; customer
善意 ぜんい good intention; favorable sense
任意の にんいの optional, voluntary, discretionary; arbitrary

❸ **MEANING, sense, intent**

意味 いみ meaning, intention, significance, purport
意義 いぎ meaning, sense, signification, significance
意訳 いやく free translation
真意 しんい true meaning [signification]; real intention
文意 ぶんい meaning (of a passage), purport
表意文字 ひょういもじ ideograph, ideographic character

INDEPENDENT

【い 意】

① **MIND, heart, thoughts, feelings; opinion**

意に介する いにかいする mind, take (something) to heart
意を強くする いをつよくする be reassured, feel encouraged

② **MIND** (to do something), intention, will, inclination, desire

意を決する いをけっする make up one's mind
人の意を受ける ひとのいをうける comply with a person's wishes

③ **MEANING**, sense, intent

意を得ない いをえない fail to make sense (of)

SYNONYMS

❶ **thought**

念 THOUGHTS →2554
考え thought →3962
意 MIND →2650
想 conception →3507

❷ **will and intention**

志 AMBITION →2725
意 MIND →2650
図 intention →3809
気 mind to do something →3960
念 thought of doing something →2554
趣 PURPOSE →4111
欲 DESIRE →1867

❸ **meaning**

義 MEANING →2948
意 MEANING →2650
訳 SENSE →1865
旨 PURPORT →2516
趣 PURPOSE →4111

NOTE

➡ see COMPOUND FORMATION for
得意 とくい → 得 0577
表意文字 ひょういもじ → 表 3083

棄

2651

2-2-11

▶**ABANDON**

キ す(てる)▲

Ⓝ 弃 Ⓒ 弃 qì

75	Jōyō	U68C4
木	S13-4-9	F1334

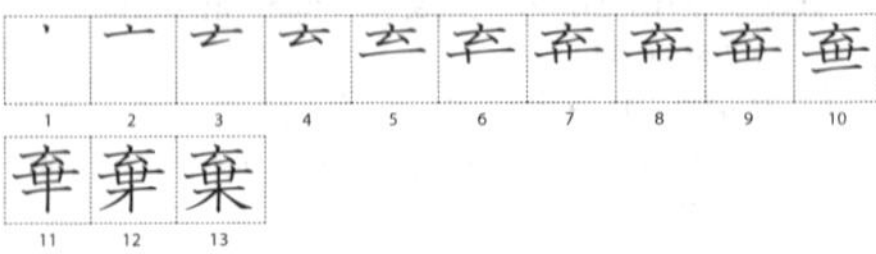

COMPOUNDS

❶ⓐ ABANDON, forsake, desert, discard
ⓑ [original meaning] **throw away; give up, ABANDON**

a 棄権する きけんする abstain from voting, abandon one's right
棄却する ききゃくする turn down, reject, renounce
放棄する ほうきする abandon, resign
破棄する はきする break (a treaty), annul
ab 廃棄 はいき discarding, abolition, annulment
b 投棄する とうきする abandon, give up, throw away

❷ [formerly 毀 2246] **destroy, ruin, damage**
破棄する はきする reverse (the original judgment)

KUN

【すてる 棄てる】[usu. 捨てる]
ⓐ discard, throw away, cast aside
ⓑ **ABANDON**, desert, discard, forsake, give up
a 棄て売り すてうり sacrifice sale
b 権利を棄てる けんりをすてる abandon one's rights

SYNONYMS

❶ discard and abandon
捨 DISCARD → 0608
棄 ABANDON → 2651
諦 GIVE UP → 2010

HOMOPHONES

すてる 捨 DISCARD → 0608

NOTE

➡ see USAGE note at 捨 0608

裏

2652

2-2-11

▶**REAR**

リ うら

Ⓝ 裡 Ⓒ 里 lǐ li

145	Jōyō-6	U88CF
衣	S13-6-7	F0580

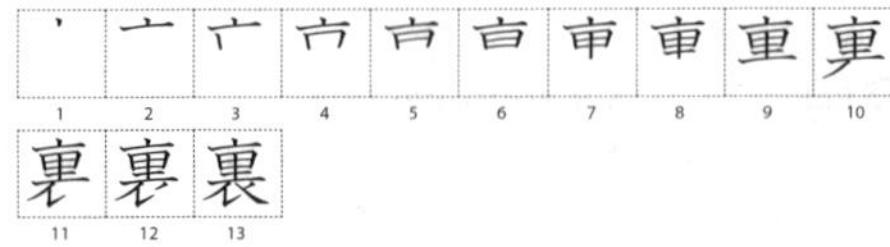

COMPOUNDS

❶ REAR, back, reverse, other side
裏面 りめん back, reverse, other side, inside; background
表裏 ひょうり front and rear, both sides (of a thing or matter); duplicity
庫裏 くり temple's kitchen; priest's living quarters

❷ inside, within, in
脳裏 のうり brain, mind, memory
胸裏 きょうり one's bosom, one's heart, one's feelings
手裏剣 しゅりけん throwing knife
禁裏 きんり the Imperial Palace

❸ [suffix] in a state of, -ly
成功裏に せいこうりに in success
暗暗裏に あんあんりに tacitly, implicitly

KUN

【うら 裏】[also prefix and suffix] **REAR, back; reverse, other side; lining (of clothes); inside, hidden part; support, backing, proof;** *baseball* **second half (of an inning), bottom**
裏通り うらどおり back street
裏庭 うらにわ rear garden
裏口 うらぐち back door, kitchen door
裏門 うらもん back gate
裏側 うらがわ back [reverse, other] side, wrong side
裏表 うらおもて both sides; two faces; reverse, opposite; the reverse; double-dealing
裏返しにする うらがえしにする turn over, turn inside out, turn upside down
裏を返す うらをかえす turn the other way, turn inside out
裏打ち うらうち lining, backing
裏付け うらづけ guarantee, endorsement; support, backing; substantiation, proof
裏切る うらぎる betray, turn traitor, double-cross
裏を掻く うらをかく counterplot, outwit, defeat
頁の裏に ぺーじのうらに overleaf
三回の裏 さんかいのうら bottom [second half] of the third inning

SYNONYMS

❶ rear
後 after- → 0431
背 BACK → 3182
裏 REAR → 2652
尻 tail end → 3766
尾 TAIL → 3799

❷ inside

内 INSIDE → 4277
裏 inside → 2652
奥 INNER PART → 3503
中 IN → 4262

稟

2653

2-2-11

▶**REPORT TO**

ヒン リン ㊔ うくる

113	Nonstandard	U7980
示	S13-5-8	F0000

alternative form → see 禀 at 2649

喪

2-2-11

incorrect classification/ stroke-count
➡ see 2-9-3: 亞 at 3504

禽

2654

2-2-11

▶**BIRD**

キン とり

Ⓒ 禽 qín

114	Names	U79BD
内	S13-5-8	F3275

COMPOUNDS

❶ BIRD, fowl

禽類 きんるい birds
禽獣 きんじゅう birds and animals
禽舎 きんしゃ poultry shed
家禽 かきん poultry, domestic fowl
猛禽 もうきん bird of prey
水禽 すいきん waterfowl, aquatic bird
野禽 やきん wild bird

❷ [archaic]

ⓐ capture, take captive
ⓑ captive

KUN

【とり 禽】[usu. 鳥] **BIRD, fowl**

SYNONYMS

❶ bird

鳥 BIRD → 4105
禽 BIRD → 2654
雛 CHICK → 2312

HOMOPHONES

とり

鳥 BIRD → 4105
鶏 CHICKEN → 2221
酉 THE ROOSTER → 4358

NOTE

➡ see USAGE note at 鳥 4105

會

2655

2-2-11

▶**MEET**
▶**SOCIETY**

カイ エ あ(う) あ(わせる)

73	Nonstandard	U6703
曰	S13-4-9	F0000

traditional form → see 会 at 2512

爺

2656

2-2-11

▶**OLD MAN**

ヤ じじ じじい じい

Ⓒ 爷 yé

88	Non-Jōyō	U723A
父	S13-4-9	F1767

COMPOUNDS

● OLD MAN

老爺 ろうや old man
好好爺 こうこうや good-natured old man

KUN

【じじ 爺】**OLD MAN**

爺臭い じじくさい old-mannish
爺婆 じじばば old man and old woman; grandfather and grandmother

【じじい 爺, 爺い】*slang* **OLD MAN, old geezer**

糞×爺 くそじじい old geezer, old fart

【じい 爺】**OLD MAN**

お爺さん おじいさん old man, grandpa
爺や じいや old man, old manservant

SYNONYMS

● old persons

老 old person → 3963
爺 OLD MAN → 2656
翁 OLD MAN → 2611
婆 OLD WOMAN → 3433
姥 OLD WOMAN → 0420

● man

男 MAN → 3147
郎 YOUNG MAN → 1641
雄 MALE → 1271
牡 MALE → 1040
夫 male adult → 4271
翁 OLD MAN → 2611
爺 OLD MAN → 2656

義慈 etc.

2-2-11

incorrect classification
➡ see 2-3-10: 䒑 at 2948

寫

2-2-11

incorrect stroke-count
➡ see 2-2-12: 冖 at 2660

2

豪

▸GREAT MAN
▸MAGNIFICENT

ゴウ えら(い)▲ ㊔ つよし たけし たけ ひで

Ⓒ 豪 háo

2657

2-2-12

152	Jōyō	U8C6A
豕	S14-7-7	F1018

COMPOUNDS

❶ **GREAT MAN, person of extraordinary powers, champion, hero**
豪傑 ごうけつ hero, great [extraordinary] man
文豪 ぶんごう great man of letters, literary master
酒豪 しゅごう great [heavy] drinker
剣豪 けんごう great swordsman, master fencer
強豪(=強剛) きょうごう veteran, champion
富豪 ふごう wealthy man, millionaire

❷ⓐ **MAGNIFICENT, grand, grandiose, great, splendid**
ⓑ bold and unrestrained, heroic, chivalrous
a 豪華な ごうかな gorgeous, splendid, pompous
豪壮な ごうそうな grand, magnificent, splendid
豪勢な ごうせいな great, grand, magnificent
b 豪快な ごうかいな exciting, heroic, largehearted
豪放な ごうほうな largehearted, openhearted
豪語する ごうごする talk big, boast, brag
豪遊 ごうゆう wild merrymaking

❸ wealthy
豪農 ごうのう wealthy farmer
豪族 ごうぞく wealthy and powerful family [clan]
豪商 ごうしょう wealthy merchant

❹ **powerful, heavy**
豪雨 ごうう heavy rain, downpour
豪雪 ごうせつ tremendous snowfall

❺ [formerly also 濠 0975] Australia
豪州 ごうしゅう Australia
日豪の にちごうの Japanese-Australian

INDEPENDENT

【ごう 豪】Australia

KUN

【えらい 豪い】[usu. 偉い]
① remarkable, extraordinary
豪さ えらさ remarkableness
豪物 えらぶつ extraordinary [able] character
② awful, serious
ど豪い どえらい terrible, very serious

SYNONYMS

❶ **great persons**
豪 GREAT MAN → 2657
傑 OUTSTANDING PERSON → 0175
雄 hero → 1271
匠 CRAFTSMAN → 3711
聖 great master → 3509

❷ⓐ **great**
偉 GREAT (of superior character) → 0167
大 BIG → 4224
宏 GRAND (large in scale) → 2728
壮 GRAND (having grandeur) → 0263
豪 MAGNIFICENT → 2657
雄 HEROIC → 1271
碩 EMINENT → 1555

ⓑ **brave**
勇 BRAVE → 2592
侠 chivalrous → 0110
赳 VALIANT → 4100
驍 VALIANT → 2327
敢 bold → 2142
豪 bold and unrestrained → 2657
雄 HEROIC → 1271
壮 heroic → 0263
義 chivalrous → 2948
凜 gallant → 0195

❸ **rich**
富 RICH → 2892
豪 wealthy → 2657

❺ **continents**
亜 Asia → 4354
阿 Africa → 0408
欧 EUROPE → 1098
米 AMERICA → 4342
豪 Australia → 2657

HOMOPHONES

えらい 偉 GREAT → 0167

NOTE

➡ see USAGE note at 偉 0167

膏

▸FAT

コウ あぶら

Ⓒ 膏 gāo gào

2658

2-2-12

130	Names	U818F
月	S14-4-10	F2852

COMPOUNDS

❶ [original meaning] **FAT, grease; greasy substance**
膏肓× こうこう(=こうもう) inmost part (of the body)
膏血 こうけつ sweat and blood

❷ [also suffix]

ⓐ **ointment, cream**
ⓑ **plaster, medicated patch (for aching muscles)**
a 軟膏 なんこう ointment, salve
b 絆創膏 ばんそうこう adhesive plaster [tape]
按摩膏 あんまこう massaging plaster
石膏 せっこう plaster, gypsum

❸ become **FAT**, become fertile
膏腴× こうゆ fertile soil [land]; fertility

KUN

【あぶら 膏】 [now usu. 脂] **FAT**, grease; greasy substance
膏汗 あぶらあせ cold sweat, greasy sweat
膏薬 あぶらぐすり(=こうやく) plaster; ointment
豚の膏 ぶたのあぶら lard, grease of a hog

SYNONYMS

❶ **fats and oils**
油 OIL → 0400
脂 FAT → 1190
肪 ANIMAL FAT → 1089
膏 FAT → 2658
蠟 WAX → 1818

HOMOPHONES

あぶら
脂 FAT → 1190
油 OIL → 0400

NOTE

➡ see USAGE note at 油 0400

齊

2659
2-2-12

▸**UNIFORM**
セイ サイ ㊔ ひとし ひさし いつき なり

210	Names	U9F4A
齊	S14-14-0	F0000

traditional form → see 斉 at 2548

RADICAL

sei 'uniform' (齋 齎×), used in characters related to uniformity or evenness
Variant: 斉 *sei* (斎)

寫

2660
2-2-12

▸**COPY**
シャ うつ(す) うつ(る)

14	Nonstandard	U51A9
冖	S14-2-12	F0000

traditional form → see 写 at 2493

福

2-2-12

incorrect classification
➡ see 1-5-9: 礻 at 1557

舞

2661
2-2-12

▸**DANCE**
ブ ま(う) -ま(う) まい

136	Nonstandard	U821E
舛	S14-6-8	F0000

traditional form → see 舞 at 2666

褒

2662
2-2-13

▸**COMMEND**
ホウ ほ(める)
Ⓝ 褒 Ⓒ 褒 bāo

145	Jōyō	U8912
衣	S15-6-9	F1984

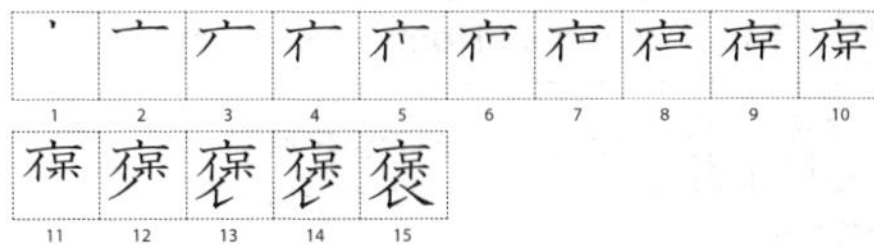

COMPOUNDS

● **COMMEND, praise, laud, award, give recognition to**
褒章 ほうしょう medal of merit
褒美 ほうび reward, prize
褒賞 ほうしょう prize, reward
過褒 かほう overpraise, excessive compliment
毀誉褒貶× きよほうへん praise and censure, criticisms

KUN

【ほめる 褒める】 [sometimes also 誉める or 賞める]
praise, COMMEND, admire, compliment, eulogize
褒め称える ほめたたえる admire, applaud, praise

SYNONYMS

● **praise**
賛 PRAISE → 3484
頌 EULOGIZE → 1319
謳 EXTOL → 2061
讃 PRAISE → 2093
美 regard as beautiful → 2817
褒 COMMEND → 2662
嘉 commend (esp. an inferior) → 2953
彰 PROCLAIM MERITS → 2337
称 acclaim → 1491
賞 express admiration → 3237
揚 EXALT → 0722

USAGE

【ほめる】
褒める
[sometimes also 誉める or 賞める] praise, commend, admire, compliment, eulogize
誉める
[usu. 褒める, sometimes also 賞める] same as 褒める

賞める
[usu. 褒める, sometimes also 誉める] same as 褒める

HOMOPHONES

ほめる
誉 HONOR → 3135
賞 PRIZE → 3237

稾

2663

2-2-13

▶**MANUSCRIPT**

コウ

115	Nonstandard	U7A3E
禾	S15-5-10	F0000

traditional form → see 稿 at 1574

養 養

2-2-13

incorrect classification
➡ see 2-3-12: ⺷ at 2998

憂

2664

2-2-13

▶**BE ANXIOUS**

ユウ うれ(える) うれ(い) う(い) う(き)

Ⓒ 忧 yōu

61	Jōyō	U6182
心	S15-4-11	F1753

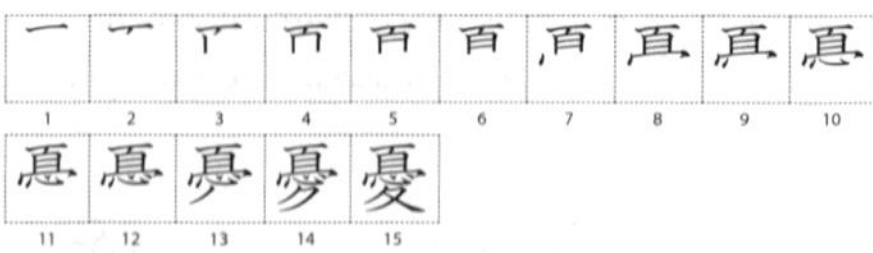

COMPOUNDS

❶ⓐ BE [feel] ANXIOUS, fear, worry, be concerned
ⓑ anxiety, fears, apprehension

a 憂慮 ゆうりょ anxiety, concern, worry
憂国 ゆうこく patriotism, concern for one's country
b 一喜一憂 いっきいちゆう alternation of joy and sorrow
杞×憂 きゆう imaginary fears

❷ grief, sorrow
憂鬱 ゆううつ melancholy, gloom
憂愁 ゆうしゅう melancholy, gloom, grief

KUN

【うれえる 憂える】**BE ANXIOUS, fear, be apprehensive**
国の将来を憂える くにのしょうらいをうれえる be anxious about the future of one's country

【うれい 憂い】**anxiety, trouble, worry; danger**
後顧の憂い こうこのうれい anxiety about the future

【うい 憂い】**melancholy, sad**
憂さ うさ gloom, melancholy
物憂い ものうい languid, melancholy

【うき 憂き】*literary* **grief, sorrow**
憂き目を見る うきめをみる have a bitter experience, have a hard time of it

SYNONYMS

❶ worry
憂 BE ANXIOUS → 2664
配 concern oneself → 1853
構う MIND → 1325
虞 FEARS (of undesirable event) → 4037

❷ sorrow
哀 SORROW → 2568
憂 grief → 2664

USAGE

❶【うれえる】
憂える
be anxious, fear, be apprehensive
愁える
grieve, lament, feel sorrow

❷【うれい】
憂い
anxiety, trouble, worry; danger
愁い
melancholy, grief, sorrow, sadness

HOMOPHONES

うれえる 愁 MELANCHOLY → 3508
うれい 愁 MELANCHOLY → 3508

魯

2665

2-2-13

▶**DULL**

ロ

Ⓒ 鲁 lǔ

195	Names	U9B6F
魚	S15-11-4	F1985

COMPOUNDS

❶ [original meaning] **DULL, stupid, foolish**
魯鈍 ろどん imbecility, stupidity
烏焉×魯魚 うえんろぎょ miswriting a word

❷ Lu, name of an ancient Chinese state

❸ [usu. 露 3495] Russia
魯国 ろこく Russia

INDEPENDENT

【ろ 魯】State of Lu

SYNONYMS

❶ foolish
愚 FOOLISH → 3513
暗 DARK → 1273
痴 STUPID → 4072
鈍 DULL → 2123
呆 DIM-WITTED → 2712
魯 DULL → 2665
闇 DARK → 4134
蒙 IGNORANCE → 2938

舞

▶DANCE

ブ　ま(う)　-ま(う)　まい

Ⓝ 舞 Ⓒ 舞 wǔ

2666

2-2-13

136	Jōyō	U821E
舛	S15-7-8	F0633

COMPOUNDS

❶ [original meaning]
ⓐ DANCE, dancing
ⓑ to DANCE

a 舞曲 ぶきょく dance music, music and dancing
剣舞 けんぶ sword dance
日舞 にちぶ Japanese dancing
歌舞伎 かぶき kabuki

b 舞踏 ぶとう dancing
舞台 ぶたい stage, the boards
舞踏会 ぶとうかい ball, dance

❷ encourage, urge
鼓舞 こぶ encouragement, stimulation

KUN

【まう　舞う】DANCE (gracefully, esp. traditional dances); flutter, fly, circle (in the sky)
舞を舞う まいをまう perform a dance, dance
舞い上がる まいあがる soar, fly high

【-まう　-舞う】verbal suffix
振る舞う ふるまう behave oneself; entertain, treat
見舞う みまう ask for, visit (a sick person)
仕舞う しまう close, finish; put away, lay away

【まい　舞】dancing, DANCE
舞扇 まいおうぎ dancer's fan
舞姫 まいひめ dancing girl, dancer

SYNONYMS

❶ &【まう】dance
踊 DANCE (energetically) → 1961
舞 DANCE (gracefully) → 2666

NOTE

➡ see COMPOUND FORMATION for 椀飯振舞 おうばんぶるまい → 椀 1250

龜

▶TURTLE

キ　かめ　㊔ ひさし　すすむ　ひさ

2667

2-2-14

213	Nonstandard	U9F9C
龜	S16-16-0	F0000

traditional form → see 亀 at 2637

RADICAL

kame 'tortoise', used in characters related to tortoises or tortoiseshells

Variant: 龜 *kame*

褒

▶COMMEND

ホウ　ほ(める)

2668

2-2-15

145	Nonstandard	U8943
衣	S17-6-11	F0000

traditional form → see 褒 at 2662

齋

▶OBSERVE RELIGIOUS ABSTINENCE

サイ　とき　㊔ ひとし　いつき

2669

2-2-15

210	Nonstandard	U9F4B
齊	S17-14-3	F0000

traditional form → see 斎 at 2622

龠

▶YAKU

2670

2-2-15

214	Radical	U9FA0
龠	S17-17-0	F0000

RADICAL

yaku 'flute', used in characters related to music or musical instruments

龜

▶TURTLE

キ　かめ　㊔ ひさし　すすむ　ひさ

2671

2-2-16

213	Nonstandard	UF907
龜	S18-18-0	F0000

alternative form → see 亀 at 2637
radical variant → see 龜 at 2667

麗

▶OF GRACEFUL BEAUTY

レイ　うるわ(しい)　うら(らか)▲　㊔ うらら

Ⓒ 丽 lì lí

2672

2-2-17

198	Jōyō	U9E97
鹿	S19-11-8	F1340

COMPOUNDS

● [original meaning] **OF GRACEFUL BEAUTY, lovely, beautiful and neat [refreshing], resplendent**
麗人 れいじん beauty, belle
麗質 れいしつ beauty, charm
奇麗(=綺麗)な きれいな beautiful, pretty; clean; fair
美麗な びれいな beautiful, gorgeous

華麗な かれいな splendid, magnificent, resplendent, gorgeous
端麗な たんれいな graceful, elegant, handsome
豊麗な ほうれいな rich (design), beautiful, splendid
鮮麗 せんれい resplendent beauty
美辞麗句 びじれいく flowery words

KUN

【うるわしい 麗しい】 **beautiful and graceful, lovely, pretty; heartwarming, tenderly moving;** (of humor or health) **good**
麗しい情景 うるわしいじょうけい heartwarming scene
見目麗しい みめうるわしい good-looking, fair
御機嫌麗しい ごきげんうるわしい be in good humor

【うららか 麗らか】
うららかな 麗らかな beautiful, lovely, bright (weather); bright (mood)
麗らかな春の日 うららかなはるのひ beautiful [lovely] spring day
麗らかな気分 うららかなきぶん feeling bright

SYNONYMS

● **beautiful**
美 BEAUTIFUL → 2817
彪 MAGNIFICENT → 4115
綺 BEAUTIFUL → 1734
娃 BEAUTIFUL → 0419
佳 FINE → 0096
瑶 EXQUISITE → 1301
麗 OF GRACEFUL BEAUTY → 2672
艶 CHARMING → 2403
妙 of marvelous beauty → 0280
華 MAGNIFICENT → 2841
絢 GORGEOUS → 1705
斐 florid → 3449

太

2673
2-3-1

▶**GREAT**
▶**THICK**
タイ タ ふと(い) ふと(る) ㊔ おう だい たか うず
Ⓒ 太 tài

37	Jōyō-2	U592A
大	S4-3-1	F0176

一 ナ 大 太
1 2 3 4

COMPOUNDS

❶ⓐ (extremely large in size or scale) **GREAT, large, big, enormous**
ⓑ [also 泰 たい 3193] **GREAT**est (in degree), most extreme
a 太陽 たいよう sun
太鼓 たいこ (big) drum; professional jester; flatterer; big obi bow
太陰 たいいん moon
太白 たいはく Venus; thick silk thread; kind of sweet potato
太古 たいこ ancient times, remote ages
太平洋 たいへいよう Pacific Ocean

❷ **of highest rank, grand, GREAT**
太子 たいし crown prince
太閤 たいこう father of the imperial adviser; Toyotomi Hideyoshi
太守 たいしゅ governor general, viceroy
太夫 たゆう chief actor in a noh play; entertainer, courtesan
太祖 たいそ founder; first emperor (of a Chinese dynasty)

❸ (great in diameter) **THICK**
丸太 まるた log

❹ ultimate source
太初 たいしょ beginning of the world

KUN

【ふとい 太い】
①ⓐ (of great diameter or width) **THICK, big; fat; broad, wide**
ⓑ **THICK** (voice), deep
a 太さ ふとさ thickness; depth (of voice)
太糸 ふといと thick thread, low count yarn
太字 ふとじ thick character, bold-faced type
太い線 ふといせん thick line
太っちょ ふとっちょ fat person
太い腕 ふというで big arm
太い鉛筆 ふといえんぴつ broad pencil

② shameless, audacious, insolent
太っ腹な ふとっぱらな generous, large-minded, big-hearted
図太い ずぶとい audacious, brazen

【ふとる 太る】 [sometimes also 肥る] **grow fat, fatten, gain weight**
太った ふとった fat, stout, plump

SPECIAL READINGS

太刀 たち long sword

SYNONYMS

❶ⓐ **big and huge**
大 BIG → 4224
太 GREAT → 2673
浩 VAST → 0525
巨 HUGE → 3773
厖 BULKY → 3725

❷ **high-ranking**
貴 NOBLE → 3220
上 upper → 4212

高 HIGH → 2601
総 GENERAL → 1743
太 of highest rank → 2673
❸ &【ふとい】①ⓐ **thick**
厚 THICK (great in depth) → 3726
太 THICK (great in diameter) → 2673
【ふとる】
◯ **fatten**
肥 FATTEN → 1091
太る grow fat → 2673

USAGE

【ふとる】
太る
[sometimes also 肥る] grow fat, fatten, gain weight
肥る
[usu. 太る] grow fat, fatten, gain weight

HOMOPHONES

ふとる 肥 FATTEN → 1091

丒

2674
⬒ 2-3-1

▶**THE OX**
チュウ うし

1	Nonstandard	U4E12
一	S4-1-3	F0000

traditional form → see 丑 at 4241

予

⬒ 2-3-1

incorrect classification
➡ see ⬒ 2-2-2: マ at 2477

今

⬒ 2-3-1

incorrect classification
➡ see ⬒ 2-2-2: 𠆢 at 2464

号

2675
⬒ 2-3-2

▶**NUMBER**
▶**DESIGNATION**
▶**SIGN**
ゴウ

Ⓝ 號 Ⓒ 号 hào háo

30△	Jōyō-3	U53F7
口	S5-3-2	F0430

丶(1) ㄇ(2) 口(3) 旦(4) 号(5)

COMPOUNDS

❶ [also suffix]
ⓐ (numerical designation or label) **NUMBER, as: room No., house No., type size No., railroad car No., route No., item [subsection] No., etc.**
ⓑ (single copy of a periodical) **NUMBER, issue**
a 号数 ごうすう number or size of periodicals or pictures, type size
番号 ばんごう number, serial number
百号室 ひゃくごうしつ room No. 100
一丁目二番地九号 いっちょうめにばんちきゅうごう 2-9, 1-chome (part of an address)
五号活字 ごごうかつじ No. 5 type, small pica
十五号車 じゅうごごうしゃ (railway) car No. 15
二号線 にごうせん Route No. 2
第二項第四号 だいにこうだいよんごう Subsection 2, Paragraph 4
b 号外 ごうがい newspaper extra
第二号 だいにごう second issue; number two
創刊号 そうかんごう inaugural number, first issue

❷ⓐ **DESIGNATION, title, name, pen name, pseudonym**
ⓑ **suffix after names of ships, trains, aircraft, horses or dogs**
a 称号 しょうごう title, degree
雅号 がごう pen name, pseudonym
屋号 やごう name of a store; stage title
年号 ねんごう name of era, reign title
b クイーンメリー号 くいーんめりーごう S.S. *Queen Mary*
ひかり号 ひかりごう *Hikari* (name of a bullet train)

❸ (arbitrary sign, esp. in mathematics) **SIGN, symbol, mark**
等号 とうごう equal sign [mark]
負号 ふごう negative sign
符号 ふごう sign, mark, symbol
記号 きごう symbol, mark, sign
暗号 あんごう code, password

❹ **SIGNal**
号砲 ごうほう signal gun
信号 しんごう signal; traffic light

❺ⓐ [original meaning] holler, call out, shout, cry, wail
ⓑ holler a command, order
a 号泣 ごうきゅう wailing, lamentation
怒号 どごう (angry) roar, outcry, bellow
b 号令 ごうれい order, command
呼号する こごうする cry out, proclaim

INDEPENDENT

【ごう 号】
① (single copy of a periodical) **NUMBER**, issue
次の号 つぎのごう next number [issue]
② **DESIGNATION**, title, name, pen name, pseudonym
. . . と云う号を名乗る …というごうをなのる assume the pseudonym of…
【ごうする 号する】name; call, declare

SYNONYMS

❶ **kinds of numbers**
数 NUMBER (mathematical unit) → 2245
員 fixed number → 2822
号 NUMBER (numerical designation) → 2675
番 No. → 3416

第 ORDINAL NUMBER PREFIX →3298
-目 ordinal number suffix →3777
次 numerical order suffix →0058
桁 DIGIT →1165

❷ **name**
名 NAME →2693
銘 name (inscribed by maker) →2158
姓 SURNAME →0334
氏 FAMILY NAME →3669
称 APPELLATION →1491
題 TITLE →4139
号 DESIGNATION →2675

❸ **marks and signs**
標 MARK (identifying sign) →1347
徽 EMBLEM →0968
痕 SCAR →4066
印 MARK (visible sign) →1023
跡 TRACE →1937
蹟 TRACE →2065
踪 FOOTPRINTS →1996
紋 print →1651
符 SYMBOL →3299
号 SIGN →2675
栞 BOOKMARK →3285

❹ **signal**
号 signal →2675
報 signal →2133

❺ⓐ **give out a call**
叫 SHOUT →0233
号 holler →2675
喝 SHOUT AT →0554
喚 call out →0666
呼 CALL →0324
鳴 CRY →0831
吠 BARK →0269

兄

2676

2-3-2

▸**OLDER BROTHER**

ケイ キョウ あに ㊔ **え**

Ⓒ 兄 xiōng

10	Jōyō-2	U5144
儿	S5-2-3	F0643

Stroke order: 1 丨 2 ロ 3 ロ 4 尸 5 兄

COMPOUNDS

❶ OLDER BROTHER
兄弟 きょうだい(=けいてい) brother
長兄 ちょうけい eldest brother
実兄 じっけい one's own older brother
義兄 ぎけい brother-in-law
父兄 ふけい one's father and older brothers; guardians

❷ **familiar title used in addressing seniors or close friends**
山田兄 やまだけい Mr. Yamada

❸ (fellow man) **brother, friend**
諸兄 しょけい dear friends
学兄 がっけい my learned friend
貴兄 きけい you

INDEPENDENT

【けい 兄】 **OLDER BROTHER;** *literary* **you**
兄たり難く弟たり難し けいたりがたくていたりがたし There is little to choose between the two

KUN

【あに 兄】 **OLDER BROTHER, big brother**
兄貴 あにき older brother; one's senior
兄弟子 あにでし senior schoolmate, senior apprentice

SPECIAL READINGS

兄さん にいさん older brother

SYNONYMS

❶ **siblings**
妹 YOUNGER SISTER →0333
姉 OLDER SISTER →0336
兄 OLDER BROTHER →2676
弟 YOUNGER BROTHER →2537

❷ **titles of address**
氏 COURTESY TITLE →3669
兄 familiar title (seniors) →2676
君 FAMILIAR TITLE (peers) →3974
嬢 Miss →0936
様 FORMAL TITLE →1332
殿 FORMAL HONORIFIC TITLE →2247
師 honorific title (clergymen) →1680
公 honorific title (noblemen) →2468

只

2677

2-3-2

▸**FREE OF CHARGE**
▸**ORDINARY**

シ ただ ただ-

Ⓒ 只 zhǐ zhī

30	Names	U53EA
口	S5-3-2	F2095

COMPOUNDS

● [original meaning, now archaic] **only, just**
只今 しこん just now

KUN

【ただ 只】
① **no charge**
只の ただの free of charge, cost-free, for nothing; ordinary, common, plain

② **ordinariness, plainness**

只の人 ただのひと common [ordinary] person, man in the street

只ならぬ ただならぬ unusual, alarming, serious

③ **doing nothing, being idle**

只では置かないぞ ただではおかないぞ You shall pay dear for that

【ただ- 只-】

① **FREE OF CHARGE, cost-free, for nothing**

只働き ただばたらき working for nothing

只乗り ただのり free ride

② **ORDINARY, common, plain**

只者 ただもの ordinary person, common mortal

只事ではない ただごとではない It is no common case

③ [also 唯] **only, just, merely, solely**

只今 ただいま at present, now; just now; soon; Hello (used by person returning home)

SYNONYMS

【ただ-】

② **ordinary**

常 NORMAL → 3203
只- ORDINARY → 2677
並 ordinary → 2793
平 common → 4291
普 common → 2919
庸 MEDIOCRE → 3881
凡 COMMONPLACE → 3656
套 TRITE → 2823

HOMOPHONES

ただ 唯 ONLY → 0556

NOTE

➡ see USAGE note at 唯 0556

去

▶GO AWAY

キョ コ さ(る) -さ(る)

Ⓒ 去 qù

2678

2-3-2

28	Jōyō-3	U53BB
厶	S5-2-3	F0544

一 (1) 十 (2) 土 (3) 去 (4) 去 (5)

COMPOUNDS

❶ⓐ **GO AWAY, leave, retire, depart from**
ⓑ (go away from this world) **pass away, die**

a 去来 きょらい coming and going; recurrence

辞去する じきょする leave, quit, retire

退去する たいきょする retreat, withdraw, evacuate

b 逝去 せいきょ death

死去する しきょする die, pass away

❷ⓐ **pass away, elapse, go by**
ⓑ **last (year, etc.)**

a 過去 かこ the past, bygone days

b 去年 きょねん last year

去月 きょげつ last month

❸ take away, remove, get rid of, eliminate

去勢 きょせい castration; enervation

除去する じょきょする rid of, remove, eliminate

撤去する てっきょする remove, dismantle (a building); evacuate (an army)

❹ falling tone in Chinese phonetics

去声 きょしょう falling tone

KUN

【さる 去る】 **GO AWAY, leave, depart, resign; be distant [away] from; pass, elapse, go by; remove, take of, get rid of; divorce; last (November)**

去る十一月 さるじゅういちがつ last November

遠くに去る とおくにさる go far away

置き去りにする おきざりにする leave (a person) behind

過ぎ去る すぎさる pass (away), elapse

取り去る とりさる take away, remove, leave out

【-さる -去る】 [verbal suffix] **completely**

忘れ去る わすれさる forget completely

SYNONYMS

❶ⓐ **leave and set forth**

去 GO AWAY → 2678
離 leave → 2364
発 START → 3174
出 GO OUT → 4310
退 RETREAT → 3838
撤 WITHDRAW → 0912

ⓑ **die**

死 DIE → 4334
萎 WITHER → 2872
没 die → 0305
亡 DECEASE → 4210
殉 DIE A MARTYR → 1177
歿 DIE → 1078
去 pass away → 2678
逝 DEPART THIS LIFE → 3850
斃 FALL DOWN DEAD → 3593
枯 WITHER → 1113

❷ⓐ **elapse**

過 PASS BY → 3891
経 pass → 1687
歴 pass → 3748
去 pass away → 2678

ⓑ **most recent**

昨 LAST → 1106
去 last → 2678
先 last → 3046

❸ **eliminate**

却 ELIMINATE → 1436
排 EXCLUDE → 0593
払う CLEAR AWAY → 0225
剥 PEEL OFF → 2105
耘 WEED → 1661
削 cross out → 1837
抹 wipe off → 0370
省 leave out → 3100
脱 REMOVE → 1225
去 take away → 2678
外す take off → 0215
除 RID OF → 0546
撤 WITHDRAW → 0912

冬

2679
2-3-2

▶**WINTER**
トウ ふゆ
Ⓝ 冬 Ⓒ 冬 dōng

15	Jōyō-2	U51AC
冫	S5-2-3	F0986

COMPOUNDS

● [original meaning] **WINTER**
冬季 とうき winter season
冬期 とうき winter, wintertime
冬至 とうじ winter solstice
冬眠 とうみん hibernation ("winter sleep")
越冬 えっとう passing the winter, wintering
初冬 しょとう early winter
立冬 りっとう first day of winter
春夏秋冬 しゅんかしゅうとう four seasons, all (the) year round

KUN

【ふゆ 冬】**WINTER**
冬めく ふゆめく become wintry
冬休み ふゆやすみ winter vacation
冬山 ふゆやま mountain in winter
冬物 ふゆもの winter clothing, winter goods
冬将軍 ふゆしょうぐん hard winter, Jack Frost
真冬 まふゆ depth of winter, midwinter

SYNONYMS

● **cold seasons**
冬 WINTER → 2679
寒 coldest season → 2894
秋 AUTUMN → 1464

冬

2680
2-3-2

▶**WINTER**
トウ ふゆ

34	Nonstandard	U2F81A
夂	S5-3-2	F0000

traditional form → see 冬 at 2679

夲

2681
2-3-2

▶**BASIS**
▶**BOOK**
▶**THIS**
ホン もと ㊔ はじめ

37	Nonstandard	U5932
大	S5-3-2	F0000

traditional form → see 本 at 4314

穴

2682
2-3-2

▶**HOLE**
ケツ あな
Ⓝ 穴 Ⓒ 穴 xué

116	Jōyō-6	U7A74
穴	S5-5-0	F1113

radical variant → see 穴 at 2684

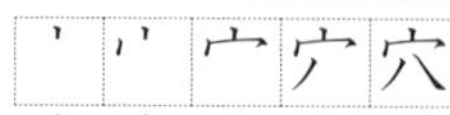

COMPOUNDS

❶ⓐ **HOLE, cavity**
ⓑ counter for **HOLE**s
ⓒ [original meaning] cave, den
a 穴隙 けつげき aperture, crevice
墓穴 ぼけつ grave
b 二穴 にけつ two holes
c 穴居 けっきょ cave dwelling, troglodytism
虎穴 こけつ tiger's den; dangerous place
❷ [also suffix] points in the human body where acupuncture or moxibustion can be applied
経穴 けいけつ points in the human body where acupuncture or moxibustion can be applied

INDEPENDENT

【けつ 穴】*vulgar* ass, fanny; tail end

KUN

【あな 穴】
①ⓐ **HOLE, opening, gap; hollow, cavity**
ⓑ [sometimes also 孔] **open or bottomless HOLE, opening, aperture, perforation**
ⓒ **cave, lair; pit**
a ボタンの穴 ぼたんのあな buttonhole
b 落とし穴 おとしあな pit, trap
c 洞穴 ほらあな cave, cavern, den
②ⓐ fault, flaw, defect
ⓑ deficit, loss
a 穴だらけだ あなだらけだ be full of holes; hold no water
b 穴を開ける あなをあける cause a loss

③ good place known to few
穴場 あなば good place known to few people
④ long shot, dark horse
大穴 おおあな big hole; *horse racing* dark horse

SYNONYMS

❶ holes and cavities
穴 HOLE → 2682
洞 CAVE → 0455
窟 CAVE → 2923
窪 HOLLOW → 2962
腔 BODY CAVITY → 1267
孔 OPEN HOLE → 0205
口 MOUTH → 4189
坑 PIT → 0277
堀 DITCH → 0561
溝 CHANNEL → 0810
壕 TRENCH → 0966
濠 MOAT → 0975
凹 concavity → 4294

USAGE

【あな】
穴
①ⓐ hole, opening, gap; hollow, cavity
ⓑ [sometimes also 孔] open or bottomless hole, opening, aperture, perforation
ⓒ cave, lair; pit
②ⓐ fault, flaw, defect
ⓑ deficit, loss
③ good place known to few
④ long shot, dark horse
孔
[usu. 穴] open or bottomless hole, opening, aperture, perforation

HOMOPHONES

あな 孔 OPEN HOLE → 0205

⺳ **2683** 2-3-2

▶***ANAKANMURI***

116	Radical	U7A74
穴	S5-5-0	F0000

radical variant → see 穴 at 2684

穴 **2684** 2-3-2

▶**HOLE**
ケツ あな

116	Nonstandard	U7A74
穴	S5-5-0	F0000

traditional form → see 穴 at 2682

RADICAL

ana 'hole', used in characters related to holes or their qualities
Top variant: ⺳ ***anakanmuri*** (空 究 突)

字 2-3-2
incorrect stroke-count
➡ see 2-3-3: 宀 at 2696

芝 2-3-2
incorrect stroke-count
➡ see 2-3-3: 艹 at 2705

矛 2-3-2
incorrect classification
➡ see 2-2-3: マ at 2501

令 2-3-2
incorrect classification
➡ see 2-2-3: 𠆢 at 2489

充 **2685** 2-3-2

▶**FILL**
ジュウ あ(てる) み(たす) ㊔ みつ みつる あつ まこと よし みち

10	Nonstandard	U5145
儿	S5-2-3	F0000

traditional form → see 充 at 2507

吊 **2686** 2-3-3

▶**SUSPEND**
チョウ つ(る) つ(り) つ(るす)
Ⓒ 吊 diào

30	Non-Jōyō	U540A
口	S6-3-3	F1841

COMPOUNDS

● [original meaning] **SUSPEND, hang, sling**
懸吊 けんちょう suspension

KUN

【つる 吊る】
① [also 釣る] **SUSPEND, hang, swing, sling**
吊り上げる つりあげる hang up, suspend; raise, lift
② **lift by the loins (in sumo wrestling)**
吊り出す つりだす hold (the opponent) in the arms and carry him out of the ring
③ [formerly 攣る] **cramp, have a cramp**
引き吊り ひきつり cramp; scar
④ [formerly 攣る] **turn up, slant upward**
吊り目 つりめ slanted [upturned] eyes

【つり 吊り】
ⓐ **suspension, hanging; SUSPENDer(s)**
ⓑ [also 釣り-] **SUSPENDed, hanging**
a 首吊り くびつり hanging (by the neck)
ズボン吊り ずぼんつり suspenders
b 吊り棚 つりだな hanging shelf
吊り革 つりかわ (hand) strap
吊り輪 つりわ flying rings

【つるす 吊るす】 **SUSPEND, hang, hang up**
吊るし上げ つるしあげ hanging up, hoisting; denouncement, severe criticism

【口】土士夂夕宀小⺌干幺彐艹云亠亡千亼

吊るし柿 つるしがき persimmon (hung to dry), dried persimmon

SYNONYMS

❶ **hang**

掛ける HANG →0596
垂 HANG DOWN →4382
懸 SUSPEND →3632
吊 SUSPEND →2686
釣り- suspended →2108

HOMOPHONES

つる
釣 ANGLE →2108
攣 CRAMP →3635
つり 釣 ANGLE →2108

NOTE

➡ see USAGE note at 釣 2108

号

2-3-3

incorrect stroke-count
➡ see 2-3-2: 口 at 2675

寺 2687

2-3-3

▶**BUDDHIST TEMPLE**

ジ てら

Ⓒ 寺 sì

41	Jōyō-2	U5BFA
寸	S6-3-3	F0403

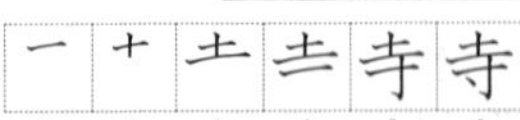

COMPOUNDS

❶ⓐ **BUDDHIST TEMPLE, temple**
ⓑ **suffix after names of BUDDHIST TEMPLEs**
ⓒ counter for **BUDDHIST TEMPLEs**

a 寺院 じいん temple
社寺 しゃじ shrines and temples
古寺 こじ old temple
b 国分寺 こくぶんじ state-established provincial temple
東大寺 とうだいじ Todaiji Temple
金閣寺 きんかくじ Temple of the Golden Pavilion
c 一箇寺 いっかじ one temple

❷ [original meaning, now archaic] public office

KUN

【てら 寺】**BUDDHIST TEMPLE, temple; (rent of a) gambling house**
寺参り てらまいり visit to a temple
寺銭 てらせん rent of a gambling house
尼寺 あまでら nunnery, convent
山寺 やまでら mountain temple

SYNONYMS

❶ **places of worship**

堂 temple building →3202
塔 pagoda →0683
寺 BUDDHIST TEMPLE →2687
刹 TEMPLE →1620
社 Shinto shrine →1042
宮 SHINTO SHRINE →2828
院 monastery →0544
教 church →1887

圭 2688

2-3-3

▶**SHARP CORNER**

ケイ ケ ㊔ たま か よし きよし きよ

Ⓒ 圭 guī

32	Names	U572D
土	S6-3-3	F1769

COMPOUNDS

❶ **SHARP CORNER (of ancient ceremonial jade tablet), point**
圭角の有る けいかくのある angular, harsh-mannered, rough
尖圭コンジローム せんけいこんじろーむ pointed condyloma

❷ [original meaning] ceremonial jade tablet with a rectangular base and pointed end used by the emperor in ancient China in appointing feudal lords
圭璧 けいへき [archaic] ritual jades worn by feudal lords in ancient China
刀圭 とうけい medicine, art of healing

SYNONYMS

❶ **corners**

角 corner →2541
圭 SHARP CORNER →2688
隅 NOOK →0760
隈 RECESS →0763

𠮷 2689

2-3-3

▶**LUCKY**

キチ キツ ㊔ よし

30	Nonstandard	U20BB7
口	S6-3-3	F0000

alternative form →see 吉 at 2691

赱 2690

2-3-3

▶**RUN**

ソウ はし(る)

32	Nonstandard	U8D71
土	S6-3-3	F0000

traditional form →see 走 at 2720

吉 2691

2-3-3

▶**LUCKY**

キチ キツ ㊔ よし

Ⓝ 吉◇ Ⓒ 吉 jí

30	Jōyō	U5409
口	S6-3-3	F0256

一 十 士 吉 吉 吉
1 2 3 4 5 6

COMPOUNDS

❶ [original meaning] **LUCKY, propitious, auspicious, favorable, good**
吉兆 きっちょう good omen, lucky sign
吉日 きちじつ(=きつじつ) lucky day
吉凶 きっきょう good or ill luck, fortune
吉事 きちじ auspicious event
大吉 だいきち excellent [good] luck
不吉 ふきつ ill omen, inauspiciousness

❷ good, excellent
吉報 きっぽう good news

INDEPENDENT

【きち 吉】good luck, good fortune, good omen
君の運勢は吉だ きみのうんせいはきちだ You were born under a lucky star

SYNONYMS

❶ **good fortune**
吉 LUCKY → 2691
嘉 HAPPY → 2953
祥 AUSPICIOUS → 1184
瑞 AUSPICIOUS OMEN → 1302
禎 PROPITIOUS OMEN → 1305
幸 GOOD FORTUNE → 2755
福 FORTUNE → 1303
倖 GOOD FORTUNE → 0134

各

2692

2-3-3

▶**EACH**
カク おのおの
Ⓒ 各 gè gě

30	Jōyō-4	U5404
口	S6-3-3	F0572

ノ ク 夂 夂 各 各
1 2 3 4 5 6

COMPOUNDS

● [also prefix] **EACH, every, every one, all, various**
各社 かくしゃ each company
各自 かくじ each one, every individual
各国 かっこく every country, each nation, various states
各般 かくはん every, various
各地 かくち every place, various parts [areas] (of the country)
各種の かくしゅの each [every] kind, various
各位 かくい gentlemen, sirs
各団体 かくだんたい each group
各大学 かくだいがく each university, all universities

INDEPENDENT

【かく 各】EACH
各一部 かくいちぶ one copy each

KUN

【おのおの 各】**EACH, every, respectively**
各方 おのおのがた all of you
各の考えで おのおののかんがえで at individual discretion

SYNONYMS

● **all**
皆 ALL → 3093
悉 THOROUGHLY → 3405
総 TOTAL → 1743
諸 VARIOUS → 1984
毎 EVERY → 2527
各 EACH → 2692
都 all → 2120
万 all → 3653
全 WHOLE → 2514
渾 ENTIRE → 0738
一 all in one → 4148
満 FULL → 0739
丸 complete(ly) → 4225
完 COMPLETE → 2727

名

2693

2-3-3

▶**NAME**
メイ ミョウ な -な
Ⓒ 名 míng

30	Jōyō-1	U540D
口	S6-3-3	F0078

ノ ク 夕 夕 名 名
1 2 3 4 5 6

COMPOUNDS

❶ⓐ [also suffix] **NAME, first name**
ⓑ (mere designation) **NAME**
a 名簿 めいぼ register [list] of names
名刺 めいし calling [business] card
名称 めいしょう appellation, name, title
名字(=苗字) みょうじ surname, family name
氏名 しめい (full) name
署名 しょめい signature, autograph
指名 しめい nomination, designation
匿名の とくめいの anonymous, incognito, pseudonymous
題名 だいめい title
本名 ほんみょう one's real name
戒名 かいみょう posthumous Buddhist name
商品名 しょうひんめい trade [brand] name
b 名目 めいもく name, title; pretext
名義 めいぎ name, title
名実 めいじつ name and reality

口 士 士 夂 【夕】 宀 小 ⺌ 干 幺 ヨ 艹 云 亠 亡 千 今

❷ (reputation, esp. good reputation) **NAME, fame, reputation**

名誉 めいよ honor, glory; dignity
名声 めいせい fame, reputation
有名な ゆうめいな famous, noted, celebrated; notorious
著名 ちょめい prominence, eminence, distinction
汚名 おめい bad name, ill fame, disgrace
功名 こうみょう great exploit; distinction, fame

❸ [also prefix]

ⓐ (of well known name) **famous, noted, celebrated**
ⓑ **first-rate, master, excellent, fine, great**

a 名物 めいぶつ specialty, noted product
名所 めいしょ noted place, sights, scenic place
名勝 めいしょう place of scenic beauty
名門 めいもん distinguished [noted] family; prestigious establishment
名場面 めいばめん famous [impressive] scene
b 名人 めいじん (past) master, master hand, expert
名作 めいさく masterpiece, fine work
名画 めいが famous picture, masterpiece; noted film
名曲 めいきょく excellent [exquisite] piece of music, famous tune
名月 めいげつ full moon, harvest moon
名投手 めいとうしゅ star pitcher
名探偵 めいたんてい great detective

❹ **counter for persons**

会員五名 かいいんごめい five members

❺ abbrev. of 名古屋 なごや: Nagoya

名大 めいだい Nagoya University

❻ persons or land of a feudal manor subject to taxation in medieval Japan

大名 だいみょう daimyo, feudal lord
小名 しょうみょう minor feudal lord

KUN

【な 名】 **NAME, first name;** (mere designation) **name;** (reputation, esp. good reputation) **name, fame, reputation; pretext, plea, justification**

名前 なまえ name, given name
名付ける なづける name, give a name to
名高い なだかい famous, well-known
名ばかりの王 なばかりのおう a king in name only
名も無い人 なもないひと nameless [insignificant] person, nobody
本の名 ほんのな name of a book
正義の名に於て せいぎのなにおいて in the name of justice

【-な -名】 [sometimes also -字] **character, letter**

仮名 かな kana, Japanese syllabary

SPECIAL READINGS

渾名▲ あだな nickname

SYNONYMS

❶ⓐ **name**

名 NAME → 2693
銘 name (inscribed by maker) → 2158
姓 SURNAME → 0334
氏 FAMILY NAME → 3669
称 APPELLATION → 1491
題 TITLE → 4139
号 DESIGNATION → 2675

❷ **repute**

声 reputation → 2724
誉 HONOR → 3135
名 NAME → 2693
望 popularity → 3408

❸ⓑ **excellent and superior**

優 SUPERIOR → 0200
絶 without match → 1711
卓 PROMINENT → 2561
快 splendid → 0289
妙 MARVELOUS → 0280
秀 EXCELLENT → 3152
英 DISTINGUISHED → 2782
尤 outstanding → 3755
傑 outstanding → 0175
穎 TALENTED → 2036
逸 exceptional → 3872
名 first-rate → 2693
上 of upper grade → 4212

❹ **counters for persons**

人 counter for people → 4175
名 counter for persons → 2693

USAGE

【-な】

-名
[sometimes also -字] character, letter

-字
[usu. -名] character, letter

HOMOPHONES

-な 字 CHARACTER → 2696

NOTE

➡ see COMPOUND FORMATION for 苗字(=名字) みょうじ → 苗 2781

多

2694

2-3-3

▶**MANY**

タ おお(い) ㊔ かず

Ⓝ 𡖄 Ⓒ 多 duō

36	Jōyō-2	U591A
夕	S6-3-3	F0112

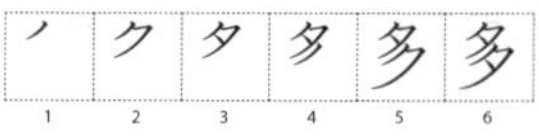

COMPOUNDS

❶ⓐ [original meaning] **MANY, much, numerous**
ⓑ [prefix] **MANY-, multi-, poly-**

a 多角 たかく many-sided, versatile; polygonal
多数 たすう large number, multitude
多量 たりょう large quantity, great deal
多面 ためん many sides, many phases
多分 たぶん probably, perhaps, maybe
多少 たしょう a little, somewhat
多大の ただいの great, considerable, a great deal of; serious
多湿 たしつ high humidity
b 多目的 たもくてき multipurpose
多神教 たしんきょう polytheism
多音節 たおんせつ polysyllable

❷ **used phonetically for *ta***
滅多に めったに rarely

INDEPENDENT

【た 多】 much, a great deal
多とする たとする appreciate, be thankful

KUN

【おおい 多い】 much, lots of, MANY, numerous; frequent
多く おおく much, many, abundantly; largely, mostly
多目に おおめに plenty, lots

SYNONYMS

❶ **plentiful**
百 numerous → 2519
沃 FERTILE → 0315
万 myriad → 3653
多 MANY → 2694
豊 PLENTIFUL → 3344
沢 plentiful → 0313
穣 YIELDING ABUNDANTLY → 1597
裕 ABUNDANT → 1530
饒 ABUNDANT → 2280
富 RICH → 2892

NOTE

➡ see USAGE note at 大 4224

安

2695

2-3-3

▶**PEACEFUL**
▶**INEXPENSIVE**

アン やす(い) やす やす(らか) やす(まる)▲
㊔ あ やすし
Ⓒ 安 ān

40	Jōyō-3	U5B89
宀	S6-3-3	F0170

Stroke order: 1–6

COMPOUNDS

❶ⓐ **PEACEFUL, tranquil, calm, quiet, gentle**
ⓑ **have peace of mind, feel contented, be at ease; give peace of mind, pacify**
ⓒ **public peace, order**

a 安住する あんじゅうする live peacefully
安泰 あんたい peace, security, tranquility
安眠 あんみん quiet sleep, peaceful slumber
安定 あんてい stability; composure
安静 あんせい rest, quiet, repose
b 安心 あんしん peace of mind, relief
不安 ふあん uneasiness, anxiety
c 治安 ちあん public peace and order
保安 ほあん preservation of public peace
公安 こうあん public peace

❷ **safe, secure**
安全 あんぜん safety, security
安否 あんぴ safety, welfare
安打 あんだ safe hit, base hit
安保条約 あんぽじょうやく (Japan-U.S.) security treaty

❸ (without effort) **easy, comfortable**
安易な あんいな easy, easygoing
安産 あんざん easy [smooth] delivery (of a baby)
安楽な あんらくな comfortable, carefree, cozy

❹ **INEXPENSIVE, cheap**
安価 あんか low price
安直な あんちょくな cheap, inexpensive; easy, simple

❺ **ammonia**
硫安 りゅうあん ammonium sulfate
液安 えきあん liquid ammonia

KUN

【やすい 安い】

① **INEXPENSIVE, cheap, low-priced**
安く やすく inexpensively
安値 やすね low price
安物 やすもの cheap article, bargain
安売り やすうり bargain sale
安っぽい やすっぽい cheapish, flashy
じり安 じりやす gradual decline of stock prices

② **PEACEFUL, quiet, tranquil**
安んじる やすんじる feel at ease, ease a person's mind
安らぎ やすらぎ peace of mind
気安い きやすい friendly

【やす 安】

① [prefix] **cheap, INEXPENSIVE, low (cost)**
安月給 やすげっきゅう low salary

② [suffix] **low price, cheap**

十円安 じゅうえんやす down 10 yen (foreign exchange market)

③ [prefix] lightheartedly, without due consideration

安請け合いする やすうけあいする promise without due consideration

【やすらか 安らか】

やすらかな 安らかな **PEACEFUL, tranquil**

安らかな眠り やすらかなねむり peaceful sleep

【やすまる 安まる】[usu. 休まる] feel rested; be set at ease

心の安まる時が無い こころのやすまるときがない have no moment of ease

SYNONYMS

❶ⓐ calm and peaceful

安 PEACEFUL →2695
康 peaceful →3877
寧 peaceful →2959
泰 TRANQUIL →3193
静 QUIET →2164
平 CALM →4291
穏 CALM →1578

ⓒ peace

和 PEACE →1450
安 public peace →2695
治 public order →0393

❸ comfortable

楽 COMFORTABLE →3505
安 easy (without effort) →2695

❸ easy

易 EASY (without difficulty) →3064
安 easy (without effort) →2695
簡 SIMPLE →3380
軽 LIGHT →1909

❹ inexpensive

安 INEXPENSIVE →2695
廉 CHEAP →3911
低 low-priced →0082

USAGE

【やすい】

安い
① inexpensive, cheap, low-priced
② peaceful, quiet, tranquil

易い
ⓐ easy, simple
ⓑ [verbal suffix] easy (to do)

HOMOPHONES

やすい 易 EASY →3064
やすまる 休 REST →0056

NOTE

➡ see also USAGE note at 休 0056

➡ see COMPOUND FORMATION for 安堵する あんどする →堵 0682

字

▶CHARACTER

ジ あざ あざな▲ -な▲

ⓒ 字 zì

2696

2-3-3

39	Jōyō-1	U5B57
子	S6-3-3	F0400

COMPOUNDS

❶ⓐ CHARACTER, letter; type; word

ⓑ Chinese CHARACTER, kanji, ideograph, logograph

ⓒ counter for (Chinese) **CHARACTER**s

a 字体 じたい character form, type
字義 じぎ character definition, meaning of a word [term]
字引 じびき dictionary
文字 もじ(=もんじ) character, letter
大文字 おおもじ capital letter
文字 もんじ character, letter; writings
ローマ字 ろーまじ Roman letters
漢字 かんじ Chinese characters, kanji
活字 かつじ movable type, printing type
数字 すうじ figure, numeral
習字 しゅうじ penmanship
赤字 あかじ deficit, red figures

b 字画 じかく stroke-count
字音 じおん Chinese-derived pronunciation of kanji, *on* reading

c 五百字 ごひゃくじ 500 (Chinese) characters

❷ nickname, pseudonym

字号 じごう nickname
名字(=苗字) みょうじ surname, family name

INDEPENDENT

【じ 字】**CHARACTER, letter; word; Chinese character, ideograph; handwriting**

字が上手である じがじょうずである have a good handwriting
細い字 ほそいじ slender character

KUN

【あざ 字】**village or town section in the Japanese addressing system**

大字片山 おおあざかたやま name of a town section

【あざな 字】pseudonym, alias; nickname

【-な -字】[usu. -名] **CHARACTER**, letter

仮字 かな kana, Japanese syllabary

SYNONYMS

❶ characters

字 CHARACTER → 2696
文 LETTER → 2458
漢 kanji → 0808
旁 RIGHT RADICAL → 2598

【あざ】

◯ **parts of towns**

区 WARD → 3681
街 CITY QUARTER → 0702
町 town section (*cho*) → 1430
丁 TOWN SUBSECTION (*chome*) → 4155
字 village or town section → 2696

HOMOPHONES

-な 名 NAME → 2693

NOTE

➡ see USAGE note at 名 2693
➡ see COMPOUND FORMATION for
苗字(=名字) みょうじ → 苗 2781
表意文字 ひょういもじ → 表 3083

守

2697

2-3-3

▸**PROTECT**

シュ ス まも(る) まも(り) もり も(り) -もり かみ▲ ㊔ もりお

Ⓒ 守 shǒu

40	Jōyō-3	U5B88
宀	S6-3-3	F0387

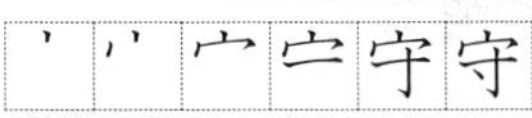

COMPOUNDS

❶ⓐ PROTECT (from, against), defend, guard, watch over
ⓑ guard, keeper

a 守備 しゅび defense; fielding
守護 しゅご protection, guard, defense, safeguard
守衛 しゅえい guard, doorkeeper
守株 しゅしゅ stupidity, lack of innovation
留守 るす absence (from home); caretaking; defending when the lord is absent
攻守 こうしゅ offense and defense; batting and fielding
死守する ししゅする defend to the last, defend desperately

b 看守 かんしゅ jailer, prison guard

❷ observe, obey, keep, adhere, abide by

順守(=遵守)する じゅんしゅする observe, obey, follow, conform to
厳守 げんしゅ strict observance
保守 ほしゅ conservatism; maintenance

❸ feudal governor, feudal lord

太守 たいしゅ governor general, viceroy
国守 こくしゅ governor of a province, feudal lord

INDEPENDENT

【しゅ 守】*baseball* fielding

KUN

【まもる 守る】

① [formerly also 護る] **PROTECT, defend, guard, watch over**
身を守る みをまもる defend oneself
見守る みまもる watch, keep watch over

②ⓐ **observe, obey, keep to, abide by**
ⓑ adhere to
ⓒ **keep (a promise), fulfill**

a 規則を守る きそくをまもる keep to the regulations

【まもり 守り】**PROTECTion, defense; good-luck charm**

守り神 まもりがみ guardian deity
お守り おまもり good-luck charm

【もり 守, 守り】**baby-sitting; nursemaid**

お守 おもり baby-sitting; baby-sitter
子守 こもり baby-sitting; baby-sitter

【-もり -守】[also suffix] **keeper**

関守 せきもり barrier keeper
灯台守 とうだいもり lighthouse keeper

【かみ 守】feudal governor, lord, baron

豊後の守 ぶんごのかみ Lord of Bungo

SYNONYMS

❶ⓐ protect

守 PROTECT (by watching over) → 2697
護 PROTECT (by safeguarding) → 2079
庇 PROTECT (by shielding) → 3802
衛 GUARD → 0938
警 GUARD AGAINST → 3595
防 defend → 0320
番 WATCH → 3416
保 PRESERVE → 0107
看 CARE FOR → 3992

ⓑ guard

哨 SENTRY → 0481
衛 GUARD → 0938
守 guard → 2697
警 guard → 3595

❷ obey

守 observe → 2697
遵 OBEY → 3929
順 OBEY → 0018
隷 be subordinate to → 2201
従 FOLLOW → 0498

USAGE

【まもる】

守る

① [formerly also 護る] protect, defend, guard, watch over

② ⓐ observe, obey, keep to, abide by

ⓑ adhere to

ⓒ keep (a promise), fulfill

護る

[now usu. 守る] protect, defend, guard, watch over

HOMOPHONES

まもる 護 PROTECT → 2079

かみ 上 UP → 4212

NOTE

➡ see also USAGE note at 上 4212

➡ see COMPOUND FORMATION for

守株 しゅしゅ → 株 1172

留守 るす → 留 3189

宅

2698

2-3-3

▸DWELLING HOUSE

タク ㊔ やけ

ⓒ 宅 zhái

40	Jōyō-6	U5B85
宀	S6-3-3	F0642

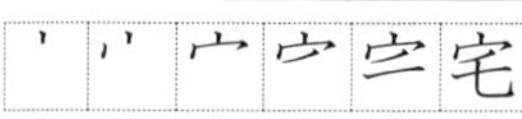

COMPOUNDS

● [also suffix] (house where one lives) **DWELLING HOUSE, home, abode, house, residence**

宅地 たくち land for housing, residential land

お宅 おたく your home, your house; you

帰宅 きたく homecoming

自宅 じたく one's house, one's home

拙宅 せったく my home, my humble abode

住宅 じゅうたく housing, dwelling house, residence

社宅 しゃたく company house

邸宅 ていたく residence, mansion

横江氏宅 よこえしたく residence of Mr. Yokoe

INDEPENDENT

【たく 宅】 home, house; my home; my husband

宅の子供 たくのこども my [our] child

宅も参ります たくもまいります My husband is going too

SYNONYMS

● **houses**

家 HOUSE → 2827

屋 HOUSE → 3842

軒 house → 1851

戸 HOUSEHOLD → 2429

宅 DWELLING HOUSE → 2698

居 residence → 3822

邸 STATELY RESIDENCE → 1451

住 housing → 0072

庵 HERMITAGE → 3876

宇

2699

2-3-3

▸UNIVERSE

ウ ㊔ たか ひろし いえ

ⓒ 宇 yǔ

40	Jōyō-6	U5B87
宀	S6-3-3	F0782

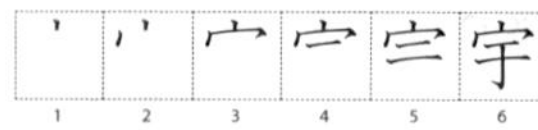

COMPOUNDS

❶ **UNIVERSE, infinite space, world**

宇宙 うちゅう universe, cosmos; (outer) space

宇内 うだい the whole universe, the whole world

❷ⓐ large building, building with large roof

ⓑ counter for temple buildings

ⓒ [original meaning] roof, eaves

a 堂宇 どうう edifice, temple, hall

b 一宇の堂 いちうのどう one temple building

c 八紘一宇 はっこういちう the whole world under one roof

❸ the whole country, realm, land

御宇 ぎょう Imperial reign

❹ heart, soul

気宇広大な きうこうだいな large-minded, magnanimous

SYNONYMS

❶ **universe and space**

宇 UNIVERSE → 2699

宙 SPACE → 2761

❷ⓐ **buildings**

閣 TALL MAGNIFICENT BUILDING → 4128

宇 large building → 2699

殿 PALACE → 2247

堂 HALL → 3202

館 PUBLIC BUILDING → 2196

舎 BUILDING → 2555

棟 BLOCK → 1248

厩 HORSE STABLE → 3746

ⓒ **roof**

屋 roof → 3842

宇 roof → 2699

尖

2700

2-3-3

▸POINT

セン とが(る) とんが(る)

ⓒ 尖 jiān

42	Names	U5C16
小	S6-3-3	F1886

COMPOUNDS

[now also 先 3046]

ⓐ (pointed end) **POINT, end, tip**

ⓑ [original meaning] **POINTed, acute**

a 尖端 せんたん pointed end, tip; spearhead; vanguard

尖兵 せんぺい advance-guard point; advance detachment

肺尖 はいせん apex of a lung

b 尖塔 せんとう pinnacle, spire

尖頭 せんとう pointed end, cusp

尖鋭な せんえいな radical; acute, sharp

KUN

【とがる 尖る】 **be POINTed, be sharp**

尖り声 とがりごえ sharp [angry] voice

尖鼠 とがりねずみ shrew

神経を尖らせる しんけいをとがらせる be uptight, be on edge

【とんがる 尖る】 same as 尖る とがる

尖り帽子 とんがりぼうし pointy hat

SYNONYMS

ⓐ **extremity**

端 END → 1564

末 end → 4317

梢 tip → 1208

先 point → 3046

尖 POINT → 2700

鋒 POINT OF A BLADE → 2172

ⓑ **sharp**

鋭 SHARP → 2171

先 pointed → 3046

尖 pointed → 2700

当

2701

2-3-3

▶**THE PRESENT**
▶**HIT**

トウ あ(たる) あ(たり)[1] あ(たり)[2] あ(てる) あ(て) まさ(に)▲ ㊔ まさ

Ⓝ 當 Ⓒ 当 dāng dàng

42△	Jōyō-2	U5F53
⺌	S6-3-3	F0068

COMPOUNDS

❶ⓐ [also prefix] **THE PRESENT, this, that, the said, the very**

ⓑ (occurring presently) **THE PRESENT, present, current**

a 当局 とうきょく the authorities concerned

当時 とうじ at that time, in those days; at the present time

当事者 とうじしゃ the person [party] concerned

当人 とうにん the one concerned, the said person

当店 とうてん this shop, we

当駅 とうえき this station

当該 とうがい the said, the concerned

当日 とうじつ the appointed day, that day

当社 とうしゃ this firm; this shrine

当営業所 とうえいぎょうしょ our [the present] business office

b 当分 とうぶん for some time, for a while, for the present, temporarily

当面の とうめんの present, immediate; urgent, pressing

❷ **proper, appropriate, fitting, applicable**

当然 とうぜん naturally, as a matter of course

当否 とうひ right or wrong, justice; propriety

正当な せいとうな just, right, due; legal

適当な てきとうな suitable, fit; irresponsible

妥当な だとうな proper, appropriate

該当する がいとうする come under, be applicable to

不当な ふとうな unfair, unreasonable, unjust

本当の ほんとうの true, real, genuine

❸ⓐ **assign, allot, appropriate**

ⓑ **be assigned, undertake, take charge of**

a 配当 はいとう apportionment, allotment

充当する じゅうとうする allot, appropriate, earmark

日当 にっとう daily allowance

勘当 かんどう disinheritance

b 当番 とうばん being on duty [guard]; person on duty

当直員 とうちょくいん person on duty

担当する たんとうする undertake, be in charge of

❹ⓐ **be elected, be selected, win**

ⓑ abbrev. of 当選 とうせん: being elected, winning an election

a 当選 とうせん election to office; winning (a lottery)

b 当確 とうかく be sure of being elected

❺ [original meaning] **be equivalent, correspond to, equal**

相当する そうとうする correspond to, be proportionate; be suitable for, become

グラム当量 ぐらむとうりょう gram equivalent

❻ **confront, come across, face**

当面する とうめんする face, confront

当惑する とうわくする be perplexed, be confused [puzzled], be embarrassed

一騎当千の武者 いっきとうせんのむしゃ matchless warrior, match for a thousand

❼ **pawn, mortgage**

抵当 ていとう mortgage, security

❽ **guess, conjecture**

見当 けんとう estimate, guess; aim

❾ unclassified compounds

弁当 べんとう box lunch, lunch, picnic lunch

芸当 げいとう feat, trick, stunt

INDEPENDENT

【とう 当】 right, justice, propriety

当を得る とうをうる be right, be in order

【とうの 当の】 this, **THE PRESENT**, that, the one in question

当の本人 とうのほんにん the person himself

KUN

【あたる 当たる】 *vi*

①ⓐ **HIT, strike**

ⓑ **HIT the mark**

ⓒ **strike against, touch, be touched, be exposed**

ⓓ (be struck by light or heat) **shine upon, strike; warm oneself, bask**

a 突き当たる つきあたる hit against, run into; come to the end of (a street)

体当たりする たいあたりする hurl oneself (at), dash oneself (against)

b 行き当たる いきあたる strike into, light on; come against

紛れ当たり まぐれあたり chance hit, fluke

c 当たり障りの無い あたりさわりのない harmless and inoffensive

口当たり くちあたり taste

手当たり次第 てあたりしだい at random

風に当たる かぜにあたる be exposed to wind

d 日当たり ひあたり exposure to the sun

火に当たる ひにあたる warm oneself at the fire

②ⓐ **HIT on, guess rightly; come true**

ⓑ **make a HIT, come off, succeed; win in a lottery**

a 思い当たる おもいあたる occur to, strike

見当たらない みあたらない not be found

心当たり こころあたり knowledge, idea, clue

b 当たり屋 あたりや lucky person, lucky batter; automobile accident faker

当たり役 あたりやく successful role

大当たり おおあたり big hit, great success, bonanza; bumper crop

籤が当たった くじがあたった I drew a prize

③ⓐ be equivalent to, be equal, correspond to

ⓑ be in relation to

a 一フィートは約一尺に当たる いちふぃーとはやくいっしゃくにあたる One foot is roughly equivalent to 1 *shaku*

b 彼は私の叔父に当たる かれはわたしのおじにあたる He is my uncle

④ be applicable to, apply

この解釈は当たっていない このかいしゃくはあたっていない This interpretation does not apply

⑤ face, confront, attack

総当たり戦 そうあたりせん round robin event

⑥ [in the form of 当たり あたり or 当たって あたって] on the occasion of, at, in

この時に当たって このときにあたって at this time [juncture]

⑦ undertake, take charge of

任に当たる にんにあたる undertake a duty

⑧ [often in the form of 当たって見る あたってみる] try, have a look, take a chance, feel out, sound

人の意向を当たって見る ひとのいこうをあたってみる sound out a person's thoughts

別の辞書に当たって見る べつのじしょにあたってみる try another dictionary

⑨ **treat (unkindly)**

当たり散らす あたりちらす find fault with everybody, make oneself disagreeable

八つ当たりする やつあたりする snarl (at the wrong person), take it out on (someone)

⑩ be assigned, be allotted; be selected

英語の時間に当たった えいごのじかんにあたった I was called on (to read aloud) in English class

⑪ lie, be located (in the direction of)

京都は東京の西に当たる きょうとはとうきょうのにしにあたる Kyoto lies to the west of Tokyo

⑫ [formerly also 中る] be poisoned, disagree with; suffer from

河豚に当たる ふぐにあたる get poisoned by swellfish

⑬ *theater jargon* next, coming

当たる日曜日 あたるにちようび next Sunday

【あたり[1] 当たり】 HIT, on-target impact; hit, success; clue, guess; manners; batting average; a bite (in fishing)

当たりを取る あたりをとる make a hit

当たりを付ける あたりをつける give it a try

人当たりが良い ひとあたりがよい have sociable manners

【あたり[2] 当たり】

① [suffix] **per**

一日当たり千円 いちにちあたりせんえん 1000 yen a day

② [in compounds] [often in the form of 当たって あたって] **at present**

差し当たり(=差し当たって) さしあたり(=さしあたって) for the time being, for the present, at present

③ [in compounds] **proper, appropriate**

当たり前 あたりまえ proper, right, just; of course

【あてる 当てる】 *vt*

①ⓐ **HIT, strike; touch**

ⓑ **HIT the mark**

ⓒ (cause to be struck) expose

a 当て逃げ あてにげ hit-and-run accident (causing property damage)

鞘当て さやあて rivalry ("touching of sheaths")
b 的を当てる まとをあてる hit the mark
c 日に当てる ひにあてる expose to the sun
②ⓐ **HIT on, guess**
ⓑ **make a HIT, succeed**
a 言い当てる いいあてる guess right
b 掘り当てる ほりあてる strike, find, dig up
③ **apply (to), put (to), lay, place**
当て嵌まる あてはまる be applicable, come under (a category), fulfill (criteria)
当て嵌める あてはめる apply, fit, adapt
手当て てあて provision; medical care, treatment
手当 てあて allowance, compensation, benefits
双眼鏡に目を当てる そうがんきょうにめをあてる put binoculars to one's eyes
座布団を当てる ざぶとんをあてる sit on a cushion
④ [usu. 充てる, but in compounds always 当てる] **allot, assign, appropriate**
割り当てる わりあてる assign, allot
⑤ [usu. 宛てる, but in compounds also 当てる] assign Chinese characters to a word (as phonetic substitutes)
当前は当て字だ とうぜんはあてじだ 当前 is written in phonetic substitute characters
⑥ call on (a pupil to answer a question)
問題を三人に当てる もんだいをさんにんにあてる ask three pupils to solve a problem
⑦ [in the form of 当てられる あてられる]
ⓐ be poisoned by, agree badly with, be affected by
ⓑ be annoyed by (flirtation)
a 暑さに当てられる あつさにあてられる be affected by heat

【あて 当て】
① **aim, end, goal**
当ても無く あてもなく aimlessly, at random
目当て めあて guide, aiming; aim
② **hopes, expectation**
当て事 あてごと expectations, hopes; guessing
当てが外れる あてがはずれる be disappointed
③ **reliance, confidence, trust**
当てにする あてにする rely upon, have trust in
④ [suffix] pad
肩当て かたあて shoulder pad

【まさに 当に】 [always followed by 可し べし] properly, naturally; it is proper to, ought to
当に人類を救う可き時だ まさにじんるいをすくうべきときだ Now is the time to save the human race

SYNONYMS

❶ⓐ **this and that**
本 THIS → 4314
爾 THAT → 4407
其れ THAT → 3255
彼 that → 0346
今 THIS (week, etc.) → 2464
当 THE PRESENT → 2701
該 the said → 1916
同 the same → 3707
之 this → 4228
是 this → 3090
此 THIS → 1017
斯 THIS → 2140
ⓑ **present**
今 PRESENT → 2464
当 THE PRESENT → 2701
現 ACTUAL → 1218
❷ **suitable**
適 SUITABLE → 3918
当 proper → 2701
宜 RIGHT → 2763
便 CONVENIENT → 0105
❸ⓐ **allot**
充 allot → 2507
当 assign → 2701
❺ **correspond to**
該 CORRESPOND TO → 1916
準 apply correspondingly → 3541
当 be equivalent → 2701
❼ **pawn**
質 pawn → 3483
当 pawn → 2701

【あたる】
①ⓐ **collide**
衝 COLLIDE → 0893
牴 COLLIDE WITH → 1134
觝 COLLIDE WITH → 1892
突 DASH → 2772
当たる HIT → 2701

【あてる】
①ⓐ **strike**
打 STRIKE → 0224
撲 DEAL A BLOW → 0903
殴 BEAT (strike a person) → 1099
蹴 KICK → 2074
撃 STRIKE → 3552
挌 STRIKE (a person) → 0448
撞 STRIKE (a ball or bell) → 0905
撥ねる strike (knock down) → 0907
当てる HIT → 2701
叩 KNOCK → 0208
拍 BEAT (strike repeatedly) → 0361
搏 BEAT (throb) → 0794

口土士夊夕宀小【⺌】干幺彐艹云亠亡千亼

口土士夂夕𭕄小【⺍】干幺彐卄云⺷亡千亼

③ **touch**
触 TOUCH → 1914
接 CONTACT → 0607
撫 STROKE → 0904
当てる apply → 2701

USAGE

❶【あたる】
当たる
vi
①ⓐ hit, strike
ⓑ hit the mark
ⓒ strike against, touch, be touched, be exposed
ⓓ (be struck by light or heat) shine upon, strike; warm oneself, bask
②ⓐ hit on, guess rightly; come true
ⓑ make a hit, come off, succeed; win in a lottery
③ⓐ be equivalent to, be equal, correspond to
ⓑ be in relation to
④ be applicable to, apply
⑤ face, confront, attack
⑥ [in the form of 当たり **あたり** or 当たって **あたって**] on the occasion of, at, in
⑦ undertake, take charge of
⑧ [often in the form of 当たって見る **あたってみる**] try, have a look, take a chance, feel out, sound
⑨ treat (unkindly)
⑩ be assigned, be allotted; be selected
⑪ lie, be located (in the direction of)
⑫ [formerly also 中る] be poisoned, disagree with; suffer from
⑬ *theater jargon* next, coming

中る
[now usu. 当たる] be poisoned, disagree with; suffer from

❷【あたり】
当たり
hit, on-target impact; hit, success; clue, guess; manners; batting average; a bite (in fishing)

辺り
①ⓐ vicinity, neighborhood, surroundings
ⓑ [also suffix] (near that place or time) thereabouts, about
② for instance

❸【あてる】
当てる
vt
①ⓐ hit, strike; touch
ⓑ hit the mark
ⓒ (cause to be struck) expose
②ⓐ hit on, guess
ⓑ make a hit, succeed
③ apply (to), put (to), lay, place
④ [usu. 充てる, but in compounds always 当てる] allot, assign, appropriate
⑤ [usu. 宛てる, but in compounds also 当てる] assign Chinese characters to a word (as phonetic substitutes)
⑥ call on (a pupil to answer a question)
⑦ [in the form of 当てられる **あてられる**]
ⓐ be poisoned by, agree badly with, be affected by
ⓑ be annoyed by (flirtation)

充てる
[sometimes also 当てる, but in compounds always 当てる] allot, assign, appropriate

宛てる
① address (a letter), direct
② [sometimes also 当てる] assign Chinese characters to a word (as phonetic substitutes)

★Both 当てる and 宛てる are used in the sense 'assigning Chinese characters', but the latter is preferred. However, in the compound あてじ 'phonetic substitute, etc.', 当て字 is the preferred form.

❹【あて】
当て
① aim, end, goal
② hopes, expectation
③ reliance, confidence, trust
④ [suffix] pad

-宛て
[suffix]
① addressed to
② per, apiece

HOMOPHONES

あたる 中 MIDDLE → 4262
あたり [2] 辺 VICINITY → 3761
あてる
充 FILL → 2507
宛 ADDRESS → 2762
あて 宛 ADDRESS → 2762
まさに
正 RIGHT → 4296
将 GENERAL OFFICER → 0551

COMPOUND FORMATION

❶【勘当 かんどう】
勘当 'disinheritance' originally meant to interrogate a criminal (勘) and assign (当 ❸ⓐ) the case to the authorities. This gave rise to the idea of finding disfavor with someone, as with one's children, which is how 勘当 acquired its current meaning.

❷【当惑 とうわく】
当惑する 'be perplexed, etc.' is to confront (当 ❻) a perplexing (惑) situation.

❸【弁当 べんとう】

The origin of 弁当 'box lunch, etc.' is not clear, but it appears that 当 ❾ is used phonetically without relation to its meaning.

❹【当たり前 あたりまえ】【当然 とうぜん】

当たり前 'proper, right, just; of course' consists of 当たり あたり[2] ③ 'proper, appropriate' and 前. It derives from 当然 とうぜん 'naturally, as a matter of course', which is a combination of 当 ❷ 'proper' and 然 'so, be definitely so'. Since 然 and 前 both have the *on* reading ゼン, the latter was mistakenly substituted for the former, and the resulting combination is pronounced in the *kun* reading, i.e., あたりまえ.

NOTE

➡ see also USAGE note at 正 4296

➡ see COMPOUND FORMATION for 相当 そうとう → 相 1120

光

2-3-3

incorrect classification

➡ see 2-4-2: ⺌ at 3043

舌

2702

2-3-3

▶**TONGUE**

ゼツ した

135	Nonstandard	U820C
舌	S6-6-0	F0000

alternative form → see 舌 at 2711

糸

2703

2-3-3

▶**THREAD**

シ いと

Ⓝ 絲 Ⓒ 丝 sī

120	Jōyō-1	U7CF8
糸	S6-6-0	F1379

く 幺 幺 糸 糸 糸
1 2 3 4 5 6

RADICAL

ito 'thread' (素 繭 辮), used in characters related to threads, ropes or their qualities

Left variant: 糸 × *itohen* (終 経 約)

COMPOUNDS

❶ⓐ [original meaning] **THREAD, yarn, filament**

ⓑ silk **THREAD**, silk

ⓒ something as thin as **THREAD**

a 綿糸 めんし cotton yarn [thread]

絹糸 けんし(=きぬいと) silk thread

抜糸 ばっし removal [extraction] of stitches

一糸も纏わずに いっしもまとわずに without a stitch of clothing on, stark-naked

b 製糸 せいし silk reeling, filature

蚕糸 さんし silk raising and reeling, sericulture

c 糸状虫 しじょうちゅう heartworm, filaria

菌糸 きんし hypha, mycelium

❷ [rare] stringed instruments

糸竹 しちく musical instruments

❸ 1/100,000

一厘二毛三糸 いちりんにもうさんし 0.00123

INDEPENDENT

【し 糸】1/100,000

KUN

【いと 糸】[also suffix] **THREAD, yarn, filament; (fish) line; string, chord (of musical instruments)**

糸巻き いとまき spool, bobbin

糸口 いとぐち [formerly also 緒] beginning, first step; clue

毛糸 けいと woolen yarn, wool

生糸 きいと raw silk (thread)

横糸 よこいと [also 緯糸 or 緯] woof

縦糸 たていと [also 経糸 or 経] warp

刺繍糸 ししゅういと embroidery thread

SYNONYMS

❶ⓐ **threads and fibers**

糸 THREAD → 2703

緯 woof → 1782

経 warp → 1687

繊 FIBER → 1789

維 FIBER → 1733

綸 THREAD → 1739

緬 FINE THREAD → 1758

HOMOPHONES

いとぐち

緒 OUTSET → 1742

糸口 → 2703, 4189

よこいと

緯 LATITUDE → 1782

横糸 → 1350, 2703

緯糸 → 1782, 2703

たていと

経 PASS THROUGH → 1687

縦糸 → 1783, 2703

経糸 → 1687, 2703

NOTE

➡ see USAGE notes at 緒 1742 and 緯 1782 and 経 1687

夛

2704

2-3-3

▶**MANY**

タ おお(い) ㊔ かず

36	Nonstandard	U591B
夕	S6-3-3	F0000

traditional form → see 多 at 2694

口 士 士 夊 夕 宀 小 ⺌ 干 幺 彐 【艹】 云 亠 亡 千 亼

芝

▶LAWN GRASS

シ▲ しば

ⓒ 芝 zhī

2705

2-3-3

140	Jōyō	U829D
艹	S6-3-3	F1318

一 ⺊ 艹 艹 芝 芝

1 2 3 4 5 6

COMPOUNDS

● [rare] purplish mushroom (traditionally considered good omen of long life)

霊芝 れいし *Fomes japonicus*

KUN

【しば 芝】

ⓐ **LAWN GRASS, zoysia**

ⓑ **lawn, turf, sod**

a 芝草 しばくさ lawn

芝地 しばち grass plot

高麗芝 こうらいしば Korean lawn grass

b 芝生 しばふ lawn, turf

芝刈り機 しばかりき lawn mower

芝居 しばい play, drama

SYNONYMS

【しば】

○ **kinds of grasses**

草 GRASS → 2813

荻 AMUR SILVERGRASS → 2844

蒲 CATTAIL → 2932

萊 GOOSEFOOT → 2878

蕨 BRACKEN → 2992

叢 grassy place → 3243

芝 LAWN GRASS → 2705

笹 BAMBOO GRASS → 3301

茅 cogongrass → 2779

萱 THATCH GRASS → 2904

藁 STRAW → 3015

芦 REED → 2743

葦 COMMON REED → 2934

菅 SEDGE → 2874

USAGE

【しば】

芝

ⓐ lawn grass, zoysia

ⓑ lawn, turf, sod

柴

brushwood, firewood

HOMOPHONES

しば 柴 BRUSHWOOD → 3287

COMPOUND FORMATION

【芝居 しばい】

芝居 'play, drama' originated from the idea of sitting (居) on the lawn (芝 しば ⓑ) to watch a play.

芋

▶POTATO

ウ▲ いも

ⓒ 芋 yù

2706

2-3-3

140	Jōyō	U828B
艹	S6-3-3	F1646

一 ⺊ 艹 艹 芋 芋

1 2 3 4 5 6

KUN

【いも 芋】

① **POTATO; sweet potato; tuber**

芋蔓 いもづる sweet potato vine

芋虫 いもむし green caterpillar

ジャガ芋 じゃがいも potato, white potato

里芋 さといも taro

薩摩芋 さつまいも sweet potato

焼き芋 やきいも baked sweet potato

② [also prefix] unrefined, rustic

芋侍 いもざむらい rustic (boorish) samurai

SYNONYMS

【いも】

① **vegetables**

菜 greens → 2880

蕪 TURNIP → 2990

芋 POTATO → 2706

豆 BEAN → 2442

蕗 BUTTERBUR → 3007

茄 EGGPLANT → 2787

芹 JAPANESE PARSLEY → 2742

瓜 GOURD → 3789

瓢 BOTTLE GOURD → 2356

芥 mustard → 2741

共

2-3-3

incorrect classification

➡ see 2-4-2: 廾 at 3045

至

▶COME TO

シ いた(る) ㊔ ゆき よし みち

ⓒ 至 zhì

2707

2-3-3

133	Jōyō-6	U81F3
至	S6-6-0	F1049

一 ㇖ 云 云 至 至

1 2 3 4 5 6

RADICAL

itaru 'arrive' (致 臻×), used in characters related to arriving or reaching

COMPOUNDS

❶ [original meaning] **COME TO, arrive at, reach**

必至だ ひっしだ be inevitable

❷ **to, as far as**

至徳島 しとくしま to Tokushima

乃至 ないし from…to…, between…and…; or

❸ **utmost, most, extreme**

至急の しきゅうの urgent, pressing

至難の しなんの most difficult

至上 しじょう supremacy

至極 しごく very, most, exceedingly, extremely

至孝 しこう supreme filial piety

❹ **solstice**

夏至 げし summer solstice

冬至 とうじ winter solstice

KUN

【いたる 至る】

① [sometimes also 到る] **COME TO, arrive at, reach; lead (to)**

至り いたり extremity, utmost limit; result

至る処 いたるところ everywhere, all over

箱根に至る道 はこねにいたるみち road leading to Hakone

② **COME TO** (do something), get to, result in

信じるに至る しんじるにいたる come to believe

大事に至る だいじにいたる develop into a serious affair

SYNONYMS

❶ **arrive**

着 ARRIVE → 4110

到 ARRIVE → 1615

至 COME TO → 2707

及 REACH TO → 4192

届く REACH → 3820

達 ATTAIN → 3893

❷ **direction indicators**

至 to → 2707

-行き bound for → 0246

-向け (bound) for → 3790

迄 UP TO → 3967

以 TO THE…OF → 0045

自 from → 4338

来 since → 4366

而 DIRECTION WORD → 2520

❸ **most**

最 MOST → 3120

至 utmost → 2707

極 EXTREME → 1243

USAGE

【いたる】

至る

① [sometimes also 到る] come to, arrive at, reach; lead (to)

② come to (do something), get to, result in

到る

[usu. 至る] arrive at, reach, come to

HOMOPHONES

いたる 到 ARRIVE → 1615

羊

▶**SHEEP**

ヨウ ひつじ

Ⓒ 羊 yáng

2708

2-3-3

123	Jōyō-3	U7F8A
羊	S6-6-0	F1720

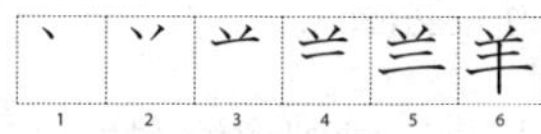

RADICAL

hitsuji 'sheep' (群 羣 羸×), used in characters related to sheep

Top variant: ⺷ ***hitsujikanmuri*** (義 着 美)

Left variant: ⺶× ***hitsujihen*** (羝× 羯× 羚)

COMPOUNDS

❶ [original meaning] **SHEEP, ram, ewe**

羊肉 ようにく mutton

羊毛 ようもう wool

羊頭狗肉 ようとうくにく using a better name to sell inferior goods, crying wine and selling vinegar

羊羹× ようかん sweet jelly of beans

牧羊 ぼくよう sheep farming

❷ something that envelops the fetus

羊水 ようすい amniotic fluid

KUN

【ひつじ 羊】 **SHEEP, ram, ewe**

羊飼い ひつじかい shepherd

羊雲 ひつじぐも floccus

子羊 こひつじ lamb

SPECIAL READINGS

羊歯▲ しだ fern

山羊▲ やぎ goat

SYNONYMS

❶ **sheep**

羊 SHEEP → 2708

未 the Ram → 4318

❶ **domesticated mammals**

牛 CATTLE → 4263

馬 HORSE → 4086

豚 PIG → 1228

口 士 士 夂 夕 宀 小 ⺌ 干 幺 彐 艹 云 【⺷】 亡 千 亼

羊 SHEEP →2708
犬 DOG →4275
猫 CAT →0651
兎 RABBIT →4374

USAGE

【ひつじ】
羊
sheep, ram, ewe
未
eighth sign of the Oriental zodiac: the Ram

HOMOPHONES

ひつじ 未 NOT YET →4318

COMPOUND FORMATION

❶【羊頭狗肉 ようとうくにく】
羊頭狗肉 'using a better name to sell inferior goods, etc.' is to sell dog (狗) meat (肉) under the pretense that it is sheep's (羊 ❶) head (頭).

❷【羊羹× ようかん】
羊羹× 'sweet jelly of beans' originally referred to a broth (羹×) of Chinese lamb (羊 ❶), but now refers to Japanese bean jelly, which resembles the former dish in shape (long and slender).

⺷

2709

2-3-3

▶***HITSUJIKANMURI***

123	Radical	U2EB7
羊	S6-6-0	F0000

radical variant →see 羊 at 2708

妄

2710

2-3-3

▶**RASH**

モウ ボウ みだ(りに)

38	Nonstandard	U5984
女	S6-3-3	F0000

traditional form →see 妄 at 2509

舌

2711

2-3-3

▶**TONGUE**

ゼツ した

Ⓝ 舌◇ Ⓒ 舌 shé

135	Jōyō-5	U820C
舌	S6-6-0	F1181

1	2	3	4	5	6
丿	二	千	千	舌	舌

RADICAL

shita 'tongue' (舒×), used in characters related to actions performed by the tongue
Left variant: 舌× ***shitahen*** (舐)

COMPOUNDS

❶ [original meaning] **TONGUE**
舌端 ぜったん tip of the tongue; speech, way of talking
舌頭 ぜっとう tip of the tongue; speech, way of talking
舌音 ぜつおん lingual sound
舌癌 ぜつがん cancer of the tongue

❷ (manner of speech) **TONGUE, speech, language, words**
舌戦 ぜっせん war of words
舌鋒 ぜっぽう (sharp) tongue
弁舌 べんぜつ speech
毒舌 どくぜつ wicked tongue, abusive language, blistering remarks
饒舌 じょうぜつ garrulity, loquacity
筆舌に尽くし難い ひつぜつにつくしがたい be beyond description

KUN

【した 舌】**TONGUE; tongue-shaped objects as a clapper or reed**
舌打ち したうち tongue clicking
舌触りが良い したざわりがよい be soft and pleasant on the tongue
舌足らずな したたらずな lisping; lame (expression)
猫舌だ ねこじただ have a tongue too sensitive to heat
二枚舌 にまいじた double-dealing

SYNONYMS

❶ **mouth parts**
唇 LIP →3401
歯 TOOTH →3124
舌 TONGUE →2711
牙 FANG →4243

❷ **speech**
言 SPEECH →2440
談 TALK →1975
舌 TONGUE →2711
口 MOUTH →4189

会合

2-3-3

incorrect classification
➡ see 2-2-4: 𠆢 at 2511

呆

2712

2-3-4

▶**DIM-WITTED**

ホウ ボウ あき(れる) ほう(ける) ぼ(ける)

Ⓒ 呆 dāi

30	Non-Jōyō	U5446
口	S7-3-4	F1508

COMPOUNDS

❶ [original meaning] **DIM-WITTED, foolish, stupid**
痴呆 ちほう imbecility, dementia
阿呆 あほう(=あほ) fool, idiot
阿呆らしい あほらしい ridiculous, absurd

❷ **be amazed, be astonished, be astounded**

呆然(=茫×然)とする ぼうぜんとする be struck dumb (with surprise), be stupefied

KUN

【あきれる 呆れる】**be amazed, be astonished, be astounded**

呆れ返る あきれかえる be utterly amazed
呆れ果てる あきれはてる be dumbfounded, be flabbergasted
呆れ顔 あきれがお amazed [stunned] expression
聞いて呆れる きいてあきれる be astonished to hear, be incredulous

【ほうける 呆ける】[also 惚ける]

①ⓐ grow senile
ⓑ be mentally slow, be befuddled

② [verbal suffix] be engrossed in (doing something)

遊び呆ける あそびほうける be absorbed in play; spend one's time in idle amusement

【ぼける 呆ける】[also 惚ける]

①ⓐ grow senile
ⓑ be mentally slow, be befuddled

ab 呆け ぼけ being out of it, dementia, senility; idiot, fool; funnyman (of a comedy duo)

② be out of focus, become unclear [indistinct]

古呆ける ふるぼける become old-looking, become worn out

SPECIAL READINGS

呆気ない あっけない disappointing, too short [quick], unexpectedly quick [easy]
呆気に取られる あっけにとられる be astonished, be amazed

SYNONYMS

❶ **foolish**

愚 FOOLISH → 3513
暗 DARK → 1273
痴 STUPID → 4072
鈍 DULL → 2123
呆 DIM-WITTED → 2712
魯 DULL → 2665
闇 DARK → 4134
蒙 IGNORANCE → 2938

HOMOPHONES

ぼける 惚 FALL IN LOVE → 0584
ほうける 惚 FALL IN LOVE → 0584

NOTE

➡ see USAGE note at 惚 0584

呂

2713

2-3-4

▸**PHONETIC [ro]**

ロ リョ▲ ㊔ なが とも おと ふえ

Ⓒ 吕 lǚ

30	Jōyō	U5442
口	S7-3-4	F1207

1 2 3 4 5 6 7

COMPOUNDS

❶ **used PHONETICally for** ***ro***

風呂 ふろ bath
語呂 ごろ sound harmony
伊呂波 いろは *iroha,* the Japanese syllabary [alphabet]

❷ ancient musical note in traditional Chinese and Japanese music

呂律 ろれつ articulation
律呂 りつりょ Chinese system of musical sounds, standard tones

❸ [original meaning, now archaic] backbone

SYNONYMS

❶ **phonetic [r]**

呂 PHONETIC [ro] → 2713
路 phonetic [ru] → 1936
羅 PHONETIC [ra] → 3244

❷ **musical elements**

韻 RHYME → 2279
律 RHYTHM → 0433
拍 BEAT → 0361
調 TONE → 1973
呂 ancient musical note → 2713

足

2714

2-3-4

▸**FOOT**
▸**SUFFICE**

ソク あし た(りる) た(る) た(す)

Ⓒ 足 zú

157	Jōyō-1	U8DB3
足	S7-7-0	F0207

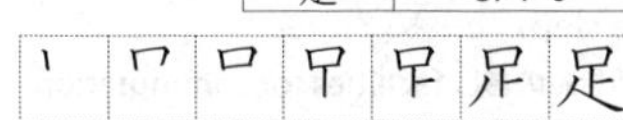

1 2 3 4 5 6 7

RADICAL

ashi 'foot' (蹬× 躄× 蹇×), used in characters related to the foot or actions using feet

Left variant: 𧾷 ***ashihen*** (路 跡 踊)

COMPOUNDS

❶ⓐ [original meaning] **FOOT, leg**
ⓑ **travel on FOOT, walk, run**

a 足跡 そくせき footprint, footmark; the course of one's life, one's achievements
義足 ぎそく artificial leg
蛇足 だそく superfluity, redundancy

b 足労 そくろう trouble of going somewhere
遠足 えんそく excursion, hike, long walk
発足 ほっそく(=はっそく) starting, inauguration
長足の進歩 ちょうそくのしんぽ rapid progress [strides]

❷ counter for steps

【口】士士夂宀小⺌⺍巛己艹⺈刃刃夂亡厶厷

一足飛び いっそくとび at a leap, at a jump

❸ **counter for pairs of FOOTwear, as shoes, slippers or socks**

靴一足 くついっそく a pair of shoes

❹ **SUFFICE, be enough, be adequate**

満足 まんぞく satisfaction, contentment

不足 ふそく insufficiency, shortage, deficit; want; dissatisfaction

自足 じそく self-sufficiency

❺ **supplement**

補足 ほそく supplement, replenishment

充足 じゅうそく sufficiency

KUN

【あし 足】

①ⓐ **leg, limb; FOOT, paw**

ⓑ [also 脚] (leg-shaped support) **leg**

ⓒ **FOOT** (of something standing), base

a 足腰 あしこし legs and loins

足首 あしくび ankle

足場 あしば scaffold, footing, foothold

足下(=足元) あしもと gait, pace, step

手足 てあし hands and feet, limbs

b 机の足 つくえのあし legs of a table

c 垂線の足 すいせんのあし foot of a perpendicular line

②ⓐ [also suffix] **walking, traveling**

ⓑ **step, stride**

ⓒ means of transportation

a 足取り あしどり one's manner of walking; trace (of a culprit's movement); (price) movement

足並み あしなみ pace, step

千鳥足 ちどりあし tottering gait

b 一足 ひとあし a step

c 通勤の足 つうきんのあし facilities for commutation

③ [also 脚] **movement, pace**

出足 であし start

雨足 あまあし density of the falling rain; pace (of the approaching shower)

④ trace

足が付く あしがつく be traced [tracked]

⑤ deficit

足が出る あしがでる exceed the budget, do not cover the expense

⑥ relation

足を洗う あしをあらう wash one's hands of, quit (the shady business); wash one's feet

足入れ あしいれ tentative marriage

【たりる 足りる】 **SUFFICE, be sufficient [enough]; serve, answer, do; be satisfied [content]; be worth (doing);** [in negative constructions] **(not) intelligent**

千円で足りる せんえんでたりる A thousand yen will suffice

事足りる ことたりる answer the purpose, be sufficient

満ち足りる みちたりる be content, have enough, be happy

物足りない ものたりない be somehow unsatisfied, feel something wanting; be unsatisfactory

一見するに足りる いっけんするにたりる be worth seeing

少少足りない しょうしょうたりない somewhat weak in the head; somewhat lacking

【たる 足る】 literary or dialect form of 足りる たりる

舌足らずな したたらずな lisping; lame (expression)

【たす 足す】 **add; supplement, make up for; do (one's business)**

足し算 たしざん addition

接ぎ足す つぎたす add, extend

用を足す ようをたす do one's business; relieve oneself

SPECIAL READINGS

足袋 たび Japanese [digitated] socks, *tabi*

百足▲ むかで centipede

SYNONYMS

❶ⓐ **leg**

足 FOOT → 2714

脚 LEG → 1226

膝 KNEE → 1359

ⓑ **walk**

歩 WALK → 3071

徒 go on foot → 0499

脚 move on foot → 1226

足 travel on foot → 2714

踏 TREAD → 1997

❸ **footwear**

靴 SHOES → 2235

沓 FOOTWEAR → 3074

駄 clogs → 2291

履 footwear → 3933

足 counter for footwear → 2714

❹ **suffice**

足 SUFFICE → 2714

満 satisfied → 0739

❺ **supplement**

補 SUPPLEMENT → 1529

足 supplement → 2714

給 SUPPLY → 1708

充 fill up (a vacancy) → 2507

【たす】

◯ **add**

加 ADD → 0042

足す add → 2714

〆る SUM → 4179

USAGE

【あし】

足

①ⓐ leg, limb; foot, paw

ⓑ [also 脚] (leg-shaped support) leg

ⓒ foot (of something standing), base

②ⓐ [also suffix] walking, traveling

ⓑ step, stride

ⓒ means of transportation

③ [also 脚] movement, pace

④ trace

⑤ deficit

⑥ relation

脚

① [also 足] (leg-shaped support) leg

② [also 足] movement, pace

③ bottom radical of Chinese characters, leg radical

HOMOPHONES

あし 脚 LEG → 1226

NOTE

➡ see COMPOUND FORMATION for 蛇足 だそく → 蛇 1701

呈

▶PRESENT

テイ

Ⓝ 呈 Ⓒ 呈 chéng

2715

2-3-4

30	Jōyō	U5448
口	S7-3-4	F1958

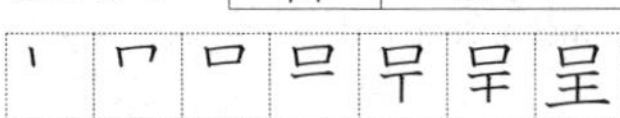

1 2 3 4 5 6 7

COMPOUNDS

❶ [also suffix] **PRESENT (a gift), give**

呈上 ていじょう presentation

進呈する しんていする proffer, present

謹呈する きんていする present, make a present

贈呈 ぞうてい presentation

案内書呈 あんないしょてい presentation of a guide-book

❷ (offer to view) **PRESENT, show, display, exhibit**

呈示する ていじする exhibit, present

呈色 ていしき color, coloring

露呈 ろてい exposure, disclosure

INDEPENDENT

【ていする 呈する】**PRESENT**, offer; present (an appearance), display, assume (a color)

苦言を呈する くげんをていする give bitter-pill advice

青色を呈する あおいろをていする assume a blue color, turn blue

SYNONYMS

❶ **give**

与 GIVE → 4229

呈 PRESENT → 2715

進 present to a superior → 3873

上 give (to superior or others) → 4212

下 give (to inferior or speaker) → 4186

呉れる give (to speaker) → 3156

授 CONFER → 0595

賜 DEIGN TO GIVE → 1994

贈 PRESENT A GIFT → 2064

賄 BRIBE → 1931

賂 BRIBE → 1930

❷ **show**

示 SHOW → 2435

見せる show → 3151

呈 PRESENT → 2715

邑

▶VILLAGE

ユウ ㊔ むら お おう さと くに

Ⓒ 邑 yì

2716

2-3-4

163	Names	U9091
邑	S7-7-0	F2645

RADICAL

mura 'city', used in characters related to place names or towns

Right variant: 阝 ***ōzato*** (部 都 郎)

COMPOUNDS

❶ **VILLAGE, town; fief**

邑落 ゆうらく [archaic] hamlet

都邑 とゆう city, town

❷ [rare] fief

采邑 さいゆう fief

SYNONYMS

❶ **villages and towns**

町 TOWN → 1430

村 VILLAGE → 1029

里 hamlet → 4356

郷 HOMETOWN → 0664

庄 FEUDAL VILLAGE → 3788

邑 VILLAGE → 2716

⻊

▶ASHIHEN

2717

2-3-4

157	Radical	U2ECA
足	S7-7-0	F0000

radical variant → see 足 at 2714

【口】 土 士 夂 宀 小 ⺌ ⺍ 巛 己 艹 ⺮ 刃 刄 久 亡 亼 厶

呈

2718

2-3-4

▶**PRESENT**

テイ

30	Nonstandard	U5448
口	S7-3-4	F0000

traditional form → see 呈 at 2715

赤

2719

2-3-4

▶**RED**

セキ シャク あか あか- あか(い) あか(らむ) あか(らめる)

Ⓒ 赤 chì

155	Jōyō-1	U8D64
赤	S7-7-0	F0482

Stroke order: 一 十 土 𡗗 𡗗 赤 赤 (1 2 3 4 5 6 7)

RADICAL

aka 'red', used in characters related to the color red
Left variant: 赤 × ***akahen*** (赦 赫 赭×)

COMPOUNDS

❶ⓐ RED, crimson, scarlet
ⓑ RED, Communist

a 赤銅 しゃくどう gold-copper alloy
赤外線 せきがいせん infrared rays
赤痢 せきり dysentery
赤十字 せきじゅうじ Red Cross
赤面する せきめんする blush [turn red] (with shame), feel ashamed

ab 赤色 せきしょく red; Communism
赤化する せっか(=せきか)する turn red; go Communist

b 赤軍 せきぐん Red Army

❷ utter, bare
赤貧 せきひん extreme poverty
赤裸裸な せきららな naked, frank

❸ sincere, loyal
赤心 せきしん one's true heart, sincerity

❹ equator
赤道 せきどう equator
赤経 せっけい right ascension

KUN

【あか 赤】 **RED, crimson, scarlet; Red, Communist**
赤ちゃん あかちゃん baby
赤紫 あかむらさき purplish red
赤線 あかせん red-light district
赤字 あかじ deficit, red figures
赤ん坊 あかんぼう baby
赤金 あかがね [also 銅] copper
赤旗 あかはた Red Flag

【あか- 赤-】
① [prefix] **RED**
赤電話 あかでんわ red public phone
② utter, total
赤裸 あかはだか stark naked

【あかい 赤い】 [sometimes also 紅い] **RED, crimson, scarlet**

【あからむ 赤らむ】 **become RED**
赤らんだ あからんだ ruddy, florid

【あからめる 赤らめる】 **blush, REDden**
顔を赤らめる かおをあからめる blush, change color

SPECIAL READINGS

真っ赤 まっか deep red

SYNONYMS

❶ⓐ red colors
赤 RED → 2719
紅 CRIMSON → 1629
緋 SCARLET → 1732
朱 VERMILION → 4344
丹 CINNABAR → 4249
茜 MADDER → 2811

ⓑ Communism
共 Communism → 3045
左 the Left → 3692
赤 RED → 2719

USAGE

❶【あかい】
赤い
[sometimes also 紅い] red, crimson, scarlet
紅い
[usu. 赤い] crimson, deep red

❷【あからむ】
赤らむ
become red
明らむ
brighten

HOMOPHONES

あかがね
銅 COPPER → 2155
赤金 → 2719, 2552
あかい 紅 CRIMSON → 1629
あからむ 明 BRIGHT → 1060

COMPOUND FORMATION

【赤ん坊 あかんぼう】

赤ん坊 'baby' derives from the red (赤 あか) state in which an infant is born. 坊 is a suffix of endearment.

NOTE

➡ see also USAGE note at 銅 2155

走

▶RUN

ソウ はし(る)

Ⓝ 赱 Ⓒ 走 zǒu

2720

▀2-3-4

156	Jōyō-2	U8D70
走	S7-7-0	F0445

一	十	土	キ	キ	赤	走
1	2	3	4	5	6	7

RADICAL

hashiru 'run', used in characters related to running or advancing quickly

Enclosure: 走 *sōnyō* (起 越 超)

COMPOUNDS

❶ⓐ [original meaning] **RUN, dash, rush**

ⓑ [suffix] **RUN**, dash

a 走者 そうしゃ runner

御馳走 ごちそう feast, treat

御馳走様 ごちそうさま Thank you (for the meal)/I've enjoyed the meal

奔走する ほんそうする bustle about, exert oneself for, devote oneself to

競走 きょうそう race, sprint

独走 どくそう running alone; easy victory, walkover

b 五十メートル走 ごじゅうめーとるそう 50 meter dash

❷ **RUN away, flee**

逃走 とうそう flight, escape

脱走する だっそうする desert, escape

❸ **travel by vehicle or craft, drive, sail**

走行 そうこう traveling, driving

暴走 ぼうそう reckless driving; running wild

滑走路 かっそうろ runway

帆走 はんそう sailing by boat

INDEPENDENT

【そう 走】*baseball* base **RUN**ning

KUN

【はしる 走る】**RUN, dash, rush; drive, ride; turn to, become; go to excess; flow**

走り はしり season's first supply (of tomatoes); running; *dialect* sink

走り書き はしりがき running script, cursive writing

四十キロで突っ走る よんじゅっきろでつっぱしる fly along at 40 kph

左翼に走る さよくにはしる turn leftist

口走る くちばしる blurt out

ペンが走る ぺんがはしる one's pen flows

SPECIAL READINGS

師走 しわす December

SYNONYMS

❶ **run**

走 RUN → 2720

奔 RUSH → 2758

馳 RUN QUICKLY → 2289

駆 gallop → 2293

❷ **escape**

逃 ESCAPE → 3839

遁 FLEE → 4027

亡 flee → 4210

走 run away → 2720

脱 ESCAPE FROM → 1225

❸ **travel by vehicle**

乗 RIDE → 4393

走 travel by vehicle → 2720

航 NAVIGATE → 1671

騎 RIDE ON HORSEBACK → 2307

COMPOUND FORMATION

【御馳走 ごちそう】

御馳走 'feast, treat' is a combination of the honorific prefix 御, 馳 'run' and 走 ❶ⓐ 'run'. The idea is that a person who prepares a feast must run around to gather ingredients.

NOTE

➡ see COMPOUND FORMATION for 師走 しわす → 師 1680

走

▶*SŌNYŌ*

2721

▀2-3-4

156	Radical	U8D70
走	S7-7-0	F0000

radical variant → see 走 at 2720

赱

▀2-3-4

incorrect stroke-count

➡ see ▀2-3-3: 土 at 2690

売

▶SELL

バイ う(る) う(れる)

Ⓝ 賣 Ⓒ 卖 mài

2722

▀2-3-4

33△	Jōyō-2	U58F2
士	S7-3-4	F0292

一	十	士	士	声	声	売
1	2	3	4	5	6	7

COMPOUNDS

❶ⓐ [original meaning] **SELL**

ⓑ **sale**

a 売買 ばいばい buying and selling, trade

売店 ばいてん booth, stand; store

売却 ばいきゃく sale

売春 ばいしゅん prostitution

商売 しょうばい trade, business, commerce

販売 はんばい sale, selling, marketing

発売する はつばいする sell, put on the market

b 即売 そくばい sale on the spot, spot sale

口 土 【土】 夂 宀 小 ⺌ ⺍ 巛 己 艹 ⺈ 刃 刄 久 亡 亽 厶

特売 とくばい special sale, bargain sale

❷ⓐ SELL (oneself to the public), make known
ⓑ SELL out (one's country)

a 売名 ばいめい self-advertisement, publicity stunt

b 売国 ばいこく selling out [betrayal] of one's own country

KUN

【うる 売る】**SELL; sell out, betray; sell (oneself to the public), make known**

売り うり sale, selling

売り上げ うりあげ sales, proceeds

売り出す うりだす put on sale; rise in fame

売り切れ うりきれ sellout; sold out

売り切れる うりきれる be sold out, go out of stock

売り込む うりこむ sell, market; push (one's wares); become well known

売り場 うりば (place where something is sold) counter, sales floor, shop

売り手 うりて seller

小売り こうり retail, sale in small quantities

卸売り おろしうり wholesale

国を売る くにをうる betray one's country (to an enemy)

名を売る なをうる make oneself famous, gain a reputation

【うれる 売れる】**SELL, be in demand, enjoy a large sale; be well known, become popular**

売れ行き うれゆき sales, demand

売れっ子 うれっこ person of great popularity

SYNONYMS

❶ⓐ & ❶ⓑ sell and trade

売 SELL → 2722

卸す WHOLESALE → 1835

販 ENGAGE IN SALES → 1869

商 TRADE → 2623

貿 TRADE → 3214

易 EXCHANGE → 3064

COMPOUND FORMATION

【売春 ばいしゅん】

売春 'prostitution' is, literally, to sell (売 ❶ⓐ) spring (春). In this instance 春 refers to lovemaking—what a picturesque way to depict prostitution!

壱

2723

2-3-4

▶ONE

イチ ㊔ い かず はじめ

Ⓝ 壹 Ⓒ 壹 yī

33	Jōyō	U58F1
士	S7-3-4	F2558

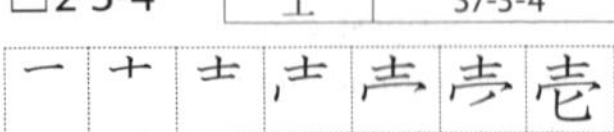

COMPOUNDS

● **ONE**—used in legal documents and checks

金壱阡×参百円也 きんいっせんさんびゃくえんなり one thousand three hundred yen

INDEPENDENT

【いち 壱】**ONE** (→●)

SYNONYMS

● **one**

一 ONE → 4148

壱 ONE (in legal documents) → 2723

片- ONE OF TWO → 4272

隻 ONE OF A PAIR → 3426

単 SINGLE → 2805

個 INDIVIDUAL → 0132

声

2724

2-3-4

▶VOICE

セイ ショウ こえ こわ-

Ⓝ 聲 Ⓒ 声 shēng

33△	Jōyō-2	U58F0
士	S7-3-4	F0145

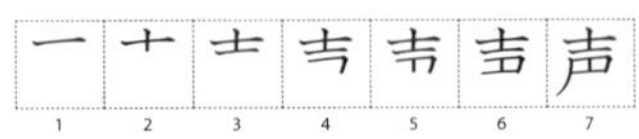

COMPOUNDS

❶ⓐ [original meaning] **VOICE, sound**
ⓑ (tone produced in singing) **VOICE**
ⓒ *phonetics* **VOICE**

a 声調 せいちょう tone of voice, style; tone (in Chinese phonetics)

声帯 せいたい vocal cords

音声 おんせい voice, sound

発声 はっせい vocalization, utterance

銃声 じゅうせい sound of gunfire

擬声語 ぎせいご onomatopoeic word

大音声 だいおんじょう very loud voice

b 声楽 せいがく vocal music

混声合唱 こんせいがっしょう mixed chorus

c 有声音 ゆうせいおん voiced sound

❷ tone in Chinese phonetics

四声 しせい the four tones (of Chinese)

第一声 だいいっせい first tone

❸ **speak out, announce, declare**

声明 せいめい declaration

声援 せいえん shout of encouragement, cheering; support

声優 せいゆう radio actor; dialogue speaker (in dubbing)

❹ **reputation**

声価 せいか reputation, fame

名声 めいせい fame, reputation

KUN

【こえ 声, こわ- 声-】[also suffix] **VOICE, sound, cry; word; opinion**

声色 こわいろ tone of voice; vocal mimicry
読者の声 どくしゃのこえ reader's voice
歌声 うたごえ singing (voice)
大声 おおごえ loud voice
掛け声 かけごえ shout to mark time, shout of encouragement
叫び声 さけびごえ shout, outcry
金切り声 かなきりごえ shrill voice, scream

SYNONYMS

❶ **kinds of sound**
音 SOUND → 2570
声 VOICE → 2724
響 reverberation → 3573
韻 melodious tone → 2279
玲 TINKLING OF JADES → 1139

❹ **repute**
声 reputation → 2724
誉 HONOR → 3135
名 NAME → 2693
望 popularity → 3408

NOTE

➡ see COMPOUND FORMATION for 擬声語 ぎせいご → 擬 0969

志 ▶AMBITION

2725

2-3-4

シ こころざ(す) こころざし しりんぐ▲
㊔ むね ゆき
Ⓒ 志 zhì

61	Jōyō-5	U5FD7
心	S7-4-3	F0597

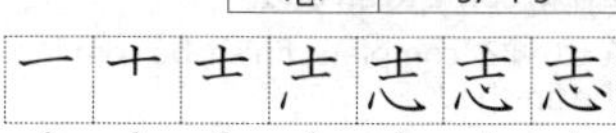

COMPOUNDS

❶ⓐ **AMBITION, aim, intention, purpose, aspiration, desire, wishes**
ⓑ [original meaning] **have AMBITION to, intend, aim, aspire to**

a 志願する しがんする volunteer, apply for
立志 りっし fixing one's aim in life
大志 たいし lofty ambition, aspiration
初志 しょし original aim [intention]
有志の ゆうしの voluntary, interested
b 志向 しこう intention, aim
志士 しし noble-minded patriot

❷ **will, mind, purpose, determination**
闘志 とうし fighting spirit, will to fight
意志 いし will, volition
同志 どうし like-minded person, comrade
遺志 いし wishes of a deceased person

❸ goodwill, kindness, benevolence
厚志 こうし kindness, kind thought [intention]
寸志 すんし little token of one's gratitude, small present
篤志家 とくしか benevolent person; volunteer, supporter

❹ *hist*
ⓐ historical record, annals; story
ⓑ record, write down

a 三国志 さんごくし Annals of the Three Kingdoms
聊×斎志異 りょうさいしい Liao Zhai Zhi I (Strange Stories from a Chinese Studio)

KUN

【こころざす 志す】**aim, have an AMBITION for, intend, aspire**
学問に志す がくもんにこころざす set one's heart on learning

【こころざし 志】**AMBITION, aspiration, intention, desire, wish; will, mind; goodwill, kindness, gift**
青雲の志 せいうんのこころざし high [lofty] ambition
本の志ですが ほんのこころざしですが Please accept this as a small token of my appreciation

【しりんぐ 志】shilling
百志 ひゃくしりんぐ 100 shillings

SYNONYMS

❶ⓐ & ❷ **will and intention**
志 AMBITION → 2725
意 MIND → 2650
図 intention → 3809
気 mind to do something → 3960
念 thought of doing something → 2554
趣 PURPOSE → 4111
欲 DESIRE → 1867

NOTE

➡ see USAGE note at 士 4213

条 ▶ARTICLE

2726

2-3-4

ジョウ ㊔ えだ
Ⓝ 條 Ⓒ 条 tiáo

75	Jōyō-5	U6761
木	S7-4-3	F0479

COMPOUNDS

❶ⓐ **ARTICLE, item, section, clause**
ⓑ (written regulations) **ARTICLEs (of law), provision, stipulation, rule, law**
ⓒ **counter for ARTICLEs or sections**

a 条項 じょうこう articles (and clauses), terms

条目 じょうもく article, stipulation
条件 じょうけん condition; item, proviso
箇条書きする かじょうがきする itemize
信条 しんじょう principle, creed, article of a religion
教条 きょうじょう tenet, dogma
b 条文 じょうぶん text (of a regulation), provision
条約 じょうやく treaty
条例 じょうれい regulations, rules, law
前条 ぜんじょう preceding article
c 憲法第九条 けんぽうだいきゅうじょう Article 9 of the constitution
百三条 ひゃくさんじょう 103 articles (of a constitution)

❷ⓐ strip, stripe, streak, vein, line, groove, thread
ⓑ strip of material (esp. metal), rod, rail
ⓒ counter for striplike slender objects
ⓓ strips of land serving as units of subdivision; avenue (esp. in Kyoto)
a 条痕 じょうこん streak
条虫 じょうちゅう tapeworm
星条旗 せいじょうき the Stars and Stripes
b 多条カム たじょうかむ multigrooved cam
鉄条網 てつじょうもう barbed wire entanglements
軌条 きじょう rails
c 一条の煙 いちじょうのけむり a wisp of smoke
d 条里制 じょうりせい system of land subdivision in ancient Japan
三条 さんじょう name of a street in Kyoto

❸ thread of presentation, line of reasoning
条理 じょうり reason, logic

❹ state of affairs
別条 べつじょう something wrong, accident
蕭×条たる しょうじょうたる bleak, dreary, lonely

❺ [original meaning, now archaic] branch, twig
柳条 りゅうじょう willow twig

INDEPENDENT

【じょう 条】
① ARTICLE
この条の規定に従い このじょうのきていにしたがい in accordance with the provisions of this article
②ⓐ although, though
ⓑ [archaic] since, as; that
a 愚鈍とは言い条 ぐどんとはいいじょう fool as he is
b 係る次第に候条 かかるしだいにそうろうじょう such being the case

SYNONYMS

❶ parts of writing
章 CHAPTER → 2624
段 passage → 1471
節 paragraph → 3336
款 ARTICLE → 2135
条 ARTICLE → 2726
項 CLAUSE → 0692
目 ITEM → 3777
箇 item → 3348

❷ⓐ line
線 LINE → 1760
筋 THREADLIKE STRUCTURE → 3319
条 strip → 2726
脈 VEIN → 1189
棒 straight line → 1237
縞 STRIPE → 1784
軸 AXIS → 1908

完

2727

2-3-4

▶COMPLETE

カン ㊔ たもつ ゆたか ひろし さだ

Ⓒ 完 wán

40	Jōyō-4	U5B8C
宀	S7-3-4	F0736

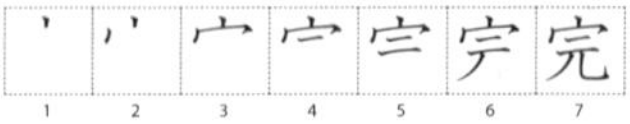

COMPOUNDS

❶ (having all its parts intact) **COMPLETE, perfect, whole, full, intact**
完全な かんぜんな perfect, complete, whole
完璧な かんぺきな perfect, flawless
完備した かんびした fully-equipped, perfect, complete
完投する かんとうする pitch a whole game
完封 かんぷう complete blockade [seal]; baseball shutout

❷ⓐ (bring to a final stage) **COMPLETE, conclude, finish, end**
ⓑ be COMPLETEd, come to an end
a 完成する かんせいする complete, finish; be completed, be finished
完結 かんけつ completion, conclusion, finish
完遂する かんすいする execute successfully, accomplish, bring to completion
b 完了する かんりょうする complete, finish; be completed, be finished
未完の みかんの incomplete, unfinished

INDEPENDENT

【かん 完】 completion, end

SYNONYMS

❶ all
皆 ALL → 3093
悉 THOROUGHLY → 3405
総 TOTAL → 1743
諸 VARIOUS → 1984
毎 EVERY → 2527
各 EACH → 2692

都 all → 2120
万 all → 3653
全 WHOLE → 2514
渾 ENTIRE → 0738
一 all in one → 4148
満 FULL → 0739
丸 complete(ly) → 4225
完 COMPLETE → 2727

❷ **end**
終 END → 1692
絶 COME TO AN END → 1711
閉 CLOSE → 4116
了 FINISH → 4157
済 SETTLE → 0634
-上げる completion suffix → 4212
完 COMPLETE → 2727
結 CONCLUDE → 1706
竣 COMPLETE → 1528

宏

2728
2-3-4

▶GRAND
コウ ㊔ ひろ ひろし ひろむ あつ
Ⓒ 宏 hóng

40	Names	U5B8F
宀	S7-3-4	F1424

COMPOUNDS

[now usu. 広 3769]
ⓐ (large in scale) **GRAND, great, magnificent**
ⓑ [original meaning] **extensive, vast**
a 宏壮な **こうそうな** grand, magnificent, imposing
宏弁 **こうべん** [rare] eloquence, fluency
b 宏遠な **こうえんな** vast and far-reaching
宏大な **こうだいな** vast, extensive, grand

SYNONYMS

ⓐ **great**
偉 GREAT (of superior character) → 0167
大 BIG → 4224
宏 GRAND (large in scale) → 2728
壮 GRAND (having grandeur) → 0263
豪 MAGNIFICENT → 2657
雄 HEROIC → 1271
碩 EMINENT → 1555

究

2729
2-3-4

▶STUDY EXHAUSTIVELY
キュウ ク▲ きわ(める)
Ⓒ 究 jiū

116	Jōyō-3	U7A76
穴	S7-5-2	F0573

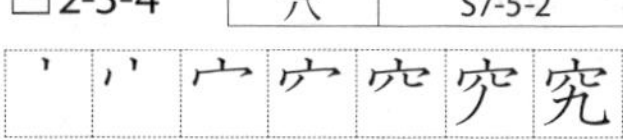

COMPOUNDS

❶ **STUDY EXHAUSTIVELY, investigate thoroughly, delve into, go to the bottom of**
究明する **きゅうめいする** investigate, study
究理 **きゅうり** study of natural laws
研究 **けんきゅう** research, study
追究する **ついきゅうする** investigate thoroughly, inquire into
学究 **がっきゅう** scholar, student
探究 **たんきゅう** investigation, search, inquiry

❷ **reach the extreme, reach the very end**
究極の **きゅうきょくの** ultimate, final
究竟×の **くっきょう(=きゅうきょう)の** excellent, superb, handy, appropriate, ideal

KUN

【きわめる 究める】[sometimes also 窮める] **investigate thoroughly, STUDY EXHAUSTIVELY, master**
奥義を究める **おうぎをきわめる** master the secrets of an art

SYNONYMS

❶ **learn and study**
学 STUDY → 3162
考 study → 3962
習 LEARN → 3306
研 RESEARCH → 1456
究 STUDY EXHAUSTIVELY → 2729
攻 specialize → 0286

❶ **investigate and examine**
閲 REVIEW → 4132
審 EXAMINE CAREFULLY → 2985
験 TEST → 2306
勘 CHECK → 2231
糾 INQUIRE INTO → 1631
究 STUDY EXHAUSTIVELY → 2729
察 INSPECT → 2961
討 STUDY → 1846
探 PROBE → 0613
検 EXAMINE → 1241
診 EXAMINE A PATIENT → 1898
調 INVESTIGATE → 1973
査 LOOK INTO → 3092

HOMOPHONES

きわめる
極 EXTREME → 1243
窮 BE IN EXTREMITY → 2983

NOTE

➡ see USAGE note at 極 1243

宋

2730
2-3-4

▶**SONG DYNASTY**
ソウ ㊔くに おき
Ⓒ 宋 sòng

40 宀	Names	U5B8B
	S7-3-4	F1866

COMPOUNDS

● **SONG DYNASTY (960-1279 A.D.)**
宋詞 そうし Song poetry
宋学 そうがく Song-period neo-Confucianism
南宋 なんそう Southern Song Dynasty
北宋 ほくそう Northern Song Dynasty

INDEPENDENT

【そう 宋】SONG DYNASTY

SYNONYMS

● **later Chinese dynasties**
唐 TANG DYNASTY → 3867
宋 SONG DYNASTY → 2730
元 Yuan Dynasty → 2428
明 Ming Dynasty → 1060
清 Qing Dynasty → 0635

宐

2731
2-3-4

▶**RIGHT**
ギ よろ(しい) よろ(しく) ㊔よし のぶ のり

40 宀	Nonstandard	U5B90
	S7-3-4	F0000

traditional form → see 宜 at 2763

肖

2732
2-3-4

▶**MODEL**
ショウ

42 小	Nonstandard	U8096
	S7-3-4	F0000

traditional form → see 肖 at 2733

肖

2733
2-3-4

▶**MODEL**
ショウ
Ⓝ 肖 Ⓒ 肖 xiào xiāo

130 月	Jōyō	U8096
	S7-4-3	F2115

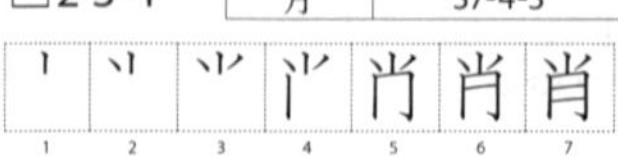

COMPOUNDS

❶ [original meaning] (make a model of) **MODEL, imitate**
肖像 しょうぞう portrait, likeness

❷ be like, resemble
不肖 ふしょう being unlike one's father; my humble self

SYNONYMS

❶ **imitate**
擬 IMITATE → 0969
倣 COPY AFTER → 0127
摸 PATTERN AFTER → 0797
模 pattern after → 1326
肖 MODEL → 2733
象 represent → 2647

学

2-3-4

incorrect classification/stroke-count
➡ see 2-5-3: ⺍ at 3162

労

2-3-4

incorrect classification
➡ see 2-5-2: ⺍ at 3155

災

2734
2-3-4

▶**NATURAL CALAMITY**
サイ わざわ(い)
Ⓒ 灾 zāi

86 火	Jōyō-5	U707D
	S7-4-3	F1245

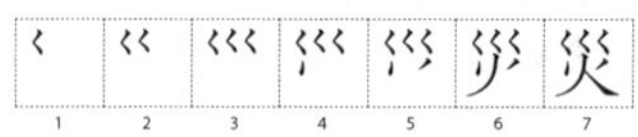

COMPOUNDS

● [original meaning] **NATURAL CALAMITY, disaster, misfortune, serious trouble**
災難 さいなん calamity, disaster, accident, misfortune
災禍 さいか accident, natural calamity, disaster, misfortune
災害 さいがい calamity, disaster, accident
災厄 さいやく calamity, disaster, accident
火災 かさい fire, conflagration
天災 てんさい natural calamity [disaster]
人災 じんさい man-made calamity
戦災 せんさい war damage
被災地 ひさいち disaster stricken area

KUN

【わざわい 災い】[formerly also 禍] **calamity, misfortune, disaster, evil, serious trouble**
災いする わざわいする be the ruin of (a person)
災い転じて福となる わざわいてんじてふくとなる Good comes out of evil
不測の災い ふそくのわざわい unexpected disaster

SYNONYMS

● **misfortune and disaster**
災 NATURAL CALAMITY → 2734
難 DISASTER → 2310
禍 CALAMITY → 1304
厄 MISFORTUNE → 3665
凶 BAD LUCK → 3679

USAGE

【わざわい】

災い

[formerly also 禍] calamity, misfortune, disaster, evil, serious trouble

禍

[now usu. 災い] calamity, misfortune, disaster, evil, serious trouble

HOMOPHONES

わざわい 禍 CALAMITY → 1304

忌

▶MOURNING
▶ABHOR

キ い(む) い(み) い(まわしい)

Ⓒ 忌 jì

2735

2-3-4

61	Jōyō	U5FCC
心	S7-4-3	F2053

Stroke order: 1–7

COMPOUNDS

❶ MOURNING, mourning period

忌中 きちゅう in mourning

忌引き きびき absence from work [school] due to mourning

忌服 きふく mourning

❷ [also suffix] **death anniversary**

忌日 きにち death anniversary

一周忌 いっしゅうき first anniversary of death

桜桃忌 おうとうき Death Anniversary of Dazai Osamu

❸ shun, avoid, abstain from

忌避 きひ evasion, shirking

忌憚× きたん reserve, scruple

禁忌 きんき taboo; contraindication

INDEPENDENT

【き 忌】MOURNING

忌が明ける きがあける come out of mourning

KUN

【いむ 忌む】

ⓐ (regard with horror) **ABHOR, loathe, detest, hate**

ⓑ (reject vehemently) **ABHOR**, shun, avoid

a 忌み嫌う いみきらう abhor, detest

忌むべき いむべき detestable, abominable

b 忌ま忌ましい いまいましい annoying

【いみ 忌み】**MOURNING; abstinence, taboo**

忌み日 いみび death anniversary; unlucky day

物忌み ものいみ abstinence; confinement to one's house on an unlucky day

【いまわしい 忌まわしい】**disgusting, detestable**

忌まわしい事件 いまわしいじけん abominable incident

SYNONYMS

❶ mourn and mourning

弔 CONDOLE → 4240

悼 MOURN → 0587

喪 MOURNING → 3504

忌 MOURNING → 2735

❷ date

日 date → 3759

忌 death anniversary → 2735

❸ avoid and abstain

避 AVOID → 3944

逃 ESCAPE → 3839

禦 WARD OFF → 3561

忌 shun → 2735

禁 abstain from → 3469

【いむ】

ⓐ **hate and dislike**

憎 HATE → 0845

悪 hate → 3413

忌む ABHOR → 2735

嫌 DISLIKE → 0781

恨 HOLD A GRUDGE → 0439

怨 HOLD A GRUDGE → 3179

厭 disagreeable → 3745

芭

▶JAPANESE FIBER BANANA

バ ㊔ はな

Ⓒ 芭 bā

2736

2-3-4

140	Names	U82AD
⺿	S7-3-4	F2373

COMPOUNDS

● JAPANESE FIBER BANANA

芭蕉 ばしょう Japanese banana plant, *Musa basjoo;* plantain

水芭蕉 みずばしょう Asian skunk cabbage, *Lysichiton camtschatcense*

SYNONYMS

● shrubs

藤 WISTERIA → 3025

蔦 JAPANESE IVY → 2972

萩 *HAGI* → 2908

茉 JASMINE → 2790

莉 JASMINE → 2843

芭 JAPANESE FIBER BANANA → 2736

芙

▶LOTUS

フ ㊔ はす

Ⓒ 芙 fú

2737

2-3-4

140	Names	U8299
⺿	S7-3-4	F2566

COMPOUNDS

❶ LOTUS

芙蓉 ふよう cotton rose; lotus

芙蓉峰 ふようほう Mt. Fuji ("lotus-shaped mountain")

SYNONYMS

❶ flowering plants

菊 CHRYSANTHEMUM → 2875

菖 IRIS → 2881

菫 VIOLET → 2877

蓮 LOTUS → 2940

葛 KUDZU → 2905

蓬 JAPANESE MUGWORT → 2973

葵 MALLOW → 2906

蓉 COTTON ROSE → 2944

芙 LOTUS → 2737

蘭 ORCHID → 3031

萩 *HAGI* → 2908

藤 WISTERIA → 3025

桜 cherry blossom → 1168

梅 *ume* blossom → 1159

芸

2738

2-3-4

▸**ART**

ゲイ ㊔ き

Ⓝ 藝 Ⓒ 艺 yì

140	Jōyō-4	U82B8
艹	S7-3-4	F0499

COMPOUNDS

❶ **ART, craft, skill**

芸術 げいじゅつ art, the arts

芸事 げいごと artistic accomplishments

工芸 こうげい technical art, technology

民芸 みんげい folkcraft

手芸 しゅげい handicrafts, manual arts

技芸 ぎげい arts, crafts, accomplishments

文芸 ぶんげい literature, literary art, art and literature

学芸 がくげい arts and sciences; culture

多芸は無芸 たげいはむげい Jack-of-all-trades and master of none

❷ [also suffix] **entertainment, performance, show business, acting**

芸能 げいのう public entertainment

芸者 げいしゃ geisha girl

芸名 げいめい stage name

芸人 げいにん artiste, entertainer

芸風 げいふう style (of one's performance)

演芸 えんげい performance, entertainments

名人芸 めいじんげい masterly performance, virtuosity

大道芸 だいどうげい street performing

❸ trick, feat, stunt

芸当 げいとう feat, trick, stunt

曲芸 きょくげい acrobatics, trick, stunt

隠し芸 かくしげい hidden talent; parlor trick

❹ [original meaning] **plant, cultivate**

園芸 えんげい gardening, horticulture

❺ abbrev. of 安芸 あき, old name for west Hiroshima Prefecture

芸備線 げいびせん Geibi Line (Hiroshima-North Okayama Railway)

INDEPENDENT

【げい 芸】**ART, craft, artistic accomplishment; trick, feat, stunt**

芸は身を助く げいはみをたすく Accomplishments are a lifelong benefit to their possessor

芸をする犬 げいをするいぬ dog that knows [does] tricks

SYNONYMS

❶ **art**

技 SKILL → 0292

倆 SKILL → 0136

術 PRACTICAL ART → 0575

芸 ART → 2738

道 the way of an art → 3888

❷ **performance**

劇 DRAMA → 2399

演 performance → 0855

芸 entertainment → 2738

芳

2739

2-3-4

▸**FRAGRANT**

ホウ かんば(しい) ㊔ よし かおる かおり か ふさ

Ⓒ 芳 fāng

140	Jōyō	U82B3
艹	S7-3-4	F1496

COMPOUNDS

❶ **FRAGRANT, aromatic, balmy**

芳香 ほうこう perfume, fragrance, aroma

芳気 ほうき fragrant scent

芳草 ほうそう fragrant herb

芳潤な ほうじゅんな aromatic, rich

❷ honorific prefix

芳名 ほうめい your (honored) name

芳志 ほうし your good wishes, your kind intentions

芳情 ほうじょう your good wishes, your kind intentions

❸ bloom of youth, esp. of a beautiful young lady
芳紀 ほうき age (of a young lady)
芳眉 ほうび eyebrows of a beautiful woman

❹ honor, reputation
遺芳 いほう honor of the deceased

KUN

【かんばしい 芳しい】**FRAGRANT, aromatic; favorable, fair**
芳しくない かんばしくない poor, unfavorable; disgraceful

SYNONYMS

❶ **smell and fragrance**
気 smell → 3960
匂い SMELL → 3662
臭 BAD SMELL → 3261
香 SWEET SMELL → 3177
馨 PERFUME → 3575
芳 FRAGRANT → 2739
薫 BALMY → 3005
郁 AROMATIC → 1640

花

2740

2-3-4

▶**FLOWER**

カ ケ▲ はな

Ⓝ 苍 花 Ⓒ 花 huā

140	Jōyō-1	U82B1
艹	S7-3-4	F0436

一 十 艹 ヰ 苄 花 花
1 2 3 4 5 6 7

COMPOUNDS

❶ [original meaning] **FLOWER, blossom**
花壇 かだん flower bed
花弁 かべん(=はなびら) petal
花瓶 かびん flower vase
花粉 かふん pollen
国花 こっか national flower
造花 ぞうか artificial flower; artificial flower making
開花する かいかする flower, blossom, come into bloom
沈丁花 じんちょうげ(=ちんちょうげ) (sweet-smelling) daphne

❷ as beautiful as a **FLOWER**
名花 めいか beautiful flower; celebrated beauty

❸ red-light district
花柳 かりゅう geisha girls, courtesans; red-light district
花柳界 かりゅうかい red-light district

KUN

【はな 花】
①ⓐ [also prefix] **FLOWER, blossom; cherry blossom**
ⓑ **FLOWER arrangement**
a 花見 はなみ flower [cherry blossom] viewing
花嫁 はなよめ bride
花火 はなび fireworks, firecrackers
花形 はながた floral pattern; star, lion; leading, popular, favorite
花時計 はなどけい flower clock
草花 くさばな flowering plant
b お花 おはな flower arrangement
②ⓐ [also 華] (figuratively) **FLOWER** (of life), essence, cream
ⓑ honor, success, glory
a 若い内が花だ わかいうちがはなだ Youth is a treasure
b 花を持たせる はなをもたせる let (a person) have the credit for (the success)
③ Japanese playing cards with floral patterns
花を引く はなをひく play *hana* cards
④ [in compounds] geisha, prostitute
花代 はなだい tip to a geisha girl
花街 はなまち red-light district

SPECIAL READINGS

浪花▲ なにわ old name for Osaka

SYNONYMS

❶ **flower**
花 FLOWER → 2740
華 flower → 2841

USAGE

【はな】
花
①ⓐ [also prefix] flower, blossom; cherry blossom
ⓑ flower arrangement
②ⓐ [also 華] (figuratively) flower (of life), essence, cream
ⓑ honor, success, glory
③ Japanese playing cards with floral patterns
④ [in compounds] geisha, prostitute
華
①ⓐ [also 花] (figuratively) flower (of life), essence, cream
ⓑ flower of youth, prime of life
② [in compounds] flowery, beautiful, gallant

HOMOPHONES

はな 華 MAGNIFICENT → 2841

NOTE

➡ see COMPOUND FORMATION for 花柳 かりゅう → 柳 1115

口 士 士 夊 宀 小 ⺌ ⺍ 巛 己 艹 ⺈ 刃 刅 久 亡 亼 厶

芥

2741
2-3-4

▶**TRASH**
カイ ケ あくた ごみ ㊔ からしな
Ⓒ 芥 jiè gài

140	Names	U82A5
艹	S7-3-4	F2215

COMPOUNDS

❶ **TRASH, garbage, rubbish, litter; dirt, dust**
雑芥 ざっかい miscellaneous trash
厨芥 ちゅうかい kitchen waste

❷ **mustard, rape**
芥子(=罌×粟) けし poppy

KUN

【あくた 芥】**TRASH, garbage, rubbish; dirt, dust**
塵芥 ちりあくた(=じんかい) trash, garbage, rubbish; worthless thing

【ごみ 芥】[usu. 塵] **TRASH**, garbage, rubbish, litter; dirt, dust
芥箱 ごみばこ trash can [bin], garbage can
芥溜め ごみため garbage dump, trash heap

SPECIAL READINGS

芥子(=辛子) からし mustard

SYNONYMS

❶ **waste**
屑 WASTE → 3861
芥 TRASH → 2741
塵 DUST → 3922

❷ **vegetables**
菜 greens → 2880
蕪 TURNIP → 2990
芋 POTATO → 2706
豆 BEAN → 2442
蕗 BUTTERBUR → 3007
茄 EGGPLANT → 2787
芹 JAPANESE PARSLEY → 2742
瓜 GOURD → 3789
瓢 BOTTLE GOURD → 2356
芥 mustard → 2741

HOMOPHONES

ごみ 塵 DUST → 3922

NOTE

➡ see USAGE note at 塵 3922

芹

2742
2-3-4

▶**JAPANESE PARSLEY**
キン ゴン せり
Ⓒ 芹 qín

140	Names	U82B9
艹	S7-3-4	F3373

COMPOUNDS

● [original meaning, now archaic] **JAPANESE PARSLEY**, cress

KUN

【せり 芹】**JAPANESE PARSLEY, *Oenanthe stolonifera*, dropwort**
オランダ芹 おらんだぜり parsley

SYNONYMS

【せり】
○ **vegetables**
菜 greens → 2880
蕪 TURNIP → 2990
芋 POTATO → 2706
豆 BEAN → 2442
蕗 BUTTERBUR → 3007
茄 EGGPLANT → 2787
芹 JAPANESE PARSLEY → 2742
瓜 GOURD → 3789
瓢 BOTTLE GOURD → 2356
芥 mustard → 2741

芦

2743
2-3-4

▶**COMMON REED**
ロ あし よし
Ⓝ 芦 蘆 Ⓒ 芦 lú lǔ

140	Names	U82A6
艹	S7-3-4	F2409

COMPOUNDS

● **COMMON REED, reed**
芦花 ろか reed flower

KUN

【あし 芦】**COMMON REED, reed**
芦毛 あしげ gray (horse coat color)

【よし 芦】**COMMON REED, reed**

SYNONYMS

● **kinds of grasses**
草 GRASS → 2813
荻 AMUR SILVERGRASS → 2844
蒲 CATTAIL → 2932
莱 GOOSEFOOT → 2878
蕨 BRACKEN → 2992
叢 grassy place → 3243
芝 LAWN GRASS → 2705
笹 BAMBOO GRASS → 3301
茅 cogongrass → 2779
萱 THATCH GRASS → 2904
藁 STRAW → 3015
芦 REED → 2743
葦 COMMON REED → 2934
菅 SEDGE → 2874

HOMOPHONES

あし 葦 COMMON REED →2934
よし 葦 COMMON REED →2934

NOTE

➡ see USAGE note at 葦 2934

芯
2744
2-3-4

▶CORE
シン
Ⓒ 芯 xīn xìn

140	Jōyō	U82AF
艹	S7-3-4	F2123

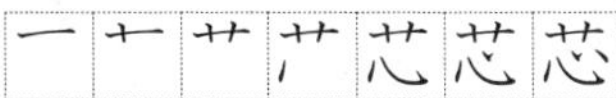

COMPOUNDS

● [sometimes also 心 0011] **CORE (of fruit); wick; lead (of a pencil); padding**
芯地 しんじ padding, lining
花芯 かしん center of a flower
空芯菜 くうしんさい water morning glory
摘芯 てきしん thinning (of buds)
灯芯 とうしん (lamp) wick
替え芯 かえしん spare lead

INDEPENDENT

【しん 芯】 [sometimes also 心 0011] **CORE (of fruit); wick; lead (of a pencil); padding**
芯が腐っている しんがくさっている be rotten to the core
芯を切る しんをきる trim a wick
鉛筆の芯 えんぴつのしん lead of a pencil

SYNONYMS

● **central parts**
核 NUCLEUS →1162
仁 kernel →0021
心 core →0011
芯 CORE →2744

NOTE

➡ see USAGE note at 心 0011

芽
2745
2-3-4

▶BUD
ガ め ㊔ めい

140	Nonstandard	U2F995
艹	S7-3-4	F0000

traditional form →see 芽 at 2784

苅
2746
2-3-4

▶CLIP
ガイ カイ か(る)

140	Nonstandard	U82C5
艹	S7-3-4	F0000

traditional form →see 刈 at 0032

苍
2747
2-3-4

▶FLOWER
カ ケ はな

140	Nonstandard	U82B2
艹	S7-3-4	F0000

traditional form →see 花 at 2740

花
2748
2-3-4

▶FLOWER
カ ケ はな

140	Nonstandard	U82B1
艹	S7-3-4	F0000

traditional form →see 花 at 2740

芦
2749
2-3-4

▶COMMON REED
ロ あし よし

140	Nonstandard	U82A6
艹	S7-3-4	F0000

traditional form →see 芦 at 2743

豸
2-3-4

incorrect classification
➡ see 2-4-3: 豸 at 3054

忍
2750
2-3-4

▶BEAR
ニン しの(ぶ) しの(ばせる) ㊔ おし
Ⓝ 忍 Ⓒ 忍 rěn

61	Jōyō	U5FCD
心	S7-4-3	F1122

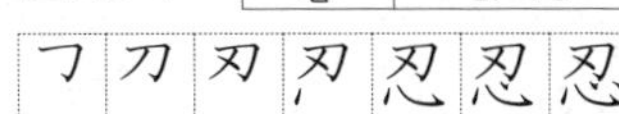

COMPOUNDS

❶ⓐ **BEAR, endure, tolerate, suffer patiently**
ⓑ forbear, restrain, repress, hold back
a 忍耐する にんたいする persevere, be patient, endure
忍従 にんじゅう submission, resignation
忍苦 にんく endurance, stoicism
b 堪忍(=勘忍) かんにん patience, forbearance; forgiveness, pardon
隠忍 いんにん patience, endurance

❷ **perform by stealth, practice the art of making oneself invisible**
忍術 にんじゅつ art of making oneself invisible
忍法 にんぽう art of making oneself invisible
忍者 にんじゃ ancient spy who mastered *ninjutsu*

❸ merciless, atrocious, truculent, cruel
残忍 ざんにん cruelty, atrocity, brutality

INDEPENDENT

【にん 忍】 endurance, forbearance, patience
...は忍の一字に尽きる …はにんのいちじにつきる Endurance is the only word to describe…

KUN

【しのぶ 忍ぶ】

① **BEAR, endure, suffer, stand, put up with**

忍び難い しのびがたい unbearable, intolerable

恥を忍ぶ はじをしのぶ abide one's shame

②ⓐ **conceal oneself, hide**

ⓑ **perform by stealth, steal one's way to (a lover)**

a 忍び しのび stealing (into); art of mystification; incognito, traveling incognito

忍び泣く しのびなく shed silent tears

b 忍び足 しのびあし tiptoeing, stealthy steps

忍び込む しのびこむ steal in, sneak in

忍びやかな しのびやかな stealthy, secret

【しのばせる 忍ばせる】 *vt* **conceal, secrete; suppress, subdue**

ポケットにナイフを忍ばせる ぽけっとにないふをしのばせる conceal a knife in one's pocket

声を忍ばせて こえをしのばせて in a subdued voice

SYNONYMS

❶ⓐ **bear and endure**

堪 ENDURE → 0680

忍 BEAR → 2750

耐 WITHSTAND → 1634

❷ **hide**

隠 HIDE → 0873

蔽 COVER → 2991

伏 lie in concealment → 0049

潜 LURK → 0922

匿 CONCEAL → 3735

忍 perform by stealth → 2750

USAGE

【しのぶ】

忍ぶ

① bear, endure, suffer, stand, put up with

②ⓐ conceal oneself, hide

ⓑ perform by stealth, steal one's way to (a lover)

偲ぶ

recall, recollect, remember, reminisce

HOMOPHONES

しのぶ 偲 RECOLLECT → 0153

忍

2751

2-3-4

▶**BEAR**

ニン しの(ぶ) しの(ばせる) ㊔ おし

61	Nonstandard	U5FCD
心	S7-4-3	F0000

traditional form → see 忍 at 2750

灸

2752

2-3-4

▶**MOXIBUSTION**

キュウ やいと

Ⓒ 灸 jiǔ

86	Names	U7078
火	S7-4-3	F3255

COMPOUNDS

❶ **MOXIBUSTION**

灸点 きゅうてん moxa treatment points

灸治 きゅうじ treatment with moxa

鍼灸(=針灸) しんきゅう acupuncture and moxibustion

温灸 おんきゅう moxibustion

INDEPENDENT

【きゅう 灸】 MOXIBUSTION

灸を据える きゅうをすえる give moxa treatment; chastise, punish [scold] someone

KUN

【やいと 灸】 MOXIBUSTION

SYNONYMS

❶ **medicines**

薬 DRUG → 3011

剤 PREPARATION → 2102

錠 PILL → 2180

丸 pill suffix → 4225

鍼 ACUPUNCTURE → 2204

灸 MOXIBUSTION → 2752

忘

2753

2-3-4

▶**FORGET**

ボウ わす(れる)

61	Nonstandard	U5FD8
心	S7-4-3	F0000

traditional form → see 忘 at 2529

含

2-3-4

incorrect classification

➡ see 2-2-5: 𠆢 at 2534

育

2754

2-3-4

▶**RAISE**

イク そだ(つ) そだ(ち) そだ(てる) はぐく(む) ㊔ やす なる

130	Nonstandard	U80B2
月	S7-4-3	F0000

traditional form → see 育 at 2544

幸

2755

2-3-5

▶**GOOD FORTUNE**

▶**HAPPINESS**

コウ さいわ(い) さち しあわ(せ) ㊔ ゆき みゆき さき よし

Ⓒ 幸 xìng

51	Jōyō-3	U5E78
干	S8-3-5	F0545

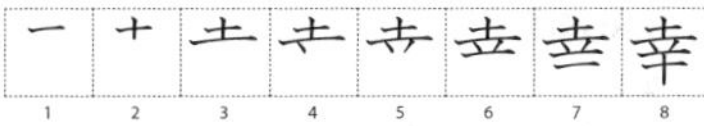

COMPOUNDS

❶ [formerly also 倖 0134]
ⓐ [original meaning] **GOOD FORTUNE, good luck**
ⓑ **HAPPINESS, well-being, felicity**

a 幸運 こううん good fortune, good luck
射幸心 しゃこうしん speculative spirit
b 幸福 こうふく happiness; good fortune
薄幸 はっこう unhappiness; sad fate, misfortune
不幸 ふこう unhappiness; misfortune; bereavement
多幸 たこう great happiness; great fortune

❷ imperial tour
行幸 ぎょうこう imperial visit
巡幸 じゅんこう imperial tour, royal progress

❸ [formerly also 倖 0134] [rare] be in the good graces of (one's ruler); bestow favor upon
寵幸 ちょうこう grace, favor

INDEPENDENT

【こう 幸】**HAPPINESS**, fortune
幸か不幸か こうかふこうか for good or for evil, luckily or unluckily

KUN

【さいわい 幸い】**HAPPINESS, blessing; good fortune**
幸いな さいわいな happy, blessed
幸いに さいわいに fortunately, luckily

【さち 幸】**HAPPINESS; good fortune; catch, game**
幸有る さちある happy, fortunate, lucky

【しあわせ 幸せ】[also 仕合わせ, formerly also 倖せ] **HAPPINESS, blessing; good fortune**
幸せな しあわせな happy, fortunate
不幸せ ふしあわせ unhappiness, misfortune, ill luck

SYNONYMS

❶ⓐ **good fortune**
吉 LUCKY → 2691
嘉 HAPPY → 2953
祥 AUSPICIOUS → 1184
瑞 AUSPICIOUS OMEN → 1302
禎 PROPITIOUS OMEN → 1305
幸 GOOD FORTUNE → 2755
福 FORTUNE → 1303
倖 GOOD FORTUNE → 0134

ⓑ **happiness**
幸 HAPPINESS → 2755
祉 BLESSEDNESS → 1087
福 FORTUNE → 1303

USAGE

【しあわせ】
幸せ
[also 仕合わせ, formerly also 倖せ] happiness, blessing; good fortune
倖せ
[now usu. 幸せ or 仕合わせ] same as 幸せ
仕合わせ
[also 幸せ, formerly also 倖せ] same as 幸せ

HOMOPHONES

しあわせ
倖せ → 0134
仕合わせ → 0037, 2511

NOTE

➡ see COMPOUND FORMATION for 仕合わせ しあわせ → 合 2511

奇

2756

2-3-5

▶**UNUSUAL**
キ く(しき)▲
Ⓝ 竒 Ⓒ 奇 qí jī

37	Jōyō	U5947
大	S8-3-5	F0858

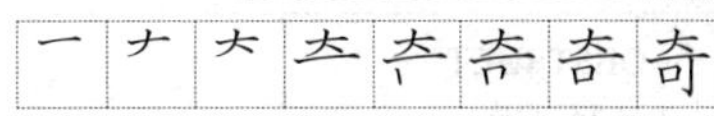

COMPOUNDS

❶ [formerly also 畸 1533]
ⓐ **UNUSUAL, strange, odd, extraordinary, queer, eccentric**
ⓑ deformity, malformation

a 奇異な きいな unusual, strange
奇人 きじん eccentric (person), queer [odd] fellow
奇妙な きみょうな strange, queer, odd
奇跡(=奇蹟) きせき miracle, wonder
奇談 きだん strange story
珍奇な ちんきな novel, curious; rare; strange
怪奇 かいき mystery, wonder
好奇心 こうきしん curiosity
偏奇 へんき eccentricity
b 奇形 きけい deformity, malformation

❷ of **UNUSUAL** excellence
奇勝 きしょう place of scenic beauty

❸ surprising, unexpected
奇襲 きしゅう surprise attack
奇遇 きぐう unexpected meeting, chance encounter

❹ [formerly 綺 1734] **beautiful, gorgeous, elegant**
奇麗な きれいな beautiful, pretty; clean; fair

❺ *math* **odd, odd number**
奇数 きすう odd number
奇偶 きぐう odd and even numbers

❻ [also 詭 1919] trick, cheat, deceive, defraud

奇弁 きべん sophism, sophistry

INDEPENDENT

【き 奇】 strangeness, oddity, eccentricity

奇を衒×う きをてらう make a display of one's originality [eccentricity]

奇なる きなる strange, odd, eccentric

KUN

【くしき 奇しき】 strange, mysterious

奇しくも くしくも mysteriously, strangely enough

SPECIAL READINGS

数奇屋(=数寄屋) すきや tea-ceremony arbor

SYNONYMS

❶ⓐ abnormal

変 ABNORMAL → 2569
奇 UNUSUAL → 2756
畸 UNUSUAL → 1533
怪 MYSTERIOUS → 0354
妖 MYSTERIOUS → 0282
妙 strange → 0280
異 not ordinary → 3195
珍 curious → 1135

奄

▶OBSTRUCT

エン ㊔ ひさ

Ⓒ 奄 yǎn

2757

2-3-5

37	Names	U5944
大	S8-3-5	F2974

COMPOUNDS

❶ⓐ OBSTRUCT (by covering), stop up

ⓑ [original meaning, now obsolete] cover

a 奄奄 えんえん gasping

気息奄奄 きそくえんえん gasping for breath, on the brink of death

❷ [archaic] suddenly

SPECIAL READINGS

奄美の黒兎 あまみのくろうさぎ Amami rabbit, Ryukyu rabbit

SYNONYMS

❶ⓐ obstruct and hinder

遮 INTERRUPT → 3916
塞 STOP UP → 2924
阻 OBSTRUCT → 0411
沮 OBSTRUCT → 0399
奄 OBSTRUCT (by covering) → 2757
妨 HINDER → 0279
障 hinder → 0875
碍 STAND IN THE WAY → 1536
害 stand in the way → 2826
梗 STOP UP → 1204

奔

▶RUSH

ホン

Ⓝ 奔 Ⓒ 奔 bēn bèn

2758

2-3-5

37	Jōyō	U5954
大	S8-3-5	F1943

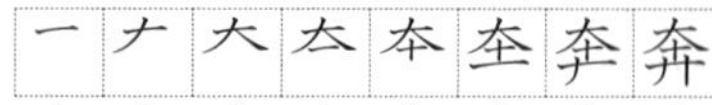

1 2 3 4 5 6 7 8

COMPOUNDS

❶ⓐ [original meaning] **RUSH, rush about, run fast, gallop, hurry**

ⓑ run away, run off

a 奔走する ほんそうする bustle about, exert oneself for, devote oneself to

奔流 ほんりゅう torrent, rapids

奔騰 ほんとう price jump, boom

奔馬 ほんば galloping horse

狂奔する きょうほんする rush around, run madly about, run wild; make frantic efforts, be very busy (in)

東奔西走する とうほんせいそうする be on the run, bustle about, bestir oneself

b 出奔 しゅっぽん abscondence, flight

❷ let one's ego run wild, do as one pleases

奔放な ほんぽうな wild, extravagant; free-spirited

淫奔 いんぽん wantonness, lustfulness, lewdness

SYNONYMS

❶ⓐ run

走 RUN → 2720
奔 RUSH → 2758
馳 RUN QUICKLY → 2289
駆 gallop → 2293

奈

▶PHONETIC [na]

ナ ナイ▲

Ⓒ 奈 nài

2759

2-3-5

37	Jōyō	U5948
大	S8-3-5	F0786

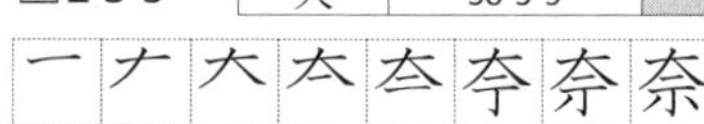

1 2 3 4 5 6 7 8

COMPOUNDS

❶ used PHONETICally for *na*, esp. in the transliteration of foreign words

奈落 ならく Hell; trap cellar

奈翁 なおう Napoleon

加奈陀 かなだ Canada

❷ [also 那 1047] element for forming interrogative words

奈辺 なへん where?

❸ [original meaning, now obsolete] crab apple tree

SPECIAL READINGS

奈良県 ならけん Nara Prefecture
奈何▲(=如何▲) いかん what; how
神奈川県 かながわけん Kanagawa Prefecture

SYNONYMS

❶ **phonetic [na]**
那 PHONETIC [na] → 1047
奈 PHONETIC [na] → 2759

❷ **interrogatives**
奈 interrogative forming element → 2759
那 interrogative forming element → 1047
何 WHAT → 0073
誰 WHO → 1986

孟

2760
2-3-5

▶MENCIUS
モウ ㊔ たけ　たけし　たける　つとむ　はじめ　おさ　はる
Ⓒ 孟 mèng

39	Names	U5B5F
子	S8-3-5	F2087

COMPOUNDS

❶ **MENCIUS**
孟子 もうし Mencius; the works of Mencius
孔孟の教え こうもうのおしえ the teachings of Confucius and Mencius

❷ⓐ first month of a season
ⓑ [archaic] firstborn [eldest] brother or sister
a 孟春 もうしゅん January (of the lunar calendar)
孟夏 もうか April (of the lunar calendar)
b 孟女 もうじょ eldest daughter

SYNONYMS

❶ **Confucius and Confucianists**
孔 Confucius → 0205
子 the Master (Confucius) → 4196
孟 MENCIUS → 2760

宙

2761
2-3-5

▶SPACE
▶MIDAIR
チュウ ㊔ ひろし
Ⓒ 宙 zhòu

40	Jōyō-6	U5B99
宀	S8-3-5	F1193

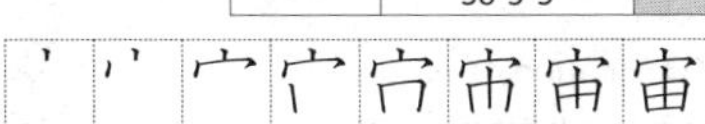

COMPOUNDS

❶ⓐ (expanse of the universe) **SPACE, outer space, heavens**
ⓑ (point above the ground) **MIDAIR, air, space**
a 宇宙 うちゅう universe, cosmos; (outer) space
航宙 こうちゅう space flight
b 宙乗り ちゅうのり aerial stunts
宙吊り ちゅうづり hanging in midair
宙返り ちゅうがえり somersault

❷ [original meaning, now archaic] infinite time, all ages

INDEPENDENT

【ちゅう 宙】**MIDAIR**, air, space; memory
宙に浮く ちゅうにうく float in the air
宙で読む ちゅうでよむ recite from memory

SYNONYMS

❶ⓐ **universe and space**
宇 UNIVERSE → 2699
宙 SPACE → 2761
ⓑ **sky**
空 SKY → 2767
昊 SKY → 3066
穹 SKY → 2768
天 HEAVEN → 4250
宙 MIDAIR → 2761

宛

2762
2-3-5

▶ADDRESS
エン▲　あ(てる)　-あ(て)　-あて　-ずつ▲　あたか(も)▲
Ⓒ 宛 wǎn

40	Jōyō	U5B9B
宀	S8-3-5	F1830

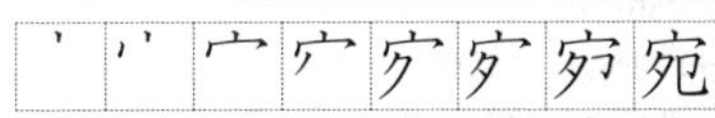

COMPOUNDS

❶ **as if, just as, just like**
宛然 えんぜん as if

❷ [original meaning, now archaic] long and winding, lithe
宛転たる えんてんたる (of eyebrows) shapely; moving smoothly

KUN

【あてる 宛てる】
① **ADDRESS (a letter), direct**
宛て先 あてさき destination, address
宛名 あてな address
手紙を宛てる てがみをあてる address [direct] a letter to a person

② [sometimes also 当てる] **assign Chinese characters to a word (as phonetic substitutes)**
宛て字 あてじ phonetic substitute, false substitute character
外来語に字を宛てる がいらいごにじをあてる assign Chinese characters to a foreign word

【-あて -宛て, -宛】[suffix]
① **ADDRESSed to**
Ａ氏宛ての手紙 えーしあてのてがみ letter addressed to Mr. A

② **per, apiece**

オレンジを一人宛て三個 おれんじをひとりあてさんこ three oranges apiece [per head]

【-ずつ -宛】 at a time, each, apiece

少し宛 すこしずつ a little for each; little by little, gradually

【あたかも 宛も】 [now usu. 恰も] as if, just as, just like

宛も月明の如し あたかもげつめいのごとし It is as bright as the moon

SYNONYMS

【あてる】

① **indicate**

指 POINT → 0452

示 SHOW → 2435

標 MARK → 1347

宛てる ADDRESS → 2762

USAGE

【あたかも】

宛も

[now usu. 恰も] as if, just as, just like

恰も

[formerly also 宛も] just like, as if

HOMOPHONES

あてる

当 THE PRESENT → 2701

充 FILL → 2507

-あて 当 THE PRESENT → 2701

あたかも 恰 JUST → 0437

NOTE

➡ see also USAGE note at 当 2701

宜

2763

2-3-5

▸**RIGHT**

ギ よろ(しい)▲ よろ(しく)▲ ㊔ よし のぶ のり

Ⓝ 冝 宐 Ⓒ 宜 yí

40 宀	Jōyō	U5B9C
	S8-3-5	F2012

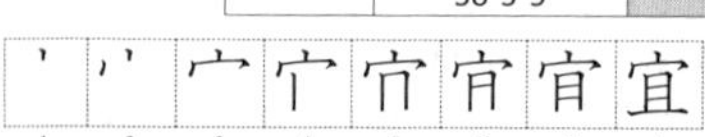

1 2 3 4 5 6 7 8

COMPOUNDS

❶ **RIGHT, just right, appropriate, suitable, opportune, good**

機宜 きぎ opportunity, occasion

便宜 べんぎ convenience, facility

適宜 てきぎ suitableness, appropriateness; suitably

時宜 じぎ right time [occasion], proper time

❷ [also 誼 1977 or 義 2948] friendship; favor, kindness

友宜 ゆうぎ friendship, fellowship

高宜 こうぎ your kindness [favor]

KUN

【よろしい 宜しい】 **all RIGHT, well; all right, OK (in answer to a request)**

宜しかったら よろしかったら if you like; if you don't mind

しても宜しい してもよろしい may (do), may as well (do), have a right (to do)

【よろしく 宜しく】 **properly, suitably, as one thinks fit; one's regards, one's best wishes;** [followed by べし] *literary* **by all means**

宜しくやる よろしくやる do at one's own discretion; make cozy with

宜しくお伝え下さい よろしくおつたえください Please send my best regards

宜しく反省すべし よろしくはんせいすべし You are to reflect on your own deed

SYNONYMS

❶ **suitable**

適 SUITABLE → 3918

当 proper → 2701

宜 RIGHT → 2763

便 CONVENIENT → 0105

NOTE

★ do not confuse with 宣 PROCLAIM → 2799

宝

2764

2-3-5

▸**TREASURE**

ホウ たから ㊔ たか とみ

Ⓝ 寶 寳 寚 Ⓒ 宝 bǎo

40 宀	Jōyō-6	U5B9D
	S8-3-5	F1033

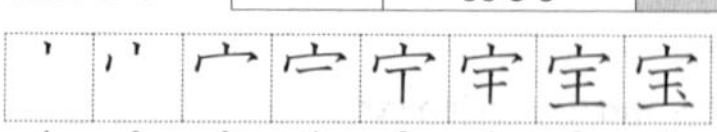

1 2 3 4 5 6 7 8

COMPOUNDS

❶ⓐ **TREASURE, treasured object**

ⓑ (something very valuable) **TREASURE, heirloom**

ⓒ **TREASURE**d, precious

a 宝庫 ほうこ treasure house, treasury

宝石 ほうせき gem, jewel

財宝 ざいほう treasure, valuables; riches, wealth

重宝 じゅうほう(=ちょうほう) priceless treasure

b 宝典 ほうてん thesaurus, treasury of words; precious book

国宝 こくほう national treasure

家宝 かほう family treasure, heirloom

c 重宝な ちょうほうな convenient, useful, handy

❷ honorific term used in reference to the emperor or Buddha

宝算 ほうさん the emperor's age

宝塔 ほうとう two-storied Buddhist tower

KUN

【たから 宝】 **TREASURE, precious thing; riches, wealth, money;** (something very valuable) **treasure, jewel**

宝物 たからもの treasure

宝船 たからぶね treasure ship; picture of a treasure ship

宝籤 たからくじ public lottery

宝捜し たからさがし treasure hunt

宝島 たからじま treasure island

子宝 こだから the treasure that is children; children

SYNONYMS

❶ⓐ & ❶ⓑ wealth

財 WEALTH → 1849

産 property → 4089

富 riches → 2892

宝 TREASURE → 2764

実

2765

▀ 2-3-5

▸REAL

ジツ み みの(る) まこと▲ ㊔ さね みち

Ⓝ 實 Ⓒ 实 shí

40	Jōyō-3	U5B9F
宀	S8-3-5	F0066

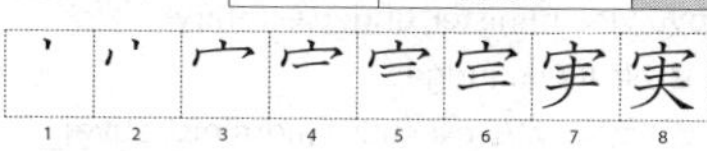

COMPOUNDS

❶ⓐ [also prefix] **REAL, actual, true**

ⓑ REALity, fact, truth

ⓒ *math* **REAL**

a 実施する じっしする carry out, enforce, execute

実現する じつげんする realize, materialize

実験 じっけん experiment

実力 じつりょく real ability [power], capability, competence

実績 じっせき (actual) result, positive achievements

実費 じっぴ actual expenses, cost price

実名 じつめい one's real name

実社会 じっしゃかい actual world

実際 じっさい truth, reality; actual state; practice

b 事実 じじつ fact, reality; as a matter of fact

現実 げんじつ actuality, reality

確実な かくじつな certain, sure, reliable; sound, solid

真実 しんじつ truth, reality

c 実関数 じつかんすう real variable function

❷ practical

実用 じつよう practical use, utility

実用的な じつようてきな practical

実務 じつむ practical business

実技 じつぎ practical technique [skill]

❸ⓐ substance, contents

ⓑ substantial, solid, full

a 充実した じゅうじつした full, complete, rich

情実 じょうじつ private circumstances, personal consideration; favoritism

口実 こうじつ excuse, pretext, pretense

b 実車 じっしゃ full-scale car (vs. model); occupied taxi

実名詞 じつめいし noun substantive

❹ faithfulness, sincerity, fidelity

実直な じっちょくな upright, honest, steady

切実な せつじつな acute, keen, earnest; urgent

誠実な せいじつな sincere, honest, faithful

忠実な ちゅうじつな faithful, devoted, honest

❺ fruit

果実 かじつ fruit, berry

結実する けつじつする bear fruit; be successful, achieve success

綿実 めんじつ cottonseed

INDEPENDENT

【じつ 実】

① **REALity, fact, truth**

実に じつに truly, surely

実は じつは to tell the truth, the fact is

② substance, contents

虚を捨てて実を取る きょをすててじつをとる discard the shadow for the substance

③ faithfulness, sincerity, fidelity

実の有る じつのある sincere, faithful

④ fruit, outcome

憲政の実を上げる けんせいのじつをあげる realize constitutionalism

⑤ *math* dividend, multiplicand

法と実 ほうとじつ divisor and dividend

KUN

【み 実】 **fruit, nut, berry, seed; substance; ingredients**

実の有る みのある substantial, solid

実入り みいり crop, harvest; income, profits

木の実 きのみ nut, berry

【みのる 実る】 [sometimes also 稔る] **bear fruit, ripen**

実り みのり crop, ripening

実っている みのっている be in bearing

実らなかった努力 みのらなかったどりょく fruitless [resultless] efforts

【まこと 実】 [usu. 誠, sometimes also 真] truth, **REALity**

実の心 まことのこころ one's real intention

実しやかに まことしやかに plausibly, as if it were true

SYNONYMS

❶ⓐ & ❶ⓑ true

真 TRUE → 2616
洵 TRULY → 0458
実 REAL → 2765
本 real → 4314
正 genuine → 4296
現 ACTUAL → 1218

❸ⓐ essential content
実 substance → 2765
体 substance → 0080
味 contents → 0325

❹ fidelity
忠 LOYALTY → 3087
義 faith → 2948
孝 FILIAL PIETY → 3973
悌 BROTHERLY LOVE → 0507
誠 SINCERITY → 1922
実 faithfulness → 2765
信 fidelity → 0115
操 constancy → 0948
節 moral integrity → 3336

❺ fruit
果 FRUIT → 4377
実 fruit → 2765

【みのる】
◯ mature
熟 MATURE → 3558
成 grow up → 4352
稔 RIPEN → 1544
爛 OVERRIPE → 1427
実る bear fruit → 2765

USAGE

❶【みのる】
実る
[sometimes also 稔る] bear fruit, ripen
稔る
[usu. 実る] bear fruit, ripen

❷【みのり】
実り
[sometimes also 稔り] crop, ripening
稔り
[usu. 実り] crop, ripening

HOMOPHONES

みのる 稔 RIPEN → 1544
みのり 稔 RIPEN → 1544
まこと
誠 SINCERITY → 1922
真 TRUE → 2616

NOTE

➡ see also USAGE note at 誠 1922

官

2766
2-3-5

▶ **GOVERNMENT**
▶ **GOVERNMENT OFFICIAL**
カン
Ⓒ 官 guān

40 宀	Jōyō-4	U5B98
	S8-3-5	F0304

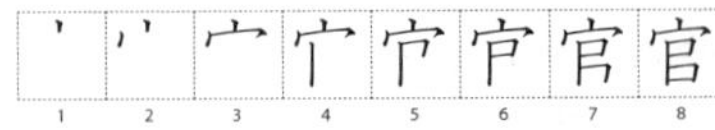

COMPOUNDS

❶ [original meaning] **GOVERNMENT, court**
官房 かんぼう secretariat
官邸 かんてい official residence
官庁 かんちょう government office [agency]
官僚 かんりょう government official(s); bureaucracy, officialdom
官製の かんせいの government manufactured
官吏 かんり government official
官女 かんじょ court lady

❷ⓐ [also suffix] **GOVERNMENT OFFICIAL, officer**
ⓑ GOVERNMENT service [post]
a 長官 ちょうかん director, administrator, chief
警官 けいかん police officer, policeman
次官 じかん vice-minister, undersecretary
裁判官 さいばんかん judge
行政官 ぎょうせいかん executive [administrative] official
b 任官 にんかん appointment to an office, commission
退官 たいかん retirement from office

❸ organ (of the body)
官能 かんのう bodily function; fleshly sense, carnal desire
器官 きかん (body) organ
五官 ごかん the five organs (of sense)

INDEPENDENT

【かん 官】**GOVERNMENT**, authorities; government service [post]
官に就く かんにつく enter the government service

SYNONYMS

❶ governments
官 GOVERNMENT → 2766
幕 SHOGUNATE → 2937
廷 COURT → 3795
朝 court → 2130
宮 Imperial Court → 2828

❷ⓐ officials
官 GOVERNMENT OFFICIAL → 2766
吏 OFFICIAL → 4351
僚 official → 0186
司 officiator → 3648

役 executive →0288
事 officer →4384

❸ **organ**
臓 INTERNAL ORGAN →1417
器 organ →3367
官 organ →2766

NOTE

➡ see COMPOUND FORMATION for 官房 かんぼう →房 2445

空

▶SKY
▶AIR
▶EMPTY

2767
2-3-5

クウ そら あ(く) あ(き) あ(ける) から す(く)▲ す(かす)▲ むな(しい)▲

Ⓒ 空 kōng kòng

116	Jōyō-1	U7A7A
穴	S8-5-3	F0253

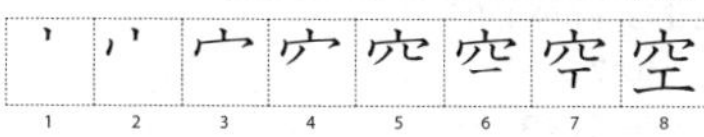

COMPOUNDS

❶ⓐ **SKY, heavens, the air, space**
ⓑ (space where aircraft operate) **AIR, airspace**
a 空中で くうちゅうで in the air [sky]
空間 くうかん space, room
天空 てんくう sky, air, firmament, heavens
虚空 こくう empty space, sky
b 東京上空 とうきょうじょうくう the skies of Tokyo
航空 こうくう aviation, aerial navigation
制空権 せいくうけん command of the air

❷ⓐ **AIRcraft, airplane**
ⓑ abbrev. of 空軍 くうぐん: **AIR force**
a 空港 くうこう airport
空軍 くうぐん air force
空輸 くうゆ air transportation
空路 くうろ air route, airway
b 空曹 くうそう noncommissioned officer of the Japanese Air Self-Defense Forces
空陸 くうりく air force and army

❸ **AIR**
空気 くうき air; atmosphere
空調 くうちょう air conditioning
空圧 くうあつ air [pneumatic] pressure

❹ [original meaning] **EMPTY, vacant, unoccupied, blank**
空車 くうしゃ vacant taxi, empty car
空砲 くうほう blank shot [cartridge]
空白 くうはく blank, empty space; void, vacuum
空席 くうせき vacant seat; vacancy
真空 しんくう vacuum

❺ⓐ (insubstantial) **EMPTY, void, vain, idle, futile, meaningless**
ⓑ *Sunyata* (Sanskrit for emptiness or void): the nonexistence of matter and self, the transcendental void (in Buddhism)
a 空虚 くうきょ emptiness, voidness; inanity
空想 くうそう fancy, fantasy; imagination
空論 くうろん abstract [impractical] theory
空費 くうひ waste
b 空性 くうしょう *Sunyata*
色即是空 しきそくぜくう Matter is void/Form [Matter] is nonsubstantial

INDEPENDENT

【くう 空】 **AIR**, airspace; air force; idleness, vanity; *Sunyata* (→❺ⓑ)
空を摑む くうをつかむ grasp at the air
空対空ミサイル くうたいくうみさいる air-to-air missile
空に帰する くうにきする come to naught

KUN

【そら 空】
① **SKY, heavens; the skies, the air**
空色 そらいろ sky blue
空を飛ぶ そらをとぶ fly in the air
曇り空 くもりぞら cloudy sky [weather]
② **weather**
空模様 そらもよう weather
女心と秋の空 おんなごころとあきのそら woman's heart and autumn weather (are both fickle)
③ memory
空で そらで from memory, by heart
④ pretense, feigning
空言 そらごと falsehood, lie
空空しい そらぞらしい false, feigned, hypocritical, transparent
⑤ absentmindedness
上の空 うわのそら absentminded, have a vacant air
⑥ vain, vague, strange
空頼み そらだのみ vain hopes
空恐ろしい そらおそろしい have a vague fear

【あく 空く】
① **become vacant, become vacated [EMPTY]**
空いている部屋 あいているへや vacant room
② become available for use
辞書が空いたら貸して下さい じしょがあいたらかしてください Let me use the dictionary when available
③ **become free [unoccupied]**
私は時間が空いている わたしはじかんがあいている I have time to spare
④ [sometimes also 明く] have (a hole or aperture) in, (a gap) is open

穴が空いている あながあいている have [be pierced with] a hole

【あき 空き】

① [sometimes also 明き] **gap, aperture, space; vacancy; free time**

空きを埋める あきをうめる fill a gap

② [prefix] **vacant, EMPTY**

空き家 あきや vacant house

空き缶 あきかん empty can

【あける 空ける】

① **EMPTY, clear, vacate, clear out**

部屋を空ける へやをあける clear a room

② **leave space, make room**

一字空ける いちじあける leave a space (between words)

③ **bore, make a hole**

穴を空ける あなをあける make a hole

④ free oneself (to do), make spare time

時間を空ける じかんをあける make oneself available [free]

【から 空】

① **emptiness, vacancy, hollow**

空の からの empty, vacant, hollow

空っぽ からっぽ empty, hollow

空手 からて karate; empty hand

② [prefix]

ⓐ (void of content) **EMPTY**

ⓑ (lacking substance) **EMPTY**, vain, bogus, false

a 空瓶 からびん empty bottle

b 空梅雨 からつゆ dry rainy season, rainless *tsuyu*

空約束 からやくそく empty promise

空手形 からてがた bad [fictitious] bill; empty promise

【すく 空く】 **become EMPTY, become less crowded**

空き すき vacancy, interval

空きっ腹 すきっぱら hunger

空いた電車 すいたでんしゃ uncrowded train

手空きの てすきの not busy, unengaged

【すかす 空かす】

① feel hungry

腹を空かす はらをすかす be hungry

② make available, make free

手を空かす てをすかす make oneself available

【むなしい 空しい】 [sometimes also 虚しい]

①ⓐ **EMPTY, void**

ⓑ **vain, futile**

a 空しさ むなしさ emptiness, futility

空しい名声 むなしいめいせい empty name

b 努力も空しく どりょくもむなしく after efforts in vain

② **dead, lifeless**

空しくなる むなしくなる die, expire

SYNONYMS

❶ sky

空 SKY → 2767
昊 SKY → 3066
穹 SKY → 2768
天 HEAVEN → 4250
宙 MIDAIR → 2761

❷ⓐ aircraft and spacecraft

機 AIRCRAFT → 1365
空 aircraft → 2767
船 spaceship → 1700

❸ gas and vapor

気 GAS → 3960
空 AIR → 2767
汽 STEAM → 0309

❹ emptiness and nothing

空 EMPTY → 2767
白 WHITE (blank) → 4305
虚 VOID → 4017
無 NOTHING → 2648

❺ⓐ vain

空 EMPTY → 2767
虚 without substance → 4017
徒 vain → 0499

USAGE

❶【から】

空

① emptiness, vacancy, hollow

② [prefix]

ⓐ (void of content) empty

ⓑ (lacking substance) empty, vain, bogus, false

殻

①ⓐ shell, crust

ⓑ husk, hull

② castoff skin, refuse

❷【むなしい】

空しい

[sometimes also 虚しい]

①ⓐ empty, void

ⓑ vain, futile

② dead, lifeless

虚しい

[usu. 空しい] same as 空しい

❸【あき】

空き

① [sometimes also 明き] gap, aperture, space; vacancy; free time

② [prefix] vacant, empty

明き

④ [usu. 空き] gap, aperture, space; vacancy; free time

HOMOPHONES

あく

明 BRIGHT → 1060

開 OPEN → 4121

あき 明 BRIGHT → 1060

あける

明 BRIGHT → 1060

開 OPEN → 4121

から 殻 SHELL → 1883

すく

透 PASS THROUGH → 3854

隙 GAP → 0826

すかす

透 PASS THROUGH → 3854

隙 GAP → 0826

むなしい 虚 VOID → 4017

NOTE

➡ see also USAGE notes at 明 1060 and 透 3854

穹

2768

2-3-5

▶**SKY**

キュウ

Ⓒ 穹 qióng

116	Names	U7A79
穴	S8-5-3	F0000

COMPOUNDS

❶ **SKY**

蒼穹 そうきゅう blue sky

❷ **bow-shaped, arched**

穹窿× きゅうりゅう yurt, circular domed tent

天穹 てんきゅう vault, dome

SYNONYMS

❶ **sky**

空 SKY → 2767

昊 SKY → 3066

穹 SKY → 2768

天 HEAVEN → 4250

宙 MIDAIR → 2761

宗

2769

2-3-5

▶**RELIGIOUS SECT**

シュウ ソウ むね▲ ㊔ むな もと とき

Ⓒ 宗 zōng

40	Jōyō-6	U5B97
宀	S8-3-5	F0540

丶 丶丶 宀 宀 宁 宇 宗 宗 (1 2 3 4 5 6 7 8)

COMPOUNDS

❶ⓐ **RELIGIOUS SECT (esp. Buddhist), denomination**

ⓑ **suffix after names of RELIGIOUS SECTs**

ⓒ **religion**

a 宗派 しゅうは religious sect, denomination

宗旨 しゅうし tenets of a religious sect; (religious) sect

b 浄土宗 じょうどしゅう *Jodo* sect (of Buddhism)

天台宗 てんだいしゅう *Tendai* sect (of Buddhism)

c 宗教 しゅうきょう religion, faith, creed

改宗 かいしゅう conversion; proselytism

❷ ancestor, originator, patriarch

宗家 そうけ head family, originator

宗主 そうしゅ suzerain

祖宗 そそう ancestors

❸ leader, great master

宗匠 そうしょう master (of an art)

詩宗 しそう master poet

❹ [original meaning] ancestral shrine

宗廟 そうびょう ancestral shrine [temple]

INDEPENDENT

【しゅう 宗】**RELIGIOUS SECT**, denomination

我宗の徒 わがしゅうのと believer of my denomination

KUN

【むね 宗】[now usu. 旨] **principle, aim**

SYNONYMS

❶ⓐ & ❶ⓑ **parties and sects**

党 PARTY → 3190

閥 CLIQUE → 4126

流 school → 0529

派 SECT → 0456

翼 WING → 3379

系 faction → 2443

門 (religious) sect → 1100

宗 RELIGIOUS SECT (esp. Buddhist) → 2769

ⓒ **religion**

教 RELIGION → 1887

宗 religion → 2769

道 the Way → 3888

HOMOPHONES

むね 旨 PURPORT → 2516

NOTE

➡ see USAGE note at 旨 2516

定

2770

2-3-5

▶**FIX**

テイ ジョウ さだ(める) さだ(まる) さだ(か)

㊔ さだむ さだお やす

Ⓒ 定 dìng

40	Jōyō-3	U5B9A
宀	S8-3-5	F0093

丶 丶丶 宀 宀 宀 宁 宇 定 (1 2 3 4 5 6 7 8)

土 大 大 子 【宀】 小 ⺌ ⺍ 山 艹 䒑 亡 亼 廾

COMPOUNDS

❶ⓐ **FIX, determine, decide, set, settle**
ⓑ **lay down, prescribe, establish**

a 決定 けってい decision, settlement, conclusion
断定 だんてい decision, conclusion
一定する いっていする fix, define, unify
確定する かくていする make a definite decision, decide upon; be decided
予定 よてい schedule, plan, prearrangement; expectation; estimate
否定 ひてい denial, negation
指定 してい designation, appointment
勘定 かんじょう calculation; account, settlement of accounts
b 制定する せいていする establish, enact
規定 きてい regulations, rules; provisions
協定 きょうてい agreement, pact

❷ⓐ (firmly in position) **FIXed, stationary**
ⓑ [also prefix] [original meaning] (unchanging) **FIXed, definite, regular, constant**

a 定着 ていちゃく fixing, fastening, fixation
定滑車 ていかっしゃ fixed pulley
固定する こていする fix, settle, be fixed
措定する そていする suppose, assume
b 定価 ていか fixed [set] price
定員 ていいん fixed number of regular personnel; capacity
定期 ていき fixed term; fixed deposit; commuter's pass; regular, periodic
定期券 ていきけん commuter's pass
定休 ていきゅう regular holiday
定休日 ていきゅうび regular holiday
定数 ていすう fixed number, constant
定則 ていそく established rule
定刻 ていこく regular [appointed] time
定形 ていけい fixed form
定食 ていしょく day's special, table d'hôte
安定した あんていした stable, steady, firm; calm

❸ pacify (a country), suppress
鎮定 ちんてい suppression, subdual
平定する へいていする suppress, subjugate, subdue

❹ certainly, definitely
必定 ひつじょう as certain as death

❺ *Buddhism* state of complete cessation of thought, meditation
入定 にゅうじょう calm contemplation
禅定 ぜんじょう Samadhi, meditative concentration

❻ **as it is; without fail**
案の定 あんのじょう as feared, sure enough

KUN

【さだめる 定める】 **FIX, determine, decide, set; lay down, prescribe, establish; pacify**
定め さだめ law; decision; destiny, karma; certainty
定めし さだめし surely
見定める みさだめる make sure of, ascertain

【さだまる 定まる】 **be decided, be settled; quiet down**
定まり さだまり custom, rule; tranquility
定まった場所 さだまったばしょ specified place
定まらない天気 さだまらないてんき changeable weather

【さだか 定か】
さだかな 定かな **certain, positive**
定かに さだかに clearly

SYNONYMS

❶ⓐ **decide**
決 DECIDE →0308
断 RESOLVE →1885
定 FIX →2770

❷ⓐ **not moving**
固 FIRM →3830
定 fixed →2770
静 still →2164
止 still →3659

ⓑ **constant**
定 fixed →2770
恒 CONSTANT →0438
常 REGULAR →3203
例 regular →0099

NOTE

➡ see COMPOUND FORMATION for 措定 そてい →措 0610

宕

2771

2-3-5

▸**UNCONSTRAINED**
トウ ㊔ とおる
Ⓒ 宕 dàng

40	Names	U5B95
宀	S8-3-5	F2975

COMPOUNDS

❶ **UNCONSTRAINED, self-willed, carefree**
豪宕な ごうとうな bold and unconstrained, magnanimous

❷ [original meaning, now obsolete] **cave**

SPECIAL READINGS

愛宕山 あたごやま name of: a mountain in Kyoto; a hill in Tokyo; a mountain in Chiba Prefecture

SYNONYMS

❶ **unrestrained**
漫 RAMBLING →0858
散 unrestrained →2137

宕 UNCONSTRAINED → 2771

突

2772

2-3-5

▶**DASH**
▶**THRUST**
トツ つ(く)

Ⓝ 突 Ⓒ 突 tū

116	Jōyō	U7A81
穴	S8-5-3	F0370

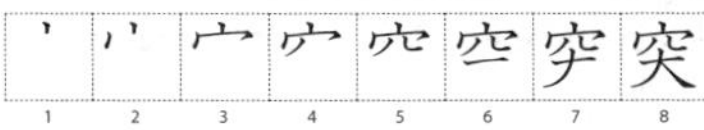

COMPOUNDS

❶ **DASH forward, thrust, charge**
突進する とっしんする dash [rush] forward, push ahead
突貫する とっかんする charge at, make a dash at (the enemy's position)
突入する とつにゅうする dash into, thrust into, rush into
突撃する とつげきする charge at, make a dash at (the enemy's position)
突破する とっぱする break [smash] through; surmount; exceed

❷ (strike with violence) **DASH against, collide, crash against**
衝突する しょうとつする collide (with), crash (into); conflict [clash] (with)
追突する ついとつする collide with from behind
激突 げきとつ crash, collision

❸ **protruding, projecting, sticking out**
突角 とっかく convex angle
突出する とっしゅつする project, protrude, stick out, jut out
突起 とっき projection, protuberance
突端 とったん tip, point
突堤 とってい pier, breakwater

❹ **abruptly, suddenly, unexpectedly**
突然 とつぜん abruptly, suddenly, unexpectedly
突如 とつじょ suddenly, unexpectedly
突風 とっぷう squall, sudden gust
突飛な とっぴな wild, extravagant, extraordinary
唐突に とうとつに abruptly

❺ **chimney**
煙突 えんとつ chimney, smokestack

KUN

【つく 突く】

① (penetrate with a pointed end) **THRUST, pierce, stab, prick**
突き刺す つきさす stab, pierce, thrust
突き殺す つきころす stab to death
突き抜く つきぬく pierce through
突き抜ける つきぬける go [push, thrust] through, penetrate
突き破る つきやぶる break [smash] through, pierce
楯突く たてつく oppose, defy; rebel

②ⓐ (strike forcibly with a pointed end) **THRUST, push, give a push [thrust]**
ⓑ [sometimes also 撞く] **poke, strike (a bell)**

a 突き つき thrust, push; lunge
突き出す つきだす thrust out, push out; push out of a sumo ring
突き当たる つきあたる hit against, run into; come to the end of (a street)
突き当たり つきあたり end [bottom] of a street
突っ込む つっこむ thrust in, ram into, stuff into; dash [run] into
突っ掛ける つっかける slip on, slip into (slippers)

b 鐘を突く かねをつく strike a bell

③ [sometimes also 衝く] attack, strike at
中堅を突く ちゅうけんをつく strike [attack] at the center [heart]

④ [sometimes also 衝く] brave, face courageously
嵐を突いて進む あらしをついてすすむ proceed in the face of a storm

⑤ [sometimes also 衝く] stimulate (the senses), be pungent
鼻を突く はなをつく assail the nostrils

SYNONYMS

❶ **move forward**
進 ADVANCE → 3873
突 DASH → 2772
這う CRAWL → 4003

❷ **collide**
衝 COLLIDE → 0893
牴 COLLIDE WITH → 1134
觝 COLLIDE WITH → 1892
突 DASH → 2772
当たる HIT → 2701

❸ **protrude and protruding**
突 protruding → 2772
凸 CONVEX → 4298
隆 protuberant → 0661
起 RISE → 4099
出る stick out → 4310

❹ **sudden**
急 SUDDEN → 2595
激 sudden → 0955
暴 sudden → 3138
俄 SUDDEN → 0106
頓 SUDDEN → 1320
勃 SUDDENLY → 1839
突 abruptly → 2772

【つく】

① **stab**
刺 STAB → 1625

突く THRUST → 2772

② **push**

押 PUSH → 0371
突く THRUST → 2772
圧 apply pressure → 3688
挨 PUSH → 0510
按 HOLD DOWN → 0444

USAGE

【つく】

突く
① (penetrate with a pointed end) **thrust, pierce, stab, prick**
②ⓐ (strike forcibly with a pointed end) **thrust, push, give a push [thrust]**
ⓑ [sometimes also 撞く] poke, strike (a bell)
③ [sometimes also 衝く] attack, strike at
④ [sometimes also 衝く] brave, face courageously
⑤ [sometimes also 衝く] stimulate (the senses), be pungent

衝く
① [usu. 突く] attack, strike at
② [usu. 突く] brave, face courageously
③ [usu. 突く] stimulate (the senses), be pungent
④ unclassified compounds

撞く
[usu. 突く] poke, strike (a bell)

HOMOPHONES

つく
衝 COLLIDE → 0893
撞 STRIKE → 0905

尙

2773
2-3-5

▸STILL
▸VALUE HIGHLY
ショウ なお ㊔ ひさ ひさし たか たかし まさ

42	Nonstandard	U5C19
小	S8-3-5	F0000

traditional form → see 尚 at 2774

尚

2774
2-3-5

▸STILL
▸VALUE HIGHLY
ショウ なお▲ ㊔ ひさ ひさし たか たかし まさ
Ⓝ 尙 Ⓒ 尚 shàng

42	Jōyō	U5C1A
⺌	S8-3-5	F1356

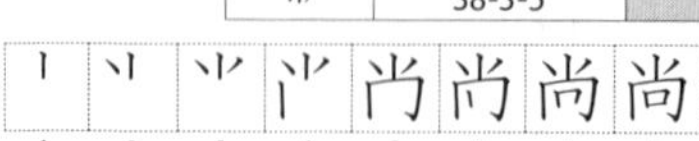

COMPOUNDS

❶ **STILL, yet**
尚早の しょうそうの premature

❷ **VALUE HIGHLY, esteem, be enthusiastically devoted**
尚古 しょうこ worship of ancient things
尚武 しょうぶ militarism, warlike spirit
好尚 こうしょう taste, fancy, fashion

❸ high, lofty, refined
高尚な こうしょうな high, noble, elegant

❹ used phonetically for *shō*
和尚 おしょう Buddhist priest [abbot] in charge of a temple

KUN

【なお 尚】[sometimes also 猶]
①ⓐ (in increasing degree) **STILL (more), all the more**
ⓑ **further, in addition, by the way**
a 尚の事 なおのこと all the more, still more
尚一層悪い事は なおいっそうわるいことは what is worse still
この方が尚良い このほうがなおよい This is still better
b 尚更 なおさら still more, all the more
尚又 なおまた further, besides
尚且つ なおかつ and yet
②ⓐ **STILL**, yet
ⓑ even, **STILL**
a 春尚浅し はるなおあさし Spring is not yet far advanced
b 昼尚暗い ひるなおくらい be dark even in the day-time
③ *literary* as, just like, no more…than
鯨の魚にあらざるは尚馬の魚にあらざるが如し くじらのさかなにあらざるはなおうまのさかなにあらざるがごとし A whale is no more a fish than a horse is

SYNONYMS

❶ **still**
未 NOT YET → 4318
尚 STILL → 2774

❷ **respect**
敬 RESPECT → 2136
尊 HONOR → 2920
畏 respect → 3170
欽 REVERE → 2124
仰 look up to → 0051
崇 REVERENCE → 2864
尚 VALUE HIGHLY → 2774
重 set value on → 4390
拝 WORSHIP → 0360
慕 ADORE → 2970

【なお】
①ⓐ **additionally**
亦 ALSO → 2504
兼 CONCURRENTLY → 2850

又 also, and →4158
而うして and →2520
及び and →4192
並びに and also →2793
傍ら besides →0166
尚 STILL →2774
更に furthermore →4355
且つ AS WELL →4297

USAGE

【なお】

尚

[sometimes also 猶]

①ⓐ (in increasing degree) still (more), all the more

ⓑ further, in addition, by the way

②ⓐ still, yet

ⓑ even, still

③ *literary* as, just like, no more…than

猶

[usu. 尚] same as 尚

HOMOPHONES

なお 猶 DELAY →0757

畄

2775

⬒2-3-5

▶KEEP
▶STAY

リュウ ル と(める) -と(める) -ど(め) と(まる) とど(まる) とど(める) るーぶる

102	Nonstandard	U7544
田	S8-5-3	F0000

handwritten form → see 留 at 3189

鼡

2776

⬒2-3-5

▶RAT

ソ ねずみ ねず

42	Nonstandard	U9F21
⺍	S8-3-5	F0000

traditional form → see 鼠 at 3340

学

⬒2-3-5

incorrect classification

➡ see ⬒2-5-3: ⺍ at 3162

岸

2777

⬒2-3-5

▶SHORE

ガン きし

Ⓒ 岸 àn

46	Jōyō-3	U5CB8
山	S8-3-5	F0799

1 2 3 4 5 6 7 8

COMPOUNDS

❶ [original meaning] **SHORE, bank, coast, beach**

岸壁 がんぺき quay (wall), wharf
沿岸 えんがん coast, shore
海岸 かいがん seashore, (sea) coast, beach
左岸 さがん left bank (of a river)
対岸 たいがん opposite bank [shore]

❷ proud, dignified

傲岸な ごうがんな arrogant, haughty

KUN

【きし 岸】**SHORE, bank, coast, beach**

岸辺に きしべに ashore, on the shore
向こう岸 むこうぎし opposite bank, farther shore

SPECIAL READINGS

河岸 かし riverside; fish market

SYNONYMS

❶ **shores and watersides**

畔 WATERSIDE →1472
-辺 -side →3761
浜 BEACH →0523
岸 SHORE →2777
浦 SEASIDE →0524
渚 STRAND →0637
磯 ROCKY BEACH →1587
汀 STRAND →0228

岩

2778

⬒2-3-5

▶ROCK

ガン いわ ㊔ いわお

Ⓒ 岩 yán

46	Jōyō-2	U5CA9
山	S8-3-5	F0772

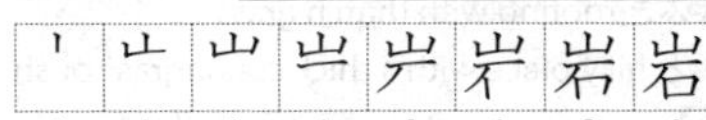

1 2 3 4 5 6 7 8

COMPOUNDS

● [sometimes also 巖 3037] [also suffix] [original meaning] **ROCK**

岩石 がんせき rock
岩層 がんそう rock formation
岩床 がんしょう bedrock
岩礁 がんしょう reef
岩塩 がんえん rock salt
火山岩 かざんがん volcanic rock, lava
花崗×岩 かこうがん granite

KUN

【いわ 岩】[formerly also 巖 or 磐] **ROCK, crag**

岩山 いわやま rocky mountain
岩屋 いわや [also 窟] cave, cavern, hole

SYNONYMS

● **rock and stone**

石 STONE →3689
岩 ROCK →2778
巖 CRAG →3037

USAGE

【いわ】

岩

[formerly also 巖 or 磐] rock, crag

磐

[usu. 岩] same as 岩

HOMOPHONES

いわ

磐 BEDROCK → 3534

巖 CRAG → 3037

いわや

窟 CAVE → 2923

岩屋 → 2778, 3842

茅

2779

2-3-5

▸THATCH GRASS

ボウ ミョウ かや ちがや ㊔ ち

Ⓒ 茅 máo

140	Names	U8305
艹	S8-3-5	F2513

COMPOUNDS

● **THATCH GRASS such as cogongrass, eulalias and other gramineous plants**

茅屋 ぼうおく thatched cottage, hovel; my humble abode

KUN

【かや 茅】[also 萱] **THATCH GRASS such as cogongrass, eulalias and other gramineous plants**

茅葺 かやぶき roofing with thatch grass

茅戸 かやと hilly place with a thick cogongrass bush

【ちがや 茅】**cogongrass, alang grass, bladygrass; *Impereta cylindrica***

SYNONYMS

● & 【かや】 **kinds of grasses**

草 GRASS → 2813

荻 AMUR SILVERGRASS → 2844

蒲 CATTAIL → 2932

萊 GOOSEFOOT → 2878

蕨 BRACKEN → 2992

叢 grassy place → 3243

芝 LAWN GRASS → 2705

笹 BAMBOO GRASS → 3301

茅 cogongrass → 2779

萱 THATCH GRASS → 2904

藁 STRAW → 3015

芦 REED → 2743

葦 COMMON REED → 2934

菅 SEDGE → 2874

USAGE

【かや】

茅

[also 萱] thatch grass such as cogongrass, eulalias and other gramineous plants

萱

[also 茅] thatch grass such as cogongrass, eulalias and other gramineous plants

HOMOPHONES

かや 萱 THATCH GRASS → 2904

NOTE

★ do not confuse with 芽 BUD → 2784

苺

2780

2-3-5

▸STRAWBERRY

ボウ バイ いちご

Ⓝ 莓 Ⓒ 莓 méi

140	Names	U82FA
艹	S8-3-5	F3483

COMPOUNDS

● [original meaning] **STRAWBERRY**

KUN

【いちご 苺】**STRAWBERRY**

木苺 きいちご bramble, *Rubus*

草苺 くさいちご *Rubus hirsutus*

蛇苺 へびいちご false strawberry, *Duchesnea chrysantha*

海老殻苺 えびがらいちご wineberry

SYNONYMS

【いちご】

○ **fruits and fruit trees**

桃 PEACH → 1174

榛 HAZEL → 1328

椎 CHINQUAPIN → 1249

柚 YUZU → 1123

椰 COCONUT → 1285

柑 CITRUS → 1112

橙 BITTER ORANGE → 1369

葡 GRAPE → 2902

萄 GRAPE → 2870

柿 PERSIMMON → 1118

檎 APPLE → 1386

李 PLUM → 3050

枇 LOQUAT → 1063

杷 LOQUAT → 1065

苺 STRAWBERRY → 2780

菱 water chestnut → 2879

杏 APRICOT → 3049

梅 JAPANESE APRICOT → 1159

橘 MANDARIN → 1366

栗 CHESTNUT → 3280

栃 JAPANESE HORSE CHESTNUT → 1122

梨 PEAR → 3412
蕉 PLANTAIN → 2994

苗

2781
2-3-5

▸**SEEDLING**
ビョウ ミョウ▲ なえ なわ- ㊔ みつ たね
Ⓒ 苗 miáo

140	Jōyō	U82D7
艹	S8-3-5	F1645

Stroke order: 1–8

COMPOUNDS

❶ [original meaning] **SEEDLING, sapling, young plant**
苗圃 びょうほ seedbed
苗字(=名字) みょうじ surname, family name
種苗 しゅびょう seedlings, seeds and saplings
育苗 いくびょう seedling culture

❷ offspring, descendants
苗裔× びょうえい offspring
痘苗 とうびょう vaccine, vaccine virus; smallpox vaccine

KUN

【なえ 苗】**SEEDLING, sapling**
苗木 なえぎ sapling, young tree
苗床 なえどこ seedbed
早苗 さなえ rice sprouts

【なわ- 苗-】**SEEDLING, rice seedling**
苗代 なわしろ bed for rice seedlings, rice nursery
苗水 なわみず water for a rice nursery

SYNONYMS

❶ **early states of plant life**
芽 BUD → 2784
蕾 BUD (of a flower) → 3006
苗 SEEDLING → 2781
種 SEED → 1560

COMPOUND FORMATION

❶【苗字(=名字) みょうじ】
According to one theory, 苗字 'surname, family name' refers to the name (字) of one's ancestors, who are likened to a seedling (苗 ❶).

❷【痘苗 とうびょう】
痘苗 'vaccine, etc.' is the offspring (苗 ❷), i.e., the virus or lymph, of a vaccine (痘).

英

2782
2-3-5

▸**DISTINGUISHED**
▸**ENGLAND**
エイ はなぶさ▲ ㊔ ひで ひでし はな すぐる あきら ふさ つね てる
Ⓒ 英 yīng

140	Jōyō-4	U82F1
艹	S8-3-5	F0439

Stroke order: 1–8

COMPOUNDS

❶ⓐ [rarely also 穎 2036] **DISTINGUISHED, outstanding, excellent, talented; wise**
ⓑ person of **DISTINGUISHED** talent, outstanding person

a 英雄 えいゆう hero
英武 えいぶ distinguished [surpassing] valor
英才 えいさい [formerly also 穎才] talent, genius; gifted person, talented person
英断 えいだん prompt decision; resolute step
英知 えいち [sometimes also 叡智] sagacity, wisdom
英姿 えいし gallant figure, majestic appearance
英気 えいき spirit, energy; vigor

b 俊英 しゅんえい talent, genius; gifted person
育英 いくえい education of the gifted or promising

❷ⓐ **ENGLAND, United Kingdom; English, British**
ⓑ Englishman
ⓒ **English (language)**

a 英国 えいこく England, Great Britain, the U.K.
英米 えいべい England and America, Anglo-American
英領 えいりょう British territory [possession]
英文学 えいぶんがく English literature

c 英数 えいすう English and mathematics
英会話 えいかいわ English conversation
英和 えいわ English-Japanese
英文 えいぶん English; English writing

❸ [original meaning] flower
石英 せきえい quartz

INDEPENDENT

【えい 英】**ENGLAND**, United Kingdom; English (language)

KUN

【はなぶさ 英】**corolla**

SPECIAL READINGS

蒲公英▲ たんぽぽ dandelion

SYNONYMS

❶ⓐ **excellent and superior**
優 SUPERIOR → 0200
絶 without match → 1711
卓 PROMINENT → 2561
快 splendid → 0289
妙 MARVELOUS → 0280
秀 EXCELLENT → 3152
英 DISTINGUISHED → 2782
尤 outstanding → 3755
傑 outstanding → 0175
穎 TALENTED → 2036

逸 exceptional → 3872
名 first-rate → 2693
上 of upper grade → 4212

❷ⓐ European countries

英 ENGLAND → 2782
独 GERMANY → 0471
仏 FRANCE → 0020
伊 ITALY → 0052
葡 PORTUGAL → 2902
西 Spain → 4333
蘭 the Netherlands → 3031
希 Greece → 2543
露 Russia → 3495
白 Belgium → 4305

苑

2783
2-3-5

▶IMPERIAL GARDEN
エン オン その
Ⓒ 苑 yuàn

140	Names	U82D1
艹	S8-3-5	F2045

COMPOUNDS

❶ [sometimes also 園 えん 3914] **IMPERIAL GARDEN, garden, park**

御苑 ぎょえん Imperial garden
内苑 ないえん inner garden of the Imperial Palace
神宮外苑 じんぐうがいえん Outer Gardens of Meiji Shrine
鹿野苑 ろくやおん The Deer Park, *Mṛgadāva* (where Buddha delivered his first sermon)

❷ⓐ collection of artists or men of letters
ⓑ collection of artistic or literary works

a 文苑 ぶんえん literary world; anthology; collection of literary masterpieces
芸苑 げいえん world of artists and men of letters
b 広辞苑 こうじえん name of a well-known Japanese-Japanese dictionary

❸ [usu. 園 えん 3914] suffix after names of business establishments such as restaurants and tea shops, esp. where there are gardens

珈琲×苑 こーひーえん name of a coffee shop

KUN

【その 苑】[usu. 園] *literary*
① **garden**
② **institution**

SYNONYMS

❶ gardens

園 GARDEN → 3914
庭 GARDEN → 3866
苑 IMPERIAL GARDEN → 2783

❸ restaurant suffixes

亭 quality restaurant suffix → 2572
閣 high-class restaurant suffix → 4128
園 restaurant suffix → 3914
苑 restaurant suffix → 2783

HOMOPHONES

その 園 GARDEN → 3914

NOTE

➡ see USAGE note at 園 3914

芽

2784
2-3-5

▶BUD
ガ め ㊔ めい
Ⓝ 芽 Ⓒ 芽 yá

140	Jōyō-4	U82BD
艹	S8-3-5	F1762

Stroke order: 1 一 2 十 3 艹 4 艹 5 芒 6 芒 7 芽 8 芽

COMPOUNDS

● [original meaning] **BUD, sprout**

芽胞 がほう spore
発芽する はつがする bud, sprout, germinate
麦芽 ばくが wheat germ, malt
萌芽 ほうが germination, beginning; sprout
胚×芽 はいが embryo bud, germ

KUN

【め 芽】**BUD, sprout, germ**

芽生える めばえる bud, sprout; begin
新芽 しんめ sprout, bud, shoot, ratoon
若芽 わかめ young bud

SYNONYMS

● early states of plant life

芽 BUD → 2784
蕾 BUD (of a flower) → 3006
苗 SEEDLING → 2781
種 SEED → 1560

HOMOPHONES

め

目 EYE → 3777
眼 EYE → 1504

NOTE

➡ see USAGE note at 目 3777
★ do not confuse with 茅 THATCH GRASS → 2779

若

2785
2-3-5

▶YOUNG
ジャク ニャク ニャ▲ わか(い) わか-
も(しくは) も(し)▲ ㊔ わかし
Ⓒ 若 ruò rě

140	Jōyō-6	U82E5
艹	S8-3-5	F0310

Stroke order: 1 一 2 十 3 艹 4 艹 5 芐 6 芐 7 若 8 若

COMPOUNDS

❶ [also 弱 じゃく 1499] **YOUNG**

若年 じゃくねん youth, early age
若輩 じゃくはい young people; greenhorn
老若男女 ろうじゃくだんじょ(=ろうにゃくなんにょ) people of all ages and both sexes

❷ **somewhat, a certain amount, a little**

若干 じゃっかん a number of, some, a little

❸ function word for forming adjectives

泰然自若たる たいぜんじじゃくたる imperturbable, self-possessed
瞠×若たらしめる どうじゃくたらしめる strike someone dumb with astonishment

❹ used phonetically for *nya,* esp. in the transliteration of Sanskrit Buddhist terms

般若 はんにゃ wisdom, *Prajñā*

❺ like, similar to

傍若無人な ぼうじゃくぶじんな overbearing, arrogant, audacious

KUN

【わかい 若い】 **YOUNG, youthful, younger, junior; immature; low (number)**

若さ わかさ youth, youthfulness
若若しい わかわかしい youthful, young-looking

【わか- 若-】 [also prefix] **YOUNG**

若手 わかて young man; young official
若者 わかもの young person [fellow], youth
若夫婦 わかふうふ young couple

【もしくは 若しくは】 **or, either...or; otherwise**

【もし 若し】 **if, in case of**

若しも もしも if; the worst
若しかしたら もしかしたら possibly, perhaps
若しかすると もしかすると possibly, perhaps

SPECIAL READINGS

若人 わこうど youth, young man

SYNONYMS

❶ **young**

若 YOUNG → 2785
弱 young → 1499
少 young → 4278
青 youthful → 3084
幼 VERY YOUNG → 0222
稚 CHILDISH → 1543

苛

2786

2-3-5

▶**HARSH**

カ いら▲ いじ(める)▲ さいな(む)▲

Ⓒ 苛 kē

140	Jōyō	U82DB
艹	S8-3-5	F1765

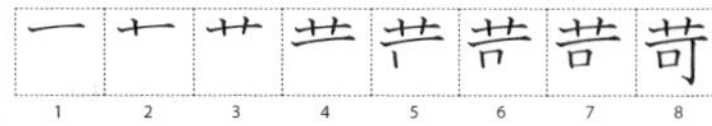

COMPOUNDS

❶ **HARSH, severe, cruel**

苛酷 かこく severe, cruel, harsh
苛烈 かれつ severe, stern
苛政 かせい tyranny, despotism

❷ **irritating, itching, stinging**

苛性 かせい caustic

KUN

【いら 苛】 irritation, frustration

苛立つ いらだつ be irritated, be nettled, be impatient
苛立たしい いらだたしい irritating, frustrating
苛苛 いらいら irritation, annoyance, edginess

【いじめる 苛める】 torment, tease, persecute

苛め いじめ bullying, teasing
苛められっ子 いじめられっこ bullied child

【さいなむ 苛む】 torment, torture, harass

責め苛む せめさいなむ treat cruelly, torment, torture

SYNONYMS

❶ **cruel**

虐 CRUEL → 3989
惨 CRUEL → 0585
酷 SEVERE → 1967
辣 SEVERE → 1965
残 RUTHLESS → 1179
凶 ATROCIOUS → 3679
苛 HARSH → 2786

【いじめる】

◯ **trouble and suffering**

困 BE IN TROUBLE → 3808
苛 torment → 2786
窮 BE IN EXTREMITY → 2983
悶 BE IN AGONY → 4119
悩 SUFFER → 0504
苦 SUFFERING → 2789
痛 PAIN → 4071
辛 HARD → 2531
煩 VEXED → 1295
難 DIFFICULT → 2310

茄

2787

2-3-5

▶**EGGPLANT**

カ ケ

Ⓒ 茄 jiā qié

140	Names	U8304
艹	S8-3-5	F2933

COMPOUNDS

❶ **EGGPLANT**

蕃茄 ばんか tomato

❷ [original meaning, now archaic] lotus, stem of lotus

SPECIAL READINGS

茄子 なす(=なすび) eggplant

SYNONYMS

❶ **vegetables**

菜 greens → 2880
蕪 TURNIP → 2990
芋 POTATO → 2706
豆 BEAN → 2442
蕗 BUTTERBUR → 3007
茄 EGGPLANT → 2787
芹 JAPANESE PARSLEY → 2742
瓜 GOURD → 3789
瓢 BOTTLE GOURD → 2356
芥 mustard → 2741

土
大
六
子
宀
小
⺌
⺍
山
【艹】
亠
亡
亼
廿

茎

▶STEM

ケイ くき

Ⓝ 莖 Ⓒ 茎 jīng

2788

2-3-5

140	Jōyō	U830E
艹	S8-3-5	F1997

一 十 艹 艼 芀 茎 茎 茎 (1–8)

COMPOUNDS

❶ [also suffix] [original meaning] **STEM, stalk**

茎葉 けいよう stems and leaves
球茎 きゅうけい corn, bulb
地下茎 ちかけい subterranean shoot, rootstock

❷ⓐ **STEM**-shaped object, esp. the male genital organ

ⓑ [rare] counter for long and narrow objects

a 陰茎 いんけい penis

b 一茎 いっけい a stem

KUN

【くき 茎】**STEM, stalk; long and narrow object; supportive structure**

長い茎の有る ながいくきのある long-stemmed
水茎 みずぐき writing brush
歯茎 はぐき gums

SYNONYMS

❶ **supporting parts of plants**

根 ROOT → 1167
株 stump → 1172
幹 TRUNK → 2152
茎 STEM → 2788

苦

▶SUFFERING
▶BITTER

ク くる(しい) -ぐる(しい) くる(しむ) くる(しめる) にが(い) にが(る)

Ⓒ 苦 kǔ

2789

2-3-5

140	Jōyō-3	U82E6
艹	S8-3-5	F0466

一 十 艹 艹 苎 苎 苦 苦 (1–8)

COMPOUNDS

❶ⓐ **SUFFERING, hardship, pain, distress**

ⓑ (characterized by suffering) **hard, painful, distressing**

ⓒ hardship, trouble, difficulty

a 苦痛 くつう pain, agony, anguish
苦悶 くもん agony, anguish
苦悩 くのう suffering, distress, anguish
苦難 くなん suffering, hardship
苦渋 くじゅう distress, affliction

b 苦境 くきょう distressing circumstances, straits
苦界 くがい bitter [hard] world; life of prostitution
苦労 くろう difficulties, trouble, hardships, labor

c 苦楽 くらく pleasure and pain, joys and sorrows
辛苦 しんく hardships, trials; labor, trouble
貧苦 ひんく hardship of poverty

❷ **hard, energetically**

苦戦 くせん hard fight, desperate battle
苦心 くしん pains, efforts, hard work
苦学する くがくする study under adversity, work one's way (through school)

❸ⓐ [original meaning] **BITTER**

ⓑ (disagreeable) **BITTER, unpleasant**

a 苦味 くみ bitter taste
苦土 くど magnesia
苦情 くじょう complaint, grievance
苦杯 くはい bitter ordeal

b 苦笑 くしょう forced [strained] smile
苦言 くげん frank advice; exhortation

INDEPENDENT

【く 苦】**SUFFERING**, hardship, pain, distress; hardships, trouble, difficulty

苦にする くにする take it seriously, distress oneself
苦も無く くもなく easily, without effort
苦は楽の種 くはらくのたね No pain, no gain

KUN

【くるしい 苦しい】**hard, painful, distressing; straitened, needy; strained, forced, awkward**

苦しさ くるしさ pain, agony; suffering, hardship
苦しがる くるしがる complain of a pain, suffer
苦しい懐 くるしいふところ tight budget

苦しい言い訳 くるしいいいわけ lame [poor] excuse
胸が苦しい むねがくるしい have a pain in one's chest

【-ぐるしい -苦しい】 [verbal suffix] **difficult to bear, disagreeable, unpleasant**
見苦しい みぐるしい dishonorable, unsightly, ugly
聞き苦しい ききぐるしい disagreeable to hear, offensive to the ear
息苦しい いきぐるしい breathe with difficulty; suffocating, choking

【くるしむ 苦しむ】 **suffer (from), groan; be troubled, be distressed; be worried; be perplexed, try hard, make efforts**
苦しみ くるしみ pain, anguish; distress, suffering, hardship
借金で苦しむ しゃっきんでくるしむ be distressed with debts

【くるしめる 苦しめる】 **torment, distress, harass; trouble, worry; inflict pain**
親を苦しめる おやをくるしめる cause one's parents distress

【にがい 苦い】
ⓐ **BITTER**
ⓑ (disagreeable) **BITTER, sour, trying, hard**
a 苦さ にがさ bitterness, bitter taste
苦い薬 にがいくすり bitter medicine
苦汁(=苦塩) にがり bittern, brine
苦味 にがみ bitter taste
b 苦苦しい にがにがしい unpleasant; shameful
苦手 にがて person that is hard to deal with; weak point
苦笑い にがわらい bitter smile
苦い経験 にがいけいけん bitter experience

【にがる 苦る】 **feel BITTER, scowl**
苦り顔 にがりがお sour [wry] face
苦り切る にがりきる look sour [disgusted]

SYNONYMS

❶ trouble and suffering
困 BE IN TROUBLE → 3808
苛 torment → 2786
窮 BE IN EXTREMITY → 2983
悶 BE IN AGONY → 4119
悩 SUFFER → 0504
苦 SUFFERING → 2789
痛 PAIN → 4071
辛 HARD → 2531
煩 VEXED → 1295
難 DIFFICULT → 2310

❸ⓐ tastes
甘 SWEET → 4306
苦 BITTER → 2789
辛 PUNGENT → 2531
辣 PUNGENT → 1965
酸 sour → 1968
渋い ASTRINGENT → 0625
鹹 SALTY → 2366

NOTE

➡ see COMPOUND FORMATION for 粒粒辛苦 りゅうりゅうしんく → 粒 1682

茉

2790
2-3-5

▸JASMINE
マツ ㊔ ま
Ⓒ 茉 mò

140	Names	U8309
艹	S8-3-5	F2826

COMPOUNDS

● JASMINE, white jasmine
茉莉 まつり jasmine, *Jasminum sambac*
茉莉花 まつりか jasmine, *Jasminum sambac*

SYNONYMS

● shrubs
藤 WISTERIA → 3025
蔦 JAPANESE IVY → 2972
萩 *HAGI* → 2908
茉 JASMINE → 2790
莉 JASMINE → 2843
芭 JAPANESE FIBER BANANA → 2736

茂

2791
2-3-5

▸GROW THICK
モ しげ(る) ㊔ もと たか
Ⓒ 茂 mào

140	Jōyō	U8302
艹	S8-3-5	F1011

1	2	3	4	5	6	7	8
一	十	艹	艿	芦	茂	茂	茂

COMPOUNDS

● GROW THICK, grow luxuriantly, be overgrown
茂林 もりん [rare] luxuriant [dense] forest
繁茂する はんもする grow thick, luxuriate

KUN

【しげる 茂る】 [formerly also 繁る] **GROW THICK, be luxuriant, be overgrown**
茂み しげみ thicket, bush
生い茂る おいしげる grow luxuriantly [thickly]

SYNONYMS

● flourish
茂 GROW THICK → 2791
繁 THRIVE → 3536

USAGE

【しげる】

茂る

[formerly also 繁る] grow thick, be luxuriant, be overgrown

繁る

[now usu. 茂る] same as 茂る

HOMOPHONES

しげる 繁 THRIVE →3536

苔

2792

2-3-5

▸MOSS

タイ こけ

Ⓒ 苔 tái tāi

140	Names	U82D4
艹	S8-3-5	F2273

COMPOUNDS

❶ⓐ MOSS, liverwort, bryophyte

ⓑ lichen

a 苔類 たいるい liverworts, *Marchantiophyta*

蘚×苔 せんたい moss, bryophyte

b 苔癬× たいせん (disease) lichen

❷ (coating resembling moss) **fur**

舌苔 ぜったい fur (on one's tongue)

KUN

【こけ 苔】

ⓐ **MOSS, liverwort, bryophyte**

ⓑ **lichen, short plants resembling MOSS**

a 苔植物 こけしょくぶつ bryophyte

水苔 みずごけ bog moss

転石苔を生ぜず てんせきこけをしょうぜず A rolling stone gathers no moss

b 苔桃 こけもも cowberry, lingonberry

SPECIAL READINGS

海苔 のり nori, laver

SYNONYMS

❶ plants

菜 VEGETABLE →2880

植 PLANT →1247

栽 garden plant →4087

茨 thorny shrub →2812

苔 MOSS →2792

蔓 VINE →2975

桔 PLANT NAME ELEMENT →1164

並

2793

2-3-5

▸LINE UP

ヘイ なみ な(み) なら(べる) なら(ぶ) なら(びに)

Ⓝ 竝 Ⓒ 并 bìng bīng

1△	Jōyō-6	U4E26
一	S8-1-7	F0675

、	丷	䒑	䒑	䒑	䒑	並	並
1	2	3	4	5	6	7	8

COMPOUNDS

ⓐ LINE UP, place in a row, place side by side, stand in a row

ⓑ [also 併 0092] [original meaning] **side by side, in line, together**

a 並立 へいりつ standing abreast

並列 へいれつ arrangement; row, parallel

b 並行(=平行) へいこう going side by side; occurring together

並置 へいち juxtaposition, placing side by side

並用する へいようする use together [jointly]

KUN

【なみ 並, 並み】

①ⓐ **medium quality, common run, average**

ⓑ [in compounds] **ordinary, common, average**

a 並の なみの ordinary, average, mediocre

並肉 なみにく meat of medium quality

b 並製品 なみせいひん common article, article of average quality

並外れて なみはずれて extraordinary, uncommonly

月並な つきなみな conventional, commonplace; trite, hackneyed

② **row, line**

並木 なみき row of trees, roadside trees

軒並み のきなみ row of houses; all round, across the board

③ [also suffix] **equal, match, peer**

人並の ひとなみの common, ordinary, average; decent

欧米並みに おうべいなみに as in Europe and America

【ならべる 並べる】 *vt* **LINE UP, arrange, put side by side, juxtapose, place in order; display (goods); set up (chess pieces); enumerate, itemize; compare with**

並べ立てる ならべたてる enumerate

並べて見ると ならべてみると in comparison

品物を並べる しなものをならべる arrange goods

五目並べ ごもくならべ gobang

【ならぶ 並ぶ】 *vi* **LINE UP, form a line, stand in a row, be parallel; rank with, rival, equal**

並び ならび line, row; side

並び無い ならびない unrivaled, unequaled

立ち並ぶ たちならぶ stand in a row; be equal to

【ならびに 並びに】 **and also, besides, and, in addition**

性別並びに国籍 せいべつならびにこくせき sex and nationality

SYNONYMS

ⓐ arrange

並 LINE UP →2793
比 rank →0029
列 arrange in a row →1018
陳 lay out (for exhibit) →0656
羅 spread out →3244
揃える arrange properly →0719
整 PUT IN ORDER →3562
理 put in order →1220

ⓑ **together**
共 JOINT →3045
同 together →3707
併 TOGETHER →0092
並 side by side →2793
兼 CONCURRENTLY →2850
倶 TOGETHER →0125

【なみ】
①ⓑ **ordinary**
常 NORMAL →3203
只- ORDINARY →2677
並 ordinary →2793
平 common →4291
普 common →2919
庸 MEDIOCRE →3881
凡 COMMONPLACE →3656
套 TRITE →2823

【ならびに】
◯ **additionally**
亦 ALSO →2504
兼 CONCURRENTLY →2850
又 also, and →4158
而うして and →2520
及び and →4192
並びに and also →2793
傍ら besides →0166
尚 STILL →2774
更に furthermore →4355
且つ AS WELL →4297

NOTE
➡ see USAGE note at 平 4291

盲

2794
2-3-5

▶**BLIND**
モウ めくら

109	Nonstandard	U76F2
目	S8-5-3	F0000

traditional form →see 盲 at 2547

命念

2-3-5

incorrect classification
➡ see 2-2-6: 𠆢 at 2552

革

2-3-5

incorrect stroke-count
➡ see 2-4-5: 廿 at 3099

品

2795
2-3-6

▶**ARTICLE**
ヒン ホン▲ しな
Ⓒ 品 pǐn

30	Jōyō-3	U54C1
口	S9-3-6	F0213

Stroke order: 1–9

COMPOUNDS

❶ [also suffix]
ⓐ [original meaning] **ARTICLE, thing**
ⓑ **ARTICLE of merchandise, goods, commodity, product**

a 品名 ひんめい name of article
作品 さくひん (piece of) work, performance, product
食品 しょくひん food, foodstuff
用品 ようひん article, supplies
薬品 やくひん medicine, drug; chemicals
貴重品 きちょうひん article of value
b 商品 しょうひん goods, commodities
製品 せいひん manufactured goods [articles], product; refined petroleum products
納品 のうひん delivery of goods; delivered goods
返品 へんぴん returning goods; returned goods, article sent back
舶来品 はくらいひん imported goods

❷ counter for courses of a meal
一品料理 いっぴんりょうり one-dish meal
五品の定食 ごひんのていしょく five-course meal

❸ⓐ **grade of excellence, quality, character**
ⓑ **refinement, grace, elegance, good character**

a 品質 ひんしつ quality
品性 ひんせい character
品位 ひんい dignity, grace, nobility; grade, quality
品格 ひんかく dignity, grace
b 上品 じょうひん elegance, refinement
気品 きひん dignity, grace, nobility

❹ **category, classification, type**
品目 ひんもく list of articles [items]
品種 ひんしゅ kind, variety, description, brand
品詞 ひんし part of speech

❺ criticize, judge, grade
品評 ひんぴょう criticism, comment

❻ *Buddhism* chapter of a sutra
普門品 ふもんぼん Fumon (name of a chapter)

❼ [archaic] rank of a prince

INDEPENDENT

【ひん 品】**refinement, grace, elegance, good character; grade of excellence, quality, character**

品の良い人 ひんのよいひと person of refined manners

KUN

【しな 品】**ARTICLE, thing; article of merchandise, goods, commodity, product, stock; quality, grade of excellence; type, kind**

品物 しなもの article, thing, goods

品切れ しなぎれ absence [exhaustion] of stock

品が良い しながいい be of good quality

手を変え品を変え てをかえしなをかえ by all possible means, by hook or by crook

SYNONYMS

❶ⓐ **object**

物 THING → 1084

品 ARTICLE → 2795

体 BODY → 0080

ⓑ **merchandise**

産 product → 4089

品 ARTICLE (of merchandise) → 2795

貨 GOODS → 3113

物 commodity → 1084

❸ⓐ **nature and character**

性 NATURE → 0357

気 temperament → 3960

質 QUALITY → 3483

品 grade of excellence → 2795

柄 CHARACTER → 1111

格 (good) character → 1161

ⓑ **flavor and elegance**

趣 FLAVOR → 4111

味 TASTE → 0325

風 elegance → 3730

品 refinement → 2795

❹ **kinds and types**

型 TYPE → 3266

類 KIND → 2275

色 kind → 2522

般 SORT → 1670

属 genus → 3901

品 category → 2795

種 VARIETY → 1560

様 variety → 1332

奎

2796

2-3-6

▶**ANDROMEDA**

ケイ キ ㊔ ふみ

Ⓒ 奎 kuí

37	Names	U594E
大	S9-3-6	F3257

COMPOUNDS

❶ [original meaning, now obsolete] **ANDROMEDA**; zodiac sign symbolizing literature

SYNONYMS

❶ **constellation**

奎 ANDROMEDA → 2796

彗 COMET → 3439

昴 PLEIADES → 3091

奔

2797

2-3-6

▶**RUSH**

ホン

37	Nonstandard	U5954
大	S9-3-6	F0000

traditional form → see 奔 at 2758

客

2798

2-3-6

▶**VISITOR**
▶**CUSTOMER**

キャク カク

Ⓒ 客 kè

40	Jōyō-3	U5BA2
宀	S9-3-6	F0405

丶 丿 宀 宀 夕 安 客 客 客
1 2 3 4 5 6 7 8 9

COMPOUNDS

❶ⓐ [original meaning] **VISITOR, caller, guest**

ⓑ (someone or something in a visiting capacity) **guest, associate**

a 客人 きゃくじん caller, visitor, company

客室 きゃくしつ guest room, stateroom

客間 きゃくま drawing room

来客 らいきゃく visitor, guest

珍客 ちんきゃく unexpected (but welcome) visitor

b 客員 きゃくいん guest [associate] member

客演 きゃくえん guest appearance

客土 きゃくど earth brought from another place to mix with the soil

❷ [also suffix] (one who pays for a product or service) **CUSTOMER, client; spectator; passenger**

客席 きゃくせき seat (in the theater); passenger seat

客船 きゃくせん passenger boat

客商売 きゃくしょうばい hotel, restaurant or entertainment business

乗客 じょうきゃく passenger, fare

観客 かんきゃく audience, spectators

観光客 かんこうきゃく sightseer, tourist, visitor

❸ **object**

客観 きゃっかん object; objective

客観的な きゃっかんてきな objective

客体 きゃくたい(=かくたい) object

主客 しゅかく host and guest; principal and auxiliary

❹ **skilled person, -er, -ian**

剣客 けんきゃく swordsman, fencer

俠客 きょうかく chivalrous person, self-styled humanitarian

刺客 しかく assassin

❺ traveler; travel

客死 かくし dying abroad

❻ last (year)

客年 かくねん last year

❼ counter for utensils, tableware, etc. used for receiving guests

吸い物椀五客 すいものわんごきゃく five soup bowls

INDEPENDENT

【きゃく 客】 **VISITOR, caller, guest; customer, client; spectator, passenger; traveler**

お客さん おきゃくさん visitor, caller, guest; customer, client; spectator; passenger; outsider

不帰の客 ふきのきゃく traveler on one's last journey, deceased person

SYNONYMS

❶ **visitor**

客 VISITOR → 2798

賓 GUEST → 2982

❹ **workers and professionals**

家 professional → 2827

婦 woman worker → 0565

嬢 (unmarried) female worker → 0936

夫 MAN LABORER → 4271

匠 CRAFTSMAN → 3711

工 workman → 4190

客 skilled person → 2798

士 PROFESSION SUFFIX → 4213

師 profession suffix → 1680

者 person who → 3980

人 person of certain category → 4175

員 MEMBER (of a staff) → 2822

屋 colloquial occupation suffix → 3842

手 OCCUPATION SUFFIX → 4267

宣

2799

2-3-6

▶**PROCLAIM**

セン　のたま(う)▲　のたま(わく)▲ ㊔ のぶ　のり　よし　わたる

Ⓒ 宣 xuān

40 宀	Jōyō-6	U5BA3
	S9-3-6	F1005

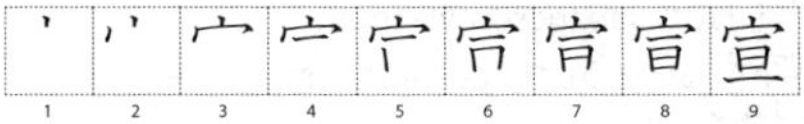

COMPOUNDS

❶ⓐ (make widely known) **PROCLAIM, declare, announce, publicize**

ⓑ (declare in public) **PROCLAIM, pronounce, declare**

a 宣伝 せんでん publicity, propaganda; advertisement

宣教 せんきょう missionary work

b 宣言 せんげん declaration, proclamation

宣戦 せんせん proclamation [declaration] of war

宣布 せんぷ proclamation, promulgation

宣告 せんこく sentence, verdict, pronouncement

宣誓 せんせい oath, swearing, vowing

❷ imperial proclamation, imperial edict

宣下 せんげ imperial proclamation

院宣 いんせん imperial command [decree]

INDEPENDENT

【せんする 宣する】 **PROCLAIM**, announce

KUN

【のたまう 宣う】 *literary* [honorific] say, be pleased to say

【のたまわく 宣わく】 [formerly 曰わく] *literary* [honorific] say that…

子宣わく しのたまわく Confucius says…

SYNONYMS

❶ **inform and communicate**

報 INFORM → 2133

通 COMMUNICATE → 3855

告 NOTIFY → 3062

届ける give notice → 3820

達 issue a notice → 3893

知 let know → 1446

申 REPORT → 4319

稟 REPORT TO → 2649

宣 PROCLAIM → 2799

❷ **imperial decree**

勅 IMPERIAL DECREE → 1841

詔 IMPERIAL EDICT → 1900

宣 imperial proclamation → 2799

USAGE

【のたまわく】

宣わく

[formerly 曰わく] *literary* [honorific] say that…

曰わく

[now also 宣わく] same as 宣わく

HOMOPHONES

のたまわく 曰 SAY THAT → 3757

NOTE

★ do not confuse with 宜 RIGHT → 2763

穿

2800

2-3-6

▶**DRILL**
▶**PUT ON**

セン　は(く)　うが(つ)　ほじく(る)　ほじ(る)

Ⓝ 穿 Ⓒ 穿 chuān

116	Names	U7A7F
穴	S9-5-4	F2179

COMPOUNDS

● [original meaning] **DRILL, bore, pierce**

穿孔 せんこう perforation, punching; rupture
穿鑿する せんさくする scrutinize, dig into
穿刺 せんし puncture, stab
穿通 せんつう penetration
穿山甲 せんざんこう pangolin

KUN

【はく 穿く】**PUT ON (trousers or socks), wear (a skirt)**

下穿き したばき undershorts, underpants
スカートを穿く すかーとをはく put on a skirt

【うがつ 穿つ】

① **DRILL, bore, pierce**

雨垂れ石を穿つ あまだれいしをうがつ Slow but steady wins the race
孔を穿つ こうをうがつ pierce a hole

② **PUT ON**, wear

③ be true to (nature), hit (the mark)

穿ちすぎた うがちすぎた farfetched

【ほじくる 穿る】

ⓐ dig, peck at, pick (as one's nose)
ⓑ pry into, dredge up

a 穿り出す ほじくりだす pick [dig] something out; pry into, expose
穿り返す ほじくりかえす dig up, expose, disclose

【ほじる 穿る】**dig, peck at, pick (as one's nose)**

掻っ穿じる かっぽじる dig up, peck at

SYNONYMS

● **dig**

掘 DIG → 0601
鑿 EXCAVATE → 3640
削 excavate → 1837
穿 DRILL → 2800

【はく】

○ **wear and put on**

着 PUT ON → 4110
装 DRESS → 3327
帯 WEAR (esp. at the belt) → 3191
穿く PUT ON → 2800
纏 put on → 1814
履く put on footwear → 3933
被る put on headgear → 1495

HOMOPHONES

はく 履 FULFILL → 3933

NOTE

➡ see USAGE note at 履 3933

窃

2801

2-3-6

▶**STEAL**

セツ

Ⓝ 竊 Ⓒ 窃 qiè

116	Jōyō	U7A83
穴	S9-5-4	F2797

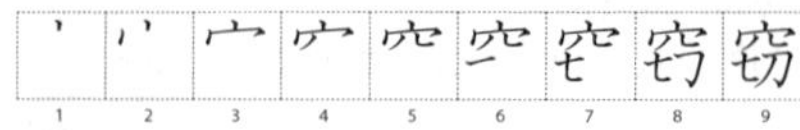

COMPOUNDS

ⓐ **STEAL, pilfer**
ⓑ [rare] by **STEAL**th, secretly

a 窃盗 せっとう theft, larceny
窃取 せっしゅ theft, larceny
剽×窃する ひょうせつする plagiarize
b 窃用する せつようする [rare] use secretly, embezzle

SYNONYMS

ⓐ **steal and rob**

盗 STEAL → 3309
窃 STEAL → 2801
取 TAKE → 1613
奪 ROB → 2956
略 plunder → 1501
掠 PLUNDER → 0605
鹵 PLUNDER → 2634

室

2802

2-3-6

▶**ROOM**

シツ　むろ　㊔ むろや

Ⓒ 室 shì

40	Jōyō-2	U5BA4
宀	S9-3-6	F0360

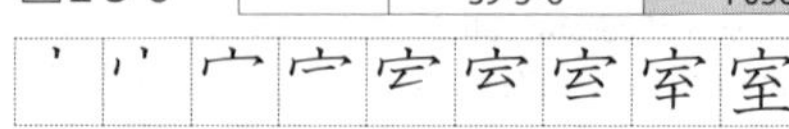

COMPOUNDS

❶ⓐ [also suffix] [original meaning] **ROOM, chamber, compartment**
ⓑ **cave, house**

a 室内 しつない indoors
教室 きょうしつ classroom, class
個室 こしつ private room, single room
寝室 しんしつ bedroom
和室 わしつ Japanese style room
一等室 いっとうしつ first-class compartment
更衣室 こういしつ changing room
b 氷室 ひょうしつ icehouse
温室 おんしつ greenhouse

❷ kinsmen, relatives, family
皇室 こうしつ Imperial Family
❸ wife, esp. of persons of rank or noblemen
正室 せいしつ legal wife
後室 こうしつ widow

INDEPENDENT

【しつ 室】**ROOM**; wife (esp. of high-ranking persons)
室を出る しつをでる leave the room

KUN

【むろ 室】**cellar**
室咲き むろざき blooming under glass

SYNONYMS

❶ⓐ **rooms**
室 ROOM → 2802
間 room → 4122
房 CHAMBER → 2445
斎 study → 2622
堂 HALL → 3202
❸ **wives of rulers**
后 EMPRESS → 3701
妃 PRINCESS → 0238
室 wife (esp. of persons of rank) → 2802
❸ **wives**
妻 WIFE → 3166
奥 wife → 3503
内 wife → 4277
室 wife (esp. of persons of rank) → 2802
嫡 legitimate wife → 0839
婦 married woman → 0565
嫁 BRIDE → 0780
寡 widow → 2957

宥

2803
2-3-6

▶**PARDON**
ユウ ウ なだ(める) ㊔ ゆたか ひろ いく すけ
Ⓒ 宥 yòu

40	Names	U5BA5
宀	S9-3-6	F2883

COMPOUNDS

● **PARDON, excuse, forgive**
宥免する ゆうめんする pardon (a crime), excuse
宥和する ゆうわする forgive and make peace

KUN

【なだめる 宥める】**soothe, calm (someone) down**
泣く子を宥める なくこをなだめる soothe a crying child

SYNONYMS

● **forgive**
赦 AMNESTY → 1870
免 EXEMPT → 2565
許す forgive → 1862
恕 FORGIVE WITH COMPASSION → 3282
宥 PARDON → 2803

突

2804
2-3-6

▶**DASH**
▶**THRUST**
トツ つ(く)

116	Names	UFA55
穴	S9-5-4	F0000

traditional form → see 突 at 2772

単

2805
2-3-6

▶**SINGLE**
タン
Ⓝ 單 Ⓒ 单 dān shàn chán

42△	Jōyō-4	U5358
⺍	S9-3-6	F0520

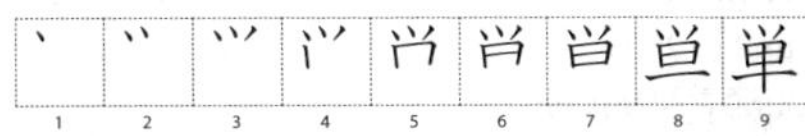

COMPOUNDS

❶ⓐ [also prefix] **SINGLE, one, lone, uni-, mono-**
ⓑ **SINGLE**s (as in tennis)
a 単一な たんいつな single, simple, sole, individual
単車 たんしゃ motorcycle, motorbike
単独の たんどくの single, independent, sole, lone
単色 たんしょく single color, monochrome
単数 たんすう *gram* singular number
単眼 たんがん one eye, ocellus
単弁 たんべん univalve
単細胞 たんさいぼう single cell, one cell
単糖類 たんとうるい monosaccharide
b 単勝式 たんしょうしき winning system (as in horse racing)
❷ **simple, uncomplicated, plain**
単純な たんじゅんな simple, uncomplicated, plain
単利 たんり simple interest
単調な たんちょうな monotonous, dull
簡単な かんたんな simple, easy, light
❸ⓐ **unit**
ⓑ term for designating size of dry cells
a 単位 たんい unit
単価 たんか unit cost, unit price
単語 たんご word
単元 たんげん unit
b 単一の電池 たんいちのでんち D size battery
❹ slip of paper, card
伝単 でんたん leaflet, handbill (in China)

INDEPENDENT

【たん 単】**SINGLE**s (as in tennis); abbrev. of 単勝式 たんしょうしき: winning system (as in horse racing)
【たんに 単に】**merely, simply**

【たんなる 単なる】**mere, simple, sheer**

SYNONYMS

❶ⓐ one

一 ONE → 4148
壱 ONE (in legal documents) → 2723
片- ONE OF TWO → 4272
隻 ONE OF A PAIR → 3426
単 SINGLE → 2805
個 INDIVIDUAL → 0132

❷ plain and simple

素 PLAIN → 3108
朴 SIMPLE (unadorned) → 1013
単 simple (uncomplicated) → 2805

❸ⓐ element

素 ELEMENT → 3108
元 element → 2428
単 unit → 2805

COMPOUND FORMATION

【単車 たんしゃ】

単車 'motorcycle, motorbike' is a vehicle (車) for a single (単 ❶ⓐ) rider.

栄

2-3-6

incorrect classification
➡ see 2-5-4: ⺍ at 3183

炭

2806

2-3-6

▶**COAL**
▶**CHARCOAL**
タン すみ

Ⓝ 炭 Ⓒ 炭 tàn

86	Jōyō-3	U70AD
火	S9-4-5	F1344

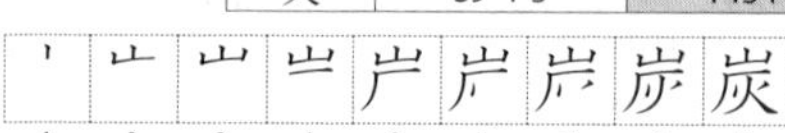

COMPOUNDS

❶ⓐ [also suffix] [original meaning] **COAL**
ⓑ abbrev. of 炭鉱 たんこう: **COAL mine**

a 炭抗 たんこう coal mine, coal pit
炭鉱 たんこう coal mine
石炭 せきたん coal
無煙炭 むえんたん anthracite, smokeless coal
b 炭労 たんろう Japan Coal Miners' Union

❷ CHARCOAL

木炭 もくたん charcoal
薪炭 しんたん firewood and charcoal
塗炭 とたん misery, distress

❸ carbon

炭素 たんそ carbon
炭水化物 たんすいかぶつ carbohydrates
炭酸 たんさん carbonic acid; seltzer
炭化 たんか carbonization

KUN

【すみ 炭】**CHARCOAL**

炭火 すみび charcoal fire
炭焼き すみやき charcoal making
消し炭 けしずみ cinders

SYNONYMS

❶ⓐ & ❷ kinds of fuel

炭 COAL, CHARCOAL → 2806
薪 FIREWOOD → 3009
油 OIL → 0400

❷ products of combustion

灰 ASH → 3699
殻 cinders → 1883
炭 CHARCOAL → 2806
煤 SOOT → 1292
煙 SMOKE → 1294

❸ lighter elements

水 hydrogen → 0010
酸 OXYGEN → 1968
窒 NITROGEN → 2853
塩 chlorine → 0774
臭 bromine → 3261
硫 SULFUR → 1519
炭 carbon → 2806

HOMOPHONES

すみ 墨 INDIA INK → 3423

NOTE

➡ see USAGE note at 墨 3423
➡ see COMPOUND FORMATION for 塗炭 とたん → 塗 3523

炭

2807

2-3-6

▶**COAL**
▶**CHARCOAL**
タン すみ

46	Nonstandard	U2F91A
山	S9-3-6	F0000

traditional form → see 炭 at 2806

茶

2808

2-3-6

▶**TEA**
チャ サ

Ⓒ 茶 chá

140	Jōyō-2	U8336
艹	S9-3-6	F0571

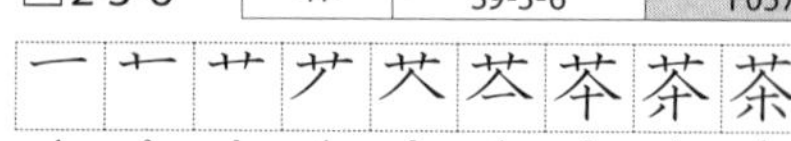

COMPOUNDS

❶ⓐ TEA (the beverage), **tea leaves**
ⓑ [original meaning] **TEA plant, tea shrub [bush]**
ⓒ TEA ceremony

a 茶菓 さか(=ちゃか) tea and cakes, refreshments
茶話会 さわかい tea party

茶碗 ちゃわん teacup; rice bowl
茶の間 ちゃのま living room
茶の湯 ちゃのゆ tea ceremony
新茶 しんちゃ new season's tea
紅茶 こうちゃ black tea
番茶 ばんちゃ coarse tea
喫茶店 きっさてん coffee shop, tea house
b 茶園 ちゃえん tea plantation, tea shop
茶摘み ちゃつみ tea-picking
c 茶室 ちゃしつ tea arbor, tea ceremony room
茶道 さどう(=ちゃどう) tea ceremony

❷ **light brown**
茶色 ちゃいろ light brown
焦げ茶 こげちゃ dark brown

❸ comicality, joke
茶番劇 ちゃばんげき burlesque, low comedy

❹ **used phonetically for *cha***
無茶な むちゃな absurd, unreasonable; reckless; excessive; disorderly
無茶苦茶な むちゃくちゃな confused; incoherent; absurd, unreasonable

INDEPENDENT

【ちゃ 茶】**TEA, green tea, tea leaves; tea ceremony; light brown**
お茶 おちゃ tea, green tea; tea ceremony

SYNONYMS

❶ⓐ **drinks**
汁 JUICE, SOUP → 0227
乳 MILK → 1823
酒 ALCOHOLIC DRINK → 0532
茶 TEA → 2808
珈 COFFEE → 1138
醇 UNDILUTED WINE → 2001
酎 SHOCHU → 1852

❷ **brown colors**
褐 BROWN → 1548
茶 light brown → 2808

茸

2809

2-3-6

▶**MUSHROOM**

ジョウ きのこ たけ

Ⓒ 茸 róng

140	Names	U8338
艹	S9-3-6	F2633

COMPOUNDS

❶ **MUSHROOM, fungus**
茸状乳頭 じじょうにゅうとう fungiform papilla

❷ **fuzz, soft hairy growth**
毛茸 もうじょう trichome
鹿茸 ろくじょう pilose antler

❸ polyp
鼻茸 びじょう(=はなたけ) nasal polyp

KUN

【きのこ 茸】**MUSHROOM, fungus**
茸狩り きのこがり mushroom gathering
茸雲 きのこぐも mushroom cloud
毒茸 どくきのこ toadstool, poisonous mushroom

【たけ 茸】
① **MUSHROOM, fungus**
松茸 まつたけ *matsutake* mushroom
椎茸 しいたけ shiitake (mushroom), *Lentinula edodes*
舞茸 まいたけ hen of the woods

② [in compounds] fuzz
耳茸 みみたけ ear polyp

SYNONYMS

❶ &【きのこ】**fungus**
黴 MOLD → 1008
茸 MUSHROOM → 2809
菌 fungus → 2876

荒

2810

2-3-6

▶**WILD**

コウ あら(い) あら- あ(れる) あ(らす) -あ(らし) すさ(む)▲ ㊔ ら あらき

Ⓒ 荒 huāng

140	Jōyō	U8352
艹	S9-3-6	F0966

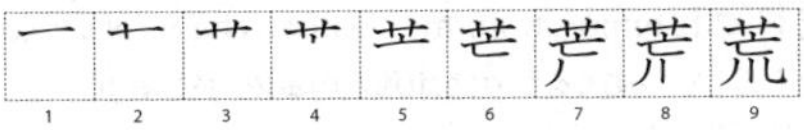

COMPOUNDS

❶ⓐ (in a primitive or uninhabited state) **WILD, barren, desolate, bleak, deserted; devastated, ruined**
ⓑ the **WILD**, frontier land, remote region
a 荒野 こうや wilderness, the wilds, wasteland
荒蕪地 こうぶち wild [waste] land, wilderness
荒廃 こうはい desolation, waste, ruin
荒涼たる こうりょうたる desolate, dreary
荒城 こうじょう ruined castle
b 八荒 はっこう national boundaries

❷ (of natural phenomena) **WILD, stormy, fierce**
荒天 こうてん stormy weather

❸ (unrestrained by reason) **WILD**, absurd, ridiculous
荒唐無稽な こうとうむけいな absurd, nonsensical
破天荒の はてんこうの record-breaking, unprecedented

❹ indulge in pleasure
荒淫 こういん sexual indulgence

❺ famine, crop failure
備荒 びこう provision against famine

KUN

【あらい 荒い】

①ⓐ (of natural phenomena) **WILD, violent, rough**
ⓑ (of behavior) **WILD, rough, rude, savage**
a 荒さ あらさ wildness, roughness; extravagance
荒い波 あらいなみ wild [raging] waves, stormy seas
b 荒荒しい あらあらしい wild, violent; rough, rude, gruff
荒っぽい あらっぽい rough, wild, rude
手荒な てあらな violent, rough
② unrestrained, lavish
金遣いの荒い かねづかいのあらい wasteful of money, extravagant

【あら- 荒-】
① (in a natural state) **WILD, barren, desolate**
荒野(=曠野) あらの(=あれの) wilderness, deserted land
②ⓐ (of natural phenomena) **WILD, violent, rough**
ⓑ [prefix] (of behavior) **WILD, rough, rude, savage**
a 荒海 あらうみ rough sea, stormy sea
b 荒武者 あらむしゃ daredevil, rowdy
③ [also 粗-] (not elaborate) coarse, rough, crude, gross
荒削りの あらけずりの roughhewn; unrefined
④ unrestrained, extravagant
荒稼ぎ あらかせぎ making easy money; robbery

【あれる 荒れる】 (of natural phenomena) **be WILD, become rough, rage;** (of people) **run wild, rage, go berserk; run waste, be devastated;** (of skin) **become rough, get chapped**
荒れ あれ tempest, stormy weather; chaps (of skin)
荒れ狂う あれくるう get stormy, rage; get angry
荒れ地 あれち wilderness
荒れた手 あれたて rough [chapped] hands

【あらす 荒らす】 **devastate, lay waste, damage; break into**
荒らし回る あらしまわる rampage; break into (houses here and there)
踏み荒らす ふみあらす trample down, devastate

【-あらし -荒らし】 [suffix]
ⓐ **robbery, burglary; intrusion**
ⓑ **robber, burglar; intruder**
a アパート荒らし あぱーとあらし apartment house robbery [robber]

【すさむ 荒む】 grow **WILD**, roughen; come to live dissolutely, be degenerated
荒んだ心 すさんだこころ hardened heart, dissolute mind
吹き荒む ふきすさむ blow violently

SYNONYMS

❶ⓐ **barren**
荒 WILD → 2810
寥 DESOLATE → 2960

❷ & 【あらい】 ①ⓐ **extreme in power**
激 VIOLENT → 0955
荒 WILD → 2810
狂 raging → 0318
烈 VEHEMENT → 3286
猛 FIERCE → 0653

❸ **rash**
滅 unreasonable → 0812
妄 RASH → 2509
盲 BLIND → 2547
暴 unrestrained → 3138
荒 WILD → 2810
濫 EXCESSIVE → 0990
乱 excessive → 1611

【あらい】
①ⓑ **violent**
暴 VIOLENT → 3138
猛 FIERCE → 0653
荒い WILD → 2810

USAGE

❶【あらい】
荒い
①ⓐ (of natural phenomena) wild, violent, rough
ⓑ (of behavior) wild, rough, rude, savage
② unrestrained, lavish
粗い
①ⓐ (not fine) coarse, rough, gross
ⓑ (not smooth) coarse, rough, rugged
ⓒ (not elaborate) coarse, rough, crude, gross
② sparse, scattered

❷【あら-】
荒-
① (in a natural state) wild, barren, desolate
②ⓐ (of natural phenomena) wild, violent, rough
ⓑ [prefix] (of behavior) wild, rough, rude, savage
③ [also 粗-] (not elaborate) coarse, rough, crude, gross
④ unrestrained, extravagant
粗-
①ⓐ [also 荒-] (not elaborate) coarse, rough, crude, gross
ⓑ (in the natural state) crude, raw, unrefined, unprocessed
② sparse, scattered

HOMOPHONES

あらい 粗 COARSE → 1683
あら- 粗 COARSE → 1683

NOTE

★ do not confuse with 慌 FLURRIED → 0707

茜 2811 2-3-6

▶**MADDER**

セン あかね ㊔ せい

Ⓒ 茜 qiàn xī

140	Names	U831C
艹	S9-3-6	F2264

KUN

【あかね 茜】

ⓐ **MADDER, *Rubia cordifolia***

ⓑ **MADDER red, crimson**

a 茜の根 あかねのね madder root

b 茜色 あかねいろ madder, crimson

茜差す空 あかねさすそら glowing sky

SYNONYMS

【あかね】

ⓑ **red colors**

赤 RED → 2719

紅 CRIMSON → 1629

緋 SCARLET → 1732

朱 VERMILION → 4344

丹 CINNABAR → 4249

茜 MADDER → 2811

茨 2812 2-3-6

▶**THORN**

シ▲ いばら

Ⓝ 茨 Ⓒ 茨 cí

140	Jōyō	U8328
艹	S9-3-6	F2356

COMPOUNDS

● **THORN**y shrub, brier

茨棘× しきょく thorn

KUN

【いばら 茨】

①ⓐ (plant with thorns) **THORN, brier; wild rose**

ⓑ (sharp process on a plant) **THORN, prickle**

a 茨城県 いばらきけん Ibaraki Prefecture

茨姫 いばらひめ Sleeping Beauty, Briar Rose

b 茨の道 いばらのみち thorny path

茨の冠 いばらのかんむり crown of thorns

② (architectural) cusp

SYNONYMS

● **plants**

菜 VEGETABLE → 2880

植 PLANT → 1247

栽 garden plant → 4087

茨 thorny shrub → 2812

苔 MOSS → 2792

蔓 VINE → 2975

桔 PLANT NAME ELEMENT → 1164

【いばら】

①ⓑ **needle**

針 NEEDLE → 2099

刺 prickle → 1625

茨 THORN → 2812

草 2813 2-3-6

▶**GRASS**

ソウ くさ くさ- -ぐさ

Ⓒ 草 cǎo

140	Jōyō-1	U8349
艹	S9-3-6	F0551

COMPOUNDS

❶ [also suffix] **GRASS, weed**

草原 そうげん grassland, prairie, savannah, pampas, steppe

草木 そうもく trees and plants, vegetation

草食の そうしょくの herbivorous

野草 やそう wild grass

雑草 ざっそう weed

海草 かいそう seaweed

除草剤 じょそうざい herbicide

一年草 いちねんそう annual plant, therophyte

❷ **draft, manuscript, outline**

草稿 そうこう outline, draft

草案 そうあん (rough) draft

起草する きそうする draft (a bill), draw up

❸ hurried, flurried, hasty

草草 そうそう closing words of a letter; hurried, flurried

❹ *sosho,* cursive style of Chinese characters

草書 そうしょ *sosho,* cursive writing

❺ crude, shabby

草堂 そうどう monk's cell; (my) humble abode

❻ beginning

草創 そうそう inauguration, beginning

INDEPENDENT

【そう 草】 *sosho* (→❹); draft, manuscript

【そうする 草する】 draft, write

KUN

【くさ 草】 [also suffix] **GRASS, weed**

草花 くさばな flowering plant

草木 くさき plants, vegetation

草叢 くさむら [also 叢] grass, grassy place

草分け くさわけ pioneer, pathfinder, originator

干し草 ほしくさ hay, dry grass

待宵草 まつよいぐさ evening primrose

【くさ- 草-】 [prefix]

① **amateur, crude**
草野球 くさやきゅう sandlot baseball
② sham, similar
草雲雀 くさひばり grass cricket
【-ぐさ -草】
① [sometimes also -種] **material, stuff**
質草 しちぐさ article for pawning
笑い草 わらいぐさ laughingstock
② [suffix] writing
徒然草 つれづれぐさ Random Thoughts from My Leisure Hours

SPECIAL READINGS
草履 ぞうり Japanese sandals, *zori*
草臥れる▲ くたびれる get tired, be worn out
煙草▲ たばこ tobacco; cigarette

SYNONYMS
❶ **kinds of grasses**
草 GRASS → 2813
荻 AMUR SILVERGRASS → 2844
蒲 CATTAIL → 2932
莱 GOOSEFOOT → 2878
蕨 BRACKEN → 2992
叢 grassy place → 3243
芝 LAWN GRASS → 2705
笹 BAMBOO GRASS → 3301
茅 cogongrass → 2779
萱 THATCH GRASS → 2904
藁 STRAW → 3015
芦 REED → 2743
葦 COMMON REED → 2934
菅 SEDGE → 2874
❷ **manuscript**
稿 MANUSCRIPT → 1574
草 draft → 2813
案 draft → 2824
❹ **styles of Chinese characters**
楷 SQUARE STYLE → 1282
行 *gyosho* → 0246
草 *sosho* → 2813

USAGE
【-ぐさ】
-草
① [sometimes also -種] material, stuff
② [suffix] writing
-種
[usu. -草] material, stuff

HOMOPHONES
-ぐさ 種 VARIETY → 1560
くさむら
叢 CROWD TOGETHER → 3243
草叢 → 2813, 3243

NOTE
➡ see also USAGE note at 早 3042

荘

2814

2-3-6

▶**VILLA**
▶**DIGNIFIED**
ソウ ショウ▲ チャン▲
N 莊 C 庄 zhuāng

140	Jōyō	U8358
艹	S9-3-6	F1423

Stroke order: 1 2 3 4 5 6 7 8 9

COMPOUNDS
❶ⓐ **VILLA, cottage**
ⓑ **suffix after names of VILLAs, inns or apartment houses**
a 別荘 べっそう villa, country cottage
山荘 さんそう mountain villa
b 山水荘 さんすいそう The Sansui Inn
❷ⓐ [sometimes also 庄 しょう 3788] manor (in feudal Japan), **VILL**Age
ⓑ used in the formation of the names of former feudal **VILL**Ages (farm villages that were formerly manors) → see also 庄 3788 ❶
a 荘園 しょうえん manor
荘司 しょうじ administrator of a manor
b 五家荘 ごかのしょう Gokanosho (place name)
❸ **DIGNIFIED, solemn, grave, sublime**
荘厳な そうごんな solemn, sublime
荘重な そうちょうな solemn, grave, impressive
❹ Zhuangzi (contemporary of Mencius)
老荘 ろうそう Laozi and Zhuangzi
❺ adorn
荘厳する しょうごんする adorn (a Buddhist statue)
❻ⓐ mahjong
ⓑ counter for mahjong games
a 連荘 れんちゃん extended game
b 一荘 いーちゃん a game of mahjong

SYNONYMS
❶ **mansions**
邸 STATELY RESIDENCE → 1451
館 stately mansion → 2196
荘 VILLA → 2814
❷ **feudal territorial divisions**
藩 FEUDAL DOMAIN → 3022
国 province (in former Japan) → 3831
領 fief → 1567
封 daimiate → 1639
荘 manor (in feudal Japan) → 2814
❸ **dignified**
荘 DIGNIFIED → 2814
威 dignified → 4394

儼 SOLEMN → 0204
厳 solemn → 4079
粛 solemnly → 4400

栄

2815

▀2-3-6

▶**FLOURISH**
▶**GLORY**

エイ さか(える) は(え) -ば(え) は(える) え
㊔ ひで しげ しげる よし

75	Nonstandard	U8363
木	S9-4-5	F0000

traditional form → see 榮 at 3183

茨

2816

▀2-3-6

▶**THORN**

シ いばら

140	Nonstandard	U8328
艹	S9-3-6	F0000

traditional form → see 茨 at 2812

革

▀2-3-6

incorrect classification
➡ see ▀2-4-5: 廿 at 3099

巷巷

▀2-3-6

incorrect classification
➡ see ▀2-4-5: 㐀 at 3097

美

2817

▀2-3-6

▶**BEAUTIFUL**

ビ ミ▲ うつく(しい) ㊔ よし はる

Ⓒ 美 měi

123	Jōyō-3	U7F8E
羊	S9-6-3	F0140

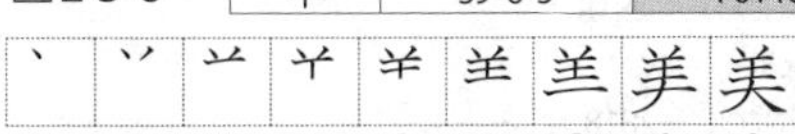

COMPOUNDS

❶ⓐ [sometimes also 媚 び 0687] [original meaning] **BEAUTIFUL, pretty, lovely**
ⓑ [also suffix] beauty

a 美人 びじん beautiful woman
美少年 びしょうねん handsome youth
美女 びじょ beautiful woman [girl]
美容院 びよういん beauty shop [parlor]
美術 びじゅつ art, fine arts
美術館 びじゅつかん art museum [gallery]
美観 びかん fine view, beautiful sight
美化 びか beautification
優美 ゆうび grace, elegance
明美な めいびな picturesque, beautiful

b 肉体美 にくたいび physical beauty

❷ abbrev. of 美術 びじゅつ: art
美大 びだい school of fine arts

❸ (very satisfactory) **BEAUTIFUL, good, superior**
美風 びふう beautiful [laudable] custom
美点 びてん point of beauty, good point
美味 びみ good flavor, delicacy
美名 びめい good name, high reputation
美徳 びとく virtue, good deed

❹ **regard as BEAUTIFUL, praise, extol**
賛美する さんびする praise, admire
嘆美する たんびする admire, adore, extol

❺ used phonetically for *mi*
美事(=見事)な みごとな splendid, admirable, beautiful

INDEPENDENT

【び 美】**beauty, grace, charm**
精神の美 せいしんのび moral beauty, mental charm

KUN

【うつくしい 美しい】**BEAUTIFUL, pretty, lovely; fine, splendid; noble-minded**
美しさ うつくしさ beauty, grace, charm

SPECIAL READINGS

美味しい▲ おいしい tasty, good; nice

SYNONYMS

❶ⓐ **beautiful**
美 BEAUTIFUL → 2817
彪 MAGNIFICENT → 4115
綺 BEAUTIFUL → 1734
娃 BEAUTIFUL → 0419
佳 FINE → 0096
瑶 EXQUISITE → 1301
麗 OF GRACEFUL BEAUTY → 2672
艶 CHARMING → 2403
妙 of marvelous beauty → 0280
華 MAGNIFICENT → 2841
絢 GORGEOUS → 1705
斐 florid → 3449

❸ **good**
良 GOOD → 4373
善 GOOD → 2921
好 FAVORABLE → 0240
順 favorable → 0018
佳 FINE → 0096
美 BEAUTIFUL → 2817

❹ **praise**
賛 PRAISE → 3484
頌 EULOGIZE → 1319
謳 EXTOL → 2061
讃 PRAISE → 2093
美 regard as beautiful → 2817
褒 COMMEND → 2662
嘉 commend (esp. an inferior) → 2953
彰 PROCLAIM MERITS → 2337

称 acclaim →1491
賞 express admiration →3237
揚 EXALT →0722

NOTE

➡ see COMPOUND FORMATION for 見事(=美事) みごと →事 4384

首

▶HEAD
▶NECK
▶LEADER

シュ くび

2818

2-3-6

Ⓒ 首 shǒu

185	Jōyō-2	U9996
首	S9-9-0	F0281

丶 丷 䒑 䒑 产 肖 首 首 首
1 2 3 4 5 6 7 8 9

RADICAL

kubi 'neck' (馘× 馗×), used in characters related to the head or neck

COMPOUNDS

❶ⓐ [original meaning] **HEAD**
ⓑ (forepart of a vessel) **HEAD**

a 首肯する しゅこうする assent, nod one's assent, consent
首級 しゅきゅう decapitated head
斬首 ざんしゅ decapitation
b 機首 きしゅ nose (of an airplane)
艦首 かんしゅ bow (of a war vessel)

❷ **NECK**
絞首刑 こうしゅけい death [execution] by hanging

❸ (person occupying a head position) **LEADER, head, chief**
首長 しゅちょう leader, chief, head
首脳 しゅのう head, leader
首相 しゅしょう prime minister
首謀者 しゅぼうしゃ ringleader, mastermind
党首 とうしゅ party chief [leader]
元首 げんしゅ ruler, sovereign

❹ⓐ (occupying a head position) **leading, top, first**
ⓑ (most important) **leading, main, principal**

ab 首席 しゅせき top seat [place]; chief, head
b 首都 しゅと capital (city)
首位 しゅい first place, leading position
首班 しゅはん head (of state or of a cabinet), prime minister

❺ beginning
首尾 しゅび beginning and end; result, issue
首章 しゅしょう beginning of a book
部首 ぶしゅ radical (of Chinese characters)

❻ⓐ poem
ⓑ counter for poems

a 落首 らくしゅ lampoon, satirical verse
b 和歌二首 わかにしゅ two tanka poems
百人一首 ひゃくにんいっしゅ One Hundred Poems by One Hundred Poets; (playing) cards of one hundred famous poems

❼ **confess**
自首 じしゅ self-surrender

KUN

【くび 首】

① [formerly also 頸]
ⓐ **NECK**
ⓑ **narrow part, NECK (of a bottle)**

a 首飾り くびかざり necklace
b 手首 てくび wrist
バイオリンの首 ばいおりんのくび neck of a violin

② **HEAD**
首を傾げる くびをかしげる put one's head on one side

③ firing, discharge
首切り くびきり firing, dismissal; decapitation
首になる くびになる be fired, be dismissed

SYNONYMS

❶ⓐ **head**
頭 HEAD →2019
首 HEAD →2818
脳 BRAIN →1227
ⓑ **front**
前 front →2819
面 FACE →2590
首 HEAD →2818

❷ **neck**
首 NECK →2818
頸 NECK →2035
項 nape →0692

❸ **leaders**
主 MASTER →2437
王 KING →4247
長 CHIEF →3163
頭 HEAD →2019
首 LEADER →2818
領 leader →1567
魁 LEADER →4125

❹ⓐ **main**
主 MAIN →2437
正 chief →4296
本 head →4314
親- PARENT →2264
首 leading →2818

USAGE

【くび】

首

① [formerly also 頸]

ⓐ neck

ⓑ narrow part, neck (of a bottle)

② head

③ firing, discharge

頸

[now usu. 首]

ⓐ [original meaning] neck

ⓑ narrow part, neck (of a bottle)

HOMOPHONES

くび 頸 NECK →2035

NOTE

➡ see COMPOUND FORMATION for 首班 しゅはん →班 1182

前

2819

2-3-6

▶**BEFORE**

ゼン まえ -まえ ㊔ さき すすむ

Ⓝ 前 Ⓒ 前 qián

18	Jōyō-2	U524D
刂	S9-2-7	F0031

Stroke order: 1 丶 2 丷 3 䒑 4 5 6 7 8 9 前

COMPOUNDS

❶ [also prefix] (in front) **BEFORE, ahead, front, fore**

前後 ぜんご before and after; order, sequence

前方 ぜんぽう front

前進 ぜんしん advance, going ahead

前面 ぜんめん front, frontage, facade

前線 ぜんせん front line, fighting front; *meteorology* front

前途 ぜんと one's future, prospects; distance yet to cover

前車輪 ぜんしゃりん front wheel

❷ⓐ [also suffix] (preceding in time) **BEFORE, ago, previous, past**

ⓑ [also prefix] (immediately preceding in order of time) **previous, former, ex-, onetime**

a 前日 ぜんじつ the day before

前年 ぜんねん the year before

前年度 ぜんねんど preceding (fiscal) year

午前 ごぜん morning, forenoon

以前 いぜん before, ago, since

寸前に すんぜんに immediately before

三年前 さんねんぜん three years ago

b 前夫 ぜんぷ former husband, ex-husband

前大統領 ぜんだいとうりょう former president

前住所 ぜんじゅうしょ one's former address

❸ⓐ (preceding in order) **former, preceding, first (of two)**

ⓑ (in an earlier part of a text) **preceding, above**

a 前者 ぜんしゃ the former

前半 ぜんはん(=ぜんぱん) first half

前編 ぜんぺん first volume; first part

前場 ぜんば morning session (of stock market)

前期 ぜんき first term, first half year; first semester

前略 ぜんりゃく Dispensing with the preliminaries... (salutation)

b 前回 ぜんかい last time

前記の ぜんきの the above-mentioned

前条 ぜんじょう preceding article

❹ in the presence of (a superior)

御前 ごぜん Your Excellency; the (Imperial) presence

面前で めんぜんで before, in the presence of

目前で もくぜんで in the face of, in the presence of

神前に誓う しんぜんにちかう pledge before God

INDEPENDENT

【ぜん 前】 in the past, previously; abbrev. of 紀元前 きげんぜん: B.C. (before Christ); abbrev. of 午前 ごぜん: morning, forenoon

前三百九年 ぜんさんびゃくきゅうねん 309 B.C.

前九時 ぜんくじ 9 a.m.

KUN

【まえ 前】

①ⓐ **front, fore part**

ⓑ presence

a 前に まえに ahead, before

前足 まえあし forelegs

前置き まえおき introductory remark

前書き まえがき preface, foreword

b 人前で ひとまえで before others

②ⓐ **BEFORE, ago, since**

ⓑ **BEFOREhand, in advance**

a 前の まえの former, previous, old

前に まえに previously, formerly

b 前以て まえもって in advance

前払い まえばらい advance payment

前借り まえがり advance payment

前売り まえうり advance sale

前売り券 まえうりけん advance ticket

前触れ まえぶれ previous notice, sign

③ private parts

前を隠す まえをかくす cover one's private parts

④ **unclassified compounds**

名前 なまえ name, given name

当たり前 あたりまえ proper, right, just; of course

【-まえ -前】 [also suffix]

①ⓐ **ago, BEFORE, since**

ⓑ **(10 minutes) to (seven), BEFORE (seven)**
a 二日前 ふつかまえ two days ago
b 十時五分前 じゅうじごふんまえ five to ten
② **in front of, BEFORE**
駅前の えきまえの in front of the station
③ **function word for forming pronouns**
お前 おまえ [belittling] you; darling, my child
手前 てまえ [humble] I; [belittling] you
④ **portion, helping, serving**
分け前 わけまえ share, portion
一人前 いちにんまえ one helping, one portion
⑤ **worthy of, becoming of**
一人前 いちにんまえ full-fledged man
男前 おとこまえ man's looks
腕前 うでまえ skill, ability, capacity
気前 きまえ generosity
⑥ honorific title after names of court ladies
玉藻の前 たまものまえ Lady Tamamo

SYNONYMS
❶ **in front**
前 BEFORE → 2819
先 AHEAD → 3046
❷ⓐ **before**
前 BEFORE → 2819
先 AHEAD → 3046
予 IN ADVANCE → 2477
ⓑ **former**
旧 FORMER → 0014
元 former → 2428
故 OLD (earlier time) → 1466
前 previous → 2819
嘗て previously → 3230
曽 previously → 2632
先 former → 3046
既 ALREADY → 1498
【まえ】
①ⓐ **front**
前 front → 2819
面 FACE → 2590
首 HEAD → 2818

COMPOUND FORMATION
❶【男前 おとこまえ】
男前 'man's looks' is looks becoming of (-前 ❺) a man (男).
❷【腕前 うでまえ】
腕前 'skill, etc.' is something worthy of (-前 ❺) one's ability (腕).
❸【気前 きまえ】
気前 'generosity' is something worthy of (-前 ❺) one's feelings (気).

NOTE
➡ see COMPOUND FORMATION for 当たり前 あたりまえ → 当 2701

前 **2820** 2-3-6

▶**BEFORE**
ゼン まえ -まえ ㊔ さき すすむ

18	Nonstandard	U524D
刂	S9-2-7	F0000

traditional form → see 前 at 2819

韋 **2821** 2-3-6

▶***NAMESHIGAWA***

178	Radical	U97CB
韋	S9-9-0	F0000

RADICAL
nameshigawa 'leather' (鞣×), used in characters related to tanned leather products
Variant: 韋 ***nameshigawa*** (韓)

食 飠 2-3-6
incorrect classification
➡ see 2-2-7: 𠆢 at 2578

員 **2822** 2-3-7

▶**MEMBER**
イン ㊔ かず
Ⓒ 员 yuán yún yùn

30	Jōyō-3	U54E1
口	S10-3-7	F0165

1	2	3	4	5	6	7	8	9	10
丶	冖	口	尸	吕	員	員	員	員	員

COMPOUNDS
❶ [also suffix]
ⓐ **MEMBER of a staff [profession], personnel, person in charge**
ⓑ **MEMBER of an organization**
a 社員 しゃいん staff member, employee
職員 しょくいん staff, employee, personnel
全員 ぜんいん all members, entire staff
係員 かかりいん clerk in charge
検査員 けんさいん inspector
会社員 かいしゃいん company employee, office worker
公務員 こうむいん public service personnel, government worker
事務員 じむいん clerk, clerical staff
警備員 けいびいん guard
b 委員 いいん committeeman; delegate
議員 ぎいん member of an assembly, assemblyman
党員 とういん party member
❷ **fixed number, capacity**

員数 いんずう(=いんすう) number, total
定員 ていいん fixed number of regular personnel; capacity
満員 まんいん full to capacity

❸ girth
幅員 ふくいん width [extent] of roads or ships

INDEPENDENT

【いん 員】 **MEMBER** of a staff
員に備わるのみ いんにそなわるのみ be a member of staff but useless as a worker

SYNONYMS

❶ⓐ person in charge
係 PERSON IN CHARGE → 0108
-方 person in charge → 2459
員 MEMBER (of a staff) → 2822

❶ⓐ workers and professionals
家 professional → 2827
婦 woman worker → 0565
嬢 (unmarried) female worker → 0936
夫 MAN LABORER → 4271
匠 CRAFTSMAN → 3711
工 workman → 4190
客 skilled person → 2798
士 PROFESSION SUFFIX → 4213
師 profession suffix → 1680
者 person who → 3980
人 person of certain category → 4175
員 MEMBER (of a staff) → 2822
屋 colloquial occupation suffix → 3842
手 OCCUPATION SUFFIX → 4267

❷ kinds of numbers
数 NUMBER (mathematical unit) → 2245
員 fixed number → 2822
号 NUMBER (numerical designation) → 2675
番 No. → 3416
第 ORDINAL NUMBER PREFIX → 3298
-目 ordinal number suffix → 3777
次 numerical order suffix → 0058
桁 DIGIT → 1165

❸ width
幅 WIDTH → 0694
員 girth → 2822
径 DIAMETER → 0347

套

2823
2-3-7

▶TRITE
トウ ㊔ なが
Ⓒ 套 tào

37	Names	U5957
大	S10-3-7	F2492

COMPOUNDS

❶ TRITE, outdated, conventional
常套手段 じょうとうしゅだん old trick, usual practice
常套句 じょうとうく cliche, hackneyed expression
旧套 きゅうとう conventionalism, old style

❷ covering, wrapping
外套 がいとう overcoat, cloak
手套 しゅとう gloves

SYNONYMS

❶ ordinary
常 NORMAL → 3203
只- ORDINARY → 2677
並 ordinary → 2793
平 common → 4291
普 common → 2919
庸 MEDIOCRE → 3881
凡 COMMONPLACE → 3656
套 TRITE → 2823

案

2824
2-3-7

▶PROPOSAL
アン
Ⓒ 案 àn

75	Jōyō-4	U6848
木	S10-4-6	F0528

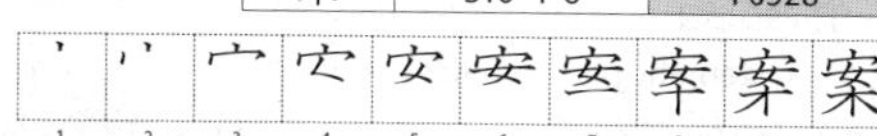

COMPOUNDS

❶ⓐ [also suffix] **PROPOSAL, plan, scheme**
ⓑ draft
a 案件 あんけん matter, case, item
提案 ていあん proposition, proposal, suggestion
法案 ほうあん bill, legislative proposal
議案 ぎあん bill, measure
原案 げんあん original bill [plan]
試案 しあん tentative plan, draft
対案 たいあん counterproposal
立案する りつあんする make a plan, devise, draft
増税案 ぞうぜいあん tax increase proposal
具体案 ぐたいあん concrete proposal
b 案内する あんないする guide, show; inform, notify
草案 そうあん (rough) draft

❷ⓐ think out, devise
ⓑ thought, idea, design
a 案出する あんしゅつする think out, contrive, devise, invent
思案 しあん thought, consideration, reflection
考案 こうあん idea, plan; project
b 懸案 けんあん pending question [problem]
名案 めいあん splendid idea
新案特許 しんあんとっきょ patent on a new device

❸ **official documents, records**

答案 とうあん examination paper; answer

❹ **expectations**

案外 あんがい contrary to one's expectations, unexpectedly

案の定 あんのじょう as feared, sure enough

❺ [formerly 按 0444] according to

案分する あんぶんする divide [distribute] proportionally

❻ [original meaning] desk, table

案下 あんか beneath the desk

INDEPENDENT

【あん 案】**plan, scheme; draft**

案を立てる あんをたてる draft a proposal

案に相違して あんにそういして contrary to one's expectations

【あんじる 案じる】**be anxious, be concerned about; think out, devise**

【あんずる 案ずる】**ponder; worry over**

SYNONYMS

❶ⓐ **plans and planning**

計 PLAN → 1828
画 DRAW UP A PLAN → 3723
案 PROPOSAL → 2824
企 PROJECT → 2513
図 systematic plan → 3809
謀 SCHEME → 2004
策 SCHEME → 3320
略 STRATEGY → 1501
揆 PLOT → 0718

ⓑ **manuscript**

稿 MANUSCRIPT → 1574
草 draft → 2813
案 draft → 2824

❷ⓐ **think and consider**

思 THINK → 3173
惟 MEDITATE → 0582
省 INTROSPECT → 3100
稽 THINK → 1573
考 THINK → 3962
存 hold an opinion → 3702
案 think out → 2824
想 CONCEIVE → 3507
慮 CONSIDER → 4050
勘 take into consideration → 2231
銓 WEIGH → 2161
量 weigh → 3119

USAGE

【あんずる】

案ずる
ponder; worry over

按ずる
investigate, consider

COMPOUND FORMATION

❶【案内 あんない】

案内 consists of 案 ❶ⓑ 'draft' and 内 'inside'. It derives from 文案の内容 ぶんあんのないよう, which literally means the contents of a draft. By extension, 案内する 'guide, etc.' means to know or let know the contents of, that is, to guide, show or inform.

❷【案外 あんがい】

案外 'contrary to one's expectations, etc.' is to be beyond (外) one's thoughts or expectation (案 ❹).

❸【案分 あんぶん】

案分する 'divide [distribute] proportionally', formerly written 按分する, is to divide (分) something in accordance with (案 ❺) or in proportion to needs.

宴

2825

2-3-7

▸**BANQUET**

エン うたげ▲

Ⓒ 宴 yàn

40	Jōyō	U5BB4
宀	S10-3-7	F1684

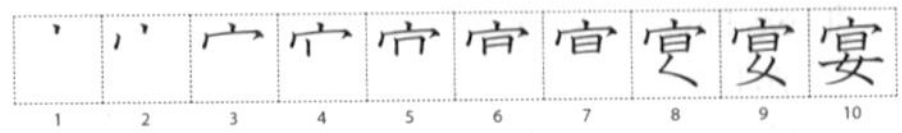

COMPOUNDS

● [also suffix] **BANQUET, feast, dinner party, dinner; entertainment**

宴会 えんかい dinner party, banquet, feast

宴席 えんせき banquet hall, dinner party

招宴 しょうえん invitation to a party; party

披露宴 ひろうえん wedding reception

饗宴 きょうえん banquet, feast, dinner

INDEPENDENT

【えん 宴】BANQUET, feast, dinner party

宴を張る えんをはる hold a banquet, give a dinner party

KUN

【うたげ 宴】BANQUET, feast, party, dinner

花見の宴 はなみのうたげ cherry-blossom viewing party

SYNONYMS

● **social gatherings**

宴 BANQUET → 2825
饗 BANQUET → 3616
会 party → 2512

NOTE

★ do not confuse with 晏 LATE → 3103

害

▶HARM
ガイ
Ⓝ 害 Ⓒ 害 hài

2826
2-3-7

40 宀	Jōyō-4	U5BB3
	S10-3-7	F0451

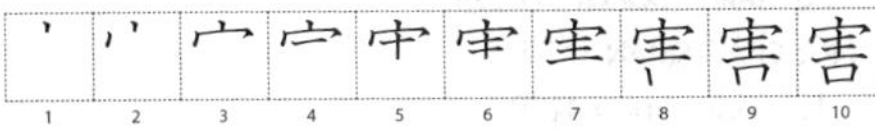

COMPOUNDS

❶ⓐ HARM, evil, ill effect
ⓑ HARM, injure, damage

a 害毒 がいどく harm, evil, evil influence
被害 ひがい damage, harm
弊害 へいがい evil, abuse, vice
有害な ゆうがいな harmful, pernicious, noxious

b 害虫 がいちゅう harmful insect
傷害 しょうがい injury, bodily harm
侵害 しんがい infringement, violation

❷ damage; pollution
公害 こうがい environmental pollution
災害 さいがい calamity, disaster, accident
損害 そんがい damage, harm
冷害 れいがい damage from cold weather
水害 すいがい flood damage

❸ [formerly also 碍 1536] [original meaning] **stand in the way, hinder, obstruct, interfere with**
障害 しょうがい obstacle, hindrance; (physical) disorder
妨害する ぼうがいする disturb, hinder, obstruct, hamper, impede, interfere
阻害する そがいする obstruct, check, impede, hinder

❹ kill
殺害する さつがい(=せつがい)する murder, kill, assassinate
自害 じがい suicide

❺ vital point
要害 ようがい stronghold, strategic position

INDEPENDENT

【がい 害】**HARM, evil, ill effect; damage**
飲酒の害 いんしゅのがい ill effects of drinking
【がいする 害する】**HARM, injure, damage**

SYNONYMS

❶ & ❷ harm and damage
害 HARM, damage → 2826
損 damage → 0801
傷 WOUND → 0179

❸ obstruct and hinder
遮 INTERRUPT → 3916
塞 STOP UP → 2924
阻 OBSTRUCT → 0411
沮 OBSTRUCT → 0399
奄 OBSTRUCT (by covering) → 2757
妨 HINDER → 0279
障 hinder → 0875
碍 STAND IN THE WAY → 1536
害 stand in the way → 2826
梗 STOP UP → 1204

家

▶HOUSE
▶FAMILY
カ ケ いえ や うち▲ ㊔ やか
Ⓒ 家 jiā jia jie

2827
2-3-7

40 宀	Jōyō-2	U5BB6
	S10-3-7	F0028

COMPOUNDS

❶ [original meaning] **HOUSE, home, dwelling**
家屋 かおく house, building
家具 かぐ furniture
人家 じんか dwelling (house), human habitation
民家 みんか private house

❷ⓐ FAMILY, house, household
ⓑ [suffix] **FAMILY, House**

a 家族 かぞく family, household
家庭 かてい home, family, household
家計 かけい household economy, family finances
家内 かない family, household; wife
家事 かじ household affairs, housework
家裁 かさい family court
実家 じっか family in which one was born; one's parents' home
良家 りょうけ good family
一家 いっか family, household; one's family; style (of established reputation)

b 将軍家 しょうぐんけ family to inherit the shogunate
徳川家 とくがわけ the Tokugawas, the House of Tokugawa
宮田家 みやたけ the Miyata family

❸ [also suffix]
ⓐ professional, member of a profession
ⓑ performer of an action or person associated with something

a 作家 さっか writer, novelist, author
画家 がか artist, painter
政治家 せいじか politician
専門家 せんもんか specialist, expert

b 勉強家 べんきょうか diligent student, studious person
財産家 ざいさんか person of wealth
儒家 じゅか Confucian, Confucianist

道家 どうか Taoist scholar

❹ **territory, country**

国家 こっか state, country, nation

邦家 ほうか one's country, the state

KUN

【いえ 家】**HOUSE, home, dwelling; family, household; family name**

家家 いえいえ houses

家を興す いえをおこす found a house; raise the reputation of one's family

家出 いえで running away from home

家柄 いえがら social standing of a family; lineage, descent; good family

家元 いえもと head [master] of a school (of noh drama players)

貧しい家 まずしいいえ poor family

【や 家】

① [also suffix] **HOUSE, home**

家主 やぬし house owner, landlord, landlady

家賃 やちん (house) rent

我が家 わがや one's home [house]

借家 しゃくや house for rent, rented house

一軒家 いっけんや solitary house; private home

② [usu. 屋] suffix after stage **FAMILY** names

林家正蔵 はやしやしょうぞう Shozo Hayashiya (name of a comic story teller)

【うち 家】[also 内]

ⓐ **HOUSE, one's home**

ⓑ **one's FAMILY, household**

a 家を建てる うちをたてる build one's house

b 家の人 うちのひと my husband; one's family

SYNONYMS

❶ **houses**

家 HOUSE → 2827

屋 HOUSE → 3842

軒 house → 1851

戸 HOUSEHOLD → 2429

宅 DWELLING HOUSE → 2698

居 residence → 3822

邸 STATELY RESIDENCE → 1451

住 housing → 0072

庵 HERMITAGE → 3876

❷ **family and relations**

族 FAMILY → 1195

家 FAMILY → 2827

門 family → 1100

氏 clan → 3669

縁 RELATION → 1754

姻 relative by marriage → 0421

親 RELATIVES → 2264

戚 RELATIVES → 4401

曽 GREAT- → 2632

❸ **workers and professionals**

家 professional → 2827

婦 woman worker → 0565

嬢 (unmarried) female worker → 0936

夫 MAN LABORER → 4271

匠 CRAFTSMAN → 3711

工 workman → 4190

客 skilled person → 2798

士 PROFESSION SUFFIX → 4213

師 profession suffix → 1680

者 person who → 3980

人 person of certain category → 4175

員 MEMBER (of a staff) → 2822

屋 colloquial occupation suffix → 3842

手 OCCUPATION SUFFIX → 4267

USAGE

【家 か 者 しゃ】

★家 and 者 both refer to the performer of an action or holder of an occupation. The former often stresses that the action is performed by a professional engaged in that work, as in 作家 さっか 'writer, novelist, author', while the latter more often denotes the performer of the action, whether by profession or not, as in 読者 どくしゃ 'reader, subscriber'. The two are sometimes used interchangeably, as in 翻訳者[家] ほんやくしゃ[か], the latter implying that the person is a professional translator.

HOMOPHONES

や 屋 HOUSE → 3842

うち

内 INSIDE → 4277

中 MIDDLE → 4262

NOTE

➡ see also USAGE notes at 屋 3842 and 内 4277

宮

2828

2-3-7

▶**ROYAL PALACE**
▶**SHINTO SHRINE**

キュウ グウ ク クウ▲ みや

Ⓒ 宮 gōng

40 宀	Jōyō-3	U5BAE
	S10-3-7	F0386

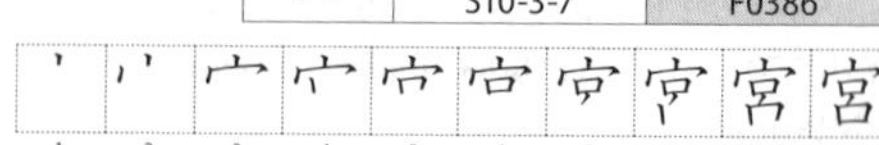

COMPOUNDS

❶ⓐ **ROYAL PALACE, imperial palace, magnificent dwelling**

ⓑ **suffix after names of palaces**

a 宮殿 きゅうでん palace (of a royal person)

王宮 おうきゅう King's palace, royal palace

離宮 りきゅう detached palace, Imperial villa

迷宮 めいきゅう labyrinth, maze; mystery

竜宮 りゅうぐう Palace of the Dragon King
b エリゼ宮 えりぜきゅう Élysée
❷ Imperial Court, court
宮廷 きゅうてい the Court, the Palace
宮中 きゅうちゅう Imperial Court
宮内庁 くないちょう Imperial Household Agency
皇宮警察 こうぐうけいさつ Imperial Guard
❸ⓐ **SHINTO SHRINE, imperial Shinto shrine**
ⓑ suffix after names of **SHINTO SHRINE**s
a 宮司 ぐうじ chief priest of a Shinto shrine
神宮 じんぐう Shinto shrine; Grand Shrine at Ise
遷宮 せんぐう transfer of a shrine
b 外宮 げくう Outer Shrine of Ise
東照宮 とうしょうぐう Toshogu Shrine
❹ (Imperial) prince or princess
中宮 ちゅうぐう Empress or second consort in Heian period
東宮 とうぐう Crown Prince
❺ⓐ sex organ, womb
ⓑ castration as a punishment in ancient China
a 子宮 しきゅう womb, uterus
b 宮刑 きゅうけい castration
❻ section of the zodiac
十二宮 じゅうにきゅう the twelve signs of the zodiac
獅子宮 ししきゅう Leo, the Lion
❼ [rare] first note of the pentatonic scale (→see APPENDIX 8)

INDEPENDENT

【きゅう 宮】[rare] first note of the pentatonic scale

KUN

【みや 宮】
① **SHINTO SHRINE**
宮参り みやまいり shrine visit
宮居 みやい shrine compound; Imperial Palace
② **Imperial Court**
宮仕え みやづかえ court service
③ⓐ member of Imperial family
ⓑ title after names of Imperial princes or princesses
a 宮様 みやさま prince, princess
b 高松の宮 たかまつのみや Prince Takamatsu

SYNONYMS

❶ **palace**
宮 ROYAL PALACE →2828
殿 PALACE →2247
閣 FEUDAL PALACE →4130
❷ **governments**
官 GOVERNMENT →2766
幕 SHOGUNATE →2937
廷 COURT →3795
朝 court →2130
宮 Imperial Court →2828
❸ **places of worship**
堂 temple building →3202
塔 pagoda →0683
寺 BUDDHIST TEMPLE →2687
刹 TEMPLE →1620
社 Shinto shrine →1042
宮 SHINTO SHRINE →2828
院 monastery →0544
教 church →1887

宰

2829
2-3-7

▸PRESIDE
サイ ㊔ つかさ
Ⓒ 宰 zǎi

40 宀	Jōyō	U5BB0
	S10-3-7	F1791

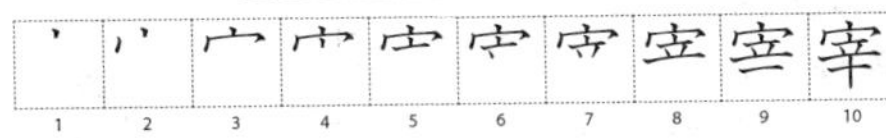

COMPOUNDS

❶ **PRESIDE (over), superintend, supervise, manage**
宰領 さいりょう supervision, management; supervisor, superintendent
主宰する しゅさいする preside (over), superintend, supervise
❷ chief minister
宰相 さいしょう prime minister, chancellor

SYNONYMS

❶ **direct and supervise**
制 CONTROL →1624
理 manage →1220
経 MANAGE →1687
管 EXERCISE CONTROL →3349
轄 EXERCISE JURISDICTION OVER →2056
掌 TAKE CHARGE OF →3215
監 OVERSEE →3535
督 SUPERVISE →3471
司 OFFICIATE →3648
宰 PRESIDE →2829
営 MANAGE →3216
❷ **high officials**
相 MINISTER →1120
宰 chief minister →2829
卿 STATE MINISTER →0769

窄

2830
2-3-7

▸NARROW
サク すぼ(む) すぼ(める) すぼ(まる)
Ⓒ 窄 zhǎi

116 穴	Names	U7A84
	S10-5-5	F3039

COMPOUNDS

ⓐ NARROW, contract
ⓑ [original meaning] NARROW, constricted
ab 狭窄 きょうさく stricture, stenosis

KUN

【すぼむ 窄む】
①ⓐ NARROW, contract
ⓑ shut, close
② lose force, dampen
尻窄み しりすぼみ tapering, weak ending

【すぼめる 窄める】
ⓐ make NARROW, contract
ⓑ shut, shrug, purse

【すぼまる 窄まる】
ⓐ become NARROW, contract
ⓑ shut, close

SYNONYMS

● narrow
狭 NARROW → 0473
窄 NARROW → 2830

宵

▶EARLY EVENING
ショウ よい
Ⓝ 宵 Ⓒ 宵 xiāo

2831
2-3-7

40 宀	Jōyō	U5BB5
	S10-3-7	F2296

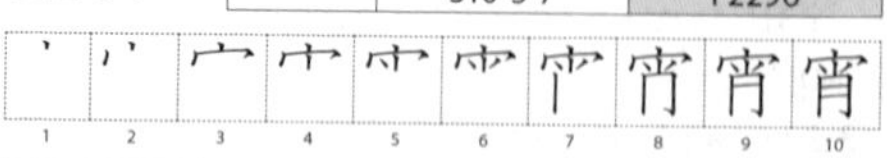

COMPOUNDS

ⓐ [original meaning] **EARLY EVENING, evening, nightfall**
ⓑ night
a 春宵 しゅんしょう spring evening
b 徹宵 てっしょう all night long, throughout the night

KUN

【よい 宵】**EARLY EVENING, early hours of the night; night**
宵の口 よいのくち early evening
宵の明星 よいのみょうじょう evening star, Venus
宵越しの よいごしの kept overnight
今宵 こよい this evening, tonight

SYNONYMS

● evening and night
夜 NIGHT → 2550
晩 EVENING → 1232
夕 EVENING → 4195
宵 EARLY EVENING → 2831
暮 DUSK → 2971

容

▶APPEARANCE
▶CONTAIN
ヨウ い(れる)▲ ㊔ まさ ひろ
Ⓒ 容 róng

2832
2-3-7

40 宀	Jōyō-5	U5BB9
	S10-3-7	F0372

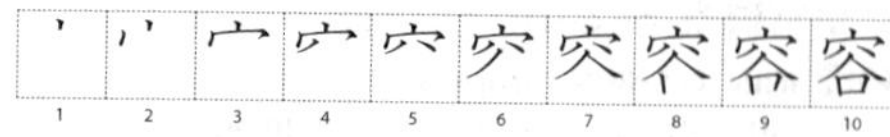

COMPOUNDS

❶ⓐ **APPEARANCE, looks, view, figure, countenance**
ⓑ shape, form, formation
a 容姿 ようし face and figure, appearance
容貌 ようぼう looks, personal appearance
容態(=容体) ようだい one's condition, one's state of health
美容 びよう beauty
威容 いよう dignified [majestic] appearance
変容 へんよう transfiguration, transformation
b 陣容 じんよう battle formation; members of a group

❷ⓐ (have within) **CONTAIN, hold, accommodate**
ⓑ **contents, substance**
a 容器 ようき receptacle, container, vessel
容量 ようりょう capacity, volume
収容する しゅうようする accommodate, receive (guests)
包容する ほうようする encompass, comprehend; imply; tolerate
b 内容 ないよう contents, import, substance

❸ **tolerate, permit, allow**
容赦する ようしゃする pardon, forgive, have mercy on
容疑者 ようぎしゃ suspected person
容共 ようきょう procommunist
容認する ようにんする admit, approve, accept
受容する じゅようする receive, accept
許容する きょようする tolerate, allow, permit

❹ **easy, simple**
容易な よういな easy, simple

INDEPENDENT

【よう 容】**APPEARANCE**, looks; shape, form
容を改む ようをあらたむ change one's appearance

KUN

【いれる 容れる】[usu. 入れる] accept, tolerate, be compatible
相容れない あいいれない incompatible

SPECIAL READINGS

容易い▲ たやすい easy, simple

SYNONYMS

❶ⓐ appearance

容 APPEARANCE → 2832
貌 APPEARANCE → 1958
姿 FIGURE → 3264
相 PHASE → 1120
体 FORM (outer appearance) → 0080
色 COLOR → 2522
風 air → 3730

❷ⓐ contain and include
含 CONTAIN (have as a part) → 2534
容 CONTAIN (have within) → 2832
包 ENCOMPASS → 3684
挟 HOLD BETWEEN → 0450

❸ agree and approve
賛 APPROVE OF → 3484
可 APPROVE → 3687
認 RECOGNIZE → 1948
諾 CONSENT → 1974
承 AGREE TO → 0016
肯 ASSENT → 3072
容 tolerate → 2832

HOMOPHONES

いれる 入 ENTER → 4177

NOTE

➡ see USAGE note at 入 4177

害

2833
2-3-7

▶**HARM**
ガイ

40	Nonstandard	U5BB3
宀	S10-3-7	F0000

traditional form → see 害 at 2826

穿

2834
2-3-7

▶**DRILL**
▶**PUT ON**
セン は(く) うが(つ) ほじく(る) ほじ(る)

116	Nonstandard	U7A7F
穴	S10-5-5	F0000

traditional form → see 穿 at 2800

宵

2835
2-3-7

▶**EARLY EVENING**
ショウ よい

40	Nonstandard	U5BB5
宀	S10-3-7	F0000

traditional form → see 宵 at 2831

党

2-3-7

incorrect classification
➡ see 2-5-5: ⺌ at 3190

挙

2-3-7

incorrect classification
➡ see 2-4-6: ⺌ at 3106

峩

2836
2-3-7

▶**HIGH AND RUGGED**
ガ

46	Nonstandard	U5CE9
山	S10-3-7	F0000

traditional form → see 峨 at 0493

峯

2837
2-3-7

▶**PEAK**
ホウ みね ㊔ お

46	Names	U5CEF
山	S10-3-7	F0000

traditional form → see 峰 at 0494

貢

2838
2-3-7

▶**TRIBUTE**
コウ ク みつ(ぐ)
Ⓒ 贡 gòng

154	Jōyō	U8CA2
貝	S10-7-3	F1707

1	2	3	4	5	6	7	8	9	10
一	丅	工	产	𢀖	青	貢	貢	貢	貢

COMPOUNDS

❶ⓐ [original meaning] **TRIBUTE**
ⓑ offer **TRIBUTE**, pay tribute
a 貢租 こうそ tribute, annual tax
年貢 ねんぐ land tax
b 入貢する にゅうこうする pay tribute
朝貢する ちょうこうする bring tribute

❷ render services to, contribute
貢献する こうけんする contribute to, serve

KUN

【みつぐ 貢ぐ】**support, finance, contribute**
貢ぎ みつぎ tribute
貢ぎ物 みつぎもの tribute

SYNONYMS

❶ⓐ offering
奠 OFFERING → 2641
幣 offering → 3582
貢 TRIBUTE → 2838

❶ⓐ tax
税 TAX → 1525
租 LAND TAX → 1492
貢 TRIBUTE → 2838
賦 levy → 1992

ⓑ offer
供 OFFER (to a person or god) → 0098
献 OFFER (esp. to a superior) → 2240
納 offer (as to a god) → 1652
提 PRESENT → 0720
貢 offer tribute → 2838
奉 DEDICATE → 3167

捧 OFFER RESPECTFULLY → 0594

莫

2839

2-3-7

▶NOT

バク ボ なか(れ)

C 莫 mò

140	Names	U83AB
艹	S10-3-7	F2126

COMPOUNDS

❶ NOT, never, no

莫大な ばくだいな vast, immense, enormous

莫逆 ばくぎゃく(=ばくげき) very close relations ("never opposing")

❷ void, empty

索莫(=索漠)たる さくばくたる dreary, bleak, desolate

落莫たる らくばくたる dreary, desolate, lonesome

KUN

【なかれ 莫れ】[usu. 勿れ] do **NOT**, not, never

SPECIAL READINGS

莫迦(=馬鹿) ばか fool, blockhead; nonsense

SYNONYMS

❶ terms of negation

不 NOT (negation) → 4242

非 IS NOT (contrariety) → 1101

無 WITHOUT (nonexistence) → 2648

没 lacking in → 0305

欠 LACK → 2481

否 OR NOT → 3058

未 NOT YET → 4318

莫 NOT → 2839

勿 DO NOT → 3661

HOMOPHONES

なかれ 勿 DO NOT → 3661

COMPOUND FORMATION

【莫大 ばくだい】

莫大な 'vast, immense, enormous' is as big (大) as no other (莫 ❶).

NOTE

➡ see USAGE note at 勿 3661

荷

2840

2-3-7

▶LOAD

カ に

C 荷 hé hè

140	Jōyō-3	U8377
艹	S10-3-7	F1068

1	2	3	4	5	6	7	8	9	10
一	十	艹	艹	芢	芢	芢	荷	荷	荷

COMPOUNDS

❶ⓐ LOAD, burden; cargo, goods

ⓑ counter for **LOAD**s or burdens

ⓒ *elec* **LOAD**

a 荷重 かじゅう load

出荷する しゅっかする forward, ship, consign

入荷 にゅうか arrival of goods (at a shop), receipt of goods

集荷 しゅうか collection of cargo, cargo booking

在荷 ざいか stock, goods on hand

b 一荷 いっか one load

c 電荷 でんか electric charge

装荷 そうか loading

❷ carry on shoulder, bear a burden

荷担(=加担) かたん assistance, support, participation

負荷 ふか load, burden

❸ [original meaning, now archaic] lotus, water lily

荷葉 かよう lotus leaves

KUN

【に 荷】**LOAD, burden; cargo, goods;** (figuratively) **load, burden**

荷を下ろす にをおろす take a load off

荷物 にもつ baggage, load

荷台 にだい carrier, bed (of a truck)

荷造り にづくり packing

荷役 にえき loading, handling cargo

荷札 にふだ tag

荷が勝つ にがかつ be unequal to the burden [job]

初荷 はつに first cargo of the New Year

積み荷 つみに load, freight, cargo

重荷 おもに heavy load; burden, encumbrance

SPECIAL READINGS

稲荷▲ いなり god of harvests; fox deity; flavored boiled rice wrapped up with fried bean curd

SYNONYMS

❶ burden

荷 LOAD → 2840

貨 freight → 3113

❷ bear

負 BEAR (on the back) → 2594

荷 carry on shoulder → 2840

担 BEAR ON SHOULDER → 0376

支 SUPPORT → 2473

華

2841

2-3-7

▶MAGNIFICENT

▶CHINA

カ ケ はな

C 华 huá huà

140	Jōyō	U83EF
艹	S10-3-7	F0820

1	2	3	4	5	6	7	8	9	10
一	十	艹	艹	芏	芏	芔	莒	華	華

COMPOUNDS

❶ **MAGNIFICENT, gorgeous, splendid, brilliant, flowery**

華麗な かれいな splendid, magnificent, resplendent, gorgeous

華言 かげん [rare] flowery words, rhetorical flourishes

豪華な ごうかな gorgeous, splendid, pompous

❷ⓐ [original meaning] **flower, blossom**

ⓑ *chem* flowers; *mining* bloom

a 華道 かどう flower arrangement

法華経 ほけきょう the Lotus Sutra

香華 こうげ incense and flowers

散華する さんげする fall as flowers do, die a glorious death

b 亜鉛華 あえんか zinc flowers, zinc oxide

❸ (best part) flower, essence, cream

華実 かじつ flowers and fruit; appearance and content

精華 せいか flower, essence, glory

詞華集 しかしゅう anthology, florilegium

❹ prosperous, flourishing

繁華 はんか prosperity, bustle

栄華 えいが prosperity, splendor, glory

❺ CHINA

華僑× かきょう Chinese merchant living abroad

華北 かほく North China

中華料理 ちゅうかりょうり Chinese food

日華 にっか Japan and China

INDEPENDENT

【か 華】 floweriness

華を去り実に就く かをさりじつにつく discard the flower for the fruit

KUN

【はな 華】

①ⓐ [also 花] (figuratively) **flower (of life), essence, cream**

ⓑ flower of youth, prime of life

a 武士道の華 ぶしどうのはな flower of chivalry [Bushido]

b 若い内が華 わかいうちがはな Youth is a treasure

② [in compounds] **flowery, beautiful, gallant**

華やかな はなやかな flowery, gay, bright, brilliant, gorgeous

華華しい はなばなしい brilliant, magnificent, spectacular

SYNONYMS

❶ **beautiful**

美 BEAUTIFUL → 2817

彪 MAGNIFICENT → 4115

綺 BEAUTIFUL → 1734

娃 BEAUTIFUL → 0419

佳 FINE → 0096

瑶 EXQUISITE → 1301

麗 OF GRACEFUL BEAUTY → 2672

艶 CHARMING → 2403

妙 of marvelous beauty → 0280

華 MAGNIFICENT → 2841

絢 GORGEOUS → 1705

斐 florid → 3449

❷ⓐ **flower**

花 FLOWER → 2740

華 flower → 2841

❺ **China**

華 CHINA → 2841

漢 CHINESE → 0808

支 China → 2473

中 People's Republic of China → 4262

胡 NATIVES OF ANCIENT CHINA → 1467

台 Taiwan → 2498

唐 Cathay → 3867

呉 KINGDOM OF WU → 3156

❺ **Asian countries**

日 JAPAN → 3759

緬 Myanmar → 1758

老 Laos → 3963

華 CHINA → 2841

蒙 Mongolia → 2938

鮮 Korea → 2355

泰 Thailand → 3193

越 Vietnam → 4108

印 India → 1023

竺 INDIA → 3248

比 Philippines → 0029

HOMOPHONES

はな 花 FLOWER → 2740

NOTE

➡ see USAGE note at 花 2740

莞

2842

2-3-7

▶**SMILE SWEETLY**

カン ガン

Ⓒ 莞 wǎn guān guǎn

140	Names	U839E
艹	S10-3-7	F3227

COMPOUNDS

❶ **SMILE SWEETLY**

莞爾たる かんじたる with a (sweet) smile

❷ [original meaning, now archaic] reed used to cover tatami; reed mat

SYNONYMS

❶ **laugh**

笑 LAUGH → 3275

莞 SMILE SWEETLY →2842

莉 2843
2-3-7

▶**JASMINE**

リ ㊔ れい

Ⓒ 莉 lì

140	Names	U8389
艹	S10-3-7	F2461

COMPOUNDS

● **JASMINE, white jasmine**

茉莉 まつり jasmine, *Jasminum sambac*

茉莉花 まつりか jasmine, *Jasminum sambac*

SYNONYMS

● **shrubs**

藤 WISTERIA →3025
蔦 JAPANESE IVY →2972
萩 *HAGI* →2908
茉 JASMINE →2790
莉 JASMINE →2843
芭 JAPANESE FIBER BANANA →2736

荻 2844
2-3-7

▶**AMUR SILVERGRASS**

テキ おぎ

Ⓒ 荻 dí

140	Names	U837B
艹	S10-3-7	F2227

COMPOUNDS

● **AMUR SILVERGRASS**

荻花 てきか flower of Amur silvergrass

KUN

【おぎ 荻】**AMUR SILVERGRASS**

荻江節 おぎえぶし type of Japanese music with shamisen and song

SYNONYMS

● **kinds of grasses**

草 GRASS →2813
荻 AMUR SILVERGRASS →2844
蒲 CATTAIL →2932
莱 GOOSEFOOT →2878
蕨 BRACKEN →2992
叢 grassy place →3243
芝 LAWN GRASS →2705
笹 BAMBOO GRASS →3301
茅 cogongrass →2779
萱 THATCH GRASS →2904
藁 STRAW →3015
芦 REED →2743
葦 COMMON REED →2934
菅 SEDGE →2874

NOTE

★ do not confuse with 萩 *HAGI* →2908

莓 2845
2-3-7

▶**STRAWBERRY**

ボウ バイ いちご

140	Nonstandard	U8393
艹	S10-3-7	F0000

traditional form → see 苺 at 2780

莖 2846
2-3-7

▶**STEM**

ケイ くき

140	Nonstandard	U8396
艹	S10-3-7	F0000

traditional form → see 茎 at 2788

萊 2847
2-3-7

▶**GOOSEFOOT**

ライ

140	Nonstandard	U83B1
艹	S10-3-7	F0000

traditional form → see 莱 at 2878

莊 2848
2-3-7

▶**VILLA**
▶**DIGNIFIED**

ソウ ショウ チャン

140	Names	U838A
艹	S10-3-7	F0000

traditional form → see 荘 at 2814

恭
2-3-7

incorrect classification
➡ see 2-4-6: 廾 at 3109

益 2849
2-3-7

▶**BENEFIT**
▶**PROFIT**

エキ ヤク ま(す)▲ ㊔ よし やす

Ⓝ 益 Ⓒ 益 yì

108	Jōyō-5	U76CA
皿	S10-5-5	F0925

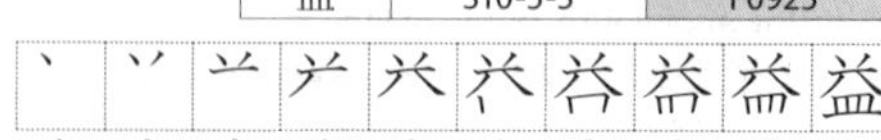

COMPOUNDS

❶ⓐ **BENEFIT, good, advantage**
ⓑ **beneficial, useful**

a 有益な ゆうえきな beneficial; profitable
公益 こうえき public benefit
実益 じつえき practical use, benefit, actual profit
御利益 ごりやく grace of God

b 益友 えきゆう useful friend
益虫 えきちゅう beneficial insect

❷ [also suffix] **PROFIT, gain**

益金 えききん profit, gain

差益 さえき marginal profits
利益 りえき profit, gains; benefit
収益 しゅうえき profit, earnings, proceeds, returns
損益 そんえき profit and loss; advantage and disadvantage
売却益 ばいきゃくえき profit on sales

❸ increase, gain
増益 ぞうえき increase in profit; increase

INDEPENDENT

【えき 益】**PROFIT**, benefit, advantage, use
益を与える人 えきをあたえるひと benefactor
【えきする 益する】be beneficial

KUN

【ます 益す】[usu. 増す] *vi* & *vt* **increase, augment, multiply**
益益 ますます increasingly

SYNONYMS

❶ **benefit**
利 ADVANTAGE → 1431
益 BENEFIT → 2849
為 SAKE → 4395
用 use(ful) → 3694
役 SERVICE → 0288

❷ **profit**
利 PROFIT → 1431
益 PROFIT → 2849
儲ける PROFIT → 0202
得 GAIN → 0577

HOMOPHONES

ます 増 INCREASE → 0836

NOTE

➡ see USAGE note at 増 0836

兼

2850

2-3-7

▶**CONCURRENTLY**
ケン か(ねる) -か(ねる)
N 兼 C 兼 jiān

12	Jōyō	U517C
丷	S10-2-8	F1351

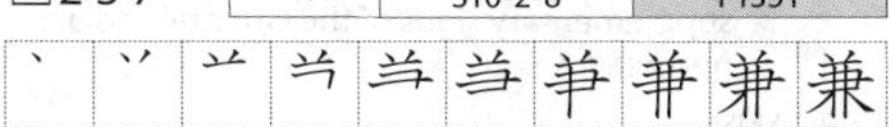

1 2 3 4 5 6 7 8 9 10

COMPOUNDS

❶ⓐ (serving two functions) **CONCURRENTLY, simultaneously, together**
ⓑ **serve two functions or hold two jobs CONCURRENTLY**

a 兼用 けんよう combined use; serving two purposes
兼備する けんびする combine (one thing with another)
兼行 けんこう doing simultaneously
b 兼任 けんにん holding two or more posts
兼務 けんむ holding another post; additional post
兼業 けんぎょう side business

❷ prepared, assigned
兼題 けんだい prepared theme for a poem

INDEPENDENT

【けん 兼】**CONCURRENTLY**, simultaneously, and, cum, in addition
総理大臣兼外務大臣 そうりだいじんけんがいむだいじん Prime Minister and (concurrently) Foreign Minister
居間兼食堂 いまけんしょくどう living-room-cum-dining-room

KUN

【かねる 兼ねる】**serve two functions, combine [unite] (one thing with another), serve as well; hold (another office) CONCURRENTLY [in addition]**
兼ね合い かねあい equilibrium, even balance
用事と遊びを兼ねて ようじとあそびをかねて on business combined with pleasure
両職を兼ねる りょうしょくをかねる hold two offices concurrently
【-かねる -兼ねる】**verbal suffix indicating hesitation, difficulty, or impatience in performing some action**
申し兼ねますが もうしかねますが Excuse me, but…
やり兼ねない やりかねない would stop at nothing, be capable of doing
見兼ねる みかねる be unable to let pass unnoticed
お待ち兼ねの おまちかねの long-waited-for

SYNONYMS

❶ⓐ **together**
共 JOINT → 3045
同 together → 3707
併 TOGETHER → 0092
並 side by side → 2793
兼 CONCURRENTLY → 2850
倶 TOGETHER → 0125

【けん】
◯ **additionally**
亦 ALSO → 2504
兼 CONCURRENTLY → 2850
又 also, and → 4158
而うして and → 2520
及び and → 4192
並びに and also → 2793
傍ら besides → 0166
尚 STILL → 2774
更に furthermore → 4355
且つ AS WELL → 4297

差

incorrect classification
➡ see 3-7-3: 𦍌 at 4104

2-3-7

倉

incorrect classification
➡ see 2-2-8: 𠆢 at 2607

2-3-7

韋

▶**TANNED LEATHER**

イ

Ⓒ 韦 wéi

2851

2-3-7

178	Non-Jōyō	U97CB
韋	S10-10-0	F0000

radical variant → see 韋 at 2821

COMPOUNDS

❶ **TANNED [dressed] LEATHER [skin], leather**
韋編 いへん leather cord

❷ **used phonetically for *i***
韋駄天 いだてん swift-running heavenly warrior; great runner

SYNONYMS

❶ **kinds of skin**
皮 SKIN (of any kind) → 3771
膚 SKIN (of the human body) → 4049
肌 SKIN (of the human body) → 1021
革 LEATHER → 3099
韋 TANNED LEATHER → 2851
鱗 SCALES → 2375

壷

▶**JAR**

コ つぼ

2852

2-3-8

33	Nonstandard	U58F7
士	S11-3-8	F0000

traditional form → see 壺 at 2890

窒

▶**CHOKE**
▶**NITROGEN**

チツ

Ⓒ 窒 zhì

2853

2-3-8

116	Jōyō	U7A92
穴	S11-5-6	F2411

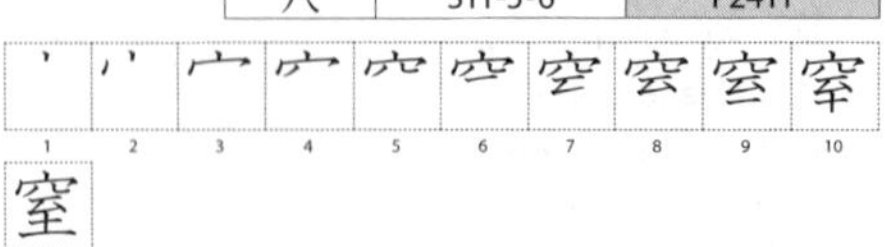

COMPOUNDS

❶ⓐ **CHOKE, suffocate**
ⓑ [original meaning, now rare] **CHOKE up, stuff up, block**
a 窒息 ちっそく suffocation, asphyxia
窒死 ちっし [rare] death from suffocation
b 窒塞する ちっそくする be blocked

❷ **NITROGEN**
窒素 ちっそ nitrogen
窒化物 ちっかぶつ nitride

SYNONYMS

❶ⓐ **kill**
殺 KILL → 1677
劉 KILL → 2398
刺 stab to death → 1625
絞 STRANGLE → 1707
窒 CHOKE → 2853

❷ **lighter elements**
水 hydrogen → 0010
酸 OXYGEN → 1968
窒 NITROGEN → 2853
塩 chlorine → 0774
臭 bromine → 3261
硫 SULFUR → 1519
炭 carbon → 2806

❷ **nitrogen**
窒 NITROGEN → 2853
硝 NITER → 1520

寅

▶**THE TIGER**

イン とら ㊔ のぶ とも

Ⓒ 寅 yín

2854

2-3-8

40	Names	U5BC5
宀	S11-3-8	F2176

COMPOUNDS

● third sign of the Oriental zodiac: **THE TIGER**—(time) 3-5 a.m., (direction) ENE, (season) January (of the lunar calendar) (→ see APPENDIX 8)

KUN

【とら 寅】third sign of the Oriental zodiac: **THE TIGER** (→ ●)
寅の刻 とらのこく around four o'clock in the morning
丑寅 うしとら [also 艮] one of the four supplementary signs of the Oriental zodiac: northeast

SYNONYMS

● **tiger**
虎 TIGER → 3981
寅 THE TIGER → 2854

HOMOPHONES

とら 虎 TIGER → 3981
うしとら
艮 NORTHEAST → 4330
丑寅 → 4241, 2854

NOTE

➡ see USAGE note at 虎 3981

寂 2855

▶LONESOME

ジャク セキ さび さび(しい) さび(れる) さみ(しい)▲

Ⓒ 寂 jì

2-3-8

40 宀	Jōyō	U5BC2
	S11-3-8	F1546

COMPOUNDS

❶ⓐ **LONESOME, lonely, desolate, deserted**

ⓑ [original meaning] **quiet, still, serene**

a 寂寥たる せきりょうたる lonely, desolate

寂然たる せきぜんたる(=じゃくねんたる) lonely, desolate

b 静寂 せいじゃく silence, quietness, stillness

閑寂 かんじゃく quietness, tranquility

❷ death of a Buddhist monk or nun

寂滅 じゃくめつ Nirvana, death

入寂 にゅうじゃく death of saint, entering Nirvana

INDEPENDENT

【じゃく 寂】indicates date of death of a Buddhist monk or nun; hush, stillness

寂とした じゃくとした hushed, still

明治四年寂 めいじよねんじゃく died 1871

【せき 寂】hush, stillness

寂とした せきとした hushed, still

KUN

【さび 寂】**patina, elegant simplicity, *sabi***

侘×と寂 わびとさび *wabi* and *sabi*, taste for the simple and quiet

【さびしい 寂しい】[sometimes also 淋しい]

ⓐ **LONESOME, lonely, desolate, deserted**

ⓑ scarce, scanty

a 寂しさ さびしさ loneliness

寂しがる さびしがる feel lonely, miss someone

b 懐が寂しい ふところがさびしい have a scanty supply of money

【さびれる 寂れる】**decline in prosperity, become desolate**

寂れた季節 さびれたきせつ dead season

【さみしい 寂しい】same as 寂しい さびしい

SYNONYMS

❶ⓐ **sad and depressed**

悲 SAD →3448

悄 BECOME DISPIRITED →0506

哀 sorrowful →2568

愁 MELANCHOLY →3508

鬱 GLOOM →3625

陰 gloomy →0657

沈 depressed →0306

寂 LONESOME →2855

淋しい LONESOME →0632

惨 MISERABLE →0585

ⓑ **quiet**

静 QUIET →2164

閑 QUIET →4123

寂 quiet →2855

幽 QUIET AND SECLUDED →3731

粛 still →4400

黙 SILENT →3554

USAGE

❶【さびしい】

寂しい

[sometimes also 淋しい]

ⓐ lonesome, lonely, desolate, deserted

ⓑ scarce, scanty

淋しい

[usu. 寂しい] same as 寂しい さびしい

❷【さみしい】

寂しい

[sometimes also 淋しい] same as 寂しい さびしい

淋しい

[usu. 寂しい] same as 寂しい さみしい

HOMOPHONES

さびしい 淋 GONORRHEA →0632

さみしい 淋 GONORRHEA →0632

寄 2856

▶CONTRIBUTE

▶DRAW NEAR

キ よ(る) -よ(り) よ(せる)

Ⓒ 寄 jì

2-3-8

40 宀	Jōyō-5	U5BC4
	S11-3-8	F0447

COMPOUNDS

❶ⓐ (give money or goods) **CONTRIBUTE, donate**

ⓑ (submit for publication) **CONTRIBUTE**

a 寄付 きふ contribution, donation

寄金 ききん contribution, donation

寄贈する きぞう(=きそう)する donate, present as a gift

寄与 きよ contribution, services

b 寄稿する きこうする contribute (to a newspaper)

寄書 きしょ contributed article

❷ **lodge at, reside temporarily, be dependent on (someone for food)**

寄宿 きしゅく lodging, boarding
寄留 きりゅう temporary residence, sojourn
寄生 きせい parasitism
寄食 きしょく parasitism, dependency

❸ call at, call on, make a short visit
寄港する きこうする call at a port
寄航する きこうする call at a(n) (air)port

❹ entrust to, consign, deposit
寄託する きたくする deposit, entrust

❺ send, deliver
寄語する きごする send word by
寄信 きしん sending a letter

KUN

【よる 寄る】
①ⓐ **DRAW NEAR, draw up, come near, approach**
ⓑ **draw aside, step aside**
a 近寄る ちかよる go near, approach
歩み寄る あゆみよる step up; compromise, meet halfway
最寄りの もよりの nearest, nearby
身寄り みより relative, relation, kinsfolk
思いも寄らない おもいもよらない unexpected, unforeseen, inconceivable
b 脇に寄る わきによる draw aside
片寄る かたよる concentrate on one side [place], go aside

② draw together, come together, gather, meet
寄り合い よりあい meeting, assembly, gathering

③ **drop in, call on**
寄り道する よりみちする drop in on the way, go out of the way
立ち寄る たちよる drop in for a short visit, call at

④ **increase, gain**
年寄り としより old [aged] person, the aged; older councilor
皺×が寄る しわがよる wrinkle, crumple

⑤ lean on, rest against
壁に寄り掛かる かべによりかかる rest against the wall

⑥ *sumo* push one's opponent while holding his belt
寄り切り よりきり pushing one's opponent out of the ring while holding his belt

⑦ (of the stock market) open
寄り付き よりつき opening of a session

【-より -寄り】[also suffix] **toward, leaning toward**
北寄りの風 きたよりのかぜ northerly wind
アメリカ寄りの外交 あめりかよりのがいこう pro-American diplomacy

【よせる 寄せる】
①ⓐ **DRAW (a thing) NEAR, allow to approach; come near**
ⓑ **draw up, bring together, gather, collect; add up**
a 寄せ付けない よせつけない keep off, keep away
車寄せ くるまよせ carriage porch
皺×寄せ しわよせ shifting (the loss) to someone else
又寄せて頂きます またよせていただきます I shall call on you again
打ち寄せる うちよせる break upon, beat upon (the shore)
引き寄せる ひきよせる draw near, pull nearer
取り寄せる とりよせる order; get, obtain
b 寄せ集め よせあつめ mixture, odds and ends
寄せ鍋 よせなべ chowder
寄せ算 よせざん addition, adding up
呼び寄せる よびよせる call, summon, send for, call together

② send (a letter), CONTRIBUTE, write
原稿を寄せる げんこうをよせる contribute an article

③ take to a person, let one's heart go out to someone
心を寄せる こころをよせる let one's heart go out to, take to

④ be dependent on, under (a person's) roof
身を寄せる みをよせる become a dependent on, live under another's roof

⑤ⓐ attack, storm, surge
ⓑ bring (a game of shogi) to a victorious end
a 攻め寄せる せめよせる make an onslaught on
b 寄せ よせ last moves, end game

⑥ liken, make a pretext of
病気に事寄せて びょうきにことよせて under the pretext of being ill

SPECIAL READINGS

寄席 よせ storyteller's hall, variety hall
数寄屋(=数奇屋) すきや tea-ceremony arbor

SYNONYMS

❶ⓐ donate
施 give alms → 1103
恵む give charity → 3293
寄 CONTRIBUTE → 2856
醵 CONTRIBUTE MONEY → 2087
献 donate → 2240

❸ visit
訪 VISIT → 1860
参 VISIT A HOLY PLACE → 2563
詣 VISIT A HOLY PLACE → 1918
寄 call at → 2856
伺 call on → 0078

【よる】
①ⓐ **approach**
寄る DRAW NEAR → 2856

迫 PRESS → 3815
近 NEAR → 3798
接 come close to → 0607
搒 PRESS → 0451

【よせる】
①ⓐ **pull**
引 DRAW → 0207
曳 DRAW → 4348
牽 DRAW → 2621
惹 DRAW ATTENTION → 2903
抽 DRAW OUT → 0359
抜 PULL OUT → 0290
控える HOLD BACK → 0600
扣える HOLD BACK → 0250
寄せる DRAW NEAR → 2856

HOMOPHONES

よる
因 CAUSE → 3792
依 DEPEND ON → 0093
拠 GROUNDS → 0369
由 REASON → 4311

かたよる
偏る → 0151
片寄る → 4272, 2856

COMPOUND FORMATION

❶【身寄り みより】
身寄り 'relative, etc.' refers to persons near (寄る ①ⓐ) one's person (身) or self.

❷【寄席 よせ】
寄席 'storyteller's hall, variety hall' refers to the gathering of (寄せる よせる ①ⓑ) people at an entertainment hall (席).

NOTE

➡ see USAGE notes at 因 3792 and 偏 0151

密

▶**CLOSE**
▶**SECRET**
ミツ ひそ(か)▲

2857

Ⓒ 密 mì

2-3-8

40 宀	Jōyō-6	U5BC6
	S11-3-8	F0558

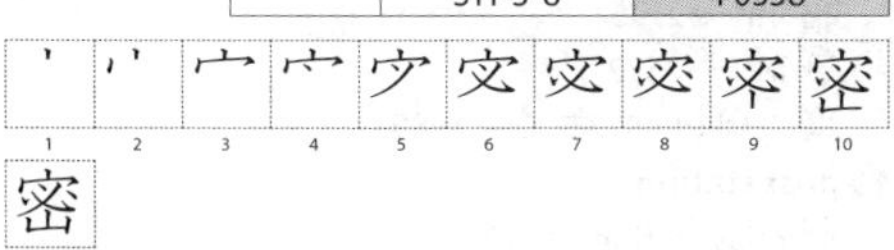

COMPOUNDS

❶ⓐ (closely crowded) **CLOSE, dense, thick, compact, tight**
ⓑ (very near in relationship) **CLOSE, intimate**
a 密集する みっしゅうする crowd, swarm, aggregate densely
密林 みつりん close thicket, dense forest, jungle
密度 みつど density
密室 みっしつ secret room [chamber]; locked room
過密な かみつな overcrowded
b 密接な みっせつな close, intimate
緊密な きんみつな close, tight
親密な しんみつな intimate, close

❷ (characterized by exacting minuteness) **CLOSE, minute, elaborate, careful**
精密 せいみつ precision, accuracy, minuteness
厳密な げんみつな strict, precise, rigid, exact
綿密な めんみつな close, minute, detailed
緻密な ちみつな minute, close, elaborate, exact

❸ [also suffix] **SECRET, private, clandestine, illegal, stealthy**
密使 みっし secret messenger
密告 みっこく secret information
密輸 みつゆ smuggling, contraband trade
密売 みつばい smuggling
密入国 みつにゅうこく illegal entry [immigration]
秘密 ひみつ secret, mystery; privacy
内密の ないみつの secret, confidential, private

❹ abbrev. of 密教 みっきょう: esoteric Buddhism
密教 みっきょう esoteric Buddhism, secret religion
台密 たいみつ esoteric Buddhism of the Japanese *Tendai* Sect

INDEPENDENT

【みつな 密な】**CLOSE**, dense, thick, crowded; close, intimate; close, minute, elaborate

KUN

【ひそか 密か】
ひそかな 密かな **SECRET**, private, hidden

SYNONYMS

❶ⓐ **dense**
濃 THICK (concentrated) → 0956
密 CLOSE → 2857
ⓑ **familiar and friendly**
親 INTIMATE → 2264
密 CLOSE → 2857
近 NEAR → 3798
睦 FRIENDLY → 1534
懇 FAMILIAR → 3606
和 HARMONIOUS → 1450

❷ **detailed**
詳 DETAILED → 1926
細 MINUTE → 1689
緻 MINUTE → 1780
密 CLOSE → 2857
精 meticulous → 1729

❸ **secret and private**

秘 SECRET → 1490
密 SECRET → 2857
暗 in the dark → 1273
私 PRIVATE → 1432
内 not public → 4277
隠 hidden from view → 0873

宿

2858

2-3-8

▶LODGE

シュク やど やど(る) やど(す)

Ⓒ 宿 sù xiǔ xiù

40	Jōyō-3	U5BBF
宀	S11-3-8	F0634

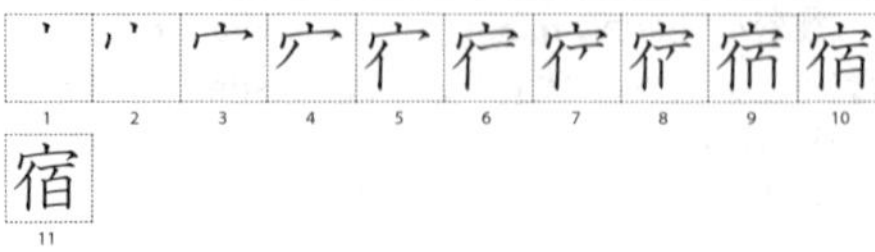

COMPOUNDS

❶ⓐ [original meaning] **LODGE, board, stay overnight**
ⓑ be contained within the body

a 宿泊する しゅくはくする lodge, stay
宿直 しゅくちょく night duty, night watch
寄宿 きしゅく lodging, boarding
合宿する がっしゅくする lodge together, stay in a camp for training
下宿 げしゅく lodging, boarding house

b 宿便 しゅくべん feces contained long in the intestines, fecal stasis

❷ **lodging, inn, hotel, lodging house**
宿舎 しゅくしゃ lodgings, quarters
宿所 しゅくしょ address, lodgings
宿営 しゅくえい billeting, camp
宿題 しゅくだい homework
民宿 みんしゅく tourist home

❸ from a previous time, remaining, old
宿根草 しゅっこんそう perennial plant
宿酔 しゅくすい hangover
宿敵 しゅくてき old enemy
宿願 しゅくがん long-cherished desire

❹ **from a previous life [incarnation]**
宿命 しゅくめい fate, destiny
宿縁 しゅくえん karma, destiny, fate

❺ post station, relay station, stage, stopping place
宿場 しゅくば post station, relay station

❻ stage along the zodiac, mansion; constellation
星宿 せいしゅく constellation
二十八宿 にじゅうはっしゅく The 28 stages along the zodiac

❼ experienced
宿老 しゅくろう old men, elders, seniors
宿将 しゅくしょう veteran general

INDEPENDENT

【しゅく 宿】 post town, relay station, stage
合いの宿 あいのしゅく town situated between two post towns

【しゅくす 宿す】 literary form of 宿る やどる

KUN

【やど 宿】 **lodging, inn, hotel; house, dwelling;** *slang* **my hubby, my good man**
宿屋 やどや inn, hotel, lodging house
宿賃 やどちん hotel charge
宿無し やどなし vagabond
宿六 やどろく my old man, my hubby
船宿 ふなやど operator of pleasure boats; shipping agent

【やどる 宿る】 **LODGE, board, stay overnight; dwell [reside] in;** (of a bird) **roost**
宿り やどり lodging abode; shelter
雨宿りする あまやどりする take shelter from the rain

【やどす 宿す】 **conceive, be pregnant with; carry, let stay**
子を宿す こをやどす be pregnant with a child
露を宿した葉 つゆをやどしたは leaf heavy with dew

SYNONYMS

❶ⓐ **stay**
滞 STAY → 0815
頓 STAY IN PLACE → 1320
留 STAY → 3189
逗 STAY → 4005
駐 STATIONED → 2297
屯 STATION TROOPS → 4268
在 reside temporarily → 3704
泊 STAY OVERNIGHT → 0389
宿 LODGE → 2858
寓 stay temporarily → 2893

❷ **temporary quarters**
舎 temporary quarters → 2555
寮 DORMITORY → 2984
宿 lodging → 2858
館 inn → 2196
亭 INN → 2572
寓 TEMPORARY ABODE → 2893

❺ **post station**
駅 relay station → 2292
逓 RELAY → 3852
宿 post station → 2858

NOTE

➡ see COMPOUND FORMATION for 下宿 げしゅく → 下 4186

窓

▶WINDOW

ソウ まど

Ⓝ 窗 Ⓒ 窗 chuāng

2859

2-3-8

116	Jōyō-6	U7A93
穴	S11-5-6	F0894

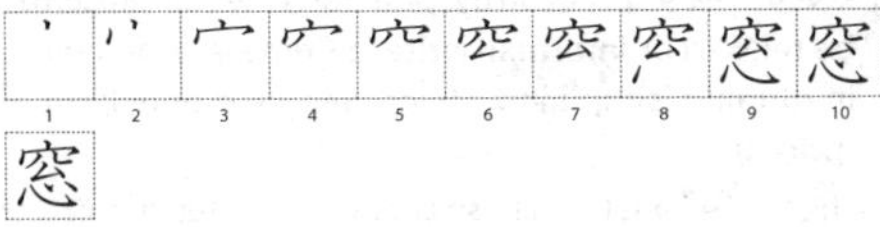

COMPOUNDS

❶ [original meaning] **WINDOW**

窓外 そうがい outside the window
車窓 しゃそう car window
舷窓 げんそう porthole

❷ **WINDOW**ed structure:

ⓐ chamber
ⓑ school

a 深窓に育つ しんそうにそだつ be brought up with tenderest care in a good family

b 学窓 がくそう school
同窓生 どうそうせい fellow student, alumnus, alumna

KUN

【まど 窓】WINDOW, porthole; windowpane

窓ガラス まどがらす windowpane
窓口 まどぐち window, wicket; clerk at a window
窓枠 まどわく window frame, sash
飾り窓 かざりまど show window, display window
出窓 でまど bow window, bay window

窑

▶KILN

ヨウ かま

2860

2-3-8

116	Nonstandard	U7A91
穴	S11-5-6	F0000

traditional form → see 窯 at 2986

常堂

incorrect classification
➡ see 2-5-6: ⺌ at 3202

2-3-8

巣

▶NEST

ソウ す

Ⓝ 巢 Ⓒ 巢 cháo

2861

2-3-8

42△	Jōyō-4	U5DE3
⺍	S11-3-8	F1683

COMPOUNDS

❶ⓐ [original meaning] (structure for birds or insects) **NEST**

ⓑ (place favoring the growth of something dangerous) **NEST** (of robbers), hangout

a 営巣 えいそう nest building
蜂巣 ほうそう beehive, hive

b 巣窟 そうくつ den, haunt, nest
病巣 びょうそう *medicine* focus, lesion

❷ place where sperm or eggs accumulate

卵巣 らんそう ovary
精巣 せいそう spermary, testis

KUN

【す 巣】[sometimes also 栖]

ⓐ (structure for birds, insects or animals) **NEST, beehive; web; lair, den**

ⓑ (place favoring the growth of something dangerous) **NEST**, den, hangout (for bandits)

a 巣箱 すばこ bird box, bird house
巣立つ すだつ leave one's nest; become independent
巣食う すくう build a nest, nest; haunt, hang out
古巣 ふるす old nest, one's former haunt

b 空き巣 あきす sneak thief

USAGE

【す】

巣

[sometimes also 栖]

ⓐ (structure for birds, insects or animals) nest, beehive; web; lair, den

ⓑ (place favoring the growth of something dangerous) nest, den, hangout (for bandits)

栖

[usu. 巣] same as 巣

HOMOPHONES

す 栖 INHABIT → 1170

蛍

incorrect classification
➡ see 2-5-6: ⺌ at 3204

2-3-8

崖

▶CLIFF

ガイ がけ

Ⓝ 崕 Ⓒ 崖 yá

2862

2-3-8

46	Jōyō	U5D16
山	S11-3-8	F1835

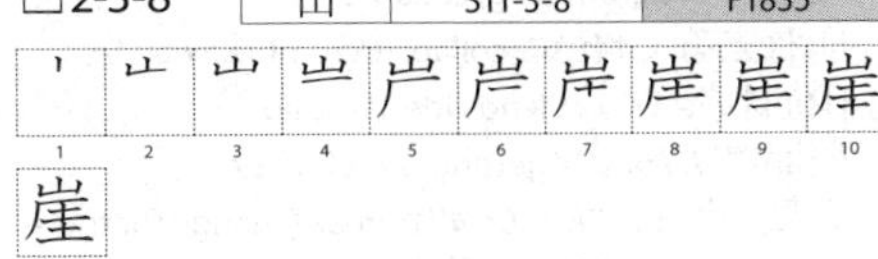

COMPOUNDS

● **CLIFF, bluff, precipice**

懸崖 けんがい overhanging cliff

断崖絶壁 だんがいぜっぺき precipitous cliff, sheer precipice

KUN

【がけ 崖】 **CLIFF, bluff, precipice**

崖崩れ がけくずれ landslide

崖っ縁 がけっぷち edge of a cliff; perilous position [state]

SYNONYMS

● **mountain parts**

頂 SUMMIT →0164

峰 PEAK →0494

嶺 RIDGE →3013

峠 MOUNTAIN PASS →0428

崖 CLIFF →2862

壁 wall-like structure →3601

崩

▶CRUMBLE

ホウ くず(れる) -くず(れ) くず(す)

Ⓝ 崩 Ⓒ 崩 bēng

2863

2-3-8

46	Jōyō	U5D29
山	S11-3-8	F1056

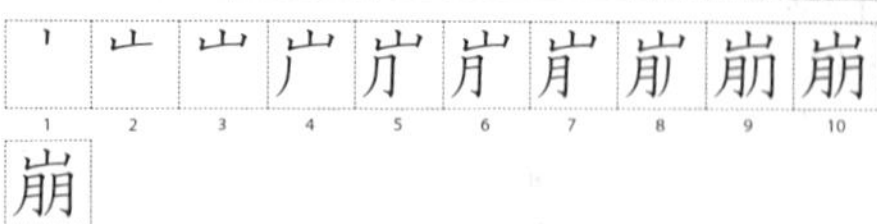

COMPOUNDS

❶ **CRUMBLE, collapse**

崩壊する ほうかいする collapse, crumble, break down, cave in

崩落 ほうらく collapse, cave-in; crash; (of the market) decline

❷ (of an emperor) **die**

崩御 ほうぎょ demise [death] of an emperor

INDEPENDENT

【ほうじる(=ほうずる) 崩じる(=崩ずる)】 (of an emperor) **demise, pass away**

KUN

【くずれる 崩れる】 *vi* **CRUMBLE, collapse, break, cave in; get out of shape; slump;** (of money) **be changeable**

崩れ くずれ crumbling, collapse

崩れ去る くずれさる collapse, crumble away

山崩れ やまくずれ landslide, landslip

型崩れ かたくずれ getting out of shape

天気の崩れ てんきのくずれ break [change for the worse] in the weather

十円玉に崩れる じゅうえんだまにくずれる can be changed into ten-yen coins

【-くずれ -崩れ】 [suffix] **delinquent, degenerate**

学生崩れ がくせいくずれ degenerate ex-student

俳優崩れ はいゆうくずれ down-and-out ex-film star

【くずす 崩す】 *vt* **destroy, pull down, level; cause to be relaxed or informal; write (a Chinese character) in running [simplified] style; change (money); cut (prices)**

崩し字 くずしじ Chinese character written in running [simplified] style

切り崩す きりくずす level (a hill); break (a strike)

持ち崩す もちくずす ruin [degrade] oneself

膝を崩す ひざをくずす sit at ease

SPECIAL READINGS

雪崩 なだれ snowslide

SYNONYMS

❶ **break**

破 BREAK →1478

拉ぐ crush →0372

崩 CRUMBLE →2863

挫 SPRAIN →0519

壊 BREAK DOWN →0934

毀す break down →2246

折 BREAK OFF →0297

割る crack →2284

裂 SPLIT →3331

砕 CRUSH UP →1458

摧 CRUSH UP →0849

潰す CRUSH →0919

❶ **collapse**

陥 FALL IN →0547

落 FALL →2907

崩 CRUMBLE →2863

没 SINK →0305

崇

▶REVERENCE

スウ あが(める)▲ ㊔ たか たかし そう しゅう

Ⓒ 崇 chóng

2864

2-3-8

46	Jōyō	U5D07
山	S11-3-8	F1438

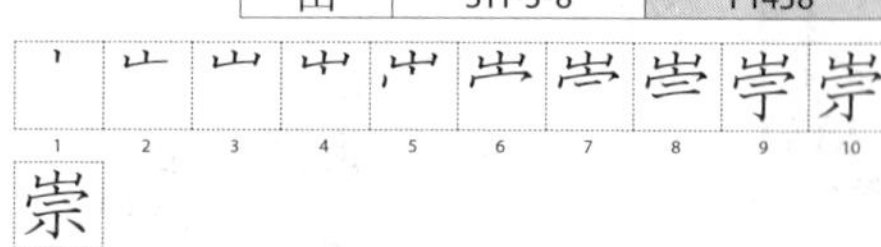

COMPOUNDS

❶ **REVERENCE, revere, worship, venerate, adore, esteem**

崇敬 すうけい reverence, admiration

崇拝 すうはい worship, adoration
崇高な すうこうな lofty, sublime, noble
尊崇 そんすう reverence, veneration

❷ [usu. 嵩 2927] [original meaning, now archaic] lofty (mountain)

KUN

【あがめる 崇める】 **REVERENCE**, revere, worship, venerate, esteem
神と崇める かみとあがめる deify

SYNONYMS

❶ respect
敬 RESPECT → 2136
尊 HONOR → 2920
畏 respect → 3170
欽 REVERE → 2124
仰 look up to → 0051
崇 REVERENCE → 2864
尚 VALUE HIGHLY → 2774
重 set value on → 4390
拝 WORSHIP → 0360
慕 ADORE → 2970

❶ pray and worship
祈 PRAY → 1086
祷 PRAY → 1224
願 pray → 2320
拝 WORSHIP → 0360
祀 WORSHIP AS GOD → 1448
崇 REVERENCE → 2864
斎 OBSERVE RELIGIOUS ABSTINENCE → 2622
呪 SPELL → 0323

崩
2865
2-3-8

▶CRUMBLE
ホウ くず(れる) -くず(れ) くず(す)

46	Nonstandard	U5D29
山	S11-3-8	F0000

traditional form → see 崩 at 2863

嵜
2866
2-3-8

▶PROMONTORY
キ さき

46	Nonstandard	U37E2
山	S11-3-8	F0000

traditional form → see 崎 at 0569

嵌
2-3-8

incorrect stroke-count
➡ see 2-3-9: 山 at 2897

巢
2867
2-3-8

▶NEST
ソウ す

47	Names	U5DE2
巛	S11-3-8	F0000

traditional form → see 巣 at 2861

菩
2868
2-3-8

▶PHONETIC [bo]
ボ
Ⓒ 菩 pú

140	Names	U83E9
艹	S11-3-8	F1834

COMPOUNDS

● used PHONETICally for *bo*, esp. in the transliteration of Sanskrit Buddhist terms
菩提 ぼだい *Bodhi*
菩提樹 ぼだいじゅ sacred fig, bo tree; linden, esp. *Tilia miqueliana*
菩提寺 ぼだいじ one's family temple
菩薩 ぼさつ *bodhisattva*
普賢菩薩 ふげんぼさつ *Samantabhadra* (a *bodhisattva*)

SYNONYMS

● phonetic [b]
毘 PHONETIC [bi] → 3169
菩 PHONETIC [bo] → 2868

著
2869
2-3-8

▶AUTHOR
▶CONSPICUOUS
チョ チャク▲ あらわ(す) いちじる(しい)
Ⓝ 著 Ⓒ 著 zhù zhe zhuó

140	Jōyō-6	U8457
艹	S11-3-8	F0688

Stroke order: 一(1) 十(2) 艹(3) 艹(4) 艹(5) 芏(6) 芓(7) 芓(8) 著(9) 著(10) 著(11)

COMPOUNDS

❶ⓐ AUTHOR, write, publish
ⓑ [suffix] AUTHORed by, by
a 著作する ちょさくする write, author
著述家 ちょじゅつか writer, author
著者 ちょしゃ author, writer
著作権 ちょさくけん copyright
共著 きょうちょ joint authorship, coauthorship
b 三島由紀夫著 みしまゆきおちょ authored by Mishima Yukio

❷ literary work, book, writing
著書 ちょしょ literary work, book
新著 しんちょ new book
拙著 せっちょ my humble work

名著 めいちょ famous book, masterpiece

❸ (since writing makes things clearly visible) (attracting attention) **CONSPICUOUS, remarkable, prominent, well-known**

著大な ちょだいな exceptionally large

著名 ちょめい prominence, eminence, distinction

顕著な けんちょな notable, conspicuous; clear, obvious

❹ [now always 着 ちゃく 4110] same as 着 4110

→see 着 4110 for compounds

INDEPENDENT

【ちょ 著】literary work, book

. . . の著 …のちょ book written by…

KUN

【あらわす 著す】**AUTHOR, write, publish**

書き著す かきあらわす publish (a book)

【いちじるしい 著しい】**remarkable, CONSPICUOUS, marked**

著しく いちじるしく remarkably, considerably, strikingly

SYNONYMS

❶ **compile**

編 COMPILE →1755
纂 COMPILE →3393
撰 COMPILE →0911
集 edit →3445
輯 EDIT →2025
著 AUTHOR →2869

❶ **compose**

著 AUTHOR →2869
作 compose →0077
書く WRITE →3292
筆 write →3317

❷ **books**

本 BOOK →4314
典 STANDARD WORK →3253
経 religious classic →1687
書 BOOK →3292
冊 bound book →4295
籍 books →3394
著 literary work →2869
巻 VOLUME →3273
編 piece of writing →1755
篇 PIECE OF WRITING →3361
鑑 REFERENCE VOLUME →2226

❸ **conspicuous**

著 CONSPICUOUS →2869
顕 MANIFEST →2274
卓 PROMINENT →2561
傑 outstanding →0175

HOMOPHONES

あらわす

表 EXPRESS →3083
現 ACTUAL →1218

NOTE

➡ see USAGE note at 表 3083 and NOTE at 着 4110

萄

2870

2-3-8

▶**GRAPE**

ドウ

Ⓒ 萄 táo

140	Names	U8404
艹	S11-3-8	F2618

COMPOUNDS

● **GRAPE, grapevine**

葡萄 ぶどう grape
葡萄酒 ぶどうしゅ (grape) wine
山葡萄 やまぶどう crimson glory vine

SPECIAL READINGS

葡萄牙 ぽるとがる Portugal
葡萄 えび grape; dark purplish red color

SYNONYMS

● **fruits and fruit trees**

桃 PEACH →1174
榛 HAZEL →1328
椎 CHINQUAPIN →1249
柚 YUZU →1123
椰 COCONUT →1285
柑 CITRUS →1112
橙 BITTER ORANGE →1369
葡 GRAPE →2902
萄 GRAPE →2870
柿 PERSIMMON →1118
檎 APPLE →1386
李 PLUM →3050
枇 LOQUAT →1063
杷 LOQUAT →1065
苺 STRAWBERRY →2780
菱 water chestnut →2879
杏 APRICOT →3049
梅 JAPANESE APRICOT →1159
橘 MANDARIN →1366
栗 CHESTNUT →3280
栃 JAPANESE HORSE CHESTNUT →1122
梨 PEAR →3412
蕉 PLANTAIN →2994

萌

2871

2-3-8

▶GERMINATE

ホウ ボウ も(える) きざ(す) ㊔ めぐみ め ほ ほの

Ⓝ 萠 Ⓒ 萌 méng

140	Names	U840C
艹	S11-3-8	F2371

COMPOUNDS

❶ⓐ GERMINATE, sprout, bud

ⓑ germination, beginning, sign, indication

a 萌芽 ほうが germination, beginning; sprout

❷ [archaic] the people, the masses

萌黎 ほうれい common people, the masses

KUN

【もえる 萌える】**sprout, bud, burst into bud**

萌え立つ もえたつ sprout, burst into leaf

萌黄色 もえぎいろ yellowish green

下萌え したもえ sprout of a plant shooting from under the soil

【きざす 萌す】**GERMINATE, sprout; spring up, dawn**

萌し きざし germination, sprouting; dawning

SYNONYMS

❶ⓐ sprout and bloom

萌 GERMINATE → 2871

咲く BLOOM → 0413

HOMOPHONES

もえる 燃 BURN → 1375

きざす 兆 OMEN → 0264

きざし 兆 OMEN → 0264

NOTE

➡ see USAGE notes at 燃 1375 and 兆 0264

萎

2872

2-3-8

▶WITHER

イ な(える) しお(れる)▲ しな(びる)▲ しぼ(む)▲

Ⓒ 萎 wěi

140	Jōyō	U840E
艹	S11-3-8	F2397

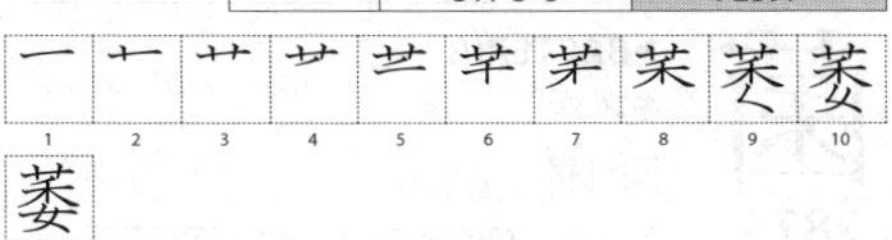

COMPOUNDS

● [now also 委 3160] [original meaning] **WITHER, weaken, decline**

萎縮 いしゅく withering, atrophy; being crestfallen

萎黄病 いおうびょう greensickness, chlorosis

陰萎 いんい impotence

KUN

【なえる 萎える】

ⓐ **WITHER, droop**

ⓑ **weaken, lose strength**

b 気持ちが萎える きもちがなえる feel discouraged, lose one's drive

手萎え てなえ [archaic] arm [hand] disability

【しおれる 萎れる】

ⓐ droop, **WITHER**

ⓑ have the blues, be downcast

a 打ち萎れる うちしおれる droop; be depressed

【しなびる 萎びる】**WITHER**, shrivel, wilt

【しぼむ 萎む】fade (away), **WITHER**, wilt, shrivel

SYNONYMS

● decay

朽 DECAY → 1015

腐 ROT → 3921

枯 WITHER → 1113

萎 WITHER → 2872

錆 RUST → 2188

● die

死 DIE → 4334

萎 WITHER → 2872

没 die → 0305

亡 DECEASE → 4210

殉 DIE A MARTYR → 1177

歿 DIE → 1078

去 pass away → 2678

逝 DEPART THIS LIFE → 3850

斃 FALL DOWN DEAD → 3593

枯 WITHER → 1113

菓

2873

2-3-8

▶CONFECTIONERY

カ

Ⓒ 果 guǒ

140	Jōyō	U83D3
艹	S11-3-8	F1676

COMPOUNDS

❶ CONFECTIONERY, confection, cake, sweets, candy

菓子 かし confectionery, cake, sweets

和菓子 わがし Japanese-style confection

糖菓 とうか sweetmeats, sweets, confection

氷菓 ひょうか ice cream, sherbet

製菓 せいか confectionery (making of confections)

茶菓 さか(=ちゃか) tea and cakes, refreshments

銘菓 めいか excellent cake, cake of an established name

冷菓 れいか ices, ice cream

❷ [original meaning] fruit

水菓子 みずがし fruit

SYNONYMS

❶ **confectionery**

菓 CONFECTIONERY → 2873
飴 CANDY → 2250

菅

2874

2-3-8

▶SEDGE

カン ケン すげ すが

Ⓒ 菅 jiān

140	Names	U83C5
艹	S11-3-8	F1926

COMPOUNDS

● **SEDGE**

菅蓋 かんがい large sedge parasol

KUN

【すげ 菅】**SEDGE**

菅笠 すげがさ sedge hat
夕菅 ゆうすげ citron daylily, *Hemerocallis citrina*
寒菅 かんすげ Japanese sedge, *Carex morrowii*

【すが 菅】**SEDGE**

菅畳 すがたたみ sedge mat
菅原 すがはら(=すげはら) field of sedge

SYNONYMS

● **kinds of grasses**

草 GRASS → 2813
荻 AMUR SILVERGRASS → 2844
蒲 CATTAIL → 2932
莱 GOOSEFOOT → 2878
蕨 BRACKEN → 2992
叢 grassy place → 3243
芝 LAWN GRASS → 2705
笹 BAMBOO GRASS → 3301
茅 cogongrass → 2779
萱 THATCH GRASS → 2904
藁 STRAW → 3015
芦 REED → 2743
葦 COMMON REED → 2934
菅 SEDGE → 2874

菊

2875

2-3-8

▶CHRYSANTHEMUM

キク

Ⓒ 菊 jú

140	Jōyō	U83CA
艹	S11-3-8	F1292

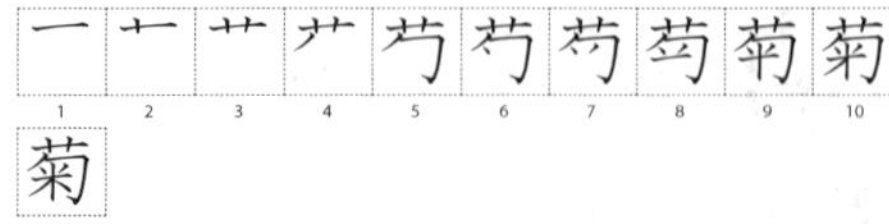

COMPOUNDS

❶ [also suffix] [original meaning] **CHRYSANTHEMUM**

菊花 きっか chrysanthemum
菊人形 きくにんぎょう chrysanthemum figure [doll]
野菊 のぎく wild chrysanthemum; aster
白菊 しらぎく white chrysanthemum
除虫菊 じょちゅうぎく pyrethrum

❷ kind of book size

菊判 きくばん small octavo, medium octavo

❸ abbrev. of 菊五郎 きくごろう, name of a kabuki actor

団菊祭 だんぎくさい kabuki performance in commemoration of Danjuro and Kikugoro

INDEPENDENT

【きく 菊】**CHRYSANTHEMUM**

菊の御紋 きくのごもん Imperial crest of the chrysanthemum

SYNONYMS

❶ **flowering plants**

菊 CHRYSANTHEMUM → 2875
菖 IRIS → 2881
菫 VIOLET → 2877
蓮 LOTUS → 2940
葛 KUDZU → 2905
蓬 JAPANESE MUGWORT → 2973
葵 MALLOW → 2906
蓉 COTTON ROSE → 2944
芙 LOTUS → 2737
蘭 ORCHID → 3031
萩 *HAGI* → 2908
藤 WISTERIA → 3025
桜 cherry blossom → 1168
梅 *ume* blossom → 1159

菌

2876

2-3-8

▶BACTERIA

キン

Ⓒ 菌 jūn jùn

140	Jōyō	U83CC
艹	S11-3-8	F1462

COMPOUNDS

❶ [also suffix] **BACTERIA, bacillus, germ, microorganism**

細菌 さいきん bacteria, germ, microbe
黴菌 ばいきん bacterium, germ
殺菌する さっきんする sterilize, pasteurize
病菌 びょうきん disease germ, virus
保菌者 ほきんしゃ germ carrier
チフス菌 ちふすきん typhoid bacillus
赤痢菌 せきりきん dysentery bacillus

❷ fungus, mushroom
菌類 きんるい fungi
菌毒 きんどく mushroom poison
菌糸 きんし hypha, mycelium

INDEPENDENT

【きん 菌】**BACTERIA, germ; fungus, mushroom**
菌を培養する きんをばいようする culture [cultivate] bacteria

SYNONYMS

❷ fungus
黴 MOLD → 1008
茸 MUSHROOM → 2809
菌 fungus → 2876

菫

2877
2-3-8

▶VIOLET
キン コン すみれ ㊔ かおる
Ⓒ 堇 jǐn

140	Names	U83EB
艹	S11-3-8	F0000

COMPOUNDS

❶ **VIOLET**
❷ [archaic] aconite; *Aconitum chinense*
❸ [archaic] rose of Sharon; alth(a)ea
❹ [archaic] celery

KUN

【すみれ 菫】**VIOLET (the flower)**
菫色 すみれいろ violet (the color)
三色菫 さんしょくすみれ(=さんしきすみれ) pansy, heartsease

SYNONYMS

❶ & 【すみれ】 flowering plants
菊 CHRYSANTHEMUM → 2875
菖 IRIS → 2881
菫 VIOLET → 2877
蓮 LOTUS → 2940
葛 KUDZU → 2905
蓬 JAPANESE MUGWORT → 2973
葵 MALLOW → 2906
蓉 COTTON ROSE → 2944
芙 LOTUS → 2737
蘭 ORCHID → 3031
萩 *HAGI* → 2908
藤 WISTERIA → 3025
桜 cherry blossom → 1168
梅 *ume* blossom → 1159

萊

2878
2-3-8

▶GOOSEFOOT
ライ
Ⓝ 莱 Ⓒ 莱 lái

140	Names	U840A
艹	S11-3-8	F3247

COMPOUNDS

❶ **GOOSEFOOT**
蓬萊 ほうらい Mt. Penglai, a mystical land in Chinese mythology

❷ overgrown with weed; wasteland
草萊 そうらい rampant weeds; wastelands, wilderness

SYNONYMS

❶ kinds of grasses
草 GRASS → 2813
荻 AMUR SILVERGRASS → 2844
蒲 CATTAIL → 2932
萊 GOOSEFOOT → 2878
蕨 BRACKEN → 2992
叢 grassy place → 3243
芝 LAWN GRASS → 2705
笹 BAMBOO GRASS → 3301
茅 cogongrass → 2779
萱 THATCH GRASS → 2904
藁 STRAW → 3015
芦 REED → 2743
葦 COMMON REED → 2934
菅 SEDGE → 2874

菱

2879
2-3-8

▶RHOMBUS
リョウ ひし ㊔ ゆう みち
Ⓝ 蔆 Ⓒ 菱 líng

140	Names	U83F1
艹	S11-3-8	F1917

COMPOUNDS

❶ **RHOMBUS, diamond shape, lozenge**
菱面体 りょうめんたい rhombohedron
菱脳 りょうのう rhombencephalon, hindbrain
菱鉄鉱 りょうてっこう siderite

❷ [original meaning] **water chestnut**
菱花 りょうか water chestnut flower

KUN

【ひし 菱】
① **RHOMBUS, diamond shape, lozenge**
菱形 ひしがた diamond shape, rhombus, lozenge
菱餅 ひしもち diamond-shaped colored rice cake

士 宀 ⺌ ⺍ 山 巛 【艹】 丷 亼 廿

花菱 はなびし family crest with a rhombus-shaped flower motif

② **water chestnut, esp. *Trapa japonica***

菱食 ひしくい bean goose, *Anser fabalis*

③ (weapon) caltrop

撒菱 まきびし caltrop

SYNONYMS

❷ **fruits and fruit trees**

桃 PEACH → 1174
榛 HAZEL → 1328
椎 CHINQUAPIN → 1249
柚 YUZU → 1123
椰 COCONUT → 1285
柑 CITRUS → 1112
橙 BITTER ORANGE → 1369
葡 GRAPE → 2902
萄 GRAPE → 2870
柿 PERSIMMON → 1118
檎 APPLE → 1386
李 PLUM → 3050
枇 LOQUAT → 1063
杷 LOQUAT → 1065
苺 STRAWBERRY → 2780
菱 water chestnut → 2879
杏 APRICOT → 3049
梅 JAPANESE APRICOT → 1159
橘 MANDARIN → 1366
栗 CHESTNUT → 3280
栃 JAPANESE HORSE CHESTNUT → 1122
梨 PEAR → 3412
蕉 PLANTAIN → 2994

菜

▸VEGETABLE

サイ な

Ⓝ 菜 Ⓒ 菜 cài

2880

2-3-8

140	Jōyō-4	U83DC
艹	S11-3-8	F1101

Stroke order: 1–11

COMPOUNDS

❶ **VEGETABLE, greens**

菜食 さいしょく vegetable diet
菜食主義 さいしょくしゅぎ vegetarianism
菜園 さいえん vegetable garden
野菜 やさい vegetables, greens
白菜 はくさい Chinese cabbage, white rape
山菜 さんさい edible wild plant

❷ⓐ **dish accompanying the rice in Japanese meals, side dish**

ⓑ counter for dishes

a 前菜 ぜんさい *hors d'oeuvre*
惣菜(=総菜) そうざい daily [household] dish, side dish

b 一汁一菜 いちじゅういっさい simple meal

INDEPENDENT

【さい 菜】side dish (→ ❷ⓐ)

粗末なお菜 そまつなおさい poor side dish

KUN

【な 菜】**greens, VEGETABLES; rape**

菜っ葉 なっぱ greens
菜種 なたね rapeseed, coleseed
青菜 あおな greens

SYNONYMS

❶ **plants**

菜 VEGETABLE → 2880
植 PLANT → 1247
栽 garden plant → 4087
茨 thorny shrub → 2812
苔 MOSS → 2792
蔓 VINE → 2975
桔 PLANT NAME ELEMENT → 1164

【な】

◯ **vegetables**

菜 greens → 2880
蕪 TURNIP → 2990
芋 POTATO → 2706
豆 BEAN → 2442
蕗 BUTTERBUR → 3007
茄 EGGPLANT → 2787
芹 JAPANESE PARSLEY → 2742
瓜 GOURD → 3789
瓢 BOTTLE GOURD → 2356
芥 mustard → 2741

NOTE

➡ see COMPOUND FORMATION for 惣菜 そうざい → 惣 3452

菖

▸IRIS

ショウ ㊔ あやめ

Ⓒ 菖 chāng

2881

2-3-8

140	Names	U83D6
艹	S11-3-8	F3228

COMPOUNDS

● **IRIS, sweet flag**

菖蒲 しょうぶ sweet flag; Japanese water iris, *Iris ensata* var. *ensata*

SYNONYMS

● **flowering plants**

菊 CHRYSANTHEMUM → 2875
菖 IRIS → 2881
菫 VIOLET → 2877
蓮 LOTUS → 2940
葛 KUDZU → 2905
蓬 JAPANESE MUGWORT → 2973
葵 MALLOW → 2906
蓉 COTTON ROSE → 2944
芙 LOTUS → 2737
蘭 ORCHID → 3031
萩 *HAGI* → 2908
藤 WISTERIA → 3025
桜 cherry blossom → 1168
梅 *ume* blossom → 1159

萃

2882

2-3-8

▶GATHER

スイ

Ⓒ 萃 cuì

140	Non-Jōyō	U8403
艹	S11-3-8	F0000

COMPOUNDS

[now replaced by 粋 1645]

ⓐ [original meaning] **GATHER, assemble**

ⓑ **GATHERing, collection**

b 抜萃 **ばっすい** extract, excerpt, selection

SYNONYMS

ⓐ **gather**

集 COLLECT → 3445
蒐 COLLECT → 2942
聚 COLLECT → 3479
収 collect → 0031
採 GATHER → 0606
采 GATHER → 3077
萃 GATHER → 2882
湊 come together → 0743

萠

2883

2-3-8

▶GERMINATE

ホウ　ボウ　も(える)　きざ(す) ㊔ めぐみ　め　ほ　ほの

140	Names	U8420
艹	S11-3-8	F0000

traditional form → see 萌 at 2871

葛

2884

2-3-8

▶KUDZU

カツ　くず　かずら ㊔ つら　かつら　ふじ　かず　かど　さち

140	Nonstandard	U845B
艹	S11-3-8	F0000

traditional form → see 葛 at 2905

菜

2885

2-3-8

▶VEGETABLE

サイ　な

140	Nonstandard	U83DC
艹	S11-3-8	F0000

traditional form → see 菜 at 2880

黄

2-3-8

incorrect classification

➡ see 2-4-7: 龷 at 3116

葉

2-3-8

incorrect stroke-count

➡ see 2-3-9: 艹 at 2912

剪

2886

2-3-8

▶PRUNE

セン　き(る)　つ(む)

Ⓒ 剪 jiǎn

18	Non-Jōyō	U526A
刀	S11-2-9	F0000

COMPOUNDS

● [original meaning] **PRUNE, trim, shear**

剪定する **せんていする** prune, trim
剪断 **せんだん** shearing, shear

KUN

【きる 剪る】[now usu. 切る] **PRUNE, trim, shear**

枝を剪る **えだをきる** prune a tree

【つむ 剪む】[also 摘む] **cut (one's hair), trim**

髪を剪む **かみをつむ** have one's hair cut [trimmed]

SPECIAL READINGS

剪刀(=鋏) **はさみ** scissors, shears

SYNONYMS

● **cut**

切 CUT → 0030
薙ぐ MOW DOWN → 3010
剪 PRUNE → 2886
削 CUT BY CHIPPING → 1837
挽く GRIND, saw → 0511
断 CUT OFF → 1885
截 CUT OFF → 4092
裁 CUT OUT → 4090
斬 CUT WITH A SWORD → 1874
割 cut with a knife → 2284
剖 DISSECT → 2103
刈る CLIP → 0032
伐 CUT DOWN → 0046

HOMOPHONES

きる

切 CUT → 0030
伐 CUT DOWN → 0046
截 CUT OFF → 4092

士 宀 ⺍ ⺌ 山 巛 艹 【䒑】 亼 廿

斬 CUT WITH A SWORD →1874
つむ 摘 PICK →0851

NOTE

➡ see USAGE notes at 切 0030 and 摘 0851

葢 2887

▶COVER

ガイ コウ ふた おお(う) けだ(し)

108	Nonstandard	U76D6
皿	S11-5-6	F0000

2-3-8 traditional form →see 蓋 at 2933

貪

2-3-8 incorrect classification
➡ see 2-2-9: 亼 at 2630

黄

2-3-8 incorrect stroke-count
➡ see 2-4-8: 廿 at 3128

堯 2888

▶YAO

ギョウ ㊔ たか たかし あき あきら

10	Names	U582F
儿	S12-2-10	F0000

2-3-9 traditional form →see 尭 at 2560

喜 2889

▶HAPPY

キ よろこ(ぶ) よろこ(ばす) ㊔ よし のぶ

Ⓝ 歖 㐂◆ Ⓒ 喜 xǐ

30	Jōyō-4	U559C
口	S12-3-9	F0605

2-3-9

COMPOUNDS

❶ⓐ [original meaning] **be HAPPY [glad], rejoice**
ⓑ joy, pleasure

a 喜悦 きえつ delight, rapture, joy
喜色 きしょく glad countenance
歓喜する かんきする rejoice, be greatly delighted

b 悲喜 ひき joy and sorrow
一喜一憂 いっきいちゆう alternation of joy and sorrow

❷ **amusing, funny**
喜劇 きげき comedy

KUN

【よろこぶ 喜ぶ】[formerly also 悦ぶ] *vi* **be HAPPY [glad], be delighted**
喜び よろこび [formerly also 悦び] joy, delight; [sometimes also 慶び] felicitation, congratulation; matter for congratulation
喜ばしい よろこばしい joyful, delightful, gratifying
喜んで よろこんで willingly, with pleasure
大喜び おおよろこび great joy, delight

【よろこばす 喜ばす】[formerly also 悦ばす] *vt* **please, gladden, make HAPPY**
親を喜ばす おやをよろこばす make one's parents happy
目を喜ばす めをよろこばす feast one's eyes (on)

SYNONYMS

❶ **pleased and pleasant**
楽 pleasurable →3505
欣 JOYFUL →1057
爽 REFRESHING →4402
快 PLEASANT →0289
朗 CHEERFUL →1679
愉 PLEASED →0710
悦 DELIGHTED →0501
嬉しい GLAD →0890
喜 HAPPY →2889
歓 JOYOUS →2342
驩 JOYOUS →2333

USAGE

❶【よろこぶ】
喜ぶ
[formerly also 悦ぶ] *vi* be happy [glad], be delighted
悦ぶ
[now usu. 喜ぶ] *vi* be happy [glad], be delighted

❷【よろこび】
喜び
ⓐ [formerly also 悦び] joy, delight
ⓑ [sometimes also 慶び] felicitation, congratulation; matter for congratulation
悦び
[now usu. 喜び] joy, delight
慶び
[usu. 喜び] felicitation, congratulation; matter for congratulation

❸【よろこばす】
喜ばす
[formerly also 悦ばす] *vt* please, gladden, make happy
悦ばす
[now usu. 喜ばす] *vt* please, gladden, make happy

HOMOPHONES

よろこぶ 悦 DELIGHTED →0501
よろこび
悦 DELIGHTED →0501
慶 FELICITATION →3936
よろこばす 悦 DELIGHTED →0501

壺

2890

2-3-9

▶**JAR**

コ つぼ

Ⓝ 壷 Ⓒ 壶 hú

33	Non-Jōyō	U58FA
士	S12-3-9	F1893

COMPOUNDS

● globular vessel: **JAR, pot, crock, vase; jug**

壺中 こちゅう inside a pot

唾壺 だこ spittoon

酒壺 しゅこ(=さかつぼ) wine jar, liquor jar

INDEPENDENT

【こ 壺】 *hu*: **ancient Chinese vase-shaped vessel**

KUN

【つぼ 壺】

① [also suffix] globular vessel: **JAR, pot, crock; vase; jug**

壺焼き つぼやき cooking in a crock; turban shell cooked in the shell

墨壺 すみつぼ inkpot, ink line (in carpentry)

骨壺 こつつぼ (cremation) urn

茶壺 ちゃつぼ urn for tea leaves

痰×壺 たんつぼ spittoon

火消し壺 ひけしつぼ charcoal extinguisher

② **dice cup**

壺振り つぼふり rolling dice (in a cup)

③ **depression, basin**

滝壺 たきつぼ pool below a waterfall

④ **pressure point, acupuncture point, moxibustion point**

足壺 あしつぼ pressure points on the foot

⑤ **key point, essence; bull's-eye**

壺を心得る つぼをこころえる understand the essence, catch the main point(s)

⑥ **one's wishes [expectations]**

思う壺 おもうつぼ one's wishes [expectations]

思う壺に嵌まる おもうつぼにはまる turn out just as one wished; play into the hands (of)

⑦ (finger) position (of a stringed instrument)

⑧ [archaic] target (when aiming an arrow)

SYNONYMS

● **containers**

箱 BOX → 3362

壺 JAR → 2890

槽 TANK → 1352

樽 BARREL → 1368

棺 COFFIN → 1240

桶 BUCKET → 1211

笈 BOX CARRIED ON THE BACK → 3274

鞘 SHEATH → 2259

篳 BAMBOO BOX → 3381

函 BOX → 3724

籠 BASKET → 3398

袋 BAG → 3201

鞄 BAG (for carrying) → 2248

器 VESSEL → 3367

瓶 BOTTLE → 1702

缶 CAN → 2526

缶 EARTHENWARE JAR → 2525

壹

2891

2-3-9

▶**ONE**

イチ ㊔ い かず はじめ

33	Nonstandard	U58F9
士	S12-3-9	F0000

traditional form → see 壱 at 2723

富

2892

2-3-9

▶**RICH**

フ フウ フッ- と(む) とみ ㊔ ひさ

Ⓝ 冨 Ⓒ 富 fù

40	Jōyō-5	U5BCC
宀	S12-3-9	F0722

(stroke order diagram: 1–12)

COMPOUNDS

❶ⓐ [original meaning] **RICH, wealthy, affluent**

ⓑ **RICHes, wealth**

ⓒ make **RICH**, enrich

a 富裕 ふゆう wealth, richness

b 富豪 ふごう wealthy man, millionaire

富農 ふのう rich farmer

富力 ふりょく wealth, riches

富貴な ふうきな(=ふっきな) wealthy and noble

c 富国強兵策 ふこくきょうへいさく measure to enrich and strengthen a country

❷ (abounding in) **RICH, abundant, plentiful**

富鉱 ふこう rich ore

豊富な ほうふな abundant, plentiful, rich

❸ Mt. Fuji

富士山 ふじさん Mt. Fuji

富岳 ふがく Mt. Fuji

KUN

【とむ 富む】 **be RICH; abound in, teem with**

富ます とます enrich, make wealthy

資源に富む しげんにとむ abound in natural resources

【とみ 富】 **wealth, RICHes; resources; lottery, lottery ticket**

富の分配 とみのぶんぱい distribution of wealth

富札 とみふだ lottery ticket

富籤 とみくじ lottery, lottery ticket

SPECIAL READINGS

富山県 とやまけん Toyama Prefecture

SYNONYMS

❶ⓐ **rich**

富 RICH → 2892
豪 wealthy → 2657

ⓑ **wealth**

財 WEALTH → 1849
産 property → 4089
富 riches → 2892
宝 TREASURE → 2764

❷ **plentiful**

百 numerous → 2519
沃 FERTILE → 0315
万 myriad → 3653
多 MANY → 2694
豊 PLENTIFUL → 3344
沢 plentiful → 0313
穣 YIELDING ABUNDANTLY → 1597
裕 ABUNDANT → 1530
饒 ABUNDANT → 2280
富 RICH → 2892

寓

2893

2-3-9

▶**TEMPORARY ABODE**

グウ ㊔ よる より

Ⓒ 寓 yù

40	Names	U5BD3
宀	S12-3-9	F2855

COMPOUNDS

❶ⓐ **TEMPORARY ABODE**

ⓑ **stay [reside] temporarily**

a 仮寓 かぐう temporary residence
b 寄寓 きぐう lodging with; temporary residence

❷ **imply, suggest**

寓話 ぐうわ fable, allegory
寓意 ぐうい hidden meaning, allegory; moral (of a story)

INDEPENDENT

【ぐうする 寓する】 reside temporarily; imply

SYNONYMS

❶ⓐ **temporary quarters**

舎 temporary quarters → 2555
寮 DORMITORY → 2984
宿 lodging → 2858
館 inn → 2196
亭 INN → 2572
寓 TEMPORARY ABODE → 2893

ⓑ **stay**

滞 STAY → 0815
頓 STAY IN PLACE → 1320
留 STAY → 3189
逗 STAY → 4005
駐 STATIONED → 2297
屯 STATION TROOPS → 4268
在 reside temporarily → 3704
泊 STAY OVERNIGHT → 0389
宿 LODGE → 2858
寓 stay temporarily → 2893

❷ **express**

表 EXPRESS → 3083
揮 WIELD → 0717
寓 imply → 2893

寒

2894

2-3-9

▶**COLD**

カン さむ(い)

Ⓝ 寒 Ⓒ 寒 hán

40	Jōyō-3	U5BD2
宀	S12-3-9	F1166

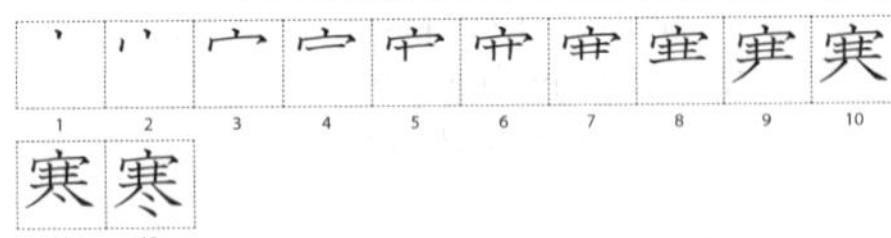

COMPOUNDS

❶ (of weather) **COLD, chilly**

寒気 かんき cold, cold weather
寒暑 かんしょ hot and cold
寒流 かんりゅう cold current
寒冷 かんれい cold, coldness, chilliness
寒波 かんぱ cold wave
寒暖計 かんだんけい thermometer

❷ **COLD**est season, cold season, midwinter

寒鮒× かんぶな crucian caught in midwinter
大寒 だいかん coldest season, midwinter

❸ poor, deserted

寒村 かんそん deserted [poor] village
素寒貧 すかんぴん dire poverty; pauper

❹ tremble, shudder

寒心すべき かんしんすべき alarming, deplorable

INDEPENDENT

【かん 寒】 **COLD**est season, midwinter

寒の入り かんのいり beginning of midwinter

KUN

【さむい 寒い】 (of weather) **COLD, chilly**

寒さ さむさ coldness, cold
寒空 さむぞら wintry sky, cold weather
寒気 さむけ chill
肌寒い はださむい chill, chilly

SYNONYMS

❶ **cold**

冷 COLD →0088
寒 COLD (weather) →2894
涼 COOL →0633
凜 SEVERELY COLD →0195

❷ cold seasons
冬 WINTER →2679
寒 coldest season →2894
秋 AUTUMN →1464

寒

2895

2-3-9

▶COLD

カン さむ(い)

40	Nonstandard	U5BD2
宀	S12-3-9	F0000

traditional form → see 寒 at 2894

窗

2896

2-3-9

▶WINDOW

ソウ まど

116	Nonstandard	U7A97
穴	S12-5-7	F0000

traditional form → see 窓 at 2859

掌

2-3-9

incorrect classification
➡ see 2-5-7: ⺌ at 3215

嘗

2-3-9

incorrect classification/
stroke-count
➡ see 2-5-8: ⺌ at 3225

営覚

2-3-9

incorrect classification
➡ see 2-5-7: ⺌ at 3216

嵌

2897

2-3-9

▶INLAY

カン ガン は(める) は(まる)

Ⓒ 嵌 qiàn kàn

46	Non-Jōyō	U5D4C
山	S12-3-9	F2560

COMPOUNDS

● [now also 眼 がん 1504] **INLAY, set in**
嵌入する かんにゅうする set in, inlay, dovetail
嵌合 かんごう fitting together, fit
象嵌 ぞうがん inlaid work, inlaying

KUN

【はめる 嵌める】[sometimes also 塡める]
①ⓐ **put in, set in, insert, fit**
ⓑ **put on, slip on**
a 嵌め込み はめこみ insertion, inlaying
② **entrap, ensnare; trick, deceive**
旨く嵌められた うまくはめられた I was cleverly taken in

【はまる 嵌まる】[sometimes also 塡まる]
① **fit, be fit for, suit**
当て嵌まる あてはまる be applicable, come under (a category), fulfill (criteria)
②ⓐ **be trapped, be ensnared**
ⓑ **be addicted, be deep (into)**
a 嵌まり込む はまりこむ get stuck in, be mired in; be addicted to
穴に嵌まる あなにはまる fall in a pit

SYNONYMS

● **put in**
入 PUT IN →4177
挿 INSERT →0517
嵌 INLAY →2897
-込む cause to move inward →3762

USAGE

❶【はめる】
嵌める
[sometimes also 塡める]
①ⓐ put in, set in, insert, fit
ⓑ put on, slip on
② entrap, ensnare; trick, deceive
塡める
[usu. 嵌める] same as 嵌める

❷【はまる】
嵌まる
[sometimes also 塡まる]
① fit, be fit for, suit
②ⓐ be trapped, be ensnared
ⓑ be addicted, be deep (into)
塡まる
[usu. 嵌まる] same as 嵌まる

HOMOPHONES

はめる 塡 FILL →0777
はまる 塡 FILL →0777

嵐

2898

2-3-9

▶STORM

ラン▲ あらし

Ⓒ 岚 lán

46	Jōyō	U5D50
山	S12-3-9	F1800

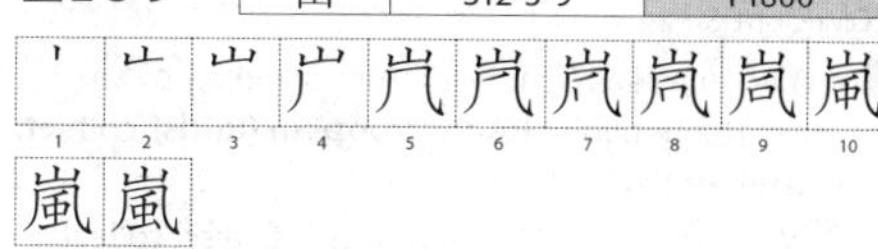

COMPOUNDS

❶ **STORM, tempest**
春嵐 しゅんらん spring storm

❷ [original meaning] **mountain air, mountain vapor, mist**
嵐気 らんき mountain air, mountain mist
晴嵐 せいらん mountain vapor

KUN

【あらし 嵐】 **STORM, tempest; stormy wind**

嵐の前の静けさ あらしのまえのしずけさ the lull [calm] before a storm
政界の嵐 せいかいのあらし political storm
砂嵐 すなあらし sandstorm
青嵐 あおあらし wind blowing through verdure, mountain air

SYNONYMS

❶ **wind**
風 WIND → 3730
嵐 STORM → 2898
颱 TYPHOON → 4138
台 typhoon → 2498
凪 CALM → 3709
颯 SOUND OF GUSTING WIND → 1563

嵜

2899
2-3-9

▶**PROMONTORY**
キ さき

46	Nonstandard	U5D5C
山	S12-3-9	F0000

traditional form → see 崎 at 0569

尋

2900
2-3-9

▶**INQUIRE**
ジン たず(ねる) ひろ ㊔ ひろし

41	Nonstandard	U5C0B
寸	S12-3-9	F0000

traditional form → see 尋 at 2918

募

2901
2-3-9

▶**RAISE**
ボ つの(る)
Ⓒ 募 mù

19	Jōyō	U52DF
力	S12-2-10	F1387

1	2	3	4	5	6	7	8	9	10	11	12
一	十	艹	艹	芇	苩	苷	苴	莫	莫	募	募

COMPOUNDS

● [original meaning] (gather persons or money by appealing to the public) **RAISE (troops or funds), collect, recruit, enlist**
募集する ぼしゅうする recruit, enlist; raise, collect
募金 ぼきん fund-raising, collection of subscriptions
募債 ぼさい raising of a loan, loan flotation
応募する おうぼする apply for, subscribe for [to], enlist for
公募 こうぼ appeal for public subscription
徴募 ちょうぼ recruitment

KUN

【つのる 募る】 *vt* **recruit, enlist, levy; RAISE (subscriptions or funds);** *vi* **grow violent, increase severity**
募って来る食欲 つのってくるしょくよく rising appetite
寄付金を募る きふきんをつのる make an appeal for contributions

SYNONYMS

● **enlist**
徴 LEVY → 0841
募 RAISE → 2901

葡

2902
2-3-9

▶**GRAPE**
▶**PORTUGAL**
ブ ホ ポ
Ⓒ 葡 pú

140	Names	U8461
艹	S12-3-9	F2478

COMPOUNDS

❶ **GRAPE, grapevine**
葡萄 ぶどう grape
葡萄酒 ぶどうしゅ (grape) wine
山葡萄 やまぶどう crimson glory vine

❷ⓐ **PORTUGAL**
ⓑ **Portuguese (language)**
a 日葡関係 にっぽかんけい Japan-Portugal relations
b 日葡辞書 にっぽじしょ *Vocabvlário da Lingoa de Iapam* (Japanese-Portuguese dictionary published 1603)
羅葡日辞典 らほにちじてん Latin-Portuguese-Japanese dictionary

INDEPENDENT

【ぽ 葡】 **PORTUGAL**

SPECIAL READINGS

葡萄牙 ぽるとがる Portugal
葡萄 えび grape; dark purplish red color

SYNONYMS

❶ **fruits and fruit trees**
桃 PEACH → 1174
榛 HAZEL → 1328
椎 CHINQUAPIN → 1249
柚 YUZU → 1123
椰 COCONUT → 1285
柑 CITRUS → 1112
橙 BITTER ORANGE → 1369
葡 GRAPE → 2902
萄 GRAPE → 2870
柿 PERSIMMON → 1118
檎 APPLE → 1386
李 PLUM → 3050

枇 LOQUAT → 1063
杷 LOQUAT → 1065
苺 STRAWBERRY → 2780
菱 water chestnut → 2879
杏 APRICOT → 3049
梅 JAPANESE APRICOT → 1159
橘 MANDARIN → 1366
栗 CHESTNUT → 3280
栃 JAPANESE HORSE CHESTNUT → 1122
梨 PEAR → 3412
蕉 PLANTAIN → 2994

❷ⓐ European countries
英 ENGLAND → 2782
独 GERMANY → 0471
仏 FRANCE → 0020
伊 ITALY → 0052
葡 PORTUGAL → 2902
西 Spain → 4333
蘭 the Netherlands → 3031
希 Greece → 2543
露 Russia → 3495
白 Belgium → 4305

惹

2903

2-3-9

▶DRAW ATTENTION

ジャク　ひ(く)

Ⓒ 惹 rě

61	Names	U60F9
心	S12-4-8	F1987

COMPOUNDS

❶ DRAW (ATTENTION or sympathy), attract, catch
惹句 じゃっく catchphrase, slogan

❷ cause, induce
惹起する じゃっきする bring about, cause, provoke

KUN

【ひく 惹く】[now usu. 引く]
ⓐ **draw (attention or sympathy), attract, catch**
ⓑ **catch (a cold)**
a 惹き付ける ひきつける attract, charm
心惹かれる こころひかれる feel attracted [fascinated] by
注意を惹く ちゅういをひく draw attention
b 風邪を惹いている かぜをひいている have a cold

SYNONYMS

❶ pull
引 DRAW → 0207
曳 DRAW → 4348
牽 DRAW → 2621
惹 DRAW ATTENTION → 2903
抽 DRAW OUT → 0359
抜 PULL OUT → 0290
控える HOLD BACK → 0600
扣える HOLD BACK → 0250
寄せる DRAW NEAR → 2856

HOMOPHONES

ひく
引 DRAW → 0207
弾 PROJECTILE → 0697
退 RETREAT → 3838
挽 GRIND → 0511
轢 RUN OVER → 2095
牽 DRAW → 2621
曳 DRAW → 4348

NOTE

➡ see USAGE note at 引 0207

萱

2904

2-3-9

▶THATCH GRASS

カン　ケン　かや　㊔まさ　ただ

Ⓒ 萱 xuān

140	Names	U8431
艹	S12-3-9	F2831

COMPOUNDS

● daylily
萱草 かんぞう(=けんぞう) daylily

KUN

【かや 萱】[also 茅] **THATCH GRASS such as cogongrass, eulalias and other gramineous plants**
萱葺き かやぶき roofing with thatch grass
萱鼠 かやねずみ harvest mouse
茅萱 ちがや cogongrass

SYNONYMS

【かや】
○ **kinds of grasses**
草 GRASS → 2813
荻 AMUR SILVERGRASS → 2844
蒲 CATTAIL → 2932
莱 GOOSEFOOT → 2878
蕨 BRACKEN → 2992
叢 grassy place → 3243
芝 LAWN GRASS → 2705
笹 BAMBOO GRASS → 3301
茅 cogongrass → 2779
萱 THATCH GRASS → 2904
藁 STRAW → 3015
芦 REED → 2743
葦 COMMON REED → 2934
菅 SEDGE → 2874

HOMOPHONES

かや 茅 THATCH GRASS → 2779

NOTE

➡ see USAGE note at 茅 2779

葛

▸KUDZU

カツ くず かずら▲ ㊔ つら かつら ふじ かず かど さち

2905

2-3-9

Ⓝ 葛 Ⓒ 葛 gě gé

140	Jōyō	U845B
艹	S12-3-9	F1657

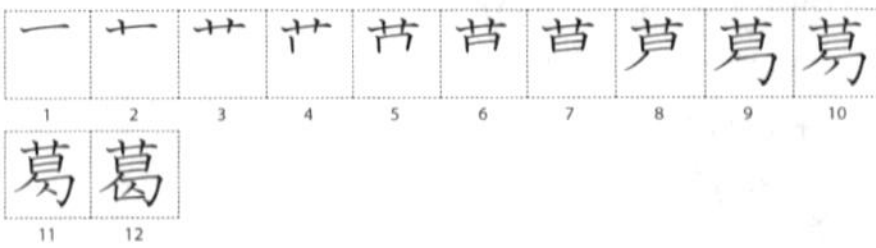

COMPOUNDS

● **KUDZU, Japanese arrowroot**

葛藤 かっとう complication, troubles, discord

葛根湯 かっこんとう antifebrile infusion

KUN

【くず 葛】**KUDZU, Japanese arrowroot**

葛布 くずふ cloth made from kudzu fiber

葛粉 くずこ arrowroot starch [flour]

葛餅 くずもち kudzu starch cake

葛餡× くずあん kudzu sauce

【かずら 葛】[sometimes also 蔓] vine, creeper

風船葛 ふうせんかずら balloon vine

SPECIAL READINGS

葛籠▲ つづら wicker hamper

SYNONYMS

● & 【くず】 **flowering plants**

菊 CHRYSANTHEMUM → 2875
菖 IRIS → 2881
菫 VIOLET → 2877
蓮 LOTUS → 2940
葛 KUDZU → 2905
蓬 JAPANESE MUGWORT → 2973
葵 MALLOW → 2906
蓉 COTTON ROSE → 2944
芙 LOTUS → 2737
蘭 ORCHID → 3031
萩 *HAGI* → 2908
藤 WISTERIA → 3025
桜 cherry blossom → 1168
梅 *ume* blossom → 1159

USAGE

【かずら】

葛
[sometimes also 蔓] vine, creeper

蔓
[usu. 葛] vine, creeper

HOMOPHONES

かずら 蔓 VINE → 2975

NOTE

➡ see COMPOUND FORMATION for 葛藤 かっとう → 藤 3025

葵

▸MALLOW

キ あおい ㊔ まもる

Ⓒ 葵 kuí

2906

2-3-9

140	Names	U8475
艹	S12-3-9	F2475

COMPOUNDS

[archaic]

❶ **MALLOW**, hollyhock

戎×葵 じゅうき hollyhock

❷ sunflower

葵花 きか sunflower

KUN

【あおい 葵】**MALLOW, hollyhock; asarabacca; asarabacca crest (esp. of Shogunate government)**

銭葵 ぜにあおい common mallow

SPECIAL READINGS

向日葵 ひまわり sunflower

SYNONYMS

❶ **flowering plants**

菊 CHRYSANTHEMUM → 2875
菖 IRIS → 2881
菫 VIOLET → 2877
蓮 LOTUS → 2940
葛 KUDZU → 2905
蓬 JAPANESE MUGWORT → 2973
葵 MALLOW → 2906
蓉 COTTON ROSE → 2944
芙 LOTUS → 2737
蘭 ORCHID → 3031
萩 *HAGI* → 2908
藤 WISTERIA → 3025
桜 cherry blossom → 1168
梅 *ume* blossom → 1159

落

▸FALL

ラク お(ちる) お(ち) お(とす)

Ⓒ 落 luò là lào

2907

2-3-9

140	Jōyō-3	U843D
艹	S12-3-9	F0247

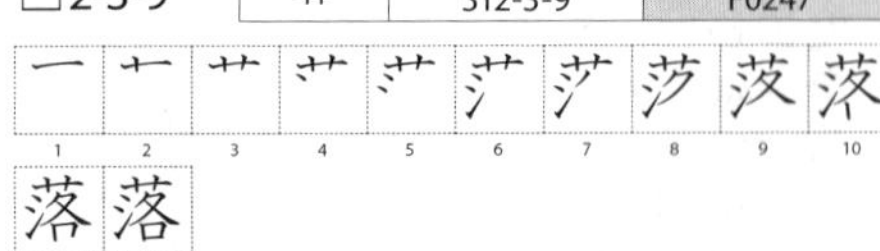

COMPOUNDS

❶ⓐ [original meaning] **FALL, fall off, drop, sink**
ⓑ **let FALL, drop**
ⓒ **FALL** in, collapse, crumble
ⓓ **FALL into (one's hands), receive**

a 落下 らっか fall, drop, descent
落馬する らくばする fall from a horse
落日 らくじつ setting sun
墜落する ついらくする fall, drop; crash
b 落球する らっきゅうする fail to catch a ball
落涙する らくるいする shed tears
落盤 らくばん cave-in
c 陥落する かんらくする fall in, cave in; surrender
d 落札する らくさつする make a successful bid

❷ (esp. of stock prices)
ⓐ (become less) **FALL, drop, decline**
ⓑ (reduction in value) **FALL**, drop

a 低落する ていらくする fall, depreciate, go down
下落 げらく fall, drop, decline; deterioration
ab 急落 きゅうらく sudden drop [fall], steep decline
暴落 ぼうらく slump, crash, heavy decline (in prices)

❸ⓐ (decline in status) **FALL, decline, decay**
ⓑ (be defeated) **FALL**, be defeated, surrender
ⓒ **FALL through, fail (an examination)**
ⓓ **FALL off, drop out, become omitted, be missing**

a 落魄 らくはく straitened [reduced] circumstances
堕落 だらく degeneration, corruption, decadence
没落 ぼつらく ruin, fall, collapse
b 落城 らくじょう fall of a castle
c 落選 らくせん election defeat; rejection
落第 らくだい failure in an examination
落伍者 らくごしゃ straggler
d 落丁 らくちょう missing page [leaf]
脱落する だつらくする be omitted; fall away [behind], drop out

❹ **be concluded, be settled, be completed**
落着する らくちゃくする be settled, come to a conclusion
落成 らくせい completion
一段落 いちだんらく pause; (figuratively) end of chapter

❺ village, town, settlement
村落 そんらく village, hamlet
部落 ぶらく community, village, hamlet

❻ **humor, jest, witticism**
落語 らくご *rakugo,* Japanese-style comic story
落書き らくがき scribbling, scrawling, graffiti

❼ perish, die
落命 らくめい death

❽ shave one's head to enter the Buddhist priesthood, take the tonsure
落髪 らくはつ tonsure

❾ lonesome, desolate
落莫たる らくばくたる dreary, desolate, lonesome

KUN

【おちる 落ちる】

①ⓐ **FALL, drop, go down; drip; sink**
ⓑ **FALL in, collapse, crumble**
ⓒ (of water) **FALL in, flow down, flow into**
ⓓ **FALL** into (one's hands), receive
ⓔ come off, be omitted, be missing

a 落ち込む おちこむ fall [cave] in; fall into depression
落ち葉 おちば fallen leaves
落ち零れ おちこぼれ student who cannot keep up with the class (in science); dropout
b 崩れ落ちる くずれおちる crumble down, tumble down
c 落ち合う おちあう gather, meet, join; flow together
d 人の手に落ちる ひとのてにおちる fall into another's hands
e 訳が落ちている やくがおちている The translation is missing

②ⓐ **FALL (in one's estimation); go down, be inferior, fall short of**
ⓑ **fail (in an examination); be defeated, surrender**

a 信用がガタ落ちだ しんようががたおちだ have a sudden fall in public estimation
気落ちする きおちする be discouraged, be dispirited
b パリが落ちた ぱりがおちた Paris has fallen

③ⓐ go down (from the capital), leave; escape
ⓑ go downstream

a 都落ち みやこおち rustication
駆け落ち かけおち elopement
b 落ち鮎 おちあゆ ayu coming down the river for spawning

④ [in compounds] **be settled**
落ち着く おちつく calm down, settle down, be steady; settle in, take up one's residence; harmonize with, match
落ち着き おちつき presence of mind, composure

⑤ (of wind) drop, abate, go down
風が落ちる かぜがおちる The wind dies away

⑥ **FALL** unconscious; die
落ち魚 おちうお dead fish

【おち 落ち】

① **omission, slip, error, fault**
落ち度 おちど fault, error; guilt
片手落ち かたておち partiality, one-sidedness, favoritism

② end, upshot; punch line [point] of a joke

馬鹿を見るのが落ちだよ ばかをみるのがおちだよ The upshot of the matter will be that you'll make a fool of yourself

③ [suffix] (stock) ex, off, less, minus

配当落ち はいとうおち ex dividend, dividend off

④ [suffix] handicap in a game of shogi

角落ち かくおち shogi game with the superior player playing without the *kaku*

【おとす 落とす】

① **drop, let FALL, throw down, dump**

落とし物 おとしもの lost article

撃ち落とす うちおとす shoot down

②ⓐ **remove, take away, clean**

ⓑ **omit, miss**

ⓒ fail to obtain

a 洗い落とす あらいおとす wash off, wash out

b 見落とし みおとし oversight, thing left unnoticed

c 単位を落とす たんいをおとす fail to earn a credit

③ⓐ debase, abase, depreciate

ⓑ lessen, decrease

a 品質を落とす ひんしつをおとす lower the quality

b 速力を落とす そくりょくをおとす slow down

④ take, capture; win (a person) over

砦を落とす とりでをおとす capture a fort

口説き落とす くどきおとす persuade, prevail upon; win a woman's heart

⑤ bid in, knock (an article) down

競り落とす せりおとす knock down, make a successful bid

⑥ scatter, spend (money)

日本人観光客が落とす金 にほんじんかんこうきゃくがおとすかね money scattered by Japanese tourists

⑦ let escape

士を奥州へ落としてやる しをおうしゅうへおとしてやる help a samurai get away to Oshu

⑧ drive away, exorcise

狐を落とす きつねをおとす exorcise a fox spirit (from a person)

SPECIAL READINGS

洒×落▲ しゃれ witticism, joke; pun, wordplay

洒×落る▲ しゃれる pun, play on words; jest, joke; dress smartly [stylishly]; make up

お洒×落▲ おしゃれ dressing up smartly [stylishly]; make up; dandy

SYNONYMS

❶ⓐ & ❶ⓑ descend and fall

落 FALL → 2907
墜 DROP DOWN → 3578
降 DESCEND → 0548
下 go down → 4186
倒 TOPPLE → 0139

ⓒ collapse

陥 FALL IN → 0547
落 FALL → 2907
崩 CRUMBLE → 2863
没 SINK → 0305

❷ decrease

減 DECREASE → 0733
耗 WEAR AWAY → 1660
削 cut down → 1837
縮 SHRINK → 1790
落 FALL → 2907
蝕 ERODE → 2258

❸ⓐ degenerate

落 FALL → 2907
衰 DECLINE → 2604
頽 DECLINE → 2039
堕 DEGENERATE → 3501
綻 UNRAVEL → 1745
破 break down → 1478

ⓒ fail

敗 fail → 1868
落 fall through → 2907
-損なう fail to (do) → 0801

❹ settle

着 settle (down) → 4110
帰 settle in place → 0148
落 be concluded → 2907

萩

2908

2-3-9

▶*HAGI*

シュウ はぎ

Ⓒ 萩 qiū

140	Names	U8429
艹	S12-3-9	F2046

COMPOUNDS

● [archaic] kind of rush

KUN

【はぎ 萩】***HAGI*, Japanese bush clover, *Lespedeza bicolor***

萩属 はぎぞく *Lespedeza*

SYNONYMS

【はぎ】

○ **shrubs**

藤 WISTERIA → 3025
蔦 JAPANESE IVY → 2972
萩 *HAGI* → 2908
茉 JASMINE → 2790
莉 JASMINE → 2843
芭 JAPANESE FIBER BANANA → 2736

○ **flowering plants**

菊 CHRYSANTHEMUM → 2875
菖 IRIS → 2881

菫 VIOLET → 2877
蓮 LOTUS → 2940
葛 KUDZU → 2905
蓬 JAPANESE MUGWORT → 2973
葵 MALLOW → 2906
蓉 COTTON ROSE → 2944
芙 LOTUS → 2737
蘭 ORCHID → 3031
萩 *HAGI* → 2908
藤 WISTERIA → 3025
桜 cherry blossom → 1168
梅 *ume* blossom → 1159

NOTE

★ do not confuse with 荻 AMUR SILVERGRASS → 2844

葺

2909

2-3-9

▶THATCH
シュウ ふ(く) -ぶき
Ⓒ 葺 qì

140	Names	U847A
艹	S12-3-9	F2746

KUN

【ふく 葺く】THATCH, cover (a roof)
葺き替える ふきかえる rethatch, reroof, retile
葺き板 ふきいた shingles

【-ぶき -葺き】
ⓐ **THATCHing [roofing] with**
ⓑ **THATCHed [covered] roof**
ab 茅葺き(=萱葺き) かやぶき roofing with thatch grass; thatched roof
藁葺き わらぶき straw thatching; straw roof
瓦葺き かわらぶき tile roofing; tile roof
板葺き いたぶき shingle roofing; shingle roof

SYNONYMS

【ふく】
◯ **cover and wrap**
覆 COVER → 3386
掩 COVER → 0592
被 cover → 1495
包 WRAP → 3684
蓋う COVER → 2933
蔽 COVER → 2991
葺く THATCH → 2909

葬

2910

2-3-9

▶FUNERAL
ソウ ほうむ(る)
Ⓝ 塟 Ⓒ 葬 zàng

140	Jōyō	U846C
艹	S12-3-9	F1453

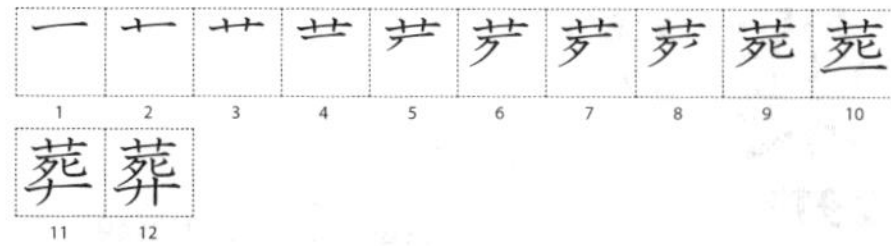

COMPOUNDS

❶ [also suffix] **FUNERAL**
葬式 そうしき funeral ceremony
葬儀 そうぎ funeral service [rites]
冠婚葬祭 かんこんそうさい ceremonial occasions (coming of age, marriage, funeral and ancestral worship)
国葬 こくそう national funeral
会社葬 かいしゃそう company funeral

❷ [original meaning] **bury (a corpse), entomb, inter**
埋葬する まいそうする bury, inter
火葬 かそう cremation
水葬 すいそう burial at sea

INDEPENDENT

【そう 葬】FUNERAL
葬の列 そうのれつ funeral procession

KUN

【ほうむる 葬る】bury (a corpse), entomb, inter; consign to oblivion, shelve
葬り去る ほうむりさる consign to oblivion

SYNONYMS

❷ **bury**
埋 BURY → 0484
葬 bury (a corpse) → 2910

董

2911

2-3-9

▶OLD TOOL
トウ ㊔ まさ しげ のぶ よし なお ただし ただす まこと しげる
Ⓒ 董 dǒng

140	Names	U8463
艹	S12-3-9	F2130

COMPOUNDS

❶ **OLD TOOL, used article**
骨董 こっとう antique, curio

❷ correct; oversee, superintend

SYNONYMS

❶ **machines and tools**
機 MACHINE → 1365
械 MECHANICAL CONTRIVANCE → 1203
具 IMPLEMENT → 3159
器 INSTRUMENT → 3367
儀 measuring instrument → 0191
鏡 OPTICAL INSTRUMENT → 2219
董 OLD TOOL → 2911

NOTE

★ do not confuse with 薫 BALMY → 3005

2

葉

▶LEAF

ヨウ は¹ は²

ⓒ 叶 yè xié

2912

2-3-9

140	Jōyō-3	U8449
艹	S12-3-9	F0202

COMPOUNDS

❶ [original meaning] **LEAF, foliage**

葉脈 ようみゃく veins of a leaf
葉緑素 ようりょくそ chlorophyll
紅葉 こうよう(=もみじ) red leaves, crimson foliage, autumn tints
落葉 らくよう fall of leaves; fallen leaves
子葉 しよう seed leaf, cotyledon
針葉樹 しんようじゅ conifer
枝葉末節 しようまっせつ unimportant details

❷ various **LEAF**like objects, as:
ⓐ (sheet of paper) **LEAF, sheet, page, paper**
ⓑ counter for leaves or sheets
ⓒ *anat* lobe, lobule
ⓓ plane (of an aircraft)

a 薄葉 うすよう Japanese tissue
前葉 ぜんよう preceding page [leaf]
b 紙二葉 かみによう two sheets of paper
三葉虫 さんようちゅう trilobite
c 肝葉 かんよう lobe of the liver
前頭葉 ぜんとうよう frontal lobe
d 単葉飛行機 たんようひこうき monoplane
複葉機 ふくようき biplane

❸ part of a historical period divided into three
初葉 しょよう initial period, beginning of an epoch

INDEPENDENT

【よう 葉】 *anat* lobe, lobule

KUN

【は¹ 葉】 **LEAF, foliage; needle; blade, spear**

葉っぱ はっぱ *colloq* leaf, foliage; needle; blade, spear
草の葉 くさのは blade of grass
松葉 まつば pine needle
落ち葉 おちば fallen leaves

【は² 葉】 [in compounds] **fragment, piece**—historically sometimes interchangeable with 端, as in the word はがき, which is now always written 葉書

葉書 はがき postcard
言葉 ことば word, term; wording; language

SPECIAL READINGS

紅葉 もみじ red leaves, crimson foliage, autumn tints; Japanese maple

SYNONYMS

❷ⓐ **paper**

紙 PAPER → 1654
葉 LEAF → 2912
丁 sheet → 4155
箋 PIECE OF PAPER → 3352
頁 PAGE → 2589
面 page (of a newspaper) → 2590

ⓑ **counters for flat things**

枚 COUNTER FOR FLAT THINGS → 1069
葉 counter for leaves → 2912
丁 counter for sheets → 4155
頁 counter for pages → 2589
通 counter for letters → 3855
竿 counter for flags → 3259

ⓓ **wings**

翼 WING (of birds or aircraft) → 3379
羽 WING (of birds or insects) → 0265
葉 plane → 2912

HOMOPHONES

は² 端 END → 1564

COMPOUND FORMATION

【言葉 ことば】

言葉 'word, etc.' consists of 言 こと 'word' and 葉 は² 'fragment, piece'. In ancient times, 言 こと referred to both a word and its meaning. Later, 葉 was attached to 言 to show that it is used in the sense of 'word'. Now, however, 言 is used only in the latter sense.

NOTE

➡ see USAGE note at 端 1564

著

▶AUTHOR
▶CONSPICUOUS

チョ チャク あらわ(す) いちじる(しい)

2913

2-3-9

140	Names	UFA5F
艹	S12-3-9	F0000

traditional form → see 著 at 2869

葢

▶COVER

ガイ コウ ふた おお(う) けだ(し)

2914

2-3-9

140	Nonstandard	U8462
艹	S12-3-9	F0000

traditional form → see 蓋 at 2933

葦

2915

2-3-9

▶COMMON REED

イ あし よし

140	Nonstandard	U8466
艹	S12-3-9	F0000

traditional form → see 葦 at 2934

萬

2916

2-3-9

▶TEN THOUSAND

マン バン よろず ㊔ かず

140	Names	U842C
艹	S12-3-9	F0000

traditional form → see 万 at 3653

葬

2917

2-3-9

▶FUNERAL

ソウ ほうむ(る)

140	Nonstandard	U585F
艹	S12-3-9	F0000

traditional form → see 葬 at 2910

蒸

2-3-9

incorrect stroke-count

➡ see 2-3-10: 艹 at 2936

蓮

2-3-9

incorrect stroke-count

➡ see 2-3-10: 艹 at 2940

蓬

2-3-9

incorrect stroke-count

➡ see 2-3-10: 艹 at 2945

尋

2918

2-3-9

▶INQUIRE

ジン たず(ねる) ひろ▲ ㊔ ひろし

Ⓝ 尋 Ⓒ 寻 xún

41	Jōyō	U5C0B
寸	S12-3-9	F1230

Stroke order: 1–12

COMPOUNDS

❶ [rare] **INQUIRE** into, investigate

討尋 とうじん thorough inquiry, minute investigation

❷ [sometimes also 訊 1842] **interrogate, question**

尋問 じんもん questioning, examination, interrogation

❸ ordinary, usual, common, normal

尋常の じんじょうの common, ordinary, normal

尋常に じんじょうに tamely; squarely; commonly, ordinarily, normally

❹ *hiro,* fathom: unit of length equiv. to approx. 1.8 m or 6 *shaku* (尺), used esp. for measuring the depth of water

千尋の谷 せんじんのたに abysmal valley

INDEPENDENT

【じん 尋】 fathom (→❹)

KUN

【たずねる 尋ねる】

①ⓐ [sometimes also 訊ねる] **INQUIRE (about, after), ask, question**

ⓑ **INQUIRE into, investigate into**

a 理由を尋ねる りゆうをたずねる ask the reason

b 由来を尋ねる ゆらいをたずねる inquire into the origin

② **search for, look for**

尋ね人 たずねびと missing person

尋ね求める たずねもとめる seek for

お尋ね者 おたずねもの wanted person, person wanted by the police

【ひろ 尋】 ***hiro,* fathom: unit of length equiv. to approx. 1.8 m or 6 *shaku* (尺), used esp. for measuring the depth of water**

SYNONYMS

❹ **length units**

寸 *sun* (3.03 cm) → 3652
浬 NAUTICAL MILE (1852 m) → 0526
反 *tan* (10.6 m) → 3663
尺 *SHAKU* (30.3 cm) → 4248
米 meter → 4342
尋 fathom (1.8 m) → 2918
間 *ken* (1.8 m) → 4122
丈 *jo* (3.03 m) → 4227
町 *cho* (109 m) → 1430
里 LEAGUE, *ri* (3.9 km) → 4356
哩 MILE (1609 m) → 0479

【たずねる】

①ⓐ **inquire**

問 QUESTION → 4117
詰 question closely → 1920
聞く ask → 4127
質 query → 3483
尋ねる INQUIRE → 2918
訊 INQUIRE → 1842
伺う INQUIRE (*humble*) → 0078
諮 CONSULT → 2009
詢 ASK FOR ADVICE → 1917

USAGE

【たずねる】

尋ねる

①ⓐ [sometimes also 訊ねる] inquire (about, after), ask, question

ⓑ inquire into, investigate into
② search for, look for
訊ねる
[usu. 尋ねる]
ⓐ question, interrogate
ⓑ inquire (about, after), ask, question
訪ねる
visit, call on, pay a visit

HOMOPHONES

たずねる
訪 VISIT → 1860
訊 INQUIRE → 1842

普 2919

▶WIDESPREAD
フ あまね(く)▲ ㊔ しん ひろ
Ⓒ 普 pǔ

2-3-9

72	Jōyō	U666E
日	S12-4-8	F0771

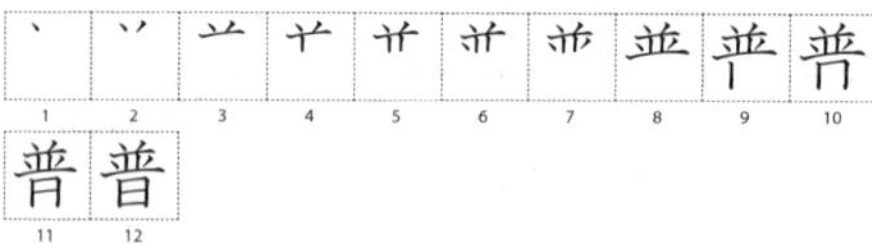

COMPOUNDS

❶ⓐ WIDESPREAD, general, universal, common
ⓑ common, ordinary

a 普及 ふきゅう diffusion, spread, propagation
普遍 ふへん universality, generality
普遍的な ふへんてきな universal, omnipresent, ubiquitous
普請 ふしん building, construction
b 普通の ふつうの normal, regular, ordinary
普選 ふせん universal suffrage
普段(=不断)の ふだんの usual, ordinary, everyday, habitual

❷ Prussia
普仏戦争 ふふつせんそう Franco-Prussian War

KUN

【あまねく 普く】[also 遍く] *literary* all over, everywhere, widely, universally
普く捜す あまねくさがす make a wide search
普く世界に知られる あまねくせかいにしられる be known all over the world

SYNONYMS

❶ⓐ widespread
普 WIDESPREAD → 2919
遍 ALL OVER → 3890
通 common → 3855
公 common (math) → 2468
ⓑ ordinary
常 NORMAL → 3203
只 ORDINARY → 2677
並 ordinary → 2793
平 common → 4291
普 common → 2919
庸 MEDIOCRE → 3881
凡 COMMONPLACE → 3656
套 TRITE → 2823

USAGE

【あまねく】
普く
[also 遍く] *literary* all over, everywhere, widely, universally
遍く
[also 普く] same as 普く

HOMOPHONES

あまねく 遍 ALL OVER → 3890

NOTE

➡ see COMPOUND FORMATION for 普請 ふしん → 請 1983
★ do not confuse with 晋 JIN DYNASTY → 3290

尊 2920

▶HONOR
ソン たっと(い) とうと(い) たっと(ぶ) とうと(ぶ) ㊔ たか たかし みこと
Ⓝ 尊 Ⓒ 尊 zūn

2-3-9

41	Jōyō-6	U5C0A
寸	S12-3-9	F1060

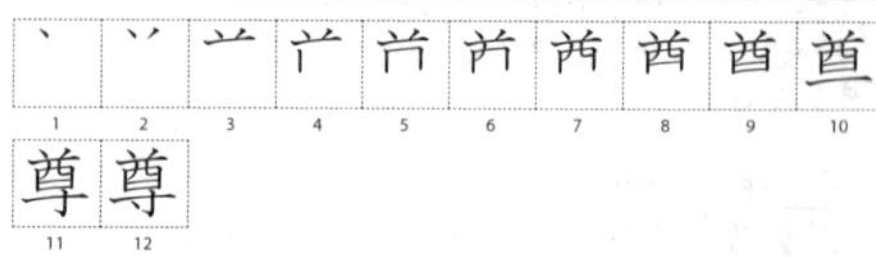

COMPOUNDS

❶ⓐ HONOR, respect, venerate, esteem
ⓑ HONORary, noble, exalted

a 尊重する そんちょうする respect, esteem, value
尊敬する そんけいする respect, esteem, honor, revere
自尊心 じそんしん (spirit of) self-respect, pride
b 尊厳 そんげん dignity, majesty, prestige
尊王 そんのう reverence for the emperor
尊称 そんしょう honorary title

❷ [honorific] **your HONORable, your**
尊顔 そんがん your countenance
尊父 そんぷ your father
尊宅 そんたく your house

❸ [also suffix] **HONORific title after names of Buddhist deities or statues**
釈尊 しゃくそん *Śākyamuni*, Buddha
本尊 ほんぞん principal image of Buddha
地蔵尊 じぞうそん (image of) *Kṣitigarbha-bodhisattva, Jizo* (guardian deity of children)

❹ haughty, arrogant

尊大な そんだいな haughty, arrogant, self-important
唯我独尊 ゆいがどくそん self-conceit; vainglory

❺ [original meaning, now archaic] kind of wine vessel used in ancient China

KUN

【たっとい 尊い】 **exalted, august, awe-inspiring, sacred**
尊い高齢 たっといこうれい sacred old age

【とうとい 尊い】 same as 尊い たっとい

【たっとぶ 尊ぶ】 **HONOR, respect, revere**
神を尊ぶ かみをたっとぶ revere God

【とうとぶ 尊ぶ】 same as 尊ぶ たっとぶ

SYNONYMS

❶ⓐ respect
敬 RESPECT → 2136
尊 HONOR → 2920
畏 respect → 3170
欽 REVERE → 2124
仰 look up to → 0051
崇 REVERENCE → 2864
尚 VALUE HIGHLY → 2774
重 set value on → 4390
拝 WORSHIP → 0360
慕 ADORE → 2970

❷ honorific prefixes
御 GENERAL HONORIFIC TERM → 0703
貴 YOUR HONORABLE → 3220
尊 your honorable → 2920
令 your honorable → 2489

HOMOPHONES

たっとい 貴 NOBLE → 3220
とうとい 貴 NOBLE → 3220
たっとぶ 貴 NOBLE → 3220
とうとぶ 貴 NOBLE → 3220

NOTE

➡ see USAGE note at 貴 3220

善

2921

2-3-9

▶GOOD
ゼン よ(い) ㊔ よし
Ⓝ 譱 Ⓒ 善 shàn

30	Jōyō-6	U5584
口	S12-3-9	F0837

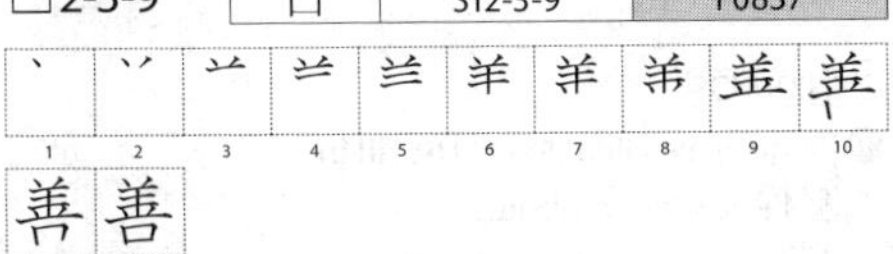

COMPOUNDS

❶ⓐ (having positive qualities) **GOOD**
ⓑ (satisfactory) **GOOD, well**

a 善意 ぜんい good intention; favorable sense
善良な ぜんりょうな good, virtuous
善政 ぜんせい good government [administration]
改善 かいぜん improvement, amelioration
最善 さいぜん best

b 善処する ぜんしょする make the best of
善戦する ぜんせんする fight well

❷ⓐ (morally excellent) **GOOD, virtuous**
ⓑ GOOD, goodness, virtue, moral excellence

a 善人 ぜんにん good people
善行 ぜんこう good deed, benevolence

b 善悪 ぜんあく good and evil
偽善 ぎぜん hypocrisy

❸ (on good terms) **GOOD, intimate**
善隣関係 ぜんりんかんけい good neighborly relations
親善 しんぜん goodwill, friendly relations

INDEPENDENT

【ぜん 善】 **GOOD, goodness, virtue**
善と悪 ぜんとあく good and evil

KUN

【よい 善い】 (morally excellent) **GOOD, good-natured, virtuous, upright**
善い行い よいおこない good deed
善く善く よくよく very carefully, very closely; exceedingly

SYNONYMS

❶ⓐ good
良 GOOD → 4373
善 GOOD → 2921
好 FAVORABLE → 0240
順 favorable → 0018
佳 FINE → 0096
美 BEAUTIFUL → 2817

❷ⓐ virtuous
正 RIGHT → 4296
義 righteous → 2948
善 GOOD → 2921
良 GOOD → 4373
鯁 UPRIGHT → 2357

ⓑ moral goodness
徳 VIRTUE → 0842
道 the way of moral conduct → 3888
善 GOOD → 2921
義 RIGHTEOUSNESS → 2948

HOMOPHONES

よい
良 GOOD → 4373
好 LIKE → 0240

NOTE

➡ see USAGE note at 良 4373

着 incorrect classification
➡ see ▢3-7-5: 兰 at 4110
2-3-9

寛 2922

2-3-10

▸**LENIENT**

カン くつろ(ぐ)▲ ㊔ ひろ ひろし

Ⓝ 寬 Ⓒ 宽 kuān

40 宀	Jōyō	U5BDB
	S13-3-10	F1346

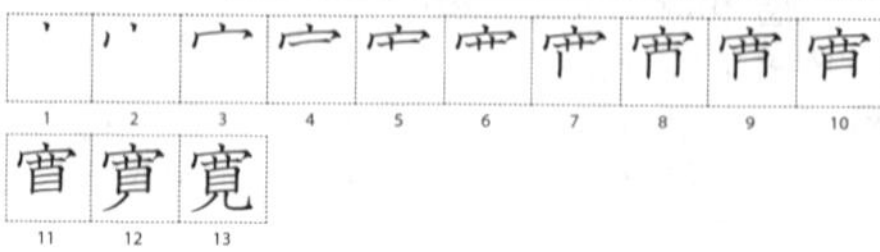

COMPOUNDS

● **LENIENT, tolerant, largehearted, generous, magnanimous, broad-minded**

寛大な かんだいな generous, magnanimous, lenient

寛容な かんような tolerant, liberal, generous

寛厳 かんげん lenity and severity

寛闊な かんかつな generous, largehearted

寛厚 かんこう kindness and largeheartedness

INDEPENDENT

【かん 寛】 leniency, generosity

人には寛 ひとにはかん leniency to others

KUN

【くつろぐ 寛ぐ】 make oneself comfortable, be at ease, relax

寛ぎ くつろぎ ease, relaxation

SYNONYMS

● **tolerant**

寛 LENIENT →2922

甘い indulgent →4306

窟 2923

2-3-10

▸**CAVE**

クツ いわや▲

Ⓒ 窟 kū

116 穴	Jōyō	U7A9F
	S13-5-8	F2050

COMPOUNDS

❶ [now also 屈 3821] [original meaning] **CAVE, cavern, hole**

洞窟 どうくつ cavern, cave

岩窟王 がんくつおう The Count of Monte Cristo

理窟 りくつ reason, logic; argument; pretext; theory

❷ [also suffix] **den**

巣窟 そうくつ den, haunt, nest

魔窟 まくつ haunts of the demon, den of iniquity; brothel, red-light district

阿片窟 あへんくつ opium den

貧民窟 ひんみんくつ slum

私娼×窟 ししょうくつ house of ill fame, brothel

KUN

【いわや 窟】 [also 岩屋] **CAVE**, cavern, hole

窟の中 いわやのなか inside of a cave

SYNONYMS

❶ **holes and cavities**

穴 HOLE →2682

洞 CAVE →0455

窟 CAVE →2923

窪 HOLLOW →2962

腔 BODY CAVITY →1267

孔 OPEN HOLE →0205

口 MOUTH →4189

坑 PIT →0277

堀 DITCH →0561

溝 CHANNEL →0810

壕 TRENCH →0966

濠 MOAT →0975

凹 concavity →4294

HOMOPHONES

いわや 岩屋 →2778, 3842

NOTE

➡ see COMPOUND FORMATION for 理屈 りくつ →屈 3821

塞 2924

2-3-10

▸**STOP UP**
▸**FORT**

サイ ソク ふさ(ぐ) ふさ(がる) せ(く)▲ とりで▲

Ⓒ 塞 sāi sài sè

32 土	Jōyō	U585E
	S13-3-10	F1525

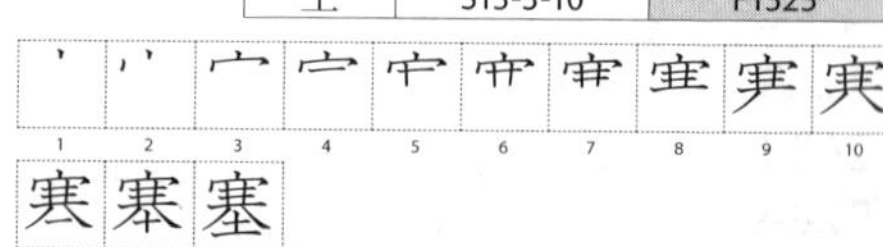

COMPOUNDS

❶ [original meaning] **STOP UP, fill in**

塞栓 そくせん embolus

閉塞 へいそく blockade, stoppage

梗塞 こうそく stoppage; tightness; infarction

❷ [sometimes also 砦 さい 3310] **FORT, fortress, stronghold**

城塞(=城砦) じょうさい fortress, stronghold, citadel
要塞 ようさい fortress, stronghold
人間万事塞翁が馬 にんげんばんじさいおうがうま Inscrutable are the ways of heaven

❸ used phonetically for *soku* in the transliteration of Sanskrit Buddhist terms
優婆塞 うばそく *upasaka,* devout male lay follower of Buddhism

KUN

【ふさぐ 塞ぐ】
①ⓐ **STOP UP, fill in**
ⓑ **obstruct, block, cover**
ⓒ occupy, take up
a 穴を塞ぐ あなをふさぐ fill a hole with earth
b 耳を塞ぐ みみをふさぐ stop [plug] one's ears
② **be in low spirits**
塞ぎ(=鬱ぎ)込む ふさぎこむ mope
③ fulfill (one's duty)

【ふさがる 塞がる】
ⓐ **get STOPped UP, become closed**
ⓑ **get blocked, be clogged**
ⓒ **be occupied, be taken**
ⓓ [verbal suffix] **get in the way**
a 開いた口が塞がらない あいたくちがふさがらない be struck speechless
b 八方塞がり はっぽうふさがり hemmed in on all sides
c 手が塞がる てがふさがる be tied up (doing something)
d 立ち塞がる たちふさがる stand in one's way

【せく 塞く】[also 堰く]
ⓐ dam up
ⓑ check, prevent
a 塞き止める せきとめる dam up, stop; check

【とりで 塞】[now usu. 砦] **FORT, fortress, stronghold**

SYNONYMS

❶ **obstruct and hinder**
遮 INTERRUPT → 3916
塞 STOP UP → 2924
阻 OBSTRUCT → 0411
沮 OBSTRUCT → 0399
奄 OBSTRUCT (by covering) → 2757
妨 HINDER → 0279
障 hinder → 0875
碍 STAND IN THE WAY → 1536
害 stand in the way → 2826
梗 STOP UP → 1204

❶ **close**
閉 CLOSE → 4116
鎖 lock up → 2213
封 SEAL → 1639
梗 STOP UP → 1204
塞 STOP UP → 2924

❷ **strongholds**
城 CASTLE → 0417
塁 SMALL FORT → 3206
塞 FORT → 2924
砦 FORT → 3310
堡 FORT → 3500

HOMOPHONES

とりで
塁 BASE → 3206
砦 FORT → 3310
せく 堰 DAM → 0676

NOTE

➡ see USAGE notes at 塁 3206 and 堰 0676

寝

▶GO TO SLEEP
シン ね(る) ね(かす) ね(かせる)
Ⓝ 寢 Ⓒ 寝 qǐn

2925
2-3-10

40 宀	Jōyō	U5BDD
	S13-3-10	F0641

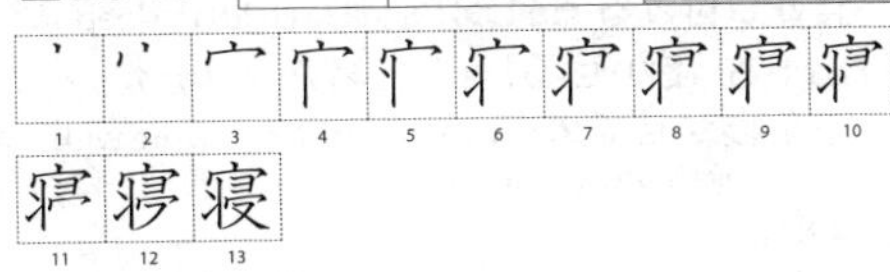

COMPOUNDS

❶ [original meaning]
ⓐ **GO TO SLEEP [bed], sleep**
ⓑ **going to bed, sleeping, sleep**
a 寝台 しんだい bed, sleeping berth
寝室 しんしつ bedroom
寝具 しんぐ bedclothes, bedding
不寝番 ふしんばん night watch
b 寝食 しんしょく eating and sleeping
就寝する しゅうしんする go to bed

❷ inner room, back room, recesses
寝殿造り しんでんづくり Heian residential architecture

INDEPENDENT

【しん 寝】 going to bed, sleeping, sleep
寝に就く しんにつく go to bed

KUN

【ねる 寝る】
①ⓐ **GO TO SLEEP [bed], retire (to bed)**
ⓑ **sleep, fall asleep**
ⓒ **be confined to one's bed, be laid up**
a 寝る時間 ねるじかん bedtime
b 寝 ね sleep
寝付く ねつく go to sleep, fall asleep
寝付き ねつき going to sleep, falling asleep

寝床 ねどこ bed
寝袋 ねぶくろ sleeping bag
寝坊 ねぼう late riser, sleepyhead; oversleeping
寝息 ねいき breathing of a sleeping person
寝顔 ねがお one's sleeping face
寝返る ねがえる turn over in bed; go over to the enemy, change sides, betray
寝返り ねがえり turning over in bed; changing sides, betray
寝惚ける ねぼける be half asleep, be half awake
寝間着 ねまき pajamas
昼寝 ひるね siesta, nap

② **lie down**
寝転ぶ ねころぶ lie down

③ sleep with, share the bed with
人妻と寝る ひとづまとねる sleep with another person's wife

④ lie idle
寝ている資本 ねているしほん dead capital

【ねかす 寝かす】 **put to sleep; bed down; lay down; let (goods) lie idle; ferment (rice malt)**
寝かし付ける ねかしつける lull (a child) to sleep

【ねかせる 寝かせる】 same as 寝かす ねかす
筆を寝かせて書く ふでをねかせてかく write with one's brush slanted

SYNONYMS

❶ **sleep**
眠 SLEEP → 1474
睡 SLEEP → 1535
寝 GO TO SLEEP → 2925

【ねる】
② **lie down**
伏 PROSTRATE → 0049
臥 LIE DOWN → 1825
寝る lie down → 2925

寚

2926
2-3-10

▶**TREASURE**
ホウ たから ㊔ たか とみ

40 宀	Nonstandard	U5BDA
	S13-3-10	F0000

traditional form → see 宝 at 2764

嘗甞

2-3-10

incorrect classification
➡ see 2-5-8: ⺍ at 3225

誉

2-3-10

incorrect classification
➡ see 2-4-9: ⺍ at 3135

嵩

2927
2-3-10

▶**BULK**
スウ かさ かさ(む) ㊔ たか たかし たけ こう だけ
Ⓒ 嵩 sōng

46 山	Names	U5D69
	S13-3-10	F2802

COMPOUNDS

ⓐ Songshan: the highest and central peak of the Five Sacred Mountains in Henan Province
ⓑ [sometimes also 崇 2864] [archaic] as lofty as Songshan

a 嵩山 すうざん Songshan
嵩高 すうこう Songshan; lofty
b 嵩呼 すうこ shouting "Long live the emperor"

KUN

【かさ 嵩】 **BULK, volume, size, quantity**
嵩に掛かって かさにかかって arrogantly, high-handedly, overbearingly
嵩張る かさばる be bulky [voluminous], bulk large
年嵩の としかさの older, aged, elderly, senior
水嵩 みずかさ volume of water
値嵩株 ねがさかぶ high-priced stocks, blue-chip shares

【かさむ 嵩む】 **increase in volume [BULK], accumulate; run up to a large sum**
借金が嵩む しゃっきんがかさむ get deeper in debt
荷嵩み にがさみ overstock, glut

SYNONYMS

【かさ】
○ **quantity and number**
量 QUANTITY → 3119
嵩 BULK → 2927
積 size → 1579
額 AMOUNT → 2273
分 content → 2466
数 NUMBER → 2245
勢 strength → 3542

嵳

2928
2-3-10

▶**RUGGED**
サ ザ シ

46 山	Nonstandard	U5D73
	S13-3-10	F0000

traditional form → see 嵯 at 0786

彙

2929
2-3-10

▶**ASSEMBLAGE**
イ
Ⓒ 汇 huì

58 彐	Jōyō	U5F59
	S13-3-10	F3015

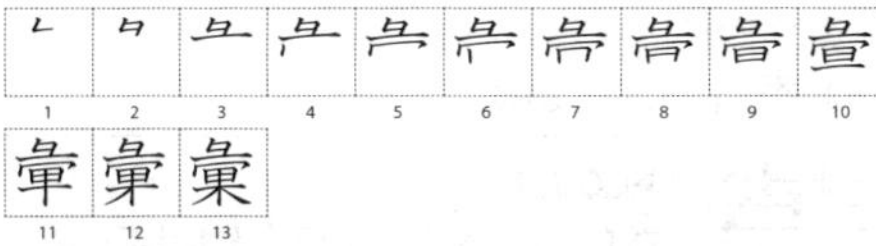

COMPOUNDS

❶ⓐ (things of the same kind) **ASSEMBLAGE, collection**

ⓑ [rare] assemble, collect

a 彙類 いるい same kind [class]; classification
語彙 ごい vocabulary
辞彙 じい dictionary
b 彙報 いほう bulletin, collection of reports

❷ [original meaning, now obsolete] hedgehog

SYNONYMS

❶ⓐ **collection**
集 collection → 3445
選 selection → 3931
彙 ASSEMBLAGE → 2929

墓

▶GRAVE
ボ はか
Ⓒ 墓 mù

2930
2-3-10

32	Jōyō-5	U5893
土	S13-3-10	F1307

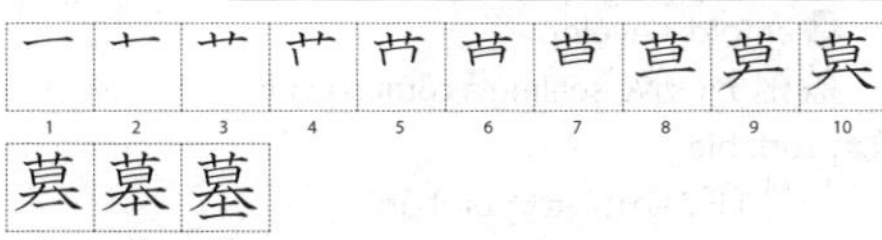

COMPOUNDS

● [original meaning] **GRAVE, tomb**
墓碑 ぼひ tombstone, gravestone
墓地 ぼち graveyard, cemetery, burial grounds
墓標 ぼひょう grave post, grave marker, gravestone
墓参 ぼさん visit to a grave

KUN

【はか 墓】**GRAVE, tomb, sepulcher; gravestone**
墓石 はかいし tombstone
墓参り はかまいり visit to a grave

SYNONYMS

● **graves**
墓 GRAVE → 2930
墳 TUMULUS → 0887
陵 IMPERIAL MAUSOLEUM → 0660
廟 MAUSOLEUM → 3935
祢 FATHER'S MAUSOLEUM → 1142
塚 grave mound → 0675

蓄

▶STORE UP
チク たくわ(える)
Ⓒ 蓄 xù

2931
2-3-10

140	Jōyō	U84C4
艹	S13-3-10	F1726

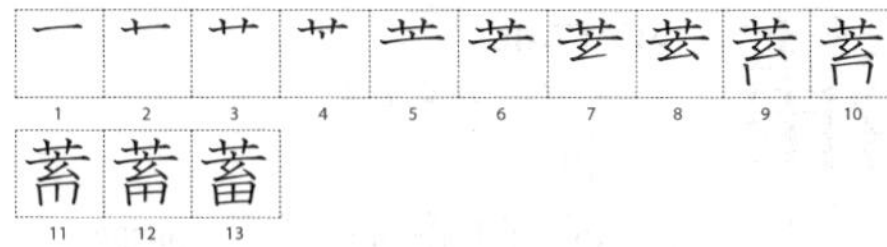

COMPOUNDS

❶ **STORE UP, accumulate, amass, lay aside**
蓄積 ちくせき accumulation, stockpiling
蓄電池 ちくでんち storage battery, accumulator
蓄音機 ちくおんき phonograph, gramophone
蓄財 ちくざい accumulation of wealth
貯蓄する ちょちくする save (money), lay aside
備蓄 びちく saving for [against] emergency, storing
含蓄 がんちく implication, significance, suggestiveness

❷ keep (a mistress)
蓄妾× ちくしょう keeping a mistress [concubine]

KUN

【たくわえる 蓄える】
① [sometimes also 貯える] **STORE UP, lay in stock, save, lay aside**
蓄え たくわえ store, reserve, stock; savings
燃料を蓄える ねんりょうをたくわえる store up fuel
知識を蓄える ちしきをたくわえる store one's mind with knowledge
② have, wear (a mustache)

SYNONYMS

❶ **store**
蔵 STORE → 2995
蓄 STORE UP → 2931
貯 LAY UP → 1903
納 PUT AWAY → 1652

USAGE

❶【たくわえる】
蓄える
① [sometimes also 貯える] store up, lay in stock, save, lay aside
② have, wear (a mustache)
貯える
[usu. 蓄える] store up, lay in stock, save, lay aside

❷【たくわえ】
蓄え
[sometimes also 貯え] store, reserve, stock; savings
貯え
[usu. 蓄え] store, reserve, stock; savings

HOMOPHONES

たくわえる 貯 LAY UP →1903
たくわえ 貯 LAY UP →1903

NOTE

★ do not confuse with 畜 LIVESTOCK →2599

蒲

2932

2-3-10

▶**CATTAIL**

フ ホ かば かま がま

Ⓒ 蒲 pú

140	Names	U84B2
艹	S13-3-10	F1906

COMPOUNDS

ⓐ CATTAIL, reed mace
ⓑ resembling a CATTAIL

a 蒲団 ふとん [now usu. 布団] futon, bedquilt
蒲柳の質 ほりゅうのしつ delicate [fragile] health
b 菖蒲 しょうぶ sweet flag; Japanese water iris, *Iris ensata* var. *ensata*

KUN

【かば 蒲】
ⓐ **CATTAIL, reed mace**
ⓑ abbrev. of 蒲色 かばいろ: **reddish yellow**
a 蒲焼き かばやき eels split and broiled in soy

【かま 蒲】 **CATTAIL, reed mace**
蒲鉾 かまぼこ steamed fish paste
蒲魚 かまとと feigning innocence [naiveté]; someone (esp. a woman) pretending to be innocent [naive]

【がま 蒲】 [also 香蒲] **CATTAIL, reed mace**

SPECIAL READINGS

蒲公英 たんぽぽ dandelion
菖蒲 あやめ iris (flower), esp. blood iris, *Iris sanguinea;* [archaic] sweet flag
香蒲 がま [also 蒲] cattail, reed mace

SYNONYMS

ⓐ kinds of grasses
草 GRASS →2813
荻 AMUR SILVERGRASS →2844
蒲 CATTAIL →2932
萊 GOOSEFOOT →2878
蕨 BRACKEN →2992
叢 grassy place →3243
芝 LAWN GRASS →2705
笹 BAMBOO GRASS →3301
茅 cogongrass →2779
萱 THATCH GRASS →2904
藁 STRAW →3015
芦 REED →2743
葦 COMMON REED →2934
菅 SEDGE →2874

HOMOPHONES

がま 香蒲 →3177, 2932

蓋

2933

2-3-10

▶**COVER**

ガイ コウ▲ ふた おお(う)▲ けだ(し)▲

Ⓝ 葢 盖 Ⓒ 盖 gài gě

140	Jōyō	U84CB
艹	S13-3-10	F1766

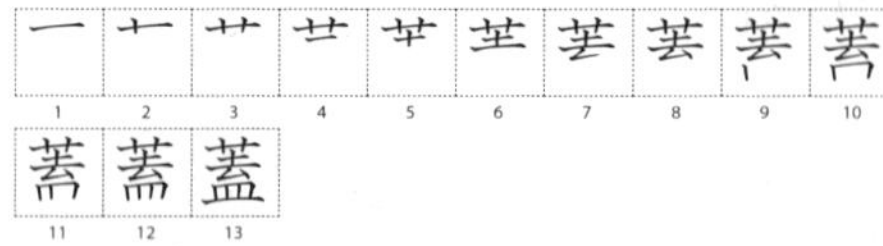

COMPOUNDS

❶ⓐ COVER, lid
ⓑ counter for lid-shaped objects such as bamboo hats
a 頭蓋骨 ずがいこつ cranium
無蓋車 むがいしゃ open freight car
天蓋 てんがい canopy; mendicant Zen priest's reed hood
口蓋 こうがい palate
b 笠三蓋 かささんがい three bamboo hats

❷ⓐ [original meaning] **COVER**, veil
ⓑ hide, conceal, screen
ⓒ enfold, envelop
a 蓋棺 がいかん sealing a coffin; death

❸ probable
蓋然性 がいぜんせい probability

KUN

【ふた 蓋】 **COVER, lid**
鍋蓋 なべぶた pot lid; *nabebuta,* "lid" radical (亠)
火蓋 ひぶた cover for a gun barrel
目蓋 まぶた eyelid
瘡×蓋 かさぶた scab
身も蓋もない みもふたもない point-blank, blunt

【おおう 蓋う】 [usu. 覆う]
ⓐ **COVER**, veil
ⓑ hide, conceal, screen
ⓒ enfold, envelop
a 空を蓋う そらをおおう cover up the sky

【けだし 蓋し】 probably

SYNONYMS

【おおう】
ⓐ **cover and wrap**
覆 COVER →3386
掩 COVER →0592
被 cover →1495
包 WRAP →3684
蓋う COVER →2933
蔽 COVER →2991

葺く THATCH →2909

HOMOPHONES

おおう

覆 COVER →3386

被 BE SUBJECTED TO →1495

蔽 COVER →2991

掩 COVER →0592

NOTE

➡ see USAGE note at 覆 3386

葦

2934

2-3-10

▶**COMMON REED**

イ あし よし

Ⓝ 葦 Ⓒ 苇 wěi

140	Names	U8466
艹	S13-3-10	F2380

COMPOUNDS

● **COMMON REED**, reed

葦岸 いがん reedy shore

一葦 いちい a boat

KUN

【あし 葦】**COMMON REED, reed**

葦毛 あしげ gray (horse coat color)

葦笛 あしぶえ reed pipe

葦船 あしぶね papyrus boat

葦辺 あしべ reedy shore

葦鹿 あしか eared seal, sea lion

【よし 葦】**COMMON REED, reed**

葦簀× よしず reed screen

葦切 よしきり reed warbler

葦鴨 よしがも falcated teal

SYNONYMS

● **kinds of grasses**

草 GRASS →2813

荻 AMUR SILVERGRASS →2844

蒲 CATTAIL →2932

萊 GOOSEFOOT →2878

蕨 BRACKEN →2992

叢 grassy place →3243

芝 LAWN GRASS →2705

笹 BAMBOO GRASS →3301

茅 cogongrass →2779

萱 THATCH GRASS →2904

藁 STRAW →3015

芦 REED →2743

葦 COMMON REED →2934

菅 SEDGE →2874

USAGE

❶【あし】

葦

common reed, reed

芦

common reed, reed

❷【よし】

葦

common reed, reed

芦

common reed, reed

HOMOPHONES

あし 芦 COMMON REED →2743

よし 芦 COMMON REED →2743

蒔

2935

2-3-10

▶**SOW**

ジ シ ま(く)

Ⓒ 莳 shì

140	Names	U8494
艹	S13-3-10	F2634

COMPOUNDS

● [original meaning, now rare] **transplant or plant**

蒔植する じしょくする transplant (vegetable)

KUN

【まく 蒔く】

① [also 播く] **sow**

種を蒔く たねをまく sow seed

② **scatter (powder)**

蒔絵 まきえ (gold [silver]) lacquer(ing)

ばら蒔く ばらまく scatter; spend recklessly

SYNONYMS

【まく】

① **farm and plant**

植 PLANT →1247

栽 PLANT (saplings) →4087

培 CULTIVATE →0558

耕 TILL →1659

作 raise crops →0077

農 farm, FARMING →3345

蒔 SOW →2935

播 SOW →0906

USAGE

【まく】

蒔く

① [also 播く] sow

② scatter (powder)

撒く

① scatter, sprinkle

② give (someone) the slip

播く

[also 蒔く] sow

HOMOPHONES

まく

撒 SCATTER →0909

播 SOW →0906

蒸

2936

2-3-10

▶STEAM
▶EVAPORATE

ジョウ セイ▲ む(す) む(れる) む(らす) ふか(す)▲

Ⓒ 蒸 zhēng

140	Jōyō-6	U84B8
艹	S13-3-10	F1659

COMPOUNDS

❶ **STEAM, heat with steam**

蒸籠 せいろう steaming basket

薫蒸する くんじょうする fumigate, smoke

❷ **EVAPORATE**

蒸発 じょうはつ evaporation, volatilization; mysterious disappearance

蒸散 じょうさん transpiration

蒸留 じょうりゅう distillation

蒸気 じょうき steam, vapor

❸ [archaic] numerous, crowded

蒸民 じょうみん the people, the masses

KUN

【むす 蒸す】

① *vt* **STEAM, heat with steam; foment**

蒸し むし steaming

蒸し菓子 むしがし steamed cake

② *vi* **be sultry, be stuffy**

蒸し暑い むしあつい sultry, sweltering

【むれる 蒸れる】*vi* **be STEAMed (to the proper degree); be stuffy; molder**

【むらす 蒸らす】*vt* **STEAM, cook by steam**

飯を蒸らす めしをむらす steam boiled rice

【ふかす 蒸かす】*vt* **STEAM**, heat with steam

SYNONYMS

❶ **cook**

煮 BOIL (cook by boiling) →3460

沸 BOIL (undergo boiling) →0387

炊 COOK →1080

蒸 STEAM →2936

焼く cook by fire →1256

揚げる fry in deep fat →0722

煎 ROAST, DECOCT →2950

❷ **vaporize**

蒸 EVAPORATE →2936

留 distill →3189

HOMOPHONES

むす

生 LIFE →4309

産 GIVE BIRTH →4089

NOTE

➡ see USAGE note at 生 4309

幕

2937

2-3-10

▶CURTAIN
▶SHOGUNATE

マク バク

Ⓒ 幕 mù

50	Jōyō-6	U5E55
巾	S13-3-10	F0716

COMPOUNDS

❶ⓐ [original meaning] **CURTAIN, screen**

ⓑ **CURTAIN**fall, end

a 幕屋 まくや tent, tabernacle; Makuya (Original Gospel Movement of Japan)

天幕 てんまく tent

垂れ幕 たれまく hanging screen, curtain

内幕 うちまく inside facts, inner workings; [original meaning] inner curtain

除幕式 じょまくしき unveiling ceremony

煙幕 えんまく smoke screen

b 幕切れ まくぎれ curtainfall, end

❷ *theater*

ⓐ **act, scene**

ⓑ counter for acts

a 開幕 かいまく rising of the curtain; opening scene of a play

序幕 じょまく opening act, curtain raiser

終幕 しゅうまく end, close, curtainfall

b 第三幕 だいさんまく Act 3

❸ (since banquets in honor of champion wrestlers were held in a curtained enclosure) first grade in sumo wrestling

幕内 まくうち first-class sumo wrestler

幕下 まくした junior-class sumo wrestler

入幕する にゅうまくする become a first-grade sumo wrestler

❹ⓐ shogun's headquarters, camp

ⓑ **SHOGUNATE, feudal government of Japan**

a 幕営 ばくえい camp, camping

b 幕僚 ばくりょう staff, staff officer

幕府 ばくふ shogunate

幕末 ばくまつ closing days of the Tokugawa shogunate

佐幕 さばく adherence to the shogunate

❺ abbrev. of 幕僚 ばくりょう: staff, staff officer

統幕 とうばく general staff headquarters

INDEPENDENT

【まく 幕】**CURTAIN;** *theater* **act; one's turn, place; first grade in sumo wrestling**

幕を引く まくをひく draw a curtain

愈×君の出る幕が来た いよいよきみのでるまくがきた This is where you come in/It's your turn now

SYNONYMS

❶ⓐ **curtain**

幕 CURTAIN → 2937

簾 BAMBOO SCREEN → 3388

帳 drapery → 0572

❷ **parts of plays**

幕 act → 2937

場 scene → 0678

❹ⓑ **governments**

官 GOVERNMENT → 2766

幕 SHOGUNATE → 2937

廷 COURT → 3795

朝 court → 2130

宮 Imperial Court → 2828

蒙 ▸IGNORANCE

モウ こうむ(る)

Ⓒ 蒙 méng mēng měng

2938

2-3-10

140	Names	U8499
艹	S13-3-10	F1986

COMPOUNDS

❶ **IGNORANCE**

蒙昧 もうまい ignorance

啓蒙 けいもう enlightenment, instruction

❷ **unclassified compounds**

蒙古 もうこ Mongolia

❸ abbrev. of 蒙古 もうこ: **Mongolia**

内蒙 ないもう Inner Mongolia

満蒙 まんもう Manchuria and Mongolia

INDEPENDENT

【もう 蒙】**IGNORANCE**

蒙を啓く もうをひらく enlighten

KUN

【こうむる 蒙る】[also 被る] **be subjected to, undergo, receive, sustain**

損害を蒙る そんがいをこうむる suffer a loss

SYNONYMS

❶ **foolish**

愚 FOOLISH → 3513

暗 DARK → 1273

痴 STUPID → 4072

鈍 DULL → 2123

呆 DIM-WITTED → 2712

魯 DULL → 2665

闇 DARK → 4134

蒙 IGNORANCE → 2938

❸ **Asian countries**

日 JAPAN → 3759

緬 Myanmar → 1758

老 Laos → 3963

華 CHINA → 2841

蒙 Mongolia → 2938

鮮 Korea → 2355

泰 Thailand → 3193

越 Vietnam → 4108

印 India → 1023

竺 INDIA → 3248

比 Philippines → 0029

HOMOPHONES

こうむる 被 BE SUBJECTED TO → 1495

NOTE

➡ see USAGE note at 被 1495

夢 ▸DREAM

ム ゆめ

Ⓝ 夢 梦◇ Ⓒ 梦 mèng

2939

2-3-10

36	Jōyō-5	U5922
夕	S13-3-10	F0712

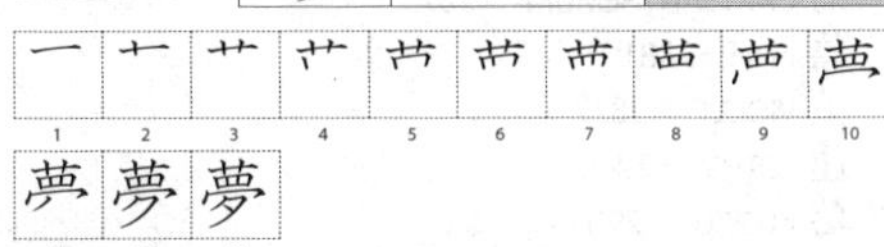

COMPOUNDS

● [original meaning] **DREAM**

夢想 むそう dream, vision; daydream

夢想家 むそうか dreamer

夢幻 むげん dream; vision; fantasy

夢中で むちゅうで like one in a dream; like one dazed; frantically

悪夢 あくむ nightmare, bad dream

白昼夢 はくちゅうむ waking dream

迷夢 めいむ illusion, delusion, fallacy

KUN

【ゆめ 夢】**DREAM; vision, fancy, illusion, delusion**

夢見る ゆめみる dream, fancy

夢占い ゆめうらない divination by means of dreams

夢枕に ゆめまくらに in a dream

夢心地 ゆめごこち ecstasy, trance

夢物語 ゆめものがたり empty dream; fantastic story

初夢 はつゆめ first dream of the New Year

正夢 まさゆめ dream which comes true, prophetic dream

SYNONYMS

● **illusory mental images**

夢 DREAM → 2939
幻 PHANTOM → 0206

蓮

▶LOTUS

レン はす はちす

Ⓝ 蓮 Ⓒ 莲 lián

2940

2-3-10

140	Names	U84EE
艹	S13-3-10	F1808

COMPOUNDS

● **LOTUS**

蓮華 れんげ lotus flower; Chinese milk vetch; Chinese (porcelain) spoon
木蓮 もくれん lily magnolia; cucumber tree; *Magnolia liliflora*

KUN

【はす 蓮】**LOTUS**

蓮池 はすいけ lotus pond

【はちす 蓮】

① *elegant* **LOTUS**
② old name for rose of Sharon, alth(a)ea

木蓮 きはちす rose of Sharon, alth(a)ea

SYNONYMS

● **&【はす】flowering plants**

菊 CHRYSANTHEMUM → 2875
菖 IRIS → 2881
菫 VIOLET → 2877
蓮 LOTUS → 2940
葛 KUDZU → 2905
蓬 JAPANESE MUGWORT → 2973
葵 MALLOW → 2906
蓉 COTTON ROSE → 2944
芙 LOTUS → 2737
蘭 ORCHID → 3031
萩 *HAGI* → 2908
藤 WISTERIA → 3025
桜 cherry blossom → 1168
梅 *ume* blossom → 1159

蓑

▶STRAW RAINCOAT

サ みの

Ⓝ 簑 簔 Ⓒ 蓑 suō

2941

2-3-10

140	Names	U84D1
艹	S13-3-10	F2997

KUN

【みの 蓑】**STRAW RAINCOAT**

蓑虫 みのむし bagworm
蓑笠子 みのかさご luna lionfish, *Pterois lunulata*
隠れ蓑 かくれみの invisibility cloak; pretext

SYNONYMS

【みの】

○ **clothing**

服 CLOTHES → 1090
袴 FORMAL DIVIDED SKIRT → 1509
蓑 STRAW RAINCOAT → 2941
-着 wear → 4110
衣 GARMENT → 2506
装 DRESS → 3327
裳 DRESS → 3231
襤 RAGS → 1607
袈 BUDDHIST SURPLICE → 3200
裟 BUDDHIST CASSOCK → 3420
襖 overgarment → 1600

蒐

▶COLLECT

シュウ ㊔ あつむ

Ⓒ 搜 sōu

2942

2-3-10

140	Names	U8490
艹	S13-3-10	F2953

COMPOUNDS

● [now replaced by 収 0031 or 集 3445] **COLLECT, gather**

蒐集(=収集)する しゅうしゅうする collect, gather, accumulate
蒐荷(=集荷) しゅうか collection of cargo, cargo booking

SYNONYMS

● **gather**

集 COLLECT → 3445
蒐 COLLECT → 2942
聚 COLLECT → 3479
収 collect → 0031
採 GATHER → 0606
采 GATHER → 3077
萃 GATHER → 2882
湊 come together → 0743

蒼

▶PALE BLUE

ソウ あお(い) ㊔ しげる

Ⓒ 苍 cāng

2943

2-3-10

140	Names	U84BC
艹	S13-3-10	F1792

COMPOUNDS

❶ [original meaning] **deep blue; green; gray**

蒼天 そうてん blue [azure] sky
蒼生 そうせい people, the masses

暮色蒼然として迫る ぼしょくそうぜんとしてせまる
Evening dusk is fast gathering

❷ (pale in appearance) **green, pale**
蒼白な そうはくな pale, pallid

❸ **old, hoary**
古色蒼然たる こしょくそうぜんたる antique-looking

❹ [now replaced by 倉 そう 2607] hurried, flurried
蒼惶(=倉皇)として そうこうとして in great haste

KUN

【あおい 蒼い】[usu. 青い] **PALE BLUE; pale; green**
顔が蒼い かおがあおい look pale [green]

SYNONYMS

【あおい】

◯ **blue and purple colors**
青 BLUE → 3084
碧 DEEP BLUE → 3515
瑠 LAPIS LAZULI (bright blue) → 1342
紺 DARK BLUE → 1688
藍 INDIGO → 3024
紫 PURPLE → 3332
蒼 PALE BLUE → 2943

HOMOPHONES

あおい 青 BLUE → 3084

NOTE

➡ see USAGE note at 青 3084

蓉

2944
▀ 2-3-10

▶**COTTON ROSE**
ヨウ ㊔ ひろ
Ⓒ 蓉 róng

140	Names	U84C9
艹	S13-3-10	F3058

COMPOUNDS

❶ **COTTON ROSE, hibiscus**
芙蓉 ふよう cotton rose; lotus

❷ lotus

SYNONYMS

❶ **flowering plants**
菊 CHRYSANTHEMUM → 2875
菖 IRIS → 2881
菫 VIOLET → 2877
蓮 LOTUS → 2940
葛 KUDZU → 2905
蓬 JAPANESE MUGWORT → 2973
葵 MALLOW → 2906
蓉 COTTON ROSE → 2944
芙 LOTUS → 2737
蘭 ORCHID → 3031
萩 *HAGI* → 2908
藤 WISTERIA → 3025
桜 cherry blossom → 1168
梅 *ume* blossom → 1159

蓬

2945
▀ 2-3-10

▶**JAPANESE MUGWORT**
ホウ よもぎ ㊔ ほ とも

140	Nonstandard	U84EC
艹	S13-3-10	F0000

traditional form → see 蓬 at 2973

慈

2946
▀ 2-3-10

▶**AFFECTIONATE**
ジ いつく(しむ) ㊔ しげ

61	Nonstandard	U2F8A6
心	S13-4-9	F0000

traditional form → see 慈 at 2949

蔣

2947
▀ 2-3-10

▶**WILD RICE**
ショウ ㊔ こも

140	Nonstandard	U848B
艹	S13-3-10	F0000

traditional form → see 蒋 at 2976

蓬

▀ 2-3-10

incorrect stroke-count
➡ see ▀ 2-3-11: 艹 at 2973

蓮

▀ 2-3-10

incorrect stroke-count
➡ see ▀ 2-3-11: 艹 at 2979

義

2948
▀ 2-3-10

▶**RIGHTEOUSNESS**
▶**MEANING**
ギ ㊔ よし のり よしみ
Ⓒ 义 yì

123	Jōyō-5	U7FA9
羊	S13-6-7	F0226

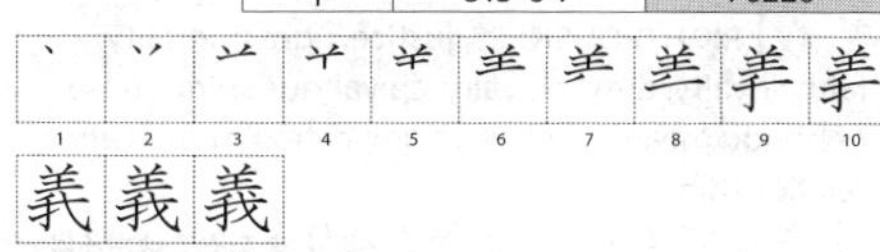

COMPOUNDS

❶ⓐ **RIGHTEOUSNESS, justice, right, morality**
ⓑ **righteous, just, upright**
a 正義 せいぎ justice, righteousness
道義 どうぎ morality, moral principles
仁義 じんぎ humanity and justice; moral code; formal greeting among gamblers
情義 じょうぎ justice and humanity
b 義人 ぎじん righteous man
義憤 ぎふん righteous indignation

❷ chivalrous, heroic, self-sacrificing, public-spirited
義侠 ぎきょう chivalry, generosity
義気 ぎき chivalry, heroism

義兵 ぎへい army in the cause of justice, volunteer corps
義捐×金(=義援金) ぎえんきん donation, contribution

❸ⓐ **faith, loyalty, duty**
ⓑ faithful, loyal

a 義務 ぎむ duty, obligation
義理 ぎり sense of duty [honor], obligation, debt of gratitude; justice; courtesy
忠義 ちゅうぎ loyalty, fidelity, devotion
信義 しんぎ fidelity, faith, loyalty
恩義 おんぎ obligation, debt of gratitude

b 義臣 ぎしん loyal retainer

❹ **MEANING, sense, signification, significance**
意義 いぎ meaning, sense, signification, significance
講義 こうぎ lecture
定義 ていぎ definition
字義 じぎ character definition, meaning of a word [term]
疑義 ぎぎ doubt, doubtful points

❺ moral principle
主義 しゅぎ principle, -ism

❻ **-in-law; step-, foster**
義父 ぎふ father-in-law; foster father, stepfather
義兄 ぎけい brother-in-law
義母 ぎぼ mother-in-law

❼ artificial
義足 ぎそく artificial leg
義眼 ぎがん artificial eye

❽ [also 宜 2763 or 誼 1977] friendship; favor, kindness
情義 じょうぎ friendship

INDEPENDENT

【ぎ 義】**RIGHTEOUSNESS**, justice, right, morality; faith, loyalty, duty; chivalry, chivalrous spirit, sense of honor; meaning, sense, signification, significance; relationship

義を見てせざるは勇無きなり ぎをみてせざるはゆうなきなり Do what is right in your sight/Knowing what is right without practicing it betrays one's cowardice
義を破る ぎをやぶる break faith with
義を重んじる ぎをおもんじる value honor
経文の義を説く きょうもんのぎをとく explain the meaning of a sutra
兄弟の義を結ぶ きょうだいのぎをむすぶ become sworn brothers

SYNONYMS

❶ⓐ **moral goodness**
徳 VIRTUE → 0842
道 the way of moral conduct → 3888
善 GOOD → 2921
義 RIGHTEOUSNESS → 2948

ⓑ **virtuous**
正 RIGHT → 4296
義 righteous → 2948
善 GOOD → 2921
良 GOOD → 4373
鯁 UPRIGHT → 2357

❷ **brave**
勇 BRAVE → 2592
侠 chivalrous → 0110
赳 VALIANT → 4100
驍 VALIANT → 2327
敢 bold → 2142
豪 bold and unrestrained → 2657
雄 HEROIC → 1271
壮 heroic → 0263
義 chivalrous → 2948
凜 gallant → 0195

❸ⓐ **fidelity**
忠 LOYALTY → 3087
義 faith → 2948
孝 FILIAL PIETY → 3973
悌 BROTHERLY LOVE → 0507
誠 SINCERITY → 1922
実 faithfulness → 2765
信 fidelity → 0115
操 constancy → 0948
節 moral integrity → 3336

❹ **meaning**
義 MEANING → 2948
意 MEANING → 2650
訳 SENSE → 1865
旨 PURPORT → 2516
趣 PURPOSE → 4111

❻ **related by marriage**
義 -in-law → 2948
継 step- → 1720

❼ **false**
虚 FALSE → 4017
仮 fake → 0053
偽 sham → 0149
擬 imitation → 0969
義 artificial → 2948

慈

2949
2-3-10

▸**AFFECTIONATE**
ジ いつく(しむ) ㊔ しげ
N 慈 C 慈 cí

61	Jōyō	U6148
心	S13-4-9	F1880

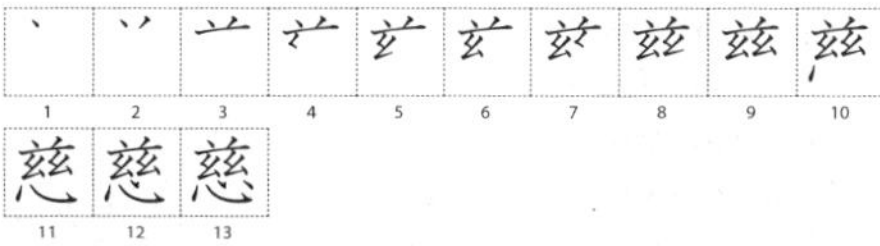

COMPOUNDS

❶ [original meaning] **AFFECTIONATE (towards one's child), tender, gentle and loving, kind**

慈愛 じあい affection, love, benevolence

慈母 じぼ affectionate [loving] mother

❷ⓐ *Buddhism* **compassion, active benevolence, universal love, loving kindness**

ⓑ compassionate, charitable, merciful

a 慈悲 じひ mercy, compassion

慈善 じぜん charity

慈雨 じう beneficial [welcome] rain

b 仁慈 じんじ benevolence

KUN

【いつくしむ 慈しむ】**be AFFECTIONATE to, treat tenderly, love**

慈しみ いつくしみ affection, love

親が子を慈しむ おやがこをいつくしむ Parents care tenderly for their children

SYNONYMS

❶ **kind**

厚 KIND → 3726

篤 cordial → 3371

懇 cordial → 3606

慈 AFFECTIONATE → 2949

温 warmhearted → 0740

渥 GRACIOUS → 0731

優 kindly → 0200

❷ⓐ **tender feelings for others**

仁 BENEVOLENCE → 0021

慈 compassion → 2949

情 sympathy → 0583

悲 mercy → 3448

哀 PITY → 2568

憐 PITY → 0945

煎

2950

2-3-10

▶ROAST

▶DECOCT

セン い(る)

Ⓝ 煎 Ⓒ 煎 jiān

86	Jōyō	U714E
灬	S13-4-9	F2516

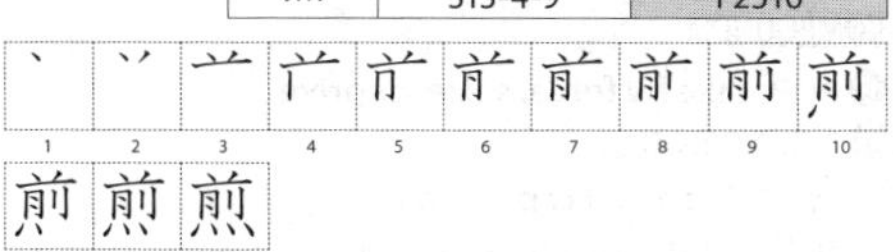

COMPOUNDS

❶ **ROAST, parch**

煎餅 せんべい rice cracker, wafer

焙×煎 ばいせん roasting (of coffee, etc.)

❷ **DECOCT, boil, brew**

煎茶 せんちゃ green tea

湯煎 ゆせん warming something by immersion in hot water

INDEPENDENT

【せんじる(=せんずる) 煎じる(=煎ずる)】**DECOCT, boil, brew**

煎じ薬 せんじぐすり (medical) decoction

煎じ詰める せんじつめる boil down

二番煎じ にばんせんじ rehash

KUN

【いる 煎る】**ROAST, parch**

煎り鍋 いりなべ roasting pan

煎り立て いりたて freshly roasted [parched]

煎り卵 いりたまご scrambled eggs

肝煎り きもいり good offices, auspices, sponsorship

SYNONYMS

❶ & ❷ **cook**

煮 BOIL (cook by boiling) → 3460

沸 BOIL (undergo boiling) → 0387

炊 COOK → 1080

蒸 STEAM → 2936

焼く cook by fire → 1256

揚げる fry in deep fat → 0722

煎 ROAST, DECOCT → 2950

COMPOUND FORMATION

【肝煎り きもいり】

肝煎り 'performing good offices, etc.' originally referred to anxiety that burns (煎 ①) one's heart or mind (肝), and thus to wholehearted consideration for and care of others.

羨

2951

2-3-10

▶BE ENVIOUS

セン ゼン▲ エン▲ うらや(む) うらや(ましい)

㊔ よし のぶ

Ⓒ 羡 xiàn

123	Jōyō	U7FA8
羊	S13-6-7	F2290

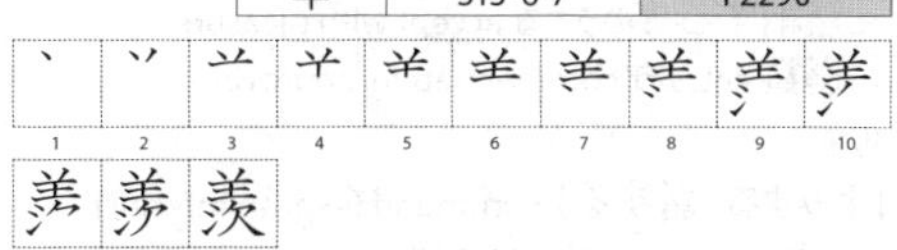

COMPOUNDS

❶ **BE ENVIOUS, be jealous**

羨望 せんぼう envy, jealousy

❷ underground path in a tomb

羨道 せんどう(=えんどう) tomb path leading to a burial chamber

KUN

【うらやむ 羨む】**BE ENVIOUS, be jealous**
彼女の幸運を皆が羨んだ かのじょのこううんをみながうらやんだ Everyone was envious of her good fortune

【うらやましい 羨ましい】**envious, jealous; enviable**

SYNONYMS

❶ **jealous and envious**
嫉 JEALOUS →0783
妬 JEALOUS →0337
羨 ENVIOUS →2951

煎

▸ROAST
▸DECOCT
セン い(る)

2952
2-3-10

86	Nonstandard	U714E
灬	S13-4-9	F0000

traditional form →see 煎 at 2950

會

2-3-10

incorrect classification
➡ see 2-2-11: 𠆢 at 2655

嘉

▸HAPPY
カ よみ(する) 名 よし よしみ ひろ
Ⓒ 嘉 jiā

2953
2-3-11

30	Names	U5609
口	S14-3-11	F1530

COMPOUNDS

❶ [also 佳 0096] **HAPPY, auspicious, lucky, good**
嘉節 かせつ happy [auspicious] occasion
嘉例 かれい happy precedent, festive annual custom
嘉日 かじつ auspicious day, good day

❷ [original meaning] good, fine, delicious
嘉言善行 かげんぜんこう good words and good deeds
嘉肴(=佳肴) かこう delicious food

❸ commend (esp. an inferior), praise, approve of, applaud
嘉納する かのうする accept with pleasure
嘉賞 かしょう commendation, approval

KUN

【よみする 嘉する】**commend (esp. an inferior), praise, approve of, applaud**
家臣の功績を嘉する かしんのこうせきをよみする approve one's retainer's achievement

SYNONYMS

❶ **good fortune**
吉 LUCKY →2691
嘉 HAPPY →2953
祥 AUSPICIOUS →1184
瑞 AUSPICIOUS OMEN →1302
禎 PROPITIOUS OMEN →1305
幸 GOOD FORTUNE →2755
福 FORTUNE →1303
倖 GOOD FORTUNE →0134

❸ **praise**
賛 PRAISE →3484
頌 EULOGIZE →1319
謳 EXTOL →2061
讃 PRAISE →2093
美 regard as beautiful →2817
褒 COMMEND →2662
嘉 commend (esp. an inferior) →2953
彰 PROCLAIM MERITS →2337
称 acclaim →1491
賞 express admiration →3237
揚 EXALT →0722

臺

▸STAND
▸COUNTER FOR VEHICLES
ダイ タイ

2954
2-3-11

133	Nonstandard	U81FA
至	S14-6-8	F0000

traditional form →see 台 at 2498

壽

▸LONGEVITY
▸CONGRATULATIONS
ジュ ス ことぶき ことほ(ぐ) 名 とし ひさ ひさし やすし かず なが

2955
2-3-11

33	Names	U58FD
士	S14-3-11	F0000

traditional form →see 寿 at 4372

奪

▸ROB
ダツ うば(う)
Ⓒ 夺 duó

2956
2-3-11

37	Jōyō	U596A
大	S14-3-11	F1128

1	2	3	4	5	6	7	8	9	10	11	12	13	14
一	ナ	大	夵	夵	夵	夵	夵	奞	奞	奞	奞	奪	奪

COMPOUNDS

ⓐ **ROB, take by force, seize, deprive**
ⓑ *baseball* **ROB**
a 奪還 だっかん recapture, recovery
奪取 だっしゅ capture, seizure
略奪 りゃくだつ pillage, plunder, looting

強奪する ごうだつする rob, seize, plunder; hijack
争奪 そうだつ scramble, contest, struggle
剝奪する はくだつする deprive, divest
b 奪三振 だつさんしん striking a batter out

KUN

【うばう 奪う】**ROB, take by force, deprive; absorb, engross, fascinate**
奪い取る うばいとる plunder
奪い返す うばいかえす take back, recapture
女に心を奪われる おんなにこころをうばわれる be fascinated [captivated] by a woman

SYNONYMS

ⓐ steal and rob
盗 STEAL → 3309
窃 STEAL → 2801
取 TAKE → 1613
奪 ROB → 2956
略 plunder → 1501
掠 PLUNDER → 0605
鹵 PLUNDER → 2634

ⓐ take forcibly
奪 ROB → 2956
拐 KIDNAP → 0365
収 take possession by force → 0031

NOTE

★ do not confuse with 奮 ROUSE UP → 3000

寡

2957
2-3-11

▶FEW
カ
Ⓒ 寡 guǎ

40	Jōyō	U5BE1
宀	S14-3-11	F2434

COMPOUNDS

❶ FEW, little
寡少の かしょうの few, little, scanty
寡占 かせん oligopoly
寡黙な かもくな silent, taciturn, reticent
寡聞 かぶん having little knowledge (of), being ill-informed
多寡 たか quantity, number, amount

❷ widow, widower, widowed spouse; widowed
寡婦 かふ(=やもめ) widow
寡居 かきょ widowhood

❸ [archaic] [humble] my unbenevolent, my humble
寡人 かじん my humble self

INDEPENDENT

【か 寡】*literary* small number of people, minority
寡は衆に敵せず かはしゅうにてきせず There is no contending against numbers

SYNONYMS

❶ few
少 LITTLE → 4278
寡 FEW → 2957
乏 SCANTY → 2432
薄 meager → 3004
微 SLIGHT → 0788
寸 A BIT OF → 3652
僅 A LITTLE → 0176
些 A BIT → 3251

❷ wives
妻 WIFE → 3166
奥 wife → 3503
内 wife → 4277
室 wife (esp. of persons of rank) → 2802
嫡 legitimate wife → 0839
婦 married woman → 0565
嫁 BRIDE → 0780
寡 widow → 2957

蜜

2958
2-3-11

▶HONEY
ミツ ビツ▲
Ⓒ 蜜 mì

142	Jōyō	U871C
虫	S14-6-8	F2003

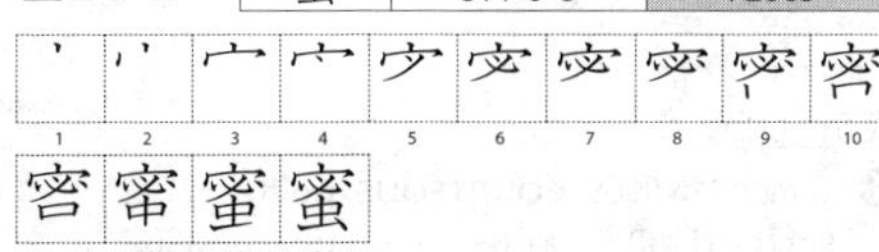

COMPOUNDS

❶ HONEY, nectar, syrup, molasses
蜜蜂 みつばち honeybee, hive bee
蜜月 みつげつ honeymoon
蜜蠟 みつろう beeswax
蜂蜜 はちみつ honey
花蜜 かみつ nectar
黒蜜 くろみつ brown sugar syrup
糖蜜 とうみつ molasses, syrup

❷ used phonetically for *mitsu* in the transliteration of Sanskrit Buddhist terms
波羅蜜 はらみつ *pāramitā*, entrance into Nirvana
般若波羅蜜多 はんにゃはらみった *Buddhism* perfection of wisdom, *prajñāpāramitā*

INDEPENDENT

【みつ 蜜】**HONEY, nectar, syrup, molasses**

SPECIAL READINGS

蜜柑▲ みかん mandarin orange, esp. Satsuma mandarin, *Citrus unshiu*

SYNONYMS

❶ **seasonings**

糖 SUGAR → 1777
塩 SALT → 0774
酢 VINEGAR → 1910
醋 VINEGAR → 2002
油 OIL → 0400
醤 FERMENTED SAUCE → 3569
噌 MISO → 0882
蜜 HONEY → 2958

❷ **phonetic [m]**

弥 PHONETIC [mi] → 0344
摩 phonetic [ma] → 3938
昧 phonetic [mai] → 1105
蜜 phonetic [mitsu] → 2958
勿 phonetic [mot] → 3661
牟 PHONETIC [mu] → 2518

寧

2959
2-3-11

▶**COURTEOUS**
ネイ むし(ろ)▲ ㊔ やす やすし
Ⓝ 寧 Ⓒ 宁 níng nìng

40 宀	Jōyō	U5BE7
	S14-3-11	F1620

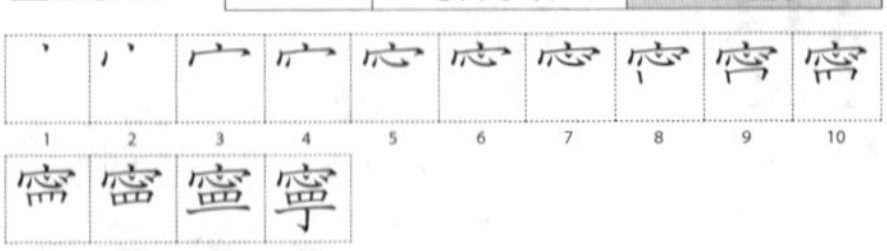

COMPOUNDS

❶ [formerly 嚀 0965] **COURTEOUS, polite**

丁寧(=叮嚀)な ていねいな polite, courteous

❷ **peaceful, quiet, tranquil**

寧日 ねいじつ peaceful day
安寧 あんねい public peace, tranquility
康寧 こうねい [rare] peacefulness, tranquility

KUN

【むしろ 寧ろ】 rather, better

彼は学者と言うより寧ろ詩人だ かれはがくしゃというよりむしろしじんだ He is not so much a scholar as a poet

SYNONYMS

❶ **courteous**

寧 COURTEOUS → 2959
鄭 COURTEOUS → 2379
叮 COURTEOUS → 0211
嚀 COURTEOUS → 0965
丁 courteous → 4155

❷ **calm and peaceful**

安 PEACEFUL → 2695
康 peaceful → 3877
寧 peaceful → 2959
泰 TRANQUIL → 3193
静 QUIET → 2164
平 CALM → 4291
穏 CALM → 1578

寥

2960
2-3-11

▶**DESOLATE**
リョウ
Ⓒ 寥 liáo

40 宀	Non-Jōyō	U5BE5
	S14-3-11	F0000

COMPOUNDS

❶ [now also 涼 0633] **DESOLATE, deserted, empty**

荒寥たる こうりょうたる desolate, dreary
寂寥たる せきりょうたる lonely, desolate

❷ [original meaning] **few, scarce**

寥寥たる りょうりょうたる few, rare; lonesome

SYNONYMS

❶ **barren**

荒 WILD → 2810
寥 DESOLATE → 2960

察

2961
2-3-11

▶**INSPECT**
▶**GUESS**
サツ
Ⓒ 察 chá

40 宀	Jōyō-4	U5BDF
	S14-3-11	F0515

COMPOUNDS

❶ⓐ (examine officially) **INSPECT, investigate, examine**

ⓑ (examine carefully) **INSPECT, observe, scrutinize, examine**

a 警察 けいさつ police, police station
視察 しさつ inspection, observation
巡察 じゅんさつ round of inspection, patrol
検察 けんさつ criminal investigation; prosecution
査察 ささつ inspection, investigation
診察 しんさつ medical examination

b 観察 かんさつ observation, supervision
洞察する どうさつする see through, penetrate

❷ **GUESS, conjecture, infer, surmise, gather, judge**

察知する さっちする infer, gather

推察する すいさつする guess, conjecture, infer, imagine
予察する よさつする [rare] guess beforehand, conjecture in advance
考察する こうさつする consider, contemplate, study

INDEPENDENT

【さつ 察】abbrev. of 警察 けいさつ: *underworld slang* cop, dick

【さっする 察する】**GUESS, conjecture, infer, gather, judge, imagine; sympathize with**
察し さっし guess, conjecture, judgment

SYNONYMS

❶ⓐ investigate and examine
閲 REVIEW → 4132
審 EXAMINE CAREFULLY → 2985
験 TEST → 2306
勘 CHECK → 2231
糾 INQUIRE INTO → 1631
究 STUDY EXHAUSTIVELY → 2729
察 INSPECT → 2961
討 STUDY → 1846
探 PROBE → 0613
検 EXAMINE → 1241
診 EXAMINE A PATIENT → 1898
調 INVESTIGATE → 1973
査 LOOK INTO → 3092

ⓑ see and look
見 SEE → 3151
看 WATCH → 3992
察 INSPECT → 2961
窺 WATCH FURTIVELY → 3002
瞥 GLANCE AT → 3592
目 look → 3777
観 VIEW → 2359
覧 LOOK OVER → 3538
眺 LOOK OUT OVER → 1503
望 LOOK AFAR → 3408
仰 LOOK UP → 0051
顧 LOOK BACK → 2394
視 REGARD → 1223

❷ conjecture
推 INFER → 0612
憶 SPECULATE → 0944
測 CONJECTURE → 0744
察 GUESS → 2961

窪

2962

2-3-11

▸HOLLOW

ワ くぼ くぼ(む) くぼ(まる)

Ⓝ 漥 Ⓒ 洼 wā

116	Names	U7AAA
穴	S14-5-9	F2146

COMPOUNDS

● [original meaning] (of the ground) become **HOLLOW**, become depressed, cave in
窪下 わか [rare] depressed place, hollow; low and depressed

KUN

【くぼ 窪】**HOLLOW, cavity, dent, depression**
窪地 くぼち depressed ground, hollow
笑窪 えくぼ dimple
盆の窪 ぼんのくぼ hollow at the nape of the neck

【くぼむ 窪む】(of the ground) **become HOLLOW, become depressed, cave in**
窪み くぼみ hollow, cavity, dent, depression
落ち窪む おちくぼむ sink in, cave in

【くぼまる 窪まる】same as 窪む くぼむ

SYNONYMS

● holes and cavities
穴 HOLE → 2682
洞 CAVE → 0455
窟 CAVE → 2923
窪 HOLLOW → 2962
腔 BODY CAVITY → 1267
孔 OPEN HOLE → 0205
口 MOUTH → 4189
坑 PIT → 0277
堀 DITCH → 0561
溝 CHANNEL → 0810
壕 TRENCH → 0966
濠 MOAT → 0975
凹 concavity → 4294

HOMOPHONES

くぼむ 凹 CONCAVE → 4294

NOTE

➡ see USAGE note at 凹 4294

賓

2963

2-3-11

▸GUEST

ヒン

40	Names	UFA64
宀	S14-3-11	F0000

traditional form → see 賓 at 2982

實

2964

2-3-11

▸REAL

ジツ み みの(る) まこと ㊔ さね みち

40	Names	U5BE6
宀	S14-3-11	F0000

traditional form → see 実 at 2765

寬

▸LENIENT

カン くつろ(ぐ) ㊔ ひろ ひろし

40 宀	Names	U5BEC
	S14-3-11	F0000

2965

2-3-11 traditional form → see 寛 at 2922

寧

▸COURTEOUS

ネイ むし(ろ) ㊔ やす やすし

40 宀	Nonstandard	UF95F
	S14-3-11	F0000

2966

2-3-11 traditional form → see 寧 at 2959

寢

▸GO TO SLEEP

シン ね(る) ね(かす) ね(かせる)

40 宀	Names	U5BE2
	S14-3-11	F0000

2967

2-3-11 traditional form → see 寝 at 2925

寫

incorrect stroke-count
➡ see 2-3-12: 宀 at 2987

2-3-11

裳 嘗

incorrect classification
➡ see 2-5-9: ⺌ at 3230

2-3-11

嶌

▸ISLAND

トウ しま

46 山	Nonstandard	U5D8C
	S14-3-11	F0000

2968

2-3-11 traditional form → see 島 at 4103

蔑

▸DESPISE

ベツ さげす(む) ないがし(ろ)▲

Ⓝ 蔑 蔑 Ⓒ 蔑 miè

140 艹	Jōyō	U8511
	S14-3-11	F1998

2969

2-3-11

COMPOUNDS

● **DESPISE, disdain, scorn, look down on**

蔑視する べっしする regard with contempt, scorn, look down on

蔑称 べっしょう disparaging [derogatory] name [term]

軽蔑 けいべつ contempt, disdain

侮蔑 ぶべつ contempt, scorn

KUN

【さげすむ 蔑む】**DESPISE, disdain, scorn, look down on**

【ないがしろ 蔑ろ】slighting, neglecting, making light of

蔑ろにする ないがしろにする slight, neglect, make light of, ignore

SYNONYMS

● **disdain**

侮 despise → 0091
軽 make light of → 1909
蔑 DESPISE → 2969
嘲 SCOFF AT → 0878

慕

▸ADORE

ボ した(う)

Ⓒ 慕 mù

61 小	Jōyō	U6155
	S14-4-10	F2164

2970

2-3-11

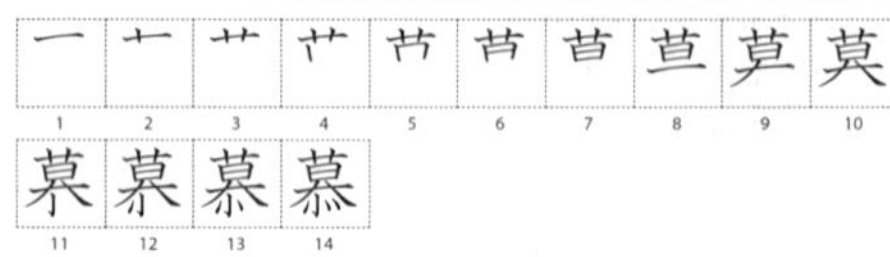

COMPOUNDS

ⓐ **ADORE, love deeply, be attached to**
ⓑ yearn for, long for

a 敬慕する けいぼする adore, love and respect, admire

恋慕 れんぼ love, attachment

b 慕情 ぼじょう longing; love, affection

思慕する しぼする love dearly, yearn for

追慕する ついぼする cherish one's memory, yearn after, sigh for

KUN

【したう 慕う】**ADORE, love deeply, be attached to; yearn for, long for; follow**

慕わしい したわしい dear, beloved

慕い寄る したいよる approach in adoration

故郷を慕う こきょうをしたう pine for home

後を慕って あとをしたって following (a person to a place)

SYNONYMS

ⓐ **respect**

敬 RESPECT → 2136
尊 HONOR → 2920
畏 respect → 3170
欽 REVERE → 2124
仰 look up to → 0051
崇 REVERENCE → 2864
尚 VALUE HIGHLY → 2774

重 set value on →4390
拝 WORSHIP →0360
慕 ADORE →2970

ⓐ love and like
愛 LOVE →3133
恋 LOVE (the opposite sex) →2602
好 LIKE →0240
慕 ADORE →2970
惚れる FALL IN LOVE →0584
玩 cherish →1085

ⓑ wish and desire
願 WISH →2320
憧 YEARN AFTER →0899
憬 YEARN AFTER →0898
貪 COVET →2630
望 HOPE →3408
希 ASPIRE →2543
懐 LONG FOR →0942
慕 yearn for →2970
渇 thirst for →0627
欲 DESIRE →1867
慾 DESIRE →3551
求 SEEK →4365

暮

2971
2-3-11

▶**DUSK**
▶**LIVE**
ボ く(れる) く(らす)
Ⓒ 暮 mù

72	Jōyō-6	U66AE
日	S14-4-10	F0665

Stroke order: 1–14

COMPOUNDS

❶ [original meaning] **DUSK, nightfall**
暮色 ぼしょく dusk, twilight scene
暮夜 ぼや night
薄暮 はくぼ nightfall, dusk, twilight

❷ towards the end (of the year), late
暮春 ぼしゅん late spring
歳暮 せいぼ end of the year; year-end present

KUN

【くれる 暮れる】**grow dark; come to an end, close; be at a loss**
暮れ くれ dusk, twilight, nightfall
日暮れ ひぐれ nightfall, dusk, evening
今年も暮れた ことしもくれた The year has come to an end
思案に暮れる しあんにくれる be lost in thought
途方に暮れる とほうにくれる be at a loss, be puzzled

【くらす 暮らす】(pass one's life) **LIVE, lead one's life, spend one's day;** (make a living) **live, earn one's livelihood**
暮らし くらし living, livelihood, subsistence; circumstances
暮らし向き くらしむき circumstances
一人暮らしをする ひとりぐらしをする live alone
その日暮らし そのひぐらし hand-to-mouth life

SYNONYMS

❶ **evening and night**
夜 NIGHT →2550
晩 EVENING →1232
夕 EVENING →4195
宵 EARLY EVENING →2831
暮 DUSK →2971

【くらす】
○ **live**
活 LIVE →0460
暮らす LIVE (pass one's life) →2971
生 live (be alive) →4309

蔦

2972
2-3-11

▶**JAPANESE IVY**
チョウ つた ㊔ かずら
Ⓒ 茑 niǎo

140	Names	U8526
艹	S14-3-11	F1755

COMPOUNDS

● [original meaning] ivy

KUN

【つた 蔦】**JAPANESE [Boston] IVY, ivy**
蔦蘿× つたかずら ivy and vine, creepers
蔦紅葉 つたもみじ scarlet-tinged ivy; maple
木蔦 きづた ivy, *Hedera rhombea*

SYNONYMS

【つた】
○ **shrubs**
藤 WISTERIA →3025
蔦 JAPANESE IVY →2972
萩 *HAGI* →2908
茉 JASMINE →2790
莉 JASMINE →2843
芭 JAPANESE FIBER BANANA →2736

蓬

2973
2-3-11

▶**JAPANESE MUGWORT**
ホウ よもぎ ㊔ ほ とも
Ⓝ 蓬 Ⓒ 蓬 péng

140	Names	U84EC
艹	S14-3-11	F2803

COMPOUNDS

❶ⓐ JAPANESE MUGWORT
ⓑ tumbleweed
a 蓬矢 ほうし arrow made of mugwort
b 転蓬 てんぽう tumbleweed
❷ⓐ disheveled, unkempt
ⓑ overgrown
a 蓬頭垢面 ほうとうこうめん unkempt hair and dirty face; being indifferent to one's appearance
弊衣蓬髪 へいいほうはつ unkempt hair and shabby clothes

士大宀⺌山【艹】

KUN

【よもぎ 蓬】JAPANESE MUGWORT
蓬餅 よもぎもち mugwort-flavored rice cake
蓬生 よもぎう area overgrown with weeds, wasteland
大蓬 おおよもぎ *Artemisia montana*

SYNONYMS

❶ flowering plants
菊 CHRYSANTHEMUM → 2875
菖 IRIS → 2881
菫 VIOLET → 2877
蓮 LOTUS → 2940
葛 KUDZU → 2905
蓬 JAPANESE MUGWORT → 2973
葵 MALLOW → 2906
蓉 COTTON ROSE → 2944
芙 LOTUS → 2737
蘭 ORCHID → 3031
萩 *HAGI* → 2908
藤 WISTERIA → 3025
桜 cherry blossom → 1168
梅 *ume* blossom → 1159

蔭 2974

▶SHADE
イン かげ
Ⓝ 蔭 Ⓒ 荫 yìn yīn

2-3-11

140	Names	U852D
艹	S14-3-11	F2133

COMPOUNDS

● [now usu. 陰 0657] [original meaning] SHADE
樹蔭 じゅいん [rare] shade of a tree
緑蔭 りょくいん shade of trees

KUN

【かげ 蔭】
① [also 陰] [in the form of お蔭 おかげ] grace, favor
お蔭で おかげで thanks to; due to
お蔭様で皆元気です おかげさまでみなげんきです We are all well and fine, thank you
② [now usu. 陰] SHADE
木蔭 こかげ shade of a tree, bower
日蔭 ひかげ the shade
③ [now usu. 陰]
ⓐ back side, reverse side
ⓑ behind the scenes
a カーテンの蔭に隠れる かーてんのかげにかくれる hide behind a curtain
b 蔭口 かげぐち backbiting

SYNONYMS

● shadow
影 SHADOW → 2381
翳 SHADOW → 3567
陰 SHADE → 0657
蔭 SHADE → 2974

HOMOPHONES

かげ
陰 SHADE → 0657
影 SHADOW → 2381

NOTE

➡ see USAGE note at 影 2381

蔓 2975

▶VINE
マン つる かずら
Ⓒ 蔓 màn wàn mán

2-3-11

140	Names	U8513
艹	S14-3-11	F2536

COMPOUNDS

❶ VINE, creeper, runner, trailer, tendril
蔓生 まんせい (of vines) creeping, running, trailing, climbing
❷ be rampant, spread
蔓延 まんえん spread, rampancy, infestation

KUN

【つる 蔓】
①ⓐ VINE, creeper, runner, trailer, tendril
ⓑ tendril
a 蔓草 つるくさ vine, creeper, runner, trailer, climber
蔓植物 つるしょくぶつ vine, creeper, runner, trailer, climber
藤蔓 ふじづる wisteria vine
芋蔓 いもづる sweet potato vine
芋蔓式に いもづるしきに one after another, in succession
② (eyeglass part) bows, earpieces
③ connections, contacts
手蔓 てづる connections, contacts, influence
金蔓 かねづる source of revenue, financial backer
【かずら 蔓】[usu. 葛] VINE, creeper
靫×蔓 うつぼかずら pitcher plant
日陰の蔓 ひかげのかずら running ground pine

SPECIAL READINGS

蔓延る はびこる spread, grow thick, run rampant, become powerful

SYNONYMS

❶ **plants**

菜 VEGETABLE → 2880
植 PLANT → 1247
栽 garden plant → 4087
茨 thorny shrub → 2812
苔 MOSS → 2792
蔓 VINE → 2975
枯 PLANT NAME ELEMENT → 1164

HOMOPHONES

かずら 葛 KUDZU → 2905

NOTE

➡ see USAGE note at 葛 2905

蔣
2976
2-3-11

▶WILD RICE
ショウ ㊔ こも
Ⓝ 蒋 Ⓒ 蒋 jiǎng

140	Names	U8523
艹	S14-3-11	F2426

COMPOUNDS

● [original meaning, now obsolete] **WILD RICE**

蔣介石 しょうかいせき Chiang Kai-shek

SYNONYMS

● **cereals**

米 RICE → 4342
麦 WHEAT → 3061
豆 BEAN → 2442
粟 FOXTAIL MILLET → 3326
黍 PROSO MILLET → 3210
蕎 BUCKWHEAT → 2993
蔣 WILD RICE → 2976

蔑
2977
2-3-11

▶DESPISE
ベツ さげす(む) ないがし(ろ)

140	Nonstandard	U8511
艹	S14-3-11	F0000

traditional form → see 蔑 at 2969

蔴
2978
2-3-11

▶HEMP
▶BECOME NUMB
マ マー あさ

140	Nonstandard	U8534
艹	S14-3-11	F0000

traditional form → see 麻 at 3878

蓮
2979
2-3-11

▶LOTUS
レン はす はちす

140	Nonstandard	UF999
艹	S14-3-11	F0000

traditional form → see 蓮 at 2940

蔆
2980
2-3-11

▶RHOMBUS
リョウ ひし ㊔ ゆう みち

140	Nonstandard	U8506
艹	S14-3-11	F0000

traditional form → see 菱 at 2879

蔵
2-3-11

incorrect stroke-count
➡ see 2-3-12: 艹 at 2995

蔭
2-3-11

incorrect stroke-count
➡ see 2-3-12: 艹 at 2997

賣
2981
2-3-12

▶SELL
バイ う(る) う(れる)

154	Names	U8CE3
貝	S15-7-8	F0000

traditional form → see 売 at 2722

賓
2982
2-3-12

▶GUEST
ヒン
Ⓝ 賓 Ⓒ 宾 bīn

154	Jōyō	U8CD3
貝	S15-7-8	F2597

COMPOUNDS

❶ [original meaning] **GUEST, visitor**

賓客 ひんきゃく(=ひんかく) guest, guest of honor
国賓 こくひん state guest
来賓 らいひん guest, visitor
迎賓館 げいひんかん guest house [palace]

❷ⓐ object of a verb
ⓑ *logic* predicate

a 賓辞 ひんじ object of a verb
b 賓位語 ひんいご *logic* predicate

SYNONYMS

❶ **visitor**

客 VISITOR → 2798
賓 GUEST → 2982

窮

▶BE IN EXTREMITY

キュウ きわ(める) きわ(まる) きわ(まり) きわ(み)

2983

2-3-12

Ⓒ 穷 qióng

116	Jōyō	U7AAE
穴	S15-5-10	F1794

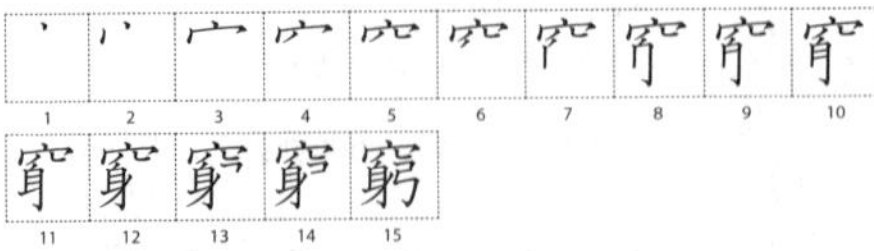

COMPOUNDS

❶ⓐ BE IN EXTREMITY, come to an extreme, be in distress

ⓑ destitute, poor

a 窮地 きゅうち predicament, difficult situation, dilemma

窮状 きゅうじょう distress, wretched condition

窮余の策 きゅうよのさく desperate measure

窮迫 きゅうはく straitened circumstances, distress

窮屈な きゅうくつな cramped, confined; formal; poor

b 窮乏 きゅうぼう destitution, poverty

窮民 きゅうみん poor people, the poor

窮措大 きゅうそだい poor student [scholar]

困窮 こんきゅう destitution, poverty, distress

貧窮 ひんきゅう poverty

❷ⓐ go to the extremity [extreme], go to the limit, reach the end

ⓑ extremity, limit, end

a 窮極の きゅうきょくの ultimate, extreme

b 無窮 むきゅう eternity, infinitude, immortality

INDEPENDENT

【きゅうする 窮する】**BE IN EXTREMITY**, come to an extreme, be in distress, be in want [need]

窮すれば通ず きゅうすればつうず Necessity is the mother of invention

返答に窮する へんとうにきゅうする be at a loss for an answer

KUN

【きわめる 窮める】

① [also 極める]

ⓐ **carry to extremity, go to extremes, be extremely (cruel)**

ⓑ **go to the extreme [end], reach an extreme, go to the highest point**

a 口を窮めて誉める くちをきわめてほめる be lavish in another's praise

b 貧困を窮める ひんこんをきわめる be reduced to extreme poverty, be extremely poor

② [usu. 究める] investigate thoroughly, study exhaustively, master

学を窮める がくをきわめる study exhaustively

【きわまる 窮まる】[sometimes also 谷まる]

ⓐ **come to an end, terminate**

ⓑ come to the end of one's tether, be at a loss

a 道が窮まる みちがきわまる come to a dead end

b 進退窮まる しんたいきわまる be at a loss

【きわまり 窮まり】[now usu. 極まり] **extremity, limit**

窮まり無い きわまりない extremely, in the extreme

【きわみ 窮み】**extremity, end, limit**

窮み無き きわみなき endless, without limit

SYNONYMS

❶ⓐ trouble and suffering

困 BE IN TROUBLE → 3808

苛 torment → 2786

窮 BE IN EXTREMITY → 2983

悶 BE IN AGONY → 4119

悩 SUFFER → 0504

苦 SUFFERING → 2789

痛 PAIN → 4071

辛 HARD → 2531

煩 VEXED → 1295

難 DIFFICULT → 2310

ⓑ poor

貧 POOR → 2631

乏 poor → 2432

窮 destitute → 2983

❷ⓑ extreme

極 EXTREME → 1243

窮 extremity → 2983

限 LIMIT → 0475

涯 OUTER LIMITS → 0623

果て end → 4377

HOMOPHONES

きわめる

極 EXTREME → 1243

究 STUDY EXHAUSTIVELY → 2729

きわまる

極 EXTREME → 1243

谷 VALLEY → 2536

きわまり 極 EXTREME → 1243

きわみ 極 EXTREME → 1243

NOTE

➡ see USAGE note at 極 1243

寮

▶DORMITORY

リョウ

2984

2-3-12

Ⓒ 寮 liáo

40	Jōyō	U5BEE
宀	S15-3-12	F1939

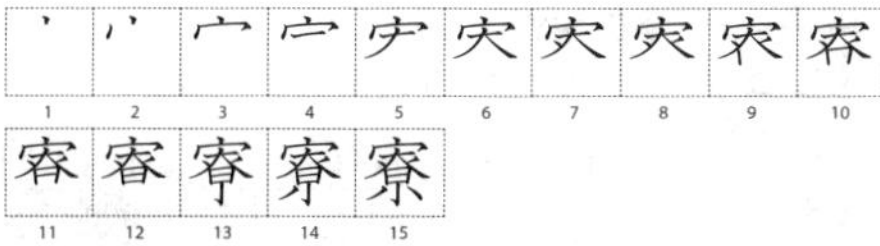

COMPOUNDS

❶ lodging accommodations or similar facilities for use by students, company employees or members of an organization:
ⓐ **student DORMITORY, hostel**
ⓑ [also suffix] **company DORMITORY, lodging house, villa**
ⓒ suffix after names of dormitories

a 寮長 りょうちょう dormitory leader
寮母 りょうぼ matron of a dormitory
寮歌 りょうか dormitory song
寮生 りょうせい boarder
学寮 がくりょう dormitory, hostel; seminary
b 工員寮 こういんりょう dormitory for factory workers
独身寮 どくしんりょう company dormitory for unmarried employees
c 若葉寮 わかばりょう Wakaba Dormitory

❷ fanciful building, pavilion
御寮人 ごりょうにん madam, mistress
茶寮 さりょう(=ちゃりょう) tea cottage, tea house

❸ former government bureau
大学寮 だいがくりょう Bureau of Education

INDEPENDENT

【りょう 寮】**DORMITORY, lodging house, villa; former government bureau**
寮に住む りょうにすむ live in a dormitory

SYNONYMS

❶ **temporary quarters**
舎 temporary quarters → 2555
寮 DORMITORY → 2984
宿 lodging → 2858
館 inn → 2196
亭 INN → 2572
寓 TEMPORARY ABODE → 2893

審

2985

2-3-12

▶**EXAMINE CAREFULLY**
▶**TRY**
シン
Ⓒ 审 shěn

40 宀	Jōyō	U5BE9
	S15-3-12	F1037

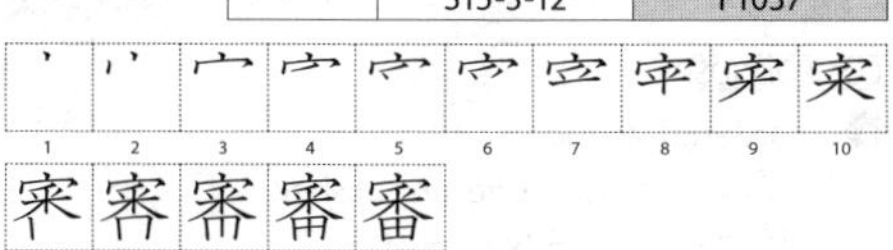

COMPOUNDS

❶ⓐ **EXAMINE CAREFULLY, investigate**
ⓑ abbrev. of 審議会 しんぎかい: (deliberative) council
ⓒ appraise, appreciate

a 審議 しんぎ deliberation, consideration, careful discussion
審査する しんさする examine, investigate, judge
審判 しんぱん(=しんばん) refereeing, judgment; referee, umpire
b 米審(=米価審議会) べいしん(=べいかしんぎかい) Rice Price Deliberative Council
c 審美 しんび appreciation of the beautiful

❷ⓐ **TRY, hold a court trial, hear, judge**
ⓑ [also suffix] trial, hearing, examination, judgment

a 審理する しんりする try, examine, inquire into
審問 しんもん trial, hearing, formal interrogation
b 結審 けっしん conclusion of a hearing
陪審 ばいしん jury
予審 よしん preliminary examination
再審 さいしん retrial, new trial, review of
第二審 だいにしん second hearing
控訴審 こうそしん hearing of an intermediate appeal

❸ umpire, referee
球審 きゅうしん *baseball* chief umpire
主審 しゅしん chief umpire
塁審 るいしん base umpire

❹ **detailed, clear**
不審 ふしん doubt, question

SYNONYMS

❶ⓐ **investigate and examine**
閲 REVIEW → 4132
審 EXAMINE CAREFULLY → 2985
験 TEST → 2306
勘 CHECK → 2231
糾 INQUIRE INTO → 1631
究 STUDY EXHAUSTIVELY → 2729
察 INSPECT → 2961
討 STUDY → 1846
探 PROBE → 0613
検 EXAMINE → 1241
診 EXAMINE A PATIENT → 1898
調 INVESTIGATE → 1973
査 LOOK INTO → 3092

❷ⓐ **judge**
判 JUDGE → 1441
裁 JUDGE → 4090
鑑 APPRAISE → 2226
評 evaluate → 1895
審 TRY → 2985

決 DECIDE → 0308
視 REGARD → 1223

NOTE

➡ see COMPOUND FORMATION for 陪審 ばいしん → 陪 0655

士 【宀】 ⺍ 艹 䒑 廿

窯 2986

▸**KILN**
ヨウ かま
Ⓝ 窰 窑 Ⓒ 窑 yáo

2-3-12

116 穴	Jōyō	U7AAF
	S15-5-10	F1993

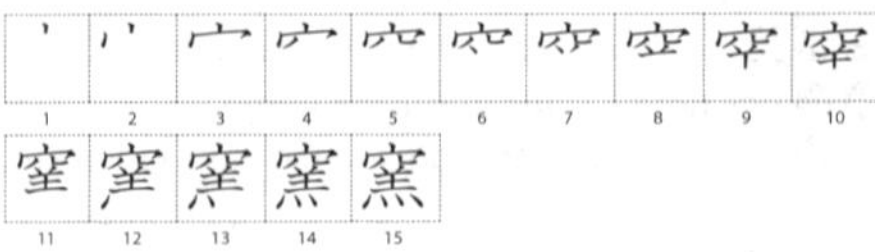

COMPOUNDS

ⓐ **KILN**, furnace
ⓑ **ceramics**
a 官窯 かんよう governmental porcelain furnace
b 窯業 ようぎょう ceramics, ceramic industry

KUN

【かま 窯】 **KILN, oven, furnace, stove; pottery**
窯元 かまもと pottery
窯印 かまじるし potter's mark

SYNONYMS

ⓐ **heating devices**
炉 FURNACE → 1079
窯 KILN → 2986
缶 steam boiler → 2526
ⓑ **ceramics ware**
陶 POTTERY → 0662
窯 ceramics → 2986
磁 porcelain → 1554

USAGE

【かま】
窯
kiln, oven, furnace, stove; pottery
釜
①ⓐ iron pot, kettle, cauldron
ⓑ boiler
② *slang* buttocks
罐
[sometimes also 缶] boiler
缶
[usu. 罐] boiler

HOMOPHONES

かま
釜 IRON POT → 2610
罐 → 1822

寫 2987

▸**COPY**
シャ うつ(す) うつ(る)

2-3-12

40 宀	Nonstandard	U5BEB
	S15-3-12	F0000

traditional form → see 写 at 2493

窰 2988

▸**KILN**
ヨウ かま

2-3-12

116 穴	Nonstandard	U7AB0
	S15-5-10	F0000

traditional form → see 窯 at 2986

賞

2-3-12

incorrect classification
➡ see 2-5-10: ⺍ at 3237

蕃 2989

▸**BARBARIAN**
バン ハン ㊔ ば しげる しげり もり みつ ふさ しく
Ⓒ 蕃 fán fān

2-3-12

140 艹	Names	U8543
	S15-3-12	F2843

COMPOUNDS

❶ⓐ [now also 蛮 2638] **BARBARIAN, savage**
ⓑ **BARBARIAN**, aboriginal; foreign
a 蕃夷 ばんい savages, barbarians
蕃族 ばんぞく savage tribe
蕃人 ばんじん savage, barbarian; aborigine
b 蕃社 ばんしゃ aborigines' village
蕃椒× ばんしょう [rare] Guinea pepper
❷ [now replaced by 繁 3536] thrive, luxuriate, grow thick
蕃殖する はんしょくする breed, propagate, increase, multiply

SYNONYMS

❶ **savage**
蛮 BARBARIAN → 2638
夷 BARBARIAN → 4349
蕃 BARBARIAN → 2989

蕪 2990

▸**TURNIP**
ブ かぶ かぶら
Ⓒ 芜 wú

2-3-12

140 艹	Names	U856A
	S15-3-12	F2978

COMPOUNDS

❶ disordered, crude
蕪雑な ぶざつな crude, unpolished
蕪辞 ぶじ my humble remarks
❷ [original meaning] wild, overrun with weeds

荒蕪地 こうぶち wild [waste] land, wilderness

KUN

【かぶ 蕪】[also 蕪菁×] **TURNIP**

赤蕪 あかかぶ red turnip

【かぶら 蕪】[also 蕪菁×] same as 蕪 かぶ

蕪菜 かぶらな turnip

SPECIAL READINGS

和布蕪 めかぶ thick *wakame* leaves from near the stalk

SYNONYMS

【かぶ】

○ & 【かぶら】 **vegetables**

菜 greens → 2880
蕪 TURNIP → 2990
芋 POTATO → 2706
豆 BEAN → 2442
蕗 BUTTERBUR → 3007
茄 EGGPLANT → 2787
芹 JAPANESE PARSLEY → 2742
瓜 GOURD → 3789
瓢 BOTTLE GOURD → 2356
芥 mustard → 2741

蔽 2991

▶**COVER**

ヘイ おお(う)▲

Ⓝ 蔽 Ⓒ 蔽 bì

2-3-12

140	Jōyō	U853D
艹	S15-3-12	F2353

1	2	3	4	5	6	7	8	9	10	11	12	13	14	15
一	十	艹	艹	艹	艹	艹	芇	茼	蔽	蔽	蔽	蔽	蔽	蔽

COMPOUNDS

● [original meaning] **COVER, screen, shield, hide**

遮蔽 しゃへい shield, cover, screen; *elec* shielding
隠蔽する いんぺいする conceal, cover up, hide
掩蔽 えんぺい cover, obscuration
建蔽率 けんぺいりつ coverage, building coverage ratio

KUN

【おおう 蔽う】[now usu. 覆う] screen, shield, hide

蔽い おおい cover, covering
事実を蔽う じじつをおおう disguise a fact

SYNONYMS

● **cover and wrap**

覆 COVER → 3386
掩 COVER → 0592
被 cover → 1495
包 WRAP → 3684
蓋う COVER → 2933
蔽 COVER → 2991
葺く THATCH → 2909

● **hide**

隠 HIDE → 0873
蔽 COVER → 2991
伏 lie in concealment → 0049
潜 LURK → 0922
匿 CONCEAL → 3735
忍 perform by stealth → 2750

HOMOPHONES

おおう

覆 COVER → 3386
被 BE SUBJECTED TO → 1495
蓋 COVER → 2933
掩 COVER → 0592

NOTE

➡ see USAGE note at 覆 3386

蕨 2992

▶**BRACKEN**

ケツ わらび

Ⓒ 蕨 jué

2-3-12

140	Names	U8568
艹	S15-3-12	F0000

KUN

【わらび 蕨】**BRACKEN, brake**

蕨粉 わらびこ bracken starch
蕨餅 わらびもち bracken-starch dumpling
蕨糊 わらびのり glue produced from bracken starch

SYNONYMS

【わらび】

○ **kinds of grasses**

草 GRASS → 2813
荻 AMUR SILVERGRASS → 2844
蒲 CATTAIL → 2932
莱 GOOSEFOOT → 2878
蕨 BRACKEN → 2992
叢 grassy place → 3243
芝 LAWN GRASS → 2705
笹 BAMBOO GRASS → 3301
茅 cogongrass → 2779
萱 THATCH GRASS → 2904
藁 STRAW → 3015
芦 REED → 2743
葦 COMMON REED → 2934
菅 SEDGE → 2874

土 冖 业 [艹] 亠 廿

蕎

2993

2-3-12

▶BUCKWHEAT

キョウ ㊔ たかし

Ⓒ 荞 qiáo

140	Names	U854E
艹	S15-3-12	F2137

COMPOUNDS

● **BUCKWHEAT**

蕎麦 きょうばく(=そば) common buckwheat

SPECIAL READINGS

蕎麦 そば Japanese buckwheat noodles, *soba;* common buckwheat

SYNONYMS

● **cereals**

米 RICE → 4342
麦 WHEAT → 3061
豆 BEAN → 2442
粟 FOXTAIL MILLET → 3326
黍 PROSO MILLET → 3210
蕎 BUCKWHEAT → 2993
蒋 WILD RICE → 2976

蕉

2994

2-3-12

▶PLANTAIN

ショウ

Ⓒ 蕉 jiāo

140	Names	U8549
艹	S15-3-12	F2408

COMPOUNDS

● **PLANTAIN**

芭蕉 ばしょう Japanese banana plant, *Musa basjoo;* plantain

SYNONYMS

● **fruits and fruit trees**

桃 PEACH → 1174
榛 HAZEL → 1328
椎 CHINQUAPIN → 1249
柚 YUZU → 1123
椰 COCONUT → 1285
柑 CITRUS → 1112
橙 BITTER ORANGE → 1369
葡 GRAPE → 2902
萄 GRAPE → 2870
柿 PERSIMMON → 1118
檎 APPLE → 1386
李 PLUM → 3050
枇 LOQUAT → 1063
杷 LOQUAT → 1065
苺 STRAWBERRY → 2780
菱 water chestnut → 2879
杏 APRICOT → 3049
梅 JAPANESE APRICOT → 1159
橘 MANDARIN → 1366
栗 CHESTNUT → 3280
栃 JAPANESE HORSE CHESTNUT → 1122
梨 PEAR → 3412
蕉 PLANTAIN → 2994

NOTE

★ do not confuse with 焦 SCORCH → 3444

蔵

2995

2-3-12

▶STORE

ゾウ くら

Ⓝ 藏 Ⓒ 藏 cáng zàng

140	Jōyō-6	U8535
艹	S15-3-12	F0392

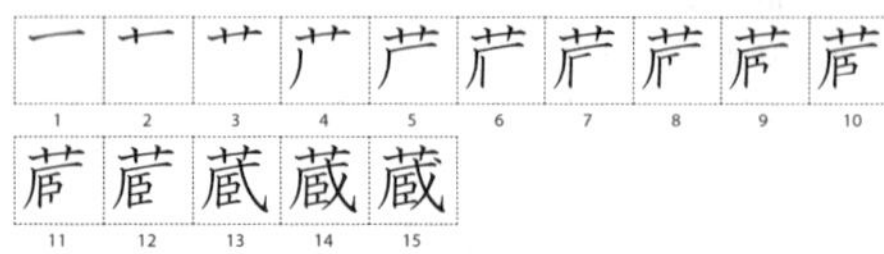

COMPOUNDS

❶ⓐ **STORE, put away, lay by**
ⓑ hide, conceal

a 貯蔵 ちょぞう storage, preservation
収蔵 しゅうぞう garnering, storage
死蔵する しぞうする hoard (up), keep (something) idle
秘蔵 ひぞう treasuring
冷蔵庫 れいぞうこ refrigerator
内蔵する ないぞうする have (a thing) within, have (something) built in

b 蔵匿する ぞうとくする [rare] conceal, shelter, harbor
埋蔵する まいぞうする bury in the ground, have (oil) deposits underground

❷ **own, possess, keep (a collection of books)**

蔵書 ぞうしょ one's library, book collection
蔵本 ぞうほん one's library
所蔵 しょぞう possession

❸ **STORE**house, storing place, treasury

土蔵 どぞう storehouse, godown
宝蔵 ほうぞう treasury
経蔵 きょうぞう scripture house

❹ abbrev. of 大蔵省 おおくらしょう: **Ministry of Finance**

蔵相 ぞうしょう Minister of Finance

❺ Tibet

漢蔵語 かんぞうご Sino-Tibetan (languages)

❻ *Buddhism* encompassing the whole universe

地蔵 じぞう (image of) *Kṣitigarbha-bodhisattva, Jizo* (guardian deity of children)

❼ collection of Buddhist sutras

三蔵 さんぞう *tripiṭaka* (three branches of Buddhist sutras)

INDEPENDENT

【ぞう 蔵】possession

中村家蔵 なかむらけぞう property of the Nakamura family

【ぞうする 蔵する】own, cherish

KUN

【くら 蔵】[also 倉, sometimes also 庫] **STOREhouse (for temporary preservation), storeroom, godown**

蔵出し くらだし delivery of goods from a storehouse

米蔵 こめぐら rice granary

大蔵省 おおくらしょう Ministry of Finance

SYNONYMS

❶ⓐ store

蔵 STORE → 2995

蓄 STORE UP → 2931

貯 LAY UP → 1903

納 PUT AWAY → 1652

❷ possess

有 HAVE → 3703

蔵 own → 2995

持 HOLD → 0447

属 BELONG TO → 3901

享 ENJOY → 2545

具 possess → 3159

❸ storehouse

倉 STOREHOUSE → 2607

蔵 storehouse → 2995

庫 STORAGE CHAMBER → 3864

HOMOPHONES

くら

倉 STOREHOUSE → 2607

庫 STORAGE CHAMBER → 3864

NOTE

➡ see USAGE note at 倉 2607

蔽

2996

2-3-12

▶COVER

ヘイ おお(う)

140	Nonstandard	U853D
艹	S15-3-12	F0000

traditional form → see 蔽 at 2991

蔭

2997

2-3-12

▶SHADE

イン かげ

140	Nonstandard	U4543
艹	S15-3-12	F0000

traditional form → see 蔭 at 2974

養

2998

2-3-12

▶FOSTER

ヨウ やしな(う)

Ⓝ 養 Ⓒ 养 yǎng

184	Jōyō-4	U990A
食	S15-9-6	F0783

COMPOUNDS

❶ⓐ FOSTER, bring up, raise to maturity, rear, support, care for

ⓑ (affording parental care) **FOSTER (parent), adopted**

ⓒ **breed, raise (animals or plants), keep**

a 養育する よういくする foster, bring up, educate

養護 ようご protective care

扶養 ふよう support, maintenance

b 養子 ようし foster [adopted] child

養父 ようふ foster father

c 養殖 ようしょく culture, cultivation, raising

養鶏 ようけい chicken raising

養毛剤 ようもうざい hair tonic

培養する ばいようする cultivate, culture, incubate

❷ⓐ FOSTER one's intellect, cultivate one's mind, train

ⓑ **FOSTER one's physical strength, nurse, cure**

a 養成する ようせいする train, educate, bring up

教養 きょうよう culture, education, cultivation

修養 しゅうよう mental culture, cultivation of the mind, character-building

b 養生 ようじょう care of health, recuperation

休養 きゅうよう rest, recuperation, relaxation

療養する りょうようする recruit one's health, recuperate, receive medical care

❸ nourishment

養分 ようぶん nourishment, nutrient

栄養 えいよう nutrition, nourishment

滋養 じよう nourishment, nutrition

KUN

【やしなう 養う】**FOSTER, bring up, raise to maturity, rear, support, care for; breed, raise animals, keep; foster (one's character), cultivate, develop; foster one's physical strength, nurse, cure**

養い やしない bringing up, nurture; nutrition, nourishment, sustenance

養い子 やしないご foster [adopted] child

養い育てる やしないそだてる foster, bring up, rear

SYNONYMS

❶ raise and nourish

育 RAISE → 2544
飼 RAISE ANIMALS → 2149
養 FOSTER → 2998
滋 NOURISH → 0734
哺 NURSE → 0478
牧 PASTURE → 1083

❷ⓐ cultivate

修 CULTIVATE → 0138
養 FOSTER (one's intellect) → 2998
練 TRAIN → 1738
錬 REFINE → 2185
鍛 train → 2206
磨 POLISH → 3946
琢 POLISH → 1222

養

▸FOSTER
ヨウ やしな(う)

2999
2-3-12

184	Nonstandard	U990A
食	S15-9-6	F0000

traditional form → see 養 at 2998

燕

2-3-12

incorrect stroke-count
➡ see 2-4-12: 廿 at 3142

奮

▸ROUSE UP
フン ふる(う)
Ⓒ 奋 fèn

3000
2-3-13

37	Jōyō-6	U596E
大	S16-3-13	F1328

COMPOUNDS

❶ⓐ ROUSE UP, rouse oneself (to action), be stirred up, be stimulated, be enlivened
ⓑ be ROUSEd UP, get excited, be angered
ⓒ energetically, strenuously, vigorously, courageously

a 奮起する ふんきする rouse [bestir] oneself, rise (to the occasion)
発奮(=発憤)する はっぷんする be stimulated, be inspired, be roused
感奮する かんぷんする be inspired, be moved to action

b 興奮(=昂奮) こうふん excitement, agitation, stimulation

c 奮戦する ふんせんする fight desperately, fight hard
奮撃 ふんげき fierce attack
奮迅 ふんじん dashing forward impetuously
奮励 ふんれい strenuous efforts [exertions]
奮然と ふんぜんと resolutely, courageously, vigorously
奮発する ふんぱつする exert oneself, make strenuous efforts; come down handsomely

❷ [original meaning, now archaic] (of birds) rouse (in the sense of take wing), spring up, fly away
奮飛する ふんぴする spring up, fly away

KUN

【ふるう 奮う】**ROUSE UP, rouse oneself, arouse**
奮って ふるって with energy, strenuously; heartily, willingly
勇気を奮い起こす ゆうきをふるいおこす muster up one's courage

SYNONYMS

❶ⓐ incite

挑 PROVOKE → 0445
唆 INSTIGATE → 0480
扇 FAN → 2449
煽 FAN → 1338
激 excite → 0955
奮 ROUSE UP → 3000
振 arouse to action → 0515
動 MOVE → 2232
起 rise to action → 4099

ⓑ elated

亢 HIGH-SPIRITED → 2460
高 high-spirited → 2601
昂 high-spirited → 3065
揚 exalted → 0722
奮 roused up → 3000

HOMOPHONES

ふるう
振 SWING → 0515
震 QUAKE → 3481
揮 WIELD → 0717

NOTE

➡ see USAGE note at 振 0515
★ do not confuse with 奪 ROB → 2956

憲

▸CONSTITUTION
ケン ㊔ のり かず とし さだ
Ⓝ 憲 Ⓒ 宪 xiàn

3001
2-3-13

61	Jōyō-6	U61B2
心	S16-4-12	F0972

COMPOUNDS

❶ⓐ CONSTITUTION, code of laws
ⓑ rules, regulations

a 憲法 けんぽう constitution, constitutional law
憲政 けんせい constitutional government
憲章 けんしょう constitution, charter
制憲する せいけんする establish a constitution
合憲的 ごうけんてき constitutional
立憲 りっけん constitutionalism
b 家憲 かけん family constitution [rules]
❷ official, authorities
憲兵 けんぺい military policeman [police]
官憲 かんけん authorities, officials; police

SYNONYMS

❶ⓐ laws and rules
法 LAW → 0391
律 LAW → 0433
典 CANON → 3253
憲 CONSTITUTION → 3001
令 ordinance → 2489
則 RULE → 1831
矩 RULE → 1475
規 REGULATION → 1231
紀 discipline → 1628

窺

3002
2-3-13

▶WATCH FURTIVELY
キ うかが(う)
ⓒ 窥 kuī

116	Names	U7ABA
穴	S16-5-11	F1980

COMPOUNDS

● WATCH FURTIVELY, peek, spy on
窺知する きちする perceive, understand

KUN

【うかがう 窺う】
①ⓐ **WATCH FURTIVELY, peek, spy on**
ⓑ **await (a chance)**
b 隙を窺う すきをうかがう watch for an unguarded moment
② **guess, infer, gather, surmise**
窺い知る うかがいしる perceive, understand

SYNONYMS

● see and look
見 SEE → 3151
看 WATCH → 3992
察 INSPECT → 2961
窺 WATCH FURTIVELY → 3002
瞥 GLANCE AT → 3592
目 look → 3777
観 VIEW → 2359
覧 LOOK OVER → 3538
眺 LOOK OUT OVER → 1503
望 LOOK AFAR → 3408
仰 LOOK UP → 0051
顧 LOOK BACK → 2394
視 REGARD → 1223

憲

3003
2-3-13

▶CONSTITUTION
ケン ㊔ のり かず とし さだ

61	Nonstandard	U61B2
心	S16-4-12	F0000

traditional form → see 憲 at 3001

薄

3004
2-3-13

▶THIN
ハク うす(い) うす- -うす うす(める) うす(まる) うす(らぐ) うす(ら)- うす(れる) すすき▲ ㊔ うすき
ⓒ 薄 báo bó bò

140	Jōyō	U8584
艹	S16-3-13	F0854

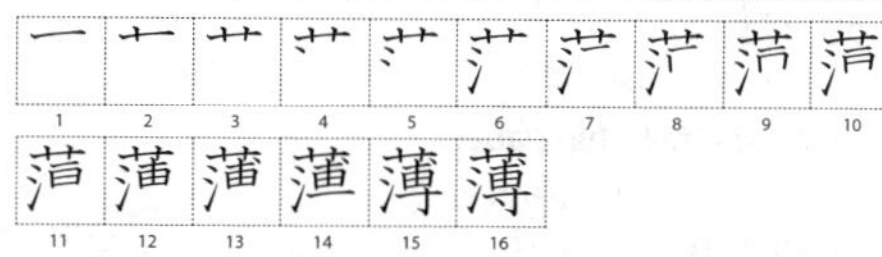

COMPOUNDS

❶ⓐ (not thick) **THIN, flimsy**
ⓑ (lacking intensity) **THIN, weak**
a 薄片 はくへん thin leaf; slice
薄氷 はくひょう thin ice; danger
厚薄 こうはく (relative) thickness
b 薄光 はっこう pale light, faint light
薄力粉 はくりきこ wheat flour of low viscosity
希薄な きはくな dilute, thin, rare, sparse
❷ⓐ meager, scanty, little, small (amount)
ⓑ **THIN** (luck), ill (fate)
a 薄給 はっきゅう meager [scanty, small] salary
薄利 はくり small profits, low interest
薄謝 はくしゃ small remuneration, small token of gratitude
薄弱な はくじゃくな weak, feeble, frail
b 薄幸(=薄倖) はっこう unhappiness; sad fate, misfortune
薄命 はくめい evil fate, misfortune
❸ⓐ frivolous, flippant, light, unthoughtful
ⓑ lacking warmth, cold, heartless
a 軽薄な けいはくな insincere, frivolous, flippant, fickle
浮薄な ふはくな frivolous, fickle, insincere
浅薄な せんぱくな shallow, superficial, flimsy
b 薄情な はくじょうな unfeeling, heartless, cruel
酷薄(=刻薄)な こくはくな cruel, inhumane
❹ close in on, press near
薄暮 はくぼ nightfall, dusk, twilight

肉薄(=肉迫)する にくはくする close in upon, press (the enemy) hard

KUN

【うすい 薄い】
① (not thick) **THIN, flimsy**
薄い板 うすいいた thin plate, sheet
薄着する うすぎする be thinly dressed
②ⓐ (not dense) **THIN, weak, watery**
ⓑ (of colors) **pale, THIN, light**
ⓒ (of taste) **light, slightly salted**
a 髪が薄い かみがうすい have thin hair
b 薄い色 うすいいろ light color
c 味が薄い あじがうすい lightly seasoned
③ meager, scanty, little
興味が薄い きょうみがうすい uninteresting
情が薄い じょうがうすい be coldhearted [hard-hearted]

【うす- 薄-】
① (not thick) **THIN**
薄紙 うすがみ thin paper
② (low in intensity or degree)
ⓐ **slightly**
ⓑ [also prefix] pale, light (color)
a 薄曇りの うすぐもりの slightly cloudy
b 薄紫色 うすむらさきいろ light purple, orchid
③ [also prefix] somehow, vaguely
薄薄 うすうす dimly, vaguely
薄気味悪い うすきみわるい weird, uncanny, eerie
薄汚い うすぎたない filthy, dirty, bedraggled

【-うす -薄】 [also suffix] **scarcity (of), shortage (of)**
品薄 しなうす scarcity of goods, shortage of stock
手薄な てうすな short of hands
期待薄だ きたいうすだ be of little hope, not to be depended on

【うすめる 薄める】 *vt* **THIN, lighten, weaken, dilute**
水で薄める みずでうすめる dilute with water, water down

【うすまる 薄まる】 *vi* **THIN out [down], be diluted**

【うすらぐ 薄らぐ】 *vi* **fade, become dim; abate, decline, lessen**
光が薄らいだ ひかりがうすらいだ The light has faded
時と共に悲しみも薄らぐ ときとともにかなしみもうすらぐ Time wears away grief

【うすら- 薄ら-】 [also prefix] (low in intensity or degree) **slightly, somewhat, rather; slight, a little, faint**
薄ら寒い うすらさむい chilly, rather cold, somewhat cold
薄ら馬鹿 うすらばか dimwit, simpleton, sluggard

【うすれる 薄れる】 same as 薄らぐ うすらぐ

【すすき 薄】 eulalia

SYNONYMS

❶ⓐ thin
薄 THIN → 3004
細 SLENDER → 1689
繊 FINE → 1789
痩 GET THIN → 4069
ⓑ less in degree
弱 WEAK → 1499
軽 LIGHT → 1909
微 SLIGHT → 0788
低 LOW → 0082
薄 THIN → 3004
浅 SHALLOW → 0464
仄 FAINT → 3664
❷ⓐ few
少 LITTLE → 4278
寡 FEW → 2957
乏 SCANTY → 2432
薄 meager → 3004
微 SLIGHT → 0788
寸 A BIT OF → 3652
僅 A LITTLE → 0176
些 A BIT → 3251

【うすい】
②ⓐ **rare and sparse**
薄い THIN → 3004
希 RARE → 2543
疎 SPARSE → 1512
粗 COARSE → 1683
稀 RARE → 1523
ⓑ **light-colored**
淡 LIGHT → 0640
浅 light → 0464
薄い pale → 3004
鈍- DULL → 2123

NOTE

★ do not confuse with 簿 RECORD BOOK → 3387

薫

3005

2-3-13

▶BALMY
クン かお(る) ㊔ しげ
Ⓝ 薰 Ⓒ 薰 xūn

140	Jōyō	U85AB
艹	S16-3-13	F2139

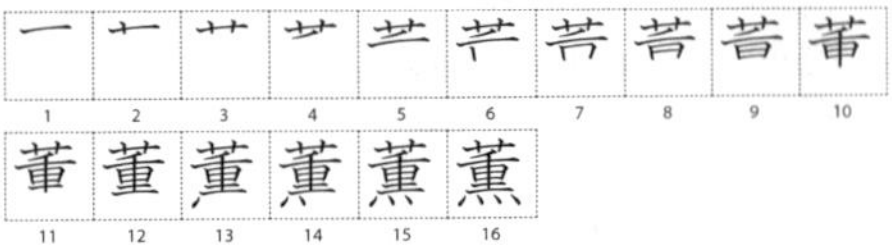

COMPOUNDS

❶ⓐ [original meaning] **BALMY, sweet-smelling, fragrant**

ⓑ fragrance, sweet smell
a 薫風 くんぷう balmy breeze
薫煙 くんえん fragrant smoke
b 余薫 よくん lingering fragrance
❷ influence, educate
薫化 くんか influencing people by one's virtue
薫育 くんいく moral education
薫陶 くんとう education, discipline
❸ [formerly also 燻 1406] smoke, fumigate, fume
薫香 くんこう incense; fragrance
薫製 くんせい smoking (fish or meat)

INDEPENDENT

【くんずる 薫ずる】be fragrant; perfume

KUN

【かおる 薫る】**look sweet-smelling [BALMY], look fragrant**
薫り かおり fragrance, aroma
若葉が薫る わかばがかおる The fresh verdure looks sweet-smelling

SYNONYMS

❶ **smell and fragrance**
気 smell → 3960
匂い SMELL → 3662
臭 BAD SMELL → 3261
香 SWEET SMELL → 3177
馨 PERFUME → 3575
芳 FRAGRANT → 2739
薫 BALMY → 3005
郁 AROMATIC → 1640
❸ **preserve food**
漬ける PICKLE → 0861
燻 SMOKE → 1406
薫 smoke → 3005

HOMOPHONES

かおる 香 SWEET SMELL → 3177
かおり 香 SWEET SMELL → 3177

NOTE

➡ see USAGE note at 香 3177
★ do not confuse with 董 OLD TOOL → 2911

蕾

3006
2-3-13

▶**BUD**
ライ つぼみ つぼ(む)
Ⓒ 蕾 lěi

140	Names	U857E
艹	S16-3-13	F2948

COMPOUNDS

● **BUD (of a flower)**
味蕾 みらい taste buds

KUN

【つぼみ 蕾】**BUD (of a flower)**
薔×薇×の蕾 ばらのつぼみ rosebud
【つぼむ 蕾む】**BUD**, set buds

SYNONYMS

● **early states of plant life**
芽 BUD → 2784
蕾 BUD (of a flower) → 3006
苗 SEEDLING → 2781
種 SEED → 1560

蕗

3007
2-3-13

▶**BUTTERBUR**
ロ ル ふき ㊔ つゆ
Ⓒ 蕗 lù

140	Names	U8557
艹	S16-3-13	F3030

COMPOUNDS

● [archaic] licorice
蕗草 ろそう licorice

KUN

【ふき 蕗】**BUTTERBUR**

SYNONYMS

【ふき】
○ **vegetables**
菜 greens → 2880
蕪 TURNIP → 2990
芋 POTATO → 2706
豆 BEAN → 2442
蕗 BUTTERBUR → 3007
茄 EGGPLANT → 2787
芹 JAPANESE PARSLEY → 2742
瓜 GOURD → 3789
瓢 BOTTLE GOURD → 2356
芥 mustard → 2741

薦

3008
2-3-13

▶**RECOMMEND**
セン すす(める) ㊔ こも
Ⓒ 荐 jiàn

140	Jōyō	U85A6
艹	S16-3-13	F2028

COMPOUNDS

❶ **RECOMMEND (a person to a post or a product)**
薦挙 せんきょ recommendation
推薦する すいせんする recommend, nominate
自薦 じせん self-recommendation
❷ [rare] straw mat
蒲薦 ほせん bulrush mat

KUN

【すすめる 薦める】RECOMMEND (a person to a post or a product to a person)

...に薦められて …にすすめられて on the recommendation of...

SYNONYMS

❶ recommend

薦 RECOMMEND →3008

推 recommend →0612

❷ mats

畳 TATAMI →3205

薦 straw mat →3008

-敷き underlay →2345

HOMOPHONES

すすめる

勧 URGE →2334

奨 ENCOURAGE →3524

進 ADVANCE →3873

NOTE

➡ see USAGE note at 進 3873

薪

3009

2-3-13

▶FIREWOOD

シン たきぎ まき▲

Ⓒ 薪 xīn

140	Jōyō	U85AA
艹	S16-3-13	F2192

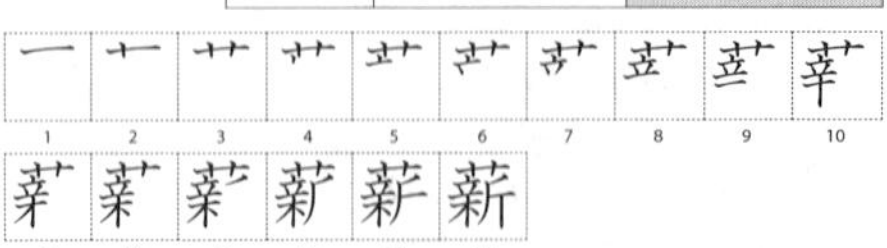

COMPOUNDS

● FIREWOOD, wood for fuel

薪炭 しんたん firewood and charcoal

薪水 しんすい cooking

KUN

【たきぎ 薪】FIREWOOD

薪拾い たきぎひろい firewood gathering

【まき 薪】FIREWOOD

薪割り まきわり wood-chopping[-splitting]; hatchet, axe

SYNONYMS

● kinds of wood

木 WOOD →4261

材 TIMBER →1031

薪 FIREWOOD →3009

柴 BRUSHWOOD →3287

● kinds of fuel

炭 COAL, CHARCOAL →2806

薪 FIREWOOD →3009

油 OIL →0400

薙

3010

2-3-13

▶MOW DOWN

テイ チ な(ぐ)

Ⓒ 薙 tì

140	Names	U8599
艹	S16-3-13	F2316

COMPOUNDS

❶ MOW DOWN (an enemy)

薙射 ちしゃ strafing

❷ shave

薙髪 ていはつ(=ちはつ) shaving one's head

KUN

【なぐ 薙ぐ】MOW DOWN

薙ぎ払う なぎはらう mow down

薙ぎ倒す なぎたおす mow down, knock down; defeat one after another

草薙の剣 くさなぎのつるぎ sword of the Imperial regalia

水薙鳥 みずなぎどり *Procellariidae, Procellariiformes*

SPECIAL READINGS

薙刀 なぎなた weapon consisting of a curved blade on a long shaft

SYNONYMS

【なぐ】

◯ cut

切 CUT →0030

薙ぐ MOW DOWN →3010

剪 PRUNE →2886

削 CUT BY CHIPPING →1837

挽く GRIND, saw →0511

断 CUT OFF →1885

截 CUT OFF →4092

裁 CUT OUT →4090

斬 CUT WITH A SWORD →1874

割 cut with a knife →2284

剖 DISSECT →2103

刈る CLIP →0032

伐 CUT DOWN →0046

薬

3011

2-3-13

▶DRUG

ヤク くすり ㊔ くす

Ⓝ 藥 Ⓒ 药 yào

140	Jōyō-3	U85AC
艹	S16-3-13	F0621

COMPOUNDS

❶ [also suffix] [original meaning] **DRUG, medicine, remedy, pharmaceutical**
薬剤 やくざい medicine, drugs
薬品 やくひん medicine, drug; chemicals
薬局 やっきょく drugstore, pharmacy
薬効 やっこう effect of a medicine
麻薬 まやく narcotic, drug
医薬 いやく medicine, drug; medical practice and dispensary
製薬 せいやく pharmaceutical manufacture
妙薬 みょうやく miracle drug, golden remedy
胃腸薬 いちょうやく medicine for the stomach and bowels

❷ **chemical, compound**
農薬 のうやく agricultural chemicals
試薬 しやく (chemical) reagent
火薬 かやく gunpowder
爆薬 ばくやく explosive compound, blasting powder

INDEPENDENT

【やく 薬】*slang* dope, narcotics
薬を打つ やくをうつ inject a unit of dope

KUN

【くすり 薬】**DRUG, medicine, remedy; powdered medicine, pill; chemical; enamel, glaze; benefit**
薬屋 くすりや drugstore
薬指 くすりゆび third finger, ring finger
薬になる くすりになる be beneficial (to), do (a person) good
飲み薬 のみぐすり medicine, internal medicine
風邪薬 かぜぐすり remedy for a cold
上薬 うわぐすり [also 釉 or 釉薬] glaze, enamel

SYNONYMS

❶ **medicines**
薬 DRUG → 3011
剤 PREPARATION → 2102
錠 PILL → 2180
丸 pill suffix → 4225
鍼 ACUPUNCTURE → 2204
灸 MOXIBUSTION → 2752

USAGE

【くすり】
薬
drug, medicine, remedy; powdered medicine, pill; chemical; enamel, glaze; benefit
釉
glaze, enamel

HOMOPHONES

うわぐすり
釉 GLAZE → 1911
釉薬 → 1911, 3011
上薬 → 4212, 3011
くすり 釉 GLAZE → 1911

薗

▶GARDEN
エン その

3012
2-3-13

140	Names	U8597
艹	S16-3-13	F0000

traditional form → see 園 at 3914

薩

2-3-13

incorrect stroke-count
➡ see 2-3-14: 艹 at 3016

舊

2-3-13

incorrect stroke-count
➡ see 2-3-14: 艹 at 3019

嶺

▶RIDGE
レイ リョウ みね ね
Ⓒ 岭 lǐng

3013
2-3-14

46	Names	U5DBA
山	S17-3-14	F2289

COMPOUNDS

ⓐ **RIDGE, ridge of a mountain, summit, peak**
ⓑ high mountain, lofty peak, mountain range
a 分水嶺 ぶんすいれい ridge, watershed
海嶺 かいれい (submarine) ridge
雪嶺 せつれい snow-capped peak
峻嶺 しゅんれい steep peak, high rugged mountain
b 鷲尾嶺 わしおりょう Washio Mountains

KUN

【みね 嶺】[usu. 峰]
①ⓐ (summit or vicinity of a summit) **peak, summit, RIDGE**
ⓑ **high mountain**
② **back of a sword**
【ね 嶺】*elegant* **peak, summit, RIDGE; high mountain**
高嶺の花 たかねのはな flower on the inaccessible heights; unattainable object

SYNONYMS

ⓐ **mountain parts**
頂 SUMMIT → 0164
峰 PEAK → 0494
嶺 RIDGE → 3013
峠 MOUNTAIN PASS → 0428
崖 CLIFF → 2862
壁 wall-like structure → 3601

HOMOPHONES

みね 峰 PEAK → 0494

NOTE

➡ see USAGE note at 峰 0494

嶽
3014
2-3-14

▶HIGH MOUNTAIN
ガク たけ ㊔ たか おか

46	Nonstandard	U5DBD
山	S17-3-14	F0000

traditional form → see 岳 at 3164

藁
3015
2-3-14

▶STRAW
コウ わら
Ⓒ 藁 gǎo

140	Names	U85C1
艹	S17-3-14	F2374

KUN
【わら 藁】STRAW
藁葺き わらぶき straw thatching; straw roof
藁人形 わらにんぎょう straw effigy [doll]
麦藁 むぎわら (wheat) straw
稲藁 いねわら(=いなわら) rice [paddy] straw
敷き藁 しきわら bed of straw, litter
溺れる者は藁をも摑む おぼれるものはわらをもつかむ A drowning man will catch at a straw

SYNONYMS
【わら】
◯ **kinds of grasses**
草 GRASS → 2813
荻 AMUR SILVERGRASS → 2844
蒲 CATTAIL → 2932
萊 GOOSEFOOT → 2878
蕨 BRACKEN → 2992
叢 grassy place → 3243
芝 LAWN GRASS → 2705
笹 BAMBOO GRASS → 3301
茅 cogongrass → 2779
萱 THATCH GRASS → 2904
藁 STRAW → 3015
芦 REED → 2743
葦 COMMON REED → 2934
菅 SEDGE → 2874

薩
3016
2-3-14

▶PHONETIC [satsu]
サツ
Ⓝ 薩 Ⓒ 萨 sà

140	Names	U85A9
艹	S17-3-14	F1388

COMPOUNDS
❶ **used PHONETICally for *satsu* in the transliteration of Sanskrit Buddhist terms**
菩薩 ぼさつ *bodhisattva*
弥勒×菩薩 みろくぼさつ *Maitreya* (a *bodhisattva*)
金剛薩埵× こんごうさった *Vajrasattva* (a *bodhisattva*)
❷ abbrev. of 薩摩 さつま, old name for Kagoshima Prefecture
薩摩芋 さつまいも sweet potato
薩長 さっちょう Satsuma and Choshu
薩英戦争 さつえいせんそう Anglo-Satsuma War

SYNONYMS
❶ **phonetic [s]/[sh]**
沙 phonetic [sha] → 0311
刹 phonetic [setsu] → 1620
遮 phonetic [sha] → 3916
叉 phonetic [sha] → 4194
世 phonetic [se] → 4308
須 phonetic [shu] → 0700
修 phonetic [shu] → 0138
西 phonetic [su] → 4333
相 phonetic [sō] → 1120
薩 phonetic [satsu] → 3016

藉
3017
2-3-14

▶TRAMPLE ON
シャ セキ
Ⓒ 藉 jí jiè

140	Non-Jōyō	U85C9
艹	S17-3-14	F2987

COMPOUNDS
❶ **TRAMPLE ON, step on**
狼藉 ろうぜき disorder; violence
❷ use (as a pretext), use (to one's advantage)
. . . に藉口して …にしゃこうして under the pretext of…
❸ [now replaced by 謝 しゃ 2048] console, solace
慰藉料 いしゃりょう consolation money
❹ [original meaning, now obsolete] lay, spread

SYNONYMS
❶ **step on**
踏 TREAD → 1997
蹈 STEP ON → 2055
藉 TRAMPLE ON → 3017

NOTE
★ do not confuse with 籍 REGISTER → 3394

薫
3018
2-3-14

▶BALMY
クン かお(る) ㊔ しげ

140	Names	U85B0
艹	S17-3-14	F0000

traditional form → see 薫 at 3005

舊
▶FORMER
キュウ

134	Nonstandard	U820A
臼	S17-6-11	F0000

3019
2-3-14

traditional form → see 旧 at 0014

薩
▶PHONETIC [satsu]
サツ

140	Nonstandard	U85A9
艹	S17-3-14	F0000

3020
2-3-14

traditional form → see 薩 at 3016

藍
2-3-14

incorrect stroke-count
➡ see 2-3-15: 艹 at 3024

薦
2-3-14

incorrect stroke-count
➡ see 2-3-13: 艹 at 3008

龠
2-3-14

incorrect classification
➡ see 2-2-15: 𠆢 at 2670

嚞
▶SAGACIOUS
▶PHILOSOPHY
テツ ㊔ さと さとし さとる あき あきら のり

30	Nonstandard	U569E
口	S18-3-15	F0000

3021
2-3-15

traditional form → see 哲 at 3402

藩
▶FEUDAL DOMAIN
ハン
Ⓒ 藩 fān

140	Jōyō	U85E9
艹	S18-3-15	F0884

3022
2-3-15

COMPOUNDS

❶ⓐ *han*: **FEUDAL DOMAIN (governed by a daimyo in Edo Japan), fief; feudal clan**
ⓑ **suffix after names of FEUDAL DOMAINs**
ⓒ feudal lord, daimyo

a 藩校 はんこう *han* school
藩内 はんない within the *han*
藩閥 はんばつ clan favoritism, clanship
廃藩 はいはん abolition of the *han* system
b 薩摩藩 さつまはん Satsuma Han
c 藩主 はんしゅ feudal lord, daimyo
藩邸 はんてい daimyo's estate in Edo
藩儒 はんじゅ daimyo's scholar

❷ [original meaning, now archaic] **hedge, fence**

INDEPENDENT

【はん 藩】*han* (→ ❶ⓐ)
藩の財政 はんのざいせい *han* finances

SYNONYMS

❶ⓐ & ❶ⓑ feudal territorial divisions
藩 FEUDAL DOMAIN → 3022
国 province (in former Japan) → 3831
領 fief → 1567
封 daimiate → 1639
荘 manor (in feudal Japan) → 2814

繭
▶COCOON
ケン まゆ
Ⓒ 茧 jiǎn

120	Jōyō	U7E6D
糸	S18-6-12	F3561

3023
2-3-15

COMPOUNDS

● [original meaning] **COCOON**
繭糸 けんし cocoon and silk-thread, silk-thread
繭価 けんか price of cocoons

KUN

【まゆ 繭】**COCOON**
繭玉 まゆだま festive cocoons
繭を掛ける まゆをかける spin a cocoon
春繭 はるまゆ spring cocoon crop

SYNONYMS

● **insect**
虫 INSECT → 4343
昆 INSECT → 3067
繭 COCOON → 3023

藍
▶INDIGO
ラン あい
Ⓒ 蓝 lán

140	Jōyō	U85CD
艹	S18-3-15	F1817

3024
2-3-15

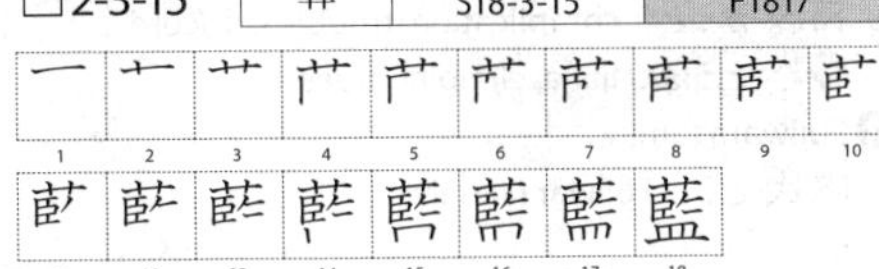

COMPOUNDS

❶ⓐ [also prefix] INDIGO blue, deep blue, blue
ⓑ INDIGO plant, indigo dye
a 藍綬×褒章 らんじゅほうしょう Blue Ribbon Medal
藍晶石 らんしょうせき cyanite
青藍 せいらん indigo blue
b 出藍の誉れ しゅつらんのほまれ surpassing one's master
❷ [now always 襤 1607] rags, tattered clothes
藍褸× らんる rags, tattered clothes

KUN

【あい 藍】 **Japanese INDIGO plant, indigo plant; indigo blue**
藍に染める あいにそめる dye deep blue
藍色 あいいろ indigo blue
人造藍 じんぞうあい synthetic indigo

SYNONYMS

❶ⓐ blue and purple colors
青 BLUE → 3084
碧 DEEP BLUE → 3515
瑠 LAPIS LAZULI (bright blue) → 1342
紺 DARK BLUE → 1688
藍 INDIGO → 3024
紫 PURPLE → 3332
蒼 PALE BLUE → 2943
ⓑ pigments
墨 INDIA INK → 3423
漆 LACQUER → 0863
藍 INDIGO → 3024
堊 WHITEWASH → 3442

藤

3025
2-3-15

▶WISTERIA
トウ ふじ
Ⓝ 籐 Ⓒ 藤 téng

140	Jōyō	U85E4
艹	S18-3-15	F0264

COMPOUNDS

❶ⓐ WISTERIA
ⓑ [original meaning] climbing plants, vines, liana
a 葛藤 かっとう complication, troubles, discord
b 藤本 とうほん liana, climbing trees
❷ Fujiwara family
藤氏 とうし Fujiwara family

KUN

【ふじ 藤】 **WISTERIA; light purple, lilac**
藤棚 ふじだな wisteria trellis [arbor]
藤色 ふじいろ light purple, lilac
上り藤 のぼりふじ lupine

SYNONYMS

❶ⓐ shrubs
藤 WISTERIA → 3025
蔦 JAPANESE IVY → 2972
萩 *HAGI* → 2908
茉 JASMINE → 2790
莉 JASMINE → 2843
芭 JAPANESE FIBER BANANA → 2736
❶ⓐ flowering plants
菊 CHRYSANTHEMUM → 2875
菖 IRIS → 2881
菫 VIOLET → 2877
蓮 LOTUS → 2940
葛 KUDZU → 2905
蓬 JAPANESE MUGWORT → 2973
葵 MALLOW → 2906
蓉 COTTON ROSE → 2944
芙 LOTUS → 2737
蘭 ORCHID → 3031
萩 *HAGI* → 2908
藤 WISTERIA → 3025
桜 cherry blossom → 1168
梅 *ume* blossom → 1159

COMPOUND FORMATION

【葛藤 かっとう】
葛藤 'complication, etc.' is something as complicated or entangled as kudzu vines (葛) and wisterias (藤 ❶ⓐ).

藝

3026
2-3-15

▶ART
ゲイ ㊔ き

140	Names	U85DD
艹	S18-3-15	F0000

traditional form → see 芸 at 2738

藥

3027
2-3-15

▶DRUG
ヤク くすり ㊔ くす

140	Names	U85E5
艹	S18-3-15	F0000

traditional form → see 薬 at 3011

藏

3028
2-3-15

▶STORE
ゾウ くら

140	Names	U85CF
艹	S18-3-15	F0000

traditional form → see 蔵 at 2995

寵

3029

2-3-16

▶**AFFECTION**

チョウ ㊔ よし うつくし うつく

Ⓒ 宠 chǒng

40	Names	U5BF5
宀	S19-3-16	F2430

COMPOUNDS

❶ **AFFECTION, love; favor, grace**

寵愛 ちょうあい affection, favor
寵幸 ちょうこう grace, favor
君寵 くんちょう favor of one's ruler [lord]
恩寵 おんちょう grace (of God), favor

❷ **favorite, beloved**

寵児 ちょうじ favorite child; popular figure, darling
寵臣 ちょうしん favored retainer

INDEPENDENT

【ちょう 寵】**AFFECTION**, favor

SYNONYMS

❶ **love**

愛 LOVE →3133
情 love →0583
恋 LOVE (for the opposite sex) →2602
艶 ROMANCE →2403
寵 AFFECTION →3029

寶

3030

2-3-16

▶**TREASURE**

ホウ たから ㊔ たか とみ

40	Nonstandard	U5BF3
宀	S19-3-16	F0000

traditional form →see 宝 at 2764

蘭

3031

2-3-16

▶**ORCHID**

ラン

Ⓒ 兰 lán

140	Names	U862D
艹	S19-3-16	F1714

COMPOUNDS

❶ **ORCHID**

蘭栽培法 らんさいばいほう orchidology

❷ⓐ Holland, the Netherlands
ⓑ Dutch (language)

a 蘭人 らんじん Dutch people
b 蘭学 らんがく study of Western science (in the Edo period) by means of the Dutch language

INDEPENDENT

【らん 蘭】**ORCHID**; Holland, the Netherlands

SYNONYMS

❶ **flowering plants**

菊 CHRYSANTHEMUM →2875
菖 IRIS →2881
菫 VIOLET →2877
蓮 LOTUS →2940
葛 KUDZU →2905
蓬 JAPANESE MUGWORT →2973
葵 MALLOW →2906
蓉 COTTON ROSE →2944
芙 LOTUS →2737
蘭 ORCHID →3031
萩 *HAGI* →2908
藤 WISTERIA →3025
桜 cherry blossom →1168
梅 *ume* blossom →1159

❷ⓐ **European countries**

英 ENGLAND →2782
独 GERMANY →0471
仏 FRANCE →0020
伊 ITALY →0052
葡 PORTUGAL →2902
西 Spain →4333
蘭 the Netherlands →3031
希 Greece →2543
露 Russia →3495
白 Belgium →4305

蘇

3032

2-3-16

▶**REVIVE**

ソ ス よみがえ(る)

Ⓝ 穌 Ⓒ 苏 sū

140	Names	U8607
艹	S19-3-16	F1745

COMPOUNDS

❶ [sometimes also 甦 そ 4109] **REVIVE, come back to life**

蘇生 そせい revival, resuscitation
蘇鉄 そてつ king sago palm, *Cycas revoluta*
屠×蘇 とそ spiced sake

❷ⓐ perilla
ⓑ sappanwood

a 紫蘇 しそ beefsteak plant, perilla, esp. *Perilla frutescens*
b 蘇芳(=蘇方、蘇枋×) すおう sappanwood; sappanwood dye

❸ used phonetically for *so*

蘇連 それん Soviet Union
耶蘇 やそ Jesus

INDEPENDENT

【そ 蘇(=酥×)】ancient food similar to cheese

KUN

【よみがえる 蘇る】[also 甦る] **REVIVE, resuscitate**

蘇り よみがえり resurrection, resuscitation

SYNONYMS

❶ **return and restore**

返 RETURN → 3797
戻 RETURN → 2441
還 RETURN → 3945
復 RETURN TO → 0701
蘇 REVIVE → 3032
甦 REVIVE → 4109

USAGE

【よみがえる】

蘇る
[also 甦る] revive, resuscitate

甦る
[also 蘇る] revive, resuscitate

HOMOPHONES

よみがえる 甦 REVIVE → 4109

藻

3033
2-3-16

▶**ALGAE**
ソウ も
Ⓒ 藻 zǎo

140	Jōyō	U85FB
艹	S19-3-16	F2340

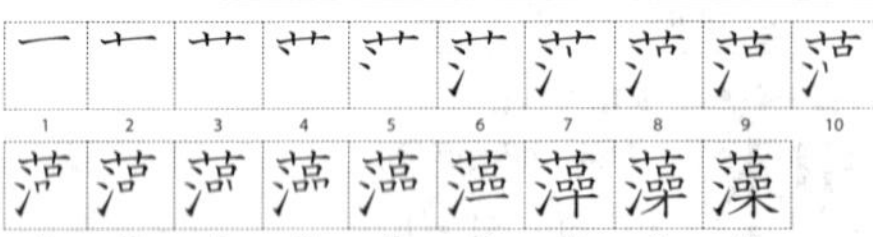

COMPOUNDS

❶ [original meaning] **ALGAE, seaweed**
藻類 そうるい algae, seaweed
海藻 かいそう marine algae, seaweed, kelp
緑藻 りょくそう green algae

❷ elegant expression, rhetorical flourish
詩藻(=詞藻) しそう florid expression, poetical talent
文藻 ぶんそう literary talent

KUN

【も 藻】 **ALGAE, duckweed, seaweed**
藻屑 もくず seaweed

蘆

3034
2-3-16

▶**COMMON REED**
ロ あし よし

140	Nonstandard	U8606
艹	S19-3-16	F0000

traditional form → see 芦 at 2743

蘓

3035
2-3-16

▶**REVIVE**
ソ ス よみがえ(る)

140	Nonstandard	U8613
艹	S19-3-16	F0000

traditional form → see 蘇 at 3032

寶

3036
2-3-17

▶**TREASURE**
ホウ たから ㊔ たか とみ

40	Nonstandard	U5BF6
宀	S20-3-17	F0000

traditional form → see 宝 at 2764

黨

2-3-17

incorrect classification
➡ see 2-5-15: 𰀪 at 3245

巌

3037
2-3-17

▶**CRAG**
ガン いわお いわ ㊔ げん たけ いつく よし
Ⓝ 巖 巗 Ⓒ 岩 yán

46	Names	U5DCC
山	S20-3-17	F2605

COMPOUNDS

❶ [usu. 岩 2778] [original meaning] **CRAG, (massive) rock**
巌頭 がんとう top of a massive rock
巌窟 がんくつ cave, rocky cavern
奇巌 きがん massive rock of unusual shape

❷ [rare] **CRAG**gy, precipitous, steep
巌巌とした がんがんとした steep (as of a mountain), craggy

KUN

【いわお 巌】 **massive rock, CRAG**
【いわ 巌】 [now usu. 岩] **rock, CRAG**

SYNONYMS

❶ **rock and stone**

石 STONE → 3689
岩 ROCK → 2778
巌 CRAG → 3037

HOMOPHONES

いわ
岩 ROCK → 2778
磐 BEDROCK → 3534

NOTE

➡ see USAGE note at 岩 2778

譱

3038
2-3-17

▶**GOOD**
ゼン よ(い) ㊔ よし

149	Nonstandard	U8B71
言	S20-7-13	F0000

traditional form → see 善 at 2921

竊

3039
2-3-19

▶**STEAL**
セツ

116	Nonstandard	U7ACA
穴	S22-5-17	F0000

traditional form → see 窃 at 2801

巖

3040

2-3-20

▶**CRAG**

ガン いわお いわ ㊔ げん たけ いつく よし

46	Names	U5DD6
山	S23-3-20	F0000

traditional form → see 巌 at 3037

旦

3041

2-4-1

▶**DAYBREAK**

タン ダン ㊔ あさ あき あきら

Ⓒ 旦 dàn

72	Jōyō	U65E6
日	S5-4-1	F1171

丨 冂 月 日 旦

1 2 3 4 5

COMPOUNDS

❶ⓐ [original meaning] **DAYBREAK, dawn, morn, morning**

ⓑ **first day, day**

a 旦暮 たんぼ morn and eve, dawn and dusk

旦夕 たんせき morning and evening, day and night

一旦 いったん once; for a while; [archaic] one morning, one day

b 元旦 がんたん New Year's Day

月旦 げったん criticism, comment; [rare] first day of the month

❷ **master, gentleman; husband**

旦那(=檀那) だんな master, husband, patron, protector; sir; [original meaning] donor

震旦 しんたん ancient Indian name for China

SYNONYMS

❶ⓐ **morning and dawn**

朝 MORNING → 2130

暁 DAWN → 1233

旦 DAYBREAK → 3041

曙 DAWN → 1384

晨 EARLY MORNING → 3110

ⓑ **days**

日 DAY → 3759

曜 DAY OF THE WEEK → 1402

昼 DAYTIME → 3841

旦 first day → 3041

朔 FIRST DAY OF THE LUNAR MONTH → 1678

晦 LAST DAY OF THE LUNAR MONTH → 1196

丞

2-4-1

incorrect stroke-count

➡ see 2-5-1: 丞 at 3146

孪

2-4-2

incorrect classification/ stroke-count

➡ see 2-2-5: 亠 at 2532

早

3042

2-4-2

▶**EARLY**

▶**QUICK**

ソウ サッ- はや(い) はや はや- はや(まる) はや(める) さ-* ㊔ はやし

Ⓒ 早 zǎo

72	Jōyō-1	U65E9
日	S6-4-2	F0347

丨 冂 日 日 旦 早

1 2 3 4 5 6

COMPOUNDS

❶ⓐ [original meaning] (near the beginning of a time period) **EARLY**

ⓑ (occurring before the usual time) **EARLY, premature**

a 早朝 そうちょう early morning

早期 そうき early stage

早春 そうしゅん early spring

早晩 そうばん sooner or later

b 早熟な そうじゅくな precocious, forward

早世 そうせい early death

早産 そうざん premature birth

早退 そうたい leaving earlier than usual

尚早の しょうそうの premature

❷ⓐ **QUICK, fast**

ⓑ hasty, rash

a 早早 そうそう quickly, without delay, immediately; early

早速 さっそく immediately

早急に さっきゅう(=そうきゅう)に urgently, pressingly, in a hurry

b 早計 そうけい rashness

❸ abbrev. of 早稲田大学 わせだだいがく: Waseda University

早明戦 そうめいせん Waseda-Meiji (baseball) game

KUN

【はやい 早い】

① **EARLY, premature**

早く はやく early, soon; early age [time]

早早と はやばやと early, promptly

お早う おはよう Good morning!

日暮れが早い ひぐれがはやい Dusk falls early

親に早く死なれる おやにはやくしなれる be orphaned while still young

② [sometimes also 速い] (requiring little time) **QUICK, prompt**

早い話が はやいはなしが in short

早い事 はやいこと quickly

耳が早い みみがはやい be quick-eared

手っ取り早く てっとりばやく expeditiously, with dispatch

【はや 早】 **already, now**

最早 もはや already; no longer
五月も早半ばだ ごがつもはやなかばだ It's already the middle of May

【はや- 早-】
① EARLY
早起き はやおき early rising
早立ち(=早発ち) はやだち early morning departure
早引き はやびき early leaving
早寝する はやねする go to bed early
②ⓐ [also prefix] [sometimes also 速-] **QUICK, fast, rapid**
ⓑ [prefix] hasty, rash
a 早見表 はやみひょう list, chart
早業 はやわざ quick work, (clever) feat
早口 はやくち fast [rapid] talking
b 早合点 はやがてん hasty conclusion
早呑み込み はやのみこみ hasty conclusion

【はやまる 早まる】
① **take place ahead of time**
梅雨明けは早まるだろう つゆあけははやまるだろう The rainy season will end early
② **be rash, be too hasty, act rashly**
早まって はやまって in one's hurry

【はやめる 早める】 **perform an action EARLY, do ahead of time**
期日を早める きじつをはやめる advance the date (of)

【さ- 早-】 **young, supple**
早乙女 さおとめ rice-planting girl; girl
早苗 さなえ rice sprouts

SPECIAL READINGS
早生▲ わせ early ripening; precocious
早稲▲ わせ early ripening rice

SYNONYMS
❷ **fast**
速 QUICK → 3851
早 QUICK → 3042
疾 fast → 4064
快 fast → 0289
急 rapid → 2595
迅 SWIFT → 3780
敏 NIMBLE → 1675
即 IMMEDIATE → 1439
捷 AGILE → 0609

USAGE
❶【はやい】
早い
① early, premature
② [sometimes also 速い] (requiring little time) quick, prompt
速い
ⓐ (acting or moving quickly) quick, speedy, fast, rapid, swift
ⓑ [usu. 早い] (requiring little time) quick, prompt

❷【はや-】
早-
① early
②ⓐ [also prefix] [sometimes also 速-] quick, fast, rapid
ⓑ [prefix] hasty, rash
速-
[usu. 早-] quick, fast, rapid
★Though 早い and 速い as independent *kun* words can be discriminated as shown above, they are often interchangeable in the formation of compounds related to speed.

❸【はやめる】
早める
perform an action early, do ahead of time
速める
vt quicken, accelerate, speed up, hasten

❹【そうそう】
早早
① quickly, without delay, immediately
② early
草草
① closing words of a letter
② hurried, flurried

❺【はやまる】
早まる
① take place ahead of time
② be rash, be too hasty, act rashly
速まる
vi quicken, accelerate, speed up

HOMOPHONES
はやい 速 QUICK → 3851
はや- 速 QUICK → 3851
はやまる 速 QUICK → 3851
はやめる 速 QUICK → 3851
さ- 小 SMALL → 0007

NOTE
➡ see also USAGE note at 小 0007

李 incorrect stroke-count
➡ see 2-4-3: 木 at 3050
2-4-2

孝 incorrect classification/stroke-count
➡ see 3-4-3: 耂 at 3973
2-4-2

考老 incorrect classification
➡ see 3-4-2: 耂 at 3962
2-4-2

交 2-4-2
incorrect classification
➡ see 2-2-4: 亠 at 2508

充 2-4-2
incorrect classification
➡ see 2-2-4: 亠 at 2507

光

3043
2-4-2

▶LIGHT

コウ ひか(る) ひかり ㊔ みつ てる あきら みつる みつし ひろし あき

Ⓒ 光 guāng

10	Jōyō-2	U5149
儿	S6-2-4	F0280

Stroke order: 1 2 3 4 5 6

COMPOUNDS

❶ⓐ [also suffix] **LIGHT, glow**
ⓑ brightness, luster

a 光線 こうせん ray (of light), beam
光熱 こうねつ light and heat
光化学 こうかがく photochemistry
日光 にっこう sunshine, sunlight
月光 げっこう moonlight, moonshine
発光する はっこうする radiate, emit light
太陽光 たいようこう sunlight

b 光沢 こうたく luster, gloss, polish

❷ [original meaning] **shine, glow, glitter**
光照 こうしょう shining
光輝有る こうきある shining, brilliant, glorious, splendid

❸ **honor, glory**
光明 こうみょう glory, hope, right future
光栄 こうえい honor, glory; privilege
栄光 えいこう glory

❹ **scenery, sight**
光景 こうけい spectacle, sight, scene
風光 ふうこう (beautiful) scenery, natural beauty
観光 かんこう sightseeing

❺ time
光陰矢の如し こういんやのごとし Time flies like an arrow
消光する しょうこうする pass one's time

❻ term of respect
光来 こうらい your visit [presence]

KUN

【ひかる 光る】**shine, emit LIGHT, glitter, sparkle**
光り輝く ひかりかがやく shine brilliantly
光り物 ひかりもの luminous body like a shooting star; any bright metal

【ひかり 光】**LIGHT, flash, sparkle, beam; glory, honor**
稲光 いなびかり lightning
親の光は七光 おやのひかりはななひかり It is a great help to have a famous parent

SYNONYMS

❶ⓐ **light**
光 LIGHT → 3043
明 light → 1060
灯 LAMP → 1019
燭 CANDLE → 1391
照 sunlight → 3506
虹 RAINBOW → 1637

❷ **shine and reflect**
輝 SHINE BRILLIANTLY → 1775
光 shine → 3043
照 ILLUMINATE → 3506
映 REFLECT → 1104
耀 SHINE BRILLIANTLY → 1812
燿 SHINE → 1407
閃 FLASH → 4114
煌 GLITTER → 1296

❸ **great respect**
栄 GLORY → 3183
誉 HONOR → 3135
光 honor → 3043

❹ **view**
景 SCENE → 3118
風 (beautiful) scenery → 3730
光 scenery → 3043
観 VIEW → 2359

兇

3044
2-4-2

▶ATROCIOUS

キョウ

Ⓒ 凶 xiōng

10	Non-Jōyō	U5147
儿	S6-2-4	F3153

COMPOUNDS

❶ [now replaced by 凶 3679]
ⓐ **ATROCIOUS, ferocious, wicked, brutal, cruel**
ⓑ **ATROCIOUS [lethal] crime, murder, wicked deed**
ⓒ wicked person, villain

a 兇悪な きょうあくな atrocious, villainous, fiendish
兇暴な きょうぼうな atrocious, ferocious, brutal
兇漢 きょうかん villain, ruffian, assailant
兇行 きょうこう violence, murder, crime

b 兇器 きょうき murder [dangerous] weapon
兇刃 きょうじん assassin's dagger [knife]

c 元兇 げんきょう ringleader, chief instigator

❷ [usu. 凶 3679] unlucky, bad, disastrous

兇変 きょうへん calamity, disaster; tragic accident

INDEPENDENT

【きょう 兇(=凶)】**bad luck**

SYNONYMS

❶ⓐ & ❶ⓑ evil

邪 EVIL → 1443
兇 ATROCIOUS → 3044
凶 ATROCIOUS → 3679
悪 BAD → 3413

共

3045

2-4-2

▶JOINT

キョウ とも とも(に) -ども

Ⓒ 共 gòng

12	Jōyō-4	U5171
八	S6-2-4	F0318

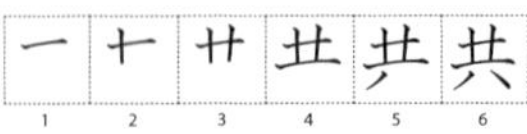

COMPOUNDS

❶ [original meaning] **JOINT, united, together, co-**

共同の きょうどうの joint; common, concerted, united; public
共通の きょうつうの common
共通語 きょうつうご common language; lingua franca
共和国 きょうわこく republic
共和制 きょうわせい republicanism
共催 きょうさい joint auspices, cosponsorship
共感 きょうかん sympathy
共演 きょうえん coacting, costarring
共産党 きょうさんとう Communist Party
共存 きょうぞん coexistence
共闘 きょうとう joint struggle, common [united] front
共著 きょうちょ joint authorship, coauthorship
共有の きょうゆうの common, joint
共用する きょうようする share, use in common
公共の こうきょうの public, common

❷ abbrev. of 共産主義 きょうさんしゅぎ or 共産党 きょうさんとう: Communism, Communist Party

反共 はんきょう anticommunist
容共 ようきょう procommunist

INDEPENDENT

【きょう 共】Communist Party

社・共 しゃきょう Social and Communist Parties

KUN

【とも 共】

① [in compounds]

ⓐ **JOINT, together, simultaneous**
ⓑ of the same quality [kind]
ⓒ **both, neither; including**

a 共稼ぎ ともかせぎ working together (for a living), working in double harness
共倒れ ともだおれ falling together, joint bankruptcy
共共 ともども together, in common
b 共布 ともぬの same cloth
c 両方共 りょうほうとも both, the two
送料共 そうりょうとも including postage

② same cloth

共のハンカチ とものはんかち handkerchief of the same cloth

【ともに 共に】

① [formerly also 倶に] **together**

共に天を戴かず ともにてんをいただかず cannot live together under the canopy of heaven

② **both, alike**

母子共に ぼしともに both mother and child

【-ども -共】**belittling or humble plural suffix**

私共 わたくしども we
大人共 おとなども adults
餓鬼共 がきども those damn kids

SYNONYMS

❶ together

共 JOINT → 3045
同 together → 3707
併 TOGETHER → 0092
並 side by side → 2793
兼 CONCURRENTLY → 2850
倶 TOGETHER → 0125

❷ &【きょう】Communism

共 Communism → 3045
左 the Left → 3692
赤 RED → 2719

【-ども】

◯ plural suffixes

-達 plural suffix → 3893
-等 plural suffix → 3321
衆 somewhat polite plural suffix → 3325
-共 belittling plural suffix → 3045
-方 polite plural suffix → 2459

USAGE

❶【ともに】

共に
① [formerly also 倶に] together
② both, alike

倶に
[now usu. 共に] together

❷【-ども】

-共
belittling or humble plural suffix

-供
plural suffix—now used only in 子供 こども without implying plurality
★Note that こども is correctly written 子供, *not* 子共.

HOMOPHONES
とも
供 OFFER →0098
友 FRIEND →3670
朋 COMRADE →1092
ともに 倶 TOGETHER →0125
-ども 供 OFFER →0098

NOTE
➡ see also USAGE note at 友 3670

先 3046

▸**AHEAD**
セン さき ま(ず)▴
Ⓒ 先 xiān
2-4-2

10	Jōyō-1	U5148
儿	S6-2-4	F0104

Stroke order: ノ 𠂉 ⺧ 生 ⺩ 先 (1–6)

COMPOUNDS
❶ⓐ [original meaning] (at the head or front) **AHEAD, fore, before, forward**
ⓑ **go AHEAD, precede**
a 先頭 せんとう forefront, head, top
先駆者 せんくしゃ pioneer, forerunner
先陣 せんじん advance guard, vanguard
先遣する せんけんする send ahead [in advance]
率先する そっせんする take the lead [initiative]
b 先行する せんこうする precede, go ahead of
先進国 せんしんこく advanced [developed] nation [country]
❷ⓐ (antecedent in time or order) **AHEAD of, in advance, first, previous, preceding, prior, beforehand**
ⓑ former, previous
ⓒ late, deceased
a 先発する せんぱつする start in advance, go ahead, precede
先着 せんちゃく first arrival
先取する せんしゅする take first, score first
先見 せんけん foresight, anticipation
先決 せんけつ previous decision, prior settlement
先入観 せんにゅうかん preconception, bias, prejudice
先番 せんばん one's turn to make the first move
先輩 せんぱい senior, superior, elder
先生 せんせい teacher; doctor
優先 ゆうせん preference, priority
b 先夫 せんぷ former husband
先主 せんしゅ former master
先君 せんくん previous ruler
c 先父 せんぷ deceased father
❸ⓐ **last (week, etc.)**
ⓑ **the other (day), recently**
a 先月 せんげつ last month
先週 せんしゅう last week
先先週 せんせんしゅう week before last
b 先日 せんじつ the other day, a few days ago
先達て せんだって the other day, some time ago; lately
❹ ancient, past
先古 せんこ ancient times
先哲 せんてつ ancient sage [wise man]
❺ [formerly also 尖 2700]
ⓐ (pointed end) **point, end, tip**
ⓑ pointed, acute
a 先端 せんたん pointed end, tip; spearhead; vanguard
先兵 せんぺい advance-guard point; advance detachment
b 先鋭な せんえいな radical; acute, sharp
❻ the other party
先方 せんぽう the other party, they; one's destination

INDEPENDENT
【せん 先】priority, precedence; former time; the first move (in a game of go)
先を越す せんをこす forestall, take the initiative
先の せんの former, previous, old, late

KUN
【さき 先】
①ⓐ (at the front) **AHEAD, away, off**
ⓑ **the head, the lead; the first; precedence**
a 三キロ先に さんきろさきに three kilometers ahead
目先 めさき before one's eyes; near future; foresight; appearance
店先 みせさき storefront
水先案内 みずさきあんない pilotage; pilot
真っ先 まっさき head, beginning
春先 はるさき early spring
切っ先 きっさき [sometimes also 鋒] point of a blade [sword]; tone of argument, force of an attack
b 先にする さきにする give priority (to)
先駆け さきがけ [sometimes also 魁] the first to charge; lead, pioneer
② [usu. followed by particle]
ⓐ **AHEAD of, in advance, prior to, previously, beforehand**
ⓑ **previous, former, ex-; recent**
a 先に さきに previously, beforehand, formerly

先んじる さきんじる go ahead, precede; forestall, get the start of
先立つ さきだつ precede, go before; die before
先払い さきばらい payment in advance, payment on delivery
b 先の総理大臣 さきのそうりだいじん former prime minister
先頃 さきごろ sometime ago, the other day

③ the future
先行き さきゆき future, future prospects
先物 さきもの (market) futures
老い先 おいさき remaining years (of one's life)

④ **point, tip, end**
先細の さきぼその tapering
爪先 つまさき tip of a toe, tiptoe, toe
ペン先 ぺんさき pen point, nib
手先 てさき fingers; tool, implement

⑤ [also suffix] **destination, place**
行き先 いきさき(=ゆきさき) one's destination
宛て先 あてさき destination, address
勤務先 きんむさき one's place of employment
連絡先 れんらくさき where to make contact

⑥ the other party
先様 さきさま the other party

⑦ sequel
話の先 はなしのさき sequel of a story

【まず 先ず】first, to begin with; nearly, hardly, on the whole; anyway; well, now

SYNONYMS

❶ⓐ in front
前 BEFORE → 2819
先 AHEAD → 3046

❷ⓐ before
前 BEFORE → 2819
先 AHEAD → 3046
予 IN ADVANCE → 2477

ⓑ former
旧 FORMER → 0014
元 former → 2428
故 OLD (earlier time) → 1466
前 previous → 2819
嘗て previously → 3230
曽 previously → 2632
先 former → 3046
既 ALREADY → 1498

❸ⓐ most recent
昨 LAST → 1106
去 last → 2678
先 last → 3046

❺ⓐ extremity
端 END → 1564
末 end → 4317
梢 tip → 1208
先 point → 3046
尖 POINT → 2700
鋒 POINT OF A BLADE → 2172

ⓑ sharp
鋭 SHARP → 2171
先 pointed → 3046
尖 pointed → 2700

HOMOPHONES

さきがけ
魁 LEADER → 4125
先駆け → 3046, 2293

きっさき
鋒 POINT OF A BLADE → 2172
切っ先 → 0030, 3046

NOTE

➡ see COMPOUND FORMATION for 先生 せんせい → 生 4309

虫

2-4-2

incorrect classification
➡ see 4-6-3 at 4343

劣

3047

2-4-2

▶**INFERIOR**
レツ おと(る)
Ⓒ 劣 liè

19	Jōyō	U52A3
力	S6-2-4	F1662

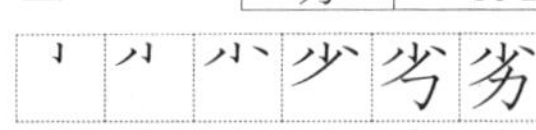

COMPOUNDS

❶ⓐ (lower in quality or status) **INFERIOR, poor, sub-grade, low-grade; weak**
ⓑ [original meaning] (of little strength) **INFERIOR,** weak

a 劣等感 れっとうかん inferiority complex
劣悪な れつあくな inferior, coarse
優劣 ゆうれつ superiority or inferiority, quality
卑劣な ひれつな mean, base, cowardly
b 劣情 れつじょう animal passion, carnal desire
劣勢 れっせい numerical inferiority
劣性 れっせい inferiority; recessiveness

❷ *math* minor
劣角 れっかく minor angle
劣弧 れっこ minor arc

INDEPENDENT

【れつ 劣】**INFERIORity**

KUN

【おとる 劣る】be INFERIOR to, be worse than, be second to

見劣りがする みおとりがする compare unfavorably [poorly] with, be not so good as
優るとも劣らぬ まさるともおとらぬ not at all inferior to

SYNONYMS

❶ⓐ **bad**
悪 BAD → 3413
劣 INFERIOR → 3047
下 of low grade → 4186
弊 shabby → 3583
粗 COARSE → 1683
駄 GOOD FOR NOTHING → 2291
廃 WASTE → 3902

孛

■2-4-3

incorrect classification
➡ see ■2-2-5: 亠 at 2532

旱

3048
■2-4-3

▶DROUGHT
カン
Ⓒ 旱 hàn

72	Non-Jōyō	U65F1
日	S7-4-3	F0000

COMPOUNDS

● [now replaced by 干 4187] **DROUGHT, dry weather**
旱魃× かんばつ drought
旱害 かんがい drought damage
旱天 かんてん drought, dry weather

SYNONYMS

● **dry**
乾 DRY → 2113
干 DRY → 4187
燥 DRY UP (desiccate) → 1392
涸 DRY UP (run dry) → 0629
渇 RUN DRY → 0627
旱 DROUGHT → 3048

杏

3049
■2-4-3

▶APRICOT
キョウ アン あんず
Ⓒ 杏 xìng

75	Names	U674F
木	S7-4-3	F2203

COMPOUNDS

● [original meaning] **APRICOT tree; apricot**
杏子 あんず apricot; apricot tree
杏仁 きょうにん apricot stone
杏林 きょうりん doctor
銀杏 ぎんなん(=いちょう) ginkgo nut, ginkgo tree

KUN

【あんず 杏】**APRICOT; apricot tree**
杏ジャム あんずじゃむ apricot jam

SYNONYMS

● **fruits and fruit trees**
桃 PEACH → 1174
榛 HAZEL → 1328
椎 CHINQUAPIN → 1249
柚 YUZU → 1123
椰 COCONUT → 1285
柑 CITRUS → 1112
橙 BITTER ORANGE → 1369
葡 GRAPE → 2902
萄 GRAPE → 2870
柿 PERSIMMON → 1118
檎 APPLE → 1386
李 PLUM → 3050
枇 LOQUAT → 1063
杷 LOQUAT → 1065
苺 STRAWBERRY → 2780
菱 water chestnut → 2879
杏 APRICOT → 3049
梅 JAPANESE APRICOT → 1159
橘 MANDARIN → 1366
栗 CHESTNUT → 3280
栃 JAPANESE HORSE CHESTNUT → 1122
梨 PEAR → 3412
蕉 PLANTAIN → 2994

COMPOUND FORMATION

【杏林 きょうりん】
杏林 'doctor' originally referred to a Chinese doctor who had an apricot tree (杏) planted as payment for his services. This is how 杏林, literally "apricot (杏) grove (林)," acquired its current meaning.

李

3050
■2-4-3

▶PLUM
リ すもも ㊔ い もも
Ⓒ 李 lǐ

75	Names	U674E
木	S7-4-3	F1468

COMPOUNDS

❶ **PLUM tree; plum**
李花 りか plum blossoms
李下に冠を正さず りかにかんむりをたださず Refrain from doing anything that may incur suspicion

❷ common Chinese family name: **Li**
李白 りはく Li Bo (one of China's greatest poets in the Tang Dynasty)

❸ **Li Dynasty of Korea**
李朝 りちょう Li Dynasty

❹ **portmanteau**
行李 こうり portmanteau, wicker trunk; luggage

文 日 木 【止】 氏 爫 爪 牛 王 歹 亟 今 去 不 天 五 丰 生 夭

KUN

【すもも 李】 **PLUM, Japanese plum, prune; plum tree**

干し李 ほしすもも prune

SYNONYMS

❶ **fruits and fruit trees**

桃 PEACH → 1174
榛 HAZEL → 1328
椎 CHINQUAPIN → 1249
柚 YUZU → 1123
椰 COCONUT → 1285
柑 CITRUS → 1112
橙 BITTER ORANGE → 1369
葡 GRAPE → 2902
萄 GRAPE → 2870
柿 PERSIMMON → 1118
檎 APPLE → 1386
李 PLUM → 3050
枇 LOQUAT → 1063
杷 LOQUAT → 1065
苺 STRAWBERRY → 2780
菱 water chestnut → 2879
杏 APRICOT → 3049
梅 JAPANESE APRICOT → 1159
橘 MANDARIN → 1366
栗 CHESTNUT → 3280
栃 JAPANESE HORSE CHESTNUT → 1122
梨 PEAR → 3412
蕉 PLANTAIN → 2994

COMPOUND FORMATION

【李下に冠を正さず りかにかんむりをたださず】

李下に冠を正さず 'Refrain from doing anything that may incur suspicion' is a proverb that literally means to avoid adjusting (正) one's hat (冠) under (下) a plum tree (李 ❶); that is, to avoid incurring the suspicion of being a plum thief.

NOTE

★ do not confuse with 季 SEASON → 3161

步 3051

2-4-3

▶**WALK**

ホ ブ フ ある(く) あゆ(む)

77	Names	U6B65
止	S7-4-3	F0000

traditional form → see 歩 at 3071

帋 3052

2-4-3

▶**PAPER**

シ かみ

50	Nonstandard	U5E0B
巾	S7-3-4	F0000

traditional form → see 紙 at 1654

妥 3053

2-4-3

▶**COME TO TERMS**

ダ

Ⓝ 妥 Ⓒ 妥 tuǒ

38	Jōyō	U59A5
女	S7-3-4	F2042

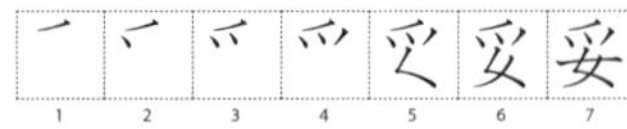

COMPOUNDS

❶ **COME TO TERMS, compromise, arrive at an understanding, agree**

妥協 だきょう compromise, agreement, understanding

妥結 だけつ compromise, agreement, understanding

❷ **appropriate, proper, satisfactory**

妥当な だとうな proper, appropriate

SYNONYMS

❶ **compromise**

妥 COME TO TERMS → 3053
譲 concede → 2080
媾 MAKE PEACE → 0782

豸 3054

2-4-3

▶***MUJINA***

153	Radical	U8C78
豸	S7-7-0	F0000

RADICAL

mujina 'wild animal' (貌 豹 貂×), used in characters related to wild animals

---

妥 3055

2-4-3

▶**COME TO TERMS**

ダ

38	Nonstandard	U59A5
女	S7-3-4	F0000

traditional form → see 妥 at 3053

吿 3056

2-4-3

▶**NOTIFY**

コク つ(げる)

30	Nonstandard	U543F
口	S7-3-4	F0000

traditional form → see 告 at 3062

弄 3057

2-4-3

▶**TOY WITH**

ロウ もてあそ(ぶ) いじ(る)▲ いじ(くる)▲

Ⓒ 弄 nòng lòng

55	Jōyō	U5F04
廾	S7-3-4	F2057

一 丅 干 王 王 弄 弄
1 2 3 4 5 6 7

COMPOUNDS

❶ TOY WITH, play with, fiddle with
玩弄する がんろうする make sport of, toy with, play with
翻弄する ほんろうする trifle with, make sport of, toss about (as of a boat)

❷ ridicule, mock, make light of
愚弄 ぐろう mockery, derision, ridicule
嘲弄 ちょうろう taunting, mockery, ridicule

INDEPENDENT

【ろうする 弄する】resort to, play (a trick)
詭弁を弄する きべんをろうする use sophistry

KUN

【もてあそぶ 弄ぶ】[sometimes also 玩ぶ]
①ⓐ **TOY [fiddle] WITH (the hands)**
ⓑ **TOY [trifle] WITH; do (with something) as one pleases**
a 髪を弄ぶ かみをもてあそぶ fiddle with one's hair
b 人の気持ちを弄ぶ ひとのきもちをもてあそぶ toy with people's feelings
② take pleasure in, appreciate, enjoy as a diversion

【いじる 弄る】
ⓐ **TOY** [fiddle] **WITH**, finger
ⓑ tinker with, tweak; tamper with
b 庭弄り にわいじり *colloq* gardening
土弄り つちいじり *colloq* playing with dirt; gardening, farming (as a hobby)

【いじくる 弄くる】*colloq* same as 弄る いじる
弄くり回す いじくりまわす fiddle with, monkey around with

SYNONYMS

❶ &【もてあそぶ】①ⓐⓑ **play**
遊 PLAY → 3896
戯 SPORT → 2351
弄 TOY WITH → 3057

USAGE

【もてあそぶ】
弄ぶ
[sometimes also 玩ぶ]
①ⓐ toy [fiddle] with (the hands)
ⓑ toy [trifle] with; do (with something) as one pleases
② take pleasure in, appreciate, enjoy as a diversion
玩ぶ
[usu. 弄ぶ]
①ⓐ toy [fiddle] with (something) with one's hands
ⓑ toy [trifle] with; do (with something) as one pleases
② take pleasure in, appreciate, enjoy as a diversion

HOMOPHONES

もてあそぶ 玩 TAKE PLEASURE IN → 1085

考 ▀2-4-3
incorrect classification/ stroke-count
➡ see □3-4-2: 耂 at 3962

孝 ▀2-4-3
incorrect classification
➡ see □3-4-3: 耂 at 3973

系 ▀2-4-3
incorrect classification
➡ see ▀2-1-6: ノ at 2443

含 ▀2-4-3
incorrect classification
➡ see ▀2-2-5: 𠆢 at 2534

弃 ▀2-4-3
incorrect classification
➡ see ▀2-2-5: 亠 at 2533

否
3058
▀2-4-3

▶**SAY NO**
▶**OR NOT**
ヒ いな いや▲
Ⓒ 否 fǒu pǐ

30	Jōyō-6	U5426
口	S7-3-4	F0946

一 ア 不 不 不 否 否
1 2 3 4 5 6 7

COMPOUNDS

❶ **SAY NO, negate, deny**
否定する ひていする deny, negate
否決 ひけつ rejection, voting down, negation
否認 ひにん denial, negation
拒否 きょひ denial, rejection

❷ⓐ **OR NOT**—used as the second element of a compound to negate the meaning of the first
ⓑ no, nay
a 良否 りょうひ good or bad, quality
当否 とうひ right or wrong, justice; propriety
賛否 さんぴ approval or disapproval; yes or no

❸ bad, evil
否運(=非運) ひうん bad luck, misfortune

INDEPENDENT

【ひ 否】no
否か応か ひかおうか yes or no

KUN

【いな 否】*literary* **no, nay**
否む いなむ refuse, decline

否めない いなめない undeniable, incontrovertible
否や いなや (whether…) or not; objection; as soon as, no sooner than

【いや 否】
ⓐ no
ⓑ being unwilling, wanting to **SAY NO**
b 否でも応でも いやでもおうでも whether one likes it or not, willy-nilly
否応無しに いやおうなしに whether one likes it or not, willy-nilly
否否 いやいや definitely [absolutely] not

SYNONYMS

❶ **refuse and reject**
拒 REFUSE → 0368
断る refuse → 1885
否 SAY NO → 3058
却 reject → 1436

❷ **terms of negation**
不 NOT (negation) → 4242
非 IS NOT (contrariety) → 1101
無 WITHOUT (nonexistence) → 2648
没 lacking in → 0305
欠 LACK → 2481
否 OR NOT → 3058
未 NOT YET → 4318
莫 NOT → 2839
勿 DO NOT → 3661

HOMOPHONES

いや
嫌 DISLIKE → 0781
厭 TIRE OF → 3745

NOTE

➡ see USAGE notes at 嫌 0781 and 不 4242

呑

3059
2-4-3

▶**SWALLOW**
ドン の(む)
Ⓝ 呑 Ⓒ 吞 tūn

30	Names	U541E
口	S7-3-4	F1372

COMPOUNDS

● [original meaning] **SWALLOW, gulp**
呑吐 どんと swallowing and vomiting
呑舟の魚 どんしゅうのうお great fish; great man; notorious man
併呑 へいどん annexation, merger

KUN

【のむ 呑む】
①ⓐ **SWALLOW, gulp**
ⓑ **SWALLOW** (one's feelings), hold back
a 呑み込み のみこみ understanding, comprehension
鵜呑み うのみ accepting (a story) unthinkingly; swallowing whole
丸呑み まるのみ swallowing whole
蛇が卵を呑んだ へびがたまごをのんだ The snake swallowed an egg
b 息を呑む いきをのむ hold one's breath, gasp
涙を呑む なみだをのむ choke back one's tears, pocket an insult
② [also 飲む] **drink (esp. alcoholic beverages)**
呑み助 のみすけ guzzler, boozer
湯呑み ゆのみ teacup
酒呑み さけのみ drinking; (heavy) drinker
乳呑み児 ちのみご unweaned baby
③ **accept**
清濁併せ呑む せいだくあわせのむ be broad-minded enough to accept both good and bad
条件を呑む じょうけんをのむ accept the conditions
④ look down on, make light of
呑んで掛かる のんでかかる hold lightly, make light of
⑤ conceal
どすを呑む どすをのむ wear a dagger in one's bosom

SPECIAL READINGS

呑気(=暢気) のんき happy-go-lucky, easygoing, carefree
呑兵衛 のんべえ guzzler, boozer
剣呑 けんのん risky, dangerous, insecure

SYNONYMS

● **ingest**
喫 INGEST → 0668
服 take → 1090
食 EAT → 2578
喰う EAT → 0670
飲 DRINK → 2127
呑 SWALLOW → 3059
啄 PECK → 0482

HOMOPHONES

のむ 飲 DRINK → 2127

COMPOUND FORMATION

【鵜呑み うのみ】
鵜呑み 'accepting (a story) unthinkingly, etc.' likens the thoughtless swallowing of information to the manner in which a cormorant (鵜) swallows (呑む) fish whole.

NOTE

➡ see USAGE note at 飲 2127
➡ see COMPOUND FORMATION for 鵜呑み うのみ → 呑 3059

吾

▶I

ゴ われ わが- あ-

Ⓒ 吾 wú

3060

2-4-3

30	Names	U543E
口	S7-3-4	F1043

COMPOUNDS

a [original meaning] **I**

b [archaic] **my**

a 吾人 ごじん *literary* we

KUN

【われ 吾】[usu. 我]

ⓐ *elegant* **I; we**

ⓑ *slang* **you**

a 吾等 われら we, I; you

【わが- 吾-】[usu. 我が-] *literary* **my; our**

吾輩 わがはい I

【あ- 吾-】*elegant* **my**

吾子 あこ my child

SYNONYMS

【われ】

ⓐ **first person pronouns**

私 I (*polite*) → 1432

我 SELF → 4362

己 ONESELF → 4188

身 ONE'S PERSON → 4368

僕 I (*familiar*) → 0185

俺 I (*intimate*) → 0124

吾 I (*elegant*) → 3060

予 I (*pompous*) → 2477

余 I (*pompous*) → 2535

麿 I (*archaic*) → 3949

朕 IMPERIAL WE → 1185

自 SELF → 4338

HOMOPHONES

われ 我 SELF → 4362

わが- 我 SELF → 4362

NOTE

➡ see USAGE note at 我 4362

麦

▶WHEAT

バク むぎ

Ⓝ 麥 Ⓒ 麦 mài

3061

2-4-3

199	Jōyō-2	U9EA6
麦	S7-7-0	F1491

radical variant → see 麥 at 3441

1	2	3	4	5	6	7
一	十	丰	圭	𡗗	麦	麦

COMPOUNDS

● **WHEAT, barley, oats, rye**

麦秋 ばくしゅう wheat harvest [season]; early summer

麦価 ばくか price of wheat

麦芽 ばくが wheat germ, malt

麦酒 ばくしゅ(=びーる) beer

米麦 べいばく rice and barley; corn

精麦 せいばく cleaning barley or wheat; polished barley or wheat

KUN

【むぎ 麦】**WHEAT, barley, oats, rye**

麦畑 むぎばたけ wheat field

小麦 こむぎ wheat

大麦 おおむぎ barley

ライ麦 らいむぎ rye

SPECIAL READINGS

蕎麦▲ そば buckwheat noodles, *soba;* buckwheat

蕎麦屋▲ そばや *soba* restaurant [vendor]

SYNONYMS

● **cereals**

米 RICE → 4342

麦 WHEAT → 3061

豆 BEAN → 2442

粟 FOXTAIL MILLET → 3326

黍 PROSO MILLET → 3210

蕎 BUCKWHEAT → 2993

蒋 WILD RICE → 2976

告

▶NOTIFY

コク つ(げる)

Ⓝ 吿 Ⓒ 告 gào

3062

2-4-3

30	Jōyō-4	U544A
口	S7-3-4	F0356

1	2	3	4	5	6	7
ノ	⺈	牛	生	牛	告	告

COMPOUNDS

1 a (let know, esp. in writing) **NOTIFY, inform, announce, advise, tell, report**

b (make widely known) **NOTIFY, announce, proclaim**

c notice, announcement, information

a 告知する こくちする notify, announce

通告する つうこくする notify, announce

報告 ほうこく report, information

申告 しんこく report, statement, notification

予告 よこく advance notice, preliminary announcement

公告 こうこく public notice

広告 こうこく public notice; advertisement

b 告示 こくじ notification, bulletin

c 布告 ふこく proclamation, declaration

❷ **advise, instruct, warn, admonish**
忠告 ちゅうこく advice; counsel, warning; admonition
警告 けいこく warning, admonition
勧告 かんこく advice, counsel, recommendation
❸ **accuse of (an offense), sue, accuse, appeal to the law**
告訴する こくそする sue, complain, accuse
告発 こくはつ prosecution, indictment, accusation
上告 じょうこく final appeal
被告 ひこく defendant, the accused
宣告 せんこく sentence, verdict, pronouncement
誣×告 ぶこく false accusation
❹ bid farewell to
告別 こくべつ leave taking, farewell
告辞 こくじ farewell address

KUN

【つげる 告げる】**tell, inform, let know; NOTIFY, announce; bid, tell, order**
お告げ おつげ oracle, revelation
告げ口 つげぐち taletelling

SYNONYMS

❶ⓐ & ❶ⓑ inform and communicate
報 INFORM → 2133
通 COMMUNICATE → 3855
告 NOTIFY → 3062
届ける give notice → 3820
達 issue a notice → 3893
知 let know → 1446
申 REPORT → 4319
稟 REPORT TO → 2649
宣 PROCLAIM → 2799
❷ warn
警 WARN → 3595
戒 CAUTION → 3972
誡 CAUTION AGAINST → 1947
諭 ADMONISH → 2012
告 advise → 3062
❸ sue
訴 SUE → 1901
訟 LITIGATE → 1864
告 accuse of → 3062
控 accuse in court → 0600

呑

3063
2-4-3

▶**SWALLOW**
ドン の(む)

30	Nonstandard	U5451
口	S7-3-4	F0000

traditional form → see 吞 at 3059

斉

2-4-4

incorrect classification
➡ see 2-2-6: 亠 at 2548

易

3064
2-4-4

▶**EASY**
▶**EXCHANGE**
エキ イ やさ(しい) やす(い)▲ ㊔ やすし
Ⓒ 易 yì

72	Jōyō-5	U6613
日	S8-4-4	F0888

1	2	3	4	5	6	7	8
丨	冂	日	日	旦	易	易	易

COMPOUNDS

❶ [also prefix] (without difficulty) **EASY, simple**
易損品 いそんひん fragile article
容易な よういな easy, simple
安易な あんいな easy, easygoing
簡易な かんいな simple, simplified; easy
平易な へいいな plain, simple, easy
❷ⓐ **EXCHANGE, trade**
ⓑ change, be transformed; be reformed
a 貿易 ぼうえき trade, commerce
交易 こうえき trade, commerce
b 不易の ふえきの immutable, unchangeable
改易 かいえき change of rank
❸ⓐ **divination, fortunetelling**
ⓑ Book of Changes, Yi Jing
a 易者 えきしゃ fortuneteller, diviner
易学 えきがく science of divination
b 易経 えききょう Book of Changes, Yi Jing

INDEPENDENT

【えき 易】divination, fortunetelling; Book of Changes, Yi Jing
易を見る えきをみる divine
易の六十四卦× えきのろくじゅうしけ the 64 hexagrams of the Book of Changes
【い 易】ease, simplicity
易より難へ進む いよりなんへすすむ proceed from the easy to the difficult

KUN

【やさしい 易しい】**EASY, simple**
易しさ やさしさ easiness
易しい文章 やさしいぶんしょう easy [simple] writing
【やすい 易い】
ⓐ **EASY, simple**
ⓑ [verbal suffix] **EASY (to do)**
a 易易と やすやすと easily, without difficulty
お易い御用 おやすいごよう easy request
b 壊れ易い こわれやすい break easily, fragile
分かり易い わかりやすい easy to understand

SYNONYMS

❶ **easy**

易 EASY (without difficulty) → 3064
安 easy (without effort) → 2695
簡 SIMPLE → 3380
軽 LIGHT → 1909

❷ⓐ **sell and trade**

売 SELL → 2722
卸す WHOLESALE → 1835
販 ENGAGE IN SALES → 1869
商 TRADE → 2623
貿 TRADE → 3214
易 EXCHANGE → 3064

ⓑ **change and replace**

変 CHANGE → 2569
替 REPLACE → 3457
代 SUBSTITUTE → 0034
迭 ALTERNATE → 3818
更 change → 4355
改 change → 0287
易 change → 3064
化 CHANGE INTO, -ize → 0022
遷 undergo transition → 3932
転 turn into → 1872
換 EXCHANGE → 0716
交 INTERCHANGE → 2508

❸ⓐ **divine**

占 DIVINE → 2496
卜 DIVINE → 4174
易 divination → 3064

HOMOPHONES

やさしい 優 SUPERIOR → 0200
やすい 安 PEACEFUL → 2695

NOTE

➡ see USAGE notes at 安 2695 and 優 0200

昂

3065

2-4-4

▸**HIGH**

コウ ㊔ たか たかし のぼる あきら あき

Ⓒ 昂 áng

72	Names	U6602
日	S8-4-4	F1940

COMPOUNDS

❶ [now usu. 高 2601 or 興 3622] **HIGH-spirited, excited, elated**

昂奮(=興奮) こうふん excitement, agitation, stimulation
昂進(=高進、亢進)する こうしんする rise, exasperate, accelerate
昂揚(=高揚)する こうようする exalt, enhance, uplift; surge up
激昂(=激高)する げっこう(=げきこう)する get excited, be exasperated, become indignant
意気軒昂(=意気軒高)として いきけんこうとして in high spirits

❷ⓐ [now replaced by 高 2601] **HIGH**

ⓑ [original meaning, now archaic] **hold one's head HIGH**

a 昂騰(=高騰) こうとう steep rise (in prices), jump

INDEPENDENT

【こうじる(=こうずる) 昂じる(=高じる、昂ずる、高ずる)】grow worse, grow in intensity

SYNONYMS

❶ **elated**

亢 HIGH-SPIRITED → 2460
高 high-spirited → 2601
昂 high-spirited → 3065
揚 exalted → 0722
奮 roused up → 3000

NOTE

★ do not confuse with 昴 PLEIADES → 3091

昊

3066

2-4-4

▸**SKY**

コウ ㊔ ひろ ひろし

Ⓒ 昊 hào

72	Names	U660A
日	S8-4-4	F0000

COMPOUNDS

● **SKY**

昊天 こうてん summer sky; wide sky, the heavens
蒼昊 そうこう [rare] blue sky

SYNONYMS

● **sky**

空 SKY → 2767
昊 SKY → 3066
穹 SKY → 2768
天 HEAVEN → 4250
宙 MIDAIR → 2761

昆

3067

2-4-4

▸**INSECT**

コン

Ⓒ 昆 kūn

72	Jōyō	U6606
日	S8-4-4	F1945

1	2	3	4	5	6	7	8
丨	冂	日	日	旦	昆	昆	昆

COMPOUNDS

❶ **INSECT; swarm of insects**

昆虫 こんちゅう insect
昆布 こんぶ(=こぶ) sea tangle, kelp

❷ [rare] progeny, posterity, descendants

後昆 こうこん posterity, grandchildren

❸ [archaic] brethren, older brother

SYNONYMS

❶ **insect**

虫 INSECT →4343
昆 INSECT →3067
繭 COCOON →3023

昇

3068

2-4-4

▶ASCEND

ショウ のぼ(る) ㊔ のり のぶ

Ⓝ 昪 Ⓒ 升 shēng

72	Jōyō	U6607
日	S8-4-4	F1095

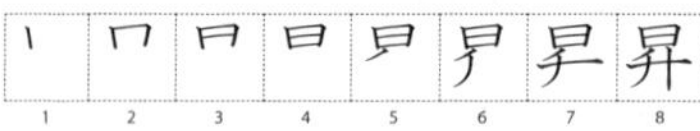

COMPOUNDS

ⓐ [original meaning] **ASCEND, rise, go up**

ⓑ [formerly also 陞 0549] **ASCEND to a higher rank, rise in rank, be promoted**

a 昇天 しょうてん the Ascension; death
昇降口 しょうこうぐち entrance, hatchway
上昇する じょうしょうする ascend, rise

b 昇順 しょうじゅん ascending order
昇格する しょうかくする be promoted [raised] to a higher status
昇進する しょうしんする be promoted, rise in rank
昇給 しょうきゅう salary raise
昇叙 しょうじょ promotion, advancement

KUN

【のぼる 昇る】

ⓐ (rise up to the sky) **ASCEND, rise**

ⓑ **ASCEND to a higher rank, rise in rank, be promoted**

a 太陽は東から昇る たいようはひがしからのぼる The sun rises in the east
煙が昇って行く けむりがのぼっていく Smoke is going up

b 位が昇る くらいがのぼる rise in rank

SYNONYMS

ⓐ **ascend**

昇 ASCEND →3068
上 go up →4212
騰 RISE (esp. in price) →1422
登 CLIMB →3208

ⓑ **rise in rank**

陞 ASCEND TO A HIGHER RANK →0549
昇 ascend to a higher rank →3068
進 advance in rank →3873

HOMOPHONES

のぼる

上 UP →4212
登 CLIMB →3208

NOTE

➡ see USAGE note at 上 4212

昌

3069

2-4-4

▶PROSPERING

ショウ ㊔ まさ あき まさし あきら あつ よし あつし さかえ

Ⓒ 昌 chāng

72	Names	U660C
日	S8-4-4	F1389

COMPOUNDS

● **PROSPERING, flourishing, prosperous, glorious**

繁昌(=繁盛) はんじょう prosperity

SYNONYMS

● **prospering and prosperity**

隆 PROSPER →0661
振 rise →0515
興 RISE TO PROSPERITY →3622
盛 PROSPEROUS →3314
昌 PROSPERING →3069
栄 FLOURISH →3183
繁 THRIVE →3536
賑 BUSTLE →1959

NOTE

★ do not confuse with 冒 RISK →3088

枩

3070

2-4-4

▶PINE

ショウ まつ

75	Nonstandard	U67A9
木	S8-4-4	F0000

traditional form →see 松 at 1075

歩

3071

2-4-4

▶WALK

ホ ブ フ ある(く) あゆ(む)

Ⓝ 步 Ⓒ 步 bù

77	Jōyō-2	U6B69
止	S8-4-4	F0271

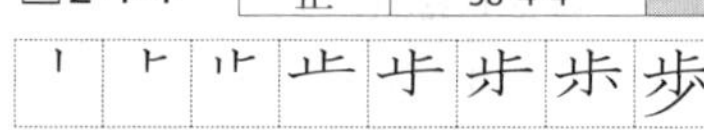

COMPOUNDS

❶ [original meaning] **WALK, go on foot**

歩行する ほこうする walk
歩行者 ほこうしゃ pedestrian
歩行者天国 ほこうしゃてんごく pedestrians' "paradise" (an area of streets temporarily closed to vehicular traffic)
歩道 ほどう sidewalk, footpath
歩兵 ほへい foot soldier, infantry
散歩する さんぽする go for a walk [stroll]
徒歩 とほ walking, going on foot

❷ⓐ **step, pace**
ⓑ **steps, progress, course, path**
ⓒ **counter for steps**

a 歩調 ほちょう pace, step, cadence
歩数 ほすう number of steps
b 進歩 しんぽ progress, advancement, improvement
初歩 しょほ first steps, rudiments, the ABCs (of)
譲歩 じょうほ concession, compromise
退歩 たいほ retrogression, backward step; deterioration
c 二歩 にほ two steps

❸ name of chess piece in shogi (Japanese chess): *fu*, pawn
敵歩 てきふ opponent's pawn

❹ **percentage, rate**
歩合 ぶあい rate, percentage; commission
歩留まり ぶどまり yield, yield rate

❺ *bu*: unit of sq. measure equiv. to approx. 3.3 sq. m or 36 sq. *shaku* (尺), used esp. for measuring fields or farms
三十歩 さんじゅうぶ 30 *bu*

INDEPENDENT

【ほ 歩】 step, pace; foot soldier; **WALK**
歩を進める ほをすすめる step forward, make progress
歩五分 ほごふん five-minutes' walk

【ぶ 歩】
① [sometimes also 分 ぶ 2466] percentage; commission
歩が悪い ぶがわるい The percentage is unfavorable
三割の歩 さんわりのぶ commission of 30%
② *bu* (→❺)

【ふ 歩】 *fu*, pawn (→❸)
歩を突く ふをつく advance a pawn

KUN

【あるく 歩く】 **WALK, go on foot, step**
歩き回る あるきまわる walk about, walk to and fro, pace around
持ち歩く もちあるく carry about

【あゆむ 歩む】 *elegant* **WALK, step**
歩み あゆみ walking; step, pace
時代と共に歩む じだいとともにあゆむ move along with the times

SYNONYMS

❶ **walk**
歩 WALK → 3071
徒 go on foot → 0499
脚 move on foot → 1226
足 travel on foot → 2714
踏 TREAD → 1997

❹ **rate**
率 RATE → 2625
割 rate → 2284
比 ratio → 0029
歩 percentage → 3071

❺ **area units**
坪 *TSUBO* (3.3 sq. m) → 0328
歩 *bu* (3.3 sq. m) → 3071
畝 *se* (0.99 ares) → 1857
反 *tan* (9.9 ares) → 3663
町 *cho* (99.2 ares) → 1430

NOTE

➡ see USAGE note at 分 2466
➡ see COMPOUND FORMATION for 歩留まり ぶどまり → 留 3189

肯

3072
2-4-4

▶**ASSENT**
コウ
Ⓒ 肯 kěn

130	Jōyō	U80AF
月	S8-4-4	F2067

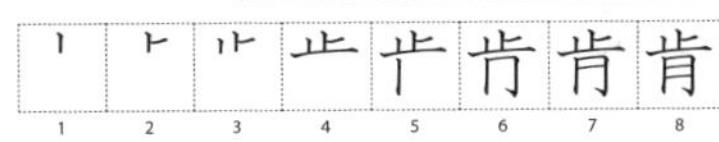

COMPOUNDS

❶ **ASSENT, nod agreement, consent, permit**
肯定 こうてい affirmation, affirmative
首肯する しゅこうする assent, nod one's assent, consent

❷ [original meaning] meat sticking to a bone
肯綮× こうけい important point, gist

SYNONYMS

❶ **agree and approve**
賛 APPROVE OF → 3484
可 APPROVE → 3687
認 RECOGNIZE → 1948
諾 CONSENT → 1974
承 AGREE TO → 0016
肯 ASSENT → 3072
容 tolerate → 2832

昏

3073
2-4-4

▶**LOSE CONSCIOUSNESS**
コン くら(い)
Ⓒ 昏 hūn

72	Names	U660F
日	S8-4-4	F2474

COMPOUNDS

❶ **LOSE CONSCIOUSNESS, faint**
昏迷 こんめい [now usu. 混迷] stupor, unconsciousness
昏倒 こんとう swoon, faint

昏睡 こんすい coma, lethargy; dead sleep
昏昏と眠っている こんこんとねむっている be sound asleep; be in coma

❷ⓐ [original meaning] **dark**
ⓑ **dusk, twilight**

a 昏冥 こんめい darkness, gloom
b 黄昏 こうこん(=たそがれ) dusk, twilight

KUN

【くらい 昏い】[usu. 暗い, sometimes also 闇い or 冥い] dark, dim; (of colors) dark; (producing gloom) dark, dreary, dismal; (concealed) dark, shadowy, shady

SYNONYMS

❷ **dark**
暗 DARK → 1273
黒 BLACK → 3406
陰 shaded → 0657
闇 DARK → 4134
晦 DARK → 1196
昏 dark → 3073
昧 DARK → 1105
冥 DARK → 2613
曖 SHADY → 1383

HOMOPHONES

くらい
暗 DARK → 1273
冥 DARK → 2613
闇 DARK → 4134

NOTE

➡ see USAGE note at 暗 1273

沓

3074

2-4-4

▶**FOOTWEAR**
トウ くつ
Ⓒ 沓 tà dá

85	Names	U6C93
水	S8-4-4	F2915

COMPOUNDS

● [now replaced by 踏 1997] **overlap, mingle; be numerous**
雑沓 ざっとう hustle and bustle, traffic jam

KUN

【くつ 沓】[usu. 靴] **FOOTWEAR, sandals, clogs**
沓脱ぎ くつぬぎ stepstone, doorstone
沓下 くつした socks
沓摺り くつずり doorsill
雪沓 ゆきぐつ straw snow boots [shoes]

SYNONYMS

【くつ】
○ **footwear**
靴 SHOES → 2235
沓 FOOTWEAR → 3074
駄 clogs → 2291
履 footwear → 3933
足 counter for footwear → 2714

HOMOPHONES

くつ 靴 SHOES → 2235

NOTE

➡ see USAGE note at 靴 2235

炎

3075

2-4-4

▶**FLAME**
▶**INFLAMMATION**
エン ほのお ㊔ ほむら
Ⓒ 炎 yán

86	Jōyō	U708E
火	S8-4-4	F1343

Stroke order: 1 2 3 4 5 6 7 8 (丶 丷 ⺌ 火 火 炏 炎 炎)

COMPOUNDS

❶ [formerly also 焰 1255]
ⓐ [original meaning] **FLAME, blaze**
ⓑ (figuratively) **FLAMEs (as of passion)**

a 火炎 かえん flames, blaze
紅炎 こうえん red blazes of flame
b 気炎を吐く きえんをはく talk big, talk a lot of hot air
情炎 じょうえん flaming desires, burning passions
妖炎 ようえん The Fires of Enchantment (movie title)

❷ⓐ go up in **FLAME**s, burn up
ⓑ (hot like a flame) scorching, sweltering, burning hot

a 炎上する えんじょうする go up in flames
b 炎暑 えんしょ scorching heat of summer
炎天下で えんてんかで under the blazing sun
炎熱 えんねつ scorching weather, extreme heat

❸ [also suffix] **INFLAMMATION, -itis**
炎症 えんしょう inflammation
脳炎 のうえん brain inflammation, encephalitis
肺炎 はいえん pneumonia, inflammation of the lungs
虫垂炎 ちゅうすいえん appendicitis

KUN

【ほのお 炎】[formerly also 焰]
ⓐ **FLAME, blaze**
ⓑ (figuratively) **FLAMEs (as of passion)**
a 炎を上げて燃える ほのおをあげてもえる flame up
b 嫉妬の炎 しっとのほのお flames of jealousy

SYNONYMS

❶ⓐ **fire**
火 FIRE → 4273
炎 FLAME → 3075
焰 FLAME → 1255

❷ⓑ **hot**

熱 HOT →3555
暑い HOT (weather) →3121
炎 scorching →3075
温 WARM →0740
暖 WARM (esp. weather) →1274

❸ **diseases and disease symptoms**
疸 SMALLPOX →4070
淋 GONORRHEA →0632
癌 CANCER →4076
熱 fever →3555
炎 INFLAMMATION →3075
痢 DIARRHEA →4068
下 diarrhea →4186

USAGE

【ほのお】
炎
[formerly also 焔]
ⓐ flame, blaze
ⓑ (figuratively) flames (as of passion)
焔
ⓐ [now replaced by 炎] flame, blaze
ⓑ [now usu. 炎] (figuratively) flames (as of passion)

HOMOPHONES

ほのお 焔 FLAME →1255

受

▶RECEIVE
ジュ う(ける) -う(け) う(かる)
Ⓒ 受 shòu

3076
2-4-4

29	Jōyō-3	U53D7
又	S8-2-6	F0183

COMPOUNDS

❶ [original meaning] **RECEIVE, accept, take, get**
受信 じゅしん reception (of radio waves); receipt of a message
受講 じゅこう attending lectures
受領 じゅりょう receipt
受注する じゅちゅうする receive an order
受納する じゅのうする accept, receive
受賞する じゅしょうする win a prize
受諾する じゅだくする receive, accept
受験する じゅけんする take an examination
受動的な じゅどうてきな passive
受話器 じゅわき (telephone) receiver
感受性 かんじゅせい sensibility

❷ be subjected to, undergo, suffer
受難 じゅなん ordeal, crucifixion
受刑者 じゅけいしゃ prisoner, convict

❸ *Buddhism* one of the five aggregates; perception
受蘊× じゅうん perception

KUN

【うける 受ける】
①ⓐ **RECEIVE, accept, get, take, catch**
ⓑ **accept (an offer)**
ⓒ **RECEIVE** (an insult), suffer, be subjected to
ⓓ [sometimes also 享ける] enjoy, be granted
a 受け取る うけとる receive, accept; understand
受取 うけとり receipt
受け付ける うけつける receive; accept
受付 うけつけ receipt, reception, acceptance; receptionist, information clerk; information office [desk]
受け身 うけみ passiveness; passive voice
b お受けしましょう おうけしましょう I will accept it
受け入れる うけいれる accept, consent to; receive, accommodate
受け持ちの うけもちの in charge of, in one's care
引き受ける ひきうける undertake; answer for, guarantee
c 被害を受ける ひがいをうける be damaged
d 恩寵を受ける おんちょうをうける enjoy (a person's) favor
② [sometimes also 承ける] **inherit, get**
受け継ぐ うけつぐ inherit, succeed to
③ parry (a blow), defend (in chess, etc.)
受けを誤る うけをあやまる make a faulty defense
受け流す うけながす ward off, elude; turn aside (a joke)
④ take, interpret
真に受ける まにうける take seriously, believe
⑤ appeal to the public, be popular
受けが良い うけがよい be popular (with)
馬鹿受け ばかうけ great hit
⑥ face, front on
南を受ける みなみをうける face the south
⑦ **be modified**

【-うけ -受け】
ⓐ **receptacle**
ⓑ support
a 郵便受け ゆうびんうけ mailbox
b 軸受け じくうけ bearing

【うかる 受かる】**pass an examination**
大学に受かる だいがくにうかる pass the entrance examination to a university

SYNONYMS

❶ **receive**
受 RECEIVE →3076
享 ENJOY →2545
領 receive →1567
収 TAKE IN →0031
納 ACCEPT →1652

貰 GET →3219
戴 RECEIVE HUMBLY →4093
頂 RECEIVE HUMBLY →0164
拝 have the honor to receive →0360

❷ **be subjected to**
被 BE SUBJECTED TO →1495
受 be subjected to →3076

USAGE

【うける】
受ける
①ⓐ receive, accept, get, take, catch
ⓑ accept (an offer)
ⓒ receive (an insult), suffer, be subjected to
ⓓ [sometimes also 享ける] enjoy, be granted
② [sometimes also 承ける] inherit, get
③ parry (a blow), defend (in chess, etc.)
④ take, interpret
⑤ appeal to the public, be popular
⑥ face, front on
⑦ be modified
享ける
[usu. 受ける] enjoy, be granted
承ける
[usu. 受ける] inherit, get
請ける
① undertake, take upon oneself
② redeem (pawned goods), ransom

HOMOPHONES

うける
享 ENJOY →2545
承 AGREE TO →0016
請 REQUEST →1983

采 3077

2-4-4

▶**GATHER**
サイ ㊔ うね あや こと
Ⓝ 采 Ⓒ 采 cǎi cài

75	Jōyō	U91C7
木	S8-4-4	F2504

Stroke order: 1–8

COMPOUNDS

❶ **GATHER; pick; select**
采詩 さいし gathering folk poetry and music in ancient China
采配を振る さいはいをふる direct, command
拍手喝采する はくしゅかっさいする applaud with hand clapping

❷ fief
采地 さいち fief

❸ beautifully colored
采色 さいしょく beautiful coloring

❹ appearance
風采 ふうさい appearance, air, mien, getup

❺ dice

INDEPENDENT

【さい 采】dice

SYNONYMS

❶ **gather**
集 COLLECT →3445
蒐 COLLECT →2942
聚 COLLECT →3479
収 collect →0031
採 GATHER →0606
采 GATHER →3077
萃 GATHER →2882
湊 come together →0743

采 3078

2-4-4

▶**GATHER**
サイ ㊔ うね あや こと

87	Nonstandard	U91C7
爫	S8-4-4	F0000

traditional form →see 采 at 3077

爭 3079

2-4-4

▶**CONTEND**
ソウ あらそ(う)

87	Names	U722D
爫	S8-4-4	F0000

traditional form →see 争 at 2523

斧 2-4-4
incorrect classification
➡ see 2-2-6: 八 at 2558

者 2-4-4
incorrect classification
➡ see 3-4-4: 耂 at 3980

苅 2-4-4
incorrect stroke-count
➡ see 2-3-4: 艹 at 2746

苍 2-4-4
incorrect stroke-count
➡ see 2-3-4: 艹 at 2747

花 2-4-4
incorrect stroke-count
➡ see 2-3-4: 艹 at 2748

芦 2-4-4
incorrect stroke-count
➡ see 2-3-4: 艹 at 2749

念 2-4-4
incorrect classification
➡ see 2-2-6: 𠆢 at 2554

育 incorrect classification
➡ see 2-2-6: 亠 at 2544
2-4-4

忽

▶IN AN INSTANT
コツ たちま(ち) ゆるが(せ)
Ⓒ 忽 hū

3080
2-4-4

61	Names	U5FFD
心	S8-4-4	F2238

COMPOUNDS

❶ **IN AN INSTANT, immediately, all of a sudden**
忽然と こつぜん(=こつねん)と suddenly; unexpectedly

❷ **neglect, disregard, slight, make light of**
粗忽 そこつ careless, thoughtless, rash

INDEPENDENT

【こつ 忽】**one hundred-thousandth; sudden**

KUN

【たちまち 忽ち】**IN AN INSTANT, immediately, all of a sudden**

【ゆるがせ 忽せ】**neglect, disregard**
勉強を忽せにする べんきょうをゆるがせにする neglect one's studies

SYNONYMS

❶ **immediate**
即 IMMEDIATE → 1439
直 straight away → 3649
忽 IN AN INSTANT → 3080

冐

▶RISK
ボウ おか(す)

3081
2-4-4

13	Nonstandard	U5190
冂	S8-2-6	F0000

traditional form → see 冒 at 3088

毒

▶POISON
ドク
Ⓒ 毒 dú

3082
2-4-4

80	Jōyō-4	U6BD2
毋	S8-4-4	F1123

1	2	3	4	5	6	7	8
一	十	丰	主	圭	責	毒	毒

COMPOUNDS

❶ [original meaning] **POISON, toxin**
毒殺 どくさつ poisoning, killing by poison
毒ガス どくがす poison gas
毒薬 どくやく poisonous drug
毒物 どくぶつ poisonous substance, toxin
有毒な ゆうどくな poisonous
中毒 ちゅうどく poisoning, toxication; addiction
消毒 しょうどく disinfection, sterilization
猛毒 もうどく deadly poison

❷ **malice, harm**
毒舌 どくぜつ wicked tongue, abusive language, blistering remarks
毒突く どくづく spit, curse, abuse

INDEPENDENT

【どく 毒】**POISON, venom, toxicant; harm, injury; malice, spite**
毒の有る どくのある poisonous; harmful, malicious
気の毒な きのどくな pitiable, miserable; regrettable, too bad

【どくする 毒する】**POISON**; do harm, injure; spoil, contaminate

表

▶EXPRESS
▶SURFACE
▶TABLE
ヒョウ おもて -おもて あらわ(す) あらわ(れる)
Ⓒ 表 biǎo

3083
2-4-4

145	Jōyō-3	U8868
衣	S8-6-2	F0143

1	2	3	4	5	6	7	8
一	十	丰	主	耒	耒	表	表

COMPOUNDS

❶ ⓐ **EXPRESS, manifest, show**
ⓑ **appear (on the surface)**
ⓒ **be made public, become open**

a 表明する ひょうめいする express, state, show, demonstrate
表現する ひょうげんする express, represent, manifest; give expression to
表示する ひょうじする indicate, show, express, manifest
表彰 ひょうしょう commendation, awarding
表彰状 ひょうしょうじょう certificate of commendation
表決 ひょうけつ decision, resolution
表意文字 ひょういもじ ideograph, ideographic character
発表する はっぴょうする announce, make public, publish
公表する こうひょうする announce officially [in public], proclaim

b 表象 ひょうしょう representation, image, idea
表情 ひょうじょう expression, look

c 代表する だいひょうする represent, stand for; typify

❷ **SURFACE, face, exterior, outside**
表面 ひょうめん surface, face, outside; appearance
表紙 ひょうし cover, binding
表皮 ひょうひ epidermis; bark, rind

表裏 ひょうり front and rear, both sides (of a thing or matter); duplicity
表記する ひょうきする write, express in writing; write on a surface
地表 ちひょう surface of the earth, ground surface
意表 いひょう limits of one's expectation

❸ [also suffix]
ⓐ TABLE, chart, diagram, schedule, tabular form
ⓑ list

a 図表 ずひょう chart, diagram
年表 ねんぴょう chronological table
時刻表 じこくひょう timetable, schedule
予定表 よていひょう schedule
b 一覧表 いちらんひょう list, table, schedule, catalog

❹ memorial to the throne, written appeal, letter
上表 じょうひょう one's opinion presented to the throne; the table above
辞表 じひょう (letter of) resignation
賀表 がひょう congratulatory address

❺ [also 標 1347] inscription, mark
表札 ひょうさつ nameplate, doorplate

❻ model, paragon
師表 しひょう model, paragon

INDEPENDENT

【ひょう 表】**TABLE, chart, diagram, schedule, tabular form; list**
表にする ひょうにする tabulate; make a list of

【ひょうする 表する】**EXPRESS**, manifest; pay (one's respects)

KUN

【おもて 表】
①ⓐ [also prefix] (front or outer side) **front side, face, outside, right side; the obverse, the head**
ⓑ **the front (of a house)**
ⓒ **superficial [outward] appearance, outside**

a 表門 おもてもん front gate
表通り おもてどおり main street, street
表日本 おもてにほん Pacific side of Japan
葉書の表 はがきのおもて front of a post card
裏表に着る うらおもてにきる wear (a coat) wrong side out
b 表の戸 おもてのと street [front] door
c 表向きの理由 おもてむきのりゆう ostensible [surface] reason

② outdoors, outside
表で遊ぶ おもてであそぶ play outside [out of doors]

③ matting
表替え おもてがえ refacing mats

④ *baseball* first half of an inning, top
五回の表 ごかいのおもて top of the fifth inning

⑤ formal, official, public
表立つ おもてだつ become public [open]

【-おもて -表】[also suffix] **quarters, place, direction**
国表 くにおもて one's native province, one's home
江戸表 えどおもて Edo

【あらわす 表す】
① **EXPRESS, manifest (one's feelings), indicate (one's character), show (anger)**
喜びを顔に表す よろこびをかおにあらわす express one's happiness, show happiness on one's face

② (put in words) **EXPRESS**, convey
言葉に表せない ことばにあらわせない inexpressible, ineffable

③ **EXPRESS in symbols, represent, stand for, symbolize**
記号で表す きごうであらわす represent by signs

【あらわれる 表れる】**be EXPRESSed, find expression in, show, become manifest**
表れ あらわれ expression, manifestation, indication
地方色の表れた小説 ちほうしょくのあらわれたしょうせつ novel with local color

SYNONYMS

❶ⓐ express
表 EXPRESS → 3083
揮 WIELD → 0717
寓 imply → 2893

❷ outside
外 OUTSIDE → 0215
表 SURFACE → 3083
面 FACE → 2590

❸ⓐ diagram
表 TABLE → 3083
図 DRAWING → 3809

USAGE

❶【おもて】

表
①ⓐ [also prefix] (front or outer side) front side, face, outside, right side; the obverse, the head
ⓑ the front (of a house)
ⓒ superficial [outward] appearance, outside
② outdoors, outside
③ matting
④ *baseball* first half of an inning, top
⑤ formal, official, public

面
①ⓐ (front of head) face
ⓑ (outer surface) face, surface (as of water)
② mask

❷【あらわす】

表す
① express, manifest (one's feelings), indicate (one's character), show (anger)

② (put in words) express, convey
③ express in symbols, represent, stand for, symbolize

現す
① cause to appear, show, display, reveal
② attain distinction, become famous

著す
author, write, publish

❸【あらわれる】

表れる
be expressed, find expression in, show, become manifest

現れる
① appear, emerge, come out, become visible, materialize
② become known, attain distinction; be exposed [found out]

❹【あらわれ】

表れ
expression, manifestation, indication

現れ
embodiment, materialization

❺【ひょうじする】

表示する
indicate, show, express, manifest

標示する
post up, declare, demonstrate

❻【ひょうきする】

表記する
write on a surface; write, express in writing

標記する
mark; write a title

HOMOPHONES

おもて 面 FACE →2590
あらわす
現 ACTUAL →1218
著 AUTHOR →2869
あらわれる 現 ACTUAL →1218
あらわれ 現 ACTUAL →1218

COMPOUND FORMATION

【表意文字 ひょういもじ】
表意文字 'ideograph, ideographic character' refers to characters (文字) that express (表 ❶ⓐ) meaning (意).

青

▶BLUE
▶GREEN

3084
2-4-4

セイ ショウ チン▲ あお あお- あお(い)
㊔ はる
Ⓝ 青 Ⓒ 青 qīng

174	Jōyō-1	U9752
青	S8-8-0	F0449

radical variant → see 青 at 3085

COMPOUNDS

❶ⓐ BLUE
ⓑ GREEN, greenish

a 青色 せいしょく blue
青天 せいてん blue sky
青色症 せいしょくしょう cyanosis
紺青 こんじょう Prussian blue, deep blue
緑青 ろくしょう verdigris, copper [green] rust
丹青 たんせい red and blue; painting
b 青松 せいしょう green pine
青椒×肉絲 ちんじゃおろーす stir-fried shredded meat and green pepper
青梗菜 ちんげんさい bok choy

❷ GREENs, vegetables
青果 せいか vegetables and fruits

❸ⓐ youthful, young
ⓑ abbrev. of 青年 せいねん youth
a 青春 せいしゅん bloom of youth
青年 せいねん youth, young man
青少年 せいしょうねん youth, young people
b 民青 みんせい Democratic Youth League of Japan

❹ *chem* cyanide
青化物 せいかぶつ cyanide
青酸 せいさん prussic acid

❺ strips of bamboo formerly used for writing
青史 せいし history, history book

KUN

【あお 青】BLUE; green; green light; bluish-gray horse
光沢の有る青 こうたくのあるあお peacock blue

【あお- 青-】
① [also prefix]
ⓐ **BLUE**
ⓑ **GREEN**
a 青色 あおいろ blue
青空 あおぞら blue sky
b 青信号 あおしんごう green light, green (traffic) signal
青草 あおくさ green grass
青物 あおもの greens, vegetables
青菜 あおな greens

② (not mature) **GREEN**, unripe
青二才 あおにさい green [immature] youth, novice, greenhorn
青臭い あおくさい inexperienced, immature; grassy-smelling

③ (pale in appearance) **GREEN, pale**
青白い あおじろい pale, pallid
青ざめる あおざめる become pale

文 日 木 止 氏 水 火 爫 爫 父 耂 艹 今 去 勿 冂 【圭】 丗 中 夳

【あおい 青い】
①ⓐ **BLUE**
ⓑ **GREEN**
a 青い旗 あおいはた blue flag
② [sometimes also 蒼い] (pale in appearance) **GREEN, pale**
顔が青い かおがあおい look pale [green]
③ (not mature) **GREEN**, unripe
青い果実 あおいかじつ unripe [green] fruit

SPECIAL READINGS

真っ青 まっさお deep blue; paleness, ghastliness

SYNONYMS

❶ⓐ blue and purple colors
青 BLUE → 3084
碧 DEEP BLUE → 3515
瑠 LAPIS LAZULI (bright blue) → 1342
紺 DARK BLUE → 1688
藍 INDIGO → 3024
紫 PURPLE → 3332
蒼 PALE BLUE → 2943

ⓑ green colors
緑 GREEN → 1741
青 GREEN → 3084
翠 JADE GREEN → 3356

❸ⓐ young
若 YOUNG → 2785
弱 young → 1499
少 young → 4278
青 youthful → 3084
幼 VERY YOUNG → 0222
稚 CHILDISH → 1543

USAGE

【あおい】
青い
①ⓐ blue
ⓑ green
② [sometimes also 蒼い] (pale in appearance) green, pale
③ (not mature) green, unripe
蒼い
[usu. 青い] pale blue; pale; green

HOMOPHONES

あおい 蒼 PALE BLUE → 2943

COMPOUND FORMATION

【青史 せいし】
青史 'history, history book' originally referred to history (史) written on bamboo strips (青 ❺).

青

3085
2-4-4

▶**BLUE**
▶**GREEN**
セイ ショウ チン あお あお- あお(い)
㊔ はる

174	Nonstandard	U9751
靑	S8-8-0	F0000

traditional form → see 靑 at 3084

RADICAL

ao 'blue' (靜), used for character classification
Variant: 青 *ao* (靖 静)

昔

3086
2-4-4

▶**FORMER TIMES**
セキ シャク むかし
Ⓒ 昔 xī

72	Jōyō-3	U6614
日	S8-4-4	F0905

一 十 廾 丗 昔 昔 昔 昔
1 2 3 4 5 6 7 8

COMPOUNDS

● [original meaning] **FORMER TIMES, ancient times, past, antiquity**
昔時 せきじ former times, old times
昔日 せきじつ ancient times, former days, bygone days
昔年 せきねん antiquity, former years
今昔 こんじゃく past and present, yesterday and today

KUN

【むかし 昔】**FORMER TIMES, old times, antiquity, bygone years; formerly, in the past**
昔話 むかしばなし legend, old tale
昔風 むかしふう old-fashioned

SYNONYMS

● old times
昔 FORMER TIMES → 3086
往 bygone days → 0348

芽苛

2-4-4

incorrect classification
➡ see 2-3-5: 艹 at 2779

忠

3087
2-4-4

▶**LOYALTY**
チュウ ㊔ ただ ただし ただす ただお
Ⓒ 忠 zhōng

61	Jōyō-6	U5FE0
心	S8-4-4	F0859

丶 冂 口 中 中 忠 忠 忠
1 2 3 4 5 6 7 8

COMPOUNDS

❶ⓐ LOYALTY, devotion, faithfulness, fidelity

ⓑ loyal, devoted, faithful
a 忠実 ちゅうじつ faithfulness, devotion, honesty
忠孝 ちゅうこう loyalty and filial piety
忠義 ちゅうぎ loyalty, fidelity, devotion
b 忠臣 ちゅうしん loyal retainer, loyal subject
忠犬 ちゅうけん faithful dog
❷ [original meaning] **sincerity, honesty**
忠告する ちゅうこくする advise; counsel, give warning; admonish

INDEPENDENT

【ちゅう 忠】**LOYALTY**, devotion; faithfulness, fidelity
忠なる ちゅうなる loyal, devoted, faithful, true
君に忠である きみにちゅうである be loyal to one's sovereign

SYNONYMS

❶ⓐ **fidelity**
忠 LOYALTY → 3087
義 faith → 2948
孝 FILIAL PIETY → 3973
悌 BROTHERLY LOVE → 0507
誠 SINCERITY → 1922
実 faithfulness → 2765
信 fidelity → 0115
操 constancy → 0948
節 moral integrity → 3336

奈
2-4-4

incorrect classification
➡ see 2-3-5: 大 at 2759

彦
2-4-5

incorrect classification
➡ see 2-2-7: 亠 at 2574

冒

3088
2-4-5

▸**RISK**
ボウ おか(す)
Ⓝ 冐 冒 Ⓒ 冒 mào

109△	Jōyō	U5192
目	S9-5-4	F1470

COMPOUNDS

❶ **RISK, brave, defy**
冒険 ぼうけん adventure, risk
冒涜×する ぼうとくする desecrate, profane
❷ affect, attack, afflict
感冒 かんぼう cold, catarrh
❸ **beginning**
冒頭 ぼうとう beginning, opening

KUN

【おかす 冒す】
①ⓐ **RISK, brave, defy**
ⓑ (risk the danger of using a great person's name) assume (another's name); bear
a 危険を冒す きけんをおかす brave [defy] a danger
b 源の姓を冒す みなもとのせいをおかす assume the clan name of Minamoto
② affect, attack, afflict
病に冒される やまいにおかされる be attacked by a disease

SYNONYMS

❶ **risk**
冒 RISK → 3088
賭 WAGER → 2021
懸 stake → 3632

HOMOPHONES

おかす
犯 OFFENSE → 0229
侵 INVADE → 0116

NOTE

➡ see USAGE note at 侵 0116
★ do not confuse with 昌 PROSPERING → 3069

星

3089
2-4-5

▸**STAR**
セイ ショウ ほし -ぼし
Ⓒ 星 xīng

72	Jōyō-2	U661F
日	S9-4-5	F0670

COMPOUNDS

❶ⓐ [also suffix] **STAR**
ⓑ **suffix after names of STARs**
a 星座 せいざ constellation
恒星 こうせい fixed star
超巨星 ちょうきょせい supergiant star
一等星 いっとうせい first magnitude star
b 北極星 ほっきょくせい Polaris
織女星 しょくじょせい Vega
❷ **celestial body, planet, satellite**
惑星 わくせい planet
衛星 えいせい satellite; moon
流星 りゅうせい shooting star, falling star
火星 かせい Mars
冥王星 めいおうせい Pluto
明星 みょうじょう Venus
❸ (prominent personage) **STAR, great man**
巨星 きょせい giant star; great person [star], big shot
将星 しょうせい general
❹ time, years
星霜 せいそう years, time

文【日】日木比耂分亣冂不卌廿少丗

KUN

【ほし 星】**STAR, heavenly body, planet; spot, dot; bull's eye; point, score; criminal**

星占い ほしうらない astrology

図星 ずぼし bull's eye, mark

【-ぼし -星】[also suffix] **STAR, heavenly body, planet**

彗×星 ほうきぼし comet

綺羅星 きらぼし glittering stars

SYNONYMS

❶ **stars**

星 STAR → 3089

座 constellation → 3868

NOTE

➡ see COMPOUND FORMATION for 織女星 しょくじょせい → 織 1801

是

3090

2-4-5

▶**RIGHT**

ぜ これ▲ ㊔ ゆき よし

Ⓒ 是 shì

72	Jōyō	U662F
日	S9-4-5	F1477

COMPOUNDS

❶ⓐ **RIGHT**

ⓑ (set right) **RIGHT, correct**

a 是非 ぜひ right and/or wrong; by all means, at any cost

是非とも ぜひとも at any cost, by some means or other

是是非非主義 ぜぜひひしゅぎ fair and unbiased policy, principle of being fair and just

是認 ぜにん approval

b 是正 ぜせい correction

❷ policy, guideline

国是 こくぜ national policy

社是 しゃぜ company policy

店是 てんぜ shop policy

❸ this

如是我聞 にょぜがもん these ears have heard; thus I hear (quote from the sutras)

INDEPENDENT

【ぜ 是】**RIGHT**, righteousness

是を是とし非を非とする ぜをぜとしひをひとする Call what is right right, and wrong wrong

KUN

【これ 是】[also 之] *pronoun* **this**

SYNONYMS

❶ⓐ **right**

正 RIGHT → 4296

是 RIGHT → 3090

尤 RIGHT → 3755

端 correct → 1564

❷ **policy**

策 policy → 3320

是 policy → 3090

綱 guiding principle → 1735

【これ】

◯ **this and that**

本 THIS → 4314

爾 THAT → 4407

其れ THAT → 3255

彼 that → 0346

今 THIS (week, etc.) → 2464

当 THE PRESENT → 2701

該 the said → 1916

同 the same → 3707

之 this → 4228

是 this → 3090

此 THIS → 1017

斯 THIS → 2140

USAGE

【これ】

是

[also 之] *pronoun* this

之

[also 是] *pronoun* this

此れ

[also 是 or 之] *pronoun* this

惟

[archaic] emphatic adverb

HOMOPHONES

これ

之 POSSESSIVE PARTICLE → 4228

此 THIS → 1017

惟 MEDITATE → 0582

昴

3091

2-4-5

▶**PLEIADES**

ボウ すばる ㊔ こう のぼる たかし

Ⓒ 昴 mǎo

72	Names	U6634
日	S9-4-5	F0000

COMPOUNDS

● **the PLEIADES**

昴宿 ぼうしゅく *literary* the Pleiades

KUN

【すばる 昴】**the PLEIADES**

昴座 すばるざ the Pleiades

SYNONYMS

● **constellation**

奎 ANDROMEDA → 2796
彗 COMET → 3439
昴 PLEIADES → 3091

NOTE

★ do not confuse with 昂 HIGH → 3065

査

3092
2-4-5

▶LOOK INTO
サ
Ⓒ 查 chá zhā

75	Jōyō-5	U67FB
木	S9-4-5	F0411

COMPOUNDS

❶ LOOK INTO, investigate, examine, check, inspect, find out, inquire into
査察 ささつ inspection, investigation
査閲 さえつ inspection, examination
査問 さもん inquiry, hearing
調査 ちょうさ investigation, examination, inquiry, survey
捜査 そうさ criminal investigation, search
検査 けんさ inspection, examination, test
審査する しんさする examine, investigate, judge
鑑査 かんさ inspection, audit

❷ investigator, examiner
主査 しゅさ chairman of an investigation
巡査 じゅんさ police, patrolman

SYNONYMS

❶ investigate and examine
閲 REVIEW → 4132
審 EXAMINE CAREFULLY → 2985
験 TEST → 2306
勘 CHECK → 2231
糾 INQUIRE INTO → 1631
究 STUDY EXHAUSTIVELY → 2729
察 INSPECT → 2961
討 STUDY → 1846
探 PROBE → 0613
検 EXAMINE → 1241
診 EXAMINE A PATIENT → 1898
調 INVESTIGATE → 1973
査 LOOK INTO → 3092

皆

3093
2-4-5

▶ALL
カイ みな みんな▲
Ⓒ 皆 jiē

106	Jōyō	U7686
白	S9-5-4	F1139

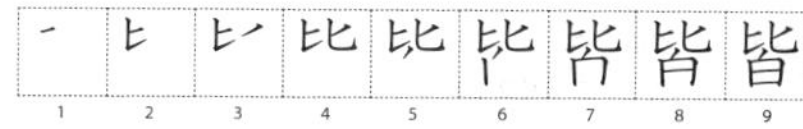

COMPOUNDS

● [original meaning] **ALL, whole, everything; everybody, everyone**
皆目 かいもく altogether, wholly; (not) at all
皆無 かいむ nothing
皆勤 かいきん perfect attendance
皆既食 かいきしょく total solar [lunar] eclipse
免許皆伝 めんきょかいでん initiation into all the mysteries of an art
国民皆兵 こくみんかいへい universal conscription
国民皆保険 こくみんかいほけん medical insurance for the whole nation

KUN

【みな 皆】**ALL, everything; everybody, everyone**
皆さん みなさん everybody; ladies and gentlemen
皆様 みなさま everybody; ladies and gentlemen
皆殺し みなごろし massacre, annihilation
【みんな 皆】colloquial form of 皆 みな

SYNONYMS

● all
皆 ALL → 3093
悉 THOROUGHLY → 3405
総 TOTAL → 1743
諸 VARIOUS → 1984
毎 EVERY → 2527
各 EACH → 2692
都 all → 2120
万 all → 3653
全 WHOLE → 2514
渾 ENTIRE → 0738
一 all in one → 4148
満 FULL → 0739
丸 complete(ly) → 4225
完 COMPLETE → 2727

者

2-4-5

incorrect classification
➡ see ☐3-4-5: 耂 at 3988

盆

2-4-5

incorrect classification
➡ see 2-2-7: 八 at 2581

彦

2-4-5

incorrect classification
➡ see ☐3-6-3: 产 at 4085

冒 3094

2-4-5

▶RISK

ボウ おか(す)

13	Nonstandard	U5192
冂	S9-2-7	F0000

traditional form → see 冒 at 3088

歪 3095

2-4-5

▶DISTORT

ワイ ゆが(める) ゆが(む) ひず(む) いびつ

Ⓒ 歪 wāi wǎi

77	Non-Jōyō	U6B6A
止	S9-4-5	F1938

COMPOUNDS

ⓐ DISTORT, warp, twist, bend
ⓑ DISTORTed, warped, bent, askew
ⓒ DISTORTion, strain, bend

a 歪力 わいりょく stress (intensity)
歪度 わいど skewness
b 歪曲 わいきょく distortion; perversion
c 磁歪 じわい magnetostriction
電歪 でんわい electrostriction

KUN

【ゆがめる 歪める】*vt* **DISTORT, warp, twist, bend; pervert**
【ゆがむ 歪む】*vi* **be DISTORTed, warp, twist, bend; be perverse**
歪み ゆがみ distortion, strain, bend
歪んだ心 ゆがんだこころ distorted mind, perverse mind
顔を歪める かおをゆがめる contort one's face
【ひずむ 歪む】be **DISTORT**ed, warp, twist, bend
歪み ひずみ distortion, strain, bend
歪んだ板 ひずんだいた warped board
【いびつ 歪】**DISTORT**ed, warped, crooked, irregular
歪な形 いびつなかたち irregular shape

SYNONYMS

ⓐ bend
曲 CURVE → 4340
彎 CURVE (become bow-shaped) → 3634
屈 BEND → 3821
折 bend → 0297
勾 be bent → 3660
歪 DISTORT → 3095

盃 3096

2-4-5

▶CUP

ハイ さかずき

108	Names	U76C3
皿	S9-5-4	F0000

traditional form → see 杯 at 1066

巷 3097

2-4-5

▶THE STREETS

コウ ちまた ㊔ さと

Ⓝ 衖 巷 Ⓒ 巷 xiàng hàng

49	Names	U5DF7
己	S9-3-6	F2694

COMPOUNDS

ⓐ THE STREETS, the town
ⓑ the public

a 陋×巷 ろうこう narrow, dirty backstreet
柳巷花街 りゅうこうかがい [archaic] red-light district
b 巷間 こうかん around town, the public, the world
巷説 こうせつ gossip, talk of the town
巷談 こうだん rumor, gossip

KUN

【ちまた 巷】
① ⓐ **THE STREETS, the town**
ⓑ **the public**
ab 巷の噂 ちまたのうわさ popular rumor, word on the street
② fork in a road, crossroads
③ scene, locale
修羅の巷 しゅらのちまた scene of carnage

SYNONYMS

ⓐ ways and routes
道 WAY (path) → 3888
径 PATH → 0347
軌 TRACK → 1832
線 LINE → 1760
澪 WATERWAY → 0957
途 WAY (route) → 3853
路 ROAD → 1936
筋 wayside → 3319
通り street → 3855
街 city street → 0702
辻 CROSSROADS → 3958
岐 forked road → 0285
巷 THE STREETS → 3097

ⓑ public
公 PUBLIC → 2468
俗 POPULAR → 0119
巷 the public → 3097

巷 3098

2-4-5

▶THE STREETS

コウ ちまた ㊔ さと

49	Nonstandard	U5DF7
己	S9-3-6	F0000

traditional form → see 巷 at 3097

茸

2-4-5

incorrect classification
➡ see 2-3-6: 艹 at 2809

革

▶LEATHER
▶REFORM
カク かわ

3099 Ⓒ 革 gé jí

2-4-5

177	Jōyō-6	U9769
革	S9-9-0	F0657

一 十 廾 廿 廿 芇 芇 苣 革
1 2 3 4 5 6 7 8 9

RADICAL

kawa 'rawhide' (䩻), used in characters related to hide or leather products

Left variant: 革 *kawahen* (靴 鞄 鞭)

COMPOUNDS

❶ **LEATHER, tanned skin**

革質の かくしつの coriaceous, leathery

皮革 ひかく leather, hides

❷ⓐ **REFORM, transform, change**

ⓑ abbrev. of 改革 かいかく: **REFORM, reformation**

a 革新 かくしん innovation, reform, renovation

革命 かくめい revolution

改革 かいかく reform, reformation

変革 へんかく change, reform, revolution

沿革 えんかく history, annals

b 保革 ほかく conservatives and reformists

行革(=行政改革) ぎょうかく(=ぎょうせいかいかく) administrative reform

❸ abbrev. of 革命 かくめい: revolution

マル革 まるかく Marxist revolution

KUN

【かわ 革】[also prefix and suffix] **LEATHER**

革靴 かわぐつ leather shoes

革手袋 かわてぶくろ leather gloves

牛革 ぎゅうかわ cowhide, oxhide

エナメル革 えなめるがわ enameled [patent] leather

SYNONYMS

❶ **kinds of skin**

皮 SKIN (of any kind) →3771

膚 SKIN (of the human body) →4049

肌 SKIN (of the human body) →1021

革 LEATHER →3099

韋 TANNED LEATHER →2851

鱗 SCALES →2375

❷ **reform**

改 REFORM →0287

革 REFORM →3099

更 RENEW →4355

新 make new →2239

HOMOPHONES

かわ 皮 SKIN →3771

NOTE

➡ see USAGE note at 皮 3771

➡ see COMPOUND FORMATION for

沿革 えんかく →沿 0386

革命 かくめい →命 2553

省

▶MINISTRY
▶SAVE
▶INTROSPECT
セイ ショウ かえり(みる) はぶ(く)

3100 Ⓒ 省 shěng xǐng

2-4-5

109	Jōyō-4	U7701
目	S9-5-4	F0591

丨 丿丨 小 少 少 省 省 省 省
1 2 3 4 5 6 7 8 9

COMPOUNDS

❶ [also suffix] **MINISTRY, government department [office]**

省庁 しょうちょう Ministries and Agencies

省令 しょうれい Ministerial ordinance

同省 どうしょう the said Ministry

文部省 もんぶしょう Ministry of Education, Science and Culture

大蔵省 おおくらしょう Ministry of Finance

❷ **SAVE, conserve**

省力 しょうりょく labor saving

省エネルギー しょうえねるぎー energy conservation

省資源 しょうしげん saving resources

❸ **leave out, omit**

省略 しょうりゃく omission, abbreviation, abridgment

❹ⓐ (examine oneself critically) **INTROSPECT, reflect upon oneself**

ⓑ [original meaning] examine carefully, scrutinize

a 反省 はんせい reflection, introspection

三省する さんせいする reflect upon oneself (three times a day), examine oneself over and over again

自省 じせい self-examination [reflection], introspection

b 省察 せいさつ reflection; self-reflection, introspection

人事不省 じんじふせい unconsciousness

❺ **pay a visit**

帰省 きせい homecoming

❻ [suffix] province in China

山東省 さんとうしょう Shandong Province

文 日 曰 木 比 耂 分 亣 冂 不 丗 廿 少 【丗】

INDEPENDENT

【しょう 省】**MINISTRY**, government department [office]; province in China

KUN

【かえりみる 省みる】**INTROSPECT, examine oneself, reflect upon oneself**

自分の行いを省みる じぶんのおこないをかえりみる reflect upon one's deeds

【はぶく 省く】**leave out, omit, exclude; SAVE, curtail, cut down, reduce**

無駄を省く むだをはぶく exclude wastefulness

労力を省く ろうりょくをはぶく save labor

SYNONYMS

❶ **parts of governments**

閣 CABINET → 4128
省 MINISTRY → 3100

❶ **public offices**

省 MINISTRY → 3100
庁 GOVERNMENT AGENCY → 3768
府 government office → 3824
公 public office → 2468
署 PUBLIC-SERVICE STATION → 3223
局 public service office → 3800
所 office → 1056

❷ **economizing and economy**

省 SAVE → 3100
節 economize → 3336
倹 FRUGAL → 0130

❸ **eliminate**

却 ELIMINATE → 1436
排 EXCLUDE → 0593
払う CLEAR AWAY → 0225
剥 PEEL OFF → 2105
耘 WEED → 1661
削 cross out → 1837
抹 wipe off → 0370
省 leave out → 3100
脱 REMOVE → 1225
去 take away → 2678
外す take off → 0215
除 RID OF → 0546
撤 WITHDRAW → 0912

❹ⓐ **think and consider**

思 THINK → 3173
惟 MEDITATE → 0582
省 INTROSPECT → 3100
稽 THINK → 1573
考 THINK → 3962
存 hold an opinion → 3702
案 think out → 2824
想 CONCEIVE → 3507
慮 CONSIDER → 4050
勘 take into consideration → 2231
銓 WEIGH → 2161
量 weigh → 3119

❻ **territorial divisions**

州 STATE → 0064
県 PREFECTURE → 3269
府 URBAN PREFECTURE → 3824
道 district of Hokkaido → 3888
都 METROPOLIS OF TOKYO → 2120
省 province in China → 3100
郡 COUNTY → 1858

HOMOPHONES

かえりみる 顧 LOOK BACK → 2394

NOTE

➡ see USAGE note at 顧 2394

帯
2-4-5

incorrect stroke-count
➡ see 2-5-5: 丗 at 3191

晃

3101
2-4-6

▸**DAZZLING**

コウ ㊔ てる あき あきら ひかる のぼる あつし

Ⓝ 晄 Ⓒ 晃 huǎng huàng

72	Names	U6643
日	S10-4-6	F1933

COMPOUNDS

● [archaic] **DAZZLING**, brilliant

晃晃たる こうこうたる dazzling, brilliant
晃朗たる こうろうたる bright and brilliant
晃曜 こうよう dazzling brightness

SYNONYMS

● **bright**

明 BRIGHT → 1060
昭 LUMINOUS → 1107
蛍 fluorescent → 3204
晃 DAZZLING → 3101
燦 BRILLIANT → 1390
赫 BLAZING → 1960
暉 radiant → 1276
熙 BRIGHT → 3559
晟 SUNNY → 3104

昪

3102
2-4-6

▸**ASCEND**

ショウ のぼ(る) ㊔ のり のぶ

72	Nonstandard	U66FB
日	S10-4-6	F0000

traditional form → see 昇 at 3068

晏

3103

2-4-6

▶**LATE**

アン エン ㊔ やす はる

Ⓒ 晏 yàn

72	Names	U664F
日	S10-4-6	F0000

COMPOUNDS

❶ [original meaning, now rare] **LATE** (hours of the day)

晏起 あんき getting up late in the morning, late rising

❷ [rare] peaceful, calm, quiet, tranquil

晏如たる あんじょたる peaceful, calm

SYNONYMS

❶ **late**

遅 LATE (delayed) → 3887

晩 late (advanced) → 1232

晏 LATE → 3103

NOTE

★ do not confuse with 宴 BANQUET → 2825

晟

3104

2-4-6

▶**SUNNY**

セイ ジョウ ㊔ あきら のぼる あき てる なり ひかる

Ⓝ 晠 晟 Ⓒ 晟 shèng

72	Names	U665F
日	S10-4-6	F0000

COMPOUNDS

● [archaic] **SUNNY**, bright, full of sunshine

SYNONYMS

● **bright**

明 BRIGHT → 1060

昭 LUMINOUS → 1107

蛍 fluorescent → 3204

晃 DAZZLING → 3101

燦 BRILLIANT → 1390

赫 BLAZING → 1960

暉 radiant → 1276

熙 BRIGHT → 3559

晟 SUNNY → 3104

NOTE

★ do not confuse with 晨 EARLY MORNING → 3110

釜

2-4-6

incorrect classification

➡ see 2-2-8: 八 at 2610

茨

2-4-6

incorrect stroke-count

➡ see 2-3-6: 艹 at 2816

翁

2-4-6

incorrect classification

➡ see 2-2-8: 八 at 2611

索

3105

2-4-6

▶**SEARCH FOR**

サク

Ⓒ 索 suǒ

120	Jōyō	U7D22
糸	S10-6-4	F1288

1	2	3	4	5	6	7	8	9	10
一	十	广	产	声	壳	玄	索	索	索

COMPOUNDS

❶ **SEARCH FOR (a word in a dictionary), look up, retrieve, locate**

索引 さくいん index

捜索する そうさくする search for, investigate

探索する たんさくする search for; inquire into, investigate

模索(=摸索)する もさくする grope for

検索する けんさくする look up (a word in a dictionary), search for, refer to

思索する しさくする think, speculate

❷ [original meaning] **cable, thick rope, cord**

索条 さくじょう cable, rope

索道 さくどう cableway, ropeway

鋼索 こうさく cable, steel wire rope

鉄索 てっさく cable, cableway

軸索 じくさく axon, axis cylinder

❸ alone, solitary

索莫(=索漠)たる さくばくたる dreary, bleak, desolate

INDEPENDENT

【さく 索】 rope, steel cable

SYNONYMS

❶ **seek**

探 SEARCH → 0613

索 SEARCH FOR → 3105

捜 LOOK FOR → 0516

求 SEEK → 4365

猟 hunt for → 0654

❷ **ropes and lines**

綱 ROPE (esp. of fiber) → 1735

絃 STRING → 1685

縄 ROPE (esp. of straw) → 1756

緒 cord → 1742

組 braid → 1693

索 cable → 3105

鎖 CHAIN → 2213

線 LINE → 1760

紐 STRING → 1647

弦 STRING → 0343

日 曰 父 艹 公 【声】 ⺌ 天 圭 𡈽

COMPOUND FORMATION

【思索 しさく】

思索する 'think, speculate' is to search for (索 ❶) by thinking about (思).

挙

3106

2-4-6

▶**NOMINATE**
▶**NOTEWORTHY ACT**
▶**RAISE**

キョ あ(げる) あ(がる) ㊔ たか

Ⓝ 擧 舉 Ⓒ 举 jǔ

64	Jōyō-4	U6319
手	S10-4-6	F0596

1	2	3	4	5	6	7	8	9	10
ヽ	ヽヽ	⺍	龸	𰀁	兴	兴	㒸	巻	挙

COMPOUNDS

❶ **NOMINATE, appoint, recommend**
挙用する きょようする appoint, promote
選挙 せんきょ election
推挙する すいきょする recommend, nominate

❷ **NOTEWORTHY ACT, deed, scheme, attempt, undertaking**
暴挙 ぼうきょ rash act, reckless attempt
壮挙 そうきょ grand scheme, heroic [daring] attempt
快挙 かいきょ brilliant achievement, heroic deed [feat]

❸ **deportment, behavior, action, conduct, bearing**
挙動 きょどう deportment, conduct, behavior, action
挙措 きょそ behavior, manner
挙止 きょし bearing, deportment

❹ⓐ [original meaning] **RAISE (one's hand), hold up, lift**
ⓑ **RAISE** (an army), recruit
a 挙手 きょしゅ raising [holding up] one's hand; salute
b 挙兵 きょへい raising an army

❺ hold a function, perform (a ceremony)
挙式 きょしき holding a ceremony
挙行する きょこうする hold, perform, celebrate

❻ cite, give (an example), mention
挙証 きょしょう presentation of proof
列挙する れっきょする enumerate, list
枚挙する まいきょする list, enumerate

❼ arrest, round up, nab
検挙する けんきょする arrest, round up

❽ **whole, entire, all**
挙国 きょこく whole nation
挙党 きょとう whole party
一挙に いっきょに at a stroke, with a single swoop

INDEPENDENT

【きょ 挙】 **NOTEWORTHY ACT**, deed, scheme, attempt, undertaking
軽率な挙 けいそつなきょ rash act

KUN

【あげる 挙げる】

①ⓐ (raise something and hold it up for display) **hold up, RAISE (one's hand or a wineglass)**
ⓑ (gather together) **RAISE** (an army), recruit
ⓒ (elevate in dignity) **RAISE** oneself, raise one's reputation
a 手を挙げろ てをあげろ Hold up!/Stick 'em up!
b 兵を挙げる へいをあげる raise an army
c 名を挙げる なをあげる make one's name, gain fame

② **cite, give (an example), mention**
例を挙げる れいをあげる cite an example

③ **hold (a function), perform (a ceremony)**
式を挙げる しきをあげる hold a ceremony

④ arrest, round up, nab
挙げられる あげられる be arrested, be caught

⑤ give birth to, have children
三人の子を挙げる さんにんのこをあげる have three children

⑥ use fully
挙げて あげて all, whole, en masse

⑦ gain (points), score
先取点を挙げる せんしゅてんをあげる score the first point

⑧ **unclassified compounds**
挙げ句(=揚句)に あげくに in the end; finally

【あがる 挙がる】

① **be cited, be mentioned, be listed**
良い例が挙がっている よいれいがあがっている A good example is given

② be arrested, be caught, be nabbed
犯人が挙がった はんにんがあがった The culprit was arrested

③ become famous
名が挙がる ながあがる become famous

④ come into possession, be recovered
証拠が挙がった しょうこがあがった Evidence turned up

SYNONYMS

❶ **appoint**
任 appoint →0057
補 appoint →1529
挙 NOMINATE →3106

❷ **acts**
行 ACT →0246
挙 NOTEWORTHY ACT →3106
業 deed →3227

❸ **behavior**

行 conduct →0246
挙 deportment →3106
動 behavior →2232

❹ⓐ **raise**

揚 RAISE HIGH →0722
掲 PUT UP →0597
挙 RAISE →3106
上 raise →4212
起 raise up →4099
擡 RAISE (one's head) →0972
立てる STAND →2486
拾う PICK UP →0454

❺ **hold an event**

催 HOLD AN EVENT →0178
挙 hold a function →3106

❻ **quote**

引 quote →0207
挙 cite →3106

HOMOPHONES

あげる

上 UP →4212
揚 RAISE HIGH →0722

あがる

上 UP →4212
揚 RAISE HIGH →0722

NOTE

➡ see USAGE note at 上 4212
★ do not confuse with 拳 FIST →3295

蚕

3107

▶**SILKWORM**

サン かいこ こ▲

Ⓝ 蠶 蠺◇ Ⓒ 蚕 cán

2-4-6

142	Jōyō-6	U8695
虫	S10-6-4	F2846

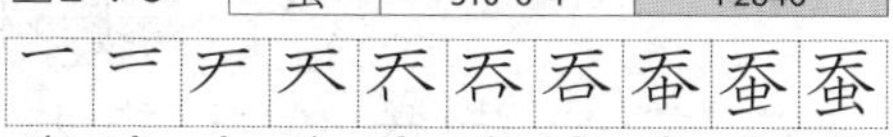

COMPOUNDS

● [original meaning] **SILKWORM**

蚕糸 さんし silk raising and reeling, sericulture
蚕室 さんしつ silkworm-raising room
蚕食する さんしょくする encroach on, make an inroad into
養蚕 ようさん sericulture, silkworm culture

KUN

【かいこ 蚕】SILKWORM

三眠蚕 さんみんかいこ three-molt silkworm

【こ 蚕】SILKWORM

春蚕 はるご spring breed of silkworm

SYNONYMS

● **insects**

蚊 MOSQUITO →1673
蛍 FIREFLY →3204
蝶 BUTTERFLY →1772
蚕 SILKWORM →3107
蟬 CICADA →1804
蜂 BEE →1728
蛔 ROUNDWORM →1717

COMPOUND FORMATION

【蚕食 さんしょく】

蚕食する 'encroach on, etc.' is to encroach on another's territory like a silkworm (蚕) nibbling (食) at the edge of a mulberry leaf.

素

3108

▶**ELEMENT**
▶**PLAIN**

ソ ス もと▲ ㊔ もとい

Ⓒ 素 sù

2-4-6

120	Jōyō-5	U7D20
糸	S10-6-4	F0416

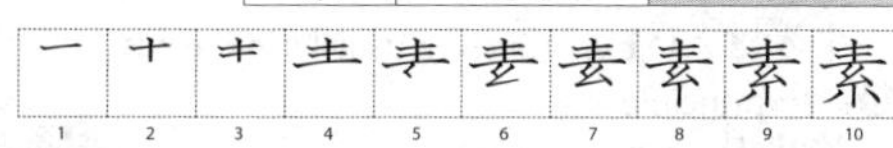

COMPOUNDS

❶ [also suffix]

ⓐ **ELEMENT, basic constituent, component**
ⓑ **chemical ELEMENT**
ⓒ (structural element of language) -eme
ⓓ (pertaining to an element) **ELEMENT**ary, elemental

a 素子 そし *elec* element
要素 ようそ (essential) element, constituent, factor
酵素 こうそ ferment; enzyme
色素 しきそ pigment, coloring matter
栄養素 えいようそ nutritive elements [substance]
葉緑素 ようりょくそ chlorophyll
元素 げんそ element, chemical element

b 酸素 さんそ oxygen
炭素 たんそ carbon

c 音素 おんそ phoneme
形態素 けいたいそ morpheme

d 素反応 そはんのう elementary reaction

❷ⓐ [also prefix] **primary, ELEMENTal, fundamental, original, primordial**
ⓑ *math* prime

a 素質 そしつ character, nature, makings, constitution
素因 そいん basic factor, predisposition
素粒子 そりゅうし elementary particle

b 素数 そすう prime (number)
素体 そたい prime field
素因数 そいんすう prime factor

❸ⓐ [also prefix] (lacking ornament) **PLAIN, simple, unpretentious, natural, unadorned, unrefined, raw, crude**
ⓑ (lacking distinction) **PLAIN, ordinary, common**
a 素材 そざい material; subject matter
素描 そびょう (rough) sketch
素朴な そぼくな simple, naive, artless
素顔 すがお face without makeup
素直な すなおな docile, obedient; honest, frank
簡素な かんそな plain, simple
質素な しっそな simple, modest, frugal
b 素通りする すどおりする pass through without stopping, pass by
素泊まり すどまり staying overnight without board
❹ **bare, naked**
素肌 すはだ bare skin
素手 すで bare hands
素足 すあし bare [naked] feet
❺ usually, formerly
素行 そこう usual behavior
素志 そし long-cherished [long-fostered] desire
平素は へいそは ordinarily, usually; in the past
❻ *chem* principle
苦味素 くみそ bitter principle
❼ **emphatic prefix**
素敵な すてきな grand, cute, fine
素晴らしい すばらしい splendid, magnificent, wonderful, excellent
素早い すばやい nimble; quick
素っ頓狂 すっとんきょう harum-scarum, hysteric
❽ [original meaning] **PLAIN** white cloth; white
素絹 そけん coarse silk
緇×素 しそ old term for Buddhist priesthood and the common people (since they used to wear black and white clothing, respectively)

INDEPENDENT

【そ 素】 *math* prime(ness); mutual indivisibility
素の その prime

KUN

【もと 素】 [now usu. 元] **raw material, base**
味の素 あじのもと AJINOMOTO (registered trademark)
スープの素 すーぷのもと soup stock

SPECIAL READINGS

素人 しろうと amateur, novice, outsider; decent woman

SYNONYMS

❶ **element**
素 ELEMENT → 3108
元 element → 2428
単 unit → 2805
ⓐ **basis**
基 BASE → 3312
本 BASIS → 4314
素 ELEMENT → 3108
礎 foundation → 1595
底 BOTTOM → 3827
根 ROOT → 1167
拠 GROUNDS → 0369
❷ **original**
素 primary → 3108
原 ORIGINAL → 3733
本 original → 4314
初 FIRST → 1433
❸ **plain and simple**
素 PLAIN → 3108
朴 SIMPLE (unadorned) → 1013
単 simple (uncomplicated) → 2805
❹ **naked**
裸 NAKED → 1550
素 bare → 3108

HOMOPHONES

もと
本 BASIS → 4314
元 ORIGIN → 2428
基 BASE → 3312
下 DOWN → 4186
許 PERMIT → 1862

NOTE

➡ see USAGE note at 元 2428

恭

3109

2-4-6

▶**RESPECTFUL**

キョウ うやうや(しい) ㊔ やす やすし ゆき たか

Ⓒ 恭 gōng

61	Jōyō	U606D
小	S10-4-6	F1876

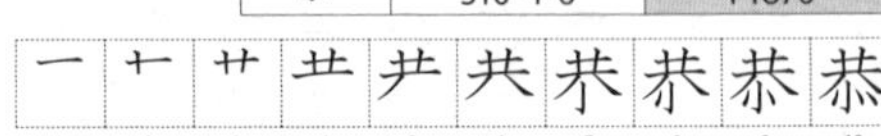

COMPOUNDS

⬤ [original meaning] **RESPECTFUL, reverent**
恭敬 きょうけい respect, reverence
恭順 きょうじゅん obedience, submission
恭賀 きょうが respectful congratulations
恭謙 きょうけん modesty, humility
恭倹 きょうけん humility, respect

KUN

【うやうやしい 恭しい】 **RESPECTFUL, reverent**
恭しく うやうやしく respectfully, reverentially

SYNONYMS

⬤ **respectful**

恭 RESPECTFUL → 3109
謹 RESPECTFULLY → 2045
奉 reverentially → 3167
拝 HUMBLY → 0360

華
▀2-4-6

incorrect classification
➡ see ▀2-3-7: 艹 at 2841

斎 產
▀2-4-7

incorrect classification
➡ see ▀2-2-9: 亠 at 2621

昇
▀2-4-7

incorrect stroke-count
➡ see ▀2-4-6: 日 at 3102

晨
3110
▀2-4-7

▶EARLY MORNING
シン ジン ㊔ あき あきら はやし とき
Ⓒ 晨 chén

72	Names	U6668
日	S11-4-7	F0000

COMPOUNDS

● [rare] **EARLY MORNING**, dawn, daybreak
清晨 せいしん a refreshing morning

SYNONYMS

● **morning and dawn**
朝 MORNING → 2130
暁 DAWN → 1233
旦 DAYBREAK → 3041
曙 DAWN → 1384
晨 EARLY MORNING → 3110

NOTE

★ do not confuse with 晟 SUNNY → 3104

晟
3111
▀2-4-7

▶SUNNY
セイ ジョウ ㊔ あきら のぼる あき てる なり ひかる

72	Nonstandard	U665F
日	S11-4-7	F0000

traditional form → see 晟 at 3104

貫
3112
▀2-4-7

▶PENETRATE
カン つらぬ(く) ぬき▲ ㊔ とおる
Ⓒ 贯 guàn

154	Jōyō	U8CAB
貝	S11-7-4	F1324

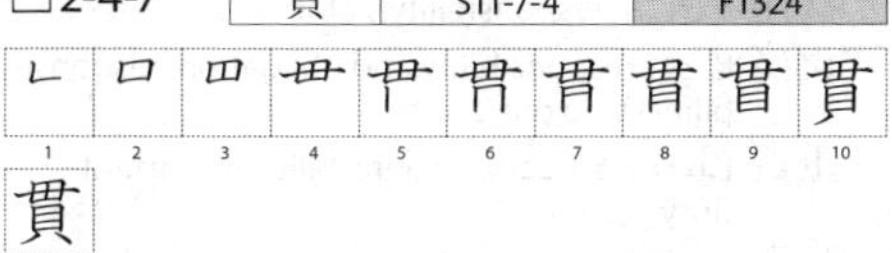

COMPOUNDS

❶ **PENETRATE, pierce through, pass through**
貫通する かんつうする penetrate, pierce, pass through
貫流する かんりゅうする flow through
貫入 かんにゅう penetration
縦貫する じゅうかんする run through, traverse
突貫 とっかん (bayonet) charge, rush

❷ **carry through, attain, carry out**
貫徹する かんてつする carry through, go through with, accomplish, attain
一貫して いっかんして consistently

❸ *kan*:
ⓐ unit of weight equiv. to 3.75 kg or 1000 momme (匁)
ⓑ former monetary unit equiv. to 1000 *mon* (文)
a 尺貫法 しゃっかんほう Japanese system of weights and measures
八貫目 はっかんめ 8 *kan*
b 貫禄 かんろく dignity; [original meaning] retainer's stipend
一貫五十文 いっかんごじゅうもん 1 *kan* 50 *mon*

❹ place of one's ancestral home (in ancient times)
貫主(=貫首) かんじゅ chief abbot (of a Buddhist temple)

INDEPENDENT

【かん 貫】*kan* (→❸)

KUN

【つらぬく 貫く】**PENETRATE, pierce, perforate, go through; carry through [out], attain**
壁を貫く かべをつらぬく penetrate the wall
目的を貫く もくてきをつらぬく accomplish [attain] one's object

【ぬき 貫】**brace; thin and narrow board**

SYNONYMS

❶ **penetrate**
透 PASS THROUGH → 3854
貫 PENETRATE → 3112
破 break through → 1478
滲 PERMEATE → 0862

❸ⓐ **weight units**
匁 MOMME (3.75 g) → 4276
斤 CATTY (600 g) → 3667
貫 *kan* (3.75 kg) → 3112
噸 TON → 0930
屯 ton → 4268

莓
▀2-4-7

incorrect stroke-count
➡ see ▀2-3-7: 艹 at 2845

莖

incorrect stroke-count
➡ see 2-3-7: 艹 at 2846

2-4-7

萊

incorrect stroke-count
➡ see 2-3-7: 艹 at 2847

2-4-7

貨

▶MONEY
▶GOODS
カ

3113

2-4-7

N 貨 C 货 huò

154	Jōyō-4	U8CA8
貝	S11-7-4	F1199

COMPOUNDS

❶ⓐ [original meaning] (legal tender) **MONEY, currency**
ⓑ **coin**
ⓒ (assets) **MONEY,** property

a 貨幣 かへい money, currency, coinage
外貨 がいか foreign currency [money]; foreign [imported] goods
通貨 つうか currency, current money
米貨 べいか American currency, U.S. dollar
b 硬貨 こうか coin, metallic currency
白銅貨 はくどうか nickel coin
鋳貨 ちゅうか coinage, mintage
c 貨殖 かしょく moneymaking

❷ **GOODS, commodity**
百貨店 ひゃっかてん department store
雑貨 ざっか sundries, general cargo; miscellaneous goods
奇貨 きか curiosity, rarity; good opportunity

❸ **freight, cargo**
貨物 かもつ freight, cargo, goods
貨車 かしゃ freight car
貨客 かきゃく freight and passengers

SYNONYMS

❶ⓐ & ❶ⓑ **money**
金 MONEY → 2552
銭 MONEY → 2159
貨 MONEY (legal tender), coin → 3113
幣 CURRENCY → 3582
銀 SILVER → 2156
財 finance → 1849
資 RESOURCES → 3342
-玉 coin suffix → 4289
札 bill → 1011

❷ **merchandise**
産 product → 4089
品 ARTICLE (of merchandise) → 2795
貨 GOODS → 3113
物 commodity → 1084

❸ **burden**
荷 LOAD → 2840
貨 freight → 3113

NOTE

★ do not confuse with 貸 LEND → 3213 and 賃 WAGE → 3341

貨

▶MONEY
▶GOODS
カ

3114

2-4-7

154	Nonstandard	U8CA8
貝	S11-7-4	F0000

traditional form → see 貨 at 3113

貧

incorrect classification
➡ see 2-2-9: 八 at 2631

2-4-7

貪

incorrect classification
➡ see 2-2-9: 𠆢 at 2630

2-4-7

産

incorrect classification
➡ see 3-6-5: 产 at 4089

2-4-7

商

incorrect classification
➡ see 2-2-9: 亠 at 2623

2-4-7

責

▶RESPONSIBILITY
▶BLAME
セキ せ(める)

3115

2-4-7

C 责 zé

154	Jōyō-5	U8CAC
貝	S11-7-4	F0832

COMPOUNDS

❶ **RESPONSIBILITY, liability**
責任 せきにん responsibility, liability
責務 せきむ responsibility and obligation, responsibility to do one's duty
重責 じゅうせき heavy responsibility, important duty
職責 しょくせき responsibilities pertaining to one's work

引責する いんせきする take responsibility upon oneself

❷ **BLAME, condemn, censure**

叱責する しっせきする reproach, scold, reprove

問責 もんせき censure, reproof

自責 じせき self-accusation

❸ [original meaning] torture, torment

INDEPENDENT

【せき 責】**RESPONSIBILITY**

責を果たす せきをはたす fulfill one's responsibility

KUN

【せめる 責める】

① **BLAME, condemn, censure, accuse, criticize, reproach**

責め せめ responsibility; blame; [also suffix] torture, persecution

人の怠慢を責める ひとのたいまんをせめる blame [denounce] a person for his [her] negligence

② **torture, persecute**

責め道具 せめどうぐ instruments of torture

責め立てる せめたてる torture severely; urge

水責め みずぜめ water torture

③ urge, press; tease

金を払えと責める かねをはらえとせめる press for payment

SYNONYMS

❶ **responsibility**

務 DUTY →1505

任 duty →0057

責 RESPONSIBILITY →3115

分 one's part →2466

❷ **blame and accuse**

責 BLAME →3115

叱 SCOLD →0210

詰 REPRIMAND →1920

難 find fault with →2310

批 CRITICIZE →0294

劾 EXPOSE CRIMES →1618

弾 impeach →0697

【せめる】

② **torture and oppress**

拷 TORTURE →0446

責める torture →3115

虐 treat cruelly →3989

迫 oppress →3815

HOMOPHONES

せめる 攻 ATTACK →0286

せめ 攻 ATTACK →0286

NOTE

➡ see USAGE note at 攻 0286

黄

3116

2-4-7

▸**YELLOW**

コウ オウ き こ-

Ⓝ 黄 Ⓒ 黄 huáng

201	Jōyō-2	U9EC4
黄	S11-11-0	F1003

radical variant → see 黄 at 3128

Stroke order: 一 十 廾 廾 丗 丗 芇 苗 茜 黄 黄 (1–11)

COMPOUNDS

❶ⓐ [original meaning] **YELLOW**

ⓑ **YELLOW**-skinned, yellow

ⓒ turn **YELLOW**

a 黄色 こうしょく(=おうしょく) yellow

黄海 こうかい the Yellow Sea

黄金 おうごん gold; money

黄鉄鉱 おうてっこう iron pyrite, fool's gold

黄熱病 おうねつびょう yellow fever

卵黄 らんおう yolk

硫黄 いおう sulfur

b 黄禍 こうか Yellow Peril

黄人 おうじん yellow race

c 黄葉する こうようする turn yellow, put on autumnal leaves

❷ *astron* ecliptic

黄緯 こうい ecliptic latitude

黄道 こうどう ecliptic

KUN

【き 黄】[also prefix] **YELLOW**

黄ばむ きばむ grow yellowish

黄色 きいろ yellow

黄八丈 きはちじょう yellow silk cloth

【こ- 黄-】**YELLOW**

黄金 こがね gold; money

SPECIAL READINGS

黄昏▲ たそがれ dusk

黄楊▲ つげ [also 柘植, sometimes also 柘] Japanese boxwood

SYNONYMS

❶ⓐ **yellow colors**

黄 YELLOW →3116

金 golden →2552

HOMOPHONES

つげ

柘 JAPANESE BOXWOOD →1117

黄楊 →3116, 1286

柘植 →1117, 1247

文日日田艹化化分今亣圭【廾】少世

菫 incorrect classification
➡ see 2-3-8: 艹 at 2877
2-4-7

雀

▶SPARROW
▶MAHJONG
ジャク ジャン すずめ
Ⓒ 雀 què qiǎo qiāo

3117
2-4-7

172	Names	U96C0
隹	S11-8-3	F1869

COMPOUNDS

❶ⓐ SPARROW
ⓑ happy like a **SPARROW**, delighted

a 燕雀 えんじゃく small birds
孔雀 くじゃく peacock
b 欣喜雀躍する きんきじゃくやくする dance [jump] for joy

❷ **unclassified compounds**
麻雀 まーじゃん mahjong

❸ abbrev. of 麻雀 まーじゃん: **MAHJONG**
雀荘 じゃんそう mahjong club
雀球 じゃんきゅう *jankyu* (combination of Japanese pinball and mahjong)
雀卓 じゃんたく mahjong board

KUN

【すずめ 雀】**SPARROW, Japanese sparrow**

SYNONYMS

❶ⓐ **birds**
鷹 HAWK → 3955
鷗 GULL → 2370
烏 CROW → 4088
雀 SPARROW → 3117
燕 SWALLOW → 3142
鴻 LARGE WILD BIRD → 0977
鳳 MALE PHOENIX → 3749
凰 FEMALE PHOENIX → 3738
鵬 MYTHICAL HUGE BIRD → 1416
鶏 CHICKEN → 2221
酉 ROOSTER → 4358
隼 FALCON → 3427
鳩 PIGEON → 0184
鷲 EAGLE → 3598
鳶 BLACK KITE → 3919
鶴 CRANE → 2326
鷺 HERON → 3621
鵜 CORMORANT → 2067
鴨 DUCK → 1582
雁 WILD GOOSE → 3741

❸ **board games**
局 board game → 3800
棋 SHOGI → 1242
碁 GO → 3346
雀 MAHJONG → 3117

貰 incorrect stroke-count
➡ see 2-5-7: 世 at 3219
2-4-7

景

▶SCENE
ケイ ㊔ かげ
Ⓒ 景 jǐng

3118
2-4-8

72	Jōyō-4	U666F
日	S12-4-8	F0492

Stroke order: 1 丶 2 冂 3 日 4 日 5 旦 6 早 7 昙 8 昙 9 景 10 景 11 景 12 景

COMPOUNDS

❶ⓐ **SCENE, scenery, view, -scape**
ⓑ *theater* **SCENE**

a 景勝 けいしょう picturesque scenery
背景 はいけい background; (stage) scenery, setting, scene; backing
夜景 やけい night view [scene]
風景 ふうけい scenery, landscape, view
光景 こうけい spectacle, sight, scene
絶景 ぜっけい superb view, picturesque scenery
情景 じょうけい scene, sight; nature and sentiment
海景 かいけい seascape
全景 ぜんけい complete view
雲景 うんけい cloudscape
b 第一景 だいいっけい first scene

❷ **business conditions, market situation, conditions, circumstances**
景気 けいき things, times; business conditions
景況 けいきょう situation, outlook
不景気 ふけいき business depression, slump, dull market

❸ premium, present
景品 けいひん premium, gift
景物 けいぶつ seasonal scenery; present, premium

❹ respect, admire
景仰する けいこう(=けいぎょう)する adore, admire, revere

❺ [rare] auspicious, great
景雲 けいうん auspicious cloud

INDEPENDENT

【けい 景】**SCENE**, view
天下の景 てんかのけい superlative view

SPECIAL READINGS

景色 けしき scenery, landscape

SYNONYMS

❶ⓐ **view**

景 SCENE → 3118
風 (beautiful) scenery → 3730
光 scenery → 3043
観 VIEW → 2359

❷ **states and situations**

態 STATE → 3529
調 TONE → 1973
様 MODE → 1332
相 PHASE → 1120
状 CONDITION → 0322
況 CONDITIONS → 0395
景 business conditions → 3118
勢 course of events → 3542
境 SITUATION → 0835
局 current situation → 3800
情 ACTUAL CONDITIONS → 0583
訳 circumstances → 1865

量

3119

2-4-8

▶**QUANTITY**

リョウ はか(る) ㊔ かず

Ⓒ 量 liàng liáng

166	Jōyō-4	U91CF
里	S12-7-5	F0514

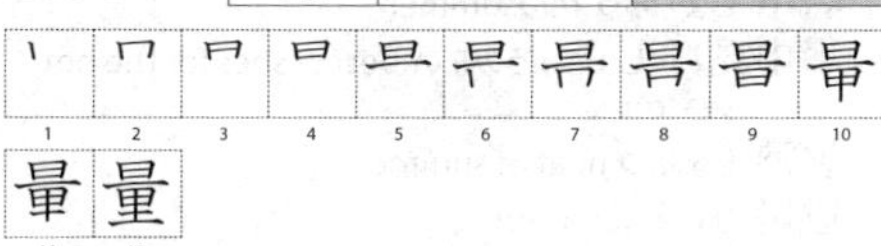

COMPOUNDS

❶ [also suffix] **QUANTITY, amount, volume, capacity, magnitude; weight**

量産 りょうさん mass production
量感 りょうかん massiveness
量子論 りょうしろん quantum theory
数量 すうりょう quantity, volume
大量 たいりょう large quantity, great volume, mass
容量 ようりょう capacity, volume
重量 じゅうりょう weight
交通量 こうつうりょう traffic volume
消費量 しょうひりょう amount of consumption

❷ⓐ [original meaning] (determine the volume, area or weight of) **measure, gauge, weigh**
ⓑ weighing instrument, balance, scale

a 測量する そくりょうする measure, survey
計量する けいりょうする measure, weigh
b 度量衡 どりょうこう weights and measures

❸ **weigh, consider, estimate, assess**

量刑 りょうけい assessment of a case
推量する すいりょうする guess, conjecture, infer
裁量 さいりょう discretion

❹ [formerly also 倆 0136] capacity, ability, skill

器量 きりょう ability, capacity; personal appearance; dignity
力量 りきりょう ability, capacity; physical strength
技量 ぎりょう skill, ability, capacity

❺ magnanimity

度量 どりょう magnanimity, generosity

INDEPENDENT

【りょう 量】**QUANTITY, amount, volume, capacity, magnitude**

量より質 りょうよりしつ quality before quantity

KUN

【はかる 量る】

① (determine the weight or volume of) **measure, weigh**

量り はかり measurements; weighing
量り売り はかりうり sale by measure; sale by weight
肉の目方を量る にくのめかたをはかる weigh the meat

② [in compounds] **guess, surmise, fathom**

推し量る おしはかる conjecture, surmise, guess

SYNONYMS

❶ **quantity and number**

量 QUANTITY → 3119
嵩 BULK → 2927
積 size → 1579
額 AMOUNT → 2273
分 content → 2466
数 NUMBER → 2245
勢 strength → 3542

❷ⓐ **measure**

測 MEASURE → 0744
量 measure → 3119

❸ **think and consider**

思 THINK → 3173
惟 MEDITATE → 0582
省 INTROSPECT → 3100
稽 THINK → 1573
考 THINK → 3962
存 hold an opinion → 3702
案 think out → 2824
想 CONCEIVE → 3507
慮 CONSIDER → 4050
勘 take into consideration → 2231
銓 WEIGH → 2161
量 weigh → 3119

HOMOPHONES

はかる

計 PLAN → 1828
測 MEASURE → 0744

日 木 止 罒 爫 父 艹 厷 丗 廿 中 夭

図 DRAWING → 3809
謀 SCHEME → 2004
諮 CONSULT → 2009

NOTE

➡ see USAGE note at 計 1828

最 3120

▶MOST

サイ もっと(も) ㊔ も

Ⓒ 最 zuì

2-4-8

73	Jōyō-4	U6700
日	S12-4-8	F0101

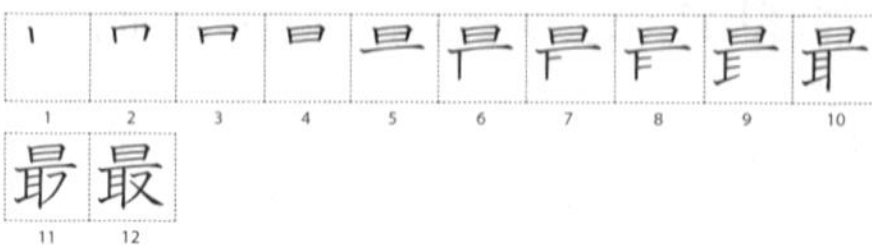

COMPOUNDS

● [also prefix] **MOST, the most, -est, -most, ultra-, extreme**—used to indicate the superlative degree

最高の さいこうの maximum, supreme, highest
最少 さいしょう smallest, minimum, least
最大の さいだいの biggest, largest, greatest
最新の さいしんの newest, latest
最中 さいちゅう in the middle [midst] of, during
最終 さいしゅう last, the end; final
最低の さいていの lowest
最南の さいなんの southernmost
最高級 さいこうきゅう highest grade, top class
最強の さいきょうの strongest
最上の さいじょうの best, the finest; highest
最先端(=最尖端) さいせんたん leading edge; forefront
最大限の さいだいげんの maximum, greatest

INDEPENDENT

【さい 最】the best, the greatest

最たる物 さいたるもの the most extreme

KUN

【もっとも 最も】**the MOST**

最も重要な事 もっともじゅうようなこと the most important thing

SPECIAL READINGS

最寄りの もよりの nearest, nearby

SYNONYMS

● **most**

最 MOST → 3120
至 utmost → 2707
極 EXTREME → 1243

USAGE

【もっとも】

最も
the most

尤も
① right, reasonable, natural
② indeed, it is true; but

HOMOPHONES

もっとも 尤 RIGHT → 3755

暑 3121

▶SUMMER HEAT
▶HOT

ショ あつ(い)

Ⓝ 暑 Ⓒ 暑 shǔ

2-4-8

72	Jōyō-3	U6691
日	S12-4-8	F1560

COMPOUNDS

● [original meaning] **SUMMER HEAT, hot weather, hottest day of summer, summer**

暑気 しょき hot weather
暑中 しょちゅう midsummer
暑中見舞 しょちゅうみまい best wishes for the hot season
暑熱 しょねつ heat of summer
避暑 ひしょ summering
炎暑 えんしょ scorching heat of summer
残暑 ざんしょ lingering summer
猛暑 もうしょ fierce heat
酷暑 こくしょ severe heat
大暑 たいしょ Japanese midsummer day

INDEPENDENT

【しょ 暑】**SUMMER HEAT**

暑を避ける しょをさける go away for the summer, summer

KUN

【あつい 暑い】**HOT (weather), warm, sultry**

暑さ あつさ heat, summer heat, hot weather
真夏の暑さ まなつのあつさ heat of high summer
蒸し暑い むしあつい sultry, sweltering

SYNONYMS

● **heat**

熱 HEAT → 3555
暑 SUMMER HEAT → 3121

● **warm seasons**

春 SPRING → 3184
夏 SUMMER → 2619

暑 SUMMER HEAT → 3121

【あつい】

◯ **hot**

熱 HOT → 3555
暑い HOT (weather) → 3121
炎 scorching → 3075
温 WARM → 0740
暖 WARM (esp. weather) → 1274

HOMOPHONES

あつい 熱 HEAT → 3555

NOTE

➡ see USAGE note at 熱 3555

晶

3122

2-4-8

▶CRYSTAL

ショウ ㊔ あき あきら まさ

Ⓒ 晶 jīng

72	Jōyō	U6676
日	S12-4-8	F1594

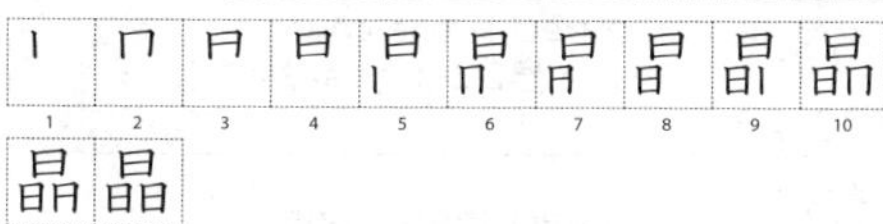

COMPOUNDS

❶ⓐ (body of crystalline structure) **CRYSTAL**
ⓑ (transparent mineral) **CRYSTAL**

a 晶化 しょうか crystallization
晶子 しょうし crystallite
結晶 けっしょう crystallization, crystal; grain; fruit(s)
氷晶 ひょうしょう ice crystal
液晶 えきしょう crystalline liquid
b 水晶 すいしょう rock crystal

❷ [original meaning] **CRYSTAL**-clear, brilliant
晶光 しょうこう brilliant light

SYNONYMS

❶ⓑ precious stones

玉 GEM → 4289
珂 WHITE AGATE → 1137
璧 DISK-SHAPED JEWEL → 3608
琥 AMBER → 1261
珀 AMBER → 1136
珠 PEARL → 1183
瑛 TRANSPARENT GEM → 1259
瑠 LAPIS LAZULI → 1342
璃 GLASSY SUBSTANCE → 1358
晶 CRYSTAL → 3122
玖 beautiful black jewel → 1041
琉 LAPIS LAZULI → 1221
琳 BEAUTIFUL GEM → 1262

森

3123

2-4-8

▶THICK WOODS

シン もり

Ⓒ 森 sēn

75	Jōyō-1	U68EE
木	S12-4-8	F0635

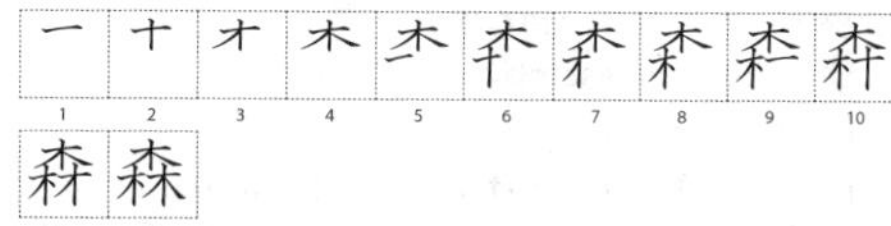

COMPOUNDS

❶ⓐ [original meaning] **THICK WOODS, forest**
ⓑ in close rows as trees in a forest, thickly wooded

a 森林 しんりん forest, woodland
b 森森 しんしん deeply forested
森羅万象 しんらばんしょう all creation, Nature

❷ⓐ solemn
ⓑ hushed, quiet

a 森厳な しんげんな solemn, grave
b 森閑とした しんかんとした quiet, still, silent as a graveyard

KUN

【もり 森】 [sometimes also 杜] **THICK WOODS, forest**
森の都 もりのみやこ tree-clad town
鎮守の森 ちんじゅのもり grove of the village shrine

SYNONYMS

❶ⓐ forest

林 FOREST, small woods → 1071
森 THICK WOODS → 3123
杜 GROVE → 1030

USAGE

【もり】

森
[sometimes also 杜] thick woods, forest

杜
[usu. 森] grove, small woods (esp. surrounding temples or shrines)

HOMOPHONES

もり 杜 GROVE → 1030

NOTE

➡ see also USAGE note at 林 1071

歯

3124

2-4-8

▶TOOTH

シ は

Ⓝ 齒 Ⓒ 齿 chǐ

211	Jōyō-3	U6B6F
歯	S12-12-0	F1065

radical variant → see 齒 at 3139

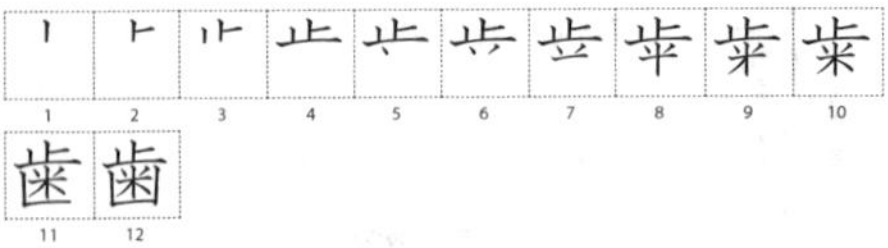

COMPOUNDS

❶ⓐ [original meaning] **TOOTH**

ⓑ something resembling a **TOOTH**

a 歯科 しか dentistry

歯石 しせき tartar (on teeth), dental calculus

抜歯 ばっし tooth extraction

永久歯 えいきゅうし permanent tooth

義歯 ぎし false tooth

b 鋸歯 きょし saw tooth

❷ age

年歯 ねんし age

INDEPENDENT

【しする 歯する】 join, become a member; fall in the same line

KUN

【は 歯】 [also prefix] **TOOTH;** (machine or tool element) **tooth, cog, dent**

歯磨(=歯磨き) はみがき toothpaste; brushing one's teeth

歯医者 はいしゃ dentist

歯ブラシ はぶらし toothbrush

歯向かう(=刃向かう) はむかう stand up to; oppose

歯痒×い はがゆい feel impatient; be irritating

歯切れの良い はぎれのよい crisp; clear and crisp (in speaking); piquant (manner)

歯車 はぐるま cog, toothed wheel

歯付ベルト はつきべると toothed belt

歯止め はどめ drag, pallet; brake

入れ歯 いれば dentures

虫歯 むしば decayed tooth

SYNONYMS

❶ⓐ **mouth parts**

唇 LIP → 3401

歯 TOOTH → 3124

舌 TONGUE → 2711

牙 FANG → 4243

NOTE

➡ see COMPOUND FORMATION for 唇歯輔車 しんしほしゃ → 輔 1963

歮

3125

2-4-8

▶**NOT GO SMOOTHLY**
▶**ASTRINGENT**

ジュウ しぶ しぶ(い) しぶ(る)

77	Nonstandard	U6B6E
止	S12-4-8	F0000

traditional form → see 渋 at 0625

舜

3126

2-4-8

▶**SHUN**

シュン ㊔ きよ みつ さとし あきら ひとし とし

136	Nonstandard	U821C
舛	S12-6-6	F0000

traditional form → see 舜 at 3134

爲

3127

2-4-8

▶**DO**
▶**SAKE**

イ ため¹ ため² な(る) な(す) す(る) な(さる)

87	Names	U7232
⺥	S12-4-8	F0000

traditional form → see 為 at 4395

爺

2-4-8

incorrect classification/stroke-count

➡ see 2-2-11: 八 at 2656

萃

2-4-8

incorrect stroke-count

➡ see 2-3-8: 艹 at 2882

葛

2-4-8

incorrect stroke-count

➡ see 2-3-8: 艹 at 2884

棄

2-4-8

incorrect classification/stroke-count

➡ see 2-2-11: 亠 at 2651

葬 茎

2-4-8

incorrect classification

➡ see 2-3-9: 艹 at 2901

黃

3128

2-4-8

▶**YELLOW**

コウ オウ き こ-

201	Names	U9EC3
黄	S12-12-0	F0000

traditional form → see 黄 at 3116

RADICAL

kiiro 'yellow' (黌×), used in characters related to the color yellow

---

貴

2-4-8

incorrect classification

➡ see 2-5-7: ⾉ at 3220

喬

3129

2-4-8

▶**TALL**

キョウ ㊔ たか たかし こう

Ⓒ 乔 qiáo

30	Names	U55AC
口	S12-3-9	F2815

COMPOUNDS

❶ **TALL**—said esp. of trees
喬木 きょうぼく tall tree, forest tree

❷ [archaic] boast
喬志 きょうし self-conceit, pride

SYNONYMS

❶ **high**
高 HIGH →2601
喬 TALL →3129
峻 high and steep →0495
峨 HIGH AND RUGGED →0493

暑

3130
2-4-9

▶**SUMMER HEAT**
▶**HOT**
ショ あつ(い)

72	Names	UFA43
日	S13-4-9	F0000

traditional form →see 暑 at 3121

歳

3131
2-4-9

▶**YEAR**
▶**AGE SUFFIX**
サイ セイ とし▲ ㊔ とせ
Ⓝ 歳 Ⓒ 岁 suì

77	Jōyō	U6B73
止	S13-4-9	F0268

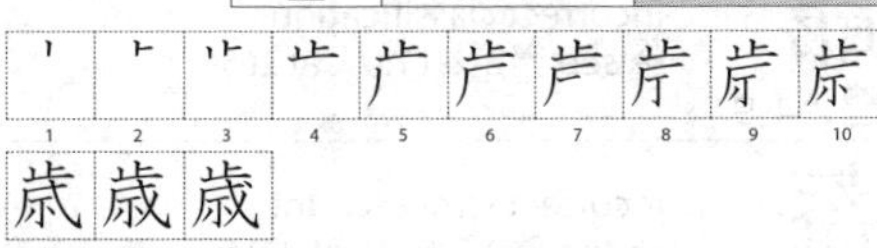

COMPOUNDS

❶ **YEAR**
歳末 さいまつ year end
歳費 さいひ annual expenditure
歳月 さいげつ time
歳入 さいにゅう revenue, annual income
歳暮 せいぼ end of the year; year-end present

❷ [also 才 さい 4218] **AGE SUFFIX**
一歳 いっさい one year old
何歳 なんさい how old, what age
万歳 ばんざい Banzai!/Hurrah!/Long live…!

❸ [rare] literary expression for Jupiter
歳星 さいせい Jupiter

KUN

【とし 歳】
ⓐ [now usu. 年] **YEAR**
ⓑ [also 年, sometimes also 齢] **one's YEARs, age**
b 歳を取る としをとる age, grow old

SPECIAL READINGS

二十歳(=二十) はたち 20 years old

SYNONYMS

❶ **year**
年 YEAR →2528
歳 YEAR →3131

❷ **age**
齢 AGE →2390
令 age →2489
年 years →2528
歳 AGE SUFFIX →3131
才 AGE SUFFIX →4218
寿 life span →4372

HOMOPHONES

とし
年 YEAR →2528
齢 AGE →2390

NOTE

➡ see USAGE note at 年 2528

歲

3132
2-4-9

▶**YEAR**
▶**AGE SUFFIX**
サイ セイ とし ㊔ とせ

77	Nonstandard	U6B72
止	S13-4-9	F0000

traditional form →see 歳 at 3131

愛

3133
2-4-9

▶**LOVE**
アイ いと(しい)▲ ㊔ まな あ なる めぐみ ちか よし
Ⓒ 爱 ài

61	Jōyō-4	U611B
心	S13-4-9	F0287

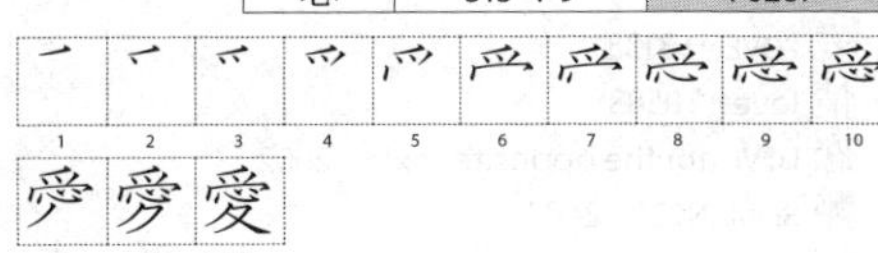

COMPOUNDS

❶ⓐ [also suffix] **LOVE, affection**
ⓑ *Buddhism* **LOVE**
a 愛情 あいじょう love, affection
愛憎 あいぞう love and hate
博愛 はくあい philanthropy
母性愛 ぼせいあい maternal love
同性愛 どうせいあい homosexual love, lesbianism
b 慈愛 じあい affection, love, benevolence

❷ⓐ **LOVE, have affection for**
ⓑ **LOVE (a person of the opposite sex), care deeply for**
a 愛児 あいじ one's beloved [favorite] child
愛犬家 あいけんか lover of dogs
愛国心 あいこくしん patriotism, nationalism

愛車 あいしゃ one's own car [bicycle]
愛妻 あいさい one's beloved wife
b 愛人 あいじん lover
愛欲 あいよく love and lust, sexual passion
恋愛 れんあい love (for the opposite sex)

❸ (have a strong liking for) **LOVE, like, be fond of**
愛好する あいこうする love, be fond of
愛用する あいようする use habitually
愛読する あいどくする read with pleasure
愛唱する あいしょうする love to sing

❹ⓐ be reluctant to part with
ⓑ cherish, treasure, hold dear
a 愛惜する あいせきする be reluctant (to part)
割愛する かつあいする part with (something), give up; omit (reluctantly)
b 愛護 あいご protection
自愛する じあいする take care of oneself

❺ used phonetically for *ai* in the transliteration of foreign words
愛蘭 あいるらんど Ireland

INDEPENDENT

【あい 愛】**LOVE, tender passion; charity**
神の愛 かみのあい divine love
【あいする 愛する】**LOVE, care for, be fond of**

KUN

【いとしい 愛しい】**darling, beloved, dear**

SPECIAL READINGS

愛媛県 えひめけん Ehime Prefecture

SYNONYMS

❶ **love**
愛 LOVE → 3133
情 love → 0583
恋 LOVE (for the opposite sex) → 2602
艶 ROMANCE → 2403
寵 AFFECTION → 3029

❷ & ❸ **love and like**
愛 LOVE → 3133
恋 LOVE (the opposite sex) → 2602
好 LIKE → 0240
慕 ADORE → 2970
惚れる FALL IN LOVE → 0584
玩 cherish → 1085

USAGE

【愛 あい 恋 れん】
★Though both 恋 and 愛 mean love, the former is mostly restricted to love between man and woman while the latter is a general term roughly equivalent to the English word *love*.

舜
3134
2-4-9

▶**SHUN**
シュン ㊔ きよ みつ さとし あきら ひとし とし
Ⓝ 舜 Ⓒ 舜 shùn

136 舛	Names	U821C
	S13-7-6	F2808

COMPOUNDS

● name of a legendary sage monarch in ancient China: **SHUN**
尭舜 ぎょうしゅん Yao and Shun (two of the most celebrated monarchs in ancient China)

INDEPENDENT

【しゅん 舜】name of a mythical holy emperor in ancient China

SYNONYMS

● **rulers**
君 RULER → 3974
王 KING → 4247
帝 EMPEROR → 2573
天 Heaven's messenger on earth → 4250
皇 EMPEROR → 3175
尭 YAO → 2560
舜 SHUN → 3134

爺
2-4-9
incorrect classification
➡ see 2-2-11: 八 at 2656

蓋
2-4-9
incorrect stroke-count
➡ see 2-3-9: 艹 at 2914

蓬
2-4-9
incorrect stroke-count
➡ see 2-3-10: 艹 at 2945

葦
2-4-9
incorrect stroke-count
➡ see 2-3-9: 艹 at 2917

棄
2-4-9
incorrect classification
➡ see 2-2-11: 亠 at 2651

誉
3135
2-4-9

▶**HONOR**
ヨ ほま(れ) ほ(める)▲ ㊔ たか たかし しげ
Ⓝ 譽 Ⓒ 誉 yù

149 言	Jōyō	U8A89
	S13-7-6	F1586

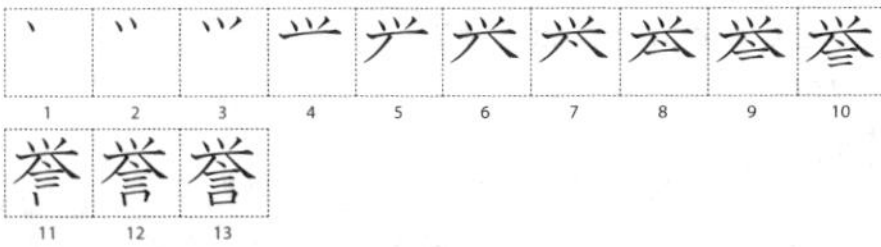

COMPOUNDS

❶ **HONOR, good reputation, fame, glory**

名誉 めいよ honor, glory; dignity
栄誉 えいよ honor, glory, distinction
声誉 せいよ fame, reputation, honor and distinction, credit

❷ praise

毀誉褒貶× きよほうへん praise and censure, criticisms

KUN

【ほまれ 誉れ】**HONOR, glory, fame**
国の誉れ くにのほまれ national glory
【ほめる 誉める】[usu. 褒める, sometimes also 賞める]
praise, commend, admire, compliment, eulogize
誉め称える ほめたたえる admire, applaud, praise

SYNONYMS

❶ **great respect**
栄 GLORY →3183
誉 HONOR →3135
光 honor →3043

❶ **repute**
声 reputation →2724
誉 HONOR →3135
名 NAME →2693
望 popularity →3408

HOMOPHONES

ほめる
賞 PRIZE →3237
褒 COMMEND →2662

NOTE

➡ see USAGE note at 褒 2662

蓬
2-4-10
incorrect stroke-count
➡ see 2-3-11: 艹 at 2973

蓑
2-4-10
incorrect stroke-count
➡ see 2-3-10: 艹 at 2941

蓬
2-4-10
incorrect stroke-count
➡ see 2-3-10: 艹 at 2945

蓮
2-4-10
incorrect stroke-count
➡ see 2-3-11: 艹 at 2979

蒋
2-4-10
incorrect stroke-count
➡ see 2-3-10: 艹 at 2947

夢
3136
2-4-10

▶**DREAM**
ム ゆめ

140	Nonstandard	U5922
艹	S14-4-10	F0000

traditional form →see 夢 at 2939

態熊
2-4-10
incorrect classification
➡ see 2-10-4: 能 at 3529

睿
3137
2-4-10

▶**PROFOUNDLY WISE**
エイ ㊔ さとし さとる あきら とおる まさ よし ただ とし

109	Nonstandard	U777F
目	S14-5-9	F0000

traditional form →see 叡 at 2405

暴
3138
2-4-11

▶**VIOLENT**
ボウ バク あば(く) あば(れる)
Ⓒ 暴 bào

72	Jōyō-5	U66B4
日	S15-4-11	F0812

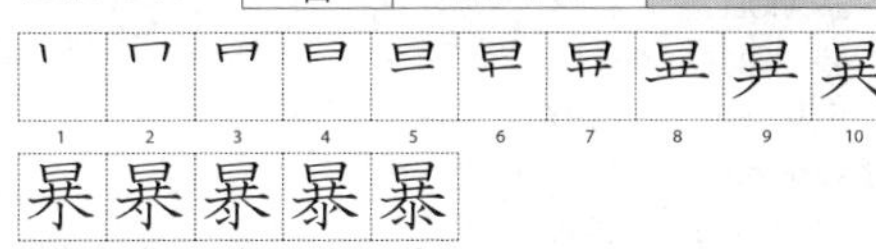

COMPOUNDS

❶ⓐ (acting with destructive force) **VIOLENT, rough, wild, cruel, harsh, tyrannical**
ⓑ **act VIOLENTly, rage about**

a 暴力 ぼうりょく violence, force
暴行 ぼうこう act of violence, assault
暴走 ぼうそう reckless driving; running wild
暴言 ぼうげん offensive [abusive] language
暴君 ぼうくん tyrant, despot
暴風 ぼうふう storm, violent wind
暴風雨 ぼうふうう tempest, rainstorm
乱暴 らんぼう violence, roughness; rape
横暴な おうぼうな arbitrary, tyrannical, despotic

b 暴動 ぼうどう riot, disturbance, uprising
暴徒 ぼうと rioters, mobsters, insurgents

❷ **sudden, abrupt**
暴落 ぼうらく slump, crash, heavy decline (in prices)
暴発 ぼうはつ spontaneous discharge, accidental gun discharge
暴騰 ぼうとう sudden (price) rise

日【止】艹 a 艹

❸ **unrestrained, inordinate, wild, excessive, irrational**
暴飲 ぼういん heavy drinking
暴利 ぼうり excessive profits, usury
❹ⓐ [formerly also 曝 ばく 1410] **disclose, divulge, expose**
ⓑ [original meaning, now archaic] expose to the sun
a 暴露 ばくろ exposure, disclosure
❺ strike with one's bare hands
暴虎馮×河 ぼうこひょうが foolhardy courage

INDEPENDENT

【ぼう 暴】violence

KUN

【あばく 暴く】[sometimes also 発く] **disclose (a secret), expose (a crime), lay bare, divulge**
秘密を暴く ひみつをあばく disclose a secret
【あばれる 暴れる】**act VIOLENTly, rage about**
暴れ回る あばれまわる rampage, run riot
暴れ出す あばれだす grow restive, begin to act violently
暴れ者 あばれもの rowdy, roughneck
暴れ馬 あばれうま restive horse, runaway

SYNONYMS

❶ⓐ **violent**
暴 VIOLENT → 3138
猛 FIERCE → 0653
荒い WILD → 2810
❷ **sudden**
急 SUDDEN → 2595
激 sudden → 0955
暴 sudden → 3138
俄 SUDDEN → 0106
頓 SUDDEN → 1320
勃 SUDDENLY → 1839
突 abruptly → 2772
❸ **rash**
滅 unreasonable → 0812
妄 RASH → 2509
盲 BLIND → 2547
暴 unrestrained → 3138
荒 WILD → 2810
濫 EXCESSIVE → 0990
乱 excessive → 1611
❹ⓐ **reveal**
発 reveal → 3174
露 EXPOSE → 3495
曝 EXPOSE → 1410
晒す EXPOSE → 1156
暴 disclose → 3138
披 OPEN OUT → 0362
顕 MANIFEST → 2274
現 cause to appear → 1218

USAGE

【あばく】
暴く
[sometimes also 発く] disclose (a secret), expose (a crime), lay bare, divulge
発く
[usu. 暴く] same as 暴く

HOMOPHONES

あばく 発 START → 3174

COMPOUND FORMATION

【暴虎馮×河 ぼうこひょうが】
暴虎馮×河 'foolhardy courage' refers to killing a tiger (虎) with one's bare hands (暴 ❺) and wading across (馮×) the river (河).

齒

3139

2-4-11

▶**TOOTH**

シ　は

211	Nonstandard	U9F52
齒	S15-15-0	F0000

traditional form → see 歯 at 3124

RADICAL

ha 'tooth' (齧×), used in characters related to teeth or actions using teeth
Left variants: 歯× 齒× *hahen* (齢 齠× 齶×)
Variant: 歯 *ha* (齢 齠× 齶×)

蓬
2-4-11
incorrect stroke-count
➡ see 2-3-11: 艹 at 2973

蔑
2-4-11
incorrect stroke-count
➡ see 2-3-11: 艹 at 2977

蔴
2-4-11
incorrect stroke-count
➡ see 2-3-11: 艹 at 2978

蓮
2-4-11
incorrect stroke-count
➡ see 2-3-11: 艹 at 2979

蔆
2-4-11
incorrect stroke-count
➡ see 2-3-11: 艹 at 2980

蔑

3140

2-4-11

▶**DESPISE**

ベツ　さげす(む)　ないがし(ろ)

140	Nonstandard	U8511
艹	S15-4-11	F0000

traditional form → see 蔑 at 2969

曇

3141

2-4-12

▶**CLOUDY**

ドン くも(る)

Ⓒ 昙 tán

72	Jōyō	U66C7
日	S16-4-12	F2035

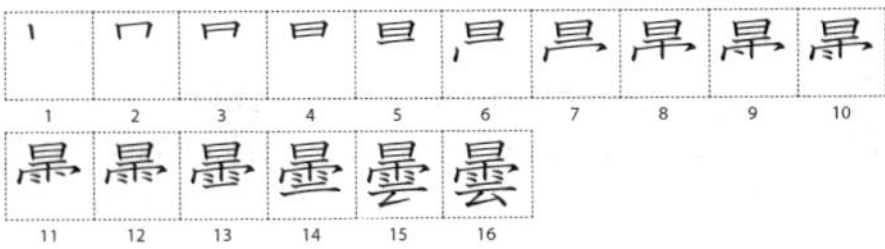

COMPOUNDS

❶ [original meaning] **CLOUDY**

曇天 どんてん cloudy weather

晴曇 せいどん fine and cloudy weather

KUN

【くもる 曇る】**cloud up, become CLOUDY; become dim, fog up, be blurred; be gloomy**

曇り(=曇) くもり cloudiness, cloudy weather

曇り空 くもりぞら cloudy sky [weather]

曇り勝ち くもりがち cloudy

曇りガラス くもりがらす frosted glass, stained glass

薄曇り うすぐもり slightly cloudy weather

花曇り はなぐもり cloudy weather in springtime

蔽

2-4-12

incorrect stroke-count

➡ see 2-3-12: 艹 at 2996

蔭

2-4-12

incorrect stroke-count

➡ see 2-3-12: 艹 at 2997

蕾

2-4-12

incorrect classification

➡ see 2-3-13: 艹 at 3006

燕

3142

2-4-12

▶**SWALLOW**

エン つばめ ㊔ やすし やす よし なる てる

Ⓒ 燕 yàn yān

86	Names	U71D5
灬	S16-4-12	F2501

COMPOUNDS

❶ **SWALLOW, martin**

燕尾服 えんびふく tailcoat

燕麦 えんばく wild oat, *Avena fatua*

燕雀 えんじゃく small birds

燕窩[×] えんか edible bird's nest

飛燕 ひえん swallow in flight

❷ name of an ancient Chinese state: Yan

燕京 えんけい(=えんきょう) Yanjing (old name for Beijing)

INDEPENDENT

【えん 燕】State of Yan

KUN

【つばめ 燕】

① **SWALLOW, martin**

燕の巣 つばめのす swallow's nest; edible bird's nest

雨燕 あまつばめ swift (bird); fork-tailed swift, *Apus pacificus*

海燕 うみつばめ storm petrel

紫燕 むらさきつばめ purple martin (bird); powdered oakblue (butterfly)

② **younger man involved with an older woman**

若い燕 わかいつばめ young lover of an older woman

SPECIAL READINGS

燕子花 かきつばた rabbit-ear iris, *Iris laevigata*

SYNONYMS

❶ **birds**

鷹 HAWK → 3955

鷗 GULL → 2370

烏 CROW → 4088

雀 SPARROW → 3117

燕 SWALLOW → 3142

鴻 LARGE WILD BIRD → 0977

鳳 MALE PHOENIX → 3749

凰 FEMALE PHOENIX → 3738

鵬 MYTHICAL HUGE BIRD → 1416

鶏 CHICKEN → 2221

酉 ROOSTER → 4358

隼 FALCON → 3427

鳩 PIGEON → 0184

鷲 EAGLE → 3598

鳶 BLACK KITE → 3919

鶴 CRANE → 2326

鷺 HERON → 3621

鵜 CORMORANT → 2067

鴨 DUCK → 1582

雁 WILD GOOSE → 3741

爵

3143

2-4-13

▶**RANK OF NOBILITY**

シャク

Ⓝ 爵 Ⓒ 爵 jué

87	Jōyō	U7235
爫	S17-4-13	F1271

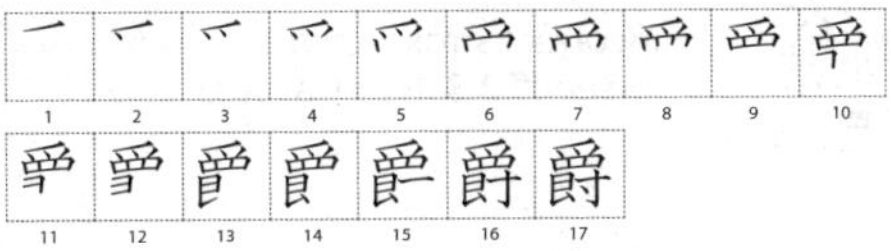

COMPOUNDS

❶ **RANK OF NOBILITY, peerage, court rank**

爵位 しゃくい rank of nobility
伯爵 はくしゃく count, earl
男爵 だんしゃく baron
授爵 じゅしゃく ennoblement

❷ [original meaning, now obsolete] ancient wine vessel with three legs and a loop handle

SYNONYMS

❶ **nobility**
爵 RANK OF NOBILITY →3143
公 nobleman →2468
侯 FEUDAL LORD →0109

舊 2-4-13
incorrect stroke-count
➡ see 2-3-14: 艹 at 3019

舊 2-4-13
incorrect stroke-count
➡ see 2-4-14: 艹 at 3145

爵
3144
2-4-14

▶RANK OF NOBILITY
シャク

87	Nonstandard	U7235
爫	S18-4-14	F0000

traditional form →see 爵 at 3143

藉 2-4-14
incorrect stroke-count
➡ see 2-3-14: 艹 at 3017

舊 2-4-14
incorrect stroke-count
➡ see 2-3-14: 艹 at 3019

薩 2-4-14
incorrect stroke-count
➡ see 2-3-14: 艹 at 3020

舊
3145
2-4-14

▶FORMER
キュウ

134	Nonstandard	U65E7
臼	S18-6-12	F0000

traditional form →see 旧 at 0014

蘆 2-4-16
incorrect stroke-count
➡ see 2-3-16: 艹 at 3034

蘊 2-4-16
incorrect stroke-count
➡ see 2-3-16: 艹 at 3035

丞
3146
2-5-1

▶AIDE
ジョウ ㊔ すけ すすむ つぐ
Ⓒ 丞 chéng

1	Names	U4E1E
一	S6-1-5	F1455

COMPOUNDS

ⓐ **AIDE, assistant officer (in ancient China)**
ⓑ [original meaning, now archaic] **aid, assist, help**
a 丞相 じょうしょう prime minister (in ancient China)

SYNONYMS

ⓐ **assistant**
補 assistant →1529
丞 AIDE →3146

男
3147
2-5-2

▶MAN
ダン ナン おとこ お▲
Ⓒ 男 nán

102	Jōyō-1	U7537
田	S7-5-2	F0084

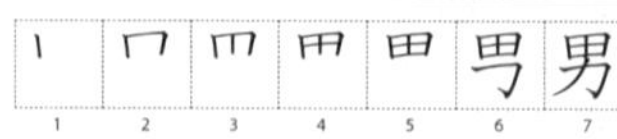

COMPOUNDS

❶ [original meaning] **MAN, male**
男子 だんし boy, young man, man
男性 だんせい male, man
男性的 だんせいてき masculine, manly
男女 だんじょ men and women, both sexes
男尊女卑 だんそんじょひ predominance of men over women, sexism
男児 だんじ boy, son; man
美男子 びだんし(=びなんし) handsome man
下男 げなん male servant, manservant

❷ **son**—used esp. to indicate order of birth
一男二女 いちなんにじょ one son and two daughters
長男 ちょうなん eldest son
三男 さんなん third son

❸ⓐ **baron**
ⓑ **title after names of barons**
a 男爵 だんしゃく baron
b 吉川男 よしかわだん Baron Yoshikawa

INDEPENDENT

【だん 男】*literary* **MAN**; son

KUN

【おとこ 男】**MAN, male; adult male; lover, paramour; manservant, fellow, guy; manliness, honor**
男らしい おとこらしい manly, masculine
男の子 おとこのこ boy, baby boy
男前 おとこまえ man's looks

男盛り おとこざかり prime of manhood
雪男 ゆきおとこ abominable snowman

【お 男】

① *elegant* **MAN, male**
男の子 おのこ man

② [in compounds] **the larger or stronger of two**
男滝(=雄滝) おだき the greater waterfall (of the two)
益荒男(=丈夫) ますらお manly [brave] man

SYNONYMS

❶ **man**
男 MAN → 3147
郎 YOUNG MAN → 1641
雄 MALE → 1271
牡 MALE → 1040
夫 male adult → 4271
翁 OLD MAN → 2611
爺 OLD MAN → 2656

❷ **offspring**
子 CHILD → 4196
仔 OFFSPRING → 0038
孤 orphan → 0426
嫡 LEGITIMATE CHILD → 0839
息 son → 3278
男 son → 3147
惣 eldest son → 3452
娘 DAUGHTER → 0488
女 daughter → 4226
姫 DAUGHTER OF NOBLE BIRTH → 0489

❸ **noblemen**
公 duke → 2468
侯 marquis → 0109
伯 COUNT → 0067
子 viscount → 4196
男 baron → 3147

HOMOPHONES

お
雄 MALE → 1271
牡 MALE → 1040

NOTE

➡ see USAGE note at 雄 1271
➡ see COMPOUND FORMATION for 男前 おとこまえ → 前 2819

甼 3148

2-5-2

▶**TOWN**
チョウ まち

102	Nonstandard	U753C
田	S7-5-2	F0000

traditional form → see 町 at 1430

皃 3149

2-5-2

▶**APPEARANCE**
ボウ かたち

106	Nonstandard	U7683
白	S7-5-2	F0000

traditional form → see 貌 at 1958

貝 3150

2-5-2

▶**SHELLFISH**
バイ▲ かい
Ⓒ 贝 bèi

154	Jōyō-1	U8C9D
貝	S7-7-0	F1850

1	2	3	4	5	6	7
丨	冂	冃	月	目	貝	貝

RADICAL

kai 'cowry' (買 貨 貴), used in characters related to valuables or money
Variant: 貝 × ***kaihen*** (財 貯 贈)

COMPOUNDS

❶ **SHELLFISH**
魚貝 ぎょばい fish and shellfish

❷ seashell, shell
貝独楽 ばいごま shell top

❸ [original meaning, now archaic] cowries used as currency in ancient China
貝貨 ばいか (ancient) shell money

INDEPENDENT

【ばい 貝】 kind of **SHELLFISH**

KUN

【かい 貝】

① [sometimes also 介] **SHELLFISH**
貝類 かいるい shellfish
貝柱 かいばしら adductor muscle
赤貝 あかがい arc shell
巻き貝 まきがい roll-shell; snail
魚貝類(=魚介類) ぎょかいるい marine products

② ⓐ **seashell, shell**
ⓑ trumpet shell
a 貝殻 かいがら shell
貝細工 かいざいく shellwork

SYNONYMS

❶ & 【かい】 ① **fish**
魚 FISH → 2636
貝 SHELLFISH → 3150

❷ & 【かい】 ② ⓐ **shells**
殻 SHELL (of any kind) → 1883
甲 SHELL (of animals) → 4293
貝 seashell → 3150
螺 SPIRAL-SHELLED GASTROPOD → 1799
瑚 CORAL → 1300

田白【目】禾穴立臼旧奴古𠮛𠮛𠮛丘此

HOMOPHONES

かい 介 MEDIATE →2463

見

▶SEE

ケン み(る) み(える) み(せる)

Ⓒ 见 jiàn

3151

2-5-2

147	Jōyō-1	U898B
見	S7-7-0	F0010

田 白 【目】 禾 穴 立 臼 旧 奴 古 当 骨 巨 丘 此

RADICAL

miru 'see' (視 覚 覧), used in characters related to seeing

COMPOUNDS

❶ⓐ [original meaning] **SEE, look at, observe**
ⓑ become SEEn, come into view, appear

a 見物 けんぶつ sightseeing, visit
見学 けんがく tour [field trip] for study and observation
見聞する けんぶんする experience, observe
拝見する はいけんする have the honor of seeing, see, look at, inspect
一見 いっけん a look, a glance; apparently
外見 がいけん outward appearance

b 見当 けんとう estimate, guess; aim
発見 はっけん discovery, revelation, detection
露見 ろけん discovery, detection, exposure

❷ (grant or be granted an audience) **SEE (someone), interview, give [be given] an audience**
会見 かいけん interview, audience
接見する せっけんする receive, give an interview
朝見 ちょうけん audience with the emperor

❸ view, personal opinion
見解 けんかい opinion, view
見地 けんち standpoint, viewpoint
意見 いけん opinion, view; admonition
偏見 へんけん prejudice, biased view, narrow view

INDEPENDENT

【けん 見】 view, opinion
皮相の見 ひそうのけん shallow view

KUN

【みる 見る】

①ⓐ **SEE, look (at), have a look**
ⓑ [sometimes also 観る] **view (flowers), watch (a movie), SEE, observe, appreciate**
ⓒ read (casually), skim through

a 見付ける みつける find (out), locate, spot, turn up
見付かる みつかる be found (out), be discovered, come to light; be caught
見出だす みいだす find out, discover
見本 みほん sample, specimen
見通し みとおし perspective, vista; prospect, outlook
見合い みあい meeting with a view to marriage; looking at each other
見当たる みあたる be found
見事(=美事)な みごとな splendid, admirable, beautiful
見送り みおくり seeing someone off
見上げる みあげる look up (at); look up to, respect
見下ろす みおろす look down; overlook
見直す みなおす reconsider, review; change one's opinion for the better; have another look
見比べる みくらべる compare (with one's eye), judge
見習う みならう learn (by observation), follow someone's example
見分け みわけ distinction; identification, recognition
見掛け みかけ looks, appearance
見渡す みわたす look out over
見落とす みおとす overlook, pass by; fail to notice
見詰める みつめる stare
見出し みだし headline, heading, caption; title; index
見舞い みまい inquiry (after a person's health); expression of sympathy; visit
見た目 みため outward appearance
見ず知らずの みずしらずの strange, unknown
見蕩×れる みとれる be fascinated by, look admiringly at
見窄らしい みすぼらしい shabby, poor-looking, miserable
見す見す みすみす before one's very eyes
見る見る みるみる in a moment [instant]
見方 みかた (point of) view, way of looking, viewpoint
見所 みどころ good point, merit; highlight
見晴らす みはらす command a view, look out onto
余所見する よそみする look away, take one's eyes off
脇見 わきみ looking aside

b 花見 はなみ flower [cherry blossom] viewing

② [sometimes also 視る] **look over, examine; look up, refer to**
見積もり みつもり estimate, assessment
見極める みきわめる see through, discern; ascertain, grasp
見届ける みとどける make sure, see with one's own eyes
下見 したみ preliminary inspection; preview
書類を見る しょるいをみる examine papers

③ **take (for), regard (as), judge, estimate**
見なす みなす regard as, presume

見込み みこみ hope, promise; prospect, possibility
見限る みかぎる give up, abandon; desert
見縊×る みくびる look down on, hold someone cheap

④ⓐ attend (to), manage
ⓑ [sometimes also 看る] **take care of, look after**

a 事務を見る じむをみる attend to business
b 面倒見が良い めんどうみがよい take good care of, be very helpful

⑤ experience, undergo
憂き目を見る うきめをみる have a bitter experience, have a hard time of it
血を見る争い ちをみるあらそい struggle with bloodshed

⑥ [following the TE-form of verbs]
ⓐ try (doing something), do and **SEE**
ⓑ [usu. in the form of 見ると] upon doing, when (the action is achieved), once

a やって見る やってみる try (to do)
聞いて見ましょう きいてみましょう Let's ask (him)
b 知って見ると詰まらない しってみるとつまらない When you know it, its charm is gone

【みえる 見える】 **be visible, be SEEn; look like, seem, appear;** [honorific] **come; be able to see**
見え みえ appearance
見栄 みえ [sometimes also 見え] show, ostentation, vanity
見得 みえ [sometimes also 見え] pose, posture
今夜は星が見える こんやはほしがみえる Stars can be seen tonight
若く見える わかくみえる look [seem] young
病気だと見える びょうきだとみえる seem to be sick
先生が見えた せんせいがみえた The teacher has come
夜でも見える目 よるでもみえるめ eyes capable of seeing in the dark

【みせる 見せる】 **show, let SEE, disclose, exhibit; make (a thing) look like, give an air of, pretend; make (a person) experience [understand];** [following the TE-form of verbs] **be determined to**
見せ物 みせもの show, exhibition
見せびらかす みせびらかす show off, display
見せ掛ける みせかける make (a thing) look like, pretend
見せしめ みせしめ lesson, warning
古く見せる ふるくみせる impart an ancient appearance
彼を負かして見せる かれをまかしてみせる I'll win him over

SYNONYMS

❶ⓐ see and look
見 SEE → 3151
看 WATCH → 3992
察 INSPECT → 2961
窺 WATCH FURTIVELY → 3002
瞥 GLANCE AT → 3592
目 look → 3777
観 VIEW → 2359
覧 LOOK OVER → 3538
眺 LOOK OUT OVER → 1503
望 LOOK AFAR → 3408
仰 LOOK UP → 0051
顧 LOOK BACK → 2394
視 REGARD → 1223

❷ meet
会 MEET → 2512
遇 ENCOUNTER → 3889
遭 MEET WITH → 3917
見 SEE → 3151
謁 BE GRANTED AN AUDIENCE → 1976
逢 MEET → 4002

❸ opinion
見 view (personal opinion) → 3151
観 VIEW (conception) → 2359
説 opinion → 1949
論 opinion → 1981

【みせる】
◯ **show**
示 SHOW → 2435
見せる show → 3151
呈 PRESENT → 2715

USAGE

❶【みる】

見る
①ⓐ see, look (at), have a look
ⓑ [sometimes also 観る] view (flowers), watch (a movie), see, observe, appreciate
ⓒ read (casually), skim through
② [sometimes also 視る] look over, examine; look up, refer to
③ take (for), regard (as), judge, estimate
④ⓐ attend (to), manage
ⓑ [sometimes also 看る] take care of, look after
⑤ experience, undergo
⑥ [following the TE-form of verbs]
ⓐ try (doing something), do and see
ⓑ [usu. in the form of 見ると] upon doing, when (the action is achieved), once

視る
[usu. 見る] look over, examine; look up, refer to

診る
examine (a patient)

観る
[usu. 見る] view (flowers), watch (a movie), see, observe, appreciate

田 白 目 【禾】 穴 立 臼 旧 奴 古 乢 呂 巨 丘 此

看る
[usu. 見る] take care of, look after

❷【みえ】

見え
① appearance
② [usu. 見栄] show, ostentation, vanity
③ [usu. 見得] pose, posture

見栄
[sometimes also 見え] show, ostentation, vanity

見得
[sometimes also 見え] pose, posture

HOMOPHONES

みる
- 観 VIEW → 2359
- 看 WATCH → 3992
- 診 EXAMINE A PATIENT → 1898
- 視 REGARD → 1223

NOTE

➡ see COMPOUND FORMATION for 見事(=美事) みごと →事 4384

秀 3152

2-5-2

▶EXCELLENT

シュウ ひい(でる) ㊔ ひで ひでし すぐる しげる さかえ みのる

Ⓒ 秀 xiù

115	Jōyō	U79C0
禾	S7-5-2	F0576

Stroke order: 1–7

COMPOUNDS

❶ EXCELLENT, supreme
- 秀逸 しゅういつ supreme excellence
- 秀歌 しゅうか excellent [superb] tanka, gem of tankas
- 秀麗な しゅうれいな graceful, beautiful, handsome
- 優秀な ゆうしゅうな excellent, superior, best

❷ genius, prodigy
- 秀才 しゅうさい (person of) genius
- 俊秀 しゅんしゅう genius, prodigy
- 閨×秀 けいしゅう accomplished lady

INDEPENDENT

【しゅう 秀】EXCELLENT (school mark), A

KUN

【ひいでる 秀でる】excel, surpass
- 英語に秀でる えいごにひいでる excel in English

SYNONYMS

❶ excellent and superior
- 優 SUPERIOR → 0200
- 絶 without match → 1711
- 卓 PROMINENT → 2561
- 快 splendid → 0289
- 妙 MARVELOUS → 0280
- 秀 EXCELLENT → 3152
- 英 DISTINGUISHED → 2782
- 尤 outstanding → 3755
- 傑 outstanding → 0175
- 穎 TALENTED → 2036
- 逸 exceptional → 3872
- 名 first-rate → 2693
- 上 of upper grade → 4212

❷ wise and talented persons
- 哲 sage → 3402
- 賢 wise man → 3518
- 博 DOCTOR → 0170
- 秀 genius → 3152
- 俊 BRILLIANT PERSON → 0117
- 才 person of talent → 4218
- 通 well-informed person → 3855

季 2-5-2
incorrect stroke-count
➡ see 2-5-3: 禾 at 3161

究 2-5-2
incorrect classification
➡ see 2-3-4: 宀 at 2729

辛 2-5-2
incorrect classification
➡ see 2-2-5: 亠 at 2531

兒 2-5-2
incorrect stroke-count
➡ see 2-6-2: 臼 at 3249

児 3153

2-5-2

▶CHILD

ジ ニ ご▲ -ご▲ -(っ)こ▲ ㊔ ちご

Ⓝ 兒 Ⓒ 儿 ér

10	Jōyō-4	U5150
儿	S7-2-5	F0774

Stroke order: 1–7

COMPOUNDS

❶ⓐ [also suffix] CHILD (of any age), youngster, youth
ⓑ [original meaning] small CHILD, infant
ⓒ (offspring of man) CHILD, son, daughter

a 児童 じどう child, juvenile
- 園児 えんじ kindergarten child
- 小児科 しょうにか (department of) pediatrics
- 健康児 けんこうじ healthy child
- 幼児 ようじ young child, infant
- 男児 だんじ boy, son; man

二歳児 にさいじ two-year old child
b 乳児 にゅうじ infant, baby, suckling
育児 いくじ infant rearing, nursing of children
胎児 たいじ embryo, fetus
c 児孫 じそん children and grandchildren; descendants
愛児 あいじ one's beloved [favorite] child

❷ [suffix] person
革命児 かくめいじ man of revolutionary temperament
熱血児 ねっけつじ hot-blooded man

KUN

【こ 児】 [now usu. 子] (boy or girl) **CHILD, kid, youngster**
良い児 いいこ good boy (or girl)
男の児 おとこのこ boy, baby boy

【-こ -児, -っこ -っ児】 [also -っこ] [usu. 子]
ⓐ person, performer of an action
ⓑ [suffix] native of a specific place
a 売り児 うりこ shopgirl, sales clerk

SPECIAL READINGS

稚児 ちご infant, child
鹿児島県 かごしまけん Kagoshima Prefecture

SYNONYMS

❶ **child**
児 CHILD (of any age) → 3153
子 CHILD → 4196
童 CHILD (young person) → 2639
幼 young child → 0222
坊 SONNY → 0274

HOMOPHONES

こ
子 CHILD → 4196
娘 DAUGHTER → 0488
仔 OFFSPRING → 0038
小 SMALL → 0007
-こ 子 CHILD → 4196

NOTE

➡ see USAGE note at 子 4196

努

3154
2-5-2

▶**EXERT**
ド つと(める) ㊔ **つとむ**
Ⓒ 努 nǔ

19	Jōyō-4	U52AA
力	S7-2-5	F1284

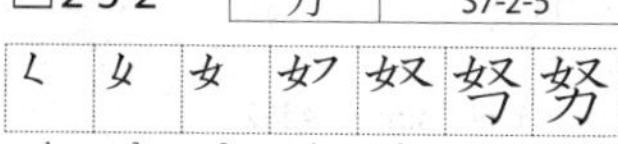

COMPOUNDS

● [original meaning] **EXERT (oneself), make efforts, endeavor**
努力 どりょく endeavor, effort, exertion
努力家 どりょくか hard worker
努力賞 どりょくしょう prize awarded for a person's effort

KUN

【つとめる 努める】 [sometimes also 勉める] **endeavor, make efforts, try hard, work diligently**
努めて つとめて with effort, as much as possible
極力努める きょくりょくつとめる do one's best

SYNONYMS

● **exert oneself**
努 EXERT → 3154
勉 ENDEAVOR → 4113
励 make efforts → 1438
勤 work diligently → 2287
尽 use all one's strength → 3786
精 put one's heart into → 1729
孜 MAKE DILIGENT EFFORTS → 0284

HOMOPHONES

つとめる
勉 ENDEAVOR → 4113
勤 SERVICE → 2287
務 DUTY → 1505

NOTE

➡ see USAGE note at 勤 2287

克

2-5-2

incorrect classification
➡ see 2-2-5: 十 at 2540

労

3155
2-5-2

▶**LABOR**
ロウ いたわ(る)▲ ねぎら(う)▲
Ⓝ 勞 Ⓒ 劳 láo

19	Jōyō-4	U52B4
力	S7-2-5	F0598

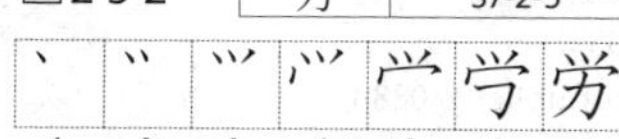

COMPOUNDS

❶ⓐ (work hard) **LABOR, toil, do manual work**
ⓑ (hard work) **LABOR, toil, work, trouble, pains**
a 労働 ろうどう (manual) labor, toil
労働者 ろうどうしゃ laborer, worker
労務 ろうむ labor, work, service
労力 ろうりょく trouble, labors, efforts
b 勤労 きんろう labor, work, service
苦労 くろう difficulties, trouble, hardships, labor

❷ abbrev. of 労働組合 ろうどうくみあい or 労働者 ろうどうしゃ: **workers' union, LABOR union, labor, laborer**
労資 ろうし capital and labor
労相 ろうしょう Labor Minister

田 白 目 禾 穴 立 臼 旧 奴 古 【学】 ⺕ 㠯 丘 此

田 白 目 禾 穴 立 臼 旧 奴 古 〔⺍〕 呉 巨 丘 此

国労 こくろう National Railway Workers' Union

❸ **fatigue, become fatigued**

疲労 ひろう fatigue

心労 しんろう cares, worries, anxiety

❹ meritorious deed, service

功労 こうろう meritorious deed, (distinguished) services

❺ express one's appreciation, reward, bring comfort to

慰労する いろうする acknowledge a person's services

❻ [formerly 撈 0908] drag for, dredge up, fish for

漁労 ぎょろう fishing, fishery

INDEPENDENT

【ろう 労】LABOR, trouble, service

労を謝する ろうをしゃする thank a person for his [her] trouble

【ろうする 労する】LABOR, exert oneself, toil

KUN

【いたわる 労る】

①ⓐ be kind to, be considerate of; sympathize with, console

ⓑ express one's appreciation

② take good care of, care for, nurse, tend

【ねぎらう 労う】express one's appreciation, reward, bring comfort to

SYNONYMS

❶ⓐ **work**

働 WORK → 0172

稼 WORK (for a living) → 1572

労 LABOR → 3155

勤める serve (in an office) → 2287

仕 SERVE → 0037

ⓑ **work and employment**

務 DUTY → 1505

任 OFFICE → 0057

役 SERVICE (esp. public) → 0288

勤 SERVICE (employment) → 2287

業 WORK → 3227

職 EMPLOYMENT → 1803

労 LABOR → 3155

❷ **organized bodies**

会 SOCIETY → 2512

協 association → 0103

団 BODY → 3791

体 BODY → 0080

組 union → 1693

労 workers' union → 3155

連 federation → 3849

講 fraternity → 2046

院 INSTITUTION → 0544

❸ **tire**

疲 TIRED → 4063

労 fatigue → 3155

倦 TIRE OF → 0131

厭 TIRE OF → 3745

学 incorrect stroke-count
➡ see 2-5-3: ⺍ at 3162

2-5-2

呉

3156

2-5-2

▶**KINGDOM OF WU**

ゴ く(れる)▲ ㊔ くれ

Ⓝ 呉 Ⓒ 吴 wú

30	Jōyō	U5449
口	S7-3-4	F1517

1 2 3 4 5 6 7

COMPOUNDS

❶ **KINGDOM OF WU, name of an ancient Chinese state in the Three Kingdom period (220-280 A.D.)**

呉国 ごこく Kingdom of Wu

呉音 ごおん Wu reading of Chinese characters

呉越 ごえつ Wu and Yue, two rival states in ancient China

呉越同舟 ごえつどうしゅう bitter enemies in the same boat

❷ **originating from China or the Chinese mainland**

呉服 ごふく dry goods; drapery

呉須 ごす asbolite; *gosu* porcelain

INDEPENDENT

【ご 呉】KINGDOM OF WU

KUN

【くれる 呉れる】give (to the speaker); give (to an inferior, animal or plant); [following the TE-form of verbs] do something for (the benefit of the speaker)

呉れ呉れも宜しく くれぐれもよろしく Give my best regards to (her)

それを呉れ それをくれ Give it to me

乞食に金を呉れてやる こじきにかねをくれてやる give money to a beggar

彼が仕事をして呉れた かれがしごとをしてくれた He did the work for me

SYNONYMS

❶ **China**

華 CHINA → 2841

漢 CHINESE → 0808

支 China → 2473

中 People's Republic of China → 4262

胡 NATIVES OF ANCIENT CHINA → 1467

台 Taiwan → 2498

唐 Cathay → 3867

【目】禾穴立西占𡿨巨丘臿𦘒夫

呉 KINGDOM OF WU →3156

【くれる】

◯ **give**

与 GIVE →4229

呈 PRESENT →2715

進 present to a superior →3873

上 give (to superior or others) →4212

下 give (to inferior or speaker) →4186

呉れる give (to speaker) →3156

授 CONFER →0595

賜 DEIGN TO GIVE →1994

贈 PRESENT A GIFT →2064

賄 BRIBE →1931

賂 BRIBE →1930

長

3157

2-5-2

▶LONG
▶CHIEF

チョウ なが(い) ㊔ おさ ながし おさむ つかさ すすむ たけ ひさ

168	Nonstandard	U9578
長	S7-7-0	F0000

alternative form →see 長 at 3163
radical variant →see 長 at 3163

兵

3158

2-5-2

▶SOLDIER

ヘイ ヒョウ ㊔ たけ

Ⓒ 兵 bīng

12	Jōyō-4	U5175
八	S7-2-5	F0171

1	2	3	4	5	6	7
ノ	𠂉	𠂒	斤	丘	乒	兵

COMPOUNDS

❶ⓐ [also suffix] **SOLDIER, private, rank and file**

ⓑ [suffix] (rank of) private

a 兵士 へいし soldier

兵卒 へいそつ private, common soldier

兵隊 へいたい soldier; troops

兵舎 へいしゃ barracks

カナダ兵 かなだへい Canadian soldier

騎兵 きへい cavalry soldier, cavalry

b 上等兵 じょうとうへい private first class

❷ⓐ **the military, army, SOLDIERy**

ⓑ military, military science

a 兵事 へいじ military affairs

兵役 へいえき military service

兵糧 ひょうろう army provisions, food

徴兵 ちょうへい conscription, enlistment, draft

b 兵学 へいがく military science, strategy, tactics

兵法 ひょうほう(=へいほう) art of war, strategy

❸ **weapons, arms; sword**

兵器 へいき arms, weapon, ordnance

造兵 ぞうへい manufacture of arms

白兵 はくへい unsheathed sword

❹ war, battle

兵備 へいび war preparations

兵禍 へいか ravages of war

INDEPENDENT

【へい 兵】**SOLDIER**; troops, army

兵を向ける へいをむける send an army

SYNONYMS

❶ **soldiers and warriors**

兵 SOLDIER →3158

卒 private →2549

士 MILITARY MAN →4213

武 warrior →3979

侍 SAMURAI →0094

❷ⓐ **armed forces**

軍 ARMY →2582

兵 the military →3158

勢 forces →3542

隊 PARTY →0762

ⓑ **military**

武 MILITARY →3979

兵 military →3158

些

2-5-2

incorrect stroke-count
➡ see 2-6-2: 此 at 3251

具

3159

2-5-3

▶IMPLEMENT

グ そな(える)▲ そな(わる)▲ ㊔ とも く

Ⓝ 具 Ⓒ 具 jù

12	Jōyō-3	U5177
八	S8-2-6	F0628

1	2	3	4	5	6	7	8
丨	冂	月	目	目	且	具	具

COMPOUNDS

❶ [also suffix]

ⓐ (utensil for work) **IMPLEMENT, tool, utensil**

ⓑ (article serving to equip) **IMPLEMENT, equipment, gear, fittings, fixtures, outfit**

a 道具 どうぐ tool, utensil, implement; furniture; theatrical appurtenances; tool, means; ingredient

器具 きぐ utensil, implement, appliance

用具 ようぐ tool, instrument, appliance; outfit

工具 こうぐ tool, implement

治具 じぐ jig

絵の具 えのぐ coloring materials, colors, oils, paint

文房具 ぶんぼうぐ stationery, writing materials

b 家具 かぐ furniture

寝具 しんぐ bedclothes, bedding

仏具 ぶつぐ Buddhist altar fittings
筆記具 ひっきぐ writing materials
装身具 そうしんぐ personal ornaments [outfit]

❷ [original meaning] **possess, be possessed of, be endowed with**
具備する ぐびする be endowed [equipped] with, possess
具象する ぐしょうする embody, express concretely
具体的な ぐたいてきな concrete, definite, specific
具足 ぐそく completeness; armor, coat of mail

❸ in detail, fully
具申書 ぐしんしょ full [detailed] report
具陳 ぐちん formal statement
具現 ぐげん incarnation, embodiment

❹ counter for sets of articles, as suits of armor
鎧一具 よろいいちぐ a suit of armor

❺ **unclassified compounds**
具合(=工合) ぐあい condition, state; health; manner, way

INDEPENDENT

【ぐ 具】 tool, means; ingredient
具の無いスープ ぐのないすーぷ soup with no ingredients
政争の具とする せいそうのぐとする make a political issue of (something)
寿司の具 すしのぐ ingredients for sushi

【ぐする 具する(=倶する)】 possess; take (retainers) with (one), be followed by

KUN

【そなえる 具える】 [also 備える] possess, be endowed with

【そなわる 具わる】 [also 備わる] be possessed of, be endowed with

SYNONYMS

❶ **machines and tools**
機 MACHINE → 1365
械 MECHANICAL CONTRIVANCE → 1203
具 IMPLEMENT → 3159
器 INSTRUMENT → 3367
儀 measuring instrument → 0191
鏡 OPTICAL INSTRUMENT → 2219
董 OLD TOOL → 2911

❷ **possess**
有 HAVE → 3703
蔵 own → 2995
持 HOLD → 0447
属 BELONG TO → 3901
享 ENJOY → 2545
具 possess → 3159

NOTE

➡ see COMPOUND FORMATION for
治具 じぐ → 治 0393
文房具 ぶんぼうぐ → 房 2445
道具 どうぐ → 道 3888

委

3160

2-5-3

▶**COMMIT**
イ ゆだ(ねる)
Ⓒ 委 wěi wēi

38	Jōyō-3	U59D4
女	S8-3-5	F0720

COMPOUNDS

❶ [original meaning] **COMMIT, entrust, leave to, delegate**
委員会 いいんかい committee
委託する いたくする entrust with, charge with, consign
委任する いにんする entrust, delegate, commit
委嘱する いしょくする charge, commission [entrust] with

❷ abbrev. of 委員 いいん or 委員会 いいんかい: **COMMITteeperson, committee**
教委 きょうい Board of Education
中労委(=中央労働委員会) ちゅうろういい(=ちゅうおうろうどういいんかい) Central Labor Relations Committee

❸ details
委細 いさい details, particulars
委曲 いきょく details, circumstances

❹ [also 萎 2872] wither, weaken, decline
委縮 いしゅく withering, atrophy; being crestfallen

❺ abandon
委棄 いき waiver

INDEPENDENT

【いする 委する】 **COMMIT**, entrust, delegate

KUN

【ゆだねる 委ねる】 **COMMIT, entrust, leave to, delegate; give [yield] oneself to**
全権を委ねる ぜんけんをゆだねる entrust (a person) with power of attorney (to do something for one)
激情に身を委ねる げきじょうにみをゆだねる yield oneself to passion

SYNONYMS

❶ **commit**
託 ENTRUST → 1845
托 ENTRUST → 0252
預 DEPOSIT → 1317
委 COMMIT → 3160
任 LEAVE TO → 0057
嘱 CHARGE WITH → 0881

季

▶SEASON

キ ㊔ すえ とし ひで

Ⓒ 季 jì

3161

2-5-3

39	Jōyō-4	U5B63
子	S8-3-5	F1102

COMPOUNDS

❶ⓐ (division of the year) **SEASON, quarter**
ⓑ (period of time) **SEASON**

a 季節 きせつ season
季候 きこう season
季刊 きかん quarterly publication
夏季 かき summer, summer season
四季 しき the four seasons
b 年季 ねんき one's term of service
雨季(=雨期) うき rainy season

❷ **feature of a SEASON term in haiku poetry, season word**
季語 きご season word (in haiku)

❸ [archaic] youngest or fourth-born child
季子 きし last child

❹ end of a period
季春 きしゅん late spring

INDEPENDENT

【き 季】**SEASON**

SYNONYMS

❶ **time periods**
時 TIME → 1155
季 SEASON (quarter) → 3161
候 SEASON (time of year) → 0133
頃 TIME → 0163
暇 FREE TIME → 1275
般 period of time → 1670
刻 POINT OF TIME → 1619
間 INTERVAL → 4122
隙 GAP → 0826
期 TERM → 2139
節 SEASON → 3336

NOTE

★ do not confuse with 李 PLUM → 3050

秀 2-5-3
incorrect stroke-count
➡ see 2-5-2: 禾 at 3152

空突 etc. 2-5-3
incorrect classification
➡ see 2-3-5: 穴 at 2761

辛 2-5-3
incorrect classification
➡ see 2-2-6: 亠 at 2551

要 2-5-3
incorrect stroke-count
➡ see 2-6-3: 襾 at 3262

桌 2-5-3
incorrect classification
➡ see 2-2-6: ⺊ at 2562

学

▶STUDY
▶EDUCATIONAL INSTITUTION

ガク まな(ぶ)

Ⓝ 學 斈◇ 斅◇ Ⓒ 学 xué

3162

2-5-3

39	Jōyō-1	U5B66
子	S8-3-5	F0047

COMPOUNDS

❶ **STUDY, learn**
学習する がくしゅうする study, learn
学力 がくりょく scholarship, scholastic ability
独学 どくがく self-study, self-teaching
留学 りゅうがく studying abroad
見学 けんがく tour [field trip] for study and observation

❷ⓐ [also suffix] **branch of STUDY, -ology**
ⓑ **learning, STUDY, education, scholarship, knowledge, science**

a 文学 ぶんがく literature, letters
医学 いがく medical science, medicine
数学 すうがく mathematics
化学 かがく chemistry
物理学 ぶつりがく physics, physical science
b 学問 がくもん learning, study
学会 がっかい institute, academy, learned society; meeting of a research organization
学識 がくしき learning, scholarship
学芸 がくげい arts and sciences; culture
学術 がくじゅつ science, learning; arts and sciences

❸ [original meaning] **EDUCATIONAL INSTITUTION, school, university, academy**
学園 がくえん educational institution, school
学校 がっこう school, college
学院 がくいん institute, academy
学長 がくちょう college president, rector; dean
学年 がくねん school year, grade
小学校 しょうがっこう elementary [primary] school
中学 ちゅうがく junior high school
大学 だいがく university, college

私学 しがく private [nongovernmental] school [college, university]
通学する つうがくする attend [go to] school
入学する にゅうがくする enter a school, matriculate

❹ **scholar, student**
学究 がっきゅう scholar, student
学生 がくせい student
学者 がくしゃ scholar, learned man
学割 がくわり student discount
学界 がっかい academic circles [world]
先学 せんがく scholars of the past, senior scholar
宿学 しゅくがく renowned scholar
後学 こうがく junior scholar; future reference
篤学 とくがく love of learning, devotion to one's studies

INDEPENDENT

【がく 学】**studies, learning**
学が有る がくがある have learning, be educated
学の独立 がくのどくりつ freedom of learning

KUN

【まなぶ 学ぶ】**learn, STUDY, take lessons**
学び まなび learning, study

SYNONYMS

❶ **learn and study**
学 STUDY → 3162
考 study → 3962
習 LEARN → 3306
研 RESEARCH → 1456
究 STUDY EXHAUSTIVELY → 2729
攻 specialize → 0286

❷ⓐ **branch of study**
科 SUBJECT OF STUDY → 1463
学 branch of study → 3162
門 field → 1100

ⓑ **learning and knowledge**
業 studies → 3227
学 learning → 3162
文 culture → 2458
識 KNOWLEDGE → 2070
知 knowledge → 1446

❸ **schools**
校 SCHOOL → 1166
学 EDUCATIONAL INSTITUTION → 3162
院 INSTITUTION → 0544
塾 PRIVATE SCHOOL → 3546
大 UNIVERSITY → 4224
高 high school → 2601
中 junior high school → 4262
小 elementary school → 0007
園 kindergarten → 3914

❹ **students and followers**
生 STUDENT → 4309
卒 graduate student → 2549
学 scholar → 3162
門 pupil → 1100
弟 disciple → 2537
徒 FOLLOWER → 0499

NOTE

➡ see COMPOUND FORMATION for 幾何学 きかがく → 何 0073

長

3163

2-5-3

▶**LONG**
▶**CHIEF**

チョウ なが(い) ㊔ おさ ながし おさむ つかさ すすむ たけ ひさ

Ⓝ 镸◇ Ⓒ 长 cháng zhǎng

168	Jōyō-2	U9577
長	S8-8-0	F0040

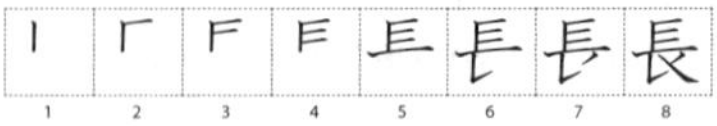

RADICAL

nagai 'long', used in characters related to longness
Left variant: 镸 ***nagai***

COMPOUNDS

❶ⓐ [also prefix] (of considerable extent) **LONG**
ⓑ **length**
ⓒ **tall**

a 長編 ちょうへん long piece, full-length work (as of a novel or a film)
長打 ちょうだ long hit
長距離 ちょうきょり long distance
長大な ちょうだいな long and massive; tall and stout

b 身長 しんちょう stature, height
測長機 そくちょうき length measuring machine

c 長身 ちょうしん tall figure, high stature

❷ [also prefix] (of considerable duration) **LONG**
長期 ちょうき long period
長寿 ちょうじゅ long life, longevity
長時間 ちょうじかん long time

❸ **grow (up), develop, prolong**
成長 せいちょう growth
延長 えんちょう extension, prolongation, continuation

❹ [also suffix] **CHIEF, head, president, director, chairman**
長官 ちょうかん director, administrator, chief
課長 かちょう section chief [head]
市長 しちょう mayor
船長 せんちょう (ship) captain
社長 しゃちょう president (of a company)

会長 かいちょう president (of a society)
議長 ぎちょう chairman, president (of the senate)
酋×長 しゅうちょう chieftain
裁判長 さいばんちょう presiding [chief] judge

❺ **strong point, merit, advantage, superiority**
長所 ちょうしょ strong point, merit
特長 とくちょう strong point, forte
一長一短 いっちょういったん merits and demerits, strong and weak points

❻ **eldest, older; old, senior**
長男 ちょうなん eldest son
長女 ちょうじょ eldest daughter
年長 ねんちょう seniority

❼ useless, wasteful
長物 ちょうぶつ useless thing, white elephant

❽ *music* major
長調 ちょうちょう major key
長音階 ちょうおんかい major scale

❾ abbrev. of 長門 ながと, old name for western Yamaguchi Prefecture
長州 ちょうしゅう Choshu, Nagato
薩長 さっちょう Satsuma and Choshu

INDEPENDENT

【ちょう 長】**CHIEF, head, leader; strong point, merit; superiority**
一家の長 いっかのちょう head of a family
. . . より一日の長が有る …よりいちじつのちょうがある be ahead of (someone)

【ちょうずる(=ちょうじる) 長ずる(=長じる)】grow; be older; excel

KUN

【ながい 長い】
ⓐ (of considerable extent) **LONG, lengthy, prolonged**
ⓑ (of considerable duration) **LONG**

a 長さ ながさ length
長袖 ながそで clothes with long sleeves
b 長らく ながらく for a long time
長引く ながびく be prolonged, drag on
長持ちする ながもちする last [keep] long, endure
長続きする ながつづきする last for a long time
長話をする ながばなしをする have a long talk

SPECIAL READINGS

長閑な▲ のどかな tranquil, peaceful

SYNONYMS

❷ **of long duration**
長 LONG →3163
永 ETERNAL →2436
久 OF LONG DURATION →4191
恒 permanent →0438

❸ **grow**
成 grow up →4352
長 grow (up) →3163
生 grow →4309
育 grow →2544
発 develop →3174
伸 expand →0079
展 UNFOLD →3862

❹ **leaders**
主 MASTER →2437
王 KING →4247
長 CHIEF →3163
頭 HEAD →2019
首 LEADER →2818
領 leader →1567
魁 LEADER →4125

USAGE

【ながい】
長い
ⓐ (of considerable extent) **long, lengthy, prolonged**
ⓑ (of considerable duration) **long**
永い
(lasting forever) **eternal, everlasting, long**

HOMOPHONES

ながい 永 ETERNAL →2436

岳

3164
2-5-3

▸**HIGH MOUNTAIN**
ガク たけ ㊔ たか おか
Ⓝ 嶽 Ⓒ 岳 yuè

46	Jōyō	U5CB3
山	S8-3-5	F1528

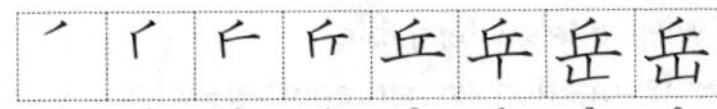

COMPOUNDS

❶ **HIGH MOUNTAIN, mountain, peak**
岳友会 がくゆうかい mountaineering club
山岳 さんがく mountains

❷ Mt. Fuji
岳麓 がくろく foot of Mt. Fuji
富岳 ふがく Mt. Fuji

❸ wife's father, father-in-law
岳父 がくふ one's wife's father

KUN

【たけ 岳】**HIGH MOUNTAIN, mountain, peak; suffix after names of mountains**
浅間の岳 あさまのたけ Mt. Asama
朝日岳 あさひだけ Mt. Asahi

SYNONYMS

❶ **mountains**
峰 PEAK →0494

岳 HIGH MOUNTAIN → 3164
山 MOUNTAIN → 3658

兎

3165 2-5-3

▶**RABBIT**

ト うさぎ ㊔ う うさ

10	Nonstandard	U514E
儿	S8-2-6	F0000

alternative form → see 兎 at 4374

兎

2-5-3

incorrect classification
➡ see 4-7-4 at 4374

妻

3166 2-5-3

▶**WIFE**

サイ つま

ⓒ 妻 qī

38	Jōyō-5	U59BB
女	S8-3-5	F0531

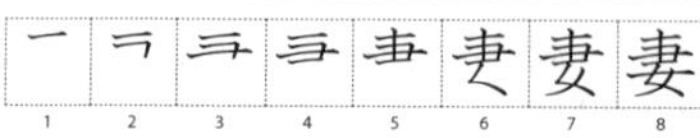

COMPOUNDS

● [original meaning] **WIFE**

妻子 さいし one's wife and children, one's family
夫妻 ふさい husband and wife, Mr. and Mrs., married couple
恐妻家 きょうさいか henpecked husband, man bossed by his wife
正妻 せいさい lawful [legal] wife

INDEPENDENT

【さい 妻】**WIFE**, my wife

KUN

【つま 妻】**WIFE, one's wife; gable**

人妻 ひとづま married woman, another's wife
稲妻 いなずま lightning
切妻 きりづま gable

SYNONYMS

● **wives**

妻 WIFE → 3166
奥 wife → 3503
内 wife → 4277
室 wife (esp. of persons of rank) → 2802
嫡 legitimate wife → 0839
婦 married woman → 0565
嫁 BRIDE → 0780
寡 widow → 2957

NOTE

➡ see COMPOUND FORMATION for 稲妻 いなずま → 稲 1561

奉

3167 2-5-3

▶**DEDICATE**

ホウ ブ たてまつ(る) ㊔ とも

ⓒ 奉 fèng

37	Jōyō	U5949
大	S8-3-5	F0921

COMPOUNDS

❶ [original meaning] **DEDICATE (esp. to a deity), offer, present, proffer**

奉納する ほうのうする dedicate (to a deity), offer
奉呈する ほうていする dedicate, present, offer (to a high personage)
奉献する ほうけんする offer (to a shrine)
奉加 ほうが donation
奉幣 ほうへい offering a wand with hemp and paper streamers to a Shinto god
奉灯 ほうとう dedicated lantern

❷ⓐ **reverentially, respectfully, humbly**—honorific term expressing respect toward the person addressed, esp. the emperor of Japan

ⓑ **serve reverentially, serve under (a master)**

a 奉読する ほうどくする read reverentially
奉還 ほうかん restoration to the emperor
奉答 ほうとう reply to the Throne
奉賀 ほうが respectful congratulation

b 奉仕する ほうしする attend, serve
奉公 ほうこう public duty [service]; domestic service, apprenticeship
奉職する ほうしょくする be in the service of

❸ obey reverentially, accept humbly

奉行 ぶぎょう magistrate, chief of an administrative department
信奉する しんぽうする believe in, have faith
遵奉(=順奉)する じゅんぽうする observe, obey, follow
供奉 ぐぶ attendance (on the emperor in his travels); attendant

❹ [formerly 捧 ほう 0594] hold in both hands

奉持する ほうじする hold up, bear

INDEPENDENT

【ほうじる(=ほうずる) 奉じる(=奉ずる)】**DEDICATE** (esp. to a deity), offer [present] respectfully; obey reverentially, accept humbly; hold in both hands

神前に舞を奉じる しんぜんにまいをほうじる dedicate a dance to a god
命を奉じる めいをほうじる obey orders
キリスト教を奉じる きりすときょうをほうじる believe in Christianity
国旗を奉じる こっきをほうじる hold up the national flag

KUN

【たてまつる 奉る】

① [honorific] **DEDICATE, offer [present] respectfully**

国王に書を奉る こくおうにしょをたてまつる address a memorial to the King

② revere at a distance

長老として奉る ちょうろうとしてたてまつる revere (a person) as one's leader; kick (a person) upstairs

③ [in compounds] do respectfully

無事の御帰国を謹んで賀し奉ります ぶじのごきこくをつつしんでがしたてまつります We respectfully tender our congratulations on your safe return home

SYNONYMS

❶ **offer**

供 OFFER (to a person or god) → 0098
献 OFFER (esp. to a superior) → 2240
納 offer (as to a god) → 1652
提 PRESENT → 0720
貢 offer tribute → 2838
奉 DEDICATE → 3167
捧 OFFER RESPECTFULLY → 0594

❷ **respectful**

恭 RESPECTFUL → 3109
謹 RESPECTFULLY → 2045
奉 reverentially → 3167
拝 HUMBLY → 0360

某

3168

2-5-4

▶A CERTAIN

ボウ なにがし▲

Ⓒ 某 mǒu

75	Jōyō	U67D0
木	S9-4-5	F1982

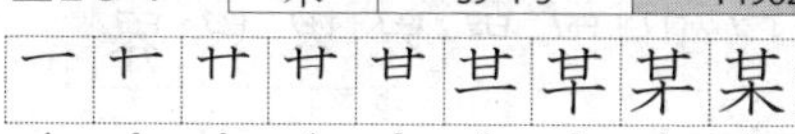

COMPOUNDS

ⓐ [also prefix] **A CERTAIN, one**

ⓑ [suffix] **A CERTAIN** person

a 某日 ぼうじつ a certain day
某氏 ぼうし a certain person
某国 ぼうこく a certain country
某女 ぼうじょ Ms. So-and-so
某某 ぼうぼう so-and-so
某所 ぼうしょ a certain place
某高校 ぼうこうこう a certain high school
某博士 ぼうはかせ Dr. X
b 山田某 やまだぼう a certain Mr. Yamada

INDEPENDENT

【ぼう 某】**A CERTAIN** person

某の仕業 ぼうのしわざ the work [doings] of so-and-so

KUN

【なにがし 某】**A CERTAIN** person; some (amount)

某かの金 なにがしかのかね some money, a certain sum of money
山田某 やまだなにがし a certain Mr. Yamada

SYNONYMS

ⓐ **a certain**

某 A CERTAIN → 3168
或る A CERTAIN → 3978
一 ONE → 4148

毘

3169

2-5-4

▶PHONETIC [bi]

ヒ ビ ㊔ のぶ よし やす まさ とも てる ひで たる すけ

Ⓝ 毗 Ⓒ 毗 pí

81	Names	U6BD8
比	S9-4-5	F2789

COMPOUNDS

❶ **used PHONETICally for *bi*, esp. in the transliteration of Sanskrit Buddhist terms**

毘沙門天 びしゃもんてん *Vaiśravaṇ*
毘盧×遮那仏 びるしゃなぶつ *Vairocana-Buddha*
金毘羅 こんぴら guardian deity of seafaring
荼×毘 だび cremation
大直毘神 おおなおびのかみ Great God of Restoration

❷ [archaic] help, assist

❸ [original meaning, now archaic] navel

SYNONYMS

❶ **phonetic [b]**

毘 PHONETIC [bi] → 3169
菩 PHONETIC [bo] → 2868

畏

3170

2-5-4

▶BE OVERAWED

イ おそ(れる) かしこ(まる)▲ かしこ(い)▲

Ⓒ 畏 wèi

102	Jōyō	U754F
田	S9-5-4	F2306

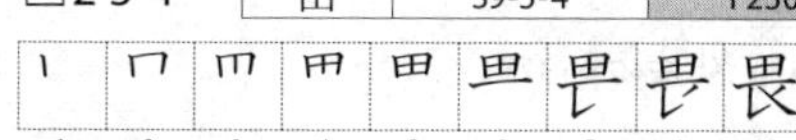

COMPOUNDS

❶ [original meaning] **BE OVERAWED, stand in awe, fear**

畏怖 いふ awe, fear, dread, fright
畏縮する いしゅくする shrink, flinch, wince
畏懼× いく reverence, awe, fear
畏服 いふく awed submission

❷ **respect, revere**

畏友 いゆう one's respected friend
畏敬 いけい awe and respect, reverence

KUN

【おそれる 畏れる】[now usu. 恐れる] **BE OVERAWED, stand in awe, fear**

畏れ おそれ fear, anxiety, awe
畏れ多くも おそれおおくも graciously
畏れ入る おそれいる be sorry, feel small; be grateful; be amazed, be stunned
神を畏れる かみをおそれる fear God

【かしこまる 畏まる】
ⓐ be awed, humble oneself, listen respectfully
ⓑ sit straight [respectfully]

a 畏まりました かしこまりました Certainly, Sir

【かしこい 畏い】 awe-inspiring, august

畏くも かしこくも graciously

SYNONYMS

❶ **fear**

怖 FEARFUL → 0353
凄 UNCANNY → 0145
恐 FEAR → 3283
惧 FEAR → 0581
慄 TREMBLE WITH FEAR → 0791
兢 BE IN FEAR → 1971
惶 BE AFRAID → 0708
畏 BE OVERAWED → 3170
臆 FEEL TIMID → 1397
怯える BE FRIGHTENED → 0355

❷ **respect**

敬 RESPECT → 2136
尊 HONOR → 2920
畏 respect → 3170
欽 REVERE → 2124
仰 look up to → 0051
崇 REVERENCE → 2864
尚 VALUE HIGHLY → 2774
重 set value on → 4390
拝 WORSHIP → 0360
慕 ADORE → 2970

HOMOPHONES

おそれる 恐 FEAR → 3283

NOTE

➡ see USAGE note at 恐 3283

胃

3171

2-5-4

▶**STOMACH**

イ

Ⓒ 胃 wèi

130	Jōyō-4	U80C3
月	S9-4-5	F1734

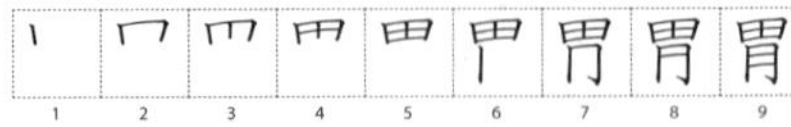

COMPOUNDS

ⓐ [original meaning] **STOMACH**
ⓑ [prefix] **gastric**

a 胃腸 いちょう stomach and intestines [bowels]
胃腸病学 いちょうびょうがく gastroenterology
胃弱 いじゃく dyspepsia, indigestion

ab 胃袋 いぶくろ stomach
胃下垂 いかすい gastric ptosis
胃炎 いえん gastritis
胃潰瘍 いかいよう stomach ulcer
胃癌 いがん gastric cancer
胃カタル いかたる gastric catarrh

INDEPENDENT

【い 胃】 **STOMACH; paunch**

SYNONYMS

● **internal organs**

心 HEART → 0011
肺 LUNG → 1147
胃 STOMACH → 3171
腸 INTESTINES → 1307
肝 LIVER → 1045
胆 GALLBLADDER → 1150
腎 KIDNEY → 3511

界

3172

2-5-4

▶**WORLD**
▶**BOUNDS**

カイ ㊔ さかい

Ⓝ 畍 Ⓒ 界 jiè

102	Jōyō-3	U754C
田	S9-5-4	F0150

COMPOUNDS

❶ [also suffix] (segment of society engaged in same activity) **WORLD, circles**

業界 ぎょうかい industry, business world
政界 せいかい political world
各界 かっかい every sphere of life, various circles
学界 がっかい academic circles [world]
経済界 けいざいかい economic world, financial circles
芸能界 げいのうかい entertainment world, world of show business

❷ⓐ (physical world) **WORLD**
ⓑ [also suffix] (sphere or realm) **WORLD, kingdom, realm**

a 世界 せかい world, universe
他界する たかいする die, pass away

外界 がいかい external world
b 界隈 かいわい neighborhood, vicinity
自然界 しぜんかい realm of nature
動物界 どうぶつかい animal kingdom
❸ *phys* field
界磁極 かいじきょく field pole
視界 しかい field of vision, visibility
電界 でんかい electric field
❹ⓐ [original meaning] **BOUNDS, boundary, border**
ⓑ *math* bound
a 界面 かいめん interface
限界 げんかい boundary, limit, bounds
境界 きょうかい boundary, border
臨界点 りんかいてん critical point [temperature]
b 下界 かかい lower bound
❺ *geol* group
古生界 こせいかい Paleozoic group

INDEPENDENT

【かい 界】 *math* bound

SYNONYMS

❶ **circles**
界 WORLD → 3172
壇 circles → 0932
❷ **world**
世 WORLD → 4308
界 WORLD → 3172
❸ **range**
程 EXTENT → 1524
範 range → 3360
域 area → 0559
圏 SPHERE → 3904
野 FIELD → 1877
界 field (*phys*) → 3172
場 field (*phys*, *psychol*) → 0678
❹ⓐ **edges and boundaries**
縁 EDGE → 1754
端 edge → 1564
辺 border → 3761
境 BOUNDARY → 0835
疆 BOUNDARY → 1810
界 BOUNDS → 3172
際 VERGE → 0874
涯 OUTER LIMITS → 0623

NOTE

★ 界 and 堺 were originally the same character.

思

▸THINK
シ おも(う)
Ⓒ 思 sī

3173
2-5-4

61	Jōyō-2	U601D
心	S9-4-5	F0023

1 2 3 4 5 6 7 8 9

COMPOUNDS

❶ⓐ [original meaning] **THINK, consider, regard, believe, feel**
ⓑ thought, idea
a 思考 しこう thinking, thought, consideration
思惟 しい thinking, speculation
思案する しあんする think, consider, reflect
思索する しさくする think, speculate
思慮 しりょ consideration, thought, discretion
思想 しそう thought, conception, idea
意思 いし intention, purpose
不思議な ふしぎな strange, mysterious, wonderful
b 思潮 しちょう trend of thought
❷ **THINK** of someone, care for, love
思慕する しぼする love dearly, yearn for
相思 そうし mutual love

KUN

【おもう 思う】
①ⓐ **THINK, consider; regard**
ⓑ (believe) **THINK, believe, hold**
ⓒ (consider likely) **THINK, expect, hope; guess**
a 思い おもい thought, idea; feelings; desire, wish; heart
思い付く おもいつく think of, hit upon
思い付き おもいつき idea, plan
思い上がる おもいあがる get conceited, get stuck-up
思い込む おもいこむ be under the impression that, be convinced that
b 私は彼が間違っていると思います わたしはかれがまちがっているとおもいます I believe that he is wrong
c 思わず おもわず unintentionally; unconsciously; unexpectedly
思い掛けない おもいがけない unexpected; accidental
② **wish, desire, want**
思惑 おもわく thought, intention, purpose
思い切る おもいきる resign oneself to, give up; resolve, determine
思い切って おもいきって boldly, decisively, daringly
思い切り おもいきり decisiveness; resignation; to one's heart content; with all one's might
思い止まる おもいとどまる abandon (an idea), refrain from (doing)

思う存分 おもうぞんぶん to one's heart's content
したいと思う したいとおもう want to do something

③ [sometimes also 想う] (recall a thought) **THINK, recollect, recall, remember**
思い出 おもいで recollections, memory, reminiscences
思い出す おもいだす recollect, recall, remember

④ **THINK of, care for, love**
思い遣り おもいやり sympathy, compassion; thoughtfulness

⑤ wonder

SYNONYMS

❶ⓐ & 【おもう】 ①ⓐ think and consider
思 THINK → 3173
惟 MEDITATE → 0582
省 INTROSPECT → 3100
稽 THINK → 1573
考 THINK → 3962
存 hold an opinion → 3702
案 think out → 2824
想 CONCEIVE → 3507
慮 CONSIDER → 4050
勘 take into consideration → 2231
銓 WEIGH → 2161
量 weigh → 3119

USAGE

【おもう】

思う
①ⓐ think, consider; regard
ⓑ (believe) think, believe, hold
ⓒ (consider likely) think, expect, hope; guess
② wish, desire, want
③ [sometimes also 想う] (recall a thought) think, recollect, recall, remember
④ think of, care for, love
⑤ wonder

想う
[usu. 思う] (recall a thought) think, recollect, recall, remember

HOMOPHONES

おもう 想 CONCEIVE → 3507

NOTE

➡ see COMPOUND FORMATION for 思索 しさく → 索 3105

発

3174

2-5-4

▶START
▶EMIT

ハツ ホツ た(つ)▲ あば(く)▲ ㊔ ひらく あきら

Ⓝ 發 Ⓒ 发 fā

105	Jōyō-3	U767A
癶	S9-5-4	F0064

COMPOUNDS

❶ (bring into being) **START, originate, initiate, give rise to, generate, produce**
発端 ほったん origin, beginning, outset
発会 はっかい opening of a meeting; first meeting
発足する ほっそく(=はっそく)する start, be inaugurated
発刊する はっかんする publish, issue
発動する はつどうする exercise, invoke; move, put in motion
発電 はつでん generation of electricity; telegraphing
発熱 はつねつ generation of heat; attack of fever
発癌 はつがん carcinogenesis, production of cancer
発想 はっそう conception; *music* expression
発明 はつめい invention, contrivance
発起人 ほっきにん originator; promoter; proposer

❷ (come into being) **START up, arise, become, occur**
発生する はっせいする occur, happen; grow, breed
発効する はっこうする become effective, take effect, come into force
発狂する はっきょうする go mad, become insane [crazy]
発奮(=発憤)する はっぷんする be stimulated, be inspired, be roused
発作 ほっさ fit, attack, seizure
自発性 じはつせい spontaneity, spontaneousness

❸ⓐ (begin forward movement) **START, depart, set out, leave**
ⓑ departure
ⓒ suffix indicating time or point of departure
a 発着 はっちゃく departure and arrival
発車する はっしゃする start, leave, depart
出発 しゅっぱつ departure, starting
先発する せんぱつする start in advance, go ahead, precede
b 始発 しはつ first departure; starting station
c 八時発の列車 はちじはつのれっしゃ train leaving at eight
ニューヨーク発の便 にゅーよーくはつのびん flight from New York

❹ⓐ (give off) **EMIT, send out, issue, discharge, dispatch, transmit**
ⓑ (put forth or distribute officially) **issue, promulgate, publish**
ⓒ suffix indicating point [time] of origin or transmission (of cables)
a 発光 はっこう radiation, luminescence
発汗 はっかん perspiring, sweating
発音 はつおん pronunciation
発火 はっか ignition; combustion

発散 はっさん emission; radiation; evaporation
発病する はつびょうする fall ill, get sick
蒸発 じょうはつ evaporation, volatilization; mysterious disappearance
b 発信 はっしん sending a letter [telegram]
発送 はっそう sending, forwarding, shipping
発言する はつげんする speak, utter
発行 はっこう publication, issue; (of bank notes) issue
発布 はっぷ proclamation, promulgation
発令する はつれいする announce officially, issue
発売する はつばいする sell, put on the market
発注 はっちゅう ordering
発禁(=発売禁止) はっきん(=はつばいきんし) prohibition of sale, suppression (of a book)
濫発(=乱発) らんぱつ excessive issue
c ロンドン発の報道 ろんどんはつのほうどう news under a London dateline

❺ⓐ [original meaning] (emit a projectile) **discharge, fire, shoot**
ⓑ (be discharged) **discharge, explode**
ⓒ counter for shots or rounds
a 発射する はっしゃする discharge, shoot, launch
発砲 はっぽう firing, discharge of a gun
連発 れんぱつ running fire, volley
暴発 ぼうはつ spontaneous discharge, accidental gun discharge
b 不発 ふはつ misfire
爆発する ばくはつする explode, burst; erupt
一触即発 いっしょくそくはつ touch-and-go situation, hair-trigger crisis
c 三発撃つ さんぱつうつ fire three shots

❻ **reveal, open up, disclose, make public, announce**
発表する はっぴょうする announce, make public, publish
発見 はっけん discovery, revelation, detection
発掘する はっくつする dig, excavate
発揮する はっきする display, exhibit, demonstrate
発露 はつろ expression, manifestation
摘発する てきはつする expose, lay bare, disclose

❼ **develop, grow**
発達 はったつ development, growth, progress
発育する はついくする grow, develop
発展する はってんする expand, grow, develop; prosper
開発する かいはつする develop, open out; enlighten

❽ counter for engines
双発機 そうはつき twin-engined plane

❾ counter for blows
一発食らわす いっぱつくらわす give a blow

❿ abbrev. of 発電所 はつでんしょ: power generation plant
原発 げんぱつ nuclear power plant

⓫ [formerly also 撥 はつ 0907] **repel, repulse, rebound**
発条 はつじょう(=ばね) spring
反発 はんぱつ repulsion, repelling; rally (of the market); opposition

⓬ [formerly 撥 はつ 0907] stir, stir up
挑発 ちょうはつ provocation, incitement, excitement, stimulation

⓭ [formerly 醱 はつ 2076] brew, ferment
発酵 はっこう fermentation, zymosis

⓮ [formerly 潑 はつ 0917] **lively, energetic**
活発な かっぱつな lively, active

⓯ collect, conscript
徴発する ちょうはつする commandeer, requisition

INDEPENDENT

【はっする 発する】**EMIT, radiate, send forth; issue (orders), promulgate; originate in; utter**
放射線を発する ほうしゃせんをはっする emit radioactive rays
喪を発する もをはっする put (the court) into mourning
源を湖水に発する みなもとをこすいにはっする rise [flow] from a lake
奇声を発する きせいをはっする raise a queer voice, squeak

KUN

【たつ 発つ】[now usu. 立つ] **START (on a journey), leave, depart**
東京を発つ とうきょうをたつ leave Tokyo

【あばく 発く】[usu. 暴く] disclose (a secret), expose (a crime), lay bare, divulge
秘密を発く ひみつをあばく disclose a secret

SYNONYMS

❶ **create**
創 CREATE → 2283
作 compose → 0077
綴 COMPOSE → 1746
生 produce → 4309
発 START → 3174
起 generate → 4099

❶ **begin**
始 BEGIN → 0335
-出す begin to do → 4310
-掛ける start doing → 0596
発 START → 3174
起 start → 4099
就 SET ABOUT → 2129
開 OPEN → 4121
創 initiate → 2283

肇 ORIGINATE → 3474

❸ⓐ leave and set forth

去 GO AWAY → 2678
離 leave → 2364
発 START → 3174
出 GO OUT → 4310
退 RETREAT → 3838
撤 WITHDRAW → 0912

❹ⓐ emit

出 PUT OUT → 4310
発 EMIT → 3174
放 radiate → 1058
排 DISCHARGE → 0593
射 SHOOT → 1850
噴 SPOUT → 0879
吐 SPEW → 0235
湧 WELL UP → 0749

❺ⓐ shoot

射 SHOOT → 1850
撃 fire → 3552
発 discharge → 3174

ⓑ explode

爆 EXPLODE → 1415
発 discharge → 3174

❻ reveal

発 reveal → 3174
露 EXPOSE → 3495
曝 EXPOSE → 1410
晒す EXPOSE → 1156
暴 disclose → 3138
披 OPEN OUT → 0362
顕 MANIFEST → 2274
現 cause to appear → 1218

❼ grow

成 grow up → 4352
長 grow (up) → 3163
生 grow → 4309
育 grow → 2544
発 develop → 3174
伸 expand → 0079
展 UNFOLD → 3862

HOMOPHONES

たつ

立 STAND → 2486
建 BUILD → 3834
起 RISE → 4099
経 PASS THROUGH → 1687

あばく 暴 VIOLENT → 3138

NOTE

➡ see USAGE notes at 立 2486 and 暴 3138

➡ see COMPOUND FORMATION for 発達 はったつ → 達 3893

皇

3175

2-5-4

▸EMPEROR

コウ オウ ㊔ すめらぎ すめら

Ⓒ 皇 huáng

106	Jōyō-6	U7687
白	S9-5-4	F0385

1 2 3 4 5 6 7 8 9

COMPOUNDS

❶ⓐ EMPEROR, sovereign
ⓑ related to the EMPEROR, imperial

a 皇帝 こうてい emperor
皇后 こうごう empress, queen
皇妃 こうひ empress, queen
皇太子 こうたいし crown prince
天皇 てんのう emperor of Japan
b 皇居 こうきょ Imperial Palace
皇室 こうしつ Imperial Family
皇子 おうじ imperial prince

❷ Japan under imperial rule

皇典 こうてん Japanese classics
皇国 こうこく the Japanese Empire

❸ Lord of Heaven, God

皇天 こうてん Heaven, Providence

❹ [formerly 惶 こう 0708] be afraid, be anxious; be flurried

倉皇として そうこうとして in great haste

SYNONYMS

❶ⓐ rulers

君 RULER → 3974
王 KING → 4247
帝 EMPEROR → 2573
天 Heaven's messenger on earth → 4250
皇 EMPEROR → 3175
尭 YAO → 2560
舜 SHUN → 3134

泉

3176

2-5-4

▸SPRING

セン いずみ ㊔ みず

Ⓒ 泉 quán

85	Jōyō-6	U6CC9
水	S9-4-5	F0425

1 2 3 4 5 6 7 8 9

COMPOUNDS

❶ⓐ (source or issue of water) **SPRING, fountain**
ⓑ [also suffix] **hot SPRING**

a 泉水 せんすい fountain, garden pond

温泉 おんせん hot spring
冷泉 れいせん cold water spring
b 鉱泉 こうせん mineral spring
源泉 げんせん fountainhead, source
硫黄泉 いおうせん sulfur spring
アルカリ泉 あるかりせん alkali spring

❷ [archaic] waterfall
飛泉 ひせん waterfall

❸ Hades, the underworld
黄泉 こうせん(=よみ) Hades, nether world

❹ money
泉貨紙(=仙花紙) せんかし reclaimed paper

❺ abbrev. of 和泉 いずみ, old name for southeast Osaka Prefecture
泉南 せんなん southern Izumi district; Sennan City

KUN

【いずみ 泉】**SPRING, fountain; fountainhead, source**
知識の泉 ちしきのいずみ source of knowledge

SYNONYMS

❶ⓐ **water sources**
源 SOURCE →0806
泉 SPRING →3176
井 WELL →4265
ⓑ **baths**
浴 bath →0533
湯 hot bath →0747
泉 hot spring →3176

県

incorrect classification
➡ see 2-6-3: 且 at 3269

2-5-4

柔

incorrect classification
➡ see 2-2-7: マ at 2591

2-5-4

香

3177

2-5-4

▸**SWEET SMELL**
コウ キョウ か かお(り) かお(る) ㊔ よし
Ⓒ 香 xiāng

186	Jōyō	U9999
香	S9-9-0	F0505

RADICAL

nioikō 'fragrance' (馨 馥×), used in characters related to fragrance or sweet smell

COMPOUNDS

❶ⓐ [original meaning] **SWEET SMELL, pleasant odor, perfume, fragrance, aroma, scent**
ⓑ **SWEET-SMELLing, fragrant**

a 香ばしい こうばしい nice-smelling, fragrant
芳香 ほうこう perfume, fragrance, aroma
b 香水 こうすい perfume
香気 こうき fragrance, perfume, scent
香油 こうゆ pomade, balm, perfumed oil
新香 しんこう pickles

❷ **SWEET-SMELL**ing substance:
ⓐ [also suffix] incense, joss stick
ⓑ spices

a 香典(=香奠) こうでん obituary [condolence] gift, incense money
焼香する しょうこうする burn [offer] incense
線香 せんこう stick of incense, joss stick
安息香 あんそくこう benzoin
b 香辛料 こうしんりょう spices, seasoning
香料 こうりょう spices; perfumes

❸ incense smelling game
香道 こうどう art of incense smelling

❹ name of chess piece in shogi (Japanese chess): *yari*, spear
香車 きょうしゃ chess piece in shogi (Japanese chess), *yari*, spear

❺ unclassified compounds
香港 ほんこん Hong Kong

INDEPENDENT

【こう 香】incense; incense smelling game
香を焚く こうをたく burn incense, cense
香を聞く こうをきく smell incense

【きょう 香】*kyo, yari* (→❹)

KUN

【か 香】**SWEET SMELL, fragrance, perfume, aroma**
花の香 はなのか fragrance of flowers
移り香 うつりが lingering [absorbed] scent
色香 いろか beauty, loveliness, feminine charms; color and scent

【かおり 香り】**SWEET SMELL, perfume, fragrance, scent**
桃の花の香り もものはなのかおり fragrance of peach blossom

【かおる 香る】**smell sweet, be fragrant**

SPECIAL READINGS

香蒲▲ がま [also 蒲] cattail, reed mace

SYNONYMS

❶ **smell and fragrance**
気 smell →3960
匂い SMELL →3662
臭 BAD SMELL →3261
香 SWEET SMELL →3177
馨 PERFUME →3575
芳 FRAGRANT →2739
薫 BALMY →3005

郁 AROMATIC → 1640

USAGE

❶【かおり】

香り

sweet smell, perfume, fragrance, scent

薫り

fragrance, aroma

❷【かおる】

香る

smell sweet, be fragrant

薫る

look sweet-smelling [balmy], look fragrant

★香 and 薫 are practically indistinguishable. Strictly speaking, 香 refers to physical perception by the olfactory organ, while 薫 is used figuratively or poetically.

HOMOPHONES

かおり 薫 BALMY → 3005

かおる 薫 BALMY → 3005

がま

蒲 CATTAIL → 2932

香蒲 → 3177, 2932

窃穿 etc. incorrect classification
➡ see 2-3-6: 宀 at 2798

2-5-4

音 incorrect classification
➡ see 2-2-7: 亠 at 2570

2-5-4

架

▶LAY ACROSS

カ か(ける) か(かる)

Ⓒ 架 jià

3178

2-5-4

75	Jōyō	U67B6
木	S9-4-5	F1760

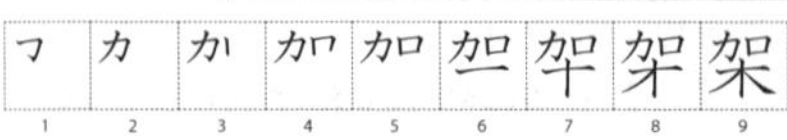

COMPOUNDS

❶ **LAY (a bridge or wire) ACROSS, build across, span (a river) with (a bridge), bridge**

架設する かせつする construct, erect, build, install

架線 かせん aerial wiring

架橋 かきょう bridge building

架空の かくうの overhead, aerial; fanciful, fictitious

高架橋 こうかきょう elevated bridge

❷ **rack, shelf, stand, mount, support, frame**

銃架 じゅうか arm rack, rifle stand

画架 がか easel

担架 たんか stretcher

十字架 じゅうじか cross, crucifix

書架 しょか bookshelf, bookstack

開架 かいか open access, open shelves

INDEPENDENT

【かする 架する】construct, erect, build, install

KUN

【かける 架ける】**LAY (a bridge or wire) ACROSS, build across, span (a river) with (a bridge), bridge**

電線を架ける でんせんをかける lay a wire

【かかる 架かる】**span,** (of cables) **be laid across, be built across**

川に架かる橋 かわにかかるはし bridge spanning a river

SYNONYMS

❶ **equip and install**

据える INSTALL → 0602

敷 LAY → 2345

架 LAY ACROSS → 3178

装 FIT OUT → 3327

設 SET UP → 1863

備 PROVIDE → 0165

❷ **flat supports**

台 STAND → 2498

座 SEAT → 3868

壇 PLATFORM → 0932

棚 SHELF → 1238

架 rack → 3178

床 BED → 3805

HOMOPHONES

かける

掛 SET → 0596

懸 SUSPEND → 3632

賭 WAGER → 2021

駆 DRIVE → 2293

翔 SOAR → 1714

かかる

掛 SET → 0596

懸 SUSPEND → 3632

係 CONNECT → 0108

繋 CONNECT → 3612

罹 FALL ILL → 3239

NOTE

➡ see USAGE note at 掛 0596

怨

▶HOLD A GRUDGE

エン オン うら(む)▲ うら(めしい)▲

Ⓒ 怨 yuàn

3179

2-5-4

61	Jōyō	U6028
心	S9-4-5	F2033

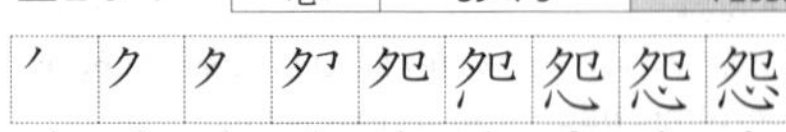

COMPOUNDS

❶ⓐ [original meaning] **HOLD A GRUDGE, feel resentment, feel bitter against**

ⓑ **grudge, hatred, malice**

a 怨恨 えんこん grudge, enmity
怨声 えんせい complaint, resentful voice
怨念 おんねん grudge
怨霊 おんりょう revengeful ghost [specter]
怨敵 おんてき sworn enemy

b 私怨 しえん personal grudge [enmity]
宿怨 しゅくえん old grudge

KUN

【うらむ 怨む】 [now usu. 恨む] **HOLD A GRUDGE**, feel resentment, feel bitter against
怨み うらみ grudge, hatred, malice
怨み言 うらみごと grudge, reproach
人を怨むより身を怨め ひとをうらむよりみをうらめ Everyone is the son of his own works

【うらめしい 怨めしい】 [now usu. 恨めしい] resentful, reproachful, indignant
怨めしや うらめしや You shall feel my wrath!

SYNONYMS

● **hate and dislike**
憎 HATE → 0845
悪 hate → 3413
忌む ABHOR → 2735
嫌 DISLIKE → 0781
恨 HOLD A GRUDGE → 0439
怨 HOLD A GRUDGE → 3179
厭 disagreeable → 3745

HOMOPHONES

うらむ
恨 HOLD A GRUDGE → 0439
憾 STRONGLY REGRET → 0943

うらみ
恨 HOLD A GRUDGE → 0439
憾 STRONGLY REGRET → 0943

うらめしい 恨 HOLD A GRUDGE → 0439

NOTE

➡ see USAGE note at 恨 0439

怒

3180

2-5-4

▶**GET ANGRY**

ド ヌ▲ いか(る) おこ(る)

Ⓒ 怒 nù

61	Jōyō	U6012
心	S9-4-5	F0758

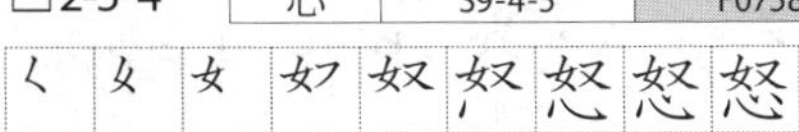

COMPOUNDS

❶ⓐ [original meaning] **GET ANGRY, be enraged**

ⓑ **anger, rage**

a 怒鳴る どなる shout, yell
憤怒 ふんど(=ふんぬ) anger, rage, resentment

b 怒気 どき anger, indignation
怒声 どせい angry voice, harsh words
怒濤× どとう raging billows [waves]
怒号 どごう (angry) roar, outcry, bellow
激怒 げきど wild rage, fury
喜怒哀楽 きどあいらく joy and anger; emotion

❷ excessive, extreme
怒張 どちょう overswelling (of a blood vessel)

KUN

【いかる 怒る】 **GET ANGRY, be enraged, get excited**
怒らす いからす offend, make angry
怒り いかり anger, rage
怒り狂う いかりくるう rage, be in a fit (of anger)

【おこる 怒る】 **GET ANGRY, be enraged, get excited; scold, rebuke**
かんかんに怒る かんかんにおこる blow one's top

SYNONYMS

❶ **anger**
怒 GET ANGRY → 3180
憤 INDIGNATION → 0897
慨 resent → 0790

NOTE

★ do not confuse with 恕 FORGIVE WITH COMPASSION → 3282

染

3181

2-5-4

▶**DYE**

セン そ(める) -ぞ(め) -ぞめ そ(まる) し(みる) -じ(みる) し(み) -し(める)▲

Ⓒ 染 rǎn

75	Jōyō-6	U67D3
木	S9-4-5	F0863

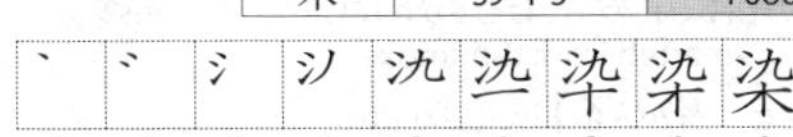

COMPOUNDS

❶ **DYE, color**
染色 せんしょく dyeing
染髪 せんぱつ hair dyeing
染織 せんしょく dyeing and weaving
染料 せんりょう dyes, dyestuffs
媒染剤 ばいせんざい mordant

❷ⓐ **be infected, contract (a disease)**

ⓑ **contaminate**

a 感染 かんせん infection
伝染病 でんせんびょう infectious disease

b 汚染 おせん pollution, contamination

KUN

【そめる 染める】

①ⓐ **DYE**

ⓑ **color, stain, tinge**

a 染め そめ dyeing, printing

染物屋 そめものや dyer

染め直す そめなおす redye

b 頬を染める ほおをそめる blush

血染めの ちぞめの bloodstained

② have a hand in, dabble in

手を染める てをそめる have a hand (in)

見染める みそめる fall in love at first glance

【-ぞめ -染め, -染】 [also suffix]

ⓐ **DYEing process**

ⓑ **DYEd fabric**

a 先染め さきぞめ yarn dyeing

b 友禅染め ゆうぜんぞめ silk printed by the *yuzen* process

【そまる 染まる】 **be DYEd, take color; be imbued [stained]**

染まり工合(=染まり具合) そまりぐあい effect of dyeing

黒く染まる くろくそまる be dyed black

悪に染まる あくにそまる steeped in vice

【しみる 染みる】 [also 滲みる]

① **soak into, permeate**

染み しみ stain, blot, spot

染み込む しみこむ soak into, permeate

染み付く しみつく be dyed in deeply, be stained

② penetrate (to the bone), come home to one's heart

身に染みる風 みにしみるかぜ piercing wind

馴染み なじみ familiarity, intimacy; old acquaintance, crony

③ smart from irritation

煙が目に染みた けむりがめにしみた My eyes smarted from the smoke

【-じみる -染みる】 [verbal suffix]

① **be imbued with, be stained with**

油染みる(=脂染みる) あぶらじみる become greasy, be oil-stained

② **have a touch of, look like**

気違い染みている きちがいじみている have a touch of insanity, be slightly crazy

【しみ 染み】 **stain, blot, spot**

インキの染み いんきのしみ ink stain

【-しめる -染める】 permeate with fluid or smoke

煮染める にしめる boil thoroughly with seasoning

焚き染める たきしめる perfume clothes by burning incense

SYNONYMS

❶ **color**

彩 color → 2115

染 DYE → 3181

❷ⓑ **dirty**

汚 DIRTY → 0258

染 contaminate → 3181

USAGE

❶【そめる】

染める

①ⓐ dye

ⓑ color, stain, tinge

② have a hand in, dabble in

-初める

[verbal suffix] begin to (occur); for the first time

❷【-ぞめ】

-染め

[also suffix]

ⓐ dyeing process

ⓑ dyed fabric

-初め

[verbal suffix] performing an action for the first time (of the year)

❸【しみる】

染みる

[also 滲みる]

① soak into, permeate

② penetrate (to the bone), come home to one's heart

③ smart from irritation

滲みる

[also 染みる] same as 染みる

凍みる

freeze, congeal

HOMOPHONES

そめる 初 FIRST → 1433

-ぞめ 初 FIRST → 1433

しみる

滲 PERMEATE → 0862

凍 FREEZE → 0146

-しめる 湿 DAMP → 0741

NOTE

➡ see also USAGE note at 湿 0741

背

3182

2-5-4

▶**BACK**

ハイ せ せい そむ(く) そむ(ける) ㊔ しろ

Ⓒ 背 bèi bēi

130	Jōyō-6	U80CC
月	S9-4-5	F0412

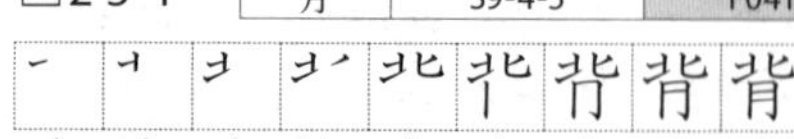

COMPOUNDS

❶ⓐ **BACK (of the body)**

❻ (backside) **BACK, reverse side, rear**
❼ abbrev. of 背泳 はいえい: **BACK**stroke
a 背部 はいぶ back
背泳 はいえい backstroke
背後 はいご back, rear
b 背面 はいめん rear, back, reverse
背景 はいけい background; (stage) scenery, setting, scene; backing
腹背 ふくはい back and front; opposition in the heart
c 百背 ひゃくはい 100 meter backstroke
❷ [formerly also 悖 0503] (turn one's back on) **go against, disobey, rebel, betray**
背反 はいはん revolt, rebellion; going against, violation
背信 はいしん breach of faith [trust], betrayal
背徳 はいとく immorality, corruption, lapse from virtue

INDEPENDENT

【はい 背】**BACK**stroke

KUN

【せ 背】
① [sometimes also 脊] **BACK; backside**
背中 せなか back
背骨 せぼね backbone, spine
背負う せおう carry on one's back, shoulder, bear
背を向ける せをむける turn one's back on, pretend not to see
② [sometimes also 脊] **stature, height**
背の順 せのじゅん order of height
③ [sometimes also 脊] **ridge**
山の背 やまのせ ridge (of a mountain)
④ **unclassified compounds**
背広 せびろ business suit

【せい 背】[sometimes also 脊] **stature, height**
背比べ せいくらべ comparison of statures
上背 うわぜい height, stature

【そむく 背く】
① [sometimes also 叛く] **go against, disobey, rebel against, violate**
約束に背く やくそくにそむく break one's promise
② **turn one's BACK on**

【そむける 背ける】**turn (one's face) away**
顔を背ける かおをそむける turn one's face away

SYNONYMS

❶❹ **trunk parts**
胸 CHEST → 1187
腹 BELLY → 1308
胴 TRUNK → 1186
腰 WAIST → 1311
背 BACK → 3182
肩 SHOULDER → 2446
股 CROTCH → 1093
脇 ARMPIT → 1188
腋 ARMPIT → 1266
❻ **rear**
後 after- → 0431
背 BACK → 3182
裏 REAR → 2652
尻 tail end → 3766
尾 TAIL → 3799
❷ **violate**
違 VIOLATE → 3907
破 BREAK → 1478
犯 offend against → 0229
反 act contrary to → 3663
悖 GO AGAINST → 0503
背 go against → 3182

【せ】
② **height**
高 height → 2601
丈 STATURE → 4227
背 stature → 3182

USAGE

【そむく】
背く
① [sometimes also 叛く] go against, disobey, rebel against, violate
② turn one's back on
叛く
[usu. 背く] rebel against, go against, disobey, violate

❶【せ】
背
① [sometimes also 脊] back; backside
② [sometimes also 脊] stature, height
③ [sometimes also 脊] ridge
④ unclassified compounds
脊
[usu. 背]
① back; backside
② stature, height
③ ridge

❷【せい】
背
[sometimes also 脊] stature, height
脊
[usu. 背] height, stature

HOMOPHONES

そむく 叛 REBEL → 1469

せ 脊 SPINE → 3297

せい 脊 SPINE → 3297

NOTE

➡ see COMPOUND FORMATION for 背広 せびろ → 広 3769

点 2-5-4

incorrect classification
➡ see 2-2-7: ⺊ at 2587

急 2-5-4

incorrect classification
➡ see 2-2-7: ⺈ at 2595

菜 2-5-4

incorrect classification
➡ see 2-2-7: 十 at 2585

栄 3183 2-5-4

▶FLOURISH
▶GLORY

エイ さか(える) は(え) -ば(え) は(える) え▲

㊔ ひで しげ しげる よし

Ⓝ 榮 荣 Ⓒ 荣 róng

75	Jōyō-4	U6804
木	S9-4-5	F0969

Stroke order: 1–9

COMPOUNDS

❶ⓐ FLOURISH, prosper, thrive, be prosperous

ⓑ [original meaning, now archaic] (grow thick) **FLOURISH**, grow luxuriantly

a 栄落 えいらく flourishing and declining

栄枯盛衰 えいこせいすい prosperity and decline, rise and fall

繁栄する はんえいする prosper, thrive, flourish

❷ GLORY, honor, splendor, fame, distinction

栄誉 えいよ honor, glory, distinction

栄光 えいこう glory

栄華 えいが prosperity, splendor, glory

栄達 えいたつ success in life, rise in the world

栄冠 えいかん honor, glory; garland, laurels

栄転 えいてん promotion

❸ [sometimes also 営 3216] **tonic, blood (in Chinese medicine)**

栄養 えいよう nutrition, nourishment

INDEPENDENT

【えい 栄】 *literary* **GLORY**, honor

身に余る栄を被る みにあまるえいをこうむる receive undeserved honor

KUN

【さかえる 栄える】 **FLOURISH, prosper, thrive, be prosperous**

栄えた時代 さかえたじだい prosperous age

国の栄え くにのさかえ prosperity of a country

【はえ 栄え】 **GLORY, splendor**

栄え有る はえある glorious, splendid

【-ばえ -栄え】

① [also -映え] **looking better**

見栄え みばえ improvement in appearance, good show

② [sometimes also -映え] **result, effect**

出来栄え できばえ result, effect, workmanship

【はえる 栄える】 [also 映える] **look better [to advantage], go well with**

栄えない色 はえないいろ dull color

その木のお蔭で庭が栄える そのきのおかげでにわがはえる The tree sets off the garden

【え 栄】 [in compounds] **GLORY, splendor**

見栄 みえ [sometimes also 見え] show, ostentation, vanity

SYNONYMS

❶ⓐ prospering and prosperity

隆 PROSPER → 0661

振 rise → 0515

興 RISE TO PROSPERITY → 3622

盛 PROSPEROUS → 3314

昌 PROSPERING → 3069

栄 FLOURISH → 3183

繁 THRIVE → 3536

賑 BUSTLE → 1959

❷ great respect

栄 GLORY → 3183

誉 HONOR → 3135

光 honor → 3043

HOMOPHONES

はえ 映 REFLECT → 1104

-ばえ 映 REFLECT → 1104

はえる 映 REFLECT → 1104

NOTE

➡ see USAGE notes at 映 1104 and 見 3151

➡ see COMPOUND FORMATION for 栄達 えいたつ → 達 3893

衷 2-5-4

incorrect classification/stroke-count
➡ see 2-2-8: 亠 at 2600

春

3184

2-5-4

▶SPRING

シュン はる ㊔ かす す はじめ

Ⓒ 春 chūn

72	Jōyō-2	U6625
日	S9-4-5	F0494

一 二 三 夫 夫 耒 春 春 春

COMPOUNDS

❶ⓐ [original meaning] **SPRING**

ⓑ **the SPRING of life, youth**

a 春季 しゅんき spring

春闘 しゅんとう spring labor offensive

春分 しゅんぶん vernal equinox

春眠 しゅんみん morning sleep in spring

春夏秋冬 しゅんかしゅうとう four seasons, all (the) year round

立春 りっしゅん first day of spring

来春 らいしゅん next spring

今春 こんしゅん this spring

b 春秋に富む しゅんじゅうにとむ be young

青春 せいしゅん bloom of youth

❷ beginning of the year

新春 しんしゅん the New Year

❸ **love, sex, sexual desire, eros**

春情 しゅんじょう sexual passion

春画 しゅんが pornography, obscene picture

売春 ばいしゅん prostitution

思春期 ししゅんき puberty, adolescence

KUN

【はる 春】**SPRING; the New Year; spring of life, youth; love, sex, sexual desire, eros**

春雨 はるさめ spring rain; sticks of bean jelly

春風 はるかぜ spring breeze

春先 はるさき early spring

春めく はるめく become springlike

春一番 はるいちばん first storm in the spring

春の目覚め はるのめざめ awakening of the spring, puberty

春を売る はるをうる become a prostitute

人生の春 じんせいのはる the spring of life, the flower [prime] of youth

初春 はつはる early spring; the New Year

SYNONYMS

❶ⓐ **warm seasons**

春 SPRING → 3184

夏 SUMMER → 2619

暑 SUMMER HEAT → 3121

❸ **sex**

性 SEX → 0357

情 (illicit) love → 0583

春 love → 3184

色 lust → 2522

淫 LEWD → 0624

NOTE

➡ see COMPOUND FORMATION for 売春 ばいしゅん → 売 2722

奏

3185

2-5-4

▶PLAY MUSIC

ソウ かな(でる)

Ⓒ 奏 zòu

37	Jōyō-6	U594F
大	S9-3-6	F1337

一 二 三 夫 夫 夫 奏 奏 奏

COMPOUNDS

❶ **PLAY MUSIC, perform (on a musical instrument)**

演奏する えんそうする perform, play

吹奏楽 すいそうがく wind instrument music

重奏 じゅうそう duet

合奏 がっそう ensemble, concert

伴奏 ばんそう accompaniment

協奏曲 きょうそうきょく concerto

❷ speak (to a ruler), report (to the throne or emperor)

奏上 そうじょう report to the emperor

奏請 そうせい petitioning the emperor

❸ achieve, accomplish

奏功 そうこう success, fruition

奏効 そうこう efficacy

INDEPENDENT

【そうする 奏する】play, perform; report to the emperor; be successful, work well

効を奏する こうをそうする take effect, work well

KUN

【かなでる 奏でる】**play on (a musical instrument), perform**

ピアノを奏でる ぴあのをかなでる play the piano

SYNONYMS

❶ **play music**

奏 PLAY MUSIC → 3185

弾 play on (stringed instruments) → 0697

吹 BLOW → 0272

NOTE

★ do not confuse with 泰 TRANQUIL → 3193 and 秦 QIN DYNASTY → 3192

柴

2-5-4

incorrect stroke-count

➡ see 2-6-4: 此 at 3287

【玄】田 白 穴 立 比 …

畜

2-5-5

incorrect classification
➡ see 2-2-8: 亠 at 2599

毘

2-5-5

incorrect stroke-count
➡ see 2-5-4: 田 at 3169

畠

3186
2-5-5

▶FIELD
はた はたけ -ばたけ
C 畠 tián (国字)

102	Names	U7560
田	S10-5-5	F2561

KUN

【はた 畠】[now usu. 畑] **(plowed or cultivated) FIELD, farm, vegetable garden, plantation**
田畠 たはた(=でんぱた) fields (of rice and other crops)

【はたけ 畠】[now usu. 畑]
① **(plowed or cultivated) FIELD, farm, vegetable garden, plantation**
畠を耕す はたけをたがやす plow a field
② one's **FIELD**, one's specialty
畠違いだ はたけちがいだ be out of one's field

【-ばたけ -畠】[now usu. 畑]
① [also suffix] **FIELD, farm, vegetable garden, plantation**
段段畠 だんだんばたけ terraced fields, terraced farm
② [suffix] one's **FIELD**, one's specialty
工学畠 こうがくばたけ engineering field

SYNONYMS

【はた】
○ &【はたけ】① **cultivated fields**
畑 FIELD → 1131
畠 FIELD → 3186
牧 PASTURE → 1083
園 GARDEN → 3914
田 RICE FIELD → 3775
佃 CULTIVATED RICE FIELD → 0066
圃 VEGETABLE GARDEN → 3871

HOMOPHONES

はた 畑 FIELD → 1131
はたけ 畑 FIELD → 1131
-ばたけ 畑 FIELD → 1131

NOTE

➡ see USAGE note at 畑 1131

皋

3187
2-5-5

▶MAY
コウ ゴウ コ ㊔ たかし さつき あきら のぼる さい

106	Nonstandard	U768B
白	S10-5-5	F0000

traditional form → see 皐 at 3198

窄 穿

2-5-5

incorrect classification
➡ see 2-3-7: 宀 at 2824

竜 竞

2-5-5

incorrect classification
➡ see 2-2-8: 亠 at 2598

皆

2-5-5

incorrect stroke-count
➡ see 2-4-5: 比 at 3093

监

3188
2-5-5

▶OVERSEE
カン

108	Nonstandard	U76D1
皿	S10-5-5	F0000

handwritten form → see 監 at 3535

留

3189
2-5-5

▶KEEP
▶STAY
リュウ ル と(める) -と(める) -ど(め) と(まる) とど(まる)▲ とど(める)▲ るーぶる▲
N 畱 畄◆ C 留 liú

102	Jōyō-5	U7559
田	S10-5-5	F0768

1	2	3	4	5	6	7	8	9	10
ノ	𠂉	𠂎	𠂎フ	卯	卯丨	卯冂	留	留	留

COMPOUNDS

❶ cause to remain in a given place or condition:
ⓐ [original meaning] **KEEP in place, keep from moving, keep in position**
ⓑ **KEEP in custody, detain**
ⓒ **KEEP for future use, leave behind**
ⓓ **KEEP** in mind, pay attention to

a 係留する けいりゅうする moor, anchor
慰留する いりゅうする dissuade from resigning
b 留置 りゅうち detention, custody, retention
抑留する よくりゅうする detain, intern, seize, arrest
c 留保する りゅうほする reserve, withhold, keep back
保留 ほりゅう reservation
遺留品 いりゅうひん article left behind, lost property
d 留意 りゅうい attention, heed, regard

❷ⓐ (remain in a given condition) **STAY, remain, continue**
ⓑ (remain in a given place) **STAY, sojourn, reside**

a 留任する りゅうにんする remain [stay] in office
留年する りゅうねんする stay more than two years in the same class
残留する ざんりゅうする stay behind
停留所 ていりゅうじょ (bus) stop, station
b 留学生 りゅうがくせい student studying abroad
留守 るす absence (from home); caretaking; defending when the lord is absent
駐留する ちゅうりゅうする be stationed at, stay
逗留する とうりゅうする stay, sojourn
在留邦人 ざいりゅうほうじん Japanese residents

❸ [formerly 溜 りゅう 0814] distill
蒸留 じょうりゅう distillation
分留 ぶんりゅう fraction, fractional distillation
乾留 かんりゅう dry distillation

INDEPENDENT

【りゅう 留】*astron* stationary (point)

KUN

【とめる 留める】
①ⓐ **KEEP in place, retain, fix, fasten**
ⓑ **KEEP** (a parcel) until called for
ⓒ **KEEP** in custody, detain
ⓓ (keep a vehicle from moving) **park**
a 留め金 とめがね clasp, latch, fastening
取り留めの無い とりとめのない wandering, rambling, incoherent
b 局留め きょくどめ poste restante
c 引き留める ひきとめる detain
足留めする あしどめする keep indoors, induce to stay
d 車を留める くるまをとめる park a car
② **KEEP in mind**
気に留める きにとめる mind, give heed to, pay attention to
③ **KEEP** (a quarrel) from intensifying, stop
留め男 とめおとこ man who stops a quarrel

【-とめる -留める】[also -止める]
① **kill**
仕留める しとめる kill, shoot dead
② **write down, register**
書留 かきとめ registered mail

【-どめ -留め】**clip, fastener, retainer**
帯留め おびどめ sash clip [fastener]
土留め どどめ sheathing, retaining (wall)

【とまる 留まる】
① **be held in position, be fastened**
釘で留まっている くぎでとまっている be fastened with a nail
②ⓐ **remain in one's perception, strike one's senses**
ⓑ [in compounds] **remain, be left over**
a 目に留まる めにとまる attract one's attention, strike the eye
b 歩留まり ぶどまり yield, yield rate
③ **perch on**
木に留まる きにとまる sit in a tree
お高く留まる おたかくとまる assume an air of importance, put on airs

【とどまる 留まる】**STAY behind, remain**
家に留まる いえにとどまる stay home

【とどめる 留める】
① **leave (behind)**
書き留める かきとどめる leave a note behind
② **make STAY, detain**
原級に留める げんきゅうにとどめる keep (a student) back (to repeat a grade)

【るーぶる 留】ruble
一留 いちるーぶる one ruble

SYNONYMS

❶ⓐ **preserve**
留 KEEP → 3189
保 PRESERVE → 0107
持 uphold → 0447
ⓑ **imprison and confine**
拘 ARREST → 0367
禁 confine → 3469
留 keep in custody → 3189
置 place in custody → 3222
錮 IMPRISON → 2182

❷ⓐ **remain**
残 REMAIN → 1179
余 REMAINING → 2535
留 STAY → 3189
滞 STAY → 0815
ⓑ **stay**
滞 STAY → 0815
頓 STAY IN PLACE → 1320
留 STAY → 3189
逗 STAY → 4005
駐 STATIONED → 2297
屯 STATION TROOPS → 4268
在 reside temporarily → 3704
泊 STAY OVERNIGHT → 0389
宿 LODGE → 2858
寓 stay temporarily → 2893

❸ **vaporize**
蒸 EVAPORATE → 2936
留 distill → 3189

❸ **refine**
錬 REFINE (crude metals) → 2185
精 REFINE (crude materials) → 1729
留 distill → 3189

玄 田 白 穴 立 比 ᐧᐧ 〔 〕 ᐧᐧ 世 ᐧᐧ 此 ᐧᐧ

HOMOPHONES

とめる

- 止 STOP →3659
- 泊 STAY OVERNIGHT →0389
- 停 HALT →0156

-とめる 止 STOP →3659

-どめ 止 STOP →3659

とまる

- 止 STOP →3659
- 泊 STAY OVERNIGHT →0389
- 停 HALT →0156

とどめる 止 STOP →3659

とどまる 止 STOP →3659

COMPOUND FORMATION

❶【留守 るす】

留守 'absence, etc.' originally meant to stay behind (留 ❷ⓑ) and defend (守) the castle during the absence of one's lord, but was extended to mean absence from the castle or home. Thus although 留 normally means to stay or remain, in this case it is used in a word related to the opposite idea of *not* to stay.

❷【歩留まり ぶどまり】

歩留まり 'yield, yield rate' is the percentage (歩) of what is left over (留まる とまる ②ⓑ).

NOTE

➡ see USAGE note at 止 3659

晉

incorrect classification

➡ see 2-1-9: 一 at 2451

2-5-5

益

incorrect classification

➡ see 2-3-7: 䒑 at 2849

2-5-5

党

▶PARTY

トウ

Ⓝ 黨 Ⓒ 党 dǎng

3190

2-5-5

10△	Jōyō-6	U515A
儿	S10-2-8	F0355

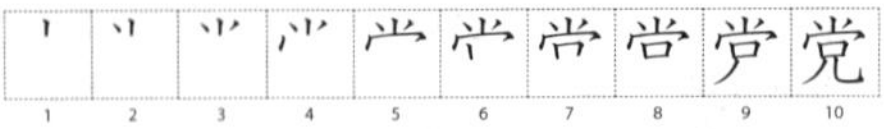

COMPOUNDS

❶ⓐ (political group) **PARTY, political party, faction**
ⓑ **suffix after names of political parties**

a 党員 とういん party member
党首 とうしゅ party chief [leader]
党大会 とうたいかい party convention
党派 とうは party, faction, clique
政党 せいとう political party
野党 やとう opposition party
粛党 しゅくとう purging disloyal elements from a party

b 共和党 きょうわとう Republican Party
社会党 しゃかいとう Socialist Party

❷ (group of persons) **PARTY**, companions, clique, fellows, fellow
一党 いっとう party, league, clique; a political party
徒党 ととう clique, faction, conspirators
残党 ざんとう remnants (of a defeated party), refugees
悪党 あくとう scoundrel, rogue

❸ person who likes a particular food or beverage, fan
辛党 からとう drinker
巨人党 きょじんとう Giants fan

INDEPENDENT

【とう 党】**political PARTY, faction**
党を脱退する とうをだったいする leave the party

SYNONYMS

❶ **parties and sects**
- 党 PARTY →3190
- 閥 CLIQUE →4126
- 流 school →0529
- 派 SECT →0456
- 翼 WING →3379
- 系 faction →2443
- 門 (religious) sect →1100
- 宗 RELIGIOUS SECT (esp. Buddhist) →2769

❷ **groups**
- 群 GROUP (of any kind) →1942
- 班 SQUAD →1182
- 軍 team →2582
- 組 group (of people) →1693
- 陣 lineup →0545
- 連 set →3849
- 族 common-interest group (*slang*) →1195
- 党 PARTY →3190
- 隊 PARTY (organized group) →0762
- 団 BODY →3791
- 伍 ranks →0050

帯

▶BELT
▶WEAR

タイ お(びる) おび

Ⓝ 帶 Ⓒ 带 dài

3191

2-5-5

50	Jōyō-4	U5E2F
巾	S10-3-7	F0574

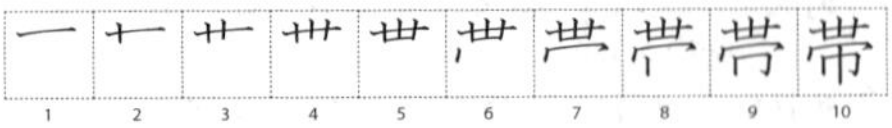

COMPOUNDS

❶ⓐ [also suffix] [original meaning] **BELT, sash, girdle, band, obi**

ⓑ *engineering* band

ⓒ [suffix] *anat* girdle

a 包帯 ほうたい bandage, dressing

腹帯 ふくたい bellyband

着帯する ちゃくたいする wear a maternity belt

止血帯 しけつたい tourniquet

b 帯域幅 たいいきはば band width

c 声帯 せいたい vocal cords

肩甲帯 けんこうたい shoulder girdle

❷ [also suffix] (geographical area) **BELT, zone, region**

帯状の おびじょう(=たいじょう)の belt-shaped

地帯 ちたい zone, area

一帯 いったい belt, zone, tract (of land), area

熱帯 ねったい tropics, torrid zone

緑地帯 りょくちたい green belt

時間帯 じかんたい time belt

バンアレン帯 ばんあれんたい Van Allen Belt

❸ **WEAR (esp. at [on] the belt), bear, carry on one's person, be armed with**

帯刀 たいとう wearing a sword

帯剣する たいけんする wear a sword, be armed with a sword

携帯する けいたいする carry, bring with one, equip oneself with

❹ⓐ **have, possess**

ⓑ be tinged with (a color), be charged with (electricity)

a 所帯(=世帯) しょたい household, home

妻帯者 さいたいしゃ married man

拐帯 かいたい abscondence with money

付帯的な ふたいてきな incidental, secondary, accessory

b 帯黄色 たいおうしょく yellowish color

帯緑の たいりょくの greenish

帯電体 たいでんたい charged body

❺ **work together, cooperate**

帯同する たいどうする be accompanied by, take (a person) along

連帯 れんたい solidarity

INDEPENDENT

【たい 帯】 *anat* girdle

【たいする 帯する】 **WEAR** (esp. at [on] the belt), bear, carry on one's person, be armed with

剣を帯する けんをたいする wear a sword

KUN

【おびる 帯びる】 **WEAR (esp. at [on] the belt), bear, carry on one's person be armed with; wear (a sad look), assume, have; be tinged with (a color), be charged with (electricity); be entrusted with, be charged with (a mission)**

剣を帯びる けんをおびる wear a sword at one's side

赤味を帯びた あかみをおびた reddish, tinged with red

憂いを帯びた顔 うれいをおびたかお sorrowful look

電気を帯びる でんきをおびる be charged with electricity

使命を帯びる しめいをおびる be charged with a mission

【おび 帯】 **BELT, sash, girdle, band; belting**

帯を締める おびをしめる do up a sash

帯止め(=帯留め) おびどめ sash clip [fastener]

帯革(=帯皮) おびかわ leather belt

帯封 おびふう half wrapper, strip of paper

袋帯 ふくろおび double-woven obi

SYNONYMS

❷ **areas and localities**

地 PLACE →0236

方 locality →2459

辺 VICINITY →3761

域 BOUNDED AREA →0559

区 DISTRICT →3681

領 TERRITORY →1567

帯 BELT →3191

圏 SPHERE →3904

❸ **wear and put on**

着 PUT ON →4110

装 DRESS →3327

帯 WEAR (esp. at the belt) →3191

穿く PUT ON →2800

纏 put on →1814

履く put on footwear →3933

被る put on headgear →1495

秦

3192

2-5-5

▶**QIN DYNASTY**

シン ジン はた ㊔ はだ

Ⓒ 秦 qín

115	Names	U79E6
禾	S10-5-5	F1919

COMPOUNDS

● **QIN DYNASTY (221-206 B.C.)**

秦の始皇帝 しんのしこうてい first emperor of Qin Dynasty

INDEPENDENT

【しん 秦】 **QIN DYNASTY** (221-206 B.C.)

玄 田 白 穴 立 比 皿 ... 世 【夫】 此 冊

KUN

【はた 秦】*Hata*: name of ancient Japanese clan of Korean origin

SYNONYMS

❶ **earlier Chinese dynasties**
- 夏 Xia Dynasty → 2619
- 商 Shang Dynasty → 2623
- 周 Zhou Dynasty → 3720
- 漢 Han Dynasty → 0808
- 晋 JIN DYNASTY → 3290
- 秦 QIN DYNASTY → 3192

NOTE

★ do not confuse with 奏 PLAY MUSIC → 3185 and 泰 TRANQUIL → 3193

泰

3193
2-5-5

▶**TRANQUIL**

タイ ㊔ やす やすし ひろ はた

Ⓒ 泰 tài

85	Jōyō	U6CF0
氺	S10-5-5	F1471

一 二 三 丰 夫 夫 秦 泰 泰 泰 (1–10)

COMPOUNDS

❶ **TRANQUIL, peaceful, composed, calm**
- 泰平 たいへい tranquility, perfect peace
- 泰然たる たいぜんたる calm, composed; firm
- 安泰 あんたい peace, security, tranquility

❷ [also 太 2673] extreme, great
- 泰西 たいせい the Occident

❸ Thailand, Siam
- 泰国 たいこく Thailand, Siam
- 泰語 たいご Thai, Siamese
- 対泰関係 たいたいかんけい relations with Thailand

❹ Mt. Taishan (sacred Chinese mountain associated with Confucius)
- 泰山 たいざん Mt. Taishan
- 泰斗 たいと leading authority

INDEPENDENT

【たい 泰】Thailand

SYNONYMS

❶ **calm and peaceful**
- 安 PEACEFUL → 2695
- 康 peaceful → 3877
- 寧 peaceful → 2959
- 泰 TRANQUIL → 3193
- 静 QUIET → 2164
- 平 CALM → 4291
- 穏 CALM → 1578

❸ **Asian countries**
- 日 JAPAN → 3759
- 緬 Myanmar → 1758
- 老 Laos → 3963
- 華 CHINA → 2841
- 蒙 Mongolia → 2938
- 鮮 Korea → 2355
- 泰 Thailand → 3193
- 越 Vietnam → 4108
- 印 India → 1023
- 竺 INDIA → 3248
- 比 Philippines → 0029

NOTE

➡ see COMPOUND FORMATION for 泰斗 たいと → 斗 3671
★ do not confuse with 奏 PLAY MUSIC → 3185 and 秦 QIN DYNASTY → 3192

砦

2-5-5

incorrect stroke-count
➡ see 2-6-5: 此 at 3310

帯

2-5-5

incorrect stroke-count
➡ see 2-6-5: 卌 at 3315

畢

3194
2-5-6

▶**END**

ヒツ おわ(る)

Ⓒ 毕 bì

102	Names	U7562
田	S11-5-6	F0000

COMPOUNDS

❶ ⓐ **END, come to an end, finish, terminate**
ⓑ **bring to an END, finish, complete**

ab 畢生 ひっせい lifetime

❷ **at last, in the END, finally**
- 畢竟× ひっきょう after all, in the end; *Buddhism atyanta*, extreme, ultimate, absolute

KUN

【おわる 畢る】[now always 終わる] **END**, come to an end, finish, terminate; end one's life, die

SYNONYMS

❶ **ends**
- 末 LAST PART → 4317
- 終 END → 1692
- 畢 END → 3194
- 尾 end → 3799
- 局 close → 3800

HOMOPHONES

おわる 終 END → 1692

NOTE

➡ see USAGE note at 終 1692

異

▶DIFFERENT

イ こと こと(なる)

N 異 C 异 yì

3195

2-5-6

102	Jōyō-6	U7570
田	S11-5-6	F0470

COMPOUNDS

❶ [also prefix]

ⓐ [original meaning] (not alike) **DIFFERENT, unlike; opposite**

ⓑ (of a different place) **foreign**

ⓒ (different or distinct from) another, other

a 異議 いぎ objection, complaint
異性 いせい opposite sex
異動 いどう shifting, reshuffle
異文化 いぶんか different cultures
差異 さい difference, disparity

b 異境 いきょう foreign country, strange land
異邦人 いほうじん foreigner, alien

c 異名 いみょう another name, alias

❷ **not ordinary: strange, unusual, abnormal, unorthodox, extraordinary, exceptional, peculiar**
異常な いじょうな abnormal, unusual, extraordinary
異端 いたん heresy, paganism, heterodoxy
異心 いしん treasonous intention, betrayal; eccentricity
異例 いれい singular case, exception
異色の いしょくの novel, unique
異才 いさい genius, prodigy
奇異な きいな unusual, strange

❸ calamity
天変地異 てんぺんちい extraordinary natural phenomenon

❹ marvel, be surprised
驚異 きょうい wonder, marvel, miracle

INDEPENDENT

【い 異】**DIFFERENT** opinion; difference; uncommonness
異を立てる いをたてる raise an objection
異な気分 いなきぶん queer feeling

KUN

【こと 異】**difference**
異にする ことにする differ, be different

【ことなる 異なる】**DIFFERENT, be different from**
二つの異なる点 ふたつのことなるてん two different points

SYNONYMS

❶ⓐ **differing and difference**
違 DIFFER → 3907
異 DIFFERENT → 3195
差 DIFFERENCE → 4104

ⓑ **foreign**
外 foreign → 0215
異 foreign → 3195

❷ **abnormal**
変 ABNORMAL → 2569
奇 UNUSUAL → 2756
畸 UNUSUAL → 1533
怪 MYSTERIOUS → 0354
妖 MYSTERIOUS → 0282
妙 strange → 0280
異 not ordinary → 3195
珍 curious → 1135

USAGE

【い 異 違】

★異 is sometimes used interchangeably with 違 in sense ❶ⓐ above in such words as 差異 さい 'difference' and 相違 そうい 'difference', which are preferably written as shown.

HOMOPHONES

こと 殊 SPECIAL → 1178

NOTE

➡ see also USAGE note at 殊 1178

累

▶CUMULATE

ルイ

C 累 lèi lěi

3196

2-5-6

120	Jōyō	U7D2F
糸	S11-6-5	F2333

COMPOUNDS

❶ⓐ **CUMULATE, accumulate, pile up**

ⓑ successive, repeated, gradual

a 累積 るいせき accumulation
累加 るいか cumulation, cumulative rise
累計 るいけい total
累増 るいぞう cumulative increase, progressive increase
累乗 るいじょう *math* involution, power
累算温度 るいさんおんど cumulative temperature

b 累累と るいるいと heaps on heaps, one upon another
累進する るいしんする successive promotions, graduated increase

累次に るいじに successively, repeatedly

❷ involvement, implication

係累 けいるい family ties, dependents

連累 れんるい implication, involvement

INDEPENDENT

【るい 累】involvement, implication, trouble

他に累を及ぼす たにるいをおよぼす involve others in trouble

SYNONYMS

❶ⓐ **accumulate**

積 ACCUMULATE → 1579

溜 ACCUMULATE → 0814

累 CUMULATE → 3196

重 pile up → 4390

盛る heap up → 3314

堆 PILED HIGH → 0563

畧

▶ABRIDGED

▶STRATEGY

リャク ほぼ

3197

2-5-6

102	Nonstandard	U7567
田	S11-5-6	F0000

alternative form → see 略 at 1501

皐

▶MAY

コウ ゴウ コ ㊔ たかし さつき あきら のぼる さい

Ⓝ 皋 Ⓒ 皋 gāo

3198

2-5-6

106	Names	U7690
白	S11-5-6	F3466

COMPOUNDS

❶ [rare] **MAY** (of the lunar calendar)

皐月 こうげつ(=さつき) May (of the lunar calendar)

❷ [original meaning, now archaic] marsh, swamp

SPECIAL READINGS

皐月(=五月) さつき *elegant* May

窓窒 etc. incorrect classification
➡ see 2-3-8: 穴 at 2853

2-5-6

章 incorrect classification
➡ see 2-2-9: 亠 at 2624

2-5-6

衆

▶MULTITUDE

シュウ シュ

3199

2-5-6

109	Nonstandard	U773E
目	S11-5-6	F0000

alternative form → see 衆 at 3325

袈

▶BUDDHIST SURPLICE

ケ カ

Ⓒ 袈 jiā

3200

2-5-6

145	Names	U8888
衣	S11-6-5	F2420

COMPOUNDS

● **BUDDHIST SURPLICE**

袈裟 けさ Buddhist surplice

大袈裟な おおげさな exaggerated, hyperbolical

SYNONYMS

● **clothing**

服 CLOTHES → 1090

袴 FORMAL DIVIDED SKIRT → 1509

蓑 STRAW RAINCOAT → 2941

-着 wear → 4110

衣 GARMENT → 2506

装 DRESS → 3327

裳 DRESS → 3231

襤 RAGS → 1607

袈 BUDDHIST SURPLICE → 3200

裟 BUDDHIST CASSOCK → 3420

襖 overgarment → 1600

袋

▶BAG

タイ ふくろ

Ⓒ 袋 dài

3201

2-5-6

145	Jōyō	U888B
衣	S11-6-5	F1112

(stroke order: 1–11)

COMPOUNDS

ⓐ [original meaning] **BAG, sack**

ⓑ counter for **BAG**s or bagfuls

a 郵袋 ゆうたい mailbag

製袋 せいたい bag manufacturing

風袋 ふうたい tare

b 二袋 にたい two sacks

KUN

【ふくろ 袋】

①ⓐ [also suffix] **BAG, sack, pouch**

ⓑ counter for **BAG**s or bagfuls

a お袋 おふくろ one's mother

袋入り ふくろいり pouched, sacked

袋帯 ふくろおび double-woven obi

紙袋 かみぶくろ paper bag

手袋 てぶくろ gloves

浮き袋 うきぶくろ air bladder

給料袋 きゅうりょうぶくろ pay envelope

b 一袋 ひとふくろ one bag

② [also prefix] cul-de-sac

袋小路 ふくろこうじ blind alley

SPECIAL READINGS

足袋 たび Japanese [digitated] socks, *tabi*

SYNONYMS

ⓐ **containers**

箱 BOX → 3362
壺 JAR → 2890
槽 TANK → 1352
樽 BARREL → 1368
棺 COFFIN → 1240
桶 BUCKET → 1211
笈 BOX CARRIED ON THE BACK → 3274
鞘 SHEATH → 2259
箪 BAMBOO BOX → 3381
函 BOX → 3724
籠 BASKET → 3398
袋 BAG → 3201
鞄 BAG (for carrying) → 2248
器 VESSEL → 3367
瓶 BOTTLE → 1702
缶 CAN → 2526
缶 EARTHENWARE JAR → 2525

ⓐ **bags**

俵 STRAW SACK → 0129
袋 BAG → 3201
鞄 BAG (for carrying) → 2248
包 wrapper → 3684
胞 MEMBRANOUS SAC → 1148

COMPOUND FORMATION

【お袋 おふくろ】

お袋 'one's mother', literally "honorable bag," is an expression indicating intimacy or respect for one's mother. The origin of this word is not clear. According to one theory, it is related to the fact that the placenta enveloping the fetus is similar in shape to a bag.

堂

3202

2-5-6

▶**HALL**

ドウ

Ⓒ 堂 táng

32	Jōyō-4	U5802
土	S11-3-8	F0651

Stroke order: 11 strokes

COMPOUNDS

❶ [also suffix] (building for public gatherings) **HALL, public building**

公会堂 こうかいどう town [public] hall

議事堂 ぎじどう assembly hall; Diet Building

❷ⓐ (large room for public gatherings) **HALL, meeting place**

ⓑ [original meaning] large reception room

a 講堂 こうどう lecture hall, auditorium

食堂 しょくどう dining hall [room]; restaurant

音楽堂 おんがくどう concert hall

b 殿堂 でんどう hall, palace, shrine; sanctuary

❸ⓐ (building or hall for worship) **temple building, temple, shrine, church**

ⓑ suffix after names of temple buildings

a 堂塔 どうとう temple buildings, temple

堂宇 どうう edifice, temple, hall

b 聖堂 せいどう shrine [temple] of Confucius; sanctuary, church

本堂 ほんどう main temple, main building (of a temple)

金色堂 こんじきどう Konjikido (name of a temple building)

❹ house, abode

草堂 そうどう monk's cell; (my) humble abode

❺ suffix for forming names of business establishments or pen names

三省堂 さんせいどう Sanseido (name of a publisher)

❻ the Court

廟堂 びょうどう the Court

❼ **dignified, majestic**

堂堂たる どうどうたる dignified, magnificent, imposing, majestic, stately

❽ honorific title for another's mother

母堂 ぼどう your [his] mother

❾ secret knowledge

堂奥 どうおう secret knowledge; interior of a temple

INDEPENDENT

【どう 堂】 temple or shrine building; **HALL**, public building; secret knowledge

堂に入る どうにいる become expert, be master at

SYNONYMS

❶ **buildings**

閣 TALL MAGNIFICENT BUILDING → 4128
宇 large building → 2699
殿 PALACE → 2247
堂 HALL → 3202
館 PUBLIC BUILDING → 2196
舎 BUILDING → 2555
棟 BLOCK → 1248
厩 HORSE STABLE → 3746

❷ rooms
室 ROOM →2802
間 room →4122
房 CHAMBER →2445
斎 study →2622
堂 HALL →3202

❸ places of worship
堂 temple building →3202
塔 pagoda →0683
寺 BUDDHIST TEMPLE →2687
刹 TEMPLE →1620
社 Shinto shrine →1042
宮 SHINTO SHRINE →2828
院 monastery →0544
教 church →1887

NOTE
★ do not confuse with 常 NORMAL →3203

常

▶NORMAL
▶REGULAR
ジョウ つね とこ- ㊔ とき ときわ
Ⓒ 常 cháng

3203
2-5-6

50	Jōyō-5	U5E38
巾	S11-3-8	F0313

COMPOUNDS
❶ NORMAL, ordinary, usual, common, regular
常識 じょうしき common sense, common knowledge
常態 じょうたい normal state [condition]
非常 ひじょう emergency, calamity
異常な いじょうな abnormal, unusual, extraordinary
正常 せいじょう normality, normalcy
通常の つうじょうの common, ordinary, usual
平常の へいじょうの ordinary, normal, usual

❷ REGULAR, habitual, standing
常務 じょうむ managing [executive] director
常連 じょうれん regular visitors [customers], frequenters
常緑樹 じょうりょくじゅ evergreen tree
常食 じょうしょく daily food, staple food
常用 じょうよう common use, daily use
常用漢字 じょうようかんじ Chinese characters designated for daily use
常時の じょうじの regular, standing
常任委員 じょうにんいいん standing committee
日常の にちじょうの daily, everyday

❸ code of morals
五常 ごじょう the five cardinal virtues (of Confucianism)
綱常 こうじょう moral principles, code of morals

❹ abbrev. of 常陸 ひたち, old name for Ibaraki Prefecture
常磐炭田 じょうばんたんでん Joban Coalfield

KUN
【つね 常】ordinary course of events, NORMAL condition
常に つねに always, at all times
世の常 よのつね the way of the world

【とこ- 常-】everlasting, unending
常夏の国 とこなつのくに land of everlasting summer

SYNONYMS
❶ ordinary
常 NORMAL →3203
只- ORDINARY →2677
並 ordinary →2793
平 common →4291
普 common →2919
庸 MEDIOCRE →3881
凡 COMMONPLACE →3656
套 TRITE →2823

❷ constant
定 fixed →2770
恒 CONSTANT →0438
常 REGULAR →3203
例 regular →0099

NOTE
★ do not confuse with 堂 HALL →3202

蛍

▶FIREFLY
ケイ ほたる
Ⓝ 螢 Ⓒ 萤 yíng

3204
2-5-6

142	Jōyō	U86CD
虫	S11-6-5	F2407

COMPOUNDS
❶ [original meaning] FIREFLY, glowfly
蛍火 けいか light of a firefly
蛍雪 けいせつ diligent study

❷ (luminous as a firefly) fluorescent
蛍光 けいこう fluorescence
蛍光灯 けいこうとう fluorescent lamp [light]
蛍石 けいせき fluorite

KUN

【ほたる 蛍】 **FIREFLY, glowfly**

蛍の光 ほたるのひかり firefly glow; *Auld Lang Syne*
蛍烏賊 ほたるいか firefly squid
土蛍 つちぼたる glowworm

SYNONYMS

❶ **insects**

蚊 MOSQUITO → 1673
蛍 FIREFLY → 3204
蝶 BUTTERFLY → 1772
蚕 SILKWORM → 3107
蟬 CICADA → 1804
蜂 BEE → 1728
蛔 ROUNDWORM → 1717

❷ **bright**

明 BRIGHT → 1060
昭 LUMINOUS → 1107
蛍 fluorescent → 3204
晃 DAZZLING → 3101
燦 BRILLIANT → 1390
赫 BLAZING → 1960
暉 radiant → 1276
煕 BRIGHT → 3559
晟 SUNNY → 3104

COMPOUND FORMATION

【蛍雪 けいせつ】

蛍雪 'diligent study' refers to studying by the light of fireflies (蛍 ❶) and snow (雪).

萃 2-5-6

incorrect classification
➡ see 2-3-8: 艹 at 2882

紫 2-5-6

incorrect stroke-count
➡ see 2-6-6: 此 at 3332

畳

3205

2-5-7

▸**TATAMI**
▸**FOLD UP**
ジョウ たた(む) たた(み)- たたみ

Ⓝ 疊 畳 曡 Ⓒ 叠 dié

102	Jōyō	U7573
田	S12-5-7	F1309

COMPOUNDS

❶ [sometimes also 帖 0342] **counter for TATAMI or (straw) mats**

畳数 じょうすう number of tatami [mats]
四畳半の部屋 よじょうはんのへや four-and-a-half-mat room

❷ⓐ reduplicate (a word), repeat, reiterate
ⓑ [original meaning] pile up, place one upon another

a 畳成語 じょうせいご reiterative
畳語 じょうご syllable repetition to indicate plurals (as 人人 ひとびと)
畳韻 じょういん repeated [recurring] rhymes (in Chinese poetry)
b 重畳たる ちょうじょうたる piled up, placed one upon another; excellent, splendid

KUN

【たたむ 畳む】 **FOLD UP, fold; shut; bear in mind; do away with**

畳まる たたまる be folded (up)
畳んでしまえ たたんでしまえ Down with him!
折り畳みの おりたたみの collapsible
家を畳む いえをたたむ shut up one's house
胸に畳む むねにたたむ bear in mind

【たたみ- 畳み-】 [prefix] **folding, collapsible**

畳み椅子 たたみいす folding [collapsible] chair
畳み地図 たたみちず folding map

【たたみ 畳】 **TATAMI, mat, straw mat**

畳表 たたみおもて mat facing
畳替え たたみがえ refacing [renewing] mats
畳敷きの部屋 たたみじきのへや straw-matted room
青畳 あおだたみ new mat

SYNONYMS

❶ & 【たたみ】 **mats**

畳 TATAMI → 3205
薦 straw mat → 3008
-敷き underlay → 2345

❷ⓐ **repeating and repetition**

再 ANOTHER TIME → 4332
又 AGAIN → 4158
復 repeat → 0701
重 DUPLICATE → 4390
畳 reduplicate → 3205
改 redo → 0287
-換える redo → 0716
-直す repetition suffix → 3649
-返す do over → 3797

【たたむ】

○ **fold**

折 FOLD → 0297
畳む FOLD UP → 3205

塁 3206

2-5-7

▶BASE
▶SMALL FORT

ルイ とりで▲

Ⓝ 壘 Ⓒ 垒 lěi

32	Jōyō	U5841
土	S12-3-9	F1911

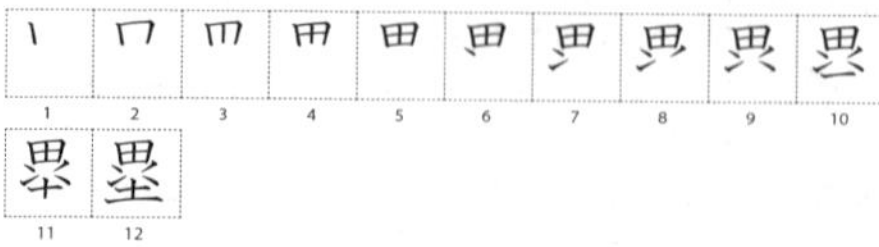

COMPOUNDS

❶ *baseball* **BASE**

塁審 るいしん base umpire
満塁 まんるい full bases
三塁 さんるい third base
本塁打 ほんるいだ home run
盗塁 とうるい base stealing, steal

❷ [original meaning] (small military fortification consisting of raised earthwork) **SMALL FORT, rampart, parapet, fortress, redoubt**

塁壁 るいへき rampart
敵塁 てきるい enemy fortress, enemy position
堅塁 けんるい strong fort(ress)
堡塁 ほうるい(=ほるい) fort, fortress, stronghold
土塁 どるい earthwork, fieldwork

INDEPENDENT

【るい 塁】 *baseball* **BASE**; fort, rampart, parapet

塁に出る るいにでる go to first
塁を守る るいをまもる defend a fort
塁を摩する るいをますする rival, run close to

KUN

【とりで 塁】 [now usu. 砦, formerly also 塞] fort, fortress, stronghold

SYNONYMS

❷ **strongholds**

城 CASTLE →0417
塁 SMALL FORT →3206
塞 FORT →2924
砦 FORT →3310
堡 FORT →3500

USAGE

【とりで】

塁
[now usu. 砦, formerly also 塞] fort, fortress, stronghold

砦
[formerly also 塁 or 塞] fort, fortress, stronghold

塞
[now usu. 砦] fort, fortress, stronghold

HOMOPHONES

とりで

砦 FORT →3310
塞 STOP UP →2924

異 3207

2-5-7

▶DIFFERENT

イ こと こと(なる)

102	Nonstandard	U7570
田	S12-5-7	F0000

traditional form →see 異 at 3195

登 3208

2-5-7

▶CLIMB

トウ ト のぼ(る) ㊔ たか すみ

Ⓒ 登 dēng

105	Jōyō-3	U767B
癶	S12-5-7	F0560

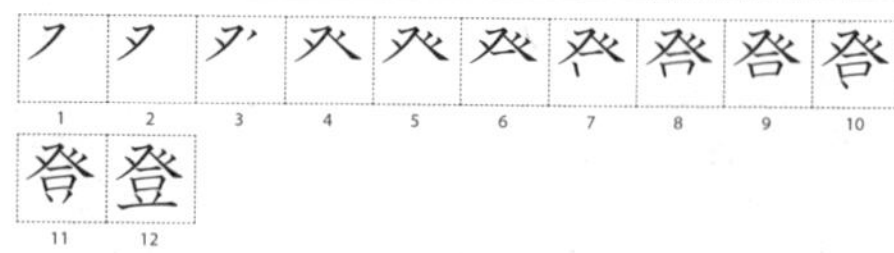

COMPOUNDS

❶ⓐ **CLIMB, ascend, mount, go up**
ⓑ **CLIMB** or promote to a higher rank or position

a 登山 とざん mountain climbing, mountaineering
登頂 とうちょう climbing to the summit
登楼する とうろうする go into a tall building; visit a brothel
登高する とうこうする climb up

b 登用する とうようする appoint, designate; promote, advance
登竜門 とうりゅうもん gateway to success, opening to honors

❷ **attend, go to, appear**

登校 とうこう attending school
登庁する とうちょうする attend a government office
登院 とういん attendance at the House
登城 とじょう attendance at a castle
登場する とうじょうする come on stage; appear

❸ **register, enter, record**

登録 とうろく registration
登記 とうき registration, registry
登載 とうさい registration, record

❹ [rare] pass (an examination)

登科 とうか passing the civil service examination
登第 とうだい passing the examination

KUN

【のぼる 登る】 (move up, esp. by using the hands and feet) **CLIMB, mount, ascend, scale**

登り のぼり climbing, ascent

登り口 のぼりぐち starting point (for the ascent of a mountain)
山登り やまのぼり mountain climbing
演壇に登る えんだんにのぼる mount the platform

SYNONYMS

❶ⓐ ascend
昇 ASCEND →3068
上 go up →4212
騰 RISE (esp. in price) →1422
登 CLIMB →3208

❷ attend
臨 BE PRESENT AT →2059
登 attend →3208
出 appear →4310

❸ write
書 WRITE →3292
筆 write →3317
写 COPY →2493
記 WRITE DOWN →1843
紀 record in writing →1628
控える note down →0600
録 RECORD →2186
登 register →3208
註 ANNOTATE →1893

HOMOPHONES

のぼる
上 UP →4212
昇 ASCEND →3068
のぼり 上 UP →4212

NOTE

➡ see USAGE note at 上 4212

發

3209
2-5-7

▶**START**
▶**EMIT**
ハツ ホツ た(つ) あば(く) ㊔ ひらく
あきら

105	Nonstandard	U767C
癶	S12-5-7	F0000

traditional form → see 発 at 3174

黍

3210
2-5-7

▶**PROSO MILLET**
ショ きび
Ⓒ 黍 shǔ

202	Non-Jōyō	U9ECD
黍	S12-12-0	F0000

RADICAL

kibi 'millet' (黎 黐×), used in characters related to millet or its qualities

COMPOUNDS

● [original meaning] **PROSO MILLET, common millet**
蜀×黍 しょくしょ(=もろこし) sorghum, Indian millet

KUN

【きび 黍】 **PROSO MILLET, common millet**
黍団子 きびだんご millet dumpling
唐黍 とうきび(=もろこし) sorghum, Indian millet
砂糖黍 さとうきび sugarcane

SPECIAL READINGS

玉蜀×黍 とうもろこし corn

SYNONYMS

● cereals
米 RICE →4342
麦 WHEAT →3061
豆 BEAN →2442
粟 FOXTAIL MILLET →3326
黍 PROSO MILLET →3210
蕎 BUCKWHEAT →2993
蔣 WILD RICE →2976

窗
2-5-7

incorrect classification
➡ see 2-3-9: 穴 at 2896

童
2-5-7

incorrect classification
➡ see 2-2-10: 亠 at 2639

買

3211
2-5-7

▶**BUY**
バイ か(う)
Ⓒ 买 mǎi

154	Jōyō-2	U8CB7
貝	S12-7-5	F0339

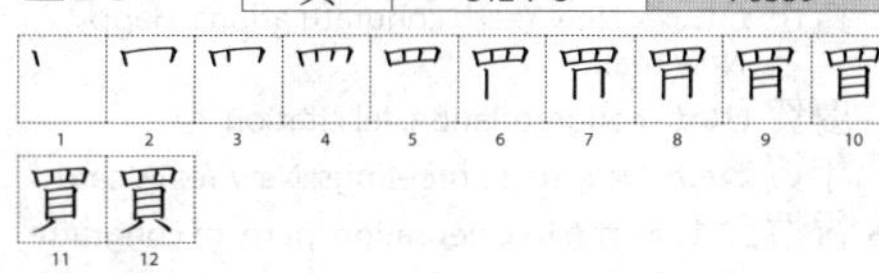

COMPOUNDS

● [original meaning] **BUY, purchase**
買収 ばいしゅう buying up, purchasing; bribing
購買 こうばい purchase, buying
売買 ばいばい buying and selling, trade

KUN

【かう 買う】
① **BUY, purchase**
買い かい buying
買い手 かいて buyer, customer
買い物 かいもの shopping, marketing; purchase
買い上げる かいあげる buy, buy up; bid up
買い入れ かいいれ purchase, buying
買い気 かいき bullish [buying] sentiment [feeling]
買い戻し かいもどし redemption, repurchase
② incur, invite

人の恨みを買う ひとのうらみをかう incur a person's enmity

③ **appreciate**

買い被る かいかぶる overrate, think too highly of

苦心を買われる くしんをかわれる have one's labor appreciated

SYNONYMS

● **buy**

買 BUY → 3211

購 PURCHASE → 2053

鼠

2-5-7

incorrect stroke-count
➡ see 2-6-7: 臼 at 3340

賀

3212

2-5-7

▶CONGRATULATE

ガ ㊔ か よし のり

Ⓒ 贺 hè

154	Jōyō-5	U8CC0
貝	S12-7-5	F0934

COMPOUNDS

ⓐ **CONGRATULATE, greet**

ⓑ **celebrate**

a 賀状 がじょう greeting card

賀詞 がし greetings, congratulations

賀正 がしょう New Year's congratulations, Happy New Year

慶賀 けいが congratulation, felicitation

年賀 ねんが New Year's greetings; New Year's card

b 祝賀会 しゅくがかい celebration, party of congratulation

INDEPENDENT

【が 賀】 celebration; congratulation, felicitations

七十の賀 しちじゅうのが celebration of one's 70th birthday

【がする 賀する】 **CONGRATULATE**, greet

SYNONYMS

● **celebrating and congratulating**

祝 CELEBRATE → 1144

慶 FELICITATION → 3936

賀 CONGRATULATE → 3212

寿 CONGRATULATIONS → 4372

貸

3213

2-5-7

▶LEND

タイ か(す) か(し)- かし-

Ⓒ 贷 dài

154	Jōyō-5	U8CB8
貝	S12-7-5	F1231

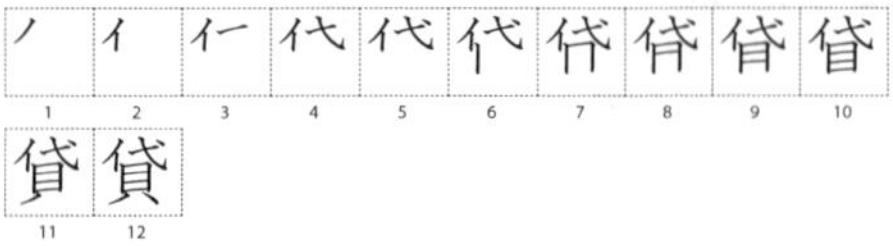

COMPOUNDS

● [original meaning] **LEND, loan; rent, hire out**

貸借 たいしゃく lending and borrowing, debt and credit, loan

貸与 たいよ loan, lending

賃貸 ちんたい lease, hiring out, charter

KUN

【かす 貸す】 **LEND, loan; rent, hire out; give credit**

貸し かし loan, lending; renting

貸し倒れ かしだおれ irrecoverable debt

貸金 かしきん loan

貸し出す かしだす lend, make a loan; rent; hire

貸し出し かしだし loan; lending service

貸し切りの かしきりの booked, reserved, chartered

貸間 かしま room for rent

高利貸し こうりがし(=こうりかし) loansharking, usury

【かし- 貸し-, 貸-】 [also prefix] **for rent, for hire**

貸し本屋 かしほんや rental library

貸し室 かししつ room for rent

貸家 かしや house for rent

貸店舗 かしてんぽ store for rent

SYNONYMS

● **lend and borrow**

借 BORROW → 0137

債 DEBT → 0177

貸 LEND → 3213

融 finance → 2303

NOTE

★ do not confuse with 貨 MONEY → 3113 and 賃 WAGE → 3341

貿

3214

2-5-7

▶TRADE

ボウ

Ⓒ 贸 mào

154	Jōyō-5	U8CBF
貝	S12-7-5	F1317

COMPOUNDS

● [original meaning] **TRADE, buy and sell, exchange**

貿易 ぼうえき trade, commerce
貿易会社 ぼうえきがいしゃ trading firm
貿易風 ぼうえきふう trade wind
貿易品 ぼうえきひん articles of commerce
貿易業 ぼうえきぎょう trading business

SYNONYMS

● **sell and trade**

売 SELL → 2722
卸す WHOLESALE → 1835
販 ENGAGE IN SALES → 1869
商 TRADE → 2623
貿 TRADE → 3214
易 EXCHANGE → 3064

嵜

2-5-7

incorrect classification
➡ see 2-3-9: 山 at 2899

掌

▶PALM
▶TAKE CHARGE OF
ショウ てのひら▲ たなごころ▲

3215

2-5-7

Ⓒ 掌 zhǎng

64	Jōyō	U638C
手	S12-4-8	F1602

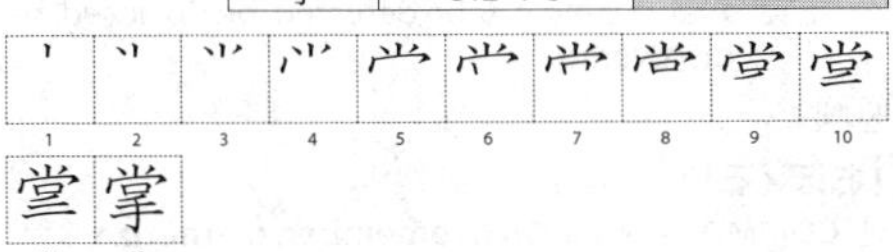

COMPOUNDS

❶ [original meaning] **PALM of the hand**

掌中本 しょうちゅうぼん pocket edition
掌握する しょうあくする hold, seize, grasp, command
合掌する がっしょうする join one's hands (in prayer)
指掌紋 ししょうもん hand print

❷ⓐ **TAKE CHARGE OF, be in charge of, supervise**
ⓑ charge, duties

a 掌理する しょうりする take charge of, preside over, manage
職掌 しょくしょう office, function
車掌 しゃしょう conductor
b 分掌 ぶんしょう division of duties
管掌 かんしょう taking charge, management

INDEPENDENT

【しょう 掌】**PALM** of the hand

KUN

【てのひら 掌】[also 手の平] **PALM of the hand**
【たなごころ 掌】**PALM** of the hand
掌を指す様に知っている たなごころをさすようにしっている know (something) like the palm of one's hand

SYNONYMS

❶ **hand and arm**

手 HAND → 4267
腕 ARM → 1269
肘 ELBOW → 1044
掌 PALM → 3215
指 FINGER → 0452
拇 THUMB → 0358
拳 FIST → 3295

❷ **direct and supervise**

制 CONTROL → 1624
理 manage → 1220
経 MANAGE → 1687
管 EXERCISE CONTROL → 3349
轄 EXERCISE JURISDICTION OVER → 2056
掌 TAKE CHARGE OF → 3215
監 OVERSEE → 3535
督 SUPERVISE → 3471
司 OFFICIATE → 3648
宰 PRESIDE → 2829
営 MANAGE → 3216

USAGE

【てのひら】
掌
[also 手の平] palm of the hand
手の平
[also 掌] palm of the hand

HOMOPHONES

てのひら 手の平 → 4267, 4291

嘗

2-5-7

incorrect stroke-count
➡ see 2-5-8: 尚 at 3225

営

▶MANAGE
▶BARRACKS
エイ いとな(む)

3216

2-5-7

Ⓝ 營 Ⓒ 营 yíng

42△	Jōyō-5	U55B6
⺍	S12-3-9	F0368

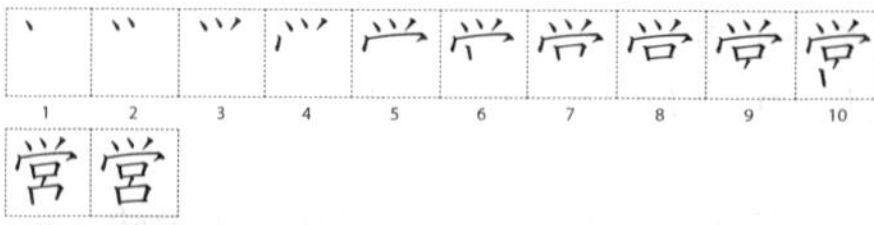

COMPOUNDS

❶ⓐ MANAGE (the affairs of an organization), conduct, administer, operate, run, engage in
ⓑ [also suffix] **MANAGEd by, operated by**

a 営業する えいぎょうする conduct [do] business, trade in
営林 えいりん forest management
経営する けいえいする manage (a firm), conduct (a business)
運営する うんえいする operate, manage
b 公営 こうえい public management
名古屋市営 なごやしえい managed by the Nagoya Municipality

❷ BARRACKS, camp, encampment; fort
兵営 へいえい barracks
陣営 じんえい camp, quarters
野営 やえい camping, campground

❸ construct, build, erect
営繕 えいぜん building and repairs, maintenance
造営 ぞうえい building, construction

❹ plan, realize (profits)
営利 えいり profit, gain

❺ [usu. 栄 3183] vitality obtained from nutriments (in Chinese medicine)
営養 えいよう nutrition, nourishment

KUN

【いとなむ 営む】**MANAGE, operate, conduct; build; perform (a religious service)**
営み いとなみ business, occupation, operation

SYNONYMS

❶ direct and supervise
制 CONTROL → 1624
理 manage → 1220
経 MANAGE → 1687
管 EXERCISE CONTROL → 3349
轄 EXERCISE JURISDICTION OVER → 2056
掌 TAKE CHARGE OF → 3215
監 OVERSEE → 3535
督 SUPERVISE → 3471
司 OFFICIATE → 3648
宰 PRESIDE → 2829
営 MANAGE → 3216

❷ camps
陣 CAMP → 0545
営 BARRACKS → 3216

覚

3217

2-5-7

▶PERCEIVE
▶COMMIT TO MEMORY

カク おぼ(える) さ(ます) さ(める) さと(る)▲
㊔ さとし あきら がく
Ⓝ 覺 Ⓒ 觉 jué jiào

147	Jōyō-4	U899A
見	S12-7-5	F0361

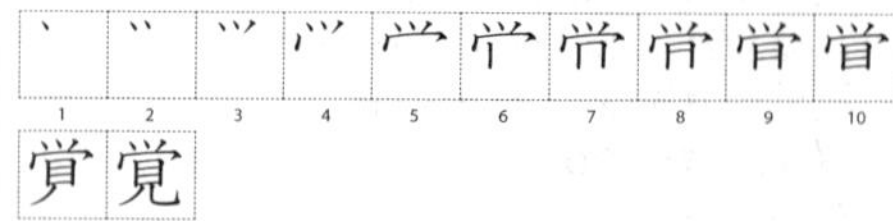

COMPOUNDS

❶ⓐ PERCEIVE, sense, discern, feel, be conscious; realize, know, comprehend
ⓑ sense, sensation

a 覚悟 かくご readiness, preparedness; resignation; resolution
知覚 ちかく perception, sensation
自覚する じかくする be conscious of, realize
b 感覚 かんかく sense, sensation, feeling
視覚 しかく sense of sight
痛覚 つうかく sense of pain

❷ⓐ awake, wake up; be disillusioned
ⓑ awake to the Truth, become enlightened

a 覚醒する かくせいする awake, wake up; be awakened, be disillusioned
覚醒剤 かくせいざい stimulant
b 覚者 かくしゃ Buddha, the awakened one

❸ be detected, be disclosed, be discovered
発覚する はっかくする be detected, be disclosed, be discovered

KUN

【おぼえる 覚える】
① **COMMIT TO MEMORY, remember, memorize**
覚え おぼえ recollection, memory; learning; favor; feeling
覚え書き おぼえがき memorandum, memo, note
見覚え みおぼえ recognition, remembrance
物覚え ものおぼえ memory
② **learn, know, acquire**
覚え易い おぼえやすい be easy to learn
③ feel, experience
痛みを覚える いたみをおぼえる feel a pain

【さます 覚ます】[also 醒ます] *vt*
① **awake, wake up**
目を覚ます めをさます awake, wake up, awaken
目覚まし めざまし alarm clock
② disillusion
③ make sober

【さめる 覚める】[also 醒める] *vi*
① **awake, wake up**

眠りから覚める ねむりからさめる awake from one's sleep

② be disillusioned

③ become sober

酔い覚め よいざめ recovering from intoxication, sobering up

【さとる 覚る】[now usu. 悟る] **awake to, be aware of, PERCEIVE, discern, realize**

覚り さとり comprehension, understanding

覚りが早い さとりがはやい be quick to understand

SYNONYMS

❶ⓐ perceive

覚 PERCEIVE →3217

知 KNOW →1446

感 FEEL →3514

認 RECOGNIZE →1948

ⓑ sense

感 SENSE →3514

覚 sense →3217

勘 INTUITIVE PERCEPTION →2231

❷ awake

悟 AWAKE TO →0502

醒 AWAKE →2033

覚 awake →3217

惺 AWAKE TO →0709

【おぼえる】

① **remember**

憶 REMEMBER →0944

覚える COMMIT TO MEMORY →3217

記 commit to memory →1843

追 reminisce →3840

顧 LOOK BACK →2394

偲 RECOLLECT →0153

USAGE

❶【さます】

覚ます

[also 醒ます] *vt*

① awake, wake up

② disillusion

③ make sober

冷ます

vt

① cool, let cool

② dampen, spoil

醒ます

[also 覚ます] same as 覚ます

❷【さめる】

覚める

[also 醒める] *vi*

① awake, wake up

② be disillusioned

③ become sober

冷める

vi

ⓐ cool off, get cold

ⓑ cool down, subside, flag, be dampened

醒める

[also 覚める] *vi*

① awake, wake up

② be disillusioned, come to one's senses

③ become sober

HOMOPHONES

さます

冷 COLD →0088

醒 AWAKE →2033

さめる

冷 COLD →0088

醒 AWAKE →2033

さとる 悟 AWAKE TO →0502

さとり 悟 AWAKE TO →0502

NOTE

➡ see also USAGE note at 悟 0502

黹

3218

2-5-7

▶*FUTSU*

204 黹	Radical	U9EF9
	S12-12-0	F0000

RADICAL

futsu 'embroidery' (黻×), used in characters related to embroidery or designs on clothing

---

貰

3219

2-5-7

▶**GET**

セイ もら(う)

Ⓒ 贳 shì

154 貝	Names	U8CB0
	S12-7-5	F1666

KUN

【もらう 貰う】

①ⓐ **GET, be given, receive, accept, take**

ⓑ **contract, pick up (a disease)**

ⓒ **buy, take, have**

ⓓ marry (a woman), adopt (a child, etc.)

a 貰い手 もらいて receiver, recipient

貰い物 もらいもの (received) present, gift

貰い泣き もらいなき crying in sympathy

物貰い ものもらい beggar; sty (on the eyelid)

b 風邪を貰う かぜをもらう pick up a cold

c このコップを貰います このこっぷをもらいます I'll take this cup

d 貰い子 もらいご adopted child, foster child

② [following the TE-form of verbs] **GET something done (by someone)**

診て貰う みてもらう see [consult] (a doctor), receive medical treatment
来て貰う きてもらう have someone come over

SYNONYMS

【もらう】
①ⓐ **receive**
受 RECEIVE → 3076
享 ENJOY → 2545
領 receive → 1567
収 TAKE IN → 0031
納 ACCEPT → 1652
貰 GET → 3219
戴 RECEIVE HUMBLY → 4093
頂 RECEIVE HUMBLY → 0164
拝 have the honor to receive → 0360

貴

3220
2-5-7

▶**NOBLE**
▶**YOUR HONORABLE**
キ たっと(い) とうと(い) たっと(ぶ) とうと(ぶ) ㊔ たか たかし あつ よし
ⓒ 贵 guì

154	Jōyō-6	U8CB4
貝	S12-7-5	F0752

COMPOUNDS

❶ⓐ (of noble rank) **NOBLE, high-ranking**
ⓑ (lofty in character) **NOBLE, exalted, honorable, dignified**
ⓒ (chemically inactive) **NOBLE**, inert
a 貴族 きぞく nobility, noble
貴婦人 きふじん lady of rank, gentlewoman
b 富貴な ふうきな(=ふっきな) wealthy and noble
高貴な こうきな high and noble
c 貴金属 ききんぞく noble metals
貴ガス きがす noble gas, inert gas
❷ⓐ [also prefix] [honorific] **YOUR HONORABLE, your, your esteemed**
ⓑ [honorific] **you**
a 貴社 きしゃ your company
貴翰 きかん your letter
b 貴下 きか you
貴殿 きでん you
貴様 きさま [belittling] you; [original meaning] sir, madam
❸ **precious, valuable, costly**
貴重な きちょうな precious, valuable
物価騰貴 ぶっかとうき rise in prices
❹ colloquial suffix expressing intimacy
兄貴 あにき older brother; one's senior
伯父貴 おじき uncle

KUN

【たっとい 貴い】
① **precious, valuable, priceless**
貴い命 たっといいのち precious life
② (of noble rank) **NOBLE, high-ranking**
貴い家柄である たっといいえがらである be of noble birth
【とうとい 貴い】 same as 貴い たっとい
【たっとぶ 貴ぶ】 **value, set a high value on, have a high regard for**
命より名を貴ぶ いのちよりなをたっとぶ value honor above life
【とうとぶ 貴ぶ】 same as 貴ぶ たっとぶ

SPECIAL READINGS

貴方▲ あなた you
貴女▲ あなた you (feminine pronoun)

SYNONYMS

❶ⓐ & ❶ⓑ **high-ranking**
貴 NOBLE → 3220
上 upper → 4212
高 HIGH → 2601
総 GENERAL → 1743
太 of highest rank → 2673
❷ⓐ **honorific prefixes**
御 GENERAL HONORIFIC TERM → 0703
貴 YOUR HONORABLE → 3220
尊 your honorable → 2920
令 your honorable → 2489
ⓑ **second person pronouns**
君 YOU (*familiar*) → 3974
汝 THOU → 0255
爾 thou → 4407
貴 you (*honorific*) → 3220
卿 you (*archaic*, *honorific*) → 0769
❸ **expensive**
貴 precious → 3220
高 high-priced → 2601

USAGE

❶【たっとい】
貴い
① precious, valuable, priceless
② (of noble rank) noble, high-ranking
尊い
exalted, august, awe-inspiring, sacred
❷【とうとい】
貴い
same as 貴い たっとい
尊い
same as 尊い たっとい

❸【たっとぶ】
貴ぶ
value, set a high value on, have a high regard for
尊ぶ
honor, respect, revere

❹【とうとぶ】
貴ぶ
same as 貴ぶ たっとぶ
尊ぶ
same as 尊ぶ たっとぶ

HOMOPHONES

たっとい 尊 HONOR → 2920
とうとい 尊 HONOR → 2920
たっとぶ 尊 HONOR → 2920
とうとぶ 尊 HONOR → 2920

費

3221

2-5-7

▶EXPENSE

ヒ つい(やす) つい(える)

Ⓒ 费 fèi

154	Jōyō-4	U8CBB
貝	S12-7-5	F0602

COMPOUNDS

❶ [also suffix] **EXPENSE, expenses, expenditure, cost**
費用 ひよう expenses, outlay
費目 ひもく item of expenditure
会費 かいひ fee, membership fee
学費 がくひ school [educational] expenses
食費 しょくひ food expenses; (charge for) board
出費 しゅっぴ expenses, expenditure, outlay
経費 けいひ expense(s), cost(s), expenditure, upkeep
生活費 せいかつひ living expenses, cost of living

❷ [original meaning] **expend, spend, consume, use up**
消費 しょうひ consumption, spending
浪費 ろうひ waste, extravagance
空費 くうひ waste

KUN

【ついやす 費やす】**expend, spend, consume, use up; waste, squander**
多くの金を費やす おおくのかねをついやす spend [expend] a lot of money
空しく費やされた時 むなしくついやされたとき time passed in vain, wasted time

【ついえる 費える】**be wasted**
費え ついえ wasteful expenses
無為に費えた年月 むいについえたとしつき years spent idly

SYNONYMS

❶ **fee and price**
料 FEE → 1644
代 CHARGE → 0034
賃 CHARGES → 3341
銭 money paid → 2159
費 EXPENSE → 3221
価 PRICE → 0095
値 price → 0123

❷ **consume**
消 SPEND → 0531
費 expend → 3221
尽 EXHAUST → 3786
耗 WEAR AWAY → 1660
銷 USE UP → 2174

USAGE

【ついえる】
費える
be wasted
潰える
ⓐ be routed, be utterly defeated
ⓑ collapse

HOMOPHONES

ついえる 潰 CRUSH → 0919

窟

2-5-8

incorrect classification
➡ see 2-3-10: 宀 at 2923

意

2-5-8

incorrect classification
➡ see 2-2-11: 亠 at 2650

置

3222

2-5-8

▶PLACE

チ お(く) -お(き)

Ⓒ 置 zhì

122	Jōyō-4	U7F6E
罒	S13-5-8	F0260

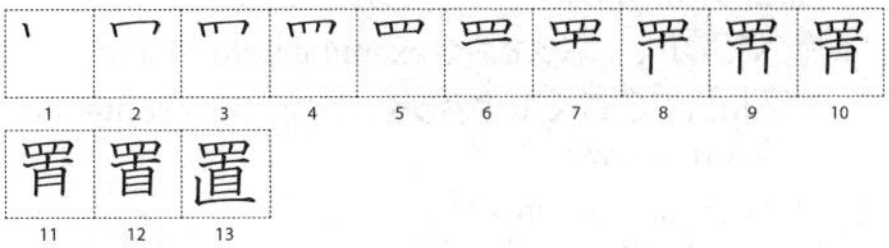

COMPOUNDS

❶ⓐ **PLACE, put, install, set**
ⓑ **PLACE** in custody, detain
ⓒ **PLACE, position**

a 置換 ちかん substitution, replacement, displacement
倒置 とうち turning upside down; *gram* inversion
配置する はいちする arrange; post (troops)

布置 ふち arrangement, grouping
前置詞 ぜんちし preposition
安置する あんちする install, lay in state
対置する たいちする oppose (a thing) to (another)
装置 そうち equipment, device, installation
b 留置 りゅうち detention, custody, retention
拘置する こうちする detain, confine, arrest
c 位置 いち position, place

❷ found, establish, set up
設置する せっちする establish, found, set up
増置する ぞうちする establish more (offices)
常置の じょうちの permanent; standing

❸ take proper steps, adopt measures, deal with
処置する しょちする dispose of, deal with
措置 そち measure, step, action

❹ leave, let (alone)
放置する ほうちする leave alone, neglect, leave as it is

KUN

【おく 置く】
①ⓐ **put, PLACE, set**
ⓑ **assign; post, station**
a 置き場 おきば storehouse, place to put something in [on]
置き時計 おきどけい table clock
置き換える おきかえる replace, rearrange, interchange
置き物 おきもの ornament
b 歩哨を置く ほしょうをおく post a sentinel
②ⓐ **leave, leave behind, leave with**
ⓑ leave (undone), let (alone)
ⓒ leave (a day or space) open
a 置き忘れる おきわすれる leave behind, forget
書き置き かきおき note [letter] left behind
b 据え置く すえおく leave as it is; defer (payment)
c 一軒置いて隣 いっけんおいてとなり next door but one
③ [following the TE-form of verbs] (perform an action and leave it in the state of having been done) do beforehand, do anyhow
調べて置く しらべておく examine beforehand
一応聞いて置く いちおうきいておく hear someone out anyway
④ establish, set up, organize
委員会を置く いいんかいをおく form a committee
⑤ engage, employ; lodge, keep
下宿人を置く げしゅくにんをおく keep boarders
⑥ (of frost or dew) be formed
霜を置いた しもをおいた frosted; gray, hoary

【-おき -置き】 [suffix] **every other, alternate**
一日置きに いちにちおきに every other [second] day
十分置きに運転する じゅっぷんおきにうんてんする operate on a ten-minute schedule

SYNONYMS

❶ⓐ put
据える INSTALL → 0602
置 PLACE → 3222
擱 LAY DOWN → 0970
掛ける SET → 0596
措 DISPOSE → 0610
ⓑ imprison and confine
拘 ARREST → 0367
禁 confine → 3469
留 keep in custody → 3189
置 place in custody → 3222
錮 IMPRISON → 2182

❷ found
立 ESTABLISH → 2486
設 SET UP → 1863
置 found → 3222

❸ deal with
扱う HANDLE → 0251
処 DEAL WITH → 3764
辦 DISPOSE OF → 2028
措 dispose of → 0610
置 take proper steps → 3222

USAGE

【おく】
置く
①ⓐ put, place, set
ⓑ assign; post, station
②ⓐ leave, leave behind, leave with
ⓑ leave (undone), let (alone)
ⓒ leave (a day or space) open
③ [following the TE-form of verbs] (perform an action and leave it in the state of having been done) do beforehand, do anyhow
④ establish, set up, organize
⑤ engage, employ; lodge, keep
⑥ (of frost or dew) be formed
措く
① desist from, discontinue
② except, set apart, lay aside
擱く
lay down (one's pen)

HOMOPHONES

おく
措 DISPOSE → 0610
擱 LAY DOWN → 0970

署 3223

▶PUBLIC-SERVICE STATION

ショ

N 署 C 署 shǔ

2-5-8

122	Jōyō-6	U7F72
罒	S13-5-8	F1281

COMPOUNDS

❶ [also suffix] **PUBLIC-SERVICE STATION or office, as a police station, fire station or tax office**

署長 しょちょう chief of police, office head
署員 しょいん member of an office, staff
警察署 けいさつしょ police station
消防署 しょうぼうしょ fire station
税務署 ぜいむしょ tax office
本署 ほんしょ chief police station, principal office
公署 こうしょ government office

❷ **sign one's name**

署名 しょめい signature, autograph
連署 れんしょ joint signature
代署する だいしょする sign for another

❸ assign duties to, post

部署 ぶしょ one's post, one's place of duty

INDEPENDENT

【しょ 署】**PUBLIC-SERVICE STATION** [office] (→❶)
【しょする 署する】sign one's name

SYNONYMS

❶ **public offices**

省 MINISTRY →3100
庁 GOVERNMENT AGENCY →3768
府 government office →3824
公 public office →2468
署 PUBLIC-SERVICE STATION →3223
局 public service office →3800
所 office →1056

罪 3224

▶CRIME

ザイ つみ

C 罪 zuì

2-5-8

122	Jōyō-5	U7F6A
罒	S13-5-8	F0739

COMPOUNDS

❶ⓐ [also suffix] **CRIME, offense** ⓑ **guilt**

a 罪状 ざいじょう offense, charges
罪人 ざいにん criminal, offender; sinner
犯罪 はんざい offense, crime
余罪 よざい other crimes [charges]
微罪 びざい minor offense, misdemeanor
破廉恥罪 はれんちざい infamous offense
b 有罪 ゆうざい guiltiness, guilt
無罪の むざいの not guilty, innocent

❷ **sin**

罪悪 ざいあく crime, sin, vice
罪業 ざいごう sin, iniquity
罪障 ざいしょう sins
原罪 げんざい original sin

❸ **fault, demerit**

功罪 こうざい merits and demerits
謝罪 しゃざい apology

❹ [also suffix] punishment, penalty

斬罪 ざんざい decapitation
流罪 るざい banishment, exile
死罪 しざい capital punishment; capital offense

KUN

【つみ 罪】**CRIME, offense; sin; sinful act; vice; punishment**

罪する つみする charge, sentence, punish
罪人 つみびと sinner
罪な事 つみなこと sinful act, trick, cruel thing
罪の無い つみのない innocent, guiltless
罪に服する つみにふくする submit to a sentence, admit an offense

SYNONYMS

❶ **crimes and offenses**

犯 OFFENSE →0229
罪 CRIME →3224
凶 atrocious crime →3679

❷ **wrongdoing and evil**

罪 sin →3224
非 wrong(doing) →1101
邪 wrong →1443
悪 evil (something bad) →3413
弊 evil(s) (something undesirable) →3583

嵩

2-5-8

incorrect classification
➡ see 2-3-10: 山 at 2927

究 立 田 ⺫ 【⺌】 丵 业

甞

3225

2-5-8

▶TASTE

ショウ ジョウ な(める) な(めずる) かつ(て) ㊔ ふる

99	Nonstandard	U751E
甘	S13-5-8	F0000

alternative form → see 嘗 at 3230

當

3226

2-5-8

▶THE PRESENT
▶HIT

トウ あ(たる) あ(たり)[1] あ(たり)[2] あ(てる) あ(て) まさ(に) ㊔ まさ

102	Nonstandard	U7576
田	S13-5-8	F0000

traditional form → see 当 at 2701

蕢

2-5-8

incorrect classification
➡ see 2-3-10: ⺾ at 2941

業

3227

2-5-8

▶WORK
▶BUSINESS
▶INDUSTRY

ギョウ ゴウ わざ ㊔ なり

Ⓒ 业 yè

75	Jōyō-3	U696D
木	S13-4-9	F0092

(stroke order 1–13)

COMPOUNDS

❶ⓐ (work as a means of livelihood) **WORK, occupation, business, employment, trade, profession**
ⓑ (operative activity or task) **WORK, operation**

a 職業 しょくぎょう occupation, vocation, profession
失業する しつぎょうする be out of work, lose one's job
生業 せいぎょう occupation, calling
生業 せいぎょう(=なりわい) livelihood; calling, occupation
従業員 じゅうぎょういん employee, workers
b 業績 ぎょうせき achievements; business results
操業する そうぎょうする operate, work, run
分業 ぶんぎょう division of labor [work]
作業 さぎょう work, operation

❷ [also suffix] **BUSINESS, trade, enterprise**

業務 ぎょうむ business, affairs, work, service
業者 ぎょうしゃ the trade, businessman
開業する かいぎょうする start a business, open a practice
商業 しょうぎょう commerce, trade, business
営業 えいぎょう business, trade
兼業 けんぎょう side business
事業 じぎょう undertaking, enterprise, business; achievement
企業 きぎょう undertaking, enterprise; business enterprise, company
印刷業 いんさつぎょう printing business

❸ [also suffix] **INDUSTRY**

業界 ぎょうかい industry, business world
業種 ぎょうしゅ type of industry, category of business
産業 さんぎょう industry
工業 こうぎょう industry, manufacturing industry
農業 のうぎょう agriculture
鉱業 こうぎょう mining (industry)
興業 こうぎょう promotion of industry
製造業 せいぞうぎょう manufacturing industry

❹ **studies, course of study, schoolwork**

学業 がくぎょう studies; scholastic attainments
授業 じゅぎょう teaching, instruction; lesson
卒業 そつぎょう graduation
修業する しゅうぎょう(=しゅぎょう)する pursue one's studies, study, complete a course

❺ⓐ deed, **WORK**, achievement
ⓑ (one's deeds as a determinant factor in one's future life) karma

a 所業 しょぎょう deed, one's doings
偉業 いぎょう great work [achievement]
b 業報 ごうほう karmic effects, fate, inevitable retribution
悪業 あくごう evil doings in one's former existence, evil karma
自業自得 じごうじとく natural consequence of one's own deeds
罪業 ざいごう sin, iniquity
非業の死 ひごうのし unnatural death

❻ resentment, vexation

業腹 ごうはら resentment, vexation, spite

INDEPENDENT

【ぎょう 業】occupation, **WORK**; business; studies, arts
医を業とする いをぎょうとする practice medicine, be a physician by profession

【ごう 業】karma, karmic effect; resentment, vexation
業が深い ごうがふかい be sinful, be past redemption
業を煮やす ごうをにやす be exasperated, lose one's temper

KUN

【わざ 業】**WORK, act, deed**
業師 わざし tricky wrestler, shrewd fellow
仕業 しわざ act, action, deed, work
人間業 にんげんわざ work of man

軽業 かるわざ acrobatics

SYNONYMS

❶ⓐ work and employment

務 DUTY → 1505
任 OFFICE → 0057
役 SERVICE (esp. public) → 0288
勤 SERVICE (employment) → 2287
業 WORK → 3227
職 EMPLOYMENT → 1803
労 LABOR → 3155

❷ & ❸ industry and business

業 BUSINESS, INDUSTRY → 3227
商 TRADE → 2623
産 industry → 4089
工 manufacturing industry → 4190

❹ learning and knowledge

業 studies → 3227
学 learning → 3162
文 culture → 2458
識 KNOWLEDGE → 2070
知 knowledge → 1446

❺ⓐ acts

行 ACT → 0246
挙 NOTEWORTHY ACT → 3106
業 deed → 3227

ⓑ fate and fortune

運 FORTUNE → 3894
命 fate → 2553
業 karma → 3227
縁 karma relation → 1754
籤 LOT → 3399

HOMOPHONES

わざ 技 SKILL → 0292

NOTE

➡ see USAGE note at 技 0292

窪

▀2-5-9

incorrect classification
➡ see ▀2-3-11: 穴 at 2962

罰

3228

▀2-5-9

▶PUNISHMENT

バツ バチ

Ⓝ 罸 Ⓒ 罚 fá

122	Jōyō	U7F70
罒	S14-5-9	F1536

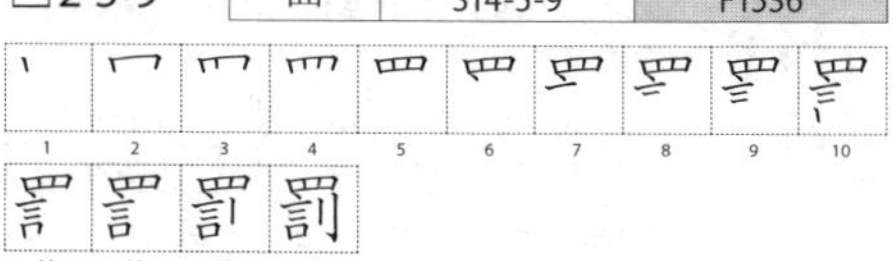

COMPOUNDS

ⓐ PUNISHMENT, penalty
ⓑ divine PUNISHMENT, Heaven's vengeance
ⓒ [original meaning] **punish, penalize**

a 罰金 ばっきん fine, penalty
罰則 ばっそく penal regulations, punitive provisions
罰点 ばってん black mark, X mark
刑罰 けいばつ penalty, punishment
b 天罰 てんばつ divine punishment
c 懲罰 ちょうばつ discipline, punishment
処罰 しょばつ punishment, penalty

INDEPENDENT

【ばつ 罰】PUNISHMENT, penalty
罰を科する ばつをかする inflict a punishment

【ばっする 罰する】punish

【ばち 罰】divine PUNISHMENT, retribution, Heaven's vengeance
罰当たり ばちあたり the damned, the cursed

SYNONYMS

● punishment

刑 PENALTY → 1024
罰 PUNISHMENT → 3228
懲 CHASTISE → 3623
処 DEAL WITH (lawbreakers) → 3764

署

3229

▀2-5-9

▶PUBLIC-SERVICE STATION

ショ

122	Names	UFA5A
罒	S14-5-9	F0000

traditional form → see 署 at 3223

嘗

3230

▀2-5-9

▶TASTE

ショウ ジョウ な(める) な(めずる) かつ(て)

㊔ ふる

Ⓝ 甞◇ Ⓒ 尝 cháng

30	Names	U5617
口	S14-3-11	F2886

COMPOUNDS

❶ TASTE, have a taste

臥薪嘗胆 がしんしょうたん perseverance; enduring hardships for the sake of vengeance

❷ try, attempt

嘗試する しょうしする try, attempt

❸ [now rare] autumn harvest festival

新嘗祭 しんじょうさい(=にいなめさい) ceremonial offering by the emperor of newly harvested rice to the deities

KUN

【なめる 嘗める】[also 舐める]

①ⓐ **TASTE, have a taste**

ⓑ **TASTE, undergo, experience (hardship, etc.)**
a 塩を嘗める しおをなめる taste the salt
b 辛酸を嘗める しんさんをなめる experience hardships

② **lick, lap, suck**
嘗め尽くす なめつくす lick thoroughly; burn to the ground
べろべろ嘗める べろべろなめる lick up with one's tongue

③ burn down, consume, devour
総嘗め そうなめ annihilation; a sweeping victory

④ make light of, treat with contempt

【なめずる 嘗めずる】[also 舐めずる] lick around (one's lips)
舌嘗めずりする したなめずりする lick one's lips; await eagerly

【かつて 嘗て】[also 曽て]
ⓐ **previously, formerly, once, before**
ⓑ [in negative constructions] (not) **ever**
a 嘗ての友 かつてのとも former friend
b 未だ嘗て いまだかつて [in negative constructions] (not) until now, (not) ever before, (not) yet

SYNONYMS

【なめる】
①ⓐ **taste**
味 TASTE (savor) → 0325
嘗める TASTE (have a taste) → 3230
舐める TASTE (have a taste) → 1669

【かつて】
ⓐ **former**
旧 FORMER → 0014
元 former → 2428
故 OLD (earlier time) → 1466
前 previous → 2819
嘗て previously → 3230
曽 previously → 2632
先 former → 3046
既 ALREADY → 1498

USAGE

❶【なめる】
嘗める
[also 舐める]
①ⓐ taste, have a taste
ⓑ taste, undergo, experience (hardship, etc.)
② lick, lap, suck
③ burn down, consume, devour
④ make light of, treat with contempt
舐める
[also 嘗める] same as 嘗める

❷【なめずる】
嘗めずる
[also 舐めずる] lick around (one's lips)
舐めずる
[also 嘗めずる] lick around (one's lips)

❸【かつて】
嘗て
[also 曽て]
ⓐ previously, formerly, once, before
ⓑ [in negative constructions] (not) ever
曽て
[also 嘗て] same as 嘗て

HOMOPHONES
なめる 舐 TASTE → 1669
なめずる 舐 TASTE → 1669
かつて 曽 GREAT- → 2632

裳
3231
2-5-9

▶**DRESS**
ショウ も
Ⓒ 裳 cháng shang

145	Names	U88F3
衣	S14-6-8	F2337

COMPOUNDS
❶ [now usu. 装 3327] **DRESS, clothing**
❷ [original meaning] long skirt worn in ancient China
a 裳階 しょうかい(=もこし) decorative pent roof
衣裳 いしょう clothes, garment, dress, costume

KUN
【も 裳】ancient skirt
裳裾 もすそ hem [cuff, train] of clothing
裳着 もぎ coming-of-age ceremony for girls in Heian period

SYNONYMS
❶ **clothing**
服 CLOTHES → 1090
袴 FORMAL DIVIDED SKIRT → 1509
蓑 STRAW RAINCOAT → 2941
-着 wear → 4110
衣 GARMENT → 2506
装 DRESS → 3327
裳 DRESS → 3231
襤 RAGS → 1607
袈 BUDDHIST SURPLICE → 3200
裟 BUDDHIST CASSOCK → 3420
襖 overgarment → 1600

盡
3232
2-5-9

▶**EXHAUST**
ジン つ(くす) -つ(くす) -づ(くし) つ(きる) つ(かす)

108	Names	U76E1
皿	S14-5-9	F0000

traditional form → see 尽 at 3786

窮窯 etc. incorrect classification
➡ see 2-3-12: 穴 at 2982
2-5-10

罵

▶ABUSE
バ ののし(る)
Ⓒ 骂 mà

3233
2-5-10

122	Jōyō	U7F75
罒	S15-5-10	F2062

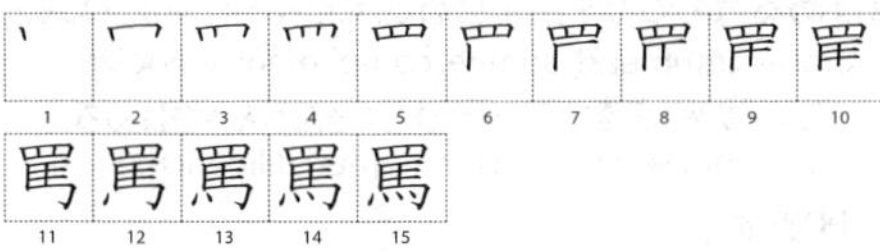

COMPOUNDS

● [original meaning] **ABUSE, revile, speak ill of, swear at, call names**
罵倒 ばとう abuse, denunciation, calling names
罵詈×雑言 ばりぞうごん vituperation, all manner of abuse
罵声 ばせい boos, jeers
面罵 めんば abusing someone to his [her] face
痛罵 つうば castigation, invective, severe abuse

KUN

【ののしる 罵る】**ABUSE, revile, speak ill of, swear at, call names**
罵り ののしり abuse, curse, swearing, insult

SYNONYMS

● **disgrace**
恥 SHAME → 1664
羞 shame → 4106
辱 HUMILIATE → 3400
侮 INSULT → 0091
罵 ABUSE → 3233
汚 defile → 0258
誹 SLANDER → 1978
譏 SLANDER → 2069

罷

▶DISMISS
ヒ まか(り)-▲ や(める)▲
Ⓒ 罢 bà ba

3234
2-5-10

122	Jōyō	U7F77
罒	S15-5-10	F2690

COMPOUNDS

❶ **DISMISS, remove from office**
罷免 ひめん dismissal, discharge
罷官 ひかん [archaic] removal from office

❷ stop working, go on strike
罷業 ひぎょう strike, walkout

KUN

【まかり- 罷り-】emphatic verbal prefix
罷り通る まかりとおる push one's way through; be unchallenged
罷り成らぬ まかりならぬ must not, not be allowed
罷り間違えば まかりまちがえば if the worst happens, if things go wrong

【やめる 罷める】[in the form of 罷めさせる やめさせる] fire, discharge
罷めさせる やめさせる fire, discharge

SYNONYMS

❶ **dismiss**
罷 DISMISS → 3234
免 discharge → 2565
解 release from office → 1913

HOMOPHONES

やめる
辞 WORD → 1726
止 STOP → 3659
已 CEASE → 4185

NOTE

➡ see USAGE note at 辞 1726

罸

▶PUNISHMENT
バツ バチ

3235
2-5-10

122	Nonstandard	U7F78
罒	S15-5-10	F0000

traditional form → see 罰 at 3228

駕

▶CARRIAGE
ガ ㊔ のり
Ⓒ 驾 jià

3236
2-5-10

187	Names	U99D5
馬	S15-10-5	F1682

COMPOUNDS

❶ⓐ **CARRIAGE, litter, vehicle**
ⓑ ride a vehicle

a 駕輿 がよ palanquin, litter, *kago*
来駕 らいが [honorific] coming, attendance, presence (of a person)
鳳駕 ほうが imperial carriage

❷ **outdo, surpass**
凌駕(=陵駕) りょうが excelling, surpassing

INDEPENDENT

【がする 駕する】ride (a vehicle, animal); outdo, surpass

SPECIAL READINGS

駕籠 かご palanquin, litter, *kago*

SYNONYMS

❶ⓐ vehicle
車 VEHICLE →4367
輛 VEHICLE →2000
乗 vehicle →4393
輪 wheeled vehicle →1999
駕 CARRIAGE →3236
輿 PALANQUIN →3626
台 COUNTER FOR VEHICLES →2498

❷ excel
勝 EXCEL →1268
抜 STAND OUT →0290
擢んでる stand out →0973
超 SURPASS →4107
越 GO BEYOND →4108
凌 SURPASS →0144
駕 outdo →3236

賞

▶PRIZE
ショウ ほ(める)▲
Ⓒ 赏 shǎng

3237
2-5-10

154	Jōyō-4	U8CDE
貝	S15-7-8	F0667

COMPOUNDS

❶ⓐ [also suffix] **PRIZE, award, reward**
ⓑ award a PRIZE
a 賞金 しょうきん prize, award, reward
賞状 しょうじょう certificate of merit
賞品 しょうひん prize, trophy
賞罰 しょうばつ reward and punishment
懸賞 けんしょう prize competition; prize, reward
受賞する じゅしょうする win a prize
b ノーベル医学・生理学賞 のーべるいがくせいりがくしょう Nobel Prize for physiology and medicine
ノーベル賞 のーべるしょう Nobel prize
アカデミー賞 あかでみーしょう Academy Award
褒賞 ほうしょう prize, reward

❷ⓐ express admiration, praise, commend
ⓑ admire, appreciate, enjoy
a 賞賛(=称賛)する しょうさんする laud, praise, admire, commend
激賞 げきしょう high praise, unbounded admiration
b 賞美する しょうびする admire, praise; prize; appreciate
賞味する しょうみする relish, appreciate
鑑賞する かんしょうする appreciate
観賞する かんしょうする admire, enjoy

INDEPENDENT

【しょう 賞】**PRIZE**
賞を受ける しょうをうける receive a prize
【しょうする 賞する】commend, praise, award

KUN

【ほめる 賞める】[usu. 褒める, sometimes also 誉める]
praise, commend, admire, compliment, eulogize
人の勤勉さを賞める ひとのきんべんさをほめる praise a person for his [her] diligence

SYNONYMS

❶ⓐ prizes
賞 PRIZE →3237
杯 prize cup →1066
章 decoration →2624

❷ⓐ praise
賛 PRAISE →3484
頌 EULOGIZE →1319
謳 EXTOL →2061
讃 PRAISE →2093
美 regard as beautiful →2817
褒 COMMEND →2662
嘉 commend (esp. an inferior) →2953
彰 PROCLAIM MERITS →2337
称 acclaim →1491
賞 express admiration →3237
揚 EXALT →0722

HOMOPHONES

ほめる
誉 HONOR →3135
褒 COMMEND →2662

NOTE

➡ see USAGE note at 褒 2662

畳

▶TATAMI
▶FOLD UP
ジョウ たた(む) たた(み)- たたみ

3238
2-5-11

102	Nonstandard	U7582
田	S16-5-11	F0000

traditional form →see 疊 at 3205

窺

incorrect classification
➡ see 2-3-13: 宀 at 3002

2-5-11

罹
3239
2-5-11

▶FALL ILL
リ かか(る)
C 罹 lí

122	Non-Jōyō	U7F79
罒	S16-5-11	F2674

COMPOUNDS

a FALL ILL, contract (a disease)
b suffer (from a calamity)

a 罹患 りかん contraction of a disease
b 罹災者 りさいしゃ sufferers, victims

KUN

【かかる 罹る】**FALL ILL, contract (a disease)**
病気に罹る びょうきにかかる contract a disease

SYNONYMS

a disease
病 ILLNESS → 4062
疾 DISEASE → 4064
風 (infectious) disease → 3730
症 PATHOLOGICAL CONDITION → 4065
患 AFFECTED BY DISEASE → 3415
疫 EPIDEMIC → 4061
罹 FALL ILL → 3239
臥 be sick in bed → 1825

HOMOPHONES

かかる
掛 SET → 0596
懸 SUSPEND → 3632
架 LAY ACROSS → 3178
係 CONNECT → 0108
繋 CONNECT → 3612

NOTE

➡ see USAGE note at 掛 0596

黛
3240
2-5-11

▶EYEBROW INK
タイ ダイ まゆずみ
N 黛 C 黛 dài

203	Names	U9EDB
黑	S16-11-5	F0000

COMPOUNDS

1 EYEBROW INK
黛眉 たいび black eyebrows
2 blackish blue
黛青 たいせい blackish blue

KUN

【まゆずみ 黛】**EYEBROW INK**
黛で眉を引く まゆずみでまゆをひく paint one's eyebrows with eyebrow ink

SYNONYMS

1 cosmetics
紅 rouge → 1629
粉 face powder → 1643
黛 EYEBROW INK → 3240

覆
2-5-12

incorrect stroke-count
➡ see 2-6-12: 覀 at 3385

黛
3241
2-5-12

▶EYEBROW INK
タイ ダイ まゆずみ

203	Nonstandard	U9EDB
黑	S17-12-5	F0000

traditional form → see 黛 at 3240

聲
2-5-12

incorrect classification
➡ see 2-11-6: 殸 at 3565

藁
2-5-12

incorrect classification
➡ see 2-3-14: 艹 at 3015

壘
3242
2-5-13

▶BASE
▶SMALL FORT
ルイ とりで

32	Names	U58D8
土	S18-3-15	F0000

traditional form → see 塁 at 3206

叢
3243
2-5-13

▶CROWD TOGETHER
ソウ むら むら(がる) くさむら
C 丛 cóng

29	Names	U53E2
又	S18-2-16	F2603

COMPOUNDS

1 [sometimes also 双 0028] **CROWD TOGETHER, meet in large numbers**
叢生する そうせいする grow in clusters
叢書(=双書) そうしょ series, library
叢談 そうだん collection of stories
叢氷 そうひょう ice pack
論叢 ろんそう collection of treatises
2 grassy place, thicket, bush
叢林 そうりん Buddhist monastery
3 [also suffix] plexus
太陽神経叢 たいようしんけいそう solar plexus

KUN

【むら 叢】[usu. 群]
a [in compounds] group, crowd, flock
b counter for groups or flocks
a 叢雲 むらくも cloud masses
竹叢(=篁×) たかむら bamboo grove

稲叢 いなむら rick, stack (of rice straw)
草叢 くさむら [also 叢] grass, grassy place
b 一叢 ひとむら a copse; a crowd, a herd

【むらがる 叢がる】[usu. 群がる] **CROWD TOGETHER, throng, flock together, swarm**
蜂が叢がる はちがむらがる be swarmed with bees

【くさむら 叢】[also 草叢] grass, grassy place

SPECIAL READINGS

叢祠× ほこら small shrine

SYNONYMS

❶ kinds of grasses
草 GRASS → 2813
荻 AMUR SILVERGRASS → 2844
蒲 CATTAIL → 2932
萊 GOOSEFOOT → 2878
蕨 BRACKEN → 2992
叢 grassy place → 3243
芝 LAWN GRASS → 2705
笹 BAMBOO GRASS → 3301
茅 cogongrass → 2779
萱 THATCH GRASS → 2904
藁 STRAW → 3015
芦 REED → 2743
葦 COMMON REED → 2934
菅 SEDGE → 2874

❷ crowd
群 GROUP → 1942
衆 MULTITUDE → 3325
叢 CROWD TOGETHER → 3243
簇 FORM A CLUSTER → 3377

HOMOPHONES

むら 群 GROUP → 1942
むらがる 群 GROUP → 1942
くさむら 草叢 → 2813, 3243

NOTE

➡ see USAGE note at 群 1942

羅

3244
2-5-14

▶PHONETIC [ra]
ラ ㊔ろ
Ⓒ 罗 luó

122	Jōyō	U7F85
罒	S19-5-14	F1233

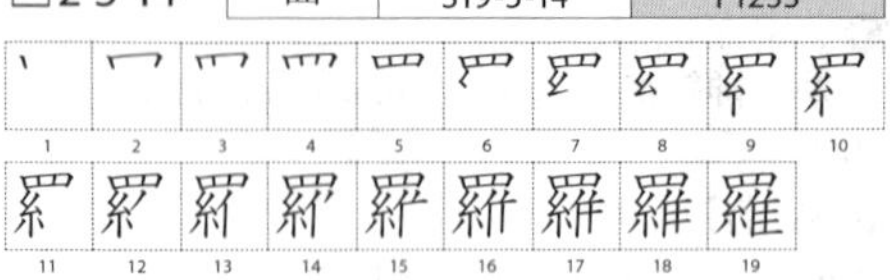

COMPOUNDS

❶ used PHONETICally for *ra* or similar sounds, esp. in the transliteration of proper names or Sanskrit Buddhist terms
羅紗 らしゃ woolen cloth
羅馬 ろーま Rome
天麩×羅 てんぷら tempura, Japanese deep-fat fried food
阿羅漢 あらかん *Arhat*, Buddhist monk who has attained Nirvana
金毘羅 こんぴら guardian deity of seafaring

❷ spread out, arrange, line up; lie in a row
羅列する られつする arrange, itemize
羅針盤 らしんばん compass
森羅万象 しんらばんしょう all creation, Nature

❸ⓐ [original meaning] bird net, net
ⓑ catch (birds) with a net
a 雀羅 じゃくら sparrow net
b 網羅する もうらする encompass, comprehend

❹ (netlike silk) silk gauze, thin silk
綺羅 きら fine clothes, gorgeous dress
一張羅 いっちょうら one's Sunday best; only suit one has

❺ abbrev. of 羅典 らてん: Latin
羅葡日辞典 らぽにちじてん Latin-Portuguese-Japanese dictionary

❻ abbrev. of 羅針盤 らしんばん: compass
羅方位 らほうい compass bearing
羅北 らほく compass north

INDEPENDENT

【ら 羅】silk gauze, thin silk

SYNONYMS

❶ phonetic [r]
呂 PHONETIC [ro] → 2713
路 phonetic [ru] → 1936
羅 PHONETIC [ra] → 3244

❷ arrange
並 LINE UP → 2793
比 rank → 0029
列 arrange in a row → 1018
陳 lay out (for exhibit) → 0656
羅 spread out → 3244
揃える arrange properly → 0719
整 PUT IN ORDER → 3562
理 put in order → 1220

❸ⓐ net
網 NET → 1737
羅 bird net → 3244

COMPOUND FORMATION

【羅針盤 らしんばん】
羅針盤 'compass' is a disk (盤) with a pointer (針) that lines up with (羅 ❷), or points to, the north.

罄

2-5-15

incorrect classification
➡ see 2-11-9: 殸 at 3575

黨
3245
⬒2-5-15

▶PARTY
トウ

203	Nonstandard	U9EE8
黑	S20-12-8	F0000

traditional form → see 党 at 3190

疊
3246
⬒2-5-17

▶TATAMI
▶FOLD UP
ジョウ たた(む) たた(み)- たたみ

102	Names	U758A
田	S22-5-17	F0000

traditional form → see 畳 at 3205

曡
3247
⬒2-5-17

▶TATAMI
▶FOLD UP
ジョウ たた(む) たた(み)- たたみ

102	Nonstandard	U7589
田	S22-5-17	F0000

traditional form → see 畳 at 3205

竊
⬒2-5-17

incorrect classification
➡ see ⬒2-3-19: 宀 at 3039

竺
3248
⬒2-6-2

▶INDIA
ジク ㊔ あつ あつし
Ⓒ 竺 zhú

118	Names	U7AFA
⺮	S8-6-2	F3300

COMPOUNDS

● INDIA
竺学 じくがく [rare] Indian [Buddhist] studies
天竺 てんじく India

SYNONYMS

● Asian countries
日 JAPAN → 3759
緬 Myanmar → 1758
老 Laos → 3963
華 CHINA → 2841
蒙 Mongolia → 2938
鮮 Korea → 2355
泰 Thailand → 3193
越 Vietnam → 4108
印 India → 1023
竺 INDIA → 3248
比 Philippines → 0029

兒
3249
⬒2-6-2

▶CHILD
ジ ニ こ -こ -(っ)こ ㊔ ちご

10	Names	U5152
儿	S8-2-6	F0000

traditional form → see 児 at 3153

呉
⬒2-6-2

incorrect stroke-count
➡ see ⬒2-5-2: 呉 at 3156

呪
3250
⬒2-6-2

▶SPELL
ジュ シュウ のろ(う) まじな(う)

30	Nonstandard	U5492
口	S8-3-5	F0000

traditional form → see 呪 at 0323

些
3251
⬒2-6-2

▶A BIT
サ いささ(か)
Ⓒ 些 xiē

7	Names	U4E9B
二	S8-2-6	F2494

COMPOUNDS

● A BIT, a little, somewhat, slightly
些細な ささいな trifling, slight, insignificant
些末な さまつな trivial, trifling
些事 さじ trivial matter, trifle
些少 さしょう a trivial amount [degree]

INDEPENDENT

【さ 些】A little BIT

KUN

【いささか 些か】A BIT, a little, somewhat, slightly

SYNONYMS

● few
少 LITTLE → 4278
寡 FEW → 2957
乏 SCANTY → 2432
薄 meager → 3004
微 SLIGHT → 0788
寸 A BIT OF → 3652
僅 A LITTLE → 0176
些 A BIT → 3251

卓
⬒2-6-2

incorrect classification
➡ see ⬒2-2-6: ⺊ at 2561

厽
⬒2-6-2

incorrect classification
➡ see ⬒2-2-6: 厶 at 2564

2

免 incorrect classification
➡ see 2-2-6: ⺈ at 2565
2-6-2

尭 incorrect classification
➡ see 2-2-6: 十 at 2560
2-6-2

卒 incorrect classification
➡ see 2-2-6: 亠 at 2549
2-6-2

受 incorrect classification
➡ see 2-4-4: ⺥ at 3076
2-6-2

具
3252
2-6-2

▸IMPLEMENT

グ そな(える) そな(わる) ㊔ とも く

12	Nonstandard	U5177
八	S8-2-6	F0000

traditional form → see 具 at 3159

典
3253
2-6-2

▸STANDARD WORK
▸CANON

テン デン▲ ㊔ のり つかさ つね ふみ すけ みち よし

Ⓒ 典 diǎn

12	Jōyō-4	U5178
八	S8-2-6	F0898

COMPOUNDS

❶ [original meaning] **STANDARD WORK** of reference or scholarship:
 ⓐ **reference book, dictionary, encyclopedia**
 ⓑ **classics, scriptures**

a 辞典 じてん dictionary
事典 じてん cyclopedia
字典 じてん Chinese character dictionary
b 原典 げんてん original text
古典 こてん classics; old book
聖典 せいてん sacred book, scriptures

❷ⓐ (standard code of laws) **CANON, code, law, rule, principle**
 ⓑ (standard of authority or evaluation) **CANON, model, standard, authority**

a 典則 てんそく regulations
法典 ほうてん code of laws, statute
刑典 けいてん penal code
b 典範 てんぱん model, standard; law, code
典型 てんけい type, pattern, model, exemplar
典型的な てんけいてきな typical, representative
典拠 てんきょ authority

❸ **formal ceremony, celebration**
典礼 てんれい formal ceremony
式典 しきてん ceremony
祭典 さいてん festival
祝典 しゅくてん celebration, festival

❹ decent, decorous, seemly, classic
典雅な てんがな refined, graceful, elegant, classic
典麗な てんれいな graceful, elegant

❺ [formerly 奠 でん 2641] **offering**
香典 こうでん obituary [condolence] gift, incense money

❻ be in charge of, supervise
典獄 てんごく prison warden

❼ used phonetically for *ten* or *den*
羅典 らてん Latin
瑞典 すうぇーでん Sweden

INDEPENDENT

【てん 典】formal ceremony, celebration
華燭の典 かしょくのてん wedding ceremony

SYNONYMS

❶ **books**
本 BOOK → 4314
典 STANDARD WORK → 3253
経 religious classic → 1687
書 BOOK → 3292
冊 bound book → 4295
籍 books → 3394
著 literary work → 2869
巻 VOLUME → 3273
編 piece of writing → 1755
篇 PIECE OF WRITING → 3361
鑑 REFERENCE VOLUME → 2226

❷ⓐ **laws and rules**
法 LAW → 0391
律 LAW → 0433
典 CANON → 3253
憲 CONSTITUTION → 3001
令 ordinance → 2489
則 RULE → 1831
矩 RULE → 1475
規 REGULATION → 1231
紀 discipline → 1628

ⓑ **model**
範 MODEL → 3360
典 CANON → 3253
模 PATTERN → 1326
程 ESTABLISHED FORM → 1524
式 form → 3785
準 STANDARD → 3541
格 NORM → 1161

❸ **ceremonies and festivities**

式 CEREMONY → 3785
儀 CEREMONY → 0191
典 formal ceremony → 3253
礼 RITE → 1012
斎 religious ritual → 2622
会 Buddhist ceremony → 2512
祭 FESTIVAL → 3311

阜

3254
2-6-2

▶**MOUND**
フ
Ⓒ 阜 fù

170	Jōyō	U961C
阜	S8-8-0	F2075

Stroke order: 1–8

RADICAL

gifunofu 'mound', used in characters related to mounds, hills or the like
Left variant: 阝 ***kozatohen*** (院 防 阪)

COMPOUNDS

● [original meaning] **MOUND**
岐阜県 ぎふけん Gifu Prefecture
陰阜 いんふ mons pubis, mons veneris

SYNONYMS

● **hills**
丘 HILL → 4307
畝 RIDGE → 1857
岡 HILL → 3719
台 heights → 2498
坂 SLOPE → 0275
阪 slope → 0321
塚 MOUND → 0675
阜 MOUND → 3254
陵 high mound → 0660
稜 RIDGE → 1545

其

3255
2-6-2

▶**THAT**
キ そ(れ) そ(の)
Ⓒ 其 qí

12	Names	U5176
八	S8-2-6	F1551

KUN

【それ 其れ】
① [sometimes also 夫れ] *pronoun* **THAT, it**
其れ其れ それぞれ respectively, each
其れから それから and then, after that
其れでも それでも nevertheless, even so
其れなりに それなりに in its own way
其れと無く それとなく indirectly, obliquely
② (interjection used to call attention) look, there

【その 其の】
①ⓐ *demonstrative* **THAT, the;** *possessive pronoun* **its**
ⓑ [archaic] his
a 其の後 そのご after that, thereafter
其のまま そのまま without change, as is; immediately; exactly like
其の上 そのうえ on top of which, furthermore
其の他 そのた etc., and so forth; the rest [others]
其の物 そのもの the very thing, itself
b 其の国に入りては其の俗に従う そのくにいりてはそのぞくにしたごう When in Rome do as the Romans do
② um, er

SPECIAL READINGS

其方 そなた there, your place; thou, you
其奴 そいつ *colloq* that person [guy]; *pronoun* that
其方 そちら that way, there, *pronoun* that; *polite* you, that person
其処(=其所) そこ that place, there; that point, that juncture

SYNONYMS

【それ】
① **this and that**
本 THIS → 4314
爾 THAT → 4407
其れ THAT → 3255
彼 that → 0346
今 THIS (week, etc.) → 2464
当 THE PRESENT → 2701
該 the said → 1916
同 the same → 3707
之 this → 4228
是 this → 3090
此 THIS → 1017
斯 THIS → 2140

HOMOPHONES

それ 夫 HUSBAND → 4271

NOTE

➡ see USAGE note at 夫 4271

券

3256
2-6-2

▶**TICKET**
▶**CERTIFICATE**
ケン
Ⓝ 劵 Ⓒ 券 quàn xuàn

18	Jōyō-5	U5238
刀	S8-2-6	F1107

Stroke order: 1–8

COMPOUNDS

[also suffix]

❶ TICKET, coupon
食券 しょっけん food ticket
乗車券 じょうしゃけん railway [passenger] ticket
入場券 にゅうじょうけん entrance [admission] ticket
定期券 ていきけん commuter's pass
❷ CERTIFICATE, voucher, bond
旅券 りょけん passport
証券 しょうけん bill, bond, securities
債券 さいけん bond, debenture
株券 かぶけん share [stock] certificate
日銀券 にちぎんけん Bank of Japan bond
INDEPENDENT
【けん 券】CERTIFICATE, voucher; ticket, coupon
SYNONYMS
❶ labels and slips
札 TAG → 1011
券 TICKET → 3256
票 SLIP → 3308
符 tally → 3299
節 token → 3336
❷ certificates
証 CERTIFICATE → 1899
券 CERTIFICATE → 3256
状 official document → 0322
免 license → 2565

巻

▸ROLL UP
▸VOLUME
カン ケン ま(く) まき ま(き)

3257
2-6-2

26	Names	U5377
㔾	S8-2-6	F0000

traditional form → see 卷 at 3273

劵

▸TICKET
▸CERTIFICATE
ケン

3258
2-6-2

18	Nonstandard	U5238
刀	S8-2-6	F0000

traditional form → see 券 at 3256

竿

▸POLE
カン さお
Ⓒ 竿 gān

3259
2-6-3

118	Names	U7AFF
⺮	S9-6-3	F2140

COMPOUNDS
ⓐ POLE, rod
ⓑ counter for POLEs or rods
a 竿頭 かんとう top [end] of a pole
三竿 さんかん (of the sun or moon) being high in the sky
b 一竿 いっかん one pole, one rod
KUN
【さお 竿】
①ⓐ POLE, rod
ⓑ beam (of a balance)
a 釣竿 つりざお fishing rod
竹竿 たけざお bamboo pole
物干し竿 ものほしざお pole on which to hang laundry
旗竿 はたざお flagstaff, flagpole; arabis, esp. tower mustard
b 竿秤 さおばかり beam balance, steelyard
② single line of flying geese
③ *vulgar* penis
④ counter for:
ⓐ flags (on poles)
ⓑ chests (of drawers)
ⓒ bar-shaped Japanese sweets, as *yokan*, etc.
SYNONYMS
ⓐ long slender objects
棒 ROD → 1237
箸 CHOPSTICKS → 3359
桟 crosspiece → 1169
軸 AXLE → 1908
錘 SPINDLE → 2191
竿 POLE → 3259
杖 STAFF → 1026
錫 Buddhist priest's staff → 2189
軛 YOKE → 1873
ⓑ counters for long objects
本 counter for cylindrical objects → 4314
筋 counter for slender objects → 3319
竿 counter for poles or rods → 3259
挺 COUNTER FOR LONG SOLID OBJECTS → 0512
【さお】
④ⓐ counters for flat things
枚 COUNTER FOR FLAT THINGS → 1069
葉 counter for leaves → 2912
丁 counter for sheets → 4155
頁 counter for pages → 2589
通 counter for letters → 3855
竿 counter for flags → 3259

笈

▸BOX CARRIED ON THE BACK
キュウ おい

3260
2-6-3

118	Nonstandard	U7B08
⺮	S9-6-3	F0000

traditional form → see 笈 at 3274

美

2-6-3
incorrect classification
➡ see 2-3-6: ⺷ at 2817

臭

3261

2-6-3

▶BAD SMELL

シュウ くさ(い) -くさ(い) にお(う) にお(い)

N 臭 C 臭 chòu xiù

132	Jōyō	U81ED
自	S9-6-3	F1217

Stroke order: 1–9

COMPOUNDS

❶ⓐ **BAD SMELL, stink**

ⓑ [also suffix] smell, odor

ⓒ **smelly, stinking**

a 臭味 しゅうみ bad smell, offensive odor; a smack of
体臭 たいしゅう body smell
悪臭 あくしゅう offensive [foul] odor, stench
防臭 ぼうしゅう deodorization
異臭 いしゅう offensive smell, stink

b 臭覚 しゅうかく sense of smell
刺激臭 しげきしゅう irritating smell [odor], irritant odor

c 臭気 しゅうき offensive [odious] smell, bad [foul] odor, stench

❷ smack, taste
俗臭 ぞくしゅう low taste, vulgarity
官僚臭 かんりょうしゅう smack of the bureaucrat

❸ bromine
臭素 しゅうそ bromine

KUN

【くさい 臭い】**ill-smelling, stinking, smelly; suspicious-looking, fishy**
臭み くさみ bad smell; fulsomeness
臭い奴 くさいやつ dubious fellow
酒臭い さけくさい reek of liquor
水臭い みずくさい not frank, reserved; watery
生臭い なまぐさい smelling of fish [blood]

【-くさい -臭い】[suffix] **smack of, look like**
人間臭い にんげんくさい quite human, full of human traits
素人臭い しろうとくさい amateurish

【におう 臭う】**stink, reek**
ガスが臭う がすがにおう There is a smell of gas

【におい 臭い】
ⓐ **stench, stink**
ⓑ **smack, inkling (of something disagreeable)**

a 臭い消し においけし deodorant

b 不正の臭い ふせいのにおい smack of evil

SYNONYMS

❶ **smell and fragrance**
気 smell →3960
匂い SMELL →3662
臭 BAD SMELL →3261
香 SWEET SMELL →3177
馨 PERFUME →3575
芳 FRAGRANT →2739
薫 BALMY →3005
郁 AROMATIC →1640

❸ **lighter elements**
水 hydrogen →0010
酸 OXYGEN →1968
窒 NITROGEN →2853
塩 chlorine →0774
臭 bromine →3261
硫 SULFUR →1519
炭 carbon →2806

USAGE

❶【におう】
臭う
stink, reek
匂う
① smell (sweet), give out a smell [fragrance]
② (of blossoms) glow, be shiningly beautiful

❷【におい】
臭い
ⓐ stench, stink
ⓑ smack, inkling (of something disagreeable)
匂い
ⓐ smell, scent, fragrance, aroma
ⓑ flavor, touch (of something agreeable)

HOMOPHONES

におう 匂 SMELL →3662
におい 匂 SMELL →3662

要

3262

2-6-3

▶IMPORTANT
▶SUMMARIZE
▶REQUIRE

ヨウ かなめ い(る) 名 とし

146	Nonstandard	U8981
襾	S9-6-3	F0000

traditional form →see 要 at 3263

要

3263

2-6-3

▶IMPORTANT
▶SUMMARIZE
▶REQUIRE

ヨウ かなめ い(る) 名 とし

N 要 C 要 yào yāo

146	Jōyō-4	U8981
襾	S9-6-3	F0153

Stroke order: 1–9

COMPOUNDS

❶ **IMPORTANT, essential, principal, leading**
要約 ようやく summary, abridged statement

要素 ようそ (essential) element, constituent, factor
要因 よういん primary factor, main cause
要件 ようけん important matter; necessary condition
要点 ようてん main [essential] point, gist
要談 ようだん important talk
要所 ようしょ important point; strategic position
重要な じゅうような important, essential, principal
主要な しゅような main, principal, essential
枢要な すうような pivotal, cardinal
肝要な かんような important, vital, essential, necessary
不要(=不用)な ふような unnecessary, useless; disused, waste

❷ⓐ SUMMARIZE (the important points), outline
ⓑ [also suffix] **summary (of important points), gist, essence**

a 要旨 ようし gist, point, essentials, summary; purport
要綱 ようこう outline, gist; general plan
要領 ようりょう gist, essentials; outline; procedure
b 概要 がいよう outline, summary, synopsis
紀要 きよう bulletin, proceedings
提要 ていよう summary, outline
哲学史要 てつがくしよう Concise History of Philosophy

❸ⓐ REQUIRE, demand, request
ⓑ [also prefix] **REQUIREd, necessary, essential**

a 要求 ようきゅう requirement, demand, request
要請 ようせい request, demand
要望 ようぼう demand, request
強要 きょうよう coercion, extortion
必要な ひつような needed, necessary
需要 じゅよう demand
所要の しょようの required, needed
b 要注意 ようちゅうい attention [care] required
要確認 ようかくにん confirmation required

❹ secret
要諦 ようてい secret, cardinal point

❺ ambush, waylay
要撃 ようげき ambush attack

❻ [original meaning, now archaic] waist, hips

INDEPENDENT

【よう 要】 **main [essential] point, secret; summary, gist; necessity, need; REQUIREd, necessary**
要は ようは the point is…; in short
要するに ようするに in a word, in short
要を得ている ようをえている be to the point
保証人要 ほしょうにんよう guarantor required

【ようする 要する】 **REQUIRE, need; ambush, waylay**
修理を要する しゅうりをようする want [need] mending

KUN

【かなめ 要】 **pivot; main point, key**
要石 かなめいし keystone, cornerstone

【いる 要る】 [sometimes also 入る]
ⓐ **need, want, REQUIRE**
ⓑ **be necessary [REQUIREd]; cost, take**

a 金が要る かねがいる I need [want] money/It takes money
b 要り いり expense(s)

SYNONYMS

❶ important
要 IMPORTANT → 3263
重 HEAVY → 4390

❷ⓐ abridge
要 SUMMARIZE → 3263
抄 EXCERPT → 0298
約 CONTRACT → 1632
略 omit → 1501

ⓑ essential part
精 ESSENCE (essential part) → 1729
粋 essence (best part) → 1645
髄 essence (vital part) → 2316
枢 PIVOT → 1076
幹 TRUNK → 2152
綱 ESSENTIAL POINTS → 1735
旨 PURPORT → 2516
要 summary → 3263

❸ⓐ request
請 REQUEST → 1983
訴 APPEAL TO → 1901
頼 ASK → 2041
嘱 CHARGE WITH → 0881
要 REQUIRE → 3263
願 ASK A FAVOR → 2320
求 SEEK → 4365
乞 BEG → 2457

ⓑ need and necessity
要 required → 3263
必 must → 0015
須 MUST → 0700
需 DEMAND → 3472
入 necessary → 4177
用 needed for (a specific use) → 3694

USAGE

❶【いる】
要る
[sometimes also 入る]
ⓐ need, want, require
ⓑ be necessary [required]; cost, take
入る
①ⓐ enter, go in, come in

ⓑ (of the sun) **set**
② **attain**
③ [usu. 要る]
ⓐ **need, want, require**
ⓑ **be necessary [required]; cost, take**

❷【いり】
要り
[also 入り] **expense(s)**
入り
[also 要り] **expense(s)**

HOMOPHONES
いる 入 ENTER →4177
いり 入 ENTER →4177

姿 3264

▶**FIGURE**
シ すがた ㊔ しな
Ⓝ 姿 Ⓒ 姿 zī

2-6-3

38	Jōyō-6	U59FF
女	S9-3-6	F0373

Stroke order: 1–9

COMPOUNDS
ⓐ [original meaning] (outer shape, esp. of the body) **FIGURE, form, shape, appearance, looks, aspect**
ⓑ **posture, bearing, pose**
a 容姿 ようし face and figure, appearance
英姿 えいし gallant figure, majestic appearance
雄姿 ゆうし brave [imposing] figure
b 姿勢 しせい posture, position, poise, attitude
姿態 したい figure, person; pose

KUN
【すがた 姿】 **FIGURE, form, shape, appearance; portrait; posture; condition, state**
姿を消す すがたをけす disappear
姿見 すがたみ full-length mirror
姿絵 すがたえ portrait
女の姿になる おんなのすがたになる disguise oneself as a woman
パジャマ姿で ぱじゃますがたで in pajamas
孤立の姿 こりつのすがた state of isolation

SYNONYMS
ⓐ **appearance**
容 APPEARANCE →2832
貌 APPEARANCE →1958
姿 FIGURE →3264
相 PHASE →1120
体 FORM (outer appearance) →0080
色 COLOR →2522
風 air →3730
ⓐ **form**
形 SHAPE →1050
状 FORM (external) →0322
体 FORM (characteristic) →0080
姿 FIGURE →3264
ⓑ **posture**
姿 posture →3264
態 attitude →3529

姿 3265

▶**FIGURE**
シ すがた ㊔ しな

2-6-3

38	Nonstandard	U59FF
女	S9-3-6	F0000

traditional form →see 姿 at 3264

型 3266

▶**TYPE**
ケイ かた -がた
Ⓒ 型 xíng

2-6-3

32	Jōyō-4	U578B
土	S9-3-6	F0501

Stroke order: 1–9

COMPOUNDS
❶ⓐ (pattern from which something is made) **TYPE, mold, model**
ⓑ (representative specimen) **TYPE, model**
a 原型 げんけい archetype, prototype, model
模型 もけい model, pattern, mold
紙型 しけい papier-mâché mold, paper mold
造型(=造形) ぞうけい molding, modeling
b 典型 てんけい type, pattern, model, exemplar
❷ (general form characterizing a class) **TYPE, kind, pattern, form**
型式 けいしき model
類型 るいけい similar type, prototype, pattern
同型 どうけい same type [pattern]
定型 ていけい type, definite form
体型 たいけい form, figure

KUN
【かた 型】
① (general form characterizing a class) **TYPE, kind, pattern, form**
型に嵌める かたにはめる squeeze into a pattern, regiment
大型 おおがた large size; large pattern
新型 しんがた new style, new model
痩せ型 やせがた slender figure
② (pattern from which something is made) **TYPE, mold, model**
型紙 かたがみ paper pattern (for a dress)
鋳型 いがた mold, cast, matrix, die

歯型 はがた impression of the teeth, tooth-mark
③ set [traditional] form, *kata* (in martial arts and plays)
空手の型 からてのかた *kata* (in karate)
【-がた -型】[also suffix] **TYPE, model**
O型 おーがた model O; blood type O
血液型 けつえきがた blood type
千九百五十四年型 せんきゅうひゃくごじゅうよねんがた 1954 model

SYNONYMS

❶ⓐ prototype
型 TYPE → 3266
儀 model → 0191
ⓑ example
例 EXAMPLE → 0099
型 TYPE → 3266
❷ kinds and types
型 TYPE → 3266
類 KIND → 2275
色 kind → 2522
般 SORT → 1670
属 genus → 3901
品 category → 2795
種 VARIETY → 1560
様 variety → 1332

USAGE

❶【かた】
型
① (general form characterizing a class) type, kind, pattern, form
② (pattern from which something is made) type, mold, model
③ set [traditional] form, *kata* (in martial arts and plays)
形
①ⓐ shape, form; pattern, design
ⓑ marks, traces
② security, pledge
❷【-がた】
-型
[also suffix] type, model
-形
[also suffix] -shaped

HOMOPHONES

かた 形 SHAPE → 1050
-がた 形 SHAPE → 1050

契

3267
2-6-3

▸MAKE AN AGREEMENT
ケイ ちぎ(る)
Ⓝ 契 Ⓒ 契 qì xiè

37	Jōyō	U5951
大	S9-3-6	F1266

一	十	キ	丰	丰7	刧	刧	契	契
1	2	3	4	5	6	7	8	9

COMPOUNDS

❶ⓐ MAKE AN AGREEMENT, agree on, pledge, promise
ⓑ agreement, contract
a 契約 けいやく contract, agreement
b 黙契 もっけい implicit agreement, tacit understanding
❷ⓐ (coincide exactly) agree with, match, coincide
ⓑ tally impression
a 契合する けいごうする coincide, agree
b 契印 けいいん impression of a seal over the joint of two papers, tally
❸ chance, opportunity
契機 けいき opportunity, chance; *philosophy* moment

INDEPENDENT

【けい 契】tally impression

KUN

【ちぎる 契る】**pledge, vow, swear, promise**
契り ちぎり pledge, vow, promise
固く契った恋人 かたくちぎったこいびと plighted lovers

SYNONYMS

❶ promise
約 PROMISE → 1632
締 CONCLUDE (a treaty) → 1761
協 reach an agreement → 0103
契 MAKE AN AGREEMENT → 3267
盟 ALLIANCE → 3468
誓 VOW → 3424

契

3268
2-6-3

▸MAKE AN AGREEMENT
ケイ ちぎ(る)

37	Nonstandard	UF909
大	S9-3-6	F0000

traditional form → see 契 at 3267

変弯

2-6-3

incorrect classification
➡ see 2-2-7: 亠 at 2568

帝

2-6-3

incorrect classification
➡ see 2-2-7: 亠 at 2573

巷巷 incorrect classification
➡ see 2-4-5: 廾 at 3097

2-6-3

県

3269

2-6-3

▶**PREFECTURE**

ケン ㊔ がた あがた

Ⓝ 縣 Ⓒ 县 xiàn

109△	Jōyō-3	U770C
目	S9-5-4	F0422

1	2	3	4	5	6	7	8	9
丨	冂	冃	月	目	㫐	𥃩	県	県

COMPOUNDS

❶ⓐ [also prefix and suffix] (largest administrative subdivision of Japan) **PREFECTURE**

ⓑ **suffix after names of PREFECTUREs**

a 県庁 けんちょう prefectural office

県警 けんけい prefectural police

県税 けんぜい prefectural tax

県立の けんりつの prefectural

県立病院 けんりつびょういん prefectural hospital

県民 けんみん citizens of a prefecture

県知事 けんちじ prefectural governor

府県 ふけん prefectures

隣接県 りんせつけん neighboring prefecture

b 香川県 かがわけん Kagawa Prefecture

❷ (administrative subdivision of China smaller than a province) county

INDEPENDENT

【けん 県】 PREFECTURE (→ ❶ⓐ)

SYNONYMS

❶ **territorial divisions**

州 STATE → 0064

県 PREFECTURE → 3269

府 URBAN PREFECTURE → 3824

道 district of Hokkaido → 3888

都 METROPOLIS OF TOKYO → 2120

省 province in China → 3100

郡 COUNTY → 1858

卑

3270

2-6-3

▶**MEAN**

ヒ いや(しい) いや(しむ) いや(しめる)

Ⓝ 卑 Ⓒ 卑 bēi

24	Jōyō	U5351
十	S9-2-7	F1710

1	2	3	4	5	6	7	8	9
′	丫	冂	巾	甶	由	由	卑	卑

COMPOUNDS

❶ⓐ (low in social status) **MEAN, lowly, humble**

ⓑ [formerly also 鄙 2338] [humble] my humble

a 卑賤 ひせん lowly position, humble condition

尊卑 そんぴ upper and lower classes, high and low

b 卑見 ひけん my humble opinion

❷ [formerly also 鄙 2338] (lacking in elevating human qualities) **MEAN, vulgar, despicable**

卑屈な ひくつな mean, mean-spirited; servile

卑劣な ひれつな mean, base, cowardly

卑怯 ひきょう cowardice, meanness, unfairness

卑語 ひご vulgarism, vulgar word

野卑 やひ vulgarity, meanness

❸ⓐ humble oneself

ⓑ despise, look down on

a 卑下 ひげ humility, self-depreciation

b 男尊女卑 だんそんじょひ predominance of men over women, sexism

❹ familiar, common

卑近 ひきん familiar, common; plain

卑金属 ひきんぞく base metals

❺ (of land) low

卑湿な ひしつな low and damp (land)

KUN

【いやしい 卑しい】

① [formerly also 賤しい] (low in social status) **MEAN, lowly, humble, inferior in position**

卑しさ いやしさ meanness, vulgarity

卑しい生まれの いやしいうまれの lowborn

② [formerly also 賤しい]

ⓐ (of poor appearance) **MEAN, shabby, seedy**

ⓑ (lacking elevating human qualities) **MEAN**, base, vulgar, despicable

a 卑しい身形 いやしいみなり shabby appearance

卑しからぬ いやしからぬ decent, respectable

b 卑しい根性 いやしいこんじょう mean spirit

卑しい笑い いやしいわらい mean smirk

③ **greedy, gluttonous**

卑しん坊 いやしんぼう greedy person, glutton

【いやしむ 卑しむ】 [formerly also 賤しむ] **despise, disdain, look down on, regard with contempt**

卑しみ いやしみ contempt

卑しむべき いやしむべき despicable

労働を卑しむ ろうどうをいやしむ despise labor

【いやしめる 卑しめる】 [formerly also 賤しめる] same as 卑しむ いやしむ

SYNONYMS

❶ⓐ **lowly**

卑 MEAN → 3270

下 of low rank → 4186

低 LOW → 0082

❷ **vulgar and unrefined**

俗 vulgar → 0119

卑 MEAN → 3270

賤 MEAN → 1993

鄙 MEAN → 2338
俚 RURAL → 0112
里 rural → 4356
粗 COARSE → 1683
野 rustic → 1877
蛮 barbaric → 2638

USAGE

❶【いやしい】

卑しい

① [formerly also 賤しい] (low in social status) mean, lowly, humble, inferior in position

② [formerly also 賤しい]

ⓐ (of poor appearance) mean, shabby, seedy

ⓑ (lacking elevating human qualities) mean, base, vulgar, despicable

③ greedy, gluttonous

賤しい

[now usu. 卑しい]

① (low in social status) mean, lowly, humble, inferior in position

②ⓐ (of poor appearance) mean, shabby, seedy

ⓑ (lacking elevating human qualities) mean, base, vulgar, despicable

❷【いやしむ】

卑しむ

[formerly also 賤しむ] despise, disdain, look down on, regard with contempt

賤しむ

[now usu. 卑しむ] same as 卑しむ いやしむ

❸【いやしめる】

卑しめる

same as 卑しむ いやしむ

賤しめる

[now usu. 卑しめる] same as 卑しめる いやしめる

HOMOPHONES

いやしい 賤 MEAN → 1993
いやしむ 賤 MEAN → 1993
いやしめる 賤 MEAN → 1993

甚

▸**EXTREMELY**

ジン はなは(だ) はなは(だしい) ㊔ しん

Ⓒ 甚 shèn shén

3271

2-6-3

99	Jōyō	U751A
甘	S9-5-4	F1631

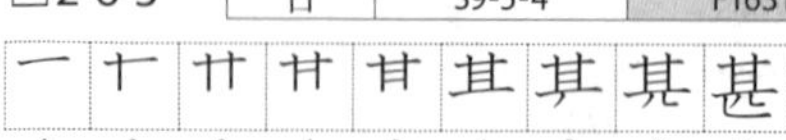

COMPOUNDS

ⓐ **EXTREMELY, very, exceedingly**

ⓑ **extreme, excessive**

a 甚大な じんだいな extremely big, very great; serious; heavy

幸甚である こうじんである be very glad, deem a favor

b 深甚な しんじんな profound; careful, mature

蝕甚(=食尽) しょくじん maximum eclipse

KUN

【はなはだ 甚だ】**EXTREMELY, very, excessively, greatly**

甚だ不親切である はなはだふしんせつである be extremely unkind

【はなはだしい 甚だしい】**extreme, excessive, intense, tremendous**

甚だしい誤解 はなはだしいごかい serious misunderstanding

SYNONYMS

● **extreme in degree**

酷 SEVERE → 1967
強 STRONG → 0574
凄い tremendous → 0145
重 HEAVY → 4390
高 HIGH → 2601
深 DEEP → 0636
大 BIG → 4224
厳 SEVERE → 4079
激 intense → 0955
極 EXTREME → 1243
痛 bitter(ly) → 4071
切 keen → 0030
甚 EXTREMELY → 3271
祁 EXTREMELY → 1447
超 super- → 4107
頗る EXCEEDINGLY → 1552

専

▸**EXCLUSIVE**

セン もっぱ(ら)

Ⓝ 專 Ⓒ 专 zhuān

3272

2-6-3

41	Jōyō-6	U5C02
寸	S9-3-6	F0763

COMPOUNDS

❶ⓐ [original meaning] **EXCLUSIVE, special, specialized**

ⓑ **take EXCLUSIVE possession of, monopolize**

a 専用 せんよう exclusive use, private use

専攻する せんこうする major in, specialize in

専門 せんもん specialty, profession

専念 せんねん close attention, concentration

専売 せんばい monopoly

b 専有 せんゆう exclusive possession, monopoly

❷ [formerly also 擅 0947] arrogate to oneself, claim arbitrarily, do something on one's own authority

専横 せんおう arbitrariness, despotism
専行 せんこう arbitrary action
専断 せんだん arbitrary decision, arbitrariness
❸ abbrev. of 専門学校 せんもんがっこう: professional school
高専 こうせん technical college
❹ abbrev. of 専攻 せんこう: specialty, major
国文専 こくぶんせん major in Japanese literature

KUN

【もっぱら 専ら】**entirely, EXCLUSIVEly, wholly, solely**
専ら...を研究する もっぱら…をけんきゅうする devote oneself to the study of...

SYNONYMS

❶ⓐ **special**
特 SPECIAL (distinct) → 1181
別 special (distinct) → 1434
殊 SPECIAL (exceptional) → 1178
専 EXCLUSIVE → 3272
ⓑ **occupy**
占 OCCUPY → 2496
拠 occupy → 0369
領 take possession of → 1567
専 take exclusive possession of → 3272
❷ **acting arbitrarily**
横 arbitrary → 1350
独 act arbitrarily → 0471
恣 SELF-INDULGENT → 3281
耽 INDULGE IN → 1665
擅 ARROGATE TO ONESELF → 0947
専 arrogate to oneself → 3272
逞 DO AS ONE PLEASES → 4004

巻 3273

▶**ROLL UP**
▶**VOLUME**

カン ケン▲ ま(く) まき ま(き)
Ⓝ 巻 Ⓒ 巻 juàn juǎn

2-6-3

49△	Jōyō-6	U5DFB
己	S9-3-6	F0371

Stroke order: 1 丶 2 丷 3 䒑 4 𠂉 5 𠔿 6 尖 7 关 8 券 9 巻

COMPOUNDS

❶ⓐ [original meaning] **ROLL UP, roll, scroll**
ⓑ counter for film reels
a 巻子本 かんしほん scroll, roll, rolled book
巻雲(=絹雲) けんうん cirrus cloud
b 五巻物 ごかんもの five-reel film
❷ⓐ **VOLUME, book**
ⓑ counter for **VOLUME**s
a 巻末 かんまつ end of a book
全巻 ぜんかん the whole volume [reel]
上中下巻 じょうちゅうげかん set of three volumes
別巻 べっかん separate volume, extra issue
b 全六巻の著作 ぜんろっかんのちょさく work in six volumes
第一巻 だいいっかん first volume, Vol. 1

INDEPENDENT

【かん 巻】scroll, hanging scroll; **VOLUME**, book

KUN

【まく 巻く】[sometimes also 捲く] **ROLL UP, roll; wind, reel; wrap**
巻き上げる まきあげる roll up; hoist, heave up; take away; blow up (dust)
巻き込む まきこむ roll (up), wrap; involve, drag in
巻き起こす まきおこす create (a sensation); give rise to
巻き付ける まきつける wind or tie around, coil
巻き返し作戦 まきかえしさくせん rollback operation
巻き添え まきぞえ involvement, entanglement
渦巻き うずまき eddy, whirlpool; coil

【まき 巻, 巻き】
①ⓐ **roll, winding**
ⓑ counter for rolls, scrolls or windings
a 巻き紙 まきがみ rolled letter paper
巻き物 まきもの scroll
葉巻 はまき cigar
b 絹布一巻 けんぷひとまき one roll of silk
② book, **VOLUME**
一の巻 いちのまき Vol. 1
虎の巻 とらのまき key, crib, pony; secret (of a trade)

SYNONYMS

❶ⓐ **wind and twine**
巻 ROLL UP → 3273
捲 ROLL UP → 0598
繰る REEL → 1806
絡 ENTWINE → 1709
纏 WIND AROUND → 1814
❷ⓐ **books**
本 BOOK → 4314
典 STANDARD WORK → 3253
経 religious classic → 1687
書 BOOK → 3292
冊 bound book → 4295
籍 books → 3394
著 literary work → 2869
巻 VOLUME → 3273
編 piece of writing → 1755
篇 PIECE OF WRITING → 3361
鑑 REFERENCE VOLUME → 2226
ⓑ **counters for books**

冊 COUNTER FOR BOOKS → 4295
巻 counter for volumes → 3273
部 counter for copies → 2111

USAGE

【まく】
巻く
[sometimes also 捲く] roll up, roll; wind, reel; wrap
捲く
[usu. 巻く] roll up, roll; wind, reel; wrap

HOMOPHONES

まく 捲 ROLL UP → 0598

笈

3274

2-6-4

▶**BOX CARRIED ON THE BACK**

キュウ おい

Ⓝ 笈 Ⓒ 笈 jí

118	Names	U7B08
⺮	S10-6-4	F3138

COMPOUNDS

● [original meaning] **BOX CARRIED ON THE BACK**
書笈 しょきゅう box for books carried on the back

INDEPENDENT

【きゅう 笈】**bookcase carried on the back**
笈を負う きゅうをおう study far from one's home

KUN

【おい 笈】**BOX CARRIED ON THE BACK** to store one's belongings
笈摺 おいずり(=おいずる) sleeveless overgarment worn by pilgrims

SYNONYMS

【おい】
◯ **containers**
箱 BOX → 3362
壺 JAR → 2890
槽 TANK → 1352
樽 BARREL → 1368
棺 COFFIN → 1240
桶 BUCKET → 1211
笈 BOX CARRIED ON THE BACK → 3274
鞘 SHEATH → 2259
箪 BAMBOO BOX → 3381
函 BOX → 3724
籠 BASKET → 3398
袋 BAG → 3201
鞄 BAG (for carrying) → 2248
器 VESSEL → 3367
瓶 BOTTLE → 1702
缶 CAN → 2526
缶 EARTHENWARE JAR → 2525

笑

3275

2-6-4

▶**LAUGH**

ショウ わら(う) え(む)

Ⓒ 笑 xiào

118	Jōyō-4	U7B11
⺮	S10-6-4	F0212

1	2	3	4	5	6	7	8	9	10
ノ	⺊	⺮	⺮	⺮	⺮	笑	笑	笑	笑

COMPOUNDS

❶ⓐ **LAUGH, smile**
ⓑ **LAUGHter, smile**
ⓒ **LAUGH** at, ridicule, deride
a 一笑する いっしょうする laugh a laugh, smile a smile
爆笑する ばくしょうする roar with laughter, burst into laughter
b 微笑 びしょう smile
苦笑 くしょう forced [strained] smile
c 冷笑 れいしょう derisive smile, sneer
嘲笑する ちょうしょうする laugh at, deride
❷ indicates humility when presenting someone with something
笑覧 しょうらん your inspection

KUN

【わらう 笑う】**LAUGH, smile; laugh at, ridicule, deride; bloom beautifully**
笑い わらい laughter, smile; sneer
笑い声 わらいごえ laughter
笑い話 わらいばなし funny [humorous] story
笑い物 わらいもの object of ridicule, subject of derision
笑い草(=笑い種) わらいぐさ laughingstock
【えむ 笑む】**smile, beam; bloom, come out**
笑み えみ smile
微笑む ほほえむ smile

SPECIAL READINGS

笑顔 えがお smiling face, smile

SYNONYMS

❶ⓐ & ❶ⓑ & 【わらう】 **laugh**
笑 LAUGH → 3275
莞 SMILE SWEETLY → 2842

笹
2-6-4

incorrect stroke-count
➡ see 2-6-5: ⺮ at 3301

笈
2-6-4

incorrect stroke-count
➡ see 2-6-3: ⺮ at 3260

差
2-6-4

incorrect classification
➡ see ◻3-7-3: 羊 at 4104

翆

3276

2-6-4

▶JADE GREEN

スイ　みどり　㊔ みす　あきら

124	Nonstandard	U7FC6
羽	S10-6-4	F0000

traditional form → see 翠 at 3356

翠

3277

2-6-4

▶JADE GREEN

スイ　みどり　㊔ みす　あきら

124	Nonstandard	U7FE0
羽	S10-6-4	F0000

traditional form → see 翠 at 3356

息

3278

2-6-4

▶BREATH

ソク　いき

Ⓒ 息 xī

61	Jōyō-3	U606F
心	S10-4-6	F0417

1	2	3	4	5	6	7	8	9	10
′	丿	白	白	自	自	自	息	息	息

COMPOUNDS

❶ [original meaning] **BREATH, respiration**

嘆息 たんそく sigh

喘×息 ぜんそく asthma

窒息 ちっそく suffocation, asphyxia

❷ **live, BREATHe, be alive**

生息(=棲息)する せいそくする inhabit, live

消息 しょうそく (personal) news, movements; letter

❸ **rest, repose**

休息 きゅうそく rest, repose

安息日 あんそくび Sabbath

❹ **son, child**

息女 そくじょ daughter

子息 しそく son

❺ **interest**

利息 りそく interest

❻ [formerly 熄 1339] go out, die out

終息する しゅうそくする cease, come to an end

INDEPENDENT

【そく　息】son

山本氏の息 やまもとしのそく Mr. Yamamoto's son

KUN

【いき　息】**BREATH; tone**

息切れ いきぎれ breathlessness

息抜き いきぬき rest, relaxation

息の合った いきのあった in good coordination

溜め息 ためいき sigh

一息 ひといき breath; pause, rest; a little bit of effort

SPECIAL READINGS

息子 むすこ son

息吹 いぶき breath

SYNONYMS

❶ **breathe and blow**

息 BREATH → 3278

気 breath → 3960

吸 BREATHE IN → 0234

呼 breathe out → 0324

吹 BLOW → 0272

❸ **rest**

休 REST → 0056

息 rest → 3278

憩 TAKE A REST → 3590

歇 TAKE A REST → 2243

❹ **offspring**

子 CHILD → 4196

仔 OFFSPRING → 0038

孤 orphan → 0426

嫡 LEGITIMATE CHILD → 0839

息 son → 3278

男 son → 3147

惣 eldest son → 3452

娘 DAUGHTER → 0488

女 daughter → 4226

姫 DAUGHTER OF NOBLE BIRTH → 0489

COMPOUND FORMATION

【消息　しょうそく】

消息 '(personal) news, movements; letter' originally referred to life (息 ❷) or death (消). This was extended to mean news about a person's state of being or movements.

臭

3279

2-6-4

▶BAD SMELL

シュウ　くさ(い)　-くさ(い)　にお(う)　にお(い)

132	Names	UFA5C
自	S10-6-4	F0000

traditional form → see 臭 at 3261

栗

3280

2-6-4

▶CHESTNUT

リツ　リ　くり　㊔ くる

Ⓒ 栗 lì

75	Names	U6817
木	S10-4-6	F1668

COMPOUNDS

❶ [original meaning] **CHESTNUT tree, Japanese chestnut tree; chestnut**

栗鼠 りす squirrel

❷ [now always 慄 りつ 0791] tremble with fear, shudder

戦戦栗栗 せんせんりつりつ trembling with fear

KUN

【くり 栗】CHESTNUT tree, Japanese chestnut tree; chestnut

栗石 くりいし cobblestone
栗毛 くりげ chestnut (horse)
勝ち栗 かちぐり dried chestnut

SYNONYMS

❶ & 【くり】 **fruits and fruit trees**

桃 PEACH → 1174
榛 HAZEL → 1328
椎 CHINQUAPIN → 1249
柚 YUZU → 1123
椰 COCONUT → 1285
柑 CITRUS → 1112
橙 BITTER ORANGE → 1369
葡 GRAPE → 2902
萄 GRAPE → 2870
柿 PERSIMMON → 1118
檎 APPLE → 1386
李 PLUM → 3050
枇 LOQUAT → 1063
杷 LOQUAT → 1065
苺 STRAWBERRY → 2780
菱 water chestnut → 2879
杏 APRICOT → 3049
梅 JAPANESE APRICOT → 1159
橘 MANDARIN → 1366
栗 CHESTNUT → 3280
栃 JAPANESE HORSE CHESTNUT → 1122
梨 PEAR → 3412
蕉 PLANTAIN → 2994

NOTE

★ do not confuse with 粟 FOXTAIL MILLET → 3326

恣

3281

2-6-4

▶SELF-INDULGENT

シ ほしいまま▲

Ⓒ 恣 zì

61	Jōyō	U6063
心	S10-4-6	F3050

1 2 3 4 5 6 7 8 9 10

COMPOUNDS

● **SELF-INDULGENT, selfish, arbitrary**

恣意 しい selfishness, arbitrariness
恣意的 しいてき arbitrary, selfish
放恣 ほうし licentiousness, self-indulgence
驕×恣 きょうし being proud and self-indulgent

KUN

【ほしいまま 恣】[sometimes also 擅] **SELF-INDULGENT**, selfish; arbitrary

SYNONYMS

● **acting arbitrarily**

横 arbitrary → 1350
独 act arbitrarily → 0471
恣 SELF-INDULGENT → 3281
耽 INDULGE IN → 1665
擅 ARROGATE TO ONESELF → 0947
専 arrogate to oneself → 3272
逞 DO AS ONE PLEASES → 4004

USAGE

【ほしいまま】

恣
[sometimes also 擅] self-indulgent, selfish; arbitrary

擅
[usu. 恣] self-indulgent, selfish; arbitrary

HOMOPHONES

ほしいまま 擅 ARROGATE TO ONESELF → 0947

恕

3282

2-6-4

▶FORGIVE WITH COMPASSION

ジョ ショ ㊔ ひろ よし ゆき ひろし ひろむ しのぶ のり くに みち はかる

Ⓒ 恕 shù

61	Names	U6055
心	S10-4-6	F0000

COMPOUNDS

❶ **FORGIVE WITH COMPASSION, pardon, tolerate**

寛恕する かんじょする forgive, pardon, tolerate

❷ **sympathetic, thoughtful**

忠恕 ちゅうじょ *literary* sincere and thoughtful

INDEPENDENT

【じょ 恕】sympathy, considerateness

SYNONYMS

❶ **forgive**

赦 AMNESTY → 1870
免 EXEMPT → 2565
許す forgive → 1862
恕 FORGIVE WITH COMPASSION → 3282
宥 PARDON → 2803

NOTE

★ do not confuse with 怒 GET ANGRY → 3180

恐

3283

2-6-4

▶FEAR

キョウ おそ(れる) おそ(る) おそ(ろしい) こわ(い)▲ こわ(がる)▲

Ⓝ 恐 Ⓒ 恐 kǒng

61	Jōyō	U6050
心	S10-4-6	F0697

1 2 3 4 5 6 7 8 9 10

COMPOUNDS

❶ⓐ [formerly also 兢 1971] [original meaning] **FEAR, be afraid of, dread**
ⓑ **FEARful, frightening**

a 恐怖 きょうふ fear
恐慌 きょうこう panic, scare, alarm
恐懼× きょうく dread, fear, awe
恐妻家 きょうさいか henpecked husband, man bossed by his wife
恐水病 きょうすいびょう hydrophobia
閉所恐怖症 へいしょきょうふしょう claustrophobia
戦戦恐恐として せんせんきょうきょうとして with fear and trembling

b 恐竜 きょうりゅう dinosaur, titanosaur

❷ **be overwhelmed (as with gratitude or astonishment)**
恐縮する きょうしゅくする feel much obliged, deeply appreciate; regret; feel embarrassed
恐悦がる きょうえつがる congratulate oneself, chuckle with delight

❸ threaten
恐喝する きょうかつする threaten, menace

KUN

【おそれる 恐れる】
ⓐ **FEAR, dread, be afraid of**
ⓑ **apprehend, be anxious about**
ⓒ [formerly also 畏れる] **be overawed, stand in awe, FEAR**

a 恐れ おそれ fear, dread, terror; [also 虞] fears (of undesirable event), danger, risk, signs, adverse chance, possibility
b 恐れていた通り おそれていたとおり as apprehended
c 恐れ多い おそれおおい gracious, august
恐れ入る おそれいる be overwhelmed [dumbfounded] (as with gratitude, shame, regret or astonishment)

【おそる 恐る】 *literary* **FEAR**
恐るべき おそるべき fearful, formidable
恐る恐る おそるおそる fearfully; cautiously, gingerly
恐らく おそらく probably

【おそろしい 恐ろしい】 **terrible, FEARful, fierce; awful, tremendous, marvelous**
恐ろしさ おそろしさ fear, terror
恐ろしく おそろしく fearfully, terribly, awfully

【こわい 恐い】 [also 怖い] **FEAR**ful, scary, uncanny; be afraid
恐さ こわさ fear, dreadfulness
犬が恐い いぬがこわい be afraid of dogs

【こわがる 恐がる】 [also 怖がる] be afraid of, be frightened
恐がり こわがり timidity; coward

SYNONYMS

❶ **fear**
怖 FEARFUL → 0353
凄 UNCANNY → 0145
恐 FEAR → 3283
惧 FEAR → 0581
慄 TREMBLE WITH FEAR → 0791
兢 BE IN FEAR → 1971
惶 BE AFRAID → 0708
畏 BE OVERAWED → 3170
臆 FEEL TIMID → 1397
怯える BE FRIGHTENED → 0355

USAGE

❶【おそれる】
恐れる
ⓐ fear, dread, be afraid of
ⓑ apprehend, be anxious about
ⓒ [formerly also 畏れる] be overawed, stand in awe, fear
畏れる
[now usu. 恐れる] be overawed, stand in awe, fear

❷【おそれ】
恐れ
① fear, dread, terror
② [also 虞] fears (of undesirable event), danger, risk, signs, adverse chance, possibility
虞
[also 恐れ] fears (of undesirable event), danger, risk, signs, adverse chance, possibility

HOMOPHONES

おそれる 畏 BE OVERAWED → 3170
おそれ 虞 FEARS → 4037
こわい
怖 FEARFUL → 0353
強 STRONG → 0574
こわがる 怖 FEARFUL → 0353

NOTE

➡ see also USAGE note at 怖 0353

恐 **3284** 2-6-4

▶**FEAR**
キョウ おそ(れる) おそ(る) おそ(ろしい) こわ(い) こわ(がる)

61	Nonstandard	U6050
心	S10-4-6	F0000

traditional form → see 恐 at 3283

栞 **3285** 2-6-4

▶**BOOKMARK**
カン しおり
Ⓒ 刊 kān

75	Names	U681E
木	S10-4-6	F0000

COMPOUNDS

● [original meaning, now archaic] twig or branch used as a waymark in a mountain path

KUN

【しおり 栞】[sometimes also 枝折り] **BOOKMARK; guidebook**

旅の栞 たびのしおり travel guidebook

SYNONYMS

● & 【しおり】 **marks and signs**

標 MARK (identifying sign) → 1347
徽 EMBLEM → 0968
痕 SCAR → 4066
印 MARK (visible sign) → 1023
跡 TRACE → 1937
蹟 TRACE → 2065
踪 FOOTPRINTS → 1996
紋 print → 1651
符 SYMBOL → 3299
号 SIGN → 2675
栞 BOOKMARK → 3285

HOMOPHONES

しおり 枝折り → 1073, 0297

NOTE

★ do not confuse with 柴 BRUSHWOOD → 3287

烈

▸VEHEMENT
レツ はげ(しい)▲
Ⓒ 烈 liè

3286
2-6-4

86	Jōyō	U70C8
灬	S10-4-6	F1287

一	ア	歹	歹	歹	列	列	列	烈	烈
1	2	3	4	5	6	7	8	9	10

COMPOUNDS

❶ⓐ **VEHEMENT, violent, strong, furious, fierce, intense**

ⓑ [original meaning] (of fire) **VEHEMENT** (flames), raging, fiery

a 烈風 れっぷう violent [strong] wind
烈震 れっしん violent [disastrous] earthquake
強烈な きょうれつな intense, severe
痛烈な つうれつな sharp, biting, scathing, cutting
猛烈な もうれつな violent, vehement, fierce
激烈な げきれつな vehement, furious, violent, severe
熱烈な ねつれつな ardent, fervent, vehement

b 烈火 れっか raging fire, vehement flames
烈日 れつじつ hot day, scorching sun

❷ staunch, virtuous, gallant, heroic

烈士 れっし patriot, hero
烈婦 れっぷ virtuous woman, heroine
壮烈な そうれつな heroic, brave

KUN

【はげしい 烈しい】[usu. 激しい]

① (acting with extreme force) violent, fierce, **VEHEMENT**

烈しさ はげしさ intensity, severity
烈しい風 はげしいかぜ strong wind

② (of great intensity) intense, violent, severe

烈しい競争 はげしいきょうそう hot competition

SYNONYMS

❶ⓐ **extreme in power**

激 VIOLENT → 0955
荒 WILD → 2810
狂 raging → 0318
烈 VEHEMENT → 3286
猛 FIERCE → 0653

HOMOPHONES

はげしい 激 VIOLENT → 0955

NOTE

➡ see USAGE note at 激 0955

柴

▸BRUSHWOOD
サイ しば
Ⓒ 柴 chái

3287
2-6-4

75	Names	U67F4
木	S10-4-6	F1406

COMPOUNDS

● [original meaning] **BRUSHWOOD, firewood**

柴戸 さいこ brushwood door; crude dwelling
柴門 さいもん gate made of woven brushwood; humble home

KUN

【しば 柴】**BRUSHWOOD, firewood**

柴刈り しばかり firewood gathering
柴垣 しばがき brushwood fence
柴犬 しばいぬ (Japanese) midget Shiba (kind of dog)

SYNONYMS

● **kinds of wood**

木 WOOD → 4261
材 TIMBER → 1031
薪 FIREWOOD → 3009
柴 BRUSHWOOD → 3287

HOMOPHONES

しば 芝 LAWN GRASS → 2705

NOTE

➡ see USAGE note at 芝 2705
★ do not confuse with 栞 BOOKMARK → 3285

桌
⬒2-6-4
incorrect classification
➡ see ⬒2-2-8: ⺊ at 2617

恋
⬒2-6-4
incorrect classification
➡ see ⬒2-2-8: 亠 at 2602

脅
⬒2-6-4
incorrect classification
➡ see ⬒2-2-8: 力 at 2614

桑
⬒2-6-4
incorrect classification
➡ see ⬒2-2-8: 又 at 2618

旁
⬒2-6-4
incorrect classification
➡ see ⬒2-2-8: 亠 at 2598

挙
⬒2-6-4
incorrect classification
➡ see ⬒2-4-6: ⺍ at 3106

案
⬒2-6-4
incorrect classification
➡ see ⬒2-3-7: 宀 at 2824

莞
⬒2-6-4
incorrect classification
➡ see ⬒2-3-7: 艹 at 2842

骨

3288
⬒2-6-4

▶**BONE**
コツ　ほね
Ⓒ 骨 gǔ gū

188	Jōyō-6	U9AA8
骨	S10-10-0	F0885

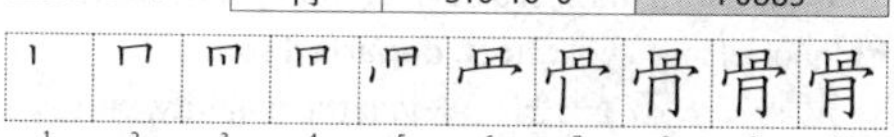
1 2 3 4 5 6 7 8 9 10

RADICAL

hone 'bone', used in characters related to bones or bone products
Left variant: 骨× ***honehen*** (髄 骼 骸)

COMPOUNDS

❶ⓐ [also suffix] [original meaning] **BONE**
ⓑ **BONE**s, body
a 骨折 こっせつ bone fracture
骨格 こっかく frame, physique; framework, skeletal structure
人骨 じんこつ human bone
肋骨 ろっこつ rib, costa
遺骨 いこつ (skeletal) remains; ashes
白骨 はっこつ bleached bone, skeleton
大腿×骨 だいたいこつ thighbone, femur
骸骨 がいこつ skeleton
b 老骨 ろうこつ old bones, old man

❷ (strength of character) backbone, spirit, grit
気骨 きこつ (moral) backbone, spirit, soul, grit
反骨の精神 はんこつのせいしん spirit of defiance, backbone

❸ remains (of a body), ashes
納骨する のうこつする lay (a person's) ashes to rest

❹ essence, gist
骨子 こっし essence, gist

❺ knack, the ropes
骨法 こっぽう knack, the ropes

INDEPENDENT

【こつ 骨】remains (of a body), ashes; knack, trick, the ropes
お骨 おこつ ashes, remains
骨を覚える こつをおぼえる get the knack, learn the ropes

KUN

【ほね 骨】**BONE, skeleton; frame, rib; backbone, spirit, grit; essence**
骨組み ほねぐみ skeleton; framework
骨休め ほねやすめ relaxation, recreation
骨っぽい ほねっぽい bony; spirited; hard to deal with
骨の有る男 ほねのあるおとこ man of spirit
骨を折る ほねをおる take pains, make efforts; break one's bone
骨が折れる ほねがおれる require much effort, be hard to do; have one's bone broken

SYNONYMS

❶ⓐ **bone**
骨 BONE → 3288
髄 MARROW → 2316
椎 SPINE → 1249
脊 SPINE → 3297
肋 RIB → 1022
骼 SKELETAL FRAME → 2302
骸 skeleton → 2301

恩

3289
⬒2-6-4

▶**GRACE**
▶**DEBT OF GRATITUDE**
オン ㊔ めぐみ
Ⓒ 恩 ēn

61	Jōyō-5	U6069
心	S10-4-6	F1371

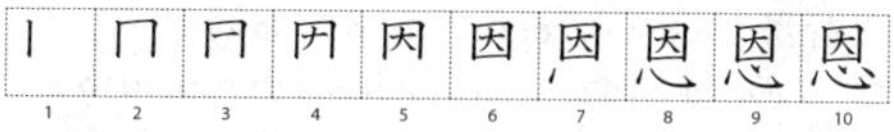
1 2 3 4 5 6 7 8 9 10

COMPOUNDS

❶ⓐ [original meaning] **GRACE, favor, kindness, benevolence, blessing**
ⓑ gracious, compassionate, benevolent

ⓒ by **GRACE** of the emperor

a 恩恵 おんけい benefit, grace, favor, blessing
恩返し おんがえし repaying another's kindness
恩人 おんじん benefactor, patron
恩寵 おんちょう grace (of God), favor

b 恩情 おんじょう compassion, affection
恩命 おんめい gracious command [words]

c 恩賜 おんし Imperial gift

❷ **DEBT OF GRATITUDE, gratitude, obligation, indebtedness**
恩義 おんぎ obligation, debt of gratitude
恩師 おんし one's respected teacher, one's former teacher
恩給 おんきゅう pension
恩知らず おんしらず ingratitude, ingrate
謝恩 しゃおん expression of gratitude
忘恩 ぼうおん ingratitude

❸ love (esp. between family members)
恩讐[×] おんしゅう love and hate

INDEPENDENT

【おん 恩】**DEBT OF GRATITUDE, gratitude, obligation, indebtedness; kindness, favor; love**
恩が有る おんがある owe a debt of gratitude
恩に着せる おんにきせる demand gratitude
恩を忘れる おんをわすれる be ungrateful

SYNONYMS

❶ⓐ **favor**
恵 FAVOR →3293
徳 act of kindness →0842
恩 GRACE →3289

❷ **thanking and gratitude**
謝 THANK →2048
礼 thanks →1012
恩 DEBT OF GRATITUDE →3289

晋

3290
2-6-4

▶**JIN DYNASTY**
シン ㊔ すすむ くに ゆき
Ⓝ 晉 Ⓒ 晋 jìn

72	Names	U664B
日	S10-4-6	F1501

COMPOUNDS

❶ⓐ **JIN DYNASTY (265-420 A.D.)**
ⓑ name of an ancient Chinese state
ⓒ another name for Shanxi Province (山西省)

a 晋書 しんじょ History of the Jin Dynasty

❷ [original meaning, now rare] advance, proceed to
晋山 しんざん taking up a new position as chief priest of a Buddhist temple

INDEPENDENT

【しん 晋】JIN DYNASTY

SYNONYMS

❶ⓐ **earlier Chinese dynasties**
夏 Xia Dynasty →2619
商 Shang Dynasty →2623
周 Zhou Dynasty →3720
漢 Han Dynasty →0808
晋 JIN DYNASTY →3290
秦 QIN DYNASTY →3192

NOTE

★ do not confuse with 普 WIDESPREAD →2919

鬼

3291
2-6-4

▶**DEVIL**
キ おに おに-
Ⓒ 鬼 guǐ

194	Jōyō	U9B3C
鬼	S10-10-0	F1057

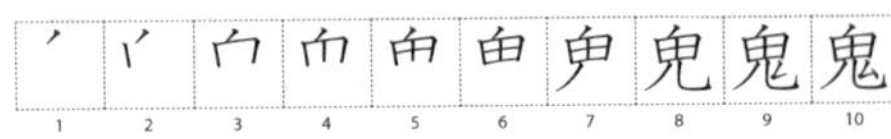

RADICAL

oni 'ghost' (魔 魂 魄), used in characters related to spirits, ghosts or demons
Enclosure: 鬼[×] *kinyō* (魅 魑[×] 魎[×])

COMPOUNDS

❶ⓐ (harmful evil spirit) **DEVIL, demon**
ⓑ (imaginary evil monster with horns) **DEVIL, ogre**

a 鬼神 きしん terrible god; departed spirit, ghost
鬼畜 きちく devil
鬼気迫る ききせまる ghastly, bloodcurdling
鬼女 きじょ demoness, witch
悪鬼 あっき devil, demon, evil spirit, goblin
疑心暗鬼 ぎしんあんき suspicion and fear

b 鬼面 きめん mask of a devil, startling appearance

❷ [original meaning] **ghost, departed spirit**
鬼籍に入る きせきにいる join the majority, pass away
餓鬼 がき hungry ghost; *slang* kid

❸ clever, artful, extremely competent
鬼才 きさい genius, wizard, prodigy
神出鬼没の しんしゅつきぼつの appearing and disappearing unexpectedly, elusive

❹ [also suffix] **DEVIL**ish or wicked person
債鬼 さいき creditor
剣鬼 けんき devilish swordsman
殺人鬼 さつじんき devilish homicide, cutthroat

KUN

【おに 鬼】(imaginary evil monster with horns) **DEVIL, demon, ogre;** (person with a demonic passion for something) **demon, fiend; tagger, "it"**
鬼婆 おにばば hag, witch
鬼ごっこ おにごっこ tag game

仕事の鬼 しごとのおに devil for work, work fiend

【おに- 鬼-】

① [prefix] **daredevil, extremely competent, inhumanly sharp**

鬼武者 おにむしゃ daredevil warrior

鬼刑事 おにけいじ crack detective

② unbecomingly large

鬼蓮 おにばす prickly water lily

鬼歯 おにば protruding tooth

SYNONYMS

❶ **supernatural and evil beings**

鬼 DEVIL → 3291

魔 DEMON → 3953

怪 monster → 0354

霊 SPIRIT → 3480

精 SPIRIT → 1729

書

▶WRITE

▶BOOK

ショ か(く) -が(き) -がき

3292

Ⓒ 书 shū

2-6-4

73	Jōyō-2	U66F8
日	S10-4-6	F0072

1 2 3 4 5 6 7 8 9 10

COMPOUNDS

❶ **WRITE**

書写 しょしゃ transcription, copying, handwriting

書記 しょき clerk, secretary

清書する せいしょする write out fair, make a fair [clean] copy

代書する だいしょする write for another

❷ⓐ **writing, art of writing, calligraphy, penmanship**

ⓑ **style of writing, calligraphic style**

ⓒ written symbols, writings, characters

a 書法 しょほう penmanship, calligraphy

書道 しょどう calligraphy, penmanship

書家 しょか calligrapher

b 書体 しょたい penmanship style, calligraphic style

楷書 かいしょ square style of Chinese characters

行書 ぎょうしょ semicursive style of Chinese characters

草書 そうしょ *sosho,* cursive writing

c 書画 しょが pictures and writings

❸ written materials:

ⓐ [also suffix] **writings, document, papers, certificate**

ⓑ (written message) **letter, note, message**

a 書類 しょるい documents, papers

書面 しょめん letter, document

文書 ぶんしょ(=もんじょ) document, letter, note

秘書 ひしょ secretary; treasured book

証明書 しょうめいしょ certificate, diploma

b 書簡 しょかん letter, correspondence

書状 しょじょう letter, note

投書 とうしょ contribution, letter (from a reader)

遺書 いしょ testamentary letter, will

私書箱 ししょばこ post office box (P.O.B.)

親展書 しんてんしょ confidential letter

一般教書 いっぱんきょうしょ State of the Union message

❹ⓐ [also suffix] **BOOK, literary work**

ⓑ history **BOOK**, chronicles, Chinese classics

ⓒ abbrev. of 書経 しょきょう: **BOOK** of Documents [History] (name of a Chinese classic)

a 書物 しょもつ book, volume

書店 しょてん bookstore

書籍 しょせき books, publications

辞書 じしょ dictionary

図書 としょ books

図書館 としょかん library

読書 どくしょ reading a book, reading

良書 りょうしょ good book, valuable work

教科書 きょうかしょ textbook, schoolbook

b 漢書 かんじょ Chronicles of the Han Dynasty; Chinese classics

四書 ししょ the Four Chinese Classics

INDEPENDENT

【しょ 書】 calligraphy, penmanship, handwriting; **BOOK**; letter

書の旨い人 しょのうまいひと excellent calligrapher

書を呈する しょをていする write a letter

座右の書 ざゆうのしょ one's desk-side book

KUN

【かく 書く】

ⓐ **WRITE, pen**

ⓑ (compose written texts) **WRITE, compose**

a 書き換える かきかえる rewrite, renew (a bill), transfer

書き順 かきじゅん stroke order (in writing Chinese characters)

書き方 かきかた how to write, way [style] of writing

書き言葉 かきことば written language

書き取り かきとり dictation

書留 かきとめ registered mail

読み書き よみかき reading and writing

b 小説を書く しょうせつをかく write a novel

【-がき -書き, -書】 writing, written document, written statement, note

横書きする よこがきする write laterally, write from left to right

覚え書き おぼえがき memorandum, memo, note
肩書き かたがき title, degree
葉書 はがき postcard

SYNONYMS

❶ **write**
書 WRITE →3292
筆 write →3317
写 COPY →2493
記 WRITE DOWN →1843
紀 record in writing →1628
控える note down →0600
録 RECORD →2186
登 register →3208
註 ANNOTATE →1893

❷ⓐ & ❸ⓐ **writing**
文 WRITINGS →2458
筆 WRITING →3317
書 writing(s) →3292
銘 INSCRIPTION →2158

❸ⓑ **written communications**
状 LETTER →0322
文 LETTER →2458
翰 LETTER →2198
書 letter →3292
信 written communication →0115
電 telegram →3465
牒 OFFICIAL NOTICE →1299

❹ⓐ **books**
本 BOOK →4314
典 STANDARD WORK →3253
経 religious classic →1687
書 BOOK →3292
冊 bound book →4295
籍 books →3394
著 literary work →2869
巻 VOLUME →3273
編 piece of writing →1755
篇 PIECE OF WRITING →3361
鑑 REFERENCE VOLUME →2226

【かく】
ⓑ **compose**
著 AUTHOR →2869
作 compose →0077
書く WRITE →3292
筆 write →3317

USAGE

【かく】
書く
ⓐ write, pen
ⓑ (compose written texts) write, compose
描く
draw, paint

HOMOPHONES

かく 描 DEPICT →0591

COMPOUND FORMATION

【秘書 ひしょ】
秘書 'secretary; treasured book' originally referred to secret (秘) documents (書 ❸ⓐ) and was extended to mean a person who handles such documents.

NOTE

➡ see COMPOUND FORMATION for
図書 としょ →図 3809
親展書 しんてんしょ →展 3862

恵

3293

2-6-4

▶**FAVOR**
ケイ エ めぐ(む) ㊔ やす さとし えい あや しげ
Ⓝ 惠 Ⓒ 惠 huì

61	Jōyō	U6075
心	S10-4-6	F0777

1 2 3 4 5 6 7 8 9 10

COMPOUNDS

❶ⓐ **FAVOR, grace, kindness**
ⓑ [original meaning] **FAVOR, bestow with a favor, show kindness to**
a 恵沢 けいたく blessing, pity, favor, benefit
恩恵 おんけい benefit, grace, favor, blessing
互恵 ごけい reciprocity, mutual benefits
特恵 とっけい special favor [benefit], preference, preferentialism
b 恵方 えほう lucky direction

❷ give, bestow, present
恵与する けいよする present, give, bestow
恵贈 けいぞう presentation

❸ [formerly 慧 え 3485] **intelligence, wisdom**
知恵 ちえ wisdom, intelligence, sagacity

KUN

【めぐむ 恵む】
① **bestow with a FAVOR, show kindness to; have mercy on, render benevolence**
恵み めぐみ favor, benefaction; blessing, grace, mercy
恵まれる めぐまれる be blessed; be privileged, be favored
恵まれた人人 めぐまれたひとびと favored [privileged] people; blessed people

② **give charity [alms]**
乞食に金を恵む こじきにかねをめぐむ give money to a beggar

SYNONYMS

❶ **favor**

恵 FAVOR → 3293
徳 act of kindness → 0842
恩 GRACE → 3289

【めぐむ】

② **donate**

施 give alms → 1103
恵む give charity → 3293
寄 CONTRIBUTE → 2856
醵 CONTRIBUTE MONEY → 2087
献 donate → 2240

曺
3294
2-6-4

▶**SERGEANT**
ソウ ゾウ

73	Nonstandard	U66FA
曰	S10-4-6	F0000

traditional form → see 曹 at 3414

拳
3295
2-6-4

▶**FIST**
ケン ゲン▲ こぶし ㊔ つとむ つよし
Ⓝ 拳 Ⓒ 拳 quán

64	Jōyō	U62F3
手	S10-4-6	F1859

COMPOUNDS

❶ **FIST**

拳銃 けんじゅう pistol, handgun
拳骨 げんこつ fist
鉄拳 てっけん clenched fist

❷ **sparring feat; boxing**

拳闘 けんとう boxing
太極拳 たいきょくけん tai chi
じゃん拳 じゃんけん *janken*: game of paper-scissors-stone

❸ (from the idea of humbly holding up something with both hands) with a humble attitude

拳拳服膺ˣする けんけんふくようする bear (a moral or lesson) in mind

INDEPENDENT

【けん 拳】 *ken*: a game played with the hands
拳を打つ けんをうつ play *ken*

KUN

【こぶし 拳】 FIST
拳を握る こぶしをにぎる make a fist

SYNONYMS

❶ **hand and arm**

手 HAND → 4267
腕 ARM → 1269
肘 ELBOW → 1044
掌 PALM → 3215
指 FINGER → 0452
拇 THUMB → 0358
拳 FIST → 3295

NOTE

★ do not confuse with 挙 NOMINATE → 3106

拳
3296
2-6-4

▶**FIST**
ケン ゲン こぶし ㊔ つとむ つよし

64	Nonstandard	U62F3
手	S10-4-6	F0000

traditional form → see 拳 at 3295

脊
3297
2-6-4

▶**SPINE**
セキ せ▲ せい▲
Ⓒ 脊 jǐ

130	Jōyō	U810A
月	S10-4-6	F2656

COMPOUNDS

● **SPINE, backbone**

脊髄 せきずい spinal cord
脊椎 せきつい spine, backbone
脊柱 せきちゅう spinal column
脊梁 せきりょう backbone, spine
脊索 せきさく notochord

KUN

【せ 脊】 [usu. 背]

① back; backside

脊骨 せぼね backbone, spine

② stature, height
③ ridge

【せい 脊】 [usu. 背] height, stature

SYNONYMS

● **bone**

骨 BONE → 3288
髄 MARROW → 2316
椎 SPINE → 1249
脊 SPINE → 3297
肋 RIB → 1022
骼 SKELETAL FRAME → 2302
骸 skeleton → 2301

HOMOPHONES

せ 背 BACK → 3182
せい 背 BACK → 3182

NOTE

➡ see USAGE note at 背 3182

【竹】 羊 羽 羽 西 次 此 叙 厶 卤 出 芸 茎 甘 聿 成 卌

第

3298

2-6-5

▸ORDINAL NUMBER PREFIX

ダイ テイ▲

N 才◇ C 第 dì

118	Jōyō-3	U7B2C
⺮	S11-6-5	F0203

COMPOUNDS

❶ **PREFIX for forming ORDINAL NUMBERs**

第五 だいご the fifth, No. 5

第一印象 だいいちいんしょう first impression

第一 だいいち the first, number one; the best; to begin with, above everything else

第三者 だいさんしゃ third party

第六感 だいろっかん the sixth sense, intuition

❷ [original meaning] **order, sequence**

次第 しだい order; circumstances, reasons; as soon as

❸ **examination (originally referred to grades into which successful candidates in the imperial examinations in China were placed)**

及第する きゅうだいする pass an examination

落第 らくだい failure in an examination

❹ *hist* mansion or residence of a high official

聚楽第 じゅらくだい(=じゅらくてい) mansion of Toyotomi Hideyoshi (16th century)

INDEPENDENT

【だい 第】examination in ancient China; mansion or residence of a high official

SYNONYMS

❶ **kinds of numbers**

数 NUMBER (mathematical unit) → 2245

員 fixed number → 2822

号 NUMBER (numerical designation) → 2675

番 No. → 3416

第 ORDINAL NUMBER PREFIX → 3298

-目 ordinal number suffix → 3777

次 numerical order suffix → 0058

桁 DIGIT → 1165

符

3299

2-6-5

▸SYMBOL

フ

C 符 fú

118	Jōyō	U7B26
⺮	S11-6-5	F1941

COMPOUNDS

❶ [also suffix]

ⓐ (arbitrary sign other than a letter representing meaning) **SYMBOL, sign, mark**

ⓑ *music* note

a 符号 ふごう sign, mark, symbol

符牒 ふちょう sign; secret price tag; password

疑問符 ぎもんふ question mark

終止符 しゅうしふ period

音符 おんぷ note; phonetic element of kanji

二分音符 にぶおんぷ half note

❷ⓐ [original meaning] **tally (of wood or bamboo) split in half used for identification (esp. in ancient China); tag**

ⓑ tally with, accord with

a 符節 ふせつ tally, check

割符 わりふ tally, check

切符 きっぷ ticket

b 符合する ふごうする coincide [agree] with, conform with

❸ charm, amulet

護符 ごふ charm, amulet

神符 しんぷ charm, talisman, amulet

INDEPENDENT

【ふ 符】paper charm

SYNONYMS

❶ⓐ **marks and signs**

標 MARK (identifying sign) → 1347

徽 EMBLEM → 0968

痕 SCAR → 4066

印 MARK (visible sign) → 1023

跡 TRACE → 1937

蹟 TRACE → 2065

踪 FOOTPRINTS → 1996

紋 print → 1651

符 SYMBOL → 3299

号 SIGN → 2675

栞 BOOKMARK → 3285

❷ⓐ **labels and slips**

札 TAG → 1011

券 TICKET → 3256

票 SLIP → 3308

符 tally → 3299

節 token → 3336

笠
3300
▀2-6-5

▸SEDGE HAT
リュウ かさ
Ⓒ 笠 lì

118	Names	U7B20
⺮	S11-6-5	F1367

COMPOUNDS

● [original meaning] **SEDGE HAT, bamboo hat, conical hat**
破笠 はりゅう torn bamboo [sedge] hat

KUN

【かさ 笠】
①ⓐ **SEDGE HAT, bamboo hat, conical hat**
ⓑ **something that protects like a hat**
a 笠雲 かさぐも cap cloud
笠の台が飛ぶ かさのだいがとぶ be decapitated; be fired
編み笠 あみがさ braided hat
陣笠 じんがさ ancient soldier's hat; party rank and file
b 父親の威光を笠に着る ちちおやのいこうをかさにきる shelter oneself under one's father's influence
② **shade (of a lamp), hood, something shaped like a SEDGE HAT**
煙突の笠 えんとつのかさ chimney cap
松笠 まつかさ pine cone

SYNONYMS

【かさ】
①ⓐ **headgear**
帽 HEADGEAR →0693
冠 CROWN →2583
笠 SEDGE HAT →3300
兜 HEADPIECE →3499

HOMOPHONES

かさ 傘 UMBRELLA →2640

NOTE

➡ see USAGE note at 傘 2640

笹
3301
▀2-6-5

▸BAMBOO GRASS
ささ
Ⓒ (国字)

118	Names	U7B39
⺮	S11-6-5	F2099

KUN

【ささ 笹】 [sometimes also 篠] **BAMBOO GRASS**
笹原 ささはら field of bamboo grass
笹舟 ささぶね toy bamboo-leaf boat
熊笹 くまざさ *Sasa albo-marginata,* low and striped bamboo

SYNONYMS

【ささ】
○ **kinds of grasses**
草 GRASS →2813
荻 AMUR SILVERGRASS →2844
蒲 CATTAIL →2932
萊 GOOSEFOOT →2878
蕨 BRACKEN →2992
叢 grassy place →3243
芝 LAWN GRASS →2705
笹 BAMBOO GRASS →3301
茅 cogongrass →2779
萱 THATCH GRASS →2904
藁 STRAW →3015
芦 REED →2743
葦 COMMON REED →2934
菅 SEDGE →2874
○ **bamboo**
竹 BAMBOO →0267
笹 BAMBOO GRASS →3301
篠 DWARF BAMBOO →3376

USAGE

【ささ】
笹
[sometimes also 篠] bamboo grass
篠
[usu. 笹] bamboo grass

HOMOPHONES

ささ 篠 DWARF BAMBOO →3376

笙
3302
▀2-6-5

▸*SHO*
ショウ ソウ セイ
Ⓒ 笙 shēng

118	Names	U7B19
⺮	S11-6-5	F2906

COMPOUNDS

● ***SHO*: free-reed mouth organ used in Japanese court music**
笙歌 しょうか(=せいか) singing and playing *sho*

INDEPENDENT

【しょう 笙】 *SHO*: free-reed mouth organ

SYNONYMS

● **musical instruments**
琴 KOTO →3455
箏 KOTO →3353
鼓 DRUM →2241
笛 FLUTE →3303
琵 LUTE →3453
琶 LUTE →3454
笙 *SHO* →3302

笛

▶FLUTE
テキ ふえ
Ⓒ 笛 dí

3303
2-6-5

118	Jōyō-3	U7B1B
⺮	S11-6-5	F1897

COMPOUNDS

❶ [original meaning] **FLUTE, pipe, recorder**
鼓笛隊 こてきたい drum and fife band
牧笛 ぼくてき shepherd's pipe
銀笛 ぎんてき flageolet
魔笛 まてき magic flute; The Magic Flute (by Mozart)

❷ **whistle, horn**
汽笛 きてき steam whistle
霧笛 むてき foghorn
警笛 けいてき alarm-whistle, horn

KUN

【ふえ 笛】**FLUTE, pipe, clarinet, oboe; whistle**
笛吹き ふえふき flute player
横笛 よこぶえ flute, fife
草笛 くさぶえ reed
麦笛 むぎぶえ oaten pipe
喉笛 のどぶえ windpipe
口笛 くちぶえ whistle

SYNONYMS

❶ **musical instruments**
琴 KOTO → 3455
箏 KOTO → 3353
鼓 DRUM → 2241
笛 FLUTE → 3303
琵 LUTE → 3453
琶 LUTE → 3454
笙 *SHO* → 3302

羞

incorrect classification
➡ see 3-7-4: 羊 at 4106
2-6-5

盖

incorrect classification
➡ see 2-3-8: 丷 at 2887
2-6-5

䨱

▶LEARN
▶CUSTOM
シュウ ジュ なら(う) なら(い)

3304
2-6-5

124	Nonstandard	U7FD2
羽	S11-6-5	F0000

traditional form → see 習 at 3306

翌

▶THE FOLLOWING
ヨク

3305
2-6-5

124	Nonstandard	U7FCC
羽	S11-6-5	F0000

traditional form → see 翌 at 3307

習

▶LEARN
▶CUSTOM
シュウ ジュ▲ なら(う) なら(い)
Ⓝ 習 Ⓒ 习 xí

3306
2-6-5

124	Jōyō-3	U7FD2
羽	S11-6-5	F0702

COMPOUNDS

❶ **LEARN, acquire, be taught, study**
習得 しゅうとく learning, acquirement
学習 がくしゅう study, learning
練習 れんしゅう practice, training
講習 こうしゅう short training course
独習 どくしゅう self-study, self-teaching
実習 じっしゅう practice, training
演習 えんしゅう exercise, practice; military maneuvers; seminar
補習 ほしゅう supplementary lessons

❷ **CUSTOM, habit, practice, tradition**
習慣 しゅうかん custom, habit
慣習 かんしゅう custom, usage, tradition
風習 ふうしゅう manners and customs
悪習 あくしゅう bad habit
奇習 きしゅう strange custom

❸ be familiar with, become attached to
近習 きんじゅ attendant

KUN

【ならう 習う】**LEARN, be taught, study; practice**
習い事 ならいごと practice
見習い みならい apprenticeship, apprentice

【ならい 習い】**habit, CUSTOM, practice**
習わし ならわし custom, practice

SYNONYMS

❶ **learn and study**

学 STUDY → 3162
考 study → 3962
習 LEARN → 3306
研 RESEARCH → 1456
究 STUDY EXHAUSTIVELY → 2729
攻 specialize → 0286

❷ **custom**
慣 HABITUAL PRACTICE → 0843
例 established practice → 0099
習 CUSTOM → 3306
風 manners → 3730
俗 popular custom → 0119
癖 HABIT → 4080
弊 EVIL PRACTICE → 3583

USAGE

【ならう】
習う
learn, be taught, study; practice
倣う
copy after, copy from, imitate, follow an example

HOMOPHONES

ならう 倣 COPY AFTER → 0127

翌

3307
2-6-5

▶**THE FOLLOWING**
ヨク
Ⓝ 翌 Ⓒ 翌 yì

124	Jōyō-6	U7FCC
羽	S11-6-5	F0915

COMPOUNDS

● **THE FOLLOWING, the next (month or year)**
翌日 よくじつ the following [next] day
翌年 よくねん the next [following] year
翌春 よくしゅん next spring
翌翌日 よくよくじつ two days after
翌朝 よくあさ the following morning

INDEPENDENT

【よく 翌】next, **THE FOLLOWING** (month or year)
翌二十日 よくはつか the following day, the 20th

SYNONYMS

● **next**
次 NEXT → 0058
明 next → 1060
翌 THE FOLLOWING → 3307
来 the coming → 4366

票

3308
2-6-5

▶**VOTE**
▶**SLIP**
ヒョウ
Ⓒ 票 piào

113	Jōyō-4	U7968
示	S11-5-6	F1236

COMPOUNDS

❶ⓐ [also suffix] **VOTE, ballot**
ⓑ counter for **VOTE**s
a 票田 ひょうでん favorable voting constituency
投票 とうひょう vote, ballot
白票 はくひょう blank ballot
得票 とくひょう number of votes obtained
開票 かいひょう official counting of votes
賛否同票 さんぴどうひょう tie vote
b 二千票 にせんびょう 2000 votes

❷ [also suffix] **SLIP, chit, voucher, card**
伝票 でんぴょう slip, chit, ticket
証票 しょうひょう voucher, chit
軍票 ぐんぴょう military scrip, army note
入金票 にゅうきんひょう deposit slip
住民票 じゅうみんひょう resident card
調査票 ちょうさひょう questionnaire

INDEPENDENT

【ひょう 票】**VOTE, ballot**
票を読む ひょうをよむ count the votes

SYNONYMS

❶ⓐ **vote and election**
票 VOTE → 3308
選 election → 3931

❷ **labels and slips**
札 TAG → 1011
券 TICKET → 3256
票 SLIP → 3308
符 tally → 3299
節 token → 3336

盗

3309
2-6-5

▶**STEAL**
トウ ぬす(む)
Ⓝ 盗 Ⓒ 盗 dào

108	Jōyō	U76D7
皿	S11-5-6	F1070

丶	冫	冫	冫	冫	次	次	咨	咨	盗
1	2	3	4	5	6	7	8	9	10

盗 11

COMPOUNDS

❶ⓐ STEAL, burglarize
ⓑ perform by **STEAL**th, steal

a 盗品 とうひん stolen article [goods]
盗癖 とうへき kleptomania
盗難 とうなん robbery, burglary, theft
窃盗 せっとう theft, larceny

b 盗作 とうさく plagiarism
盗聴 とうちょう wire tapping, unlicensed radio listening

❷ thief, burglar, robber
盗賊 とうぞく thief, robber, bandit
怪盗 かいとう mysterious thief
群盗 ぐんとう group [gang] of robbers
夜盗 やとう night thief

❸ *baseball* **STEAL**
盗塁 とうるい base stealing, steal
重盗 じゅうとう double steal

KUN

【ぬすむ 盗む】**STEAL, rob; plagiarize;** *baseball* **steal**
盗み ぬすみ theft
盗人 ぬすびと(=ぬすっと) thief
盗み聞き ぬすみぎき eavesdropping, tapping
盗み出す ぬすみだす steal (from a person)

SYNONYMS

❶ⓐ steal and rob
盗 STEAL → 3309
窃 STEAL → 2801
取 TAKE → 1613
奪 ROB → 2956
略 plunder → 1501
掠 PLUNDER → 0605
鹵 PLUNDER → 2634

❷ thieves
盗 thief → 3309
泥 petty thief → 0384
賊 BANDIT → 1932

砦

▶FORT
サイ とりで
Ⓒ 砦 zhài

3310
2-6-5

112	Names	U7826
石	S11-5-6	F2271

COMPOUNDS

● [usu. 塞 さい 2924] **FORT, fortress, stronghold**
城砦(=城塞) じょうさい fortress, stronghold, citadel
山砦 さんさい mountain stronghold

KUN

【とりで 砦】[formerly also 塁 or 塞] **FORT, fortress, stronghold**
砦を築く とりでをきずく construct a fort

SYNONYMS

● strongholds
城 CASTLE → 0417
塁 SMALL FORT → 3206
塞 FORT → 2924
砦 FORT → 3310
堡 FORT → 3500

HOMOPHONES

とりで
塁 BASE → 3206
塞 STOP UP → 2924

NOTE

➡ see USAGE note at 塁 3206

祭

▶FESTIVAL
サイ まつ(る) まつ(り) まつり
Ⓒ 祭 jì

3311
2-6-5

113	Jōyō-3	U796D
示	S11-5-6	F1110

ノ	ク	タ	タ	タ	奴	奴	祭	祭	祭
1	2	3	4	5	6	7	8	9	10

祭 11

COMPOUNDS

❶ⓐ [also suffix] **FESTIVAL, feast, celebration, holiday**
ⓑ religious **FESTIVAL**, rite

a 祭日 さいじつ national holiday, festival [feast] day
祝祭日 しゅくさいじつ national holiday, festival [feast] day
文化祭 ぶんかさい cultural festival
芸術祭 げいじゅつさい art festival
前夜祭 ぜんやさい eve

b 祭礼 さいれい festival, feast, rituals
祭祀 さいし religious service; festival

❷ [original meaning] offer a sacrifice, worship a god
祭壇 さいだん altar
祭神 さいじん the enshrined deity
祭司 さいし priest

KUN

【まつる 祭る】[formerly also 祀る]
ⓐ **worship as god, deify**
ⓑ **enshrine**

a 先祖を祭る せんぞをまつる worship one's ancestors

【まつり 祭り, 祭】[also suffix] **FESTIVAL, celebration, feast day**
夏祭り なつまつり summer festival
雛祭り ひなまつり Doll Festival (March 3)

SYNONYMS

❶ **ceremonies and festivities**
式 CEREMONY → 3785
儀 CEREMONY → 0191
典 formal ceremony → 3253
礼 RITE → 1012
斎 religious ritual → 2622
会 Buddhist ceremony → 2512
祭 FESTIVAL → 3311

USAGE

【まつる】
祭る
[formerly also 祀る]
ⓐ worship as god, deify
ⓑ enshrine
祀る
[now usu. 祭る] same as 祭る

HOMOPHONES

まつる 祀 WORSHIP AS GOD → 1448

参
⬒2-6-5
incorrect classification
➡ see ⬒2-2-9: 厶 at 2635

离
⬒2-6-5
incorrect classification
➡ see ⬒2-2-9: 亠 at 2627

崇
⬒2-6-5
incorrect classification
➡ see ⬒2-3-8: 山 at 2864

菅
⬒2-6-5
incorrect classification
➡ see ⬒2-3-8: 艹 at 2874

菱
⬒2-6-5
incorrect classification
➡ see ⬒2-3-8: 艹 at 2879

基

3312
⬒2-6-5

▶**BASE**
キ もと もとい ㊔ もとし もとえ
Ⓒ 基 jī

32	Jōyō-5	U57FA
土	S11-3-8	F0404

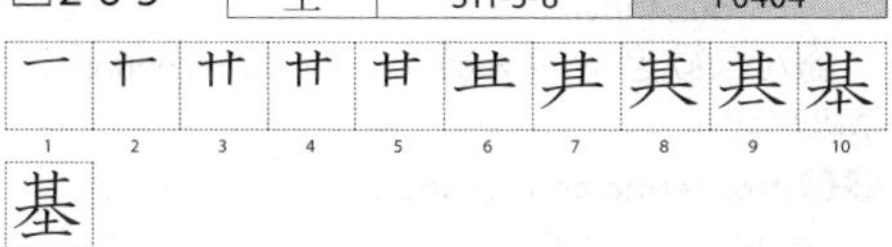

COMPOUNDS

❶ⓐ (physical support) **BASE, basis, foundation**
ⓑ [also suffix] *chem* **BASE**; radical, group
ⓒ *math* **BASE**, radix
ⓓ [suffix] **BASE** material
a 基礎 きそ basis, foundation
基盤 きばん bedrock, base, foundation
基底 きてい base, basis, foundation; *math* base
基石 きせき foundation stone
基地 きち base
開基 かいき foundation of a temple
b 塩基 えんき base
水酸基 すいさんき hydroxyl group [radical]
遊離基 ゆうりき free radical
c 根基 こんき radical
d 培養基 ばいようき (culture) medium

❷ⓐ (nonphysical support) **BASE, basis, foundation, ground**
ⓑ basic, fundamental, cardinal
ⓒ be **BASE**d on, be founded on
a 基本 きほん basis, foundation
基準 きじゅん standard, criterion, basis
基幹 きかん mainstay, nucleus
基金 ききん fund, foundation, endowment
基調 きちょう keynote, underlying tone, basis
b 基音 きおん fundamental tone
基点 きてん cardinal point, reference point
c 基因する きいんする cause

❸ counter for mounted objects, esp. lanterns, gravestones, heavy machinery, torii (shrine archways) or large wreaths of flowers
石塔二基 せきとうにき two tombstones
エレベーター三基 えれべーたーさんき three elevators

❹ Christianity
基教 ききょう Christianity

❺ origin
基源 きげん origin

INDEPENDENT

【き 基】*math* radix; **BASE**; *chem* radical; (nonphysical) basis, base

KUN

【もと 基】(underlying support) **basis, foundation, grounds, authority**
基づく もとづく be based on, be grounded on; originate, be due to
資料を基にする しりょうをもとにする on the basis [grounds] of the data

【もとい 基】**(nonphysical) basis, foundation, essence**
信仰を基とする しんこうをもといとする be based on faith

SPECIAL READINGS

基督▲ きりすと Jesus Christ

SYNONYMS

❶ⓐ **bottoms and bases**

底 BOTTOM → 3827
柢 BOTTOM → 1121
下 lower part → 4186
基 BASE → 3312
礎 FOUNDATION STONE → 1595
麓 FOOT OF MOUNTAIN → 3494
磐 BEDROCK → 3534
盤 bedrock → 3533
床 BED → 3805

❷ⓐ **basis**

基 BASE → 3312
本 BASIS → 4314
素 ELEMENT → 3108
礎 foundation → 1595
底 BOTTOM → 3827
根 ROOT → 1167
拠 GROUNDS → 0369

HOMOPHONES

もと

本 BASIS → 4314
元 ORIGIN → 2428
下 DOWN → 4186
素 ELEMENT → 3108
許 PERMIT → 1862

NOTE

➡ see USAGE note at 元 2428

晝

▶DAYTIME

チュウ ひる

3313

2-6-5

72	Names	U665D
日	S11-4-7	F0000

traditional form → see 昼 at 3841

盛

▶PROSPEROUS

セイ ジョウ も(る) さか(る) さか(ん)

㊔ しげ さかえ

Ⓝ 盛 Ⓒ 盛 shèng chéng

3314

2-6-5

108	Jōyō-6	U76DB
皿	S11-5-6	F0766

Stroke order: ノ 厂 厅 成 成 成 成 咸 咸 盛 盛 (1–11)

COMPOUNDS

❶ⓐ **PROSPEROUS, flourishing, successful, booming**

ⓑ at the height of, in the midst of

a 盛衰 せいすい ups and downs, rise and fall, prosperity and decline
盛況 せいきょう prosperity, boom, success
繁盛(=繁昌)する はんじょうする prosper, flourish, thrive
隆盛 りゅうせい prosperity

b 盛夏 せいか midsummer
最盛期 さいせいき height of prosperity

❷ **grand, splendid, great, excellent**

盛大な せいだいな grand, magnificent, prosperous
盛儀 せいぎ grand ceremony
盛装 せいそう gala dress, beautiful attire

KUN

【もる 盛る】

①ⓐ **heap up (sand), pile (up)**

ⓑ **fill (a bowl with rice), serve food**

a 盛り上がり もりあがり climax (of a story), upsurge
盛り上げる もりあげる pile up, heap up; stir up, bring to a climax
盆に胡桃を盛る ぼんにくるみをもる heap a tray with walnuts

b 盛り もり helping, serving; quantity
盛り付ける もりつける dish up
山盛り やまもり a heap, a full measure
酒盛り さかもり drinking bout, merrymaking

② administer (medicine), prescribe

毒を盛る どくをもる kill with poison

③ **put into**

盛り込む もりこむ incorporate, include

④ **mark out (in degrees), graduate**

目盛り めもり division, scale, graduations

【さかる 盛る】 **prosper, thrive, flourish;** (of animals) **copulate**

盛り さかり height, peak, prime; heat, rut
盛り場 さかりば public resort, bustling place
盛りが付く さかりがつく rut, get on heat
働き盛り はたらきざかり prime of life

【さかん 盛ん】

さかんな 盛んな [also 旺んな] **PROSPEROUS, flourishing; vigorous, energetic, active; hearty, cordial, enthusiastic, furious; keen; extensive, large; popular**

盛んに さかんに vigorously, energetically, actively; heartily, enthusiastically
盛んな商売 さかんなしょうばい thriving business
盛んになる さかんになる prosper, grow prosperous, thrive
盛んな歓迎 さかんなかんげい cordial reception

SYNONYMS

❶ⓐ **prospering and prosperity**

隆 PROSPER → 0661

振 rise → 0515
興 RISE TO PROSPERITY → 3622
盛 PROSPEROUS → 3314
昌 PROSPERING → 3069
栄 FLOURISH → 3183
繁 THRIVE → 3536
賑 BUSTLE → 1959

【もる】

①ⓐ **accumulate**

積 ACCUMULATE → 1579
溜 ACCUMULATE → 0814
累 CUMULATE → 3196
重 pile up → 4390
盛る heap up → 3314
堆 PILED HIGH → 0563

USAGE

【さかんな】

盛んな

③ [also 旺んな] prosperous, flourishing; vigorous, energetic, active; hearty, cordial, enthusiastic, furious; keen; extensive, large; popular

旺んな

[also 盛んな] vigorous, energetic, lively

HOMOPHONES

さかんな 旺 ENERGETIC → 1061

帯

▶BELT
▶WEAR
タイ お(びる) おび

3315
2-6-5

50	Names	U5E36
巾	S11-3-8	F0000

traditional form → see 帶 at 3191

筑

▶OLD NAME FOR KYUSHU
チク ㊔ つき

Ⓒ 筑 zhù

3316
2-6-6

118	Names	U7B51
⺮	S12-6-6	F2088

COMPOUNDS

❶ abbrev. of 筑紫 つくし: **OLD NAME FOR KYUSHU or west Fukuoka Prefecture**

筑前煮 ちくぜんに chicken stew with root vegetables

❷ [original meaning, now obsolete] ancient Chinese instrument

SPECIAL READINGS

筑子(=小切子) こきりこ clave-like folk instrument made of bamboo
筑紫鴨 つくしがも common shelduck

筆

▶BRUSH
▶WRITING
ヒツ ふで

Ⓒ 笔 bǐ

3317
2-6-6

118	Jōyō-3	U7B46
⺮	S12-6-6	F0922

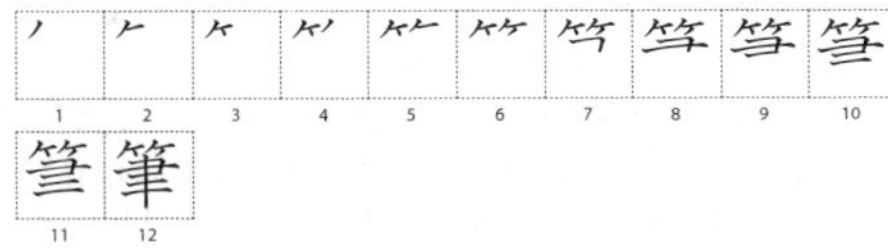

COMPOUNDS

❶ [original meaning] **BRUSH, writing brush, paintbrush**

毛筆 もうひつ (writing or painting) brush
画筆 がひつ paintbrush

❷ **WRITING instrument, pen, pencil**

鉛筆 えんぴつ pencil
万年筆 まんねんひつ fountain pen
鉄筆 てっぴつ steel pen, stencil pen
潤筆料 じゅんぴつりょう fee for writing or painting

❸ⓐ **WRITING, literary profession**
ⓑ art of **WRITING**, calligraphy, penmanship
ⓒ (something written) **WRITINGs, handwriting, writing, composition**

a 文筆業 ぶんぴつぎょう literary profession, writing
b 筆力 ひつりょく power of the pen; ability to write
筆才 ひっさい literary talent
筆法 ひっぽう style of penmanship
筆跡 ひっせき handwriting, holograph
c 自筆 じひつ one's own handwriting
随筆 ずいひつ essay; stray notes

❹ⓐ **write**
ⓑ writer

a 筆者 ひっしゃ writer
筆記する ひっきする take notes of, write down
筆記試験 ひっきしけん written examination
筆記用具 ひっきようぐ writing materials, pens and pencils
執筆 しっぴつ writing
特筆する とくひつする mention specially
b 主筆 しゅひつ chief editor

❺ subdivision of land

分筆 ぶんぴつ subdivision of a lot

INDEPENDENT

【ひつ 筆】**WRITING**; written by

これは弘法大師の筆だそうです これはこうぼうだいしのひつだそうです This writing is ascribed to Saint Kobo

KUN

【ふで 筆】**writing BRUSH, paintbrush; WRITING, painting handwriting, penmanship; literary work, painting**

筆先 ふでさき brush tip
筆不精 ふでぶしょう poor correspondent
筆を置く ふでをおく put down one's pen, stop writing, close (a letter)
絵筆 えふで paintbrush, drawing pen
弘法筆を選ばず こうぼうふでをえらばず The cunning workman does not quarrel with his tools
一筆 ひとふで a stroke (of the pen or brush)
雪舟の筆 せっしゅうのふで work of Sesshu

SYNONYMS

❸ **writing**
文 WRITINGS → 2458
筆 WRITING → 3317
書 writing(s) → 3292
銘 INSCRIPTION → 2158

❹ⓐ **compose**
著 AUTHOR → 2869
作 compose → 0077
書く WRITE → 3292
筆 write → 3317

❹ⓐ **write**
書 WRITE → 3292
筆 write → 3317
写 COPY → 2493
記 WRITE DOWN → 1843
紀 record in writing → 1628
控える note down → 0600
録 RECORD → 2186
登 register → 3208
註 ANNOTATE → 1893

NOTE

➡ see COMPOUND FORMATION for
随筆 ずいひつ → 随 0765
潤筆料 じゅんぴつりょう → 潤 0918

筈

3318
2-6-6

▶OUGHT TO
カツ はず
Ⓒ 筈 kuò

118	Names	U7B48
⺮	S12-6-6	F1761

KUN

【はず 筈】

①ⓐ (be a matter of course) **OUGHT TO, sure to, bound to, should, must**
ⓑ (be scheduled) **OUGHT TO, expected to, due to, supposed to, should**

a 出来る筈 できるはず should be able to
b 手筈 てはず arrangements, plan
今夜届く筈 こんやとどくはず expected to arrive tonight

② nock of an arrow [bow]
矢筈 やはず nock of an arrow; forked tool used for hanging scrolls
弓筈 ゆみはず(=ゆはず) nock of a bow

SYNONYMS

【はず】
① **certain**
必 WITHOUT FAIL → 0015
確 CERTAIN → 1571
筈 OUGHT TO → 3318

筋

3319
2-6-6

▶MUSCLE
▶THREADLIKE STRUCTURE
キン すじ
Ⓒ 筋 jīn

118	Jōyō-6	U7B4B
⺮	S12-6-6	F0833

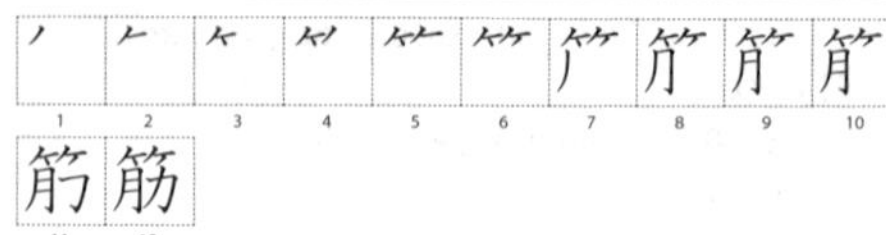

COMPOUNDS

❶ [also suffix] [original meaning] **MUSCLE**
筋肉 きんにく muscle, sinews
筋骨 きんこつ sinews and bones
筋炎 きんえん myositis, inflammation of a muscle
心筋 しんきん myocardium, heart muscle
腹筋 ふっきん abdominal muscle
上腕筋 じょうわんきん brachial muscle

❷ reinforcement
鉄筋コンクリート てっきんこんくりーと reinforced concrete, ferroconcrete
補強筋 ほきょうきん reinforcement bar

INDEPENDENT

【きん 筋】**MUSCLE**

KUN

【すじ 筋】

① **MUSCLE; tendon, sinew**
筋張った すじばった sinewy, brawny; stringy
筋違い すじちがい cramp, sprain; misplacement, irrelevance

② **THREADLIKE STRUCTURE**, as:
ⓐ **line, stripe, strip, streak**
ⓑ vein
ⓒ fiber (of a plant), string; grain
ⓓ counter for long, slender objects

a 背筋 せすじ spinal column, spine; seam in the back
金筋 きんすじ gold stripes

b 青筋 あおすじ veins bulging along the temples
c 豆の筋を取る まめのすじをとる string peas
d 一筋の涙 ひとすじのなみだ a trickle of tears

③ lineage, descent
血筋 ちすじ blood relationship, lineage
長生きの筋 ながいきのすじ long-lived family

④ **thread, coherence, reason, logic**
筋合い すじあい reason
筋道 すじみち reason, thread (of an argument), coherence; systematic method, due formality
筋の通った すじのとおった logical, rational, coherent
本筋 ほんすじ right course (of action); main thread
大筋 おおすじ outline

⑤ **plot**
筋書き すじがき plot (of a play), synopsis, outline; plan, scheme
芝居の筋 しばいのすじ plot of a play

⑥ [also suffix] **quarters, circles, source, channel**
その筋 そのすじ authorities concerned
政府筋 せいふすじ official quarters
消息筋 しょうそくすじ informed circles

⑦ aptitude, nature
手筋 てすじ aptitude; handwriting; apt move (in a go or shogi game)

⑧ [in compounds] wayside, roadside, route, way
道筋 みちすじ route, course, way
東海道筋の町 とうかいどうすじのまち towns on the Tokaido
川筋 かわすじ course of a river; land along a river

SYNONYMS

❶ **flesh**
肉 FLESH → 3966
筋 MUSCLE → 3319

【すじ】

②ⓐ **line**
線 LINE → 1760
筋 THREADLIKE STRUCTURE → 3319
条 strip → 2726
脈 VEIN → 1189
棒 straight line → 1237
縞 STRIPE → 1784
軸 AXIS → 1908

ⓓ **counters for long objects**
本 counter for cylindrical objects → 4314
筋 counter for slender objects → 3319
竿 counter for poles or rods → 3259
挺 COUNTER FOR LONG SOLID OBJECTS → 0512

④ **reasoning**
理 REASON → 1220
筋 thread → 3319
脈 VEIN → 1189

⑧ **ways and routes**
道 WAY (path) → 3888
径 PATH → 0347
軌 TRACK → 1832
線 LINE → 1760
澪 WATERWAY → 0957
途 WAY (route) → 3853
路 ROAD → 1936
筋 wayside → 3319
通り street → 3855
街 city street → 0702
辻 CROSSROADS → 3958
岐 forked road → 0285
巷 THE STREETS → 3097

策

3320

2-6-6

▶SCHEME
▶MEASURE
サク

Ⓒ 策 cè

118	Jōyō-6	U7B56
⺮	S12-6-6	F0535

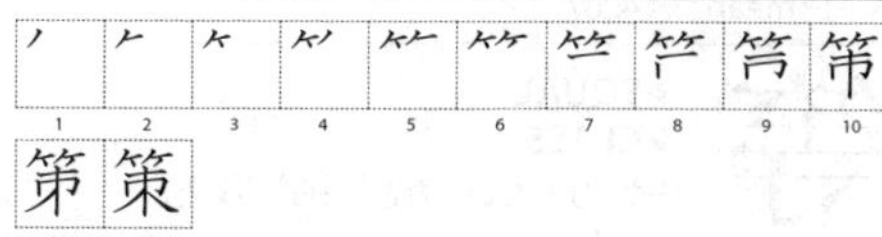

COMPOUNDS

❶ⓐ (clever plan of action) **SCHEME, device, plan, stratagem**
ⓑ [also suffix] **policy**
a 策謀 さくぼう artifice, stratagem
策士 さくし tactician; schemer, machinator
b 政策 せいさく policy, political measures
方策 ほうさく plan, policy, scheme
国策 こくさく national policy
強硬策 きょうこうさく hard-line policy, drastic measures

❷ [also suffix] **MEASURE, means, step, resource**
対策 たいさく countermeasure, counterplan
施策 しさく enforcement of a policy
万策 ばんさく all means [measures]
失策 しっさく blunder, slip, error
善後策 ぜんごさく remedial [relief] measure, countermeasure

❸ⓐ [original meaning, now rare] whip
ⓑ walking stick
a 策励 さくれい whipping (up), urging
b 散策する さんさくする go for a walk

INDEPENDENT

【さく 策】**SCHEME, device, plan, stratagem; policy; measure, means, step, resource**

策を講ずる さくをこうずる take [adopt] measures
最善の策 さいぜんのさく the best policy [measure]

【さくする 策する】plan

SYNONYMS

❶ⓐ plans and planning
計 PLAN → 1828
画 DRAW UP A PLAN → 3723
案 PROPOSAL → 2824
企 PROJECT → 2513
図 systematic plan → 3809
謀 SCHEME → 2004
策 SCHEME → 3320
略 STRATEGY → 1501
揆 PLOT → 0718

ⓑ policy
策 policy → 3320
是 policy → 3090
綱 guiding principle → 1735

❷ means
策 MEASURE → 3320
段 STEP → 1471
手 means → 4267

等

3321

2-6-6

▶EQUAL
▶CLASS

トウ ひと(しい) など▲ -ら▲ ㊔ とし

Ⓒ 等 děng

118	Jōyō-3	U7B49
⺮	S12-6-6	F0538

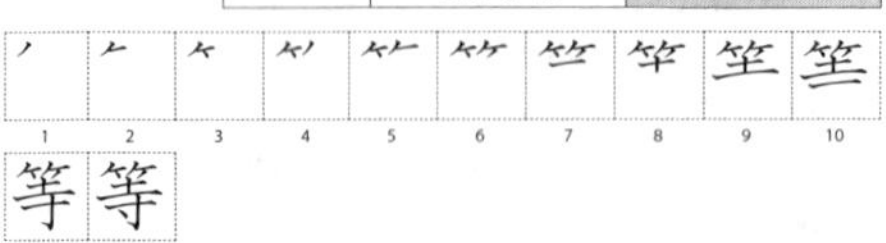

COMPOUNDS

❶ [also prefix] [original meaning] **EQUAL, same, alike**
等号 とうごう equal sign [mark]
等分する とうぶんする divide equally
等価 とうか equivalence, equal value; parity
平等 びょうどう equality, impartiality
均等 きんとう equality, uniformity
二等辺三角形 にとうへんさんかっけい equilateral [isosceles] triangle

❷ [also suffix] **CLASS, grade, rank, degree, place, magnitude (of a star)**
等級 とうきゅう class, grade, rank, magnitude
高等な こうとうな higher, high-grade, advanced
上等の じょうとうの first-class, superior
劣等 れっとう inferiority
中等 ちゅうとう middle-class, secondary grade
一等 いっとう first class; first place
三等星 さんとうせい third magnitude star

❸ et cetera, and the like, and so forth
等等 とうとう et cetera, and so forth

INDEPENDENT

【とう 等】CLASS, grade; et cetera, and the like, and so forth
等を分ける とうをわける classify, grade
家具等 かぐとう furniture and the like

KUN

【ひとしい 等しい】**EQUAL, same, alike**
Ｘは２Ｙに等しい えっくすはにわいにひとしい X equals 2Y

【など 等】and the like, and what not, et cetera
等等 などなど et cetera, et cetera
飛行機等 ひこうきなど airplanes and the like
私等には わたくしなどには for the likes of me

【-ら -等】[suffix]
① **and others, and the like, et al.**
山田等 やまだら Yamada and the others
② **plural suffix with deprecatory overtones**
奴等 やつら those guys, they

SPECIAL READINGS

等閑にする▲ なおざりにする disregard, neglect

SYNONYMS

❶ same and uniform
等 EQUAL → 3321
平 equal → 4291
均 EVEN → 0276
斉 UNIFORM → 2548
同 SAME → 3707
一 same → 4148

❷ class
級 GRADE → 1630
段 grade → 1471
位 RANK → 0069
階 RANK → 0761
身 social status → 4368
格 STATUS → 1161
等 CLASS → 3321
流 class → 0529
層 STRATUM → 3920

【-ら】
② **plural suffixes**
-達 plural suffix → 3893
-等 plural suffix → 3321
衆 somewhat polite plural suffix → 3325
-共 belittling plural suffix → 3045
-方 polite plural suffix → 2459

答 3322

▶ANSWER

トウ こた(える) こた(え)

Ⓒ 答 dá dā

2-6-6

118	Jōyō-2	U7B54
⺮	S12-6-6	F0463

COMPOUNDS

ⓐ [original meaning] **ANSWER (a question), reply, respond**
ⓑ **ANSWER (to a question), reply**
ⓒ **ANSWER, solve**
ⓓ **ANSWER (to a problem), solution**

a 答礼 とうれい return salute
答申 とうしん report, reply (to the jury)
答弁 とうべん reply, answer; defending oneself
b 応答 おうとう answer, response, reply
回答 かいとう reply, answer
確答 かくとう definite answer [reply]
返答 へんとう reply, answer
問答 もんどう questions and answers, catechism
c 答案 とうあん examination paper; answer
d 解答 かいとう solution, answer

KUN

【こたえる 答える】
ⓐ **ANSWER (a question), reply, respond**
ⓑ **ANSWER (a problem), solve**
a 質問に答える しつもんにこたえる answer a question

【こたえ 答え】**ANSWER (to a question), reply; answer (to a problem), solution**
受け答え うけこたえ reply, response

SYNONYMS

● **answer**
答 ANSWER → 3322
解 solve → 1913
返 reply → 3797
応 RESPOND → 3804

USAGE

【こたえる】
答える
ⓐ answer (a question), reply, respond
ⓑ answer (a problem), solve
応える
① come home to (one), strike home, have effect on; be a great strain
② repay, reward

HOMOPHONES

こたえる 応 RESPOND → 3804

筒 3323

▶TUBE

トウ つつ

Ⓒ 筒 tǒng

2-6-6

118	Jōyō	U7B52
⺮	S12-6-6	F1445

COMPOUNDS

ⓐ [also suffix] [original meaning] **TUBE, cylinder, pipe**
ⓑ **TUBE-shaped encasement**

a 円筒 えんとう cylinder
発煙筒 はつえんとう smoke ball [bomb]
b 水筒 すいとう canteen
封筒 ふうとう envelope

KUN

【つつ 筒】**TUBE, cylinder, pipe; tube-shaped encasement; gun barrel; gun; well curb**
筒形 つつがた cylindrical, tube-shaped
筒袖 つつそで tight-sleeved kimono
筒抜け つつぬけ passing directly through
茶筒 ちゃづつ tea caddy
短筒 たんづつ revolver, pistol
井筒 いづつ well curb

SYNONYMS

● **tubular passages**
管 PIPE → 3349
筒 TUBE → 3323
道 passage → 3888
脈 VEIN → 1189
樋 WATER PIPE → 1353

ⓐ **three-dimensional shapes**
錐 CONE → 2190
筒 cylinder → 3323
角 cube → 2541
球 sphere → 1219

箋 3324

▶PIECE OF PAPER

セン

2-6-6

118	Nonstandard	U41F3
⺮	S12-6-6	F0000

traditional form → see 箋 at 3352

着

2-6-6

incorrect classification
➡ see □3-7-5: 羊 at 4110

竹 【羊】 血 西 艹 壮 皿 罒 巴 廿 列 此 亦 厶 色 芇 苗 ⾉ 卌 甘 聿 ⽾

羊 【血】 壯 巴 列 此 亦 厽

衆

3325

2-6-6

▶**MULTITUDE**

シュウ シュ

N 眾◇ C 众 zhòng

143	Jōyō-6	U8846
血	S12-6-6	F0759

COMPOUNDS

1a the MULTITUDE(s), populace, the masses, the public

b (large crowd) **MULTITUDE, crowd**

c (great number) **MULTITUDE,** numerous, many

a 民衆 みんしゅう populace, the people, the masses
大衆 たいしゅう the masses, populace
公衆 こうしゅう the public

b 群衆 ぐんしゅう crowd of people, multitude
観衆 かんしゅう audience
アメリカ合衆国 あめりかがっしゅうこく United States of America

c 衆多 しゅうた great numbers, multitude

2 abbrev. of 衆議院 しゅうぎいん: **Lower House, House of Representatives**
衆参両院 しゅうさんりょういん both Houses (of the Diet)
衆院 しゅういん Lower House, House of Representatives

3 all kinds, various
衆説 しゅうせつ various theories

4 somewhat polite plural suffix
旦那衆 だんなしゅう(=だんなしゅ) gentlemen, gents

5 Buddhist priest
衆徒 しゅと many Buddhist priests

INDEPENDENT

【しゅう 衆】 the **MULTITUDE**(s), populace; crowd
衆に先んじる しゅうにさきんじる go ahead of the crowd

SYNONYMS

1a the people
民 PEOPLE → 3770
衆 the multitude(s) → 3325
庶 the masses → 3880
公 PUBLIC → 2468

b crowd
群 GROUP → 1942
衆 MULTITUDE → 3325
叢 CROWD TOGETHER → 3243
簇 FORM A CLUSTER → 3377

4 plural suffixes
-達 plural suffix → 3893
-等 plural suffix → 3321
衆 somewhat polite plural suffix → 3325
-共 belittling plural suffix → 3045
-方 polite plural suffix → 2459

粟

3326

2-6-6

▶**FOXTAIL MILLET**

ゾク あわ

C 粟 sù

119	Names	U7C9F
米	S12-6-6	F2644

COMPOUNDS

● **FOXTAIL MILLET**
粟粒 ぞくりゅう millet grain

KUN

【あわ 粟】 **FOXTAIL MILLET, Italian millet**
粟粒 あわつぶ millet grain
粟餅 あわもち millet mochi
粟立つ あわだつ have gooseflesh
濡れ手で粟 ぬれてであわ easy profit ("Grabbing millet with wet hands")

SPECIAL READINGS

罌×粟(=芥子) けし poppy

SYNONYMS

● **cereals**
米 RICE → 4342
麦 WHEAT → 3061
豆 BEAN → 2442
粟 FOXTAIL MILLET → 3326
黍 PROSO MILLET → 3210
蕎 BUCKWHEAT → 2993
蒋 WILD RICE → 2976

NOTE

★ do not confuse with 栗 CHESTNUT → 3280

萃

2-6-6

incorrect classification/ stroke-count

➡ see 2-3-8: ++ at 2882

装

3327

2-6-6

▶**DRESS**

▶**FIT OUT**

ソウ ショウ よそお(う)

N 裝 C 装 zhuāng

145	Jōyō-6	U88C5
衣	S12-6-6	F0588

COMPOUNDS

❶ⓐ **DRESS, put on clothes**
ⓑ **DRESS up, disguise, play the part**
ⓒ **DRESS, outfit, attire, ornaments**

a 正装する せいそうする dress up
b 装身具 そうしんぐ personal ornaments [outfit]
男装する だんそうする disguise oneself as a man, wear men's clothes
変装する へんそうする disguise oneself
仮装する かそうする disguise oneself, dress up (as)
c 装束 しょうぞく costume, attire
服装 ふくそう dress, garments, attire
旅装 りょそう traveling outfit
和装 わそう Japanese dress, kimono
衣装(=衣裳) いしょう clothes, garment, dress, costume

❷ **FIT OUT, equip, outfit, furnish, install**
装備する そうびする equip, fit out, furnish
装置 そうち equipment, device, installation
艤×装する ぎそうする fit out (a ship), equip
武装 ぶそう armament, equipment

❸ⓐ (decorate) **DRESS (up), ornament, trim**
ⓑ **coat, lay on**
a 装飾する そうしょくする ornament, adorn, decorate
新装 しんそう refurbishment, redecoration
改装 かいそう remodeling, refurbishing
b 塗装 とそう painting, coating
舗装 ほそう paving

❹ⓐ **load (a gun), charge; pack**
ⓑ load (as of gunpowder), charge
a 装填する そうてんする load, charge
包装 ほうそう wrapping, packing
b 口装 こうそう muzzle loading gun
二連装 にれんそう double load

❺ [also suffix] **binding**
装丁(=装幀) そうてい binding, format
革装 かわそう leather binding

INDEPENDENT

【そう 装】**DRESS**, outfit, attire; appearance
装を新たにする そうをあらたにする renew one's dress; refurbish

KUN

【よそおう 装う】**DRESS [attire] oneself, wear; make up; pretend**
装い よそおい dress, outfit; equipment

SYNONYMS

❶ⓐ **wear and put on**
着 PUT ON → 4110
装 DRESS → 3327
帯 WEAR (esp. at the belt) → 3191
穿く PUT ON → 2800
纏 put on → 1814
履く put on footwear → 3933
被る put on headgear → 1495

ⓑ **disguise**
装 dress up → 3327
化 change oneself into → 0022

ⓒ **clothing**
服 CLOTHES → 1090
袴 FORMAL DIVIDED SKIRT → 1509
蓑 STRAW RAINCOAT → 2941
-着 wear → 4110
衣 GARMENT → 2506
装 DRESS → 3327
裳 DRESS → 3231
襤 RAGS → 1607
袈 BUDDHIST SURPLICE → 3200
裟 BUDDHIST CASSOCK → 3420
襖 overgarment → 1600

❷ **equip and install**
据える INSTALL → 0602
敷 LAY → 2345
架 LAY ACROSS → 3178
装 FIT OUT → 3327
設 SET UP → 1863
備 PROVIDE → 0165

❸ⓐ **decorate**
飾 DECORATE → 2150
粧 APPLY MAKEUP → 1703
粉 apply face powder → 1643
装 DRESS → 3327

單

3328

2-6-6

▶**SINGLE**

タン

30	Names	U55AE
口	S12-3-9	F0000

traditional form → see 単 at 2805

巽

3329

2-6-6

▶**SOUTHEAST**

ソン たつみ ㊔ せん ゆずる

Ⓝ 巽 Ⓒ 巽 xùn

49	Names	U5DFD
己	S12-3-9	F0000

COMPOUNDS

❶ [rare] one of the four supplementary signs of the Oriental zodiac: **SOUTHEAST**
巽位 そんい one of the four supplementary signs of the Oriental zodiac

❷ [original meaning, now archaic] make an offering (on an altar)

KUN

【たつみ 巽】[also 辰巳]

① **SOUTHEAST**
巽の方角 たつみのほうがく southeast direction
② **old name of *Yoshiwara*** (prostitute quarters in Edo Era)
巽上がり たつみあがり speaking in a high-pitched voice or a graceless manner

SYNONYMS

【たつみ】
① **cardinal points**
東 EAST → 4385
西 WEST → 4333
北 NORTH → 0230
南 SOUTH → 2584
巽 SOUTHEAST → 3329
艮 NORTHEAST → 4330

HOMOPHONES

たつみ 辰巳 → 3713, 4197

巽 3330

2-6-6

▶SOUTHEAST
ソン たつみ ㊔ せん ゆずる

49	Nonstandard	U2F884
己	S12-3-9	F0000

traditional form → see 巽 at 3329

喆

2-6-6

incorrect classification
➡ see 1-6-6: 吉 at 1718

裂 3331

2-6-6

▶SPLIT
レツ さ(く) さ(ける) -ぎ(れ)▲
Ⓒ 裂 liè liě

145	Jōyō	U88C2
衣	S12-6-6	F1229

Stroke order: 1–12

COMPOUNDS

❶ⓐ [original meaning] (separate or become separated into pieces) **SPLIT, tear, crack**
ⓑ crack, fissure
a 破裂 はれつ explosion, bursting
核分裂 かくぶんれつ nuclear fission
b 裂傷 れっしょう lacerated wound
亀裂 きれつ crack, fissure
❷ (sever relations) **SPLIT up, separate, break off**
分裂する ぶんれつする be divided, split, break up, be disrupted
決裂 けつれつ breakdown, rupture
四分五裂 しぶんごれつ disruption

KUN

【さく 裂く】 *vt*
① **SPLIT, tear, rend, rip**
引き裂く ひきさく tear off, tear to pieces, split; separate, estrange, sever
八つ裂きにする やつざきにする tear (a person) limb from limb, tear to pieces
② (sever relations) **SPLIT up, separate, break off**
夫婦の仲を裂く ふうふのなかをさく bring about marital separation
【さける 裂ける】 *vi* **SPLIT, tear, crack, burst**
裂け目 さけめ rent, tear, crack, split, cleft, rip
張り裂ける はりさける burst (open), break, split
【-ぎれ -裂れ】 [also suffix] fragment (of old textile), strip
縁裂れ ふちぎれ border strip
古代裂れ こだいぎれ ancient cloth fragment

SYNONYMS

❶ **break**
破 BREAK → 1478
拉ぐ crush → 0372
崩 CRUMBLE → 2863
挫 SPRAIN → 0519
壊 BREAK DOWN → 0934
毀す break down → 2246
折 BREAK OFF → 0297
割る crack → 2284
裂 SPLIT → 3331
砕 CRUSH UP → 1458
摧 CRUSH UP → 0849
潰す CRUSH → 0919

USAGE

【さく】
裂く
① split, tear, rend, rip
② (sever relations) split up, separate, break off
割く
① spare (time), set [put] aside
② cede, alienate

HOMOPHONES

さく 割 DIVIDE → 2284
-ぎれ 切 CUT → 0030

NOTE

➡ see also USAGE note at 切 0030

紫 3332

2-6-6

▶PURPLE
シ むらさき
Ⓒ 紫 zǐ

120	Jōyō	U7D2B
糸	S12-6-6	F1459

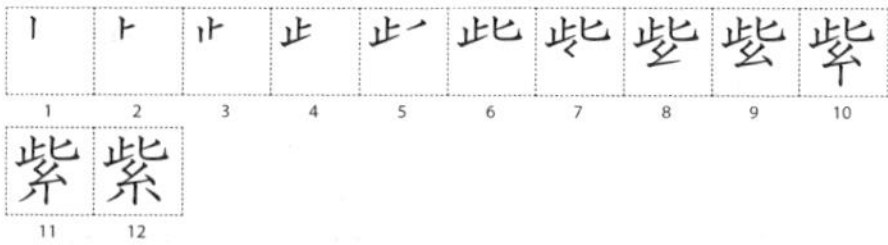

COMPOUNDS

❶ [original meaning] **PURPLE, violet**
紫紺 しこん purplish blue
紫外線 しがいせん ultraviolet rays
紫斑病 しはんびょう purpura

❷ related to a monarch or supernatural being
紫宸×殿 ししんでん Hall for State Ceremonies

KUN

【むらさき 紫】**PURPLE, amethyst; gromwell; soy**
紫色 むらさきいろ purple color, purple
赤紫 あかむらさき purplish red

SYNONYMS

❶ **blue and purple colors**
青 BLUE →3084
碧 DEEP BLUE →3515
瑠 LAPIS LAZULI (bright blue) →1342
紺 DARK BLUE →1688
藍 INDIGO →3024
紫 PURPLE →3332
蒼 PALE BLUE →2943

蛮 2-6-6
incorrect classification
➡ see 2-2-10: 亠 at 2638

叅 2-6-6
incorrect classification
➡ see 2-2-10: 厶 at 2646

象 2-6-6
incorrect classification
➡ see 2-2-10: ⺈ at 2647

萓 2-6-6
incorrect classification
➡ see 2-3-9: 艹 at 2904

葺 2-6-6
incorrect classification
➡ see 2-3-9: 艹 at 2909

景 2-6-6
incorrect classification
➡ see 2-4-8: 日 at 3118

舜 2-6-6
incorrect classification
➡ see 2-4-8: ⺤ at 3126

朞 3333 2-6-6

▶**TERM**
▶**EXPECT**
キ ゴ

74	Nonstandard	U671E
月	S12-4-8	F0000

traditional form →see 期 at 2139

棊 3334 2-6-6

▶**SHOGI**
キ

75	Nonstandard	U68CA
木	S12-4-8	F0000

alternative form →see 棋 at 1242

畫 3335 2-6-6

▶**PICTURE**
▶**DRAW UP A PLAN**
ガ カク え えが(く)

102	Nonstandard	U756B
田	S12-5-7	F0000

traditional form →see 画 at 3723

登 2-6-6
incorrect classification
➡ see 2-5-7: 癶 at 3208

節 3336 2-6-7

▶**JOINT**
▶**SEASON**
セツ セチ ふし -ぶし のっと▲ ㊔ たかし
まこと とき さだ みさお
Ⓝ 節 節◇ Ⓒ 节 jié jiē

118	Jōyō-4	U7BC0
⺮	S13-6-7	F0842

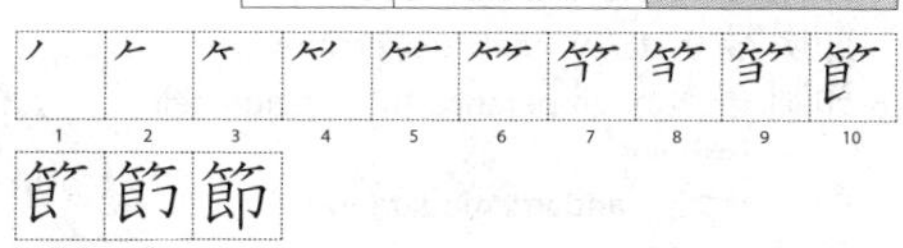

COMPOUNDS

❶ⓐ [also suffix] *anat* **JOINT, knuckle, node**
ⓑ [original meaning] *bot* **JOINT (as in a bamboo), node, knot**
ⓒ link (for transmitting motion in a machine)
a 節足動物 せっそくどうぶつ arthropod
関節 かんせつ joint
結節 けっせつ node, knotting, knot
リンパ節 りんぱせつ lymph node
神経節 しんけいせつ ganglion
b 末節 まっせつ minor details, nonessentials
c 単節 たんせつ simple link

❷ⓐ **SEASON [division] of the year, season, turning of the seasons**
ⓑ (fixed time in the year) **SEASON, time, occasion**
a 節分 せつぶん eve of the beginning of spring, close of winter

【⺮】⺶ 臼 任 次 兴 艹 罒 曲 甘

節季 せっき end of year, year end
季節 きせつ season
b 時節 じせつ season, times; occasion
当節 とうせつ these days

❸ [also suffix] **festival, annual festival**
節句 せっく seasonal festival
節会 せちえ [rare] seasonal court banquet
お節料理 おせちりょうり festive food for the New Year
佳節 かせつ happy [auspicious] occasion
紀元節 きげんせつ Empire Day

❹ⓐ [also suffix] (subdivision, as of a text) **paragraph, passage, section, part**
ⓑ (subdivision of a poem) **stanza, verse**
ⓒ [also suffix] (subdivision of a sentence) **clause**
a 章節 しょうせつ chapter and verse
第二節 だいにせつ Paragraph 2
小節 しょうせつ bar, measure
b 音節 おんせつ syllable
c 主節 しゅせつ principal clause
従属節 じゅうぞくせつ subordinate clause

❺ **tune, air, melody**
節奏 せっそう rhythm
曲節 きょくせつ tune, air

❻ⓐ **economize, save, be frugal**
ⓑ **be moderate, be temperate**
a 節約する せつやくする economize, save
節減 せつげん curtailment, economy
節水 せっすい water economy
節電 せつでん economy of electric power
節炭器 せったんき coal [fuel] economizer
b 節制 せっせい temperance, moderation, self-restraint
節度 せつど standard; moderation
節煙 せつえん moderation in smoking
節食 せっしょく moderation in eating, spare diet
お節介な おせっかいな meddlesome, nosy
調節 ちょうせつ regulation, adjustment; modulation, tuning

❼ **moral integrity, principle, fidelity, loyalty**
節操 せっそう constancy, fidelity, integrity, honor
貞節 ていせつ chastity, virtue; constancy, principle
忠節 ちゅうせつ loyalty, allegiance, fidelity

❽ **token or bamboo tally used in ancient times as credentials**
使節 しせつ envoy, ambassador
符節 ふせつ tally, check

INDEPENDENT

【せつ 節】
① **time, occasion**
この節 このせつ now, at present, in these days

②ⓐ (subdivision, as of a text) **paragraph, passage, section, part**
ⓑ (subdivision of a poem) **stanza, verse**
ⓒ (subdivision of a sentence) **clause**
a 前の節で まえのせつで in the former section [stanza]

③ moral integrity, principle, fidelity, loyalty
節を曲げない せつをまげない stick by one's principles, remain firm

【せっする 節する】 be moderate [temperate], control; save, curtail
酒を節する さけをせっする be temperate in drinking
時間を節する じかんをせっする save time

【おせち お節】 dishes for the New Year

KUN

【ふし 節】
①ⓐ **JOINT, knuckle**
ⓑ **JOINT (as of a bamboo), node, knot**
ⓒ knot (of a thread), burl
a 節節 ふしぶし joints
指の節 ゆびのふし knuckle
b 竹の節 たけのふし node [joint] of a bamboo
c 節糸 ふしいと knotted silk

② (subdivision of a poem) stanza, verse
一節歌う ひとふしうたう sing a tune

③ point
疑わしい節 うたがわしいふし dubious points

④ **tune, air, melody**
節回し ふしまわし melody, intonation
節付け ふしづけ setting to music, composition

⑤ time, occasion
折節 おりふし occasionally, at times

【-ぶし -節】 **suffix after names of (traditional) Japanese folk songs**
ソーラン節 そーらんぶし *Soran-bushi* (Hokkaido folk song)

【のっと 節】 [also 浬] knot, nautical mile
時速二十節 じそくにじゅうのっと speed of 20 knots per hour

SYNONYMS

❶ⓐ & ❶ⓑ **joint**
節 JOINT → 3336
関 connection → 4129

❷ⓐ **time periods**
時 TIME → 1155
季 SEASON (quarter) → 3161
候 SEASON (time of year) → 0133
頃 TIME → 0163
暇 FREE TIME → 1275
般 period of time → 1670
刻 POINT OF TIME → 1619

間 INTERVAL → 4122
隙 GAP → 0826
期 TERM → 2139
節 SEASON → 3336
ⓑ **occasions**
際 OCCASION → 0874
折 occasion → 0297
時 timely occasion → 1155
機 OPPORTUNITY → 1365
節 time → 3336
❹ⓐ **parts of writing**
章 CHAPTER → 2624
段 passage → 1471
節 paragraph → 3336
款 ARTICLE → 2135
条 ARTICLE → 2726
項 CLAUSE → 0692
目 ITEM → 3777
箇 item → 3348
ⓒ **sentence and sentence parts**
句 PHRASE → 3685
文 sentence → 2458
節 clause → 3336
❺ **music and songs**
楽 MUSIC → 3505
音 sound of music → 2570
節 tune → 3336
調べ melody → 1973
曲 MUSICAL COMPOSITION → 4340
歌 SONG → 2296
謡 POPULAR SONG → 2011
唄 DITTY → 0477
❻ **economizing and economy**
省 SAVE → 3100
節 economize → 3336
倹 FRUGAL → 0130
❼ **fidelity**
忠 LOYALTY → 3087
義 faith → 2948
孝 FILIAL PIETY → 3973
悌 BROTHERLY LOVE → 0507
誠 SINCERITY → 1922
実 faithfulness → 2765
信 fidelity → 0115
操 constancy → 0948
節 moral integrity → 3336
❽ **labels and slips**
札 TAG → 1011
券 TICKET → 3256
票 SLIP → 3308
符 tally → 3299
節 token → 3336

USAGE

【のっと】
節
[also 浬] knot, nautical mile
浬
[also 節] nautical mile per hour, knot

HOMOPHONES

のっと 浬 NAUTICAL MILE → 0526

COMPOUND FORMATION

【使節 しせつ】
使節 'envoy, ambassador' is a messenger (使) bearing a tally (節 ❽) of identification when going abroad.

箁 3337

▶**RECORD BOOK**
ボ

118	Nonstandard	U7C3F
⺮	S13-6-7	F0000

2-6-7
handwritten form → see 簿 at 3387

篆 3338

▶**DWARF BAMBOO**
ショウ しの ささ

118	Nonstandard	U7B7F
⺮	S13-6-7	F0000

2-6-7
traditional form → see 篠 at 3376

筱 3339

▶**DWARF BAMBOO**
ショウ しの ささ

118	Nonstandard	U7B71
⺮	S13-6-7	F0000

2-6-7
traditional form → see 篠 at 3376

義羨

2-6-7
incorrect classification
➡ see 2-3-10: ⺍ at 2948

鼠 3340

▶**RAT**
ソ ねずみ ねず
Ⓝ 鼡 Ⓒ 鼠 shǔ

208	Non-Jōyō	U9F20
鼠	S13-13-0	F2277

2-6-7

RADICAL

nezumi 'rat', used in characters related to rats, mice or similar animals
Enclosure: 鼠[×] ***nezuminyō*** (鼬[×])

COMPOUNDS

❶ [original meaning] **RAT, mouse**
鼠蹊[×]部 そけいぶ inguinal region
窮鼠 きゅうそ cornered mouse
殺鼠剤 さっそざい rat poison

❷ injurious person

鼠賊 そぞく sneak thief

鼠輩 そはい insignificant fellow, small fry

KUN

【ねずみ 鼠】

① **RAT, mouse**

鼠入らず ねずみいらず meat safe

鼠色 ねずみいろ dark gray, slate color

鼠算 ねずみざん geometrical progression

二十日鼠 はつかねずみ mouse

② **dark gray, slate color**

【ねず 鼠】 same as 鼠 ねずみ

銀鼠 ぎんねず silver gray

SPECIAL READINGS

海鼠 なまこ sea cucumber

栗鼠 りす squirrel

SYNONYMS

❶ **undomesticated mammals**

虎 TIGER → 3981
猿 MONKEY → 0824
鯨 WHALE → 2361
犀 RHINOCEROS → 3900
狼 WOLF → 0541
狐 FOX → 0472
羚 SEROW → 1695
鼠 RAT → 3340
獅 LION → 0825
豹 LEOPARD → 1847
熊 BEAR → 3530
象 ELEPHANT → 2647
麒 MALE CHINESE UNICORN → 2363
麟 FEMALE CHINESE UNICORN → 2376
猪 WILD BOAR → 0652
鹿 DEER → 3879

賃

3341

2-6-7

▶**WAGE**
▶**CHARGES**

チン

Ⓒ 赁 lìn

154	Jōyō-6	U8CC3
貝	S13-7-6	F1479

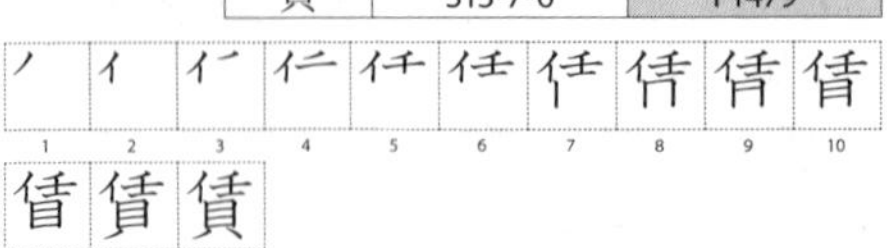

COMPOUNDS

❶ⓐ **WAGE, wages, salary, pay**

ⓑ [original meaning] **hire for WAGEs, employ**

a 賃上げ ちんあげ wage increase

労賃 ろうちん wages, pay

工賃 こうちん wage, wages, pay

手間賃 てまちん wages [charge] for labor

最賃法 さいちんほう Minimum Wages Act

b 賃金(=賃銀) ちんぎん wages, pay

❷ [also suffix] **CHARGES (for rental or transportation), fare, rent, hire, fee**

賃貸し ちんがし lease, hire

家賃 やちん (house) rent

運賃 うんちん freight [shipping] expense, passenger fare

船賃 ふなちん boat fare, passage; shipping charges

無賃の むちんの charge-free

借り賃 かりちん rent, hire

SYNONYMS

❶ⓐ **pay and earnings**

給 PAY → 1708
賃 WAGE → 3341
料 FEE → 1644
俸 SALARY → 0128
禄 RETAINER'S STIPEND → 1264
収 income → 0031

❷ **fee and price**

料 FEE → 1644
代 CHARGE → 0034
賃 CHARGES → 3341
銭 money paid → 2159
費 EXPENSE → 3221
価 PRICE → 0095
値 price → 0123

NOTE

★ do not confuse with 貸 LEND → 3213 and 貨 MONEY → 3113

資

3342

2-6-7

▶**RESOURCES**

シ ㊔ もと よし すけ

Ⓝ 資 Ⓒ 资 zī

154	Jōyō-5	U8CC7
貝	S13-7-6	F0312

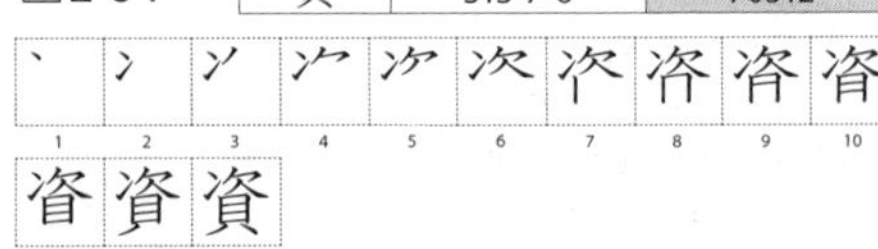

COMPOUNDS

❶ⓐ [original meaning] **monetary RESOURCES, funds, capital, money**

ⓑ **material RESOURCES, materials, means**

ⓒ supply with monetary or material **RESOURCES**, provide

a 資金 しきん funds, capital

資本 しほん funds, capital

資本主義 しほんしゅぎ capitalism
資本家 しほんか capitalist
資産 しさん property, assets, fortune
投資 とうし investment
融資 ゆうし financing, advance of funds, loan
増資 ぞうし increase of capital, capital increase
出資 しゅっし investment, financing
外資 がいし foreign capital
学資 がくし school expenses, education fund
b 資料 しりょう materials, data
資源 しげん resources
資材 しざい materials
物資 ぶっし commodities, goods, resources
師資 しし relying on someone as one's teacher

❷ natural ability, qualification
資格 しかく qualifications, competence, capacity
資質 ししつ nature, disposition

❸ abbrev. of 資本家 しほんか: capitalist
労資 ろうし capital and labor

INDEPENDENT

【し 資】monetary **RESOURCES**, funds, capital, money; material resources, materials, means; natural ability
資を投ずる しをとうずる invest in, lay out (one's money) in
生活の資 せいかつのし means of living
天与の資 てんよのし natural endowment [ability]

【しする 資する】contribute to, be conductive to, be helpful
問題の解決に資する もんだいのかいけつにしする contribute to solving a problem

SYNONYMS

❶ⓐ money
金 MONEY → 2552
銭 MONEY → 2159
貨 MONEY (legal tender), coin → 3113
幣 CURRENCY → 3582
銀 SILVER → 2156
財 finance → 1849
資 RESOURCES → 3342
-玉 coin suffix → 4289
札 bill → 1011

ⓑ matter
質 MATTER → 3483
物 substance → 1084
材 MATERIAL → 1031
料 MATERIALS → 1644
資 material resources → 3342

資 3343

▀2-6-7

▶**RESOURCES**
シ ㊔もと よし すけ

154	Nonstandard	U8CC7
貝	S13-7-6	F0000

traditional form → see 資 at 3342

誉 ▀2-6-7
incorrect classification
➡ see ▀2-4-9: ⺍ at 3135

蓉 ▀2-6-7
incorrect classification
➡ see ▀2-3-10: 艹 at 2944

愛舜 ▀2-6-7
incorrect classification
➡ see ▀2-4-9: ⺤ at 3133

豊 3344

▀2-6-7

▶**PLENTIFUL**
ホウ ブ▲ ゆた(か) ㊔とよ と ぶん
みのる て のぼる
Ⓝ 豐 Ⓒ 丰 fēng

151	Jōyō-5	U8C4A
豆	S13-7-6	F0801

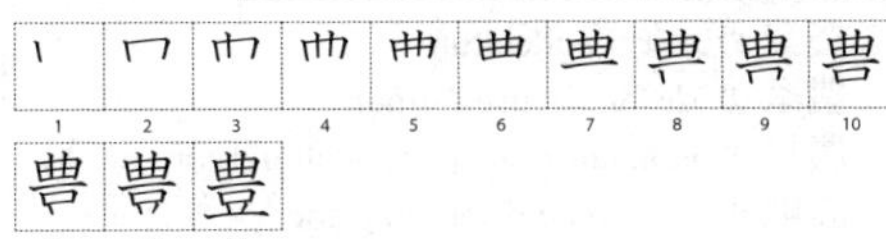

COMPOUNDS

❶ PLENTIFUL, abundant, ample, rich
豊富な ほうふな abundant, plentiful, rich
豊水 ほうすい abundance of water
豊潤な ほうじゅんな rich and prosperous, luxurious
豊麗な ほうれいな rich (design), beautiful, splendid
豊満な ほうまんな plump, corpulent

❷ abundant harvest, good crop
豊作 ほうさく good [abundant] harvest
豊年 ほうねん fruitful year
豊凶 ほうきょう rich or poor harvest
豊穣 ほうじょう abundant crop, rich harvest

❸ old name for northeast Kyushu
豊前 ぶぜん Buzen
築豊炭田 ちくほうたんでん Chikuho Coalfield

KUN

【ゆたか 豊か】
ゆたかな 豊かな **abundant, PLENTIFUL, ample, rich**
資源の豊かな国 しげんのゆたかなくに country rich in natural resources

SYNONYMS

❶ plentiful
百 numerous → 2519

竺 羊 臼 任 次 关 芇 𠔿 【曲】 甘

沃 FERTILE → 0315
万 myriad → 3653
多 MANY → 2694
豊 PLENTIFUL → 3344
沢 plentiful → 0313
穣 YIELDING ABUNDANTLY → 1597
裕 ABUNDANT → 1530
饒 ABUNDANT → 2280
富 RICH → 2892

農

3345
2-6-7

▶**FARMING**
ノウ ㊔ みのる みのり
Ⓒ 农 nóng

161	Jōyō-3	U8FB2
辰	S13-7-6	F0753

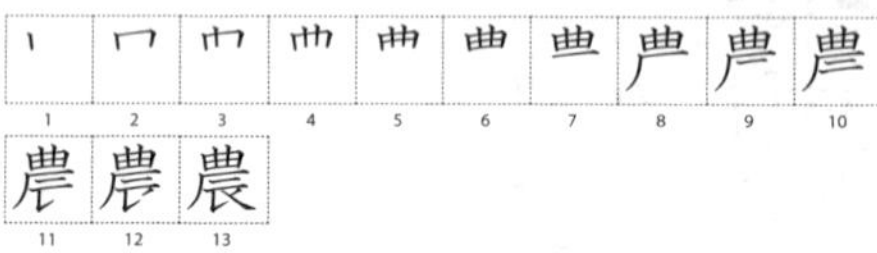

COMPOUNDS

❶ⓐ **FARMING, agriculture**
ⓑ [original meaning] **farm, till**

a 農業 のうぎょう agriculture
農家 のうか farmhouse, farmer
農村 のうそん farm village, agricultural community
農地 のうち farmland, farming land
農場 のうじょう farm
農協 のうきょう agricultural cooperative
農政 のうせい agricultural administration
農閑期 のうかんき leisure season for farmers
農具 のうぐ farming implements
離農 りのう giving up farming
酪農 らくのう dairy farming
b 農作 のうさく land cultivation
農婦 のうふ farmerette
農民 のうみん peasants, farmers

❷ⓐ abbrev. of 農学 のうがく: (science of) agriculture
ⓑ abbrev. of 農学部 のうがくぶ, 農業高校 のうぎょうこうこう or 農業大学 のうぎょうだいがく: department of agriculture, agricultural high school, agricultural college

a 農博 のうはく doctor of agriculture
b 東大農卒 とうだいのうそつ graduated from the department of agriculture of the University of Tokyo
瀬田農入学資格 せたのうにゅうがくしかく requirements for admission to Seta Agricultural High School

❸ **farmer**
豪農 ごうのう wealthy farmer
貧農 ひんのう needy peasant
自作農 じさくのう owner farmer
篤農家 とくのうか exemplary good farmer
士農工商 しのうこうしょう warriors, farmers, artisans and tradesmen (the four classes of Tokugawa Japan)

INDEPENDENT

【のう 農】 agriculture
農を業とする のうをぎょうとする be occupied with agriculture

SYNONYMS

❶ **farm and plant**
植 PLANT → 1247
栽 PLANT (saplings) → 4087
培 CULTIVATE → 0558
耕 TILL → 1659
作 raise crops → 0077
農 farm, FARMING → 3345
蒔 SOW → 2935
播 SOW → 0906

碁

3346
2-6-7

▶**GO**
ゴ
Ⓒ 棋 qí

112	Jōyō	U7881
石	S13-5-8	F1907

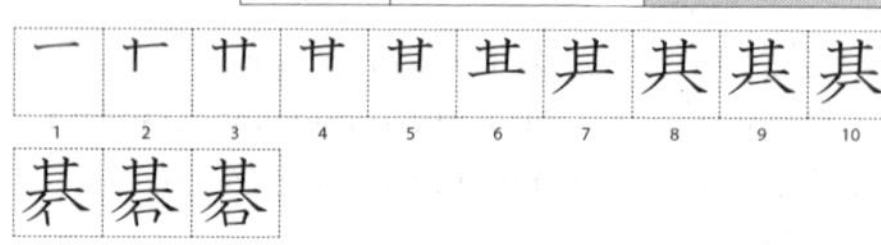

COMPOUNDS

● [original meaning] **GO, Japanese checkers**
碁石 ごいし go stone
碁盤 ごばん go board, checkerboard
碁会所 ごかいしょ commercial go playing parlor
囲碁 いご (the game of) go
西洋碁 せいようご checkers

INDEPENDENT

【ご 碁】 GO
碁を打つ ごをうつ play (a game of) go

SYNONYMS

● **board games**
局 board game → 3800
棋 SHOGI → 1242
碁 GO → 3346
雀 MAHJONG → 3117

箔

▸FOIL
ハク
Ⓒ 箔 bó

3347
2-6-8

118	Names	U7B94
⺮	S14-6-8	F3040

COMPOUNDS

❶ⓐ [original meaning] **FOIL, leaf, gilt, gilding**
ⓑ prestige, luster
a 箔押し はくおし covering [tooling, stamping] with foil, hot stamping, foil stamping
金箔 きんぱく gold foil, gold leaf
銅箔 どうはく copper foil
アルミ箔 あるみはく aluminum foil, tinfoil
❷ⓐ bamboo blind
ⓑ frame on which silkworms are made to spin cocoons
b 蚕箔 さんぱく basket [box, frame] for raising silkworms

INDEPENDENT

【はく 箔】**FOIL, leaf, gilt, gilding; prestige, luster**
箔が付く はくがつく increase in value, gain prestige

箇

▸COUNTER FOR ITEMS
カ コ▲
Ⓝ 个◇ ケ◇ Ⓒ 个 gè

3348
2-6-8

118	Jōyō	U7B87
⺮	S14-6-8	F1972

COMPOUNDS

❶ⓐ **COUNTER FOR ITEMS, places or units of time**
ⓑ [sometimes also 個 か 0132] **item, place**
a 二箇所 にかしょ two places
一箇月 いっかげつ one month
b 箇条 かじょう items, articles
箇条書き かじょうがき itemization
不通箇所 ふつうかしょ tied-up places [spots]
❷ [usu. 個 こ 0132] individual, single unit, person or thing
箇箇に ここに individually, separately

SYNONYMS

❶ⓐ **general counters**
丁 MISCELLANEOUS COUNTER → 4155
個 GENERAL COUNTER → 0132
箇 COUNTER FOR ITEMS → 3348
点 counter for articles → 2587
件 counter for cases → 0054

ⓑ **parts of writing**
章 CHAPTER → 2624
段 passage → 1471
節 paragraph → 3336
款 ARTICLE → 2135
条 ARTICLE → 2726
項 CLAUSE → 0692
目 ITEM → 3777
箇 item → 3348

USAGE

【か, こ】
箇
① ⓐ counter for items, places or units of time
ⓑ [sometimes also 個 か] item, place
② [usu. 個 こ] individual, single unit, person or thing
個
① [sometimes also 箇 こ] individual, single unit, person or thing
② general counter for things or articles
③ [usu. 箇 か] item, place

★箇 is easily confused with 個, to which it is similar in shape, sound and meaning. 箇, often simplified to ヶ, is restricted to counting items, places or units of time (mostly months), while 個 is a counter for things or articles in general. Strictly speaking, 箇 should be read か and 個 should be read こ, but in practice both have both readings and are sometimes used interchangeably.

管

▸PIPE
▸EXERCISE CONTROL
カン くだ ㊔ すが
Ⓒ 管 guǎn

3349
2-6-8

118	Jōyō-4	U7BA1
⺮	S14-6-8	F0654

COMPOUNDS

❶ [also suffix]
ⓐ (tubular conveyance) **PIPE, tube, duct**
ⓑ *anat* (tubular part or organ) **tube, PIPE, duct**
a 管状の かんじょうの tubular
鋼管 こうかん steel pipe [tubing]
配管 はいかん piping
真空管 しんくうかん vacuum tube
試験管 しけんかん test tube
b 血管 けっかん blood vessel
気管 きかん trachea, windpipe
❷ⓐ wind instrument, **PIPE**

ⓑ counter for wind instruments

a 管弦 かんげん wind and string instruments

管楽器 かんがっき wind instruments

木管 もっかん woodwind (instrument); wood pipe

b 二管の笛 にかんのふえ two flutes

❸ⓐ EXERCISE CONTROL [jurisdiction] over, control, manage, administer, take charge of

ⓑ control, jurisdiction

a 管理する かんりする administer, supervise, manage, exercise control [jurisdiction] over

管轄 かんかつ jurisdiction, control

管制 かんせい control

保管する ほかんする take custody [charge] of, keep

移管 いかん transfer of control [jurisdiction]

選管 せんかん Election Administration Commission

b 管内 かんない within (the area of) the jurisdiction

八管 はちかん 8th District

INDEPENDENT

【かん 管】**PIPE, tube, duct**

KUN

【くだ 管】**tube, PIPE; drunken talk**

管を巻く くだをまく grumble over one's wine cups

ゴムの管 ごむのくだ rubber tube

SYNONYMS

❶ tubular passages

管 PIPE → 3349

筒 TUBE → 3323

道 passage → 3888

脈 VEIN → 1189

樋 WATER PIPE → 1353

❷ⓐ musical instrument

管 wind instrument → 3349

弦 string instrument → 0343

❸ⓐ direct and supervise

制 CONTROL → 1624

理 manage → 1220

経 MANAGE → 1687

管 EXERCISE CONTROL → 3349

轄 EXERCISE JURISDICTION OVER → 2056

掌 TAKE CHARGE OF → 3215

監 OVERSEE → 3535

督 SUPERVISE → 3471

司 OFFICIATE → 3648

宰 PRESIDE → 2829

営 MANAGE → 3216

箕

3350

2-6-8

▶**WINNOW**

キ み ㊔ みる

Ⓒ 箕 jī

118	Names	U7B95
⺮	S14-6-8	F2391

COMPOUNDS

● WINNOW

箕宿 きしゅく(=みぼし) the Winnowing Basket, one of the twenty-eight stages along the Chinese zodiac

KUN

【み 箕】**WINNOW**

箕星 みぼし(=きしゅく) the Winnowing Basket, one of the twenty-eight stages along the Chinese zodiac

箕作鮫 みつくりざめ goblin shark

唐箕 とうみ fan winnowing machine

爪で拾って箕で零す つめでひろってみでこぼす Penny-wise and pound foolish

算

3351

2-6-8

▶**CALCULATE**

サン そろ▲ ㊔ かず

Ⓒ 算 suàn

118	Jōyō-2	U7B97
⺮	S14-6-8	F0481

1	2	3	4	5	6	7	8	9	10	11	12	13	14
ノ	⺊	⺮	⺮	⺮	⺮	竹	笪	笪	笪	笪	笪	算	算

COMPOUNDS

❶ⓐ CALCULATE, compute reckon, count

ⓑ [also suffix] **calculation, arithmetical operation**

a 算出する さんしゅつする compute, calculate

算数 さんすう arithmetic; calculation

算術 さんじゅつ arithmetic

計算 けいさん computation, calculation

換算表 かんさんひょう conversion table

b 採算 さいさん (commercial) profit

概算 がいさん approximation, rough estimate [calculation]

清算 せいさん settlement, liquidation; clearing (off)

暗算 あんざん mental arithmetic [calculation]

予算 よさん budget; estimate, calculation

電算機 でんさんき electronic computer

足し算 たしざん addition

読み上げ算 よみあげざん calculation by abacus, having the figures read aloud by another person

❷ calculating device, divining stick

算木 さんぎ calculating device, divining stick

珠算 しゅざん calculation on the abacus

❸ CALCULATE (one's chances), take into account, foretell; scheme, infer

算段する さんだんする contrive, manage

打算 ださん calculation, self-interest, selfishness

❹ probability, chance

公算 こうさん probability

勝算 しょうさん chance of success, prospects of victory

❺ age (esp. of the emperor)

聖算 せいさん emperor's age

INDEPENDENT

【さん 算】calculating device, divining stick; calculation, counting

算を置く さんをおく divine; calculate

KUN

【そろ 算】[in compounds] Japanese abacus, *soroban*

算盤 そろばん Japanese abacus, *soroban*

電算 でんそろ electronic calculator combined with a *soroban*

SYNONYMS

❶ **calculate and count**

算 CALCULATE → 3351

計 COMPUTE → 1828

数 count → 2245

箋

3352

2-6-8

▶**PIECE OF PAPER**

セン

Ⓝ 箋 Ⓒ 笺 jiān

118	Jōyō	U7B8B
⺮	S14-6-8	F2630

(stroke order 1–14)

COMPOUNDS

❶ **PIECE OF PAPER, label**

便箋 びんせん letter paper, stationery, writing paper

付箋 ふせん tag, label, sticky note

用箋 ようせん stationery, writing paper

処方箋 しょほうせん prescription

❷ annotation, note, comment

箋注 せんちゅう annotation, note, commentary

SYNONYMS

❶ **paper**

紙 PAPER → 1654

葉 LEAF → 2912

丁 sheet → 4155

箋 PIECE OF PAPER → 3352

頁 PAGE → 2589

面 page (of a newspaper) → 2590

箏

3353

2-6-8

▶**KOTO**

ソウ こと

Ⓒ 筝 zhēng

118	Non-Jōyō	U7B8F
⺮	S14-6-8	F0000

COMPOUNDS

● [original meaning] **KOTO, (Japanese) zither**

箏曲 そうきょく koto music

INDEPENDENT

【そう 箏】**(Japanese) zither**

KUN

【こと 箏】[usu. 琴] **KOTO, (Japanese) zither**

SYNONYMS

● **musical instruments**

琴 KOTO → 3455

箏 KOTO → 3353

鼓 DRUM → 2241

笛 FLUTE → 3303

琵 LUTE → 3453

琶 LUTE → 3454

笙 *SHO* → 3302

HOMOPHONES

こと 琴 KOTO → 3455

NOTE

➡ see USAGE note at 琴 3455

箸

3354

2-6-8

▶**CHOPSTICKS**

チョ はし ㊔ つく あきら あき

118	Nonstandard	U7BB8
⺮	S14-6-8	F0000

traditional form → see 箸 at 3359

翠

3355

2-6-8

▶**JADE GREEN**

スイ みどり ㊔ みす あきら

124	Nonstandard	U7FE0
羽	S14-6-8	F0000

traditional form → see 翠 at 3356

翠

3356

2-6-8

▶**JADE GREEN**

スイ みどり ㊔ みす あきら

Ⓝ 翠 翠 翠 Ⓒ 翠 cuì

124	Names	U7FE0
羽	S14-6-8	F2452

COMPOUNDS

❶ **JADE GREEN, emerald green, verdure, yellowish green**

翠色 すいしょく verdure, emerald green

翠玉 すいぎょく emerald, jade
翡×翠色 ひすいいろ jade green
❷ [original meaning] kingfisher
翡×翠 ひすい green jadeite, jade; kingfisher

KUN

【みどり 翠】[usu. 緑]
① **green; verdure**
② *elegant* **young leaves**

SYNONYMS

❶ **green colors**
緑 GREEN → 1741
青 GREEN → 3084
翠 JADE GREEN → 3356

HOMOPHONES

みどり 緑 GREEN → 1741

NOTE

➡ see USAGE note at 緑 1741

鼻

3357
2-6-8

▶**NOSE**
ビ はな
Ⓝ 鼻 Ⓒ 鼻 bí

209	Jōyō-3	U9F3B
鼻	S14-14-0	F1030

radical variant → see 鼻 at 3358

COMPOUNDS

❶ **NOSE**
鼻音 びおん nasal sound
鼻孔 びこう nostrils
鼻炎 びえん nasal inflammation
鼻下長 びかちょう amorous man, spoony
耳鼻 じび nose and ears
❷ **beginning**
鼻祖 びそ founder, originator

KUN

【はな 鼻】
①ⓐ **NOSE, snout, trunk**
ⓑ [also 端] end, protruded point
a 鼻血 はなぢ nosebleed
鼻水 はなみず nasal discharge
鼻柱 はなばしら bridge of the nose; self-assertion
鼻息 はないき snorting; temper; vigor
鼻紙 はながみ tissue paper (for wiping the nose)
鼻摘まみ はなつまみ disgusting fellow
鼻が高い はながたかい be proud (have one's nose up)
鼻持ちならない はなもちならない be intolerable; stink
目鼻が付く めはながつく take a concrete shape, materialize
② [also 端] beginning
出鼻 ではな outset, start; point of going out

SYNONYMS

❶ **face orifices**
口 MOUTH → 4189
鼻 NOSE → 3357
耳 EAR → 4329
目 EYE → 3777

USAGE

【はな】
鼻
①ⓐ nose, snout, trunk
ⓑ [also 端] end, protruded point
② [also 端] beginning
端
[also 鼻]
① outset, beginning
② end, protruded point

HOMOPHONES

はな 端 END → 1564

鼻

3358
2-6-8

▶**NOSE**
ビ はな

209	Nonstandard	U9F3B
鼻	S14-14-0	F0000

traditional form → see 鼻 at 3357

RADICAL

hana 'nose', used in characters related to the nose
Left variant: 鼻× ***hanahen*** (鼾×)

蕢
2-6-8
incorrect classification/ stroke-count
➡ see 2-3-10: ⺾ at 2941

鞏
2-6-8
incorrect stroke-count
➡ see 2-6-9: 巩 at 3369

箸

3359
2-6-9

▶**CHOPSTICKS**
チョ▲ はし ㊔ つく あきら あき
Ⓝ 箸 Ⓒ 箸 zhù

118	Jōyō	U7BB8
⺮	S15-6-9	F1976

COMPOUNDS

● [original meaning] **CHOPSTICKS**

匕箸 ひちょ spoon and chopsticks

KUN

【はし 箸】**CHOPSTICKS**

箸置き はしおき chopstick rest

箸使い はしづかい chopstick usage

箸休め はしやすめ palate-cleansing side dish

箸にも棒にも掛からない はしにもぼうにもかからない incorrigible, hopeless

割り箸 わりばし half-split (disposable) chopsticks

火箸 ひばし tongs

握り箸 にぎりばし gripping both chopsticks in one's fist

SYNONYMS

● **long slender objects**

棒 ROD → 1237

箸 CHOPSTICKS → 3359

桟 crosspiece → 1169

軸 AXLE → 1908

錘 SPINDLE → 2191

竿 POLE → 3259

杖 STAFF → 1026

錫 Buddhist priest's staff → 2189

軛 YOKE → 1873

HOMOPHONES

はし

橋 BRIDGE → 1367

端 END → 1564

梯 LADDER → 1210

NOTE

➡ see USAGE note at 橋 1367

範 3360

▶**MODEL**

ハン ㊔ のり

Ⓒ 范 fàn

⬒2-6-9

118	Jōyō	U7BC4
⺮	S15-6-9	F1195

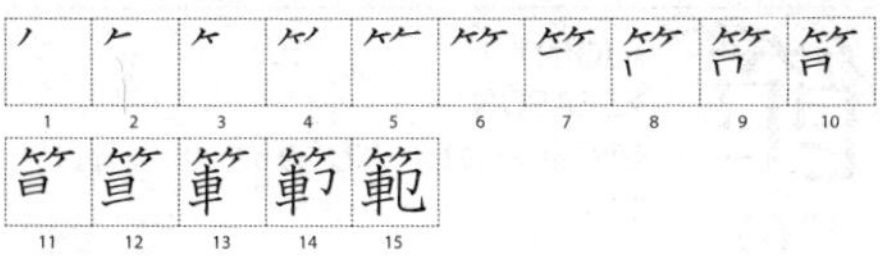

COMPOUNDS

❶ (something to be followed) **MODEL, example, pattern, standard**

模範 もはん model, pattern, example

軌範 きはん standard, norm

師範 しはん teacher, master, coach

典範 てんぱん model, standard; law, code

❷ⓐ **range, limits, scope, sphere**

ⓑ [formerly 汎 0254] extensive, wide-ranging

a 範囲 はんい range, scope

範疇× はんちゅう category

b 広範な こうはんな extensive, wide-ranging, comprehensive

INDEPENDENT

【はん 範】**MODEL**, example, pattern

範を垂れる はんをたれる give an example

SYNONYMS

❶ **model**

範 MODEL → 3360

典 CANON → 3253

模 PATTERN → 1326

程 ESTABLISHED FORM → 1524

式 form → 3785

準 STANDARD → 3541

格 NORM → 1161

❷ⓐ **range**

程 EXTENT → 1524

範 range → 3360

域 area → 0559

圏 SPHERE → 3904

野 FIELD → 1877

界 field (*phys*) → 3172

場 field (*phys*, *psychol*) → 0678

篇 3361

▶**PIECE OF WRITING**

ヘン

Ⓝ 篇 Ⓒ 篇 piān

⬒2-6-9

118	Names	U7BC7
⺮	S15-6-9	F1790

COMPOUNDS

[now usu. 編 1755]

❶ⓐ [also suffix] **PIECE OF WRITING, literary work; film**

ⓑ **volume, book**

ⓒ **chapter, section, part, canto**

a 巨篇 きょへん great literary work

短篇 たんぺん short piece

予告篇 よこくへん preview, trailer

詩篇 しへん book of poetry; Psalms

b 続篇 ぞくへん sequel, supplementary volume

bc 前篇 ぜんぺん first volume; first part

❷ **counter for PIECEs OF WRITING such as volumes, chapters, parts or poems**

一篇の詩 いっぺんのし one poem

第二篇 だいにへん chapter 2, canto 2

千篇一律 せんぺんいちりつ humdrum, monotony, lack of variety ("thousand poems, one rhythm")

INDEPENDENT

【へん 篇】 **chapter, section, part; compilation, editing**

SYNONYMS

❶ⓐ books

本 BOOK → 4314
典 STANDARD WORK → 3253
経 religious classic → 1687
書 BOOK → 3292
冊 bound book → 4295
籍 books → 3394
著 literary work → 2869
巻 VOLUME → 3273
編 piece of writing → 1755
篇 PIECE OF WRITING → 3361
鑑 REFERENCE VOLUME → 2226

箱

3362

2-6-9

▶BOX

ソウ▲ はこ

Ⓒ 箱 xiāng

118	Jōyō-3	U7BB1
⺮	S15-6-9	F1105

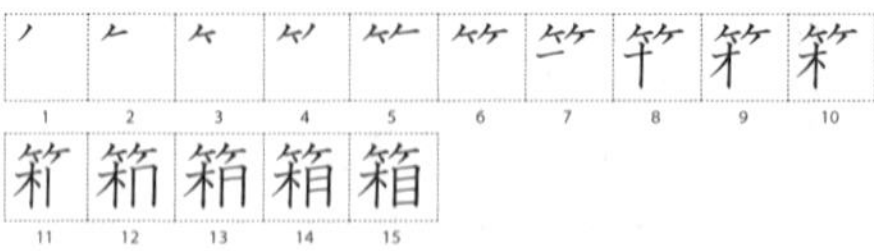

KUN

【はこ 箱】

①ⓐ [sometimes also 函] [also suffix] **BOX, case, chest, bin**

ⓑ counter for **BOX**es

a 箱入りの はこいりの cased, boxed
箱入り娘 はこいりむすめ innocent [naive] girl of a good family
小箱 こばこ small box; casket
郵便箱 ゆうびんばこ mailbox
巣箱 すばこ bird box, bird house
本箱 ほんばこ bookcase
救急箱 きゅうきゅうばこ first-aid kit

b 二箱 ふたはこ two boxes

② *slang* railway car
箱師 はこし train pickpocket

③ *slang* shamisen

SYNONYMS

【はこ】

① **containers**

箱 BOX → 3362
壺 JAR → 2890
槽 TANK → 1352
樽 BARREL → 1368
棺 COFFIN → 1240
桶 BUCKET → 1211
笈 BOX CARRIED ON THE BACK → 3274
鞘 SHEATH → 2259
箪 BAMBOO BOX → 3381
函 BOX → 3724
籠 BASKET → 3398
袋 BAG → 3201
鞄 BAG (for carrying) → 2248
器 VESSEL → 3367
瓶 BOTTLE → 1702
缶 CAN → 2526
缶 EARTHENWARE JAR → 2525

USAGE

【はこ】

箱
①ⓐ [sometimes also 函] [also suffix] **box, case, chest, bin**
ⓑ counter for boxes
② *slang* railway car
③ *slang* shamisen

函
[now usu. 箱] box, case, mailbox

HOMOPHONES

はこ 函 BOX → 3724

篇

3363

2-6-9

▶PIECE OF WRITING

ヘン

118	Nonstandard	U7BC7
⺮	S15-6-9	F0000

traditional form → see 篇 at 3361

節

3364

2-6-9

▶JOINT
▶SEASON

セツ セチ ふし -ぶし のっと ㊔ たかし まこと とき さだ みさお

118	Names	UFA56
⺮	S15-6-9	F0000

traditional form → see 節 at 3336

節

3365

2-6-9

▶JOINT
▶SEASON

セツ セチ ふし -ぶし のっと ㊔ たかし まこと とき さだ みさお

118	Nonstandard	U7BC0
⺮	S15-6-9	F0000

alternative form → see 節 at 3336

簞

3366

▀2-6-9

▶**BAMBOO BOX**

タン

118	Nonstandard	U7BAA
⺮	S15-6-9	F0000

traditional form → see 箪 at 3381

養

▀2-6-9

incorrect classification

➡ see ▀2-3-12: ⺷ at 2998

器

3367

▀2-6-9

▶**VESSEL**
▶**INSTRUMENT**

キ うつわ

Ⓝ 器 噐 Ⓒ 器 qì

30	Jōyō-4	U5668
口	S15-3-12	F0467

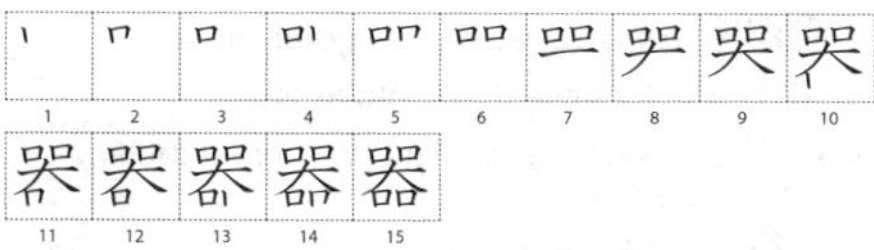

COMPOUNDS

❶ [original meaning] **VESSEL, receptacle, container**

容器 ようき receptacle, container, vessel
陶器 とうき pottery, porcelain, chinaware
便器 べんき toilet bowl, urinal
食器 しょっき tableware, dinner set
花器 かき flower vase [bowl]

❷ [also suffix] **INSTRUMENT, device, appliance, implement, utensil**

器具 きぐ utensil, implement, appliance
器械 きかい instrument, apparatus, appliance
楽器 がっき musical instrument
機器 きき machinery and tools, apparatus
計器 けいき meter, gauge; instrument
兵器 へいき arms, weapon, ordnance
注射器 ちゅうしゃき syringe
消火器 しょうかき fire extinguisher
電熱器 でんねつき electric heater, electric cooker

❸ [also suffix] **organ (of the body)**

器官 きかん (body) organ
臓器 ぞうき internal organs, viscera
呼吸器 こきゅうき respiratory organs
消化器 しょうかき digestive organs

❹ **capacity, ability, talent**

器量 きりょう ability, capacity; personal appearance; dignity
器用な きような skillful, clever, ingenious
大器 たいき person of great talent

INDEPENDENT

【き 器】capacity, ability; person of capability
宰相の器 さいしょうのき person qualified for prime minister

KUN

【うつわ 器】**VESSEL, receptacle; capacity, ability**
奇麗な器 きれいなうつわ beautiful bowl
その器ではない そのうつわではない not be fit for, not be equal to

SYNONYMS

❶ **containers**

箱 BOX → 3362
壺 JAR → 2890
槽 TANK → 1352
樽 BARREL → 1368
棺 COFFIN → 1240
桶 BUCKET → 1211
笈 BOX CARRIED ON THE BACK → 3274
鞘 SHEATH → 2259
箪 BAMBOO BOX → 3381
函 BOX → 3724
籠 BASKET → 3398
袋 BAG → 3201
鞄 BAG (for carrying) → 2248
器 VESSEL → 3367
瓶 BOTTLE → 1702
缶 CAN → 2526
缶 EARTHENWARE JAR → 2525

❷ **machines and tools**

機 MACHINE → 1365
械 MECHANICAL CONTRIVANCE → 1203
具 IMPLEMENT → 3159
器 INSTRUMENT → 3367
儀 measuring instrument → 0191
鏡 OPTICAL INSTRUMENT → 2219
董 OLD TOOL → 2911

❸ **organ**

臓 INTERNAL ORGAN → 1417
器 organ → 3367
官 organ → 2766

噐

3368

▀2-6-9

▶**VESSEL**
▶**INSTRUMENT**

キ うつわ

30	Nonstandard	U5650
口	S15-3-12	F0000

traditional form → see 器 at 3367

鞏

3369

▀2-6-9

▶**TOUGH**

キョウ

Ⓒ 巩 gǒng

177	Non-Jōyō	U978F
革	S15-9-6	F0000

COMPOUNDS

● [now also 強 0574] **TOUGH, firm, solid, strong, hard**
鞏固な きょうこな firm, stable, solid, strong
鞏膜 きょうまく sclera

SYNONYMS

● **hard**
硬 HARD → 1518
堅 FIRM → 3502
鞏 TOUGH → 3369
固 SOLID → 3830
剛 TOUGH → 2107
強 STRONG → 0574
勁 STRONG → 1833

築

▶CONSTRUCT
チク きず(く) ㊔ つき
Ⓝ 築 Ⓒ 筑 zhù zhú

3370
2-6-10

118	Jōyō-5	U7BC9
⺮	S16-6-10	F0902

COMPOUNDS

● [original meaning] **CONSTRUCT, erect, build**
築港 ちっこう harbor construction
築城 ちくじょう castle construction
建築 けんちく construction, building, architecture
建築家 けんちくか architect
構築 こうちく construction, building
新築 しんちく new building [construction]
増築 ぞうちく enlargement of a building

KUN

【きずく 築く】 **build, CONSTRUCT, erect, throw up**
築き上げる きずきあげる build up, establish (one's reputation)
堤防を築く ていぼうをきずく construct an embankment

SPECIAL READINGS

築山 つきやま artificial hill

SYNONYMS

● **build**
建 BUILD (a building) → 3834
造 build (various structures) → 3856
築 CONSTRUCT → 3370
設 SET UP → 1863

篤

▶DEVOTED
トク あつ(い)▲ ㊔ あつ あつし
Ⓒ 笃 dǔ

3371
2-6-10

118	Jōyō	U7BE4
⺮	S16-6-10	F2086

COMPOUNDS

❶ⓐ **DEVOTED, fervent, sincere**
ⓑ **cordial, warmhearted, affectionate**
a 篤信 とくしん devoutness
篤学 とくがく love of learning, devotion to one's studies
篤農家 とくのうか exemplary good farmer
篤実 とくじつ sincerity, faithfulness
b 篤志家 とくしか benevolent person; volunteer, supporter
篤行 とっこう good deed
懇篤な こんとくな cordial, kind

❷ (of an illness) **critical, serious, dangerous**
危篤である きとくである be dangerously ill, be in critical condition

KUN

【あつい 篤い】
① [now usu. 厚い] cordial, kind, hearty, warm, deep
篤い持てなし あついもてなし cordial reception
篤い友情 あついゆうじょう warm friendship
篤い信仰 あついしんこう deep faith
② (of an illness) critical, serious, dangerous
病が篤い やまいがあつい be seriously ill

SYNONYMS

❶ⓐ **eager**
懇 EARNEST → 3606
切 eager → 0030
摯 SERIOUS → 3556
篤 DEVOTED → 3371
熱 HOT → 3555
ⓑ **kind**
厚 KIND → 3726
篤 cordial → 3371
懇 cordial → 3606
慈 AFFECTIONATE → 2949
温 warmhearted → 0740
渥 GRACIOUS → 0731
優 kindly → 0200

HOMOPHONES

あつい 厚 THICK →3726

NOTE

➡ see USAGE note at 厚 3726

築

3372

2-6-10

▶CONSTRUCT

チク きず(く) ㊔ つき

118	Nonstandard	U7BC9
⺮	S16-6-10	F0000

traditional form →see 築 at 3370

篭

3373

2-6-10

▶BASKET

ロウ かご こ(もる) こ(める)

118	Nonstandard	U7BED
⺮	S16-6-10	F0000

alternative form →see 籠 at 3398

簑

3374

2-6-10

▶STRAW RAINCOAT

サ みの

118	Nonstandard	U7C11
⺮	S16-6-10	F0000

traditional form →see 蓑 at 2941

器

3375

2-6-10

▶VESSEL

▶INSTRUMENT

キ うつわ

30	Names	UFA38
口	S16-3-13	F0000

traditional form →see 器 at 3367

篠

3376

2-6-11

▶DWARF BAMBOO

ショウ しの ささ

Ⓝ 筿 筱 Ⓒ 筱 xiǎo

118	Names	U7BE0
⺮	S17-6-11	F1651

KUN

【しの 篠】

① **thin-culmed DWARF BAMBOO growing in clusters**

篠竹 しのだけ thin-culmed dwarf bamboo growing in clusters

篠笛 しのぶえ Japanese transverse bamboo flute

篠突く雨 しのつくあめ driving rain

② **sliver, strand of textile fibers**

【ささ 篠】 [usu. 笹] **bamboo grass**

SYNONYMS

【しの】

① **bamboo**

竹 BAMBOO →0267

笹 BAMBOO GRASS →3301

篠 DWARF BAMBOO →3376

HOMOPHONES

ささ 笹 BAMBOO GRASS →3301

NOTE

➡ see USAGE note at 笹 3301

簇

3377

2-6-11

▶FORM A CLUSTER

ゾク ソウ

Ⓒ 簇 cù

118	Non-Jōyō	U7C07
⺮	S17-6-11	F0000

COMPOUNDS

● [now also 族 ぞく 1195] [original meaning] **FORM A CLUSTER**

簇生する ぞくせい(=そうせい)する (of plants) grow in clusters

簇出する ぞくしゅつ(=そうしゅつ)する spring up in clusters

SYNONYMS

● **crowd**

群 GROUP →1942

衆 MULTITUDE →3325

叢 CROWD TOGETHER →3243

簇 FORM A CLUSTER →3377

簔

3378

2-6-11

▶STRAW RAINCOAT

サ みの

118	Nonstandard	U7C14
⺮	S17-6-11	F0000

traditional form →see 蓑 at 2941

翼

3379

2-6-11

▶WING

ヨク つばさ

Ⓝ 翼 Ⓒ 翼 yì

124	Jōyō	U7FFC
羽	S17-6-11	F1472

COMPOUNDS

❶ⓐ [original meaning] **WING of a bird, wings**

ⓑ [also suffix] **WING of an aircraft, airfoil**

a 翼状 よくじょう wing shape

羽翼 うよく wings; assistance

b 主翼 しゅよく wing (of an aircraft)

水平翼 すいへいよく horizontal plane

補助翼 ほじょよく aileron

❷ⓐ something resembling a **WING** in structure, function or appearance

ⓑ **(political) WING, faction; (army) wing, flank**

a 翼棟 よくとう wing (of a building)
b 左翼 さよく left wing [flank]; left wing [faction]; left field
両翼 りょうよく both flanks; two wings

❸ assist, help (as if taking someone under one's wings)
翼賛する よくさんする support, countenance, assist
輔翼する ほよくする aid, assist
❹ respectful, reverent
小心翼翼と しょうしんよくよくと timidly, nervously

INDEPENDENT

【よく 翼】**WING**; aircraft wing, airfoil

KUN

【つばさ 翼】**WING; airfoil**
翼を広げる つばさをひろげる spread the wings

SYNONYMS

❶ **wings**
翼 WING (of birds or aircraft) → 3379
羽 WING (of birds or insects) → 0265
葉 plane → 2912
❷ⓑ **parties and sects**
党 PARTY → 3190
閥 CLIQUE → 4126
流 school → 0529
派 SECT → 0456
翼 WING → 3379
系 faction → 2443
門 (religious) sect → 1100
宗 RELIGIOUS SECT (esp. Buddhist) → 2769

簡 3380

▶**SIMPLE**
カン
Ⓝ 簡 Ⓒ 简 jiǎn

2-6-12

118	Jōyō-6	U7C21
⺮	S18-6-12	F0995

COMPOUNDS

❶ⓐ **SIMPLE, easy, light**
ⓑ **simplified, brief, concise**
a 簡単な かんたんな simple, easy, light
簡素な かんそな plain, simple
簡易な かんいな simple, simplified; easy
b 簡明な かんめいな terse, concise
簡略 かんりゃく simplicity, brevity, conciseness; informality
簡潔な かんけつな brief, concise
簡裁 かんさい summary court
❷ [formerly also 翰 2198] letter, note
書簡 しょかん letter, correspondence
手簡 しゅかん letter
❸ [original meaning] bamboo strips used for writing in ancient China
簡札 かんさつ wooden tag
竹簡 ちくかん bamboo writing strip
❹ [archaic] select
簡抜 かんばつ selection

INDEPENDENT

【かん 簡】simplicity, brevity
簡にして要を得た かんにしてようをえた brief, succinct

SYNONYMS

❶ⓐ **easy**
易 EASY (without difficulty) → 3064
安 easy (without effort) → 2695
簡 SIMPLE → 3380
軽 LIGHT → 1909
ⓑ **short and shortened**
短 SHORT → 1515
簡 simplified → 3380
略 ABRIDGED → 1501
❸ **writing strips**
簡 bamboo writing strips → 3380
竹 bamboo writing tablets → 0267

簞 3381

▶**BAMBOO BOX**
タン
Ⓝ 簞 Ⓒ 箪 dān

2-6-12

118	Names	U7C1E
⺮	S18-6-12	F2287

COMPOUNDS

● [original meaning] **BAMBOO BOX [basket]**
簞笥× たんす chest of drawers, cabinet, dresser
瓢簞 ひょうたん bottle gourd, calabash

SYNONYMS

● **containers**
箱 BOX → 3362
壺 JAR → 2890
槽 TANK → 1352
樽 BARREL → 1368
棺 COFFIN → 1240
桶 BUCKET → 1211
笈 BOX CARRIED ON THE BACK → 3274
鞘 SHEATH → 2259
簞 BAMBOO BOX → 3381
函 BOX → 3724
籠 BASKET → 3398
袋 BAG → 3201

簡

3382

2-6-12

▶**SIMPLE**

カン

118	Nonstandard	U7C21
⺮	S18-6-12	F0000

traditional form → see 簡 at 3380

翼

3383

2-6-12

▶**WING**

ヨク つばさ

124	Nonstandard	U7FFC
羽	S18-6-12	F0000

traditional form → see 翼 at 3379

蟲

3384

2-6-12

▶**INSECT**

チュウ むし

142	Nonstandard	U87F2
虫	S18-6-12	F0000

traditional form → see 虫 at 4343

覆

3385

2-6-12

▶**COVER**
▶**OVERTURN**

フク おお(う) くつがえ(す) くつがえ(る)

146	Nonstandard	U8986
西	S18-6-12	F0000

traditional form → see 覆 at 3386

覆

3386

2-6-12

▶**COVER**
▶**OVERTURN**

フク おお(う) くつがえ(す) くつがえ(る)

Ⓝ 覆 Ⓒ 覆 fù

146	Jōyō	U8986
西	S18-6-12	F1397

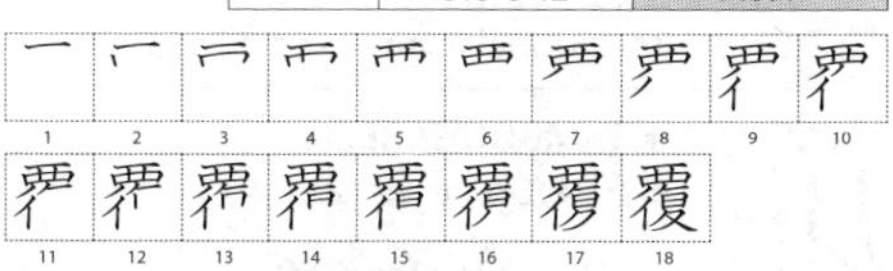

COMPOUNDS

❶ [original meaning] **COVER**
覆面 ふくめん mask, veil
覆土 ふくど covering up seeds with soil
被覆 ひふく covering, coating

❷ **OVERTURN, upset, turn over**
覆没する ふくぼつする capsize and sink
覆水盆に返らず ふくすいぼんにかえらず It is no use crying over spilt milk
転覆する てんぷくする overturn, turn over, upset; overthrow

❸ [usu. 復 0701] reproduce, repeat
覆刻する ふっこくする republish, reissue
反覆する はんぷくする repeat, do over again

KUN

【おおう 覆う】 [sometimes also 被う or 蓋う, formerly also 蔽う or 掩う]
ⓐ **COVER, veil**
ⓑ **hide, conceal, screen**
ⓒ enfold, envelop
a 覆い おおい cover, mantle
顔を覆う かおをおおう cover one's face
b 事実を覆う じじつをおおう disguise a fact
日覆い ひおおい sunscreen
c 霧に覆われる きりにおおわれる be enveloped in mist

【くつがえす 覆す】 *vt* **OVERTURN, upset, turn over, capsize; overthrow, undermine; overrule, reverse**
現体制を覆す げんたいせいをくつがえす overthrow the present regime
判決を覆す はんけつをくつがえす overrule a decision

【くつがえる 覆る】 *vi* **OVERTURN, upset, topple over, capsize; fall, be overthrown; be reversed, be overruled**
覆った説 くつがえったせつ overthrown theory
大きな船も覆る程の波 おおきなふねもくつがえるほどのなみ wave so high as to capsize a big ship

SYNONYMS

❶ **cover and wrap**
覆 COVER → 3386
掩 COVER → 0592
被 cover → 1495
包 WRAP → 3684
蓋う COVER → 2933
蔽 COVER → 2991
葺く THATCH → 2909

❷ **overturn**
覆 OVERTURN → 3386
翻 TURN OVER → 2391
反 turn over → 3663
顛 TURN [roll] OVER → 2317
転 turn [roll] over → 1872
倒 TOPPLE → 0139
轢 RUN OVER → 2095

USAGE

【おおう】
覆う
[sometimes also 被う or 蓋う, formerly also 蔽う or 掩う]
ⓐ cover, veil

ⓑ hide, conceal, screen
ⓒ enfold, envelop

被う
[usu. 覆う] cover, veil

蓋う
[usu. 覆う] same as 覆う

蔽う
[now usu. 覆う] screen, shield, hide

掩う
[now usu. 覆う]
ⓐ cover, veil
ⓑ hide, conceal, screen

HOMOPHONES

おおう
被 BE SUBJECTED TO → 1495
蓋 COVER → 2933
蔽 COVER → 2991
掩 COVER → 0592

覇
2-6-12
incorrect stroke-count
➡ see 2-6-13: 襾 at 3392

嚞
2-6-12
incorrect classification
➡ see 2-3-15: 士 at 3021

簿
3387
2-6-13

▶RECORD BOOK
ボ
Ⓝ 簿 箔◆ Ⓒ 簿 bù

118	Jōyō	U7C3F
⺮	S19-6-13	F1757

COMPOUNDS

❶ [also suffix] **RECORD BOOK, book(s), account book, register**
簿記 ぼき bookkeeping
帳簿 ちょうぼ account book, ledger, register
名簿 めいぼ register [list] of names
計算簿 けいさんぼ account book
登記簿 とうきぼ register
家計簿 かけいぼ housekeeping account book
通知簿 つうちぼ report card [book]

❷ Imperial procession, cortege
鹵簿 ろぼ imperial cortege [procession]

SYNONYMS

❶ **notebook**
帳 NOTEBOOK → 0572
帖 NOTEBOOK → 0342
簿 RECORD BOOK → 3387
籍 REGISTER → 3394

NOTE

★ do not confuse with 薄 THIN → 3004

簾
3388
2-6-13

▶BAMBOO SCREEN
レン すだれ す ㊔ せん きよし
Ⓝ 簾 Ⓒ 帘 lián

118	Names	U7C3E
⺮	S19-6-13	F2288

COMPOUNDS

● **BAMBOO SCREEN [blind], reed screen**
暖簾 のれん shop curtain, *noren;* credit, reputation
珠暖簾 たまのれん bead curtain
鋤×簾 じょれん long-handled winnow used to sift earth [sand]

KUN

【すだれ 簾】 **BAMBOO SCREEN [blind], reed screen**
板簾 いたすだれ Venetian blind

【す 簾】 **BAMBOO SCREEN [blind], reed screen**
御簾 みす bamboo blind
巻き簾(=巻き簀×) まきす bamboo mat used in preparing sushi rolls and other food
葦簾(=葦簀×) よしず reed screen

SYNONYMS

● **curtain**
幕 CURTAIN → 2937
簾 BAMBOO SCREEN → 3388
帳 drapery → 0572

NOTE

➡ see COMPOUND FORMATION for 暖簾 のれん → 暖 1274

簿
3389
2-6-13

▶RECORD BOOK
ボ

118	Nonstandard	U7C3F
⺮	S19-6-13	F0000

traditional form → see 簿 at 3387

簾
3390
2-6-13

▶BAMBOO SCREEN
レン すだれ す ㊔ せん きよし

118	Nonstandard	U7C3E
⺮	S19-6-13	F0000

traditional form → see 簾 at 3388

覇
3391
2-6-13

▶SUPREMACY
ハ

146	Nonstandard	U8987
襾	S19-6-13	F0000

alternative form → see 覇 at 3392

霸

▶SUPREMACY

ハ

Ⓝ 霸 覇◇ Ⓒ 霸 bà

3392

2-6-13

146	Jōyō	U8987
襾	S19-6-13	F1955

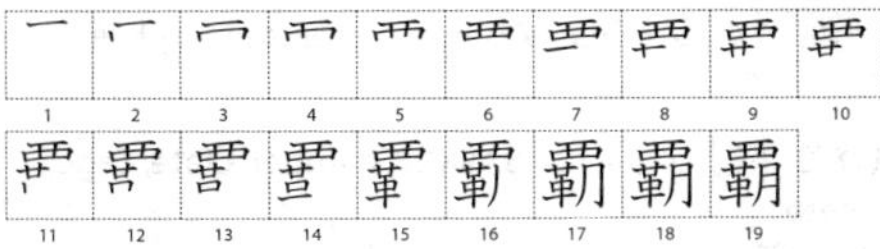

COMPOUNDS

❶ⓐ **SUPREMACY, mastery, hegemony, domination, leadership**

ⓑ **SUPREMACY** in a contest, victory, championship

a 覇権 はけん supremacy, mastery, hegemony, supreme power

覇道 はどう military government [rule]

制覇する せいはする conquer, dominate, gain supremacy; win the championship

b 覇気 はき ambitious spirit, aspiration

争覇 そうは contending for victory, struggling for supremacy

連覇 れんぱ successive victories

❷ [original meaning] supreme ruler, chief of the feudal lords

覇者 はしゃ supreme ruler; champion

INDEPENDENT

【は 覇】**SUPREMACY**, leadership, domination, hegemony; victory, championship

覇を唱える はをとなえる assume the leadership [hegemony], reign supreme, dominate

SYNONYMS

❶ⓐ **power and authority**

力 POWER → 4178

威 MIGHT → 4394

勢 POWER (to influence) → 3542

権 POWER (to control) → 1348

覇 SUPREMACY → 3392

纂

▶COMPILE

サン

Ⓒ 纂 zuǎn

3393

2-6-14

120	Names	U7E82
糸	S20-6-14	F2709

COMPOUNDS

● **COMPILE, edit**

編纂 へんさん compilation, editing

雑纂 ざっさん miscellaneous collection

類纂 るいさん collection of similar objects, classification by similarity

SYNONYMS

● **compile**

編 COMPILE → 1755

纂 COMPILE → 3393

撰 COMPILE → 0911

集 edit → 3445

輯 EDIT → 2025

著 AUTHOR → 2869

籍

▶REGISTER

セキ

Ⓝ 籍 Ⓒ 籍 jí

3394

2-6-14

118	Jōyō	U7C4D
竹	S20-6-14	F1273

COMPOUNDS

❶ⓐ **REGISTER, family [domiciliary] register; record**

ⓑ **one's domicile, nationality**

ⓒ **membership**

a 戸籍 こせき family register

軍籍 ぐんせき army register

移籍 いせき transfer of one's name in the register

入籍 にゅうせき entry in the family register

b 国籍 こくせき nationality, citizenship

本籍 ほんせき one's legal domicile, one's permanent residence

c 在籍する ざいせきする be on the register, be a member of

党籍 とうせき party membership

❷ **books, written works, records**

書籍 しょせき books, publications

史籍 しせき history books

漢籍 かんせき Chinese books, Chinese classics

典籍 てんせき classical books, books

INDEPENDENT

【せき 籍】domiciliary **REGISTER**, one's domicile; membership

籍を入れる せきをいれる have a name entered in the family register

SYNONYMS

❶ⓐ **notebook**

帳 NOTEBOOK → 0572

帖 NOTEBOOK → 0342

簿 RECORD BOOK → 3387

籍 REGISTER → 3394

❷ **books**

本 BOOK → 4314

典 STANDARD WORK → 3253
経 religious classic → 1687
書 BOOK → 3292
冊 bound book → 4295
籍 books → 3394
著 literary work → 2869
巻 VOLUME → 3273
編 piece of writing → 1755
篇 PIECE OF WRITING → 3361
鑑 REFERENCE VOLUME → 2226

NOTE

★ do not confuse with 藉 TRAMPLE ON → 3017

籍

3395

2-6-14

▶REGISTER

セキ

118	Nonstandard	U7C4D
⺮	S20-6-14	F0000

traditional form → see 籍 at 3394

嚴

3396

2-6-14

▶SEVERE

ゲン ゴン おごそ(か) きび(しい)
いか(めしい) ㊔ いわお いつき いわ

30	Names	U56B4
口	S20-3-17	F0000

traditional form → see 厳 at 4079

籐

3397

2-6-15

▶WISTERIA

トウ ふじ

118	Nonstandard	U7C50
⺮	S21-6-15	F0000

traditional form → see 藤 at 3025

籠

3398

2-6-16

▶BASKET

ロウ かご こ(もる) こ(める)▲

Ⓒ 笼 lóng lǒng

118	Jōyō	U7C60
⺮	S22-6-16	F1204

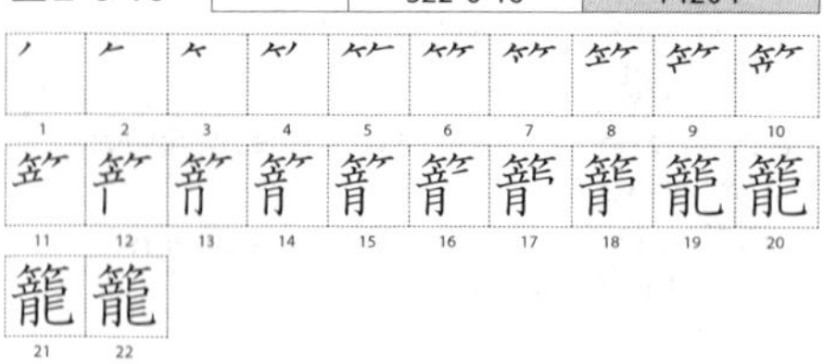

COMPOUNDS

❶ [original meaning] **BASKET, cage, coop, case**

籠球 ろうきゅう basketball
灯籠 とうろう garden lantern; hanging lantern
薬籠 やくろう medicine chest [container]

❷ **be confined in, shut oneself, seclude oneself**

籠城 ろうじょう confinement, keeping inside; holding a castle, sustaining a siege
籠居 ろうきょ living in seclusion, retirement
参籠 さんろう confinement in a temple [shrine] to pray

❸ cajole, entice

籠絡する ろうらくする inveigle, ensnare, entice

KUN

【かご 籠】 [also suffix] **BASKET, hamper, crate, cage, case**

屑籠 くずかご wastebasket
鳥籠 とりかご bird cage
果物籠 くだものかご fruit basket

【こもる 籠もる】

ⓐ **be confined in, shut oneself up, seclude oneself**
ⓑ **be pregnant [filled] with, be fraught with**
ⓒ (be prevented from free outflow) **be heavy [thick], be stuffy [close]**

a 書斎に籠もる しょさいにこもる shut oneself up in one's study
b 憎悪の籠もった目 ぞうおのこもっため eyes fraught with hatred
c 籠もった声 こもったこえ thick voice
煙草の煙が籠もっている たばこのけむりがこもっている be heavy with tobacco smoke

【こめる 籠める】 [now usu. 込める]

① concentrate on, devote oneself to
心を籠めて こころをこめて with all one's heart, wholeheartedly

② impregnate with, imply
警告の意味を籠めて けいこくのいみをこめて with an implication of warning

③ hang over, envelop, shroud
霧が立ち籠めた港 きりがたちこめたみなと harbor wrapped in a mist

SYNONYMS

❶ & 【かご】 **containers**

箱 BOX → 3362
壺 JAR → 2890
槽 TANK → 1352
樽 BARREL → 1368
棺 COFFIN → 1240
桶 BUCKET → 1211
笈 BOX CARRIED ON THE BACK → 3274
鞘 SHEATH → 2259
箪 BAMBOO BOX → 3381
函 BOX → 3724
籠 BASKET → 3398
袋 BAG → 3201
鞄 BAG (for carrying) → 2248
器 VESSEL → 3367
瓶 BOTTLE → 1702

缶 CAN → 2526
缶 EARTHENWARE JAR → 2525

HOMOPHONES

こめる 込 MOVE INWARD → 3762

NOTE

➡ see USAGE note at 込 3762

籤

3399

2-6-17

▶**LOT**

セン くじ

Ⓒ 签 qiān

118	Non-Jōyō	U7C64
⺮	S23-6-17	F0000

COMPOUNDS

● [now also 選 3931] **LOT, lottery**

抽籤 ちゅうせん drawing of lots
当籤する とうせんする win a prize, draw a lucky number

KUN

【くじ 籤】**LOT, lottery**

籤引き くじびき drawing of lots
籤運 くじうん luck with lotteries
御神籤 おみくじ written fortune

SYNONYMS

● **fate and fortune**

運 FORTUNE → 3894
命 fate → 2553
業 karma → 3227
縁 karma relation → 1754
籤 LOT → 3399

貞

2-7-2

incorrect classification
➡ see 2-2-7: ⺊ at 2586

頁

2-7-2

incorrect classification
➡ see 2-2-7: 亠 at 2589

負

2-7-2

incorrect classification
➡ see 2-2-7: ⺈ at 2594

勇

2-7-2

incorrect classification
➡ see 2-2-7: マ at 2592

辱

3400

2-7-3

▶**HUMILIATE**

ジョク はずかし(める)

Ⓒ 辱 rǔ

161	Jōyō	U8FB1
辰	S10-7-3	F1799

一 厂 尸 戸 尼 辰 辰 辰 辱 辱 (1–10)

COMPOUNDS

❶ **HUMILIATE, disgrace, dishonor, insult**

侮辱する ぶじょくする insult, treat with contempt
屈辱 くつじょく humiliation, disgrace, insult
恥辱 ちじょく disgrace, dishonor, shame
雪辱する せつじょくする vindicate one's honor, get revenge for one's defeat
凌辱する りょうじょくする insult, disgrace; rape

❷ grateful, thankful

辱知 じょくち friend (that one is grateful to have)

KUN

【はずかしめる 辱める】**HUMILIATE, put to shame; disgrace, insult, dishonor; rape, violate**

辱め はずかしめ shame, disgrace; being raped
家名を辱める かめいをはずかしめる bring disgrace upon one's family name

SYNONYMS

❶ **disgrace**

恥 SHAME → 1664
羞 shame → 4106
辱 HUMILIATE → 3400
侮 INSULT → 0091
罵 ABUSE → 3233
汚 defile → 0258
誹 SLANDER → 1978
譏 SLANDER → 2069

唇

3401

2-7-3

▶**LIP**

シン くちびる

Ⓝ 脣◇ Ⓒ 唇 chún

30	Jōyō	U5507
口	S10-3-7	F1120

一 厂 尸 戸 尼 辰 辰 辰 唇 唇 (1–10)

COMPOUNDS

● [original meaning] **LIP, lips, labium, labia**

唇音 しんおん labial sound
陰唇 いんしん labium
口唇 こうしん lips, labia

INDEPENDENT

【しん 唇】**LIP**, labium

KUN

【くちびる 唇】**LIP, lips**

上唇 うわくちびる upper lip

SYNONYMS

● **mouth parts**

唇 LIP → 3401

歯 TOOTH → 3124
舌 TONGUE → 2711
牙 FANG → 4243

NOTE

➡ see COMPOUND FORMATION for 唇歯輔車 しんしほしゃ → 輔 1963

辰 【折】 言 百 色

哲 3402

2-7-3

▶SAGACIOUS
▶PHILOSOPHY

テツ ㊔ さと さとし さとる あき あきら のり

Ⓝ 喆 悊 嚞 晢 Ⓒ 哲 zhé

30	Jōyō	U54F2
口	S10-3-7	F1017

一 十 才 扌 扩 扩 折 折 哲 哲 (1–10)

COMPOUNDS

❶ⓐ [original meaning] **SAGACIOUS, wise, intelligent**
ⓑ sage, philosopher, wise man

a 明哲 めいてつ wisdom, sagacity; wise man
賢哲 けんてつ sage, wise man
b 哲人 てつじん philosopher, sage
西哲 せいてつ Western philosopher
先哲 せんてつ ancient sage [wise man]
十哲 じってつ ten sages

❷ PHILOSOPHY
哲学 てつがく philosophy
哲理 てつり philosophy (of something)
中哲 ちゅうてつ Chinese philosophy
印哲 いんてつ Indian philosophy

❸ used phonetically for *tetsu*
何の変哲も無い なんのへんてつもない plain, commonplace

SYNONYMS

❶ⓐ **intelligent and wise**
賢 WISE → 3518
俊 brilliant → 0117
鋭 SHARP → 2171
敏 NIMBLE → 1675
叡 PROFOUNDLY WISE → 2405
智 wise → 3458
慧 INTELLIGENT → 3485
伶 CLEVER → 0356
悧 CLEVER → 0505
俐 CLEVER → 0113
哲 SAGACIOUS → 3402
明 clear-sighted → 1060
聡 SHARP-WITTED → 1750

ⓑ **wise and talented persons**
哲 sage → 3402
賢 wise man → 3518
博 DOCTOR → 0170
秀 genius → 3152
俊 BRILLIANT PERSON → 0117
才 person of talent → 4218
通 well-informed person → 3855

❷ **wisdom**
識 KNOWLEDGE → 2070
知 knowledge → 1446
智 WISDOM → 3458
慧 prajna (transcendental wisdom) → 3485
哲 PHILOSOPHY → 3402

真

2-7-3

incorrect classification
➡ see 2-2-8: 十 at 2616

夏

2-7-3

incorrect classification
➡ see 2-2-8: 一 at 2619

奐

2-7-3

incorrect classification
➡ see 2-2-8: ⺈ at 2620

軣 3403

2-7-4

▶**RESOUND**

ゴウ とどろ(く)

159	Nonstandard	U8EE3
車	S11-7-4	F0000

traditional form → see 轟 at 3425

脣 3404

2-7-4

▶**LIP**

シン くちびる

130	Nonstandard	U8123
月	S11-4-7	F0000

alternative form → see 唇 at 3401

悉 3405

2-7-4

▶**THOROUGHLY**

シツ ことごと(く)

Ⓒ 悉 xī

61	Names	U6089
心	S11-4-7	F2907

COMPOUNDS

❶ **THOROUGHLY, completely, entirely**
悉皆 しっかい all, to the last
知悉する ちしつする have thorough knowledge

❷ used phonetically for *shit* in the transliteration of Sanskrit Buddhist terms
悉曇 しったん *Sīddhaṃ* characters

KUN

【ことごとく 悉く】 **THOROUGHLY, completely, entirely, altogether, without exception**

SYNONYMS

❶ **all**

皆 ALL → 3093
悉 THOROUGHLY → 3405
総 TOTAL → 1743
諸 VARIOUS → 1984
毎 EVERY → 2527
各 EACH → 2692
都 all → 2120
万 all → 3653
全 WHOLE → 2514
渾 ENTIRE → 0738
一 all in one → 4148
満 FULL → 0739
丸 complete(ly) → 4225
完 COMPLETE → 2727

黒 3406

2-7-4

▶**BLACK**
コク くろ くろ(い)
N 黑 C 黑 hēi

203	Jōyō-2	U9ED2
黑	S11-11-0	F0415

radical variant → see 黑 at 3462

Stroke order: 1–11

COMPOUNDS

❶ⓐ [also suffix] [original meaning] **BLACK, blackish**
ⓑ (lacking light) **BLACK**, dark

a 黒海 こっかい Black Sea
黒板 こくばん blackboard
黒点 こくてん black [dark] spot, sunspot
黒人 こくじん black, Negro
黒褐色 こっかっしょく blackish brown
漆黒 しっこく pitch black
b 暗黒 あんこく darkness

❷ **BLACK**, evil, wicked
黒白 こくびゃく right and wrong; black and white

KUN

【くろ 黒】**BLACK**
黒豆 くろまめ black soybean
黒髪 くろかみ black hair
黒字 くろじ the black, surplus
黒ずむ くろずむ blacken, darken
白黒 しろくろ black and white; right or wrong
真っ黒な まっくろな deep-black, jet-black

【くろい 黒い】**BLACK; dark(-colored)**
腹黒い はらぐろい blackhearted, malicious
浅黒い あさぐろい dark-complexioned, tanned, swarthy

SYNONYMS

❶ⓐ **black colors**
黒 BLACK → 3406
漆 pitch-black → 0863
黎 BLACK → 3487

ⓑ **dark**
暗 DARK → 1273
黒 BLACK → 3406
陰 shaded → 0657
闇 DARK → 4134
晦 DARK → 1196
昏 dark → 3073
昧 DARK → 1105
冥 DARK → 2613
曖 SHADY → 1383

悠 3407

2-7-4

▶**LEISURELY**
ユウ 名 しのぶ
C 悠 yōu

61	Jōyō	U60A0
心	S11-4-7	F1408

Stroke order: 1–11

COMPOUNDS

❶ **LEISURELY, at ease, relaxed, composed, serene**
悠悠と ゆうゆうと calmly, leisurely; easily, without difficulty; boundlessly
悠長な ゆうちょうな leisurely, easygoing; tedious
悠然として ゆうぜんとして with an air of perfect composure

❷ [original meaning] (remote in space or time) **far-off**, faraway, remote, distant
悠遠 ゆうえん remoteness
悠久な ゆうきゅうな eternal, everlasting, permanent

SYNONYMS

❶ **leisurely**
悠 LEISURELY → 3407
閑 idle → 4123

❷ **distant**
遠 DISTANT → 3906
遥 FAR → 3895
悠 far-off → 3407
遼 FARAWAY → 3930
隔 APART → 0827
離 separated → 2364
迂 ROUNDABOUT → 3969

望

▶HOPE
▶LOOK AFAR

ボウ モウ のぞ(む) もち▲ ㊔ み

3408

2-7-4

Ⓝ 望 Ⓒ 望 wàng

74	Jōyō-4	U671B
月	S11-4-7	F0517

車 辰 釆 里 攸 【朗】 朗 沕 折 利 色 岗 亲 亜 曲 串 奴

COMPOUNDS

❶ **HOPE, expect, wish, aspire to, desire**
- 望外の ぼうがいの unexpected, unanticipated
- 希望する きぼうする hope, wish, aspire to
- 要望 ようぼう demand, request
- 絶望 ぜつぼう despair, hopelessness
- 失望する しつぼうする be disappointed, lose hope
- 欲望 よくぼう desire, craving
- 志望する しぼうする desire, wish, aspire to
- 待望の たいぼうの hoped-for, long-awaited
- 有望な ゆうぼうな promising, hopeful
- 本望 ほんもう one's long cherished desire; satisfaction
- 大望 たいもう(=たいぼう) ambition, aspiration
- 懇望する こんもうする entreat, solicit, beg earnestly

❷ **LOOK AFAR, gaze into the distance, command a view of**
- 望見する ぼうけんする watch from afar
- 望郷 ぼうきょう homesickness, nostalgia
- 望遠鏡 ぼうえんきょう telescope
- 展望する てんぼうする have a view of
- 眺望 ちょうぼう view, prospect, outlook

❸ popularity, reputation
- 信望 しんぼう prestige, popularity
- 人望 じんぼう popularity, popular favor
- 声望 せいぼう popularity, reputation

❹ [original meaning] full moon
- 既望 きぼう [archaic] moon 16 days old; 16th night (of the lunar month)

KUN

【のぞむ 望む】

①ⓐ **desire, wish, crave for**
ⓑ **HOPE (for), expect, look forward to**

a 望み のぞみ desire, wish; hope, expectation, prospect; preference
望ましい のぞましい desirable, welcome
平和を望む へいわをのぞむ crave for peace
b 成功を望む せいこうをのぞむ hope to succeed
待ち望む まちのぞむ expect, look forward to

② **expect (a person) to do, ask for**
自重を望む じちょうをのぞむ ask for prudence

③ **LOOK AFAR**, gaze into the distance, command a view of
富士を望む家 ふじをのぞむいえ house commanding a view of Mt. Fuji

【もち 望】 *elegant* full moon
望月 もちづき full moon

SYNONYMS

❶ **wish and desire**
- 願 WISH → 2320
- 憧 YEARN AFTER → 0899
- 憬 YEARN AFTER → 0898
- 貪 COVET → 2630
- 望 HOPE → 3408
- 希 ASPIRE → 2543
- 懐 LONG FOR → 0942
- 慕 yearn for → 2970
- 渇 thirst for → 0627
- 欲 DESIRE → 1867
- 慾 DESIRE → 3551
- 求 SEEK → 4365

❷ **see and look**
- 見 SEE → 3151
- 看 WATCH → 3992
- 察 INSPECT → 2961
- 窺 WATCH FURTIVELY → 3002
- 瞥 GLANCE AT → 3592
- 目 look → 3777
- 観 VIEW → 2359
- 覧 LOOK OVER → 3538
- 眺 LOOK OUT OVER → 1503
- 望 LOOK AFAR → 3408
- 仰 LOOK UP → 0051
- 顧 LOOK BACK → 2394
- 視 REGARD → 1223

❸ **repute**
- 声 reputation → 2724
- 誉 HONOR → 3135
- 名 NAME → 2693
- 望 popularity → 3408

USAGE

【のぞむ】

望む
①ⓐ desire, wish, crave for
ⓑ hope (for), expect, look forward to
② expect (a person) to do, ask for
③ look afar, gaze into the distance, command a view of

臨む
① be present at, be on the spot, attend, come to, visit

②come face to face, meet, be confronted with
③overlook, face, border on

HOMOPHONES
のぞむ 臨 BE PRESENT AT →2059

朢

3409
2-7-4

▶HOPE
▶LOOK AFAR
ボウ モウ のぞ(む) もち ㊔ み

74	Nonstandard	U671B
月	S11-4-7	F0000

traditional form → see 望 at 3408

樑

3410
2-7-4

▶BEAM
リョウ はり やな ㊔ むね やね たかし
Ⓒ 梁 liáng

75	Names	U6881
木	S11-4-7	F1853

COMPOUNDS
❶ⓐ **BEAM, crossbeam, girder**
ⓑ **something resembling a BEAM or girder**
a 棟梁 とうりょう chief support, pillar (of a nation), chief, leader, foreman
臥梁 がりょう perimeter beam
b 鼻梁 びりょう bridge of the nose
脊梁 せきりょう backbone, spine
❷ⓐ **bridge**
ⓑ something resembling a bridge
a 橋梁 きょうりょう bridge
石梁 せきりょう stone bridge
b 脳梁 のうりょう corpus callosum
❸ [original meaning] weir, fish trap
跳梁 ちょうりょう rampancy, domination; [original meaning] jumping about
❹ⓐ name of an ancient Chinese state; another name for Wei (魏× c. 362 B.C.)
ⓑ Liang Dynasty (502-557 A.D.)
ⓒ Later Liang Dynasty (907-923 A.D.)
ⓓ Chinese family name: Liang
b 後梁 こうりょう Later Liang Dynasty (907-923 A.D.)
d 梁山泊 りょうざんぱく gathering place of ambitious men

INDEPENDENT
【りょう 梁】Liang Dynasty; Later Liang Dynasty; another name for Wei

KUN
【はり 梁】**BEAM, crossbeam, girder**
横梁 よこばり crossbeam, stringer, trave
片持ち梁 かたもちばり cantilever
【やな 梁】**weir, fish trap**

SYNONYMS
❶ **supporting structures**
柱 PILLAR →1109
礎 FOUNDATION STONE →1595
桁 BEAM →1165
梁 BEAM →3410

NOTE
➡ see COMPOUND FORMATION for 梁山泊 りょうざんぱく →泊 0389

悊

3411
2-7-4

▶SAGACIOUS
▶PHILOSOPHY
テツ ㊔ さと さとし さとる あき あきら のり

61	Nonstandard	U608A
心	S11-4-7	F0000

traditional form → see 哲 at 3402

梨

3412
2-7-4

▶PEAR
リ* なし
Ⓝ 棃 Ⓒ 梨 lí

75	Jōyō	U68A8
木	S11-4-7	F1673

COMPOUNDS
❶ **PEAR tree; pear**
梨花 りか pear blossoms
梨果 りか pome
❷ theatrical world
梨園 りえん theatrical world; pear orchard

KUN
【なし 梨】**PEAR; pear tree**
梨の実 なしのみ pear
梨の礫× なしのつぶて no communication

SYNONYMS
❶ **fruits and fruit trees**
桃 PEACH →1174
榛 HAZEL →1328
椎 CHINQUAPIN →1249
柚 YUZU →1123
椰 COCONUT →1285
柑 CITRUS →1112
橙 BITTER ORANGE →1369
葡 GRAPE →2902
萄 GRAPE →2870
柿 PERSIMMON →1118
檎 APPLE →1386
李 PLUM →3050
枇 LOQUAT →1063

車 辰 釆 里 攸

杷 LOQUAT → 1065
苺 STRAWBERRY → 2780
菱 water chestnut → 2879
杏 APRICOT → 3049
梅 JAPANESE APRICOT → 1159
橘 MANDARIN → 1366
栗 CHESTNUT → 3280
栃 JAPANESE HORSE CHESTNUT → 1122
梨 PEAR → 3412
蕉 PLANTAIN → 2994

魚 2-7-4
incorrect classification
➡ see 2-2-9: ⺈ at 2636

曽 2-7-4
incorrect classification
➡ see 2-2-9: ⺍ at 2632

牽 2-7-4
incorrect classification
➡ see 2-2-9: 亠 at 2621

悪
3413
2-7-4

▶**BAD**
アク オ わる(い) わる- あ(し)*
N 惡 C 恶 è ě wù

61	Jōyō-3	U60AA
心	S11-4-7	F0273

COMPOUNDS

❶ [also prefix]
ⓐ (morally evil) **BAD, evil, wicked, immoral**
ⓑ (inferior in quality) **BAD, inferior, poor, unsatisfactory**
ⓒ (disagreeable) **BAD, unpleasant**

a 悪魔 あくま devil, demon, satan
悪徳 あくとく vice, corruption, immorality
悪事 あくじ evil deed
悪化する あっかする worsen, aggravate, deteriorate
悪用 あくよう abuse, misuse, improper use
悪人 あくにん wicked person, scoundrel
悪女 あくじょ wicked woman; ugly woman
b 悪質な あくしつな bad, malicious; malignant
悪筆 あくひつ poor handwriting
悪日 あくにち(=あくび) unlucky day
悪循環 あくじゅんかん vicious circle
悪条件 あくじょうけん bad terms
最悪 さいあく the worst
c 悪臭 あくしゅう offensive [foul] odor, stench
悪寒 おかん chill
悪天候 あくてんこう bad weather

❷ [also suffix] (something bad) **evil, BADness, vice**
善悪 ぜんあく good and evil
諸悪 しょあく various evils
社会悪 しゃかいあく social ills
必要悪 ひつようあく necessary evil

❸ **hate, bear ill will, despise**
悪意 あくい malicious intent
憎悪 ぞうお abhorrence, hatred
嫌悪 けんお hatred, dislike, repugnance

❹ intense, hard
悪戦苦闘する あくせんくとうする fight desperately, fight against heavy odds

INDEPENDENT

【あく 悪】**evil, BADness, vice; villain's part (in a play)**
悪に染まる あくにそまる steeped in vice
彼は悪だ かれはあくだ He is the villain

KUN

【わるい 悪い】
①ⓐ **BAD, evil, wicked, immoral**
ⓑ (inferior in quality) **BAD, inferior, poor, unsatisfactory**
ⓒ (disagreeable) **BAD, unpleasant**
a 悪 わる bad fellow, knave
悪い行い わるいおこない bad [evil] deed
b 頭が悪い あたまがわるい weak-headed, slow
c 悪い評判 わるいひょうばん unsavory rumor
決まり悪い きまりわるい awkward, embarrassed
②ⓐ (causing harm) **BAD, injurious, harmful**
ⓑ **BAD (luck), ill (omen)**
a 悪い風邪 わるいかぜ bad cold
目に悪い めにわるい bad for the eyes
b 悪い知らせ わるいしらせ bad news
③ (of the body) **BAD (eyesight), sick, ill**
目が悪い めがわるい have bad eyesight
④ **blamable, in fault**
悪かった わるかった I'm sorry/It's my fault
私が悪い わたくしがわるい I am to blame/It is my fault

【わる- 悪-】
① **BAD, evil**
悪気 わるぎ malice
悪賢い わるがしこい cunning, artful, sly, crafty
悪知恵 わるぢえ cunning, craft, serpentine wisdom
悪口 わるくち(=あっこう) slander, abuse, foul language
② disagreeably excessive
悪酔い わるよい drunken sickness
悪ふざけ わるふざけ prank, horseplay, practical joke

悪乗りする わるのりする overdo, do (something) to death, run (something) into the ground

【あし 悪し】*elegant* **BAD, evil, wrong**

悪しからず あしからず I beg you to understand my position

善し悪し よしあし good or bad [evil], right or wrong

SPECIAL READINGS

悪戯▲ いたずら mischief, prank, practical joke

悪阻▲ つわり(=おそ) morning sickness

SYNONYMS

❶ⓐ evil

邪 EVIL → 1443

兇 ATROCIOUS → 3044

凶 ATROCIOUS → 3679

悪 BAD → 3413

ⓑ bad

悪 BAD → 3413

劣 INFERIOR → 3047

下 of low grade → 4186

弊 shabby → 3583

粗 COARSE → 1683

駄 GOOD FOR NOTHING → 2291

廃 WASTE → 3902

❷ wrongdoing and evil

罪 sin → 3224

非 wrong(doing) → 1101

邪 wrong → 1443

悪 evil (something bad) → 3413

弊 evil(s) (something undesirable) → 3583

❸ hate and dislike

憎 HATE → 0845

悪 hate → 3413

忌む ABHOR → 2735

嫌 DISLIKE → 0781

恨 HOLD A GRUDGE → 0439

怨 HOLD A GRUDGE → 3179

厭 disagreeable → 3745

HOMOPHONES

いたずら

徒 FOLLOWER → 0499

悪戯 → 3413, 2351

NOTE

➡ see USAGE note at 戯 2351

曹

3414

2-7-4

▶SERGEANT

ソウ ゾウ▲

Ⓝ 曺 Ⓒ 曹 cáo

73	Jōyō	U66F9
日	S11-4-7	F1246

COMPOUNDS

❶ SERGEANT, petty officer

曹長 そうちょう sergeant officer, sergeant major

軍曹 ぐんそう sergeant

海曹 かいそう petty officer (navy)

陸曹 りくそう noncommissioned officer

❷ soda

曹達 そーだ soda

重曹 じゅうそう bicarbonate of soda

❸ officials, government office

法曹 ほうそう legal profession, judicial officer, lawyer

❹ chamber in the Imperial court

御曹司 おんぞうし son of a noble family

❺ [original meaning] friends, companions

INDEPENDENT

【そう 曹】friends, companions

SYNONYMS

❶ military officers and ranks

曹 SERGEANT → 3414

尉 COMPANY OFFICER → 2119

佐 FIELD OFFICER → 0076

将 GENERAL OFFICER → 0551

督 COMMANDER → 3471

帥 COMMANDER IN CHIEF → 1642

患

3415

2-7-4

▶AFFECTED BY DISEASE

カン わずら(う)

Ⓒ 患 huàn

61	Jōyō	U60A3
心	S11-4-7	F1036

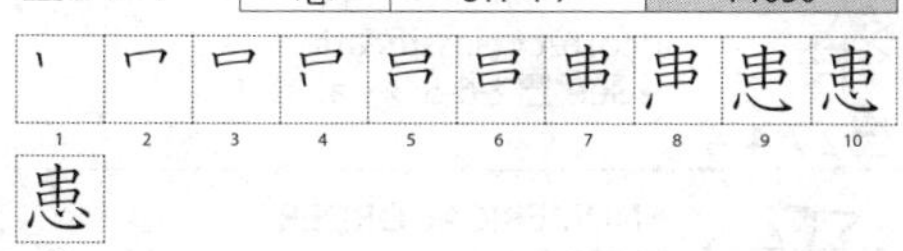

COMPOUNDS

❶ⓐ AFFECTED BY DISEASE, diseased, sick

ⓑ affection, disease

a 患者 かんじゃ patient

患部 かんぶ diseased part, affected area

b 罹患 りかん contraction of a disease

疾患 しっかん disease, ailment, trouble, disorder

❷ abbrev. of 患者 かんじゃ: patient

急患 きゅうかん emergency case, acutely sick patient

新患 しんかん new patient

❸ [original meaning] trouble, worry, anxiety

内憂外患 ないゆうがいかん troubles from within and without

後患 こうかん future trouble

憂患 ゆうかん sorrow, grief, distress

KUN

【わずらう 患う】**fall ill, be afflicted with**

患い わずらい illness, sickness

長患い ながわずらい lingering sickness

胸を患う むねをわずらう have trouble in one's lungs, suffer from pulmonary tuberculosis

SYNONYMS

❶ **disease**

病 ILLNESS →4062

疾 DISEASE →4064

風 (infectious) disease →3730

症 PATHOLOGICAL CONDITION →4065

患 AFFECTED BY DISEASE →3415

疫 EPIDEMIC →4061

罹 FALL ILL →3239

臥 be sick in bed →1825

USAGE

❶【わずらう】

患う
fall ill, be afflicted with

煩う
worry about, feel anxious, be vexed

❷【わずらい】

患い
illness, sickness

煩い
worry, agony, vexation

HOMOPHONES

わずらう 煩 VEXED →1295

わずらい 煩 VEXED →1295

祭

2-7-4

incorrect classification
➡ see 2-6-5: 夕 at 3311

番

3416

2-7-5

▶**NUMERICAL ORDER**
▶**WATCH**

バン つが(い)▲

Ⓒ 番 fān pān

102	Jōyō-2	U756A
田	S12-5-7	F0246

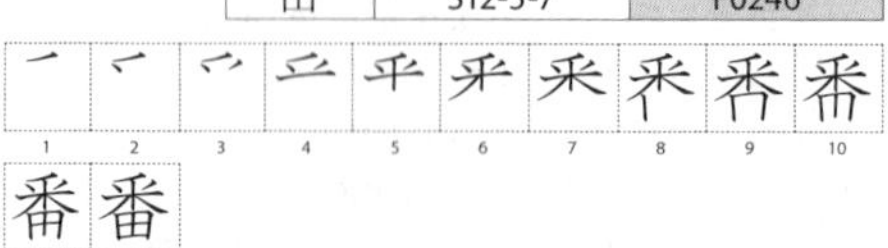

COMPOUNDS

❶ⓐ suffix for expressing **NUMERICAL ORDER** or forming ordinal numbers: **No., number**
ⓑ **NUMERICAL ORDER, order, ranking, place**

a 一番 いちばん first, first place; first verse; most, best; a game, a round, a bout; a number, a piece

三番線 さんばんせん Track No. 3

b 番号 ばんごう number, serial number

番地 ばんち lot [house] number, address

番組 ばんぐみ (TV) program

番付 ばんづけ ranking list

番頭 ばんとう (head) clerk

番狂わせ ばんくるわせ upsetting of arrangements, upset, surprise

先番 せんばん one's turn to make the first move

本番 ほんばん acting for the audience, take, going on the air

順番 じゅんばん order, turn

❷ⓐ [also suffix] **WATCH, vigil, guard, lookout**
ⓑ **WATCH**man, guard, keeper

a 番人 ばんにん watchman, guard, caretaker

番犬 ばんけん watchdog

留守番 るすばん caretaking (during a person's absence); caretaker

b 門番 もんばん gatekeeper, janitor

下足番 げそくばん caretaker of footwear

❸ **(one's) turn, duty, shift**

交番 こうばん police box

出番 でばん one's turn, one's time

当番 とうばん being on duty [guard]; person on duty

非番 ひばん off duty

輪番 りんばん turn, rotation

❹ coarse

番茶 ばんちゃ coarse tea

番傘 ばんがさ coarse oilpaper umbrella

❺ counter for number of games, dances or kabuki plays

三番勝負 さんばんしょうぶ three-game match

十八番 じゅうはちばん repertoire comprising 18 classical kabuki pieces; one's specialty

INDEPENDENT

【ばん 番】**one's turn, duty, shift; WATCH, vigil, guard, lookout**

番に当たる ばんにあたる be on duty, have one's inning

【ばんする 番する】keep **WATCH**, guard

KUN

【つがい 番い】couple, brace, pair

一番いの鴨 ひとつがいのかも a brace of ducks

蝶番い ちょうつがい hinge

SYNONYMS

❶ⓐ kinds of numbers
数 NUMBER (mathematical unit) → 2245
員 fixed number → 2822
号 NUMBER (numerical designation) → 2675
番 No. → 3416
第 ORDINAL NUMBER PREFIX → 3298
-目 ordinal number suffix → 3777
次 numerical order suffix → 0058
桁 DIGIT → 1165

ⓑ order
序 ORDER (sequence/arrangement) → 3803
順 ORDER (sequence) → 0018
次 order (sequence) → 0058
番 NUMERICAL ORDER → 3416
秩 ORDER (methodical arrangement) → 1489

❷ⓐ protect
守 PROTECT (by watching over) → 2697
護 PROTECT (by safeguarding) → 2079
庇 PROTECT (by shielding) → 3802
衛 GUARD → 0938
警 GUARD AGAINST → 3595
防 defend → 0320
番 WATCH → 3416
保 PRESERVE → 0107
看 CARE FOR → 3992

COMPOUND FORMATION

【番組 ばんぐみ】

番組 '(TV) program' is a scheduled or planned out (組) order (番 ❶ⓑ) of events of some public presentation, such as a TV or radio program.

盗 **3417** 2-7-5

▶**STEAL**
トウ ぬす(む)

108	Names	U76DC
皿	S12-5-7	F0000

traditional form → see 盜 at 3309

募葛 2-7-5

incorrect classification
➡ see 2-3-9: 艹 at 2901

喬 2-7-5

incorrect classification
➡ see 2-4-8: 夭 at 3129

黍 2-7-5

incorrect classification
➡ see 2-5-7: 禾 at 3210

畱 **3418** 2-7-5

▶**KEEP**
▶**STAY**
リュウ ル と(める) -と(める) -ど(め) と(まる) とど(まる) とど(める) るーぶる

102	Nonstandard	U7571
田	S12-5-7	F0000

traditional form → see 留 at 3189

盛 **3419** 2-7-5

▶**PROSPEROUS**
セイ ジョウ も(る) さか(る) さか(ん)
㊔ しげ さかえ

108	Nonstandard	U76DB
皿	S12-5-7	F0000

traditional form → see 盛 at 3314

箸 2-7-5

incorrect classification
➡ see 2-6-9: ⺮ at 3359

裟 **3420** 2-7-6

▶**BUDDHIST CASSOCK**
サ シャ
ⓒ 裟 shā

145	Names	U88DF
衣	S13-6-7	F2367

COMPOUNDS

● BUDDHIST CASSOCK
袈裟 けさ Buddhist surplice
大袈裟な おおげさな exaggerated, hyperbolical

SYNONYMS

● clothing
服 CLOTHES → 1090
袴 FORMAL DIVIDED SKIRT → 1509
蓑 STRAW RAINCOAT → 2941
-着 wear → 4110
衣 GARMENT → 2506
装 DRESS → 3327
裳 DRESS → 3231
襤 RAGS → 1607
袈 BUDDHIST SURPLICE → 3200
裟 BUDDHIST CASSOCK → 3420
襖 overgarment → 1600

裝 **3421** 2-7-6

▶**DRESS**
▶**FIT OUT**
ソウ ショウ よそお(う)

145	Names	U88DD
衣	S13-6-7	F0000

traditional form → see 装 at 3327

幕墓 2-7-6

incorrect classification
➡ see 2-3-10: 艹 at 2930

沙 壯 艹 【君】

羣

3422

2-7-6

▶GROUP

グン　む(れる)　む(れ)　むら　むら(がる)

123	Nonstandard	U7FA3
羊	S13-6-7	F0000

alternative form → see 群 at 1942

墨

3423

2-7-7

▶INDIA INK

ボク　すみ

Ⓝ 墨 Ⓒ 墨 mò

32	Jōyō	U58A8
土	S14-3-11	F1848

COMPOUNDS

❶ **INDIA INK, Chinese ink, ink stick**

墨汁 ぼくじゅう India ink, black writing fluid

水墨画 すいぼくが India ink drawing, painting in India ink

❷ⓐ something written in **INDIA INK**

ⓑ something used like or resembling **INDIA INK**

a 墨痕 ぼっこん handwriting; ink marks

遺墨 いぼく autographs of a departed person

b 石墨 せきぼく graphite, black lead

白墨 はくぼく chalk

筆墨 ひつぼく pen and ink; writing materials, stationery

❸ [rare] tattooing, ancient Chinese punishment by tattooing

墨刑 ぼっけい punishment by tattooing

❹ Mexico

日墨 にちぼく Japan and Mexico

❺ Mozi (name of a Chinese philosopher)

墨子 ぼくし Mozi

墨守 ぼくしゅ strict adherence ("defending like Mozi")

KUN

【すみ 墨】

ⓐ **INDIA INK, Chinese ink, ink stick**

ⓑ (black substance) ink, soot, black dye

a 墨色 すみいろ India ink color

墨絵 すみえ India ink drawing, painting in India ink

お墨付き おすみつき handwriting; certificate, authorization; paper bearing the signature of the shogun or feudal lord

b 墨染め すみぞめ dyeing black; (Buddhist priest's) black robe

眉墨 まゆずみ eyebrow pencil

入れ墨 いれずみ tattooing, tattoo, tattoo marks

SYNONYMS

❶ **pigments**

墨 INDIA INK → 3423

漆 LACQUER → 0863

藍 INDIGO → 3024

堊 WHITEWASH → 3442

USAGE

【すみ】

墨

ⓐ India ink, Chinese ink, ink stick

ⓑ (black substance) ink, soot, black dye

炭

charcoal

HOMOPHONES

すみ 炭 COAL → 2806

誓

3424

2-7-7

▶VOW

セイ　ちか(う)

Ⓒ 誓 shì

149	Jōyō	U8A93
言	S14-7-7	F1752

COMPOUNDS

● [original meaning] **VOW, swear, pledge, make [take] an oath**

誓約する せいやくする vow, pledge, make [take] an oath, swear

誓願 せいがん oath, vow, pledge

宣誓する せんせいする make [take] an oath, swear, vow

KUN

【ちかう 誓う】**VOW, swear, pledge, make [take] an oath**

誓い ちかい vow, oath, pledge

誓って ちかって upon my word, by Jove

誓い交わす ちかいかわす vow to each other

SYNONYMS

● **promise**

約 PROMISE → 1632

締 CONCLUDE (a treaty) → 1761

協 reach an agreement → 0103

契 MAKE AN AGREEMENT → 3267

盟 ALLIANCE → 3468

誓 VOW → 3424

暮慕 incorrect classification

➡ see 2-3-11: 艹 at 2969

2-7-7

魯 2-7-8

incorrect classification
➡ see 2-2-13: ⺈ at 2665

篇 2-7-8

incorrect classification
➡ see 2-6-9: ⺮ at 3363

蘆 2-7-12

incorrect classification
➡ see 2-3-16: 艹 at 3034

轟 **3425** 2-7-14

▶**RESOUND**

ゴウ とどろ(く)

Ⓝ 軣 Ⓒ 轰 hōng

159	Names	U8F5F
車	S21-7-14	F2310

COMPOUNDS

● **RESOUND, reverberate, boom; roar, rumble, roll**
轟音 ごうおん thundering noise, roar, rumble
轟轟 ごうごう thunderous, rumbling
轟沈 ごうちん sinking (a ship) instantly

KUN

【とどろく 轟く】

① **RESOUND, reverberate, boom; roar, rumble, roll**
轟き とどろき roar, rumble, boom; pounding, throbbing

② **be famous**

③ **palpitate, throb**

SYNONYMS

● **make sound or noise**
鳴 SOUND →0831
響 REVERBERATE →3573
騒 CLAMOR →2308
轟 RESOUND →3425

昼 2-8-1

incorrect classification
➡ see 3-3-6: 尸 at 3841

隻 **3426** 2-8-2

▶**ONE OF A PAIR**
▶**COUNTER FOR SHIPS**

セキ

Ⓒ 只 zhī

172	Jōyō	U96BB
隹	S10-8-2	F1995

1	2	3	4	5	6	7	8	9	10
ノ	イ	イ'	亻丶	什	仵	隹	隹	隻	隻

COMPOUNDS

❶ⓐ [original meaning] **ONE OF A PAIR, esp. when the second member is absent**
ⓑ one only, single, lone
a 隻手 せきしゅ one arm, one hand
隻眼 せきがん one eye
b 隻影 せきえい a single shadow; a speck (of cloud)

❷ just a little, a bit
隻語 せきご just a few words
隻句 せっく a few words

❸ **COUNTER FOR SHIPS**
一隻 いっせき one ship
数隻 すうせき several ships

SYNONYMS

❶ **one**
一 ONE →4148
壱 ONE (in legal documents) →2723
片- ONE OF TWO →4272
隻 ONE OF A PAIR →3426
単 SINGLE →2805
個 INDIVIDUAL →0132

❸ **boats and ships**
船 SHIP →1700
舶 OCEANGOING SHIP →1699
艦 WARSHIP →1817
潜 submarine →0922
舟 SMALL BOAT →4353
艇 BOAT →1727
隻 COUNTER FOR SHIPS →3426

隼 **3427** 2-8-2

▶**FALCON**

シュン はやぶさ ㊔ **はや はやし じゅん**

Ⓒ 隼 sǔn

172	Names	U96BC
隹	S10-8-2	F2370

COMPOUNDS

● [original meaning, now archaic] **FALCON**
鷹隼 ようしゅん hawk and falcon

KUN

【はやぶさ 隼】

ⓐ **FALCON, peregrine falcon, duck hawk**
ⓑ as fast and brave as a **FALCON**
a 隼科 はやぶさか *Falconidae*
大隼 おおはやぶさ gerfalcon

SYNONYMS

● **birds**
鷹 HAWK →3955
鷗 GULL →2370
烏 CROW →4088
雀 SPARROW →3117
燕 SWALLOW →3142
鴻 LARGE WILD BIRD →0977
鳳 MALE PHOENIX →3749
凰 FEMALE PHOENIX →3738

鵬 MYTHICAL HUGE BIRD → 1416
鶏 CHICKEN → 2221
酉 ROOSTER → 4358
隼 FALCON → 3427
鳩 PIGEON → 0184
鷲 EAGLE → 3598
鳶 BLACK KITE → 3919
鶴 CRANE → 2326
鷺 HERON → 3621
鵜 CORMORANT → 2067
鴨 DUCK → 1582
雁 WILD GOOSE → 3741

勢

3428

2-8-2

▶POWER

セイ ゼイ いきお(い) ㊔ なり

19	Nonstandard	U351F
力	S10-2-8	F0000

traditional form → see 勢 at 3542

鬯

3429

2-8-2

▶*CHŌ*

192	Radical	U9B2F
鬯	S10-10-0	F0000

RADICAL

chō 'fragrant wine', used in characters related to fragrant wine or fragrance

---

雫

3430

2-8-3

▶DROP

ダ しずく

Ⓒ 雫 nǎ (国字)

173	Names	U96EB
雨	S11-8-3	F3213

KUN

【しずく 雫】[also 滴]

ⓐ (liquid globule) **DROP**

ⓑ counter for **DROP**s

a 露の雫 つゆのしずく dewdrop

b 一雫 ひとしずく a drop

SYNONYMS

【しずく】

ⓐ **small water masses**

滴 DROP → 0866
雫 DROP → 3430
泡 BUBBLE → 0392
沫 BUBBLE → 0397

HOMOPHONES

しずく 滴 DROP → 0866

NOTE

➡ see USAGE note at 滴 0866

雪

3431

2-8-3

▶SNOW

セツ ゆき

Ⓝ 雪 Ⓒ 雪 xuě

173	Jōyō-2	U96EA
雨	S11-8-3	F0780

COMPOUNDS

❶ⓐ SNOW, snowfall

ⓑ as white (and pure) as **SNOW**

a 雪上車 せつじょうしゃ snowmobile
豪雪 ごうせつ tremendous snowfall
降雪 こうせつ snowfall, snow
積雪 せきせつ (fallen) snow
新雪 しんせつ fresh snow
蛍雪 けいせつ diligent study

b 雪白の せっぱくの snow-white; pure, immaculate

❷ wipe out (disgrace), vindicate

雪辱 せつじょく vindication of honor, revenge

KUN

【ゆき 雪】**SNOW, snowfall**

雪合戦 ゆきがっせん snowball fight
雪焼け ゆきやけ snow-tan
雪祭り ゆきまつり Snow Festival
初雪 はつゆき first snow of the season

SPECIAL READINGS

雪崩 なだれ snowslide
吹雪 ふぶき snowstorm

SYNONYMS

❶ⓐ kinds of frozen water

氷 ICE → 0043
雪 SNOW → 3431

❶ⓐ kinds of precipitation

雨 RAIN → 4378
露 DEW → 3495
霜 FROST → 3491
雪 SNOW → 3431

NOTE

➡ see COMPOUND FORMATION for 蛍雪 けいせつ → 蛍 3204

雪

3432

2-8-3

▶SNOW

セツ ゆき

173	Nonstandard	U96EA
雨	S11-8-3	F0000

traditional form → see 雪 at 3431

婆

3433

2-8-3

▶**OLD WOMAN**

バ ばば▲ ばあ▲

Ⓒ 婆 pó

38	Jōyō	U5A46
女	S11-3-8	F1527

Stroke order: 1–11

COMPOUNDS

❶ **OLD WOMAN, old maid, old mother; woman**

老婆 ろうば old woman
妖婆 ようば witch, hag
老婆心 ろうばしん grandmotherly solicitude
産婆 さんば midwife

❷ used phonetically for *ba,* esp. in the transliteration of Sanskrit Buddhist terms

婆羅門 ばらもん Brahman
娑×婆 しゃば this world, outside world (as viewed from prison)
卒塔婆 そとば wooden grave tablet; stupa, dagoba

KUN

【ばば 婆】**OLD WOMAN**; joker (in playing cards); something detestable

婆あ ばばあ *slang* old woman, hag
婆抜き ばばぬき Old Maid; living without one's mother-in-law
鬼婆 おにばば hag, witch

【ばあ 婆】[in compounds] **OLD WOMAN, old wife**

婆や ばあや old housekeeper; wet nurse
お婆さん おばあさん old woman, old wife, grandma

SYNONYMS

❶ **old persons**

老 old person → 3963
爺 OLD MAN → 2656
翁 OLD MAN → 2611
婆 OLD WOMAN → 3433
姥 OLD WOMAN → 0420

❶ **woman**

女 WOMAN → 4226
婦 ADULT WOMAN → 0565
婆 OLD WOMAN → 3433
嬢 YOUNG LADY → 0936
娘 GIRL → 0488
雌 FEMALE → 1337
牝 FEMALE → 1020
媛 DAMSEL → 0688

啓

3434

2-8-3

▶**ENLIGHTEN**

ケイ ひら(く)▲ ㊔ ひろ ひろし ひら あきら よし

Ⓝ 啓 Ⓒ 启 qǐ

30	Jōyō	U5553
口	S11-3-8	F1661

Stroke order: 1–11

COMPOUNDS

❶ⓐ **ENLIGHTEN, edify, awaken, educate**
ⓑ reveal

a 啓蒙 けいもう enlightenment, instruction
啓発する けいはつする enlighten, develop, edify
b 啓示 けいじ revelation
天啓 てんけい divine revelation

❷ **address respectfully**—used esp. in polite salutations

啓上する けいじょうする speak respectfully
拝啓 はいけい Dear Sir, Dear Madam
謹啓 きんけい Dear Sirs, Gentlemen

❸ [original meaning] open (a door)

中啓 ちゅうけい ceremonial folding fan

❹ favor with one's presence, deign to come

行啓 ぎょうけい attendance (of the Empress)

KUN

【ひらく 啓く】[usu. 開く] **ENLIGHTEN**, edify

蒙を啓く もうをひらく enlighten (a person's mind)

SYNONYMS

❶ **teach**

教 TEACH → 1887
啓 ENLIGHTEN → 3434
諄 TEACH WITH CARE → 1979
授 teach → 0595
育 educate → 2544
練 TRAIN → 1738
訓 INSTRUCT → 1844
誨 INSTRUCT → 1946
諭 ADMONISH → 2012
導 GUIDE → 3587
迪 EDIFY → 3817

❷ **speak humbly**

申す SPEAK HUMBLY → 4319
啓 address respectfully → 3434

HOMOPHONES

ひらく

開 OPEN → 4121
拓 OPEN UP → 0375

NOTE

➡ see USAGE note at 開 4121

啓
3435
2-8-3

▶**ENLIGHTEN**
ケイ ひら(く) ㊔ ひろ ひろし ひら あきら よし

30	Nonstandard	U5553
口	S11-3-8	F0000

traditional form → see 啓 at 3434

梦
3436
2-8-3

▶**DREAM**
ム ゆめ

36	Nonstandard	U68A6
夕	S11-3-8	F0000

alternative form → see 夢 at 2939

埜
3437
2-8-3

▶**FIELD**
ヤ の の- ㊔ のう ぬ

32	Names	U57DC
土	S11-3-8	F0000

traditional form → see 野 at 1877

哲
3438
2-8-3

▶**SAGACIOUS**
▶**PHILOSOPHY**
テツ ㊔ さと さとし さとる あき あきら のり

30	Nonstandard	U5560
口	S11-3-8	F0000

traditional form → see 哲 at 3402

彗
3439
2-8-3

▶**COMET**
スイ ズイ エイ エ ㊔ けい
Ⓒ 彗 huì

58	Names	U5F57
⺕	S11-3-8	F3035

COMPOUNDS

❶ **COMET**
彗星 **すいせい** comet

❷ [original meaning, now archaic] broom

SYNONYMS

❶ **constellation**
奎 ANDROMEDA → 2796
彗 COMET → 3439
昴 PLEIADES → 3091

NOTE

★ do not confuse with 慧 INTELLIGENT → 3485

菱
2-8-3

incorrect classification
➡ see 2-3-8: 艹 at 2879

基
2-8-3

incorrect classification
➡ see 2-6-5: 甘 at 3312

麦
3440
2-8-3

▶***BAKUNYŌ***

199	Radical	U9EA5
麥	S11-11-0	F0000

radical variant → see 麥 at 3441

麥
3441
2-8-3

▶**WHEAT**
バク むぎ

199	Nonstandard	U9EA5
麥	S11-11-0	F0000

traditional form → see 麦 at 3061

RADICAL

baku 'wheat', used in characters related to wheat or foods made of wheat
Enclosures: 麦 麦× ***bakunyō*** (麩× 麺 麹×)

堊
3442
2-8-3

▶**WHITEWASH**
アク ア
Ⓒ 垩 è

32	Non-Jōyō	U580A
土	S11-3-8	F0000

COMPOUNDS

● [now also 亜 あ 4354] **WHITEWASH**
白堊 **はくあ** chalk; white wall

SYNONYMS

● **pigments**
墨 INDIA INK → 3423
漆 LACQUER → 0863
藍 INDIGO → 3024
堊 WHITEWASH → 3442

專
3443
2-8-3

▶**EXCLUSIVE**
セン もっぱ(ら)

41	Names	U5C08
寸	S11-3-8	F0000

traditional form → see 専 at 3272

隋
2-8-3

incorrect stroke-count
➡ see 2-9-3: 隋 at 3501

臤
2-8-3

incorrect stroke-count
➡ see 2-9-3: 臤 at 3502

焦

3444

2-8-4

▶SCORCH
▶BE IMPATIENT

ショウ こ(げる) こ(がす) こ(がれる) あせ(る)

Ⓒ 焦 jiāo

86	Jōyō	U7126
灬	S12-4-8	F1454

ノ 亻 亻' 亻˝ 什 仹 隹 隹 隹 焦 焦 焦
1 2 3 4 5 6 7 8 9 10 11 12

COMPOUNDS

❶ⓐ [original meaning] **SCORCH, burn**
ⓑ [also prefix] pyro-

a 焦点 しょうてん focus, focal point; (photographic) focus
焦土 しょうど scorched earth
焦熱 しょうねつ scorching heat
焦眉 しょうび emergency, urgency, imminence
b 焦性硫酸 しょうせいりゅうさん pyrosulfuric acid
焦電気 しょうでんき pyroelectricity

❷ **BE IMPATIENT, be too eager, burn to do something**
焦燥 しょうそう fretfulness, impatience
焦慮 しょうりょ impatience; worry
焦心 しょうしん impatience

KUN

【こげる 焦げる】*vi* **SCORCH, burn, singe**
焦げ臭い こげくさい smell burnt
焦げ茶色 こげちゃいろ dark brown, olive brown
【こがす 焦がす】*vt* **SCORCH, burn, char**
【こがれる 焦がれる】**pine for, yearn for; be deeply in love with**
恋い焦がれる こいこがれる pine for, burn with passion
【あせる 焦る】**BE IMPATIENT, be hasty, be in a hurry, be too eager**
焦り あせり impatience
焦るなよ あせるなよ Don't be in such a hurry/Take your time

SYNONYMS

❶ **burn**
焼 BURN → 1256
燃 BURN (undergo combustion) → 1375
焚く BURN (build a fire) → 3450
焦 SCORCH → 3444
灼 SCORCH → 1036
炮 ROAST → 1132
燎 SET ON FIRE → 1376

❷ **impatient**
焦 BE IMPATIENT → 3444
躁 RESTLESS → 2083
燥 restless → 1392

COMPOUND FORMATION

【焦点 しょうてん】
焦点 'focus, etc.' is the point (点) of burning (焦 ❶ⓐ), i.e., a point of great significance or focal point.

NOTE

★ do not confuse with 蕉 PLANTAIN → 2994

集

3445

2-8-4

▶COLLECT

シュウ あつ(まる) あつ(める) つど(う)

Ⓒ 集 jí

172	Jōyō-3	U96C6
隹	S12-8-4	F0163

ノ 亻 亻' 亻˝ 什 仹 隹 隹 隹 隼 集 集
1 2 3 4 5 6 7 8 9 10 11 12

COMPOUNDS

❶ [formerly also 聚 3479 or 蒐 2942]
ⓐ (bring together) **COLLECT, gather, concentrate, assemble, recruit**
ⓑ [original meaning] (come together) **COLLECT, gather, congregate**
ⓒ **gathering, meeting, assembly; COLLECTion**

a 集金 しゅうきん collecting money
集配 しゅうはい collection and delivery
集貨 しゅうか collection of freight
採集する さいしゅうする collect, gather
収集(=蒐集)する しゅうしゅうする collect, gather, accumulate
招集する しょうしゅうする call, summon, convene
募集する ぼしゅうする recruit, enlist; raise, collect
徴集する ちょうしゅうする levy, recruit
b 集中する しゅうちゅうする concentrate, focus; converge
集合する しゅうごうする gather, meet, assemble; summon, call together
集落 しゅうらく community, settlement, town, village; colony
結集する けっしゅうする concentrate, marshal
c 集会 しゅうかい gathering, meeting, assembly
集団 しゅうだん group, body, mass, crowd
群集 ぐんしゅう crowd, mob; forming a large group (of people)

❷ [also suffix] **COLLECTion of literary works, anthology, series**
詩集 ししゅう anthology of poems
川端全集 かわばたぜんしゅう the complete works of Kawabata

万葉集 まんようしゅう(=まんにょうしゅう) Japan's oldest anthology of poems
書簡集 しょかんしゅう collection of letters

❸ [formerly also 輯 2025]
ⓐ (collect written materials) **edit, compile**
ⓑ **edition, series**
a 集録 しゅうろく compilation, editing
編集する へんしゅうする edit, compile
b 特集 とくしゅう special edition
第一集 だいいっしゅう first series

INDEPENDENT

【しゅう 集】**COLLECT**ion of literary works, anthology

KUN

【あつまる 集まる】*vi* **gather, COLLECT, meet, crowd, flock;** (of money) **be collected; center, converge, focus**
集まり あつまり gathering, meeting, assembly; collection
寄り集まる よりあつまる gather, assemble

【あつめる 集める】*vt* **COLLECT, gather, assemble, recruit; raise (funds); focus, concentrate**
掻き集める かきあつめる gather up, scrape up together
切手集め きってあつめ stamp collecting

【つどう 集う】*vi* **gather, COLLECT, meet**
集い つどい meeting, gathering, get-together

SYNONYMS

❶ⓐ & ❶ⓑ **gather**
集 COLLECT → 3445
蒐 COLLECT → 2942
聚 COLLECT → 3479
収 collect → 0031
採 GATHER → 0606
采 GATHER → 3077
萃 GATHER → 2882
湊 come together → 0743
ⓒ **assembly**
会 meeting → 2512
集 gathering → 3445
❷ **collection**
集 collection → 3445
選 selection → 3931
彙 ASSEMBLAGE → 2929
❸ⓐ **compile**
編 COMPILE → 1755
纂 COMPILE → 3393
撰 COMPILE → 0911
集 edit → 3445
輯 EDIT → 2025
著 AUTHOR → 2869

NOTE

➡ see USAGE note at 微 0841

雰

3446

2-8-4

▶**ATMOSPHERE**

フン

Ⓒ 氛 fēn

173	Jōyō	U96F0
雨	S12-8-4	F1805

COMPOUNDS

❶ **ATMOSPHERE**
雰囲気 ふんいき atmosphere, mood
❷ [original meaning, now archaic] **mist, fog**

SYNONYMS

❶ **atmosphere**
雰 ATMOSPHERE → 3446
気 atmosphere → 3960

雲

3447

2-8-4

▶**CLOUD**

ウン くも -ぐも

Ⓒ 云 yún

173	Jōyō-2	U96F2
雨	S12-8-4	F0950

COMPOUNDS

❶ⓐ [original meaning] **CLOUD**
ⓑ something resembling a **CLOUD**
a 雲海 うんかい sea of clouds
雲霧 うんむ clouds and fog
雲泥の差 うんでいのさ great difference (as between clouds and mud)
積乱雲 せきらんうん cumulonimbus
b 風雲 ふううん state of affairs, situation
星雲 せいうん nebula
❷ (figuratively) as high as the **CLOUD**s
青雲の志 せいうんのこころざし high [lofty] ambition

KUN

【くも 雲】**CLOUD**
雲隠れする くもがくれする vanish behind the clouds; disappear, run away
雲間 くもま rift between clouds
浮き雲 うきぐも cloud drift

【-ぐも -雲】[suffix] **CLOUD**

入道雲 にゅうどうぐも gigantic columns of clouds (in summer), cumulonimbus
キノコ雲 きのこぐも mushroom cloud (from a nuclear blast)

SPECIAL READINGS

雲雀▲ ひばり skylark

SYNONYMS

❶ **kinds of atmospheric vapor**
霧 FOG → 3493
霞 MIST → 3490
雲 CLOUD → 3447

悲

▸SAD

ヒ かな(しい) かな(しむ)

Ⓒ 悲 bēi

3448

2-8-4

61	Jōyō-3	U60B2
心	S12-4-8	F0829

Stroke order: 1–12

COMPOUNDS

❶ⓐ **SAD, sorrowful, pathetic**
ⓑ [original meaning] feel **SAD**, feel sorrow
ⓒ sorrow, grief

a 悲痛な ひつうな sad, grievous
悲惨な ひさんな miserable, wretched, tragic, pitiable
悲壮な ひそうな pathetic, tragic
悲劇 ひげき tragedy, tragic drama
悲鳴 ひめい shriek, scream
悲観する ひかんする be pessimistic, lose heart
悲観的な ひかんてきな pessimistic
b 悲嘆 ひたん grief, sorrow, lamentation
悲哀 ひあい sorrow, sadness
c 悲喜 ひき joy and sorrow

❷ⓐ *Buddhism* **mercy, compassion**
ⓑ merciful, compassionate

a 慈悲 じひ mercy, compassion
大慈大悲 だいじだいひ great mercy and compassion
b 悲願 ひがん one's pathetic wish; vows resulting from the compassion of the Buddhas

INDEPENDENT

【ひ 悲】 *Buddhism* mercy, compassion

KUN

【かなしい 悲しい】
ⓐ (low in spirit) **SAD, unhappy, sorrowful**
ⓑ [sometimes also 哀しい] (causing sorrow) **SAD, sorrowful, pathetic**

a 悲しさ かなしさ sadness, sorrow, grief
悲しげに かなしげに sadly, with a sad look
b 悲しがる かなしがる be sad, feel sorrow

【かなしむ 悲しむ】 **feel [be] SAD, grieve, feel sorrow; lament, regret**
悲しみ かなしみ grief, sadness
悲しむべき境遇 かなしむべききょうぐう pitiable condition

SYNONYMS

❶ⓐ & ❶ⓒ **sad and depressed**
悲 SAD → 3448
悄 BECOME DISPIRITED → 0506
哀 sorrowful → 2568
愁 MELANCHOLY → 3508
鬱 GLOOM → 3625
陰 gloomy → 0657
沈 depressed → 0306
寂 LONESOME → 2855
淋しい LONESOME → 0632
惨 MISERABLE → 0585

ⓑ **grieve**
慨 DEPLORE → 0790
嘆 SIGH → 0773
悼 MOURN → 0587
傷 grieve → 0179
悲 feel sad → 3448
悄 BECOME DISPIRITED → 0506

❷ⓐ **tender feelings for others**
仁 BENEVOLENCE → 0021
慈 compassion → 2949
情 sympathy → 0583
悲 mercy → 3448
哀 PITY → 2568
憐 PITY → 0945

USAGE

【かなしい】
悲しい
ⓐ (low in spirit) **sad, unhappy, sorrowful**
ⓑ [sometimes also 哀しい] (causing sorrow) **sad, sorrowful, pathetic**

哀しい
[now usu. 悲しい] (causing sorrow) **sad, sorrowful, pathetic**

HOMOPHONES

かなしい 哀 SORROW → 2568

斐

▸PHONETIC [i]

ヒ イ ㊔ あや

Ⓒ 斐 fěi

3449

2-8-4

67	Names	U6590
文	S12-4-8	F2041

佳 雫 非 【林】 炏 物 玨 炏 㚘 知 矛 無 侖 並 其 直 侖 者 或 里 亞 東 臤 禺

COMPOUNDS

❶ **used PHONETICally for *i***

甲斐(=詮)が有る かいがある fruitful, effective, worth, worthwhile

❷ [archaic] florid, embellished, beautiful

斐然たる ひぜんたる florid, beautiful

SYNONYMS

❶ **phonetic [i]**

伊 PHONETIC [i] → 0052
斐 PHONETIC [i] → 3449

❷ **beautiful**

美 BEAUTIFUL → 2817
彪 MAGNIFICENT → 4115
綺 BEAUTIFUL → 1734
娃 BEAUTIFUL → 0419
佳 FINE → 0096
瑶 EXQUISITE → 1301
麗 OF GRACEFUL BEAUTY → 2672
艶 CHARMING → 2403
妙 of marvelous beauty → 0280
華 MAGNIFICENT → 2841
絢 GORGEOUS → 1705
斐 florid → 3449

焚

3450

2-8-4

▶**BURN**

フン た(く)

Ⓒ 焚 fén

86	Names	U711A
火	S12-4-8	F2103

COMPOUNDS

● [original meaning] **BURN, kindle, build a fire**

焚書 ふんしょ book burning
焚刑 ふんけい burning at the stake

KUN

【たく 焚く】**BURN, kindle, build a fire**

焚き火 たきび bonfire
焚き付け たきつけ kindling, fire lighter
焚き付ける たきつける kindle, build a fire; instigate, stir up
空焚き からだき heating a pan or bathtub without water in it
追い焚き おいだき reheating (of bath)

SYNONYMS

【たく】

◯ **burn**

焼 BURN → 1256
燃 BURN (undergo combustion) → 1375
焚く BURN (build a fire) → 3450
焦 SCORCH → 3444
灼 SCORCH → 1036
炮 ROAST → 1132
燎 SET ON FIRE → 1376

HOMOPHONES

たく 炊 COOK → 1080

NOTE

➡ see USAGE note at 炊 1080

勞

3451

2-8-4

▶**LABOR**

ロウ いたわ(る) ねぎら(う)

19	Nonstandard	U52DE
力	S12-2-10	F0000

traditional form → see 労 at 3155

惣

3452

2-8-4

▶**GENERAL**

ソウ ㊔ のぶ みち ふさ

Ⓒ 总 zǒng

61	Names	U60E3
心	S12-4-8	F1908

COMPOUNDS

[now usu. 総 1743]

❶ (applicable to the whole or the usual) **GENERAL, overall; ordinary**

惣菜 そうざい daily [household] dish, side dish
惣社 そうじゃ shrine enshrining several gods
惣嫁 そうか streetwalker (in the Edo period)

❷ⓐ (of supreme rank) **GENERAL**, supreme, chief
ⓑ [archaic] exercise **GENERAL** control, administer, govern

a 惣管領 そうかんりょう *hist* governor-general
b 惣領する そうりょうする govern, administer (a fief)

❸ eldest son, eldest child—used esp. in names

惣領 そうりょう eldest son, eldest child

SYNONYMS

❶ **general**

総 GENERAL → 1743
惣 GENERAL → 3452
汎 OVERALL → 0254

❸ **offspring**

子 CHILD → 4196
仔 OFFSPRING → 0038
孤 orphan → 0426
嫡 LEGITIMATE CHILD → 0839
息 son → 3278
男 son → 3147
惣 eldest son → 3452
娘 DAUGHTER → 0488
女 daughter → 4226
姫 DAUGHTER OF NOBLE BIRTH → 0489

USAGE

【そう 惣総】

★The function of 惣 in Japanese is vague and does not lend itself to logical analysis. Originally it was a corrupt form of 総 (core meanings GENERAL and TOTAL), but is now restricted mostly to personal names, esp. of an eldest son. It can be said that 惣 is actually a *variant* of 総, *not* a different character with the same meanings.

COMPOUND FORMATION

【惣菜 そうざい】【惣社 そうじゃ】【惣嫁 そうか】

惣菜 and 惣社, the only compounds including 惣 that one is likely to encounter, are now normally written 総菜 and 総社. 惣菜 'daily [household] dish, side dish' can be interpreted as an ordinary (惣 ❶) side dish (菜), and 惣社 'shrine enshrining several gods' as a general (惣 ❶) shrine (社), i.e., a shrine not limited in scope to one deity, while 惣嫁, a colorful word to describe a streetwalker, is a general (惣 ❶) bride (嫁), i.e., "a bride to be shared by everyone."

琵

3453

2-8-4

▶LUTE

ビ

Ⓒ 琵 pí

96	Names	U7435
王	S12-4-8	F2292

COMPOUNDS

❶ LUTE, Japanese lute

琵琶 びわ *biwa,* Japanese lute

琵琶湖 びわこ Lake Biwa

琵琶行 びわこう Biwa Song

❷ pluck forward

SYNONYMS

❶ musical instruments

琴 KOTO → 3455
箏 KOTO → 3353
鼓 DRUM → 2241
笛 FLUTE → 3303
琵 LUTE → 3453
琶 LUTE → 3454
笙 *SHO* → 3302

琶

3454

2-8-4

▶LUTE

ハ ワ

Ⓒ 琶 pá

96	Names	U7436
王	S12-4-8	F2282

COMPOUNDS

❶ LUTE, Japanese lute

琵琶 びわ *biwa,* Japanese lute

琵琶湖 びわこ Lake Biwa

琵琶行 びわこう Biwa Song

❷ strum downward

SYNONYMS

❶ musical instruments

琴 KOTO → 3455
箏 KOTO → 3353
鼓 DRUM → 2241
笛 FLUTE → 3303
琵 LUTE → 3453
琶 LUTE → 3454
笙 *SHO* → 3302

琴

3455

2-8-4

▶KOTO

キン こと

Ⓒ 琴 qín

96	Jōyō	U7434
王	S12-4-8	F1595

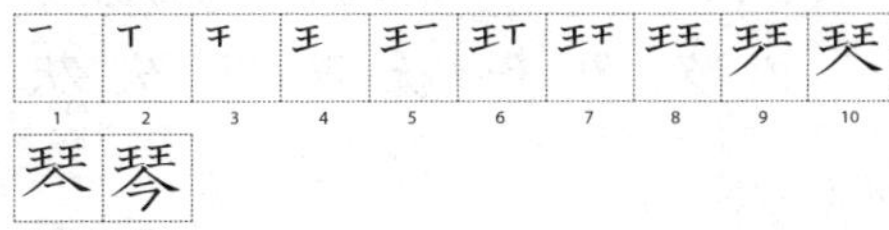

COMPOUNDS

ⓐ [original meaning] **KOTO, (Japanese) zither**

ⓑ general term for certain musical instruments

a 琴曲 きんきょく koto music

弾琴 だんきん playing on the koto

b 琴線 きんせん heartstrings

木琴 もっきん xylophone

風琴 ふうきん organ, accordion

提琴 ていきん violin

INDEPENDENT

【きん 琴】Chinese zither

KUN

【こと 琴】[sometimes also 箏] [also suffix] **KOTO, (Japanese) zither, harp, lute**

琴爪 ことづめ artificial fingernail [plectrum] of ivory used in playing the koto

竪琴 たてごと harp

大正琴 たいしょうごと taishogoto, Nagoya harp

SYNONYMS

ⓐ musical instruments

琴 KOTO → 3455
箏 KOTO → 3353
鼓 DRUM → 2241
笛 FLUTE → 3303
琵 LUTE → 3453
琶 LUTE → 3454
笙 *SHO* → 3302

USAGE

【こと】

琴

[sometimes also 箏] [also suffix] koto, (Japanese) zither, harp, lute

箏

[usu. 琴] koto, (Japanese) zither

HOMOPHONES

こと 箏 KOTO →3353

然

3456

2-8-4

▶MODIFIER FORMING SUFFIX
▶SO

ゼン ネン しか▲ しか(り)▲ しか(し)▲ しか(して)▲ さ▲

Ⓒ 然 rán

86	Jōyō-4	U7136
灬	S12-4-8	F0205

Stroke order: 1–12

COMPOUNDS

❶ⓐ SUFFIX for FORMING MODIFIERs (noun adjectives and adverbs); suffix attached to a one-character base to express a state of being or quality

ⓑ suffix after nouns to express likeness: -like, smack of

a 突然 とつぜん abruptly, suddenly, unexpectedly
公然の こうぜんの open, public
平然と へいぜんと calmly, quietly, with composure
純然たる じゅんぜんたる pure, sheer; absolute
憤然として ふんぜんとして indignantly, wrathfully, in a rage
全然 ぜんぜん wholly, totally, completely; (not) at all
断然 だんぜん resolutely, decisively
茫×然(=呆然)とする ぼうぜんとする be struck dumb (with surprise), be stupefied

b 学者然としている がくしゃぜんとしている be quite like a scholar

❷ⓐ SO, be definitely so, be as it is

ⓑ just SO, just as you say, yes

a 天然の てんねんの natural
自然 しぜん nature
偶然 ぐうぜん chance, accident, coincidence
当然 とうぜん naturally, as a matter of course
依然 いぜん still, as yet

b 然諾する ぜんだくする consent, say yes

KUN

【しか 然】SO, thus; yes, aye

然も しかも [formerly also 而も] moreover, furthermore; and yet, nevertheless

【しかり 然り】just SO, just as you say, yes

然るに しかるに however, still, but
然るべき しかるべき due, proper, appropriate

【しかし 然し】[also 併し] however, but, nevertheless

然しながら しかしながら however, nevertheless

【しかして 然して】[usu. 而して] and, and then

【さ 然】so

然る さる a certain; so
然り気ない さりげない unconcerned, nonchalant

SYNONYMS

❶ modifier suffixes

然 MODIFIER FORMING SUFFIX →3456
乎 MODIFIER FORMING SUFFIX →4316
如 modifier suffix →0239
爾 adjective suffix →4407
的 ADJECTIVAL SUFFIX →1444

❷ terms of assent

然 SO →3456
諾 yes →1974

【しかし】

◯ **conditional conjunctions**

但し PROVIDED THAT →0081
然し however →3456

USAGE

【しかも】

然も

[formerly also 而も]

ⓐ moreover, furthermore
ⓑ and yet, nevertheless

而も

[now usu. 然も] same as 然も

HOMOPHONES

しかも 而 DIRECTION WORD →2520
しかして 而 DIRECTION WORD →2520

COMPOUND FORMATION

【自然 しぜん】

自然 'nature' is to be (然 ❷ⓐ) in a spontaneous or natural (自) state.

NOTE

➡ see also USAGE note at 而 2520
➡ see COMPOUND FORMATION for 当然 とうぜん →当 2701

替

3457

2-8-4

▶REPLACE

タイ か(える) か(え)- か(わる)

Ⓒ 替 tì

73	Jōyō	U66FF
曰	S12-4-8	F0880

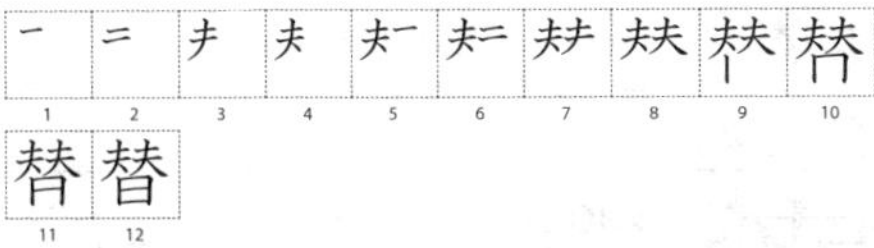

COMPOUNDS

❶ [original meaning] **REPLACE (one thing or person by another), change places, substitute, change**

代替 だいたい substitution

交替(=交代) こうたい alternation, shift, change

❷ decline, decay

隆替 りゅうたい rise and decline

KUN

【かえる 替える】

①ⓐ **REPLACE (one thing or person by another), renew, change**

ⓑ **change to something new (as a job or set of clothes), change over to**

a 替え かえ replacement, spare

畳の表を替える たたみのおもてをかえる replace the covers of old mats with new ones

塗り替える ぬりかえる repaint

取り替える とりかえる change, renew, replace, substitute

両替 りょうがえ money changing, exchange of money

b 商売を替える しょうばいをかえる change to a new business

着替える きがえる change clothes

② [usu. 換える] **exchange, interchange, trade, barter, change (money), convert**

引き替える ひきかえる exchange, change, convert

【かえ- 替え-】 **substitute, spare, extra**

替え玉 かえだま substitute, double

替え刃 かえば extra blades

替え着 かえぎ spare (change of) clothes

【かわる 替わる】 **be REPLACEd, change places with, replace, take turns, relieve, change**

替わり かわり turn, shift; replacement (for a maid); substitute program (of a kabuki play)

替わってくれないか かわってくれないか Could you take over, please?

立ち替わる たちかわる take turns, alternate

入れ替わり いれかわり replacement, substitution, change, shifting

校長が替わった こうちょうがかわった A new school principal took over the job

SPECIAL READINGS

為替 かわせ money order, exchange

SYNONYMS

❶ **change and replace**

変 CHANGE → 2569

替 REPLACE → 3457

代 SUBSTITUTE → 0034

迭 ALTERNATE → 3818

更 change → 4355

改 change → 0287

易 change → 3064

化 CHANGE INTO, -ize → 0022

遷 undergo transition → 3932

転 turn into → 1872

換 EXCHANGE → 0716

交 INTERCHANGE → 2508

HOMOPHONES

かえる

変 CHANGE → 2569

換 EXCHANGE → 0716

代 SUBSTITUTE → 0034

かえ-

変 CHANGE → 2569

換 EXCHANGE → 0716

代 SUBSTITUTE → 0034

かわる

変 CHANGE → 2569

換 EXCHANGE → 0716

代 SUBSTITUTE → 0034

かわり

変 CHANGE → 2569

換 EXCHANGE → 0716

代 SUBSTITUTE → 0034

NOTE

➡ see USAGE note at 変 2569

➡ see COMPOUND FORMATION for 為替 かわせ → 為 4395

智

3458

▀ 2-8-4

▶**WISDOM**

チ ㊔ とも さとし さと さとる とし のり あきら まさる さとり

Ⓒ 智 zhì

72	Names	U667A
日	S12-4-8	F0989

COMPOUNDS

❶ [now replaced by 知 1446]

ⓐ **WISDOM, intelligence**

ⓑ [original meaning] **wise, clever, resourceful**

a 智能 ちのう intelligence, mental capacity

智慧(=知恵) ちえ wisdom, intelligence, sagacity

智識 ちしき wisdom; Buddhist priest of renown

智謀 ちぼう resources, artifice

無智 むち ignorance, stupidity

b 智慮 ちりょ foresight

智者 ちしゃ wise man; learned priest

智将 ちしょう resourceful general

❷ Chile

智日 ちにち Chile and Japan

隹 雨 非 林 炊 物 玨 殀 炔 知 【秎】 無 侖 並 其 直 侖 者 或 里 亞 叀 臤 禺

INDEPENDENT

【ち 智(=知)】**WISDOM**, intellect, intelligence, sense; stratagem

智を磨く ちをみがく cultivate wisdom

SYNONYMS

❶ⓐ wisdom

識 KNOWLEDGE → 2070
知 knowledge → 1446
智 WISDOM → 3458
慧 prajna (transcendental wisdom) → 3485
哲 PHILOSOPHY → 3402

ⓑ intelligent and wise

賢 WISE → 3518
俊 brilliant → 0117
鋭 SHARP → 2171
敏 NIMBLE → 1675
叡 PROFOUNDLY WISE → 2405
智 wise → 3458
慧 INTELLIGENT → 3485
怜 CLEVER → 0356
悧 CLEVER → 0505
俐 CLEVER → 0113
哲 SAGACIOUS → 3402
明 clear-sighted → 1060
聡 SHARP-WITTED → 1750

棃

3459

2-8-4

▶**PEAR**

リ なし

75	Nonstandard	U68C3
木	S12-4-8	F0000

traditional form → see 梨 at 3412

無

2-8-4

incorrect classification
➡ see 2-2-10: 𠂉 at 2648

禽

2-8-4

incorrect classification/ stroke-count
➡ see 2-2-11: 𠆢 at 2654

普

2-8-4

incorrect classification
➡ see 2-3-9: 䒑 at 2919

棊 朞

2-8-4

incorrect classification
➡ see 2-6-6: 甚 at 3333

悳

2-8-4

incorrect classification
➡ see 2-2-10: 十 at 2645

曾

2-8-4

incorrect classification
➡ see 2-2-10: 八 at 2642

煮

3460

2-8-4

▶**BOIL**

シャ に(る) -に に(える) に(やす)

Ⓝ 煮 Ⓒ 煮 zhǔ

86	Jōyō	U716E
灬	S12-4-8	F1495

Stroke order: 一 十 土 耂 耂 者 者 者 者 者 煮 煮 (1–12)

COMPOUNDS

● [original meaning] (cook by boiling) **BOIL, cook**

煮沸 しゃふつ boiling

KUN

【にる 煮る】*vt* **BOIL, cook, do**

煮込む にこむ boil well; stew, cook together
煮立つ にたつ boil up, begin to boil
煮詰める につめる boil down
煮豆 にまめ boiled (cooked) beans

【-に -煮】[suffix] **BOILed food, boiling**

甘露煮 かんろに sweet boiled food

【にえる 煮える】*vi* **BOIL, be boiled, be cooked**

煮え切らない にえきらない half-cooked; vague, halfhearted
煮え湯 にえゆ boiling water
煮え湯を飲まされる にえゆをのまされる be betrayed

【にやす 煮やす】*vt* **BOIL down, wear out**

業を煮やす ごうをにやす be exasperated, lose one's temper

SYNONYMS

● cook

煮 BOIL (cook by boiling) → 3460
沸 BOIL (undergo boiling) → 0387
炊 COOK → 1080
蒸 STEAM → 2936
焼く cook by fire → 1256
揚げる fry in deep fat → 0722
煎 ROAST, DECOCT → 2950

【-に】

○ **cooked dishes**

-焼き roasted, baked or fried food → 1256
-揚げ fried food → 0722
-煮 boiled food → 3460

惑 3461

2-8-4

▶BEWILDERED
ワク まど(う)
Ⓒ 惑 huò

61 心	Jōyō S12-4-8	U60D1 F0918

COMPOUNDS

❶ⓐ [original meaning] **BEWILDERED, perplexed, puzzled, confused**
ⓑ **mislead, lead astray, entice**

a 惑乱 わくらん bewilderment, confusion
迷惑 めいわく trouble, annoyance
当惑 とうわく perplexity, confusion, embarrassment
困惑 こんわく embarrassment, perplexity, confusion

b 魅惑 みわく fascination, enchantment, charm
誘惑 ゆうわく temptation, seduction
眩×惑 げんわく dazzle, daze, bewilderment

❷ wander
惑星 わくせい planet

❸ doubt, suspect
疑惑 ぎわく doubt, suspicion

❹ *Buddhism* illusion
三惑 さんわく three kinds of illusion

❺ used phonetically for *waku*
思惑 おもわく thought, intention, purpose

KUN

【まどう 惑う】**be BEWILDERED, be puzzled;** [in compounds] **do something in confusion, be at a loss**
惑い まどい delusion, illusion, infatuation; bewilderment, perplexity
惑わす まどわす mislead, lead astray, entice; fascinate; bewilder, perplex, puzzle
戸惑い とまどい loss of orientation, bewilderment
逃げ惑う にげまどう run about trying to escape

SYNONYMS

❶ⓐ **bewildered**
迷 PERPLEXED → 3836
惑 BEWILDERED → 3461

ⓑ **deceive**
欺 DECEIVE → 2138
騙 DECEIVE → 2314
詐 SWINDLE → 1896
惑 mislead → 3461
拐 defraud → 0365
偽 FALSIFY → 0149
詭 TRICK → 1919

NOTE

➡ see COMPOUND FORMATION for 当惑 とうわく → 当 2701

黑 3462

2-8-4

▶BLACK
コク くろ くろ(い)

203 黑	Names S12-12-0	U9ED1 F0000

traditional form → see 黒 at 3406

RADICAL

kuroi 'black' (黴), used in characters related to blackness
Variant: 黒 *kuroi* (黙)

惡 3463

2-8-4

▶BAD
アク オ わる(い) わる- あ(し)

61 心	Names S12-4-8	U60E1 F0000

traditional form → see 悪 at 3413

惠 3464

2-8-4

▶FAVOR
ケイ エ めぐ(む) ㊔ やす さとし えい あや しげ

61 心	Names S12-4-8	U60E0 F0000

traditional form → see 恵 at 3293

胥

2-8-4

incorrect stroke-count
➡ see 2-9-4: 臤 at 3511

禺

2-8-4

incorrect stroke-count
➡ see 2-9-4: 禺 at 3513

電 3465

2-8-5

▶ELECTRICITY
デン
Ⓒ 电 diàn

173 雨	Jōyō-2 S13-8-5	U96FB F0214

COMPOUNDS

❶ ELECTRICITY
電気 でんき electricity; electric light
電子 でんし electron
電力 でんりょく electric power, electricity
電車 でんしゃ train, electric train, trolley
電波 でんぱ electromagnetic waves, radio waves
電話 でんわ telephone; phone call

電話帳 でんわちょう telephone book [directory]
電報 でんぽう telegram
電算機 でんさんき electronic computer
電源 でんげん power source [supply]
発電する はつでんする generate electricity; telegraph
停電 ていでん stoppage of electric power, power failure

❷ various devices operated by **ELECTRICITY**, as:
ⓐ abbrev. of 電車 でんしゃ: **electric railway, train**
ⓑ abbrev. of 電話 でんわ: **telephone**
ⓒ abbrev. of 電報 でんぽう: [also suffix] **telegram**

a 終電 しゅうでん last train
国電 こくでん National Railway
b 電電公社 でんでんこうしゃ Nippon Telegraph and Telephone Public Corporation (defunct)
c 外電 がいでん foreign telegram, cablegram
打電する だでんする send a telegram, telegraph
ロイター電 ろいたーでん Reuters dispatch

❸ [original meaning] lightning
電光 でんこう lightning; electric light
雷電 らいでん thunder and lightning, thunderbolt

SYNONYMS

❶ **electricity and magnetism**
電 ELECTRICITY →3465
流 electric current →0529
磁 MAGNETISM →1554

❷ⓐ **kinds of railway**
鉄 railway →2147
電 electric railway →3465
車 railway car →4367
両 counter for railway cars →4331
輛 counter for railway cars →2000

ⓒ **written communications**
状 LETTER →0322
文 LETTER →2458
翰 LETTER →2198
書 letter →3292
信 written communication →0115
電 telegram →3465
牒 OFFICIAL NOTICE →1299

❸ **atmospheric discharges**
雷 THUNDER →3466
電 lightning →3465

雷

3466
2-8-5

▶**THUNDER**
ライ かみなり
Ⓒ 雷 léi

173	Jōyō	U96F7
雨	S13-8-5	F1613

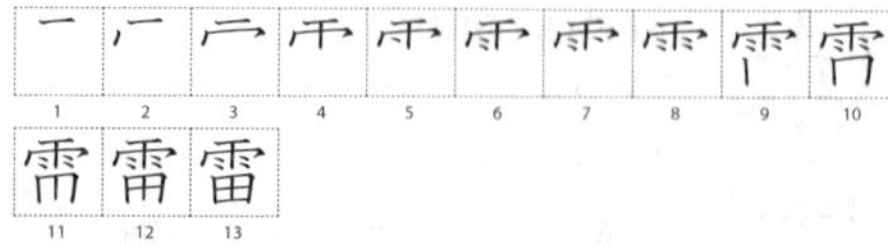

COMPOUNDS

❶ⓐ [original meaning] **THUNDER**
ⓑ lightning
a 雷電 らいでん thunder and lightning, thunderbolt
雷雲 らいうん thunder cloud
雷神 らいじん god of thunder
b 落雷 らくらい strike of a thunderbolt
避雷針 ひらいしん lightning rod

❷ explosive device, mine, torpedo
雷撃 らいげき torpedo attack
機雷 きらい mine
地雷 じらい land mine
水雷 すいらい torpedo, mine

❸ fame, renown
雷名 らいめい renown, fame, great name

INDEPENDENT

【らい 雷】**THUNDER**

KUN

【かみなり 雷】**THUNDER, thunderbolt; lightning; thunderous rebuke, thundering at (a person); roaring sound**
雷親父 かみなりおやじ irascible old man
雷族 かみなりぞく Thunder Herd, hot-rodders

SYNONYMS

❶ **atmospheric discharges**
雷 THUNDER →3466
電 lightning →3465

❷ **projectiles and bombs**
弾 PROJECTILE →0697
丸 round projectile →4225
矢 ARROW →2502
槍 SPEAR →1329
爆 bomb →1415
雷 explosive device →3466

零

3467
2-8-5

▶**ZERO**
レイ ぜろ▲ こぼ(す)▲ こぼ(れる)▲
Ⓒ 零 líng

173	Jōyō	U96F6
雨	S13-8-5	F2121

COMPOUNDS

❶ **ZERO, naught**

零度 れいど zero, freezing point
零下 れいか below zero, sub-zero
零時 れいじ twelve o'clock
零敗 れいはい whitewash, being shut out
零点 れいてん zero, no marks

❷ few, scanty, infinitesimal

零細な れいさいな small, trifling, petty
零砕 れいさい [rare] a tiny bit

❸ⓐ [original meaning, now rare] fall, drip (as of rain)
ⓑ fall low, go to ruin

a 零露 れいろ dripping dew
b 零落 れいらく downfall, ruin

INDEPENDENT

【れい 零】**ZERO, naught**

KUN

【ぜろ 零】**ZERO** (the number)
零戦 ぜろせん Zero fighter

【こぼす 零す】*vt*
① spill, drop; shed (tears)
② let out (a smile)
③ complain, grumble

【こぼれる 零れる】*vi*
① spill, drop, fall; overflow
② (issue involuntarily from) escape, find vent, break out

SYNONYMS

❶ **zero**

零 ZERO → 3467
○ ZERO → 4149

USAGE

【ぜろ】
零
zero (the number)
○
zero (the numeral)

❶【こぼす】
零す
vt
① spill, drop; shed (tears)
② let out (a smile)
③ complain, grumble
溢す
①ⓐ spill
ⓑ shed (tears)
② grumble

❷【こぼれる】
零れる
vi
① spill, drop, fall; overflow
② (issue involuntarily from) escape, find vent, break out
溢れる
①ⓐ spill, fall out
ⓑ overflow
②ⓐ leak out (as of light)
ⓑ show (as of a smile)

HOMOPHONES

ぜろ ○ ZERO → 4149
こぼす 溢 OVERFLOW → 0807
こぼれる 溢 OVERFLOW → 0807

NOTE

➡ see NOTE at ○ 4149

盟

3468
2-8-5

▸**ALLIANCE**
メイ
Ⓒ 盟 méng

108	Jōyō-6	U76DF
皿	S13-5-8	F1053

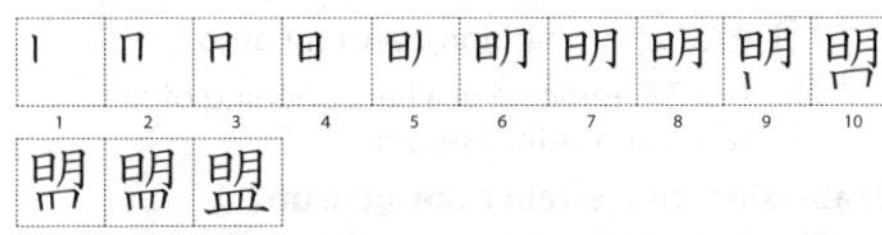

COMPOUNDS

❶ **ALLIANCE, league, pledge, pact**

盟約 めいやく pledge, pact, alliance, league
盟邦 めいほう ally, allied powers
盟友 めいゆう sworn friend
同盟 どうめい alliance, league, union
連盟 れんめい union, federation, league
加盟 かめい participation, affiliation

❷ [original meaning] make a blood pledge by drinking sacrificial blood from a plate

血盟 けつめい blood pledge

INDEPENDENT

【めい 盟】**ALLIANCE**
盟を結ぶ めいをむすぶ form an alliance

SYNONYMS

❶ **promise**

約 PROMISE → 1632
締 CONCLUDE (a treaty) → 1761
協 reach an agreement → 0103
契 MAKE AN AGREEMENT → 3267
盟 ALLIANCE → 3468
誓 VOW → 3424

禁

3469

2-8-5

▶PROHIBIT

キン

Ⓒ 禁 jìn jīn

113	Jōyō-5	U7981
示	S13-5-8	F0974

1	2	3	4	5	6	7	8	9	10	11	12	13
一	十	オ	木	木一	村	材	林	林	埜	埜	禁	禁

COMPOUNDS

❶ⓐ PROHIBIT, forbid, ban
ⓑ PROHIBITion, ban, embargo

a 禁止する **きんしする** prohibit, forbid, ban
禁煙 **きんえん** NO SMOKING; giving up smoking
禁句 **きんく** tabooed word
厳禁する **げんきんする** prohibit strictly, taboo
発禁 **はっきん** prohibition of sale, suppression (of a book)

b 禁令 **きんれい** prohibition, ban, embargo
解禁 **かいきん** removal of a ban; opening of the fishing [hunting] season

❷ abstain from, refrain from, give up
禁酒する **きんしゅする** abstain from [give up] drinking
禁欲的な **きんよくてきな** abstentious, self-denying, ascetic

❸ (prohibited place) Imperial Palace, the Court
禁中 **きんちゅう** the Court, the Imperial Palace
禁裏 **きんり** the Imperial Palace

❹ confine, imprison
禁固 **きんこ** imprisonment
監禁する **かんきんする** imprison, confine
拘禁 **こうきん** detention, confinement, imprisonment

INDEPENDENT

【きん 禁】**PROHIBIT**ion, ban, embargo
禁を犯す **きんをおかす** violate the ban, break the prohibition (law)

【きんじる(=きんずる) 禁じる(=禁ずる)】**PROHIBIT, forbid; suppress, restrain**

SYNONYMS

❶ⓐ restrain
制 CONTROL (restrain) → 1624
禁 PROHIBIT → 3469
限 LIMIT → 0475
抑 SUPPRESS → 0301
束 TIE UP → 4369
縛 BIND → 1779
控える HOLD BACK → 0600
扣える HOLD BACK → 0250
渋る hang [hold] back → 0625

❷ avoid and abstain
避 AVOID → 3944
逃 ESCAPE → 3839
禦 WARD OFF → 3561
忌 shun → 2735
禁 abstain from → 3469

❹ imprison and confine
拘 ARREST → 0367
禁 confine → 3469
留 keep in custody → 3189
置 place in custody → 3222
錮 IMPRISON → 2182

楚

3470

2-8-5

▶NEAT AND TRIM

ソ しもと ㊔ たか うばら

Ⓒ 楚 chǔ

75	Names	U695A
木	S13-4-9	F2135

COMPOUNDS

❶ NEAT AND TRIM
楚楚 **そそ** graceful, neat
清楚 **せいそ** neat and clean

❷ Chu, name of an ancient Chinese state
四面楚歌 **しめんそか** being surrounded by enemies on all sides

INDEPENDENT

【そ 楚】Kingdom of Chu

KUN

【しもと 楚】[archaic] (flogging implement) switch

SYNONYMS

❶ clean and purified
浄 CLEAN → 0457
清 clean → 0635
純 PURE → 1649
潔 IMMACULATE → 0920
粋 REFINED (free from impurities) → 1645
精 refined (purified) → 1729
楚 NEAT AND TRIM → 3470

琵

2-8-5

incorrect stroke-count
➡ see 2-8-4: 珏 at 3453

督

3471

2-8-5

▶SUPERVISE
▶COMMANDER

トク ㊔ まさ すけ

Ⓒ 督 dū

109	Jōyō	U7763
目	S13-5-8	F0723

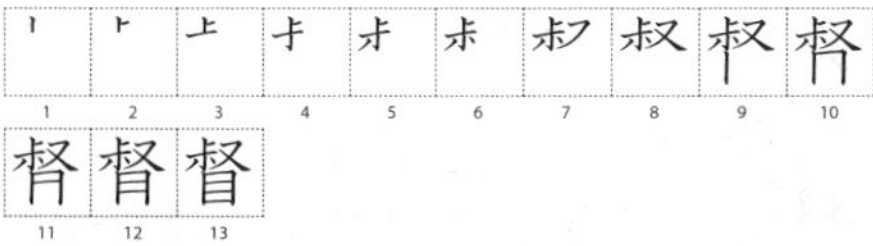

COMPOUNDS

❶ [original meaning] **SUPERVISE, oversee, superintend**

督学官 とくがくかん school inspector

監督 かんとく supervision, superintendence; supervisor; film director

❷ⓐ **COMMANDER, governor-general, viceroy**

ⓑ command (troops), lead

a 総督 そうとく governor-general, viceroy

都督 ととく governor general

提督 ていとく admiral

❸ **urge, press, demand**

督促する とくそくする urge, press, demand

督戦する とくせんする urge soldiers to fight more vigorously

❹ **inheritor of an estate**

家督 かとく headship of a family, family estate

SYNONYMS

❶ **direct and supervise**

制 CONTROL → 1624
理 manage → 1220
経 MANAGE → 1687
管 EXERCISE CONTROL → 3349
轄 EXERCISE JURISDICTION OVER → 2056
掌 TAKE CHARGE OF → 3215
監 OVERSEE → 3535
督 SUPERVISE → 3471
司 OFFICIATE → 3648
宰 PRESIDE → 2829
営 MANAGE → 3216

❷ⓐ **military officers and ranks**

曹 SERGEANT → 3414
尉 COMPANY OFFICER → 2119
佐 FIELD OFFICER → 0076
将 GENERAL OFFICER → 0551
督 COMMANDER → 3471
帥 COMMANDER IN CHIEF → 1642

禽 2-8-5
incorrect classification
➡ see 2-2-11: 𠆢 at 2654

夢 2-8-5
incorrect classification
➡ see 2-3-10: 艹 at 2939

蓄 2-8-5
incorrect classification
➡ see 2-3-10: 艹 at 2931

碁 2-8-5
incorrect classification
➡ see 2-6-7: 甘 at 3346

竪 2-8-5
incorrect stroke-count
➡ see 2-9-5: 豎 at 3516

需
3472
2-8-6

▸**DEMAND**

ジュ

Ⓒ 需 xū

173	Jōyō	U9700
雨	S14-8-6	F1572

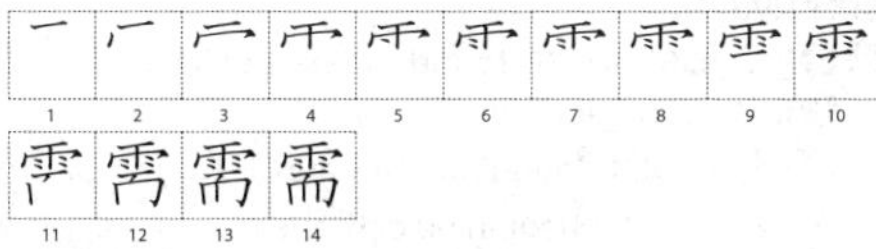

COMPOUNDS

ⓐ **DEMAND, needs, requirements**

ⓑ **need, require**

a 需給 じゅきゅう supply and demand

特需 とくじゅ emergency demand, special procurements

軍需品 ぐんじゅひん war supplies

実需 じつじゅ actual demand

民需 みんじゅ private demands, civilian requirements

外需 がいじゅ foreign demand

b 需要 じゅよう demand

必需品 ひつじゅひん necessaries, necessities

SYNONYMS

● **need and necessity**

要 required → 3263
必 must → 0015
須 MUST → 0700
需 DEMAND → 3472
入 necessary → 4177
用 needed for (a specific use) → 3694

蜚
3473
2-8-6

▸**FLY**

ヒ

Ⓒ 蜚 fēi fěi

142	Non-Jōyō	U871A
虫	S14-6-8	F0000

COMPOUNDS

❶ [now replaced by 飛 4389] **FLY; flying**

蜚鳥 ひちょう flying bird

蜚語 ひご false report, flying rumor
❷ [archaic] cockroach
SYNONYMS
❶ **fly**
飛 FLY → 4389
蜚 FLY → 3473
翔 SOAR → 1714
航 NAVIGATE → 1671

肇
3474
⬒2-8-6

▶**ORIGINATE**
チョウ ㊔ はつ はじめ はじむ とし けい ただし
Ⓝ 肇 Ⓒ 肇 zhào

129	Names	U8087
聿	S14-6-8	F2952

COMPOUNDS
❶ⓐ [rare] **ORIGINATE**, found, create, begin
ⓑ [archaic] beginning
a 肇国 ちょうこく founding of a state
b 肇歳 ちょうさい beginning of the year
❷ [archaic] make right, adjust
SYNONYMS
❶ⓐ **begin**
始 BEGIN → 0335
-出す begin to do → 4310
-掛ける start doing → 0596
発 START → 3174
起 start → 4099
就 SET ABOUT → 2129
開 OPEN → 4121
創 initiate → 2283
肇 ORIGINATE → 3474

肈
3475
⬒2-8-6

▶**ORIGINATE**
チョウ ㊔ はつ はじめ はじむ とし けい ただし

129	Nonstandard	U8087
聿	S14-6-8	F0000

traditional form → see 肇 at 3474

榮
3476
⬒2-8-6

▶**FLOURISH**
▶**GLORY**
エイ さか(える) は(え) -ば(え) は(える) え
㊔ ひで しげ しげる よし

75	Names	U69AE
木	S14-4-10	F0000

traditional form → see 栄 at 3183

聟
3477
⬒2-8-6

▶**SON-IN-LAW**
セイ むこ

128	Nonstandard	U805F
耳	S14-6-8	F0000

alternative form → see 婿 at 0689

製
3478
⬒2-8-6

▶**MANUFACTURE**
セイ
Ⓒ 制 zhì

145	Jōyō-5	U88FD
衣	S14-6-8	F0611

COMPOUNDS
❶ⓐ **MANUFACTURE, make, produce, fabricate; bind (books); refine (oil)**
ⓑ [also suffix] **indicates place or agent of MANUFACTURE**
a 製造業 せいぞうぎょう manufacturing industry
製作 せいさく manufacture, production
製品 せいひん manufactured goods [articles], product; refined petroleum products
製薬 せいやく pharmaceutical manufacture
製本 せいほん bookbinding
製図 せいず drafting, drawing
精製 せいせい refining; careful manufacture
特製の とくせいの specially made [manufactured]
手製の てせいの handmade
b 官製の かんせいの government manufactured
日本製の にほんせいの made in Japan
❷ [also suffix] indicates material composition
木製の もくせいの wooden, made of wood
金属製の きんぞくせいの made of metal
INDEPENDENT
【せいする 製する】**MANUFACTURE**, produce
SYNONYMS
❶ **make**
作 MAKE → 0077
造 MAKE → 3856
成 FORM → 4352
工 MANUFACTURE → 4190
製 MANUFACTURE → 3478
産 PRODUCE → 4089
調 PREPARE → 1973
組む ASSEMBLE → 1693
構 CONSTRUCT → 1325

USAGE

【せいさく】
製作
manufacture, production
制作
production (of a film), (literary) work

聚

▶COLLECT
シュウ ジュ
Ⓒ 聚 jù

3479
2-8-6

128	Non-Jōyō	U805A
耳	S14-6-8	F2631

COMPOUNDS

[now replaced by 集 3445]

❶ COLLECT, gather
聚散 しゅうさん collection and distribution
類聚 るいじゅ(=るいじゅう) collection of similar objects

❷ village, settlement
聚落 しゅうらく colony, community, village

SYNONYMS

❶ gather
集 COLLECT →3445
蒐 COLLECT →2942
聚 COLLECT →3479
収 collect →0031
採 GATHER →0606
采 GATHER →3077
萃 GATHER →2882
湊 come together →0743

舞

2-8-6
incorrect classification
➡ see 2-2-12: 𠂉 at 2661

蔑蔑

2-8-6
incorrect classification
➡ see 2-3-11: 艹 at 2969

緊

2-8-6
incorrect stroke-count
➡ see 2-9-6: 臤 at 3517

霊

▶SPIRIT
レイ リョウ たま
Ⓝ 靈 Ⓒ 灵 líng

3480
2-8-7

173	Jōyō	U970A
雨	S15-8-7	F1155

(stroke order diagram, strokes 1–15)

COMPOUNDS

❶ⓐ departed SPIRIT, ghost
ⓑ [also suffix] (supernatural being) SPIRIT, ghost
a 霊園 れいえん cemetery park
霊前に れいぜんに before the spirit of the departed
霊魂 れいこん spirit, soul
慰霊祭 いれいさい memorial service
幽霊 ゆうれい ghost, apparition
亡霊 ぼうれい departed spirit, ghost
英霊 えいれい spirit of the war dead
精霊 しょうりょう spirit of a dead person
b 神霊 しんれい divine spirit
悪霊 あくりょう evil spirit
聖霊 せいれい Holy Ghost, Holy Spirit
守護霊 しゅごれい guardian spirit

❷ (incorporeal part of man) SPIRIT, soul
霊長類 れいちょうるい Primates
霊的な れいてきな spiritual, incorporeal
心霊 しんれい spirit
全身全霊 ぜんしんぜんれい body and soul; one's best

❸ miraculous, sacred, divine
霊場 れいじょう holy ground, sacred place
霊峰 れいほう sacred mountain
霊験 れいげん(=れいけん) miracle, miraculous virtue
霊感 れいかん inspiration, extrasensory perception
霊水 れいすい miracle-working water
霊妙な れいみょうな miraculous, wonderful

INDEPENDENT

【れい 霊】SPIRIT, soul; departed spirit
霊と肉 れいとにく flesh and spirit
祖先の霊を祭る そせんのれいをまつる perform religious services for the departed souls of one's ancestors

KUN

【たま 霊】[also 魂] soul, SPIRIT, ghost
霊送り たまおくり sending off the spirits of the dead
御霊屋 みたまや mausoleum

SYNONYMS

❶ supernatural and evil beings
鬼 DEVIL →3291
魔 DEMON →3953
怪 monster →0354
霊 SPIRIT →3480
精 SPIRIT →1729

❷ psyche
心 HEART →0011
霊 SPIRIT (soul) →3480
魂 SOUL, spirit →1346
魄 SOUL →1570

腹 heart → 1308
衷 INNER HEART → 2600
襟 inner mind → 1599
胸 breast → 1187
懐 BOSOM → 0942
神 MIND → 1143
気 SPIRIT (consciousness) → 3960
精 SPIRIT (mind) → 1729

❸ **holy**
聖 HOLY → 3509
神 divine → 1143
霊 miraculous → 3480

HOMOPHONES

たま 魂 SOUL → 1346

NOTE

➡ see USAGE note at 魂 1346

震

▶QUAKE
シン ふる(う) ふる(える)
Ⓒ 震 zhèn

3481
2-8-7

173	Jōyō	U9707
雨	S15-8-7	F0822

COMPOUNDS

❶ⓐ **QUAKE, shake, vibrate**
ⓑ **QUAKE, earthquake, shock, tremor**

a 震動 しんどう shock, tremor, vibration
地震 じしん earthquake
b 震源 しんげん earthquake [seismic] center
震度 しんど seismic intensity
震災 しんさい earthquake disaster
弱震 じゃくしん weak earthquake, minor tremor

❷ **QUAKE** with (fear), tremble, shudder
震撼×させる しんかんさせる shake, shock
震駭×させる しんがいさせる terrify, frighten, shock

❸ fourth of the eight trigrams in the Book of Changes: east, thunder
震旦 しんたん ancient Indian name for China

KUN

【ふるう 震う】 **tremble, quiver, shudder**
震い ふるい trembling, shaking, shivering
身震い みぶるい shivering

【ふるえる 震える】 **tremble, quiver, shake, vibrate, shudder**
震え ふるえ trembling, shaking, shivering
震え声 ふるえごえ trembling voice
震え上がる ふるえあがる tremble violently, shudder

SYNONYMS

❶ⓐ **shake**
振 SWING → 0515
震 QUAKE → 3481
揺 SHAKE → 0723

HOMOPHONES

ふるう
振 SWING → 0515
奮 ROUSE UP → 3000
揮 WIELD → 0717

NOTE

➡ see USAGE note at 振 0515

輩

▶FELLOW
ハイ -ばら▲ やから▲
Ⓒ 辈 bèi

3482
2-8-7

159	Jōyō	U8F29
車	S15-7-8	F1279

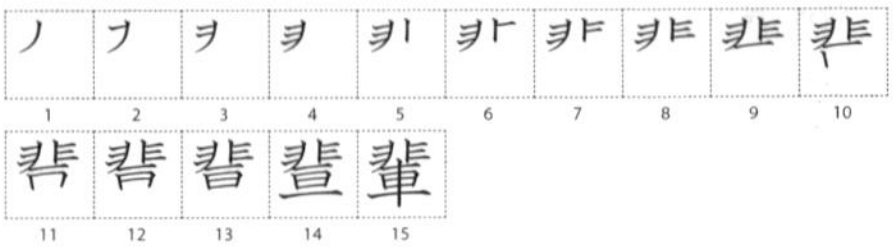

COMPOUNDS

❶ⓐ **FELLOW(s), companion, comrade**
ⓑ [also suffix] [belittling] **FELLOW, guy**

a 先輩 せんぱい senior, superior, elder
後輩 こうはい one's junior, younger generation, peer
同輩 どうはい fellow, comrade, colleague
朋輩 ほうばい comrade, friend, associate
若輩 じゃくはい young people; greenhorn
b 鼠輩 そはい insignificant fellow, small fry
徒輩 とはい set, company, fellows
我が輩(=吾輩) わがはい I
中野輩 なかのはい the likes of Nakano

❷ plural suffix
青年輩 せいねんはい young people

❸ [original meaning] successively
輩出する はいしゅつする appear successively

INDEPENDENT

【はい 輩】 *literary* **FELLOW**, people

KUN

【-ばら -輩】 [belittling] plural suffix
奴輩 やつばら fellows, guys

【やから 輩】 [belittling] **FELLOW**s, guys; family; kinsmen

SYNONYMS

❶ⓐ **friends and associates**

僚 COLLEAGUE → 0186
輩 FELLOW → 3482
朋 COMRADE → 1092
友 FRIEND → 3670
侶 COMPANION → 0114
ⓑ fellow
奴 GUY → 0217
漢 FELLOW → 0808
輩 FELLOW (*belittling*) → 3482
徒 fellows → 0499
棒 tough guy → 1237
坊 COLLOQUIAL PERSON SUFFIX → 0274
屋 colloquial person suffix → 3842
物 character → 1084

質

▸QUALITY
▸MATTER

シツ　シチ　チ　たち▲　ただ(す)▲　㊔ ただ

3483

Ⓝ 貭◆　Ⓒ 质 zhì

2-8-7

154	Jōyō-5	U8CEA
貝	S15-7-8	F0352

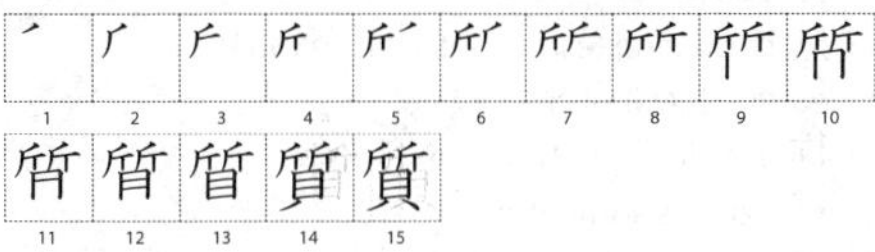

COMPOUNDS

❶ⓐ [also suffix] (natural attribute) **QUALITY, nature, character, property, temperament, disposition**
ⓑ (degree of excellence) **QUALITY, grade**
a 本質 ほんしつ essence, reality
性質 せいしつ nature, temperament, character; (characteristic) property, quality
体質 たいしつ physical constitution
素質 そしつ character, nature, makings, constitution
実質 じっしつ substance, essence
特質 とくしつ characteristic, property, quality
神経質 しんけいしつ nervous temperament
b 品質 ひんしつ quality
悪質な あくしつな bad, malicious; malignant
音質 おんしつ sound [tone] quality

❷ⓐ MATTER, substance, material
ⓑ [suffix] (specific substance or constituent) **MATTER**
a 質量 しつりょう *phys* mass; quality and quantity
物質 ぶっしつ matter, substance
b 植物質 しょくぶつしつ vegetable matter
蛋×白質 たんぱくしつ protein, albuminous substance

❸ query, question, verify, confront
質問 しつもん question
質疑 しつぎ question, interrogation
対質する たいしつする confront, cross-examine

❹ⓐ (thing serving as security) **pawn, pledge**
ⓑ (person serving as security) **pawn, hostage**
a 質屋 しちや pawnshop
質草 しちぐさ article for pawning
質入れ しちいれ pawning
b 言質 げんち pledge, promise
人質 ひとじち hostage, prisoner

❺ simple, unadorned
質素 しっそ simplicity, modesty, frugality
質実 しつじつ plainness, simplicity

INDEPENDENT

【しつ 質】**QUALITY; nature, disposition;** *logic* (positive or negative character of a proposition) **quality**
質を良くする しつをよくする improve the quality
量より質だ りょうよりしつだ Quality matters more than quantity

【しち 質】**pawn, pledge**
質に入れる しちにいれる pawn, pledge

KUN

【たち 質】**QUALITY**, nature, character, disposition, inclination
質の良い たちのよい of good quality

【ただす 質す】
ⓐ query, question, consult, inquire
ⓑ ascertain, verify
a 専門家に質す せんもんかにただす consult an expert
b 子細を質す しさいをただす verify details

SYNONYMS

❶ nature and character
性 NATURE → 0357
気 temperament → 3960
質 QUALITY → 3483
品 grade of excellence → 2795
柄 CHARACTER → 1111
格 (good) character → 1161

❷ matter
質 MATTER → 3483
物 substance → 1084
材 MATERIAL → 1031
料 MATERIALS → 1644
資 material resources → 3342

❸ inquire
問 QUESTION → 4117
詰 question closely → 1920
聞く ask → 4127
質 query → 3483
尋ねる INQUIRE → 2918
訊 INQUIRE → 1842
伺う INQUIRE (*humble*) → 0078

諮 CONSULT →2009
詢 ASK FOR ADVICE →1917

❹ⓐ **pawn**
質 pawn →3483
当 pawn →2701

HOMOPHONES

ただす
正 RIGHT →4296
糾 INQUIRE INTO →1631

NOTE

➡ see USAGE note at 正 4296

賛

▸APPROVE OF
▸PRAISE
サン

3484
Ⓝ 贊 Ⓒ 赞 zàn
2-8-7

154	Jōyō-5	U8CDB
貝	S15-7-8	F1378

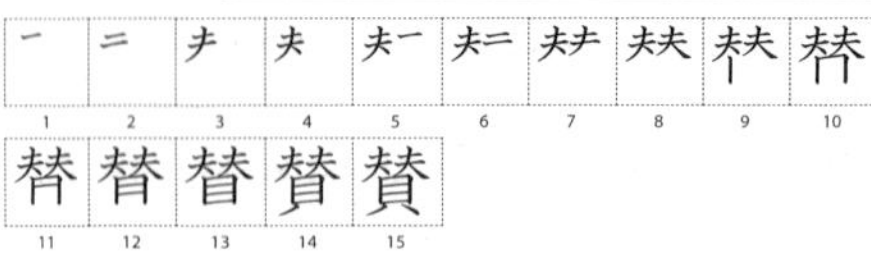

COMPOUNDS

❶ⓐ **APPROVE OF, agree with**
ⓑ **back up, give support, assist, help**

a 賛成 さんせい approval, agreement, support
賛否 さんぴ approval or disapproval; yes or no
賛意 さんい approval
賛同 さんどう approval, endorsement
b 賛助 さんじょ backing, support, approval
協賛 きょうさん support, cooperation
翼賛 よくさん support, countenance, assistance

❷ [formerly also 讃 2093] **PRAISE, laud, admire, commend**
賛辞 さんじ eulogy, praise, compliment
賛美 さんび praise, admiration
賛嘆 さんたん praise, admiration
賞賛(=称賛)する しょうさんする laud, praise, admire, commend
絶賛 ぜっさん great admiration
礼賛 らいさん worship, adoration, glorification

❸ [formerly also 讃 2093] legend or inscription on a picture
画賛 がさん legend [writing] on a picture
自画自賛 じがじさん painting with the eulogy written in by the artist himself; self-praise

INDEPENDENT

【さん 賛(=讃)】 legend or inscription on a picture; a style of Chinese poetry
画に賛をする えにさんをする write a legend on a picture

SYNONYMS

❶ⓐ **agree and approve**
賛 APPROVE OF →3484
可 APPROVE →3687
認 RECOGNIZE →1948
諾 CONSENT →1974
承 AGREE TO →0016
肯 ASSENT →3072
容 tolerate →2832

ⓑ **support**
支 SUPPORT →2473
擁 SUPPORT →0949
扶 LEND SUPPORT TO →0291
賛 back up →3484

❷ **praise**
賛 PRAISE →3484
頌 EULOGIZE →1319
謳 EXTOL →2061
讃 PRAISE →2093
美 regard as beautiful →2817
褒 COMMEND →2662
嘉 commend (esp. an inferior) →2953
彰 PROCLAIM MERITS →2337
称 acclaim →1491
賞 express admiration →3237
揚 EXALT →0722

慧

▸INTELLIGENT
ケイ エ ㊔ さとし さと さとる とし えい あきら めぐみ

3485
Ⓝ 慧 Ⓒ 慧 huì
2-8-7

61	Names	U6167
心	S15-4-11	F2637

COMPOUNDS

❶ⓐ [original meaning] **INTELLIGENT, wise, bright, clever, cunning**
ⓑ [now replaced by 恵 え 3293] **intelligence, wisdom**

a 慧眼 けいがん discerning [quick] eye, keen insight
慧敏な けいびんな [rare] clever, of quick intellect
b 智慧(=知恵) ちえ wisdom, intelligence, sagacity

❷ *Buddhism* prajna, transcendental wisdom—often used in the names of Buddhist priests
慧遠 えおん Hui-Yuan (Chinese priest of the Jin Dynasty)

INDEPENDENT

【え 慧】 *Buddhism* transcendental wisdom, prajna

SYNONYMS

❶ⓐ **intelligent and wise**
賢 WISE →3518
俊 brilliant →0117

鋭 SHARP →2171
敏 NIMBLE →1675
叡 PROFOUNDLY WISE →2405
智 wise →3458
慧 INTELLIGENT →3485
怜 CLEVER →0356
悧 CLEVER →0505
俐 CLEVER →0113
哲 SAGACIOUS →3402
明 clear-sighted →1060
聡 SHARP-WITTED →1750

❷ **wisdom**

識 KNOWLEDGE →2070
知 knowledge →1446
智 WISDOM →3458
慧 prajna (transcendental wisdom) →3485
哲 PHILOSOPHY →3402

NOTE

★ do not confuse with 彗 COMET →3439

慧

3486

2-8-7

▶**INTELLIGENT**

ケイ エ ㊔ さとし さと さとる とし えい あきら めぐみ

61	Nonstandard	U6167
心	S15-4-11	F0000

traditional form →see 慧 at 3485

黎

3487

2-8-7

▶**BLACK**

レイ ライ リ

Ⓒ 黎 lí

202	Names	U9ECE
黍	S15-12-3	F2590

COMPOUNDS

❶ **BLACK, dark**

黎明 れいめい dawn, daybreak, beginning (of a new age)

❷ [rare] many, various, all

黎元 れいげん the (common) people, the masses

SYNONYMS

❶ **black colors**

黒 BLACK →3406
漆 pitch-black →0863
黎 BLACK →3487

憂

2-8-7

incorrect classification
➡ see 2-2-13: 亠 at 2664

舞

2-8-7

incorrect classification
➡ see 2-2-13: 𠂉 at 2666

養

2-8-7

incorrect classification
➡ see 2-3-12: 䒑 at 2998

暴

2-8-7

incorrect classification
➡ see 2-4-11: 日 at 3138

墨

3488

2-8-7

▶**INDIA INK**

ボク すみ

32	Names	UFA3A
土	S15-3-12	F0000

traditional form →see 墨 at 3423

賢

2-8-7

incorrect stroke-count
➡ see 2-9-7: 臤 at 3518

豎

2-8-7

incorrect stroke-count
➡ see 2-9-7: 臤 at 3519

螢

3489

2-8-8

▶**FIREFLY**

ケイ ほたる

142	Nonstandard	U87A2
虫	S16-6-10	F0000

traditional form →see 蛍 at 3204

篭 簑

2-8-8

incorrect classification
➡ see 2-6-10: ⺮ at 3370

霞

3490

2-8-9

▶**MIST**

カ かすみ かす(む)

Ⓒ 霞 xiá

173	Names	U971E
雨	S17-8-9	F2107

COMPOUNDS

❶ **MIST, haze**

煙霞 えんか mist [haze] and smoke; beauties of nature
雲霞の如く うんかのごとく in swarms
朝霞 ちょうか morning mist [haze]; [archaic] morning glow

❷ [original meaning, now archaic] morning or evening glow

KUN

【かすみ 霞】**MIST, haze; dimness of sight, mist; Japanese mist net**

霞を食う かすみをくう live on air
霞ケ関 かすみがせき Japanese Foreign Ministry
春霞 はるがすみ spring haze

【かすむ 霞む】

ⓐ **haze, be hazy, MIST**
ⓑ [formerly 翳む] **have dim sight**
a 遠くに霞む とおくにかすむ loom in the distance
b 年で霞んだ目 としでかすんだめ eyes dimmed with age

SYNONYMS

❶ **kinds of atmospheric vapor**
霧 FOG → 3493
霞 MIST → 3490
雲 CLOUD → 3447

USAGE

【かすむ】
霞む
ⓐ haze, be hazy, mist
ⓑ [formerly 翳む] have dim sight
翳む
[now usu. 霞む] have dim sight

HOMOPHONES

かすむ 翳 SHADOW → 3567

COMPOUND FORMATION

【霞ケ関 かすみがせき】
霞ケ関 'Japanese Foreign Ministry' is so called because it is located in Kasumigaseki, Tokyo.

霜

3491
2-8-9

▶**FROST**
ソウ しも
Ⓒ 霜 shuāng

173	Jōyō	U971C
雨	S17-8-9	F2482

COMPOUNDS

❶ [original meaning] **FROST, hoarfrost**
霜害 そうがい frost damage
霜雪 そうせつ frost and snow
降霜 こうそう (fall of) frost
❷ years, time
星霜 せいそう years, time

KUN

【しも 霜】**FROST, hoarfrost**
霜柱 しもばしら frost columns
霜焼け しもやけ frostbite, chilblains
霜降り しもふり pepper-and-salt; marbled meat
遅霜 おそじも late frosting

SYNONYMS

❶ **kinds of precipitation**
雨 RAIN → 4378
露 DEW → 3495
霜 FROST → 3491
雪 SNOW → 3431

營

3492
2-8-9

▶**MANAGE**
▶**BARRACKS**
エイ いとな(む)

86	Nonstandard	U71DF
火	S17-4-13	F0000

traditional form → see 営 at 3216

簑

2-8-9

incorrect classification
➡ see 2-6-11: ⺮ at 3378

霧

3493
2-8-11

▶**FOG**
ム きり
Ⓒ 雾 wù

173	Jōyō	U9727
雨	S19-8-11	F1559

COMPOUNDS

❶ [original meaning] **FOG, mist**
霧笛 むてき foghorn
霧氷 むひょう rime, hoarfrost, silver frost
濃霧 のうむ dense [thick] fog
煙霧 えんむ smog
雲散霧消する うんさんむしょうする scatter and vanish, vanish like mist
❷ spray
噴霧器 ふんむき sprayer, vaporizer, atomizer

KUN

【きり 霧】**FOG, mist; spray**
霧雨 きりさめ(=きりあめ) drizzle, misting rain
霧吹き きりふき sprayer, atomizer
夜霧 よぎり night fog [mist]

SYNONYMS

❶ **kinds of atmospheric vapor**
霧 FOG → 3493
霞 MIST → 3490
雲 CLOUD → 3447

麓

3494
2-8-11

▶**FOOT OF MOUNTAIN**
ロク ふもと
Ⓒ 麓 lù

198	Jōyō	U9E93
鹿	S19-11-8	F2153

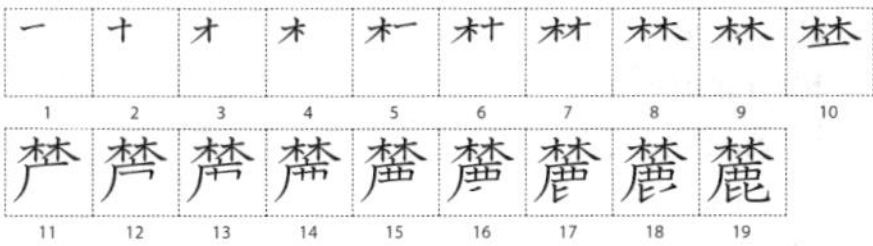

COMPOUNDS

● FOOT [base] OF a MOUNTAIN

山麓 さんろく foot [base] of a mountain
岳麓 がくろく foot of Mt. Fuji

KUN

【ふもと 麓】 **FOOT [base] OF a MOUNTAIN**

SYNONYMS

● **bottoms and bases**

底 BOTTOM → 3827
柢 BOTTOM → 1121
下 lower part → 4186
基 BASE → 3312
礎 FOUNDATION STONE → 1595
麓 FOOT OF MOUNTAIN → 3494
磐 BEDROCK → 3534
盤 bedrock → 3533
床 BED → 3805

麗 2-8-11

incorrect classification
➡ see 2-2-17: 一 at 2672

霸 2-8-12

incorrect stroke-count
➡ see 2-8-13: 雨 at 3496

露 3495

2-8-13

▶**DEW**
▶**EXPOSE**
ロ ロウ つゆ

Ⓒ 露 lù lòu

173	Jōyō	U9732
雨	S21-8-13	F0947

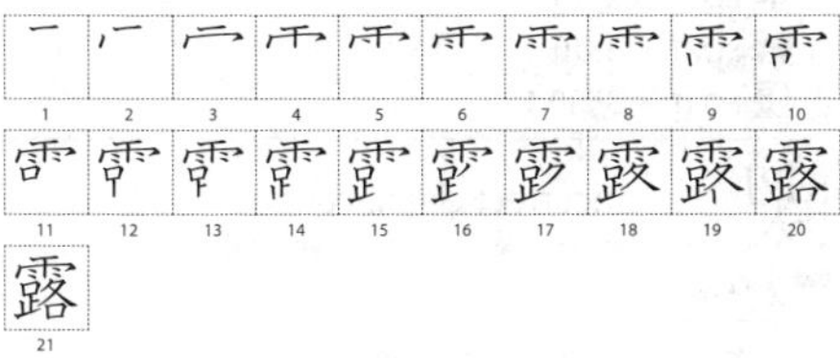

COMPOUNDS

❶ⓐ [original meaning] **DEW, dewdrop**
ⓑ as evanescent as the **DEW**, transient

a 露滴 ろてき dewdrop
露点 ろてん dew point
雨露 うろ rain and dew
b 露命 ろめい transient life

❷ⓐ **EXPOSE, bare to view, disclose**
ⓑ **EXPOSEd, uncovered, open**

a 露出 ろしゅつ exposure, disclosure; (photographic) exposure
露呈 ろてい exposure, disclosure
露顕(=露見) ろけん discovery, detection, exposure
b 露骨な ろこつな candid, plainspoken; indecent
露天 ろてん open air, the open
露店 ろてん roadside stand
披露 ひろう announcement; introduction
お披露目(=お広め) おひろめ début
暴露 ばくろ exposure, disclosure

❸ⓐ [sometimes also 魯 2665] Russia
ⓑ Russian (language)

a 露帝 ろてい Czar, Russian emperor
日露戦争 にちろせんそう Russo-Japanese war (of 1904-05)
b 露語 ろご Russian (language)

INDEPENDENT

【ろ 露】 Russia

KUN

【つゆ 露】 **DEW, dewdrop; tears; evanescence, frailty;** [in negative constructions] **(not) in the least, (not) at all**

露に濡れた つゆにぬれた dewy, wet with dew
露払い つゆはらい herald; heralding, ushering
露の命 つゆのいのち life as evanescent as the dew
露知らず つゆしらず not knowing at all
夜露 よつゆ evening dew
袖の露 そでのつゆ tears falling onto the sleeve

SYNONYMS

❶ⓐ **kinds of precipitation**

雨 RAIN → 4378
露 DEW → 3495
霜 FROST → 3491
雪 SNOW → 3431

❷ⓐ **reveal**

発 reveal → 3174
露 EXPOSE → 3495
曝 EXPOSE → 1410
晒す EXPOSE → 1156
暴 disclose → 3138
披 OPEN OUT → 0362
顕 MANIFEST → 2274
現 cause to appear → 1218

❸ⓐ **European countries**

英 ENGLAND → 2782
独 GERMANY → 0471
仏 FRANCE → 0020
伊 ITALY → 0052
葡 PORTUGAL → 2902
西 Spain → 4333
蘭 the Netherlands → 3031

希 Greece → 2543
露 Russia → 3495
白 Belgium → 4305

【雨】

霸 ▶SUPREMACY
ハ

3496
2-8-13

173	Nonstandard	U9738
雨	S21-8-13	F0000

traditional form → see 覇 at 3392

靈 ▶SPIRIT
レイ リョウ たま

3497
2-8-16

173	Nonstandard	U9748
雨	S24-8-16	F0000

traditional form → see 霊 at 3480

蠶 ▶SILKWORM
サン かいこ こ

3498
2-8-16

142	Nonstandard	U8695
虫	S24-6-18	F0000

alternative form → see 蚕 at 3107

兜 ▶HEADPIECE
ト トウ かぶと
N 兠 C 兜 dōu

3499
2-9-2

10	Names	U515C
儿	S11-2-9	F2577

COMPOUNDS

❶ **HEADPIECE, headgear**
兜巾(=頭巾、頭襟) ときん headgear worn by mountain ascetics

❷ used phonetically for *to,* esp. in the transliteration of Sanskrit Buddhist terms
兜率天 とそつてん *Buddhism Tuṣita* Heaven

KUN

【かぶと 兜】 **helmet (of armor), HEADPIECE**
兜虫 かぶとむし rhinoceros beetle, esp. Japanese rhinoceros beetle
兜蟹 かぶとがに horseshoe crab
鉄兜 てつかぶと steel helmet
鳥兜 とりかぶと aconite, wolfsbane, monkshood; hat used in *bugaku* dance

SYNONYMS

❶ **headgear**
帽 HEADGEAR → 0693
冠 CROWN → 2583
笠 SEDGE HAT → 3300
兜 HEADPIECE → 3499

【かぶと】
○ **protective coverings**
盾 SHIELD → 3729
楯 SHIELD → 1281
鎧 ARMOR → 2211
甲 armor → 4293
縅 BRAID OF ARMOR → 1759
面 mask → 2590
兜 helmet → 3499
幌 COVERING FOR VEHICLES → 0787

率
2-9-2
incorrect classification
➡ see 2-2-9: 亠 at 2625

黄
2-9-2
incorrect classification
➡ see 2-4-7: 艹 at 3116

異
2-9-2
incorrect classification
➡ see 2-5-6: 田 at 3195

堡 ▶FORT
ホ ホウ
C 堡 bǎo bǔ pù

3500
2-9-3

32	Non-Jōyō	U5821
土	S12-3-9	F2930

COMPOUNDS

● [now also 保 0107] **FORT**
堡塁 ほうるい(=ほるい) fort, fortress, stronghold
堡礁 ほしょう barrier reef
海堡 かいほう coast battery; breakwater
橋頭堡 きょうとうほ bridgehead, beachhead

SYNONYMS

● **strongholds**
城 CASTLE → 0417
塁 SMALL FORT → 3206
塞 FORT → 2924
砦 FORT → 3310
堡 FORT → 3500

喫
2-9-3
incorrect classification
➡ see 1-3-9: 口 at 0668

堕 ▶DEGENERATE
ダ
N 墮 C 堕 duò

3501
2-9-3

32	Jōyō	U5815
土	S12-3-9	F2237

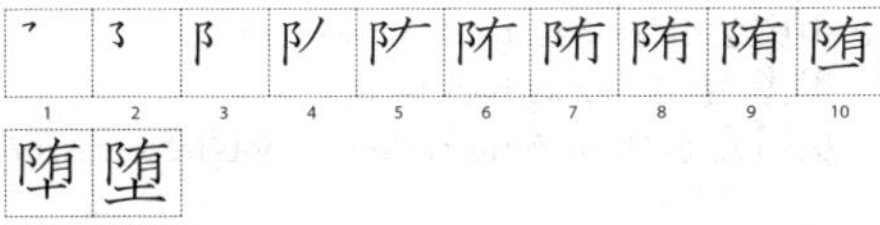

COMPOUNDS

❶ **DEGENERATE, become degraded into, sink into evil ways, descend to**

堕落 だらく degeneration, corruption, decadence
堕罪 ざい sinking into sin

❷ cause to fall, drop, abort

堕胎 だたい abortion

INDEPENDENT

【だする 堕する】descend to, lapse into, become degraded into

SYNONYMS

❶ **degenerate**

落 FALL → 2907
衰 DECLINE → 2604
頽 DECLINE → 2039
堕 DEGENERATE → 3501
綻 UNRAVEL → 1745
破 break down → 1478

堅

3502

2-9-3

▸FIRM

ケン かた(い) -がた(い) ㊔ かたし

Ⓒ 坚 jiān

32	Jōyō	U5805
土	S12-3-9	F1513

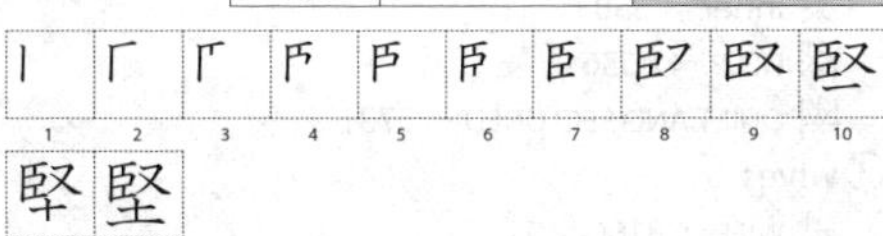

COMPOUNDS

❶ [original meaning] (resisting deformation) **FIRM, hard, solid, sturdy**

堅材 けんざい hard wood
堅牢×な けんろうな solid, durable, fast
堅果 けんか nut (hard fruit)

❷ⓐ (of a person's character) **FIRM, steadfast, trustworthy**

ⓑ (unfluctuating) **FIRM, steady, stable**

ⓒ **FIRM**ly, resolutely

a 堅固な けんごな strong, secure, firm, steadfast
堅実な けんじつな steady, sound, reliable
堅志 けんし iron purpose
中堅 ちゅうけん the mainstay, nucleus (of a company)

b 堅調 けんちょう bullish, firm (market)

c 堅持する けんじする maintain firmly, hold fast to

❸ strong (defenses), secure, **FIRM**

堅守 けんしゅ strong defense
堅陣 けんじん stronghold

INDEPENDENT

【けん 堅】**FIRM**ness, hardness

敵の堅を破る てきのけんをやぶる break the strong defenses of the enemy

KUN

【かたい 堅い, -がたい -堅い】

① (resisting deformation) **FIRM, hard (lumber)**

堅さ かたさ firmness, hardness; steadiness, honesty
堅い材木 かたいざいもく hard lumber
堅パン かたぱん hardtack, hard biscuits

② **steady (market or business), sound (investment)**

堅い商売 かたいしょうばい sound business
底堅い そこがたい steady undertone (of the market)
手堅い てがたい steady (market); safe; trustworthy

③ⓐ steadfast, reliable, trustworthy

ⓑ honest, honorable, upright, serious, chaste

a 堅気な かたぎな honest, respectable
堅人 かたじん trustworthy person

b 堅い女 かたいおんな chaste woman

④ **stiff, formal, bookish**

堅苦しい かたくるしい formal, stiff-mannered
堅物 かたぶつ straight-laced person
堅い言葉 かたいことば stiff speech

SYNONYMS

❶ **hard**

硬 HARD → 1518
堅 FIRM → 3502
鞏 TOUGH → 3369
固 SOLID → 3830
剛 TOUGH → 2107
強 STRONG → 0574
勁 STRONG → 1833

❷ **firm and obstinate**

堅 FIRM → 3502
固 FIRM, stiff → 3830
確 firm → 1571
毅 RESOLUTE → 2341
剛 TOUGH → 2107
頑 STUBBORN → 1315
硬 hard-line → 1518

HOMOPHONES

かたい

固 SOLID → 3830
硬 HARD → 1518
難 DIFFICULT → 2310

NOTE

➡ see USAGE note at 固 3830

善
incorrect classification
➡ see 2-3-9: 䒑 at 2921
2-9-3

尊
incorrect classification
➡ see 2-3-9: 䒑 at 2920
2-9-3

葬
incorrect classification
➡ see 2-3-9: 艹 at 2910
2-9-3

堯
incorrect classification
➡ see 2-3-9: 土 at 2888
2-9-3

奥 3503

▶**INNER PART**
オウ オク▲ おく
Ⓝ 奧 Ⓒ 奥 ào

2-9-3

37	Jōyō	U5965
大	S12-3-9	F0452

Stroke order: 1–12

COMPOUNDS

❶ⓐ inmost, mysterious, deep, profound
ⓑ inmost part, innermost, mystery, inner depths

a 奥義 おうぎ(=おくぎ) secret principles, secrets, hidden mysteries
胸奥 きょうおう one's heart of hearts, the depths of one's mind
b 深奥 しんおう esoteric doctrines, mysteries, depth
内奥 ないおう inner part, depths, recesses

❷ old name for Tohoku district
奥州 おうしゅう old name for Tohoku district

KUN

【おく 奥】

①ⓐ **INNER PART, interior, the back, the heart, the depths, the recesses**
ⓑ [also prefix] **the interior (of a country), inland, back country**
ⓒ **interior room, inner chamber, parlor**
ⓓ [in compounds] **inner, interior**

a 奥まる おくまる extend far back, lie deep in
奥行き おくゆき depth, length
山奥 やまおく deep in the mountains, in the recesses of a mountain
森の奥 もりのおく deep in the forest
b 奥地 おくち interior, hinterland, backwoods
c 奥の間 おくのま back room
大奥 おおおく inner palace; place where shogun's wife resided
d 奥庭 おくにわ inner garden, backyard
奥歯 おくば molars, back teeth
奥日光 おくにっこう the secluded spots [recesses] of Nikko
奥座敷 おくざしき inner room [chamber]

② **INNER**most **PART**, mystery, inner depths
奥床しい おくゆかしい refined, graceful, modest
奥の手 おくのて last resort; secrets
心の奥 こころのおく inner heart

③ (from the idea that the wife of a nobleman lives in the inner chambers) **wife**
奥さん おくさん married lady, Mrs.; your wife
奥様 おくさま married lady, Mrs.; your wife
奥方 おくがた wife of a nobleman

SYNONYMS

❶ **profound**
玄 PROFOUND → 2485
幽 deep hidden → 3731
奥 inmost → 3503
深 DEEP → 0636
滉 DEEP AND VAST → 0811

【おく】

①ⓐ **inside**
内 INSIDE → 4277
裏 inside → 2652
奥 INNER PART → 3503
中 IN → 4262

ⓓ **inner**
奥 inner → 3503
深 DEEP → 0636
幽 QUIET AND SECLUDED → 3731

③ **wives**
妻 WIFE → 3166
奥 wife → 3503
内 wife → 4277
室 wife (esp. of persons of rank) → 2802
嫡 legitimate wife → 0839
婦 married woman → 0565
嫁 BRIDE → 0780
寡 widow → 2957

NOTE

★ The reading おく is both the *on* and *kun* reading of 奥, but as an *on* reading it is not in the Jōyō Kanji list. When read おく, 奥 forms compounds in the *kun* reading.

喪 3504

▶**MOURNING**
ソウ も
Ⓒ 丧 sāng sàng

2-9-3

30	Jōyō	U55AA
口	S12-3-9	F1847

COMPOUNDS

❶ [original meaning, now rare] **MOURNING**
喪家 そうか family in mourning
大喪 たいそう Imperial mourning

❷ **lose, be deprived of**
喪失 そうしつ loss, forfeit
喪神する そうしんする lose consciousness
阻喪(=沮喪) そそう loss of spirit, dejection

KUN

【も 喪】**MOURNING**
喪服 もふく mourning dress
喪主 もしゅ chief mourner
喪中 もちゅう in mourning
服喪 ふくも mourning

SYNONYMS

❶ **mourn and mourning**
弔 CONDOLE →4240
悼 MOURN →0587
喪 MOURNING →3504
忌 MOURNING →2735

❷ **losing and loss**
失 LOSE →4325
喪 lose →3504
逸 LET SLIP →3872
損 LOSS, lose →0801
佚 LOST →0070

惡 incorrect stroke-count
➡ see 2-8-4: 亞 at 3463
2-9-4

楽 3505

2-9-4

▶**PLEASURE**
▶**COMFORTABLE**
▶**MUSIC**

ガク ラク たの(しい) たの(しむ)

Ⓝ 樂 Ⓒ 乐 lè yuè

75	Jōyō-2	U697D
木	S13-4-9	F0266

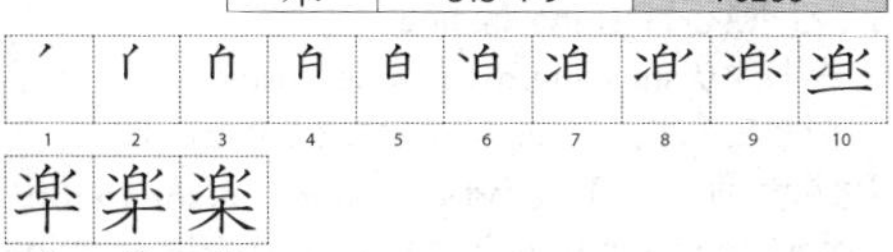

COMPOUNDS

❶ⓐ **PLEASURE, joy**
ⓑ **pleasurable, pleasant, merry**
a 享楽 きょうらく enjoyment
快楽 かいらく pleasure, enjoyment
娯楽 ごらく amusement, pastime
行楽 こうらく excursion, outing, holidaymaking
b 楽園 らくえん paradise

❷ **COMFORTABLE, easy**
楽観する らっかんする be optimistic, take a hopeful view
楽観的な らっかんてきな optimistic
楽隠居 らくいんきょ comfortable life in retirement
楽楽と らくらくと comfortably; very easily
楽勝 らくしょう easy victory, walkaway
楽天的 らくてんてき optimistic
安楽な あんらくな comfortable, carefree, cozy

❸ⓐ [also suffix] **MUSIC, musical composition**
ⓑ suffix after names of Japanese court **MUSIC** compositions
ⓒ play **MUSIC** compositions
a 楽譜 がくふ (sheet of) music, musical score
楽器 がっき musical instrument
音楽 おんがく music
邦楽 ほうがく Japanese music
b 越天楽 えてんらく Etenraku (name of a Japanese court music composition)
c 吹奏楽 すいそうがく wind instrument music

❹ end of public performance
千秋楽の日 せんしゅうらくのひ closing day of a show

❺ hand-molded earthenware
楽焼き らくやき hand-molded pottery

❻ unclassified compounds
文楽 ぶんらく Japanese puppet show, *bunraku*

INDEPENDENT

【らく 楽】**comfort, ease; relief; closing day (of a public performance); hand-molded pottery**
楽な らくな easy, light; comfortable
楽に暮らす らくにくらす live in comfort

【がく 楽】**MUSIC**
楽を奏する がくをそうする play music

KUN

【たのしい 楽しい】[sometimes also 愉しい] **pleasurable, pleasant, enjoyable, merry**
楽しさ たのしさ pleasure, joy; pleasantness
楽しい思い出 たのしいおもいで happy [sweet] memory

【たのしむ 楽しむ】[sometimes also 愉しむ] **take PLEASURE in, enjoy (oneself)**
楽しみ たのしみ pleasure, enjoyment; amusement, diversion, hobby; expectation
映画を楽しむ えいがをたのしむ enjoy a movie

SPECIAL READINGS

神楽 かぐら sacred (Shinto) music and dancing

独楽▲ こま top

SYNONYMS

❶ⓐ **pleasure**
楽 PLEASURE → 3505
娯 ENJOYMENT → 0487
興 AMUSEMENT → 3622
玩 TAKE PLEASURE IN → 1085
ⓑ **pleased and pleasant**
楽 pleasurable → 3505
欣 JOYFUL → 1057
爽 REFRESHING → 4402
快 PLEASANT → 0289
朗 CHEERFUL → 1679
愉 PLEASED → 0710
悦 DELIGHTED → 0501
嬉しい GLAD → 0890
喜 HAPPY → 2889
歓 JOYOUS → 2342
驩 JOYOUS → 2333

❷ **comfortable**
楽 COMFORTABLE → 3505
安 easy (without effort) → 2695

❸ⓐ & ❸ⓑ **music and songs**
楽 MUSIC → 3505
音 sound of music → 2570
節 tune → 3336
調べ melody → 1973
曲 MUSICAL COMPOSITION → 4340
歌 SONG → 2296
謡 POPULAR SONG → 2011
唄 DITTY → 0477

USAGE

❶【たのしい】
楽しい
[sometimes also 愉しい] pleasurable, pleasant, enjoyable, merry
愉しい
[usu. 楽しい] same as 楽しい

❷【たのしむ】
楽しむ
[sometimes also 愉しむ] take pleasure in, enjoy (oneself)
愉しむ
[usu. 楽しむ] same as 楽しむ

❸【たのしみ】
楽しみ
① [sometimes also 愉しみ]
ⓐ pleasure, enjoyment
ⓑ amusement, diversion, hobby
② expectation
愉しみ
[usu. 楽しみ]
ⓐ pleasure, enjoyment
ⓑ amusement, diversion, hobby

HOMOPHONES

たのしい 愉 PLEASED → 0710
たのしむ 愉 PLEASED → 0710
たのしみ 愉 PLEASED → 0710

COMPOUND FORMATION

【文楽 ぶんらく】
The word 文楽 'Japanese puppet show, *bunraku*' originates from the name of its founder, 植村文楽軒 うえむらぶんらくけん.

照

3506

2-9-4

▸**ILLUMINATE**

ショウ て(る) て(らす) て(れる)

Ⓒ 照 zhào

86	Jōyō-4	U7167
灬	S13-4-9	F0889

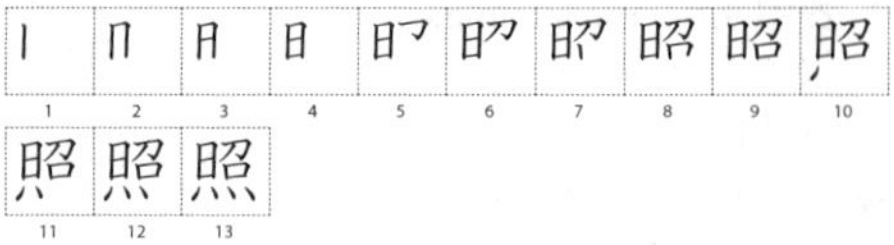

COMPOUNDS

❶ [original meaning] **ILLUMINATE, shine, reflect**
照明 しょうめい illumination, lighting
照射 しょうしゃ irradiation
照度 しょうど intensity of illumination
日照権 にっしょうけん right to sunshine

❷ sunlight, light
返照 へんしょう reflection of light [sunlight]
晩照 ばんしょう sunset, setting sun

❸ **check (one thing) against (another), collate, examine by comparison, refer**
照査する しょうさする check against [up], examine by reference, verify
照合する しょうごうする verify, compare, collate
照会する しょうかいする inquire, apply for information
対照 たいしょう contrast, comparison; control

❹ picture
照映 しょうえい portrait

KUN

【てる 照る】*vi* **shine; be fine**
照り てり sunshine; dry weather; luster
降っても照っても ふってもてっても rain or shine

【てらす 照らす】**ILLUMINATE, shine on, shed light; check (one thing) against another, collate, examine by comparison, refer**
照らし合わせる てらしあわせる check by comparison, collate, verify
事実に照らして じじつにてらして in view of the facts

亞 凶 昭 相 【秋】 耶 取 兹 前 者 禺 咸 配

【てれる 照れる】**feel shy, be abashed; feel awkward, become self-conscious, be ill at ease**
照れ臭い てれくさい embarrassed

SYNONYMS

❶ **shine and reflect**
輝 SHINE BRILLIANTLY → 1775
光 shine → 3043
照 ILLUMINATE → 3506
映 REFLECT → 1104
耀 SHINE BRILLIANTLY → 1812
燿 SHINE → 1407
閃 FLASH → 4114
煌 GLITTER → 1296

❷ **light**
光 LIGHT → 3043
明 light → 1060
灯 LAMP → 1019
燭 CANDLE → 1391
照 sunlight → 3506
虹 RAINBOW → 1637

❸ **compare**
比 COMPARE → 0029
較 COMPARE → 1939
譬 COMPARE TO → 3613
校 COLLATE → 1166
照 check against → 3506
対 OPPOSE (contrast) → 1025
参 refer → 2563

想

3507
2-9-4

▸**CONCEIVE**
ソウ ソ おも(う)▲
Ⓒ 想 xiǎng

61	Jōyō-3	U60F3
心	S13-4-9	F0302

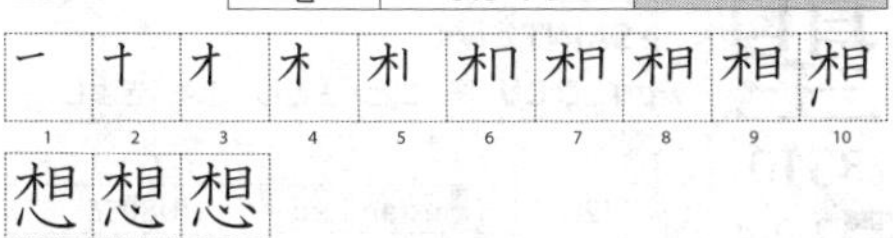

COMPOUNDS

❶ⓐ **CONCEIVE, think of, think, contemplate, imagine**
ⓑ **think of the past, recollect, reminisce**
a 想像 そうぞう imagination
想定 そうてい hypothesis, supposition, assumption
予想 よそう prospect, expectation, conjecture
感想 かんそう thoughts, impressions
連想 れんそう association (of ideas)
b 想起する そうきする remember, recollect
回想 かいそう recollection, reminiscence

❷ **conception, idea, thought, image, concept**
思想 しそう thought, conception, idea
構想 こうそう conception, idea; plot, plan
理想 りそう ideal
幻想 げんそう fantasy, illusion
愛想 あいそ(=あいそう) civility, hospitality
発想 はっそう conception; *music* expression

INDEPENDENT

【そう 想】conception, idea, thought
想を練る そうをねる think deeply, turn (a matter) over in one's mind

KUN

【おもう 想う】[usu. 思う] (recall a thought) **think, recollect, recall, remember**
昔を想う むかしをおもう recall the old days

SYNONYMS

❶ⓐ **think and consider**
思 THINK → 3173
惟 MEDITATE → 0582
省 INTROSPECT → 3100
稽 THINK → 1573
考 THINK → 3962
存 hold an opinion → 3702
案 think out → 2824
想 CONCEIVE → 3507
慮 CONSIDER → 4050
勘 take into consideration → 2231
銓 WEIGH → 2161
量 weigh → 3119

❷ **thought**
念 THOUGHTS → 2554
考え thought → 3962
意 MIND → 2650
想 conception → 3507

HOMOPHONES

おもう 思 THINK → 3173

NOTE

➡ see USAGE note at 思 3173

愁

3508
2-9-4

▸**MELANCHOLY**
シュウ うれ(える) うれ(い)
Ⓒ 愁 chóu

61	Jōyō	U6101
心	S13-4-9	F2312

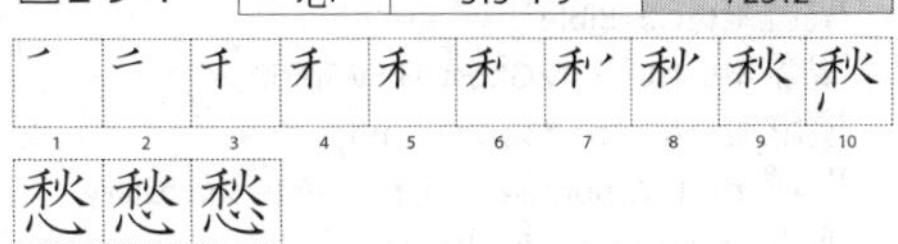

COMPOUNDS

ⓐ **MELANCHOLY, sad, gloomy, worried**
ⓑ **MELANCHOLY, sadness, grief, sorrow, loneliness**

a 愁眉 しゅうび worried look, melancholy air
憂愁 ゆうしゅう melancholy, gloom, grief
b 哀愁 あいしゅう sadness, sorrow, pensiveness
郷愁 きょうしゅう homesickness, nostalgia
旅愁 りょしゅう loneliness on a journey

KUN

【うれえる 愁える】**grieve, lament, feel sorrow**
友の死を愁える とものしをうれえる grieve for the death of a friend

【うれい 愁い】**MELANCHOLY, grief, sorrow, sadness**
愁い顔 うれいがお sad face

SYNONYMS

● **sad and depressed**
悲 SAD → 3448
悄 BECOME DISPIRITED → 0506
哀 sorrowful → 2568
愁 MELANCHOLY → 3508
鬱 GLOOM → 3625
陰 gloomy → 0657
沈 depressed → 0306
寂 LONESOME → 2855
淋しい LONESOME → 0632
惨 MISERABLE → 0585

HOMOPHONES

うれえる 憂 BE ANXIOUS → 2664
うれい 憂 BE ANXIOUS → 2664

NOTE

➡ see USAGE note at 憂 2664

聖

3509
2-9-4

▶**HOLY**
▶**SAINT**

セイ ひじり▲ ㊔ さと さとし きよ きよし さとる

Ⓝ 聖 Ⓒ 圣 shèng

128	Jōyō-6	U8056
耳	S13-6-7	F0897

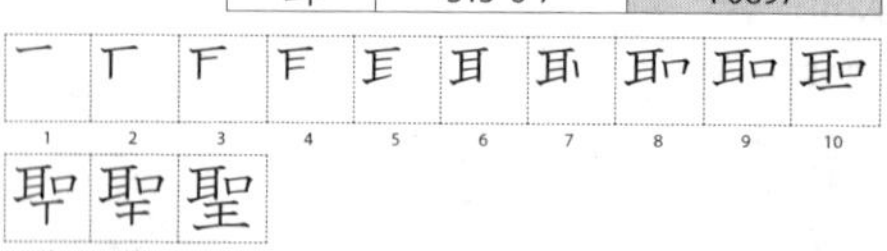

COMPOUNDS

❶ **HOLY, sacred, divine**
聖書 せいしょ Bible
聖霊 せいれい Holy Ghost, Holy Spirit
聖歌 せいか sacred song, hymn
聖域 せいいき holy [sacred] precincts, sanctuary
聖火 せいか sacred fire [torch]
神聖な しんせいな holy, sacred, divine

❷ⓐ SAINT
ⓑ title before names of **SAINT**s: **St.**
ⓒ (Confucian) sage
a 聖賢 せいけん saints and sages
b 聖ペテロ せいぺてろ St. Peter
聖路加病院 せいろかびょういん St. Luke Hospital
c 四聖 しせい the four greatest sages of the world

❸ great master
楽聖ベートーベン がくせいべーとーべん Beethoven, the great musician
棋聖 きせい great master of go [shogi]

❹ [honorific] imperial, emperor's
聖断 せいだん emperor's decision
聖恩 せいおん imperial favor

INDEPENDENT

【せいなる 聖なる】**HOLY**

KUN

【ひじり 聖】**SAINT; master; emperor**
聖の御代 ひじりのみよ emperor's reign
高野聖 こうやひじり saint living at Koyasan

SYNONYMS

❶ **holy**
聖 HOLY → 3509
神 divine → 1143
霊 miraculous → 3480

❷ⓐ & ❷ⓑ **religious persons**
聖 SAINT → 3509
仙 IMMORTAL MOUNTAIN FAIRY → 0036

❸ **great persons**
豪 GREAT MAN → 2657
傑 OUTSTANDING PERSON → 0175
雄 hero → 1271
匠 CRAFTSMAN → 3711
聖 great master → 3509

聖

3510
2-9-4

▶**HOLY**
▶**SAINT**

セイ ひじり ㊔ さと さとし きよ きよし さとる

128	Nonstandard	U8056
耳	S13-6-7	F0000

traditional form → see 聖 at 3509

腎

3511
2-9-4

▶**KIDNEY**

ジン シン▲

Ⓒ 肾 shèn

130	Jōyō	U814E
月	S13-4-9	F2275

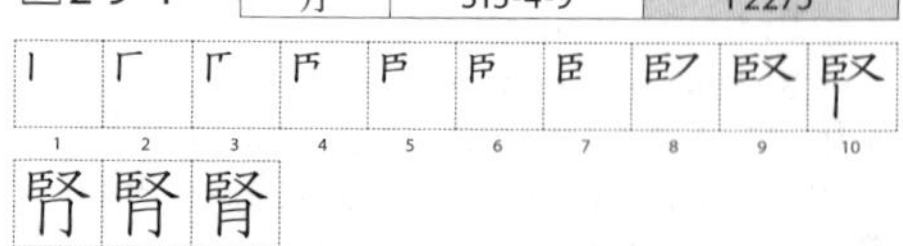

COMPOUNDS

❶ [original meaning] **KIDNEY**
腎臓 じんぞう kidneys
腎炎 じんえん nephritis
腎盂× じんう renal pelvis
副腎 ふくじん adrenal glands

❷ [now usu. 心 0011] **heart of a matter, vital point**
肝腎な かんじんな vital, essential, main

INDEPENDENT

【じん 腎】**KIDNEY**

SYNONYMS

❶ **internal organs**
心 HEART → 0011
肺 LUNG → 1147
胃 STOMACH → 3171
腸 INTESTINES → 1307
肝 LIVER → 1045
胆 GALLBLADDER → 1150
腎 KIDNEY → 3511

慈 2-9-4
incorrect classification
➡ see 2-3-10: 䒑 at 2949

煎 2-9-4
incorrect classification
➡ see 2-3-10: 䒑 at 2950

煮 3512

2-9-4

▶**BOIL**

シャ に(る) -に に(える) に(やす)

86	Names	UFA48
灬	S13-4-9	F0000

traditional form → see 煮 at 3460

愚 3513

2-9-4

▶**FOOLISH**

グ おろ(か)

Ⓒ 愚 yú

61	Jōyō	U611A
心	S13-4-9	F1179

Stroke order: 1–13

COMPOUNDS

❶ [original meaning] **FOOLISH, stupid, ignorant**
愚劣な ぐれつな stupid, silly, foolish
愚痴 ぐち idle complaint, grumble; querulousness
愚人 ぐじん fool
愚鈍な ぐどんな stupid, silly
愚問 ぐもん silly question

❷ [humble] my **FOOLISH**, my humble
愚息 ぐそく my (foolish) son
愚妻 ぐさい my (foolish) wife
愚案 ぐあん my humble opinion, my (foolish) plan

INDEPENDENT

【ぐ 愚】**FOOLISH**ness, folly, stupidity
愚な ぐな foolish, silly, stupid

KUN

【おろか 愚か】
おろかな 愚かな **FOOLISH, stupid, dull, silly**
愚かさ おろかさ foolishness, stupidity
愚かしい おろかしい foolish, stupid, dull, silly
愚か者 おろかもの fool, dunce

SYNONYMS

❶ **foolish**
愚 FOOLISH → 3513
暗 DARK → 1273
痴 STUPID → 4072
鈍 DULL → 2123
呆 DIM-WITTED → 2712
魯 DULL → 2665
闇 DARK → 4134
蒙 IGNORANCE → 2938

❷ **humble prefixes**
小 my little (*humble*) → 0007
弊 our [my] humble → 3583
拙 my humble → 0373
愚 my foolish → 3513

感 3514

2-9-4

▶**SENSE**
▶**FEEL**

カン

Ⓒ 感 gǎn

61	Jōyō-3	U611F
心	S13-4-9	F0090

Stroke order: 1–13

COMPOUNDS

❶ⓐ [also suffix] **SENSE, feeling, sensation, sentiment, emotion**
ⓑ (faculty of perception) **SENSE**
ⓒ (detect) **SENSE**, be sensitive to

a 感情 かんじょう feelings, emotion, sentiment
感想 かんそう thoughts, impressions
同感 どうかん same sentiment, sympathy
劣等感 れっとうかん inferiority complex
責任感 せきにんかん sense of responsibility
親近感 しんきんかん feeling of intimacy

b 五感 ごかん the five senses

亜 淅 昭 相 秋 聑 叡 兹 前 者 禺 咸 【熈】

第六感 だいろっかん the sixth sense, intuition
敏感な びんかんな sensitive
c 感光板 かんこうばん sensitive plate
感熱剤 かんねつざい heat sensitizer

❷ⓐ FEEL, perceive
ⓑ [original meaning] **FEEL deeply, feel admiration, be moved, be affected, be impressed**

a 感覚 かんかく sense, sensation, feeling
感知する かんちする perceive, become aware of
感応作用 かんのうさよう induction
共感する きょうかんする sympathize with, feel sympathy (for)
実感する じっかんする feel actually; realize, experience personally
b 感動する かんどうする be moved, be impressed
感銘 かんめい deep impression
感激 かんげき deep emotion
感心 かんしん admiration

❸ be affected, be influenced, be struck by, contract
感電 かんでん electric shock
感染 かんせん infection
流感(=流行性感冒) りゅうかん(=りゅうこうせいかんぼう) cold, influenza

❹ FEEL gratitude, thank
感謝 かんしゃ gratitude, thanks

INDEPENDENT

【かん 感】 **FEEL**ing, sensation, sentiment, sense, emotion; impression
隔世の感が有る かくせいのかんがある be poles apart

【かんじる(=かんずる) 感じる(=感ずる)】 **be conscious of, suffer, be sensible to, have a FEELing that; be impressed, be struck**
感じ かんじ feeling, sense, sensation, touch, feel; impression, sentiment

SYNONYMS

❶ⓐ feeling
感 SENSE (feeling) →3514
情 EMOTION →0583
心 HEART →0011
気 spirits →3960
ⓑ sense
感 SENSE →3514
覚 sense →3217
勘 INTUITIVE PERCEPTION →2231
ⓒ detect
検 detect →1241
感 SENSE →3514
嗅 SMELL →0772

❷ⓐ perceive
覚 PERCEIVE →3217
知 KNOW →1446
感 FEEL →3514
認 RECOGNIZE →1948
ⓑ feel deeply
感 feel deeply →3514
動 be moved →2232
嘆 sigh in admiration →0773

熈

2-9-4

incorrect stroke-count
➡ see 2-10-4: 熙 at 3531

碧 3515

2-9-5

▶**DEEP BLUE**
ヘキ ㊔ みどり あお あおい
Ⓒ 碧 bì

112	Names	U78A7
石	S14-5-9	F2737

COMPOUNDS

❶ [original meaning] **DEEP BLUE, azure, blue**
碧水 へきすい blue water
碧空 へきくう blue sky
金髪碧眼の外人 きんぱつへきがんのがいじん foreigner with golden hair and blue eyes
紺碧 こんぺき deep blue, azure

❷ green, verdant, emerald green
碧山 へきざん green mountains
碧玉 へきぎょく jasper

SYNONYMS

❶ blue and purple colors
青 BLUE →3084
碧 DEEP BLUE →3515
瑠 LAPIS LAZULI (bright blue) →1342
紺 DARK BLUE →1688
藍 INDIGO →3024
紫 PURPLE →3332
蒼 PALE BLUE →2943

竪 3516

2-9-5

▶**VERTICAL**
ジュ たて-
Ⓝ 豎 Ⓒ 竖 shù

117	Names	U7AEA
立	S14-5-9	F2899

COMPOUNDS

❶ VERTICAL, upright
竪立 じゅりつ stand upright

❷ [archaic] boy, child
竪子 じゅし stripling, greenhorn

KUN

【たて- 竪-】
ⓐ [now usu. 縦-] **VERTICAL, upright**

ⓑ [now usu. 立て-] **VERTICAL**, upright

a 竪琴 たてごと harp
竪縞 たてじま vertical stripes
竪穴 たてあな pit
竪樋 たてどい downspout

SYNONYMS

【たて-】

ⓐ **vertical**
縦 VERTICAL → 1783
竪- VERTICAL → 3516
垂 perpendicular → 4382
立て- standing → 2486
直 STRAIGHT → 3649

HOMOPHONES

たて
立 STAND → 2486
縦 VERTICAL → 1783
建 BUILD → 3834

NOTE

➡ see USAGE note at 立 2486

夢
▀2-9-5
incorrect classification
➡ see ▀2-4-10: 艹 at 3136

管
▀2-9-5
incorrect classification
➡ see ▀2-6-8: ⺮ at 3349

監
▀2-9-5
incorrect stroke-count
➡ see ▀2-10-5: 臣 at 3535

緊

3517
▀2-9-6

▶TIGHTEN
▶EXIGENT
キン
Ⓒ 紧 jǐn

120	Jōyō	U7DCA
糸	S15-6-9	F1118

COMPOUNDS

❶ⓐ [original meaning] **TIGHTEN, make tight [tense], become tight [tense]**
ⓑ tight, close, tense

a 緊縛する きんばくする bind tightly
緊張する きんちょうする become tense, be strained, be keyed up
緊縮 きんしゅく contraction, shrinkage; strict economy

b 緊密な きんみつな close, tight

❷ EXIGENT, urgent, pressing, imminent
緊急な きんきゅうな urgent, pressing, emergent
緊要な きんような important, momentous; exigent, urgent
緊迫した きんぱくした tense, strained
緊切な きんせつな urgent, pressing
喫緊事 きっきんじ urgent [pressing] matter

SYNONYMS

❶ⓐ tighten
締める TIGHTEN → 1761
緊 TIGHTEN → 3517
張 STRAIN → 0573

❷ urgent
急 URGENT → 2595
緊 EXIGENT → 3517
迫 pressing → 3815

蔑
▀2-9-6
incorrect classification
➡ see ▀2-4-11: 艹 at 3140

賢

3518
▀2-9-7

▶WISE
ケン かしこ(い) ㊔ さとし まさる まさかた よし まこと たか
Ⓝ 賢 Ⓒ 贤 xián

154	Jōyō	U8CE2
貝	S16-7-9	F1487

COMPOUNDS

❶ⓐ WISE, intelligent, sagacious, bright
ⓑ WISE man, sage

a 賢明な けんめいな wise, intelligent; sensible
賢者 けんじゃ wise man
賢母 けんぼ wise mother

b 賢哲 けんてつ sage, wise man

❷ capable, talented
賢才 けんさい man of ability

❸ [honorific] your
賢察 けんさつ your discernment
諸賢 しょけん gentlemen

KUN

【かしこい 賢い】**WISE, intelligent, sagacious, bright**
賢さ かしこさ wisdom, intelligence, sagacity
悪賢い わるがしこい cunning, artful, sly, crafty
狡×賢い ずるがしこい sly, cunning

SYNONYMS

❶ⓐ intelligent and wise

賢 WISE → 3518
俊 brilliant → 0117
鋭 SHARP → 2171
敏 NIMBLE → 1675
叡 PROFOUNDLY WISE → 2405
智 wise → 3458
慧 INTELLIGENT → 3485
伶 CLEVER → 0356
悧 CLEVER → 0505
俐 CLEVER → 0113
哲 SAGACIOUS → 3402
明 clear-sighted → 1060
聡 SHARP-WITTED → 1750

ⓑ wise and talented persons

哲 sage → 3402
賢 wise man → 3518
博 DOCTOR → 0170
秀 genius → 3152
俊 BRILLIANT PERSON → 0117
才 person of talent → 4218
通 well-informed person → 3855

竪

3519

2-9-7

▶VERTICAL

ジュ たて-

151	Nonstandard	U8C4E
豆	S16-7-9	F0000

traditional form → see 竪 at 3516

覽

2-9-7

incorrect stroke-count
➡ see 2-10-7: 臣 at 3538

鍫

3520

2-9-8

▶HOE

シュウ くわ

167	Nonstandard	U936B
金	S17-8-9	F0000

traditional form → see 鍬 at 2205

爵

2-9-8

incorrect classification
➡ see 2-4-13: 爫 at 3143

凖

3521

2-10-2

▶STANDARD
▶QUASI-

ジュン なぞら(える)

15	Nonstandard	U51D6
冫	S12-2-10	F0000

alternative form → see 準 at 3541

兜

3522

2-10-2

▶HEADPIECE

ト トウ かぶと

10	Nonstandard	U5160
儿	S12-2-10	F0000

traditional form → see 兜 at 3499

募

2-10-2

incorrect classification
➡ see 2-3-9: 艹 at 2901

異

2-10-2

incorrect classification
➡ see 2-5-7: 田 at 3207

勞

2-10-2

incorrect classification
➡ see 2-8-4: 𤇾 at 3451

奧

2-10-2

incorrect classification
➡ see 2-9-3: 㑹 at 3503

堊

2-10-3

incorrect stroke-count
➡ see 2-8-3: 亞 at 3442

塗

3523

2-10-3

▶APPLY ON A SURFACE

ト ぬ(る) ぬ(り) まみ(れる)▲

Ⓒ 涂 tú

32	Jōyō	U5857
土	S13-3-10	F1415

1	2	3	4	5	6	7	8	9	10	11	12	13
丶	冫	氵	氵	沦	汵	泠	浛	涂	涂	涂	塗	塗

COMPOUNDS

❶ [original meaning] **APPLY ON A SURFACE, lay on, spread on, coat, paint**

塗装 とそう painting, coating
塗料 とりょう paint
塗布する とふする apply (an ointment)
塗工 とこう painter

❷ mud

塗炭 とたん misery, distress

KUN

【ぬる 塗る】**lay on, spread on, paint, coat; blame someone, pin a crime on**

塗り付ける ぬりつける daub, smear
塗り絵 ぬりえ picture for coloring

【ぬり 塗り】[also suffix] **coating, painting; painted or lacquered product**

上塗り うわぬり final coating of paint

一塗り ひとぬり one coat of paint
輪島塗り わじまぬり Wajima lacquer

【まみれる 塗れる】 be covered, be smeared, be stained
泥に塗れる どろにまみれる be covered with mud

SYNONYMS

❶ **spread**
散 SCATTER → 2137
布 SPREAD → 3691
敷く LAY → 2345
舗 PAVE → 2177
塗 APPLY ON A SURFACE → 3523
抹 wipe over → 0370
撒 SCATTER → 0909

COMPOUND FORMATION

【塗炭 とたん】
塗炭 'misery, distress' is, literally, to be smeared with mud (塗 ❷) and burned with charcoal (炭); that is, to be in a totally miserable state.

奨

3524
2-10-3

▶**ENCOURAGE**
ショウ すす(める)^ ㊔ すすむ
Ⓝ 奬 奬 Ⓒ 奖 jiǎng

37	Jōyō	U5968
大	S13-3-10	F2021

COMPOUNDS

❶ (stimulate by assistance) **ENCOURAGE, promote, stimulate**
奨励 しょうれい encouragement, promotion, stimulation, incitement
奨学金 しょうがくきん scholarship (grant)
報奨 ほうしょう reward, compensation

❷ praise, commend, reward
推奨する すいしょうする recommend, commend, praise
選奨 せんしょう recommendation

KUN

【すすめる 奨める】 [usu. 勧める] **ENCOURAGE**, promote, stimulate
学問の奨め がくもんのすすめ encouragement of learning

SYNONYMS

❶ **advance**
進 ADVANCE → 3873
興 cause to rise → 3622
奨 ENCOURAGE → 3524
勧 encourage → 2334

HOMOPHONES

すすめる
勧 URGE → 2334
薦 RECOMMEND → 3008
進 ADVANCE → 3873

NOTE

➡ see USAGE note at 進 3873

塑

3525
2-10-3

▶**MODEL**
ソ
Ⓝ 塑 Ⓒ 塑 sù

32	Jōyō	U5851
土	S13-3-10	F3276

COMPOUNDS

❶ⓐ [original meaning] (make by shaping a plastic material, esp. clay) **MODEL, mold, sculpt**
ⓑ figure **MODEL**ed of clay or plaster, plastic figure
a 塑造 そぞう modeling, molding
彫塑 ちょうそ carving and modeling, plastic arts; clay model
b 塑像 そぞう plastic image, clay figure

❷ *phys* plastic
塑性変形 そせいへんけい plastic deformation
塑弾性 そだんせい plasto-elasticity
可塑材 かそざい plastic material

SYNONYMS

❶ⓐ **form and carve**
刻 ENGRAVE → 1619
彫 CARVE → 2117
塑 MODEL → 3525
鋳 CAST → 2170

❷ **soft**
柔 SOFT (supple and yielding) → 2591
軟 SOFT (not hard) → 1871
塑 plastic → 3525

塐

3526
2-10-3

▶**MODEL**
ソ

32	Nonstandard	U5851
土	S13-3-10	F0000

traditional form → see 塑 at 3525

幕墓

2-10-3

incorrect classification
➡ see 2-3-10: 艹 at 2930

奧 3527 2-10-3

▶INNER PART

オウ オク おく

37	Names	U5967
大	S13-3-10	F0000

traditional form → see 奥 at 3503

㙷 2-10-3

incorrect stroke-count
➡ see 2-11-3: 孰 at 3546

髮 3528 2-10-4

▶HAIR

ハツ かみ

Ⓝ 髮 Ⓒ 发 fà

190	Jōyō	U9AEA
髟	S14-10-4	F0867

COMPOUNDS

ⓐ **HAIR (on the head)**
ⓑ **HAIRsbreadth**

a 頭髮 とうはつ hair, head hair
毛髮 もうはつ hair
散髮 さんぱつ haircut
白髮 はくはつ white [gray] hair
b 一髮 いっぱつ a hairsbreadth; a hair
危機一髮の脱出 ききいっぱつのだっしゅつ escape by a hairsbreadth

INDEPENDENT

【はつ 髮】 *literary* **HAIR**sbreadth
間、髮を入れず かん,はつをいれず in a flash, in no time

KUN

【かみ 髮】 **HAIR (of the head);** [also suffix] **hairstyle, coiffeur**
髮の毛 かみのけ hair
髮結い かみゆい hairdresser; hairdressing
日本髮 にほんがみ Japanese coiffeur

SPECIAL READINGS

白髮 しらが white [gray] hair

SYNONYMS

ⓐ **hair**
毛 HAIR (of any kind) → 4264
髮 HAIR (on the head) → 3528
辮 PLAIT → 2085
羽 FEATHER → 0265
眉 EYEBROW → 3991
鬚 BEARD → 3539

惡 2-10-4

incorrect stroke-count
➡ see 2-8-4: 亞 at 3463

態 3529 2-10-4

▶STATE

タイ わざ(と)▲

Ⓒ 态 tài

61	Jōyō-5	U614B
心	S14-4-10	F0367

COMPOUNDS

❶ [also suffix] **STATE, condition, situation; form, appearance**
状態 じょうたい state, condition, appearance, situation, aspect
生態 せいたい ecology; mode of life
実態 じったい actual conditions, state
重態(=重体) じゅうたい serious condition, critical state
事態 じたい situation, state of affairs
形態(=形体) けいたい shape, form, structure, morphology
姿態 したい figure, person; pose

❷ [original meaning] **attitude, posture**
態度 たいど attitude, manner
態勢 たいせい attitude, preparedness, condition

❸ [suffix] *gram* **voice**
受動態 じゅどうたい passive voice
能動態 のうどうたい active voice

KUN

【わざと 態と】 **on purpose, intentionally**
態態 わざわざ on purpose, purposely; expressly

SYNONYMS

❶ **states and situations**
態 STATE → 3529
調 TONE → 1973
様 MODE → 1332
相 PHASE → 1120
状 CONDITION → 0322
況 CONDITIONS → 0395
景 business conditions → 3118
勢 course of events → 3542
境 SITUATION → 0835
局 current situation → 3800
情 ACTUAL CONDITIONS → 0583
訳 circumstances → 1865

❷ **posture**

姿 posture →3264
態 attitude →3529

熊

▶BEAR
ユウ* くま
Ⓒ 熊 xióng

3530
2-10-4

86	Jōyō	U718A
灬	S14-4-10	F1141

COMPOUNDS

● [rare] **BEAR**

熊掌 ゆうしょう bear's paw (as a rare Chinese delicacy)

KUN

【くま 熊】**BEAR;** [in compounds] **as fierce or big as a bear**

熊手 くまで rake, fork, bamboo rake
熊蜂 くまばち hornet
熊笹 くまざさ *Sasa albo-marginata*, low and striped bamboo
熊の胆 くまのい bear's gall (used as medicine for the stomach)
白熊 しろくま sea bear, polar bear

SYNONYMS

● **undomesticated mammals**

虎 TIGER →3981
猿 MONKEY →0824
鯨 WHALE →2361
犀 RHINOCEROS →3900
狼 WOLF →0541
狐 FOX →0472
羚 SEROW →1695
鼠 RAT →3340
獅 LION →0825
豹 LEOPARD →1847
熊 BEAR →3530
象 ELEPHANT →2647
麒 MALE CHINESE UNICORN →2363
麟 FEMALE CHINESE UNICORN →2376
猪 WILD BOAR →0652
鹿 DEER →3879

熈

▶BRIGHT
キ ㊔ ひろ ひろし ひろむ のり よし

3531
2-10-4

86	Nonstandard	U7155
灬	S14-4-10	F0000

traditional form →see 熙 at 3559

齊 incorrect classification
➡ see 2-2-12: 亠 at 2659
2-10-4

暮慕 incorrect classification
➡ see 2-3-11: 艹 at 2969
2-10-4

滎 incorrect classification
➡ see 2-8-6: 𤇾 at 3476
2-10-4

熈 incorrect stroke-count
➡ see 2-11-4: 煕 at 3547
2-10-4

甜 incorrect stroke-count
➡ see 2-11-4: 甛 at 3550
2-10-4

熟 incorrect stroke-count
➡ see 2-11-4: 孰 at 3558
2-10-4

熙 incorrect stroke-count
➡ see 2-11-4: 熈 at 3559
2-10-4

髮

▶HAIR
ハツ かみ

3532
2-10-5

190	Names	U9AEE
髟	S15-10-5	F0000

traditional form →see 髪 at 3528

盤

▶DISK
▶BOARD
バン ㊔ いわ いわお
Ⓒ 盘 pán

3533
2-10-5

108	Jōyō	U76E4
皿	S15-5-10	F1244

COMPOUNDS

❶ⓐ **DISK, round plate**
ⓑ [also suffix] **phonograph DISK, record**

a 円盤 えんばん disk; flying saucer
吸盤 きゅうばん sucker, sucking disk
羅針盤 らしんばん compass
胎盤 たいばん placenta
b 音盤 おんばん disk, record
輸入盤 ゆにゅうばん foreign [imported] record

❷ⓐ [also suffix] (flat surface for specific purpose) **BOARD (as for shogi or chess), panel, plate**
ⓑ **BOARD** game, esp. shogi or go

a 将棋盤 しょうぎばん chessboard
鍵盤 けんばん keyboard
算盤 そろばん Japanese abacus, *soroban*
制御盤 せいぎょばん control panel
配電盤 はいでんばん distributing board [panel], switchboard
b 序盤 じょばん opening (in the game of go)

❸ⓐ dish, plate, tray, platter
ⓑ [original meaning] basin, pan, tub, bowl

a 杯盤 はいばん glasses and plates
銀盤 ぎんばん silver plate; surface of ice, skating rink
b 水盤 すいばん basin; flower bowl
銅盤 どうばん bronze bowl
骨盤 こつばん pelvis

❹ [formerly also 磐 3534] **bedrock, base rock, base, foundation**
盤石 ばんじゃく huge rock; firmness
基盤 きばん bedrock, base, foundation
岩盤 がんばん bedrock, base rock
地盤 じばん ground, foundation, base
落盤 らくばん cave-in

❺ [also suffix] machine tool
旋盤 せんばん lathe
フライス盤 ふらいすばん milling machine
研削盤 けんさくばん grinding machine

❻ entwine, twist about
盤根 ばんこん entwined roots

INDEPENDENT

【ばん 盤】 go **BOARD**, shogi board, chessboard; phonograph disk, record
将棋の盤 しょうぎのばん shogi board, Japanese chessboard

SYNONYMS

❶ⓐ **circular objects**
環 RING → 1395
輪 WHEEL, RING → 1999
車 WHEEL → 4367
盤 DISK → 3533
釧 ARMLET → 2109

❷ⓐ **boards and plates**
板 BOARD, PLATE → 1067
盤 BOARD → 3533

❸ **vessels and receptacles**
盤 dish → 3533
鍋 POT → 2202
釜 IRON POT → 2610
鼎 TRIPOD CAULDRON → 4405
臼 MORTAR → 4341
碓 MORTAR → 1537
托 RECEPTACLE → 0252
皿 PLATE → 4286
盆 TRAY → 2581
膳 LEGGED TRAY → 1381
杯 CUP → 1066
鉢 BOWL → 2144
椀 WOODEN BOWL → 1250
碗 CERAMIC BOWL → 1539
丼 LARGE BOWL → 4323

❹ **bottoms and bases**
底 BOTTOM → 3827
柢 BOTTOM → 1121
下 lower part → 4186
基 BASE → 3312
礎 FOUNDATION STONE → 1595
麓 FOOT OF MOUNTAIN → 3494
磐 BEDROCK → 3534
盤 bedrock → 3533
床 BED → 3805

NOTE

➡ see COMPOUND FORMATION for 羅針盤 らしんばん → 羅 3244

磐 3534

▶**BEDROCK**
バン いわ
Ⓒ 磐 pán

2-10-5

112	Names	U78D0
石	S15-5-10	F2509

COMPOUNDS

❶ [now usu. 盤 3533] **BEDROCK, base rock, base, foundation**
磐石 ばんじゃく huge rock; firmness
落磐 らくばん cave-in
大磐石である だいばんじゃくである be as firm as rock

❷ abbrev. of 磐城 いわき, old name for eastern Fukushima Prefecture
常磐炭田 じょうばんたんでん Joban Coalfield

KUN

【いわ 磐】 [now usu. 岩] **rock, crag**
磐座 いわくら dwelling place of a god

SPECIAL READINGS

常磐 ときわ unchanging rock; everlastingness, eternity; evergreen

SYNONYMS

❶ **bottoms and bases**
底 BOTTOM → 3827
柢 BOTTOM → 1121
下 lower part → 4186
基 BASE → 3312

礎 FOUNDATION STONE → 1595
麓 FOOT OF MOUNTAIN → 3494
磐 BEDROCK → 3534
盤 bedrock → 3533
床 BED → 3805

HOMOPHONES

いわ
岩 ROCK → 2778
巌 CRAG → 3037

NOTE

➡ see USAGE note at 岩 2778

監

▶OVERSEE
カン
Ⓝ 监◆ Ⓒ 监 jiān jiàn

3535
2-10-5

108	Jōyō	U76E3
皿	S15-5-10	F0589

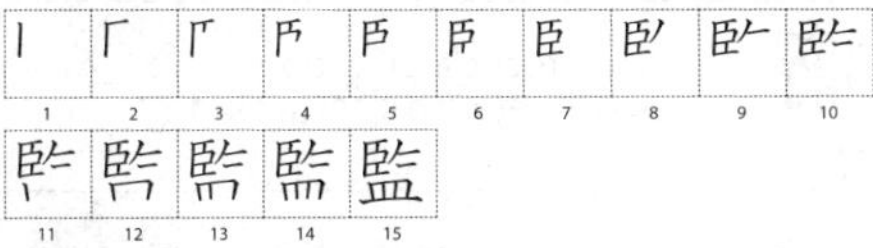

COMPOUNDS

❶ⓐ **OVERSEE, supervise, overlook, watch over, superintend, inspect**
ⓑ OVERSEEr, supervisor, inspector
a 監督する かんとくする supervise, superintend; direct (a film)
監視する かんしする watch, keep under observation, exercise surveillance
監査 かんさ inspection; inspector, supervisor
監修 かんしゅう (editorial) supervision
b 総監 そうかん governor-general, inspector general
舎監 しゃかん dormitory inspector [superintendent]
学監 がっかん school superintendent [overseer]; dean

❷ **prison**
監獄 かんごく prison, jail
監禁 かんきん imprisonment, confinement
監房 かんぼう cell, ward

SYNONYMS

❶ⓐ **direct and supervise**
制 CONTROL → 1624
理 manage → 1220
経 MANAGE → 1687
管 EXERCISE CONTROL → 3349
轄 EXERCISE JURISDICTION OVER → 2056
掌 TAKE CHARGE OF → 3215
監 OVERSEE → 3535
督 SUPERVISE → 3471
司 OFFICIATE → 3648
宰 PRESIDE → 2829
営 MANAGE → 3216

❷ **prison**
獄 PRISON → 0872
監 prison → 3535

蕎

2-10-5

incorrect classification
➡ see 2-3-12: 艹 at 2993

繁

▶THRIVE
ハン しげ(る)▲ しげ(く)▲
Ⓝ 繁 Ⓒ 繁 fán pó

3536
2-10-6

120	Jōyō	U7E41
糸	S16-6-10	F1249

COMPOUNDS

❶ [formerly also 蕃 2989] (grow vigorously) **THRIVE, luxuriate, grow thick**
繁殖する はんしょくする breed, propagate, increase, multiply
繁茂 はんも luxuriant growth

❷ⓐ (enjoy prosperity) **THRIVE, prosper, flourish**
ⓑ **bustling, busy**
a 繁栄する はんえいする prosper, thrive, flourish
繁華 はんか prosperity, bustle
繁盛(=繁昌)する はんじょうする prosper, flourish, thrive
b 繁忙 はんぼう pressure of business, business
繁閑 はんかん press and slack of business
農繁期 のうはんき busy farming season

❸ **numerous, frequent**
頻繁に ひんぱんに frequently, very often

❹ complicated, complex, intricate
繁雑な はんざつな complicated, intricate, confused
繁簡 はんかん complexity and simplicity

KUN

【しげる 繁る】[now usu. 茂る] **grow thick, be luxuriant, be overgrown**
【しげく 繁く】frequently, often
繁繁 しげしげ very frequently; (look) steadily

SYNONYMS

❶ **flourish**
茂 GROW THICK → 2791
繁 THRIVE → 3536

❷ⓐ **prospering and prosperity**
隆 PROSPER → 0661
振 rise → 0515

興 RISE TO PROSPERITY → 3622
盛 PROSPEROUS → 3314
昌 PROSPERING → 3069
栄 FLOURISH → 3183
繁 THRIVE → 3536
賑 BUSTLE → 1959

ⓑ busy

忙 BUSY → 0248
繁 bustling → 3536
慌てる FLURRIED → 0707

❹ complex

繁 complicated → 3536
煩 vexatious → 1295

HOMOPHONES

しげる 茂 GROW THICK → 2791

NOTE

➡ see USAGE note at 茂 2791

螢

2-10-6

incorrect classification
➡ see 2-8-8: 𤇾 at 3489

醬

3537

2-10-7

▸**FERMENTED SAUCE**

ショウ ジャン ひしお

164	Nonstandard	U91A4
酉	S17-7-10	F0000

traditional form → see 醤 at 3569

覽

3538

2-10-7

▸**LOOK OVER**

ラン

Ⓝ 覽 Ⓒ 览 lǎn

147	Jōyō-6	U89A7
見	S17-7-10	F1541

COMPOUNDS

ⓐ [original meaning] **LOOK OVER (a wide area), look at, glance at, view, see**

ⓑ (make an overall inspection of) **LOOK OVER, inspect, read**

a 御覧 ごらん [honorific] look, see; try
一覧 いちらん a look, a glance, a reading; summary, synopsis
一覧する いちらんする look, glance through, inspect
観覧車 かんらんしゃ Ferris wheel

b 展覧する てんらんする exhibit, show
博覧会 はくらんかい exhibition, fair, exposition
閲覧室 えつらんしつ reading room
便覧 べんらん(=びんらん) handbook, manual
要覧 ようらん survey, outline, handbook

SYNONYMS

● see and look

見 SEE → 3151
看 WATCH → 3992
察 INSPECT → 2961
窺 WATCH FURTIVELY → 3002
瞥 GLANCE AT → 3592
目 look → 3777
観 VIEW → 2359
覧 LOOK OVER → 3538
眺 LOOK OUT OVER → 1503
望 LOOK AFAR → 3408
仰 LOOK UP → 0051
顧 LOOK BACK → 2394
視 REGARD → 1223

齋

2-10-7

incorrect classification
➡ see 2-2-15: 亠 at 2669

營

2-10-7

incorrect classification
➡ see 2-8-9: 𤇾 at 3492

嚮饗

2-10-9

incorrect stroke-count
➡ see 2-11-9: 郷 at 3573

競

2-10-10

incorrect classification
➡ see 1-10-10: 竟 at 2322

鬚

3539

2-10-12

▸**BEARD**

シュ ひげ

Ⓒ 须 xū

190	Non-Jōyō	U9B1A
髟	S22-10-12	F3181

COMPOUNDS

● [rarely also 須 しゅ 0700] [original meaning] **BEARD**
鬚髯× しゅぜん beard

KUN

【ひげ 鬚】**BEARD**
顎鬚 あごひげ beard
鯨鬚 くじらひげ whalebone, baleen

SYNONYMS

● hair

毛 HAIR (of any kind) → 4264
髪 HAIR (on the head) → 3528
辮 PLAIT → 2085
羽 FEATHER → 0265

眉 EYEBROW →3991
鬚 BEARD →3539

競 incorrect classification
➡ see 1-11-11: 竟 at 2369
2-10-12

蠶 ▶SILKWORM
サン かいこ こ
3540

142	Nonstandard	U8836
虫	S26-6-20	F0000

2-10-16 traditional form →see 蚕 at 3107

準 ▶STANDARD
▶QUASI-
ジュン なぞら(える)▲
3541 Ⓝ 準◇ Ⓒ 准 zhǔn

85	Jōyō-5	U6E96
氵	S13-3-10	F0719

2-11-2

COMPOUNDS

❶ **STANDARD, norm, criterion**
準則 じゅんそく regulations, standard
水準 すいじゅん level, standard; water level
基準 きじゅん standard, criterion, basis
標準 ひょうじゅん standard, norm, criterion
平準 へいじゅん level; equality

❷ [original meaning] **water level** (the instrument)
準縄 じゅんじょう level and inked string; rule, standard

❸ [also prefix] **QUASI-, semi-, associate**
準急 じゅんきゅう local express, semi-express (train)
準星 じゅんせい quasar
準決勝 じゅんけっしょう semifinal
準会員 じゅんかいいん associate member

❹ **apply correspondingly, conform to, be proportionate**
準拠 じゅんきょ conformity
準用する じゅんようする apply correspondingly

❺ **prepare, provide for**
準備する じゅんびする provide for [against], prepare for [against]

INDEPENDENT

【じゅんじる(=じゅんずる) 準じる(=準ずる)】be treated [regarded] correspondingly; apply correspondingly, be proportionate to

KUN

【なぞらえる 準える】**compare to, model after**
人生は大河に準えられる じんせいはたいがになぞらえられる Life can be compared to a mighty river.

SYNONYMS

❶ **model**
範 MODEL →3360
典 CANON →3253
模 PATTERN →1326
程 ESTABLISHED FORM →1524
式 form →3785
準 STANDARD →3541
格 NORM →1161

❸ **subordinate**
副 SECONDARY →2230
次 secondary →0058
従 subordinate →0498
亜 SUB- →4354
準 QUASI- →3541
半 semi- →4313
准 JUNIOR →0143
助 assistant →1440

❹ **correspond to**
該 CORRESPOND TO →1916
準 apply correspondingly →3541
当 be equivalent →2701

勢 ▶POWER
セイ ゼイ▲ いきお(い) ㊔ なり
Ⓝ 勢 Ⓒ 势 shì
3542

19	Jōyō-5	U52E2
力	S13-2-11	F0348

2-11-2

COMPOUNDS

❶ⓐ (ability to influence) **POWER to influence, influence, strength, authority**
ⓑ **spiritual energy or POWER, vigor, spirit, dash**
a 勢力 せいりょく influence, power, might; force (of a typhoon)
勢門 せいもん influential family
権勢 けんせい power, influence, authority
党勢 とうせい strength of a party
優勢な ゆうせいな superior, leading, predominant
豪勢な ごうせいな great, grand, magnificent
虚勢 きょせい bluff, bluster, false show of power
b 気勢 きせい spirit, ardor
威勢 いせい spirits, dash; power

❷ⓐ **physical POWER, force; momentum; energy**
ⓑ procreative **POWER**, male genitals

a 火勢 かせい force of the fire, flames
強勢 きょうせい emphasis, stress, accent
筆勢 ひっせい stroke [dash] of the pen
余勢 よせい surplus power, reserve energy
b 去勢する きょせいする castrate; enervate
❸ⓐ (numerical force) **strength, number (of soldiers or people), large numbers**
ⓑ [also suffix] forces, army
ⓒ [also suffix] party, group
a 多勢 たぜい great numbers, superiority in number
大勢の おおぜいの great number of, multitude of
b 勢揃いする せいぞろいする assemble in full force, muster
加勢する かせいする held, aid, assist
軍勢 ぐんぜい army, force; number of soldiers
総勢 そうぜい the whole army
徳川勢 とくがわぜい Tokugawa forces
c 同勢 どうぜい company, party
外国勢 がいこくぜい (group of) foreigners
埼玉勢 さいたまぜい the Saitama group
❹ⓐ **course of events, state of affairs, situation, condition, circumstances**
ⓑ **trend of events, drift, tendency**
a 形勢 けいせい situation, state of affairs; prospects
情勢 じょうせい state of things, situation
態勢 たいせい attitude, preparedness, condition
国勢 こくせい state [condition] of a country
b 勝勢である しょうせいである stand a good chance of winning the game
大勢 たいせい general trend [tendency]
時勢 じせい trend of the times, spirit of the age
運勢 うんせい one's star, fortune, luck
❺ **outward appearance**
地勢 ちせい geographical features, topography
姿勢 しせい posture, position, poise, attitude
体勢 たいせい posture, stance
❻ abbrev. of 伊勢 いせ, old name for Mie Prefecture
紀勢本線 きせいほんせん Kisei Main Line (Wakayama-Mie Railway)

INDEPENDENT

【せい 勢】army, force; strength, number of soldiers
【ぜい 勢】same as 勢 せい
敵の勢 てきのぜい enemy's strength [forces]

KUN

【いきおい 勢い】**force, vigor, POWER, energy, spirit; momentum, impetus; influence, power; course of events, trend, tendency; naturally, necessarily**
勢い良く いきおいよく forcibly, with vigor
勢い込む いきおいこむ brace oneself up
勢い付く いきおいづく gain strength, take heart
勢いを振るう いきおいをふるう exercise authority, wield power
自然の勢いで しぜんのいきおいで by force of circumstances

SYNONYMS

❶ⓐ **power and authority**
力 POWER → 4178
威 MIGHT → 4394
勢 POWER (to influence) → 3542
権 POWER (to control) → 1348
覇 SUPREMACY → 3392
❷ⓐ **energy and force**
力 POWER, force → 4178
勢 physical power → 3542
気 energy → 3960
圧 PRESSURE → 3688
鋒 brunt → 2172
❸ⓐ **quantity and number**
量 QUANTITY → 3119
嵩 BULK → 2927
積 size → 1579
額 AMOUNT → 2273
分 content → 2466
数 NUMBER → 2245
勢 strength → 3542
ⓑ **armed forces**
軍 ARMY → 2582
兵 the military → 3158
勢 forces → 3542
隊 PARTY → 0762
❹ⓐ **states and situations**
態 STATE → 3529
調 TONE → 1973
様 MODE → 1332
相 PHASE → 1120
状 CONDITION → 0322
況 CONDITIONS → 0395
景 business conditions → 3118
勢 course of events → 3542
境 SITUATION → 0835
局 current situation → 3800
情 ACTUAL CONDITIONS → 0583
訳 circumstances → 1865
ⓑ **tendency**
向 tendency → 3790
性 NATURE → 0357
勢 trend → 3542
傾 inclination → 0174
潮 TIDE → 0916
流 CURRENT → 0529

零

▬2-11-2

incorrect classification
➡ see ▬2-8-5: 雫 at 3467

與

3543

▬2-11-2

▶**GIVE**

ヨ あた(える) あずか(る) ㊔ よし とも

134	Names	U8207
臼	S13-7-6	F0000

traditional form → see 与 at 4229

嶌

3544

▬2-11-3

▶**ISLAND**

トウ しま

46	Nonstandard	U3800
山	S14-3-11	F0000

traditional form → see 島 at 4103

奬

3545

▬2-11-3

▶**ENCOURAGE**

ショウ すす(める) ㊔ すすむ

37	Names	U596C
大	S14-3-11	F0000

traditional form → see 奨 at 3524

塾

3546

▬2-11-3

▶**PRIVATE SCHOOL**

ジュク

Ⓒ 塾 shú

32	Jōyō	U587E
土	S14-3-11	F1636

Stroke order: 1–14

COMPOUNDS

● [also suffix] **PRIVATE SCHOOL, school run outside normal school hours, cram school**

塾長 じゅくちょう principal of a private school
塾生 じゅくせい private school student
入塾 にゅうじゅく entering a private school
英語塾 えいごじゅく private school for the study of English

INDEPENDENT

【じゅく 塾】**PRIVATE SCHOOL**

塾を開いている じゅくをひらいている run a private school

SYNONYMS

● **schools**

校 SCHOOL → 1166
学 EDUCATIONAL INSTITUTION → 3162
院 INSTITUTION → 0544
塾 PRIVATE SCHOOL → 3546
大 UNIVERSITY → 4224
高 high school → 2601
中 junior high school → 4262
小 elementary school → 0007
園 kindergarten → 3914

奪

▬2-11-3

incorrect classification
➡ see ▬2-3-11: 大 at 2956

隧

▬2-11-3

incorrect stroke-count
➡ see ▬2-12-3: 隊 at 3578

隨

▬2-11-3

incorrect stroke-count
➡ see ▬2-12-3: 隋 at 3580

導

▬2-11-3

incorrect stroke-count
➡ see ▬2-12-3: 道 at 3587

熈

3547

▬2-11-4

▶**BRIGHT**

キ ㊔ ひろ ひろし ひろむ のり よし

86	Nonstandard	U7188
灬	S15-4-11	F0000

traditional form → see 熙 at 3559

樂

3548

▬2-11-4

▶**PLEASURE**
▶**COMFORTABLE**
▶**MUSIC**

ガク ラク たの(しい) たの(しむ)

75	Names	U6A02
木	S15-4-11	F0000

traditional form → see 楽 at 3505

獎

3549

▬2-11-4

▶**ENCOURAGE**

ショウ すす(める) ㊔ すすむ

94	Nonstandard	U734E
犬	S15-4-11	F0000

traditional form → see 奨 at 3524

憇

3550

▬2-11-4

▶**TAKE A REST**

ケイ いこ(い) いこ(う)

61	Nonstandard	U6187
心	S15-4-11	F0000

traditional form → see 憩 at 3590

慾

3551

▬2-11-4

▶**DESIRE**

ヨク

Ⓒ 欲 yù

61	Non-Jōyō	U617E
心	S15-4-11	F0000

COMPOUNDS

● [now replaced by 欲 1867] [also suffix] [original meaning] **DESIRE, craving; avarice, greed**

性慾 せいよく sexual desire, lust
愛慾 あいよく love and lust, sexual passion
物慾 ぶつよく worldly desires
無慾 むよく freedom from avarice
色慾 しきよく sexual appetite
食慾 しょくよく appetite (for food)
名誉慾 めいよよく love of fame

INDEPENDENT

【よく 慾】 **DESIRE**, craving; avarice, greed

SYNONYMS

● **wish and desire**

願 WISH →2320
憧 YEARN AFTER →0899
憬 YEARN AFTER →0898
貪 COVET →2630
望 HOPE →3408
希 ASPIRE →2543
懐 LONG FOR →0942
慕 yearn for →2970
渇 thirst for →0627
欲 DESIRE →1867
慾 DESIRE →3551
求 SEEK →4365

熈 絲絲 將 甜 欲 【毄】 斬 默 埶 執 尉 孰 熙 動 魚 窒 蕪 涸

擊

▸**STRIKE**
ゲキ う(つ)
Ⓝ 撃 軎◆ Ⓒ 击 jī

3552
2-11-4

64 手	Jōyō	U6483
	S15-4-11	F0423

(Stroke order 1–15)

COMPOUNDS

❶ **STRIKE, make a military attack, destroy**

撃破する げきはする defeat, rout; destroy
攻撃 こうげき attack, assault; criticism; *baseball* batting
爆撃 ばくげき bombing, bombardment
反撃する はんげきする counterattack, strike [fight] back
襲撃する しゅうげきする raid, attack, assault

❷ **fire, shoot, discharge**

撃墜する げきついする shoot down
撃沈する げきちんする attack and sink a ship
射撃する しゃげきする shoot, fire at
銃撃 じゅうげき shooting, gunning (down)

❸ⓐ [original meaning] **STRIKE, beat**
ⓑ come in contact with

a 打撃 だげき blow, strike; batting, hitting
直撃 ちょくげき direct hit
衝撃 しょうげき impact, shock, impulse
目撃者 もくげきしゃ eyewitness
電撃 でんげき electric shock; lightning attack, blitz

KUN

【うつ 撃つ】

① **fire, shoot, discharge**

撃ち落とす うちおとす shoot down
早撃ち はやうち quick [snap] shooting; quick [snap] shot [draw]

② [sometimes also 打つ or 討つ] **attack, STRIKE, assault**

撃ち破る うちやぶる defeat, crush
迎え撃つ むかえうつ fight the attack of an enemy

SYNONYMS

❶ **attack**

攻 ATTACK →0286
撃 STRIKE →3552
襲 RAID →3633
侵 INVADE →0116
爆 bomb →1415

❷ **shoot**

射 SHOOT →1850
撃 fire →3552
発 discharge →3174

❸ⓐ **strike**

打 STRIKE →0224
撲 DEAL A BLOW →0903
殴 BEAT (strike a person) →1099
蹴 KICK →2074
撃 STRIKE →3552
挌 STRIKE (a person) →0448
撞 STRIKE (a ball or bell) →0905
撥ねる strike (knock down) →0907
当てる HIT →2701
叩 KNOCK →0208
拍 BEAT (strike repeatedly) →0361
搏 BEAT (throb) →0794

HOMOPHONES

うつ

討 STUDY →1846
打 STRIKE →0224

NOTE

➡ see USAGE note at 打 0224

暫

▶SHORT WHILE
ザン しばら(く)▲
Ⓒ 暂 zàn

3553
2-11-4

72	Jōyō	U66AB
日	S15-4-11	F2108

COMPOUNDS

ⓐ [original meaning] **SHORT WHILE, a while**
ⓑ **for the time being, temporary, provisional**

a 暫時 ざんじ short while, a moment
b 暫定の ざんていの provisional, tentative
暫定案 ざんていあん provisional plan

KUN

【しばらく 暫く】**awhile, a moment; good while, long time; for the time being**
暫くですね しばらくですね It's been a while

SYNONYMS

ⓐ **short time periods**
頃 moment → 0163
瞬 INSTANT → 1594
秒 SECOND → 1462
分 MINUTE → 2466
時 hour → 1155
暫 SHORT WHILE → 3553

ⓑ **temporary**
仮 TEMPORARY → 0053
暫 for the time being → 3553

NOTE

★ do not confuse with 漸 GRADUALLY → 0867

黙

▶SILENT
モク だま(る) もだ(す)▲
Ⓝ 默 Ⓒ 默 mò

3554
2-11-4

203	Jōyō	U9ED9
黑	S15-11-4	F0839

COMPOUNDS

ⓐ **SILENT, taciturn**
ⓑ (unexpressed) **SILENT, tacit**

a 黙秘する もくひする keep silent, keep secret
黙祷 もくとう silent prayer
黙読する もくどくする read silently
沈黙 ちんもく silence, reticence, taciturnity
寡黙な かもくな silent, taciturn, reticent
b 黙認 もくにん tacit [silent] approval, toleration
黙許 もっきょ tacit permission
暗黙の あんもくの tacit

INDEPENDENT

【もくする 黙する】keep **SILENT**

KUN

【だまる 黙る】**become SILENT, shut one's mouth**
黙り だんまり silence; taciturnity; refusing explanation; pantomime
黙り込む だまりこむ sink into silence

【もだす 黙す】be **SILENT**; leave something unattended
黙し難い もだしがたい be unable to decline

SYNONYMS

ⓐ **quiet**
静 QUIET → 2164
閑 QUIET → 4123
寂 quiet → 2855
幽 QUIET AND SECLUDED → 3731
粛 still → 4400
黙 SILENT → 3554

熱

▶HEAT
▶HOT
ネツ あつ(い)
Ⓒ 热 rè

3555
2-11-4

86	Jōyō-4	U71B1
灬	S15-4-11	F0534

COMPOUNDS

❶ⓐ (source of warmth) **HEAT**
ⓑ [also prefix] **HEAT** energy, thermo-
ⓒ **HEAT, make hot**

a 高熱 こうねつ intense heat; high fever
加熱 かねつ heating
光熱費 こうねつひ fuel and electricity expenses
地熱 じねつ(=ちねつ) terrestrial heat
耐熱性 たいねつせい heat-resisting property
b 熱機関 ねつきかん heat engine, thermomotor
熱原子核 ねつげんしかく thermal nucleus
c 過熱する かねつする overheat, superheat

❷ [also suffix] (abnormal bodily heat) **fever, temperature**
熱病 ねつびょう fever
発熱 はつねつ generation of heat; attack of fever
微熱 びねつ slight fever

産褥×熱 さんじょくねつ puerperal fever

❸ [original meaning] **HOT, boiling**

熱湯 ねっとう boiling water

熱帯 ねったい tropics, torrid zone

熱気 ねっき hot air, heat; fevered air, enthusiasm

灼熱 しゃくねつ heat

❹ (showing intense feeling) **HOT (with excitement), fervent, passionate, ardent, enthusiastic, earnest**

熱意 ねつい zeal, ardor, enthusiasm

熱心に ねっしんに enthusiastically, zealously, fervently, earnestly

熱戦 ねっせん hot contest, hard fight

熱中する ねっちゅうする be absorbed in, become enthusiastic

熱望 ねつぼう fervent hope, earnest desire

熱烈な ねつれつな ardent, fervent, vehement

熱血漢 ねっけつかん hot-blooded man

情熱 じょうねつ passion, enthusiasm

❺ [suffix] fever, craze, enthusiasm, mania

野球熱 やきゅうねつ baseball fever, enthusiasm for baseball

海外留学熱 かいがいりゅうがくねつ craze for studying abroad

投機熱 とうきねつ speculation fever

INDEPENDENT

【ねつ 熱】 **HEAT; fever; enthusiasm, passion**

熱を上げる ねつをあげる become enthusiastic

勉強に熱が入る べんきょうにねつがはいる become very keen on one's studies

【ねっする 熱する】 **HEAT, make hot; become hot, get excited**

熱し易い ねっしやすい excitable

KUN

【あつい 熱い】

① **HOT (to the touch), heated**

熱さ あつさ heat

熱いコーヒー あついこーひー hot coffee

②ⓐ **HOT (with excitement), passionate**

ⓑ be madly in love

b 熱い仲だ あついなかだ be sweet on each other

SYNONYMS

❶ⓐ **heat**

熱 HEAT → 3555

暑 SUMMER HEAT → 3121

ⓒ **raise the temperature**

暖 WARM (the air) → 1274

煖 WARM (the air) → 1293

温める WARM (a thing) → 0740

熱 HEAT → 3555

❷ **diseases and disease symptoms**

痘 SMALLPOX → 4070

淋 GONORRHEA → 0632

癌 CANCER → 4076

熱 fever → 3555

炎 INFLAMMATION → 3075

痢 DIARRHEA → 4068

下 diarrhea → 4186

❸ **hot**

熱 HOT → 3555

暑い HOT (weather) → 3121

炎 scorching → 3075

温 WARM → 0740

暖 WARM (esp. weather) → 1274

❹ **eager**

懇 EARNEST → 3606

切 eager → 0030

摯 SERIOUS → 3556

篤 DEVOTED → 3371

熱 HOT → 3555

❺ **mania and maniacs**

痴 infatuated → 4072

狂 maniac → 0318

魔 maniac → 3953

熱 fever → 3555

USAGE

【あつい】

熱い

① hot (to the touch), heated

②ⓐ hot (with excitement), passionate

ⓑ be madly in love

暑い

hot (weather), warm, sultry

HOMOPHONES

あつい 暑 SUMMER HEAT → 3121

摯

3556

2-11-4

▶**SERIOUS**

シ

Ⓒ 摯 zhì

64	Jōyō	U646F
手	S15-4-11	F2730

COMPOUNDS

● **SERIOUS, sincere**

真摯 しんし sincerity, earnestness

SYNONYMS

● **eager**

懇 EARNEST → 3606

切 eager → 0030

摯 SERIOUS → 3556
篤 DEVOTED → 3371
熱 HOT → 3555

慰

▶CONSOLE
イ なぐさ(める) なぐさ(む)
Ⓒ 慰 wèi

3557
2-11-4

61	Jōyō	U6170
心	S15-4-11	F1670

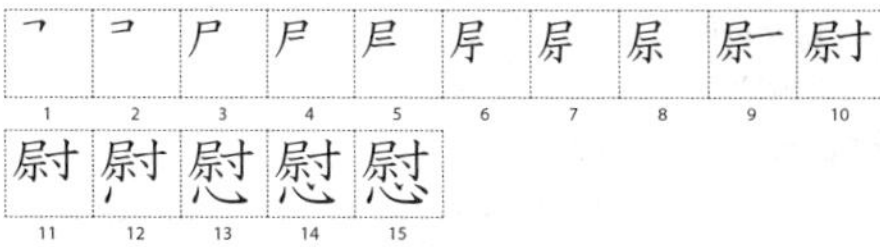

COMPOUNDS

ⓐ [original meaning] **CONSOLE, comfort; show sympathy to**
ⓑ divert, amuse; amuse oneself sexually

a 慰問 いもん inquiring after a person's health; consolation
慰霊 いれい comforting the spirits of the dead
慰謝料 いしゃりょう consolation money
慰労 いろう recognition of services
b 慰安 いあん solace, consolation; recreation
弔慰 ちょうい condolence, sympathy
自慰 じい self-consolation; masturbation

INDEPENDENT

【いする 慰する】 CONSOLE, comfort

KUN

【なぐさめる 慰める】 **CONSOLE, comfort, cheer up**
慰め なぐさめ consolation, comfort
慰め顔 なぐさめがお comforting look
酒は心を慰める さけはこころをなぐさめる Drink comforts the soul

【なぐさむ 慰む】 **be diverted (by); make fun of; make a plaything of, play around with (an innocent girl)**
慰み なぐさみ amusement, pastime, pleasure; fooling around
慰み半分 なぐさみはんぶん half for fun
慰んだ挙句に捨てる なぐさんだあげくにすてる throw a girl away after making her one's plaything
何の慰みも無い毎日 なんのなぐさみもないまいにち a pleasureless life

SYNONYMS

ⓐ **console**
慰 CONSOLE → 3557
弔 CONDOLE → 4240

熟

▶MATURE
ジュク う(れる)
Ⓒ 熟 shú shóu

3558
2-11-4

86	Jōyō-6	U719F
灬	S15-4-11	F1330

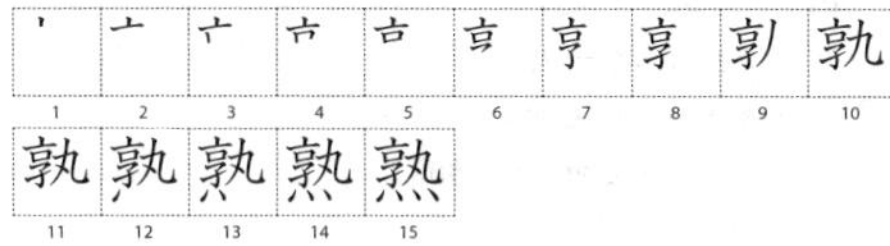

COMPOUNDS

❶ (become ripe, as of fruit) **MATURE, ripen**
熟柿 じゅくし ripe persimmon
未熟な みじゅくな unripe, immature; unskilled, poor

❷ⓐ (become fully developed) **MATURE, ripen, attain full growth**
ⓑ **become skilled, attain proficiency**

a 熟成 じゅくせい aging, ripening, maturation
成熟する せいじゅくする mature, ripen, attain full growth
早熟な そうじゅくな precocious, forward
b 熟練 じゅくれん skill, dexterity
熟達する じゅくたつする attain proficiency, become expert
円熟した えんじゅくした mature, mellow, ripe, fully developed
習熟する しゅうじゅくする get skilled (in), become practiced (in)

❸ [original meaning] boiled, cooked
熟食 じゅくしょく [rare] well-cooked[-boiled] food
半熟卵 はんじゅくたまご soft boiled egg

❹ thoroughly, carefully, completely
熟読 じゅくどく careful reading
熟睡 じゅくすい sound sleep
熟知 じゅくち thorough knowledge
熟考 じゅっこう due consideration, mature reflection

❺ (of words) **get into popular use, come to sound natural**
熟語 じゅくご compound word (esp. in Japanese); phrase, idiom

INDEPENDENT

【じゅくす 熟す】 (become ripe, as of fruit) **MATURE**, ripen, be ripe for; get into popular use
機が熟すのを待つ きがじゅくすのをまつ wait for a ripe moment

KUN

【うれる 熟れる】 **ripen, become ripe, mellow, MATURE**
熟れ うれ ripeness, maturity
熟れ過ぎ うれすぎ overripeness
熟れた果実 うれたかじつ mellow [ripe] fruit

巸
𢇍
將
甜
欲
毄
斬
猒
埶
執
尉
孰
【巸】
動
魚
窐
蕪
凞

SYNONYMS

❶ & ❷ⓐ mature

熟 MATURE → 3558
成 grow up → 4352
稔 RIPEN → 1544
爛 OVERRIPE → 1427
実る bear fruit → 2765

❷ⓑ attain proficiency

達 attain proficiency → 3893
熟 become skilled → 3558

熙

3559
2-11-4

▶**BRIGHT**

キ ㊔ ひろ ひろし ひろむ のり よし

Ⓝ 凞 凞 熈 熈 Ⓒ 熙 xī

86	Names	U7199
灬	S15-4-11	F3042

COMPOUNDS

ⓐ **BRIGHT, prosperous; glorious, peaceful**
ⓑ happiness, joy, enjoyment

ab 熙熙たる きぎたる *literary* in a delightful manner; extensive, vast; (of traffic) busy

SYNONYMS

ⓐ **bright**

明 BRIGHT → 1060
昭 LUMINOUS → 1107
蛍 fluorescent → 3204
晃 DAZZLING → 3101
燦 BRILLIANT → 1390
赫 BLAZING → 1960
暉 radiant → 1276
熙 BRIGHT → 3559
晟 SUNNY → 3104

勲

3560
2-11-4

▶**MERITORIOUS SERVICE**

クン いさお▲ ㊔ いさ いさむ

Ⓝ 勳 Ⓒ 勋 xūn

19	Jōyō	U52F2
力	S15-2-13	F2089

1	2	3	4	5	6	7	8	9	10	11	12	13	14	15
一	二	亍	呈	旨	旨	亘	重	重	動	動	動	勲	勲	勲

COMPOUNDS

ⓐ **MERITORIOUS [distinguished] SERVICE, merit, meritorious deed, exploits**
ⓑ order of merit, decoration

a 勲功 くんこう distinguished services, merit
勲章 くんしょう decoration, order, medal
殊勲 しゅくん meritorious deeds, distinguished service
武勲 ぶくん deeds of arms, distinguished military service

b 勲記 くんき decoration diploma, diploma
叙勲 じょくん decoration, bestowal of an order

INDEPENDENT

【くん 勲】 order of merit
勲一等 くんいっとう First Order of Merit

KUN

【いさお 勲】 [also 功] *elegant* **MERITORIOUS SERVICE, merit**

SYNONYMS

ⓐ **accomplishment**

績 ACHIEVEMENTS → 1788
功 MERIT → 0218
勲 MERITORIOUS SERVICE → 3560

USAGE

【いさお】

勲
[also 功] *elegant* meritorious service, merit

功
[also 勲] *elegant* meritorious service, merit

HOMOPHONES

いさお 功 MERIT → 0218

魯

2-11-4

incorrect classification
➡ see 2-2-13: ⺈ at 2665

窯

2-11-4

incorrect classification
➡ see 2-3-12: 宀 at 2986

蕪

2-11-4

incorrect classification
➡ see 2-3-12: 艹 at 2990

凞

2-11-4

incorrect stroke-count
➡ see 2-12-4: 凞 at 3589

禦

3561
2-11-5

▶**WARD OFF**

ギョ ふせ(ぐ)

Ⓒ 御 yù

113	Non-Jōyō	U79A6
示	S16-5-11	F3296

COMPOUNDS

[now replaced by 御 0703]

❶ [original meaning] **WARD OFF, resist, keep out**

防禦する ぼうぎょする defend, protect, safeguard

❷ **handle, control**

制禦する せいぎょする control, govern, suppress

KUN

【ふせぐ 禦ぐ】[now replaced by 防ぐ] **WARD OFF, prevent, keep off; defend, protect, resist**

侵略を禦ぐ しんりゃくをふせぐ defend against an invasion

SYNONYMS

❶ **avoid and abstain**

避 AVOID → 3944
逃 ESCAPE → 3839
禦 WARD OFF → 3561
忌 shun → 2735
禁 abstain from → 3469

HOMOPHONES

ふせぐ 防 PREVENT → 0320

NOTE

➡ see USAGE note at 防 0320

整

3562

2-11-5

▶**PUT IN ORDER**

セイ ととの(える) ととの(う) ㊔ ひとし

Ⓒ 整 zhěng

66	Jōyō-3	U6574
攵	S16-4-12	F0757

一	𠂉	𠃍	𠃍	申	申	束	束	束	束
1	2	3	4	5	6	7	8	9	10

敕	敕	敕	敕	整	整
11	12	13	14	15	16

COMPOUNDS

ⓐ [original meaning] **PUT IN ORDER, arrange, adjust properly, make straight**

ⓑ **in good order, well-arranged, proper, intact**

a 整理する せいりする put in order, arrange; liquidate, disorganize; retrench; cut, dispose of
整備 せいび maintenance, servicing, preparation
整風 せいふう rectification
整形外科 せいけいげか orthopedic surgery, orthopedics
整列する せいれつする stand in a row, line up
整地 せいち leveling of ground, soil preparation
整頓 せいとん proper arrangement
調整 ちょうせい regulation, adjustment

b 整然たる せいぜんたる orderly, systematic
整数 せいすう integer
均整(=均斉) きんせい symmetry

KUN

【ととのえる 整える】(put in order) **arrange, tidy up, adjust (clothes), regulate**

髪を整える かみをととのえる arrange [tidy up] one's hair
調子を整える ちょうしをととのえる put in tune

【ととのう 整う】**be in order, be adjusted [regulated], be made up properly**

整った ととのった in good order, well-ordered, well-regulated; well-featured
服装が整っている ふくそうがととのっている be properly dressed

SYNONYMS

ⓐ **arrange**

並 LINE UP → 2793
比 rank → 0029
列 arrange in a row → 1018
陳 lay out (for exhibit) → 0656
羅 spread out → 3244
揃える arrange properly → 0719
整 PUT IN ORDER → 3562
理 put in order → 1220

HOMOPHONES

ととのえる 調 TONE → 1973
ととのう 調 TONE → 1973

NOTE

➡ see USAGE note at 調 1973

奮

2-11-5

incorrect classification
➡ see 2-3-13: 大 at 3000

蕾

2-11-5

incorrect classification
➡ see 2-3-13: 艹 at 3006

篭

2-11-5

incorrect classification
➡ see 2-6-10: ⺮ at 3373

舉

3563

2-11-5

▶**NOMINATE**
▶**NOTEWORTHY ACT**
▶**RAISE**

キョ あ(げる) あ(がる) ㊔ たか

134	Nonstandard	U8209
臼	S16-7-9	F0000

traditional form → see 挙 at 3106

繫

3564

2-11-6

▶**CONNECT**

ケイ つな(ぐ) つな(がる) つな(げる) かか(る)

120	Nonstandard	U7E4B
糸	S17-6-11	F0000

traditional form → see 繋 at 3612

聲

3565

2-11-6

▶**VOICE**

セイ ショウ こえ こわ-

128	Nonstandard	U8072
耳	S17-6-11	F0000

traditional form → see 声 at 2724

軗 殼 【敏】 殹 齟

繫
3566
⬒2-11-6

▶**THRIVE**
ハン　しげ(る)　しげ(く)

120	Names	UFA59
糸	S17-6-11	F0000

traditional form → see 繁 at 3536

翳
3567
⬒2-11-6

▶**SHADOW**
エイ　かげ(る)　かす(む)　かざ(す)
Ⓒ 翳 yì

124	Non-Jōyō	U7FF3
羽	S17-6-11	F2468

COMPOUNDS

● [now replaced by 影 2381] **SHADOW, shade**
暗翳 あんえい shadow, gloom
陰翳 いんえい shadow

KUN

【かげる　翳る】[also 陰る] **darken, be clouded**
翳り かげり shade; gloom
翳りの有る顔 かげりのあるかお face shaded with pensiveness
【かすむ　翳む】[now usu. 霞む] **have dim sight**
【かざす　翳す】**hold up over one's head, hold aloft; hold one's hands out (toward a fire)**
振り翳す ふりかざす brandish (a sword) over one's head

SYNONYMS

● **shadow**
影 SHADOW → 2381
翳 SHADOW → 3567
陰 SHADE → 0657
蔭 SHADE → 2974

HOMOPHONES

かげり 陰 SHADE → 0657
かげる 陰 SHADE → 0657
かすむ 霞 MIST → 3490

NOTE

➡ see USAGE notes at 陰 0657 and 霞 3490

擧
3568
⬒2-11-6

▶**NOMINATE**
▶**NOTEWORTHY ACT**
▶**RAISE**
キョ　あ(げる)　あ(がる) ㊔ たか

64	Nonstandard	U64E7
手	S17-4-13	F0000

traditional form → see 挙 at 3106

醬
3569
⬒2-11-7

▶**FERMENTED SAUCE**
ショウ　ジャン　ひしお
Ⓝ 醤 Ⓒ 酱 jiàng

164	Names	U91AC
酉	S18-7-11	F2575

COMPOUNDS

● **FERMENTED SAUCE [paste]; kind of miso**
醬油 しょうゆ soy sauce
魚醬 ぎょしょう fish sauce
豆板醬 とうばんじゃん chili bean paste
ＸＯ醬 えっくすおーじゃん XO sauce

KUN

【ひしお　醬】kind of miso

SPECIAL READINGS

醬蝦 あみ opossum shrimp

SYNONYMS

● **seasonings**
糖 SUGAR → 1777
塩 SALT → 0774
酢 VINEGAR → 1910
醋 VINEGAR → 2002
油 OIL → 0400
醬 FERMENTED SAUCE → 3569
噌 MISO → 0882
蜜 HONEY → 2958

毉
3570
⬒2-11-7

▶**MEDICINE**
▶**DOCTOR**
イ

79	Nonstandard	U6BC9
殳	S18-4-14	F0000

traditional form → see 医 at 3715

醫
3571
⬒2-11-7

▶**MEDICINE**
▶**DOCTOR**
イ

164	Nonstandard	U91AB
酉	S18-7-11	F0000

traditional form → see 医 at 3715

叢
⬒2-11-7

incorrect classification
➡ see ⬒2-5-13: 䒑 at 3243

豐
3572
⬒2-11-7

▶**PLENTIFUL**
ホウ　ブ　ゆた(か) ㊔ とよ　と　ぶん　みのる　て　のぼる

151	Nonstandard	U8C50
豆	S18-7-11	F0000

traditional form → see 豊 at 3344

響 3573

2-11-9

▶REVERBERATE

キョウ ひび(く)

Ⓝ 響 响 響◇ Ⓒ 响 xiǎng

180 音	Jōyō	U97FF
	S20-9-11	F0694

COMPOUNDS

❶ⓐ [original meaning] **REVERBERATE, resound, echo, ring**

ⓑ **reverberation, echo, sound**

a 反響する はんきょうする echo, reverberate

反響 はんきょう echo, reverberation; response, repercussions

影響 えいきょう influence, effect

b 音響 おんきょう sound

交響 こうきょう reverberation

無響室 むきょうしつ anechoic room

交響曲 こうきょうきょく symphony

❷ abbrev. of 交響楽団 こうきょうがくだん: symphony orchestra

Ｎ響 えぬきょう NHK Symphony Orchestra

ボストン響 ぼすとんきょう Boston Symphony Orchestra

KUN

【ひびく 響く】**REVERBERATE, resound; ring, sound; vibrate; affect, have an unfavorable influence; get known**

響き ひびき sound, echo; vibration; influence

鳴り響く なりひびく reverberate, echo, resound

地響き じひびき earth tremor

暮らしに響く くらしにひびく affect the cost of living

名が響いている ながひびいている be famous

SYNONYMS

❶ⓐ **make sound or noise**

鳴 SOUND →0831

響 REVERBERATE →3573

騒 CLAMOR →2308

轟 RESOUND →3425

ⓑ **kinds of sound**

音 SOUND →2570

声 VOICE →2724

響 reverberation →3573

韻 melodious tone →2279

玲 TINKLING OF JADES →1139

NOTE

➡ see COMPOUND FORMATION for 影響 えいきょう →影 2381

饗 3574

2-11-9

▶BANQUET

キョウ ㊔ あえ

184 食	Nonstandard	U9957
	S20-9-11	F0000

traditional form → see 饗 at 3616

馨 3575

2-11-9

▶PERFUME

ケイ キョウ ㊔ かおる かおり はじめ

Ⓒ 馨 xīn

186 香	Names	U99A8
	S20-9-11	F2950

COMPOUNDS

● [original meaning, now archaic] **PERFUME**, fragrance, aroma

馨香 けいこう(=けいきょう) perfume, fragrance, aroma; honor, fame

SYNONYMS

● **smell and fragrance**

気 smell →3960

匂い SMELL →3662

臭 BAD SMELL →3261

香 SWEET SMELL →3177

馨 PERFUME →3575

芳 FRAGRANT →2739

薫 BALMY →3005

郁 AROMATIC →1640

轝 3576

2-11-9

▶PALANQUIN

ヨ こし

159 車	Nonstandard	U8F5D
	S20-7-13	F0000

traditional form → see 輿 at 3626

譽 3577

2-11-9

▶HONOR

ヨ ほま(れ) ほ(める) ㊔ たか たかし しげ

149 言	Nonstandard	U8B7D
	S20-7-13	F0000

traditional form → see 誉 at 3135

與

2-12-2

incorrect stroke-count

➡ see 2-11-2: 與 at 3543

學

2-12-2

incorrect stroke-count

➡ see 2-12-3: 與 at 3588

堊

2-12-3

incorrect stroke-count

➡ see 2-8-3: 亞 at 3442

亞 【隊】 隊 隋 林 敝 敝 道 與

墜

▶DROP DOWN

ツイ

Ⓝ 墜 Ⓒ 坠 zhuì

3578

2-12-3

32	Jōyō	U589C
土	S15-3-12	F2208

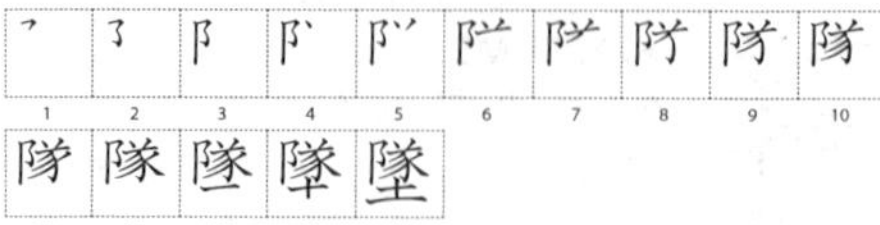

COMPOUNDS

❶ⓐ [original meaning] (fall suddenly from a great height) **DROP DOWN, drop, fall down, crash down**

ⓑ **cause to DROP DOWN, drop**

a 墜落 ついらく fall, crash

墜死する ついしする fall to one's death (as from a cliff)

b 撃墜する げきついする shoot down

❷ fall to ruin, decline, lose

失墜 しっつい loss, fall

SYNONYMS

❶ **descend and fall**

落 FALL → 2907

墜 DROP DOWN → 3578

降 DESCEND → 0548

下 go down → 4186

倒 TOPPLE → 0139

墬

▶DROP DOWN

ツイ

3579

2-12-3

32	Nonstandard	U589C
土	S15-3-12	F0000

traditional form → see 墜 at 3578

墮

▶DEGENERATE

ダ

3580

2-12-3

32	Nonstandard	U58AE
土	S15-3-12	F0000

traditional form → see 堕 at 3501

壄

▶FIELD

ヤ の の- ㊔ のう ぬ

3581

2-12-3

32	Nonstandard	U58C4
土	S15-3-12	F0000

traditional form → see 野 at 1877

幣

▶CURRENCY

ヘイ ぬさ▲ ㊔ しで

Ⓝ 幣 幣 Ⓒ 币 bì

3582

2-12-3

50	Jōyō	U5E63
巾	S15-3-12	F1970

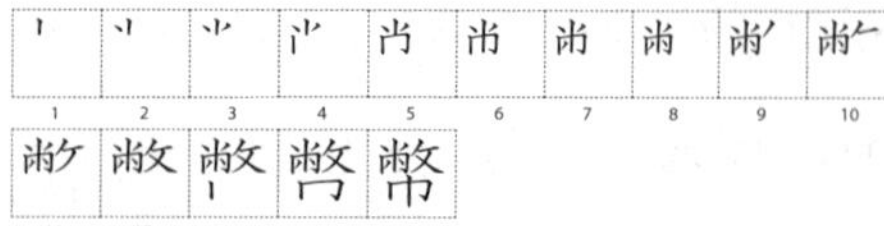

COMPOUNDS

❶ **CURRENCY, money, coins, legal tender**

幣制 へいせい currency [monetary] system

貨幣 かへい money, currency, coinage

造幣 ぞうへい coinage, mintage

紙幣 しへい paper currency, bank note, bill

❷ⓐ **offering of cloth or paper to the gods, esp. in Shinto rituals**

ⓑ offering (to a ruler or guest), tribute, present

a 幣帛× へいはく Shinto offering of cloth (or paper)

御幣 ごへい pendant paper strips in a Shinto shrine, sacred staff with cut paper

奉幣 ほうへい offering a wand with hemp and paper streamers to a Shinto god

b 幣物 へいもつ(=へいぶつ) Shinto offerings; present to a guest

幣貢 へいこう tribute, offering

INDEPENDENT

【へい 幣】Shinto offering of cloth or paper; tribute, present

KUN

【ぬさ 幣】offering of cloth or paper to the gods, esp. in Shinto rituals

幣を奉る ぬさをたてまつる offer a wand with hemp and paper streamers to a Shinto god

SYNONYMS

❶ **money**

金 MONEY → 2552

銭 MONEY → 2159

貨 MONEY (legal tender), coin → 3113

幣 CURRENCY → 3582

銀 SILVER → 2156

財 finance → 1849

資 RESOURCES → 3342

-玉 coin suffix → 4289

札 bill → 1011

❷ **offering**

奠 OFFERING → 2641

幣 offering → 3582

貢 TRIBUTE → 2838

NOTE

★ do not confuse with 弊 EVIL PRACTICE → 3583

弊

3583

2-12-3

▶**EVIL PRACTICE**

ヘイ

Ⓝ 弊 Ⓒ 弊 bì

55	Jōyō	U5F0A
廾	S15-3-12	F2332

COMPOUNDS

❶ⓐ **EVIL [corrupt] PRACTICE, bad habit, defect**
ⓑ (something undesirable) **evil(s), abuse**

a 弊習 へいしゅう corrupt custom, bad habit
弊政 へいせい misgovernment, maladministration
積弊 せきへい deep-rooted evil

b 弊害 へいがい evil, abuse, vice
悪弊 あくへい evil, vice, abuse
語弊 ごへい defects in expression, improper word
党弊 とうへい party evils

❷ shabby, worn-out, ragged, poor, impoverished
弊衣破帽 へいいはぼう shabby clothes and an old hat
弊履 へいり worn-out sandals [shoes]

❸ [humble] **our [my] humble**
弊社 へいしゃ our firm
弊店 へいてん our shop

INDEPENDENT

【へい 弊】**EVIL** [corrupt] **PRACTICE**, bad habit, defect; (something undesirable) **evil(s)**, abuse
飲酒の弊 いんしゅのへい bad habit of drinking
時代の弊 じだいのへい abuses of the times

SYNONYMS

❶ⓐ **custom**
慣 HABITUAL PRACTICE → 0843
例 established practice → 0099
習 CUSTOM → 3306
風 manners → 3730
俗 popular custom → 0119
癖 HABIT → 4080
弊 EVIL PRACTICE → 3583

ⓑ **wrongdoing and evil**
罪 sin → 3224
非 wrong(doing) → 1101
邪 wrong → 1443
悪 evil (something bad) → 3413
弊 evil(s) (something undesirable) → 3583

❷ **bad**
悪 BAD → 3413
劣 INFERIOR → 3047
下 of low grade → 4186
弊 shabby → 3583
粗 COARSE → 1683
駄 GOOD FOR NOTHING → 2291
廃 WASTE → 3902

❸ **humble prefixes**
小 my little (*humble*) → 0007
弊 our [my] humble → 3583
拙 my humble → 0373
愚 my foolish → 3513

NOTE

★ do not confuse with 幣 CURRENCY → 3582

幣

3584

2-12-3

▶**CURRENCY**

ヘイ ぬさ ㊔ しで

50	Nonstandard	U5E64
巾	S15-3-12	F0000

traditional form → see 幣 at 3582

弊

3585

2-12-3

▶**EVIL PRACTICE**

ヘイ

55	Nonstandard	U5F0A
廾	S15-3-12	F0000

traditional form → see 弊 at 3583

幣

3586

2-12-3

▶**CURRENCY**

ヘイ ぬさ ㊔ しで

50	Nonstandard	U5E63
巾	S15-3-12	F0000

traditional form → see 幣 at 3582

導

3587

2-12-3

▶**GUIDE**

ドウ みちび(く) ㊔ みち

Ⓝ 導 Ⓒ 导 dǎo

41	Jōyō-5	U5C0E
寸	S15-3-12	F0625

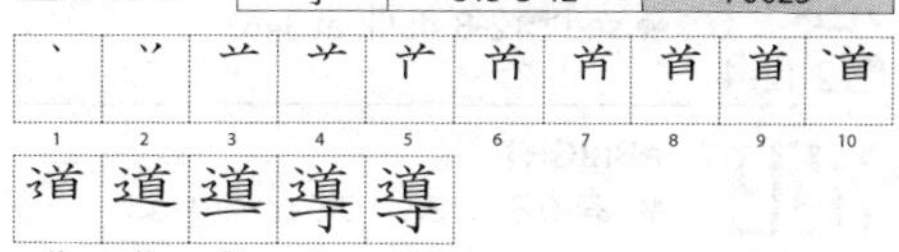

COMPOUNDS

❶ⓐ (show the way) **GUIDE, lead, conduct**
ⓑ (give guidance to) **GUIDE, teach, instruct, direct**

a 導入する どうにゅうする lead into, bring into
導因 どういん inducement, incentive
主導権 しゅどうけん leadership, initiative
誘導する ゆうどうする induce, incite; guide, lead
盲導犬 もうどうけん guide dog, Seeing Eye dog

b 指導する しどうする guide, lead, instruct
教導する きょうどうする instruct, teach, train

❷ (serve as a medium) **conduct, transmit**
導火線 どうかせん fuse; cause, incentive
伝導 でんどう conduction, transmission
半導体 はんどうたい semiconductor

KUN

【みちびく 導く】**GUIDE, lead, conduct, usher**
導き みちびき guidance
導き出す みちびきだす draw (a conclusion), deduce
導き手 みちびきて guide

SYNONYMS

❶ⓐ lead and escort
率 LEAD → 2625
引 lead → 0207
導 GUIDE → 3587
連 take along → 3849

ⓑ teach
教 TEACH → 1887
啓 ENLIGHTEN → 3434
諄 TEACH WITH CARE → 1979
授 teach → 0595
育 educate → 2544
練 TRAIN → 1738
訓 INSTRUCT → 1844
誨 INSTRUCT → 1946
諭 ADMONISH → 2012
導 GUIDE → 3587
迪 EDIFY → 3817

亞 隊 隊 隋 𣟗 敝 敝 道 【𦥯】

學

3588
2-12-3

▶**STUDY**
▶**EDUCATIONAL INSTITUTION**
ガク まな(ぶ)

39	Nonstandard	U5B66
子	S15-3-12	F0000

alternative form → see 学 at 3162

惡

2-12-4

incorrect stroke-count
➡ see 2-8-4: 亞 at 3463

凞

3589
2-12-4

▶**BRIGHT**
キ ㊔ ひろ ひろし ひろむ のり よし

86	Nonstandard	UFA15
灬	S16-4-12	F0000

traditional form → see 熙 at 3559

憩

3590
2-12-4

▶**TAKE A REST**
ケイ いこ(い) いこ(う)
Ⓝ 憩 Ⓒ 憩 qì

61	Jōyō	U61A9
心	S16-4-12	F2244

COMPOUNDS

● **TAKE A REST, repose, relax, rest**
憩室 けいしつ diverticulum
休憩する きゅうけいする rest, repose
小憩 しょうけい short rest, brief recess

KUN

【いこい 憩い】**rest, repose, relaxation, vacation**
憩いの場 いこいのば place for relaxation and refreshment

【いこう 憩う】**TAKE A REST, repose, relax, rest**
木陰に憩う こかげにいこう take a rest under a tree

SYNONYMS

● **rest**
休 REST → 0056
息 rest → 3278
憩 TAKE A REST → 3590
歇 TAKE A REST → 2243

凞

2-12-4

incorrect stroke-count
➡ see 2-13-4: 凞 at 3605

禦

2-12-5

incorrect stroke-count
➡ see 2-11-5: 御 at 3561

舉

2-12-5

incorrect stroke-count
➡ see 2-11-5: 𦦙 at 3563

瞥

3591
2-12-5

▶**GLANCE AT**
ベツ

109	Nonstandard	U77A5
目	S17-5-12	F0000

traditional form → see 瞥 at 3592

瞥

3592
2-12-5

▶**GLANCE AT**
ベツ
Ⓝ 瞥 Ⓒ 瞥 piē

109	Names	U77A5
目	S17-5-12	F2653

COMPOUNDS

● **GLANCE AT, look at**

瞥見する べっけんする glance at, take a brief look

一瞥 いちべつ a glance, a look

SYNONYMS

● **see and look**

見 SEE → 3151
看 WATCH → 3992
察 INSPECT → 2961
窺 WATCH FURTIVELY → 3002
瞥 GLANCE AT → 3592
目 look → 3777
観 VIEW → 2359
覧 LOOK OVER → 3538
眺 LOOK OUT OVER → 1503
望 LOOK AFAR → 3408
仰 LOOK UP → 0051
顧 LOOK BACK → 2394
視 REGARD → 1223

擧 2-12-6

incorrect stroke-count
➡ see 2-11-6: 舉 at 3568

斃

3593
2-12-6

▶**FALL DOWN DEAD**
ヘイ たお(す) たお(れる)
Ⓒ 毙 bì

66	Non-Jōyō	U6583
攵	S18-4-14	F2961

COMPOUNDS

❶ [original meaning] **FALL DOWN DEAD, perish, die**

斃死する へいしする fall dead, perish

❷ **kill**

KUN

【たおす 斃す】[now usu. 倒す] **kill**

敵を斃す てきをたおす kill one's enemy [opponent]

【たおれる 斃れる】[now usu. 倒れる] **FALL DOWN DEAD, perish, die**

凶弾に斃れる きょうだんにたおれる be shot to death by an assassin

SYNONYMS

❶ **die**

死 DIE → 4334
萎 WITHER → 2872
没 die → 0305
亡 DECEASE → 4210
殉 DIE A MARTYR → 1177
歿 DIE → 1078
去 pass away → 2678
逝 DEPART THIS LIFE → 3850
斃 FALL DOWN DEAD → 3593
枯 WITHER → 1113

HOMOPHONES

たおれる 倒 TOPPLE → 0139
たおす 倒 TOPPLE → 0139

NOTE

➡ see USAGE note at 倒 0139

嚮 2-12-6

incorrect stroke-count
➡ see 2-13-6: 嚮 at 3609

嚮 2-12-6

incorrect stroke-count
➡ see 2-13-6: 嚮 at 3610

賛

3594
2-12-7

▶**APPROVE OF**
▶**PRAISE**
サン

154	Nonstandard	U8D0A
貝	S19-7-12	F0000

traditional form → see 贊 at 3484

警

3595
2-12-7

▶**GUARD AGAINST**
▶**WARN**
ケイ いまし(める)▲
Ⓝ 警 Ⓒ 警 jǐng

149	Jōyō-6	U8B66
言	S19-7-12	F0435

1	2	3	4	5	6	7	8	9	10
11	12	13	14	15	16	17	18	19	

COMPOUNDS

❶ⓐ **GUARD AGAINST, protect, police, watch**
ⓑ **guard, watchman, police officer**

a 警察 けいさつ police, police station
警官 けいかん police officer, policeman
警視庁 けいしちょう Metropolitan Police Office
警戒 けいかい caution, precaution, warning; watch, guard, vigilance
警備 けいび guard, defense
警手 けいしゅ guard, attendant

b 夜警 やけい night watch; night watchman
婦警 ふけい policewoman

❷ abbrev. of 警察 けいさつ: **police (force)**

警部 けいぶ police inspector
警務 けいむ police affairs
県警 けんけい prefectural police
京都府警 きょうとふけい Kyoto Prefectural Police

❸ [original meaning] **WARN, admonish**

警告 けいこく warning, admonition
警報 けいほう warning signal, alarm

警鐘 けいしょう alarm bell, warning

❹ witty, smart, original, extraordinary

警句 けいく witticism

警抜な けいばつな scintillating, extraordinarily excellent

KUN

【いましめる 警める】[usu. 戒める]

ⓐ [sometimes also 誡める] caution against, admonish, **WARN**

ⓑ take caution (against), take precautions, **GUARD AGAINST**

a 警め いましめ caution, admonition, warning; caution, guard; commandment, precept

b 自ら警める みずからいましめる take precautions, guard against

SYNONYMS

❶ⓐ protect

守 PROTECT (by watching over) → 2697
護 PROTECT (by safeguarding) → 2079
庇 PROTECT (by shielding) → 3802
衛 GUARD → 0938
警 GUARD AGAINST → 3595
防 defend → 0320
番 WATCH → 3416
保 PRESERVE → 0107
看 CARE FOR → 3992

❶ⓐ take precautions

戒 take caution → 3972
警 GUARD AGAINST → 3595

ⓑ guard

哨 SENTRY → 0481
衛 GUARD → 0938
守 guard → 2697
警 guard → 3595

❸ warn

警 WARN → 3595
戒 CAUTION → 3972
誡 CAUTION AGAINST → 1947
諭 ADMONISH → 2012
告 advise → 3062

HOMOPHONES

いましめる

戒 CAUTION → 3972
誡 CAUTION AGAINST → 1947

いましめ 戒 CAUTION → 3972

NOTE

➡ see USAGE note at 戒 3972
★ do not confuse with 驚 SURPRISE → 3597

譽 incorrect stroke-count
➡ see 2-11-9: 臽 at 3577
2-12-9

轝 incorrect stroke-count
➡ see 2-11-9: 臽 at 3576
2-12-9

饗響 incorrect stroke-count
➡ see 2-13-9: 郷 at 3618
2-12-9

鬻

3596

2-12-10

▶RICE GRUEL

シュク かゆ

193	Nonstandard	U9B3B
鬲	S22-10-12	F0000

traditional form → see 粥 at 0698

驚

3597

2-12-10

▶SURPRISE

キョウ おどろ(く) おどろ(かす)

N 驚 C 惊 jīng

187	Jōyō	U9A5A
馬	S22-10-12	F0784

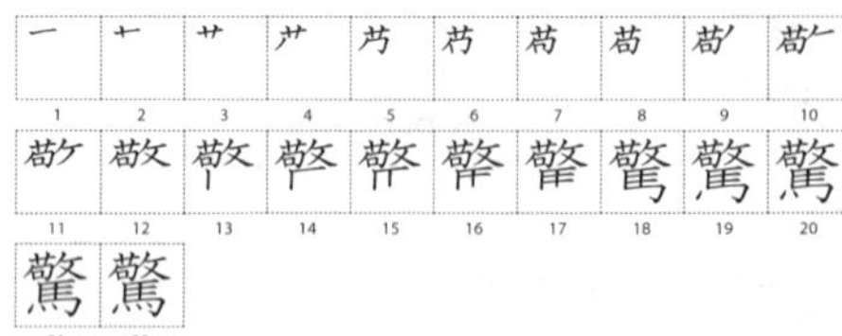

COMPOUNDS

ⓐ **SURPRISE, startle, astonish, frighten**

ⓑ [original meaning] **be SURPRISEd, be startled, be astonished**

a 驚愕× きょうがく astonishment, surprise, fright, shock

驚天動地 きょうてんどうち world-shaking, astounding

b 驚嘆する きょうたんする admire, wonder, be struck with admiration

驚異 きょうい wonder, marvel, miracle

驚喜 きょうき pleasant surprise

KUN

【おどろく 驚く】**be SURPRISEd, be astonished, be startled; be frightened**

驚き おどろき surprise, astonishment, amazement; fright

驚くべき おどろくべき astonishing, amazing, surprising, wonderful

【おどろかす 驚かす】**SURPRISE, astonish, amaze; frighten**

驚かされる おどろかされる be surprised

世人を驚かす せじんをおどろかす strike terror in people's hearts

NOTE

★ do not confuse with 警 GUARD AGAINST → 3595

鷲

3598

2-12-11

▶EAGLE

シュウ ジュ わし ㊔ す

Ⓒ 鹫 jiù

196 鳥	Names	U9DF2
	S23-11-12	F2303

KUN

【わし 鷲】 EAGLE

鷲鼻 わしばな hooked [aquiline] nose

鷲摑みにする わしづかみにする grab

鷲座 わしざ Aquila

大鷲 おおわし Steller's sea eagle

白頭鷲 はくとうわし bald eagle

SYNONYMS

【わし】

○ birds

鷹 HAWK → 3955
鷗 GULL → 2370
烏 CROW → 4088
雀 SPARROW → 3117
燕 SWALLOW → 3142
鴻 LARGE WILD BIRD → 0977
鳳 MALE PHOENIX → 3749
凰 FEMALE PHOENIX → 3738
鵬 MYTHICAL HUGE BIRD → 1416
鶏 CHICKEN → 2221
酉 ROOSTER → 4358
隼 FALCON → 3427
鳩 PIGEON → 0184
鷲 EAGLE → 3598
鳶 BLACK KITE → 3919
鶴 CRANE → 2326
鷺 HERON → 3621
鵜 CORMORANT → 2067
鴨 DUCK → 1582
雁 WILD GOOSE → 3741

NOTE

★ do not confuse with 鷺 HERON → 3621

欝

3599

2-12-13

▶GLOOM

ウツ

75 木	Nonstandard	U6B1D
	S25-4-21	F0000

traditional form → see 鬱 at 3625

鬱

3600

2-12-15

▶GLOOM

ウツ

192 鬯	Nonstandard	U9B30
	S27-10-17	F0000

traditional form → see 鬱 at 3625

質

2-13-2

incorrect classification

➡ see 2-8-7: 斦 at 3483

賛

2-13-2

incorrect classification

➡ see 2-8-7: 兟 at 3484

學

2-13-2

incorrect stroke-count

➡ see 2-13-3: 𦥯 at 3604

壁

3601

2-13-3

▶WALL

ヘキ かべ

Ⓒ 壁 bì

32 土	Jōyō	U58C1
	S16-3-13	F0872

(stroke order 1–16)

COMPOUNDS

[also suffix]

❶ [original meaning] **WALL, partition, fence, barrier**

壁画 へきが wall painting, fresco

障壁 しょうへき [formerly also 牆壁] fence, wall; barrier

防火壁 ぼうかへき fire wall

❷ **any WALL-like structure such as a cliff or precipice**

絶壁 ぜっぺき precipice, cliff

岸壁 がんぺき quay (wall), wharf

胃壁 いへき walls of the stomach

北壁 ほくへき northern cliff

氷壁 ひょうへき ice ridge

城壁 じょうへき castle wall, rampart

火口壁 かこうへき crater wall

KUN

【かべ 壁】 **WALL, partition, barrier**

壁紙 かべがみ wallpaper

壁塗り かべぬり plastering

壁新聞 かべしんぶん wall newspaper; wall poster

言葉の壁 ことばのかべ language barrier

SYNONYMS

❶ **fences and walls**

壁 WALL → 3601
塀 FENCE (for screening) → 0677
垣 FENCE (for partitioning) → 0416
墻 FENCE (for partitioning) → 1393
柵 FENCE (with spaced pickets) → 1116
堵 FENCE (made of earth) → 0682

囲い enclosure →3807
欄 railing →1419

❷ **mountain parts**
頂 SUMMIT →0164
峰 PEAK →0494
嶺 RIDGE →3013
峠 MOUNTAIN PASS →0428
崖 CLIFF →2862
壁 wall-like structure →3601

NOTE

★ do not confuse with 璧 DISK-SHAPED JEWEL →3608

墾

3602
2-13-3

▶**RECLAIM**
コン ㊔ ひらく
Ⓒ 垦 kěn

32	Jōyō	U58BE
土	S16-3-13	F3056

COMPOUNDS

● [original meaning] **RECLAIM (wasteland), open up new land for farming, clear land, cultivate**
墾田 こんでん new rice field
開墾 かいこん clearing, reclamation
未墾の みこんの uncultivated, wild

SYNONYMS

● **reclaim**
拓 OPEN UP →0375
墾 RECLAIM →3602
開 OPEN →4121

NOTE

★ do not confuse with 懇 EARNEST →3606

舉

2-13-3

incorrect classification
➡ see 2-11-5: 𦥑 at 3563

導

3603
2-13-3

▶**GUIDE**
ドウ みちび(く) ㊔ みち

41	Nonstandard	U5C0E
寸	S16-3-13	F0000

traditional form →see 導 at 3587

學

3604
2-13-3

▶**STUDY**
▶**EDUCATIONAL INSTITUTION**
ガク まな(ぶ)

39	Nonstandard	U5B78
子	S16-3-13	F0000

traditional form →see 学 at 3162

凞

3605
2-13-4

▶**BRIGHT**
キ ㊔ ひろ ひろし ひろむ のり よし

15	Nonstandard	U51DE
冫	S17-2-15	F0000

traditional form →see 熙 at 3559

懇

3606
2-13-4

▶**EARNEST**
▶**FAMILIAR**
コン ねんご(ろ)
Ⓒ 恳 kěn

61	Jōyō	U61C7
心	S17-4-13	F1949

COMPOUNDS

❶ⓐ **EARNEST, fervent, sincere**
ⓑ cordial, kindly, kind

a 懇願する こんがんする beg earnestly, implore, entreat
懇望 こんもう entreaty, solicitation, earnest request
懇請する こんせいする request earnestly, solicit, entreat
懇懇と こんこんと earnestly, repeatedly

b 懇切な こんせつな kind, cordial; exhaustive
懇篤 こんとく cordiality, kindness
懇書 こんしょ your kind letter
懇情 こんじょう kindliness

❷ **FAMILIAR, friendly, intimate**
懇談 こんだん familiar talk [chat]
懇談会 こんだんかい social gathering; round table conference
懇意 こんい intimacy, friendship; kindness
懇親 こんしん friendship, intimacy
懇話 こんわ friendly [familiar] chat [talk]
別懇 べっこん intimacy

❸ abbrev. of 懇談会 こんだんかい: round table conference, consultation
米懇 べいこん Round Table Conference on Rice Price

KUN

【ねんごろ 懇ろ】
ねんごろな 懇ろな **cordial, kind, hearty; polite, courteous; FAMILIAR, intimate**
懇ろに葬る ねんごろにほうむる bury with due ceremony
懇ろになる ねんごろになる become acquainted; become intimate

SYNONYMS

❶ⓐ **eager**

懇 EARNEST → 3606
切 eager → 0030
摯 SERIOUS → 3556
篤 DEVOTED → 3371
熱 HOT → 3555
ⓑ kind
厚 KIND → 3726
篤 cordial → 3371
懇 cordial → 3606
慈 AFFECTIONATE → 2949
温 warmhearted → 0740
渥 GRACIOUS → 0731
優 kindly → 0200
❷ familiar and friendly
親 INTIMATE → 2264
密 CLOSE → 2857
近 NEAR → 3798
睦 FRIENDLY → 1534
懇 FAMILIAR → 3606
和 HARMONIOUS → 1450

NOTE
★ do not confuse with 墾 RECLAIM → 3602

擊

▶STRIKE
ゲキ う(つ)

3607
2-13-4

64	Names	U64CA
手	S17-4-13	F0000

traditional form → see 撃 at 3552

擧

incorrect classification
➡ see 2-11-6: 𦦙 at 3568

2-13-4

璧

▶DISK-SHAPED JEWEL
ヘキ たま▲
Ⓒ 璧 bì

3608
2-13-5

96	Jōyō	U74A7
玉	S18-5-13	F2073

1	2	3	4	5	6	7	8	9	10
㇇	コ	尸	尸	吊	启	启	启	启	启

11	12	13	14	15	16	17	18
启	辟	辟	辟	辟	辟	璧	璧

COMPOUNDS
❶ⓐ DISK-SHAPED JEWEL with a hole in the center
ⓑ jewel, beautiful jewel
a 完璧な かんぺきな perfect, flawless
b 圭璧 けいへき [archaic] ritual jades worn by feudal lords in ancient China
❷ something as excellent or as beautiful as a jewel
双璧 そうへき two matchless authorities [jewels]

INDEPENDENT
【へき 璧】**DISK-SHAPED JEWEL** with a hole in the center
KUN
【たま 璧】[now usu. 玉, formerly also 珠] gem, jewel, precious stone, pearl, bead
SYNONYMS
❶ⓐ precious stones
玉 GEM → 4289
珂 WHITE AGATE → 1137
璧 DISK-SHAPED JEWEL → 3608
琥 AMBER → 1261
珀 AMBER → 1136
珠 PEARL → 1183
瑛 TRANSPARENT GEM → 1259
瑠 LAPIS LAZULI → 1342
璃 GLASSY SUBSTANCE → 1358
晶 CRYSTAL → 3122
玖 beautiful black jewel → 1041
琉 LAPIS LAZULI → 1221
琳 BEAUTIFUL GEM → 1262
HOMOPHONES
たま
玉 GEM → 4289
弾 PROJECTILE → 0697
珠 PEARL → 1183
球 BALL → 1219
NOTE
➡ see USAGE note at 玉 4289
★ do not confuse with 壁 WALL → 3601

嚮

▶GO TOWARD
コウ キョウ

3609
2-13-6

30	Nonstandard	U56AE
口	S19-3-16	F0000

traditional form → see 嚮 at 3610

嚮

▶GO TOWARD
コウ キョウ
Ⓒ 向 xiàng

3610
2-13-6

30	Non-Jōyō	U56AE
口	S19-3-16	F0000

COMPOUNDS
❶ [original meaning] **GO TOWARD, head toward**
嚮導する きょうどうする guide, conduct, lead
❷ [now replaced by 向 3790] turn toward, be inclined toward, lean toward
意嚮 いこう intention, inclination
SYNONYMS
❶ go and come

行 GO →0246
徠 COME →0576
往 GO ON →0348
出 go to →4310
参 go somewhere →2563
来 COME →4366
通 go to and from →3855
向 head toward →3790
赴 PROCEED TO →4095
嚮 GO TOWARD →3610

蟹

3611
2-13-6

▸CRAB
カイ かに
Ⓝ 蠏 Ⓒ 蟹 xiè

142	Names	U87F9
虫	S19-6-13	F2189

COMPOUNDS

● **CRAB**
蟹行する かいこうする walk sideways

KUN

【かに 蟹】**CRAB**
蟹味噌 かにみそ crab guts
蟹座 かにざ Cancer, the Crab (constellation)
蟹工船 かにこうせん crab-canning boat
蟹缶 かにかん canned crab
蟹股 がにまた bowlegged
毛蟹 けがに hair crab, horsehair crab
ずわい蟹 ずわいがに snow crab, *Chionoecetes opilio*

SYNONYMS

● **crustaceans**
蝦 SHRIMP →1773
蟹 CRAB →3611

繫

3612
2-13-6

▸CONNECT
ケイ つな(ぐ) つな(がる) つな(げる) かか(る)
Ⓝ 繫 Ⓒ 系 jì xì

120	Names	U7E6B
糸	S19-6-13	F1756

COMPOUNDS

[now replaced by 係 0108]
ⓐ [original meaning] **CONNECT, link, bind, fasten, anchor, moor**
ⓑ **be CONNECTed with, relate to**
a 繫船 けいせん mooring a ship
繫留 けいりゅう mooring, anchorage
b 繫属 けいぞく pendency (of a legal case); relationship
繫争 けいそう dispute, contention (of a legal case); lawsuit
連繫 れんけい connection, linking, contact

KUN

【つなぐ 繫ぐ】
ⓐ **CONNECT, link, bind, fasten, anchor, moor**
ⓑ [also suffix] sustain, keep something going
a 繫ぎ つなぎ stopgap measure, filler; binding agent (in cooking); overalls
繫ぎ止める つなぎとめる fasten, hitch; keep (someone) engaged
繫ぎ目 つなぎめ knot, joint
手を繫ぐ てをつなぐ join hands (with)
b 食い繫ぐ くいつなぐ survive on (some food); eke out a living, scrape by

【つながる 繫がる】**be CONNECTed with, relate to**
繫がり つながり connection, link, relationship

【つなげる 繫げる】**CONNECT, link, fasten, tie together**

【かかる 繫る】[now usu. 掛かる] anchor, moor
沖に繫る船 おきにかかるふね ship mooring off the coast

SYNONYMS

ⓐ **join**
結 TIE →1706
繫 CONNECT →3612
縛 BIND →1779
綴 BIND →1746
繃 BIND UP →1787
束 TIE UP →4369
梱 PACK →1205
連 LINK →3849
係 CONNECT →0108
接 join →0607

HOMOPHONES

かかる
掛 SET →0596
懸 SUSPEND →3632
架 LAY ACROSS →3178
係 CONNECT →0108
罹 FALL ILL →3239

NOTE

➡ see USAGE note at 掛 0596

譬

3613
2-13-7

▸COMPARE TO
ヒ たと(える)
Ⓒ 譬 pì

149	Non-Jōyō	U8B6C
言	S20-7-13	F3374

COMPOUNDS

● [now also 比 0029] **COMPARE TO, liken**
譬喩 ひゆ simile, metaphor, allegory

KUN

【たとえる 譬える】[also 喩える] **COMPARE TO, liken, speak figuratively**

譬え(=喩え、例え) たとえ simile, metaphor, allegory

譬え話 たとえばなし fable, allegory

死を眠りに譬える しをねむりにたとえる compare death to sleep

SYNONYMS

● **compare**

比 COMPARE → 0029

較 COMPARE → 1939

譬 COMPARE TO → 3613

校 COLLATE → 1166

照 check against → 3506

対 OPPOSE (contrast) → 1025

参 refer → 2563

HOMOPHONES

たとえる

例 EXAMPLE → 0099

喩 METAPHOR → 0671

NOTE

➡ see USAGE note at 例 0099

警

3614

2-13-7

▶**GUARD AGAINST**
▶**WARN**

ケイ いまし(める)

149	Nonstandard	U8B66
言	S20-7-13	F0000

traditional form → see 警 at 3595

譽輩

2-13-7

incorrect classification

➡ see 2-11-9: 蛆 at 3576

覺

3615

2-13-7

▶**PERCEIVE**
▶**COMMIT TO MEMORY**

カク おぼ(える) さ(ます) さ(める) さと(る)

㊔ さとし あきら がく

147	Nonstandard	U89BA
見	S20-7-13	F0000

traditional form → see 覚 at 3217

饗

3616

2-13-9

▶**BANQUET**

キョウ ㊔ あえ

N 饗 饗 C 飨 xiǎng

184	Names	U9957
食	S22-9-13	F3085

COMPOUNDS

● [now also 供 0098] [original meaning] **BANQUET, treat, provide dinner for, entertain**

饗応 きょうおう treat, feast, banquet

饗宴 きょうえん banquet, feast, dinner

INDEPENDENT

【きょうする 饗する】treat, provide dinner for

SYNONYMS

● **social gatherings**

宴 BANQUET → 2825

饗 BANQUET → 3616

会 party → 2512

響

3617

2-13-9

▶**REVERBERATE**

キョウ ひび(く)

180	Names	UFA69
音	S22-9-13	F0000

traditional form → see 響 at 3573

響

3618

2-13-9

▶**REVERBERATE**

キョウ ひび(く)

180	Nonstandard	U97FF
音	S22-9-13	F0000

alternative form → see 響 at 3573

饗

3619

2-13-9

▶**BANQUET**

キョウ ㊔ あえ

184	Nonstandard	U9957
食	S22-9-13	F0000

traditional form → see 饗 at 3616

驚

3620

2-13-10

▶**SURPRISE**

キョウ おどろ(く) おどろ(かす)

187	Nonstandard	U9A5A
馬	S23-10-13	F0000

traditional form → see 驚 at 3597

鷺

3621

2-13-11

▶**HERON**

ロ さぎ

C 鹭 lù

196	Names	U9DFA
鳥	S24-11-13	F3326

COMPOUNDS

● **HERON**

烏鷺 うろ crows and herons; black and white

KUN

【さぎ 鷺】**HERON**

鷺草 さぎそう white egret orchid

鷺苔 さぎごけ creeping mazus, *Mazus miquelii*

白鷺 しらさぎ(=はくろ) generic term for herons with all-white plumage

黒鷺 くろさぎ Pacific reef heron

SPECIAL READINGS

朱鷺 とき(=しゅろ) crested ibis

SYNONYMS

● **birds**

鷹 HAWK → 3955
鴎 GULL → 2370
烏 CROW → 4088
雀 SPARROW → 3117
燕 SWALLOW → 3142
鴻 LARGE WILD BIRD → 0977
鳳 MALE PHOENIX → 3749
凰 FEMALE PHOENIX → 3738
鵬 MYTHICAL HUGE BIRD → 1416
鶏 CHICKEN → 2221
酉 ROOSTER → 4358
隼 FALCON → 3427
鳩 PIGEON → 0184
鷲 EAGLE → 3598
鳶 BLACK KITE → 3919
鶴 CRANE → 2326
鷺 HERON → 3621
鵜 CORMORANT → 2067
鴨 DUCK → 1582
雁 WILD GOOSE → 3741

NOTE

★ do not confuse with 鷲 EAGLE → 3598

興

3622

2-14-2

▶**RISE TO PROSPERITY**
▶**AMUSEMENT**

コウ キョウ おこ(る) おこ(す) ㊔ おき とも

Ⓒ 兴 xīng xìng

134	Jōyō-5	U8208
臼	S16-7-9	F0579

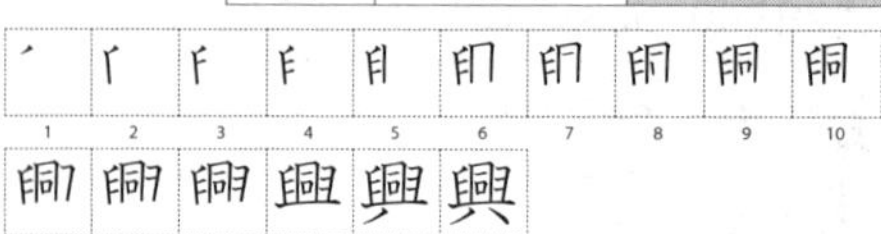

COMPOUNDS

❶ **RISE TO PROSPERITY, rise, prosper, flourish**

興隆 こうりゅう prosperity, rise
興亡 こうぼう rise and fall, ups and downs
興起する こうきする rise, be in the ascendant; rouse, stir
新興の しんこうの rising, newly-established
勃興 ぼっこう sudden rise, sudden increase in power

❷ⓐ **cause to rise (to prosperity), promote, further, advance, develop**

ⓑ [formerly also 昂 こう 3065 or 亢 こう 2460] **rouse up, be stirred, be excited**

a 興業 こうぎょう promotion of industry
興国 こうこく making a country prosperous
興信所 こうしんじょ private inquiry agency, credit bureau
振興 しんこう promotion, furtherance, rousing
復興する ふっこうする revive, restore to the original state, reconstruct
再興する さいこうする revive, restore
作興する さっこうする promote; awaken, arouse, enhance

b 興奮する こうふんする get excited, be agitated, be aroused

❸ **AMUSEMENT, entertainment, fun, interest, desire to enjoy**

興味 きょうみ interest
興行 こうぎょう public entertainment, show business
余興 よきょう entertainment, side show
遊興 ゆうきょう merrymaking, spree
感興 かんきょう interest, fun, inspiration
一興 いっきょう amusement, fun

INDEPENDENT

【きょう 興】**interest, fun, AMUSEMENT**

興が有る きょうがある be interesting, be fun

【きょうじる(=きょうずる) 興じる(=興ずる)】
amuse oneself, have fun, make merry

KUN

【おこる 興る】

① **RISE TO PROSPERITY, prosper, thrive, flourish**

国が興る くにがおこる The country prospers

② [also 起こる] (come into existence) **rise, spring up, be established**

新しい産業が興った あたらしいさんぎょうがおこった A new industry has sprung up

【おこす 興す】**cause to rise (to prosperity), promote, further, advance, develop**

工業を興す こうぎょうをおこす promote industry
廃れた家を興す すたれたいえをおこす restore a family to its former prosperity

SYNONYMS

❶ **prospering and prosperity**

隆 PROSPER → 0661
振 rise → 0515
興 RISE TO PROSPERITY → 3622
盛 PROSPEROUS → 3314
昌 PROSPERING → 3069
栄 FLOURISH → 3183
繁 THRIVE → 3536
賑 BUSTLE → 1959

❷ⓐ **advance**

進 ADVANCE → 3873
興 cause to rise → 3622
奨 ENCOURAGE → 3524
勧 encourage → 2334

❸ **pleasure**

楽 PLEASURE → 3505
娯 ENJOYMENT → 0487
興 AMUSEMENT → 3622
玩 TAKE PLEASURE IN → 1085

HOMOPHONES

おこる 起 RISE → 4099
おこす 起 RISE → 4099

NOTE

➡ see USAGE note at 起 4099

舉 2-14-3
incorrect classification/stroke-count
➡ see 2-11-5: 𦥑 at 3563

擧 2-14-4
incorrect classification/stroke-count
➡ see 2-11-6: 𦥑 at 3568

懲

3623 2-14-4

▶**CHASTISE**

チョウ こ(りる) こ(らす) こ(らしめる)

Ⓝ 懲 Ⓒ 惩 chéng

61	Jōyō	U61F2
心	S18-4-14	F1964

COMPOUNDS

● [original meaning] **CHASTISE, punish, discipline**

懲悪 ちょうあく chastisement, punishment
懲罰 ちょうばつ discipline, punishment
懲戒 ちょうかい official reprimand, discipline
懲役 ちょうえき penal servitude, imprisonment with hard labor

KUN

【こりる 懲りる】**learn by experience, learn a lesson; have had enough of, be sick of**

懲り懲りする こりごりする learn to one's sorrow
性懲りも無く しょうこりもなく incorrigibly

【こらす 懲らす】**CHASTISE, punish, discipline**

悪を懲らす あくをこらす punish the wicked

【こらしめる 懲らしめる】same as 懲らす こらす

懲らしめ こらしめ chastisement

SYNONYMS

● **punishment**

刑 PENALTY → 1024
罰 PUNISHMENT → 3228
懲 CHASTISE → 3623
処 DEAL WITH (lawbreakers) → 3764

璽

3624 2-14-5

▶**IMPERIAL SEAL**

ジ

Ⓒ 玺 xǐ

96	Jōyō	U74BD
玉	S19-5-14	F3729

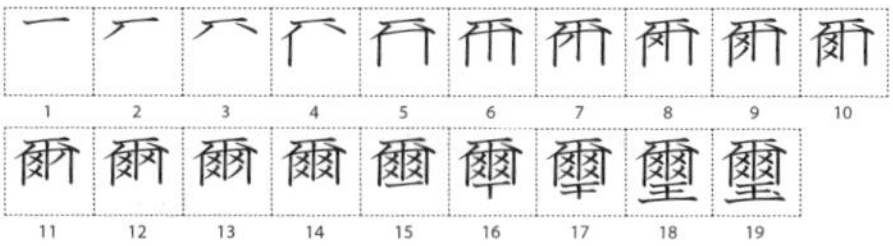

COMPOUNDS

❶ⓐ **IMPERIAL SEAL**

ⓑ [original meaning] seal

a 御璽 ぎょじ Imperial seal
b 国璽 こくじ seal of state

❷ sacred comma-shaped bead signifying Imperial sovereignty

神璽 しんじ Yasakani no Magatama (one of the three insignia of the Imperial throne); Imperial seal

INDEPENDENT

【じ 璽】seal (of state)

SYNONYMS

❶ **seals**

印 SEAL → 1023
判 personal seal → 1441
璽 IMPERIAL SEAL → 3624

譽 2-14-7
incorrect classification/stroke-count
➡ see 2-11-9: 𦥑 at 3577

轝 2-14-7
incorrect classification/stroke-count
➡ see 2-11-9: 𦥑 at 3576

覽 2-14-7
incorrect stroke-count
➡ see 2-15-7: 臨 at 3628

贒 2-14-7
incorrect stroke-count
➡ see 2-15-7: [illegible] at 3629

鑒 2-14-8
incorrect stroke-count
➡ see 2-15-8: 臨 at 3630

鬱

3625 2-14-15

▶**GLOOM**

ウツ

Ⓝ 欝 鬰 Ⓒ 郁 yù

192	Jōyō	U9B31
鬯	S29-10-19	F1803

COMPOUNDS

❶ **GLOOM, depression, melancholy**
鬱陶しい うっとうしい gloomy, depressing; dull, cloudy
憂鬱 ゆううつ melancholy, gloom
陰鬱 いんうつ gloominess, melancholy
抑鬱 よくうつ depression, dejection
躁鬱病 そううつびょう manic-depressive psychosis
抗鬱剤 こううつざい antidepressant

❷ **stagnate, be blocked up**
鬱血 うっけつ congestion (of blood)
鬱積する うっせきする be pent up, accumulate (as of negative emotions)
鬱憤 うっぷん frustration, pent-up anger

❸ grow thick
鬱蒼とした うっそうとした thick, dense (as of forests)
鬱然とした うつぜんとした thick, dense (as of forests)

❹ fragrant spice
鬱金香 うっこんこう tulip
鬱金 うこん turmeric

INDEPENDENT

【うつ 鬱】**depression, GLOOM**
鬱を散じる うつをさんじる chase one's gloom away

SYNONYMS

❶ **sad and depressed**
悲 SAD → 3448
悄 BECOME DISPIRITED → 0506
哀 sorrowful → 2568
愁 MELANCHOLY → 3508
鬱 GLOOM → 3625
陰 gloomy → 0657
沈 depressed → 0306
寂 LONESOME → 2855
淋しい LONESOME → 0632
惨 MISERABLE → 0585

輿

3626
2-15-2

▶**PALANQUIN**
ヨ こし
Ⓝ 轝 Ⓒ 舆 yú

159	Names	U8F3F
車	S17-7-10	F2338

COMPOUNDS

❶ [original meaning] **PALANQUIN, litter**
輿丁 よてい palanquin bearer
駕輿 がよ palanquin, litter, *kago*
鸞×輿 らんよ imperial palanquin

❷ the Earth, the world
輿地 よち the Earth, the world

❸ multitude, numerous, many
輿論(=世論) よろん public opinion
輿望 よぼう popularity, public esteem [reputation, confidence]

KUN

【こし 輿】**PALANQUIN, litter; bier**
輿入れ こしいれ wedding, marriage (into a family)
玉の輿 たまのこし marriage to a man of wealth
前輿(=先輿) さきごし front carrier of a palanquin

SPECIAL READINGS

神輿(=御輿) みこし portable shrine, sacred palanquin

SYNONYMS

❶ **vehicle**
車 VEHICLE → 4367
輛 VEHICLE → 2000
乗 vehicle → 4393
輪 wheeled vehicle → 1999
駕 CARRIAGE → 3236
輿 PALANQUIN → 3626
台 COUNTER FOR VEHICLES → 2498

徵

3627
2-15-4

▶**CHASTISE**
チョウ こ(りる) こ(らす) こ(らしめる)

61	Names	UFA40
心	S19-4-15	F0000

traditional form → see 懲 at 3623

覽

3628
2-15-7

▶**LOOK OVER**
ラン

147	Names	U89BD
見	S22-7-15	F0000

traditional form → see 覧 at 3538

贒

3629
2-15-7

▶**WISE**
ケン かしこ(い) ㊔ さとし まさる まさ かた よし まこと たか

154	Nonstandard	U8D12
貝	S22-7-15	F0000

traditional form → see 賢 at 3518

鑒

3630

2-15-8

▶APPRAISE
▶REFERENCE VOLUME

カン かんが(みる) かがみ

167	Nonstandard	U9452
金	S23-8-15	F0000

traditional form → see 鑑 at 2226

雙

3631

2-16-2

▶SET OF TWO

ソウ ふた ㊔ もろ なみ

172	Nonstandard	U96D9
隹	S18-8-10	F0000

traditional form → see 双 at 0028

懸

3632

2-16-4

▶SUSPEND

ケン ケ か(ける) か(かる)

Ⓒ 悬 xuán

61	Jōyō	U61F8
心	S20-4-16	F1241

COMPOUNDS

❶ **SUSPEND, be suspended (in midair), hang (over), overhang**

懸垂 けんすい suspension, pendency; chinning exercises

懸架 けんが suspension (of an automobile)

懸吊 けんちょう suspension

懸濁 けんだく *chem* suspension

懸崖 けんがい overhanging cliff

❷ **pending, unsettled, unresolved**

懸案 けんあん pending question [problem]

❸ **occupy the mind, be anxious**

懸念 けねん anxiety, concern, fear

懸想 けそう falling in love, attachment

❹ **stake, risk**

一生懸命(=一所懸命)に いっしょうけんめい(=いっしょけんめい)に for life, with all one's might

❺ **offer [set] a prize**

懸賞 けんしょう prize competition; prize, reward

❻ be (greatly) different from, be far apart

懸隔 けんかく difference, discrepancy

懸絶 けんぜつ great difference

懸軍 けんぐん expeditionary army

KUN

【かける 懸ける】

① [sometimes also 賭ける] **stake (one's life), risk**

命懸けで いのちがけで at the risk of one's life

② **offer [set] a prize**

賞金を懸ける しょうきんをかける offer a prize

③ [in compounds] be (greatly) different from, be far apart

懸け離れる かけはなれる be far apart; be greatly different from

【かかる 懸かる】

① **be SUSPENDed in midair (as of the moon), hang**

月が空に懸かる つきがそらにかかる The moon hangs in the sky

② **have a prize offered, have a reward (set on one's head)**

犯人の首に賞金が懸かっている はんにんのくびにしょうきんがかかっている There is a reward on the criminal's head

SYNONYMS

❶ **hang**

掛ける HANG → 0596
垂 HANG DOWN → 4382
懸 SUSPEND → 3632
吊 SUSPEND → 2686
釣り- suspended → 2108

❹ **risk**

冒 RISK → 3088
賭 WAGER → 2021
懸 stake → 3632

HOMOPHONES

かける

掛 SET → 0596
架 LAY ACROSS → 3178
駆 DRIVE → 2293
賭 WAGER → 2021
翔 SOAR → 1714

かかる

掛 SET → 0596
架 LAY ACROSS → 3178
係 CONNECT → 0108
繋 CONNECT → 3612
罹 FALL ILL → 3239

NOTE

➡ see USAGE note at 掛 0596

➡ see COMPOUND FORMATION for 一生懸命(=一所懸命) いっしょうけんめい(=いっしょけんめい) → 生 4309

襲

3633

2-16-6

▶RAID

シュウ おそ(う)

Ⓒ 袭 xí

145	Jōyō	U8972
衣	S22-6-16	F0963

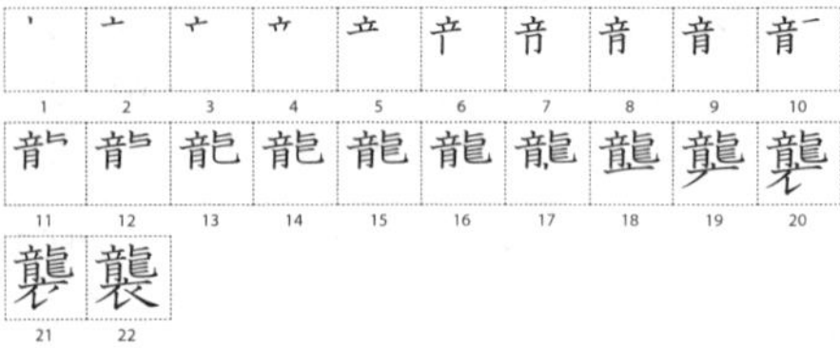

COMPOUNDS

❶ⓐ **RAID, make a surprise attack on, assault, invade**
ⓑ **RAID, surprise attack**

ab 襲撃 しゅうげき raid, attack, assault
来襲 らいしゅう attack, invasion, raid
急襲 きゅうしゅう raid, surprise attack
空襲 くうしゅう air raid
奇襲 きしゅう surprise attack
逆襲 ぎゃくしゅう counterattack

❷ⓐ inherit old customs, carry on without change
ⓑ succeed, take over

a 踏襲 とうしゅう following (former policies)
因襲(=因習) いんしゅう conventions
b 襲名 しゅうめい succession to another's professional name
世襲 せしゅう heredity, descent

❸ [original meaning, now archaic] wear one garment over another
襲衣する しゅういする wear one garment over another

KUN

【おそう 襲う】**RAID, attack, invade; inherit, succeed**
襲い掛かる おそいかかる assault, pounce upon, sweep down on (a person)
城を襲う しろをおそう raid a fort
大統領の後を襲う だいとうりょうのあとをおそう succeed to the presidency

SYNONYMS

❶ **attack**
攻 ATTACK → 0286
撃 STRIKE → 3552
襲 RAID → 3633
侵 INVADE → 0116
爆 bomb → 1415

彎

▶**CURVE**
ワン
Ⓝ 弯 Ⓒ 弯 wān

3634
2-19-3

57	Non-Jōyō	U5F4E
弓	S22-3-19	F0000

COMPOUNDS

● [now replaced by 湾 0748] [original meaning] **CURVE**
彎曲 わんきょく curve, crook, bend
彎入する わんにゅうする curve in
彎月 わんげつ crescent moon

SYNONYMS

● **bend**
曲 CURVE → 4340
彎 CURVE (become bow-shaped) → 3634
屈 BEND → 3821
折 bend → 0297
勾 be bent → 3660
歪 DISTORT → 3095

攣

▶**CRAMP**
レン つ(る)
Ⓒ 挛 luán

3635
2-19-4

64	Non-Jōyō	U6523
手	S23-4-19	F2398

COMPOUNDS

● [original meaning] **CRAMP, have a cramp**
攣縮 れんしゅく spasm
痙×攣 けいれん convulsions, cramp

KUN

【つる 攣る】[now usu. 吊る]
① **CRAMP, have a cramp**
引き攣り ひきつり cramp; scar
足が攣る あしがつる have one's leg cramp
② **turn up, slant upward**
攣り目 つりめ slanted [upturned] eyes

SYNONYMS

● **contract and shrink**
縮 SHRINK → 1790
約 CONTRACT → 1632
攣 CRAMP → 3635

HOMOPHONES

つる
釣 ANGLE → 2108
吊 SUSPEND → 2686

NOTE

➡ see USAGE note at 釣 2108

變

▶**CHANGE**
▶**ABNORMAL**
ヘン か(わる) か(わり) か(える)

3636
2-19-4

149	Nonstandard	U8B8A
言	S23-7-16	F0000

traditional form → see 変 at 2569

戀 3637

2-19-4

▶LOVE

レン こ(う) こい こい(しい)

61	Nonstandard	U6200
心	S23-4-19	F0000

traditional form → see 恋 at 2602

鹽

2-19-5

incorrect stroke-count

➡ see 2-20-5: 鹽 at 3639

蠻 3638

2-19-6

▶BARBARIAN

バン

142	Nonstandard	U883B
虫	S25-6-19	F0000

traditional form → see 蛮 at 2638

鹽 3639

2-20-5

▶SALT

エン しお

197	Nonstandard	U9E7D
鹵	S25-11-14	F0000

traditional form → see 塩 at 0774

鑿 3640

2-20-8

▶EXCAVATE

▶CHISEL

サク のみ

Ⓒ 凿 záo

167	Non-Jōyō	U947F
金	S28-8-20	F2889

COMPOUNDS

❶ [now also 削 1837] **EXCAVATE, drill, bore, dig**

鑿岩機 さくがんき rock drill
鑿井 さくせい well drilling
開鑿 かいさく excavation, cutting, digging
掘鑿する くっさくする dig out, excavate
穿鑿する せんさくする scrutinize, dig into

❷ [original meaning] **CHISEL**

斧鑿 ふさく [archaic] elaboration; lucubration; chisel and axe
平鑿 へいさく flat chisel

KUN

【のみ 鑿】CHISEL

丸鑿 まるのみ gouge

SYNONYMS

❶ **dig**

掘 DIG → 0601
鑿 EXCAVATE → 3640
削 excavate → 1837
穿 DRILL → 2800

❷ **cutting instruments**

刀 cutting tool → 3642
鎌 SICKLE → 2212
刃 BLADE → 3646
鋏 SCISSORS → 2173
鋸 SAW → 2184
斧 AXE → 2558
鍬 HOE → 2205
錐 DRILL → 2190
鑿 CHISEL → 3640

〔匚〕
⺆
⺄
乀

口 3
ENCLOSURE
囲み型

匕

3641
口3-1-1

▶**SPOON**
ヒ
Ⓒ 匕 bǐ

21	Non-Jōyō	U5315
匕	S2-2-0	F2742

RADICAL

sajinohi 'spoon' (北 化 匙×), used in characters related to spoons or people

COMPOUNDS

❶ [original meaning, now archaic] **SPOON**
匕箸 ひちょ spoon and chopsticks

❷ **dagger**
匕首 ひしゅ(=あいくち) dagger, dirk

SYNONYMS

❶ **spoons**
斗 DIPPER → 3671
杓 DIPPER → 1028
匕 SPOON → 3641

刀

3642
口3-1-1

▶**SWORD**
トウ かたな ㊔ たち
Ⓒ 刀 dāo

18	Jōyō-2	U5200
刀	S2-2-0	F0796

Stroke order: 1 ㇇ 2 刀

RADICAL

katana 'sword' (分 切 剪), used in characters related to swords, cutting tools or cutting
Right variant: 刂 ***rittō*** (利 判 別)

COMPOUNDS

[also suffix]

ⓐ [original meaning] (single-edged) **SWORD**

ⓑ **cutting tool, knife, blade, -tome**

a 刀剣 とうけん sword
刀身 とうしん sword blade
名刀 めいとう excellent blade, famous sword
日本刀 にほんとう Japanese sword
短刀 たんとう dagger
b 彫刻刀 ちょうこくとう graver, chisel

INDEPENDENT

【とう 刀】**SWORD**, saber; burin
刀を帯びる とうをおびる wear a sword

KUN

【かたな 刀】**SWORD, blade**
刀鍛冶 かたなかじ sword smith
小刀 こがたな pocketknife
守り刀 まもりがたな sword for self-defense
懐刀 ふところがたな dagger; one's right-hand man, henchman
手刀 てがたな hand used like a sword in striking

SPECIAL READINGS

太刀 たち long sword
竹刀 しない bamboo sword
剃×刀▲ かみそり razor

SYNONYMS

ⓐ **cutting weapons**
刀 SWORD (single-edged) → 3642
剣 SWORD (double-edged) → 2104
矛 HALBERD → 2501
戟 HALBERD → 2131
鉾 DECORATIVE HALBERD → 2154
戈 DAGGER-AX → 4274

ⓑ **cutting instruments**
刀 cutting tool → 3642
鎌 SICKLE → 2212
刃 BLADE → 3646
鋏 SCISSORS → 2173
鋸 SAW → 2184
斧 AXE → 2558

鍬 HOE → 2205
錐 DRILL → 2190
鑿 CHISEL → 3640

乃 ▶POSSESSIVE PARTICLE
ナイ ダイ の すなわ(ち) ㊔ おさむ
Ⓒ 乃 nǎi

3643
□3-1-1

4	Names	U4E43
丿	S2-1-1	F1237

COMPOUNDS

❶ otherwise
乃至 ないし from...to..., between...and...; or

❷ thou, you; your—also functions as a reflexive pronoun
乃父 だいふ [rare] your father, father
乃公 だいこう I

KUN

【の 乃】POSSESSIVE PARTICLE
日乃丸 ひのまる Rising Sun flag
波乃花 なみのはな crest of a wave; salt

【すなわち 乃ち】
ⓐ thereupon, whereupon, accordingly
ⓑ and then
a 戦えば乃ち勝つ たたかえばすなわちかつ win every battle (that is fought)

SYNONYMS

【の】
○ possessive particles
之 POSSESSIVE PARTICLE → 4228
乃 POSSESSIVE PARTICLE → 3643

HOMOPHONES

の 之 POSSESSIVE PARTICLE → 4228
すなわち 即 IMMEDIATE → 1439

NOTE

➡ see USAGE notes at 之 4228 and 即 1439

八 ▶EIGHT
ハチ や や(つ) やっ(つ) よう
Ⓝ 八 Ⓒ 八 bā

3644
□3-1-1

12	Jōyō-1	U516B
八	S2-2-0	F0144

ノ(1) 八(2)

RADICAL

hachigashira 'eight' (兮ˣ), used for character classification
Variant: 八 *hachi* (六 共 具)
Top variant: ᐟᐠ *hachigashira* (兼)

COMPOUNDS

● EIGHT, eighth
八十 はちじゅう 80
八面 はちめん eight faces
八苦 はっく the eight sufferings (of Buddhism)
尺八 しゃくはち bamboo flute

INDEPENDENT

【はち 八】EIGHT

KUN

【や 八】[in compounds] **many, varied**
八重桜 やえざくら double flowered cherry tree
八百屋 やおや greengrocer; jack-of-all-trades
八百長 やおちょう rigged affair, fixed game

【やつ 八つ】EIGHT; 2 o'clock (in former time system)
八つ切り やつぎり cutting into eight parts; octavo
八つ当たり やつあたり unjustified outburst of anger
お八つ おやつ afternoon tea, refreshments

【やっつ 八つ】EIGHT; eight years old

【よう 八】[in compounds] EIGHT; many
八日 ようか eight days; 8th of the month

SYNONYMS

● small numbers
一 ONE → 4148
十 TEN → 4172
廿 TWENTY → 4258
二 TWO → 2421
三 THREE → 2423
四 FOUR → 3778
五 FIVE → 4244
六 SIX → 2461
七 SEVEN → 4169
八 EIGHT → 3644
九 NINE → 4176

NOTE

➡ see COMPOUND FORMATION for 尺八 しゃくはち → 尺 4248

入 □3-1-1
incorrect classification
➡ see ■4-2-4 at 4177

巳 □3-1-2
incorrect classification
➡ see ■4-3-1 at 4197

亾 ▶DECEASE
ボウ モウ な(い) な(き)- ほろ(びる) ほろ(ぶ) ほろ(ぼす)

3645
□3-1-2

11	Nonstandard	U5166
入	S3-2-1	F0000

traditional form → see 亡 at 4210

刃

▶BLADE

ジン ニン▲ は やいば▲

Ⓝ 刅 刄◇ Ⓒ 刃 rèn

3646

□3-1-2

18	Jōyō	U5203
刀	S3-2-1	F1555

フ 刀 刃

COMPOUNDS

❶ⓐ [original meaning] (part for cutting) **BLADE, edge**
ⓑ (weapon for cutting) **BLADE, sword, dagger, knife**

b 白刃 はくじん drawn sword
凶刃 きょうじん assassin's dagger [knife]
利刃 りじん sharp sword
兵刃 へいじん sword

❷ cut
刃傷 にんじょう bloodshed
自刃 じじん suicide by sword

INDEPENDENT

【じん 刃】**BLADE**

KUN

【は 刃】**BLADE, edge;** [in compounds] **sword**
刃物 はもの edged tool, cutlery; sword
刃先 はさき edge of a blade
刃渡り はわたり length of a sword; walking on the edge of a sword
両刃の りょうばの double-edged

【やいば 刃】**BLADE;** sword
刃を交える やいばをまじえる cross swords (with)
氷の刃 こおりのやいば gleaming sword

SYNONYMS

❶ **cutting instruments**
刀 cutting tool →3642
鎌 SICKLE →2212
刃 BLADE →3646
鋏 SCISSORS →2173
鋸 SAW →2184
斧 AXE →2558
鍬 HOE →2205
錐 DRILL →2190
鑿 CHISEL →3640

刄

▶BLADE

ジン ニン は やいば

3647

□3-1-2

18	Nonstandard	U5203
刀	S3-2-1	F0000

traditional form →see 刃 at 3646

巴

incorrect classification
➡ see ■4-4-1 at 4246

□3-1-3

司

▶OFFICIATE

シ つかさど(る)▲ ㊔ つかさ つとむ おさむ もり

Ⓒ 司 sī

3648

□3-1-4

30	Jōyō-4	U53F8
口	S5-3-2	F0559

㇆ ㇆ 𠃌 㕜 司

COMPOUNDS

❶ [original meaning] **OFFICIATE, administer, take charge of, manage**
司法 しほう administration of justice
司書 ししょ librarian
司祭 しさい Catholic priest, rabbi
司直 しちょく administration of justice; judicial authorities
司令官 しれいかん commander
司会する しかいする preside at, take the chair, officiate; emcee (a show)

❷ [also suffix] **officiator, officer, official, administrator**
上司 じょうし superior officer; superior
行司 ぎょうじ sumo umpire
保護司 ほごし probation officer

❸ **used phonetically for *shi***
寿司 すし sushi (raw fish and vinegared rice)

KUN

【つかさどる 司る】administer, **OFFICIATE**, take charge of, manage, preside over
国政を司る こくせいをつかさどる administer the affairs of state

SYNONYMS

❶ **direct and supervise**
制 CONTROL →1624
理 manage →1220
経 MANAGE →1687
管 EXERCISE CONTROL →3349
轄 EXERCISE JURISDICTION OVER →2056
掌 TAKE CHARGE OF →3215
監 OVERSEE →3535
督 SUPERVISE →3471
司 OFFICIATE →3648
宰 PRESIDE →2829
営 MANAGE →3216

❷ **officials**
官 GOVERNMENT OFFICIAL →2766
吏 OFFICIAL →4351

僚 official →0186
司 officiator →3648
役 executive →0288
事 officer →4384

迅 ☐3-1-5
incorrect classification
➡ see ☐3-3-3: 辶 at 3780

迅 ☐3-1-6
incorrect classification
➡ see ☐3-4-3: 辶 at 3970

直 3649 ☐3-1-7

▸STRAIGHT
▸FIX
チョク ジキ ジカ▲ ただ(ちに) なお(す) -なお(す) なお(る) なお(き) す(ぐ)▲
㊔ なお ただし すなお まさ ま
Ⓒ 直 zhí

109	Jōyō-2	U76F4
目	S8-5-3	F0216

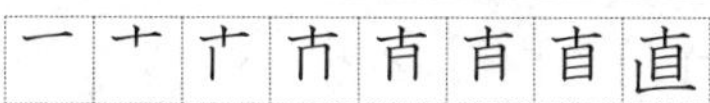
1 2 3 4 5 6 7 8

COMPOUNDS

❶ⓐ [original meaning] (unbent) **STRAIGHT**
ⓑ (upright) **STRAIGHT, vertical, perpendicular, right**
a 直線 ちょくせん straight line
直球 ちょっきゅう straight ball [pitch]
直進する ちょくしんする go straight on
直滑降 ちょっかっこう straight descent, schuss
直径 ちょっけい diameter
直視する ちょくしする look in the face, look straight at
硬直 こうちょく stiffness, rigidity
b 直立する ちょくりつする stand erect [upright], rise perpendicularly
直角 ちょっかく right angle
直円柱 ちょくえんちゅう right cylinder
垂直の すいちょくの vertical, perpendicular

❷ⓐ **STRAIGHT away, immediately**
ⓑ [also prefix] **direct, personal**
a 直後 ちょくご immediately after
直答 ちょくとう prompt answer; direct answer
直答 じきとう direct answer
直流 ちょくりゅう direct current
直通 ちょくつう direct communication [service]; through service [traffic]
直感 ちょっかん intuition
直前に ちょくぜんに just [immediately] before
直列 ちょくれつ *elec* (in) series
直観 ちょっかん intuition
b 直結する ちょっけつする connect directly with
直面する ちょくめんする face, confront
直訳 ちょくやく literal translation
直喩 ちょくゆ simile
直筆 じきひつ autograph, one's own handwriting
直輸入 ちょくゆにゅう direct import [importation]
直談判 じかだんぱん personal negotiations, direct bargaining

❸ **STRAIGHTforward, straight, upright, honest**
正直な しょうじきな honest, upright, frank
実直な じっちょくな upright, honest, steady
愚直な ぐちょくな honest to a fault, stupidly honest
曲直 きょくちょく right and wrong
司直 しちょく administration of justice; judicial authorities

❹ duty, watch
当直する とうちょくする be on duty
宿直 しゅくちょく night duty, night watch

❺ price, cost
安直な あんちょくな cheap, inexpensive; easy, simple
高直な こうじきな expensive

❻ *baseball* liner, line drive
左直 さちょく left liner

INDEPENDENT

【じき 直】**at once, soon**
直に じきに at once, soon, on the spot; easily
【じかに 直に】**directly, at first hand; personally**
【ちょくな 直な】openhearted; free and easy; cheap

KUN

【ただちに 直ちに】**at once, immediately; directly**
直ちに返事する ただちにへんじする replay immediately

【なおす 直す】
①ⓐ **FIX, repair, mend, set right**
ⓑ **FIX** up, adjust, put in order
a 直し物 なおしもの mending, thing to be mended
パンクを直す ぱんくをなおす fix a flat tire
b 化粧直し けしょうなおし adjusting one's makeup
② **correct, rectify, remedy, reform, cure (a bad habit)**
誤りを直す あやまりをなおす correct an error
行儀を直す ぎょうぎをなおす mend one's manners
③ⓐ **alter, change**
ⓑ **convert**
ⓒ **render, translate**
a 時間割りを直す じかんわりをなおす alter the schedule
b キロをポンドに直す きろをぽんどになおす convert kilograms to pounds
c 日本語に直す にほんごになおす render into Japanese

【-なおす -直す】verbal suffix indicating repetition: **do over again**
やり直す やりなおす do over again
書き直す かきなおす rewrite
思い直す おもいなおす reconsider, think better of
焼き直し やきなおし rebaking; adaptation (from)
やり直し やりなおし doing over again, redoing

【なおる 直る】
① **be FIXed, be mended, be repaired**
直らない なおらない irreparable, beyond repair
② **be corrected, be reformed, be cured (of a bad habit)**
悪癖が直る あくへきがなおる get over a bad habit
③ⓐ **be restored, return to normal**
ⓑ improve in status, change for the better
a 仲直り なかなおり reconciliation
立ち直る たちなおる regain one's footing, recover; (of the market) improve
b 開き直る ひらきなおる switch to a defiant attitude

【なおき 直き】*elegant* **STRAIGHT, upright, honest**
素直な すなおな docile, obedient; honest, frank

【すぐ 直ぐ】**at once, immediately, directly; soon; easily, readily; just, right**
真っ直ぐに まっすぐに dead straight; honestly

SYNONYMS

❶ⓐ **straight**
直 STRAIGHT → 3649
棒 straight → 1237
ⓑ **vertical**
縦 VERTICAL → 1783
竪- VERTICAL → 3516
垂 perpendicular → 4382
立て- standing → 2486
直 STRAIGHT → 3649
❷ⓐ **immediate**
即 IMMEDIATE → 1439
直 straight away → 3649
忽 IN AN INSTANT → 3080
❸ **purehearted**
純 PURE → 1649
淳 PUREHEARTED → 0626
清 clean → 0635
潔 IMMACULATE → 0920
廉 INCORRUPT → 3911
敦 HONEST → 2128
惇 SINCERE → 0588
直 straightforward → 3649
侃 FORTHRIGHT → 0097

【なおす】
①ⓐ **repair**
直す FIX → 3649
修 REPAIR → 0138
繕 MEND → 1802
② **correct**
正 RIGHT → 4296
直す correct → 3649
訂 REVISE → 1829
改 REFORM → 0287
矯 RECTIFY → 1586
匡 RECTIFY → 3710
◯ **repeating and repetition**
再 ANOTHER TIME → 4332
又 AGAIN → 4158
復 repeat → 0701
重 DUPLICATE → 4390
畳 reduplicate → 3205
改 redo → 0287
-換える redo → 0716
-直す repetition suffix → 3649
-返す do over → 3797

USAGE

❶【なおす】
直す
①ⓐ fix, repair, mend, set right
ⓑ fix up, adjust, put in order
② correct, rectify, remedy, reform, cure (a bad habit)
③ⓐ alter, change
ⓑ convert
ⓒ render, translate
治す
cure, heal

❷【なおる】
直る
① be fixed, be mended, be repaired
② be corrected, be reformed, be cured (of a bad habit)
③ⓐ be restored, return to normal
ⓑ improve in status, change for the better
治る
be cured, get well, recover

HOMOPHONES

なおす 治 GOVERN → 0393
なおる 治 GOVERN → 0393

置
□ 3-1-12
incorrect classification
➡ see ⬒2-5-8: 罒 at 3222

厂
□ 3-2-0
incorrect classification
➡ see ■4-2-1 at 4166

勺

3650

□3-2-1

▶*SHAKU*

シャク

Ⓝ 勺 Ⓒ 勺 sháo

20	Names	U52FA
勺	S3-2-1	F3753

COMPOUNDS

❶ *SHAKU*:

ⓐ **former unit of capacity equiv. to approx. 0.018 liters or 1/10 of a *go* (合)**

ⓑ unit of sq. measure equiv. to approx. 0.033 sq. m or 1/100 of a *tsubo* (坪)

ⓒ 1/100 of the height of a given mountain

ab 一勺 いっしゃく 1 *shaku*

❷ [now always 杓 1028] dipper, ladle, spoon

INDEPENDENT

【しゃく 勺】*SHAKU* (→❶)

SYNONYMS

❶ⓐ **capacity units**

勺 *SHAKU* (0.018 liters) →3650

合 *go* (0.18 liters) →2511

立 liter →2486

升 *SHO* (1.8 liters) →4266

斗 *TO* (18 liters) →3671

石 *koku* (180 liters) →3689

勺

3651

□3-2-1

▶*SHAKU*

シャク

20	Nonstandard	U2F828
勺	S3-2-1	F0000

traditional form → see 勺 at 3650

乃

□3-2-1

incorrect stroke-count

➡ see □3-1-1: 乃 at 3643

寸

3652

□3-2-1

▶A BIT OF

スン

Ⓒ 寸 cùn

41	Jōyō-6	U5BF8
寸	S3-3-0	F1478

一 (1) 寸 (2) 寸 (3)

RADICAL

sun 'inch' (対 寺 将), used for character classification

COMPOUNDS

❶ⓐ (of small amount) **A BIT OF, very little, small, brief**

ⓑ (of small size) **A BIT OF, very little, small**

a 寸前に すんぜんに immediately before

寸時 すんじ a moment, a minute

b 寸劇 すんげき skit, short play

寸描 すんびょう thumbnail [brief] sketch

寸断する すんだんする cut into pieces [shreds]

❷ ***sun*, (Japanese) inch: unit of length equiv. to approx. 3.03 cm or 1/10 of a *shaku* (尺)**

二寸 にすん 2 *sun*

❸ **measurement, measure, dimensions, length, size**

寸法 すんぽう measurements, size; plan

原寸 げんすん full [actual] size

採寸 さいすん taking measurements

❹ [rare] rule, law

INDEPENDENT

【すん 寸】measure, length; *sun* (→❷)

寸が足りない すんがたりない be too short

SPECIAL READINGS

一寸▲ ちょっと just a moment; just a little, a bit; [in negative constructions] easily, readily

SYNONYMS

❶ⓐ **few**

少 LITTLE →4278

寡 FEW →2957

乏 SCANTY →2432

薄 meager →3004

微 SLIGHT →0788

寸 A BIT OF →3652

僅 A LITTLE →0176

些 A BIT →3251

ⓑ **small and tiny**

小 SMALL →0007

豆- miniature →2442

微 SLIGHT →0788

細 MINUTE →1689

寸 A BIT OF →3652

❷ **length units**

寸 *sun* (3.03 cm) →3652

浬 NAUTICAL MILE (1852 m) →0526

反 *tan* (10.6 m) →3663

尺 *SHAKU* (30.3 cm) →4248

米 meter →4342

尋 fathom (1.8 m) →2918

間 *ken* (1.8 m) →4122

丈 *jo* (3.03 m) →4227

町 *cho* (109 m) →1430

里 LEAGUE, *ri* (3.9 km) →4356

哩 MILE (1609 m) →0479

❸ **size**

寸 measurement →3652

大 size →4224

万 3653

□3-2-1

▶TEN THOUSAND

マン バン よろず▲ ㊔ かず

Ⓝ 萬 Ⓒ 万 wàn mò

1△	Jōyō-2	U4E07
一	S3-1-2	F0193

一 丂 万

COMPOUNDS

❶ TEN THOUSAND

万年 まんねん 10,000 years, eternity

万一 まんいち(=まんいつ) if by any chance

一万 いちまん 10,000

❷ⓐ myriad, multitude, many
ⓑ all

a 万緑 ばんりょく myriad green leaves

万歳 ばんざい Banzai!/Hurrah!/Long live…!

巨万 きょまん myriads, millions, vast fortune

b 万国 ばんこく all nations

万病 まんびょう all kinds of diseases

万全の ばんぜんの perfect, infallible, absolutely secure

万能 ばんのう omnipotence

万事 ばんじ all things, everything

万人 ばんにん(=ばんじん) all people

❸ used phonetically for *man*

万引き まんびき shoplifting; shoplifter

❹ [original meaning, now obsolete] scorpion

INDEPENDENT

【まん 万】TEN THOUSAND

【ばん 万】by any chance

万已むを得なければ ばんやむをえなければ if necessary

KUN

【よろず 万】TEN THOUSAND, myriad; all things, everything

万屋 よろずや general dealer; jack-of-all-trades

SYNONYMS

❶ large numbers

百 HUNDRED → 2519
千 THOUSAND → 4219
万 TEN THOUSAND → 3653
億 HUNDRED MILLION → 0192
兆 TRILLION → 0264
京 ten quadrillion → 2546

❷ⓐ plentiful

百 numerous → 2519
沃 FERTILE → 0315
万 myriad → 3653
多 MANY → 2694
豊 PLENTIFUL → 3344
沢 plentiful → 0313
穣 YIELDING ABUNDANTLY → 1597
裕 ABUNDANT → 1530
饒 ABUNDANT → 2280
富 RICH → 2892

ⓑ all

皆 ALL → 3093
悉 THOROUGHLY → 3405
総 TOTAL → 1743
諸 VARIOUS → 1984
毎 EVERY → 2527
各 EACH → 2692
都 all → 2120
万 all → 3653
全 WHOLE → 2514
渾 ENTIRE → 0738
一 all in one → 4148
満 FULL → 0739
丸 complete(ly) → 4225
完 COMPLETE → 2727

尢 3654

□3-2-1

▶*MAGEASHI*

43	Radical	U5C22
尢	S3-3-0	F0000

RADICAL

mageashi 'lame' (就 尤 尨×), used in characters related to lameness or physical disability

丬 3655

□3-2-1

▶*SHŌHEN*

90	Radical	U4E2C
爿	S3-3-0	F0000

radical variant → see 爿 at 4279

凡 3656

□3-2-1

▶COMMONPLACE

ボン ハン およ(そ)▲ おおよ(そ)▲ すべ(て)▲
㊔ なみ つね おうし

Ⓝ 凢 凣 Ⓒ 凡 fán

16	Jōyō	U51E1
几	S3-2-1	F1779

丿 几 凡

COMPOUNDS

❶ [also prefix] COMMONPLACE, mediocre, ordinary, common

凡庸な ぼんような commonplace, mediocre, banal

凡才 ぼんさい mediocrity, ordinary ability; (man of) mediocrity, man of no genius

凡夫 ぼんぷ(=ぼんぶ) ordinary man; *Buddhism* common mortal
凡人 ぼんじん (man of) mediocrity, ordinary person
凡俗 ぼんぞく mediocrity, commonplaceness; (man of) mediocrity, ordinary person
凡フライ ぼんふらい easy fly (in baseball)
凡試合 ぼんしあい dull game (of baseball)
平凡な へいぼんな common, ordinary, commonplace, mediocre
非凡な ひぼんな rare, unique, extraordinary

❷ **every, all**
凡百の ぼんぴゃくの many, many kinds of
凡例 はんれい introductory remarks, explanatory notes, legend

INDEPENDENT

【ぼん 凡】mediocrity
凡ならざる人物 ぼんならざるじんぶつ remarkable man, man of unusual ability

KUN

【およそ, おおよそ 凡そ】generally, on the whole; approximately, almost; quite, entirely
凡そ正しい およそただしい be right on the whole
凡その見当 およそのけんとう rough estimation
凡そ百人 およそひゃくにん about 100 people
凡そ無意味だ およそむいみだ be quite meaningless

【すべて 凡て】[also 全て or 総べて]
①ⓐ all, everything, the whole
ⓑ entirely, wholly
a 凡ての すべての all, entire, whole
② generally, as a rule

SYNONYMS

❶ **ordinary**
常 NORMAL → 3203
只- ORDINARY → 2677
並 ordinary → 2793
平 common → 4291
普 common → 2919
庸 MEDIOCRE → 3881
凡 COMMONPLACE → 3656
套 TRITE → 2823

USAGE

【すべて】
凡て
[also 全て or 総べて]
①ⓐ all, everything, the whole
ⓑ entirely, wholly
② generally, as a rule
全て
[also 凡て or 総べて] same as 凡て
総べて
[also 凡て or 全て] same as 凡て

HOMOPHONES

すべて
全 WHOLE → 2514
総 TOTAL → 1743

凡 3657 口3-2-1

▶**COMMONPLACE**
ボン ハン およ(そ) おおよ(そ) すべ(て)
㊔ なみ つね おうし

16	Nonstandard	U51E1
几	S3-2-1	F0000

traditional form → see 凡 at 3656

山 3658 口3-2-1

▶**MOUNTAIN**
サン セン▲ やま
Ⓒ 山 shān

46	Jōyō-1	U5C71
山	S3-3-0	F0060

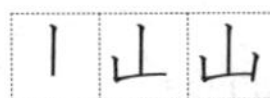
1 2 3

RADICAL

yama 'mountain' (島 岡 岳), used in characters related to mountains
Left variant: 山× ***yamahen*** (崎 峰 岬)
Top variant: 山× ***yamakanmuri*** (岩 岸 崩)

COMPOUNDS

❶ⓐ [original meaning] **MOUNTAIN**
ⓑ **suffix after names of MOUNTAINs**
a 山岳 さんがく mountains
山脈 さんみゃく mountain range
登山 とざん mountain climbing, mountaineering
火山 かざん volcano
b 富士山 ふじさん Mt. Fuji
須弥山 しゅみせん Mt. Sumeru (in Buddhism, said to be the highest mountain rising in the center of the world)

❷ **mine**
鉱山 こうざん mine
閉山 へいざん closing a mine; closing of the climbing season

❸ⓐ Buddhist temple
ⓑ suffix after names of Buddhist temples
a 山門 さんもん main temple gate
本山 ほんざん head temple; this temple
b 高野山 こうやさん name of a Buddhist temple

KUN

【やま 山】**MOUNTAIN, peak; heap, pile; crown (of a hat); speculation; climax; forest; mine**
山山 やまやま mountains; very much
山場 やまば climax, turning point
岩山 いわやま rocky mountain
トマト一山 とまとひとやま a pile of tomatoes

硫黄山 いおうやま sulfur mine

SPECIAL READINGS

山車 だし festival car, float
山羊▲ やぎ goat

SYNONYMS

❶ **mountains**
峰 PEAK → 0494
岳 HIGH MOUNTAIN → 3164
山 MOUNTAIN → 3658

❷ **mine**
坑 PIT → 0277
鉱 MINE → 2145
礦 MINE → 1606
山 mine → 3658

NOTE

➡ see COMPOUND FORMATION for 梁山泊 りょうざんぱく → 泊 0389

込辺 etc.

incorrect stroke-count
➡ see □3-3-2: 辶 at 3761

□3-2-2

止

3659
□3-2-2

▶**STOP**

シ と(まる) -ど(まり) と(める) -と(める) -ど(め) とど(める)▲ とど(め)▲ とど(まる)▲ や(める)▲ や(む)▲ -や(む)▲ よ(す)▲ -さ(す)▲ -さ(し)▲ ㊔ とどむ

Ⓒ 止 zhǐ

77	Jōyō-2	U6B62
止	S4-4-0	F0393

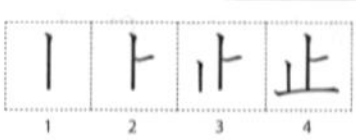

RADICAL

tomeru 'stop' (正 歩 武), used in characters related to feet or actions using feet
Left variant: ⺊× ***tomehen*** (此)

COMPOUNDS

❶ⓐ (cease moving) **STOP, come to a standstill, halt; stop over**
ⓑ (motionless) **still, quiet**
a 止宿 ししゅく lodging
停止する ていしする stop, stand still; suspend, put to an end
静止する せいしする stand still, come to a standstill
b 止水 しすい still water
黙止する もくしする keep quiet; take no measures

❷ⓐ (cease acting) **STOP, cease, discontinue**
ⓑ **cause to STOP, arrest, discontinue, suspend**
a 終止 しゅうし termination, cessation
休止 きゅうし pause, standstill, dormancy; rest
b 止血する しけつする stop [arrest] bleeding
中止する ちゅうしする suspend, stop, discontinue
廃止する はいしする abolish, abandon, discontinue

❸ **STOP an action from occurring, check, deter, dissuade**
止音器 しおんき (piano) damper
抑止する よくしする deter, check, hold back
阻止する そしする obstruct, check, hinder
制止する せいしする control, check, stop (a person) from (doing)
禁止 きんし prohibition, forbiddance, ban
防止 ぼうし prevention, check
諫×止する かんしする dissuade

❹ behavior, manner
挙止 きょし bearing, deportment

❺ *śamatha*: concentrating the mind, calming oneself (in Buddhism)
止観 しかん giving up illusions and attaining enlightenment

❻ unclassified compounds
笑止千万 しょうしせんばん be highly ridiculous, quite absurd

INDEPENDENT

【し 止】*śamatha* (→❺); OFF (marking on taps or valves)

KUN

【とまる 止まる】
①ⓐ **come to a STOP, stop, halt**
ⓑ [sometimes also 停まる] (of vehicles) **roll to a STOP, stop (at a station)**
ⓒ be **STOP**ped up
a 止まり とまり stop, stoppage; end
止まり木 とまりぎ perch, roost; footrail
立ち止まる たちどまる stop, halt, stand still
b 駅に止まる えきにとまる stop at a station
② (cease acting) **STOP, cease; be suspended, be interrupted**
行き止まり いきどまり dead end, blind alley, *cul-de-sac*
血が止まる ちがとまる stop bleeding

【-どまり -止まり】[suffix]
① **STOP, stopping, last stop**
品川止まり しながわどまり train whose last stop is Shinagawa Station
② limit, extreme
高いと言っても一万円止まりだ たかいといってもいちまんえんどまりだ Ten thousand yen is as high as the price will go
あいつは課長止まりだ あいつはかちょうどまりだ The likes of him will never be promoted beyond section chief

【とめる 止める】
①ⓐ (arrest motion) **STOP, bring to a standstill, arrest**

ⓑ [sometimes also 停める] (bring a vehicle to a temporary halt) **STOP (a bus or train), bring to a halt, brake**

a 呼び止める よびとめる stop, call to stop
受け止める うけとめる stop, catch; receive
塞き止める せきとめる dam up, stop; check
b 車を止める くるまをとめる bring a car to a halt

② (cause an action to cease) **STOP (an engine), turn off; arrest, stop, hold**
止め処無く とめどなく endlessly, ceaselessly
ガスを止める がすをとめる turn off the gas
通行止め つうこうどめ suspension of traffic
消し止める けしとめる put out, extinguish
客止め きゃくどめ full house
打ち止め うちどめ close, end

③ⓐ **STOP an action from occurring, check, arrest**
ⓑ **STOP a person from doing, dissuade**
a 食い止める くいとめる check, hold back
b 差し止める さしとめる prohibit, forbid; suspend (a paper)
口止めする くちどめする forbid to mention, hush up

【-とめる -止める】 [also -留める] **kill**
射止める いとめる shoot to death; win, acquire
突き止める つきとめる ascertain, run to the ground; [archaic] stab [thrust] to death

【-どめ -止め】
① **device for STOPping, stopper**
車止め くるまどめ bumping post, bumper
歯止め はどめ drag, pallet; brake
滑り止め すべりどめ tire chains; creepers; taking the entrance examination to a university as a safety measure in case one fails at other universities

② something that prevents, preventive
咳×止め せきどめ cough medicine
錆止め さびどめ anticorrosive, rust preventive

【とどめる 止める】
① (arrest motion) **STOP**, arrest
押し止める おしとどめる stop, check, keep back
② confine (oneself) to, be restricted to
. . . と言うだけに止めよう …というだけにとどめよう Suffice it to say that…

【とどめ 止め】 finishing blow, *coup de grâce*
止めを刺す とどめをさす finish by a stab in the neck; put an end to
花は桜に止めを刺す はなはさくらにとどめをさす Of all flowers cherry blossom is the best

【とどまる 止まる】
① come to a **STOP**, stop, halt
思い止まる おもいとどまる abandon (an idea), refrain from (doing)
② be limited [confined] to
単に希望を述べたに止まる たんにきぼうをのべたにとどまる I simply expressed my desire

【やめる 止める】 [sometimes also 已める]
①ⓐ **STOP (performing an action), cease, discontinue**
ⓑ **give up, abandon, quit**
a 仕事を止める しごとをやめる stop [leave off] work
b 止めになる やめになる be discontinued, be given up
取り止める とりやめる cancel, call off
煙草を止める たばこをやめる give up smoking
② **abolish, do away with**

【やむ 止む】
①ⓐ [sometimes also 已む] **STOP, cease, come to an end**
ⓑ **abate, die away**
b 嵐が止んだ あらしがやんだ The storm has calmed down
② [also 已む] **cease, discontinue; not do**
止むを得ない やむをえない unavoidable, cannot be helped

【-やむ -止む】 [verbal suffix] **STOP**, come to an end
泣き止む なきやむ stop crying, cry oneself out
雨が降り止んだ あめがふりやんだ It stopped raining

【よす 止す】 **STOP**, drop, give up
止せ よせ Cut it out!

【-さす -止す】 [verbal suffix] leave something unfinished, **STOP** in the middle
言い止す いいさす break off, stop (in the middle of a sentence)

【-さし -止し】 [verbal suffix] leaving something unfinished
読み止しの本 よみさしのほん unfinished book

SPECIAL READINGS
波止場 はとば wharf, quay

SYNONYMS
❶ⓐ stop
止 STOP → 3659
停 HALT → 0156
駐 park → 2297
ⓑ not moving
固 FIRM → 3830
定 fixed → 2770
静 still → 2164
止 still → 3659
❷ discontinue
絶 BREAK OFF → 1711
廃 ABOLISH → 3902
断 CUT OFF → 1885
止 STOP → 3659
休 suspend → 0056

停 suspend →0156
已む CEASE →4185

❸ **prevent**
防 PREVENT →0320
止 STOP →3659

USAGE

❶【とまる】

止まる
①ⓐ come to a stop, stop, halt
ⓑ [sometimes also 停まる] (of vehicles) **roll to a stop, stop (at a station)**
ⓒ be stopped up
② (cease acting) **stop, cease; be suspended, be interrupted**

留まる
① be held in position, be fastened
②ⓐ remain in one's perception, strike one's senses
ⓑ [in compounds] **remain, be left over**
③ perch on

泊まる
① stay overnight, lodge, stay at
② stay at anchor
③ be on night duty

停まる
[now usu. 止まる] (of vehicles) **roll to a stop, stop (at a station)**

❷【とまり】

止まり
ⓐ stop, stoppage
ⓑ end

泊まり
①ⓐ stopover, stay
ⓑ night duty
② anchorage

❸【とめる】

止める
①ⓐ (arrest motion) **stop, bring to a standstill, arrest**
ⓑ [sometimes also 停める] (bring a vehicle to a temporary halt) **stop (a bus or train), bring to a halt, brake**
② (cause an action to cease) **stop (an engine), turn off; arrest, stop, hold**
③ⓐ stop an action from occurring, check, arrest
ⓑ stop a person from doing, dissuade

留める
①ⓐ keep in place, retain, fix, fasten
ⓑ keep (a parcel) until called for
ⓒ keep in custody, detain
ⓓ (keep a vehicle from moving) **park**
② keep in mind
③ keep (a quarrel) from intensifying, stop

泊める
① lodge, give shelter, accommodate
② anchor a ship

停める
[now usu. 止める] (bring a vehicle to a temporary halt) **stop (a bus or train), bring to a halt, brake**

❹【-とめる】

-止める
[also -留める] **kill**

-留める
[also -止める]
① kill
② write down, register

★Both forms are used in compounds in the sense of kill, but -留める is preferred in the word 仕留める しとめる 'kill, shoot dead'. とめる is not used independently in this sense.

❺【-どめ】

-止め
① device for stopping, stopper
② something that prevents, preventive

-留め
clip, fastener, retainer

❻【とどめる】

止める
① (arrest motion) **stop, arrest**
② confine (oneself) to, be restricted to

留める
① leave (behind)
② make stay, detain

❼【とどまる】

止まる
① come to a stop, stop, halt
② be limited [confined] to

留まる
stay behind, remain

❽【やむ】

止む
①ⓐ [sometimes also 已む] **stop, cease, come to an end**
ⓑ abate, die away
② [also 已む] **cease, discontinue; not do**

已む
ⓐ [also 止む] (bring to an end) **cease, discontinue; not do**
ⓑ [usu. 止む] (come to an end) **cease, stop**

HOMOPHONES

とまる
留 KEEP →3189
泊 STAY OVERNIGHT →0389
停 HALT →0156

とまり 泊 STAY OVERNIGHT →0389
とめる
　留 KEEP →3189
　泊 STAY OVERNIGHT →0389
　停 HALT →0156
-とめる 留 KEEP →3189
-どめ 留 KEEP →3189
とどめる 留 KEEP →3189
とどまる 留 KEEP →3189
やめる
　辞 WORD →1726
　罷 DISMISS →3234
　已 CEASE →4185
やむ 已 CEASE →4185
-さす
　差 DIFFERENCE →4104
　指 FINGER →0452
　刺 STAB →1625
　挿 INSERT →0517
　注 POUR →0383
　射 SHOOT →1850
-さし
　差 DIFFERENCE →4104
　刺 STAB →1625
　指 FINGER →0452

NOTE

➡ see also USAGE notes at 辞 1726 and 差 4104

勾

▶**ARREST**

コウ　まがり(り)▲

Ⓒ 勾 gōu gòu

3660

□3-2-2

20	Jōyō	U52FE
勹	S4-2-2	F2541

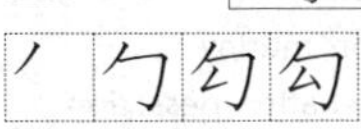

COMPOUNDS

❶ [now also 拘 0367] **ARREST, detain, confine**
　勾引 こういん arrest, custody
　勾留 こうりゅう detention for investigation
❷ **be bent, be hooked, be curved**
　勾配 こうばい slope, incline; gradient

KUN

【まがり　勾り】[usu. 曲がり] curvature, warp
　勾玉(=曲玉) まがたま comma-shaped bead

SPECIAL READINGS

　勾引かす▲(=拐す) かどわかす kidnap

SYNONYMS

❶ **catch a criminal**
　捕 CATCH →0514
　逮 CATCH A CRIMINAL →3875
　拘 ARREST →0367
　勾 ARREST →3660
❷ **bend**
　曲 CURVE →4340
　彎 CURVE (become bow-shaped) →3634
　屈 BEND →3821
　折 bend →0297
　勾 be bent →3660
　歪 DISTORT →3095

HOMOPHONES

まがり 曲 MUSICAL COMPOSITION →4340

勿

▶**DO NOT**

モチ　モッ-　ブツ　なか(れ)

Ⓒ 勿 wù

3661

□3-2-2

20	Names	U52FF
勹	S4-2-2	F2187

COMPOUNDS

❶ **DO NOT, not, never**
　勿論 もちろん of course, no doubt, naturally
❷ [sometimes also 物 もつ 1084] **used phonetically for *mot-***
　勿体 もったい air of importance, superior airs
　勿体無い もったいない wasteful; be more than one deserves
　勿怪の幸い もっけのさいわい piece of good luck, windfall

KUN

【なかれ　勿れ】[sometimes also 莫れ] **DO NOT**, not, never
　勿れ主義の道徳 なかれしゅぎのどうとく negative virtues
　事勿れ主義 ことなかれしゅぎ peace-at-any-price principle
　恐るる勿れ おそるるなかれ Be not afraid!

SPECIAL READINGS

　勿忘草 わすれなぐさ forget-me-not

SYNONYMS

❶ **terms of negation**
　不 NOT (negation) →4242
　非 IS NOT (contrariety) →1101
　無 WITHOUT (nonexistence) →2648
　没 lacking in →0305
　欠 LACK →2481
　否 OR NOT →3058
　未 NOT YET →4318
　莫 NOT →2839
　勿 DO NOT →3661
❷ **phonetic [m]**
　弥 PHONETIC [mi] →0344
　摩 phonetic [ma] →3938

昧 phonetic [mai] → 1105
蜜 phonetic [mitsu] → 2958
勿 phonetic [mot] → 3661
牟 PHONETIC [mu] → 2518

USAGE

【なかれ】
勿れ
[sometimes also 莫れ] do not, not, never
莫れ
[usu. 勿れ] do not, not, never

HOMOPHONES

なかれ 莫 NOT → 2839

NOTE

➡ see COMPOUND FORMATION for 勿論 もちろん → 論 1981

匂 3662

▶SMELL
にお(う) にお(い) にお(わせる) にお(わす)
Ⓒ (国字)
口3-2-2

20	Jōyō	U5302
勹	S4-2-2	F1289

ノ 勹 匀 匂 (1 2 3 4)

KUN

【におう 匂う】
① **SMELL (sweet), give out a smell [fragrance]**
匂い立つ においたつ be enveloped in a smell; be radiant, be attractive
香水が髪から匂った こうすいがかみからにおった Her hair emitted a fragrance
② (of blossoms) **glow, be shiningly beautiful**
桜が咲き匂う さくらがさきにおう Cherry trees are in beautiful bloom

【におい 匂い】
ⓐ **SMELL, scent, fragrance, aroma**
ⓑ **flavor, touch (of something agreeable)**
a 匂い袋 においぶくろ sachet
b 文学的な匂い ぶんがくてきなにおい literary flavor

【におわせる 匂わせる】
ⓐ **give out an odor [scent]**
ⓑ **drop a hint, give an inkling (of)**
b 介入を匂わせる かいにゅうをにおわせる hint at one's intervention

【におわす 匂わす】 same as 匂わせる におわせる

SYNONYMS

【におい】
◯ **smell and fragrance**
気 smell → 3960
匂い SMELL → 3662
臭 BAD SMELL → 3261
香 SWEET SMELL → 3177
馨 PERFUME → 3575
芳 FRAGRANT → 2739
薫 BALMY → 3005
郁 AROMATIC → 1640

HOMOPHONES

におう 臭 BAD SMELL → 3261
におい 臭 BAD SMELL → 3261

NOTE

➡ see USAGE note at 臭 3261

反 3663

▶COUNTER
ハン ホン タン ホ▲ そ(る) そ(らす) かえ(す)▲ かえ(る)▲ -かえ(る)▲
Ⓒ 反 fǎn
口3-2-2

29	Jōyō-3	U53CD
又	S4-2-2	F0276

一 厂 反 反 (1 2 3 4)

COMPOUNDS

❶ⓐ **COUNTER, oppose, go against**
ⓑ **act contrary to (the rule), act against, violate, infringe**
ⓒ [formerly also 叛 はん, ほん 1469] **rebel, revolt**
a 反対する はんたいする oppose, object (to)
反抗 はんこう resistance, opposition, defiance
反目 はんもく antagonism, hostility, feud
反則 はんそく violation of rules, infringement, foul
反感 はんかん ill feeling, antipathy
b 違反(=違犯)する いはんする violate (the law), infringe; act contrary to
背反する はいはんする revolt, rebel; go against, violate
c 反乱 はんらん rebellion, revolt
反逆 はんぎゃく revolt, rebellion, mutiny
離反 りはん estrangement, alienation, desertion
謀反 むほん rebellion, revolt, treason

❷ [also prefix] **COUNTER, counter-, anti-, opposite, reverse, inverse**
反発する はんぱつする repulse, repel; rally; oppose
反論 はんろん counterargument, refutation
反撃 はんげき counterattack
反動 はんどう backlash, recoil, reaction
反戦 はんせん antiwar
反米 はんべい anti-America
反日 はんにち anti-Japanese
反落 はんらく reactionary fall (in stock prices)
反比例 はんぴれい inverse proportion
反政府 はんせいふ anti-government
反作用 はんさよう reaction

❸ⓐ [original meaning] **turn over, reverse**

ⓑ return in the original direction, reflect, be reflected; react

a 反転する はんてんする turn around, reverse, roll over

反側する はんそくする turn over in bed

b 反応 はんのう reaction, response

反響 はんきょう echo, reverberation; response, repercussions

反射 はんしゃ reflection

反射的 はんしゃてき reflective, reflexive

反省 はんせい reflection, introspection

❹ repeat

反復 はんぷく [sometimes also 反覆] repetition, reiteration

反芻[×] はんすう chewing the cud, rumination

❺ *tan*:

ⓐ unit for measuring cloth equiv. to approx. 10.6 m in length and 34 cm in width

ⓑ [formerly also 段 たん 1471] unit of sq. measure equiv. to approx. 9.9 ares or 300 *bu* (歩)

ⓒ former unit of length equiv. to approx. 10.9 m or 6 *ken* (間)

a 反物 たんもの cloth, textiles, dry goods

木綿三反 もめんさんたん three *tan* of cotton cloth

b 土地四反 とちよんたん a lot of 4 *tan* (approx. 1 acre)

❻ unclassified compounds

反古(=反故) ほご(=ほぐ) wastepaper, scrap of paper

INDEPENDENT

【はん 反】 antithesis

正と反 せいとはん thesis and antithesis

【はんする 反する】 **oppose, be opposed to, go against; act contrary to (the rule), act against, violate, infringe**

【たん 反】 *tan* (→❺)

KUN

【そる 反る】 *vi* **bend, curve, warp, lean backwards**

反り そり curve, bend, warp; disposition, natural inclination

反った板 そったいた warped board

反り返る そりかえる warp, bend backwards; throw back one's head

【そらす 反らす】 *vt* **bend (backward), curve, warp**

体を反らす からだをそらす bend oneself backward

胸を反らす むねをそらす throw out one's chest, be puffed up with pride

【かえす 反す】 *vt* turn over, overturn, upset, reverse

干し草を反す ほしくさをかえす turn over hay

【かえる 反る】 *vi* turn over, become overturned

スカートの裾が反る すかーとのすそがかえる The hem of the skirt turns over

【-かえる -反る】 [also -返る] [emphatic verbal suffix] utterly, completely

呆れ反る あきれかえる be utterly amazed

SYNONYMS

❶ⓐ resist

抗 RESIST → 0296

抵 RESIST → 0377

耐 WITHSTAND → 1634

対 OPPOSE → 1025

反 COUNTER → 3663

逆 rebel → 3835

撥 REPEL → 0907

叛 REBEL → 1469

ⓑ violate

違 VIOLATE → 3907

破 BREAK → 1478

犯 offend against → 0229

反 act contrary to → 3663

悖 GO AGAINST → 0503

背 go against → 3182

❷ opposite

対 OPPOSITE → 1025

反 COUNTER → 3663

逆 REVERSE → 3835

倒 upside-down → 0139

❸ⓐ overturn

覆 OVERTURN → 3386

翻 TURN OVER → 2391

反 turn over → 3663

顛 TURN [roll] OVER → 2317

転 turn [roll] over → 1872

倒 TOPPLE → 0139

轢 RUN OVER → 2095

ⓑ spring back

弾 SPRING BACK → 0697

反 return in original direction → 3663

❺ⓐ length units

寸 *sun* (3.03 cm) → 3652

浬 NAUTICAL MILE (1852 m) → 0526

反 *tan* (10.6 m) → 3663

尺 *SHAKU* (30.3 cm) → 4248

米 meter → 4342

尋 fathom (1.8 m) → 2918

間 *ken* (1.8 m) → 4122

丈 *jo* (3.03 m) → 4227

町 *cho* (109 m) → 1430

里 LEAGUE, *ri* (3.9 km) → 4356

哩 MILE (1609 m) → 0479

ⓑ area units

坪 *TSUBO* (3.3 sq. m) → 0328

歩 *bu* (3.3 sq. m) → 3071

畝 *se* (0.99 ares) → 1857
反 *tan* (9.9 ares) → 3663
町 *cho* (99.2 ares) → 1430

USAGE

【そらす】
反らす
vt bend (backward), curve, warp
逸らす
① let slip, miss, lose, let go, let pass
② (cause to deviate) divert, avert, dodge, evade

HOMOPHONES

そらす 逸 LET SLIP → 3872
かえす
返 RETURN → 3797
帰 RETURN → 0148
かえる
返 RETURN → 3797
帰 RETURN → 0148
還 RETURN → 3945
-かえる 返 RETURN → 3797

NOTE

➡ see also USAGE notes at 返 3797 and 帰 0148

仄 3664

□ 3-2-2

▶**FAINT**

ソク ほの(か) ほの- ほの(めかす) ほの(めく)

Ⓒ 仄 zè

9	Non-Jōyō	U4EC4
人	S4-2-2	F2807

COMPOUNDS

❶ **FAINT, vague, indistinct**
❷ [now also 側 0155] **from the side**
仄聞する そくぶんする learn by hearsay
❸ **oblique (tone)**
平仄 ひょうそく different tones in which characters are pronounced in Chinese; consistency

KUN

【ほのか 仄か】**FAINT, vague, indistinct**
仄かな ほのかな faint, vague, indistinct
【ほの- 仄-】**FAINTly, vaguely**
仄白い ほのじろい dimly white
仄暗い ほのぐらい dim, dusky, gloomy
仄仄と ほのぼのと dimly, faintly; heartwarming
【ほのめかす 仄めかす】**hint, allude, show FAINTly**
仄めかし ほのめかし hint, intimation
【ほのめく 仄めく】**appear FAINTly, be seen dimly**

SYNONYMS

❶ **less in degree**
弱 WEAK → 1499
軽 LIGHT → 1909
微 SLIGHT → 0788
低 LOW → 0082
薄 THIN → 3004
浅 SHALLOW → 0464
仄 FAINT → 3664

厄 3665

□ 3-2-2

▶**MISFORTUNE**

ヤク

Ⓒ 厄 è

27	Jōyō	U5384
厂	S4-2-2	F1942

一 厂 厅 厄
1 2 3 4

COMPOUNDS

❶ **MISFORTUNE, trouble, evil, ill luck**
厄除け やくよけ warding off evil fortune; talisman against evils
厄日 やくび unlucky day, critical day
厄年 やくどし climacteric [critical] age, unlucky year
厄介 やっかい trouble, annoyance
大厄 たいやく great misfortune [calamity]; grand climacteric
災厄 さいやく calamity, disaster, accident
❷ abbrev. of 厄年 やくどし: climacteric [critical] age, unlucky year
前厄 まえやく the year preceding a critical age, the year before one's grand climacteric

INDEPENDENT

【やく 厄】**MISFORTUNE**, ill luck, evil
厄を落とす やくをおとす escape evil; exorcise

SYNONYMS

❶ **misfortune and disaster**
災 NATURAL CALAMITY → 2734
難 DISASTER → 2310
禍 CALAMITY → 1304
厄 MISFORTUNE → 3665
凶 BAD LUCK → 3679

NOTE

➡ see COMPOUND FORMATION for 厄介 やっかい → 介 2463

不

□ 3-2-2

incorrect classification
➡ see ■4-4-1 at 4242

及 3666

□ 3-2-2

▶**REACH TO**

キュウ およ(ぶ) およ(び) および およ(ぼす)
㊔ おい

29	Nonstandard	U53CA
又	S4-2-2	F0000

traditional form → see 及 at 4192

斤

3667

□3-2-2

▶**CATTY**

キン

Ⓒ 斤 jīn

69	Jōyō	U65A4
斤	S4-4-0	F3357

RADICAL

ono 'ax' (斥 新 断), used in characters related to cutting or chopping

COMPOUNDS

❶ **CATTY, *kin*: unit of weight equiv. to 600 g or 160 momme (匁)**

斤目 きんめ weight (in catties)

斤量 きんりょう weight

パン三斤 ぱんさんぎん three catties of bread

❷ [original meaning, now archaic] **axe**

斧斤 ふきん axe

INDEPENDENT

【きん 斤】CATTY, *kin* (→❶)

SYNONYMS

❶ **weight units**

匁 MOMME (3.75 g) →4276

斤 CATTY (600 g) →3667

貫 *kan* (3.75 kg) →3112

噸 TON →0930

屯 ton →4268

戶

3668

□3-2-2

▶**DOOR**

▶**HOUSEHOLD**

コ と¹ と² ㊔べ ど へ

63	Nonstandard	U6236
戶	S4-4-0	F0000

traditional form →see 戸 at 2429

RADICAL

tobiranoto 'door' (扁 扈×), used in characters related to doors or houses

Enclosure: 戸 ***tobiranoto*** (戻 房 扇)

氏

3669

□3-2-2

▶**COURTESY TITLE**

▶**FAMILY NAME**

シ うじ -うじ

Ⓒ 氏 shì zhī

83	Jōyō-4	U6C0F
氏	S4-4-0	F0177

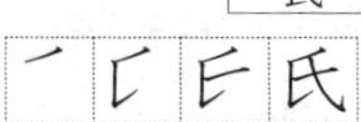

RADICAL

uji 'family name' (民 氓×), used for character classification

COMPOUNDS

❶ⓐ **COURTESY TITLE** after family names: **Mr., Mister**

ⓑ [polite] **person**

a 田中氏 たなかし Mr. Tanaka

b 某氏 ぼうし a certain person

同氏 どうし the said person, he

無名氏 むめいし anonymous person, a nobody

❷ⓐ **FAMILY NAME, surname**

ⓑ [archaic] suffix after a married woman's maiden name: **née**

a 氏名 しめい (full) name

氏姓制度 しせいせいど former naming system

b 夫人李氏 ふじんりし his wife née Li

❸ⓐ **clan, family**

ⓑ **suffix after names of clans or families**

a 氏族 しぞく clan, family

b 源氏 げんじ the Genji family, the Minamotos

平氏 へいし the Heike [Taira] clan [family], the Heikes

❹ **suffix for temperature scales**

摂氏(=セ氏) せっし(=せし) centigrade

華氏 かし Fahrenheit

❺ **he**

彼氏 かれし he; lover, beau

INDEPENDENT

【し 氏】[polite] **third person pronoun, he; FAMILY NAME**

氏の意見 しのいけん his opinion

KUN

【うじ 氏】**FAMILY NAME, surname; lineage, stock, birth**

氏素性 うじすじょう (a person's) family background

氏神 うじがみ tutelary god

氏より育ち うじよりそだち Birth is much, but breeding is more

【-うじ -氏】honorific **COURTESY TITLE**: **Mr.**

加藤氏 かとううじ Mr. Kato

SYNONYMS

❶ⓐ **titles of address**

氏 COURTESY TITLE →3669

兄 familiar title (seniors) →2676

君 FAMILIAR TITLE (peers) →3974

嬢 Miss →0936

様 FORMAL TITLE →1332

殿 FORMAL HONORIFIC TITLE →2247

師 honorific title (clergymen) →1680

公 honorific title (noblemen) →2468

ⓑ **person**

人 HUMAN BEING →4175

者 PERSON →3980

方 person (*honorific*) →2459

氏 person (*polite*) → 3669

❷ⓐ **name**

名 NAME → 2693
銘 name (inscribed by maker) → 2158
姓 SURNAME → 0334
氏 FAMILY NAME → 3669
称 APPELLATION → 1491
題 TITLE → 4139
号 DESIGNATION → 2675

❸ **family and relations**

族 FAMILY → 1195
家 FAMILY → 2827
門 family → 1100
氏 clan → 3669
縁 RELATION → 1754
姻 relative by marriage → 0421
親 RELATIVES → 2264
戚 RELATIVES → 4401
曽 GREAT- → 2632

【し】

○ **third person pronouns**

彼 THIRD PERSON PRONOUN (*neutral*) → 0346
氏 third person pronoun (*polite*) → 3669
奴 third person pronoun (*slang*) → 0217

友

3670

□3-2-2

▶**FRIEND**

ユウ とも

Ⓒ 友 yǒu

29	Jōyō-2	U53CB
又	S4-2-2	F0458

一 ナ 方 友 (1 2 3 4)

COMPOUNDS

ⓐ **FRIEND, comrade**
ⓑ **FRIEND**ly
ⓒ **be FRIEND**s **with**

a 友人 ゆうじん friend
友情 ゆうじょう friendship, fellowship
親友 しんゆう close [intimate] friend
朋友 ほうゆう friend, companion
僚友 りょうゆう comrade, colleague, fellow worker
戦友 せんゆう comrade-in-arms
b 友軍 ゆうぐん allied army, friendly troops
c 友好 ゆうこう friendship, amity

KUN

【とも 友】[sometimes also 朋] **FRIEND, companion, pal**

友達 ともだち friend, companion
竹馬の友 ちくばのとも childhood friend, old playmate

SYNONYMS

ⓐ **friends and associates**

僚 COLLEAGUE → 0186
輩 FELLOW → 3482
朋 COMRADE → 1092
友 FRIEND → 3670
侶 COMPANION → 0114

USAGE

【とも】

友
[sometimes also 朋] friend, companion, pal

朋
[usu. 友] same as 友

供
attendant, retinue

共
① [in compounds]
ⓐ joint, together, simultaneous
ⓑ of the same quality [kind]
ⓒ both, neither; including
② same cloth

HOMOPHONES

とも

供 OFFER → 0098
共 JOINT → 3045
朋 COMRADE → 1092

NOTE

➡ see COMPOUND FORMATION for 竹馬の友 ちくばのとも → 竹 0267

斗

3671

□3-2-2

▶**DIPPER**
▶***TO***

ト トウ▲

Ⓒ 斗 dǒu dòu

68	Jōyō	U6597
斗	S4-4-0	F2010

丶 ⺀ 三 斗 (1 2 3 4)

RADICAL

tomasu 'measure' (料 斜 斡), used in characters related to measures, measuring or scooping

COMPOUNDS

❶ⓐ [original meaning] **DIPPER, ladle**
ⓑ **the Big DIPPER**

a 漏斗 ろうと funnel ("dipper for leaking")
b 斗南 となん [archaic] south of the Big Dipper; the whole world
北斗七星 ほくとしちせい the Big Dipper
泰斗 たいと leading authority
南斗 なんと [rare] constellation in Sagittarius

❷ *TO*: **unit of capacity equiv. to approx. 18 liters or 10 *sho* (升), used esp. for sake or rice**
斗酒 としゅ a *to* of sake, big supply of sake
二斗 にと 2 *to*
❸ [usu. 闘 とう 4136] fight (with)
→ see 闘 4136 for compounds

INDEPENDENT

【と 斗】 *to* (→❷); one-*to* measure
胆、斗の如し たんとのごとし be as bold as a lion

SYNONYMS

❶ⓐ **spoons**
斗 DIPPER → 3671
杓 DIPPER → 1028
匕 SPOON → 3641
❷ **capacity units**
勺 *SHAKU* (0.018 liters) → 3650
合 *go* (0.18 liters) → 2511
立 liter → 2486
升 *SHO* (1.8 liters) → 4266
斗 *TO* (18 liters) → 3671
石 *koku* (180 liters) → 3689

COMPOUND FORMATION

【泰斗 たいと】
泰斗 'leading authority' is someone as great as Mt. Taishan (泰), one of the Five Sacred Mountains in China, and as eminent as the Big Dipper (斗 ❶ⓑ).

NOTE

➡ see NOTE at 闘 4136

斗

3672

□3-2-2

▶**FIGHT**
トウ たたか(う)

68	Nonstandard	U6597
斗	S4-4-0	F0000

alternative form → see 闘 at 4136

円

3673

□3-2-2

▶**CIRCLE**
▶**YEN**
エン まる(い) まる ㊔ つぶら まどか まど
Ⓝ 圓 Ⓒ 圆 yuán

13△	Jōyō-1	U5186
冂	S4-2-2	F0208

丨 冂 门 円
1 2 3 4

COMPOUNDS

❶ⓐ CIRCLE
ⓑ [also prefix] **circular, round**
a 円周 えんしゅう circumference
楕円形 だえんけい ellipse
同心円 どうしんえん concentric circles
b 円卓 えんたく round table
円盤 えんばん disk; flying saucer
円軌道 えんきどう circular orbit
❷ **rounded out, whole, complete; smooth**
円満な えんまんな perfect, harmonious, well-rounded
円滑な えんかつな smooth, harmonious
円熟 えんじゅく maturity, perfection
❸ vicinity, whole district
関東一円 かんとういちえん whole district of Kanto
❹ [also prefix and suffix] **YEN, ¥**
円貨 えんか yen currency
円高 えんだか appreciation of the yen
円安 えんやす low yen rate, depreciation of the yen
円相場 えんそうば yen exchange rate
五百円 ごひゃくえん 500 yen

INDEPENDENT

【えん 円】 **CIRCLE; yen**
円を描く えんをえがく draw a circle
円の騰貴 えんのとうき rise of the yen

KUN

【まるい 円い】 [also 丸い] (shaped like a circle) **circular, round**
円さ まるさ roundness
円く輪になって踊る まるくわになっておどる dance in a circle

【まる 円】
① [usu. 丸] **CIRCLE**
円で囲む まるでかこむ enclose (a word) with a circle
② *slang* money, dough—used in telegrams

SYNONYMS

❶ⓐ **circle**
円 CIRCLE → 3673
圏 circle → 3904
丸 round or spherical shape → 4225
楕 ELLIPSE → 1279
ⓑ **round**
丸い ROUND → 4225
円 circular → 3673
❹ **Japanese money denominations**
文 *mon* → 2458
両 *ryo* → 4331
厘 *RIN* → 3727
銭 sen → 2159
円 YEN → 3673

HOMOPHONES

まるい 丸 ROUND → 4225
まる
丸 ROUND → 4225
〇 ZERO → 4149

辶 𠃊 勹 厂 ⺁ 𠃌 尸 厂 匚 ナ 十 【冂】 八 凵 匚 匸 ユ

NOTE

➡ see USAGE note at 丸 4225

月 3674

☐3-2-2

▶MOON
▶MONTH

ゲツ ガツ つき

Ⓝ 月 Ⓒ 月 yuè

74	Jōyō-1	U6708
月	S4-4-0	F0049

radical variant → see 月 at 3677

丿 1 | 冂 2 | 月 3 | 月 4

COMPOUNDS

❶ [original meaning] **MOON**

月光 げっこう moonlight, moonshine
月面 げつめん lunar surface
月齢 げつれい moon's age
月食(=月蝕) げっしょく lunar eclipse
満月 まんげつ full moon

❷ⓐ **MONTH**
ⓑ **suffix after names of the MONTHs**
ⓒ **MONTHly**

a 月日 がっぴ date
月末 げつまつ end of the month
今月 こんげつ this month
来月 らいげつ next month
二箇月 にかげつ two months
正月 しょうがつ New Year, New Year's day; January
生年月日 せいねんがっぴ date of birth

b 二月 にがつ February

c 月賦 げっぷ monthly installments
月給 げっきゅう monthly pay [salary]
月刊の げっかんの published monthly

❸ **Monday**

月曜(日) げつよう(び) Monday
月水金 げっすいきん Mondays, Wednesdays and Fridays

INDEPENDENT

【げつ 月】**Monday**

KUN

【つき 月】

① **MOON**

月夜 つきよ moonlit night
月見をする つきみをする view the moon, enjoy the moonlight
三日月 みかづき new moon

② **MONTH**

月日 つきひ time, days
月初めに つきはじめに in the beginning of the month
毎月 まいつき every month
年月 としつき time, years

SPECIAL READINGS

五月雨 さみだれ early summer rain

SYNONYMS

❶ **moon**

月 MOON → 3674
陰 moon → 0657

❷ **weeks and months**

週 WEEK → 3874
旬 TEN-DAY PERIOD → 3698
月 MONTH → 3674

❸ **days of the week**

日 Sunday → 3759
月 Monday → 3674
火 Tuesday → 4273
水 Wednesday → 0010
木 Thursday → 4261
金 Friday → 2552
土 Saturday → 4211

月 3675

☐3-2-2

▶*TSUKI*

74	Radical	U2EBC
月	S4-4-0	F0000

radical variant → see 月 at 3677

月 3676

☐3-2-2

▶*NIKUZUKI*

130	Radical	U6708
月	S4-4-0	F0000

radical variant → see 肉 at 3966

月 3677

☐3-2-2

▶MOON
▶MONTH

ゲツ ガツ つき

74	Nonstandard	U6708
月	S4-4-0	F0000

traditional form → see 月 at 3674

RADICAL

tsuki 'moon' (望), used in characters related to the moon or time

Variants: 月 月 *tsuki* (服 朝 朋)

𠘨 3678

☐3-2-2

▶WIND
▶MANNER

フウ フ かぜ かざ- -かぜ

16	Nonstandard	U98A8
几	S4-2-2	F0000

handwritten form → see 風 at 3730

凶

▶BAD LUCK
▶ATROCIOUS
キョウ

3679
□3-2-2

Ⓒ 凶 xiōng

17	Jōyō	U51F6
凵	S4-2-2	F1772

ノ 乂 区 凶
1 2 3 4

COMPOUNDS

❶ⓐ BAD LUCK, misfortune, calamity
ⓑ unlucky, bad, disastrous

a 吉凶 きっきょう good or ill luck, fortune
b 凶事 きょうじ calamity, misfortune
凶報 きょうほう bad news
凶日 きょうじつ unlucky day
凶変(=兇変) きょうへん calamity, disaster; tragic accident

❷ [original meaning] bad harvest
凶作 きょうさく bad harvest
凶年 きょうねん bad year, bad harvest

❸ [formerly also 兇 3044]
ⓐ ATROCIOUS, ferocious, wicked, brutal, cruel
ⓑ ATROCIOUS [lethal] crime, murder, wicked deed
ⓒ wicked person, villain

a 凶悪な きょうあくな atrocious, villainous, fiendish
凶暴な きょうぼうな atrocious, ferocious, brutal
凶漢 きょうかん villain, ruffian, assailant
凶行 きょうこう violence, murder, crime
b 凶器 きょうき murder [dangerous] weapon
凶刃 きょうじん assassin's dagger [knife]
c 元凶 げんきょう ringleader, chief instigator

INDEPENDENT

【きょう 凶】BAD LUCK
お神籤は凶と出た おみくじはきょうとでた The written oracle read "unlucky"

SYNONYMS

❶ misfortune and disaster
災 NATURAL CALAMITY → 2734
難 DISASTER → 2310
禍 CALAMITY → 1304
厄 MISFORTUNE → 3665
凶 BAD LUCK → 3679

❸ⓐ evil
邪 EVIL → 1443
兇 ATROCIOUS → 3044
凶 ATROCIOUS → 3679
悪 BAD → 3413

❸ⓐ cruel
虐 CRUEL → 3989
惨 CRUEL → 0585
酷 SEVERE → 1967
辣 SEVERE → 1965
残 RUTHLESS → 1179
凶 ATROCIOUS → 3679
苛 HARSH → 2786

ⓑ crimes and offenses
犯 OFFENSE → 0229
罪 CRIME → 3224
凶 atrocious crime → 3679

匹

▶COUNTER FOR ANIMALS
ヒツ ひき

3680
□3-2-2

Ⓝ 匹 Ⓒ 匹 pǐ

23	Jōyō	U5339
匸	S4-2-2	F1577

一 ア 兀 匹
1 2 3 4

COMPOUNDS

❶ match, be a match for
匹敵する ひってきする match, rival

❷ coarse, plain
匹夫 ひっぷ coarse man, man of low rank

❸ shaped like the buttocks of a horse
馬匹 ばひつ horses

KUN

【ひき 匹】
① [formerly also 疋] **COUNTER FOR ANIMALS**
犬五匹 いぬごひき five dogs
数匹 すうひき several animals
② [also 疋] *hiki*: unit of measure for cloth equiv. to 2 *tan* (反)
絹一匹 きぬいっぴき one *hiki* of silk

SYNONYMS

【ひき】
① counters for animals
匹 COUNTER FOR ANIMALS → 3680
頭 counter for large animals → 2019
羽 counter for birds → 0265
疋 counter for animals → 4292

USAGE

【ひき】
匹
① [formerly also 疋] counter for animals
② [also 疋] *hiki*: unit of measure for cloth equiv. to 2 *tan* (反)
疋
① *hiki*:
ⓐ [also 匹] unit of measure for cloth equiv . to 2 *tan* (反)

ⓑ former monetary unit equiv. to 10 (later 25) *mon* (文)
② [now usu. 匹] counter for animals

HOMOPHONES
ひき 疋 UNIT OF MEASURE FOR CLOTH →4292

区

▶DISTRICT
▶WARD
ク

3681
□3-2-2

Ⓝ 區 Ⓒ 区 qū ōu

23	Jōyō-3	U533A
匚	S4-2-2	F0541

一 ア 又 区
1 2 3 4

COMPOUNDS
❶ⓐ [also suffix] **DISTRICT, zone, region, area, section**
ⓑ *biogeography* region
a 区域 くいき zone, area; limits
区間 くかん section, territory
地区 ちく district, area, region, lot
管区 かんく district (under jurisdiction); parish
学区 がっく school district [area]
選挙区 せんきょく electoral district, precinct
禁漁区 きんりょうく game preserve, wildlife sanctuary
b 新熱帯区 しんねったいく neotropical region
❷ⓐ (major subdivision of a city, esp. in Japan) **WARD, municipal [urban] district, borough**
ⓑ **suffix after names of WARDs or municipal districts**
ⓒ counter for WARDs
a 区役所 くやくしょ ward office
区長 くちょう ward headman, borough mayor
区立の くりつの established by the ward
区会 くかい ward assembly
b 新宿区 しんじゅくく Shinjuku Ward
クイーンズ区 くいーんずく Queens Borough
c 東京二十三区 とうきょうにじゅうさんく the 23 wards of Tokyo
❸ⓐ [original meaning] **divide into sections, partition**
ⓑ **divided, in little pieces**
a 区分する くぶんする divide, section, subdivide
区別する くべつする distinguish; classify, divide
b 区区たる くくたる various, diverse; irregular
区切る(=句切る) くぎる punctuate, mark off by a comma

INDEPENDENT
【く 区】WARD (→❷ⓐ)
区の財政 くのざいせい ward finances

SYNONYMS
❶ⓐ **areas and localities**
地 PLACE →0236
方 locality →2459
辺 VICINITY →3761
域 BOUNDED AREA →0559
区 DISTRICT →3681
領 TERRITORY →1567
帯 BELT →3191
圏 SPHERE →3904
❷ **parts of towns**
区 WARD →3681
街 CITY QUARTER →0702
町 town section (*cho*) →1430
丁 TOWN SUBSECTION (*chome*) →4155
字 village or town section →2696

巨

□3-2-2

incorrect stroke-count
➡ see □3-3-2: 匚 at 3773

匹

▶COUNTER FOR ANIMALS
ヒツ ひき

3682
□3-2-2

23	Nonstandard	U5339
匚	S4-2-2	F0000

traditional form → see 匹 at 3680

丑

▶THE OX
チュウ うし

3683
□3-2-2

1	Nonstandard	U4E11
一	S4-1-3	F0000

alternative form → see 丑 at 4241

巡迅 etc.

□3-2-3

incorrect stroke-count
➡ see □3-3-3: 辶 at 3780

包

▶WRAP
▶ENCOMPASS
ホウ つつ(む) ㊔ かね

3684
□3-2-3

Ⓝ 包 Ⓒ 包 bāo

20	Jōyō-4	U5305
勹	S5-2-3	F0956

丿 勹 匂 匂 包
1 2 3 4 5

COMPOUNDS
❶ⓐ [formerly also 繃 1787] **WRAP, pack, envelop, cover**
ⓑ **WRAP(per), package, parcel**
ⓒ counter for packets of powder medicine
a 包装 ほうそう wrapping, packing
梱包 こんぽう packing, packaging; package
b 包帯 ほうたい bandage, dressing
c 二包 にほう two packets (of medicine)

❷ cartridge
薬包 やくほう cartridge; chartula
空包 くうほう blank cartridge
❸ⓐ (hold within) **ENCOMPASS, include, envelop, contain; include hidden meanings, imply**
ⓑ [original meaning] (surround with) **ENCOMPASS, surround, encircle**
a 包含する ほうがんする include, encompass, cover; imply
包容する ほうようする encompass, comprehend; imply; tolerate
包蔵する ほうぞうする contain, comprehend; imply; cherish
内包 ないほう connotation, intention, comprehension
b 包括的 ほうかつてき inclusive, comprehensive
包囲する ほういする surround, encircle, envelop
❹ [formerly 庖 3825] **kitchen**
包丁 ほうちょう kitchen knife, carving knife

KUN

【つつむ 包む】**WRAP, pack; cover, envelop, enshroud; conceal**
包み つつみ bundle, wrapper, package, parcel
包み込む つつみこむ wrap up
包み紙 つつみがみ wrapping paper
包み隠す つつみかくす conceal, keep secret
小包 こづつみ parcel, package
霧に包まれる きりにつつまれる be shrouded in mist

SYNONYMS

❶ⓐ **cover and wrap**
覆 COVER → 3386
掩 COVER → 0592
被 cover → 1495
包 WRAP → 3684
蓋う COVER → 2933
蔽 COVER → 2991
葺く THATCH → 2909
ⓑ **bags**
俵 STRAW SACK → 0129
袋 BAG → 3201
鞄 BAG (for carrying) → 2248
包 wrapper → 3684
胞 MEMBRANOUS SAC → 1148
❸ⓐ **contain and include**
含 CONTAIN (have as a part) → 2534
容 CONTAIN (have within) → 2832
包 ENCOMPASS → 3684
挟 HOLD BETWEEN → 0450
ⓑ **surround**
囲む ENCLOSE → 3807
環 SURROUND → 1395

包 ENCOMPASS → 3684

NOTE

➡ see COMPOUND FORMATION for 庖丁(=包丁) ほうちょう → 丁 4155

句

3685
☐3-2-3

▶**PHRASE**
▶**HAIKU**
ク
Ⓒ 句 jù gōu

30	Jōyō-5	U53E5
口	S5-3-2	F0927

ノ 勹 勺 句 句
1 2 3 4 5

COMPOUNDS

❶ [also suffix]
ⓐ **PHRASE, expression, set phrase**
ⓑ *gram* (sentence subdivision) **PHRASE, clause**
a 語句 ごく words and phrases
文句 もんく phrase, expression; complaint
慣用句 かんようく idiom, common phrase
b 句読点 くとうてん punctuation marks
句法 くほう phraseology, diction
名詞句 めいしく noun phrase
❷ line of poetry, verse, poem, stanza
起句 きく opening line of a Chinese quatrain
❸ⓐ **HAIKU, 17-syllable poem**
ⓑ counter for **HAIKU** poems
a 句会 くかい gathering of haiku
句集 くしゅう collection of haiku poems
俳句 はいく haiku
発句 ほっく haiku, hokku
b 三句 さんく three haiku poems

INDEPENDENT

【く 句】**PHRASE, set phrase; clause; verse; haiku**
句を切る くをきる punctuate a sentence
句を作る くをつくる compose a haiku poem
上の句 かみのく first half of a tanka poem

SYNONYMS

❶ⓐ **words and expressions**
語 WORD → 1944
辞 WORD → 1726
詞 WORDS → 1897
句 PHRASE → 3685
諺 PROVERB → 2006
喩 METAPHOR → 0671
ⓑ **sentence and sentence parts**
句 PHRASE → 3685
文 sentence → 2458
節 clause → 3336
❸ⓐ **poetry**

詩 POETRY → 1924
歌 Japanese poetry → 2296
俳 HAIKU → 0126
句 HAIKU → 3685

包

▶WRAP
▶ENCOMPASS
ホウ つつ(む) ㊔ かね

3686
口3-2-3

20	Nonstandard	U5305
勹	S5-2-3	F0000

traditional form → see 包 at 3684

可

▶-ABLE
▶APPROVE
カ -べ(し)▲ ㊔ よし
Ⓒ 可 kě kè

3687
口3-2-3

30	Jōyō-5	U53EF
口	S5-3-2	F0366

一 丅 可 可 可
1 2 3 4 5

COMPOUNDS

❶ [also prefix] **-ABLE, -ible, possible, can**
可能な かのうな possible, potential, practical
可動の かどうの movable
可溶性 かようせい solubility
可視光線 かしこうせん visible ray
可処分の かしょぶんの disposable
可燃物 かねんぶつ combustibles, (in)flammable materials
不可解な ふかかいな incomprehensible, inexplicable, baffling

❷ [original meaning] **APPROVE, be in favor of, permit**
可決 かけつ approval [adoption] of a bill
可否 かひ right or wrong, propriety
許可する きょかする permit, approve, authorize
認可 にんか approval, authorization, permission

❸ **be worthy of**
可憐な かれんな cute, sweet, pretty; tiny
可愛い かわいい dear, darling, charming, lovely, sweet
可愛がる かわいがる love, make a pet of, treat with affection; caress
可愛らしい かわいらしい lovely, charming, cute, sweet
可哀相な かわいそうな poor, pitiable, pathetic

INDEPENDENT

【か 可】fair, passable, grade C; approval
可の評点 かのひょうてん Passable, grade C
可とする かとする approve (of), be in favor of

KUN

【-べし -可し】[auxiliary] *literary* can; should, must, ought to; expected to; perhaps, maybe
見る可き成果 みるべきせいか noticeable [remarkable] result
行く可し ゆくべし Go!
風雨強かる可し ふううつよかるべし It will be stormy

SYNONYMS

❶ **possible**
可 -ABLE → 3687
能 possible → 1676

❷ **agree and approve**
賛 APPROVE OF → 3484
可 APPROVE → 3687
認 RECOGNIZE → 1948
諾 CONSENT → 1974
承 AGREE TO → 0016
肯 ASSENT → 3072
容 tolerate → 2832

圧

▶PRESSURE
アツ お(す)▲
Ⓝ 壓 Ⓒ 压 yā

3688
口3-2-3

32	Jōyō-5	U5727
土	S5-3-2	F0740

一 厂 圧 圧 圧
1 2 3 4 5

COMPOUNDS

❶ⓐ **PRESSURE**
ⓑ [original meaning] **apply PRESSURE, press down**
a 水圧 すいあつ water pressure
気圧 きあつ atmospheric [air] pressure
血圧 けつあつ blood pressure
電圧 でんあつ voltage, electric pressure
b 圧力 あつりょく pressure
圧縮する あっしゅくする compress, constrict
圧搾する あっさくする press, compress
圧砕 あっさい crushing

❷ **PRESSURE, bring pressure to bear on, press, suppress**
圧迫する あっぱくする press, oppress, pressure
圧制 あっせい oppression, coercion
抑圧する よくあつする oppress, repress, suppress
弾圧する だんあつする oppress, suppress

❸ **overwhelming**
圧倒する あっとうする overwhelm, overpower, crush
圧勝 あっしょう overwhelming victory
圧巻 あっかん the best part, masterpiece

INDEPENDENT

【あつ 圧】PRESSURE

【あっする 圧する】press (down), oppress; overpower, overwhelm

KUN

【おす 圧す】[now usu. 押す] press down, press; compress, squash

圧し おし pressing down; weight; authority, commanding presence

気圧される けおされる be overawed [overpowered]

SYNONYMS

❶ⓐ energy and force

力 POWER, force → 4178
勢 physical power → 3542
気 energy → 3960
圧 PRESSURE → 3688
鋒 brunt → 2172

ⓑ push

押 PUSH → 0371
突く THRUST → 2772
圧 apply pressure → 3688
挨 PUSH → 0510
按 HOLD DOWN → 0444

❶ⓑ squeeze

搾 SQUEEZE → 0798
絞る WRING → 1707
圧 apply pressure → 3688

❷ compel and press

圧 PRESSURE → 3688
迫 PRESS → 3815
強 force → 0574
押す PUSH → 0371

HOMOPHONES

おす

押 PUSH → 0371
推 INFER → 0612
捺 AFFIX A SEAL → 0603

おし 押 PUSH → 0371

NOTE

➡ see USAGE note at 押 0371
★ do not confuse with 庄 FEUDAL VILLAGE → 3788

石

3689

☐3-2-3

▸STONE

セキ シャク コク いし ㊔ し いわ いそ あきら

Ⓒ 石 shí dàn

112	Jōyō-1	U77F3
石	S5-5-0	F0233

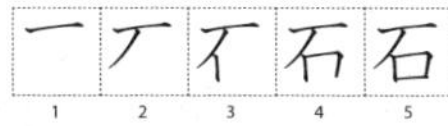

RADICAL

ishi 'stone' (碧 磐 磨), used in characters related to stones, minerals or their qualities

Left variant: 石 ✕ ***ishihen*** (研 破 確)

COMPOUNDS

❶ⓐ [also suffix] [original meaning] **STONE, rock**

ⓑ playing **STONE** in a game of go

a 石像 せきぞう stone statue
石炭 せきたん coal
石鹸✕ せっけん soap
石油 せきゆ petroleum, oil
岩石 がんせき rock
宝石 ほうせき gem, jewel
磁石 じしゃく magnet; compass
大理石 だいりせき marble

b 定石 じょうせき set [standard] moves in the game of go

❷ counter for jewels of a watch, transistors or diodes

二十一石の時計 にじゅういっせきのとけい 21-jewel watch
五石ラジオ ごせきらじお five-transistor radio

❸ *koku*:

ⓐ former unit of capacity equiv. to approx. 180 liters or 10 *to* (斗), used esp. as unit of rice stipends in feudal Japan

ⓑ former unit of capacity equiv. to approx. 278 liters or 10 cubic *shaku* (尺), used esp. for measuring lumber

a 石高 こくだか yield, fief, stipend
二千石 にせんごく stipend of 2000 *koku* in rice

ab 一石 いっこく 1 *koku*

INDEPENDENT

【こく 石】*koku* (→❸)

KUN

【いし 石】[also suffix] **STONE, small rock, pebble; playing stone in a game of go; transistor; silicon chip**

石ころ いしころ piece of stone, pebble
石頭 いしあたま hard head, obstinate person
小石 こいし pebble, stone
土台石 どだいいし foundation stone, cornerstone
碁石 ごいし go stone

SYNONYMS

❶ⓐ rock and stone

石 STONE → 3689
岩 ROCK → 2778
巌 CRAG → 3037

❸ⓐ capacity units

勺 *SHAKU* (0.018 liters) → 3650

合 *go* (0.18 liters) → 2511
立 liter → 2486
升 *SHO* (1.8 liters) → 4266
斗 *TO* (18 liters) → 3671
石 *koku* (180 liters) → 3689

斥

3690
□3-2-3

▶EXPEL
セキ しりぞ(ける)▲
Ⓒ 斥 chì

69	Jōyō	U65A5
斥	S5-4-1	F2766

丿 厂 𠂆 斤 斥
1 2 3 4 5

COMPOUNDS

❶ **EXPEL, repel, reject, exclude**
斥力 せきりょく repulsion, repulsive force
排斥する はいせきする expel, reject, exclude, ostracize
擯×斥 ひんせき rejection, ostracism

❷ survey, scout, patrol
斥候 せっこう scout, patrol, reconnoitering soldier

KUN

【しりぞける 斥ける】[usu. 退ける] reject, refuse, turn down
提案を斥ける ていあんをしりぞける turn down a proposal

SYNONYMS

❶ **drive out**
斥 EXPEL → 3690
排 EXCLUDE → 0593
追 chase away → 3840
退 cause to retreat → 3838
駆 drive away → 2293
逐 DRIVE OUT → 3848
払う clear out → 0225

HOMOPHONES

しりぞける 退 RETREAT → 3838

NOTE

➡ see USAGE note at 退 3838

布

3691
□3-2-3

▶CLOTH
▶SPREAD
フ ぬの きれ▲
Ⓒ 布 bù

50	Jōyō-5	U5E03
巾	S5-3-2	F0696

ノ ナ 才 右 布
1 2 3 4 5

COMPOUNDS

❶ [original meaning] **CLOTH, textile**
布巾 ふきん dishcloth, napkin
毛布 もうふ blanket
綿布 めんぷ cotton cloth
財布 さいふ purse, wallet

❷ distribute over a surface:
ⓐ [also 敷 2345] **SPREAD, lay out, apply**
ⓑ **SPREAD** out, arrange, line up
a 塗布する とふする apply (an ointment)
散布する さんぷ(=さっぷ)する scatter, sprinkle, spray
配布 はいふ wide distribution
頒布 はんぷ distribution, circulation
b 布陣 ふじん lineup
布石 ふせき arrangement of go stones; preparation

❸ (become or cause to become widely known) **SPREAD, disseminate, distribute**
布告する ふこくする proclaim, declare
布教 ふきょう propagation, missionary work
布令 ふれい official notice, proclamation, announcement
公布する こうふする promulgate, proclaim
流布する るふする circulate, disseminate, spread

❹ [formerly 蒲 2932] **cattail, reed mace**
布団 ふとん *futon*, bedquilt

INDEPENDENT

【ふ 布】CLOTH; coin used in ancient China

KUN

【ぬの 布】CLOTH
布地 ぬのじ cloth
麻布 あさぬの hemp cloth, linen

【きれ 布】[also 切れ] CLOTH

SPECIAL READINGS

若布▲ わかめ *wakame* (kind of seaweed)

SYNONYMS

❶ **fabric**
布 CLOTH → 3691
地 fabric → 0236
巾 CLOTH → 4217

❷ⓐ **spread**
散 SCATTER → 2137
布 SPREAD → 3691
敷く LAY → 2345
舗 PAVE → 2177
塗 APPLY ON A SURFACE → 3523
抹 wipe over → 0370
撒 SCATTER → 0909

❸ **make widely known**
布 SPREAD → 3691
流 spread → 0529
伝 spread → 0048
広 spread → 3769

弘 DISSEMINATE (esp. Buddhism) →0223
及 REACH TO →4192

NOTE

➡ see COMPOUND FORMATION for 布団 ふとん →団 3791

左 ▶LEFT

サ シャ▲ ひだり ㊔ すけ

Ⓒ 左 zuǒ

3692

☐3-2-3

48	Jōyō-1	U5DE6
工	S5-3-2	F0384

一 ナ 左 左 左 (1 2 3 4 5)

COMPOUNDS

❶ⓐ [original meaning] **LEFT**

ⓑ abbrev. of 左翼手 さよくしゅ: **LEFT** fielder

a 左方 さほう left side
左折する させつする turn to the left
左記 さき undermentioned (statement), following
左表 さひょう chart at the left
左右 さゆう right and left
左右する さゆうする command, dominate, control

b 左中間 さちゅうかん between left and center fielders
左直 さちょく left liner

❷ the LEFT, leftist
左派 さは left wing, left faction
左翼 さよく left wing [flank]; left wing [faction]; left field

❸ low rank
左遷 させん relegation, demotion

❹ drunkard, drinker
左党 さとう drinker, wine lover; left (wing), leftist

❺ supporting evidence
証左 しょうさ evidence, proof

❻ used phonetically for *sa* or *sha*
左様 さよう such; yes; let me see
左様なら さようなら goodbye, farewell
左官 さかん(=しゃかん) plasterer

INDEPENDENT

【さ 左】**LEFT**; the following
左の通り さのとおり as following

KUN

【ひだり 左】**LEFT; left hand; leftist; drinking**
左側 ひだりがわ left side
左手 ひだりて left hand
左向き ひだりむき turning to the left
左利き ひだりきき left-handedness; left-hander; drinker, wine lover
左寄り ひだりより tending to the left
左党 ひだりとう drinker, wine lover

SYNONYMS

❶ⓐ left and right
右 RIGHT →3693
左 LEFT →3692

❷ Communism
共 Communism →3045
左 the Left →3692
赤 RED →2719

右 ▶RIGHT

ウ ユウ みぎ ㊔ すけ

Ⓒ 右 yòu

3693

☐3-2-3

30	Jōyō-1	U53F3
口	S5-3-2	F0341

ノ ナ 大 右 右 (1 2 3 4 5)

COMPOUNDS

❶ⓐ [original meaning] **RIGHT**

ⓑ abbrev. of 右翼手 うよくしゅ: **RIGHT** fielder

a 右折 うせつ right turn
右往左往する うおうさおうする go this way and that
右岸 うがん right bank
左右 さゆう right and left
座右に ざゆうに at one's (right) hand; by one's side

b 右中間 うちゅうかん between right and center fielders

❷ the RIGHT, right wing
右派 うは right wing
右翼 うよく right wing; right field
極右 きょくう extreme right

❸ [also 祐 ゆう 1146] **help, assist**
右筆 ゆうひつ amanuensis, private secretary

❹ regard highly
右文 ゆうぶん respect for literary culture

KUN

【みぎ 右】[also prefix] **RIGHT; the above mentioned; superiority**
右側 みぎがわ(=うそく) right side
右手 みぎて right hand
右の通り みぎのとおり as above mentioned
右寄り みぎより tending to the Right
右に出る みぎにでる be superior to

SYNONYMS

❶ⓐ left and right
右 RIGHT →3693
左 LEFT →3692

存 incorrect stroke-count
➡ see □3-2-4: ナ at 3702
□3-2-3

用

▶EMPLOY
▶THINGS TO DO
ヨウ　もち(いる)

3694
□3-2-3

Ⓒ 用 yòng

101	Jōyō-2	U7528
用	S5-5-0	F0083

丿 冂 月 月 用
1 2 3 4 5

RADICAL
mochiiru 'use' (甫 甬×), used for character classification

COMPOUNDS

❶ⓐ EMPLOY, use, make use of, utilize, apply
ⓑ [also suffix] **used for, for**
a 用意する よういする prepare, ready oneself, make arrangements
用語 ようご terminology; diction, wording; vocabulary
用途 ようと use, service, application
用法 ようほう usage, directions for use, use
用心 ようじん care; caution
用心深い ようじんぶかい careful; cautious; watchful
利用する りようする utilize, make use of, avail oneself of
使用する しようする use, employ, apply
採用 さいよう adoption, acceptance; employment, appointment
適用 てきよう application
運用する うんようする make use of; invest in; apply to
b 乗用車 じょうようしゃ passenger car, automobile
家庭用 かていよう for domestic use
返信用 へんしんよう for reply

❷ [formerly also 傭 0181 or 庸 3881] **EMPLOY (a person), engage**
用人 ようにん steward, manager
雇用(=雇傭) こよう employment, hire

❸ⓐ be useful, be effective, work
ⓑ use, usefulness, utility
a 作用 さよう action, operation, function; effect
信用 しんよう trust, credit, confidence
効用 こうよう use, usefulness, effect
b 無用の むようの useless; unnecessary; forbidden
有用な ゆうような useful, serviceable

❹ THINGS TO DO, business, task, errand
用事 ようじ things to do, errand, business, engagement
用件 ようけん matter (of business), things to be done
用談 ようだん business talk
用足し ようたし taking care of business, running an errand; relieving oneself
所用 しょよう things to do, errand, business, engagement
公用 こうよう official business [duty], official mission; public use
私用 しよう private business; private use

❺ needed for (a specific use), required
用紙 ようし blank form, stationery
用地 ようち land, lot, site
用具 ようぐ tool, instrument, appliance; outfit
不用な ふような unnecessary, useless; disused, waste
入用 にゅうよう need, demand, necessity
学校用品 がっこうようひん school requisites [supplies]

❻ expenses, expenditures
用度 ようど expenditure, office expenses; supplies
費用 ひよう expenses, outlay

❼ answering nature's call
用便 ようべん defecation, urination

INDEPENDENT

【よう 用】
① **THINGS TO DO, business, task, errand**
用が有る ようがある have things to do
② **use, usefulness, utility**
用に立つ ようにたつ be of use [service]
用に足りない ようにたりない be useless, be of no use
③ [archaic] expenses, expenditures
用を節する ようをせっする save expenses
④ answering nature's call
用を足す ようをたす do one's business; relieve oneself

KUN

【もちいる 用いる】**EMPLOY, use, make use of, utilize, apply; employ, engage**
広く用いる ひろくもちいる be in wide use
重く用いる おもくもちいる give an important position

SYNONYMS

❶ⓐ use
使 USE → 0100
用 EMPLOY → 3694
❷ employ
雇 EMPLOY → 2454
用 EMPLOY → 3694
使う employ → 0100
傭 HIRE → 0181

役 press into service →0288

❸ **benefit**

利 ADVANTAGE →1431
益 BENEFIT →2849
為 SAKE →4395
用 use(ful) →3694
役 SERVICE →0288

❹ **affairs**

用 THINGS TO DO →3694
事 affairs →4384
務 affairs →1505

❺ **need and necessity**

要 required →3263
必 must →0015
須 MUST →0700
需 DEMAND →3472
入 necessary →4177
用 needed for (a specific use) →3694

NOTE

➡ see COMPOUND FORMATION for 用途 ようと →途 3853

回

3695
□3-2-3

▶**TURN ROUND**
▶**TIME**
カイ エ まわ(る) -まわ(る) -まわ(り) まわ(す) -まわ(す) まわ(し)- -まわ(し)
㊔ めぐり

13	Nonstandard	U56D8
冂	S5-2-3	F0000

alternative form →see 回 at 3793

凧

3696
□3-2-3

▶**KITE**
たこ いかのぼり
Ⓒ (国字)

16	Names	U51E7
几	S5-2-3	F3211

KUN

【たこ 凧】**KITE**

凧揚げ たこあげ kite flying
奴凧 やっこだこ kite shaped like a footman
引っ張り凧 ひっぱりだこ very popular, in great demand

【いかのぼり 凧】**KITE**

廷
□3-2-4

incorrect stroke-count
➡ see □3-3-4: 廴 at 3795

近返 etc.
□3-2-4

incorrect stroke-count
➡ see □3-3-4: 辶 at 3796

旭

3697
□3-2-4

▶**RISING SUN**
キョク あさひ ㊔ あき あきら てる のぼる
Ⓒ 旭 xù

72	Names	U65ED
日	S6-4-2	F2241

COMPOUNDS

● [original meaning] **RISING SUN, morning sun**

旭日 きょくじつ rising sun
旭日章 きょくじつしょう Order of the Rising Sun
旭光 きょっこう rays of the morning [rising] sun

INDEPENDENT

【きょく 旭】abbrev. of 旭日章: Order of the **RISING SUN**

KUN

【あさひ 旭】[usu. 朝日] **RISING SUN, morning sun; rays of the morning sun**

SYNONYMS

● **sun**

日 SUN →3759
陽 SUN →0764
旭 RISING SUN →3697

USAGE

【あさひ】

旭
[usu. 朝日] rising sun, morning sun; rays of the morning sun

朝日
[sometimes also 旭] rising sun, morning sun; rays of the morning sun

HOMOPHONES

あさひ 朝日 →2130, 3759

旬

3698
□3-2-4

▶**TEN-DAY PERIOD**
ジュン シュン
Ⓒ 旬 xún

72	Jōyō	U65EC
日	S6-4-2	F1567

1	2	3	4	5	6
ノ	勹	勺	旬	旬	旬

COMPOUNDS

ⓐ [original meaning] **TEN-DAY PERIOD**
ⓑ [rare] ten years (in counting age)

a 旬日 じゅんじつ ten-day period
旬刊 じゅんかん published every ten days
旬報 じゅんぽう ten-day report
上旬 じょうじゅん first ten days of a month
中旬 ちゅうじゅん middle [second] ten days of a month
b 齢七旬 よわいしちじゅん three score and ten

INDEPENDENT

【しゅん 旬】season (for specific products), the best season (for sports)

旬の魚 しゅんのさかな fish in season

SYNONYMS

ⓐ weeks and months

週 WEEK → 3874

旬 TEN-DAY PERIOD → 3698

月 MONTH → 3674

灰

3699

口3-2-4

▶ASH

カイ はい

Ⓝ 灰 Ⓒ 灰 huī

86	Jōyō-6	U7070
火	S6-4-2	F1538

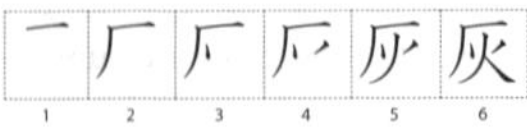

COMPOUNDS

❶ⓐ [original meaning] **ASH, ashes**

ⓑ ASHen, gray, grayish

a 灰燼[×] かいじん ashes, ashes and cinder

灰分 かいぶん ash content

重灰 じゅうかい dense ash

b 灰白色 かいはくしょく ash color, light gray

灰緑色 かいりょくしょく greenish gray

❷ lime

石灰 せっかい lime

苦灰石 くかいせき dolomite

❸ lifeless, spiritless

死灰 しかい as lifeless as cold ashes

KUN

【はい 灰】ASHes

灰皿 はいざら ashtray

灰色の はいいろの ashen, gray

死の灰 しのはい lethal radioactive fallout, atomic dust

ソーダ灰 そーだばい soda ash

火山灰 かざんばい volcano ashes

SPECIAL READINGS

灰汁[▲] あく lye, ash; harshness, harsh taste

SYNONYMS

❶ⓐ products of combustion

灰 ASH → 3699

殻 cinders → 1883

炭 CHARCOAL → 2806

煤 SOOT → 1292

煙 SMOKE → 1294

厤

3700

口3-2-4

▶PERSONAL HISTORY

レキ レッキ

77	Nonstandard	U6B74
止	S6-4-2	F0000

handwritten form → see 歴 at 3748

后

3701

口3-2-4

▶EMPRESS

コウ ゴ[▲] きさき[▲] ㊔ み

Ⓒ 后 hòu

30	Jōyō-6	U540E
口	S6-3-3	F1735

COMPOUNDS

❶ (wife of an emperor) **EMPRESS, queen**

后妃 こうひ queen consort, empress, queen

皇后 こうごう empress, queen

皇太后 こうたいこう empress dowager, queen mother

❷ [usu. 後 ご 0431] after, later

午后 ごご afternoon

KUN

【きさき 后】EMPRESS, queen; consort

SYNONYMS

❶ wives of rulers

后 EMPRESS → 3701

妃 PRINCESS → 0238

室 wife (esp. of persons of rank) → 2802

存

3702

口3-2-4

▶EXIST

ソン ゾン ㊔ あり

Ⓒ 存 cún

39	Jōyō-6	U5B58
子	S6-3-3	F0358

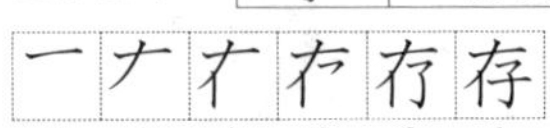

COMPOUNDS

❶ⓐ (have actuality) **EXIST, be**

ⓑ (have life) **EXIST, live, remain alive**

a 存在 そんざい existence, being

存否 そんぴ existence; life or death

存続 そんぞく continuation, maintenance

存亡 そんぼう destiny; life or death

共存 きょうぞん coexistence

依存 いぞん(=いそん) dependence, reliance

既存の きそんの existing

現存の げんぞん(=げんそん)の existing, living

残存する ざんそん(=ざんぞん)する survive, subsist, be extant

実存 じつぞん existence

b 存命中 ぞんめいちゅう (while) in life, in one's lifetime

生存する せいぞんする exist, live, survive

❷ **keep, preserve, maintain**

保存する ほぞんする preserve, conserve, maintain, store, keep

温存する おんぞんする preserve, retain

❸ⓐ **hold an opinion, believe, think**

ⓑ know

a 存外 ぞんがい contrary to one's expectations; beyond expectation

存分に ぞんぶんに to one's heart's content, freely

所存 しょぞん one's opinion [view], intention

異存 いぞん objection

b 存知 ぞんち having knowledge of

INDEPENDENT

【そんする 存する】(have actuality) **EXIST**, be; (have life) exist, live, remain alive; consist in, rest with

猶疑問が存する なおぎもんがそんする A doubt still remains

幸福は満足に存する こうふくはまんぞくにそんする Happiness consists in contentment

【ぞんじる(=ぞんずる) 存じる(=存ずる)】[humble] **think, believe; know, be aware of, be acquainted with**

御存じ(=御存知) ごぞんじ your knowledge; your acquaintance

お元気の事と存じます おげんきのこととぞんじます I trust you are in good health

SYNONYMS

❶ⓐ **exist and be**

在 BE → 3704

存 EXIST → 3702

有 exist → 3703

居 be present → 3822

臨 BE PRESENT AT → 2059

也 CLASSICAL COPULA → 4214

❸ⓐ **think and consider**

思 THINK → 3173

惟 MEDITATE → 0582

省 INTROSPECT → 3100

稽 THINK → 1573

考 THINK → 3962

存 hold an opinion → 3702

案 think out → 2824

想 CONCEIVE → 3507

慮 CONSIDER → 4050

勘 take into consideration → 2231

銓 WEIGH → 2161

量 weigh → 3119

有

3703

□3-2-4

▶**HAVE**

ユウ ウ あ(る) ㊔ なり

Ⓝ 有 Ⓒ 有 yǒu yòu

74	Jōyō-3	U6709
月	S6-4-2	F0254

ノ ナ 冇 有 有 有 (1 2 3 4 5 6)

COMPOUNDS

❶ⓐ [also prefix] **HAVE, possess, own, retain**

ⓑ **having the characteristic [property] of**

a 有産階級 ゆうさんかいきゅう propertied [proprietary] classes, bourgeoisie

有意義な ゆういぎな significant, useful, worthwhile

有資格者 ゆうしかくしゃ eligible person, qualified person

所有する しょゆうする have, own, possess

保有 ほゆう possession, maintenance

b 有望な ゆうぼうな promising, hopeful

有害な ゆうがいな harmful, pernicious, noxious

有利な ゆうりな advantageous, favorable; profitable

有名な ゆうめいな famous, noted, celebrated; notorious

有効な ゆうこうな effective, valid

有力な ゆうりょくな powerful, influential

有限の ゆうげんの limited; finite

有料の ゆうりょうの fee-charging, pay, toll

❷ⓐ **exist, be, be present**

ⓑ existence; *bhava*, existence (in Buddhism)

a 有無 うむ existence, presence; yes or no

現有の げんゆうの present, existing

b 仮有 けう temporary existence

❸ again; in addition to

十有五年 じゅうゆうごねん 15 years

❹ [archaic] used before one-character names of countries or groups of people

有衆 ゆうしゅう the people, the multitudes

有夏 ゆうか Mainland China

INDEPENDENT

【ゆう 有】existence; possession

. . . の有に帰する …のゆうにきする come into possession of…

【ゆうする 有する】**HAVE, possess, own**

【う 有】existence (→❷ⓑ)

KUN

【ある 有る】

① **be, exist, be present, there is**

有り様 ありさま condition, state of affairs; sight

有り難う ありがとう thank you

有り難い ありがたい welcome, appreciated; precious
有りの儘×の ありのままの as it is, plain, bare
有り合わせの ありあわせの available, in [on] hand
有り触れた ありふれた common, run-of-the-mill, trite
月にはクレーターが有る つきにはくれーたーがある There are craters on the moon

② **HAVE, possess, own**
有り金 ありがね money on hand, ready cash
彼女には子供が二人有る かのじょにはこどもがふたりある She has two children

③ **HAVE the experience of doing something**
フランスに行った事が有るか ふらんすにいったことがあるか Have you ever been to France?

④ (have a magnitude of) **number, cover, weigh, measure**
あの農場は二百平方メートル有る あののうじょうはにひゃくへいほうめーとるある That farm covers 200 sq. meters

⑤ **happen, occur, take place**
事故が有った じこがあった There was an accident
昨日会議が有った きのうかいぎがあった The conference was held yesterday

⑥ consist [lie] in, depend on
幸福は満足に有る こうふくはまんぞくにある Happiness consists in contentment

⑦ [in the form of transitive verb followed by て有る てある] describes a state resulting from an action
部屋が暖めて有る へやがあたためてある The room is kept [has been made] warm

SYNONYMS

❶ **possess**
有 HAVE → 3703
蔵 own → 2995
持 HOLD → 0447
属 BELONGING TO → 3901
享 ENJOY → 2545
具 possess → 3159

❷ⓐ **exist and be**
在 BE → 3704
存 EXIST → 3702
有 exist → 3703
居 be present → 3822
臨 BE PRESENT AT → 2059
也 CLASSICAL COPULA → 4214

USAGE

【ある】
有る
① be, exist, be present, there is
② have, possess, own
③ have the experience of doing something
④ (have a magnitude of) number, cover, weigh, measure
⑤ happen, occur, take place
⑥ consist [lie] in, depend on
⑦ [in the form of transitive verb followed by て有る てある] describes a state resulting from an action

在る
① (exist in a specified place) be at [in], be situated in, be sited
② be alive, live

HOMOPHONES

ある 在 BE → 3704

COMPOUND FORMATION

【有り難う ありがとう】
有り難う 'thank you' literally means "I find it difficult (難) to exist (有る ①)"; that is, "I could never be content until I have shown you my gratitude." Another interpretation is "the kindness you have shown me is so rare as to seldom exist."

在

▶**BE**
ザイ あ(る)
Ⓒ 在 zài

3704
□ 3-2-4

32	Jōyō-5	U5728
土	S6-3-3	F0209

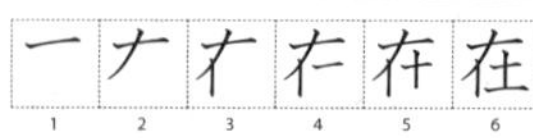

COMPOUNDS

❶ [also prefix] [original meaning] (exist in a specified place) **BE at [in], be situated in, be sited**
在庫 ざいこ stock, stockpile
在学する ざいがくする be in school
在校する ざいこうする be in school
在宅する ざいたくする be in, be at home
在東京 ざいとうきょう situated in Tokyo
不在 ふざい absence
所在 しょざい whereabouts, position, situation

❷ⓐ **reside [live] temporarily, stay**
ⓑ [prefix] **resident in**
a 在日の ざいにちの (staying) in Japan
在外の ざいがいの overseas
在住する ざいじゅうする live, reside, dwell
在米中 ざいべいちゅう while resident in America
在留する ざいりゅうする reside, stay, be resident
駐在 ちゅうざい residence, stay
滞在 たいざい stay, sojourn
b 在ベルリン邦人 ざいべるりんほうじん Japanese (resident) in Berlin

❸ⓐ (exist in actuality) **BE, exist**
ⓑ **BE** alive, live

a 現在の げんざいの present time, now; present tense; actually
存在する そんざいする exist, be
自在に じざいに freely, unrestrictedly, at will
実在 じつざい real [actual] existence, entity
b 在世中 ざいせいちゅう during one's lifetime
健在だ けんざいだ be well, be in good health
❹ the country; outskirts, suburbs
在郷 ざいごう rural districts
在所 ざいしょ the country; one's residence
近在 きんざい neighboring villages, suburban districts

INDEPENDENT

【ざい 在】 the country; outskirts, suburbs
練馬の在 ねりまのざい the Nerima countryside

KUN

【ある 在る】
① (exist in a specified place) **BE at [in], be situated in, be sited**
机の上に本が在る つくえのうえにほんがある There is a book on the desk
② **BE** alive, live
在りし日 ありしひ the days when one was alive; bygone days

SYNONYMS

❶ & ❸ⓐ exist and be
在 BE → 3704
存 EXIST → 3702
有 exist → 3703
居 be present → 3822
臨 BE PRESENT AT → 2059
也 CLASSICAL COPULA → 4214
❷ stay
滞 STAY → 0815
頓 STAY IN PLACE → 1320
留 STAY → 3189
逗 STAY → 4005
駐 STATIONED → 2297
屯 STATION TROOPS → 4268
在 reside temporarily → 3704
泊 STAY OVERNIGHT → 0389
宿 LODGE → 2858
寓 stay temporarily → 2893

HOMOPHONES

ある 有 HAVE → 3703

NOTE

➡ see USAGE note at 有 3703

灰

▶ASH
カイ はい

3705
口3-2-4

86 火	Nonstandard / S6-4-2	U7070 / F0000

traditional form → see 灰 at 3699

有

▶HAVE
ユウ ウ あ(る) ㊔ なり

3706
口3-2-4

74 月	Nonstandard / S6-4-2	U6709 / F0000

traditional form → see 有 at 3703

同

▶SAME
ドウ おな(じ)
Ⓝ 仝◇ Ⓒ 同 tóng tòng

3707
口3-2-4

30 口	Jōyō-2 / S6-3-3	U540C / F0062

丨 冂 冂 同 同 同 (1 2 3 4 5 6)

COMPOUNDS

❶ [also prefix]
ⓐ SAME, similar, equal
ⓑ (the one previously mentioned) **the SAME (as above), the said, the aforementioned**
a 同一 どういつ sameness, identity
同様の どうようの similar
同好 どうこう similar tastes
同盟 どうめい alliance, league, union
同胞 どうほう brothers; brethren, fellow country-men
同窓会 どうそうかい alumni association
同意 どうい consent, approval
同音の どうおんの of the same sound, homophonous
同音語 どうおんご homophone, homonym
同等 どうとう equality
同期 どうき same period
同上 どうじょう as above, ditto
同性の どうせいの of the same sex
同列 どうれつ same rank
b 同日 どうじつ the same day, the said day
同氏 どうし the said person, he
同国 どうこく the same country, the said country
同委員会 どういいんかい the same committee
❷ⓐ together, in common
ⓑ come together, gather
a 同居する どうきょする live together
同情 どうじょう sympathy, compassion
同封する どうふうする enclose (in a letter)
同棲 どうせい cohabitation, living together

共同する きょうどうする work together, cooperate
一同 いちどう all (of us), all persons concerned
ｂ 合同 ごうどう combination, union, joint, merger; congruence
❸ abbrev. of 同志社大学 どうししゃだいがく: Doshisha University
同大 どうだい Doshisha University; the said university

INDEPENDENT

【どうずる 同ずる】agree
和して同ぜず わしてどうぜず harmonize but not agree

KUN

【おなじ 同じ】**SAME, identical, similar; common**
同じく おなじく in the same way, similarly
同い年 おないどし same age
同じ様に おなじように in the same way

SYNONYMS

❶ⓐ same and uniform
等 EQUAL → 3321
平 equal → 4291
均 EVEN → 0276
斉 UNIFORM → 2548
同 SAME → 3707
一 same → 4148

ⓑ this and that
本 THIS → 4314
爾 THAT → 4407
其れ THAT → 3255
彼 that → 0346
今 THIS (week, etc.) → 2464
当 THE PRESENT → 2701
該 the said → 1916
同 the same → 3707
之 this → 4228
是 this → 3090
此 THIS → 1017
斯 THIS → 2140

❷ⓐ together
共 JOINT → 3045
同 together → 3707
併 TOGETHER → 0092
並 side by side → 2793
兼 CONCURRENTLY → 2850
倶 TOGETHER → 0125

NOTE

➡ see COMPOUND FORMATION for 同胞 どうほう → 胞 1148

The symbol 々, which indicates a repetition of the previous kanji (人人=人々), originates from the alternative form, 仝.

网

3708

□3-2-4

▶*AMIGASHIRA*

122	Radical	U7F51
网	S6-6-0	F0000

RADICAL

amigashira 'net', used in characters related to nets or their qualities

Top variants: 罒 ⺳ ***yonkashira*** (置 署 罕×)

肉

□3-2-4

incorrect classification
➡ see □3-4-2: 内 at 3966

凪

3709

□3-2-4

▶**CALM**

な(ぐ) なぎ ㊔ なぎさ

Ⓒ (国字)

16	Names	U51EA
几	S6-2-4	F2970

KUN

【なぐ 凪ぐ】(of the wind) **become CALM, calm down, abate, drop**
風が凪ぐ かぜがなぐ The wind drops

【なぎ 凪】(of the wind) **CALM, lull**
夕凪 ゆうなぎ evening calm

SYNONYMS

【なぐ】
◯ &【なぎ】wind
風 WIND → 3730
嵐 STORM → 2898
颱 TYPHOON → 4138
台 typhoon → 2498
凪 CALM → 3709
颯 SOUND OF GUSTING WIND → 1563

匡

3710

□3-2-4

▶**RECTIFY**

キョウ ㊔ まさ ただ ただし ただす まさし くに

Ⓒ 匡 kuāng

22	Names	U5321
匚	S6-2-4	F3152

COMPOUNDS

❶ RECTIFY, correct, reform
匡正する きょうせいする reform (bad customs)

❷ [rare] save, deliver
匡救する きょうきゅうする deliver from sin; succor

SYNONYMS

❶ correct
正 RIGHT → 4296
直す correct → 3649

訂 REVISE → 1829
改 REFORM → 0287
矯 RECTIFY → 1586
匡 RECTIFY → 3710

匠 3711 □3-2-4

▸CRAFTSMAN
ショウ たくみ▲
Ⓒ 匠 jiàng

22	Jōyō	U5320
匚	S6-2-4	F1425

Stroke order: 一 ア ア 斤 斤 匠 (1–6)

COMPOUNDS

❶ⓐ (skilled workman) **CRAFTSMAN, artisan, workman**
ⓑ (master of an art) **CRAFTSMAN, master, artist**
a 工匠 こうしょう artisan, mechanic
名匠 めいしょう skilled craftsman
b 師匠 ししょう master, teacher
巨匠 きょしょう great master, maestro
❷ idea, design, ingenuity
匠気 しょうき affectation, showmanship
意匠 いしょう design, idea

KUN

【たくみ 匠】 **artisan; woodworker, carpenter**

SYNONYMS

❶ⓐ **workers and professionals**
家 professional → 2827
婦 woman worker → 0565
嬢 (unmarried) female worker → 0936
夫 MAN LABORER → 4271
匠 CRAFTSMAN → 3711
工 workman → 4190
客 skilled person → 2798
士 PROFESSION SUFFIX → 4213
師 profession suffix → 1680
者 person who → 3980
人 person of certain category → 4175
員 MEMBER (of a staff) → 2822
屋 colloquial occupation suffix → 3842
手 OCCUPATION SUFFIX → 4267
ⓑ **great persons**
豪 GREAT MAN → 2657
傑 OUTSTANDING PERSON → 0175
雄 hero → 1271
匠 CRAFTSMAN → 3711
聖 great master → 3509

HOMOPHONES

たくみ 巧 SKILLFUL → 0219

NOTE

➡ see USAGE note at 巧 0219

臣 3712 □3-2-4

▸RETAINER
シン ジン ㊔ おみ とみ

131	Nonstandard	U81E3
臣	S6-6-0	F0000

alternative form → see 臣 at 3806

RADICAL

shin 'retainer', used for character classification
Left variant: 臣 *shin* (臨 臥)

延廹 □3-2-5

incorrect stroke-count
➡ see □3-3-5: 廴 at 3812

述廹 etc. □3-2-5

incorrect stroke-count
➡ see □3-3-5: 辶 at 3815

辰 3713 □3-2-5

▸THE DRAGON
シン たつ ㊔ よし とき のぶ のぶる
Ⓒ 辰 chén

161	Names	U8FB0
辰	S7-7-0	F1523

RADICAL

shinnotatsu 'the Dragon' (農 辱), used in characters related to agriculture

COMPOUNDS

❶ fifth sign of the Oriental zodiac: **THE DRAGON**—(time) 7-9 a.m., (direction) ESE, (season) March (of the lunar calendar) (→ see APPENDIX 8)
戊辰 ぼしん fifth of the sexagenary cycle
❷ time, day
誕辰 たんしん birthday
❸ celestial body
星辰 せいしん stars, celestial bodies

KUN

【たつ 辰】 fifth sign of the Oriental zodiac: **THE DRAGON** (→ ❶)
辰の年 たつのとし the year of the Dragon
辰の刻 たつのこく the fifth hour, 8 a.m.; the Hour of the Dragon
辰巳 たつみ [also 巽] southeast

SYNONYMS

❶ **mythical animals**
竜 DRAGON → 2603
辰 THE DRAGON → 3713
麒 MALE CHINESE UNICORN → 2363

麟 FEMALE CHINESE UNICORN → 2376
鵬 MYTHICAL HUGE BIRD → 1416
鳳 MALE PHOENIX → 3749
凰 FEMALE PHOENIX → 3738

❶ **dragon**
竜 DRAGON → 2603
辰 THE DRAGON → 3713

HOMOPHONES

たつ 竜 DRAGON → 2603
たつみ
巽 SOUTHEAST → 3329
辰巳 → 3713, 4197

NOTE

➡ see USAGE note at 竜 2603

乕

3714
口3-2-5

▶**TIGER**
コ とら ㊔ たけ

4	Nonstandard	U4E55
丿	S7-1-6	F0000

traditional form → see 虎 at 3981

医

3715
口3-2-5

▶**MEDICINE**
▶**DOCTOR**
イ
Ⓝ 醫 毉 Ⓒ 医 yī

23△	Jōyō-3	U533B
匚	S7-2-5	F0391

一 丆 𠂉 三 矢 医 医
1 2 3 4 5 6 7

COMPOUNDS

❶ **MEDICINE, medical science, art of healing**
医道 いどう art of medicine
医大 いだい medical college
医化学 いかがく medical chemistry
法医学 ほういがく legal medicine

❷ [also suffix] **DOCTOR, physician**
医師 いし doctor, physician, surgeon
医局 いきょく medical staff room, medical office
獣医 じゅうい veterinarian
女医 じょい woman doctor
歯科医 しかい dentist

❸ **cure**
医学 いがく medical science, medicine
医療 いりょう medical treatment [care]
医者 いしゃ doctor
医薬 いやく medicine, drug; medical practice and dispensary
医薬品 いやくひん pharmaceuticals, medicines
医院 いいん clinic

INDEPENDENT

【い 医】**MEDICINE**, art of medicine, medical practice
医は仁術 いはじんじゅつ Medicine is a benevolent art

【いする 医する】treat, heal, cure

SYNONYMS

❸ **cure and recover**
療 TREAT → 4078
治 CURE → 0393
医 cure → 3715
癒 HEAL → 4081
快 recover → 0289

建 廻

口3-2-6

incorrect stroke-count
➡ see 口3-3-6: 廴 at 3833

送 追 etc.

口3-2-6

incorrect stroke-count
➡ see 口3-3-6: 辶 at 3835

厚

口3-2-6

incorrect stroke-count
➡ see 口3-2-7: 厂 at 3726

房

3716
口3-2-6

▶**CHAMBER**
ボウ ふさ ㊔ のぶ

63	Nonstandard	U623F
戶	S8-4-4	F0000

traditional form → see 房 at 2445

肩

3717
口3-2-6

▶**SHOULDER**
ケン かた

130	Nonstandard	U80A9
月	S8-4-4	F0000

traditional form → see 肩 at 2446

戾

3718
口3-2-6

▶**RETURN**
レイ もど(す) もど(る)

63	Nonstandard	U623E
戶	S8-4-4	F0000

traditional form → see 戻 at 2441

岡

3719
口3-2-6

▶**HILL**
コウ▲ おか
Ⓝ 堽 Ⓒ 冈 gāng

46	Jōyō	U5CA1
山	S8-3-5	F0532

丨 冂 冂 冂 冃 冈 岡 岡
1 2 3 4 5 6 7 8

COMPOUNDS

❶ [archaic] **HILL**

岡陵 こうりょう hill

❷ [original meaning, now archaic] ridge (of a mountain)

KUN

【おか 岡】

① [usu. 丘] **HILL, hillock, mound**—used chiefly in proper names

岡山県 おかやまけん Okayama Prefecture
岡野 おかの surname
静岡県 しずおかけん Shizuoka Prefecture
福岡県 ふくおかけん Fukuoka Prefecture

② [sometimes also 傍-] [in compounds] **outsider, third party, bystander**

岡っ引き おかっぴき detective, secret policeman (in Edo Japan)
岡惚れ おかぼれ illicit love

SYNONYMS

❶ **hills**

丘 HILL → 4307
畝 RIDGE → 1857
岡 HILL → 3719
台 heights → 2498
坂 SLOPE → 0275
阪 slope → 0321
塚 MOUND → 0675
阜 MOUND → 3254
陵 high mound → 0660
稜 RIDGE → 1545

HOMOPHONES

おか

丘 HILL → 4307
陸 LAND → 0659
傍 BESIDE → 0166

NOTE

➡ see USAGE note at 丘 4307

周

3720

口3-2-6

▶**PERIPHERY**

シュウ まわ(り) ㊔ ちか まこと あまね かね す のり

Ⓝ 周 Ⓒ 周 zhōu

30	Jōyō-4	U5468
口	S8-3-5	F0552

丿 冂 月 円 用 周 周 周
1 2 3 4 5 6 7 8

COMPOUNDS

❶ **PERIPHERY, circumference, perimeter**

周囲 しゅうい circumference, periphery; surroundings
周辺 しゅうへん environs, outskirts; circumference
周回 しゅうかい circumference, girth, surroundings
円周 えんしゅう circumference
四周 ししゅう circumference, periphery

❷ⓐ **circuit, cycle, circle**
ⓑ **counter for circuits or laps**
ⓒ [rarely also 週 3874] **circuit, circle, go round**

a 周波 しゅうは cycle
半周 はんしゅう semicircle, hemicycle
b 三周 さんしゅう three rounds [laps]
一周する いっしゅうする make a round, circuit; sail round, revolve
c 周期 しゅうき period, cycle
周遊 しゅうゆう (circular) tour, pleasure [round] trip

❸ anniversary

周年 しゅうねん anniversary; whole year
三周忌 さんしゅうき second anniversary of death

❹ throughout, everywhere

周知 しゅうち common knowledge
周到な しゅうとうな scrupulous, cautious, circumspect

❺ Zhou Dynasty (approx. 1100-256 B.C.)

周王朝 しゅうおうちょう Zhou Dynasty

INDEPENDENT

【しゅう 周】**PERIPHERY**; Zhou Dynasty

周五百メートル しゅうごひゃくめーとる periphery of 500 meters

KUN

【まわり 周り】

ⓐ **PERIPHERY, surroundings, circumference**
ⓑ border, fringe

a 周りの人 まわりのひと surrounding people
地球の周り ちきゅうのまわり circumference of the earth; space around the earth
b 池の周りを一回りする いけのまわりをひとまわりする go round a pond

SYNONYMS

❶ **periphery**

周 PERIPHERY → 3720
囲 circumference → 3807
郭 OUTER ENCLOSURE → 2112
廓 OUTER ENCLOSURE → 3923

❺ **earlier Chinese dynasties**

夏 Xia Dynasty → 2619
商 Shang Dynasty → 2623
周 Zhou Dynasty → 3720
漢 Han Dynasty → 0808
晋 JIN DYNASTY → 3290
秦 QIN DYNASTY → 3192

HOMOPHONES

まわり

回 TURN ROUND → 3793
廻 TURN ROUND → 3833

NOTE

➡ see USAGE note at 回 3793

夂 辶 厂 广 【冂】 几 凵

周 ▶PERIPHERY
シュウ まわ(り) ㊔ ちか まこと あまね かね す のり

3721
口3-2-6

13	Nonstandard	U2F83F
冂	S8-2-6	F0000

traditional form → see 周 at 3720

凬 ▶WIND ▶MANNER
フウ フ かぜ かざ- -かぜ

3722
口3-2-6

16	Nonstandard	U51EE
几	S8-2-6	F0000

traditional form → see 風 at 3730

画 ▶PICTURE ▶DRAW UP A PLAN
ガ カク え▲ えが(く)▲

3723
口3-2-6

Ⓝ 畫 Ⓒ 画 huà

102	Jōyō-2	U753B
田	S8-5-3	F0168

一 丆 冂 币 再 亩 画 画
1 2 3 4 5 6 7 8

COMPOUNDS

❶ⓐ [also suffix] **PICTURE, drawing, painting**
ⓑ **draw, paint**
ⓒ abbrev. of 映画 えいが: **film, movie, motion PICTURE**
ⓓ (television) **field**

a 画廊 がろう picture gallery
画用紙 がようし drawing paper
絵画 かいが pictures, paintings, drawings
漫画 まんが cartoon, comic strip
名画 めいが famous picture, masterpiece; noted film
映画 えいが cinema, film, movie
日本画 にほんが picture in the Japanese style
b 画家 がか artist, painter
c 洋画 ようが foreign film; Western painting
邦画 ほうが Japanese film [movie]; Japanese painting
d 画面 がめん picture; television field; screen

❷ [formerly also 劃 かく 2378] [original meaning] **mark off, draw a line, demarcate, partition**
画期的な かっきてきな epoch-making, epochal
画一的な かくいつてきな uniform, standardized
画定 かくてい demarcation
区画する くかくする divide, draw a line, mark off

❸ [formerly also 劃 かく 2378]
ⓐ **DRAW UP A PLAN, plan, design**
ⓑ **plan**

a 画策する かくさくする plan, scheme
b 計画 けいかく plan, project
企画 きかく plan, project
参画 さんかく participation in planning

❹ⓐ **stroke of a Chinese character**
ⓑ **counter for strokes**

a 画数 かくすう stroke-count
b 四画の字 よんかくのじ four-stroke character

INDEPENDENT

【かくする 画する(=劃する)】 **mark off; plan**

KUN

【え 画】
ⓐ [usu. 絵] [also suffix] **PICTURE**, painting, drawing, sketch, illustration, cut, (woodcut) print
ⓑ [sometimes also 絵] television field

a 本に画を入れる ほんにえをいれる illustrate a book with pictures
似顔画 にがおえ likeness, portrait

【えがく 画く】 [usu. 描く] draw, paint
油絵を画く あぶらえをえがく paint in oil

SYNONYMS

❶ⓐ **picture**
絵 PICTURE → 1704
画 PICTURE → 3723
図 DRAWING → 3809
ⓑ **draw**
描 DEPICT → 0591
画 draw → 3723
ⓒ **motion picture**
映 motion picture → 1104
画 film → 3723

❷ **mark**
印 imprint → 1023
押 seal → 0371
劃 MARK OFF → 2378
画 mark off → 3723
捺 AFFIX A SEAL → 0603

❸ **plans and planning**
計 PLAN → 1828
画 DRAW UP A PLAN → 3723
案 PROPOSAL → 2824
企 PROJECT → 2513
図 systematic plan → 3809
謀 SCHEME → 2004
策 SCHEME → 3320
略 STRATEGY → 1501
揆 PLOT → 0718

HOMOPHONES

え 絵 PICTURE → 1704

えがく 描 DEPICT → 0591

NOTE

➡ see USAGE notes at 絵 1704 and 描 0591

函 3724 ☐3-2-6

▶BOX

カン はこ

Ⓝ 凾 Ⓒ 函 hán

17	Names	U51FD
凵	S8-2-6	F2272

COMPOUNDS

❶ [original meaning] **BOX, case, mailbox**

函蓋 かんがい box and cover

書函 しょかん letterbox; book chest

投函する とうかんする mail (a letter), put in the post

潜函病 せんかんびょう caisson disease

❷ [now also 関 4129] **used phonetically for the Chinese sound *han***

函数 かんすう *math* function

❸ abbrev. of 函館 はこだて: **name of a city in Hokkaido**

青函トンネル せいかんとんねる Seikan Tunnel

KUN

【はこ 函】[now usu. 箱] **BOX**, case, mailbox

私書函 ししょばこ post office box (P.O.B.)

暗函 あんばこ camera obscura

通い函 かよいばこ reusable shipping carton

SYNONYMS

❶ **containers**

箱 BOX → 3362

壺 JAR → 2890

槽 TANK → 1352

樽 BARREL → 1368

棺 COFFIN → 1240

桶 BUCKET → 1211

笈 BOX CARRIED ON THE BACK → 3274

鞘 SHEATH → 2259

簞 BAMBOO BOX → 3381

函 BOX → 3724

籠 BASKET → 3398

袋 BAG → 3201

鞄 BAG (for carrying) → 2248

器 VESSEL → 3367

瓶 BOTTLE → 1702

缶 CAN → 2526

缶 EARTHENWARE JAR → 2525

HOMOPHONES

はこ 箱 BOX → 3362

NOTE

➡ see USAGE note at 箱 3362

凾 ☐3-2-6 incorrect stroke-count
➡ see ☐3-2-7: 凵 at 3732

廻 ☐3-2-7 incorrect stroke-count
➡ see ☐3-3-7: 廴 at 3847

通連 etc. ☐3-2-7 incorrect stroke-count
➡ see ☐3-3-7: 辶 at 3848

厖 3725 ☐3-2-7

▶BULKY

ボウ

Ⓝ 厐 Ⓒ 庞 páng

27	Non-Jōyō	U5396
厂	S9-2-7	F0000

COMPOUNDS

● [now replaced by 膨 1380] **BULKY, extensive**

厖大な ぼうだいな bulky, massive, extensive

SYNONYMS

● **big and huge**

大 BIG → 4224

太 GREAT → 2673

浩 VAST → 0525

巨 HUGE → 3773

厖 BULKY → 3725

厚 3726 ☐3-2-7

▶THICK

▶KIND

コウ あつ(い) ㊔ あつし

Ⓒ 厚 hòu

27	Jōyō-5	U539A
厂	S9-2-7	F0981

一 厂 厂 戶 戸 戸 戸 厚 厚 (1–9)

COMPOUNDS

❶ⓐ (great in depth) **THICK, deep**

ⓑ **THICK, rich, plentiful**

a 厚薄 こうはく (relative) thickness

b 濃厚な のうこうな thick, dense, heavy, rich

重厚 じゅうこう profoundness, depth, seriousness

❷ **KIND, cordial, hearty, heartfelt, kindhearted, warm**

厚意 こうい kindness, favor

厚情 こうじょう kindness, favor, hospitality

厚志 こうし kindness, kind thought [intention]

厚遇 こうぐう cordial welcome, kind treatment

温厚な おんこうな gentle, courteous

❸ **make plentiful, enrich**

厚生 こうせい public welfare, health promotion

夂 辶 [厂] 厂 八 凵

厚生省 こうせいしょう Ministry of Health and Welfare

❹ abbrev. of 厚生省 こうせいしょう: Ministry of Health and Welfare

厚相 こうしょう Minister of Health and Welfare

❺ great, excessive

厚恩 こうおん great favor [kindness]

厚顔な こうがんな impudent, shameless, brazen

KUN

【あつい 厚い】

① (great in depth) **THICK, bulky, deep**

厚さ あつさ thickness

厚板 あついた thick board, plank

厚かましい あつかましい unabashed, brazen

厚着する あつぎする be heavily clothed

分厚い ぶあつい bulky, massive

② [formerly also 篤い] cordial, **KIND**, hearty, warm, deep

厚い持てなし あついもてなし cordial reception

厚く礼を述べる あつくれいをのべる thank (a person) heartily

手厚い てあつい warm, hearty, cordial

下に厚く したにあつく more generously for the lower-paid

SYNONYMS

❶ⓐ thick

厚 THICK (great in depth) → 3726

太 THICK (great in diameter) → 2673

❷ kind

厚 KIND → 3726

篤 cordial → 3371

懇 cordial → 3606

慈 AFFECTIONATE → 2949

温 warmhearted → 0740

渥 GRACIOUS → 0731

優 kindly → 0200

USAGE

【あつい】

厚い

① (great in depth) thick, bulky, deep

② [formerly also 篤い] cordial, kind, hearty, warm, deep

篤い

① [now usu. 厚い] cordial, kind, hearty, warm, deep

② (of an illness) critical, serious, dangerous

HOMOPHONES

あつい 篤 DEVOTED → 3371

厘

3727

□ 3-2-7

▶*RIN*

リン

Ⓒ 厘 lí

27	Jōyō	U5398
厂	S9-2-7	F2776

一 厂 厂 戶 戶 戶 厍 厘 厘
1 2 3 4 5 6 7 8 9

COMPOUNDS

RIN:

❶ former monetary unit equiv. to 1/1000 of a yen (円)

一厘 いちりん 1 *rin*

❷ⓐ former unit of length equiv. to approx. 0.3 mm or 1/100 of a *sun* (寸)

ⓑ former unit of weight equiv. to 37.5 mg or 1/100 of a momme (匁)

a 一分一厘も違わず いちぶいちりんもたがわず be exactly alike

b 厘毛の軽重無し りんもうのけいちょうなし be equal in weight [significance]

❸ⓐ 1/100

ⓑ 1/100 of 10%: 0.001

a 九分九厘 くぶくりん ten to one, in all probability

b 年利六分五厘 ねんりろくぶごりん annual interest of 6.5%

SYNONYMS

❶ Japanese money denominations

文 *mon* → 2458

両 *ryo* → 4331

厘 *RIN* → 3727

銭 sen → 2159

円 YEN → 3673

扁

3728

□ 3-2-7

▶**FLAT**

ヘン

Ⓝ 扁 Ⓒ 扁 biǎn piān

63	Non-Jōyō	U6241
戶	S9-4-5	F2909

COMPOUNDS

❶ FLAT

扁平な へんぺいな flat

扁桃 へんとう almond; tonsils

❷ small, little

扁舟 へんしゅう little boat

❸ [now usu. 偏 0151] left-side radical of Chinese characters, left radical

扁旁 へんぼう left and right radicals

SYNONYMS

❶ flat

平 FLAT → 4291

扁 FLAT → 3728
坦 LEVEL → 0329

盾

▸SHIELD
ジュン たて
Ⓒ 盾 dùn

3729
□3-2-7

109	Jōyō	U76FE
目	S9-5-4	F1665

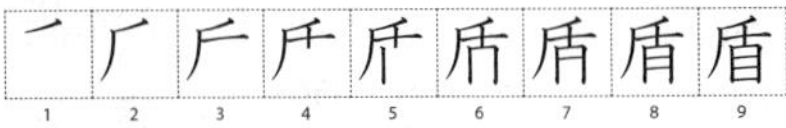

COMPOUNDS

● [original meaning] **SHIELD**
矛盾 むじゅん contradiction
矛盾する むじゅんする be contradictory, be at variance

KUN

【たて 盾】[sometimes also 楯] **SHIELD, escutcheon**
盾突く たてつく oppose, defy, rebel
盾座 たてざ the Shield, Scutum
法律を盾に取って ほうりつをたてにとって on the authority of law

SYNONYMS

● **protective coverings**
盾 SHIELD → 3729
楯 SHIELD → 1281
鎧 ARMOR → 2211
甲 armor → 4293
縅 BRAID OF ARMOR → 1759
面 mask → 2590
兜 helmet → 3499
幌 COVERING FOR VEHICLES → 0787

USAGE

【たて】
盾
[sometimes also 楯] shield, escutcheon
楯
[usu. 盾] shield, escutcheon

HOMOPHONES

たて 楯 SHIELD → 1281

NOTE

➡ see COMPOUND FORMATION for 矛盾 むじゅん → 矛 2501

風

▸WIND
▸MANNER
フウ フ かぜ かざ- -かぜ
Ⓝ 凬 凨◆ Ⓒ 风 fēng

3730
□3-2-7

182	Jōyō-2	U98A8
風	S9-9-0	F0231

RADICAL

kaze 'wind' (颯 飄× 颪×), used in characters related to wind or its qualities
Left variant: 風× ***kaze*** (颱 颶×)

COMPOUNDS

❶ [also suffix] **WIND, breeze**
風速 ふうそく wind velocity
風波 ふうは wind and waves, rough seas, storm
風力 ふうりょく force of the wind; wind power
台風(=颱風) たいふう typhoon
強風 きょうふう strong [high] wind
扇風機 せんぷうき electric fan
季節風 きせつふう seasonal wind, periodic wind

❷ (trend of events) **WIND, trend, movement, tendency**
風潮 ふうちょう tide, trend, tendency
風雲 ふううん state of affairs, situation

❸ (prevailing customs) **MANNERs, customs, tradition**
風俗 ふうぞく manners, customs; popular [public] morals
風習 ふうしゅう manners and customs
家風 かふう family traditions [customs]

❹ [also suffix] (characteristic style) **MANNER, style, school**
整風 せいふう rectification
洋風 ようふう Western [foreign] style
歌風 かふう style of poetry
日本風 にほんふう Japanese style
鷗外風に おうがいふうに in [after] the manner of Ogai

❺ [also suffix] **air, airs, appearance, MANNER, bearing, atmosphere**
風格 ふうかく (distinctive) character, (admirable) appearance; style, race
風采 ふうさい appearance, air, mien, getup
風体 ふうてい(=ふうたい) appearance, looks; posture
軍人風の ぐんじんふうの of military bearing

❻ **elegance, charm, taste**
風味 ふうみ flavor, taste
風雅 ふうが elegance, refinement, daintiness
風流 ふうりゅう refined elegance, taste
風情 ふぜい appearance, air, taste, elegance

❼ **(beautiful) scenery**
風景 ふうけい scenery, landscape, view
風物 ふうぶつ natural objects [features], scenery; scenes and manners
風光 ふうこう (beautiful) scenery, natural beauty
風土記 ふどき topography

❽ spread a rumor
風説 ふうせつ rumor, hearsay

風評 ふうひょう rumor, report
風聞 ふうぶん rumor, hearsay

❾ (infectious) disease, serious disease

風疹× ふうしん German measles, rubella
中風 ちゅうぶ(=ちゅうぶう, ちゅうふう) palsy, paralysis
破傷風 はしょうふう tetanus

❿ [formerly also 諷 ふう 2005] **insinuate, hint, satirize**

風刺 ふうし satire, sarcasm
風喩 ふうゆ hint, insinuation, allegory

⓫ influence, educate

風靡×する ふうびする overwhelm, dominate, sweep

⓬ **used phonetically for *fu***

風呂 ふろ bath
風呂屋 ふろや bathhouse; public bath
風呂場 ふろば bathroom
風呂敷 ふろしき wrapping cloth

INDEPENDENT

【ふう 風】

① (prevailing customs) **MANNERs, customs, tradition**

勤倹の風 きんけんのふう custom [habit] of diligence and thrift

② tendency, inclination

小成に安んじる風 しょうせいにやすんじるふう tendency to be content with small successes

③ (characteristic style) **MANNER, style, school**

こんな風に こんなふうに in this way

④ **air, airs, appearance, MANNER, mien, bearing, atmosphere**

偉そうな風 えらそうなふう air of importance

⑤ **type, kind**

こんな風な物 こんなふうなもの things of this kind

KUN

【かぜ 風, かざ- 風-】**WIND, breeze, draft, current; turn of events**

風車 かざぐるま(=ふうしゃ) windmill; pinwheel
風向き かざむき wind direction
風上の かざかみの windward, upwind
風当りが強い かぜあたりがつよい be windswept; receive harsh treatment
風の吹き回しで かぜのふきまわしで by a (curious) turn of events
北風 きたかぜ north wind
神風 かみかぜ providential [divine] wind; suicide plane, kamikaze
そよ風 そよかぜ gentle breeze, soft wind

【-かぜ -風】[suffix] **air, airs; touch of**

先輩風を吹かす せんぱいかぜをふかす put on a patronizing air
臆病風 おくびょうかぜ panic, funk

SPECIAL READINGS

風邪 かぜ(=ふうじゃ) (common) cold

SYNONYMS

❶ **wind**

風 WIND → 3730
嵐 STORM → 2898
颱 TYPHOON → 4138
台 typhoon → 2498
凪 CALM → 3709
颯 SOUND OF GUSTING WIND → 1563

❸ **custom**

慣 HABITUAL PRACTICE → 0843
例 established practice → 0099
習 CUSTOM → 3306
風 manners → 3730
俗 popular custom → 0119
癖 HABIT → 4080
弊 EVIL PRACTICE → 3583

❹ **way and style**

風 MANNER → 3730
様 MODE → 1332
方 WAY → 2459
途 WAY → 3853
法 METHOD → 0391
流 STYLE → 0529
式 STYLE → 3785
調 TONE → 1973

❺ **appearance**

容 APPEARANCE → 2832
貌 APPEARANCE → 1958
姿 FIGURE → 3264
相 PHASE → 1120
体 FORM (outer appearance) → 0080
色 COLOR → 2522
風 air → 3730

❻ **flavor and elegance**

趣 FLAVOR → 4111
味 TASTE → 0325
風 elegance → 3730
品 refinement → 2795

❼ **view**

景 SCENE → 3118
風 (beautiful) scenery → 3730
光 scenery → 3043
観 VIEW → 2359

❾ **disease**

病 ILLNESS → 4062
疾 DISEASE → 4064
風 (infectious) disease → 3730
症 PATHOLOGICAL CONDITION → 4065
患 AFFECTED BY DISEASE → 3415

疫 EPIDEMIC → 4061
罹 FALL ILL → 3239
臥 be sick in bed → 1825

幽

3731
□3-2-7

▶QUIET AND SECLUDED
ユウ
Ⓒ 幽 yōu

52	Jōyō	U5E7D
幺	S9-3-6	F1778

COMPOUNDS

❶ⓐ QUIET AND SECLUDED, deep and remote
ⓑ seclude, confine, imprison
a 幽棲(=幽栖)する ゆうせいする live a quiet life in seclusion away from the masses
幽谷 ゆうこく deep ravine, secluded valley
幽寂な ゆうじゃくな quiet, sequestered
b 幽居 ゆうきょ hermitage, retirement, seclusion
幽閉 ゆうへい house arrest, confinement
幽囚 ゆうしゅう imprisonment
❷ deep hidden, profound
幽玄な ゆうげんな subtle and profound, quiet and beautiful, occult
幽愁 ゆうしゅう deep contemplation
❸ world of the dead, the other world, Hades
幽霊 ゆうれい ghost, apparition
幽冥 ゆうめい Hades, realm of the dead
幽界 ゆうかい Hades, realm of the dead
幽鬼 ゆうき departed soul, spirit of the dead
❹ [original meaning] dim, indistinct
幽暗 ゆうあん gloom, darkness

INDEPENDENT

【ゆう 幽】quietness and seclusion; invisible world
【ゆうする 幽する】confine (to a house), imprison

SYNONYMS

❶ⓐ inner
奥 inner → 3503
深 DEEP → 0636
幽 QUIET AND SECLUDED → 3731
❶ⓐ quiet
静 QUIET → 2164
閑 QUIET → 4123
寂 quiet → 2855
幽 QUIET AND SECLUDED → 3731
粛 still → 4400
黙 SILENT → 3554
❷ profound
玄 PROFOUND → 2485
幽 deep hidden → 3731
奥 inmost → 3503
深 DEEP → 0636
淵 DEEP AND VAST → 0811
❸ posthumous worlds
天 HEAVEN → 4250
幽 world of the dead → 3731
獄 hell → 0872

凾

3732
□3-2-7

▶BOX
カン はこ

17	Nonstandard	U51FE
凵	S9-2-7	F0000

traditional form → see 函 at 3724

凾

□3-2-7

incorrect stroke-count
➡ see □3-2-6: 凵 at 3724

進週 etc.

□3-2-8

incorrect stroke-count
➡ see □3-3-8: ⻌ at 3872

遊遇

□3-2-8

incorrect stroke-count
➡ see □3-3-9: ⻌ at 3887

原

3733
□3-2-8

▶PLAIN
▶ORIGINAL
ゲン はら ㊔ ばる もと
Ⓒ 原 yuán

27	Jōyō-2	U539F
厂	S10-2-8	F0133

COMPOUNDS

❶ [also suffix] PLAIN, field, plateau
原野 げんや vast plain, wilderness, field
高原 こうげん plateau, tableland, heights
草原 そうげん grassland, prairie, savannah, pampas, steppe
平原 へいげん plain, prairie
氷原 ひょうげん ice field
火口原 かこうげん crater basin
❷ⓐ [also prefix] ORIGINAL, primary, primitive
ⓑ [original meaning] origin, source, root
ⓒ in the ORIGINAL state, raw, crude
a 原因 げんいん cause, origin
原則 げんそく principle, general rule
原作 げんさく original (work)
原子 げんし atom
原案 げんあん original bill [plan]
原始 げんし primitive; primeval

原始的な げんしてきな primitive, primeval
原色 げんしょく primary color
原告 げんこく plaintiff
原判決 げんはんけつ original decision [judgment]
原書 げんしょ the original (work)
原点 げんてん starting point, origin
原稿用紙 げんこうようし manuscript paper; writing pad
b 病原体 びょうげんたい pathogen
抗原 こうげん antigen
c 原料 げんりょう raw material
原油 げんゆ crude oil
❸ abbrev. of 原子力 げんしりょく: **atomic energy**
原爆 げんばく atomic bomb
原発 げんぱつ nuclear power plant

KUN

【はら 原】**PLAIN, field, plateau**
原っぱ はらっぱ open field, empty lot
野原 のはら field, plain
海原 うなばら sea, ocean

SPECIAL READINGS

河原(=川原) かわら dry riverbed, river beach

SYNONYMS

❶ **uncultivated expanses of land**
野 FIELD → 1877
原 PLAIN → 3733
漠 DESERT → 0804
❷ⓐ **original**
素 primary → 3108
原 ORIGINAL → 3733
本 original → 4314
初 FIRST → 1433
ⓒ **natural**
地 natural → 0236
野 wild → 1877
粗 crude → 1683
原 in the original state → 3733

辱 唇 incorrect classification
➡ see 2-7-3: 辰 at 3400
口 3-2-8

扇

3734
口 3-2-8

▶**FAN**
セン おうぎ あお(ぐ)

63	Nonstandard	U6247
戸	S10-4-6	F0000

traditional form → see 扇 at 2449

匿

3735
口 3-2-8

▶**CONCEAL**
トク かくま(う)▲
Ⓝ 匿 Ⓒ 匿 nì

23	Jōyō	U533F
匚	S10-2-8	F2175

(stroke order 1–10)

COMPOUNDS

● [original meaning] **CONCEAL, hide**
匿名 とくめい anonymity, incognito, pseudonym
隠匿 いんとく concealment; misprision
秘匿する ひとくする hide, conceal
蔵匿する ぞうとくする [rare] conceal, shelter, harbor

KUN

【かくまう 匿う】shelter (a prisoner), harbor, give refuge
犯人を匿う はんにんをかくまう shelter a criminal

SYNONYMS

● **hide**
隠 HIDE → 0873
蔽 COVER → 2991
伏 lie in concealment → 0049
潜 LURK → 0922
匿 CONCEAL → 3735
忍 perform by stealth → 2750

匿

3736
口 3-2-8

▶**CONCEAL**
トク かくま(う)

23	Nonstandard	U533F
匚	S10-2-8	F0000

traditional form → see 匿 at 3735

遜 incorrect stroke-count
➡ see 口 3-3-10: 辶 at 3910
口 3-2-9

道 運 etc. incorrect stroke-count
➡ see 口 3-3-9: 辶 at 3887
口 3-2-9

脣 incorrect classification
➡ see 2-7-4: 辰 at 3404
口 3-2-9

貭

3737
口 3-2-9

▶**QUALITY**
▶**MATTER**
シツ シチ チ たち ただ(す) ㊔ ただ

154	Nonstandard	U8CAD
貝	S11-7-4	F0000

handwritten form → see 質 at 3483

凰
3738
☐3-2-9

▶FEMALE PHOENIX
オウ
Ⓒ 凰 huáng

16	Names	U51F0
几	S11-2-9	F2448

COMPOUNDS

● FEMALE PHOENIX, mythical Chinese phoenix
鳳凰 ほうおう male and female Chinese phoenixes
鳳凰座 ほうおうざ the Phoenix (constellation)

SYNONYMS

● birds
鷹 HAWK →3955
鷗 GULL →2370
烏 CROW →4088
雀 SPARROW →3117
燕 SWALLOW →3142
鴻 LARGE WILD BIRD →0977
鳳 MALE PHOENIX →3749
凰 FEMALE PHOENIX →3738
鵬 MYTHICAL HUGE BIRD →1416
鶏 CHICKEN →2221
酉 ROOSTER →4358
隼 FALCON →3427
鳩 PIGEON →0184
鷲 EAGLE →3598
鳶 BLACK KITE →3919
鶴 CRANE →2326
鷺 HERON →3621
鵜 CORMORANT →2067
鴨 DUCK →1582
雁 WILD GOOSE →3741
● mythical animals
竜 DRAGON →2603
辰 THE DRAGON →3713
麒 MALE CHINESE UNICORN →2363
麟 FEMALE CHINESE UNICORN →2376
鵬 MYTHICAL HUGE BIRD →1416
鳳 MALE PHOENIX →3749
凰 FEMALE PHOENIX →3738

區
3739
☐3-2-9

▶DISTRICT
▶WARD
ク

23	Nonstandard	U5340
匚	S11-2-9	F0000

traditional form →see 区 at 3681

匿
☐3-2-9

incorrect stroke-count
➡ see ☐3-2-8: 匚 at 3736

違遠 etc.
☐3-2-10

incorrect stroke-count
➡ see ☐3-3-10: 辶 at 3906

厨
3740
☐3-2-10

▶KITCHEN
チュウ ズ くりや
Ⓝ 廚 Ⓒ 厨 chú

27	Names	U53A8
厂	S12-2-10	F2322

COMPOUNDS

❶ KITCHEN
厨房 ちゅうぼう kitchen, galley
庖厨 ほうちゅう kitchen
❷ chest, case, box
厨子 ずし case used for keeping revered objects in a temple; case for storing books, food, etc.

KUN

【くりや 厨】*hist* KITCHEN

SYNONYMS

❶ kitchen
厨 KITCHEN →3740
庖 KITCHEN →3825

雁
3741
☐3-2-10

▶WILD GOOSE
ガン かり かりがね
Ⓝ 鴈 Ⓒ 雁 yàn

172	Names	U96C1
隹	S12-8-4	F2514

COMPOUNDS

❶ WILD GOOSE
雁行 がんこう flight formation of geese; forming an echelon
雁首 がんくび *colloq* neck, head; bowl of a Japanese smoking pipe
雁擬き がんもどき deep-fried tofu mixed with thinly sliced vegetables
雁木 がんぎ zigzag; steps of a pier; large-toothed saw; rasp
落雁 らくがん wild geese descending on a pond; candy made of rice or other flour mixed with sugar
❷ unclassified compounds
雁字搦×め がんじがらめ bound hand and foot; hedged in
雁皮 がんぴ *Diplomorpha sikokiana;* abbrev. of 雁皮紙 がんぴし: paper made from fiber of this plant

INDEPENDENT

【がん 雁】WILD GOOSE

KUN

【かり 雁】WILD GOOSE

雁首 かりくび (something resembling a) goose's neck; *colloq* glans, head of a penis
雁の文 かりのふみ (message) letter
雁が音(=雁金) かりがね [also 雁 or 雁金] *elegant* cry of the wild goose; wild goose

【かりがね 雁】[also 雁が音 or 雁金] *elegant*
ⓐ cry of the **WILD GOOSE**
ⓑ **WILD GOOSE**

SYNONYMS

❶ **birds**
鷹 HAWK → 3955
鷗 GULL → 2370
烏 CROW → 4088
雀 SPARROW → 3117
燕 SWALLOW → 3142
鴻 LARGE WILD BIRD → 0977
鳳 MALE PHOENIX → 3749
凰 FEMALE PHOENIX → 3738
鵬 MYTHICAL HUGE BIRD → 1416
鶏 CHICKEN → 2221
酉 ROOSTER → 4358
隼 FALCON → 3427
鳩 PIGEON → 0184
鷲 EAGLE → 3598
鳶 BLACK KITE → 3919
鶴 CRANE → 2326
鷺 HERON → 3621
鵜 CORMORANT → 2067
鴨 DUCK → 1582
雁 WILD GOOSE → 3741

HOMOPHONES

かりがね
雁が音 → 3741, 2570
雁金 → 3741, 2552

厩
3742
□3-2-10

▶**HORSE STABLE**
キュウ うまや

27	Nonstandard	U53A9
厂	S12-2-10	F0000

alternative form → see 廐 at 3746

扉
3743
□3-2-10

▶**HINGED DOOR**
ヒ とびら

63	Nonstandard	U6249
戸	S12-4-8	F0000

traditional form → see 扉 at 2453

雇
3744
□3-2-10

▶**EMPLOY**
コ やと(う)

172	Nonstandard	U96C7
隹	S12-8-4	F0000

traditional form → see 雇 at 2454

適遺 etc.
□3-2-11
incorrect stroke-count
➡ see □3-3-11: 辶 at 3916

廐
□3-2-11
incorrect stroke-count
➡ see □3-2-12: 厂 at 3746

選遺 etc.
□3-2-12
incorrect stroke-count
➡ see □3-3-12: 辶 at 3928

厭
3745
□3-2-12

▶**TIRE OF**
エン オン いや あ(きる) いと(う)
Ⓒ 厌 yàn

27	Non-Jōyō	U53AD
厂	S14-2-12	F2191

COMPOUNDS

ⓐ **TIRE OF, weary of, lose interest in**
ⓑ **be disgusted with, detest, dislike**
a 厭世観 えんせいかん pessimism
厭戦 えんせん war-weariness
倦厭する けんえんする weary of
b 厭離 おんり *Buddhism* depart from (in disdain)
厭人 えんじん misanthropy

KUN

【いや 厭】[now usu. 嫌] **disagreeable, unpleasant, detestable**
厭な いやな disagreeable, repulsive
厭厭 いやいや grudgingly, unwillingly; (of children) shaking of the head in refusal
厭がる いやがる dislike, hate
厭がらせ いやがらせ harassment

【あきる 厭きる】[usu. 飽きる, sometimes also 倦きる]
grow TIREd OF, lose interest in
厭き厭きする あきあきする be sick (of), be bored (with)
厭き性 あきしょう fickle [capricious] nature, get soon wearied of

【いとう 厭う】
① **dislike; be disgusted with**
厭わしい いとわしい detestable, disagreeable
危険を厭わない きけんをいとわない do not mind running a risk
② **take (good) care of**
身を厭う みをいとう take good care of oneself

SYNONYMS

ⓐ **tire**

疲 TIRED →4063
労 fatigue →3155
倦 TIRE OF →0131
厭 TIRE OF →3745

【いや】

◯ **hate and dislike**

憎 HATE →0845
悪 hate →3413
忌む ABHOR →2735
嫌 DISLIKE →0781
恨 HOLD A GRUDGE →0439
怨 HOLD A GRUDGE →3179
厭 disagreeable →3745

HOMOPHONES

いや

嫌 DISLIKE →0781
否 SAY NO →3058

あきる

飽 SATIATED →2148
倦 TIRE OF →0131

NOTE

➡ see USAGE notes at 嫌 0781 and 飽 2148

厩

3746

□3-2-12

▶**HORSE STABLE**

キュウ うまや

Ⓝ 廏 廐◇ 厩◇ Ⓒ 厩 jiù

27	Names	U53A9
厂	S14-2-12	F2814

COMPOUNDS

● **HORSE STABLE, horse barn**

厩舎 きゅうしゃ barn, stable
厩務員 きゅうむいん stable hand, groom

KUN

【うまや 厩】[also 馬屋] **HORSE STABLE, horse barn**

厩肥 うまやごえ(=きゅうひ) stable [barnyard] manure

SYNONYMS

● **buildings**

閣 TALL MAGNIFICENT BUILDING →4128
宇 large building →2699
殿 PALACE →2247
堂 HALL →3202
館 PUBLIC BUILDING →2196
舎 BUILDING →2555
棟 BLOCK →1248
厩 HORSE STABLE →3746

HOMOPHONES

うまや 馬屋 →4086, 3842

暦

3747

□3-2-12

▶**CALENDAR**

レキ こよみ

Ⓝ 曆 Ⓒ 历 lì

72	Jōyō	U66A6
日	S14-4-10	F1787

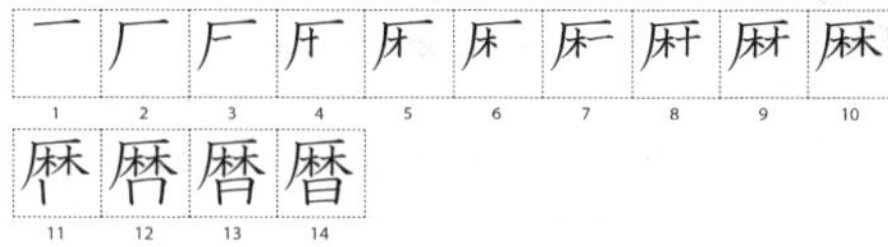

COMPOUNDS

❶ [also suffix] **CALENDAR**

暦年 れきねん calendar year
太陽暦 たいようれき solar calendar
旧暦 きゅうれき old [lunar] calendar
西暦 せいれき Christian Era, A.D.
陰暦 いんれき lunar calendar

❷ years, time

還暦 かんれき 60th anniversary of one's birthday

INDEPENDENT

【れき 暦】**CALENDAR**, almanac

KUN

【こよみ 暦】**CALENDAR, almanac**

花暦 はなごよみ floral calendar

SYNONYMS

❶ **calendars**

暦 CALENDAR →3747
新 new calendar →2239
旧 old calendar →0014

NOTE

★ do not confuse with 歴 PERSONAL HISTORY →3748

歴

3748

□3-2-12

▶**PERSONAL HISTORY**

レキ レッキ▲

Ⓝ 歷 厤◆ 厯◆ Ⓒ 历 lì

77	Jōyō-4	U6B74
止	S14-4-10	F0577

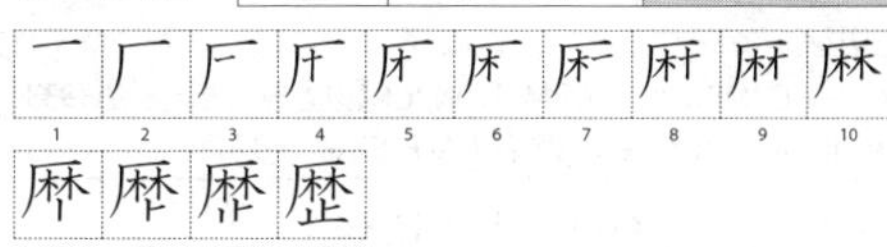

COMPOUNDS

❶ [also suffix] **PERSONAL HISTORY, one's career, experience, personal record**

履歴 りれき personal history, career
学歴 がくれき academic career
経歴 けいれき personal history
病歴 びょうれき case history
逮捕歴 たいほれき criminal record

一輪車歴 いちりんしゃれき one's experience as a unicyclist

❷ **pass, elapse, pass through, experience**

歴史 れきし history

歴戦 れきせん long record of active service

遍歴 へんれき travels, pilgrimage

❸ successive, successively, one by one

歴任 れきにん successive service in various posts

歴訪する れきほうする make a round of calls

歴代 れきだい successive reigns

❹ **clear, plain, obvious**

歴然たる れきぜんたる clear, obvious, plain

お歴歴 おれきれき notables, distinguished persons

❺ [also 瀝 れき 0996]

ⓐ drip, trickle

ⓑ pour

a 歴青炭 れきせいたん bituminous coal

b 披歴する ひれきする express (one's opinion), reveal (one's thoughts)

INDEPENDENT

【れっきとした 歴とした】clear, plain; respectable, decent

SYNONYMS

❶ **history**

史 HISTORY → 4324

伝 biography → 0048

歴 PERSONAL HISTORY → 3748

❷ **elapse**

過 PASS BY → 3891

経 pass → 1687

歴 pass → 3748

去 pass away → 2678

❸ **in succession**

連 IN SUCCESSION → 3849

歴 successive → 3748

逐 ONE BY ONE → 3848

逓 progressively → 3852

漸 GRADUALLY → 0867

NOTE

➡ see COMPOUND FORMATION for 履歴 りれき → 履 3933

★ do not confuse with 暦 CALENDAR → 3747

鳳

3749

口3-2-12

▶**MALE PHOENIX**

ホウ ブウ おおとり ㊔ とり ぽう

Ⓒ 凤 fèng

196	Names	U9CF3
鳥	S14-11-3	F2190

COMPOUNDS

❶ **MALE PHOENIX, mythical Chinese phoenix**

鳳凰 ほうおう male and female Chinese phoenixes

白鳳時代 はくほうじだい name of an archaic Japanese era

❷ [archaic] symbolic expression of an emperor or son of Heaven

鳳輦× ほうれん archaic Imperial sedan, Imperial carriage

KUN

【おおとり 鳳】

① [also 大鳥 or 鴻] **large wild bird such as a crane or white stork**

② [also 大鳥 or 鵬] **huge bird such as a mythical Chinese phoenix**

SYNONYMS

❶ **birds**

鷹 HAWK → 3955

鷗 GULL → 2370

烏 CROW → 4088

雀 SPARROW → 3117

燕 SWALLOW → 3142

鴻 LARGE WILD BIRD → 0977

鳳 MALE PHOENIX → 3749

凰 FEMALE PHOENIX → 3738

鵬 MYTHICAL HUGE BIRD → 1416

鶏 CHICKEN → 2221

酉 ROOSTER → 4358

隼 FALCON → 3427

鳩 PIGEON → 0184

鷲 EAGLE → 3598

鳶 BLACK KITE → 3919

鶴 CRANE → 2326

鷺 HERON → 3621

鵜 CORMORANT → 2067

鴨 DUCK → 1582

雁 WILD GOOSE → 3741

❶ **mythical animals**

竜 DRAGON → 2603

辰 THE DRAGON → 3713

麒 MALE CHINESE UNICORN → 2363

麟 FEMALE CHINESE UNICORN → 2376

鵬 MYTHICAL HUGE BIRD → 1416

鳳 MALE PHOENIX → 3749

凰 FEMALE PHOENIX → 3738

USAGE

【おおとり】

鳳

① [also 大鳥 or 鴻] large wild bird such as a crane or white stork

② [also 大鳥 or 鵬] huge bird such as a mythical Chinese phoenix

鵬

[also 大鳥 or 鳳] huge bird such as a mythical Chinese phoenix

鴻
[also 大鳥 or 鳳] large wild bird such as a crane or white stork

HOMOPHONES

おおとり
鵬 MYTHICAL HUGE BIRD → 1416
鴻 LARGE WILD BIRD → 0977
大鳥 → 4224, 4105

避還 incorrect stroke-count
➡ see ☐3-3-13: 辶 at 3944
☐3-2-13

鴈
3750
☐3-2-13

▶**WILD GOOSE**
ガン かり かりがね

196 鳥	Nonstandard	U9D08
	S15-11-4	F0000

traditional form → see 雁 at 3741

厤
3751
☐3-2-14

▶**CALENDAR**
レキ こよみ

72 日	Names	U66C6
	S16-4-12	F0000

traditional form → see 暦 at 3747

歷
3752
☐3-2-14

▶**PERSONAL HISTORY**
レキ レッキ

77 止	Names	U6B77
	S16-4-12	F0000

traditional form → see 歴 at 3748

壓
3753
☐3-2-15

▶**PRESSURE**
アツ お(す)

32 土	Nonstandard	U58D3
	S17-3-14	F0000

traditional form → see 圧 at 3688

冂 incorrect classification
➡ see ■4-3-4 at 4239
☐3-3-0

口 incorrect classification
➡ see ■4-3-1 at 4189
☐3-3-0

囗 incorrect classification
➡ see ■4-3-1 at 4199
☐3-3-0

辷 incorrect stroke-count
➡ see ☐3-4-1: 辶 at 3957
☐3-3-1

弌
3754
☐3-3-1

▶**ONE**
イチ イツ ひと- ひと(つ) ㊔ かず ひ はじめ おさむ まこと すすむ かつ くに

56 弋	Nonstandard	U5F0C
	S4-3-1	F0000

traditional form → see 一 at 4148

牙 incorrect classification
➡ see ■4-4-1 at 4243
☐3-3-1

尺 incorrect classification
➡ see ■4-4-1 at 4248
☐3-3-1

不 incorrect classification
➡ see ■4-4-1 at 4242
☐3-3-1

斤 incorrect classification
➡ see ☐3-2-2: 厂 at 3667
☐3-3-1

尤
3755
☐3-3-1

▶**RIGHT**
ユウ もっと(も)
Ⓒ 尤 yóu

43 尢	Names	U5C24
	S4-3-1	F2920

COMPOUNDS

❶ outstanding, excellent
尤物 ゆうぶつ superfine thing; beauty, belle

❷ **RIGHT**, reasonable, natural
尤度 ゆうど plausibility, likelihood

INDEPENDENT

【ゆうなる 尤なる】 best, most excellent

KUN

【もっとも 尤も】

① **RIGHT, reasonable, natural**
尤もらしい もっともらしい plausible, specious
御尤も ごもっとも You are quite right

② **indeed, it is true; but**
尤も例外は有る もっともれいがいはある There are, indeed, some exceptions

SYNONYMS

❶ **excellent and superior**
優 SUPERIOR → 0200
絶 without match → 1711
卓 PROMINENT → 2561
快 splendid → 0289
妙 MARVELOUS → 0280
秀 EXCELLENT → 3152
英 DISTINGUISHED → 2782

尤 outstanding → 3755
傑 outstanding → 0175
穎 TALENTED → 2036
逸 exceptional → 3872
名 first-rate → 2693
上 of upper grade → 4212
❷ **right**
正 RIGHT → 4296
是 RIGHT → 3090
尤 RIGHT → 3755
端 correct → 1564

HOMOPHONES
もっとも 最 MOST → 3120

NOTE
➡ see USAGE note at 最 3120

方
□ 3-3-1
incorrect classification
➡ see ▭2-2-2: 亠 at 2459

片
□ 3-3-1
incorrect classification
➡ see ■4-4-4 at 4272

爪
3756
□ 3-3-1

▶**NAIL**
ソウ▲ つめ つま
Ⓒ 爪 zhǎo zhuǎ

87	Jōyō	U722A
爪	S4-4-0	F1796

Stroke order: 1 2 3 4

RADICAL
tsume 'claw' (爫×), used in characters related to grasping or pulling
Top variant: 爫 ***notsu*** (爵)
Top variant: ⺥ ***tsumekanmuri*** (争)

COMPOUNDS
● [original meaning] **NAIL, claw, talon, hoof**
爪牙 そうが claws and tusks, devious design; right-hand man
距爪 きょそう cockspur
有爪動物 ゆうそうどうぶつ velvet worms, *Onychophora*

KUN
【つめ 爪】
① **NAIL, claw, talon, hoof**
爪切り つめきり nail clipper [nipper]
爪痕 つめあと scratch, nail mark; ravages, after effects
深爪 ふかづめ cutting a fingernail to the quick
蹴爪 けづめ cockspur
② **plectrum, pick**
琴爪 ことづめ artificial fingernail [plectrum] of ivory used in playing the koto
③ pawl, catch, hook
爪クラッチ つめくらっち claw clutch
④ [in compounds]
ⓐ fingertip
ⓑ tiptoe
a 爪印 つめいん thumbprint, thumb impression
【つま 爪】[in compounds]
①ⓐ **fingertip**
ⓑ **tiptoe**
a 爪弾く つまびく pluck the strings (of a guitar)
爪弾き つまはじき fillip; ostracism; black sheep (of a family)
爪楊枝(=爪楊子) つまようじ toothpick; [rare] willow-made toothbrush
b 爪先 つまさき tip of a toe, tiptoe, toe
爪立つ つまだつ stand on tiptoe
② plectrum, pick
爪音 つまおと sound of a koto; clang of hoofs

SYNONYMS
● **ungual**
爪 NAIL → 3756
蹄 HOOF → 2022

NOTE
★ do not confuse with 瓜 GOURD → 3789

曰
3757
□ 3-3-1

▶**SAY THAT**
エツ いわ(く) のたま(わく)
Ⓒ 曰 yuē

73	Non-Jōyō	U66F0
曰	S4-4-0	F2537

RADICAL
hirabi 'say', used for character classification
Variant: 曰 ***hirabi*** (書 最 曲)

KUN
【いわく 曰く】
① *literary* **SAY THAT…**
曰く言い難し いわくいいがたし It is hard to say
② **reason, pretext; history**
曰く付きの いわくつきの with a history [story]
【のたまわく 曰わく】[now also 宣わく] [honorific] *literary* **SAY THAT…**
子曰わく しのたまわく Confucius says…

SYNONYMS
【いわく】
① **speak and say**
言 SAY → 2440
語る TELL → 1944
談 TALK → 1975
喋 TALK → 0665

諷 INSINUATE → 2005
謂う REFER TO → 2007
云 say → 2430
曰 SAY THAT → 3757
話 SPEAK → 1928
口 give mouth to → 4189
申す SPEAK HUMBLY → 4319
述 STATE → 3816
陳 SET FORTH → 0656
弁 SPEAK ELOQUENTLY → 2497

HOMOPHONES

のたまわく 宣 PROCLAIM → 2799

NOTE

➡ see USAGE note at 宣 2799
★ do not confuse with 日 DAY → 3759

曰

3758

☐ 3-3-1

▶ ***HIRABI***

73	Radical	U66F0
曰	S4-4-0	F0000

radical variant → see 曰 at 3757

日

3759

☐ 3-3-1

▶ **DAY**
▶ **SUN**
▶ **JAPAN**

ニチ ジツ ひ -び -か

N 日 C 日 rì

72	Jōyō-1	U65E5
日	S4-4-0	F0003

radical variant → see 曰 at 3760

丨 冂 月 日
1 2 3 4

COMPOUNDS

❶ⓐ (period of light) **DAY**
ⓑ [also suffix] (24-hour period) **DAY, daily**
ⓒ **counter for DAYs**
ⓓ **suffix for DAYs of the month**
a 日夜 にちや day and night
日中 にっちゅう during the day
b 日給 にっきゅう daily wage
日数 にっすう number of days
日運動 にちうんどう daily motion
日用品 にちようひん daily necessities
日刊の にっかんの published daily
毎日 まいにち every day
今日 こんにち today, these days
一日 いちにち a day; all day
本日 ほんじつ today
平日 へいじつ weekday
太陽日 たいようじつ solar day
c 五十日 ごじゅうにち 50 days
d 十一月三十日 じゅういちがつさんじゅうにち November 30
❷ (day on which something occurs) **date, DAY, anniversary**
日時 にちじ date, time
期日 きじつ (fixed) date, due date
命日 めいにち anniversary of death
❸ [original meaning] **SUN, sunlight**
日光 にっこう sunshine, sunlight
日没 にちぼつ sunset
日食 にっしょく solar eclipse
日月 じつげつ sun and moon; time, days, years
落日 らくじつ setting sun
❹ **SUNday**
日曜(日) にちよう(び) Sunday
土日 どにち Saturday and Sunday, weekend
❺ⓐ **JAPAN**
ⓑ **JAPANese (language)**
a 日本 にほん(=にっぽん) Japan
日銀 にちぎん Bank of Japan
日米 にちべい Japan and U.S.
日韓 にっかん Japan and (South) Korea
日ソ にっそ Soviet-Japanese, Japanese-Soviet
日本酒 にほんしゅ sake, rice wine
来日する らいにちする come to Japan
b 日英通訳 にちえいつうやく Japanese-English interpreting
❻ abbrev. of 日向 ひゅうが, old name for Miyazaki Prefecture
日豊本線 にっぽうほんせん Nippo Main Line (Kagoshima-Miyazaki-Fukuoka Railway)
日南海岸 にちなんかいがん Nichinan coastline

INDEPENDENT

【にち 日】**JAPAN; Sunday**

KUN

【ひ 日】
① [sometimes also 陽] **SUN, sunlight**
日の丸 ひのまる Rising Sun Flag
日時計 ひどけい sundial
日の出 ひので sunrise
日の入り ひのいり sunset
日陰 ひかげ the shade
日影 ひかげ sunshine; shadow
日向 ひなた sunshine, sunny place
日差し ひざし rays of the sun, sunlight
朝日 あさひ [sometimes also 旭] rising sun, morning sun; rays of the morning sun
② **DAY, date, time**
日日 ひび daily; days
日日 ひにち date; number of days
日付 ひづけ date, dating

日頃 ひごろ usually; always
日替わり ひがわり changing on a daily basis
日に日に ひにひに day by day, every day
曜日 ようび day of the week
生年月日 せいねんがっぴ date of birth

【-び -日】 [suffix] **DAY**
誕生日 たんじょうび birthday
記念日 きねんび memorial day, anniversary
最終日 さいしゅうび the last day

【-か -日】
ⓐ **counter for DAYs**
ⓑ **suffix for DAYs of the month**
a 三日前 みっかまえ three days ago
ab 二十日 はつか 20 days; 20th of the month
二日 ふつか two days; 2nd of the month
b 十月十日 じゅうがつとおか October 10

SPECIAL READINGS
今日 きょう today
一日 ついたち [sometimes also 朔] 1st of the month
明日 あす tomorrow
明日▲ あした tomorrow
昨日 きのう yesterday
晦日▲ つごもり [also 晦] last day of the month

SYNONYMS
❶ **days**
日 DAY → 3759
曜 DAY OF THE WEEK → 1402
昼 DAYTIME → 3841
旦 first day → 3041
朔 FIRST DAY OF THE LUNAR MONTH → 1678
晦 LAST DAY OF THE LUNAR MONTH → 1196

❷ **date**
日 date → 3759
忌 death anniversary → 2735

❸ **sun**
日 SUN → 3759
陽 SUN → 0764
旭 RISING SUN → 3697

❹ **days of the week**
日 Sunday → 3759
月 Monday → 3674
火 Tuesday → 4273
水 Wednesday → 0010
木 Thursday → 4261
金 Friday → 2552
土 Saturday → 4211

❺ⓐ **Japan**
日 JAPAN → 3759
和 JAPAN → 1450
邦 JAPAN → 1051
国 Japanese → 3831
倭 ANCIENT NAME FOR JAPAN → 0140

❺ⓐ **Asian countries**
日 JAPAN → 3759
緬 Myanmar → 1758
老 Laos → 3963
華 CHINA → 2841
蒙 Mongolia → 2938
鮮 Korea → 2355
泰 Thailand → 3193
越 Vietnam → 4108
印 India → 1023
竺 INDIA → 3248
比 Philippines → 0029

USAGE
【ひ】
日
① [sometimes also 陽] sun, sunlight
② day, date, time
陽
[usu. 日] sun, sunlight

HOMOPHONES
ひ 陽 SUN → 0764
あさひ
旭 RISING SUN → 3697
朝日 → 2130, 3759
ついたち
朔 FIRST DAY OF THE LUNAR MONTH → 1678
一日 → 4148, 3759
つごもり
晦 DARK → 1196
晦日 → 1196, 3759

NOTE
➡ see also USAGE notes at 旭 3697 and 朔 1678
➡ see COMPOUND FORMATION for 日本 にほん(=にっぽん) → 本 4314
★ do not confuse with 曰 SAY THAT → 3757

日

3760
口 3-3-1

▶**DAY**
▶**SUN**
▶**JAPAN**
ニチ ジツ ひ -び -か

72	Nonstandard	U65E5
日	S4-4-0	F0000

traditional form → see 日 at 3759

RADICAL
hi 'sun', used in characters related to the sun, sunlight or time
Variant: 日 *hi* (明 春 星)

辺

3761

口3-3-2

▶VICINITY
▶BORDERLAND

ヘン あた(り) -べ ㊔ なべ

Ⓝ 邊 邉 Ⓒ 边 biān

162	Jōyō-4	U8FBA
⻌	S5-3-2	F0606

フ 刀 `刀 刃 辺
1 2 3 4 5

COMPOUNDS

❶ⓐ [also suffix] (nearby area) **VICINITY, surroundings, neighborhood, environs, outskirts**
ⓑ (space next to something, as a body of water) **-side**

a 周辺 しゅうへん environs, outskirts; circumference
身辺 しんぺん one's person, one's immediate surroundings
近辺 きんぺん vicinity, neighborhood
官辺 かんぺん government [official] circles, official quarters
東京辺で とうきょうへんで in the vicinity of Tokyo
b 水辺 すいへん waterside, shore

❷ *math*
ⓐ **side**
ⓑ **member**

a 一辺 いっぺん a side (of a triangle)
二等辺三角形 にとうへんさんかっけい equilateral [isosceles] triangle
b 右辺 うへん right member

❸ⓐ [original meaning] border, edge, periphery, fringe
ⓑ **BORDERLAND, frontier, remote region, outer regions, deep rural areas**

a 広大無辺な こうだいむへんな boundless, infinite
縁辺 えんぺん border, edge; relations
b 辺地 へんち remote place
辺境 へんきょう frontier (district), remote region, border(land)
辺鄙な へんぴな out-of-the-way, unfrequented, remote

INDEPENDENT

【へん 辺】

①ⓐ **VICINITY, neighborhood, part, locality, quarters**
ⓑ **VICINITY** (of a figure), approximate level

a この辺に このへんに in this neighborhood
どの辺 どのへん where, whereabout
b 五百円の辺で ごひゃくえんのへんで in the vicinity of 500 yen

② *math* side
多角形の辺 たかっけいのへん side of a polygon

KUN

【あたり 辺り】

①ⓐ **VICINITY, neighborhood, surroundings**
ⓑ [also suffix] (near that place or time) **thereabouts, about**

a 家の辺りに いえのあたりに around the house
b 一昨年辺り いっさくねんあたり the year before last or thereabouts

② for instance
ロンドン辺りなら ろんどんあたりなら in the case of London, for instance

【-べ -辺】

①ⓐ (space next to something) **-side, VICINITY, surroundings**
ⓑ (space next to a body of water) **-side, waterside, bank**

a 窓辺で まどべで near the window
道辺 みちべ roadside
b 海辺 うみべ seaside, beach, seashore
川辺 かわべ riverside, edge of a river
岸辺に きしべに ashore, on the shore

② **indefinite term referring to a person or thing**
知る辺 しるべ acquaintance, friend
寄る辺 よるべ person to depend on, one's resort

SYNONYMS

❶ⓐ **areas and localities**
地 PLACE → 0236
方 locality → 2459
辺 VICINITY → 3761
域 BOUNDED AREA → 0559
区 DISTRICT → 3681
領 TERRITORY → 1567
帯 BELT → 3191
圏 SPHERE → 3904

ⓑ **side**
側 SIDE → 0155
脇 SIDE → 1188
方 side → 2459
辺 -side → 3761
面 side → 2590
傍 BESIDE → 0166
横 SIDEWAYS → 1350

❷ⓐ **lines and line segments**
線 LINE → 1760
弧 ARC → 0430
弦 chord → 0343
径 DIAMETER → 0347
辺 side → 3761

❸ⓐ **edges and boundaries**
縁 EDGE → 1754
端 edge → 1564
辺 border → 3761
境 BOUNDARY → 0835
疆 BOUNDARY → 1810

界 BOUNDS → 3172
際 VERGE → 0874
涯 OUTER LIMITS → 0623
ⓑ the country
郊 SUBURB → 1638
里 COUNTRYSIDE → 4356
鄙 THE COUNTRY → 2338
郷 the country → 0664
辺 BORDERLAND → 3761

【あたり】
①ⓑ **approximately**
約 APPROXIMATELY → 1632
概 GENERAL → 1322
大 in substance → 4224
-頃 ABOUT → 0163
位 about → 0069
-方 about → 2459
-程 …or thereabouts → 1524
辺り thereabouts → 3761

【-べ】
①ⓑ **shores and watersides**
畔 WATERSIDE → 1472
-辺 -side → 3761
浜 BEACH → 0523
岸 SHORE → 2777
浦 SEASIDE → 0524
渚 STRAND → 0637
磯 ROCKY BEACH → 1587
汀 STRAND → 0228

HOMOPHONES
あたり 当 THE PRESENT → 2701

NOTE
➡ see USAGE note at 当 2701

込

▶MOVE INWARD
▶EMPHATIC VERBAL SUFFIX
-こ(む) こ(む) こ(み) -こ(み) こ(める)

3762
□ 3-3-2

Ⓝ 込 Ⓒ (国字)

162	Jōyō	U8FBC
辶	S5-3-2	F0181

1	2	3	4	5
ノ	入	`入	込	込

KUN

【-こむ -込む】
①ⓐ [original meaning] **MOVE INWARD, get in, come in**
ⓑ **cause to MOVE INWARD, put in, bring in**—used as a verbal suffix to indicate action directed inward
a 乗り込む のりこむ board, go on board; march into
迷い込む まよいこむ stray [wander] into
割り込み わりこみ breaking into a queue, wedging oneself in
b 払い込む はらいこむ pay in, pay up
吸い込む すいこむ inhale, breathe in; suck in
持ち込む もちこむ carry [bring] in; propose, refer to; bring (a matter) to
②ⓐ **EMPHATIC VERBAL SUFFIX indicating intense involvement in an activity (similar to *up* in *polish up*)**
ⓑ verbal suffix indicating continuation of present state
a 眠り込む ねむりこむ fall asleep
黙り込む だまりこむ sink into silence
b 住み込みの すみこみの live-in
泊まり込み とまりこみ staying in (to do one's job)

【こむ 込む】
① [sometimes also 混む] **be crowded, be congested, be packed**
込み合う こみあう be crowded, be packed, be jammed
込み上げる こみあげる fill (one's heart); feel nausea
人込み ひとごみ crowd [throng] (of people)
② be intricate
込み入った こみいった complicated, intricate

【こみ 込み】**inclusiveness; handicap (in the game of go)**
込みで買う こみでかう buy in bulk, buy the whole lot

【-こみ -込み】[also suffix] **including**
税込み四万円 ぜいこみよんまんえん 40,000 yen, tax included
運賃込みで うんちんこみで freight included [pre-paid]

【こめる 込める】
① [also verbal suffix] **put in, coop in, shut up**
閉じ込める とじこめる shut in [up], lock in [up]
引っ込める ひっこめる put [pull, move] back
② load (a gun), charge
元込め銃 もとごめじゅう breechloading rifle, breechloader
③ⓐ include, count in
ⓑ [formerly also 籠める] impregnate with, imply
a 一切を込めた宿泊料 いっさいをこめたしゅくはくりょう all-inclusive hotel charges
b 警告の意味を込めて けいこくのいみをこめて with an implication of warning
④ [formerly also 籠める] **concentrate on, devote oneself to**
心を込めて こころをこめて with all one's heart, wholeheartedly
⑤ [formerly also 籠める] hang over, envelop, shroud
霧が立ち込めた港 きりがたちこめたみなと harbor wrapped in a mist

SYNONYMS

【-こむ】

①ⓐ **enter**

入 ENTER →4177

-込む MOVE INWARD →3762

ⓑ **put in**

入 PUT IN →4177

挿 INSERT →0517

嵌 INLAY →2897

-込む cause to move inward →3762

USAGE

❶【こむ】

込む

① [sometimes also 混む] be crowded, be congested, be packed

② be intricate

混む

[usu. 込む] be crowded, be congested, be packed

❷【こめる】

込める

① [also verbal suffix] put in, coop in, shut up

② load (a gun), charge

③ⓐ include, count in

ⓑ [formerly also 籠める] impregnate with, imply

④ [formerly also 籠める] concentrate on, devote oneself to

⑤ [formerly also 籠める] hang over, envelop, shroud

籠める

[now usu. 込める]

① concentrate on, devote oneself to

② impregnate with, imply

③ hang over, envelop, shroud

HOMOPHONES

こむ 混 MIX →0631

こめる 籠 BASKET →3398

辻

3763

口3-3-2

▶**CROSSROADS**

つじ

162	Nonstandard	U8FBB
辶	S5-3-2	F0000

traditional form →see 辻 at 3958

辻込

口3-3-2

incorrect stroke-count

➡ see 口3-4-2: 辶 at 3958

処

3764

口3-3-2

▶**DEAL WITH**

ショ ところ▲ -こ▲

Ⓝ 處 Ⓒ 处 chù chǔ

16△	Jōyō-6	U51E6
几	S5-2-3	F0600

ノ ク 夂 夗 処 (strokes 1 2 3 4 5)

COMPOUNDS

❶ⓐ **DEAL WITH, dispose of, manage, cope with, treat**

ⓑ **DEAL WITH (lawbreakers), punish**

a 処理する しょりする manage, deal with, dispose of; process, treat

処置 しょち disposal, measure, treatment

処方箋 しょほうせん prescription

処分 しょぶん disposal, measure; punishment

対処する たいしょする cope [deal] with, meet

善処する ぜんしょする make the best of

b 処刑 しょけい execution, punishment

処罰 しょばつ punishment, penalty

❷ [usu. 所 1056] place, proper place, location

処処 しょしょ several places

❸ [original meaning] stay in one's place, stay home, as:

ⓐ **stay home and not get married**

ⓑ stay home and not take on a government post, remain civilian

a 処女 しょじょ virgin, maiden

b 出処進退 しゅっしょしんたい one's move, course of action (whether one gets a government job or not)

❹ act, behave, conduct

処世術 しょせいじゅつ how to get on in the world

INDEPENDENT

【しょする 処する】**DEAL WITH**, dispose of, manage; sentence, condemn; act, behave

KUN

【ところ 処】[also suffix] **place (for a specific purpose, as eating or resting)**

お食事処 おしょくじどころ (Japanese) restaurant

【-こ -処】suffix for forming demonstratives

何処 どこ where?

此処 ここ here, this place

SYNONYMS

❶ⓐ **deal with**

扱う HANDLE →0251

処 DEAL WITH →3764

辦 DISPOSE OF →2028

措 dispose of →0610

置 take proper steps →3222

ⓑ **punishment**

辶 辷 【込】 弋 户 广 戸 戶 庐 𠂇 户 八 匚 口 囗 口 且 口

刑 PENALTY → 1024
罰 PUNISHMENT → 3228
懲 CHASTISE → 3623
処 DEAL WITH (lawbreakers) → 3764

❷ places and positions

所 PLACE → 1056
処 place → 3764
場 PLACE (for specific activity) → 0678
地 PLACE (particular location) → 0236
席 meeting place → 3865
位 POSITION → 0069
点 POINT → 2587
座 place → 3868

HOMOPHONES

ところ 所 PLACE → 1056

NOTE

➡ see USAGE note at 所 1056

弐

3765

□3-3-2

▶TWO

ニ ふた ふた(つ) ㊔ つぎ つぐ かず

56	Nonstandard	U5F0D
弋	S5-3-2	F0000

traditional form → see 二 at 2421

尻

3766

□3-3-2

▶BUTTOCKS

コウ▲ しり

Ⓝ 尻 Ⓒ 尻 kāo

44	Jōyō	U5C3B
尸	S5-3-2	F1157

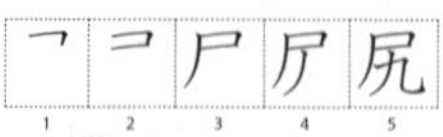

COMPOUNDS

● [original meaning, now archaic] **BUTTOCKS**

尻座 こうざ crouching

KUN

【しり 尻】

①ⓐ **BUTTOCKS, hips, the rear, ass**
ⓑ **bottom, base**

a お尻 おしり buttocks; backside (of a kettle)
尻に帆掛けて逃げる しりにほかけてにげる take to one's heels ("stick a sail in one's ass and take off like the devil")
尻の軽い女 しりのかるいおんな wanton girl
尻尾 しっぽ tail; one's true colors
b 鍋尻 なべじり bottom of a pan

② **tail end, end, back part, rear**

尻取り しりとり capping (verses)
尻切れ蜻×蛉× しりきれとんぼ unfinished ending
尻上がり しりあがり rising intonation; head over heels; rising market
尻込みする しりごみする flinch, shrink back
尻窄み しりつぼみ tapering, weak ending
尻目に懸ける しりめにかける look askance (contemptuously)
台尻 だいじり butt end (of a gun)
縄尻 なわじり end of a rope
どん尻 どんじり tail end; tailender
言葉尻を捉える ことばじりをとらえる cavil at a person's words

③ **aftermath, consequence**

尻拭い しりぬぐい bearing the consequences of someone else's error
喧嘩の尻 けんかのしり aftermath of a quarrel [failure]

SYNONYMS

【しり】

①ⓐ **buttocks**

尻 BUTTOCKS → 3766
肛 ANUS → 1046

② **rear**

後 after- → 0431
背 BACK → 3182
裏 REAR → 2652
尻 tail end → 3766
尾 TAIL → 3799

尼

3767

□3-3-2

▶BUDDHIST NUN

ニ あま

Ⓒ 尼 ní

44	Jōyō	U5C3C
尸	S5-3-2	F2004

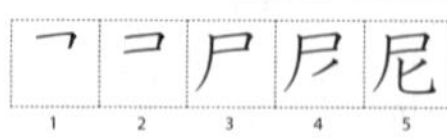

COMPOUNDS

❶ⓐ BUDDHIST NUN [priestess], sister
ⓑ title after names of **BUDDHIST NUN**s

a 尼僧 にそう nun, sister; (Buddhist) priestess
僧尼 そうに monks and nuns
禅尼 ぜんに Zen nun
修道尼 しゅうどうに nun
b 蓮月尼 れんげつに name of a famous Buddhist nun

❷ used phonetically for *ni*, esp. in the transliteration of Sanskrit Buddhist terms

陀羅尼 だらに *dhāraṇi*, mystic Buddhist incantation

KUN

【あま 尼】BUDDHIST NUN, sister

尼寺 あまでら nunnery, convent

SYNONYMS

❶ⓐ clergymen

僧 BONZE → 0180

坊 Buddhist priest → 0274
尼 BUDDHIST NUN → 3767
父 FATHER → 2467

庁

▶**GOVERNMENT AGENCY**

チョウ

Ⓝ 廳 廰 Ⓒ 厅 tīng

3768

□3-3-2

53	Jōyō-6	U5E81
广	S5-3-2	F0957

丶 亠 广 庁 庁
1 2 3 4 5

COMPOUNDS

● [also suffix] [original meaning] **GOVERNMENT AGENCY, government [public] office**
庁舎 ちょうしゃ government building
官庁 かんちょう government office [agency]
都庁 とちょう Tokyo Metropolitan Government Office
県庁 けんちょう prefectural office
警視庁 けいしちょう Metropolitan Police Office
環境庁 かんきょうちょう Environment Agency

INDEPENDENT

【ちょう 庁】**public office**
閻×魔の庁 えんまのちょう judgment seat of *Yama*

SYNONYMS

● **public offices**
省 MINISTRY → 3100
庁 GOVERNMENT AGENCY → 3768
府 government office → 3824
公 public office → 2468
署 PUBLIC-SERVICE STATION → 3223
局 public service office → 3800
所 office → 1056

広

▶**WIDE**

コウ ひろ(い) ひろ(まる) ひろ(める) ひろ(がる) ひろ(げる) ㊔ ひろし ひろむ

Ⓝ 廣 Ⓒ 广 guǎng

3769

□3-3-2

53	Jōyō-2	U5E83
广	S5-3-2	F0274

丶 亠 广 広 広
1 2 3 4 5

COMPOUNDS

❶ⓐ [original meaning] (extending over a large area) **WIDE, broad, vast, extensive, large, spacious**
ⓑ [also prefix] (having great scope) **WIDE, wide-ranging**
a 広大な こうだいな vast, extensive, grand
広域 こういき wide area
広野 こうや [formerly also 曠野] vast plain, prairie
b 広角 こうかく wide angle
広義 こうぎ broad sense, broader application
広範囲 こうはんい wide scope, vast range

❷ **spread, disseminate**
広告 こうこく public notice; advertisement
広報(=弘報) こうほう (public) information, public relations

❸ [formerly also 宏 2728] **grand, great, magnificent**
広壮な こうそうな grand, magnificent, imposing

KUN

【ひろい 広い】**WIDE, broad, vast, extensive, large, spacious; wide-ranging; generous**
広さ ひろさ area, extent
広広とした ひろびろとした spacious, open, extensive
手広く てびろく extensively, widely, on an extensive scale
幅広い はばひろい wide, broad
心の広い こころのひろい broad-minded, generous
背広 せびろ business suit

【ひろまる 広まる】[sometimes also 弘まる] **spread, be diffused, be in general circulation, become popular**
広まり ひろまり spread
噂が広まった うわさがひろまった A rumor went about [spread]

【ひろめる 広める】[sometimes also 弘める] **spread, disseminate; extend, broaden, WIDEn**
お広め(=お披露目) おひろめ début
仏教を広める ぶっきょうをひろめる propagate Buddhism
知識を広める ちしきをひろめる extend one's knowledge

【ひろがる 広がる】[sometimes also 拡がる] *vi*
ⓐ **spread out, stretch, unfold**
ⓑ **expand, extend**
ⓒ **spread, reach, go about**
a 広がった枝 ひろがったえだ spreading branches
b 広がり ひろがり extent, expanse, stretch, spread
c 火が燃え広がった ひがもえひろがった The fire spread

【ひろげる 広げる】[sometimes also 拡げる] *vt*
①ⓐ **spread (out), outstretch**
ⓑ **unfold, unroll, open**
a 地図を広げる ちずをひろげる spread a map
b 広げた腕 ひろげたうで outstretched arms
本を広げる ほんをひろげる open a book
繰り広げる くりひろげる roll out, unfold, spread out; develop
② **WIDEn, enlarge, expand, extend**
運動場を広げる うんどうじょうをひろげる enlarge the playground

SYNONYMS

❶ **wide and extensive**

広 WIDE →3769
紘 WIDE-RANGING →1650
博 EXTENSIVE →0170
恢 EXTENSIVE →0436
浩 VAST →0525
洸 VAST (expanse of water) →0462
滉 DEEP AND VAST →0811
曠 SPACIOUS →1411
闊 BROAD →4135

❷ **make widely known**

布 SPREAD →3691
流 spread →0529
伝 spread →0048
広 spread →3769
弘 DISSEMINATE (esp. Buddhism) →0223
及 REACH TO →4192

【ひろげる】

①ⓐ **expand**

脹 SWELL →1265
膨 EXPAND →1380
張 SPREAD →0573
氾 SPREAD OUT →0226
広げる spread (out) →3769
拡 ENLARGE →0366
伸 STRETCH →0079
延 EXTEND →3812

USAGE

❶【ひろまる】

広まる
[sometimes also 弘まる] spread, be diffused, be in general circulation, become popular

弘まる
[usu. 広まる] same as 広まる

❷【ひろめる】

広める
[sometimes also 弘める] spread, disseminate; extend, broaden, widen

弘める
[usu. 広める] same as 広める

❸【ひろがる】

広がる
[sometimes also 拡がる] *vi*
ⓐ spread out, stretch, unfold
ⓑ expand, extend
ⓒ spread, reach, go about

拡がる
[usu. 広がる] same as 広がる

❹【ひろげる】

広げる
[sometimes also 拡げる] *vt*
①ⓐ spread (out), outstretch
ⓑ unfold, unroll, open
② widen, enlarge, expand, extend

拡げる
[usu. 広げる] same as 広げる

❺【こうほう】

広報
(public) information, public relations

弘報
(public) information, public relations

公報
public [official] report [bulletin]

HOMOPHONES

ひろまる 弘 DISSEMINATE →0223
ひろめる 弘 DISSEMINATE →0223
ひろがる 拡 ENLARGE →0366
ひろげる 拡 ENLARGE →0366

COMPOUND FORMATION

【背広 せびろ】

背広 'business suit' is a corruption either of "civil clothes" or of "Savile Row," the name of a famous street of tailors in London.

斥

□3-3-2

incorrect classification
➡ see □3-2-3: 厂 at 3690

民

3770
□3-3-2

▶**PEOPLE**
ミン たみ ㊔ み ひと
ⓒ 民 mín

83	Jōyō-4	U6C11
氏	S5-4-1	F0105

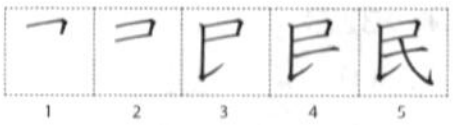

COMPOUNDS

❶ [also suffix]
ⓐ **PEOPLE, nation, race**
ⓑ **the PEOPLE, populace, folk, civilians, citizens, inhabitants**

a 民族 みんぞく race, people, nation
民衆 みんしゅう populace, the people, the masses
国民 こくみん people, nation; the people
選民 せんみん chosen people
b 民主 みんしゅ democracy
民主主義 みんしゅしゅぎ democracy
民謡 みんよう folk song [ballad]
民間 みんかん private citizens, civilians
民営 みんえい private management
民法 みんぽう civil law [code]
人民 じんみん the people, populace, subjects
住民 じゅうみん residents, dwellers

庶民 しょみん common people, the masses
県民 けんみん citizens of a prefecture
農漁民 のうぎょみん the fishing and agrarian populace

❷ subjects
臣民 しんみん subjects

INDEPENDENT

【みん 民】 civilians, private citizens
官と民の協力 かんとみんのきょうりょく cooperation between the private and public sectors

KUN

【たみ 民】 **PEOPLE, nation, race; subjects**
民草 たみぐさ(=たみくさ) subjects
流浪の民 るろうのたみ wandering people, the Jews

SYNONYMS

❶ⓐ people
民 PEOPLE → 3770
族 race → 1195

ⓑ the people
民 PEOPLE → 3770
衆 the multitude(s) → 3325
庶 the masses → 3880
公 PUBLIC → 2468

皮

3771
□3-3-2

▸SKIN
ヒ かわ
Ⓒ 皮 pí

107	Jōyō-3	U76AE
皮	S5-5-0	F0982

ノ 厂 广 皮 皮 (1 2 3 4 5)

RADICAL

kegawa 'skin' (皺× 皰× 皸×), used in characters related to the skin

COMPOUNDS

❶ⓐ [original meaning] **SKIN (of human beings or animals), hide, pelt; fur; leather**
ⓑ SKIN (of plants), bark, peel, husk, shell
a 皮膚 ひふ skin
皮革 ひかく leather, hides
皮下注射 ひかちゅうしゃ hypodermic injection
皮肉 ひにく cynicism, sarcasm; irony
脱皮 だっぴ ecdysis; self-renewal
b 樹皮 じゅひ bark

❷ appearance
皮相 ひそう outward look; superficiality

KUN

【かわ 皮】
①ⓐ **SKIN, hide, pelt; fur; leather**
ⓑ **SKIN, bark, peel, husk, shell**
a 皮財布 かわざいふ leather wallet
牛皮 ぎゅうかわ cowhide, oxhide
毛皮 けがわ fur
鰐×皮 わにがわ crocodile skin [hide]
b バナナの皮 ばななのかわ banana peel

②ⓐ outer covering of articles
ⓑ outward appearance, veneer
a 薄皮 うすかわ thin skin film
布団皮(=蒲団皮) ふとんがわ ticking, quilting
b 皮切り かわきり beginning, start
化けの皮を現わす ばけのかわをあらわす expose one's true colors [character]

SYNONYMS

❶ kinds of skin
皮 SKIN (of any kind) → 3771
膚 SKIN (of the human body) → 4049
肌 SKIN (of the human body) → 1021
革 LEATHER → 3099
韋 TANNED LEATHER → 2851
鱗 SCALES → 2375

USAGE

【かわ】
皮
①ⓐ skin, hide, pelt; fur; leather
ⓑ skin, bark, peel, husk, shell
②ⓐ outer covering of articles
ⓑ outward appearance, veneer

革
[also prefix and suffix] leather

HOMOPHONES

かわ 革 LEATHER → 3099

COMPOUND FORMATION

【皮肉 ひにく】
皮肉 'cynicism, etc.' originally referred to the skin (皮 ❶ⓐ) and flesh (肉), i.e., the human body. It is not clear how it acquired its current meaning.

存

□3-3-2

incorrect classification/stroke-count
➡ see □3-2-4: 𠂇 at 3702

片

□3-3-2

incorrect classification
➡ see ■4-5-4 at 4328

瓜

3772
□3-3-2

▸GOURD
カ うり

97	Nonstandard	U74DC
瓜	S5-5-0	F0000

alternative form → see 瓜 at 3789

RADICAL

uri 'gourd' (瓠× 瓢), used in characters related to gourds, melons or cucumbers
Variant: 瓜 *uri* (瓠× 瓢)

巨 **▶HUGE**
キョ ㊔ お おう こ なお み
Ⓝ 巨 Ⓒ 巨 jù

3773
口3-3-2

7	Jōyō	U5DE8
二	S5-2-3	F0864

Stroke order: 1–5

COMPOUNDS

❶ⓐ (of extraordinary size) **HUGE, enormous, giant, big, large, great**
ⓑ (of extraordinary quantity) **HUGE**, enormous, great

a 巨大な きょだいな huge, gigantic, enormous
巨人 きょじん giant; great person
巨星 きょせい giant star; great person [star], big shot
巨象 きょぞう gigantic elephant
巨岩 きょがん huge rock, crag
巨視的 きょしてき macroscopic, all-inclusive
b 巨額 きょがく enormous sum
巨費 きょひ great expenditure

❷ great, grand
巨匠 きょしょう great master, maestro

SYNONYMS

❶ **big and huge**
大 BIG →4224
太 GREAT →2673
浩 VAST →0525
巨 HUGE →3773
厖 BULKY →3725

巨 **▶HUGE**
キョ ㊔ お おう こ なお み

3774
口3-3-2

48	Nonstandard	U5DE8
工	S5-3-2	F0000

traditional form →see 巨 at 3773

田 **▶RICE FIELD**
デン た
Ⓒ 田 tián

3775
口3-3-2

102	Jōyō-1	U7530
田	S5-5-0	F0050

Stroke order: 1–5

RADICAL

ta 'field' (町 男 畑), used in characters related to fields, rice fields or surfaces

COMPOUNDS

❶ⓐ **RICE FIELD, paddy field**
ⓑ [original meaning] **field, farmland**

a 田畑 でんぱた(=たはた) fields and rice paddies
田地 でんち land, farm, rice fields
田作 でんさく rice-field tilling
乾田 かんでん dry rice field
水田 すいでん paddy field, rice field
b 田園 でんえん fields and gardens, rural districts

❷ (land area yielding or worked for a natural resource) **field**
油田 ゆでん oil field
塩田 えんでん salt field
炭田 たんでん coal field

❸ country, rural district
田家 でんか rural cottage
田夫野人 でんぷやじん rustic, boor, hick

KUN

【た 田】**RICE FIELD, paddy field**
田植え たうえ rice planting
田圃 たんぼ rice field
稲田 いなだ rice field

SPECIAL READINGS

田舎 いなか country, rural district

SYNONYMS

❶ **cultivated fields**
畑 FIELD →1131
畠 FIELD →3186
牧 PASTURE →1083
園 GARDEN →3914
田 RICE FIELD →3775
佃 CULTIVATED RICE FIELD →0066
圃 VEGETABLE GARDEN →3871

囚 **▶PRISONER**
シュウ とら(われる)▲
Ⓒ 囚 qiú

3776
口3-3-2

31	Jōyō	U56DA
口	S5-3-2	F2063

Stroke order: 1–5

COMPOUNDS

❶ [also suffix] **PRISONER, convict, criminal**
囚人 しゅうじん prisoner, convict
囚衣 しゅうい prison uniform
女囚 じょしゅう female convict
虜囚 りょしゅう captive, prisoner
死刑囚 しけいしゅう criminal condemned to death
脱獄囚 だつごくしゅう jail-breaker, escaped prisoner

❷ [original meaning] arrest, imprison

幽囚 ゆうしゅう imprisonment

INDEPENDENT

【しゅう 囚】 imprisonment, captivity

囚を解く しゅうをとく be relieved from captivity

KUN

【とらわれる 囚われる】 [also 捕らわれる]

① be imprisoned, be taken captive

囚われ とらわれ captive, imprisonment

② adhere to (tradition), be swayed by

囚われた考え とらわれたかんがえ conventional ideas, prejudiced opinion

SYNONYMS

❶ **prisoner**

虜 CAPTIVE →4038

囚 PRISONER →3776

HOMOPHONES

とらわれる 捕 CATCH →0514

NOTE

➡ see USAGE note at 捕 0514

皿 incorrect classification ➡ see ■4-5-1 at 4286

口3-3-2

目

3777

口3-3-2

▶EYE
▶ITEM

モク ボク め -め ま- ㊔ さっか

Ⓒ 目 mù

109	Jōyō-1	U76EE
目	S5-5-0	F0039

1 2 3 4 5

RADICAL

me 'eye' (直 相 眠), used in characters related to the eye, seeing or perceiving

COMPOUNDS

❶ⓐ [original meaning] **EYE**

ⓑ (perform an action with the eyes) **look, EYE, gaze, glance, keep an eye on**

ⓒ **before one's EYEs, right now**

a 目前の もくぜんの before one's eyes, imminent

盲目 もうもく blindness

耳目 じもく eyes and ears; one's attention

b 目撃する もくげきする observe, witness, see

目測 もくそく eye measurement

目礼する もくれいする nod, greet

目送する もくそうする follow with one's eyes, gaze after

注目 ちゅうもく attention, notice

一目瞭然の いちもくりょうぜんの quite obvious, as clear as day

c 目下 もっか now, at present

❷ⓐ point, pivot

ⓑ **aim, object, objective**

a 眼目 がんもく main object [point], gist, essence

b 目標 もくひょう mark, target, goal, object

目的 もくてき object, purpose

目的地 もくてきち destination, goal

❸ⓐ [also suffix] **ITEM, subdivision, subitem, category**

ⓑ **counter for ITEMs**

ⓒ **list of ITEMs, list, catalog**

ⓓ **ITEM heading, title, name**

a 項目 こうもく clause, item, provision

種目 しゅもく item; event (as a race)

細目 さいもく details, specified items

科目 かもく school subject; subdivision, items

b 第一目 だいいちもく item one

c 目録 もくろく catalog

目次 もくじ table of contents

品目 ひんもく list of articles [items]

d 曲目 きょくもく number; program, selection (for a concert)

名目 めいもく name, title; pretext

題目 だいもく title, heading; theme; prayer of the Nichiren sect

❹ *biol* order

食肉目 しょくにくもく Carnivora

半翅[×]目 はんしもく Hemiptera

❺ⓐ cross of a go board, go piece

ⓑ counter for crosses of a go board or go pieces

a 小目 こもく cross next to the star

b 一目置く いちもくおく put a stone, give a piece; acknowledge another's superiority

五目の勝ち ごもくのかち win by five crosses

❻ **bearing, attitude**

面目 めんぼく(=めんもく) face, honor, prestige

❼ head, chief

頭目 とうもく chief, head, boss

❽ forecast, estimate, planning for the future

目算 もくさん expectations, anticipation, calculation

目論見 もくろみ plan, scheme; intention

INDEPENDENT

【もく 目】 ITEM, subdivision; *biol* order

同じ目に属する おなじもくにぞくする co-ordinal (animals)

【もくする 目する】 look upon, regard as

KUN

【め 目】

①ⓐ [sometimes also 眼] **EYE; eyesight**

ⓑ **looking, seeing, watching**

ⓒ **look, stare, expression**
ⓓ **point of view**

a 目玉 めだま eyeball; loss leader (of merchandise)
目先 めさき before one's eyes; near future; foresight; appearance
目薬 めぐすり eye lotion, eyewash, eyedrops
目覚める めざめる wake (up); come to one's senses; be awakened
目覚ましい めざましい striking, remarkable, phenomenal; marvelous
目覚まし時計 めざましどけい alarm clock
目眩× めまい dizziness, giddiness
b 目印 めじるし mark, sign, landmark
目処 めど aim, goal; prospects, outlook
お目に掛かる おめにかかる [humble] see, meet; have the honor of seeing
目指す(=目差す) めざす aim for, have an eye on
一目 ひとめ a look, a glimpse
c 非難の目を向ける ひなんのめをむける turn a look of reproach
d 外人の目から見ると がいじんのめからみると from a foreigner's point of view

②ⓐ **watchful EYE, attention, notice**
ⓑ **discerning EYE, judgment, an eye for**

a 目に触れる めにふれる catch the eye, attract attention
目をくらます めをくらます blind the eyes of; deceive
b 目立つ めだつ stand out, be conspicuous
目が効く めがきく have an eye for
大目に見る おおめにみる overlook
素人目 しろうとめ untrained eye

③ experience, treatment
憂き目を見る うきめをみる have a bitter experience, have a hard time of it
酷い目に遇う ひどいめにあう have a bad time

④ (linear pattern) **texture, weave; grain (of wood); mesh (of a net)**
目の粗い めのあらい coarse (texture or grain)
編み目 あみめ stitch
網目 あみめ meshes (of a net)

⑤ **cross of a go board; territory (in a go game)**
相手の目 あいてのめ the opponent's territory
駄目 だめ *go* cross that does not constitute a territory; no good, useless; No!

⑥ pip, spot (of dice); [in compounds] chances (of winning in dice or the like)
裏目 うらめ the reverse side of a dice; disappointment
勝ち目 かちめ good chance of winning

⑦ tooth (of a saw)
目立て めたて setting of a saw

⑧ **graduations (of a scale)**
目盛り めもり division, scale, graduations

⑨ **EYE** (of a typhoon)
台風の目 たいふうのめ eye of a typhoon

⑩ **weight**
目減り めべり loss of weight
目方 めかた weight

⑪ **unclassified compounds**
目安 めやす standard, criterion; aim
お目出度う おめでとう Congratulations!

【-め -目】

① **suffix indicating ordinal numbers or order**
五十年目 ごじゅうねんめ 50th year
二番目 にばんめ second

② adjectival suffix indicating that the quality in question is slightly greater than normal: **rather, -ish, on the (large) side**
軽目 かるめ rather light, lighter
控え目な ひかえめな modest, temperate, reserved

③ **dividing point, border line**
変わり目 かわりめ turning point
切れ目 きれめ rift, gap, break; end, pause, interval

④ momme (匁): unit of weight equiv. to 3.75 g
百目蠟燭 ひゃくめろうそく big candle (weighing 100 momme)

⑤ **degree, extent**
効き目 ききめ effect, efficacy

⑥ **things (to do), role**
役目 やくめ duty, function; role

【ま- 目-】 EYE
目の当たりに まのあたりに before one's eyes; personally; actually
目蓋 まぶた eyelid

SYNONYMS

❶ⓐ face orifices
口 MOUTH → 4189
鼻 NOSE → 3357
耳 EAR → 4329
目 EYE → 3777

❶ⓐ eye
目 EYE → 3777
眼 EYE → 1504
眸 EYE → 1502
瞳 PUPIL → 1583

ⓑ see and look
見 SEE → 3151
看 WATCH → 3992
察 INSPECT → 2961
窺 WATCH FURTIVELY → 3002
瞥 GLANCE AT → 3592
目 look → 3777
観 VIEW → 2359

覧 LOOK OVER → 3538
眺 LOOK OUT OVER → 1503
望 LOOK AFAR → 3408
仰 LOOK UP → 0051
顧 LOOK BACK → 2394
視 REGARD → 1223

❷ⓑ target

的 TARGET → 1444
標 MARK → 1347
狙 AIM → 0406
目 aim → 3777

❸ⓐ parts of writing

章 CHAPTER → 2624
段 passage → 1471
節 paragraph → 3336
款 ARTICLE → 2135
条 ARTICLE → 2726
項 CLAUSE → 0692
目 ITEM → 3777
箇 item → 3348

【-め】

① **kinds of numbers**

数 NUMBER (mathematical unit) → 2245
員 fixed number → 2822
号 NUMBER (numerical designation) → 2675
番 No. → 3416
第 ORDINAL NUMBER PREFIX → 3298
-目 ordinal number suffix → 3777
次 numerical order suffix → 0058
桁 DIGIT → 1165

USAGE

【め】

目

①ⓐ [sometimes also 眼] eye; eyesight
ⓑ looking, seeing, watching
ⓒ look, stare, expression
ⓓ point of view
②ⓐ watchful eye, attention, notice
ⓑ discerning eye, judgment, an eye for
③ experience, treatment
④ (linear pattern) texture, weave; grain (of wood); mesh (of a net)
⑤ cross of a go board; territory (in a go game)
⑥ pip, spot (of dice); [in compounds] chances (of winning in dice or the like)
⑦ tooth (of a saw)
⑧ graduations (of a scale)
⑨ eye (of a typhoon)
⑩ weight
⑪ unclassified compounds

眼

[usu. 目] eye

芽

bud, sprout, germ

HOMOPHONES

め

眼 EYE → 1504
芽 BUD → 2784

目 incorrect classification
➡ see ■4-5-1 at 4297
口3-3-2

四

3778

口3-3-2

▶FOUR

シ よ よ(つ) よっ(つ) よん

Ⓒ 四 sì

31	Jōyō-1	U56DB
口	S5-3-2	F0103

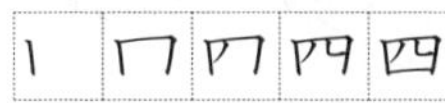

1 2 3 4 5

COMPOUNDS

❶ⓐ FOUR

ⓑ FOUR times

a 四角 しかく square, quadrilateral
四月 しがつ April
四球 しきゅう base on balls
四季 しき the four seasons
四角い しかくい square, four-sided
十四 じゅうし 14

b 再三再四 さいさんさいし again and again

❷ in all directions

四方八方 しほうはっぽう in all directions
四海 しかい the whole world; the seven seas

INDEPENDENT

【し 四】 FOUR; base on balls

KUN

【よ 四】 [in compounds] **FOUR**

四人 よにん four people
四時 よじ four o'clock

【よつ 四つ】 FOUR; 10 o'clock (in former time system); *sumo* **cross grips**

四つ角 よつかど street corner, intersection
四日 よっか four days; 4th of the month

【よっつ 四つ】 FOUR; four years old

四つ目 よっつめ fourth

【よん 四】 FOUR

四回 よんかい four times
四階 よんかい 4th floor

SYNONYMS

❶ⓐ small numbers

一 ONE → 4148
十 TEN → 4172

廿 TWENTY → 4258
二 TWO → 2421
三 THREE → 2423
四 FOUR → 3778
五 FIVE → 4244
六 SIX → 2461
七 SEVEN → 4169
八 EIGHT → 3644
九 NINE → 4176

罒

3779
□ 3-3-2

▶*YONKASHIRA*

122	Radical	U7F52
罒	S5-5-0	F0000

radical variant → see 网 at 3708

迅

3780
□ 3-3-3

▶**SWIFT**
ジン
N 迅 C 迅 xùn

162	Jōyō	U8FC5
辶	S6-3-3	F2200

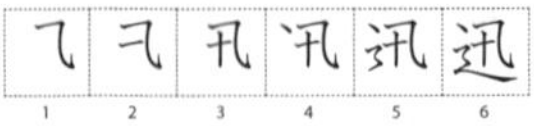

COMPOUNDS

a [original meaning] **SWIFT, fast, rapid**
b sudden, violent

a 迅速な じんそくな swift, rapid
b 迅雷 じんらい sudden peal of thunder, thunderclap
疾風迅雷 しっぷうじんらい swiftly, as quick as the wind and as swift as thunder
獅子奮迅の勢いで ししふんじんのいきおいで with irresistible force

SYNONYMS

a fast
速 QUICK → 3851
早 QUICK → 3042
疾 fast → 4064
快 fast → 0289
急 rapid → 2595
迅 SWIFT → 3780
敏 NIMBLE → 1675
即 IMMEDIATE → 1439
捷 AGILE → 0609

巡

3781
□ 3-3-3

▶**MAKE THE ROUNDS**
ジュン めぐ(る) めぐ(り)
N 巡 C 巡 xún

47	Jōyō	U5DE1
巛	S6-3-3	F1213

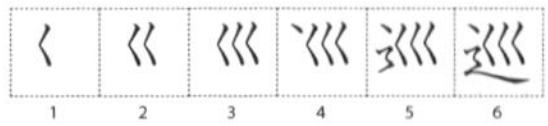

COMPOUNDS

1 MAKE THE ROUNDS, patrol, make a round of inspection, go round
巡査 じゅんさ police, patrolman
巡視 じゅんし inspection tour
巡回 じゅんかい round, patrol
巡洋艦 じゅんようかん cruiser
巡察する じゅんさつする make a round of inspection, patrol
巡航 じゅんこう cruise, cruising
一巡する いちじゅんする make a round

2 tour around, visit, make a pilgrimage
巡業 じゅんぎょう provincial tour
巡歴 じゅんれき tour, trip
巡礼 じゅんれい pilgrimage; pilgrim
巡行 じゅんこう round, patrol, tour
巡拝 じゅんぱい circuit pilgrimage

KUN

【めぐる 巡る】**go round, turn round, revolve; circulate; tour, visit, make a pilgrimage**
巡らす めぐらす enclose (with), surround (with), encircle
巡り歩く めぐりあるく travel around; walk around
巡り会う(=巡り合う) めぐりあう come across, meet by chance

【めぐり 巡り】**going round, circulation; tour; circumference; turn of the fortune wheel, fate**
堂堂巡り どうどうめぐり roll-call vote; going round and round, vicious circle
血の巡り ちのめぐり circulation of blood
お寺巡り おてらめぐり pilgrimage to famous temples

SPECIAL READINGS

お巡りさん おまわりさん policeman

SYNONYMS

1 turn
旋 GYRATE → 1194
転 TURN → 1872
回 TURN ROUND → 3793
廻 TURN ROUND → 3833
巡 MAKE THE ROUNDS → 3781
循 CIRCULATE → 0704
斡 REVOLVE → 2168
捻 TWIST → 0604

2 journey
旅 TRAVEL → 1153
行 trip → 0246
遊 tour → 3896
巡 tour around → 3781

辿
3782
☐3-3-3

▶UP TO
キツ まで

162	Nonstandard	U8FC4
辶	S6-3-3	F0000

alternative form →see 迄 at 3967

辿
3783
☐3-3-3

▶FOLLOW
テン たど(る)

162	Nonstandard	U8FBF
辶	S6-3-3	F0000

traditional form →see 辿 at 3968

迂
3784
☐3-3-3

▶ROUNDABOUT
ウ ㊔ ゆき とお

162	Nonstandard	U8FC2
辶	S6-3-3	F0000

traditional form →see 迂 at 3969

辿迂 etc. incorrect stroke-count
➡ see ☐3-4-3: 辶 at 3967
☐3-3-3

式
3785
☐3-3-3

▶STYLE
▶CEREMONY
シキ
Ⓒ 式 shì

56	Jōyō-3	U5F0F
弋	S6-3-3	F0351

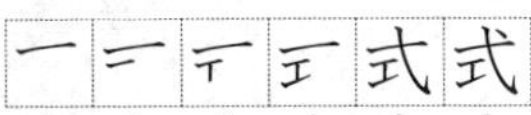
1 2 3 4 5 6

COMPOUNDS

❶ [also suffix]
ⓐ **STYLE, type, form, sort, manner**
ⓑ (way of doing) **STYLE, method, system, way**
a 様式 ようしき mode, manner; style, order
旧式 きゅうしき old style, old type
株式 かぶしき stocks, shares
ドリス式 どりすしき Doric style (architecture)
和式 わしき Japanese style
b 方式 ほうしき formula, mode; method
電動式 でんどうしき electric, electrically operated
ヘボン式ローマ字 へぼんしきろーまじ Hepburn romanization system
山本式 やまもとしき Yamamoto's way (of doing things)

❷ [also suffix] **CEREMONY, rite, rituals, celebration, exercises**
式典 しきてん ceremony
儀式 ぎしき ceremony, rite, ritual
挙式 きょしき holding a ceremony
葬式 そうしき funeral ceremony
結婚式 けっこんしき wedding ceremony
卒業式 そつぎょうしき graduation ceremony

❸ⓐ **form, prescribed regulation, model, law, standard**
ⓑ [also suffix] detailed regulations, code of laws
a 形式 けいしき form, model, formality
正式に せいしきに formally, regularly
略式の りゃくしきの informal, summary
b 律令格式 りつりょうきゃくしき codes of laws and ethics

❹ [also suffix] **formula, expression**
公式 こうしき formula; formality
方程式 ほうていしき equation
無理式 むりしき irrational expression
化学式 かがくしき chemical formula

INDEPENDENT

【しき 式】
①ⓐ **STYLE, type, form, sort, manner**
ⓑ (way of doing) **STYLE, method, system, way**
a ...の式に …のしきに after the fashion [manner] of
他の式の銃 たのしきのじゅう another type of gun
b ...と云った式のやり方 …といったしきのやりかた a method in the style of...
② **CEREMONY, rite, ritual, celebration, exercises**
式を挙げる しきをあげる hold a ceremony
③ⓐ formula, expression, equation
ⓑ *logic* form
a 式を立てる しきをたてる formularize (a theory)

SYNONYMS

❶ **way and style**
風 MANNER →3730
様 MODE →1332
方 WAY →2459
途 WAY →3853
法 METHOD →0391
流 STYLE →0529
式 STYLE →3785
調 TONE →1973

❷ **ceremonies and festivities**
式 CEREMONY →3785
儀 CEREMONY →0191
典 formal ceremony →3253
礼 RITE →1012
斎 religious ritual →2622
会 Buddhist ceremony →2512
祭 FESTIVAL →3311

❸ⓐ **model**
範 MODEL →3360
典 CANON →3253
模 PATTERN →1326
程 ESTABLISHED FORM →1524

辶 辶 弋 【夕】 尸 广 斤 ナ 𠂇 八 冂 口

式 form →3785
準 STANDARD →3541
格 NORM →1161

COMPOUND FORMATION

【株式 かぶしき】

株式 'stocks, shares' signifies the mode (式 ❶ⓐ) of capital investiture, i.e., by stock (株) issuance.

NOTE

★ do not confuse with 弐 TWO →3961

名多 incorrect classification
➡ see ▀2-3-3: 夕 at 2693
□3-3-3

尽

3786
□3-3-3

▶**EXHAUST**

ジン つ(くす) -つ(くす) -づ(くし) つ(きる) つ(かす)

Ⓝ 盡 Ⓒ 尽 jìn jǐn

44△	Jōyō	U5C3D
尸	S6-3-3	F1247

(stroke order) 1 2 3 4 5 6

COMPOUNDS

❶ⓐ **EXHAUST, use up completely, finish**
ⓑ **be EXHAUSTed, come to an end**
ⓒ **EXHAUST** one's days, end one's life, die

a 蕩×尽する とうじんする squander, dissipate
理不尽な りふじんな unreasonable, unjust, absurd
大尽 だいじん millionaire, magnate; seeker of riotous pleasures; last day of 31-day month

b 無尽 むじん inexhaustibility; mutual financing association
無尽蔵 むじんぞう inexhaustible supply

c 自尽 じじん suicide

❷ **use [EXHAUST] all one's strength (in the performance of one's duties), make utmost efforts, exert oneself**

尽力 じんりょく efforts, assistance
尽忠報国 じんちゅうほうこく loyalty and patriotism
不尽 ふじん Yours sincerely

❸ wholly, completely, all

尽日 じんじつ whole day; last day of a month [year]
食尽(=蝕甚) しょくじん maximum eclipse
一網打尽にする いちもうだじんにする catch the whole group with one throw

❹ [suffix] last day of a month

十月尽 じゅうがつじん last day of October

KUN

【つくす 尽くす】 **use [EXHAUST] all one's strength (in the performance of one's duties), make utmost efforts, exert oneself**

心尽くし こころづくし kindness, consideration, solicitude
最善を尽くす さいぜんをつくす do something to the best of one's ability, do one's best
手段を尽くす しゅだんをつくす leave no stone unturned, try everything
人類の為に尽くす じんるいのためにつくす render a service to humanity

【-つくす -尽くす】 [verbal suffix]

ⓐ **EXHAUST, use up completely**
ⓑ **do to the utmost**

a 食べ尽くす たべつくす eat up
言い尽くす いいつくす tell all, exhaust a subject

b し尽くす しつくす do everything possible, exhaust

【-づくし -尽くし】 [also suffix] **full enumeration of**

国尽くし くにづくし enumeration of the names of countries

【つきる 尽きる】 **be EXHAUSTed, be used up, be consumed; come to an end, terminate**

尽き果てる つきはてる be exhausted
尽きない つきない inexhaustible, everlasting
食料が尽きた しょくりょうがつきた The provisions have run out

【つかす 尽かす】 **run out of, use up**

愛想を尽かす あいそをつかす run out of patience, be disgusted with, fall out of love

SYNONYMS

❶ⓐ **consume**

消 SPEND →0531
費 expend →3221
尽 EXHAUST →3786
耗 WEAR AWAY →1660
銷 USE UP →2174

ⓑ **come to an end**

尽 be exhausted →3786
絶 COME TO AN END →1711

❷ & 【つくす】 **exert oneself**

努 EXERT →3154
勉 ENDEAVOR →4113
励 make efforts →1438
勤 work diligently →2287
尽 use all one's strength →3786
精 put one's heart into →1729
孜 MAKE DILIGENT EFFORTS →0284

COMPOUND FORMATION

❶【理不尽 りふじん】

理不尽な 'unreasonable, unjust, absurd' is not (不) fully using (尽 ❶ⓐ) one's reason (理).

❷【不尽 ふじん】

不尽 'Yours sincerely' is a sort of apology for not (不) having made sufficient efforts (尽 ❷) in expressing one's intentions.

屁

3787

☐3-3-3

▶**BUTTOCKS**

コウ しり

44	Nonstandard	U378D
尸	S6-3-3	F0000

traditional form → see 尻 at 3766

庄

3788

☐3-3-3

▶**FEUDAL VILLAGE**

ショウ ソウ ㊔ まさ

Ⓒ 庄 zhuāng

53	Names	U5E84
广	S6-3-3	F1492

COMPOUNDS

❶ⓐ **FEUDAL farm VILLAGE, hamlet or district in Edo period that used to be a manor until the end of Muromachi period**

ⓑ used chiefly in the formation of names of former **FEUDAL VILLAGE**s → see also 荘 2814 ❷

a 庄屋 しょうや village headman

b 院庄 いんのしょう Innosho (place name)

❷ [usu. 荘 2814] manor (in feudal Japan)

庄園 しょうえん manor

❸ [archaic] farmhouse

村庄 そんしょう countryside, village; country house

SYNONYMS

❶ⓐ **villages and towns**

町 TOWN → 1430
村 VILLAGE → 1029
里 hamlet → 4356
郷 HOMETOWN → 0664
庄 FEUDAL VILLAGE → 3788
邑 VILLAGE → 2716

NOTE

★ do not confuse with 圧 PRESSURE → 3688

后

☐3-3-3

incorrect classification
➡ see ☐3-2-4: 厂 at 3701

衣

☐3-3-3

incorrect classification
➡ see ⬒2-2-4: 亠 at 2506

在存

☐3-3-3

incorrect classification
➡ see ☐3-2-4: ナ at 3702

瓜

3789

☐3-3-3

▶**GOURD**

カ うり

Ⓝ 瓜◇ Ⓒ 瓜 guā

97	Names	U74DC
瓜	S6-6-0	F2285

radical variant → see 瓜 at 3772

COMPOUNDS

● [original meaning] **GOURD, melon**

瓜田に履を納れず かでんにくつをいれず Refrain from doing anything that may incur suspicion

西瓜(=水瓜) すいか watermelon

冬瓜 とうが(=とうがん) wax gourd, winter melon

破瓜 はか age 16 (for girls), age 64 (for men); deflowering

KUN

【うり 瓜】**GOURD, melon**

瓜科 うりか gourd family, *Cucurbitaceae*

瓜二つ うりふたつ as alike as two peas

瓜実顔 うりざねがお oval face

瓜坊 うりぼう wild boar piglet

苦瓜 にがうり bitter melon

真桑瓜 まくわうり Oriental melon, *Cucumis melo* var. *makuwa*

SPECIAL READINGS

南瓜 かぼちゃ pumpkin

胡瓜(=黄瓜) きゅうり cucumber

糸瓜(=天糸瓜) へちま sponge gourd, dishcloth gourd, loofah; sponge cucumber; something useless

木瓜 ぼけ flowering quince, *Chaenomeles speciosa*

SYNONYMS

【うり】

○ **vegetables**

菜 greens → 2880
蕪 TURNIP → 2990
芋 POTATO → 2706
豆 BEAN → 2442
蕗 BUTTERBUR → 3007
茄 EGGPLANT → 2787
芹 JAPANESE PARSLEY → 2742
瓜 GOURD → 3789
瓢 BOTTLE GOURD → 2356
芥 mustard → 2741

COMPOUND FORMATION

【破瓜 はか】

破瓜 'age 16 (for girls), age 64 (for men), etc.' is so called because the character 瓜 can be broken apart (破) into two parts, each resembling 八 'eight'.

NOTE

★ do not confuse with 爪 NAIL → 3756

瓜

☐3-3-3

incorrect stroke-count
➡ see ☐3-3-2: 𠂢 at 3772

向

▶TURN TOWARD

コウ む(く) む(き) -む(き) む(ける) -む(け) む(かう) む(こう) む(こう)-

3790

□3-3-3

ⓒ 向 xiàng

30	Jōyō-3	U5411
口	S6-3-3	F0119

丿 丨丿 冂 向 向 向
1 2 3 4 5 6

COMPOUNDS

❶ⓐ TURN TOWARD, face, look toward
  ⓑ turn (one's heart or mind) to
  ⓒ (meet face to face) **face, confront**

a 向日性 こうじつせい disposition (in flowers) to turn toward the sun, heliotropism
b 向上心 こうじょうしん ambition, aspiration
向学心 こうがくしん desire for learning, intellectual appetite
c 向寒 こうかん facing the winter
対向車 たいこうしゃ car (running) on the opposite lane

❷ head toward, go toward, proceed to
向心力 こうしんりょく central force, centripetal force
出向する しゅっこうする proceed to, leave for, be temporarily transferred to
下向する げこうする go away from the capital, go down (to a province)

❸ direction, orientation
方向 ほうこう direction, bearing; course
転向 てんこう turn, conversion, about-face
指向する しこうする point to
風向 ふうこう direction of the wind
偏向 へんこう deviation, deflection

❹ [formerly also 嚮 3610] **tendency, inclination, turn**
傾向 けいこう tendency, trend; disposition
意向 いこう intention, inclination
動向 どうこう trend, tendency, movement
性向 せいこう inclination, disposition
趣向 しゅこう idea, contrivance, plan

❺ pro-
向米的な こうべいてきな pro-American

❻ in the future
向後 こうご hence(forth), hereafter

KUN

【むく 向く】 *vi* **face, front, look upon; TURN TOWARD, look toward; tend toward, be inclined to; suit, be fit, be geared for**
北に向いた窓 きたにむいたまど window to the north
上向く うわむく look upward; turn upward, rise
運が向く うんがむく be in luck's way
気が向かない きがむかない be not inclined (to do)
教師に向いている きょうしにむいている be cut out for a teacher

【むき 向き】
①ⓐ **direction, turn**
ⓑ (manner of facing) aspect, exposure, situation
a 風の向き かぜのむき direction of the wind
b 家の向き いえのむき aspect of a house
② suitability
向き不向きが有る むきふむきがある have one's own field of work
③ purport, intention, inclination
その向きを伝える そのむきをつたえる tell (a person) the purport as such
④ those (who), some people
御希望の向きは ごきぼうのむきは those who want it
⑤ [followed by に成る になる] become serious, get hot
向きに成って怒る むきになっておこる flare up

【-むき -向き】
① **facing toward**
前向きに まえむきに facing forward; positively, constructively
② [suffix] suitable for, fit for
万人向きである ばんにんむきである suit all tastes

【むける 向ける】 *vt* **TURN TOWARD, look toward; point at, aim at, direct; send (a messenger) to; apply, appropriate**
背を向ける せをむける turn one's back on, pretend not to see
仰向ける あおむける turn up (one's face)
我我に向けられた非難 われわれにむけられたひなん criticism leveled against us
差し向ける さしむける send, dispatch
振り向ける ふりむける apply [appropriate] (money) toward

【-むけ -向け】 [suffix] **(bound) for, meant for**
国内向けの こくないむけの for domestic use

【むかう 向かう】 *vi* **face, front, look upon; confront, oppose; head toward, go toward, proceed to; near, approach**
向かい むかい opposite side
向かって左に むかってひだりに on the left as one faces (it)
向かい風 むかいかぜ head wind, adverse wind
立ち向かう たちむかう stand against; head for
. . . に向かっている …にむかっている be going (toward), be headed (for)
寒さに向かうと さむさにむかうと as winter approaches

【むこう 向こう】 **the other side, the opposite direction; the other party; opponent; abroad, overseas; beyond, across; destination**
向こう側 むこうがわ other side

向こうから来る むこうからくる come from the opposite direction
向こうが悪い むこうがわるい He is in the wrong
向こうに回して むこうにまわして in opposition to
向こうで暮らす むこうでくらす live overseas
向こうに着いたら むこうについたら when you get to the destination

【むこう- 向こう-】[prefix]
① (days) **to come, coming, next**
向こう十日間 むこうとおかかん for the next ten days
② facing, opposite
向こう三軒 むこうさんげん three houses on the opposite side

SYNONYMS

❶ **face**
向 TURN TOWARD → 3790
面 FACE → 2590
対 face (each other) → 1025

❷ **go and come**
行 GO → 0246
徠 COME → 0576
往 GO ON → 0348
出 go to → 4310
参 go somewhere → 2563
来 COME → 4366
通 go to and from → 3855
向 head toward → 3790
赴 PROCEED TO → 4095
嚮 GO TOWARD → 3610

❸ **direction**
方 DIRECTION → 2459
向 direction → 3790

❹ **tendency**
向 tendency → 3790
性 NATURE → 0357
勢 trend → 3542
傾 inclination → 0174
潮 TIDE → 0916
流 CURRENT → 0529

【-むけ】
○ **direction indicators**
至 to → 2707
-行き bound for → 0246
-向け (bound) for → 3790
迄 UP TO → 3967
以 TO THE…OF → 0045
自 from → 4338
来 since → 4366
而 DIRECTION WORD → 2520

団

▶**BODY**
ダン トン
Ⓝ 團 Ⓒ 团 tuán

3791
口 3-3-3

31	Jōyō-5	U56E3
口	S6-3-3	F0333

丨 冂 冃 団 団 団
1 2 3 4 5 6

COMPOUNDS

❶ⓐ [also suffix] (collective group) **BODY, corps, group, party**
ⓑ **gather in one BODY, form a group**
a 団体 だんたい group, party, body, corps; corporation, organization
団長 だんちょう leader [head] of a body [party]
団交 だんこう collective bargaining
集団 しゅうだん group, body, mass, crowd
一団 いちだん body, group, party, troupe
星団 せいだん star cluster
観光団 かんこうだん sightseeing party
外交団 がいこうだん diplomatic corps [body]
顧問団 こもんだん advisory body
b 団地 だんち (public) housing development
団結 だんけつ unity, union, solidarity

❷ (organized entity) **BODY, corporation, organization, association**
公団 こうだん public corporation
劇団 げきだん dramatic company, theatrical troupe
師団 しだん army division
社団 しゃだん corporation, association
財団 ざいだん foundation, consortium, endowment; syndicate
軍団 ぐんだん army corps, corps
経団連(=経済団体連合会) けいだんれん(=けいざいだんたいれんごうかい) Federation of Economic Organizations

❸ⓐ [original meaning] **round**
ⓑ perfect; harmonious
a 団子 だんご dumpling
布団 ふとん [sometimes also 蒲団] *futon*, bedquilt
大団円 だいだんえん (grand) finale, dénouement, conclusion
b 団欒× だんらん family circle; harmony

INDEPENDENT

【だん 団】(collective group) **BODY**, corps, group, party
団の精神 だんのせいしん spirit of the corps, esprit de corps

SYNONYMS

❶ⓐ **groups**
群 GROUP (of any kind) → 1942
班 SQUAD → 1182
軍 team → 2582

組 group (of people) →1693
陣 lineup →0545
連 set →3849
族 common-interest group (*slang*) →1195
党 PARTY →3190
隊 PARTY (organized group) →0762
団 BODY →3791
伍 ranks →0050
❷ **organized bodies**
会 SOCIETY →2512
協 association →0103
団 BODY →3791
体 BODY →0080
組 union →1693
労 workers' union →3155
連 federation →3849
講 fraternity →2046
院 INSTITUTION →0544

COMPOUND FORMATION

【布団 ふとん】
布団 '*futon*, bedquilt' originally referred to a round (団 ❸ⓐ) mat made of cattail (布). 布 is a phonetic substitute for 蒲 'cattail'.

因

3792
口3-3-3

▶CAUSE
イン よ(る) ちな(む)▲
Ⓒ 因 yīn

31	Jōyō-5	U56E0
口	S6-3-3	F0821

Stroke order: 1 2 3 4 5 6

COMPOUNDS

❶ⓐ CAUSE, reason, origin, factor
ⓑ *Buddhism* **direct CAUSE, connection, relation, affinity**
a 因果 いんが cause and effect; karma
因子 いんし *math* factor
因数 いんすう *math* factor
死因 しいん cause of death
原因 げんいん cause, origin
要因 よういん primary factor, main cause
b 因縁 いんねん karma, fate; direct and indirect causes; connection, affinity; pretext; origin
❷ follow (customs), be based on
因習(=因襲) いんしゅう conventions
❸ abbrev. of 因幡 いなば, old name for east Tottori Prefecture
因美線 いんびせん Inbi Line (East Okayama Railway)

INDEPENDENT

【いん 因】**CAUSE**, origin, factor
因をなす いんをなす cause, give rise to

KUN

【よる 因る】[formerly also 由る] **be CAUSEd by, be due to**
風邪に因る発熱 かぜによるはつねつ fever caused by a cold
【ちなむ 因む】be related, be connected
因みに ちなみに in this connection, by the way
それは仏教に因んでいる それはぶっきょうにちなんでいる It comes from Buddhism

SYNONYMS

❶ⓐ cause and reason
因 CAUSE →3792
由 REASON →4311
為 because →4395
故 reason →1466
訳 reason →1865

USAGE

【よる】
因る
[formerly also 由る] be caused by, be due to
由る
[now usu. 因る] be caused by, be due to
依る
① depend on, rely on, hang on
② do by (means of), resort to, have recourse to
拠る
① be based on, be grounded on
② occupy (a fortress), hold
寄る
①ⓐ draw near, draw up, come near, approach
ⓑ draw aside, step aside
② draw together, come together, gather, meet
③ drop in, call on
④ increase, gain
⑤ lean on, rest against
⑥ *sumo* push one's opponent while holding his belt
⑦ (of the stock market) open

HOMOPHONES

よる
由 REASON →4311
依 DEPEND ON →0093
拠 GROUNDS →0369
寄 CONTRIBUTE →2856

NOTE

★ do not confuse with 困 BE IN TROUBLE →3808

回

3793

口3-3-3

▸**TURN ROUND**
▸**TIME**

カイ エ まわ(る) -まわ(る) -まわ(り) まわ(す) -まわ(す) まわ(し)- -まわ(し)

㊔ めぐり

Ⓝ 囬◇ 囘◇ Ⓒ 回 huí

31	Jōyō-2	U56DE
口	S6-3-3	F0141

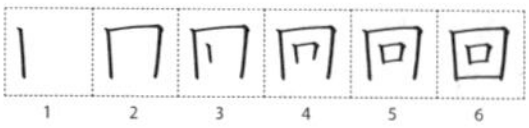

COMPOUNDS

❶ [formerly 廻 かい 3833]
ⓐ [original meaning] **TURN ROUND, revolve, rotate, circulate**
ⓑ **go round, make the rounds; circulate, make a circular tour**

a 回転する かいてんする revolve, rotate, turn
転回 てんかい turning over; revolution, rotation
旋回 せんかい revolution, rotation, circling, swiveling
b 回診 かいしん make a round of visits (to one's patients)
回路 かいろ (electric) circuit
回覧する かいらんする circulate, send round
巡回する じゅんかいする go round, make the rounds, patrol
徘×回(=徘×徊)する はいかいする loiter, wander about

❷ [formerly also 廻 かい, え 3833]
ⓐ **turn back, return, come round**
ⓑ **turn (something) back, return, reply, bring back**

a 回復 かいふく [formerly also 恢復] recovery, restoration; rehabilitation
回帰 かいき revolution, recurrence, regression
回忌 かいき death anniversary
回向 えこう Buddhist memorial service
輪回 りんね *Buddhism* transmigration of souls, *saṃsāra*
b 回答 かいとう reply, answer
回収する かいしゅうする collect, recover; withdraw
回心 かいしん(=えしん) conversion
撤回する てっかいする withdraw, retract

❸ [formerly 廻 かい 3833] send round, forward, transport
回送 かいそう forwarding
回漕業 かいそうぎょう shipping business
回船 かいせん lighter, cargo vessel

❹ **turn one's thoughts back to, look back, retrospect**
回想 かいそう recollection, reminiscence
回顧する かいこする look back on, retrospect

❺ turn away, avert, avoid
回避する かいひする evade, dodge, avoid
迂回する うかいする take a long way around, make a detour

❻ⓐ [also suffix] **TIME; round, game; inning**
ⓑ **counter for number of TIMEs, rounds or innings**

a 回数 かいすう frequency, number of times
回数券 かいすうけん book of tickets
今回 こんかい this time; lately
最終回 さいしゅうかい last time; last inning
b 百回 ひゃっかい 100 times
八回裏 はちかいうら second half of the eighth inning

❼ Mohammedanism, Islam
回教 かいきょう Mohammedanism, Islam

❽ *anat* gyrus, convolution
海馬回 かいばかい hippocampal gyrus

❾ *music* volta
二回 にかい *due volte*

❿ [formerly 蛔 かい 1717] roundworm, ascarid
回虫 かいちゅう roundworm, ascarid

INDEPENDENT

【かい 回】**TIME**, round; inning
回を重ねる かいをかさねる repeat; (of a baseball game) advance
次の回 つぎのかい next time; next inning

KUN

【まわる 回る】[formerly 廻る]
①ⓐ **TURN ROUND, revolve, rotate**
ⓑ **go round, circulate, make a round**
ⓒ **detour, go round (to)**

a 回り まわり rotation; detour; close surroundings; spreading (of flames); efficacy
回り舞台 まわりぶたい rotative stage
b 見回る みまわる make one's rounds
c 回りくどい まわりくどい roundabout, circuitous, indirect
回り道 まわりみち roundabout [long] way, detour

② **swing over to, come round to, be transferred**
反対に回る はんたいにまわる go into opposition

③ be past (a certain hour)
もう十一時を回った もうじゅういちじをまわった It is already past 11

④ pass (from hand to hand), circulate, spread; take effect
火が回る ひがまわる Fire spreads
酔いが回る よいがまわる get drunk, become tipsy

⑤ yield interest
利回り りまわり (investment) yield, interest, profits

【-まわる -回る】[verbal suffix]
① **about, around, to and fro**

歩き回る あるきまわる walk about, walk to and fro, pace around
飛び回る とびまわる fly about, jump about, rush around
出回る でまわる appear on the market, be moving
②reach, attain
上回る うわまわる exceed, be more than
下回る したまわる be less than, fall below

【-まわり -回り】[also suffix]
①ⓐ **indicates direction of turning**
ⓑ **counter for rounds**
a 時計回りの とけいまわりの clockwise
西回り にしまわり west circuit
b 三回り みまわり three rounds
② **a size (larger or smaller)**
一回り小さな ひとまわりちいさな a size smaller
③ **via, by way of**
欧州回りで合衆国へ行く おうしゅうまわりでがっしゅうこくへいく go to the U.S. via Europe
④cycle of 12 years
彼は私より一回り若い かれはわたくしよりひとまわりわかい He is my junior by 12 years
⑤girth, circumference
胴回り どうまわり girth

【まわす 回す】[formerly 廻す]
① **TURN (ROUND), rotate**
独楽を回す こまをまわす spin a top
②ⓐ **send [pass] around, circulate; forward, transfer**
ⓑ send round, forward, transfer
a 回し まわし sumo wrestler's loincloth; gang rape
塩を回して下さい しおをまわしてください Pass me the salt, please
③lend money at interest
金を上手く回す かねをうまくまわす invest one's money profitably
④arrange, prepare
手回し てまわし preparations
⑤perform gang rape

【-まわす -回す】[emphatic verbal suffix] **about, around**
追い回す おいまわす chase about, follow about
乗り回す のりまわす drive about, ride around
言い回し いいまわし expression, manner [turn] of expression
掻き回す かきまわす stir (up); ransack, throw into confusion

【まわし- 回し-】
① **by turns, alternately**
回し飲み まわしのみ drinking in turn from one cup
回し読み まわしよみ reading a book in turn
②turning, swivel
回し金 まわしがね lathe dog

【-まわし -回し】 **turning, rotating**
ねじ回し ねじまわし screwdriver
盥[×]回し たらいまわし passing the buck; balancing a spinning washtub

SYNONYMS

❶ **turn**
旋 GYRATE → 1194
転 TURN → 1872
回 TURN ROUND → 3793
廻 TURN ROUND → 3833
巡 MAKE THE ROUNDS → 3781
循 CIRCULATE → 0704
斡 REVOLVE → 2168
捻 TWIST → 0604

❷ⓐ **return**
帰 RETURN → 0148
還 RETURN → 3945
回 turn back → 3793
廻 turn back → 3833
戻る RETURN → 2441
復 RETURN TO → 0701

❸ **send**
送 SEND → 3837
投 SEND IN → 0300
回 send round → 3793
遣 DISPATCH → 3908
派 DISPATCH → 0456

❻ **time and time counters**
回 TIME → 3793
度 TIME → 3844
遍 counter for number of times → 3890
返 counter for number of times → 3797

USAGE

❶【まわる】
回る
[formerly 廻る]
①ⓐturn round, revolve, rotate
ⓑgo round, circulate, make a round
ⓒdetour, go round (to)
②swing over to, come round to, be transferred
③be past (a certain hour)
④pass (from hand to hand), circulate, spread; take effect
⑤yield interest
廻る
[now usu. 回る] same as 回る

❷【まわり】
回り
[formerly 廻り]
①ⓐrotation

ⓑ detour
② close surroundings
③ spreading (of flames)
④ efficacy
廻り
[now usu. 回り] same as 回り
周り
ⓐ periphery, surroundings, circumference
ⓑ border, fringe
❸【まわす】
回す
[formerly 廻す]
① turn (round), rotate
②ⓐ send [pass] around, circulate; forward, transfer
ⓑ send round, forward, transfer
③ lend money at interest
④ arrange, prepare
⑤ perform gang rape
廻す
[now usu. 回す] same as 回す

HOMOPHONES

まわる 廻 TURN ROUND →3833
まわり
廻 TURN ROUND →3833
周 PERIPHERY →3720
まわす 廻 TURN ROUND →3833

延

3794
口3-3-4

▶EXTEND
▶POSTPONE
エン の(びる) の(べる) の(べ) の(ばす)
㊔ のぶ

54	Nonstandard	U5EF6
廴	S7-3-4	F0000

traditional form →see 延 at 3812

廷

3795
口3-3-4

▶COURT
テイ
Ⓒ 廷 tíng

54	Jōyō	U5EF7
廴	S7-3-4	F1458

Stroke order: 1 ㇀ 2 二 3 千 4 壬 5 ㇋壬 6 廷 7 廷

COMPOUNDS

❶ [also suffix] **COURT of law**
廷内で ていないで in the court
法廷 ほうてい law court
開廷 かいてい opening of a court, trial
出廷 しゅってい appearance in court
公判廷 こうはんてい court, public trial court
❷ [rarely also 庭 3866] **COURT, Imperial Court**
廷臣 ていしん court official
朝廷 ちょうてい Imperial Court
宮廷 きゅうてい the Court, the Palace

SYNONYMS

❶ **court**
廷 COURT →3795
裁 court →4090
❷ **governments**
官 GOVERNMENT →2766
幕 SHOGUNATE →2937
廷 COURT →3795
朝 court →2130
宮 Imperial Court →2828

NOTE

★ do not confuse with 延 EXTEND →3812

迎

3796
口3-3-4

▶WELCOME
ゲイ むか(える)
Ⓝ 迎 Ⓒ 迎 yíng

162	Jōyō	U8FCE
⻌	S7-3-4	F0827

Stroke order: 1 ノ 2 𠂉 3 卬 4 卬 5 ゛卬 6 迎 7 迎

COMPOUNDS

❶ⓐ **WELCOME, greet, receive**
ⓑ [original meaning] **go (out) to meet, meet face to face**
a 迎賓 げいひん welcoming guests
歓迎する かんげいする welcome
送迎する そうげいする welcome and send off
b 迎撃 げいげき interception, counter
❷ flatter, curry favor with
迎合する げいごうする flatter, curry favor with, ingratiate oneself with

KUN

【むかえる 迎える】**WELCOME, greet, receive, play host; meet, go out to meet; invite, call, send for; meet (an occasion); cater to, ingratiate**
迎え むかえ meeting; person sent to pick up an arrival
迎え酒 むかえざけ another drink in the morning
迎え入れる むかえいれる receive (a person), usher
迎え撃つ むかえうつ fight the attack of an enemy
意を迎える いをむかえる cater to another's wish

SYNONYMS

❶ⓐ **treat and welcome**
遇 TREAT →3889
待 treat →0434
扱う HANDLE →0251
款 treat cordially →2135

夂 夊 【辶】 辶 尸 广 门 匚 口

接 receive → 0607
迎 WELCOME → 3796

返 3797

□3-3-4

▶RETURN
ヘン かえ(す) -かえ(す) かえ(る) -かえ(る)
Ⓝ 返 Ⓒ 返 fǎn

162	Jōyō-3	U8FD4
辶	S7-3-4	F0263

一 厂 万 反 `反 㱿 返 (1 2 3 4 5 6 7)

COMPOUNDS

❶ⓐ RETURN, give back, send back, repay
ⓑ [original meaning] **RETURN, go back**

a 返還 へんかん return, restoration, repayment
返上する へんじょうする return, send back
返戻する へんれいする return, give back
返品 へんぴん returning goods; returned goods, article sent back
返送する へんそうする send back, return
返却 へんきゃく return
返金 へんきん repayment
返報 へんぽう requital, retaliation, revenge

❷ reply, answer
返信 へんしん reply, answer
返事 へんじ answer, reply
返電 へんでん reply telegram
返答 へんとう reply, answer

❸ [usu. 遍 3890] counter for number of times
二返 にへん two times

INDEPENDENT

【へん 返】 abbrev. of 返事 へんじ: reply (in telegrams)

KUN

【かえす 返す】
①ⓐ **RETURN, send back, put back, give back, repay**
ⓑ **RETURN (a kindness), repay**
a お返し おかえし return present; answer, reply; revenge; change (for money)
b 恩返し おんがえし repaying another's kindness
② dismiss, discharge, divorce

【-かえす -返す】 [verbal suffix]
① **do over, redo, re-**
繰り返す くりかえす repeat, do over again
読み返す よみかえす reread, read again
②ⓐ **do back, do in RETURN**
ⓑ **take back, recover**
a 仕返し しかえし doing over, tit for tat, revenge
言い返す いいかえす talk back, retort
b 取り返す とりかえす take back, regain
引き返す ひきかえす turn back, retrace one's steps
③ **turn over, overturn, reverse**
ひっくり返す ひっくりかえす turn over, upset
裏返す うらがえす turn over, turn inside out

【かえる 返る】
① **be restored to, RETURN to (the original state)**
返り咲き かえりざき second bloom; a comeback (in business)
振り返る ふりかえる turn one's head, turn round
生き返る いきかえる revive, come to oneself; be restored to life
② be given back

【-かえる -返る】 [also -反る] [emphatic verbal suffix]
utterly, completely
静まり返る しずまりかえる become still as death
呆れ返る あきれかえる be utterly amazed

SYNONYMS

❶ⓐ return and restore
返 RETURN → 3797
戻 RETURN → 2441
還 RETURN → 3945
復 RETURN TO → 0701
蘇 REVIVE → 3032
甦 REVIVE → 4109

❷ answer
答 ANSWER → 3322
解 solve → 1913
返 reply → 3797
応 RESPOND → 3804

❸ time and time counters
回 TIME → 3793
度 TIME → 3844
遍 counter for number of times → 3890
返 counter for number of times → 3797

【-かえす】
① **repeating and repetition**
再 ANOTHER TIME → 4332
又 AGAIN → 4158
復 repeat → 0701
重 DUPLICATE → 4390
畳 reduplicate → 3205
改 redo → 0287
-換える redo → 0716
-直す repetition suffix → 3649
-返す do over → 3797

USAGE

❶【かえす】
返す
①ⓐ return, send back, put back, give back, repay
ⓑ return (a kindness), repay
② dismiss, discharge, divorce

-返す

[verbal suffix]

① do over, redo, re-

②ⓐ do back, do in return

ⓑ take back, recover

③ turn over, overturn, reverse

帰す

let (someone) return, see out, send (someone) home, dismiss

反す

vt turn over, overturn, upset, reverse

★In the sense of overturn, かえす should be written 反す, though this reading is not approved. However, as a verbal suffix meaning to overturn, かえす is written 返す, as in 裏返す うらがえす 'turn over, turn inside out'.

❷【-かえる】

-返る

[also -反る] [emphatic verbal suffix] utterly, completely

-反る

[also -返る] same as -返る

HOMOPHONES

かえす

帰 RETURN →0148

反 COUNTER →3663

かえる

帰 RETURN →0148

反 COUNTER →3663

還 RETURN →3945

-かえる 反 COUNTER →3663

NOTE

➡ see also USAGE note at 帰 0148

近

▶NEAR
▶RECENT

キン コン▲ ちか(い)

3798

□3-3-4

Ⓝ 近 Ⓒ 近 jìn

162	Jōyō-2	U8FD1
辶	S7-3-4	F0127

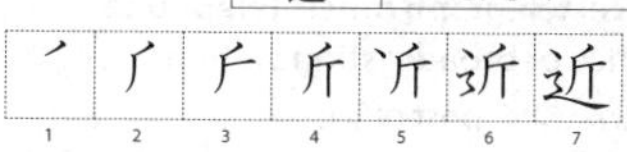

COMPOUNDS

❶ⓐ (close in space) **NEAR, close, nearby, neighboring**

ⓑ [original meaning] (come close) **NEAR, approach**

a 近視 きんし nearsightedness, shortsightedness

近郊 きんこう suburbs, outskirts

近所 きんじょ neighborhood

近隣 きんりん neighborhood

近県 きんけん neighboring prefectures

近距離 きんきょり short distance

付近 ふきん neighborhood, environs, vicinity

b 接近する せっきんする approach, draw near, come close

❷ (close in time) **RECENT, near, modern**

近況 きんきょう recent condition [situation]

近影 きんえい one's recent photograph

近年 きんねん recent years, late years

近世 きんせい modern ages

近代 きんだい modern [recent] times

近代的な きんだいてきな modern

近日 きんじつ soon, shortly, one of these days

最近の さいきんの late, recent

❸ (close in relationship) **NEAR**, close, personal; intimate

近親 きんしん near relative

近衛 このえ Imperial Guards

親近感 しんきんかん feeling of intimacy

側近 そっきん close associate, aide

❹ abbrev. of 近畿 きんき: Kinki district

近鉄 きんてつ Kinki Nippon Railway

KUN

【ちかい 近い】**NEAR (in space), close, not far; near (in time), early, soon; near (in relationship), close; akin to, close to**

近さ ちかさ nearness

近くの ちかくの nearby, neighboring

近付く ちかづく approach, near, get near; get acquainted

近付ける ちかづける bring [put] close (to)

近寄せる ちかよせる bring close to

近道 ちかみち shortcut

近頃 ちかごろ recently, nowadays

身近な みぢかな near oneself, close to one, familiar

SYNONYMS

❶ⓐ **near**

近 NEAR →3798

隣 neighboring →0961

傍 BESIDE →0166

旁 BESIDE →2598

沿 ALONG →0386

ⓑ **approach**

寄る DRAW NEAR →2856

迫 PRESS →3815

近 NEAR →3798

接 come close to →0607

拶 PRESS →0451

❷ **recent**

近 RECENT →3798

新 NEW →2239

❸ **familiar and friendly**

親 INTIMATE →2264

密 CLOSE →2857

近 NEAR → 3798
睦 FRIENDLY → 1534
懇 FAMILIAR → 3606
和 HARMONIOUS → 1450

近返 etc. incorrect stroke-count
➡ see □3-4-3: 辶 at 3967
□3-3-4

尾

3799
□3-3-4

▶TAIL
ビ お
Ⓒ 尾 wěi yǐ

44	Jōyō	U5C3E
尸	S7-3-4	F0647

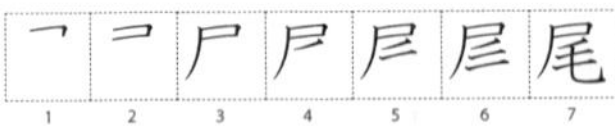

COMPOUNDS

❶ⓐ [original meaning] **TAIL**
ⓑ buttocks
a 有尾類 ゆうびるい tailed amphibians
b 尾骶×骨 びていこつ coccyx
❷ⓐ (rear part) **TAIL, rear**
ⓑ **end**
a 尾部 びぶ tail, tail section
尾翼 びよく tail, tail plane
尾灯 びとう taillight
尾行 びこう following, shadowing
船尾 せんび stern, poop
b 首尾 しゅび beginning and end; result, issue
竜頭蛇尾 りゅうとうだび bright start, dull finish
巻尾 かんび end of a book
末尾 まつび end, close
語尾 ごび ending of a word
❸ counter for fish
鮪×二十尾 まぐろにじゅうび 20 tunnies
❹ copulate, mate
交尾 こうび copulation, coupling
❺ abbrev. of 尾張 おわり, old name for west Aichi Prefecture
濃尾平野 のうびへいや Nobi Plain

KUN

【お 尾】**TAIL, scut, caudal fin; trail (as of a meteor); ridge**
尾長猿 おながざる long-tailed monkey
尾頭付き おかしらつき fish served whole [complete with head and tail]
尾鰭× おひれ(=おびれ) tail and fin
尾を引く おをひく leave a trail; leave a lasting effect
尾根 おね mountain ridge

SPECIAL READINGS

尻尾 しっぽ tail; one's true colors

SYNONYMS

❶ⓐ **body projections**
角 HORN → 2541
尾 TAIL → 3799
❷ⓐ **rear**
後 after- → 0431
背 BACK → 3182
裏 REAR → 2652
尻 tail end → 3766
尾 TAIL → 3799
ⓑ **ends**
末 LAST PART → 4317
終 END → 1692
畢 END → 3194
尾 end → 3799
局 close → 3800

局

3800
□3-3-4

▶BUREAU
▶LIMITED PART
キョク つぼね▲
Ⓒ 局 jú

44	Jōyō-3	U5C40
尸	S7-3-4	F0441

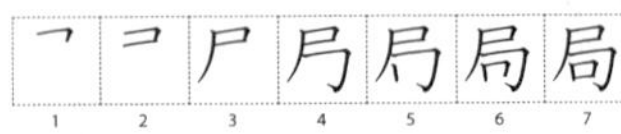

COMPOUNDS

❶ [also suffix] **BUREAU, department (esp. of a government office)**
局長 きょくちょう bureau chief, director, postmaster
部局 ぶきょく department, bureau
水道局 すいどうきょく Water Works Bureau
法制局 ほうせいきょく Legislative Bureau
総務局 そうむきょく General Affairs Bureau
薬局 やっきょく drugstore, pharmacy
事務局 じむきょく secretariat
当局 とうきょく the authorities concerned
❷ [also suffix] **public service office or station, as a post office, telegraph office, telephone exchange office or broadcasting station**
郵便局 ゆうびんきょく post office
電報局 でんぽうきょく telegraph office
放送局 ほうそうきょく radio broadcasting station
支局 しきょく branch office
テレビ局 てれびきょく TV station
電話局 でんわきょく telephone exchange office
❸ [suffix] telephone office number, exchange number
４２局２０１２番 よんじゅうにきょくにせんじゅうにばん 42-2012 (phone number)
❹ **LIMITED PART, portion (of space), locality**
局限する きょくげんする localize, limit, set limits to

局部 きょくぶ limited part, section; affected part
局所 きょくしょ (limited) part, section
局地的 きょくちてき local

❺ current situation, state of affairs

局面 きょくめん situation, aspect of an affair; position (in a chess game)
時局 じきょく situation, circumstances
戦局 せんきょく state of the war, war situation
難局 なんきょく difficult [delicate] situation, deadlock
政局 せいきょく political situation

❻ close, end, conclusion

終局 しゅうきょく end, conclusion, termination; end of a game
結局 けっきょく after all, finally, in conclusion

❼ⓐ board game (as chess or shogi)
ⓑ counter for board games

a 対局 たいきょく game of go [shogi]
b 一局 いっきょく a game (of go or shogi)
チェス十二局 ちぇすじゅうにきょく 12 chess games

INDEPENDENT

【きょく 局】**BUREAU, department; public service office (→ ❷); affair, situation; close, end, conclusion**

局に当たる きょくにあたる take charge of an affair, deal with a situation
局を結ぶ きょくをむすぶ come to a close [an end], be settled
同じ局 おなじきょく same (radio) station

KUN

【つぼね 局】apartment of a court lady; court lady, lady in waiting

SYNONYMS

❶ divisions of organizations

課 SECTION → 1980
部 department → 2111
局 BUREAU → 3800

❷ public offices

省 MINISTRY → 3100
庁 GOVERNMENT AGENCY → 3768
府 government office → 3824
公 public office → 2468
署 PUBLIC-SERVICE STATION → 3223
局 public service office → 3800
所 office → 1056

❹ part

分 PART → 2466
部 SECTION → 2111
局 LIMITED PART → 3800
片 FRAGMENT → 4272

❺ states and situations

態 STATE → 3529
調 TONE → 1973
様 MODE → 1332
相 PHASE → 1120
状 CONDITION → 0322
況 CONDITIONS → 0395
景 business conditions → 3118
勢 course of events → 3542
境 SITUATION → 0835
局 current situation → 3800
情 ACTUAL CONDITIONS → 0583
訳 circumstances → 1865

❻ ends

末 LAST PART → 4317
終 END → 1692
畢 END → 3194
尾 end → 3799
局 close → 3800

❼ board games

局 board game → 3800
棋 SHOGI → 1242
碁 GO → 3346
雀 MAHJONG → 3117

尿

3801

口3-3-4

▶URINE

ニョウ

Ⓒ 尿 niào suī

44	Jōyō	U5C3F
尸	S7-3-4	F1748

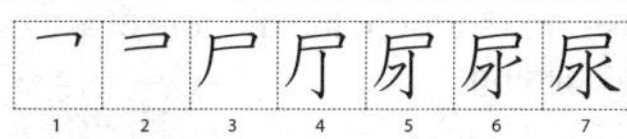

COMPOUNDS

● [original meaning] **URINE**

尿素 にょうそ urea
尿酸 にょうさん uric acid
排尿 はいにょう urination
検尿 けんにょう urinalysis
糖尿病 とうにょうびょう diabetes
夜尿症 やにょうしょう bed wetting, nocturia

INDEPENDENT

【にょう 尿】**URINE**

尿の検査 にょうのけんさ urinalysis

SYNONYMS

● excreta

便 EXCRETA → 0105
尿 URINE → 3801
汗 SWEAT → 0256

庇

▶PROTECT
▶EAVES
ヒ かば(う) ひさし
Ⓒ 庇 bì

3802
囗3-3-4

53	Names	U5E87
广	S7-3-4	F2160

COMPOUNDS

❶ **PROTECT, cover, shield**
庇護 ひご patronage, protection
曲庇 きょくひ bending the truth [law] to protect someone

❷ [original meaning] **EAVES**
雪庇 せっぴ(=ゆきびさし) overhanging snow

KUN

【かばう 庇う】
ⓐ **PROTECT, harbor, take under one's wing**
ⓑ **stand up for, stick up for, cover up for**
ⓒ cover, shield; avoid using (an injured limb)
b 庇い立て かばいだて protect (someone), defend

【ひさし 庇】
① **EAVES**
庇を貸して母屋を取られる ひさしをかしておもやをとられる Give him an inch and he'll take an ell
② **visor, peak**
庇髪 ひさしがみ classic Japanese women's low pompadour hairstyle
目庇 まびさし visor, eyeshade
③ narrow aisle-like area surrounding the core of a *shinden-zukuri* building

SYNONYMS

❶ **protect**
守 PROTECT (by watching over) → 2697
護 PROTECT (by safeguarding) → 2079
庇 PROTECT (by shielding) → 3802
衛 GUARD → 0938
警 GUARD AGAINST → 3595
防 defend → 0320
番 WATCH → 3416
保 PRESERVE → 0107
看 CARE FOR → 3992

❷ **roof parts**
軒 EAVES → 1851
庇 EAVES → 3802
棟 ridge → 1248
瓦 roof tile → 4288

序

▶INTRODUCTORY PART
▶ORDER
ジョ つい(で)▲
Ⓒ 序 xù

3803
囗3-3-4

53	Jōyō-5	U5E8F
广	S7-3-4	F1475

丶 亠 广 户 户 序 序 (stroke order 1–7)

COMPOUNDS

❶ⓐ **INTRODUCTORY PART** of something: **opening, beginning, inception, first stage**
ⓑ **INTRODUCTORY PART** of a book: **preface, introduction, foreword**
ⓒ **INTRODUCTORY** [first] **PART** of a traditional Japanese performance
a 序盤 じょばん opening (in the game of go)
序曲 じょきょく prelude, overture
序説 じょせつ introduction
序幕 じょまく opening act, curtain raiser
b 自序 じじょ author's preface
c 序破急 じょはきゅう artistic modulations in traditional Japanese performances; opening, middle and climax [end]

❷ⓐ **ORDER, precedence, sequence**
ⓑ **ORDER(liness), methodical arrangement**
ⓒ [archaic] **ORDER**, arrange in order
a 序列 じょれつ rank, grade, order
序次 じょじ order, sequence
順序 じゅんじょ order, sequence; system, procedure
b 秩序 ちつじょ order, discipline; method, system
花序 かじょ inflorescence
c 序歯 じょし [archaic] arranging seats by seniority

INDEPENDENT

【じょ 序】**INTRODUCTORY PART**, opening, beginning, the first stage; order, precedence; preface; first part of a play
序の口 じょのくち start, the first stage
長幼序有り ちょうようじょあり elders first

KUN

【ついで 序で】occasion, opportunity
序でが有る ついでがある have occasion to do
序でに ついでに while, on the occasion

SYNONYMS

❶ **beginnings**
緒 OUTSET → 1742
序 INTRODUCTORY PART → 3803
端 start → 1564
始 beginning → 0335
初 beginning → 1433
元 ORIGIN → 2428

本 origin →4314
根 ROOT →1167
源 SOURCE →0806

❷ **order**

序 ORDER (sequence/arrangement) →3803
順 ORDER (sequence) →0018
次 order (sequence) →0058
番 NUMERICAL ORDER →3416
秩 ORDER (methodical arrangement) →1489

応

3804

☐3-3-4

▶RESPOND

オウ -ノウ▲ こた(える)

Ⓝ 應 Ⓒ 应 yìng yīng

61	Jōyō-5	U5FDC
心	S7-4-3	F0336

Stroke order: 1–7

COMPOUNDS

❶ (act in return) **RESPOND to (a situation), react, act in accordance with, cope with**

応募 おうぼ application, subscription, enlistment
応援する おうえんする aid, reinforce; support; cheer
応酬する おうしゅうする respond, reply; counter
応接 おうせつ reception
応力 おうりょく *phys* stress
反応する はんのうする react, respond
対応する たいおうする correspond to, answer to; be equivalent; deal [cope] with
適応する てきおうする adapt (oneself) to, adjust (things) to
順応 じゅんのう adaptation, accommodation, adjustment

❷ (make a reply) **RESPOND, answer, reply**

応答 おうとう answer, response, reply
呼応して こおうして in concert, in response

❸ [original meaning] comply with, accede to, consent

応諾する おうだくする consent, assent

❹ **suitable, appropriate**

応用 おうよう practical application
応分の おうぶんの appropriate, reasonable (in view of one's position), within one's power [means]
相応する そうおうする be suitable, befit, correspond

❺ **used phonetically for ō**

一応(=一往) いちおう once; in outline; tentatively; for the time being

INDEPENDENT

【おう 応】 yes, all right

応と答える おうとこたえる say yes

【おうじる(=おうずる) 応じる(=応ずる)】 (act in return) **RESPOND to (a situation), act in accordance with;** (make a reply) **respond, answer; comply with, accede to, consent; be suitable [appropriate]**

力に力で応じる ちからにちからでおうじる meet force with force
求めに応じる もとめにおうじる answer a request
場合に応じて ばあいにおうじて in accordance with the situation

KUN

【こたえる 応える】

① **come home to (one), strike home, have effect on; be a great strain**

暑さが応える あつさがこたえる feel the heat very much

② **repay, reward**

親切に応える しんせつにこたえる repay a kindness

SYNONYMS

❷ **answer**

答 ANSWER →3322
解 solve →1913
返 reply →3797
応 RESPOND →3804

HOMOPHONES

こたえる 答 ANSWER →3322

COMPOUND FORMATION

【一応(=一往) いちおう】

一応 'once, etc.', formerly written 一往, originally meant to proceed (往) one time (一). Later, 応 ❺ was phonetically substituted for 往.

NOTE

➡ see USAGE note at 答 3322

床

3805

☐3-3-4

▶BED
▶FLOOR

ショウ とこ ゆか

Ⓒ 床 chuáng

53	Jōyō	U5E8A
广	S7-3-4	F0970

Stroke order: 1–7

COMPOUNDS

❶ⓐ **BED, sickbed**
ⓑ counter for BEDs

a 起床する きしょうする get up, rise
臨床医 りんしょうい clinician
b 百床病院 ひゃくしょうびょういん hospital with 100 beds

❷ (bed-shaped support or underlying part) **BED, foundation or ore deposit**

温床 おんしょう hotbed

夂 夊 辶 辶 尸 广 【冂】 匚 囗

岩床 がんしょう bedrock
視床 ししょう thalamus
銃床 じゅうしょう gunstock
鉱床 こうしょう ore deposit
❸ [original meaning] campstool
床几(=床机) しょうぎ campstool, folding stool

KUN

【とこ 床】**BED, sickbed; bed (as of flowers); alcove; barber**
床に就く とこにつく go to bed; be sick in bed, be laid up
床の間 とこのま alcove
床屋 とこや barber; barbershop
寝床 ねどこ bed
川床 かわどこ riverbed

【ゆか 床】**FLOOR; platform for *joruri* music players; floor exercises**
床下 ゆかした under the floor
床で金メダルを取る ゆかできんめだるをとる win a gold medal for one's floor exercise performance

SYNONYMS

❶ **flat supports**
台 STAND → 2498
座 SEAT → 3868
壇 PLATFORM → 0932
棚 SHELF → 1238
架 rack → 3178
床 BED → 3805

❷ **bottoms and bases**
底 BOTTOM → 3827
柢 BOTTOM → 1121
下 lower part → 4186
基 BASE → 3312
礎 FOUNDATION STONE → 1595
麓 FOOT OF MOUNTAIN → 3494
磐 BEDROCK → 3534
盤 bedrock → 3533
床 BED → 3805

伺

□3-3-4

incorrect classification
➡ see ◧1-2-5: 亻 at 0078

臣

3806
□3-3-4

▶**RETAINER**
シン ジン ㊔ おみ とみ
Ⓝ 臣◇ Ⓒ 臣 chén

131	Jōyō-4	U81E3
臣	S7-7-0	F0746

radical variant → see 臣 at 3712

COMPOUNDS

ⓐ **RETAINER, subject, vassal**
ⓑ first person pronoun used by **RETAINER**s
a 臣下 しんか retainer, subject, vassal
臣民 しんみん subjects
家臣 かしん retainer, vassal
君臣 くんしん sovereign and subject, lord and vassal
忠臣 ちゅうしん loyal retainer, loyal subject
大臣 だいじん minister (of state)

INDEPENDENT

【しん 臣】**RETAINER**, subject

SYNONYMS

ⓐ **servants**
僕 MANSERVANT → 0185
奴 SLAVE → 0217
隷 UNDERLING → 2201
臣 RETAINER → 3806
従 follower → 0498
供 attendant → 0098

囲

3807
□3-3-4

▶**ENCLOSE**
イ かこ(む) かこ(う) かこ(い)
Ⓝ 圍 Ⓒ 围 wéi

31	Jōyō-4	U56F2
囗	S7-3-4	F0604

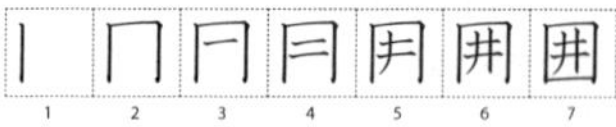

COMPOUNDS

ⓐ [original meaning] **ENCLOSE, encircle, surround**
ⓑ **circumference, surroundings**
a 囲碁 いご (the game of) go
包囲する ほういする surround, encircle, envelop
範囲 はんい range, scope
b 雰囲気 ふんいき atmosphere, mood
周囲 しゅうい circumference, periphery; surroundings
胸囲 きょうい chest measurement
外囲 がいい surroundings, periphery

KUN

【かこむ 囲む】**ENCLOSE, encircle, surround; enclose with a fence, fence in; besiege**
囲み かこみ enclosure; siege
取り囲む とりかこむ enclose, encircle

【かこう 囲う】**ENCLOSE, fence; preserve (food), keep (a mistress)**
庭を垣で囲う にわをかきでかこう enclose a garden with a fence

【かこい 囲い】**enclosure, fence**

囲いに入れる かこいにいれる place in an enclosure

SYNONYMS

ⓐ &【かこむ】 **surround**

囲む ENCLOSE → 3807

環 SURROUND → 1395

包 ENCOMPASS → 3684

ⓑ **periphery**

周 PERIPHERY → 3720

囲 circumference → 3807

郭 OUTER ENCLOSURE → 2112

廓 OUTER ENCLOSURE → 3923

【かこい】

○ **fences and walls**

壁 WALL → 3601

塀 FENCE (for screening) → 0677

垣 FENCE (for partitioning) → 0416

牆 FENCE (for partitioning) → 1393

柵 FENCE (with spaced pickets) → 1116

堵 FENCE (made of earth) → 0682

囲い enclosure → 3807

欄 railing → 1419

困

▶BE IN TROUBLE

コン こま(る)

Ⓒ 困 kùn

3808

囗3-3-4

31	Jōyō-6	U56F0
囗	S7-3-4	F0845

Stroke order: 1–7

COMPOUNDS

❶ [original meaning] **BE IN TROUBLE, be hard-pressed, be distressed, suffer**

困難 こんなん difficulty, trouble, distress, hardship

困惑 こんわく embarrassment, perplexity, confusion

困窮 こんきゅう destitution, poverty, distress

困苦 こんく hardships, privation

貧困 ひんこん poverty, indigence, destitution; lack, shortage

❷ tired, exhausted

困憊× こんぱい exhaustion, fatigue

KUN

【こまる 困る】 **BE IN TROUBLE, be distressed, be annoyed, be embarrassed, be perplexed; be destitute**

困らせる こまらせる annoy, embarrass

困り者 こまりもの good-for-nothing, scapegrace, nuisance, trouble

困り果てる こまりはてる be hard up, be at one's wit's end, be in a bad fix

生活に困る せいかつにこまる live in want

SYNONYMS

❶ **trouble and suffering**

困 BE IN TROUBLE → 3808

苛 torment → 2786

窮 BE IN EXTREMITY → 2983

悶 BE IN AGONY → 4119

悩 SUFFER → 0504

苦 SUFFERING → 2789

痛 PAIN → 4071

辛 HARD → 2531

煩 VEXED → 1295

難 DIFFICULT → 2310

NOTE

★ do not confuse with 因 CAUSE → 3792

図

▶DRAWING

ズ ト はか(る)

Ⓝ 圖 Ⓒ 图 tú

3809

囗3-3-4

31	Jōyō-2	U56F3
囗	S7-3-4	F0408

Stroke order: 1–7

COMPOUNDS

❶ [also suffix]

ⓐ **DRAWING, plan, diagram, figure, illustration, picture**

ⓑ [original meaning] **map, chart**

a 図面 ずめん drawing, plan, map, sketch

図形 ずけい figure, diagram

図表 ずひょう chart, diagram

図鑑 ずかん picture [illustrated] book

図書 としょ books

図書室 としょしつ library

図示 ずし illustration, graphic(al) representation

設計図 せっけいず plan, blueprint

b 地図 ちず map, atlas

版図 はんと territory

天気図 てんきず weather chart

市街図 しがいず city map

❷ⓐ **systematic plan, scheme, attempt**

ⓑ **intention**

a 壮図 そうと grand scheme

企図する きとする plan, scheme, intend

雄図 ゆうと ambitious enterprise, grand project

b 意図 いと intention, aim

合図 あいず signal, sign

❸ [emphatic prefix] **extraordinary, outrageous, audacious**

図太い ずぶとい audacious, brazen

図抜けている ずぬけている be outstanding

図図しい ずうずうしい cheeky, impudent
図体 ずうたい body, frame
❹ limits, bounds (of common sense)
野放図な のほうずな unrestrained, unruly
❺ expectation
図星 ずぼし bull's eye, mark

INDEPENDENT

【ず 図】
① **DRAWING, plan, figure, illustration, diagram; map, chart**
図を描く ずをかく draw a diagram
② *slang* sight; situation
滅多に見られない図 めったにみられないず seldom seen sight
③ *slang* expectation, intention
図に当たる ずにあたる hit the bull's eye, go as expected
図に乗る ずにのる push a good thing too far

KUN

【はかる 図る】
① **strive for, work for, promote, look to, provide for, seek**
相互理解を図る そうごりかいをはかる strive for mutual understanding
公益を図る こうえきをはかる labor for the public good
安全を図る あんぜんをはかる provide for safety
② **bring about, attempt**
便宜を図る べんぎをはかる accommodate, suit the convenience of
自殺を図る じさつをはかる attempt suicide
③ [in negative constructions] expect, look forward to
図らずも はからずも unexpectedly

SYNONYMS

❶ⓐ diagram
表 TABLE →3083
図 DRAWING →3809
❶ⓐ picture
絵 PICTURE →1704
画 PICTURE →3723
図 DRAWING →3809
❷ⓐ plans and planning
計 PLAN →1828
画 DRAW UP A PLAN →3723
案 PROPOSAL →2824
企 PROJECT →2513
図 systematic plan →3809
謀 SCHEME →2004
策 SCHEME →3320
略 STRATEGY →1501
揆 PLOT →0718
ⓑ will and intention
志 AMBITION →2725
意 MIND →2650
図 intention →3809
気 mind to do something →3960
念 thought of doing something →2554
趣 PURPOSE →4111
欲 DESIRE →1867

HOMOPHONES

はかる
計 PLAN →1828
謀 SCHEME →2004
量 QUANTITY →3119
測 MEASURE →0744
諮 CONSULT →2009

COMPOUND FORMATION

❶【図書 としょ】
図書 'books' formerly meant drawings (図 ❶ⓐ) and books (書).
❷【合図 あいず】
合図 'signal, sign' is the transmission of an agreed upon (合) intention (図 ❷ⓑ).

NOTE

➡ see USAGE note at 計 1828

圂
3810
□3-3-4

▸**DEEP WATER**
エン ふち ㊔ のぶ ひろ ふか ふかし なみ すけ すえ しずか

31	Nonstandard	U56E6
口	S7-3-4	F0000

traditional form →see 淵 at 0732

囘
3811
□3-3-4

▸**TURN ROUND**
▸**TIME**
カイ エ まわ(る) -まわ(る) -まわ(り) まわ(す) -まわ(す) まわ(し)- -まわ(し)
㊔ めぐり

31	Nonstandard	U56DE
口	S7-3-4	F0000

alternative form →see 回 at 3793

延
3812
□3-3-5

▸**EXTEND**
▸**POSTPONE**
エン の(びる) の(べる) の(べ) の(ばす)
㊔ のぶ
Ⓝ 延 Ⓒ 延 yán

54	Jōyō-6	U5EF6
廴	S8-3-5	F1039

1	2	3	4	5	6	7	8
一	丆	下	正	正	⺄正	廴正	延

COMPOUNDS

❶ⓐ [original meaning] **EXTEND (in space or time), prolong, spread**
ⓑ *metallurgy* (cause to extend) **flatten out, roll**

a 延長 えんちょう extension, prolongation, continuation
延焼 えんしょう spread of a fire
延延たる えんえんたる lengthy
延髄 えんずい medulla oblongata

b 熱延 ねつえん hot rolling
圧延鋼 あつえんこう rolled steel

❷ **POSTPONE, delay, defer**
延期 えんき postponement, deferment
延納 えんのう delayed [deferred] payment
延着 えんちゃく delayed arrival
延発 えんぱつ postponement of departure, delayed departure
延会 えんかい adjournment [postponement] of a meeting
延滞 えんたい arrear, arrearage
遅延 ちえん delay, retardation

KUN

【のびる 延びる】*vi*

① **EXTEND (in space or time), be extended, be prolonged**
延び のび extension; postponement
延び率 のびりつ growth rate
この鉄道は国境迄延びている このてつどうはこっきょうまでのびている This railway extends as far as the frontier

② **be POSTPONEd, be delayed**
延び延び のびのび repeated delays, dragging on and on
出発が延びた しゅっぱつがのびた The departure was postponed

【のべる 延べる】

① [also 伸べる]
ⓐ **EXTEND, stretch out (one's arm)**
ⓑ spread out (bedding)

a 手を延べる てをのべる stretch one's arm

② **POSTPONE, delay**
日延べ ひのべ postponement, adjournment

【のべ 延べ】

① [also prefix] **total, aggregate**
延べ時間 のべじかん total man hours

② deferment
延べ払い のべばらい deferred payment

【のばす 延ばす】*vt*

① **EXTEND (in space or time), prolong, spread**
引き延ばす ひきのばす extend, draw out; enlarge; prolong, filibuster
寿命を延ばす じゅみょうをのばす prolong one's life
期限を延ばす きげんをのばす extend the term

② **POSTPONE, delay, defer**
返事を延ばす へんじをのばす delay one's answer

SYNONYMS

❶ **expand**
脹 SWELL →1265
膨 EXPAND →1380
張 SPREAD →0573
氾 SPREAD OUT →0226
広げる spread (out) →3769
拡 ENLARGE →0366
伸 STRETCH →0079
延 EXTEND →3812

❷ **be late and delay**
遅 be late →3887
後 fall behind →0431
滞 fall into arrears →0815
延 POSTPONE →3812
猶 DELAY →0757

HOMOPHONES

のびる 伸 STRETCH →0079
のび 伸 STRETCH →0079
のべる 伸 STRETCH →0079
のばす 伸 STRETCH →0079

NOTE

➡ see USAGE note at 伸 0079
★ do not confuse with 廷 COURT →3795

廹

3813
□3-3-5

▶**PRESS**
ハク せま(る) ㊔ さこ せこ はさみ はざま はさま

54	Nonstandard	U8FEB
廴	S8-3-5	F0000

traditional form →see 迫 at 3815

廻

3814
□3-3-5

▶**TURN ROUND**
カイ エ まわ(る) まわ(す)

54	Nonstandard	U5EFB
廴	S8-3-5	F0000

traditional form →see 迴 at 3833

迫

3815
□3-3-5

▶**PRESS**
ハク せま(る) ㊔ さこ せこ はさみ はざま はさま

Ⓝ 廹 迫 Ⓒ 迫 pò pǎi

162	Jōyō	U8FEB
辶	S8-3-5	F0891

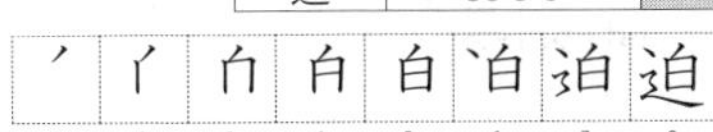

1 2 3 4 5 6 7 8

COMPOUNDS

❶ⓐ [original meaning] (close in on) **PRESS on, close in, draw near**

ⓑ **PRESSing, urgent, imminent, impending, close**

a 迫撃 はくげき close attack

迫真の はくしんの true to life, realistic

切迫する せっぱくする draw near, press; become acute, grow tense

b 急迫した きゅうはくした pressing, urgent, imminent

緊迫する きんぱくする become tense, grow strained

❷ⓐ (force to action) **PRESS upon, press for, urge, force, compel**

ⓑ (cause distress) **oppress, PRESS hard, persecute**

ⓒ **hard-PRESSed, in distress**

a 迫力 はくりょく power, force, punch, appeal

脅迫する きょうはくする threaten, intimidate, menace

強迫 きょうはく coercion, compulsion

圧迫する あっぱくする press, oppress, pressure

bc 迫害 はくがい persecution, oppression

窮迫 きゅうはく straitened circumstances, distress

逼×迫する ひっぱくする be tight, get stringent

❸ [also 魄 1570] soul, spirit

気迫 きはく spirit, soul, vigor

KUN

【せまる 迫る】 **PRESS (a person), urge, compel; close in on, press, draw near; be imminent**

辞職を迫る じしょくをせまる urge to resign

真に迫る しんにせまる be true to nature [life], be lifelike

差し迫る さしせまる be imminent, be impending

SYNONYMS

❶ⓐ **approach**

寄る DRAW NEAR →2856

迫 PRESS →3815

近 NEAR →3798

接 come close to →0607

拶 PRESS →0451

ⓑ **urgent**

急 URGENT →2595

緊 EXIGENT →3517

迫 pressing →3815

❷ⓐ **compel and press**

圧 PRESSURE →3688

迫 PRESS →3815

強 force →0574

押す PUSH →0371

ⓑ **torture and oppress**

拷 TORTURE →0446

責める torture →3115

虐 treat cruelly →3989

迫 oppress →3815

COMPOUND FORMATION

【迫力 はくりょく】

迫力 'power, etc.' is the power (力) to compel (迫 ❷ⓐ) or influence a person.

述

3816

□3-3-5

▶**STATE**

ジュツ の(べる)

Ⓝ 述 Ⓒ 述 shù

162	Jōyō-5	U8FF0
辶	S8-3-5	F0843

1	2	3	4	5	6	7	8
一	十	才	木	朮	朮	𨑐	述

COMPOUNDS

❶ⓐ **STATE orally, expound, mention, declare**

ⓑ **STATE [express] in writing**

a 述懐 じゅっかい effusion of one's thoughts (and feelings), reminiscence

述語 じゅつご predicate

供述 きょうじゅつ testimony, statement; confession

口述する こうじゅつする state orally, dictate

陳述 ちんじゅつ statement, declaration

叙述 じょじゅつ description, depiction

詳述 しょうじゅつ (detailed) expatiation, full account

前述の通り ぜんじゅつのとおり as stated [mentioned] above

b 述作 じゅっさく writing a book; literary work

記述する きじゅつする describe, give an account, write

著述 ちょじゅつ writing (of books); book, literary work

❷ *gram* abbrev. of 述語 じゅつご: predicate

主述 しゅじゅつ subject and predicate

❸ hand down, transmit

祖述 そじゅつ exposition [propagation] of one's master's doctrines

INDEPENDENT

【じゅつ 述】 **STATE**ment

先生の述 せんせいのじゅつ teacher's statement [expounding]

KUN

【のべる 述べる】 **STATE orally (or in writing), expound, mention, declare; relate, tell**

述べ立てる のべたてる dwell eloquently (on), relate at great length

詳しく述べる くわしくのべる expound

申し述べる もうしのべる state, mention, tell

SYNONYMS

❶ⓐ **speak and say**

言 SAY →2440

語る TELL →1944

談 TALK → 1975
喋 TALK → 0665
諷 INSINUATE → 2005
謂う REFER TO → 2007
云 say → 2430
曰 SAY THAT → 3757
話 SPEAK → 1928
口 give mouth to → 4189
申す SPEAK HUMBLY → 4319
述 STATE → 3816
陳 SET FORTH → 0656
弁 SPEAK ELOQUENTLY → 2497

迪 3817 ☐3-3-5

▶EDIFY
テキ ㊔みち すすむ
Ⓝ 迪 Ⓒ 迪 dí

162	Names	U8FEA
辶	S8-3-5	F0000

COMPOUNDS

❶ [rare] **EDIFY**, enlighten, guide, teach
啓迪する けいてきする edify, enlighten, guide
訓迪 くんてき guide, teach; master

❷ [archaic] advance, proceed

❸ [original meaning, now obsolete] way, path

SYNONYMS

❶ **teach**
教 TEACH → 1887
啓 ENLIGHTEN → 3434
諄 TEACH WITH CARE → 1979
授 teach → 0595
育 educate → 2544
練 TRAIN → 1738
訓 INSTRUCT → 1844
誨 INSTRUCT → 1946
諭 ADMONISH → 2012
導 GUIDE → 3587
迪 EDIFY → 3817

迭 3818 ☐3-3-5

▶ALTERNATE
テツ
Ⓝ 迭 Ⓒ 迭 dié

162	Jōyō	U8FED
辶	S8-3-5	F3027

Stroke order: 1 ノ 2 ⺈ 3 𠂉 4 ⺧ 5 失 6 ˋ失 7 迭 8 迭

COMPOUNDS

● [original meaning] **ALTERNATE, change, take turns**
更迭する こうてつする reshuffle, change (as of government officials), exchange places

SYNONYMS

● **change and replace**
変 CHANGE → 2569
替 REPLACE → 3457
代 SUBSTITUTE → 0034
迭 ALTERNATE → 3818
更 change → 4355
改 change → 0287
易 change → 3064
化 CHANGE INTO, -ize → 0022
遷 undergo transition → 3932
転 turn into → 1872
換 EXCHANGE → 0716
交 INTERCHANGE → 2508

● **alternate**
迭 ALTERNATE → 3818
交 INTERCHANGE → 2508
輪 take turns → 1999

NOTE

★ do not confuse with 送 SEND → 3837

迦 3819 ☐3-3-5

▶PHONETIC [ka]
カ

162	Nonstandard	U8FE6
辶	S8-3-5	F0000

traditional form → see 迦 at 3982

述迫 etc. ☐3-3-5

incorrect stroke-count
➡ see ☐3-4-5: 辶 at 3982

届 3820 ☐3-3-5

▶DELIVER
▶REACH
カイ▲ とど(ける) -とど(け) とど(く)
Ⓝ 届 Ⓒ 届 jiè

44	Jōyō-6	U5C4A
尸	S8-3-5	F1007

Stroke order: 1 ㇕ 2 コ 3 尸 4 尸 5 屆 6 屆 7 届 8 届

KUN

【とどける 届ける】

① **DELIVER (a letter or goods), send, forward**
届け先 とどけさき destination, address
送り届ける おくりとどける send to, deliver; escort (a person) home
付け届け つけとどけ present, tip; bribe

② **give notice (to the authorities), report, notify, file notice**
届け とどけ report, notice; delivery, forwarding
届け出る とどけでる report, notify
無届けの むとどけの without notice

【-とどけ -届け】[suffix] **report, notice; notification**
被害届け ひがいとどけ report of damage
出生届け しゅっしょうとどけ register of birth

【とどく 届く】
①ⓐ (succeed in touching) **REACH, get at**
ⓑ (be delivered) **REACH (a destination), arrive, be received**
a 手の届く所 てのとどくところ within one's reach
目の届く限り めのとどくかぎり as far as the eye can reach
b 届かない手紙 とどかないてがみ letter that fails to reach its destination
② be attained, be fulfilled, be realized
届かぬ願い とどかぬねがい unfulfilled wish
③ **be attentive, be careful**
行き届く ゆきとどく(=いきとどく) be scrupulous, be attentive, be prudent; be complete, be thorough
不届きな ふとどきな insolent, outrageous

SYNONYMS

【とどける】
① **transmit and deliver**
伝 TRANSMIT →0048
逓 RELAY →3852
届ける DELIVER →3820
達 deliver →3893
② **inform and communicate**
報 INFORM →2133
通 COMMUNICATE →3855
告 NOTIFY →3062
届ける give notice →3820
達 issue a notice →3893
知 let know →1446
申 REPORT →4319
稟 REPORT TO →2649
宣 PROCLAIM →2799

【とどく】
① **arrive**
着 ARRIVE →4110
到 ARRIVE →1615
至 COME TO →2707
及 REACH TO →4192
届く REACH →3820
達 ATTAIN →3893

屈

3821
□3-3-5

▶**BEND**
クツ かが(む)▲ かが(める)▲
Ⓒ 屈 qū

44	Jōyō	U5C48
尸	S8-3-5	F1090

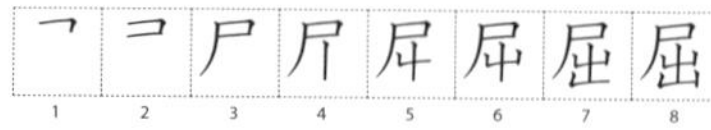

COMPOUNDS

❶ⓐ [original meaning] **BEND, flex, crouch**
ⓑ crooked
a 屈伸 くっしん bending and stretching, extension and contraction
屈折 くっせつ bending, turn; refraction
屈曲する くっきょくする bend, wind
屈指の くっしの leading, foremost
前屈 ぜんくつ bending forward, anteflexion
b 偏屈な へんくつな eccentric, narrow-minded, obstinate
❷ **BEND in submission, bow, submit to, yield**
屈伏(=屈服)する くっぷくする bend in submission, submit to, surrender, yield to
屈従 くつじゅう servile submission, subservience
屈辱 くつじょく humiliation, disgrace, insult
不屈の ふくつの indomitable, unyielding
卑屈な ひくつな mean, mean-spirited; servile
❸ **be in an uncomfortable position, be cramped, reach the limit**
屈託 くったく worry, vexation
退屈な たいくつな tedious, boring
窮屈な きゅうくつな cramped, confined; formal; poor
❹ strong, robust
屈強な くっきょうな strong, sturdy, robust
❺ [formerly 窟 2923] **cave, cavern**
理屈 りくつ reason, logic; argument; pretext; theory

INDEPENDENT

【くっする 屈する】**BEND, flex; bend in submission, bow, submit to, yield**

KUN

【かがむ 屈む】*vi* stoop, lean over; crouch
屈み込む かがみこむ lean in, lean over
前屈み まえかがみ slouch
【かがめる 屈める】*vt* **BEND** (one's legs), bow (one's knee), incline (one's head)
腰を屈めて歩く こしをかがめてあるく walk with a stoop

SYNONYMS

❶ⓐ **bend**
曲 CURVE →4340
彎 CURVE (become bow-shaped) →3634
屈 BEND →3821
折 bend →0297
勾 be bent →3660
歪 DISTORT →3095
❷ **submit and surrender**
服 SUBMIT →1090

伏 submit →0049
屈 bend in submission →3821
降 surrender →0548

COMPOUND FORMATION

【理屈 りくつ】

According to one theory, 理屈 'reason, etc.' originally referred to a cave (屈 ❺) for amassing truth or reason (理).

居

▶RESIDE

キョ い(る) -い お(る)▲ 名 すえ

Ⓒ 居 jū

3822

口3-3-5

44	Jōyō-5	U5C45
尸	S8-3-5	F0395

Stroke order: 1–8

COMPOUNDS

❶ⓐ RESIDE, live, dwell
ⓑ RESIDEnce, dwelling, address

a 居住する きょじゅうする live, dwell, reside
居留地 きょりゅうち settlement, concession
同居する どうきょする live together
別居 べっきょ separation, limited divorce
群居する ぐんきょする live gregariously
b 住居 じゅうきょ house, dwelling, residence
皇居 こうきょ Imperial Palace
入居する にゅうきょする move into (a flat)
転居する てんきょする move, change one's residence

❷ⓐ (of living beings) **be present, be, be found, stay**
ⓑ be still, do nothing

a 家居する かきょする stay at home
b 居然たる きょぜんたる still, doing nothing

❸ [original meaning] **sit**
起居 ききょ one's daily life

❹ [rare] ordinary, usual
居常 きょじょう daily life

INDEPENDENT

【きょ 居】**RESIDEnce, dwelling**
居を構える きょをかまえる take up one's residence

KUN

【いる 居る】

① **be present, exist, be found**—said esp. of living things
居合わせる いあわせる happen to be present
居候 いそうろう hanger-on, parasite

②ⓐ **RESIDE, live, dwell, inhabit**
ⓑ (of animals) inhabit, live

a 居所 いどころ one's address [residence], one's whereabouts

③ **sit**
居眠り いねむり doze, nap
居並ぶ いならぶ sit in a row, be arrayed
居間 いま living [sitting] room
居酒屋 いざかや bar, pub

④ [following the TE-form of verbs] **be...-ing, be engaged in**
笑って居る わらっている be smiling [laughing]

【-い -居】

① **presence; someone present**
長居 ながい long visit [stay]
仲居 なかい parlormaid, waitress
留守居 るすい caretaker, janitor; caretaking (during a person's absence)

② **sitting; seat**
芝居 しばい play, drama

【おる 居る】**variant of** 居る いる
父は居りません ちちはおりません Father is not home

SPECIAL READINGS

居士 こじ lay scholar
一言居士 いちげんこじ ready critic, one ready to comment on any and every subject

SYNONYMS

❶ⓐ reside
住 LIVE →0072
居 RESIDE →3822
棲 INHABIT (said of animals), live →1246
栖 INHABIT (said of animals), live →1170
生 inhabit →4309
植 colonize →1247

ⓑ houses
家 HOUSE →2827
屋 HOUSE →3842
軒 house →1851
戸 HOUSEHOLD →2429
宅 DWELLING HOUSE →2698
居 residence →3822
邸 STATELY RESIDENCE →1451
住 housing →0072
庵 HERMITAGE →3876

❷ⓐ exist and be
在 BE →3704
存 EXIST →3702
有 exist →3703
居 be present →3822
臨 BE PRESENT AT →2059
也 CLASSICAL COPULA →4214

❸ sit
座 SIT →3868
坐 SIT →4361

居 sit → 3822

NOTE

➡ see COMPOUND FORMATION for
仲居 なかい → 仲 0047
居候 いそうろう → 候 0133
芝居 しばい → 芝 2705

屆

▶DELIVER
▶REACH
カイ とど(ける) -とど(け) とど(く)

3823
□3-3-5

44 尸	Nonstandard	U5C46
	S8-3-5	F0000

traditional form → see 届 at 3820

府

▶URBAN PREFECTURE
フ
Ⓒ 府 fǔ

3824
□3-3-5

53 广	Jōyō-4	U5E9C
	S8-3-5	F0369

Stroke order: 丶 亠 广 广 庐 庐 府 府 (1–8)

COMPOUNDS

❶ **URBAN [metropolitan] PREFECTURE (limited to Kyoto and Osaka prefectures)**
府庁 ふちょう urban prefectural office
府警 ふけい prefectural police
府税 ふぜい urban prefectural tax
府立の ふりつの prefectural
京都府 きょうとふ Kyoto Prefecture

❷ⓐ **capital, metropolis**
ⓑ Edo in feudal Japan
a 府下 ふか suburban districts (of a metropolis)
首府 しゅふ capital, metropolis
b 御府内 ごふない within the town limits of Edo

❸ **government office, seat of government**
政府 せいふ government, administration
総理府 そうりふ Prime Minister's Office
国府 こくふ National Government (of China); provincial capital
幕府 ばくふ shogunate

❹ center, focus (as of learning)
学府 がくふ academic center

❺ [original meaning, now rare] storehouse, treasury, archives
府庫 ふこ treasury

INDEPENDENT

【ふ 府】URBAN PREFECTURE (→❶); center, focus
禍の府 わざわいのふ sink of iniquity
文教の府 ぶんきょうのふ fountainhead of culture; Ministry of Education

SYNONYMS

❶ **territorial divisions**
州 STATE → 0064
県 PREFECTURE → 3269
府 URBAN PREFECTURE → 3824
道 district of Hokkaido → 3888
都 METROPOLIS OF TOKYO → 2120
省 province in China → 3100
郡 COUNTY → 1858

❸ **public offices**
省 MINISTRY → 3100
庁 GOVERNMENT AGENCY → 3768
府 government office → 3824
公 public office → 2468
署 PUBLIC-SERVICE STATION → 3223
局 public service office → 3800
所 office → 1056

庖

▶KITCHEN
ホウ
Ⓝ 庖 Ⓒ 庖 páo

3825
□3-3-5

53 广	Non-Jōyō	U5E96
	S8-3-5	F3176

COMPOUNDS

● [now also 包 3684] [original meaning] **KITCHEN**
庖厨 ほうちゅう kitchen
庖丁 ほうちょう kitchen knife, carving knife

SYNONYMS

● **kitchen**
厨 KITCHEN → 3740
庖 KITCHEN → 3825

NOTE

➡ see COMPOUND FORMATION for 庖丁(=包丁) ほうちょう → 丁 4155

庚

▶SEVENTH CALENDAR SIGN
コウ かのえ ㊔ か やす つぐ みち
Ⓒ 庚 gēng

3826
□3-3-5

53 广	Names	U5E9A
	S8-3-5	F3402

COMPOUNDS

● **SEVENTH CALENDAR SIGN**
庚申 こうしん 57th of the sexagenary cycle

INDEPENDENT

【こう 庚】SEVENTH CALENDAR SIGN

KUN

【かのえ 庚】SEVENTH CALENDAR SIGN

SYNONYMS

● **calendar signs**

戊 FIFTH CALENDAR SIGN → 4321
庚 SEVENTH CALENDAR SIGN → 3826
壬 NINTH CALENDAR SIGN → 4257

底

3827
□3-3-5

▶BOTTOM
テイ そこ
Ⓒ 底 dǐ de

53 广	Jōyō-4	U5E95
	S8-3-5	F0676

丶 亠 广 广 庀 庀 底 底
1 2 3 4 5 6 7 8

COMPOUNDS

❶ⓐ **BOTTOM, base**
ⓑ *math* base, radix
a 底流 ていりゅう bottom current, undercurrent
海底 かいてい sea bottom
心底 しんてい bottom of one's heart, inmost thoughts
b 底数 ていすう base, radix
底角 ていかく base angle
底辺 ていへん base (in geometry)
❷ [formerly also 柢 1121] (fundamental part) **BOTTOM, basis, origin**
底本 ていほん original text
根底 こんてい root, basis, foundation
基底 きてい base, basis, foundation; *math* base
徹底 てってい thoroughness, completeness

INDEPENDENT

【てい 底】 **BOTTOM**, base; base, radix; kind, sort
この底の本 このていのほん this sort of book

KUN

【そこ 底】 **BOTTOM, sole, bed; bottom (as of one's heart), depths; bowels (of the earth)**
底革 そこがわ sole, sole leather
底値 そこね bottom price
箱の底 はこのそこ bottom of a box
川底 かわぞこ riverbed
どん底 どんぞこ rock bottom, depths
心の奥底 こころのおくそこ innermost depths of one's heart
地の底深く ちのそこふかく deep in the bowels of the earth

SYNONYMS

❶ⓐ **bottoms and bases**
底 BOTTOM → 3827
柢 BOTTOM → 1121
下 lower part → 4186
基 BASE → 3312
礎 FOUNDATION STONE → 1595
麓 FOOT OF MOUNTAIN → 3494
磐 BEDROCK → 3534
盤 bedrock → 3533
床 BED → 3805
❷ **basis**
基 BASE → 3312
本 BASIS → 4314
素 ELEMENT → 3108
礎 foundation → 1595
底 BOTTOM → 3827
根 ROOT → 1167
拠 GROUNDS → 0369

店

3828
□3-3-5

▶SHOP
テン みせ たな▲
Ⓒ 店 diàn

53 广	Jōyō-2	U5E97
	S8-3-5	F0275

丶 亠 广 广 庐 庐 店 店
1 2 3 4 5 6 7 8

COMPOUNDS

ⓐ [also suffix] [original meaning] **SHOP, store; stall**
ⓑ [also suffix] **(small) business establishment, as a bank or restaurant**
ⓒ counter for **SHOP**s or firms
a 店員 てんいん clerk
店舗 てんぽ shop, store
店頭 てんとう shop [store] front
商店 しょうてん shop, store
書店 しょてん bookstore
売店 ばいてん booth, stand; store
百貨店 ひゃっかてん department store
ab 支店 してん branch (office), branch (store)
本店 ほんてん head [main] office [store]
b 店屋物 てんやもの dishes from a caterer
代理店 だいりてん agency, agent
特約店 とくやくてん special [sole] agency [agent]
喫茶店 きっさてん coffee shop, tea house
c 五十店 ごじゅってん 50 shops [branch offices]

KUN

【みせ 店】 **SHOP, store**
店屋 みせや shop, store
店先 みせさき storefront
店開き みせびらき opening of a business
茶店 ちゃみせ tea stall, rest house
出店 でみせ branch (store)
【たな 店】
① **SHOP**, store
店卸し(=棚卸し) たなおろし inventory
大店 おおだな large store
② house for rent

夂 辶 辶 尸 【广】 疒 口

店子 たなこ tenant

SYNONYMS

● **places of business**

店 SHOP (of any kind) → 3828
舗 SHOP (esp. traditional) → 2177
屋 SMALL SHOP → 3842
社 COMPANY → 1042

USAGE

【たな】

店
① shop, store
② house for rent

棚
ⓐ [also suffix] shelf, rack, ledge, mantelpiece
ⓑ (natural shelflike structure) shelf, ledge (of rock)
ⓒ continental shelf

HOMOPHONES

たな 棚 SHELF → 1238

庖

3829
口3-3-5

▶**KITCHEN**
ホウ

53	Nonstandard	U5E96
广	S8-3-5	F0000

traditional form → see 庖 at 3825

度

口3-3-5

incorrect stroke-count
➡ see 口3-3-6: 广 at 3844

庇

口3-3-5

incorrect stroke-count
➡ see 口3-3-4: 广 at 3802

夜

口3-3-5

incorrect classification
➡ see 亠2-2-6: 亠 at 2550

固

3830
口3-3-5

▶**SOLID**
▶**FIRM**
コ かた(める) かた(まる) かた(まり) かた(い)

ⓒ 固 gù

31	Jōyō-4	U56FA
口	S8-3-5	F0862

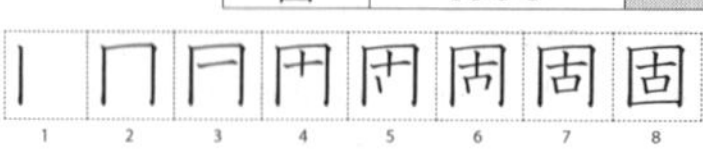

COMPOUNDS

❶ⓐ **SOLID**
ⓑ **SOLIDify, harden**

a 固体 こたい solid, solid matter
固溶体 こようたい solid solution
固形の こけいの solid
b 固化 こか solidification
凝固 ぎょうこ solidification, coagulation, congelation

❷ⓐ [original meaning] (fixed in place) **FIRM, fixed, immovable, stable**
ⓑ (having determination) **FIRM, resolute, determined**
ⓒ defend **FIRM**ly, hold firm

a 固定された こていされた fixed, stationary, permanent
固着する こちゃくする adhere to, stick fast
b 固辞する こじする decline positively, decline firmly
堅固な けんごな strong, secure, firm, steadfast
強固な きょうこな firm, stable, solid, strong
c 固守する こしゅする defend stubbornly [firmly], keep to old customs

❸ **FIRMly persistent, stiff, unyielding, stubborn**

固執する こしつ(=こしゅう)する adhere to, persist in
頑固な がんこな stubborn, obstinate, bigoted

❹ **intrinsically, originally**

固有の こゆうの peculiar to, characteristic, inborn

❺ [also 乎 こ 4316] suffix for forming modifiers

断固たる だんこたる firm, conclusive, determined
確固たる かっこたる firm, sure, resolute

❻ [also 錮 2182] imprison, hold in custody

禁固 きんこ imprisonment

KUN

【かためる 固める】*vt* **harden, SOLIDify; tamp; strengthen, make secure, establish oneself; fortify, defend**

固め かため hardening; defense, fortifying; pledge
土を固める つちをかためる harden earth into a mass
国境を固める こっきょうをかためる fortify the frontier
決心を固める けっしんをかためる make a firm resolution

【かたまる 固まる】*vi* **harden, SOLIDify, congeal; become firm, become stiff; gather, huddle; be devoted to; become certain**

固く固まる かたくかたまる form a hard mass
思想が固まっていない しそうがかたまっていない have no fixed ideas
隅っこに固まる すみっこにかたまる huddle in a corner
凝り固まる こりかたまる be fanatical; coagulate, clot

【かたまり 固まり】

① [sometimes also 塊] **lump, mass, clod; ingot**
鉄の固まり てつのかたまり iron ingot
② [usu. 塊] group, crowd, cluster
③ [sometimes also 塊] devotee, worshiper; incarnation (of selfishness), personification

欲の固まり よくのかたまり incarnation of selfishness
拝金主義の固まり はいきんしゅぎのかたまり money worshiper

【かたい 固い】
①ⓐ (glutinous or not flexible) **stiff, FIRM, thick**
ⓑ (not easily moved) **stiff, tight, fast**
a 固さ かたさ stiffness
固練りコンクリート かたねりこんくりーと stiff-consistency concrete
固いカラー かたいからー stiff collar
ドアが固い どあがかたい The door sticks [has stiff hinges]
b 固い結び目 かたいむすびめ tight knot
固い握り かたいにぎり tight grip
②ⓐ (unshakable) **stiff, FIRM, resolute, strong**
ⓑ (unyielding) **stiff (stand), obstinate, stubborn, inflexible**
a 固い約束 かたいやくそく solemn promise
決意が固い けついがかたい be firmly determined
団結が固い だんけつがかたい be strongly united
b 固苦しい かたくるしい formal, stiff, strained; strict; rigid
頭が固い あたまがかたい obstinate, thickheaded, inflexible
③ rigid, strict, stern
固く戒める かたくいましめる admonish sternly
④ certain, sure
合格は固い ごうかくはかたい He is certain to pass the exam

SYNONYMS

❶ⓐ hard
硬 HARD → 1518
堅 FIRM → 3502
鞏 TOUGH → 3369
固 SOLID → 3830
剛 TOUGH → 2107
強 STRONG → 0574
勁 STRONG → 1833
ⓑ solidify and coagulate
固 solidify → 3830
凝 CONGEAL → 0198
結 form into a mass → 1706
凍 FREEZE → 0146
❷ⓐ not moving
固 FIRM → 3830
定 fixed → 2770
静 still → 2164
止 still → 3659
ⓑ & ❸ firm and obstinate
堅 FIRM → 3502
固 FIRM, stiff → 3830
確 firm → 1571
毅 RESOLUTE → 2341
剛 TOUGH → 2107
頑 STUBBORN → 1315
硬 hard-line → 1518

USAGE

❶【かたまり】
固まり
① [sometimes also 塊] lump, mass, clod; ingot
② [usu. 塊] group, crowd, cluster
③ [sometimes also 塊] devotee, worshiper; incarnation (of selfishness), personification
塊
① [usu. 固まり] lump, mass, clod; ingot
② [sometimes also 固まり] group, crowd, cluster
③ [usu. 固まり] devotee, worshiper; incarnation (of selfishness), personification

❷【かたい】
固い
①ⓐ (glutinous or not flexible) stiff, firm, thick
ⓑ (not easily moved) stiff, tight, fast
②ⓐ (unshakable) stiff, firm, resolute, strong
ⓑ (unyielding) stiff (stand), obstinate, stubborn, inflexible
③ rigid, strict, stern
④ certain, sure
硬い
① (resisting pressure) hard, tough, strong (esp. metals or stone)
②ⓐ stiff (style), uninteresting
ⓑ stiff (facial expression)
堅い
① (resisting deformation) firm, hard (lumber)
② steady (market or business), sound (investment)
③ⓐ steadfast, reliable, trustworthy
ⓑ honest, honorable, upright, serious, chaste
④ stiff, formal, bookish
難い
difficult, hard

★かたい is a source of confusion to all users of Japanese, with many dictionaries disagreeing with each other. Though the information here is lexically "correct," it is not always reliable for determining meaning in actual occurrences, esp. in reference to physical hardness. Study the equivalents and examples under each entry. In the ordinary sense of hard, 硬い is used, esp. in reference to metals or stone. In reference to wood, 堅い is the correct choice, though the two are often used interchangeably. 固い implies stickiness, as in pasty substances, resistance to motion (stiff hinges) or tightness (tight knot or grip). It does *not* mean solid, despite the fact that it has that meaning in *on* compounds. In figurative uses, 堅い is basically positive (steadfast, trustworthy, upright, chaste), while 固い has negative overtones (stiff, obstinate). However, 固い is also used positively (solemn promise, firm determination). In reference to speech or writing, 硬い means uninteresting or unpolished, while 堅い means formal (style) or bookish. The verbs かためる and かたまる are always written 固める and 固まる. 難い is a literary expression for difficult or a verbal suffix meaning hard to do. It is never interchangeable with the above three.

HOMOPHONES

かたまり 塊 LUMP →0775

かたい
- 硬 HARD →1518
- 堅 FIRM →3502
- 難 DIFFICULT →2310

国

3831

囗3-3-5

▶**COUNTRY**

コク くに

Ⓝ 國 囯 囶◇ 囗◇

Ⓒ 国 guó

31	Jōyō-2	U56FD
囗	S8-3-5	F0011

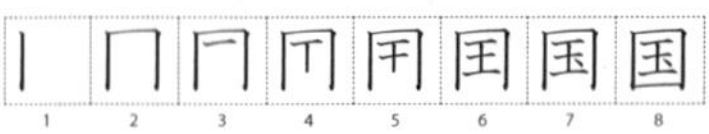

COMPOUNDS

❶ⓐ [also suffix] **COUNTRY, nation, state**
ⓑ **national, government-operated**

a 国家 こっか state, country, nation
国会 こっかい National Diet; national assembly, congress
国際 こくさい international
国際的な こくさいてきな international
国旗 こっき national flag
国防 こくぼう national defense
国民 こくみん people, nation; the people
国境 こっきょう (national) boundary [border]
国外の こくがいの foreign, external
国際化 こくさいか internationalization
国名 こくめい country name
全国 ぜんこく the whole country
外国 がいこく foreign country
傾国 けいこく beautiful woman; courtesan
先進国 せんしんこく advanced [developed] nation [country]

b 国債 こくさい national bonds; national debt [loan]
国立 こくりつ national (park, etc.)
国鉄 こくてつ Japanese National Railways (defunct)
国道 こくどう national highway
国費 こくひ national expenditure
国営 こくえい government-managed; state-operated
国税 こくぜい national tax
国有の こくゆうの state-owned, nationalized
国力 こくりょく national power; national resources

❷ native **COUNTRY**, homeland
郷国 きょうこく one's native country [land]

❸ (unit of administration in former Japan equiv. to modern prefecture) province
国司 こくし provincial governor
国府 こくふ National Government (of China); provincial capital

❹ⓐ abbrev. of 国鉄 こくてつ: Japanese National Railways
ⓑ abbrev. of 国会 こっかい: National Diet

a 国労 こくろう National Railway Workers' Union
b 国対(=国会対策委員会) こくたい(=こっかいたいさくいいんかい) Committee of the National Diet

❺ⓐ (of Japan) **Japanese**
ⓑ abbrev. of 国語 こくご: Japanese language

a 国語 こくご national language; Japanese
国文学 こくぶんがく Japanese literature
国史 こくし Japanese history
b 国漢 こっかん Japanese and Chinese
英数国 えいすうこく English, Mathematics and Japanese

❻ distinguished in one's **COUNTRY**
国手 こくしゅ noted doctor; master
国士 こくし distinguished citizen; patriot

KUN

【くに 国】**COUNTRY, state, nation, land, territory, realm; one's native country, homeland, home town; province** (→❸)
国境 くにざかい (national, state or provincial) boundary [border]
国国 くにぐに nations
国自慢 くにじまん provincial pride
国侍 くにざむらい provincial samurai
島国 しまぐに island country
大和の国 やまとのくに Japan, Yamato

SYNONYMS

❶ⓐ **country**
国 COUNTRY →3831
邦 STATE →1051
土 land →4211
ⓑ **national**
国 national →3831
内 internal →4277

❸ **feudal territorial divisions**
藩 FEUDAL DOMAIN →3022
国 province (in former Japan) →3831
領 fief →1567
封 daimiate →1639

荘 manor (in feudal Japan) → 2814

❺ⓐ **Japan**

日 JAPAN → 3759

和 JAPAN → 1450

邦 JAPAN → 1051

国 Japanese → 3831

倭 ANCIENT NAME FOR JAPAN → 0140

NOTE

➡ see COMPOUND FORMATION for 傾国 けいこく → 傾 0174

囶

3832

口3-3-5

▶**COUNTRY**

コク くに

31	Nonstandard	U56F6
口	S8-3-5	F0000

traditional form → see 国 at 3831

廻

3833

口3-3-6

▶**TURN ROUND**

カイ エ まわ(る) まわ(す)

Ⓝ 廽 廻 Ⓒ 回 huí

54	Names	U5EFB
廴	S9-3-6	F1386

COMPOUNDS

❶ [now usu. 回 3793]

ⓐ **TURN ROUND, revolve, rotate, circulate**

ⓑ **go round, make the rounds; circulate, make a circular tour**

a 廻転する かいてんする revolve, rotate, turn

旋廻 せんかい revolution, rotation, circling, swiveling

b 廻覧する かいらんする circulate, send round

廻状 かいじょう circular (letter)

廻文 かいぶん palindrome; circular

廻廊 かいろう corridor, gallery

❷ [now usu. 回 3793]

ⓐ **turn back, return, come back**

ⓑ **turn (something) back, return, reply, bring back**

a 廻向 えこう Buddhist memorial service

輪廻 りんね *Buddhism* transmigration of souls, *saṃsāra*

b 廻心 かいしん(=えしん) conversion

❸ [now replaced by 回 かい 3793] send round, forward, transmit

廻送 かいそう forwarding

廻漕業 かいそうぎょう shipping business

廻船 かいせん lighter, cargo vessel

KUN

【まわる 廻る】[now usu. 回る]

①ⓐ **TURN ROUND, revolve, rotate**

ⓑ **go round, circulate, make a round**

ⓒ **detour, go round (to)**

a 廻り まわり rotation; detour; close surroundings; spreading (of flames); efficacy

② **swing over to, come round to, be transferred**

③ be past (a certain hour)

④ pass (from hand to hand), circulate, spread; take effect

⑤ yield interest

【まわす 廻す】[now usu. 回す]

① **TURN (ROUND), rotate**

② **send [pass] around, circulate; forward, transfer**

③ lend money at interest

④ arrange, prepare

⑤ perform gang rape

SYNONYMS

❶ **turn**

旋 GYRATE → 1194

転 TURN → 1872

回 TURN ROUND → 3793

廻 TURN ROUND → 3833

巡 MAKE THE ROUNDS → 3781

循 CIRCULATE → 0704

斡 REVOLVE → 2168

捻 TWIST → 0604

❷ⓐ **return**

帰 RETURN → 0148

還 RETURN → 3945

回 turn back → 3793

廻 turn back → 3833

戻る RETURN → 2441

復 RETURN TO → 0701

HOMOPHONES

まわる 回 TURN ROUND → 3793

まわり

回 TURN ROUND → 3793

周 PERIPHERY → 3720

まわす 回 TURN ROUND → 3793

NOTE

➡ see USAGE note at 回 3793

建

3834

口3-3-6

▶**BUILD**

ケン コン た(てる) た(て) -だ(て) た(つ)

㊔ たけ たけし たける たつる

Ⓒ 建 jiàn

54	Jōyō-4	U5EFA
廴	S9-3-6	F0377

1	2	3	4	5	6	7	8	9
㇇	⺕	⺕	⺕	⺕	聿	𢗲	𢗲	建

COMPOUNDS

❶ⓐ **BUILD (a building), construct, erect, put up**

ⓑ establish (a nation)

a 建築 けんちく construction, building, architecture
建設する けんせつする construct, build, erect
建造 けんぞう building, construction
建碑 けんぴ erection of a monument
建立 こんりゅう erection, building (as a temple)
再建 さいけん reconstruction, rehabilitation
b 建国 けんこく establishing a nation
❷ propose, suggest, petition
建議 けんぎ proposal, suggestion
建白 けんぱく petition, memorial
建策 けんさく recommendation, suggestion

KUN

【たてる 建てる】
ⓐ **BUILD, construct, erect, put up**
ⓑ establish (a nation)
a 建物 たてもの building, structure
建て前 たてまえ erection of house framework; principle, rule, one's position; one's words (as opposed to one's real intentions)
b 建て直し たてなおし rebuilding, re-erection
【たて 建て】[in compounds] **business commitment, sales contract**
建て値 たてね official quotations, rates of exchange, market
【-だて -建て】[also suffix]
① **way of BUILDing, method of construction**
二階建ての家 にかいだてのいえ two-storied house
② currency of exchange
ドル建て どるだて quotation in dollars
③ average number of pages (of a newspaper or magazine)
十六頁建ての新聞 じゅうろくぺーじだてのしんぶん 16-page newspaper
【たつ 建つ】**be built, be erected, be established**
銅像が建った どうぞうがたった A bronze statue was erected

SYNONYMS

❶ⓐ **build**
建 BUILD (a building) →3834
造 build (various structures) →3856
築 CONSTRUCT →3370
設 SET UP →1863

HOMOPHONES

たてる
立 STAND →2486
点 POINT →2587
閉 CLOSE →4116
たて
立 STAND →2486
縦 VERTICAL →1783
竪 VERTICAL →3516
-だて 立 STAND →2486
たつ
立 STAND →2486
起 RISE →4099
発 START →3174
経 PASS THROUGH →1687

NOTE

➡ see USAGE note at 立 2486

逆

3835
口3-3-6

▶**REVERSE**
ギャク ゲキ▲ さか さか(さ) さか(らう)
Ⓝ 逆 Ⓒ 逆 nì

162	Jōyō-5	U9006
辶	S9-3-6	F0764

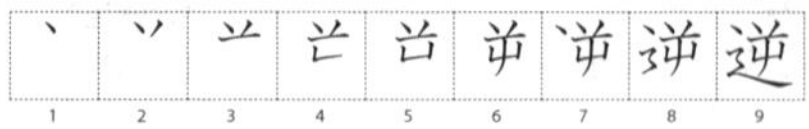

COMPOUNDS

❶ [also prefix] **REVERSE, inverse, backward, contrary, counter**
逆転 ぎゃくてん reversal, turnabout, inversion; reverse rotation
逆流 ぎゃくりゅう countercurrent, adverse tide; regurgitation (of blood)
逆戻り ぎゃくもどり retrogression, reversal, going back
逆数 ぎゃくすう reciprocal number
逆説 ぎゃくせつ paradox
逆効果 ぎゃくこうか counter result, reverse effect
逆比例 ぎゃくひれい inverse proportion
❷ **contrary, adverse, unfavorable**
逆境 ぎゃっきょう adversity, adverse [unfavorable] circumstances
逆風 ぎゃくふう adverse [contrary] wind
❸ **rebel, defy, disobey**
逆徒 ぎゃくと rebel, traitor
反逆する はんぎゃくする revolt [rebel] against, rise in mutiny
❹ receive, welcome
逆旅 げきりょ inn

INDEPENDENT

【ぎゃく 逆】**REVERSE, inverse, contrariness;** *math* **converse**
逆な ぎゃくな contrary, adverse; reverse, inverse

KUN

【さか 逆】
ⓐ [in compounds] **REVERSE, inverse**
ⓑ **upside-down**
a 逆立ち さかだち handstand
逆立つ さかだつ stand on end, stand up, bristle up
逆上る さかのぼる [usu. 遡る] go upstream; go back (to the past); retroact

b 逆子 さかご foot presentation
逆様の さかさまの upside-down, reverse
逆になる さかになる turn upside down

【さかさ 逆さ】**REVERSE, inversion**
逆さの さかさの inverted, upside-down, reverse
逆さに さかさに bottom up, upside-down

【さからう 逆らう】**act contrary to, go against, oppose, disobey, defy**
親に逆らう おやにさからう disobey one's parents

SPECIAL READINGS

逆上せる▲ のぼせる have a rush of blood to the head, feel dizzy; get excited; run mad after; become conceited

SYNONYMS

❶ **opposite**
対 OPPOSITE →1025
反 COUNTER →3663
逆 REVERSE →3835
倒 upside-down →0139

❸ **resist**
抗 RESIST →0296
抵 RESIST →0377
耐 WITHSTAND →1634
対 OPPOSE →1025
反 COUNTER →3663
逆 rebel →3835
撥 REPEL →0907
叛 REBEL →1469

USAGE

【さかのぼる】
逆上る
[usu. 遡る]
ⓐ go upstream
ⓑ go back (to the past); retroact
遡る
[sometimes also 逆上る] same as 逆上る

HOMOPHONES

さかのぼる
遡る →4040
逆上る →3835, 4212
のぼせる
上せる →4212
逆上せる →3835, 4212

NOTE

➡ see also USAGE note at 上 4212
➡ see COMPOUND FORMATION for 逆鱗 げきりん →鱗 2375

迷 3836

□3-3-6

▶**PERPLEXED**
メイ まよ(う)
Ⓝ 迷 Ⓒ 迷 mí

162	Jōyō-5	U8FF7
⻌	S9-3-6	F1024

Stroke order: 1–9

COMPOUNDS

❶ (be at a loss at what to do) **be PERPLEXED, be puzzled, be bewildered; hesitate**
迷惑 めいわく trouble, annoyance
迷信 めいしん superstition
混迷 こんめい confusion, bewilderment; [formerly 昏迷] stupor, unconsciousness
低迷する ていめいする hang low; (of the market) be sluggish

❷ [original meaning] **lose one's way, get lost, go astray**
迷路 めいろ maze, labyrinth
迷宮 めいきゅう labyrinth, maze; mystery
迷鳥 めいちょう stray bird

❸ absurd, ridiculous, bizarre, fantastic
迷論 めいろん fallacy, absurd opinion
迷答 めいとう ridiculous answer, boner

KUN

【まよう 迷う】**be PERPLEXED, be puzzled; hesitate; get lost, lose one's way; be tempted, be seduced, be misguided; turn in one's grave**
迷い まよい bewilderment, doubt, indecision; infatuation; *Buddhism* maya
迷わす まよわす perplex, puzzle; fascinate, infatuate; lead astray
迷い込む まよいこむ stray [wander] into
血迷う ちまよう lose control of oneself

SPECIAL READINGS

迷子 まいご lost child

SYNONYMS

❶ **bewildered**
迷 PERPLEXED →3836
惑 BEWILDERED →3461

送 3837

□3-3-6

▶**SEND**
ソウ おく(る)
Ⓝ 送 Ⓒ 送 sòng

162	Jōyō-3	U9001
⻌	S9-3-6	F0329

Stroke order: 1–9

COMPOUNDS

❶ⓐ [original meaning] **SEND, dispatch, deliver, mail**

❻ **transmit**

a 送金 そうきん remittance
送付 そうふ sending, remittance
送検する そうけんする commit for trial, send to the prosecutors office
送料 そうりょう postage, carriage
郵送する ゆうそうする mail, send by mail
輸送 ゆそう transport, conveyance
発送する はっそうする send out, dispatch, ship
b 送電 そうでん electrical transmission
送信 そうしん transmission (of a message)
放送 ほうそう broadcasting

❷ **SEND off, see off, escort**

送迎する そうげいする welcome and send off
送別 そうべつ farewell, send-off
送別会 そうべつかい farewell [seeing-off] party
護送 ごそう safeguard, convoy, escort

❸ give as a present

送呈する そうていする send a book as a present

INDEPENDENT

【そう 送】postage
送五百円 そうごひゃくえん postage 500 yen

KUN

【おくる 送る】

① **SEND, ship, dispatch, mail; transmit**
送り先 おくりさき destination; receiver, consignee
送り込む おくりこむ send into
申し送る もうしおくる send word to, hand over (one's business to another)

②ⓐ **see off, SEND off**
ⓑ escort, take a person (home)
a 送り おくり seeing off; funeral; sending
見送る みおくる see off
b 送り届ける おくりとどける send to, deliver; escort (a person) home

③ spend (time), lead (one's life)
空しく日を送る むなしくひをおくる spend days in vain

④ **add kana affixes to Chinese characters**
送り仮名 おくりがな *okurigana,* kana affixes (→ see APPENDIX 6)

SYNONYMS

❶ **send**
送 SEND → 3837
投 SEND IN → 0300
回 send round → 3793
遣 DISPATCH → 3908
派 DISPATCH → 0456

USAGE

【おくる】
送る
① send, ship, dispatch, mail; transmit
②ⓐ see off, send off
ⓑ escort, take a person (home)
③ spend (time), lead (one's life)
④ add kana affixes to Chinese characters
贈る
① present (a gift), give (a present)
② bestow on, confer upon

HOMOPHONES

おくる 贈 PRESENT A GIFT → 2064

NOTE

★ do not confuse with 迭 ALTERNATE → 3818

退

3838

□3-3-6

▶**RETREAT**

タイ しりぞ(く) しりぞ(ける) ひ(く)▲ ど(く)▲ ど(ける)▲ ど(かす)▲ の(く)▲ の(ける)▲

Ⓝ 退 Ⓒ 退 tuì

162	Jōyō-5	U9000
辶	S9-3-6	F0601

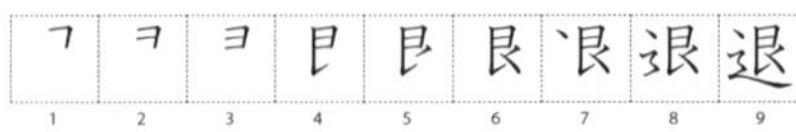

COMPOUNDS

❶ⓐ [original meaning] **RETREAT, move back, withdraw, leave**
ⓑ **cause to RETREAT, drive back, repulse**
a 退場する たいじょうする leave, exit
退去 たいきょ retreat, withdrawal, evacuation
退出 たいしゅつ leaving, withdrawal
退院 たいいん discharge from a hospital
撤退する てったいする withdraw, evacuate, pull out
後退する こうたいする retreat, recede
脱退 だったい withdrawal, secession
b 退学 たいがく leave school; be expelled from school
撃退する げきたいする repulse, drive back; reject, repulse

❷ (retreat from public life) **retire, resign, leave**
退職 たいしょく retirement, resignation
引退する いんたいする retire, go into retirement
隠退 いんたい retirement, seclusion from the world

❸ **keep one's distance, hesitate**
辞退する じたいする decline, refuse

❹ [formerly also 頽 2039] **decline, decay**
退廃 たいはい degeneration, decadence, deterioration
退廃的 たいはいてき decadent, degenerating
退勢 たいせい one's declining fortunes, decay
衰退 すいたい decline, decay, degeneration

❺ **become spiritless, be languid**

退屈 たいくつ tedium, boredom

❻ [formerly also 褪 1577] fade, discolor

退色 たいしょく fading, faded color

KUN

【しりぞく 退く】RETREAT, recede, back; withdraw, leave; retire, resign

一歩退く いっぽしりぞく take a step backward

御前を退く ごぜん(=おまえ)をしりぞく withdraw from the presence (of the emperor)

職を退く しょくをしりぞく resign from one's post

【しりぞける 退ける】

① (cause to retreat) **drive away, repel, expel, keep away**

要職から退ける ようしょくからしりぞける expel (a person) from an important position

人を退ける ひとをしりぞける keep others away

② **defeat, beat**

敵の攻撃を退ける てきのこうげきをしりぞける beat off an attack by the enemy

③ [sometimes also 斥ける] **reject, refuse, turn down**

提案を退ける ていあんをしりぞける turn down a proposal

【ひく 退く】 [also 引く]

①ⓐ **RETREAT**, withdraw

ⓑ retire, resign

a 後へ退く あとへひく retreat, recede

b 役所を退く やくしょをひく leave office, resign one's post in an office

② subside, abate, go down

熱が退く ねつがひく The fever abates

【どく 退く】 move out of the way, make way [room] (for), step aside, step back

【どける 退ける】 get out of the way, remove

【どかす 退かす】 same as 退ける どける

【のく 退く】

ⓐ same as 退く どく

ⓑ leave, retire (from), withdrraw (from)

a 立ち退く たちのく leave, depart, evacuate; take refuge; vacate, leave, quit

【のける 退ける】

① [also 除ける] same as 退ける どける

② [usu. in the form of て退ける] (do something bold or difficult) pull off, dare to, venture to

SYNONYMS

❶ⓐ leave and set forth

去 GO AWAY → 2678

離 leave → 2364

発 START → 3174

出 GO OUT → 4310

退 RETREAT → 3838

撤 WITHDRAW → 0912

ⓑ drive out

斥 EXPEL → 3690

排 EXCLUDE → 0593

追 chase away → 3840

退 cause to retreat → 3838

駆 drive away → 2293

逐 DRIVE OUT → 3848

払う clear out → 0225

❷ resign

辞 RESIGN → 1726

退 retire → 3838

USAGE

【しりぞける】

退ける

① (cause to retreat) drive away, repel, expel, keep away

② defeat, beat

③ [sometimes also 斥ける] reject, refuse, turn down

斥ける

[usu. 退ける] reject, refuse, turn down

HOMOPHONES

しりぞける 斥 EXPEL → 3690

ひく

引 DRAW → 0207

弾 PROJECTILE → 0697

惹 DRAW ATTENTION → 2903

挽 GRIND → 0511

轢 RUN OVER → 2095

牽 DRAW → 2621

曳 DRAW → 4348

NOTE

➡ see also USAGE note at 引 0207

逃

3839

口3-3-6

▶ESCAPE

トウ に(げる) に(がす) のが(す) のが(れる)

Ⓝ 迯 逃 Ⓒ 逃 táo

162	Jōyō	U9003
辶	S9-3-6	F0614

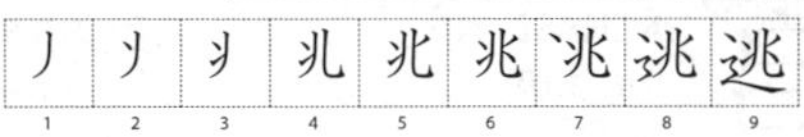

COMPOUNDS

❶ [original meaning] **ESCAPE, run away, flee**

逃亡する とうぼうする escape, abscond, desert

逃走 とうそう flight, escape

❷ (succeed in avoiding) **ESCAPE, evade, shirk**

逃避 とうひ escape, evasion, flight

KUN

【にげる 逃げる】ESCAPE, run away, flee; escape, evade, shirk

逃げ にげ escape, evasion

逃げ出す にげだす make a break, run off, make off
逃げ道 にげみち way of escape
逃げ足 にげあし flight, running away
轢き逃げする ひきにげする hit and run

【にがす 逃がす】**let go, set free; let ESCAPE; let slip, miss**
取り逃がす とりにがす fail to catch, let slip

【のがす 逃す】same as 逃がす にがす
見逃す みのがす overlook, miss
好機を逃す こうきをのがす let an opportunity slip

【のがれる 逃れる】**ESCAPE, get away; get clear of; escape, evade, shirk**
責任を逃れる せきにんをのがれる shirk one's responsibility
言い逃れ いいのがれ evasion, subterfuge, excuse

SYNONYMS

❶ **escape**
逃 ESCAPE →3839
遁 FLEE →4027
亡 flee →4210
走 run away →2720
脱 ESCAPE FROM →1225

❷ **avoid and abstain**
避 AVOID →3944
逃 ESCAPE →3839
禦 WARD OFF →3561
忌 shun →2735
禁 abstain from →3469

USAGE

【のがれる】
逃れる
escape, get away; get clear of; escape, evade, shirk
遁れる
flee, escape; evade, shirk away

HOMOPHONES

のがれる 遁 FLEE →4027

追

▶CHASE
ツイ お(う)
Ⓝ 追 Ⓒ 追 zhuī

3840
□3-3-6

162	Jōyō-3	U8FFD
辶	S9-3-6	F0409

Stroke order: 1–9

COMPOUNDS

❶ⓐ **CHASE, pursue, follow, seek**
ⓑ **CHASE away, drive out, expel**
a 追跡する ついせきする pursue, chase, follow up
追突 ついとつ rear-end collision
追求する ついきゅうする pursue
追及する ついきゅうする pursue, seek after, follow, press (a person) hard
追究 ついきゅう thorough investigation, close inquiry
追随する ついずいする follow (in the wake of)
追従 ついしょう flattery, sycophancy
猛追 もうつい hot chase [pursuit]
b 追放する ついほうする banish, purge, exile
追儺× ついな ceremony of driving out the devils

❷ⓐ **add, perform in addition to**
ⓑ [also prefix] **additional, supplementary**
a 追加 ついか addition, appendix, supplement
追刊 ついかん additional publication
b 追徴金 ついちょうきん additional imposition
追試験 ついしけん supplementary exam

❸ⓐ post-, subsequent(ly), afterwards
ⓑ posthumous
a 追記 ついき postscript
追体験する ついたいけんする experience for oneself what another person has gone through
追認 ついにん ratification, confirmation
b 追贈する ついぞうする confer court rank posthumously

❹ⓐ reminisce, recollect, recall the past
ⓑ **remember the dead, mourn**
a 追想 ついそう recollection, reminiscence
b 追悼 ついとう mourning
追善 ついぜん mass for the dead

KUN

【おう 追う】**CHASE, pursue, follow; drive away**
追って おって later, afterwards, by and by
追い掛ける(=追っ掛ける) おいかける(=おっかける) chase, run after
追い詰める おいつめる corner, drive to the wall, run down
追い付く おいつく overtake, catch up with
追い越す おいこす outrun, pass; overtake
追い抜く おいぬく pass, overtake
追い込む おいこむ drive [chase] (into a corner); run on (in printing)
追い込み おいこみ last spurt, final lap
追い出す おいだす turn [drive, throw] out; discharge; evict
追い払う(=追っ払う) おいはらう(=おっぱらう) drive away, expel, exorcise

SYNONYMS

❶ⓐ **follow and pursue**
従 FOLLOW →0498
随 FOLLOW →0765
辿る FOLLOW (a path) →3968
追 CHASE →3840

ⓑ **drive out**

斥 EXPEL → 3690
排 EXCLUDE → 0593
追 chase away → 3840
退 cause to retreat → 3838
駆 drive away → 2293
逐 DRIVE OUT → 3848
払う clear out → 0225

❷ⓐ **add to**

付 ATTACH → 0035
附 ATTACH → 0410
加 ADD → 0042
追 add → 3840
添 ADD TO → 0641

ⓑ **additional**

追 additional → 3840
補 supplementary → 1529
副 accessory → 2230

❹ⓐ **remember**

憶 REMEMBER → 0944
覚える COMMIT TO MEMORY → 3217
記 commit to memory → 1843
追 reminisce → 3840
顧 LOOK BACK → 2394
偲 RECOLLECT → 0153

飛

□3-3-6

incorrect classification
➡ see ■4-9-1 at 4389

昼

3841
□3-3-6

▶**DAYTIME**
チュウ ひる
Ⓝ 晝 Ⓒ 昼 zhòu

72	Jōyō-2	U663C
日	S9-4-5	F0978

COMPOUNDS

❶ [original meaning] **DAYTIME**

昼間 ちゅうかん daytime, day
昼夜 ちゅうや day and night

❷ **midday, noon**

昼食 ちゅうしょく lunch
白昼 はくちゅう daytime, broad daylight

KUN

【ひる 昼】**DAYTIME; midday, noon; lunch**

昼間 ひるま daytime, day
昼寝 ひるね siesta, nap
昼前 ひるまえ in the morning, before noon
昼過ぎ ひるすぎ early afternoon
昼時 ひるどき noon, lunch time
昼休み ひるやすみ noon recess, lunch break
真昼 まひる noon

SYNONYMS

❶ **days**

日 DAY → 3759
曜 DAY OF THE WEEK → 1402
昼 DAYTIME → 3841
旦 first day → 3041
朔 FIRST DAY OF THE LUNAR MONTH → 1678
晦 LAST DAY OF THE LUNAR MONTH → 1196

❷ **noon**

午 NOON → 2478
昼 midday → 3841

屋

3842
□3-3-6

▶**HOUSE**
▶**SMALL SHOP**
オク や
Ⓒ 屋 wū

44	Jōyō-3	U5C4B
尸	S9-3-6	F0089

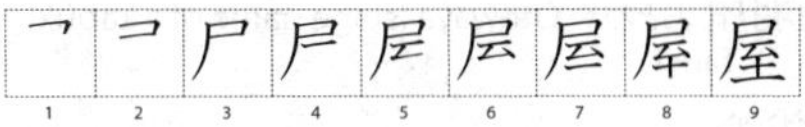

COMPOUNDS

❶ **HOUSE, building**

屋外 おくがい outdoors, open air, exterior of a house
屋内 おくない indoors
家屋 かおく house, building
社屋 しゃおく office building
廃屋 はいおく deserted house

❷ [original meaning] **roof**

屋上 おくじょう housetop, roof

INDEPENDENT

【おく 屋】roof; **HOUSE**

屋上屋を架す おくじょうおくをかす gild refined gold, paint the lily

KUN

【や 屋】

① [in compounds] **HOUSE, dwelling house**

屋敷 やしき [sometimes also 邸] mansion, residence; residential lot
小屋 こや cottage, hut, cabin; playhouse
部屋 へや room, chamber
母屋(=母家) おもや main house [wing]
馬屋 うまや [also 厩] horse stable, horse barn

② [in compounds] **roof**

屋根 やね roof
岩屋 いわや [also 窟] cave, cavern, hole

③ⓐ [also suffix] **SMALL SHOP or place of business, store**

ⓑ [suffix] **shopkeeper, dealer**
ⓒ **suffix for forming names of business establishments**
a 屋台 やたい stall, stand; float, festival car
店屋 みせや shop, store
料理屋 りょうりや restaurant
ab 魚屋 さかなや fish shop; fish dealer
花屋 はなや flower shop; florist
本屋 ほんや bookstore; bookseller
不動産屋 ふどうさんや real estate agent, Realtor
c 松坂屋 まつざかや Matsuzakaya Department Store
④ colloquial occupation suffix—sometimes indicates slight contempt or humility
事務屋 じむや clerk, office worker
何でも屋 なんでもや jack-of-all-trades
⑤ **colloquial suffix indicating the peculiarity or idiosyncrasy of a person**
気取り屋 きどりや affected person, snob
分からず屋 わからずや obstinate person, hardhead
恥ずかしがり屋 はずかしがりや shy person
⑥ [sometimes also 家] suffix after stage family names
音羽屋 おとわや Otowaya (stage name of a kabuki family)

SYNONYMS

❶ **houses**
家 HOUSE → 2827
屋 HOUSE → 3842
軒 house → 1851
戸 HOUSEHOLD → 2429
宅 DWELLING HOUSE → 2698
居 residence → 3822
邸 STATELY RESIDENCE → 1451
住 housing → 0072
庵 HERMITAGE → 3876
❷ **roof**
屋 roof → 3842
宇 roof → 2699
【や】
③ⓐ **places of business**
店 SHOP (of any kind) → 3828
舗 SHOP (esp. traditional) → 2177
屋 SMALL SHOP → 3842
社 COMPANY → 1042
ⓑ **merchant**
屋 shopkeeper → 3842
商 merchant → 2623
④ **workers and professionals**
家 professional → 2827
婦 woman worker → 0565
嬢 (unmarried) female worker → 0936
夫 MAN LABORER → 4271
匠 CRAFTSMAN → 3711
工 workman → 4190
客 skilled person → 2798
士 PROFESSION SUFFIX → 4213
師 profession suffix → 1680
者 person who → 3980
人 person of certain category → 4175
員 MEMBER (of a staff) → 2822
屋 colloquial occupation suffix → 3842
手 OCCUPATION SUFFIX → 4267
⑤ **fellow**
奴 GUY → 0217
漢 FELLOW → 0808
輩 FELLOW (*belittling*) → 3482
徒 fellows → 0499
棒 tough guy → 1237
坊 COLLOQUIAL PERSON SUFFIX → 0274
屋 colloquial person suffix → 3842
物 character → 1084
⑥ **pseudonym suffixes**
亭 PSEUDONYM SUFFIX → 2572
屋 stage name suffix → 3842

USAGE

【や】
屋
① [in compounds] house, dwelling house
② [in compounds] roof
③ⓐ [also suffix] small shop or place of business, store
ⓑ [suffix] shopkeeper, dealer
ⓒ suffix for forming names of business establishments
④ colloquial occupation suffix
⑤ colloquial suffix indicating the peculiarity or idiosyncrasy of a person
⑥ [sometimes also 家] suffix after stage family names
家
① [also suffix] house, home
② [usu. 屋] suffix after stage family names
★Both 屋 and 家 refer to a house or dwelling, but they are not used interchangeably in the same compounds.

HOMOPHONES

や 家 HOUSE → 2827
やしき
邸 STATELY RESIDENCE → 1451
屋敷 → 3842, 2345
いわや
窟 CAVE → 2923
岩屋 → 2778, 3842
うまや
厩 HORSE STABLE → 3746

馬屋 →4086, 3842

NOTE

➡ see also USAGE note at 邸 1451

屍
3843
□3-3-6

▶**CORPSE**
シ しかばね
Ⓒ 尸 shī

44	Non-Jōyō	U5C4D
尸	S9-3-6	F2458

COMPOUNDS

● [now also 死 4334] [original meaning] **CORPSE, dead body**
屍体 したい corpse
屍蠟 しろう adipocere
屍姦× しかん necrophilia, necrophilism
死屍 しし corpse

KUN

【しかばね 屍】[sometimes also 尸] **CORPSE**
生ける屍 いけるしかばね living corpse, living dead

SYNONYMS

● **body**
体 BODY →0080
身 BODY (esp. vs. mind) →4368
肉 FLESH →3966
屍 CORPSE →3843
尸 CORPSE →4198
骸 DEAD BODY →2301

HOMOPHONES

しかばね 尸 CORPSE →4198

度
3844
□3-3-6

▶**DEGREE**
▶**TIME**
ド ト タク たび -た(い)▲ 名 わたる のり
Ⓒ 度 dù duó

53	Jōyō-3	U5EA6
广	S9-3-6	F0073

Stroke order: 1 丶 2 亠 3 广 4 户 5 庐 6 庐 7 庐 8 庹 9 度

COMPOUNDS

❶ [also suffix] **DEGREE, extent**
度合 どあい degree, extent, rate
程度 ていど degree, extent, standard
高度 こうど altitude, height; high degree
震度 しんど seismic intensity
限度 げんど limit, bounds
速度 そくど speed, velocity
精度 せいど precision, accuracy
透明度 とうめいど transparency, degree of clearness
知名度 ちめいど publicity

❷ⓐ (unit of angular measure, latitude, longitude, etc.) **DEGREE**
ⓑ (unit of temperature or humidity) **DEGREE**
ⓒ *optics* **DEGREE** (of refraction), diopter unit
ⓓ *music* **DEGREE**
ⓔ (strength of a liquor) **proof**
a 度数 どすう degree
角度 かくど angle, angular measure, degree
緯度 いど latitude
経度 けいど longitude
二度三十分 にどさんじゅっぷん 2°30′
b 温度 おんど temperature
湿度 しつど humidity
体温三十八度 たいおんさんじゅうはちど 38°(of fever)
c 十八度 じゅうはちど 18 diopter units
d 三度の和音 さんどのわおん triad, common chord
e 四十度のウイスキー よんじゅうどのういすきー 80-proof whisky

❸ⓐ **TIME, occasion**
ⓑ **counter for number of TIMEs**
a 度数 どすう number of times
今度 こんど this time; next time, another time; recently
何度 なんど how many degrees; how many times
毎度 まいど every [each] time, always
b 二度 にど two times [degrees]

❹ **standard of propriety, limit**
度外視する どがいしする leave out of account, neglect
制度 せいど system, organization, institution
節度 せつど standard; moderation
落ち度 おちど fault, error; guilt
過度の かどの excessive
法度 はっと law, ordinance, prohibition

❺ **period, term**
年度 ねんど year, fiscal year; school year; term

❻ generosity, liberality
度量 どりょう magnanimity, generosity
度胸 どきょう courage, pluck, heart
襟度 きんど magnanimity, generosity

❼ **manner, bearing, attitude**
態度 たいど attitude, manner

❽ⓐ conjecture, guess
ⓑ [original meaning] **measure**
a 忖×度 そんたく conjecture, surmise
b 支度する したくする arrange, prepare; [original meaning, now archaic] measure, estimate

❾ measuring instrument, ruler
度量衡 どりょうこう weights and measures

❿ provisions, necessary supplies
調度 ちょうど personal effects, furnishings, supplies

用度 ようど expenditure, office expenses; supplies

⓫ save, redeem

済度 さいど *Buddhism* salvation

⓬ become a bonze

得度 とくど entering of Buddhist priesthood

⓭ **unclassified compounds**

度忘れ どわすれ slip of memory

丁度 ちょうど [sometimes also 恰度] just, exactly; as if

INDEPENDENT

【ど 度】

① **DEGREE, extent**

緊張の度 きんちょうのど degree of tenseness

② *optics* **DEGREE (of refraction), diopter unit**

度の強い眼鏡 どのつよいめがね powerful spectacles

③ **TIME**s, frequency

度を重ねる どをかさねる repeat

④ standard of propriety, limit

度が過ぎる どがすぎる go to excess, carry too far

度を失う どをうしなう lose one's presence of mind

【どする 度する】 save, redeem

KUN

【たび 度】 **TIME, occasion; counter for number of times**

度度 たびたび often

見る度に みるたびに whenever [each time] one sees (it)

一度 ひとたび one time

【-たい -度い】 [desiderative verbal suffix] want [wish] to do

行き度い いきたい want to go

し度くない したくない do not want to do (it)

SYNONYMS

❶ **degree**

程 EXTENT → 1524

度 DEGREE → 3844

分 relative degree → 2466

❷ⓐ **angle and angular measure**

角 ANGLE → 2541

度 DEGREE → 3844

❸ **time and time counters**

回 TIME → 3793

度 TIME → 3844

遍 counter for number of times → 3890

返 counter for number of times → 3797

NOTE

➡ see COMPOUND FORMATION for 支度 したく → 支 2473

麻

3845

□3-3-6

▶**DEER**

ロク しか か ㊔ かの

53	Nonstandard	U22218
广	S9-3-6	F0000

traditional form → see 鹿 at 3879

席

□3-3-6

incorrect stroke-count

➡ see □3-3-7: 广 at 3865

庭

□3-3-6

incorrect stroke-count

➡ see □3-3-7: 广 at 3866

囶

3846

□3-3-6

▶**COUNTRY**

コク くに

31	Nonstandard	U5700
口	S9-3-6	F0000

alternative form → see 国 at 3831

廻

3847

□3-3-7

▶**TURN ROUND**

カイ エ まわ(る) まわ(す)

54	Nonstandard	U5EFD
廴	S10-3-7	F0000

traditional form → see 廻 at 3833

逐

3848

□3-3-7

▶**ONE BY ONE**
▶**DRIVE OUT**

チク

Ⓝ 逐 Ⓒ 逐 zhú

162	Jōyō	U9010
辶	S10-3-7	F2202

1	2	3	4	5	6	7	8	9	10
一	㇇	豕	豕	豕	豕	豕	豕	逐	逐

COMPOUNDS

❶ **ONE BY ONE, successively, one after another**

逐一 ちくいち one by one, in detail

逐次 ちくじ one by one, successively

逐条審議 ちくじょうしんぎ article-by-article discussion

逐語訳 ちくごやく word for word translation

逐日 ちくじつ day after day, every day

逐年 ちくねん annually, year by year

❷ⓐ **DRIVE OUT, expel**

ⓑ [original meaning] pursue, chase after

a 放逐する ほうちくする expel, banish, expatriate

駆逐する くちくする drive away, drive out, expel

❸ compete, contend

角逐する かくちくする compete with, vie with

SYNONYMS

❶ **in succession**

連 IN SUCCESSION →3849
歴 successive →3748
逐 ONE BY ONE →3848
逓 progressively →3852
漸 GRADUALLY →0867

❷ **drive out**
斥 EXPEL →3690
排 EXCLUDE →0593
追 chase away →3840
退 cause to retreat →3838
駆 drive away →2293
逐 DRIVE OUT →3848
払う clear out →0225

NOTE

★ do not confuse with 遂 ACCOMPLISH →3892

連 3849 口3-3-7

▶LINK
▶IN SUCCESSION
レン つら(なる) つら(ねる) つ(れる) -づ(れ) ㊔ むらじ

Ⓝ 連 Ⓒ 连 lián

162	Jōyō-4	U9023
辶	S10-3-7	F0131

Stroke order: 一 丆 冖 币 百 亘 車 `車 漣 連 (1–10)

COMPOUNDS

❶ [formerly also 聯 1797]
ⓐ (join together) **LINK, join**
ⓑ (connect as if by linking) **LINK, connect, join, unite**

a 連結 れんけつ connection, coupling, linking
連辞 れんじ copula
連鎖 れんさ chain (as of reasoning), link, series; connection
連星 れんせい binary star

b 連絡 れんらく connection, contact; communication
連立 れんりつ alliance, coalition
連係 れんけい connection, linking, contact
連帯 れんたい solidarity
連合 れんごう combination, union, alliance; association
連盟 れんめい union, federation, league
関連 かんれん connection, relation, association

❷ **federation, union, alliance, league**
ソ連 それん Soviet Union
国連 こくれん United Nations
全学連 ぜんがくれん All-Japan Federation of Student Self-Government Associations

❸ⓐ **IN SUCCESSION, in series, continually, repeatedly**
ⓑ [also prefix] **successive, in a row, consecutive, continued**

a 連発する れんぱつする fire in rapid succession, fire in volleys
連載する れんさいする serialize, publish serially
連続する れんぞくする continue, occur in succession
連戦 れんせん series of battles [games], every battle [game]
五連敗 ごれんぱい five-game losing streak

b 連休 れんきゅう consecutive holidays
連日 れんじつ day after day, everyday
連山 れんざん mountain range
連分数 れんぶんすう continued fraction

❹ [also suffix] **set, party, company, gang, clique**
連中 れんちゅう(=れんじゅう) party, company, clique; those fellows [guys]
常連 じょうれん regular visitors [customers], frequenters
愚連隊 ぐれんたい hooligans, hoodlums
文士連 ぶんしれん the literary set
ハイカラ連 はいかられん the smart set

❺ take along, bring along, accompany
連行する れんこうする take a suspect to the police

❻ counter for:
ⓐ reams (of paper)
ⓑ miscellaneous **LINK**ed objects or sets of objects such as chains, necklaces, etc.

a 一連 いちれん one ream
b 数珠一連 じゅずいちれん a string of beads, a rosary

KUN

【つらなる 連なる】**range, stand in a row; attend**
山は南北に連なっている やまはなんぼくにつらなっている The mountains range north and south

【つらねる 連ねる】**put in a row, join, put together**
名を連ねる なをつらねる have one's name entered (in a list)

【つれる 連れる】**take along, bring along, accompany**
連れ つれ companion
連れ合い つれあい spouse, mate
連れ立つ つれだつ accompany
連れて行く つれていく take [bring] along (with one); take (person) away
連れて来る つれてくる bring, fetch (a person)
引き連れる ひきつれる take [bring, have] along (with one)

【-づれ -連れ】[suffix] **with, accompanied by**
二人連れ ふたりづれ party of two
子供連れ こどもづれ accompanied by children

SYNONYMS

❶ⓐ join

結 TIE → 1706
繫 CONNECT → 3612
縛 BIND → 1779
綴 BIND → 1746
繃 BIND UP → 1787
束 TIE UP → 4369
梱 PACK → 1205
連 LINK → 3849
係 CONNECT → 0108
接 join → 0607

ⓑ relate

関 CONCERN → 4129
係 CONNECT → 0108
絡 INTERLINK → 1709
渉 HAVE RELATIONS WITH → 0638
連 LINK → 3849
聯 LINK → 1797

❷ organized bodies

会 SOCIETY → 2512
協 association → 0103
団 BODY → 3791
体 BODY → 0080
組 union → 1693
労 workers' union → 3155
連 federation → 3849
講 fraternity → 2046
院 INSTITUTION → 0544

❸ continue

続 CONTINUE → 1722
継 SUCCEED → 1720
連 IN SUCCESSION → 3849
持 HOLD → 0447

❸ in succession

連 IN SUCCESSION → 3849
歴 successive → 3748
逐 ONE BY ONE → 3848
逓 progressively → 3852
漸 GRADUALLY → 0867

❹ groups

群 GROUP (of any kind) → 1942
班 SQUAD → 1182
軍 team → 2582
組 group (of people) → 1693
陣 lineup → 0545
連 set → 3849
族 common-interest group (*slang*) → 1195
党 PARTY → 3190
隊 PARTY (organized group) → 0762
団 BODY → 3791
伍 ranks → 0050

❺ lead and escort

率 LEAD → 2625
引 lead → 0207
導 GUIDE → 3587
連 take along → 3849

逝

3850
□3-3-7

▶DEPART THIS LIFE
セイ ゆ(く) い(く)
Ⓝ 逝 Ⓒ 逝 shì

162	Jōyō	U901D
辶	S10-3-7	F2317

1	2	3	4	5	6	7	8	9	10
一	十	扌	扌	扩	折	折	逝	逝	逝

COMPOUNDS

ⓐ DEPART THIS LIFE, pass away, die suddenly
ⓑ [original meaning, now archaic] **depart, be gone, leave**

a 逝去する せいきょする pass away, die
急逝する きゅうせいする die suddenly
長逝 ちょうせい death, passing

KUN

【ゆく 逝く】DEPART THIS LIFE, pass away, die
【いく 逝く】DEPART THIS LIFE, pass away, die

SYNONYMS

ⓐ die

死 DIE → 4334
萎 WITHER → 2872
没 die → 0305
亡 DECEASE → 4210
殉 DIE A MARTYR → 1177
歿 DIE → 1078
去 pass away → 2678
逝 DEPART THIS LIFE → 3850
斃 FALL DOWN DEAD → 3593
枯 WITHER → 1113

HOMOPHONES

ゆく 行 GO → 0246
いく 行 GO → 0246

NOTE

➡ see USAGE note at 行 0246

速

3851
□3-3-7

▶QUICK
ソク はや(い) はや- はや(める) はや(まる) すみ(やか) ㊔ はやみ
Ⓝ 速 Ⓒ 速 sù

162	Jōyō-3	U901F
辶	S10-3-7	F0631

1	2	3	4	5	6	7	8	9	10
一	𠃌	币	㠯	申	束	束	束	速	速

COMPOUNDS

❶ⓐ [original meaning] **QUICK, speedy, fast, rapid, swift, prompt, hasty**
ⓑ **QUICKly, swiftly**
a 速球 そっきゅう fast ball
速射 そくしゃ quick firing
速達便 そくたつびん special delivery, express mail
速報 そくほう prompt report, news flash
快速 かいそく high speed; fast (local) train
急速な きゅうそくな rapid, swift, prompt
迅速な じんそくな swift, rapid
b 速記 そっき shorthand, stenography
速断 そくだん hasty conclusion; prompt decision
早速 さっそく immediately
❷ **speed, velocity**
速度 そくど speed, velocity
時速 じそく speed per hour
風速 ふうそく wind velocity
変速機 へんそくき speed change gear

KUN

【はやい 速い】
ⓐ (acting or moving quickly) **QUICK, speedy, fast, rapid, swift**
ⓑ [usu. 早い] (requiring little time) **QUICK, prompt**
a 速さ はやさ speed
足速い あしばやい swift-footed, light-footed
b 素速い すばやい quick, nimble, agile
耳が速い みみがはやい be quick-eared
【はや- 速-】 [usu. 早-] **QUICK, fast, rapid**
速口 はやくち fast [rapid] talking
速業 はやわざ quick work, (clever) feat
速分かり はやわかり quick understanding; guide, handbook
【はやめる 速める】 *vt* **QUICKen, accelerate, speed up, hasten**
足を速める あしをはやめる quicken one's pace [steps]
【はやまる 速まる】 *vi* **QUICKen, accelerate, speed up**
速まる鼓動 はやまるこどう quickening heartbeat
【すみやか 速やか】
すみやかな 速やかな **swift, QUICK, prompt**
速やかに すみやかに swiftly, quickly, promptly, immediately
速やかさ すみやかさ swiftness, promptness

SYNONYMS

❶ **fast**
速 QUICK → 3851
早 QUICK → 3042
疾 fast → 4064
快 fast → 0289
急 rapid → 2595
迅 SWIFT → 3780
敏 NIMBLE → 1675
即 IMMEDIATE → 1439
捷 AGILE → 0609

USAGE

【そく】
速
quick, speedy, fast, rapid, swift, prompt, hasty
即
immediate, prompt, instant, on the spot

HOMOPHONES

はやい 早 EARLY → 3042
はや- 早 EARLY → 3042
はやめる 早 EARLY → 3042
はやまる 早 EARLY → 3042

NOTE

➡ see also USAGE note at 早 3042

逓

3852
□3-3-7

▶**RELAY**
テイ
Ⓝ 遞 Ⓒ 递 dì

162	Jōyō	U9013
辶	S10-3-7	F3183

1	2	3	4	5	6	7	8	9	10
一	厂	𠂆	戶	斤	肩	虒	𠃊虒	㡯	逓

COMPOUNDS

❶ⓐ (transmit by stages) **RELAY, forward**
ⓑ (place where fresh horses are posted) **RELAY, post station**
a 逓伝する ていでんする relay (a message)
逓信 ていしん communications
逓送 ていそう forwarding
b 駅逓 えきてい transportation from post to post; postal service in Meiji era
❷ **progressively, successively, gradually, in order**
逓増する ていぞうする increase progressively [gradually]
逓減する ていげんする diminish successively, decrease in order
逓次 ていじ in order, successively
逓降変圧器 ていこうへんあつき step-down transformer

SYNONYMS

❶ⓐ **transmit and deliver**
伝 TRANSMIT → 0048
逓 RELAY → 3852
届ける DELIVER → 3820
達 deliver → 3893
ⓑ **post station**
駅 relay station → 2292

逓 RELAY →3852
宿 post station →2858

❷ **in succession**
連 IN SUCCESSION →3849
歴 successive →3748
逐 ONE BY ONE →3848
逓 progressively →3852
漸 GRADUALLY →0867

途

3853
3-3-7

▸**WAY**
ト ㊔ みち
Ⓝ 途 Ⓒ 途 tú

162	Jōyō	U9014
辶	S10-3-7	F0733

COMPOUNDS

❶ [original meaning] **WAY, route, course, road, path**
途中で とちゅうで on the way
途上で とじょうで on the way
中途で ちゅうとで halfway, in the middle
発展途上国 はってんとじょうこく developing countries
前途 ぜんと one's future, prospects; distance yet to cover
帰途 きと one's way home, return trip

❷ (method of doing) **WAY, means**
方途 ほうと means, way, measure
用途 ようと use, service, application
金の使途 かねのしと how money is used

❸ [formerly also 杜 1030] **shut out, stop, prevent**
途絶 とぜつ stoppage, interruption, cessation

INDEPENDENT

【と 途】**WAY**
帰国の途に就く きこくのとにつく leave for home

SYNONYMS

❶ **ways and routes**
道 WAY (path) →3888
径 PATH →0347
軌 TRACK →1832
線 LINE →1760
澪 WATERWAY →0957
途 WAY (route) →3853
路 ROAD →1936
筋 wayside →3319
通り street →3855
街 city street →0702
辻 CROSSROADS →3958
岐 forked road →0285
巷 THE STREETS →3097

❷ **way and style**
風 MANNER →3730
様 MODE →1332
方 WAY →2459
途 WAY →3853
法 METHOD →0391
流 STYLE →0529
式 STYLE →3785
調 TONE →1973

COMPOUND FORMATION

【用途 ようと】
用途 'use, service, application' is the way (途 ❷) of using (用) something.

透

3854
3-3-7

▸**PASS THROUGH**
▸**TRANSPARENT**
トウ す(く) す(かす) す(ける) とお(る)▲ とお(す)▲
Ⓝ 透 Ⓒ 透 tòu

162	Jōyō	U900F
辶	S10-3-7	F1333

COMPOUNDS

❶ (move through something) **PASS THROUGH, let through, permeate, penetrate**
透過 とうか penetration, transmission
透析 とうせき *chem* dialysis
透磁性 とうじせい magnetic permeability
浸透 しんとう permeation, penetration

❷ⓐ (allow light to pass through) **be TRANSPARENT, be seen through**
ⓑ see through
a 透明な とうめいな transparent
透視図 とうしず perspective drawing, transparent view
透徹した とうてつした lucid, clear, penetrating
b 透視 とうし seeing through; clairvoyance
透察 とうさつ insight

KUN

【すく 透く】
① **be TRANSPARENT, be seen through**
見え透く みえすく be easily seen, be obvious
②ⓐ become sparse
ⓑ [formerly also 隙く] leave a gap
a 透いた枝 すいたえだ thinned branches
b 透き(=隙) すき gap, interval
透き間(=隙間) すきま gap, opening; crack, crevice

【すかす 透かす】
①ⓐ **make TRANSPARENT**
ⓑ **look through, peer into**

a 透かし すかし watermark; openwork
b 闇を透かす やみをすかす peer into the darkness
② [formerly also 隙かす] leave a space [opening], thin (out)
透かさず すかさず without a moment's delay
木を透かす きをすかす thin trees
③ *slang* break wind noiselessly
【すける 透ける】**be [grow] TRANSPARENT**
透けるブラウス すけるぶらうす sheer blouse
【とおる 透る】[also 通る]
ⓐ **be TRANSPARENT, be pervious to (light)**
ⓑ **penetrate, pierce, permeate**
a 透り とおり penetration (as of light)
光が透るカーテン ひかりがとおるかーてん curtain pervious to light
b 透る声 とおるこえ carrying voice
【とおす 透す】[also 通す] be **TRANSPARENT**, be pervious to (light)
光を透す ひかりをとおす be pervious to light

SYNONYMS

❶ **penetrate**
透 PASS THROUGH →3854
貫 PENETRATE →3112
破 break through →1478
滲 PERMEATE →0862
❷ **clear**
透 TRANSPARENT →3854
澄 LIMPID →0915
清 CLEAR (liquid) →0635
明 CLEAR (unclouded) →1060
朗 CLEAR (sky) →1679
冴える CRISP AND CLEAR →0087

USAGE

❶【すく】
透く
① be transparent, be seen through
②ⓐ become sparse
ⓑ [formerly also 隙く] leave a gap
空く
become empty, become less crowded
隙く
[now usu. 透く] leave a gap
❷【すき】
透き
[also 隙] gap, interval
隙
① [also 透き] gap, interval
② chance, unguarded moment
❸【すかす】
透かす
①ⓐ make transparent
ⓑ look through, peer into
② [formerly also 隙かす] leave a space [opening], thin (out)
③ *slang* break wind noiselessly
空かす
① feel hungry
② make available, make free
隙かす
[now usu. 透かす] leave a space [opening], thin (out)

HOMOPHONES

すく
空 SKY →2767
隙 GAP →0826
すき 隙 GAP →0826
すかす
空 SKY →2767
隙 GAP →0826
とおる 通 PASS →3855
とおり 通 PASS →3855
とおす 通 PASS →3855

NOTE

➡ see also USAGE note at 通 3855

通

3855
☐3-3-7

▶**PASS**
▶**COMMUNICATE**
ツウ ツ とお(る) とお(り) -とお(り) -どお(り) とお(す) とお(し) -どお(し) かよ(う) ㊔ みち ゆき
Ⓝ 通 Ⓒ 通 tōng tòng

162	Jōyō-2	U901A
辶	S10-3-7	F0086

1	2	3	4	5	6	7	8	9	10
㇇	㇇	了	了	甬	甬	甬	㴞	通	通

COMPOUNDS

❶ⓐ [original meaning] **PASS (by), pass through**
ⓑ **PASS current, pass for**
a 通過 つうか passing, passage
通行 つうこう passing, passage, transit, traffic
通路 つうろ passage, pathway, alley, aisle
開通する かいつうする be opened to [for] traffic
不通 ふつう impassability, interruption, stoppage, tie-up
b 通用する つうようする pass, circulate, pass [go] current, hold good
通貨 つうか currency, current money
流通 りゅうつう circulation of money or goods; flow of water; ventilation
❷ **go to and from, go back and forth, commute**
通勤 つうきん commuting, commutation, attending office
通学 つうがく attending school, going to school

通商 つうしょう commerce, trade, commercial relation [intercourse]

❸ⓐ (transmit or interchange information) **COMMUNICATE, exchange information, let know**
ⓑ **interpret (from a foreign language)**
ⓒ (form a connecting passage) **COMMUNICATE (with), lead to**

a 通信 つうしん correspondence, communication, information
通達する つうたつする communicate, notify; attain proficiency
通告 つうこく notice, notification, announcement
通話 つうわ telephone call
文通 ぶんつう correspondence, exchange of letters

b 通訳 つうやく interpreting; interpreter
通弁 つうべん interpreter (in Edo period)

c 直通 ちょくつう direct communication [service]; through service [traffic]

❹ **through, from beginning to end**
通算 つうさん sum total, aggregate
通読する つうどくする read through
通巻 つうかん consecutive number of volumes
通夜 つや vigil, deathwatch

❺ **common, general, universal, popular**
通常の つうじょうの common, ordinary, usual
通称 つうしょう popular [common] name
通念 つうねん common idea, generally accepted idea
通説 つうせつ common opinion, popular view
通俗的 つうぞくてき popular, common
普通の ふつうの normal, regular, ordinary
共通の きょうつうの common

❻ⓐ **know [understand] thoroughly, be thoroughly familiar with, master**
ⓑ [also suffix] well-informed person, authority, expert

a 通人 つうじん man of the world, man about town; dilettante
精通する せいつうする be well versed in, have thorough knowledge of

b 食通 しょくつう gourmet
消息通 しょうそくつう well-informed person, insider

❼ have sexual intercourse
密通 みっつう illicit intercourse, misconduct
姦×通 かんつう adultery, illicit intercourse

❽ counter for letters or documents
手紙二通 てがみにつう two letters

❾ occult [magic] powers
神通力 じんつうりき occult [supernatural] power, divine power

INDEPENDENT

【つう 通】 man of the world, man about town, dilettante; thorough knowledge; occult powers
通を気取る つうをきどる set up for a man about town

【つうじる(=つうずる) 通じる(=通ずる)】
①ⓐ **PASS, run, be opened to, communicate with**
ⓑ **PASS electric current, transmit**

a 通じ つうじ passage, evacuation; movement of the bowels
通じて つうじて through; through(out)

② put through (a call)
③ be understood [comprehensible]
④ be versed in, know thoroughly
⑤ **COMMUNICATE** secretly with; have sexual intercourse

KUN

【とおる 通る】
①ⓐ **PASS (by), go along [past], get through**
ⓑ **PASS for [as], be known as, pass current**

a 通り掛かる とおりかかる happen to pass by
通り道 とおりみち path
町を通る まちをとおる pass through town

b 本物で通る ほんものでとおる pass for [as] genuine

② [also 透る]
ⓐ penetrate, pierce, permeate
ⓑ **be transparent, be pervious to (light)**

a 通る声 とおるこえ carrying voice

b 透き通る すきとおる be transparent

③ⓐ **PASS** (an examination)
ⓑ **PASS**, be admissible

a 議案が通った ぎあんがとおった The bill passed (the House)

b そんな言い訳は通らない そんないいわけはとおらない Such excuses will not do

④ come in, be ushered into
客間に通る きゃくまにとおる enter the parlor

⑤ be understood [comprehensible]
意味が通らない いみがとおらない not make sense, be incomprehensible

【とおり 通り】
①ⓐ **PASSage; drainage**
ⓑ **street traffic, coming and going**

a 通りが良い とおりがよい pass [run] well

b 人通り ひとどおり traffic

② **street, avenue, road**
大通り おおどおり main street

③ reputation; favor
世間の通り せけんのとおり reputation

④ **accordance, agreement, conformity**
約束の通り やくそくのとおり true to one's promise, as promised

【-とおり -通り】
ⓐ **counter for kinds**
ⓑ **counter for ways (of doing)**
ab 三通り みとおり(=さんとおり) three kinds; three ways
【-どおり -通り】
① **suffix after names of streets [avenues]**
青山通り あおやまどおり Aoyama Street
② [also suffix] **as, according to, in accordance with**
型通り かたどおり formally, in due form
注文通り ちゅうもんどおり as ordered
③ degree, proportion
九分通り くぶどおり nine parts, almost
【とおす 通す】
①ⓐ **let PASS, let go by; run (a thread) through**
ⓑ **let in, admit, usher**
ⓒ **PASS through, penetrate, pierce**
a 通せん坊 とおせんぼう barring (a person's) way
先に通す さきにとおす let (a person) pass first
b 客を通す きゃくをとおす show a guest in
c 千枚通し せんまいどおし eyeleteer
水を通さない みずをとおさない be impervious to water
② [also 透す] **be transparent, be pervious to (light)**
光を通す ひかりをとおす be pervious to light
③ **PASS [carry] (a bill)**
議案を通す ぎあんをとおす pass [see] a bill (through the House)
④ [also verbal suffix] **carry through, stick to**
押し通す おしとおす push through, carry it through, hold out to the end
⑤ [also verbal suffix] continue, keep doing, remain
三日通して みっかとおして for three days on end
泣き通す なきとおす keep crying
⑥ do (something) through an intermediary
仲人を通して なこうどをとおして through a go-between
【とおし 通し】
① **letting PASS; showing in**
お通ししなさい おとおししなさい Ask [Show] him in
風通し かぜとおし ventilation
② **through, consecutive, straight**
通しで とおしで right through, direct, straight
通し切符 とおしきっぷ through ticket
見通し みとおし perspective, vista; prospect, outlook
切り通し きりどおし sunken road, excavation; open-cut
【-どおし -通し】 **continuing**
夜通し よどおし all through the night
立ち通しである たちどおしである keep standing (all the way)

【かよう 通う】 **go to and from, go back and forth, commute; frequent a place, visit often; circulate, ventilate; resemble closely**
通い かよい going back and forth, commuting; living out; passbook
学校へ通う がっこうへかよう attend school
血の通った ちのかよった blood-circulating; warm, compassionate
心が通う こころがかよう call forth response in another's heart
似通う にかよう resemble closely

SYNONYMS

❶ **pass**
通 PASS → 3855
過 PASS BY → 3891
経 PASS THROUGH → 1687
疏 LET PASS → 1511

❷ **go and come**
行 GO → 0246
徠 COME → 0576
往 GO ON → 0348
出 go to → 4310
参 go somewhere → 2563
来 COME → 4366
通 go to and from → 3855
向 head toward → 3790
赴 PROCEED TO → 4095
嚮 GO TOWARD → 3610

❸ⓐ **inform and communicate**
報 INFORM → 2133
通 COMMUNICATE → 3855
告 NOTIFY → 3062
届ける give notice → 3820
達 issue a notice → 3893
知 let know → 1446
申 REPORT → 4319
稟 REPORT TO → 2649
宣 PROCLAIM → 2799

❹ **throughout**
通 through → 3855
徹 all through → 0894
終 from beginning to end → 1692
中 throughout → 4262

❺ **widespread**
普 WIDESPREAD → 2919
遍 ALL OVER → 3890
通 common → 3855
公 common (math) → 2468

❻ⓐ **know and understand**
知 KNOW → 1446
通 know thoroughly → 3855

夂【辶】辶 ⻌ 尸 广 口

得 gain understanding of →0577
分かる understand →2466
解 understand →1913
諒 UNDERSTAND →1982
了 COMPREHEND →4157
悟 AWAKE TO →0502
惺 AWAKE TO →0709
ⓑ wise and talented persons
哲 sage →3402
賢 wise man →3518
博 DOCTOR →0170
秀 genius →3152
俊 BRILLIANT PERSON →0117
才 person of talent →4218
通 well-informed person →3855
❽ counters for flat things
枚 COUNTER FOR FLAT THINGS →1069
葉 counter for leaves →2912
丁 counter for sheets →4155
頁 counter for pages →2589
通 counter for letters →3855
竿 counter for flags →3259
【とおり】
②&【-どおり】① **ways and routes**
道 WAY (path) →3888
径 PATH →0347
軌 TRACK →1832
線 LINE →1760
澪 WATERWAY →0957
途 WAY (route) →3853
路 ROAD →1936
筋 wayside →3319
通り street →3855
街 city street →0702
辻 CROSSROADS →3958
岐 forked road →0285
巷 THE STREETS →3097
【-どおり】
② **similar**
類 similar →2275
様 like →1332
如 AS →0239
-通り as →3855
云 SUCH →2430

USAGE

❶【とおる】
通る
①ⓐ pass (by), go along [past], get through
ⓑ pass for [as], be known as, pass current
② [also 透る]
ⓐ penetrate, pierce, permeate
ⓑ be transparent, be pervious to (light)
③ⓐ pass (an examination)
ⓑ pass, be admissible
④ come in, be ushered into
⑤ be understood [comprehensible]
透る
[also 通る]
ⓐ be transparent, be pervious to (light)
ⓑ penetrate, pierce, permeate
❷【とおり】
通り
①ⓐ passage; drainage
ⓑ street traffic, coming and going
② street, avenue, road
③ reputation; favor
④ accordance, agreement, conformity
透り
penetration (as of light)
❸【とおす】
通す
①ⓐ let pass, let go by; run (a thread) through
ⓑ let in, admit, usher
ⓒ pass through, penetrate, pierce
② [also 透す] be transparent, be pervious to (light)
③ pass [carry] (a bill)
④ [also verbal suffix] carry through, stick to
⑤ [also verbal suffix] continue, keep doing, remain
⑥ do (something) through an intermediary
透す
[also 通す] be transparent, be pervious to (light)

HOMOPHONES

とおる 透 PASS THROUGH →3854
とおり 透 PASS THROUGH →3854
とおす 透 PASS THROUGH →3854

造

▶MAKE
ゾウ つく(る) つく(り) -づく(り)
Ⓝ 造 Ⓒ 造 zào

3856
口3-3-7

162	Jōyō-5	U9020
辶	S10-3-7	F0394

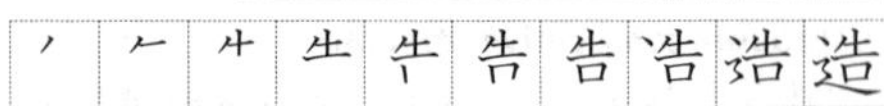
1 2 3 4 5 6 7 8 9 10

COMPOUNDS

❶ⓐ MAKE, produce, manufacture, shape, coin
ⓑ build (various structures as building or ships), construct
a 造血 ぞうけつ blood making, hematosis
造花 ぞうか artificial flower; artificial flower making
造形(=造型) ぞうけい molding, modeling
造幣 ぞうへい coinage, mintage

製造 せいぞう production, manufacture
改造 かいぞう remodeling; reorganization
構造 こうぞう structure, construction, framework
創造 そうぞう creation
酒造 しゅぞう sake brewing; distilling
b 造船 ぞうせん shipbuilding
造成する ぞうせいする create, clear, reclaim
築造 ちくぞう building, construction

❷ suffix indicating material composition
木造の もくぞうの wooden
石造の せきぞうの stone-built

❸ reach, attain
造詣 ぞうけい attainments, scholarship

❹ fleeting
造次 ぞうじ moment, very short time

KUN

【つくる 造る】
①ⓐ MAKE (as an object that requires time and skill), manufacture, fabricate, fashion
ⓑ build (ships or buildings), construct
b 船を造る ふねをつくる build a ship
② MAKE (wine), brew
酒造り さけづくり sake brewing
③ coin, mint
新語を造る しんごをつくる coin a new word

【つくり 造り】
ⓐ making, building, constructing (as buildings or ships)
ⓑ MAKE, structure, construction
a 造り付けの つくりつけの built-in
b 造りの頑丈な家 つくりのがんじょうないえ house of solid structure

【-づくり -造り】 [also suffix]
ⓐ MAKE, structure; style of building
ⓑ building, constructing, developing
a 防火造り ぼうかづくり fireproof construction
数寄屋造り(=数奇屋造り) すきやづくり *sukiya* style of building, style of a tea-ceremony arbor
b 別荘地造り べっそうちづくり developing a villa site

SYNONYMS

❶ⓐ make
作 MAKE → 0077
造 MAKE → 3856
成 FORM → 4352
工 MANUFACTURE → 4190
製 MANUFACTURE → 3478
産 PRODUCE → 4089
調 PREPARE → 1973
組む ASSEMBLE → 1693
構 CONSTRUCT → 1325

ⓑ build
建 BUILD (a building) → 3834
造 build (various structures) → 3856
築 CONSTRUCT → 3370
設 SET UP → 1863

【つくり】
ⓑ structure
構 structure → 1325
造り MAKE → 3856

HOMOPHONES

つくる
作 MAKE → 0077
創 CREATE → 2283
つくり 作 MAKE → 0077
-づくり 作 MAKE → 0077

NOTE

➡ see USAGE note at 作 0077

逢
3857
□3-3-7

▶MEET
ホウ あ(う)

162	Nonstandard	U9022
辶	S10-3-7	F0000

traditional form → see 逢 at 4002

這
3858
□3-3-7

▶CRAWL
シャ は(う) ㊔ これ ちか

162	Nonstandard	U9019
辶	S10-3-7	F0000

traditional form → see 這 at 4003

逞
3859
□3-3-7

▶DO AS ONE PLEASES
▶ROBUST
テイ たくま(しい) ㊔ たく とし とおる たくむ よし ゆた ゆき

162	Nonstandard	U901E
辶	S10-3-7	F0000

traditional form → see 逞 at 4004

逗
3860
□3-3-7

▶STAY
トウ

162	Nonstandard	U9017
辶	S10-3-7	F0000

traditional form → see 逗 at 4005

這逢 etc. incorrect stroke-count
➡ see □3-4-7: 辶 at 4002
□3-3-7

眞 incorrect classification
➡ see ▀2-2-8: 匕 at 2615
□3-3-7

屑

3861

口3-3-7

▶WASTE

セツ くず ㊔ きよ

Ⓝ 屑 Ⓒ 屑 xiè

44	Names	U5C51
尸	S10-3-7	F2547

COMPOUNDS

● **WASTE, rubbish, trash, scraps, junk, dust**

砕屑物 さいせつぶつ clastic material

KUN

【くず 屑】

ⓐ **WASTE, trash, scraps, junk, dust**

ⓑ worthless person, scum

a 屑籠 くずかご wastebasket
屑鉄 くずてつ scrap iron
屑拾い くずひろい rag picking; ragpicker
紙屑 かみくず waste paper
糸屑 いとくず lint, waste thread
星屑 ほしくず stardust
藻屑 もくず seaweed

SYNONYMS

● **waste**

屑 WASTE →3861
芥 TRASH →2741
塵 DUST →3922

展

3862

口3-3-7

▶UNFOLD
▶DISPLAY

テン ㊔ のぶ ひろ ひらく

Ⓒ 展 zhǎn

44	Jōyō-6	U5C55
尸	S10-3-7	F0660

1	2	3	4	5	6	7	8	9	10
㇐	㇕	尸	尸	屈	屈	屈	屈	展	展

COMPOUNDS

❶ **UNFOLD, develop, expand, evolve**

展開 てんかい unfolding, development, evolution; deployment
発展 はってん expansion, growth, development; prosperity
進展 しんてん development, progress
伸展する しんてんする expand, extend

❷ⓐ (open) **UNFOLD, spread out, open (a letter)**

ⓑ [original meaning] extend, flatten

a 親展書 しんてんしょ confidential letter

b 展性 てんせい malleability

❸ⓐ (spread out before the view of the public) **DISPLAY, exhibit, put on display**

ⓑ [also suffix] abbrev. of 展覧会 てんらんかい: **exhibition, exhibit**

a 展示する てんじする put on display, exhibit
展覧会 てんらんかい exhibition
展観する てんかんする exhibit

b 個展 こてん personal exhibition
デザイン展 でざいんてん design exhibition
ダリ展 だりてん exhibition of Dali's paintings

❹ **take an extensive view of**

展望 てんぼう view, outlook, prospect

❺ visit

展墓 てんぼ visiting a grave

SYNONYMS

❶ **grow**

成 grow up →4352
長 grow (up) →3163
生 grow →4309
育 grow →2544
発 develop →3174
伸 expand →0079
展 UNFOLD →3862

❷ⓐ **open**

開 OPEN →4121
展 UNFOLD →3862
披 open and read →0362

❸ⓐ **display**

展 DISPLAY →3862
陳 lay out (for exhibit) →0656
掲 PUT UP →0597

ⓑ **public display**

展 exhibition →3862
博 exposition →0170

COMPOUND FORMATION

【親展書 しんてんしょ】

親展書 'confidential letter' is a letter (書) to be opened (展 ❷ⓐ) only by the person himself (親).

屑

3863

口3-3-7

▶WASTE

セツ くず ㊔ きよ

44	Nonstandard	U5C51
尸	S10-3-7	F0000

traditional form →see 屑 at 3861

庫

3864

口3-3-7

▶STORAGE CHAMBER

コ ク くら▲

Ⓒ 库 kù

53	Jōyō-3	U5EAB
广	S10-3-7	F0747

1	2	3	4	5	6	7	8	9	10
㇔	亠	广	庐	庐	肩	肩	肩	庫	庫

COMPOUNDS

❶ [also suffix] [original meaning] **STORAGE CHAMBER, esp. a large structure for storing vehicles; storehouse, warehouse**

倉庫 そうこ warehouse, storehouse
金庫 きんこ strong box, cashbox
車庫 しゃこ car shed, garage
艇庫 ていこ boathouse
宝庫 ほうこ treasure house, treasury
文庫 ぶんこ library; collection of literary works; box for stationery
在庫 ざいこ stock, stockpile
国庫 こっこ (National) Treasury
公庫 こうこ municipal [state] treasury
格納庫 かくのうこ hangar, airplane shed

❷ temple's kitchen; priest's living quarters

庫裏 くり temple's kitchen; priest's living quarters

KUN

【くら 庫】[usu. 倉, sometimes also 蔵] **warehouse (for merchandise), storeroom**

庫入れ くらいれ warehousing

SYNONYMS

❶ **storehouse**

倉 STOREHOUSE →2607
蔵 storehouse →2995
庫 STORAGE CHAMBER →3864

HOMOPHONES

くら

蔵 STORE →2995
倉 STOREHOUSE →2607

NOTE

➡ see USAGE note at 倉 2607

席

3865

□3-3-7

▶**SEAT**

セキ むしろ▲

Ⓒ 席 xí

50	Jōyō-4	U5E2D
巾	S10-3-7	F0629

1	2	3	4	5	6	7	8	9	10
丶	亠	广	户	庐	庐	庐	庐	席	席

COMPOUNDS

❶ⓐ [also suffix] **SEAT, one's place**

ⓑ [original meaning] reed mat, rush mat

a 席次 せきじ order of seats, seating precedence; class standing
座席 ざせき seat
議席 ぎせき seat (in an assembly house)
即席の そくせきの impromptu, offhand
打席 だせき batter's box; one's turn at bat
主席 しゅせき top seat; the Chairman
指定席 していせき reserved seat
一般席 いっぱんせき general admission seat

b 席巻する せっけんする sweep over (the whole land); make a conquest

❷ **meeting place, hall; meeting**

席上で せきじょうで at the meeting; on the occasion
出席 しゅっせき attendance, presence
欠席 けっせき absence, nonattendance
会席 かいせき meeting place
宴席 えんせき banquet hall, dinner party

❸ entertainment hall, variety hall, club

定席 じょうせき regular hall; entertainment hall
碁席 ごせき go club

INDEPENDENT

【せき 席】**SEAT, one's place; meeting place, room; occasion; vaudeville theater**

席に着く せきにつく take a seat
公開の席で こうかいのせきで in public

KUN

【むしろ 席】mat, straw mat

SPECIAL READINGS

寄席 よせ storyteller's hall, variety hall

SYNONYMS

❶ⓐ **seat**

席 SEAT →3865
座 SEAT →3868
椅 CHAIR →1239
鞍 SADDLE →2255

❷ **places and positions**

所 PLACE →1056
処 place →3764
場 PLACE (for specific activity) →0678
地 PLACE (particular location) →0236
席 meeting place →3865
位 POSITION →0069
点 POINT →2587
座 place →3868

NOTE

➡ see COMPOUND FORMATION for 寄席 よせ →寄 2856

庭

3866

□3-3-7

▶**COURT**
▶**GARDEN**

テイ にわ ㊔ ば

Ⓒ 庭 tíng

53	Jōyō-3	U5EAD
广	S10-3-7	F0653

1	2	3	4	5	6	7	8	9	10
丶	亠	广	广	庄	库	庄	庭	庭	庭

COMPOUNDS

❶ⓐ [original meaning] **COURT, courtyard, yard**

ⓑ (sports) **COURT**, tennis court
a 校庭 こうてい schoolyard, campus
b 庭球 ていきゅう tennis

❷ **GARDEN, ornamental garden**
庭園 ていえん garden, park
庭前 ていぜん garden
石庭 せきてい rock garden

❸ [now always 廷 3795] the **COURT**, Imperial Court
宮庭 きゅうてい the Court, the Palace

❹ **home, family**
庭訓 ていきん [archaic] home education
家庭 かてい home, family, household

KUN

【にわ 庭】 **GARDEN; court, courtyard;** *elegant* **place**
庭木 にわき garden tree, shrub
庭師 にわし gardener
中庭 なかにわ courtyard
学びの庭 まなびのにわ school
戦いの庭 たたかいのにわ battlefield

SYNONYMS

❶ⓑ **sports fields**
場 ground(s) → 0678
庭 COURT → 3866
野 baseball field → 1877

❷ **gardens**
園 GARDEN → 3914
庭 GARDEN → 3866
苑 IMPERIAL GARDEN → 2783

唐

3867
口 3-3-7

▸**TANG DYNASTY**
トウ から
Ⓝ 唐 Ⓒ 唐 táng

30	Jōyō	U5510
口	S10-3-7	F1258

COMPOUNDS

❶ **TANG DYNASTY (618-907 A.D.)**
唐朝 とうちょう Tang Dynasty
唐詩 とうし Tang poetry

❷ **Cathay, China; foreign countries in general**
唐人 とうじん Chinese; foreigner
唐音 とうおん Tang reading of Chinese characters
唐辛子 とうがらし red pepper
毛唐 けとう *slang* foreigner, Westerner

❸ abrupt
唐突に とうとつに abruptly

❹ wild talk, nonsense
荒唐無稽 こうとうむけい absurdity, nonsense

INDEPENDENT

【とう 唐】 **TANG DYNASTY**

KUN

【から 唐】
ⓐ **elegant term for China, Cathay**
ⓑ [also 韓] foreign countries
a 唐様 からよう Chinese style [design]
b 唐草模様 からくさもよう arabesque design
唐獅子 からじし imaginary animal similar to a lion

SYNONYMS

❶ **later Chinese dynasties**
唐 TANG DYNASTY → 3867
宋 SONG DYNASTY → 2730
元 Yuan Dynasty → 2428
明 Ming Dynasty → 1060
清 Qing Dynasty → 0635

❷ **China**
華 CHINA → 2841
漢 CHINESE → 0808
支 China → 2473
中 People's Republic of China → 4262
胡 NATIVES OF ANCIENT CHINA → 1467
台 Taiwan → 2498
唐 Cathay → 3867
呉 KINGDOM OF WU → 3156

USAGE

【から】
唐
ⓐ elegant term for China, Cathay
ⓑ [also 韓] foreign countries
韓
ⓐ elegant term for Korea
ⓑ [also 唐] foreign countries

HOMOPHONES

から 韓 SOUTH KOREA → 2218

COMPOUND FORMATION

【毛唐 けとう】
毛唐 'foreigner, Westerner', literally a "hairy (毛) Chinaman (唐 ❷)," is a derogatory term referring to foreigners of Western origin.

座

3868
口 3-3-7

▸**SEAT**
▸**SIT**
ザ すわ(る) ㊔ くら
Ⓒ 座 zuò

53	Jōyō-6	U5EA7
广	S10-3-7	F0401

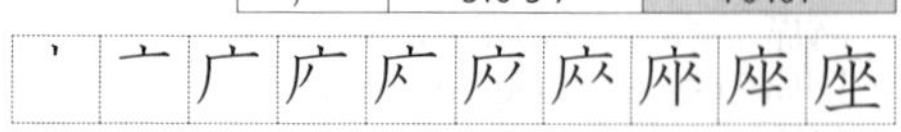

COMPOUNDS

❶ [formerly also 坐 4361]
ⓐ [original meaning] (place for sitting) **SEAT**
ⓑ (part on which one sits) **SEAT, bottom**

a 座席 ざせき seat
座右の書 ざゆうのしょ one's desk-side book
座敷 ざしき drawing room, parlor; Japanese-style room
座布団 ざぶとん (floor) cushion
王座 おうざ throne
上座 かみざ(=じょうざ) top seat, seat of honor

b 便座 べんざ toilet seat

❷ (supporting base) **SEAT, mount, base, platform, stand**
座金 ざがね (metal) washer
台座 だいざ pedestal, base, stand
弁座 べんざ valve seat
機関座 きかんざ seat of an engine

❸ⓐ (one's position) **SEAT, status, (social) position**
ⓑ **place, position**

a 司教権座 しきょうけんざ the episcopal seat
講座 こうざ lectureship, (professor's) chair; course of study

b 座標 ざひょう coordinates
即座に そくざに immediately, promptly, at once
口座 こうざ (bank) account
当座 とうざ the present, the time being; current account

❹ [formerly also 坐 4361]
ⓐ **SIT, take a seat, sit down**
ⓑ **SIT** still without doing anything, not stir

a 座臥 ざが sitting and lying down
座禅 ざぜん Zen meditation
座礁する ざしょうする run aground, be stranded
正座する せいざする sit upright [straight]

b 座視する ざしする remain an idle spectator, look on idly [doing nothing]

❺ **company, gathering, party**
座談会 ざだんかい round-table talk, symposium
座興 ざきょう amusement of the company

❻ⓐ theater, theatrical company [troupe]
ⓑ **suffix after names of theaters**

a 座長 ざちょう leader of a troupe; chairman, president
同座 どうざ same theater

b 明治座 めいじざ the Meijiza Theater
文学座 ぶんがくざ the Bungaku Company

❼ religious organization, temple, shrine
座主 ざす head priest of a temple, abbot
遷座 せんざ transfer of an object of worship

❽ⓐ **constellation**
ⓑ suffix after names of constellations

a 星座 せいざ constellation

b 大熊座 おおくまざ the Big Bear

❾ *hist* guild in medieval times
鉄砲座 てっぽうざ gunmakers guild

❿ mint (during the Edo period)
銀座 ぎんざ the Ginza; mint (during Edo period)

⓫ counter for:
ⓐ Shinto deities or sedentary statues (seated figures)
ⓑ high mountains or forests

a 仏像二座 ぶつぞうにざ two images of Buddha

b 高峰八座 こうほうはちざ eight lofty peaks

⓬ [formerly also 坐 4361] be accused of a crime
連座する れんざする be implicated [involved] in (a crime)

⓭ [formerly also 坐 4361] travel (by ship)
座乗する ざじょうする go on board (a ship)

⓮ **used phonetically for *za***
御座る ござる go, come; be in love; rot
御座います ございます [polite] be, exist

INDEPENDENT

【ざ 座】**SEAT**, seat (of a chair), bottom; seat (of power), status, position; company, gathering, party
座が白けた ざがしらけた A chill was cast over the party
天子の座 てんしのざ throne
権力の座 けんりょくのざ position of power
妻の座 つまのざ status of wifehood

【ざする 座する(=坐する)】**SIT** down, take a seat; be implicated [involved] in (a crime)

KUN

【すわる 座る】[formerly also 坐る] **SIT, take a seat, sit down**
座り すわり stability
座り込み すわりこみ sit-in, sit-down (strike)
居座る いすわる settle down, stay on; remain in the same position unwantedly

SYNONYMS

❶ **seat**
席 SEAT → 3865
座 SEAT → 3868
椅 CHAIR → 1239
鞍 SADDLE → 2255

❷ **flat supports**
台 STAND → 2498
座 SEAT → 3868
壇 PLATFORM → 0932
棚 SHELF → 1238
架 rack → 3178
床 BED → 3805

❸ⓑ **places and positions**

所 PLACE →1056
処 place →3764
場 PLACE (for specific activity) →0678
地 PLACE (particular location) →0236
席 meeting place →3865
位 POSITION →0069
点 POINT →2587
座 place →3868

❹ⓐ **sit**
座 SIT →3868
坐 SIT →4361
居 sit →3822

❽ **stars**
星 STAR →3089
座 constellation →3868

USAGE

❶【すわる】
座る
[formerly also 坐る] sit, take a seat, sit down
坐る
[now usu. 座る] sit, take a seat, sit down
据わる
be set

❷【すわり】
座り
[formerly also 坐り] stability
坐り
[now usu. 座り] stability

HOMOPHONES

すわる
坐 SIT →4361
据 INSTALL →0602
すわり 坐 SIT →4361

COMPOUND FORMATION

❶【即座 そくざ】
即座に 'immediately, etc.' refers to performing an action right on (即) the spot (座 ❸ⓑ).

❷【口座 こうざ】
口座 '(bank) account' refers to the place (座 ❸ⓑ) where account items (口) are recorded.

❸【銀座 ぎんざ】
銀座 'the Ginza; mint (during Edo period)' refers to a former mint (座 ❿) where silver coins (銀) were made. The famous Ginza district in Tokyo is so named since it was formerly the location of such a mint.

庬
3869
口3-3-7

▶**BULKY**
ボウ

53	Nonstandard	U5EAC
广	S10-3-7	F0000

traditional form →see 厖 at 3725

唐
3870
口3-3-7

▶**TANG DYNASTY**
トウ から

53	Nonstandard	U5510
广	S10-3-7	F0000

traditional form →see 唐 at 3867

庶
口3-3-7

incorrect stroke-count
➡ see 口3-3-8: 广 at 3880

圃
3871
口3-3-7

▶**VEGETABLE GARDEN**
ホ
Ⓒ 圃 pǔ

31	Names	U5703
口	S10-3-7	F2667

COMPOUNDS

❶ [sometimes also 甫 4363] [original meaning] **VEGETABLE GARDEN; rice nursery**
圃場 ほじょう cultivated land [field]
田圃 でんぽ fields and rice paddies
苗圃 びょうほ seedbed

❷ unclassified compounds
玄圃梨 けんぽなし Japanese raisin tree

SPECIAL READINGS

田圃 たんぼ rice field

SYNONYMS

❶ **cultivated fields**
畑 FIELD →1131
畠 FIELD →3186
牧 PASTURE →1083
園 GARDEN →3914
田 RICE FIELD →3775
佃 CULTIVATED RICE FIELD →0066
圃 VEGETABLE GARDEN →3871

逸
3872
口3-3-8

▶**LET SLIP**
イツ そ(れる)▲ そ(らす)▲ ㊔ はやる はや
Ⓝ 逸 Ⓒ 逸 yì

162	Jōyō	U9038
辶	S11-3-8	F1587

1	2	3	4	5	6	7	8	9	10	11
ノ	⺈	〔stroke 3〕	〔stroke 4〕	〔stroke 5〕	〔stroke 6〕	〔stroke 7〕	免	〔stroke 9〕	〔stroke 10〕	逸

COMPOUNDS

❶ⓐ **LET SLIP, miss, lose, let go, let pass**
ⓑ [formerly also 佚 0070] lost, missing
a 逸球 いっきゅう muffed ball, missed ball
逸機する いっきする miss a chance, lose an opportunity

後逸する こういつする let (a ball) pass, miss (a grounder)
b 逸書 いっしょ lost book
散逸する さんいつする be lost and scattered

❷ⓐ [original meaning] slip away, run (away), escape
ⓑ escape from the world, seclude oneself, be secluded

a 逸走する いっそうする escape, scamper away
逸話 いつわ uncommon tale, anecdote
b 隠逸 いんいつ seclusion

❸ **deviate from the norm, swerve from a course**
逸脱 いつだつ deviation, departure from the norm
放逸 ほういつ self-indulgence, looseness, dissoluteness

❹ **exceptional, superb, outstanding, excellent**
逸品 いっぴん superb article
逸材 いつざい person of (exceptional) talent
秀逸 しゅういつ supreme excellence

❺ [formerly also 佚 0070] indulge in idle pleasure
逸楽 いつらく idle pursuit of pleasure
安逸 あんいつ (idle) ease, idleness, indolence

INDEPENDENT

【いつ 逸】ease
逸を以て労を待つ いつをもってろうをまつ wait for the enemy to tire at ease

【いっする 逸する】**LET SLIP**, miss, lose, let go, let pass; deviate from the norm, swerve from a course
好機を逸する こうきをいっする miss a chance
常軌を逸した じょうきをいっした aberrant

KUN

【それる 逸れる】deviate from, swerve from (a course), miss
針路を逸れる しんろをそれる swerve from the course
的を逸れる まとをそれる miss the target

【そらす 逸らす】
① **LET SLIP**, miss, lose, let go, let pass
ボールを逸らす ぼーるをそらす miss a ball, let a ball pass
注意を逸らす ちゅういをそらす distract a person's attention
② (cause to deviate) divert, avert, dodge, evade
目を逸らす めをそらす avert one's eyes, look away

SYNONYMS

❶ⓐ **losing and loss**
失 LOSE →4325
喪 lose →3504
逸 LET SLIP →3872
損 LOSS, lose →0801
佚 LOST →0070

❸ **deviate**
逸 deviate →3872
外れる miss →0215

❹ **excellent and superior**
優 SUPERIOR →0200
絶 without match →1711
卓 PROMINENT →2561
快 splendid →0289
妙 MARVELOUS →0280
秀 EXCELLENT →3152
英 DISTINGUISHED →2782
尤 outstanding →3755
傑 outstanding →0175
穎 TALENTED →2036
逸 exceptional →3872
名 first-rate →2693
上 of upper grade →4212

HOMOPHONES

そらす 反 COUNTER →3663

NOTE

➡ see USAGE note at 反 3663

進

3873
□3-3-8

▶**ADVANCE**
シン　すす(む)　すす(める)　㊔ のぶ
Ⓝ 進 Ⓒ 进 jìn

162	Jōyō-3	U9032
辶	S11-3-8	F0235

Stroke order: 1–11

COMPOUNDS

❶ⓐ [original meaning] (move forward in position) **ADVANCE, go forward, proceed**
ⓑ (move forward in rank) **ADVANCE in rank, become promoted**

a 進行する しんこうする advance, make progress, go forward
進路 しんろ course, route
進出 しんしゅつ advance, march; debouchment
進入する しんにゅうする penetrate, go into, enter
前進する ぜんしんする advance, go ahead
行進する こうしんする march, parade
突進する とっしんする dash [rush] forward, push ahead
二進する にしんする advance to second (base)
b 進学 しんがく entering a school of higher grade
進級 しんきゅう promotion (to a higher grade)
昇進 しょうしん promotion, advancement

❷ⓐ (make progress) **ADVANCE, make progress, improve**
ⓑ (aid the progress of) **ADVANCE, promote, further**

【辶】 辶 广 口

a 進歩 しんぽ progress, advancement, improvement
進展 しんてん development, progress
進化 しんか evolution, progress
先進国 せんしんこく advanced [developed] nation [country]
躍進 やくしん rapid advance [progress]
b 推進する すいしんする propel, drive; promote
促進する そくしんする promote, spur on, facilitate
増進する ぞうしんする promote, improve, advance

❸ⓐ present to a superior, proffer, offer
ⓑ do something for someone, esp. a superior
a 進呈する しんていする proffer, present
進物 しんもつ gift
寄進 きしん contribution, donation
b 進言 しんげん counsel, advice (to a superior)
進講 しんこう lecturing to the emperor
注進 ちゅうしん information, report (to a superior)

KUN

【すすむ 進む】
①ⓐ (move forward in position) **ADVANCE, go forward**
ⓑ (of clocks) **go too fast**
a 進み出る すすみでる step forward
② (make progress) **ADVANCE, make progress, be promoted**
進み すすみ progress
文明が進むに連れて ぶんめいがすすむにつれて with the advance of civilization
大学へ進む だいがくへすすむ enter a university
③ feel inclined to
食が進む しょくがすすむ have a good appetite

【すすめる 進める】
①ⓐ (cause to move forward in position) **ADVANCE, move forward**
ⓑ (raise in rank) **ADVANCE, raise, promote**
ⓒ **set (a clock) ahead**
a 軍を進める ぐんをすすめる move troops forward
②ⓐ (aid the progress of) **ADVANCE, promote, further**
ⓑ stimulate, hasten
a 計画を進める けいかくをすすめる carry a plan forward
b 工事を進める こうじをすすめる hasten [speed up] the works

SYNONYMS

❶ⓐ move forward
進 ADVANCE → 3873
突 DASH → 2772
這う CRAWL → 4003
ⓑ rise in rank
陞 ASCEND TO A HIGHER RANK → 0549
昇 ascend to a higher rank → 3068
進 advance in rank → 3873
❷ⓐ make progress
進 ADVANCE → 3873
亨 GO SMOOTHLY → 2530
捗 MAKE PROGRESS → 0513
ⓑ advance
進 ADVANCE → 3873
興 cause to rise → 3622
奨 ENCOURAGE → 3524
勧 encourage → 2334
❸ⓐ give
与 GIVE → 4229
呈 PRESENT → 2715
進 present to a superior → 3873
上 give (to superior or others) → 4212
下 give (to inferior or speaker) → 4186
呉れる give (to speaker) → 3156
授 CONFER → 0595
賜 DEIGN TO GIVE → 1994
贈 PRESENT A GIFT → 2064
賄 BRIBE → 1931
賂 BRIBE → 1930

USAGE

【すすめる】
進める
①ⓐ (cause to move forward in position) advance, move forward
ⓑ (raise in rank) advance, raise, promote
ⓒ set (a clock) ahead
②ⓐ (aid the progress of) advance, promote, further
ⓑ stimulate, hasten
勧める
①ⓐ urge, persuade, advise
ⓑ [sometimes also 奨める] encourage, promote, stimulate
② offer, present
奨める
[usu. 勧める] encourage, promote, stimulate
薦める
recommend (a person to a post or a product to a person)

HOMOPHONES

すすめる
勧 URGE → 2334
奨 ENCOURAGE → 3524
薦 RECOMMEND → 3008

週
3874
□3-3-8

▶WEEK
シュウ
Ⓝ 週 Ⓒ 周 zhōu

162	Jōyō-2	U9031
辶	S11-3-8	F0679

丿	冂	冂	冂	用	用	周	周	周	调
1	2	3	4	5	6	7	8	9	10

週 11

COMPOUNDS

❶ⓐ **WEEK, weekly**
ⓑ counter for order of **WEEK**s within a month
a 週間 しゅうかん week
週刊 しゅうかん weekly publication, weekly
今週 こんしゅう this week
二週間 にしゅうかん two weeks
b 五月の第二週 ごがつのだいにしゅう second week of May

❷ [now always 周 3720] [original meaning] go round
週期 しゅうき period, cycle

INDEPENDENT

【しゅう 週】**WEEK**
週に三回 しゅうにさんかい three times a week

SYNONYMS

❶ⓐ **weeks and months**
週 WEEK → 3874
旬 TEN-DAY PERIOD → 3698
月 MONTH → 3674

逮

▶CATCH A CRIMINAL
タイ
Ⓝ 逮 Ⓒ 逮 dǎi dài

3875
□3-3-8

162 辶	Jōyō	U902E
	S11-3-8	F1341

㇇	⺕	⺕	聿	聿	隶	隶	隶	逮	逮
1	2	3	4	5	6	7	8	9	10

逮 11

COMPOUNDS

❶ [original meaning] (chase after and reach out to capture) **CATCH A CRIMINAL, capture**
逮捕 たいほ arrest, capture
逮捕状 たいほじょう warrant of arrest

❷ reach
逮夜 たいや eve of death anniversary

SYNONYMS

❶ **catch a criminal**
捕 CATCH → 0514
逮 CATCH A CRIMINAL → 3875
拘 ARREST → 0367
勾 ARREST → 3660

遇 □3-3-8
incorrect stroke-count
➡ see □3-3-9: 辶 at 3889

透 □3-3-8
incorrect stroke-count
➡ see □3-3-7: 辶 at 3854

遊 □3-3-8
incorrect stroke-count
➡ see □3-3-9: 辶 at 3896

逸進 etc. □3-3-8
incorrect stroke-count
➡ see □3-4-8: 辶 at 4020

庵

▶HERMITAGE
アン いおり
Ⓒ 庵 ān

3876
□3-3-8

53 广	Names	U5EB5
	S11-3-8	F1571

COMPOUNDS

● **HERMITAGE, retreat**
庵主 あんしゅ owner of a hermitage; abbess, prioress, nun in charge of a Buddhist convent
庵室 あんしつ hermit's cell, retreat
沢庵(=沢庵漬け) たくあん(=たくあんづけ) pickled daikon [Japanese radish]
草庵 そうあん thatched hut
僧庵 そうあん priest's hermitage

INDEPENDENT

【あん 庵】**HERMITAGE, retreat**

KUN

【いおり 庵】**HERMITAGE, retreat**
庵点 いおりてん symbol indicating that the following words are taken from a song or that the person saying the words is singing

SYNONYMS

● **houses**
家 HOUSE → 2827
屋 HOUSE → 3842
軒 house → 1851
戸 HOUSEHOLD → 2429
宅 DWELLING HOUSE → 2698
居 residence → 3822
邸 STATELY RESIDENCE → 1451
住 housing → 0072
庵 HERMITAGE → 3876

康

▶HEALTHY
コウ ㊔ やす やすし
Ⓒ 康 kāng

3877
□3-3-8

53 广	Jōyō-4	U5EB7
	S11-3-8	F0568

stroke order: 1–11 (康)

COMPOUNDS

❶ **HEALTHY, robust**

健康 けんこう health

健康な けんこうな healthy, sound, well

❷ (free from danger or hardship) **peaceful, secure, safe**

康寧 こうねい [rare] peacefulness, tranquility

小康 しょうこう lull, respite, breathing spell (of peace)

SYNONYMS

❶ **strong**

強 STRONG → 0574

壮 VIGOROUS → 0263

丈 STOUT → 4227

健 ROBUST (healthy) → 0152

逞しい ROBUST (sturdy) → 4004

康 HEALTHY → 3877

旺 ENERGETIC → 1061

潑 LIVELY → 0917

❶ **healthy**

康 HEALTHY → 3877

健 ROBUST → 0152

生 health → 4309

❷ **calm and peaceful**

安 PEACEFUL → 2695

康 peaceful → 3877

寧 peaceful → 2959

泰 TRANQUIL → 3193

静 QUIET → 2164

平 CALM → 4291

穏 CALM → 1578

麻 3878

□3-3-8

▶**HEMP**
▶**BECOME NUMB**

マ マー▲ あさ

Ⓝ 蔴 痲 Ⓒ 麻 má mā

200	Jōyō	U9EBB
麻	S11-11-0	F0881

radical variant → see 麻 at 3884

stroke order: 1–11 (麻)

COMPOUNDS

❶ⓐ [original meaning] **HEMP, flax or other similar plants**

ⓑ **HEMP fiber, flax fiber**

a 亜麻 あま flax

ab 黄麻 こうま(=おうま) jute

製麻 せいま hemp dressing, flax [hemp] spinning

大麻 たいま hemp; paper amulet used in Shinto rites

❷ sesame

胡麻 ごま sesame

❸ **BECOME NUMB, become palsied**

麻酔 ますい anesthesia

麻薬 まやく narcotic, drug

麻痺× まひ paralysis, palsy, numbness, anesthesia

❹ pockmarks

蕁×麻疹× じんましん hives, urticaria

❺ **unclassified compounds**

麻雀 まーじゃん mahjong

INDEPENDENT

【ま 麻】**HEMP**

KUN

【あさ 麻】**HEMP, flax, jute; hemp fiber, flax fiber**

麻布 あさぬの hemp cloth, linen

麻袋 あさぶくろ jute bag

マニラ麻 まにらあさ Manila hemp

SPECIAL READINGS

麻疹×▲ はしか measles

SYNONYMS

❶ⓐ **fiber-producing plants**

麻 HEMP → 3878

綿 COTTON → 1736

ⓑ & 【あさ】 **fabrics**

織 woven fabric → 1801

紬 PONGEE → 1684

紗 GAUZE → 1653

絹 SILK → 1721

綾 TWILL → 1740

綿 COTTON → 1736

棉 COTTON → 1244

麻 HEMP → 3878

毛 wool → 4264

錦 BROCADE → 2181

❸ **become stupefied**

酔 BECOME INTOXICATED → 1875

麻 BECOME NUMB → 3878

鹿 3879

□3-3-8

▶**DEER**

ロク▲ しか か ㊔ かの

Ⓝ 廘 Ⓒ 鹿 lù

198	Jōyō	U9E7F
鹿	S11-11-0	F1022

' 亠 广 户 庐 庐 庐 庐 鹿 鹿 鹿
1 2 3 4 5 6 7 8 9 10 11

RADICAL

shika 'deer' (麗 麟), used in characters related to deers or similar animals

COMPOUNDS

● [original meaning, now rare] **DEER**

鹿砦 ろくさい abatis

KUN

【しか 鹿】**DEER, stag, hind**

鹿皮 しかがわ deerskin

【か 鹿】

① [in compounds] **DEER**

鹿の子 かのこ dapples, pattern of white spots; fawn

② **used phonetically for *ka***

馬鹿 ばか fool, blockhead; nonsense

SPECIAL READINGS

鹿児島県 かごしまけん Kagoshima Prefecture

SYNONYMS

【しか】

○ **undomesticated mammals**

虎 TIGER → 3981
猿 MONKEY → 0824
鯨 WHALE → 2361
犀 RHINOCEROS → 3900
狼 WOLF → 0541
狐 FOX → 0472
羚 SEROW → 1695
鼠 RAT → 3340
獅 LION → 0825
豹 LEOPARD → 1847
熊 BEAR → 3530
象 ELEPHANT → 2647
麒 MALE CHINESE UNICORN → 2363
麟 FEMALE CHINESE UNICORN → 2376
猪 WILD BOAR → 0652
鹿 DEER → 3879

NOTE

➡ see COMPOUND FORMATION for 馬鹿 ばか → 馬 4086

庶

▶MANIFOLD

ショ ㊔ ちか

Ⓒ 庶 shù

3880

☐3-3-8

53	Jōyō	U5EB6
广	S11-3-8	F1775

' 亠 广 广 庐 庐 府 庐 庐 庶 庶
1 2 3 4 5 6 7 8 9 10 11

COMPOUNDS

❶ **MANIFOLD, many, numerous, various, general**

庶務 しょむ general affairs
庶事(=諸事) しょじ various matters
庶政(=諸政) しょせい all phases of government

❷ **the masses, common people, populace**

庶民 しょみん common people, the masses
衆庶 しゅうしょ common people, the masses

❸ illegitimate (child), born of a concubine

庶子 しょし illegitimate child
庶出 しょしゅつ illegitimate birth

❹ desire, hope for

庶機する しょきする desire, hope

SYNONYMS

❶ **various**

諸 VARIOUS → 1984
庶 MANIFOLD → 3880
雑 MISCELLANEOUS → 1752

❷ **the people**

民 PEOPLE → 3770
衆 the multitude(s) → 3325
庶 the masses → 3880
公 PUBLIC → 2468

庸

▶MEDIOCRE

ヨウ ㊔ のぶ やす つね

Ⓒ 庸 yōng

3881

☐3-3-8

53	Jōyō	U5EB8
广	S11-3-8	F2491

' 亠 广 户 庐 庐 庐 肩 肩 肩 庸
1 2 3 4 5 6 7 8 9 10 11

COMPOUNDS

❶ **MEDIOCRE, commonplace, common, ordinary, banal; stupid**

庸才 ようさい mediocre talent
庸愚 ようぐ mediocrity, imbecility
庸君 ようくん stupid ruler
凡庸な ぼんような commonplace, mediocre, banal
中庸 ちゅうよう the (golden) mean, the middle path

❷ [now usu. 用 3694] employ (a person), engage

登庸 とうよう appointment, promotion

❸ tax paid in labor during the Asuka period

租庸調 そようちょう taxes in kind or service (former tax system), corvée

SYNONYMS

❶ **ordinary**
常 NORMAL →3203
只- ORDINARY →2677
並 ordinary →2793
平 common →4291
普 common →2919
庸 MEDIOCRE →3881
凡 COMMONPLACE →3656
套 TRITE →2823

NOTE

★ do not confuse with 傭 HIRE →0181

麻

3882
口3-3-8

▶***ASAKANMURI***

200	Radical	U9EBB
麻	S11-11-0	F0000

radical variant →see 麻 at 3884

庿

3883
口3-3-8

▶**MAUSOLEUM**
ビョウ ㊔ いえ

53	Nonstandard	U5EBF
广	S11-3-8	F0000

traditional form →see 廟 at 3935

麻

3884
口3-3-8

▶**HEMP**
▶**BECOME NUMB**
マ マー あさ

200	Nonstandard	U9EBB
麻	S11-11-0	F0000

traditional form →see 麻 at 3878

RADICAL

asa 'hemp' (痲×), used in characters related to hemp or flax
Enclosures: 麻 麻× ***asakanmuri*** (麿 麾)

廊

口3-3-8

incorrect stroke-count
➡ see 口3-3-9: 广 at 3903

圏

3885
口3-3-8

▶**SPHERE**
ケン

31	Names	U5708
口	S11-3-8	F0000

traditional form →see 圈 at 3904

國

3886
口3-3-8

▶**COUNTRY**
コク くに

31	Names	U570B
口	S11-3-8	F0000

traditional form →see 国 at 3831

遅

3887
口3-3-9

▶**SLOW**
▶**LATE**
チ おく(れる) おく(らす) おそ(い)
Ⓝ 遲 Ⓒ 迟 chí

162	Jōyō	U9045
辶	S12-3-9	F0994

1	2	3	4	5	6	7	8	9	10	11	12
㇕	コ	尸	尸	尸	尸	层	屋	犀	犀	遅	遅

COMPOUNDS

❶ⓐ [original meaning] (not fast) **SLOW, tardy**
ⓑ (mentally dull) **SLOW, dull**
a 遅遅たる ちちたる slow, lagging, tardy
遅脈 ちみゃく slow pulse
b 遅鈍 ちどん dull, stupid

❷ⓐ (delayed) **LATE, tardy**
ⓑ **be LATE, be tardy, be delayed**
a 遅延 ちえん delay, retardation
遅配 ちはい delay in rationing
b 遅刻 ちこく tardiness, lateness
遅参 ちさん lateness, tardiness

KUN

【おくれる 遅れる】
ⓐ **be LATE, be tardy, be delayed**
ⓑ (of clocks) **go SLOW, lose**
a 遅れ おくれ being late; (of clocks) going slow
遅れ馳せの おくればせの belated, eleventh-hour
知恵遅れ ちえおくれ mental retardation
乗り遅れる のりおくれる miss [fail to catch] (a train)

【おくらす 遅らす】 **delay, put off, retard**
返事を遅らす へんじをおくらす defer one's reply
時計を一時間遅らせる とけいをいちじかんおくらせる turn back a watch one hour

【おそい 遅い】 (not fast) **SLOW, tardy;** (delayed) **late, tardy**
遅生まれの おそうまれの born after April 1 (school entrance date)
遅咲き おそざき late blooming, late flower
足が遅い あしがおそい be slow-footed

SYNONYMS

❶ⓐ **slow**
徐 SLOWLY →0497
遅 SLOW →3887

緩 SLACK → 1757
慢 SLUGGISH → 0844

❷ⓐ late
遅 LATE (delayed) → 3887
晩 late (advanced) → 1232
晏 LATE → 3103

ⓑ be late and delay
遅 be late → 3887
後 fall behind → 0431
滞 fall into arrears → 0815
延 POSTPONE → 3812
猶 DELAY → 0757

HOMOPHONES

おくれる 後 AFTER → 0431
おくれ 後 AFTER → 0431

NOTE

➡ see USAGE note at 後 0431

道

3888
□3-3-9

▶WAY
ドウ トウ みち ㊔ おさむ わたる とおる
Ⓝ 道 Ⓒ 道 dào

162	Jōyō-2	U9053
辶	S12-3-9	F0096

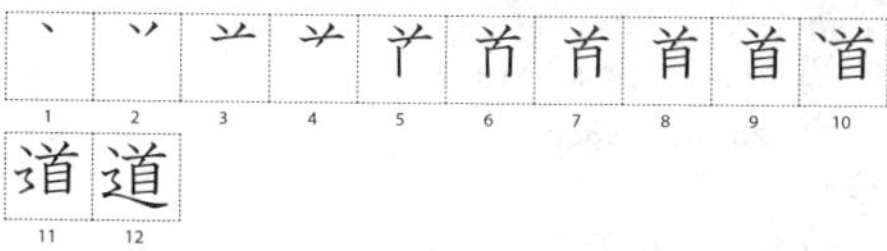

COMPOUNDS

❶ [also suffix]
ⓐ [original meaning] **WAY, path, road, track**
ⓑ **passage, duct**

a 道路 どうろ road, street, way
道程 どうてい distance, journey, itinerary; process
鉄道 てつどう railway
街道 かいどう thoroughfare, highway
軌道 きどう track, railway; planetary orbit; beaten track
歩道 ほどう sidewalk, footpath

b 地下道 ちかどう underpass, underground passage
水道 すいどう water service [supply]; channel
気道 きどう air passage
食道 しょくどう esophagus
外耳道 がいじどう external auditory meatus

❷ **the WAY of moral conduct, moral principles, morality, right way of life (esp. according to Confucian precepts), truth**
道徳 どうとく morality, morals
道理 どうり reason, right, justice, truth
道義 どうぎ morality, moral principles
正道 せいどう path of righteousness, right track
人道的な じんどうてきな humane, humanitarian

❸ **the WAY, Tao, *Do*** —a basic concept in Oriental religion and philosophy:
ⓐ *Taoism* **unitary first principle of existence, Taoism**
ⓑ *Confucianism* ultimate principle of cosmic reason
ⓒ *Buddhism* **the WAY of the Buddha, the teachings of Buddha**
ⓓ *other religions* **the WAY, religious teachings**

a 道教 どうきょう Taoism
道家 どうか Taoist scholar

b 道学 どうがく Confucian philosophy; Taoism

c 道具 どうぐ tool, utensil, implement; furniture; theatrical appurtenances; tool, means; ingredient
道心 どうしん faith (in Buddha), piety; bonze, priest; sense of morality
入道する にゅうどうする become a bonze, renounce the world

d 神道 しんとう Shinto, the Way of the Gods
伝道 でんどう gospel preaching, missionary work, evangelism

❹ [also suffix] **the WAY of an art, esp. the principles of training and mental discipline of an art (as a martial art); art, way of life**
道場 どうじょう *dojo*, gymnasium
柔道 じゅうどう judo
武道 ぶどう martial arts
書道 しょどう calligraphy, penmanship
茶道 さどう(=ちゃどう) tea ceremony
武士道 ぶしどう Bushido (samurai code of behavior)
陰陽道 おんみょうどう(=おんようどう) art of divining

❺ⓐ [also prefix] **District of Hokkaido** (northern island of Japan)
ⓑ [also suffix] former administrative division of Japan

a 道民 どうみん people of Hokkaido
道議会 どうぎかい Hokkaido Prefectural Assembly
北海道 ほっかいどう Hokkaido
都道府県 とどうふけん urban and rural prefectures

b 七道 しちどう the seven districts of ancient Japan
東海道 とうかいどう Tokaido district; Tokaido highway

❻ **say, convey**
道破 どうは declaration
報道 ほうどう news, report, information
言語道断な ごんごどうだんな inexcusable, outrageous, absurd

❼ [also suffix] *Buddhism* posthumous world
六道 ろくどう six posthumous worlds
餓鬼道 がきどう world of hungry spirits

〔辶〕 辶 弋 尸 广 口

INDEPENDENT

【どう 道】District of Hokkaido; former administrative division of Japan

道の将来 どうのしょうらい future of Hokkaido

KUN

【みち 道】

①ⓐ [formerly also 路] [also prefix and suffix] **WAY, road, path, street; highway, track**

ⓑ (distance in general) **WAY, distance, journey**

ⓒ **halfway**

a 道端 みちばた roadside, wayside

道順 みちじゅん route, itinerary

道案内 みちあんない guiding, guide; guidepost

道草を食う みちくさをくう loiter, dawdle; waste one's time on the way

坂道 さかみち slope

筋道 すじみち reason, thread (of an argument), coherence; systematic method, due formality

散歩道 さんぽみち walk, promenade, esplanade

b 五キロの道 ごきろのみち distance of five kilometers

c 帰り道で かえりみちで on one's way home

② **WAY of doing, means, course of action**

自活の道 じかつのみち independent living

地道な じみちな steady, straight, fair

使い道 つかいみち use, application

③ **the WAY of moral conduct, path of righteousness, moral principles, morality, right way of life**

道ならぬ みちならぬ improper, illicit

人たる道に背く ひとたるみちにそむく stray from the path of righteousness

④ art, line (of work), career

剣の道 けんのみち swordsmanship

歌の道 うたのみち art of tanka poetry

その道 そのみち the line (of business), the profession, the art, the field

SPECIAL READINGS

非道い▲ ひどい [also 酷い] cruel, harsh, rough; severe, intense, heavy

SYNONYMS

❶ⓐ ways and routes

道 WAY (path) → 3888

径 PATH → 0347

軌 TRACK → 1832

線 LINE → 1760

澪 WATERWAY → 0957

途 WAY (route) → 3853

路 ROAD → 1936

筋 wayside → 3319

通り street → 3855

街 city street → 0702

辻 CROSSROADS → 3958

岐 forked road → 0285

巷 THE STREETS → 3097

ⓑ tubular passages

管 PIPE → 3349

筒 TUBE → 3323

道 passage → 3888

脈 VEIN → 1189

樋 WATER PIPE → 1353

❷ moral goodness

徳 VIRTUE → 0842

道 the way of moral conduct → 3888

善 GOOD → 2921

義 RIGHTEOUSNESS → 2948

❷ moral principles

倫 MORALS → 0135

道 the way of moral conduct → 3888

❸ religion

教 RELIGION → 1887

宗 religion → 2769

道 the Way → 3888

ⓐ religions and sects

仏 Buddhism → 0020

法 Buddha's teachings → 0391

禅 ZEN → 1306

儒 CONFUCIANISM → 0197

道 Taoism → 3888

❹ art

技 SKILL → 0292

倆 SKILL → 0136

術 PRACTICAL ART → 0575

芸 ART → 2738

道 the way of an art → 3888

❺ⓐ territorial divisions

州 STATE → 0064

県 PREFECTURE → 3269

府 URBAN PREFECTURE → 3824

道 district of Hokkaido → 3888

都 METROPOLIS OF TOKYO → 2120

省 province in China → 3100

郡 COUNTY → 1858

USAGE

【みち】

道

①ⓐ [formerly also 路] [also prefix and suffix] way, road, path, street; highway, track

ⓑ (distance in general) way, distance, journey

ⓒ halfway

② way of doing, means, course of action

③ the way of moral conduct, path of righteousness, moral principles, morality, right way of life

④ art, line (of work), career

路

[now usu. 道] road, avenue, boulevard

HOMOPHONES

みち 路 ROAD → 1936

ひどい

酷い → 1967

非道い → 1101, 3888

COMPOUND FORMATION

【道具 どうぐ】

道具 'tool, etc.' originally referred to the implements (具) used in performing Buddhist (道 ❸❻) ceremonies.

NOTE

➡ see also USAGE note at 酷 1967

遇

3889

口3-3-9

▶TREAT
▶ENCOUNTER

グウ あ(う)▲

Ⓝ 遇 Ⓒ 遇 yù

162	Jōyō	U9047
辶	S12-3-9	F1432

COMPOUNDS

❶ **TREAT, entertain, receive, deal with**

待遇する たいぐうする treat, receive, entertain

処遇する しょぐうする treat, deal with

冷遇 れいぐう cold treatment, frigid reception

知遇 ちぐう favor, warm friendship

優遇する ゆうぐうする treat favorably, receive warmly

❷ (meet by chance) **ENCOUNTER, happen to meet, come across, meet with**

遭遇する そうぐうする encounter, come across

奇遇 きぐう unexpected meeting, chance encounter

千載一遇の せんざいいちぐうの experienced once in a thousand years, very rare

❸ **fate, luck, one's lot**

遇不遇 ぐうふぐう happiness and sorrows

不遇 ふぐう misfortune, ill luck

境遇 きょうぐう one's lot, circumstances, situation in life

INDEPENDENT

【ぐうする 遇する】 TREAT, entertain

KUN

【あう 遇う】 [also 遭う] (come upon, esp. by accident) meet with, ENCOUNTER, be confronted

酷い目に遇う ひどいめにあう have a bad time

SYNONYMS

❶ **treat and welcome**

遇 TREAT → 3889

待 treat → 0434

扱う HANDLE → 0251

款 treat cordially → 2135

接 receive → 0607

迎 WELCOME → 3796

❷ **meet**

会 MEET → 2512

遇 ENCOUNTER → 3889

遭 MEET WITH → 3917

見 SEE → 3151

謁 BE GRANTED AN AUDIENCE → 1976

逢 MEET → 4002

HOMOPHONES

あう

遭 MEET WITH → 3917

会 MEET → 2512

合 COMBINE → 2511

逢 MEET → 4002

NOTE

➡ see USAGE note at 会 2512

遍

3890

口3-3-9

▶ALL OVER

ヘン あまね(く)▲

Ⓝ 遍 Ⓒ 遍 biàn

162	Jōyō	U904D
辶	S12-3-9	F1852

COMPOUNDS

❶ **ALL OVER, everywhere, universal, ubiquitous, widespread**

遍在 へんざい omnipresence, ubiquity

遍歴 へんれき travels, pilgrimage

遍路 へんろ pilgrim

普遍的な ふへんてきな universal, omnipresent, ubiquitous

満遍無く(=万遍無く) まんべんなく evenly, equally; without exception; all over

❷ [sometimes also 返 3797] **counter for number of times**

五遍 ごへん five times

何遍 なんべん how many times

何遍も なんべんも several [many] times, very often

KUN

【あまねく 遍く】[also 普く] *literary* **ALL OVER**, everywhere, widely, universally

遍く捜す あまねくさがす make a wide search

遍く世界に知られる あまねくせかいにしられる be known all over the world

SYNONYMS

❶ **widespread**

普 WIDESPREAD → 2919

遍 ALL OVER → 3890

通 common → 3855

公 common (math) → 2468

❷ **time and time counters**

回 TIME → 3793

度 TIME → 3844

遍 counter for number of times → 3890

返 counter for number of times → 3797

HOMOPHONES

あまねく 普 WIDESPREAD → 2919

NOTE

➡ see USAGE note at 普 2919

過

3891

3-3-9

▶**PASS BY**

▶**EXCEED**

カ す(ぎる) -す(ぎる) -す(ぎ) す(ごす)
あやま(つ) あやま(ち)

Ⓝ 過 Ⓒ 过 guò

162	Jōyō-5	U904E
辶	S12-3-9	F0295

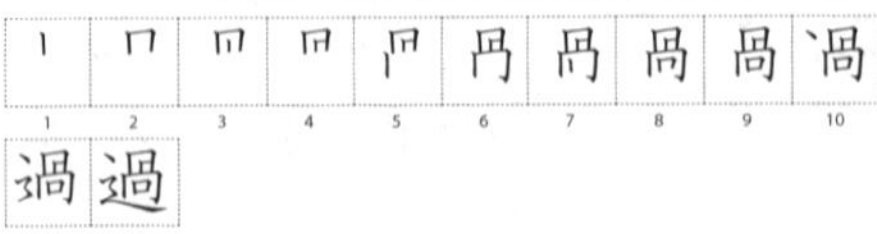

COMPOUNDS

❶ [original meaning] **PASS BY, go past, pass through**

過程 かてい process, course

過渡期 かとき transitional period [stage]

通過する つうかする pass through, carry (a resolution)

経過 けいか progress, course, development; lapse, passage

一過性の いっかせいの temporary, transitory

❷ (of time) **PASS BY [away], elapse**

過去 かこ the past, bygone days

過日 かじつ the other day, some days ago

❸ⓐ **EXCEED, be above, be over**

ⓑ [prefix] **excessive, over-, too much, super-**

a 過剰 かじょう surplus, excess

過密 かみつ overcrowding

過当な かとうな excessive, undue, unreasonable

過熱する かねつする overheat, superheat

過労 かろう overwork

超過する ちょうかする exceed, be in excess, be above

b 過半数 かはんすう majority, more than half

過保護 かほご overprotectiveness

❹ⓐ **error, fault, mistake, slip**

ⓑ err, make a mistake

a 過失 かしつ error, fault, mistake; negligence

大過 たいか serious error, gross mistake

罪過 ざいか fault

b 過誤 かご mistake, error, fault

❺ *chem* per-

過酸化水素 かさんかすいそ hydrogen peroxide

過硫酸 かりゅうさん persulfuric acid

❻ *Buddhism* past

過現未 かげんみ past, present and future, three temporal states of existence

KUN

【すぎる 過ぎる】**PASS BY, go past, pass through;** (of time) **pass by [away], elapse, expire; exceed, be above, go too far**

過ぎ去る すぎさる pass (away), elapse

過ぎた事 すぎたこと the past, bygones, past event

通り過ぎる とおりすぎる go past, pass

五十を過ぎる ごじゅうをすぎる be above 50

冗談が過ぎる じょうだんがすぎる carry a joke too far

【-すぎる -過ぎる】[verbal suffix] **over-, too, to excess, to a fault**

食べ過ぎる たべすぎる overeat oneself

利口過ぎる りこうすぎる be too clever

【-すぎ -過ぎ】

① [suffix] **past, after**

二時過ぎに にじすぎに after two o'clock

② [verbal suffix] **over-, too much, excessive**

飲み過ぎ のみすぎ overdrinking

【すごす 過ごす】

① **pass [spend] (time), tide over, get through**

一日を過ごす いちにちをすごす pass a day

冬を過ごす ふゆをすごす go through the winter

②ⓐ [verbal suffix] **let pass, leave alone**

ⓑ [also verbal suffix] **go too far, overdo**

a やり過ごす やりすごす let (a person) go past

見過ごす みすごす let go by, let pass; overlook, miss

b 寝過ごす ねすごす oversleep

【あやまつ 過つ】**err, make a mistake**

過って あやまって be mistaken, in error; by accident

【あやまち 過ち】**fault; error, mistake**

過ちを改める あやまちをあらためる correct a fault

SYNONYMS

❶ **pass**

通 PASS → 3855
過 PASS BY → 3891
経 PASS THROUGH → 1687
疏 LET PASS → 1511

❷ **elapse**

過 PASS BY → 3891
経 pass → 1687
歴 pass → 3748
去 pass away → 2678

❸ **exceeding and excess**

過 EXCEED → 3891
超 SURPASS → 4107
越 GO BEYOND → 4108
濫 EXCESSIVE → 0990
余 EXCESS → 2535
剰 SURPLUS → 2233
冗 REDUNDANT → 2470

❹ⓐ **mistakes and mistaking**

過 error → 3891
失 SLIP → 4325
誤 MISTAKE → 1945
謬 MISTAKE → 2060
錯 mistaken → 2187
-違える mis- → 3907

遂

3892
◻3-3-9

▶ACCOMPLISH
スイ と(げる) つい(に)▲
Ⓝ 遂 Ⓒ 遂 suì suí

162	Jōyō	U9042
辶	S12-3-9	F1469

(stroke order 1–12)

COMPOUNDS

● (complete successfully) **ACCOMPLISH, achieve, attain, complete, carry out, execute, commit, perform**

遂行する すいこうする accomplish, execute, perform, carry out
完遂する かんすいする execute successfully, accomplish, bring to completion
未遂の みすいの attempted (suicide, etc.)

KUN

【とげる 遂げる】**ACCOMPLISH, achieve, attain, fulfill, realize, carry out**

成し遂げる なしとげる complete, carry out, accomplish
遣り遂げる やりとげる carry out, complete; achieve

【ついに 遂に】[sometimes also 終に] **at last, at length, in the end, finally**

SYNONYMS

● **execute**

執 EXECUTE → 2114
行 ACT → 0246
履 FULFILL → 3933
施 CARRY OUT → 1103
践 IMPLEMENT → 1938
果たす effect → 4377
遂 ACCOMPLISH → 3892

● **accomplish**

達 ATTAIN → 3893
遂 ACCOMPLISH → 3892
成 ACHIEVE → 4352
徹 GO THROUGH → 0894
破 carry through with → 1478
叶 BE FULFILLED → 0209

USAGE

【ついに】

遂に
[sometimes also 終に] at last, at length, in the end, finally
終に
[usu. 遂に] same as 遂に

HOMOPHONES

ついに 終 END → 1692

NOTE

★ do not confuse with 遂 ONE BY ONE → 3848

達

3893
◻3-3-9

▶ATTAIN
タツ ダ▲ **-たち**▲ ㊔ とおる さとる だて さと みち
Ⓝ 達 達 Ⓒ 达 dá

162	Jōyō-4	U9054
辶	S12-3-9	F0382

(stroke order 1–12)

COMPOUNDS

❶ⓐ (arrive at) **ATTAIN, reach, arrive, come up to, gain**

ⓑ (succeed in reaching a goal) **ATTAIN, achieve, reach, realize**

a 到達 とうたつ arrival; attainment
先達 せんだつ guide, precursor, pioneer, leader
発達する はったつする develop, grow, make progress
b 達成する たっせいする attain, achieve, accomplish

調達 ちょうたつ supply, procurement; execution (of an order); raising (money)
栄達 えいたつ success in life, rise in the world

❷ **ATTAIN proficiency or maturity, understand thoroughly, be versed in, be skillful**
達観 たっかん philosophic view [ripeness]; far-sighted view
達人 たつじん expert, master
達筆 たっぴつ good handwriting
達者な たっしゃな expert, proficient, clever; healthy, well, strong, robust
上達する じょうたつする make progress, attain proficiency
熟達する じゅくたつする attain proficiency, become expert

❸ **deliver, convey**
達意 たつい intelligibility, perspicuity
配達 はいたつ delivery
速達 そくたつ special delivery, express mail
伝達 でんたつ transmission, conveyance, communication; propagation
送達 そうたつ conveyance, delivery, dispatch

❹ **issue a notice, issue [deliver] orders, notify**
通達 つうたつ communication, notification; proficiency
示達 じたつ(=したつ) instructions, directions
上意下達する じょういかたつする convey the will of the governing to the governed
執達吏 しったつり bailiff

❺ [original meaning] **extend to, reach to**
四通八達 しつうはったつ traffic network extending in all directions
闊達な かったつな openhearted, frank, broad-minded

❻ **used phonetically for *da* or similar sounds**
達磨 だるま Bodhidharma; tumbler
曹達 そーだ soda

INDEPENDENT

【たっする 達する】(arrive at) **ATTAIN, reach, arrive, come up to, amount to;** (succeed in reaching a goal) **attain, achieve, reach, realize; issue a notice, issue [deliver] orders, notify**
頂上に達する ちょうじょうにたっする attain the summit
成年に達する せいねんにたっする come of age
目的を達する もくてきをたっする attain one's aim, achieve one's purpose

【たっし 達し】government notice

KUN

【-たち -達】[suffix]
① **suffix, often polite, for forming the plural of pronouns, people or animals**
私達 わたくしたち we
動物達 どうぶつたち animals
② **...and the others**
山田さん達 やまださんたち Mr. Yamada and the others

SPECIAL READINGS

友達 ともだち friend, companion

SYNONYMS

❶ⓐ **arrive**
着 ARRIVE → 4110
到 ARRIVE → 1615
至 COME TO → 2707
及 REACH TO → 4192
届く REACH → 3820
達 ATTAIN → 3893

ⓑ **accomplish**
達 ATTAIN → 3893
遂 ACCOMPLISH → 3892
成 ACHIEVE → 4352
徹 GO THROUGH → 0894
破 carry through with → 1478
叶 BE FULFILLED → 0209

❷ **attain proficiency**
達 attain proficiency → 3893
熟 become skilled → 3558

❸ **transmit and deliver**
伝 TRANSMIT → 0048
逓 RELAY → 3852
届ける DELIVER → 3820
達 deliver → 3893

❹ **inform and communicate**
報 INFORM → 2133
通 COMMUNICATE → 3855
告 NOTIFY → 3062
届ける give notice → 3820
達 issue a notice → 3893
知 let know → 1446
申 REPORT → 4319
稟 REPORT TO → 2649
宣 PROCLAIM → 2799

❻ **phonetic [d]**
陀 PHONETIC [da] → 0409
達 phonetic [da] → 3893
提 phonetic [dai] → 0720
胴 phonetic [dō] → 1186

【-たち】
① **plural suffixes**
-達 plural suffix → 3893
-等 plural suffix → 3321
衆 somewhat polite plural suffix → 3325
-共 belittling plural suffix → 3045
-方 polite plural suffix → 2459

COMPOUND FORMATION

❶【発達 はったつ】

発達する 'develop, grow, make progress' is to grow (発) and attain (達 ❶ⓑ) perfection gradually.

❷【栄達 えいたつ】

栄達 'success in life, rise in the world' is the attainment (達 ❶ⓑ) of glory (栄) or worldly fame.

運

3894

口3-3-9

▶CARRY
▶MOVE
▶FORTUNE

ウン はこ(ぶ)

Ⓝ 運 Ⓒ 运 yùn

162	Jōyō-3	U904B
辶	S12-3-9	F0259

COMPOUNDS

❶ⓐ (move something from one place to another in one's hands or in a vehicle) **CARRY, transport, ship**

ⓑ **carriage, transport, transportation**

a 運輸 うんゆ transport(ation), conveyance
運送 うんそう shipping, transportation
運搬する うんぱんする carry, transport, convey, deliver
海運 かいうん marine transportation, merchant shipping
陸運 りくうん land transportation [carriage]
舟運 しゅううん transportation by water

b 運賃 うんちん freight [shipping] expense, passenger fare
運河 うんが canal

❷ⓐ [original meaning] **MOVE, revolve**

ⓑ **control MOVEment skillfully, handle, set in motion**

a 運動 うんどう motion, movement; exercise; campaign
運動会 うんどうかい sports meeting, meet
運航 うんこう navigation; (airline or shipping) service
運行する うんこうする revolve, orbit; operate
運休 うんきゅう suspension of (bus) service

b 運転する うんてんする operate, drive, run
運転士 うんてんし officer, mate; driver
運営する うんえいする operate, manage
運用する うんようする make use of; invest in; apply to
運筆 うんぴつ handling the brush

❸ **FORTUNE, luck, fate, destiny, chance**

運命 うんめい fate, fortune, destiny
運良く うんよく fortunately, luckily
好運 こううん good luck
不運 ふうん misfortune, bad luck
社運 しゃうん fortune of the company

❹ [formerly 耘 1661] weed, remove weeds

耕運機 こううんき cultivator, tiller

INDEPENDENT

【うん 運】**FORTUNE, luck, fate, destiny, chance**

運が悪い うんがわるい out of luck
運に任せる うんにまかせる trust to luck

KUN

【はこぶ 運ぶ】**CARRY, transport; progress, advance, go on (well)**

運び はこび carriage; step, pace; progress, development; stage
運び出す はこびだす bring out, carry out
すらすらと運ぶ すらすらとはこぶ go smoothly

SYNONYMS

❶ **carry**

運 CARRY →3894
搬 CARRY →0795
輸 TRANSPORT →2026

❷ⓐ **move**

動 MOVE →2232
運 MOVE →3894
滑 SLIDE →0809
辷る SLIP →3957
移 SHIFT →1508
転 remove →1872
遷 TRANSFER →3932
繰る SHIFT ONWARD →1806

ⓑ **handle**

扱う HANDLE →0251
馭 HANDLE →2282
操 MANIPULATE →0948
揮 WIELD →0717
運 control movement skillfully →3894

❸ **fate and fortune**

運 FORTUNE →3894
命 fate →2553
業 karma →3227
縁 karma relation →1754
籤 LOT →3399

NOTE

➡ see COMPOUND FORMATION for 運転 うんてん →転 1872

遥 ▶FAR

ヨウ　はる(か)

Ⓝ 遙 Ⓒ 遥 yáo

[辶] 辶 弋 尸 广 囗

3895

□3-3-9

162	Names	U9065
辶	S12-3-9	F2182

COMPOUNDS

❶ **FAR, faraway, far-off, distant, remote**

遥拝 ようはい worshiping from afar

遥遠な ようえんな [rare] very far-off, remote

❷ walk about, wander about

逍×遥学派 しょうようがくは Peripatetic school (of philosophy)

KUN

【はるか 遥か】

はるかな 遥かな **FAR, faraway, far-off, distant, remote**

遥か彼方の はるかかなたの faraway, far-off

遥か昔 はるかむかし long ago

遥かに はるかに far, far off, in the distance; a long time ago; by far

遥遥 はるばる from afar, all the way; at a great distance

SYNONYMS

❶ **distant**

遠 DISTANT → 3906

遥 FAR → 3895

悠 far-off → 3407

遼 FARAWAY → 3930

隔 APART → 0827

離 separated → 2364

迂 ROUNDABOUT → 3969

遊 ▶PLAY

ユウ　ユ　あそ(ぶ)　あそ(ばす)

Ⓝ 遊 Ⓒ 游 yóu

3896

□3-3-9

162	Jōyō-3	U904A
辶	S12-3-9	F0682

Stroke order: 1 丶, 2 亠, 3 方, 4 方, 5 方, 6 方, 7 方, 8 斿, 9 斿, 10 斿, 11 游, 12 遊

COMPOUNDS

❶ⓐ **PLAY, amuse oneself**

ⓑ **PLAY** around with (the opposite sex), flirt

ⓒ associate intimately with

a 遊戯 ゆうぎ game, pastime, amusement

遊興 ゆうきょう merrymaking, spree

遊園地 ゆうえんち amusement park

b 遊女 ゆうじょ harlot, prostitute

遊里 ゆうり licensed quarters, red-light district

c 交遊 こうゆう companionship, friendship

❷ be idle, be unemployed

遊民 ゆうみん idle people, the unemployed

遊休施設 ゆうきゅうしせつ idle facilities

遊食する ゆうしょくする live in idleness

遊資 ゆうし idle capital

❸ **tour, take a pleasure trip or excursion, make a study tour**

遊学 ゆうがく traveling to study

遊山 ゆさん excursion, outing, picnic

遊説 ゆうぜい electioneering tour; campaign speech

外遊 がいゆう foreign tour, trip abroad

歴遊 れきゆう traveling, tour, pleasure trip

❹ⓐ move about freely, wander, roam

ⓑ mobile, free moving

a 遊星 ゆうせい wandering star, planet

遊牧 ゆうぼく nomadism

遊離する ゆうりする isolate, separate

b 遊撃 ゆうげき attack by a mobile unit

浮遊物 ふゆうぶつ floating matter, suspended particles

❺ [sometimes also 游 ゆう 0750] swim

遊泳する ゆうえいする swim

回遊 かいゆう excursion, circular tour; migration (of fish)

❻ *baseball* abbrev. of 遊撃手 ゆうげきしゅ: shortstop

遊失 ゆうしつ shortstop error

KUN

【あそぶ 遊ぶ】 **PLAY, amuse oneself; play around with, flirt; be idle, loaf; be not in use; be unemployed; make an excursion, take a trip; visit**

遊び あそび play, sport; amusement, fun; diversion; visit; outing; dissipation; play (of a wheel)

遊び場 あそびば playground

遊び人 あそびにん gambler; playboy

【あそばす 遊ばす】 [honorific] **be pleased to, deign, condescend**

遊ばせ言葉 あそばせことば polite language used by women

SYNONYMS

❶ⓐ & ❶ⓑ **play**

遊 PLAY → 3896

戯 SPORT → 2351

弄 TOY WITH → 3057

❸ **journey**

旅 TRAVEL → 1153

行 trip → 0246

遊 tour → 3896

巡 tour around → 3781

❹ⓐ **wander**

浪 WANDER → 0527
遊 move about freely → 3896
漂 drift about → 0857
流 drift → 0529
低 WANDER ABOUT → 0350
徊 MOVE TO AND FRO → 0432

選

3897
☐3-3-9

▶**CHOOSE**
セン　えら(ぶ)　よ(る)

162	Nonstandard	U9078
辶	S12-3-9	F0000

handwritten form → see 選 at 3931

遁

3898
☐3-3-9

▶**FLEE**
トン　のが(れる)

162	Nonstandard	U9041
辶	S12-3-9	F0000

traditional form → see 遁 at 4027

遜

☐3-3-9

incorrect stroke-count
➡ see ☐3-3-10: 辶 at 3910

遜

☐3-3-9

incorrect stroke-count
➡ see ☐3-4-10: 辶 at 4041

遁道 etc.

☐3-3-9

incorrect stroke-count
➡ see ☐3-4-9: 辶 at 4027

貳

3899
☐3-3-9

▶**TWO**
ニ

154	Nonstandard	U8CB3
貝	S12-7-5	F0000

traditional form → see 弐 at 3961

犀

3900
☐3-3-9

▶**RHINOCEROS**
サイ　セイ　㊔ かた
Ⓒ 犀 xī

93	Names	U7280
牛	S12-4-8	F2784

COMPOUNDS

❶ **RHINOCEROS**
犀角 さいかく rhinoceros horn
黒犀 くろさい black rhinoceros
一角犀 いっかくさい great one-horned rhinoceros
金木犀 きんもくせい orange osmanthus, *Osmanthus fragrans* var. *aurantiacus*

❷ⓐ firm, hard
ⓑ sharp, keen, acute
b 犀利 さいり sharp, keen

INDEPENDENT

【さい 犀】RHINOCEROS

SYNONYMS

❶ **undomesticated mammals**
虎 TIGER → 3981
猿 MONKEY → 0824
鯨 WHALE → 2361
犀 RHINOCEROS → 3900
狼 WOLF → 0541
狐 FOX → 0472
羚 SEROW → 1695
鼠 RAT → 3340
獅 LION → 0825
豹 LEOPARD → 1847
熊 BEAR → 3530
象 ELEPHANT → 2647
麒 MALE CHINESE UNICORN → 2363
麟 FEMALE CHINESE UNICORN → 2376
猪 WILD BOAR → 0652
鹿 DEER → 3879

COMPOUND FORMATION

【金木犀　きんもくせい】
金木犀 'orange osmanthus' is a tree (木) with bark that resembles the skin of the rhinoceros (犀 ❶) and flowers the color of gold (金).

属

3901
☐3-3-9

▶**BELONG TO**
ゾク　ショク▲ ㊔ さっか
Ⓝ 屬 Ⓒ 属 shǔ zhǔ

44	Jōyō-5	U5C5E
尸	S12-3-9	F0928

COMPOUNDS

❶ⓐ **BELONG TO, pertain to, be one of**
ⓑ **be subordinate to, depend upon**
a 付属する ふぞくする be attached to, belong to
所属する しょぞくする belong to, be attached to
専属する せんぞくする belong exclusively to
軍属 ぐんぞく army civilian employee
b 属領 ぞくりょう possession, dependency, dominion
属国 ぞっこく vassal state, dependency
従属 じゅうぞく subordination, dependency

❷ [also suffix] **subordinate official**
属官 ぞっかん subordinate, government clerk
配属する はいぞくする assign, attach
部属 ぶぞく section, division

辶 辶 弋 尸 【广】 口

文部属山本氏 もんぶぞくやまもとし Mr. Yamamoto, clerk of the Ministry of Education, Science and Culture

❸ⓐ genus, kind, sort, family; category
ⓑ *biol* **genus**

a 金属 きんぞく metal
尊属 そんぞく ascendant
b 属名 ぞくめい generic name
属差 ぞくさ generic difference
猫属 ねこぞく the cat genus

❹ [usu. 嘱 しょく 0881] charge, entrust
属託する しょくたくする entrust with

❺ [usu. 嘱 しょく 0881] fasten one's attention upon
属目する しょくもくする pay attention to

INDEPENDENT

【ぞく 属】genus, kind, sort, family; *biol* genus
【ぞくする 属する】**BELONG TO, pertain to, be one of, be associated with**
政党に属する せいとうにぞくする belong to a political party

SYNONYMS

❶ⓐ possess
有 HAVE → 3703
蔵 own → 2995
持 HOLD → 0447
属 BELONG TO → 3901
享 ENJOY → 2545
具 possess → 3159

❸ⓐ kinds and types
型 TYPE → 3266
類 KIND → 2275
色 kind → 2522
般 SORT → 1670
属 genus → 3901
品 category → 2795
種 VARIETY → 1560
様 variety → 1332

廃
3902
□3-3-9

▸**ABOLISH**
▸**WASTE**
ハイ すた(れる) すた(る)
Ⓝ 廢 Ⓒ 废 fèi

53 广	Jōyō	U5EC3
	S12-3-9	F1074

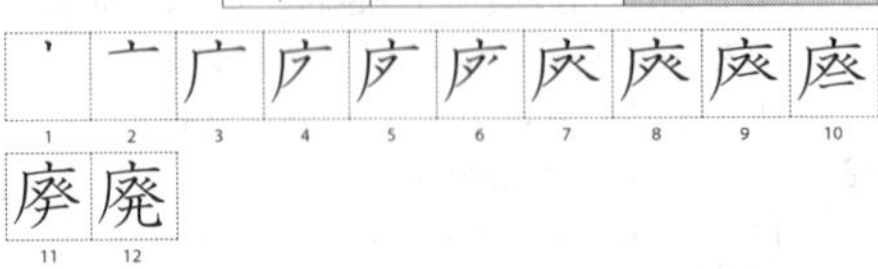

COMPOUNDS

❶ ABOLISH, abandon, discontinue, give up
廃止する はいしする abolish, abandon, discontinue
廃案 はいあん rejected bill [project]
廃刊 はいかん discontinuance of publication
廃棄 はいき discarding, abolition, annulment
廃藩 はいはん abolition of the *han* system
廃絶 はいぜつ extinction
全廃 ぜんぱい (total) abolition
撤廃 てっぱい abolition, removal

❷ⓐ WASTE, useless, discarded, abandoned, obsolete
ⓑ [formerly also 癈 4077] disabled, crippled

a 廃品 はいひん waste articles, junk
廃ガス はいがす waste gas
廃熱 はいねつ waste heat
廃坑 はいこう abandoned mine
廃語 はいご obsolete word
荒廃 こうはい desolation, waste, ruin
b 廃疾 はいしつ disablement
廃人 はいじん invalid, crippled person

INDEPENDENT

【はいする 廃する】**ABOLISH**, abandon; annul, repeal; dethrone, depose

KUN

【すたれる 廃れる】**go out of use, fall into disuse, be outmoded**
廃れた すたれた disused, out of date, obsolete
【すたる 廃る】same as 廃れる すたれる
廃り すたり waste, wastage, waster

SYNONYMS

❶ discontinue
絶 BREAK OFF → 1711
廃 ABOLISH → 3902
断 CUT OFF → 1885
止 STOP → 3659
休 suspend → 0056
停 suspend → 0156
已む CEASE → 4185

❷ⓐ bad
悪 BAD → 3413
劣 INFERIOR → 3047
下 of low grade → 4186
弊 shabby → 3583
粗 COARSE → 1683
駄 GOOD FOR NOTHING → 2291
廃 WASTE → 3902

廊
3903
□3-3-9

▸**CORRIDOR**
ロウ
Ⓝ 廊 Ⓒ 廊 láng

53 广	Jōyō	U5ECA
	S12-3-9	F1275

丶	亠	广	广	庐	庐	庐	底	底	底
1	2	3	4	5	6	7	8	9	10
廊	廊								
11	12								

COMPOUNDS

● [original meaning] **CORRIDOR, gallery, passageway, hall**
廊下 ろうか corridor, gallery, passage
画廊 がろう picture gallery
回廊 かいろう corridor, gallery
歩廊 ほろう corridor, gallery; platform

廓 口3-3-9

incorrect stroke-count
➡ see 口3-3-11: 广 at 3923

圏

3904 口3-3-9

▶**SPHERE**
ケン
N 圏 C 圈 quān juān juàn

31	Jōyō	U570F
口	S12-3-9	F1506

丨	冂	冂	冂	円	冎	冎	罔	罔	圏
1	2	3	4	5	6	7	8	9	10
圏	圏								
11	12								

COMPOUNDS

[also suffix]
❶ⓐ (spherical domain of action) **SPHERE, realm, circle, domain, zone, radius, range**
ⓑ **circle**
a 対流圏 たいりゅうけん troposphere
生物圏 せいぶつけん biosphere
暴風圏 ぼうふうけん storm zone
通信圏外 つうしんけんがい out of the range of communication
ポンド圏 ぽんどけん sterling zone
ab 北極圏 ほっきょくけん arctic zone; Arctic Circle
b 圏点 けんてん circle (for emphasis)
大圏コース たいけんこーす great circle route
❷ (domain of influence) **SPHERE, circle, domain**
影響圏 えいきょうけん sphere of influence
共産圏 きょうさんけん the Communist bloc

SYNONYMS

❶ⓐ **areas and localities**
地 PLACE → 0236
方 locality → 2459
辺 VICINITY → 3761
域 BOUNDED AREA → 0559
区 DISTRICT → 3681
領 TERRITORY → 1567
帯 BELT → 3191
圏 SPHERE → 3904
❶ⓐ & ❷ **range**
程 EXTENT → 1524
範 range → 3360
域 area → 0559
圏 SPHERE → 3904
野 FIELD → 1877
界 field (*phys*) → 3172
場 field (*phys*, *psychol*) → 0678
ⓑ **circle**
円 CIRCLE → 3673
圏 circle → 3904
丸 round or spherical shape → 4225
楕 ELLIPSE → 1279

圍

3905 口3-3-9

▶**ENCLOSE**
イ かこ(む) かこ(う) かこ(い)

31	Nonstandard	U570D
口	S12-3-9	F0000

traditional form → see 囲 at 3807

遠

3906 口3-3-10

▶**DISTANT**
エン オン とお(い)
N 遠 C 远 yuǎn

162	Jōyō-2	U9060
辶	S13-3-10	F0496

一	十	土	土	吉	吉	吉	声	袁	袁
1	2	3	4	5	6	7	8	9	10
遠	遠	遠							
11	12	13							

COMPOUNDS

❶ⓐ **DISTANT (in space), far, remote**
ⓑ **DISTANT (in time), far-off, remote**
ⓒ **become DISTANT**
a 遠隔の えんかくの distant, remote, far
遠景 えんけい distant view, perspective
遠方 えんぽう great distance; distant place
遠足 えんそく excursion, hike, long walk
遠征 えんせい (punitive) expedition, invasion; tour
遠視 えんし farsightedness
遠距離 えんきょり long distance
望遠鏡 ぼうえんきょう telescope
b 永遠 えいえん eternity
久遠 くおん eternity
c 遠心力 えんしんりょく centrifugal force
❷ **DISTANT (in relationship), estranged**
遠慮 えんりょ reserve; hesitation; forethought, prudence

敬遠する けいえんする keep at a respectful distance; avoid
疎遠 そえん estrangement, alienation, neglect

❸ profound, deep
深遠な しんえんな profound, deep

KUN

【とおい 遠い】 **far(-off), DISTANT, remote (in time or space); distant (in relationship); hard of hearing**
遠ざかる とおざかる become distant; keep away
遠く とおく great distance
遠回り とおまわり roundabout way
遠い昔 とおいむかし remote past
遠からず とおからず in the offing
遠縁 とおえん distant relation
耳が遠い みみがとおい hard of hearing

SYNONYMS

❶ **distant**
遠 DISTANT → 3906
遥 FAR → 3895
悠 far-off → 3407
遼 FARAWAY → 3930
隔 APART → 0827
離 separated → 2364
迂 ROUNDABOUT → 3969

❷ **estrange**
疎 ESTRANGE → 1512
離 separate from → 2364
遠 DISTANT → 3906

違

3907
口3-3-10

▶**DIFFER**
▶**VIOLATE**
イ ちが(う) ちが(い) ちが(える) -ちが(える) たが(う)▲ たが(える)▲
Ⓝ 違 Ⓒ 违 wéi

162	Jōyō	U9055
辶	S13-3-10	F0255

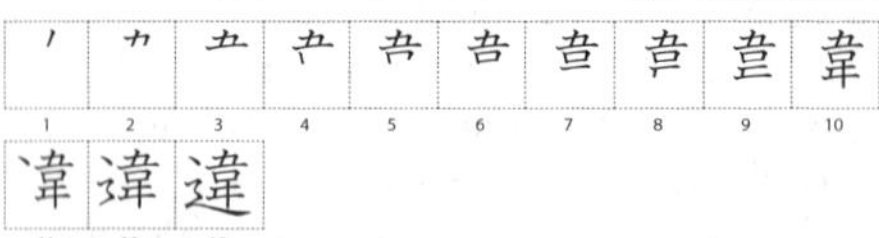

COMPOUNDS

❶ **DIFFER, be different**
違和感 いわかん feeling of being out of place, incongruity
相違 そうい difference, disparity

❷ **VIOLATE, break, disobey**
違反(=違犯) いはん violation (of the law), infringement; breach
違法 いほう illegality, unlawfulness
違憲 いけん unconstitutionality, violation of the constitution
違約 いやく breach of promise

❸ mistake, error
違算 いさん miscalculation, misjudgment

KUN

【ちがう 違う】
① **DIFFER, be different; differ in opinion, disagree**
違う ちがう No (that's not true)!
話が違う はなしがちがう That's a different story
② **be mistaken, be wrong**
間違う まちがう be mistaken, be incorrect
③ cross, go by
擦れ違う すれちがう pass by each other, brush past

【ちがい 違い】
① **DIFFERence**
食い違い くいちがい difference (in opinion), cross-purposes; cross
② [also suffix] **mistake**
違い無い ちがいない no mistaking it, for certain
勘違いする かんちがいする be under the wrong impression
計算違い けいさんちがい miscalculation

【ちがえる 違える】
① **change, alter**
話し方を違える はなしかたをちがえる disguise one's speech
② **mistake, make a mistake**
間違える まちがえる mistake, confuse
③ break, fail to keep, **VIOLATE**
約束を違える やくそくをちがえる break a promise
④ sprain, wrench
首筋を違える くびすじをちがえる wrench one's neck

【-ちがえる -違える】 [verbal suffix] **mis-, make a mistake in performing an action**
言い違える いいちがえる mistake, make a slip
見違える みちがえる mistake, fail to recognize
薬を飲み違える くすりをのみちがえる take the wrong medicine

【たがう 違う】 same as 違う ちがう
【たがえる 違える】 same as 違える ちがえる

SYNONYMS

❶ **differing and difference**
違 DIFFER → 3907
異 DIFFERENT → 3195
差 DIFFERENCE → 4104

❷ **violate**
違 VIOLATE → 3907
破 BREAK → 1478
犯 offend against → 0229
反 act contrary to → 3663
悖 GO AGAINST → 0503

背 go against →3182

【-ちがえる】

○ **mistakes and mistaking**

過 error →3891

失 SLIP →4325

誤 MISTAKE →1945

謬 MISTAKE →2060

錯 mistaken →2187

-違える mis- →3907

NOTE

➡ see USAGE note at 異 3195

遣

3908

☐3-3-10

▸DISPATCH

ケン つか(う) -つか(い) -づか(い) つか(わす) や(る)▲

Ⓝ 遣 Ⓒ 遣 qiǎn

162	Jōyō	U9063
辶	S13-3-10	F1008

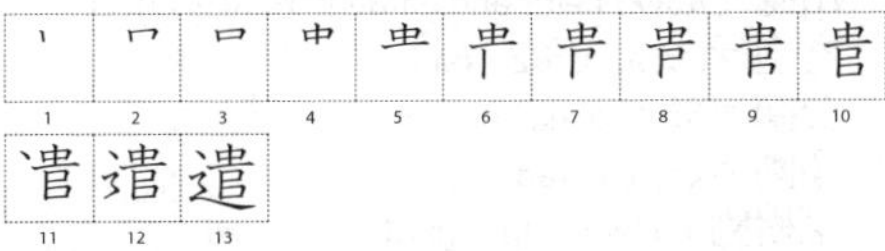

COMPOUNDS

❶ **DISPATCH, send**

遣外の けんがいの dispatched abroad

遣唐使 けんとうし Japanese envoy to Tang China

遣米 けんべい sending to America

派遣する はけんする dispatch, send

分遣 ぶんけん detachment, detail

先遣する せんけんする send ahead [in advance]

❷ [rare] banish, drive away

遣悶する けんもんする drive away melancholy

KUN

【つかう 遣う】

① [sometimes also 使う] **spend, use (time or money)**

金を遣う かねをつかう spend money

② **be anxious, worry**

気遣う きづかう feel anxious about, worry about, have apprehensions of

③ use (language properly), spell

正しい言葉を遣う ただしいことばをつかう use the correct word

④ manipulate

人形を遣う にんぎょうをつかう manipulate puppets

【-つかい, -づかい -遣い】

① **spending, spending money**

無駄遣い むだづかい wasting money

小遣い こづかい pocket money, spending money

② **worrying, being anxious**

心遣い こころづかい consideration, anxiety

③ **use (of language), spelling**

仮名遣い かなづかい kana orthography, use of kana

④ manipulating

人形遣い にんぎょうつかい puppet manipulator

【つかわす 遣わす】 **DISPATCH, send; present, bestow;** [following the TE-form of verbs] **do something for someone**

使者を遣わす ししゃをつかわす dispatch a messenger

誉めて遣わす ほめてつかわす You have my praise

【やる 遣る】 give (to an inferior); send (a person); do, perform; perform, act, play; perform an action for the benefit of an inferior; drink alcohol

使いに遣る つかいにやる send a person on an errand

おもちゃを買って遣る おもちゃをかってやる buy a toy (for a child)

SYNONYMS

❶ **send**

送 SEND →3837

投 SEND IN →0300

回 send round →3793

遣 DISPATCH →3908

派 DISPATCH →0456

HOMOPHONES

つかう 使 USE →0100

-つかい 使 USE →0100

NOTE

➡ see USAGE note at 使 0100

★ do not confuse with 遺 LEAVE BEHIND →3928

遡

3909

☐3-3-10

▸GO UPSTREAM

ソ さかのぼ(る)

162	Nonstandard	U9061
辶	S13-3-10	F0000

alternative form →see 遡 at 4040

遜

3910

☐3-3-10

▸HUMBLE

ソン へりくだ(る) ㊔ ゆずる やす

162	Nonstandard	U905C
辶	S13-3-10	F0000

alternative form →see 遜 at 4041

遮

☐3-3-10

incorrect stroke-count

➡ see ☐3-3-11: 辶 at 3916

遡遜 etc.

☐3-3-10

incorrect stroke-count

➡ see ☐3-4-10: 辶 at 4040

廉

3911
□3-3-10

▶INCORRUPT
▶CHEAP
レン ㊔ やす かど やすし
Ⓝ 廉 Ⓒ 廉 lián

53	Jōyō	U5EC9
广	S13-3-10	F2542

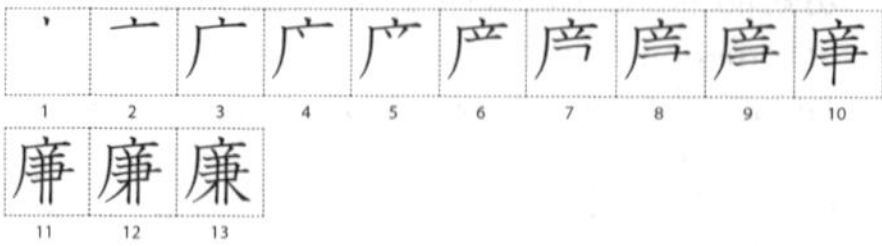

COMPOUNDS

❶ **INCORRUPT, honest and clean, upright, clean-handed**
廉直 れんちょく integrity, uprightness
廉潔な れんけつな honest, incorruptible
清廉な せいれんな incorruptible, honest, upright
破廉恥な はれんちな shameless, infamous, impudent

❷ **CHEAP, low-priced, bargain-priced, inexpensive**
廉価な れんかな cheap, low-priced
廉売 れんばい bargain sale
低廉な ていれんな cheap, inexpensive

SYNONYMS

❶ **purehearted**
純 PURE → 1649
淳 PUREHEARTED → 0626
清 clean → 0635
潔 IMMACULATE → 0920
廉 INCORRUPT → 3911
敦 HONEST → 2128
惇 SINCERE → 0588
直 straightforward → 3649
侃 FORTHRIGHT → 0097

❷ **inexpensive**
安 INEXPENSIVE → 2695
廉 CHEAP → 3911
低 low-priced → 0082

廉

3912
□3-3-10

▶INCORRUPT
▶CHEAP
レン ㊔ やす かど やすし

53	Nonstandard	UF9A2
广	S13-3-10	F0000

traditional form → see 廉 at 3911

廊

3913
□3-3-10

▶CORRIDOR
ロウ

53	Names	UF928
广	S13-3-10	F0000

traditional form → see 廊 at 3903

廓

□3-3-10

incorrect stroke-count
➡ see □3-3-11: 广 at 3923

園

3914
□3-3-10

▶GARDEN
エン その
Ⓝ 薗 Ⓒ 园 yuán

31	Jōyō-2	U5712
囗	S13-3-10	F0622

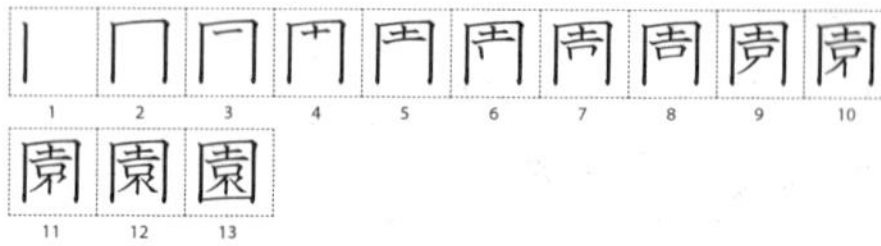

COMPOUNDS

❶ [sometimes also 苑 2783] [also suffix] [original meaning] **GARDEN, park, plantation, farm**
園芸 えんげい gardening, horticulture
田園 でんえん fields and gardens, rural districts
庭園 ていえん garden, park
公園 こうえん park, public garden
楽園 らくえん paradise
果樹園 かじゅえん fruit garden, orchard

❷ **public premises, institution**
学園 がくえん educational institution, school
動物園 どうぶつえん zoo
遊園地 ゆうえんち amusement park
幼稚園 ようちえん kindergarten

❸ ⓐ abbrev. of 幼稚園 ようちえん: **kindergarten**
ⓑ counter for kindergartens
a 園児 えんじ kindergarten child
入園 にゅうえん entering kindergarten
b 四百園 よんひゃくえん 400 kindergartens

❹ [sometimes also 苑 2783] **suffix after names of business establishments such as restaurants and tea shops, esp. where there are GARDENs**
永谷園 ながたにえん Nagatanien (name of a food company)

INDEPENDENT

【えん 園】 kindergarten; park; zoo
園の方針 えんのほうしん policy of our kindergarten

KUN

【その 園】 [sometimes also 苑] *literary*
① **GARDEN**
花園 はなぞの flower garden
② **institution**
学びの園 まなびのその educational institution

SYNONYMS

❶ **cultivated fields**
畑 FIELD → 1131
畠 FIELD → 3186

牧 PASTURE → 1083
園 GARDEN → 3914
田 RICE FIELD → 3775
佃 CULTIVATED RICE FIELD → 0066
圃 VEGETABLE GARDEN → 3871

❶ **gardens**
園 GARDEN → 3914
庭 GARDEN → 3866
苑 IMPERIAL GARDEN → 2783

❸ **schools**
校 SCHOOL → 1166
学 EDUCATIONAL INSTITUTION → 3162
院 INSTITUTION → 0544
塾 PRIVATE SCHOOL → 3546
大 UNIVERSITY → 4224
高 high school → 2601
中 junior high school → 4262
小 elementary school → 0007
園 kindergarten → 3914

❹ **restaurant suffixes**
亭 quality restaurant suffix → 2572
閣 high-class restaurant suffix → 4128
園 restaurant suffix → 3914
苑 restaurant suffix → 2783

USAGE

❶【えん】
園
[sometimes also 苑] [also suffix] garden, park, plantation, farm
苑
[sometimes also 園] Imperial garden, garden, park

★苑, now mostly replaced by 園, was formerly used in the sense of garden or farm, but is now more or less limited to the imperial garden and proper names, such as 神宮外苑 じんぐうがいえん.

❷【その】
園
[sometimes also 苑] *literary*
① garden
② institution
苑
[usu. 園] same as 園

HOMOPHONES

その 苑 IMPERIAL GARDEN → 2783

圓

3915
口3-3-10

▸CIRCLE
▸YEN
エン まる(い) まる ㊔ つぶら まどか まど

31	Names	U5713
囗	S13-3-10	F0000

traditional form → see 円 at 3673

遮

3916
口3-3-11

▸INTERRUPT
シャ さえぎ(る)
Ⓝ 遮 Ⓒ 遮 zhē

162	Jōyō	U906E
⻌	S14-3-11	F1992

Stroke order: 1–14

COMPOUNDS

❶ⓐ **INTERRUPT, block (off), intercept, obstruct**
ⓑ shield, screen, cover
a 遮断する しゃだんする intercept, interrupt, block, blockade, isolate
b 遮蔽 しゃへい shield, cover, screen; *elec* shielding
遮光する しゃこうする shield [shade] light

❷ used phonetically for *sha,* esp. in the transliteration of Sanskrit Buddhist terms
遮二無二 しゃにむに recklessly, madly
毘盧ˣ遮那仏 びるしゃなぶつ *Vairocana-Buddha*

INDEPENDENT

【しゃ 遮】name of chess piece in shogi (Japanese chess): *hisha*, rook

KUN

【さえぎる 遮る】**INTERRUPT, block (off), intercept, obstruct; shield, screen, cover**
道を遮る みちをさえぎる block the way
光線を遮る こうせんをさえぎる intercept the light
話を遮る はなしをさえぎる interrupt (a person)

SYNONYMS

❶ⓐ **obstruct and hinder**
遮 INTERRUPT → 3916
塞 STOP UP → 2924
阻 OBSTRUCT → 0411
沮 OBSTRUCT → 0399
奄 OBSTRUCT (by covering) → 2757
妨 HINDER → 0279
障 hinder → 0875
碍 STAND IN THE WAY → 1536
害 stand in the way → 2826
梗 STOP UP → 1204

❷ **phonetic [s]/[sh]**
沙 phonetic [sha] → 0311
刹 phonetic [setsu] → 1620
遮 phonetic [sha] → 3916
叉 phonetic [sha] → 4194
世 phonetic [se] → 4308
須 phonetic [shu] → 0700
修 phonetic [shu] → 0138
西 phonetic [su] → 4333

⻌ 弋 尸 广 口

相 phonetic [sō] → 1120
薩 phonetic [satsu] → 3016

【辶】弋尸广口

遭

▶MEET WITH
ソウ あ(う) あ(わせる)
Ⓝ 遭 Ⓒ 遭 zāo

3917
□3-3-11

162	Jōyō	U906D
辶	S14-3-11	F1600

一 𠂆 冂 𠘨 𠚇 曲 曲 曹 曹 曹 曹 ˋ曹 漕 遭 (stroke order 1–14)

COMPOUNDS

● [original meaning] (come upon, esp. by accident) **MEET WITH (disaster)**
遭難する そうなんする meet with disaster
遭遇する そうぐうする encounter, come across

KUN

【あう 遭う】[also 遇う] (come upon, esp. by accident) **MEET WITH, encounter, be confronted**
酷い目に遭う ひどいめにあう have a bad time

【あわせる 遭わせる】**subject to (an unfavorable experience), expose to**
痛い目に遭わせる いたいめにあわせる make (a person) pay for (something)

SYNONYMS

● **meet**
会 MEET → 2512
遇 ENCOUNTER → 3889
遭 MEET WITH → 3917
見 SEE → 3151
謁 BE GRANTED AN AUDIENCE → 1976
逢 MEET → 4002

HOMOPHONES

あう
遇 TREAT → 3889
会 MEET → 2512
合 COMBINE → 2511
逢 MEET → 4002

あわせる
会 MEET → 2512
合 COMBINE → 2511
併 TOGETHER → 0092

NOTE

➡ see USAGE notes at 会 2512 and 合 2511

適

▶SUITABLE
テキ かな(う)▲
Ⓝ 適 Ⓒ 适 shì

3918
□3-3-11

162	Jōyō-5	U9069
辶	S14-3-11	F0908

(stroke order 1–14)

COMPOUNDS

❶ⓐ **SUITABLE, fit, proper, appropriate, right**
ⓑ **suit, fit**

a 適当な てきとうな suitable, fit; irresponsible
適正な てきせいな proper, appropriate, reasonable, right
適切な てきせつな appropriate, adequate, proper
適時の てきじの timely, opportune
適宜 てきぎ suitableness, appropriateness; suitably
適量 てきりょう proper quantity
適者 てきしゃ suitable person
適度 てきど moderate, proper
適齢期 てきれいき marriageable age
最適な さいてきな optimum

b 適用する てきようする apply
適法 てきほう legality, lawfulness
適応 てきおう adaptation, adjustment
適合する てきごうする suit, be fit, conform (to)
適性 てきせい aptitude

❷ agreeable
快適な かいてきな comfortable, pleasant, agreeable
悠悠自適の生活 ゆうゆうじてきのせいかつ life free from worldly cares

INDEPENDENT

【てきする 適する】**suit, fit; be SUITABLE [appropriate]; be qualified [competent]**

KUN

【かなう 適う】
ⓐ suit, serve (the purpose)
ⓑ agree with, be consistent with
a 道理に適う どうりにかなう stand to reason

SYNONYMS

❶ⓐ **suitable**
適 SUITABLE → 3918
当 proper → 2701
宜 RIGHT → 2763
便 CONVENIENT → 0105
ⓑ **fit**
合 FIT → 2511
填まる fit → 0777
適 suit → 3918

揃える MAKE UNIFORM →0719

USAGE

【かなう】

適う

ⓐ suit, serve (the purpose)

ⓑ agree with, be consistent with

敵う

① be a match for, compare with

② stand, bear

叶う

① (of a wish) be fulfilled, be realized, be granted

② be able to, can (do)

HOMOPHONES

かなう

敵 ENEMY →2340

叶 BE FULFILLED →0209

鳶

▶BLACK KITE

エン とび とんび

Ⓒ 鸢 yuān

3919

口3-3-11

196	Names	U9CF6
鳥	S14-11-3	F2586

COMPOUNDS

● **BLACK KITE** (kind of bird)

鳶目兎耳 えんもくとじ sharp eyes and ears ("eyes of a black kite and ears of a rabbit")

KUN

【とび 鳶】

①ⓐ **BLACK KITE (kind of bird)**

ⓑ abbrev. of 鳶口 とびぐち: firefighter's hook

ⓒ abbrev. of 鳶色 とびいろ: reddish brown color

② abbrev. of 鳶職 とびしょく: **scaffolding [construction] worker**

鳶ズボン とびずぼん construction worker's baggy trousers

【とんび 鳶】

ⓐ (bird) **BLACK KITE**

ⓑ abbrev. of 鳶ガッパ とんびがっぱ: Inverness cape

ⓒ casual thief

a 鳶が鷹を生む とんび(=とび)がたかをうむ A black hen lays a white egg

c 昼鳶 ひるとんび(=ひるとび) sneak thief, pickpocket

SYNONYMS

● **birds**

鷹 HAWK →3955

鷗 GULL →2370

烏 CROW →4088

雀 SPARROW →3117

燕 SWALLOW →3142

鴻 LARGE WILD BIRD →0977

鳳 MALE PHOENIX →3749

凰 FEMALE PHOENIX →3738

鵬 MYTHICAL HUGE BIRD →1416

鶏 CHICKEN →2221

酉 ROOSTER →4358

隼 FALCON →3427

鳩 PIGEON →0184

鷲 EAGLE →3598

鳶 BLACK KITE →3919

鶴 CRANE →2326

鷺 HERON →3621

鵜 CORMORANT →2067

鴨 DUCK →1582

雁 WILD GOOSE →3741

層

▶STRATUM

ソウ

Ⓝ 層 Ⓒ 层 céng

3920

口3-3-11

44	Jōyō-6	U5C64
尸	S14-3-11	F0892

COMPOUNDS

❶ [also suffix]

ⓐ **STRATUM, layer**

ⓑ *geol* **STRATUM**, measures; seam, bed

ⓒ *biol* **STRATUM**

ⓓ counter for layers

a 層状 そうじょう stratiform, stratified

成層圏 せいそうけん stratosphere

電離層 でんりそう ionosphere

b 地層 ちそう layer, stratum

鉱層 こうそう ore bed

断層 だんそう dislocation, fault

c 高木層 こうぼくそう tree stratum

d 一層目 いっそうめ first layer

❷ [also suffix] **social STRATUM, class, bracket**

階層 かいそう social stratum, class; tier

下層 かそう lower classes

社会層 しゃかいそう stratum of society

知識層 ちしきそう the intellectual class

読者層 どくしゃそう class of readers [subscribers]

❸ⓐ **story (of a building)**

ⓑ counter for stories

a 高層 こうそう high altitude; tall (building)

b 三層楼 さんそうろう three-storied house [building]

INDEPENDENT

【そう 層】**STRATUM**, layer; seam, bed; stratum, class

石炭の層 せきたんのそう coal bed, coal seam

SYNONYMS

❷ **class**
- 級 GRADE → 1630
- 段 grade → 1471
- 位 RANK → 0069
- 階 RANK → 0761
- 身 social status → 4368
- 格 STATUS → 1161
- 等 CLASS → 3321
- 流 class → 0529
- 層 STRATUM → 3920

❸ **floor**
- 階 FLOOR → 0761
- 層 story → 3920

腐

3921

□3-3-11

▸ROT

フ くさ(る) -くさ(る) くさ(れる) くさ(れ) くさ(らす) くさ(す)▲

Ⓒ 腐 fǔ

130	Jōyō	U8150
肉	S14-6-8	F1414

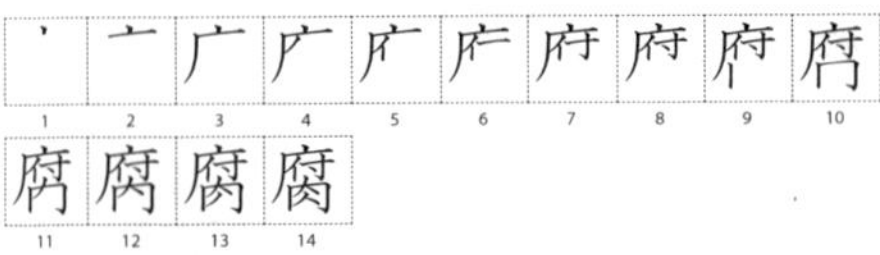

COMPOUNDS

❶ [original meaning] **ROT, decay, decompose; corrode**
- 腐敗する ふはいする rot, decay; become corrupt
- 腐朽 ふきゅう deterioration, decay
- 腐食 ふしょく corrosion; erosion
- 防腐 ぼうふ preservation from decay
- 豆腐 とうふ tofu (Japanese bean curd)

❷ **worn-out, worthless, useless, old**
- 腐儒 ふじゅ pedant, worthless scholar
- 陳腐な ちんぷな old-fashioned, trite, worn-out

❸ worry, be anxious
- 腐心する ふしんする rack one's brains

❹ [rare] castration (as a punishment in ancient China)
- 腐刑 ふけい castration

KUN

【くさる 腐る】**ROT, decay, decompose; corrode; feel blue; be corrupted**
- 腐り くさり rottenness, decay; corruption
- 腐るな くさるな Cheer up!
- 腐り果てる くさりはてる be completely rotten; be corrupted to the bottom

【-くさる -腐る】**suffix indicating speaker's spite**
- 威張り腐る いばりくさる be puffed up, throw one's weight around

【くされる 腐れる】**go ROTten; become worthless**
- 不貞腐れる ふてくされる have a fit of the sulks; become desperate

【くされ 腐れ】[in compounds]

① **becoming ROTten, rottenness**
- 宝の持ち腐れ たからのもちぐされ pearls thrown before swine
- 不貞腐れ ふてくされ sulkiness

② **base, despicable, worthless**
- 腐れ縁 くされえん unhappy yet inseparable relation; fatal bonds
- 腐れ金 くされがね paltry sum (of money)

【くさらす 腐らす】**ROT, spoil, decay; corrode; be depressed**
- 野菜を腐らす やさいをくさらす spoil the vegetables
- 気を腐らす きをくさらす be depressed, be in the blues

【くさす 腐す】speak ill of, disparage, slander
- 作品を腐す さくひんをくさす speak ill of a person's work

SYNONYMS

❶ **decay**
- 朽 DECAY → 1015
- 腐 ROT → 3921
- 枯 WITHER → 1113
- 萎 WITHER → 2872
- 錆 RUST → 2188

塵

3922

□3-3-11

▸DUST

ジン ちり ごみ

Ⓒ 尘 chén

32	Non-Jōyō	U5875
土	S14-3-11	F2165

COMPOUNDS

❶ [also suffix] **DUST; trash, garbage, rubbish, litter**
- 塵肺 じんぱい pneumoconiosis
- 塵埃× じんあい dust, dirt; this drab world, worldly squalor
- 粉塵 ふんじん dust
- 砂塵 さじん cloud of sand
- 吸塵 きゅうじん dust vacuuming
- 宇宙塵 うちゅうじん cosmic dust
- 微塵 みじん particle, atom; pieces, fragments; [in negative constructions] the slightest bit
- 後塵を拝する こうじんをはいする play second fiddle (to), be outdone (by)

❷ **worldliness, mundanity; worldly, mundane**
- 塵界 じんかい this drab world
- 戦塵 せんじん tumult of war; dust of battle
- 俗塵 ぞくじん the world, worldly affairs

❸ [rare] 1/1,000,000,000

一塵 いちじん 1/1,000,000,000

INDEPENDENT

【じん 塵】[rare] 1/1,000,000,000

KUN

【ちり 塵】DUST

塵取り ちりとり dustpan

塵紙 ちりがみ tissue paper, toilet paper

塵芥 ちりあくた(=じんかい) trash, garbage, rubbish; worthless thing

【ごみ 塵】[sometimes also 芥] **trash, garbage, rubbish, litter; dirt, DUST**

塵箱 ごみばこ trash can [bin], garbage can

塵溜め ごみため garbage dump, trash heap

粗大塵 そだいごみ bulk trash, oversized garbage

SYNONYMS

❶ **waste**

屑 WASTE → 3861

芥 TRASH → 2741

塵 DUST → 3922

USAGE

【ごみ】

塵

[sometimes also 芥] trash, garbage, rubbish, litter; dirt, dust

芥

[usu. 塵] trash, garbage, rubbish, litter; dirt, dust

HOMOPHONES

ごみ 芥 TRASH → 2741

廓

3923

□3-3-11

▶OUTER ENCLOSURE

カク くるわ

Ⓒ 廓 kuò

53	Non-Jōyō	U5ED3
广	S14-3-11	F2568

COMPOUNDS

[now usu. 郭 2112]

❶ **OUTER ENCLOSURE** [walls], outline, contour

外廓 がいかく outer block [enclosure]; outline, contour

輪廓 りんかく contour, outline, profile

城廓 じょうかく castle, fortress; castle walls, enclosure

❷ district; red-light district

一廓 いっかく a block

遊廓 ゆうかく licensed quarters, red-light district

❸ open, wide, empty

廓清する かくせいする purify, clean up, purge

KUN

【くるわ 廓】[now usu. 郭]

① red-light district

② area enclosed by earthwork

SYNONYMS

❶ **periphery**

周 PERIPHERY → 3720

囲 circumference → 3807

郭 OUTER ENCLOSURE → 2112

廓 OUTER ENCLOSURE → 3923

HOMOPHONES

くるわ 郭 OUTER ENCLOSURE → 2112

NOTE

➡ see USAGE note at 郭 2112

廐

3924

□3-3-11

▶HORSE STABLE

キュウ うまや

53	Nonstandard	U5ED0
广	S14-3-11	F0000

alternative form → see 厩 at 3746

廏

3925

□3-3-11

▶HORSE STABLE

キュウ うまや

53	Nonstandard	U5ECF
广	S14-3-11	F0000

traditional form → see 厩 at 3746

廣

□3-3-11

incorrect stroke-count

➡ see □3-3-12: 广 at 3942

團

3926

□3-3-11

▶BODY

ダン トン

31	Names	U5718
囗	S14-3-11	F0000

traditional form → see 団 at 3791

圖

3927

□3-3-11

▶DRAWING

ズ ト はか(る)

31	Nonstandard	U5716
囗	S14-3-11	F0000

traditional form → see 図 at 3809

遺

3928

□3-3-12

▶LEAVE BEHIND

イ ユイ

Ⓝ 遗 Ⓒ 遗 yí wèi

162	Jōyō-6	U907A
辶	S15-3-12	F0617

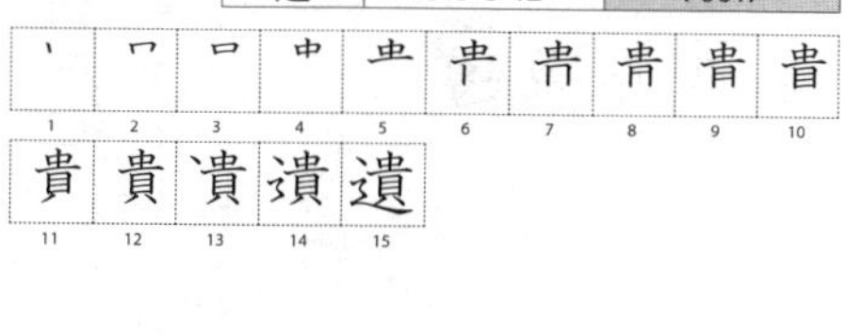

COMPOUNDS

❶ⓐ LEAVE BEHIND (at one's death), bequeath, bestow; be left behind, remain
ⓑ [original meaning] **LEAVE (a thing) BEHIND, forget**

a 遺産 いさん inheritance, bequest
遺族 いぞく bereaved family
遺骨 いこつ (skeletal) remains; ashes
遺憾な いかんな regrettable
遺伝 いでん hereditary transmission
遺体 いたい remains, body, corpse
遺品 いひん article left by the deceased, article left behind
遺賢 いけん able men left out of office
遺言 ゆいごん(=いごん) will, testament
後遺症 こういしょう sequela, aftereffect (of a disease)

b 遺失物 いしつぶつ lost article

❷ omit, be negligent
遺漏 いろう omission, oversight, neglect

❸ discharge involuntarily from the penis, urinate
遺尿 いにょう bed wetting
遺精 いせい involuntary emission of semen

SYNONYMS

❶ⓐ leave
遺 LEAVE BEHIND → 3928
残す leave → 1179
ⓑ forget
忘 FORGET → 2529
遺 LEAVE BEHIND → 3928

COMPOUND FORMATION

【遺伝 いでん】
遺伝 'hereditary transmission' means to leave behind (遺 ❶ⓐ) and transmit (伝) one's characteristics to posterity.

NOTE

★ do not confuse with 遣 DISPATCH → 3908

遵 ▶OBEY
ジュン
Ⓝ 遵 Ⓒ 遵 zūn
3929
□3-3-12

162 辶	Jōyō	U9075
	S15-3-12	F2827

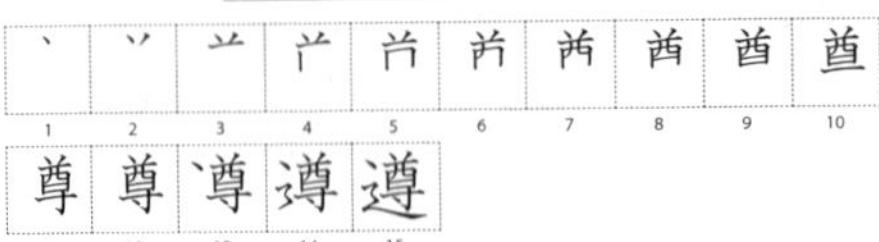

COMPOUNDS

● [also 順 0018] [original meaning] **OBEY, observe, abide by, follow**
遵守する じゅんしゅする observe, obey, follow, conform to
遵法 じゅんぽう law observance
遵奉する じゅんぽうする observe, obey, follow

SYNONYMS

● obey
守 observe → 2697
遵 OBEY → 3929
順 OBEY → 0018
隷 be subordinate to → 2201
従 FOLLOW → 0498

遼 ▶FARAWAY
リョウ ㊔ はるか
Ⓝ 遼 Ⓒ 辽 liáo
3930
□3-3-12

162 辶	Names	U907C
	S15-3-12	F2659

COMPOUNDS

❶ FARAWAY, remote, distant, stretching a great distance
遼遠な りょうえんな remote, far-off

❷ⓐ Liao River in Manchuria
ⓑ Liao Dynasty (916-1125 A.D.)

a 遼東半島 りょうとうはんとう Liaotung Peninsula
遼東の豕 りょうとうのいのこ being self-complacent
b 西遼 せいりょう Western Liao Dynasty

SYNONYMS

❶ distant
遠 DISTANT → 3906
遥 FAR → 3895
悠 far-off → 3407
遼 FARAWAY → 3930
隔 APART → 0827
離 separated → 2364
迂 ROUNDABOUT → 3969

COMPOUND FORMATION

【遼東の豕 りょうとうのいのこ】
遼東の豕 'being self-complacent' refers literally to the pigs (豕) of Liaotung province (遼東 ❷ⓐ). An ancient tradition says that the residents of Liaotung province in ancient China thought that the white-headed pigs born in their district must be extremely rare, yet in the neighboring province white-headed pigs were commonplace. The saying 遼東の豕 came to denote self-complacence because of the false confidence they had in their mistaken belief.

選 3931

□3-3-12

▶CHOOSE

セン えら(ぶ) よ(る)▲

Ⓝ 選 選◆ Ⓒ 选 xuǎn

162	Jōyō-4	U9078
⻌	S15-3-12	F0222

COMPOUNDS

❶ⓐ [sometimes also 撰 せん 0911] [original meaning] CHOOSE, select, elect

ⓑ [also suffix] selection, anthology

a 選択する せんたくする select, choose

選抜 せんばつ selection, choice

選民 せんみん chosen people

選者 せんじゃ judge, selector

選考(=銓衡)する せんこうする select, screen

選挙 せんきょ election

選出する せんしゅつする elect

選手 せんしゅ representative athlete [player]

選任 せんにん assignment, nomination

選定する せんていする select, choose

予選 よせん preliminary match; primary election

b 名作選 めいさくせん selection of masterpieces

❷ [also suffix] **election**

当選 とうせん election to office; winning (a lottery)

公選 こうせん public election, election by popular vote

再選 さいせん reelection

市長選 しちょうせん mayoral election

❸ [also 籤 3399] **lot, lottery**

抽選 ちゅうせん drawing of lots

INDEPENDENT

【せん 選】selection, choice

選に入る せんにはいる be chosen, be selected

KUN

【えらぶ 選ぶ】

①ⓐ **CHOOSE, prefer, select**

ⓑ **elect**

a 選び出す えらびだす select, pick out

上手に選ぶ じょうずにえらぶ make a good choice

ab 選ばれる えらばれる be chosen; be elected

② [usu. 撰ぶ] **compile, edit**

【よる 選る】CHOOSE, select, pick out

SYNONYMS

❶ⓐ **choose**

選 CHOOSE → 3931

撰 choose → 0911

択 SELECT → 0299

採 PICK → 0606

摘 pick out → 0851

擢 SINGLE OUT → 0973

抜 single out → 0290

汰 SIFT OUT → 0312

ⓑ **collection**

集 collection → 3445

選 selection → 3931

彙 ASSEMBLAGE → 2929

❷ **vote and election**

票 VOTE → 3308

選 election → 3931

HOMOPHONES

えらぶ 撰 COMPILE → 0911

遷 3932

□3-3-12

▶TRANSFER

セン

Ⓝ 遷 Ⓒ 迁 qiān

162	Jōyō	U9077
⻌	S15-3-12	F2149

COMPOUNDS

❶ⓐ **TRANSFER, relocate, move**

ⓑ **TRANSFER (an official) to**

a 遷座 せんざ transfer of an object of worship

遷宮 せんぐう transfer of a shrine

遷都 せんと transfer of the capital

b 左遷 させん relegation, demotion

❷ **undergo transition, change, elapse, pass by**

遷移 せんい transition, change

遷延 せんえん delay, procrastination

変遷 へんせん changes, vicissitudes

❸ [archaic] drive away, exile

遷客 せんかく exiled person

❹ [original meaning, now archaic] rise (up to heaven)

升遷 しょうせん rising up

SYNONYMS

❶ⓐ **move**

動 MOVE → 2232

運 MOVE → 3894

滑 SLIDE → 0809

辷る SLIP → 3957

移 SHIFT → 1508

転 remove → 1872

遷 TRANSFER → 3932

繰る SHIFT ONWARD → 1806

❷ **change and replace**

変 CHANGE → 2569
替 REPLACE → 3457
代 SUBSTITUTE → 0034
迭 ALTERNATE → 3818
更 change → 4355
改 change → 0287
易 change → 3064
化 CHANGE INTO, -ize → 0022
遷 undergo transition → 3932
転 turn into → 1872
換 EXCHANGE → 0716
交 INTERCHANGE → 2508

履

3933
□3-3-12

▶**FULFILL**
リ　は(く)
Ⓒ 履 lǚ

44	Jōyō	U5C65
尸	S15-3-12	F1644

Stroke order: 1–15

COMPOUNDS

❶ (carry out an obligation) **FULFILL, carry out, execute, perform, complete**

履行する りこうする fulfill, perform, carry out
履歴 りれき personal history, career
履歴書 りれきしょ résumé, personal history
履修 りしゅう completion (of a course), taking (a course)

❷ **footwear, footgear; sandals, shoes, clogs**

草履 ぞうり Japanese sandals, *zori*
弊履 へいり worn-out sandals [shoes]

❸ [original meaning, now archaic] **tread, step, trample**

KUN

【はく 履く】**put on footwear, wear (shoes)**

履物 はきもの footwear, footgear; clogs, sandals
履き違える はきちがえる put on another's shoes; be mistaken

SYNONYMS

❶ **execute**

執 EXECUTE → 2114
行 ACT → 0246
履 FULFILL → 3933
施 CARRY OUT → 1103
践 IMPLEMENT → 1938
果たす effect → 4377
遂 ACCOMPLISH → 3892

❷ **footwear**

靴 SHOES → 2235
沓 FOOTWEAR → 3074
駄 clogs → 2291
履 footwear → 3933
足 counter for footwear → 2714

【はく】

◯ **wear and put on**

着 PUT ON → 4110
装 DRESS → 3327
帯 WEAR (esp. at the belt) → 3191
穿く PUT ON → 2800
纏 put on → 1814
履く put on footwear → 3933
被る put on headgear → 1495

USAGE

【はく】

履く
put on footwear, wear (shoes)

穿く
put on (trousers or socks), wear (a skirt)

HOMOPHONES

はく 穿 DRILL → 2800

COMPOUND FORMATION

❶【履歴　りれき】

履歴 'personal history, career' is the history (歴) of the deeds one has performed (履 ❶).

❷【履修　りしゅう】

履修 'completion (of a course), etc.' is to complete or carry out (履 ❶) one's studies (修).

層

3934
□3-3-12

▶**STRATUM**
ソウ

44	Names	UFA3B
尸	S15-3-12	F0000

traditional form → see 層 at 3920

廟

3935
□3-3-12

▶**MAUSOLEUM**
ビョウ ㊔ いえ
Ⓝ 庿 廟 Ⓒ 庙 miào

53	Names	U5EDF
广	S15-3-12	F2604

COMPOUNDS

❶ [original meaning] **MAUSOLEUM, ancestral mausoleum [shrine]**

霊廟 れいびょう mausoleum
帝廟 ていびょう imperial mausoleum
宗廟 そうびょう ancestral shrine [temple]

❷ shrine
古廟 こびょう old shrine
聖廟 せいびょう Confucian temple; temple dedicated to Sugawara no Michizane
❸ palace, court
廟堂 びょうどう the Court

INDEPENDENT

【びょう 廟】 **MAUSOLEUM, ancestral mausoleum [shrine]; shrine**

SYNONYMS

❶ **graves**
墓 GRAVE → 2930
墳 TUMULUS → 0887
陵 IMPERIAL MAUSOLEUM → 0660
廟 MAUSOLEUM → 3935
祢 FATHER'S MAUSOLEUM → 1142
塚 grave mound → 0675

慶

3936
□3-3-12

▶**FELICITATION**
ケイ よろこ(び)▲ ㊔ よし ちか のり やす
Ⓒ 庆 qìng

61	Jōyō	U6176
心	S15-4-11	F1218

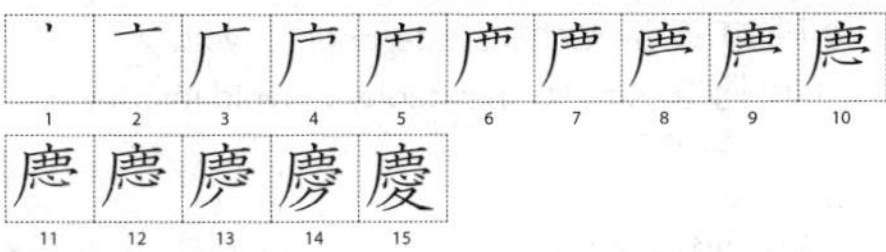

COMPOUNDS

❶ **FELICITATION, congratulation; celebration, rejoicing**
慶祝 けいしゅく celebration, congratulation
慶弔 けいちょう congratulations and condolences
慶事 けいじ happy [auspicious] event
同慶 どうけい (matter of) mutual congratulations
国慶 こっけい National day (of China)
❷ abbrev. of 慶応大学 けいおうだいがく: Keio University
慶大 けいだい Keio University
早慶戦 そうけいせん Waseda-Keio (baseball) game

INDEPENDENT

【けいする 慶する】 felicitate, congratulate

KUN

【よろこび 慶び】 [usu. 喜び] **FELICITATION**, congratulation; matter for congratulation

SYNONYMS

❶ **celebrating and congratulating**
祝 CELEBRATE → 1144
慶 FELICITATION → 3936
賀 CONGRATULATE → 3212
寿 CONGRATULATIONS → 4372

HOMOPHONES

よろこび
喜 HAPPY → 2889
悦 DELIGHTED → 0501

NOTE

➡ see USAGE note at 喜 2889

麾

3937
□3-3-12

▶**COMMAND**
キ
Ⓒ 麾 huī

200	Non-Jōyō	U9EBE
麻	S15-11-4	F3000

COMPOUNDS

❶ [now also 旗 1321] **COMMAND**
麾下の きかの under one's command, under the banner (of)
❷ [archaic] flag, banner, standard

SYNONYMS

❶ **command**
令 COMMAND → 2489
麾 COMMAND → 3937
命 ORDER → 2553

摩

3938
□3-3-12

▶**RUB AGAINST**
マ さす(る)▲
Ⓝ 摩 Ⓒ 摩 mó mā

64	Jōyō	U6469
手	S15-4-11	F1291

COMPOUNDS

❶ [also 磨 3946] **RUB AGAINST, rub, chafe, scrape, wear away**
摩擦 まさつ friction; rubbing, chafing
摩耗 まもう wear, abrasion
摩滅 まめつ wear, defacement
摩損 まそん wear and tear, friction loss, abrasion
❷ graze, scrape, nearly touch
摩天楼 まてんろう skyscraper
❸ [original meaning] stroke gently, pat
按摩 あんま massage; massager, masseur, masseuse
❹ used phonetically for *ma* in the transliteration of Sanskrit Buddhist terms
摩利支天 まりしてん *Marīci*, god of war
護摩 ごま *homa*, Buddhist rite of cedar-stick burning

INDEPENDENT

【まする 摩する】 graze, scrape, nearly touch

塁を摩する るいをまする rival, run close to

KUN

【さする 摩る】[also 擦る] rub (with the hands), stroke

SYNONYMS

❶ **polish and rub**

磨 POLISH → 3946
擦 RUB → 0971
摩 RUB AGAINST → 3938
摺 RUB AGAINST → 0850
研 GRIND → 1456
削 CUT BY CHIPPING → 1837
瑳 POLISH → 1343

❹ **phonetic [m]**

弥 PHONETIC [mi] → 0344
摩 phonetic [ma] → 3938
昧 phonetic [mai] → 1105
蜜 phonetic [mitsu] → 2958
刎 phonetic [mot] → 3661
牟 PHONETIC [mu] → 2518

NOTE

★ do not confuse with 磨 POLISH → 3946

廟
3939
□3-3-12

▶**MAUSOLEUM**
ビョウ ㊔ いえ

53	Nonstandard	U5EDF
广	S15-3-12	F0000

traditional form → see 廟 at 3935

廚
3940
□3-3-12

▶**KITCHEN**
チュウ ズ くりや

53	Nonstandard	U5EDA
广	S15-3-12	F0000

traditional form → see 厨 at 3740

廢
3941
□3-3-12

▶**ABOLISH**
▶**WASTE**
ハイ すた(れる) すた(る)

53	Nonstandard	U5EE2
广	S15-3-12	F0000

traditional form → see 廃 at 3902

廣
3942
□3-3-12

▶**WIDE**
コウ ひろ(い) ひろ(まる) ひろ(める) ひろ(がる) ひろ(げる) ㊔ ひろし ひろむ

53	Names	U5EE3
广	S15-3-12	F0000

traditional form → see 広 at 3769

摩
3943
□3-3-12

▶**RUB AGAINST**
マ さす(る)

53	Nonstandard	U6469
广	S15-3-12	F0000

traditional form → see 摩 at 3938

避
3944
□3-3-13

▶**AVOID**
ヒ さ(ける) よ(ける)▲
Ⓝ 避 Ⓒ 避 bì

162	Jōyō	U907F
辶	S16-3-13	F1042

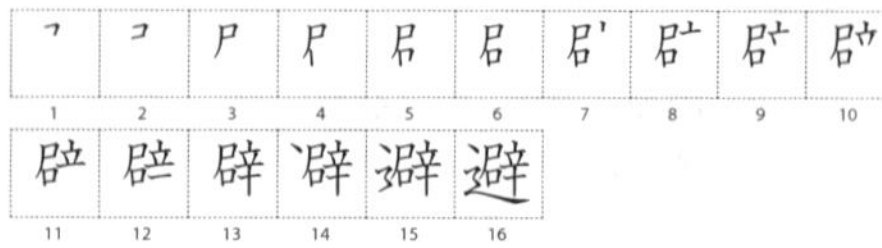

COMPOUNDS

● [original meaning] **AVOID, evade, shirk**

避暑 ひしょ summering
避妊 ひにん contraception
避難 ひなん refuge, shelter, evacuation
逃避 とうひ escape, evasion, flight
退避 たいひ taking refuge, evacuation
回避する かいひする evade, dodge, avoid
不可避な ふかひな inevitable, unavoidable, inescapable

KUN

【さける 避ける】**AVOID, evade, shirk**

人の目を避ける ひとのめをさける avert people's eyes
責任を避ける せきにんをさける shirk a responsibility
ラッシュ時を避ける らっしゅじをさける avoid the rush hours

【よける 避ける】[also 除ける] **AVOID**, shun, evade; avert, ward off

車を避ける くるまをよける dodge a car
日射しを避ける ひざしをよける keep out of the sun

SYNONYMS

● **avoid and abstain**

避 AVOID → 3944
逃 ESCAPE → 3839
禦 WARD OFF → 3561
忌 shun → 2735
禁 abstain from → 3469

還

3945

☐3-3-13

▶**RETURN**

カン　かえ(る)▲

Ⓝ 還 Ⓒ 还 huán hái

162	Jōyō	U9084
辶	S16-3-13	F1208

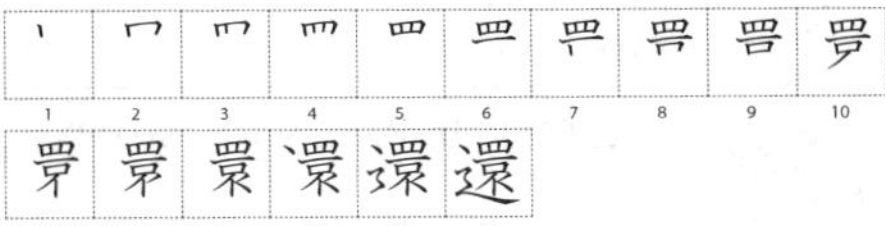

COMPOUNDS

ⓐ [original meaning] **RETURN, come back, come round**

ⓑ **RETURN, give back, restore**

a 還流 かんりゅう return current; convection

帰還する きかんする return, come home, be repatriated

償還 しょうかん repayment, refunding, reimbursement

生還する せいかんする return alive; *baseball* reach the home plate

b 還付する かんぷする return, restore, refund

還元 かんげん restoration; reduction, deoxidization

返還 へんかん return, restoration, repayment

送還 そうかん sending back, repatriation

奪還 だっかん recapture, recovery

KUN

【かえる　還る】[usu. 帰る]

ⓐ **RETURN** (to one's original position), come back, come home

ⓑ go back [home], take one's leave

a 家に還る いえにかえる go back home

SYNONYMS

ⓐ **return**

帰 RETURN → 0148

還 RETURN → 3945

回 turn back → 3793

廻 turn back → 3833

戻る RETURN → 2441

復 RETURN TO → 0701

ⓑ **return and restore**

返 RETURN → 3797

戻 RETURN → 2441

還 RETURN → 3945

復 RETURN TO → 0701

蘇 REVIVE → 3032

甦 REVIVE → 4109

HOMOPHONES

かえる

帰 RETURN → 0148

返 RETURN → 3797

反 COUNTER → 3663

NOTE

➡ see USAGE note at 帰 0148

還避 etc. incorrect stroke-count

➡ see ☐3-4-13: 辶 at 4057

☐3-3-13

磨

3946

☐3-3-13

▶**POLISH**

マ　みが(く)　す(る)▲　㊔ とぎ

Ⓝ 磨 Ⓒ 磨 mó mò

112	Jōyō	U78E8
石	S16-5-11	F1557

COMPOUNDS

[also 摩 3938]

❶ⓐ [original meaning] **POLISH, grind**

ⓑ wear down, rub away, abrade

a 磨滅 まめつ wear, defacement

研磨する けんまする grind, polish; study hard, brush up

b 消磨 しょうま abrasion, wearing out

❷ **POLISH** [improve] (one's skill), cultivate, train

錬磨 れんま training, practice, cultivation

❸ used phonetically for *ma* in the transliteration of Sanskrit Buddhist terms

達磨 だるま Bodhidharma; tumbler

KUN

【みがく　磨く】**POLISH, grind, burnish, rub; polish [improve] (one's skill), cultivate, train**

磨き みがき polish, burnishing

磨き上げる みがきあげる polish up

歯磨き はみがき toothpaste; brushing one's teeth

【する　磨る】**POLISH**, file, rub down

磨りガラス すりがらす frosted glass

磨り減らす すりへらす wear away [out]; exhaust

SYNONYMS

❶ **polish and rub**

磨 POLISH → 3946

擦 RUB → 0971

摩 RUB AGAINST → 3938

摺 RUB AGAINST → 0850

研 GRIND → 1456

削 CUT BY CHIPPING → 1837

瑳 POLISH → 1343

❷ **cultivate**

修 CULTIVATE → 0138

養 FOSTER (one's intellect) → 2998

練 TRAIN → 1738
錬 REFINE → 2185
鍛 train → 2206
磨 POLISH → 3946
琢 POLISH → 1222

HOMOPHONES

する
擦 RUB → 0971
摺 RUB AGAINST → 0850
刷 PRINT → 1623

NOTE

➡ see USAGE note at 擦 0971
★ do not confuse with 摩 RUB AGAINST → 3938

磿

3947
□3-3-13

▶POLISH
マ みが(く) す(る) ㊔ とぎ

53	Nonstandard	U78E8
广	S16-3-13	F0000

traditional form → see 磨 at 3946

應

3948
□3-3-14

▶RESPOND
オウ -ノウ こた(える)

61	Names	U61C9
心	S17-4-13	F0000

traditional form → see 応 at 3804

麿

3949
□3-3-15

▶CLASSICAL MALE NAME SUFFIX
まろ
Ⓝ 麿 Ⓒ (国字)

200	Names	U9EBF
麻	S18-11-7	F1923

KUN

【まろ 麿】
① **CLASSICAL SUFFIX for forming MALE NAMEs**
坂上田村麿 さかのうえのたむらまろ Sakanoue Tamuramaro
② [archaic] I—used esp. by noblemen mainly in the Heian period

SYNONYMS

【まろ】
① **name suffixes**
郎 MALE NAME SUFFIX → 1641
麿 CLASSICAL MALE NAME SUFFIX → 3949
彦 MALE NAME ELEMENT → 4085
-子 female name element → 4196
② **first person pronouns**
私 I (*polite*) → 1432
我 SELF → 4362
己 ONESELF → 4188
身 ONE'S PERSON → 4368
僕 I (*familiar*) → 0185
俺 I (*intimate*) → 0124
吾 I (*elegant*) → 3060
予 I (*pompous*) → 2477
余 I (*pompous*) → 2535
麿 I (*archaic*) → 3949
朕 IMPERIAL WE → 1185
自 SELF → 4338

麿

3950
□3-3-15

▶CLASSICAL MALE NAME SUFFIX
まろ

53	Nonstandard	U9EBF
广	S18-3-15	F0000

traditional form → see 麿 at 3949

厡

□3-3-16

incorrect classification
➡ see ◧1-10-9: 原 at 2320

廳

3951
□3-3-17

▶GOVERNMENT AGENCY
チョウ

53	Nonstandard	U5EF0
广	S20-3-17	F0000

traditional form → see 庁 at 3768

屬

3952
□3-3-18

▶BELONG TO
ゾク ショク ㊔ さっか

44	Nonstandard	U5C6C
尸	S21-3-18	F0000

traditional form → see 属 at 3901

魔

3953
□3-3-18

▶DEMON
マ
Ⓝ 魔 Ⓒ 魔 mó

194	Jōyō	U9B54
鬼	S21-10-11	F0993

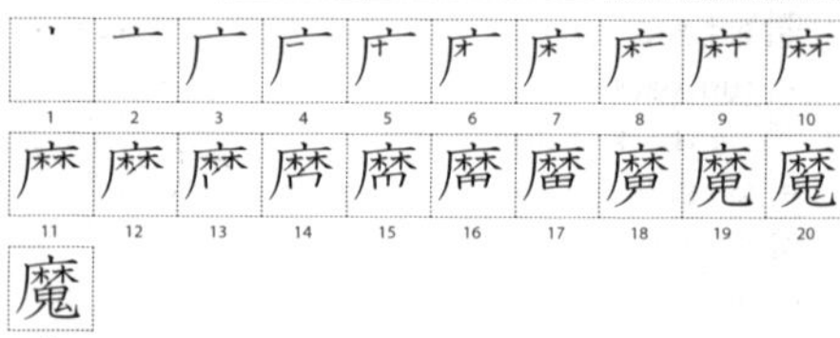

COMPOUNDS

❶ **DEMON, devil, evil spirit**
魔神 まじん evil spirit, devil
魔物 まもの goblin, apparition
悪魔 あくま devil, demon, satan
病魔 びょうま demon of ill health; disease
邪魔 じゃま hindrance, obstruction, impediment
❷ (related to the powers of a demon) **magic(al), evil**
魔法 まほう magic, sorcery, witchcraft

魔法瓶 まほうびん thermos bottle
魔術 まじゅつ magic, sorcery, witchcraft
魔力 まりょく magical powers
魔女 まじょ witch, sorceress
魔笛 まてき magic flute; The Magic Flute (by Mozart)
魔手 ましゅ evil power

❸ [also suffix] (person with excessive passion for something) maniac
放火魔 ほうかま pyromaniac
収集魔 しゅうしゅうま collecting maniac
通り魔 とおりま phantom killer [robber]

INDEPENDENT

【ま 魔】**DEMON**, evil spirit, evil influence
魔が差す まがさす be tempted by an evil spirit
魔の海峡 まのかいきょう dangerous strait

SYNONYMS

❶ **supernatural and evil beings**
鬼 DEVIL →3291
魔 DEMON →3953
怪 monster →0354
霊 SPIRIT →3480
精 SPIRIT →1729

❷ **miraculous**
妙 MARVELOUS →0280
魔 magic(al) →3953

❸ **mania and maniacs**
痴 infatuated →4072
狂 maniac →0318
魔 maniac →3953
熱 fever →3555

COMPOUND FORMATION

❶【邪魔 じゃま】
邪魔 'hindrance, etc.' originally represented an evil (邪) demon (魔 ❶) that stood in the way of Buddhist righteousness.

❷【魔法瓶 まほうびん】
魔法瓶 'thermos bottle' is a bottle (瓶) that keeps water warm by "magical" (魔 ❷) means (法).

魔 3954
□3-3-18

▶**DEMON**
マ

53 广	Nonstandard	U9B54
	S21-3-18	F0000

traditional form → see 魔 at 3953

鷹 3955
□3-3-21

▶**HAWK**
ヨウ オウ たか
Ⓒ 鹰 yīng

196 鳥	Names	U9DF9
	S24-11-13	F1509

COMPOUNDS

ⓐ [original meaning] **HAWK, falcon**
ⓑ as unhurried and calm as the flight of a **HAWK**
a 放鷹 ほうよう hawking, falconry
b 鷹揚(=大様)な おうような(=おおような) largehearted, generous

KUN

【たか 鷹】**HAWK, falcon**
鷹匠 たかじょう falconer, hawker
夜鷹 よたか Japanese goatsucker; nightwalker

SYNONYMS

ⓐ **birds**
鷹 HAWK →3955
鷗 GULL →2370
烏 CROW →4088
雀 SPARROW →3117
燕 SWALLOW →3142
鴻 LARGE WILD BIRD →0977
鳳 MALE PHOENIX →3749
凰 FEMALE PHOENIX →3738
鵬 MYTHICAL HUGE BIRD →1416
鶏 CHICKEN →2221
酉 ROOSTER →4358
隼 FALCON →3427
鳩 PIGEON →0184
鷲 EAGLE →3598
鳶 BLACK KITE →3919
鶴 CRANE →2326
鷺 HERON →3621
鵜 CORMORANT →2067
鴨 DUCK →1582
雁 WILD GOOSE →3741

廳 3956
□3-3-22

▶**GOVERNMENT AGENCY**
チョウ

53 广	Names	U5EF3
	S25-3-22	F0000

traditional form → see 庁 at 3768

辷 3957
□3-4-1

▶**SLIP**
すべ(る)
Ⓒ (国字)

162 辶	Non-Jōyō	U8FB7
	S5-4-1	F0000

KUN

【すべる 辷る】[now usu. 滑る]
① **SLIP**
辷らす すべらす let slip, slide, glide
地辷り じすべり landslide
口が辷る くちがすべる make a slip of the tongue

② flunk an (entrance) examination

辷り止め すべりどめ tire chains; creepers; taking the entrance examination to a university as a safety measure in case one fails at other universities

SYNONYMS

【すべる】

① **move**

動 MOVE → 2232
運 MOVE → 3894
滑 SLIDE → 0809
辷る SLIP → 3957
移 SHIFT → 1508
転 remove → 1872
遷 TRANSFER → 3932
繰る SHIFT ONWARD → 1806

HOMOPHONES

すべる 滑 SLIDE → 0809

NOTE

➡ see USAGE note at 滑 0809

牙

incorrect classification

➡ see ■4-5-1 at 4304

□3-4-1

辻

3958

□3-4-2

▸CROSSROADS

つじ

Ⓝ 辻 Ⓒ 辻 shí (国字)

162	Names	U8FBB
辶	S6-4-2	F1863

KUN

【つじ 辻】

ⓐ [original meaning] **CROSSROADS, crossing, intersection**

ⓑ **street, roadside, street corner**

a 四つ辻 よつつじ crossroads, intersection

b 辻占 つじうら slip of paper with a fortune-telling message

辻辻に つじつじに at every crossing, at every street corner

辻君 つじぎみ streetwalker, nightwalker

辻説法 つじせっぽう street preaching

辻店 つじみせ street stall

SYNONYMS

【つじ】

◯ **ways and routes**

道 WAY (path) → 3888
径 PATH → 0347
軌 TRACK → 1832
線 LINE → 1760
澪 WATERWAY → 0957
途 WAY (route) → 3853
路 ROAD → 1936
筋 wayside → 3319
通り street → 3855
街 city street → 0702
辻 CROSSROADS → 3958
岐 forked road → 0285
巷 THE STREETS → 3097

込

3959

□3-4-2

▸MOVE INWARD
▸EMPHATIC VERBAL SUFFIX

-こ(む) こ(む) こ(み) -こ(み) こ(める)

162	Nonstandard	U8FBC
辶	S6-4-2	F0000

traditional form → see 込 at 3762

気

3960

□3-4-2

▸GAS
▸SPIRIT

キ ケ

Ⓝ 氣 Ⓒ 气 qì

84	Jōyō-1	U6C17
气	S6-4-2	F0025

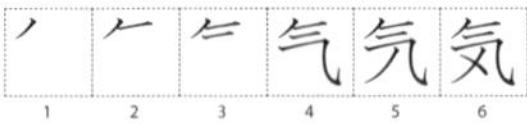

COMPOUNDS

❶ⓐ [original meaning] **GAS, vapor**

ⓑ **air**

a 気体 きたい gas, vapor, gaseous body

気化 きか gasification, evaporation

空気 くうき air; atmosphere

排気 はいき exhaust, used steam; exhaustion, evacuation

b 気流 きりゅう air [atmospheric] current, air stream

気団 きだん air mass

冷気 れいき cold air; cold, chill

換気 かんき ventilation

❷ⓐ **atmosphere**

ⓑ (psychological environment) **atmosphere, tone**

a 気圧 きあつ atmospheric [air] pressure

気温 きおん (atmospheric) temperature

大気 たいき the atmosphere

b 気運 きうん luck, tendency, opportunity

景気 けいき things, times; business conditions

雰囲気 ふんいき atmosphere, mood

殺気 さっき menace of death, reek of murder

熱気 ねっき hot air, heat; fevered air, enthusiasm

❸ **breath**

気管 きかん trachea, windpipe

気息 きそく breathing; breath

一気に いっきに at a breath, in one breath; on [at] a stretch [stroke]

❹ⓐ **vital energy, SPIRIT, breath of life, vitality**

ⓑ vital energy in Chinese medicine: *ki, chi*

a 気力 きりょく energy, spirit, vitality, pluck, guts
気勢 きせい spirit, ardor
病気 びょうき illness, sickness, disease
元気 げんき vigor, energy; spirits; health
意気盛んだ いきさかんだ be in high spirits
勇気 ゆうき courage, valor, bravery, nerve
活気 かっき vigor, spirit, animation
精気 せいき spirit, energy, essence

❺ **energy, force**
電気 でんき electricity; electric light
磁気 じき magnetism

❻ **natural phenomenon**
気象 きしょう atmospheric phenomena, weather conditions
気候 きこう climate, weather; season
天気 てんき weather, atmospheric conditions; fine weather

❼ⓐ **SPIRIT, mind, consciousness**
ⓑ (emotional state) **SPIRITs, one's feelings, mood, frame of mind**

a 気付く きづく notice, become aware of, find out
気の毒な きのどくな pitiable, miserable; regrettable, too bad
気構え きがまえ readiness of mind, preparedness; expectation
気絶 きぜつ fainting
気違い きちがい insanity; insane person, lunatic
正気 しょうき consciousness; sanity, reason
狂気 きょうき insanity, madness

b 気持 きもち feeling, sensation, mood
気分 きぶん feeling, mood; atmosphere
気前 きまえ generosity
気軽な きがるな lighthearted, cheerful; ready
人気 にんき popularity; temperament of the people; business conditions
平気 へいき nonchalance, unconcern; composure
本気 ほんき seriousness, earnestness
呆気に取られる あっけにとられる be astonished, be amazed

❽ [also suffix] **temperament, temper, disposition, one's nature, character**
気質 きしつ temperament, disposition
気性 きしょう disposition, nature, temper
気難しい きむずかしい moody, hard to please
気紛れ きまぐれ whim, caprice
強気の つよきの strong, firm, bullish
短気な たんきな short-tempered, hot-tempered
負けん気 まけんき unyielding [competitive] spirit
移り気 うつりぎ caprice, fickleness, frivolity

❾ **mind to do something, intention, will**
気儘×な きままな willful, selfish
気乗りしない きのりしない halfhearted, indisposed
気楽な きらくな easygoing; comfortable, easy, carefree
買い気 かいき bullish [buying] sentiment [feeling]
やる気 やるき mind to do something, determination to do
眠気 ねむけ sleepiness
吐き気 はきけ nausea
何気無い なにげない casually, unconcernedly

❿ **care, attention, precaution**
気遣う きづかう feel anxious about, worry about, have apprehensions of
気配り きくばり attention to detail
気付 きづけ c/o (care of)
気兼ねする きがねする feel hesitant, be ill at ease, be afraid of giving trouble

⓫ [also suffix] **sign, indication, symptom, trace, air**
気配 けはい sign, indication
気品 きひん dignity, grace, nobility
気取る きどる make an affected pose, assume airs
気高い けだかい noble, lofty, high-minded
人気が無い ひとけがない no sign of life
色気 いろけ sex appeal, sensuality; fancifulness; inclination, interest; shade of color
飾り気 かざりけ affectation, love of display
得意気に とくいげに with an air of expertise
惜し気に おしげに grudgingly

⓬ⓐ smell, odor
ⓑ **flavor, a dash of**

a 香気 こうき fragrance, perfume, scent
臭気 しゅうき offensive [odious] smell, bad [foul] odor, stench

b 気味 きみ feeling, sensation; a touch [tinge] (of)
味気無い あじけない(=あじきない) wearisome, insipid
塩気 しおけ salty
湿気 しっけ(=しっき) moisture, dampness, humidity

⓭ [prefix] somehow, in some way or other
気だるい けだるい listless, languid, languish
気圧される けおされる be overawed [overpowered]

⓮ period of 15 days
節気 せっき seasonal turning point (that comes every 15 days)

⓯ unclassified compounds
中気 ちゅうき palsy, paralysis
脚気 かっけ beriberi

INDEPENDENT

【き 気】

①ⓐ **SPIRIT, mind, consciousness**
ⓑ (emotional state) **SPIRITs, one's feelings, mood, frame of mind**

辶【气】弋乡广𠂉𠮛尸少丙尺内

a 気が狂う きがくるう go mad [insane]
気に掛かる きにかかる weigh on one's mind
気にする きにする take to heart, be concerned
気に入る きにいる like, be pleased with
気が付く きがつく notice, become aware; be attentive
b 気が重い きがおもい be heavyhearted, be dispirited
気の詰まる きのつまる stuffy
気がする きがする have a feeling [hunch]

② **temperament, temper, disposition, one's nature, character**
気が強い きがつよい strong of heart
気が短い きがみじかい quick-tempered
気の向く儘×に きのむくままに at one's fancy [whim]
気を悪くする きをわるくする take offense, feel hurt

③ **mind to do something, intention, will**
気が変わる きがかわる change one's mind
何の気無しに なんのきなしに unintentionally, casually
したい気がする したいきがする feel like doing

④ **care, attention, precaution**
気を付ける きをつける take care of, pay attention to
気を許す きをゆるす be off one's guard
気が利く きがきく be smart [tactful]

⑤ ⓐ atmosphere, air
ⓑ (psychological environment) atmosphere, tone
a 山の気 やまのき mountain air
b 清新の気 せいしんのき general mood of freshness

⑥ sign, indication, symptom, trace, air
復興の気 ふっこうのき signs of revival

⑦ flavor, savor, dash of
気が抜ける きがぬける become stale, lose flavor

⑧ vital energy in Chinese medicine: *ki, chi*

【け 気】

① sign, indication, symptom, trace, air
火の気 ひのけ trace of fire
風邪の気 かぜのけ signs of a cold

② flavor, savor, dash of
酒の気が有る さけのけがある smack of wine

SPECIAL READINGS

気質▲ かたぎ spirit, character
意気地 いくじ(=いきじ) pride, (a sense of) honor, self-respect

SYNONYMS

❶ **gas and vapor**
気 GAS → 3960
空 AIR → 2767
汽 STEAM → 0309

❷ **atmosphere**
雰 ATMOSPHERE → 3446
気 atmosphere → 3960

❸ **breathe and blow**
息 BREATH → 3278
気 breath → 3960
吸 BREATHE IN → 0234
呼 breathe out → 0324
吹 BLOW → 0272

❹ⓐ **life energy**
精 SPIRIT → 1729
気 vital energy → 3960

❺ **energy and force**
力 POWER, force → 4178
勢 physical power → 3542
気 energy → 3960
圧 PRESSURE → 3688
鋒 brunt → 2172

❻ **phenomenon**
象 PHENOMENON → 2647
気 natural phenomenon → 3960
物 physical phenomena → 1084

❼ⓐ **psyche**
心 HEART → 0011
霊 SPIRIT (soul) → 3480
魂 SOUL, spirit → 1346
魄 SOUL → 1570
腹 heart → 1308
衷 INNER HEART → 2600
襟 inner mind → 1599
胸 breast → 1187
懐 BOSOM → 0942
神 MIND → 1143
気 SPIRIT (consciousness) → 3960
精 SPIRIT (mind) → 1729

ⓑ **feeling**
感 SENSE (feeling) → 3514
情 EMOTION → 0583
心 HEART → 0011
気 spirits → 3960

❽ **nature and character**
性 NATURE → 0357
気 temperament → 3960
質 QUALITY → 3483
品 grade of excellence → 2795
柄 CHARACTER → 1111
格 (good) character → 1161

❾ **will and intention**
志 AMBITION → 2725
意 MIND → 2650
図 intention → 3809

気 mind to do something → 3960
念 thought of doing something → 2554
趣 PURPOSE → 4111
欲 DESIRE → 1867

⑩ attention

気 care → 3960
念 attention → 2554

⑪ signs

候 indication → 0133
徴 SYMPTOM → 0841
症 symptom (of a disease) → 4065
気 sign → 3960
兆 OMEN → 0264

⑫ⓐ smell and fragrance

気 smell → 3960
匂い SMELL → 3662
臭 BAD SMELL → 3261
香 SWEET SMELL → 3177
馨 PERFUME → 3575
芳 FRAGRANT → 2739
薫 BALMY → 3005
郁 AROMATIC → 1640

NOTE

➡ see COMPOUND FORMATION for
元気 げんき → 元 2428
気前 きまえ → 前 2819

弐

▶TWO

ニ

Ⓝ 貳 貮◇ Ⓒ 贰 弍 èr

3961

□3-4-2

56△	Jōyō	U5F10
弋	S6-3-3	F3446

Stroke order: 1–6

COMPOUNDS

● [original meaning] **TWO**—used in legal documents and checks

金弐阡×円 きんにせんえん the sum of two thousand yen

INDEPENDENT

【に 弐】TWO (→ ●)

SYNONYMS

● two

二 TWO → 2421
弐 TWO (in legal documents) → 3961
双 SET OF TWO → 0028
対 pair → 1025
偶 COUPLE → 0150
両 BOTH → 4331

NOTE

★ do not confuse with 式 STYLE → 3785

考

▶THINK

コウ かんが(える) かんが(え) ㊔ たか たかし

Ⓒ 考 kǎo

3962

□3-4-2

125	Jōyō-2	U8003
耂	S6-4-2	F0118

Stroke order: 1–6

COMPOUNDS

❶ THINK, give thought to, consider, reflect

考慮 こうりょ consideration, deliberation, careful thought
考察する こうさつする consider, contemplate, study
考案 こうあん idea, plan; project
思考 しこう thinking, thought, consideration
一考 いっこう consideration, thought

❷ⓐ study, investigate, research

ⓑ [also suffix] **study, treatise, monograph**

a 考査 こうさ consideration, test, quiz
考証 こうしょう investigation, research
考古学 こうこがく archaeology
参考 さんこう reference, consultation
選考(=銓衡)する せんこうする select, screen

b 論考 ろんこう study (on English literature)
万葉考 まんようこう A Study of Manyoshu

❸ one's deceased father

先考 せんこう one's deceased father

KUN

【かんがえる 考える】**THINK, consider, reflect, deliberate; imagine, suppose; invent, devise; expect, hope; intend, mean; be prepared for**

考え深い かんがえぶかい deep-thinking, thoughtful
考えられない かんがえられない unimaginable
考え出す かんがえだす think out, devise, invent; begin to think
万一を考える まんいちをかんがえる be prepared for the worst

【かんがえ 考え】**thought, THINKing, consideration, reflection, deliberation; thought, view, opinion; idea, fancy, imagination; intention, resolution**

考えを伝える かんがえをつたえる convey one's thoughts

SYNONYMS

❶ think and consider

思 THINK → 3173
惟 MEDITATE → 0582
省 INTROSPECT → 3100
稽 THINK → 1573

考 THINK → 3962
存 hold an opinion → 3702
案 think out → 2824
想 CONCEIVE → 3507
慮 CONSIDER → 4050
勘 take into consideration → 2231
銓 WEIGH → 2161
量 weigh → 3119

❷ⓐ learn and study
学 STUDY → 3162
考 study → 3962
習 LEARN → 3306
研 RESEARCH → 1456
究 STUDY EXHAUSTIVELY → 2729
攻 specialize → 0286

【かんがえ】
○ thought
念 THOUGHTS → 2554
考え thought → 3962
意 MIND → 2650
想 conception → 3507

NOTE
★ do not confuse with 老 OLD → 3963

老

▶OLD
ロウ お(いる) ふ(ける)
Ⓒ 老 lǎo

3963
口3-4-2

125	Jōyō-4	U8001
老	S6-6-0	F0426

一 十 土 耂 耂 老 (1 2 3 4 5 6)

RADICAL
oi 'old person' (耆× 耄× 耋×), used in characters related to old people
Top variant: 耂 ***oikanmuri*** or ***oigashira*** (者 考)

COMPOUNDS
❶ⓐ [also prefix] (not young) **OLD, aged**
ⓑ grow OLD, degenerate
a 老人 ろうじん old person, old folks
老年 ろうねん old age
老齢 ろうれい old age
老木 ろうぼく old tree
老後 ろうご one's old age
老眼 ろうがん presbyopia, farsightedness due to old age
老政治家 ろうせいじか venerable statesman
b 老化 ろうか aging
老衰 ろうすい senility
老朽化した ろうきゅうかした outworn, deteriorated

❷ⓐ [original meaning] **OLD person**
ⓑ honorific suffix after names of **OLD** men
a 老若 ろうにゃく(=ろうじゃく) the old and the young
敬老 けいろう respect for the aged
古老(=故老) ころう elder, old man; old-timer
b 野村老 のむらろう old Mr. Nomura

❸ⓐ (of long experience) **OLD**, experienced, veteran
ⓑ elder, senior member, chief vassal
a 老練な ろうれんな experienced, veteran
老巧な ろうこうな veteran, experienced
老成する ろうせいする mature, become precocious
b 長老 ちょうろう elder, senior; superior priest
元老 げんろう elder [senior] statesman; senior member

❹ (not new) **OLD**
老舗 ろうほ(=しにせ) old [long-established] shop
老酒 らおちゅー vintage wine (esp. rice wine made in Shaoxing)

❺ Laozi (legendary founder of Taoism)
老子 ろうし Laozi; the works of Laozi
老荘 ろうそう Laozi and Zhuangzi

❻ Laos
老日辞書 ろうにちじしょ Lao-Japanese Dictionary

INDEPENDENT
【ろう 老】OLD age; old person
老と病 ろうとびょう old age and sickness
老を労わる ろうをいたわる be kind to old people

KUN
【おいる 老いる】grow OLD
老い おい old age; old person
老い先 おいさき remaining years (of one's life)
老い込む おいこむ grow old, weaken with age

【ふける 老ける】grow OLD
老け役 ふけやく role of an aged person

SPECIAL READINGS
海老▲ えび lobster, shrimp

SYNONYMS
❶ⓐ old
古 OLD (not new) → 2495
老 OLD (not young) → 3963
故 OLD (of the past) → 1466
旧 old → 0014

❷ⓐ old persons
老 old person → 3963
爺 OLD MAN → 2656
翁 OLD MAN → 2611
婆 OLD WOMAN → 3433
姥 OLD WOMAN → 0420
ⓑ honorific suffixes
翁 honorific suffix → 2611
老 honorific suffix → 3963

❻ Asian countries

日 JAPAN → 3759
緬 Myanmar → 1758
老 Laos → 3963
華 CHINA → 2841
蒙 Mongolia → 2938
鮮 Korea → 2355
泰 Thailand → 3193
越 Vietnam → 4108
印 India → 1023
竺 INDIA → 3248
比 Philippines → 0029

NOTE

★ do not confuse with 考 THINK → 3962

孝 □3-4-2

incorrect stroke-count
➡ see □3-4-3: 耂 at 3973

虍 ▶*TORAKANMURI*

3964 □3-4-2

141	Radical	U864D
虍	S6-6-0	F0000

RADICAL

torakanmuri 'tiger' (虚 虜 虐), used in characters related to tigers or their qualities
Variant: 虍× ***torakanmuri*** (劇)

危 ▶DANGEROUS

キ　あぶ(ない)　あや(うい)　あや(ぶむ)
Ⓝ 危 Ⓒ 危 wēi

3965 □3-4-2

26	Jōyō-6	U5371
㔾	S6-2-4	F0668

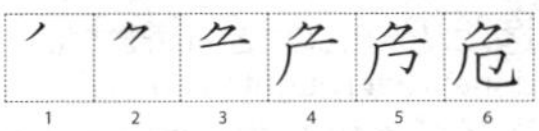

COMPOUNDS

❶ [original meaning] **DANGEROUS, precarious**
危険な きけんな dangerous
危機 きき crisis, emergency
危害 きがい injury, harm; danger, risk
危難 きなん danger, distress, hazard
危篤 きとく on the verge of death, critical condition
安危 あんき safety or danger, fate, welfare

❷ **fear, apprehend**
危惧(=危虞) きぐ fear, misgivings

KUN

【あぶない　危ない】**DANGEROUS, perilous, risky; critical, serious, uncertain, insecure; limping; narrow, close; Watch out!**
危ながる あぶながる be afraid, be apprehensive, doubt
彼の命が危ない かれのいのちがあぶない His life is in danger

【あやうい　危うい】same as 危ない あぶない
危うく あやうく almost, nearly, in imminent danger of

【あやぶむ　危ぶむ】**fear, apprehend**

SYNONYMS

❶ **danger**
危 DANGEROUS → 3965
殆 dangerous → 1130
険 DANGER → 0658

NOTE

★ The symbol 危 is used on fuel trucks and the like: DANGER!

衣 □3-4-2

incorrect classification
➡ see ▀2-2-4: 亠 at 2506

艮 □3-4-2

incorrect classification
➡ see ■4-6-1 at 4330

劣 □3-4-2

incorrect classification
➡ see ▀2-4-2: 少 at 3047

而 □3-4-2

incorrect classification
➡ see ▀2-2-4: 一 at 2520

尽 □3-4-2

incorrect classification
➡ see □3-3-3: 尸 at 3786

肉 ▶FLESH

ニク
Ⓒ 肉 ròu

3966 □3-4-2

130	Jōyō-2	U8089
肉	S6-6-0	F0550

RADICAL

niku 'flesh' (腐 臠×), used in characters related to the flesh, body or body parts
Variant: 月 ***nikuzuki*** (育 能 腕)
Variants: 月 月 ***tsuki*** (育 能 腕)

COMPOUNDS

❶ⓐ [original meaning] **FLESH (of humans or animals)**
ⓑ **FLESH** (of fruit), pulp
ⓒ (article of food) **FLESH, meat**

a 肉腫 にくしゅ sarcoma
肉離れ にくばなれ torn muscle
筋肉 きんにく muscle, sinews

皮肉 ひにく cynicism, sarcasm; irony
b 果肉 かにく flesh, pulp
c 肉食 にくしょく meat diet
牛肉 ぎゅうにく beef
食肉 しょくにく meat
挽き肉 ひきにく ground [minced] meat
羊頭狗肉 ようとうくにく using a better name to sell inferior goods, crying wine and selling vinegar

❷ⓐ (degree of fatness) **FLESH**, weight
ⓑ thickness
a 中肉中背の ちゅうにくちゅうぜいの of medium build
b 肉付け にくづけ modeling; giving body and substance
肉太 にくぶと boldface (type)

❸ **the FLESH (versus the spirit)**
肉体 にくたい body, flesh
肉欲 にくよく lusts of the flesh, animal passions

❹ **one's FLESH and blood, one's kindred**
肉親 にくしん blood relation
骨肉 こつにく one's own flesh and blood, kinsmen

❺ **unaided by mechanical devices, in the natural state; in person**
肉眼 にくがん naked eye
肉声 にくせい natural voice
肉筆 にくひつ one's own handwriting, autograph

❻ ink pad
印肉 いんにく ink pad

INDEPENDENT

【にく 肉】
①ⓐ **FLESH (of humans or animals)**
ⓑ **FLESH** (of fruit), pulp
ⓒ (article of food) **FLESH, meat**
a 人間の肉 にんげんのにく human flesh
②ⓐ (degree of fatness) **FLESH**, weight
ⓑ thickness
a 肉の厚い にくのあつい thick
③ the **FLESH** (versus the spirit)
霊と肉 れいとにく flesh and spirit
④ ink pad

SYNONYMS

❶ⓐ **flesh**
肉 FLESH → 3966
筋 MUSCLE → 3319
ⓒ **meat**
肉 FLESH → 3966
身 meat → 4368
脩 DRIED MEAT → 0154
❸ **body**
体 BODY → 0080
身 BODY (esp. vs. mind) → 4368
肉 FLESH → 3966
屍 CORPSE → 3843
尸 CORPSE → 4198
骸 DEAD BODY → 2301

NOTE

➡ see COMPOUND FORMATION for
羊頭狗肉 ようとうくにく → 羊 2708
皮肉 ひにく → 皮 3771

迄

3967

□3-4-3

▶UP TO

キツ まで

Ⓝ 辿◇ Ⓒ 迄 qì

162	Names	U8FC4
辶	S7-4-3	F2777

KUN

【まで 迄】
①ⓐ (as far as a designated place) **UP TO, as far as**
ⓑ (as far as a designated time) **UP TO, till, until, to**
a 京都迄の切符 きょうとまでのきっぷ ticket to Kyoto
b 今迄 いままで till now, so far, up to the present
百歳迄生きる ひゃくさいまでいきる live to be a hundred
② (to the limit of) **UP TO, to the extent [limit] of**
五十迄数える ごじゅうまでかぞえる count up to fifty
盗み迄する ぬすみまでする go to the extent of committing theft
親に迄見放される おやにまでみはなされる be the despair of one's parents
③ [followed by に] **by, by the time, before**
次の日曜迄に つぎのにちようまでに by next Sunday
年末迄に ねんまつまでに before the end of this year
④ **only, merely, just**
当然の事をした迄だ とうぜんのことをしたまでだ I simply have done what I ought to do
君が言うから来た迄だ きみがいうからきたまでだ I came just because you asked me to
⑤ [in negative constructions]
ⓐ **(no) need (to)**
ⓑ **even (not) so**
a 言う迄も無い いうまでもない There is no need to say so/But of course
b 全部ではない迄も ぜんぶではないまでも though all of them may not be included

SYNONYMS

【まで】
① **direction indicators**
至 to → 2707
-行き bound for → 0246
-向け (bound) for → 3790
迄 UP TO → 3967
以 TO THE…OF → 0045

自 from →4338
来 since →4366
而 DIRECTION WORD →2520

辿

▸FOLLOW
テン たど(る)
Ⓝ 辿 Ⓒ 辿 chān

3968
口3-4-3

162	Names	U8FBF
辶	S7-4-3	F2074

KUN

【たどる 辿る】
ⓐ **FOLLOW (a path), pursue (a course)**
ⓑ **retrace**
a 辿り着く たどりつく work one's way (to), arrive somewhere

SYNONYMS

【たどる】
ⓐ **follow and pursue**
従 FOLLOW →0498
随 FOLLOW →0765
辿る FOLLOW (a path) →3968
追 CHASE →3840

迂

▸ROUNDABOUT
ウ ㊔ ゆき とお
Ⓝ 迂 Ⓒ 迂 yū

3969
口3-4-3

162	Names	U8FC2
辶	S7-4-3	F2444

COMPOUNDS

❶ **ROUNDABOUT, circuitous**
迂回 うかい detour
迂闊 うかつ careless, absentminded
迂遠な うえんな roundabout, devious
迂曲する うきょくする meander
❷ **ignorant of worldly affairs**
迂愚 うぐ stupid, ignorant
迂生 うせい [humble] I (used by men in writing)

SYNONYMS

❶ **distant**
遠 DISTANT →3906
遥 FAR →3895
悠 far-off →3407
遼 FARAWAY →3930
隔 APART →0827
離 separated →2364
迂 ROUNDABOUT →3969

迅

▸SWIFT
ジン

3970
口3-4-3

162	Nonstandard	U8FC5
辶	S7-4-3	F0000

traditional form →see 迅 at 3780

巡

▸MAKE THE ROUNDS
ジュン めぐ(る) めぐ(り)

3971
口3-4-3

162	Nonstandard	U5DE1
辶	S7-4-3	F0000

traditional form →see 巡 at 3781

呉

口3-4-3

incorrect classification
➡ see ▀2-5-2: 呉 at 3156

戒

▸CAUTION
カイ いまし(める) ㊔ えびす
Ⓒ 戒 jiè

3972
口3-4-3

62	Jōyō	U6212
戈	S7-4-3	F1390

1	2	3	4	5	6	7
一	二	于	开	戒	戒	戒

COMPOUNDS

❶ⓐ [formerly also 誡 1947] **CAUTION against, admonish, warn, give warning**
ⓑ [original meaning] **take CAUTION (against), guard against, be careful**
a 戒告 かいこく caution, warning, reprimand
訓戒する くんかいする admonish, warn
自戒する じかいする admonish oneself
b 戒厳令 かいげんれい martial law
戒心 かいしん caution, precaution, care
戒慎する かいしんする be cautious, be discreet
警戒 けいかい caution, precaution, warning; watch, guard, vigilance
❷ commandment, Buddhist commandment, *śīla*, precept
戒律 かいりつ commandments, precepts
十戒 じっかい the ten precepts of Buddhism
破戒 はかい offense against the Buddhist commandments
❸ [formerly 誨 1946 or 誡 1947] instruct, teach
教戒 きょうかい exhortation, preaching

INDEPENDENT

【かい 戒】[formerly also 誡 1947] Buddhist commandment
戒を破る かいをやぶる break the Buddhist commandments

KUN

【いましめる 戒める】

① [sometimes also 警める]
ⓐ [sometimes also 誡める] **CAUTION against, admonish, warn**
ⓑ **take CAUTION (against), take precautions, guard against**

a 戒め いましめ caution, admonition, warning; caution, guard; commandment, precept; binding, bondage
不心得を戒める ふこころえをいましめる caution a person against misconduct
b 自ら戒める みずからいましめる take precautions, guard against

② **bind, restrict**
後ろ手に戒める うしろでにいましめる bind a person's hands behind his back

SYNONYMS

❶ⓐ warn
警 WARN → 3595
戒 CAUTION → 3972
誡 CAUTION AGAINST → 1947
諭 ADMONISH → 2012
告 advise → 3062

ⓑ take precautions
戒 take caution → 3972
警 GUARD AGAINST → 3595

❷ precept
戒 commandment → 3972
訓 precept → 1844

USAGE

❶【いましめる】
戒める
① [sometimes also 警める]
ⓐ [sometimes also 誡める] caution against, admonish, warn
ⓑ take caution (against), take precautions, guard against
② bind, restrict
誡める
[usu. 戒める, sometimes also 警める] caution against, admonish, warn
警める
[usu. 戒める]
ⓐ [sometimes also 誡める] caution against, admonish, warn
ⓑ take caution (against), take precautions, guard against

❷【いましめ】
戒め
① [sometimes also 警め]
ⓐ caution, admonition, warning
ⓑ caution, guard
ⓒ commandment, precept
② binding, bondage
警め
[usu. 戒め]
ⓐ caution, admonition, warning
ⓑ caution, guard
ⓒ commandment, precept

❸【じっかい】
十戒
the ten precepts of Buddhism
十誡
the Ten Commandments (of Moses)

HOMOPHONES

いましめる
警 GUARD AGAINST → 3595
誡 CAUTION AGAINST → 1947
いましめ 警 GUARD AGAINST → 3595

戻

□3-4-3

incorrect classification
➡ see ▀2-1-6: 乛 at 2441

孝

3973

□3-4-3

▶FILIAL PIETY
コウ キョウ▲ ㊔ たか たかし のり ゆき なり もと よし
Ⓒ 孝 xiào

39	Jōyō-6	U5B5D
子	S7-3-4	F1297

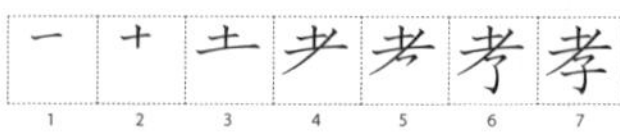

COMPOUNDS

● FILIAL PIETY, filial devotion
孝行 こうこう filial piety
孝心 こうしん filial devotion [affection]
孝養 こうよう discharge of filial duties
孝子 こうし filial child, good son
忠孝 ちゅうこう loyalty and filial piety
不孝 ふこう(=ふきょう) lack of filial piety, undutifulness

INDEPENDENT

【こう 孝】**FILIAL PIETY**, filial devotion
孝は百行の本 こうはひゃっこうのもと Filial devotion is the basis of human conduct

SYNONYMS

● fidelity
忠 LOYALTY → 3087
義 faith → 2948
孝 FILIAL PIETY → 3973
悌 BROTHERLY LOVE → 0507
誠 SINCERITY → 1922
実 faithfulness → 2765
信 fidelity → 0115
操 constancy → 0948

節 moral integrity → 3336

考 incorrect stroke-count
➡ see □3-4-2: 耂 at 3962
□3-4-3

希 incorrect classification
➡ see 2-2-5: メ at 2543
□3-4-3

君
3974
□3-4-3

▶RULER
▶FAMILIAR TITLE
▶YOU

クン きみ -ぎみ

Ⓒ 君 jūn

30	Jōyō-3	U541B
口	S7-3-4	F0512

Stroke order: 1 2 3 4 5 6 7

COMPOUNDS

❶ [original meaning] **RULER, sovereign, monarch, king; lord**
君主 くんしゅ monarch, sovereign
君臨する くんりんする reign, rule over, dominate
暴君 ぼうくん tyrant, despot
主君 しゅくん one's lord, one's master
名君 めいくん wise ruler, enlightened monarch, benevolent lord

❷ **FAMILIAR TITLE used in addressing peers, friends or inferiors (usu. restricted to men)**
山田君 やまだくん Mr. Yamada
太郎君 たろうくん Taro

❸ **term of respect used in addressing family members, peers or men of rank**
君子 くんし man of virtue, wise man
諸君 しょくん Ladies and Gentlemen, my friends, you
父君 ふくん (your) father

KUN

【きみ 君】
① **RULER, sovereign, emperor, one's master [lord]**
君が代 きみがよ Imperial reign; title of Japanese national anthem
我が君 わがきみ my lord
大君 おおきみ sovereign, emperor

② **YOU, old boy**—familiar second person pronoun used in addressing friends, peers or inferiors
君達 きみたち you (plural)
君の きみの your

【-ぎみ -君】 **former title of respect used in addressing parents, ancestors and men of rank**
母君 ははぎみ mother
姫君 ひめぎみ princess, highborn young lady

SYNONYMS

❶ **rulers**
君 RULER → 3974
王 KING → 4247
帝 EMPEROR → 2573
天 Heaven's messenger on earth → 4250
皇 EMPEROR → 3175
尭 YAO → 2560
舜 SHUN → 3134

❷ **titles of address**
氏 COURTESY TITLE → 3669
兄 familiar title (seniors) → 2676
君 FAMILIAR TITLE (peers) → 3974
嬢 Miss → 0936
様 FORMAL TITLE → 1332
殿 FORMAL HONORIFIC TITLE → 2247
師 honorific title (clergymen) → 1680
公 honorific title (noblemen) → 2468

【きみ】
② **second person pronouns**
君 YOU (*familiar*) → 3974
汝 THOU → 0255
爾 thou → 4407
貴 you (*honorific*) → 3220
卿 you (*archaic*, *honorific*) → 0769

何 incorrect classification
➡ see 1-2-5: 亻 at 0073
□3-4-3

角 incorrect classification
➡ see 2-2-5: ⺈ at 2541
□3-4-3

局 incorrect classification
➡ see □3-3-4: 尸 at 3800
□3-4-3

迎
3975
□3-4-4

▶WELCOME

ゲイ むか(える)

162	Nonstandard	U8FCE
辶	S8-4-4	F0000

traditional form → see 迎 at 3796

返
3976
□3-4-4

▶RETURN

ヘン かえ(す) -かえ(す) かえ(る) -かえ(る)

162	Nonstandard	U8FD4
辶	S8-4-4	F0000

traditional form → see 返 at 3797

近

3977
□3-4-4

▶NEAR
▶RECENT
キン コン ちか(い)

162	Nonstandard	U8FD1
⻌	S8-4-4	F0000

traditional form → see 近 at 3798

迄

□3-4-4

incorrect stroke-count
➡ see □3-4-3: ⻌ at 3967

或

3978
□3-4-4

▶A CERTAIN
ワク あ(る) ある(いは)
Ⓒ 或 huò

62	Names	U6216
戈	S8-4-4	F1816

COMPOUNDS

● A CERTAIN, some
或問 わくもん questions and answers

KUN

【ある 或る】A CERTAIN, some
或る日 あるひ a certain day, one day
或る程度 あるていど a certain extent, some extent
或る種 あるしゅ certain, some kind, some sort
或る人 あるひと someone
と或る とある a certain

【あるいは 或いは】
① or
② possibly

SYNONYMS

【ある】
◯ a certain
某 A CERTAIN → 3168
或る A CERTAIN → 3978
一 ONE → 4148
◯ some
幾- SOME → 4403
何- several → 0073
数 several → 2245
或る A CERTAIN → 3978

武

3979
□3-4-4

▶MILITARY
ブ ム ㊔ たけ たけし
Ⓒ 武 wǔ

77	Jōyō-5	U6B66
止	S8-4-4	F0317

1	2	3	4	5	6	7	8
一	二	亍	干	亓	正	武	武

COMPOUNDS

❶ⓐ MILITARY, martial; military affairs, military might
ⓑ MILITARY [martial] arts, science of war, Bushido
a 武力 ぶりょく military power, armed might
武術 ぶじゅつ military [martial] arts
b 武道 ぶどう martial arts
文武 ぶんぶ literary and military arts

❷ warrior, samurai; MILITARY man, officer
武士 ぶし samurai, warrior
武者 むしゃ warrior, soldier
武官 ぶかん military officer

❸ (military equipment) armaments, weapons
武装する ぶそうする arm, bear arms
武器 ぶき weapon, arms

❹ war
武運 ぶうん fortunes of war

❺ brave, chivalrous, valiant
武勇 ぶゆう bravery, valor

❻ abbrev. of 武蔵 むさし, old name for Tokyo-Saitama area
総武線 そうぶせん Sobu Line (Chiba-Tokyo Railway)

INDEPENDENT

【ぶ 武】MILITARY [martial] arts, Bushido; military power, arms
武を練る ぶをねる train oneself in military arts

SYNONYMS

❶ military
武 MILITARY → 3979
兵 military → 3158

❷ soldiers and warriors
兵 SOLDIER → 3158
卒 private → 2549
士 MILITARY MAN → 4213
武 warrior → 3979
侍 SAMURAI → 0094

房戻 etc.

□3-4-4

incorrect classification
➡ see □3-2-6: 厂 at 3716

房肩

□3-4-4

incorrect classification
➡ see ⬒2-1-7: 一 at 2445

者

3980
□3-4-4

▶PERSON
シャ もの
Ⓝ 者 Ⓒ 者 zhě

125	Jōyō-3	U8005
耂	S8-4-4	F0019

一	十	土	耂	耂	者	者	者
1	2	3	4	5	6	7	8

COMPOUNDS

❶ⓐ PERSON

ⓑ PERSON concerned, party

a 弱者 じゃくしゃ weak person, the weak
死者 ししゃ dead person, the deceased
b 三者会談 さんしゃかいだん tripartite conference
第三者 だいさんしゃ third party

❷ [also suffix] **PERSON** [one] who performs an action or holds an occupation: **-er (as in *reader*)**
読者 どくしゃ reader, subscriber
学者 がくしゃ scholar, learned man
記者 きしゃ journalist, reporter; editor
著者 ちょしゃ author, writer
医者 いしゃ doctor
打者 だしゃ batter, hitter
賛成者 さんせいしゃ approver, supporter
被爆者 ひばくしゃ victim of atomic air raid
科学者 かがくしゃ scientist

❸ **used to designate a thing or PERSON**
前者 ぜんしゃ the former
後者 こうしゃ the latter
両者 りょうしゃ both

KUN

【もの 者】**PERSON, fellow, somebody**
若者 わかもの young person [fellow], youth
怠け者 なまけもの idle [lazy] fellow
悪者 わるもの bad fellow, ruffian

SPECIAL READINGS

猛者 もさ stalwart; veteran

SYNONYMS

❶ⓐ **person**
人 HUMAN BEING → 4175
者 PERSON → 3980
方 person (*honorific*) → 2459
氏 person (*polite*) → 3669

❷ **workers and professionals**
家 professional → 2827
婦 woman worker → 0565
嬢 (unmarried) female worker → 0936
夫 MAN LABORER → 4271
匠 CRAFTSMAN → 3711
工 workman → 4190
客 skilled person → 2798
士 PROFESSION SUFFIX → 4213
師 profession suffix → 1680
者 person who → 3980
人 person of certain category → 4175
員 MEMBER (of a staff) → 2822
屋 colloquial occupation suffix → 3842
手 OCCUPATION SUFFIX → 4267

HOMOPHONES

もの 物 THING → 1084

NOTE

➡ see USAGE notes at 物 1084 and 家 2827
➡ see COMPOUND FORMATION for 候補者 こうほしゃ → 補 1529

虎

3981
口3-4-4

▶**TIGER**
コ とら ㊔ たけ
Ⓝ 虎 Ⓒ 虎 hǔ

141	Jōyō	U864E
虍	S8-6-2	F1109

丨	⺊	广	广	庐	虍	虎	虎
1	2	3	4	5	6	7	8

COMPOUNDS

● [original meaning] **TIGER**
虎穴 こけつ tiger's den; dangerous place
虎口 ここう tiger's den; dangerous place
虎視眈×眈× こしたんたん on the alert, eye covetously
竜虎の争い りゅうこのあらそい well matched contest ("serpent and tiger fight")
暴虎馮×河 ぼうこひょうが foolhardy courage

KUN

【とら 虎】
① **TIGER**
虎の巻 とらのまき key, crib, pony; secret (of a trade)
② **drunkard**

SYNONYMS

● **tiger**
虎 TIGER → 3981
寅 THE TIGER → 2854

● **undomesticated mammals**
虎 TIGER → 3981
猿 MONKEY → 0824
鯨 WHALE → 2361
犀 RHINOCEROS → 3900
狼 WOLF → 0541
狐 FOX → 0472
羚 SEROW → 1695
鼠 RAT → 3340
獅 LION → 0825
豹 LEOPARD → 1847
熊 BEAR → 3530
象 ELEPHANT → 2647
麒 MALE CHINESE UNICORN → 2363
麟 FEMALE CHINESE UNICORN → 2376
猪 WILD BOAR → 0652
鹿 DEER → 3879

USAGE

【とら】

虎
① tiger
② drunkard

寅
third sign of the Oriental zodiac: the Tiger

HOMOPHONES

とら 寅 THE TIGER → 2854

NOTE

➡ see COMPOUND FORMATION for 暴虎馮×河 ぼうこひょうが → 暴 3138

夜 口3-4-4
incorrect classification
➡ see 2-2-6: 亠 at 2550

肴 口3-4-4
incorrect classification
➡ see 2-2-6: メ at 2567

迦 3982 口3-4-5

▶PHONETIC [ka]

カ

Ⓝ 迦 Ⓒ 迦 jiā

162	Names	U8FE6
辶	S9-4-5	F2229

COMPOUNDS

● **used PHONETICally for *ka*, esp. in the transliteration of Sanskrit Buddhist terms**

迦楼羅 かるら *Garud¥.a,* man-bird deity in Hindu-Buddhist myth

釈迦 しゃか *Śākyamuni, Gautama*

宇迦御魂 うかのみたま god of foodstuffs, esp. of rice

SPECIAL READINGS

莫迦(=馬鹿) ばか fool, blockhead; nonsense

SYNONYMS

● **phonetic [k]/[g]**

迦 PHONETIC [ka] → 3982

珈 phonetic [kō] → 1138

伽 PHONETIC [ga] → 0074

瓦 phonetic [ga] → 4288

祇 phonetic [gi] → 1459

迫 3983 口3-4-5

▶PRESS

ハク せま(る) ㊔ さこ せこ はさみ はざま はさま

162	Nonstandard	U8FEB
辶	S9-4-5	F0000

traditional form → see 迫 at 3815

述 3984 口3-4-5

▶STATE

ジュツ の(べる)

162	Nonstandard	U8FF0
辶	S9-4-5	F0000

traditional form → see 述 at 3816

迪 3985 口3-4-5

▶EDIFY

テキ ㊔ みち すすむ

162	Nonstandard	U8FEA
辶	S9-4-5	F0000

traditional form → see 迪 at 3817

迭 3986 口3-4-5

▶ALTERNATE

テツ

162	Nonstandard	U8FED
辶	S9-4-5	F0000

traditional form → see 迭 at 3818

迯 3987 口3-4-5

▶ESCAPE

トウ に(げる) に(がす) のが(す) のが(れる)

162	Nonstandard	U8FEF
辶	S9-4-5	F0000

traditional form → see 逃 at 3839

県 口3-4-5
incorrect classification
➡ see 2-6-3: 目 at 3269

扁 口3-4-5
incorrect classification
➡ see 口3-2-7: 厂 at 3728

扁 口3-4-5
incorrect classification
➡ see 2-1-8: 一 at 2447

者 3988 口3-4-5

▶PERSON

シャ もの

125	Names	UFA5B
耂	S9-4-5	F0000

traditional form → see 者 at 3980

虐 3989 口3-4-5

▶CRUEL

ギャク しいた(げる)

Ⓝ 虐 Ⓒ 虐 nüè

141	Jōyō	U8650
虍	S9-6-3	F1502

1	2	3	4	5	6	7	8	9
丨	卜	广	广	卢	虍	虐	虐	虐

COMPOUNDS

ⓐ **CRUEL, savage, tyrannical, oppressive**

ⓑ [original meaning] **treat CRUELly, oppress, tyrannize**

a 虐待 ぎゃくたい maltreatment, abuse, cruelty
残虐な ざんぎゃくな cruel, atrocious, brutal, inhuman
悪虐無道の あくぎゃくむどうの treacherous, heinous
暴虐な ぼうぎゃくな tyrannical, cruel, atrocious
b 虐政 ぎゃくせい oppressive [tyrannical] government
虐殺 ぎゃくさつ massacre, butchery, genocide

KUN

【しいたげる 虐げる】 **oppress, persecute, tyrannize, grind down**
虐げられた人人 しいたげられたひとびと downtrodden people, the oppressed

SYNONYMS

ⓐ **cruel**
虐 CRUEL → 3989
惨 CRUEL → 0585
酷 SEVERE → 1967
辣 SEVERE → 1965
残 RUTHLESS → 1179
凶 ATROCIOUS → 3679
苛 HARSH → 2786

ⓑ **torture and oppress**
拷 TORTURE → 0446
責める torture → 3115
虐 treat cruelly → 3989
迫 oppress → 3815

虐
3990
☐3-4-5

▶**CRUEL**
ギャク しいた(げる)

141	Nonstandard	U8650
虍	S9-6-3	F0000

traditional form → see 虐 at 3989

盾
☐3-4-5

incorrect classification
➡ see ☐3-2-7: 厂 at 3729

眉
3991
☐3-4-5

▶**EYEBROW**
ビ ミ まゆ
Ⓒ 眉 méi

109	Jōyō	U7709
目	S9-5-4	F1409

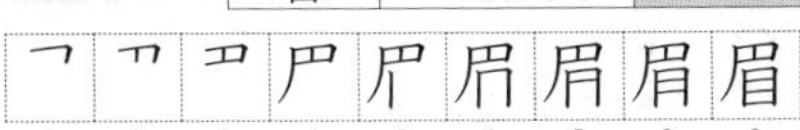

COMPOUNDS

● **EYEBROW**
焦眉の急 しょうびのきゅう urgent need

KUN

【まゆ 眉】 **EYEBROW**
眉毛 まゆげ eyebrows
眉をひそめる まゆをひそめる knit one's brows, frown

SYNONYMS

● **hair**
毛 HAIR (of any kind) → 4264
髪 HAIR (on the head) → 3528
辮 PLAIT → 2085
羽 FEATHER → 0265
眉 EYEBROW → 3991
鬚 BEARD → 3539

省
☐3-4-5

incorrect classification
➡ see ▀2-4-5: 少 at 3100

看
3992
☐3-4-5

▶**WATCH**
▶**CARE FOR**
カン み(る)▲
Ⓒ 看 kàn kān

109	Jōyō-6	U770B
目	S9-5-4	F1149

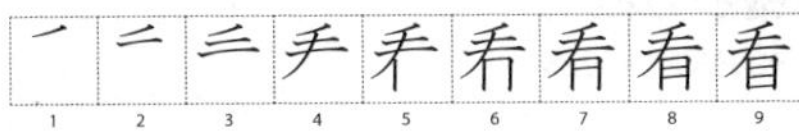

COMPOUNDS

❶ [original meaning] (look carefully) **WATCH, look, see, observe**
看板 かんばん signboard, sign
看破する かんぱする see through, penetrate, read (another's thoughts)
看取する かんしゅする perceive, detect; see through

❷ⓐ (keep a watchful eye on) **CARE FOR (the sick), watch, look after, nurse**
ⓑ abbrev. of 看護婦 かんごふ: nurse

a 看病する かんびょうする nurse, care for
看護婦 かんごふ nurse
看守 かんしゅ jailer, prison guard
b 准看 じゅんかん practical nurse

❸ **read**
看経 かんきん silent reading of sutra

KUN

【みる 看る】 [usu. 見る] take care of, look after
看取る みとる nurse, tend [care for] (the sick)

SYNONYMS

❶ **see and look**
見 SEE → 3151
看 WATCH → 3992
察 INSPECT → 2961
窺 WATCH FURTIVELY → 3002

辶 ⻌ 戶 戸 耂 虍 庘 尸 少 手 【冂】 尺

瞥 GLANCE AT → 3592
目 look → 3777
観 VIEW → 2359
覧 LOOK OVER → 3538
眺 LOOK OUT OVER → 1503
望 LOOK AFAR → 3408
仰 LOOK UP → 0051
顧 LOOK BACK → 2394
視 REGARD → 1223

❷ⓐ protect

守 PROTECT (by watching over) → 2697
護 PROTECT (by safeguarding) → 2079
庇 PROTECT (by shielding) → 3802
衛 GUARD → 0938
警 GUARD AGAINST → 3595
防 defend → 0320
番 WATCH → 3416
保 PRESERVE → 0107
看 CARE FOR → 3992

HOMOPHONES

みる

見 SEE → 3151
診 EXAMINE A PATIENT → 1898
観 VIEW → 2359
視 REGARD → 1223

NOTE

➡ see USAGE note at 見 3151

南
□3-4-5

incorrect classification
➡ see ▀2-2-7: 十 at 2584

昼
□3-4-5

incorrect classification
➡ see □3-3-6: 尸 at 3841

逆
3993
□3-4-6

▶REVERSE

ギャク ゲキ さか さか(さ) さか(らう)

162	Nonstandard	U9006
⻌	S10-4-6	F0000

traditional form → see 逆 at 3835

迷
3994
□3-4-6

▶PERPLEXED

メイ まよ(う)

162	Nonstandard	U8FF7
⻌	S10-4-6	F0000

traditional form → see 迷 at 3836

迹
3995
□3-4-6

▶TRACE

セキ あと

162	Nonstandard	U8FF9
⻌	S10-4-6	F0000

alternative form → see 跡 at 1937

送
3996
□3-4-6

▶SEND

ソウ おく(る)

162	Nonstandard	U9001
⻌	S10-4-6	F0000

traditional form → see 送 at 3837

退
3997
□3-4-6

▶RETREAT

タイ しりぞ(く) しりぞ(ける) ひ(く) ど(く) ど(ける) ど(かす) の(く) の(ける)

162	Nonstandard	U9000
⻌	S10-4-6	F0000

traditional form → see 退 at 3838

逃
3998
□3-4-6

▶ESCAPE

トウ に(げる) に(がす) のが(す) のが(れる)

162	Nonstandard	U9003
⻌	S10-4-6	F0000

traditional form → see 逃 at 3839

追
3999
□3-4-6

▶CHASE

ツイ お(う)

162	Nonstandard	U8FFD
⻌	S10-4-6	F0000

traditional form → see 追 at 3840

氣
4000
□3-4-6

▶GAS
▶SPIRIT

キ ケ

84	Names	U6C23
气	S10-4-6	F0000

traditional form → see 気 at 3960

扇
□3-4-6

incorrect classification
➡ see ▀2-1-9: 一 at 2449

虐
□3-4-6

incorrect stroke-count
➡ see □3-4-5: 虍 at 3989

毬
4001
□3-4-7

▶BALL

キュウ グ まり いが

Ⓒ 球 qiú

82	Names	U6BEC
毛	S11-4-7	F3225

COMPOUNDS

❶ **BALL**

打毬 だきゅう ancient Japanese polo

❷ **BALL**-shaped object

毬果 きゅうか cone (of a plant)

KUN

【まり 毬】[also 鞠] **BALL**

毬歌 まりうた (children's) handball song

【いが 毬】**burr**

毬栗 いがぐり chestnuts in burrs; close-cropped head

毬栗頭 いがぐりあたま close-cropped head

SYNONYMS

❶ & ❷ & 【まり】**spherical object**

玉 spherical object → 4289
球 BALL → 1219
丸 round body → 4225
鞠 BALL → 2268
毬 BALL → 4001

HOMOPHONES

まり 鞠 BALL → 2268

NOTE

➡ see USAGE note at 鞠 2268

逢

4002

□3-4-7

▶**MEET**

ホウ あ(う)

Ⓝ 逢 Ⓒ 逢 féng

162	Names	U9022
辶	S11-4-7	F1843

COMPOUNDS

● (encounter by chance) **MEET, see, encounter**

逢着する ほうちゃくする encounter, face

KUN

【あう 逢う】(encounter by chance or arrangement) **MEET, see, encounter**—used esp. in reference to romantic encounters

逢わせる あわせる have (a person) meet (another), allow (a person) to see (someone)

逢い引き あいびき (lovers') date, rendezvous

逢瀬 おうせ meeting, date

出逢う であう meet (by chance), encounter

忍び逢い しのびあい clandestine meeting, rendezvous

SYNONYMS

● **meet**

会 MEET → 2512
遇 ENCOUNTER → 3889
遭 MEET WITH → 3917
見 SEE → 3151
謁 BE GRANTED AN AUDIENCE → 1976
逢 MEET → 4002

HOMOPHONES

あう

会 MEET → 2512
合 COMBINE → 2511
遇 TREAT → 3889
遭 MEET WITH → 3917

NOTE

➡ see USAGE note at 会 2512

這

4003

□3-4-7

▶**CRAWL**

シャ は(う) ㊔ これ ちか

Ⓝ 這 Ⓒ 这 zhè

162	Names	U9019
辶	S11-4-7	F1518

COMPOUNDS

ⓐ *pronoun* this

ⓑ *demonstrative* this

b 這般 しゃはん *demonstrative* these

KUN

【はう 這う】

①ⓐ **CRAWL, creep**

ⓑ (of plants) **creep, trail**

a 這い上がる はいあがる crawl up, creep up, climb up

這い這い はいはい crawling (of babies)

這い蹲×る はいつくばる grovel, go down on one's hands and knees

横這い よこばい crawling sideways; remain at the same level

四つん這い よつんばい on all fours, on one's hands and feet

b 這松 はいまつ Japanese stone pine, creeping pine

② unclassified compounds

夜這い よばい sneaking nocturnal visit (to make love); [archaic] proposal of marriage

SYNONYMS

【はう】

①ⓐ **move forward**

進 ADVANCE → 3873
突 DASH → 2772
這う CRAWL → 4003

逞

4004

□3-4-7

▶**DO AS ONE PLEASES**

▶**ROBUST**

テイ たくま(しい) ㊔ たく とし とおる たくむ よし ゆた ゆき

Ⓝ 逞 逞 Ⓒ 逞 chěng

162	Names	U901E
辶	S11-4-7	F2493

毛【辶】弋户戶少

COMPOUNDS

● DO AS ONE PLEASES, be self-indulgent
不逞 ふてい recalcitrance, outlawry, insubordination
不逞の輩 ふていのやから lawless people [gang], malcontents, recalcitrants

KUN

【たくましい 逞しい】
ⓐ (sturdy) **ROBUST, brawny, strapping**
ⓑ (indefatigable) **ROBUST, resilient, hardy**
ⓒ (energetic) **ROBUST, vigorous**
a 逞しい体付き たくましいからだつき sturdy build
b 逞しい雑草 たくましいざっそう hardy weeds
c 想像力が逞しい そうぞうりょくがたくましい have a robust imagination

SYNONYMS

● **acting arbitrarily**
横 arbitrary → 1350
独 act arbitrarily → 0471
恣 SELF-INDULGENT → 3281
耽 INDULGE IN → 1665
擅 ARROGATE TO ONESELF → 0947
専 arrogate to oneself → 3272
逞 DO AS ONE PLEASES → 4004

【たくましい】
ⓐ **strong**
強 STRONG → 0574
壮 VIGOROUS → 0263
丈 STOUT → 4227
健 ROBUST (healthy) → 0152
逞しい ROBUST (sturdy) → 4004
康 HEALTHY → 3877
旺 ENERGETIC → 1061
潑 LIVELY → 0917

逗 4005
□3-4-7

▶**STAY**
トウ
Ⓝ 逗 Ⓒ 逗 dòu

162	Names	U9017
辶	S11-4-7	F2838

COMPOUNDS

● (remain in a given place) **STAY, sojourn, reside**
逗留 とうりゅう staying, sojourn

SYNONYMS

● **stay**
滞 STAY → 0815
頓 STAY IN PLACE → 1320
留 STAY → 3189
逗 STAY → 4005
駐 STATIONED → 2297
屯 STATION TROOPS → 4268
在 reside temporarily → 3704
泊 STAY OVERNIGHT → 0389
宿 LODGE → 2858
寓 stay temporarily → 2893

逐 4006
□3-4-7

▶**ONE BY ONE**
▶**DRIVE OUT**
チク

162	Nonstandard	U9010
辶	S11-4-7	F0000

traditional form → see 逐 at 3848

逕 4007
□3-4-7

▶**PATH**
▶**DIAMETER**
ケイ ㊔ みち

162	Nonstandard	U9015
辶	S11-4-7	F0000

traditional form → see 径 at 0347

連 4008
□3-4-7

▶**LINK**
▶**IN SUCCESSION**
レン つら(なる) つら(ねる) つ(れる) -づ(れ) ㊔ むらじ

162	Nonstandard	UF99A
辶	S11-4-7	F0000

traditional form → see 連 at 3849

逝 4009
□3-4-7

▶**DEPART THIS LIFE**
セイ ゆ(く) い(く)

162	Nonstandard	U901D
辶	S11-4-7	F0000

traditional form → see 逝 at 3850

速 4010
□3-4-7

▶**QUICK**
ソク はや(い) はや- はや(める) はや(まる) すみ(やか) ㊔ はやみ

162	Nonstandard	U901F
辶	S11-4-7	F0000

traditional form → see 速 at 3851

逞 4011
□3-4-7

▶**DO AS ONE PLEASES**
▶**ROBUST**
テイ たくま(しい) ㊔ たく とし とおる たくむ よし ゆた ゆき

162	Nonstandard	U901E
辶	S11-4-7	F0000

traditional form → see 逞 at 4004

途 4012
□3-4-7

▶**WAY**
ト ㊔ みち

162	Nonstandard	U9014
辶	S11-4-7	F0000

traditional form → see 途 at 3853

透

4013
□3-4-7

▶PASS THROUGH
▶TRANSPARENT
トウ す(く) す(かす) す(ける) とお(る) とお(す)

162	Nonstandard	U900F
辶	S11-4-7	F0000

traditional form → see 透 at 3854

通

4014
□3-4-7

▶PASS
▶COMMUNICATE
ツウ ツ とお(る) とお(り) -とお(り) -どお(り) とお(す) とお(し) -どお(し) かよ(う) ㊔ みち ゆき

162	Nonstandard	U901A
辶	S11-4-7	F0000

traditional form → see 通 at 3855

造

4015
□3-4-7

▶MAKE
ゾウ つく(る) つく(り) -づく(り)

162	Nonstandard	U9020
辶	S11-4-7	F0000

traditional form → see 造 at 3856

貳

4016
□3-4-7

▶TWO
ニ

56	Nonstandard	U8CAE
弋	S11-3-8	F0000

alternative form → see 弐 at 3961

虛

4017
□3-4-7

▶VOID
▶FALSE
キョ コ むな(しい)▲ うつ(ろ)▲
Ⓝ 虚 虚 Ⓒ 虚 xū

141	Jōyō	U865A
虍	S11-6-5	F1283

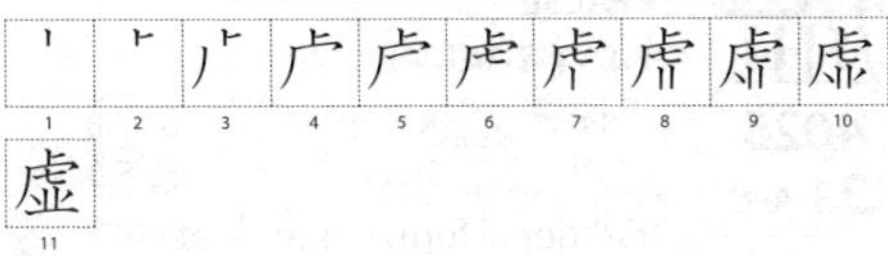

COMPOUNDS

❶ (containing nothing) **VOID, empty, vacant, hollow**
虚無 きょむ nothingness; nihility
虚無僧 こむそう flute-playing Zen mendicant priest
虚脱 きょだつ (physical) collapse, prostration; absentmindedness
虚空 こくう empty space, sky
空虚な くうきょな empty, void; inane

❷ **without substance, in name only, empty, vain, inane, hollow, VOID**
虚栄 きょえい vanity, vainglory
虚栄心 きょえいしん vanity
虚勢 きょせい bluff, bluster, false show of power
虚飾 きょしょく ostentation, affectation, show
虚礼 きょれい empty [useless] formalities

❸ **FALSE, sham, untrue, feigned**
虚偽 きょぎ falsehood, lie, fallacy
虚言 きょげん falsehood
虚報 きょほう false alarm
虚構 きょこう fabrication, fiction
虚虚実実の戦い きょきょじつじつのたたかい match between persons equal in shrewdness

❹ *math* imaginary
虚数 きょすう imaginary number
虚式 きょしき imaginary expression

❺ **openhearted, humble**
虚心 きょしん disinterestedness, freedom from prejudice
謙虚な けんきょな humble, modest

❻ weak, feeble
虚弱な きょじゃくな weak, feeble, sickly

❼ [also 墟 きょ 0888] ruins
廃虚 はいきょ ruins, remains

INDEPENDENT

【きょ 虚】 insubstantiality, emptiness, inanity, **VOID**; unguarded position, unpreparedness; *math* imaginary unit
虚を衝く きょをつく attack the enemy in his unguarded moment

KUN

【むなしい 虚しい】 [usu. 空しい]
① ⓐ empty, **VOID**
ⓑ vain, futile
a 虚しさ むなしさ emptiness, futility
虚しい名声 むなしいめいせい empty name
b 努力も虚しく どりょくもむなしく after efforts in vain
② dead, lifeless
虚しくなる むなしくなる die, expire

【うつろ 虚ろ】 hollow, cavity, **VOID**, vacant
虚ろな目 うつろなめ vacant eyes
木の虚ろ きのうつろ hollow in a tree

SYNONYMS

❶ **emptiness and nothing**
空 EMPTY → 2767
白 WHITE (blank) → 4305
虚 VOID → 4017
無 NOTHING → 2648

❷ **vain**
空 EMPTY → 2767
虚 without substance → 4017
徒 vain → 0499

❸ **false**
虚 FALSE → 4017

毛 辶 弋 【虍】 尸 少

仮 fake → 0053
偽 sham → 0149
擬 imitation → 0969
義 artificial → 2948

❼ **ruins**

墟 RUINS → 0888
虚 ruins → 4017

HOMOPHONES

むなしい 空 SKY → 2767

NOTE

➡ see USAGE note at 空 2767

虗

4018
□3-4-7

▶VOID
▶FALSE
キョ コ むな(しい) うつ(ろ)

141	Nonstandard	U8657
虍	S11-6-5	F0000

traditional form → see 虚 at 4017

處

4019
□3-4-7

▶DEAL WITH
ショ ところ -こ

141	Nonstandard	U8655
虍	S11-6-5	F0000

traditional form → see 処 at 3764

質

□3-4-7

incorrect classification
➡ see □3-2-9: 厂 at 3737

雀

□3-4-7

incorrect classification
➡ see ▀2-4-7: 少 at 3117

逸

4020
□3-4-8

▶LET SLIP
イツ そ(れる) そ(らす) ㊔ はやる はや

162	Names	UFA67
辶	S12-4-8	F0000

traditional form → see 逸 at 3872

進

4021
□3-4-8

▶ADVANCE
シン すす(む) すす(める) ㊔ のぶ

162	Nonstandard	U9032
辶	S12-4-8	F0000

traditional form → see 進 at 3873

週

4022
□3-4-8

▶WEEK
シュウ

162	Nonstandard	U9031
辶	S12-4-8	F0000

traditional form → see 週 at 3874

逮

4023
□3-4-8

▶CATCH A CRIMINAL
タイ

162	Nonstandard	U902E
辶	S12-4-8	F0000

traditional form → see 逮 at 3875

達

4024
□3-4-8

▶ATTAIN
タツ ダ -たち ㊔ とおる さとる だて さと みち

162	Nonstandard	U9039
辶	S12-4-8	F0000

traditional form → see 達 at 3893

遇

□3-4-8

incorrect stroke-count
➡ see □3-4-9: 辶 at 4029

透

□3-4-8

incorrect stroke-count
➡ see □3-4-7: 辶 at 4013

遊

□3-4-8

incorrect stroke-count
➡ see □3-4-9: 辶 at 4036

雇扉

□3-4-8

incorrect classification
➡ see □3-2-10: 厂 at 3743

雇扉

□3-4-8

incorrect classification
➡ see ▀2-1-11: 一 at 2453

煮

□3-4-8

incorrect classification
➡ see ▀2-8-4: 者 at 3460

虛

4025
□3-4-8

▶VOID
▶FALSE
キョ コ むな(しい) うつ(ろ)

141	Names	U865B
虍	S12-6-6	F0000

traditional form → see 虚 at 4017

虜

4026
□3-4-8

▶CAPTIVE
リョ とりこ

141	Names	UF936
虍	S12-6-6	F0000

traditional form → see 虜 at 4038

遁

▶FLEE

トン のが(れる)

Ⓝ 遁 Ⓒ 遁 dùn

4027

口3-4-9

162	Names	U9041
⻌	S13-4-9	F2530

COMPOUNDS

● **FLEE, escape, evade; shirk away**

遁走 とんそう fleeing, escape

遁世 とんせい seclusion from the world

遁術 とんじゅつ ninja art of escape

隠遁 いんとん retirement (from the world), seclusion

水遁 すいとん ninja art of water-escape

KUN

【のがれる 遁れる】**FLEE**, escape; evade, shirk away

SYNONYMS

● **escape**

逃 ESCAPE → 3839

遁 FLEE → 4027

亡 flee → 4210

走 run away → 2720

脱 ESCAPE FROM → 1225

HOMOPHONES

のがれる 逃 ESCAPE → 3839

NOTE

➡ see USAGE note at 逃 3839

道

▶WAY

ドウ トウ みち ㊔ おさむ わたる とおる

4028

口3-4-9

162	Nonstandard	U9053
⻌	S13-4-9	F0000

traditional form → see 道 at 3888

遇

▶TREAT

▶ENCOUNTER

グウ あ(う)

4029

口3-4-9

162	Nonstandard	U9047
⻌	S13-4-9	F0000

traditional form → see 遇 at 3889

遍

▶ALL OVER

ヘン あまね(く)

4030

口3-4-9

162	Nonstandard	U904D
⻌	S13-4-9	F0000

traditional form → see 遍 at 3890

違

▶DIFFER

▶VIOLATE

イ ちが(う) ちが(い) ちが(える) -ちが(える) たが(う) たが(える)

4031

口3-4-9

162	Nonstandard	U9055
⻌	S13-4-9	F0000

traditional form → see 違 at 3907

過

▶PASS BY

▶EXCEED

カ す(ぎる) -す(ぎる) -す(ぎ) す(ごす) あやま(つ) あやま(ち)

4032

口3-4-9

162	Nonstandard	U904E
⻌	S13-4-9	F0000

traditional form → see 過 at 3891

遂

▶ACCOMPLISH

スイ と(げる) つい(に)

4033

口3-4-9

162	Nonstandard	U9042
⻌	S13-4-9	F0000

traditional form → see 遂 at 3892

達

▶ATTAIN

タツ ダ -たち ㊔ とおる さとる だて さと みち

4034

口3-4-9

162	Nonstandard	U9054
⻌	S13-4-9	F0000

traditional form → see 達 at 3893

運

▶CARRY

▶MOVE

▶FORTUNE

ウン はこ(ぶ)

4035

口3-4-9

162	Nonstandard	U904B
⻌	S13-4-9	F0000

traditional form → see 運 at 3894

遊

▶PLAY

ユウ ユ あそ(ぶ) あそ(ばす)

4036

口3-4-9

162	Nonstandard	U904A
⻌	S13-4-9	F0000

traditional form → see 遊 at 3896

遜

口3-4-9

incorrect stroke-count

➡ see 口3-4-10: ⻌ at 4041

煮

口3-4-9

incorrect classification

➡ see ▀2-9-4: 者 at 3512

虞

辶 歩 【广】

4037

口3-4-9

▶**FEARS**

グ▲ おそれ

Ⓝ 虞 Ⓒ 虞 yú

141	Jōyō	U865E
虍	S13-6-7	F3315

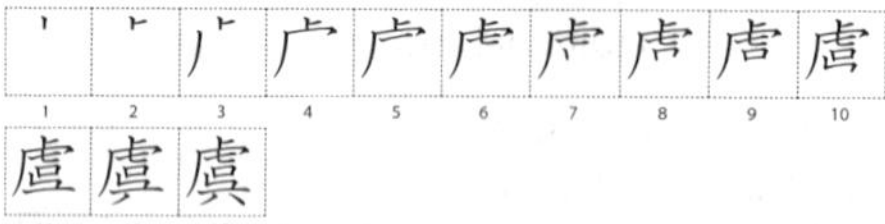

COMPOUNDS

● [original meaning, now rare] be anxious, be apprehensive

危虞(=危惧) きぐ fear, misgivings

憂虞 ゆうぐ fear, anxiety

KUN

【おそれ 虞】[also 恐れ] **FEARS (of undesirable event), danger, risk, signs, adverse chance, possibility**

失敗の虞 しっぱいのおそれ risk of failure

雨の虞が有る あめのおそれがある There is some fear of rain

感染の虞を無くす かんせんのおそれをなくす preclude the possibility of infection

SYNONYMS

【おそれ】

○ **worry**

憂 BE ANXIOUS → 2664

配 concern oneself → 1853

構う MIND → 1325

虞 FEARS (of undesirable event) → 4037

HOMOPHONES

おそれ 恐 FEAR → 3283

NOTE

➡ see USAGE note at 恐 3283

虜

4038

口3-4-9

▶**CAPTIVE**

リョ とりこ▲

Ⓝ 虜 Ⓒ 虏 lǔ

141	Jōyō	U865C
虍	S13-6-7	F1870

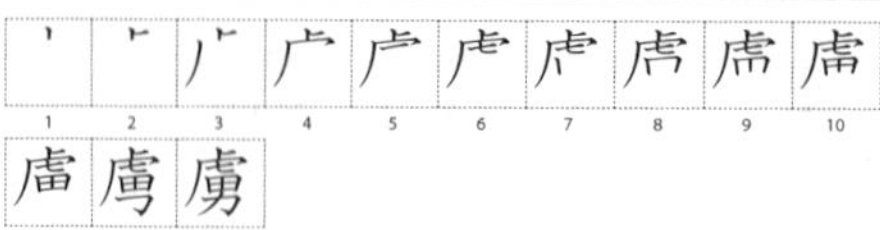

COMPOUNDS

● [original meaning] **CAPTIVE, prisoner**

虜囚 りょしゅう captive, prisoner

捕虜 ほりょ prisoner of war, captive

俘×虜 ふりょ prisoner, POW, captive

KUN

【とりこ 虜】**CAPTIVE**; victim, slave

美貌の虜になる びぼうのとりこになる be enslaved by a woman's beauty

SYNONYMS

● **prisoner**

虜 CAPTIVE → 4038

囚 PRISONER → 3776

NOTE

★ do not confuse with 慮 CONSIDER → 4050

虞

4039

口3-4-9

▶**FEARS**

グ おそれ

141	Nonstandard	U865E
虍	S13-6-7	F0000

traditional form → see 虞 at 4037

遡

4040

口3-4-10

▶**GO UPSTREAM**

ソ さかのぼ(る)

Ⓝ 泝 溯 遡◈ Ⓒ 溯 sù

162	Jōyō	U9061
辶	S14-4-10	F2462

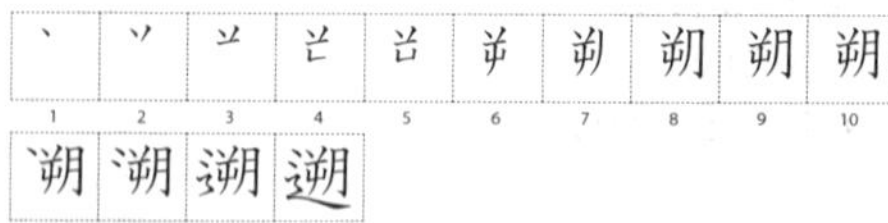

COMPOUNDS

ⓐ [original meaning] **GO UPSTREAM**

ⓑ **go back (to the past); retroact**

a 遡上 そじょう going upstream

遡求 そきゅう (request for repayment) recourse

遡河魚 そかぎょ anadromous fish

b 遡及する そきゅうする retroact

KUN

【さかのぼる 遡る】[sometimes also 逆上る]

ⓐ **GO UPSTREAM, go back (to the past)**

ⓑ **retroact**

a 鮭×は川を遡る さけはかわをさかのぼる Salmon swim up the river

キリスト教の伝来は十六世紀に遡る きりすときょうのでんらいはじゅうろくせいきにさかのぼる The introduction of Christianity goes back to the sixteenth century

b 五月一日に遡って ごがつついたちにさかのぼって retroactive to May 1

SYNONYMS

● **move through water**

泳 SWIM → 0385

游 SWIM → 0750

渉 wade → 0638

遡 GO UPSTREAM → 4040

漕 ROW →0864

HOMOPHONES

さかのぼる 逆上る →3835, 4212

NOTE

➡ see USAGE note at 逆 3835

遜

4041

口3-4-10

▶HUMBLE

ソン へりくだ(る)▲ ㊔ ゆずる やす

Ⓝ 遜◈ Ⓒ 逊 xùn

162 辶	Jōyō	U905C
	S14-4-10	F2533

COMPOUNDS

❶ **HUMBLE, modest**

謙遜 けんそん humility, modesty

不遜 ふそん arrogance, insolence

❷ inferior, subgrade

遜色のない そんしょくのない favorably comparing with, bearing comparison to, not inferior to

KUN

【へりくだる 遜る】[also 謙る] be **HUMBLE**, be modest

SYNONYMS

❶ **humble**

謙 HUMBLE →2044

遜 HUMBLE →4041

拝 HUMBLY →0360

USAGE

【へりくだる】

遜る

[also 謙る] be humble, be modest

謙る

[also 遜る] be humble, be modest

HOMOPHONES

へりくだる 謙 HUMBLE →2044

遠

4042

口3-4-10

▶DISTANT

エン オン とお(い)

162 辶	Nonstandard	U9060
	S14-4-10	F0000

traditional form →see 遠 at 3906

遣

4043

口3-4-10

▶DISPATCH

ケン つか(う) -つか(い) -づか(い) つか(わす) や(る)

162 辶	Nonstandard	U9063
	S14-4-10	F0000

traditional form →see 遣 at 3908

遞

4044

口3-4-10

▶RELAY

テイ

162 辶	Nonstandard	U905E
	S14-4-10	F0000

traditional form →see 逓 at 3852

遙

4045

口3-4-10

▶FAR

ヨウ はる(か)

162 辶	Names	U9059
	S14-4-10	F0000

traditional form →see 遥 at 3895

遮

口3-4-10

incorrect stroke-count

➡ see 口3-4-11: 辶 at 4046

虞

口3-4-10

incorrect stroke-count

➡ see 口3-4-9: 广 at 4037

遮

4046

口3-4-11

▶INTERRUPT

シャ さえぎ(る)

162 辶	Nonstandard	U906E
	S15-4-11	F0000

traditional form →see 遮 at 3916

遭

4047

口3-4-11

▶MEET WITH

ソウ あ(う) あ(わせる)

162 辶	Nonstandard	U906D
	S15-4-11	F0000

traditional form →see 遭 at 3917

適

4048

口3-4-11

▶SUITABLE

テキ かな(う)

162 辶	Nonstandard	U9069
	S15-4-11	F0000

traditional form →see 適 at 3918

膚

4049

口3-4-11

▶SKIN

フ はだ▲

Ⓒ 肤 fū

130 月	Jōyō	U819A
	S15-4-11	F1731

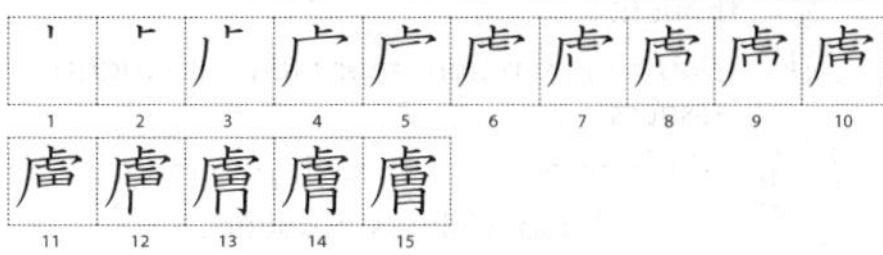

COMPOUNDS

● **SKIN (of the human body)**

皮膚 ひふ skin

完膚無き迄 かんぷなきまで thoroughly, beyond recognition; scathingly

KUN

【はだ 膚】[now usu. 肌]

①ⓐ **SKIN**, body
ⓑ surface; grain (of wood)

a 膚身 はだみ body
赤膚 あかはだ abraded skin
山膚 やまはだ surface of a mountain
b 膚の美しい材 はだのうつくしいざい wood of fine grain

②ⓐ disposition, temperament
ⓑ [suffix] turn of mind

a 学者膚 がくしゃはだ scholarly bent of mind

SYNONYMS

● **kinds of skin**
皮 SKIN (of any kind) →3771
膚 SKIN (of the human body) →4049
肌 SKIN (of the human body) →1021
革 LEATHER →3099
韋 TANNED LEATHER →2851
鱗 SCALES →2375

HOMOPHONES

はだ 肌 SKIN →1021

NOTE

➡ see USAGE note at 肌 1021

慮

4050
□3-4-11

▶**CONSIDER**
リョ おもんぱか(る)▲
Ⓒ 虑 lǜ

61	Jōyō	U616E
心	S15-4-11	F1174

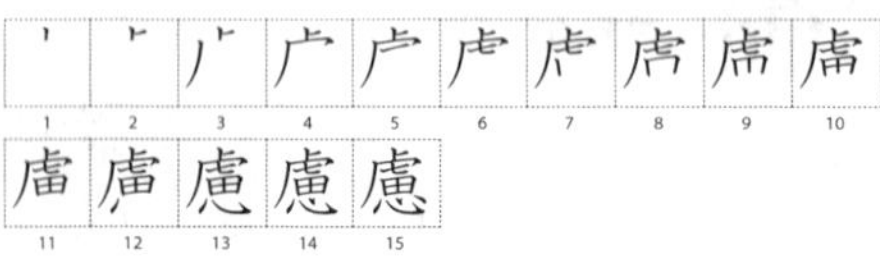

COMPOUNDS

ⓐ [original meaning] **CONSIDER, think over, deliberate**
ⓑ **show CONSIDERation, be prudent, be discreet**
ⓒ **CONSIDER**ation, concern

a 考慮する こうりょする consider, deliberate, give thought to
浅慮 せんりょ indiscretion, imprudence, thoughtlessness
思慮 しりょ consideration, thought, discretion
深慮 しんりょ thoughtfulness, prudence
b 遠慮する えんりょする be reserved; hesitate; refrain
顧慮 こりょ regard, consideration
配慮 はいりょ consideration, care, concern
c 憂慮 ゆうりょ anxiety, concern, worry

KUN

【おもんぱかる 慮る】**CONSIDER**, take thought of; fear, apprehend
慮り おもんぱかり thought, consideration; fears

SYNONYMS

ⓐ **think and consider**
思 THINK →3173
惟 MEDITATE →0582
省 INTROSPECT →3100
稽 THINK →1573
考 THINK →3962
存 hold an opinion →3702
案 think out →2824
想 CONCEIVE →3507
慮 CONSIDER →4050
勘 take into consideration →2231
銓 WEIGH →2161
量 weigh →3119

NOTE

★ do not confuse with 虜 CAPTIVE →4038

遲

4051
□3-4-12

▶**SLOW**
▶**LATE**
チ おく(れる) おく(らす) おそ(い)

162	Nonstandard	U9072
辶	S16-4-12	F0000

traditional form →see 遅 at 3887

遺

4052
□3-4-12

▶**LEAVE BEHIND**
イ ユイ

162	Nonstandard	U907A
辶	S16-4-12	F0000

traditional form →see 遺 at 3928

遵

4053
□3-4-12

▶**OBEY**
ジュン

162	Nonstandard	U9075
辶	S16-4-12	F0000

traditional form →see 遵 at 3929

遼

4054
□3-4-12

▶**FARAWAY**
リョウ ㊔ はるか

162	Nonstandard	UF9C3
辶	S16-4-12	F0000

traditional form →see 遼 at 3930

選

4055
□3-4-12

▶**CHOOSE**
セン えら(ぶ) よ(る)

162	Nonstandard	U9078
辶	S16-4-12	F0000

traditional form →see 選 at 3931

遷

▶TRANSFER

セン

4056

□3-4-12

162	Nonstandard	U9077
辶	S16-4-12	F0000

traditional form → see 遷 at 3932

邉

▶VICINITY
▶BORDERLAND

ヘン あた(り) -べ ㊔ なべ

4057

□3-4-13

162	Nonstandard	U9089
辶	S17-4-13	F0000

traditional form → see 辺 at 3761

避

▶AVOID

ヒ さ(ける) よ(ける)

4058

□3-4-13

162	Nonstandard	U907F
辶	S17-4-13	F0000

traditional form → see 避 at 3944

還

▶RETURN

カン かえ(る)

4059

□3-4-13

162	Nonstandard	U9084
辶	S17-4-13	F0000

traditional form → see 還 at 3945

邊

▶VICINITY
▶BORDERLAND

ヘン あた(り) -べ ㊔ なべ

4060

□3-4-15

162	Nonstandard	U908A
辶	S19-4-15	F0000

traditional form → see 辺 at 3761

戊 □3-5-1
incorrect classification
➡ see ■4-6-4 at 4350

成 □3-5-1
incorrect classification
➡ see ■4-6-4 at 4352

芦 □3-5-2
incorrect classification
➡ see ⬒2-3-4: 艹 at 2743

良 □3-5-2
incorrect classification
➡ see ■4-7-4 at 4373

肖 □3-5-2
incorrect classification
➡ see ⬒2-3-4: ⺌ at 2733

成 □3-5-2
incorrect classification
➡ see ■4-7-4 at 4376

呉 □3-5-3
incorrect classification/
stroke-count
➡ see ⬒2-5-2: 旦 at 3156

奇 □3-5-3
incorrect classification
➡ see ⬒2-3-5: 大 at 2756

苛 □3-5-3
incorrect classification
➡ see ⬒2-3-5: 艹 at 2786

尚 □3-5-3
incorrect classification
➡ see ⬒2-3-5: ⺌ at 2774

為 □3-5-4
incorrect classification
➡ see ■4-9-4 at 4395

疫

▶EPIDEMIC

エキ ヤク

Ⓒ 疫 yì

4061

□3-5-4

104	Jōyō	U75AB
疒	S9-5-4	F1849

1 丶 2 亠 3 广 4 广 5 疒 6 疒 7 疒 8 疫 9 疫

COMPOUNDS

● [original meaning] **EPIDEMIC, disease**

疫病 えきびょう epidemic, plague
疫学 えきがく epidemiology
疫病神 やくびょうがみ God of the plagues; abominable person, pest
免疫 めんえき immunity (from a disease)
検疫 けんえき quarantine, medical inspection
防疫 ぼうえき prevention of epidemics

SYNONYMS

● **disease**

病 ILLNESS → 4062
疾 DISEASE → 4064
風 (infectious) disease → 3730
症 PATHOLOGICAL CONDITION → 4065
患 AFFECTED BY DISEASE → 3415
疫 EPIDEMIC → 4061
罹 FALL ILL → 3239
臥 be sick in bed → 1825

炭 □3-5-4
incorrect classification
➡ see ⬒2-3-6: 山 at 2806

威 □3-5-4
incorrect classification
➡ see ■4-9-4 at 4394

面 incorrect classification
➡ see ▀2-2-7: 𠆢 at 2590
□3-5-4

為 疒 广 戊 【百】

病
4062
□3-5-5

▶**ILLNESS**
ビョウ ヘイ や(む) -や(み) やまい
ⓒ 病 bìng

104 疒	Jōyō-3	U75C5
	S10-5-5	F0344

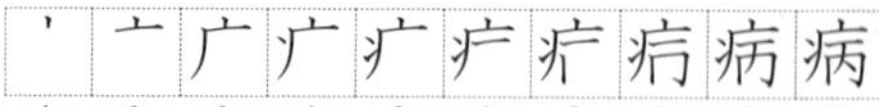
1 2 3 4 5 6 7 8 9 10

COMPOUNDS

❶ⓐ [also suffix] [original meaning] **ILLNESS, sickness, disease**
ⓑ **sick, ill, weak**

a 病気 びょうき illness, sickness, disease
病院 びょういん hospital
病室 びょうしつ patient [sick] room
病死 びょうし death of sickness
疾病 しっぺい sickness, disease
看病 かんびょう nursing, nursing care
難病 なんびょう incurable [intractable] disease
肺病 はいびょう lung disease; pulmonary tuberculosis
精神病 せいしんびょう mental disease
高山病 こうざんびょう altitude sickness
臆病 おくびょう cowardice, timidity
b 病身 びょうしん weak constitution, ill health
病人 びょうにん patient, invalid
病弱な びょうじゃくな weak, weakly, sickly
病躯× びょうく sick body, sickly constitution

❷ bad habit, weakness, blemish
病癖 びょうへき peculiarity, weakness, morbid habit
病根 びょうこん root of an evil
病弊 びょうへい evil, ill effect

KUN

【やむ 病む】**fall ill, be taken ill, suffer from**
病み付く やみつく be taken ill; be addicted to, become absorbed in, give oneself up [to]
病み付き やみつき infatuation, beginning (of a bad habit)
病み上がり やみあがり convalescence

【-やみ -病み】[suffix] **patient affected with…**
肺病病み はいびょうやみ patient with pulmonary tuberculosis

【やまい 病】**sickness, disease; bad habit, weakness, blemish**
病膏肓×に入る やまいこうこう(=こうもう)にいる become a slave of a habit (膏肓× こうこう is sometimes incorrectly pronounced こうもう)
不治の病 ふじ(=ふち)のやまい incurable illness

SYNONYMS

❶ⓐ **disease**
病 ILLNESS →4062
疾 DISEASE →4064
風 (infectious) disease →3730
症 PATHOLOGICAL CONDITION →4065
患 AFFECTED BY DISEASE →3415
疫 EPIDEMIC →4061
罹 FALL ILL →3239
臥 be sick in bed →1825

疲
4063
□3-5-5

▶**TIRED**
ヒ つか(れる) -づか(れ) つか(らす)▲
ⓒ 疲 pí

104 疒	Jōyō	U75B2
	S10-5-5	F1191

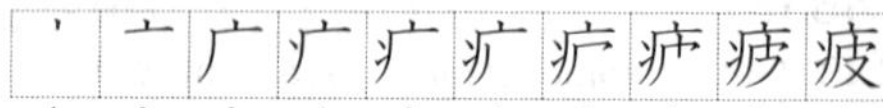
1 2 3 4 5 6 7 8 9 10

COMPOUNDS

● [original meaning] **TIRED, fatigued**
疲労 ひろう fatigue
疲弊 ひへい exhaustion; impoverishment

KUN

【つかれる 疲れる】*vi* **get TIRED, become fatigued**
疲れ つかれ fatigue, exhaustion
疲れ果てる つかれはてる be tired out
気疲れ きづかれ nervous strain, worry
歩き疲れる あるきつかれる be tired from walking

【-づかれ -疲れ】[suffix] **fatigue**
旅行疲れ りょこうづかれ fatigue from traveling

【つからす 疲らす】*vt* tire, fatigue, exhaust
心を疲らす こころをつからす fatigue one's mind

SYNONYMS

● **tire**
疲 TIRED →4063
労 fatigue →3155
倦 TIRE OF →0131
厭 TIRE OF →3745

疾
4064
□3-5-5

▶**DISEASE**
シツ と(く)▲
ⓒ 疾 jí

104 疒	Jōyō	U75BE
	S10-5-5	F1635

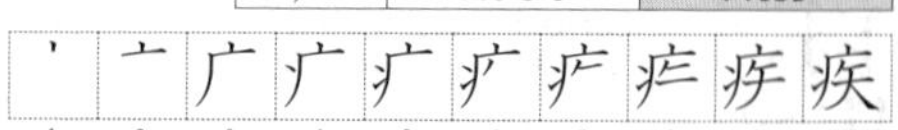
1 2 3 4 5 6 7 8 9 10

COMPOUNDS

❶ [original meaning] **DISEASE, illness**
疾患 しっかん disease, ailment, trouble, disorder

疾病 しっぺい sickness, disease
悪疾 あくしつ malignant disease
痼×疾 こしつ chronic disease
廃疾 はいしつ disablement

❷ **fast, swift, at full speed**
疾走 しっそう sprint, dash
疾駆する しっくする ride fast, drive a horse fast
疾風 しっぷう gale, strong wind

❸ [rare] suffering, distress
疾苦 しっく suffering, affliction

❹ [rare] hate, detest
疾視 しっし spiteful gaze

KUN

【とく 疾く】 fast, promptly; already, long since
疾っくに とっくに long since, long ago; well (past)
疾っくの昔 とっくのむかし long ago, a long time ago

SYNONYMS

❶ **disease**
病 ILLNESS →4062
疾 DISEASE →4064
風 (infectious) disease →3730
症 PATHOLOGICAL CONDITION →4065
患 AFFECTED BY DISEASE →3415
疫 EPIDEMIC →4061
罹 FALL ILL →3239
臥 be sick in bed →1825

❷ **fast**
速 QUICK →3851
早 QUICK →3042
疾 fast →4064
快 fast →0289
急 rapid →2595
迅 SWIFT →3780
敏 NIMBLE →1675
即 IMMEDIATE →1439
捷 AGILE →0609

症

4065
□3-5-5

▶**PATHOLOGICAL CONDITION**
ショウ
Ⓒ 症 zhèng zhēng

104	Jōyō	U75C7
疒	S10-5-5	F0900

Stroke order: 1–10

COMPOUNDS

[also suffix]

❶ **PATHOLOGICAL CONDITION, illness, disease, -osis, -ia**
神経症 しんけいしょう neurosis, nervous disease
既往症 きおうしょう previous illness, medical history
不眠症 ふみんしょう insomnia
尿毒症 にょうどくしょう uremia
重症 じゅうしょう serious illness

❷ [original meaning] **symptom, nature of a disease, syndrome**
症状 しょうじょう symptom
症候 しょうこう symptom
後遺症 こういしょう sequela, aftereffect (of a disease)
ダウン症 だうんしょう Down's syndrome

SYNONYMS

❶ **disease**
病 ILLNESS →4062
疾 DISEASE →4064
風 (infectious) disease →3730
症 PATHOLOGICAL CONDITION →4065
患 AFFECTED BY DISEASE →3415
疫 EPIDEMIC →4061
罹 FALL ILL →3239
臥 be sick in bed →1825

❷ **signs**
候 indication →0133
徴 SYMPTOM →0841
症 symptom (of a disease) →4065
気 sign →3960
兆 OMEN →0264

痕

4066
□3-5-6

▶**SCAR**
コン あと
Ⓒ 痕 hén

104	Jōyō	U75D5
疒	S11-5-6	F1927

Stroke order: 1–11

COMPOUNDS

ⓐ **SCAR**
ⓑ **trace(s), mark, trail**

a 瘢×痕組織 はんこんそしき scar tissue
聖痕 せいこん stigmata (in Christianity)
b 痕跡 こんせき trace, vestige
弾痕 だんこん bullet hole [mark]
墨痕 ぼっこん handwriting; ink marks
血痕 けっこん bloodstain

KUN

【あと 痕】 [also 跡] **SCAR**
傷痕 きずあと scar, cicatrix

爪痕 つめあと scratch, nail mark; ravages, after effects

SPECIAL READINGS

痘痕▲ あばた(=とうこん) pockmark

SYNONYMS

● **marks and signs**
標 MARK (identifying sign) → 1347
徽 EMBLEM → 0968
痕 SCAR → 4066
印 MARK (visible sign) → 1023
跡 TRACE → 1937
蹟 TRACE → 2065
踪 FOOTPRINTS → 1996
紋 print → 1651
符 SYMBOL → 3299
号 SIGN → 2675
栞 BOOKMARK → 3285

HOMOPHONES

あと
後 AFTER → 0431
跡 TRACE → 1937
蹟 TRACE → 2065

NOTE

➡ see USAGE note at 後 0431

疵 4067 □3-5-6

▶**DEFECT**
シ きず
Ⓒ 疵 cī

104 疒	Non-Jōyō	U75B5
	S11-5-6	F2810

COMPOUNDS

● **DEFECT, flaw, crack, fault, weak point**
疵瑕× しか flaw, blemish, defect
瑕×疵 かし defect, flaw

KUN

【きず 疵】[now usu. 傷] **DEFECT, flaw, crack, fault, weak point**
疵物 きずもの defective article; deflowered girl
玉に疵(=玉に瑕×) たまにきず flaw in the crystal, fly in the ointment
脛×に疵持つ すねにきずもつ have a guilty conscience

SYNONYMS

● **faults and flaws**
難 fault → 2310
短 shortcoming → 1515
疵 DEFECT → 4067
陥 defect → 0547
欠 incompleteness → 2481

HOMOPHONES

きず 傷 WOUND → 0179

NOTE

➡ see USAGE note at 傷 0179

崖 □3-5-6

incorrect classification
➡ see ▀2-3-8: 山 at 2862

戚 □3-5-6

incorrect classification
➡ see ■4-11-4 at 4401

痢 4068 □3-5-7

▶**DIARRHEA**
リ
Ⓒ 痢 lì

104 疒	Jōyō	U75E2
	S12-5-7	F2612

1	2	3	4	5	6	7	8	9	10	11	12
丶	亠	广	广	疒	疒	疒	疒	疒	疒	痢	痢

COMPOUNDS

● **DIARRHEA**
下痢 げり diarrhea
赤痢 せきり dysentery
疫痢 えきり children's dysentery

INDEPENDENT

【り 痢】**DIARRHEA**

SYNONYMS

● **diseases and disease symptoms**
痘 SMALLPOX → 4070
淋 GONORRHEA → 0632
癌 CANCER → 4076
熱 fever → 3555
炎 INFLAMMATION → 3075
痢 DIARRHEA → 4068
下 diarrhea → 4186

痩 4069 □3-5-7

▶**GET THIN**
ソウ シュウ▲ や(せる) こ(ける)▲
Ⓝ 痩 瘦 Ⓒ 瘦 shòu

104 疒	Jōyō	U75E9
	S12-5-7	F2911

1	2	3	4	5	6	7	8	9	10	11	12
丶	亠	广	广	疒	疒	疒	疒	疒	疒	痩	痩

COMPOUNDS

ⓐ **GET THIN, slim [thin] down, lose weight**

❻ thin, slim, slender, lean

a 痩身 そうしん slimming; slim [lean] figure

b 痩躯× そうく slim [lean] figure

KUN

【やせる 痩せる】

① **GET THIN, slim [thin] down, lose weight**

痩せた やせた thin, skinny; barren, infertile

痩せ衰える やせおとろえる become emaciated, grow thin and worn out

痩せ型 やせがた slender figure

痩せ我慢 やせがまん fake stoicism, pretended endurance

着痩せする きやせする look slender in clothing

② become barren [infertile]

痩せ地 やせち barren soil

【こける 痩ける】 become hollow, become scrawny

頬が痩ける ほおがこける get sunken cheeks

SYNONYMS

ⓐ thin

薄 THIN →3004

細 SLENDER →1689

繊 FINE →1789

痩 GET THIN →4069

痘

4070

□3-5-7

▶SMALLPOX

トウ

Ⓒ 痘 dòu

104	Jōyō	U75D8
疒	S12-5-7	F3277

COMPOUNDS

❶ [original meaning] **SMALLPOX**

痘瘡× とうそう smallpox

痘苗 とうびょう vaccine, vaccine virus; smallpox vaccine

天然痘 てんねんとう smallpox

種痘 しゅとう vaccination against smallpox

❷ pox

牛痘 ぎゅうとう cow pox, vaccinia

水痘 すいとう chicken pox, varicella

SYNONYMS

❶ & ❷ diseases and disease symptoms

痘 SMALLPOX →4070

淋 GONORRHEA →0632

癌 CANCER →4076

熱 fever →3555

炎 INFLAMMATION →3075

痢 DIARRHEA →4068

下 diarrhea →4186

NOTE

➡ see COMPOUND FORMATION for 痘苗 とうびょう →苗 2781

痛

4071

□3-5-7

▶PAIN

ツウ いた(い) いた(む) いた(ましい) いた(める)

Ⓒ 痛 tòng

104	Jōyō-6	U75DB
疒	S12-5-7	F0721

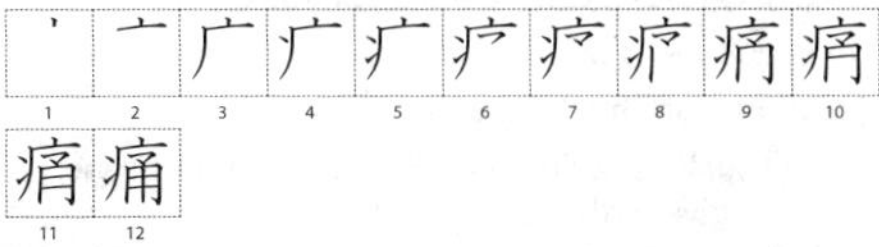

COMPOUNDS

❶ⓐ [also suffix] [original meaning] (physical suffering) **PAIN, ache**

ⓑ (mental suffering) **PAIN**, agony, grief, sadness

a 痛覚 つうかく sense of pain

苦痛 くつう pain, agony, anguish

頭痛 ずつう headache

鎮痛剤 ちんつうざい anodyne, painkiller

神経痛 しんけいつう neuralgia

筋肉痛 きんにくつう muscular pain

b 痛痒× つうよう interest, concern; pain and tickling

心痛 しんつう mental agony, heartache

悲痛な ひつうな sad, grievous

沈痛な ちんつうな grave, serious, sad

❷ bitter(ly), severe(ly), vehement(ly), keen(ly)

痛言 つうげん bitter criticism, harsh words

痛烈な つうれつな sharp, biting, scathing, cutting

痛感する つうかんする feel strongly, take to heart

痛快 つうかい thrill, keen pleasure

痛切に つうせつに keenly, acutely

痛打 つうだ hard blow, severe attack

痛恨 つうこん deep regret, great sorrow

KUN

【いたい 痛い】 **PAINful, sore; hard to bear, trying**

痛さ いたさ pain, ache

痛痛しい いたいたしい pitiful, pathetic

痛い目に遭わす いたいめにあわす make a person sweat for it

痛い損失 いたいそんしつ painful loss

歯痛 はいた toothache

手痛い ていたい severe, hard, heavy

【いたむ 痛む】

① **feel PAIN, hurt, ache**

痛み いたみ (physical or mental suffering) pain, ache
痛み止め いたみどめ painkiller, analgesic
② be **PAIN**ed, be grieved at heart
痛み入る いたみいる be greatly obliged; be very sorry
懐が痛む ふところがいたむ suffer in one's pocket [purse]
胸が痛む様な出来事 むねがいたむようなできごと painful incident

【いたましい 痛ましい】 **sad, piteous, miserable, heartbreaking, pathetic**
痛ましさ いたましさ sadness, piteousness

【いためる 痛める】
① **inflict PAIN, hurt, injure**
腹を痛める はらをいためる have a stomachache; give birth to
心を痛める こころをいためる be grieved at heart
② **PAIN, bother, worry, afflict**
痛め付ける いためつける rebuke, taunt; give a good shaking, knock about

SYNONYMS

❶ **trouble and suffering**
困 BE IN TROUBLE → 3808
苛 torment → 2786
窮 BE IN EXTREMITY → 2983
悶 BE IN AGONY → 4119
悩 SUFFER → 0504
苦 SUFFERING → 2789
痛 PAIN → 4071
辛 HARD → 2531
煩 VEXED → 1295
難 DIFFICULT → 2310

❷ **extreme in degree**
酷 SEVERE → 1967
強 STRONG → 0574
凄い tremendous → 0145
重 HEAVY → 4390
高 HIGH → 2601
深 DEEP → 0636
大 BIG → 4224
厳 SEVERE → 4079
激 intense → 0955
極 EXTREME → 1243
痛 bitter(ly) → 4071
切 keen → 0030
甚 EXTREMELY → 3271
祁 EXTREMELY → 1447
超 super- → 4107
頗る EXCEEDINGLY → 1552

USAGE

❶【いたむ】
痛む
① feel pain, hurt, ache
② be pained, be grieved at heart
傷む
① be damaged, be spoiled, wear out
② rot, spoil
悼む
mourn, grieve over, be grieved at

❷【いためる】
痛める
① inflict pain, hurt, injure
② pain, bother, worry, afflict
傷める
damage, spoil

HOMOPHONES

いたむ
傷 WOUND → 0179
悼 MOURN → 0587
いためる 傷 WOUND → 0179

痴

▶**STUPID**
チ し(れる)▲
Ⓝ 癡 Ⓒ 痴 chī

4072
□3-5-8

104	Jōyō	U75F4
疒	S13-5-8	F1896

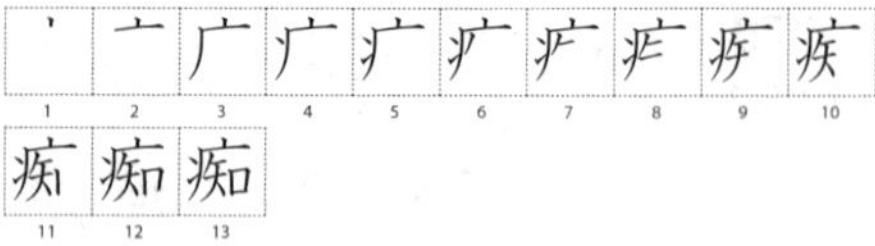

COMPOUNDS

❶ⓐ [original meaning] **STUPID, foolish, silly**
ⓑ lacking ability, slow
a 痴呆 ちほう imbecility, dementia
痴人 ちじん fool, simpleton, idiot, dunce
白痴 はくち idiocy, idiot
愚痴 ぐち idle complaint, grumble; querulousness
b 音痴 おんち tone deafness
運痴 うんち *colloq* slow in one's movements

❷ **infatuated, crazy about, blindly in love, amorous**
痴漢 ちかん molester of women, masher
痴情 ちじょう blind love, infatuation, amorous passion; jealousy
痴話 ちわ lover's talk, sweet nothings
情痴 じょうち love foolery

KUN

【しれる 痴れる】 *literary* be infatuated
痴れ者 しれもの fool, dunce, idiot
酔い痴れる よいしれる be fuddled [drunk] (with)

SYNONYMS

❶ **foolish**

愚 FOOLISH → 3513
暗 DARK → 1273
痴 STUPID → 4072
鈍 DULL → 2123
呆 DIM-WITTED → 2712
魯 DULL → 2665
闇 DARK → 4134
蒙 IGNORANCE → 2938

❷ **mania and maniacs**

痴 infatuated → 4072
狂 maniac → 0318
魔 maniac → 3953
熱 fever → 3555

瘦
☐3-5-8

incorrect stroke-count
➡ see ☐3-5-9: 疒 at 4074

導
☐3-5-9

incorrect classification/ stroke-count
➡ see ⬒2-12-3: 道 at 3587

瘍

4073
☐3-5-9

▶**SWELLING**
ヨウ
Ⓒ 疡 yáng

104 疒	Jōyō	U760D
	S14-5-9	F2242

Stroke order: 1–14

COMPOUNDS

● **SWELLING, boil, malignant growth [tumor]**

潰瘍 かいよう ulcer
腫瘍 しゅよう tumor, neoplasm, growth
腫瘍学 しゅようがく oncology
膿×瘍 のうよう abscess, boil

SYNONYMS

● **swell and swelling**

脹 SWELL → 1265
腫 SWELLING → 1310
瘍 SWELLING → 4073
爛 break out in sores → 1427

瘦

4074
☐3-5-9

▶**GET THIN**
ソウ シュウ や(せる) こ(ける)

104 疒	Nonstandard	U75E9
	S14-5-9	F0000

traditional form → see 痩 at 4069

瘦
☐3-5-9

incorrect stroke-count
➡ see ☐3-5-10: 疒 at 4075

瘦

4075
☐3-5-10

▶**GET THIN**
ソウ シュウ や(せる) こ(ける)

104 疒	Names	U7626
	S15-5-10	F0000

traditional form → see 痩 at 4069

蕨
☐3-5-10

incorrect classification
➡ see ⬒2-3-12: 艹 at 2992

癌

4076
☐3-5-12

▶**CANCER**
ガン
Ⓒ 癌 ái

104 疒	Non-Jōyō	U764C
	S17-5-12	F2326

COMPOUNDS

● [also suffix] [original meaning] **CANCER; cancerous**

癌腫 がんしゅ carcinoma
癌細胞 がんさいぼう cancer cell
癌遺伝子 がんいでんし oncogene, cancer gene
抗癌剤 こうがんざい anticancer drug
肺癌 はいがん lung cancer
乳癌 にゅうがん breast cancer
発癌 はつがん carcinogenesis, production of cancer
末期癌 まっきがん terminal cancer

INDEPENDENT

【がん 癌】 CANCER

SYNONYMS

● **diseases and disease symptoms**

痘 SMALLPOX → 4070
淋 GONORRHEA → 0632
癌 CANCER → 4076
熱 fever → 3555
炎 INFLAMMATION → 3075
痢 DIARRHEA → 4068
下 diarrhea → 4186

癈

4077
☐3-5-12

▶**DISABLED**
ハイ
Ⓒ 废 fèi

104 疒	Non-Jōyō	U7648
	S17-5-12	F0000

COMPOUNDS

● [now also 廃 3902] [original meaning] **DISABLED, crippled**

癈疾 はいしつ disablement

癈人 はいじん invalid, crippled person
癈兵 はいへい disabled soldier, crippled soldier

SYNONYMS

● **weak**
弱 WEAK → 1499
柔 SOFT → 2591
脆 FRAGILE → 1191
癈 DISABLED → 4077

療

▶TREAT
リョウ
Ⓒ 疗 liáo

4078
□3-5-12

104	Jōyō	U7642
疒	S17-5-12	F0644

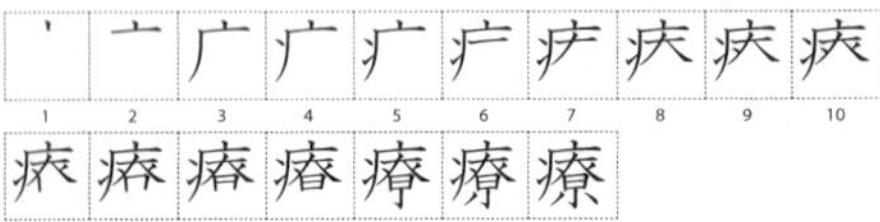

COMPOUNDS

ⓐ [original meaning] **TREAT, care for**
ⓑ **medical TREATment**
a 治療する ちりょうする treat, cure
診療 しんりょう diagnosis and treatment
b 療法 りょうほう method of treatment, cure, remedy
療養中 りょうようちゅう under medical care, in recuperation
医療 いりょう medical treatment [care]
施療 せりょう gratuitous treatment, free medical treatment
物療 ぶつりょう physiotherapy, physical treatment

SYNONYMS

● **cure and recover**
療 TREAT → 4078
治 CURE → 0393
医 cure → 3715
癒 HEAL → 4081
快 recover → 0289

厳

▶SEVERE
ゲン ゴン おごそ(か) きび(しい)
いか(めしい)▲ ㊔ いわお いつき いわ
Ⓝ 嚴 Ⓒ 严 yán

4079
□3-5-12

42△	Jōyō-6	U53B3
⺍	S17-3-14	F0849

COMPOUNDS

❶ [original meaning] **strict, SEVERE, stern, rigorous, harsh**
厳格な げんかくな strict, stern, severe, rigorous
厳密な げんみつな strict, precise, rigid, exact
厳正 げんせい exactness, strictness, rigor
厳重な げんじゅうな strict, severe, close; secure, firm, strong
厳守 げんしゅ strict observance
厳罰 げんばつ severe punishment
厳選 げんせん careful selection
戒厳令 かいげんれい martial law
❷ (of great intensity) **SEVERE, intense, extreme**
厳寒 げんかん severe [intense] cold
厳冬 げんとう severe winter
❸ [formerly also 儼 げん 0204] **solemn, grave, awe-inspiring, dignified**
厳然たる げんぜんたる solemn, grave, majestic, stern
厳粛な げんしゅくな grave, solemn, austere
威厳 いげん solemn dignity
謹厳な きんげんな stern, grave, solemn
荘厳な そうごんな solemn, sublime
❹ [honorific] father
厳父 げんぷ your honored father

INDEPENDENT

【げん 厳】 **SEVERE**ness, strictness, rigor
厳として げんとして strictly
警戒を厳にする けいかいをげんにする take strict precautions

KUN

【おごそか 厳か】
おごそかな 厳かな **solemn, grave, awe-inspiring, dignified**
厳かな儀式 おごそかなぎしき solemn ceremony
【きびしい 厳しい】 **SEVERE, strict, stern, rigorous, harsh;** (of great intensity) **severe, intense, extreme**
厳しさ きびしさ severity, strictness; intensity
厳しい批評 きびしいひひょう severe criticism
厳しい暑さ きびしいあつさ intense heat
【いかめしい 厳めしい】 grave, stern, dignified, majestic
厳めしい顔付き いかめしいかおつき grave [stern] look

SYNONYMS

❶ **strict**
厳 strict → 4079
酷 SEVERE → 1967
辣 SEVERE → 1965
峻 STERN → 0495
❷ **extreme in degree**

酷 SEVERE →1967
強 STRONG →0574
凄い tremendous →0145
重 HEAVY →4390
高 HIGH →2601
深 DEEP →0636
大 BIG →4224
厳 SEVERE →4079
激 intense →0955
極 EXTREME →1243
痛 bitter(ly) →4071
切 keen →0030
甚 EXTREMELY →3271
祁 EXTREMELY →1447
超 super- →4107
頗る EXCEEDINGLY →1552

❸ **dignified**
荘 DIGNIFIED →2814
威 dignified →4394
儼 SOLEMN →0204
厳 solemn →4079
粛 solemnly →4400

NOTE

➡ see COMPOUND FORMATION for 厳格 げんかく →格 1161

癖

4080
□3-5-13

▶HABIT
ヘキ くせ くせ(に)
Ⓒ 癖 pǐ

104	Jōyō	U7656
疒	S18-5-13	F1674

Stroke order: 1–18

COMPOUNDS

● [also suffix] **HABIT, habitual practice, propensity, peculiarity, weakness**
悪癖 あくへき bad habit, vice
性癖 せいへき one's natural disposition, propensity, mental habit
習癖 しゅうへき (bad) habit, habitual practice
病癖 びょうへき peculiarity, weakness, morbid habit
潔癖 けっぺき love of cleanliness, fastidiousness
飲酒癖 いんしゅへき inebriety, drinking habit
放浪癖 ほうろうへき vagrant habits, vagabondism

INDEPENDENT

【へき 癖】**HABIT**
奇矯な癖 ききょうなへき eccentric habit

KUN

【くせ 癖】**HABIT, habitual practice, propensity, peculiarity, weakness; mannerism, affectation; curl, kink**
癖の有る文章 くせのあるぶんしょう mannered style
癖毛 くせげ kinky hair
口癖 くちぐせ way [habit] of saying, one's favorite phrase
難癖 なんくせ fault, blemish
無くて七癖 なくてななくせ Every man has his own peculiar habits
爪を噛む癖 つめをかむくせ habit of biting one's nails

【くせに 癖に】**though, in spite of**
新米の癖に しんまいのくせに though (one is) only a beginner
知ってる癖に しってるくせに As if you didn't know!

SYNONYMS

● **custom**
慣 HABITUAL PRACTICE →0843
例 established practice →0099
習 CUSTOM →3306
風 manners →3730
俗 popular custom →0119
癖 HABIT →4080
弊 EVIL PRACTICE →3583

癒

4081
□3-5-13

▶HEAL
ユ い(える) い(やす)
Ⓝ 癒 Ⓒ 愈 yù

104	Jōyō	U7652
疒	S18-5-13	F1802

Stroke order: 1–18

COMPOUNDS

ⓐ [original meaning] **HEAL, recover**
ⓑ **HEAL (a wound), cure**
a 治癒 ちゆ healing, cure, recovery
平癒 へいゆ recovery, restoration to health
b 癒着 ゆちゃく adhesion, conglutination; connection, collusion
癒傷組織 ゆしょうそしき wound-healing tissue

KUN

【いえる 癒える】*poetic* **be cured, recover**
【いやす 癒やす】*poetic* **HEAL, cure, restore**
病を癒やす やまいをいやす cure an illness [a disease]

SYNONYMS

● **cure and recover**

療 TREAT → 4078
治 CURE → 0393
医 cure → 3715
癒 HEAL → 4081
快 recover → 0289

癒
4082
□3-5-13

▶**HEAL**
ユ い(える) い(やす)

104	Nonstandard	U7652
疒	S18-5-13	F0000

traditional form → see 癒 at 4081

繭
□3-5-13

incorrect classification
➡ see 2-3-15: 艹 at 3023

癡
4083
□3-5-14

▶**STUPID**
チ し(れる)

104	Nonstandard	U7661
疒	S19-5-14	F0000

traditional form → see 痴 at 4072

虎
□3-6-2

incorrect classification
➡ see □3-4-4: 虍 at 3981

芦
□3-6-2

incorrect classification/ stroke-count
➡ see 2-3-4: 艹 at 2743

啇
□3-6-3

incorrect classification
➡ see 2-2-7: 亠 at 2575

哉
4084
□3-6-3

▶**EXCLAMATORY PARTICLE**
サイ かな や ㊔ なり はじめ すけ ちか とし
Ⓒ 哉 zāi

30	Names	U54C9
口	S9-3-6	F1774

COMPOUNDS

● **EXCLAMATORY PARTICLE**

快哉を叫ぶ かいさいをさけぶ shout for joy, shout with exultation
善哉 ぜんざい Well done!/That's it!; thick bean-meal soup (with sugar and rice cake)

KUN

【かな 哉】 *literary* **EXCLAMATORY PARTICLE**, used esp. in classical texts: **Alas! Oh! How...! What...!**
悲しい哉 かなしいかな Alas!/How sad!
天なる哉、命なる哉 てんなるかな, めいなるかな All is decreed by Heaven

【や 哉】 [also 也 or 耶] **classical interrogative or rhetorical particle like modern か**
君迷える哉 きみまよえるや Did you lose your way?

SYNONYMS

● **classical particles**

耶 INTERROGATIVE PARTICLE → 1635
也 rhetorical particle → 4214
哉 EXCLAMATORY PARTICLE → 4084

HOMOPHONES

や

也 CLASSICAL COPULA → 4214
耶 INTERROGATIVE PARTICLE → 1635

NOTE

➡ see USAGE note at 也 4214

虐
□3-6-3

incorrect classification
➡ see □3-4-5: 虍 at 3989

彦
4085
□3-6-3

▶**MALE NAME ELEMENT**
ゲン ひこ ㊔ ひろ よし やす
Ⓝ 彥 Ⓒ 彦 yàn

59	Names	U5F66
彡	S9-3-6	F0886

COMPOUNDS

● [rare] gifted and virtuous man, man of fine character; handsome man; possessing laudable masculine qualities

俊彦 しゅんげん [rare] gifted [accomplished] man
諸彦 しょげん [rare] many accomplished persons

KUN

【ひこ 彦】
ⓐ **ELEMENT for forming MALE NAMEs**
ⓑ [archaic] handsome man, prince

SYNONYMS

【ひこ】

○ **name suffixes**

郎 MALE NAME SUFFIX → 1641
麿 CLASSICAL MALE NAME SUFFIX → 3949
彦 MALE NAME ELEMENT → 4085
-子 female name element → 4196

馬
4086
□3-6-4

▶**HORSE**
バ マ˄ メ˄ うま うま- ま ㊔ は
Ⓒ 马 mǎ

187	Jōyō-2	U99AC
馬	S10-10-0	F0298

丨	厂					馬	馬	馬	馬
1	2	3	4	5	6	7	8	9	10

RADICAL

uma 'horse' (驚 騰 駕), used in characters related to horses or their qualities
Left variant: 馬× ***umahen*** (験 駅 駐)

COMPOUNDS

❶ [also suffix] [original meaning] **HORSE**
馬車 ばしゃ horse-drawn carriage, coach, wagon
馬力 ばりき horsepower; energy, effort; cart, wagon
馬身 ばしん horse's length
馬肉 ばにく horsemeat
乗馬 じょうば horse riding
競馬 けいば horse racing
竹馬の友 ちくばのとも childhood friend, old playmate
関西馬 かんさいば Kansai horse

❷ name of chess piece in shogi (Japanese chess): *keima*, knight; *narikaku*, promoted bishop
桂馬 けいま *keima*, knight
竜馬 りゅうめ *narikaku*, promoted bishop

❸ **candidate (for an election)**
出馬する しゅつばする come forward as a candidate; go in person
有力馬 ゆうりょくば hopeful [promising, strong] candidate

❹ **used phonetically for *ba* or *ma***
馬鹿 ばか fool, blockhead; nonsense
馬克 まるく (German) mark

KUN

【うま 馬】
①ⓐ **HORSE, pony**
ⓑ **vaulting HORSE**
a 馬が合う うまがあう get on well (with a person)
馬屋 うまや [also 厩] horse stable, horse barn
勝馬 かちうま winning horse
竹馬 たけうま(=ちくば) stilts
② *keima, narikaku* (shogi chess pieces) (→❷)
③ stepping ladder
④ person who accompanies a reveler home to collect payment
付け馬 つけうま person who accompanies a reveler home to collect payment

【うま- 馬-】 **the larger of a species of animals or plants**
馬蠅× うまばえ horse botfly

【ま 馬】 [in compounds] **HORSE**
馬子 まご packhorse driver
絵馬 えま votive picture of a horse

SYNONYMS

❶ **horse**
馬 HORSE →4086
駒 HORSE (*elegant*) →2298
駿 FLEET STEED →2304
午 the Horse →2478

❶ **domesticated mammals**
牛 CATTLE →4263
馬 HORSE →4086
豚 PIG →1228
羊 SHEEP →2708
犬 DOG →4275
猫 CAT →0651
兎 RABBIT →4374

USAGE

【うま】
馬
①ⓐ horse, pony
ⓑ vaulting horse
② *keima, narikaku* (shogi chess pieces)
③ stepping ladder
④ person who accompanies a reveler home to collect payment

午
seventh sign of the Oriental zodiac: **the Horse**

HOMOPHONES

うま 午 NOON →2478
うまや
厩 HORSE STABLE →3746
馬屋 →4086, 3842

COMPOUND FORMATION

【馬鹿 ばか】
馬鹿 'fool, blockhead; nonsense' is unrelated to its constituent elements of 馬 ❶ 'horse' and 鹿 'deer', but is a transliteration of the Sanskrit word *moha* 'ignorance'.

NOTE

➡ see COMPOUND FORMATION for 竹馬 たけうま(=ちくば) →竹 0267

栽

4087
□3-6-4

▶**PLANT**
サイ
Ⓒ 栽 zāi

75	Jōyō	U683D
木	S10-4-6	F2036

一	十	土						栽	栽
1	2	3	4	5	6	7	8	9	10

COMPOUNDS

❶ **PLANT (saplings), transplant, grow, raise**
栽培 さいばい cultivation, raising, growing
植栽 しょくさい raising trees and plants
輪栽 りんさい rotation of crops
果樹栽培 かじゅさいばい fruit culture, pomiculture

❷ **garden PLANT, potted plant**

盆栽 ぼんさい bonsai (potted dwarf tree)

前栽 せんざい *elegant* trees and flowers in a garden; garden

SYNONYMS

❶ **farm and plant**

植 PLANT → 1247

栽 PLANT (saplings) → 4087

培 CULTIVATE → 0558

耕 TILL → 1659

作 raise crops → 0077

農 farm, FARMING → 3345

蒔 SOW → 2935

播 SOW → 0906

❷ **plants**

菜 VEGETABLE → 2880

植 PLANT → 1247

栽 garden plant → 4087

茨 thorny shrub → 2812

苔 MOSS → 2792

蔓 VINE → 2975

桔 PLANT NAME ELEMENT → 1164

烏

4088

□3-6-4

▶**CROW**

ウ オ からす

Ⓒ 乌 wū wù

86	Names	U70CF
灬	S10-4-6	F2060

COMPOUNDS

❶ **CROW, raven**

烏合の衆 うごうのしゅう disorderly crowd, mob

烏鷺 うろ crows and herons; black and white

烏滸×がましい おこがましい presumptuous, impertinent; ridiculous, absurd

❷ **black**

烏木(=烏文木) うぼく(=うぶんぼく) ebony

烏龍茶 うーろんちゃ oolong tea

❸ how, why

烏有 うゆう nonexistence ("how could it be")

❹ used phonetically for *u* in the transliteration of Sanskrit Buddhist terms

烏枢沙摩明王 うすさまみょうおう *Ucchuṣma* (a king of wisdom in Buddhism)

KUN

【からす 烏】

① **CROW, raven**

烏の行水 からすのぎょうずい quick bath

烏口 からすぐち ruling pen

海烏 うみがらす common murre, common guillemot

旅烏 たびがらす wanderer; stranger

三羽烏 さんばがらす trio, triumvirate

② [prefix] **black**

烏蛇 からすへび all-black variant of Japanese striped snake

烏揚羽 からすあげは Chinese peacock

SPECIAL READINGS

烏賊 いか cuttlefish, squid

烏帽子 えぼし black-lacquered headgear originally worn by court nobles in ancient Japan

烏玉 ぬばたま seed of the leopard lily; peyote

SYNONYMS

❶ **birds**

鷹 HAWK → 3955

鷗 GULL → 2370

烏 CROW → 4088

雀 SPARROW → 3117

燕 SWALLOW → 3142

鴻 LARGE WILD BIRD → 0977

鳳 MALE PHOENIX → 3749

凰 FEMALE PHOENIX → 3738

鵬 MYTHICAL HUGE BIRD → 1416

鶏 CHICKEN → 2221

酉 ROOSTER → 4358

隼 FALCON → 3427

鳩 PIGEON → 0184

鷲 EAGLE → 3598

鳶 BLACK KITE → 3919

鶴 CRANE → 2326

鷺 HERON → 3621

鵜 CORMORANT → 2067

鴨 DUCK → 1582

雁 WILD GOOSE → 3741

NOTE

★ do not confuse with 鳥 BIRD → 4105

虚處 etc.

incorrect classification

➡ see □3-4-7: 𠂆 at 4017

□3-6-5

産

4089

□3-6-5

▶**GIVE BIRTH**

▶**PRODUCE**

サン う(む) う(まれる) うぶ- む(す)▲

Ⓝ 產 Ⓒ 产 chǎn

100	Jōyō-4	U7523
生	S11-5-6	F0242

COMPOUNDS

❶ⓐ **GIVE BIRTH (to), deliver, bear, breed**

ⓑ **be born**

❻ childbirth, delivery

a 産婦 さんぷ woman in childbirth
産卵 さんらん egg-laying, spawning
産婦人科 さんふじんか obstetrics and gynecology
出産する しゅっさんする give birth (to), deliver, bear (a child)

b 産制 さんせい birth control

c 安産 あんざん easy [smooth] delivery (of a baby)
死産 しざん stillbirth

❷❹ PRODUCE, yield
❻ [also suffix] production

a 産出する さんしゅつする produce, yield
産業 さんぎょう industry
産地 さんち place of production; place of birth
産物 さんぶつ product, produce

b 国産 こくさん home [domestic] production

❸ product, PRODUCE
水産 すいさん marine products, fisheries
物産 ぶっさん product, produce
名産 めいさん noted product

❹ abbrev. of 産業 さんぎょう: **industry**
産別会議 さんべつかいぎ Congress of Industrial Organizations (CIO)
通産省 つうさんしょう Ministry of International Trade and Industry

❺ property, fortune, wealth
財産 ざいさん property, fortune, wealth
資産 しさん property, assets, fortune
倒産 とうさん insolvency, bankruptcy; breech birth
破産 はさん bankruptcy
共産主義 きょうさんしゅぎ Communism
不動産 ふどうさん immovable property, real estate

❻ suffix indicating place of origin or of birth
フロリダ産のオレンジ ふろりだざんのおれんじ oranges grown in Florida

INDEPENDENT

【さん 産】childbirth; native of...; product; property, fortune, wealth
お産 おさん childbirth, delivery
産を成す さんをなす amass a fortune
京都の産 きょうとのさん native of Kyoto

【さんする 産する】**PRODUCE, grow**

KUN

【うむ 産む】(produce offspring) **GIVE BIRTH to, bear offspring, beget, breed; spawn**
産み うみ (physical) birth
産み出す うみだす begin to give birth to
産み月 うみづき last month of pregnancy
彼女は子供を五人産んだ かのじょはこどもをごにんうんだ She gave birth to five children

【うまれる 産まれる】(undergo the physical act of birth) **be born**
赤ん坊が産まれた あかんぼうがうまれた The baby was born

【うぶ- 産-】**related to birth, as when born**
産声 うぶごえ baby's first cry
産毛 うぶげ downy hair

【むす 産す】[also 生す] grow
苔産した こけむした moss-grown, mossy

SPECIAL READINGS

土産 みやげ souvenir

SYNONYMS

❶ give birth
生 BE BORN →4309
誕 BE BORN →1987
産 GIVE BIRTH →4089
娩 GIVE BIRTH →0486
殖 MULTIPLY →1253

❷❹ make
作 MAKE →0077
造 MAKE →3856
成 FORM →4352
工 MANUFACTURE →4190
製 MANUFACTURE →3478
産 PRODUCE →4089
調 PREPARE →1973
組む ASSEMBLE →1693
構 CONSTRUCT →1325

❸ merchandise
産 product →4089
品 ARTICLE (of merchandise) →2795
貨 GOODS →3113
物 commodity →1084

❹ industry and business
業 BUSINESS, INDUSTRY →3227
商 TRADE →2623
産 industry →4089
工 manufacturing industry →4190

❺ wealth
財 WEALTH →1849
産 property →4089
富 riches →2892
宝 TREASURE →2764

USAGE

❶【うむ】
産む
(produce offspring) give birth to, bear offspring, beget, breed; spawn
彼女は子供を五人産んだ かのじょはこどもをごにんうんだ She gave birth to five children

生む

① have children

② produce, bring forth, give rise to, yield

彼女は子供を五人生んだ かのじょはこどもをごにんうんだ She has five children

★These verbs share the meaning of giving birth. 産む, the more common form, refers to the physical act of bearing offspring, while 生む is used in the more abstract sense of having children. The principal use of 生む is in the sense of producing or giving rise to.

❷【うみ】

産み

(physical) birth

生み

production, bringing into the world

❸【うまれる】

産まれる

(undergo the physical act of birth) be born

男の子が産まれた おとこのこがうまれた A boy was born

生まれる

ⓐ (of persons) (come into being) be born, come into existence

ⓑ (of things in general) appear, see the light, be a result (of)

彼はアメリカで生まれた かれはあめりかでうまれた He was born in America

★産まれる is used in the narrow sense of being born, referring to the physical act of birth. 生まれる is used in the broader sense of a person coming into the world.

HOMOPHONES

うむ 生 LIFE → 4309

うみ 生 LIFE → 4309

うまれる 生 LIFE → 4309

むす

生 LIFE → 4309

蒸 STEAM → 2936

NOTE

➡ see also USAGE note at 生 4309

商

3-6-5

incorrect classification

➡ see 2-2-9: 亠 at 2623

裁

4090

3-6-6

▶CUT OUT

▶JUDGE

サイ た(つ) さば(く)

Ⓒ 裁 cái

145	Jōyō-6	U88C1
衣	S12-6-6	F0706

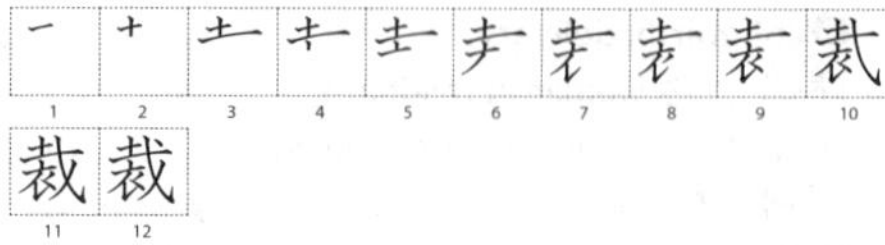

COMPOUNDS

❶ⓐ [original meaning] **CUT OUT (a garment)**

ⓑ abbrev. of 裁縫 さいほう: **sewing, dressmaking**

a 裁縫 さいほう sewing, needlework, dressmaking

裁断師 さいだんし (tailor's) cutter

b 洋裁 ようさい foreign-style dressmaking

和裁 わさい Japanese dressmaking

❷ (pass judgment) **JUDGE, decide, try, arbitrate**

裁判 さいばん trial, judgment, decision

裁定 さいてい decision, ruling, arbitration

裁決 さいけつ decision, ruling

裁量 さいりょう discretion

制裁 せいさい sanction, punishment, discipline

仲裁 ちゅうさい arbitration, mediation

❸ abbrev. of 裁判所 さいばんしょ: court

最高裁 さいこうさい Supreme Court

家裁 かさい family court

❹ **rule, administer, manage**

総裁 そうさい president, governor

独裁 どくさい dictatorship, autocracy

❺ **form, style**

体裁 ていさい decency, form, style, appearance

KUN

【たつ 裁つ】**CUT OUT (a garment), cut (paper)**

裁ち出す たちだす cut out (a dress) from cloth

裁ち縫い たちぬい cutting and sewing

裁ち板 たちいた (tailor's) cutting board

【さばく 裁く】**JUDGE, pass judgment, decide**

裁き さばき judgment, decision, verdict

裁きの庭 さばきのにわ law court

SYNONYMS

❶ⓐ **cut**

切 CUT → 0030

薙ぐ MOW DOWN → 3010

剪 PRUNE → 2886

削 CUT BY CHIPPING → 1837

挽く GRIND, saw → 0511

断 CUT OFF → 1885

截 CUT OFF → 4092

裁 CUT OUT → 4090

斬 CUT WITH A SWORD → 1874

割 cut with a knife → 2284

剖 DISSECT → 2103

刈る CLIP → 0032

伐 CUT DOWN → 0046

❷ **judge**
判 JUDGE → 1441
裁 JUDGE → 4090
鑑 APPRAISE → 2226
評 evaluate → 1895
審 TRY → 2985
決 DECIDE → 0308
視 REGARD → 1223
❸ **court**
廷 COURT → 3795
裁 court → 4090
HOMOPHONES
たつ
断 CUT OFF → 1885
絶 BREAK OFF → 1711
NOTE
➡ see USAGE note at 断 1885

虚 虜 incorrect classification
➡ see □3-4-8: 产 at 4025
□3-6-6

載

▸**LOAD**
▸**PUT IN PRINT**
サイ の(せる) の(る)
Ⓒ 载 zài zǎi

4091
□3-6-7

159	Jōyō	U8F09
車	S13-7-6	F0693

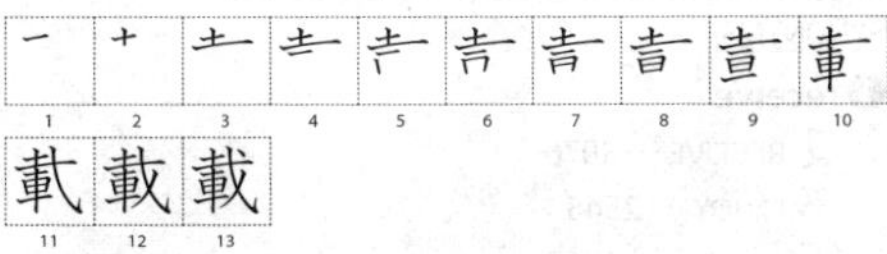

COMPOUNDS
❶ [original meaning] **LOAD (a vehicle or ship with cargo), lade, carry**
満載する まんさいする be loaded to capacity (with)
積載する せきさいする load (a vehicle or ship with cargo), carry
搭載 とうさい loading, embarkation
混載 こんさい mixed loading
❷ⓐ **PUT IN PRINT, publish, carry, put on record**
ⓑ **appear in print, be published**
a 載録する さいろくする record
掲載 けいさい publication, insertion, printing
記載する きさいする record, state, mention
ab 連載 れんさい serialization, serial publication
転載する てんさいする reproduce, reprint
登載する とうさいする register, record
❸ year
千載一遇 せんざいいちぐう once in a thousand years
❹ [archaic] one hundred tredecillion (10^{44})
KUN
【のせる 載せる】
① **LOAD (a vehicle or ship with cargo), lade, carry**
船に貨物を載せる ふねにかもつをのせる load a ship with cargo
② **place on, put on**
棚に本を載せる たなにほんをのせる place a book on a shelf
③ **PUT IN PRINT, publish, carry, put on record**
記録に載せる きろくにのせる put on record
【のる 載る】
① **appear in print, be published, be recorded**
新聞に載る しんぶんにのる appear in the newspaper
② **be placed upon**
棚の上に載っている たなのうえにのっている be [lie] on a shelf
③ be **LOAD**ed (on a vehicle)
SYNONYMS
❶ **load**
載 LOAD → 4091
積む load → 1579
搭 load on board → 0721
❷ **print and publish**
刷 PRINT → 1623
印 print → 1023
植 typeset → 1247
刊 PUBLISH → 0221
版 PUBLISHING → 1082
載 PUT IN PRINT → 4091
掲 display in writing → 0597
幀 BOOKBINDING → 0695
HOMOPHONES
のせる 乗 RIDE → 4393
のる 乗 RIDE → 4393
NOTE
➡ see USAGE note at 乗 4393
★ do not confuse with 戴 RECEIVE HUMBLY → 4093

虜 虞 etc. incorrect classification
➡ see □3-4-9: 产 at 4037
□3-6-7

截

▸**CUT OFF**
セツ サイ き(る)
Ⓒ 截 jié

4092
□3-6-8

62	Non-Jōyō	U622A
戈	S14-4-10	F3193

COMPOUNDS
● [now also 切 せつ 0030] [original meaning] **CUT OFF, sever**

截断 せつだん cutting
截然たる せつぜんたる distinct, clear-cut, sharp
直截な ちょくせつ(=ちょくさい)な direct, plain, straightforward

戈【产】

KUN

【きる 截る】[now usu. 切る] **cut (flat things such as cloth or paper)**
布を截る ぬのをきる cut cloth

SYNONYMS

● **cut**
切 CUT → 0030
薙ぐ MOW DOWN → 3010
剪 PRUNE → 2886
削 CUT BY CHIPPING → 1837
挽く GRIND, saw → 0511
断 CUT OFF → 1885
截 CUT OFF → 4092
裁 CUT OUT → 4090
斬 CUT WITH A SWORD → 1874
割 cut with a knife → 2284
剖 DISSECT → 2103
刈る CLIP → 0032
伐 CUT DOWN → 0046

HOMOPHONES

きる
切 CUT → 0030
伐 CUT DOWN → 0046
剪 PRUNE → 2886
斬 CUT WITH A SWORD → 1874

NOTE

➡ see USAGE note at 切 0030

麻
☐3-6-8
incorrect classification
➡ see ▀2-3-11: 艹 at 2978

導
☐3-6-9
incorrect classification
➡ see ▀2-12-3: 道 at 3587

慮膚
☐3-6-9
incorrect classification
➡ see ☐3-4-11: 广 at 4049

薦
☐3-6-10
incorrect classification
➡ see ▀2-3-13: 艹 at 3008

戴

4093
☐3-6-11

▶**RECEIVE HUMBLY**
タイ いただ(く)▲
Ⓝ 戴 Ⓒ 戴 dài

62	Jōyō	U6234
戈	S17-4-13	F2008

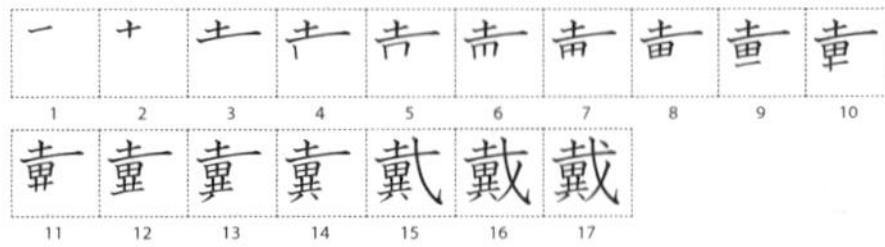

COMPOUNDS

❶ **RECEIVE HUMBLY, accept with thanks**
頂戴する ちょうだいする [humble] receive, accept, take; eat, drink

❷ have over, be presided over by, live under (a ruler)
推戴する すいたいする have over, be presided over by
奉戴する ほうたいする have over, be presided over by, live under
不倶戴天 ふぐたいてん cannot live together under the canopy of heaven

❸ [original meaning] be crowned with, wear (a crown)
戴冠式 たいかんしき coronation (ceremony)
戴白 たいはく becoming gray haired; old people

KUN

【いただく 戴く】[usu. 頂く] [humble]
① ⓐ **RECEIVE HUMBLY, accept with thanks, be given, be favored with**
ⓑ **eat, drink**
ⓒ **trouble someone to do something, have something done**
② have over, be presided over by, live under (a ruler)
③ wear (a crown); be crowned (with snow)
→ see 頂 0164 for compounds

SYNONYMS

❶ **receive**
受 RECEIVE → 3076
享 ENJOY → 2545
領 receive → 1567
収 TAKE IN → 0031
納 ACCEPT → 1652
貰 GET → 3219
戴 RECEIVE HUMBLY → 4093
頂 RECEIVE HUMBLY → 0164
拝 have the honor to receive → 0360

HOMOPHONES

いただく 頂 SUMMIT → 0164

NOTE

➡ see USAGE note at 頂 0164
★ do not confuse with 載 LOAD → 4091

戴
☐3-6-11
incorrect stroke-count
➡ see ☐3-6-12: 戈 at 4094

戴 4094

□3-6-12

▶RECEIVE HUMBLY

タイ いただ(く)

62	Nonstandard	U6234
戈	S18-4-14	F0000

traditional form → see 戴 at 4093

赴 4095

□3-7-2

▶PROCEED TO

フ おもむ(く)

Ⓒ 赴 fù

156	Jōyō	U8D74
走	S9-7-2	F1988

1	2	3	4	5	6	7	8	9
一	+	土	キ	キ	未	走	赴	赴

COMPOUNDS

● **PROCEED TO (as a new appointment), go to, head for, attend**

赴任 ふにん proceeding to a new post

KUN

【おもむく 赴く】[sometimes also 趣く]

① **PROCEED TO, go to, head for**

死地に赴く しちにおもむく ride into the jaws of death

② become, tend towards

快方に赴く かいほうにおもむく get better, improve, convalesce

SYNONYMS

● **go and come**

行 GO → 0246
徠 COME → 0576
往 GO ON → 0348
出 go to → 4310
参 go somewhere → 2563
来 COME → 4366
通 go to and from → 3855
向 head toward → 3790
赴 PROCEED TO → 4095
嚮 GO TOWARD → 3610

USAGE

【おもむく】

赴く
[sometimes also 趣く]
① proceed to, go to, head for
② become, tend towards

趣く
[usu. 赴く] same as 赴く

HOMOPHONES

おもむく 趣 FLAVOR → 4111

赳 4096

□3-7-2

▶VALIANT

キュウ ㊔ たけ たけし つよし いさむ

156	Nonstandard	U8D73
走	S9-7-2	F0000

traditional form → see 赳 at 4100

剋 4097

□3-7-2

▶OVERCOME

コク

Ⓝ 尅 Ⓒ 克 kè 剋 kēi kè

18	Non-Jōyō	U524B
刂	S9-2-7	F3192

COMPOUNDS

● [now usu. 克 2540] [original meaning] **OVERCOME, conquer, win**

下剋上 げこくじょう the lower dominating the upper

相剋する そうこくする struggle with each other, conflict

SYNONYMS

● **win**

勝 WIN → 1268
克 OVERCOME → 2540
剋 OVERCOME → 4097
征 CONQUER → 0349
破 BREAK → 1478
凱 TRIUMPH → 2286

勉 4098

□3-7-2

▶ENDEAVOR

ベン つと(める) ㊔ つとむ

19	Names	UFA33
力	S9-2-7	F0000

traditional form → see 勉 at 4113

起 4099

□3-7-3

▶RISE

キ お(きる) お(こる) お(こす) た(つ)▲

Ⓝ 起 Ⓒ 起 qǐ

156	Jōyō-3	U8D77
走	S10-7-3	F0258

1	2	3	4	5	6	7	8	9	10
一	+	土	キ	キ	未	走	起	起	起

COMPOUNDS

❶ⓐ [original meaning] (assume a standing position) **RISE (to one's feet), stand up**

ⓑ (get out of bed) **RISE, get up**

a 起立する きりつする stand up, rise

起居 ききょ one's daily life

b 起床 きしょう getting up, rising

起座する きざする sit up in bed

❷ⓐ (project upward) **RISE, protrude**

ⓑ **raise up, lift**

【走】克 鳥 羊 苻

a 起伏 きふく ups and downs, undulations
突起する とっきする project, protrude
隆起 りゅうき protuberance, elevation
b 起重機 きじゅうき crane, derrick

❸ **used in forming verbal compounds**—roughly equiv. to *up* in *bring up*
提起する ていきする raise (a question), bring forward
喚起する かんきする awaken, rouse, arouse
想起する そうきする remember, recollect

❹ call into office
起用 きよう appointment, employment

❺ **RISE [rouse oneself] to action, spring up, be stirred up**
奮起する ふんきする rouse [bestir] oneself, rise (to the occasion)
決起する けっきする rise to action, spring up
再起 さいき comeback, recovery, restoration

❻ⓐ **start, begin, initiate, promote**
ⓑ **starting point, beginning, origin**
ⓒ first stanza in a Chinese quatrain; the opening line
a 起訴 きそ prosecution, indictment, litigation
起草する きそうする draft (a bill), draw up
起工 きこう start of construction work
起爆 きばく priming (in explosives)
b 起点 きてん starting point, terminus
起源 きげん origin, beginning
起因する きいんする originate in, be attributable to
縁起 えんぎ origin, history; omen, luck
c 起承転結 きしょうてんけつ introduction, development, turn and conclusion (of a Chinese quatrain)
起句 きく opening line of a Chinese quatrain

❼ generate, produce
起電 きでん generation of electricity
起磁力 きじりょく magnetomotive force
励起 れいき excitation

KUN

【おきる 起きる】
①ⓐ **RISE to one's feet, get up**
ⓑ **RISE (from one's bed), get out of bed**
a 起き上がる おきあがる get up, rise
b 早起き はやおき early rising
② **wake up, awake**
遅く迄起きている おそくまでおきている stay up late
③ **happen, take place, occur, break out**
クーデターが起きた くーでたーがおきた A coup d'état broke out
④ begin to burn, be kindled
良く起きた火 よくおきたひ blazing fire

【おこる 起こる】
① **happen, occur, take place**
沸き起こる わきおこる arise
② [also 興る] (come into existence) **RISE, spring up, be established**
新たに起こった国 あらたにおこったくに newly established country
③ **arise from, originate in, result from**
起こり おこり origin, source, beginning; cause, genesis
不眠から起こる疲労 ふみんからおこるひろう fatigue resulting from insomnia
④ (of heat or electricity) **be generated, be produced**
摩擦で起こった熱 まさつでおこったねつ heat generated from friction
⑤ (of diseases) **develop, have an attack of**
喘×息が起こる ぜんそくがおこる have an attack of asthma
⑥ be kindled
赤赤と起こった火 あかあかとおこったひ blazing fire

【おこす 起こす】
① **raise up, set upright**
抱き起こす だきおこす lift (a person) in one's arms, help (a person) sit up
② **wake up, awake, arouse**
揺り起こす ゆりおこす shake up, wake by shaking
③ **give RISE to, bring about, raise**
引き起こす ひきおこす bring about, cause, provoke; pull up
④ⓐ start, begin, launch, inaugurate
ⓑ establish, set up
a 書き起こす かきおこす begin [start] writing
b 会社を起こす かいしゃをおこす set up a company
⑤ (of heat or electricity) **produce, generate**
水力で電気を起こす すいりょくででんきをおこす generate electricity by hydraulic power
⑥ plow
畑を起こす はたけをおこす plow a field

【たつ 起つ】[now usu. 立つ] **RISE** (to action), rouse oneself
起ち居 たちい one's movement
祖国の為に起つ そこくのためにたつ rise to the rescue of one's country

SYNONYMS

❶ **assume upright position**
立 STAND → 2486
起 RISE → 4099

❷ⓐ **protrude and protruding**
突 protruding → 2772
凸 CONVEX → 4298
隆 protuberant → 0661
起 RISE → 4099

出る stick out →4310
ⓑ raise
揚 RAISE HIGH →0722
掲 PUT UP →0597
挙 RAISE →3106
上 raise →4212
起 raise up →4099
擡 RAISE (one's head) →0972
立てる STAND →2486
拾う PICK UP →0454
❺ incite
挑 PROVOKE →0445
唆 INSTIGATE →0480
扇 FAN →2449
煽 FAN →1338
激 excite →0955
奮 ROUSE UP →3000
振 arouse to action →0515
動 MOVE →2232
起 rise to action →4099
❻ⓐ begin
始 BEGIN →0335
-出す begin to do →4310
-掛ける start doing →0596
発 START →3174
起 start →4099
就 SET ABOUT →2129
開 OPEN →4121
創 initiate →2283
肇 ORIGINATE →3474
❼ create
創 CREATE →2283
作 compose →0077
綴 COMPOSE →1746
生 produce →4309
発 START →3174
起 generate →4099

USAGE

❶【おこる】
起こる
① happen, occur, take place
② [also 興る] (come into existence) rise, spring up, be established
③ arise from, originate in, result from
④ (of heat or electricity) be generated, be produced
⑤ (of diseases) develop, have an attack of
⑥ be kindled
興る
① rise to prosperity, prosper, thrive, flourish
② [also 起こる] (come into existence) rise, spring up, be established

❷【おこす】
起こす
① raise up, set upright
② wake up, awake, arouse
③ give rise to, bring about, raise
④ⓐ start, begin, launch, inaugurate
ⓑ establish, set up
⑤ (of heat or electricity) produce, generate
⑥ plow
興す
cause to rise (to prosperity), promote, further, advance, develop

HOMOPHONES

おこる 興 RISE TO PROSPERITY →3622
おこす 興 RISE TO PROSPERITY →3622
たつ
立 STAND →2486
建 BUILD →3834
発 START →3174
経 PASS THROUGH →1687

NOTE

➡ see also USAGE note at 立 2486

赳

4100
□3-7-3

▶**VALIANT**
キュウ ㊔ たけ たけし つよし いさむ
Ⓝ 赳 Ⓒ 赳 jiū

156	Names	U8D73
走	S10-7-3	F3117

COMPOUNDS

● [rare] **VALIANT**, brave and strong, gallant
赳赳たる武夫 きゅうきゅうたるぶふ soldier of dauntless courage

SYNONYMS

● **brave**
勇 BRAVE →2592
侠 chivalrous →0110
赳 VALIANT →4100
驍 VALIANT →2327
敢 bold →2142
豪 bold and unrestrained →2657
雄 HEROIC →1271
壮 heroic →0263
義 chivalrous →2948
凜 gallant →0195

起

4101
□3-7-3

▶**RISE**
キ お(きる) お(こる) お(こす) た(つ)

156	Nonstandard	U8D77
走	S10-7-3	F0000

traditional form →see 起 at 4099

走 【克】 鳥 羊 芇

尅 4102

□3-7-3

▶**OVERCOME**

コク

41	Nonstandard	U5C05
寸	S10-3-7	F0000

traditional form → see 剋 at 4097

島 4103

□3-7-3

▶**ISLAND**

トウ しま

Ⓝ 嶋 㠀 嶌 陦 Ⓒ 岛 dǎo

46	Jōyō-3	U5CF6
山	S10-3-7	F0184

1	2	3	4	5	6	7	8	9	10
′	亻	户	户	自	自	鳥	鳥	島	島

COMPOUNDS

ⓐ [also suffix] [original meaning] **ISLAND**
ⓑ suffix after names of **ISLAND**s

a 島嶼× とうしょ islands
島民 とうみん islanders
諸島 しょとう archipelago
半島 はんとう peninsula
列島 れっとう archipelago
無人島 むじんとう uninhabited island
b 色丹島 しこたんとう Shikotan Island

KUN

【しま 島】[also suffix] **ISLAND, isle, islet**
島国 しまぐに island country
島巡り しまめぐり tour of the islands, tour of an island
離れ島 はなれじま solitary island
宝島 たからじま treasure island
八丈島 はちじょうじま Hachijo Island

SYNONYMS

● **elevations in water**
島 ISLAND → 4103
州 sandbar → 0064
礁 REEF → 1588
洲 SANDBAR → 0467

USAGE

【しま】
島
[also suffix] island, isle, islet
縞
stripe, streak

HOMOPHONES

しま 縞 STRIPE → 1784

差 4104

□3-7-3

▶**DIFFERENCE**

サ さ(す) さ(し)

Ⓒ 差 chà chā chāi cī

48	Jōyō-4	U5DEE
工	S10-3-7	F0464

1	2	3	4	5	6	7	8	9	10
`	ˊˋ	䒑	䒑	羊	羊	差	差	差	差

COMPOUNDS

❶ [also suffix]
ⓐ [original meaning] **DIFFERENCE, discrepancy, inequality, differential**
ⓑ (quantitative) **DIFFERENCE;** *math* **remainder**

a 差異 さい difference, disparity
差別 さべつ discrimination
大差 たいさ big difference
格差 かくさ difference in quality [price]
個人差 こじんさ individual differences
b 差額 さがく difference (in prices), balance
時差 じさ time difference

❷ [formerly 叉 4194] **cross, intersect**
交差 こうさ crossing, intersection
三差路 さんさろ three-forked road

❸ dispatch, expedite
差遣する さけんする dispatch, send
差配人 さはいにん real estate agent

INDEPENDENT

【さ 差】**DIFFERENCE;** *math* **remainder**
差を付ける さをつける discriminate; establish a lead
賃金の差 ちんぎんのさ wage difference

KUN

【さす 差す】
① **offer, present, provide**
杯を差す さかずきをさす offer a cup (of sake)
② **hold up, spread (over one's hand)**
傘を差す かさをさす hold an umbrella
③ **wear in one's belt or hair**
刀を差す かたなをさす wear a sword
④ become tinged with
赤味が差している あかみがさしている tinged red
⑤ (of water) rise, flow
潮が差す しおがさす The tide comes in
⑥ be struck by
魔が差す まがさす be tempted by an evil spirit
⑦ [sometimes also 注す] pour (into), fill up
器に水を差す うつわにみずをさす fill a pitcher with water
⑧ [sometimes also 注す] color
⑨ [also 射す] shine on

障子に影が差す しょうじにかげがさす A shadow is cast on the *shoji* (paper sliding door)

【さし 差し】

①ⓐ [emphatic or polite prefix] **do, execute**

ⓑ [verbal prefix] **send, present**

a 差し当たり(=差し当たって) さしあたり(=さしあたって) for the time being, for the present, at present

差し上げる さしあげる give (to superior)

差し控える さしひかえる be moderate in; withhold, desist from, refrain from

差し止める さしとめる prohibit, forbid; suspend (a paper)

差し掛かる さしかかる come near, approach

差し引き さしひき balance (of an account); ebb and flow

差し支え さしつかえ hindrance, complications; objections

b 差し回す さしまわす send (a car) around

差し出す さしだす present, submit, send; stretch, reach

差し出し先 さしだしさき address

② [in compounds] **measure, measuring**

物差し ものさし ruler

③ [in compounds] vessel for pouring

水差し みずさし pitcher, jug

④ counter for dances

⑤ sumo move

⑥ tête-à-tête

差しで さしで between two persons, face to face

⑦ **unclassified compounds**

眼差し まなざし look, expression

SYNONYMS

❶ **differing and difference**

違 DIFFER → 3907

異 DIFFERENT → 3195

差 DIFFERENCE → 4104

❷ **intercross**

交 intercross → 2508

差 cross → 4104

USAGE

❶【さす】

差す

① offer, present, provide

② hold up, spread (over one's hand)

③ wear in one's belt or hair

④ become tinged with

⑤ (of water) rise, flow

⑥ be struck by

⑦ [sometimes also 注す] pour (into), fill up

⑧ [sometimes also 注す] color

⑨ [also 射す] shine on

指す

①ⓐ point to, point at, indicate

ⓑ aim at, have in view

② appoint, nominate; finger, accuse

③ play board games (esp. shogi)

刺す

①ⓐ stab, pierce, prick, thrust

ⓑ sting, bite

② sew, stitch

③ *baseball* catch (a runner) out

挿す

ⓐ insert, put into, stick between

ⓑ insert seedlings, plant

注す

[usu. 差す]

① pour (into), fill up

② color

射す

[also 差す] shine on

-止す

[verbal suffix] leave something unfinished, stop in the middle

★The relationship between the above seven verbs is complicated, and lexicographers disagree as to their proper usage. Their recommended, but not necessarily universal, usage is as shown. Study the equivalents and examples under the respective entries. It is interesting to note that さす can be written in a total of 91 different ways!

❷【さし】

差し

①ⓐ [emphatic or polite prefix] do, execute

ⓑ [verbal prefix] send, present

② [in compounds] measure, measuring

③ [in compounds] vessel for pouring

④ counter for dances

⑤ sumo move

⑥ tête-à-tête

⑦ unclassified compounds

刺し

① stabbing, piercing, pricking

② stitch

③ *sashimi,* sliced raw flesh (esp. of fish)

-指し

[suffix] player (of shogi)

-止し

[verbal suffix] leaving something unfinished

HOMOPHONES

さす

指 FINGER → 0452

刺 STAB → 1625

挿 INSERT → 0517

注 POUR → 0383

射 SHOOT → 1850

止 STOP →3659

さし

刺 STAB →1625

指 FINGER →0452

止 STOP →3659

荷 incorrect classification
➡ see ▀2-3-7: 艹 at 2840
□3-7-3

鳥

▶BIRD
チョウ とり
Ⓒ 鸟 niǎo diǎo

4105
□3-7-4

196	Jōyō-2	U9CE5
鳥	S11-11-0	F0848

Stroke order: 1–11

RADICAL

tori 'bird' (鷹 鴬× 鷲), used in characters related to bird names

Right variant: 鳥× *tori* (鳴 鶏 鳩)

COMPOUNDS

● [also suffix] [original meaning] **BIRD, fowl**

鳥類 ちょうるい birds, fowls
野鳥 やちょう wild fowl, wild bird
愛鳥週間 あいちょうしゅうかん Bird Week
保護鳥 ほごちょう protected bird
益鳥 えきちょう beneficial bird
害鳥 がいちょう injurious bird
白鳥 はくちょう swan
七面鳥 しちめんちょう turkey
雷鳥 らいちょう snow grouse
一石二鳥 いっせきにちょう killing two birds with one stone

KUN

【とり 鳥】

ⓐ [sometimes also 禽] **BIRD, fowl**
ⓑ [also 鶏] **chicken; fowl, poultry**

a 鳥居 とりい torii, Shinto shrine archway (开)
海鳥 うみどり seabird
小鳥 ことり small [little] bird
渡り鳥 わたりどり migratory bird
水鳥 みずとり waterfowl
大鳥 おおとり [also 鳳, 鴻 or 鵬] large wild bird such as crane or white stork; huge bird such as a mythical Chinese phoenix

b 鳥肉 とりにく chicken
鳥屋 とりや bird dealer; poulterer
雌鳥 めんどり hen

SPECIAL READINGS

鳥取県 とっとりけん Tottori Prefecture

SYNONYMS

● **bird**

鳥 BIRD →4105
禽 BIRD →2654
雛 CHICK →2312

USAGE

【とり】

鳥
ⓐ [sometimes also 禽] bird, fowl
ⓑ [also 鶏] chicken; fowl, poultry

鶏
[also 鳥] chicken; fowl, poultry

禽
[usu. 鳥] bird, fowl

酉
tenth sign of the Oriental zodiac: the Rooster (→●)

HOMOPHONES

とり

鶏 CHICKEN →2221
酉 THE ROOSTER →4358
禽 BIRD →2654

おおとり

鳳 MALE PHOENIX →3749
鴻 LARGE WILD BIRD →0977
鵬 MYTHICAL HUGE BIRD →1416
大鳥 →4224, 4105

NOTE

★ do not confuse with 烏 CROW →4088

羞

▶SHY
シュウ は(じる)▲ はじ▲ は(じらう)▲ は(ずかしい)▲
Ⓒ 羞 xiū

4106
□3-7-4

123	Jōyō	U7F9E
羊	S11-6-5	F2419

Stroke order: 1–11

COMPOUNDS

❶ⓐ **SHY, abashed**
ⓑ **be SHY, be abashed**
ⓒ put to shame, disgrace

ab 羞恥 しゅうち shyness; sense of shame
含羞 がんしゅう shyness, bashfulness
嬌×羞 きょうしゅう charming coyness

c 閉月羞花 へいげつしゅうか Such beauty as to make the moon hide and shame flowers (as of a woman)

❷ [original meaning, now archaic] **offer, dedicate, present**
時羞 じしゅう foods in season offered to the gods

KUN

【はじる 羞じる】[usu. 恥じる] **feel ashamed**
【はじ 羞】[usu. 恥] **shame, disgrace, humiliation**
【はじらう 羞じらう】[usu. 恥じらう] **be SHY, be coy, look abashed**
羞じらい はじらい shyness
【はずかしい 羞ずかしい】[usu. 恥ずかしい] **SHY; ashamed; shameful, disgraceful**

SPECIAL READINGS

含羞む▲ はにかむ be shy [bashful]

SYNONYMS

❶ⓒ **disgrace**
恥 SHAME → 1664
羞 shame → 4106
辱 HUMILIATE → 3400
侮 INSULT → 0091
罵 ABUSE → 3233
汚 defile → 0258
誹 SLANDER → 1978
譏 SLANDER → 2069

HOMOPHONES

はじる 恥 SHAME → 1664
はじ 恥 SHAME → 1664
はじらう 恥 SHAME → 1664
はずかしい 恥 SHAME → 1664

NOTE

➡ see USAGE note at 恥 1664

著 □3-7-4

incorrect classification
➡ see 2-3-8: 艹 at 2869

超

4107 □3-7-5

▶**SURPASS**
チョウ こ(える) こ(す)
Ⓒ 超 chāo

156	Jōyō	U8D85
走	S12-7-5	F0800

一 十 土 キ キ 走 走 起 起 超 超 超 (strokes 1–12)

COMPOUNDS

❶ⓐ (go beyond the limit) **SURPASS, transcend, excel**
ⓑ [also prefix] **super-, ultra-**
a 超越する ちょうえつする transcend, surpass
超絶 ちょうぜつ transcendence; excellence, superiority
超然たる ちょうぜんたる transcendental, standing aloof
b 超人 ちょうじん superman
超自然的な ちょうしぜんてきな supernatural
超国家的な ちょうこっかてきな ultranationalistic
超音速 ちょうおんそく supersonic speed
超大型 ちょうおおがた extra-large
超特急 ちょうとっきゅう superexpress (train)
❷ⓐ (go beyond in quantity or degree) **SURPASS, exceed, be over**
ⓑ [suffix] **excess, in excess of, over**
a 超過 ちょうか excess
入超 にゅうちょう excess of imports over exports
b 五千円超 ごせんえんちょう 5000 yen in excess
払い超 はらいちょう deficit in long-term capital
❸ [original meaning, now archaic] **jump over (an obstacle), cross over**

KUN

【こえる 超える】
ⓐ (go beyond in quantity or degree) **exceed, SURPASS, be over**
ⓑ (go beyond the limit) **SURPASS, excel, be above, transcend**
a 限度を超える げんどをこえる pass the limit, go beyond the limit
観客は百人を超えた かんきゃくはひゃくにんをこえた The audience exceeded 100
b 人知を超えた じんちをこえた beyond human understanding
【こす 超す】(go beyond in quantity or degree) **SURPASS, exceed, rise above, be over**
一万人を超す人人 いちまんにんをこすひとびと more than 10,000 people

SYNONYMS

❶ⓐ **excel**
勝 EXCEL → 1268
抜 STAND OUT → 0290
擢んでる stand out → 0973
超 SURPASS → 4107
越 GO BEYOND → 4108
凌 SURPASS → 0144
駕 outdo → 3236
ⓑ **extreme in degree**
酷 SEVERE → 1967
強 STRONG → 0574
凄い tremendous → 0145
重 HEAVY → 4390
高 HIGH → 2601
深 DEEP → 0636
大 BIG → 4224
厳 SEVERE → 4079
激 intense → 0955

極 EXTREME → 1243
痛 bitter(ly) → 4071
切 keen → 0030
甚 EXTREMELY → 3271
祁 EXTREMELY → 1447
超 super- → 4107
頗る EXCEEDINGLY → 1552

❷ⓐ **exceeding and excess**
過 EXCEED → 3891
超 SURPASS → 4107
越 GO BEYOND → 4108
濫 EXCESSIVE → 0990
余 EXCESS → 2535
剰 SURPLUS → 2233
冗 REDUNDANT → 2470

HOMOPHONES
こえる 越 GO BEYOND → 4108
こす 越 GO BEYOND → 4108

NOTE
➡ see USAGE note at 越 4108

越

4108
□3-7-5

▶GO BEYOND
エツ オツ▲ こ(す) -こ(す) -ご(し) こ(える) -ご(え) ㊔ えち おこし
Ⓒ 越 yuè

156	Jōyō	U8D8A
走	S12-7-5	F0554

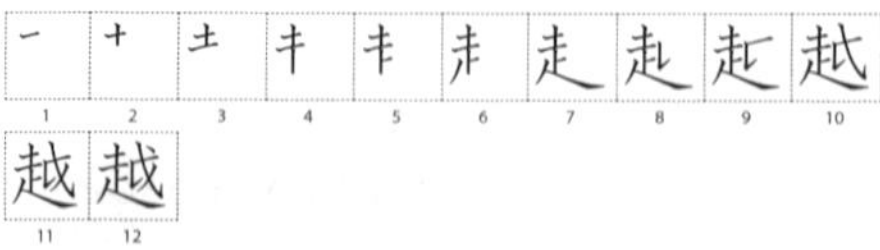

COMPOUNDS

❶ⓐ **GO BEYOND** or over a physical or abstract boundary: **go over, skip over, jump over**
ⓑ **GO BEYOND** the bounds of propriety or authority: **transgress, overstep, exceed**
a 飛越する ひえつする jump over (a hurdle), clear (a fence)
b 越訴 えっそ(=おっそ) appeal made directly to a senior official without going through formalities
越境 えっきょう border transgression, violation of the border
越権 えっけん going beyond one's authority
僭×越な せんえつな presumptuous, arrogant

❷ⓐ **GO** or be **BEYOND** in degree: **be more than, exceed, surpass**
ⓑ **GO BEYOND** the bounds of the ordinary: **be better than, transcend, surpass, excel**
a 激越な げきえつな violent, vehement
超越する ちょうえつする transcend, surpass
b 優越 ゆうえつ superiority, supremacy
卓越する たくえつする excel, surpass

❸ pass, spend (time)
越冬 えっとう passing the winter, wintering
越年草本 えつねんそうほん biennial herb

❹ⓐ Yue, name of an ancient Chinese state
ⓑ abbrev. of 越南 えつなん: Vietnam
a 呉越 ごえつ Wu and Yue, two rival states in ancient China
b 中越紛争 ちゅうえつふんそう dispute between China and Vietnam
反越 はんえつ anti-Vietnam

❺ Esshu, old name for Niigata, Toyama and east Fukui prefectures
越後 えちご Echigo, old name for Niigata Prefecture
信越本線 しんえつほんせん Shinetsu Main Line (Gunma-Nagano-Niigata Railway)

INDEPENDENT
【えつ 越】Yue (→ ❹ⓐ)

KUN
【こす 越す】
①ⓐ **go over, cross over, pass, go across**
ⓑ **surmount, pass through, overcome**
a 通り越す とおりこす go beyond, pass through
乗り越す のりこす ride past
b 山を越す やまをこす go across a mountain; surmount a difficulty

②ⓐ **be better than, surpass**
ⓑ **outstrip, outrun**
a それに越した事は無い それにこしたことはない Nothing could be better
勝ち越す かちこす have more wins than losses; lead (someone) by (three) matches
b 追い越す おいこす outrun, pass; overtake

③ pass, spend (time)
年越し としこし welcoming the new year

④ **move, change quarters**
引っ越す ひっこす move, change quarters

⑤ go, come
斎藤さんがお越しです さいとうさんがおこしです Mr. Saito has come

【-こす -越す】**shift over, shift onward**
持ち越す もちこす carry forward, bring over, defer
繰り越す くりこす transfer, bring forward, carry over
見越す みこす anticipate, speculate (on), foresee
寄越す よこす send; give, hand over

【-ごし -越し】[also suffix]
ⓐ **across, over, beyond**
ⓑ **after, over**
a 垣根越しに見る かきねごしにみる look over the fence

b 十年越しの付き合い じゅうねんごしのつきあい acquaintance of ten years' standing

【こえる 越える】**go over, go across, GO BEYOND, jump over**

乗り越える のりこえる get over, climb over; surmount, overcome

川を越える かわをこえる cross a river

【-ごえ -越え】

ⓐ **crossing over, going over**

ⓑ [suffix] road across (a place or mountain)

a バンカー越えの一打 ばんかーごえのいちだ a shot over the bunker

b 伊賀越え いがごえ road across Iga

SYNONYMS

❶ⓐ cross

渡 CROSS →0746

渉 wade →0638

越 GO BEYOND →4108

❷ⓐ exceeding and excess

過 EXCEED →3891

超 SURPASS →4107

越 GO BEYOND →4108

濫 EXCESSIVE →0990

余 EXCESS →2535

剰 SURPLUS →2233

冗 REDUNDANT →2470

ⓑ excel

勝 EXCEL →1268

抜 STAND OUT →0290

擢んでる stand out →0973

超 SURPASS →4107

越 GO BEYOND →4108

凌 SURPASS →0144

駕 outdo →3236

❹ⓑ Asian countries

日 JAPAN →3759

緬 Myanmar →1758

老 Laos →3963

華 CHINA →2841

蒙 Mongolia →2938

鮮 Korea →2355

泰 Thailand →3193

越 Vietnam →4108

印 India →1023

竺 INDIA →3248

比 Philippines →0029

USAGE

❶【こす】

越す

①ⓐ go over, cross over, pass, go across

ⓑ surmount, pass through, overcome

②ⓐ be better than, surpass

ⓑ outstrip, outrun

③ pass, spend (time)

④ move, change quarters

⑤ go, come

超す

(go beyond in quantity or degree) surpass, exceed, rise above, be over

❷【こえる】

越える

go over, go across, go beyond, jump over

超える

ⓐ (go beyond in quantity or degree) exceed, surpass, be over

ⓑ (go beyond the limit) surpass, excel, be above, transcend

★The differences between the above verbs are subtle, and they are easily confused. Make a careful study of the equivalents and examples under each entry. There is no consensus among lexicographers as to their correct usage.

HOMOPHONES

こす 超 SURPASS →4107

こえる 超 SURPASS →4107

甦 4109

□3-7-5

▸REVIVE

ソ コウ よみがえ(る)

Ⓒ 苏 sū

100	Non-Jōyō	U7526
生	S12-5-7	F2488

COMPOUNDS

● [now usu. 更 こう 4355 or 蘇 そ 3032] [original meaning] **REVIVE, come back to life**

甦生する そせい(=こうせい)する revive, resuscitate

KUN

【よみがえる 甦る】[also 蘇る] **REVIVE, resuscitate**

SYNONYMS

● return and restore

返 RETURN →3797

戻 RETURN →2441

還 RETURN →3945

復 RETURN TO →0701

蘇 REVIVE →3032

甦 REVIVE →4109

HOMOPHONES

よみがえる 蘇 REVIVE →3032

NOTE

➡ see USAGE note at 蘇 3032

走 更 【羊】

着

4110
□3-7-5

▶PUT ON
▶ARRIVE
▶STICK

チャク ジャク き(る) -ぎ き(せる) -き(せ) つ(く) つ(ける)

Ⓒ 着 zhe zháo zhuó zhāo

123	Jōyō-3	U7740
羊	S12-6-6	F0217

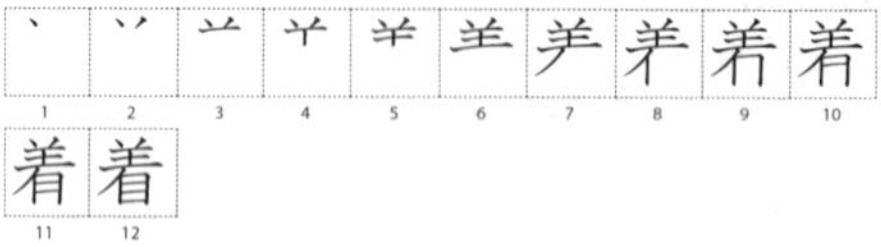

COMPOUNDS

❶ⓐ PUT ON (clothes), don, dress, wear
ⓑ counter for suits of clothes or garments

a 着用する ちゃくようする wear, have on
着衣 ちゃくい one's clothes [clothing]
着帽 ちゃくぼう putting on one's hat
b ズボン二着 ずぼんにちゃく two pairs of trousers

❷ [rarely also 著 2869]
ⓐ ARRIVE at, reach, come to hand
ⓑ land
ⓒ suffix indicating time, place or order of arrival

a 着駅 ちゃくえき destination station
着信 ちゃくしん arrival of mail
着米 ちゃくべい arriving in America
到着 とうちゃく arrival
先着順 せんちゃくじゅん order of arrival
帰着する きちゃくする return, come back; arrive at, result in
発着 はっちゃく departure and arrival
b 着陸 ちゃくりく landing, alighting
着地 ちゃくち landing
着水 ちゃくすい alighting [landing] on the water
c 五時着の列車 ごじちゃくのれっしゃ train due at five o'clock
東京着の時間 とうきょうちゃくのじかん time of arrival in Tokyo
第一着 だいいっちゃく first to arrive

❸ⓐ STICK, adhere, become attached
ⓑ (figuratively) STICK to, adhere to, hold fast to

a 付着 ふちゃく adhesion, agglutination; cohesion
密着 みっちゃく close adhesion
吸着 きゅうちゃく adsorption
接着 せっちゃく adhesion, gluing
癒着 ゆちゃく adhesion, conglutination; connection, collusion
粘着する ねんちゃくする stick to, be glued to, adhere to
b 執着 しゅうちゃく(=しゅうじゃく) attachment; tenacity
愛着 あいちゃく(=あいじゃく) attachment, affection; love
無頓着な むとんちゃくな indifferent, unmindful, careless

❹ apply, coat, cover, attach to

着色 ちゃくしょく color, coloring
装着する そうちゃくする fit, install

❺ⓐ (come to rest in one place) settle (down), settle [seat] oneself, become situated, settle down (in a place)
ⓑ (reach a decision) settle, come to a settlement
ⓒ settle down, become calm [composed], become steady

a 着席する ちゃくせきする take one's seat
着座 ちゃくざ taking a seat
着氷 ちゃくひょう icing (on a plane); ice formed by icing
着床 ちゃくしょう implantation
土着の どちゃくの native, indigenous, aboriginal
b 決着 けっちゃく conclusion, decision
落着 らくちゃく settlement, conclusion
c 着着と ちゃくちゃくと steadily, step by step
着実な ちゃくじつな steady, solid, sound
横着な おうちゃくな impudent, brazen; idle, lazy
沈着 ちんちゃく composure, self-possession

❻ set about, start, commence

着工 ちゃっこう starting construction
着手 ちゃくしゅ start, commencement

❼ bring one's attention to, come to one's attention, think of

着眼 ちゃくがん viewpoint, observation
着想 ちゃくそう idea, conception
着意 ちゃくい idea, conception; caution

❽ be ignited

着火する ちゃっかする be ignited, be kindled, catch (fire)

❾ play board games (esp. go)

勝着 しょうちゃく winning move (in a go game)

❿ take upon oneself

着服 ちゃくふく embezzlement, misappropriation

⓫ auxiliary particle

瞞×着 まんちゃく deception, cheating, trickery
悶着 もんちゃく trouble(s), difficulty, dispute

INDEPENDENT

【ちゃく 着】 **arrival**
早朝の着 そうちょうのちゃく early morning arrival

【ちゃくする 着する】 PUT ON clothes, dress, don, wear
法衣を着する ほうい(=ほうえ)をちゃくする put on a priest's robe

KUN

【きる 着る】*vi*

① **PUT ON clothes, dress, don, wear**

着物 きもの clothes, kimono
着付け きつけ dressing, fitting
着こなす きこなす wear [dress (oneself)] stylishly
着飾る きかざる dress up
着替え きがえ change of clothes
コートを着る こーとをきる put on [don] one's coat

② be charged with (a crime), take upon oneself

罪を着る つみをきる be accused of, take (another's guilt) on oneself
恩に着る おんにきる feel oneself indebted to

【-ぎ -着】[sometimes also -衣] [also suffix] **wear, clothes, dress, suit**

晴れ着 はれぎ one's best (clothes), gala [holiday] dress
肌着 はだぎ underwear
上着 うわぎ outer garment, coat, jacket
水着 みずぎ bathing [swimming] suit
不断着(=普段着) ふだんぎ everyday wear [clothes], home wear
訪問着 ほうもんぎ visiting [gala] dress

【きせる 着せる】*vt*

①ⓐ **dress (a person), PUT ON clothes, clothe**
ⓑ coat, plate

a 手伝って着せる てつだってきせる help (a person) dress
お仕着せ おしきせ clothes provided by the employer; livery
b 金を着せた指輪 きんをきせたゆびわ ring plated with gold

② charge, pin a crime on, fix

罪を着せる つみをきせる pin a crime on

【-きせ -着せ】**coated with**

銀着せの ぎんきせの silver-plated

【つく 着く】

①ⓐ **ARRIVE at, reach, come to hand**
ⓑ (succeed in touching) **reach, come in contact with, touch**

a 駅に着く えきにつく arrive at the station
行き着く いきつく arrive at, get to
b 船着き場 ふなつきば harbor; landing place
追い着く おいつく catch up with

② (come to rest in a position) **settle, settle [seat] oneself, become situated, settle down (in a place)**

席に着く せきにつく take a seat
帰途に着く きとにつく leave for home
落ち着く おちつく calm down, settle down, be steady; settle in, take up one's residence; harmonize with, match

【つける 着ける】

① (cause to arrive) **bring (a vehicle or boat) alongside, put ashore, berth**

ボートを岸に着ける ぼーとをきしにつける put a boat ashore
車を門に着ける くるまをもんにつける pull a car up at the gate

② **PUT ON clothes, don, wear, be dressed**

面を着ける めんをつける put a mask on

③ (place a person in a position) settle, settle [seat] a person, situate, steady

落ち着ける おちつける calm (down); settle (down)

④ set about, start, commence

手を着ける てをつける start; set one's hand to

SYNONYMS

❶ⓐ **wear and put on**

着 PUT ON → 4110
装 DRESS → 3327
帯 WEAR (esp. at the belt) → 3191
穿く PUT ON → 2800
纏 put on → 1814
履く put on footwear → 3933
被る put on headgear → 1495

❷ **arrive**

着 ARRIVE → 4110
到 ARRIVE → 1615
至 COME TO → 2707
及 REACH TO → 4192
届く REACH → 3820
達 ATTAIN → 3893

❸ⓐ **stick**

着 STICK → 4110
貼 STICK → 1904
付 attach itself to → 0035
附 attach itself to → 0410

ⓑ **adhere to**

執 adhere to → 2114
着 stick to → 4110

❺ **settle**

着 settle (down) → 4110
帰 settle in place → 0148
落 be concluded → 2907

【-ぎ】

◯ **clothing**

服 CLOTHES → 1090
袴 FORMAL DIVIDED SKIRT → 1509
蓑 STRAW RAINCOAT → 2941
-着 wear → 4110
衣 GARMENT → 2506
装 DRESS → 3327
裳 DRESS → 3231
襤 RAGS → 1607

袈 BUDDHIST SURPLICE → 3200
裟 BUDDHIST CASSOCK → 3420
襖 overgarment → 1600

USAGE

【-ぎ】

-着
[sometimes also -衣] [also suffix] wear, clothes, dress, suit

-衣
[usu. -着] outer garment, clothes, wear

HOMOPHONES

-ぎ 衣 GARMENT → 2506

つく
付 ATTACH → 0035
附 ATTACH → 0410
就 SET ABOUT → 2129
即 IMMEDIATE → 1439
点 POINT → 2587

つける
付 ATTACH → 0035
附 ATTACH → 0410
就 SET ABOUT → 2129
即 IMMEDIATE → 1439
点 POINT → 2587
漬 PICKLE → 0861

NOTE

➡ see also USAGE note at 付 0035
★ 着 was originally a variant of 著 2869

趣

▸FLAVOR
▸PURPOSE
シュ おもむき おもむ(く)▲

4111
□3-7-8

Ⓒ 趣 qù

156	Jōyō	U8DA3
走	S15-7-8	F1286

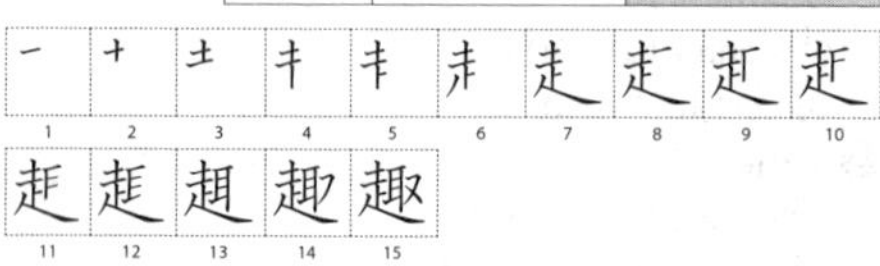

COMPOUNDS

❶ⓐ FLAVOR, distinctive charm, elegance, taste, beauty, sentiment
ⓑ interest, taste, hobby

a 情趣 じょうしゅ mood, sentiment, artistic effects, charms
野趣 やしゅ charms of the countryside, rural beauty
興趣 きょうしゅ taste, elegance, flavor
b 趣味 しゅみ hobby, interest, taste
俗趣 ぞくしゅ vulgar taste

❷ PURPOSE, aim, motive, object, meaning, purport
趣旨 しゅし purpose, aim; purport, meaning
趣意 しゅい purpose, motive, aim; purport, meaning, point
趣向 しゅこう idea, contrivance, plan
意趣 いしゅ spite, grudge, enmity; [original meaning] purpose, meaning

❸ appearance, air, complexion
異趣 いしゅ extraordinary appearance

❹ *Buddhism* lower levels of the ten realms of living beings
三悪趣 さんあくしゅ(=さんなくしゅ) three evil worlds: hell, the world of hungry spirits and the world of animals

KUN

【おもむき 趣】 **purport, effect, meaning, tenor, gist; FLAVOR, distinctive charm, taste, elegance; appearance, air, aspect**
趣の有る おもむきのある tasteful, zestful, elegant
趣を異にする おもむきをことにする differ in features, be unlike
お手紙の趣承知しました おてがみのおもむきしょうちしました I have duly noted the contents of your letter

【おもむく 趣く】 [usu. 赴く]
① proceed to, go to, head for
死地に趣く しちにおもむく ride into the jaws of death
② become, tend towards
盛大に趣く せいだいにおもむく grow in prosperity

SYNONYMS

❶ flavor and elegance
趣 FLAVOR → 4111
味 TASTE → 0325
風 elegance → 3730
品 refinement → 2795

❷ will and intention
志 AMBITION → 2725
意 MIND → 2650
図 intention → 3809
気 mind to do something → 3960
念 thought of doing something → 2554
趣 PURPOSE → 4111
欲 DESIRE → 1867

❷ meaning
義 MEANING → 2948
意 MEANING → 2650
訳 SENSE → 1865
旨 PURPORT → 2516
趣 PURPOSE → 4111

HOMOPHONES

おもむく 赴 PROCEED TO → 4095

NOTE

➡ see USAGE notes at 旨 2516 and 赴 4095

蘼
口3-7-8

incorrect classification/ stroke-count
➡ see 2-3-11: 艹 at 2978

麺

▶NOODLES

メン ベン▲

Ⓝ 麵 麪◇ Ⓒ 面 miàn

4112
口3-7-9

199	Jōyō	U9EBA
麦	S16-7-9	F3224

COMPOUNDS

❶ [original meaning] **NOODLES**

麺類 めんるい noodles
麺棒 めんぼう rolling pin
製麺 せいめん noodle making
乾麺 かんめん dried noodles
拉麺 らーめん ramen, Chinese-style soup noodles
素麺(=索麺) そうめん thin wheat noodles
カップ麺 かっぷめん cup-type instant noodles

❷ wheat flour

甜×麺醬 てんめんじゃん sweet flour paste

INDEPENDENT

【めん 麺】**NOODLES**

導
口3-7-9

incorrect classification
➡ see 2-13-3: 道 at 3603

門
口3-8-0

incorrect classification
➡ see 1-4-4: 𠂆 at 1100

勉

▶ENDEAVOR

ベン つと(める)▲ ㊔ つとむ

Ⓝ 勉 Ⓒ 勉 miǎn

4113
口3-8-2

19	Jōyō-3	U52C9
力	S10-2-8	F1301

COMPOUNDS

❶ [original meaning] **ENDEAVOR, make efforts, work diligently, exert oneself**

勉励 べんれい diligence, industry
勉強 べんきょう study; selling cheap; [rare] diligence
勉学 べんがく study
勤勉な きんべんな diligent, assiduous, industrious, hardworking

❷ study

ガリ勉 がりべん [belittling] studying hard, digging; diligent student, grind

KUN

【つとめる 勉める】[usu. 努める] **ENDEAVOR,** make efforts, try hard, work diligently

勉めて つとめて with effort, as much as possible
極力勉める きょくりょくつとめる do one's best

SYNONYMS

❶ **exert oneself**

努 EXERT → 3154
勉 ENDEAVOR → 4113
励 make efforts → 1438
勤 work diligently → 2287
尽 use all one's strength → 3786
精 put one's heart into → 1729
孜 MAKE DILIGENT EFFORTS → 0284

HOMOPHONES

つとめる

努 EXERT → 3154
勤 SERVICE → 2287
務 DUTY → 1505

NOTE

➡ see USAGE note at 勤 2287
➡ see COMPOUND FORMATION for 勉強 べんきょう → 強 0574

閃

▶FLASH

セン ひらめ(く) ひらめ(かす)

Ⓒ 闪 shǎn

4114
口3-8-2

169	Names	U9583
門	S10-8-2	F2431

COMPOUNDS

● **FLASH, flicker, glitter**

閃光 せんこう flash, glint
閃緑岩 せんりょくがん diorite
一閃 いっせん a flash (of light)
角閃石 かくせんせき amphibole

KUN

【ひらめく 閃く】

①ⓐ **FLASH, flicker, glitter**
ⓑ **FLASH to mind, occur to someone, hit on (an idea)**

ab 閃き ひらめき flare, flash; inspiration; fluttering

② **wave, flutter**

【ひらめかす 閃かす】

①ⓐ **FLASH, make flash**
ⓑ **show a glimpse of**

② **make (a flag) flutter**

SYNONYMS

● **shine and reflect**

輝 SHINE BRILLIANTLY → 1775
光 shine → 3043
照 ILLUMINATE → 3506
映 REFLECT → 1104
耀 SHINE BRILLIANTLY → 1812
燿 SHINE → 1407
閃 FLASH → 4114
煌 GLITTER → 1296

彪

▸MAGNIFICENT

ヒョウ ヒュウ ㊔ たけ たけし あきら つよし あや とら

4115

Ⓒ 彪 biāo

□ 3-8-3

59	Names	U5F6A
彡	S11-3-8	F3493

COMPOUNDS

ⓐ [original meaning, now archaic] **tiger stripes**
ⓑ [archaic] as **MAGNIFICENT** and gorgeous as tiger stripes

SYNONYMS

ⓑ **beautiful**
美 BEAUTIFUL → 2817
彪 MAGNIFICENT → 4115
綺 BEAUTIFUL → 1734
娃 BEAUTIFUL → 0419
佳 FINE → 0096
瑶 EXQUISITE → 1301
麗 OF GRACEFUL BEAUTY → 2672
艶 CHARMING → 2403
妙 of marvelous beauty → 0280
華 MAGNIFICENT → 2841
絢 GORGEOUS → 1705
斐 florid → 3449

閉

▸CLOSE

ヘイ と(じる) と(ざす) し(める) し(まる) た(てる)[▲]

4116

Ⓝ 閇 Ⓒ 闭 bì

□ 3-8-3

169	Jōyō-6	U9589
門	S11-8-3	F0856

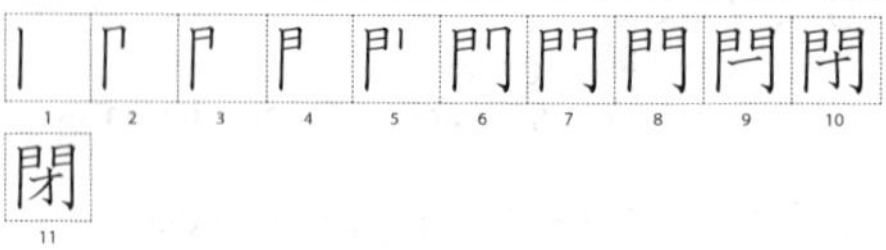

COMPOUNDS

❶ⓐ [original meaning] (move into closed position) **CLOSE, shut, confine**
ⓑ (plug up) **CLOSE**, stop up

a 閉鎖 へいさ closing, closure, shutdown
閉口する へいこうする be dumbfounded [stumped], be silenced
開閉する かいへいする open and shut [close]; make and break (circuits)
密閉する みっぺいする close up tightly, seal hermetically

b 閉塞 へいそく blockade, stoppage

❷ (bring to an end) **CLOSE (a shop), adjourn, end**
閉会 へいかい closing (of a meeting), adjournment
閉店 へいてん closing the shop
閉幕となる へいまくとなる come to a close [end]
閉校 へいこう closing a school

INDEPENDENT

【へい 閉】OFF, **CLOSE** (marking on switches or taps)

KUN

【とじる 閉じる】*vi* & *vt*
① **CLOSE, shut**
閉じ込める とじこめる shut in [up], lock in [up]
閉じ籠もる とじこもる shut oneself up (in a room)
② (come or bring to an end) **CLOSE (a meeting)**
幕を閉じる まくをとじる close the curtain; come to an end

【とざす 閉ざす】*vt* **shut, CLOSE, fasten, lock; cause to be buried (in grief)**
門戸を閉ざす もんこをとざす close the door to, exclude
悲しみに閉ざされる かなしみにとざされる be buried in grief

【しめる 閉める】*vt* (move into closed position) **shut, CLOSE**
蓋を閉める ふたをしめる shut the lid

【しまる 閉まる】*vi* **be shut, be CLOSEd, shut, close**
閉まり しまり shutting, closing
戸が閉まった とがしまった The door shut [closed]

【たてる 閉てる】[sometimes also 立てる] shut (as a paper sliding door)
開け閉て あけたて opening and shutting

SYNONYMS

❶ⓐ **close**
閉 CLOSE → 4116
鎖 lock up → 2213
封 SEAL → 1639
梗 STOP UP → 1204
塞 STOP UP → 2924

❷ **end**
終 END → 1692
絶 COME TO AN END → 1711
閉 CLOSE → 4116
了 FINISH → 4157
済 SETTLE → 0634
-上げる completion suffix → 4212

完 COMPLETE → 2727
結 CONCLUDE → 1706
竣 COMPLETE → 1528

USAGE

【とじる】
閉じる
vi & vt
① close, shut
② (come or bring to an end) close (a meeting)
綴じる
ⓐ bind, file
ⓑ sew up, stitch together; mend

HOMOPHONES

とじる 綴 BIND → 1746
しめる
締 CONCLUDE → 1761
〆 SUM → 4179
絞 STRANGLE → 1707
しまる
締 CONCLUDE → 1761
絞 STRANGLE → 1707
たてる
立 STAND → 2486
建 BUILD → 3834
点 POINT → 2587

NOTE

➡ see also USAGE notes at 締 1761 and 立 2486

問

4117
口 3-8-3

▶**QUESTION**
モン と(う) と(い) とん
ⓒ 问 wèn

30	Jōyō-3	U554F
口	S11-3-8	F0132

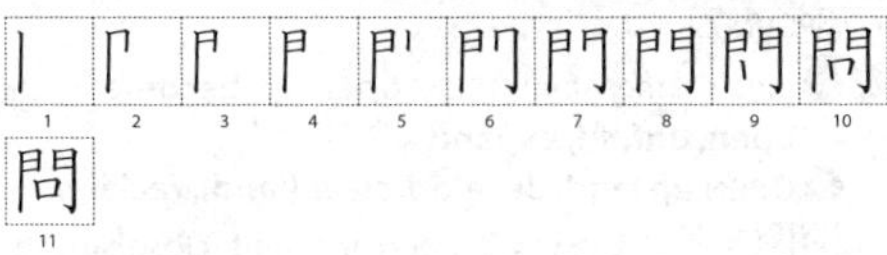

COMPOUNDS

❶ⓐ [original meaning] **QUESTION, ask, inquire**
ⓑ **QUESTION, inquiry, problem**
ⓒ counter for **QUESTION**s

a 質問 しつもん question
尋問する じんもんする question, examine, interrogate
詰問する きつもんする cross-examine, cross-question, question closely
顧問 こもん adviser, consultant

b 問題 もんだい problem, question, issue, matter
問答 もんどう questions and answers, catechism
難問 なんもん difficult problem [question]

c 第一問 だいいちもん first question [problem]

❷ **call on, pay a visit**
訪問 ほうもん visit
慰問 いもん inquiring after a person's health; consolation

❸ accuse, charge
問罪 もんざい accusation, indictment

❹ care, mind
不問 ふもん regardless, irrespective

KUN

【とう 問う】
① **ask, QUESTION, inquire**
問い合わせる といあわせる inquire, make a reference, apply
問い質す といただす inquire, question
問い詰める といつめる press a question, cross-examine

② accuse, charge
殺人罪に問われて さつじんざいにとわれて on a charge of murder

③ care, mind
経験を問わず けいけんをとわず no experience necessary

【とい 問い】 **QUESTION, query, inquiry, interrogation**
問いを掛ける といをかける ask a question of (a person)

【とん 問】 [in compounds] **unclassified compounds**
問屋 とんや(=といや) wholesale store, wholesaler, commission agent

SYNONYMS

❶ⓐ **inquire**
問 QUESTION → 4117
詰 question closely → 1920
聞く ask → 4127
質 query → 3483
尋ねる INQUIRE → 2918
訊 INQUIRE → 1842
伺う INQUIRE (*humble*) → 0078
諮 CONSULT → 2009
詢 ASK FOR ADVICE → 1917

ⓑ **question**
題 PROBLEM → 4139
問 QUESTION (inquiry) → 4117
論 question (issue) → 1981
謎 RIDDLE → 2047

USAGE

【とう】
問う
① ask, question, inquire
② accuse, charge
③ care, mind

訪う
call on, visit

HOMOPHONES

とう 訪 VISIT →1860

NOTE

➡ see COMPOUND FORMATION for 顧問 こもん →顧 2394

閇

4118

口3-8-3

▶CLOSE

ヘイ と(じる) と(ざす) し(める) し(まる) た(てる)

169 門	Nonstandard	U9587
	S11-8-3	F0000

traditional form →see 閉 at 4116

啇

口3-8-3

incorrect classification
➡ see 亠2-2-9: 亠 at 2623

髙

口3-8-3

incorrect classification
➡ see 亠2-2-9: 亠 at 2626

暑

口3-8-4

incorrect classification
➡ see 日2-4-8: 日 at 3121

悶

4119

口3-8-4

▶BE IN AGONY

モン もだ(える)

Ⓒ 闷 mēn mèn

61 心	Non-Jōyō	U60B6
	S12-4-8	F2185

COMPOUNDS

● [original meaning] **BE IN AGONY, worry, fret**

悶着 もんちゃく trouble(s), difficulty, dispute
悶悶とする もんもんとする worry endlessly, suffer mental agony
悶絶する もんぜつする faint in agony
苦悶 くもん agony, anguish
煩悶 はんもん anguish, worry
遣悶する けんもんする drive away melancholy

KUN

【もだえる 悶える】**BE IN AGONY, worry; writhe**

悶え苦しむ もだえくるしむ writhe in agony
悶え死に もだえじに death in agony
身悶える みもだえる writhe (in agony)

SYNONYMS

● **trouble and suffering**

困 BE IN TROUBLE →3808
苛 torment →2786
窮 BE IN EXTREMITY →2983
悶 BE IN AGONY →4119
悩 SUFFER →0504
苦 SUFFERING →2789
痛 PAIN →4071
辛 HARD →2531
煩 VEXED →1295
難 DIFFICULT →2310

閏

4120

口3-8-4

▶INTERCALARY

ジュン うるう ㊔ うる

Ⓒ 闰 rùn

169 門	Names	U958F
	S12-8-4	F3332

COMPOUNDS

❶ **INTERCALARY, leap (day)**

正閏 せいじゅん normal and leap years; legitimate and illegitimate dynasties [lineages]

❷ illegitimate throne

KUN

【うるう 閏】**INTERCALARY, leap (day)**

閏年 うるうどし leap year
閏日 うるうび leap day
閏秒 うるうびょう leap second

開

4121

口3-8-4

▶OPEN

カイ ひら(く) ひら(き) -びら(き) ひら(ける) あ(く) あ(ける)

Ⓒ 开 kāi

169 門	Jōyō-3	U958B
	S12-8-4	F0123

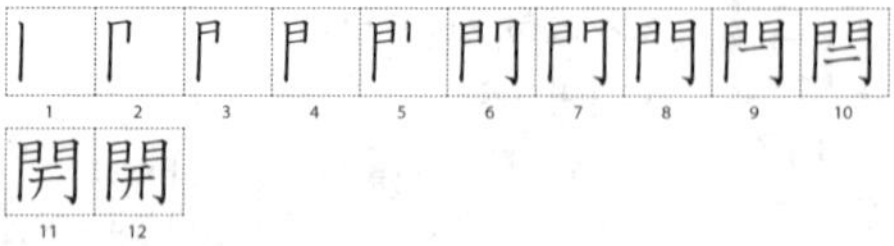

COMPOUNDS

❶ⓐ [original meaning] **OPEN, open up, become open, unfold, expand**
ⓑ **OPEN up land, develop, clear (land), reclaim**

a 開閉する かいへいする open and shut [close]; make and break (circuits)
開封する かいふうする open (a letter), unseal
開通 かいつう opening to [for] traffic
展開 てんかい unfolding, development, evolution; deployment
公開 こうかい opening to the public

b 開発する かいはつする develop, open out; enlighten
開拓 かいたく reclamation, opening up, clearing; exploitation
新開地 しんかいち newly opened land

❷ⓐ **OPEN** to the benefits of civilization, become enlightened [civilized], be developed

❻ **OPEN** oneself to eternal truths, become enlightened

a 開化 かいか civilization; enlightenment

b 開悟 かいご enlightenment, wisdom

❸ **OPEN, commence, establish**

開始する かいしする begin, commence, open

開会 かいかい opening a meeting

開祖 かいそ founder, originator

開運 かいうん beginning of good luck

開催する かいさいする hold an event, open (an exhibition)

開店する かいてんする open a store [shop]; set up a business

再開する さいかいする reopen, resume

❹ *math* root extraction

開方 かいほう extraction of roots

開平 かいへい square root extraction

❺ state, mention

開陳する かいちんする state, express (one's opinion)

INDEPENDENT

【かい 開】ON, **OPEN** (marking on switches or taps)

KUN

【ひらく 開く】

①ⓐ **OPEN, open up; unfold, flower**

ⓑ **OPEN up, commence operations**

ⓒ **OPEN (a conference), hold (a meeting)**

a 開き直る ひらきなおる switch to a defiant attitude

b 店を開く みせをひらく open a business

c パーティーを開く ぱーてぃーをひらく give a party

② [sometimes also 拓く] **OPEN** up (land), clear, reclaim, develop

道を切り開く みちをきりひらく open a path

③ differ, widen the margin between

距離を開く きょりをひらく open the distance

④ [sometimes also 啓く] enlighten, edify

蒙を開く もうをひらく enlighten (a person's mind)

【ひらき 開き】**OPENing; aperture; hinged door; split and dried fish; adjournment, breakup (of a wedding);** *navigation* **tack**

開き鯵× ひらきあじ split and dried saurel

お開き おひらき breakup of a wedding

【-びらき -開き】

① **OPENing**

両開き りょうびらき double door

② **OPEN**ing, commencement, first day of the season

スキー開き すきーびらき opening of the skiing season

【ひらける 開ける】**widen, become OPENed up; develop, become civilized; be up-to-date**

街が開けている まちがひらけている The town is opened up

【あく 開く】

ⓐ **OPEN, become open**

ⓑ (of a shop) **OPEN, begin**

a ドアが開いている どあがあいている The door is open

幕開き まくあき raising of the curtains; beginning

b 十時に開く じゅうじにあく (the shop) opens ten o'clock

【あける 開ける】**OPEN, unlock**

戸を開ける とをあける open the door

SYNONYMS

❶ⓐ **open**

開 OPEN →4121

展 UNFOLD →3862

披 open and read →0362

❻ **reclaim**

拓 OPEN UP →0375

墾 RECLAIM →3602

開 OPEN →4121

❸ **begin**

始 BEGIN →0335

-出す begin to do →4310

-掛ける start doing →0596

発 START →3174

起 start →4099

就 SET ABOUT →2129

開 OPEN →4121

創 initiate →2283

肇 ORIGINATE →3474

USAGE

【ひらく】

開く

①ⓐ open, open up; unfold, flower

ⓑ open up, commence operations

ⓒ open (a conference), hold (a meeting)

② [sometimes also 拓く] open up (land), clear, reclaim, develop

③ differ, widen the margin between

④ [sometimes also 啓く] enlighten, edify

拓く

[usu. 開く] open up (land), clear, reclaim, develop

啓く

[usu. 開く] enlighten, edify

HOMOPHONES

ひらく

拓 OPEN UP →0375

啓 ENLIGHTEN →3434

あく

空 SKY →2767

明 BRIGHT →1060

あける

空 SKY →2767

明 BRIGHT → 1060

NOTE

➡ see also USAGE note at 明 1060

間

▶INTERVAL
▶BETWEEN

カン ケン あいだ ま あい▴ ㊔ はざま

4122

□3-8-4

Ⓝ 間 Ⓒ 间 jiān jiàn

169	Jōyō-2	U9593
門	S12-8-4	F0021

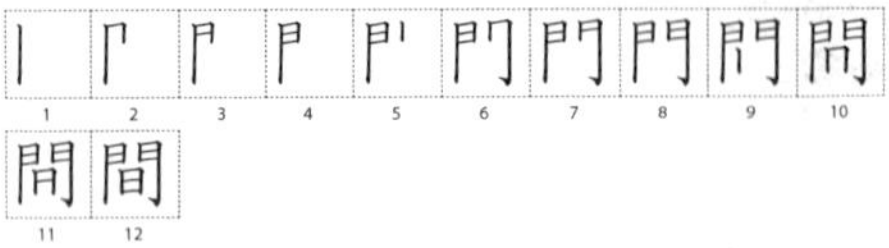

COMPOUNDS

❶ [also suffix] (space between) **INTERVAL, space, opening, distance**

間隔 かんかく interval, space
間接 かんせつ indirect
空間 くうかん space, room
区間 くかん section, territory
東京大阪間 とうきょうおおさかかん between Tokyo and Osaka

❷ [also suffix]
ⓐ (time between) **INTERVAL, duration of time, period**
ⓑ **for an INTERVAL of, during**

a 時間 じかん time, period; hour
夜間に やかんに at night
期間 きかん term, period
週間 しゅうかん week
b 十年間 じゅうねんかん for ten years

❸ [also suffix] **BETWEEN, among, midway**

間食 かんしょく eating between meals; snack
中間 ちゅうかん middle, midway
民間の みんかんの private, nongovernmental, civil
世間 せけん world, society; the public, people
人間 にんげん human being, man; people, mankind
三遊間 さんゆうかん *baseball* between third and shortstop
友人間に ゆうじんかんに among one's friends

❹ *ken*: unit of length equiv. to approx. 1.8 m or 6 *shaku* (尺)

間数 けんすう length in *ken*
三間 さんげん 3 *ken*

❺ spy on

間者 かんじゃ spy

❻ [usu. 閑 4123] idleness, leisure, spare time

間居 かんきょ idle life, quiet retreat

❼ separate, divide

離間 りかん alienation, estrangement

INDEPENDENT

【かん 間】 (space between) **INTERVAL, space, opening, distance;** (time between) **interval, duration of time, period**

間一髪 かんいっぱつ by a hairbreadth
間、髪を入れず かん,はつをいれず in a flash, in no time
指呼の間 しこのかん hailing distance
この間 このかん during this period

【けん 間】 *ken* (→❹)

KUN

【あいだ 間】

① (space between) **INTERVAL, space, opening, distance**

間を空ける あいだをあける leave space (between)
数キロの間 すうきろのあいだ for several kilometers

② (time between) **INTERVAL, duration of time, period**

間を置いて あいだをおいて at intervals (of), intermittently
長い間 ながいあいだ long time
この間 このあいだ the other day, recently

③ (something between) **middle; BETWEEN, among, midway; relationship, terms**

間柄 あいだがら relation, terms
間を取る あいだをとる take the middle (between the two)
本の間に ほんのあいだに between two books; between the pages
我我の間で われわれのあいだで among ourselves

【ま 間】

① (space between) **INTERVAL, space, opening**

谷間 たにま valley, gorge
隙間 すきま gap, opening; crack, crevice

② (time between) **INTERVAL, duration of time, period**

間も無く まもなく soon, in a short time
間近に まぢかに nearby, close at hand
昼間 ひるま daytime, day
手間 てま labor, trouble; time (required for a task)

③ **BETWEEN, among**

仲間 なかま company, fellow, comrade, associate

④ **timing, situation, occasion**

間に合う まにあう be in time; answer the purpose; can do without
間に合わせる まにあわせる manage, make do, make shift; have (something) ready (by a certain time)
間に合わせ まにあわせ makeshift, temporary expedient
間が良い まがいい be lucky
間違い まちがい mistake, error
間抜け まぬけ stupid fellow, bonehead, nitwit
鈍間 のろま dull fellow

⑤ⓐ **room, chamber**
ⓑ counter for rooms
a 居間 いま living [sitting] room
茶の間 ちゃのま living room
応接間 おうせつま drawing room, guest room
孔雀の間 くじゃくのま the Peacock Room
b 二間 ふたま two rooms

【あい 間】 [also 合い or 合]
① (space between) **INTERVAL**, space, opening
間の戸 あいのと door between the rooms
②ⓐ [also prefix] (time between) **INTERVAL**, intermission
ⓑ **BETWEEN** seasons
a 間の手 あいのて interlude
間狂言 あいきょうげん interlude (in a noh drama)
幕間 まくあい intermission, interval
b 間服 あいふく between-season wear
③ [in compounds] mixed (blood)
間の子 あいのこ *derogatory* person of mixed parentage; crossbreed

SYNONYMS

❶ **distance and interval**
距 DISTANCE → 1905
間 INTERVAL → 4122
程 EXTENT → 1524
隙 GAP → 0826

❷ⓐ **time periods**
時 TIME → 1155
季 SEASON (quarter) → 3161
候 SEASON (time of year) → 0133
頃 TIME → 0163
暇 FREE TIME → 1275
般 period of time → 1670
刻 POINT OF TIME → 1619
間 INTERVAL → 4122
隙 GAP → 0826
期 TERM → 2139
節 SEASON → 3336

ⓑ **during**
間 for an interval of → 4122
中 IN (the course of) → 4262
内 within (a given period) → 4277

❸ **between**
中 MIDDLE → 4262
仲 intermediate → 0047
間 BETWEEN → 4122
際 inter- → 0874

❹ **length units**
寸 *sun* (3.03 cm) → 3652
浬 NAUTICAL MILE (1852 m) → 0526
反 *tan* (10.6 m) → 3663
尺 *SHAKU* (30.3 cm) → 4248
米 meter → 4342
尋 fathom (1.8 m) → 2918
間 *ken* (1.8 m) → 4122
丈 *jo* (3.03 m) → 4227
町 *cho* (109 m) → 1430
里 LEAGUE, *ri* (3.9 km) → 4356
哩 MILE (1609 m) → 0479

【ま】
⑤ⓐ **rooms**
室 ROOM → 2802
間 room → 4122
房 CHAMBER → 2445
斎 study → 2622
堂 HALL → 3202

HOMOPHONES

あい
相 PHASE → 1120
合 COMBINE → 2511

COMPOUND FORMATION

【人間 にんげん】【世間 せけん】
人間 'human being, etc.' and 世間 'world, society, etc.' originally meant among (間 ❸) the people (人) and among (間 ❸) society (世).

NOTE

➡ see USAGE note at 相 1120

閑

4123
口3-8-4

▶**LEISURE**
▶**QUIET**
カン ㊔しず
Ⓒ 闲 xián

169	Jōyō	U9591
門	S12-8-4	F2038

丨 1, 𠃌 2, 𠂋 3, 𠁣 4, 門 5, 門 6, 門 7, 門 8, 閂 9, 閂 10, 閑 11, 閑 12

COMPOUNDS

❶ⓐ **LEISURE, idleness, spare time**
ⓑ **idle, LEISURELy, idly**
a 閑暇 かんか leisure
閑散 かんさん leisure, inactivity
農閑期 のうかんき leisure season for farmers
b 閑居 かんきょ [sometimes also 間居] idle life, quiet retreat
閑職 かんしょく leisurely post, do-nothing job
安閑と あんかんと idly, in idleness

❷ idle, trifling, rambling
閑談 かんだん idle talk
閑話休題 かんわきゅうだい to return to the subject

❸ **QUIET, tranquil**
閑静な かんせいな quiet, tranquil
閑寂な かんじゃくな quiet, tranquil
森閑とした しんかんとした quiet, still, silent as a graveyard
❹ neglect, make slight of
閑却する かんきゃくする neglect, disregard
等閑 とうかん negligence, neglect, disregard

INDEPENDENT

【かん 閑】**LEISURE**, idleness, spare time
忙中閑有り ぼうちゅうかんあり find odd moments of leisure in one's busy life

SYNONYMS

❶ⓐ leisure
暇 FREE TIME → 1275
閑 LEISURE → 4123
ⓑ leisurely
悠 LEISURELY → 3407
閑 idle → 4123
❸ quiet
静 QUIET → 2164
閑 QUIET → 4123
寂 quiet → 2855
幽 QUIET AND SECLUDED → 3731
粛 still → 4400
黙 SILENT → 3554

COMPOUND FORMATION

【閑話休題 かんわきゅうだい】
閑話休題 'to return to the subject' means "we have been engaging in idle (閑 ❷) talk (話) and have stopped (休) the main topic (題), so let's get back to the subject."

間

4124
□3-8-4

▶**INTERVAL**
▶**BETWEEN**
カン ケン あいだ ま あい ㊔ はざま

169	Nonstandard	U9592
門	S12-8-4	F0000

traditional form → see 間 at 4122

爲

□3-8-4

incorrect classification
➡ see ▀2-4-8: 爫 at 3127

筒

□3-8-4

incorrect classification
➡ see ▀2-6-6: ⺮ at 3323

暑

□3-8-5

incorrect classification
➡ see ▀2-4-9: 日 at 3130

魁

4125
□3-8-6

▶**LEADER**
カイ さきがけ ㊔ いさむ いさお はじめ すぐる つとむ
ⓒ 魁 kuí

194	Names	U9B41
鬼	S14-10-4	F2741

COMPOUNDS

ⓐ LEADER, chief, head, the highest
ⓑ as great or eminent as a LEADER
a 魁首 かいしゅ leader; top candidate for the classical examinations in ancient China
首魁 しゅかい leader; forerunner, pioneer
b 魁傑 かいけつ (of one's body) stout, sturdy, muscular; eminent person
魁偉な かいいな gigantic, large-boned and impressive
魁梧 かいご (of one's body) stout, sturdy, muscular

KUN

【さきがけ 魁】[usu. 先駆け]
ⓐ **the lead, the initiative**
ⓑ **pioneer, forerunner; herald, sign**
a 流行の魁となる りゅうこうのさきがけとなる lead the fashion, take the lead
b 春の魁 はるのさきがけ harbinger of spring

SYNONYMS

ⓐ leaders
主 MASTER → 2437
王 KING → 4247
長 CHIEF → 3163
頭 HEAD → 2019
首 LEADER → 2818
領 leader → 1567
魁 LEADER → 4125

HOMOPHONES

さきがけ 先駆け → 3046, 2293

閥

4126
□3-8-6

▶**CLIQUE**
バツ
ⓒ 阀 fá

169	Jōyō	U95A5
門	S14-8-6	F1831

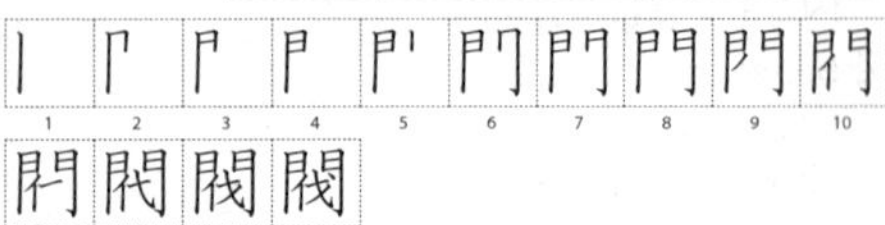

COMPOUNDS

❶ [also suffix] **CLIQUE, clan, power group**
派閥 はばつ clique, faction, coterie
財閥 ざいばつ financial clique [combine], *zaibatsu*
学閥 がくばつ academic clique, academic cliquism

軍閥 ぐんばつ military clique
藩閥 はんばつ clan favoritism, clanship
薩摩閥 さつまばつ Satsuma clan

❷ [original meaning] pedigree, lineage, descent
閥族 ばつぞく clan, clique
門閥 もんばつ (renowned) lineage, pedigree

INDEPENDENT

【ばつ 閥】 **CLIQUE**, faction
閥を作る ばつをつくる form a clique

SYNONYMS

❶ **parties and sects**
党 PARTY → 3190
閥 CLIQUE → 4126
流 school → 0529
派 SECT → 0456
翼 WING → 3379
系 faction → 2443
門 (religious) sect → 1100
宗 RELIGIOUS SECT (esp. Buddhist) → 2769

聞

▶HEAR
ブン モン き(く) き(こえる)
Ⓒ 闻 wén

4127
口3-8-6

128	Jōyō-2	U805E
耳	S14-6-8	F0115

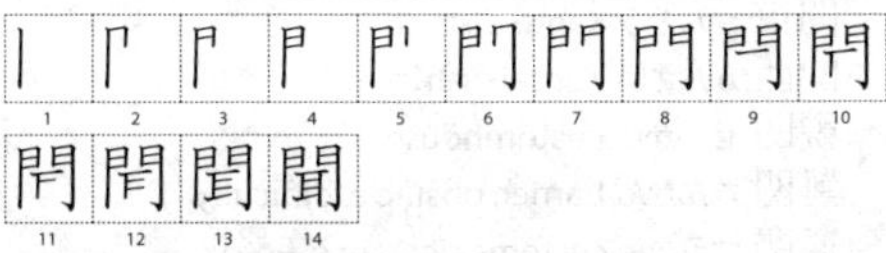

COMPOUNDS

❶ⓐ (perceive by ear) **HEAR**
ⓑ (learn by being told) **HEAR of, be told**
a 見聞 けんぶん experience, observation, knowledge
b 上聞 じょうぶん imperial hearing
聴聞会 ちょうもんかい hearing
前代未聞の ぜんだいみもんの unheard-of, unprecedented

❷ⓐ **HEARsay, rumor, news**
ⓑ fame, reputation
a 伝聞 でんぶん hearsay, rumor, report
風聞 ふうぶん rumor, hearsay
新聞 しんぶん newspaper
旧聞 きゅうぶん old news
b 醜聞 しゅうぶん scandal, ill fame

KUN

【きく 聞く】
①ⓐ **HEAR**
ⓑ **HEAR of, be informed**
a 聞き苦しい ききぐるしい disagreeable to hear, offensive to the ear
聞き手 ききて listener, audience
聞き取る ききとる catch, follow, understand
聞き取り ききとり aural comprehension
盗み聞き ぬすみぎき eavesdropping, tapping
b 聞かせる(=聞かす) きかせる(=きかす) inform, tell; read to, play for, sing for

② obey, follow
親の言う事を聞く おやのいうことをきく obey one's parents

③ [formerly also 訊く] **ask, inquire**
聞き返す ききかえす inquire again
道を聞く みちをきく ask the way

【きこえる 聞こえる】 **HEAR, be heard [audible]; sound, seem; be known [famed]**
声が聞こえる こえがきこえる I hear a voice

SYNONYMS

❶ **hear**
聞 HEAR → 4127
聴 LISTEN → 1796

【きく】
③ **inquire**
問 QUESTION → 4117
詰 question closely → 1920
聞く ask → 4127
質 query → 3483
尋ねる INQUIRE → 2918
訊 INQUIRE → 1842
伺う INQUIRE (*humble*) → 0078
諮 CONSULT → 2009
詢 ASK FOR ADVICE → 1917

USAGE

【きく】
聞く
①ⓐ hear
ⓑ hear of, be informed
② obey, follow
③ [formerly also 訊く] ask, inquire

聴く
listen (to), give an ear to

訊く
[now usu. 聞く] ask, inquire

HOMOPHONES

きく
聴 LISTEN → 1796
訊 INQUIRE → 1842

兜 【門】

閣

4128

▶TALL MAGNIFICENT BUILDING
▶CABINET

カク

Ⓒ 阁 gé

□3-8-6

169 門	Jōyō-6	U95A3
	S14-8-6	F0977

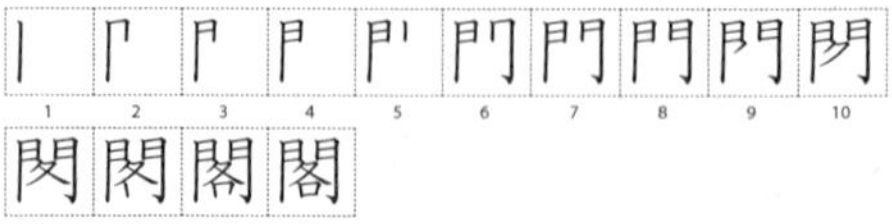

COMPOUNDS

❶ⓐ TALL MAGNIFICENT BUILDING, tower, pavilion, stately mansion, palace
ⓑ suffix after names of magnificent buildings such as high-class restaurants

a 閣下 かっか Your [His] Excellency
楼閣 ろうかく multistoried building
天守閣 てんしゅかく castle-tower; dungeon, keep
仏閣 ぶっかく Buddhist temple
銀閣寺 ぎんかくじ Ginkaku Temple
b 山水閣 さんすいかく Sansuikaku (restaurant's name)

❷ CABINET (of a government)
閣僚 かくりょう cabinet members
閣議 かくぎ cabinet conference
内閣 ないかく cabinet

SYNONYMS

❶ⓐ buildings
閣 TALL MAGNIFICENT BUILDING →4128
宇 large building →2699
殿 PALACE →2247
堂 HALL →3202
館 PUBLIC BUILDING →2196
舎 BUILDING →2555
棟 BLOCK →1248
厩 HORSE STABLE →3746

❶ⓐ tall buildings
閣 TALL MAGNIFICENT BUILDING →4128
楼 TALL BUILDING →1284
塔 TOWER →0683
台 observatory →2498

ⓑ restaurant suffixes
亭 quality restaurant suffix →2572
閣 high-class restaurant suffix →4128
園 restaurant suffix →3914
苑 restaurant suffix →2783

❷ parts of governments
閣 CABINET →4128
省 MINISTRY →3100

関

4129

▶CONCERN
▶BARRIER

カン せき -ぜき かか(わる)

Ⓝ 關 Ⓒ 关 guān

□3-8-6

169 門	Jōyō-4	U95A2
	S14-8-6	F0087

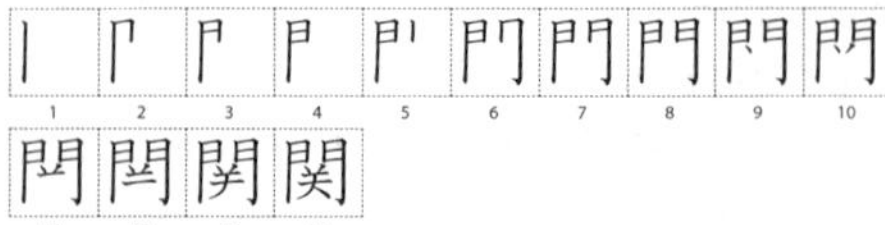

COMPOUNDS

❶ CONCERN (oneself), be concerned (with), relate, involve, be connected with
関係 かんけい relation, relationship, connection
関連 かんれん connection, relation, association
関心 かんしん concern, interest
関与する かんよする take part in, participate in, be concerned in
関知する かんちする be concerned (with), have a concern (in)
相関 そうかん mutual relationship, correlation

❷ⓐ BARRIER, customs barrier, checkpoint
ⓑ entranceway, gateway

a 関税 かんぜい customs, custom duty
関門 かんもん barrier, gateway
関東 かんとう Kanto district
関西 かんさい Kansai district
税関 ぜいかん customhouse
難関 なんかん barrier, obstacle, difficulty
通関 つうかん customs clearance, entry
b 玄関 げんかん entrance, (front) door

❸ connection, link; turning point
関節 かんせつ joint
機関 きかん engine, machine; agency, facilities, institution

❹ [also 函 3724] used phonetically for *kan*
関数 かんすう *math* function

❺ abbrev. of 関西 かんさい: Kansai district
関大 かんだい Kansai University

INDEPENDENT

【かんする 関する】**CONCERN, relate to, be connected with; affect, involve**

KUN

【せき 関】**BARRIER, checkpoint;** [in compounds] **champion wrestler, sumo wrestler**
関所 せきしょ barrier, checkpoint
関取 せきとり ranking sumo wrestler
箱根の関 はこねのせき Barrier of Hakone
霞ケ関 かすみがせき Japanese Foreign Ministry
大関 おおぜき sumo wrestler of second highest rank

【-ぜき -関】 **suffix after names of sumo wrestlers**
輪島関 わじまぜき Champion Wajima (sumo wrestler)
【かかわる 関わる】 [also 係わる]
① **be CONCERNed in, be involved**
関わり かかわり relation, connection
事件に関わる じけんにかかわる be involved in a case
② **influence (adversely), affect**
命に関わる いのちにかかわる be threatening to one's life, be a matter of life and death, fatal

SYNONYMS
❶ **relate**
関 CONCERN →4129
係 CONNECT →0108
絡 INTERLINK →1709
渉 HAVE RELATIONS WITH →0638
連 LINK →3849
聯 LINK →1797
❷ⓐ **obstacle**
障 HINDRANCE →0875
関 BARRIER →4129
❸ **joint**
節 JOINT →3336
関 connection →4129

HOMOPHONES
かかわる
係 CONNECT →0108
拘 ARREST →0367

COMPOUND FORMATION
❶【関東 かんとう】
関東 'Kanto district', a major district centered around Tokyo, originally meant 'east (東) of the barrier (関 ❷ⓐ)'. The reference is to an ancient barrier located in the Hakone area.
❷【関西 かんさい】
関西 'Kansai district' is similar in origin to 関東 above.

NOTE
➡ see USAGE note at 係 0108
➡ see COMPOUND FORMATION for
関取 せきとり →取 1613
玄関 げんかん →玄 2485
霞ケ関 かすみがせき →霞 3490

閤
4130
☐3-8-6
▶**FEUDAL PALACE**
コウ
Ⓒ 合 hé

169	Names	U95A4
門	S14-8-6	F2520

COMPOUNDS
❶ⓐ **FEUDAL PALACE**
ⓑ [archaic] government office
a 閤下 こうか [archaic] Your [His] Excellency
太閤 たいこう father of the imperial adviser; Toyotomi Hideyoshi
❷ [original meaning, now archaic] small side gate

SYNONYMS
❶ⓐ **palace**
宮 ROYAL PALACE →2828
殿 PALACE →2247
閣 FEUDAL PALACE →4130

魅
4131
☐3-8-7
▶**CHARM**
ミ
Ⓒ 魅 mèi

194	Jōyō	U9B45
鬼	S15-10-5	F1265

Stroke order: 1–15

COMPOUNDS
❶ **CHARM, bewitch, enchant, fascinate**
魅力 みりょく charm, glamour, appeal
魅惑 みわく fascination, enchantment, charm
魅了する みりょうする charm, fascinate
❷ [original meaning] evil spirit, mischievous ghost
魑×魅 ちみ mountain demon

INDEPENDENT
【みする 魅する】 CHARM, bewitch
魅せられる みせられる be charmed, be enchanted

SYNONYMS
❶ **charm**
魅 CHARM →4131
幻 bewitch →0206
媚 FAWN UPON →0687

閲
4132
☐3-8-7
▶**REVIEW**
エツ けみ(する)▲
Ⓝ 閲 Ⓒ 阅 yuè

169	Jōyō	U95B2
門	S15-8-7	F2247

Stroke order: 1–15

兒【門】

COMPOUNDS

❶ⓐ **REVIEW manuscripts, read carefully, look over, revise, edit**
ⓑ [suffix] **REVIEWed by, revised by**
ⓒ [original meaning] **REVIEW (troops), inspect, examine**

a 閲覧する えつらんする read, pursue
検閲 けんえつ censorship; inspection, review
校閲 こうえつ revision, reviewing, editing
b 部長閲 ぶちょうえつ revised by section chief
c 閲兵 えっぺい inspection [review] of troops
観閲 かんえつ inspection of troops

❷ elapse, pass
閲歴 えつれき one's career

INDEPENDENT

【えつ 閲】 revision, inspection
閲を請う えつをこう ask for a revision
【えっする 閲する】 **REVIEW**, revise, look over

KUN

【けみする 閲する】 examine, inspect; pass, elapse

SYNONYMS

❶ⓐ **revise**
訂 REVISE → 1829
閲 REVIEW → 4132
校 COLLATE → 1166
ⓒ **investigate and examine**
閲 REVIEW → 4132
審 EXAMINE CAREFULLY → 2985
験 TEST → 2306
勘 CHECK → 2231
糾 INQUIRE INTO → 1631
究 STUDY EXHAUSTIVELY → 2729
察 INSPECT → 2961
討 STUDY → 1846
探 PROBE → 0613
検 EXAMINE → 1241
診 EXAMINE A PATIENT → 1898
調 INVESTIGATE → 1973
査 LOOK INTO → 3092

閱

4133
□3-8-7

▸**REVIEW**
エツ けみ(する)

169	Nonstandard	U95B1
門	S15-8-7	F0000

traditional form → see 閲 at 4132

闇

4134
□3-8-9

▸**DARK**
アン▲ やみ くら(い)▲
Ⓒ 暗 àn

169	Jōyō	U95C7
門	S17-8-9	F1197

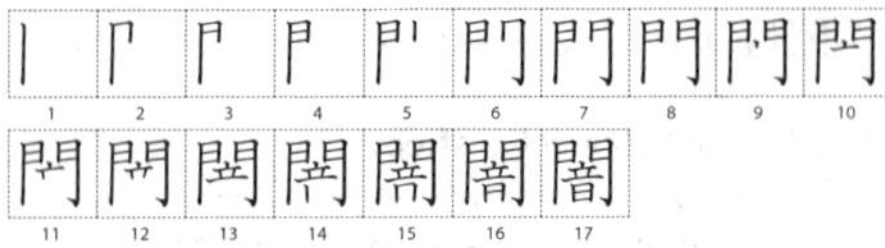

COMPOUNDS

[now usu. 暗 1273]

❶ⓐ [original meaning] **DARK, dim**
ⓑ **DARKness**

a 闇夜 あんや dark night
闇黒 あんこく darkness
闇然とした あんぜんとした dark, black, unclear; doleful, dispirited
b 諒闇 りょうあん court [national] mourning

❷ (lacking wisdom) **DARK**, ignorant, foolish
闇愚 あんぐ imbecility, feeblemindedness

KUN

【やみ 闇】
①ⓐ **DARKness**
ⓑ [in compounds] **DARK, dim**

a 闇討ち やみうち attacking under cover of darkness, surprise attack
真の闇 しんのやみ pitch-darkness
暗闇 くらやみ in darkness
夕闇 ゆうやみ dusk, twilight
b 闇夜 やみよ dark night
闇雲に やみくもに recklessly, blindly, at random

② [also prefix] **shady, illegal**
闇市 やみいち black market
闇金(=闇金融) やみきん(=やみきんゆう) black-market lending, illegal loan

③ unclassified compounds
無闇に むやみに rashly, thoughtlessly; excessively; needlessly

【くらい 闇い】 [usu. 暗い, sometimes also 昏い or 冥い] **DARK**, dim; (of colors) **dark**; (producing gloom) **dark**, dreary, dismal; (concealed) **dark**, shadowy, shady

SYNONYMS

❶ **dark**
暗 DARK → 1273
黒 BLACK → 3406
陰 shaded → 0657
闇 DARK → 4134
晦 DARK → 1196
昏 dark → 3073
昧 DARK → 1105

冥 DARK → 2613
曖 SHADY → 1383

❷ **foolish**

愚 FOOLISH → 3513
暗 DARK → 1273
痴 STUPID → 4072
鈍 DULL → 2123
呆 DIM-WITTED → 2712
魯 DULL → 2665
闇 DARK → 4134
蒙 IGNORANCE → 2938

HOMOPHONES

くらい

暗 DARK → 1273
冥 DARK → 2613
昏 LOSE CONSCIOUSNESS → 3073

NOTE

➡ see USAGE note at 暗 1273
➡ see COMPOUND FORMATION for 諒闇 りょうあん → 諒 1982

闊

4135
□3-8-9

▶**BROAD**
カツ
Ⓝ 濶 Ⓒ 阔 kuò

169	Non-Jōyō	U95CA
門	S17-8-9	F2623

COMPOUNDS

❶ⓐ [original meaning] **BROAD, wide**
ⓑ [now also 活 0460] **BROAD-minded, generous**

a 闊葉樹 かつようじゅ broadleaf tree
闊歩する かっぽする stride, swagger
b 闊達な かったつな openhearted, frank, broad-minded
快闊な かいかつな cheerful, lively, lighthearted
迂闊な うかつな thoughtless, careless

❷ **be separated, live apart**

久闊 きゅうかつ silence, neglecting to write

SYNONYMS

❶ⓐ **wide and extensive**

広 WIDE → 3769
紘 WIDE-RANGING → 1650
博 EXTENSIVE → 0170
恢 EXTENSIVE → 0436
浩 VAST → 0525
洸 VAST (expanse of water) → 0462
滉 DEEP AND VAST → 0811
曠 SPACIOUS → 1411
闊 BROAD → 4135

闘

4136
□3-8-10

▶**FIGHT**
トウ たたか(う)
Ⓝ 鬭 鬪 鬦◇ 斗◇
Ⓒ 斗 dòu dǒu

169△	Jōyō	U95D8
門	S18-8-10	F0830

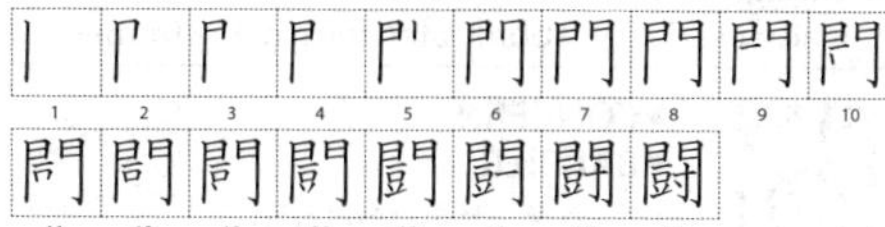

1 2 3 4 5 6 7 8 9 10 11 12 13 14 15 16 17 18

COMPOUNDS

[sometimes also 斗 3671]

❶ⓐ **FIGHT (with)**
ⓑ **FIGHT, fighting, struggle**

a 闘牛 とうぎゅう bullfight, fighting bull
ab 奮闘 ふんとう hard fighting
乱闘 らんとう free-for-all [confused] fight, melee
戦闘 せんとう battle, fight, combat
決闘 けっとう duel

❷ (struggle with) **FIGHT (against), contend with, compete with**

闘争 とうそう fight, conflict
闘士 とうし fighter, boxer
闘技 とうぎ competition, contest
健闘 けんとう good fight; strenuous efforts
春闘 しゅんとう spring labor offensive

KUN

【たたかう 闘う】(struggle with) **FIGHT (against), contend with, strive against**

闘い たたかい struggle, conflict
困難と闘う こんなんとたたかう contend with difficulties

SYNONYMS

❶ⓐ **fight and war**

闘 FIGHT → 4136
戦 WAR → 2242
征 go on a military expedition → 0349

ⓑ **warfare and rebellions**

戦 WAR → 2242
軍 war → 2582
役 war → 0288
陣 battle → 0545
乱 rebellion → 1611
変 uprising → 2569
闘 FIGHT → 4136

❷ **compete**

競 COMPETE → 2322
戦う contest → 2242
闘 FIGHT → 4136

争 CONTEND →2523

HOMOPHONES

たたかう 戦 WAR →2242
たたかい 戦 WAR →2242

NOTE

➡ see USAGE note at 戦 2242
★ Though 鬭 and 斗 are distinct characters, the latter is also used as an abbreviated form of the former.

關

4137
口3-8-11

▶CONCERN
▶BARRIER
カン せき -ぜき かか(わる)

169 門	Nonstandard	U95DC
	S19-8-11	F0000

traditional form →see 関 at 4129

巖

口3-8-12

incorrect classification
➡ see ▀2-3-17: 山 at 3037

嚴

口3-8-12

incorrect classification
➡ see ▀2-6-14: 口口 at 3396

署

口3-9-4

incorrect classification
➡ see ▀2-5-8: 罒 at 3223

颱

4138
口3-9-5

▶TYPHOON
タイ
Ⓒ 台 tái

182 風	Non-Jōyō	U98B1
	S14-9-5	F0000

COMPOUNDS

● [now replaced by 台 2498] **TYPHOON**
颱風 たいふう typhoon

SYNONYMS

● **wind**
風 WIND →3730
嵐 STORM →2898
颱 TYPHOON →4138
台 typhoon →2498
凪 CALM →3709
颯 SOUND OF GUSTING WIND →1563

署

口3-9-5

incorrect classification
➡ see ▀2-5-9: 罒 at 3229

題

4139
口3-9-9

▶TITLE
▶TOPIC
▶PROBLEM
ダイ
Ⓒ 题 tí

181 頁	Jōyō-3	U984C
	S18-9-9	F0192

1	2	3	4	5	6	7	8	9	10	11	12	13	14	15	16	17	18
丨	冂	日	日	旦	早	早	昰	是	是	是	是	題	題	題	題	題	題

COMPOUNDS

❶ **TITLE, caption, heading, headline**
題目 だいもく title, heading; theme; prayer of the Nichiren sect
題名 だいめい title
表題 ひょうだい title, heading, caption
改題 かいだい change of title

❷ **TOPIC, subject, theme**
題材 だいざい subject matter, theme
主題 しゅだい subject, theme
話題 わだい topic [subject] of conversation
演題 えんだい subject of a speech, speech title
議題 ぎだい topic for discussion
閑話休題 かんわきゅうだい to return to the subject

❸ⓐ **PROBLEM, question**
ⓑ counter for **PROBLEMs**
a 問題 もんだい problem, question, issue, matter
課題 かだい task, assignment; problem
難題 なんだい difficult problem [question]
出題する しゅつだいする set a problem
宿題 しゅくだい homework
b 五題 ごだい five problems [questions]

❹ [original meaning, now archaic] **forehead**

INDEPENDENT

【だい 題】**TITLE, caption; topic, subject, theme**
題を付ける だいをつける entitle
作文の題 さくぶんのだい subject of a composition

【だいする 題する】entitle

SYNONYMS

❶ **name**
名 NAME →2693
銘 name (inscribed by maker) →2158
姓 SURNAME →0334
氏 FAMILY NAME →3669
称 APPELLATION →1491
題 TITLE →4139
号 DESIGNATION →2675

❸ⓐ **question**
題 PROBLEM →4139

問 QUESTION (inquiry) → 4117
論 question (issue) → 1981
謎 RIDDLE → 2047

NOTE

➡ see COMPOUND FORMATION for 閑話休題 かんわきゅうだい → 閑 4123

簾簾 □3-9-10
incorrect classification
➡ see 2-6-13: ⺮ at 3387

魁 □3-10-4
incorrect classification
➡ see □3-8-6: 鬼 at 4125

鳶 □3-10-4
incorrect classification
➡ see □3-3-11: 弋 at 3919

箸 □3-10-4
incorrect classification
➡ see 2-6-8: ⺮ at 3354

鬦 4140 □3-10-4
▶FIGHT
トウ たたか(う)

191	Nonstandard	U9B26
鬥	S14-10-4	F0000

traditional form → see 闘 at 4136

魅 □3-10-5
incorrect classification
➡ see □3-8-7: 鬼 at 4131

鬪 4141 □3-10-10
▶FIGHT
トウ たたか(う)

191	Nonstandard	U9B2A
鬥	S20-10-10	F0000

alternative form → see 闘 at 4136

鬭 □3-10-14
incorrect stroke-count
➡ see □3-10-15: 鬥 at 4142

鬭 4142 □3-10-15
▶FIGHT
トウ たたか(う)

191	Nonstandard	U9B2D
鬥	S25-10-15	F0000

traditional form → see 闘 at 4136

麪 4143 □3-11-4
▶NOODLES
メン ベン

199	Nonstandard	U9EAA
麥	S15-11-4	F0000

alternative form → see 麺 at 4112

摩 □3-11-4
incorrect classification
➡ see □3-3-12: 广 at 3938

麾摩 □3-11-4
incorrect classification
➡ see □3-3-12: 广 at 3935

磨 □3-11-5
incorrect classification
➡ see □3-3-13: 广 at 3946

麿 □3-11-7
incorrect classification
➡ see □3-3-15: 广 at 3949

麓 □3-11-8
incorrect classification
➡ see 2-8-11: 林 at 3494

蘭 □3-11-8
incorrect classification
➡ see 2-3-16: ⺾ at 3031

麵 4144 □3-11-9
▶NOODLES
メン ベン

199	Nonstandard	U9EB5
麥	S20-11-9	F0000

traditional form → see 麺 at 4112

魔 □3-11-10
incorrect classification
➡ see □3-3-18: 广 at 3953

巖 □3-11-12
incorrect classification
➡ see 2-3-20: 山 at 3040

簡 □3-14-4
incorrect classification
➡ see 2-6-12: ⺮ at 3380

■ 4

SOLID
全体型

乙

4145

■4-1-1

▶SECOND

オツ イツ▲ おと-▲ きのと▲ ㊔ と

Ⓒ 乙 yǐ

5	Jōyō	U4E59
乙	S1-1-0	F1861

乙

RADICAL

otsu 'hook' (九 乞 乾), used for character classification

Variant:乚 *re* (乱 乳 也)

COMPOUNDS

ⓐ the SECOND, B; second class, grade B; the latter

ⓑ SECOND calendar sign (→see APPENDIX 8)

a 乙種 おつしゅ second grade

甲乙 こうおつ first and second, former and latter

b 乙卯 いつぼう 52nd of the sexagenary cycle

INDEPENDENT

【おつ 乙】**the SECOND, B; the latter; second calendar sign; bass (in traditional Japanese music)**

【おつな 乙な】queer, strange, odd; smartish, chic; nice, fanciful, delicate; romantic

乙な味 おつなあじ delicate flavor

乙に澄ます おつにすます pose affectedly serene

KUN

【おと- 乙-】(of girls) **young, youngest**

乙女 おとめ virgin, maiden

乙姫 おとひめ Princess of the Dragon Palace; younger princess

【きのと 乙】SECOND calendar sign

SYNONYMS

ⓐ second

乙 SECOND →4145

次 second →0058

後 AFTER (latter) →0431

中 MIDDLE →4262

NOTE

➡ see 甲 4293 FIRST, 丙 4290 THIRD and 丁 4155 fourth

了

■4-1-1

incorrect stroke-count

➡ see ■4-2-1 at 4157

乚

4146

■4-1-2

▶*RE*

5	Radical	U4E5A
乚	S1-1-0	F0000

radical variant →see 乙 at 4145

乚

4147

■4-1-2

▶HIDE

イン オン かく(す) かく(し)- かく(れる)

5	Nonstandard	U4E5A
乚	S1-1-0	F0000

traditional form →see 隠 at 0873

一

4148

■4-1-4

▶ONE

イチ イツ ひと- ひと(つ) ㊔ かず ひ はじめ おさむ まこと すすむ かつ くに

Ⓝ 弌 Ⓒ 一 yī

1	Jōyō-1	U4E00
一	S1-1-0	F0002

一

RADICAL

ichi 'one' (丁 七 上), used in characters related to numbers or horizontal things

COMPOUNDS

❶ⓐ [also prefix] [original meaning] **ONE, unity, first**

ⓑ ONE time, once

ⓒ make ONE, unify, become one

a 一方 いっぽう one side, one hand; a party, the other party; in the meantime; only
一部 いちぶ part, portion, section; a copy (of a book)
一緒に いっしょに together; at the same time; in a lump
一番 いちばん first, first place; first verse; most, best; a game, a round, a bout; a number, a piece
一千 いっせん 1000
一体 いったい one body; a style, a form; (why, what) on earth, (what, why) in the world
一家 いっか family, household; one's family; style (of established reputation)
一応(=一往) いちおう once; in outline; tentatively; for the time being
一月 いちがつ January
一瞬 いっしゅん instant, moment
一生懸命(=一所懸命)に いっしょうけんめい(=いっしょけんめい)に for life, with all one's might
一大事 いちだいじ matter of great importance
一一 いちいち one by one; in detail
一層 いっそう more, even more, all the more
一度に いちどに at a time, all at once
一部分 いちぶぶん part, portion, section
一円 いちえん the entire region [district]; one yen
第一 だいいち the first, number one; the best; to begin with, above everything else
唯一の ゆいいつの the only, the sole
b 一敗 いっぱい one defeat
一遍に いっぺんに once
c 一括 いっかつ one lump, summing up
統一する とういつする unify, coordinate, standardize

❷ [also prefix] (a certain) **ONE, a, an, another**
一夜 いちや(=ひとよ) one night, a night
一説 いっせつ another view, another version [report]
一日本人 いちにほんじん one [a] Japanese
一要素 いちようそ one factor, one element
一員 いちいん member

❸ **(one and the) same, identical**
一致 いっち accord, agreement
一律 いちりつ uniformity, equality
均一 きんいつ uniformity, equality, evenness

❹ **all in ONE, everything, the whole**
一般の いっぱんの general, universal, widespread
一切の いっさいの all, entire, whole
一掃する いっそうする clean out, wipe out, dispel, eradicate
一同 いちどう all (of us), all persons concerned
一座 いちざ the whole company, all present
一天 いってん the whole sky

❺ **ONE and only, sole, exclusive**
一途に いちずに with all one's might; blindly
一意専心 いちいせんしん wholeheartedly, single-mindedly
一向(に) いっこう(に) (not) at all, (not) in the least
一心に いっしんに wholeheartedly, with one's whole heart

❻ **the best**
一流の いちりゅうの first-rate; peculiar
日本一 にほんいち(=にっぽんいち) best in Japan

❼ **ONE little bit, slight amount**
一見 いっけん a look, a glance; apparently
一時 いちじ for a time, temporarily; once; one o'clock
一風変わった いっぷうかわった odd, queer; eccentric

❽ *baseball* first base, first baseman
一飛 いちひ first fly

INDEPENDENT

【いち 一】**ONE, unity**
一、二、三、四. . . いち, に, さん, し… one, two, three, four…
七分の一 ななぶんのいち one seventh

【いつ 一】(one and the) same, identical
軌を一にする きをいつにする have the same way of doing

【いつに 一に】solely, wholly, entirely; in part, partially; besides; **ONE**

KUN

【ひと- 一-】

① **ONE, one time**
一人 ひとり one person; only (child, son or daughter)
一人一人 ひとりひとり one by one, one at a time
一月目 ひとつきめ first month
一勝負 ひとしょうぶ one round
一晩中 ひとばんじゅう all night (long)
一先ず ひとまず for the time being, for the present
一重の ひとえの single (layer)
一通り ひととおり briefly, in a general way
一休みする ひとやすみする take a (short) rest
一握り ひとにぎり a handful (of rice)

② **at ONE time, once**
一頃 ひところ at one time, once
一昔 ひとむかし age, generation; decade

③ just a little
一筆書く ひとふで(=いっぴつ)かく drop a few lines
一息 ひといき breath; pause, rest; a little bit of effort

【ひとつ 一つ】**ONE; the same; just**
一つ目の ひとつめの one-eyed; first
一つ頼む ひとつたのむ I want to ask you for a favor

一〔〇〕丨丶丿㇀亅〆

SPECIAL READINGS

一日 ついたち [sometimes also 朔] 1st of the month
一昨年▲ おととし(=いっさくねん) year before last

SYNONYMS

❶ⓐ small numbers
一 ONE → 4148
十 TEN → 4172
廿 TWENTY → 4258
二 TWO → 2421
三 THREE → 2423
四 FOUR → 3778
五 FIVE → 4244
六 SIX → 2461
七 SEVEN → 4169
八 EIGHT → 3644
九 NINE → 4176

❶ⓐ one
一 ONE → 4148
壱 ONE (in legal documents) → 2723
片- ONE OF TWO → 4272
隻 ONE OF A PAIR → 3426
単 SINGLE → 2805
個 INDIVIDUAL → 0132

❷ a certain
某 A CERTAIN → 3168
或る A CERTAIN → 3978
一 ONE → 4148

❸ same and uniform
等 EQUAL → 3321
平 equal → 4291
均 EVEN → 0276
斉 UNIFORM → 2548
同 SAME → 3707
一 same → 4148

❹ all
皆 ALL → 3093
悉 THOROUGHLY → 3405
総 TOTAL → 1743
諸 VARIOUS → 1984
毎 EVERY → 2527
各 EACH → 2692
都 all → 2120
万 all → 3653
全 WHOLE → 2514
渾 ENTIRE → 0738
一 all in one → 4148
満 FULL → 0739
丸 complete(ly) → 4225
完 COMPLETE → 2727

❺ only
唯 ONLY → 0556
一 one and only → 4148

HOMOPHONES

ひとり
独り → 0471
一人 → 4148, 4175

ついたち
朔 FIRST DAY OF THE LUNAR MONTH → 1678
一日 → 4148, 3759

NOTE

➡ see USAGE note at 独 0471
➡ see USAGE note at 朔 1678
➡ see COMPOUND FORMATION for
一律 いちりつ → 律 0433
一緒 いっしょ → 緒 1742
一応(=一往) いちおう → 応 3804
一生懸命(=一所懸命) いっしょうけんめい (=いっしょけんめい) → 生 4309

〇

4149
■ 4-1-4

▶**ZERO**
レイ まる ぜろ
Ⓒ 〇 líng

31	Non-Jōyō	U3007
口	S1-1-0	F0000

COMPOUNDS

❶ ZERO (the numeral)
電話二三〇の九四一一 でんわにさんれいのきゅうよんいちいち Phone 230-9411
九〇字 きゅうじゅうじ 90 characters

❷ indicates omitted or unprintable letters [characters]
お〇んこ お—んこ c—t; f—king

KUN

【まる 〇】
① ZERO (the numeral)
一〇一号室 いちまるいちごうしつ room 101
② [also 丸] **check mark for correct answers (similar to ✓)**
〇×式の試験 まるばつしきのしけん examination paper in which correct answers are to be marked with circles and the wrong ones with crosses
③ indicates omitted or unprintable letters [characters]
〇〇氏 まるまるし Mr. X

【ぜろ 〇】**ZERO (the numeral)**
ゼッケン三〇一四番 ぜっけんさんぜろいちよんばん bib number 3014

SYNONYMS

❶ zero
零 ZERO → 3467
〇 ZERO → 4149

HOMOPHONES

ぜろ 零 ZERO →3467

まる

丸 ROUND →4225

円 CIRCLE →3673

NOTE

➡ see USAGE notes at 零 3467 and 丸 4225

★ The character 〇 is not recorded in any Japanese character dictionary, though it is used very frequently. Since 〇 has *on* and *kun* readings, it is clear that it is a kanji, no matter how the latter term is defined. The editor has therefore decided to include it in this dictionary.

丨

▶*BŌ*

4150

■4-1-4

2	Radical	U4E28
丨	S1-1-0	F0000

RADICAL

bō 'downstroke' (中 个 串), used for character classification

丶

▶*TEN*

4151

■4-1-4

3	Radical	U4E36
丶	S1-1-0	F0000

RADICAL

ten 'dot' (丸 丹 主), used for character classification

丿

▶*NO*

4152

■4-1-4

4	Radical	U4E3F
丿	S1-1-0	F0000

RADICAL

no 'left stroke' (乃 及 久), used for character classification

Top variant: ノ ***no*** (乏 乎 乗)

丿

▶*NO*

4153

■4-1-4

4	Radical	U4E3F
丿	S1-1-0	F0000

radical variant → see 丿 at 4152

亅

▶*HANEBŌ*

4154

■4-1-4

6	Radical	U4E85
亅	S1-1-0	F0000

RADICAL

hanebō 'hooked stroke' (事 予 了), used for character classification

---

〆

■4-1-4

incorrect stroke-count

➡ see ■4-2-4 at 4179

丁

▶**TOWN SUBSECTION**

▶**MISCELLANEOUS COUNTER**

チョウ テイ チン▲ ひのと▲

4155

■4-2-1

Ⓒ 丁 dīng

1	Jōyō-3	U4E01
一	S2-1-1	F0971

一 丁
1 2

COMPOUNDS

❶ⓐ (minor subdivision in the Japanese addressing system) **TOWN SUBSECTION, *chome*, subsection of a 町 ちょう (town section)**

ⓑ counter for town blocks

a 二丁目 にちょうめ 2-chome

国府町三丁目 こくふちょうさんちょうめ 3-chome, Kokufu-cho

b 二丁 にちょう two blocks

❷ **COUNTER for MISCELLANEOUS things, as:**

ⓐ **cakes (of bean curd)**

ⓑ **servings (as of cutlet, noodles, etc.)**

ⓒ carpenter's tools

ⓓ [also 挺 ちょう 0512] guns

a 豆腐一丁 とうふいっちょう one cake of bean curd

b ラーメン三丁 らーめんさんちょう three bowls of Chinese noodles

c 鋸二丁 のこぎりにちょう two saws

d ピストル五丁 ぴすとるごちょう five pistols

❸ⓐ full-fledged man, adult, young man

ⓑ **worker, servant**

a 丁年 ていねん full age, conscription age

壮丁 そうてい young man of conscription age

b 馬丁 ばてい batman, footman

園丁 えんてい gardener

庖丁(=包丁) ほうちょう kitchen knife, carving knife

❹ [sometimes also 恰 ちょう 0437] **just, exactly**

丁度 ちょうど just, exactly; as if

❺ⓐ the fourth, D; fourth class, grade D

ⓑ fourth calendar sign (→see APPENDIX 8)

a 甲乙丙丁 こうおつへいてい first, second, third and fourth; A, B, C and D
b 丁亥 ていがい 24th of the sexagenary cycle
❻ [formerly 叮 てい 0211 or 鄭 てい 2379] **courteous**
丁寧(=叮嚀)な ていねいな polite, courteous
丁重(=鄭重)に ていちょうに politely, courteously
❼ [formerly 釘 てい 2100 or 幀 てい 0695] bookbinding
装丁する そうていする bind (a book)
❽ⓐ sheet or leaf, esp. of books bound in the Japanese style
ⓑ counter for such sheets (1 丁 = 2 pages)
a 丁数 ちょうすう number of pages; paging
丁付け ちょうづけ pagination, numbering
落丁 らくちょう missing page [leaf]
b 五丁 ごちょう five sheets
❾ T-shaped
丁字形の ていじけいの T-shaped
丁定規 ていじょうぎ T-square
❿ even number
丁半 ちょうはん odd and even (numbers); gambling
⓫ [formerly 牒 ちょう 1299] wooden placard, label, tag
符丁 ふちょう sign; secret price tag; password
⓬ [usu. 町 ちょう 1430] *cho*: former unit of length equiv. to approx. 109 m or 60 *ken* (間)
⓭ [rare] used phonetically for *chin* in the transliteration of foreign words
沃度丁幾 よーどちんき iodine tincture
⓮ [original meaning, now obsolete] nail

INDEPENDENT

【ちょう 丁】even number; *cho* (→⓬)
丁か半か ちょうかはんか even or odd
【てい 丁】the fourth, D; fourth calendar sign

KUN

【ひのと 丁】fourth calendar sign

SYNONYMS

❶ⓐ parts of towns
区 WARD →3681
街 CITY QUARTER →0702
町 town section (*cho*) →1430
丁 TOWN SUBSECTION (*chome*) →4155
字 village or town section →2696
❷ general counters
丁 MISCELLANEOUS COUNTER →4155
個 GENERAL COUNTER →0132
箇 COUNTER FOR ITEMS →3348
点 counter for articles →2587
件 counter for cases →0054
❻ courteous
寧 COURTEOUS →2959
鄭 COURTEOUS →2379
叮 COURTEOUS →0211
嚀 COURTEOUS →0965
丁 courteous →4155
❽ⓐ paper
紙 PAPER →1654
葉 LEAF →2912
丁 sheet →4155
箋 PIECE OF PAPER →3352
頁 PAGE →2589
面 page (of a newspaper) →2590
ⓑ counters for flat things
枚 COUNTER FOR FLAT THINGS →1069
葉 counter for leaves →2912
丁 counter for sheets →4155
頁 counter for pages →2589
通 counter for letters →3855
竿 counter for flags →3259

COMPOUND FORMATION

【庖丁(=包丁) ほうちょう】
庖丁 'kitchen knife, carving knife' originally meant a worker (丁 ❸ⓑ) of the kitchen (庖), i.e., a cook. It acquired its current meaning since a cook uses a kitchen knife in his work.

NOTE

➡ see 甲 4293 FIRST, 乙 4145 SECOND and 丙 4290 THIRD

几 4156

■4-2-1

▶**DESK**
キ
Ⓒ 几 jī

16	Non-Jōyō	U51E0
几	S2-2-0	F2610

RADICAL

tsukue 'table' (凡 処 凱), used in characters related to laying on, leaning against or wind
Enclosure: 几 ***kazagamae*** (凧 凰 凪)

COMPOUNDS

● [original meaning] **DESK, small table**
几案 きあん [rare] desk
几下(=机下) きか under the desk
几帳 きちょう screen
几帳面な きちょうめんな exact, precise, punctual
浄几(=浄机) じょうき clean [tidy] writing desk
床几(=床机) しょうぎ campstool, folding stool

SYNONYMS

● tables and stands
卓 TABLE →2561
机 DESK →1014
几 DESK →4156
台 STAND →2498

了

4157

■4-2-1

▶**FINISH**
▶**COMPREHEND**

リョウ

Ⓒ 了 liǎo le

6	Jōyō	U4E86
亅	S2-1-1	F1168

乛 了
1 2

COMPOUNDS

❶ **FINISH, complete, conclude**

議了する ぎりょうする finish discussion, close a debate

未了 みりょう unfinished, incomplete

完了する かんりょうする complete, finish; be completed, be finished

終了する しゅうりょうする end, conclude, complete; expire

修了 しゅうりょう completion (of a course)

満了する まんりょうする expire, become due

❷ [sometimes also 諒 1982 or 領 1567]

ⓐ **COMPREHEND, know clearly, understand**

ⓑ show understanding, be sympathetic, acknowledge

a 了解 りょうかい understanding, comprehension; consent

了承する りょうしょうする acknowledge, understand, note

了知する りょうちする know, understand, appreciate

b 了察する りょうさつする consider, take into account, sympathize with

INDEPENDENT

【りょう 了】end (following the end of a novel or thesis); [usu. 諒 1982] understanding, comprehension

了とする(=諒とする) りょうとする understand, appreciate; excuse

SYNONYMS

❶ **end**

終 END → 1692

絶 COME TO AN END → 1711

閉 CLOSE → 4116

了 FINISH → 4157

済 SETTLE → 0634

-上げる completion suffix → 4212

完 COMPLETE → 2727

結 CONCLUDE → 1706

竣 COMPLETE → 1528

❷ **know and understand**

知 KNOW → 1446

通 know thoroughly → 3855

得 gain understanding of → 0577

分かる understand → 2466

解 understand → 1913

諒 UNDERSTAND → 1982

了 COMPREHEND → 4157

悟 AWAKE TO → 0502

惺 AWAKE TO → 0709

又

4158

■4-2-1

▶**AGAIN**

ユウ▲ また また- また(の)-

Ⓝ 又 Ⓒ 又 yòu

29	Jōyō	U53C8
又	S2-2-0	F1187

radical variant → see 又 at 4167

フ 又
1 2

KUN

【また 又】

① [formerly also 復] **AGAIN, once more [again], repeatedly**

又会う日迄 またあうひまで till we meet again

又しても またしても once again

② [formerly also 亦] [often preceded by も] **also, too, as well**

私も又 わたくしもまた I also, me too

それも又結構だ それもまたけっこうだ That's also good

③ ⓐ and, besides, further

ⓑ on the other hand

ⓒ [often followed by particle は] **or, in other words**

a 勝利又勝利 しょうりまたしょうり victory after victory

b 夫は病弱だが妻は又元気が良い おっとはびょうじゃくだがつまはまたげんきがよい The husband is invalid, while the wife is robust

c 又は または or, in other words

言っても良いし、又言わなくても良い いってもよいし,またいわなくてもよい You can either say it or not say it

④ adverb expressing surprise or doubt

これは又何の騒ぎだ これはまたなんのさわぎだ Well, what's this row?

そりゃ又酷い話だ そりゃまたひどいはなしだ What a shame!

【また- 又-】[also prefix] **indirect, through an intermediary**

又貸し またがし underlease, sublease

又聞き またぎき hearsay, secondhand information

又従兄弟 またいとこ second cousin

【またの- 又の-】**another, next**

又の名 またのな another name, alias

又の日 またのひ the next day; another day, some other day

SYNONYMS

【また】

① **repeating and repetition**

再 ANOTHER TIME → 4332
又 AGAIN → 4158
復 repeat → 0701
重 DUPLICATE → 4390
畳 reduplicate → 3205
改 redo → 0287
-換える redo → 0716
-直す repetition suffix → 3649
-返す do over → 3797

② & ③ⓐ **additionally**

亦 ALSO → 2504
兼 CONCURRENTLY → 2850
又 also, and → 4158
而うして and → 2520
及び and → 4192
並びに and also → 2793
傍ら besides → 0166
尚 STILL → 2774
更に furthermore → 4355
且つ AS WELL → 4297

USAGE

【また】

又

① [formerly also 復] again, once more [again], repeatedly
② [formerly also 亦] [often preceded by も] also, too, as well
③ⓐ and, besides, further
ⓑ on the other hand
ⓒ [often followed by particle は] or, in other words
④ adverb expressing surprise or doubt

亦

[now usu. 又] [often preceded by も] also, too, as well

復

[now replaced by 又] again, once more [again], repeatedly

HOMOPHONES

また

亦 ALSO → 2504
復 RETURN TO → 0701

冂

▶ ***KEIGAMAE***

4159
■4-2-1

13	Radical	U5182
冂	S2-2-0	F0000

RADICAL

keigamae 'border' (内 円 再), used for character classification

冖

▶ ***WAKANMURI***

4160
■4-2-1

14	Radical	U5196
冖	S2-2-0	F0000

RADICAL

wakanmuri 'cover' (写 冠 冗), used in characters related to covering or covers

---

⺇

▶ ***KAZAGAMAE***

4161
■4-2-1

16	Radical	U2E87
⺇	S2-2-0	F0000

radical variant → see 几 at 4156

匚

▶ ***HAKOGAMAE***

4162
■4-2-1

22	Radical	U531A
匚	S2-2-0	F0000

RADICAL

hakogamae 'box' (匠 匡 匪×), used in characters related to boxes or receptacles

---

匸

▶ ***KAKUSHIGAMAE***

4163
■4-2-1

23	Radical	U5338
匸	S2-2-0	F0000

RADICAL

kakushigamae 'enclose' (匿), used in characters related to concealing or enclosing
Enclosure: 匸× ***kakushigamae*** (区 匹)

㔾

▶ ***FUSHIZUKURI***

4164
■4-2-1

26	Radical	U353E
㔾	S2-2-0	F0000

radical variant → see 卩 at 4165

卩

▶ ***FUSHIZUKURI***

4165
■4-2-1

26	Radical	U5369
卩	S2-2-0	F0000

RADICAL

fushizukuri 'seal' (印 卵 卸), used in characters related to actions performed while kneeling
Variant: 㔾 ***fushizukuri*** (危 卮× 巻)

厂 ▶***GANDARE***

4166
■4-2-1

27	Radical	U5382
厂	S2-2-0	F0000

RADICAL

gandare 'cliff' (原 厚 厘), used in characters related to cliffs, rocks or stones

---

㕛 ▶**AGAIN**
ユウ また また- また(の)-

4167
■4-2-1

29	Nonstandard	U53C8
又	S2-2-0	F0000

traditional form → see 又 at 4158

RADICAL

mata 'right hand' (又), used in characters related to actions performed by the hand
Variant: 又 ***mata*** (反 双)

厂 ▶**PERSONAL HISTORY**
レキ レッキ

4168
■4-2-1

27	Nonstandard	U5382
厂	S2-2-0	F0000

handwritten form → see 歴 at 3748

乃
■4-2-1
incorrect classification
➡ see □3-1-1: 乃 at 3643

乙
■4-2-1
incorrect stroke-count
➡ see ■4-1-1 at 4145

子
■4-2-1
incorrect stroke-count
➡ see ■4-3-1 at 4196

刀
■4-2-1
incorrect classification
➡ see □3-1-1: 刀 at 3642

廴
■4-2-1
incorrect stroke-count
➡ see ■4-3-1 at 4202

廴
■4-2-1
incorrect stroke-count
➡ see ■4-3-1 at 4203

阝
■4-2-1
incorrect stroke-count
➡ see ■4-3-1 at 4206

阝
■4-2-1
incorrect stroke-count
➡ see ■4-3-1 at 4207

七 ▶**SEVEN**
シチ なな なな(つ) なの ㊔ な
Ⓒ 七 qī

4169
■4-2-2

1	Jōyō-1	U4E03
一	S2-1-1	F0199

一 七
1 2

COMPOUNDS

● **SEVEN, seventh**
七曜表 しちようひょう calendar
七月 しちがつ July
十七日 じゅうしちにち 17 days; 17th of the month

INDEPENDENT

【しち 七】 **SEVEN**

KUN

【なな 七】 **SEVEN**
七週間 ななしゅうかん seven weeks
七草 ななくさ the seven spring herbs, the seven autumnal flowers
【ななつ 七つ】 **SEVEN; seven years old; 4 o'clock** (in former time system)
七つ目 ななつめ seventh
【なの 七】 [in compounds] **SEVEN**
七日 なのか(=なぬか) seven days; 7th of the month

SPECIAL READINGS

七夕 たなばた Festival of the Weaver [Star Vega]; the Star Festival

SYNONYMS

● **small numbers**
一 ONE → 4148
十 TEN → 4172
廿 TWENTY → 4258
二 TWO → 2421
三 THREE → 2423
四 FOUR → 3778
五 FIVE → 4244
六 SIX → 2461
七 SEVEN → 4169
八 EIGHT → 3644
九 NINE → 4176

亠 ▶*NABEBUTA*

4170
■4-2-2

8	Radical	U4EA0
亠	S2-2-0	F0000

RADICAL

nabebuta 'lid' (亡 亢 亦), used for character classification

凵 ▶*KANNYŌ, UKEBAKO*

4171
■4-2-2

17	Radical	U51F5
凵	S2-2-0	F0000

RADICAL

kannyō or ***ukebako*** 'receptacle' (出 凶 函), used for character classification

十 ▶TEN

ジュウ ジッ- ジュッ- **とお と** ㊔ そ

Ⓒ 十 shí

4172
■4-2-3

24	Jōyō-1	U5341
十	S2-2-0	F0027

一 十
1 2

RADICAL

jū 'ten' (千 南 卓), used for character classification
Left variant: 十 ***jūhen*** (協 博)

COMPOUNDS

❶ⓐ TEN, tenth
ⓑ TEN times

a 十時 じゅうじ ten o'clock
七十 しちじゅう 70
第十 だいじゅう tenth
二十 にじゅう [sometimes also 廿] 20
b 十回 じっかい(=じゅっかい) ten times
十進法 じっしんほう decimal system

❷ complete, completely, perfect
十分(=充分)な じゅうぶんな full, enough, sufficient; plentiful
十全の じゅうぜんの perfect, absolute

❸ many
十目 じゅうもく all eyes

❹ cross
十字架 じゅうじか cross, crucifix
十文字 じゅうもんじ cross
十字路 じゅうじろ crossroads

INDEPENDENT

【じゅう 十】**TEN**
一から十迄 いちからじゅうまで without exception

KUN

【とお 十】**TEN, tenth**
十日 とおか ten days; 10th of the month

【と 十】**TEN**
十重 とえ tenfold
十人十色 じゅうにんといろ So many men, so many minds

SPECIAL READINGS

十重二十重 とえはたえ manifold, multitude
二十(=二十歳) はたち 20 years old
二十日 はつか 20 days; 20th of the month

SYNONYMS

❶ⓐ small numbers
一 ONE →4148
十 TEN →4172
廿 TWENTY →4258
二 TWO →2421
三 THREE →2423
四 FOUR →3778
五 FIVE →4244
六 SIX →2461
七 SEVEN →4169
八 EIGHT →3644
九 NINE →4176

❶ⓐ ten
十 TEN →4172
拾 ten (in legal documents) →0454

HOMOPHONES

にじゅう
廿 TWENTY →4258
二十 →2421, 4172

十 ▶*JŪHEN*

4173
■4-2-3

24	Radical	U5341
十	S2-2-0	F0000

radical variant →see 十 at 4172

卜 ▶DIVINE

ボク **うらな(う) うらない**

Ⓒ 卜 bǔ bo

4174
■4-2-4

25	Names	U535C
卜	S2-2-0	F2818

RADICAL

bokunoto 'divine' (卦×), used in characters related to divination
Variant: ⺊× ***bokunoto*** (占)

COMPOUNDS

● [original meaning] **DIVINE, tell (a person's) fortune, augur**

卜者 ぼくしゃ fortuneteller, diviner
卜占 ぼくせん augury
卜筮× ぼくぜい fortunetelling, divination
卜居 ぼっきょ choosing a homesite by divination
亀卜 きぼく divination by tortoiseshells
売卜 ばいぼく fortunetelling (as an occupation)

INDEPENDENT

【ぼくする 卜する】tell (a person's) fortune, **DIVINE**; fix, choose

KUN

【うらなう 卜う】[now usu. 占う] **DIVINE**, tell (a person's) fortune, augur
【うらない 卜】[now usu. 占い] divination, fortunetelling

SYNONYMS

● **divine**

占 DIVINE → 2496
卜 DIVINE → 4174
易 divination → 3064

HOMOPHONES

うらなう 占 OCCUPY → 2496
うらない 占 OCCUPY → 2496

NOTE

➡ see USAGE note at 占 2496

人

4175

■ 4-2-4

▶HUMAN BEING

ジン ニン ひと -り* -と*

Ⓒ 人 rén

9	Jōyō-1	U4EBA
人	S2-2-0	F0001

丿 人
1 2

RADICAL

hito 'person' (仄 以 來), used in characters related to human beings
Left variant: 亻 *ninben* (仏 仁 代)
Top variant: 𠆢 *hitoyane* (今 令 会)

COMPOUNDS

❶ⓐ [also suffix] [original meaning] **HUMAN BEING, person, man; people, mankind**
ⓑ **counter for people**

a 人間 にんげん human being, man; people, mankind
人類 じんるい mankind, humankind
人工の じんこうの artificial
人為 じんい human work, artificiality
人造の じんぞうの artificial, man-made
人民 じんみん the people, populace, subjects
人生 じんせい human life, life
人気 にんき popularity; temperament of the people; business conditions
人名 じんめい personal name
人道主義 じんどうしゅぎ humanitarianism
夫人 ふじん wife, married lady, Mrs.
商人 しょうにん merchant, trader, tradesman
他人 たにん another person, other people; stranger
個人 こじん individual
現代人 げんだいじん modern person [people]

b 人数 にんずう number of people
二十人 にじゅうにん 20 people

❷ [suffix]
ⓐ **person of specific geographical origin, nationality or race**
ⓑ person of certain category, as the performer of an action or holder of an occupation: **-er (as in *manager*)**

a アメリカ人 あめりかじん American
外国人 がいこくじん foreigner, alien

b 見物人 けんぶつにん spectator, sightseer
料理人 りょうりにん cook
支配人 しはいにん manager, executive
芸能人 げいのうじん performing artist

❸ [rare] other people, others
人我 じんが oneself and others

❹ **personality, character, disposition**
人格 じんかく character, personality

INDEPENDENT

【にん 人】*literary* person; character

KUN

【ひと 人】
①ⓐ **man, HUMAN BEING, person, mankind**
ⓑ **people, men**

a 人殺し ひとごろし murder; murderer
人質 ひとじち hostage, prisoner
人人 ひとびと people
人違い ひとちがい mistaken identity
恋人 こいびと lover, sweetheart

b 人出 ひとで turnout, crowd
人だかりがする ひとだかりがする be crowded with people
人だかり ひとだかり crowd, throng

② **other people, others**
人事 ひとごと other people's affairs
人の金 ひとのかね other people's money
人見知りする ひとみしりする be shy of strangers
人目 ひとめ attention, public notice

③ man of talent, able man
人を得る ひとをえる employ the right person

④ **nature, character, personality**

人柄 ひとがら character, personality
人の良い ひとのよい good natured, kindhearted
お人好し おひとよし good-natured person; credulous person

【-り -人】counter for people

一人 ひとり one person; only (child, son or daughter)
二人 ふたり two persons

【-と -人】person

玄人 くろうと expert, master hand; prostitute
素人 しろうと amateur, novice, outsider; decent woman
仲人 なこうど go-between, matchmaker
若人 わこうど youth, young man

SPECIAL READINGS

大人 おとな adult

SYNONYMS

❶ⓐ person

人 HUMAN BEING → 4175
者 PERSON → 3980
方 person (*honorific*) → 2459
氏 person (*polite*) → 3669

ⓑ counters for persons

人 counter for people → 4175
名 counter for persons → 2693

❷ⓑ workers and professionals

家 professional → 2827
婦 woman worker → 0565
嬢 (unmarried) female worker → 0936
夫 MAN LABORER → 4271
匠 CRAFTSMAN → 3711
工 workman → 4190
客 skilled person → 2798
士 PROFESSION SUFFIX → 4213
師 profession suffix → 1680
者 person who → 3980
人 person of certain category → 4175
員 MEMBER (of a staff) → 2822
屋 colloquial occupation suffix → 3842
手 OCCUPATION SUFFIX → 4267

HOMOPHONES

ひとり

独り → 0471
一人 → 4148, 4175

NOTE

➡ see USAGE note at 独 0471
➡ see COMPOUND FORMATION for
人間 にんげん → 間 4122
夫人 ふじん → 夫 4271

九

4176

■4-2-4

▶NINE

キュウ ク ここの ここの(つ) ㊔ ひさし ひさ

Ⓒ 九 jiǔ

5	Jōyō-1	U4E5D
乙	S2-1-1	F0137

ノ 九
1 2

COMPOUNDS

❶ NINE

九百 きゅうひゃく 900
九回 きゅうかい nine times
九星術 きゅうせいじゅつ astrology
九月 くがつ September
九人 きゅうにん nine people

❷ many

九死に一生を得る きゅうしにいっしょうをうる have a narrow escape from death
九拝 きゅうはい bowing many times (in apology)

❸ abbrev. of 九州 きゅうしゅう: Kyushu district

九大 きゅうだい Kyushu University

INDEPENDENT

【きゅう 九】NINE
【く 九】NINE

KUN

【ここの 九】[in compounds] **NINE**

九日 ここのか nine days; 9th of the month
九重 ここのえ ninefold; Imperial Palace

【ここのつ 九つ】NINE; nine years old; 12 o'clock (in former time system)

SYNONYMS

❶ small numbers

一 ONE → 4148
十 TEN → 4172
廿 TWENTY → 4258
二 TWO → 2421
三 THREE → 2423
四 FOUR → 3778
五 FIVE → 4244
六 SIX → 2461
七 SEVEN → 4169
八 EIGHT → 3644
九 NINE → 4176

❶ nine

九 NINE → 4176
玖 NINE → 1041

入

▶ENTER
▶PUT IN
ニュウ ニッ-▲ い(る) -い(る) -い(り)
い(れる) -い(れ) はい(る)

4177
■4-2-4

Ⓒ 入 rù

11	Jōyō-1	U5165
入	S2-2-0	F0034

ノ 入
1 2

RADICAL

iru 'enter' (全 兪× 兩), used for character classification

COMPOUNDS

❶ [original meaning] **ENTER, come in, go in**
入場 にゅうじょう entrance, admission
入国 にゅうこく entry [entrance] into a country
入室する にゅうしつする enter a room; join (a laboratory)
収入 しゅうにゅう income, earnings, receipts
侵入する しんにゅうする invade, raid, trespass, intrude
介入 かいにゅう intervention

❷ⓐ (become a member of) **ENTER, join, be admitted**
ⓑ abbrev. of 入学 にゅうがく: **ENTERing a school**
a 入学する にゅうがくする enter a school, matriculate
入門する にゅうもんする become a pupil of, enter a private school
入閣する にゅうかくする join the Cabinet, become a Cabinet member
入賞 にゅうしょう winning a prize
入選する にゅうせんする be accepted, be selected
加入する かにゅうする enter, join
b 入試 にゅうし entrance examination

❸ **PUT IN, insert, enter, admit**
入札 にゅうさつ tender, bidding
入手する にゅうしゅする obtain, get, come by, procure
入力 にゅうりょく input; power input
入金 にゅうきん receipt of money; money received
記入する きにゅうする enter, write in, record
注入 ちゅうにゅう pouring into, injection
輸入 ゆにゅう import, importation
導入 どうにゅう introduction

❹ necessary
入用 にゅうよう need, demand, necessity
入費 にゅうひ expense(s)

❺ **ENTER**ing tone in Chinese phonetics
入声 にっしょう(=にっせい) entering tone

INDEPENDENT

【にゅう 入】ON (marking on switches)
切—入 せつにゅう OFF-ON (marking on switches)

KUN

【いる 入る】
①ⓐ **ENTER, go in, come in**
ⓑ (of the sun) **set**
a 入り いり setting (of the sun); attendance; beginning; income
入り口 いりぐち entrance
押し入る おしいる enter by force, break into
b 入り日 いりひ setting sun
② attain
老境に入る ろうきょうにいる be advanced in age
③ [usu. 要る]
ⓐ need, want, require
ⓑ be necessary [required]; cost, take
b 入り いり expense(s)
入り用 いりよう need, want

【-いる -入る】**emphatic verbal suffix**
恐れ入る おそれいる be overwhelmed [dumbfounded] (as with gratitude, shame, regret or astonishment)
聞き入る ききいる listen attentively to, be lost in

【-いり -入り】[also suffix]
①ⓐ **ENTERing**
ⓑ **be encased, be placed in**
a 出入り でいり going in and out; frequentation, usual visit (as by a merchant); indentations; incomings and outgoings; trouble, fight
立ち入り たちいり entering
b 箱入りの はこいりの cased, boxed
② (be accepted as a member) **ENTER, join, enroll**
プロ入り ぷろいり turning professional
仲間入り なかまいり joining the ranks of
③ⓐ including, accompanied by
ⓑ containing, having a capacity of
a 蜂蜜入りの はちみついりの containing honey
鳴り物入りで なりものいりで with a flourish of trumpets
b 一リットル入りの瓶 いちりっとるいりのびん bottle holding a liter

【いれる 入れる】
①ⓐ **PUT IN, enter, insert, fit; add to**
ⓑ **let in, admit, show in**
a 入れ替え いれかえ replacement, shifting; switching
ポケットに入れる ぽけっとにいれる put (a thing) in one's pocket
②ⓐ (cause to enter) **send, deliver, extend**
ⓑ (permit to enter or join) take in, admit; hire, employ
ⓒ (put into action or use) **exercise (care), exert**
a 申し入れる もうしいれる propose; make representations to
b 患者を入れる かんじゃをいれる admit a patient
c 手入れ ていれ care, repairs, trimming; (police) raid

③ **accommodate, hold, contain**
入れ物 いれもの receptacle, container
受け入れ うけいれ reception; acceptance
乗り入れ のりいれ extension (of a railway line) into
取り入れる とりいれる take in; harvest; accept, adopt, introduce
押し入れ おしいれ closet; wall-cupboard

④ include, count in
数に入れる かずにいれる include in the number

⑤ make (tea), brew (coffee)

⑥ [sometimes also 容れる] **accept, tolerate, be compatible**
受け入れる うけいれる accept, consent to; receive, accommodate
相入れない あいいれない incompatible
聞き入れる ききいれる comply with, accept

【-いれ -入れ】 [suffix] **receptacle, container**
小銭入れ こぜにいれ change purse

【はいる 入る】 **ENTER, come in, go in; break in; enter (a school), join, go into; contain, hold, accommodate; have, get, receive; begin, set in**
入り込む はいりこむ get in, come in, enter
クラブに入る くらぶにはいる join a club
千人入る講堂 せんにんはいるこうどう auditorium with a seating capacity of 1000
金が手に入る かねがてにはいる get hold of money
梅雨に入った つゆにはいった The rainy season has set in

SYNONYMS

❶ **enter**
入 ENTER →4177
-込む MOVE INWARD →3762

❷ⓐ **participate and join**
参 PARTICIPATE →2563
与 take part in →4229
加 join →0042
入 ENTER →4177

❸ **put in**
入 PUT IN →4177
挿 INSERT →0517
嵌 INLAY →2897
-込む cause to move inward →3762

❹ **need and necessity**
要 required →3263
必 must →0015
須 MUST →0700
需 DEMAND →3472
入 necessary →4177
用 needed for (a specific use) →3694

USAGE

【いれる】
入れる
①ⓐ put in, enter, insert, fit; add to
ⓑ let in, admit, show in
②ⓐ (cause to enter) send, deliver, extend
ⓑ (permit to enter or join) take in, admit; hire, employ
ⓒ (put into action or use) exercise (care), exert
③ accommodate, hold, contain
④ include, count in
⑤ make (tea), brew (coffee)
⑥ [sometimes also 容れる] accept, tolerate, be compatible

容れる
[usu. 入れる] accept, tolerate, be compatible

HOMOPHONES

いる 要 IMPORTANT →3263
いり 要 IMPORTANT →3263
いれる 容 APPEARANCE →2832

NOTE

➡ see also USAGE note at 要 3263

力

4178

4-2-4

▶POWER
リョク リキ リー▲ ちから ㊔ つとむ いさむ
Ⓒ 力 lì

19	Jōyō-1	U529B
力	S2-2-0	F0077

フ 力
1 2

RADICAL

chikara 'strength' (加 勢 功), used in characters related to strength, work or effort

COMPOUNDS

❶ⓐ [also suffix] [original meaning] **muscular POWER, physical strength, force, might**
ⓑ **military POWER, armed force**
ⓒ (power in general) **POWER to influence, strength, influence, authority**

a 人力 じんりょく human power [strength]
筋力 きんりょく muscular strength [power]
体力 たいりょく physical strength, strength of one's body
暴力 ぼうりょく violence, force
強力(=剛力) ごうりき Herculean strength; mountain carrier [guide]
省力化 しょうりょくか labor savings
全力で ぜんりょくで with all one's might, to the best of one's ability
苦力 くーりー coolie

五人力が有る ごにんりきがある have the strength of five men
b 兵力 へいりょく military force; strength of an army
主力 しゅりょく main force, main body
武力 ぶりょく military power, armed might
c 権力 けんりょく power, authority, influence
勢力 せいりょく influence, power, might; force (of a typhoon)
威力 いりょく power, might, authority, influence
迫力 はくりょく power, force, punch, appeal
有力者 ゆうりょくしゃ influential person, man of importance
金力 きんりょく power of money
強力な きょうりょくな strong, powerful, mighty

2a (source of energy) **POWER, energy; motive power**
b *phys* **force**
a 力織機 りきしょっき power loom
電力 でんりょく electric power, electricity
原子力 げんしりょく atomic energy, nuclear power
馬力 ばりき horsepower; energy, effort; cart, wagon
動力源 どうりょくげん power source
出力 しゅつりょく generating power, output
b 重力 じゅうりょく gravity, force of gravity
圧力 あつりょく pressure
表面張力 ひょうめんちょうりょく surface tension

3a [also suffix] (ability to do or act) **POWER, ability, faculty**
b **mental POWER, vigor, vitality**
a 能力 のうりょく ability, capacity, faculty
実力 じつりょく real ability [power], capability, competence
理解力 りかいりょく comprehensive faculty, power to understand
戦力 せんりょく war potentials, fighting power
学力 がくりょく scholarship, scholastic ability
魅力 みりょく charm, glamour, appeal
効力 こうりょく effect, efficacy; effect (as of a law), validity
弾力 だんりょく elasticity, spring
極力 きょくりょく to the utmost, to the best of one's power
b 気力 きりょく energy, spirit, vitality, pluck, guts
念力 ねんりき will power; psychokinesis
活力 かつりょく vital power [force], vitality, energy

4 **POWER**ful(ly), all-out, hard, strenuously
力泳 りきえい powerful swimming
力投 りきとう all-out pitching
力漕する りきそうする row hard
力作 りきさく labored work, masterpiece
力説する りきせつする emphasize, lay stress on, insist upon

5a **efforts, endeavors**
b **assistance, help**
a 努力 どりょく endeavor, effort, exertion
死力を尽くす しりょくをつくす make frantic efforts
独力 どくりょく one's own efforts
b 協力する きょうりょくする cooperate, collaborate, work together
他力 たりき help from without
助力 じょりょく help, aid, support, cooperation

INDEPENDENT

【りき 力】physical strength
【りきむ 力む】**strain (oneself); swagger, brag**
力んで見せる りきんでみせる show a bold front

KUN

【ちから 力】
①ⓐ **muscular strength, POWER, force**
ⓑ (physical) **force; POWER, energy**
ⓒ (power in general) **POWER, authority, influence, force, emphasis**
a 力持ち ちからもち man of great strength, muscleman
力一杯 ちからいっぱい with full force, with all one's might
力ずくで ちからずくで by force, by sheer strength
力強い ちからづよい powerful, vigorous, reassuring
力仕事 ちからしごと heavy work
馬鹿力 ばかぢから great physical power, animal strength
b 力の場 ちからのば field of force
c 力関係 ちからかんけい power relationship
②ⓐ (ability to perform) **POWER, ability, faculty; proficiency**
ⓑ **vigor, spirit, energy**
a 力試し ちからだめし test of one's ability [strength]
底力 そこぢから latent power
語学の力 ごがくのちから one's linguistic ability
b 力付ける ちからづける encourage, cheer up, support
力落とし ちからおとし disappointment, sorrow, grief
③ⓐ **efforts, endeavors**
ⓑ assistance, aid, help
a 力を尽くす ちからをつくす make efforts, exert oneself
b 力添え ちからぞえ aid, help, assistance
④ efficacy, effectiveness
薬の力 くすりのちから efficacy of a drug

SYNONYMS

1c **power and authority**
力 POWER →4178
威 MIGHT →4394
勢 POWER (to influence) →3542

権 POWER (to control) → 1348
覇 SUPREMACY → 3392

❷ **energy and force**

力 POWER, force → 4178
勢 physical power → 3542
気 energy → 3960
圧 PRESSURE → 3688
鋒 brunt → 2172

❸ⓐ **skill**

力 POWER → 4178
能 ABILITY → 1676
技 SKILL → 0292
倆 SKILL → 0136
腕 skill → 1269
才 TALENT → 4218

NOTE

➡ see COMPOUND FORMATION for 迫力 はくりょく → 迫 3815

ト 人 九 入 力 【〆 ヘ イ 勹 ム メ ヒ 之】 七

〆

4179
■4-2-4

▶**SUM**
しめ(る) しめ
Ⓝ メ Ⓒ (国字)

4	Non-Jōyō	U3006
丿	S2-1-1	F0000

KUN

【しめる 〆る】[also 締める]

① **SUM, sum [add] up; close the account**
〆て しめて in all, all told

② [in compounds] **fasten, lock (a door or window), shut**
〆切(=締め切り) しめきり closing day, deadline; Closed, No Entrance

③ **finish off a bout of eating and drinking (with a closing dish)**

④ **pickle, marinate (fish) (with vinegar)**
鯖×を酢で〆る さばをすでしめる marinate mackerel with vinegar

【しめ 〆】

① [also 締め] **SUMming up**
〆切日 しめきりび closing day, deadline, time limit

② [also 締め] **finishing dish, closing dish**
〆の蕎麦 しめのそば buckwheat noodles to finish

③ [also 締め] **counter for reams or bundles of paper**
紙二〆 かみふたしめ two reams of paper

④ **mark on envelope seal**

SYNONYMS

【しめる】

① **add**

加 ADD → 0042
足す add → 2714
〆る SUM → 4179

HOMOPHONES

しめる

締 CONCLUDE → 1761
閉 CLOSE → 4116
絞 STRANGLE → 1707

NOTE

➡ see USAGE note at 締 1761

𠆢

4180
■4-2-4

▶***HITOYANE***

9	Radical	U201A2
人	S2-2-0	F0000

radical variant → see 人 at 4175

イ

4181
■4-2-4

▶***NINBEN***

9	Radical	U4EBB
イ	S2-2-0	F0000

radical variant → see 人 at 4175

勹

4182
■4-2-4

▶***TSUTSUMIGAMAE***

20	Radical	U52F9
勹	S2-2-0	F0000

RADICAL

tsutsumigamae 'wrap' (勺 匆 包), used in characters related to enclosing

---

ム

4183
■4-2-4

▶***MU***

28	Radical	U53B6
ム	S2-2-0	F0000

RADICAL

mu 'oneself' (参 去), used for character classification

メ

4184
■4-2-4

▶**SUM**
しめ(る) しめ

4	Nonstandard	U3006
丿	S2-1-1	F0000

traditional form → see 〆 at 4179

ヒ

■4-2-4

incorrect classification
➡ see □3-1-1: 乚 at 3641

之

■4-2-4

incorrect stroke-count
➡ see ■4-3-4 at 4228

七 incorrect classification
➡ see ■4-2-2 at 4169
■4-2-4

已

4185
■4-3-1

▶**CEASE**
イ や(む) や(める) すで(に)
Ⓒ 已 yǐ

49	Names	U5DF2
己	S3-3-0	F3002

COMPOUNDS

❶ **already**
已然形 いぜんけい *gram* realis form
生滅滅已 しょうめつめつい ending the cycle of life and death and entering Nirvana

❷ [now usu. 以 0045] directional preposition placed before localizers to indicate the point of reference in compounds related to direction, time or range: to the…of, -ward
已下 いか or less than, not more than, under; and downward; the following
已後 いご after this, from now on, in future; after that, thereafter

KUN

【やむ 已む】
ⓐ [also 止む] (bring to an end) **CEASE, discontinue; not do**
ⓑ [usu. 止む] (come to an end) **CEASE**, stop
a 已むを得ない やむをえない unavoidable, cannot be helped
已む無く やむなく unavoidably, out of necessity
已むに已まれぬ事情 やむにやまれぬじじょう circumstances beyond one's control
b 已んぬる哉 やんぬるかな I give up!
死して後已む ししてのちやむ I am determined to do or die

【やめる 已める】[usu. 止める]
①ⓐ stop (performing an action), **CEASE**, discontinue
ⓑ give up, abandon, quit
② abolish, do away with

【すでに 已に】[now usu. 既に] already
時已に遅し ときすでにおそし It is too late now

SYNONYMS

【やむ】
ⓐ **discontinue**
絶 BREAK OFF →1711
廃 ABOLISH →3902
断 CUT OFF →1885
止 STOP →3659
休 suspend →0056
停 suspend →0156
已む CEASE →4185

HOMOPHONES

やむ 止 STOP →3659
すでに 既 ALREADY →1498
やめる
辞 WORD →1726
罷 DISMISS →3234
止 STOP →3659

NOTE

➡ see USAGE notes at 止 3659 and 既 1498 and 辞 1726
★ do not confuse with 己 ONESELF →4188 and 巳 THE SERPENT →4197

下

4186
■4-3-1

▶**DOWN**
カ ゲ した[1] した[2] しも もと さ(げる) さ(がる) くだ(る) くだ(り) くだ(す) -くだ(す) くだ(さる) お(ろす) お(りる)
Ⓒ 下 xià

1	Jōyō-1	U4E0B
一	S3-1-2	F0044

一 丅 下
1 2 3

COMPOUNDS

❶ⓐ [also suffix] **DOWN, under, below; lower part**
ⓑ [also prefix] (in a lower position) **lower, under-, sub-**
a 下線 かせん underline
下記の かきの following, undermentioned
上下 じょうげ upper and lower parts [sides], high and low; going up and down, rise and fall; first and second volumes
地下 ちか underground
投下する とうかする throw down, drop, airdrop; invest
廊下 ろうか corridor, gallery, passage
以下 いか or less than, not more than, under; and downward; the following
氷点下 ひょうてんか below the freezing point
b 下流 かりゅう downstream, lower reaches of a stream
下部 かぶ lower part
下段 げだん lowest step; lower berth
下駄 げた geta, wooden clogs
下半身 かはんしん lower half of one's body
下意識 かいしき subconsciousness

❷ⓐ **of low rank, inferior**
ⓑ **of low grade, low-class, humble**
ⓒ **persons of low rank, juniors, inferiors, the people**
a 下位 かい lower rank [grade], subordinate position
下院 かいん Lower House
下級 かきゅう lower grade [class]
b 下等な かとうな low, lower, inferior, mean

下宿 げしゅく lodging, boarding house
下水 げすい sewerage, drainage; foul water
下品な げひんな vulgar; low; mean; dirty
c 下男 げなん male servant, manservant
下劣な げれつな base, mean, vulgar
下情 かじょう conditions of the common people
下克上 げこくじょう the lower dominating the upper
部下 ぶか subordinate

❸ [also suffix] (subject to the influence of) **under (the rule of), in a state of**
眼下の がんかの under one's eyes
灯下で とうかで by lamplight
管下の かんかの under the jurisdiction of
治下の ちかの under the rule of
城下 じょうか castle town, capital of a daimyo's fief
県下 けんか throughout the prefecture
目下 もっか now, at present
戦時下 せんじか in times of war

❹ⓐ (proceed to or as if to a lower place) **go DOWN, descend, drop, sink**
ⓑ go DOWN or away from a central place (as the capital), withdraw, leave
ⓒ **get DOWN from (a horse or vehicle), dismount, alight**
ⓓ (cause to go down) **bring DOWN, lower**
a 下降する かこうする descend, go down; subside
下山する げざんする descend a mountain; leave a temple
落下する らっかする fall, drop, descend
低下する ていかする fall, sink, lower, go down
南下する なんかする go down south
b 下阪する げはんする go down to Osaka
下校する げこうする leave school, come home from school
c 下車する げしゃする alight, get off
下馬 げば dismounting
d 却下する きゃっかする reject, dismiss, turn down

❺ⓐ **give to an inferior, grant**
ⓑ give a command, issue orders
a 下賜 かし imperial grant
下付する かふする grant, issue
b 下命する かめいする order, command

❻ honorific indicating respect without referring directly to a superior
閣下 かっか Your [His] Excellency
陛下 へいか His [Her, Your] Majesty; [original meaning] at the palace steps
貴下 きか you

❼ **last (in a series of two or three)**
下旬 げじゅん last ten days of a month
下巻 げかん second [third] volume

❽ **diarrhea**
下痢 げり diarrhea
下剤 げざい purgative, laxative
下血 げけつ bloody bowel discharge

INDEPENDENT

【げ 下】**low class, inferiority; last volume**
下の下 げのげ the lowest of its kind

KUN

【した[1] 下】
①ⓐ [in the form of 下 した + particle] **DOWN, under, below, underneath**
ⓑ **lower part, bottom, foot**
ⓒ **DOWNstairs**
a 下の したの under, lower
真下に ましたに just under, directly below
靴下 くつした socks, stockings
机の下に つくえのしたに under the desk
b 坂の下に さかのしたに at the foot of a slope
c 下の部屋 したのへや downstairs room
② (of lower rank, grade or degree) **lower, under, below, inferior, younger**
下回る したまわる be less than, fall below
下火になる したびになる burn low; decline
下手 したて humble position
手下 てした subordinate, underling
年下の とししたの younger, junior
目下 めした one's inferiors [subordinates]
③ part payment
下取りする したどりする take a trade-in

【した[2] 下】
① [in compounds]
ⓐ **lower, under-**
ⓑ **of lower rank or degree, inferior**
a 下唇 したくちびる lower lip
下着 したぎ underwear
下心 したごころ underlying motive, secret intention
b 下値 したね lower price
下請け したうけ subcontract
② [also prefix] **preliminary**
下調べ したしらべ preliminary examination [inquiry], preparation
下準備 したじゅんび prearrangement
下書き したがき draft (of a manuscript)
版下 はんした camera-ready copy, mechanical; block copy

【しも 下】
①ⓐ **lower part, bottom, foot**
ⓑ **lower stream**
ⓒ [also prefix] Lower—used before place names
a 下に しもに below, down, downward
b 風下 かざしも leeward, lee side

川下 かわしも lower part of a river
c 下エジプト しもえじぷと Lower Egypt
② [also prefix] **last (in a series of two or three)**
下の句 しものく second half of a tanka poem
下半期 しもはんき second half of the year
下二桁 しもふたけた last two figures of a number
③ persons of lower rank:
ⓐ inferiors, servants
ⓑ the governed, the ruled, the people, the lower classes
a 下座 しもざ seat for inferiors
b 下下 しもじも lower classes, the masses
④ lower part of the body, the genitals
下掛かった話をする しもがかったはなしをする talk about indecent things

【もと 下】
① **lower part, bottom**
木の下に きのもとに under a tree
② [in the form of 下に もとに] (subject to the influence of) **under (the supervision of)**
ナポレオンの指揮の下に なぽれおんのしきのもとに under the command of Napoleon
一撃の下に いちげきのもとに by a single blow

【さげる 下げる】
①ⓐ (move downward) **lower, bring DOWN, drop**
ⓑ (lower the level of) **lower (the price), bring DOWN, cut**
ⓒ **reduce to lower rank, demote**
a 頭を下げる あたまをさげる bow one's head
掘り下げる ほりさげる dig down; investigate, probe, delve into
b 値下げ ねさげ reduction in price
c 引き下げる ひきさげる lower, reduce, put back; pull down
格下げ かくさげ degradation
② **hang (down), suspend**
お下げ おさげ hair hanging down the back, pigtail
ぶら下げる ぶらさげる hang, suspend, dangle
③ⓐ move back [backwards]
ⓑ let (a person) go away, dismiss
a お膳を下げる おぜんをさげる clear the table
b 下げ渡す さげわたす grant, release
取り下げる とりさげる withdraw, dismiss
④ withdraw (one's deposit from the bank)
貯金を下げる ちょきんをさげる withdraw one's savings
⑤ (of tides) ebb
下げ潮 さげしお ebb tide

【さがる 下がる】
①ⓐ **come DOWN, go down**
ⓑ **hang DOWN, dangle, sag**
a 彼女の靴下が下がる かのじょのくつしたがさがる Her socks slip down
b 垂れ下がる たれさがる hang, dangle
ぶら下がる ぶらさがる hang down, dangle
②ⓐ (decline in level or intensity) **go DOWN, fall, drop, decline**
ⓑ (decline in rank, status or quality) **sink DOWN (to a lower level), drop, be degraded, decline, deteriorate**
a 上がり下がり あがりさがり rise and fall, ups and downs, fluctuations
ab 下がり さがり lowering; sagging; decline, fall
b 値下がり ねさがり fall in price, depreciation of price
成り下がる なりさがる degrade oneself, fall low, come down in the world
③ⓐ draw back, step back
ⓑ **withdraw, leave**
a 一歩下がる いっぽさがる take a step backward
b お下がり おさがり clothes handed down, hand-me-downs; withdrawn offering
引き下がる ひきさがる retire, withdraw; disclaim
④ **elapse, pass**
昼下がり ひるさがり early afternoon

【くだる 下る】
①ⓐ **go DOWN, descend, step down from; go downstream**
ⓑ **go DOWN or away from a central place (as the capital)**
ⓒ (decline in level or grade) fall, drop, be inferior
a 丘を下る おかをくだる go down a hill
川を下る かわをくだる descend a river
駆け下る かけくだる run down
b 九州へ下る きゅうしゅうへくだる go down to Kyushu
野に下る やにくだる leave the government service
c 下らない くだらない be no less than; trifling, worthless; absurd
② be given (orders), be issued
判決が下る はんけつがくだる Sentence is passed
③ have loose bowels
腹が下る はらがくだる have loose bowels
④ elapse, pass
時代が更に下って じだいがさらにくだって later in the period

【くだり 下り】
①ⓐ [also prefix] **DOWNhill, descend, going down**
ⓑ [also suffix] going **DOWN**stream
a 下り坂 くだりざか downward path; decline, ebb
b 球磨川下り くまがわくだり shooting down the Kuma Rapids
② **going DOWN (away from the capital, esp. Tokyo), outbound**
下り線 くだりせん down line (away from Tokyo)

東下り あずまくだり going down to the eastern provinces

③ diarrhea

下り腹 くだりばら loose bowels

【くだす 下す】

① **bring DOWN, lower**

位を下す くらいをくだす lower in rank, degrade

見下す みくだす look down upon, think lightly of

②ⓐ **give to an inferior, grant, bestow**

ⓑ **give a command, issue orders**

a 神の下し給うた物 かみのくだしたもうたもの heavenly gift, godsend

b 進軍の命令を下す しんぐんのめいれいをくだす give a marching order

③ **pass (judgment), hand DOWN (a decision)**

結論を下す けつろんをくだす draw a conclusion

④ [sometimes also 降す] subjugate, subdue; defeat, beat

⑤ have loose bowels

腹下し はらくだし diarrhea, laxity; purgative (medicine), evacuant

【-くだす -下す】 **perform an action smoothly**

書き下す かきくだす write down; transliterate [read] classical Chinese (into Japanese)

読み下す よみくだす transliterate classical Chinese into Japanese

【くださる 下さる】

ⓐ [honorific] **give, confer (to the speaker or speaker's group)**

ⓑ [following the TE-form of verbs] perform an action for the benefit of the speaker: **favor with, oblige, do (a courtesy)**

a それを私に下さい それをわたしにください Give it to me

b その人は親切に道を教えて下さった そのひとはしんせつにみちをおしえてくださった The man kindly told me the way

お心安くして下さる方 おこころやすくしてくださるかた gentleman who favors me with friendship

【おろす 下ろす】

① **bring DOWN, take down, let down, lower, pull down**

振り下ろす ふりおろす swing downward

雪下ろし ゆきおろし removing snow from the roof of a house

ボートを下ろす ぼーとをおろす lower a boat

根を下ろす ねをおろす take root

② wear for the first time

仕立て下ろし したておろし brand-new clothes

③ have an abortion performed

下ろし薬 おろしぐすり aborticide

④ withdraw (one's savings)

貯金を下ろす ちょきんをおろす withdraw one's savings

⑤ lock up

錠を下ろす じょうをおろす fasten a lock, lock

⑥ grate (vegetables)

下ろし おろし grated radish; vegetable grater

下ろし金 おろしがね vegetable grater

【おりる 下りる】

① (move downward) **go DOWN, come down(stairs), descend (from a mountain)**

駆け下りる かけおりる run down

坂を下りる さかをおりる go down a slope, go downhill

幕が下りる まくがおりる The curtain falls

② be discharged; abort

下り物 おりもの discharge from the womb

③ be granted, be issued

免許が下りた めんきょがおりた The license was granted

④ be locked

錠が下りている じょうがおりている be locked

SPECIAL READINGS

下手な へたな unskillful, unskilled, poor, clumsy

SYNONYMS

❶ⓐ &【した¹】①ⓑ **bottoms and bases**

底 BOTTOM → 3827

柢 BOTTOM → 1121

下 lower part → 4186

基 BASE → 3312

礎 FOUNDATION STONE → 1595

麓 FOOT OF MOUNTAIN → 3494

磐 BEDROCK → 3534

盤 bedrock → 3533

床 BED → 3805

ⓑ **low**

低 LOW → 0082

下 lower → 4186

❷ⓐ **lowly**

卑 MEAN → 3270

下 of low rank → 4186

低 LOW → 0082

ⓑ **bad**

悪 BAD → 3413

劣 INFERIOR → 3047

下 of low grade → 4186

弊 shabby → 3583

粗 COARSE → 1683

駄 GOOD FOR NOTHING → 2291

廃 WASTE → 3902

❹ⓐ **descend and fall**

落 FALL → 2907

墜 DROP DOWN → 3578

降 DESCEND → 0548

下 go down → 4186
倒 TOPPLE → 0139
c get off
降 alight → 0548
下 get down → 4186
d & 【さげる】 ①ⓐ lower
低 lower → 0082
下 bring down → 4186
5a & 【くださる】 ⓐ give
与 GIVE → 4229
呈 PRESENT → 2715
進 present to a superior → 3873
上 give (to superior or others) → 4212
下 give (to inferior or speaker) → 4186
呉れる give (to speaker) → 3156
授 CONFER → 0595
賜 DEIGN TO GIVE → 1994
贈 PRESENT A GIFT → 2064
賄 BRIBE → 1931
賂 BRIBE → 1930
8 diseases and disease symptoms
痘 SMALLPOX → 4070
淋 GONORRHEA → 0632
癌 CANCER → 4076
熱 fever → 3555
炎 INFLAMMATION → 3075
痢 DIARRHEA → 4068
下 diarrhea → 4186

USAGE

1 【さげる】

下げる
①ⓐ (move downward) lower, bring down, drop
ⓑ (lower the level of) lower (the price), bring down, cut
ⓒ reduce to lower rank, demote
② hang (down), suspend
③ⓐ move back [backwards]
ⓑ let (a person) go away, dismiss
④ withdraw (one's deposit from the bank)
⑤ (of tides) ebb

提げる
carry in hand, take (a thing) with (a person)

2 【くだる】

下る
①ⓐ go down, descend, step down from; go downstream
ⓑ go down or away from a central place (as the capital)
ⓒ (decline in level or grade) fall, drop, be inferior
② be given (orders), be issued
③ have loose bowels
④ elapse, pass

降る
surrender, submit to

3 【くだす】

下す
① bring down, lower
②ⓐ give to an inferior, grant, bestow
ⓑ give a command, issue orders
③ pass (judgment), hand down (a decision)
④ [sometimes also 降す] subjugate, subdue; defeat, beat
⑤ have loose bowels

降す
[usu. 下す] subjugate, subdue; defeat, beat

4 【おろす】

下ろす
① bring down, take down, let down, lower, pull down
② wear for the first time
③ have an abortion performed
④ withdraw (one's savings)
⑤ lock up
⑥ grate (vegetables)

降ろす
① set (a passenger) down, discharge, unload
② demote, deprive (someone) of (his) role

卸す
wholesale, sell wholesale

★In the sense of grating vegetables, おろす is sometimes mistakenly written 卸す.

5 【おりる】

下りる
① (move downward) go down, come down(stairs), descend (from a mountain)
② be discharged; abort
③ be granted, be issued
④ be locked

降りる
①ⓐ (dismount) alight, get off, disembark
ⓑ (come down from a high place) alight, land, swoop
ⓒ (of frost or rain) fall, come down
② retire (from a position), withdraw, drop out (of a program), quit

HOMOPHONES

もと
元 ORIGIN → 2428
本 BASIS → 4314
基 BASE → 3312
許 PERMIT → 1862
素 ELEMENT → 3108

さげる 提 PRESENT →0720
くだる 降 DESCEND →0548
くだす 降 DESCEND →0548
おろす
　降 DESCEND →0548
　卸 WHOLESALE →1835
おろし 卸 WHOLESALE →1835
おりる 降 DESCEND →0548

COMPOUND FORMATION

【下宿 げしゅく】

下宿 'lodging, boarding house' originally referred to an inn or lodging (宿) of low class (下 ❷ⓑ).

NOTE

➡ see also USAGE notes at 元 2428 and 卸 1835
➡ see COMPOUND FORMATION for 李下に冠を正さず りかにかんむりをたださず →李 3050

干

▶DRY
カン　ほ(す)　ほ(し)-　-ぼ(し)　ひ(る)

Ⓒ 干 gān

4187
■4-3-1

51	Jōyō-6	U5E72
干	S3-3-0	F1260

一 二 干
1 2 3

RADICAL

hosu 'shield' (年 幹 幸), used for character classification

COMPOUNDS

❶ⓐ DRY, dry up, desiccate
　ⓑ (of tides) **ebb, recede**
　ⓒ [formerly 旱 3048] **drought, DRY weather**

a 干拓する かんたくする reclaim by drainage
　干魚(=乾魚) かんぎょ dried fish
b 干潮 かんちょう ebb tide
　干満 かんまん ebb and flow, tide
c 干害 かんがい drought damage
　干天 かんてん drought, dry weather

❷ concern oneself in, interfere, intervene
　干渉する かんしょうする interfere, intervene

❸ offend against
　干犯 かんぱん infringement, violation

❹ sexagenary cycle, calendar signs (→see APPENDIX 8)
　干支 かんし sexagenary cycle
　十干 じっかん the ten calendar signs

❺ somewhat, a little
　若干 じゃっかん a number of, some, a little

❻ defend
　干城 かんじょう bulwark, defender, safeguard

❼ rail, handrail
　欄干 らんかん railing, handrail, balustrade

❽ shield
　干戈 かんか arms, weapons

KUN

【ほす 干す】 *vt*

① **DRY (up), desiccate, air (clothes)**
　干し物 ほしもの clothes for drying
　物干し ものほし clotheshorse, clothes-drier
　日干しの ひぼしの sun-dried

② [formerly also 乾す]
　ⓐ draw off (liquids), drain off
　ⓑ drink up, drain DRY

a 役を干される やくをほされる be deprived of one's role
b 飲み干す のみほす drink up

【ほし- 干し-】 [also prefix] **dried**
　干し草 ほしくさ hay, dry grass
　干し柿 ほしがき dried persimmons

【-ぼし -干し】 [also suffix]

① **sunning, DRYing, airing**
　甲羅干し こうらぼし basking in the sun
　土用干し どようぼし summer airing

② **dried food**
　梅干し うめぼし pickled *ume*
　白子干し しらすぼし dried young sardines

【ひる 干る】 *vi*

① [formerly also 乾る] **get DRY, parch**
　干魚 ひうお(=ほしざかな) dried fish
　干涸びる ひからびる dry up completely
　干上がる ひあがる dry up, parch; ebb away

② (of tides) **ebb, recede**
　潮干狩り しおひがり shell gathering (at low tide)

SYNONYMS

❶ⓐ dry
　乾 DRY →2113
　干 DRY →4187
　燥 DRY UP (desiccate) →1392
　涸 DRY UP (run dry) →0629
　渇 RUN DRY →0627
　旱 DROUGHT →3048

【-ぼし】

② **preserved foods**
　-漬け pickles →0861
　-干し dried food →4187

USAGE

❶【ほす】
　干す
　　vt
　　① dry (up), desiccate, air (clothes)
　　② [formerly also 乾す]
　　　ⓐ draw off (liquids), drain off
　　　ⓑ drink up, drain dry

乾す
[now usu. 干す] *vt*
ⓐ draw off (liquids), drain off
ⓑ drink up, drain dry
❷【ひる】
干る
vi
① [formerly also 乾る] get dry, parch
② (of tides) ebb, recede
乾る
[now usu. 干る] *vi* get dry, parch

HOMOPHONES

ほす 乾 DRY →2113
ひる 乾 DRY →2113

NOTE

★ do not confuse with 千 THOUSAND →4219

己

4188
■4-3-1

▶**ONESELF**
コ キ おのれ つちのと▲
Ⓒ 己 jǐ

49	Jōyō-6	U5DF1
己	S3-3-0	F0991

Stroke order: 1 2 3

RADICAL

onore 'self' (巻), used for character classification
Variant: 巳 *mi* (巴 巽 巷)

COMPOUNDS

❶ **ONESELF, self**
自己 じこ oneself, self, ego
利己主義 りこしゅぎ egoism
克己 こっき self-denial, self-control
知己 ちき acquaintance; intimate friend
❷ sixth calendar sign (→see APPENDIX 8)
己巳 きし sixth of the sexagenary cycle

KUN

【おのれ 己】**myself;** *slang* **you; You wretch!**
己を捨てる おのれをすてる rise above oneself
【つちのと 己】sixth calendar sign

SYNONYMS

❶ **first person pronouns**
私 I (*polite*) →1432
我 SELF →4362
己 ONESELF →4188
身 ONE'S PERSON →4368
僕 I (*familiar*) →0185
俺 I (*intimate*) →0124
吾 I (*elegant*) →3060
予 I (*pompous*) →2477
余 I (*pompous*) →2535
麿 I (*archaic*) →3949
朕 IMPERIAL WE →1185
自 SELF →4338

NOTE

★ do not confuse with 已 CEASE →4185 and 巳 THE SERPENT →4197

口

4189
■4-3-1

▶**MOUTH**
コウ ク くち
Ⓒ 口 kǒu

30	Jōyō-1	U53E3
口	S3-3-0	F0108

Stroke order: 1 2 3

RADICAL

kuchi 'mouth' (只 台 和), used in characters related to actions performed by the mouth
Left variant: 𠮛 × *kuchihen* (叱 吸 吐)

COMPOUNDS

❶ [original meaning] (oral cavity) **MOUTH**
口腔 こうくう(=こうこう) mouth, oral cavity
口内 こうない in the mouth
口角 こうかく corners of one's mouth
経口の けいこうの oral
閉口する へいこうする be dumbfounded [stumped], be silenced
❷ [also suffix] (mouthlike opening) **MOUTH, opening, hole, aperture**
口径 こうけい caliber, bore; diameter
河口 かこう river mouth, estuary
火口 かこう crater
銃口 じゅうこう muzzle (of a rifle)
排気口 はいきこう exhaust port
突破口 とっぱこう breach, breakthrough
❸ⓐ **give MOUTH to, mouth, speak, talk**
ⓑ (expression in words) **MOUTH, speech**
a 口論 こうろん argument
口語 こうご colloquial language
口外する こうがいする tell, divulge
口実 こうじつ excuse, pretext, pretense
口調 くちょう tone, expression
口説く くどく persuade; seduce
口述 こうじゅつ oral statement, dictation
b 悪口 あっこう(=わるくち) slander, abuse, foul language
異口同音に いくどうおんに with one voice, unanimously
利口(=悧巧)な りこうな clever, bright, sharp, shrewd
❹ **number of persons** (mouths to feed)
人口 じんこう population

戸口 ここう houses and inhabitants, population

❺ⓐ subdivision of a whole, unit, item
ⓑ counter for swords

a 口座 こうざ (bank) account
口銭 こうせん commission
b 一口の剣 いっこうのけん a sword

KUN

【くち 口】

①ⓐ (oral cavity) **MOUTH**
ⓑ **counter for MOUTHfuls**
ⓒ (one's) taste, (one's) palate

a 口の小さい くちのちいさい small mouthed
口元(=口許) くちもと mouth, shape of the mouth
口紅 くちべに lipstick, rouge
口先 くちさき lips, mouth; lip service
b 一口食べる ひとくちたべる eat a mouthful
c 口に合う くちにあう suit one's taste, be palatable
口当たり くちあたり taste

②ⓐ (mouthlike opening) **MOUTH (as of a receptacle or river), opening, hole**
ⓑ [also suffix] **entrance, exit, entranceway, doorway, gateway, door**

a 急須の口 きゅうすのくち spout of a teapot
b 口金 くちがね metal clasp, snap; metal cap
窓口 まどぐち window, wicket; clerk at a window
間口 まぐち frontage, front; width
入り口 いりぐち entrance
西口 にしぐち westside entrance [exit]
非常口 ひじょうぐち emergency exit
改札口 かいさつぐち ticket barrier [gate], wicket

③ (expression in words) **MOUTH, tongue, speech, talk, words**

口が巧い(=口が上手い) くちがうまい honey-mouthed, fair-spoken
口を出す くちをだす butt [chip] in
口口に くちぐちに individually, severally; unanimously
口癖 くちぐせ way [habit] of saying, one's favorite phrase
口喧嘩 くちげんか quarrel
口籠もる くちごもる mumble, be stuck for a word, stammer
口先の巧い くちさきのうまい smooth-tongued; fair-spoken
口出しする くちだしする butt in, interfere
口数 くちかず number of dependents; speech, words; number of shares
口答え くちごたえ back talk
無駄口 むだぐち idle talk
無口 むくち taciturnity, reticence

④ⓐ (place from which an ascent to a mountain is made) **route, ascent**
ⓑ suffix after names of ascents

a 登山口 とざんぐち place where an ascent to a mountain is made
b 吉田口 よしだぐち Yoshida route [ascent]

⑤ **MOUTH**s to feed, number of persons

口が多い くちがおおい have a large family to support
口減らし くちべらし reducing the mouths to feed

⑥ⓐ employment, job, position; vacancy
ⓑ call, engagement

a 口が無い くちがない be unable to find a job
就職口 しゅうしょくぐち employment, work
b 口を掛ける くちをかける call for (a doctor); apply for (a job)

⑦ⓐ share, item, lot
ⓑ counter for shares, items or lots
ⓒ kind, sort

a 小口 こぐち small lot, small sum [amount]; end, edge
大口 おおぐち large amount; big mouth; tall talk
b 一口 ひとくち an item, a share, a unit
品物が十口 しなものがじゅっくち goods of ten lots
c 手口 てぐち way of doing, method, trick
この口の品 このくちのしな this kind of goods

⑧ beginning

糸口 いとぐち [formerly also 緒] beginning, first step; clue

SPECIAL READINGS

口惜しい▲ くやしい [also 悔しい] vexing, mortifying, regrettable

SYNONYMS

❶ face orifices

口 MOUTH → 4189
鼻 NOSE → 3357
耳 EAR → 4329
目 EYE → 3777

❷ holes and cavities

穴 HOLE → 2682
洞 CAVE → 0455
窟 CAVE → 2923
窪 HOLLOW → 2962
腔 BODY CAVITY → 1267
孔 OPEN HOLE → 0205
口 MOUTH → 4189
坑 PIT → 0277
堀 DITCH → 0561
溝 CHANNEL → 0810
壕 TRENCH → 0966
濠 MOAT → 0975
凹 concavity → 4294

❸ⓐ speak and say

言 SAY → 2440

語る TELL →1944
談 TALK →1975
喋 TALK →0665
諷 INSINUATE →2005
謂う REFER TO →2007
云 say →2430
曰 SAY THAT →3757
話 SPEAK →1928
口 give mouth to →4189
申す SPEAK HUMBLY →4319
述 STATE →3816
陳 SET FORTH →0656
弁 SPEAK ELOQUENTLY →2497

ⓑ **speech**
言 SPEECH →2440
談 TALK →1975
舌 TONGUE →2711
口 MOUTH →4189

【くち】
②ⓑ **doors**
戸 DOOR →2429
扉 HINGED DOOR →2453
門 GATE →1100
口 entrance (or exit) →4189
襖 OPAQUE SLIDING DOOR →1600

HOMOPHONES

くやしい
悔しい →0435
口惜しい →4189, 0586

いとぐち
緒 OUTSET →1742
糸口 →2703, 4189

NOTE

➡ see USAGE notes at 悔 0435 and 緒 1742
➡ see COMPOUND FORMATION for 口座 こうざ →座 3868

工

4190

■4-3-1

▶**MANUFACTURE**
▶**CONSTRUCTION**

コウ ク グ▲ ㊔ たくみ

Ⓒ 工 gōng

48	Jōyō-2	U5DE5
工	S3-3-0	F0402

一 丅 工
1 2 3

RADICAL

takumi 'work' (左 差 巫×), used in characters related to working or building
Left variant: 工× ***takumihen*** (巧)

COMPOUNDS

❶ (make by tools or machinery) **MANUFACTURE, process, fabricate, construct**
工作する こうさくする make; construct, build; maneuver, scheme
工場 こうじょう(=こうば) factory, plant, workshop
工具 こうぐ tool, implement
工芸 こうげい technical art, technology
工学 こうがく engineering
工学部 こうがくぶ department of engineering
工業 こうぎょう industry, manufacturing industry
工員 こういん industrial worker
加工 かこう processing, manufacturing

❷ⓐ abbrev. of 工業 こうぎょう: **manufacturing industry**
ⓑ abbrev. of 工学 こうがく: engineering technology
ⓒ abbrev. of 工業高校 こうぎょうこうこう: suffix after names of technical high schools
a 商工 しょうこう commerce and industry
重工 じゅうこう heavy industry
b 工大 こうだい technical college
工科 こうか department of engineering
工博 こうはく Doctor of Engineering
c 小倉工 こくらこう Kokura Technical High School

❸ **CONSTRUCTION, building, engineering project**
工事 こうじ construction
工務 こうむ engineering
工費 こうひ cost of construction
施工する せこう(=しこう)する execute (a building contract), carry out
着工する ちゃっこうする start (construction) work

❹ⓐ [also suffix] **workman, worker, artisan, craftsman, mechanic**
ⓑ **workmanship, craftsmanship, work**
a 工人 こうじん workman, craftsman
職工 しょっこう workman, mechanic, (factory) hand
大工 だいく carpenter
石工 いしく(=せっこう) stonemason, mason
印刷工 いんさつこう printer
熟練工 じゅくれんこう skilled workman, master mechanic
b 細工 さいく work, craftsmanship; artifice, tactics

❺ **used phonetically for *ku* or *gu***
工夫 くふう device, contrivance; scheme, resources
工面する くめんする contrive, manage, make shift; raise (money)
工合(=具合) ぐあい condition, state; health; manner, way

INDEPENDENT

【こう 工】CONSTRUCTION, building; abbrev. of 工学部 こうがくぶ: faculty of technology, department of engineering

SYNONYMS

❶ **make**
作 MAKE →0077

造 MAKE → 3856
成 FORM → 4352
工 MANUFACTURE → 4190
製 MANUFACTURE → 3478
産 PRODUCE → 4089
調 PREPARE → 1973
組む ASSEMBLE → 1693
構 CONSTRUCT → 1325

❷ⓐ industry and business

業 BUSINESS, INDUSTRY → 3227
商 TRADE → 2623
産 industry → 4089
工 manufacturing industry → 4190

❹ⓐ workers and professionals

家 professional → 2827
婦 woman worker → 0565
嬢 (unmarried) female worker → 0936
夫 MAN LABORER → 4271
匠 CRAFTSMAN → 3711
工 workman → 4190
客 skilled person → 2798
士 PROFESSION SUFFIX → 4213
師 profession suffix → 1680
者 person who → 3980
人 person of certain category → 4175
員 MEMBER (of a staff) → 2822
屋 colloquial occupation suffix → 3842
手 OCCUPATION SUFFIX → 4267

久

4191

■4-3-1

▶OF LONG DURATION

キュウ ク ひさ(しい) ㊔ ひさし はる

Ⓒ 久 jiǔ

4	Jōyō-5	U4E45
丿	S3-1-2	F0518

ノ ク 久
1 2 3

COMPOUNDS

● OF LONG DURATION, longstanding, lasting for a long time

久遠 くおん eternity
永久の えいきゅうの permanent, eternal, lasting
恒久の こうきゅうの lasting, everlasting, permanent, eternal
耐久性 たいきゅうせい durability, persistence, lasting quality
悠久な ゆうきゅうな eternal, everlasting, permanent

KUN

【ひさしい 久しい】(of long duration) **long, longstanding**

久しい昔 ひさしいむかし a long time ago
久久に ひさびさに after a long time, for the first time in a long period
久し振りに ひさしぶりに after a long time [interval]

SYNONYMS

● of long duration

長 LONG → 3163
永 ETERNAL → 2436
久 OF LONG DURATION → 4191
恒 permanent → 0438

及

4192

■4-3-1

▶REACH TO

キュウ およ(ぶ) およ(び) および およ(ぼす)

㊔ おい

Ⓝ 及 Ⓒ 及 jí

4	Jōyō	U53CA
丿	S3-1-2	F0762

ノ 乃 及
1 2 3

COMPOUNDS

❶ⓐ [original meaning] (go as far as or arrive at a goal) **REACH TO, come up to (a standard), attain (successful results)**

ⓑ (extend as far as) **REACH TO, extend over, range over**

a 及第する きゅうだいする pass an examination
及落 きゅうらく passing or failing an examination
追及する ついきゅうする pursue, seek after, follow, press (a person) hard
企及する ききゅうする try to attain (something)

b 普及 ふきゅう diffusion, spread, propagation
波及する はきゅうする be propagated; extend, spread; affect
遡及的な そきゅうてき(=さっきゅうてき)な retroactive

❷ refer to, mention

言及する げんきゅうする refer to, mention, touch upon
論及する ろんきゅうする mention, refer to

KUN

【およぶ 及ぶ】(go as far as or arrive at a goal) **REACH TO, come up to, amount to; come up with; equal to, match**

及び腰で およびごしで with one's back bent; unconfidently
及びも付かぬ およびもつかぬ not at all equal, far beyond one's power
数百万に及ぶ すうひゃくまんにおよぶ reach [range] into the millions
聞き及ぶ ききおよぶ hear of, learn of
遠く及ばない とおくおよばない be no equal [match] for, fall far short of

【および 及び, 及】**and, as well as**

太陽及び地球 たいようおよびちきゅう the sun and the earth

【およぼす 及ぼす】**exert (influence upon), cause (harm), extend (benefits)**

害を及ぼす がいをおよぼす cause harm (to)

SYNONYMS

❶ⓐ arrive

着 ARRIVE → 4110
到 ARRIVE → 1615
至 COME TO → 2707
及 REACH TO → 4192
届く REACH → 3820
達 ATTAIN → 3893

ⓑ extend over

亘 EXTEND OVER → 2438
及 REACH TO → 4192
跨 STRADDLE → 1935

❶ⓑ make widely known

布 SPREAD → 3691
流 spread → 0529
伝 spread → 0048
広 spread → 3769
弘 DISSEMINATE (esp. Buddhism) → 0223
及 REACH TO → 4192

【および】

◯ **additionally**

亦 ALSO → 2504
兼 CONCURRENTLY → 2850
又 also, and → 4158
而うして and → 2520
及び and → 4192
並びに and also → 2793
傍ら besides → 0166
尚 STILL → 2774
更に furthermore → 4355
且つ AS WELL → 4297

弓

4193

■4-3-1

▶BOW

キュウ ゆみ ㊔ ゆ ゆげ

Ⓒ 弓 gōng

57	Jōyō-2	U5F13
弓	S3-3-0	F1604

1 2 3

RADICAL

yumi 'bow' (弟 弔 彎), used in characters related to bows or actions performed with bows

Left variant: 弓× *yumihen* (強 引 張)

COMPOUNDS

❶ⓐ [original meaning] **BOW**

ⓑ violin BOW

a 弓道 きゅうどう archery
弓状の きゅうじょうの bow-shaped, arched
弓術 きゅうじゅつ archery
洋弓 ようきゅう Western archery

b 胡弓 こきゅう Chinese fiddle

❷ [suffix] *anat* arch

内臓弓 ないぞうきゅう visceral arch

INDEPENDENT

【きゅう 弓】violin **BOW**

KUN

【ゆみ 弓】**BOW; archery; bow (of a violin)**

弓矢 ゆみや bow and arrow
弓弦 ゆみづる(=ゆづる) bowstring
弓形 ゆみなり arch, curve
弓取り式 ゆみとりしき conferment of the championship bow (in sumo)
真弓 まゆみ [also 檀] spindle tree, *Euonymus sieboldiana*

SYNONYMS

❶ⓐ weapons for shooting

銃 GUN (portable firearm) → 2157
砲 HEAVY GUN → 1479
火 firearms → 4273
弓 BOW → 4193

HOMOPHONES

まゆみ

檀 SPINDLE TREE → 1385
真弓 → 2616, 4193

叉

4194

■4-3-1

▶FORK

サ シャ また

Ⓒ 叉 chā chá chǎ chà

29	Names	U53C9
叉	S3-2-1	F2427

COMPOUNDS

❶ (place of furcation) **FORK (as of a road), crotch (as of a tree)**

音叉 おんさ tuning fork
蹄叉 ていさ fourchette
轍×叉 てっさ *railway* frog

❷ [now usu. 差 4104] **cross, intersect**

交叉 こうさ crossing, intersection
三叉路 さんさろ three-forked road

❸ used phonetically for *sha*

夜叉 やしゃ *yakṣa*, demon

❹ [original meaning] hold between

叉手網 さであみ scoop net

KUN

【また 叉】[usu. 股, sometimes also 俣] (place of furcation) **crotch (of a tree), FORK (of a road)**

木の叉 きのまた crotch of a tree
二叉 ふたまた bifurcation; *slang* two-timing
三つ叉 みつまた three-pronged fork, trident, trifurcation

SYNONYMS

❶ **furcation**
叉 FORK → 4194
俣 BIFURCATION → 0111
股 CROTCH → 1093
岐 forked road → 0285

❸ **phonetic [s]/[sh]**
沙 phonetic [sha] → 0311
刹 phonetic [setsu] → 1620
遮 phonetic [sha] → 3916
叉 phonetic [sha] → 4194
世 phonetic [se] → 4308
須 phonetic [shu] → 0700
修 phonetic [shu] → 0138
西 phonetic [su] → 4333
相 phonetic [sō] → 1120
薩 phonetic [satsu] → 3016

HOMOPHONES

また
股 CROTCH → 1093
俣 BIFURCATION → 0111

NOTE

➡ see USAGE note at 股 1093

夕 4195

■ 4-3-1

▶**EVENING**
セキ ゆう ㊔ ゆ
Ⓒ 夕 xī

36	Jōyō-1	U5915
夕	S3-3-0	F0861

ノ (1) ク (2) 夕 (3)

RADICAL

yūbe 'evening' (外 多 夢), used in characters related to nighttime

COMPOUNDS

● [original meaning] **EVENING, dusk, night**
今夕 こんせき this evening, tonight
一朝一夕に いっちょういっせきに in one day, in a short time
旦夕 たんせき morning and evening, day and night

KUN

【ゆう 夕】**EVENING, dusk**
夕べ ゆうべ evening
夕方 ゆうがた evening
夕闇 ゆうやみ dusk, twilight
夕暮れ ゆうぐれ evening, twilight
夕日(=夕陽) ゆうひ setting sun
夕食 ゆうしょく supper
夕刊 ゆうかん evening edition [paper]

SPECIAL READINGS

七夕 たなばた Festival of the Weaver [Star Vega]; the Star Festival

SYNONYMS

● **evening and night**
夜 NIGHT → 2550
晩 EVENING → 1232
夕 EVENING → 4195
宵 EARLY EVENING → 2831
暮 DUSK → 2971

子 4196

■ 4-3-1

▶**CHILD**
▶**NOUN SUFFIX**
シ ス ツ▲ こ -こ -(っ)こ ね▲ ㊔ たね
Ⓒ 子 zǐ zi

39	Jōyō-1	U5B50
子	S3-3-0	F0009

フ (1) 了 (2) 子 (3)

RADICAL

ko 'child' (字 孝 孟), used in characters related to children
Left variant: 子× *kohen* (孫 孔 孤)

COMPOUNDS

❶ⓐ [original meaning] (offspring of man) **CHILD, son, daughter, offspring**
ⓑ **boy, young man**
a 子女 しじょ children, sons and daughters
子息 しそく son
子音 しいん(=しおん) consonant ("child sound")
母子 ぼし mother and child
養子 ようし foster [adopted] child
b 太子 たいし crown prince
男子 だんし boy, young man, man
弟子 でし disciple, pupil, apprentice

❷ (offspring of plants or animals) **seed, egg, fruit**
種子 しゅし seed, pit, stone
卵子 らんし ovum, ovule, egg

❸ term of respect for men:
ⓐ **gentleman, man of learning**—sometimes used as familiar second person pronoun
ⓑ (male) member of a group or profession
ⓒ honorific after names of Chinese sages or their works, esp. authors of the Chinese classics
ⓓ the Master, esp. Confucius
a 君子 くんし man of virtue, wise man
遊子 ゆうし wanderer, traveler
b 編集子 へんしゅうし member of editorial staff

c 老子 ろうし Laozi; the works of Laozi
孟子 もうし Mencius; the works of Mencius
諸子 しょし Chinese sages or their works (except for Confucius and Mencius); gentlemen, you
d 孔子 こうし Confucius

❹ **SUFFIX after NOUNs, esp. names of small objects:**
ⓐ **various articles and fixtures, esp. furniture**
ⓑ **small entities such as particles, esp. nuclear particles**
ⓒ **various abstract concepts**

a 障子 しょうじ paper sliding-door, *shoji*
椅子 いす chair
菓子 かし confectionery, cake, sweets
柚子 ゆず [also 柚] yuzu
帽子 ぼうし cap, hat
b 粒子 りゅうし particle, grain
原子 げんし atom
電子 でんし electron
遺伝子 いでんし gene
晶子 しょうし crystallite
c 骨子 こっし essence, gist
調子 ちょうし tone, tune; key, note; condition, state (of health); manner, way
様子 ようす situation, aspect, circumstances; appearance, looks; sign, indication
面子 めんつ face, honor

❺ ("offspring" of money) **interest**
利子 りし interest
金子 きんす money, funds

❻ first sign of the Oriental zodiac: **the Rat**—(time) midnight (11 p.m.-1 a.m.), (direction) north, (season) November (of the lunar calendar) (→see APPENDIX 8)
子午線 しごせん meridian
正子 しょうし midnight

❼ viscount
子爵 ししゃく viscount

❽ⓐ counter for go pieces
ⓑ go pieces
a 三子 さんし three go pieces

❾ [sometimes also 仔 し 0038] minute, fine, small
子細 しさい particulars; reasons, circumstances

INDEPENDENT

【し 子】viscount; Confucius, the Master
子曰く しいわく Confucius said

KUN

【こ 子】
① offspring of humans or animals:
ⓐ **CHILD, son, daughter**
ⓑ [formerly also 仔] **offspring, youngling; puppy; cub; roe**
ⓒ [sometimes also 児] (boy or girl) **CHILD, kid, youngster**

a 子供 こども child, kid; son, daughter
親子 おやこ(=しんし) parent and child
息子 むすこ son
b 子犬 こいぬ puppy
c 男の子 おとこのこ boy, baby boy
迷子 まいご lost child

② [also 娘 or コ] girl, gal
あいつは行ける子だ あいつはいけるこだ She's a nice gal [good-looking broad]

③ interest

【-こ -子, -っこ -っ子】
① [also suffix] [also -っこ] **CHILD, kid, boy, girl**
継子 ままこ stepchild
悪戯っ子 いたずらっこ mischievous kid

② [also -っこ] [sometimes also 児]
ⓐ **person, performer of an action**
ⓑ [suffix] native of a specific place
a 売り子 うりこ shopgirl, sales clerk
踊り子 おどりこ dancer, dancing girl
売れっ子歌手 うれっこかしゅ popular singer
b 江戸っ子 えどっこ Edoite, Tokyoite
神戸っ子 こうべっこ native of Kobe

③ [also -っこ] **NOUN forming SUFFIX, esp. for small objects**
振り子 ふりこ pendulum
玉子 たまご [also 卵] egg
根っ子 ねっこ root; stump, stub
梯子 はしご ladder

④ **element for forming female names**
恵子 けいこ Keiko
典子 のりこ Noriko

【ね 子】first sign of the Oriental zodiac: the Rat (→❻)
子の刻 ねのこく midnight

SPECIAL READINGS

餃×子▲ ぎょうざ dumplings (stuffed with meat and vegetables)
捻子▲ ねじ screw; spring, mainspring

SYNONYMS

❶ⓐ **offspring**
子 CHILD →4196
仔 OFFSPRING →0038
孤 orphan →0426
嫡 LEGITIMATE CHILD →0839
息 son →3278
男 son →3147
惣 eldest son →3452
娘 DAUGHTER →0488
女 daughter →4226
姫 DAUGHTER OF NOBLE BIRTH →0489

❸ⓐ **gentleman**
紳 GENTLEMAN →1690

巳 下 干 己 口 工 久 及 弓 叉 夕 【子】 巳 尸 口 夂 夊 彑 彐 卩 阝 刄 口 万 乃 刃

子 gentleman →4196
士 man of learning and virtue →4213
ⓓ Confucius and Confucianists
孔 Confucius →0205
子 the Master (Confucius) →4196
孟 MENCIUS →2760
❹ nominalizers
所 PARTICLE OF NOMINALIZATION →1056
事 nominalization word →4384
子 NOUN SUFFIX →4196
性 -ITY →0357
ⓑ particle
粒 GRAIN →1682
子 particle suffix →4196
核 NUCLEUS →1162
❺ interest and dividend
利 interest →1431
子 interest →4196
配 dividend →1853
❼ noblemen
公 duke →2468
侯 marquis →0109
伯 COUNT →0067
子 viscount →4196
男 baron →3147
【こ】
①ⓒ **child**
児 CHILD (of any age) →3153
子 CHILD →4196
童 CHILD (young person) →2639
幼 young child →0222
坊 SONNY →0274
【-こ】
④ **name suffixes**
郎 MALE NAME SUFFIX →1641
麿 CLASSICAL MALE NAME SUFFIX →3949
彦 MALE NAME ELEMENT →4085
-子 female name element →4196

USAGE

❶【こ】

子
①offspring of humans or animals:
ⓐchild, son, daughter
ⓑ[formerly also 仔] offspring, youngling; puppy; cub; roe
ⓒ[sometimes also 児] (boy or girl) child, kid, youngster
②[also 娘 or コ] girl, gal
③interest

児
[now usu. 子] (boy or girl) child, kid, youngster

娘
[also 子 or コ] girl, gal

仔
[now usu. 子] animal offspring such as a puppy, cub or roe

小-
[also prefix]
①ⓐ(less in size or quantity) small, little, short
ⓑ(less in intensity) small, light, slight
②ⓐ(of secondary importance) secondary, sub-
ⓑ[belittling] small, petty, little
③[emphatic preceding adjectives or verbs] a little, slightly, very
④nearly, almost

❷【-こ】

-子
①[also suffix] [also -っこ] child, kid, boy, girl
②[also -っこ] [sometimes also 児]
ⓐperson, performer of an action
ⓑ[suffix] native of a specific place
③[also -っこ] noun forming suffix, esp. for small objects
④element for forming female names

-児
[usu. 子]
ⓐperson, performer of an action
ⓑ[suffix] native of a specific place

HOMOPHONES

こ
児 CHILD →3153
娘 DAUGHTER →0488
仔 OFFSPRING →0038
小 SMALL →0007
-こ 児 CHILD →3153
たまご
卵 EGG →1054
玉子 →4289, 4196
はしご
梯 LADDER →1210
梯子 →1210, 4196
ゆず
柚 YUZU →1123
柚子 →1123, 4196

COMPOUND FORMATION

【子午線 しごせん】
子午線 'meridian' is a line (線) going from north (子❻) to south (午).

NOTE

➡ see also USAGE note at 卵 1054

巳

4197
■4-3-1

▶**THE SERPENT**
シ み
Ⓒ 巳 sì

49	Names	U5DF3
己	S3-3-0	F2083

radical variant →see 已 at 4188

COMPOUNDS

● sixth sign of the Oriental zodiac: **THE SERPENT**—(time) 9-11 a.m., (direction) SSE, (season) April (of the lunar calendar) (→see APPENDIX 8)

上巳 じょうし March 3rd of the lunar calendar (one of the five annual festivals)

KUN

【み 巳】sixth sign of the Oriental zodiac: **THE SERPENT** (→●)

初巳 はつみ first Serpent day of the year

辰巳 たつみ [also 巽] southeast

SYNONYMS

● **snake**

蛇 SNAKE →1701

巳 THE SERPENT →4197

HOMOPHONES

たつみ

巽 SOUTHEAST →3329

辰巳 →3713, 4197

NOTE

★ do not confuse with 已 CEASE →4185 and 己 ONESELF →4188

尸

4198
■4-3-1

▶**CORPSE**
シ しかばね
Ⓒ 尸 shī

44	Non-Jōyō	U5C38
尸	S3-3-0	F0000

RADICAL

shikabane 'corpse' (尺 局 展), used in characters related to the human body or buttocks

COMPOUNDS

❶ [original meaning] **CORPSE**

尸諫×(=屍諫×)する しかんする admonish (one's master) at the cost of one's life

❷ [archaic] personator of the dead at sacrifices

尸位素餐× しいそさん neglecting the duties of an office while taking pay

KUN

【しかばね 尸】[usu. 屍] **CORPSE**

SYNONYMS

❶ **body**

体 BODY →0080

身 BODY (esp. vs. mind) →4368

肉 FLESH →3966

屍 CORPSE →3843

尸 CORPSE →4198

骸 DEAD BODY →2301

HOMOPHONES

しかばね 屍 CORPSE →3843

囗

4199
■4-3-1

▶***KUNIGAMAE***

31	Radical	U56D7
囗	S3-3-0	F0000

RADICAL

kunigamae 'enclosure' (回 四 ◯), used in characters related to enclosures, enclosing or encircling

夂

4200
■4-3-1

▶***FUYUGASHIRA***

34	Radical	U5902
夂	S3-3-0	F0000

RADICAL

fuyugashira 'descend' (変), used in characters related to things descending or coming down

夊

4201
■4-3-1

▶***SUINYŌ***

35	Radical	U590A
夊	S3-3-0	F0000

RADICAL

suinyō 'move slowly', used for character classification
Bottom variant: 夂× ***natsuashi*** (夏)

廴

4202
■4-3-1

▶***ENNYŌ***

54	Radical	U5EF4
廴	S3-3-0	F0000

RADICAL

ennyō 'proceed' (建× 延 廷×), used in characters related to advancing or going
Enclosure: 廴 ***ennyō*** (建 延 廷)

廴

4203
■4-3-1

▶***ENNYŌ***

54	Radical	U5EF4
廴	S3-3-0	F0000

radical variant →see 廴 at 4202

已下千己口工久及弓叉夕子巳尸口夂夊夂夊【彐ヨ阝阝刃口万乃刄】

彐

▶*KEIGASHIRA*

4204

■4-3-1

58	Radical	U2E95
彐	S3-3-0	F0000

radical variant → see ヨ at 4205

ヨ

▶*KEIGASHIRA*

4205

■4-3-1

58	Radical	U5F50
ヨ	S3-3-0	F0000

RADICAL

keigashira 'pig's head', used for character classification

Variants: 彐 彑 ***keigashira*** (彗 彙 彖×)

阝

▶*ŌZATO*

4206

■4-3-1

163	Radical	U2ECF
阝	S3-3-0	F0000

radical variant → see 邑 at 2716

阝

▶*KOZATOHEN*

4207

■4-3-1

170	Radical	U961D
阝	S3-3-0	F0000

radical variant → see 阜 at 3254

刃

▶BLADE

ジン ニン は やいば

4208

■4-3-1

18	Nonstandard	U5204
刀	S3-2-1	F0000

alternative form → see 刃 at 3646

口

▶COUNTRY

コク くに

4209

■4-3-1

31	Nonstandard	U56D7
口	S3-3-0	F0000

alternative form → see 国 at 3831

万

■4-3-1

incorrect classification

➡ see □3-2-1: 丆 at 3653

乃

■4-3-1

incorrect classification/ stroke-count

➡ see □3-1-1: ㇋ at 3643

刄刃

■4-3-1

incorrect classification

➡ see □3-1-2: 𠃌 at 3646

亡

▶DECEASE

ボウ モウ な(い) な(き)- ほろ(びる)▲ ほろ(ぶ)▲ ほろ(ぼす)▲

4210

■4-3-2

Ⓝ 亾 亡 Ⓒ 亡 wáng

8	Jōyō-6	U4EA1
亠	S3-2-1	F0749

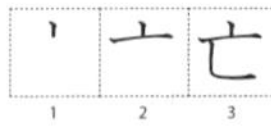

COMPOUNDS

❶ⓐ DECEASE, die, pass away, perish

ⓑ [also prefix] **DECEASEd, one's late**

a 亡霊 ぼうれい departed spirit, ghost

死亡する しぼうする die

存亡 そんぼう destiny; life or death

未亡人 みぼうじん widow, widowed lady

b 亡父 ぼうふ deceased father

亡妻 ぼうさい deceased wife

亡者 もうじゃ the dead

亡祖父 ぼうそふ deceased [one's late] grandfather

❷ [original meaning] (become destroyed) **perish, go to ruin, cease to exist**

亡国 ぼうこく ruined country, national ruin

滅亡する めつぼうする go to ruin, fall

衰亡 すいぼう ruin, fall, collapse

❸ flee, escape

亡命 ぼうめい exile

逃亡 とうぼう escape, abscondence, desertion

❹ lose

亡失 ぼうしつ loss

KUN

【ない 亡い】 **not in this world, dead**

亡くす なくす lose (a parent), be bereft of

亡くなる なくなる die, pass away, breathe one's last

【なき- 亡き-】 **DECEASEd, the late**

亡き人 なきひと the deceased

亡き母 なきはは dead mother

亡骸 なきがら remains, corpse, body

【ほろびる 亡びる】 [usu. 滅びる] go to ruin, meet with destruction, cease to exist; be overthrown

亡びて行く民族 ほろびていくみんぞく dying race

【ほろぶ 亡ぶ】 [usu. 滅ぶ] literary form of 亡びる ほろびる

【ほろぼす 亡ぼす】 [usu. 滅ぼす] destroy, ruin, annihilate; overthrow

敵を亡ぼす てきをほろぼす destroy the enemy

SYNONYMS

❶ⓐ die

死 DIE → 4334

萎 WITHER → 2872

没 die →0305
亡 DECEASE →4210
殉 DIE A MARTYR →1177
歿 DIE →1078
去 pass away →2678
逝 DEPART THIS LIFE →3850
斃 FALL DOWN DEAD →3593
枯 WITHER →1113
ⓑ dead
故 THE LATE →1466
亡 deceased →4210
❷ destroy
滅 DESTROY →0812
毀 DESTROY →2246
亡 perish →4210
消 EXTINGUISH →0531
剿 EXTERMINATE →2335
❸ escape
逃 ESCAPE →3839
遁 FLEE →4027
亡 flee →4210
走 run away →2720
脱 ESCAPE FROM →1225

HOMOPHONES

ない 無 WITHOUT →2648
なくす 無 WITHOUT →2648
なくなる 無 WITHOUT →2648
ほろびる 滅 DESTROY →0812
ほろぶ 滅 DESTROY →0812
ほろぼす 滅 DESTROY →0812

NOTE

➡ see USAGE notes at 無 2648 and 滅 0812

土

▶SOIL
ド ト つち ㊔ ひじ は はに
Ⓝ 圡 圠 Ⓒ 土 tǔ

4211
■4-3-2

32	Jōyō-1	U571F
土	S3-3-0	F0284

一 十 土
1 2 3

RADICAL

tsuchi 'earth' (型 圧 坐), used in characters related to earth or things built on the ground
Left variant: 扌× ***tsuchihen*** (地 場 坂)

COMPOUNDS

❶ⓐ [also suffix] [original meaning] **SOIL, earth, mud, sand, clay**
ⓑ **earthen**
ⓒ the third of the five elements: earth (→see APPENDIX 8)

a 土砂 どしゃ earth and sand
土壌 どじょう soil, earth
土俵 どひょう sumo (wrestling) ring; sandbag
土台 どだい foundation, base, basis; utterly
土木 どぼく engineering works
土砂降り どしゃぶり pouring rain, downpour
土壇場 どたんば the last moment
土足で どそくで with one's shoes on
土手 どて bank, embankment
土間 どま earth floor, dirt floor; pit
粘土 ねんど clay
耕土 こうど arable soil
珪×藻土 けいそうど diatomite, silicious marl
アルカリ土類 あるかりどるい alkaline earths
b 土器 どき earthenware
土瓶 どびん earthen teapot, pipkin
土用 どよう midsummer

❷ⓐ land, ground, territory, country
ⓑ of the land, local, native

a 土地 とち land
国土 こくど country, territory, realm
領土 りょうど territory, domain
本土 ほんど mainland; the country proper
風土 ふうど natural features (of a region), climate
郷土 きょうど one's birthplace
b 土俗 どぞく local customs
土着民 どちゃくみん natives, aborigines

❸ Saturday
土曜(日) どよう(び) Saturday
土日 どにち Saturday and Sunday, weekend

❹ Saturn
土星 どせい Saturn

❺ abbrev. of 土佐 とさ, old name for Kochi Prefecture
土讃線 どさんせん Dosan Line (Kochi-Kagawa Railway)

❻ Turkey
土国 どこく Turkey

❼ *colloq* emphatic prefix
土根性 どこんじょう disposition
土真ん中 どまんなか right in the center
土偉い どえらい immense, great; hell of a lot

INDEPENDENT

【ど 土】Saturday; land, country; the third of the five elements: **earth**

KUN

【つち 土】
①ⓐ **SOIL, earth, mud, clay; ground**
ⓑ mother earth

a 土色 つちいろ earth color
土壁 つちかべ mud wall

肥えた土 こえたつち rich [fertile] soil
盛り土 もりつち earth pile
b 土に帰る つちにかえる return to mother earth, die
② *sumo* defeat
土付かず つちつかず clean record, no defeat

SPECIAL READINGS
土産 みやげ souvenir

SYNONYMS
❶ⓐ & ❶ⓑ land and soil
土 SOIL → 4211
地 GROUND → 0236
壌 ARABLE SOIL → 0933
泥 MUD → 0384
陸 LAND → 0659
埴 CLAY → 0562
❷ⓐ country
国 COUNTRY → 3831
邦 STATE → 1051
土 land → 4211
❸ days of the week
日 Sunday → 3759
月 Monday → 3674
火 Tuesday → 4273
水 Wednesday → 0010
木 Thursday → 4261
金 Friday → 2552
土 Saturday → 4211

COMPOUND FORMATION
【土壇場 どたんば】
土壇場 'the last moment' originally referred to a place (場) of execution where there is a mound (壇) of earth (土 ❶ⓐ).

NOTE
★ do not confuse with 士 MILITARY MAN → 4213

上

4212
■4-3-2

▶UP
ジョウ ショウ シャン* うえ -うえ うわ-
かみ あ(げる) -あ(げる) あ(がる) -あ(がる)
あ(がり) -あ(がり) のぼ(る) のぼ(り)
のぼ(せる) のぼ(す) ㊔ かど
Ⓒ 上 shàng shang

1	Jōyō-1	U4E0A
一	S3-1-2	F0013

丨 ⺊ 上
1 2 3

COMPOUNDS
❶ⓐ UPper part, top; up, above
ⓑ [also prefix] **UPper, higher, outer**
ⓒ [also suffix] **on top of, over; on, at; aboard**

a 上下 じょうげ upper and lower parts [sides], high and low; going up and down, rise and fall; first and second volumes
頂上 ちょうじょう summit, peak, top; climax
屋上 おくじょう housetop, roof
b 上部 じょうぶ upper part [section], top; surface
上空 じょうくう skies, upper air
上記の じょうきの above-mentioned
上流 じょうりゅう upper stream (of a river); upper class
上皮 じょうひ outer skin, epidermis
上甲板 じょうかんぱん upper deck
上半身 じょうはんしん upper part of the body
以上 いじょう or more than, not less than; beyond; the above-mentioned; now that; that's all
c 陸上 りくじょう land, ground; shore; track and field
海上の かいじょうの maritime
紙上で しじょうで on paper, in print; by letter
発展途上国 はってんとじょうこく developing countries
席上で せきじょうで at the meeting; on the occasion
地球上の ちきゅうじょうの on the earth

❷ⓐ (of higher rank or position) **UPper, higher, superior, advanced**
ⓑ [also prefix] **of UPper grade, top-quality, first-class, excellent, best, good**

a 上位 じょうい higher rank, precedence
上級 じょうきゅう higher grade, advanced class, high class
上官 じょうかん higher officer, senior
上院 じょういん Upper House
上人 しょうにん Buddhist saint
b 上水 じょうすい water supply; tap water
上手な じょうずな skilled, dexterous, good at
上等の じょうとうの first-class, superior
上製 じょうせい superior make; superior (book) binding
上白 じょうはく first-class rice; first-class sugar
上出来 じょうでき good performance, master stroke
上天気 じょうてんき fine weather, splendid weather

❸ proceed **UP**ward:
ⓐ (proceed to or as if to a higher place) **go UP, rise, ascend; board, get on**
ⓑ **go UP [proceed] to the capital**
ⓒ **go UP in value or quality, rise, advance, make progress**
ⓓ (cause to move upward) **raise**

a 上昇する じょうしょうする ascend, rise
上陸する じょうりくする land, disembark
上船する じょうせんする embark
浮上する ふじょうする surface, rise [float] to the surface

遡上する そじょうする go upstream; retroact, retrospect
北上する ほくじょうする go up north
b 上京する じょうきょうする go to Tokyo
c 上進 じょうしん advance, progress
上達する じょうたつする make progress, attain proficiency
向上 こうじょう elevation, improvement, progress
d 上棟式 じょうとうしき ceremony of raising the ridgepole

❹ [also suffix] **from the viewpoint of, -ly, by reasons of**
史上 しじょう historically, from the historical point of view
身上 しんじょう one's history; one's merit
身上 しんしょう fortune, property
事実上 じじつじょう actually, as a matter of fact
便宜上 べんぎじょう for convenience' sake

❺ⓐ **present something before a superior or higher authority; perform an action for a superior**
ⓑ **present for consideration, introduce; take UP, deal with**
ⓒ **present before the public, exhibit, make public**
a 上納 じょうのう payment (to the authorities)
上奏する じょうそうする report to the Throne
献上する けんじょうする present (a gift to a superior)
参上する さんじょうする go to see, call on, pay one's respects
b 上告する じょうこくする appeal to a higher court
上程する じょうていする introduce on the agenda, lay [introduce] a bill before the Diet
上場する じょうじょうする list (stocks)
c 上演 じょうえん stage performance
上映する じょうえいする screen, show, project

❻ **first (in a series of two or three)**
上巻 じょうかん first book [volume]
上旬 じょうじゅん first ten days of a month

❼ early, ancient
上代 じょうだい ancient times, remote ages
上古の じょうこの ancient, of remote ages

❽ have blood rush **UP** to one's head, get dizzy
上気する じょうきする have a rush of blood to the head
逆上する ぎゃくじょうする be driven to frenzy, explode

❾ emperor, shogun; imperial
上意 じょうい command of the emperor
上使 じょうし shogun's envoy
主上 しゅじょう emperor

❿ verbal intensifier expressing a state of completion (as *up* in *add up*)
炎上する えんじょうする go up in flames
計上する けいじょうする sum up, appropriate (a sum for some purpose)

⓫ abbrev. of 上野 こうずけ, old name for Gunma Prefecture
上越線 じょうえつせん Joetsu Line (Gunma-Niigata Railway)

⓬ rising tone in Chinese phonetics
上声 じょうしょう(=じょうせい) rising tone

INDEPENDENT

【じょう 上】 **first class, the best; first book [volume];** (marking on gift wrapper) **With one's compliments**
上の じょうの first, best, excellent
上の巻 じょうのまき volume I

KUN

【うえ 上】
①ⓐ [in the form of 上 うえ + particle] **UP, over, above, on**
ⓑ **UPside, upper part, top, summit; the surface**
a 上の うえの upward, upper, higher (than)
机の上の本 つくえのうえのほん book on the desk
b 上下 うえした up and down, above and below
上を向く うえをむく look upward

②ⓐ (of higher rank, position or grade) **UPper, higher, above, better, greater, older**
ⓑ (persons of) **higher rank, superiors, nobility**
a 上の地位 うえのちい higher position
上の子 うえのこ the older child
目上 めうえ one's superiors, one's seniors; one's elders
b 上からの命令 うえからのめいれい order from above

③ **as far as...is concerned, concerning**
身の上 みのうえ one's career, one's condition, one's fortune
理屈の上では正しい りくつのうえではただしい It's correct as far as the theory goes

④ **besides, moreover, in addition**
その上 そのうえ on top of that, what is more, moreover
金が有る上に美男子だ かねがあるうえにびだんしだ be handsome as well as rich

⑤ after, on, **UP**on
照合の上 しょうごうのうえ after checking up

【-うえ -上】
① **honorific title for addressing persons of superior rank, esp. family members**
母上 ははうえ my dear mother
② honorific title after names of court ladies
葵の上 あおいのうえ Lady Aoi

亡土【上】士也乍亡廿山

亡土【上】士也𠀋亡廿山

【うわ- 上-】
①ⓐ **UPper, top, upward**
ⓑ (of higher rank, grade or quantity) **UPper, higher, better, greater**
a 上唇 うわくちびる upper lip
b 上手 うわて upper part; better hand, superior
上回る うわまわる exceed, be more than
②ⓐ **outer, external**
ⓑ superficial, shallow; careless
a 上着 うわぎ outer garment, coat, jacket
上辺 うわべ outward appearance; exterior, surface
上薬 うわぐすり [also 釉 or 釉薬] glaze, enamel
b 上っ調子な うわっちょうしな flippant, shallow
上滑りな うわすべりな superficial, shallow, careless

【かみ 上】
①ⓐ **UPper part, top, head**
ⓑ **UPper stream**
ⓒ [also prefix before place names] **UPper, Northern**
a 上手 かみて upper part, upper reaches; left stage
b 川上 かわかみ upstream, upriver
c 上カプアス山脈 かみかぷあすさんみゃく Upper Kapuas Mountains
② first (in a series of two or three)
上の句 かみのく first half of a tanka poem
上半期 かみはんき first half of the (fiscal) year
③ persons of superior rank:
ⓐ **superiors, high rank**
ⓑ **government, authorities**
ⓒ **emperor, sovereign**
a 上下 かみしも superiors and inferiors
b お上 おかみ government, authorities; emperor; wife, madam, landlady

【あげる 上げる】
①ⓐ (cause to move upward) **raise, elevate, lift UP**
ⓑ (increase the level of) **raise, increase, hike**
ⓒ (elevate in rank) **raise, promote, elevate**
ⓓ **raise one's voice, shout**
ⓔ (raise the quality of) **improve (one's skill), advance**
a 顔を上げる かおをあげる raise one's face
引き上げる ひきあげる draw [pull] up; promote; increase
棚上げする たなあげする shelve (up), pigeonhole
b 上げ あげ rise in price; making a tuck
値上げする ねあげする raise [increase] the price
賃上げ ちんあげ wage increase
c 格上げする かくあげする raise to higher status, promote to a higher rank
d 声を上げる こえをあげる raise one's voice
e 腕を上げる うでをあげる improve one's skill
②ⓐ **give, offer, present, hand (to a superior, equal or others, not the speaker)**
ⓑ offer, make an offering (to a deity)
a 彼に本を上げた かれにほんをあげた I gave him a book
b 仏壇に花を上げる ぶつだんにはなをあげる offer flowers before the family Buddhist altar
③ [following the TE-form of verbs] **perform an action for (the benefit of) someone, do for a person**
本を読んで上げよう ほんをよんであげよう I'll read a book for you
席を譲って上げる せきをゆずってあげる offer a seat to someone
④ **complete, finish**
仕事を上げる しごとをあげる finish the work
⑤ **achieve (results), gain (profits)**
良い成績を上げる よいせいせきをあげる achieve satisfactory results
売り上げ うりあげ sales, proceeds
⑥ show in, usher in, admit
芸者を上げる げいしゃをあげる call in a geisha
⑦ send, enter (a child in school)
子供を学校に上げる こどもをがっこうにあげる send one's child to school
⑧ manage (to do something)
安く上げる やすくあげる make it less expensive
⑨ praise
上げたり下げたり あげたりさげたり praising and blaming; raising and lowering
⑩ dress **UP**
髪を上げる かみをあげる put up one's hair
⑪ throw **UP**, vomit
上げてしまった あげてしまった I threw up
⑫ (of tides) rise
上げ潮 あげしお rising [flowing] tide

【-あげる -上げる】
① **UP, upward**
持ち上げる もちあげる raise, lift up; flatter
積み上げる つみあげる pile [heap] up, accumulate
打ち上げ うちあげ letting off, launching; close (of a run of performances)
取り上げる とりあげる take [pick] up; take away, confiscate; deliver a baby; accept, listen to; adopt (a proposal)
繰り上げる くりあげる advance, move up
②ⓐ **emphatic verbal suffix (as *up* in *stir up*)**
ⓑ **verbal suffix indicating completion of an action**
a 縛り上げる しばりあげる bind [tie] up
磨き上げる みがきあげる polish up
買い上げる かいあげる buy, buy up; bid up
b 作り上げる つくりあげる make up, build up, complete
仕上げる しあげる finish, complete, perfect
書き上げる かきあげる finish writing
③ **honorific verbal suffix**

申し上げる もうしあげる tell, say, speak humbly; (have the honor to) do

【あがる 上がる】
①ⓐ **go UP, come up, rise, climb**
ⓑ **go UP in price, rise, jump**
ⓒ go **UP** in rank or quality: rise, be promoted; make progress, advance
a 屋根に上がる やねにあがる go up on the roof
風呂から上がる ふろからあがる step out of the bath
b 月給が上がる げっきゅうがあがる get a raise in salary
c 腕が上がる うでがあがる gain in skill
②ⓐ **be completed, be finished**
ⓑ **come to an end, stop (raining); die, die out**
ⓒ (of games like Japanese parcheesi) come to the finish
a 原稿が上がった げんこうがあがった The manuscript is completed
b 雨が上がった あめがあがった It stopped raining
商売が上がったりだ しょうばいがあがったりだ My business is ruined
c 一番で上がる いちばんであがる win the first place
③ **issue, accrue, be derived**
効果が上がる こうかがあがる take effect, bear fruit
④ lose control of oneself, get excited, be nervous, get stage fright
試験で上がる しけんであがる get nervous at an examination
⑤ [honorific] **take, have; eat, drink**
ワインを召し上がれ わいんをめしあがれ Please help yourself to the wine
⑥ be sufficient
安く上がる やすくあがる cost little
⑦ⓐ **come in, enter (a house), be admitted to (a school)**
ⓑ [honorific] **call on, visit**
a 上がり込む あがりこむ enter, come in, step in
b 駅迄お迎えに上がります えきまでおむかえにあがります I'll go to the station to meet you
⑧ land, go ashore
上がり場 あがりば landing place
⑨ be offered
灯明が上がっている とうみょうがあがっている Sacred candles are lighted (before a household shrine)

【-あがる -上がる】
① **UP, upward**
立ち上がる たちあがる stand up, rise to one's feet; take action
盛り上がる もりあがる swell, rise; upsurge; be brought to climax
浮かび上がる うかびあがる rise to the surface
②ⓐ **emphatic verbal suffix (as *up* in *stir up*)**
ⓑ **verbal suffix indicating completion of an action**
a 縮み上がる ちぢみあがる cringe, wince, flinch
b 煮上がる にあがる boil up, be thoroughly cooked
出来上がる できあがる be completed, be finished

【あがり 上がり】
① **rise, advance; ascent**
値上がり ねあがり rise in price
② **finish, completion**
仕上がり しあがり finish, completion; result
③ⓐ proceeds, income, return
ⓑ crop, yield
a 店の上がり みせのあがり income from a shop
b 蚕の上がりが良い かいこのあがりがよい Silkworms are spinning well
④ tea, green tea (esp. in sushi shops)
上がり一丁 あがりいっちょう One tea!

【-あがり -上がり】 [also suffix]
① **just after the completion of an action**
雨上がりの虹 あめあがりのにじ rainbow after the rain
風呂上がり ふろあがり just out of the bath
② ex-
軍人上がりの実業家 ぐんじんあがりのじつぎょうか businessman who was once a military man

【のぼる 上る】
①ⓐ **go UP (stairs), walk up (a hill); go [swim] upstream**
ⓑ go **UP** to the capital
a 階段を上る かいだんをのぼる go up the stairs
煙が立ち上る けむりがたちのぼる Smoke ascends to the sky
逆上る さかのぼる [usu. 遡る] go upstream; go back (to the past); retroact
鮭×が川を上る さけがかわをのぼる Salmon run up the rivers
b 京に上る きょうにのぼる go up to Kyoto
② reach, amount to, add **UP** to
かなりの数に上る かなりのかずにのぼる amount to a considerable number
③ come **UP**, be brought up (for discussion)
噂に上る うわさにのぼる be gossiped about

【のぼり 上り】
ⓐ **going UP, going upstream**
ⓑ **ascent, UPhill road**
ⓒ **UP**ward-bound train, Tokyo-bound train
a 上り下り のぼりくだり going up and down
b 上り坂 のぼりざか ascent, upward slope
上り勾配 のぼりこうばい upgrade, uphill grade
c 上り列車 のぼりれっしゃ up train [line]

【のぼせる 上せる】
ⓐ **bring UP (a proposal for discussion)**

ⓑ enter, put on record
a 梓に上せる しにのぼせる publish, bring (a book) into the world

【のぼす 上す】same as 上せる のぼせる
議題に上す ぎだいにのぼす bring up for discussion

SPECIAL READINGS

上手い▲(=巧い、旨い) うまい skillful, clever; splendid, excellent
逆上せる▲ のぼせる have a rush of blood to the head, feel dizzy; get excited; run mad after; become conceited

SYNONYMS

❶ⓐ &【うえ】①ⓑ tops
上 upper part → 4212
頂 SUMMIT → 0164
頭 HEAD → 2019
ⓑ high
高 HIGH → 2601
上 upper → 4212
峻 LOFTY → 0570
❷ⓐ high-ranking
貴 NOBLE → 3220
上 upper → 4212
高 HIGH → 2601
総 GENERAL → 1743
太 of highest rank → 2673
ⓑ excellent and superior
優 SUPERIOR → 0200
絶 without match → 1711
卓 PROMINENT → 2561
快 splendid → 0289
妙 MARVELOUS → 0280
秀 EXCELLENT → 3152
英 DISTINGUISHED → 2782
尤 outstanding → 3755
傑 outstanding → 0175
穎 TALENTED → 2036
逸 exceptional → 3872
名 first-rate → 2693
上 of upper grade → 4212
❸ⓐ &【あがる】①ⓐ ascend
昇 ASCEND → 3068
上 go up → 4212
騰 RISE (esp. in price) → 1422
登 CLIMB → 3208
ⓓ &【あげる】①ⓐ raise
揚 RAISE HIGH → 0722
掲 PUT UP → 0597
挙 RAISE → 3106
上 raise → 4212
起 raise up → 4099
擡 RAISE (one's head) → 0972
立てる STAND → 2486
拾う PICK UP → 0454
❹ aspect
面 side → 2590
上 from the viewpoint of → 4212
柄 considering the character of → 1111
❺ⓐ &【あげる】②ⓐ give
与 GIVE → 4229
呈 PRESENT → 2715
進 present to a superior → 3873
上 give (to superior or others) → 4212
下 give (to inferior or speaker) → 4186
呉れる give (to speaker) → 3156
授 CONFER → 0595
賜 DEIGN TO GIVE → 1994
贈 PRESENT A GIFT → 2064
賄 BRIBE → 1931
賂 BRIBE → 1930

【-あげる】
②ⓑ end
終 END → 1692
絶 COME TO AN END → 1711
閉 CLOSE → 4116
了 FINISH → 4157
済 SETTLE → 0634
-上げる completion suffix → 4212
完 COMPLETE → 2727
結 CONCLUDE → 1706
竣 COMPLETE → 1528

USAGE

❶【かみ】
上
①ⓐ upper part, top, head
ⓑ upper stream
ⓒ [also prefix before place names] upper, Northern
② first (in a series of two or three)
③ persons of superior rank:
ⓐ superiors, high rank
ⓑ government, authorities
ⓒ emperor, sovereign
守
feudal governor, lord, baron

❷【あげる】
上げる
①ⓐ (cause to move upward) raise, elevate, lift up
ⓑ (increase the level of) raise, increase, hike
ⓒ (elevate in rank) raise, promote, elevate
ⓓ raise one's voice, shout
ⓔ (raise the quality of) improve (one's skill), advance

②ⓐ give, offer, present, hand (to a superior, equal or others, not the speaker)
ⓑ offer, make an offering (to a deity)
③ [following the TE-form of verbs] perform an action for (the benefit of) someone, do for a person
④ complete, finish
⑤ achieve (results), gain (profits)
⑥ show in, usher in, admit
⑦ send, enter (a child in school)
⑧ manage (to do something)
⑨ praise
⑩ dress up
⑪ throw up, vomit
⑫ (of tides) rise

挙げる
①ⓐ (raise something and hold it up for display) hold up, raise (one's hand or a wineglass)
ⓑ (gather together) raise (an army), recruit
ⓒ (elevate in dignity) raise oneself, raise one's reputation
② cite, give (an example), mention
③ hold (a function), perform (a ceremony)
④ arrest, round up, nab
⑤ give birth to, have children
⑥ use fully
⑦ gain (points), score
⑧ unclassified compounds

揚げる
① (cause to rise high or float in the air) raise (a flag), send up, hoist, lift, fly (a kite), shoot up (fireworks)
② fry in deep fat
③ land, unload, disembark

❸【あげ】

上げ
① rise in price
② making a tuck

-揚げ
ⓐ [also suffix] fried food, fry
ⓑ fried bean curd

❹【あがる】

上がる
①ⓐ go up, come up, rise, climb
ⓑ go up in price, rise, jump
ⓒ go up in rank or quality: rise, be promoted; make progress, advance
②ⓐ be completed, be finished
ⓑ come to an end, stop (raining); die, die out
ⓒ (of games like Japanese parcheesi) come to the finish
③ issue, accrue, be derived
④ lose control of oneself, get excited, be nervous, get stage fright
⑤ [honorific] take, have; eat, drink
⑥ be sufficient
⑦ⓐ come in, enter (a house), be admitted to (a school)
ⓑ [honorific] call on, visit
⑧ land, go ashore
⑨ be offered

挙がる
① be cited, be mentioned, be listed
② be arrested, be caught, be nabbed
③ become famous
④ come into possession, be recovered

揚がる
① (rise high or float in the air) (of kites or flags) be up, fly, be flying; (of fireworks) be shot up, be set off
② be fried, fry
③ (of appearance) stand out, improve
④ become elated, get into high spirits

❺【のぼる】

上る
①ⓐ go up (stairs), walk up (a hill); go [swim] upstream
ⓑ go up to the capital
② reach, amount to, add up to
③ come up, be brought up (for discussion)

登る
(move up, esp. by using the hands and feet) climb, mount, ascend, scale

昇る
ⓐ (rise up to the sky) ascend, rise
ⓑ ascend to a higher rank, rise in rank, be promoted

★In the sense of moving upwards, the above three verbs are easily confused. Whereas 上る refers only to the process of going up (as a hill or steps), 登る implies that an effort is made to reach the top, as when climbing a mountain. 昇る refers to something rising toward the sky, such as smoke or the rising sun, or a soul rising to heaven.

❻【のぼり】

上り
ⓐ going up, going upstream
ⓑ ascent, uphill road
ⓒ upward-bound train, Tokyo-bound train

登り
climbing, ascent

❼【のぼせる】

上せる
ⓐ bring up (a proposal for discussion)
ⓑ enter, put on record

逆上せる
① have a rush of blood to the head, feel dizzy
② get excited; run mad after; become conceited

❽【ひきあげる】
引き上げる
draw [pull] up; promote; increase
引き揚げる
withdraw, leave, return, repatriate

HOMOPHONES

かみ 守 PROTECT →2697
あげる
挙 NOMINATE →3106
揚 RAISE HIGH →0722
あげ 揚 RAISE HIGH →0722
あがる
挙 NOMINATE →3106
揚 RAISE HIGH →0722
のぼる
登 CLIMB →3208
昇 ASCEND →3068
さかのぼる
遡る →4040
逆上る →3835, 4212
のぼり 登 CLIMB →3208
のぼせる 逆上せる →3835, 4212
うまい
旨い →2516
巧い →0219
甘い →4306
上手い →4212, 4267
うわぐすり
釉 GLAZE →1911
釉薬 →1911, 3011
上薬 →4212, 3011

NOTE

➡ see also USAGE notes at 逆 3835 and 旨 2516

士

▶MILITARY MAN
▶PROFESSION SUFFIX
シ ㊔ お まもる こと ひと

4213 Ⓒ 士 shì

■4-3-2

33	Jōyō-4	U58EB
士	S3-3-0	F0262

一 十 士
1 2 3

RADICAL

samurai 'knight' (壬 声 壮), used for character classification

COMPOUNDS

❶ⓐ **MILITARY MAN, warrior, soldier, knight; officer**
ⓑ warrior class of feudal Japan: **samurai, retainer**
ⓒ private (military rank of Japanese Self-Defense Forces)
a 士官 しかん officer
士気 しき fighting spirit
兵士 へいし soldier
騎士 きし knight
武士 ぶし samurai, warrior
b 士族 しぞく descendant of samurai
士分 しぶん status of samurai
士農工商 しのうこうしょう warriors, farmers, artisans and tradesmen (the four classes of Tokugawa Japan)
四十七士 しじゅうしちし Forty-Seven Loyal Retainers
c 一等陸士 いっとうりくし private first class

❷ⓐ **man of learning and virtue, gentleman, scholar, man of good breeding**
ⓑ [original meaning] man, man of full age
a 士君子 しくんし man of learning and virtue, gentleman
博士 はくし doctor, Ph.D.
紳士 しんし gentleman
名士 めいし man of distinction, big name
国士 こくし distinguished citizen; patriot
同士 どうし fellow (as in 学生同士 がくせいどうし "fellow students")
b 士女 しじょ men and women

❸ **SUFFIX for members of a PROFESSION, esp. a licensed profession**
弁護士 べんごし lawyer, attorney
力士 りきし sumo wrestler
棋士 きし professional go [shogi] player

❹ suffix for academic degrees
文学士 ぶんがくし Bachelor of Arts
理学修士 りがくしゅうし Master of Science

INDEPENDENT

【し 士】 man of learning and virtue, gentleman; samurai
篤学の士 とくがくのし diligent student, devoted scholar

SPECIAL READINGS

博士 はかせ expert, learned man; doctor, Ph.D.
居士 こじ lay scholar
一言居士 いちげんこじ ready critic, one ready to comment on any and every subject
海士 あま diver

SYNONYMS

❶ **soldiers and warriors**
兵 SOLDIER →3158
卒 private →2549
士 MILITARY MAN →4213
武 warrior →3979
侍 SAMURAI →0094
❷ⓐ **gentleman**
紳 GENTLEMAN →1690

子 gentleman →4196
士 man of learning and virtue →4213

❸ **workers and professionals**
家 professional →2827
婦 woman worker →0565
嬢 (unmarried) female worker →0936
夫 MAN LABORER →4271
匠 CRAFTSMAN →3711
工 workman →4190
客 skilled person →2798
士 PROFESSION SUFFIX →4213
師 profession suffix →1680
者 person who →3980
人 person of certain category →4175
員 MEMBER (of a staff) →2822
屋 colloquial occupation suffix →3842
手 OCCUPATION SUFFIX →4267

USAGE

【どうし】
同士
fellow (as in 学生同士 がくせいどうし "fellow students")
同志
like-minded person, comrade

NOTE

★ do not confuse with 土 SOIL →4211

也

4214
■4-3-2

▶CLASSICAL COPULA
ヤ なり や
Ⓒ 也 yě

5	Names	U4E5F
乚	S3-1-2	F1034

KUN

【なり 也】**CLASSICAL COPULA** equiv. to である: **be**
金十円也 きんじゅうえんなり ten yen
【や 也】[also 哉 or 耶] *classical particle* **rhetorical or interrogative particle like modern か**
これは何ぞ也 これはなんぞや What can this be?

SYNONYMS

【なり】
◯ **exist and be**
在 BE →3704
存 EXIST →3702
有 exist →3703
居 be present →3822
臨 BE PRESENT AT →2059
也 CLASSICAL COPULA →4214
【や】
◯ **classical particles**
耶 INTERROGATIVE PARTICLE →1635
也 rhetorical particle →4214
哉 EXCLAMATORY PARTICLE →4084

USAGE

【や】
也
[also 哉 or 耶] *classical particle* rhetorical or interrogative particle like modern か
哉
[also 也 or 耶] classical interrogative or rhetorical particle like modern か
耶
[also 哉 or 也] classical rhetorical or exclamatory particle

HOMOPHONES

や
哉 EXCLAMATORY PARTICLE →4084
耶 INTERROGATIVE PARTICLE →1635

彑

4215
■4-3-2

▶*KEIGASHIRA*

58	Radical	U5F51
彐	S3-3-0	F0000

radical variant →see 彐 at 4205

亡

4216
■4-3-2

▶DECEASE
ボウ モウ な(い) な(き)- ほろ(びる) ほろ(ぶ) ほろ(ぼす)

8	Nonstandard	U4EA1
亠	S3-2-1	F0000

traditional form →see 亡 at 4210

廿

■4-3-2

incorrect stroke-count
➡ see ■4-4-2 at 4258

山

■4-3-2

incorrect classification
➡ see □3-2-1: 凵 at 3658

巾

4217
■4-3-3

▶CLOTH
キン はば▲
Ⓒ 巾 jīn

50	Jōyō	U5DFE
巾	S3-3-0	F2051

丨	冂	巾
1	2	3

RADICAL

haba 'cloth' (布 帳 師), used in characters related to fabrics or their qualities

COMPOUNDS

❶ [original meaning] **CLOTH, napkin**
巾着 きんちゃく purse

雑巾 ぞうきん rag; mop
布巾 ふきん dishcloth, napkin
茶巾 ちゃきん tea cloth [napkin]
三角巾 さんかくきん triangle bandage

❷ **headgear**
頭巾 ずきん hood, kerchief

❸ [usu. 幅 0694] width, breadth, range
→ see 幅 0694 for compounds

❹ unclassified compounds
金巾 かなきん *canequim* (Portuguese), unbleached muslin, calico

INDEPENDENT

【きん 巾】CLOTH, napkin

KUN

【はば 巾】[usu. 幅] **width, breadth, range**
半巾 はんはば half-width (approx. 18 cm)

SPECIAL READINGS

脛×巾▲ はばき leggings

SYNONYMS

❶ **fabric**
布 CLOTH → 3691
地 fabric → 0236
巾 CLOTH → 4217

HOMOPHONES

はば 幅 WIDTH → 0694

NOTE

➡ see USAGE note and NOTE at 幅 0694

才

▶**TALENT**
▶**AGE SUFFIX**
サイ ㊔ とし
Ⓒ 才 cái

4218
■4-3-3

64	Jōyō-2	U624D
扌	S3-3-0	F1038

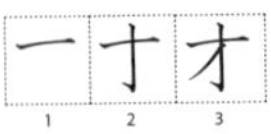

COMPOUNDS

❶ⓐ **TALENT, natural ability, gift, genius**
ⓑ **person of TALENT, man of ability, capable person**

a 才能 さいのう talent, ability
才気 さいき talent
才知 さいち wit and intelligence
英才 えいさい [formerly also 穎才] talent, genius; gifted person, talented person
詩才 しさい poetic genius
商才 しょうさい business ability [talent]

b 俊才 しゅんさい genius, person of exceptional talent
天才 てんさい (person of) genius
秀才 しゅうさい (person of) genius

❷ [also 歳 3131] **AGE SUFFIX**
十二才 じゅうにさい 12 years old
何才 なんさい how old, what age

❸ *sai*:
ⓐ unit of volume equiv. to approx. 0.0278 cubic cm or 1 cubic *shaku* (尺), used esp. for measuring lumber or freight
ⓑ unit of capacity equiv. to approx. 1/10 of a *shaku* (勺)
ⓒ unit of sq. measure equiv. to approx. 1 sq. foot, used for measuring textiles

❹ **used phonetically for *sai***
漫才 まんざい comic dialogue, comic backchat, *manzai*

INDEPENDENT

【さい 才】TALENT, ability, gift; wit; *sai* (→❸)
語学の才 ごがくのさい talent for languages
外交の才 がいこうのさい diplomatic talent

SYNONYMS

❶ⓐ **skill**
力 POWER → 4178
能 ABILITY → 1676
技 SKILL → 0292
倆 SKILL → 0136
腕 skill → 1269
才 TALENT → 4218

ⓑ **wise and talented persons**
哲 sage → 3402
賢 wise man → 3518
博 DOCTOR → 0170
秀 genius → 3152
俊 BRILLIANT PERSON → 0117
才 person of talent → 4218
通 well-informed person → 3855

❷ **age**
齢 AGE → 2390
令 age → 2489
年 years → 2528
歳 AGE SUFFIX → 3131
才 AGE SUFFIX → 4218
寿 life span → 4372

千

▶**THOUSAND**
セン ち ㊔ かず ゆき
Ⓒ 千 qiān

4219
■4-3-3

24	Jōyō-1	U5343
十	S3-2-1	F0307

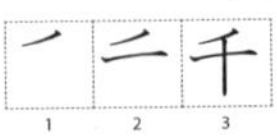

COMPOUNDS

❶ **THOUSAND**

千円 せんえん 1000 yen
五千 ごせん 5000

❷ a large number
千差万別 せんさばんべつ infinite variety
千秋 せんしゅう a thousand years, many years

INDEPENDENT

【せん 千】**THOUSAND**

KUN

【ち 千】[in compounds] **THOUSAND**
千代 ちよ a thousand years, a very long period
千草 ちぐさ various flowering plants
千千に ちぢに in pieces
千鳥足 ちどりあし tottering gait
千切る ちぎる tear (to pieces), tear off
千切れる ちぎれる be torn off, come off

SYNONYMS

❶ **large numbers**
百 HUNDRED → 2519
千 THOUSAND → 4219
万 TEN THOUSAND → 3653
億 HUNDRED MILLION → 0192
兆 TRILLION → 0264
京 ten quadrillion → 2546

NOTE

★ do not confuse with 干 DRY → 4187

屮

4220
■4-3-3

▶***TETSU***

45	Radical	UFA3C
屮	S3-3-0	F0000

RADICAL

tetsu 'sprout' (屯), used for character classification

廾

4221
■4-3-3

▶***NIJŪASHI***

55	Radical	U5EFE
廾	S3-3-0	F0000

RADICAL

nijūashi 'clasp hands' (弁 弊 弄), used in characters related to offering or presenting

---

扌

4222
■4-3-3

▶***TEHEN***

64	Radical	U624C
扌	S3-3-0	F0000

radical variant → see 手 at 4267

艹

4223
■4-3-3

▶***KUSAKANMURI***

140	Radical	U8279
艹	S3-3-0	F0000

radical variant → see 艸 at 0241

寸

■4-3-3

incorrect classification
➡ see □3-2-1: 寸 at 3652

大

4224
■4-3-4

▶**BIG**
▶**UNIVERSITY**

ダイ タイ おお- おお(きい) おお(いに)
㊔ ひろし ひろ ふとし まさる たかし はじめ ゆたか とも
Ⓒ 大 dà dài

37	Jōyō-1	U5927
大	S3-3-0	F0004

一 ナ 大
1 2 3

RADICAL

ōkii or ***dai*** 'big' (太 天 契), used in characters related to standing persons or largeness
Top variant: 大 ***ōkii*** or ***dai*** (奪 奮 奔)

COMPOUNDS

❶ⓐ [also prefix] (great in size, extent or quantity) **BIG, large, great, major, grand, vast, numerous**
ⓑ [prefix] (before place names) Great, Greater
ⓒ [suffix] size

a 大小 だいしょう large and small; size; long and short swords
大会 たいかい mass meeting, rally; meet, tournament
大陸 たいりく continent
大衆 たいしゅう the masses, populace
大量 たいりょう large quantity, great volume, mass
大規模 だいきぼ large scale
大金 たいきん large sum of money
大正 たいしょう Taisho era
拡大する かくだいする magnify, enlarge, expand
最大の さいだいの biggest, largest, greatest
巨大な きょだいな huge, gigantic, enormous
莫大な ばくだいな vast, immense, enormous

b 大ニューヨーク だいにゅーよーく Greater New York
大ブリテン島 だいぶりてんとう Great Britain

c 卵大の たまごだいの egg-sized
２０ｃｍ×２０ｃｍ大 にじゅっせんちかけるにじゅっせんちだい 20 cm by 20 cm in size

❷ [also prefix] (of great intensity or degree) **BIG, great, extreme, intense, severe, loud**
大変な たいへんな awful, terrible; serious, grave
大病 たいびょう serious illness, dangerous disease

大切な たいせつな important, weighty; valuable
大丈夫 だいじょうぶ safe, sure, all right
大地震 だいじしん big earthquake
大歓迎 だいかんげい warm welcome
大層 たいそう very, greatly, highly, very much
大嫌いだ だいきらいだ hate, detest
大好きだ だいすきだ like very much, be very fond of
大戦 たいせん world war; great war

❸ⓐ (characterized by greatness) **BIG, great, grand, important, chief, prominent, excellent**
ⓑ **BIG-hearted, generous, kindly**

a 大使 たいし ambassador
大統領 だいとうりょう president
大臣 だいじん minister (of state)
大学 だいがく university, college
大学生 だいがくせい university student; undergraduate
大国 たいこく world power, great country; large country
大事 だいじ great thing, serious affair; importance
大家 たいか great master, authority
大前提 だいぜんてい major premise
偉大な いだいな great, mighty, grand
重大な じゅうだいな important, serious, grave

b 寛大な かんだいな generous, magnanimous, lenient

❹ⓐ abbrev. of 大学 だいがく: **UNIVERSITY, college**
ⓑ **suffix after names of universities**

a 大卒 だいそつ university graduate
女子大生 じょしだいせい female university student
短大 たんだい junior college

b オックスフォード大 おっくすふぉーどだい Oxford University
東大 とうだい Tokyo University

❺ **in substance, on the whole, in general, for the most part**

大意 たいい substance, gist, general outline
大概 たいがい generally, mostly; probably, maybe
大勢 たいせい general trend [tendency]
大体 だいたい outline, substance; generally, roughly, on the whole
大抵 たいてい generally, mostly, for the most part
大半 たいはん the greater part, majority
大部分 だいぶぶん most, greater part; mostly, for the most part
大分 だいぶ(=だいぶん) very, greatly, considerably
大多数 だいたすう majority, greater part

❻ [honorific prefix]
ⓐ great, honorable
ⓑ imperial

a 大西郷 だいさいごう the Great Saigo

b 大政奉還 たいせいほうかん restoration of imperial rule

❼ⓐ senior, older, eldest
ⓑ (one generation removed) **great-, grand-**

a 大兄 たいけい older brother; honorific title for someone a little older

b 大祖父 だいそふ great-grandfather

INDEPENDENT

【だい 大】**BIGness, largeness; large size, large; adult; greatness; long month (of 31 days)**
大は小を兼ねる だいはしょうをかねる The greater serves for the lesser
ビールの大 びーるのだい large beer

【だいの 大の】passionate, confirmed; (of months) long; **BIG**, large
大の猫好き だいのねこずき ardent cat lover [fancier]

【たい 大】abbrev. of 大正 たいしょう: Taisho era

【たいした 大した】**enormous, great, grand; important, serious**

【たいして 大して】**(not) very, greatly**

KUN

【おお- 大-】[also prefix]

①ⓐ (of considerable extent or intensity) **BIG, large, great, extreme, severe**
ⓑ **grand, great, BIG, magnificent**
ⓒ **many, much**

a 大形 おおがた large size
大目に おおめに rather large
大手 おおて major companies
大急ぎで おおいそぎで in a great [urgent] hurry, against time
大水 おおみず flood, inundation
大雪 おおゆき heavy snow
大幅に おおはばに sharply, by a large margin
大盛り おおもり large helping [serving]

b 大蔵省 おおくらしょう Ministry of Finance
大物 おおもの great man, big shot
大家 おおや owner, proprietor, landlord
大鳥 おおとり [also 鳳, 鴻 or 鵬] large wild bird such as crane or white stork; huge bird such as a mythical Chinese phoenix

c 大勢の おおぜいの great number of, multitude of
大助かり おおだすかり big help

② **main, chief, representative**
大詰め おおづめ finale, end
大晦日 おおみそか last day of the year, December 31

③ (one generation removed) **great-**
大伯母 おおおば great-aunt

④ honorific prefix
大宮人 おおみやびと courtier

大御代 おおみよ glorious reign of the emperor

⑤ **more or less**

大方 おおかた almost, nearly; probably

大まかな おおまかな rough, general, broad

大筋 おおすじ outline

大雑把な おおざっぱな rough, broad, sketchy

【おおきい 大きい】**BIG, large, extensive; massive, enormous; great, grand**

大きな おおきな noun adjective form of 大きい おおきい

大きさ おおきさ size, dimensions

【おおいに 大いに】**very, greatly, highly, exceedingly**

大いに喜ぶ おおいによろこぶ be highly pleased

SPECIAL READINGS

大人 おとな adult

大人しい▲ おとなしい gentle, meek

大和 やまと [also 倭] Yamato (old name for Japan)

大分県 おおいたけん Oita Prefecture

SYNONYMS

❶ⓐ big and huge

大 BIG →4224

太 GREAT →2673

浩 VAST →0525

巨 HUGE →3773

厖 BULKY →3725

ⓒ size

寸 measurement →3652

大 size →4224

❷ extreme in degree

酷 SEVERE →1967

強 STRONG →0574

凄い tremendous →0145

重 HEAVY →4390

高 HIGH →2601

深 DEEP →0636

大 BIG →4224

厳 SEVERE →4079

激 intense →0955

極 EXTREME →1243

痛 bitter(ly) →4071

切 keen →0030

甚 EXTREMELY →3271

祁 EXTREMELY →1447

超 super- →4107

頗る EXCEEDINGLY →1552

❸ⓐ great

偉 GREAT (of superior character) →0167

大 BIG →4224

宏 GRAND (large in scale) →2728

壮 GRAND (having grandeur) →0263

豪 MAGNIFICENT →2657

雄 HEROIC →1271

碩 EMINENT →1555

❹ schools

校 SCHOOL →1166

学 EDUCATIONAL INSTITUTION →3162

院 INSTITUTION →0544

塾 PRIVATE SCHOOL →3546

大 UNIVERSITY →4224

高 high school →2601

中 junior high school →4262

小 elementary school →0007

園 kindergarten →3914

❺ approximately

約 APPROXIMATELY →1632

概 GENERAL →1322

大 in substance →4224

-頃 ABOUT →0163

位 about →0069

-方 about →2459

-程 …or thereabouts →1524

辺り thereabouts →3761

USAGE

【おお- 大- 多-】

★大 is a word-forming element meaning big or large, but in some compounds it is used in the sense of many, as in 大勢 おおぜい 'crowd of people' and 大人数 おおにんずう 'many people'. Though 多い おおい also means much or many, the prefix おお- in the sense of many is written 大-, not 多-. However, compare the following words:

大目に おおめに rather large

多目に おおめに plenty, lots

HOMOPHONES

やまと

倭 ANCIENT NAME FOR JAPAN →0140

大和 →4224, 1450

おおとり

鳳 MALE PHOENIX →3749

鴻 LARGE WILD BIRD →0977

鵬 MYTHICAL HUGE BIRD →1416

大鳥 →4224, 4105

NOTE

➡ see COMPOUND FORMATION for

大切 たいせつ →切 0030

大変 たいへん →変 2569

莫大 ばくだい →莫 2839

大丈夫 だいじょうぶ →夫 4271

大【丸】女丈之与弋夨女宀幺广彡凢ケ円乏亡久夕也夂夊尢

丸

4225

■4-3-4

▸ROUND

ガン まる¹ まる² まる(い) まる(める)

Ⓒ 丸 wán

3	Jōyō-2	U4E38
丶	S3-1-2	F0637

ノ 九 丸
1 2 3

COMPOUNDS

❶ⓐ ROUND body, pellet, ball
ⓑ ROUND projectile, ball
a 丸薬 がんやく pill
一丸となって いちがんとなって in a body [lump]
b 砲丸 ほうがん cannonball
弾丸 だんがん shot, bullet, shell
銃丸 じゅうがん bullet
❷ suffix after names of pills
救命丸 きゅうめいがん Kyumeigan (name of pill)

KUN

【まる¹ 丸】
①ⓐ **ROUND or spherical shape**
ⓑ [sometimes also 円] **circle**
a 日の丸 ひのまる Rising Sun Flag
② **wholeness, completeness**
丸の儘× まるのまま whole, in its entirety
丸で まるで just like; completely, perfectly
③ [also ◯] **check mark for correct answers (similar to ✓)**
丸を付ける まるをつける mark a correct answer with a circle
④ **small circle corresponding to a period in a sentence**
⑤ within the castle walls
二の丸 にのまる outworks of a castle
本丸 ほんまる keep of a castle, donjon

【まる² 丸】
① [in compounds] **ROUND, circular, spherical**
丸顔 まるがお round face, moon face
丸丸と太った まるまるとふとった plump, rotund, chubby
② [also prefix] **complete(ly), total(ly), perfect(ly)**
丸っきり まるっきり just like; completely, perfectly
丸丸 まるまる completely, entirely
丸儲け まるもうけ clear profit
丸二日 まるふつか for a full two days
丸焼けになった まるやけになった completely burned
魚を丸ごと食べる さかなをまるごとたべる eat a fish whole
③ suffix after names of ships—formerly also used after names of swords, children or dogs
南海丸 なんかいまる *Nankaimaru* (name of ship)
日吉丸 ひよしまる name of Toyotomi Hideyoshi during his youth

【まるい 丸い】
①ⓐ (shaped like a ball) **ROUND, spherical**
ⓑ [also 円い] (shaped like a circle) **ROUND, circular**
a 丸み まるみ roundness
背が丸い せがまるい round-backed
b 丸くなって まるくなって in a circle [ring]
② **ROUND**ed, amicable, harmonious
丸く治まる まるくおさまる become reconciled, settle peacefully

【まるめる 丸める】**ROUND, make round, roll up; cajole, coax, wheedle**
丸め込む まるめこむ cajole, coax, wheedle
雪を丸める ゆきをまるめる make a snowball

SYNONYMS

❶ⓐ spherical object
玉 spherical object →4289
球 BALL →1219
丸 round body →4225
鞠 BALL →2268
毬 BALL →4001
ⓑ projectiles and bombs
弾 PROJECTILE →0697
丸 round projectile →4225
矢 ARROW →2502
槍 SPEAR →1329
爆 bomb →1415
雷 explosive device →3466
❷ medicines
薬 DRUG →3011
剤 PREPARATION →2102
錠 PILL →2180
丸 pill suffix →4225
鍼 ACUPUNCTURE →2204
灸 MOXIBUSTION →2752

【まる¹】
① **circle**
円 CIRCLE →3673
圏 circle →3904
丸 round or spherical shape →4225
楕 ELLIPSE →1279

【まる²】
② **all**
皆 ALL →3093
悉 THOROUGHLY →3405
総 TOTAL →1743
諸 VARIOUS →1984
毎 EVERY →2527
各 EACH →2692
都 all →2120

万 all →3653
全 WHOLE →2514
渾 ENTIRE →0738
一 all in one →4148
満 FULL →0739
丸 complete(ly) →4225
完 COMPLETE →2727

【まるい】
① **round**
丸い ROUND →4225
円 circular →3673

USAGE

❶【まる¹】
丸
①ⓐ round or spherical shape
ⓑ [sometimes also 円] circle
② wholeness, completeness
③ [also ○] check mark for correct answers (similar to ✓)
④ small circle corresponding to a period in a sentence
⑤ within the castle walls

円
① [usu. 丸] circle
② *slang* money, dough—used in telegrams

○
① zero (the numeral)
② [also 丸] check mark for correct answers (similar to ✓)
③ indicates omitted or unprintable letters [characters]

❷【まるい】
丸い
①ⓐ (shaped like a ball) round, spherical
ⓑ [also 円い] (shaped like a circle) round, circular
② rounded, amicable, harmonious

円い
[also 丸い] (shaped like a circle) circular, round

HOMOPHONES

まる¹
円 CIRCLE →3673
○ ZERO →4149
まるい 円 CIRCLE →3673

女

4226

■4-3-4

▶WOMAN

ジョ ニョ ニョウ おんな め

Ⓒ 女 nǚ

38	Jōyō-1	U5973
女	S3-3-0	F0029

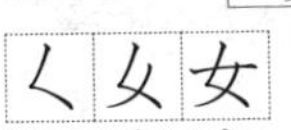

RADICAL

onna 'woman' (姿 姦× 威), used in characters related to women, marriage or sex
Left variant: 女 ***onnahen*** (好 妙 妹)

COMPOUNDS

❶ [also prefix and suffix]
ⓐ [original meaning] **WOMAN, female**
ⓑ **girl, maiden**

a 女性 じょせい woman, female; feminine gender
女性的 じょせいてき feminine, womanly
女子 じょし woman, girl
女優 じょゆう actress
女王 じょおう(=じょうおう) queen; belle, mistress
女人 にょにん woman
女房 にょうぼう wife; court lady
女中 じょちゅう maidservant, maid
彼女 かのじょ she; one's sweetheart
男女 だんじょ men and women, both sexes
修道女 しゅうどうじょ nun, sister

b 女生徒 じょせいと schoolgirl, girl student
少女 しょうじょ girl
処女 しょじょ virgin, maiden
織女星 しょくじょせい Vega

❷ **daughter**—used esp. to indicate order of birth
長女 ちょうじょ eldest daughter
養女 ようじょ adopted daughter, stepdaughter
三女 さんじょ third daughter

❸ suffix after names of women, esp. haiku poetesses
千代女 ちよじょ name of a haiku poetess

INDEPENDENT

【じょ 女】WOMAN; girl; daughter

KUN

【おんな 女】[also prefix] **WOMAN, lady, female; girl; mistress**
女の子 おんなのこ girl, daughter
女らしい おんならしい womanly, ladylike; feminine
女手 おんなで hiragana, woman's handwriting; woman in a family
女歌舞伎 おんなかぶき girls' kabuki

【め 女】
① *elegant* **the fair sex, WOMAN, female**
女神 めがみ goddess
賤の女 しずのめ woman of lowly birth
② [in compounds] the weaker or smaller of two
女女しい めめしい effeminate, unmanly
女波 めなみ the smaller waves
女滝(=雌滝) めだき the smaller waterfall (of the two)

SPECIAL READINGS

女将▲ おかみ mistress, landlady, proprietress
海女 あま woman diver

巫×女▲ みこ maiden in the service of a shrine; medium
貴女▲ あなた you (feminine pronoun)

SYNONYMS

❶ woman

女 WOMAN → 4226
婦 ADULT WOMAN → 0565
婆 OLD WOMAN → 3433
嬢 YOUNG LADY → 0936
娘 GIRL → 0488
雌 FEMALE → 1337
牝 FEMALE → 1020
媛 DAMSEL → 0688

❷ offspring

子 CHILD → 4196
仔 OFFSPRING → 0038
孤 orphan → 0426
嫡 LEGITIMATE CHILD → 0839
息 son → 3278
男 son → 3147
惣 eldest son → 3452
娘 DAUGHTER → 0488
女 daughter → 4226
姫 DAUGHTER OF NOBLE BIRTH → 0489

HOMOPHONES

め

雌 FEMALE → 1337
牝 FEMALE → 1020

NOTE

➡ see USAGE note at 雌 1337
➡ see COMPOUND FORMATION for
織女星 しょくじょせい → 織 1801
女房 にょうぼう → 房 2445
女中 じょちゅう → 中 4262

丈

4227

■4-3-4

▶**STOUT**
▶**STATURE**

ジョウ たけ だけ▲ ㊔ たけし

Ⓝ 丈 Ⓒ 丈 zhàng

1	Jōyō	U4E08
一	S3-1-2	F1001

一 ナ 丈
1 2 3

COMPOUNDS

❶ STOUT, robust, strong, tough

丈夫な じょうぶな healthy, strong, robust; stout, solid
気丈な きじょうな stouthearted, courageous
頑丈な がんじょうな solid, firm; strong

❷ STATURE, height

偉丈夫 いじょうふ towering [great] man; hero
大丈夫 だいじょうぶ safe, sure, all right

❸ [original meaning] *jo*: unit of length equiv. to approx. 3.03 m or 10 *shaku* (尺)

一丈一尺 いちじょういっしゃく 1 *jo* 1 *shaku*
方丈 ほうじょう 10 sq. feet; abbot's chamber; chief priest
万丈 ばんじょう unfathomable height

❹ title after names of artists

団十郎丈 だんじゅうろうじょう Mr. Danjuro (kabuki actor)

INDEPENDENT

【じょう 丈】*jo* (→❸)

KUN

【たけ 丈】**STATURE, height; length, measure; all (one has)**

丈比べ たけくらべ comparison of statures
背丈 せたけ stature, height
思いの丈 おもいのたけ one's inmost heart

【だけ 丈】only, merely; as much; the more...the more

一度丈 いちどだけ only once

SYNONYMS

❶ strong

強 STRONG → 0574
壮 VIGOROUS → 0263
丈 STOUT → 4227
健 ROBUST (healthy) → 0152
逞しい ROBUST (sturdy) → 4004
康 HEALTHY → 3877
旺 ENERGETIC → 1061
溌 LIVELY → 0917

❷ height

高 height → 2601
丈 STATURE → 4227
背 stature → 3182

❸ length units

寸 *sun* (3.03 cm) → 3652
浬 NAUTICAL MILE (1852 m) → 0526
反 *tan* (10.6 m) → 3663
尺 *SHAKU* (30.3 cm) → 4248
米 meter → 4342
尋 fathom (1.8 m) → 2918
間 *ken* (1.8 m) → 4122
丈 *jo* (3.03 m) → 4227
町 *cho* (109 m) → 1430
里 LEAGUE, *ri* (3.9 km) → 4356
哩 MILE (1609 m) → 0479

NOTE

➡ see COMPOUND FORMATION for 大丈夫 だいじょうぶ → 夫 4271

之

▶POSSESSIVE PARTICLE

シ の これ ㊔ ゆき いたる

Ⓒ 之 zhī

4228

■4-3-4

3	Names	U4E4B
丶	S3-1-2	F0375

COMPOUNDS

❶ shaped like the character ⻌

之繞× しんにょう(=しんにゅう) *shinnyo*, 'advance' radical (⻌)

❷ [original meaning, now archaic] go, proceed toward

KUN

【の 之】**POSSESSIVE PARTICLE**

鳥之巣 とりのす bird's nest

実業之日本社 じつぎょうのにほんしゃ Jitsugyo no Nihon Sha (name of a publisher)

【これ 之】[also 是] *pronoun* **this**

之は何ですか これはなんですか What is this?

SYNONYMS

【の】

◯ **possessive particles**

之 POSSESSIVE PARTICLE →4228

乃 POSSESSIVE PARTICLE →3643

【これ】

◯ **this and that**

本 THIS →4314

爾 THAT →4407

其れ THAT →3255

彼 that →0346

今 THIS (week, etc.) →2464

当 THE PRESENT →2701

該 the said →1916

同 the same →3707

之 this →4228

是 this →3090

此 THIS →1017

斯 THIS →2140

USAGE

【の】

之

possessive particle

乃

possessive particle

HOMOPHONES

の 乃 POSSESSIVE PARTICLE →3643

これ

是 RIGHT →3090

此 THIS →1017

惟 MEDITATE →0582

NOTE

➡ see also USAGE note at 是 3090

与

▶GIVE

ヨ あた(える) あずか(る)▲ ㊔ よし とも

Ⓝ 與 Ⓒ 与 yǔ yù

4229

■4-3-4

1△	Jōyō	U4E0E
一	S3-1-2	F0477

一 与 与
1 2 3

COMPOUNDS

❶ **GIVE, present, grant**

与件 よけん postulate, given conditions

供与する きょうよする offer, present, submit

給与する きゅうよする allow, grant; pay (a salary)

授与する じゅよする grant, give, confer

寄与する きよする contribute, render services to

贈与する ぞうよする donate, present

❷ **take part in, participate in, side with**

与党 よとう party in power

与野党 よやとう both parties, parties in and out of power

与国 よこく ally

参与する さんよする participate in, take part in

関与する かんよする take part in, participate in, be concerned in

INDEPENDENT

【よ 与】[archaic] and, together with

KUN

【あたえる 与える】**GIVE, present, grant, award; provide (with food); cause, inflict (damage)**

分け与える わけあたえる distribute, hand out

【あずかる 与る】

① participate in, take part in, share in

相談に与る そうだんにあずかる be consulted

② enjoy, receive

招待に与る しょうたいにあずかる receive an invitation

SYNONYMS

❶ **give**

与 GIVE →4229

呈 PRESENT →2715

進 present to a superior →3873

上 give (to superior or others) →4212

下 give (to inferior or speaker) →4186

呉れる give (to speaker) →3156

授 CONFER →0595

賜 DEIGN TO GIVE →1994

贈 PRESENT A GIFT →2064

賄 BRIBE →1931

賂 BRIBE →1930

❷ **participate and join**

参 PARTICIPATE →2563

与 take part in →4229
加 join →0042
入 ENTER →4177

HOMOPHONES

あずかる 預 DEPOSIT →1317

NOTE

➡ see USAGE note at 預 1317

弋

4230
■4-3-4

▶**CATCH**
ヨク
Ⓒ 弋 yì

56	Non-Jōyō	U5F0B
弋	S3-3-0	F0000

RADICAL

shikigamae 'spike' (式 弐 弑×), used for character classification

COMPOUNDS

❶ **CATCH, capture**
遊弋する ゆうよくする cruise, patrol

❷ [original meaning, now archaic] arrow with a string for **CATCH**ing birds
弋人 よくじん archer, hunter

SYNONYMS

❶ **hunt and fish**
猟 HUNTING →0654
狩 HUNT →0474
獲 CATCH GAME →0959
漁 FISH →0856
釣 ANGLE →2108
弋 CATCH →4230

大

4231
■4-3-4

▶***ŌKII, DAI***

37	Radical	U5927
大	S3-3-0	F0000

radical variant →see 大 at 4224

女

4232
■4-3-4

▶***ONNAHEN***

38	Radical	U5973
女	S3-3-0	F0000

radical variant →see 女 at 4226

宀

4233
■4-3-4

▶***UKANMURI***

40	Radical	U5B80
宀	S3-3-0	F0000

RADICAL

ukanmuri 'roof' (実 家 定), used in characters related to roofs or houses

---

幺

4234
■4-3-4

▶***ITOGASHIRA***

52	Radical	U5E7A
幺	S3-3-0	F0000

RADICAL

itogashira 'tiny' (幼 幾 幽), used in characters related to threads, dimness or slightness

---

广

4235
■4-3-4

▶***MADARE***

53	Radical	U5E7F
广	S3-3-0	F0000

RADICAL

madare 'roof' (府 広 庁), used in characters related to roofs or buildings

---

犭

4236
■4-3-4

▶***KEMONOHEN***

94	Radical	U72AD
犭	S3-3-0	F0000

radical variant →see 犬 at 4275

凢

4237
■4-3-4

▶**COMMONPLACE**
ボン ハン およ(そ) おおよ(そ) すべ(て)
㊔ なみ つね おうし

16	Nonstandard	U51E2
几	S3-2-1	F0000

traditional form →see 凡 at 3656

ケ

4238
■4-3-4

▶**COUNTER FOR ITEMS**
カ コ

1	Nonstandard	U30F6
一	S3-1-2	F0000

alternative form →see 箇 at 3348

门

4239
■4-3-4

▶**GATE**
モン かど ㊔ と

13	Nonstandard	U95E8
冂	S3-2-1	F0000

handwritten form →see 門 at 1100

乏

■4-3-4

incorrect classification/ stroke-count
➡ see ■2-1-3: ノ at 2432

亡
■4-3-4
incorrect classification
➡ see ■4-3-2 at 4210

久
■4-3-4
incorrect classification
➡ see ■4-3-1 at 4191

夕
■4-3-4
incorrect classification
➡ see ■4-3-1 at 4195

也
■4-3-4
incorrect classification
➡ see ■4-3-2 at 4214

夂
■4-3-4
incorrect classification
➡ see ■4-3-1 at 4200

攵
■4-3-4
incorrect classification
➡ see ■4-3-1 at 4201

尢
■4-3-4
incorrect classification
➡ see □3-2-1: 𠂇 at 3654

弔 4240 ■4-4-1

▸**CONDOLE**
チョウ とむら(う)
Ⓒ 吊 diào

57	Jōyō	U5F14
弓	S4-3-1	F2593

COMPOUNDS

ⓐ **CONDOLE, offer one's condolences to a bereaved person, console, mourn**
ⓑ **CONDOLE**nce, condolences, funeral condolences

a 弔辞 ちょうじ message of condolence
弔電 ちょうでん telegram of condolence
弔問 ちょうもん condolence call
弔慰 ちょうい condolence, sympathy
b 慶弔 けいちょう congratulations and condolences

KUN

【とむらう 弔う】**mourn, CONDOLE (with a bereaved family); perform a memorial service, hold a Buddhist mass**
弔い とむらい funeral service; mass for the dead; condolence

SYNONYMS

ⓐ **mourn and mourning**
弔 CONDOLE →4240
悼 MOURN →0587
喪 MOURNING →3504
忌 MOURNING →2735

ⓐ **console**
慰 CONSOLE →3557
弔 CONDOLE →4240

丑 4241 ■4-4-1

▸**THE OX**
チュウ うし
Ⓝ 刃 丑◇ Ⓒ 丑 chǒu

1	Names	U4E11
一	S4-1-3	F2606

COMPOUNDS

● second sign of the Oriental zodiac: **THE OX**—(time) 1-3 a.m., (direction) NNE, (season) December (of the lunar calendar) (→see APPENDIX 8)
癸×丑 きちゅう 50th of the sexagenary cycle

KUN

【うし 丑】second sign of the Oriental zodiac: **THE OX** (→●)
丑の刻 うしのこく two o'clock in the morning
丑の年 うしのとし Year of the Ox
丑三つ時 うしみつどき in the dead of night
丑寅 うしとら [also 艮] one of the four supplementary signs of the Oriental zodiac: northeast

SYNONYMS

● **cattle**
牛 CATTLE →4263
丑 THE OX →4241

HOMOPHONES

うし 牛 CATTLE →4263
うしとら
艮 NORTHEAST →4330
丑寅 →4241, 2854

NOTE

➡ see USAGE note at 牛 4263

不 4242 ■4-4-1

▸**NOT**
フ ブ
Ⓒ 不 bù bu

1	Jōyō-4	U4E0D
一	S4-1-3	F0107

COMPOUNDS

● [also prefix] **NOT, un-, in-, non-, dis-**—element of negation usu. placed before nouns or noun adjectives
不足 ふそく insufficiency, shortage, deficit; want; dissatisfaction
不安 ふあん uneasiness, anxiety

不動の ふどうの immobile
不況 ふきょう depression, slump, recession
不運 ふうん misfortune, bad luck
不満 ふまん dissatisfaction, discontent
不思議 ふしぎ mystery, wonder
不尽 ふじん Yours sincerely
不気味な ぶきみな uncanny, weird, ghastly
不器用な ぶきような clumsy, unskillful
不用心 ぶようじん insecurity; carelessness
不平 ふへい discontent, dissatisfaction, complaint
不利 ふり disadvantage
不意に ふいに suddenly, unexpectedly
不時着する ふじちゃくする make an emergency landing; ditch
不順な ふじゅんな unseasonable; irregular
不純な ふじゅんな impure; mixed
不燃物 ふねんぶつ incombustibles
不備 ふび defect, imperfection
不法 ふほう unlawfulness, illegality, wrong
不本意に ふほんいに reluctantly, unwillingly
不慮の ふりょの unexpected, unforeseen; accidental
不親切な ふしんせつな unkind, unfriendly; inattentive
不安定 ふあんてい instability
不可能な ふかのうな impossible
不完全 ふかんぜん imperfection, incompleteness
不機嫌 ふきげん bad mood, displeasure
不規則な ふきそくな irregular
不合格 ふごうかく failure, disqualification
不公平な ふこうへいな unfair, unjust
不自然な ふしぜんな unnatural, artificial
不自由 ふじゆう inconvenience; disability; poverty
不十分 ふじゅうぶん insufficiency, lack
不確かな ふたしかな unreliable, uncertain
不注意 ふちゅうい carelessness, inattention
不得意 ふとくい one's weak point
不必要な ふひつような unnecessary; superfluous
不平等な ふびょうどうな unequal, unfair
不可 ふか F, fail(ure); improper; inadvisable
不合理な ふごうりな irrational, unreasonable
不始末 ふしまつ mismanagement, irregularity
不条理 ふじょうり absurdity
不相応な ふそうおうな unsuited, unbecoming
不都合 ふつごう inconvenience; misconduct
不透明な ふとうめいな opaque
不慣れな ふなれな inexperienced, unfamiliar
不変な ふへんな unchanging, invariable; eternal
不利益 ふりえき disadvantage

SPECIAL READINGS

不味い▲ まずい bad-tasting, unpalatable; poor, clumsy; unwise, foolish

SYNONYMS

● **terms of negation**

不 NOT (negation) →4242
非 IS NOT (contrariety) →1101
無 WITHOUT (nonexistence) →2648
没 lacking in →0305
欠 LACK →2481
否 OR NOT →3058
未 NOT YET →4318
莫 NOT →2839
勿 DO NOT →3661

USAGE

【ふ 不】
[also prefix] not, un-, in-, non-, dis-—element of negation usu. placed before nouns or noun adjectives

【ひ 非】
[also prefix] is not, not, non-, un-, in-—element of contrariety usu. placed before nouns

【む 無】
[also prefix] without, -less, non-, un-, in-, no—element indicating nonexistence or lack

【ぼつ 没】
[prefix] lacking in, not, un-

【けつ 欠】
lack, be short of, be deficient

【み 未】
[also prefix] not yet, un- (as in *unpublished*)

【ひ 否】
or not—used as the second element of a compound to negate the meaning of the first

★不, 非 and 無 are comparable to English prefixes of negation such as *non-*, *un-*, *in-*, *dis-*, etc. 非 is best described as a prefix of contrariety with strong negative overtones. It is equivalent to the *in-* of *inhuman* (非人間的な ひにんげんてきな) and to the *un-* of *unscientific* (非科学的な ひかがくてきな). 不 is the general prefix of negation like the *un-* of *unhappy* (不幸な ふこうな) or the *dis-* of *disagreement* (不一致 ふいっち). 不, the most frequently used, is usu. placed before nouns or noun adjectives, while 非 is rather restricted to nouns. 無 usu. stresses mere lack and implies nothing further, much like the English *non-* in *nonpoisonous* (無毒の むどくの). 没, the less frequently used prefix, implies a complete lack of something, as in 没個性 ぼつこせい 'lack of individuality'. 未 is equivalent to *un-* in the sense of 'not yet', as 未完の みかんの 'uncompleted' and 未婚の みこんの 'unmarried'. The whole question is rather complicated and only idiom will tell which choice is correct in each case.

NOTE

➡ see COMPOUND FORMATION for 理不尽 りふじん →尽 3786

牙

▶FANG

ガ ゲ きば ㊔ かび

Ⓝ 牙◇ Ⓒ 牙 yá

4243

■4-4-1

92	Jōyō	U7259
牙	S4-4-0	F2198

一 1 ㄷ 2 㸦 3 牙 4

RADICAL

kiba 'sharp tooth', used in characters related to teeth

Left variant: 牙 *kiba*

COMPOUNDS

❶ **FANG, tusk**

歯牙 しが teeth

毒牙 どくが poison fang

爪牙 そうが claws and tusks, devious design; right-hand man

象牙 ぞうげ ivory

❷ standard of a military leader

牙城 がじょう stronghold, inner citadel

KUN

【きば 牙】**FANG, tusk**

牙を剝く きばをむく bare one's fangs

SPECIAL READINGS

西班牙▲ すぺいん Spain

葡萄牙▲ ぽるとがる Portugal

SYNONYMS

❶ **mouth parts**

唇 LIP →3401

歯 TOOTH →3124

舌 TONGUE →2711

牙 FANG →4243

五

▶FIVE

ゴ いつ いつ(つ) ㊔ い

Ⓒ 五 wǔ

4244

■4-4-1

7	Jōyō-1	U4E94
二	S4-2-2	F0075

一 1 丆 2 五 3 五 4

COMPOUNDS

ⓐ [original meaning] **FIVE, fifth**

ⓑ **FIVE** times

a 五百 ごひゃく 500

五十音 ごじゅうおん Japanese syllabary

五感 ごかん the five senses

五指 ごし the five fingers

五分 ごぶ half, 50 percent

五分五分 ごぶごぶ evenly matched; tie

五輪旗 ごりんき five-ringed Olympic flag

五目飯 ごもくめし Japanese pilaf

五月 ごがつ May

五階 ごかい fifth floor

b 五回 ごかい five times

INDEPENDENT

【ご 五】**FIVE, fifth**

五の組 ごのくみ fifth group

ダイヤの五 だいやのご five of diamonds

KUN

【いつ 五】[in compounds] **FIVE**

五日 いつか five days; 5th of the month

五月 いつつき five months

【いつつ 五つ】**FIVE**

五つ児 いつつご quintuplets

SPECIAL READINGS

五月晴れ さつきばれ fine weather in early summer [during the rainy season]

五月雨 さみだれ early summer rain

五月 さつき May

SYNONYMS

ⓐ **small numbers**

一 ONE →4148

十 TEN →4172

廿 TWENTY →4258

二 TWO →2421

三 THREE →2423

四 FOUR →3778

五 FIVE →4244

六 SIX →2461

七 SEVEN →4169

八 EIGHT →3644

九 NINE →4176

ⓐ **five**

五 FIVE →4244

伍 five (in legal documents) →0050

互

▶RECIPROCAL

ゴ たが(い)

Ⓒ 互 hù

4245

■4-4-1

7	Jōyō	U4E92
二	S4-2-2	F1029

一 1 ㄷ 2 互 3 互 4

COMPOUNDS

● [original meaning] **RECIPROCAL, mutual, each other**

互恵 ごけい reciprocity, mutual benefits
互助 ごじょ mutual aid, cooperation
互角 ごかく equality; good match
互選 ごせん co-optation, mutual election
相互の そうごの mutual, reciprocal
交互に こうごに mutually, reciprocally, alternately

KUN

【たがい 互い】**RECIPROCALity**
互いの たがいの mutual, reciprocal
互いに たがいに mutually, reciprocally
互い違いに たがいちがいに alternately

SYNONYMS

● **mutual**
相 MUTUAL → 1120
互 RECIPROCAL → 4245

巴

4246
■4-4-1

▶CIRCULAR COMMA PATTERN
ハ ともえ ㊔ とも
Ⓒ 巴 bā

49	Names	U5DF4
己	S4-3-1	F2638

COMPOUNDS

❶ used phonetically for *ha* or *pa*
巴旦杏 はたんきょう plum
巴里 ぱり Paris
❷ [archaic] ancient name for east Sichuan Province
巴人 はじん resident of ancient Sichuan; uneducated bumpkin

KUN

【ともえ 巴】**CIRCULAR COMMA PATTERN, eddy, whirl ()**
巴瓦 ともえがわら comma pattern tile
三つ巴 みつどもえ circular pattern of three commas; three-sided fight
卍×巴と まんじともえと in whirls

SYNONYMS

❶ **phonetic [ha]**
巴 phonetic [ha] → 4246
波 phonetic [ha] → 0388

王

4247
■4-4-1

▶KING
オウ -ノウ▲
Ⓒ 王 wáng wàng

96	Jōyō-1	U738B
王	S4-4-0	F0433

radical variant → see 玉 at 4289

1	2	3	4
一	丅	干	王

COMPOUNDS

❶ⓐ **KING, monarch, ruler, emperor**
ⓑ [also suffix] (the most powerful of a group) **KING, magnate, baron**
a 王様 おうさま king
王国 おうこく kingdom, monarchy
王座 おうざ throne
王子 おうじ prince
王女 おうじょ royal princess, princess
国王 こくおう king, monarch
女王 じょおう(=じょうおう) queen; belle, mistress
帝王 ていおう monarch, emperor
b 王者 おうじゃ king, monarch, champion
法王 ほうおう pope
海賊王 かいぞくおう pirate king
石油王 せきゆおう oil magnate
❷ name of chess piece in shogi (Japanese chess) or chess: **KING**
王将 おうしょう king (in shogi)
王手 おうて Check!
❸ imperial prince
親王 しんのう imperial prince
勤王 きんのう loyalty to the emperor

INDEPENDENT

【おう 王】**KING, monarch;** (the most powerful of a group) **king, magnate; king** (→ ❷)
王を立てる おうをたてる enthrone a king
王を詰める おうをつめる checkmate the king
百獣の王 ひゃくじゅうのおう king of beasts

SYNONYMS

❶ⓐ **rulers**
君 RULER → 3974
王 KING → 4247
帝 EMPEROR → 2573
天 Heaven's messenger on earth → 4250
皇 EMPEROR → 3175
堯 YAO → 2560
舜 SHUN → 3134
ⓑ **leaders**
主 MASTER → 2437
王 KING → 4247
長 CHIEF → 3163
頭 HEAD → 2019
首 LEADER → 2818
領 leader → 1567
魁 LEADER → 4125

尺

▸*SHAKU*
シャク
Ⓒ 尺 chǐ chě

4248
■4-4-1

44	Jōyō-6	U5C3A
尸	S4-3-1	F1534

1 ㇕ 2 ㇕ 3 尸 4 尺

COMPOUNDS

❶ ***SHAKU*: unit of length equiv. to approx. 30.3 cm or 10 *sun* (寸)**

尺貫法 しゃっかんほう Japanese system of weights and measures
尺八 しゃくはち bamboo flute
一尺 いっしゃく 1 *shaku*

❷ⓐ [also suffix] **rule, measure, scale**
ⓑ length

a 尺度 しゃくど linear measure; standard
巻き尺 まきじゃく measuring tape
計算尺 けいさんじゃく slide rule
b 尺取り虫 しゃくとりむし measuring worm
間尺に合わない ましゃくにあわない do not pay, be not worth (one's) while

❸ slight amount

尺地 しゃくち small plot of land

INDEPENDENT

【しゃく 尺】*SHAKU* (→❶); rule, measure, scale; length

尺を当てる しゃくをあてる measure with a rule
尺を取る しゃくをとる measure (the length)

SYNONYMS

❶ **length units**

寸 *sun* (3.03 cm) → 3652
浬 NAUTICAL MILE (1852 m) → 0526
反 *tan* (10.6 m) → 3663
尺 *SHAKU* (30.3 cm) → 4248
米 meter → 4342
尋 fathom (1.8 m) → 2918
間 *ken* (1.8 m) → 4122
丈 *jo* (3.03 m) → 4227
町 *cho* (109 m) → 1430
里 LEAGUE, *ri* (3.9 km) → 4356
哩 MILE (1609 m) → 0479

❷ⓐ **measuring devices**

枡 MEASURE → 1070
尺 rule → 4248
計 meter → 1828
衡 scales → 0939
秤 BALANCE → 1488

COMPOUND FORMATION

【尺八 しゃくはち】

尺八 'bamboo flute' is so called because it is 1 *shaku* (尺 ❶) and 8 (八) *sun* (寸) in length.

丹

▸CINNABAR
タン に▲ ㊔ あか あかし にい まこと あきら
Ⓒ 丹 dān

4249
■4-4-1

3	Jōyō	U4E39
丶	S4-1-3	F1209

1 丿 2 冂 3 円 4 丹

COMPOUNDS

❶ **CINNABAR red, vermilion, red**

丹朱 たんしゅ vermilion, red; cinnabar
丹青 たんせい red and blue; painting
丹花 たんか red flower
牡丹 ぼたん peony, *Paeonia suffruticosa*

❷ [original meaning] **CINNABAR**, minium, red lead

丹砂 たんしゃ cinnabar
鉛丹 えんたん red lead, minium

❸ **wholeheartedly, sincerely, devotedly**

丹精(=丹誠) たんせい efforts, pains
丹念な たんねんな painstaking, assiduous, diligent

❹ⓐ pill, medicine (esp. in Chinese medicine)
ⓑ suffix after names of pills

a 煉丹 れんたん elixir of life (prepared from cinnabar in ancient China)

❺ old name for Kyoto Prefecture

丹後 たんご old name for north Kyoto Prefecture

❻ used phonetically for *tan* in the transliteration of foreign words

切支丹 きりしたん early Christianity in Japan; Jesuitism

KUN

【に 丹】**CINNABAR red, vermilion**

丹塗りの にぬりの red-painted, vermilion-lacquered

SYNONYMS

❶ **red colors**

赤 RED → 2719
紅 CRIMSON → 1629
緋 SCARLET → 1732
朱 VERMILION → 4344
丹 CINNABAR → 4249
茜 MADDER → 2811

NOTE

★ do not confuse with 舟 SMALL BOAT → 4353

天

4250

■4-4-1

▶HEAVEN

テン あめ あま- ㊔ たかし

Ⓒ 天 tiān

37	Jōyō-1	U5929
大	S4-3-1	F0159

COMPOUNDS

❶ⓐ HEAVEN(s), sky, celestial sphere
ⓑ (state of the) weather, look of the sky

a 天地 てんち heaven and earth; top and bottom
天空 てんくう sky, air, firmament, heavens
天体 てんたい heavenly body
天文学 てんもんがく astronomy
天下 てんか the whole country [empire], the world
天衣無縫 てんいむほう perfect beauty with no trace of artifice
衝天 しょうてん high spirits
b 天気 てんき weather, atmospheric conditions; fine weather
天気予報 てんきよほう weather forecast
天候 てんこう weather
晴天 せいてん fine [fair] weather, cloudless sky
雨天 うてん rainy weather, rainy day

❷ (abode of God and blessed souls) **HEAVEN, paradise**
天国 てんごく Kingdom of Heaven, Paradise
天使 てんし angel
昇天 しょうてん the Ascension; death

❸ⓐ HEAVEN, the Creator, Ruler of the Universe, God
ⓑ HEAVEN's will, fate, destiny

a 天帝 てんてい Lord of Heaven, the Creator
天主 てんしゅ Lord of Heaven, God
b 天罰 てんばつ divine punishment
天命 てんめい providence, fate, Heaven's will
天運 てんうん fate, destiny, fortune

❹ⓐ HEAVEN's messenger on earth, the emperor
ⓑ imperial

a 天皇 てんのう emperor of Japan
天子 てんし son of Heaven, emperor
天顔 てんがん emperor's countenance
b 天覧 てんらん imperial inspection

❺ⓐ nature, laws of nature
ⓑ by nature, innate

a 天然 てんねん nature
天災 てんさい natural calamity [disaster]
b 天才 てんさい (person of) genius
天性 てんせい nature, one's innate disposition
先天的な せんてんてきな native, inborn

❻ *Buddhism* deva, divine being
梵×天 ぼんてん Brahma-Deva
帝釈天 たいしゃくてん *Śakra devānām Indra*

❼ [also 纏 1814] put on, be wrapped in
半天 はんてん short coat, workman's livery coat

❽ [original meaning] **top, head**
天辺 てっぺん top, summit
脳天 のうてん crown of the head

❾ abbrev. of 天麩×羅 てんぷら: tempura, Japanese deep-fat fried food
天つゆ てんつゆ sauce for tempura

INDEPENDENT

【てん 天】**HEAVENs, sky; Heaven, God; Heaven's will, providence; fate, destiny**
天から降りる てんからおりる fall from heaven [the sky]
天に坐します我等の父 てんにましますわれらのちち our Father who art in Heaven…
天なり命なり てんなりめいなり It is Heaven's will

KUN

【あめ 天, あま- 天-】*literary* **HEAVEN, sky**
天が下 あめがした the world
天の川 あまのがわ Milky Way

SYNONYMS

❶ⓐ sky
空 SKY → 2767
昊 SKY → 3066
穹 SKY → 2768
天 HEAVEN → 4250
宙 MIDAIR → 2761

ⓑ weather
候 SEASONAL WEATHER → 0133
天 weather → 4250
晴 FINE WEATHER → 1234

❷ posthumous worlds
天 HEAVEN → 4250
幽 world of the dead → 3731
獄 hell → 0872

❸ⓐ god
神 GOD → 1143
帝 the Supreme Being → 2573
天 HEAVEN → 4250
主 Lord → 2437
祇 EARTHLY GOD → 1459

❹ rulers
君 RULER → 3974
王 KING → 4247
帝 EMPEROR → 2573
天 Heaven's messenger on earth → 4250
皇 EMPEROR → 3175
尭 YAO → 2560
舜 SHUN → 3134

NOTE

➡ see COMPOUND FORMATION for
衝天 しょうてん → 衝 0893
天衣無縫 てんいむほう → 縫 1781

无 ▶*MUNYŌ*

4251
■4-4-1

71	Radical	U65E0
无	S4-4-0	F0000

RADICAL

munyō 'without', used in characters related to surfeit or choking

Right variants: 旡 旡 ***sudenotsukuri*** (旣 既)

旡 ▶*SUDENOTSUKURI*

4252
■4-4-1

71	Radical	U65E1
无	S4-4-0	F0000

radical variant → see 无 at 4251

歹 ▶*GATSUHEN*

4253
■4-4-1

78	Radical	U6B79
歹	S4-4-0	F0000

RADICAL

gatsuhen 'death' (死 残 殊), used in characters related to death or serious injury

毌 ▶*HAHA, NAKARE*

4254
■4-4-1

80	Radical	U6BCC
毋	S4-4-0	F0000

radical variant → see 毋 at 4255

毋 ▶*NAKARE*

4255
■4-4-1

80	Radical	U6BCB
毋	S4-4-0	F0000

RADICAL

nakare 'mother' (毎 毒), used in characters related to mothers or for classification

Variant: 毌 ***haha*** or ***nakare*** (毎 毒)

⺩ ▶*TAMAHEN*

4256
■4-4-1

96	Radical	U2EA9
王	S4-4-0	F0000

radical variant → see 玉 at 4289

反 ■4-4-1
incorrect classification
➡ see □3-2-2: 厂 at 3663

弖 ■4-4-1
incorrect stroke-count
➡ see ■4-3-1 at 4193

及 ■4-4-1
incorrect stroke-count
➡ see ■4-3-1 at 4192

日 ■4-4-1
incorrect classification
➡ see □3-3-1: 囗 at 3759

凹 ■4-4-1
incorrect stroke-count
➡ see ■4-5-1 at 4294

凸 ■4-4-1
incorrect stroke-count
➡ see ■4-5-1 at 4298

疋 ■4-4-1
incorrect stroke-count
➡ see ■4-5-1 at 4300

及 ■4-4-1
incorrect classification
➡ see □3-2-2: ㇇ at 3666

曰日 ■4-4-1
incorrect classification
➡ see □3-3-1: 囗 at 3757

月円 etc. ■4-4-1
incorrect classification
➡ see □3-2-2: 冂 at 3673

壬 ▶NINTH CALENDAR SIGN

ジン みずのえ ㊔ み みず よし てい つぐ おおい まさ あきら

Ⓒ 壬 rén

4257
■4-4-2

33	Names	U58EC
士	S4-3-1	F3047

COMPOUNDS

● NINTH CALENDAR SIGN

壬申 じんしん ninth of the sexagenary cycle

INDEPENDENT

【じん 壬】NINTH CALENDAR SIGN

KUN

【みずのえ 壬】NINTH CALENDAR SIGN

SPECIAL READINGS

壬生 みぶ name of a neighborhood in Kyoto

SYNONYMS

● **calendar signs**

戊 FIFTH CALENDAR SIGN → 4321
庚 SEVENTH CALENDAR SIGN → 3826
壬 NINTH CALENDAR SIGN → 4257

廿

4258
■4-4-2

▶**TWENTY**
ジュウ　ニュウ　にじゅう
Ⓒ 廿 niàn

24	Names	U5EFF
十	S4-2-2	F3114

COMPOUNDS

● [original meaning] **TWENTY**

KUN

【にじゅう　廿】[usu. 二十] **TWENTY**
廿五日 にじゅうごにち 25 days; 25th of the month

SPECIAL READINGS

廿日 はつか 20 days; 20th of the month

SYNONYMS

【にじゅう】
○ **small numbers**

一 ONE → 4148
十 TEN → 4172
廿 TWENTY → 4258
二 TWO → 2421
三 THREE → 2423
四 FOUR → 3778
五 FIVE → 4244
六 SIX → 2461
七 SEVEN → 4169
八 EIGHT → 3644
九 NINE → 4176

HOMOPHONES

にじゅう 二十 → 2421, 4172

NOTE

★ Though 廿 has the *on* readings ジュウ and ニュウ, they do not appear to have ever been in actual use. Historically, 念 ねん has frequently been used in place of 廿, such as when indicating dates. The latter, however, is never read ねん.

𡈼

4259
■4-4-2

▶**SOIL**
ド　ト　つち ㊔ ひじ　は　はに

32	Nonstandard	U2123D
土	S4-3-1	F0000

traditional form → see 土 at 4211

圡

4260
■4-4-2

▶**SOIL**
ド　ト　つち ㊔ ひじ　は　はに

32	Nonstandard	U5721
土	S4-3-1	F0000

traditional form → see 土 at 4211

甘
■4-4-2

incorrect stroke-count
➡ see ■4-5-2 at 4306

世
■4-4-2

incorrect stroke-count
➡ see ■4-5-2 at 4308

止
■4-4-2

incorrect classification
➡ see □3-2-2: 丄 at 3659

丗
■4-4-2

incorrect stroke-count
➡ see ■4-5-2 at 4312

圭
■4-4-2

incorrect classification/ stroke-count
➡ see ⬒2-2-3: 亠 at 2488

木

4261
■4-4-3

▶**TREE**
▶**WOOD**
ボク　モク　き　こ-
Ⓒ 木 mù

75	Jōyō-1	U6728
木	S4-4-0	F0162

一 十 才 木
1 2 3 4

RADICAL

ki 'tree' (本 査 某), used in characters related to trees, wood or wooden objects
Left variant: 木 *kihen* (梅 校 株)

COMPOUNDS

❶ [also suffix] [original meaning] **TREE**
木石 ぼくせき trees and stones, inanimate objects
樹木 じゅもく tree; trees and shrubs
草木 そうもく trees and plants, vegetation
大木 たいぼく gigantic tree
香木 こうぼく fragrant wood; aromatic tree

❷ⓐ **WOOD, timber**
ⓑ **WOODen**
ⓒ the first of the five elements: **WOOD** (→ see APPENDIX 8)

a 木材 もくざい wood, timber, lumber
木目 もくめ wood grain
木工 もっこう woodworking, woodworker
原木 げんぼく material wood; pulpwood

土木 どぼく engineering works

b 木刀 ぼくとう wooden sword

木製の もくせいの wooden, made of wood

木造の もくぞうの wooden

❸ **Thursday**

木曜(日) もくよう(び) Thursday

火木 かもく Tuesdays and Thursdays

❹ Jupiter

木星 もくせい Jupiter

INDEPENDENT

【ぼく 木】 (old gnarled) **TREE**, trunk

見事な木 みごとなぼく magnificent tree

【もく 木】 Thursday; grain of wood; the first of the five elements: **WOOD**

KUN

【き 木】

① [sometimes also 樹] **TREE**

木登り きのぼり tree climbing

植木 うえき garden plant, shrub, pot plant

苗木 なえぎ sapling, young tree

並木 なみき row of trees, roadside trees

正木 まさき [also 柾] spindle tree

② **WOOD, timber, lumber**

木切れ きぎれ piece of wood, splinter

木彫り きぼり woodcarving

白木 しらき plain wood

頸木 くびき [also 軛] yoke

③ **WOOD**en clappers

【こ- 木-】 **TREE**

木陰 こかげ shade of a tree, bower

木立ち こだち clump of trees, thicket

木の葉 このは foliage of trees

SPECIAL READINGS

木綿 もめん cotton, cotton cloth

桧木▲ ひのき [also 桧] Japanese cypress, *hinoki*

SYNONYMS

❶ **tree**

木 TREE → 4261

樹 STANDING TREE → 1363

❷ⓐ & ❷ⓑ **kinds of wood**

木 WOOD → 4261

材 TIMBER → 1031

薪 FIREWOOD → 3009

柴 BRUSHWOOD → 3287

❸ **days of the week**

日 Sunday → 3759

月 Monday → 3674

火 Tuesday → 4273

水 Wednesday → 0010

木 Thursday → 4261

金 Friday → 2552

土 Saturday → 4211

USAGE

【き】

木

① [sometimes also 樹] tree

② wood, timber, lumber

③ wooden clappers

樹

[usu. 木] standing tree, tree

HOMOPHONES

き 樹 STANDING TREE → 1363

まさき

柾 STRAIGHT GRAIN → 1114

正木 → 4296, 4261

くびき

軛 YOKE → 1873

頸木 → 2035, 4261

ひのき

桧 JAPANESE CYPRESS → 1160

桧木 → 1160, 4261

NOTE

➡ see COMPOUND FORMATION for 金木犀 きんもくせい → 犀 3900

中

4262

■4-4-3

▸**MIDDLE**

▸**IN**

チュウ ジュウ なか うち▲ あた(る)▲

㊔ なかば

Ⓒ 中 zhōng zhòng

2	Jōyō-1	U4E2D
丨	S4-1-3	F0008

丨 冂 口 中
1 2 3 4

COMPOUNDS

❶ lying between two extremes of space:

ⓐ [original meaning] **MIDDLE, center, midway**

ⓑ **MIDDLE, Middle, mid-, central, intermediate**

a 中間 ちゅうかん middle, midway

中心 ちゅうしん center, middle

中核 ちゅうかく core, nucleus; kernel

集中する しゅうちゅうする concentrate, focus; converge

b 中点 ちゅうてん middle point

中部 ちゅうぶ central [middle] part

中衛 ちゅうえい middle guard

中耳 ちゅうじ middle ear, *auris media*

中欧 ちゅうおう Central Europe

中東 ちゅうとう Middle East

4

木【中】牛毛井升手屯牜才午市爪水斗

中労委(=中央労働委員会) ちゅうろうい(=ちゅうおうろうどういいんかい) Central Labor Relations Committee
中継する ちゅうけいする relay, rebroadcast

❷ⓐ (of time) **MIDDLE, medieval, Middle**
ⓑ **in the MIDDLE, halfway**

a 中年 ちゅうねん middle age
中古の ちゅうこの medieval
中世 ちゅうせい Middle [Medieval] Ages
中石器時代 ちゅうせっきじだい Mesolithic period
中期 ちゅうき middle period; metaphase

b 中止する ちゅうしする suspend, stop, discontinue
中断 ちゅうだん interruption, discontinuance, suspension
中退する ちゅうたいする drop out of [quit] school
途中で とちゅうで on the way

❸ⓐ [also prefix] (of intermediate size, quality or extent) **MIDDLE, medium, intermediate, average**
ⓑ (being at neither extreme) **MIDDLE (course), moderate, neutral, medial**

a 中型 ちゅうがた medium size
中肉中背の ちゅうにくちゅうぜいの of medium build
中ヒール ちゅうひーる medium-high heel
中小企業 ちゅうしょうきぎょう small-to-medium-sized enterprises
中細の ちゅうぼその medium-fine
中古の ちゅうこ(=ちゅうぶる)の secondhand, used
中波 ちゅうは medium waves
中辞典 ちゅうじてん medium-sized dictionary
中産階級 ちゅうさんかいきゅう middle class, bourgeoisie
中学 ちゅうがく junior high school
中学校 ちゅうがっこう junior high school
中学生 ちゅうがくせい junior high school student
中級の ちゅうきゅうの middle-class [grade], intermediate

b 中庸 ちゅうよう the (golden) mean, the middle path
中立 ちゅうりつ neutrality; neutralization
中和する ちゅうわする neutralize; counteract
中道 ちゅうどう middle road, golden mean

❹ second in a series of three: **MIDDLE, second**
中編 ちゅうへん second part [volume]; medium-length story
中旬 ちゅうじゅん middle [second] ten days of a month
中元 ちゅうげん midyear gift; July 15th (lunar calendar)

❺ [also suffix] within the confines of a given range:
ⓐ **IN, within, inside, interior**
ⓑ (indicates one of many) **IN, one of, among**

a 空中で くうちゅうで in the air [sky]
水中眼鏡 すいちゅうめがね swimming goggles
市中銀行 しちゅうぎんこう city bank
暗中模索 あんちゅうもさく groping in the dark
意中の人 いちゅうのひと person one is thinking of; man of one's heart
一酸化炭素中で いっさんかたんそちゅうで in an atmosphere of carbon monoxide

b 十中八九 じっちゅうはっく nine cases out of ten
連中 れんちゅう(=れんじゅう) party, company, clique; those fellows [guys]
女中 じょちゅう maidservant, maid
乗客中の一人 じょうきゃくちゅうのひとり one of the passengers

❻ [also suffix] within the confines of a given period:
ⓐ **IN, in the course of, during, while**
ⓑ **IN the process of, in progress, under**

a 午前中 ごぜんちゅう in the morning
今週中に こんしゅうちゅうに in the course of the week, before the week is over
授業中 じゅぎょうちゅう while in class

b 建築中 けんちくちゅう under construction
修繕中 しゅうぜんちゅう during repairs, in the process of being repaired

❼ [also suffix]
ⓐ (in every part) **throughout, all over, everywhere**
ⓑ (during the entire time) **throughout (the night), all through**

a 国中で くにじゅうで all over the country
東京中 とうきょうじゅう all over Tokyo

b 一年中 いちねんじゅう throughout the year, always
一日中 いちにちじゅう all day long

❽ⓐ **People's Republic of China, China**
ⓑ **Modern Chinese, Mandarin**

a 中華 ちゅうか Middle Kingdom, China; Chinese food
中共 ちゅうきょう Communist China
訪中 ほうちゅう visit to China
日中友好協会 にっちゅうゆうこうきょうかい Japan-China Amity Association

b 中日辞典 ちゅうにちじてん Chinese-Japanese dictionary

❾ⓐ abbrev. of 中学校 ちゅうがっこう: junior high school, **MIDDLE** school
ⓑ suffix after names of junior high schools

a 中二 ちゅうに second year of junior high
中卒 ちゅうそつ junior high graduate

b 武蔵中 むさしちゅう Musashi Junior High School

❿ **hit the target [mark]**
的中する てきちゅうする hit the mark, hit (on) it
命中する めいちゅうする hit the mark [target]

⓫ **be absorbed IN, be immersed**
熱中 ねっちゅう absorption, enthusiasm
夢中で むちゅうで like one in a dream; like one dazed; frantically

⓬ **be subjected to the harmful effects of (poison); suffer from**

中毒する ちゅうどくする get poisoned; be addicted
中風 ちゅうぶ(=ちゅうぶう, ちゅうふう) palsy, paralysis
中傷する ちゅうしょうする slander, libel
⓭ abbrev. of 中堅手 ちゅうけんしゅ: center fielder
中飛 ちゅうひ center fly
左中間 さちゅうかん between left and center fielders

INDEPENDENT

【ちゅう 中】**MIDDLE, medium; medium size, medium quality; mediocrity, average; second (volume of three); China**
中の ちゅうの medium, mediocre
中以上 ちゅういじょう above average
ビールの中 びーるのちゅう medium-sized beer

KUN

【なか 中】
① **INside, interior**
中へ入る なかへはいる step into, go [come] inside, enter
中味 なかみ interior, content, substance
中庭 なかにわ courtyard
②ⓐ **MIDDLE, the second**
ⓑ **MIDDLE course, mean**
a 中の兄 なかのあに middle brother
中指 なかゆび middle finger
中継ぎ(=中次ぎ) なかつぎ intermediation; agent; relay
真ん中 まんなか center, middle
背中 せなか back
b 中を取る なかをとる take the middle course [mean]
③ⓐ **within the confines of a given range**
ⓑ amidst an undesirable event
a 中に なかに in; in the middle of; between, among
中には なかには some (of them), among (them)
町中で まちなかで in the streets
夜中 よなか midnight, dead of night
世の中 よのなか the world, society, life
多くの中から選ぶ おおくのなかからえらぶ choose among many things
b 雨の中で あめのなかで in the rain

【うち 中】[usu. 内]
① **IN**side, interior
心の中で こころのうちで in one's mind
② within (a given period), **IN** the course of, while, during
一週間の中に いっしゅうかんのうちに within a week
③ among, between
両者の中 りょうしゃのうち between the two

【あたる 中る】[now usu. 当たる] **be poisoned, disagree with; suffer from**
河豚に中る ふぐにあたる get poisoned by swellfish

SYNONYMS

❶ⓐ middle
中 MIDDLE→4262
央 CENTER→4322
心 HEART→0011
核 NUCLEUS→1162
ⓑ & ❷ & ❸ between
中 MIDDLE→4262
仲 intermediate→0047
間 BETWEEN→4122
際 inter-→0874
❹ second
乙 SECOND→4145
次 second→0058
後 AFTER (latter)→0431
中 MIDDLE→4262
❺ⓐ inside
内 INSIDE→4277
裏 inside→2652
奥 INNER PART→3503
中 IN→4262
❻ during
間 for an interval of→4122
中 IN (the course of)→4262
内 within (a given period)→4277
❼ⓑ throughout
通 through→3855
徹 all through→0894
終 from beginning to end→1692
中 throughout→4262
❽ⓐ China
華 CHINA→2841
漢 CHINESE→0808
支 China→2473
中 People's Republic of China→4262
胡 NATIVES OF ANCIENT CHINA→1467
台 Taiwan→2498
唐 Cathay→3867
呉 KINGDOM OF WU→3156
ⓑ Chinese
漢 CHINESE (language)→0808
中 Modern Chinese→4262
❾ schools
校 SCHOOL→1166
学 EDUCATIONAL INSTITUTION→3162
院 INSTITUTION→0544
塾 PRIVATE SCHOOL→3546
大 UNIVERSITY→4224
高 high school→2601
中 junior high school→4262

小 elementary school →0007
園 kindergarten →3914

USAGE

【なか】
中
① inside, interior
②ⓐ middle, the second
ⓑ middle course, mean
③ⓐ within the confines of a given range
ⓑ amidst an undesirable event
仲
① personal relations, relationship, (familiar) terms, fellowship, friendship
② intermediary, go-between
③ [in compounds] inner, middle

HOMOPHONES

なか 仲 INTERMEDIARY →0047
うち
内 INSIDE →4277
家 HOUSE →2827
あたる 当 THE PRESENT →2701

COMPOUND FORMATION

【女中 じょちゅう】
女中 'maidservant, maid' originally meant one woman (女) among many (中 ❺ⓑ).

NOTE

➡ see also USAGE notes at 当 2701 and 内 4277

牛

4263
■4-4-3

▶CATTLE
ギュウ うし ぎっ-▲
Ⓒ 牛 niú

93	Jōyō-2	U725B
牛	S4-4-0	F1127

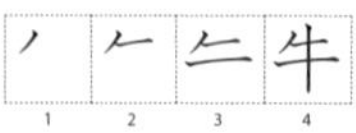

RADICAL

ushi 'cattle' (牢× 牽 犂×), used in characters related to cattle or related animals
Left variant: 牛 ***ushihen*** (物 特 牧)

COMPOUNDS

ⓐ [original meaning] (any bovine animal) **CATTLE, cow, bull, ox**
ⓑ beef
a 牛乳 ぎゅうにゅう (cow's) milk
牛肉 ぎゅうにく beef
牛皮(=牛革) ぎゅうかわ cowhide, oxhide
牛飲馬食する ぎゅういんばしょくする gorge and swill, drink like a cow and eat like a horse
牛歩戦術 ぎゅうほせんじゅつ cow's-pace tactics
乳牛 にゅうぎゅう(=ちちうし) milch cow, dairy cattle
闘牛 とうぎゅう bullfight, fighting bull
b 牛脂 ぎゅうし beef tallow

INDEPENDENT

【ぎゅう 牛】 beef; cowhide
牛百グラム ぎゅうひゃくぐらむ 100 g of beef
牛の鞄 ぎゅうのかばん cowhide bag

KUN

【うし 牛】 [also suffix] **CATTLE, cow, bull, ox**
小牛 こうし calf
去勢牛 きょせいうし bullock
【ぎっ- 牛-】 ox, cow
牛車 ぎっしゃ cow carriage (for noblemen in Heian period)

SYNONYMS

ⓐ domesticated mammals
牛 CATTLE →4263
馬 HORSE →4086
豚 PIG →1228
羊 SHEEP →2708
犬 DOG →4275
猫 CAT →0651
兎 RABBIT →4374
ⓐ cattle
牛 CATTLE →4263
丑 THE OX →4241

USAGE

【うし】
牛
[also suffix] cattle, cow, bull, ox
丑
second sign of the Oriental zodiac: the Ox

HOMOPHONES

うし 丑 THE OX →4241

毛

4264
■4-4-3

▶HAIR
モウ け
Ⓒ 毛 máo

82	Jōyō-2	U6BDB
毛	S4-4-0	F0775

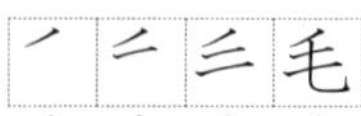

RADICAL

ke 'hair' (毫× 氈×), used in characters related to hair or fur
Enclosure: 毛× ***ke*** (毬×)

COMPOUNDS

❶ⓐ [original meaning] **HAIR (of humans or animals), fur, feather**
ⓑ HAIR (of plants)
a 毛髪 もうはつ hair
毛筆 もうひつ (writing or painting) brush

羊毛 ようもう wool
羽毛 うもう feathers, plumage, down
b 毛茸 もうじょう trichome

❷ **wool**
毛製品 もうせいひん woolen goods
毛布 もうふ blanket
純毛 じゅんもう pure wool, all wool
原毛 げんもう raw wool

❸ as thin as **HAIR**, slight
毛頭 もうとう (not) in the least, (not) a bit
毛管 もうかん capillary (tube)

❹ **vegetation**
不毛の ふもうの barren; infertile
二毛作 にもうさく two crops a year, semiannual crop

❺ⓐ 1/1000
ⓑ 1/1000 of 10%: 0.0001
a 三分五厘二毛 さんぶごりんにもう 0.0352

❻ *mo*:
ⓐ former unit of length equiv. to approx. 0.03 mm or 1/1000 of a *sun* (寸)
ⓑ former unit of weight equiv. to 3.75 mg or 1/1000 of a momme (匁)
ⓒ former monetary unit equiv. to 1/10,000 of a yen (円)
ab 三毛 さんもう 3 *mo*

INDEPENDENT

【もう 毛】 *mo* (→❻); 0.0001 (→❺ⓑ)

KUN

【け 毛】 **HAIR, fur; trichome; wool**
毛深い けぶかい hairy, thickly haired
毛糸 けいと woolen yarn, wool
毛織 けおり woolen fabric, woolen cloth
毛唐 けとう *slang* foreigner, Westerner
髪の毛 かみのけ hair
鼻毛 はなげ hairs of the nostril
赤毛 あかげ red hair, carroty hair

SYNONYMS

❶ **hair**
毛 HAIR (of any kind) → 4264
髪 HAIR (on the head) → 3528
辮 PLAIT → 2085
羽 FEATHER → 0265
眉 EYEBROW → 3991
鬚 BEARD → 3539

❷ **fabrics**
織 woven fabric → 1801
紬 PONGEE → 1684
紗 GAUZE → 1653
絹 SILK → 1721
綾 TWILL → 1740
綿 COTTON → 1736
棉 COTTON → 1244
麻 HEMP → 3878
毛 wool → 4264
錦 BROCADE → 2181

NOTE

➡ see COMPOUND FORMATION for 毛唐 けとう → 唐 3867

井

4265
■4-4-3

▶**WELL**
セイ ショウ い
Ⓒ 井 jǐng

7	Jōyō	U4E95
二	S4-2-2	F0272

一 二 井 井
1 2 3 4

COMPOUNDS

❶ [original meaning] **WELL**
油井 ゆせい oil well
鑿井 さくせい well drilling
ガス井 がすせい gas well

❷ **something resembling a WELL crib**
井目 せいもく the nine principal points in a game of go
天井 てんじょう ceiling

❸ town, community
市井 しせい the streets

KUN

【い 井】 **WELL**
井戸 いど (water) well
井の中の蛙大海を知らず いのなかのかわずたいかいをしらず A frog in the well knows nothing of the great ocean/have limited views [opinions]
井桁 いげた well crib; parallel crosses

SYNONYMS

❶ **water sources**
源 SOURCE → 0806
泉 SPRING → 3176
井 WELL → 4265

升

4266
■4-4-3

▶***SHO***
ショウ ます
Ⓒ 升 shēng

24	Jōyō	U5347
十	S4-2-2	F2564

丿 丿 升 升
1 2 3 4

COMPOUNDS

● ***SHO*: unit of capacity equiv. to approx. 1.8 liters or 10 *go* (合), used esp. for sake or rice**

一升瓶 いっしょうびん 1-*sho* bottle

INDEPENDENT

【しょう 升】*SHO* (→●)

KUN

【ます 升】[formerly also 枡]

①ⓐ **measure, measuring box**

ⓑ **box (seat)**

a 升目 ますめ measure; square (of graph paper)

五升升 ごしょうます 5-*sho* measure

② square (as of graph paper)

升形 ますがた square (shape)

SYNONYMS

● **capacity units**

勺 *SHAKU* (0.018 liters) →3650

合 *go* (0.18 liters) →2511

立 liter →2486

升 *SHO* (1.8 liters) →4266

斗 *TO* (18 liters) →3671

石 *koku* (180 liters) →3689

USAGE

【ます】

升

[formerly also 枡]

①ⓐ measure, measuring box

ⓑ box (seat)

② square (as of graph paper)

枡

[now usu. 升] same as 升

HOMOPHONES

ます 枡 MEASURE →1070

手

▶**HAND**
▶**OCCUPATION SUFFIX**

シュ ズ* て て- -て た-

4267

Ⓒ 手 shǒu

■4-4-3

64	Jōyō-1	U624B
手	S4-4-0	F0016

一 二 三 手
1 2 3 4

RADICAL

te 'hand' (挙 承 摩), used in characters related to hands or actions using hands

Left variant: 扌 *tehen* (打 投 招)

COMPOUNDS

❶ⓐ [original meaning] **HAND, palm, arm**

ⓑ [rare] hold in the HANDs

a 手中に しゅちゅうに in the hands

握手 あくしゅ handshake, handshaking

拍手 はくしゅ applause, clapping

義手 ぎしゅ artificial arm [hand]

入手する にゅうしゅする obtain, get, come by, procure

b 手燭 しゅしょく(=てしょく) portable candlestick

❷ **perform an action with one's HANDs**

手術 しゅじゅつ surgical operation

手芸 しゅげい handicrafts, manual arts

手記 しゅき note, memorandum; memoirs

手話 しゅわ talking with the hands; sign language

❸ⓐ [also suffix] holder of an **OCCUPATION** or performer of an action: **-er (as in *singer*)**

ⓑ skilled person

a 歌手 かしゅ singer

騎手 きしゅ rider, horseman, jockey

選手 せんしゅ representative athlete [player]

投手 とうしゅ pitcher

助手 じょしゅ assistant, helper

運転手 うんてんしゅ driver

b 名手 めいしゅ master, expert

❹ⓐ **means, method**

ⓑ move (as in shogi)

a 手段 しゅだん means, way, step

手法 しゅほう technique, mechanism, style

b 好手 こうしゅ good move

❺ **skill, proficiency**

手腕 しゅわん ability, skill

手練 しゅれん skill, dexterity

上手な じょうずな skilled, dexterous, good at

KUN

【て 手】

① **HAND, palm, arm**

手の平(=掌) てのひら palm of the hand

手足 てあし hands and feet, limbs

手首 てくび wrist

手に入れる てにいれる obtain

手形 てがた promissory note; hand print

手元(=手許) てもと at hand, within reach; cash at hand

手応え てごたえ response, reaction; resistance; effect

手品 てじな sleight of hand, magic

手摺り てすり handrail, railing

手拭い てぬぐい Japanese (hand) towel

手こずる てこずる not know what to do with (a person)

手引き てびき guidance; introduction; guide book, handbook

手振り てぶり gesture (of one's hand), movement

② **HANDle, knob**

取っ手(=把っ手) とって handle, knob

③ⓐ **HAND, help**

ⓑ subordinate

a 手分けする てわけする divide (work among several people), split
手が足りない てがたりない be short of hands
人手 ひとで hand, manpower; another's hand
b 手の者 てのもの one's subordinate
④ **labor, trouble, care, charge**
手の込んだ てのこんだ elaborate, intricate
手間 てま labor, trouble; time (required for a task)
手数 てすう(=てかず) trouble, bother, pains
手当 てあて allowance, compensation, benefits
手当て てあて provision; medical care, treatment
手遅れ ておくれ being too late
手落ち ておち omission, slip; error
⑤ **HAND**writing
女の手 おんなのて feminine handwriting
⑥ **achievement, skill**
手柄 てがら meritorious deed, merit; achievement
手が上がる てがあがる improve one's skill
手際 てぎわ skill, dexterity; workmanship
手際良く てぎわよく skillfully, cleverly
⑦ⓐ **means, device, trick**
ⓑ move (as in shogi); **HAND** (of a game)
a 手を変える てをかえる resort to other means
手続き てつづき procedure, formalities
奥の手 おくのて last resort; secrets
b 決め手 きめて decisive factor, clincher; trump card, winning move
先手 せんて moving first; forestalling
⑧ kind, type, line
薄手の うすでの of thin make, light
大手 おおて major companies
⑨ injury, damage
痛手 いたで severe wound; home thrust, heavy blow
⑩ direction, side, part
山の手 やまのて hilly section
⑪ connection
手切れ てぎれ severance of connections; solatium for severing connections

【て- 手-】
① [also prefix] **performed with one's HANDs, manually handled**
手製の てせいの handmade
手編み てあみ hand-knitting
手荷物 てにもつ hand baggage, personal effects
手仕事 てしごと handwork, manual labor
② emphatic before certain adjectives
手広く てびろく extensively, widely, on an extensive scale
手厳しい てきびしい severe, unsparing, harsh

【-て -手】
① **performer of an action, holder of an occupation**
相手 あいて partner; opponent
買い手 かいて buyer, customer
語り手 かたりて narrator, storyteller
② counter for moves in shogi or go
次の一手 つぎのいって next move

【た- 手-】 **performed with one's HANDs, manually handled**
手綱 たづな bridle, reins
手繰る たぐる pull in hand over hand, draw in, reel in; retrace

SPECIAL READINGS
下手な へたな unskillful, unskilled, poor, clumsy
上手い▲(=巧い、旨い) うまい skillful, clever; splendid, excellent

SYNONYMS
❶ⓐ hand and arm
手 HAND → 4267
腕 ARM → 1269
肘 ELBOW → 1044
掌 PALM → 3215
指 FINGER → 0452
拇 THUMB → 0358
拳 FIST → 3295
❸ workers and professionals
家 professional → 2827
婦 woman worker → 0565
嬢 (unmarried) female worker → 0936
夫 MAN LABORER → 4271
匠 CRAFTSMAN → 3711
工 workman → 4190
客 skilled person → 2798
士 PROFESSION SUFFIX → 4213
師 profession suffix → 1680
者 person who → 3980
人 person of certain category → 4175
員 MEMBER (of a staff) → 2822
屋 colloquial occupation suffix → 3842
手 OCCUPATION SUFFIX → 4267
❹ⓐ means
策 MEASURE → 3320
段 STEP → 1471
手 means → 4267

【て】
② **handles**
柄 HANDLE → 1111
手 handle → 4267
把 GRIP → 0293

HOMOPHONES
てのひら
掌 PALM → 3215

木 中 牛 毛 井 升 手 【屯 牛 才 午 市 爪 水 斗】

手の平 →4267, 4291

うまい

旨い →2516

巧い →0219

甘い →4306

上手い →4212, 4267

NOTE

➡ see USAGE notes at 旨 2516 and 掌 3215

➡ see COMPOUND FORMATION for 手数 てすう(=てかず) →数 2245

屯

4268

■4-4-3

▶**STATION TROOPS**

トン

Ⓒ 屯 tún zhūn

45	Jōyō	U5C6F
屮	S4-3-1	F2446

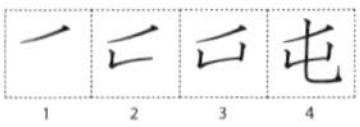

COMPOUNDS

❶ⓐ **STATION TROOPS, encamp, post**

ⓑ military station, post

a 駐屯する ちゅうとんする be stationed, occupy

b 屯田 とんでん stationing an army in the countryside to engage in farming (during the Meiji period)

屯営 とんえい military camp station, barracks, camping

屯所 とんしょ post, quarters, military station; police station

❷ [also 噸 0930]

ⓐ ton, tonnage

ⓑ shipping ton

a 五屯 ごとん 5 tons

英屯 えいとん British [long] ton

SYNONYMS

❶ⓐ **stay**

滞 STAY →0815

頓 STAY IN PLACE →1320

留 STAY →3189

逗 STAY →4005

駐 STATIONED →2297

屯 STATION TROOPS →4268

在 reside temporarily →3704

泊 STAY OVERNIGHT →0389

宿 LODGE →2858

寓 stay temporarily →2893

❷ **weight units**

匁 MOMME (3.75 g) →4276

斤 CATTY (600 g) →3667

貫 *kan* (3.75 kg) →3112

噸 TON →0930

屯 ton →4268

牜

4269

■4-4-3

▶***USHIHEN***

93	Radical	U725C
牛	S4-4-0	F0000

radical variant →see 牛 at 4263

才

4270

■4-4-3

▶**ORDINAL NUMBER PREFIX**

ダイ テイ

3	Nonstandard	U3427
丶	S4-1-3	F0000

alternative form →see 第 at 3298

午

■4-4-3

incorrect classification

➡ see ▀2-2-2: 𠂉 at 2478

市

■4-4-3

incorrect classification/ stroke-count

➡ see ▀2-2-3: 亠 at 2487

爪

■4-4-3

incorrect classification

➡ see □3-3-1: 八 at 3756

水

■4-4-3

incorrect classification

➡ see ◧1-1-3: フ at 0010

斗

■4-4-3

incorrect classification

➡ see □3-2-2: 十 at 3671

夫

4271

■4-4-4

▶**HUSBAND**

▶**MAN LABORER**

フ フウ ブ▲ おっと そ(れ)▲ ㊔ お

Ⓒ 夫 fū fú

37	Jōyō-4	U592B
大	S4-3-1	F0220

COMPOUNDS

❶ **HUSBAND**

夫婦 ふうふ husband and wife, married couple

夫妻 ふさい husband and wife, Mr. and Mrs., married couple

夫人 ふじん wife, married lady, Mrs.

前夫 ぜんぷ former husband, ex-husband

❷ [also suffix] **MAN LABORER, male worker**

農夫 のうふ peasant, plowman

人夫 にんぷ coolie, porter, laborer

煙突掃除夫 えんとつそうじふ chimney sweeper [cleaner]

❸ **male adult, man**

凡夫 ぼんぷ(=ぼんぶ) ordinary man; *Buddhism* common mortal

大丈夫 だいじょうぶ safe, sure, all right

❹ **unclassified compounds**

工夫 くふう device, contrivance; scheme, resources

義太夫 ぎだゆう *gidayu* (a form of ballad drama)

KUN

【おっと 夫】HUSBAND

夫の権利 おっとのけんり marital rights

愛する夫 あいするおっと lord of one's bosom

【それ 夫れ】

① [archaic] emphatic adverb at the beginning of a sentence

夫れ、秦王虎狼之心有り それ, しんのうころうのこころあり The King of Chin had the heart of tigers and wolves

② [usu. 其れ] *pronoun* that, it

夫れ夫れ それぞれ respectively, each

SPECIAL READINGS

膳夫▲ かしわで [also 膳] [archaic] cooks for the imperial court in ancient Japan; serving of meals on trays

SYNONYMS

❶ **husband**

夫 HUSBAND → 4271

主 master of the house → 2437

❷ **workers and professionals**

家 professional → 2827

婦 woman worker → 0565

嬢 (unmarried) female worker → 0936

夫 MAN LABORER → 4271

匠 CRAFTSMAN → 3711

工 workman → 4190

客 skilled person → 2798

士 PROFESSION SUFFIX → 4213

師 profession suffix → 1680

者 person who → 3980

人 person of certain category → 4175

員 MEMBER (of a staff) → 2822

屋 colloquial occupation suffix → 3842

手 OCCUPATION SUFFIX → 4267

❸ **man**

男 MAN → 3147

郎 YOUNG MAN → 1641

雄 MALE → 1271

牡 MALE → 1040

夫 male adult → 4271

翁 OLD MAN → 2611

爺 OLD MAN → 2656

USAGE

【それ】

夫れ

① [archaic] emphatic adverb at the beginning of a sentence

② [usu. 其れ] *pronoun* that, it

其れ

① [sometimes also 夫れ] *pronoun* that, it

② (interjection used to call attention) look, there

HOMOPHONES

それ 其 THAT → 3255

かしわで

膳 LEGGED TRAY → 1381

膳夫 → 1381, 4271

COMPOUND FORMATION

❶【夫人 ふじん】

夫人 'wife, etc.' was originally written 扶人, meaning a person (人) who helps or assists (扶). 扶 was later replaced by 夫 ❶.

❷【大丈夫 だいじょうぶ】

大丈夫 'safe, sure, all right' is a man (夫 ❸) of great (大) height (丈). Since such a man symbolizes security and stability, 大丈夫 acquired its current meaning.

片

4272

■4-4-4

▶**FRAGMENT**
▶**ONE OF TWO**

ヘン かた- かた

Ⓝ 片◇ Ⓒ 片 piàn piān

91	Jōyō-6	U7247
片	S4-4-0	F0674

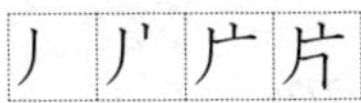

1 2 3 4

RADICAL

kata 'board' (版 牒 牌×), used in characters related to boards or things made of boards

COMPOUNDS

❶ⓐ [also suffix] **FRAGMENT, (flat thin) piece, slice, chip, flake**

ⓑ counter for **FRAGMENT**s or flakes

a 片雲 へんうん scattered clouds

断片 だんぺん fragment, piece

破片 はへん fragment, broken piece, scrap

木片 もくへん block, chip [piece] of wood

一片 いっぺん piece, bit, fragment, scrap

雪片 せっぺん snowflake

紙片 しへん piece [scrap, bit] of paper

金属片 きんぞくへん piece of metal

b 五片 ごへん five fragments [pieces]

❷ a bit, a slight amount

片言 へんげん a word, few words

KUN

【かた- 片-】 [also prefix]
ⓐ **ONE OF TWO, one, single**
ⓑ **one side, one part, one way**

a 片一方 かたいっぽう one side, the other one
片面 かためん one side, one face
片手 かたて one hand
片道 かたみち one way
片側 かたがわ one side
b 片言 かたこと imperfect speech, baby talk
片寄る かたよる concentrate on one side [place], go aside
片貿易 かたぼうえき one way [unbalanced] trade
片思い かたおもい unrequited [unreciprocated] love
片仮名 かたかな katakana

【かた 片】 **settlement, conclusion**
片付く かたづく be put in order; be settled; be cleared; get married
片付ける かたづける put in order, tidy up, clear away; dispose of, deal with, bring to a conclusion; do away with, kill; give one's daughter in marriage

SYNONYMS

❶ⓐ **part**
分 PART →2466
部 SECTION →2111
局 LIMITED PART →3800
片 FRAGMENT →4272

【かた-】
ⓐ **one**
一 ONE →4148
壱 ONE (in legal documents) →2723
片- ONE OF TWO →4272
隻 ONE OF A PAIR →3426
単 SINGLE →2805
個 INDIVIDUAL →0132

ⓑ **one side**
片- one side →4272
偏 ONE-SIDED →0151
頗 one-sided →1552

HOMOPHONES

かたよる
偏る →0151
片寄る →4272, 2856

NOTE

➡ see USAGE note at 偏 0151

火

4273

4-4-4

▶**FIRE**

カ ひ -び ほ-

Ⓒ 火 huǒ

86	Jōyō-1	U706B
火	S4-4-0	F0465

(stroke order) 1 2 3 4

RADICAL

hi 'fire' (災 灰 炎), used in characters related to firelight, heat or fire qualities
Left variant: 火 × *hihen* (灯 炊 燃)
Bottom variant: 灬 *rekka* (点 為 無)

COMPOUNDS

❶ⓐ [original meaning] **FIRE**
ⓑ the second of the five elements: **FIRE** (→see APPENDIX 8)
ⓒ (figuratively) **FIRE**, burning passion

a 火災 かさい fire, conflagration
火事 かじ fire
火炎 かえん flames, blaze
火力 かりょく caloric force; firepower
点火 てんか ignition, lighting
出火 しゅっか outbreak of fire
大火 たいか great fire, conflagration
消火 しょうか fire fighting
c 情火 じょうか fire of passion, passion of love

❷ light
灯火 とうか light, lamplight

❸ⓐ **FIRE**arms
ⓑ (discharge of firearms) **FIRE**, firing

a 火器 かき firearms
地雷火 じらいか (land) mine
b 十字砲火 じゅうじほうか cross fire

❹ **Tuesday**
火曜(日) かよう(び) Tuesday

❺ **Mars**
火星 かせい Mars

❻ urgent, pressing
火急の かきゅうの urgent, pressing

INDEPENDENT

【か 火】 Tuesday; the second of the five elements: **FIRE**

KUN

【ひ 火, -び -火】
①ⓐ [also prefix and suffix] **FIRE, flame**
ⓑ **FIRE**light

a 火元 ひもと origin [source] of a fire
火花 ひばな spark
火加減 ひかげん condition of the fire
灯火 ともしび [also 灯, sometimes also 燭] light, lamp, flame

花火 はなび fireworks, firecrackers
口火 くちび fuse; pilot burner; cause (of a war)
不審火 ふしんび suspected case of arson

②**heat**
火を通す ひをとおす heat, cook

【ほ- 火-】[also 灯-] **FIRE**
火影(=灯影) ほかげ shadows from firelight
火照る ほてる feel hot, flush

SPECIAL READINGS

火傷▲ やけど burn

SYNONYMS

❶ⓐ fire
火 FIRE → 4273
炎 FLAME → 3075
焰 FLAME → 1255

❸ⓐ weapons for shooting
銃 GUN (portable firearm) → 2157
砲 HEAVY GUN → 1479
火 firearms → 4273
弓 BOW → 4193

❹ days of the week
日 Sunday → 3759
月 Monday → 3674
火 Tuesday → 4273
水 Wednesday → 0010
木 Thursday → 4261
金 Friday → 2552
土 Saturday → 4211

USAGE

❶【ひ】
火
①ⓐ [also prefix and suffix] **fire, flame**
ⓑ **firelight**
② **heat**
灯
(source of illumination) **light, lantern, lamp**

❷【ほ-】
火-
[also 灯-] fire
灯-
[also 火-] fire

HOMOPHONES

ともしび
灯 LAMP → 1019
灯火 → 1019, 4273
燭 CANDLE → 1391
ひ 灯 LAMP → 1019
ほ- 灯 LAMP → 1019

戈

4274
■4-4-4

▸DAGGER-AX
カ ほこ
Ⓒ 戈 gē

62	Non-Jōyō	U6208
戈	S4-4-0	F3396

RADICAL

kanohoko 'spear' (戦 成 戒), used in characters related to weapons or fighting

COMPOUNDS

● [original meaning] **ancient Chinese DAGGER-AX (consisting of a long shaft with a double-edged blade attached crosswise to its end)**
干戈 かんか arms, weapons
兵戈 へいか swords and halberds, arms; warfare

INDEPENDENT

【か 戈】**ancient Chinese weapon**

KUN

【ほこ 戈】[now usu. 矛] **arms**
戈を収める ほこをおさめる lay down arms, sheathe one's sword

SYNONYMS

● cutting weapons
刀 SWORD (single-edged) → 3642
剣 SWORD (double-edged) → 2104
矛 HALBERD → 2501
戟 HALBERD → 2131
鉾 DECORATIVE HALBERD → 2154
戈 DAGGER-AX → 4274

HOMOPHONES

ほこ
矛 HALBERD → 2501
鉾 DECORATIVE HALBERD → 2154
戟 HALBERD → 2131
鋒 POINT OF A BLADE → 2172

NOTE

➡ see USAGE note at 矛 2501

犬

4275
■4-4-4

▸DOG
ケン いぬ いぬ-
Ⓒ 犬 quǎn

94	Jōyō-1	U72AC
犬	S4-4-0	F0851

一	ナ	大	犬
1	2	3	4

RADICAL

inu 'dog' (状 献 獣), used in characters related to dogs, related animals or qualities
Left variant: 犭 ***kemonohen*** (独 猫 獲)

COMPOUNDS

ⓐ [also suffix] [original meaning] **DOG, hound**

ⓑ [humble] as worthless as a **DOG**

a 忠犬 ちゅうけん faithful dog
番犬 ばんけん watchdog
猟犬 りょうけん hound, hunting dog
野犬 やけん stray dog
コリー犬 こりーけん collie
盲導犬 もうどうけん guide dog, Seeing Eye dog

b 犬儒学派 けんじゅがくは the Cynics
犬馬の労 けんばのろう rendering what little service one can

KUN

【いぬ 犬】 [formerly also 狗]

① **DOG, hound, puppy**
飼い犬 かいいぬ house dog
小犬 こいぬ little dog, puppy

② spy
警察の犬 けいさつのいぬ police spy

【いぬ- 犬-】

① [prefix] pseudo-
犬黄楊 いぬつげ Japanese holly

② **worthless, shameless**
犬侍 いぬざむらい shameless [depraved] samurai
犬死にする いぬじにする die in vain

SYNONYMS

ⓐ **domesticated mammals**
牛 CATTLE →4263
馬 HORSE →4086
豚 PIG →1228
羊 SHEEP →2708
犬 DOG →4275
猫 CAT →0651
兎 RABBIT →4374

ⓐ **dog**
犬 DOG →4275
狗 DOG →0405
戌 THE DOG →4350

USAGE

【いぬ】

犬
[formerly also 狗]
① dog, hound, puppy
② spy

狗
[now usu. 犬]
① dog (esp. of small variety)
② spy

戌
11th sign of the Oriental zodiac: the Dog

HOMOPHONES

いぬ
狗 DOG →0405
戌 THE DOG →4350

匁

▶MOMME
もんめ
Ⓒ (国字)

4276
■4-4-4

20	Names	U5301
勹	S4-2-2	F3237

KUN

【もんめ 匁】

ⓐ **MOMME: unit of weight equiv. to 3.75 g or 1/1000 of a *kan* (貫), now used esp. for weighing pearls**

ⓑ **MOMME**: former monetary unit equiv. to 1/60 of a *ryo* (両)

a 一匁 いちもんめ 1 momme

SYNONYMS

【もんめ】

ⓐ **weight units**
匁 MOMME (3.75 g) →4276
斤 CATTY (600 g) →3667
貫 *kan* (3.75 kg) →3112
噸 TON →0930
屯 ton →4268

内

▶INSIDE
ナイ ダイ うち
Ⓝ 内 Ⓒ 内 nèi

4277
■4-4-4

13△	Jōyō-2	U5185
冂	S4-2-2	F0061

丨 冂 内 内
1 2 3 4

COMPOUNDS

❶ⓐ [also prefix] [original meaning] (inner side or part) **INSIDE, interior, within, internal, inner**

ⓑ [also suffix] (inside a given range) **within, within the scope of, in**

ⓒ place **INSIDE** (the body), take in

a 内容 ないよう contents, import, substance
内部 ないぶ interior, inner parts
内外 ないがい inside and outside; approximately
内科 ないか (department of) internal medicine
内出血 ないしゅっけつ internal hemorrhage
内分泌 ないぶんぴつ internal secretion
内心 ないしん one's inmost heart; one's real intention; *math* inner center
内陸 ないりく inland, interior
内向 ないこう introversion
内向的 ないこうてき introversive
内面 ないめん inside, interior
案内する あんないする guide, show; inform, notify

b 国内の こくないの domestic, internal, inland

境内 けいだい grounds [premises] (of a shrine or temple)
以内 いない within, less than
権限内に けんげんないに within the scope of authority
都内で となないで in Tokyo Metropolis
c 内服する ないふくする take (a medicine) internally

❷ (pertaining to the affairs of a country) **internal, domestic**
内政 ないせい domestic administration, internal affairs
内戦 ないせん civil war
内紛 ないふん internal trouble [strife]; storm in a teacup
内務 ないむ internal [domestic] affairs
内需 ないじゅ domestic demand

❸ **not public, private, secret, unofficial, informal**
内内の ないないの private, informal; secret, confidential
内定 ないてい informal decision
内申 ないしん unofficial report
内規 ないき private rules [regulations], bylaws
内報 ないほう secret report [information]
内密の ないみつの secret, confidential, private

❹ (person inside the house) **wife**
内助 ないじょ wife's help
内儀 ないぎ other's wife
家内 かない family, household; wife

❺ **Imperial Palace, Imperial Court; center of politics**
内裏 だいり Imperial Palace
内閣 ないかく cabinet
参内 さんだい attendance at the Imperial Court

❻ **pertaining to Buddhism**
内典 ないてん Buddhist literature [sutras]

KUN

【うち 内】

① [sometimes also 中] [also prefix and suffix] **INSIDE, interior**
内側 うちがわ inside, interior
内幕 うちまく inside facts, inner workings; [original meaning] inner curtain
内訳 うちわけ items (of an account), details, breakdown
内ポケット うちぽけっと inside pocket
内気な うちきな shy, bashful
仲間内の なかまうちの private, informal, among one's people [group]

② [sometimes also 中] **within (a given period), in the course of, while, during**
一週間の内に いっしゅうかんのうちに within a week
若い内 わかいうち while young
その内 そのうち before long, one of these days, sooner or later; in the meantime

③ [sometimes also 中] **among, between**
両者の内 りょうしゃのうち between the two

④ [also 家]
ⓐ **house, one's home**
ⓑ **one's family, household**
a 内を建てる うちをたてる build one's house
b 内の人 うちのひと my husband; one's family
内中 うちじゅう whole family; all over the house
内弟子 うちでし pupil boarding in his master's home, apprentice

⑤ (group or organization one belongs to) **we; ourselves; our group, our company**
内の会社 うちのかいしゃ our company
内内で うちうちで among ourselves
身内 みうち relations, relative

SYNONYMS

❶ⓐ & ❶ⓑ inside
内 INSIDE → 4277
裏 inside → 2652
奥 INNER PART → 3503
中 IN → 4262

❷ national
国 national → 3831
内 internal → 4277

❸ secret and private
秘 SECRET → 1490
密 SECRET → 2857
暗 in the dark → 1273
私 PRIVATE → 1432
内 not public → 4277
隠 hidden from view → 0873

❹ wives
妻 WIFE → 3166
奥 wife → 3503
内 wife → 4277
室 wife (esp. of persons of rank) → 2802
嫡 legitimate wife → 0839
婦 married woman → 0565
嫁 BRIDE → 0780
寡 widow → 2957

【うち】

② **during**
間 for an interval of → 4122
中 IN (the course of) → 4262
内 within (a given period) → 4277

USAGE

【うち】

内

① [sometimes also 中] [also prefix and suffix] inside, interior

② [sometimes also 中] within (a given period), in the course of, while, during

③ [sometimes also 中] among, between

④ [also 家]

ⓐ house, one's home

ⓑ one's family, household

⑤ (group or organization one belongs to) we; ourselves; our group, our company

中

[usu. 内]

① inside, interior

② within (a given period), in the course of, while, during

③ among, between

家

[also 内]

ⓐ house, one's home

ⓑ one's family, household

HOMOPHONES

うち

中 MIDDLE →4262

家 HOUSE →2827

NOTE

➡ see COMPOUND FORMATION for 案内 あんない →案 2824

少

4278

■4-4-4

▸LITTLE

ショウ　すく(ない)　すこ(し)

Ⓒ 少 shǎo shào

42	Jōyō-2	U5C11
小	S4-3-1	F0152

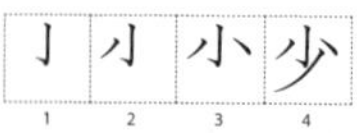

COMPOUNDS

❶ⓐ (of small quantity or number) **LITTLE, few, small**

ⓑ [original meaning] **reduce in quantity**

a 少少 しょうしょう a little, a few, slightly

少数 しょうすう small number, minority

少量(=小量) しょうりょう small quantity [amount]

少額 しょうがく small sum

多少 たしょう a little, somewhat

軽少の けいしょうの little, slight, trifling

僅少差 きんしょうさ narrow [slim] margin

b 減少 げんしょう decrease, reduction, lessening

❷ⓐ young

ⓑ the young, youth

a 少年 しょうねん boy

少女 しょうじょ girl

年少の ねんしょうの young, juvenile

b 幼少 ようしょう infancy, childhood

❸ performing a secondary function

少尉 しょうい second lieutenant

KUN

【すくない　少ない】(of small quantity or number) **LITTLE, few, limited, insufficient**

少なからず すくなからず not a little [few]

少なくとも すくなくとも at least

少ない時間 すくないじかん limited time

【すこし　少し】(of small quantity) **a LITTLE, a few, some; a bit, somewhat; a little while; short distance**

少しも すこしも (not) at all

少しずつ すこしずつ little by little

SYNONYMS

❶ⓐ few

少 LITTLE →4278

寡 FEW →2957

乏 SCANTY →2432

薄 meager →3004

微 SLIGHT →0788

寸 A BIT OF →3652

僅 A LITTLE →0176

些 A BIT →3251

❷ⓐ young

若 YOUNG →2785

弱 young →1499

少 young →4278

青 youthful →3084

幼 VERY YOUNG →0222

稚 CHILDISH →1543

爿

4279

■4-4-4

▸SHŌHEN

90	Radical	U723F
爿	S4-4-0	F0000

RADICAL

shōhen 'stand' (牆 牀×), used in characters related to stands, frames or enclosures

---

ネ

4280

■4-4-4

▸NEHEN, SHIMESUHEN

113	Radical	U793B
ネ	S4-4-0	F0000

radical variant →see 示 at 2435

冃

4281

■4-4-4

▶*GŪNOASHI*

114	Radical	U79B8
冃	S5-5-0	F0000

RADICAL

gūnoashi 'track' (禹× 禺× 禽), used for character classification

耂

4282

■4-4-4

▶*OIKANMURI, OIGASHIRA*

125	Radical	U8002
耂	S4-4-0	F0000

radical variant →see 老 at 3963

丈

4283

■4-4-4

▶**STOUT**
▶**STATURE**

ジョウ たけ だけ ㊔ たけし

1	Nonstandard	U2000B
一	S4-1-3	F0000

traditional form →see 丈 at 4227

户

4284

■4-4-4

▶**DOOR**
▶**HOUSEHOLD**

コ と[1] と[2] ㊔ べ ど へ

63	Nonstandard	U6238
戶	S4-4-0	F0000

alternative form →see 戸 at 2429

內

4285

■4-4-4

▶**INSIDE**

ナイ ダイ うち

11	Nonstandard	U5167
入	S4-2-2	F0000

traditional form →see 内 at 4277

乏
■4-4-4
incorrect classification
➡ see ⬒2-1-3: ノ at 2432

欠
■4-4-4
incorrect classification
➡ see ⬒2-2-2: ⺈ at 2481

毛
■4-4-4
incorrect classification
➡ see ■4-4-3 at 4264

勿
■4-4-4
incorrect classification
➡ see □3-2-2: 勹 at 3661

世
■4-4-4
incorrect classification/stroke-count
➡ see ■4-5-2 at 4308

氏
■4-4-4
incorrect classification
➡ see □3-2-2: 𠂆 at 3669

之
■4-4-4
incorrect stroke-count
➡ see ■4-3-4 at 4228

心
■4-4-4
incorrect classification
➡ see ◧1-1-3: ⼂ at 0011

太
■4-4-4
incorrect classification
➡ see ⬒2-3-1: 大 at 2673

屯
■4-4-4
incorrect classification
➡ see ■4-4-3 at 4268

与
■4-4-4
incorrect stroke-count
➡ see ■4-3-4 at 4229

友
■4-4-4
incorrect classification
➡ see □3-2-2: 𠂇 at 3670

尤
■4-4-4
incorrect classification
➡ see □3-3-1: 尢 at 3755

攵
■4-4-4
incorrect classification
➡ see ⬒2-2-2: 𠂉 at 2479

斤 戶
■4-4-4
incorrect classification
➡ see □3-2-2: 𠂆 at 3667

皿

4286

■4-5-1

▶**PLATE**

ベイ▲ さら

ⓒ 皿 mǐn

108	Jōyō-3	U76BF
皿	S5-5-0	F1521

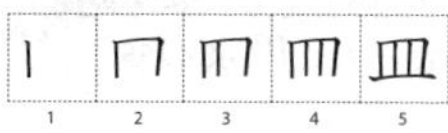

RADICAL

sara 'dish' (監 盟 盛), used in characters related to dishes, vessels or their uses

KUN

【さら 皿】

① [also suffix] [original meaning] (shallow container for holding food) **PLATE, dish**

皿洗い さらあらい dishwashing; dishwasher

皿回し さらまわし dish-spinning

スープ皿 すーぷざら soup plate
受け皿 うけざら saucer
蒸発皿 じょうはつざら evaporating dish
製氷皿 せいひょうざら ice-making pan

②ⓐ (food served in a plate) **PLATE (of vegetables), dish, helping, course**
ⓑ **counter for PLATEs or helpings**

a 最初の皿 さいしょのさら first course
b 野菜一皿 やさいひとさら a dish of vegetables

③ various **PLATE**like objects, as:
ⓐ scale, bowl (of scales)
ⓑ kneecap, patella
ⓒ *slang* record, disk

a 皿秤 さらばかり balance
b 膝の皿 ひざのさら kneecap
c お皿 おさら record, disk

SYNONYMS

【さら】

① **vessels and receptacles**
盤 dish →3533
鍋 POT →2202
釜 IRON POT →2610
鼎 TRIPOD CAULDRON →4405
臼 MORTAR →4341
碓 MORTAR →1537
托 RECEPTACLE →0252
皿 PLATE →4286
盆 TRAY →2581
膳 LEGGED TRAY →1381
杯 CUP →1066
鉢 BOWL →2144
椀 WOODEN BOWL →1250
碗 CERAMIC BOWL →1539
丼 LARGE BOWL →4323

母

4287
■4-5-1

▸**MOTHER**
ボ はは も▲
ⓒ 母 mǔ

80	Jōyō-2	U6BCD
毋	S5-5-0	F0238

radical variant →see 毋 at 4255

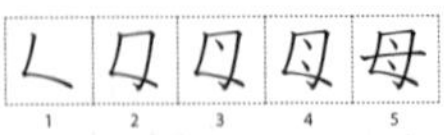

COMPOUNDS

❶ [original meaning] (female parent) **MOTHER**
母子 ぼし mother and child
母乳 ぼにゅう mother's milk
母音 ぼいん vowel ("mother sound")
母細胞 ぼさいぼう mother cell
父母 ふぼ father and mother, parents
祖母 そぼ grandmother
聖母 せいぼ Holy Mother, Virgin Mary

❷ⓐ (relating to one's birthplace) **MOTHER, native**
ⓑ (relating to the place of origin or base) **MOTHER, home**
ⓒ abbrev. of 母艦 ぼかん: **MOTHER** ship, carrier

a 母国 ぼこく one's mother country, homeland
母国語 ぼこくご one's mother tongue, native language
母校 ぼこう one's alma mater, one's old school
b 母港 ぼこう home port
母船 ぼせん mother ship
c 空母 くうぼ (airplane) carrier, flattop

❸ **base material**
母材 ぼざい *welding* base metal
母型 ぼけい matrix
酵母 こうぼ yeast; ferment
分母 ぶんぼ denominator

❹ [formerly 姆 0331] wet nurse, amah
保母 ほぼ nurse, kindergarten teacher

❺ [also 拇 0358] thumb
母印 ぼいん thumbprint

KUN

【はは 母】 (female parent) **MOTHER; cause, motive**
母の愛 はははのあい maternal love
母親 ははおや mother
母鳥 ははどり mother bird
必要は発明の母 ひつようははつめいのはは Necessity is the mother of invention

【も 母】

① [in compounds] **MOTHER**, main
入母屋 いりもや style of roof construction with eaves under the gable

② unclassified compounds
雲母 うんも mica, isinglass

SPECIAL READINGS

お母さん おかあさん mother
母屋 おもや main house [wing]
母家 おもや main house [wing]
伯母 おば aunt (older than one's parent)
叔母 おば aunt (younger than one's parent)
お祖母さん▲ おばあさん grandmother
乳母 うば [rarely also 姆] wet nurse

SYNONYMS

❶ **parents**
親 PARENT →2264
父 FATHER →2467
母 MOTHER →4287

HOMOPHONES

うば

姆 GOVERNESS → 0331

乳母 → 1823, 4287

瓦

▶**TILE**

ガ かわら ぐらむ▲

ⓒ 瓦 wǎ wà

4288

■4-5-1

98	Jōyō	U74E6
瓦	S5-5-0	F1846

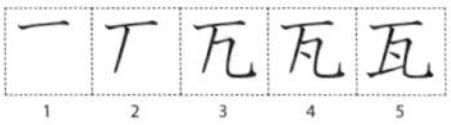

RADICAL

kawara 'tile' (瓶 甓×), used in characters related to earthenware, ceramics or tiles

COMPOUNDS

❶ⓐ [original meaning] **TILE, roof tile**

ⓑ **as fragile as a TILE, easily broken**

a 瓦礫× がれき tiles and pebbles; trash

煉瓦 れんが brick

b 瓦解する がかいする collapse, break up, fall to pieces

❷ **used phonetically for *ga***

瓦斯 がす gas

KUN

【かわら 瓦】**TILE, roof tile**

瓦版 かわらばん tile block print (newspaper in Tokugawa period)

瓦煎餅 かわらせんべい tile-shaped rice cracker

瓦屋根 かわらやね tiled roof

鬼瓦 おにがわら tile with the figure of a devil

【ぐらむ 瓦】**gram**

五十瓦 ごじゅうぐらむ 50 g

SYNONYMS

❶ⓐ **roof parts**

軒 EAVES → 1851

庇 EAVES → 3802

棟 ridge → 1248

瓦 roof tile → 4288

❷ **phonetic [k]/[g]**

迦 PHONETIC [ka] → 3982

珈 phonetic [kō] → 1138

伽 PHONETIC [ga] → 0074

瓦 phonetic [ga] → 4288

祇 phonetic [gi] → 1459

玉

▶**GEM**

ギョク たま たま- -だま

ⓒ 玉 yù

4289

■4-5-1

96	Jōyō-1	U7389
玉	S5-5-0	F0818

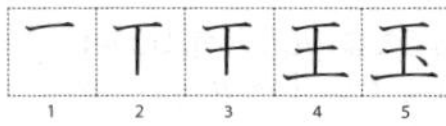

RADICAL

tama 'gem' (璽 琴), used in characters related to gems, jewels or treasures

Left variant: 𤣩 ***tamahen*** (現 理 球)

COMPOUNDS

❶ⓐ **GEM, jewel(ry), precious stone**

ⓑ [original meaning] jade

a 玉石混淆(=玉石混交) ぎょくせきこんこう mixture of good and bad, jumble of wheat and tares

宝玉 ほうぎょく jewel, gem, precious stone

珠玉 しゅぎょく jewel, gem

硬玉 こうぎょく jadeite

b 玉杯 ぎょくはい jade cup

❷ as beautiful as a jewel, exquisite

玉露 ぎょくろ refined green tea

玉砕 ぎょくさい death for honor

❸ [honorific]

ⓐ imperial

ⓑ your

a 玉音 ぎょくおん emperor's voice

玉顔 ぎょくがん imperial face

b 玉稿 ぎょっこう your manuscript

❹ engagements, stock bought or sold

玉整理 ぎょくせいり liquidation of speculative accounts

売り玉 うりぎょく short account, short interest

❺ geisha

玉代 ぎょくだい time charge for a geisha

❻ name of chess piece in shogi (Japanese chess): *gyoku*, white king

自玉 じぎょく one's own king

INDEPENDENT

【ぎょく 玉】jewel, **GEM**; jade; geisha, time charge for a geisha; *gyoku* (→❻); egg, egg roll

KUN

【たま 玉】

①ⓐ [formerly also 珠 or 璧] **GEM, jewel, precious stone, pearl; bead**

ⓑ something as beautiful or precious as a jewel

a 玉に疵(=玉に瑕×) たまにきず flaw in the crystal, fly in the ointment

勾玉(=曲玉) まがたま comma-shaped bead

b 玉の輿 たまのこし marriage to a man of wealth

掌中の玉 しょうちゅうのたま apple of one's eye

② various spherical objects, as:
ⓐ **ball, globe; lump of noodles; egg; lens**
ⓑ *slang* **testicles**
a 玉突き たまつき billiards; serial collisions (of cars)
玉子 たまご [also 卵] egg
目玉 めだま eyeball; loss leader (of merchandise)
鉄砲玉(=鉄砲弾) てっぽうだま gunshot, bullet; lost [truant] messenger; bull's-eye
b 金玉 きんたま testicles, balls
③ *slang*
ⓐ **guy, chap**
ⓑ **pretty girl, doll**
a 親玉 おやだま big shot, kingpin
表六玉(=兵六玉) ひょうろくだま nincompoop, simpleton
大変な玉だ たいへんなたまだ He's a caution!
b 上玉 じょうだま pretty girl

【たま- 玉-】 [also prefix]
①ⓐ **beautiful, exquisite**
ⓑ **sacred, precious**
a 玉手箱 たまてばこ Pandora's box; treasured casket
b 玉垣 たまがき shrine fence
② **round, spherical**
玉葱[×] たまねぎ onion
玉砂利 たまじゃり gravel

【-だま -玉】
① **coin suffix**
十円玉 じゅうえんだま 10-yen coin
五セント玉 ごせんとだま nickel
② [also suffix] **round or spherical object**
シャボン玉 しゃぼんだま soap bubble
疳[×]癪[×]玉 かんしゃくだま firecracker; temper, fit of rage

SYNONYMS

❶ⓐ precious stones
玉 GEM → 4289
珂 WHITE AGATE → 1137
璧 DISK-SHAPED JEWEL → 3608
琥 AMBER → 1261
珀 AMBER → 1136
珠 PEARL → 1183
瑛 TRANSPARENT GEM → 1259
瑠 LAPIS LAZULI → 1342
璃 GLASSY SUBSTANCE → 1358
晶 CRYSTAL → 3122
玖 beautiful black jewel → 1041
琉 LAPIS LAZULI → 1221
琳 BEAUTIFUL GEM → 1262

【たま】
② **spherical object**
玉 spherical object → 4289
球 BALL → 1219
丸 round body → 4225
鞠 BALL → 2268
毬 BALL → 4001

【-だま】
① **money**
金 MONEY → 2552
銭 MONEY → 2159
貨 MONEY (legal tender), coin → 3113
幣 CURRENCY → 3582
銀 SILVER → 2156
財 finance → 1849
資 RESOURCES → 3342
-玉 coin suffix → 4289
札 bill → 1011

USAGE

【たま】
玉
①ⓐ [formerly also 珠 or 璧] gem, jewel, precious stone, pearl; bead
ⓑ something as beautiful or precious as a jewel
② various spherical objects, as:
ⓐ ball, globe; lump of noodles; egg; lens
ⓑ *slang* testicles
③ *slang*
ⓐ guy, chap
ⓑ pretty girl, doll
弾
bullet, shot, shell
珠
[now usu. 玉, formerly also 璧] gem, jewel, precious stone, pearl; bead
球
ⓐ ball (in a sports game)
ⓑ light bulb
璧
[now usu. 玉, formerly also 珠] gem, jewel, precious stone, pearl, bead

HOMOPHONES

たま
珠 PEARL → 1183
球 BALL → 1219
弾 PROJECTILE → 0697
璧 DISK-SHAPED JEWEL → 3608
たまご
卵 EGG → 1054
玉子 → 4289, 4196

NOTE

➡ see also USAGE note at 卵 1054

丙

4290

4-5-1

▶THIRD

ヘイ ひのえ▲

Ⓝ 丙 Ⓒ 丙 bǐng

1	Jōyō	U4E19
一	S5-1-4	F3330

COMPOUNDS

ⓐ the THIRD, C; third class, grade C
ⓑ THIRD calendar sign (→see APPENDIX 8)

a 丙種 へいしゅ third class, class C
甲乙丙 こうおつへい 1st, 2nd and 3rd; A, B and C
b 丙午 へいご 43rd of the sexagenary cycle

INDEPENDENT

【へい 丙】the THIRD, C; third calendar sign

KUN

【ひのえ 丙】THIRD calendar sign
丙午 ひのえうま 43rd of the sexagenary cycle

NOTE

➡ see 甲 4293 FIRST, 乙 4145 SECOND and 丁 4155 fourth

平

4291

4-5-1

▶FLAT
▶CALM

ヘイ ビョウ ヒョウ▲ たい(ら) -だいら ひら ひら- ㊔ ぺい なり

Ⓝ 平 Ⓒ 平 píng

51	Jōyō-3	U5E73
干	S5-3-2	F0120

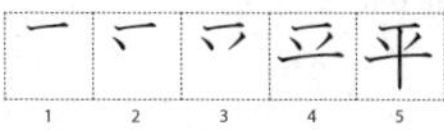

COMPOUNDS

❶ⓐ [original meaning] **FLAT, level, even**
ⓑ **FLAT** on the ground, low

a 平方 へいほう square (measure); square (of a number)
平野 へいや plain(s), open field
平面 へいめん level surface, plain
平坦な へいたんな flat, level, even
水平の すいへいの horizontal, level, even
b 平伏する へいふくする prostrate oneself (before), kiss the ground

❷ **equal, impartial, fair**

平均 へいきん average, (arithmetical) mean; equilibrium, balance
平行 へいこう parallelism, parallel; going side by side; occurring together
平等 びょうどう equality, impartiality
公平 こうへい impartiality, fairness

❸ **common, ordinary, average**

平日 へいじつ weekday
平凡な へいぼんな common, ordinary, commonplace, mediocre
平年 へいねん normal [average] year, common year
平常の へいじょうの ordinary, normal, usual

❹ simple, plain

平易 へいい plainness, simplicity, easiness
平明な へいめいな clear, simple

❺ⓐ **CALM, peaceful, quiet**
ⓑ bring peace to, pacify

a 平和 へいわ peace, harmony
平気 へいき nonchalance, unconcern; composure
平穏 へいおん calmness, quiet, tranquility
平静な へいせいな calm, serene
平安 へいあん calmness, peace, quietness, tranquility; Heian period
平成 へいせい Heisei era
和平 わへい peace
太平(=泰平) たいへい tranquility, perfect peace
b 平定 へいてい suppression, subjugation, subdual

❻ⓐ abbrev. of 平方 へいほう: square (measure)
ⓑ abbrev. of 平方根 へいほうこん: square root

a 平米 へいべい sq. meter
b 開平 かいへい square root extraction

❼ abbrev. of 平家 へいけ: Taira Family

平語 へいご The Tale of the Taira Clan
源平 げんぺい Genji and Heike clans; two opposing sides

❽ first tone in old Chinese phonetics

平声 ひょうしょう first tone in old Chinese phonetics
平上去入 ひょうじょうきょにゅう the four tones in old Chinese phonetics

❾ unclassified compounds

助平 すけべい lewd person; Peeping Tom

KUN

【たいら 平ら】
たいらな 平らな **FLAT, even, level, smooth; calm, peaceful, tranquil**
平らな道 たいらなみち level road
平らげる たいらげる eat up, finish, consume; quell, subdue, put down
心の平らな こころのたいらな even-tempered

【-だいら -平】**suffix after names of FLATs or plains**
日本平 にほんだいら Nihon Plain

【ひら 平】**common [ordinary] member(ship) of an organization; the broad [FLAT] (of a hand); shallow bowl; breaststroke**
平の社員 ひらのしゃいん mere clerk
平泳ぎ ひらおよぎ breast stroke
手の平(=掌) てのひら palm of the hand

【ひら- 平-】[also prefix]

4
皿 母 瓦 玉 丙 平【疋 甲】凹 冊 正 且 凸 旡 疋 平 丙 册 牙 田 互 丞 民 目 冬 用 西 四

① **FLAT, not elevated**
平たい ひらたい flat, even, level; simple, plain
平屋 ひらや one-story house
平地 ひらち flat [level] ground
平仮名 ひらがな hiragana, cursive kana characters
平屋根 ひらやね flat roof

② **common, ordinary, plain**
平幕 ひらまく plain sumo wrestler of senior grade
平教員 ひらきょういん common teacher
平党員 ひらとういん rank-and-file party member

SYNONYMS

❶ⓐ flat
平 FLAT → 4291
扁 FLAT → 3728
坦 LEVEL → 0329

❷ same and uniform
等 EQUAL → 3321
平 equal → 4291
均 EVEN → 0276
斉 UNIFORM → 2548
同 SAME → 3707
一 same → 4148

❷ impartial
公 impartial → 2468
平 equal → 4291

❸ ordinary
常 NORMAL → 3203
只- ORDINARY → 2677
並 ordinary → 2793
平 common → 4291
普 common → 2919
庸 MEDIOCRE → 3881
凡 COMMONPLACE → 3656
套 TRITE → 2823

❺ⓐ calm and peaceful
安 PEACEFUL → 2695
康 peaceful → 3877
寧 peaceful → 2959
泰 TRANQUIL → 3193
静 QUIET → 2164
平 CALM → 4291
穏 CALM → 1578

❻ⓐ mathematical power
乗 power → 4393
方 SQUARE → 2459
平 square (measure) → 4291

USAGE

【へいこう】
平行
① parallelism, parallel
②ⓐ going side by side
ⓑ occurring together
並行
ⓐ going side by side
ⓑ occurring together

HOMOPHONES

てのひら
掌 PALM → 3215
手の平 → 4267, 4291

NOTE

➡ see also USAGE note at 掌 3215
★ do not confuse with 乎 MODIFIER FORMING SUFFIX → 4316

疋

4292
■4-5-1

▶**UNIT OF MEASURE FOR CLOTH**
ヒキ
Ⓒ 疋 pǐ

103	Names	U758B
疋	S5-5-0	F3123

RADICAL

hiki 'animal counter' (疑), used for character classification
Left variant: 𤴔 *hikihen* (疎 疏)

COMPOUNDS

❶ *hiki*:
ⓐ [also 匹 3680] **UNIT OF MEASURE FOR CLOTH equiv. to 2 *tan* (反)**
ⓑ former monetary unit equiv. to 10 (later 25) *mon* (文)
a 絹五疋 きぬごひき five *hiki* of silk fabrics

❷ [now usu. 匹 3680] **counter for animals**
猫三疋 ねこさんびき three cats

SYNONYMS

❷ counters for animals
匹 COUNTER FOR ANIMALS → 3680
頭 counter for large animals → 2019
羽 counter for birds → 0265
疋 counter for animals → 4292

HOMOPHONES

ひき 匹 COUNTER FOR ANIMALS → 3680

NOTE

➡ see USAGE note at 匹 3680

甲

4293
■4-5-1

▶**SHELL**
▶**FIRST**
コウ カン カ▲ きのえ▲ ㊔ かぶと き
Ⓒ 甲 jiǎ

102	Jōyō	U7532
田	S5-5-0	F0882

1 2 3 4 5

COMPOUNDS

❶ **SHELL (of animals); carapace, tortoise carapace**
甲殻 こうかく carapace, shell, crust
甲羅 こうら shell, carapace
甲骨文 こうこつぶん ancient inscriptions of Chinese characters on oracle bones and carapaces
甲虫 こうちゅう beetle
甲板 かんぱん(=こうはん) deck
亀甲 きっこう carapace of a turtle, tortoiseshell

❷ armor; helmet
甲鉄 こうてつ armor plate
甲冑× かっちゅう armor and helmet
装甲部隊 そうこうぶたい armored corps

❸ⓐ **the FIRST, A; first class, grade A; the former**
ⓑ FIRST calendar sign (→see APPENDIX 8)
a 甲乙 こうおつ first and second, former and latter
甲種 こうしゅ grade A, first grade
b 甲子 かっし first of the sexagenary cycle

❹ high tone, treble
甲高い かんだかい high-pitched, shrill

❺ back of the hand, instep
甲高な こうだかな high-backed, high in the instep

❻ **used phonetically for *ka***
甲斐(=詮)が有る かいがある fruitful, effective, worth, worthwhile

❼ abbrev. of 甲斐 かい, old name for Yamanashi Prefecture
甲州 こうしゅう old name for Yamanashi Prefecture

INDEPENDENT

【こう 甲】**SHELL, tortoiseshell; armor; back of the hand, instep; the first, A; the former; first calendar sign**
甲と乙 こうとおつ A and B, the former and the latter
手の甲 てのこう back of the hand

【かん 甲】high tone (in traditional Japanese music)

KUN

【きのえ 甲】FIRST calendar sign

SYNONYMS

❶ **shells**
殻 SHELL (of any kind) → 1883
甲 SHELL (of animals) → 4293
貝 seashell → 3150
螺 SPIRAL-SHELLED GASTROPOD → 1799
瑚 CORAL → 1300

❷ **protective coverings**
盾 SHIELD → 3729
楯 SHIELD → 1281
鎧 ARMOR → 2211
甲 armor → 4293
縅 BRAID OF ARMOR → 1759
面 mask → 2590
兜 helmet → 3499
幌 COVERING FOR VEHICLES → 0787

❸ⓐ **first**
甲 FIRST → 4293
初 FIRST → 1433

NOTE

➡ see 乙 4145 SECOND, 丙 4290 THIRD and 丁 4155 fourth

凹

4294

■4-5-1

▸**CONCAVE**
オウ くぼ(む)▲ へこ(む)▲ ぼこ*
Ⓒ 凹 āo

17	Jōyō	U51F9
凵	S5-2-3	F2669

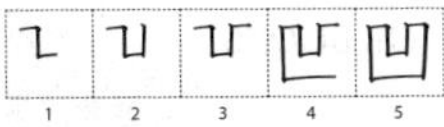

COMPOUNDS

● [original meaning] **CONCAVE, hollow, indented**
凹面鏡 おうめんきょう concave mirror
凹地 おうち hollow, pit
凹凸 おうとつ unevenness, irregularities
凹レンズ おうれんず concave lens
凹版印刷 おうはんいんさつ intaglio printing
凸凹紙 とつおうし embossed paper

KUN

【くぼむ 凹む】[in compounds] (of things) become hollow, become depressed
凹目 くぼめ sunken [deep-set] eyes

【へこむ 凹む】
① **get dented, cave in**
② *colloq* **get depressed, feel down**

【ぼこ 凹】[in compounds] **concavity**
凸凹 でこぼこ unevenness, roughness; imbalance
穴凹 あなぼこ hole, hollow

SYNONYMS

● **bowed**
凹 CONCAVE → 4294
凸 CONVEX → 4298
嵯 RUGGED → 0786

【ぼこ】
○ **holes and cavities**
穴 HOLE → 2682
洞 CAVE → 0455
窟 CAVE → 2923
窪 HOLLOW → 2962
腔 BODY CAVITY → 1267
孔 OPEN HOLE → 0205
口 MOUTH → 4189
坑 PIT → 0277
堀 DITCH → 0561

溝 CHANNEL → 0810
壕 TRENCH → 0966
濠 MOAT → 0975
凹 concavity → 4294

USAGE

【くぼむ】

凹む

[in compounds] (of things) become hollow, become depressed

窪む

(of the ground) become hollow, become depressed, cave in

HOMOPHONES

くぼむ 窪 HOLLOW → 2962

冊

4295

■4-5-1

▶COUNTER FOR BOOKS

サツ サク

Ⓝ 册◇ Ⓒ 册 cè

13	Jōyō-6	U518A
冂	S5-2-3	F1377

丨 冂 冂 冊 冊
1 2 3 4 5

COMPOUNDS

❶ⓐ COUNTER FOR BOOKS, volumes or copies
ⓑ bound book, volume, copy

a 冊数 さっすう number of books
四冊 よんさつ four volumes

b 小冊子 しょうさっし booklet, pamphlet
分冊 ぶんさつ separate volume
大冊 たいさつ great volume, bulky book
各冊 かくさつ each book [volume, copy]
別冊 べっさつ separate volume, extra issue

❷ ancient form of book consisting of bamboo strips strung together

短冊 たんざく strip of fancy paper for writing tanka poetry

❸ formal writ conferring honors or stipends

冊立 さくりつ installation, investiture (of the Crown Prince)

INDEPENDENT

【さつ 冊】 bound book, volume

SYNONYMS

❶ⓐ counters for books

冊 COUNTER FOR BOOKS → 4295
巻 counter for volumes → 3273
部 counter for copies → 2111

ⓑ books

本 BOOK → 4314
典 STANDARD WORK → 3253
経 religious classic → 1687
書 BOOK → 3292
冊 bound book → 4295
籍 books → 3394
著 literary work → 2869
巻 VOLUME → 3273
編 piece of writing → 1755
篇 PIECE OF WRITING → 3361
鑑 REFERENCE VOLUME → 2226

正

4296

■4-5-1

▶RIGHT

セイ ショウ ただ(しい) ただ(す) まさ まさ(に) ㊔ ただし まさし

Ⓒ 正 zhèng zhēng

77	Jōyō-1	U6B63
止	S5-4-1	F0135

一 丅 下 下 正
1 2 3 4 5

COMPOUNDS

❶ⓐ (not mistaken) **RIGHT, correct, proper**
ⓑ (set right) **RIGHT, correct, rectify**

a 正解 せいかい right answer, correct solution
正味の しょうみの net, full, clear
適正な てきせいな proper, appropriate, reasonable, right

b 改正する かいせいする revise, amend
訂正する ていせいする correct, amend, revise
修正する しゅうせいする amend, revise, correct; retouch
是正する ぜせいする correct
校正 こうせい proofreading
綱紀粛正 こうきしゅくせい enforcing discipline (among government officials)

❷ⓐ [also prefix] (in a precise manner) **RIGHT, accurate, exact(ly), just, due (north)**
ⓑ net

a 正確な せいかくな accurate, precise, exact
正午 しょうご noon, noontime
正北 せいほく due north
正反対 せいはんたい exactly opposite
正六時に しょうろくじに at six sharp

b 正札 しょうふだ net price

❸ (morally correct) **RIGHT, righteous, just, upright**

正邪 せいじゃ right and wrong
正義 せいぎ justice, righteousness
正当な せいとうな just, right, due; legal
正論 せいろん sound argument
正直な しょうじきな honest, upright, frank
公正な こうせいな just, fair, impartial
不正 ふせい injustice, wrong, illegality

❹ **RIGHT side, front**

正面 しょうめん front, frontage, facade
正攻法 せいこうほう regular tactics for attack

正視する せいしする look in the face; confront

❺ⓐ [also prefix] **regular, full, normal, proper, formal, orthodox; legitimate, legal**

ⓑ **genuine, authentic, pure**

a 正規の せいきの regular, formal, legitimate

正式の せいしきの formal, regular

正統の せいとうの legitimate, orthodox, traditional

正常な せいじょうな normal, regular

正座する せいざする sit upright [straight]

正気 しょうき consciousness; sanity, reason

正妻 せいさい lawful [legal] wife

正会員 せいかいいん regular member

正教授 せいきょうじゅ full professor

b 正真正銘の しょうしんしょうめいの true, genuine, authentic

正史 せいし authentic history

正体 しょうたい one's natural [true] shape; consciousness

❻ [also prefix]

ⓐ *math* (of equal sides or congruent faces) **regular**

ⓑ *chem* normal, ortho-

a 正方形 せいほうけい square

正多面体 せいためんたい regular polyhedron

b 正塩 せいえん normal salt

正安息香酸 せいあんそくこうさん orthobenzoic acid

❼ⓐ [also prefix] **chief, main, principal**

ⓑ (person of highest rank) chief

a 正使 せいし senior envoy, chief

正犯 せいはん principal offender

正副議長 せいふくぎちょう chairman and vice-chairman

正門 せいもん main gate, main entrance

正編 せいへん main part of a book

正弦 せいげん sine (of an angle)

正三位 しょうさんみ senior grade of the third court rank

b 検事正 けんじせい chief public prosecutor

僧正 そうじょう bishop

❽ original

正副二通 せいふくにつう original and duplicate

❾ⓐ *math* positive

ⓑ *elec* positive

a 正数 せいすう positive number

正号 せいごう plus sign

正比例 せいひれい direct proportion

b 正電気 せいでんき positive electricity

❿ **first month of the year, January**

正月 しょうがつ New Year, New Year's day; January

賀正 がしょう New Year's congratulations, Happy New Year

⓫ [archaic] ten duodecillion (10^{40})

INDEPENDENT

【せい 正】**RIGHT, righteousness, justice; first volume (as opposed to the sequel);** *math, elec* **positiveness**

正の せいの *math, elec* positive

KUN

【ただしい 正しい】**correct, RIGHT, accurate, exact; right, righteous, just; lawful, legitimate**

正しさ ただしさ rightness, righteousness, lawfulness; correctness, propriety

正しい答え ただしいこたえ correct answer

正しい行い ただしいおこない right conduct

規則正しい きそくただしい regular, systematic

礼儀正しい れいぎただしい courteous, decorous, polite

【ただす 正す】

ⓐ **correct, rectify**

ⓑ **set RIGHT, reform, redress**

a 誤りが有れば正せ あやまりがあればただせ Correct mistakes, if any

b 姿勢を正す しせいをただす straighten oneself

【まさ 正】[in compounds] **just, exact, definite**

正夢 まさゆめ dream which comes true, prophetic dream

正木 まさき [also 柾] spindle tree

【まさに 正に】**just, exactly; surely, certainly; really**

正に春だ まさにはるだ Spring is really here

SYNONYMS

❶ⓐ **right**

正 RIGHT → 4296

是 RIGHT → 3090

尤 RIGHT → 3755

端 correct → 1564

ⓑ **correct**

正 RIGHT → 4296

直す correct → 3649

訂 REVISE → 1829

改 REFORM → 0287

矯 RECTIFY → 1586

匡 RECTIFY → 3710

❷ⓐ **exact**

確 CERTAIN → 1571

正 RIGHT → 4296

真- right → 2616

恰 JUST → 0437

❸ **virtuous**

正 RIGHT → 4296

義 righteous → 2948

善 GOOD → 2921

良 GOOD → 4373

鯁 UPRIGHT → 2357

皿 毋 瓦 玉 丙 平 疋 甲 凹 冊 正 【且 凸】 旡 孒 丕 两 册 牙 田 互 丞 民 目 冬 用 襾 四

❺ⓐ regular

正 regular → 4296
本 regular → 4314

ⓑ true

真 TRUE → 2616
洵 TRULY → 0458
実 REAL → 2765
本 real → 4314
正 genuine → 4296
現 ACTUAL → 1218

❼ⓐ main

主 MAIN → 2437
正 chief → 4296
本 head → 4314
親- PARENT → 2264
首 leading → 2818

❾ positive

陽 positive → 0764
正 positive → 4296

USAGE

❶【ただす】

正す
ⓐ correct, rectify
ⓑ set right, reform, redress

質す
ⓐ query, question, consult, inquire
ⓑ ascertain, verify

糾す
inquire into, investigate into, examine

❷【まさに】

正に
just, exactly; surely, certainly; really

当に
[always followed by 可し べし] properly, naturally; it is proper to, ought to

将に
be about to, on the verge of

HOMOPHONES

ただす
質 QUALITY → 3483
糾 INQUIRE INTO → 1631

まさに
当 THE PRESENT → 2701
将 GENERAL OFFICER → 0551

まさき
柾 STRAIGHT GRAIN → 1114
正木 → 4296, 4261

COMPOUND FORMATION

【正弦 せいげん】【余弦 よげん】

The trigonometric function 正弦 'sine' refers to the principal (正 ❼ⓐ) arc (弦), whereas 余弦 'cosine' refers to the complementary (余) arc (弦).

NOTE

➡ see COMPOUND FORMATION for
正味 しょうみ → 味 0325
李下に冠を正さず りかにかんむりをたださず → 李 3050

且

4297

■ 4-5-1

▸AS WELL

ショ▲ ソ▲ か(つ)

Ⓒ 且 qiě

1	Jōyō	U4E14
一	S5-1-4	F2348

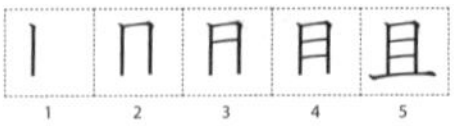

KUN

【かつ 且つ】**AS WELL (as), at the same time, besides, moreover, both…and**

且つ又 かつまた moreover
且つ飲み且つ歌う かつのみかつうたう drink as well as sing, drink and sing at the same time
彼は英語を話し且つ書く かれはえいごをはなしかつかく He speaks English and writes it as well

SYNONYMS

【かつ】

○ **additionally**

亦 ALSO → 2504
兼 CONCURRENTLY → 2850
又 also, and → 4158
而うして and → 2520
及び and → 4192
並びに and also → 2793
傍ら besides → 0166
尚 STILL → 2774
更に furthermore → 4355
且つ AS WELL → 4297

凸

4298

■ 4-5-1

▸CONVEX

トツ でこ*

Ⓒ 凸 tū

17	Jōyō	U51F8
凵	S5-2-3	F2647

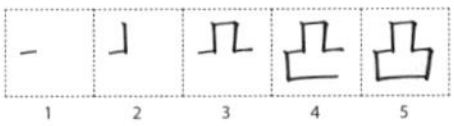

COMPOUNDS

● [original meaning] **CONVEX, gibbous, protruding**

凸レンズ とつれんず convex lens
凸面 とつめん convex surface
凸角 とっかく convex angle
凸版 とっぱん letterpress, relief printing
凹凸 おうとつ unevenness, irregularities

KUN

【でこ 凸】[in compounds] **CONVEXity**

お凸 おでこ brow, forehead

凸凹 でこぼこ unevenness, roughness; imbalance

SYNONYMS

● **protrude and protruding**

突 protruding → 2772

凸 CONVEX → 4298

隆 protuberant → 0661

起 RISE → 4099

出る stick out → 4310

● **bowed**

凹 CONCAVE → 4294

凸 CONVEX → 4298

嵯 RUGGED → 0786

旡

4299

■4-5-1

▸***SUDENOTSUKURI***

71	Radical	U65E1
无	S5-5-0	F0000

radical variant → see 无 at 4251

疋

4300

■4-5-1

▸***HIKIHEN***

103	Radical	U2EAA
疋	S5-5-0	F0000

radical variant → see 疋 at 4292

平

4301

■4-5-1

▸**FLAT**
▸**CALM**

ヘイ ビョウ ヒョウ たい(ら) -だいら ひら ひら- ㊔ へい なり

51	Nonstandard	U5E73
干	S5-3-2	F0000

traditional form → see 平 at 4291

丙

4302

■4-5-1

▸**THIRD**

ヘイ ひのえ

1	Nonstandard	U4E19
一	S5-1-4	F0000

traditional form → see 丙 at 4290

册

4303

■4-5-1

▸**COUNTER FOR BOOKS**

サツ サク

13	Nonstandard	U518C
冂	S5-2-3	F0000

alternative form → see 冊 at 4295

牙

4304

■4-5-1

▸**FANG**

ガ ゲ きば ㊔ かび

92	Nonstandard	U7259
牙	S5-5-0	F0000

alternative form → see 牙 at 4243

radical variant → see 牙 at 4243

田

■4-5-1

incorrect classification

➡ see □3-3-2: 囗 at 3775

互

■4-5-1

incorrect stroke-count

➡ see ■4-4-1 at 4245

丞

■4-5-1

incorrect classification/ stroke-count

➡ see ⬒2-5-1: 氶 at 3146

民

■4-5-1

incorrect classification

➡ see □3-3-2: 尸 at 3770

目

■4-5-1

incorrect classification

➡ see □3-3-2: 囗 at 3777

冬

■4-5-1

incorrect classification

➡ see ⬒2-3-2: 夂 at 2679

用

■4-5-1

incorrect classification

➡ see □3-2-3: 冂 at 3694

両

■4-5-1

incorrect stroke-count

➡ see ■4-6-1 at 4336

四 罒

■4-5-1

incorrect classification

➡ see □3-3-2: 囗 at 3778

白

4305

■4-5-2

▸**WHITE**

ハク ビャク しろ しら- しろ(い)

Ⓒ 白 bái

106	Jōyō-1	U767D
白	S5-5-0	F0196

1 2 3 4 5

RADICAL

shiro 'white' (的 百 皇), used in characters related to white, clarity or stating

COMPOUNDS

❶ⓐ [also prefix] **WHITE**

ⓑ WHITEn, become white

a 白人 はくじん white man, Caucasian
白鳥 はくちょう swan
白書 はくしょ white paper [book]
白色 はくしょく white
白墨 はくぼく chalk
白衣 はくい(=びゃくえ) white robe [dress]; white coat
白蓮 びゃくれん white lotus
白血球 はっけっきゅう leucocyte
白線 はくせん white line; warning line (on station platform)

b 漂白する ひょうはくする bleach, decolor

❷ (not written or printed upon) **WHITE, blank**

白紙 はくし blank sheet, flyleaf; clean slate
白票 はくひょう blank ballot
白痴 はくち idiocy, idiot
白文 はくぶん unpunctuated Chinese text
空白 くうはく blank, empty space; void, vacuum

❸ (free from blemish) **WHITE, morally pure, innocent, clean**

潔白な けっぱくな innocent, pure, upright
黒白 こくびゃく right and wrong; black and white

❹ⓐ **clear, bright**
ⓑ **clean, plain, distinct**

a 白熱 はくねつ white heat [glow]; climax
白昼 はくちゅう daytime, broad daylight

b 明白な めいはくな clear, plain, obvious

❺ **state clearly, confess, admit**

白状 はくじょう confession
告白 こくはく confession, admission, declaration
自白 じはく confession

❻ speech, words, one's line

科白 かはく(=せりふ) speech, words (in a play); one's remarks
独白 どくはく monologue, soliloquy

❼ Belgium

日白 にっぱく Japan and Belgium

❽ unclassified compounds

白寿 はくじゅ 99 years old, one's 99th birthday

INDEPENDENT

【はく 白】**WHITE**, whiteness; Belgium

KUN

【しろ 白】[also prefix] **WHITE; white pieces (of a chess or go game); innocence**

白黒 しろくろ black and white; right or wrong
白地 しろじ white (back)ground
白金 しろがね [usu. 銀] silver; silver coin
白鉢巻 しろはちまき white headband
白の帽子 しろのぼうし white hat
白バイ しろばい white police motorcycle; motorcycle policeman
白だと判る しろだとわかる be found innocent
真っ白 まっしろ pure [immaculate] white
色白の いろじろの fair, light-complexioned

【しら- 白-】**WHITE**

白む しらむ grow light, turn gray; (of the atmosphere) become chilled
白髪 しらが white [gray] hair

【しろい 白い】**WHITE; gray (hair); blank, white**

白い物 しろいもの something white; snow; gray hair
白いままの紙 しろいままのかみ blank [unwritten] paper
白さ しろさ whiteness
青白い あおじろい pale, pallid
面白い おもしろい interesting, amusing, pleasant

SPECIAL READINGS

白粉▲ おしろい (face) powder

SYNONYMS

❶ⓐ **white colors**

白 WHITE → 4305
皓 BRIGHT WHITE → 1513
銀 SILVER → 2156

❷ **emptiness and nothing**

空 EMPTY → 2767
白 WHITE (blank) → 4305
虚 VOID → 4017
無 NOTHING → 2648

❼ **European countries**

英 ENGLAND → 2782
独 GERMANY → 0471
仏 FRANCE → 0020
伊 ITALY → 0052
葡 PORTUGAL → 2902
西 Spain → 4333
蘭 the Netherlands → 3031
希 Greece → 2543
露 Russia → 3495
白 Belgium → 4305

HOMOPHONES

しろがね

銀 SILVER → 2156
白金 → 4305, 2552

COMPOUND FORMATION

❶【白寿 はくじゅ】

白寿 '99 years old, etc.' refers to the celebration (寿) of one's 99th (白 ❽) birthday. 白 denotes 99 since it consists of 百 'one hundred' minus 一 'one'.

❷【面白い おもしろい】

面白い 'interesting, amusing, pleasant' is said to have originally expressed a state of brightness (白 ❹ⓐ) in front of one's face (面) or eyes. The idea is that when all is bright and rosy, things become interesting.

NOTE

➡ see USAGE note at 金 2552

甘

▶SWEET

カン あま(い) あま(える) あま(やかす) うま(い)▲

4306

■4-5-2

Ⓒ 甘 gān

99	Jōyō	U7518
甘	S5-5-0	F1045

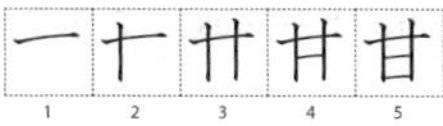

RADICAL

amai 'sweet' (甚 甜×), used in characters related to sweetness

COMPOUNDS

❶ (of sugary taste) **SWEET**

甘味料 かんみりょう sweetener
甘薯× かんしょ sweet potato
甘露 かんろ nectar, honeydew
甘蔗× かんしょ sugar cane
甘酸 かんさん sweet and bitter; pain and pleasure

❷ (pleasing to the feelings) **SWEET**, pleasant, satisfying

甘言 かんげん sweet words, flattery
甘美な かんびな sweet (dream or music)
甘夢 かんむ sweet [pleasant] dreams
甘心 かんしん satisfaction

❸ be resigned to, submit tamely

甘受する かんじゅする submit to, put up with

KUN

【あまい 甘い】

①ⓐ **SWEET, sugary**
ⓑ **SWEET** [honeyed] (words)

a 甘味 あまみ sweetness, sugary taste
甘栗 あまぐり broiled sweet chestnuts
甘口の あまくちの sweet (wine), mild (tobacco)

②ⓐ **indulgent, lenient, generous**
ⓑ **overoptimistic, easygoing**
ⓒ soft, mild, loose

a 甘んじる あまんじる be resigned to (one's fate), be contented [satisfied] with (one's lot)
子供に甘い こどもにあまい be indulgent to (one's) children

③ sentimental

甘い小説 あまいしょうせつ sentimental novel

【あまえる 甘える】play the baby (to), be coquettish; fawn on (a person); presume upon (another's love); take advantage of

甘え あまえ *amae*, dependence
甘えた調子で あまえたちょうしで in a coquettish tone
甘えっ子 あまえっこ spoilt child

【あまやかす 甘やかす】be indulgent to, spoil, pamper

甘やかして育てる あまやかしてそだてる bring up indulgently

【うまい 甘い】 [also 旨い] delicious, tasty; **SWEET**

甘さ うまさ deliciousness, relish
甘い料理 うまいりょうり tasty dish

SYNONYMS

❶ **tastes**

甘 SWEET → 4306
苦 BITTER → 2789
辛 PUNGENT → 2531
辣 PUNGENT → 1965
酸 sour → 1968
渋い ASTRINGENT → 0625
鹹 SALTY → 2366

【あまい】

②ⓐ **tolerant**

寛 LENIENT → 2922
甘い indulgent → 4306

HOMOPHONES

うまい

旨い → 2516
巧い → 0219
上手い → 4212, 4267

NOTE

➡ see USAGE note at 旨 2516

丘

▶HILL

キュウ おか

4307

■4-5-2

Ⓒ 丘 qiū

1	Jōyō	U4E18
一	S5-1-4	F1399

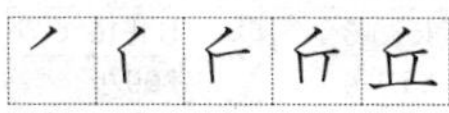

COMPOUNDS

❶ [original meaning] **HILL**

丘陵 きゅうりょう hill, hillock
砂丘 さきゅう sand dune, sand hill
段丘 だんきゅう terrace, bench (in geography)
円丘 えんきゅう knoll
火口丘 かこうきゅう volcanic cone

❷ [rare] grave mound

墳丘 ふんきゅう grave mound, tumulus

KUN

【おか 丘】 [sometimes also 岡] **HILL, hillock, mound**

丘辺 おかべ vicinity of a hill

白甘丘【世】生出由世包圭臼立主

SYNONYMS

❶ **hills**

丘 HILL → 4307
畝 RIDGE → 1857
岡 HILL → 3719
台 heights → 2498
坂 SLOPE → 0275
阪 slope → 0321
塚 MOUND → 0675
阜 MOUND → 3254
陵 high mound → 0660
稜 RIDGE → 1545

USAGE

【おか】

丘
[sometimes also 岡] hill, hillock, mound

岡
① [usu. 丘] hill, hillock, mound
② [sometimes also 傍-] [in compounds] outsider, third party, bystander

陸
land, shore

傍-
[usu. 岡] outsider, third party, bystander

★丘 and 岡 have the same meaning. The former is used in both common nouns and place names, while the latter is used chiefly in the writing of proper names.

HOMOPHONES

おか

岡 HILL → 3719
陸 LAND → 0659
傍 BESIDE → 0166

世

▸**WORLD**
▸**AGE**
セイ せ よ

4308
Ⓝ 世◇ 卋◇ Ⓒ 世 shì

■4-5-2

1	Jōyō-3	U4E16
一	S5-1-4	F0070

一 十 卄 廿 世
1 2 3 4 5

COMPOUNDS

❶ⓐ (human society) **WORLD, society, community, public**
ⓑ **WORLDly, earthly, public, popular**

a 世間 せけん world, society; the public, people
世論 せろん(=よろん) public opinion
出世 しゅっせ success in life; promotion
b 世事 せじ worldly affairs
世話 せわ help, aid, good offices; care; everyday affairs
世評 せひょう public opinion; reputation
世俗の せぞくの common, worldly

❷ⓐ (physical world) **WORLD, universe**
ⓑ (spiritual world) this **WORLD**, this life, living, existence

a 世界 せかい world, universe
創世記 そうせいき Genesis
b 世銀(=世界銀行) せぎん(=せかいぎんこう) World Bank
現世 げんせ this world, this life
来世 らいせ future life, world to come

❸ⓐ **AGE, period, century, era, the times**
ⓑ geological epoch

a 世紀 せいき century
中世 ちゅうせい Middle [Medieval] Ages
近世 きんせい modern ages
乱世 らんせい turbulent times
b 洪積世 こうせきせい diluvial epoch

❹ⓐ **generation, family line**
ⓑ of previous generations, hereditary
ⓒ **counter for generations or reign periods**

a 世代 せだい generation
b 世襲 せしゅう heredity, descent
c 二世 にせい second-generation [American-born] Japanese, nisei
ナポレオン三世 なぽれおんさんせい Napoleon III

❺ **used phonetically for *se***

世帯 せたい household, home
仲見世通り なかみせどおり shopping street in the precincts of a shrine [temple]

KUN

【よ 世】

①ⓐ **WORLD, society, public**
ⓑ **this WORLD, life, existence**

a 世の中 よのなか the world, society, life
b この世 このよ this world, present life
あの世 あのよ the other world, world of the dead

② the times, **AGE**

世に遅れる よにおくれる fall behind the times

SYNONYMS

❶ⓐ **society**

社 SOCIETY → 1042
世 WORLD → 4308
公 PUBLIC → 2468

ⓑ **worldly**

世 worldly → 4308
俗 worldly → 0119

❷ⓐ **world**

世 WORLD → 4308
界 WORLD → 3172

❸ⓐ **long time periods**

時 TIME → 1155
代 age → 0034
紀 ERA → 1628
世 AGE → 4308
朝 dynastic period → 2130
期 period → 2139
劫 KALPA → 1435

❹ generation

代 GENERATION → 0034
世 generation → 4308

❺ phonetic [s]/[sh]

沙 phonetic [sha] → 0311
刹 phonetic [setsu] → 1620
遮 phonetic [sha] → 3916
叉 phonetic [sha] → 4194
世 phonetic [se] → 4308
須 phonetic [shu] → 0700
修 phonetic [shu] → 0138
西 phonetic [su] → 4333
相 phonetic [sō] → 1120
薩 phonetic [satsu] → 3016

USAGE

【よ】

世
①ⓐ world, society, public
ⓑ this world, life, existence
② the times, age

代
① era of rule, age
② reign, rule

★The word よ has a somewhat poetic flavor. Whereas 世 refers to age or times in general, 代 is restricted to a specific era of rule, as under the reign of a particular emperor.

HOMOPHONES

よ 代 SUBSTITUTE → 0034

NOTE

➡ see COMPOUND FORMATION for
世話 せわ → 話 1928
世間 せけん → 間 4122

生

4309
■4-5-2

▶LIFE
▶BE BORN
▶STUDENT

セイ ショウ い(きる) い(かす) い(ける) う(まれる) う(まれ) うまれ う(む) お(う) は(える) は(やす) き なま なま- な(る)▲ な(す)▲ む(す)▲ -う▲ ㊔ いく うぶ お ぶ み ふ たか

Ⓒ 生 shēng

100	Jōyō-1	U751F
生	S5-5-0	F0015

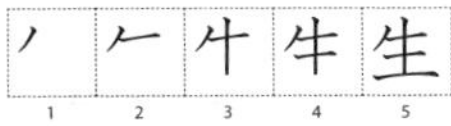

RADICAL

umareru 'birth' (産 甦 甥), used in characters related to birth

COMPOUNDS

❶ⓐ (act of being alive) **LIFE, existence**
ⓑ (interval between birth and death) **LIFEtime, life**

a 生命 せいめい life
生保(=生命保険) せいほ(=せいめいほけん) life insurance
生死 せいし life and death
生涯 しょうがい life, lifetime, career; for life
人生 じんせい human life, life

b 生前 せいぜん during one's lifetime
一生 いっしょう a lifetime
終生 しゅうせい all one's life
余生 よせい one's remaining years
平生は へいぜいは in ordinary days

❷ⓐ (living organisms) **LIFE, living things**
ⓑ bio-, -zoic

a 生物 せいぶつ living thing, life, organism
生理学 せいりがく physiology
生態 せいたい ecology; mode of life
原生動物 げんせいどうぶつ protozoan
幼生 ようせい larva
抗生物質 こうせいぶっしつ antibiotic
殺生 せっしょう destruction of life; cruelty
畜生 ちくしょう beast; Damn it!
写生する しゃせいする sketch [draw] from nature; portray

b 生化学 せいかがく biochemistry
新生代 しんせいだい Cenozoic era

❸ⓐ livelihood, living
ⓑ health, welfare

a 生計 せいけい livelihood, living
生活 せいかつ life, existence; livelihood
生協 せいきょう cooperative association [society]
生業 せいぎょう occupation, calling

b 衛生 えいせい hygiene, sanitation, preservation of health
摂生 せっせい preservation of one's health
厚生 こうせい public welfare, health promotion
民生 みんせい public welfare, people's livelihood

❹ⓐ (be alive) **live, exist**
ⓑ living, alive
ⓒ lively, vivid, fresh

a 生存する せいぞんする exist, live, survive
生別 せいべつ separation, parting
寄生 きせい parasitism
蘇生 そせい revival, resuscitation

白甘丘世【生】出由册包圭臼立主

野生の やせいの wild, feral
b 生還する せいかんする return alive; *baseball* reach the home plate
生体 せいたい living body, organism
生者 しょうじゃ living things, animate nature
c 生鮮な せいせんな fresh
生彩 せいさい life, vividness
生気 せいき animation, vitality, spirit

❺ [formerly 棲 せい 1246 or 栖 せい 1170] (of animals) (occupy a habitat) inhabit, live
生息する せいそくする inhabit, live
水生の すいせいの aquatic, living in the water
両生類 りょうせいるい Amphibia, amphibian

❻ⓐ **BE BORN**
ⓑ **bear, give birth to**
ⓒ birth
a 生家 せいか house where one was born
生年月日 せいねんがっぴ date of birth
誕生する たんじょうする be born, come into the world
更生する こうせいする be born again, start one's life all over; recycle
再生 さいせい reclamation; regeneration, resuscitation; playback
双生児 そうせいじ twins
往生する おうじょうする pass away; be at a loss
b 生母 せいぼ one's (biological) mother
生殖 せいしょく reproduction, procreation, generation
卵生の らんせいの oviparous
c 生後二週間 せいごにしゅうかん two weeks after one's birth
生滅 しょうめつ birth and death

❼ (bring into existence) **produce, give rise to**
生産 せいさん production
生成する せいせいする create, generate; be created

❽ inborn, natural, innate
生得の しょうとく(=せいとく)の natural, inborn, innate
生得権 せいとくけん one's birthright
生来 せいらい by nature [birth], congenitally

❾ⓐ **raw, uncooked, crude**
ⓑ immature
a 生乳 せいにゅう raw milk
生薬 しょうやく crude drug
生石灰 せいせっかい quicklime, unslaked lime
b 生硬な せいこうな crude, immature, unpolished

❿ⓐ [original meaning] (of plants) **grow**
ⓑ suffix indicating number of years of growth
a 生育する せいいくする grow, vegetate
生長(=成長) せいちょう (physical) growth
自生する じせいする grow wild [naturally]
群生する ぐんせいする grow gregariously [in crowds]
実生 みしょう seedling, plant raised from the seed
晩生植物 ばんせいしょくぶつ slow grower
対生葉 たいせいよう opposite leaves
b 多年生植物 たねんせいしょくぶつ perennial plant

⓫ **occur, happen**
生起する せいきする occur, take place
発生する はっせいする occur, happen; grow, breed

⓬ⓐ [also suffix] **STUDENT, pupil; scholar**
ⓑ person, people
a 生徒 せいと pupil, student
学生 がくせい student
高校生 こうこうせい high school student
同級生 どうきゅうせい classmate
門下生 もんかせい disciple, pupil
教生 きょうせい student teacher
先生 せんせい teacher; doctor
儒生 じゅせい Confucianist, student of Confucianism
b 筆生 ひっせい copyist, amanuensis
衆生 しゅじょう living things; the people

⓭ⓐ [humble] I
ⓑ suffix indicating humility on part of speaker
a 小生 しょうせい I
b 山田生 やまだせい Your humble servant, Yamada

⓮ unclassified compounds
一生懸命(=一所懸命)に いっしょうけんめい(=いっしょけんめい)に for life, with all one's might

INDEPENDENT

【せい 生】**LIFE, living;** [humble] **I**
生を享ける せいをうける be born, live

【しょうじる(=しょうずる) 生じる(=生ずる)】**happen, arise, be produced; produce, create, cause; grow**
変化が生じた へんかがしょうじた Change took place
根を生じる ねをしょうじる put forth roots, take root

KUN

【いきる 生きる】
①ⓐ (be alive) **live, exist**
ⓑ (make a living) **live (on), subsist**
a 生き いき freshness; stet
生き物 いきもの living creature
生き方 いきかた way of life, lifestyle
生き甲斐が有る いきがいがある worthwhile living
生ける屍 いけるしかばね living corpse, living dead
生き字引き いきじびき walking dictionary
長生き ながいき long life, longevity

b 人はパンのみにて生くるに非ず ひとはぱんのみにていくるにあらず Man does not live by bread alone

② [formerly also 活きる] **be enlivened**
生き生きと いきいきと lively, vividly
その一語で文章が生きる そのいちごでぶんしょうがいきる That single word gives life to the style

③ *baseball* be safe
一塁に生きる いちるいにいきる be safe on first base

【いかす 生かす】
①ⓐ **let live, keep alive**
ⓑ **revive; stet**
a あいつは生かして置けない あいつはいかしておけない I can't let him live
b 死者を生かす ししゃをいかす revive the dead

② [formerly also 活かす] make the most of
学問を生かす がくもんをいかす put one's learning to practical use

③ [formerly also 活かす] put **LIFE** [vividness] into, vivify
絵を生かす えをいかす put life into a painting

【いける 生ける】
① [mainly in compounds] keep alive
生け捕る いけどる catch [capture] alive
生け贄× いけにえ victims, sacrifice

② [formerly also 活ける] **arrange (flowers)**
生け花 いけばな flower arrangement

【うまれる 生まれる】
ⓐ (of persons) (come into being) **BE BORN, come into existence**
ⓑ (of things in general) appear, see the light, be a result (of)
a 生まれ付き うまれつき one's nature; by nature
生まれて初めて うまれてはじめて for the first time in one's life
生まれ乍×らの詩人 うまれながらのしじん born poet
彼はアメリカで生まれた かれはあめりかでうまれた He was born in America
貧乏に生まれる びんぼうにうまれる be born poor
持って生まれた もってうまれた natural, inborn, innate
b 同情から愛が生まれた どうじょうからあいがうまれた Sympathy engendered love

【うまれ 生まれ, 生】[also suffix] **birth; origin, lineage**
生まれの良い うまれのよい wellborn, of noble birth
昭和三十二年三月五日生 しょうわさんじゅうにねんさんがついつかうまれ born on March 5, 1957
どちらのお生まれですか どちらのおうまれですか Where do you come from?
良家の生まれである りょうけのうまれである be of good family
ドイツ生まれのユダヤ人 どいつうまれのゆだやじん German Jew

【うむ 生む】
① **have children**
生み うみ production, bringing into the world
生みの親 うみのおや one's real parent; creator
彼女は子供を五人生んだ かのじょはこどもをごにんうんだ She has five children

② **produce, bring forth, give rise to, yield**
生み出す うみだす bring forth, produce, yield

【おう 生う】[in compounds] **grow**
生い茂る おいしげる grow luxuriantly [thickly]
生い立ち おいたち one's upbringing, one's childhood
相生の松 あいおいのまつ twin pines, double pine

【はえる 生える】**grow, spring up; grow (hair or wings), cut (a tooth)**
生え抜きの はえぬきの native-born, trueborn
生え際 はえぎわ borders of the hair, (receding) hairline
芽生える めばえる bud, sprout; begin

【はやす 生やす】**grow (a beard), cultivate**
鬚を生やしている ひげをはやしている have [wear] a beard

【き 生】[also prefix]
ⓐ **pure, genuine**
ⓑ **raw**
a 生で飲む きでのむ drink (whisky) straight
生粋の きっすいの trueborn, pure, genuine
生地 きじ one's true color [character]; (plain) cloth, texture; unglazed pottery
生醤油 きじょうゆ pure soy, raw soy
生一本な きいっぽんな straightforward, honest
生娘 きむすめ virgin, innocent girl
b 生糸 きいと raw silk (thread)
生蠟 きろう crude Japan wax
生紙 きがみ unsized paper

【なま 生】**raw, uncooked, green, fresh, live; impudence, cheek; hard cash; draft beer**
生で食べる なまでたべる eat raw [fresh]
生生しい なまなましい green, fresh, vivid
生の情報 なまのじょうほう firsthand information
生意気な なまいきな impudent, audacious, conceited, affected
生を言うんじゃない なまをいうんじゃない None of your cheek
現生 げんなま real money

【なま- 生-】
①ⓐ **raw, uncooked, green, fresh; crude**
ⓑ [also prefix] **live**
a 生物 なまもの uncooked food; perishables
生水 なまみず unboiled water

b 生身 なまみ living body; raw meat [fish]
生唾 なまつば saliva (in one's mouth)
生ワク なまわく live vaccine
生演奏 なまえんそう live performance
② [also prefix] **imperfect, half-, slight, little**
生焼けの なまやけの half-roasted[-baked], rare
生暖かい なまあたたかい lukewarm, tepid
生温い なまぬるい lukewarm; halfway; halfhearted
生易しい なまやさしい simple, easy
生学問 なまがくもん imperfect [superficial] knowledge
生返事 なまへんじ vague answer, reluctant answer
生欠伸 なまあくび slight yawn

白甘丘世【生】出由冊包圭臼立主

【なる 生る】**bear fruit, fruit**
生り年 なりどし year of large crop
生業 なりわい(=せいぎょう) livelihood; calling, occupation
末生り うらなり fruit grown near the top end of the vine; pale-faced man
鈴生りに生る すずなりになる grow in clusters

【なす 生す】give birth, bear
生さぬ仲の なさぬなかの with no blood relation

【むす 生す】[also 産す] grow
苔生した こけむした moss-grown, mossy

【-う -生】**place overgrown with vegetation**
蓬生 よもぎう area overgrown with weeds, wasteland
浅茅生 あさじう [rare] broad field of sparsely growing cogon grass

SPECIAL READINGS

生憎▲ あいにく unfortunately, unluckily; I am sorry, but…
生絹▲ すずし raw silk goods
芝生 しばふ lawn, turf
弥生 やよい third month (of the lunar calendar), March

SYNONYMS

❶ **life**
生 LIFE →4309
命 LIFE →2553
寿 LONGEVITY →4372

❷ⓐ **animal**
獣 BEAST →2384
畜 LIVESTOCK →2599
生 LIFE →4309
物 living thing →1084

❸ⓑ **healthy**
康 HEALTHY →3877
健 ROBUST →0152
生 health →4309

❹ **live**
活 LIVE →0460
暮らす LIVE (pass one's life) →2971
生 live (be alive) →4309

❺ **reside**
住 LIVE →0072
居 RESIDE →3822
棲 INHABIT (said of animals), live →1246
栖 INHABIT (said of animals), live →1170
生 inhabit →4309
植 colonize →1247

❻ **give birth**
生 BE BORN →4309
誕 BE BORN →1987
産 GIVE BIRTH →4089
娩 GIVE BIRTH →0486
殖 MULTIPLY →1253

❼ **create**
創 CREATE →2283
作 compose →0077
綴 COMPOSE →1746
生 produce →4309
発 START →3174
起 generate →4099

❾ⓐ **new**
新 NEW →2239
鮮 FRESH →2355
生 raw →4309

❿ⓐ **grow**
成 grow up →4352
長 grow (up) →3163
生 grow →4309
育 grow →2544
発 develop →3174
伸 expand →0079
展 UNFOLD →3862

⓬ⓐ **students and followers**
生 STUDENT →4309
卒 graduate student →2549
学 scholar →3162
門 pupil →1100
弟 disciple →2537
徒 FOLLOWER →0499

USAGE

❶【いきる】
生きる
①ⓐ (be alive) live, exist
ⓑ (make a living) live (on), subsist
② [formerly also 活きる] be enlivened
③ *baseball* be safe
活きる
[now usu. 生きる] be enlivened

❷【いかす】
生かす
①ⓐ let live, keep alive
ⓑ revive; stet
② [formerly also 活かす] make the most of
③ [formerly also 活かす] put life [vividness] into, vivify
活かす
[now usu. 生かす]
① make the most of
② put life [vividness] into, vivify
❸【いける】
生ける
① [mainly in compounds] keep alive
② [formerly also 活ける] arrange (flowers)
活ける
[now usu. 生ける] arrange (flowers)
埋ける
bury; bury coals in ashes
❹【むす】
生す
[also 産す] grow
産す
[also 生す] grow
蒸す
① *vt* steam, heat with steam; foment
② *vi* be sultry, be stuffy

HOMOPHONES

いきる 活 ACTIVE →0460
いかす 活 ACTIVE →0460
いける
活 ACTIVE →0460
埋 BURY →0484
うまれる 産 GIVE BIRTH →4089
うむ 産 GIVE BIRTH →4089
うみ 産 GIVE BIRTH →4089
なる
成 FORM →4352
為 DO →4395
なす
成 FORM →4352
為 DO →4395
むす
産 GIVE BIRTH →4089
蒸 STEAM →2936

COMPOUND FORMATION

❶【先生 せんせい】
先生 'teacher; doctor' is a scholar (生 ⓬ⓐ) who studied ahead (先) of others.
❷【一生懸命(=一所懸命) いっしょうけんめい (=いっしょけんめい)】
一生懸命に 'for life, with all one's might', originally written 一所懸命に, is to risk (懸) one's life (命) in protecting a single (一) place (所), i.e., the territory of one's feudal lord. 所 was mistakenly replaced by 生 ⓮, which is more common today.

NOTE

➡ see also USAGE notes at 産 4089 and 成 4352
➡ see COMPOUND FORMATION for 生涯 しょうがい →涯 0623
★ 生 is said to have a total of more than 200 readings, which is more than any other character.

出

4310
■4-5-2

▶GO OUT
▶PUT OUT
シュツ スイ で(る) -で だ(す) -だ(す)
い(でる)▲ い(だす)▲ ㊔ いで いず いずる
Ⓒ 出 chū

17	Jōyō-1	U51FA
凵	S5-2-3	F0006

丨 1 屮 2 屮 3 出 4 出 5

COMPOUNDS

❶ⓐ [original meaning] (of persons) **GO OUT, come out; depart, leave**
ⓑ **cause to GO OUT (on a military expedition), dispatch (troops)**
ⓒ (of things) **come out, issue, flow out**
a 出国する しゅっこくする go out of a country
出発 しゅっぱつ departure, starting
出港する しゅっこうする leave port, set sail
出張する しゅっちょうする travel on official business
出動する しゅつどうする take the field, be dispatched, turn out
脱出する だっしゅつする escape, extricate
外出する がいしゅつする go out
b 出兵する しゅっぺいする dispatch troops
派出所 はしゅつじょ branch office; police box
c 出血する しゅっけつする bleed; hemorrhage
流出する りゅうしゅつする flow out, effuse
❷ⓐ (come into view or existence) **come out, appear, emerge, occur**
ⓑ **come from, originate**
a 出現 しゅつげん appearance, emergence
出火 しゅっか outbreak of fire
神出鬼没の しんしゅつきぼつの appearing and disappearing unexpectedly, elusive
初出 しょしゅつ first appearance
続出する ぞくしゅつする appear in succession
露出 ろしゅつ exposure, disclosure; (photographic) exposure
b 出所 しゅっしょ origin, source; release from prison
出身 しゅっしん coming from; graduate from
出身地 しゅっしんち one's native place

出典 しゅってん source, authority

❸ⓐ **go to, proceed to, come to**
ⓑ **appear, attend, be present at**

a 出漁する しゅつりょうする go (off) fishing
出馬する しゅつばする come forward as a candidate; go in person
出世する しゅっせする succeed in life; be promoted
進出する しんしゅつする advance, go [march] into; debouch

b 出席 しゅっせき attendance, presence
出勤する しゅっきんする attend one's office, go to work
出頭する しゅっとうする attend, present oneself
出演する しゅつえんする appear on stage, perform, play
出場する しゅつじょうする take part, participate
出願する しゅつがんする make an application

❹ cause to move toward or as if toward an outward direction:
ⓐ **PUT OUT, give out, discharge, send out, take out**
ⓑ **put on display, exhibit**

a 出荷する しゅっかする forward, ship, consign
出超 しゅっちょう excess of exports over imports
放出する ほうしゅつする release, discharge, emit
検出する けんしゅつする detect, find
選出する せんしゅつする elect
救出する きゅうしゅつする rescue, relieve, deliver
輸出 ゆしゅつ export
提出する ていしゅつする present, submit, turn in

b 出版する しゅっぱんする publish
出品する しゅっぴんする exhibit, show, display

❺ **expend, spend, pay**
出資する しゅっしする invest, finance
出納 すいとう receipts and expenses, incomings and outgoings
支出 ししゅつ expenditure, disbursement, outgo
歳出 さいしゅつ annual expenditure

❻ (bring into being) **PUT OUT, produce, beget**
出炭 しゅったん coal production
出産 しゅっさん birth, delivery
出生 しゅっしょう birth
産出する さんしゅつする produce, yield
演出する えんしゅつする produce (a play); represent
案出する あんしゅつする think out, contrive, devise, invent

❼ stand out, excel
出色の しゅっしょくの prominent, excellent, outstanding
傑出する けっしゅつする excel, stand out

❽ (of the sun or moon) rise
日出 にっしゅつ sunrise

INDEPENDENT

【しゅつ 出】 origin, birth; abbrev. of 出席 しゅっせき: presence
藤原氏の出 ふじわらしのしゅつ of Fujiwara descent

KUN

【でる 出る】

①ⓐ **GO OUT, come out; leave, go away**
ⓑ **depart, start**
ⓒ (of things) **come out, issue, flow out**

a 出 で coming [going] out; outflow; rising (of the sun or moon); graduate (of); one's turn to appear on stage
出入り でいり going in and out; frequentation, usual visit (as by a merchant); indentations; incomings and outgoings; trouble, fight
出入口 でいりぐち doorway, gateway
出迎え でむかえ meeting (someone at the station), receiving
出会う であう (happen to) meet; transact
出口 でぐち exit; exit ramp
出前 でまえ delivering dishes to order

b 出掛ける でかける go out, set off; be about to go out
良い出足 よいであし good start; good turnout of people

c 水の出が悪い みずのでがわるい The water does not come out well

② go beyond the limit:
ⓐ **stick out, protrude, project**
ⓑ **intrude, interfere**
ⓒ **be more than, exceed**

a 出っ張る でっぱる project, protrude
出っ歯 でっぱ projecting teeth
突き出る つきでる project, stick out, stand out

b 出しゃばる でしゃばる intrude, butt in

c 十年を出ない内に じゅうねんをでないうちに within ten years
抜きん出る ぬきんでる [sometimes also 擢ん出る] excel, stand out, be preeminent
食み出る はみでる protrude; project

③ⓐ (come into view) **come out, appear, emerge, turn up; be revealed; be found;** (of dishes) **be served**
ⓑ **appear (in print), come out; be published**

a 出揃う でそろう appear all together, come out fully
出回る でまわる appear on the market, be moving
お化けが出る おばけがでる A ghost haunts the place
無くした時計が出て来た なくしたとけいがでてきた The lost watch was found
思い出 おもいで recollections, memory, reminiscences
ビフテキが出た びふてきがでた Beefsteak was served

b 新聞に出ている しんぶんにでている It is in the papers

④ⓐ **attend, be present, appear; go to (work)**
ⓑ **take part in, join**

a 出稼ぎする でかせぎする work away from home
会社に出ている かいしゃにでている work for a company

b レースに出る れーすにでる run in a race

⑤ⓐ **go to, proceed to; lead to**
ⓑ **go forth into (the world), enter upon**

a 東京へ出る とうきょうへでる go to Tokyo
この道は海に出る このみちはうみにでる This path leads to the sea

b 世に出る よにでる go out into the world, come to the front
選挙に出る せんきょにでる run for election

⑥ⓐ **come from, originate, arise; graduate**
ⓑ **break out, occur, originate**
ⓒ (results) **come out, work out**

a 出来る できる be made, be completed, come into being; can; be good at (a subject)
出来るだけ できるだけ as much [far] as possible
出来上がり できあがり completion, finish
彼女は京都の出だ かのじょはきょうとのでだ She is from Kyoto
このモーターは百馬力出る このもーたーはひゃくばりきでる This motor has an output of 100 hp
大学を出る だいがくをでる graduate from a university

b 火が出た ひがでた A fire started

⑦ sell
この本は良く出る このほんはよくでる This book is a good seller

⑧ assume [take] (an attitude)
出方 でかた one's attitude, move; theater attendant, usher

⑨ draw, infuse (properly)
このティーバッグは良く出る このてぃーばっぐはよくでる This tea bag draws well

⑩ **unclassified compounds**
出鱈×目な でたらめな random, haphazard
目出度い(=芽出度い) めでたい happy, propitious, joyous

【-で -出】

① [suffix] **graduate (of)**
大学出の人 だいがくでのひと university graduate

② substance
使い出が有る つかいでがある bear long use

【だす 出す】

①ⓐ **PUT OUT, push [thrust] out, send out, hold out**
ⓑ **take out, bring out**

a 舌を出す したをだす put out one's tongue
芽を出す めをだす put forth buds, sprout
舟を出す ふねをだす put [take] out a boat
手を出す てをだす reach out one's hand, turn one's hand to
旗を出す はたをだす hang out a flag
手紙を出す てがみをだす mail a letter

b 財布を出す さいふをだす draw [take] out one's purse

②ⓐ (bring into being) **PUT OUT, produce, yield**
ⓑ (issue printed material) **PUT OUT, publish; print, insert**

a 生み出す うみだす bring forth, produce, yield
作り出す つくりだす make, turn out, create
五十キロを出す ごじっきろをだす drive 50 kph

b 辞書を出す じしょをだす publish a dictionary

③ **pay, put up, invest**
資金を出す しきんをだす furnish with funds

④ⓐ **PUT OUT (a dish), serve**
ⓑ **present, submit; tender**

a 朝食を出す ちょうしょくをだす serve breakfast

b レポートを出す れぽーとをだす turn in a report

⑤ⓐ **expose, lay bare**
ⓑ **put on display, exhibit**

a 背中を出す せなかをだす bare one's back

b 展覧会に出す てんらんかいにだす send to an exhibition
名前を出したくない なまえをだしたくない I want to remain anonymous

⑥ **utter**
大声を出す おおごえをだす shout, raise one's voice

【-だす -出す】 [verbal suffix]

① proceed or cause to proceed outward:
ⓐ **GO OUT, come out; put out, send out; jut out**
ⓑ come out, appear

a 飛び出す とびだす fly out, run out, jump out; project
乗り出す のりだす lean forward; start, set out; embark on, launch into
送り出す おくりだす send out, forward; show (a person) out
売り出す うりだす put on sale; rise in fame
取り出す とりだす take out, pick out, extract
持ち出す もちだす take out, carry out; run away with; advance (one's opinion); begin to have
引き出し ひきだし drawer; withdrawal (of money)
思い出す おもいだす recollect, recall, remember
張り出す はりだす project, jut out
食み出す はみだす protrude; project

b 浮き出す うきだす come up to the surface, loom

② **begin to do, start doing**
勉強し出す べんきょうしだす begin to study
雨が降り出した あめがふりだした It began to rain
逃げ出す にげだす make a break, run off, make off

打ち出す うちだす set out [forth], work out, hammer out; strike out, emboss; announce

【いでる 出でる】literary form of 出る でる

出で立ち いでたち dress, outfit

出で湯 いでゆ hot spring

お出で おいで being; coming; going; Come here!

日出ずる国 ひいずるくに Land of the Rising Sun

届け出でる とどけいでる submit notice, give notice

申し出で もうしいで offer, proposal, application

【いだす 出だす】literary form of 出す だす

見出だす みいだす find out, discover

SYNONYMS

❶&【でる】① leave and set forth

去 GO AWAY → 2678

離 leave → 2364

発 START → 3174

出 GO OUT → 4310

退 RETREAT → 3838

撤 WITHDRAW → 0912

❷ⓐ appear

現 APPEAR → 1218

出 come out → 4310

顕 MANIFEST → 2274

❸ⓐ go and come

行 GO → 0246

徠 COME → 0576

往 GO ON → 0348

出 go to → 4310

参 go somewhere → 2563

来 COME → 4366

通 go to and from → 3855

向 head toward → 3790

赴 PROCEED TO → 4095

嚮 GO TOWARD → 3610

ⓑ attend

臨 BE PRESENT AT → 2059

登 attend → 3208

出 appear → 4310

❹ⓐ emit

出 PUT OUT → 4310

発 EMIT → 3174

放 radiate → 1058

排 DISCHARGE → 0593

射 SHOOT → 1850

噴 SPOUT → 0879

吐 SPEW → 0235

湧 WELL UP → 0749

【でる】

②ⓐ protrude and protruding

突 protruding → 2772

凸 CONVEX → 4298

隆 protuberant → 0661

起 RISE → 4099

出る stick out → 4310

【-だす】

② begin

始 BEGIN → 0335

-出す begin to do → 4310

-掛ける start doing → 0596

発 START → 3174

起 start → 4099

就 SET ABOUT → 2129

開 OPEN → 4121

創 initiate → 2283

肇 ORIGINATE → 3474

HOMOPHONES

ぬきんでる

擢 SINGLE OUT → 0973

抜きん出る → 0290, 4310

NOTE

➡ see COMPOUND FORMATION for 出張 しゅっちょう → 張 0573

由

4311

■4-5-2

▸REASON

ユ ユウ ユイ よし よ(る)▴

Ⓒ 由 yóu

102	Jōyō-3	U7531
田	S5-5-0	F0286

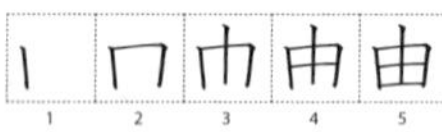

COMPOUNDS

❶ⓐ REASON (for what has happened), cause, origin, derivation

ⓑ be caused by, originate in, derive from, be based on

a 由来 ゆらい origin, source, cause; history

由緒 ゆいしょ history, lineage

理由 りゆう reason, cause, ground

事由 じゆう reason, cause, ground

来由 らいゆ(=らいゆう) cause, origin

b 自由 じゆう freedom

❷ pass through

経由 けいゆ via, through

KUN

【よし 由】**REASON, ground, cause; means, way; effect, point, purport**

由無き よしなき senseless, meaningless, absurd

...の由です ...のよしです hear that.../It is said that...

【よる 由る】[now usu. 因る] be caused by, be due to

不注意に由る ふちゅういによる be due to carelessness

SYNONYMS

❶ⓐ cause and reason
因 CAUSE →3792
由 REASON →4311
為 because →4395
故 reason →1466
訳 reason →1865

HOMOPHONES

よる
因 CAUSE →3792
依 DEPEND ON →0093
拠 GROUNDS →0369
寄 CONTRIBUTE →2856

COMPOUND FORMATION

【自由 じゆう】
自由 'freedom' is a state resulting from (由 ❶ⓑ) following one's own heart or free will (自).

NOTE

➡ see USAGE note at 因 3792

丗

4312
■4-5-2

▶**WORLD**
▶**AGE**
セイ セ よ

1 一	Nonstandard S5-1-4	U4E17 F0000

alternative form →see 世 at 4308

包
■4-5-2

incorrect classification
➡ see □3-2-3: 勹 at 3684

圭
■4-5-2

incorrect classification/ stroke-count
➡ see ▀2-3-3: 土 at 2688

臼
■4-5-2

incorrect stroke-count
➡ see ■4-6-2 at 4341

立
■4-5-2

incorrect classification
➡ see ▀2-2-3: 亠 at 2486

主
■4-5-2

incorrect classification
➡ see ▀2-1-4: 丶 at 2437

半

4313
■4-5-3

▶**HALF**
ハン なか(ば)
Ⓝ 半 Ⓒ 半 bàn

24 十	Jōyō-2 S5-2-3	U534A F0250

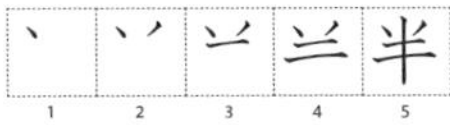

COMPOUNDS

❶ⓐ [also suffix] **HALF, ...and a half**
ⓑ [also prefix] **HALF (of), semi-, hemi-, demi-, bi-**
ⓒ split in **HALF**, halve

a 半分 はんぶん half
前半 ぜんはん(=ぜんぱん) first half
夜半 やはん midnight
大半 たいはん the greater part, majority
二年半 にねんはん two years and a half

b 半面 はんめん profile; one side
半額 はんがく half price, half amount
半球 はんきゅう hemisphere
半径 はんけい radius, semidiameter
半世紀 はんせいき half a century
半袖 はんそで short-sleeved shirt
半日 はんにち half a day
半月 はんつき half a month
半減 はんげん 50 percent reduction
半身 はんしん half the body, one side of the body
半数 はんすう half the number

c 折半 せっぱん halving

❷ⓐ **HALFway, half-done, uncompleted**
ⓑ [also prefix] (not fully) **semi-, quasi-, partly**

a 半端な はんぱな fragmentary, odd; half-done, incomplete; noncommittal
半途 はんと halfway, unfinished
半島 はんとう peninsula
半熟の はんじゅくの half-boiled; half ripe

b 半製品 はんせいひん semimanufactured goods
半導体 はんどうたい semiconductor
半永久的 はんえいきゅうてき semipermanent

❸ odd number
丁半 ちょうはん odd and even (numbers); gambling

INDEPENDENT

【はん 半】odd number

KUN

【なかば 半ば】**HALF; semi; middle, halfway; in part, partially**
半ば眠っている なかばねむっている half asleep
半ばまぐれで なかばまぐれで partly due to luck
月半ばに つきなかばに in the middle of the month

SYNONYMS

❷ⓑ subordinate
副 SECONDARY →2230
次 secondary →0058
従 subordinate →0498
亜 SUB- →4354
準 QUASI- →3541

半 semi- →4313
准 JUNIOR →0143
助 assistant →1440

本

▶BASIS
▶BOOK
▶THIS

4314
4-5-3

ホン もと 名 はじめ

N 夲 C 本 běn

75	Jōyō-1	U672C
木	S5-4-1	F0007

一 十 才 木 本
1 2 3 4 5

COMPOUNDS

1 a BASIS, base, foundation
b (basic funds) **principal, capital**

a 本拠 ほんきょ base, stronghold, headquarters
本位 ほんい (monetary) standard; standard, basis; original standing
基本 きほん basis, foundation
国本 こくほん foundation of a country
抜本的な ばっぽんてきな radical, drastic
根本 こんぽん basis, foundation; origin, source
農本主義 のうほんしゅぎ "agriculture-first" principle
b 資本 しほん funds, capital
元本 がんぽん capital, principal

2 a origin, source, root, beginning
b original, inherent, inborn
c originally, from the start

a 本源 ほんげん source, origin; principle
本初 ほんしょ origin, beginning, start
日本 にほん(=にっぽん) Japan
b 本質 ほんしつ essence, reality
本能 ほんのう instinct
本国 ほんごく one's native country, fatherland
本場 ほんば home, habitat, center
c 本来 ほんらい originally, essentially, naturally

3 the original, model, sample

見本 みほん sample, specimen
手本 てほん model, example, pattern
写本 しゃほん manuscript, written copy

4 *baseball* home base, home plate

本盗 ほんとう home steal
三本間 さんぼんかん between third and home base

5 a [also suffix] (source of knowledge) **BOOK, volume, work, magazine**
b playbook, script

a 本屋 ほんや bookstore; bookseller
読本 とくほん reader, reading book
絵本 えほん picture book
ビニ本 びにぼん vinyl-covered porno magazine
単行本 たんこうぼん separate volume, independent volume
b 脚本 きゃくほん script, playbook, drama, scenario
台本 だいほん playbook, script, scenario

6 [also prefix] **THIS, the same, the present, in question**

本日 ほんじつ today
本年 ほんねん this year
本書 ほんしょ this book
本紙 ほんし this newspaper
本人 ほんにん the person himself, the said person
本年度 ほんねんど the current fiscal year

7 [also prefix] **head, main, principal**

本部 ほんぶ head office, headquarters, administrative building
本店 ほんてん head [main] office [store]
本社 ほんしゃ head office, this office; head shrine, this shrine
本土 ほんど mainland; the country proper
本予算 ほんよさん main budget
本文 ほんぶん(=ほんもん) (main part of a text) text, body; this sentence [passage, article]
本線 ほんせん main line, trunk line

8 a real, true, genuine
b [also prefix] **regular, proper, formal, legal, full-fledged**

a 本体 ほんたい substance, thing itself; object of worship; main part
本当の ほんとうの true, real, genuine
本当に ほんとうに really, truly, indeed
本物 ほんもの real thing [stuff], genuine article; expert performance
本名 ほんみょう one's real name
本心 ほんしん one's true mind, one's real intention; one's conscience
b 本格 ほんかく fundamental rules, propriety
本番 ほんばん acting for the audience, take, going on the air
本会議 ほんかいぎ plenary session, regular session

9 counter for:
a cylindrical objects, as bottles, pencils, etc.
b rounds or points of a match (as of karate)
c movies
d *baseball* safety hits

a 八本の鉛筆 はっぽんのえんぴつ eight pencils
ビール二本 びーるにほん two bottles of beer
b 一本取る いっぽんとる gain a point; beat, upset
c 二本立ての映画 にほんだてのえいが double feature movie

10 a [original meaning] root
b plant

a 一年生草本 いちねんせいそうほん annual herb

INDEPENDENT

【ほん 本】**BOOK, volume, work, reading magazine; playbook, script;** abbrev. of 本塁打 ほんるいだ: **home run**

本を出す ほんをだす publish a book

【ほんの 本の】mere, slight; just, but, only

本の推測に過ぎない ほんのすいそくにすぎない It's mere guesswork

本の少し ほんのすこし just a little

本の五分 ほんのごふん just five minutes

KUN

【もと 本】

① (the most important thing) **BASIS, essential thing, principle**

国の本 くにのもと foundation of the country, national principles

②ⓐ root (of a tree)

ⓑ **counter for plants with roots**

a 木の本に きのもとに at the root of a tree

b 一本の草 ひともとのくさ a blade of grass

③ first half of a tanka poem

SYNONYMS

❶ⓐ basis

基 BASE → 3312
本 BASIS → 4314
素 ELEMENT → 3108
礎 foundation → 1595
底 BOTTOM → 3827
根 ROOT → 1167
拠 GROUNDS → 0369

❷ⓐ beginnings

緒 OUTSET → 1742
序 INTRODUCTORY PART → 3803
端 start → 1564
始 beginning → 0335
初 beginning → 1433
元 ORIGIN → 2428
本 origin → 4314
根 ROOT → 1167
源 SOURCE → 0806

ⓑ original

素 primary → 3108
原 ORIGINAL → 3733
本 original → 4314
初 FIRST → 1433

❺ⓐ books

本 BOOK → 4314
典 STANDARD WORK → 3253
経 religious classic → 1687
書 BOOK → 3292
冊 bound book → 4295
籍 books → 3394
著 literary work → 2869
巻 VOLUME → 3273
編 piece of writing → 1755
篇 PIECE OF WRITING → 3361
鑑 REFERENCE VOLUME → 2226

❻ this and that

本 THIS → 4314
爾 THAT → 4407
其れ THAT → 3255
彼 that → 0346
今 THIS (week, etc.) → 2464
当 THE PRESENT → 2701
該 the said → 1916
同 the same → 3707
之 this → 4228
是 this → 3090
此 THIS → 1017
斯 THIS → 2140

❼ main

主 MAIN → 2437
正 chief → 4296
本 head → 4314
親- PARENT → 2264
首 leading → 2818

❽ⓐ true

真 TRUE → 2616
洵 TRULY → 0458
実 REAL → 2765
本 real → 4314
正 genuine → 4296
現 ACTUAL → 1218

ⓑ regular

正 regular → 4296
本 regular → 4314

❾ⓐ counters for long objects

本 counter for cylindrical objects → 4314
筋 counter for slender objects → 3319
竿 counter for poles or rods → 3259
挺 COUNTER FOR LONG SOLID OBJECTS → 0512

HOMOPHONES

もと

元 ORIGIN → 2428
基 BASE → 3312
下 DOWN → 4186
素 ELEMENT → 3108
許 PERMIT → 1862

COMPOUND FORMATION

【日本 にほん(=にっぽん)】

日本 'Japan' is the source (本 ❷ⓐ) of the sun (日)—often expressed in the form "Land of the Rising Sun."

NOTE

➡ see USAGE note at 元 2428

禾

4315
■4-5-3

▶CEREAL
カ
Ⓒ 禾 hé

115	Names	U79BE
禾	S5-5-0	F0000

RADICAL

nogi 'growing grain' (秀 穀 穎), used in characters related to grains or rice plants

Left variant: 禾× *nogihen* (私 税 科)

COMPOUNDS

ⓐ **CEREAL, grain**
ⓑ [archaic] rice; foxtail millet

a 禾本科 かほんか *Gramineae*
禾穀類 かこくるい cereal crops

SPECIAL READINGS

禾偏(=ノ木偏) のぎへん *nogihen*, 'growing grain' radical

SYNONYMS

● **cereal**
穀 CEREAL → 2294
禾 CEREAL → 4315
粉 flour → 1643

乎

4316
■4-5-3

▶MODIFIER FORMING SUFFIX
コ ヲ か
Ⓒ 乎 hū

4	Names	U4E4E
丿	S5-1-4	F2866

COMPOUNDS

❶ [now also 固 こ 3830] **MODIFIER FORMING SUFFIX**
断乎たる だんこたる firm, conclusive, determined
確乎たる かっこたる firm, sure, resolute
醇乎たる じゅんこたる sheer, pure

❷ [now usu. を] objective case particle
乎古止点 をことてん aid marks for construing classical Chinese
弖×爾乎波(=天爾乎波) てにをは particles, postpositions (i.e., て, に, を, は)

KUN

【か 乎】[formerly also 耶, now always か] interrogative particle
管仲は倹なる乎 かんちゅうはけんなるか Is Guan Zhong thrifty?

SPECIAL READINGS

嗟×乎(=於乎、嗚×呼) ああ ah!, oh!; hey; yeah, OK

SYNONYMS

❶ **modifier suffixes**
然 MODIFIER FORMING SUFFIX → 3456
乎 MODIFIER FORMING SUFFIX → 4316
如 modifier suffix → 0239
爾 adjective suffix → 4407
的 ADJECTIVAL SUFFIX → 1444

HOMOPHONES

か 耶 INTERROGATIVE PARTICLE → 1635

NOTE

➡ see USAGE note at 耶 1635
★ do not confuse with 平 FLAT → 4291

末

4317
■4-5-3

▶LAST PART
マツ バツ すえ
Ⓒ 末 mò

75	Jōyō-4	U672B
木	S5-4-1	F0539

1 2 3 4 5

COMPOUNDS

❶ **LAST PART, last stage, termination, end**
末尾 まつび end, close
年末 ねんまつ end of year
期末 きまつ end of term
週末 しゅうまつ weekend
結末 けつまつ termination, end, close, conclusion
始末 しまつ management, dealing, disposal; circumstances; result, outcome

❷ⓐ **last in time, terminal, final**
ⓑ (relating to the terminal stage) last (days), closing (years)
ⓒ **last (child), youngest**

a 末日 まつじつ last day
末期 まっき closing years, final stage
末期的 まっきてき decadent; terminal (patient)
末葉 まつよう end [close] of an epoch; descendant
末期 まつご hour of death, one's last moments
末路 まつろ last days; fate

b 末世 まっせ these latter days, degenerate [corrupt] age

c 末弟 まってい(=ばってい) youngest brother
末子 まっし(=ばっし) youngest child

❸ posterity, descendants
末裔× まつえい descendant, offspring
末代 まつだい all generations, all ages to come

❹ⓐ **last in importance, trivial, insignificant**
ⓑ last in place, subordinate, secondary

a 末節 まっせつ minor details, nonessentials
粗末な そまつな coarse, crude, inferior, humble

本末 ほんまつ root and branch, means and end
b 末席 まっせき lowest seat
末寺 まつじ secondary temple
末輩 まっぱい underling, rank and file

❺ end, tip
末端 まったん end, tip, termination
末梢 まっしょう tip, end; tip of a twig; *anat* periphery
端末 たんまつ terminal

❻ⓐ powder
ⓑ suffix after names of powders
a 粉末 ふんまつ powder
b 硼×酸末 ほうさんまつ borax powder

KUN

【すえ 末】LAST PART, last stage, termination, end; last (child), youngest; descendant, offspring; trifles, trivialities; lower [outer] end, bounds; future
末っ子 すえっこ youngest child
末の問題 すえのもんだい a mere trifle
末広がりの すえひろがりの widening toward the end
末頼もしい すえたのもしい promising (future)
三月の末 さんがつのすえ end of March
議論の末に ぎろんのすえに after a heated discussion
平家の末 へいけのすえ descendant of the Taira family
場末 ばすえ squalid outskirts

SYNONYMS

❶ ends
末 LAST PART → 4317
終 END → 1692
畢 END → 3194
尾 end → 3799
局 close → 3800

❷ⓐ last
末 last in time → 4317
終 last → 1692

❸ descendant
孫 GRANDCHILD, descendant → 0492
胤 PROGENY → 0017
末 posterity → 4317

❹ⓐ unimportant
細 MINUTE → 1689
微 SLIGHT → 0788
小 SMALL → 0007
末 last in importance → 4317

❺ extremity
端 END → 1564
末 end → 4317
梢 tip → 1208
先 point → 3046
尖 POINT → 2700
鋒 POINT OF A BLADE → 2172

❻ powder
粉 POWDER → 1643
末 powder → 4317

NOTE

➡ see COMPOUND FORMATION for 始末 しまつ → 始 0335
★ do not confuse with 未 NOT YET → 4318

未

4318

■4-5-3

▶NOT YET

ミ ビ▲ いま(だ)▲ ま(だ)▲ ひつじ▲

Ⓒ 未 wèi

75	Jōyō-4	U672A
木	S5-4-1	F0565

一 二 キ 才 未 (1 2 3 4 5)

COMPOUNDS

❶ [also prefix] **NOT YET, un- (as in *unpublished*)**
未満 みまん less than
未来 みらい future
未練 みれん lingering affection, reluctance to give up
未完成 みかんせい incompletion
未知の みちの unknown
未刊の みかんの unpublished
未定の みていの undecided, pending
未払いの みはらいの unpaid
未婚の みこんの unmarried
未成年の みせいねんの minor, underage
未開の みかいの primitive, uncivilized; savage
未然に みぜんに before it happens, beforehand, previously
前代未聞の ぜんだいみもんの unheard-of, unprecedented

❷ *Buddhism* the world to come, future existence
過現未 かげんみ past, present and future, three temporal states of existence

❸ eighth sign of the Oriental zodiac: the Ram—(time) 1-3 p.m., (direction) SSW, (season) June (of the lunar calendar) (→see APPENDIX 8)
癸×未 きび 20th of the sexagenary cycle

KUN

【いまだ 未だ】yet, as yet, never; up to now
未だ嘗て無い偉大な人 いまだかつてないいだいなひと the greatest man that ever lived

【まだ 未だ】(not) **yet, still; more, besides**
彼は未だ来ていない かれはまだきていない He has not come yet

【ひつじ 未】 eighth sign of the Oriental zodiac: the Ram (→❸)

半 本 禾 乎 末 未 【申】 半 氷 氺 尓 册

SYNONYMS

❶ terms of negation

不 NOT (negation) → 4242
非 IS NOT (contrariety) → 1101
無 WITHOUT (nonexistence) → 2648
没 lacking in → 0305
欠 LACK → 2481
否 OR NOT → 3058
未 NOT YET → 4318
莫 NOT → 2839
勿 DO NOT → 3661

❶ still

未 NOT YET → 4318
尚 STILL → 2774

❸ sheep

羊 SHEEP → 2708
未 the Ram → 4318

HOMOPHONES

ひつじ 羊 SHEEP → 2708

NOTE

➡ see USAGE notes at 不 4242 and 羊 2708
➡ see COMPOUND FORMATION for 未練 みれん → 練 1738
★ do not confuse with 末 LAST PART → 4317

申

4319

■4-5-3

▸**REPORT**
▸**SPEAK HUMBLY**
シン もう(す) もう(し)- さる▲ ㊔ のぶ

Ⓒ 申 shēn

102	Jōyō-3	U7533
田	S5-5-0	F0489

1 2 3 4 5

COMPOUNDS

❶ REPORT (to a superior), state, submit a report

申告 しんこく report, statement, notification
上申する じょうしんする report (to a superior official)
答申する とうしんする submit a report [reply]
内申 ないしん unofficial report
追申 ついしん [usu. 追伸] postscript

❷ apply, appeal

申請 しんせい application, petition, request

❸ ninth sign of the Oriental zodiac: **the Monkey**—(time) 3-5 p.m., (direction) WSW, (season) July (of the lunar calendar) (→ see APPENDIX 8)

庚申 こうしん 57th of the sexagenary cycle

KUN

【もうす 申す】[humble]

①ⓐ **SPEAK HUMBLY, say, tell, speak of, talk about**
ⓑ **state humbly, declare, affirm, assert**

a 主人もそう申しております しゅじんもそうもうしております My husband also says so
b 申し述べる もうしのべる state, mention, tell
申し訳 もうしわけ excuse, apology, explanation
申し訳無い もうしわけない I am sorry/Excuse me
申し訳有りません もうしわけありません I am very sorry/Please excuse me
申し分の無い もうしぶんのない perfect, impeccable
申し上げる もうしあげる tell, say, speak humbly; (have the honor to) do

② call, name; express (in a foreign language)

私は荒木一郎と申します わたくしはあらきいちろうともうします My name is Ichiro Araki

③ (have the honor to) do

私が御案内申し上げます わたくしがごあんないもうしあげます I will show you the way

【もうし- 申し-】 **apply, appeal**

申し込む もうしこむ apply, make an application; make a proposal
申し込み もうしこみ application; proposal, request
申し出る もうしでる offer; propose; apply; report
申し子 もうしご child born in answer to one's prayer

【さる 申】 ninth sign of the Oriental zodiac: **the Monkey** (→❸)

SYNONYMS

❶ inform and communicate

報 INFORM → 2133
通 COMMUNICATE → 3855
告 NOTIFY → 3062
届ける give notice → 3820
達 issue a notice → 3893
知 let know → 1446
申 REPORT → 4319
稟 REPORT TO → 2649
宣 PROCLAIM → 2799

❸ monkey

猿 MONKEY → 0824
申 the Monkey → 4319

【もうす】

①ⓐ **speak and say**

言 SAY → 2440
語る TELL → 1944
談 TALK → 1975
喋 TALK → 0665
諷 INSINUATE → 2005
謂う REFER TO → 2007
云 say → 2430
曰 SAY THAT → 3757
話 SPEAK → 1928
口 give mouth to → 4189
申す SPEAK HUMBLY → 4319

述 STATE → 3816
陳 SET FORTH → 0656
弁 SPEAK ELOQUENTLY → 2497

①ⓐ **speak humbly**
申す SPEAK HUMBLY → 4319
啓 address respectfully → 3434

HOMOPHONES

さる 猿 MONKEY → 0824

NOTE

➡ see USAGE note at 猿 0824

半
4320
■4-5-3

▶HALF
ハン なか(ば)

24	Nonstandard	U534A
十	S5-2-3	F0000

traditional form → see 半 at 4313

氷
■4-5-3

incorrect classification
➡ see ◧1-2-3: 氵 at 0043

氺
■4-5-3

incorrect classification
➡ see ◧1-2-3: 冫 at 0041

尓
■4-5-3

incorrect classification
➡ see ⬒2-2-3: 𠂉 at 2503

册
■4-5-3

incorrect classification
➡ see ■4-5-1 at 4303

戊
4321
■4-5-4

▶FIFTH CALENDAR SIGN
ボ つちのえ ㊔ しげ しげる さかる
Ⓒ 戊 wù

62	Names	U620A
戈	S5-4-1	F2934

COMPOUNDS

● **FIFTH CALENDAR SIGN**
戊辰 ぼしん fifth of the sexagenary cycle
戊戌 ぼじゅつ 35th of the sexagenary cycle
戊夜 ぼや fifth division of the night (around four o'clock in the morning)

INDEPENDENT

【ぼ 戊】 **FIFTH CALENDAR SIGN**

KUN

【つちのえ 戊】 **FIFTH CALENDAR SIGN**

SYNONYMS

● **calendar signs**
戊 FIFTH CALENDAR SIGN → 4321
庚 SEVENTH CALENDAR SIGN → 3826
壬 NINTH CALENDAR SIGN → 4257

NOTE

★ do not confuse with 戌 THE DOG → 4350

央
4322
■4-5-4

▶CENTER
オウ ㊔ ひろ ひろし なか ちか てる お ひさ
Ⓒ 央 yāng

37	Jōyō-4	U592E
大	S5-3-2	F0883

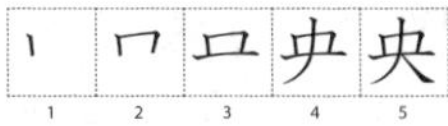

COMPOUNDS

● [original meaning] **CENTER, middle**
中央 ちゅうおう center
月央 げつおう middle of the month
震央 しんおう epicenter (of an earthquake)
中央線 ちゅうおうせん Chuo Line (central railway line in Tokyo)
道央 どうおう central Hokkaido

SYNONYMS

● **middle**
中 MIDDLE → 4262
央 CENTER → 4322
心 HEART → 0011
核 NUCLEUS → 1162

丼
4323
■4-5-4

▶LARGE BOWL
セイ▲ タン▲ トン▲ どんぶり どん
Ⓒ 丼 jǐng dǎn

3	Jōyō	U4E3C
丶	S5-1-4	F2233

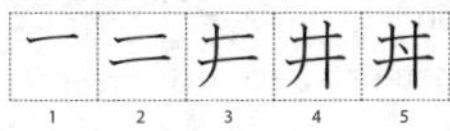

KUN

【どんぶり 丼】

①ⓐ **LARGE BOWL**
ⓑ [also suffix] **bowl of rice with food on top**
a 丼飯 どんぶりめし rice in a large bowl
ラーメン丼 らーめんどんぶり Chinese noodle bowl
b 丼物 どんぶりもの rice bowl dishes
鉄火丼 てっかどんぶり bowl of vinegared rice topped with sliced raw tuna
親子丼 おやこどんぶり bowl of rice topped with chicken and egg

② large pocket on the front of a workman's apron
丼勘定 どんぶりかんじょう sloppy accounting

【どん 丼】 [in compounds] abbrev. of 丼 どんぶり: **bowl of rice with food on top**
牛丼 ぎゅうどん beef bowl

カツ丼 かつどん bowl of rice topped with deep-fried pork cutlet
天丼 てんどん bowl of rice topped with tempura
鰻×丼 うなどん bowl of rice topped with grilled eel

SYNONYMS

【どんぶり】

①ⓐ **vessels and receptacles**

盤 dish → 3533
鍋 POT → 2202
釜 IRON POT → 2610
鼎 TRIPOD CAULDRON → 4405
臼 MORTAR → 4341
碓 MORTAR → 1537
托 RECEPTACLE → 0252
皿 PLATE → 4286
盆 TRAY → 2581
膳 LEGGED TRAY → 1381
杯 CUP → 1066
鉢 BOWL → 2144
椀 WOODEN BOWL → 1250
碗 CERAMIC BOWL → 1539
丼 LARGE BOWL → 4323

史

▸HISTORY

シ ㊔ ふみ ひさし あや ひと ちか

Ⓒ 史 shǐ

4324

■4-5-4

30	Jōyō-4	U53F2
口	S5-3-2	F0362

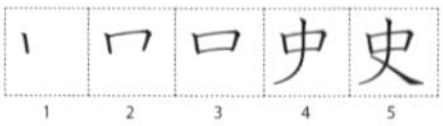

COMPOUNDS

ⓐ [also suffix] **HISTORY, chronicles; history book**
ⓑ [original meaning] historian

a 史料 しりょう historical materials [records]
史書 ししょ history book
史跡 しせき historic spot [remains]
史学者 しがくしゃ historian
史上に例を見ない しじょうにれいをみない be unparalleled in history
歴史 れきし history
青史 せいし history, history book
世界史 せかいし world history
日本史 にほんし Japanese history
b 女史 じょし madame, Mrs.; Miss

INDEPENDENT

【し 史】**HISTORY**; history book
史に名を留める しになをとどめる inscribe one's name in history

SYNONYMS

ⓐ **records**

記 written account → 1843
録 RECORD → 2186
譜 SYSTEMATIC RECORD → 2068
誌 records → 1950
史 HISTORY → 4324
伝 biography → 0048

ⓐ **history**

史 HISTORY → 4324
伝 biography → 0048
歴 PERSONAL HISTORY → 3748

NOTE

➡ see COMPOUND FORMATION for 青史 せいし → 青 3084

失

▸LOSE
▸SLIP

シツ うしな(う) う(せる)▲

Ⓒ 失 shī

4325

■4-5-4

37	Jōyō-4	U5931
大	S5-3-2	F0424

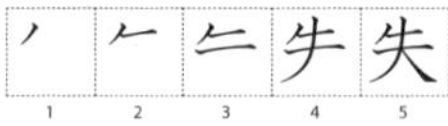

COMPOUNDS

❶ⓐ **LOSE, miss**
ⓑ **LOSE** one's memory, forget

a 失業する しつぎょうする be out of work, lose one's job
失礼 しつれい impoliteness, rudeness; bad manners; I beg your pardon/Goodbye
失望する しつぼうする be disappointed, lose hope
紛失 ふんしつ loss
喪失 そうしつ loss, forfeit
遺失する いしつする lose, leave behind
b 失念 しつねん lapse of memory, oblivion

❷ abbrev. of 失業 しつぎょう: loss of employment, unemployment

失保 しつほ unemployment insurance
失対 しったい measure against unemployment

❸ⓐ **SLIP (up), make a slip, make a mistake**
ⓑ **SLIP, oversight, mistake, error**
ⓒ *baseball* error

a 失言 しつげん slip of the tongue
失笑する しっしょうする burst out laughing
失策 しっさく blunder, slip, error
失敗 しっぱい failure, mistake
b 過失 かしつ error, fault, mistake; negligence
c 捕失 ほしつ catcher's error

❹ improper, mis-

栄養失調 えいようしっちょう malnutrition

❺ disappear, vanish

消失する しょうしつする disappear, vanish; die away

INDEPENDENT

【しつ 失】loss; error, fault
【しっする 失する】**LOSE**, miss; forget; be excessive

KUN

【うしなう 失う】**LOSE, miss, be deprived of**
見失う みうしなう lose sight of
両親を失う りょうしんをうしなう be bereft of one's parents
【うせる 失せる】disappear, vanish, be gone; be lost, be missing
失せろ うせろ Get out of my sight!/Beat it!

SYNONYMS

❶ **losing and loss**
失 LOSE → 4325
喪 lose → 3504
逸 LET SLIP → 3872
損 LOSS, lose → 0801
佚 LOST → 0070

❸ **mistakes and mistaking**
過 error → 3891
失 SLIP → 4325
誤 MISTAKE → 1945
謬 MISTAKE → 2060
錯 mistaken → 2187
-違える mis- → 3907

疒

▶*YAMAIDARE*

4326
■4-5-4

104 疒	Radical S5-5-0	U7592 F0000

RADICAL

yamaidare 'illness' (病 痛 療), used in characters related to illness, diseases or injury

---

衤

▶*KOROMOHEN*

4327
■4-5-4

145 衤	Radical S5-5-0	U8864 F0000

radical variant → see 衣 at 2506

片

▶**FRAGMENT**
▶**ONE OF TWO**
ヘン かた- かた

4328
■4-5-4

91 片	Nonstandard S5-5-0	U7247 F0000

alternative form → see 片 at 4272

乏

■4-5-4

incorrect classification/stroke-count
➡ see ⬒2-1-3: ノ at 2432

永

■4-5-4

incorrect classification
➡ see ⬒2-1-4: 丶 at 2436

皮

■4-5-4

incorrect classification
➡ see □3-3-2: 广 at 3771

必

■4-5-4

incorrect classification
➡ see ◧1-1-4: 丿 at 0015

世

■4-5-4

incorrect classification
➡ see ■4-5-2 at 4308

斥

■4-5-4

incorrect classification
➡ see □3-2-3: 厂 at 3690

失

■4-5-4

incorrect classification
➡ see ⬒2-2-3: 𠂉 at 2502

夲

■4-5-4

incorrect classification
➡ see ⬒2-3-2: 大 at 2681

耳

▶**EAR**
ジ みみ
Ⓒ 耳 ěr

4329
■4-6-1

128 耳	Jōyō-1 S6-6-0	U8033 F0735

Stroke order: 一 丅 𠃊 ... 耳 (1–6)

RADICAL

mimi 'ear' (聞 聖 聚), used in characters related to the ear or actions using ears
Left variant: 耳 *mimihen* (職 聴 聡)

COMPOUNDS

● [original meaning] **EAR**
耳目 じもく eyes and ears; one's attention
耳鼻咽喉 じびいんこう nose, ear and throat
耳鼻科 じびか otorhinology
中耳炎 ちゅうじえん otitis media; tympanitis
外耳 がいじ external ear, concha

KUN

【みみ 耳】
① ⓐ **EAR**
ⓑ **hearing**
a 耳元で みみもとで close to one's ears
耳障りな みみざわりな offensive to the ear, rough, rasping
左耳 ひだりみみ left ear

片耳 かたみみ one ear
b 耳新しい みみあたらしい novel; new
耳寄りな みみよりな welcome (news)
耳学問 みみがくもん picked-up knowledge
早耳の はやみみの quick-eared
初耳 はつみみ something heard of for the first time
② edge, border; selvage
耳の折れた本 みみのおれたほん dog-eared book
パンの耳 ぱんのみみ crust of bread

SYNONYMS

● **face orifices**
口 MOUTH → 4189
鼻 NOSE → 3357
耳 EAR → 4329
目 EYE → 3777

艮

4330
■ 4-6-1

▶**NORTHEAST**
コン ゴン うしとら
Ⓒ 艮 gěn gèn

138	Non-Jōyō	U826E
艮	S6-6-0	F0000

RADICAL

kon or ***ushitora*** 'northeast' (艮), used for character classification
Variant: 艮× ***kon*** or ***ushitora*** (艱×)

COMPOUNDS

❶ [rare] one of the four supplementary signs of the Oriental zodiac: **NORTHEAST**
❷ **seventh of the eight trigrams in the Book of Changes**
艮下艮上 ごんかごんしょう one of the 64 trigrams
❸ **used phonetically for *gon***
儒艮 じゅごん dugong

INDEPENDENT

【ごん 艮】**seventh of the eight trigrams in the Book of Changes**

KUN

【うしとら 艮】[also 丑寅] one of the four supplementary signs of the Oriental zodiac: **NORTHEAST**
艮の方角に うしとらのほうがくに in the direction of northeast

SYNONYMS

❶ **cardinal points**
東 EAST → 4385
西 WEST → 4333
北 NORTH → 0230
南 SOUTH → 2584
巽 SOUTHEAST → 3329
艮 NORTHEAST → 4330

HOMOPHONES

うしとら 丑寅 → 4241, 2854

両

4331
■ 4-6-1

▶**BOTH**
リョウ ㊔ もろ
Ⓝ 兩 两 Ⓒ 两 liǎng 辆 liàng

1△	Jōyō-3	U4E21
一	S6-1-5	F0331

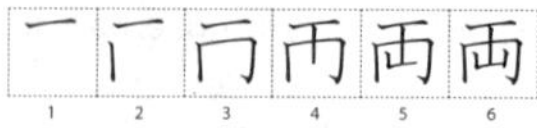

COMPOUNDS

❶ [also prefix] **BOTH, two**
両方 りょうほう both
両側 りょうがわ both sides
両院 りょういん both Houses
両手 りょうて both hands
両用 りょうよう dual use
両親 りょうしん parents
両雄 りょうゆう two great men
両性的 りょうせいてき bisexual
両義 りょうぎ double meaning, two meanings
❷ [formerly also 輛 2000]
ⓐ **vehicle, railway car**
ⓑ counter for railway cars
a 車両 しゃりょう vehicle, car; rolling stock
b 三両 さんりょう three cars, three coaches
❸ ***ryo*:**
ⓐ **former monetary unit equiv. to 4 *kan* (貫)**
ⓑ former unit of weight equiv. to 37.5 g or 1/16 of a *kin* (斤)
a 両替 りょうがえ money changing, exchange of money
千両箱 せんりょうばこ chest containing a thousand pieces of gold
銀五両 ぎんごりょう 5 *ryo* of silver
ab 十両 じゅうりょう 10 *ryo*
❹ *slang* yen
二十両 にじゅうりょう 20 yen

INDEPENDENT

【りょう 両】*ryo* (→❸); *slang* yen; *literary* **BOTH**
両の手 りょうのて both hands

SYNONYMS

❶ **two**
二 TWO → 2421
弐 TWO (in legal documents) → 3961
双 SET OF TWO → 0028
対 pair → 1025
偶 COUPLE → 0150
両 BOTH → 4331
❷ⓑ **kinds of railway**

鉄 railway → 2147
電 electric railway → 3465
車 railway car → 4367
両 counter for railway cars → 4331
輛 counter for railway cars → 2000

❸ⓐ Japanese money denominations
文 *mon* → 2458
両 *ryo* → 4331
厘 *RIN* → 3727
銭 sen → 2159
円 YEN → 3673

再

4332
■4-6-1

▸ANOTHER TIME
サイ サ ふたた(び)
Ⓒ 再 zài

13	Jōyō-5	U518D
冂	S6-2-4	F0459

COMPOUNDS

❶ [also prefix] **ANOTHER TIME, re-, again, a second time, another**
再度 さいど another time, a second time
再開 さいかい reopening, resumption
再来 さいらい return, second coming; Second Advent
再現する さいげんする reenact, reproduce
再三 さいさん again and again, repeatedly
再興 さいこう revival, restoration
再生 さいせい reclamation; regeneration, resuscitation; playback
再訂版 さいていばん second revised edition
再婚 さいこん remarriage, second marriage
再検討 さいけんとう reexamination, restudying

❷ [prefix] **after next**
再来週 さらいしゅう the week after next
再来月 さらいげつ the month after next
再来年 さらいねん the year after next

KUN

【ふたたび 再び】 **again, twice, a second time, once more**
再び読む ふたたびよむ read again, reread

SYNONYMS

❶ repeating and repetition
再 ANOTHER TIME → 4332
又 AGAIN → 4158
復 repeat → 0701
重 DUPLICATE → 4390
畳 reduplicate → 3205
改 redo → 0287
-換える redo → 0716
-直す repetition suffix → 3649
-返す do over → 3797

西

4333
■4-6-1

▸WEST
セイ サイ ス▲ にし ㊔ いり
Ⓒ 西 xī

146	Jōyō-2	U897F
西	S6-6-0	F0291

radical variant → see 覀 at 4336

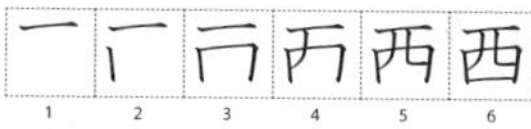

COMPOUNDS

❶ⓐ **WEST, western**
ⓑ **the WEST, the Occident; Western**
a 西部 せいぶ western part; the West
西経 せいけい west longitude
西洋人 せいようじん Westerner
関西 かんさい Kansai district
東西 とうざい east and west
北西 ほくせい northwest
b 西欧 せいおう West Europe, the Occident
西暦 せいれき Christian Era, A.D.
泰西 たいせい the Occident

❷ⓐ Spain
ⓑ Spanish (language)
a 米西戦争 べいせいせんそう Spanish-American War
b 日西辞典 にっせいじてん Japanese-Spanish dictionary

❸ used phonetically for *su*, esp. in the transliteration of foreign place names
仏蘭西 ふらんす France

INDEPENDENT

【せい 西】 Spain

KUN

【にし 西】 [also prefix] **WEST, western**
西側 にしがわ west side; west European countries and America
西半球 にしはんきゅう Western Hemisphere
西陣織 にしじんおり *Nishijin* brocade

SPECIAL READINGS

西瓜▲ すいか watermelon

SYNONYMS

❶ⓐ cardinal points
東 EAST → 4385
西 WEST → 4333
北 NORTH → 0230
南 SOUTH → 2584
巽 SOUTHEAST → 3329
艮 NORTHEAST → 4330

ⓑ west
洋 WESTERN → 0468
西 the West → 4333
❷ⓐ European countries
英 ENGLAND → 2782
独 GERMANY → 0471
仏 FRANCE → 0020
伊 ITALY → 0052
葡 PORTUGAL → 2902
西 Spain → 4333
蘭 the Netherlands → 3031
希 Greece → 2543
露 Russia → 3495
白 Belgium → 4305
❸ phonetic [s]/[sh]
沙 phonetic [sha] → 0311
刹 phonetic [setsu] → 1620
遮 phonetic [sha] → 3916
叉 phonetic [sha] → 4194
世 phonetic [se] → 4308
須 phonetic [shu] → 0700
修 phonetic [shu] → 0138
西 phonetic [su] → 4333
相 phonetic [sō] → 1120
薩 phonetic [satsu] → 3016

NOTE
➡ see COMPOUND FORMATION for
西陣織 にしじんおり → 陣 0545
関西 かんさい → 関 4129

死

4334
■4-6-1

▶DIE
シ し(ぬ) し(に)-
Ⓒ 死 sǐ

78	Jōyō-3	U6B7B
歹	S6-4-2	F0169

一 丆 歹 歹 歹 死
1 2 3 4 5 6

COMPOUNDS
❶ⓐ [original meaning] **DIE, perish, come to an end**
ⓑ [also suffix] **death, demise**
ⓒ [formerly also 屍 3843] [original meaning] **dead body, corpse**
ⓓ (no longer useful) dead, obsolete, useless
a 死亡 しぼう death
死刑 しけい capital punishment, death penalty
死後 しご after one's death
死去 しきょ death, passing away
b 戦死する せんしする die in battle
即死 そくし instant death, death on the spot
焼死 しょうし death by fire
中毒死 ちゅうどくし death from poisoning
c 死体 したい corpse
死人 しにん dead person, corpse
d 死語 しご dead language; obsolete word
❷ struggle to the death, desperation
死守する ししゅする defend to the last, defend desperately
必死に ひっしに for one's dear life, desperately
❸ *baseball* out; dead (ball)
死球 しきゅう dead ball
無死満塁 むしまんるい bases are loaded with no outs

INDEPENDENT
【し 死】 **death;** *baseball* **out; dead ball**
死を覚悟する しをかくごする be ready to die
【しする 死する】 **DIE**

KUN
【しぬ 死ぬ】 **DIE, pass away; commit suicide;** *baseball* **be put out; be captured (in go or chess)**
死ぬ迄戦う しぬまでたたかう fight to the last [death]
【しに- 死に-】 [also verbal prefix] **dying, death**
死に絶える しにたえる die out, become extinct
死に金 しにがね wasted money, idle capital
死に物狂いで しにものぐるいで desperately, frantically

SYNONYMS
❶ⓐ & ❶ⓑ die
死 DIE → 4334
萎 WITHER → 2872
没 die → 0305
亡 DECEASE → 4210
殉 DIE A MARTYR → 1177
歿 DIE → 1078
去 pass away → 2678
逝 DEPART THIS LIFE → 3850
斃 FALL DOWN DEAD → 3593
枯 WITHER → 1113

襾

4335
■4-6-1

▶*NISHI*

146	Radical	U8980
襾	S6-6-0	F0000

radical variant → see 覀 at 4336

覀

4336
■4-6-1

▶*NISHI*

146	Radical	U897E
覀	S6-6-0	F0000

RADICAL

nishi 'cover' (覃× 覈× 覊×), used in characters related to covering

Top variant: 覀 *nishi* (要 覆 覇)

亙

4337

■4-6-1

▶**EXTEND OVER**

コウ わた(る) ㊔ のぶ せん つね

7	Names	U4E99
二	S6-2-4	F0000

traditional form → see 亘 at 2438

丞 ■4-6-1

incorrect classification

➡ see ▀2-5-1: 氶 at 3146

各 ■4-6-1

incorrect classification

➡ see ▀2-3-3: 夂 at 2692

名 ■4-6-1

incorrect classification

➡ see ▀2-3-3: 夕 at 2693

凹 ■4-6-1

incorrect stroke-count

➡ see ■4-5-1 at 4294

凸 ■4-6-1

incorrect stroke-count

➡ see ■4-5-1 at 4298

百而 ■4-6-1

incorrect classification

➡ see ▀2-2-4: 一 at 2519

自

4338

■4-6-2

▶**SELF**

ジ シ みずか(ら) おの(ずから)▲ おの(ずと)▲ ㊔ より

Ⓒ 自 zì

132	Jōyō-2	U81EA
自	S6-6-0	F0017

(stroke order: 1 2 3 4 5 6)

RADICAL

mizukara 'self' (臭), used in characters related to the nose

COMPOUNDS

❶ⓐ [also prefix] **SELF, oneself**

ⓑ **one's own, one's**

a 自分 じぶん self, oneself

自己 じこ oneself, self, ego

自身 じしん self, oneself; itself

自信 じしん self-confidence

自殺 じさつ suicide

自供 じきょう (voluntary) confession

自衛 じえい self-defense, self-protection

自慢 じまん pride, self-praise, vanity

自習 じしゅう self-study, self-teaching

自営の じえいの independent, self-employed

自問する じもんする question oneself

自営業 じえいぎょう self-employment

独自の どくじの original; personal, individual

b 自宅 じたく one's house, one's home

自国 じこく one's own country

❷ **by itself, naturally, spontaneously**

自然 しぜん nature

自然に しぜんに naturally, instinctively

自然科学 しぜんかがく natural science

自動車 じどうしゃ automobile

自転 じてん rotation (of the earth)

自発的 じはつてき spontaneous, voluntary

自主的 じしゅてき independent, autonomous; active

自転車 じてんしゃ bicycle

自明の じめいの self-evident, obvious

❸ **as one pleases**

自由 じゆう freedom

自在に じざいに freely, unrestrictedly, at will

自適 じてき easy and comfortable living

❹ [also prefix] from, as of, since

自今 じこん hereafter

自東京 じとうきょう from Tokyo

❺ abbrev. of 自由民主党 じゆうみんしゅとう: Liberal Democratic Party

自公民 じこうみん Liberal Democratic Party, Komeito and Democratic Socialist Party

❻ abbrev. of 自動車 じどうしゃ: automobile

自販 じはん automobile sales

自工 じこう automobile industry

❼ intransitive verb

自他 じた oneself and others; transitive and intransitive

❽ [original meaning, now obsolete] nose

KUN

【みずから 自ら】**oneself; in person, personally**

自らの みずからの one's own, personal

【おのずから 自ずから】**naturally, by itself, spontaneously**

自ずから明かな おのずからあきらかな self-evident

【おのずと 自ずと】naturally, by itself, spontaneously

SPECIAL READINGS

自棄▲ やけ desperation

自惚れる▲ うぬぼれる be vain, be conceited

自惚れ▲ うぬぼれ self-conceit, vanity

SYNONYMS

❶ **first person pronouns**

私 I (*polite*) → 1432
我 SELF → 4362
己 ONESELF → 4188
身 ONE'S PERSON → 4368
僕 I (*familiar*) → 0185
俺 I (*intimate*) → 0124
吾 I (*elegant*) → 3060
予 I (*pompous*) → 2477
余 I (*pompous*) → 2535
麿 I (*archaic*) → 3949
朕 IMPERIAL WE → 1185
自 SELF → 4338

❹ **direction indicators**

至 to → 2707
-行き bound for → 0246
-向け (bound) for → 3790
迄 UP TO → 3967
以 TO THE…OF → 0045
自 from → 4338
来 since → 4366
而 DIRECTION WORD → 2520

NOTE

➡ see COMPOUND FORMATION for
自然 しぜん → 然 3456
自由 じゆう → 由 4311

血

4339
■4-6-2

▶**BLOOD**
ケツ ち
Ⓒ 血 xuè xiě

143	Jōyō-3	U8840
血	S6-6-0	F0471

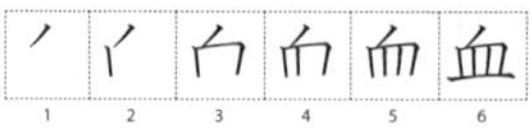

RADICAL

chi 'blood' (衆), used in characters related to blood
Left variant: 血× ***chihen*** (衄×)

COMPOUNDS

❶ [also suffix] [original meaning] **BLOOD**
血液 けつえき blood
血管 けっかん blood vessel
血圧 けつあつ blood pressure
献血 けんけつ blood donation
貧血 ひんけつ anemia
出血 しゅっけつ bleeding; hemorrhage; sacrifice

❷ hot-**BLOOD**ed, lively
血気 けっき hot blood of youth, youthful vigor
冷血な れいけつな cold-blooded, coldhearted, heartless
熱血漢 ねっけつかん hot-blooded man

❸ **BLOOD (relation), lineage**
血族 けつぞく blood relative
血統 けっとう lineage, blood, bloodline
混血 こんけつ mixed-blood, racial mixture

KUN

【ち 血】**BLOOD; blood (relation), lineage**
血眼 ちまなこ bloodshot eye
血塗れの ちまみれの bloodstained, bloody
血筋 ちすじ blood relationship, lineage
血の繋がり ちのつながり blood relationship
鼻血 はなぢ nosebleed

SYNONYMS

❸ **lineage**
系 LINEAGE → 2443
血 BLOOD → 4339

曲

4340
■4-6-2

▶**MUSICAL COMPOSITION**
▶**CURVE**
キョク ま(がる) ま(げる) ㊔ くま
Ⓒ 曲 qū qǔ

73	Jōyō-3	U66F2
曰	S6-4-2	F0734

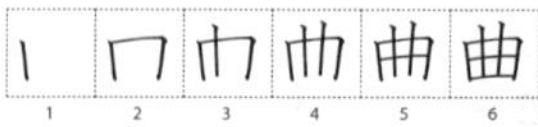

COMPOUNDS

❶ⓐ [also suffix] **MUSICAL COMPOSITION, (piece of) music, melody, tune, song**
ⓑ counter for **MUSICAL COMPOSITION**s

a 曲調 きょくちょう melody, tune
曲節 きょくせつ tune, air
曲名 きょくめい title of a musical composition [song]
曲目 きょくもく number; program, selection (for a concert)
楽曲 がっきょく musical piece, composition, tune
作曲 さっきょく composition
編曲 へんきょく arrangement (of a melody)
名曲 めいきょく excellent [exquisite] piece of music, famous tune
新曲 しんきょく new musical composition, new tune [song]
舞曲 ぶきょく dance music, music and dancing
戯曲 ぎきょく drama, play
歌謡曲 かようきょく popular song
交響曲 こうきょうきょく symphony

b 五曲 ごきょく five compositions

❷ⓐ **CURVE, bend**
ⓑ **CURVEd, bent**

a 曲折する きょくせつする bend, wind; zigzag
曲率 きょくりつ curvature

曲度 きょくど curvature
湾曲 わんきょく curve, crook, bend
屈曲 くっきょく bending, winding
婉×曲な えんきょくな roundabout, indirect; euphemistic
b 曲線 きょくせん curve, curved line
曲管 きょくかん curved pipe, siphon

❸ wrong, not right, perverse
曲事 きょくじ wickedness, injustice
曲解する きょっかい(=きょくかい)する misinterpret, distort
曲直 きょくちょく right and wrong
歪曲 わいきょく distortion; perversion

❹ acrobatics
曲芸 きょくげい acrobatics, trick, stunt
曲乗り きょくのり trick riding

❺ detailed
同工異曲である どうこういきょくである be practically the same, be equally excellent in workmanship though different in style

INDEPENDENT

【きょく 曲】**MUSICAL COMPOSITION, (piece of) music, melody, tune, song; interest, fun, pleasure; wrong; injustice**
曲を付ける きょくをつける write music for a song
曲の無い きょくのない dull, uninteresting

KUN

【まがる 曲がる】*vi* **bend, CURVE; warp, get crooked; turn (to the left); be perverse**
曲がり まがり [sometimes also 勾り] curvature, warp
曲がりくねる まがりくねる turn and twist, zigzag
曲がり角 まがりかど street corner, turning
曲がりなりにも まがりなりにも somehow, though imperfect
左に曲がる ひだりにまがる turn to the left

【まげる 曲げる】*vt* **bend, CURVE; pervert, depart from; pawn, hock**
曲げ まげ bending, flexure
曲げ物 まげもの round chip [bent wood] box
事実を曲げる じじつをまげる falsify a fact

SPECIAL READINGS

曲尺▲(=矩尺) かねじゃく carpenter's square; regular *shaku* (尺) (approx. 12 in.)

SYNONYMS

❶ⓐ **music and songs**
楽 MUSIC → 3505
音 sound of music → 2570
節 tune → 3336
調べ melody → 1973
曲 MUSICAL COMPOSITION → 4340
歌 SONG → 2296
謡 POPULAR SONG → 2011
唄 DITTY → 0477

❷ **bend**
曲 CURVE → 4340
彎 CURVE (become bow-shaped) → 3634
屈 BEND → 3821
折 bend → 0297
勾 be bent → 3660
歪 DISTORT → 3095

HOMOPHONES

まがり 勾 ARREST → 3660

臼

4341

■4-6-2

▸**MORTAR**
キュウ うす
Ⓒ 臼 jiù

134	Jōyō	U81FC
臼	S6-6-0	F2392

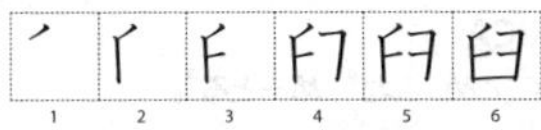

RADICAL

usu 'mortar' (舂× 舅×), used in characters related to mortars or lifting with both hands
Variant: 𦥑 ***usu*** (臾× 興)

COMPOUNDS

ⓐ [original meaning] **MORTAR; hand mill**
ⓑ **something resembling a MORTAR**
a 臼砲 きゅうほう (trench) mortar
b 臼歯 きゅうし molar (tooth)
脱臼 だっきゅう dislocation

KUN

【うす 臼】[sometimes also 碓] **MORTAR; hand mill**
石臼 いしうす stone mortar [mill]
碾×き臼 ひきうす hand mill, quern
茶臼 ちゃうす tea-grinding mill

SYNONYMS

ⓐ **vessels and receptacles**
盤 dish → 3533
鍋 POT → 2202
釜 IRON POT → 2610
鼎 TRIPOD CAULDRON → 4405
臼 MORTAR → 4341
碓 MORTAR → 1537
托 RECEPTACLE → 0252
皿 PLATE → 4286
盆 TRAY → 2581
膳 LEGGED TRAY → 1381
杯 CUP → 1066
鉢 BOWL → 2144
椀 WOODEN BOWL → 1250
碗 CERAMIC BOWL → 1539

丼 LARGE BOWL → 4323

USAGE

【うす】

臼

[sometimes also 碓] mortar; hand mill

碓

[usu. 臼] mortar; trip-hammer mill

HOMOPHONES

うす 碓 MORTAR → 1537

羊

incorrect classification
➡ see ▀2-3-3: 䒑 at 2709

■4-6-2

缶 缶

incorrect classification
➡ see ▀2-2-4: 𠂉 at 2525

■4-6-2

米

▶RICE
▶AMERICA
ベイ マイ こめ よね▲ めーとる▲

4342

Ⓒ 米 mǐ

■4-6-3

119	Jōyō-2	U7C73
米	S6-6-0	F0308

RADICAL

kome 'rice' (粟 粥 粤×), used in characters related to rice or rice products

Left variant: 米× *komehen* (精 糖 粉)

COMPOUNDS

❶ [also suffix] **RICE**

米穀 べいこく rice
米価 べいか price of rice
米作 べいさく rice crop
米飯 べいはん cooked rice
玄米 げんまい unpolished rice
精米 せいまい rice polishing; polished [white] rice
外米 がいまい foreign [imported] rice
配給米 はいきゅうまい rationed rice
新潟米 にいがたまい Niigata rice

❷ⓐ **AMERICA, United States; American**
ⓑ **continent of AMERICA**

a 米国 べいこく U.S.A.
米軍 べいぐん American armed forces
米貨 べいか American currency, U.S. dollar
日米 にちべい Japan and U.S.
b 渡米 とべい going to America
欧米 おうべい Europe and America
南米 なんべい South America

❸ meter

❹ unclassified compounds

米寿 べいじゅ 88 years old, one's 88th birthday

INDEPENDENT

【べい 米】**AMERICA**, United States

米の介入 べいのかいにゅう intervention of America

KUN

【こめ 米】**RICE**

米粒 こめつぶ grain of rice
米俵 こめだわら (straw) rice bag
米屋 こめや rice merchant

【よね 米】*elegant* **RICE**

【めーとる 米】meter

百米 ひゃくめーとる 100 m

SYNONYMS

❶ **rice**

米 RICE → 4342
飯 COOKED RICE → 2126
稲 RICE PLANT → 1561
籾 UNHULLED RICE → 1626
餅 RICE CAKE → 2256
粥 RICE GRUEL → 0698

❶ **cereals**

米 RICE → 4342
麦 WHEAT → 3061
豆 BEAN → 2442
粟 FOXTAIL MILLET → 3326
黍 PROSO MILLET → 3210
蕎 BUCKWHEAT → 2993
蒋 WILD RICE → 2976

❷ⓐ **North American countries**

米 AMERICA → 4342
加 Canada → 0042

ⓑ **continents**

亜 Asia → 4354
阿 Africa → 0408
欧 EUROPE → 1098
米 AMERICA → 4342
豪 Australia → 2657

❸ **length units**

寸 *sun* (3.03 cm) → 3652
浬 NAUTICAL MILE (1852 m) → 0526
反 *tan* (10.6 m) → 3663
尺 *SHAKU* (30.3 cm) → 4248
米 meter → 4342
尋 fathom (1.8 m) → 2918
間 *ken* (1.8 m) → 4122
丈 *jo* (3.03 m) → 4227
町 *cho* (109 m) → 1430
里 LEAGUE, *ri* (3.9 km) → 4356
哩 MILE (1609 m) → 0479

COMPOUND FORMATION

【米寿 べいじゅ】

米寿 '88 years old, etc.' refers to one's 88th birthday since 米 can be split into ソ (variant of 八), 十 and 八, i.e., 八十八 or 88.

虫

4343

■4-6-3

▶**INSECT**

チュウ むし

Ⓝ 蟲 Ⓒ 虫 chóng

142	Jōyō-1	U866B
虫	S6-6-0	F1192

丶 冂 口 中 虫 虫

1 2 3 4 5 6

RADICAL

mushi 'bug' (融 蛮 蛍), used in characters related to insects, reptiles or small animals

Left variant: 虫× *mushihen* (虹 蚊 蛇)

COMPOUNDS

● [also suffix] **INSECT, worm, bug**

虫類 ちゅうるい insects and worms

虫害 ちゅうがい insect damage

虫垂 ちゅうすい appendix

昆虫 こんちゅう insect

防虫加工の ぼうちゅうかこうの mothproof

殺虫剤 さっちゅうざい insecticide, vermicide

寄生虫 きせいちゅう parasite

KUN

【むし 虫】

① [also suffix] **INSECT, worm; bug; roundworm**

虫下し むしくだし vermifuge, anthelmintic

虫が付く むしがつく become verminous; begin to keep bad company; have an (unfavorable) lover

毛虫 けむし hairy caterpillar

油虫 あぶらむし cockroach

貝殻虫 かいがらむし scale insect

② **worm-eaten; in an unfavorable condition**

虫歯 むしば decayed tooth

水虫 みずむし athlete's foot, dermatophytosis

③ feeling; temper; self-seeking

虫の知らせ むしのしらせ premonition, hunch

虫の居所が悪い むしのいどころがわるい be in a cross mood

虫が良い むしがいい selfish, asking too much

④ enthusiastic fan (as of books)

本の虫 ほんのむし bookworm

⑤ [also suffix] **belittling term indicating a negative quality in a person**

弱虫 よわむし weakling

泣き虫 なきむし blubberer, crybaby

点取り虫 てんとりむし grinder, dig

⑥ *elec* valve core

弁の虫 べんのむし valve core

SPECIAL READINGS

虫食む▲ むしばむ [also 蝕む] (of worms) eat in; undermine, affect

SYNONYMS

● **insect**

虫 INSECT → 4343

昆 INSECT → 3067

繭 COCOON → 3023

HOMOPHONES

むしばむ

蝕 ERODE → 2258

虫食む → 4343, 2578

朱

4344

■4-6-3

▶**VERMILION**

シュ あけ▲ ㊔ じゅ あか

Ⓒ 朱 zhū

75	Jōyō	U6731
木	S6-4-2	F1539

丿 𠂉 二 牛 牛 朱

1 2 3 4 5 6

COMPOUNDS

❶ **VERMILION, red**

朱顔 しゅがん flushed face

朱色 しゅいろ vermilion, Chinese red

朱肉 しゅにく red ink pad

朱書する しゅしょする write in red

丹朱 たんしゅ vermilion, red; cinnabar

❷ cinnabar

朱筆 しゅひつ cinnabar brush

朱墨 しゅずみ cinnabar stick

❸ *shu*: former monetary unit equiv. to 1/16 of a *ryo* (両)

一朱銀 いっしゅぎん type of silver coin in Edo period

❹ Zhu Xi, great scholar of the Song Dynasty

朱子学 しゅしがく doctrines of Zhu Xi; neo-Confucianism

INDEPENDENT

【しゅ 朱】 **VERMILION**, red; cinnabar stick; *shu* (→❸)

朱を入れる しゅをいれる correct, retouch

KUN

【あけ 朱】 [sometimes also 緋] **red, blood red**

朱に染まる あけにそまる welter in blood

SYNONYMS

❶ **red colors**

赤 RED → 2719

紅 CRIMSON → 1629

緋 SCARLET → 1732

米 虫 朱 【耒 聿 耒 年 羊】

朱 VERMILION → 4344
丹 CINNABAR → 4249
茜 MADDER → 2811

USAGE

【あけ】

朱
[sometimes also 緋] red, blood red

緋
[usu. 朱] same as 朱

HOMOPHONES

あけ 緋 SCARLET → 1732

耒 ▶*RAISUKI*

4345
4-6-3

127	Radical	U8012
耒	S6-6-0	F0000

RADICAL

raisuki 'plow', used in characters related to farm implements or farming
Left variant: 耒[×] ***raihen*** (耕 耗)
Left variant: 耒[×] ***sukihen*** (耘 耡[×])

聿 ▶*FUDEZUKURI*

4346
4-6-3

129	Radical	U807F
聿	S6-6-0	F0000

RADICAL

fudezukuri 'brush' (粛 肇 肆[×]), used in characters related to writing with a brush

---

来 ▶**COME**

ライ タイ く(る) きた(る) きた(す)

4347
4-6-3

75	Nonstandard	U6765
木	S6-4-2	F0000

alternative form → see 來 at 4366

年 incorrect classification
➡ see 2-2-4: 𠂉 at 2528
4-6-3

羊 incorrect classification
➡ see 2-3-3: 䒑 at 2708
4-6-3

曳 ▶**DRAW**

エイ ひ(く) ㊔ のぶ とお

Ⓝ 曳[◇] Ⓒ 曳 yè

4348
4-6-4

73	Names	U66F3
曰	S6-4-2	F2369

COMPOUNDS

ⓐ **DRAW, pull, haul, tug**
ⓑ **drag, trail**

a 曳航 えいこう towing (of a ship)
曳船 えいせん tugboat; towing
b 曳光弾 えいこうだん tracer bullet, star shell
揺曳 ようえい flutter, linger

KUN

【ひく 曳く】[now usu. 引く]
ⓐ [sometimes also 牽く] **DRAW, pull, haul, tug**
ⓑ **drag, trail**

a 曳山 ひきやま festival float
曳き船 ひきふね tugboat, towing
綱曳き つなひき tug of war; forward puller (of a rickshaw)
b 曳き網 ひきあみ dragnet, seine

SYNONYMS

● **pull**

引 DRAW → 0207
曳 DRAW → 4348
牽 DRAW → 2621
惹 DRAW ATTENTION → 2903
抽 DRAW OUT → 0359
抜 PULL OUT → 0290
控える HOLD BACK → 0600
扣える HOLD BACK → 0250
寄せる DRAW NEAR → 2856

HOMOPHONES

ひく

引 DRAW → 0207
挽 GRIND → 0511
弾 PROJECTILE → 0697
轢 RUN OVER → 2095
牽 DRAW → 2621
惹 DRAW ATTENTION → 2903
退 RETREAT → 3838

NOTE

➡ see USAGE note at 引 0207

夷 ▶**BARBARIAN**

イ えびす ㊔ ひな やすし ひら

Ⓒ 夷 yí

4349
4-6-4

37	Names	U5937
大	S6-3-3	F1798

COMPOUNDS

❶ⓐ **BARBARIAN, savage**
ⓑ **foreigner**

a 夷狄[×] いてき barbarians, aliens
夷人 いじん barbarian, savage

征夷大将軍 せいいたいしょうぐん Commander in Chief of the Expeditionary Force Against the Barbarians

b 攘×夷 じょうい expulsion of foreigners

❷ **demolish, wipe out**

焼夷弾 しょういだん incendiary bomb

❸ used phonetically for *i* in the transliteration of Sanskrit Buddhist terms

優婆夷 うばい *upasika,* devout female lay follower of Buddhism

KUN

【えびす 夷】

① peoples formerly of northern Japan with distinct language and culture

②ⓐ hick, provincial person

ⓑ brutish [unsophisticated] warrior

ⓒ foreigner, **BARBARIAN**

b 東夷 あずまえびす crude warrior from eastern Japan

③ god of fishing and commerce

SPECIAL READINGS

蝦夷 えぞ peoples formerly of northern Japan with distinct language and culture; Ezo, Yezo

蝦夷 えみし old name of 蝦夷 えぞ

辛夷 こぶし Kobushi magnolia, Northern Japanese magnolia

SYNONYMS

❶ **savage**

蛮 BARBARIAN → 2638

夷 BARBARIAN → 4349

蕃 BARBARIAN → 2989

戌

4350

■4-6-4

▶**THE DOG**

ジュツ いぬ

Ⓒ 戌 xū

62	Non-Jōyō	U620C
戈	S6-4-2	F3335

COMPOUNDS

● 11th sign of the Oriental zodiac: **THE DOG**—(time) 7-9 p.m., (direction) WNW, (season) September (of the lunar calendar) (→ **see APPENDIX 8**)

戊戌 ぼじゅつ 35th of the sexagenary cycle

KUN

【いぬ 戌】 11th sign of the Oriental zodiac: **THE DOG**—(time) 7-9 p.m., (direction) WNW, (season) September (of the lunar calendar)

戌年 いぬどし Year of the Dog

戌亥(=乾) いぬい one of the four supplementary signs of the Oriental zodiac: northwest

SYNONYMS

● **dog**

犬 DOG → 4275

狗 DOG → 0405

戌 THE DOG → 4350

HOMOPHONES

いぬ

犬 DOG → 4275

狗 DOG → 0405

NOTE

➡ see USAGE note at 犬 4275

★ do not confuse with 戊 FIFTH CALENDAR SIGN → 4321

吏

4351

■4-6-4

▶**OFFICIAL**

り

Ⓒ 吏 lì

30	Jōyō	U540F
口	S6-3-3	F2266

COMPOUNDS

● [also suffix] [original meaning] **OFFICIAL, officer**

吏人 りじん officials

吏員 りいん official

吏臭 りしゅう officialdom, red tape

官吏 かんり government official

公吏 こうり public official

税関吏 ぜいかんり customs officer

INDEPENDENT

【り 吏】 **OFFICIAL**, officer

SYNONYMS

● **officials**

官 GOVERNMENT OFFICIAL → 2766

吏 OFFICIAL → 4351

僚 official → 0186

司 officiator → 3648

役 executive → 0288

事 officer → 4384

成

4352

■4-6-4

▶**FORM**

▶**ACHIEVE**

セイ ジョウ な(る) な(す) -な(す) ㊔ しげ まさ みのる

Ⓝ 成 Ⓒ 成 chéng

62	Jōyō-4	U6210
戈	S6-4-2	F0121

COMPOUNDS

❶ⓐ [original meaning] (become formed) **FORM, constitute, be completed, come into existence**

ⓑ (give form to) **FORM, make, create, bring to completion**

曳夷戌吏【成】舟孝肉劣糸考

Ⓒ established, existing, completed

a 成分 せいぶん ingredient, component, constituent
成立する せいりつする come into existence, materialize; be formed, be organized; be concluded
形成する けいせいする form, make up, mold
生成文法 せいせいぶんぽう generative grammar
b 完成する かんせいする complete, finish; be completed, be finished
合成する ごうせいする compose, compound, synthesize
編成する へんせいする form, compose, compile
結成する けっせいする form, organize
構成 こうせい composition, construction, formation, organization
c 成句 せいく set phrase
既成の きせいの established, existing

❷ⓐ ACHIEVE, attain, accomplish, succeed
ⓑ ACHIEVEment, success

a 成功する せいこうする succeed, be successful
成果 せいか result, fruit, outcome
成績 せいせき results, record, achievement
成就する じょうじゅする accomplish, achieve, attain
成仏する じょうぶつする enter Nirvana, attain Buddhahood; die
成算 せいさん prospects of success
b 成否 せいひ success or failure, result

❸ⓐ grow up, mature
ⓑ fully grown, adult

a 成長する せいちょうする grow up
成熟 せいじゅく maturity, ripeness, full growth
成育する せいいくする grow (up), be brought up
養成する ようせいする train, educate, bring up
促成栽培の野菜 そくせいさいばいのやさい forced vegetables
b 成人 せいじん adult, grownup
成虫 せいちゅう imago, adult (insect)
成年 せいねん full [adult] age

❹ acceptable

賛成する さんせいする approve of, agree, support

❺ become, turn into

成空 せいくう come to nothingness

KUN

【なる 成る】

① **be accomplished, succeed, be attained, materialize**

成るべく なるべく as…as possible, if possible
成程 なるほど I see, really, indeed
工事が成った こうじがなった The work was finished
丸で成ってない まるでなってない not good at all

② **FORM, constitute, consist of, be composed of**

成り立つ なりたつ consist of; be realized, be concluded, materialize
成り行き なりゆき course [turn] of events, issue
委員会は五人から成る いいんかいはごにんからなる The committee consists of five members

③ honorific auxiliary verb

山田さんがお見えに成りました やまださんがおみえになりました Mr. Yamada is here to see you

④ bear, put up with

そんな事をされて成る物か そんなことをされてなるものか I can't put up with such a thing

⑤ (of chessmen) be promoted

成り駒 なりこま promoted chessman
成り上がる なりあがる suddenly rise to a higher position

【なす 成す】

① **FORM, make, constitute**

円を成す えんをなす form a circle
山成す やまなす mountainlike, a mountain of

② **ACHIEVE, accomplish, succeed**

成し遂げる なしとげる complete, carry out, accomplish
名を成す なをなす make a name, become famous

【-なす -成す】[verbal suffix] **perform an action deliberately**

取り成す とりなす mediate, intercede; recommend
持て成す もてなす entertain, show hospitality

SYNONYMS

❶ⓑ make

作 MAKE → 0077
造 MAKE → 3856
成 FORM → 4352
工 MANUFACTURE → 4190
製 MANUFACTURE → 3478
産 PRODUCE → 4089
調 PREPARE → 1973
組む ASSEMBLE → 1693
構 CONSTRUCT → 1325

❷ⓐ accomplish

達 ATTAIN → 3893
遂 ACCOMPLISH → 3892
成 ACHIEVE → 4352
徹 GO THROUGH → 0894
破 carry through with → 1478
叶 BE FULFILLED → 0209

❸ⓐ grow

成 grow up → 4352
長 grow (up) → 3163
生 grow → 4309
育 grow → 2544
発 develop → 3174
伸 expand → 0079

展 UNFOLD → 3862

❸ⓐ mature

熟 MATURE → 3558
成 grow up → 4352
稔 RIPEN → 1544
爛 OVERRIPE → 1427
実る bear fruit → 2765

USAGE

❶【なる】

成る
① be accomplished, succeed, be attained, materialize
② form, constitute, consist of, be composed of
③ honorific auxiliary verb
④ bear, put up with
⑤ (of chessmen) be promoted

為る
①ⓐ become, turn into, grow, get
ⓑ begin to (do), come to (do)
②ⓐ result in, turn out
ⓑ amount [come] to
③ⓐ (of seasons) come, set in
ⓑ elapse, pass
④ serve [act] as

生る
bear fruit, fruit

❷【なす】

成す
① form, make, constitute
② achieve, accomplish, succeed

為す
do, perform, carry out

生す
give birth, bear

HOMOPHONES

なる
為 DO → 4395
生 LIFE → 4309

なす
為 DO → 4395
生 LIFE → 4309

NOTE

➡ see COMPOUND FORMATION for 成程 なるほど → 程 1524

舟

4353
■4-6-4

▶**SMALL BOAT**
シュウ ふね ふな- -ぶね
Ⓒ 舟 zhōu

137	Jōyō	U821F
舟	S6-6-0	F1196

RADICAL

fune 'ship', used in characters related to ships, boats or their parts
Left variant: 舟 × ***funehen*** (船 航 般)

COMPOUNDS

● [original meaning] **(SMALL) BOAT, ship**
舟艇 しゅうてい boat, craft
舟行 しゅうこう navigation, going by ship
舟運 しゅううん transportation by water
呉越同舟 ごえつどうしゅう bitter enemies in the same boat

KUN

【ふね 舟】**SMALL BOAT [craft], (row)boat**
小舟 こぶね small craft

【ふな- 舟-】[also 船-] [also prefix] **SMALL BOAT**
舟着き場 ふなつきば wharf
舟人 ふなびと sailor
舟大工 ふなだいく boatbuilder

【-ぶね -舟】[also -船] [also suffix] **SMALL BOAT**
釣り舟 つりぶね fishing boat
渡し舟 わたしぶね ferryboat

SYNONYMS

●&【ふね】**boats and ships**
船 SHIP → 1700
舶 OCEANGOING SHIP → 1699
艦 WARSHIP → 1817
潜 submarine → 0922
舟 SMALL BOAT → 4353
艇 BOAT → 1727
隻 COUNTER FOR SHIPS → 3426

HOMOPHONES

ふね
船 SHIP → 1700
槽 TANK → 1352
ふな- 船 SHIP → 1700
-ぶね 船 SHIP → 1700

NOTE

➡ see USAGE note at 船 1700
★ do not confuse with 丹 CINNABAR → 4249

孝

■4-6-4

incorrect classification/ stroke-count
➡ see ☐3-4-3: 耂 at 3973

肉

■4-6-4

incorrect classification
➡ see ☐3-4-2: 内 at 3966

劣 ■4-6-4
incorrect classification
➡ see ▀2-4-2: 少 at 3047

糸 ■4-6-4
incorrect classification
➡ see ▀2-3-3: 幺 at 2703

考老 ■4-6-4
incorrect classification
➡ see ☐3-4-2: 耂 at 3962

亜 4354 ■4-7-1

▶SUB-
▶PHONETIC [a]
ア ㊔ つぐ
Ⓝ 亞 Ⓒ 亚 yà

7	Jōyō	U4E9C
二	S7-2-5	F1210

COMPOUNDS

❶ [also prefix]
ⓐ **SUB-, subordinate**
ⓑ *chem* **SUB-**, -ite, -ous
a 亜熱帯 あねったい subtropics
亜科 あか suborder
亜麻 あま flax
亜鉛 あえん zinc
b 亜炭化物 あたんかぶつ subcarbide
亜硫酸ナトリウム ありゅうさんなとりうむ sodium sulfite
亜硝酸 あしょうさん nitrous acid
❷ⓐ **used PHONETICally for *a*, esp. in the transliteration of foreign place names**
ⓑ Argentina
a 亜米利加 あめりか America
b 亜爾然丁 あるぜんちん Argentina
亜国 あこく Argentina
❸ **Asia**
東亜 とうあ East Asia
興亜 こうあ development of Asia
❹ [also 堊 3442] whitewash
白亜 はくあ chalk; white wall

INDEPENDENT

【あ 亜】**Asia**

SYNONYMS

❶ⓐ **subordinate**
副 SECONDARY → 2230
次 secondary → 0058
従 subordinate → 0498
亜 SUB- → 4354
準 QUASI- → 3541
半 semi- → 4313
准 JUNIOR → 0143
助 assistant → 1440
❷ⓐ **phonetic [a]**
亜 PHONETIC [a] → 4354
阿 PHONETIC [a] → 0408
❸ **continents**
亜 Asia → 4354
阿 Africa → 0408
欧 EUROPE → 1098
米 AMERICA → 4342
豪 Australia → 2657

更 4355 ■4-7-1

▶RENEW
コウ さら さら(に) ふ(ける) ふ(かす)
Ⓒ 更 gèng gēng

73	Jōyō	U66F4
日	S7-4-3	F1052

COMPOUNDS

❶ⓐ **RENEW, replace, change, alter**
ⓑ **change, exchange, alternate**
a 更新する こうしんする renew, renovate, innovate
更改 こうかい renewal, renovation
更正 こうせい correction, revision, rectification
更生 こうせい rebirth, rehabilitation; recycling
更衣する こういする change one's clothes
変更する へんこうする alter, change, modify, shift
b 更迭 こうてつ reshuffle, change, exchanging places
❷ watches of the night, lateness of the night
深更 しんこう dead of night, midnight
初更 しょこう first watch of the night
三更 さんこう midnight, in the dead of night
❸ [formerly 甦 4109] revive, come back to life
更生する こうせいする revive, resuscitate

INDEPENDENT

【こう 更】watches of the night, lateness of the night

KUN

【さら 更】*literary* **of course, naturally;** [in compounds] **furthermore, moreover; still more**
尚更 なおさら still more, all the more
今更 いまさら now, after so long a time
満更 まんざら (not) wholly, (not) altogether
【さらに 更に】**furthermore, moreover; still more; anew, afresh, again; (not) in the least**
更に一歩を進める さらにいっぽをすすめる go a step further
【ふける 更ける】*vi* **grow late, advance, wear on**
秋更けて あきふけて late in autumn

【ふかす 更かす】*vt* **sit up till late (at night)**
夜更かし よふかし sitting up late at night, keeping late hours

SYNONYMS

❶ⓐ **reform**
改 REFORM → 0287
革 REFORM → 3099
更 RENEW → 4355
新 make new → 2239

ⓑ **change and replace**
変 CHANGE → 2569
替 REPLACE → 3457
代 SUBSTITUTE → 0034
迭 ALTERNATE → 3818
更 change → 4355
改 change → 0287
易 change → 3064
化 CHANGE INTO, -ize → 0022
遷 undergo transition → 3932
転 turn into → 1872
換 EXCHANGE → 0716
交 INTERCHANGE → 2508

【さらに】
○ **additionally**
亦 ALSO → 2504
兼 CONCURRENTLY → 2850
又 also, and → 4158
而うして and → 2520
及び and → 4192
並びに and also → 2793
傍ら besides → 0166
尚 STILL → 2774
更に furthermore → 4355
且つ AS WELL → 4297

里

▶**COUNTRYSIDE**
▶**LEAGUE**
り さと
Ⓒ 里 lǐ li

4356
■4-7-1

166	Jōyō-2	U91CC
里	S7-7-0	F0737

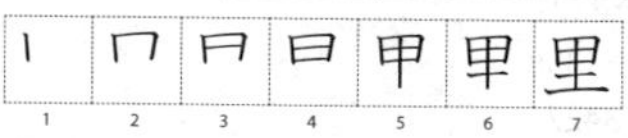

RADICAL

sato 'hamlet' (重 量 釐×), used for character classification
Left variant: 里× *satohen* (野)

COMPOUNDS

❶ⓐ **COUNTRYSIDE, country, rural district**
ⓑ [formerly also 俚 0112] (of the countryside) **rural, rustic, vulgar**
a 郷里 きょうり one's old home, native place
b 里謡 りよう ballad, folk song
里言 りげん dialect

❷ⓐ **hamlet, village**
ⓑ *ri*: unit of administration in ancient Japan similar to a hamlet
a 里人 りじん villagers, countryfolk
遊里 ゆうり licensed quarters, red-light district

❸ⓐ (former unit of distance) **LEAGUE, mile, *ri***
ⓑ *ri*, Japanese **LEAGUE**: unit of length equiv. to approx. 3.9 km or 36 *cho* (町)
a 里程 りてい mileage
海里 かいり [also 浬] nautical mile
一里塚 いちりづか milepost, milestone
万里の長城 ばんりのちょうじょう Great Wall of China
b 千里の道も一歩から せんりのみちもいっぽから A journey of a thousand miles starts with but a single step

❹ used phonetically for *ri*, esp. in the transliteration of foreign words
巴里 ぱり Paris

INDEPENDENT

【り 里】*ri*, Japanese **LEAGUE** (→ ❸ⓑ)

KUN

【さと 里】
① **hamlet, village**
里芋 さといも taro
村里 むらざと village
古里(=故郷) ふるさと hometown, birthplace
山里 やまざと mountain hamlet [village]

② **COUNTRYSIDE**

③ⓐ one's parents' home
ⓑ [sometimes also 郷] hometown, one's birthplace
b 里心 さとごころ homesickness

SYNONYMS

❶ⓐ **the country**
郊 SUBURB → 1638
里 COUNTRYSIDE → 4356
鄙 THE COUNTRY → 2338
郷 the country → 0664
辺 BORDERLAND → 3761

ⓑ **vulgar and unrefined**
俗 vulgar → 0119
卑 MEAN → 3270
賤 MEAN → 1993
鄙 MEAN → 2338
俚 RURAL → 0112
里 rural → 4356
粗 COARSE → 1683
野 rustic → 1877

蛮 barbaric →2638

❷ⓐ villages and towns

町 TOWN →1430
村 VILLAGE →1029
里 hamlet →4356
郷 HOMETOWN →0664
庄 FEUDAL VILLAGE →3788
邑 VILLAGE →2716

❸ⓐ & ❸ⓑ length units

寸 *sun* (3.03 cm) →3652
浬 NAUTICAL MILE (1852 m) →0526
反 *tan* (10.6 m) →3663
尺 *SHAKU* (30.3 cm) →4248
米 meter →4342
尋 fathom (1.8 m) →2918
間 *ken* (1.8 m) →4122
丈 *jo* (3.03 m) →4227
町 *cho* (109 m) →1430
里 LEAGUE, *ri* (3.9 km) →4356
哩 MILE (1609 m) →0479

USAGE

【さと】

里
① hamlet, village
② countryside
③ⓐ one's parents' home
ⓑ [sometimes also 郷] hometown, one's birthplace

郷
[usu. 里] hometown, one's birthplace

HOMOPHONES

さと 郷 HOMETOWN →0664

かいり
浬 NAUTICAL MILE →0526
海里 →0459, 4356

豕

4357

■4-7-1

▶SWINE

シ いのこ

Ⓒ 豕 shǐ

152	Non-Jōyō	U8C55
豕	S7-7-0	F0000

RADICAL

inoko 'pig' (象 豪 豢×), used in characters related to pigs, boars or similar animals

Variant: 豕× ***inokohen*** (豬)

COMPOUNDS

● [original meaning] **SWINE, pig, hog, boar**

魯魚亥豕 ろぎょがいし miswriting a word

KUN

【いのこ 豕】 [archaic] **SWINE**, pig, hog, boar

遼東の豕 りょうとうのいのこ being self-complacent

SYNONYMS

● swine

豚 PIG →1228
豕 SWINE →4357
猪 WILD BOAR →0652
亥 THE BOAR →2505

NOTE

➡ see COMPOUND FORMATION for 遼東の豕 りょうとうのいのこ →遼 3930

酉

4358

■4-7-1

▶THE ROOSTER

ユウ とり ㊔ なが みのる

Ⓒ 酉 yǒu

164	Names	U9149
酉	S7-7-0	F0000

RADICAL

hiyominotori 'wine' (酒 醤), used in characters related to alcoholic beverages or the like

Left variant: 酉× ***torihen*** (配 酔 酸)

COMPOUNDS

● tenth sign of the Oriental zodiac: **the Rooster**—(time) 5-7 p.m., (direction) west, (season) August (of the lunar calendar) (→see APPENDIX 8)

丁酉 ていゆう 34th of the sexagenary cycle

KUN

【とり 酉】 tenth sign of the Oriental zodiac: **THE ROOSTER** (→●)

酉年 とりどし Year of the Rooster
酉の方角 とりのほうがく west

SYNONYMS

● birds

鷹 HAWK →3955
鷗 GULL →2370
烏 CROW →4088
雀 SPARROW →3117
燕 SWALLOW →3142
鴻 LARGE WILD BIRD →0977
鳳 MALE PHOENIX →3749
凰 FEMALE PHOENIX →3738
鵬 MYTHICAL HUGE BIRD →1416
鶏 CHICKEN →2221
酉 ROOSTER →4358
隼 FALCON →3427
鳩 PIGEON →0184
鷲 EAGLE →3598
鳶 BLACK KITE →3919
鶴 CRANE →2326
鷺 HERON →3621
鵜 CORMORANT →2067
鴨 DUCK →1582
雁 WILD GOOSE →3741

HOMOPHONES

とり

鳥 BIRD → 4105
鶏 CHICKEN → 2221
禽 BIRD → 2654

NOTE

➡ see USAGE note at 鳥 4105

呉

4359

■4-7-1

▶KINGDOM OF WU

ゴ く(れる) ㊔ くれ

30	Nonstandard	U5433
口	S7-3-4	F0000

traditional form → see 吳 at 3156

两

4360

■4-7-1

▶BOTH

リョウ ㊔ もろ

1	Nonstandard	U4E24
一	S7-1-6	F0000

traditional form → see 兩 at 4331

条

■4-7-1

incorrect classification
➡ see ⬒2-3-4: 夂 at 2726

君

■4-7-1

incorrect classification
➡ see ◘3-4-3: 尹 at 3974

呂

■4-7-1

incorrect classification
➡ see ⬒2-3-4: 囗 at 2713

承

■4-7-1

incorrect classification/
stroke-count
➡ see ◧1-1-7: フ at 0016

镸

■4-7-1

incorrect classification
➡ see ⬒2-5-2: 𠀐 at 3157

坐

4361

■4-7-2

▶SIT

ザ すわ(る)

Ⓒ 坐 zuò

32	Names	U5750
土	S7-3-4	F1363

COMPOUNDS

[now usu. 座 3868]

❶ⓐ [original meaning] **SIT, take a seat, sit down**

ⓑ **SIT still without doing anything, not stir**

a 坐像 ざぞう sedentary statue [image]
坐禅 ざぜん Zen meditation
坐礁する ざしょうする run aground, be stranded
正坐する せいざする sit upright [straight]
行住坐臥 ぎょうじゅうざが the four cardinal behaviors (walking, stopping [standing], sitting and lying); daily life

b 坐視する ざしする remain an idle spectator, look on idly [doing nothing]
坐食の徒 ざしょくのと idler, drone

❷ⓐ (place for sitting) **seat**

ⓑ (part on which one sits) **seat, bottom**

a 単坐 たんざ single seat

b 坐薬 ざやく suppository

❸ be accused of a crime

連坐する れんざする be implicated [involved] in (a crime)

❹ travel (by ship)

坐乗する ざじょうする go on board (a ship)

INDEPENDENT

【ざする 坐する(=座する)】 SIT down, take a seat; be implicated [involved] in (a crime)

KUN

【すわる 坐る】 [now usu. 座る] **SIT, take a seat, sit down**

坐り すわり stability
坐り込む すわりこむ sit down (for a prolonged time); do a sit-in

SPECIAL READINGS

胡坐 あぐら sitting cross-legged

SYNONYMS

❶ⓐ **sit**

座 SIT → 3868
坐 SIT → 4361
居 sit → 3822

HOMOPHONES

すわる

座 SEAT → 3868
据 INSTALL → 0602

すわり 座 SEAT → 3868

NOTE

➡ see USAGE note at 座 3868

我

4362

■4-7-3

▶SELF

ガ われ わ わ(が)- わが-

Ⓒ 我 wǒ

62	Jōyō-6	U6211
戈	S7-4-3	F0687

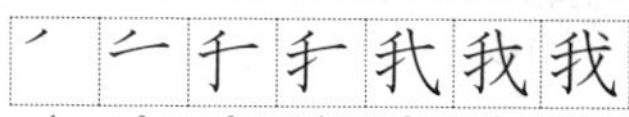

COMPOUNDS

❶ⓐ **SELF, one's own self**

ⓑ **ego, SELF**

a 我慢 がまん patience, endurance; self-restraint
我流 がりゅう self-taught method, one's own way

【我】甫串求来車身束釆事弟

b 自我 じが self, ego
無我 むが self-effacement; *Buddhism* nonself, none-go

❷ **SELFishness, egotism**
我欲 がよく selfishness
我利 がり one's own interests, self-interest
我執 がしゅう egoistic attachment, egotism

❸ one's own, my
我田引水 がでんいんすい seeking one's own interests

❹ **used phonetically for *ga***
怪我 けが injury, wound; accident

INDEPENDENT

【が 我】**SELF**, ego; selfishness, egotism, egoism
我が強い がつよい egoistic, selfish, self-willed
我を通す がをとおす persist in one's own way

KUN

【われ 我】
① **oneself, SELF, ego**
我知らず われしらず in spite of oneself, unconsciously
② [sometimes also 吾]
ⓐ **I; we**
ⓑ *slang* you
a 我我 われわれ we

【わ 我】[archaic] I

【わが- 我が-, 我-】[sometimes also 吾-] *literary* **my; our**
我が輩(=吾輩) わがはい I
我が儘× わがまま selfishness, willfulness
我が国 わがくに our country, Japan
我が家 わがや one's home [house]

SYNONYMS

❶ **first person pronouns**
私 I (*polite*) → 1432
我 SELF → 4362
己 ONESELF → 4188
身 ONE'S PERSON → 4368
僕 I (*familiar*) → 0185
俺 I (*intimate*) → 0124
吾 I (*elegant*) → 3060
予 I (*pompous*) → 2477
余 I (*pompous*) → 2535
麿 I (*archaic*) → 3949
朕 IMPERIAL WE → 1185
自 SELF → 4338

USAGE

❶【われ】
我
① oneself, self, ego
② [sometimes also 吾]
ⓐ I; we
ⓑ *slang* you
吾
[usu. 我]
ⓐ *elegant* I; we
ⓑ *slang* you

❷【わが-】
我が-
[sometimes also 吾-] *literary* my; our
吾-
[usu. 我が-] *literary* my; our

HOMOPHONES

われ 吾 I → 3060
わが- 吾 I → 3060

NOTE

➡ see COMPOUND FORMATION for 我慢 がまん → 慢 0844

甫

4363

■4-7-3

▶**BARELY**

ホ フ **はじ(めて)** ㊔ すけ もと とし うら たすく なみ

Ⓒ 甫 fǔ

101	Names	U752B
用	S7-5-2	F2643

COMPOUNDS

❶ [usu. 圃 ほ 3871] large, wide
田甫 たんぼ rice field

❷ beginning
新甫 しんぽ new futures on the first trading session of the month

❸ [archaic]
ⓐ courtesy title for elderly men
ⓑ man's courtesy name, pseudonym
a 尼甫 じほ Confucius
b 台甫 たいほ your personal name

KUN

【はじめて 甫めて】*literary* **BARELY, just**
我齢は甫めて九つなるに わがよわいははじめてここのつなるに I was barely nine years old

SYNONYMS

【はじめて】
◯ **almost**
殆ど ALMOST → 1130
瀕 ON THE VERGE OF → 0994
甫めて BARELY → 4363
辛い bare → 2531

HOMOPHONES

はじめて
初 FIRST → 1433
始 BEGIN → 0335

NOTE

➡ see USAGE note at 初 1433

串

▶SKEWER

カン^▲ セン^▲ くし

Ⓒ 串 chuàn

4364

■4-7-3

2	Jōyō	U4E32
丨	S7-1-6	F2585

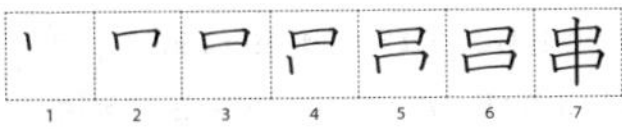

KUN

【くし 串】

① **SKEWER, spit**

串焼き くしやき grilling on a skewer; grilled skewered food

串刺し くしざし skewered

竹串 たけぐし bamboo skewer

② branch of a sacred tree

玉串 たまぐし branch of a sacred tree

SYNONYMS

【くし】

① **perforators**

針 NEEDLE → 2099

串 SKEWER → 4364

杭 STAKE → 1068

釘 NAIL → 2100

求

▶SEEK

キュウ グ^▲ もと(める) ㊔ もとむ

Ⓒ 求 qiú

4365

■4-7-3

85	Jōyō-4	U6C42
氺	S7-5-2	F0526

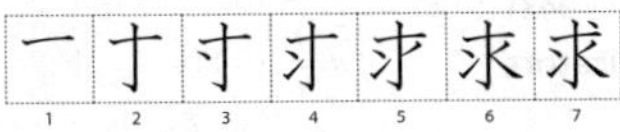

COMPOUNDS

❶ (go in search of) **SEEK (for), search, pursue; wish for, desire**

求人 きゅうじん job offer

求職 きゅうしょく seeking employment

求道 きゅうどう(=ぐどう) seeking for truth; seeking for enlightenment

探求する たんきゅうする investigate, search (for), pursue

追求 ついきゅう pursuit

欣求浄土 ごんぐじょうど seeking rebirth in the Pure Land

欲求 よっきゅう want(s), desire, wish

❷ (ask for) **SEEK, request, demand**

求婚 きゅうこん proposal of marriage

求刑する きゅうけいする demand a sentence (for the accused)

要求する ようきゅうする require, demand, request

請求 せいきゅう demand, request, claim

KUN

【もとめる 求める】(go in search of) **SEEK (for), search, pursue; wish for, desire;** (ask for) **seek, request, demand; buy**

求め もとめ request, appeal, claim, demand

追い求める おいもとめる seek after, pursue

幸福を求めて こうふくをもとめて in search [pursuit] of happiness

買い求める かいもとめる buy

SYNONYMS

❶ **seek**

探 SEARCH → 0613

索 SEARCH FOR → 3105

捜 LOOK FOR → 0516

求 SEEK → 4365

猟 hunt for → 0654

❶ **wish and desire**

願 WISH → 2320

憧 YEARN AFTER → 0899

憬 YEARN AFTER → 0898

貪 COVET → 2630

望 HOPE → 3408

希 ASPIRE → 2543

懐 LONG FOR → 0942

慕 yearn for → 2970

渇 thirst for → 0627

欲 DESIRE → 1867

慾 DESIRE → 3551

求 SEEK → 4365

❷ **request**

請 REQUEST → 1983

訴 APPEAL TO → 1901

頼 ASK → 2041

嘱 CHARGE WITH → 0881

要 REQUIRE → 3263

願 ASK A FAVOR → 2320

求 SEEK → 4365

乞 BEG → 2457

来

▶COME

ライ タイ^▲ く(る) きた(る) きた(す)

Ⓝ 來 耒^◇ Ⓒ 来 lái

4366

■4-7-3

75^△	Jōyō-2	U6765
木	S7-4-3	F0052

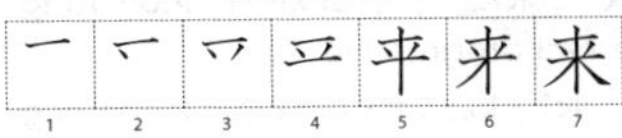

COMPOUNDS

❶ⓐ **COME, come to**

ⓑ **COME from, derive**

a 来訪 らいほう visit, call

来日 らいにち coming to Japan
来客 らいきゃく visitor, guest
到来する とうらいする come, arrive
伝来する でんらいする be transmitted, be imported
舶来の はくらいの imported, foreign-made
在来の ざいらいの ordinary, common, usual
往来 おうらい come-and-go, traffic; road, street
b 由来 ゆらい origin, source, cause; history
生来 せいらい by nature [birth], congenitally

❷ⓐ the coming, the following, the next
ⓑ coming generations, the future

a 来年 らいねん next year
来週 らいしゅう next week
来学期 らいがっき next school term
b 未来 みらい future
将来 しょうらい future; in the future

❸ [also suffix] **since, as of, from**

以来 いらい as of, since then, from that time on
従来は じゅうらいは hitherto, so far
本来 ほんらい originally, essentially, naturally
古来 こらい from ancient times
昨年来 さくねんらい since last year

❹ bring about, cause

招来する しょうらいする bring about, give rise to, cause
出来する しゅったいする happen, occur, take place

❺ used phonetically for *rai*

家来 けらい retainer, vassal, follower
矢来 やらい palisade, stockade, barrier

KUN

【くる 来る】

①ⓐ **COME (over), come near, arrive**
ⓑ **COME to see, call on, visit**
ⓒ (seasons) **COME (round), set in**
ⓓ **COME from, derive from, be due to**

a 帰って来る かえってくる come back, return
やって来る やってくる come (along), turn up
b 又遊びに来て下さい またあそびにきてください Come and see me again
c 春が来た はるがきた Spring has come
d ギリシャ語から来た言葉 ぎりしゃごからきたことば word derived from Greek

②ⓐ [auxiliary following the TE-form] **COME to be, become, grow**
ⓑ [in the form of て来た てきた] **auxiliary indicating present perfect progressive**

a 暖かくなって来た あたたかくなってきた It's getting warmer
b 酷く質素な生活を送って来た ひどくしっそなせいかつをおくってきた We have been living in the simplest way

③ assume (an attitude), take (a move)

そう来なくっちゃ そうこなくっちゃ That's the idea

【きたる 来る】

① **COME, arrive**

オバマ大統領来る おばまだいとうりょうきたる President Obama Arrives

② the coming, next, to **COME**

来る木曜日 きたるもくようび next Thursday

【きたす 来す】**bring about, cause, give rise to; result in**

破綻を来す はたんをきたす fail, be ruined; go bankrupt

SYNONYMS

❶ⓐ go and come

行 GO → 0246
徠 COME → 0576
往 GO ON → 0348
出 go to → 4310
参 go somewhere → 2563
来 COME → 4366
通 go to and from → 3855
向 head toward → 3790
赴 PROCEED TO → 4095
嚮 GO TOWARD → 3610

❷ⓐ next

次 NEXT → 0058
明 next → 1060
翌 THE FOLLOWING → 3307
来 the coming → 4366

ⓑ future

来 coming generations → 4366
後 afteryears → 0431

❸ direction indicators

至 to → 2707
-行き bound for → 0246
-向け (bound) for → 3790
迄 UP TO → 3967
以 TO THE…OF → 0045
自 from → 4338
来 since → 4366
而 DIRECTION WORD → 2520

車

4367

▶**VEHICLE**
▶**WHEEL**
シャ くるま
Ⓒ 车 chē jū

4-7-3

159	Jōyō-1	U8ECA
車	S7-7-0	F0234

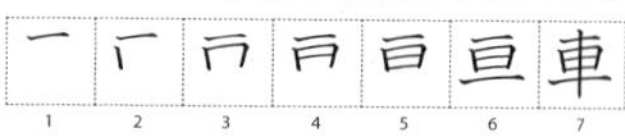

RADICAL

kuruma 'vehicle' (軍 輩 轟), used in characters related to wheeled vehicles or their qualities

Left variant: 車 × ***kurumahen*** (転 輪 軽)

COMPOUNDS

❶ [also suffix] any wheeled vehicle:

ⓐ [original meaning] **VEHICLE, cart, wagon**

ⓑ **motor VEHICLE, car, automobile**

ⓒ **railway car, train**

ⓓ suffix for wheeled **VEHICLE**s, -cycle

a 馬車 ばしゃ horse-drawn carriage, coach, wagon
唇歯輔車 しんしほしゃ mutual dependence
人力車 じんりきしゃ rickshaw, man-pulled cart

ab 戦車 せんしゃ tank; chariot

b 車道 しゃどう road, roadway
単車 たんしゃ motorcycle, motorbike
自動車 じどうしゃ automobile
駐車 ちゅうしゃ parking
救急車 きゅうきゅうしゃ ambulance

bc 車両 しゃりょう vehicle, car; rolling stock
車内 しゃない inside a vehicle (as a car or train)
下車する げしゃする alight, get off
停車 ていしゃ stoppage (of a vehicle)

c 電車 でんしゃ train, electric train, trolley
列車 れっしゃ (railway) train
客車 きゃくしゃ passenger car
機関車 きかんしゃ locomotive

d 三輪車 さんりんしゃ tricycle, three-wheeler

❷ **WHEEL**
車輪 しゃりん wheel
水車 すいしゃ water wheel
拍車 はくしゃ spur, rowel spur

KUN

【くるま 車】**WHEEL, caster; wheeled vehicle, esp. cars or taxis; rickshaw**
車椅子 くるまいす wheelchair
車酔い くるまよい car sickness
車屋 くるまや rickshawman; rickshaw station
風車 かざぐるま(=ふうしゃ) windmill; pinwheel
荷車 にぐるま cart, wagon

SPECIAL READINGS

山車 だし festival car, float

SYNONYMS

❶ **vehicle**
車 VEHICLE → 4367
輌 VEHICLE → 2000
乗 vehicle → 4393
輪 wheeled vehicle → 1999
駕 CARRIAGE → 3236
輿 PALANQUIN → 3626
台 COUNTER FOR VEHICLES → 2498

ⓒ **kinds of railway**
鉄 railway → 2147
電 electric railway → 3465
車 railway car → 4367
両 counter for railway cars → 4331
輌 counter for railway cars → 2000

❷ **circular objects**
環 RING → 1395
輪 WHEEL, RING → 1999
車 WHEEL → 4367
盤 DISK → 3533
釧 ARMLET → 2109

NOTE

➡ see COMPOUND FORMATION for
唇歯輔車 しんしほしゃ → 輔 1963
単車 たんしゃ → 単 2805

身

4368

■4-7-3

▶**BODY**
▶**ONE'S PERSON**

シン み

Ⓒ 身 shēn

158	Jōyō-3	U8EAB
身	S7-7-0	F0106

RADICAL

mi 'body', used in characters related to the body

Left variant: 身 × ***mihen*** (躬× 躾×)

COMPOUNDS

❶ⓐ **(material) BODY, human body (esp. vs. mind), one's person, the flesh**

ⓑ **BODY** length, height

a 身体 しんたい body
身長 しんちょう stature, height
身障者 しんしょうしゃ physically handicapped person, disabled person
全身 ぜんしん the whole body
心身 しんしん mind and body
焼身 しょうしん burning oneself (to death), self-immolation
変身 へんしん transformation, metamorphosis

b 馬身 ばしん horse's length
艇身 ていしん boat's length
長身 ちょうしん tall figure, high stature

❷ **BODY** or main part of a thing, esp. a sword or gun
刀身 とうしん sword blade
銃身 じゅうしん barrel of a gun, gun barrel

❸ **ONE'S PERSON, one's own person, oneself, self**
身辺 しんぺん one's person, one's immediate surroundings

我 甫 串 求 来 車【身】束 釆 事 弟

自身 じしん self, oneself; itself
出身地 しゅっしんち one's native place
独身 どくしん single life; celibacy
単身 たんしん alone, by oneself, unaccompanied
前身 ぜんしん one's former self, one's past life; predecessor
保身 ほしん self-protection
献身 けんしん self-sacrifice, devotion

❹ social status, social standing
身代 しんだい fortune, one's property
立身する りっしんする establish oneself in life
小身 しょうしん humble position

❺ life
終身 しゅうしん all through life
捨身 しゃしん becoming a priest; risking one's life for others

KUN

【み 身】

① **BODY, one's person**
身に着ける みにつける put on, wear
身の回り みのまわり one's person, one's appearance
身軽な みがるな light, agile, nimble
身形 みなり dress, clothing; one's appearance
細身 ほそみ slender figure; narrow blade
不死身 ふじみ immortality, invulnerability

② **BODY or main part of a thing**
中身 なかみ content, substance; interior
黄身 きみ yolk, vitellus
抜き身 ぬきみ naked sword

③ **ONE'S PERSON, one's own person, oneself, self**
身の上 みのうえ one's career, one's condition, one's fortune
身近な みぢかな near oneself, close to one, familiar
身元(=身許) みもと one's birth, one's identity, one's background
身寄り みより relative, relation, kinsfolk
身投げ みなげ suicide by drowning or jumping from a high place
身柄 みがら one's person; social standing
身勝手 みがって selfishness, egoism, egotism

④ **(one's) social status, one's station in life; one's position**
身の程 みのほど one's social position, one's own place
身分 みぶん social position [standing]; circumstances; rank, identity

⑤ heart, soul, mind
身を入れる みをいれる devote oneself to, exert oneself
身に染みる みにしみる go to one's heart, come home to

⑥ **meat, flesh**
脂身 あぶらみ fat, fatty meat
刺身 さしみ *sashimi*, sliced raw flesh (esp. of fish)

⑦ life
身を捨てる みをすてる throw away one's life

SYNONYMS

❶ⓐ body
体 BODY → 0080
身 BODY (esp. vs. mind) → 4368
肉 FLESH → 3966
屍 CORPSE → 3843
尸 CORPSE → 4198
骸 DEAD BODY → 2301

❸ &【み】③ first person pronouns
私 I (*polite*) → 1432
我 SELF → 4362
己 ONESELF → 4188
身 ONE'S PERSON → 4368
僕 I (*familiar*) → 0185
俺 I (*intimate*) → 0124
吾 I (*elegant*) → 3060
予 I (*pompous*) → 2477
余 I (*pompous*) → 2535
麿 I (*archaic*) → 3949
朕 IMPERIAL WE → 1185
自 SELF → 4338

❹ class
級 GRADE → 1630
段 grade → 1471
位 RANK → 0069
階 RANK → 0761
身 social status → 4368
格 STATUS → 1161
等 CLASS → 3321
流 class → 0529
層 STRATUM → 3920

【み】

⑥ **meat**
肉 FLESH → 3966
身 meat → 4368
脩 DRIED MEAT → 0154

NOTE

➡ see COMPOUND FORMATION for 身寄り みより → 寄 2856

束

4369

■4-7-3

▶TIE UP
▶BUNDLE

ソク たば たば(ねる) つか▲ つか(ねる)▲

Ⓒ 束 shù

75	Jōyō-4	U675F
木	S7-4-3	F0869

COMPOUNDS

❶ⓐ [original meaning] **TIE UP (in a bundle), bundle, bind**

ⓑ (restrict the freedom of) **TIE (a person) UP, restrain, bind**

a 束髪 そくはつ bundled hair, hair done up in a bun
束帯 そくたい old ceremonial court dress
装束 しょうぞく costume, attire

b 束縛する そくばくする restrain, restrict, bind, fetter
約束する やくそくする promise, vow, pledge
拘束 こうそく restriction, restraint, binding
結束する けっそくする band together, unite

❷ technical term for various **BUNDLE**like clusters:

ⓐ [also suffix] *anat, biol* **BUNDLE**

ⓑ *chem, math* lattice

ⓒ [also suffix] *phys, biol* flux

a 繊維束 せんいそく fiber bundle, fascicle
維管束 いかんそく vascular bundle

b 束群 そくぐん lattice group

c 磁束 じそく magnetic flux
中性子束 ちゅうせいしそく neutron flux

❸ counter for various items in **BUNDLE**s or batches, as: fagots, sheaves (of straw), reams (of 200 sheets of Japanese paper)
薪五束 まきごそく five bundles of firewood
二束三文の にそくさんもんの dirt-cheap, dog-cheap

❹ⓐ unit of 100 items (esp. fish)

ⓑ arrow length unit (measured in hand breadths)

INDEPENDENT

【そく 束】 *anat* **BUNDLE**; *math* lattice; *phys* flux

KUN

【たば 束】 **BUNDLE, bunch, batch, sheaf; counter for bundles**
束になって たばになって in a bunch; in a group
花束 はなたば bunch of flowers
札束 さつたば bundle of (bank) notes, wad of bills
一束十円 ひとたばじゅうえん 10 yen a bundle

【たばねる 束ねる】 **TIE UP in a bundle, BUNDLE; control, manage**
束ね たばね bundle; management

【つか 束】
① **hand breadth**
束の間 つかのま brief space of time, moment
② short support
③ bulk (of a book)

【つかねる 束ねる】 **BUNDLE**, tie up
手を束ねて てをつかねて folding one's arms, doing nothing

SYNONYMS

❶ⓐ **join**
結 TIE → 1706
繋 CONNECT → 3612
縛 BIND → 1779
綴 BIND → 1746
繃 BIND UP → 1787
束 TIE UP → 4369
梱 PACK → 1205
連 LINK → 3849
係 CONNECT → 0108
接 join → 0607

ⓑ **restrain**
制 CONTROL (restrain) → 1624
禁 PROHIBIT → 3469
限 LIMIT → 0475
抑 SUPPRESS → 0301
束 TIE UP → 4369
縛 BIND → 1779
控える HOLD BACK → 0600
扣える HOLD BACK → 0250
渋る hang [hold] back → 0625

❷ **bundles and clusters**
束 BUNDLE → 4369
房 tuft → 2445

HOMOPHONES

つか 柄 CHARACTER → 1111

NOTE

➡ see USAGE note at 柄 1111

釆

4370

■4-7-3

▶***NOGOME***

165	Radical	U91C6
釆	S7-7-0	F0000

RADICAL

nogome 'separate', used in characters related to separating

Left variant: 釆ˣ ***nogomehen*** (釈 釉 釋)

事

4371

■4-7-3

▶**AFFAIR**
▶**ABSTRACT THING**
ジ ズ こと

6	Nonstandard	U4E8A
亅	S7-1-6	F0000

handwritten form → see 事 at 4384

弟

■4-7-3

incorrect classification
➡ see ▀2-2-5: ソ at 2537

寿

4372
4-7-4

▶**LONGEVITY**
▶**CONGRATULATIONS**

ジュ ス▲ ことぶき ことほ(ぐ)▲ ㊔ とし ひさ ひさし やすし かず なが

Ⓝ 壽 Ⓒ 寿 shòu

41△	Jōyō	U5BFF
寸	S7-3-4	F1097

COMPOUNDS

❶ⓐ [original meaning] **LONGEVITY, long life, old age**
ⓑ celebration of **LONGEVITY**, birthday in one's old age

a 寿老人 じゅろうじん God of Longevity
長寿 ちょうじゅ long life, longevity
b 白寿 はくじゅ 99 years old, one's 99th birthday

❷ **life span, age, natural life**
寿命 じゅみょう life span
天寿 てんじゅ one's natural life span

❸ **used phonetically for *su***
寿司 すし sushi (raw fish and vinegared rice)

INDEPENDENT

【じゅ 寿】life span, age; **LONGEVITY**; celebration
百歳の寿 ひゃくさいのじゅ 100 years of age

KUN

【ことぶき 寿】**CONGRATULATIONS, felicitation, celebration, greetings; longevity**
寿教室 ことぶききょうしつ culture courses for the aged
新年の寿 しんねんのことぶき New Year's greetings

【ことほぐ 寿ぐ】*elegant* congratulate, felicitate, extend one's best wishes

SYNONYMS

❶ⓐ **life**
生 LIFE → 4309
命 LIFE → 2553
寿 LONGEVITY → 4372

❷ **age**
齢 AGE → 2390
令 age → 2489
年 years → 2528
歳 AGE SUFFIX → 3131
才 AGE SUFFIX → 4218
寿 life span → 4372

【ことぶき】
○ **celebrating and congratulating**
祝 CELEBRATE → 1144
慶 FELICITATION → 3936
賀 CONGRATULATE → 3212
寿 CONGRATULATIONS → 4372

NOTE

➡ see COMPOUND FORMATION for
傘寿 さんじゅ → 傘 2640
白寿 はくじゅ → 白 4305
米寿 べいじゅ → 米 4342

良

4373
4-7-4

▶**GOOD**

リョウ よ(い) -よ(い) い(い)▲ -い(い)▲
㊔ よし なが つかさ まこと ら ろう

Ⓒ 良 liáng

138	Jōyō-4	U826F
艮	S7-6-1	F0427

COMPOUNDS

❶ⓐ (having positive qualities) **GOOD, fine, favorable, excellent**
ⓑ (characterized by good luck) **GOOD**, lucky, auspicious, happy

a 良好な りょうこうな good, fine, excellent, favorable
良質の りょうしつの of fine quality, superior
良否 りょうひ good or bad, quality
良導体 りょうどうたい good conductor
最良の さいりょうの best, superfine, most excellent
優良な ゆうりょうな superior, excellent
改良する かいりょうする improve, reform, make better
純良品 じゅんりょうひん genuine article
不良 ふりょう badness, inferiority; delinquency; juvenile delinquent
b 良日 りょうじつ lucky [auspicious] day

❷ⓐ (having good character or moral excellence) **GOOD, good-natured, virtuous**
ⓑ (well-behaved) **GOOD**, obedient, law-abiding

a 良心 りょうしん conscience
良識 りょうしき good sense
善良な ぜんりょうな good, virtuous
b 良民 りょうみん good citizens, law-abiding people
順良な じゅんりょうな good and obedient, gentle, meek
温良な おんりょうな obedient, meek

❸ innate, natural, inborn
良知 りょうち innate intellect [intelligence]
良能 りょうのう natural ability

❹ [archaic] (considerable) **GOOD** (while), fairly
良久 りょうきゅう for a good while

INDEPENDENT

【りょう 良】(school mark) **GOOD, B; good, fine**
数学の成績は良だった すうがくのせいせきはりょうだった I got a B in math

KUN

【よい 良い】[sometimes also 好い]

①ⓐ **GOOD, fine, nice, pleasant, excellent**

ⓑ **GOOD-looking, handsome, beautiful, pretty**

ⓒ **GOOD for (one's health), beneficial**

ⓓ (of considerable amount) **GOOD** (price)

a 良さ よさ merit, virtue, good quality, good point

良く よく well, right(ly), thoroughly, skillfully, carefully, closely; much, usually, often

良い天気 よいてんき fine [fair] weather

良かったら よかったら if you like

ああ良かった ああよかった Thank God!

気分が良い きぶんがよい feel good [pleasant]

b 良い男 よいおとこ handsome man

c 健康に良い けんこうによい be good for the health

d 良い値で よいねで at a good price

② **suitable, proper, fitting; useful**

丁度良い時に ちょうどよいときに just at the right moment

これで良いか これでよいか Will this do?

盗むのは良くない ぬすむのはよくない It's wrong to steal

③ lucky, auspicious

良い日を選ぶ よいひをえらぶ choose a lucky [auspicious] day

④ **intimate, friendly**

仲良し なかよし intimacy, familiar terms; bosom friend

⑤ⓐ **preferable, better**

ⓑ **I wish, I hope**

a 君はここに居ない方が良い きみはここにいないほうがよい You had better not stay here

b 助けてくれても良かったのに たすけてくれてもよかったのに You might have helped me

⑥ [following the TE-form of verbs]

ⓐ **may, can, be allowed**

ⓑ **need not (do), do not have to**

a 入っても良い はいってもよい You may enter

b 君は行かなくて良い きみはいかなくてよい You need not go

⑦ do not mind (doing), have no objection

やって見ても良い やってみてもよい I wouldn't mind trying it

【-よい -良い】[verbal suffix] **easy**

読み良い よみよい easy to read

【いい 良い】[sometimes also 好い] colloquial form of 良い よい

良い資料 よいしりょう valuable material

良い気味だ いいきみだ Serves you right!

良いですか いいですか Is it all right?/You see?

天気が良くなってくれれば良いのだが てんきがよくなってくれればいいのだが I wish the weather would improve

車をお借りして良いですか くるまをおかりしていいですか May I use your car?

行っても良い いってもいい I wouldn't mind going there

【-いい -良い】same as -良い -よい

SPECIAL READINGS

野良 のら the fields

奈良県 ならけん Nara Prefecture

SYNONYMS

❶ⓐ good

良 GOOD →4373

善 GOOD →2921

好 FAVORABLE →0240

順 favorable →0018

佳 FINE →0096

美 BEAUTIFUL →2817

❷ⓐ virtuous

正 RIGHT →4296

義 righteous →2948

善 GOOD →2921

良 GOOD →4373

鯁 UPRIGHT →2357

USAGE

❶【よい】

良い

[sometimes also 好い]

①ⓐ good, fine, nice, pleasant, excellent

ⓑ good-looking, handsome, beautiful, pretty

ⓒ good for (one's health), beneficial

ⓓ (of considerable amount) good (price)

② suitable, proper, fitting; useful

③ lucky, auspicious

④ intimate, friendly

⑤ⓐ preferable, better

ⓑ I wish, I hope

⑥ [following the TE-form of verbs]

ⓐ may, can, be allowed

ⓑ need not (do), do not have to

⑦ do not mind (doing), have no objection

善い

(morally excellent) good, good-natured, virtuous, upright

好い

[now usu. 良い] same as 良い

❷【いい】

良い

[sometimes also 好い] colloquial form of 良い よい

好い

[now usu. 良い] colloquial form of 好い よい

HOMOPHONES

よい

善 GOOD →2921

好 LIKE →0240
いい好 LIKE →0240

兎

4374
■4-7-4

▶**RABBIT**
ト うさぎ ㊔ う うさ
Ⓝ 兎 兎◇ 兔◇ Ⓒ 兔 tù

10	Names	U514E
儿	S7-2-5	F2156

COMPOUNDS

❶ [original meaning] **RABBIT, hare**
家兎 かと tame rabbit
野兎病 やとびょう tularemia
脱兎の如く だっとのごとく with lightning speed ("like a fleeing rabbit")
二兎を追う者は一兎をも得ず にとをおうものはいっとをもえず If you run after two hares, you will catch neither

❷ unclassified compounds
兎角 とかく this and that; being apt to; somehow or other, anyhow
兎に角 とにかく anyhow, in any case; regardless
兎や角言う とやかくいう say this and that

KUN

【うさぎ 兎】**RABBIT, hare**
兎耳 うさぎみみ long ears; (figuratively) someone with long [big] ears
兎跳び うさぎとび hopping forward from a squatting position
野兎 のうさぎ hare
雪兎 ゆきうさぎ mountain hare

SYNONYMS

❶ **rabbit**
兎 RABBIT →4374
卯 THE HARE →0231

【うさぎ】
◯ **domesticated mammals**
牛 CATTLE →4263
馬 HORSE →4086
豚 PIG →1228
羊 SHEEP →2708
犬 DOG →4275
猫 CAT →0651
兎 RABBIT →4374

曳

4375
■4-7-4

▶**DRAW**
エイ ひ(く) ㊔ のぶ とお

73	Nonstandard	U66F5
曰	S7-4-3	F0000

alternative form →see 曵 at 4348

成

4376
■4-7-4

▶**FORM**
▶**ACHIEVE**
セイ ジョウ な(る) な(す) -な(す) ㊔ しげ まさ みのる

62	Nonstandard	U2F8B2
戈	S7-4-3	F0000

traditional form →see 成 at 4352

我

■4-7-4

incorrect classification
➡ see ■4-7-3 at 4362

系

■4-7-4

incorrect classification
➡ see ⬒2-1-6: ノ at 2443

希

■4-7-4

incorrect classification
➡ see ⬒2-2-5: メ at 2543

考

■4-7-4

incorrect classification/stroke-count
➡ see ◻3-4-2: 耂 at 3962

孝

■4-7-4

incorrect classification
➡ see ◻3-4-3: 耂 at 3973

身

■4-7-4

incorrect classification
➡ see ■4-7-3 at 4368

呉

■4-7-4

incorrect classification
➡ see ■4-7-1 at 4359

果

4377
■4-8-1

▶**FRUIT**
カ は(たす) -は(たす) は(てる) -は(てる) は(て)
Ⓒ 果 guǒ

75	Jōyō-4	U679C
木	S8-4-4	F0314

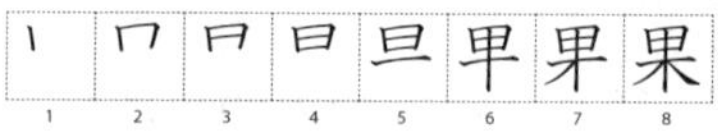

COMPOUNDS

❶ⓐ [original meaning] **FRUIT**
ⓑ counter for **FRUIT**s, jewels or seals
a 果実 かじつ fruit, berry
果汁 かじゅう fruit juice
青果 せいか vegetables and fruits
摘果 てきか thinning out superfluous fruit
b 林檎一果 りんごいっか one apple

❷ **FRUIT, result, outcome; effect**
結果 けっか result, outcome, consequence

成果 せいか result, fruit, outcome
効果 こうか effect, efficacy; result
因果 いんが cause and effect; karma
戦果 せんか fruit of battle, war results

❸ resolutely, decisively
果断な かだんな resolute, decisive
果敢な かかんな bold, daring; resolute

❹ really; as was expected
果然 かぜん as was expected

INDEPENDENT

【か 果】result; effect; satori
因となり果となる いんとなりかとなる constitute the cause and effect

KUN

【はたす 果たす】*vt* **effect, carry out, discharge, accomplish; realize (one's wishes); kill**
果たして はたして as was expected, sure enough; really
果たし合い はたしあい duel, fight to death
使命を果たす しめいをはたす carry out one's mission

【-はたす -果たす】**emphatic verbal suffix indicating completeness**
使い果たす つかいはたす use up, spend all

【はてる 果てる】*vi* **end, be finished; be exhausted; die**
宴が果てる うたげがはてる The party has ended
異境に果てる いきょうにはてる die in a strange land

【-はてる -果てる】**emphatic verbal suffix indicating completeness**
朽ち果てる くちはてる decay completely, rot away; rust away; rusticate oneself
絶え果てる たえはてる be extinguished, be exterminated; cease completely

【はて 果て】**end, extremity, limit; result**
果てしない はてしない endless, boundless, everlasting
世界の果て せかいのはて end of the world
挙げ句の果てに あげくのはてに in the end, on top of all this

SPECIAL READINGS

果物 くだもの fruit

SYNONYMS

❶ **fruit**
果 FRUIT → 4377
実 fruit → 2765

【はたす】
○ **execute**
執 EXECUTE → 2114
行 ACT → 0246
履 FULFILL → 3933
施 CARRY OUT → 1103
践 IMPLEMENT → 1938
果たす effect → 4377
遂 ACCOMPLISH → 3892

【はて】
○ **extreme**
極 EXTREME → 1243
窮 extremity → 2983
限 LIMIT → 0475
涯 OUTER LIMITS → 0623
果て end → 4377

雨

4378

■ 4-8-1

▶**RAIN**
ウ あめ あま- -さめ*
Ⓒ 雨 yǔ yù

173	Jōyō-1	U96E8
雨	S8-8-0	F0798

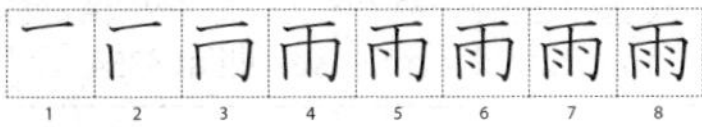

RADICAL

ame 'rain', used in characters related to precipitation
Top variant: ⻗ ***amekanmuri*** (雪 霧 雫)

COMPOUNDS

● [original meaning] **RAIN, rainfall**
雨量 うりょう rain, rainfall
雨期(=雨季) うき rainy season
降雨 こうう rainfall, rain
豪雨 ごうう heavy rain, downpour
梅雨(=黴雨) ばいう rainy season (of early summer)
風雨 ふうう wind and rain, storm

KUN

【あめ 雨, あま- 雨-】**RAIN**
雨戸 あまど shutter
雨水 あまみず rainwater
雨雲 あまぐも rain cloud
雨曇 あまぐもり overcast weather
雨上がり あめあがり just after a rainfall
雨具 あまぐ raingear, rainwear
雨降り あめふり rainfall; rainy weather
大雨 おおあめ heavy rain
俄雨 にわかあめ (rain) shower

【-さめ -雨】**RAIN**
春雨 はるさめ spring rain; sticks of bean jelly
小雨 こさめ drizzle
霧雨 きりさめ(=きりあめ) drizzle, misting rain

SPECIAL READINGS

五月雨 さみだれ early summer rain
時雨 しぐれ late fall or early winter rain

梅雨 つゆ rainy season (of early summer)

SYNONYMS

● **kinds of precipitation**

雨 RAIN → 4378
露 DEW → 3495
霜 FROST → 3491
雪 SNOW → 3431

⻗

4379

■4-8-1

▶ ***AMEKANMURI***

173	Radical	U2ED7
雨	S8-8-0	F0000

radical variant → see 雨 at 4378

亞

4380

■4-8-1

▶ **SUB-**
▶ **PHONETIC [a]**

ア ㊔ つぐ

7	Names	U4E9E
二	S8-2-6	F0000

traditional form → see 亜 at 4354

兩

4381

■4-8-1

▶ **BOTH**

リョウ ㊔ もろ

11	Nonstandard	U5169
入	S8-2-6	F0000

traditional form → see 両 at 4331

長

■4-8-1

incorrect classification
➡ see ▀2-5-3: ⾂ at 3163

承

■4-8-1

incorrect classification
➡ see ◧1-1-7: フ at 0016

吳

■4-8-1

incorrect stroke-count
➡ see ■4-7-1 at 4359

垂

4382

■4-8-2

▶ **HANG DOWN**

スイ た(れる) た(らす) た(れ) -た(れ)

㊔ たる

Ⓝ 埀 Ⓒ 垂 chuí

32	Jōyō-6	U5782
土	S8-3-5	F1441

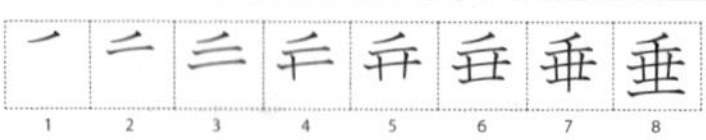

COMPOUNDS

❶ⓐ **HANG DOWN, hang, droop, dangle**
ⓑ drip, drop

a 懸垂 けんすい suspension, pendency; chinning exercises
口蓋垂 こうがいすい uvula
b 垂涎×する すいぜん(=すいえん)する covet

❷ **perpendicular, vertical**

垂直の すいちょくの vertical, perpendicular
垂線 すいせん perpendicular line

❸ hand down, leave to posterity

垂迹 すいじゃく Shinto god who is the reincarnation of a Buddha or bodhisattva

❹ confer, bestow, grant

垂範する すいはんする set an example
山上の垂訓 さんじょうのすいくん the Sermon on the Mount

❺ [rare] nearly, almost, on the verge of

垂死 すいし on the verge of dying

KUN

【たれる 垂れる】**HANG DOWN, hang, droop; drip, drop; leave to posterity; confer, bestow, grant;** *slang* **evacuate (as excreta or wind)**

垂れ下がる たれさがる hang, dangle
雨垂れ あまだれ raindrops
教訓を垂れる きょうくんをたれる give a lesson, lecture

【たらす 垂らす】**HANG DOWN, suspend; drop, drip**

髪を垂らす かみをたらす let one's hair hang down
床に水を垂らす ゆかにみずをたらす spill water on the floor

【たれ 垂れ】**sauce, gravy; lappet, flap, tassel; hanging, straw curtain; hanging radical (of Chinese characters), enclosure radicals**

胡麻垂れ ごまだれ sesame sauce
籠の垂れ かごのたれ hanging of a palanquin
病垂れ やまいだれ *yamaidare*, 'illness' radical (疒)

【-たれ -垂れ】**suffix for forming swearwords**

糞×っ垂れ くそったれ You swine!
しみっ垂れ しみったれ stinginess; miser
阿呆垂れ あほたれ You ass!

SYNONYMS

❶ⓐ **hang**

掛ける HANG → 0596
垂 HANG DOWN → 4382
懸 SUSPEND → 3632
吊 SUSPEND → 2686
釣り- suspended → 2108

❷ **vertical**

縦 VERTICAL → 1783
竪- VERTICAL → 3516
垂 perpendicular → 4382
立て- standing → 2486
直 STRAIGHT → 3649

隹

▶*FURUTORI*

4383

■4-8-2

172	Radical	U96B9
隹	S8-8-0	F0000

RADICAL

furutori 'small bird' (集 雅 雀), used in characters related to small birds or their qualities

奄

■4-8-2

incorrect classification
➡ see ⬒2-3-5: 大 at 2757

者

■4-8-2

incorrect classification
➡ see □3-4-4: 耂 at 3980

巻

■4-8-2

incorrect classification
➡ see ⬒2-6-2: 龹 at 3257

事

▶**AFFAIR**
▶**ABSTRACT THING**
ジ ズ こと
Ⓝ 事◆ Ⓒ 事 shì

4384

■4-8-3

6	Jōyō-3	U4E8B
亅	S8-1-7	F0022

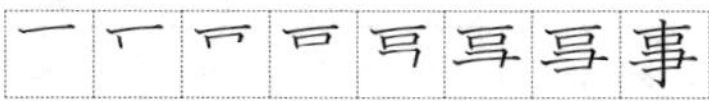
1 2 3 4 5 6 7 8

COMPOUNDS

❶ [also suffix]
ⓐ (something that is done) **AFFAIR, something, matter, thing, fact**
ⓑ (something that occurs) **AFFAIR, something, event, occurrence, incident, unexpected event, accident**

a 事物 じぶつ things, affairs
事実 じじつ fact, reality; as a matter of fact
事項 じこう matters, facts; articles, items
返事 へんじ answer, reply
房事 ぼうじ sex, lovemaking
記事 きじ news, article; account
食事 しょくじ meal, dinner, board
b 事件 じけん affair, incident, case, event
事故 じこ accident, incident, trouble
事情 じじょう circumstances, conditions, situation
事態 じたい situation, state of affairs
無事に ぶじに safely, without accident, successfully; peacefully, amicably
火事 かじ fire
好事家 こうずか dilettante, person of fantastic taste
関心事 かんしんじ matter of concern and interest

❷ (business matters) **AFFAIRs, business, work**
事務 じむ business, clerical work, duties of an office
事務室 じむしつ office
事業 じぎょう undertaking, enterprise, business; achievement
用事 ようじ things to do, errand, business, engagement
家事 かじ household affairs, housework
軍事 ぐんじ naval and military affairs
工事 こうじ construction
人事 じんじ human affairs, personnel affairs

❸ serve, be in the service of
事大主義 じだいしゅぎ worship of the powerful
師事する しじする study under, look up to (a person) as one's teacher

❹ **officer, official, public officer [servant]**
知事 ちじ (prefectural) governor
刑事 けいじ (police) detective
判事 はんじ judge
幹事 かんじ manager, secretary; organizer
領事 りょうじ consul, consular representative
理事 りじ director, trustee

KUN

【こと 事】

①ⓐ [also suffix] **ABSTRACT THING, affair, matter, fact**
ⓑ **ABSTRACT THING or act**—word used for the nominalization of verbs, adjectives or phrases

a 事柄 ことがら matter, affair, circumstances
明白な事 めいはくなこと obvious fact
学校の事を話す がっこうのことをはなす speak about the school, talk about school affairs
物事 ものごと things, matter; everything
勝負事 しょうぶごと gambling, competition, game
b 考える事 かんがえること what one thinks
. . . する事にしている …することにしている make a point of (doing), be in the habit of (doing)
永い事 ながいこと for a long time
. . . との事である …とのことである It is said that…/ They say that…/I hear that…

② (event of special import) **AFFAIR, something, incident, case, occurrence; trouble**
事を起こす ことをおこす cause trouble [a disturbance]
事勿れ主義 ことなかれしゅぎ peace-at-any-price principle
どんな事にも準備が出来ている どんなことにもじゅんびができている be ready for any contingency
大変な事が起こった たいへんなことがおこった A terrible accident occurred
出来事 できごと occurrence, happening; affair, incident; accident

③ (business matters) **AFFAIRs, business, work, duty**

事を成し遂げる ことをなしとげる achieve a task
事を運ぶ ことをはこぶ proceed, go ahead, carry on
毎日の事 まいにちのこと daily affairs, daily routine
仕事 しごと work, employment, business

④ⓐ **things, occasions, circumstances, details, particulars**
ⓑ cause, reason, account

a 事と次第で こととしだいで under certain circumstances, if things permit
どんな事が有っても どんなことがあっても under any circumstances
彼は学校を遅刻する事が有る かれはがっこうをちこくすることがある He is sometimes late for school

b 事を分ける ことをわける reason with (a person)

⑤ⓐ need, necessity
ⓑ **worthwhileness**

a 事が足りる ことがたりる answer the purpose, be sufficient
事欠く ことかく lack, be in need of
急ぐ事は無い いそぐことはない There is no need for haste

b 漢字を勉強しただけの事は有る かんじをべんきょうしただけのことはある I didn't study kanji for nothing
見事(=美事)な みごとな splendid, admirable, beautiful

⑥ **experience**
京都に行った事が有りますか きょうとにいったことがありますか Have you ever been to Kyoto?
行った事は行ったが会えなかった いったことはいったがあえなかった I did go, but I could not see him

⑦ⓐ exclamatory particle
ⓑ indicates imperative mood

a まあ親切な事 まあしんせつなこと How nice [kind] of you!

b ごみを捨てない事 ごみをすてないこと No litter please

⑧ alias, viz
鷗外事森林太郎 おうがいこともりりんたろう Mori Rintaro alias Ogai

SYNONYMS

❶ⓐ **affair**
事 AFFAIR → 4384
儀 affair → 0191
件 MATTER → 0054

ⓑ & 【こと】② **incident**
事 AFFAIR → 4384
故 incident → 1466
変 unexpected event → 2569

❷ **affairs**
用 THINGS TO DO → 3694
事 affairs → 4384
務 affairs → 1505

❹ **officials**
官 GOVERNMENT OFFICIAL → 2766
吏 OFFICIAL → 4351
僚 official → 0186
司 officiator → 3648
役 executive → 0288
事 officer → 4384

【こと】
①ⓐ **abstract thing**
事 ABSTRACT THING → 4384
物 THING → 1084

ⓑ **nominalizers**
所 PARTICLE OF NOMINALIZATION → 1056
事 nominalization word → 4384
子 NOUN SUFFIX → 4196
性 -ITY → 0357

COMPOUND FORMATION

【見事(=美事) みごと】
見事な 'splendid, admirable, beautiful' refers to something that is worthwhile (事 こと ⑤ⓑ) seeing (見).

NOTE

➡ see COMPOUND FORMATION for
事柄 ことがら → 柄 1111
房事 ぼうじ → 房 2445

東

4385
■ 4-8-3

▶**EAST**
トウ ひがし ㊔ あずま はる はじめ
Ⓒ 东 dōng

75	Jōyō-2	U6771
木	S8-4-4	F0110

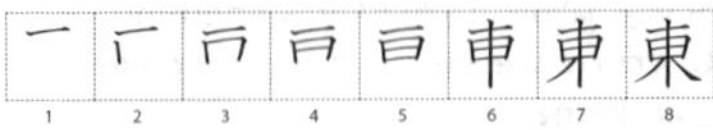

COMPOUNDS

❶ⓐ **EAST, eastern**
ⓑ go **EAST**ward

a 東方 とうほう east, eastward
東南 とうなん southeast
東亜 とうあ East Asia
東洋 とうよう Orient
東部 とうぶ eastern part; the East (of the United States)
東西南北 とうざいなんぼく north, south, east and west
関東 かんとう Kanto district
中東 ちゅうとう Middle East
遼東の豕 りょうとうのいのこ being self-complacent

b 東征 とうせい eastern expedition

❷ **Tokyo**
東京 とうきょう Tokyo

東上 とうじょう going up to Tokyo
東名高速道路 とうめいこうそくどうろ Tokyo-Nagoya Expressway

❸ abbrev. of 東京大学 とうきょうだいがく: University of Tokyo
早東戦 そうとうせん (baseball) game between Waseda and Tokyo universities

KUN

【ひがし 東】[also prefix] **EAST, eastern**
東側 ひがしがわ eastern side
東口 ひがしぐち east exit
東半球 ひがしはんきゅう Eastern Hemisphere

SYNONYMS

❶ⓐ **cardinal points**
東 EAST → 4385
西 WEST → 4333
北 NORTH → 0230
南 SOUTH → 2584
巽 SOUTHEAST → 3329
艮 NORTHEAST → 4330

❷ **Kanto region**
京 TOKYO → 2546
東 Tokyo → 4385
都 METROPOLIS OF TOKYO → 2120
浜 Yokohama → 0523
埼 SAITAMA → 0560
湘 SHONAN → 0742

NOTE

➡ see COMPOUND FORMATION for
遼東の豕 りょうとうのいのこ → 遼 3930
関東 かんとう → 関 4129

隶

4386
■4-8-3

▶ ***REIZUKURI***

171	Radical	U96B6
隶	S8-8-0	F0000

RADICAL

reizukuri 'capture' (隸), used in characters related to capturing

---

來

4387
■4-8-3

▶ **COME**
ライ タイ く(る) きた(る) きた(す)

9	Names	U4F86
人	S8-2-6	F0000

traditional form → see 来 at 4366

奄

■4-8-3

incorrect classification
➡ see ▀2-3-5: 大 at 2757

卑

4388
■4-8-4

▶ **MEAN**
ヒ いや(しい) いや(しむ) いや(しめる)

24	Names	UFA35
十	S8-2-6	F0000

traditional form → see 卑 at 3270

武

■4-8-4

incorrect classification
➡ see □3-4-4: 弋 at 3979

奉

■4-8-4

incorrect classification
➡ see ▀2-5-3: 夫 at 3167

奔

■4-8-4

incorrect classification
➡ see ▀2-3-5: 大 at 2758

券

■4-8-4

incorrect classification
➡ see ▀2-6-2: 龹 at 3256

肴

■4-8-4

incorrect classification
➡ see ▀2-2-6: 乂 at 2567

斉

■4-8-4

incorrect classification
➡ see ▀2-2-6: 亠 at 2548

哭

■4-8-4

incorrect classification/
stroke-count
➡ see ■4-7-1 at 4359

飛

4389
■4-9-1

▶ **FLY**
ヒ と(ぶ) と(ばす) -と(ばす)
Ⓒ 飞 fēi

183	Jōyō-4	U98DB
飛	S9-9-0	F0364

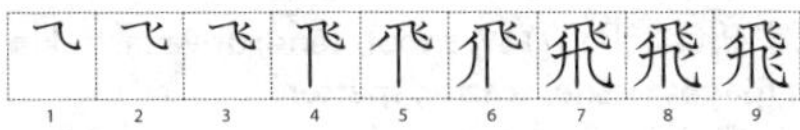

RADICAL

tobu 'fly', used in characters related to flying

COMPOUNDS

❶ⓐ [formerly also 蜚 3473] **FLY**
ⓑ **FLY** about, scatter
ⓒ *baseball* **FLY**

a 飛行 ひこう flight, aviation
飛行機 ひこうき airplane
飛行場 ひこうじょう airport, airfield
飛来する ひらいする come flying, come by air
飛鳥 ひちょう flying bird
雄飛する ゆうひする launch out, embark upon (a career)

b 飛沫 ひまつ splash, spray
飛散する ひさんする disperse, scatter, fly
c 飛球 ひきゅう fly ball
犠飛 ぎひ sacrifice fly
中飛 ちゅうひ center fly
❷ⓐ **FLY**ing, swift, quick, urgent
ⓑ [formerly 蜚 3473] **FLY**ing (rumor), unfounded
a 飛脚 ひきゃく express messenger; postman (in former times)
飛報 ひほう urgent message
b 流言飛語 りゅうげんひご false report, flying rumor
❸ **leap, spring up, jump**
飛躍する ひやくする leap, jump
突飛な とっぴな wild, extravagant, extraordinary
❹ name of chess piece in shogi (Japanese chess): *hisha*, rook
飛車 ひしゃ *hisha*
敵飛 てきひ opponent's *hisha*
❺ [archaic] high
飛簷× ひえん high roof, upturned eaves
飛瀑× ひばく waterfall

INDEPENDENT

【ひ 飛】*hisha* (→❹)

KUN

【とぶ 飛ぶ】
①ⓐ **FLY; travel by air**
ⓑ rush [**FLY**] (to the scene)
ⓒ **FLY** about, be scattered
a 飛び上がる とびあがる fly up, jump up
飛び込む とびこむ down, jump from, jump [leap] in; dive into
飛び切り とびきり exceptionally, by far
飛び魚 とびうお flying fish
② skip (pages), skip over
二頁から四頁へ飛ぶ にページからよんページへとぶ skip from page two to page four

【とばす 飛ばす】*vt* **FLY; shoot, send; drive fast; skip over (pages); issue; scatter, spatter**
鳩を飛ばす はとをとばす fly a pigeon
檄×を飛ばす げきをとばす issue a manifesto
水を飛ばす みずをとばす splash water

【-とばす -飛ばす】[emphatic verbal suffix] **off, away, recklessly**
叱り飛ばす しかりとばす scold away, rebuke strongly
書き飛ばす かきとばす write [dash] off

SYNONYMS

❶ⓐ **fly**
飛 FLY → 4389
蜚 FLY → 3473
翔 SOAR → 1714
航 NAVIGATE → 1671

USAGE

【とぶ】
飛ぶ
①ⓐ fly; travel by air
ⓑ rush [fly] (to the scene)
ⓒ fly about, be scattered
② skip (pages), skip over
翔ぶ
soar, fly
跳ぶ
ⓐ jump, leap, spring
ⓑ jump [leap] over, vault

★Though when used independently 飛ぶ means to fly and 跳ぶ to leap or jump, both 飛 and 跳 can mean to jump when used as components of compounds, as for example 飛び掛かる とびかかる 'spring [jump] upon'. 翔ぶ and 飛ぶ both mean to fly, but the former has a more poetic or elegant flavor.

HOMOPHONES

とぶ
翔 SOAR → 1714
跳 JUMP → 1934

重

4390

■4-9-2

▶**HEAVY**
▶**DUPLICATE**

ジュウ チョウ え おも(い) おも(り) かさ(ねる) かさ(なる) おも▲ ㊔ しげ しげる

Ⓒ 重 zhòng chóng

166	Jōyō-3	U91CD
里	S9-7-2	F0158

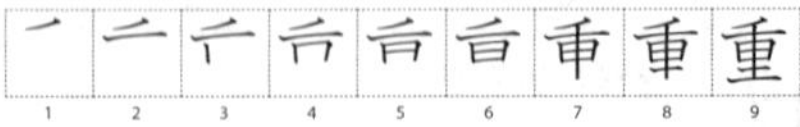

COMPOUNDS

❶ⓐ [also prefix] [original meaning] **HEAVY, weighty**
ⓑ *phys* (designating a heavier isotope) **HEAVY**
ⓒ [also prefix] *chem* **HEAVY**
ⓓ **weight, heaviness, load, gravity**
a 重油 じゅうゆ fuel oil
重金属 じゅうきんぞく heavy metal
過重な かじゅうな too heavy
b 重水素 じゅうすいそ heavy hydrogen
c 重液分離 じゅうえきぶんり heavy media [liquid] separation
d 重量 じゅうりょう weight
重力 じゅうりょく gravity, force of gravity
体重 たいじゅう body weight
比重 ひじゅう specific gravity, density; relative importance
荷重 かじゅう load
❷ [also prefix]

ⓐ (involving large-scale manufacture) **HEAVY**
ⓑ (great in degree) **HEAVY, serious, severe**
a 重爆 じゅうばく heavy bomber
重工業 じゅうこうぎょう heavy industry
重電機 じゅうでんき heavy electric apparatus
重騎兵 じゅうきへい heavy cavalry
b 重傷 じゅうしょう heavy [serious] wound, severe injury
重態(=重体) じゅうたい serious condition, critical state
重税 じゅうぜい heavy taxation
重労働 じゅうろうどう heavy labor
厳重に げんじゅうに strictly, severely, closely; securely, firmly

❸ⓐ (great in importance) **HEAVY, weighty, important, grave**
ⓑ **set value on, value, attach importance to, esteem**
a 重要な じゅうような important, essential, principal
重点 じゅうてん important point; importance, emphasis, stress; priority
重大な じゅうだいな important, serious, grave
重視する じゅうしする attach importance to, think much of
重任 じゅうにん heavy responsibility, important duty; reappointment
重宝 ちょうほう convenience, usefulness, handiness
重文(=重要文化財) じゅうぶん(=じゅうようぶんかざい) important cultural property; compound sentence
貴重な きちょうな precious, valuable
b 重商主義 じゅうしょうしゅぎ mercantilism
尊重する そんちょうする respect, esteem, value
偏重する へんちょうする attach too much importance, overemphasize
珍重する ちんちょうする value highly, treasure

❹ **dignified, composed, solemn**
重厚さ じゅうこうさ profoundness, depth, seriousness
慎重 しんちょう prudence, discretion, circumspection
自重する じちょうする be prudent [circumspect]; take care of oneself
荘重な そうちょうな solemn, grave, impressive

❺ⓐ **pile up, heap up, stack**
ⓑ **-fold, layer, story (of a building)**
a 重箱 じゅうばこ nest [tier] of boxes
重奏 じゅうそう duet
重合 じゅうごう polymerization
重積する じゅうせきする pile up
重層的 じゅうそうてき multilayered, stratified
重畳たる ちょうじょうたる piled up, placed one upon another; excellent, splendid
b 多重の たじゅうの multiple, multiplex
三重の さんじゅうの threefold, triple

❻ⓐ **DUPLICATE, repeat, redo**
ⓑ **DUPLICATE, double, multiple**
ⓒ [prefix] *chem* bi-
a 重重 じゅうじゅう repeatedly; extremely, very much
重複 ちょうふく(=じゅうふく) duplication, overlapping; repetition
b 重盗 じゅうとう double steal
重訳 じゅうやく retranslation
重版 じゅうはん second printing, reprint; second edition
重婚 じゅうこん bigamy
c 重炭酸ソーダ じゅうたんさんそーだ sodium bicarbonate, baking soda

❼ cordial, hospitable, liberal
丁重(=鄭重)な ていちょうな polite, courteous

❽ abbrev. of 重箱 じゅうばこ: nest [tier] of boxes; box lunch
天重 てんじゅう box lunch with tempura

INDEPENDENT

【じゅう 重】 nest [tier] of boxes
お重 おじゅう nest [tier] of boxes

KUN

【え 重】 [in compounds] **fold, layer, row**
幾重 いくえ(=いくじゅう) many folds
二重の ふたえ(=にじゅう)の twofold
八重咲きの やえざきの double-flowering
十重二十重 とえはたえ manifold, multitude

【おもい 重い】
①ⓐ **HEAVY, weighty**
ⓑ (difficult to move) **HEAVY, slow to move**
a 重さ おもさ weight
重たい おもたい heavy
重み おもみ weight; importance; dignity
重荷 おもに heavy load; burden, encumbrance
b 腰が重い こしがおもい be slow to act, be slow in starting work
② (weighed with concern) **HEAVY, depressed**
重苦しい おもくるしい heavy, oppressed, gloomy
③ (great in degree) **HEAVY, serious, severe**
重い罪 おもいつみ serious [grave] crime
④ (great in importance) **HEAVY, weighty, important, grave**
重い任務 おもいにんむ important task

【おもり 重り】 [also 錘] **weight, plumb, sinker, plummet**
糸に重りを付ける いとにおもりをつける weight a line

【かさねる 重ねる】 *vt* **pile up, heap up, stack in layers; repeat, add**

重ね かさね pile, heap; lapping over; suit
重ねて かさねて repeatedly, again
積み重ねる つみかさねる pile up, heap up, stack in layers

【かさなる 重なる】*vi* **be piled up, lie on top of one another; fall on, coincide with; come one after another, happen in succession**

重なり かさなり pile, piling; overlapping
折り重なる おりかさなる lie on top of one another, be in a heap
不幸が重なる ふこうがかさなる have a series of misfortunes

【おも 重】

おもな 重な [usu. 主な] **chief, principal, main, foremost**

重んじる(=重んずる) おもんじる(=おもんずる) hold in high regard; think much of
重立った おもだった principal, leading, chief, main

SYNONYMS

❷ⓑ extreme in degree

酷 SEVERE → 1967
強 STRONG → 0574
凄い tremendous → 0145
重 HEAVY → 4390
高 HIGH → 2601
深 DEEP → 0636
大 BIG → 4224
厳 SEVERE → 4079
激 intense → 0955
極 EXTREME → 1243
痛 bitter(ly) → 4071
切 keen → 0030
甚 EXTREMELY → 3271
祁 EXTREMELY → 1447
超 super- → 4107
頗る EXCEEDINGLY → 1552

❸ⓐ important

要 IMPORTANT → 3263
重 HEAVY → 4390

ⓑ respect

敬 RESPECT → 2136
尊 HONOR → 2920
畏 respect → 3170
欽 REVERE → 2124
仰 look up to → 0051
崇 REVERENCE → 2864
尚 VALUE HIGHLY → 2774
重 set value on → 4390
拝 WORSHIP → 0360
慕 ADORE → 2970

❺ⓐ accumulate

積 ACCUMULATE → 1579
溜 ACCUMULATE → 0814
累 CUMULATE → 3196
重 pile up → 4390
盛る heap up → 3314
堆 PILED HIGH → 0563

ⓑ -fold

倍 TIMES → 0122
重 -fold → 4390

❻ⓐ repeating and repetition

再 ANOTHER TIME → 4332
又 AGAIN → 4158
復 repeat → 0701
重 DUPLICATE → 4390
畳 reduplicate → 3205
改 redo → 0287
-換える redo → 0716
-直す repetition suffix → 3649
-返す do over → 3797

ⓑ compound

複 COMPOUND → 1565
倍 DOUBLE → 0122
重 DUPLICATE → 4390

USAGE

【おもり】

重り
[also 錘] weight, plumb, sinker, plummet

錘
[also 重り] weight, plumb, sinker, plummet

HOMOPHONES

おもり 錘 SPINDLE → 2191
おも 主 MAIN → 2437

NOTE

➡ see also USAGE note at 主 2437

韭

4391
■ 4-9-2

▶*NIRA*

179	Radical	U97ED
韭	S9-9-0	F0000

RADICAL

nira 'leek', used in characters related to plants resembling leeks

---

叀

4392
■ 4-9-2

▶STRIKE
ゲキ う(つ)

159	Nonstandard	U6483
車	S9-7-2	F0000

handwritten form → see 撃 at 3552

巻 incorrect classification
➡ see ▀2-6-3: 龹 at 3273
■4-9-2

看 incorrect classification
➡ see ◻3-4-5: 手 at 3992
■4-9-2

巷 incorrect classification
➡ see ▀2-4-5: 共 at 3097
■4-9-2

省 incorrect classification
➡ see ▀2-4-5: 少 at 3100
■4-9-2

春 incorrect classification
➡ see ▀2-5-4: 夫 at 3184
■4-9-2

者 incorrect classification
➡ see ◻3-4-5: 耂 at 3988
■4-9-2

乗

4393
■4-9-3

▶RIDE
▶GET ON
ジョウ の(る) -の(り) の(せる)

Ⓝ 乘 Ⓒ 乘 chéng shèng

4	Jōyō-3	U4E57
丿	S9-1-8	F0332

1 2 3 4 5 6 7 8 9

COMPOUNDS

❶ **RIDE, ride in, travel**
乗用車 じょうようしゃ passenger car, automobile
乗客 じょうきゃく passenger, fare
乗務員 じょうむいん trainman, crewman
乗馬する じょうばする ride a horse; mount a horse
同乗する どうじょうする ride together
試乗 しじょう trial ride
警乗する けいじょうする police (a train)
便乗する びんじょうする take advantage of an opportunity; go on board

❷ [original meaning] (take a place on a vehicle or animal) **GET ON, board, go aboard, mount**
乗車する じょうしゃする take a train, get aboard, get on
乗船する じょうせんする embark, go on board
乗降 じょうこう boarding and alighting, getting on and off

❸ⓐ vehicle
ⓑ *literary* counter for vehicles
a 下乗する げじょうする alight from a vehicle; get off a horse
b 万乗 ばんじょう ten thousand chariots; throne, sovereignty

❹ *Buddhism* Vehicle (Buddhist path to salvation)
大乗 だいじょう Mahayana (the Great Vehicle)
小乗 しょうじょう Hinayana (the Lesser Vehicle)

❺ *math*
ⓐ multiply
ⓑ **power**
a 乗法 じょうほう multiplication
相乗作用 そうじょうさよう synergism
b 自乗(=二乗) じじょう square, second power
二乗する にじょうする raise to the second power

❻ annals, chronicle, a history
史乗 しじょう history book, chronicle

INDEPENDENT

【じょうじる(=じょうずる) 乗じる(=乗ずる)】take advantage of, avail oneself of; multiply
人の無知に乗じる ひとのむちにじょうじる abuse [take advantage of] another's ignorance

KUN

【のる 乗る】

①ⓐ **RIDE, ride in, travel**
ⓑ (be carried) **RIDE** (the winds), be borne
a 乗組員 のりくみいん crew
乗り入れ のりいれ extension (of a railway line) into
乗り換え のりかえ change, transfer
乗り越し のりこし riding past one's stop
乗っ取る のっとる take possession of; capture, hijack
乗り物 のりもの vehicle, conveyance
電車に乗る でんしゃにのる take a train
b 風に乗る かぜにのる ride upon the winds

② (take a place on a vehicle or animal) **GET ON, board, mount**
乗り込む のりこむ board, go on board; march into
馬に乗る うまにのる get on (mount) a horse

③ (move or be placed on something) **GET ON, step on, mount**
乗り出す のりだす lean forward; start, set out; embark on, launch into
踏み台に乗る ふみだいにのる step on a footstool

④ join, participate in, get a share in
相談に乗る そうだんにのる take part in a consultation

⑤ be deceived, be taken in
計略に乗る けいりゃくにのる play into another's hands, fall into a trap

⑥ **feel like doing**
乗り気になる のりきになる get enthusiastic about, be keen to do
乗り気 のりき keenness [enthusiasm] to do

気乗りする きのりする be interested in, feel like (doing)

⑦ be in harmony with

歌が曲に乗る うたがきょくにのる The song is in harmony with the melody

⑧ be spread on

乗り のり spread

乗りが良い のりがいい spread well

【-のり -乗り】

① **suffix indicating passenger capacity**

五人乗りの車 ごにんのりのくるま five-seater (car)

②ⓐ riding

ⓑ RIDEr

a 只乗り ただのり free ride

波乗り なみのり surfriding, surfing

b ブランコ乗り ぶらんこのり trapeze performer

【のせる 乗せる】

① **take (a person) on board, carry (passengers), pick up (passengers)**

乗客を乗せる じょうきゃくをのせる take passengers on board

② let (a person) take part in (a scheme)

その仕事に私も一口乗せてくれないか そのしごとにわたしもひとくちのせてくれないか Let me in on that job, won't you?

③ take in, impose upon

そんな話に乗せられる物か そんなはなしにのせられるものか You can't come round me with such yarns

④ bring into harmony

SYNONYMS

❶ **travel by vehicle**

乗 RIDE → 4393

走 travel by vehicle → 2720

航 NAVIGATE → 1671

騎 RIDE ON HORSEBACK → 2307

❷ **get on**

乗 GET ON → 4393

搭 BOARD → 0721

❸ **vehicle**

車 VEHICLE → 4367

輌 VEHICLE → 2000

乗 vehicle → 4393

輪 wheeled vehicle → 1999

駕 CARRIAGE → 3236

輿 PALANQUIN → 3626

台 COUNTER FOR VEHICLES → 2498

❺ⓐ **multiply**

乗 multiply → 4393

掛ける multiply → 0596

ⓑ **mathematical power**

乗 power → 4393

方 SQUARE → 2459

平 square (measure) → 4291

USAGE

❶【のる】

乗る

①ⓐ ride, ride in, travel

ⓑ (be carried) ride (the winds), be borne

② (take a place on a vehicle or animal) get on, board, mount

③ (move or be placed on something) get on, step on, mount

④ join, participate in, get a share in

⑤ be deceived, be taken in

⑥ feel like doing

⑦ be in harmony with

⑧ be spread on

載る

① appear in print, be published, be recorded

② be placed upon

③ be loaded (on a vehicle)

❷【のせる】

乗せる

① take (a person) on board, carry (passengers), pick up (passengers)

② let (a person) take part in (a scheme)

③ take in, impose upon

④ bring into harmony

載せる

① load (a vehicle or ship with cargo), lade, carry

② place on, put on

③ put in print, publish, carry, put on record

HOMOPHONES

のる 載 LOAD → 4091

のせる 載 LOAD → 4091

威

4394

■4-9-4

▶**MIGHT**

▶**THREATEN BY FORCE**

イ おど(す)▲ おど(し)▲ おど(かす)▲

㊔ たけ たけし

Ⓒ 威 wēi

38	Jōyō	U5A01
女	S9-3-6	F1088

1 2 3 4 5 6 7 8 9

COMPOUNDS

❶ **MIGHT, impressive strength, power, authority, influence**

威力 いりょく power, might, authority, influence

威勢 いせい spirits, dash; power

威張る いばる put on airs, be haughty; boast, brag

権威 けんい authority, power

示威 じい show of force

猛威 もうい fierceness, fury, vehemence
球威の有る投球 きゅういのあるとうきゅう *baseball* powerful delivery
神威 しんい might of Heaven

❷ⓐ dignified, majestic, imposing
ⓑ dignity, prestige

a 威厳 いげん solemn dignity
威風 いふう majesty, dignity
威容 いよう dignified [majestic] appearance
威儀 いぎ dignity, dignified manner
威信 いしん prestige, dignity, authority
b 国威 こくい national prestige

❸ THREATEN BY FORCE, dominate by power
威圧 いあつ coercion, high-handedness
威嚇する いかくする intimidate, threaten, menace
脅威 きょうい threat, menace

INDEPENDENT

【い 威】 dignity; power, authority, influence
威有って猛からず いあってたけからず dignified without being overbearing
威を振るう いをふるう exercise authority

KUN

【おどす 威す】 [now usu. 脅す] threaten, menace, intimidate
敵を威す てきをおどす threaten the enemy

【おどし 威し】
①ⓐ [now usu. 脅し] threat, menace, intimidation
ⓑ [in compounds] something that scares or startles
b 鳥威し とりおどし scarecrow
② [usu. 縅し] braid or thread of Japanese armor

【おどかす 威かす】
ⓐ [now usu. 脅かす] threaten, menace, intimidate
ⓑ startle
a 威かして金を取る おどかしてかねをとる scare money out of (a person)

SYNONYMS

❶ power and authority
力 POWER → 4178
威 MIGHT → 4394
勢 POWER (to influence) → 3542
権 POWER (to control) → 1348
覇 SUPREMACY → 3392

❷ⓐ dignified
荘 DIGNIFIED → 2814
威 dignified → 4394
儼 SOLEMN → 0204
厳 solemn → 4079
粛 solemnly → 4400

❸ threaten
脅 THREATEN → 2614
劫 threaten → 1435
威 THREATEN BY FORCE → 4394
嚇 INTIMIDATE → 0964
喝 shout threats at → 0554

HOMOPHONES

おどす 脅 THREATEN → 2614
おどし
脅 THREATEN → 2614
縅 BRAID OF ARMOR → 1759
おどかす
脅 THREATEN → 2614
嚇 INTIMIDATE → 0964

COMPOUND FORMATION

【威張る いばる】
威張る 'put on airs, etc.' is to spread (張) authority or impressive strength (威 ❶); that is, to flaunt prestige.

NOTE

➡ see USAGE note at 脅 2614

為

4395
■4-9-4

▸DO
▸SAKE
イ ため¹▲ ため²▲ な(る)▲ な(す)▲ す(る)▲ な(さる)▲

Ⓝ 爲 Ⓒ 为 wéi wèi

86△	Jōyō	U70BA
灬	S9-4-5	F0791

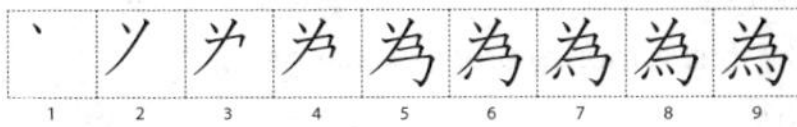

COMPOUNDS

❶ DO, make; act, behave
為政家 いせいか politician
行為 こうい act, deed, conduct, transaction
無為 むい inactivity; *Buddhism* that which is not created
作為 さくい artificiality, intention; commission (of a crime)

❷ that which is produced through causation
有為 うい vicissitudes of life; *Buddhism* perpetual change caused by karma; that which is made

KUN

【ため¹ 為】
①ⓐ **SAKE, benefit, advantage, profit**
ⓑ [often followed by に] **for the SAKE [purpose] of, on behalf of, so that**
a 人の為を思う ひとのためをおもう wish someone well
b 自分の為に じぶんのために for one's own sake, for oneself
...しない為に …しないために so as not to
② [often followed by に] **because (of), owing to, as a result of**
雨の為に あめのために because of the rain

【ため² 為】[in compounds] **exchange**
為銀 ためぎん exchange bank
外為 がいため foreign exchange

【なる 為る】
①ⓐ become, turn into, grow, get
ⓑ begin to (do), come to (do)
a 病気に為る びょうきになる fall [be taken] ill
b 泳げる様に為る およげるようになる learn how to swim
②ⓐ result in, turn out
ⓑ amount [come] to
b 幾らに為りますか いくらになりますか How much will that be?
③ⓐ (of seasons) come, set in
ⓑ elapse, pass
④ serve [act] as

【なす 為す】**DO, perform, carry out**
不善を為す ふぜんをなす do evil, commit vice

【する 為る】**DO**, perform, carry out; make, convert; cost; elapse
馬鹿な事を為る ばかなことをする do a silly thing
水を水蒸気に為る みずをすいじょうきにする change water into steam
数時間為れば すうじかんすれば in a few hours

【なさる 為さる】[honorific] **DO**, perform, carry out

SPECIAL READINGS

為替 かわせ money order, exchange

SYNONYMS

❶ **do and act**
為 DO → 4395
仕 DO → 0037
致す DO HUMBLY → 1668
行 ACT → 0246
作 WORK → 0077

【ため¹】
①ⓐ **benefit**
利 ADVANTAGE → 1431
益 BENEFIT → 2849
為 SAKE → 4395
用 use(ful) → 3694
役 SERVICE → 0288

② **cause and reason**
因 CAUSE → 3792
由 REASON → 4311
為 because → 4395
故 reason → 1466
訳 reason → 1865

HOMOPHONES

なる
成 FORM → 4352
生 LIFE → 4309

なす
成 FORM → 4352
生 LIFE → 4309

COMPOUND FORMATION

❶【外為 がいため】
外為 'foreign exchange' is an abbreviation of 外国為替 がいこくかわせ 'foreign exchange'.

❷【為替 かわせ】
為替 'money order, exchange' consists of 為 (為る する) 'let do, allow' and 替 'exchange'; that is, to allow someone to exchange money.

NOTE

➡ see USAGE note at 成 4352
★ This character has various old readings that form many compounds, including なる, なす, する 'become, do', all of which are now written in hiragana.

美
■4-9-4
incorrect classification
➡ see ▀2-3-6: 䒑 at 2817

哉
■4-9-4
incorrect classification
➡ see □3-6-3: 𢦏 at 4084

奏
■4-9-4
incorrect classification
➡ see ▀2-5-4: 𡗗 at 3185

奔
■4-9-4
incorrect classification
➡ see ▀2-3-6: 大 at 2797

馬
■4-10-1
incorrect classification
➡ see □3-6-4: 馬 at 4086

亞
■4-10-1
incorrect stroke-count
➡ see ■4-8-1 at 4380

垂
4396
■4-10-2

▶**HANG DOWN**
スイ た(れる) た(らす) た(れ) -た(れ)
㊔ たる

32 土	Nonstandard S10-3-7	U57C0 F0000

traditional form → see 垂 at 4382

畂
4397
■4-10-3

▶**RIDGE**
ボウ うね せ ㊔ あぜ

102 田	Nonstandard S10-5-5	U755E F0000

traditional form → see 畝 at 1857

乗

4398

■4-10-3

▶RIDE
▶GET ON
ジョウ の(る) -の(り) の(せる)

4	Names	U4E58
丿	S10-1-9	F0000

traditional form → see 乘 at 4393

兼

4399

■4-10-3

▶CONCURRENTLY
ケン か(ねる) -か(ねる)

12	Nonstandard	U517C
八	S10-2-8	F0000

traditional form → see 兼 at 2850

畢

■4-10-3

incorrect classification/stroke-count
➡ see ⬒2-5-6: 田 at 3194

華

■4-10-4

incorrect classification
➡ see ⬒2-3-7: 艹 at 2841

拳

■4-10-4

incorrect classification
➡ see ⬒2-6-4: 龹 at 3295

栽

■4-10-4

incorrect classification
➡ see □3-6-4: 𢦏 at 4087

脊

■4-10-4

incorrect classification
➡ see ⬒2-6-4: 𠔉 at 3297

島

■4-10-4

incorrect classification
➡ see □3-7-3: 鳥 at 4103

烏

■4-10-4

incorrect classification
➡ see □3-6-4: 烏 at 4088

拳

■4-10-4

incorrect classification
➡ see ⬒2-6-4: 龹 at 3296

泰秦

■4-10-4

incorrect classification
➡ see ⬒2-5-5: 𡗗 at 3192

畢

■4-11-1

incorrect classification
➡ see ⬒2-5-6: 田 at 3194

雀

■4-11-2

incorrect classification
➡ see ⬒2-4-7: 少 at 3117

粛

4400

■4-11-3

▶PURGE
シュク
Ⓝ 肅 Ⓒ 肃 sù

129	Jōyō	U7C9B
聿	S11-6-5	F2061

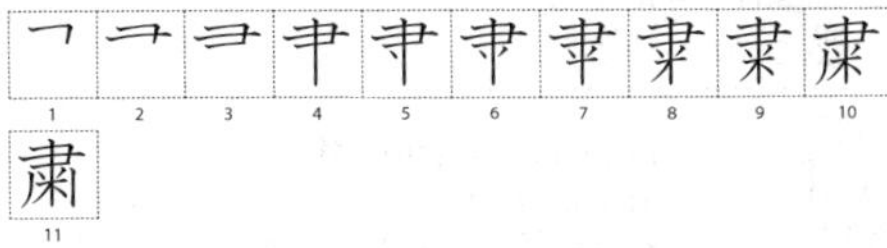

COMPOUNDS

❶ⓐ **PURGE (a political party), clean up, reform**
ⓑ restrain oneself

a 粛清する しゅくせいする purge (a political party), clean up, liquidate
粛正する しゅくせいする regulate, enforce (discipline)
粛党 しゅくとう purging disloyal elements from a party
粛学 しゅくがく purge of disloyal elements from a school

b 自粛 じしゅく self-discipline

❷ **solemnly, with profound awe; reverently, respectfully**
粛然と しゅくぜんと quietly, silently; solemnly; reverently
厳粛な げんしゅくな grave, solemn, austere

❸ **still, hushed, quiet**
粛粛と しゅくしゅくと in solemn silence
静粛 せいしゅく silence, stillness

INDEPENDENT

【しゅくとして 粛として】solemnly; silently

SYNONYMS

❶ⓐ **clean and wash**
洗 WASH → 0465
漱 RINSE → 0865
拭 WIPE → 0453
滌 WASH → 0854
濯 RINSE → 0978
浴 BATHE → 0533
浄 cleanse → 0457
粛 PURGE → 4400
清 CLEAR → 0635
払 CLEAR AWAY → 0225
掃 SWEEP → 0611

❷ **dignified**
荘 DIGNIFIED → 2814
威 dignified → 4394
儼 SOLEMN → 0204
厳 solemn → 4079
粛 solemnly → 4400

【粛】番

❸ **quiet**

静 QUIET → 2164
閑 QUIET → 4123
寂 quiet → 2855
幽 QUIET AND SECLUDED → 3731
粛 still → 4400
黙 SILENT → 3554

番 incorrect classification/stroke-count
■4-11-3
➡ see ▀2-7-5: 釆 at 3416

戚

▶**RELATIVES**

セキ ㊔ ちか

Ⓒ 戚 qī

4401
■4-11-4

62	Jōyō	U621A
戈	S11-4-7	F1978

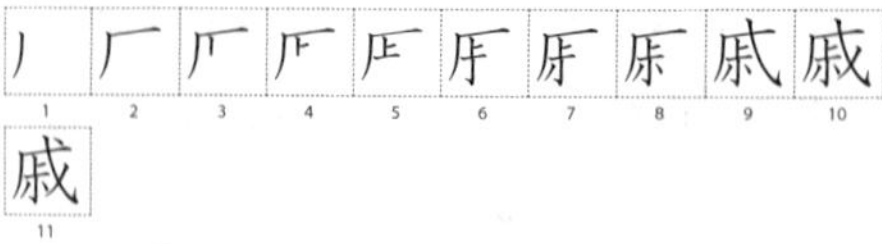

COMPOUNDS

❶ **RELATIVES, kin, relations (by marriage)**

親戚 しんせき relative
姻戚 いんせき relatives by marriage, in-laws
遠戚 えんせき distant relative
外戚 がいせき maternal relative

❷ grieve, lament, mourn

休戚 きゅうせき weal and woe
憂戚 ゆうせき grief

SYNONYMS

❶ **family and relations**

族 FAMILY → 1195
家 FAMILY → 2827
門 family → 1100
氏 clan → 3669
縁 RELATION → 1754
姻 relative by marriage → 0421
親 RELATIVES → 2264
戚 RELATIVES → 4401
曽 GREAT- → 2632

爽

▶**REFRESHING**

ソウ ショウ▲ さわ(やか) ㊔ さ あきら さやか

Ⓒ 爽 shuǎng

4402
■4-11-4

89	Jōyō	U723D
爻	S11-4-7	F2112

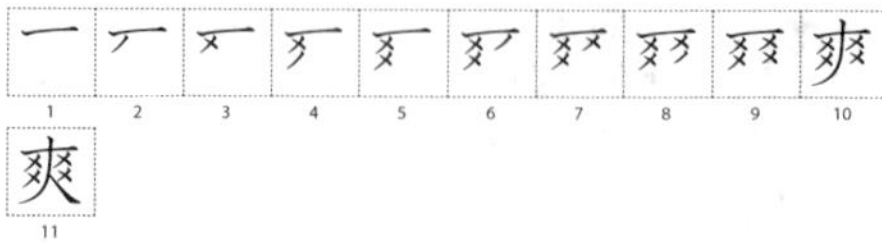

COMPOUNDS

❶ **REFRESHING, fresh**

爽快な そうかいな refreshing, invigorating, exhilarating

❷ [original meaning] **dawn; bright**

昧爽 まいそう *literary* dawn, daybreak

KUN

【さわやか 爽やか】
さわやかな 爽やかな

① **REFRESHING, fresh**

爽やかな風 さわやかなかぜ refreshing [bracing] wind

② **clear, distinct (voice); fluent, flowing**

弁舌爽やか べんぜつさわやか fluent [eloquent] in speech

SYNONYMS

❶ **pleased and pleasant**

楽 pleasurable → 3505
欣 JOYFUL → 1057
爽 REFRESHING → 4402
快 PLEASANT → 0289
朗 CHEERFUL → 1679
愉 PLEASED → 0710
悦 DELIGHTED → 0501
嬉しい GLAD → 0890
喜 HAPPY → 2889
歓 JOYOUS → 2342
驩 JOYOUS → 2333

鳥 incorrect classification
■4-11-4
➡ see ◻3-7-4: 鳥 at 4105

亀 incorrect classification
■4-11-4
➡ see ▀2-2-9: ⺈ at 2637

斎 incorrect classification
■4-11-4
➡ see ▀2-2-9: 亠 at 2622

悉 incorrect classification
■4-11-4
➡ see ▀2-7-4: 釆 at 3405

麥 incorrect classification
■4-11-4
➡ see ▀2-8-3: 來 at 3441

亞
■4-12-1
incorrect stroke-count
➡ see ■4-8-1 at 4380

雷
■4-12-1
incorrect classification
➡ see ⬒2-7-5: rP at 3418

幾

4403
■4-12-4

▶HOW MANY
▶SOME
キ いく- いく(つ) いく(ら)
Ⓒ 几 jǐ jī

52	Jōyō	U5E7E
幺	S12-3-9	F1350

COMPOUNDS

❶ **HOW MANY, how much**
幾何(学) きか(がく) geometry

❷ desire, hope
庶幾 しょき desire, hope

KUN

【いく- 幾-】[also suffix]
① **HOW MANY, how much**
幾時間 いくじかん how many hours
幾箱要りますか いくはこいりますか How many boxes do you want?
②ⓐ (being of indefinite number or quantity) **SOME, several**
ⓑ (being of considerable number) **SOME, very many**
a 幾夜も いくよも for several nights
幾分 いくぶん partially, somewhat, in a way
幾千と云う人 いくせんというひと thousands of people
b 幾日も いくにちも for some days, for many days
幾度も いくど(=いくたび)も many times, frequently

【いくつ 幾つ】**HOW MANY; how old**
幾つ欲しいのか いくつほしいのか How many do you want?
幾つになっても いくつになっても however old one may be
お幾つですか おいくつですか How old are you?

【いくら 幾ら】**how much, HOW MANY; no matter how much [many], however; even, with all (something)**
幾らか いくらか some, something, anything; somewhat, a little, in part
幾ら勉強しても いくらべんきょうしても however hard one may work
幾らでも いくらでも as many [much] as one likes
幾許(=幾何)も無く いくばくもなく not long after, before long
幾ら欠点が有っても いくらけってんがあっても with all one's faults
数は幾らか かずはいくらか How many are there?
これは幾らですか これはいくらですか How much does this cost?

SYNONYMS

❶ **how many**
幾 HOW MANY → 4403
何- HOW MANY → 0073

【いく-】
②ⓐ **some**
幾- SOME → 4403
何- several → 0073
数 several → 2245
或る A CERTAIN → 3978

NOTE

➡ see COMPOUND FORMATION for 幾何学 きかがく → 何 0073

奧
■4-12-4
incorrect classification
➡ see ⬒2-9-3: 㒳 at 3503

裁
■4-12-4
incorrect classification
➡ see ◻3-6-6: 𢦏 at 4090

黽

4404
■4-13-1

▶FROG
ボウ ビン ベン
Ⓒ 黾 miǎn

205	Non-Jōyō	U9EFD
黽	S13-13-0	F0000

RADICAL

ben 'frog' (鼃× 鼈×), used in characters related to frogs or toads

COMPOUNDS

❶ [original meaning] **FROG, toad**
蛙黽 あぼう [archaic] tree frog [toad]

❷ [archaic] make an effort, exert oneself
黽勉 びんべん working [trying] hard

SPECIAL READINGS

水黽 あめんぼ pond skater, water strider

SYNONYMS

❶ **reptiles and amphibians**
亀 TURTLE → 2637
蛇 SNAKE → 1701
竜 DRAGON → 2603
蛙 FROG → 1716
黽 FROG → 4404

鼎 4405 ■4-13-1

▶TRIPOD CAULDRON
テイ かなえ
Ⓒ 鼎 dǐng

206	Names	U9F0E
鼎	S13-13-0	F3052

RADICAL

kanae 'ritual cauldron', used in characters related to ritual cauldrons or tripod vessels

COMPOUNDS

❶ [original meaning] TRIPOD CAULDRON
鼎足 ていそく legs of a tripod cauldron; three-legged (vessel)

❷ [archaic] symbol of dynasty [the throne]
鼎革 ていかく change of dynasty

❸ (involving three parts or things) **triangular, three-party**
鼎立 ていりつ triangular [three-party] confrontation
鼎談 ていだん three-man talk, tricornered conversation
鼎坐する ていざする sit in a triangle

KUN

【かなえ 鼎】TRIPOD CAULDRON
鼎の軽重を問う かなえのけいちょうをとう weigh one's ability, call one's ability into question

SYNONYMS

❶ **vessels and receptacles**
盤 dish →3533
鍋 POT →2202
釜 IRON POT →2610
鼎 TRIPOD CAULDRON →4405
臼 MORTAR →4341
碓 MORTAR →1537
托 RECEPTACLE →0252
皿 PLATE →4286
盆 TRAY →2581
膳 LEGGED TRAY →1381
杯 CUP →1066
鉢 BOWL →2144
椀 WOODEN BOWL →1250
碗 CERAMIC BOWL →1539
丼 LARGE BOWL →4323

❸ **three**
三 THREE →2423
参 three (in legal documents) →2563
鼎 triangular →4405

鼏 4406 ■4-13-3

▶PURGE
シュク

129	Nonstandard	U8085
聿	S13-6-7	F0000

traditional form → see 粛 at 4400

截 ■4-13-4

incorrect classification
➡ see □3-6-7: 戈 at 4091

爾 4407 ■4-14-1

▶THAT
ジ ニ なんじ ㊔ ちか しか みつる あきら
Ⓝ 尒 尓° Ⓒ 尔 ěr

89	Names	U723E
爻	S14-4-10	F2546

COMPOUNDS

❶ THAT
爾来 じらい from that time on, ever since
爾後 じご from this [that] time onward, henceforth, thereafter

❷ thou, you
爾汝 じじょ addressing someone familiarly in the second person or without using a title

❸ suffix after adjectives
徒爾 とじ uselessness
莞爾として かんじとして with a smile

❹ used phonetically for *ni*
天爾乎波 てにおは particles, postpositions (i.e., て, に, を, は)

KUN

【なんじ 爾】[usu. 汝] **thou, you**

SYNONYMS

❶ **this and that**
本 THIS →4314
爾 THAT →4407
其れ THAT →3255
彼 that →0346
今 THIS (week, etc.) →2464
当 THE PRESENT →2701
該 the said →1916
同 the same →3707
之 this →4228
是 this →3090
此 THIS →1017
斯 THIS →2140

❷ **second person pronouns**
君 YOU (*familiar*) →3974
汝 THOU →0255
爾 thou →4407
貴 you (*honorific*) →3220

卿 you (*archaic*, *honorific*) → 0769

❸ modifier suffixes

然 MODIFIER FORMING SUFFIX → 3456
乎 MODIFIER FORMING SUFFIX → 4316
如 modifier suffix → 0239
爾 adjective suffix → 4407
的 ADJECTIVAL SUFFIX → 1444

HOMOPHONES

なんじ 汝 THOU → 0255

NOTE

➡ see USAGE note at 汝 0255

鳶

■4-14-4

incorrect classification
➡ see □3-3-11: 弋 at 3919

截

■4-14-4

incorrect classification
➡ see □3-6-8: 戈 at 4092

器

■4-15-1

incorrect classification
➡ see ⬒2-6-9: 吅 at 3367

畿

4408

■4-15-4

▸CAPITAL

キ ㊔ ちか

Ⓒ 畿 jī

102	Jōyō	U757F
田	S15-5-10	F2295

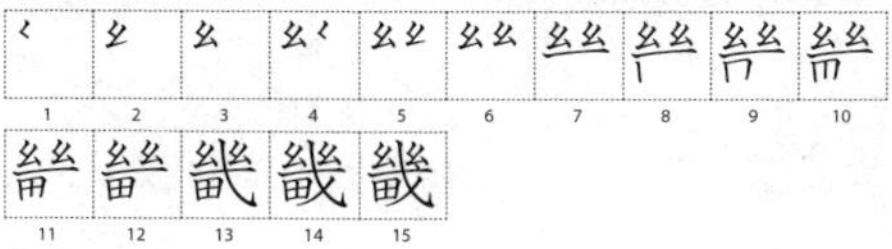

COMPOUNDS

ⓐ CAPITAL

ⓑ suburbs of a CAPITAL

a 畿内 きない territories near the capital [imperial palace]; the Five Home Provinces

b 近畿(=近畿地方) きんき(=きんきちほう) Kinki region

SYNONYMS

● cities and towns

都 METROPOLIS → 2120
京 CAPITAL → 2546
畿 CAPITAL → 4408
市 CITY → 2487
町 TOWN → 1430

器

■4-16-1

incorrect classification
➡ see ⬒2-6-10: 吅 at 3375

龜

■4-16-4

incorrect classification
➡ see ⬒2-2-14: ⺈ at 2667

齋

■4-17-4

incorrect classification
➡ see ⬒2-2-15: 亠 at 2669

龜

■4-18-4

incorrect classification
➡ see ⬒2-2-16: ⺈ at 2671

戴

■4-18-4

incorrect classification
➡ see □3-6-12: 戈 at 4094

譱

■4-20-3

incorrect classification
➡ see ⬒2-3-17: 羊 at 3038

APPENDIXES
付 録

APPENDIX 1

OUTLINE OF THE JAPANESE WRITING SYSTEM
日本語表記の概要

1 THE ORIGIN OF CHINESE CHARACTERS

1.1 The Birth of a Pictographic Script

Until recently, it was believed that the earliest examples of Chinese characters were those found on oracle bones used in divination rites dating back to the eighteenth century B.C. However, excavations made in China in 1986 have shown that at that time the Chinese characters had already had a history of 1200 years, which means that the Chinese script first appeared almost 5000 years ago.

The earliest characters were simple pictures of the things they represented. Although all the principal writing systems of the world began with pictures, these were in almost all cases simplified to abstract symbols that were eventually used for their sound values, giving rise to the major alphabet systems of the world. This happened everywhere but in China, where the primary function of the characters has always been to express both meaning and sound, rather than just sound.

Typical Pictographs

Early Forms	Modern Character	Meaning
	木	tree, wood
	林	woods
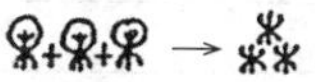	森	forest
	本	root, origin
	日	sun
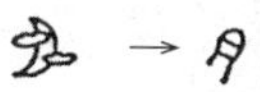	月	moon
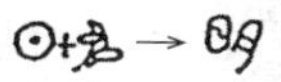	明	bright
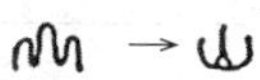	山	mountain
	鳥	bird
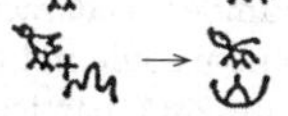	島	island

The table shows examples of early character forms and their modern counterparts. The earliest characters were pictographs, which were simple pictures of things. Pictographs may be combined to form new characters, especially characters that express complex or abstract ideas. Thus 木 'tree' is combined with 木 to give 林 'woods' while three trees give 森 'forest'; a line added to the bottom of a tree gives 本, which means 'root' or 'origin'; and so on.

The shapes of the characters underwent a great deal of change over the several thousand years of their history. Many calligraphic styles, character forms, and typeface styles have evolved over the years; furthermore, the character forms were simplified as a result of various language reforms in China and Japan. The chart below shows various forms and styles for the characters 女 and 楽.

Character Forms and Styles

tortoiseshell writing	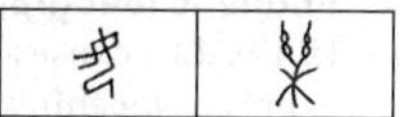	
bronze inscription	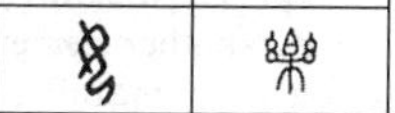	
seal style	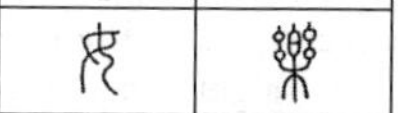	
ancient square style	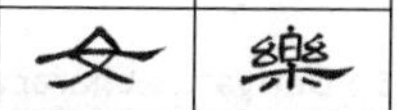	
square style	女	楽
semicursive style	女	樂
cursive style	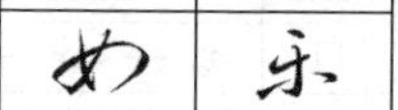	
simplified handwritten abbreviation	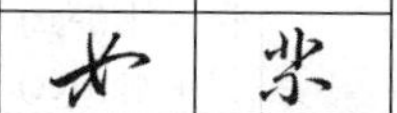	
Ming typeface	女	楽
Gothic typeface	女	楽
traditional form	女	樂
alternative form	—	—
handwritten abbreviation	—	—
modern Chinese	女	乐

1.2 Formation of Chinese Characters

Traditionally, Chinese characters are classified into six categories known as 六書 りくしょ. Introduced some 1900 years ago in the classic Chinese dictionary 説文解字 せつもんかいじ, these have played a central role in Chinese lexicography. The first four categories are based on the character formation process; the last two are based on usage.

1. **Pictographs** (象形文字 しょうけいもじ) are simple hieroglyphs that are rough sketches of the things they represent. Example:  (modern 目 もく) 'eye'.

2. **Simple ideographs** (指事文字 しじもじ) suggest the meanings of abstract ideas, such as numerals and directions. Example: 三 さん 'three'.

3. **Compound ideographs** (会意文字 かいいもじ) consist of two or more elements, each of which contributes to the meaning of the whole. Example: 休 きゅう 'rest' (person 人 resting under a tree 木).

4. **Phonetic-ideographic characters** (形声文字 けいせいもじ) consist of one element that roughly expresses meaning (usually called the **radical**), and another element that represents sound and often also meaning. Example: 茎 けい 'stem, stalk' consists of the radical 艹 'plants' and 圣 けい 'straight', i.e., the straight part of a plant.

5. **Derivative characters** (転注文字 てんちゅうもじ) are characters used in an extended, derived, or figurative sense. Example: 令 れい changed from its original meaning 'command, order' to 'person who gives orders' to 'administrator, governor'.

6. **Phonetic loans** (仮借文字 かしゃもじ) are characters borrowed to represent words phonetically without direct relation to their original meanings, or characters used erroneously. Example: 豆 とう originally referred to an ancient sacrificial vessel, but is now used in the borrowed sense of 'bean'.

The great majority of characters are phonetic-ideographic (type 4 above). 民, for example, originally a picture of an eye pierced by a needle (), represented a slave blinded by his master to keep him from escaping, but later changed to 'ignorant masses' or 'people' in general. As a phonetic-ideographic element in the formation of other characters, it represents the sound みん and has a basic meaning of 'sightlessness' or 'darkness'. For example, 民 (abbreviated to 氏) is combined with 日 'sun' to give 昏 'darkness, dusk'; 眠 'sleep' consists of an eye (目) in a state of sightlessness (民). An interesting example is 婚 'marriage', which consists of 女 'woman' + 昏 'darkness'. According to one theory, this is because wedding ceremonies were held at night. In this way, a basic unit like 民 contributes its shape, its reading, and its meaning to the formation of other characters.

The table below shows several groups of characters that share the basic element 目 'eye':

Typical Atom in Periodic Table of Chinese Characters					
Atom	**Formation**	**Molecule**	**Reading**	**Basic Meaning**	**Compounds**
目	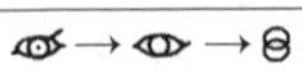 →目		もく	eye	
	目 + 儿 (legs)	見	けん	see	現
	目 + 木 (tree)	相	そう	face each other	箱
	目 + 乚 (object) + 十 (straight)	直	ちょく	straight	植
	直 + 心 (heart)	悳	とく	virtuous	徳
	目 + 斤	盾	じゅん	shield	循

Groups of characters sharing the same "molecule" element are closely interrelated. They share three important features: (1) a basic element of the same **shape,** (2) approximately the same **reading,** and (3) a common **meaning** on the character formation level. Chinese characters thus consist of logically interrelated parts that form a systematic body of symbols to express meaning and sound.

In addition to the six traditional categories, there is a seventh one limited to a small number of characters coined in Japan. When the Japanese could not find an appropriate character to represent a particular word, they sometimes created new characters, called 国字 こくじ 'national characters', on the model of the Chinese ones. Most of these have only *kun* readings (Japanese-derived pronunciations); some, such as 働

どう 'work', have both *on* (Chinese-derived) and *kun* readings, while others, such as 腺 せん 'gland', have only *on* readings. In rare instances, as in the case of 腺, a character created in Japan was "exported" back to Chinese.

2 INTRODUCTION OF CHINESE CHARACTERS TO JAPAN

2.1 Early Stages

In the early centuries of the Christian era, the Japanese did not have a writing system of their own. As the Japanese began to interact with the Chinese, they adopted Chinese institutions and adapted them to their own needs. Chinese characters were introduced to Japan via the Korean peninsula in the fourth century A.D. In the next two centuries, Chinese books on philosophy and Buddhism were brought to Japan and studied by the Japanese aristocracy.

Initially, the Japanese used the characters for writing in authentic Chinese or a hybrid Japanese-Chinese style. A good example of the latter is the 古事記 こじき (Ancient Chronicles) written in 712. Since the Japanese did not have their own script, they soon began to use the characters to write the Japanese language as well. In the early stages, they employed the characters purely for their phonetic values. For example, the native Japanese word やま 'mountain' was written 也麻, with the first character representing や and the second ま. This method of writing is referred to as 万葉仮名 まんようがな because it was used extensively in the 万葉集 まんようしゅう, an eighth-century anthology of Japanese poems.

Because of the markedly different linguistic structures of Chinese and Japanese, the Chinese characters were not well suited for writing Japanese. Whereas classical Chinese is basically a monosyllabic language with no inflected words, Japanese is a polysyllabic language with various elements attached to the stems of words to express grammatical meanings.

2.2 *On* and *Kun* Readings

These circumstances led to an extremely interesting method of writing Japanese: the Chinese characters were used for their meanings. The characters were used to write words of Chinese origin, or to write native Japanese words with Chinese characters representing the same or similar meanings. The grammatical elements continued to be written phonetically, but eventually the characters used for their phonetic values were simplified, giving rise to two sets of syllabic scripts, ***hiragana*** and ***katakana,*** in which each character represents a syllable. For example, the character 安 あん 'peaceful' gave rise to the hiragana character あ, whereas 阿 あ was simplified to the katakana character ア (see **Appendix 5**).

Characters used to represent meaning were pronounced in two ways: (1) the 音読み おんよみ or 'phonetic reading' and (2) the 訓読み くんよみ or 'explanatory reading'. This phonetic duality of the Chinese characters is fundamental to the nature of the Japanese script. Let us briefly examine how it arose.

In the first method, which is often called the "Sino-Japanese reading" or "Chinese-derived pronunciation," the characters represent Chinese-derived words or word elements. This method of reading the characters is referred to as the ***on* reading.** The reading assigned to each character was a rough approximation of the original Chinese pronunciation. For example, the character 山 'mountain' was assigned the reading さん based on its old Chinese pronunciation (modern Chinese is shān). *On* readings are found more frequently in compound words (e.g., 連山 れんざん 'mountain range') than in independent words (e.g., 天 てん 'heaven').

Since the Japanese often had native words to express the meanings represented by Chinese characters, they began to associate the characters not only with Chinese words but also with purely Japanese ones. 山 'mountain', for example, was used to represent the native Japanese word やま 'mountain' with no regard to its Chinese-derived reading さん. This method of reading the characters is referred to as the ***kun* reading.**

Originally, the *kun* reading was a kind of explanation assigned to a character that was used to interpret its meaning in a Chinese text. In other words, it was a native Japanese word that was essentially a translation of the concept represented by the Chinese character. Over the years, certain words became so well established as the translation for a given character that they were considered to be the standard reading or readings for that character. In this manner, 山 acquired the reading やま, which eventually became established as its standard accepted pronunciation along with its *on* reading さん.

A distinctive feature of Chinese characters as used in Japanese is their multiple readings. Since the characters entered Japan over different historical periods and originated from different geographical regions, many characters have acquired multiple *on* and/or *kun* readings. In extreme cases, a character may have more than 100 readings (生 has over 200). *On* and *kun* readings may be combined in four possible ways: *on-on, kun-kun, on-kun,* and *kun-on*. Unfortunately, there is no reliable rule for determining if a character is to be read in the *on* or *kun,* or for deciding which of several possible readings to select in a particular instance. A rough guideline is that *on-on* or *kun-kun* readings are used in compounds, and *kun* readings in independent words, but there are many exceptions. For example, 毎朝 **まいあさ** 'every morning' is an *on-kun* compound, though 毎 has the *kun* reading **ごと** and 朝 the *on* reading **ちょう**.

2.3 Classification of *On* Readings

Traditionally, *on* readings are classified into four types:

1. **漢音 かんおん** 'Han reading', the most frequent and the most productive *on* reading, was introduced to Japan during the seventh and eighth centuries. It is based on the pronunciation current during the Tang Dynasty in northwestern China. Example: 行 **こう**.

2. **呉音 ごおん** 'Wu reading', which is commonly assumed to originate from the Wu region in the lower Yangtze River area near Shanghai, was introduced up to the sixth and seventh centuries along with Buddhist writings. It is used mostly in Buddhist terms. Example: 行 **ぎょう**.

3. **唐音 とうおん** 'Tang reading' was introduced between the thirteenth century and the Edo period (1600-1868). It is based on the pronunciation current in the Song Dynasty and after, and is used mostly for borrowed words and technological terms. Example: 行 **あん**.

4. **慣用音 かんようおん** 'popular reading' developed as a result of erroneous pronunciations that came into popular use and gained general acceptance. Example: 立 **りつ**.

During the compilation of this dictionary, several types of *on* readings that cannot be classified under the traditional categories were found. (The terms used to describe these categories below were coined by the editor.)

1. **中音 ちゅうおん** 'modern Chinese reading' is an *on* reading based on modern Chinese. 荘, for example, is pronounced **ちゃん** in such words as 一荘 **いいちゃん** 'a game of mahjong', on the basis of its Mandarin pronunciation yīzhuāng.

2. **外音 がいおん** 'foreign reading' is an *on* reading derived from foreign languages other than Chinese. For example, 仙 **せん** is pronounced **せんと** in the sense of 'cent'. Particularly interesting is a growing trend to create readings based on English, such as 高技 **はいてく** 'high technology'.

3. **和音 わおん** 'Japanese reading' is an *on* reading assigned to *kokuji* (characters coined in Japan) on the model of Chinese characters. For example, 働 'work' is a character coined in Japan but has a "Chinese-derived" reading of **どう**, which is the reading of its principal component 動 'move'.

2.4 Special Uses

In addition to the standard *on* and *kun* readings, there are a few special ways in which characters can be used. The most important of these are:

1. **当て字 あてじ** 'phonetic substitutes' refers to characters used phonetically with little or no relation to their meanings. These are often used to transliterate Sanskrit Buddhist terms, such as 阿修羅 **あしゅら** 'Asura' (fighting demon), and other foreign words such as 倶楽部 **くらぶ** 'club'.

2. **熟字訓 じゅくじくん** 'special reading' refers to a reading of a single word consisting of two or more characters assigned to the word on the basis of its meaning without direct relation to the normal readings of each constituent character. For example, 大人 'adult' consists of 大 'big', normally pronounced **だい** or **おおきい**, and 人 'human being', normally pronounced **じん** or **ひと**, but together they function as a single unit pronounced **おとな**.

2.5 Language Reforms

Shortly after World War II, the Japanese government implemented language reforms aimed at limiting the number of characters and simplifying their forms, among other things. At the same time, kana orthography underwent extensive reforms to reflect actual pronunciation. For example, the sound **きゅう** was historically written by such combinations as **きう** and **きふ**, but is now written **きゅう**. Large-scale language reforms also took place in China to limit the number of characters and drastically simplify their forms. As a result, many modern Chinese forms are totally different from their corresponding traditional and modern Japanese forms. For example, the traditional form of 發 **はつ** 'start; emit' was simplified to 発 in Japanese but to 发 in Chinese.

We will not dwell on China, but will briefly examine the language reforms that took place in Japan. In 1946, a list of characters known as **Tōyō Kanji** (当用漢字) was published, in which the number of characters for general use was limited to 1850. Various amendments and additions followed in the ensuing years. In 1948, for example, an appendix listing 881 characters to be learned in the first six years of compulsory schooling was published, and the number of readings of many characters was reduced. In 1949, the forms of many characters were greatly simplified, while in 1951 a supplementary list of 92 characters was approved for use in personal names, bringing the total to 1942.

In spite of these changes, there was much dissatisfaction among the public, who wanted the number of characters increased. In 1973, 28 more characters for general use were added, while in 1976, 28 name characters were added, followed by an additional 54 in 1981 and 118 in 1990. Meanwhile, cultural organizations and the public at large pressed for greater freedom in the use of Chinese characters in general, as a result of which an expanded list of 1945 characters known as **Jōyō Kanji** (常用漢字) was published in 1981. This brought the total number of characters that can be used in names to 2229.

Public pressure led to further expansion of the personal name character list in 1997 (1 character), 2004 (698 characters), and 2009 (2 characters). As a result of these revisions, the number of characters allowed for use in names increased to 2930.

In 2010 the Jōyō Kanji list saw the addition of 196 further characters and the removal of 5, leaving it with a total of 2136 characters. With this change the number of characters permitted for use in names rose to 2997.

The general trend to increase the number of characters took place in the schools as well. In 1977, the number of characters to be learned during the first six years of compulsory schooling was increased to 996, and in 1989 this number was again increased to 1006 in line with the Ministry of Education's policy to place greater emphasis on reading and writing.

Currently (early 2013), the most important official lists approved by the Japanese government as part of the postwar language reforms are:

1. **Revised Jōyō Kanji** The 改定常用漢字表 **かいていじょうようかんじひょう**, or "Revised List of Characters in Common Use," is an official list (published in 2010) of 2136 characters widely used in the mass media, government and general publications, and education.

2. **Education Kanji** The 学年別漢字配当表 **がくねんべつかんじはいとうひょう**, or "List of Characters Classified by School Grade," is an official list of 1006 characters that must be learned in the first six years of compulsory schooling. The list, which is commonly referred to as 教育漢字 **きょういくかんじ** ("Education Kanji"), was promulgated on March 15, 1989. The number of characters taught in each grade is as follows:

Grade	1977 List	1989 List
First	76	80
Second	145	160
Third	195	200
Fourth	195	200
Fifth	195	185
Sixth	190	181
Total	996	1006

The principal change introduced in the new list was the moving of 60 characters from higher to lower grades. For example, 14 third-grade characters became second-grade characters. Moreover, 20 new characters were added to the list, while 10 characters were deleted, as shown below:

Additions (20)	皿 昔 笛 豆 箱 札 松 巣 束 梅 桜 枝 飼 夢 激 盛 装 誕 並 暮
Deletions (10)	歓 称 壱 勧 兼 釈 需 是 俗 弐

See **Appendix 11. Jōyō Kanji List** for a full listing of the Education Kanji.

3. **Jinmei Kanji** The 人名用漢字表 **じんめいようかんじひょう**, or "List of Name Characters," is an official list (published in 2010) of 861 characters approved for use in personal names in addition to the Jōyō Kanji list.

The promulgation of the Jōyō/Tōyō Kanji lists as part of the postwar reforms made it necessary to adopt various measures to ensure their smooth implementation. One problem was that it became impossible to write certain common words that included characters not in the official list. To solve this problem, the government published a list of simpler characters and words, called 同音の漢字による書きかえ **どうおんのかんじによるかきかえ**, that may be used to replace the characters not in the list. These characters, which we will call **phonetic replacement characters,** have the same sound and, often, the same (or a similar) meaning as the characters being replaced. The latter will be called **phonetically replaced characters.**

For example, the character 繋 (phonetically replaced character) in 連繋 **れんけい** 'connection, linking, contact' was replaced by 係 (phonetic replacement character), which has the same *on* reading and is similar to it in meaning, so that the word is now written 連係. In addition to the 170 phonetic replacement characters appearing in the aforementioned list, there are many others which are in common use. For example, 混 replaces 渾 in the word 渾沌 こんとん 'chaos'.

3 CHINESE CHARACTERS IN JAPANESE

3.1 The Japanese Script

The Japanese writing system is composed of two syllabic scripts, called ***hiragana*** (平仮名) and ***katakana*** (片仮名), and thousands of Chinese characters, called ***kanji*** (漢字).

The three scripts basically have different functions. Hiragana is used mostly to write grammatical elements, such as inflectional verb endings, and sometimes to write native Japanese words. For example, in 見た みた the kanji 見 represents the stem of the verb 見る みる 'see' and た is a verb ending for forming the past tense. The kana endings attached to a kanji base or stem are called ***okurigana*** (送り仮名). Katakana is used mostly to write Western loanwords, such as プリンター 'printer', and onomatopoeic words, such as カチッと 'with a click'.

Kanji are used to write the core of the Japanese vocabulary. This includes words, especially nouns, of Chinese origin and words coined in Japan on the Chinese model, such as 山脈 さんみゃく 'mountain range', as well as native Japanese words, such as 山 やま 'mountain'. Kanji have three basic properties: form, sound, and meaning. Each character may be pronounced according to its Chinese-derived *on* reading, or one of several native Japanese *kun* readings, and each reading may have numerous meanings associated with it.

A running Japanese text consists of a mixture of kanji and kana, with the latter normally outnumbering the former. For example:

> 漢字を組み合わせることによって多数の熟語が作り出せます。
>
> かんじをくみあわせることによってたすうのじゅくごがつくりだせます。
>
> Numerous compound words can be formed by combining Chinese characters.

In the above sentence, particles such as を (object marker), as well as verb endings (-わせる in 組み合わせる くみあわせる 'combine'), are written in hiragana, whereas nouns, such as 熟語 じゅくご 'compound word', are written in kanji. Hiragana characters serve as natural borderlines that help the reader segment the text into meaningful units. For this reason, a Japanese text is easier to read than a running Chinese text, which consists of Chinese characters only.

3.2 Functions of Kanji

One of the most important characteristics of Chinese characters is their ability to convey meaning. Just how they do this is the subject of a vast literature full of conflicting theories. Chinese characters have been described by such terms as *logographic* (symbols for words), *ideographic* (symbols for ideas), and *morphographic* (symbols for morphemes). Scholars disagree over the precise terminology and function of the characters.

According to one extreme view, the characters convey meaning phonetically and their ideographic nature is nothing but a myth. According to another view, the characters can convey meaning directly; that is, with little or no dependence on their pronunciations. Alphabetic symbols, on the other hand, are one step removed from that which is ultimately represented because they normally stand for the sounds of speech, which are in turn associated with meaning. Various other theories take intermediate positions between these two extremes. The whole question is highly controversial, but it is generally accepted that, whatever linguistic units the characters actually correspond to, their essential nature is to convey both meaning and sound, not just sound.

Another important characteristic of Chinese characters is their high productivity. By combining a stock of a few thousand characters, countless compound words are generated. 戦 せん 'war', for example, is combined with other characters to form numerous compound words related to war, such as 戦友 せんゆう 'comrade-in-arms' and many others. Chinese characters in Japanese function much the same way as Latin and Greek roots do in English. Each character has one or more distinct meanings, and often functions as a highly productive word-building element.

hydrophobia	(Greek)	恐水病	きょうすいびょう	fear-water-illness
aquarium	(Latin)	水族館	すいぞくかん	water-family-building
waterwheel	(Anglo-Saxon)	水車	みずぐるま	water-wheel

In English, the relationship between the above words is somewhat obscured by the fact that the concept of water is expressed in three different written forms, i.e., *hydr, aqua,* and *water.* In Japanese, on the other hand, although 水 has different phonetic forms, i.e., an *on* reading of すい and a *kun* reading of みず, it has only one *graphic* form, i.e., 水. The kanji thus provides a *visual link* that transcends the different pronunciations. This ability of kanji to represent a given meaning with little or no dependence on their pronunciations is perhaps one of the most distinctive features of the Japanese script.

A further characteristic of Chinese characters is their *semantic transparency.* As each component of a compound word conveys a distinct meaning, the meaning of the resulting word is often self-evident. For example, 好奇心 こうきしん "like + strangeness + heart (mind)" means 'curiosity', 貧血症 ひんけつしょう "little + blood + illness" means 'anemia', and 閉所恐怖症 へいしょきょうふしょう "closed + place + fear + illness" means 'claustrophobia'. Once the meanings of the components are known, relatively little effort is needed to learn these words.

Finally, Japanese has a large number of **homophones** (words that sound the same but are written differently). こうき and きこう, for instance, represent about a dozen words in common use, and there are many more less frequent ones. Since each character has a distinct form (and meaning), kanji serve to distinguish such words from each other. Thus, 機構 きこう 'mechanism' is easily distinguished from 帰港 きこう 'returning to the harbor'.

In summary, the principal features of the Japanese script are:

1. The Japanese writing system consists of three scripts, each of which has a different function. Each kanji has form, sound, and meaning.
2. One of the most important characteristics of kanji is their ability to convey meaning.
3. Kanji can be combined with each other to form numerous compound words.
4. Kanji provide a visual link that transcends their different pronunciations.
5. Compound words are often semantically transparent; that is, their meanings are more or less evident from their components.
6. Since each character has a distinct form (and meaning), kanji serve to distinguish homophones from each other.

3.3 Word Formation

Languages differ in the processes by which they form new words. The Japanese language is *agglutinative;* that is, it forms words by putting together basic elements, called *morphemes,* that retain their original forms and meanings with little change during the combination process. A morpheme is a distinctive linguistic unit of relatively stable meaning that cannot be divided into smaller meaningful parts. As a rule, each Chinese character represents one morpheme.

Compounding and *derivation* are among the most important word-formation processes in Japanese. Compounding consists of combining two or more words or word elements having their own lexical meaning (having a substantial meaning of their own) to produce a new unit that functions as a single word. Since the Chinese characters are extremely productive in their ability to generate new words, compounding plays a major role in Japanese word formation. By combining a stock of a few thousand characters, hundreds of thousands of compound words are created.

Traditionally, a compound word is considered to be a combination of two or more free forms, such as *headwaiter,* which consists of *head* and *waiter.* In Japanese, a compound may be any combination of free forms, combining forms, and affixes that together function as a single word. The resulting compound is distinct from, but related to, its constituent components. For example, the compound 造船所 ぞうせんじょ 'shipyard' consists of the free form 造船 'shipbuilding' (造 'make; build' + 船 'ship') followed by the suffix 所 'place' (see **§4.4 Linguistic Functions** on p. 32a for more details).

Derivation refers to creating a new word by adding to a stem a word element such as a suffix that expresses grammatical meaning but has no lexical meaning. For example, the noun 黒 くろ 'black' is combined with the adjective-forming suffix い to form the adjective 黒い くろい 'black'. Derivation should not be confused with *inflection,* which consists of adding word endings or modifying the form of a word in order to indicate various grammatical functions, such as tense. The resulting word is another *form* of the original word, not a new word in itself. For example, the last syllable of the verb 帰る かえる 'to return' is inflected to yield 帰れ かえれ, the imperative form. Inflectional word endings in Japanese are usually written in hiragana.

The precise distinctions between compounding, derivation, and inflection involve complex theoretical problems that need not concern the nonspecialist.

3.4 Orthographic Variation

The Japanese orthography is highly irregular, significantly more so than any other major language. A major factor is the interaction between kana and kanji, resulting in countless words written in unpredictable ways, and the lack of a standardized orthography. For example, ***toriatsukai*** 'handling' can be written in six ways, 取り扱い, 取扱い, 取扱, とり扱い, 取りあつかい and とりあつかい, all of identical meaning. Often, some or all the meanings depend on the orthography; e.g. in the case of ***umai,*** 旨い means 'delicious; successful, skillful', 甘い means 'delicious' and 巧い means 'skillful'.

One of the most common types of orthographic variation in Japanese occurs in kana endings, called *okurigana,* that are attached to a kanji stem. For example, ***kakiarawasu*** can be written in four ways, 書き著す, 書き著わす, 書著す and 書著わす, all meaning, 'write, publish'. *Okurigana* variants are numerous and unpredictable, as shown below.

The CJK Dictionary Institute, headed by the author, maintains comprehensive databases of orthographic variants that are used in Japanese natural language processing.

3.5 Meaning of Kanji

As we have seen above, kanji may be read in one of two ways: the *on* reading and the *kun* reading. For each reading, a character may function as an independent word (any free form that can be used on its own) or as a word element (bound form used only in combinations). Since a character may have a different sense associated with each reading and each function, the meaning of a character can be said to operate on four distinct but related levels:

1. As an *on* independent word (as 明 めい 'discernment' in 先見の明 せんけんのめい 'foresight').
2. As an *on* word element (as 明 'clear, obvious' in 明確な めいかくな 'clear, distinct').
3. As an independent *kun* word (as 明るい あかるい 'bright, light').
4. As a *kun* word element (as -明け 'end' in 忌明け いみあけ 'end of mourning').

Each character may have numerous meanings on one or more of the four levels, and the levels may interact in a complex way. On each level, the characters may be combined in various ways, such as bound + free, bound + bound, free + free, etc., and may have several, sometimes a dozen or more, different meanings. Each character may have several *on* and *kun* readings, and each reading may have several derived words associated with it, which in turn have many meanings; or the character may function as a word element with one or more meanings.

In some cases, on each level the meanings are totally different; in others, they may be similar but not quite the same. Often there is partial overlapping of some meanings but total inequality of others. For example, the *on* word element 山 さん and the independent *kun* word as well as *kun* word element 山 やま share the meaning 'mountain', but the *on* word element さん also means 'Buddhist temple', as in 本山 ほんざん 'head temple', a meaning which is not shared by やま.

Generally, the more common a character is, the more numerous are its meanings and the more complex is the relationship between them. An extreme example is 上 じょう 'up; go up'. This dictionary lists a total of 114 meanings for 上, subdivided into 16 subentries. It has 27 meanings as an *on* word element, 3 meanings as an independent *on* word, 17 meanings for 5 *kun* word elements, and 67 meanings for 9 independent *kun* words. Although 上 is a very long entry and is hardly typical, many characters do have more than ten *on* and *kun* meanings combined.

The Japanese script is now in a state of flux, and is being constantly adapted to the needs of the times. In this brief outline we have only touched upon its most important aspects, especially the role of Chinese characters, to the extent deemed necessary for using this dictionary effectively.

APPENDIX 2

SYSTEM OF KANJI INDEXING BY PATTERNS
字型式検字法

QUICK GUIDE TO SKIP

The **System of Kanji Indexing by Patterns** (SKIP) can be used to locate character entries with great speed and little effort. If you are in a hurry to know the bare essentials of the system, do as follows:

1. Read section **§2.1 Overview of SKIP** on p. 1785.
2. Refer to the charts inside the front and back covers.

To get a more thorough understanding, carefully read the sections below. Pay special attention to **§3.1 SKIP Method**, which gives detailed instructions for locating entries.

1 INTRODUCTION

1.1 Historical Background

The lack of an efficient system for ordering Chinese characters has long been a source of frustration to learners and even native speakers of Chinese and Japanese, posing a major obstacle to the effective use of character dictionaries. The traditional method of looking up characters presupposes a knowledge of kanji elements known as **radicals.** Looking up by radicals is a time-consuming, laborious, and unreliable process that may require weeks of practice to learn. Although many alternative systems have been devised, none have achieved the speed and simplicity required to meet the practical needs of the learner.

1.1.1 The Radical System The traditional radical system is based on a table consisting of 214 elements plus about 150 variants used for classifying the characters into groups in Chinese-character dictionaries (see **Appendix 7** for details). The radical system is complex and difficult to master. To use it effectively requires much experience, some knowledge of character etymology, the ability to identify the original radical from its variants, and familiarity with old character forms. Even experienced users must often resort to guesswork and repeated false attempts. The main reasons that the traditional radical system is difficult to use are:

1. A radical may have several variants of totally different form and/or stroke-count. Often, the variant cannot be recognized without prior knowledge. For example, 氵 is a three-stroke variant of the four-stroke 'water' radical 水.
2. Some radicals have almost exactly the same forms, and are easily confused. For example, 匚 (Radical 22) is the radical of 匠, while 匸 (Radical 23) is the radical of 匹.
3. Since some radicals have totally disappeared from the modern forms of characters, a knowledge of old forms is sometimes necessary. For example, 医 is classified under 酉 according to its old form 醫.
4. A character often includes several radical elements and one must choose between them; e.g., 副 consists of the four elements 一, 口, 田, and 刂, all of which are radicals (in this case 刂 is the correct choice).
5. A character that is itself a radical sometimes includes other radicals. For example, the 高 radical includes three radical elements: 亠, 口, and 冂.
6. The radical is sometimes "embedded" in the character and is difficult to identify. For example, 乙 is the radical of 也.

7. The radical sometimes appears in unpredictable positions. For example, the radical of characters with 禾 in the left position is usually 禾, but the radical of 和 is 口.

Although various attempts have been made to simplify and improve the system, it is basically cumbersome and difficult to use. Nevertheless, the time-honored radical system, which is in widespread use in character dictionaries and reference works, is important and should be learned by the serious student of Chinese or Japanese.

1.1.2 Alternative Systems To overcome the problems inherent in the radical system, numerous alternative systems have been devised throughout the long history of Chinese and Japanese lexicography. The most important of these can be classified into five types, which are briefly described below. The list includes the radical system for comparison purposes.

1. **Traditional radical system** The traditional method of ordering entries in character dictionaries lists the characters according to their historical radicals and additional strokes. To use it effectively requires much experience, some knowledge of character etymology, familiarity with the 214 radicals and their variants, and a knowledge of old forms. Its main advantage is its widespread use in character dictionaries and reference works.

2. **Simplified radical systems** Since the traditional radical system is cumbersome, many attempts have been made to simplify it by such devices as (1) reducing the number of radicals, (2) basing the radical on new rather than old character forms, and (3) assigning the radical in a consistent manner. A good example of this is the Radical Priority System introduced in Andrew Nelson's well-known character dictionary. These simplified systems are a considerable improvement over the historical radicals. Their chief disadvantage is that the user must become familiar with yet another set of radicals, and that they lack standardization—every dictionary uses a somewhat different variation.

3. **Reading indexes** The most widespread of these are the *on-kun* index and romanized index, which list the characters phonetically by their *on* and *kun* readings for Japanese and their Mandarin pronunciations for Chinese. This type of index suffers from two major drawbacks: (1) the user must have prior knowledge of the character's reading, and (2) dozens or even hundreds of entries may appear under a common reading such as こう.

4. **Stroke-count indexes** Most Japanese character dictionaries include a stroke-count index, which lists the characters by total stroke-count. These indexes are difficult to use because (1) many characters, sometimes over 500, appear in the same stroke-count section, (2) they require the user to count strokes accurately—no cross-references appear at incorrect locations, and (3) finding an entry is very slow. The characters are often further classified by radical, which requires familiarity with the radical system. The only advantage of this index is that, if one has patience, it serves as a last resort when all other means fail.

5. **Character and stroke form systems** Many systems classify the characters on the basis of form. They usually define a table of elements based on various criteria such as stroke form or structure, stroke position, or structure of character parts (such as the top or corners). Some systems, such as the well-known Four Corner System, assign a numerical code to each character, and are fairly efficient once learned. Their main disadvantage is that they presuppose a knowledge of character form and/or stroke structure, which the beginner does not have, and often require one to memorize complex rules.

6. **Stroke order systems** Some systems classify the characters on the basis of stroke order. Although there are general stroke order principles, such as "first left then right," the rules are not strict enough to serve as a basis for an efficient lookup system. The main disadvantage of these systems is that they presuppose a knowledge of stroke order, which makes them unsuitable for learners.

One might well ask why, with so many systems in existence, there is a need for yet another system. The answer is that past and existing systems often suffer from a number of serious drawbacks, the most important of which are as follows:

1. Locating an entry can be a time-consuming, laborious process.
2. Some systems are difficult to learn, sometimes requiring rote memorization of many complex elements and weeks of practice.
3. Prior knowledge of kanji, such as of radicals, stroke order, stroke form, and character reading, is often required. In effect, the user is unable to look up a character without already knowing something about it.

4. Poor cross-referencing often requires going back and forth between entries.
5. Some systems are unreliable and inconsistent, requiring guesswork and repeated false attempts.
6. Poor entry distribution between subgroups means that some indexes may have hundreds of entries in one subsection.

Because of these drawbacks, previous systems are inadequate for meeting the practical needs of the learner.

1.2 System of Kanji Indexing by Patterns

1.2.1 New Indexing System To overcome the shortcomings of the traditional methods of ordering characters, this dictionary introduces a new scheme, called the **System of Kanji Indexing by Patterns** or **SKIP,** that can be used to locate entries as quickly and as accurately as in alphabetical dictionaries. The system, which can be learned in a very short time, is based on a new concept: **the direct identification of geometrical patterns.** With the help of simple rules, each character is unambiguously classified under one of four easy-to-identify **patterns:** **◧1** left-right, **⬒2** up-down, **◻3** enclosure, and **■4** solid. For example, 相 is classified under pattern **◧1** since it can be divided into left and right parts (木 and 目).

Classification by patterns is not merely a variation of an existing system—it is, as we shall see below, a new *type* of lookup system based on an entirely new idea. The user need only identify the *pattern* formed by visual elements, and needs no prior knowledge of the character or its constituents.

Characters belonging to the first three patterns, the **divisible characters,** are arranged in ascending order of hyphenated numerals that indicate stroke-count. The first numeral indicates the number of strokes in the shaded segment of the pattern symbol, and the second the number of strokes in the nonshaded segment. The pattern number followed by these hyphenated numerals is referred to as the **SKIP number** for that character. The SKIP number for the **indivisible characters** (pattern **■4**) is formed according to a somewhat different principle.

The character entries are ordered by their SKIP numbers. Locating a character is simply a matter of determining its SKIP number and then finding the corresponding entry. To locate a divisible character, identify the pattern to which it belongs to determine the first part of the SKIP number, then divide it and count the strokes of each part to determine the second and third parts of that number. For example, 相 can be divided into left and right parts and is thus classified under pattern **◧1**. Since it contains four strokes in the **shaded part** (木) and five strokes in the **blank part** (目), its SKIP number is ◧1-4-5.

To achieve maximum lookup speed, characters sharing the same SKIP number are further subdivided into progressively smaller groups, while characters that may be difficult to locate are systematically cross-referenced at locations where they might be mistakenly looked for.

1.2.2 Advantages of SKIP The **System of Kanji Indexing by Patterns** is a great improvement over its predecessors. To overcome the six shortcomings of traditional lookup systems listed in **§1.1.2** above, SKIP offers the following six advantages:

1. **Entries can be located with great speed and little effort.** Once the system has been mastered, the user can look up entries as quickly and as effortlessly as in alphabetically arranged dictionaries. The experienced user can often locate an entry in less than twenty seconds.

2. **The basic principles of the system can be learned in a few minutes.** Since SKIP rules are based on intuition, they are easy to learn in a short time. Tests have confirmed that after only ten to fifteen minutes of learning the rules, beginners can locate entries with an accuracy of 90 to 100 percent. Although it may take some time to master the finer details, this is a small price to pay considering the total amount of time saved in looking up entries over the many years during which the dictionary is used.

3. **No prior knowledge of kanji elements is required.** The system relies on the direct identification of the *pattern* formed by kanji elements, not the *forms* of the elements themselves. Thus no prior knowledge of the character or its constituents, such as its radical, reading, stroke order, or stroke form, is needed.

4. **A cross-reference system practically eliminates dead-end searching** by placing difficult-to-find characters at locations where they might be mistakenly looked for.

5. **The system is reliable and logically consistent.** The user need not engage in guesswork and repeated false attempts. A proper understanding and application of the rules will always lead to the correct location on the first try.

6. **The distribution of characters among the four patterns is fairly uniform.** Moreover, there is no overconcentration of characters in the subdivisions into which each pattern section is divided.

As should be clear from the above, since no prior knowledge of the character or its constituents is required, one need not waste time in learning to recognize the *shapes* of an arbitrary set of elements—the user need only identify the *arrangement* of elements in relation to each other. In this sense, classification by patterns is intrinsically different from other systems—it is not merely a new variation of an existing system.

SKIP is a product of seven years of computer-assisted research and experimentation on how kanji elements are intuitively perceived in terms of their parts. Since the system can be learned in a very short time and is easy to use, it has been praised by educators as an important breakthrough in Chinese-character lexicography. At the very least, it represents a radical departure from all traditional systems for ordering characters in both China and Japan.

1.2.3 SKIP Rules Since the rules for classifying characters by patterns are essentially simple, it is often possible to identify the pattern correctly even with only a superficial knowledge of the rules. Inevitably, a small number of characters will be difficult to locate even if you know the rules. To eliminate dead-end searching, many of these problem characters are systematically cross-referenced at one or more locations where they might be mistakenly looked for.

Intuition and cross-references, however, cannot be relied upon all the time. To use the system effectively, a knowledge of the rules is necessary. In the initial stages, a brief glance at the pattern chart inside the back cover, which has been designed as an aid to locating entries without a detailed knowledge of the rules, will no doubt be most helpful. Once you become familiar with the rules and gain a little experience, you should normally be able to quickly locate a desired entry without referring to the chart.

1.3 Pattern Selection Criteria

The four SKIP patterns were selected on the basis of a study of the structure and geometrical properties of kanji elements, and an investigation of how combinations of such elements are intuitively perceived in terms of their parts. There are many other ways in which characters could conceivably be classified by patterns, such as triangular divisions (e.g., 春 under ⧄) or division into three parts (e.g., 指 under ⊞). Our computer-aided research has shown that the SKIP patterns are ideally suited as a scheme for ordering entries in character dictionaries. The principal reasons for this are (1) they are in harmony with the way the characters are intuitively perceived, and (2) they often coincide with etymologically meaningful parts.

1.3.1 Psychologistics of Pattern Recognition

There are countless ways in which combinations of visual elements may be perceived. Even a simple figure like a square can be divided up in numerous ways:

1. Four line segments of equal length:

2. Four **L**-shaped components:

3. Many short line segments:

4. Two **U**-shaped components:

Dozens of other divisions are possible. The larger the components into which a structure is divided, the simpler is the relationship between them. Dividing into smaller parts results in more complex relations. That a structure can be broken up into certain parts does not mean that it has been assembled from those parts. In fact, no division is intrinsically superior to any other—all are equally arbitrary. The best division is the one that most aptly describes the figure for a particular purpose. However, some divisions are more "intuitive" than others. For example, most people perceive a square as consisting of four line segments—few would regard it as a combination of **L**-shapes.

The perceptual principles of organizing groups of elements into larger units form a fascinating branch of psychology. This is not the place to discuss these principles in detail. The point is that Chinese characters, many of which are of highly complex structure, can be divided in countless ways, but only some of these will seem "natural"—that is, will be in harmony with the way the character is *intuitively* perceived. "Intuitively" here refers to the manner in which the absolute majority of people tend to perceive a character in terms of its parts. For example, most people perceive 宗 as consisting of 宀 and 示

stacked one over another, 国 as consisting of 囗 enclosing the internal element 玉, and so on.

SKIP rules are based on an extensive analysis of how the characters are intuitively perceived as geometrical patterns. We have developed a set of objective criteria that closely reflect the *psychologistic* principles of recognizing the patterns formed by kanji elements. Massive volumes of kanji pattern data were analyzed by computer and subjected to many tests with both beginners and experienced users over a period of several years. The result of these efforts is a set of accurate and reliable rules that are, on the one hand, in close harmony with intuition and, on the other, strike a good balance between component size and simplicity of relationship between parts.

Although we have done everything possible to ensure that the rules reflect intuition, some exceptions are inevitable. For example, some people may find it more natural to divide 真 into 直 and 八, rather than into 十 and 具. That a small number of divisions conflict with intuition is a small price to pay considering the speed, consistency, and ease with which characters can be located by following the rules.

Since SKIP rules are based on intuition, it follows that they are easy to learn in a short time. It also follows that most people will tend to intuitively divide characters according to these rules even if they do not know them. In conclusion, the firm psychological basis of SKIP patterns makes them well suited for lexicographic classification.

1.3.2 Etymological Integrity A second reason for adopting SKIP patterns is their etymological integrity; that is, dividing a character by SKIP rules often yields etymologically meaningful parts such as radicals, which are usually familiar kanji elements contributing to the character's meaning. For example, 休 きゅう 'rest', which is classified under pattern **◧1**, is a left-right character divided into 亻 'human being' and 木 もく 'tree', both of which are radicals.

However, it is important to note that SKIP rules do not *depend* on radicals or etymology; etymological integrity is merely a by-product that may be of benefit to the user familiar with the radical system. Since division by patterns is based on a precise set of rules, the division of many characters will of course not conform to division by radicals. For example, SKIP rules call for dividing 勝 into 月 and 劵, whereas division by radicals gives 朕 and 力, which is far less obvious.

2 DESCRIPTION OF THE SYSTEM

2.1 Overview of SKIP

The central idea of the **System of Kanji Indexing by Patterns** is the classification of characters into four major categories on the basis of easy-to-identify geometrical **patterns: ◧1 left-right** (相), **⬒2 up-down** (字), **□3 enclosure** (進), and **■4 solid** (下).

SKIP	Acronym of "**System of Kanji Indexing by Patterns.**" A system of classifying characters by geometrical patterns used for the rapid location of entries in this dictionary.

Characters belonging to the first three categories, referred to as the **divisible characters,** are arranged in ascending order of hyphenated numerals called the **subsection number.** The first numeral indicates the number of strokes in the **shaded part,** which corresponds to the shaded segment of the **pattern symbol,** and the second the number of strokes in the **blank part,** which corresponds to the nonshaded segment. The **pattern number** followed by the subsection number is referred to as the **SKIP number.**

To locate a divisible character, first identify the pattern to which it belongs to determine the first part of the SKIP number, then divide it and count the strokes of each part to determine the second and third parts of that number (the subsection number). For example, 格 can be divided into left and right parts and is thus classified under pattern **◧1**. Since it contains four strokes in the shaded part (木) and six strokes in the blank part (各), its SKIP number is ◧1-4-6. It thus appears under pattern **◧1**, subsection 4-6, along with other characters that share the same SKIP number such as 時 and 脂.

Divisible characters in the same **subsection** are divided into **subgroups** containing a shared element (such as 日 and 月), called the **subgroup element,** for maximum lookup speed. The characters within each subgroup are further subdivided into progressively smaller groups until each character is assigned its own position.

Characters that cannot be divided by SKIP rules, called the **indivisible characters,** are classified under pattern ■**4** solid. These are arranged by total stroke-count and subclassified into four **solid subpatterns** on the basis of easy-to-identify lines: □**1 top line** (下), □**2 bottom line** (上), □**3 through line** (中), and □**4 others** (人). The first part of the subsection number for these characters represents their total stroke-counts, and the second part represents the number of the solid subpattern. 下, for example, is a three-stroke character containing a top line, and is thus classified under pattern ■**4**, subsection 3-1 (SKIP number ■4-3-1).

The character entries in the main part of the dictionary are ordered according to the above scheme. To attain greater lookup speed and flexibility, they are also listed in exactly the same order in the **Pattern Index.** Thus, once you have determined the SKIP number, you have a choice of two lookup methods: (1) locating the entry in the **Pattern Index,** or (2) locating the entry directly without using the index. In addition, there is a special shortcut called the **Scan Method** that makes it possible to locate entries quickly without determining their SKIP numbers.

Although SKIP rules are simple, a small number of characters may be difficult to locate. To eliminate dead-end searching, many of these are systematically cross-referenced at one or more locations where they might be mistakenly looked for. Moreover, various guides printed in the outer corners and margins of the page facilitate the rapid location of entries to achieve maximum lookup speed.

The above overview describes the most important elements of the system. Since it is essentially simple, you should be able to look up entries even on the basis of this brief description. Sections **§2.2** through **§7** below explain the details of looking up entries, summarize the rules for identifying the pattern and dividing the character, and define technical terms.

It is most important that you acquire a clear understanding of the various terms used in a technical sense, particularly the term **division point.** The definitions of technical terms are enclosed in boxes, while terms appearing in the text are printed in **sanserif boldface** whenever it is necessary to draw attention to them, especially the first time they are used in a topic of discussion. All SKIP terms are briefly defined in **§7 Glossary.**

2.2 SKIP Patterns

The **System of Kanji Indexing by Patterns** classifies the characters into four major categories on the basis of easy-to-identify geometrical **patterns:** ◧**1** left-right, ⬒**2** up-down, ◻**3** enclosure, and ■**4** solid. Each pattern is identified by a **pattern symbol** and **pattern number.** The charts below illustrate and define the various parts and terms associated with SKIP patterns.

Structure of SKIP Patterns

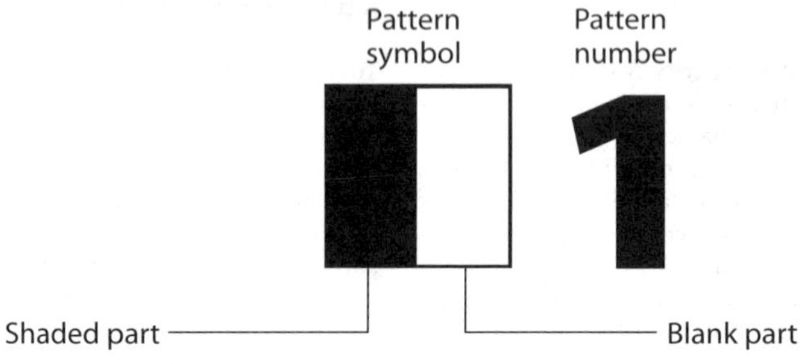

Pattern	A configuration of elements that characterizes the four major groups in the SKIP classification scheme; i.e., ◧**1 left-right,** ⬒**2 up-down,** ◻**3 enclosure,** and ■**4 solid.**
Pattern number	A number that identifies one of the four patterns in the SKIP classification scheme; i.e., **1** = ◧, **2** = ⬒, **3** = ◻, and **4** = ■.
Pattern symbol	A symbol that identifies one of the four patterns in the SKIP classification scheme; i.e., ◧ = **1**, ⬒ = **2**, ◻ = **3**, and ■ = **4**. The shaded segment of the first three pattern symbols corresponds to the **shaded part** of the **divisible characters,** and the non-shaded segment to the **blank part** of these characters.

The table below briefly describes the four SKIP patterns. Rules on how to identify each pattern are given in **§4 How to Identify the Pattern.**

SKIP Patterns

Pattern Number	Pattern Symbol	Pattern Name	Description
1	◧	LEFT-RIGHT	Character elements placed side by side. The elements are separated from each other by a **space** (保). The left-right pattern is basically of vertical construction.
2	⬒	UP-DOWN	Character elements stacked more or less one on top of the other. The elements are separated from each other by a **space** (示), a **horizontal line** (赤), or a **frame element** (古). Although the up-down pattern is basically of horizontal construction, triangular (合) and diagonal (多) divisions are allowed.
3	□	ENCLOSURE	A completely exterior element enclosing the rest of a character on two or more sides. The **enclosure element** may be separated from the rest of the character by a **space** (広), or may be in full physical contact (田) with it. The enclosure pattern, which is basically of rectangular construction, is subdivided into **enclosure subpatterns** (see **§4.2 Enclosure Subpatterns**).
4	■	SOLID	A character element or combination of elements that does not constitute a left-right, up-down, or enclosure pattern. Solid characters, such as 口, 由, and 求, cannot be divided according to SKIP rules. Many cannot be divided without breaking through **indivisible units.** The solid pattern is subclassified into **solid subpatterns.** (see **§6.2 Solid Subpatterns**).

The chart below has been carefully designed to provide you with a good understanding of SKIP patterns and subpatterns. Since these are intuitively easy to identify, a glance at the chart will often enable you to locate a character even without a detailed knowledge of SKIP rules. For ready reference, this chart also appears inside the back cover.

SKIP Patterns Chart

No.	Pattern	Classification	Examples
1	◧ LEFT-RIGHT	clear space	相 4-5, 代 2-3, 情 3-8, 小 1-2, 川 1-2, 州 2-4, 順 1-11, 傾 2-11
		conceptual space	扱 3-3, 級 6-3, 歓 11-4, 街 3-9, 町 5-2, 翻 12-6, 髄 10-9, 伺 2-5
2	⬒ UP-DOWN	clear space	示 1-4, 二 1-1, 三 1-2, 言 1-6, 公 2-2, 谷 2-5, 父 2-2, 多 3-3
		conceptual space	芳 3-4, 合 2-4, 響 11-9, 桑 2-8, 系 1-6, 雀 4-7, 券 6-2, 春 5-4
		horizontal line	寺 3-3, 空 3-5, 文 2-2, 亭 2-7, 忘 2-5, 学 5-3, 索 4-6, 義 3-10
		frame element	古 2-3, 点 2-7, 免 2-6, 早 4-2, 尭 2-6, 当 3-3, 南 2-7, 支 2-2

3	**ENCLOSURE**		進 3-8	辻 4-2	起 7-3	延 3-5	魅 8-7	直 1-7	匕 1-1	止 2-2
			旬 2-4	載 6-7	刀 1-1	司 1-4	可 2-3	戒 4-3	鳥 7-4	馬 6-4
			麻 3-8	圧 2-3	尾 3-4	病 5-5	石 2-3	考 4-2	着 7-5	斗 2-2
			間 8-4	岡 2-6	風 2-7	向 3-3	肉 4-2	凶 2-2	山 2-1	画 2-6
			医 2-5	臣 3-4	匿 2-9	丑 2-2				
			回 3-3	国 3-5	田 3-2	日 3-1	目 3-2	四 3-2	皿 3-2	
4	**SOLID**	1 top line	下 3-1	耳 6-1	雨 8-1	子 3-1	凸 5-1	口 3-1	亜 7-1	爾 14-1
		2 bottom line	上 3-2	七 2-2	亡 3-2	丘 5-2	由 5-2	自 6-2	坐 7-2	重 9-2
		3 through line	中 4-3	十 2-3	手 4-3	本 5-3	求 7-3	乗 9-3	毛 4-3	粛 11-3
		4 others	人 2-4	九 2-4	女 3-4	火 4-4	犬 4-4	成 6-4	寿 7-4	為 9-4

As should be clear from the chart, a pattern is essentially a spatial arrangement of elements. It is important to understand that it is the *position* of the elements in relation to each other, *not their forms,* that determines the pattern. For example, 休 consists of two elements, 亻 and 木, placed side by side and thus constitutes a left-right pattern. The shape of the element 亻, or the fact that it is a radical, is totally irrelevant. Any other elements arranged in a similar manner would equally qualify as a left-right pattern. The pattern is thus independent of the character's form, radical, reading, stroke order, stroke-count, etc. Thus, the user need only identify the *arrangement* of the elements, not their *forms.*

2.3 Divisible and Indivisible Characters

From the point of view of SKIP rules, the characters are classified into two major groups: **divisible** and **indivisible.** The divisible characters are divided into two parts: the **shaded part,** which corresponds to the shaded segment of the **pattern symbol,** and the **blank part,** which corresponds to the nonshaded segment. The rules for dividing the divisible characters are described in **§5 How to Divide the Character.**

Characters that cannot be divided are referred to as **indivisible** or **solid characters.** These are subclassified according to a principle described in **§6 How to Subclassify the Solid Pattern.**

Divisible characters	Characters that can be divided according to SKIP rules; i.e., characters classified under patterns ◧**1**, ⬒**2**, and ◻**3**, such as 相, 字, and 広.
Indivisible characters	Characters that cannot be divided according to SKIP rules; i.e., characters classified under pattern ■**4**, such as 雨, 本, and 九.
Shaded part	The part of a **divisible character** corresponding to the shaded segment of the **pattern symbol;** i.e., the part removed at the first **division point.** For example, 木 is the shaded part of 相 (SKIP number ◧1-4-5). The stroke-count of this part corresponds to the second part of the **SKIP number** and the first part of the **subsection number.**
Blank part	The part of a **divisible character** corresponding to the nonshaded segment of the **pattern symbol;** i.e., the part remaining after the shaded part is removed. For example, 目 is the blank part of 相 (SKIP number ◧1-4-5). The stroke-count of this part corresponds to the third part of the **SKIP number** and the second part of the **subsection number.**

Structure of Divisible Characters

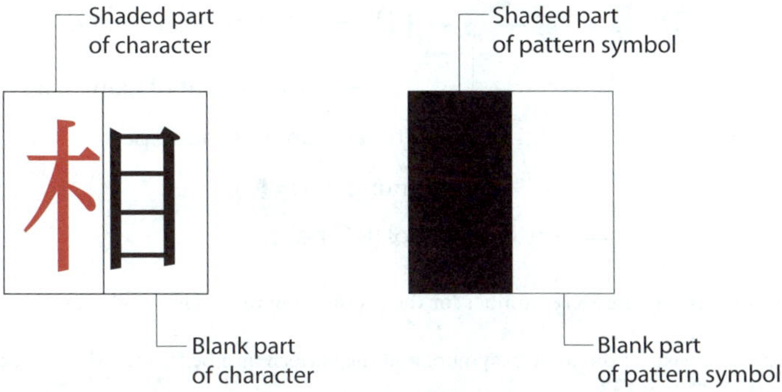

Structure of Indivisible Characters

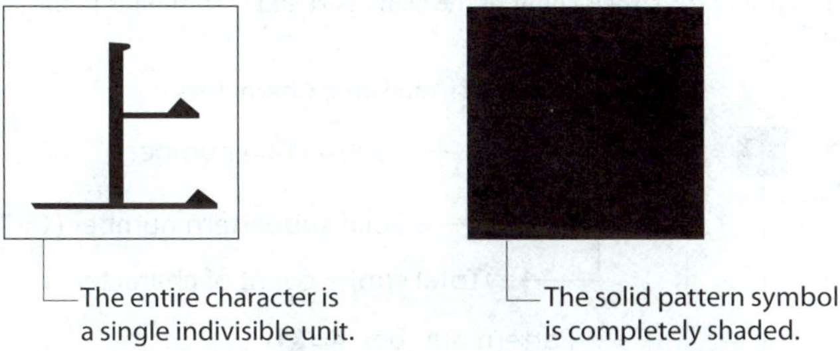

2.4 SKIP Number

The **SKIP number** consists of a **pattern symbol** followed by hyphenated numerals used to locate characters according to SKIP rules. The second and third parts of this number are called the **subsection number.** Since the entries of this dictionary are ordered according to the SKIP number, it is important to get a thorough understanding of how it is formed.

SKIP number	A **pattern symbol** followed by hyphenated numerals consisting of three parts: for the divisible characters, (1) the **pattern number,** (2) the stroke-count of the **shaded part,** and (3) the stroke-count of the **blank part;** for the indivisible characters, (1) the **pattern number,** (2) the total stroke-count, and (3) the **solid subpattern number.** For example, 相 is classified under pattern ◧**1** and divided into 木 (shaded part, 4 strokes) and 目 (blank part, 5 strokes), giving a SKIP number of ◧1-4-5. 下 is a three-stroke solid character containing a **top line** (solid subpattern □**1**), giving a SKIP number of ■4-3-1.
Subsection number	Hyphenated numerals used to identify a **subsection** and corresponding to the second and third parts of the SKIP number. For example, the subsection number for 相 (SKIP number ◧1-4-5) is 4-5. This number helps you quickly locate a desired subsection in the **Pattern Index** or in the main part of the dictionary.

SKIP Number of Divisible Characters

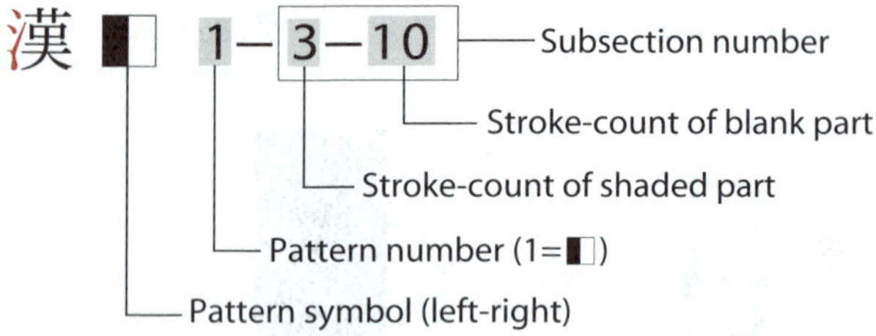

The principle for forming the SKIP number for the divisible characters is as follows:

1. The first part consists of the pattern symbol and the pattern number under which the character is classified; i.e., ◧**1**, ⬒**2**, or ▣**3**.
2. The second part indicates the stroke-count of the shaded part and corresponds to the first part of the subsection number.
3. The third part indicates the stroke-count of the blank part and corresponds to the second part of the subsection number.

SKIP Number of Indivisible Characters

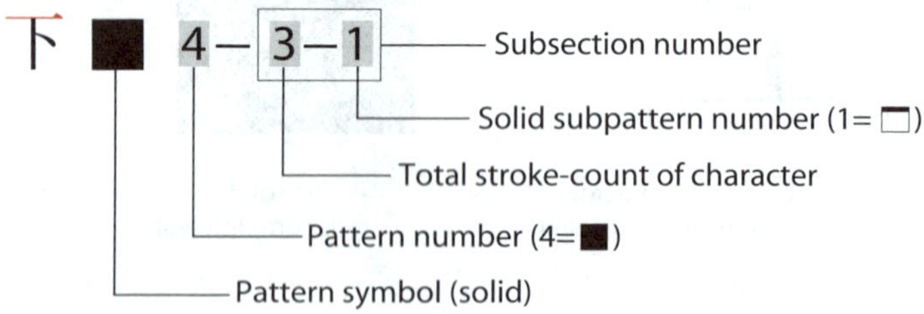

The principle for forming the SKIP number for the indivisible characters is as follows:

1. The first part consists of the pattern symbol and the pattern number for the solid pattern; i.e., ■**4**.
2. The second part indicates the total stroke-count of the character and corresponds to the first part of the subsection number.
3. The third part indicates the number of the solid subpattern under which the character is subclassified; i.e., ▔**1**, ▁**2**, ◫**3**, or □**4** (see **§6.2** for details). It corresponds to the second part of the subsection number.

The table below shows the relationship between the SKIP number and the subsection number:

SKIP Number and Subsection Number

		SKIP Number	Subsection Number
Divisible characters	漢 字 広	◧1-3-10 ⬒2-3-3 ▣3-3-2	3-10 3-3 3-2
Indivisible characters	下 上 中 丸	■4-3-1 ■4-3-2 ■4-4-3 ■4-3-4	3-1 3-2 4-3 3-4

2.5 Classification Scheme

2.5.1 Order of Entries The order of entries in this dictionary is based on a new classification scheme. The characters are grouped into four major categories on the basis of geometrical **patterns**: ◧**1** left-right, ⬒**2** up-down, □**3** enclosure, and ■**4** solid. The characters within each category are divided into **subsections**, which are in turn subdivided into **subgroups**. The subgroups are further subdivided according to various classification keys into progressively smaller groups until each character is assigned its own position. The chart below shows the most important of these subdivisions (see p. 2012 for a more detailed chart).

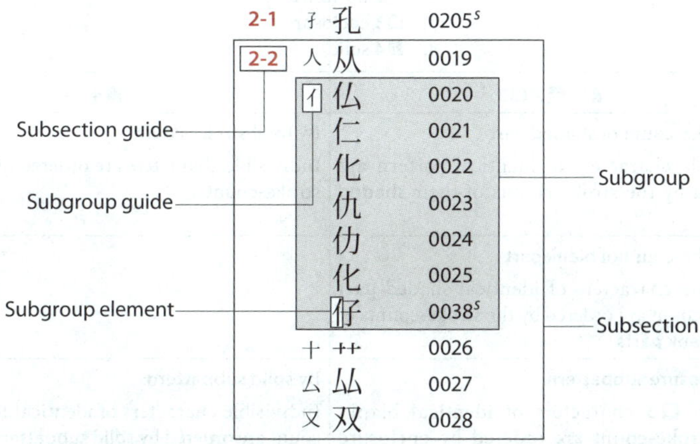

Subsection	A subdivision of the main part of the dictionary or of the **Pattern Index** in which the divisible characters are classified by **subgroup element** and the indivisible characters are classified by **entry type.** The subsections are arranged in ascending order of hyphenated numerals referred to as the **subsection number** (see **§2.4**). In the Pattern Index, each subsection is headed by a **subsection guide** for quick reference.
Subgroup	A subdivision of a **subsection** in which a group of **divisible characters** share a common **subgroup element.** In the Pattern Index, each subgroup is headed by a **subgroup guide,** which indicates the **subgroup element** for quick reference.
Subgroup element	The shared element of a **subgroup,** which corresponds to the **shaded part** of a divisible character. For example, 忄 is the subgroup element for the subgroup consisting of 怖 怪 怜 etc. Many subgroup elements, like 忄 above, are also radicals; others, like 君 in 群, are not. The subgroup elements that are radicals, which are ordered by their radical numbers, precede those that are not.

2.5.2 Classification Keys The complete scheme of SKIP classification keys is shown in the chart below. *Key* refers to any item, such as stroke-count, that is used as a criterion in ordering the entries. The **divisible characters** are subdivided according to the following eight keys: (1) by pattern, (2) by stroke-count of shaded part, (3) by stroke-count of blank part, (4) by enclosure subpattern, (5) by subgroup element, (6) by entry type, (7) by principal reading, and (8) by frequency. The **indivisible characters** are subdivided according to the following six keys: (1) by pattern, (2) by total stroke-count, (3) by solid subpattern, (4) by entry type, (5) by principal reading, and (6) by frequency.

The chart below is given for reference only—there is no need to understand all the details. For practical purposes, only the first three keys are important since they are used for forming the SKIP number. See **§3.3 Hints for Speed** for an explanation of how the various keys can help you speed up the lookup process.

The keys for the divisible characters differ somewhat from those for the indivisible characters. When these are the same, the key description extends over the entire width of the chart; when they differ, the left column refers to the former and the right column to the latter.

SKIP Classification Keys

<table>
<tr><th colspan="3">All Entries</th></tr>
<tr><td>❶</td><td colspan="2">By SKIP pattern
The entry characters are divided into four major categories by SKIP pattern:
1. ◧1 left-right
2. ⬒2 up-down
3. □3 enclosure
4. ■4 solid</td></tr>
<tr><td></td><td>◧1 ⬒2 □3</td><td>■4</td></tr>
<tr><td>❷</td><td>By stroke-count of shaded part
Divisible characters of identical pattern are ordered by the stroke-counts of their shaded parts.</td><td>By total stroke-count
Indivisible characters are ordered by their total stroke-counts.</td></tr>
<tr><td>❸</td><td>By stroke-count of blank part
Divisible characters of identical shaded-part stroke-count are ordered by the stroke-counts of their blank parts.</td><td></td></tr>
<tr><td>❹</td><td>By enclosure subpattern:
Pattern □3 characters of identical blank-part stroke-count are ordered by enclosure subpattern:
1. two sides: □ □ □ □
2. three sides: □ □ □ □
3. four sides: □ □ □</td><td>By solid subpattern:
Indivisible characters of identical total stroke-count are ordered by solid subpattern:
1. □1 top line
2. □2 bottom line
3. □3 through line
4. □4 others</td></tr>
<tr><td>❺</td><td>By subgroup element:
Divisible characters of identical blank-part stroke-count (and enclosure subpattern) are grouped by subgroup element in the following order:
1. radical elements by radical number
2. nonradical elements by stroke-count and SKIP number</td><td></td></tr>
<tr><td>❻</td><td>By entry type:
Divisible characters of identical subgroup element are grouped by entry type in the following order:</td><td>By entry type:
Indivisible characters of identical solid subpattern are grouped by entry type in the following order:</td></tr>
<tr><td></td><td colspan="2">1. standard entries
2. nonstandard entries
3. cross-reference entries</td></tr>
<tr><td>❼</td><td colspan="2">By principal reading:
Characters of the same entry type are ordered by their principal readings.</td></tr>
<tr><td>❽</td><td colspan="2">By frequency:
Characters sharing the same principal reading are ordered by their frequency of occurrence (see Appendix 10 on p. 1850).</td></tr>
</table>

2.6 Cross-References

Finding entries by SKIP rules is normally speedy and reliable. However, difficulties may arise in unusual cases, such as characters whose patterns are difficult to identify, or characters whose strokes are difficult to count. For example, 児 is an up-down character that may be mistakenly classified as a left-right character by dividing it into 丬 and 巳, whereas 子 is a three-stroke element that may be incorrectly counted as a two-stroke element.

Characters like the above are systematically placed at one or more *incorrect* SKIP locations—that is, locations where they might be mistakenly looked for—and are followed by a cross-reference to their corresponding correct locations. To ensure maximum usefulness and accuracy, the kinds of mistakes likely to occur were systematically analyzed and tested, and a network of **cross-reference entries** was generated and checked by computer.

Cross-reference entry	A character entry in the main part of the dictionary or in the **Pattern Index** appearing at an **incorrect location** with a cross-reference to the corresponding correct location.

The cross-references greatly enhance the value of the system, since they practically eliminate dead-end searching. Moreover, they inform you of the kind of mistake you have made; that is, whether you have arrived at an incorrect pattern classification, an incorrect stroke-count, or both. This helps you learn from your mistakes and thus avoid similar ones.

Cross-reference entries appear in both the main part of the dictionary and in the **Pattern Index** (see chart on p. 2012).

2.6.1 Cross-Reference Types Cross-reference entries are of two kinds:

1. **Single-character** cross-reference entries are cross-references for one character at an incorrect location. The correct location is indicated by the entry number to be referred to:

   究 ⬒2-5-2 — incorrect classification ➡ see ⬒2-3-4: 穴 at 2729

   In the example, 究 appears under the incorrect classification ⬒2-5-2, and the cross-reference points to 2729, the entry number under the correct classification ⬒2-3-4.

2. **Multiple-character** cross-reference entries are cross-references for a group of two or more characters of similar structure (pattern classification or stroke-count) at an incorrect location. The correct location is indicated by the pattern and subsection number to be referred to:

   恒 悔 etc. ◧1-1-8 — incorrect classification ➡ see ◧1-3-6: 忄 at 0435

If the group consists of two characters, both are given. If the group consists of three or more characters, the first two are given and are followed by **etc.** This indicates that the other members of the group have the same structure as the first two and can also be found at the same correct location. In the example above, **etc.** indicates that, in addition to 恒 and 悔, other left-right characters sharing the subgroup element 忄, such as 恢 and 恰, can also be found at the correct location ◧3-6.

2.6.2 Incorrect Location refers to a location where a character might be mistakenly looked for. Incorrect locations are of two kinds: (1) locations under an incorrect pattern classification, and (2) locations under an incorrect stroke-count. On rare occasions, an incorrect location may be a combination of both types:

棄 ⬒2-4-8 — incorrect classification/stroke-count ➡ see ⬒2-2-11: 亠 at 2651

In the main part of the dictionary, the kind of incorrect location is indicated by the brief description preceding the arrow ➡, and in the index by the following superscript symbols:

- ***p*** incorrect pattern classification
- ***s*** incorrect stroke-count
- ***ps*** incorrect pattern classification and incorrect stroke-count

2.7 SKIP Guides

One feature that makes the **System of Kanji Indexing by Patterns** convenient to the user is a **system of guides.** The various guides printed in the outer corners and margins of the page have been carefully designed and laid out to facilitate the speedy location of entries. They are particularly useful for finding an entry directly from its **SKIP number** without consulting the **Pattern Index** (see **§3.1.3 Direct Method** for details).

The guides in the main part of the dictionary are of the following kinds: (1) the **pattern guide,** (2) the

subsection guide, (3) the **subgroup guide,** and (4) the **entry number guide.** These and other relevant elements are illustrated and described below. For a description of the guides in the **Pattern Index,** see p. 2012.

SKIP Guides

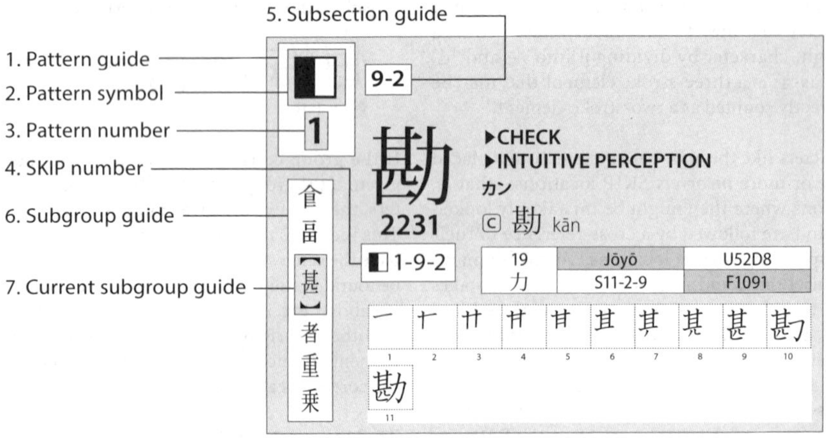

1. Pattern guide	A guide in the upper, outer corner of a page that indicates the **pattern** and **pattern number** for that page.
2. Pattern symbol	A symbol that identifies one of the four patterns in the SKIP classification scheme.
3. Pattern number	A number that identifies the SKIP pattern.
4. SKIP number	A **pattern symbol** followed by hyphenated numerals used to locate characters according to SKIP rules.
5. Subsection guide	Boldface numerals in the upper corner of a page that indicate the **subsection number** for that page. The pattern guides and subsection guides in the upper left indicate the SKIP number for the first entry in left-hand pages, while those in the upper right indicate the SKIP number for the last entry in right-hand pages. Together they indicate the SKIP number range for both pages.
6. Subgroup guide	A guide in the outer margin of a page used to locate the **subgroup element** corresponding to the **shaded part** of **divisible characters.** It lists the subgroup elements for the SKIP number of the first (left-hand page) or last (right-hand page) entry character on that page.
7. Current subgroup guide	The **subgroup element** of the first (left-hand page) or last (right-hand page) entry character on that page is enclosed in heavy square brackets 【 】 within the **subgroup guide.** The brackets move up and down as you turn the pages, allowing rapid location of your subgroup element within the subgroup guide.
8. Entry guide	A guide in the outer margin of a page used to locate **indivisible characters** sharing the same SKIP number. It lists all the **entry characters** (not just those on that page) for the **current SKIP number;** that is, the SKIP number of the first (left-hand page) or last (right-hand page) entry character on that page.
9. Current entry guide	All the **indivisible entry characters** on a page that share the same **current SKIP number** are enclosed in heavy square brackets 【 】 within the **entry guide.** The brackets move up and down as you turn the pages, allowing rapid location of your entry character within the entry guide.

3 INSTRUCTIONS FOR USE

There are two methods of locating entries by SKIP rules:

1. The **SKIP Method** consists of determining the **SKIP number** of your character, then locating it in the main part of the dictionary. This is the method recommended for ordinary use.
2. The **Scan Method** is a special shortcut that enables you to locate a character without determining its SKIP number. This method is only effective for characters containing elements of high stroke-count.

The sections below present detailed instructions for locating entries by the above methods. To use these instructions effectively, be sure you understand the material covered in **§2 Description of the System.** Although the instructions are very thorough, don't be overwhelmed by the details. Remember that the system is essentially simple—with just a little practice, you should be able to find entries with great speed and little effort.

3.1 SKIP Method

Finding an entry by the **SKIP Method** consists of two major steps:

1. Determine the **SKIP number** of your character.
2. Locate the character entry in the main part of the dictionary.

Once you know the SKIP number of your character, locating the character entry is a straightforward, largely mechanical process. To make the system as flexible as possible, there are two ways to do this: (1) the **Index Method,** by which you first find the entry number of your character in the **Pattern Index,** and (2) the **Direct Method,** by which you locate your character entry directly from its SKIP number. The second method is on the average faster than the first (see **§3.3 Hints for Speed** for details).

3.1.1 How to Determine the SKIP Number To locate a character by the SKIP Method, you must first determine its SKIP number. Since determining this number quickly is the key to using the system effectively, you should get a thorough understanding of how it is formed (see **§2.4 SKIP Number**). The gist of the method is as follows:

Identify the **pattern** to get the first part of the SKIP number. To get the second and third parts, count the strokes of the **shaded part** and **blank part** of the divisible characters, or count the total stroke-count and determine the **solid subpattern** of the indivisible characters.

The chart below gives detailed instructions for determining the SKIP number, and includes references to other sections that explain each step in greater detail. Understanding this chart is of crucial importance, so study carefully the examples appearing right after the chart. For quick reference, this chart also appears inside the front cover.

How to Determine the SKIP Number

DETERMINE THE SKIP NUMBER OF YOUR CHARACTER		
STEP 1	**IDENTIFY PATTERN** Determine to which of the four **patterns** your character belongs to get the first part of the SKIP number (the **pattern number**). If your character belongs to pattern ◧**1**, ⬒**2**, or □**3**, carry out the steps in the left column; if it belongs to pattern ■**4**, carry out the steps in the right column. ➡§4 How to Identify the Pattern	
	◧1 ⬒2 □3	■4
STEP 2	**DIVIDE CHARACTER** Divide the character into two parts at the first **division point.** ➡§5 How to Divide the Character	**OMIT** Since **solid characters** cannot be divided, go to STEP 3.

STEP 3	**COUNT STROKES OF SHADED PART** Count the strokes of the **shaded part** to get the second part of the SKIP number. ➡Appendix 3. How to Count Strokes	**DETERMINE TOTAL STROKE-COUNT** Determine the total stroke-count of your character to get the second part of the SKIP number. ➡Appendix 3. How to Count Strokes
STEP 4	**COUNT STROKES OF BLANK PART** Count the strokes of the **blank part** to get the third part of the SKIP number. ➡Appendix 3. How to Count Strokes	**IDENTIFY SOLID SUBPATTERN** Determine to which of the four **solid subpatterns** your character belongs to get the third part of the SKIP number. Select from: □**1**, □**2**, ◫**3**, or □**4**. ➡§6 How to Subclassify the Solid Pattern

Example: Determine the SKIP Number of 棚

STEP 1	**IDENTIFY PATTERN**	Since 棚 can be divided into left and right parts, we identify it as belonging to pattern ◧**1** left-right. This gives the first part of the SKIP number as 1: 棚 → ◧1
STEP 2	**DIVIDE CHARACTER**	Dividing 棚 into two parts at the first **division point** yields 木, the **shaded part,** and 朋, the **blank part**: 棚 → 木 + 朋
STEP 3	**COUNT STROKES OF SHADED PART**	Counting the strokes of the **shaded part** (木) yields a stroke-count of 4. This gives the second part of the SKIP number as 4: 棚 → ◧1-4-
STEP 4	**COUNT STROKES OF BLANK PART**	Counting the strokes of the **blank part** (朋) yields a stroke-count of 8. This gives the third part of the SKIP number as 8: 棚 → ◧1-4-8
SKIP number of 棚: ◧1-4-8		

Example: Determine the SKIP Number of 下

STEP 1	**IDENTIFY PATTERN**	Since 下 cannot be divided into parts, we identify it as an **indivisible character** belonging to pattern ■**4** solid. This gives the first part of the SKIP number as 4: 下 → ■4
STEP 2	**OMIT**	Since 下 cannot be divided, go to STEP 3.
STEP 3	**DETERMINE TOTAL STROKE-COUNT**	Counting the strokes of the entire character yields a stroke-count of 3. This gives the second part of the SKIP number as 3: 下 → ■4-3-
STEP 4	**IDENTIFY SOLID SUBPATTERN**	Since 下 contains a line on top, we identify it as belonging to subpattern □**1 top line.** This gives the third part of the SKIP number as 1: 下 → ■4-3-1
SKIP number of 下: ■4-3-1		

3.1.2 Index Method After determining the SKIP number of your character, you must locate the entry character in the main part of the dictionary. The surest way to do this is by the **Index Method,** the gist of which is as follows:

Flip through the **Pattern Index** until you locate the **pattern number** and **subsection number** for your character. Scan the **subgroup guides** to locate your **shaded part,** then find your character and its **entry number.** Finally, turn the pages of the dictionary until you find your entry number.

The chart below gives detailed instructions for locating character entries by the Index Method.

How to Use the Index Method

<table>
<tr><th colspan="3">DETERMINE THE ENTRY NUMBER IN THE PATTERN INDEX, THEN LOCATE YOUR ENTRY CHARACTER</th></tr>
<tr><td>STEP 1</td><td colspan="2">LOCATE PATTERN
Turn the pages of the Pattern Index until you locate the pattern number (the first part of the SKIP number) which corresponds to your character. Use the pattern guides in the upper, outer corners of the pages.
➡How to Use the Pattern Index on p. 2012</td></tr>
<tr><td>STEP 2</td><td colspan="2">LOCATE SUBSECTION
Continue turning the pages until you locate the subsection number (the second and third parts of the SKIP number) which corresponds to your character. Use the red subsection guides in the left part of the column.
➡How to Use the Pattern Index on p. 2012</td></tr>
<tr><td></td><td>◧1 ⬒2 ◻3</td><td>■4</td></tr>
<tr><td>STEP 3</td><td>LOCATE SUBGROUP
Scan the column of subgroup guides until you locate the one which corresponds to the shaded part of your character.
➡Pattern Index on p. 2014</td><td>OMIT
Since solid characters cannot be divided, they are not grouped by subgroup elements.</td></tr>
<tr><td>STEP 4</td><td colspan="2">DETERMINE ENTRY NUMBER
Scan the column of characters until you locate your character and its entry number.</td></tr>
<tr><td>STEP 5</td><td colspan="2">LOCATE ENTRY CHARACTER
Turn the pages of the dictionary until you locate the one which includes your entry number, then scan that page until you locate your entry character. Use the entry number guides in the lower, outer corners of the pages.
➡§2.7 SKIP Guides</td></tr>
</table>

3.1.3 Direct Method After determining the SKIP number of your character, there is a second method for locating your entry in the main part of the dictionary. This is called the **Direct Method,** and is usually faster than the **Index Method.** The gist of the Direct Method is as follows:

Turn the pages of the dictionary (*without* referring to the **Pattern Index**) until you locate the **pattern number** and **subsection number** for your character. Scan the **subgroup guides** to locate your **shaded part,** then continue flipping the pages until you locate your character.

The chart below gives detailed instructions for locating character entries by the Direct Method.

How to Use the Direct Method

<table>
<tr><td colspan="3">LOCATE YOUR ENTRY CHARACTER DIRECTLY FROM ITS SKIP NUMBER</td></tr>
<tr><td>STEP 1</td><td colspan="2">LOCATE PATTERN
Turn the pages of the dictionary until you locate the pattern number (the first part of the SKIP number) which corresponds to your character. Use the pattern guides in the upper, outer corners of the pages.
➡§2.7 SKIP Guides</td></tr>
<tr><td>STEP 2</td><td colspan="2">LOCATE SUBSECTION
Continue turning the pages until you locate the subsection number (the second and third parts of the SKIP number) which corresponds to your character. Use the subsection guides in the upper, outer corners of the pages.
➡§2.7 SKIP Guides</td></tr>
<tr><td></td><td>◧1 ⬒2 □3</td><td>■4</td></tr>
<tr><td>STEP 3</td><td>LOCATE SUBGROUP
Continue turning the pages until your subgroup element is enclosed in brackets within the subgroup guide in the outer margins.
HINT: Subgroup elements that are radicals are ordered by radical number.
➡§2.7 SKIP Guides
➡§2.5 Classification Scheme
➡§3.3 Hints for Speed</td><td>OMIT
Since solid characters are not grouped by subgroup element, go to STEP 4.</td></tr>
<tr><td>STEP 4</td><td>LOCATE CHARACTER
Continue turning the pages until you locate your entry character.</td><td>LOCATE CHARACTER
Continue turning the pages until your entry character is enclosed in brackets within the entry guide in the outer margins.</td></tr>
<tr><td></td><td colspan="2">HINT: The divisible characters in a given subgroup and the indivisible characters in a given subsection are further classified by entry type and ordered alphabetically by their principal readings.
➡§2.5 Classification Scheme
➡§3.3 Hints for Speed</td></tr>
</table>

3.2 Scan Method

3.2.1 A Powerful Shortcut To locate an entry character, it is normally necessary to count the strokes of the character's components to determine its SKIP number. While mastering the techniques explained in **Appendix 3. How to Count Strokes** helps, counting the strokes of complex characters could be an error-prone, laborious task.

The **Scan Method** is a powerful shortcut that makes it possible to dispense with counting the strokes of elements of high stroke-count. Since such characters are relatively few and appear close together, it is only necessary to find their **approximate location** and then scan the vicinity. For complex characters, this is much faster than counting strokes to determine the SKIP number.

The Scan Method is used for locating **divisible characters** that have shaded or blank parts of high stroke-count, or **indivisible characters** of high total stroke-count. Basically, "high stroke-count" refers to approximately twelve or more strokes. It is not sufficient for the *total* stroke-count of a divisible character to be high; one of its *parts* must have twelve or more strokes. For example, although 償 (blank part fifteen strokes) is ideally suited for this method, 騎 (total eighteen strokes) is not, since neither 馬 (ten strokes) nor 奇 (eight strokes) has twelve strokes.

The higher the stroke-count is, the shorter the scanning distance and the better the method works. If the shaded part has, for instance, fifteen or more strokes, characters can be located almost immediately.

Finding a character by the Scan Method consists of four steps:

1. **Identify the pattern** See **§4 How to Identify the Pattern** for details.
2. **Divide the character** In the case of divisible characters, divide the character to determine the shaded part. In the case of indivisible characters, omit this step. **Don't count strokes.** See **§5 How to Divide the Character** for details.
3. **Find the approximate location** To find a divisible character by the Scan Method, it is first necessary to determine the **approximate location** from where to begin the scan. This is the vicinity where the **subsection numbers** begin with or end in 14; that is, 14-1, 14-2, 14-3 for characters with shaded parts of high stroke-count, or 1-14, 2-14, 3-14 for characters with blank parts of high stroke-count. Be sure to use the **subsection guides** to find your subsection as quickly as possible.

   Though 14 is often the optimal approximate location, you can start the search at, for instance, 16 or 13, if that seems more appropriate. With a little practice you should soon be able to find the approximate location in a few seconds.
4. **Scan** Scan the **subgroup guides** to locate the **shaded part** of your character by turning the pages until you find your **subgroup element,** then scan the entry characters within that **subgroup** until you locate your character.

3.2.2 Instruction Chart Essentially, the Scan Method consists of turning to the approximate location and scanning until you locate your character. The chart below is a step-by-step example of how to locate 襲 by scanning.

The Scan Method can be carried out in the following two ways:

1. Determine the entry number of your character by scanning the Pattern Index. This is similar to the Index Method.
2. Locate your entry directly by scanning the main part of the dictionary without using the Pattern Index. This is similar to the Direct Method.

In either case, **there is no need** to determine the subsection number, nor to count strokes, since you locate your subsection by finding the approximate location and then scanning.

Example: Find 襲 by the Scan Method

INSTRUCTIONS	EXAMPLE: Find 襲
❶ **IDENTIFY PATTERN** ➡§4 How to Identify the Pattern	Since 襲 can be divided into up-down parts, we identify it as belonging to pattern ⬒**2**.
❷ **DIVIDE CHARACTER** If your character belongs to pattern ◧**1**, ⬒**2**, or □**3**, divide it into two parts. ➡§5 How to Divide the Character	Dividing 襲 into up-down parts yields 龍, the shaded part, and 衣, the blank part.
❸ **FIND APPROXIMATE LOCATION** Using the **pattern** and **subsection guides,** turn to your pattern section and go to the vicinity where the **subsection numbers** begin with 14; i.e., 14-1, 14-2, 14-3, etc.	Turn to the subsection numbers beginning with 14 under pattern ⬒**2**. This can be done quickly by finding the beginning of the pattern □**3** section and working your way backwards.
❹ **LOCATE CHARACTER BY SCANNING** Using the **subgroup guides,** scan until you locate your entry character.	Scanning the subgroup guides quickly leads you to 龍, the shaded part of 襲. You then easily locate your entry character in subsection 16-6.

The Scan Method can also be used for locating indivisible characters of high stroke-count, especially over ten. Simply turn to the very end of the Pattern Index or of the dictionary, and search the vicinity until you find it. As there are very few characters of this kind, you should find your entry almost immediately.

The Scan Method may sound complicated on paper, but it is actually very simple to use. There is no need to think of it as consisting of distinct steps. Essentially, you swiftly move from one subgroup to another using the subgroup guides as visual signposts. For characters of high stroke-count, you can even scan the entry characters directly without using the subgroup guides, since the scanning distance is short.

Don't bother using the Scan Method unless it suits your taste—any character can always be found reliably with the Index Method.

3.3 Hints for Speed

Every effort has been made to eliminate guesswork and make SKIP an efficient and reliable lookup system. Below are various time-saving hints and shortcuts that will help you locate entries with maximum speed and minimum effort. To use these hints effectively, refer also to the chart in **§2.5.2 Classification Keys.**

1. **Pattern identification** Since SKIP rules are based on intuition, you can often identify the correct pattern at once by merely looking at the character. When in doubt, your best guide will be the SKIP patterns chart appearing inside the back cover. This chart has been designed to help you quickly identify the pattern without thinking about the rules.

2. **Counting strokes** The ability to count strokes quickly and accurately will help you determine the SKIP number faster. Although many cross-references appear at locations where you might mistakenly look for your character, it will be worth your while to learn the stroke counting techniques explained in **Appendix 3. How to Count Strokes.** Particularly effective is memorizing the stroke-counts of high-frequency radicals and difficult-to-count elements.

3. **SKIP vs. Scan** The **SKIP Method** (**§3.1**), in which you must first determine the SKIP number, is a safe method that works reliably all the time. It is the method that you should normally use in most of your dictionary work. The **Scan Method** (**§3.2**), on the other hand, is much more limited in scope. Its main advantage is that it dispenses with the need for counting the strokes of complex elements. For characters containing parts of twelve or more strokes (e.g., 襲), it could be considerably faster than the SKIP Method, but for characters containing parts of medium stroke-count (say seven or eight) it is inefficient or totally useless. In conclusion: if you want a reliable, safe method free of guesswork, use the SKIP Method. If you prefer a rough, speedy shortcut, use the Scan Method when appropriate.

4. **Scanning** If you cannot find your character from its SKIP number, there is a good chance that you have miscounted the number of strokes by one. Rather than count again, you might save time by looking for your character in the next or in the previous subsection. For example, if you look for 暗 under ◧1-4-10 and cannot find it, try at the previous subsection ◧1-4-9 or at the next subsection ◧1-4-11 (see **§3.2 Scan Method**).

5. **Index vs. Direct** The main advantage of the **Direct Method** (**§3.1.3**) is that it dispenses with the need for searching through the **Pattern Index.** When using the SKIP Method, the Direct Method is usually faster, sometimes considerably faster, than the **Index Method** (**§3.1.2**), but for some characters the reverse may be true. A distinct advantage of the Index Method is its high reliability; once you locate the entry number of your character in the index, you can find your entry with great speed and no hesitation. When using the Scan Method, the difference in speed between the two methods is not very great. Try both and use the one that best suits your personal taste.

6. **SKIP guides** Be sure to make full use of the various **SKIP guides** (**§2.7**), which are designed to facilitate speedy lookup. Particularly useful are the **subsection guides** (printed in red in the **Pattern Index**) and the **subgroup guides,** which help you swiftly move from one **subsection** or **subgroup** to another.

7. **Enclosure subpatterns** Although the enclosure characters are grouped by **enclosure subpattern** (**§4.2**), you may totally disregard this when looking for your entry. The enclosure pattern constitutes a single category, just like the left-right or up-down pattern.

8. **Subgroup elements** The divisible characters in a given **subsection** are grouped by **subgroup element** (**§2.5.1**). If you are using the Index Method, you can quickly locate your subgroup element

without worrying about their order. Since the number of subgroup elements in a given subsection is small, you can quickly locate your element by skimming through the **subgroup guides** of the **Pattern Index.** If, on the other hand, you are using the Direct Method, you may speed up the search by keeping in mind that the subgroup elements that are radicals appear in order of their radical numbers. Ignore this feature if you do not know the radical system really well.

9. **Entry types** The divisible characters in a given **subgroup** and the indivisible characters in a given **subsection** are further classified by **entry type** (see **§1.2 Types of Entries** on p. 42a). The entries that you are most likely to look for—the standard entries—appear first, and the nonstandard and cross-reference entries, which are the least needed, follow. This is not something that you need to be consciously aware of (except possibly when deliberately searching for a nonstandard form)—it is merely an auxiliary device that automatically speeds up the lookup process.

10. **Principal reading** Characters of the same entry type are ordered alphabetically by their **principal readings,** which is usually the most common *on* reading (see **§3 Character Readings** on p. 42a). If you know the reading of your character, this may help you find it more quickly, especially when using the Direct Method.

11. **Frequency** Characters sharing the same principal reading are ordered by their **frequency** of occurrence (see **§5 Reference Data Box** on p. 44a), so that the more frequent characters appear first. This may slightly contribute to lookup speed if you are looking for a high-frequency character.

4 HOW TO IDENTIFY THE PATTERN

4.1 Pattern Identification

To locate a character according to SKIP rules, the first task you face is to determine to which of the four patterns your character belongs. The **pattern number** will constitute the first part of the three-part **SKIP number** of your character. For example, 宙 is classified under the up-down pattern ⬒**2**, so the first part of its SKIP number is 2. See **§2.4 SKIP Number** for details.

To identify the pattern, just *look* at the character (or imagine it in your mind's eye) and decide to which pattern it belongs. Most of the time, your intuition will lead you to the correct classification at once. For example, 好, 充, and 尾 look like they belong to patterns ◧**1**, ⬒**2**, and ◻**3** respectively, while 下 and 曲 look like they are indivisible and therefore belong to pattern ■**4**. If you have trouble classifying your character, a glance at the pattern chart inside the back cover should usually enable you to easily identify the pattern without referring to the rules given below.

In actual practice, you normally identify the pattern of a character and divide it or subclassify it more or less simultaneously. When you see a character like 相, for example, you identify it as a left-right pattern and, at the same time, decide that it can be divided into 木 and 目. Nevertheless, for the sake of clarity and convenience of presentation, pattern identification and character division are treated here as separate topics (**§4.3** and **§5.3** respectively).

A formal statement of the rules for identifying the pattern is given in **§4.3** below.

4.2 Enclosure Subpatterns

To make it easier to identify the **enclosure pattern,** it is desirable to understand the concepts **enclosure element** and **enclosure subpattern.** The latter are illustrated in the chart below:

Enclosure Subpatterns

Sides	Subpattern Symbol	Examples
2	└	進
	┐	句
	┌	麻
	┘	斗
3	⊓	閉
	⊔	凶
	⊏	医
	⊐	丑
4	□	団
	▯	目
	▭	四

It is important to keep in mind that the enclosure pattern constitutes a single category, just like the left-right or up-down pattern. Any enclosure character, regardless of its subpattern, is classified under the enclosure pattern, and it is not necessary to be particularly aware of the subpattern. The subpattern symbols are merely visual aids that help describe the structure of enclosure elements.

Some enclosure elements may be difficult to identify. If you have trouble, refer to the charts inside the front and back covers.

Enclosure element	A completely exterior element enclosing the rest of a character on two or more sides. The enclosure pattern is subdivided into **enclosure subpatterns.**
Enclosure subpattern	One of the eleven groups into which the enclosure pattern is subdivided according to the number of sides of the enclosure element and its position along the exterior of the character.
Enclosure subpattern symbol	A symbol that identifies one of the eleven enclosure subpatterns.

4.3 Pattern Identification Rules

	Right	Wrong
❶ DETERMINE TO WHICH OF THE FOUR PATTERNS YOUR CHARACTER BELONGS		
◧1 CHARACTERS THAT CAN BE DIVIDED INTO LEFT AND RIGHT PARTS (*a*) The resulting parts must be separated by a **space.** (*b*) The resulting division must be more or less vertical.	相 4-5 小 1-2 順 1-11 体 2-5 吹 3-4 扱 3-3	片 1-3 用 1-4 隹 2-6 可 3-2 延 3-5 多 3-3
⬒2 CHARACTERS THAT CAN BE DIVIDED INTO TOP AND BOTTOM PARTS (*a*) The resulting parts must be separated by a **space, horizontal line,** or **frame element.** (*b*) The resulting division need not be horizontal.	二 1-1 寺 3-3 古 2-3 会 2-4 字 3-3 春 5-4	万 1-2 考 4-2 間 8-4 坐 4-3 凶 2-2
□3 CHARACTERS THAT CAN BE DIVIDED BY AN **ENCLOSURE ELEMENT** (*a*) The resulting parts may be separated by a **space** or be in full physical contact. (*b*) The resulting division must be more or less rectangular.	進 3-8 問 8-3 国 3-5 可 2-3 広 3-2 凶 2-2	入 1-1 伺 3-4 呉 4-3 吹 4-3 名 3-3 為 5-4
■4 CHARACTERS THAT CANNOT BE CLASSIFIED UNDER **PATTERNS** ◧**1**, ⬒**2**, OR □**3**	雨 8-1 丘 5-2 中 4-3 与 3-4	刀 2-1 日 4-1 水 4-3
❷ IF A CHARACTER CAN BE CLASSIFIED UNDER MORE THAN ONE PATTERN, SELECT THE ONE THAT FOLLOWS THE NATURAL CONSTRUCTION OF THE CHARACTER	児 ⬒2-5-2 箱 ⬒2-6-9	児 ◧1-2-5 箱 ◧1-7-8
❸ DO NOT VIOLATE THE PRINCIPLE OF ELEMENT INTEGRITY		
1. NEVER BREAK THROUGH STROKES	口 ■4-3-1	口 ⬒2-1-3
2. NEVER BREAK THROUGH **INDIVISIBLE UNITS**	情 ◧1-3-8	情 ◧1-1-10
3. NEVER MAKE **UNNATURAL DIVISIONS**	箱 ⬒2-6-9	箱 ◧1-7-8

5 HOW TO DIVIDE THE CHARACTER

5.1 Character Division

Once you have determined to which of the four patterns your character belongs, you must divide it or subclassify it in order to determine the second and third parts of the **SKIP number.** Characters that can be divided into two or more parts are classified under the first three patterns, i.e., **◧1**, **⬒2**, and **◻3**. This section explains how to divide these **divisible characters.** Characters that cannot be classified under the above patterns are subclassified according to a different principle described in **§6.1 Subclassification of Solid Pattern.**

The imaginary line that divides the character splits it into a pattern whose shape roughly resembles the pattern symbol. The divisible characters are divided into two parts: the **shaded part** and the **blank part.** The second part of the SKIP number indicates the stroke-count of the former, whereas the third part indicates that of the latter. For example, 相 is divided into 木 (4 strokes) and 目 (5 strokes), giving a SKIP number of **◧**1-4-5. See **§2.4 SKIP Number** for details.

In the great majority of cases, you should have no problem in identifying the pattern and, at the same time, deciding at which point to divide the character. Sometimes, however, you may identify a character as belonging to a particular pattern but not be sure at which point the division should be made. That is, some characters, like 川, 三, and 磨, may contain several points at which a division could conceivably be made.

To divide such characters correctly and without hesitation, it is important that you get a clear understanding of the concept of **division points.** A brief description of these is given in **§5.2** below. The most important thing to remember is: **if there is more than one way to divide a character, divide at the first division point.**

When dividing a character, be sure not to violate the principle of **element integrity.** This rule prohibits breaking through strokes or **indivisible units.** For example, you must not divide characters like 口 into 丨 and コ, or characters like 情 into 丶 and 情. It also prohibits making **unnatural divisions.** For example, 鬪 should be classified under **◻3**, and not be divided into left and right parts, i.e., 丨 and 鬪.

A formal statement of the rules for dividing the divisible characters is given in **§5.3** below.

5.2 Division Points

The first rule for dividing the pattern is: DIVIDE THE CHARACTER INTO TWO PARTS AT THE *FIRST* DIVISION POINT. That is, if there are several ways in which a character can be divided, always divide at the *first* place possible.

Division point	A **space, horizontal line, frame element,** or **enclosure element** at which it may be possible to divide a character.

A division point is not necessarily the point at which a character is actually divided according to SKIP rules. Whether a character can or cannot be divided at a given point depends on its structure and the particular SKIP rule applying to it.

Space A gap or breaking point between elements. A **clear space** is a clearly visible gap, especially one formed by parallel strokes or elements. A **conceptual space** is a natural breaking point where one would expect a gap; i.e., a gap that may not be visible because the elements are crowded closely together.	川 1-2 州 2-4 傾 2-11 三 1-2 言 1-6 公 2-2 街 3-9 町 5-2 翻 12-6 桑 2-8 系 1-6 雀 4-7

Attachment One or more usually short strokes, stroke segments, or elements in physical contact, or almost in physical contact, with the main body of an element. **Top attachments** are never separated from a main element except when dividing by **frame element. Side** or **end attachments** are never separated from the main element. Top attachments Side attachments End attachments	 字 学 美 業 骨 危 度 年 午 台 情 疒 旬 軍 字 岩 民
Horizontal line A horizontal, or almost horizontal, stroke not intersected by any other strokes. Division by horizontal line applies only to pattern ⬒**2**.	寺 3-3 空 3-5 文 2-2 亭 2-7 学 5-3 義 3-10
Frame element A combination of strokes or stroke segments forming a figure enclosed on two, three, or four sides. Division by frame element applies only to pattern ⬒**2**.	古 2-3 免 2-6 早 4-2 当 3-3 南 2-7 支 2-2
Enclosure element A completely exterior element that encloses the rest of a character on two or more sides. Division by enclosure element applies only to pattern ◻**3**.	進 3-8 旬 2-4 麻 3-8 間 8-4 医 2-5 回 3-3

5.3 Character Division Rules

MAIN RULES	Right	Wrong
❶ **DIVIDE THE CHARACTER INTO TWO PARTS AT THE FIRST DIVISION POINT** ◧**1** GOING FROM LEFT TO RIGHT, DIVIDE AT THE FIRST **SPACE** Divide at the first **clear** or **conceptual space.**	明 4-4 小 1-2 扱 3-3	小 2-1 街 9-3
⬒**2** GOING FROM TOP TO BOTTOM, DIVIDE AT THE FIRST **SPACE, HORIZONTAL LINE,** OR **FRAME ELEMENT,** WHICHEVER COMES FIRST		
(*a*) Divide at the first **clear** or **conceptual space.**	三 1-2 会 2-4 脅 2-8	三 2-1 会 3-3 脅 6-4
(*b*) Divide after the first **horizontal line.** The horizontal line, along with its side, top, and end **attachments,** goes to the top.	赤 3-4 空 3-5 業 5-8 年 2-4	赤 2-5 空 5-3 業 8-5
(*c*) Divide at the first point where the first **frame element** is encountered. **Top attachments** become part of the top (shaded) part.	古 2-3 当 3-3 南 2-7 早 4-2	呂 4-3 免 6-2
(*d*) When dividing by **horizontal line** or by **frame element,** each part must have at least two strokes.	京 2-6 方 2-2 午 2-2 予 2-2	下 1-2 亡 2-1 了 1-1 白 1-4

▣3 GOING FROM THE OUTSIDE TOWARD THE INSIDE, DIVIDE AFTER THE FIRST **ENCLOSURE ELEMENT** Separate the first **enclosure element** from the rest of the character, whether it is separated from it by a **clear** or **conceptual space,** or is in full physical contact with it.	度 3-6 進 3-8 閉 8-3 目 3-2	度 7-2 磨 11-5
❷ DO NOT VIOLATE THE PRINCIPLE OF ELEMENT INTEGRITY 1. NEVER BREAK THROUGH STROKES 2. NEVER BREAK THROUGH **INDIVISIBLE UNITS** 3. NEVER MAKE **UNNATURAL DIVISIONS**	凶 ▣3-2-2 情 ◧1-3-8 気 ▣3-4-2 漢 ◧1-3-10	凶 ◧1-1-4 情 ◧1-1-10 気 ⬒2-2-4 漢 ⬒2-4-9
COROLLARIES ❶ EACH PART MUST HAVE AT LEAST ONE STROKE ❷ THE **SHADED PART** MUST NOT BE FURTHER DIVISIBLE UNDER THE SAME **PATTERN**	門 ◧1-4-4 口 ■4-3-1 測 ◧1-3-9 順 ◧1-1-11	門 ▣3-8-0 口 ▣3-3-0 測 ◧1-10-2 順 ◧1-3-9

6 HOW TO SUBCLASSIFY THE SOLID PATTERN

6.1 Subclassification of Solid Pattern

Characters that cannot be divided according to SKIP rules are referred to as **indivisible** or **solid characters** and are classified under pattern **■4.** The second and third parts of the **SKIP number** of the divisible characters, i.e., the characters classified under patterns **◧1**, **⬒2**, or **▣3**, are determined by dividing the character into two parts and counting the strokes of each part. Since the solid characters are, by definition, indivisible, a different principle is required for subclassifying them.

The indivisible characters are arranged in ascending order of their total stroke-counts and are subclassified into four **solid subpatterns** (see **§6.2** below). The second part of the SKIP number indicates the total stroke-count of the character, whereas the third part indicates one of the four solid subpatterns. 下, for example, is a three-stroke character containing a **top line** (subpattern □1), giving a SKIP number of ■4-3-1. See **§2.4 SKIP Number** for details.

6.2 Solid Subpatterns

The solid pattern is classified into four **solid subpatterns** on the basis of easy-to-identify lines located on the top, at the bottom, or in the middle of a character.

Solid subpattern	One of the four groups into which the solid characters are subdivided according to the presence or absence of prominent lines; i.e., **□1 top line, □2 bottom line, □3 through line,** and **□4 others.**
Solid subpattern number	A number that identifies one of the four solid subpatterns; i.e., **1** = □, **2** = □, **3** = □, and **4** = □.
Solid subpattern symbol	A symbol that identifies one of the four solid subpatterns; i.e., □ = **1**, □ = **2**, □ = **3**, and □ = **4**.

A formal definition of each subpattern is given below.

	Solid Subpattern	Examples
□1	**Top line** A horizontal, or almost horizontal, stroke or stroke segment extending across the very top of a solid character.	下 3-1 耳 6-1 雨 8-1 子 3-1 久 3-1 凸 5-1 口 3-1 亜 7-1 爾 14-1
□2	**Bottom line** A horizontal, or almost horizontal, stroke or stroke segment extending across the very bottom of a solid character.	七 2-2 上 3-2 亡 3-2 丘 5-2 由 5-2 自 6-2 血 6-2 垂 8-2 重 9-2
□3	**Through line** A perfectly vertical stroke or stroke segment intersecting another stroke of a solid character and extending over its entire, or almost its entire, length.	中 4-3 十 2-3 手 4-3 本 5-3 米 6-3 車 7-3 求 7-3 乗 9-3 粛 11-3
□4	**Others** Solid characters that cannot be classified under subpatterns □1, □2, or □3.	人 2-4 九 2-4 女 3-4 火 4-4 犬 4-4 史 5-4 成 6-4 舟 6-4 為 9-4

6.3 Pattern Subclassification Rules

	Right	Wrong
❶ **DETERMINE TO WHICH OF THE FOUR SOLID SUBPATTERNS YOUR CHARACTER BELONGS** □1 CHARACTERS THAT CONTAIN A **TOP LINE** □2 CHARACTERS THAT CONTAIN A **BOTTOM LINE** □3 CHARACTERS THAT CONTAIN A **THROUGH LINE** □4 CHARACTERS THAT DO NOT CONTAIN A **TOP LINE, BOTTOM LINE,** OR **THROUGH LINE**	雨 8-1 下 3-1 耳 6-1 果 8-1 上 3-2 丘 5-2 垂 8-2 中 4-3 東 8-3 毛 4-3 与 3-4 大 3-4 寿 7-4	刀 2-1 千 3-1 垂 8-1 丘 5-1 山 3-2 包 5-2 者 8-2 水 4-3 寸 3-3 午 4-3 弟 7-3 糸 6-4 久 3-4 友 4-4 劣 6-4
❷ **IF A CHARACTER CAN BE CLASSIFIED UNDER MORE THAN ONE SUBPATTERN, THE SUBPATTERN WITH THE SMALLEST NUMBER TAKES PRECEDENCE**	王 4-1 己 3-1 酉 7-1 果 8-1 出 5-2 生 5-2 甲 5-1	王 4-2 己 3-2 酉 7-2 果 8-3 出 5-3 生 5-3 甲 5-3

7 GLOSSARY

To use the SKIP classification scheme effectively, it is important to get a clear understanding of the various terms used in a technical sense. These terms have been selected to render their meanings as self-evident as possible. The glossary below conveniently brings all SKIP terms together for quick reference. The brief definitions given here should be sufficient for most purposes.

The headwords, which are followed by their Japanese equivalents in parentheses, are arranged in alphabetical order and followed by a definition and examples in square brackets. At the end of some entries is an arrow ➡ followed by a reference to a more detailed explanation of that term. The technical terms used within the definitions are printed in **boldface,** which indicates that these terms can be found at their own alphabetical locations in the glossary.

attachment (付随物)
one or more usually short strokes, stroke segments, or elements in physical contact, or almost in physical contact, with the main body of an element [字 年 軍]

blank part (白部・従部)
the part of a **divisible character** corresponding to the blank segment of the **pattern symbol;** i.e., the part remaining after the **shaded part** is removed [従 単 医]
➡§2.3 Divisible and Indivisible Characters

bottom line (下線)
a horizontal, or almost horizontal, stroke or stroke segment extending across the very bottom of a **solid** character [世 由 丘]

branch (枝)
a stroke or stroke segment that abuts with other strokes or stroke segments at a point of **tangential contact** [古 京 井]

clear space (完全空白)
a clearly visible gap, especially one formed by parallel strokes or elements [三 川 公]

conceptual space (疑似空白)
a natural breaking point where one would expect a gap; i.e., a gap that may not be visible because the elements are crowded closely together [桑 矛 春]

cross-reference entry (相互参照項目)
a character entry or an entry in the **Pattern Index** appearing at an *incorrect* SKIP location with a cross-reference to the corresponding correct location
➡§2.6 Cross-References

divisible characters (可分漢字)
characters that can be divided according to SKIP rules; i.e., characters classified under **patterns** ◧**1**, ⬒**2**, or ⧈**3** [相 字 広]
➡§2.3 Divisible and Indivisible Characters

division point (可分点)
a **space** [川 芳], **horizontal line** [文 忘], **frame element** [古 当], or **enclosure element** [送 凶] at which it may be possible to divide a character

element integrity (字形素分割禁止)
a principle that consists of three parts: (1) never break through strokes, (2) never break through **indivisible units**, and (3) never make **unnatural divisions**

enclosure (囲み型)
➡enclosure pattern

enclosure element (囲み要素)
a completely exterior element enclosing the rest of a character on two or more sides [広 同 団]

enclosure pattern (囲み型)
a configuration of character elements in which an exterior element encloses the rest of a character on two or more sides (pattern ⧈**3**) [進 可 医 田]
➡§2.2 SKIP Patterns

enclosure subpattern (囲み型副パターン)
one of the eleven groups into which the **enclosure pattern** is subdivided according to the number of sides of the **enclosure element** and its position along the exterior of the character
➡§4.2 Enclosure Subpatterns

enclosure subpattern symbol (囲み型副パターン記号)
a symbol that identifies one of the eleven **enclosure subpatterns**; i.e., □ □ □ □ □ □ □ □ □ ▯ ▭
➡§4.2 Enclosure Subpatterns

end attachment (端部付随物)
one or more relatively short strokes or stroke segments in physical contact, or almost in physical contact, with the end of the main body of an element [軍 岩 字]

entry number (親字番)
a serial number that uniquely identifies the numbered character entries of the dictionary
➡§2.7 SKIP Guides

entry number guide (親字番案内)
boldface numerals in the lower, outer corner of a page that indicate the **entry number** or range of entry numbers for that page
➡§2.7 SKIP Guides

frame element (枠要素)
a combination of strokes or stroke segments forming a figure enclosed on two, three, or four sides [古 早 肖]

horizontal line (横線)
a horizontal, or almost horizontal, stroke not intersected by any other strokes [赤 学 業]

independent element (独立要素)
a stroke, or a combination of strokes that intersect or come in **tangential contact** with each other, that forms a self-contained unit [桑 系 名]

indivisible characters (不可分漢字)
characters that cannot be divided according to SKIP rules; i.e., characters classified under pattern ■**4** [雨 本 九]
➡§2.3 Divisible and Indivisible Characters

indivisible unit (不可分字形素)
a combination of strokes regarded as an indivisible whole [尺 口 情]

left-right (左右型)
➡left-right pattern

left-right pattern (左右型)
a configuration of character elements placed side by side (pattern ◧**1**) [川 保 殴]
➡§2.2 SKIP Patterns

natural construction (自然構成)
an arrangement of character elements that is in harmony with the way a character is intuitively

perceived as a combination of certain constituent parts

others (その他)
solid characters that cannot be classified under **subpatterns** ▔**1**, ▁**2**, or ◫**3** [人 大 寿]

pattern (パターン・字型・型)
a configuration of elements that characterizes the four major groups in the SKIP classification scheme; i.e., **◧1 left-right, ⬒2 up-down, ◻3 enclosure,** and **■4 solid**
➡§2.2 SKIP Patterns

pattern guide (パターン案内)
a guide in the upper, outer corner of a page that indicates the **pattern** and **pattern number** for that page
➡§2.7 SKIP Guides

pattern number (パターン番号)
a number that identifies one of the four **patterns** in the SKIP classification scheme; i.e., **1** = ◧, **2** = ⬒, **3** = ◻, and **4** = ■
➡§2.2 SKIP Patterns

pattern symbol (パターン記号)
a symbol that identifies one of the four **patterns** in the SKIP classification scheme; i.e., ◧ = **1,** ⬒ = **2,** ◻ = **3,** and ■ = **4**
➡§2.2 SKIP Patterns

shaded part (黒部・主部)
the part of a **divisible character** corresponding to the shaded segment of the **pattern symbol;** i.e., the part removed at the first **division point** [相 安 回]
➡§2.3 Divisible and Indivisible Characters

side attachment (側部付随物)
one or more relatively short strokes or stroke segments in physical contact, or almost in physical contact, with the side of the main body of an element [年 台 句]

SKIP (「字型式検字法」の略称)
acronym of "**System of Kanji Indexing by Patterns**"
➡§2.1 Overview of SKIP

SKIP number (ＳＫＩＰ番号)
a **pattern symbol** followed by hyphenated numerals consisting of three parts; for the **divisible characters,** (1) the **pattern number,** (2) the stroke-count of the **shaded part,** and (3) the stroke-count of the **blank part;** for the **indivisible characters,** (1) the **pattern number,** (2) the total stroke-count, and (3) the **solid subpattern number** [相: ◧1-4-5]
➡§2.4 SKIP Number

solid (全体型)
➡solid pattern

solid pattern (全体型)
a character element or combination of elements that does not constitute a **left-right, up-down,** or **enclosure pattern** (pattern **■4**) [下 由 本 力]
➡§2.2 SKIP Patterns

solid subpattern (全体型副パターン)
one of the four groups into which the **solid** characters are subdivided according to the presence or absence of prominent lines; i.e., ▔**1 top line,** ▁**2 bottom line,** ◫**3 through line,** and □**4 others**
➡§6.2 Solid Subpatterns

solid subpattern number (全体型副パターン番号)
a number that identifies one of the four **solid subpatterns**; i.e., **1** = ▔, **2** = ▁, **3** = ◫, and **4** = □
➡§6.2 Solid Subpatterns

solid subpattern symbol (全体型副パターン記号)
a symbol that identifies one of the four **solid subpatterns**; i.e., ▔ = **1,** ▁ = **2,** ◫ = **3,** and □ = **4**
➡§6.2 Solid Subpatterns

space (空白・スペース)
a gap [三 小] or breaking point [会 桑] between elements

stroke (点画・画)
a character element such as a dot or line segment traditionally written with one sweep of the brush or pen [正 口 弓 主]
➡Appendix 3. How to Count Strokes

subgroup (下位グループ)
a subdivision of a **subsection** consisting of **divisible characters** sharing a common **subgroup element**
➡§2.5 Classification Scheme

subgroup element (主字素・字素)
the shared element of a **subgroup,** which corresponds to the **shaded part** of a **divisible character** [阪 岸 奔]
➡§2.5 Classification Scheme

subgroup guide (主字素案内)
1. in the main part of the dictionary, a guide in the outer margin of a page that indicates the **subgroup element** for each entry character
➡§2.7 SKIP Guides
2. a guide to the left of the character column in the **Pattern Index** that indicates the **subgroup element** for that **subgroup**
➡How to Use the Pattern Index on p. 2012

subpattern (副パターン)
1. **➡enclosure subpattern**
2. **➡solid subpattern**

subpattern number (副パターン番号)
➡solid subpattern number

subpattern symbol (副パターン記号)
1. **➡enclosure subpattern symbol**
2. **➡solid subpattern symbol**

subsection (下位部)
a subdivision of the main part of the dictionary or of the **Pattern Index** in which the **divisible characters** are classified by **subgroup element** and the **indivisible characters** are classified by entry type
➡§2.5 Classification Scheme

subsection guide (下位部案内)
1. in the main part of the dictionary, boldface numerals in the upper corner of a page that indicate the **subsection number** for that page
2. red hyphenated numerals in the left part of the **Pattern Index** column that indicate the **subsection number** for each **subsection**
➡§2.7 SKIP Guides, ➡How to Use the Pattern Index on p. 2012

subsection number (下位部番号)
hyphenated numerals used to identify a **subsection** and corresponding to the second and third parts of the **SKIP number**
➡§2.4 SKIP Number

System of Kanji Indexing by Patterns (字型式検字法)
a system of classifying characters by geometrical **pattern**s used for the rapid location of entries in this dictionary
➡§2.1 Overview of SKIP

tangential contact (枝点接触)
full physical contact between strokes or stroke segments that join at one point without intersecting [口 年 美]

three-branch tangential contact (三枝点接触)
tangential contact in which three **branch**es (strokes or stroke segments) join at one point [文 年]

through line (通線)
a perfectly vertical stroke or stroke segment intersecting another stroke of a **solid** character and extending over its entire, or almost its entire, length [中 才 我]

top attachment (上部付随物)
one or more usually short strokes, stroke segments, or elements in physical contact, or almost in physical contact, with the top of the main body of an element [字 骨 學]

top line (上線)
a horizontal, or almost horizontal, stroke or stroke segment extending across the very top of a **solid** character [里 疋 平]

two-branch tangential contact (二枝点接触)
tangential contact in which two **branch**es (strokes or stroke segments) join at one point [口 弓 冖]

unnatural division (不自然分割)
division of a character in a manner that is in conflict with the way it is intuitively perceived as a combination of certain constituent parts [漢 箱 導]

up-down (上下型)
➡up-down pattern

up-down pattern (上下型)
a configuration of character elements stacked more or less one on top of the other (pattern ⬒**2**) [京 音 当 早]
➡§2.2 SKIP Patterns

APPENDIX 3

HOW TO COUNT STROKES

画数の数え方

1 Introduction

Chinese characters consist of one or more interconnected line segments called **strokes.** Most character dictionaries, including this one, require the user to count strokes. This appendix briefly explains the principles of counting strokes, and includes several supplementary charts to help speed up the counting process.

The ability to count strokes quickly and accurately is useful in two ways: (1) it helps you use character dictionaries more efficiently, and (2) it helps you write the characters correctly by making you aware of where one stroke ends and the next one begins.

Stroke counting may be difficult for two reasons:

1. The standard typeface used in Japan often includes ornamental serifs that make a character appear to have a stroke-count different from its handwritten form. For example, 表 appears to have nine strokes in its printed form, but has only eight strokes in its written form (表).
2. For the beginner, it is sometimes difficult to tell where one stroke ends and the next one begins. An element such as 口, for example, may be viewed as consisting of four separate line segments, of two **L**-shaped components (㇄ + ㇕), of one continuous line, or of three segments (丨 + ㇕ + 一). Only the last division is considered correct according to the traditional method of counting strokes.

In this dictionary, we have made every effort to ease the task of locating difficult-to-count characters by cross-referencing them at common incorrect stroke-count locations. For example, 子 is a three-stroke character cross-referenced under two strokes. Nevertheless, to attain maximum speed, it is worthwhile to master the stroke counting principles given below.

2 Stroke Counting Principles

To count strokes with complete accuracy, a knowledge of how to write the characters is necessary (see **Appendix 4. How to Write Kanji**). For practical purposes, however, the guidelines below will enable even the complete beginner to count strokes accurately with just a little practice.

1. **Learn to recognize the basic strokes.** A **stroke** is defined as a character element such as a dot or line segment traditionally written with one sweep of the brush or pen. To rephrase: if a line or element is written continuously without lifting the pen or brush, it is considered a single stroke. To the beginner, however, it may not always be obvious what constitutes "one sweep," or when to lift the pen. It is thus necessary to learn to recognize the basic stroke types. Strokes may be straight (一 丨), diagonal (丿 ㇏), or bent (㇕ ㇄ ㇉). The chart below shows elements that must always be counted as single strokes.

Basic Strokes

Strokes	Examples
1 ㇐	㇐ in 五
2 ㇀ ㇕ ㇇ ㇈ ㇉	㇉ in 弓
3 ㇑ ㇓ ㇒ ㇚ ㇁	㇚ in 予
4 ㇙ ㇙ ㇜ ㇛	㇙ in 民
5 ㇗ ㇄ ㇗	㇄ in 礼
6 ㇠ ㇈ ㇅	㇅ in 呉
7 ㇔ ㇏ ㇏ ㇃	㇃ in 恩
8 ㇋ ㇌ ㇋	㇋ in 辺

2. **Ignore serifs.** There are various flips, hooks, and protrusions sometimes found at the ends of strokes that must be ignored when counting. Many of these are merely ornamental serifs (shown by small circles in the chart below) appearing in the printed form that are not considered strokes in their own right. It is the handwritten form (square style), not the printed form (Ming typeface), that forms the basis for stroke counting. The chart below lists typical characters of this kind.

Apparent and Actual Stroke-Counts

Ming Typeface	Apparent Stroke-Count	Square Style	Actual Stroke-Count
表	9	表	8
民	6	民	5
良	8	良	7
長	9	長	8
号	6	号	5
留	11	留	10
比	5	比	4
氏	5	氏	4

3. **Count element by element, rather than stroke by stroke.** Do not count all the strokes of a complex character in one pass. It is easier to break the character up into several components, count the strokes of each component, then add the subtotals to get the total stroke-count. For example, to determine the stroke-count of 筋, count as follows: ⺮ (6) + 月 (4) + 力 (2) = 12. This method is especially effective if you have memorized the stroke-counts of the important radicals.

4. **Memorize the stroke-counts of important radicals.** Since certain radicals occur very frequently as character components, memorizing the stroke-counts of high-frequency radicals will help you count strokes faster. The most frequently occurring radicals are listed below in increasing order of their stroke-counts. The numeral to the right of each radical is its **radical number,** which is followed by a typical character in which the radical occurs.

Important Radicals

Count	Radical	Example
1	一 1	一
2	亠 8	京
	亻 9	仁
	儿 10	元
	八 2	公
	刂 18	利
	力 19	加
	十 24	博
	卩 26	印
	厂 27	原
3	口 30	叱
	囗 31	回
	土 32	地
	大 37	奈
	女 38	好
	子 39	孫
	宀 40	実
	寸 41	寺
	尸 44	尺
	山 46	峰
	山 46	岩
	巾 50	帳
	广 53	広
	弓 57	強
	彳 60	得

Count	Radical	Example
	忄 61	忙
	扌 64	打
	氵 85	決
	犭 94	独
	艹 140	花
	辶 162	込
	阝 163	部
	阝 170	防
4	戈 62	戦
	攵 66	放
	日 72	明
	月 74	朝
	木 75	校
	欠 76	次
	火 86	炊
	灬 86	煮
	牛 93	物
	王 96	現
	礻 113	福
	月 130	腕
5	田 102	畑
	疒 104	病
	目 109	相
	石 112	研
	禾 115	穂

Count	Radical	Example
	穴 116	空
	罒 122	置
	衤 145	被
6	⺮ 118	笛
	米 119	粉
	糸 120	経
	耳 128	聴
	舟 137	船
	虫 142	蚊
7	言 149	訓
	貝 154	責
	貝 154	貯
	足 157	跡
	車 159	転
	酉 164	酔
8	金 167	鉄
	門 169	間
	隹 172	雀
	雨 173	雪
	食 184	飲
9	頁 181	順
10	馬 187	駅
11	魚 195	鯛

5. **Memorize the stroke-counts of difficult-to-count elements.** The stroke-count of some elements is difficult to determine without some knowledge of how to write them. For example, 子 (Radical 39) is a three-stroke element that is often miscounted as a two-stroke element.

The most common elements of this kind are listed below, accompanied by their correct and incorrect stroke-counts and typical character examples, which are followed by their total stroke-counts. Pay special attention to the elements marked by an asterisk. Memorizing their stroke-counts will help you count strokes with greater speed and accuracy. The **Variant** column gives a variant of the element (usually an old form) that slightly differs from it in form and consequently often in stroke-count.

Incorrect Stroke-Counts

Element	Right	Wrong	Example	Variant
㇉	1	2	与 3	
乙	1	2	乞 3	
了	2	1	了 2	
阝	3	2	阪 7	
阝	3	2	邦 7	
孑	3	2	孔 4	
丬	2	3	収 4	丩 2
辶*	3	2	込 5	辶 4
之	3	2 or 4	芝 6	
廴	3	2	廷 7	
夂	3	4	変 9	夊 4
及*	3	4	扱 6	
囗*	3	4	困 7	
弓*	3	4	引 4	
廿	4	3	革 9	
𠫓	4	3	育 8	𠫓 3
㐄*	4	3	降 10	㐄 3
艹	3	4	花 7	
⺿	4	3	芯 8	
巨	5	4	距 12	
世	5	4	笹 11	
牙	5	4	芽 8	牙 4
𤴔	5	4	疎 12	
此	6	5	柴 10	
臼	6	5	舊 18	
臣*	7	6	臨 18	
禺	9	8	偶 11	

As a further aid to learning how to count strokes, you may wish to check the stroke-counts of individual characters. Refer to the **reference data box** for your entry character, which gives detailed stroke-count data (see **§5** on p. 44a).

APPENDIX 4

HOW TO WRITE KANJI

漢字の書き方

The serious student of Japanese will no doubt want to learn how to write the characters. A knowledge of stroke order is essential for learning how to write the characters correctly, and is a prerequisite for the study of calligraphy. It is also an effective way to master stroke counting.

The guidelines below will enable the student to write most characters in the correct stroke order without referring to the diagrams given for each main entry character. Although there are general principles for writing the characters in the proper stroke order, in some cases a character can be written in more than one way, while in others reference works disagree as to the correct sequence. The basic principle of stroke direction and stroke order is: from left to right and from top to bottom.

The only official guidelines were published by the Japanese Ministry of Education under the title 筆順指導の手びき ひつじゅんしどうのてびき in March 1958. Given below is an unabridged translation of the above publication, reproduced here with the author's permission from **The Study of Kanji** (Hokuseido Press, Tokyo, revised edition 1984, pp. 277-286), by Michael Pye, which is an excellent introduction to the Japanese writing system. The characters are presented in the handwritten form of the 楷書 かいしょ or square style. The object of the said government publication is to explain the principles of stroke order; it is not meant to be an introduction to calligraphy, which is a separate study in itself.

The following terms and symbols appear in the text:

hen	left-side radical (亻 in 休)
tsukuri	right-side radical (阝 in 都)
nyō	bottom-left enclosure radical (辶 in 進)
＊	indicates that the element is not used as an independent character

See also the **Radical Chart** on p. 1837 for more information on radicals and **§3 Writing** on p. 30a.

PRINCIPLES OF STROKE ORDER IN THE PRESENT WORK

The stroke orders given in the present work have been classified under the Major Principles 1 and 2 and the more detailed Principles 1 to 8 shown below. Furthermore, we have also explained our attitude in cases where 2 or more different stroke orders are widely current.

MAJOR PRINCIPLE 1

FROM TOP TO BOTTOM

Write from top to bottom or from the top part to the bottom part.

a. Begin with the top stroke.

三(一 二 三)言

工(一 丅 工)

b. Begin with the upper part.

喜(士 吉 吉 壴 喜)

客(宀 安 客)

築(⺮ 筑 築)

MAJOR PRINCIPLE 2

FROM LEFT TO RIGHT

Write from left to right or from the left-hand part to the right-hand part.

a. Begin with the left-hand stroke.

川(丿 川 川)順州

学(丶 丷 ⺍)挙魚 (1 2 3 4)

帯(十 卄 卌 卌)

脈(厂 斤 𠂢)

b. Begin with the left-hand part.

The ***hen*** comes first and the ***tsukuri*** afterwards. (Characters of this kind are very numerous.)

竹(个 竹)羽

休(亻 休)林語

Write across from the left in cases with 3 parts.

例(亻 侈 例)

側湖術

PRINCIPLE 1

HORIZONTAL STROKES FIRST

When horizontal and vertical strokes cross, the horizontals are usually written first.

(For cases in which horizontals come afterwards, see Principle 2.)

a. Horizontal, vertical;

十(一 十)

計古支草

土(一 十 土)

圧至舎周

士(一 十 士)

志吉喜

even if the vertical curves after crossing the horizontal;

七(一 七)切

大(一 ナ 大)太

and when additional strokes precede or follow.

告(丿 𠂉 ⺧ 生)

先任庭

木(一 十 木)述

寸(一 十 寸)寺

b. Horizontal, vertical, vertical; cases with only 2 following verticals;

共(一 卄 丗)散港

編(冂 冃 冊)

花(一 艹)荷

算(一 廾)形鼻

and cases with 3 or more verticals.

帯(一 十 卌 卌)

無(𠂉 無 無)

c. Horizontal, horizontal, vertical; cases with only 2 horizontals;

用(冂 月 用)通

even when additional strokes precede or follow;

末未妹

cases with 3 or more horizontals;

耕(三 丰 耒)

even if the vertical curves after crossing the horizontal.

夫(二 夫 夫)春実

d. Horizontal, horizontal, vertical, vertical; cases in which there are 2 of each.

耕(二 井)囲

PRINCIPLE 2

HORIZONTAL STROKES AFTERWARDS

When horizontal and vertical strokes cross, the horizontals come afterwards in the following cases only.

a. 田.

田(冂 冂 田 田)

男異町細

b. Elements based on 田.

由(冂 巾 由 由)

油黄横画

曲(冂 巾 曲 曲 曲)

豊農

角(⺆ 冂 用 用)解

再(冂 币 再 再)構

c. 王.

王(一 丁 干 王)玉

主美差義

d. Elements based on 王; even if there are 2 horizontals in the middle;

王*(一 丁 干 王 王)

進(亻 什 隹 隹)

雑集確観

馬(厂 卩 馬 馬)駅

even if the vertical protrudes at the top;

主*(一 十 丰 主)生

麦表清星

even if there are 2 verticals.

井*(一 十 卄 井 井)

寒構

PRINCIPLE 3

CENTER FIRST

When there is a center part flanked on left and right by 1 or 2 strokes, the center is written first.

小(亅 小 小)少京

示宗 糸細

当（丨 丬 ⺌）光常

水（亅 才 水）氷永

氺*（亅 ㇆ 氺）緑暴

氺*（亻 𠂉 氺）衆

This holds good if the center consists of 2 strokes;

業（丷 丵 业 业）

赤（丿 小 小）変

or is a little complicated.

楽（白 泊 泺）薬

承（了 孑 承）率

Exceptions

There are 2 exceptions to Principle 3.

忄（丶 丷 忄）性

火（丷 火）火

秋炭 焼

PRINCIPLE 4

OUTSIDE FIRST

When there is an enclosing shape such as *kunigamae*, it is written first.

国（冂 国 国）因

同（冂 同） 円

内（冂 内）肉納

司（𠃌 司）詞羽

Cases such as 日, 月, etc. may be considered to fall under this principle.

日月目田

N.B. 区 is written as shown; similarly 医.

区（一 㐅 区）

PRINCIPLE 5

STROKES WHICH CURVE AWAY TO THE LEFT COME FIRST

When slanting strokes cross, the one which curves away to the left comes first.

文（亠 ナ 文）父

故支収処

The same holds good when they abut.

人入欠金

PRINCIPLE 6

A THROUGH-GOING VERTICAL COMES LAST

A vertical which runs right through the character is to be written last;

中（口 中）申神

車半事建

even if it is closed off at the bottom;

書（⺕ 聿）妻

or at the top.

平（丷 平）評

羊洋達拝

手（三 手）争

When the vertical protrudes neither at the top nor at the bottom, the order is: top part, vertical, bottom part.

里（日 甲 里）野黒

重（亩 亩 重）動

謹（艹 节 堇）勤

N.B. the difference between 堇 and 莫.

漢（艹 茣 莫）難

PRINCIPLE 7

A THROUGH-GOING HORIZONTAL COMES LAST

A horizontal which runs right through the character is to be written last.

女(く 女)安努
子(了 子)字存
母 每海 慣
舟→舟船 与

N.B. The only exception is 世.

世(一 卄 世)

PRINCIPLE 8

HORIZONTALS AND STROKES WHICH CURVE AWAY TO THE LEFT

When the horizontal is long and the slanting stroke short, the slanting stroke is to be written first.

右(ノ ナ 右)
有布希

When the horizontal is short and the slanting stroke long, the horizontal is to be written first.

左(一 ナ 左)
友在存抜

CASES TO BE SPECIALLY NOTED

A. Cases in which there are 2 or more widely current stroke orders.

1. The characters marked (a) have always had only the stroke order indicated.

(a) 止正足走武
(丨 ト)

Those marked (b) have 2 possibilities, (i) and (ii); we prefer (i) in conformity with (a) above.

(b) 上点店
(丨 ト)……(i)
(・ ト)……(ii)

N.B. (ii) is more frequently used in ***gyōsho*** however.

上点店

2. The character 耳 (a) is usually written as indicated.

(a) 耳 (下 耳)

As a left radical (b) it has 2 possibilities, (i) and (ii); we prefer (i) in conformity with (a) above.

(b) 取最職厳
(下 耳)……(i)
(丌 耳)……(ii)

3. 必 has several possibilities. We strongly reject (iii), and since (i) gives a good form more easily than (ii), we prefer (i).

必
(丶 ソ 义 义 必)…(i)
(ノ 乂 义 义 必)…(ii)
(心 必)……………(iii)
and others

4. ***Hatsugashira*** has several possibilities. In (i) the right-hand part is symmetrical with the left and is also more natural; we therefore prefer (i).

発登
(ﾌ 癶 癶)……(i)
(入 癶 癶)……(ii)
(ﾌ ﾌ 癶)……(iii)

N.B. The top of 祭 is written as indicated, following Principle 5.

祭(夕' 夗)

5. 感 has 2 possibilities, (i) and (ii). In conformity with the standardized form we prefer (i), following Major Principle 1.

感
(后 咸 感)…… (i)
(后 㥛 感)…… (ii)

N.B. 盛 is not in the Education Kanji list, but note that the same considerations apply.

盛
(万 成 盛)…… (i)
(万 盄 盛)…… (ii)

6. 馬 has (i), (ii) and others; we prefer (i) in accordance with Major Principle 1.

馬
(厂 𠥓 肝 馬)…… (i)
(厂 F 𠥼 馬)…… (ii)

N.B. In this way it is also brought into line with 隹.

隹*(𠂉 什 隹 隹)

7. 無 has (i), (ii) and others; we prefer (i) in accordance with Major Principle 1.

無
(𠂉 無 無)…… (i)
(𠂉 𠂤 無)…… (ii)

8. 興 might be thought of as in (i) or as in (ii); we prefer (i) in accordance with Major Principle 2.

興
(𦥑 舶 㬰)…… (i)
(月 舶 㬰)…… (ii)

B. Characters which cannot be explained according to the above principles.

1. Some *nyō* are written first (a), and some afterwards (b).

(a) 夂走免是
处起勉題

(b) 辶廴乚
近建直

2. Some strokes which curve away to the left are written first (a) and some afterwards (b).

(a) 九及

(b) 力刀万方別

APPENDIX 5

KANA AND ROMANIZATION
仮名とローマ字

The Japanese writing system uses two phonetic syllabaries, called 平仮名 ***hiragana*** and 片仮名 ***katakana.*** Hiragana is used primarily to write grammatical elements and certain native Japanese words. Katakana is mostly used to write Western loanwords. A description of kana and romanization appears below.

1 Kana Syllabary

The basic kana syllables are arranged in a table called the 五十音図 ***gojūonzu*** 'table of fifty sounds' (though it only has forty-eight syllables). The table of basic sounds, which consists of ten columns arranged in five rows, can be written in either hiragana or katakana. In the tables below, the **Hepburn** romanization of each syllable is followed by hiragana and katakana immediately below. In either system, the symbols represent the same sounds.

Basic Sounds

a あ ア	**ka** か カ	**sa** さ サ	**ta** た タ	**na** な ナ	**ha** は ハ	**ma** ま マ	**ya** や ヤ	**ra** ら ラ	**wa** わ ワ	**n** ん ン
i い イ	**ki** き キ	**shi** し シ	**chi** ち チ	**ni** に ニ	**hi** ひ ヒ	**mi** み ミ		**ri** り リ	**i** [ゐ] [ヰ]	
u う ウ	**ku** く ク	**su** す ス	**tsu** つ ツ	**nu** ぬ ヌ	**fu** ふ フ	**mu** む ム	**yu** ゆ ユ	**ru** る ル		
e え エ	**ke** け ケ	**se** せ セ	**te** て テ	**ne** ね ネ	**he** へ ヘ	**me** め メ		**re** れ レ	**e** [ゑ] [ヱ]	
o お オ	**ko** こ コ	**so** そ ソ	**to** と ト	**no** の ノ	**ho** ほ ホ	**mo** も モ	**yo** よ ヨ	**ro** ろ ロ	**o** を ヲ	

[ ] indicates obsolete characters

REMARKS:

1. The syllables し ***shi,*** ち ***chi,*** つ ***tsu,*** ふ ***fu,*** and を ***o*** are not phonetically uniform with the other syllables in the same column.
2. Although へ and は are normally pronounced ***he*** and ***ha,*** they are pronounced ***e*** and ***wa*** when used as particles, e.g., 彼は海へ行く is pronounced ***kare wa umi e iku.***

2 Voiced Sounds

The voiceless consonants ***k, s, t,*** and ***h*** are turned into the **voiced sounds *g, z, d,*** and ***b*** (濁音 ***dakuon***) by adding a diacritical mark called 濁点 ***dakuten*** or 濁り ***nigori*** (ﾞ) to the right of the kana character. Another mark, called 半濁点 ***handakuten*** (ﾟ), is used to write the ***p*** sound. (Phonetically, ***p*** is a voiceless consonant, but traditionally it is treated together with the ***b*** sounds.)

Voiced Sounds

ga が ガ	**za** ざ ザ	**da** だ ダ	**ba** ば バ	**pa** ぱ パ
gi ぎ ギ	**ji** じ ジ	**ji** ぢ ヂ	**bi** び ビ	**pi** ぴ ピ
gu ぐ グ	**zu** ず ズ	**zu** づ ヅ	**bu** ぶ ブ	**pu** ぷ プ
ge げ ゲ	**ze** ぜ ゼ	**de** で デ	**be** べ ベ	**pe** ぺ ペ
go ご ゴ	**zo** ぞ ゾ	**do** ど ド	**bo** ぼ ボ	**po** ぽ ポ

3 Palatalized Sounds

Syllables ending in ***i*** can be followed by a small ゃ ***ya,*** ゅ ***yu,*** or ょ ***yo*** to form new combinations pronounced as a single syllable. For example, き is combined with ゃ to give きゃ ***kya.*** These contracted or **palatalized sounds** are called 拗音 ***yōon*** in Japanese.

Palatalized Sounds

kya きゃ キャ	**sha** しゃ シャ	**cha** ちゃ チャ	**nya** にゃ ニャ	**hya** ひゃ ヒャ	**mya** みゃ ミャ	**rya** りゃ リャ
kyu きゅ キュ	**shu** しゅ シュ	**chu** ちゅ チュ	**nyu** にゅ ニュ	**hyu** ひゅ ヒュ	**myu** みゅ ミュ	**ryu** りゅ リュ
kyo きょ キョ	**sho** しょ ショ	**cho** ちょ チョ	**nyo** にょ ニョ	**hyo** ひょ ヒョ	**myo** みょ ミョ	**ryo** りょ リョ

Voiced sounds are also combined in a similar manner to form the syllables shown below:

Palatalized Voiced Sounds

gya ぎゃ ギャ	**ja** じゃ ジャ	**ja** ぢゃ ヂャ	**bya** びゃ ビャ	**pya** ぴゃ ピャ
gyu ぎゅ ギュ	**ju** じゅ ジュ	**ju** ぢゅ ヂュ	**byu** びゅ ビュ	**pyu** ぴゅ ピュ
gyo ぎょ ギョ	**jo** じょ ジョ	**jo** ぢょ ヂョ	**byo** びょ ビョ	**pyo** ぴょ ピョ

4 Long Vowels

Japanese vowels are of two kinds: **short vowels** (短音 ***tan'on***) and **long vowels** (長音 ***chōon***). A long vowel is pronounced approximately twice as long as a short vowel. Except in katakana loanwords, sounds ending in ***a, i,*** or ***u*** are lengthened by adding the kana character for the corresponding vowel:

か + あ →	かあ	***kā***
き + い →	きい	***kii***
く + う →	くう	***kū***

Sounds ending in ***o*** are normally lengthened by adding the vowel う, as in こう ***kō,*** but in a small number of exceptions, as in おおきい (大きい) ***ōkii*** 'big', お is used instead of う for historical reasons.

Sounds ending in ***e*** are sometimes lengthened by adding え, as in ねえ ***nē,*** but more often by adding い, as in けい ***kei.*** The vowel of a palatalized sound is lengthened in the same way as an ordinary sound, as in きょう ***kyō.***

The main difference between hiragana and katakana is that in writing katakana loanwords long vowels are indicated by adding to the previous character a dash-like symbol called 長音符 ***chōonfu***:

カ + ー → カー	***kā***	ケ + ー → ケー	***kē***
キ + ー → キー	***kī***	コ + ー → コー	***kō***
ク + ー → クー	***kū***	ギャ + ー → ギャー	***gyā***

5 Double Consonants

The consonants ***k, s, sh, t, ch,*** and ***p*** can be doubled. In katakana loanwords, other consonants, such as ***d*** and ***g,*** are sometimes doubled.

Double consonants (促音 ***sokuon***) are indicated by a small っ placed before the consonant to be doubled, and by /Q/ in phonemic transcription. Both basic sounds and palatalized sounds can be doubled, as shown below.

けっか	結果	***kekka***	けっとう	決闘	***kettō***
はっちゅう	発注	***hatchū***	けっきょく	結局	***kekkyoku***
かっさい	喝采	***kassai***	けっぱく	潔白	***keppaku***
はっしゃ	発射	***hassha***	ベッド		***beddo***

A double consonant lasts twice as long as an ordinary consonant, with a slight pause in the middle. However, in the case of ***sh*** and ***ch,*** it is pronounced as shown by the romanized spellings above.

6 Origin of Hiragana

The hiragana characters are derived from Chinese characters having the same or similar pronunciations. For example, あ originates from the character 安 ***あん.*** Hiragana is based on the cursive form of Chinese characters, so that the characters have rounded, smoothly flowing contours and an elegant appearance. The table below shows the original Chinese characters from which hiragana is derived.

Derivation of Hiragana

あ	安	い	以	う	宇	え	衣	お	於
か	加	き	幾	く	久	け	計	こ	己
さ	左	し	之	す	寸	せ	世	そ	曽
た	太	ち	知	つ	川	て	天	と	止
な	奈	に	仁	ぬ	奴	ね	祢	の	乃
は	波	ひ	比	ふ	不	へ	部	ほ	保
ま	末	み	美	む	武	め	女	も	毛
や	也			ゆ	由			よ	与
ら	良	り	利	る	留	れ	礼	ろ	呂
わ	和	ゐ	為			ゑ	恵	を	遠
ん	无								

7 Origin of Katakana

The katakana characters are derived from Chinese characters having the same or similar pronunciations. For example, ア originates from the character 阿 あ. Unlike hiragana, which is based on simplifications of whole Chinese characters, most katakana characters originate from single character components. Since katakana is based on the square style of Chinese characters, the characters have square, angular contours and a clean appearance. The table below shows the original Chinese characters from which katakana is derived.

Derivation of Katakana

ア	阿	イ	伊	ウ	宇	エ	江	オ	於
カ	加	キ	幾	ク	久	ケ	介	コ	己
サ	散	シ	之	ス	須	セ	世	ソ	曽
タ	多	チ	千	ツ	川	テ	天	ト	止
ナ	奈	ニ	仁	ヌ	奴	ネ	祢	ノ	乃
ハ	八	ヒ	比	フ	不	ヘ	部	ホ	保
マ	末	ミ	三	ム	牟	メ	女	モ	毛
ヤ	也			ユ	由			ヨ	與
ラ	良	リ	利	ル	流	レ	礼	ロ	呂
ワ	和	ヰ	井			ヱ	恵	ヲ	乎
ン	尔								

8 Ordering Scheme

Most modern Japanese dictionaries and reference works order words according to a scheme based on the kana table called アイウエオ順 あいうえおじゅん or 五十音順 ごじゅうおんじゅん. The table (see **§1 Kana Syllabary** above) is read from top to bottom starting with the first column on the right, i.e.: ***a, i, u, e, o, ka, ki, ku, ke, ko, sa, shi…*** The details of the scheme, which are fairly complex, can be found in the introduction to most Japanese dictionaries.

Formerly, a scheme called いろは順 いろはじゅん, based on a Buddhist poem, was in use. Presently, it is used mostly like ordinal numbers in lists and the like. Note that ん ***n*** was not included in this poem since it was written む ***mu*** at the time.

The IROHA Arrangement

i い	ro ろ	ha は	ni に	ho ほ	he へ	to と
chi ち	ri り	nu ぬ	ru る	o を		
wa わ	ka か	yo よ	ta た	re れ	so そ	
tsu つ	ne ね	na な	ra ら	mu む		
u う	i ゐ	no の	o お	ku く	ya や	ma ま
ke け	fu ふ	ko こ	e え	te て		
a あ	sa さ	ki き	yu ゆ	me め	mi み	shi し
e ゑ	hi ひ	mo も	se せ	su す		

9 Romanization Systems

There are several systems for romanizing Japanese, the most important of which are the **Hepburn system** (ヘボン式 ***hebonshiki***) and the **Kunrei system** (訓令式 ***kunreishiki***). The **Nippon system** from the late nineteenth century is not much used today and has been replaced by the Kunrei system.

With the rapid spread of word processors, a new "system" evolved, which for lack of a better name will be referred to as the **Wāpuro system** (from ワードプロセサー ***wādopurosesā*** 'word processor'). This is actually more of an input system, rather than a romanization system, and has many variants. Only the most important variants are shown here.

The tables below show the main differences between the three systems. Syllables not appearing in these tables are romanized in the same way in all three systems.

Basic and Voiced Sounds

Kana	Hepburn	Kunrei	Wāpuro
し	shi	si	shi/si
じ	ji	zi	ji/zi
ち	chi	ti	chi/ti
ぢ	ji	zi	di
つ	tsu	tu	tsu/tu
づ	zu	zu	du
ふ	fu	hu	fu/hu
を	o	o	wo
ん	n	n	n/nn

Palatalized Sounds

Kana	Hepburn	Kunrei	Wāpuro
しゃ	sha	sya	sha/sya
しゅ	shu	syu	shu/syu
しょ	sho	syo	sho/syo
じゃ	ja	zya	ja/zya
じゅ	ju	zyu	ju/zyu
じょ	jo	zyo	jo/zyo
ちゃ	cha	tya	cha/tya
ちゅ	chu	tyu	chu/tyu
ちょ	cho	tyo	cho/tyo
ぢゃ	ja	zya	dya
ぢゅ	ju	zyu	dyu
ぢょ	jo	zyo	dyo

Long Vowels

Kana	Hepburn	Kunrei	Wāpuro
ああ	ā	â	aa
いい	ii	ii	ii
うう	ū	û	uu
ええ	ē	ê	ee
えい	ei	ei	ei
おう	ō	ô	ou
おお	ō	ô	oo
アー	ā	â	a-
イー	ī	î	i-
ウー	ū	û	u-
エー	ē	ê	e-
オー	ō	ô	o-

10 Guide to Japanese Pronunciation

A kanji dictionary is not the place for a detailed treatment of Japanese pronunciation, but for the convenience of the user, here is a description of the Japanese sounds and how to pronounce them.

The basic Japanese sounds (phonemes) are given between slashes in Hepburn romanization. Syllabic ん is represented by /N/, as opposed to ordinary /n/. Double consonants are considered separate sounds and are represented by /Q/.

Those who know the International Phonetic Alphabet (IPA) can get a much better idea of the sounds from the IPA transcription given inside the square brackets. You can also point your browser to the KDPS website at www.kanji.org to hear the actual sounds.

/a/	[ɑ]	approx. like *a* in *father,* but shorter
/i/	[i]	approx. like *ee* in *sheet,* but shorter
	[i̥]	at word end or between voiceless consonants /k/, /t/, /p/, /s/, /sh/, /h/, /f/, often becomes almost silent (voiceless) when unstressed
/u/	[ɯ̈]	approx. like *oo* in *look,* pronounced by compressing the sides of the lips without rounding them
	[ɯ̥]	at word end or between voiceless consonants /k/, /t/, /p/, /s/, /sh/, /h/, /f/, often becomes almost silent (voiceless) when unstressed
/e/	[e]	approx. like *e* in *set*
/o/	[o]	approx. like the first half of *oa* in *soar*
/k/	[k]	like *k* in *karate*
/g/	[ɡ]	like *g* in *game*
	[ŋ]	in noninitial position, sometimes like *ng* in *sing*
/s/	[s]	approx. like *s* in *see*
/sh/	[ɕ]	approx. like *sh* in *sheet,* but produced farther back
/j/	[dʑ]	approx. like *j* in *Jim,* but produced farther back
	[ʑ]	between vowels, after /N/, and after /Q/, approx. like *g* in *mirage*
/z/	[dz]	in initial position, after /N/, and after /Q/, like *ds* in *words*
	[z]	between vowels, like *z* in *zoo*
/t/	[t]	like *t* in *tin*
/ch/	[tɕ]	approx. like *ch* in *cheer,* but produced farther back
/ts/	[ts]	like *ts* in *cats* but pronounced as a single sound
/d/	[d]	like *d* in *dart*
/n/	[n]	like *n* in *net*
	[ɲ]	before /y/, and sometimes before /i/, approx. like Spanish /ñ/

/h/	[h]	like *h* in *heart*
	[ç]	before /i/ and /y/, like *ch* in German *ich*
/f/	[ɸ]	like /h/, but with lips only slightly apart; upper teeth must not touch lower lips as in English /f/
/b/	[b]	like *b* in *barn*
/p/	[p]	like *p* in *part*
/m/	[m]	like *m* in *market*
/y/	[j]	like *y* in *yard*
/r/	[ɾ]	produced with quick tap of the tongue against the upper gum; like **American** English *tt* in *butter* or Spanish *r* in *pero*
/w/	[w]	like *w* in *want,* but unrounded; occurs mostly in わ ***wa,*** but can occasionally occur in other positions
/N/	[m]	before /m/, /b/, and /p/, like *m* in *market*
	[n]	before /t/, /d/, /n/, /ch/, /ts/, [dʑ], [dz], and /r/, like *n* in *nation*
	[ɲ]	before [ɲ] (i.e., before /nya/, /nyu/, /nyo/, and sometimes /ni/), approx. like Spanish /ñ/
	[ŋ]	before /k/ and /g/, approx. like *ng* in *sing*
	[ɴ]	at word end (before a pause), like *ng* in *sing* but farther back, with back of tongue against the uvula
	[Ṽ]	before vowels, /y/, /w/, /s/, /h/, /sh/, and /f/, becomes a nasalized vowel of varying quality depending on the previous vowel; e.g., /boN/ sounds like French *bon*
/Q/		double consonant represented by っ. See **§5** above.

REMARKS:

1. The consonants /t/, /ts/, /d/, /n/, /s/, /z/, /sh/, /ch/, and /j/ differ from their English counterparts in that they are produced with the *blade,* not the tip, of the tongue against or near the upper gums (alveolar ridge). These sounds are produced farther back than in English, with the tip of the tongue hanging loose behind the lower teeth.
2. An apostrophe (') is placed after ***n*** representing syllabic /N/ (ん) if it is followed by a vowel or by /y/. This is done to show that the /N/ is not part of the following syllable:

たんい	単位	***tan'i***	たに	谷	***tani***
きんゆう	金融	***kin'yū***	きにゅう	記入	***kinyū***

In the example, the apostrophe of ***tan'i*** serves to distinguish between たんい and たに.

APPENDIX 6

RULES FOR OKURIGANA
送り仮名の付け方

Inflected words of Japanese origin normally consist of a kanji base or stem to which kana inflections are added, or *affixed*. These kana affixes are called *okurigana* (送り仮名). For example, the verb kaku 書く かく 'to write' consists of the kanji stem 書 and the *okurigana* ending く.

One difficulty faced by students learning how to write the language is that *okurigana* orthography is not completely standardized; that is, there are different ways to "spell" the same word. For example, ゆき- 'bound for' is written either 行き or 行, depending on editorial policy or personal preference. To help the student, the *okurigana* of all *kun* readings is indicated in parentheses in the entry-head data, and the Japanese words in this dictionary conform to the standard *okurigana* orthography (except for special contexts).

As part of the postwar language reforms, the Japanese Ministry of Education issued guidelines aimed at standardizing kana orthography. The principles for the affixing of *okurigana* currently in effect were approved by the cabinet on June 18, 1973, and underwent some minor revisions as a result of the promulgation of the Jōyō Kanji list in 1981. This appendix presents a translation of the revised edition published on October 1, 1981 entitled 送り仮名の付け方 おくりがなのつけかた, "The Affixation of *Okurigana*." Except for some minor changes, it is a faithful translation of the official document.

See also **3 Character Readings** on p. 42a.

THE AFFIXATION OF OKURIGANA

1 Introduction

1. "**The Affixation of Okurigana**" describes the principles governing the affixation of *okurigana* in the writing of modern Japanese in accordance with the *on-kun* readings of the Jōyō Kanji list as it applies to the public at large in such areas as law, official documents, newspapers, magazines, and broadcasting.

2. This document does not apply to the orthography used in the various branches of learning, such as science, technology, the arts, and other fields, nor to personal writings.

3. This document does not apply to the use of kanji as symbols, to the use of kanji in charts, nor to the writing of proper nouns.

2 Guide to the Main Text

1. The structure of the Main Text of this document is as follows:

One-Character Words

(*a*) **Inflected Words**

General Rule 1: (Words affixed with inflectional endings)
General Rule 2: (Words that, in consideration of their derived and corresponding forms, are affixed at a point before their inflectional endings begin)

(*b*) **Uninflected Words**

General Rule 3: (Nouns that are not affixed with *okurigana*)

General Rule 4: (Nouns that are formed by nominalizing inflected words, and whose *okurigana* conforms to that of the original inflected word)
General Rule 5: (Adverbs, uninflected adjectives, and conjunctions)

Compound Words

General Rule 6: (Affixing *okurigana* on the basis of one-character words)
General Rule 7: (Omitting *okurigana* in conformity with popular usage)

Words in Appendix

1. (Words affixed with *okurigana*)
2. (Words not affixed with *okurigana*)

2. The term "General Rule" refers to a basic principle of affixing *okurigana* on the basis of distinctions between such categories as one-character words and compound words, inflected words and uninflected words, etc. When necessary, exceptional items and alternative forms have been included.

   Consequently, for each General Rule, in addition to the Standard Orthography, both Exceptions and Alternatives are given when necessary. However, because of the large number of exceptions to General Rule 6, a separate category, General Rule 7, was established to embrace those exceptions.

3. The meanings of the terms used in this document are as follows:

One-character words	Words written with a single kanji, using either the *on* or *kun* reading.
Compound words	Words written with two or more kanji, pronounced in various combinations of readings such as *kun* + *kun*, *on* + *kun*, etc.
Words in appendix	Of the words that appear in the appendix to the Jōyō Kanji list, those that present some problem in the affixing of *okurigana*.
Inflected words	Verbs, adjectives, and adjectival nouns.
Uninflected words	Nouns, adverbs, uninflected adjectives, and conjunctions.
Standard Orthography	A rule that is considered to be a basic principle in the affixation of *okurigana*.
Exceptions	Words whose *okurigana* does not conform to the Standard Orthography but that conforms to popular usage. The popular orthography of such words is acceptable although it deviates from the Standard Orthography.
Alternatives	Words whose *okurigana* conforms to the Standard Orthography but that have an alternative form conforming to popular usage. The popular orthography of such words is acceptable in addition to the version conforming to the Standard Orthography.

4. Since *okurigana* is not required for the parts of one-character words or compound words that are read in the *on* reading, such words are not covered here unless necessary.

5. Under each General Rule, words that have alternative orthographies may be written according to the Standard Orthography or according to the Alternatives. If when applying the rules to individual cases it is difficult to judge whether the Alternatives apply, the Standard Orthography shall take precedence.

3 MAIN TEXT

3.1 One-Character Words

3.1.1 Inflected Words

GENERAL RULE 1

Standard Orthography: The *okurigana* of inflected words (except for words to which General Rule 2 applies) begins at their inflectional endings.

Examples:

書く	かく	賢い	かしこい
考える	かんがえる	主だ	おもだ

Exceptions:

1. For adjectives whose stems end in し, the *okurigana* begins with し.

   Examples:

著しい	いちじるしい	珍しい	めずらしい

2. For adjectival nouns whose inflectional endings are preceded by か, やか, or らか, the *okurigana* begins with those syllables.

   Examples:

静かだ	しずかだ	明らかだ	あきらかだ
和やかだ	なごやかだ		

3. The *okurigana* of the following words is affixed as shown.

   Examples:

明らむ	あからむ	危うい	あやうい
味わう	あじわう	大きい	おおきい
哀れむ	あわれむ	少ない	すくない
慈しむ	いつくしむ	小さい	ちいさい
教わる	おそわる	冷たい	つめたい
脅かす	おどかす	平たい	ひらたい
脅かす	おびやかす	新ただ	あらただ
食らう	くらう	同じだ	おなじだ
異なる	ことなる	盛んだ	さかんだ
逆らう	さからう	平らだ	たいらだ
捕まる	つかまる	懇ろだ	ねんごろだ
群がる	むらがる	惨めだ	みじめだ
和らぐ	やわらぐ	哀れだ	あわれだ
揺する	ゆする	幸いだ	さいわいだ
明るい	あかるい	幸せだ	しあわせだ
危ない	あぶない	巧みだ	たくみだ

Alternatives: The *okurigana* of the following words can also begin at the syllable before their inflectional endings, as shown in parentheses:

表す(表わす)	あらわす	行う(行なう)	おこなう
現れる(現われる)	あらわれる	断る(断わる)	ことわる

NOTE: The *okurigana* of verbs whose stems and inflectional endings cannot be separated, such as 着る きる, 寝る ねる, and 来る くる, is affixed as shown.

GENERAL RULE 2

Standard Orthography: The *okurigana* of words that embed another word in a part other than their inflectional endings conforms to the *okurigana* of the embedded word. (The embedded word is shown in square brackets.)

Examples:

1. The inflected forms of verbs, and other words based on those forms:

照らす　てらす [照る てる]
生まれる　うまれる [生む うむ]
聞こえる　きこえる [聞く きく]
混ざる・混じる　まざる, まじる [混ぜる まぜる]

2. Words embedding the stems of adjectives or adjectival nouns:

重んずる　おもんずる [重い おもい]
確かめる　たしかめる [確かだ たしかだ]
清らかだ　きよらかだ [清い きよい]

3. Words that embed nouns:

春めく　はるめく [春 はる]
男らしい　おとこらしい [男 おとこ]
後ろめたい　うしろめたい [後ろ うしろ]

Alternatives: When there is no danger of misreading, the *okurigana* of parts of words other than the inflectional endings can be omitted, as shown by the forms in parentheses.

Examples:

生まれる(生れる)　うまれる　　終わる(終る)　おわる
当たる(当る)　あたる

NOTE: The following words are not considered to embed the words shown in square brackets. Their *okurigana* conforms to General Rule 1.

明るい　あかるい [明ける あける]
荒い　あらい [荒れる あれる]
悔しい　くやしい [悔いる くいる]
恋しい　こいしい [恋う こう]

3.1.2 Uninflected Words

GENERAL RULE 3

Standard Orthography: Nouns (except for those to which General Rule 4 applies) are not affixed with *okurigana.*

Examples:

山　やま　　彼　かれ

Exceptions: 1. The *okurigana* of the following words begins at their last syllable:

辺り　あたり　　便り　たより

哀れ	あわれ	半ば	なかば
勢い	いきおい	情け	なさけ
幾ら	いくら	斜め	ななめ
後ろ	うしろ	独り	ひとり
傍ら	かたわら	誉れ	ほまれ
幸い	さいわい	自ら	みずから
幸せ	しあわせ	災い	わざわい
互い	たがい		

2. The *okurigana* of nouns used for counting containing the syllable つ begins at the つ.

Examples:

一つ	ひとつ	幾つ	いくつ

GENERAL RULE 4

Standard Orthography: The *okurigana* of nouns derived from inflected words, and of nouns formed by adding suffixes such as さ, み, and げ to inflected words, conforms to the *okurigana* of the original words from which they are derived.

Examples:

1. Words derived from inflected words:

願い	ねがい	答え	こたえ
当たり	あたり	初め	はじめ
向かい	むかい	遠く	とおく

2. Words suffixed with さ, み, げ, etc.:

正しさ	ただしさ	惜しげ	おしげ
明るみ	あかるみ		

Exceptions: *Okurigana* is not affixed to the following words:

印	しるし	折	おり
恋	こい	係	かかり
次	つぎ	掛	かかり
話	はなし	組	くみ
光	ひかり		

NOTE: The word 組 くみ given above is the くみ used in such expressions as 花の組 はなのくみ ['bouquet of flowers'] and 赤の組 あかのくみ ['the red team']; it does not refer to cases like 活字の組みがゆるむ かつじのくみがゆるむ ['the setting of the type loosens']. This also applies to other similar words such as 光 ひかり, 折 おり, and 係 かかり, for which this exception does not apply if the verbal sense is strong. Therefore, in such cases *okurigana* is affixed in accordance with the Standard Orthography.

Alternatives: When there is no danger of misreading, *okurigana* may be omitted, as shown by the forms in parentheses.

Examples:

届け(届)	とどけ	問い(問)	とい
当たり(当り)	あたり	祭り(祭)	まつり
答え(答)	こたえ		

GENERAL RULE 5

Standard Orthography: The *okurigana* of adverbs, uninflected adjectives, and conjunctions begins at their last syllable.

Examples:

少し	すこし	及び	および
去る	さる	但し	ただし

Exceptions:

1. The *okurigana* of the following words is affixed as shown:

明くる	あくる	並びに	ならびに
大いに	おおいに	若しくは	もしくは
直ちに	ただちに		

2. *Okurigana* is not affixed to the following word:

又　また

3. The *okurigana* of words that are embedded in another word conforms to the *okurigana* of the embedded word. (The embedded word is shown in square brackets.)

Examples:

至って	いたって [至る いたる]
例えば	たとえば [例える たとえる]
少なくとも	すくなくとも [少ない すくない]
互いに	たがいに [互い たがい]
必ずしも	かならずしも [必ず かならず]

3.2 Compound Words

GENERAL RULE 6

Standard Orthography: The *okurigana* of compound words (except for those to which General Rule 7 applies) is affixed to each kanji in conformity with the *okurigana* of the individual one-character words having the respective *on* and *kun* readings.

Examples:

1. Inflected words:

打ち合わせる	うちあわせる	気軽だ	きがるだ
聞き苦しい	ききぐるしい		

2. Uninflected words:

竹馬	たけうま	取り扱い	とりあつかい
後ろ姿	うしろすがた	申し込み	もうしこみ
長生き	ながいき	落書き	らくがき
落ち葉	おちば	常常	つねづね
売り上げ	うりあげ	休み休み	やすみやすみ
呼び出し電話	よびだし-でんわ		

Alternatives: When there is no danger of misreading, *okurigana* may be omitted, as shown by the forms in parentheses:

Examples:

打ち合わせる(打ち合せる・打合せる)	うちあわせる
聞き苦しい(聞苦しい)	ききぐるしい
取り扱い(取扱い・取扱)	とりあつかい
申し込み(申込み・申込)	もうしこみ
呼び出し電話(呼出し電話・呼出電話)	よびだし-でんわ

NOTE: In words such as こけら落とし (こけら落し) こけらおとし, さび止め さびどめ, 洗いざらし あらいざらし, and 打ちひも うちひも, whose first or second parts are written in kana, the *okurigana* of the remaining part conforms to that of the corresponding one-character word.

GENERAL RULE 7

Of the compound words, the following types of nouns are written without *okurigana* in conformity with popular usage.

Examples:

1. Words used in specific fields whose orthography is considered to be fixed by popular usage:

(*a*) Titles indicating rank, status, managerial position, etc.:

関取	せきとり	取締役	とりしまりやく

(*b*) Words used for names of craftworks, such as 織 おり ['woven fabric, brocade'], 染 ぞめ ['dyed fabric'], and 塗 ぬり ['lacquered product']:

((博多))織	はかたおり	((鎌倉))彫	かまくらぼり
((型絵))染	かたえぞめ	((備前))焼	びぜんやき
((春慶))塗	しゅんけいぬり		

(c) Others:

書留	かきとめ	繰越(金)	くりこしきん
両替	りょうがえ	乗換(駅)	のりかええき
組合	くみあい	乗組(員)	のりくみいん
作付面積	さくつけ-めんせき	待合(室)	まちあいしつ
売上(高)	うりあげだか	申込(書)	もうしこみしょ

2. In general, words whose orthography is considered to be fixed by popular usage:

字引	じびき	建物	たてもの
日付	ひづけ	受付	うけつけ
役割	やくわり	受取	うけとり
貸家	かしや	絵巻物	えまきもの

NOTE:

1. This General Rule applies to the words appearing above in the form ((博多))織 はかたおり, ((売上))高 うりあげだか, etc., even if the part enclosed in double parentheses is replaced by other kanji.
2. The items above to which General Rule 7 applies are only examples, not an exhaustive list. Therefore, this rule shall apply by analogy to other words of a similar kind whose orthography is considered to be fixed by popular usage. When it is difficult to determine whether General Rule 7 applies, General Rule 6 takes precedence.

3.3 Words in Appendix

The *okurigana* of the following "problem words" appearing in the appendix to the Jōyō Kanji list is affixed as shown below.:

1. The *okurigana* of the following words is affixed as shown:

浮つく	うわつく	立ち退く	たちのく
お巡りさん	おまわりさん	手伝う	てつだう
差し支える	さしつかえる	最寄り	もより
五月晴れ	さつきばれ		

The *okurigana* of the following words may be omitted, as shown by the forms in parentheses:

差し支える(差支える)	さしつかえる
五月晴れ(五月晴)	さつきばれ
立ち退く(立退く)	たちのく

2. *Okurigana* is not affixed to the following words:

息吹	いぶき	築山	つきやま	吹雪	ふぶき
桟敷	さじき	名残	なごり	迷子	まいご
時雨	しぐれ	雪崩	なだれ	行方	ゆくえ

APPENDIX 7

THE RADICALS

部首

1 History and Background

The traditional method of ordering entries in Chinese and Japanese character dictionaries is known as the **radical system.** This system is based on a table of 214 elements (plus about 150 variants) called **radicals.** A radical is a frequently recurring graphic component used for classifying characters into groups sharing a common element. The radicals are listed in increasing order of their stroke-counts. Characters sharing the same radical are further grouped in increasing order of the stroke-counts of their *nonradical* elements.

The radical broadly suggests the area of meaning of the character, and is often related to the character's etymology. For example, 木 'tree; wood' is found in many characters designating the names of trees or wooden objects, e.g., 梅 ばい 'plum tree'. Often, however, the radical is merely an element used for classification purposes and is unrelated to the character's meaning, e.g., 寸 in the characters 対 and 将.

The radical system was first introduced some 1900 years ago in the well-known classic Chinese dictionary 説文解字 せつもんかいじ (Chinese: shuōwén jiězì), in which the characters were classified under 540 categories. In 1716, a comprehensive character dictionary called 康熙字典 こうきじてん (Chinese: kāngxī zìdiǎn) was published in China, reducing the number of radicals to 214. The latter has served as a model for all later character dictionaries, and the radical system it introduced is still in use as the most widespread scheme of lexicographic classification today.

The original forms of the 214 traditional radicals are referred to here as the **parent form.** A radical may also have one or more **variant forms** of considerably different shape and/or stroke-count. For example, 氵 is a three-stroke variant of the four-stroke 'water' radical 水 (Radical 85). On the other hand, the difference between some variants is merely a slight variation in proportion. For example, the parent form 弓 of Radical 57 (as in 彎) has the left-side variant 弓 (as in 弾).

The position of many radicals is constant in relation to the other elements of the character. Traditionally, the radicals are classified into categories according to their position within the character, as shown in the table below:

Types of Radicals

◧	偏	***hen***	left	亻 in 使
◨	旁	***tsukuri***	right	欠 in 欧
⬒	冠	***kanmuri***	top	宀 in 定
⬓	脚	***ashi***	bottom	儿 in 兄
◰	垂	***tare***	top-left	广 in 広
◱	繞	***nyō***	left-bottom	廴 in 廷
▢	構	***kamae***	enclosure	門 in 問

The radical system is complex and difficult to master. One problem is that the simplification of the characters that took place with the introduction of the Tōyō Kanji and Jōyō Kanji lists in the postwar period has resulted in the disappearance of the radical element from some characters. For example, 並 is traditionally classified under 立 (Radical 117) based on its old form 竝, but 立 has completely disappeared from the abbreviated form 並. (The traditional radical of these "lost-radical" characters can be determined by looking the character up in the **Radical Index.**)

Another problem is that some characters include several radical elements and one must choose between them. For example, 副 consists of four elements, all of which are radicals (see **§1.1.1 The Radical System** on p. 1781 for details). Because of these difficulties, determining which element of a character is the radical can be a laborious task. Some useful guidelines can be found in **§4 How to Determine the Radical** on p. 1982.

Despite these problems, the time-honored radical system, which is still in widespread use today, is important and should be learned by the serious student. A knowledge of radicals is useful for looking up characters in dictionaries and reference works based on the radical system, and helps the learner understand character etymology.

2 Radical Chart

The **Radical Chart** below gives a full list of radical forms, variants, names, and cross-references. It includes the following information:

1. **Radical** The **radicals** and their **variant forms** are listed in increasing order of the stroke-counts of their parent forms, and are numbered consecutively from 1 to 214 according to the traditional historical arrangement. The **radical number** is a serial number assigned to each radical that is widely used in character dictionaries and reference works for identification. The left part of the **Radical** column gives the radical number; the right part gives the radical. Note that the radical and radical number for each entry character appear in the main part of the dictionary (see **§5 Reference Data Box** on p. 44a).
2. **Radical name** When talking about the components of Chinese characters it is convenient to describe them by naming their constituent radicals. For example, we can say that 洋 consists of さんずい (the 'water' radical) on the left and ひつじ (the 'sheep' radical) on the right. Most radicals have well-established names in Japanese. The left part of the **Radical Name** column gives the romanized version of the most common name in Japanese; the right part gives the name in Japanese script. If a radical has more than one name, the less common one appears after a comma.
3. **English name** Some common radicals, such as 水 the 'water' radical, have well-established names in English, but many others are called by different names in different works. The names appearing in the **English Name** column are based primarily on tradition, where such tradition exists, and on the meaning and/or function of the radical as a character-building element.
4. **Parent and variant forms** The **Form** column indicates if the radical is a **parent form** or a **variant form.** If it is a variant form, the column shows the position in which it normally appears within the character, as explained below:

Parent	parent radical in its full traditional form (心 in 必) (this form may appear in various positions)
Left	variant normally appearing on the left (忄 in 情)
Right	variant normally appearing on the right (刂 in 削)
Top	variant normally appearing at the top (山 in 岩)
Bottom	variant normally appearing at the bottom (⺗ in 慕)
Enclosure	variant normally enclosing the remainder of the character (戸 in 戻)
Variant	variant appearing in a position other than the above (羽 in 習)

For a given radical, the parent form appears first, followed by its variants. It should be noted that some variants are more common than their parent forms. For example, 辶 (Radical 162) is now the common form while the original parent form 辵 is never used.

5. **Number** The **Number** column indicates the **entry number** where the radical appears as an entry character in the body of the dictionary. That entry includes the RADICAL section, which gives further information about the radical, such as a description of its meaning and function, and examples of characters in which the parent and variant forms appear as a radical. See **§7 Radical Section** on p. 44a for details.

RADICAL CHART

Radical		Radical Name		English Name	Form	Number
1 STROKE						
1	一	*ichi*	一	one	parent	4148
2	丨	*bō*	丨	downstroke	parent	4150
3	丶	*ten*	丶	dot	parent	4151
4	丿	*no*	丿	left stroke	parent	4152
	㇒	*no*	㇒		top	4153
5	乙	*otsu*	乙	hook	parent	4145
	乚	*re*	乚		variant	4146
6	亅	*hanebō*	亅	hooked stroke	parent	4154
2 STROKES						
7	二	*ni*	二	two	parent	2421
8	亠	*nabebuta*	亠	lid	parent	4170
9	人	*hito*	人	person	parent	4175
	亻	*ninben*	亻		left	4181
	𠆢	*hitoyane*	𠆢		top	4180
10	儿	*ninnyō, hitoashi*	儿	legs	parent	0003
11	入	*iru*	入	enter	parent	4177
12	八	*hachigashira*	八	eight	parent	3644
	八	*hachi*	八		variant	0004
	丷	*hachigashira*	丷		top	0002
13	冂	*keigamae*	冂	border	parent	4159
14	冖	*wakanmuri*	冖	cover	parent	4160
15	冫	*nisui*	冫	ice	parent	2422
16	几	*tsukue*	几	table	parent	4156
	𠘨	*kazagamae*	𠘨		enclosure	4161
17	凵	*kannyō, ukebako*	凵	receptacle	parent	4171
18	刀	*katana*	刀	sword	parent	3642
	刂	*rittō*	刂		right	0001
19	力	*chikara*	力	strength	parent	4178
20	勹	*tsutsumigamae*	勹	wrap	parent	4182
21	匕	*sajinohi*	匕	spoon	parent	3641
22	匚	*hakogamae*	匚	box	parent	4162
23	匸	*kakushigamae*	匸	enclose	parent	4163
	匸	*kakushigamae*	匸		enclosure	—
24	十	*jū*	十	ten	parent	4172
	十	*jūhen*	十		left	4173
25	卜	*bokunoto*	卜	divine	parent	4174
	⺊	*bokunoto*	⺊		variant	—
26	卩	*fushizukuri*	卩	seal	parent	4165
	㔾	*fushizukuri*	㔾		variant	4164
27	厂	*gandare*	厂	cliff	parent	4166
28	厶	*mu*	厶	oneself	parent	4183

Radical		Radical Name		English Name	Form	Number
29	又	*mata*	又	right hand	parent	4167
	又	*mata*	又		variant	4158
3 STROKES						
30	口	*kuchi*	口	mouth	parent	4189
	口	*kuchihen*	口		left	—
31	囗	*kunigamae*	囗	enclosure	parent	4199
32	土	*tsuchi*	土	earth	parent	4211
	土	*tsuchihen*	土		left	—
33	士	*samurai*	士	knight	parent	4213
34	夂	*fuyugashira*	夂	descend	parent	4200
35	夊	*suinyō*	夊	move slowly	parent	4201
	夂	*natsuashi*	夂		bottom	—
36	夕	*yūbe*	夕	evening	parent	4195
37	大	*ōkii, dai*	大	big	parent	4224
	大	*ōkii, dai*	大		top	4231
38	女	*onna*	女	woman	parent	4226
	女	*onnahen*	女		left	4232
39	子	*ko*	子	child	parent	4196
	子	*kohen*	子		left	—
40	宀	*ukanmuri*	宀	roof	parent	4233
41	寸	*sun*	寸	inch	parent	3652
42	小	*chiisai*	小	small	parent	0007
	⺌	*naogashira*	⺌		top	0005
	⺍	*naogashira*	⺍		top	—
43	尢	*mageashi*	尢	lame	parent	3654
44	尸	*shikabane*	尸	corpse	parent	4198
45	屮	*tetsu*	屮	sprout	parent	4220
46	山	*yama*	山	mountain	parent	3658
	山	*yamahen*	山		left	—
	山	*yamakanmuri*	山		top	—
47	巛	*magarigawa*	巛	river	parent	0009
	川	*sanbongawa*	川		variant	0006
48	工	*takumi*	工	work	parent	4190
	工	*takumihen*	工		left	—
49	己	*onore*	己	self	parent	4188
	巳	*mi*	巳		variant	4197
50	巾	*haba*	巾	cloth	parent	4217
51	干	*hosu*	干	shield	parent	4187
52	幺	*itogashira*	幺	tiny	parent	4234
53	广	*madare*	广	roof	parent	4235
54	廴	*ennyō*	廴	proceed	parent	4202
	廴	*ennyō*	廴		enclosure	4203
55	廾	*nijūashi*	廾	clasp hands	parent	4221
56	弋	*shikigamae*	弋	spike	parent	4230

Radical		Radical Name		English Name	Form	Number
57	弓	*yumi*	弓	bow	parent	4193
	弓	*yumihen*	弓		left	—
58	彐	*keigashira*	彐	pig's head	parent	4205
	彐	*keigashira*	彐		variant	4204
	彑	*keigashira*	彑		variant	4215
59	彡	*sanzukuri*	彡	decoration	parent	2426
60	彳	*gyōninben*	彳	locomotion	parent	2427
			4 STROKES			
61	心	*kokoro*	心	heart	parent	0011
	忄	*risshinben*	忄		left	0008
	⺗	*shitagokoro*	⺗		bottom	0012
62	戈	*kanohoko*	戈	spear	parent	4274
63	戶	*tobiranoto*	戶	door	parent	3668
	戸	*tobiranoto*	戸		enclosure	2429
64	手	*te*	手	hand	parent	4267
	扌	*tehen*	扌		left	4222
65	支	*shinyō, jūmata*	支	branch	parent	2474
	支	*shinyō, jūmata*	支		right	2473
66	攴	*bokuzukuri, tomata*	攴	strike	parent	2475
	攵	*nobun*	攵		right	2479
67	文	*bun, bunnyō*	文	pattern	parent	2462
	文	*bun, bunnyō*	文		variant	2458
68	斗	*tomasu*	斗	measure	parent	3671
69	斤	*ono*	斤	ax	parent	3667
70	方	*kata*	方	square	parent	2459
71	无	*munyō*	无	without	parent	4251
	旡	*sudenotsukuri*	旡		right	4252
	旡	*sudenotsukuri*	旡		right	4299
72	日	*hi*	日	sun	parent	3760
	日	*hi*	日		variant	3759
73	曰	*hirabi*	曰	say	parent	3757
	曰	*hirabi*	曰		variant	3758
74	月	*tsuki*	月	moon	parent	3677
	月	*tsuki*	月		variant	3674
	月	*tsuki*	月		variant	3675
75	木	*ki*	木	tree	parent	4261
	木	*kihen*	木		left	—
76	欠	*akubi*	欠	yawn	parent	2481
77	止	*tomeru*	止	stop	parent	3659
	止	*tomehen*	止		left	—
78	歹	*gatsuhen*	歹	death	parent	4253
79	殳	*rumata, hokozukuri*	殳	club	parent	2472
80	毋	*nakare*	毋	mother	parent	4255
	毌	*haha, nakare*	毌		variant	4254
	母	*haha*	母	-	variant	4287

Radical		Radical Name		English Name	Form	Number
81	比	*kuraberu, hi*	比	compare	parent	0029
82	毛	*ke*	毛	hair	parent	4264
	毛	*ke*	毛		enclosure	—
83	氏	*uji*	氏	family name	parent	3669
84	气	*kigamae*	气	vapor	parent	2480
85	水	*mizu*	水	water	parent	0010
	氵	*sanzui*	氵		left	2424
	氺	*shitamizu*	氺		bottom	0041
86	火	*hi*	火	fire	parent	4273
	火	*hihen*	火		left	—
	灬	*rekka*	灬		bottom	0013
87	爪	*tsume*	爪	claw	parent	3756
	⺤	*notsu*	⺤		top	2434
	爫	*tsumekanmuri*	爫		top	2433
88	父	*chichi*	父	father	parent	2469
	父	*chichi*	父	-	variant	2467
89	爻	*meme*	爻	crisscross	parent	2482
	爻	*meme*	爻		variant	2483
90	爿	*shōhen*	爿	stand	parent	4279
	丬	*shōhen*	丬		variant	3655
91	片	*kata*	片	board	parent	4272
92	牙	*kiba*	牙	sharp tooth	parent	4243
	牙	*kiba*	牙		left	4304
93	牛	*ushi*	牛	cattle	parent	4263
	牜	*ushihen*	牜		left	4269
94	犬	*inu*	犬	dog	parent	4275
	犭	*kemonohen*	犭		left	4236
5 STROKES						
95	玄	*gen*	玄	dark	parent	2485
96	玉	*tama*	玉	gem	parent	4289
	𤣩	*tamahen*	𤣩		left	4256
	王	*ō*	王		variant	4247
97	瓜	*uri*	瓜	gourd	parent	3772
	瓜	*uri*	瓜	gourd	variant	3789
98	瓦	*kawara*	瓦	tile	parent	4288
99	甘	*amai*	甘	sweet	parent	4306
100	生	*umareru*	生	birth	parent	4309
101	用	*mochiiru*	用	use	parent	3694
102	田	*ta*	田	field	parent	3775
103	疋	*hiki*	疋	animal counter	parent	4292
	𤴔	*hikihen*	𤴔		left	4300
104	疒	*yamaidare*	疒	illness	parent	4326
105	癶	*hatsugashira*	癶	spread legs	parent	0044
106	白	*shiro*	白	white	parent	4305
107	皮	*kegawa*	皮	skin	parent	3771

Radical		Radical Name		English Name	Form	Number
108	皿	***sara***	皿	dish	parent	4286
109	目	***me***	目	eye	parent	3777
110	矛	***hoko***	矛	lance	parent	2501
111	矢	***ya***	矢	arrow	parent	2502
	矢	***yahen***	矢		left	—
112	石	***ishi***	石	stone	parent	3689
	石	***ishihen***	石		left	—
113	示	***shimesu***	示	deity	parent	2435
	礻	***nehen, shimesuhen***	礻		left	4280
	示	***shimesuhen***	示		left	—
114	禸	***gūnoashi***	禸	track	parent	4281
115	禾	***nogi***	禾	growing grain	parent	4315
	禾	***nogihen***	禾		left	—
116	穴	***ana***	穴	hole	parent	2684
	穴	***anakanmuri***	穴		top	2683
	穴	***ana***	穴	-	variant	2682
117	立	***tatsu***	立	stand	parent	2486
	立	***tatsuhen***	立		left	—
6 STROKES						
118	竹	***take***	竹	bamboo	parent	0267
	⺮	***takekanmuri***	⺮		top	0268
119	米	***kome***	米	rice	parent	4342
	米	***komehen***	米		left	—
120	糸	***ito***	糸	thread	parent	2703
	糸	***itohen***	糸		left	—
121	缶	***hotogi***	缶	earthenware	parent	2525
122	网	***amigashira***	网	net	parent	3708
	罒	***yonkashira***	罒		top	3779
	穴	***yonkashira***	穴		top	2471
123	羊	***hitsuji***	羊	sheep	parent	2708
	羊	***hitsujikanmuri***	羊		top	2709
	羊	***hitsujihen***	羊		left	—
124	羽	***hane***	羽	wing	parent	0266
	羽	***hane***	羽		variant	0265
125	老	***oi***	老	old person	parent	3963
	耂	***oikanmuri, oigashira***	耂		top	4282
126	而	***shikashite***	而	beard	parent	2520
127	耒	***raisuki***	耒	plow	parent	4345
	耒	***raihen***	耒		left	—
	耒	***sukihen***	耒		left	—
128	耳	***mimi***	耳	ear	parent	4329
	耳	***mimihen***	耳		left	—
129	聿	***fudezukuri***	聿	brush	parent	4346

Radical		Radical Name		English Name	Form	Number
130	肉	***niku***	肉	flesh	parent	3966
	月	***nikuzuki***	月		variant	3676
	月	***tsuki***	月		variant	3675
131	臣	***shin***	臣	retainer	parent	3712
	臣	***shin***	臣		left	3806
132	自	***mizukara***	自	self	parent	4338
133	至	***itaru***	至	arrive	parent	2707
134	臼	***usu***	臼	mortar	parent	4341
	臼	***usu***	臼		variant	1049
135	舌	***shita***	舌	tongue	parent	2711
	舌	***shitahen***	舌		left	—
136	舛	***masu***	舛	dancing	parent	0237
	舛	***maiashi***	舛		bottom	0278
137	舟	***fune***	舟	ship	parent	4353
	舟	***funehen***	舟		left	—
138	艮	***kon, ushitora***	艮	northeast	parent	4330
	艮	***kon, ushitora***	艮		variant	—
139	色	***iro***	色	color	parent	2522
	色	***irozukuri***	色		right	—
140	艸	***kusa***	艸	plants	parent	0241
	艹	***kusakanmuri***	艹		top	4223
	艹	***kusakanmuri***	艹		top	0026
	艹	***kusakanmuri***	艹		top	0033
141	虍	***torakanmuri***	虍	tiger	parent	3964
	虍	***torakanmuri***	虍	tiger	variant	—
142	虫	***mushi***	虫	bug	parent	4343
	虫	***mushihen***	虫		left	—
143	血	***chi***	血	blood	parent	4339
	血	***chihen***	血		left	—
144	行	***gyō***	行	road	parent	0246
	行	***gyōgamae***	行		enclosure	0247
145	衣	***koromo***	衣	clothes	parent	2506
	衤	***koromohen***	衤		left	4327
	𧘇	***koromo***	𧘇		variant	2510
146	襾	***nishi***	襾	cover	parent	4336
	覀	***nishi***	覀		top	4335
	西	***nishi***	西	-	variant	4333
7 STROKES						
147	見	***miru***	見	see	parent	3151
148	角	***tsuno***	角	horn	parent	2541
	角	***tsunohen***	角		left	—
149	言	***kotoba***	言	speech	parent	2440
	訁	***gonben***	訁		left	—
150	谷	***tani***	谷	valley	parent	2536
	谷	***tanihen***	谷		left	—

Radical		Radical Name		English Name	Form	Number
151	豆	*mame*	豆	ritual vessel	parent	2442
	豆	*mamehen*	豆		left	—
152	豕	*inoko*	豕	pig	parent	4357
	豕	*inokohen*	豕		variant	—
153	豸	*mujina*	豸	wild animal	parent	3054
154	貝	*kai*	貝	cowry	parent	3150
	貝	*kaihen*	貝		variant	—
155	赤	*aka*	赤	red	parent	2719
	赤	*akahen*	赤		left	—
156	走	*hashiru*	走	run	parent	2720
	走	*sōnyō*	走		enclosure	2721
157	足	*ashi*	足	foot	parent	2714
	𧾷	*ashihen*	𧾷		left	2717
158	身	*mi*	身	body	parent	4368
	身	*mihen*	身		left	—
159	車	*kuruma*	車	vehicle	parent	4367
	車	*kurumahen*	車		left	—
160	辛	*karai*	辛	acrid	parent	2531
	辛	*karai*	辛		left	—
161	辰	*shinnotatsu*	辰	the Dragon	parent	3713
162	辵	*shinnyō, shinnyū*	辵	advance	parent	2444
	辶	*shinnyō, shinnyū*	辶		enclosure	2425
	辶	*shinnyō, shinnyū*	辶		enclosure	2431
163	邑	*mura*	邑	city	parent	2716
	阝	*ōzato*	阝		right	4206
164	酉	*hiyominotori*	酉	wine	parent	4358
	酉	*torihen*	酉		left	—
165	釆	*nogome*	釆	separate	parent	4370
	釆	*nogomehen*	釆		left	—
166	里	*sato*	里	hamlet	parent	4356
	里	*satohen*	里		left	—
8 STROKES						
167	金	*kane*	金	metal	parent	2552
	金	*kanehen*	金		left	—
168	長	*nagai*	長	long	parent	3163
	镸	*nagai*	镸		left	3157
169	門	*mon, mongamae*	門	gate	parent	1100
170	阜	*gifunofu*	阜	mound	parent	3254
	阝	*kozatohen*	阝		left	4207
171	隶	*reizukuri*	隶	capture	parent	4386
172	隹	*furutori*	隹	small bird	parent	4383
173	雨	*ame*	雨	rain	parent	4378
	雨	*amekanmuri*	雨		top	4379
174	靑	*ao*	靑	blue	parent	3085
	青	*ao*	青		variant	3084

Radical		Radical Name		English Name	Form	Number
175	非	***arazu***	非	not	parent	1101
9 STROKES						
176	面	***men***	面	face	parent	2590
177	革	***kawa***	革	rawhide	parent	3099
	革	***kawahen***	革		left	—
178	韋	***nameshigawa***	韋	leather	parent	2821
	韋	***nameshigawa***	韋		variant	2851
179	韭	***nira***	韭	leek	parent	4391
180	音	***oto***	音	sound	parent	2448
	音	***oto***	音		variant	2570
181	頁	***ōgai***	頁	head	parent	2589
182	風	***kaze***	風	wind	parent	3730
	風	***kaze***	風		left	—
183	飛	***tobu***	飛	fly	parent	4389
184	食	***shoku***	食	food	parent	2580
	飠	***shokuhen***	飠		left	2556
	𩙿	***shokuhen***	𩙿		left	2579
	食	***shoku***	食		variant	2578
185	首	***kubi***	首	neck	parent	2818
186	香	***nioikō***	香	fragrance	parent	3177
10 STROKES						
187	馬	***uma***	馬	horse	parent	4086
	馬	***umahen***	馬		left	—
188	骨	***hone***	骨	bone	parent	3288
	骨	***honehen***	骨		left	—
189	高	***takai***	高	high	parent	2601
190	髟	***kamikanmuri***	髟	hair	parent	1856
191	鬥	***tōgamae***	鬥	fight	parent	1497
192	鬯	***chō***	鬯	fragrant wine	parent	3429
193	鬲	***kaku***	鬲	ritual tripod	parent	2450
	鬲	***kaku***	鬲		variant	—
194	鬼	***oni***	鬼	ghost	parent	3291
	鬼	***kinyō***	鬼		enclosure	—
11 STROKES						
195	魚	***uo***	魚	fish	parent	2636
	魚	***uohen***	魚		left	—
196	鳥	***tori***	鳥	bird	parent	4105
	鳥	***tori***	鳥		right	—
197	鹵	***ro***	鹵	salt	parent	2634
198	鹿	***shika***	鹿	deer	parent	3879
199	麥	***baku***	麥	wheat	parent	3441
	麥	***bakunyō***	麥		enclosure	3440
	麦	***bakunyō***	麦		enclosure	—
	麦	***mugi***	麦	-	variant	3061

Radical		Radical Name		English Name	Form	Number
200	麻	*asa*	麻	hemp	parent	3884
	麻	*asakanmuri*	麻		enclosure	3882
	麻	*asakanmuri*	麻		enclosure	—
	麻	*asa*	麻	-	variant	3878
12 STROKES						
201	黃	*kiiro*	黃	yellow	parent	3128
	黄	*kiiro*	黄	-	variant	3116
202	黍	*kibi*	黍	millet	parent	3210
203	黑	*kuroi*	黑	black	parent	3462
	黒	*kuroi*	黒		variant	3406
204	黹	*futsu*	黹	embroidery	parent	3218
13 STROKES						
205	黽	*ben*	黽	frog	parent	4404
206	鼎	*kanae*	鼎	ritual cauldron	parent	4405
207	鼓	*tsuzumi*	鼓	drum	parent	2241
208	鼠	*nezumi*	鼠	rat	parent	3340
	鼠	*nezuminyō*	鼠		enclosure	—
14 STROKES						
209	鼻	*hana*	鼻	nose	parent	3358
	鼻	*hanahen*	鼻		left	—
	鼻	*hana*	鼻	-	variant	3357
210	齊	*sei*	齊	uniform	parent	2659
	斉	*sei*	斉		variant	2548
15 STROKES						
211	齒	*ha*	齒	tooth	parent	3139
	齒	*hahen*	齒		left	—
	齒	*hahen*	齒		left	—
	歯	*ha*	歯		variant	3124
16 STROKES						
212	龍	*ryū*	龍	dragon	parent	2266
	竜	*ryū*	竜	-	variant	2603
	龍	*ryū*	龍	-	variant	2265
213	龜	*kame*	龜	tortoise	parent	2667
	龜	*kame*	龜		variant	2671
	亀	*kame*	亀	-	variant	2637
17 STROKES						
214	龠	*yaku*	龠	flute	parent	2670

APPENDIX 8

HISTORICAL TABLES

各種参考表

This appendix presents various historical tables, such as the signs of the Oriental zodiac and the calendar signs, which are useful for reading historical texts and for general reference.

1 The Signs of the Oriental Zodiac

The 十二支 じゅうにし, literally 'the twelve branches', is an ancient set of twelve symbols that were formerly used to indicate time and direction. Later, the symbols became associated with the names of animals and began to be used as a system of divination similar to the signs of the zodiac used in Western astrology. In this dictionary, the 十二支 is referred to as **the signs of the Oriental zodiac.**

The twelve signs were marked on a circle clockwise beginning with 子 ね 'the Rat', and were used to designate time in two-hour intervals. For example, 午の刻 うまのこく indicates "the hour of the Horse" (from 11 a.m. to 1 p.m.). Each sign was also associated with a direction and a month of the year, as shown in the charts below.

The Signs of the Oriental Zodiac

Sign	Entry No.	Reading		English	Time	Direction	Month
		On	*Kun*				
1 子	4196	シ	ね	the Rat	11 p.m.-1 a.m.	north	November
2 丑	4241	チュウ	うし	the Ox	1-3 a.m.	NNE	December
3 寅	2854	イン	とら	the Tiger	3-5 a.m.	ENE	January
4 卯	0231	ボウ	う	the Hare	5-7 a.m.	east	February
5 辰	3713	シン	たつ	the Dragon	7-9 a.m.	ESE	March
6 巳	4197	シ	み	the Serpent	9-11 a.m.	SSE	April
7 午	2478	ゴ	うま	the Horse	11 a.m.-1 p.m.	south	May
8 未	4318	ビ	ひつじ	the Ram	1-3 p.m.	SSW	June
9 申	4319	シン	さる	the Monkey	3-5 p.m.	WSW	July
10 酉	4358	ユウ	とり	the Rooster	5-7 p.m.	west	August
11 戌	4350	ジュツ	いぬ	the Dog	7-9 p.m.	WNW	September
12 亥	2505	ガイ	い	the Boar	9-11 p.m.	NNW	October

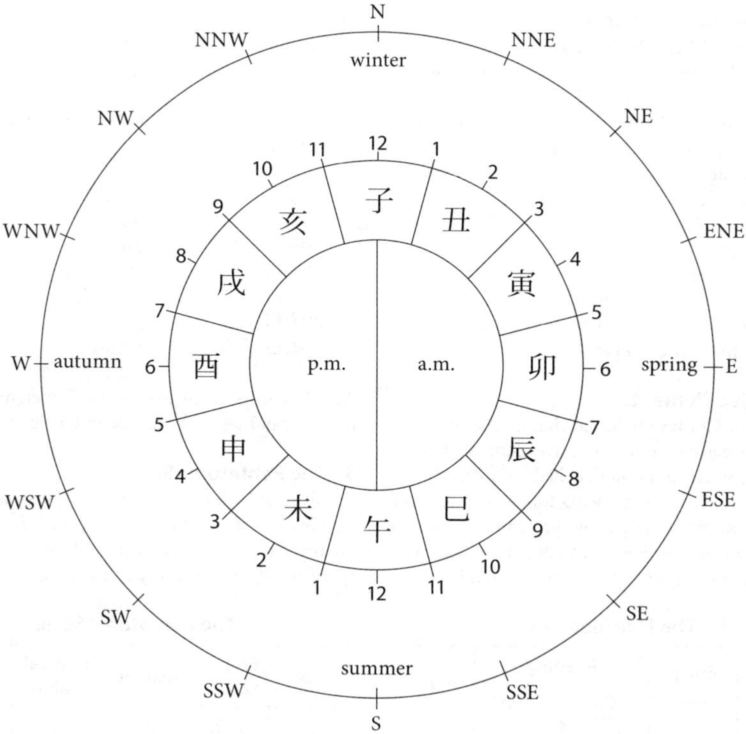

Formerly, the twelve signs were used as the basis of various methods of divination. They are still used today to designate the names of years. The year 1989, for example, is the Year of the Serpent, and the Serpent is believed to be the guardian angel of those born in that year. Another important use of the twelve signs is in conjunction with the ten calendar signs to form the sixty combinations of the sexagenary cycle (see below).

2 The Ten Calendar Signs

The 十干 じっかん, literally 'the ten stems', is an ancient Chinese set of ten symbols formerly used in conjunction with the twelve signs of the zodiac to form the sixty combinations of the sexagenary cycle (see below). Today, their chief use, especially of the first four, is as ordinal numbers to indicate grade or rank, as for example in the word 甲種 こうしゅ 'grade A, first grade'.

The ten calendar signs have two sets of names in Japanese. The first uses the *on* readings of the characters, as shown in the chart below. The second is formed by combining the five elements (see below) with the two forces, *yin* and *yang*, which are respectively represented by 兄え 'older brother' and 弟と 'younger brother'. For example, 甲 きのえ 'wood-*yang*' derives from the first element, 木 き, combined with *yang* represented by 兄え.

The Ten Calendar Signs

Sign		Entry No.	Reading		Ranking
			On	*Kun*	
1	甲	4293	コウ	きのえ	first
2	乙	4145	オツ	きのと	second
3	丙	4290	ヘイ	ひのえ	third
4	丁	4155	テイ	ひのと	fourth
5	戊	4321	ボ	つちのえ	fifth
6	己	4188	キ	つちのと	sixth
7	庚	3826	コウ	かのえ	seventh
8	辛	2531	シン	かのと	eighth
9	壬	4257	ジン	みずのえ	ninth
10	癸	—	キ	みずのと	tenth

3 The Sexagenary Cycle

The ancient Chinese had a calendar system, based on the 十干 and 十二支 described above, which was used in both China and Japan to count days, months, and years in cycles of sixty. Called 干支 かんし or えと in Japanese, the system is usually referred to as the sexagenary cycle in English. By combining the two sets of symbols a total of sixty two-character combinations is obtained. For example, the third calendar sign, 丙 ひのえ, is combined with the eleventh zodiac sign, 戌 いぬ, to give 丙戌 ひのえいぬ 'fire-*yang* dog', the twenty-third unit in the cycle. The combinations may also be read in their *on* readings, as for example 丙戌 へいじゅつ.

4 The Five Elements

The ancient Chinese believed that all the things in the universe are composed of five elements (wood, fire, earth, metal, and water), called 五行 ごぎょう, that interact with the two opposing forces, *yin* (陰) and *yang* (陽), the passive and active principles in Chinese dualistic philosophy. Each element is associated with a direction, time, planet, body organ, sound, etc.

The Five Elements

Element	Entry no.	Reading		English
		On	*Kun*	
木	4261	モク	き	wood
火	4273	カ	ひ	fire
土	4211	ド	つち	earth
金	2552	ゴン	かね	metal
水	0010	すい	みず	water

The five elements are used to designate the names of the planets, i.e., 木星 もくせい Jupiter, 火星 かせい Mars, 土星 どせい Saturn, 金星 きんせい Venus, and 水星 すいせい Mercury. They are also used along with the names for the sun (日 にち) and the moon (月 げつ) to form the names of the days of the week:

日曜日	にちようび	Sunday
月曜日	げつようび	Monday
火曜日	かようび	Tuesday
水曜日	すいようび	Wednesday
木曜日	もくようび	Thursday
金曜日	きんようび	Friday
土曜日	どようび	Saturday

Another important use of the five elements is to form the names of the ten calendar signs.

5 The Pentatonic Scale

Traditional Chinese and Japanese music is based on a scale consisting of five notes, called 五音 ごいん in Japanese or pentatonic scale in English. Each note corresponds to one of the five elements.

The Pentatonic Scale

Note	Entry no.	Reading	Musical Value	Element
宮	2828	キュウ	C	土
商	2623	ショウ	D	金
角	2541	カク	E	木
徵	0841	チ	G	火
羽	0265	ウ	A	水

APPENDIX 9

ABBREVIATIONS OF PLACE NAMES
国名・地名の略称表

This appendix lists one-character abbreviations of foreign place names, especially country names, in alphabetical order of their English equivalents. 独 どく, for example, is an abbreviation for Germany and is commonly used in such compound words as 日独 にちどく 'Japan and Germany'. Abbreviations in common use are marked by an asterisk after the character. Others are less common or only rarely used. Each place name is followed by the **entry number** for the character or by a dash if that character is not listed in the dictionary.

阿	あ	Africa	0408
留	りゅう	Algeria	3189
米*	べい	America	4342
亜	あ	Argentina	4354
亜*	あ	Asia	4354
豪*	ごう	Australia	2657
墺	おう	Austria	—
白	はく	Belgium	4305
不	ふ	Bhutan	4242
戊	ぼ	Bolivia	4321
伯	はく	Brazil	0067
勃	ぼつ	Bulgaria	1839
加	か	California	0042
加*	か	Canada	0042
智	ち	Chile	3458
中*	ちゅう	China	4262
漢	かん	China	0808
玖	きゅう	Cuba	1041
捷	しょう	Czech	0609
丁	ちょう	Denmark	4155
埃	あい	Egypt	—
得	とく	El Salvador	0577
欧*	おう	Europe	1098
仏*	ふつ	France	0020
独*	どく	Germany	0471
希	き	Greece	2543
銀	ぎん	Guinea	2156
香	こう	Hong Kong	3177
洪	こう	Hungary	0461
氷	ひょう	Iceland	0043
印*	いん	India	1023
愛	あい	Ireland	3133
伊*	い	Italy	0052
日*	にち	Japan	3759
邦	ほう	Japan	1051
和*	わ	Japan	1450
倭	わ	Japan	0140
約	やく	Jordan	1632
猶	ゆう	Judea	0757
鮮	せん	Korea	2355
老	ろう	Laos	3963
緬	めん	Myanmar	1758
蘭*	らん	the Netherlands	3031
朝	ちょう	North Korea	2130
韓*	かん	South Korea	2218
馬	ば	Malaysia	4086
満	まん	Manchuria	0739
墨	ぼく	Mexico	3423
蒙	もう	Mongolia	2938
新	しん	New Zealand	2239
児	じ	Nicaragua	3153
諾	だく	Norway	1974
巴	は	Panama	4246
秘	ひ	Peru	1490
比*	ひ	Philippines	0029
波	ぽ	Poland	0388
葡	ぽ, ほ	Portugal	2902
普	ふ	Prussia	2919
露*	ろ	Russia	3495
星	せい	Singapore	3089
西*	せい	Spain	4333
錫	しゃく	Sri Lanka	2189
叙	じょ	Syria	1834
瑞	ずい	Sweden	1302
瑞	ずい	Switzerland	1302
台*	たい	Taiwan	2498
泰	たい	Thailand	3193
蔵	ぞう	Tibet	2995
突	とつ	Tunisia	2772
土	と	Turkey	4211
英*	えい	United Kingdom	2782
瓦	が	Vanuatu	4288
委	い	Venezuela	3160
越	えつ	Vietnam	4108

APPENDIX 10

CORE MEANINGS ARRANGED BY FREQUENCY

使用頻度順中心義一覧

This appendix lists all main entry characters in order of frequency of occurrence along with their core meanings for ready reference. The **core meaning** is a concise keyword that defines the most dominant character meaning. The **frequency** is a number that expresses the relative frequency of occurrence of a character in Modern Japanese.

This appendix can be highly useful to both student and teacher in at least three ways: (1) it enables the student of kanji to know the relative importance of each character, (2) it helps the developer of teaching materials compile graded lessons, and (3) it enables the student to review the core meanings of the most frequent characters in a convenient, easy-to-read format.

The characters are listed in increasing order of their frequency numbers. The numerals to the left of the character column indicate the frequency; the numerals to the right are the **entry numbers.**

For more information on core meanings and frequency, see **§1.1 Core Meaning** on p. 25a and **§4.1 Character Importance** on p. 32a.

1	人	HUMAN BEING	4175
2	一	ONE	4148
3	日	DAY	3759
		SUN	
		JAPAN	
4	大	BIG	4224
		UNIVERSITY	
5	年	YEAR	2528
6	出	GO OUT	4310
		PUT OUT	
7	本	BASIS	4314
		BOOK	
		THIS	
8	中	MIDDLE	4262
		IN	
9	子	CHILD	4196
		NOUN SUFFIX	
10	見	SEE	3151
11	国	COUNTRY	3831
12	言	SAY	2440
		SPEECH	
13	上	UP	4212
14	分	DIVIDE	2466
		PART	
		MINUTE	
15	生	LIFE	4309
		BE BORN	
		STUDENT	
16	手	HAND	4267
		OCCUPATION SUFFIX	
17	自	SELF	4338
18	行	GO	0246
		ACT	
		LINE	
19	者	PERSON	3980
20	二	TWO	2421
21	間	INTERVAL	4122
		BETWEEN	
22	事	AFFAIR	4384
		ABSTRACT THING	
23	思	THINK	3173
24	時	TIME	1155
25	気	GAS	3960
		SPIRIT	
26	会	MEET	2512
		SOCIETY	
27	十	TEN	4172
28	家	HOUSE	2827
		FAMILY	
29	女	WOMAN	4226
30	三	THREE	2423
31	前	BEFORE	2819
32	的	TARGET	1444
		ADJECTIVAL SUFFIX	
33	方	DIRECTION	2459
		WAY	
		SQUARE	
34	入	ENTER	4177
		PUT IN	
35	小	SMALL	0007
36	地	GROUND	0236
		PLACE	
37	合	COMBINE	2511
		FIT	
38	後	AFTER	0431
39	目	EYE	3777
		ITEM	
40	長	LONG	3163

		CHIEF	
41	場	PLACE	0678
42	代	SUBSTITUTE	0034
		GENERATION	
		CHARGE	
43	私	PRIVATE	1432
		I	
44	下	DOWN	4186
45	立	STAND	2486
		ESTABLISH	
46	部	SECTION	2111
47	学	STUDY	3162
		EDUCATIONAL INSTITUTION	
48	物	THING	1084
49	月	MOON	3674
		MONTH	
50	田	RICE FIELD	3775
51	何	WHAT	0073
		HOW MANY	
52	来	COME	4366
53	彼	THIRD PERSON PRONOUN	0346
54	話	SPEAK	1928
55	体	BODY	0080
		FORM	
56	動	MOVE	2232
57	社	COMPANY	1042
		SOCIETY	
58	知	KNOW	1446
59	理	REASON	1220
		BASIC PRINCIPLE	
60	山	MOUNTAIN	3658
61	内	INSIDE	4277
62	同	SAME	3707
63	心	HEART	0011
64	発	START	3174
		EMIT	
65	高	HIGH	2601
66	実	REAL	2765
67	作	MAKE	0077
		WORK	
68	当	THE PRESENT	2701
		HIT	
69	新	NEW	2239
70	世	WORLD	4308
		AGE	
71	今	PRESENT	2464
		THIS	
72	書	WRITE	3292
		BOOK	
73	度	DEGREE	3844
		TIME	
74	明	BRIGHT	1060
		CLEAR	
75	五	FIVE	4244
76	戦	WAR	2242
77	力	POWER	4178
78	名	NAME	2693
79	金	METAL	2552
		GOLD	
		MONEY	
80	性	NATURE	0357
		SEX	
		-ITY	
81	対	OPPOSITE	1025
		OPPOSE	
82	意	MIND	2650
		MEANING	
83	用	EMPLOY	3694
		THINGS TO DO	
84	男	MAN	3147
85	主	MAIN	2437
		MASTER	
86	通	PASS	3855
		COMMUNICATE	
87	関	CONCERN	4129
		BARRIER	
88	文	LETTER	2458
		WRITINGS	
89	屋	HOUSE	3842
		SMALL SHOP	
90	感	SENSE	3514
		FEEL	
91	郎	YOUNG MAN	1641
		MALE NAME SUFFIX	
92	業	WORK	3227
		BUSINESS	
		INDUSTRY	
93	定	FIX	2770
94	政	POLITICAL ADMINISTRATION	1468
95	持	HOLD	0447
96	道	WAY	3888
97	外	OUTSIDE	0215
98	取	TAKE	1613
99	所	PLACE	1056
		PARTICLE OF NOMINALIZATION	
100	現	ACTUAL	1218
		APPEAR	
101	最	MOST	3120
102	化	CHANGE INTO	0022
103	四	FOUR	3778
104	先	AHEAD	3046
105	民	PEOPLE	3770
106	身	BODY	4368
		ONE'S PERSON	
107	不	NOT	4242
108	口	MOUTH	4189
109	川	RIVER	0006
110	東	EAST	4385
111	相	PHASE	1120
		MUTUAL	

		MINISTER	
112	多	MANY	2694
113	法	LAW	0391
		METHOD	
114	全	WHOLE	2514
115	聞	HEAR	4127
116	情	EMOTION	0583
		ACTUAL CONDITIONS	
117	野	FIELD	1877
118	考	THINK	3962
119	向	TURN TOWARD	3790
120	平	FLAT	4291
		CALM	
121	成	FORM	4352
		ACHIEVE	
122	軍	ARMY	2582
123	開	OPEN	4121
124	教	TEACH	1887
		RELIGION	
125	経	PASS THROUGH	1687
		MANAGE	
126	信	BELIEVE	0115
		MESSAGE	
127	近	NEAR	3798
		RECENT	
128	以	TO THE…OF	0045
		BY MEANS OF	
129	語	LANGUAGE	1944
		WORD	
		TELL	
130	面	FACE	2590
131	連	LINK	3849
		IN SUCCESSION	
132	問	QUESTION	4117
133	原	PLAIN	3733
		ORIGINAL	
134	顔	FACE	2277
135	正	RIGHT	4296
136	機	MACHINE	1365
		AIRCRAFT	
		OPPORTUNITY	
137	九	NINE	4176
138	次	NEXT	0058
139	数	NUMBER	2245
140	美	BEAUTIFUL	2817
141	回	TURN ROUND	3793
		TIME	
142	食	EAT	2578
		FOOD	
143	表	EXPRESS	3083
		SURFACE	
		TABLE	
144	八	EIGHT	3644
145	声	VOICE	2724
146	水	WATER	0010
147	報	INFORM	2133
		REQUITE	
148	真	TRUE	2616
149	味	TASTE	0325
150	界	WORLD	3172
		BOUNDS	
151	無	WITHOUT	2648
		NOTHING	
152	少	LITTLE	4278
153	要	IMPORTANT	3263
		SUMMARIZE	
		REQUIRE	
154	海	SEA	0459
155	変	CHANGE	2569
		ABNORMAL	
156	結	TIE	1706
		CONCLUDE	
157	切	CUT	0030
158	重	HEAVY	4390
		DUPLICATE	
159	天	HEAVEN	4250
160	神	GOD	1143
		MIND	
161	記	WRITE DOWN	1843
162	木	TREE	4261
		WOOD	
163	集	COLLECT	3445
164	和	HARMONIOUS	1450
		PEACE	
		JAPAN	
165	員	MEMBER	2822
166	引	DRAW	0207
167	公	PUBLIC	2468
168	画	PICTURE	3723
		DRAW UP A PLAN	
169	死	DIE	4334
170	安	PEACEFUL	2695
		INEXPENSIVE	
171	兵	SOLDIER	3158
172	親	PARENT	2264
		RELATIVES	
		INTIMATE	
173	六	SIX	2461
174	治	GOVERN	0393
		CURE	
175	決	DECIDE	0308
176	太	GREAT	2673
		THICK	
177	氏	COURTESY TITLE	3669
		FAMILY NAME	
178	衛	GUARD	0938
179	強	STRONG	0574
180	使	USE	0100
		ENVOY	
181	込	MOVE INWARD	3762

		EMPHATIC VERBAL SUFFIX	
182	朝	MORNING	2130
		DYNASTY	
183	受	RECEIVE	3076
184	島	ISLAND	4103
185	解	TAKE APART	1913
		DISSOLVE	
		CLARIFY	
186	市	CITY	2487
		MARKET	
187	期	TERM	2139
		EXPECT	
188	様	MODE	1332
		FORMAL TITLE	
189	村	VILLAGE	1029
190	活	ACTIVE	0460
		LIVE	
191	頭	HEAD	2019
192	題	TITLE	4139
		TOPIC	
		PROBLEM	
193	万	TEN THOUSAND	3653
194	組	ORGANIZE	1693
		ASSEMBLE	
195	仕	SERVE	0037
		DO	
196	白	WHITE	4305
197	指	FINGER	0452
		POINT	
198	説	EXPLAIN	1949
		THEORY	
199	七	SEVEN	4169
200	能	ABILITY	1676
201	京	CAPITAL	2546
		TOKYO	
		KYOTO	
202	葉	LEAF	2912
203	第	ORDINAL NUMBER PREFIX	3298
204	流	FLOW	0529
		CURRENT	
		STYLE	
205	然	MODIFIER FORMING SUFFIX	3456
		SO	
206	初	FIRST	1433
207	足	FOOT	2714
		SUFFICE	
208	円	CIRCLE	3673
		YEN	
209	在	BE	3704
210	門	GATE	1100
211	調	TONE	1973
		INVESTIGATE	
		PREPARE	
212	笑	LAUGH	3275
213	品	ARTICLE	2795
214	電	ELECTRICITY	3465
215	議	DISCUSS	2078
		LEGISLATIVE BODY	
216	直	STRAIGHT	3649
		FIX	
217	着	PUT ON	4110
		ARRIVE	
		STICK	
218	保	PRESERVE	0107
219	別	SEPARATE	1434
		ANOTHER	
220	夫	HUSBAND	4271
		MAN LABORER	
221	音	SOUND	2570
222	選	CHOOSE	3931
223	元	ORIGIN	2428
224	権	RIGHT	1348
		POWER	
225	特	SPECIAL	1181
226	義	RIGHTEOUSNESS	2948
		MEANING	
227	父	FATHER	2467
228	利	ADVANTAGE	1431
		PROFIT	
229	制	SYSTEM	1624
		CONTROL	
230	続	CONTINUE	1722
231	風	WIND	3730
		MANNER	
232	北	NORTH	0230
233	石	STONE	3689
234	車	VEHICLE	4367
		WHEEL	
235	進	ADVANCE	3873
236	夜	NIGHT	2550
237	伝	TRANSMIT	0048
238	母	MOTHER	4287
239	加	ADD	0042
240	助	HELP	1440
241	点	POINT	2587
242	産	GIVE BIRTH	4089
		PRODUCE	
243	務	DUTY	1505
244	件	MATTER	0054
245	命	ORDER	2553
		LIFE	
246	番	NUMERICAL ORDER	3416
		WATCH	
247	落	FALL	2907
248	付	ATTACH	0035
249	得	ACQUIRE	0577
		GAIN	
250	半	HALF	4313
251	戸	DOOR	2429
		HOUSEHOLD	

252	好	LIKE	0240
		FAVORABLE	
253	空	SKY	2767
		AIR	
		EMPTY	
254	有	HAVE	3703
255	違	DIFFER	3907
		VIOLATE	
256	吉	LUCKY	2691
257	殺	KILL	1677
258	起	RISE	4099
259	運	CARRY	3894
		MOVE	
		FORTUNE	
260	置	PLACE	3222
261	料	FEE	1644
		MATERIALS	
262	士	MILITARY MAN	4213
		PROFESSION SUFFIX	
263	返	RETURN	3797
264	藤	WISTERIA	3025
265	論	ARGUE	1981
		THEORY	
266	楽	PLEASURE	3505
		COMFORTABLE	
		MUSIC	
267	際	VERGE	0874
		OCCASION	
268	歳	YEAR	3131
		AGE SUFFIX	
269	色	COLOR	2522
270	帰	RETURN	0148
271	歩	WALK	3071
272	井	WELL	4265
273	悪	BAD	3413
274	広	WIDE	3769
275	店	SHOP	3828
276	反	COUNTER	3663
277	町	TOWN	1430
278	形	SHAPE	1050
279	百	HUNDRED	2519
280	光	LIGHT	3043
281	首	HEAD	2818
		NECK	
		LEADER	
282	勝	WIN	1268
		EXCEL	
283	必	WITHOUT FAIL	0015
284	土	SOIL	4211
285	係	CONNECT	0108
		PERSON IN CHARGE	
286	由	REASON	4311
287	愛	LOVE	3133
288	都	METROPOLIS	2120
		METROPOLIS OF TOKYO	
289	住	LIVE	0072
290	江	INLET	0257
291	西	WEST	4333
292	売	SELL	2722
293	放	LET GO	1058
294	確	CERTAIN	1571
295	過	PASS BY	3891
		EXCEED	
296	張	SPREAD	0573
		STRAIN	
297	約	PROMISE	1632
		CONTRACT	
		APPROXIMATELY	
298	馬	HORSE	4086
299	状	FORM	0322
		CONDITION	
		LETTER	
300	待	WAIT	0434
301	古	OLD	2495
302	想	CONCEIVE	3507
303	始	BEGIN	0335
304	官	GOVERNMENT	2766
		GOVERNMENT OFFICIAL	
305	交	INTERCOURSE	2508
		INTERCHANGE	
306	読	READ	1943
307	千	THOUSAND	4219
308	米	RICE	4342
		AMERICA	
309	配	DISTRIBUTE	1853
310	若	YOUNG	2785
311	終	END	1692
312	資	RESOURCES	3342
313	常	NORMAL	3203
		REGULAR	
314	果	FRUIT	4377
315	呼	CALL	0324
316	校	SCHOOL	1166
		COLLATE	
317	武	MILITARY	3979
318	共	JOINT	3045
319	計	PLAN	1828
		COMPUTE	
320	残	REMAIN	1179
		RUTHLESS	
321	判	JUDGE	1441
322	役	SERVICE	0288
323	城	CASTLE	0417
324	院	INSTITUTION	0544
325	他	OTHER	0039
326	総	TOTAL	1743
		GENERAL	
327	術	PRACTICAL ART	0575
328	支	BRANCH	2473
		SUPPORT	

329	送	SEND	3837
330	族	FAMILY	1195
331	両	BOTH	4331
332	乗	RIDE	4393
		GET ON	
333	団	BODY	3791
334	松	PINE	1075
335	映	REFLECT	1104
		PROJECT	
336	応	RESPOND	3804
337	済	SETTLE	0634
		RELIEVE	
338	線	LINE	1760
339	買	BUY	3211
340	設	SET UP	1863
341	右	RIGHT	3693
342	供	OFFER	0098
343	格	NORM	1161
		STATUS	
344	病	ILLNESS	4062
345	打	STRIKE	0224
346	視	REGARD	1223
347	早	EARLY	3042
		QUICK	
348	勢	POWER	3542
349	御	GENERAL HONORIFIC TERM	0703
350	断	CUT OFF	1885
		RESOLVE	
351	式	STYLE	3785
		CEREMONY	
352	質	QUALITY	3483
		MATTER	
353	師	MASTER	1680
354	台	STAND	2498
		COUNTER FOR VEHICLES	
355	党	PARTY	3190
356	告	NOTIFY	3062
357	深	DEEP	0636
358	存	EXIST	3702
359	争	CONTEND	2523
360	室	ROOM	2802
361	覚	PERCEIVE	3217
		COMMIT TO MEMORY	
362	史	HISTORY	4324
363	側	SIDE	0155
364	飛	FLY	4389
365	参	PARTICIPATE	2563
		VISIT A HOLY PLACE	
366	可	-ABLE	3687
		APPROVE	
367	態	STATE	3529
368	営	MANAGE	3216
		BARRACKS	
369	府	URBAN PREFECTURE	3824
370	突	DASH	2772
		THRUST	
371	巻	ROLL UP	3273
		VOLUME	
372	容	APPEARANCE	2832
		CONTAIN	
373	姿	FIGURE	3264
374	育	RAISE	2544
375	之	POSSESSIVE PARTICLE	4228
376	介	MEDIATE	2463
377	建	BUILD	3834
378	南	SOUTH	2584
379	構	CONSTRUCT	1325
		MIND	
380	認	RECOGNIZE	1948
381	位	RANK	0069
		POSITION	
382	達	ATTAIN	3893
383	転	TURN	1872
384	左	LEFT	3692
385	皇	EMPEROR	3175
386	宮	ROYAL PALACE	2828
		SHINTO SHRINE	
387	守	PROTECT	2697
388	満	FULL	0739
389	消	EXTINGUISH	0531
		SPEND	
390	任	OFFICE	0057
		LEAVE TO	
391	医	MEDICINE	3715
		DOCTOR	
392	蔵	STORE	2995
393	止	STOP	3659
394	造	MAKE	3856
395	居	RESIDE	3822
396	離	SEPARATE	2364
397	根	ROOT	1167
398	予	IN ADVANCE	2477
399	路	ROAD	1936
400	字	CHARACTER	2696
401	座	SEAT	3868
		SIT	
402	工	MANUFACTURE	4190
		CONSTRUCTION	
403	寺	BUDDHIST TEMPLE	2687
404	基	BASE	3312
405	客	VISITOR	2798
		CUSTOMER	
406	急	URGENT	2595
		HURRY	
		SUDDEN	
407	船	SHIP	1700
408	図	DRAWING	3809
409	追	CHASE	3840
410	隊	PARTY	0762
411	査	LOOK INTO	3092

412	背	BACK	3182
413	観	VIEW	2359
414	誰	WHO	1986
415	黒	BLACK	3406
416	素	ELEMENT	3108
		PLAIN	
417	息	BREATH	3278
418	価	PRICE	0095
		VALUE	
419	将	GENERAL OFFICER	0551
420	伊	PHONETIC [i]	0052
		ITALY	
421	改	REFORM	0287
422	県	PREFECTURE	3269
423	撃	STRIKE	3552
424	失	LOSE	4325
		SLIP	
425	泉	SPRING	3176
426	老	OLD	3963
427	良	GOOD	4373
428	示	SHOW	2435
429	振	SWING	0515
430	号	NUMBER	2675
		DESIGNATION	
		SIGN	
431	像	IMAGE	0187
432	職	EMPLOYMENT	1803
433	王	KING	4247
434	識	DISCRIMINATE	2070
		KNOWLEDGE	
435	警	GUARD AGAINST	3595
		WARN	
436	花	FLOWER	2740
437	優	SUPERIOR	0200
		ACTOR	
438	投	THROW	0300
		SEND IN	
439	英	DISTINGUISHED	2782
		ENGLAND	
440	細	SLENDER	1689
		MINUTE	
441	局	BUREAU	3800
		LIMITED PART	
442	難	DIFFICULT	2310
		DISASTER	
443	種	VARIETY	1560
		SEED	
444	証	PROVE	1899
		CERTIFICATE	
445	走	RUN	2720
446	念	THOUGHTS	2554
447	寄	CONTRIBUTE	2856
		DRAW NEAR	
448	商	TRADE	2623
449	青	BLUE	3084
		GREEN	
450	谷	VALLEY	2536
451	害	HARM	2826
452	奥	INNER PART	3503
453	派	SECT	0456
		DISPATCH	
454	僕	I	0185
		MANSERVANT	
455	佐	ASSIST	0076
		FIELD OFFICER	
456	頼	RELY ON	2041
		ASK	
457	横	SIDEWAYS	1350
458	友	FRIEND	3670
459	再	ANOTHER TIME	4332
460	増	INCREASE	0836
461	紀	ERA	1628
462	統	UNITE	1710
		INTERCONNECTED SYSTEM	
463	答	ANSWER	3322
464	差	DIFFERENCE	4104
465	火	FIRE	4273
466	苦	SUFFERING	2789
		BITTER	
467	器	VESSEL	3367
		INSTRUMENT	
468	収	TAKE IN	0031
469	段	STEP	1471
470	異	DIFFERENT	3195
471	血	BLOOD	4339
472	護	PROTECT	2079
473	紙	PAPER	1654
474	俺	I	0124
475	歌	SONG	2296
476	渡	CROSS	0746
477	与	GIVE	4229
478	注	POUR	0383
		CONCENTRATE	
479	条	ARTICLE	2726
480	演	PERFORM	0855
481	算	CALCULATE	3351
482	赤	RED	2719
483	備	PROVIDE	0165
484	独	ALONE	0471
		GERMANY	
485	象	PHENOMENON	2647
		ELEPHANT	
486	清	CLEAR	0635
487	技	SKILL	0292
488	州	STATE	0064
489	申	REPORT	4319
		SPEAK HUMBLY	
490	例	EXAMPLE	0099
491	働	WORK	0172
492	景	SCENE	3118

493	領	TERRITORY	1567
494	春	SPRING	3184
495	抜	PULL OUT	0290
		STAND OUT	
496	遠	DISTANT	3906
497	橋	BRIDGE	1367
498	源	SOURCE	0806
499	芸	ART	2738
500	影	SHADOW	2381
501	型	TYPE	3266
502	絶	BREAK OFF	1711
		COME TO AN END	
503	館	PUBLIC BUILDING	2196
504	眼	EYE	1504
505	香	SWEET SMELL	3177
506	負	BEAR	2594
		LOSE	
507	福	FORTUNE	1303
508	企	PROJECT	2513
509	旅	TRAVEL	1153
510	球	BALL	1219
511	酒	ALCOHOLIC DRINK	0532
512	君	RULER	3974
		FAMILIAR TITLE	
		YOU	
513	験	TEST	2306
514	量	QUANTITY	3119
515	察	INSPECT	2961
		GUESS	
516	写	COPY	2493
517	望	HOPE	3408
		LOOK AFAR	
518	久	OF LONG DURATION	4191
519	婚	MARRY	0566
520	単	SINGLE	2805
521	押	PUSH	0371
522	割	DIVIDE	2284
523	限	LIMIT	0475
524	戻	RETURN	2441
525	科	SUBJECT OF STUDY	1463
526	求	SEEK	4365
527	津	HARBOR	0466
528	案	PROPOSAL	2824
529	談	TALK	1975
530	降	DESCEND	0548
531	妻	WIFE	3166
532	岡	HILL	3719
533	境	BOUNDARY	0835
		SITUATION	
534	熱	HEAT	3555
		HOT	
535	策	SCHEME	3320
		MEASURE	
536	浮	FLOAT	0522
537	階	FLOOR	0761
		RANK	
538	等	EQUAL	3321
		CLASS	
539	末	LAST PART	4317
540	宗	RELIGIOUS SECT	2769
541	区	DISTRICT	3681
		WARD	
542	波	WAVE	0388
543	提	PRESENT	0720
544	去	GO AWAY	2678
545	幸	GOOD FORTUNE	2755
		HAPPINESS	
546	研	GRIND	1456
		RESEARCH	
547	移	SHIFT	1508
548	域	BOUNDED AREA	0559
549	飲	DRINK	2127
550	肉	FLESH	3966
551	草	GRASS	2813
552	周	PERIPHERY	3720
553	昭	LUMINOUS	1107
554	越	GO BEYOND	4108
555	服	CLOTHES	1090
		SUBMIT	
556	接	CONTACT	0607
557	鉄	IRON	2147
558	密	CLOSE	2857
		SECRET	
559	司	OFFICIATE	3648
560	登	CLIMB	3208
561	頃	TIME	0163
		ABOUT	
562	銀	SILVER	2156
563	類	KIND	2275
564	検	EXAMINE	1241
565	未	NOT YET	4318
566	材	TIMBER	1031
		MATERIAL	
567	個	INDIVIDUAL	0132
		GENERAL COUNTER	
568	康	HEALTHY	3877
569	沢	MARSH	0313
570	協	COOPERATE	0103
571	茶	TEA	2808
572	各	EACH	2692
573	究	STUDY EXHAUSTIVELY	2729
574	帯	BELT	3191
		WEAR	
575	規	REGULATION	1231
576	秀	EXCELLENT	3152
577	歴	PERSONAL HISTORY	3748
578	編	COMPILE	1755
		KNIT	
579	興	RISE TO PROSPERITY	3622
		AMUSEMENT	

580	裏	REAR	2652
581	精	REFINE	1729
		ESSENCE	
		SPIRIT	
582	洋	OCEAN	0468
		WESTERN	
583	率	RATE	2625
		LEAD	
584	抱	HUG	0363
585	比	COMPARE	0029
586	坂	SLOPE	0275
587	評	COMMENT	1895
588	装	DRESS	3327
		FIT OUT	
589	監	OVERSEE	3535
590	崎	PROMONTORY	0569
591	省	MINISTRY	3100
		SAVE	
		INTROSPECT	
592	鮮	FRESH	2355
		VIVID	
593	税	TAX	1525
594	激	VIOLENT	0955
595	徳	VIRTUE	0842
596	挙	NOMINATE	3106
		NOTEWORTHY ACT	
		RAISE	
597	志	AMBITION	2725
598	労	LABOR	3155
599	競	COMPETE	2322
600	処	DEAL WITH	3764
601	退	RETREAT	3838
602	費	EXPENSE	3221
603	非	IS NOT	1101
604	囲	ENCLOSE	3807
605	喜	HAPPY	2889
606	辺	VICINITY	3761
		BORDERLAND	
607	敷	LAY	2345
608	系	SYSTEM	2443
		LINEAGE	
609	河	RIVER	0394
610	織	WEAVE	1801
611	製	MANUFACTURE	3478
612	娘	DAUGHTER	0488
		GIRL	
613	端	END	1564
614	逃	ESCAPE	3839
615	探	PROBE	0613
		SEARCH	
616	極	EXTREME	1243
		POLE	
617	遺	LEAVE BEHIND	3928
618	防	PREVENT	0320
619	低	LOW	0082
620	犯	OFFENSE	0229
621	薬	DRUG	3011
622	園	GARDEN	3914
623	疑	DOUBT	1970
624	林	FOREST	1071
625	導	GUIDE	3587
626	緒	OUTSET	1742
627	静	QUIET	2164
628	具	IMPLEMENT	3159
629	席	SEAT	3865
630	房	CHAMBER	2445
631	速	QUICK	3851
632	街	CITY QUARTER	0702
633	舞	DANCE	2666
634	宿	LODGE	2858
635	森	THICK WOODS	3123
636	程	EXTENT	1524
		ESTABLISHED FORM	
637	丸	ROUND	4225
638	胸	CHEST	1187
639	陸	LAND	0659
640	倒	TOPPLE	0139
641	寝	GO TO SLEEP	2925
642	宅	DWELLING HOUSE	2698
643	兄	OLDER BROTHER	2676
644	療	TREAT	4078
645	絵	PICTURE	1704
646	諸	VARIOUS	1984
647	尾	TAIL	3799
648	株	STOCK	1172
649	破	BREAK	1478
650	秋	AUTUMN	1464
651	堂	HALL	3202
652	従	FOLLOW	0498
653	庭	COURT	3866
		GARDEN	
654	管	PIPE	3349
		EXERCISE CONTROL	
655	婦	ADULT WOMAN	0565
656	仲	INTERMEDIARY	0047
		PERSONAL RELATIONS	
657	革	LEATHER	3099
		REFORM	
658	余	REMAINING	2535
		EXCESS	
659	敵	ENEMY	2340
660	展	UNFOLD	3862
		DISPLAY	
661	訪	VISIT	1860
662	担	BEAR ON SHOULDER	0376
		UNDERTAKE	
663	冷	COLD	0088
664	効	EFFECT	1617
665	暮	DUSK	2971
		LIVE	

666	腹	BELLY	1308
667	賞	PRIZE	3237
668	危	DANGEROUS	3965
669	毎	EVERY	2527
670	星	STAR	3089
671	許	PERMIT	1862
672	復	RETURN TO	0701
673	似	RESEMBLE	0071
674	片	FRAGMENT	4272
		ONE OF TWO	
675	並	LINE UP	2793
676	底	BOTTOM	3827
677	険	DANGER	0658
		STEEP	
678	描	DEPICT	0591
679	週	WEEK	3874
680	修	CULTIVATE	0138
		REPAIR	
681	財	WEALTH	1849
682	遊	PLAY	3896
683	温	WARM	0740
684	軽	LIGHT	1909
685	録	RECORD	2186
686	腰	WAIST	1311
687	我	SELF	4362
688	著	AUTHOR	2869
		CONSPICUOUS	
689	乱	DISORDERED	1611
690	章	CHAPTER	2624
		BADGE	
691	雑	MISCELLANEOUS	1752
		MIXED	
692	殿	PALACE	2247
		FORMAL HONORIFIC TITLE	
693	載	LOAD	4091
		PUT IN PRINT	
694	響	REVERBERATE	3573
695	秘	SECRET	1490
696	布	CLOTH	3691
		SPREAD	
697	恐	FEAR	3283
698	攻	ATTACK	0286
699	値	VALUE	0123
700	角	ANGLE	2541
		HORN	
701	暗	DARK	1273
702	習	LEARN	3306
		CUSTOM	
703	健	ROBUST	0152
704	仏	BUDDHA	0020
		FRANCE	
705	積	ACCUMULATE	1579
706	裁	CUT OUT	4090
		JUDGE	
707	試	TRY	1925
708	夏	SUMMER	2619
709	隠	HIDE	0873
710	永	ETERNAL	2436
711	誌	MAGAZINE	1950
712	夢	DREAM	2939
713	環	RING	1395
		SURROUND	
714	援	AID	0715
715	故	OLD	1466
		THE LATE	
716	幕	CURTAIN	2937
		SHOGUNATE	
717	減	DECREASE	0733
718	略	ABRIDGED	1501
		STRATEGY	
719	準	STANDARD	3541
		QUASI-	
720	委	COMMIT	3160
721	痛	PAIN	4071
722	富	RICH	2892
723	督	SUPERVISE	3471
		COMMANDER	
724	倉	STOREHOUSE	2607
725	弟	YOUNGER BROTHER	2537
726	刻	ENGRAVE	1619
		POINT OF TIME	
727	鳴	CRY	0831
		SOUND	
728	令	COMMAND	2489
729	刊	PUBLISH	0221
730	施	CARRY OUT	1103
731	焼	BURN	1256
732	欲	DESIRE	1867
733	途	WAY	3853
734	曲	MUSICAL COMPOSITION	4340
		CURVE	
735	耳	EAR	4329
736	完	COMPLETE	2727
737	里	COUNTRYSIDE	4356
		LEAGUE	
738	願	WISH	2320
		ASK A FAVOR	
739	罪	CRIME	3224
740	圧	PRESSURE	3688
741	額	AMOUNT	2273
742	印	MARK	1023
		SEAL	
743	嫌	DISLIKE	0781
744	池	POND	0253
745	陽	SUN	0764
746	臣	RETAINER	3806
747	庫	STORAGE CHAMBER	3864
748	継	SUCCEED	1720
749	亡	DECEASE	4210
750	散	SCATTER	2137

751	障	HINDRANCE	0875
752	貴	NOBLE	3220
		YOUR HONORABLE	
753	農	FARMING	3345
754	掛	SET	0596
		HANG	
755	板	BOARD	1067
		PLATE	
756	昨	YESTERDAY	1106
		LAST	
757	整	PUT IN ORDER	3562
758	怒	GET ANGRY	3180
759	衆	MULTITUDE	3325
760	恋	LOVE	2602
761	羽	FEATHER	0265
		WING	
762	及	REACH TO	4192
763	専	EXCLUSIVE	3272
764	逆	REVERSE	3835
765	腕	ARM	1269
766	盛	PROSPEROUS	3314
767	玄	PROFOUND	2485
768	留	KEEP	3189
		STAY	
769	礼	ETIQUETTE	1012
		RITE	
770	短	SHORT	1515
771	普	WIDESPREAD	2919
772	岩	ROCK	2778
773	竹	BAMBOO	0267
774	児	CHILD	3153
775	毛	HAIR	4264
776	列	ROW	1018
777	恵	FAVOR	3293
778	版	PRINTING PLATE	1082
		PUBLISHING	
779	授	CONFER	0595
780	雪	SNOW	3431
781	弾	PROJECTILE	0697
		SPRING BACK	
782	宇	UNIVERSE	2699
783	養	FOSTER	2998
784	驚	SURPRISE	3597
785	払	CLEAR AWAY	0225
		PAY	
786	奈	PHONETIC [na]	2759
787	推	INFER	0612
788	給	SUPPLY	1708
		PAY	
789	況	CONDITIONS	0395
790	樹	STANDING TREE	1363
791	為	DO	4395
		SAKE	
792	阿	PHONETIC [a]	0408
793	敗	BE DEFEATED	1868
794	雄	MALE	1271
		HEROIC	
795	捕	CATCH	0514
796	刀	SWORD	3642
797	被	BE SUBJECTED TO	1495
798	雨	RAIN	4378
799	岸	SHORE	2777
800	超	SURPASS	4107
801	豊	PLENTIFUL	3344
802	忘	FORGET	2529
803	含	CONTAIN	2534
804	弁	SPEAK ELOQUENTLY	2497
		VALVE	
805	植	PLANT	1247
806	妙	MARVELOUS	0280
807	模	PATTERN	1326
808	補	SUPPLEMENT	1529
809	抗	RESIST	0296
810	級	GRADE	1630
811	休	REST	0056
812	暴	VIOLENT	3138
813	課	SECTION	1980
		LESSON	
814	瞬	INSTANT	1594
815	称	APPELLATION	1491
816	跡	TRACE	1937
817	触	TOUCH	1914
818	玉	GEM	4289
819	晴	FINE WEATHER	1234
820	華	MAGNIFICENT	2841
		CHINA	
821	因	CAUSE	3792
822	震	QUAKE	3481
823	折	BREAK OFF	0297
		FOLD	
824	億	HUNDRED MILLION	0192
825	肩	SHOULDER	2446
826	劇	DRAMA	2399
827	迎	WELCOME	3796
828	傷	WOUND	0179
829	悲	SAD	3448
830	闘	FIGHT	4136
831	港	PORT	0737
832	責	RESPONSIBILITY	3115
		BLAME	
833	筋	MUSCLE	3319
		THREADLIKE STRUCTURE	
834	訳	TRANSLATE	1865
		SENSE	
835	除	RID OF	0546
836	射	SHOOT	1850
837	善	GOOD	2921
838	刺	STAB	1625
839	黙	SILENT	3554
840	柄	CHARACTER	1111

		HANDLE	
841	刑	PENALTY	1024
842	節	JOINT	3336
		SEASON	
843	述	STATE	3816
844	輪	WHEEL	1999
		RING	
845	困	BE IN TROUBLE	3808
846	脱	REMOVE	1225
		ESCAPE FROM	
847	浅	SHALLOW	0464
848	鳥	BIRD	4105
849	厳	SEVERE	4079
850	純	PURE	1649
851	犬	DOG	4275
852	博	EXTENSIVE	0170
		DOCTOR	
853	陣	BATTLE FORMATION	0545
		CAMP	
854	薄	THIN	3004
855	阪	OSAKA	0321
856	閉	CLOSE	4116
857	吸	SUCK	0234
		BREATHE IN	
858	奇	UNUSUAL	2756
859	忠	LOYALTY	3087
860	韓	SOUTH KOREA	2218
861	夕	EVENING	4195
862	固	SOLID	3830
		FIRM	
863	染	DYE	3181
864	巨	HUGE	3773
865	講	LECTURE	2046
866	微	SLIGHT	0788
867	髪	HAIR	3528
868	標	MARK	1347
869	束	TIE UP	4369
		BUNDLE	
870	縁	RELATION	1754
		EDGE	
871	眠	SLEEP	1474
872	壁	WALL	3601
873	午	NOON	2478
874	般	SORT	1670
875	湯	HOT WATER	0747
876	訊	INQUIRE	1842
877	捨	DISCARD	0608
878	駆	DRIVE	2293
879	衣	GARMENT	2506
880	替	REPLACE	3457
881	麻	HEMP	3878
		BECOME NUMB	
882	甲	SHELL	4293
		FIRST	
883	央	CENTER	4322
884	藩	FEUDAL DOMAIN	3022
885	骨	BONE	3288
886	彦	MALE NAME ELEMENT	4085
887	齢	AGE	2390
888	易	EASY	3064
		EXCHANGE	
889	照	ILLUMINATE	3506
890	云	SUCH	2430
891	迫	PRESS	3815
892	層	STRATUM	3920
893	踏	TREAD	1997
894	窓	WINDOW	2859
895	弱	WEAK	1499
896	討	STUDY	1846
		SUPPRESS BY ARMED FORCE	
897	聖	HOLY	3509
		SAINT	
898	典	STANDARD WORK	3253
		CANON	
899	剣	SWORD	2104
900	症	PATHOLOGICAL CONDITION	4065
901	祖	ANCESTOR	1145
902	築	CONSTRUCT	3370
903	納	PAY	1652
		ACCEPT	
		PUT AWAY	
904	勤	SERVICE	2287
905	昔	FORMER TIMES	3086
906	脳	BRAIN	1227
907	便	CONVENIENT	0105
		POST	
		EXCRETA	
908	適	SUITABLE	3918
909	弥	PHONETIC [mi]	0344
910	融	FUSE	2303
911	航	NAVIGATE	1671
912	快	PLEASANT	0289
913	浜	BEACH	0523
914	郷	HOMETOWN	0664
915	翌	THE FOLLOWING	3307
916	旧	FORMER	0014
917	吹	BLOW	0272
918	惑	BEWILDERED	3461
919	柳	WILLOW	1115
920	拠	GROUNDS	0369
921	奉	DEDICATE	3167
922	筆	BRUSH	3317
		WRITING	
923	壊	BREAK DOWN	0934
924	換	EXCHANGE	0716
925	益	BENEFIT	2849
		PROFIT	
926	群	GROUP	1942
927	句	PHRASE	3685
		HAIKU	

928	属	BELONG TO	3901
929	候	SEASON	0133
		SEASONAL WEATHER	
930	爆	EXPLODE	1415
931	功	MERIT	0218
932	捜	LOOK FOR	0516
933	帝	EMPEROR	2573
934	賀	CONGRATULATE	3212
935	魚	FISH	2636
936	堀	DITCH	0561
937	油	OIL	0400
938	怖	FEARFUL	0353
939	叫	SHOUT	0233
940	伸	STRETCH	0079
941	創	CREATE	2283
942	辞	WORD	1726
		RESIGN	
943	泣	CRY	0396
944	憶	SPECULATE	0944
		REMEMBER	
945	幹	TRUNK	2152
946	否	SAY NO	3058
		OR NOT	
947	露	DEW	3495
		EXPOSE	
948	矢	ARROW	2502
949	承	AGREE TO	0016
950	雲	CLOUD	3447
951	握	GRASP	0714
952	練	TRAIN	1738
953	儀	CEREMONY	0191
954	紹	INTRODUCE	1691
955	聴	LISTEN	1796
956	包	WRAP	3684
		ENCOMPASS	
957	庁	GOVERNMENT AGENCY	3768
958	測	MEASURE	0744
		CONJECTURE	
959	占	OCCUPY	2496
		DIVINE	
960	混	MIX	0631
961	倍	TIMES	0122
		DOUBLE	
962	乳	MILK	1823
963	襲	RAID	3633
964	借	BORROW	0137
965	徴	LEVY	0841
		SYMPTOM	
966	荒	WILD	2810
967	詰	REPRIMAND	1920
		STUFF	
968	飯	COOKED RICE	2126
		MEAL	
969	栄	FLOURISH	3183
		GLORY	
970	床	BED	3805
		FLOOR	
971	丁	TOWN SUBSECTION	4155
		MISCELLANEOUS COUNTER	
972	憲	CONSTITUTION	3001
973	則	RULE	1831
974	禁	PROHIBIT	3469
975	順	ORDER	0018
		OBEY	
976	駅	STATION	2292
977	閣	TALL MAGNIFICENT BUILDING	4128
		CABINET	
978	昼	DAYTIME	3841
979	枚	COUNTER FOR FLAT THINGS	1069
980	救	SAVE	1891
981	厚	THICK	3726
		KIND	
982	皮	SKIN	3771
983	陰	SHADE	0657
984	繰	REEL	1806
		SHIFT ONWARD	
985	那	PHONETIC [na]	1047
986	冬	WINTER	2679
987	輸	TRANSPORT	2026
988	操	MANIPULATE	0948
989	智	WISDOM	3458
990	騒	CLAMOR	2308
991	己	ONESELF	4188
992	濃	THICK	0956
993	魔	DEMON	3953
994	遅	SLOW	3887
		LATE	
995	簡	SIMPLE	3380
996	撮	PHOTOGRAPH	0910
997	携	CARRY IN HAND	0796
998	姉	OLDER SISTER	0336
999	隣	NEIGHBOR	0961
1000	孫	GRANDCHILD	0492

APPENDIX 11

JŌYŌ KANJI LIST

常用漢字表

The Japanese government has implemented various language reforms aimed at simplifying the Japanese writing system. The most important of these is the **Jōyō Kanji** list, an official list of 2136 characters widely used in general publications and education. Of these, the 1006 **Education Kanji** must be learned in the first six years of compulsory schooling (see **§2.5 Language Reforms** on p. 1776 for details).

This appendix lists the Jōyō Kanji classified by school grade for speedy reference. This enables the student to know the relative importance of each character, and can help the developer of teaching materials compile graded lessons (see **§4.1 Character Importance** on p. 32a).

The characters are grouped under seven sections. The first six list the 1006 Education Kanji classified by school grade; the seventh lists the remaining 1130 general-use characters. The number of characters for each section is indicated under the section heading. Within each section the characters are listed in *a-i-u-e-o* order by their principal readings, and further grouped by total stroke-count. The numerals to the right of the character column are the **entry numbers.**

GRADE 1

(80)

イ	一	4148
ウ	右	3693
	雨	4378
エ	円	3673
オ	王	4247
	音	2570
カ	下	4186
	火	4273
	花	2740
ガ	学	3162
キ	気	3960
	九	4176
	休	0056
	金	2552
ギ	玉	4289
ク	空	2767
ケ	犬	4275
	見	3151
ゲ	月	3674
コ	口	4189
	校	1166
ゴ	五	4244
サ	左	3692
	三	2423
	山	3658
シ	子	4196
	四	3778
	糸	2703
	七	4169
	車	4367
	手	4267
	出	4310
	小	0007
	森	3123
ジ	字	2696
	耳	4329
	十	4172
	女	4226
	上	4212
	人	4175
ス	水	0010
セ	正	4296
	生	4309
	青	3084
	夕	4195
	石	3689
	赤	2719
	川	0006
	千	4219
	先	3046
ソ	早	3042
	草	2813
	足	2714
	村	1029
ダ	大	4224
	男	3147
チ	竹	0267
	中	4262
	虫	4343
	町	1430
テ	天	4250
デ	田	3775
ド	土	4211
ニ	二	2421
	日	3759
	入	4177
ネ	年	2528
ハ	白	4305
	八	3644
バ	貝	3150
ヒ	百	2519
ブ	文	2458
ホ	本	4314
ボ	木	4261
メ	名	2693
モ	目	3777
リ	立	2486
	力	4178
	林	1071
ロ	六	2461

GRADE 2

(160)

イ	引	0207
ウ	羽	0265
	雲	3447
エ	遠	3906
	園	3914
カ	何	0073
	科	1463
	夏	2619
	家	2827
	歌	2296
	会	2512
	回	3793
	海	0459
	絵	1704
	角	2541
	活	0460
	間	4122
ガ	画	3723
	外	0215
	楽	3505
	丸	4225
	岩	2778
	顔	2277
キ	汽	0309
	帰	0148
	記	1843
	弓	4193
	京	2546
	強	0574
	教	1887
	近	3798
ギ	牛	4263
	魚	2636
ケ	兄	2676
	形	1050
	計	1828
ゲ	元	2428
	言	2440
	原	3733
コ	戸	2429
	古	2495
	工	4190
	公	2468
	広	3769
	行	0246
	交	2508
	光	3043
	考	3962
	高	2601
	黄	3116
	谷	2536
	国	3831
	黒	3406
	今	2464
ゴ	午	2478
	後	0431
	語	1944
	合	2511
サ	才	4218
	細	1689
	作	0077
	算	3351
シ	止	3659
	市	2487
	矢	2502
	姉	0336
	思	3173
	紙	1654
	室	2802
	社	1042
	首	2818
	秋	1464
	週	3874
	春	3184
	書	3292
	少	4278
	色	2522
	食	2578
	心	0011
	新	2239
	親	2264
ジ	寺	2687
	自	4338
	時	1155
	弱	1499
	場	0678
ス	数	2245
ズ	図	3809
セ	西	4333
	声	2724
	星	3089
	晴	1234

	切	0030
	雪	3431
	船	1700
	線	1760
ゼ	前	2819
ソ	組	1693
	走	2720
タ	多	2694
	太	2673
	体	0080
ダ	台	2498
チ	地	0236
	池	0253
	知	1446
	茶	2808
	昼	3841
	長	3163
	鳥	4105
	朝	2130
	直	3649
ツ	通	3855
テ	弟	2537
	店	3828
	点	2587
デ	電	3465
ト	刀	3642
	冬	2679
	当	2701
	東	4385
	答	3322
	頭	2019
ド	同	3707
	道	3888
	読	1943
ナ	内	4277
	南	2584
ニ	肉	3966
ハ	半	4313
バ	馬	4086
	売	2722
	買	3211
	麦	3061
	番	3416
フ	父	2467
	風	3730
ブ	分	2466
	聞	4127
ベ	米	4342
ホ	歩	3071
	方	2459
	北	0230
ボ	母	4287
マ	毎	2527
	妹	0333
	万	3653
メ	明	1060
	鳴	0831
モ	毛	4264
	門	1100
ヤ	夜	2550
	野	1877
ユ	友	3670
ヨ	用	3694
	曜	1402
ラ	来	4366
リ	里	4356
	理	1220
ワ	話	1928

GRADE 3
(200)

ア	悪	3413
	安	2695
	暗	1273
イ	医	3715
	委	3160
	意	2650
	育	2544
	院	0544
	員	2822
	飲	2127
ウ	運	3894
エ	泳	0385
	駅	2292
オ	横	1350
	屋	3842
	温	0740
カ	化	0022
	荷	2840
	界	3172
	階	0761
	開	4121
	寒	2894
	漢	0808
	感	3514
	館	2196
ガ	岸	2777
キ	起	4099
	期	2139
	客	2798
	究	2729
	級	1630
	急	2595
	宮	2828
	球	1219
	去	2678
	橋	1367
	曲	4340
	局	3800
ギ	業	3227
	銀	2156
ク	区	3681
	苦	2789
	君	3974
グ	具	3159
ケ	係	0108
	軽	1909
	血	4339
	決	0308
	研	1456
	県	3269
コ	庫	3864
	湖	0736
	向	3790
	幸	2755
	港	0737
	根	1167
ゴ	号	2675
サ	祭	3311
シ	仕	0037
	死	4334
	使	0100
	始	0335
	指	0452
	歯	3124
	詩	1924
	式	3785
	写	2493
	者	3980
	主	2437
	守	2697
	取	1613
	酒	0532
	州	0064
	拾	0454
	終	1692
	習	3306
	集	3445
	宿	2858
	所	1056
	暑	3121
	昭	1107
	消	0531
	商	2623
	章	2624
	勝	1268
	植	1247
	申	4319
	身	4368
	神	1143
	真	2616
	深	0636
	進	3873
ジ	次	0058
	事	4384
	持	0447
	実	2765
	受	3076
	住	0072
	重	4390
	助	1440
	乗	4393
セ	世	4308
	整	3562
	昔	3086
ゼ	全	2514
ソ	相	1120
	送	3837
	想	3507
	箱	3362
	息	3278
	速	3851
ゾ	族	1195
タ	他	0039
	対	1025
	待	0434
	炭	2806
	短	1515
ダ	打	0224
	代	0034
	第	3298
	題	4139
	談	1975
チ	着	4110
	注	0383
	柱	1109
	丁	4155
	帳	0572
	調	1973
ツ	追	3840
テ	定	2770
	庭	3866
	笛	3303
	鉄	2147
	転	1872
ト	都	2120
	投	0300
	豆	2442
	島	4103
	湯	0747
	登	3208
	等	3321
ド	度	3844
	動	2232
	童	2639
ノ	農	3345
ハ	波	0388
	配	1853
	畑	1131
	発	3174
	反	3663
	坂	0275
	板	1067
バ	倍	0122
ヒ	皮	3771
	悲	3448
	筆	3317
	氷	0043
	表	3083
	品	2795
ビ	美	2817
	鼻	3357
	秒	1462
	病	4062
フ	負	2594
	服	1090
	福	1303
ブ	部	2111
	物	1084
ヘ	平	4291
	返	3797
ベ	皿	4286
	勉	4113
ホ	放	1058
ミ	味	0325
メ	命	2553
	面	2590
モ	問	4117
ヤ	役	0288
	薬	3011
ユ	由	4311
	油	0400
	有	3703
	遊	3896
ヨ	予	2477
	羊	2708
	洋	0468
	陽	0764
	葉	2912
	様	1332
ラ	落	2907
リ	流	0529
	旅	1153
	両	4331
	緑	1741
レ	礼	1012
	列	1018
	練	1738
ロ	路	1936
ワ	和	1450

GRADE 4
(200)

ア	愛	3133
	案	2824
イ	以	0045
	衣	2506
	位	0069
	囲	3807
	胃	3171
	印	1023
エ	英	2782
	栄	3183
	塩	0774
オ	央	4322
	億	0192
カ	加	0042
	果	4377
	貨	3113
	課	1980
	改	0287
	械	1203

	各	2692
	覚	3217
	完	2727
	官	2766
	管	3349
	関	4129
	観	2359
ガ	芽	2784
	害	2826
	街	0702
	願	2320
キ	希	2543
	季	3161
	紀	1628
	喜	2889
	旗	1321
	器	3367
	機	1365
	求	4365
	泣	0396
	救	1891
	給	1708
	挙	3106
	共	3045
	協	0103
	鏡	2219
	競	2322
	極	1243
ギ	議	2078
	漁	0856
ク	訓	1844
グ	軍	2582
	郡	1858
ケ	径	0347
	型	3266
	景	3118
	欠	2481
	結	1706
	建	3834
	健	0152
	験	2306
ゲ	芸	2738
コ	固	3830
	功	0218
	好	0240
	候	0133
	航	1671
	康	3877
	告	3062

サ	差	4104
	菜	2880
	最	3120
	昨	1106
	札	1011
	刷	1623
	殺	1677
	察	2961
	参	2563
	産	4089
	散	2137
ザ	材	1031
	残	1179
シ	士	4213
	氏	3669
	司	3648
	史	4324
	試	1925
	失	4325
	借	0137
	種	1560
	周	3720
	祝	1144
	初	1433
	松	1075
	笑	3275
	唱	0555
	焼	1256
	象	2647
	照	3506
	賞	3237
	臣	3806
	信	0115
ジ	児	3153
	治	0393
	辞	1726
	順	0018
セ	成	4352
	省	3100
	清	0635
	静	2164
	席	3865
	積	1579
	折	0297
	節	3336
	説	1949
	浅	0464
	戦	2242
	選	3931

ゼ	然	3456
ソ	争	2523
	倉	2607
	巣	2861
	束	4369
	側	0155
	卒	2549
	孫	0492
ゾ	続	1722
タ	帯	3191
	隊	0762
	達	3893
	単	2805
チ	置	3222
	仲	0047
	貯	1903
	兆	0264
	腸	1307
テ	低	0082
	底	3827
	停	0156
	的	1444
	典	3253
デ	伝	0048
ト	徒	0499
	灯	1019
	特	1181
	得	0577
ド	努	3154
	堂	3202
	働	0172
	毒	3082
ネ	熱	3555
	念	2554
ハ	敗	1868
	博	0170
	飯	2126
バ	梅	1159
ヒ	飛	4389
	費	3221
	必	0015
	票	3308
	標	1347
フ	不	4242
	夫	4271
	付	0035
	府	3824
	副	2230
	粉	1643

ヘ	兵	3158
	辺	3761
	変	2569
ベ	別	1434
	便	0105
ホ	包	3684
	法	0391
ボ	望	3408
	牧	1083
マ	末	4317
	満	0739
ミ	未	4318
	脈	1189
	民	3770
ム	無	2648
ヤ	約	1632
ユ	勇	2592
ヨ	要	3263
	養	2998
	浴	0533
リ	利	1431
	陸	0659
	良	4373
	料	1644
	量	3119
	輪	1999
ル	類	2275
レ	令	2489
	冷	0088
	例	0099
	歴	3748
	連	3849
ロ	老	3963
	労	3155
	録	2186

GRADE 5
(185)

ア	圧	3688
イ	移	1508
	因	3792
エ	永	2436
	営	3216
	衛	0938
	易	3064
	益	2849
	液	0622
	演	0855

オ	応	3804
	往	0348
	桜	1168
	恩	3289
カ	可	3687
	仮	0053
	価	0095
	河	0394
	過	3891
	快	0289
	解	1913
	格	1161
	確	1571
	刊	0221
	幹	2152
	慣	0843
ガ	賀	3212
	額	2273
	眼	1504
キ	規	1231
	寄	2856
	基	3312
	久	4191
	旧	0014
	居	3822
	許	1862
	境	0835
	均	0276
	禁	3469
ギ	技	0292
	義	2948
	逆	3835
ク	句	3685
グ	群	1942
ケ	経	1687
	潔	0920
	件	0054
	券	3256
	険	0658
	検	1241
ゲ	限	0475
	現	1218
	減	0733
コ	故	1466
	個	0132
	効	1617
	厚	3726
	耕	1659
	鉱	2145

	構	1325
	興	3622
	講	2046
	混	0631
ゴ	護	2079
サ	査	3092
	再	4332
	災	2734
	妻	3166
	採	0606
	際	0874
	酸	1968
	賛	3484
ザ	在	3704
	財	1849
	罪	3224
	雑	1752
シ	支	2473
	志	2725
	枝	1073
	師	1680
	飼	2149
	資	3342
	識	2070
	質	3483
	舎	2555
	謝	2048
	修	0138
	承	0016
	招	0374
	証	1899
	織	1801
	職	1803
ジ	示	2435
	似	0071
	授	0595
	述	3816
	術	0575
	準	3541
	序	3803
	状	0322
	条	2726
	情	0583
	常	3203
セ	性	0357
	制	1624
	政	1468
	勢	3542
	精	1729

	製	3478
	責	3115
	績	1788
	接	0607
	設	1863
	銭	2159
ゼ	税	1525
	舌	2711
	絶	1711
ソ	祖	1145
	素	3108
	総	1743
	則	1831
	測	0744
	率	2625
	損	0801
ゾ	造	3856
	像	0187
	増	0836
	属	3901
タ	退	3838
	貸	3213
	態	3529
ダ	団	3791
	断	1885
チ	築	3370
	張	0573
テ	提	0720
	程	1524
	適	3918
	敵	2340
ト	統	1710
	徳	0842
ド	銅	2155
	導	3587
	独	0471
ニ	任	0057
ネ	燃	1375
ノ	能	1676
ハ	破	1478
	犯	0229
	判	1441
	版	1082
ヒ	比	0029
	肥	1091
	非	1101
	俵	0129
	評	1895
	貧	2631
ビ	備	0165
フ	布	3691
	婦	0565
	富	2892
	復	0701
	複	1565
ブ	武	3979
	仏	0020
ヘ	編	1755
ベ	弁	2497
ホ	保	0107
	報	2133
	豊	3344
ボ	墓	2930
	防	0320
	貿	3214
	暴	3138
ム	務	1505
	夢	2939
メ	迷	3836
	綿	1736
ユ	輸	2026
ヨ	余	2535
	預	1317
	容	2832
リ	略	1501
	留	3189
	領	1567

GRADE 6
(181)

イ	異	3195
	遺	3928
	域	0559
ウ	宇	2699
エ	映	1104
	沿	0386
	延	3812
カ	灰	3699
	届	3820
	拡	0366
	革	3099
	閣	4128
	割	2284
	干	4187
	巻	3273
	看	3992
	簡	3380
ガ	我	4362
キ	机	1014
	危	3965
	揮	0717
	貴	3220
	吸	0234
	供	0098
	胸	1187
	郷	0664
	勤	2287
	筋	3319
ギ	疑	1970
ケ	系	2443
	敬	2136
	警	3595
	穴	2682
	絹	1721
	権	1348
	憲	3001
ゲ	劇	2399
	激	0955
	源	0806
	厳	4079
コ	己	4188
	呼	0324
	后	3701
	孝	3973
	紅	1629
	皇	3175
	降	0548
	鋼	2183
	刻	1619
	穀	2294
	骨	3288
	困	3808
ゴ	誤	1945
サ	砂	1457
	済	0634
	裁	4090
	策	3320
	冊	4295
	蚕	3107
ザ	座	3868
シ	至	2707
	私	1432
	姿	3264
	視	1223
	詞	1897
	誌	1950
	射	1850
	捨	0608
	尺	4248
	株	1172
	収	0031
	宗	2769
	就	2129
	衆	3325
	縮	1790
	処	3764
	署	3223
	諸	1984
	将	0551
	傷	0179
	障	0875
	針	2099
ジ	磁	1554
	若	2785
	樹	1363
	従	0498
	縦	1783
	熟	3558
	純	1649
	除	0546
	城	0417
	蒸	2936
	仁	0021
ス	垂	4382
	推	0612
	寸	3652
セ	盛	3314
	誠	1922
	聖	3509
	洗	0465
	宣	2799
	泉	3176
	染	3181
	専	3272
ゼ	善	2921
ソ	奏	3185
	窓	2859
	創	2283
	装	3327
	層	3920
	操	0948
	存	3702
	尊	2920
ゾ	蔵	2995
	臓	1417
タ	宅	2698
	担	0376
	探	0613
	誕	1987
ダ	段	1471
	暖	1274
チ	値	0123
	宙	2761
	忠	3087
	著	2869
	庁	3768
	頂	0164
	潮	0916
	賃	3341
ツ	痛	4071
テ	展	3862
ト	討	1846
	党	3190
	糖	1777
ナ	難	2310
ニ	乳	1823
	認	1948
ノ	納	1652
	脳	1227
ハ	派	0456
	拝	0360
	肺	1147
	背	3182
	俳	0126
	班	1182
バ	晩	1232
ヒ	批	0294
	否	3058
	秘	1490
フ	腹	1308
	奮	3000
ヘ	並	2793
	陛	0543
	閉	4116
	片	4272
ホ	補	1529
	宝	2764
	訪	1860
ボ	暮	2971
	亡	4210
	忘	2529
	棒	1237
マ	枚	1069
	幕	2937
ミ	密	2857
メ	盟	3468
モ	模	1326
ヤ	訳	1865
ユ	郵	2121
	優	0200
ヨ	幼	0222
	欲	1867
	翌	3307
ラ	卵	1054
	乱	1611
	覧	3538
リ	裏	2652
	律	0433
	臨	2059
ロ	朗	1679
	論	1981

GENERAL
(1130)

ア	亜	4354
	哀	2568
	挨	0510
	曖	1383
	握	0714
	闇	4134
イ	依	0093
	為	4395
	威	4394
	畏	3170
	尉	2119
	萎	2872
	偉	0167
	椅	1239
	違	3907
	彙	2929
	維	1733
	慰	3557
	緯	1782
	壱	2723
	逸	3872
	姻	0421
	咽	0412
	陰	0657
	淫	0624
	隠	0873
	韻	2279
ウ	芋	2706

鬱 3625
エ 詠 1894
鋭 2171
影 2381
疫 4061
悦 0501
越 4108
謁 1976
閲 4132
宛 2762
炎 3075
垣 0416
怨 3179
俺 0124
宴 2825
媛 0688
援 0715
猿 0824
煙 1294
鉛 2143
縁 1754
艶 2403
オ 汚 0258
凹 4294
押 0371
旺 1061
殴 1099
欧 1098
翁 2611
奥 3503
憶 0944
臆 1397
乙 4145
穏 1578
カ 佳 0096
苛 2786
架 3178
華 2841
菓 2873
渦 0735
嫁 0780
暇 1275
禍 1304
靴 2235
寡 2957
箇 3348
稼 1572
鍋 2202
介 2463
戒 3972
怪 0354
拐 0365
悔 0435
皆 3093
掛 0596
塊 0775
楷 1282
潰 0919
壊 0934
懐 0942
諧 2008
核 1162
殻 1883
郭 2112
隔 0827
較 1939
獲 0959
嚇 0964
穫 1598
鶴 2326
括 0449
喝 0554
渇 0627
葛 2905
滑 0809
褐 1548
轄 2056
甘 4306
汗 0256
缶 2526
肝 1045
串 4364
冠 2583
陥 0547
乾 2113
勘 2231
貫 3112
患 3415
喚 0666
堪 0680
換 0716
棺 1240
款 2135
敢 2142
閑 4123
勧 2334
寛 2922
緩 1757
歓 2342
監 3535
憾 0943
還 3945
環 1395
韓 2218
艦 1817
鑑 2226
ガ 牙 4243
瓦 4288
雅 1532
餓 2176
刈 0032
劾 1618
涯 0623
崖 2862
慨 0790
該 1916
蓋 2933
概 1322
骸 2301
岳 3164
顎 2276
含 2534
玩 1085
頑 1315
キ 伎 0055
肌 1021
企 2513
岐 0285
忌 2735
祈 1086
奇 2756
軌 1832
姫 0489
既 1498
飢 2101
鬼 3291
崎 0569
亀 2637
埼 0560
棋 1242
幾 4403
棄 2651
毀 2246
輝 1775
畿 4408
騎 2307
菊 2875
吉 2691
喫 0668
詰 1920
却 1436
脚 1226
及 4192
丘 4307
朽 1015
臼 4341
糾 1631
嗅 0772
窮 2983
巨 3773
拒 0368
拠 0369
据 0602
虚 4017
距 1905
裾 1549
凶 3679
叫 0233
狂 0318
況 0395
享 2545
峡 0427
挟 0450
狭 0473
脅 2614
恭 3109
恐 3283
脇 1188
頬 2043
矯 1586
響 3573
驚 3597
巾 4217
斤 3667
菌 2876
琴 3455
僅 0176
緊 3517
錦 2181
謹 2045
襟 1599
ギ 宜 2763
偽 0149
欺 2138
儀 0191
戯 2351
擬 0969
犠 1394
虐 3989
御 0703
仰 0051
暁 1233
凝 0198
吟 0271
ク 駆 2293
駒 2298
屈 3821
堀 0561
掘 0601
窟 2923
勲 3560
薫 3005
グ 惧 0581
愚 3513
虞 4037
偶 0150
隅 0760
遇 3889
ケ 刑 1024
茎 2788
契 3267
恵 3293
頃 0163
掲 0597
渓 0628
蛍 3204
啓 3434
傾 0174
携 0796
継 1720
詣 1918
慶 3936
稽 1573
憬 0898
憩 3590
鶏 2221
傑 0175
肩 2446
倹 0130
軒 1851
剣 2104
兼 2850
拳 3295
堅 3502
圏 3904
嫌 0781
献 2240
遣 3908
賢 3518
謙 2044
鍵 2203
顕 2274
繭 3023
懸 3632
ゲ 迎 3796
鯨 2361
隙 0826
撃 3552
幻 0206
玄 2485
弦 0343
舷 1698
コ 虎 3981
股 1093
孤 0426
弧 0430
枯 1113
雇 2454
誇 1921
鼓 2241
錮 2182
顧 2394
孔 0205
勾 3660
巧 0219
尻 3766
甲 4293
江 0257
坑 0277
攻 0286
抗 0296
更 4355
岬 0340
拘 0367
肯 3072
岡 3719
侯 0109
恒 0438
洪 0461
虹 1637
郊 1638
荒 2810
香 3177
貢 2838

	桁	1165
	控	0600
	梗	1204
	項	0692
	慌	0707
	硬	1518
	絞	1707
	喉	0669
	溝	0810
	綱	1735
	酵	1966
	稿	1574
	衡	0939
	購	2053
	克	2540
	酷	1967
	乞	2457
	込	3762
	昆	3067
	恨	0439
	婚	0566
	紺	1688
	痕	4066
	魂	1346
	墾	3602
	懇	3606
ゴ	互	4245
	呉	3156
	娯	0487
	悟	0502
	碁	3346
	拷	0446
	剛	2107
	傲	0173
	豪	2657
	獄	0872
サ	佐	0076
	沙	0311
	唆	0480
	詐	1896
	鎖	2213
	采	3077
	砕	1458
	宰	2829
	栽	4087
	彩	2115
	斎	2622
	債	0177
	催	0178
	歳	3131
	載	4091
	塞	2924
	削	1837
	柵	1116
	索	3105
	酢	1910
	搾	0798
	錯	2187
	刹	1620
	拶	0451
	撮	0910
	擦	0971
	杉	1027
	桟	1169
	惨	0585
	傘	2640
ザ	挫	0519
	剤	2102
	斬	1874
	暫	3553
シ	旨	2516
	芝	2705
	伺	0078
	祉	1087
	肢	1094
	刺	1625
	施	1103
	茨	2812
	柿	1118
	脂	1190
	恣	3281
	紫	3332
	嗣	2153
	漬	0861
	雌	1337
	賜	1994
	摯	3556
	諮	2009
	叱	0210
	疾	4064
	執	2114
	湿	0741
	嫉	0783
	漆	0863
	膝	1359
	卸	1835
	赦	1870
	斜	1878
	煮	3460
	遮	3916
	酌	1854
	釈	1876
	爵	3143
	朱	4344
	狩	0474
	殊	1178
	珠	1183
	腫	1310
	趣	4111
	囚	3776
	舟	4353
	秀	3152
	臭	3261
	袖	1496
	羞	4106
	酬	1941
	愁	3508
	醜	2058
	蹴	2074
	襲	3633
	叔	1622
	淑	0639
	粛	4400
	俊	0117
	瞬	1594
	且	4297
	庶	3880
	緒	1742
	升	4266
	召	2494
	扱	0251
	匠	3711
	抄	0298
	肖	2733
	床	3805
	沼	0398
	尚	2774
	昇	3068
	咲	0413
	祥	1184
	称	1491
	宵	2831
	症	4065
	渉	0638
	紹	1691
	訟	1864
	硝	1520
	粧	1703
	詔	1900
	晶	3122
	掌	3215
	焦	3444
	詳	1926
	奨	3524
	彰	2337
	衝	0893
	憧	0899
	償	0199
	礁	1588
	鐘	2222
	拭	0453
	殖	1253
	触	1914
	飾	2150
	嘱	0881
	伸	0079
	辛	2531
	芯	2744
	侵	0116
	津	0466
	娠	0490
	振	0515
	浸	0530
	唇	3401
	紳	1690
	診	1898
	慎	0792
	寝	2925
	審	2985
	震	3481
	薪	3009
ジ	侍	0094
	滋	0734
	慈	2949
	餌	2257
	璽	3624
	軸	1908
	邪	1443
	蛇	1701
	寂	2855
	寿	4372
	呪	0323
	需	3472
	儒	0197
	汁	0227
	充	2507
	柔	2591
	渋	0625
	銃	2157
	獣	2384
	塾	3546
	旬	3698
	巡	3781
	盾	3729
	准	0143
	殉	1177
	循	0704
	潤	0918
	遵	3929
	如	0239
	叙	1834
	徐	0497
	丈	4227
	冗	2470
	浄	0457
	娘	0488
	剰	2233
	畳	3205
	縄	1756
	壌	0933
	嬢	0936
	錠	2180
	譲	2080
	醸	2086
	辱	3400
	刃	3646
	迅	3780
	尽	3786
	甚	3271
	陣	0545
	尋	2918
	腎	3511
ス	須	0700
	吹	0272
	炊	1080
	帥	1642
	粋	1645
	衰	2604
	酔	1875
	遂	3892
	睡	1535
	穂	1575
	誰	1986
	枢	1076
	崇	2864
ズ	随	0765
	髄	2316
セ	井	4265
	丼	4323
	姓	0334
	征	0349
	斉	2548
	牲	1133
	逝	3850
	凄	0145
	婿	0689
	誓	3424
	請	1983
	醒	2033
	斥	3690
	析	1072
	隻	3426
	脊	3297
	惜	0586
	戚	4401
	跡	1937
	潟	0921
	籍	3394
	拙	0373
	窃	2801
	摂	0799
	仙	0036
	占	2496
	栓	1171
	扇	2449
	旋	1194
	腺	1309
	践	1938
	詮	1923
	羨	2951
	煎	2950
	箋	3352
	潜	0922
	遷	3932
	薦	3008
	繊	1789
	鮮	2355
ゼ	是	3090
	禅	1306
	漸	0867
	膳	1381
	繕	1802
ソ	阻	0411
	狙	0406

	租	1492
	措	0610
	粗	1683
	疎	1512
	訴	1901
	塑	3525
	遡	4040
	礎	1595
	双	0028
	爪	3756
	壮	0263
	荘	2814
	挿	0517
	捜	0516
	桑	2618
	掃	0611
	曹	3414
	爽	4402
	曽	2632
	葬	2910
	喪	3504
	痩	4069
	僧	0180
	遭	3917
	槽	1352
	踪	1996
	燥	1392
	霜	3491
	騒	2308
	繰	1806
	藻	3033
	即	1439
	促	0118
	捉	0518
	遜	4041
ゾ	憎	0845
	贈	2064
	俗	0119
	賊	1932
タ	汰	0312
	胎	1149
	耐	1634
	怠	2588
	泰	3193
	袋	3201
	逮	3875
	堆	0563
	替	3457
	滞	0815
	戴	4093
	択	0299
	沢	0313
	拓	0375
	卓	2561
	託	1845
	濯	0978
	丹	4249
	旦	3041
	但	0081
	胆	1150
	淡	0640
	嘆	0773
	端	1564
	綻	1745
	鍛	2206
ダ	妥	3053
	唾	0553
	惰	0706
	堕	3501
	駄	2291
	諾	1974
	濁	0953
	脱	1225
	奪	2956
	弾	0697
	壇	0932
チ	恥	1664
	致	1668
	遅	3887
	稚	1543
	痴	4072
	緻	1780
	畜	2599
	逐	3848
	蓄	2931
	秩	1489
	窒	2853
	嫡	0839
	沖	0307
	肘	1044
	抽	0359
	衷	2600
	酎	1852
	鋳	2170
	駐	2297
	箸	3359
	弔	4240
	挑	0445
	眺	1503
	釣	2108
	彫	2117
	塚	0675
	超	4107
	貼	1904
	跳	1934
	徴	0841
	澄	0915
	嘲	0878
	聴	1796
	懲	3623
	勅	1841
	捗	0513
	沈	0306
	枕	1064
	珍	1135
	朕	1185
	陳	0656
	鎮	2210
ツ	椎	1249
	墜	3578
テ	呈	2715
	廷	3795
	抵	0377
	邸	1451
	訂	1829
	亭	2572
	帝	2573
	貞	2586
	逓	3852
	偵	0157
	堤	0681
	艇	1727
	締	1761
	諦	2010
	摘	0851
	滴	0866
	迭	3818
	哲	3402
	徹	0894
	撤	0912
	添	0641
	塡	0777
デ	泥	0384
	溺	0805
	殿	2247
ト	斗	3671
	吐	0235
	妬	0337
	途	3853
	渡	0746
	塗	3523
	賭	2021
	到	1615
	逃	3839
	倒	0139
	凍	0146
	桃	1174
	透	3854
	唐	3867
	悼	0587
	陶	0662
	盗	3309
	塔	0683
	搭	0721
	棟	1248
	筒	3323
	痘	4070
	稲	1561
	踏	1997
	謄	1398
	藤	3025
	闘	4136
	騰	1422
	峠	0428
	匿	3735
	督	3471
	篤	3371
	栃	1122
	凸	4298
	突	2772
	屯	4268
	豚	1228
	頓	1320
ド	奴	0217
	怒	3180
	洞	0455
	胴	1186
	瞳	1583
	貪	2630
	鈍	2123
	曇	3141
ナ	那	1047
	奈	2759
	軟	1871
ニ	尼	3767
	弐	3961
	匂	3662
	尿	3801
	妊	0281
	忍	2750
ネ	寧	2959
	粘	1681
	捻	0604
ノ	悩	0504
	濃	0956
ハ	把	0293
	覇	3392
	杯	1066
	排	0593
	廃	3902
	輩	3482
	伯	0067
	拍	0361
	泊	0389
	迫	3815
	剝	2105
	舶	1699
	薄	3004
	鉢	2144
	髪	3528
	氾	0226
	帆	0242
	汎	0254
	伴	0068
	阪	0321
	畔	1472
	般	1670
	販	1869
	斑	1260
	搬	0795
	煩	1295
	頒	1318
	範	3360
	繁	3536
	藩	3022
バ	婆	3433
	罵	3233
	唄	0477
	培	0558
	陪	0655
	媒	0686
	賠	1991
	漠	0804
	縛	1779
	爆	1415
	伐	0046
	抜	0290
	罰	3228
	閥	4126
	蛮	2638
	盤	3533
ヒ	妃	0238
	彼	0346
	披	0362
	卑	3270
	被	1495
	疲	4063
	扉	2453
	碑	1553
	罷	3234
	避	3944
	匹	3680
	泌	0390
	漂	0857
	浜	0523
	賓	2982
	頻	2209
ビ	尾	3799
	眉	3991
	微	0788
	苗	2781
	描	0591
	猫	0651
	敏	1675
	瓶	1702
フ	扶	0291
	怖	0353
	附	0410
	阜	3254
	赴	4095
	訃	1827
	浮	0522
	釜	2610
	符	3299
	普	2919
	腐	3921
	賦	1992
	敷	2345
	膚	4049
	譜	2068
	封	1639
	伏	0049
	幅	0694
	覆	3386

	払	0225
	沸	0387
	紛	1648
	雰	3446
	噴	0879
	墳	0887
	憤	0897
ブ	侮	0091
	舞	2666
	蚊	1673
ヘ	丙	4290
	併	0092
	坪	0328
	柄	1111
	塀	0677
	弊	3583
	幣	3582
	蔽	2991
	餅	2256
	壁	3601
	癖	4080
	璧	3608
	偏	0151
	遍	3890
ベ	蔑	2969
ホ	捕	0514
	浦	0524
	哺	0478
	舗	2177
	邦	1051
	芳	2739
	抱	0363
	泡	0392
	奉	3167
	胞	1148
	倣	0127
	俸	0128
	峰	0494
	砲	1479
	崩	2863
	飽	2148
	褒	2662
	縫	1781
	棚	1238
	蜂	1728
	奔	2758
	翻	2391
ボ	募	2901
	慕	2970
	簿	3387
	乏	2432
	忙	0248
	坊	0274
	妨	0279
	肪	1089
	房	2445
	冒	3088
	某	3168
	紡	1646
	畝	1857
	剖	2103
	傍	0166
	帽	0693
	貌	1958
	膨	1380
	謀	2004
	朴	1013
	睦	1534
	僕	0185
	墨	3423
	撲	0903
	没	0305
	勃	1839
	凡	3656
	盆	2581
マ	麻	3878
	摩	3938
	磨	3946
	魔	3953
	昧	1105
	埋	0484
	膜	1345
	抹	0370
	慢	0844
	漫	0858
ミ	弥	0344
	魅	4131
	蜜	2958
	妙	0280
	眠	1474
ム	矛	2501
	霧	3493
メ	冥	2613
	銘	2158
	謎	2047
	滅	0812
	免	2565
	麺	4112
モ	茂	2791
	妄	2509
	盲	2547
	耗	1660
	猛	0653
	網	1737
	黙	3554
	紋	1651
ヤ	冶	0089
	厄	3665
	躍	2090
ユ	愉	0710
	喩	0671
	諭	2012
	癒	4081
	唯	0556
	又	4158
	幽	3731
	悠	3407
	湧	0749
	猶	0757
	雄	1271
	裕	1530
	誘	1952
	熊	3530
	憂	2664
	融	2303
ヨ	与	4229
	誉	3135
	妖	0282
	庸	3881
	揚	0722
	揺	0723
	溶	0816
	腰	1311
	踊	1961
	瘍	4073
	窯	2986
	擁	0949
	謡	2011
	抑	0301
	沃	0315
	翼	3379
ラ	拉	0372
	裸	1550
	羅	3244
	雷	3466
	頼	2041
	瀬	0995
	絡	1709
	酪	1940
	辣	1965
	嵐	2898
	濫	0990
	藍	3024
	欄	1419
リ	吏	4351
	梨	3412
	痢	4068
	璃	1358
	履	3933
	離	2364
	慄	0791
	柳	1115
	竜	2603
	隆	0661
	粒	1682
	硫	1519
	侶	0114
	虜	4038
	慮	4050
	了	4157
	涼	0633
	猟	0654
	陵	0660
	僚	0186
	寮	2984
	瞭	1584
	療	4078
	糧	1800
	厘	3727
	倫	0135
	隣	0961
ル	瑠	1342
	涙	0528
	累	3196
	塁	3206
レ	励	1438
	戻	2441
	鈴	2146
	零	3467
	霊	3480
	隷	2201
	齢	2390
	麗	2672
	暦	3747
	劣	3047
	烈	3286
	裂	3331
	恋	2602
	廉	3911
	錬	2185
	鎌	2212
ロ	呂	2713
	炉	1079
	賂	1930
	露	3495
	弄	3057
	郎	1641
	浪	0527
	廊	3903
	滝	0813
	楼	1284
	漏	0860
	籠	3398
	鹿	3879
	麓	3494
ワ	賄	1931
	枠	1077
	惑	3461
	湾	0748
	腕	1269

IMPORTANT VARIANTS
重要な異体字一覧

This appendix lists 390 variants or **nonstandard forms** of kanji. This refers mostly to the **traditional forms** (正字 せいじ) used in prewar literature and in names, but also includes some **alternative forms** (異体字 いたいじ). A knowledge of variants is essential for reading prewar publications, classical literature, and proper names.

All the variants of **Jinmei Kanji** and **Jōyō Kanji** officially sanctioned for use in names, as well as all the variants appearing in the **Jōyō Kanji** list, are given here. The nonstandard forms, which appear to the left of the arrow, are listed in increasing order of their SKIP numbers. The corresponding standard forms, followed by their **entry numbers,** appear to the right of the arrow.

◧1 LEFT-RIGHT

2-4	收→収	0031
2-5	佛→仏	0020
2-7	侮→侮	0091
2-8	倂→併	0092
	凉→涼	0633
2-9	條→条	2726
	假→仮	0053
2-11	傳→伝	0048
2-12	僞→偽	0149
	僧→僧	0180
2-13	價→価	0095
	儉→倹	0130
	凜→凛	0195
3-5	拔→抜	0290
	拂→払	0225
3-6	恆→恒	0438
3-7	峽→峡	0427
	徑→径	0347
	悔→悔	0435
	挾→挟	0450
	海→海	0459
	涉→渉	0638
	狹→狭	0473
3-8	從→従	0498
	淨→浄	0457
	淚→涙	0528
	淺→浅	0464
	陷→陥	0547
3-9	喝→喝	0554
	惱→悩	0504
	揭→掲	0597
	搜→捜	0516
	插→挿	0517
	渴→渇	0627
	渚→渚	0637
	猪→猪	0652
	隆→隆	0661
3-10	塚→塚	0675
	愼→慎	0792
	搖→揺	0723
	溪→渓	0628
	溫→温	0740
	鄕→郷	0664
3-11	嘆→嘆	0773
	塀→塀	0677
	嶋→島	4103
	慘→惨	0585
	漢→漢	0808
	滿→満	0739
	滯→滞	0815
3-12	增→増	0836
	彈→弾	0697
	徵→徴	0841
	德→徳	0842
	慨→慨	0790
	憎→憎	0845
	澁→渋	0625
	潛→潜	0922
3-13	衞→衛	0938
	據→拠	0369
	擇→択	0299
	擔→担	0376
	澤→沢	0313
	獨→独	0471
	險→険	0658
	隨→随	0765
3-14	彌→弥	0344
	濱→浜	0523
	濟→済	0634
	濕→湿	0741
	隱→隠	0873
3-15	擴→拡	0366
	獵→猟	0654
3-16	壞→壊	0934
	懷→懐	0942
	瀨→瀬	0995
	瀧→滝	0813
3-17	壤→壌	0933
	孃→嬢	0936
3-18	攝→摂	0799
3-21	囑→嘱	0881
3-22	灣→湾	0748
4-3	壯→壮	0263
4-4	狀→状	0322
4-5	拜→拝	0360
4-6	晄→晃	3101
4-7	晚→晩	1232
	梅→梅	1159
	將→将	0551
4-8	棧→桟	1169
	殘→残	1179
	琢→琢	1222
4-9	腦→脳	1227
	甁→瓶	1702
4-10	槇→槙	1330
4-11	樓→楼	1284
	樞→枢	1076
	樣→様	1332

4-12	曉→暁	1233
	槪→概	1322
	橫→横	1350
	燒→焼	1256
	燈→灯	1019
	豫→予	2477
4-13	檜→桧	1160
	檢→検	1241
	膽→胆	1150
4-16	爐→炉	1079
	犧→犠	1394
4-17	權→権	1348
	櫻→桜	1168
	欄→欄	1419
4-18	臟→臓	1417
5-3	社→社	1042
5-4	祈→祈	1086
	祉→祉	1087
5-5	祕→秘	1490
	神→神	1143
	祝→祝	1144
	祖→祖	1145
	祐→祐	1146
	竝→並	2793
5-6	硏→研	1456
	祥→祥	1184
5-7	視→視	1223
5-8	碑→碑	1553
	碎→砕	1458
	祿→禄	1264
	號→号	2675
5-9	福→福	1303
	禍→禍	1304
	禎→禎	1305
	稱→称	1491
	褐→褐	1548
5-10	稻→稲	1561
5-12	禪→禅	1306
	穗→穂	1575
5-13	禮→礼	1012
5-14	禰→祢	1142
	禱→祷	1224
	穩→穏	1578
5-17	穰→穣	1597
6-4	缺→欠	2481
	效→効	1617
6-6	絲→糸	2703
6-7	經→経	1687
6-8	粹→粋	1645
	綠→緑	1741
6-9	緣→縁	1754
	練→練	1738
	緖→緒	1742
6-11	縱→縦	1783
	總→総	1743
6-13	繩→縄	1756
	繪→絵	1704
6-14	繼→継	1720
6-15	續→続	1722
6-17	纖→繊	1789
	罐→缶	2526
7-2	卽→即	1439
7-3	郞→郎	1641
7-4	敍→叙	1834
	殺→殺	1677
	敏→敏	1675
	朗→朗	1679
	敕→勅	1841
7-5	旣→既	1498
7-7	輕→軽	1909
7-8	踐→践	1938
	醉→酔	1875
7-9	謁→謁	1976
	諸→諸	1984
	辨→弁	2497
	頻→頻	2209
	賴→頼	2041
7-10	謠→謡	2011
7-11	謹→謹	2045
	轉→転	1872
7-12	證→証	1899
	贈→贈	2064
	瓣→弁	2497
7-13	觸→触	1914
	譯→訳	1865
	釋→釈	1876
7-14	辯→弁	2497
7-15	讀→読	1943
7-17	讓→譲	2080
	釀→醸	2086
8-4	殼→殻	1883
8-8	錄→録	2186
	錢→銭	2159
	靜→静	2164
8-9	鍊→錬	2185
8-10	鎭→鎮	2210
8-13	鐵→鉄	2147
8-14	鑄→鋳	2170
8-15	鑛→鉱	2145
9-3	都→都	2120
9-7	餘→余	2535
	龍→竜	2603
	縣→県	3269
9-8	餠→餅	2256
10-2	剩→剰	2233
10-5	駈→駆	2293
10-8	雜→雑	1752
	歸→帰	0148
10-9	類→類	2275
10-10	騷→騒	2308
10-11	驅→駆	2293
	鷄→鶏	2221
10-12	聽→聴	1796
10-13	驛→駅	2292
	驗→験	2306
	體→体	0080
	髓→髄	2316
11-2	勤→勤	2287
11-3	對→対	1025
11-4	穀→穀	2294
	數→数	2245
	歐→欧	1098
	毆→殴	1099
11-8	難→難	2310
12-1	亂→乱	1611
12-4	默→黙	3554
	戰→戦	2242
12-5	點→点	2587
12-7	辭→辞	1726
12-9	飜→翻	2391
13-2	劍→剣	2104
13-4	戲→戯	2351
14-2	劑→剤	2102
	勳→勲	3560
	勵→励	1438
14-4	斷→断	1885
14-9	顯→顕	2274
15-4	獸→獣	2384
15-5	齡→齢	2390
16-4	獻→献	2240

17-2	勸→勧	2334
17-4	歡→歓	2342
17-7	觀→観	2359
18-6	艷→艶	2403

▀2 UP-DOWN

2-5	免→免	2565
	每→毎	2527
2-8	眞→真	2616
2-9	冨→富	2892
	參→参	2563
2-10	曾→曽	2632
2-11	會→会	2512
2-12	齊→斉	2548
2-14	龜→亀	2637
2-15	襃→褒	2662
	齋→斎	2622
3-6	突→突	2772
3-7	峯→峰	0494
	莖→茎	2788
	莊→荘	2814
3-8	巢→巣	2861
	萠→萌	2871
3-9	堯→尭	2560
	壹→壱	2723
	著→著	2869
	萬→万	3653
3-11	臺→台	2498
	壽→寿	4372
	賓→賓	2982
	實→実	2765
	寬→寛	2922
	寢→寝	2925
3-12	賣→売	2722
	寫→写	2493
3-13	薗→園	3914
3-14	嶽→岳	3164
	薰→薫	3005
	舊→旧	0014
3-15	藝→芸	2738
	藥→薬	3011
	藏→蔵	2995
3-17	寶→宝	2764
3-19	竊→窃	2801
3-20	巖→巌	3037
4-3	步→歩	3071
4-4	爭→争	2523
4-5	盃→杯	1066
4-8	爲→為	4395
	黃→黄	3116
4-9	暑→暑	3121
4-11	齒→歯	3124
5-7	發→発	3174
5-8	當→当	2701
5-9	署→署	3223
	盡→尽	3786
5-13	壘→塁	3206
5-15	黨→党	3190
5-17	疊→畳	3205
6-2	兒→児	3153
	卷→巻	3273
6-4	臭→臭	3261
6-5	晝→昼	3841
	帶→帯	3191
6-6	單→単	2805
	畫→画	3723
6-9	節→節	3336
6-10	器→器	3367
6-12	蟲→虫	4343
6-14	嚴→厳	4079
7-5	盜→盗	3309
7-6	裝→装	3327
8-3	埜→野	1877
	麥→麦	3061
	專→専	3272
8-4	勞→労	3155
	黑→黒	3406
	惡→悪	3413
	惠→恵	3293
8-6	榮→栄	3183
8-7	墨→墨	3423
8-8	螢→蛍	3204
8-9	營→営	3216
8-13	霸→覇	3392
8-16	靈→霊	3480
9-4	煮→煮	3460
10-3	奧→奥	3503
10-5	髮→髪	3528
10-16	蠶→蚕	3107
11-2	與→与	4229
11-3	奬→奨	3524
11-4	樂→楽	3505
11-6	聲→声	2724
	繁→繁	3536
	擧→挙	3106
11-7	醫→医	3715
	豐→豊	3344
11-9	譽→誉	3135
12-3	墮→堕	3501
12-7	贊→賛	3484
13-3	學→学	3162
13-4	擊→撃	3552
13-7	覺→覚	3217
13-9	響→響	3573
15-4	徵→徴	3623
15-7	覽→覧	3538
16-2	雙→双	0028
19-4	變→変	2569
	戀→恋	2602
19-6	蠻→蛮	2638
20-5	鹽→塩	0774

□3 ENCLOSURE

2-6	戾→戻	2441
2-9	區→区	3681
2-14	曆→暦	3747
	歷→歴	3748
2-15	壓→圧	3688
3-5	屆→届	3820
3-8	圈→圏	3904
	國→国	3831
3-9	貳→弐	3961
	圍→囲	3807
3-10	廊→廊	3903
	圓→円	3673
3-11	團→団	3791
	圖→図	3809
3-12	層→層	3920
	廢→廃	3902
	廣→広	3769
3-14	應→応	3804
3-18	屬→属	3901
3-22	廳→庁	3768
4-5	者→者	3980
4-6	氣→気	3960
4-7	處→処	3764
4-8	逸→逸	3872
	虛→虚	4017
	虜→虜	4038
4-10	遞→逓	3852

	遙→遥	3895
4-12	遲→遅	3887
4-15	邊→辺	3761
5-10	瘦→痩	4069
5-14	癡→痴	4072
7-2	勉→勉	4113
8-11	關→関	4129
10-15	鬭→闘	4136
11-9	麵→麺	4112

■4

SOLID

6-1	亙→亘	2438
8-1	亞→亜	4354
	兩→両	4331
8-3	來→来	4366
8-4	卑→卑	3270
10-3	乘→乗	4393
13-3	肅→粛	4400

APPENDIX 13

LIST OF KANJI SYNONYM GROUPS
類義漢字系列一覧

This appendix classifies the characters into semantic categories called **synonym groups.** For quick reference, the groups are listed alphabetically by their **headwords,** a concise keyword that normally expresses the meaning shared by the group members. In the main part of the dictionary, synonym groups are given for the principal senses of each main entry character; here, the groups are brought together in one convenient listing.

1 Benefits

This appendix could be useful in three principal ways:

1. It enables the learner to study the differences and similarities between closely related characters together, rather than as isolated units, in an easy-to-read format.
2. It serves as a simple thesaurus that helps the student composing texts select the word most appropriate to the context.
3. It enables the user to look up an unknown character from its meaning, rather than from its form or reading.

This appendix could be used in various other ways. Even browsing through it at random could be highly rewarding and provide much insight into the semantic relations between characters.

2 Format and Order

Each synonym group begins with a boldface headword, and the groups are ordered alphabetically by their headwords. Each group lists the kanji synonyms roughly in order of semantic proximity. Each character is followed by its **synonym keyword** and **entry number.** Capitals distinguish keywords that are core meanings from those that are not. Cross-references, followed by an arrow →, point to the headword where the desired group appears.

3 Lookup by Meaning

To a limited extent, it is possible to use this appendix to locate a character from its meaning. Since this is merely a semantically classified list, not a real thesaurus, it is not particularly efficient as a lookup tool. Use it when you cannot recall the form or reading of your character but have some idea of what it looks like.

For example, to find characters related to *break,* consult the entries in the SYNONYMS section for 破 in the main part of the dictionary or under **break** in this appendix, where such synonyms as 砕 CRUSH UP and 崩 CRUMBLE can be found. Follow the procedure below:

1. Try to guess the headword under which your character may be classified. Think of general conceptual categories, rather than of specific terms. For example, for 'pear' try 'fruits'; for 'outstanding' try 'excellent', etc.
2. Look for your tentative headword in the listing. If it is there, there is a good chance that your character will be in that group. If it is not, repeat step 1. The cross-references may help.
3. The number to the right of the synonym keyword is the entry number of your character.

4 Semantic Relationships

Below is some of the linguistic background related to kanji synonyms. Several categories of semantic relationships exist among the synonym group members and the SYNONYMS headword, as explained below (these categories are not necessarily mutually exclusive).

1. *Class-inclusion,* or *kind of,* is a relationship in which the SYNONYMS headword (*superordinate word*) is a general term that includes the meanings of the specific terms (*hyponyms*) represented by the individual group members:

   graves
   墓 GRAVE
   墳 TUMULUS
   陵 IMPERIAL MAUSOLEUM
   塚 grave mound

2. *Synonymy,* a relationship in which the group members share a basic meaning or are similar or identical in meaning, is often indicated by a SYNONYMS headword given in the singular form:

   matter
   質 MATTER
   物 substance
   材 MATERIAL
   料 MATERIALS
   資 material resources

3. *Part-whole,* a relationship in which the meanings of the group members are part of each other or of the thing represented by the SYNONYMS headword, is often indicated by a headword in the form "parts of..." or "... parts":

parts of towns
区 WARD
街 CITY QUARTER
町 town section (*cho*)
丁 TOWN SUBSECTION (*chome*)
字 village or town section

4. *Complementarity* is a relationship in which the meanings of the group members contrast with each other and are mutually exclusive:

siblings
妹 YOUNGER SISTER
姉 OLDER SISTER
兄 OLDER BROTHER
弟 YOUNGER BROTHER

Groups of complementary characters are only given in special cases in which it was necessary to draw attention to closely-related characters.

See also **§12 Synonyms Section** on p. 46a and **§1.9 Discriminating Synonyms** on p. 27a.

A

abandon→DISCARD AND ABANDON

abnormal

変	ABNORMAL	2569
奇	UNUSUAL	2756
畸	UNUSUAL	1533
怪	MYSTERIOUS	0354
妖	MYSTERIOUS	0282
妙	strange	0280
異	not ordinary	3195
珍	curious	1135

abridge

要	SUMMARIZE	3263
抄	EXCERPT	0298
約	CONTRACT	1632
略	omit	1501

abstain→AVOID AND ABSTAIN

abstract thing

事	ABSTRACT THING	4384
物	THING	1084

accompany

伴	ACCOMPANY	0068
添	accompany	0641
陪	ACCOMPANY A SUPERIOR	0655
侍	ATTEND UPON	0094
従	FOLLOW	0498
随	FOLLOW	0765

accomplish

達	ATTAIN	3893
遂	ACCOMPLISH	3892
成	ACHIEVE	4352
徹	GO THROUGH	0894
破	carry through with	1478
叶	BE FULFILLED	0209

accomplishment

績	ACHIEVEMENTS	1788
功	MERIT	0218
勲	MERITORIOUS SERVICE	3560

accumulate

積	ACCUMULATE	1579
溜	ACCUMULATE	0814
累	CUMULATE	3196
重	pile up	4390
盛る	heap up	3314
堆	PILED HIGH	0563

accuse→BLAME AND ACCUSE

a certain

某	A CERTAIN	3168
或る	A CERTAIN	3978
一	ONE	4148

act→DO AND ACT

acting arbitrarily

横	arbitrary	1350
独	act arbitrarily	0471
恣	SELF-INDULGENT	3281
耽	INDULGE IN	1665
擅	ARROGATE TO ONESELF	0947
専	arrogate to oneself	3272
逞	DO AS ONE PLEASES	4004

active

活	ACTIVE	0460
動	dynamic	2232

acts

行	ACT	0246
挙	NOTEWORTHY ACT	3106
業	deed	3227

add

加	ADD	0042
足す	add	2714
〆る	SUM	4179

additional

追	additional	3840
補	supplementary	1529
副	accessory	2230

additionally

亦	ALSO	2504
兼	CONCURRENTLY	2850
又	also, and	4158
而うして	and	2520
及び	and	4192
並びに	and also	2793
傍ら	besides	0166
尚	STILL	2774
更に	furthermore	4355
且つ	AS WELL	4297

add to

付	ATTACH	0035
附	ATTACH	0410
加	ADD	0042
追	add	3840
添	ADD TO	0641

adhere to

執	adhere to	2114
着	stick to	4110

advance

進	ADVANCE	3873
興	cause to rise	3622
奨	ENCOURAGE	3524
勧	encourage	2334

advocate

唱	advocate	0555
説	preach	1949

affair

事	AFFAIR	4384
儀	affair	0191
件	MATTER	0054

affairs

用	THINGS TO DO	3694
事	affairs	4384
務	affairs	1505

after

後	AFTER	0431
余	after	2535

age

齢	AGE	2390
令	age	2489
年	years	2528
歳	AGE SUFFIX	3131
才	AGE SUFFIX	4218
寿	life span	4372

agents

使	ENVOY	0100
偵	SPY	0157

agree and approve

賛	APPROVE OF	3484
可	APPROVE	3687
認	RECOGNIZE	1948
諾	CONSENT	1974
承	AGREE TO	0016
肯	ASSENT	3072
容	tolerate	2832

aircraft and spacecraft

機	AIRCRAFT	1365
空	aircraft	2767
船	spaceship	1700

all

皆	ALL	3093
悉	THOROUGHLY	3405
総	TOTAL	1743
諸	VARIOUS	1984
毎	EVERY	2527
各	EACH	2692
都	all	2120
万	all	3653
全	WHOLE	2514
渾	ENTIRE	0738
一	all in one	4148
満	FULL	0739
丸	complete(ly)	4225
完	COMPLETE	2727

allot

充	allot	2507
当	assign	2701

almost

殆ど	ALMOST	1130
瀕	ON THE VERGE OF	0994
甫めて	BARELY	4363
辛い	bare	2531

alone

独	ALONE	0471
孤	SOLITARY	0426

alternate

迭	ALTERNATE	3818
交	INTERCHANGE	2508
輪	take turns	1999

amphibians→**REPTILES AND AMPHIBIANS**

anger

怒	GET ANGRY	3180
憤	INDIGNATION	0897
慨	resent	0790

angle and angular measure

角	ANGLE	2541
度	DEGREE	3844

angular measure→**ANGLE AND ANGULAR MEASURE**

animal

獣	BEAST	2384
畜	LIVESTOCK	2599
生	LIFE	4309
物	living thing	1084

answer

答	ANSWER	3322
解	solve	1913

返	reply	3797
応	RESPOND	3804

apologize

謝	APOLOGIZE	2048
詫びる	APOLOGIZE	1927

appear

現	APPEAR	1218
出	come out	4310
顕	MANIFEST	2274

appearance

容	APPEARANCE	2832
貌	APPEARANCE	1958
姿	FIGURE	3264
相	PHASE	1120
体	FORM (outer appearance)	0080
色	COLOR	2522
風	air	3730

appoint

任	appoint	0057
補	appoint	1529
挙	NOMINATE	3106

approach

寄る	DRAW NEAR	2856
迫	PRESS	3815
近	NEAR	3798
接	come close to	0607
拶	PRESS	0451

approve→**AGREE AND APPROVE**

approximately

約	APPROXIMATELY	1632
概	GENERAL	1322
大	in substance	4224
-頃	ABOUT	0163
位	about	0069
-方	about	2459
-程	...or thereabouts	1524
辺り	thereabouts	3761

areas and localities

地	PLACE	0236
方	locality	2459
辺	VICINITY	3761
域	BOUNDED AREA	0559
区	DISTRICT	3681
領	TERRITORY	1567
帯	BELT	3191
圏	SPHERE	3904

area units

坪	*TSUBO* (3.3 sq. m)	0328
歩	*bu* (3.3 sq. m)	3071
畝	*se* (0.99 ares)	1857
反	*tan* (9.9 ares)	3663
町	*cho* (99.2 ares)	1430

argue and discuss

議	DISCUSS	2078
争	CONTEND	2523
論	ARGUE	1981
弁	argue (for)	2497
諏	CONSULT	1985

arm→**HAND AND ARM**

armed forces

軍	ARMY	2582
兵	the military	3158
勢	forces	3542
隊	PARTY	0762

arrange

並	LINE UP	2793
比	rank	0029
列	arrange in a row	1018
陳	lay out (for exhibit)	0656
羅	spread out	3244
揃える	arrange properly	0719
整	PUT IN ORDER	3562
理	put in order	1220

arrive

着	ARRIVE	4110
到	ARRIVE	1615
至	COME TO	2707
及	REACH TO	4192
届く	REACH	3820
達	ATTAIN	3893

arrogance→**BOASTING AND ARROGANCE**

art

技	SKILL	0292
倆	SKILL	0136
術	PRACTICAL ART	0575
芸	ART	2738
道	the way of an art	3888

ascend

昇	ASCEND	3068
上	go up	4212
騰	RISE (esp. in price)	1422
登	CLIMB	3208

Asian countries

日	JAPAN	3759
緬	Myanmar	1758
老	Laos	3963
華	CHINA	2841
蒙	Mongolia	2938
鮮	Korea	2355
泰	Thailand	3193
越	Vietnam	4108
印	India	1023
竺	INDIA	3248
比	Philippines	0029

aspect

面	side	2590
上	from the viewpoint of	4212
柄	considering the character of	1111

assembly
- 会 meeting 2512
- 集 gathering 3445

assistant
- 補 assistant 1529
- 丞 AIDE 3146

associates→FRIENDS AND ASSOCIATES

assume upright position
- 立 STAND 2486
- 起 RISE 4099

atmosphere
- 雰 ATMOSPHERE 3446
- 気 atmosphere 3960

atmospheric discharges
- 雷 THUNDER 3466
- 電 lightning 3465

attack
- 攻 ATTACK 0286
- 撃 STRIKE 3552
- 襲 RAID 3633
- 侵 INVADE 0116
- 爆 bomb 1415

attain proficiency
- 達 attain proficiency 3893
- 熟 become skilled 3558

attend
- 臨 BE PRESENT AT 2059
- 登 attend 3208
- 出 appear 4310

attention
- 気 care 3960
- 念 attention 2554

authority→POWER AND AUTHORITY

avoid and abstain
- 避 AVOID 3944
- 逃 ESCAPE 3839
- 禦 WARD OFF 3561
- 忌 shun 2735
- 禁 abstain from 3469

awake
- 悟 AWAKE TO 0502
- 醒 AWAKE 2033
- 覚 awake 3217
- 惺 AWAKE TO 0709

B

bad
- 悪 BAD 3413
- 劣 INFERIOR 3047
- 下 of low grade 4186
- 弊 shabby 3583
- 粗 COARSE 1683
- 駄 GOOD FOR NOTHING 2291
- 廃 WASTE 3902

bags
- 俵 STRAW SACK 0129
- 袋 BAG 3201
- 鞄 BAG (for carrying) 2248
- 包 wrapper 3684
- 胞 MEMBRANOUS SAC 1148

bamboo
- 竹 BAMBOO 0267
- 笹 BAMBOO GRASS 3301
- 篠 DWARF BAMBOO 3376

bank
- 銀 bank 2156
- 行 bank 0246

barren
- 荒 WILD 2810
- 寥 DESOLATE 2960

bases→BOTTOMS AND BASES

basis
- 基 BASE 3312
- 本 BASIS 4314
- 素 ELEMENT 3108
- 礎 foundation 1595
- 底 BOTTOM 3827
- 根 ROOT 1167
- 拠 GROUNDS 0369

baths
- 浴 bath 0533
- 湯 hot bath 0747
- 泉 hot spring 3176

bays→INLETS AND BAYS

be→EXIST AND BE

bear
- 負 BEAR (on the back) 2594
- 荷 carry on shoulder 2840
- 担 BEAR ON SHOULDER 0376
- 支 SUPPORT 2473

bear and endure
- 堪 ENDURE 0680
- 忍 BEAR 2750
- 耐 WITHSTAND 1634

beautiful
- 美 BEAUTIFUL 2817
- 彪 MAGNIFICENT 4115
- 綺 BEAUTIFUL 1734
- 娃 BEAUTIFUL 0419
- 佳 FINE 0096
- 瑶 EXQUISITE 1301
- 麗 OF GRACEFUL BEAUTY 2672
- 艶 CHARMING 2403
- 妙 of marvelous beauty 0280
- 華 MAGNIFICENT 2841
- 絢 GORGEOUS 1705

斐	florid	3449

become stupefied

酔	BECOME INTOXICATED	1875
麻	BECOME NUMB	3878

before

前	BEFORE	2819
先	AHEAD	3046
予	IN ADVANCE	2477

begin

始	BEGIN	0335
-出す	begin to do	4310
-掛ける	start doing	0596
発	START	3174
起	start	4099
就	SET ABOUT	2129
開	OPEN	4121
創	initiate	2283
肇	ORIGINATE	3474

beginnings

緒	OUTSET	1742
序	INTRODUCTORY PART	3803
端	start	1564
始	beginning	0335
初	beginning	1433
元	ORIGIN	2428
本	origin	4314
根	ROOT	1167
源	SOURCE	0806

behavior

行	conduct	0246
挙	deportment	3106
動	behavior	2232

be late and delay

遅	be late	3887
後	fall behind	0431
滞	fall into arrears	0815
延	POSTPONE	3812
猶	DELAY	0757

bells

鈴	BELL (that jingles or rings)	2146
鐘	BELL (that tolls)	2222

bend

曲	CURVE	4340
彎	CURVE (become bow-shaped)	3634
屈	BEND	3821
折	bend	0297
勾	be bent	3660
歪	DISTORT	3095

benefit

利	ADVANTAGE	1431
益	BENEFIT	2849
為	SAKE	4395
用	use(ful)	3694
役	SERVICE	0288

be subjected to

被	BE SUBJECTED TO	1495
受	be subjected to	3076

between

中	MIDDLE	4262
仲	intermediate	0047
間	BETWEEN	4122
際	inter-	0874

bewildered

迷	PERPLEXED	3836
惑	BEWILDERED	3461

big and huge

大	BIG	4224
太	GREAT	2673
浩	VAST	0525
巨	HUGE	3773
厖	BULKY	3725

bird

鳥	BIRD	4105
禽	BIRD	2654
雛	CHICK	2312

birds

鷹	HAWK	3955
鷗	GULL	2370
烏	CROW	4088
雀	SPARROW	3117
燕	SWALLOW	3142
鴻	LARGE WILD BIRD	0977
鳳	MALE PHOENIX	3749
凰	FEMALE PHOENIX	3738
鵬	MYTHICAL HUGE BIRD	1416
鶏	CHICKEN	2221
酉	ROOSTER	4358
隼	FALCON	3427
鳩	PIGEON	0184
鷲	EAGLE	3598
鳶	BLACK KITE	3919
鶴	CRANE	2326
鷺	HERON	3621
鵜	CORMORANT	2067
鴨	DUCK	1582
雁	WILD GOOSE	3741

bite

嚙	BITE	0988
啄	PECK	0482

black colors

黒	BLACK	3406
漆	pitch-black	0863
黎	BLACK	3487

blame and accuse

責	BLAME	3115
叱	SCOLD	0210
詰	REPRIMAND	1920
難	find fault with	2310

批	CRITICIZE	0294
劾	EXPOSE CRIMES	1618
弾	impeach	0697

bloom→**SPROUT AND BLOOM**

blow→**BREATHE AND BLOW**

blue and purple colors

青	BLUE	3084
碧	DEEP BLUE	3515
瑠	LAPIS LAZULI (bright blue)	1342
紺	DARK BLUE	1688
藍	INDIGO	3024
紫	PURPLE	3332
蒼	PALE BLUE	2943

board games

局	board game	3800
棋	SHOGI	1242
碁	GO	3346
雀	MAHJONG	3117

boards and plates

板	BOARD, PLATE	1067
盤	BOARD	3533

boasting and arrogance

誇	BOAST	1921
慢	ARROGANT	0844
傲	ARROGANT	0173

boats and ships

船	SHIP	1700
舶	OCEANGOING SHIP	1699
艦	WARSHIP	1817
潜	submarine	0922
舟	SMALL BOAT	4353
艇	BOAT	1727
隻	COUNTER FOR SHIPS	3426

bodies

体	BODY	0080
塊	LUMP	0775
球	BALL	1219

bodily secretions

乳	MILK	1823
精	sperm	1729
汗	SWEAT	0256
涙	TEAR	0528
唾	SALIVA	0553

body

体	BODY	0080
身	BODY (esp. vs. mind)	4368
肉	FLESH	3966
屍	CORPSE	3843
尸	CORPSE	4198
骸	DEAD BODY	2301

body projections

角	HORN	2541
尾	TAIL	3799

bombs→**PROJECTILES AND BOMBS**

bone

骨	BONE	3288
髄	MARROW	2316
椎	SPINE	1249
脊	SPINE	3297
肋	RIB	1022
骼	SKELETAL FRAME	2302
骸	skeleton	2301

books

本	BOOK	4314
典	STANDARD WORK	3253
経	religious classic	1687
書	BOOK	3292
冊	bound book	4295
籍	books	3394
著	literary work	2869
巻	VOLUME	3273
編	piece of writing	1755
篇	PIECE OF WRITING	3361
鑑	REFERENCE VOLUME	2226

borrow→**LEND AND BORROW**

bottoms and bases

底	BOTTOM	3827
柢	BOTTOM	1121
下	lower part	4186
基	BASE	3312
礎	FOUNDATION STONE	1595
麓	FOOT OF MOUNTAIN	3494
磐	BEDROCK	3534
盤	bedrock	3533
床	BED	3805

boundaries→**EDGES AND BOUNDARIES**

bow

礼	courtesy bow	1012
拝	bow in veneration	0360

bowed

凹	CONCAVE	4294
凸	CONVEX	4298
嵯	RUGGED	0786

branch

支	BRANCH	2473
分	branch	2466

branches and twigs

枝	BRANCH	1073
梢	TIP OF A TWIG	1208

branch of study

科	SUBJECT OF STUDY	1463
学	branch of study	3162
門	field	1100

brave

勇	BRAVE	2592
侠	chivalrous	0110
赳	VALIANT	4100
驍	VALIANT	2327

敢	bold	2142
豪	bold and unrestrained	2657
雄	HEROIC	1271
壮	heroic	0263
義	chivalrous	2948
凜	gallant	0195

break

破	BREAK	1478
拉ぐ	crush	0372
崩	CRUMBLE	2863
挫	SPRAIN	0519
壊	BREAK DOWN	0934
毀す	break down	2246
折	BREAK OFF	0297
割る	crack	2284
裂	SPLIT	3331
砕	CRUSH UP	1458
摧	CRUSH UP	0849
潰す	CRUSH	0919

break into small pieces

砕	CRUSH UP	1458
抹	pulverize	0370

breathe and blow

息	BREATH	3278
気	breath	3960
吸	BREATHE IN	0234
呼	breathe out	0324
吹	BLOW	0272

brew and ferment

醸	BREW	2086
醱	BREW	2076
酵	FERMENT	1966

bridges

橋	BRIDGE	1367
桟	PLANK BRIDGE	1169

bright

明	BRIGHT	1060
昭	LUMINOUS	1107
蛍	fluorescent	3204
晃	DAZZLING	3101
燦	BRILLIANT	1390
赫	BLAZING	1960
暉	radiant	1276
熙	BRIGHT	3559
晟	SUNNY	3104

brown colors

褐	BROWN	1548
茶	light brown	2808

Buddha

仏	BUDDHA	0020
釈	Sakyamuni	1876

build

建	BUILD (a building)	3834
造	build (various structures)	3856
築	CONSTRUCT	3370
設	SET UP	1863

buildings

閣	TALL MAGNIFICENT BUILDING	4128
宇	large building	2699
殿	PALACE	2247
堂	HALL	3202
館	PUBLIC BUILDING	2196
舎	BUILDING	2555
棟	BLOCK	1248
厩	HORSE STABLE	3746

bundles and clusters

束	BUNDLE	4369
房	tuft	2445

burden

荷	LOAD	2840
貨	freight	3113

burn

焼	BURN	1256
燃	BURN (undergo combustion)	1375
焚く	BURN (build a fire)	3450
焦	SCORCH	3444
灼	SCORCH	1036
炮	ROAST	1132
燎	SET ON FIRE	1376

bury

埋	BURY	0484
葬	bury (a corpse)	2910

business→**INDUSTRY AND BUSINESS**

busy

忙	BUSY	0248
繁	bustling	3536
慌てる	FLURRIED	0707

buttocks

尻	BUTTOCKS	3766
肛	ANUS	1046

buy

買	BUY	3211
購	PURCHASE	2053

C

calculate and count

算	CALCULATE	3351
計	COMPUTE	1828
数	count	2245

calendars

暦	CALENDAR	3747
新	new calendar	2239
旧	old calendar	0014

calendar signs

戊	FIFTH CALENDAR SIGN	4321
庚	SEVENTH CALENDAR SIGN	3826

- 壬 NINTH CALENDAR SIGN 4257

call and invite

- 呼ぶ CALL 0324
- 喚 CALL 0666
- 召 SUMMON 2494
- 招 INVITE 0374

calm and peaceful

- 安 PEACEFUL 2695
- 康 peaceful 3877
- 寧 peaceful 2959
- 泰 TRANQUIL 3193
- 静 QUIET 2164
- 平 CALM 4291
- 穏 CALM 1578

camps

- 陣 CAMP 0545
- 営 BARRACKS 3216

capacity units

- 勺 *SHAKU* (0.018 liters) 3650
- 合 *go* (0.18 liters) 2511
- 立 liter 2486
- 升 *SHO* (1.8 liters) 4266
- 斗 *TO* (18 liters) 3671
- 石 *koku* (180 liters) 3689

cardinal points

- 東 EAST 4385
- 西 WEST 4333
- 北 NORTH 0230
- 南 SOUTH 2584
- 巽 SOUTHEAST 3329
- 艮 NORTHEAST 4330

careful

- 慎 PRUDENT 0792
- 謹 carefully 2045
- 精 meticulous 1729

carry

- 運 CARRY 3894
- 搬 CARRY 0795
- 輸 TRANSPORT 2026

carve→**FORM AND CARVE**

catch a criminal

- 捕 CATCH 0514
- 逮 CATCH A CRIMINAL 3875
- 拘 ARREST 0367
- 勾 ARREST 3660

cattle

- 牛 CATTLE 4263
- 丑 THE OX 4241

cause

- 致 BRING ABOUT 1668
- 誘 INDUCE 1952

cause and reason

- 因 CAUSE 3792
- 由 REASON 4311
- 為 because 4395
- 故 reason 1466
- 訳 reason 1865

cavities→**HOLES AND CAVITIES**

celebrating and congratulating

- 祝 CELEBRATE 1144
- 慶 FELICITATION 3936
- 賀 CONGRATULATE 3212
- 寿 CONGRATULATIONS 4372

central parts

- 核 NUCLEUS 1162
- 仁 kernel 0021
- 心 core 0011
- 芯 CORE 2744

ceramics ware

- 陶 POTTERY 0662
- 窯 ceramics 2986
- 磁 porcelain 1554

cereal

- 穀 CEREAL 2294
- 禾 CEREAL 4315
- 粉 flour 1643

cereals

- 米 RICE 4342
- 麦 WHEAT 3061
- 豆 BEAN 2442
- 粟 FOXTAIL MILLET 3326
- 黍 PROSO MILLET 3210
- 蕎 BUCKWHEAT 2993
- 蔣 WILD RICE 2976

ceremonies and festivities

- 式 CEREMONY 3785
- 儀 CEREMONY 0191
- 典 formal ceremony 3253
- 礼 RITE 1012
- 斎 religious ritual 2622
- 会 Buddhist ceremony 2512
- 祭 FESTIVAL 3311

certain

- 必 WITHOUT FAIL 0015
- 確 CERTAIN 1571
- 筈 OUGHT TO 3318

certificates

- 証 CERTIFICATE 1899
- 券 CERTIFICATE 3256
- 状 official document 0322
- 免 license 2565

change and replace

- 変 CHANGE 2569
- 替 REPLACE 3457
- 代 SUBSTITUTE 0034
- 迭 ALTERNATE 3818
- 更 change 4355
- 改 change 0287

易	change	3064
化	CHANGE INTO, -ize	0022
遷	undergo transition	3932
転	turn into	1872
換	EXCHANGE	0716
交	INTERCHANGE	2508

character → **NATURE AND CHARACTER**

characters

字	CHARACTER	2696
文	LETTER	2458
漢	kanji	0808
旁	RIGHT RADICAL	2598

charm

魅	CHARM	4131
幻	bewitch	0206
媚	FAWN UPON	0687

chastity

貞	CHASTE	2586
操	chastity	0948

chest

胸	CHEST	1187
乳	breast	1823

child

児	CHILD (of any age)	3153
子	CHILD	4196
童	CHILD (young person)	2639
幼	young child	0222
坊	SONNY	0274

China

華	CHINA	2841
漢	CHINESE	0808
支	China	2473
中	People's Republic of China	4262
胡	NATIVES OF ANCIENT CHINA	1467
台	Taiwan	2498
唐	Cathay	3867
呉	KINGDOM OF WU	3156

Chinese

漢	CHINESE (language)	0808
中	Modern Chinese	4262

choose

選	CHOOSE	3931
撰	choose	0911
択	SELECT	0299
採	PICK	0606
摘	pick out	0851
擢	SINGLE OUT	0973
抜	single out	0290
汰	SIFT OUT	0312

circle

円	CIRCLE	3673
圏	circle	3904
丸	round or spherical shape	4225
楕	ELLIPSE	1279

circles

界	WORLD	3172
壇	circles	0932

circular objects

環	RING	1395
輪	WHEEL, RING	1999
車	WHEEL	4367
盤	DISK	3533
釧	ARMLET	2109

cities and towns

都	METROPOLIS	2120
京	CAPITAL	2546
畿	CAPITAL	4408
市	CITY	2487
町	TOWN	1430

class

級	GRADE	1630
段	grade	1471
位	RANK	0069
階	RANK	0761
身	social status	4368
格	STATUS	1161
等	CLASS	3321
流	class	0529
層	STRATUM	3920

classical particles

耶	INTERROGATIVE PARTICLE	1635
也	rhetorical particle	4214
哉	EXCLAMATORY PARTICLE	4084

class in school

組	class	1693
級	GRADE	1630

clean and purified

浄	CLEAN	0457
清	clean	0635
純	PURE	1649
潔	IMMACULATE	0920
粋	REFINED (free from impurities)	1645
精	refined (purified)	1729
楚	NEAT AND TRIM	3470

clean and wash

洗	WASH	0465
漱	RINSE	0865
拭	WIPE	0453
滌	WASH	0854
濯	RINSE	0978
浴	BATHE	0533
浄	cleanse	0457
粛	PURGE	4400
清	CLEAR	0635
払	CLEAR AWAY	0225
掃	SWEEP	0611

clear

透	TRANSPARENT	3854

澄	LIMPID	0915
清	CLEAR (liquid)	0635
明	CLEAR (unclouded)	1060
朗	CLEAR (sky)	1679
冴える	CRISP AND CLEAR	0087

clergymen

僧	BONZE	0180
坊	Buddhist priest	0274
尼	BUDDHIST NUN	3767
父	FATHER	2467

close

閉	CLOSE	4116
鎖	lock up	2213
封	SEAL	1639
梗	STOP UP	1204
塞	STOP UP	2924

clothing

服	CLOTHES	1090
袴	FORMAL DIVIDED SKIRT	1509
蓑	STRAW RAINCOAT	2941
-着	wear	4110
衣	GARMENT	2506
装	DRESS	3327
裳	DRESS	3231
襤	RAGS	1607
袈	BUDDHIST SURPLICE	3200
裟	BUDDHIST CASSOCK	3420
襖	overgarment	1600

clusters→**BUNDLES AND CLUSTERS**

coagulate→**SOLIDIFY AND COAGULATE**

cold

冷	COLD	0088
寒	COLD (weather)	2894
涼	COOL	0633
凜	SEVERELY COLD	0195

cold seasons

冬	WINTER	2679
寒	coldest season	2894
秋	AUTUMN	1464

collapse

陥	FALL IN	0547
落	FALL	2907
崩	CRUMBLE	2863
没	SINK	0305

collection

集	collection	3445
選	selection	3931
彙	ASSEMBLAGE	2929

collide

衝	COLLIDE	0893
牴	COLLIDE WITH	1134
觝	COLLIDE WITH	1892
突	DASH	2772
当たる	HIT	2701

color

色	COLOR	2522
彩	BEAUTIFUL COLORING	2115

color

彩	color	2115
染	DYE	3181

comb

櫛	COMB	1413
梳	COMB	1209

combine

合	COMBINE	2511
結	TIE	1706
統	UNITE	1710
括	LUMP TOGETHER	0449
総	integrate	1743
併	join together	0092
綜	INTEGRATE	1744
纏める	PUT TOGETHER	1814

come→**GO AND COME**

come off

脱	get out of place	1225
外れる	come off	0215
剥	PEEL OFF	2105

come to an end

尽	be exhausted	3786
絶	COME TO AN END	1711

comfortable

楽	COMFORTABLE	3505
安	easy (without effort)	2695

comic

漫	COMIC	0858
戯	sportive	2351

command

令	COMMAND	2489
麾	COMMAND	3937
命	ORDER	2553

comment upon

批	CRITICIZE	0294
評	COMMENT	1895

commit

託	ENTRUST	1845
托	ENTRUST	0252
預	DEPOSIT	1317
委	COMMIT	3160
任	LEAVE TO	0057
嘱	CHARGE WITH	0881

communicate→**INFORM AND COMMUNICATE**

Communism

共	Communism	3045
左	the Left	3692
赤	RED	2719

compare

比	COMPARE	0029
較	COMPARE	1939

譬	COMPARE TO	3613
校	COLLATE	1166
照	check against	3506
対	OPPOSE (contrast)	1025
参	refer	2563

compel and press

圧	PRESSURE	3688
迫	PRESS	3815
強	force	0574
押す	PUSH	0371

compensate

償	RECOMPENSE	0199
賠	COMPENSATE	1991
酬	RECIPROCATE	1941
報	REQUITE	2133

compete

競	COMPETE	2322
戦う	contest	2242
闘	FIGHT	4136
争	CONTEND	2523

compile

編	COMPILE	1755
纂	COMPILE	3393
撰	COMPILE	0911
集	edit	3445
輯	EDIT	2025
著	AUTHOR	2869

complex

繁	complicated	3536
煩	vexatious	1295

compose

著	AUTHOR	2869
作	compose	0077
書く	WRITE	3292
筆	write	3317

compound

複	COMPOUND	1565
倍	DOUBLE	0122
重	DUPLICATE	4390

compromise

妥	COME TO TERMS	3053
譲	concede	2080
媾	MAKE PEACE	0782

conceive

妊	BECOME PREGNANT	0281
娠	CONCEIVE	0490

concentrate on

注	CONCENTRATE	0383
傾	devote oneself to	0174

conditional conjunctions

但し	PROVIDED THAT	0081
然し	however	3456

confectionery

菓	CONFECTIONERY	2873

飴	CANDY	2250

confine→IMPRISON AND CONFINE

Confucianists→CONFUCIUS AND CONFUCIANISTS

Confucius and Confucianists

孔	Confucius	0205
子	the Master (Confucius)	4196
孟	MENCIUS	2760

congratulating→CELEBRATING AND CONGRATULATING

conjecture

推	INFER	0612
憶	SPECULATE	0944
測	CONJECTURE	0744
察	GUESS	2961

conquer and suppress

征	CONQUER	0349
討	SUPPRESS BY ARMED FORCE	1846
伐	CUT DOWN	0046
鎮	QUELL	2210
靖	PACIFY	1546

consider→THINK AND CONSIDER

console

慰	CONSOLE	3557
弔	CONDOLE	4240

conspicuous

著	CONSPICUOUS	2869
顕	MANIFEST	2274
卓	PROMINENT	2561
傑	outstanding	0175

constant

定	fixed	2770
恒	CONSTANT	0438
常	REGULAR	3203
例	regular	0099

constellation

奎	ANDROMEDA	2796
彗	COMET	3439
昴	PLEIADES	3091

consume

消	SPEND	0531
費	expend	3221
尽	EXHAUST	3786
耗	WEAR AWAY	1660
銷	USE UP	2174

contain and include

含	CONTAIN (have as a part)	2534
容	CONTAIN (have within)	2832
包	ENCOMPASS	3684
挟	HOLD BETWEEN	0450

containers

箱	BOX	3362
壺	JAR	2890
槽	TANK	1352
樽	BARREL	1368

棺	COFFIN	1240
桶	BUCKET	1211
笈	BOX CARRIED ON THE BACK	3274
鞘	SHEATH	2259
箪	BAMBOO BOX	3381
函	BOX	3724
籠	BASKET	3398
袋	BAG	3201
鞄	BAG (for carrying)	2248
器	VESSEL	3367
瓶	BOTTLE	1702
缶	CAN	2526
缶	EARTHENWARE JAR	2525
continents		
亜	Asia	4354
阿	Africa	0408
欧	EUROPE	1098
米	AMERICA	4342
豪	Australia	2657
continue		
続	CONTINUE	1722
継	SUCCEED	1720
連	IN SUCCESSION	3849
持	HOLD	0447
contract and shrink		
縮	SHRINK	1790
約	CONTRACT	1632
攣	CRAMP	3635
cook		
煮	BOIL (cook by boiling)	3460
沸	BOIL (undergo boiling)	0387
炊	COOK	1080
蒸	STEAM	2936
焼く	cook by fire	1256
揚げる	fry in deep fat	0722
煎	ROAST, DECOCT	2950
cooked dishes		
-焼き	roasted, baked or fried food	1256
-揚げ	fried food	0722
-煮	boiled food	3460
cooperate		
協	COOPERATE	0103
携	join hands	0796
調	harmonize	1973
copy		
写	COPY	2493
謄	TRANSCRIBE	1398
複	duplicate	1565
拓	copy by rubbing	0375
corners		
角	corner	2541
圭	SHARP CORNER	2688
隅	NOOK	0760
隈	RECESS	0763
correct		
正	RIGHT	4296
直す	correct	3649
訂	REVISE	1829
改	REFORM	0287
矯	RECTIFY	1586
匡	RECTIFY	3710
correspond to		
該	CORRESPOND TO	1916
準	apply correspondingly	3541
当	be equivalent	2701
cosmetics		
紅	rouge	1629
粉	face powder	1643
黛	EYEBROW INK	3240
count→CALCULATE AND COUNT		
counters for animals		
匹	COUNTER FOR ANIMALS	3680
頭	counter for large animals	2019
羽	counter for birds	0265
疋	counter for animals	4292
counters for books		
冊	COUNTER FOR BOOKS	4295
巻	counter for volumes	3273
部	counter for copies	2111
counters for flat things		
枚	COUNTER FOR FLAT THINGS	1069
葉	counter for leaves	2912
丁	counter for sheets	4155
頁	counter for pages	2589
通	counter for letters	3855
竿	counter for flags	3259
counters for houses		
軒	COUNTER FOR HOUSES	1851
戸	counter for households	2429
棟	counter for buildings	1248
counters for long objects		
本	counter for cylindrical objects	4314
筋	counter for slender objects	3319
竿	counter for poles or rods	3259
挺	COUNTER FOR LONG SOLID OBJECTS	0512
counters for persons		
人	counter for people	4175
名	counter for persons	2693
country		
国	COUNTRY	3831
邦	STATE	1051
土	land	4211
courage		
勇	bravery	2592
胆	pluck	1150
court		
廷	COURT	3795
裁	court	4090

courteous

寧	COURTEOUS	2959
鄭	COURTEOUS	2379
叮	COURTEOUS	0211
嚀	COURTEOUS	0965
丁	courteous	4155

cover and wrap

覆	COVER	3386
掩	COVER	0592
被	cover	1495
包	WRAP	3684
蓋う	COVER	2933
蔽	COVER	2991
葺く	THATCH	2909

create

創	CREATE	2283
作	compose	0077
綴	COMPOSE	1746
生	produce	4309
発	START	3174
起	generate	4099

crimes and offenses

犯	OFFENSE	0229
罪	CRIME	3224
凶	atrocious crime	3679

cross

渡	CROSS	0746
渉	wade	0638
越	GO BEYOND	4108

crowd

群	GROUP	1942
衆	MULTITUDE	3325
叢	CROWD TOGETHER	3243
簇	FORM A CLUSTER	3377

cruel

虐	CRUEL	3989
惨	CRUEL	0585
酷	SEVERE	1967
辣	SEVERE	1965
残	RUTHLESS	1179
凶	ATROCIOUS	3679
苛	HARSH	2786

crustaceans

蝦	SHRIMP	1773
蟹	CRAB	3611

cry and sigh

泣	CRY	0396
嘆	SIGH	0773
歎	SIGH	2344

cultivate

修	CULTIVATE	0138
養	FOSTER (one's intellect)	2998
練	TRAIN	1738
錬	REFINE	2185
鍛	train	2206
磨	POLISH	3946
琢	POLISH	1222

cultivated fields

畑	FIELD	1131
畠	FIELD	3186
牧	PASTURE	1083
園	GARDEN	3914
田	RICE FIELD	3775
佃	CULTIVATED RICE FIELD	0066
圃	VEGETABLE GARDEN	3871

cure and recover

療	TREAT	4078
治	CURE	0393
医	cure	3715
癒	HEAL	4081
快	recover	0289

curtain

幕	CURTAIN	2937
簾	BAMBOO SCREEN	3388
帳	drapery	0572

custom

慣	HABITUAL PRACTICE	0843
例	established practice	0099
習	CUSTOM	3306
風	manners	3730
俗	popular custom	0119
癖	HABIT	4080
弊	EVIL PRACTICE	3583

cut

切	CUT	0030
薙ぐ	MOW DOWN	3010
剪	PRUNE	2886
削	CUT BY CHIPPING	1837
挽く	GRIND, saw	0511
断	CUT OFF	1885
截	CUT OFF	4092
裁	CUT OUT	4090
斬	CUT WITH A SWORD	1874
割	cut with a knife	2284
剖	DISSECT	2103
刈る	CLIP	0032
伐	CUT DOWN	0046

cutting instruments

刀	cutting tool	3642
鎌	SICKLE	2212
刃	BLADE	3646
鋏	SCISSORS	2173
鋸	SAW	2184
斧	AXE	2558
鍬	HOE	2205
錐	DRILL	2190
鑿	CHISEL	3640

cutting weapons

刀	SWORD (single-edged)	3642

剣	SWORD (double-edged)	2104
矛	HALBERD	2501
戟	HALBERD	2131
鉾	DECORATIVE HALBERD	2154
戈	DAGGER-AX	4274

D

dairy products

酪	DAIRY PRODUCTS	1940
乳	MILK	1823
醍	CREAM	2031
醐	CREAM	2032

damage→**HARM AND DAMAGE**

dance

踊	DANCE (energetically)	1961
舞	DANCE (gracefully)	2666

danger

危	DANGEROUS	3965
殆	dangerous	1130
険	DANGER	0658

dark

暗	DARK	1273
黒	BLACK	3406
陰	shaded	0657
闇	DARK	4134
晦	DARK	1196
昏	dark	3073
昧	DARK	1105
冥	DARK	2613
曖	SHADY	1383

dark-colored

暗	DARK	1273
濃	dark	0956
深	DEEP	0636

date

日	date	3759
忌	death anniversary	2735

dawn→**MORNING AND DAWN**

days

日	DAY	3759
曜	DAY OF THE WEEK	1402
昼	DAYTIME	3841
旦	first day	3041
朔	FIRST DAY OF THE LUNAR MONTH	1678
晦	LAST DAY OF THE LUNAR MONTH	1196

days of the week

日	Sunday	3759
月	Monday	3674
火	Tuesday	4273
水	Wednesday	0010
木	Thursday	4261
金	Friday	2552
土	Saturday	4211

dead

故	THE LATE	1466
亡	deceased	4210

deal with

扱う	HANDLE	0251
処	DEAL WITH	3764
辦	DISPOSE OF	2028
措	dispose of	0610
置	take proper steps	3222

decay

朽	DECAY	1015
腐	ROT	3921
枯	WITHER	1113
萎	WITHER	2872
錆	RUST	2188

deceive

欺	DECEIVE	2138
騙	DECEIVE	2314
詐	SWINDLE	1896
惑	mislead	3461
拐	defraud	0365
偽	FALSIFY	0149
詭	TRICK	1919

decide

決	DECIDE	0308
断	RESOLVE	1885
定	FIX	2770

decorate

飾	DECORATE	2150
粧	APPLY MAKEUP	1703
粉	apply face powder	1643
装	DRESS	3327

decrease

減	DECREASE	0733
耗	WEAR AWAY	1660
削	cut down	1837
縮	SHRINK	1790
落	FALL	2907
蝕	ERODE	2258

degenerate

落	FALL	2907
衰	DECLINE	2604
頽	DECLINE	2039
堕	DEGENERATE	3501
綻	UNRAVEL	1745
破	break down	1478

degree

程	EXTENT	1524
度	DEGREE	3844
分	relative degree	2466

deliver→**TRANSMIT AND DELIVER**

dense

濃	THICK (concentrated)	0956
密	CLOSE	2857

depressed→SAD AND DEPRESSED

descend and fall

- 落 FALL 2907
- 墜 DROP DOWN 3578
- 降 DESCEND 0548
- 下 go down 4186
- 倒 TOPPLE 0139

descendant

- 孫 GRANDCHILD, descendant 0492
- 胤 PROGENY 0017
- 末 posterity 4317

describe

- 叙 DESCRIBE 1834
- 抒 DESCRIBE 0295
- 描 DEPICT 0591
- 写 portray 2493

desire→WISH AND DESIRE

destroy

- 滅 DESTROY 0812
- 毀 DESTROY 2246
- 亡 perish 4210
- 消 EXTINGUISH 0531
- 剿 EXTERMINATE 2335

detailed

- 詳 DETAILED 1926
- 細 MINUTE 1689
- 緻 MINUTE 1780
- 密 CLOSE 2857
- 精 meticulous 1729

detect

- 検 detect 1241
- 感 SENSE 3514
- 嗅 SMELL 0772

deviate

- 逸 deviate 3872
- 外れる miss 0215

diagram

- 表 TABLE 3083
- 図 DRAWING 3809

die

- 死 DIE 4334
- 萎 WITHER 2872
- 没 die 0305
- 亡 DECEASE 4210
- 殉 DIE A MARTYR 1177
- 歿 DIE 1078
- 去 pass away 2678
- 逝 DEPART THIS LIFE 3850
- 斃 FALL DOWN DEAD 3593
- 枯 WITHER 1113

difference→DIFFERING AND DIFFERENCE

differing and difference

- 違 DIFFER 3907
- 異 DIFFERENT 3195
- 差 DIFFERENCE 4104

dig

- 掘 DIG 0601
- 鑿 EXCAVATE 3640
- 削 excavate 1837
- 穿 DRILL 2800

dignified

- 荘 DIGNIFIED 2814
- 威 dignified 4394
- 儼 SOLEMN 0204
- 厳 solemn 4079
- 粛 solemnly 4400

direct and supervise

- 制 CONTROL 1624
- 理 manage 1220
- 経 MANAGE 1687
- 管 EXERCISE CONTROL 3349
- 轄 EXERCISE JURISDICTION OVER 2056
- 掌 TAKE CHARGE OF 3215
- 監 OVERSEE 3535
- 督 SUPERVISE 3471
- 司 OFFICIATE 3648
- 宰 PRESIDE 2829
- 営 MANAGE 3216

direction

- 方 DIRECTION 2459
- 向 direction 3790

direction indicators

- 至 to 2707
- -行き bound for 0246
- -向け (bound) for 3790
- 迄 UP TO 3967
- 以 TO THE…OF 0045
- 自 from 4338
- 来 since 4366
- 而 DIRECTION WORD 2520

dirty

- 汚 DIRTY 0258
- 染 contaminate 3181

dirty

- 汚 DIRTY 0258
- 濁 TURBID 0953

disappear

- 消 disappear 0531
- 没 disappear 0305

disaster→MISFORTUNE AND DISASTER

discard and abandon

- 捨 DISCARD 0608
- 棄 ABANDON 2651
- 諦 GIVE UP 2010

discernment

- 識 power of discrimination 2070
- 眼 EYE 1504

discharge from mouth

吐	SPEW	0235
吹	BLOW	0272

discolor

褪	FADE	1577
晒す	BLEACH	1156

discontinue

絶	BREAK OFF	1711
廃	ABOLISH	3902
断	CUT OFF	1885
止	STOP	3659
休	suspend	0056
停	suspend	0156
已む	CEASE	4185

discriminate

識	DISCRIMINATE	2070
弁	distinguish	2497
分	tell apart	2466

discuss→ARGUE AND DISCUSS

disdain

侮	despise	0091
軽	make light of	1909
蔑	DESPISE	2969
嘲	SCOFF AT	0878

disease

病	ILLNESS	4062
疾	DISEASE	4064
風	(infectious) disease	3730
症	PATHOLOGICAL CONDITION	4065
患	AFFECTED BY DISEASE	3415
疫	EPIDEMIC	4061
罹	FALL ILL	3239
臥	be sick in bed	1825

diseases and disease symptoms

痘	SMALLPOX	4070
淋	GONORRHEA	0632
癌	CANCER	4076
熱	fever	3555
炎	INFLAMMATION	3075
痢	DIARRHEA	4068
下	diarrhea	4186

disease symptoms→DISEASES AND DISEASE SYMPTOMS

disgrace

恥	SHAME	1664
羞	shame	4106
辱	HUMILIATE	3400
侮	INSULT	0091
罵	ABUSE	3233
汚	defile	0258
誹	SLANDER	1978
譏	SLANDER	2069

disguise

装	dress up	3327
化	change oneself into	0022

dislike→HATE AND DISLIKE

dismiss

罷	DISMISS	3234
免	discharge	2565
解	release from office	1913

disordered

紛	CONFUSED	1648
乱	DISORDERED	1611
錯	MIXED UP	2187
混	mixed up	0631
雑	mixed up	1752
沌	PRIMEVAL CHAOS	0314

disperse

解	DISSOLVE	1913
散	SCATTER	2137

display

展	DISPLAY	3862
陳	lay out (for exhibit)	0656
掲	PUT UP	0597

distance and interval

距	DISTANCE	1905
間	INTERVAL	4122
程	EXTENT	1524
隙	GAP	0826

distant

遠	DISTANT	3906
遥	FAR	3895
悠	far-off	3407
遼	FARAWAY	3930
隔	APART	0827
離	separated	2364
迂	ROUNDABOUT	3969

distribute

配	DISTRIBUTE	1853
頒	DISTRIBUTE WIDELY	1318
分	DIVIDE	2466

diverge

岐	DIVERGE	0285
分	branch off	2466

divide

除	divide	0546
割る	DIVIDE	2284

dividend→INTEREST AND DIVIDEND

divine

占	DIVINE	2496
卜	DIVINE	4174
易	divination	3064

divisions of organizations

課	SECTION	1980
部	department	2111
局	BUREAU	3800

do and act

為	DO	4395

仕	DO	0037
致す	DO HUMBLY	1668
行	ACT	0246
作	WORK	0077

dog

犬	DOG	4275
狗	DOG	0405
戌	THE DOG	4350

domesticated mammals

牛	CATTLE	4263
馬	HORSE	4086
豚	PIG	1228
羊	SHEEP	2708
犬	DOG	4275
猫	CAT	0651
兎	RABBIT	4374

donate

施	give alms	1103
恵む	give charity	3293
寄	CONTRIBUTE	2856
醵	CONTRIBUTE MONEY	2087
献	donate	2240

doors

戸	DOOR	2429
扉	HINGED DOOR	2453
門	GATE	1100
口	entrance (or exit)	4189
襖	OPAQUE SLIDING DOOR	1600

doubt

疑	DOUBT	1970
怪しむ	suspect	0354

dragon

竜	DRAGON	2603
辰	THE DRAGON	3713

draw

描	DEPICT	0591
画	draw	3723

drinks

汁	JUICE, SOUP	0227
乳	MILK	1823
酒	ALCOHOLIC DRINK	0532
茶	TEA	2808
珈	COFFEE	1138
醇	UNDILUTED WINE	2001
酎	SHOCHU	1852

drip→FLOW AND DRIP

drive out

斥	EXPEL	3690
排	EXCLUDE	0593
追	chase away	3840
退	cause to retreat	3838
駆	drive away	2293
逐	DRIVE OUT	3848
払う	clear out	0225

dry

乾	DRY	2113
干	DRY	4187
燥	DRY UP (desiccate)	1392
涸	DRY UP (run dry)	0629
渇	RUN DRY	0627
旱	DROUGHT	3048

during

間	for an interval of	4122
中	IN (the course of)	4262
内	within (a given period)	4277

E

eager

懇	EARNEST	3606
切	eager	0030
摯	SERIOUS	3556
篤	DEVOTED	3371
熱	HOT	3555

earlier Chinese dynasties

夏	Xia Dynasty	2619
商	Shang Dynasty	2623
周	Zhou Dynasty	3720
漢	Han Dynasty	0808
晋	JIN DYNASTY	3290
秦	QIN DYNASTY	3192

early states of animal life

胎	FETUS	1149
卵	EGG	1054

early states of plant life

芽	BUD	2784
蕾	BUD (of a flower)	3006
苗	SEEDLING	2781
種	SEED	1560

earnings→PAY AND EARNINGS

easy

易	EASY (without difficulty)	3064
安	easy (without effort)	2695
簡	SIMPLE	3380
軽	LIGHT	1909

economizing and economy

省	SAVE	3100
節	economize	3336
倹	FRUGAL	0130

economy→ECONOMIZING AND ECONOMY

edges and boundaries

縁	EDGE	1754
端	edge	1564
辺	border	3761
境	BOUNDARY	0835
疆	BOUNDARY	1810
界	BOUNDS	3172
際	VERGE	0874

涯	OUTER LIMITS	0623
editions		
版	edition	1082
刊	publication	0221
訂	revision	1829
刷	printing	1623
elapse		
過	PASS BY	3891
経	pass	1687
歴	pass	3748
去	pass away	2678
elated		
亢	HIGH-SPIRITED	2460
高	high-spirited	2601
昂	high-spirited	3065
揚	exalted	0722
奮	roused up	3000
election→VOTE AND ELECTION		
electricity and magnetism		
電	ELECTRICITY	3465
流	electric current	0529
磁	MAGNETISM	1554
elegance→FLAVOR AND ELEGANCE		
elegant		
雅	ELEGANT	1532
淑	GRACEFUL	0639
優	graceful	0200
粋	REFINED	1645
彬	REFINED AND GENTLE	1201
element		
素	ELEMENT	3108
元	element	2428
単	unit	2805
elevations in water		
島	ISLAND	4103
州	sandbar	0064
礁	REEF	1588
洲	SANDBAR	0467
eliminate		
却	ELIMINATE	1436
排	EXCLUDE	0593
払う	CLEAR AWAY	0225
剝	PEEL OFF	2105
耘	WEED	1661
削	cross out	1837
抹	wipe off	0370
省	leave out	3100
脱	REMOVE	1225
去	take away	2678
外す	take off	0215
除	RID OF	0546
撤	WITHDRAW	0912
embankment		
堤	EMBANKMENT	0681
防	dike	0320
堰	DAM	0676
embrace		
抱	HUG	0363
擁	embrace	0949
emit		
出	PUT OUT	4310
発	EMIT	3174
放	radiate	1058
排	DISCHARGE	0593
射	SHOOT	1850
噴	SPOUT	0879
吐	SPEW	0235
湧	WELL UP	0749
employ		
雇	EMPLOY	2454
用	EMPLOY	3694
使う	employ	0100
傭	HIRE	0181
役	press into service	0288
employment→WORK AND EMPLOYMENT		
emptiness and nothing		
空	EMPTY	2767
白	WHITE (blank)	4305
虚	VOID	4017
無	NOTHING	2648
end		
終	END	1692
絶	COME TO AN END	1711
閉	CLOSE	4116
了	FINISH	4157
済	SETTLE	0634
-上げる	completion suffix	4212
完	COMPLETE	2727
結	CONCLUDE	1706
竣	COMPLETE	1528
ends		
末	LAST PART	4317
終	END	1692
畢	END	3194
尾	end	3799
局	close	3800
endure→BEAR AND ENDURE		
enemy		
敵	ENEMY	2340
仇	FOE	0023
energy and force		
力	POWER, force	4178
勢	physical power	3542
気	energy	3960
圧	PRESSURE	3688
鋒	brunt	2172
enlist		
徴	LEVY	0841

募 RAISE 2901

enter

入 ENTER 4177
-込む MOVE INWARD 3762

envious→**JEALOUS AND ENVIOUS**

equip and install

据える INSTALL 0602
敷 LAY 2345
架 LAY ACROSS 3178
装 FIT OUT 3327
設 SET UP 1863
備 PROVIDE 0165

escape

逃 ESCAPE 3839
遁 FLEE 4027
亡 flee 4210
走 run away 2720
脱 ESCAPE FROM 1225

escort→**LEAD AND ESCORT**

essential content

実 substance 2765
体 substance 0080
味 contents 0325

essential part

精 ESSENCE (essential part) 1729
粋 essence (best part) 1645
髄 essence (vital part) 2316
枢 PIVOT 1076
幹 TRUNK 2152
綱 ESSENTIAL POINTS 1735
旨 PURPORT 2516
要 summary 3263

estrange

疎 ESTRANGE 1512
離 separate from 2364
遠 DISTANT 3906

etiquette

礼 ETIQUETTE 1012
儀 CEREMONY 0191

European countries

英 ENGLAND 2782
独 GERMANY 0471
仏 FRANCE 0020
伊 ITALY 0052
葡 PORTUGAL 2902
西 Spain 4333
蘭 the Netherlands 3031
希 Greece 2543
露 Russia 3495
白 Belgium 4305

evening and night

夜 NIGHT 2550
晩 EVENING 1232
夕 EVENING 4195
宵 EARLY EVENING 2831
暮 DUSK 2971

evident

明 CLEAR 1060
鮮 VIVID 2355
亮 LUCID 2571
顕 MANIFEST 2274
瞭 CLEAR 1584

evil→**WRONGDOING AND EVIL**

evil

邪 EVIL 1443
兇 ATROCIOUS 3044
凶 ATROCIOUS 3679
悪 BAD 3413

evil beings→**SUPERNATURAL AND EVIL BEINGS**

exact

確 CERTAIN 1571
正 RIGHT 4296
真- right 2616
恰 JUST 0437

examination

検 examination 1241
試 examination (school test) 1925

examine→**INVESTIGATE AND EXAMINE**

example

例 EXAMPLE 0099
型 TYPE 3266

exceeding and excess

過 EXCEED 3891
超 SURPASS 4107
越 GO BEYOND 4108
濫 EXCESSIVE 0990
余 EXCESS 2535
剰 SURPLUS 2233
冗 REDUNDANT 2470

excel

勝 EXCEL 1268
抜 STAND OUT 0290
擢んでる stand out 0973
超 SURPASS 4107
越 GO BEYOND 4108
凌 SURPASS 0144
駕 outdo 3236

excellent and superior

優 SUPERIOR 0200
絶 without match 1711
卓 PROMINENT 2561
快 splendid 0289
妙 MARVELOUS 0280
秀 EXCELLENT 3152
英 DISTINGUISHED 2782
尤 outstanding 3755
傑 outstanding 0175
穎 TALENTED 2036

逸	exceptional	3872
名	first-rate	2693
上	of upper grade	4212

excess→EXCEEDING AND EXCESS

excreta

便	EXCRETA	0105
尿	URINE	3801
汗	SWEAT	0256

execute

執	EXECUTE	2114
行	ACT	0246
履	FULFILL	3933
施	CARRY OUT	1103
践	IMPLEMENT	1938
果たす	effect	4377
遂	ACCOMPLISH	3892

exert oneself

努	EXERT	3154
勉	ENDEAVOR	4113
励	make efforts	1438
勤	work diligently	2287
尽	use all one's strength	3786
精	put one's heart into	1729
孜	MAKE DILIGENT EFFORTS	0284

exist and be

在	BE	3704
存	EXIST	3702
有	exist	3703
居	be present	3822
臨	BE PRESENT AT	2059
也	CLASSICAL COPULA	4214

expand

脹	SWELL	1265
膨	EXPAND	1380
張	SPREAD	0573
氾	SPREAD OUT	0226
広げる	spread (out)	3769
拡	ENLARGE	0366
伸	STRETCH	0079
延	EXTEND	3812

expect

期	EXPECT	2139
待	wait for	0434

expensive

貴	precious	3220
高	high-priced	2601

explain

説	EXPLAIN	1949
明	make clear	1060
釈	ELUCIDATE	1876
詮	EXPOUND	1923
講	expound	2046
解	CLARIFY	1913
注	annotate	0383

explanatory remarks

注	annotation	0383
評	COMMENT	1895

explode

爆	EXPLODE	1415
発	discharge	3174

express

表	EXPRESS	3083
揮	WIELD	0717
寓	imply	2893

expression

顔	FACE	2277
色	COLOR	2522

expressions→WORDS AND EXPRESSIONS

extend over

亘	EXTEND OVER	2438
及	REACH TO	4192
跨	STRADDLE	1935

extensive→WIDE AND EXTENSIVE

extinguish

消	EXTINGUISH	0531
熄	GO OUT	1339
滅	go out	0812

extreme

極	EXTREME	1243
窮	extremity	2983
限	LIMIT	0475
涯	OUTER LIMITS	0623
果て	end	4377

extreme in degree

酷	SEVERE	1967
強	STRONG	0574
凄い	tremendous	0145
重	HEAVY	4390
高	HIGH	2601
深	DEEP	0636
大	BIG	4224
厳	SEVERE	4079
激	intense	0955
極	EXTREME	1243
痛	bitter(ly)	4071
切	keen	0030
甚	EXTREMELY	3271
祁	EXTREMELY	1447
超	super-	4107
頗る	EXCEEDINGLY	1552

extreme in power

激	VIOLENT	0955
荒	WILD	2810
狂	raging	0318
烈	VEHEMENT	3286
猛	FIERCE	0653

extremity

端	END	1564

末	end	4317
梢	tip	1208
先	point	3046
尖	POINT	2700
鋒	POINT OF A BLADE	2172

eye

目	EYE	3777
眼	EYE	1504
眸	EYE	1502
瞳	PUPIL	1583

F

fabric

布	CLOTH	3691
地	fabric	0236
巾	CLOTH	4217

fabrics

織	woven fabric	1801
紬	PONGEE	1684
紗	GAUZE	1653
絹	SILK	1721
綾	TWILL	1740
綿	COTTON	1736
棉	COTTON	1244
麻	HEMP	3878
毛	wool	4264
錦	BROCADE	2181

face

向	TURN TOWARD	3790
面	FACE	2590
対	face (each other)	1025

face orifices

口	MOUTH	4189
鼻	NOSE	3357
耳	EAR	4329
目	EYE	3777

fail

敗	fail	1868
落	fall through	2907
-損なう	fail to (do)	0801

fall → DESCEND AND FALL

false

虚	FALSE	4017
仮	fake	0053
偽	sham	0149
擬	imitation	0969
義	artificial	2948

falsehood

偽	falsehood	0149
嘘	LIE	0880

familiar and friendly

親	INTIMATE	2264
密	CLOSE	2857
近	NEAR	3798
睦	FRIENDLY	1534
懇	FAMILIAR	3606
和	HARMONIOUS	1450

family and relations

族	FAMILY	1195
家	FAMILY	2827
門	family	1100
氏	clan	3669
縁	RELATION	1754
姻	relative by marriage	0421
親	RELATIVES	2264
戚	RELATIVES	4401
曽	GREAT-	2632

farm and plant

植	PLANT	1247
栽	PLANT (saplings)	4087
培	CULTIVATE	0558
耕	TILL	1659
作	raise crops	0077
農	farm, FARMING	3345
蒔	SOW	2935
播	SOW	0906

fast

速	QUICK	3851
早	QUICK	3042
疾	fast	4064
快	fast	0289
急	rapid	2595
迅	SWIFT	3780
敏	NIMBLE	1675
即	IMMEDIATE	1439
捷	AGILE	0609

fate and fortune

運	FORTUNE	3894
命	fate	2553
業	karma	3227
縁	karma relation	1754
籤	LOT	3399

fats and oils

油	OIL	0400
脂	FAT	1190
肪	ANIMAL FAT	1089
膏	FAT	2658
蠟	WAX	1818

fatten

肥	FATTEN	1091
太る	grow fat	2673

faults and flaws

難	fault	2310
短	shortcoming	1515
疵	DEFECT	4067
陥	defect	0547
欠	incompleteness	2481

favor

恵	FAVOR	3293
徳	act of kindness	0842
恩	GRACE	3289

fear

怖	FEARFUL	0353
凄	UNCANNY	0145
恐	FEAR	3283
惧	FEAR	0581
慄	TREMBLE WITH FEAR	0791
兢	BE IN FEAR	1971
惶	BE AFRAID	0708
畏	BE OVERAWED	3170
臆	FEEL TIMID	1397
怯える	BE FRIGHTENED	0355

fee and price

料	FEE	1644
代	CHARGE	0034
賃	CHARGES	3341
銭	money paid	2159
費	EXPENSE	3221
価	PRICE	0095
値	price	0123

feel deeply

感	feel deeply	3514
動	be moved	2232
嘆	sigh in admiration	0773

feeling

感	SENSE (feeling)	3514
情	EMOTION	0583
心	HEART	0011
気	spirits	3960

fellow

奴	GUY	0217
漢	FELLOW	0808
輩	FELLOW (*belittling*)	3482
徒	fellows	0499
棒	tough guy	1237
坊	COLLOQUIAL PERSON SUFFIX	0274
屋	colloquial person suffix	3842
物	character	1084

fences and walls

壁	WALL	3601
塀	FENCE (for screening)	0677
垣	FENCE (for partitioning)	0416
牆	FENCE (for partitioning)	1393
柵	FENCE (with spaced pickets)	1116
堵	FENCE (made of earth)	0682
囲い	enclosure	3807
欄	railing	1419

ferment→**BREW AND FERMENT**

festivities→**CEREMONIES AND FESTIVITIES**

feudal territorial divisions

藩	FEUDAL DOMAIN	3022
国	province (in former Japan)	3831
領	fief	1567
封	daimiate	1639
荘	manor (in feudal Japan)	2814

few

少	LITTLE	4278
寡	FEW	2957
乏	SCANTY	2432
薄	meager	3004
微	SLIGHT	0788
寸	A BIT OF	3652
僅	A LITTLE	0176
些	A BIT	3251

fiber-producing plants

麻	HEMP	3878
綿	COTTON	1736

fibers→**THREADS AND FIBERS**

fidelity

忠	LOYALTY	3087
義	faith	2948
孝	FILIAL PIETY	3973
悌	BROTHERLY LOVE	0507
誠	SINCERITY	1922
実	faithfulness	2765
信	fidelity	0115
操	constancy	0948
節	moral integrity	3336

fight and war

闘	FIGHT	4136
戦	WAR	2242
征	go on a military expedition	0349

fill

充	FILL	2507
湛	BE FULL OF	0745
填	FILL	0777
満	fill	0739
詰める	STUFF	1920

fire

火	FIRE	4273
炎	FLAME	3075
焰	FLAME	1255

firm and obstinate

堅	FIRM	3502
固	FIRM, stiff	3830
確	firm	1571
毅	RESOLUTE	2341
剛	TOUGH	2107
頑	STUBBORN	1315
硬	hard-line	1518

first

甲	FIRST	4293
初	FIRST	1433

first person pronouns

私	I (*polite*)	1432
我	SELF	4362

己	ONESELF	4188
身	ONE'S PERSON	4368
僕	I (*familiar*)	0185
俺	I (*intimate*)	0124
吾	I (*elegant*)	3060
予	I (*pompous*)	2477
余	I (*pompous*)	2535
麿	I (*archaic*)	3949
朕	IMPERIAL WE	1185
自	SELF	4338
fish		
魚	FISH	2636
貝	SHELLFISH	3150
fish→**HUNT AND FISH**		
fishes		
鯉	CARP	2358
鮎	AYU	2352
鯛	TAI	2360
鰯	SARDINE	2367
鱒	TROUT	2371
鮫	SHARK	2354
fit		
合	FIT	2511
填まる	fit	0777
適	suit	3918
揃える	MAKE UNIFORM	0719
five		
五	FIVE	4244
伍	five (in legal documents)	0050
flag		
旗	FLAG	1321
幡	LONG FLAG	0891
旒	COUNTER FOR FLAGS	1272
flat		
平	FLAT	4291
扁	FLAT	3728
坦	LEVEL	0329
flat supports		
台	STAND	2498
座	SEAT	3868
壇	PLATFORM	0932
棚	SHELF	1238
架	rack	3178
床	BED	3805
flavor and elegance		
趣	FLAVOR	4111
味	TASTE	0325
風	elegance	3730
品	refinement	2795
flaws→**FAULTS AND FLAWS**		
flesh		
肉	FLESH	3966
筋	MUSCLE	3319
float		
漂	DRIFT	0857
浮	FLOAT	0522
floor		
階	FLOOR	0761
層	story	3920
flourish		
茂	GROW THICK	2791
繁	THRIVE	3536
flow and drip		
流	FLOW	0529
注	POUR	0383
濫	overflow	0990
溢	OVERFLOW	0807
漏	LEAK	0860
滴	DROP	0866
泌	SECRETE	0390
瀝	DRIP	0996
flower		
花	FLOWER	2740
華	flower	2841
flowering plants		
菊	CHRYSANTHEMUM	2875
菖	IRIS	2881
菫	VIOLET	2877
蓮	LOTUS	2940
葛	KUDZU	2905
蓬	JAPANESE MUGWORT	2973
葵	MALLOW	2906
蓉	COTTON ROSE	2944
芙	LOTUS	2737
蘭	ORCHID	3031
萩	*HAGI*	2908
藤	WISTERIA	3025
桜	cherry blossom	1168
梅	*ume* blossom	1159
fly		
飛	FLY	4389
蜚	FLY	3473
翔	SOAR	1714
航	NAVIGATE	1671
-fold		
倍	TIMES	0122
重	-fold	4390
fold		
折	FOLD	0297
畳む	FOLD UP	3205
follow and pursue		
従	FOLLOW	0498
随	FOLLOW	0765
辿る	FOLLOW (a path)	3968
追	CHASE	3840
followers→**STUDENTS AND FOLLOWERS**		

food

飯	MEAL	2126
膳	MEAL	1381
食	FOOD, meal	2578
糧	FOOD PROVISIONS	1800
餌	ANIMAL FEED	2257
肴	ACCOMPANIMENT FOR DRINKS	2567

foolish

愚	FOOLISH	3513
暗	DARK	1273
痴	STUPID	4072
鈍	DULL	2123
呆	DIM-WITTED	2712
魯	DULL	2665
闇	DARK	4134
蒙	IGNORANCE	2938

footwear

靴	SHOES	2235
沓	FOOTWEAR	3074
駄	clogs	2291
履	footwear	3933
足	counter for footwear	2714

force→ **ENERGY AND FORCE**

force to move

推	propel	0612
駆	DRIVE	2293
押す	PUSH	0371

foreign

外	foreign	0215
異	foreign	3195

forest

林	FOREST, small woods	1071
森	THICK WOODS	3123
杜	GROVE	1030

forget

忘	FORGET	2529
遺	LEAVE BEHIND	3928

forgive

赦	AMNESTY	1870
免	EXEMPT	2565
許す	forgive	1862
恕	FORGIVE WITH COMPASSION	3282
宥	PARDON	2803

form

形	SHAPE	1050
状	FORM (external)	0322
体	FORM (characteristic)	0080
姿	FIGURE	3264

form and carve

刻	ENGRAVE	1619
彫	CARVE	2117
塑	MODEL	3525
鋳	CAST	2170

former

旧	FORMER	0014
元	former	2428
故	OLD (earlier time)	1466
前	previous	2819
嘗て	previously	3230
曽	previously	2632
先	former	3046
既	ALREADY	1498

fortune→ **FATE AND FORTUNE**

found

立	ESTABLISH	2486
設	SET UP	1863
置	found	3222

fragrance→ **SMELL AND FRAGRANCE**

frames

枠	FRAME	1077
骼	SKELETAL FRAME	2302
格	framework	1161
額	picture frame	2273

friendly→ **FAMILIAR AND FRIENDLY**

friends and associates

僚	COLLEAGUE	0186
輩	FELLOW	3482
朋	COMRADE	1092
友	FRIEND	3670
侶	COMPANION	0114

front

前	front	2819
面	FACE	2590
首	HEAD	2818

front parts of head

顔	FACE	2277
面	FACE	2590
額	forehead	2273
顎	chin	2276
頬	CHEEK	2043
吻	PROBOSCIS	0270

fruit

果	FRUIT	4377
実	fruit	2765

fruits and fruit trees

桃	PEACH	1174
榛	HAZEL	1328
椎	CHINQUAPIN	1249
柚	YUZU	1123
椰	COCONUT	1285
柑	CITRUS	1112
橙	BITTER ORANGE	1369
葡	GRAPE	2902
萄	GRAPE	2870
柿	PERSIMMON	1118
檎	APPLE	1386
李	PLUM	3050

枇	LOQUAT	1063
杷	LOQUAT	1065
苺	STRAWBERRY	2780
菱	water chestnut	2879
杏	APRICOT	3049
梅	JAPANESE APRICOT	1159
橘	MANDARIN	1366
栗	CHESTNUT	3280
栃	JAPANESE HORSE CHESTNUT	1122
梨	PEAR	3412
蕉	PLANTAIN	2994

fruit trees→FRUITS AND FRUIT TREES

full

満	FULL	0739
飽	SATIATED	2148

fungus

黴	MOLD	1008
茸	MUSHROOM	2809
菌	fungus	2876

furcation

叉	FORK	4194
俣	BIFURCATION	0111
股	CROTCH	1093
岐	forked road	0285

future

来	coming generations	4366
後	afteryears	0431

G

game

技	game	0292
戦	match	2242

gardens

園	GARDEN	3914
庭	GARDEN	3866
苑	IMPERIAL GARDEN	2783

garment parts

襟	COLLAR	1599
袖	SLEEVE	1496
懐	BOSOM	0942
衿	COLLAR	1465
裾	HEM	1549

gas and vapor

気	GAS	3960
空	AIR	2767
汽	STEAM	0309

gather

集	COLLECT	3445
蒐	COLLECT	2942
聚	COLLECT	3479
収	collect	0031
採	GATHER	0606
采	GATHER	3077
萃	GATHER	2882
湊	come together	0743

general

総	GENERAL	1743
惣	GENERAL	3452
汎	OVERALL	0254

general counters

丁	MISCELLANEOUS COUNTER	4155
個	GENERAL COUNTER	0132
箇	COUNTER FOR ITEMS	3348
点	counter for articles	2587
件	counter for cases	0054

generation

代	GENERATION	0034
世	generation	4308

genitals

陰	sex organ	0657
胎	WOMB	1149
恥	private parts	1664

gentle

優しい	gentle	0200
穏	MILD	1578
柔	SOFT	2591

gentleman

紳	GENTLEMAN	1690
子	gentleman	4196
士	man of learning and virtue	4213

get

得	ACQUIRE	0577
拾	PICK UP	0454
獲	obtain	0959
収	TAKE IN	0031
取	TAKE	1613

get off

降	alight	0548
下	get down	4186

get on

乗	GET ON	4393
搭	BOARD	0721

give

与	GIVE	4229
呈	PRESENT	2715
進	present to a superior	3873
上	give (to superior or others)	4212
下	give (to inferior or speaker)	4186
呉れる	give (to speaker)	3156
授	CONFER	0595
賜	DEIGN TO GIVE	1994
贈	PRESENT A GIFT	2064
賄	BRIBE	1931
賂	BRIBE	1930

give birth

生	BE BORN	4309
誕	BE BORN	1987

- 産 GIVE BIRTH 4089
- 娩 GIVE BIRTH 0486
- 殖 MULTIPLY 1253

give out a call

- 叫 SHOUT 0233
- 号 holler 2675
- 喝 SHOUT AT 0554
- 喚 call out 0666
- 呼 CALL 0324
- 鳴 CRY 0831
- 吠 BARK 0269

go and come

- 行 GO 0246
- 徠 COME 0576
- 往 GO ON 0348
- 出 go to 4310
- 参 go somewhere 2563
- 来 COME 4366
- 通 go to and from 3855
- 向 head toward 3790
- 赴 PROCEED TO 4095
- 嚮 GO TOWARD 3610

god

- 神 GOD 1143
- 帝 the Supreme Being 2573
- 天 HEAVEN 4250
- 主 Lord 2437
- 祇 EARTHLY GOD 1459

good

- 良 GOOD 4373
- 善 GOOD 2921
- 好 FAVORABLE 0240
- 順 favorable 0018
- 佳 FINE 0096
- 美 BEAUTIFUL 2817

good fortune

- 吉 LUCKY 2691
- 嘉 HAPPY 2953
- 祥 AUSPICIOUS 1184
- 瑞 AUSPICIOUS OMEN 1302
- 禎 PROPITIOUS OMEN 1305
- 幸 GOOD FORTUNE 2755
- 福 FORTUNE 1303
- 倖 GOOD FORTUNE 0134

govern

- 治 GOVERN 0393
- 統 rule 1710

government

- 政 POLITICAL ADMINISTRATION 1468
- 治 government 0393

governments

- 官 GOVERNMENT 2766
- 幕 SHOGUNATE 2937
- 廷 COURT 3795
- 朝 court 2130
- 宮 Imperial Court 2828

gratitude→**THANKING AND GRATITUDE**

graves

- 墓 GRAVE 2930
- 墳 TUMULUS 0887
- 陵 IMPERIAL MAUSOLEUM 0660
- 廟 MAUSOLEUM 3935
- 祢 FATHER'S MAUSOLEUM 1142
- 塚 grave mound 0675

great

- 偉 GREAT (of superior character) 0167
- 大 BIG 4224
- 宏 GRAND (large in scale) 2728
- 壮 GRAND (having grandeur) 0263
- 豪 MAGNIFICENT 2657
- 雄 HEROIC 1271
- 碩 EMINENT 1555

great persons

- 豪 GREAT MAN 2657
- 傑 OUTSTANDING PERSON 0175
- 雄 hero 1271
- 匠 CRAFTSMAN 3711
- 聖 great master 3509

great respect

- 栄 GLORY 3183
- 誉 HONOR 3135
- 光 honor 3043

green colors

- 緑 GREEN 1741
- 青 GREEN 3084
- 翠 JADE GREEN 3356

grieve

- 慨 DEPLORE 0790
- 嘆 SIGH 0773
- 悼 MOURN 0587
- 傷 grieve 0179
- 悲 feel sad 3448
- 悄 BECOME DISPIRITED 0506

groups

- 群 GROUP (of any kind) 1942
- 班 SQUAD 1182
- 軍 team 2582
- 組 group (of people) 1693
- 陣 lineup 0545
- 連 set 3849
- 族 common-interest group (*slang*) 1195
- 党 PARTY 3190
- 隊 PARTY (organized group) 0762
- 団 BODY 3791
- 伍 ranks 0050

grow

- 成 grow up 4352
- 長 grow (up) 3163
- 生 grow 4309
- 育 grow 2544

発	develop	3174
伸	expand	0079
展	UNFOLD	3862

guard

哨	SENTRY	0481
衛	GUARD	0938
守	guard	2697
警	guard	3595

H

hair

毛	HAIR (of any kind)	4264
髪	HAIR (on the head)	3528
辮	PLAIT	2085
羽	FEATHER	0265
眉	EYEBROW	3991
鬚	BEARD	3539

hand and arm

手	HAND	4267
腕	ARM	1269
肘	ELBOW	1044
掌	PALM	3215
指	FINGER	0452
拇	THUMB	0358
拳	FIST	3295

handle

扱う	HANDLE	0251
馭	HANDLE	2282
操	MANIPULATE	0948
揮	WIELD	0717
運	control movement skillfully	3894

handles

柄	HANDLE	1111
手	handle	4267
把	GRIP	0293

hang

掛ける	HANG	0596
垂	HANG DOWN	4382
懸	SUSPEND	3632
吊	SUSPEND	2686
釣り-	suspended	2108

happiness

幸	HAPPINESS	2755
祉	BLESSEDNESS	1087
福	FORTUNE	1303

hard

硬	HARD	1518
堅	FIRM	3502
鞏	TOUGH	3369
固	SOLID	3830
剛	TOUGH	2107
強	STRONG	0574
勁	STRONG	1833

harm and damage

害	HARM, damage	2826
損	damage	0801
傷	WOUND	0179

harvest

採	PICK	0606
摘	PICK	0851
穫	HARVEST	1598
刈る	reap	0032

hate and dislike

憎	HATE	0845
悪	hate	3413
忌む	ABHOR	2735
嫌	DISLIKE	0781
恨	HOLD A GRUDGE	0439
怨	HOLD A GRUDGE	3179
厭	disagreeable	3745

head→**FRONT PARTS OF HEAD**

head

頭	HEAD	2019
首	HEAD	2818
脳	BRAIN	1227

headgear

帽	HEADGEAR	0693
冠	CROWN	2583
笠	SEDGE HAT	3300
兜	HEADPIECE	3499

healthy

康	HEALTHY	3877
健	ROBUST	0152
生	health	4309

hear

聞	HEAR	4127
聴	LISTEN	1796

heat

熱	HEAT	3555
暑	SUMMER HEAT	3121

heating devices

炉	FURNACE	1079
窯	KILN	2986
缶	steam boiler	2526

height

高	height	2601
丈	STATURE	4227
背	stature	3182

help

助	HELP	1440
佑	HELP (said esp. of God)	0083
祐	DIVINE HELP	1146
援	AID	0715
佐	ASSIST	0076
補	assist	1529
輔	ASSIST	1963
済	RELIEVE	0634

hide

隠	HIDE	0873
蔽	COVER	2991
伏	lie in concealment	0049
潜	LURK	0922
匿	CONCEAL	3735
忍	perform by stealth	2750

high

高	HIGH	2601
喬	TALL	3129
峻	high and steep	0495
峨	HIGH AND RUGGED	0493

high

高	HIGH	2601
上	upper	4212
崚	LOFTY	0570

high officials

相	MINISTER	1120
宰	chief minister	2829
卿	STATE MINISTER	0769

high-ranking

貴	NOBLE	3220
上	upper	4212
高	HIGH	2601
総	GENERAL	1743
太	of highest rank	2673

hills

丘	HILL	4307
畝	RIDGE	1857
岡	HILL	3719
台	heights	2498
坂	SLOPE	0275
阪	slope	0321
塚	MOUND	0675
阜	MOUND	3254
陵	high mound	0660
稜	RIDGE	1545

hinder→**OBSTRUCT AND HINDER**

history

史	HISTORY	4324
伝	biography	0048
歴	PERSONAL HISTORY	3748

hold

持	HOLD	0447
提	carry in hand	0720
携	CARRY IN HAND	0796
捧	hold up in both hands	0594

hold an event

催	HOLD AN EVENT	0178
挙	hold a function	3106

hold in the mind

持	HOLD	0447
抱	HUG	0363
懐	embosom	0942

holes and cavities

穴	HOLE	2682
洞	CAVE	0455
窟	CAVE	2923
窪	HOLLOW	2962
腔	BODY CAVITY	1267
孔	OPEN HOLE	0205
口	MOUTH	4189
坑	PIT	0277
堀	DITCH	0561
溝	CHANNEL	0810
壕	TRENCH	0966
濠	MOAT	0975
凹	concavity	4294

holiday

休	holiday	0056
暇	leave of absence	1275

holy

聖	HOLY	3509
神	divine	1143
霊	miraculous	3480

honorific prefixes

御	GENERAL HONORIFIC TERM	0703
貴	YOUR HONORABLE	3220
尊	your honorable	2920
令	your honorable	2489

honorific suffixes

翁	honorific suffix	2611
老	honorific suffix	3963

horse

馬	HORSE	4086
駒	HORSE (*elegant*)	2298
駿	FLEET STEED	2304
午	the Horse	2478

hot

熱	HOT	3555
暑い	HOT (weather)	3121
炎	scorching	3075
温	WARM	0740
暖	WARM (esp. weather)	1274

houses

家	HOUSE	2827
屋	HOUSE	3842
軒	house	1851
戸	HOUSEHOLD	2429
宅	DWELLING HOUSE	2698
居	residence	3822
邸	STATELY RESIDENCE	1451
住	housing	0072
庵	HERMITAGE	3876

how many

幾	HOW MANY	4403
何-	HOW MANY	0073

huge→**BIG AND HUGE**

humble
謙 HUMBLE 2044
遜 HUMBLE 4041
拝 HUMBLY 0360

humble prefixes
小 my little (*humble*) 0007
弊 our [my] humble 3583
拙 my humble 0373
愚 my foolish 3513

hunger and thirst
渇 THIRST 0627
餓 STARVED 2176
飢 STARVE 2101
饑 STARVE 2281

hunt and fish
猟 HUNTING 0654
狩 HUNT 0474
獲 CATCH GAME 0959
漁 FISH 0856
釣 ANGLE 2108
弋 CATCH 4230

hurry
急 HURRY 2595
促 HASTEN 0118

husband
夫 HUSBAND 4271
主 master of the house 2437

I

illusory mental images
夢 DREAM 2939
幻 PHANTOM 0206

image
像 IMAGE 0187
影 SHADOW 2381

images
像 IMAGE 0187
仏 Buddhist image 0020
偶 figure 0150

imitate
擬 IMITATE 0969
倣 COPY AFTER 0127
摸 PATTERN AFTER 0797
模 pattern after 1326
肖 MODEL 2733
象 represent 2647

immediate
即 IMMEDIATE 1439
直 straight away 3649
忽 IN AN INSTANT 3080

impartial
公 impartial 2468
平 equal 4291

impatient
焦 BE IMPATIENT 3444
躁 RESTLESS 2083
燥 restless 1392

imperial decree
勅 IMPERIAL DECREE 1841
詔 IMPERIAL EDICT 1900
宣 imperial proclamation 2799

important
要 IMPORTANT 3263
重 HEAVY 4390

impose
徴 LEVY 0841
課 impose 1980

imprison and confine
拘 ARREST 0367
禁 confine 3469
留 keep in custody 3189
置 place in custody 3222
錮 IMPRISON 2182

incident
事 AFFAIR 4384
故 incident 1466
変 unexpected event 2569

incite
挑 PROVOKE 0445
唆 INSTIGATE 0480
扇 FAN 2449
煽 FAN 1338
激 excite 0955
奮 ROUSE UP 3000
振 arouse to action 0515
動 MOVE 2232
起 rise to action 4099

inclining→OBLIQUENESS AND INCLINING

inclining toward
偏 ONE-SIDED 0151
傾 incline toward 0174

include→CONTAIN AND INCLUDE

increase
加 add to 0042
増 INCREASE 0836
殖 MULTIPLY 1253
倍 DOUBLE 0122

indicate
指 POINT 0452
示 SHOW 2435
標 MARK 1347
宛てる ADDRESS 2762

industry and business
業 BUSINESS, INDUSTRY 3227
商 TRADE 2623
産 industry 4089

工	manufacturing industry	4190

inexpensive

安	INEXPENSIVE	2695
廉	CHEAP	3911
低	low-priced	0082

inflorescences

穂	SPIKE	1575
穎	GLUME	2036

inform and communicate

報	INFORM	2133
通	COMMUNICATE	3855
告	NOTIFY	3062
届ける	give notice	3820
達	issue a notice	3893
知	let know	1446
申	REPORT	4319
稟	REPORT TO	2649
宣	PROCLAIM	2799

information

報	information	2133
信	MESSAGE	0115
訃	NEWS OF DEATH	1827

in front

前	BEFORE	2819
先	AHEAD	3046

ingest

喫	INGEST	0668
服	take	1090
食	EAT	2578
喰う	EAT	0670
飲	DRINK	2127
呑	SWALLOW	3059
啄	PECK	0482

inheritors

嫡	LEGITIMATE CHILD	0839
嗣	HEIR	2153

injury

傷	WOUND	0179
創	wound (cut)	2283
-擦れ	sore	0971

in-laws

婿	SON-IN-LAW	0689
嫁	daughter-in-law	0780
姑	MOTHER-IN-LAW	0332

inlets and bays

江	INLET	0257
浦	coastal indentation	0524
湾	BAY	0748
峡	narrows	0427

inner

奥	inner	3503
深	DEEP	0636
幽	QUIET AND SECLUDED	3731

inquire

問	QUESTION	4117
詰	question closely	1920
聞く	ask	4127
質	query	3483
尋ねる	INQUIRE	2918
訊	INQUIRE	1842
伺う	INQUIRE (*humble*)	0078
諮	CONSULT	2009
詢	ASK FOR ADVICE	1917

insect

虫	INSECT	4343
昆	INSECT	3067
繭	COCOON	3023

insects

蚊	MOSQUITO	1673
蛍	FIREFLY	3204
蝶	BUTTERFLY	1772
蚕	SILKWORM	3107
蟬	CICADA	1804
蜂	BEE	1728
蛔	ROUNDWORM	1717

inside

内	INSIDE	4277
裏	inside	2652
奥	INNER PART	3503
中	IN	4262

insignia

紋	CREST	1651
章	BADGE	2624

install→ **EQUIP AND INSTALL**

instruct

訓	INSTRUCT	1844
指	direct	0452

instruments for beating or pounding

槌	HAMMER	1331
杵	WOODEN PESTLE	1074
砧	BLOCK FOR BEATING CLOTH	1477

in succession

連	IN SUCCESSION	3849
歴	successive	3748
逐	ONE BY ONE	3848
逓	progressively	3852
漸	GRADUALLY	0867

intelligent and wise

賢	WISE	3518
俊	brilliant	0117
鋭	SHARP	2171
敏	NIMBLE	1675
叡	PROFOUNDLY WISE	2405
智	wise	3458
慧	INTELLIGENT	3485
怜	CLEVER	0356

悧 CLEVER 0505
俐 CLEVER 0113
哲 SAGACIOUS 3402
明 clear-sighted 1060
聡 SHARP-WITTED 1750

intention→**WILL AND INTENTION**

intercross

交 intercross 2508
差 cross 4104

interest and dividend

利 interest 1431
子 interest 4196
配 dividend 1853

internal organs

心 HEART 0011
肺 LUNG 1147
胃 STOMACH 3171
腸 INTESTINES 1307
肝 LIVER 1045
胆 GALLBLADDER 1150
腎 KIDNEY 3511

interrogatives

奈 interrogative forming element 2759
那 interrogative forming element 1047
何 WHAT 0073
誰 WHO 1986

interval→**DISTANCE AND INTERVAL**

investigate and examine

閲 REVIEW 4132
審 EXAMINE CAREFULLY 2985
験 TEST 2306
勘 CHECK 2231
糾 INQUIRE INTO 1631
究 STUDY EXHAUSTIVELY 2729
察 INSPECT 2961
討 STUDY 1846
探 PROBE 0613
検 EXAMINE 1241
診 EXAMINE A PATIENT 1898
調 INVESTIGATE 1973
査 LOOK INTO 3092

invite→**CALL AND INVITE**

iron and steel

鉄 IRON 2147
銑 PIG IRON 2160
鋼 STEEL 2183

J

Japan

日 JAPAN 3759
和 JAPAN 1450
邦 JAPAN 1051
国 Japanese 3831
倭 ANCIENT NAME FOR JAPAN 0140

Japanese money denominations

文 *mon* 2458
両 *ryo* 4331
厘 *RIN* 3727
銭 sen 2159
円 YEN 3673

jealous and envious

嫉 JEALOUS 0783
妬 JEALOUS 0337
羨 ENVIOUS 2951

join→**PARTICIPATE AND JOIN**

join

結 TIE 1706
繋 CONNECT 3612
縛 BIND 1779
綴 BIND 1746
繃 BIND UP 1787
束 TIE UP 4369
梱 PACK 1205
連 LINK 3849
係 CONNECT 0108
接 join 0607

joint

節 JOINT 3336
関 connection 4129

journey

旅 TRAVEL 1153
行 trip 0246
遊 tour 3896
巡 tour around 3781

judge

判 JUDGE 1441
裁 JUDGE 4090
鑑 APPRAISE 2226
評 evaluate 1895
審 TRY 2985
決 DECIDE 0308
視 REGARD 1223

jump

跳 JUMP 1934
躍 LEAP 2090
蹶 SPRING TO ONE'S FEET 2073

K

Kansai cities

阪 OSAKA 0321
神 Kobe 1143
京 KYOTO 2546
洛 KYOTO 0463

Kanto region

京 TOKYO 2546
東 Tokyo 4385

都	METROPOLIS OF TOKYO	2120
浜	Yokohama	0523
埼	SAITAMA	0560
湘	SHONAN	0742

keys→LOCKS AND KEYS

kill

殺	KILL	1677
劉	KILL	2398
刺	stab to death	1625
絞	STRANGLE	1707
窒	CHOKE	2853

kind

厚	KIND	3726
篤	cordial	3371
懇	cordial	3606
慈	AFFECTIONATE	2949
温	warmhearted	0740
渥	GRACIOUS	0731
優	kindly	0200

kinds and types

型	TYPE	3266
類	KIND	2275
色	kind	2522
般	SORT	1670
属	genus	3901
品	category	2795
種	VARIETY	1560
様	variety	1332

kinds of atmospheric vapor

霧	FOG	3493
霞	MIST	3490
雲	CLOUD	3447

kinds of frozen water

氷	ICE	0043
雪	SNOW	3431

kinds of fuel

炭	COAL, CHARCOAL	2806
薪	FIREWOOD	3009
油	OIL	0400

kinds of grasses

草	GRASS	2813
荻	AMUR SILVERGRASS	2844
蒲	CATTAIL	2932
莱	GOOSEFOOT	2878
蕨	BRACKEN	2992
叢	grassy place	3243
芝	LAWN GRASS	2705
笹	BAMBOO GRASS	3301
茅	cogongrass	2779
萱	THATCH GRASS	2904
藁	STRAW	3015
芦	REED	2743
葦	COMMON REED	2934
菅	SEDGE	2874

kinds of numbers

数	NUMBER (mathematical unit)	2245
員	fixed number	2822
号	NUMBER (numerical designation)	2675
番	No.	3416
第	ORDINAL NUMBER PREFIX	3298
-目	ordinal number suffix	3777
次	numerical order suffix	0058
桁	DIGIT	1165

kinds of precipitation

雨	RAIN	4378
露	DEW	3495
霜	FROST	3491
雪	SNOW	3431

kinds of railway

鉄	railway	2147
電	electric railway	3465
車	railway car	4367
両	counter for railway cars	4331
輛	counter for railway cars	2000

kinds of skin

皮	SKIN (of any kind)	3771
膚	SKIN (of the human body)	4049
肌	SKIN (of the human body)	1021
革	LEATHER	3099
韋	TANNED LEATHER	2851
鱗	SCALES	2375

kinds of sound

音	SOUND	2570
声	VOICE	2724
響	reverberation	3573
韻	melodious tone	2279
玲	TINKLING OF JADES	1139

kinds of stone

硯	INKSTONE	1517
砥	WHETSTONE	1480

kinds of water

水	WATER	0010
湯	HOT WATER	0747
汽	STEAM	0309
氷	ICE	0043
淵	DEEP WATER	0732

kinds of wood

木	WOOD	4261
材	TIMBER	1031
薪	FIREWOOD	3009
柴	BRUSHWOOD	3287

kitchen

厨	KITCHEN	3740
庖	KITCHEN	3825

know and understand

知	KNOW	1446
通	know thoroughly	3855
得	gain understanding of	0577

分かる understand 2466
解 understand 1913
諒 UNDERSTAND 1982
了 COMPREHEND 4157
悟 AWAKE TO 0502
惺 AWAKE TO 0709

knowledge→LEARNING AND KNOWLEDGE

Korea
鮮 Korea 2355
朝 North Korea 2130
韓 SOUTH KOREA 2218

L

labels and slips
札 TAG 1011
券 TICKET 3256
票 SLIP 3308
符 tally 3299
節 token 3336

lakes and marshes
沢 MARSH 0313
沼 MUDDY POND 0398
湖 LAKE 0736
池 POND 0253
潟 LAGOON 0921

land and soil
土 SOIL 4211
地 GROUND 0236
壌 ARABLE SOIL 0933
泥 MUD 0384
陸 LAND 0659
埴 CLAY 0562

language
語 LANGUAGE 1944
弁 dialect 2497

large numbers
百 HUNDRED 2519
千 THOUSAND 4219
万 TEN THOUSAND 3653
億 HUNDRED MILLION 0192
兆 TRILLION 0264
京 ten quadrillion 2546

last
末 last in time 4317
終 last 1692

late
遅 LATE (delayed) 3887
晩 late (advanced) 1232
晏 LATE 3103

late and delay→BE LATE AND DELAY
late and delay→BE LATE AND DELAY

later Chinese dynasties
唐 TANG DYNASTY 3867
宋 SONG DYNASTY 2730
元 Yuan Dynasty 2428
明 Ming Dynasty 1060
清 Qing Dynasty 0635

latitude and longitude
緯 LATITUDE 1782
経 longitude 1687

laugh
笑 LAUGH 3275
莞 SMILE SWEETLY 2842

laws and rules
法 LAW 0391
律 LAW 0433
典 CANON 3253
憲 CONSTITUTION 3001
令 ordinance 2489
則 RULE 1831
矩 RULE 1475
規 REGULATION 1231
紀 discipline 1628

lazy
惰 LAZY 0706
怠 REMISS 2588
慢 SLUGGISH 0844

lead and escort
率 LEAD 2625
引 lead 0207
導 GUIDE 3587
連 take along 3849

leaders
主 MASTER 2437
王 KING 4247
長 CHIEF 3163
頭 HEAD 2019
首 LEADER 2818
領 leader 1567
魁 LEADER 4125

learn and study
学 STUDY 3162
考 study 3962
習 LEARN 3306
研 RESEARCH 1456
究 STUDY EXHAUSTIVELY 2729
攻 specialize 0286

learning and knowledge
業 studies 3227
学 learning 3162
文 culture 2458
識 KNOWLEDGE 2070
知 knowledge 1446

leave

遺	LEAVE BEHIND	3928
残す	leave	1179

leave and set forth

去	GO AWAY	2678
離	leave	2364
発	START	3174
出	GO OUT	4310
退	RETREAT	3838
撤	WITHDRAW	0912

left and right

右	RIGHT	3693
左	LEFT	3692

leg

足	FOOT	2714
脚	LEG	1226
膝	KNEE	1359

legislature

議	LEGISLATIVE BODY	2078
会	assembly	2512
院	House	0544

leisure

暇	FREE TIME	1275
閑	LEISURE	4123

leisurely

悠	LEISURELY	3407
閑	idle	4123

lend and borrow

借	BORROW	0137
債	DEBT	0177
貸	LEND	3213
融	finance	2303

length units

寸	*sun* (3.03 cm)	3652
浬	NAUTICAL MILE (1852m)	0526
反	*tan* (10.6 m)	3663
尺	*SHAKU* (30.3 cm)	4248
米	meter	4342
尋	fathom (1.8 m)	2918
間	*ken* (1.8 m)	4122
丈	*jo* (3.03 m)	4227
町	*cho* (109 m)	1430
里	LEAGUE, *ri* (3.9 km)	4356
哩	MILE (1609m)	0479

less in degree

弱	WEAK	1499
軽	LIGHT	1909
微	SLIGHT	0788
低	LOW	0082
薄	THIN	3004
浅	SHALLOW	0464
仄	FAINT	3664

let do

放	LET GO	1058
随	let do	0765

lie down

伏	PROSTRATE	0049
臥	LIE DOWN	1825
寝る	lie down	2925

life

生	LIFE	4309
命	LIFE	2553
寿	LONGEVITY	4372

life energy

精	SPIRIT	1729
気	vital energy	3960

light

光	LIGHT	3043
明	light	1060
灯	LAMP	1019
燭	CANDLE	1391
照	sunlight	3506
虹	RAINBOW	1637

light-colored

淡	LIGHT	0640
浅	light	0464
薄い	pale	3004
鈍-	DULL	2123

lighter elements

水	hydrogen	0010
酸	OXYGEN	1968
窒	NITROGEN	2853
塩	chlorine	0774
臭	bromine	3261
硫	SULFUR	1519
炭	carbon	2806

like→**LOVE AND LIKE**

limbs

肢	LIMB	1094
腕	ARM	1269
脚	LEG	1226

line

線	LINE	1760
筋	THREADLIKE STRUCTURE	3319
条	strip	2726
脈	VEIN	1189
棒	straight line	1237
縞	STRIPE	1784
軸	AXIS	1908

lineage

系	LINEAGE	2443
血	BLOOD	4339

linear arrangements

伍	RANK	0050
列	ROW	1018
行	LINE (esp. of print)	0246
欄	COLUMN	1419

lines→**ROPES AND LINES**

lines and line segments

線	LINE	1760
弧	ARC	0430
弦	chord	0343
径	DIAMETER	0347
辺	side	3761

line segments→LINES AND LINE SEGMENTS

liquefy

溶	DISSOLVE, MELT	0816
熔	MELT (metals)	1340
鎔	MELT (metals)	2214
解	DISSOLVE	1913
融	FUSE	2303

liquid

液	LIQUID	0622
汁	fluid	0227
水	WATER	0010

live

活	LIVE	0460
暮らす	LIVE (pass one's life)	2971
生	live (be alive)	4309

load

載	LOAD	4091
積む	load	1579
搭	load on board	0721

localities→AREAS AND LOCALITIES

locks and keys

鍵	KEY	2203
錠	LOCK	2180

longitude→LATITUDE AND LONGITUDE

long slender objects

棒	ROD	1237
箸	CHOPSTICKS	3359
桟	crosspiece	1169
軸	AXLE	1908
錘	SPINDLE	2191
竿	POLE	3259
杖	STAFF	1026
錫	Buddhist priest's staff	2189
軛	YOKE	1873

long time periods

時	TIME	1155
代	age	0034
紀	ERA	1628
世	AGE	4308
朝	dynastic period	2130
期	period	2139
劫	KALPA	1435

look→SEE AND LOOK

loosen

弛	SLACKEN	0245
緩	SLACK	1757

lose

負	LOSE	2594
敗	BE DEFEATED	1868

losing and loss

失	LOSE	4325
喪	lose	3504
逸	LET SLIP	3872
損	LOSS, lose	0801
佚	LOST	0070

loss→LOSING AND LOSS

loud

高い	loud	2601
朗	CLEAR (voice)	1679
騒	clamorous	2308
喧	BOISTEROUS	0667
嘩	BOISTEROUS	0771

love

愛	LOVE	3133
情	love	0583
恋	LOVE (for the opposite sex)	2602
艶	ROMANCE	2403
寵	AFFECTION	3029

love and like

愛	LOVE	3133
恋	LOVE (the opposite sex)	2602
好	LIKE	0240
慕	ADORE	2970
惚れる	FALL IN LOVE	0584
玩	cherish	1085

low

低	LOW	0082
下	lower	4186

lower

低	lower	0082
下	bring down	4186

lowly

卑	MEAN	3270
下	of low rank	4186
低	LOW	0082

luster

艶	gloss	2403
沢	luster	0313

M

machines and tools

機	MACHINE	1365
械	MECHANICAL CONTRIVANCE	1203
具	IMPLEMENT	3159
器	INSTRUMENT	3367
儀	measuring instrument	0191
鏡	OPTICAL INSTRUMENT	2219
董	OLD TOOL	2911

magnetism→ELECTRICITY AND MAGNETISM

mail

郵	MAIL	2121

便	POST	0105

main

主	MAIN	2437
正	chief	4296
本	head	4314
親-	PARENT	2264
首	leading	2818

make

作	MAKE	0077
造	MAKE	3856
成	FORM	4352
工	MANUFACTURE	4190
製	MANUFACTURE	3478
産	PRODUCE	4089
調	PREPARE	1973
組む	ASSEMBLE	1693
構	CONSTRUCT	1325

make progress

進	ADVANCE	3873
亨	GO SMOOTHLY	2530
捗	MAKE PROGRESS	0513

make sound or noise

鳴	SOUND	0831
響	REVERBERATE	3573
騒	CLAMOR	2308
轟	RESOUND	3425

make widely known

布	SPREAD	3691
流	spread	0529
伝	spread	0048
広	spread	3769
弘	DISSEMINATE (esp. Buddhism)	0223
及	REACH TO	4192

man

男	MAN	3147
郎	YOUNG MAN	1641
雄	MALE	1271
牡	MALE	1040
夫	male adult	4271
翁	OLD MAN	2611
爺	OLD MAN	2656

mania and maniacs

痴	infatuated	4072
狂	maniac	0318
魔	maniac	3953
熱	fever	3555

maniacs→MANIA AND MANIACS

mansions

邸	STATELY RESIDENCE	1451
館	stately mansion	2196
荘	VILLA	2814

manuscript

稿	MANUSCRIPT	1574
草	draft	2813
案	draft	2824

mark

印	imprint	1023
押	seal	0371
劃	MARK OFF	2378
画	mark off	3723
捺	AFFIX A SEAL	0603

market

市	MARKET	2487
場	market	0678

marks and signs

標	MARK (identifying sign)	1347
徽	EMBLEM	0968
痕	SCAR	4066
印	MARK (visible sign)	1023
跡	TRACE	1937
蹟	TRACE	2065
踪	FOOTPRINTS	1996
紋	print	1651
符	SYMBOL	3299
号	SIGN	2675
栞	BOOKMARK	3285

marriage→MARRYING AND MARRIAGE

marrying and marriage

嫁	WED A MAN	0780
婚	MARRY	0566
姻	MARRIAGE	0421
縁	marriage relation	1754

marshes→LAKES AND MARSHES

mathematical power

乗	power	4393
方	SQUARE	2459
平	square (measure)	4291

mats

畳	TATAMI	3205
薦	straw mat	3008
-敷き	underlay	2345

matter

質	MATTER	3483
物	substance	1084
材	MATERIAL	1031
料	MATERIALS	1644
資	material resources	3342

mature

熟	MATURE	3558
成	grow up	4352
稔	RIPEN	1544
爛	OVERRIPE	1427
実る	bear fruit	2765

meaning

義	MEANING	2948
意	MEANING	2650
訳	SENSE	1865
旨	PURPORT	2516

趣 PURPOSE 4111

means

策 MEASURE 3320
段 STEP 1471
手 means 4267

measure

測 MEASURE 0744
量 measure 3119

measuring devices

枡 MEASURE 1070
尺 rule 4248
計 meter 1828
衡 scales 0939
秤 BALANCE 1488

meat

肉 FLESH 3966
身 meat 4368
脩 DRIED MEAT 0154

mediating and mediators

紹 INTRODUCE 1691
介 MEDIATE 2463
媒 INTERMEDIATE 0686
仲 INTERMEDIARY 0047

mediators→MEDIATING AND MEDIATORS

medicines

薬 DRUG 3011
剤 PREPARATION 2102
錠 PILL 2180
丸 pill suffix 4225
鍼 ACUPUNCTURE 2204
灸 MOXIBUSTION 2752

meet

会 MEET 2512
遇 ENCOUNTER 3889
遭 MEET WITH 3917
見 SEE 3151
謁 BE GRANTED AN AUDIENCE 1976
逢 MEET 4002

merchandise

産 product 4089
品 ARTICLE (of merchandise) 2795
貨 GOODS 3113
物 commodity 1084

merchant

屋 shopkeeper 3842
商 merchant 2623

metal

金 METAL 2552
鉱 ORE 2145
礦 ORE 1606
鈑 SHEET METAL 2122

metals

金 GOLD 2552
銀 SILVER 2156
銅 COPPER 2155
鉄 IRON 2147
鉛 LEAD 2143
錫 TIN 2189

middle

中 MIDDLE 4262
央 CENTER 4322
心 HEART 0011
核 NUCLEUS 1162

military

武 MILITARY 3979
兵 military 3158

military officers and ranks

曹 SERGEANT 3414
尉 COMPANY OFFICER 2119
佐 FIELD OFFICER 0076
将 GENERAL OFFICER 0551
督 COMMANDER 3471
帥 COMMANDER IN CHIEF 1642

mine

坑 PIT 0277
鉱 MINE 2145
礦 MINE 1606
山 mine 3658

miraculous

妙 MARVELOUS 0280
魔 magic(al) 3953

misfortune and disaster

災 NATURAL CALAMITY 2734
難 DISASTER 2310
禍 CALAMITY 1304
厄 MISFORTUNE 3665
凶 BAD LUCK 3679

mistakes and mistaking

過 error 3891
失 SLIP 4325
誤 MISTAKE 1945
謬 MISTAKE 2060
錯 mistaken 2187
-違える mis- 3907

mistaking→MISTAKES AND MISTAKING

mix

混 MIX 0631
淆 INTERMINGLE 0630
交 intermingle 2508
雑 MIXED 1752
錯 MIXED UP 2187

model

範 MODEL 3360
典 CANON 3253
模 PATTERN 1326
程 ESTABLISHED FORM 1524
式 form 3785
準 STANDARD 3541

格	NORM	1161

modifier suffixes

然	MODIFIER FORMING SUFFIX	3456
乎	MODIFIER FORMING SUFFIX	4316
如	modifier suffix	0239
爾	adjective suffix	4407
的	ADJECTIVAL SUFFIX	1444

moisten

潤	moisten	0918
浸	SOAK	0530
漬ける	immerse	0861

monetary gifts

謝	monetary gift of thanks	2048
礼	monetary gift	1012

money

金	MONEY	2552
銭	MONEY	2159
貨	MONEY (legal tender), coin	3113
幣	CURRENCY	3582
銀	SILVER	2156
財	finance	1849
資	RESOURCES	3342
-玉	coin suffix	4289
札	bill	1011

monkey

猿	MONKEY	0824
申	the Monkey	4319

months→WEEKS AND MONTHS

moon

月	MOON	3674
陰	moon	0657

moral goodness

徳	VIRTUE	0842
道	the way of moral conduct	3888
善	GOOD	2921
義	RIGHTEOUSNESS	2948

moral principles

倫	MORALS	0135
道	the way of moral conduct	3888

morning and dawn

朝	MORNING	2130
暁	DAWN	1233
旦	DAYBREAK	3041
曙	DAWN	1384
晨	EARLY MORNING	3110

most

最	MOST	3120
至	utmost	2707
極	EXTREME	1243

most recent

昨	LAST	1106
去	last	2678
先	last	3046

motion

動	motion	2232
惰	inertia	0706

motion picture

映	motion picture	1104
画	film	3723

mountain parts

頂	SUMMIT	0164
峰	PEAK	0494
嶺	RIDGE	3013
峠	MOUNTAIN PASS	0428
崖	CLIFF	2862
壁	wall-like structure	3601

mountains

峰	PEAK	0494
岳	HIGH MOUNTAIN	3164
山	MOUNTAIN	3658

mourn and mourning

弔	CONDOLE	4240
悼	MOURN	0587
喪	MOURNING	3504
忌	MOURNING	2735

mourning→MOURN AND MOURNING

mouth parts

唇	LIP	3401
歯	TOOTH	3124
舌	TONGUE	2711
牙	FANG	4243

move

動	MOVE	2232
運	MOVE	3894
滑	SLIDE	0809
辷る	SLIP	3957
移	SHIFT	1508
転	remove	1872
遷	TRANSFER	3932
繰る	SHIFT ONWARD	1806

move forward

進	ADVANCE	3873
突	DASH	2772
這う	CRAWL	4003

move through water

泳	SWIM	0385
游	SWIM	0750
渉	wade	0638
遡	GO UPSTREAM	4040
漕	ROW	0864

multiply

乗	multiply	4393
掛ける	multiply	0596

musical elements

韻	RHYME	2279
律	RHYTHM	0433
拍	BEAT	0361

調	TONE	1973
呂	ancient musical note	2713

musical instrument

管	wind instrument	3349
弦	string instrument	0343

musical instruments

琴	KOTO	3455
箏	KOTO	3353
鼓	DRUM	2241
笛	FLUTE	3303
琵	LUTE	3453
琶	LUTE	3454
笙	*SHO*	3302

music and songs

楽	MUSIC	3505
音	sound of music	2570
節	tune	3336
調べ	melody	1973
曲	MUSICAL COMPOSITION	4340
歌	SONG	2296
謡	POPULAR SONG	2011
唄	DITTY	0477

mutual

相	MUTUAL	1120
互	RECIPROCAL	4245

mythical animals

竜	DRAGON	2603
辰	THE DRAGON	3713
麒	MALE CHINESE UNICORN	2363
麟	FEMALE CHINESE UNICORN	2376
鵬	MYTHICAL HUGE BIRD	1416
鳳	MALE PHOENIX	3749
凰	FEMALE PHOENIX	3738

N

naked

裸	NAKED	1550
素	bare	3108

name

名	NAME	2693
銘	name (inscribed by maker)	2158
姓	SURNAME	0334
氏	FAMILY NAME	3669
称	APPELLATION	1491
題	TITLE	4139
号	DESIGNATION	2675

name

呼	CALL	0324
言う	call	2440
称	name	1491

name suffixes

郎	MALE NAME SUFFIX	1641
麿	CLASSICAL MALE NAME SUFFIX	3949
彦	MALE NAME ELEMENT	4085
-子	female name element	4196

narrow

狭	NARROW	0473
窄	NARROW	2830

national

国	national	3831
内	internal	4277

natural

地	natural	0236
野	wild	1877
粗	crude	1683
原	in the original state	3733

nature and character

性	NATURE	0357
気	temperament	3960
質	QUALITY	3483
品	grade of excellence	2795
柄	CHARACTER	1111
格	(good) character	1161

near

近	NEAR	3798
隣	neighboring	0961
傍	BESIDE	0166
旁	BESIDE	2598
沿	ALONG	0386

necessity→NEED AND NECESSITY

neck

首	NECK	2818
頸	NECK	2035
項	nape	0692

need and necessity

要	required	3263
必	must	0015
須	MUST	0700
需	DEMAND	3472
入	necessary	4177
用	needed for (a specific use)	3694

needle

針	NEEDLE	2099
刺	prickle	1625
茨	THORN	2812

negative

負	negative	2594
陰	negative	0657

net

網	NET	1737
羅	bird net	3244

new

新	NEW	2239
鮮	FRESH	2355
生	raw	4309

next

次	NEXT	0058

明	next	1060
翌	THE FOLLOWING	3307
来	the coming	4366

night→**EVENING AND NIGHT**

nine

九	NINE	4176
玖	NINE	1041

nitrogen

窒	NITROGEN	2853
硝	NITER	1520

nobility

爵	RANK OF NOBILITY	3143
公	nobleman	2468
侯	FEUDAL LORD	0109

noblemen

公	duke	2468
侯	marquis	0109
伯	COUNT	0067
子	viscount	4196
男	baron	3147

nominalizers

所	PARTICLE OF NOMINALIZATION	1056
事	nominalization word	4384
子	NOUN SUFFIX	4196
性	-ITY	0357

noon

午	NOON	2478
昼	midday	3841

North American countries

米	AMERICA	4342
加	Canada	0042

notebook

帳	NOTEBOOK	0572
帖	NOTEBOOK	0342
簿	RECORD BOOK	3387
籍	REGISTER	3394

nothing→**EMPTINESS AND NOTHING**

not moving

固	FIRM	3830
定	fixed	2770
静	still	2164
止	still	3659

nourish→**RAISE AND NOURISH**

number→**QUANTITY AND NUMBER**

O

obey

守	observe	2697
遵	OBEY	3929
順	OBEY	0018
隷	be subordinate to	2201
従	FOLLOW	0498

object

物	THING	1084
品	ARTICLE	2795
体	BODY	0080

obliqueness and inclining

斜	OBLIQUE	1878
傾	INCLINE	0174

obstacle

障	HINDRANCE	0875
関	BARRIER	4129

obstinate→**FIRM AND OBSTINATE**

obstruct and hinder

遮	INTERRUPT	3916
塞	STOP UP	2924
阻	OBSTRUCT	0411
沮	OBSTRUCT	0399
奄	OBSTRUCT (by covering)	2757
妨	HINDER	0279
障	hinder	0875
碍	STAND IN THE WAY	1536
害	stand in the way	2826
梗	STOP UP	1204

occasions

際	OCCASION	0874
折	occasion	0297
時	timely occasion	1155
機	OPPORTUNITY	1365
節	time	3336

occupy

占	OCCUPY	2496
拠	occupy	0369
領	take possession of	1567
専	take exclusive possession of	3272

offenses→**CRIMES AND OFFENSES**

offer

供	OFFER (to a person or god)	0098
献	OFFER (esp. to a superior)	2240
納	offer (as to a god)	1652
提	PRESENT	0720
貢	offer tribute	2838
奉	DEDICATE	3167
捧	OFFER RESPECTFULLY	0594

offering

奠	OFFERING	2641
幣	offering	3582
貢	TRIBUTE	2838

offer wine

酌	POUR WINE	1854
献	offer wine	2240
酬	reciprocate wineglasses	1941

officials

官	GOVERNMENT OFFICIAL	2766
吏	OFFICIAL	4351
僚	official	0186

司 officiator 3648
役 executive 0288
事 officer 4384

offspring

子 CHILD 4196
仔 OFFSPRING 0038
孤 orphan 0426
嫡 LEGITIMATE CHILD 0839
息 son 3278
男 son 3147
惣 eldest son 3452
娘 DAUGHTER 0488
女 daughter 4226
姫 DAUGHTER OF NOBLE BIRTH 0489

offspring of siblings

甥 NEPHEW 1510
姪 NIECE 0422

of long duration

長 LONG 3163
永 ETERNAL 2436
久 OF LONG DURATION 4191
恒 permanent 0438

oils→**FATS AND OILS**

old

古 OLD (not new) 2495
老 OLD (not young) 3963
故 OLD (of the past) 1466
旧 old 0014

old persons

老 old person 3963
爺 OLD MAN 2656
翁 OLD MAN 2611
婆 OLD WOMAN 3433
姥 OLD WOMAN 0420

old times

昔 FORMER TIMES 3086
往 bygone days 0348

omit

漏 omit 0860
脱 leave out by mistake 1225
抜く leave out 0290
欠 missing 2481

one

一 ONE 4148
壱 ONE (in legal documents) 2723
片- ONE OF TWO 4272
隻 ONE OF A PAIR 3426
単 SINGLE 2805
個 INDIVIDUAL 0132

one side

片- one side 4272
偏 ONE-SIDED 0151
頗 one-sided 1552

only

唯 ONLY 0556
一 one and only 4148

on the verge of

-掛かる be on the verge of 0596
将 on the verge of 0551
-際 on the verge of 0874
臨 on the point of 2059

open

開 OPEN 4121
展 UNFOLD 3862
披 open and read 0362

opinion

見 view (personal opinion) 3151
観 VIEW (conception) 2359
説 opinion 1949
論 opinion 1981

opposite

対 OPPOSITE 1025
反 COUNTER 3663
逆 REVERSE 3835
倒 upside-down 0139

oppress→**TORTURE AND OPPRESS**

order

序 ORDER (sequence/arrangement) 3803
順 ORDER (sequence) 0018
次 order (sequence) 0058
番 NUMERICAL ORDER 3416
秩 ORDER (methodical arrangement) 1489

ordinary

常 NORMAL 3203
只- ORDINARY 2677
並 ordinary 2793
平 common 4291
普 common 2919
庸 MEDIOCRE 3881
凡 COMMONPLACE 3656
套 TRITE 2823

organ

臓 INTERNAL ORGAN 1417
器 organ 3367
官 organ 2766

organize

組 ORGANIZE 1693
結 form 1706
編 put together 1755

organized bodies

会 SOCIETY 2512
協 association 0103
団 BODY 3791
体 BODY 0080
組 union 1693
労 workers' union 3155
連 federation 3849

講	fraternity	2046
院	INSTITUTION	0544

original

素	primary	3108
原	ORIGINAL	3733
本	original	4314
初	FIRST	1433

other

他	OTHER	0039
余	other	2535
別	ANOTHER	1434

outside

外	OUTSIDE	0215
表	SURFACE	3083
面	FACE	2590

overturn

覆	OVERTURN	3386
翻	TURN OVER	2391
反	turn over	3663
顛	TURN [roll] OVER	2317
転	turn [roll] over	1872
倒	TOPPLE	0139
轢	RUN OVER	2095

P

palace

宮	ROYAL PALACE	2828
殿	PALACE	2247
閣	FEUDAL PALACE	4130

paper

紙	PAPER	1654
葉	LEAF	2912
丁	sheet	4155
箋	PIECE OF PAPER	3352
頁	PAGE	2589
面	page (of a newspaper)	2590

parents

親	PARENT	2264
父	FATHER	2467
母	MOTHER	4287

part

分	PART	2466
部	SECTION	2111
局	LIMITED PART	3800
片	FRAGMENT	4272

part company

別	SEPARATE	1434
離	SEPARATE	2364
訣	SEPARATE	1861

participate and join

参	PARTICIPATE	2563
与	take part in	4229
加	join	0042
入	ENTER	4177

particle

粒	GRAIN	1682
子	particle suffix	4196
核	NUCLEUS	1162

parties and sects

党	PARTY	3190
閥	CLIQUE	4126
流	school	0529
派	SECT	0456
翼	WING	3379
系	faction	2443
門	(religious) sect	1100
宗	RELIGIOUS SECT (esp. Buddhist)	2769

parts of boats and ships

舵	STEERING DEVICE	1697
梶	steering device	1199
櫓	SCULL	1412
櫂	OAR	1405
舷	GUNWALE	1698
艙	SHIP'S HOLD	1786

parts of governments

閣	CABINET	4128
省	MINISTRY	3100

parts of periodicals

欄	COLUMN	1419
面	page (of a newspaper)	2590

parts of plays

幕	act	2937
場	scene	0678

parts of towns

区	WARD	3681
街	CITY QUARTER	0702
町	town section (*cho*)	1430
丁	TOWN SUBSECTION (*chome*)	4155
字	village or town section	2696

parts of writing

章	CHAPTER	2624
段	passage	1471
節	paragraph	3336
款	ARTICLE	2135
条	ARTICLE	2726
項	CLAUSE	0692
目	ITEM	3777
箇	item	3348

pass

通	PASS	3855
過	PASS BY	3891
経	PASS THROUGH	1687
疏	LET PASS	1511

pattern

模	PATTERN (decorative design)	1326
文	decorative pattern	2458
柄	pattern (on cloth)	1111

様	pattern	1332
紋	figure	1651

pawn

質	pawn	3483
当	pawn	2701

pay

払う	PAY	0225
納	PAY (to the authorities)	1652
済	settle accounts	0634
支	pay out	2473
賦	INSTALLMENT	1992
償	RECOMPENSE	0199

pay and earnings

給	PAY	1708
賃	WAGE	3341
料	FEE	1644
俸	SALARY	0128
禄	RETAINER'S STIPEND	1264
収	income	0031

peace

和	PEACE	1450
安	public peace	2695
治	public order	0393

peaceful→CALM AND PEACEFUL

penetrate

透	PASS THROUGH	3854
貫	PENETRATE	3112
破	break through	1478
滲	PERMEATE	0862

people

民	PEOPLE	3770
族	race	1195

perceive

覚	PERCEIVE	3217
知	KNOW	1446
感	FEEL	3514
認	RECOGNIZE	1948

perforators

針	NEEDLE	2099
串	SKEWER	4364
杭	STAKE	1068
釘	NAIL	2100

performance

劇	DRAMA	2399
演	performance	0855
芸	entertainment	2738

performers

優	ACTOR	0200
俳	actor	0126
伶	MUSICIAN	0075
伎	PERFORMER	0055

periodicals

誌	MAGAZINE	1950
紙	newspaper	1654
報	bulletin	2133

periphery

周	PERIPHERY	3720
囲	circumference	3807
郭	OUTER ENCLOSURE	2112
廓	OUTER ENCLOSURE	3923

permit

許	PERMIT	1862
免	license	2565
准	grant permission	0143
允	GIVE CONSENT	2476

person

人	HUMAN BEING	4175
者	PERSON	3980
方	person (*honorific*)	2459
氏	person (*polite*)	3669

personal relations

縁	RELATION	1754
交	INTERCOURSE	2508
好	friendship	0240
仲	PERSONAL RELATIONS	0047
誼	FRIENDSHIP	1977
絆	BONDS	1686

person in charge

係	PERSON IN CHARGE	0108
-方	person in charge	2459
員	MEMBER (of a staff)	2822

phenomenon

象	PHENOMENON	2647
気	natural phenomenon	3960
物	physical phenomena	1084

phonetic [a]

亜	PHONETIC [a]	4354
阿	PHONETIC [a]	0408

phonetic [b]

毘	PHONETIC [bi]	3169
菩	PHONETIC [bo]	2868

phonetic [d]

陀	PHONETIC [da]	0409
達	phonetic [da]	3893
提	phonetic [dai]	0720
胴	phonetic [dō]	1186

phonetic [ha]

巴	phonetic [ha]	4246
波	phonetic [ha]	0388

phonetic [i]

伊	PHONETIC [i]	0052
斐	PHONETIC [i]	3449

phonetic [k]/[g]

迦	PHONETIC [ka]	3982
珈	phonetic [kō]	1138
伽	PHONETIC [ga]	0074
瓦	phonetic [ga]	4288
祇	phonetic [gi]	1459

phonetic [m]

弥 PHONETIC [mi] 0344
摩 phonetic [ma] 3938
昧 phonetic [mai] 1105
蜜 phonetic [mitsu] 2958
勿 phonetic [mot] 3661
牟 PHONETIC [mu] 2518

phonetic [na]

那 PHONETIC [na] 1047
奈 PHONETIC [na] 2759

phonetic [r]

呂 PHONETIC [ro] 2713
路 phonetic [ru] 1936
羅 PHONETIC [ra] 3244

phonetic [s]/[sh]

沙 phonetic [sha] 0311
刹 phonetic [setsu] 1620
遮 phonetic [sha] 3916
叉 phonetic [sha] 4194
世 phonetic [se] 4308
須 phonetic [shu] 0700
修 phonetic [shu] 0138
西 phonetic [su] 4333
相 phonetic [sō] 1120
薩 phonetic [satsu] 3016

photograph

撮 PHOTOGRAPH 0910
写 shoot 2493

picture

絵 PICTURE 1704
画 PICTURE 3723
図 DRAWING 3809

pigments

墨 INDIA INK 3423
漆 LACQUER 0863
藍 INDIGO 3024
堊 WHITEWASH 3442

places and positions

所 PLACE 1056
処 place 3764
場 PLACE (for specific activity) 0678
地 PLACE (particular location) 0236
席 meeting place 3865
位 POSITION 0069
点 POINT 2587
座 place 3868

places for landing or stopping

港 PORT 0737
湊 PORT 0743
津 HARBOR (*elegant*) 0466
駅 STATION 2292
停 stopping place 0156

places of business

店 SHOP (of any kind) 3828
舗 SHOP (esp. traditional) 2177
屋 SMALL SHOP 3842
社 COMPANY 1042

places of worship

堂 temple building 3202
塔 pagoda 0683
寺 BUDDHIST TEMPLE 2687
刹 TEMPLE 1620
社 Shinto shrine 1042
宮 SHINTO SHRINE 2828
院 monastery 0544
教 church 1887

plain and simple

素 PLAIN 3108
朴 SIMPLE (unadorned) 1013
単 simple (uncomplicated) 2805

planning→PLANS AND PLANNING

plans and planning

計 PLAN 1828
画 DRAW UP A PLAN 3723
案 PROPOSAL 2824
企 PROJECT 2513
図 systematic plan 3809
謀 SCHEME 2004
策 SCHEME 3320
略 STRATEGY 1501
揆 PLOT 0718

plant→FARM AND PLANT

plants

菜 VEGETABLE 2880
植 PLANT 1247
栽 garden plant 4087
茨 thorny shrub 2812
苔 MOSS 2792
蔓 VINE 2975
桔 PLANT NAME ELEMENT 1164

plants→SUPPORTING PARTS OF PLANTS

plates→BOARDS AND PLATES

play

遊 PLAY 3896
戯 SPORT 2351
弄 TOY WITH 3057

play music

奏 PLAY MUSIC 3185
弾 play on (stringed instruments) 0697
吹 BLOW 0272

pleasant→PLEASED AND PLEASANT

pleased and pleasant

楽 pleasurable 3505
欣 JOYFUL 1057
爽 REFRESHING 4402
快 PLEASANT 0289
朗 CHEERFUL 1679
愉 PLEASED 0710
悦 DELIGHTED 0501

嬉しい GLAD 0890
喜 HAPPY 2889
歓 JOYOUS 2342
驩 JOYOUS 2333

pleasure

楽 PLEASURE 3505
娯 ENJOYMENT 0487
興 AMUSEMENT 3622
玩 TAKE PLEASURE IN 1085

plentiful

百 numerous 2519
沃 FERTILE 0315
万 myriad 3653
多 MANY 2694
豊 PLENTIFUL 3344
沢 plentiful 0313
穣 YIELDING ABUNDANTLY 1597
裕 ABUNDANT 1530
饒 ABUNDANT 2280
富 RICH 2892

plural suffixes

-達 plural suffix 3893
-等 plural suffix 3321
衆 somewhat polite plural suffix 3325
-共 belittling plural suffix 3045
-方 polite plural suffix 2459

poetry

詩 POETRY 1924
歌 Japanese poetry 2296
俳 HAIKU 0126
句 HAIKU 3685

points of land

岬 CAPE 0340
崎 PROMONTORY 0569
埼 promontory 0560

policy

策 policy 3320
是 policy 3090
綱 guiding principle 1735

polish and rub

磨 POLISH 3946
擦 RUB 0971
摩 RUB AGAINST 3938
摺 RUB AGAINST 0850
研 GRIND 1456
削 CUT BY CHIPPING 1837
瑳 POLISH 1343

poor

貧 POOR 2631
乏 poor 2432
窮 destitute 2983

positions→**PLACES AND POSITIONS**

positive

陽 positive 0764
正 positive 4296

possess

有 HAVE 3703
蔵 own 2995
持 HOLD 0447
属 BELONG TO 3901
享 ENJOY 2545
具 possess 3159

possessive particles

之 POSSESSIVE PARTICLE 4228
乃 POSSESSIVE PARTICLE 3643

possible

可 -ABLE 3687
能 possible 1676

posthumous worlds

天 HEAVEN 4250
幽 world of the dead 3731
獄 hell 0872

post station

駅 relay station 2292
逓 RELAY 3852
宿 post station 2858

posture

姿 posture 3264
態 attitude 3529

potency

効 EFFECT 1617
験 efficacy 2306
能 action 1676
機 function 1365

powder

粉 POWDER 1643
末 powder 4317

power and authority

力 POWER 4178
威 MIGHT 4394
勢 POWER (to influence) 3542
権 POWER (to control) 1348
覇 SUPREMACY 3392

praise

賛 PRAISE 3484
頌 EULOGIZE 1319
謳 EXTOL 2061
讃 PRAISE 2093
美 regard as beautiful 2817
褒 COMMEND 2662
嘉 commend (esp. an inferior) 2953
彰 PROCLAIM MERITS 2337
称 acclaim 1491
賞 express admiration 3237
揚 EXALT 0722

pray and worship

祈 PRAY 1086
祷 PRAY 1224

願	pray	2320
拝	WORSHIP	0360
祀	WORSHIP AS GOD	1448
崇	REVERENCE	2864
斎	OBSERVE RELIGIOUS ABSTINENCE	2622
呪	SPELL	0323

precept

戒	commandment	3972
訓	precept	1844

precious stones

玉	GEM	4289
珂	WHITE AGATE	1137
璧	DISK-SHAPED JEWEL	3608
琥	AMBER	1261
珀	AMBER	1136
珠	PEARL	1183
瑛	TRANSPARENT GEM	1259
瑠	LAPIS LAZULI	1342
璃	GLASSY SUBSTANCE	1358
晶	CRYSTAL	3122
玖	beautiful black jewel	1041
琉	LAPIS LAZULI	1221
琳	BEAUTIFUL GEM	1262

prepare

備	PROVIDE	0165
調	PREPARE	1973

present

今	PRESENT	2464
当	THE PRESENT	2701
現	ACTUAL	1218

preserve

留	KEEP	3189
保	PRESERVE	0107
持	uphold	0447

preserved foods

-漬け	pickles	0861
-干し	dried food	4187

preserve food

漬ける	PICKLE	0861
燻	SMOKE	1406
薫	smoke	3005

press→COMPEL AND PRESS

prevent

防	PREVENT	0320
止	STOP	3659

price→FEE AND PRICE

principle

律	LAW	0433
理	BASIC PRINCIPLE	1220

print and publish

刷	PRINT	1623
印	print	1023
植	typeset	1247
刊	PUBLISH	0221
版	PUBLISHING	1082
載	PUT IN PRINT	4091
掲	display in writing	0597
幀	BOOKBINDING	0695

printing plate

版	PRINTING PLATE	1082
梓	printing block	1207

prison

獄	PRISON	0872
監	prison	3535

prisoner

虜	CAPTIVE	4038
囚	PRISONER	3776

private→SECRET AND PRIVATE

prizes

賞	PRIZE	3237
杯	prize cup	1066
章	decoration	2624

products of combustion

灰	ASH	3699
殻	cinders	1883
炭	CHARCOAL	2806
煤	SOOT	1292
煙	SMOKE	1294

professionals→WORKERS AND PROFESSIONALS

profit

利	PROFIT	1431
益	PROFIT	2849
儲ける	PROFIT	0202
得	GAIN	0577

profound

玄	PROFOUND	2485
幽	deep hidden	3731
奥	inmost	3503
深	DEEP	0636
涅	DEEP AND VAST	0811

project

映	PROJECT	1104
写	project	2493

projectiles and bombs

弾	PROJECTILE	0697
丸	round projectile	4225
矢	ARROW	2502
槍	SPEAR	1329
爆	bomb	1415
雷	explosive device	3466

promise

約	PROMISE	1632
締	CONCLUDE (a treaty)	1761
協	reach an agreement	0103
契	MAKE AN AGREEMENT	3267
盟	ALLIANCE	3468

誓 VOW 3424

prospering and prosperity

隆 PROSPER 0661
振 rise 0515
興 RISE TO PROSPERITY 3622
盛 PROSPEROUS 3314
昌 PROSPERING 3069
栄 FLOURISH 3183
繁 THRIVE 3536
賑 BUSTLE 1959

prosperity→PROSPERING AND PROSPERITY

protect

守 PROTECT (by watching over) 2697
護 PROTECT (by safeguarding) 2079
庇 PROTECT (by shielding) 3802
衛 GUARD 0938
警 GUARD AGAINST 3595
防 defend 0320
番 WATCH 3416
保 PRESERVE 0107
看 CARE FOR 3992

protective coverings

盾 SHIELD 3729
楯 SHIELD 1281
鎧 ARMOR 2211
甲 armor 4293
縅 BRAID OF ARMOR 1759
面 mask 2590
兜 helmet 3499
幌 COVERING FOR VEHICLES 0787

prototype

型 TYPE 3266
儀 model 0191

protrude and protruding

突 protruding 2772
凸 CONVEX 4298
隆 protuberant 0661
起 RISE 4099
出る stick out 4310

protruding→PROTRUDE AND PROTRUDING

pseudonym suffixes

亭 PSEUDONYM SUFFIX 2572
屋 stage name suffix 3842

psyche

心 HEART 0011
霊 SPIRIT (soul) 3480
魂 SOUL, spirit 1346
魄 SOUL 1570
腹 heart 1308
衷 INNER HEART 2600
襟 inner mind 1599
胸 breast 1187
懐 BOSOM 0942
神 MIND 1143
気 SPIRIT (consciousness) 3960
精 SPIRIT (mind) 1729

public

公 PUBLIC 2468
俗 POPULAR 0119
巷 the public 3097

public display

展 exhibition 3862
博 exposition 0170

public offices

省 MINISTRY 3100
庁 GOVERNMENT AGENCY 3768
府 government office 3824
公 public office 2468
署 PUBLIC-SERVICE STATION 3223
局 public service office 3800
所 office 1056

publish→PRINT AND PUBLISH

pull

引 DRAW 0207
曳 DRAW 4348
牽 DRAW 2621
惹 DRAW ATTENTION 2903
抽 DRAW OUT 0359
抜 PULL OUT 0290
控える HOLD BACK 0600
扣える HOLD BACK 0250
寄せる DRAW NEAR 2856

punishment

刑 PENALTY 1024
罰 PUNISHMENT 3228
懲 CHASTISE 3623
処 DEAL WITH (lawbreakers) 3764

purehearted

純 PURE 1649
淳 PUREHEARTED 0626
清 clean 0635
潔 IMMACULATE 0920
廉 INCORRUPT 3911
敦 HONEST 2128
惇 SINCERE 0588
直 straightforward 3649
侃 FORTHRIGHT 0097

purified→CLEAN AND PURIFIED

purple colors→BLUE AND PURPLE COLORS

pursue→FOLLOW AND PURSUE

push

押 PUSH 0371
突く THRUST 2772
圧 apply pressure 3688
挨 PUSH 0510
按 HOLD DOWN 0444

put

据える INSTALL 0602
置 PLACE 3222

- 擱 LAY DOWN 0970
- 掛ける SET 0596
- 措 DISPOSE 0610

put in
- 入 PUT IN 4177
- 挿 INSERT 0517
- 嵌 INLAY 2897
- -込む cause to move inward 3762

put on→WEAR AND PUT ON

Q

quantity and number
- 量 QUANTITY 3119
- 嵩 BULK 2927
- 積 size 1579
- 額 AMOUNT 2273
- 分 content 2466
- 数 NUMBER 2245
- 勢 strength 3542

question
- 題 PROBLEM 4139
- 問 QUESTION (inquiry) 4117
- 論 question (issue) 1981
- 謎 RIDDLE 2047

quiet
- 静 QUIET 2164
- 閑 QUIET 4123
- 寂 quiet 2855
- 幽 QUIET AND SECLUDED 3731
- 粛 still 4400
- 黙 SILENT 3554

quote
- 引 quote 0207
- 挙 cite 3106

R

rabbit
- 兎 RABBIT 4374
- 卯 THE HARE 0231

raise
- 揚 RAISE HIGH 0722
- 掲 PUT UP 0597
- 挙 RAISE 3106
- 上 raise 4212
- 起 raise up 4099
- 擡 RAISE (one's head) 0972
- 立てる STAND 2486
- 拾う PICK UP 0454

raise and nourish
- 育 RAISE 2544
- 飼 RAISE ANIMALS 2149
- 養 FOSTER 2998
- 滋 NOURISH 0734
- 哺 NURSE 0478
- 牧 PASTURE 1083

raise the temperature
- 暖 WARM (the air) 1274
- 煖 WARM (the air) 1293
- 温める WARM (a thing) 0740
- 熱 HEAT 3555

range
- 程 EXTENT 1524
- 範 range 3360
- 域 area 0559
- 圏 SPHERE 3904
- 野 FIELD 1877
- 界 field (*phys*) 3172
- 場 field (*phys*, *psychol*) 0678

ranks→MILITARY OFFICERS AND RANKS

rare
- 珍 RARE 1135
- 希 RARE 2543
- 稀 RARE 1523

rare and sparse
- 薄い THIN 3004
- 希 RARE 2543
- 疎 SPARSE 1512
- 粗 COARSE 1683
- 稀 RARE 1523

rash
- 滅 unreasonable 0812
- 妄 RASH 2509
- 盲 BLIND 2547
- 暴 unrestrained 3138
- 荒 WILD 2810
- 濫 EXCESSIVE 0990
- 乱 excessive 1611

rate
- 率 RATE 2625
- 割 rate 2284
- 比 ratio 0029
- 歩 percentage 3071

rear
- 後 after- 0431
- 背 BACK 3182
- 裏 REAR 2652
- 尻 tail end 3766
- 尾 TAIL 3799

reason
- 理 REASON 1220
- 訳 SENSE 1865

reason→CAUSE AND REASON

reasoning
- 理 REASON 1220
- 筋 thread 3319

- 脈 VEIN 1189

rebellions→WARFARE AND REBELLIONS

receive

- 受 RECEIVE 3076
- 享 ENJOY 2545
- 領 receive 1567
- 収 TAKE IN 0031
- 納 ACCEPT 1652
- 貰 GET 3219
- 戴 RECEIVE HUMBLY 4093
- 頂 RECEIVE HUMBLY 0164
- 拝 have the honor to receive 0360

recent

- 近 RECENT 3798
- 新 NEW 2239

receptacles→VESSELS AND RECEPTACLES

recite

- 吟 RECITE 0271
- 誦 RECITE 1951
- 唱 chant 0555
- 読 READ 1943
- 詠 RECITE POETRY 1894

reclaim

- 拓 OPEN UP 0375
- 墾 RECLAIM 3602
- 開 OPEN 4121

recommend

- 薦 RECOMMEND 3008
- 推 recommend 0612

records

- 記 written account 1843
- 録 RECORD 2186
- 譜 SYSTEMATIC RECORD 2068
- 誌 records 1950
- 史 HISTORY 4324
- 伝 biography 0048

recover→CURE AND RECOVER

red colors

- 赤 RED 2719
- 紅 CRIMSON 1629
- 緋 SCARLET 1732
- 朱 VERMILION 4344
- 丹 CINNABAR 4249
- 茜 MADDER 2811

reduce the temperature

- 凍 FREEZE 0146
- 冷 cool 0088

refine

- 錬 REFINE (crude metals) 2185
- 精 REFINE (crude materials) 1729
- 留 distill 3189

reflect→SHINE AND REFLECT

reform

- 改 REFORM 0287
- 革 REFORM 3099
- 更 RENEW 4355
- 新 make new 2239

refuse and reject

- 拒 REFUSE 0368
- 断る refuse 1885
- 否 SAY NO 3058
- 却 reject 1436

regret

- 惜 REGRET 0586
- 恨 regret 0439
- 憾 STRONGLY REGRET 0943
- 悔 REPENT 0435

regular

- 正 regular 4296
- 本 regular 4314

reject→REFUSE AND REJECT

relate

- 関 CONCERN 4129
- 係 CONNECT 0108
- 絡 INTERLINK 1709
- 渉 HAVE RELATIONS WITH 0638
- 連 LINK 3849
- 聯 LINK 1797

related by marriage

- 義 -in-law 2948
- 継 step- 1720

relations→FAMILY AND RELATIONS

release

- 放 LET GO 1058
- 釈 release 1876

religion

- 教 RELIGION 1887
- 宗 religion 2769
- 道 the Way 3888

religions and sects

- 仏 Buddhism 0020
- 法 Buddha's teachings 0391
- 禅 ZEN 1306
- 儒 CONFUCIANISM 0197
- 道 Taoism 3888

religious persons

- 聖 SAINT 3509
- 仙 IMMORTAL MOUNTAIN FAIRY 0036

rely on

- 頼 RELY ON 2041
- 依 DEPEND ON 0093

remain

- 残 REMAIN 1179
- 余 REMAINING 2535
- 留 STAY 3189
- 滞 STAY 0815

remember

- 憶 REMEMBER 0944

覚える	COMMIT TO MEMORY	3217
記	commit to memory	1843
追	reminisce	3840
顧	LOOK BACK	2394
偲	RECOLLECT	0153

repair

直す	FIX	3649
修	REPAIR	0138
繕	MEND	1802

repeating and repetition

再	ANOTHER TIME	4332
又	AGAIN	4158
復	repeat	0701
重	DUPLICATE	4390
畳	reduplicate	3205
改	redo	0287
-換える	redo	0716
-直す	repetition suffix	3649
-返す	do over	3797

repetition→REPEATING AND REPETITION

replace→CHANGE AND REPLACE

reproductive cells

卵	ovum	1054
精	sperm	1729

reptiles and amphibians

亀	TURTLE	2637
蛇	SNAKE	1701
竜	DRAGON	2603
蛙	FROG	1716
黽	FROG	4404

repute

声	reputation	2724
誉	HONOR	3135
名	NAME	2693
望	popularity	3408

request

請	REQUEST	1983
訴	APPEAL TO	1901
頼	ASK	2041
嘱	CHARGE WITH	0881
要	REQUIRE	3263
願	ASK A FAVOR	2320
求	SEEK	4365
乞	BEG	2457

rescue

救	SAVE	1891
済	RELIEVE	0634

resemble

似	RESEMBLE	0071
類	be similar	2275

reside

住	LIVE	0072
居	RESIDE	3822
棲	INHABIT (said of animals), live	1246
栖	INHABIT (said of animals), live	1170
生	inhabit	4309
植	colonize	1247

resign

辞	RESIGN	1726
退	retire	3838

resist

抗	RESIST	0296
抵	RESIST	0377
耐	WITHSTAND	1634
対	OPPOSE	1025
反	COUNTER	3663
逆	rebel	3835
撥	REPEL	0907
叛	REBEL	1469

resolutely

敢	BOLDLY	2142
断	resolutely	1885
決	decisively	0308

respect

敬	RESPECT	2136
尊	HONOR	2920
畏	respect	3170
欽	REVERE	2124
仰	look up to	0051
崇	REVERENCE	2864
尚	VALUE HIGHLY	2774
重	set value on	4390
拝	WORSHIP	0360
慕	ADORE	2970

respectful

恭	RESPECTFUL	3109
謹	RESPECTFULLY	2045
奉	reverentially	3167
拝	HUMBLY	0360

responsibility

務	DUTY	1505
任	duty	0057
責	RESPONSIBILITY	3115
分	one's part	2466

rest

休	REST	0056
息	rest	3278
憩	TAKE A REST	3590
歇	TAKE A REST	2243

restaurant suffixes

亭	quality restaurant suffix	2572
閣	high-class restaurant suffix	4128
園	restaurant suffix	3914
苑	restaurant suffix	2783

restore→RETURN AND RESTORE

restrain

制	CONTROL (restrain)	1624
禁	PROHIBIT	3469

限	LIMIT	0475
抑	SUPPRESS	0301
束	TIE UP	4369
縛	BIND	1779
控える	HOLD BACK	0600
扣える	HOLD BACK	0250
渋る	hang [hold] back	0625

return

帰	RETURN	0148
還	RETURN	3945
回	turn back	3793
廻	turn back	3833
戻る	RETURN	2441
復	RETURN TO	0701

return and restore

返	RETURN	3797
戻	RETURN	2441
還	RETURN	3945
復	RETURN TO	0701
蘇	REVIVE	3032
甦	REVIVE	4109

reveal

発	reveal	3174
露	EXPOSE	3495
曝	EXPOSE	1410
晒す	EXPOSE	1156
暴	disclose	3138
披	OPEN OUT	0362
顕	MANIFEST	2274
現	cause to appear	1218

revise

訂	REVISE	1829
閲	REVIEW	4132
校	COLLATE	1166

rice

米	RICE	4342
飯	COOKED RICE	2126
稲	RICE PLANT	1561
籾	UNHULLED RICE	1626
餅	RICE CAKE	2256
粥	RICE GRUEL	0698

rich

富	RICH	2892
豪	wealthy	2657

right→**LEFT AND RIGHT**

right

正	RIGHT	4296
是	RIGHT	3090
尤	RIGHT	3755
端	correct	1564

rise in rank

陞	ASCEND TO A HIGHER RANK	0549
昇	ascend to a higher rank	3068
進	advance in rank	3873

risk

冒	RISK	3088
賭	WAGER	2021
懸	stake	3632

rivers and streams

川	RIVER	0006
河	RIVER	0394
江	large river	0257
渓	mountain stream	0628
流	stream	0529

rob→**STEAL AND ROB**

rock and stone

石	STONE	3689
岩	ROCK	2778
巌	CRAG	3037

roof

屋	roof	3842
宇	roof	2699

roof parts

軒	EAVES	1851
庇	EAVES	3802
棟	ridge	1248
瓦	roof tile	4288

rooms

室	ROOM	2802
間	room	4122
房	CHAMBER	2445
斎	study	2622
堂	HALL	3202

ropes and lines

綱	ROPE (esp. of fiber)	1735
絃	STRING	1685
縄	ROPE (esp. of straw)	1756
緒	cord	1742
組	braid	1693
索	cable	3105
鎖	CHAIN	2213
線	LINE	1760
紐	STRING	1647
弦	STRING	0343

round

丸い	ROUND	4225
円	circular	3673

routes→**WAYS AND ROUTES**
rub→**POLISH AND RUB**

ruins

墟	RUINS	0888
虚	ruins	4017

rulers

君	RULER	3974
王	KING	4247
帝	EMPEROR	2573
天	Heaven's messenger on earth	4250
皇	EMPEROR	3175

堯	YAO	2560
舜	SHUN	3134

rules→LAWS AND RULES

run

走	RUN	2720
奔	RUSH	2758
馳	RUN QUICKLY	2289
駆	gallop	2293

running water

流	CURRENT	0529
潮	TIDE	0916
汐	TIDE	0259
瀬	rapids	0995
滝	WATERFALL	0813
洪	FLOOD	0461
渦	WHIRLPOOL	0735

S

sacrifice

犠	SACRIFICE	1394
牲	SACRIFICE	1133

sad and depressed

悲	SAD	3448
悄	BECOME DISPIRITED	0506
哀	sorrowful	2568
愁	MELANCHOLY	3508
鬱	GLOOM	3625
陰	gloomy	0657
沈	depressed	0306
寂	LONESOME	2855
淋しい	LONESOME	0632
惨	MISERABLE	0585

same and uniform

等	EQUAL	3321
平	equal	4291
均	EVEN	0276
斉	UNIFORM	2548
同	SAME	3707
一	same	4148

sand

砂	SAND (fine)	1457
沙	SAND (granular)	0311

savage

蛮	BARBARIAN	2638
夷	BARBARIAN	4349
蕃	BARBARIAN	2989

say→SPEAK AND SAY

schools

校	SCHOOL	1166
学	EDUCATIONAL INSTITUTION	3162
院	INSTITUTION	0544
塾	PRIVATE SCHOOL	3546
大	UNIVERSITY	4224
高	high school	2601
中	junior high school	4262
小	elementary school	0007
園	kindergarten	3914

sea

海	SEA	0459
洋	OCEAN	0468
沖	OFFING	0307
灘	OPEN SEA	1006

seals

印	SEAL	1023
判	personal seal	1441
璽	IMPERIAL SEAL	3624

seasonings

糖	SUGAR	1777
塩	SALT	0774
酢	VINEGAR	1910
醋	VINEGAR	2002
油	OIL	0400
醤	FERMENTED SAUCE	3569
噌	MISO	0882
蜜	HONEY	2958

seat

席	SEAT	3865
座	SEAT	3868
椅	CHAIR	1239
鞍	SADDLE	2255

second

乙	SECOND	4145
次	second	0058
後	AFTER (latter)	0431
中	MIDDLE	4262

second person pronouns

君	YOU (*familiar*)	3974
汝	THOU	0255
爾	thou	4407
貴	you (*honorific*)	3220
卿	you (*archaic*, *honorific*)	0769

secret and private

秘	SECRET	1490
密	SECRET	2857
暗	in the dark	1273
私	PRIVATE	1432
内	not public	4277
隠	hidden from view	0873

sects→RELIGIONS AND SECTS

sects→PARTIES AND SECTS

securities

株	STOCK	1172
債	BOND	0177

see and look

見	SEE	3151
看	WATCH	3992
察	INSPECT	2961

窺	WATCH FURTIVELY	3002
瞥	GLANCE AT	3592
目	look	3777
観	VIEW	2359
覧	LOOK OVER	3538
眺	LOOK OUT OVER	1503
望	LOOK AFAR	3408
仰	LOOK UP	0051
顧	LOOK BACK	2394
視	REGARD	1223

seek

探	SEARCH	0613
索	SEARCH FOR	3105
捜	LOOK FOR	0516
求	SEEK	4365
猟	hunt for	0654

sell and trade

売	SELL	2722
卸す	WHOLESALE	1835
販	ENGAGE IN SALES	1869
商	TRADE	2623
貿	TRADE	3214
易	EXCHANGE	3064

send

送	SEND	3837
投	SEND IN	0300
回	send round	3793
遣	DISPATCH	3908
派	DISPATCH	0456

sense

感	SENSE	3514
覚	sense	3217
勘	INTUITIVE PERCEPTION	2231

sentence and sentence parts

句	PHRASE	3685
文	sentence	2458
節	clause	3336

sentence parts→SENTENCE AND SENTENCE PARTS

separate

割	DIVIDE	2284
分	DIVIDE	2466
解	TAKE APART	1913
析	ANALYZE	1072
別	SEPARATE	1434
離	SEPARATE	2364
隔	partition	0827

servants

僕	MANSERVANT	0185
奴	SLAVE	0217
隷	UNDERLING	2201
臣	RETAINER	3806
従	follower	0498
供	attendant	0098

set forth→LEAVE AND SET FORTH

set in motion

動	MOVE	2232
駆	DRIVE	2293
掛ける	set going	0596

settle

着	settle (down)	4110
帰	settle in place	0148
落	be concluded	2907

sew→WEAVE AND SEW

sex

性	SEX	0357
情	(illicit) love	0583
春	love	3184
色	lust	2522
淫	LEWD	0624

shadow

影	SHADOW	2381
翳	SHADOW	3567
陰	SHADE	0657
蔭	SHADE	2974

shake

振	SWING	0515
震	QUAKE	3481
揺	SHAKE	0723

sharp

鋭	SHARP	2171
先	pointed	3046
尖	pointed	2700

sheep

羊	SHEEP	2708
未	the Ram	4318

shells

殻	SHELL (of any kind)	1883
甲	SHELL (of animals)	4293
貝	seashell	3150
螺	SPIRAL-SHELLED GASTROPOD	1799
瑚	CORAL	1300

shine and reflect

輝	SHINE BRILLIANTLY	1775
光	shine	3043
照	ILLUMINATE	3506
映	REFLECT	1104
耀	SHINE BRILLIANTLY	1812
燿	SHINE	1407
閃	FLASH	4114
煌	GLITTER	1296

ships→BOATS AND SHIPS

ships→PARTS OF BOATS AND SHIPS

shoals

瀬	SHALLOWS	0995
州	sandbar	0064
礁	REEF	1588

shoot

射	SHOOT	1850

撃 fire 3552
発 discharge 3174

shores and watersides

畔 WATERSIDE 1472
-辺 -side 3761
浜 BEACH 0523
岸 SHORE 2777
浦 SEASIDE 0524
渚 STRAND 0637
磯 ROCKY BEACH 1587
汀 STRAND 0228

short and shortened

短 SHORT 1515
簡 simplified 3380
略 ABRIDGED 1501

shortened→SHORT AND SHORTENED

short time periods

頃 moment 0163
瞬 INSTANT 1594
秒 SECOND 1462
分 MINUTE 2466
時 hour 1155
暫 SHORT WHILE 3553

show

示 SHOW 2435
見せる show 3151
呈 PRESENT 2715

shrink→CONTRACT AND SHRINK

shrubs

藤 WISTERIA 3025
蔦 JAPANESE IVY 2972
萩 *HAGI* 2908
茉 JASMINE 2790
莉 JASMINE 2843
芭 JAPANESE FIBER BANANA 2736

siblings

妹 YOUNGER SISTER 0333
姉 OLDER SISTER 0336
兄 OLDER BROTHER 2676
弟 YOUNGER BROTHER 2537

siblings of parents

叔 YOUNGER SIBLING OF PARENT 1622
伯 OLDER SIBLING OF PARENT 0067

side

側 SIDE 0155
脇 SIDE 1188
方 side 2459
辺 -side 3761
面 side 2590
傍 BESIDE 0166
横 SIDEWAYS 1350

sigh→CRY AND SIGH

signal

号 signal 2675
報 signal 2133

signs→MARKS AND SIGNS

signs

候 indication 0133
徴 SYMPTOM 0841
症 symptom (of a disease) 4065
気 sign 3960
兆 OMEN 0264

similar

類 similar 2275
様 like 1332
如 AS 0239
-通り as 3855
云 SUCH 2430

simple→PLAIN AND SIMPLE

sing

唱 SING 0555
歌 sing 2296

sink

没 SINK 0305
沈 SINK 0306
潜 SUBMERGE 0922
溺 DROWN 0805

sit

座 SIT 3868
坐 SIT 4361
居 sit 3822

situations→STATES AND SITUATIONS

six

六 SIX 2461
陸 six (in legal documents) 0659

size

寸 measurement 3652
大 size 4224

skill

力 POWER 4178
能 ABILITY 1676
技 SKILL 0292
倆 SKILL 0136
腕 skill 1269
才 TALENT 4218

skillful

巧 SKILLFUL 0219
能 able 1676

sky

空 SKY 2767
昊 SKY 3066
穹 SKY 2768
天 HEAVEN 4250
宙 MIDAIR 2761

sleep

眠 SLEEP 1474
睡 SLEEP 1535
寝 GO TO SLEEP 2925

slips→LABELS AND SLIPS

slow

徐	SLOWLY	0497
遅	SLOW	3887
緩	SLACK	1757
慢	SLUGGISH	0844

small and tiny

小	SMALL	0007
豆-	miniature	2442
微	SLIGHT	0788
細	MINUTE	1689
寸	A BIT OF	3652

small numbers

一	ONE	4148
十	TEN	4172
廿	TWENTY	4258
二	TWO	2421
三	THREE	2423
四	FOUR	3778
五	FIVE	4244
六	SIX	2461
七	SEVEN	4169
八	EIGHT	3644
九	NINE	4176

small water masses

滴	DROP	0866
雫	DROP	3430
泡	BUBBLE	0392
沫	BUBBLE	0397

smell and fragrance

気	smell	3960
匂い	SMELL	3662
臭	BAD SMELL	3261
香	SWEET SMELL	3177
馨	PERFUME	3575
芳	FRAGRANT	2739
薫	BALMY	3005
郁	AROMATIC	1640

smooth

流	flowing	0529
暢	FLUENT	1569
滑	SMOOTH	0809

snake

蛇	SNAKE	1701
巳	THE SERPENT	4197

social gatherings

宴	BANQUET	2825
饗	BANQUET	3616
会	party	2512

society

社	SOCIETY	1042
世	WORLD	4308
公	PUBLIC	2468

soft

柔	SOFT (supple and yielding)	2591
軟	SOFT (not hard)	1871
塑	plastic	3525

soil→LAND AND SOIL

soldiers and warriors

兵	SOLDIER	3158
卒	private	2549
士	MILITARY MAN	4213
武	warrior	3979
侍	SAMURAI	0094

solidify and coagulate

固	solidify	3830
凝	CONGEAL	0198
結	form into a mass	1706
凍	FREEZE	0146

some

幾-	SOME	4403
何-	several	0073
数	several	2245
或る	A CERTAIN	3978

songs→MUSIC AND SONGS

sorrow

哀	SORROW	2568
憂	grief	2664

sour substances

酢	VINEGAR	1910
酸	ACID	1968

space→UNIVERSE AND SPACE

spacecraft→AIRCRAFT AND SPACECRAFT

sparse→RARE AND SPARSE

speak and say

言	SAY	2440
語る	TELL	1944
談	TALK	1975
喋	TALK	0665
諷	INSINUATE	2005
謂う	REFER TO	2007
云	say	2430
曰	SAY THAT	3757
話	SPEAK	1928
口	give mouth to	4189
申す	SPEAK HUMBLY	4319
述	STATE	3816
陳	SET FORTH	0656
弁	SPEAK ELOQUENTLY	2497

speak humbly

申す	SPEAK HUMBLY	4319
啓	address respectfully	3434

speak in public

講	LECTURE	2046
演	make a speech	0855

special

特	SPECIAL (distinct)	1181
別	special (distinct)	1434
殊	SPECIAL (exceptional)	1178
専	EXCLUSIVE	3272

speech

言	SPEECH	2440
談	TALK	1975
舌	TONGUE	2711
口	MOUTH	4189

spherical object

玉	spherical object	4289
球	BALL	1219
丸	round body	4225
鞠	BALL	2268
毬	BALL	4001

spoons

斗	DIPPER	3671
杓	DIPPER	1028
匕	SPOON	3641

sports fields

場	ground(s)	0678
庭	COURT	3866
野	baseball field	1877

spread

散	SCATTER	2137
布	SPREAD	3691
敷く	LAY	2345
舗	PAVE	2177
塗	APPLY ON A SURFACE	3523
抹	wipe over	0370
撒	SCATTER	0909

spring back

弾	SPRING BACK	0697
反	return in original direction	3663

sprout and bloom

萌	GERMINATE	2871
咲く	BLOOM	0413

spy

偵	SPY	0157
探	spy on	0613

square

方	SQUARE	2459
角	square	2541

squeeze

搾	SQUEEZE	0798
絞る	WRING	1707
圧	apply pressure	3688

stab

刺	STAB	1625
突く	THRUST	2772

stagnate

滞	STAGNATE	0815
淀む	STAGNATE	0621
澱	SETTLE	0954
渋	NOT GO SMOOTHLY	0625
吃	STAMMER	0232

stagnating water

淵	DEEP WATER	0732
淀	pool	0621
澱	pool	0954

standpoint

地	one's ground	0236
立	standpoint	2486

stands→**TABLES AND STANDS**

stars

星	STAR	3089
座	constellation	3868

states and situations

態	STATE	3529
調	TONE	1973
様	MODE	1332
相	PHASE	1120
状	CONDITION	0322
況	CONDITIONS	0395
景	business conditions	3118
勢	course of events	3542
境	SITUATION	0835
局	current situation	3800
情	ACTUAL CONDITIONS	0583
訳	circumstances	1865

stay

滞	STAY	0815
頓	STAY IN PLACE	1320
留	STAY	3189
逗	STAY	4005
駐	STATIONED	2297
屯	STATION TROOPS	4268
在	reside temporarily	3704
泊	STAY OVERNIGHT	0389
宿	LODGE	2858
寓	stay temporarily	2893

steal and rob

盗	STEAL	3309
窃	STEAL	2801
取	TAKE	1613
奪	ROB	2956
略	plunder	1501
掠	PLUNDER	0605
鹵	PLUNDER	2634

steel→**IRON AND STEEL**

steep

険	STEEP	0658
嶮	STEEP	0937
岨	STEEP	0341
急	steep	2595
峻	high and steep	0495

step on

踏	TREAD	1997

踏 STEP ON 2055
藉 TRAMPLE ON 3017

steps

段 STEP 1471
階 stairs 0761
陛 IMPERIAL PALACE STEPS 0543
梯 LADDER 1210

stick

着 STICK 4110
貼 STICK 1904
付 attach itself to 0035
附 attach itself to 0410

still

未 NOT YET 4318
尚 STILL 2774

stone→**ROCK AND STONE**

stop

止 STOP 3659
停 HALT 0156
駐 park 2297

stoppers

栓 STOPPER 1171
弁 VALVE 2497

store

蔵 STORE 2995
蓄 STORE UP 2931
貯 LAY UP 1903
納 PUT AWAY 1652

storehouse

倉 STOREHOUSE 2607
蔵 storehouse 2995
庫 STORAGE CHAMBER 3864

stories

話 story 1928
談 account 1975
語 tale 1944
説 narrative 1949
噂 RUMOR 0883

straight

直 STRAIGHT 3649
棒 straight 1237

streams→**RIVERS AND STREAMS**

strict

厳 strict 4079
酷 SEVERE 1967
辣 SEVERE 1965
峻 STERN 0495

strike

打 STRIKE 0224
撲 DEAL A BLOW 0903
殴 BEAT (strike a person) 1099
蹴 KICK 2074
撃 STRIKE 3552
挌 STRIKE (a person) 0448
撞 STRIKE (a ball or bell) 0905
撥ねる strike (knock down) 0907
当てる HIT 2701
叩 KNOCK 0208
拍 BEAT (strike repeatedly) 0361
搏 BEAT (throb) 0794

strong

強 STRONG 0574
壮 VIGOROUS 0263
丈 STOUT 4227
健 ROBUST (healthy) 0152
逞しい ROBUST (sturdy) 4004
康 HEALTHY 3877
旺 ENERGETIC 1061
潑 LIVELY 0917

strongholds

城 CASTLE 0417
塁 SMALL FORT 3206
塞 FORT 2924
砦 FORT 3310
堡 FORT 3500

structure

構 structure 1325
造り MAKE 3856

students and followers

生 STUDENT 4309
卒 graduate student 2549
学 scholar 3162
門 pupil 1100
弟 disciple 2537
徒 FOLLOWER 0499

study→**LEARN AND STUDY**

style→**WAY AND STYLE**

styles of Chinese characters

楷 SQUARE STYLE 1282
行 *gyosho* 0246
草 *sosho* 2813

subjected to→**BE SUBJECTED TO**

submit and surrender

服 SUBMIT 1090
伏 submit 0049
屈 bend in submission 3821
降 surrender 0548

subordinate

副 SECONDARY 2230
次 secondary 0058
従 subordinate 0498
亜 SUB- 4354
準 QUASI- 3541
半 semi- 4313
准 JUNIOR 0143
助 assistant 1440

substitute

代 SUBSTITUTE 0034

摂	ACT AS REGENT	0799

subtract

減	subtract	0733
引く	subtract	0207
控	HOLD BACK	0600
扣	HOLD BACK	0250

succeed

継	SUCCEED	1720
承	succeed to	0016
嗣	inherit	2153

sudden

急	SUDDEN	2595
激	sudden	0955
暴	sudden	3138
俄	SUDDEN	0106
頓	SUDDEN	1320
勃	SUDDENLY	1839
突	abruptly	2772

sue

訴	SUE	1901
訟	LITIGATE	1864
告	accuse of	3062
控	accuse in court	0600

suffering→**TROUBLE AND SUFFERING**

suffice

足	SUFFICE	2714
満	satisfied	0739

suitable

適	SUITABLE	3918
当	proper	2701
宜	RIGHT	2763
便	CONVENIENT	0105

sun

日	SUN	3759
陽	SUN	0764
旭	RISING SUN	3697

superior→**EXCELLENT AND SUPERIOR**

supernatural and evil beings

鬼	DEVIL	3291
魔	DEMON	3953
怪	monster	0354
霊	SPIRIT	3480
精	SPIRIT	1729

supervise→**DIRECT AND SUPERVISE**

supplement

補	SUPPLEMENT	1529
足	supplement	2714
給	SUPPLY	1708
充	fill up (a vacancy)	2507

supply

供	supply	0098
給	SUPPLY	1708
納	deliver goods to a customer	1652

support

支	SUPPORT	2473
擁	SUPPORT	0949
扶	LEND SUPPORT TO	0291
賛	back up	3484

supporting parts of plants

根	ROOT	1167
株	stump	1172
幹	TRUNK	2152
茎	STEM	2788

supporting structures

柱	PILLAR	1109
礎	FOUNDATION STONE	1595
桁	BEAM	1165
梁	BEAM	3410

suppress→**CONQUER AND SUPPRESS**

surrender→**SUBMIT AND SURRENDER**

surround

囲む	ENCLOSE	3807
環	SURROUND	1395
包	ENCOMPASS	3684

swell and swelling

脹	SWELL	1265
腫	SWELLING	1310
瘍	SWELLING	4073
爛	break out in sores	1427

swelling→**SWELL AND SWELLING**

swine

豚	PIG	1228
豕	SWINE	4357
猪	WILD BOAR	0652
亥	THE BOAR	2505

system

系	SYSTEM	2443
制	SYSTEM	1624
統	INTERCONNECTED SYSTEM	1710
網	network	1737

T

tables and stands

卓	TABLE	2561
机	DESK	1014
几	DESK	4156
台	STAND	2498

take

把	GRIP	0293
握	GRASP	0714
捉	GRASP	0518
執	SEIZE	2114
摑む	GRASP	0848
捕	CATCH	0514

取 TAKE 1613
持 HOLD 0447

take forcibly

奪 ROB 2956
拐 KIDNAP 0365
収 take possession by force 0031

take from water

撈 DREDGE 0908
掬 SCOOP UP 0599
汲 DRAW WATER 0310

take in

収 TAKE IN 0031
摂 TAKE IN 0799
喫 INGEST 0668
吸 SUCK 0234

take precautions

戒 take caution 3972
警 GUARD AGAINST 3595

talented persons→WISE AND TALENTED PERSONS

tall buildings

閣 TALL MAGNIFICENT BUILDING 4128
楼 TALL BUILDING 1284
塔 TOWER 0683
台 observatory 2498

target

的 TARGET 1444
標 MARK 1347
狙 AIM 0406
目 aim 3777

taste

味 TASTE (savor) 0325
嘗める TASTE (have a taste) 3230
舐める TASTE (have a taste) 1669

tastes

甘 SWEET 4306
苦 BITTER 2789
辛 PUNGENT 2531
辣 PUNGENT 1965
酸 sour 1968
渋い ASTRINGENT 0625
鹹 SALTY 2366

tax

税 TAX 1525
租 LAND TAX 1492
貢 TRIBUTE 2838
賦 levy 1992

teach

教 TEACH 1887
啓 ENLIGHTEN 3434
諄 TEACH WITH CARE 1979
授 teach 0595
育 educate 2544
練 TRAIN 1738
訓 INSTRUCT 1844
誨 INSTRUCT 1946
諭 ADMONISH 2012
導 GUIDE 3587
迪 EDIFY 3817

temporary

仮 TEMPORARY 0053
暫 for the time being 3553

temporary quarters

舎 temporary quarters 2555
寮 DORMITORY 2984
宿 lodging 2858
館 inn 2196
亭 INN 2572
寓 TEMPORARY ABODE 2893

ten

十 TEN 4172
拾 ten (in legal documents) 0454

tendency

向 tendency 3790
性 NATURE 0357
勢 trend 3542
傾 inclination 0174
潮 TIDE 0916
流 CURRENT 0529

tender feelings for others

仁 BENEVOLENCE 0021
慈 compassion 2949
情 sympathy 0583
悲 mercy 3448
哀 PITY 2568
憐 PITY 0945

terms of assent

然 SO 3456
諾 yes 1974

terms of negation

不 NOT (negation) 4242
非 IS NOT (contrariety) 1101
無 WITHOUT (nonexistence) 2648
没 lacking in 0305
欠 LACK 2481
否 OR NOT 3058
未 NOT YET 4318
莫 NOT 2839
勿 DO NOT 3661

territorial divisions

州 STATE 0064
県 PREFECTURE 3269
府 URBAN PREFECTURE 3824
道 district of Hokkaido 3888
都 METROPOLIS OF TOKYO 2120
省 province in China 3100
郡 COUNTY 1858

thanking and gratitude

謝 THANK 2048

礼 thanks 1012
恩 DEBT OF GRATITUDE 3289

that→THIS AND THAT

the country

郊 SUBURB 1638
里 COUNTRYSIDE 4356
鄙 THE COUNTRY 2338
郷 the country 0664
辺 BORDERLAND 3761

theory

論 THEORY (systematic knowledge) 1981
説 THEORY (proposed explanation) 1949

the people

民 PEOPLE 3770
衆 the multitude(s) 3325
庶 the masses 3880
公 PUBLIC 2468

thick

厚 THICK (great in depth) 3726
太 THICK (great in diameter) 2673

thieves

盗 thief 3309
泥 petty thief 0384
賊 BANDIT 1932

thin

薄 THIN 3004
細 SLENDER 1689
繊 FINE 1789
痩 GET THIN 4069

think and consider

思 THINK 3173
惟 MEDITATE 0582
省 INTROSPECT 3100
稽 THINK 1573
考 THINK 3962
存 hold an opinion 3702
案 think out 2824
想 CONCEIVE 3507
慮 CONSIDER 4050
勘 take into consideration 2231
銓 WEIGH 2161
量 weigh 3119

third person pronouns

彼 THIRD PERSON PRONOUN (*neutral*) 0346
氏 third person pronoun (*polite*) 3669
奴 third person pronoun (*slang*) 0217

thirst→HUNGER AND THIRST

this and that

本 THIS 4314
爾 THAT 4407
其れ THAT 3255
彼 that 0346
今 THIS (week, etc.) 2464
当 THE PRESENT 2701
該 the said 1916
同 the same 3707
之 this 4228
是 this 3090
此 THIS 1017
斯 THIS 2140

thought

念 THOUGHTS 2554
考え thought 3962
意 MIND 2650
想 conception 3507

threads and fibers

糸 THREAD 2703
緯 woof 1782
経 warp 1687
繊 FIBER 1789
維 FIBER 1733
綸 THREAD 1739
緬 FINE THREAD 1758

threaten

脅 THREATEN 2614
劫 threaten 1435
威 THREATEN BY FORCE 4394
嚇 INTIMIDATE 0964
喝 shout threats at 0554

three

三 THREE 2423
参 three (in legal documents) 2563
鼎 triangular 4405

three-dimensional shapes

錐 CONE 2190
筒 cylinder 3323
角 cube 2541
球 sphere 1219

throat

咽 THROAT 0412
喉 THROAT 0669

throughout

通 through 3855
徹 all through 0894
終 from beginning to end 1692
中 throughout 4262

throw

投 THROW 0300
抛 TOSS 0364
放 toss 1058

tiger

虎 TIGER 3981
寅 THE TIGER 2854

tighten

締める TIGHTEN 1761
緊 TIGHTEN 3517
張 STRAIN 0573

time and time counters

回	TIME	3793
度	TIME	3844
遍	counter for number of times	3890
返	counter for number of times	3797

time counters→TIME AND TIME COUNTERS

time periods

時	TIME	1155
季	SEASON (quarter)	3161
候	SEASON (time of year)	0133
頃	TIME	0163
暇	FREE TIME	1275
般	period of time	1670
刻	POINT OF TIME	1619
間	INTERVAL	4122
隙	GAP	0826
期	TERM	2139
節	SEASON	3336

tiny→SMALL AND TINY

tire

疲	TIRED	4063
労	fatigue	3155
倦	TIRE OF	0131
厭	TIRE OF	3745

titles of address

氏	COURTESY TITLE	3669
兄	familiar title (seniors)	2676
君	FAMILIAR TITLE (peers)	3974
嬢	Miss	0936
様	FORMAL TITLE	1332
殿	FORMAL HONORIFIC TITLE	2247
師	honorific title (clergymen)	1680
公	honorific title (noblemen)	2468

today→YESTERDAY AND TODAY

together

共	JOINT	3045
同	together	3707
併	TOGETHER	0092
並	side by side	2793
兼	CONCURRENTLY	2850
俱	TOGETHER	0125

tolerant

寛	LENIENT	2922
甘い	indulgent	4306

tools→MACHINES AND TOOLS

tops

上	upper part	4212
頂	SUMMIT	0164
頭	HEAD	2019

torture and oppress

拷	TORTURE	0446
責める	torture	3115
虐	treat cruelly	3989
迫	oppress	3815

total

総	TOTAL	1743
計	total	1828
和	sum	1450

touch

触	TOUCH	1914
接	CONTACT	0607
撫	STROKE	0904
当てる	apply	2701

towns→CITIES AND TOWNS

towns→VILLAGES AND TOWNS

trace

軌	TRACK	1832
跡	TRACE	1937

trade→SELL AND TRADE

transfer

譲	CEDE	2080
渡	hand over	0746
付	deliver	0035
附	deliver	0410

translate

訳	TRANSLATE	1865
翻	RENDER	2391

transmit and deliver

伝	TRANSMIT	0048
逓	RELAY	3852
届ける	DELIVER	3820
達	deliver	3893

travel by vehicle

乗	RIDE	4393
走	travel by vehicle	2720
航	NAVIGATE	1671
騎	RIDE ON HORSEBACK	2307

treat and welcome

遇	TREAT	3889
待	treat	0434
扱う	HANDLE	0251
款	treat cordially	2135
接	receive	0607
迎	WELCOME	3796

tree

木	TREE	4261
樹	STANDING TREE	1363

trees

桜	CHERRY	1168
桐	PAULOWNIA	1173
桂	AROMATIC TREE, katsura tree	1163
梓	CATALPA	1207
桑	MULBERRY	2618
漆	Japanese lacquer tree	0863
樺	BIRCH	1324
椛	BIRCH	1202
梧	CHINESE PARASOL TREE	1200
檀	SPINDLE TREE	1385

椿 CAMELLIA 1278
柳 WILLOW 1115
柊 HOLLY 1119
椋 *APHANANTHE ASPERA* 1245
柾 spindle tree 1114
槻 ZELKOVA 1349
楢 OAK 1287
樫 EVERGREEN OAK 1364
柏 CYPRESS, JAPANESE EMPEROR OAK 1110
榎 HACKBERRY 1323
梶 PAPER MULBERRY 1199
柘 JAPANESE BOXWOOD 1117
楊 WILLOW 1286
桧 JAPANESE CYPRESS 1160
梛 *NAGEIA NAGI* 1206
榊 SACRED SHINTO TREE 1327
楓 MAPLE 1280
松 PINE 1075
杉 CRYPTOMERIA 1027
槙 PODOCARPUS 1330
楠 CAMPHOR TREE 1283
樟 CAMPHOR TREE 1351

trouble and suffering

困 BE IN TROUBLE 3808
苛 torment 2786
窮 BE IN EXTREMITY 2983
悶 BE IN AGONY 4119
悩 SUFFER 0504
苦 SUFFERING 2789
痛 PAIN 4071
辛 HARD 2531
煩 VEXED 1295
難 DIFFICULT 2310

true

真 TRUE 2616
洵 TRULY 0458
実 REAL 2765
本 real 4314
正 genuine 4296
現 ACTUAL 1218

trunk parts

胸 CHEST 1187
腹 BELLY 1308
胴 TRUNK 1186
腰 WAIST 1311
背 BACK 3182
肩 SHOULDER 2446
股 CROTCH 1093
脇 ARMPIT 1188
腋 ARMPIT 1266

try

試 TRY 1925
験 TEST 2306

tubular passages

管 PIPE 3349
筒 TUBE 3323
道 passage 3888
脈 VEIN 1189
樋 WATER PIPE 1353

turn

旋 GYRATE 1194
転 TURN 1872
回 TURN ROUND 3793
廻 TURN ROUND 3833
巡 MAKE THE ROUNDS 3781
循 CIRCULATE 0704
斡 REVOLVE 2168
捻 TWIST 0604

twigs→**BRANCHES AND TWIGS**

twine→**WIND AND TWINE**

two

二 TWO 2421
弐 TWO (in legal documents) 3961
双 SET OF TWO 0028
対 pair 1025
偶 COUPLE 0150
両 BOTH 4331

types→**KINDS AND TYPES**

U

uncultivated expanses of land

野 FIELD 1877
原 PLAIN 3733
漠 DESERT 0804

understand→**KNOW AND UNDERSTAND**

undertake

負 BEAR 2594
担 UNDERTAKE 0376

undomesticated mammals

虎 TIGER 3981
猿 MONKEY 0824
鯨 WHALE 2361
犀 RHINOCEROS 3900
狼 WOLF 0541
狐 FOX 0472
羚 SEROW 1695
鼠 RAT 3340
獅 LION 0825
豹 LEOPARD 1847
熊 BEAR 3530
象 ELEPHANT 2647
麒 MALE CHINESE UNICORN 2363
麟 FEMALE CHINESE UNICORN 2376
猪 WILD BOAR 0652
鹿 DEER 3879

ungual

爪 NAIL 3756
蹄 HOOF 2022

uniform→SAME AND UNIFORM

unimportant

- 細 MINUTE 1689
- 微 SLIGHT 0788
- 小 SMALL 0007
- 末 last in importance 4317

units of learning

- 課 LESSON 1980
- 科 course 1463
- 講 LECTURE 2046

universe and space

- 宇 UNIVERSE 2699
- 宙 SPACE 2761

unrefined→VULGAR AND UNREFINED

unrestrained

- 漫 RAMBLING 0858
- 散 unrestrained 2137
- 宕 UNCONSTRAINED 2771

urge

- 勧 URGE 2334
- 催 PRESS FOR 0178
- 促 HASTEN 0118
- 誘 INDUCE 1952
- 励 ENCOURAGE 1438
- 侑 URGE TO EAT 0101

urgent

- 急 URGENT 2595
- 緊 EXIGENT 3517
- 迫 pressing 3815

use

- 使 USE 0100
- 用 EMPLOY 3694

V

vain

- 空 EMPTY 2767
- 虚 without substance 4017
- 徒 vain 0499

valley

- 谷 VALLEY 2536
- 渓 RAVINE 0628
- 峡 GORGE 0427

value

- 値 VALUE 0123
- 価 VALUE 0095

vapor→GAS AND VAPOR

vaporize

- 蒸 EVAPORATE 2936
- 留 distill 3189

various

- 諸 VARIOUS 1984
- 庶 MANIFOLD 3880
- 雑 MISCELLANEOUS 1752

vegetables

- 菜 greens 2880
- 蕪 TURNIP 2990
- 芋 POTATO 2706
- 豆 BEAN 2442
- 蕗 BUTTERBUR 3007
- 茄 EGGPLANT 2787
- 芹 JAPANESE PARSLEY 2742
- 瓜 GOURD 3789
- 瓢 BOTTLE GOURD 2356
- 芥 mustard 2741

vehicle

- 車 VEHICLE 4367
- 輛 VEHICLE 2000
- 乗 vehicle 4393
- 輪 wheeled vehicle 1999
- 駕 CARRIAGE 3236
- 輿 PALANQUIN 3626
- 台 COUNTER FOR VEHICLES 2498

vertical

- 縦 VERTICAL 1783
- 竪- VERTICAL 3516
- 垂 perpendicular 4382
- 立て- standing 2486
- 直 STRAIGHT 3649

vessels and receptacles

- 盤 dish 3533
- 鍋 POT 2202
- 釜 IRON POT 2610
- 鼎 TRIPOD CAULDRON 4405
- 臼 MORTAR 4341
- 碓 MORTAR 1537
- 托 RECEPTACLE 0252
- 皿 PLATE 4286
- 盆 TRAY 2581
- 膳 LEGGED TRAY 1381
- 杯 CUP 1066
- 鉢 BOWL 2144
- 椀 WOODEN BOWL 1250
- 碗 CERAMIC BOWL 1539
- 丼 LARGE BOWL 4323

view

- 景 SCENE 3118
- 風 (beautiful) scenery 3730
- 光 scenery 3043
- 観 VIEW 2359

villages and towns

- 町 TOWN 1430
- 村 VILLAGE 1029
- 里 hamlet 4356
- 郷 HOMETOWN 0664
- 庄 FEUDAL VILLAGE 3788
- 邑 VILLAGE 2716

violate
- 違 VIOLATE 3907
- 破 BREAK 1478
- 犯 offend against 0229
- 反 act contrary to 3663
- 悖 GO AGAINST 0503
- 背 go against 3182

violent
- 暴 VIOLENT 3138
- 猛 FIERCE 0653
- 荒い WILD 2810

virtuous
- 正 RIGHT 4296
- 義 righteous 2948
- 善 GOOD 2921
- 良 GOOD 4373
- 鯁 UPRIGHT 2357

visit
- 訪 VISIT 1860
- 参 VISIT A HOLY PLACE 2563
- 詣 VISIT A HOLY PLACE 1918
- 寄 call at 2856
- 伺 call on 0078

visitor
- 客 VISITOR 2798
- 賓 GUEST 2982

vivid
- 明 BRIGHT 1060
- 鮮 VIVID 2355

vote and election
- 票 VOTE 3308
- 選 election 3931

vulgar and unrefined
- 俗 vulgar 0119
- 卑 MEAN 3270
- 賤 MEAN 1993
- 鄙 MEAN 2338
- 俚 RURAL 0112
- 里 rural 4356
- 粗 COARSE 1683
- 野 rustic 1877
- 蛮 barbaric 2638

W

wait
- 待 WAIT 0434
- 控える be in waiting 0600

walk
- 歩 WALK 3071
- 徒 go on foot 0499
- 脚 move on foot 1226
- 足 travel on foot 2714
- 踏 TREAD 1997

walls→FENCES AND WALLS

wander
- 浪 WANDER 0527
- 遊 move about freely 3896
- 漂 drift about 0857
- 流 drift 0529
- 彽 WANDER ABOUT 0350
- 徊 MOVE TO AND FRO 0432

war→FIGHT AND WAR

warfare and rebellions
- 戦 WAR 2242
- 軍 war 2582
- 役 war 0288
- 陣 battle 0545
- 乱 rebellion 1611
- 変 uprising 2569
- 闘 FIGHT 4136

warm seasons
- 春 SPRING 3184
- 夏 SUMMER 2619
- 暑 SUMMER HEAT 3121

warn
- 警 WARN 3595
- 戒 CAUTION 3972
- 誡 CAUTION AGAINST 1947
- 諭 ADMONISH 2012
- 告 advise 3062

warriors→SOLDIERS AND WARRIORS

wash→CLEAN AND WASH

waste
- 屑 WASTE 3861
- 芥 TRASH 2741
- 塵 DUST 3922

watersides→SHORES AND WATERSIDES

water sources
- 源 SOURCE 0806
- 泉 SPRING 3176
- 井 WELL 4265

waves
- 波 WAVE 0388
- 浪 BILLOW 0527
- 漣 RIPPLES 0859

way and style
- 風 MANNER 3730
- 様 MODE 1332
- 方 WAY 2459
- 途 WAY 3853
- 法 METHOD 0391
- 流 STYLE 0529
- 式 STYLE 3785
- 調 TONE 1973

ways and routes
- 道 WAY (path) 3888
- 径 PATH 0347

軌 TRACK 1832
線 LINE 1760
澪 WATERWAY 0957
途 WAY (route) 3853
路 ROAD 1936
筋 wayside 3319
通り street 3855
街 city street 0702
辻 CROSSROADS 3958
岐 forked road 0285
巷 THE STREETS 3097

weak

弱 WEAK 1499
柔 SOFT 2591
脆 FRAGILE 1191
癈 DISABLED 4077

weaken

衰 DECLINE 2604
弱 weaken 1499

wealth

財 WEALTH 1849
産 property 4089
富 riches 2892
宝 TREASURE 2764

weapons for shooting

銃 GUN (portable firearm) 2157
砲 HEAVY GUN 1479
火 firearms 4273
弓 BOW 4193

wear and put on

着 PUT ON 4110
装 DRESS 3327
帯 WEAR (esp. at the belt) 3191
穿く PUT ON 2800
纏 put on 1814
履く put on footwear 3933
被る put on headgear 1495

weather

候 SEASONAL WEATHER 0133
天 weather 4250
晴 FINE WEATHER 1234

weave and sew

織 WEAVE 1801
紡 SPIN 1646
績 spin 1788
縫 SEW 1781
編 KNIT 1755
辮 PLAIT 2085
組 braid 1693
繍 EMBROIDER 1805

weeks and months

週 WEEK 3874
旬 TEN-DAY PERIOD 3698
月 MONTH 3674

weight

錘 weight 2191
鎮 weight 2210
碇 ANCHOR 1538

weight units

匁 MOMME (3.75 g) 4276
斤 CATTY (600 g) 3667
貫 *kan* (3.75 kg) 3112
噸 TON 0930
屯 ton 4268

welcome→**TREAT AND WELCOME**

west

洋 WESTERN 0468
西 the West 4333

wet

湿 DAMP 0741
潤 MOIST 0918
濡れる GET WET 0976

white colors

白 WHITE 4305
皓 BRIGHT WHITE 1513
銀 SILVER 2156

wide and extensive

広 WIDE 3769
紘 WIDE-RANGING 1650
博 EXTENSIVE 0170
恢 EXTENSIVE 0436
浩 VAST 0525
洸 VAST (expanse of water) 0462
滉 DEEP AND VAST 0811
曠 SPACIOUS 1411
闊 BROAD 4135

widespread

普 WIDESPREAD 2919
遍 ALL OVER 3890
通 common 3855
公 common (math) 2468

width

幅 WIDTH 0694
員 girth 2822
径 DIAMETER 0347

will and intention

志 AMBITION 2725
意 MIND 2650
図 intention 3809
気 mind to do something 3960
念 thought of doing something 2554
趣 PURPOSE 4111
欲 DESIRE 1867

win

勝 WIN 1268
克 OVERCOME 2540
剋 OVERCOME 4097
征 CONQUER 0349

破	BREAK	1478
凱	TRIUMPH	2286
wind		
風	WIND	3730
嵐	STORM	2898
颱	TYPHOON	4138
台	typhoon	2498
凪	CALM	3709
颯	SOUND OF GUSTING WIND	1563
wind and twine		
巻	ROLL UP	3273
捲	ROLL UP	0598
繰る	REEL	1806
絡	ENTWINE	1709
纏	WIND AROUND	1814
wings		
翼	WING (of birds or aircraft)	3379
羽	WING (of birds or insects)	0265
葉	plane	2912
wisdom		
識	KNOWLEDGE	2070
知	knowledge	1446
智	WISDOM	3458
慧	prajna (transcendental wisdom)	3485
哲	PHILOSOPHY	3402
wise→INTELLIGENT AND WISE		
wise and talented persons		
哲	sage	3402
賢	wise man	3518
博	DOCTOR	0170
秀	genius	3152
俊	BRILLIANT PERSON	0117
才	person of talent	4218
通	well-informed person	3855
wish and desire		
願	WISH	2320
憧	YEARN AFTER	0899
憬	YEARN AFTER	0898
貪	COVET	2630
望	HOPE	3408
希	ASPIRE	2543
懐	LONG FOR	0942
慕	yearn for	2970
渇	thirst for	0627
欲	DESIRE	1867
慾	DESIRE	3551
求	SEEK	4365
wives		
妻	WIFE	3166
奥	wife	3503
内	wife	4277
室	wife (esp. of persons of rank)	2802
嫡	legitimate wife	0839
婦	married woman	0565
嫁	BRIDE	0780
寡	widow	2957
wives of rulers		
后	EMPRESS	3701
妃	PRINCESS	0238
室	wife (esp. of persons of rank)	2802
woman		
女	WOMAN	4226
婦	ADULT WOMAN	0565
婆	OLD WOMAN	3433
嬢	YOUNG LADY	0936
娘	GIRL	0488
雌	FEMALE	1337
牝	FEMALE	1020
媛	DAMSEL	0688
words and expressions		
語	WORD	1944
辞	WORD	1726
詞	WORDS	1897
句	PHRASE	3685
諺	PROVERB	2006
喩	METAPHOR	0671
work		
働	WORK	0172
稼	WORK (for a living)	1572
労	LABOR	3155
勤める	serve (in an office)	2287
仕	SERVE	0037
work and employment		
務	DUTY	1505
任	OFFICE	0057
役	SERVICE (esp. public)	0288
勤	SERVICE (employment)	2287
業	WORK	3227
職	EMPLOYMENT	1803
労	LABOR	3155
workers and professionals		
家	professional	2827
婦	woman worker	0565
嬢	(unmarried) female worker	0936
夫	MAN LABORER	4271
匠	CRAFTSMAN	3711
工	workman	4190
客	skilled person	2798
士	PROFESSION SUFFIX	4213
師	profession suffix	1680
者	person who	3980
人	person of certain category	4175
員	MEMBER (of a staff)	2822
屋	colloquial occupation suffix	3842
手	OCCUPATION SUFFIX	4267
work metals		
錬	REFINE (crude metals)	2185
煉	REFINE (crude metals)	1297
鍛	FORGE	2206
鋳	CAST	2170

- 焼き annealing 1256
- 冶 WORK METALS 0089

world

- 世 WORLD 4308
- 界 WORLD 3172

worldly

- 世 worldly 4308
- 俗 worldly 0119

worry

- 憂 BE ANXIOUS 2664
- 配 concern oneself 1853
- 構う MIND 1325
- 虞 FEARS (of undesirable event) 4037

worship→PRAY AND WORSHIP

wrap→COVER AND WRAP

write

- 書 WRITE 3292
- 筆 write 3317
- 写 COPY 2493
- 記 WRITE DOWN 1843
- 紀 record in writing 1628
- 控える note down 0600
- 録 RECORD 2186
- 登 register 3208
- 註 ANNOTATE 1893

writing

- 文 WRITINGS 2458
- 筆 WRITING 3317
- 書 writing(s) 3292
- 銘 INSCRIPTION 2158

writing strips

- 簡 bamboo writing strips 3380
- 竹 bamboo writing tablets 0267

written communications

- 状 LETTER 0322
- 文 LETTER 2458
- 翰 LETTER 2198
- 書 letter 3292
- 信 written communication 0115
- 電 telegram 3465
- 牒 OFFICIAL NOTICE 1299

wrongdoing and evil

- 罪 sin 3224
- 非 wrong(doing) 1101
- 邪 wrong 1443
- 悪 evil (something bad) 3413
- 弊 evil(s) (something undesirable) 3583

Y

yang→YIN AND YANG

year

- 年 YEAR 2528
- 歳 YEAR 3131

yellow colors

- 黄 YELLOW 3116
- 金 golden 2552

yesterday and today

- 今 today 2464
- 昨 YESTERDAY 1106

yin and yang

- 陰 yin 0657
- 陽 yang 0764

young

- 若 YOUNG 2785
- 弱 young 1499
- 少 young 4278
- 青 youthful 3084
- 幼 VERY YOUNG 0222
- 稚 CHILDISH 1543

Z

zero

- 零 ZERO 3467
- 〇 ZERO 4149

INDEXES
索 引

ON-KUN INDEX
音訓索引

The **On-Kun Index** lists the characters alphabetically by their ***on*** (Chinese-derived) and ***kun*** (native Japanese) readings. It offers a quick way to look up a character from its reading.

1. **Scope** This index lists all the ordinary readings appearing in the **entry-head data** for each entry character (see **§3** on p. 42a); it does not list readings used exclusively in names (***nanori***). Readings identical in form (は[1],は[2]) or readings differing only in *okurigana* (ゆ(き),ゆき) appear only once.
2. **Format** *On* readings are set in katakana, *kun* readings in hiragana. *Okurigana* endings are not shown in parentheses. The tiny numerals to the left of the character column indicate the total stroke-count if a reading block has more than ten items; the numerals to the right are the **entry numbers.**
3. **Order of entries** The characters are listed in *a-i-u-e-o* order of their readings. They appear in the following order: (1) *on* readings precede *kun* readings (アク,あく), (2) ordinary readings precede prefixes and suffixes (あい,あい-,-あい). Characters having the same reading are listed in increasing order of their total stroke-counts, and further grouped by radical number.
4. **Hints for speed** Since there are often many characters under a given *on* reading, but only one or a few under the *kun* readings, it is usually faster to look up by *kun* reading. When there are many entries under a given reading, you might save time by estimating the stroke-count of your character and using the tiny numerals as a rough guide for finding it more quickly.

あ

— い —

う

え

お

か

が

き

ぎ

ご

さ

ざ

し

ず

せ

ぜ

そ

ぞ

た

だ

ち

— づ —

— て —

ど

な

ば

ひ

ぶ

へ

べ

ぺ

ほ

み

む

ら

り

る

れ

HOW TO USE THE RADICAL INDEX
部首索引の使い方

For those familiar with the radical system, we have included the **Radical Index,** which lists the characters according to their traditional radicals and additional strokes. It is best not to use this index unless you are well acquainted with the traditional radical system, which is based on the 214 radicals introduced by the 康熙字典 こうきじてん (Chinese: kāngxī zìdiǎn), a comprehensive character dictionary published in China in 1716.

1 Format of Radical Index

1.1 Scope The **Radical Index** lists all the main entry characters. It also lists nonstandard forms in cases where the original radicals have been lost (see **§3** below).

1.2 Format The heading at the beginning of each section consists of the **radical number** and the **parent radical** in its full traditional form. **Variant forms** are given in parentheses only in cases where the difference between the parent and variant forms is so great as to be difficult to recognize.

For example, Radical 64 手 (扌) includes the variant in parentheses, but Radical 75 木, which has the very common left-side variant 木, does not, since both forms are so similar that no confusion is likely to arise. The small numerals to the left of the character column indicate the stroke-count of the **nonradical element;** the numerals to the right are the **entry numbers.**

1.3 Order of Entries The radicals appear in order of increasing stroke-count and are numbered from 1 to 214 according to the traditional historical arrangement. Characters sharing the same radical are listed in increasing order of the stroke-counts of their nonradical elements. The characters within a given stroke-count subsection are listed in alphabetical order of their principal *on* readings or, in cases where no *on* reading exists, their principal *kun* readings.

2 Instructions for Use

STEP 1	Determine the **radical** and **radical number** of your character: *(a)* Determine the radical. See **§4 How to Determine the Radical** below. *(b)* Determine the stroke-count of the radical. See **Appendix 3. How to Count Strokes** on p. 1810. *(c)* Determine the radical number using the **Quick Reference Radical Chart** on p. 1984. **NOTE:** If you have memorized the number of the radical in question, skip steps *(b)* and *(c)*.
STEP 2	Determine the stroke-count of the nonradical element.
STEP 3	Turn to the section of the **Radical Index** that corresponds to your radical number.
STEP 4	Locate your character under the stroke-count of the nonradical element with the aid of the small numerals on the left of the character column. The main entry number appears to the right of the character.

Example: Determine the Radical of 像

STEP 1	Carrying out STEP 1 as described, we determine that the radical of 像 is the 2-stroke element 人 (亻), Radical 9.
STEP 2	Counting the strokes of the nonradical element 象 yields a stroke-count of 12.
STEP 3	Turn to the section headed **Radical 9** 人 (亻).
STEP 4	Under the nonradical stroke-count of 12 appears the character 像, entry number 0187.

3 Cross-References

The simplification of characters that took place in the postwar period has resulted in the disappearance of the radical element from some characters. For example, 会 is traditionally classified under 曰 (Radical 73) based on its old form 會, but 曰 has completely disappeared from the simplified form 会. These **lost-radical** characters are listed under their traditional radicals, followed by the old form in parentheses. For example, the index entry for 会 appears at its traditional radical 曰 (Radical 73):

会(會)　　2512°

In addition, the lost-radical characters are cross-referenced under another radical based on their simplified forms, which is followed by the number of the traditional radical in square brackets. For example, 会 is cross-referenced under its new radical 人 (Radical 9):

会 [RAD.73]　　2512°

The entry numbers of all lost-radical characters, both at their traditional radicals and at their new radicals, are followed by a small superscript circle (°).

4 How to Determine the Radical

To determine which element of a character is the radical can be a laborious task. The following guidelines should be of help.

4.1 Radical Position The position of the radical within a character may be difficult to predict. A character may contain several radical elements, and to choose between them may require a knowledge of character etymology. 奮, for example, consists of 大, 隹, and 田, all of which are radicals. The general rule is: take the left radical in left-right characters (such as 亻 in 休), the top radical in up-down characters (such as 宀 in 完), and the enclosing radical in characters containing enclosures (as 广 in 広).

The **Important Radicals** chart below lists the most important radicals, classified by their position within the character. The radicals are shown in the form in which they occur most frequently. The position of many radicals is constant in relation to the rest of the character (though there are exceptions). These are classified in the chart below under the headings **left, right,** etc. The position of other radicals, classified under the heading **others,** is variable.

4.2 Important Radicals Memorizing the most important radicals and their numbers will greatly speed up the lookup process. Since many Japanese and Chinese character dictionaries follow the traditional radical system, those making extensive use of radical indexes will find it worthwhile to memorize the table below.

4.3 Stroke Counting Since the characters within a given radical group are arranged in increasing order of the stroke-counts of their nonradical elements, it is important to learn how to count strokes accurately. Refer to **Appendix 3. How to Count Strokes** on p. 1810.

4.4 Variant Forms Radicals may occur in their unabbreviated **parent form,** or in an abbreviated **variant form.** For example, 犬 (Radical 94) appears in its parent form in 獣, but in its abbreviated form of 犭 in 独. Some radicals, such as 艸 (Radical 140), always occur in their variant forms (in this case 艹). To use the **Radical Index** effectively, one needs the ability to identify the parent radical from its variant forms. See the **Quick Reference Radical Chart** on p. 1984 for information on parent forms and their variants.

4.5 Lost Radicals Since the radicals of some characters are based on the old forms of the characters, a knowledge of the latter may sometimes be necessary in order to identify the radical. See **§3** above for details on how this problem is overcome in this dictionary.

4.6 Quick Reference Radical Chart This chart, which appears on p. 1984 immediately before the **Radical Index,** is the quickest way to determine the radical number.

Important Radicals

LEFT RADICALS
偏 へん

9	亻
24	十
30	口
32	土
38	女
39	子
46	山
57	弓
60	彳
61	忄
64	扌
75	木
85	氵
86	火
93	牛
94	犭
96	王
112	石
113	礻
115	禾
119	米
120	糸
128	耳
130	月
137	舟
142	虫
145	衤
149	言
154	貝
157	足
159	車
164	酉
167	金
170	阝
184	食
187	馬
195	魚

RIGHT RADICALS
旁 つくり

18	刂
26	卩
62	戈
66	攵
76	欠
163	阝
181	頁

TOP RADICALS
冠 かんむり

8	亠
37	大
40	宀
46	山
116	穴
118	⺮
122	罒
140	艹
173	雨

BOTTOM RADICALS
脚 あし

10	儿
12	八
86	灬
154	貝

ENCLOSURES
囲 かこい

27	厂
31	口
44	尸
53	广
104	疒
162	辶
169	門

OTHERS

1	一
19	力
41	寸
50	巾
72	日
74	月
102	田
109	目
172	隹

QUICK REFERENCE RADICAL CHART

部首早見一覧

The **Quick Reference Radical Chart** helps the user quickly look up radical numbers as an aid to using the **Radical Index** efficiently.

1. **Format** The left part of each column gives the **radical number** in boldface; the right part shows the **radical** in its **parent form,** followed by the **radical name.**
2. **Order of entries** The radicals and their variants are listed in order of increasing stroke-count of their parent forms. These are numbered consecutively from 1 to 214 according to the traditional historical arrangement. When a radical has more than one form, the parent form is given first, followed by all its variants.
3. **Radical names** When talking about the components of Chinese characters, it is convenient to describe them by naming their constituent radicals. For example, we can say that 洋 consists of 氵 ***sanzui*** (the 'water' radical) on the left and 羊 ***hitsuji*** (the 'sheep' radical) on the right. Each radical is followed by a romanized version of its most common name in Japanese.
4. **Cross-references** If the stroke-count of a variant differs from that of its parent form, it is cross-referenced under the variant stroke-count to its corresponding parent form. The cross-references appear at the end of a given stroke-count section, and are distinguished by radical numbers in square brackets. For example, Radical 162 has the seven-stroke parent form 辵, one three-stroke variant 辶, and one four-stroke variant 辶. All three forms are listed together under Radical 162, but the variants also appear at the end of the three- and four-stroke sections, respectively.

1 STROKE

1	一	*ichi*
2	丨	*bō*
3	丶	*ten*
4	丿	*no*
	ノ	*no*
5	乙	*otsu*
	乚	*re*
6	亅	*hanebō*

2 STROKES

7	二	*ni*
8	亠	*nabebuta*
9	人	*hito*
	亻	*ninben*
	𠆢	*hitoyane*
10	儿	*ninnyō, hitoashi*
11	入	*iru*
12	八	*hachigashira*
	八	*hachi*
	丷	*hachigashira*
13	冂	*keigamae*
14	冖	*wakanmuri*
15	冫	*nisui*
16	几	*tsukue*
	几	*kazagamae*
17	凵	*kannyō, ukebako*
18	刀	*katana*
	刂	*rittō*
19	力	*chikara*
20	勹	*tsutsumigamae*
21	匕	*sajinohi*
22	匚	*hakogamae*
23	匸	*kakushigamae*
	匸	*kakushigamae*
24	十	*jū*
	十	*jūhen*
25	卜	*bokunoto*
	⺊	*bokunoto*
26	卩	*fushizukuri*
	㔾	*fushizukuri*
27	厂	*gandare*
28	厶	*mu*
29	又	*mata*
	又	*mata*

3 STROKES

30	口	*kuchi*
	口	*kuchihen*
31	囗	*kunigamae*
32	土	*tsuchi*
	土	*tsuchihen*
33	士	*samurai*
34	夂	*fuyugashira*
35	夊	*suinyō*
	夊	*natsuashi*
36	夕	*yūbe*
37	大	*ōkii, dai*
	大	*ōkii, dai*
38	女	*onna*
	女	*onnahen*
39	子	*ko*
	子	*kohen*
40	宀	*ukanmuri*
41	寸	*sun*
42	小	*chiisai*
	⺌	*naogashira*
	⺍	*naogashira*
43	尢	*mageashi*
44	尸	*shikabane*
45	屮	*tetsu*
46	山	*yama*
	山	*yamahen*
	山	*yamakanmuri*

47	巛	*magarigawa*
	川	*sanbongawa*
48	工	*takumi*
	工	*takumihen*
49	己	*onore*
	巳	*mi*
50	巾	*haba*
51	干	*hosu*
52	幺	*itogashira*
53	广	*madare*
54	廴	*ennyō*
	廴	*ennyō*
55	廾	*nijūashi*
56	弋	*shikigamae*
57	弓	*yumi*
	弓	*yumihen*
58	彐	*keigashira*
	⺕	*keigashira*
	彑	*keigashira*
59	彡	*sanzukuri*
60	彳	*gyōninben*
[61]	忄	*risshinben*
[64]	扌	*tehen*
[85]	氵	*sanzui*
[90]	丬	*shōhen*
[94]	犭	*kemonohen*
[140]	艹	*kusakanmuri*
[162]	辶	*shinnyō, shinnyū*
[163]	阝	*ōzato*
[170]	阝	*kozatohen*

4 STROKES

61	心	*kokoro*
	忄	*risshinben*
	⺗	*shitagokoro*
62	戈	*kanohoko*
63	戶	*tobiranoto*
	戸	*tobiranoto*
64	手	*te*
	扌	*tehen*
65	支	*shinyō, jūmata*
	支	*shinyō, jūmata*
66	攴	*bokuzukuri, tomata*
	攵	*nobun*
67	文	*bun, bunnyō*
	文	*bun, bunnyō*
68	斗	*tomasu*
69	斤	*ono*
70	方	*kata*
71	无	*munyō*
	旡	*sudenotsukuri*
	旡	*sudenotsukuri*
72	日	*hi*
	日	*hi*
73	曰	*hirabi*
	曰	*hirabi*
74	月	*tsuki*
	月	*tsuki*
	月	*tsuki*
75	木	*ki*
	木	*kihen*
76	欠	*akubi*
77	止	*tomeru*
	止	*tomehen*
78	歹	*gatsuhen*
79	殳	*rumata, hokozukuri*
80	毋	*nakare*
	毋	*haha, nakare*
	母	*haha*
81	比	*kuraberu, hi*
82	毛	*ke*
	毛	*ke*
83	氏	*uji*
84	气	*kigamae*
85	水	*mizu*
	氵	*sanzui*
	氺	*shitamizu*
86	火	*hi*
	火	*hihen*
	灬	*rekka*
87	爪	*tsume*
	爫	*notsu*
	⺤	*tsumekanmuri*
88	父	*chichi*
	父	*chichi*
89	爻	*meme*
	爻	*meme*
90	爿	*shōhen*
	丬	*shōhen*
91	片	*kata*
92	牙	*kiba*
	牙	*kiba*
93	牛	*ushi*
	牜	*ushihen*
94	犬	*inu*
	犭	*kemonohen*
[96]	王	*tamahen*
	王	*ō*
[113]	礻	*nehen, shimesuhen*
[122]	罒	*yonkashira*
[125]	耂	*oikanmuri, oigashira*
[130]	月	*nikuzuki*
	月	*tsuki*
[140]	艹	*kusakanmuri*
	艹	*kusakanmuri*
[162]	辶	*shinnyō, shinnyū*

5 STROKES

95	玄	*gen*
96	玉	*tama*
	王	*tamahen*
	王	*ō*
97	瓜	*uri*
	瓜	*uri*
98	瓦	*kawara*
99	甘	*amai*
100	生	*umareru*
101	用	*mochiiru*
102	田	*ta*
103	疋	*hiki*
	⺪	*hikihen*
104	疒	*yamaidare*
105	癶	*hatsugashira*
106	白	*shiro*
107	皮	*kegawa*
108	皿	*sara*
109	目	*me*
110	矛	*hoko*
111	矢	*ya*
	矢	*yahen*
112	石	*ishi*
	石	*ishihen*

113 示 *shimesu*
礻 *nehen, shimesuhen*
示 *shimesuhen*
114 禸 *gūnoashi*
115 禾 *nogi*
禾 *nogihen*
116 穴 *ana*
穴 *anakanmuri*
穴 *ana*
117 立 *tatsu*
立 *tatsuhen*
[71] 旡 *sudenotsukuri*
[80] 母 *haha*
[85] 氺 *shitamizu*
[92] 牙 *kiba*
[122] 罒 *yonkashira*
[145] 衤 *koromohen*

6 STROKES

118 竹 *take*
⺮ *takekanmuri*
119 米 *kome*
米 *komehen*
120 糸 *ito*
糸 *itohen*
121 缶 *hotogi*
122 网 *amigashira*
罒 *yonkashira*
⺳ *yonkashira*
123 羊 *hitsuji*
⺷ *hitsujikanmuri*
羊 *hitsujihen*
124 羽 *hane*
羽 *hane*
125 老 *oi*
耂 *oikanmuri, oigashira*
126 而 *shikashite*
127 耒 *raisuki*
耒 *raihen*
耒 *sukihen*
128 耳 *mimi*
耳 *mimihen*
129 聿 *fudezukuri*
130 肉 *niku*
月 *nikuzuki*
月 *tsuki*
131 臣 *shin*
臣 *shin*
132 自 *mizukara*
133 至 *itaru*
134 臼 *usu*
臼 *usu*
135 舌 *shita*
舌 *shitahen*
136 舛 *masu*
舛 *maiashi*
137 舟 *fune*
舟 *funehen*
138 艮 *kon, ushitora*
艮 *kon, ushitora*
139 色 *iro*
色 *irozukuri*
140 艸 *kusa*
艹 *kusakanmuri*
艹 *kusakanmuri*
艹 *kusakanmuri*
141 虍 *torakanmuri*
虍 *torakanmuri*
142 虫 *mushi*
虫 *mushihen*
143 血 *chi*
血 *chihen*
144 行 *gyō*
行 *gyōgamae*
145 衣 *koromo*
衤 *koromohen*
衣 *koromo*
146 襾 *nishi*
覀 *nishi*
西 *nishi*
[97] 瓜 *uri*

7 STROKES

147 見 *miru*
148 角 *tsuno*
角 *tsunohen*
149 言 *kotoba*
言 *gonben*
150 谷 *tani*
谷 *tanihen*
151 豆 *mame*
豆 *mamehen*
152 豕 *inoko*
豕 *inokohen*
153 豸 *mujina*
154 貝 *kai*
貝 *kaihen*
155 赤 *aka*
赤 *akahen*
156 走 *hashiru*
走 *sōnyō*
157 足 *ashi*
⻊ *ashihen*
158 身 *mi*
身 *mihen*
159 車 *kuruma*
車 *kurumahen*
160 辛 *karai*
辛 *karai*
161 辰 *shinnotatsu*
162 辵 *shinnyō, shinnyū*
⻌ *shinnyō, shinnyū*
⻍ *shinnyō, shinnyū*
163 邑 *mura*
阝 *ōzato*
164 酉 *hiyominotori*
酉 *torihen*
165 釆 *nogome*
釆 *nogomehen*
166 里 *sato*
里 *satohen*
[131] 臣 *shin*
[134] 臼 *usu*
[136] 舛 *maiashi*
[168] 镸 *nagai*
[199] 麦 *bakunyō*
麦 *mugi*

8 STROKES

167 金 *kane*
金 *kanehen*
168 長 *nagai*

長 *nagai*
169 門 *mon, mongamae*
170 阜 *gifunofu*
阝 *kozatohen*
171 隶 *reizukuri*
172 隹 *furutori*
173 雨 *ame*
⻗ *amekanmuri*
174 靑 *ao*
青 *ao*
175 非 *arazu*
[184] 飠 *shokuhen*
[210] 斉 *sei*

9 STROKES

176 面 *men*
177 革 *kawa*
革 *kawahen*
178 韋 *nameshigawa*
韋 *nameshigawa*
179 韭 *nira*
180 音 *oto*
音 *oto*
181 頁 *ōgai*
182 風 *kaze*
風 *kaze*
183 飛 *tobu*
184 食 *shoku*
飠 *shokuhen*
𩙿 *shokuhen*
食 *shoku*
185 首 *kubi*
186 香 *nioikō*

10 STROKES

187 馬 *uma*
馬 *umahen*
188 骨 *hone*
骨 *honehen*
189 高 *takai*
190 髟 *kamikanmuri*
191 鬥 *tōgamae*
192 鬯 *chō*
193 鬲 *kaku*
鬲 *kaku*
194 鬼 *oni*
鬼 *kinyō*
[178] 韋 *nameshigawa*
[212] 竜 *ryū*

11 STROKES

195 魚 *uo*
魚 *uohen*
196 鳥 *tori*
鳥 *tori*
197 鹵 *ro*
198 鹿 *shika*
199 麥 *baku*
麦 *bakunyō*
麦 *bakunyō*
麦 *mugi*
200 麻 *asa*
麻 *asakanmuri*
麻 *asakanmuri*
麻 *asa*
[201] 黄 *kiiro*
[203] 黒 *kuroi*
[213] 亀 *kame*

12 STROKES

201 黃 *kiiro*
黄 *kiiro*
202 黍 *kibi*
203 黑 *kuroi*
黒 *kuroi*
204 黹 *futsu*
[211] 歯 *hahen*
歯 *ha*

13 STROKES

205 黽 *ben*
206 鼎 *kanae*
207 鼓 *tsuzumi*
208 鼠 *nezumi*
鼠 *nezuminyō*

14 STROKES

209 鼻 *hana*
鼻 *hanahen*
鼻 *hana*
210 齊 *sei*
斉 *sei*

15 STROKES

211 齒 *ha*
歯 *hahen*
齒 *hahen*
歯 *ha*

16 STROKES

212 龍 *ryū*
竜 *ryū*
龍 *ryū*
213 龜 *kame*
龜 *kame*
亀 *kame*

17 STROKES

214 龠 *yaku*

18 STROKES

[213] 龜 *kame*

RADICAL INDEX
部 首 索 引

1 STROKE

2 STROKES

	佳		0096
	侃		0097
	供		0098
	侠		0102
	來		4387
	来(來)		2975°
	例		0099
	舍	[RAD.135]	2555°
	使		0100
	侑		0101
7	便		0105
	侮		0120
	俄		0106
	保		0107
	係		0108
	侯		0109
	俠		0110
	俣		0111
	俚		0112
	俐		0113
	侶		0114
	信		0115
	侵		0116
	侵		0121
	俊		0117
	促		0118
	俗		0119
8	倍		0122
	値		0123
	俺		0124
	倶		0125
	俱		0141
	俳		0126
	併		0142
	倣		0127
	俸		0128
	俵		0129
	倹		0130
	倦		0131
	個		0132
	候		0133
	倖		0134
	倫		0135
	倆		0136
	借		0137
	修		0138
	倉		2607
	倒		0139
	倭		0140
9	偽		0149
	偶		0150
	偏		0151
	偏		0158
	偉		0159
	假		0161
	健		0152
	倦		0162
	偲		0153
	側		0155
	停		0156
	偵		0157
10	備		0165
	傍		0166
	偉		0167
	傑		0168
	傘		2640
11	傳		0182
	働		0172
	傲		0173
	傾		0174
	傑		0175
	僅		0169
	僅		0176
	債		0177
	催		0178
	傷		0179
	僧		0180
	傭		0181
12	僕		0185
	僞		0188
	僚		0186
	僧		0190
	像		0187
13	儀		0191
	舖	[RAD.135]	2177°
	價		0193
	儉		0194
	億		0192
14	儒		0197
15	儲		0201
	償		0199
	優		0200
16	儲		0202
17	儼		0203
20	儼		0204

RADICAL 10 儿

0	儿		0003
2	元		2428
	允		2476
3	充		2685
	兄		2676
4	兆		0264
	充		2507
	光		3043
	兇		3044
	先		3046
5	児		3153
	克		2540
	免		2539
	兎		4374
6	兒		3249
	免		2565
	兔		2559
	兔		2566
	兎		3165
8	党	[RAD.203]	3190°
9	兜		3499
10	堯		2888
	兆		3522
12	兢		1971

RADICAL 11 入

0	入		4177
1	亾		3645
2	內		4285
	内(內)		2914°
4	全		2515
	全(仝)		1743°
6	兩		4381
	両(兩)		2949°

RADICAL 12 八 (丷)

0	八		0004
	八		3644
	丷		0002
2	公		2468
	六		2461
4	共		3045
5	兵		3158
6	具		3159
	具		3252
	其		3255
	典		3253
8	兼		2850
	兼		4399

RADICAL 13 冂

0	冂		4159
1	冂		4239
2	円	[RAD.31]	3673°
	内	[RAD.11]	4277°
3	冋		3695
	冊		4295
	册		4303
4	再		4332
6	冐		3081
	周		3721
7	冒		3094
	冒(冒)		2155°

RADICAL 14 冖

0	冖		4160
2	冗		2470
3	写	[RAD.40]	2493°
5	冝		2538
7	冠		2583
8	冥		2613
9	冨		2633
12	寫		2660

RADICAL 15 冫

0	冫		2422
3	冬		2679
4	冲		0059
	冴		0060
	冰		0061
	决		0063
5	冴		0087
	况		0090
	冷		0088
	冶		0089
8	准		0143
	凉		0147
	凌		0144
	凄		0145
	凍		0146
10	凖		3521
13	凜		0195
	凛		0196
14	凝		0198
15	凞		3605

RADICAL 16 几

0	几		4156
	凢		4161
1	凡		3656
	凡		3657
	凣		4237
2	凨		3678
3	処	[RAD.141]	3764°
	凧		3696
4	凪		3709
6	凮		3722
9	凰		3738
10	凱		2286

RADICAL 17 凵

0	凵		4171
2	凶		3679
3	凹		4294
	出		4310

	凸	4298
6	函	3724
7	圅	3732

RADICAL 18 刀 (刂)

0	刀	3642
	刂	0001
1	刃	3646
	刄	3647
	刅	4208
2	分	2466
	刈	0032
	切	0030
3	刊	0221
	刌	0220
	切	0214
4	刑	1024
	列	1018
5	別	1434
	判	1441
	判	1442
	刼	1437
	利	1431
	初	1433
6	刵	1616
	券	3256
	劵	3258
	刻	1619
	刹	1620
	刷	1623
	制	1624
	刺	1625
	到	1615
7	剋	4097
	削	1837
	削	1838
	則	1831
	前	2819
	前	2820
8	剖	2103
	剛	2107
	剝	2105
	剥	2106
	剣	2104
	帰 [RAD.77]	0148°
	剤	2102
9	副	2230
	剩	2233
	剪	2886
10	剰	2288
	割	2284
	割	2285
	創	2283
11	剿	2335
12	劃	2378
13	劇	2399
	劍	2397
	劉	2398
14	辦	2030
	劔	2400
	劒	2401
	劑	2404

RADICAL 19 力

0	力	4178
3	加	0042
	功	0218
4	劣	3047
5	努	3154
	助	1440
	劫	1435
	励	1438
	労	3155
6	劾	1618
	効	1617
7	勉	4098
	勃	1839
	勅	1841
	勁	1833
	勇	2592
	勇	2593
8	勉	4113
	勢	3428
9	動	2232
	勘	2231
	務	1505
10	募	2901
	勤	2287
	勞	3451
	勝	1268
	勝	1270
11	勧	2334
	勤	2336
	勢	3542
13	勲	3560
14	勳	2406
	勵	2407
17	勸	2413
18	勸	2417

RADICAL 20 勹

0	勹	4182
1	勺	3650
	勺	3651
2	勾	3660
	勿	3661
	匁	4276
	匂	3662
3	包	3684
	包	3686

RADICAL 21 匕

0	匕	3641
2	化	0022
3	北	0230

RADICAL 22 匚

0	匚	4162
4	匡	3710
	匠	3711

RADICAL 23 匸

0	匸	4163
2	匹	3680
	匹	3682
	区	3681
5	医 [RAD.164]	3715°
8	匿	3735
	匿	3736
9	區	3739

RADICAL 24 十

0	十	4172
	十	4173
1	千	4219
2	午	2478
	廿	4258
	升	4266
	卆	2484
3	半	4313
	半	4320
4	古	2517
6	卑	4388
	協	0103
	協	0104
	卒	2549
	卓	2561
7	卑	3270
	南	2584
10	博	0170
	博	0171

RADICAL 25 卜

0	卜	4174
3	占	2496

RADICAL 26 卩 (㔾)

0	卩	4165
	㔾	4164
3	夗	0216
	卯	0231
4	印	1023
	危	2524
	危	3965
5	却	1436
	卵	1054
	即	1439
6	巻	3257
	巻(卷)	2298°
	卸	1621
7	卻	1830
	卸	1835
	卽	1840
8	卿	0552
10	卿	0769
	卿	0770

RADICAL 27 厂

0	厂	4166
	厂	4168
2	厄	3665
7	厖	3725
	厚	3726
	厘	3727
8	原	3733
10	厨	3740
	厩	3742
12	厭	3745
	厩	3746

RADICAL 28 厶

0	厶	4183
2	厸	0027
3	去	2678
6	参	2563
9	參	2635
10	叅	2646

RADICAL 29 又

0	又	4167
	又	4158
1	叉	4194
2	反	3663
	及	3666
	及(及)	2868°
	収 [RAD.66]	0031°
	双 [RAD.172]	0028°
	友	3670
6	受	3076
	取	1613
	叔	1622
7	叛	1469

3 STROKES

RADICAL 30 口

RADICAL 31 囗

RADICAL 32 土

	執		2114
	埴		0562
	堆		0563
	堵		0564
	埜		3437
9	塚		0675
	堕		3501
	堰		0676
	塀		0677
	堡		3500
	報		2133
	場		0678
	堺		0679
	堪		0680
	堅		3502
	堽		0684
	塁		3206
	堤		0681
	堵		0682
	塔		0683
10	墓		2930
	塚		0778
	塩	[RAD.197]	0774°
	塊		0775
	塙		0776
	塞		2924
	塑		3525
	塑		3526
	塡		0777
	填		0779
	塗		3523
11	墨		3423
	塀		0837
	塵		3922
	塲		0838
	塾		3546
	境		0835
	増		0836
12	墨		3488
	墮		3580
	墳		0887
	墟		0888
	墜		3578
	墜		3579
	壄		3581
	增		0889
13	壇		0932
	墳		0935
	壁		3601
	壌		0933
	壊		0934
	墾		3602
14	壓		3753
	壕		0966
15	壘		3242
16	壞		0992
17	壤		1000

RADICAL 33 士

0	士		4213
1	壬		4257
3	壮		0263
4	売	[RAD.154]	2722°
	壱		2723
	声	[RAD.128]	2724°
	壯		1038
8	壷		2852
9	壹		2891
	壺		2890
	壻		0685
11	壽		2955
	寿(壽)		2979°

RADICAL 34 夂

0	夂		4200
2	冬		2680
6	変	[RAD.149]	2569°

RADICAL 35 夊

0	夊		4201
7	夏		2619

RADICAL 36 夕

0	夕		4195
2	外		0215
3	多		2694
	夛		2704
5	夜		2550
8	梦		3436
10	夢		2939

RADICAL 37 大

0	大		4224
	𡗒		4231
1	夫		4271
	太		2673
	天		4250
2	夲		2681
	央		4322
	失		4325
3	夷		4349
5	奄		2757
	奔		2758
	奉		3167
	奇		2756
	奈		2759
	臭	[RAD.203]	2562°
6	奔		2797
	奎		2796
	契		3267
	契		3268
	奏		3185
7	套		2823
9	奥		3503
	奠		2641
	奠		2644
10	奧		3527
	奨		3524
11	奪		2956
	獎		3545
13	奮		3000

RADICAL 38 女

0	女		4226
	女		4232
2	奴		0217
3	妃		0238
	如		0239
	好		0240
	妄		2509
	妄		2710
4	妨		0279
	妥		3053
	妥		3055
	妙		0280
	妊		0281
	妒		0283
	妖		0282
5	姆		0331
	委		3160
	姑		0332
	妹		0333
	妻		3166
	姓		0334
	始		0335
	姉		0336
	姊		0338
	妬		0337
6	娃		0419
	姥		0420
	威		4394
	姻		0421
	姫		0423
	婋		0424
	姙		0425
	姿		3264
	姿		3265
	姪		0422
7	娩		0486
	娯		0487
	娛		0491
	娘		0488
	姬		0489
	娠		0490
8	婆		3433
	娩		0567
	婦		0565
	婦		0568
	婚		0566
9	媒		0686
	媚		0687
	媛		0688
	媛		0690
	婿		0689
10	嫁		0780
	嫌		0781
	嫌		0784
	媾		0785
	媾		0782
	嫉		0783
11	嫡		0839
12	嬉		0890
13	嬢		0936
17	孃		1001

RADICAL 39 子

0	子		4196
1	孔		0205
3	字		2696
	存		3702
4	孛		2532
	孝		3973
	孜		0284
5	学		3162
	季		3161
	孤		0339
	孟		2760
6	孤		0426
7	孫		0492
12	學		3588
13	學		3604

RADICAL 40 宀

0	宀		4233
3	安		2695
	守		2697
	宅		2698
	宇		2699
4	宐		2731
	完		2727
	宏		2728
	宋		2730

4 STROKES

	挺	0512
	捕	0514
	挾	0520
	捞	0521
	振	0515
	捉	0518
	捜	0516
	挿	0517
	挫	0519
8	挽	0614
	描	0591
	捗	0615
	掩	0592
	排	0593
	捧	0594
	授	0595
	掛	0596
	掴	0616
	掲	0597
	捲	0598
	掬	0599
	控	0600
	掘	0601
	据	0602
	捺	0603
	捻	0604
	掠	0605
	採	0606
	採	0617
	接	0607
	捨	0608
	捨	0618
	捷	0609
	掌	3215
	措	0610
	掃	0611
	掻	0619
	掃	0620
	推	0612
	探	0613
9	握	0714
	援	0715
	援	0724
	換	0716
	掲	0725
	捲	0726
	揮	0717
	揆	0718
	揃	0719
	揃	0727
	揷	0728
	搜	0729
	插	0730
	提	0720
	搭	0721
	揚	0722
	揺	0723
10	搏	0794
	搬	0795
	携	0796
	摸	0797
	搾	0798
	摂	0799
	損	0801
	搔	0800
	搜	0802
	搖	0803
11	撃	3552
	摑	0848
	摩	3938
	摧	0849
	摯	3556
	摺	0850
	摺	0852
	摠	0853
	摘	0851
12	撲	0903
	撫	0904
	撞	0905
	播	0906
	撥	0907
	擕	0913
	撈	0908
	撒	0909
	撮	0910
	撰	0911
	撰	0914
	撤	0912
13	擊	3607
	據	0950
	擧	3568
	擅	0947
	操	0948
	擇	0951
	擔	0952
	擁	0949
14	擬	0969
	擱	0970
	擦	0971
	擡	0972
	擢	0973
	擢	0974
15	擴	0989
18	攜	1003
	攝	1004
19	攣	3635

RADICAL 65 支

0	支	2474
	支	2473

RADICAL 66 攴 (攵)

0	攴	2475
	攵	2479
2	收	0065
	収(收)	0016°
3	改	0287
	攻	0286
4	放	1058
5	故	1466
	政	1468
6	敏	1675
	效	1674
7	敏	1882
	敕	1890
	敗	1868
	敍	1879
	叙(敍)	1314°
	敘	1880
	教	1887
	敎	1888
	救	1891
8	敢	2142
	敬	2136
	散	2137
	敦	2128
9	敬	2244
	数	2245
11	敷	2345
	敷	2346
	敺	2348
	數	2347
	敵	2340
12	整	3562
14	斃	3593

RADICAL 67 文

0	文	2462
	文	2458
8	斑	1260
	斐	3449

RADICAL 68 斗

0	斗	3671
	斗	3672
6	料	1644
7	斜	1878
10	斡	2168

RADICAL 69 斤

0	斤	3667
1	斥	3690
4	斧	2558
7	断	1885
	斬	1874
8	斯	2140
9	新	2239
14	斷	2408

RADICAL 70 方

0	方	2459
4	於	1059
5	施	1103
6	旁	2598
	旅	1153
	旅	1154
7	旋	1194
	族	1195
9	旒	1272
10	旗	1321

RADICAL 71 无

0	无	4251
	旡	4252
	旡	4299
5	既	1498
7	旣	1884
	既	1912

RADICAL 72 日

0	日	3760
	日	3759
1	旧 [RAD.134]	0014°
	旦	3041
2	旬	3698
	旭	3697
	旨	2516
	早	3042
3	旱	3048
4	易	3064
	昆	3067
	昏	3073
	昂	3065
	昊	3066
	明	1060
	明	1062
	旺	1061
	昔	3086
	昇	3068
	昌	3069
5	昴	3091

RADICAL 73 曰

RADICAL 74 月

RADICAL 75 木

	决	0308
	汽	0309
	汲	0310
	沙	0311
	汰	0312
	沢	0313
	沌	0314
	沓	3074
	沃	0315
5	注	0383
	注	0401
	泥	0384
	泳	0385
	沿	0386
	沸	0387
	波	0388
	泊	0389
	泌	0390
	法	0391
	泡	0392
	泡	0402
	治	0393
	河	0394
	況	0395
	泣	0396
	沫	0397
	泪	0403
	泉	3176
	沼	0398
	沮	0399
	泝	0404
	泰	3193
	油	0400
6	洞	0455
	派	0456
	派	0469
	浄	0457
	洵	0458
	海	0459
	活	0460
	洪	0461
	洸	0462
	洛	0463
	流	0470
	浅	0464
	洗	0465
	津	0466
	洲	0467
	洋	0468
7	浮	0522
	浮	0534
	浜	0523
	浦	0524
	海	0535
	浩	0525
	浩	0536
	浬	0526
	浪	0527
	涙	0528
	流	0529
	浸	0530
	浸	0537
	消	0531
	涉	0538
	消	0539
	浴	0533
	涌	0540
8	淀	0621
	液	0622
	渕	0642
	淵	0643
	涯	0623
	淫	0624
	淫	0644
	淨	0645
	淳	0626
	渋	0625
	渇	0627
	渓	0628
	涸	0629
	混	0631
	淆	0630
	淋	0632
	淚	0646
	涼	0633
	済	0634
	清	0635
	淸	0647
	淺	0648
	深	0636
	滲	0649
	渚	0637
	涉	0638
	淑	0639
	淡	0640
	添	0641
	添	0650
9	渥	0731
	淵	0732
	減	0733
	澆	0751
	滋	0734
	滋	0752
	渦	0735
	渴	0753
	湖	0736
	渾	0738
	港	0737
	港	0754
	満	0739
	温	0740
	湿	0741
	渚	0755
	湘	0742
	測	0744
	湊	0743
	湛	0745
	渡	0746
	湯	0747
	湾	0748
	湧	0749
	游	0750
	湧	0756
10	漠	0804
	溺	0805
	溺	0817
	源	0806
	溢	0807
	溢	0818
	準	3541
	漢	0808
	滑	0809
	溪	0819
	溝	0810
	滉	0811
	溝	0820
	滅	0812
	溫	0821
	漣	0822
	滝	0813
	溜	0814
	溯	0823
	滞	0815
	溶	0816
11	滌	0854
	演	0855
	漁	0856
	漂	0857
	漢	0868
	漫	0858
	滿	0869
	漣	0859
	漏	0860
	漬	0861
	滲	0862
	漆	0863
	漕	0864
	漱	0865
	滯	0870
	滴	0866
	漥	0871
	漸	0867
12	澄	0915
	潮	0916
	澂	0923
	潮	0924
	潑	0917
	潤	0918
	澁	0925
	潰	0919
	潔	0920
	潔	0926
	澑	0927
	潟	0921
	潜	0922
	潛	0928
13	濁	0953
	澱	0954
	激	0955
	濃	0956
	澪	0957
	澤	0958
14	濠	0975
	濵	0979
	濱	0980
	濡	0976
	澀	0981
	濶	0982
	鴻	0977
	濟	0983
	濕	0984
	濯	0978
	濯	0985
15	濫	0990
16	瀕	0994
	瀬	0995
	瀨	0997
	瀝	0996
	瀧	0998
	瀦	0999
17	瀕	1002
18	灘	1005
19	灘	1006
22	灣	1010

RADICAL 86 火 (灬)

0	火	4273
	灬	0013
2	灰	3699
	灰	3705
	灯	1019
3	灸	2752

RADICAL 87 爪 (爫)

RADICAL 88 父

RADICAL 89 爻

RADICAL 90 爿

RADICAL 91 片

RADICAL 92 牙

RADICAL 93 牛 (牜)

RADICAL 94 犬 (犭)

5 STROKES

RADICAL 95 玄

RADICAL 96 玉 (王)

RADICAL 97 瓜

RADICAL 98 瓦

RADICAL 99 甘

RADICAL 100 生

RADICAL 101 用

RADICAL 102 田

RADICAL 103 疋

RADICAL 104 疒

RADICAL 105 癶

RADICAL 106 白

RADICAL 107 皮

RADICAL 108 皿

RADICAL 109 目

RADICAL 110 矛

RADICAL 111 矢

RADICAL 112 石

RADICAL 113 示 (礻)

RADICAL 114 禸

RADICAL 115 禾

RADICAL 116 穴

RADICAL 117 立

6 STROKES

RADICAL 118 竹 (⺮)

RADICAL 126 而

RADICAL 127 耒

RADICAL 128 耳

RADICAL 129 聿

RADICAL 130 肉 (月)

RADICAL 131 臣

RADICAL 132 自

RADICAL 133 至

RADICAL 134 臼

RADICAL 135 舌

RADICAL 136 舛

RADICAL 137 舟

RADICAL 138 艮

RADICAL 139 色

RADICAL 140 艸 (艹)

RADICAL 141 虍

RADICAL 142 虫

RADICAL 143 血

RADICAL 144 行

RADICAL 145 衣 (衤)

RADICAL 155 赤

RADICAL 156 走

RADICAL 157 足

RADICAL 158 身

RADICAL 159 車

RADICAL 160 辛

RADICAL 161 辰

RADICAL 162 辵 (辶)

RADICAL 182 風

RADICAL 183 飛

RADICAL 184 食(飠)

RADICAL 185 首

RADICAL 186 香

10 STROKES

RADICAL 187 馬

RADICAL 188 骨

RADICAL 189 高

RADICAL 190 髟

RADICAL 191 鬥

RADICAL 192 鬯

RADICAL 193 鬲

RADICAL 194 鬼

11 STROKES

RADICAL 195 魚

RADICAL 196 鳥

RADICAL 197 鹵

RADICAL 198 鹿

RADICAL 199 麥(麦)

HOW TO USE THE PATTERN INDEX
字型索引の使い方

The key to using this dictionary effectively is the **Pattern Index,** which allows you to quickly locate a character from its SKIP pattern.

Incorrect locations are indicated by the superscript symbols *p, s,* and *ps,* and are followed by cross-references to the correct locations (see **§2.6** on p. 1793 for details). The order of entries is exactly the same as that of the entry characters in the body of the dictionary (see **§2.5** on p. 1791).

Detailed instructions for using the **Pattern Index** are given in **§3.1** on p. 1795. The gist of the method is as follows:

1. Determine the **SKIP number** of your character.
2. Determine the **entry number** by locating your character in the **Pattern Index.** Use the **subsection guides** and **subgroup guides.**
3. Locate your character entry from the entry number.

Pattern Index

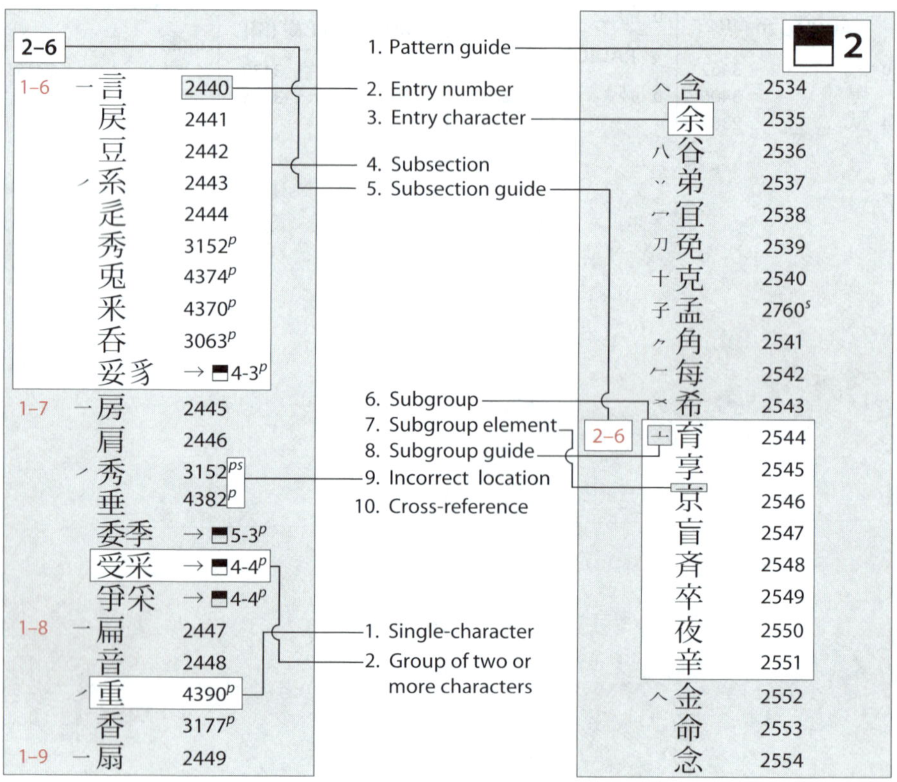

Pattern Index Elements and Guides

1. Pattern guide	A guide in the upper, outer corner of a page that indicates the **pattern** and **pattern number** for that page.
2. Entry number	A number that uniquely identifies the entry characters of the dictionary. After locating the entry number in the index, turn the pages until you find the corresponding entry character.
3. Entry character	The character that heads an index entry.
4. Subsection	A subdivision of the **Pattern Index.** The subsections are arranged in ascending order of their **subsection numbers.**
5. Subsection guide	1. Boldface numerals in the upper corner of a page that indicate the **subsection number** for that page. The upper-right guide (on a left page) indicates the subsection number for the first subsection, while the upper-left guide (on a right page) indicates the subsection number for the last subsection on that page. Together they indicate the subsection number range for both pages. 2. Red hyphenated numerals in the left part of a column that indicate the subsection number for each subsection. Scanning through the subsection guides enables you to quickly locate the subsection number corresponding to your character.
6. Subgroup	A subdivision of a **subsection** in which a group of **divisible characters** share a common **subgroup element.**
7. Subgroup element	The shared element of a **subgroup,** which corresponds to the **shaded part** of a **divisible character.**
8. Subgroup guide	A guide to the left of the character column that indicates the **subgroup element** for each subgroup. Scanning through the subgroup guides enables you to locate quickly the one corresponding to the **shaded part** of your character.
9. Incorrect location	Location where a character might be mistakenly looked for: *p* incorrect pattern classification *s* incorrect stroke-count *ps* incorrect pattern classification and incorrect stroke-count
10. Cross-reference entry	An entry appearing at an **incorrect location** with a cross-reference to the corresponding correct location. These are of two kinds: 1. Cross-reference for a single character. 2. Cross-references for a group of two or more characters.

PATTERN INDEX

字 型 索 引

◧ LEFT-RIGHT

		伴	0068
		位	0069
		佚	0070
		似	0071
		住	0072
		何	0073
		伽	0074
		伶	0075
		佐	0076
		作	0077
		伺	0078
		伸	0079
		体	0080
		但	0081
		低	0082
		佑	0083
		佛	0084
		伴	0085
		住	0086
	冫	冴	0087
		冷	0088
		冶	0089
		况	0090
	孑	孤	0426^{s}
	阝	阻附etc	→ ◧3-5^{s}
	ﾘ	児	3153^{p}
2-6	亻	侮	0091
		併	0092
		依	0093
		侍	0094
		価	0095
		佳	0096
		侃	0097
		供	0098
		例	0099
		使	0100
		侑	0101
		侠	0102
		隹	4383^{p}
	十	協	0103
		恊	0104
	孑	孤	0426^{s}
	阝	限降	→ ◧3-6^{s}
2-7	亻	便	0105
		俄	0106
		保	0107
		係	0108
		侯	0109
		俠	0110
		俣	0111
		俚	0112
		俐	0113
		侶	0114
		信	0115
		侵	0116
		俊	0117
		促	0118
		俗	0119
		侮	0120
		侵	0121
	孑	孫	0492^{s}
	阝	陷	0663^{s}
		院除etc	→ ◧3-7^{s}
2-8	亻	倍	0122
		値	0123
		俺	0124
		倶	0125
		俳	0126
		倣	0127
		俸	0128
		俵	0129
		倹	0130
		倦	0131
		個	0132
		候	0133
		倖	0134
		倫	0135
		倆	0136
		借	0137
		修	0138
		倒	0139
		倭	0140
		俱	0141
		併	0142
		偶	0150^{s}
		健	0152^{s}
	冫	准	0143
		凌	0144
		凄	0145
		凍	0146
		凉	0147
	阝	隅随	→ ◧3-9^{s}
		陸険etc	→ ◧3-8^{s}
	ﾘ	帰	0148
2-9	亻	偽	0149
		偶	0150
		偏	0151
		健	0152
		偲	0153
		脩	0154
		側	0155
		停	0156
		偵	0157
		偏	0158
		偉	0159
		條	0160
		假	0161
		倦	0162
	匕	頃	0163
	阝	階隊etc	→ ◧3-9^{s}
	丁	頂	0164
2-10	亻	備	0165
		傍	0166
		偉	0167
		傑	0168
		僅	0169
		僅	0176^{s}
	十	博	0170
		博	0171
	阝	隔隙etc	→ ◧3-10^{s}
2-11	亻	働	0172
		傲	0173
		傾	0174
		傑	0175
		僅	0176
		債	0177
		催	0178
		傷	0179
		僧	0180
		傭	0181
		傳	0182
	阝	際障etc	→ ◧3-11^{s}

	丬	臨	0183
	九	鳩	0184
2-12	亻	僕	0185
		僚	0186
		像	0187
		僞	0188
		僱	0189
		僧	0190
	阝	隣	0929[s]
2-13	亻	儀	0191
		億	0192
		價	0193
		儉	0194
	冫	凜	0195
		凛	0196
	阝	隣險etc	→ ◧3-13[s]
2-14	亻	儒	0197
	冫	凝	0198
	阝	隱	0987[s]
2-15	亻	償	0199
		優	0200
		儲	0201
2-16	亻	儲	0202
2-17	亻	儼	0203
2-20	亻	儼	0204
3-1	孑	孔	0205
	幺	幻	0206
	弓	引	0207
3-2	口	叩	0208
		叶	0209
		叱	0210
		叮	0211
		叫	0212
		叱	0213
	土	圠	0214
	夕	外	0215
		夘	0216
	女	奴	0217
		好	0240[s]
	工	功	0218
		巧	0219
		叻	0220
	干	刊	0221
	幺	幼	0222
	弓	弘	0223
	扌	打	0224
		払	0225
	止	此	1017[s]
	氵	氾	0226
		汁	0227
		汀	0228
	犭	犯	0229
	匕	比	0029[s]
	丩	収	0031[s]
	レ	以	0045[p]
	丬	北	0230
	卯	卯	0231
	E	印	1023[s]
3-3	口	吃	0232
		叫	0233
		吸	0234
		吐	0235
	土	地	0236
	夕	舛	0237
	女	妃	0238
		如	0239
		好	0240
	中	艸	0241
	工	巧	0219[s]
	巾	帆	0242
		帆	0243
		帆	0244
	弓	弛	0245
	彳	行	0246
		行	0247
	忄	忙	0248
		忙	0249
	扌	扣	0250
		扱	0251
		托	0252
	氵	池	0253
		汎	0254
		汝	0255
		汗	0256
		江	0257
		汚	0258
		汐	0259
		汲	0260
		汙	0261
		污	0262
	丬	壮	0263
	丬	兆	0264
	羽	羽	0265
	羽	羽	0266
	竹	竹	0267
		⺮	0268
	E	臼	1049[s]
3-4	口	吠	0269
		吻	0270
		吟	0271
		吹	0272
		吸	0273
		吃	0232[s]
		吸	0234[s]
	土	坊	0274
		坂	0275
		均	0276
		坑	0277
	夕	舛	0278
	女	妨	0279
		妙	0280
		妊	0281
		妖	0282
		妒	0283
		姉	0336[s]
		姊	0338[s]
	孑	孜	0284
	山	岐	0285
	工	攻	0286
	己	改	0287
	彳	役	0288
		往	0352[s]
	忄	快	0289
	扌	抜	0290
		扶	0291
		技	0292
		把	0293
		批	0294
		抒	0295
		抗	0296
		折	0297
		抄	0298

		扟	0299
		投	0300
		抑	0301
		抛	0302
		抅	0303
		扱	0304
		拒	0368[s]
		扱	0251[s]
	氵	没	0305
		沈	0306
		沖	0307
		決	0308
		汽	0309
		汲	0310
		沙	0311
		汰	0312
		沢	0313
		沌	0314
		沃	0315
		沒	0316
		沉	0317
		汚	0258[s]
		注	0401[s]
		汲	0260[s]
	犭	狂	0318
		犹	0319
	阝	防	0320
		阪	0321
	丩	收	0065[s]
	丬	状	0322
3-5	口	呪	0323
		呼	0324
		味	0325
		咏	0326
		味	0327
	土	坪	0328
		坦	0329
		坪	0330
	女	姆	0331
		姑	0332
		妹	0333
		姓	0334
		始	0335
		姉	0336

		姤	0337
		姉	0338
	子	孤	0339
	山	岬	0340
		岨	0341
	巾	帖	0342
	弓	弦	0343
		弥	0344
		弧	0345
	彳	彼	0346
		径	0347
		往	0348
		征	0349
		徃	0350
		徃	0351
		往	0352
	忄	怖	0353
		怪	0354
		怯	0355
		怜	0356
		性	0357
	扌	拇	0358
		抽	0359
		拝	0360
		拍	0361
		披	0362
		抱	0363
		抛	0364
		拐	0365
		拡	0366
		拘	0367
		拒	0368
		抛	0369
		抹	0370
		押	0371
		拉	0372
		拙	0373
		招	0374
		拓	0375
		担	0376
		抵	0377
		拔	0378
		拂	0379
		抱	0380

		拐	0381
		拒	0382
	氵	注	0383
		泥	0384
		泳	0385
		沿	0386
		沸	0387
		波	0388
		泊	0389
		泌	0390
		法	0391
		泡	0392
		治	0393
		河	0394
		況	0395
		泣	0396
		沫	0397
		沼	0398
		沮	0399
		油	0400
		注	0401
		泡	0402
		泪	0403
		泝	0404
	犭	狗	0405
		狙	0406
		狐	0407
	阝	阿	0408
		陀	0409
		附	0410
		阻	0411
3-6	口	咽	0412
		咲	0413
		响	0414
		咲	0415
	土	垣	0416
		城	0417
		垢	0418
	女	娃	0419
		姥	0420
		姻	0421
		姪	0422
		姫	0423
		娍	0424

	姙	0425
子	孤	0426
山	峡	0427
	峠	0428
干	形	0429
弓	弧	0430
彳	後	0431
	徊	0432
	律	0433
	待	0434
忄	悔	0435
	恢	0436
	恰	0437
	恒	0438
	恨	0439
	恠	0440
	恢	0441
	恆	0442
	恊	0443
	悖	0503^{s}
扌	按	0444
	挑	0445
	拷	0446
	持	0447
	挌	0448
	括	0449
	挟	0450
	拶	0451
	指	0452
	拭	0453
	拾	0454
	挺	0512^{s}
氵	洞	0455
	派	0456
	浄	0457
	洵	0458
	海	0459
	活	0460
	洪	0461
	洸	0462
	洛	0463
	浅	0464
	洗	0465
	津	0466

	洲	0467
	洋	0468
	派	0469
	流	0470
	浮	0522^{s}
犭	独	0471
	狐	0472
	狭	0473
	狩	0474
	狐	0407^{s}
阝	限	0475
	降	0476
3-7 口	唄	0477
	哺	0478
	哩	0479
	唆	0480
	哨	0481
	啄	0482
	哨	0483
土	埋	0484
	城	0485
女	娩	0486
	娯	0487
	娘	0488
	姫	0489
	娠	0490
	娯	0491
子	孫	0492
山	峨	0493
	峰	0494
	峻	0495
	峡	0496
彳	徐	0497
	従	0498
	徒	0499
	徑	0500
忄	悦	0501
	悟	0502
	悖	0503
	悩	0504
	悧	0505
	悄	0506
	悌	0507
	悦	0508

	悔	0509
	惇	0588^{s}
扌	挨	0510
	挽	0511
	挺	0512
	捗	0513
	捕	0514
	振	0515
	捜	0516
	挿	0517
	捉	0518
	挫	0519
	挾	0520
	捞	0521
	拷	0446^{s}
氵	浮	0522
	浜	0523
	浦	0524
	浩	0525
	浬	0526
	浪	0527
	涙	0528
	流	0529
	浸	0530
	消	0531
	酒	0532
	浴	0533
	浮	0534
	海	0535
	浩	0536
	浸	0537
	渉	0538
	消	0539
	涌	0540
	淳	0626^{s}
犭	狼	0541
	狭	0542
	猛	0653^{s}
阝	陛	0543
	院	0544
	陣	0545
	除	0546
	陥	0547
	降	0548

	陞	0549
	陦	0550
	陷	0663^s
丬	将	0551
亻	修候	→ ◧2-8^p
乡	鄉	0664^s
卯	卿	0552
3-8 口	唖	0553
	喝	0554
	唱	0555
	唯	0556
	啄	0557
	喋	0665^s
土	培	0558
	域	0559
	埼	0560
	堀	0561
	埴	0562
	堆	0563
	堵	0564
女	婦	0565
	婚	0566
	娩	0567
	婦	0568
	娩	0486^s
	娯	0487^s
山	崎	0569
	崚	0570
	崕	0571
巾	帳	0572
弓	張	0573
	強	0574
彳	術	0575
	徠	0576
	得	0577
	御	0578
	従	0579
	術	0580
忄	惧	0581
	惟	0582
	情	0583
	惚	0584
	惨	0585
	惜	0586

	悼	0587
	惇	0588
	惧	0589
	情	0590
扌	描	0591
	掩	0592
	排	0593
	捧	0594
	授	0595
	掛	0596
	掲	0597
	捲	0598
	掬	0599
	控	0600
	掘	0601
	据	0602
	捺	0603
	捻	0604
	掠	0605
	採	0606
	接	0607
	捨	0608
	捷	0609
	措	0610
	掃	0611
	推	0612
	探	0613
	挽	0614
	捗	0615
	掴	0616
	採	0617
	捨	0618
	掻	0619
	掃	0620
	挽	0511^s
	插	0730^s
	揷	0728^s
氵	淀	0621
	液	0622
	涯	0623
	淫	0624
	渋	0625
	淳	0626
	渇	0627

	渓	0628
	涸	0629
	淆	0630
	混	0631
	淋	0632
	涼	0633
	済	0634
	清	0635
	深	0636
	渚	0637
	渉	0638
	淑	0639
	淡	0640
	添	0641
	渕	0642
	淵	0643
	淫	0644
	淨	0645
	涙	0646
	清	0647
	淺	0648
	滲	0649
	添	0650
	渡	0746^s
	游	0750^s
犭	猫	0651
	猪	0652
	猛	0653
	猟	0654
阝	陪	0655
	陳	0656
	陰	0657
	険	0658
	陸	0659
	陵	0660
	隆	0661
	陶	0662
	陥	0663
	隅	0760^s
	随	0765^s
亻	脩條	→ ◧2-9^p
亻	悠	3407^p
乡	郷	0664
3-9 口	喋	0665

	喚	0666
	喧	0667
	喫	0668
	喉	0669
	喰	0670
	喩	0671
	喝	0672
	喫	0673
	喻	0674
土	塚	0675
	堰	0676
	塀	0677
	場	0678
	堺	0679
	堪	0680
	堤	0681
	堵	0682
	塔	0683
	堤	0684
	埥	0685
女	媒	0686
	媚	0687
	媛	0688
	婿	0689
	媛	0690
山	崎	0691
川	順	0018[p]
工	項	0692
巾	帽	0693
	幅	0694
	幀	0695
	帽	0696
弓	弾	0697
	粥	0698
	强	0699
彡	須	0700
彳	復	0701
	街	0702
	御	0703
	循	0704
	衖	0705
忄	惰	0706
	慌	0707
	惶	0708

	惺	0709
	愉	0710
	慌	0711
	惱	0712
	愉	0713
扌	握	0714
	援	0715
	換	0716
	揮	0717
	揆	0718
	揃	0719
	提	0720
	搭	0721
	揚	0722
	揺	0723
	援	0724
	掲	0725
	捲	0726
	揃	0727
	揷	0728
	搜	0729
	插	0730
	搜	0802[s]
氵	渥	0731
	淵	0732
	減	0733
	滋	0734
	渦	0735
	湖	0736
	港	0737
	渾	0738
	満	0739
	温	0740
	湿	0741
	湘	0742
	湊	0743
	測	0744
	湛	0745
	渡	0746
	湯	0747
	湾	0748
	湧	0749
	游	0750
	澆	0751

		滋	0752
		渴	0753
		港	0754
		渚	0755
		湧	0756
		漣	0822[s]
	犭	猶	0757
		猪	0758
		猶	0759
	阝	隅	0760
		階	0761
		隊	0762
		隈	0763
		陽	0764
		随	0765
		陰	0766
		隆	0767
		隊	0768
	乡	郷	0830[s]
		鄉	0829[s]
	卯	卿	0769
		卿	0770
3-10	口	嘩	0771
		嗅	0772
		嘆	0773
	土	塩	0774
		塊	0775
		塙	0776
		塡	0777
		塚	0778
		填	0779
		堰	0676[s]
	女	嫁	0780
		嫌	0781
		媾	0782
		嫉	0783
		嫌	0784
		媾	0785
	山	嵯	0786
	巾	幌	0787
	彳	微	0788
		微	0789
	忄	慨	0790
		慄	0791

		慎	0792
		愼	0793
		慌	0711[s]
	扌	搏	0794
		搬	0795
		携	0796
		摸	0797
		搾	0798
		摂	0799
		搔	0800
		損	0801
		搜	0802
		搖	0803
	止	雌	1337[s]
	氵	漠	0804
		溺	0805
		源	0806
		溢	0807
		漢	0808
		滑	0809
		溝	0810
		滉	0811
		滅	0812
		滝	0813
		溜	0814
		滞	0815
		溶	0816
		溺	0817
		溢	0818
		溪	0819
		溝	0820
		溫	0821
		漣	0822
		溯	0823
		漣	0859[s]
		満	0869[s]
	犭	猿	0824
		獅	0825
	阝	隙	0826
		隔	0827
		隔	0828
	乡	郷	0829
		鄉	0830
3-11	口	鳴	0831

	嘘	0832
	噌	0833
	嘆	0834
土	境	0835
	増	0836
	塀	0837
	塲	0838
女	嫡	0839
山	嶋	0840
彳	徴	0841
	徳	0842
忄	慣	0843
	慢	0844
	憎	0845
	慨	0846
	慘	0847
扌	摑	0848
	摧	0849
	摺	0850
	摘	0851
	摺	0852
	摠	0853
	携	0796[s]
	摸	0797[s]
氵	滌	0854
	演	0855
	漁	0856
	漂	0857
	漫	0858
	漣	0859
	漏	0860
	漬	0861
	滲	0862
	漆	0863
	漕	0864
	漱	0865
	滴	0866
	漸	0867
	漢	0868
	滿	0869
	滯	0870
	漥	0871
	淵	0732[s]
	潟	0921[s]

	犭	獄	0872
	阝	隠	0873
		際	0874
		障	0875
		隙	0876
		隟	0877
3-12	口	嘲	0878
		嘖	0879
		嘘	0880
		嘱	0881
		噌	0882
		噂	0883
		嘲	0884
		噛	0885
		噂	0886
	土	墳	0887
		墟	0888
		增	0889
	女	嬉	0890
	巾	幡	0891
	弓	彈	0892
	彳	衝	0893
		徹	0894
		徵	0895
		德	0896
	忄	憤	0897
		憬	0898
		憧	0899
		慨	0900
		憐	0901
		憎	0902
	扌	撲	0903
		撫	0904
		撞	0905
		播	0906
		撥	0907
		撈	0908
		撒	0909
		撮	0910
		撰	0911
		撤	0912
		擕	0913
		撰	0914
	氵	澄	0915

		潮	0916
		潑	0917
		潤	0918
		潰	0919
		潔	0920
		潟	0921
		潜	0922
		澂	0923
		潮	0924
		澁	0925
		潔	0926
		澑	0927
		潛	0928
	阝	隣	0929
		隨	0963^s
3-13	口	噸	0930
		噴	0931
	土	壇	0932
		壌	0933
		壊	0934
		墳	0935
	女	嬢	0936
	山	嶮	0937
	彳	衛	0938
		衡	0939
		衞	0940
		徽	0941
	忄	懐	0942
		憾	0943
		憶	0944
		憐	0945
		憤	0946
	扌	擅	0947
		操	0948
		擁	0949
		據	0950
		擇	0951
		擔	0952
		携	0913^s
	氵	濁	0953
		澱	0954
		激	0955
		濃	0956
		濤	0957

		澤	0958
	犭	獲	0959
		獨	0960
	阝	隣	0961
		險	0962
		隨	0963
3-14	口	嚇	0964
		嚀	0965
	土	壕	0966
	弓	彌	0967
	彳	徽	0968
	扌	擬	0969
		擱	0970
		擦	0971
		擡	0972
		擢	0973
		擢	0974
		擴	0989^s
	氵	濠	0975
		濡	0976
		鴻	0977
		濯	0978
		濵	0979
		濱	0980
		澀	0981
		濶	0982
		濟	0983
		濕	0984
		濯	0985
		濫	0990^s
	犭	獲	0986
	阝	隱	0987
3-15	口	嚙	0988
	扌	擴	0989
	氵	濫	0990
	犭	獵	0991
3-16	土	壞	0992
	忄	懷	0993
	氵	瀕	0994
		瀨	0995
		瀝	0996
		瀬	0997
		瀧	0998
		潛	0999

3-17	土	壤	1000
	女	孃	1001
	氵	瀕	1002
3-18	扌	攜	1003
		攝	1004
	氵	灘	1005
		灘	1006^s
3-19	氵	灘	1006
3-20	山	巖	1007
	彳	黴	1008
3-21	口	囑	1009
3-22	氵	灣	1010
4-1	木	札	1011
	礻	礼	1012
4-2	木	朴	1013
		机	1014
		朽	1015
		杈	1016
	止	此	1017
	歹	列	1018
	火	灯	1019
	牙	邪	1039^s
	牛	牝	1020
	礻	祁	1043^s
	月	肌	1021
		肋	1022
	刃	那	1047^s
	巳	印	1023
	开	刑	1024
	丰	邦	1051^s
	屯	邨	1053^s
4-3	文	対	1025
	木	杖	1026
		杉	1027
		杓	1028
		村	1029
		杜	1030
		材	1031
		杦	1032
		杓	1033
		杓	1034
		杤	1035
		朽	1015^s
	火	灼	1036

		灼	1037
	爿	壯	1038
	牙	邪	1039
	牛	牡	1040
	王	玖	1041
	ネ	社	1042
		祁	1043
	月	肘	1044
		肝	1045
		肛	1046
	冄	那	1047
	冄	那	1048
	臼	臼	1049
	开	形	1050
	丰	邦	1051
	丰	邦	1052
	屯	邨	1053
	卯	卵	1054
4-4	戸	所	1055
	戸	所	1056
	斤	欣	1057
	方	放	1058
		於	1059
	日	明	1060
		旺	1061
		明	1062
	木	枇	1063
		枕	1064
		杷	1065
		杯	1066
		板	1067
		杭	1068
		枚	1069
		枅	1070
		林	1071
		析	1072
		枝	1073
		杵	1074
		松	1075
		枢	1076
		枠	1077
		柑	1112s
		柿	1118s
		柱	1124s
	歹	殁	1078
	火	炉	1079
		炊	1080
	爿	狀	1081
	片	版	1082
	牛	牧	1083
		物	1084
	王	玩	1085
	ネ	祈	1086
		祉	1087
		祇	1088
	月	肪	1089
		服	1090
		肥	1091
		朋	1092
		股	1093
		肢	1094
		肺	1095
	月	服	1096
		朋	1097
	区	欧	1098
		殴	1099
	門	門	1100
	非	非	1101
4-5	手	拜	1102
	方	施	1103
	日	映	1104
		昧	1105
		昨	1106
		昭	1107
		旺	1108
	木	柱	1109
		柏	1110
		柄	1111
		柑	1112
		枯	1113
		柾	1114
		柳	1115
		柵	1116
		柘	1117
		柿	1118
		柊	1119
		相	1120
		柢	1121
		栃	1122
		柚	1123
		柱	1124
		柄	1125
		栁	1126
		柗	1127
		柊	1128
		柠	1129
		枇	1063s
	歹	殆	1130
	火	畑	1131
		炮	1132
	牛	牲	1133
		牴	1134
	王	珍	1135
		珀	1136
		珂	1137
		珈	1138
		玲	1139
		珊	1140
		珎	1141
	ネ	祢	1142
		神	1143
		祝	1144
		祖	1145
		祐	1146
	月	肺	1147
		胞	1148
		胎	1149
		胆	1150
		胞	1151
		脉	1152
4-6	方	旅	1153
		旅	1154
	日	時	1155
		晒	1156
		晦	1157
		晄	1158
		晠	1198s
	木	梅	1159
		桧	1160
		格	1161
		核	1162
		桂	1163

		楢	1287
		楳	1288
		榊	1289
		槌	1290
		楢	1291
		極	1243^{s}
		槌	1331^{s}
		樋	1336^{s}
	火	煤	1292
		煖	1293
		煙	1294
		煩	1295
		煌	1296
		煉	1297
		煙	1298
	片	牒	1299
	王	瑚	1300
		瑶	1301
		瑞	1302
	ネ	福	1303
		禍	1304
		禎	1305
		禅	1306
	月	腸	1307
		腹	1308
		腺	1309
		腫	1310
		腰	1311
		腳	1312
		腦	1313
		腰	1314
	元	頑	1315
	扌	瓶	1316
	予	預	1317
	分	頒	1318
	公	頌	1319
	屯	頓	1320
4-10	方	旗	1321
	木	概	1322
		榎	1323
		樺	1324
		構	1325
		模	1326
		榊	1327

		榛	1328
		槍	1329
		槙	1330
		槌	1331
		様	1332
		構	1333
		槁	1334
		槇	1335
		樋	1336
	止	雌	1337
	火	煽	1338
		熄	1339
		熔	1340
		煽	1341
	王	瑠	1342
		瑳	1343
		瑤	1344
		璃	1358^{s}
	月	膜	1345
	云	魂	1346
4-11	木	標	1347
		権	1348
		槻	1349
		横	1350
		樟	1351
		槽	1352
		樋	1353
		槪	1354
		樓	1355
		樞	1356
		樣	1357
		樫	1364^{s}
		橢	1370^{s}
	王	璃	1358
	月	膝	1359
		膓	1360
	区	鴎	1361
4-12	日	暁	1362
	木	樹	1363
		樫	1364
		機	1365
		橘	1366
		橋	1367
		樽	1368

		橙	1369
		橢	1370
		槪	1371
		橫	1372
		樽	1373
		構	1374
		檎	1386^{s}
	火	燃	1375
		燎	1376
		燒	1377
		燈	1378
	王	璢	1379
	月	膨	1380
		膳	1381
		膸	1400^{s}
	予	豫	1382
4-13	日	曖	1383
		曙	1384
	木	檀	1385
		檎	1386
		檜	1387
		檢	1388
		櫛	1389
		構	1374^{s}
	火	燦	1390
		燭	1391
		燥	1392
	爿	牆	1393
	牛	犧	1394
	王	環	1395
		環	1396
	月	臆	1397
		謄	1398
		膽	1399
		膸	1400
	月	謄	1401
4-14	日	曜	1402
		曙	1403
		曜	1404
		曠	1411^{s}
	木	櫂	1405
	火	燻	1406
		燿	1407
		燿	1408

	光	輝	1775
	夹	頬	1776
6-10	米	糖	1777
		糖	1778
	糸	縛	1779
		緻	1780
		縫	1781
		緯	1782
		縦	1783
		縞	1784
		縛	1785
		緻	1762S
	舟	艙	1786
6-11	糸	繃	1787
		績	1788
		織	1789
		縮	1790
		繃	1791
		縫	1792
		縱	1793
		繍	1794
		總	1795
	耳	聴	1796
		聯	1797
		聰	1798
	臣	臨	2059S
	虫	螺	1799
6-12	米	糧	1800
	糸	織	1801
		繕	1802
		繩	1807S
	耳	職	1803
	虫	蟬	1804
6-13	糸	繡	1805
		繰	1806
		繩	1807
		繪	1808
	虫	蠏	1809
	弓	疆	1810
6-14	糸	繼	1811
	舟	艦	1817S
	光	耀	1812
		耀	1813
6-15	糸	纏	1814
		纖	1815
		續	1816
		繡	1805S
	舟	艦	1817
	虫	蠟	1818
6-16	糸	纓	1819
6-17	糸	纖	1820
	缶	罐	1821
6-18	缶	罐	1822
7-1	孚	乳	1823
	孚	乳	1824
7-2	臣	臥	1825
		卧	1826
	言	訃	1827
		計	1828
		訂	1829
	谷	卻	1830
	貝	則	1831
	車	軌	1832
	巠	勁	1833
	余	叙	1834
	缶	卸	1835
	亩	畝	1836
	肖	削	1837
	肖	削	1838
	孛	勃	1839
	皀	卽	1840
	君	郡	1858S
	良	郎	1859S
	束	勅	1841
	享	郭	2112S
7-3	言	訊	1842
		記	1843
		訓	1844
		託	1845
		討	1846
	豸	豹	1847
		豹	1848
	貝	財	1849
	身	射	1850
	車	軒	1851
	酉	酎	1852
		配	1853
		酌	1854
		酌	1855
	長	髟	1856
	亩	畝	1857
	君	郡	1858
	良	郎	1859
	享	郭	2112S
7-4	言	訪	1860
		訣	1861
		許	1862
		設	1863
		訟	1864
		訳	1865
		謳	1866
		註	1893S
	谷	欲	1867
	貝	敗	1868
		販	1869
	赤	赦	1870
	足	距	1905S
	車	軟	1871
		転	1872
		軛	1873
		斬	1874
	酉	酔	1875
	釆	釈	1876
	里	野	1877
	余	斜	1878
		敍	1879
		敘	1880
	杀	殺	1881
	毎	敏	1882
	壳	殻	1883
	皀	既	1884
	㡭	断	1885
	囧	朙	1886
	孝	教	1887
	孝	敎	1888
	良	朗	1889
	束	敕	1890
	求	救	1891
	享	敦	2128S
7-5	角	觝	1892
	言	註	1893
		詠	1894

		謎	2015
		諮	2016
		諸	2017
		諭	2018
		謎	2047^{s}
	豆	頭	2019
	豕	豬	2020
	貝	賭	2021
	足	蹄	2022
		蹈	2023
		踴	2024
		蹈	2055^{s}
	車	輯	2025
		輸	2026
		輸	2027
	辛	辨	2028
		辨	2029
		辦	2030
	酉	醍	2031
		醐	2032
		醒	2033
		醗	2034
	巠	頸	2035
	𥝌	穎	2036
	𥝌	頴	2037
	步	頻	2038
	禿	頹	2039
		頽	2040
	束	頼	2041
		頼	2042
	夾	頰	2043
7-10	言	謙	2044
		謹	2045
		講	2046
		謎	2047
		謝	2048
		謹	2049
		謙	2050
		講	2051
		謡	2052
	貝	購	2053
		購	2054
	足	蹈	2055
	車	轄	2056

		轄	2057
	酉	醜	2058
7-11	臣	臨	2059
	言	謬	2060
		謳	2061
		謬	2062
		謹	2063
	貝	贈	2064
	足	蹟	2065
	車	轉	2066
	弟	鵜	2067
7-12	言	譜	2068
		譏	2069
		識	2070
		證	2071
	貝	贈	2072
	足	蹶	2073
		蹴	2074
	辛	辦	2075
	酉	醱	2076
7-13	角	觸	2077
	言	議	2078
		護	2079
		譲	2080
		譜	2081
		譯	2082
	足	躁	2083
	身	軆	2084
	辛	辮	2085
	酉	醸	2086
		醵	2087
	釆	釋	2088
7-14	言	護	2089
	足	躍	2090
		躍	2091
	辛	辯	2092
7-15	言	讃	2093
		讀	2094
	車	轢	2095
7-17	言	讓	2096
	酉	釀	2097
7-19	言	讚	2098
8-2	金	針	2099
		釘	2100

	食	飢	2101
	斉	剤	2102
	音	剖	2103
		部	2111^{s}
	享	郭	2112^{s}
	僉	剣	2104
	彔	剥	2105
	录	剝	2106
	岡	剛	2107
	者	都	2120^{s}
	垂	郵	2121^{s}
8-3	金	釣	2108
		釧	2109
		釣	2110
	林	彬	1201^{p}
	音	部	2111
	享	郭	2112
	卓	乾	2113
	幸	執	2114
	采	彩	2115
	采	彩	2116
	周	彫	2117
	周	彫	2118
	𡰪	尉	2119
	者	都	2120
	垂	郵	2121
8-4	金	鈑	2122
		鈍	2123
		欽	2124
		鉛	2125
	革	靴	2235^{s}
	食	飯	2126
		飲	2127
	享	敦	2128
	京	就	2129
	卓	朝	2130
		戟	2131
		朝	2132
		乾	2113^{s}
	幸	報	2133
	壳	殻	2134
	[illegible]	款	2135
	苟	敬	2136
	昔	散	2137

9-6	革	鞍	2255
	食	餅	2256
		餌	2257
		蝕	2258
9-7	革	鞘	2259
		鞘	2260
	食	餓	2261
		餝	2262
		餘	2263
	亲	親	2264
	音	龍	2265
	音	龍	2266
	県	縣	2267
9-8	革	鞠	2268
	食	餠	2269
		館	2270
	隶	隷	2271
9-9	革	鞭	2272
	客	額	2273
	显	顕	2274
	类	類	2275
	咢	顎	2276
	彦	顔	2277
	彥	顏	2278
9-10	音	韻	2279
	[illegible]	關	4137^{p}
9-12	食	饒	2280
		饑	2281
10-2	馬	馭	2282
	倉	創	2283
	害	割	2284
	害	割	2285
	豈	凱	2286
	堇	勤	2287
	乘	剩	2288
10-3	馬	馳	2289
		馴	2290
10-4	馬	駄	2291
		駅	2292
		駆	2293
		駐	2299^{s}
	殻	穀	2294
	莫	歎	2295
	哥	歌	2296

	莫	歎	2344^{s}
10-5	馬	駐	2297
		駒	2298
		駐	2299
		駈	2300
10-6	骨	骸	2301
		骼	2302
	鬲	融	2303
10-7	馬	駿	2304
	谷	谿	2305
	毉	醫	3567^{p}
10-8	馬	験	2306
		騎	2307
		騒	2308
	骨	髄	2316^{s}
	离	離	2364^{s}
	杂	雜	2309
	莫	難	2310
	奚	雞	2311
	芻	雛	2312
	𠂤	歸	2313
10-9	馬	騙	2314
		騙	2315
	骨	髄	2316
	眞	顚	2317
	真	顛	2318
	类	類	2319
	原	願	2320
10-10	馬	騷	2321
	竟	競	2322
10-11	馬	驅	2323
	奚	鷄	2324
	芻	鶵	2325
	隺	鶴	2326
10-12	馬	驍	2327
	骨	髓	2332^{s}
	髟	鬚	3539^{p}
	耳	聽	2328
10-13	馬	驛	2329
		驗	2330
	骨	體	2331
		髓	2332
10-17	馬	驩	2333
11-2	雚	勸	2334

	啚	鄙	2338^{s}
	巢	剿	2335
	堇	勤	2336
11-3	章	彰	2337
	啚	鄙	2338
	丵	對	2339
11-4	啇	敵	2340
	豙	毅	2341
	雚	歡	2342
	殻	穀	2343
	莫	歎	2344
	専	敷	2345
	専	敷	2346
	婁	數	2347
	區	毆	2348
		歐	2349
		毆	2350
	虚	戯	2351
11-5	魚	鮎	2352
	票	瓢	2353
		瓢	2356^{s}
11-6	魚	鮫	2354
		鮮	2355
	票	瓢	2356
11-7	魚	鯁	2357
		鯉	2358
	雚	観	2359
	[illegible]	鬪	4136^{p}
11-8	魚	鯛	2360
		鯨	2361
		鯛	2362
	鹿	麒	2363
	离	離	2364
	莫	難	2365
11-9	鹵	鹹	2366
11-10	魚	鰯	2367
		鰯	2368
11-11	竟	競	2369
	區	鷗	2370
11-12	魚	鱒	2371
		鱗	2372
		鱒	2373
	鹿	麟	2374
11-13	魚	鱗	2375

	鹿	麟	2376
12-1	𤔔	亂	2377
12-2	奠	鄭	2379[s]
	奠	鄭	2380[s]
	粦	鄰	2382[s]
	畫	劃	2378
12-3	奠	鄭	2379
	奠	鄭	2380
	景	影	2381
	粦	鄰	2382
12-4	黑	默	2383
	嘼	獸	2384
	喜	歖	2385
	單	戰	2386
	虛	戲	2387
12-5	黍	黏	2388
	黑	點	2389
	齒	齡	2390
12-6	番	翻	2391
		翻	2392
12-7	𤔔	辭	2393
12-8	鹿	麒	2363[s]
12-9	雇	顧	2394
	雇	顧	2395
	番	飜	2396
13-2	僉	劍	2397
	留	劉	2398
	豦	劇	2399
13-3	僉	劒	2400
		劒	2401
13-4	虘	戲	2402
13-6	豊	艶	2403
14-2	齊	劑	2404
	睿	叡	2405
	熏	勳	2406
	厲	勵	2407
14-4	㡭	斷	2408
14-9	㬎	顯	2409
15-4	嘼	獸	2410
15-5	齒	齡	2411
16-4	鬳	獻	2412
17-2	雚	勸	2413
17-4	雚	歡	2414
17-5	龠	龢	2415
17-7	雚	觀	2416
18-2	雈	勧	2417
18-4	雈	歓	2418
18-6	豐	艷	2419
18-7	雈	観	2420

⬒ UP-DOWN

1-1	一	二	2421
	丶	冫	2422
		辶	2425[s]
1-2	一	三	2423
	丶	氵	2424
		辶	2425
	ノ	彡	2426
		彳	2427
		廴	2432[s]
		凢	4237[p]
1-3	一	元	2428
		戸	2429
		云	2430
	丶	辶	2431
	ノ	廴	2432
		爫	2433
		⺤	2434
		壬	4257[p]
		毛	4264[p]
		手	4267[p]
1-4	一	示	2435
	丶	永	2436
		主	2437
	ノ	禾	4315[p]
		乎	4316[p]
1-5	一	亘	2438
		亥	2439
	ノ	舌	2711[p]
1-6	一	言	2440
		戻	2441
		豆	2442
	ノ	系	2443
		辵	2444
		秀	3152[p]
		兎	4374[p]
		釆	4370[p]
		呑	3063[p]
		妥 豸	→ ⬒4-3[p]
1-7	一	房	2445
		肩	2446
	ノ	秀	3152[ps]
		垂	4382[p]
		兎	3165[p]
		委 季	→ ⬒5-3[p]
		受 采	→ ⬒4-4[p]
		争 采	→ ⬒4-4[p]
1-8	一	扁	2447
		音	2448
	ノ	重	4390[p]
		香	3177[p]
1-9	一	扇	2449
		鬲	2450
		晉	2451
	ノ	垂	4396[p]
1-10	一	商	2452
	ノ	悉	3405[p]
1-11	一	扉	2453
		雇	2454
	ノ	番	3416[p]
		黍	3210[p]
		爲	3127[p]
1-12	ノ	愛 舜	→ ⬒4-9[p]
1-16	ノ	爵	3143[p]
2-1	亠	亡	4210[p]
	人	个	2455
		个	2456
	𠂉	乞	2457
		ケ	4238[p]
	𠂉	廴	2432[ps]
2-2	亠	文	2458
		方	2459
		亢	2460
		六	2461
		文	2462
	人	介	2463
		今	2464
		仐	2465
	八	分	2466
		父	2467

		公	2468
		父	2469
	冖	冗	2470
		冘	2471
	几	殳	2472
	十	支	2473
		攴	2474
	⺊	攴	2475
	ム	允	2476
	マ	予	2477
	𠂉	午	2478
		攵	2479
		气	2480
		乞	2457[s]
	⺈	欠	2481
	丆	乏	2432[p]
	メ	爻	2482
		爻	2483
	九	卆	2484
2-3	亠	玄	2485
		立	2486
		市	2487
		圭	2488
	𠆢	令	2489
		仝	2490
		尒	2491
		令	2492
	冖	写	2493
	刀	召	2494
	十	古	2495
		吉	2517[s]
	⺊	占	2496
	ム	弁	2497
		台	2498
	又	圣	2499
		圣	2500
	亠	主	2437[p]
	マ	矛	2501
	𠂉	矢	2502
		尔	2503
2-4	亠	亦	2504
		亥	2505
		衣	2506
		充	2507
		交	2508
		妄	2509
		衣	2510
		亨	2530[s]
		孛	2532[s]
	𠆢	合	2511
		会	2512
		企	2513
		全	2514
	入	全	2515
	ソ	羊𦍌	→ ■3-3[p]
	冖	写	2493[s]
	匕	旨	2516
	十	吉	2517
	ム	牟	2518
	丆	百	2519
		而	2520
	七	乇	2521
	⺈	色	2522
		争	2523
		危	3965[p]
	⺈	危	2524
	𠂉	缶	2525
		缶	2526
		毎	2527
		年	2528
		気	3960[p]
2-5	亠	忘	2529
		亨	2530
		辛	2531
		孛	2532
		弃	2533
		享	2545[s]
	𠆢	含	2534
		余	2535
	八	谷	2536
	ソ	弟	2537
	冖	冝	2538
	刀	兎	2539
	十	克	2540
	子	孟	2760[s]
	⺈	角	2541
	𠂉	每	2542
	メ	希	2543
2-6	亠	育	2544
		享	2545
		京	2546
		盲	2547
		斉	2548
		卒	2549
		夜	2550
		辛	2551
	𠆢	金	2552
		命	2553
		念	2554
		舎	2555
		飠	2556
		舍	2557
	八	斧	2558
		巻券	→ ■6-2[p]
	ソ	並	2793[p]
	刀	兎	2559
	十	尭	2560
		直	3649[p]
	⺊	卓	2561
		臭	2562
	ム	参	2563
		叄	2564
	⺈	免	2565
		兔	2566
	メ	肴	2567
2-7	亠	哀	2568
		変	2569
		音	2570
		亮	2571
		亭	2572
		帝	2573
		彦	2574
		啇	2575
		京	2576
		弯	2577
		彦	4085[p]
	𠆢	食	2578
		飠	2579
		食	2580
	八	益	2581
	ソ	前首etc	→ ■3-6[p]
	冖	軍	2582

		吉	2689
		吉	2690
	士	吉	2691
	夂	各	2692
	夕	名	2693
		多	2694
	宀	安	2695
		字	2696
		守	2697
		宅	2698
		宇	2699
	小	尖	2700
	⺌	当	2701
		光	3043p
	干	舌	2702
	幺	糸	2703
	ヨ	寻	2704
	艹	芝	2705
		芋	2706
		共	3045p
	𠫔	至	2707
	䒑	羊	2708
		羊	2709
	亡	妄	2710
	千	舌	2711
	亼	会合	→ ■2-4p
3-4	口	呆	2712
		呂	2713
		足	2714
		呈	2715
		邑	2716
		足	2717
		呈	2718
	土	赤	2719
		走	2720
		走	2721
		吉	2690s
	士	壳	2722
		壱	2723
		声	2724
		志	2725
	夂	条	2726
	宀	完	2727
		宏	2728

		究	2729
		宋	2730
		宜	2731
	小	肖	2732
	⺌	肖	2733
	⺍	学	3162ps
		労	3155p
	巛	災	2734
	己	忌	2735
	艹	芭	2736
		芙	2737
		芸	2738
		芳	2739
		花	2740
		芥	2741
		芹	2742
		芦	2743
		芯	2744
		芽	2745
		苅	2746
		苍	2747
		花	2748
		芦	2749
	⺈	豸	3054p
	刃	忍	2750
	刅	忍	2751
	久	灸	2752
	亡	忘	2753
	亼	含	2534p
	𠫓	育	2754
3-5	土	幸	2755
	大	奇	2756
	大	奄	2757
		奔	2758
		奈	2759
	子	孟	2760
	宀	宙	2761
		宛	2762
		宜	2763
		宝	2764
		実	2765
		官	2766
		空	2767
		穹	2768

		宗	2769
		定	2770
		宕	2771
		突	2772
	小	尙	2773
	⺌	尚	2774
	⺍	甾	2775
		巣	2776
		学	3162p
	山	岸	2777
		岩	2778
	艹	茅	2779
		苺	2780
		苗	2781
		英	2782
		苑	2783
		芽	2784
		若	2785
		苛	2786
		茄	2787
		茎	2788
		苦	2789
		茉	2790
		茂	2791
		苔	2792
	䒑	並	2793
	亡	盲	2794
	亼	命念	→ ■2-6p
	廿	革	3099s
3-6	口	品	2795
	大	奎	2796
		奔	2797
	宀	客	2798
		宣	2799
		穿	2800
		窃	2801
		室	2802
		宥	2803
		突	2804
	⺍	単	2805
		栄	3183p
	山	炭	2806
		炭	2807
	艹	茶	2808

⬒2

		茸	2809
		荒	2810
		茜	2811
		茨	2812
		草	2813
		荘	2814
		荣	2815
		茨	2816
		革	3099^{p}
		巷巷	→ ⬒4-5^{p}
	䒑	美	2817
		首	2818
		前	2819
		前	2820
	𠀎	韋	2821
	亼	食 飠	→ ⬒2-7^{p}
3-7	口	員	2822
	大	套	2823
	宀	案	2824
		宴	2825
		害	2826
		家	2827
		宮	2828
		宰	2829
		窄	2830
		宥	2831
		容	2832
		害	2833
		穿	2834
		宵	2835
	⺌	党	3190^{p}
	⺍	挙	3106^{p}
	山	峩	2836
		峯	2837
	工	貢	2838
	艹	莫	2839
		荷	2840
		華	2841
		莞	2842
		莉	2843
		荻	2844
		莓	2845
		莖	2846
		莱	2847
		莊	2848
		恭	3109^{p}
	䒑	益	2849
		兼	2850
		差	4104^{p}
	亼	倉	2607^{p}
	𠀎	韋	2851
3-8	士	壷	2852
	宀	窒	2853
		寅	2854
		寂	2855
		寄	2856
		密	2857
		宿	2858
		窓	2859
		窑	2860
	⺌	常堂	→ ⬒5-6^{p}
	⺍	巣	2861
		蛍	3204^{p}
	山	崖	2862
		崩	2863
		崇	2864
		崩	2865
		嵜	2866
		嵌	2897^{s}
	巛	巢	2867
	艹	菩	2868
		著	2869
		萄	2870
		萌	2871
		萎	2872
		菓	2873
		菅	2874
		菊	2875
		菌	2876
		菫	2877
		萊	2878
		菱	2879
		菜	2880
		菖	2881
		萃	2882
		萠	2883
		葛	2884
		荣	2885
		黄	3116^{p}
		葉	2912^{s}
	䒑	剪	2886
		盖	2887
	亼	貪	2630^{p}
	廿	黃	3128^{s}
3-9	土	堯	2888
	士	喜	2889
		壺	2890
		壹	2891
	宀	富	2892
		寓	2893
		寒	2894
		寒	2895
		窗	2896
	⺌	掌	3215^{p}
		嘗	3225^{ps}
	⺍	営覚	→ ⬒5-7^{p}
	山	嵌	2897
		嵐	2898
		嵜	2899
	⺕	尋	2900
	艹	募	2901
		葡	2902
		惹	2903
		萱	2904
		葛	2905
		葵	2906
		落	2907
		萩	2908
		葺	2909
		葬	2910
		董	2911
		葉	2912
		著	2913
		葢	2914
		葦	2915
		萬	2916
		莖	2917
		蒸	2936^{s}
		蓮	2940^{s}
		蓬	2945^{s}
	ヨ	尋	2918
	䒑	普	2919

		尊	2920
		善	2921
		着	4110[p]
3-10	宀	寛	2922
		窟	2923
		塞	2924
		寝	2925
		害	2926
	⺌	當営	→ □5-8[p]
	⺍	誉	3135[p]
	山	嵩	2927
		嵳	2928
	彑	彙	2929
	艹	墓	2930
		蓄	2931
		蒲	2932
		蓋	2933
		葦	2934
		蒔	2935
		蒸	2936
		幕	2937
		蒙	2938
		夢	2939
		蓮	2940
		蓑	2941
		蒐	2942
		蒼	2943
		蓉	2944
		蓬	2945
		慈	2946
		蒋	2947
		蓬	2973[s]
		蓮	2979[s]
	䒑	義	2948
		慈	2949
		煎	2950
		羨	2951
		煎	2952
	亼	會	2655[p]
3-11	士	嘉	2953
		臺	2954
		壽	2955
	大	奪	2956
	宀	寡	2957

		蜜	2958
		寧	2959
		寥	2960
		察	2961
		窪	2962
		賓	2963
		實	2964
		寛	2965
		寧	2966
		寢	2967
		寫	2987[s]
	⺌	裳営	→ □5-9[p]
	山	嶌	2968
	艹	蔑	2969
		慕	2970
		暮	2971
		蔦	2972
		蓬	2973
		蔭	2974
		蔓	2975
		蔣	2976
		蔑	2977
		蔴	2978
		蓮	2979
		蔆	2980
		蔵	2995[s]
		蔭	2997[s]
3-12	士	賣	2981
	宀	賓	2982
		窮	2983
		寮	2984
		審	2985
		窯	2986
		寫	2987
		窰	2988
	⺌	賞	3237[p]
	艹	蕃	2989
		蕪	2990
		蔽	2991
		蕨	2992
		蕎	2993
		蕉	2994
		蔵	2995
		蔽	2996

		蔭	2997
	䒑	養	2998
		養	2999
	廿	燕	3142[s]
3-13	大	奮	3000
	宀	憲	3001
		窺	3002
		憲	3003
	艹	薄	3004
		薫	3005
		蕾	3006
		蕗	3007
		薦	3008
		薪	3009
		薙	3010
		薬	3011
		薗	3012
		薩	3016[s]
		舊	3019[s]
3-14	山	嶺	3013
		嶽	3014
	艹	藁	3015
		薩	3016
		藉	3017
		薰	3018
		舊	3019
		薩	3020
		藍	3024[s]
		薦	3008[s]
	亼	龠	2670[p]
3-15	士	嚞	3021
	艹	藩	3022
		藺	3023
		藍	3024
		藤	3025
		藝	3026
		藥	3027
		藏	3028
3-16	宀	寵	3029
		寶	3030
	艹	蘭	3031
		蘇	3032
		藻	3033
		蘆	3034

		穮	3035
3-17	宀	寶	3036
	⺌	黨	3245^{p}
	山	巌	3037
	⺶	譱	3038
3-19	宀	竊	3039
3-20	山	巖	3040
4-1	日	旦	3041
	氶	丞	3146^{s}
4-2	文	斈	2532^{ps}
	日	早	3042
	木	李	3050^{s}
	耂	孝	3973^{ps}
		考老	→ □4-2^{p}
	六	交	2508^{p}
	𠫓	充	2507^{p}
	⺌	光	3043
	凶	兇	3044
	龷	共	3045
	⺧	先	3046
	中	虫	4343^{p}
	少	劣	3047
4-3	文	斈	2532^{p}
	日	旱	3048
	木	杏	3049
		李	3050
	止	步	3051
	氏	帋	3052
	⺤	妥	3053
		豸	3054
	爫	𡚸	3055
	牛	告	3056
	王	弄	3057
	耂	考	3962^{ps}
		孝	3973^{p}
	幺	系	2443^{p}
	今	含	2534^{p}
	𠫓	弃	2533^{p}
	不	否	3058
	天	吞	3059
	五	吾	3060
	龶	麦	3061
	⺧	告	3062
	夭	呑	3063
4-4	文	斉	2548^{p}
	日	易	3064
		昂	3065
		昊	3066
		昆	3067
		昇	3068
		昌	3069
	木	杳	3070
	止	歩	3071
		肯	3072
	氏	昏	3073
	水	沓	3074
	火	炎	3075
	⺤	受	3076
		采	3077
	爫	桵	3078
		争	3079
	父	斧	2558^{p}
	耂	者	3980^{p}
	艹	苅	2746^{s}
		苍	2747^{s}
		花	2748^{s}
		芦	2749^{s}
	今	念	2554^{p}
	𠫓	育	2544^{p}
	勿	忽	3080
	冃	冐	3081
	龶	毒	3082
		表	3083
		青	3084
		靑	3085
	龷	昔	3086
		芽苛	→ ⬒3-5^{p}
	中	忠	3087
	大	奈	2759^{p}
4-5	文	彥	2574^{p}
	日	冒	3088
		星	3089
		是	3090
	日	昴	3091
	木	査	3092
	比	皆	3093
	耂	者	3988^{p}
	分	盆	2581^{p}
	亠	彦	4085^{p}
	冃	冒	3094
	不	歪	3095
		盃	3096
	龷	巷	3097
		巻	3098
		茸	2809^{p}
	廿	革	3099
	少	省	3100
	卌	帯	3191^{s}
4-6	日	晃	3101
		舁	3102
	曰	晏	3103
		晟	3104
	父	釜	2610^{p}
	艹	茨	2816^{s}
	公	翁	2611^{p}
	十冖	索	3105
	⺍	挙	3106
	天	蚕	3107
	龶	素	3108
	龷	恭	3109
		華	2841^{p}
4-7	文	斎産	→ ⬒2-9^{p}
	日	舁	3102^{s}
	曰	晨	3110
		晟	3111
	毌	貫	3112
	艹	莓	2845^{s}
		莖	2846^{s}
		莱	2847^{s}
	化	貨	3113
	化	貨	3114
	分	貧	2631^{p}
	今	貪	2630^{p}
	亠	産	4089^{p}
		商	2623^{p}
	龶	責	3115
	龷	黄	3116
		菫	2877^{p}
	少	雀	3117
	世	貰	3219^{s}
4-8	日	景	3118
		量	3119

		最	3120
		暑	3121
		晶	3122
	木	森	3123
	止	歯	3124
		齒	3125
	爫	舜	3126
	爫	爲	3127
	父	爺	2656^{ps}
	艹	萃	2882^{s}
		葛	2884^{s}
	𠫓	棄	2651^{ps}
	丗	葬莖	→ ■3-9^{p}
	廿	黄	3128
	中	貴	3220^{p}
	夭	喬	3129
4-9	日	暑	3130
	止	歳	3131
		歲	3132
	爫	愛	3133
		舜	3134
	父	爺	2656^{p}
	艹	蓋	2914^{s}
		蓬	2945^{s}
		莖	2917^{s}
	𠫓	棄	2651^{p}
	⺍	誉	3135
4-10	艹	蓬	2973^{s}
		蓑	2941^{s}
		蓬	2945^{s}
		蓮	2979^{s}
		蒋	2947^{s}
	卝	夢	3136
	𠂢	態熊	→ ■10-4^{p}
	目	睿	3137
4-11	日	暴	3138
	止	齒	3139
	艹	蓬	2973^{s}
		蔑	2977^{s}
		蔴	2978^{s}
		蓮	2979^{s}
		蔆	2980^{s}
	卝	蔑	3140
4-12	日	曇	3141
	艹	蔽	2996^{s}
		蔭	2997^{s}
	丗	蕾	3006^{p}
	廿	燕	3142
4-13	爫	爵	3143
	艹	舊	3019^{s}
	卝	舊	3145^{s}
4-14	爫	爵	3144
	艹	藉	3017^{s}
		舊	3019^{s}
		薩	3020^{s}
	卝	舊	3145
4-16	艹	蘆	3034^{s}
		蘓	3035^{s}
5-1	丞	丞	3146
5-2	田	男	3147
		甼	3148
	白	皃	3149
	目	貝	3150
		見	3151
	禾	秀	3152
		季	3161^{s}
	穴	究	2729^{p}
	立	辛	2531^{p}
	臼	兒	3249^{s}
	旧	児	3153
	奴	努	3154
	古	克	2540^{p}
	⺍	労	3155
		学	3162^{s}
	吅	呉	3156
	镸	镸	3157
	丘	兵	3158
	此	些	3251^{s}
5-3	目	具	3159
	禾	委	3160
		季	3161
		秀	3152^{s}
	穴	空突etc	→ ■3-5^{p}
	立	辛	2551^{p}
	覀	要	3262^{s}
	占	奌	2562^{p}
	⺍	学	3162
	镸	長	3163
	丘	岳	3164
	覀	兎	3165
		兔	4374^{p}
	𠫓	妻	3166
	𡗗	奉	3167
5-4	甘	某	3168
	田	毘	3169
		畏	3170
		胃	3171
		界	3172
		思	3173
	癶	発	3174
	白	皇	3175
		泉	3176
	目	県	3269^{p}
	矛	柔	2591^{p}
	禾	香	3177
	穴	窃穿etc	→ ■3-6^{p}
	立	音	2570^{p}
	加	架	3178
	夗	怨	3179
	奴	怒	3180
	氿	染	3181
	北	背	3182
	占	点	2587^{p}
	刍	急	2595^{p}
	卉	桒	2585^{p}
	⺍	栄	3183
	覀	衷	2600^{ps}
	𡗗	春	3184
		奏	3185
	此	柴	3287^{s}
5-5	玄	畜	2599^{p}
	田	毘	3169^{s}
	白	皛	3186
		皐	3187
	穴	窄穿	→ ■3-7^{p}
	立	竜竞	→ ■2-8^{p}
	比	皆	3093^{s}
	𠂉	监	3188
	丣	留	3189
	亞	晉	2451^{p}
	䒑	益	2849^{p}
	⺍	党	3190

	世	帯	3191
	夫	秦	3192
		泰	3193
	此	砦	3310^{s}
	卌	帶	3315^{s}
5-6	田	畢	3194
		異	3195
		累	3196
		畧	3197
	白	皐	3198
	穴	窓窒etc	→ ⬒3-8^{p}
	立	章	2624^{p}
	罒	眾	3199
	加	架	3200
	代	袋	3201
	⺌	堂	3202
		常	3203
	⺌	蛍	3204
	艹	萃	2882^{p}
	此	紫	3332^{s}
5-7	田	畳	3205
		塁	3206
		異	3207
	癶	登	3208
		發	3209
	禾	黍	3210
	穴	窗	2896^{p}
	立	童	2639^{p}
	罒	買	3211
	臼	鼠	3340^{s}
	加	賀	3212
	代	貸	3213
	卯	貿	3214
	山	嵜	2899^{p}
	⺌	掌	3215
		甞	3225^{s}
	⺌	営	3216
		覚	3217
	卌	黹	3218
	世	貰	3219
	串	貴	3220
	弗	費	3221
5-8	穴	窟	2923^{p}
	立	意	2650^{p}
	罒	置	3222
		署	3223
		罪	3224
	山	嵩	2927^{p}
	⺌	甞	3225
		當	3226
	艹	蓑	2941^{p}
	业	業	3227
5-9	穴	窪	2962^{p}
	罒	罰	3228
		署	3229
	⺌	營	3230
		裳	3231
	聿	盡	3232
5-10	穴	窮窯etc	→ ⬒3-12^{p}
	罒	罵	3233
		罷	3234
		罸	3235
	加	駕	3236
	⺌	賞	3237
5-11	田	疊	3238
	穴	窺	3002^{p}
	罒	罹	3239
	代	黛	3240
5-12	襾	覆	3385^{s}
	代	黛	3241
	殸	聲	3565^{p}
	艹	藁	3015^{p}
5-13	田	壘	3242
	业	叢	3243
5-14	罒	羅	3244
5-15	殸	馨	3575^{p}
	⺌	黨	3245
5-17	田	疊	3246
		疉	3247
	穴	竊	3039^{p}
6-2	竹	竺	3248
	臼	兒	3249
	旦	県	3156^{s}
	吅	咒	3250
	此	些	3251
	卣	卓	2561^{p}
	厽	垒	2564^{p}
	缶	免	2565^{p}
	垚	尭	2560^{p}
	从	卒	2549^{p}
	爫	受	3076^{p}
	且	具	3252
	曲	典	3253
	白	阜	3254
	甘	其	3255
	龹	券	3256
	龹	卷	3257
		劵	3258
6-3	竹	竿	3259
		笈	3260
	羊	美	2817^{p}
	自	臭	3261
	西	要	3262
	襾	要	3263
	次	姿	3264
		姿	3265
	刑	型	3266
	㓞	契	3267
	㓞	契	3268
	亦	変弯	→ ⬒2-7^{p}
	产	帝	2573^{p}
	共	巷巷	→ ⬒4-5^{p}
	目	県	3269
	由	卑	3270
	甚	甚	3271
	甫	専	3272
	龹	巻	3273
6-4	竹	笈	3274
		笑	3275
		笹	3301^{s}
		笈	3260^{s}
	羊	差	4104^{p}
	羽	翌	3276
	羽	翠	3277
	自	息	3278
		臭	3279
	西	栗	3280
	次	恣	3281
	如	恕	3282
	巩	恐	3283
	巩	恐	3284
	幵	栞	3285

	西	覆	3385
	西	覆	3386
		覇	3392s
	吉	嘉	3021p
6-13	⺮	簿	3387
		簾	3388
		簿	3389
		簾	3390
	西	覇	3391
	西	覇	3392
6-14	⺮	纂	3393
		籍	3394
		籍	3395
	吅	嚴	3396
6-15	⺮	籐	3397
6-16	⺮	籠	3398
6-17	⺮	籤	3399
7-2	卣	貞	2586p
	百	頁	2589p
	⺈	負	2594p
	甬	勇	2592p
7-3	辰	辱	3400
		唇	3401
	折	哲	3402
	直	真	2616p
	百	夏	2619p
	⺈	奐	2620p
7-4	車	専	3403
	辰	脣	3404
	釆	悉	3405
	里	黒	3406
	攸	悠	3407
	亡月	望	3408
	亡月	望	3409
	汈	梁	3410
	折	悊	3411
	利	梨	3412
	⺈	魚	2636p
	八	曽	2632p
	玄	牽	2621p
	亜	悪	3413
	曲	曹	3414
	串	患	3415
	夕又	祭	3311p
7-5	釆	番	3416
	次	盜	3417
	艹	募葛	→ ⬒3-9p
	呑	喬	3129p
	黍	黍	3210p
	卯	畱	3418
	成	盛	3419
	竺	箸	3359p
7-6	沙	裟	3420
	壯	裝	3421
	莫	幕墓	→ ⬒3-10p
	君	羣	3422
7-7	里	墨	3423
	折	誓	3424
	莫	暮慕	→ ⬒3-11p
7-8	魚	魯	2665p
	⺮	篇	3363p
7-12	芦	蘆	3034p
	車	轟	3425
8-1	昼	昼	3841p
8-2	隹	隻	3426
		隼	3427
	埶	勢	3428
	圖	圖	3429
8-3	雨	雫	3430
		雪	3431
		雪	3432
	波	婆	3433
	啟	啓	3434
	啟	啓	3435
	林	梦	3436
		埜	3437
	所	晢	3438
	丰丰	彗	3439
	䒑	菱	2879p
	其	基	3312p
	夾	麦	3440
		麥	3441
	亞	堊	3442
	叀	專	3443
	隋	堕	3501s
	臤	堅	3502s
8-4	隹	焦	3444
		集	3445
	雨	雰	3446
		雲	3447
	非	悲	3448
		斐	3449
	林	焚	3450
	炏	労	3451
	物	惣	3452
	玨	琵	3453
		琶	3454
		琴	3455
	肰	然	3456
	夫夫	替	3457
	知	智	3458
	黍	黎	3459
	無	無	2648p
	禽	禽	2654ps
	並	普	2919p
	其	棊朞	→ ⬒6-6p
	直	悳	2645p
	曾	曾	2642p
	者	煮	3460
	或	惑	3461
	里	黒	3462
	亞	惡	3463
	叀	惠	3464
	臤	腎	3511s
	禺	愚	3513s
8-5	雨	電	3465
		雷	3466
		零	3467
	明	盟	3468
	林	禁	3469
		楚	3470
	玨	琵	3453s
	叔	督	3471
	禽	禽	2654p
	苗	夢	2939p
	畜	蓄	2931p
	其	碁	3346p
	臤	豎	3516s
8-6	雨	需	3472
	非	蜚	3473
	啟	肇	3474
	啟	肇	3475

	炏	縈	3476
	知	智	3477
	制	製	3478
	取	聚	3479
	無	舞	2661^{p}
	苜	蔑蔑	→⬒3-11^{p}
	臤	緊	3517^{s}
8-7	雨	霊	3480
		震	3481
	非	輩	3482
	斦	質	3483
	㚘	賛	3484
	丰丰	慧	3485
		慧	3486
	𥝢	黎	3487
	𦣻	憂	2664^{p}
	無	舞	2666^{p}
	𦍌	養	2998^{p}
	昱	暴	3138^{p}
	黒	墨	3488
	臤	賢	3518^{s}
		豎	3519^{s}
8-8	炏	螢	3489
	竺	篭簑	→⬒6-10^{p}
8-9	雨	霞	3490
		霜	3491
	炏	營	3492
	竺	簑	3378^{p}
8-11	雨	霧	3493
	林	麓	3494
	丽	麗	2672^{p}
8-12	雨	覇	3496^{s}
8-13	雨	露	3495
		霸	3496
8-16	雨	靈	3497
	𧖟	蠶	3498
9-2	由	兜	3499
	𢆶	率	2625^{p}
	苗	黄	3116^{p}
	里	異	3195^{p}
9-3	保	堡	3500
	㓞	喫	0668^{p}
	隋	隨	3501
	臤	堅	3502
	羊	善	2921^{p}
	酋	尊	2920^{p}
	茻	葬	2910^{p}
	垚	堯	2888^{p}
	奥	奧	3503
	亜	喪	3504
9-4	亞	惡	3463^{s}
	楽	楽	3505
	昭	照	3506
	相	想	3507
	秋	愁	3508
	耶	聖	3509
		聖	3510
	臤	腎	3511
	兹	慈	2949^{p}
	前	煎	2950^{p}
	者	煮	3512
	禺	愚	3513
	咸	感	3514
	配	熙	3531^{s}
9-5	珀	碧	3515
	臤	竪	3516
	苜	夢	3136^{p}
	竺	管	3349^{p}
	臣	監	3535^{s}
9-6	臤	緊	3517
	苜	蔑	3140^{p}
9-7	臤	賢	3518
		豎	3519
	臣	覧	3538^{s}
9-8	秋	鍫	3520
	爫	爵	3143^{p}
10-2	准	準	3521
	兆	兆	3522
	莫	募	2901^{p}
	里	異	3207^{p}
	炏	勞	3451^{p}
	奥	奧	3503^{p}
10-3	亞	堊	3442^{s}
	涂	塗	3523
	将	奨	3524
	朔	塑	3525
	朔	塑	3526
	莫	幕墓	→⬒3-10^{p}
	奥	奧	3527
	孰	塾	3546^{s}
10-4	髟	髪	3528
	亞	惡	3463^{s}
	能	態	3529
		熊	3530
	配	熙	3531
	斉	齊	2659^{p}
	莫	暮慕	→⬒3-11^{p}
	炏	榮	3476^{p}
	配	熈	3547^{s}
	甜	憇	3550^{s}
	孰	熟	3558^{s}
	配	熙	3559^{s}
10-5	髟	髮	3532
	般	盤	3533
		磐	3534
	臣	監	3535
	𠅃	蕎	2993^{p}
10-6	敏	繁	3536
	炏	螢	3489^{p}
10-7	将	醤	3537
	臣	覧	3538
	斉	齋	2669^{p}
	炏	營	3492^{p}
10-9	郷	響饗	→⬒11-9^{s}
10-10	竝	競	2322^{p}
10-12	髟	鬚	3539
	竝	競	2369^{p}
10-16	𧖟	蠶	3540
11-2	淮	準	3541
	埶	勢	3542
	雯	零	3467^{p}
	䑕	與	3543
11-3	島	島	3544
	將	獎	3545
	孰	塾	3546
	奞	奪	2956^{p}
	隊	墜	3578^{s}
	隋	墮	3580^{s}
	道	導	3587^{s}
11-4	配	熈	3547
	幺幺	樂	3548
	將	獎	3549

ENCLOSURE

	㇋	乃	3643
	㇏	八	3644
		入	4177^{p}
1-2	㇄	巳	4197^{p}
	㇗	亾	3645
	㇆	刄	3646
		刃	3647
1-3	㇄	巴	4246^{p}
1-4	㇆	司	3648
1-5	㇈	迅	3780^{p}
1-6	㇈	迅	3970^{p}
1-7	㇗	直	3649
1-12	㇗	置	3222^{p}
2-0	厂	厂	4168^{p}
2-1	勹	勺	3650
		勻	3651
	㇋	乃	3643^{s}
	亍	寸	3652
	丆	万	3653
	ナ	尢	3654
	丬	丬	3655
	几	凡	3656
		凡	3657
	凵	山	3658
2-2	辶	込辺etc	→ □3-2^{s}
	㇗	止	3659
	勹	勾	3660
		勿	3661
		匂	3662
	厂	反	3663
		仄	3664
		厄	3665
	丆	不	4242^{p}
	ア	及	3666
	厂	斤	3667
		戸	3668
	𠃊	氏	3669
	ナ	友	3670
	十	斗	3671
		斗	3672
	冂	円	3673
		月	3674
		月	3675
		月	3676
		月	3677
	八	风	3678
	凵	凶	3679
	匚	匹	3680
		区	3681
		巨	3773^{s}
	𠃊	匹	3682
	ユ	丑	3683
2-3	辶	巡迅etc	→ □3-3^{s}
	勹	包	3684
		句	3685
		包	3686
	丁	可	3687
	厂	圧	3688
	丆	石	3689
	厂	斥	3690
	ナ	布	3691
		左	3692
		右	3693
		存	3702^{s}
	冂	用	3694
		回	3695
	八	凧	3696
2-4	廴	廷	3795^{s}
	辶	近返etc	→ □3-4^{s}
	九	旭	3697
	勹	旬	3698
	厂	灰	3699
		圧	3700
	厂	后	3701
	ナ	存	3702
		有	3703
		在	3704
		灰	3705
		有	3706
	冂	同	3707
		网	3708
		肉	3966^{p}
	八	凪	3709
	匚	匡	3710
		匠	3711
	𠃊	臣	3712
2-5	廴	延廹	3812^{s}
	辶	述迫etc	→ □3-5^{s}
	厂	辰	3713
	厂	帍	3714
	匚	医	3715
2-6	廴	建廻	→ □3-6^{s}
	辶	送追etc	→ □3-6^{s}
	厂	厚	3726^{s}
	厂	房	3716
		肩	3717
		戾	3718
	冂	岡	3719
		周	3720
		周	3721
	八	凬	3722
	凵	画	3723
		函	3724
		凾	3732^{s}
2-7	廴	廽	3847^{s}
	辶	通連etc	→ □3-7^{s}
	厂	彨	3725
		厚	3726
		厘	3727
	厂	扁	3728
		盾	3729
	八	風	3730
	凵	幽	3731
		凾	3732
		函	3724^{s}
2-8	辶	進週etc	→ □3-8^{s}
		遊遇	→ □3-9^{s}
	厂	原	3733
		辱唇	→ ⬒7-3^{p}
	厂	扇	3734
	匚	匿	3735
	𠃊	匿	3736
2-9	辶	遜	3910^{s}
		道運etc	→ □3-9^{s}
	厂	脣	3404^{p}
	厂	質	3737
	八	凰	3738
	匚	區	3739
	𠃊	匿	3736^{s}
2-10	辶	違遠etc	→ □3-10^{s}
	厂	厨	3740
		雁	3741

Pattern	Element	Kanji	No.
		既	3742
	厂	扉	3743
		雇	3744
2-11	辶	適遭etc	→ □3-11^{s}
	厂	厩	3746^{s}
2-12	辶	選遺etc	→ □3-12^{s}
	厂	厭	3745
		厩	3746
		暦	3747
		歴	3748
	八	鳳	3749
2-13	辶	避還	→ □3-13^{s}
	厂	鴈	3750
2-14	厂	曆	3751
		歷	3752
2-15	厂	壓	3753
3-0	冂	冂	4239^{p}
	口	口	4189^{p}
	囗	囗	4209^{p}
3-1	辶	辷	3957^{s}
	弋	弍	3754
	牙	牙	4243^{p}
	尸	尺	4248^{p}
	不	不	4242^{p}
	斤	斤	3667^{p}
	尢	尤	3755
	方	方	2459^{p}
	片	片	4272^{p}
	八	爪	3756
	口	曰	3757
		日	3758
	口	日	3759
		日	3760
3-2	辶	辺	3761
		込	3762
		辻	3763
	辶	辻込	3958^{s}
	夂	処	3764
	弋	弐	3765
	尸	尻	3766
		尼	3767
	广	庁	3768
		広	3769
	斤	斥	3690^{p}
	尸	民	3770
	广	皮	3771
	𠂇	存	3702^{ps}
	片	片	4328^{p}
	八	瓜	3772
	匚	巨	3773
		巨	3774
	囗	田	3775
		囚	3776
	皿	皿	4286^{p}
	目	目	3777
	且	且	4297^{p}
	口	四	3778
		罒	3779
3-3	辶	迅	3780
		巡	3781
		辿	3782
		辿	3783
		迂	3784
	辶	辿迂etc	→ □4-3^{s}
	弋	式	3785
	夕	名多	→ ◪3-3^{p}
	尸	尽	3786
		凧	3787
	广	庄	3788
	斤	后	3701^{p}
	𠂉	衣	2506^{p}
	𠂇	在存	→ □2-4^{p}
	八	瓜	3789
		瓜	3772^{s}
	冂	向	3790
	囗	団	3791
		因	3792
		回	3793
3-4	廴	延	3794
	廴	廷	3795
	辶	迎	3796
		返	3797
		近	3798
	辶	近返etc	3967^{s}
	尸	尾	3799
		局	3800
		尿	3801
	广	庇	3802
		序	3803
		応	3804
		床	3805
	冂	伺	0078^{p}
	匚	臣	3806
	囗	囲	3807
		困	3808
		図	3809
		囦	3810
		田	3811
3-5	廴	延	3812
		廹	3813
		廻	3814
	辶	迫	3815
		述	3816
		迪	3817
		迭	3818
		迦	3819
	辶	述迫etc	→ □4-5^{s}
	尸	届	3820
		屈	3821
		居	3822
		屆	3823
	广	府	3824
		庖	3825
		庚	3826
		底	3827
		店	3828
		庖	3829
		度	3844^{s}
		庇	3802^{s}
	亠	夜	2550^{p}
	囗	固	3830
		国	3831
		囯	3832
3-6	廴	廻	3833
		建	3834
	辶	逆	3835
		迷	3836
		送	3837
		退	3838
		逃	3839
		追	3840
	飞	飛	4389^{p}

	尸	昼	3841
		屋	3842
		屍	3843
	广	度	3844
		庲	3845
		席	3865^{s}
		庭	3866^{s}
	囗	圀	3846
3-7	廴	廻	3847
	辶	逐	3848
		連	3849
		逝	3850
		速	3851
		逓	3852
		途	3853
		透	3854
		通	3855
		造	3856
		逢	3857
		這	3858
		逞	3859
		逗	3860
	辶	這逢etc	→ □4-7^{s}
	乚	眞	2615^{p}
	尸	屑	3861
		展	3862
		屑	3863
	广	庫	3864
		席	3865
		庭	3866
		唐	3867
		座	3868
		庬	3869
		唐	3870
		庶	3880^{s}
	囗	圃	3871
3-8	辶	逸	3872
		進	3873
		週	3874
		逮	3875
		遇	3889^{s}
		透	3854^{s}
		遊	3896^{s}
	辶	逸進etc	→ □4-8^{s}
	广	庵	3876
		康	3877
		麻	3878
		鹿	3879
		庶	3880
		庸	3881
		⿸广森	3882
		庿	3883
		⿸广林	3884
		廊	3903^{s}
	囗	圈	3885
		國	3886
3-9	辶	遅	3887
		道	3888
		遇	3889
		遍	3890
		過	3891
		遂	3892
		達	3893
		運	3894
		遥	3895
		遊	3896
		迸	3897
		遁	3898
		遜	3910^{s}
	辶	遜	4041^{s}
		遁道etc	4027^{s}
	弋	貳	3899
	尸	屖	3900
		属	3901
	广	廃	3902
		廊	3903
		廓	3923^{s}
	囗	圈	3904
		圍	3905
3-10	辶	遠	3906
		違	3907
		遣	3908
		遡	3909
		遜	3910
		遮	3916^{s}
	辶	遡遜etc	→ □4-10^{s}
	广	廉	3911
		廉	3912
		廊	3913
		廓	3923^{s}
	囗	園	3914
		圓	3915
3-11	辶	遮	3916
		遭	3917
		適	3918
	弋	鳶	3919
	尸	層	3920
	广	腐	3921
		塵	3922
		廓	3923
		廐	3924
		廏	3925
		廣	3942^{s}
	囗	團	3926
		圖	3927
3-12	辶	遺	3928
		遵	3929
		遼	3930
		選	3931
		遷	3932
	尸	履	3933
		層	3934
	广	廟	3935
		慶	3936
		麾	3937
		摩	3938
		廟	3939
		廚	3940
		廢	3941
		廣	3942
		摩	3943
3-13	辶	避	3944
		還	3945
	辶	邊避etc	4057^{s}
	广	磨	3946
		磨	3947
3-14	广	應	3948
3-15	广	麿	3949
		麿	3950
3-16	广	願	2320^{p}
3-17	广	廳	3951
3-18	尸	屬	3952

	虍	虞	4037^{s}
4-11	辶	遮	4046
		遭	4047
		適	4048
	虍	膚	4049
		慮	4050
4-12	辶	遲	4051
		遺	4052
		遵	4053
		遼	4054
		選	4055
		遷	4056
4-13	辶	邉	4057
		避	4058
		還	4059
4-15	辶	邊	4060
5-1	戊	戌	4350^{p}
		成	4352^{p}
5-2	芦	芦	2743^{p}
	良	良	4373^{p}
	肖	肖	2733^{p}
	戊	成	4376^{p}
5-3	呉	呉	3156^{ps}
	奇	奇	2756^{p}
	苛	苛	2786^{p}
	尚	尚	2774^{p}
5-4	為	為	4395^{p}
	疒	疫	4061
	山	炭	2806^{p}
	戊	威	4394^{p}
	面	面	2590^{p}
5-5	疒	病	4062
		疲	4063
		疾	4064
		症	4065
5-6	疒	痕	4066
		疵	4067
	山	崖	2862^{p}
	戊	戚	4401^{p}
5-7	疒	痢	4068
		痩	4069
		痘	4070
		痛	4071
5-8	疒	痴	4072
		瘦	4074^{s}
5-9	導	導	3587^{ps}
	疒	瘍	4073
		瘦	4074
		瘦	4075^{s}
5-10	疒	瘦	4075
	艹	蕨	2992^{p}
5-12	疒	癌	4076
		癈	4077
		療	4078
	山	厳	4079
5-13	疒	癖	4080
		癒	4081
		癒	4082
	艹	繭	3023^{p}
5-14	疒	癡	4083
6-2	虍	虎	3981^{p}
	艹	芦	2743^{ps}
6-3	奇	奇	2575^{p}
	戈	哉	4084
	虍	虐	3989^{p}
	产	彦	4085
6-4	馬	馬	4086
	戈	栽	4087
	烏	烏	4088
6-5	虍	虚處etc	→ □4-7^{p}
	产	産	4089
	商	商	2623^{p}
6-6	戈	裁	4090
	虍	虚虜	→ □4-8^{p}
6-7	戈	載	4091
	虍	虜虞etc	→ □4-9^{p}
6-8	戈	截	4092
	艹	蔗	2978^{p}
6-9	導	導	3587^{p}
	虍	慮膚	→ □4-11^{p}
6-10	艹	薦	3008^{p}
6-11	戈	戴	4093
		戴	4094^{s}
6-12	戈	戴	4094
7-2	走	赴	4095
		赳	4096
	克	剋	4097
	免	勉	4098
7-3	走	起	4099
		赳	4100
		起	4101
	克	尅	4102
	鳥	島	4103
	羊	差	4104
	何	荷	2840^{p}
7-4	鳥	鳥	4105
	羊	羞	4106
	者	著	2869^{p}
7-5	走	超	4107
		越	4108
	更	甦	4109
	羊	着	4110
7-8	走	趣	4111
	艹	蔗	2978^{ps}
7-9	麦	麺	4112
	導	導	3603^{p}
8-0	門	門	1100^{p}
8-2	免	勉	4113
	門	閃	4114
8-3	虎	彪	4115
	門	閉	4116
		問	4117
		閇	4118
	商	商	2623^{p}
	高	高	2626^{p}
8-4	暑	暑	3121^{p}
	門	悶	4119
		閏	4120
		開	4121
		間	4122
		閑	4123
		閒	4124
	爲	爲	3127^{p}
	竹	筒	3323^{p}
8-5	暑	暑	3130^{p}
8-6	鬼	魁	4125
	門	閥	4126
		聞	4127
		閣	4128
		関	4129
		閤	4130
8-7	鬼	魅	4131

	門	閲	4132
		閱	4133
8-9	門	闇	4134
		闊	4135
8-10	門	闘	4136
8-11	門	關	4137
8-12	产	巌	3037^{p}
	严	嚴	3396^{p}
9-4	罒	署	3223^{p}
9-5	風	颱	4138
	罒	署	3229^{p}
9-9	是	題	4139
9-10	产	簾簾	→ □6-13^{p}
10-4	鬼	魁	4125^{p}
	鳶	鳶	3919^{p}
	笋	箸	3354^{p}
	鬥	鬨	4140
10-5	鬼	魅	4131^{p}
10-10	鬥	鬪	4141
10-14	鬥	鬭	4142^{s}
10-15	鬥	鬭	4142
11-4	麦	麪	4143
	麻	摩	3938^{p}
	麻	麾摩	→ □3-12^{p}
11-5	麻	磨	3946^{p}
11-7	麻	磿	3949^{p}
11-8	林	麓	3494^{p}
	門	蘭	3031^{p}
11-9	麦	麵	4144
11-10	麻	魔	3953^{p}
11-12	严	巖	3040^{p}
14-4	简	簡	3380^{p}

■ SOLID

1-1	□	乙	4145
		了	4157^{s}
1-2	□	乚	4146
		乚	4147
1-4	□	一	4148
		○	4149
		丨	4150
		丶	4151
		丿	4152
		㇒	4153
		亅	4154
		〆	4179^{s}
2-1	□	丁	4155
		几	4156
		了	4157
		又	4158
		冂	4159
		冖	4160
		几	4161
		匚	4162
		匸	4163
		㔾	4164
		卩	4165
		厂	4166
		又	4167
		厂	4168
		乃	3643^{p}
		乙	4145^{s}
		子	4196^{s}
		刀	3642^{p}
		廴	4202^{s}
		廴	4203^{s}
		阝	4206^{s}
		阝	4207^{s}
2-2	□	七	4169
		丄	4170
		凵	4171
2-3	□	十	4172
		十	4173
2-4	□	卜	4174
		人	4175
		九	4176
		入	4177
		力	4178
		〆	4179
		へ	4180
		亻	4181
		勹	4182
		厶	4183
		メ	4184
		匕	3641^{p}
		之	4228^{s}
		七	4169^{p}
3-1	□	已	4185
		下	4186
		干	4187
		己	4188
		口	4189
		工	4190
		久	4191
		及	4192
		弓	4193
		叉	4194
		夕	4195
		子	4196
		巳	4197
		尸	4198
		囗	4199
		夂	4200
		夊	4201
		廴	4202
		廴	4203
		彐	4204
		⺕	4205
		阝	4206
		阝	4207
		刄	4208
		囗	4209
		万	3653^{p}
		乃	3643^{ps}
		刃刃	→ □1-2^{p}
3-2	□	亡	4210
		土	4211
		上	4212
		士	4213
		也	4214
		彑	4215
		亡	4216
		廿	4258^{s}
		山	3658^{p}
3-3	□	巾	4217
		才	4218
		千	4219
		中	4220
		廾	4221
		扌	4222

		艹	4223
		寸	3652^{p}
3-4	□	大	4224
		丸	4225
		女	4226
		丈	4227
		之	4228
		与	4229
		弋	4230
		亣	4231
		女	4232
		亠	4233
		幺	4234
		广	4235
		豸	4236
		九	4237
		ケ	4238
		冂	4239
		乏	2432^{ps}
		亡	4210^{p}
		久	4191^{p}
		夕	4195^{p}
		也	4214^{p}
		夂	4200^{p}
		夊	4201^{p}
		尢	3654^{p}
4-1	□	弔	4240
		丑	4241
		不	4242
		牙	4243
		五	4244
		互	4245
		巴	4246
		王	4247
		尺	4248
		丹	4249
		天	4250
		无	4251
		旡	4252
		歹	4253
		毌	4254
		毋	4255
		王	4256
		反	3663^{p}

		弓	4193^{s}
		及	4192^{s}
		日	3759^{p}
		凹	4294^{s}
		凸	4298^{s}
		𤴔	4300^{s}
		及	3666^{p}
		曰日	→ □3-1^{p}
		月円etc	→ □2-2^{p}
4-2	□	壬	4257
		廿	4258
		丰	4259
		圡	4260
		甘	4306^{s}
		世	4308^{s}
		止	3659^{p}
		卌	4312^{s}
		主	2488^{ps}
4-3	□	木	4261
		中	4262
		牛	4263
		毛	4264
		井	4265
		升	4266
		手	4267
		屯	4268
		牜	4269
		才	4270
		午	2478^{p}
		市	2487^{ps}
		爪	3756^{p}
		水	0010^{p}
		斗	3671^{p}
4-4	□	夫	4271
		片	4272
		火	4273
		戈	4274
		犬	4275
		匆	4276
		内	4277
		少	4278
		爿	4279
		礻	4280
		禸	4281

		耂	4282
		式	4283
		户	4284
		內	4285
		乏	2432^{p}
		欠	2481^{p}
		毛	4264^{p}
		勿	3661^{p}
		世	4308^{ps}
		氏	3669^{p}
		之	4228^{s}
		心	0011^{p}
		太	2673^{p}
		屯	4268^{p}
		与	4229^{s}
		友	3670^{p}
		尤	3755^{p}
		攵	2479^{p}
		斤戶	→ □2-2^{p}
5-1	□	皿	4286
		母	4287
		瓦	4288
		玉	4289
		丙	4290
		平	4291
		疋	4292
		甲	4293
		凹	4294
		冊	4295
		正	4296
		且	4297
		凸	4298
		旡	4299
		𤴔	4300
		平	4301
		丙	4302
		册	4303
		牙	4304
		田	3775^{p}
		互	4245^{s}
		丞	3146^{ps}
		民	3770^{p}
		目	3777^{p}
		冬	2679^{p}

SYSTEM OF KANJI INDEXING BY PATTERNS

HOW TO LOCATE AN ENTRY

<table>
<tr><th colspan="3">DETERMINE THE SKIP NUMBER OF YOUR CHARACTER</th></tr>
<tr><td>STEP 1</td><td colspan="2">IDENTIFY PATTERN
Determine to which of the four patterns your character belongs to get the first part of the SKIP number (the pattern number). If your character belongs to pattern ◧1, ⬒2, or ▣3, carry out the steps in the left column; if it belongs to pattern ■4, carry out the steps in the right column.
➡§4 How to Identify the Pattern</td></tr>
<tr><td></td><td>◧1 ⬒2 ▣3</td><td>■4</td></tr>
<tr><td>STEP 2</td><td>DIVIDE CHARACTER
Divide the character into two parts at the first division point.
➡§5 How to Divide the Character</td><td>OMIT
Since solid characters cannot be divided, go to STEP 3.</td></tr>
<tr><td>STEP 3</td><td>COUNT STROKES OF SHADED PART
Count the strokes of the shaded part to get the second part of the SKIP number.
➡Appendix 3. How to Count Strokes</td><td>DETERMINE TOTAL STROKE-COUNT
Determine the total stroke-count of your character to get the second part of the SKIP number.
➡Appendix 3. How to Count Strokes</td></tr>
<tr><td>STEP 4</td><td>COUNT STROKES OF BLANK PART
Count the strokes of the blank part to get the third part of the SKIP number.
➡Appendix 3. How to Count Strokes</td><td>IDENTIFY SOLID SUBPATTERN
Determine to which of the four solid subpatterns your character belongs to get the third part of the SKIP number. Select from: ☐1, ☐2, ◫3, or ☐4.
➡§6 How to Subclassify the Solid Pattern</td></tr>
</table>

After determining the SKIP number, locate your entry character in one of two ways:

1. Determine the entry number in the **Pattern Index** beginning on p. 2014, then locate your character in the main part of the dictionary. See **§3.1.2 Index Method** for details.
2. Locate your character entry directly (without referring to the Pattern Index) from its SKIP number. See **§3.1.3 Direct Method** for details.

NOTE: All references preceded by a section mark (§) refer to **Appendix 2. System of Kanji Indexing by Patterns** beginning on p. 1781.